2008 Standard Catalog of® WORLD COINS 1901-2000

35th OFFICIAL Edition

Colin R. Bruce II
Senior Editor

Thomas Michael
Market Analyst

George Cuhaj
Editor

Merna Dudley
Coordinating Editor

Deborah McCue
Database Specialist

Harry Miller
U.S. Market Analyst

Fred J. Borgmann
New Issues Editor

Randy Thern
Numismatic Cataloging Supervisor

Special Contributors
David Harrison
Ton Jacobs
Benjamin Swagerty

Bullion Value (BV) Market Valuations

Valuations for all platinum, gold, palladium and silver coins of the more common, basically bullion types, or those possessing only modest numismatic premiums are presented in this edition based on the market ranges of:

$1,150 - $1,350 per ounce for **platinum**

$650 - $670 per ounce for **gold**

$330 - $350 per ounce for **palladium**

$13.50 - $15.00 per ounce for **silver**

Published by

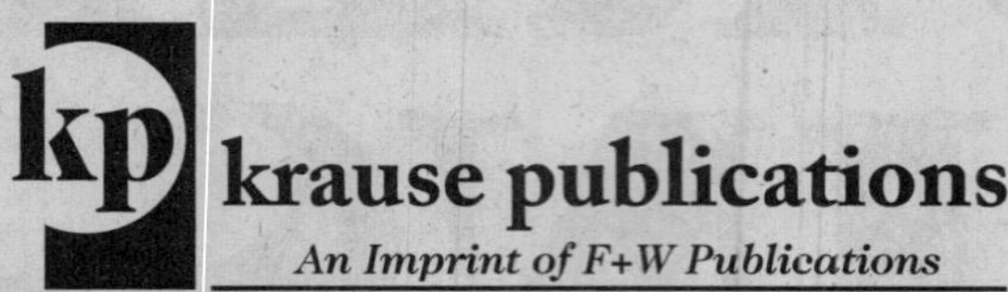

700 East State Street • Iola, WI 54990-0001
715-445-2214 • 888-457-2873
www.krausebooks.com

Our toll-free number to place an order or obtain a free catalog is (800) 258-0929.

Library of Congress Catalog Number: 1556-2263

ISBN: 978-0-89689-500-3

Designed by: Sandra Morrison

Edited by: Randy Thern

Printed in the United States of America

PROFESSIONAL NUMISMATISTS GUILD · INC

ANA
1891
MEMBER

krause publications
2005
CSA
20 YEAR
CUSTOMER SERVICE AWARD

STANDARD INTERNATIONAL NUMERAL SYSTEMS

Prepared especially for the ***Standard Catalog of World Coins***© 2007 by Krause Publications

Western	0	½	1	2	3	4	5	6	7	8	9	10	50	100	500	1000
Roman			I	II	III	IV	V	VI	VII	VIII	IX	X	L	C	D	M
Arabic-Turkish	٠	١/٢	١	٢	٣	٤	٥	٦	٧	٨	٩	١٠	٥٠	١٠٠	٥٠٠	١٠٠٠
Malay-Persian	۰	۱/۲	۱	۲	۳	۴	۵	٦ or ۶	۷	۸	۹	۱۰	۵۰	۱۰۰	۵۰۰	۱۰۰۰
Eastern Arabic	۰	½	۱	۲	۳	۴	۵	۶	۷	۸	۹	۱۰	۵۰	۱۰۰	۵۰۰	۱۰۰۰
Hyderabad Arabic	٠	١/٢	١	٢	٣	۴	٥	٦	٧	٨	٩	١٠	٥٠	١٠٠	٥٠٠	١٠٠٠
Indian (Sanskrit)	०	१/२	१	२	३	४	५	६	७	८	९	१०	५०	१००	५००	१०००
Assamese	০	১/২	১	২	৩	৪	৫	৬	৭	৮	৯	১০	৫০	১০০	৫০০	১০০০
Bengali	০	১/২	১	২	৩	৪	৫	৬	৭	৮	৯	১০	৫০	১০০	৫০০	১০০০
Gujarati	૦	૧/૨	૧	૨	૩	૪	૫	૬	૭	૮	૯	૧૦	૫૦	૧૦૦	૫૦૦	૧૦૦૦
Kutch	०	१/२	१	२	३	४	५	६	७	८	९	१०	५०	१००	५००	१०००
Devavnagri	०	१/२	१	२	३	४	५	६ or ६	७	८	९ or ९	१०	५०	१००	५००	१०००
Nepalese	०	१/२	१	२	३	४	५	६	७	८	९	१०	५०	१००	५००	१०००
Tibetan	༠	༡/༢	༡	༢	༣	༤	༥	༦	༧	༨	༩	༡༠	༥༠	༡༠༠	༥༠༠	༡༠༠༠
Mongolian	᠐	᠑/᠒	᠑	᠒	᠓	᠔	᠕	᠖	᠗	᠘	᠙	᠑᠐	᠕᠐	᠑᠐᠐	᠕᠐᠐	᠑᠐᠐᠐
Burmese	၀	၁/၂	၁	၂	၃	၄	၅	၆	၇	၈	၉	၁၀	၅၀	၁၀၀	၅၀၀	၁၀၀၀
Thai-Lao	๐	๑/๒	๑	๒	๓	๔	๕	๖	๗	๘	๙	๑๐	๕๐	๑๐๐	๕๐๐	๑๐๐๐
Lao-Laotian	໐		໑	໒	໓	໔	໕	໖	໗	໘	໙	໑໐				
Javanese	꧐		꧑	꧒	꧓	꧔	꧕	꧖	꧗	꧘	꧙	꧑꧐	꧕꧐	꧑꧐꧐	꧕꧐꧐	꧑꧐꧐꧐
Ordinary Chinese Japanese-Korean	零	半	一	二	三	四	五	六	七	八	九	十	十五	百	百五	千
Official Chinese			壹	貳	叁	肆	伍	陸	柒	捌	玖	拾	拾伍	佰	佰伍	仟
Commercial Chinese			〡	〢	〣	〤	〥	〦	〧	〨	〩	十	〥十	〡百	〥百	〡千
Korean		반	일	이	삼	사	오	육	칠	팔	구	십	오십	백	오백	천
Georgian			ა	ბ	გ	დ	ე	ვ	ზ	ჱ	თ	ი	ნ	რ	ფ	ჩ
			11 ია	20 კ	30 ლ	40 მ	60 ჲ	70 ო	80 პ	90 ჟ	200 ს	300 ტ	400 უ	600 ქ	700 ღ	800 ყ
Ethiopian	◆		፩	፪	፫	፬	፭	፮	፯	፰	፱	፲	፶	፻	፭፻	፲፻
				20 ፳	30 ፴	40 ፵	60 ፷	70 ፸	80 ፹	90 ፺						
Hebrew			א	ב	ג	ד	ה	ו	ז	ח	ט	י	נ	ק	תק	
				20 כ	30 ל	40 מ	60 ס	70 ע	80 פ	90 צ	200 ר	300 ש	400 ת	600 תר	700 תש	800 תת
Greek			Α	Β	Γ	Δ	Ε	Τ	Ζ	Η	Θ	Ι	Ν	Ρ	Φ	Α
				20 Κ	30 Λ	40 Μ	60 Ξ	70 Ο	80 Π		200 Σ	300 Τ	400 Υ	600 Χ	700 Ψ	800 Ω

ACKNOWLEDGMENTS

Many individuals have contributed countless changes, which have been incorporated into previous and now this thirty fifth edition. While all may not be acknowledged, special appreciation is extended to the following who have exhibited a special enthusiasm for this edition.

Dr. Lawrence A. Adams
David Addey
Esko Ahlroth
Stephen Album
Antonio Alessandrini
Don Bailey
Paul Baker
Oksana Bandrivska
Mitchell A. Battino
Albert Beck
Richard Benson
Peter Berger
Allen G. Berman
Sharon Blocker
Joseph Boling
Klaus Bronny
Mahdi Bseiso
John T. Bucek
Chris Budesa
Doru Calin
K. H. Chan
Peter A. Chase
Scott E. Cordry
Jerry Crain
Vincent Craven-Bartle
Jed Crump
Raymond E. Czahor
Howard A. Daniel III
Eric G. Dawson, M.D.
Jean-Paul Divo
Yossi Dotan
James R. Douglas
Graham P. Dyer
Dr. Jan M. Dyroff
Wilhelm R. Eglseer
Jack Erb
Thomas F. Fitzgerald
Joe Flores
Eugene Freeman
Arthur Friedberg
K. M. Froseth
Tom Galway
Dennis Gill
Mark E. Goldberg
David R. Gotkin
Ron Guth
Marcel Häberling
Edmond Hakimian
Brian Hannon
Flemming Lyngbeck Hansen
David Harrison
Martin Rodney Hayter
Serge Huard
Clyde Hubbard
Charles Huff
Nelva G. Icaza
Dennis H. Irving
Ton Jacobs
A. K. Jain
Hector Carlos Janson
Robert W. Julian
Børge R. Juul
Alex Kaglyan
John Kallman
Melvyn Kassenoff
Craig Keplinger
E. James Kindrake
Peter Kraneveld
Ronachai Krisadaolarn
Matti Kuronen
Samson Kin Chiu Lai
Joseph E. Lang
Thomas Lautz
Alex Lazarovici
Jan Lingen
Richard Lobel
Rudi Lotter
Ma Tak Wo
Enrico Manara
Ranko Mandic
Miguel Angel Pratt Mayans
Robert McKay
Franck Medina
Dimitar Mihov
Jürgen Mikeska
Juozas Minikevicius
Robert Mish
Ing. Benjamin M. Mizrachi R.
Dr. Richard Montrey
Paul Montz
Edward Moschetti
Horst-Dieter Müller
Hitoshi Nagai
Arkady Nakhimovsky
N. Douglas Nicol
Michael G. Nielsen
Bill Noyes
Gus A. Pappas
Frank Passic
Marc Pelletier
Juan Pena
Kirsten F. Petersen
Jens Pilegaard
Carlo Pileri
Gastone Polacco
Luis R. Ponte Puigbo
Richard Ponterio
Kent Ponterio
Elena Pop
Michel Prier
Martin Purdy
Frank Putrow
Yahya Qureshi
Dr. Dennis G. Rainey
Tony Raymond
Bob Reis
Dr. Kerry A. Rodgers
William M. Rosenblum
Egon Conti Rossini
Remy Said
Leon Saryan
Erwin Schaffer
Gunter Schön
Dr. Wolfgang Schuster
Alexander Shapiro
Ladislav Sin
Nik Sharplin
Ole Sjoelund
Gylfi Snorrason
Evzen Sknouril
Jorgen Sømod
Benjamin Swagerty
Vladimir Suchy
Barry Tabor
Steven Tan
Mehmet Tolga Taner
M. Louis Teller
Tonin Thaci
Frank Timmermann
Anthony Tumonis
J. J. Van Grover
Erik J. Van Loon
Carmen Viciedo
Helen Wallace
Justin Wang
Paul Welz
Stewart Westdal
J. Brix Westergaard
J. Hugh Witherow
Joseph Zaffern
Roy Zukerman

AUCTION HOUSES AND DISTRIBUTORS

Dixon-Noonan-Webb
Heritage World Coin Auctions
Hess-Divo Ltd.
Gerhard Hirsch
Thomas Høiland Møntauktion
Fritz Rudolf Künker
Leu Numismatik AG
Münzenhandlung Harald Möller, GmbH
Noble Numismatics, Pty. Ltd.
Omni Trading B. V.
Ponterio & Associates
Stack's
UBS, AG
World Wide Coins of California

SOCIETIES, INSTITUTIONS AND INTERNATIONAL MINTS

Africa Mint
American Numismatic Association
American Numismatic Society
Austrian Mint
British Museum
British Royal Mint
Casa de la Moneda de Cuba
Central Bank of The Russian Federation
Mint of Finland
Numismatics International
Pobjoy Mint
Royal Dutch Mint
Singapore Mint
Smithsonian Institution

PUBLICATIONS

The Statesman's Yearbook, 2004.
The Politics, Cultures and Economies of the World 140th Edition
edited by Barry Turner, Palgrave Macmillan Ltd
Houndmills, Basingstoke,
Hampshire, RG21 6XS, England

The World Factbook 2003.
By Central Intelligence Agency

COUNTRY INDEX

HEJIRA DATE CONVERSION CHART

JEHIRA DATE CHART

HEJIRA (Hijira, Hegira), the name of the Muslim era (A.H. = Anno Hegirae) dates back to the Christian year 622 when Mohammed "fled" from Mecca, escaping to Medina to avoid persecution from the Koreish tribemen. Based on a lunar year the Muslim year is 11 days shorter.

*=Leap Year (Christian Calendar)

AH Hejira	AD Christian Date
1010	1601, July 2
1011	1602, June 21
1012	1603, June 11
1013	1604, May 30
1014	1605, May 19
1015	1606, May 19
1016	1607, May 9
1017	1608, April 28
1018	1609, April 6
1017	1608, April 28
1018	1609, April 6
1019	1610, March 26
1020	1611, March 16
1021	1612, March 4
1022	1613, February 21
1023	1614, February 11
1024	1615, January 31
1025	1616, January 20
1026	1617, January 9
1027	1617, December 29
1028	1618, December 19
1029	1619, December 8
1030	1620, November 26
1031	1621, November 16
1032	1622, November 5
1033	1623, October 25
1034	1624, October 14
1035	1625, October 3
1036	1626, September 22
1037	1627, Septembe 12
1038	1628, August 31
1039	1629, August 21
1040	1630, July 10
1041	1631, July 30
1042	1632, July 19
1043	1633, July 8
1044	1634, June 27
1045	1635, June 17
1046	1636, June 5
1047	1637, May 26
1048	1638, May 15
1049	1639, May 4
1050	1640, April 23
1051	1641, April 12
1052	1642, April 1
1053	1643, March 22
1054	1644, March 10
1055	1645, February 27
1056	1646, February 17
1057	1647, February 6
1058	1648, January 27
1059	1649, January 15
1060	1650, January 4
1061	1650, December 25
1062	1651, December 14
1063	1652, December 2
1064	1653, November 22
1065	1654, November 11
1066	1655, October 31
1067	1656, October 20
1068	1657, October 9
1069	1658, September 29
1070	1659, September 18
1071	1660, September 6
1072	1661, August 27
1073	1662, August 16
1074	1663, August 5
1075	1664, July 25
1076	1665, July 14
1077	1666, July 4
1078	1667, June 23
1079	1668, June 11
1080	1669, June 1
1081	1670, May 21
1082	1671, may 10
1083	1672, April 29
1084	1673, April 18
1085	1674, April 7

AH Hejira	AD Christian Date
1086	1675, March 28
1087	1676, March 16*
1088	1677, March 6
1089	1678, February 23
1090	1679, February 12
1091	1680, February 2*
1092	1681, January 21
1093	1682, January 10
1094	1682, December 31
1095	1683, December 20
1096	1684, December 8*
1097	1685, November 28
1098	1686, November 17
1099	1687, November 7
1100	1688, October 26*
1101	1689, October 15
1102	1690, October 5
1103	1691, September 24
1104	1692, September 12*
1105	1693, September 2
1106	1694, August 22
1107	1695, August 12
1108	1696, July 31*
1109	1697, July 20
1110	1698, July 10
1111	1699, June 29
1112	1700, June 18
1113	1701, June 8
1114	1702, May 28
1115	1703, May 17
1116	1704, May 6*
1117	1705, April 25
1118	1706, April 15
1119	1707, April 4
1120	1708, March 23*
1121	1709, March 13
1122	1710, March 2
1123	1711, February 19
1124	1712, Feburary 9*
1125	1713, January 28
1126	1714, January 17
1127	1715, January 7
1128	1715, December 27
1129	1716, December 16*
1130	1717, December 5
1131	1718, November 24
1132	1719, November 14
1133	1720, November 2*
1134	1721, October 22
1135	1722, October 12
1136	1723, October 1
1137	1724, September 19
1138	1725, September 9
1139	1726, August 29
1140	1727, August 19
1141	1728, August 7*
1142	1729, July 27
1143	1730, July 17
1144	1731, July 6
1145	1732, June 24*
1146	1733, June 14
1147	1734, June 3
1148	1735, May 24
1149	1736, May 12*
1150	1737, May 1
1151	1738, April 21
1152	1739, April 10
1153	1740, March 29*
1154	1741, March 19
1155	1742, March 8
1156	1743, Febuary 25
1157	1744, February 15*
1158	1745, February 3
1159	1746, January 24
1160	1747, January 13
1161	1748, January 2
1162	1748, December 22*
1163	1749, December 11
1164	1750, November 30
1165	1751, November 20
1166	1752, November 8*
1167	1753, October 29
1168	1754, October 18
1169	1755, October 7
1170	1756, September 26*
1171	1757, September 15
1172	1758, September 4
1173	1759, August 25
1174	1760, August 13*
1175	1761, August 2
1176	1762, July 23

AH Hejira	AD Christian Date
1177	1763, July 12
1178	1764, July 1*
1179	1765, June 20
1180	1766, June 9
1181	1767, May 30
1182	1768, May 18*
1183	1769, May 7
1184	1770, April 27
1185	1771, April 16
1186	1772, April 4*
1187	1773, March 25
1188	1774, March 14
1189	1775, March 4
1190	1776, February 21*
1191	1777, February 91
1192	1778, January 30
1193	1779, January 19
1194	1780, January 8*
1195	1780, December 28*
1196	1781, December 17
1197	1782, December 7
1198	1783, November 26
1199	1784, November 14*
1200	1785, November 4
1201	1786, October 24
1202	1787, October 13
1203	1788, October 2*
1204	1789, September 21
1205	1790, September 10
1206	1791, August 31
1207	1792, August 19*
1208	1793, August 9
1209	1794, July 29
1210	1795, July 18
1211	1796, July 7*
1212	1797, June 26
1213	1798, June 15
1214	1799, June 5
1215	1800, May 25
1216	1801, May 14
1217	1802, May 4
1218	1803, April 23
1219	1804, April 12*
1220	1805, April 1
1221	1806, March 21
1222	1807, March 11
1223	1808, February 28*
1224	1809, February 16
1225	1810, Febauary 6
1226	1811, January 26
1227	1812, January 16*
1228	1813, Janaury 26
1229	1813, December 24
1230	1814, December 14
1231	1815, December 3
1232	1816, November 21*
1233	1817, November 11
1234	1818, October 31
1235	1819, October 20
1236	1820, October 9*
1237	1821, September 28
1238	1822, September 18
1239	1823, September 18
1240	1824, August 26*
1241	1825, August 16
1242	1826, August 5
1243	1827, July 25
1244	1828, July 14*
1245	1829, July 3
1246	1830, June 22
1247	1831, June 12
1248	1832, May 31*
1249	1833, May 21
1250	1834, May 10
1251	1835, April 29
1252	1836, April 18*
1253	1837, April 7
1254	1838, March 27
1255	1839, March 17
1256	1840, March 5*
1257	1841, February 23
1258	1842, February 12
1259	1843, February 1
1260	1844, January 22*
1261	1845, January 10
1262	1845, December 30
1263	1846, December 20
1264	1847, December 9
1265	1848, November 27*
1266	1849, November 17
1267	1850, November 6

AH Hejira	AD Christian Date
1268	1851, October 27
1269	1852, October 15*
1270	1853, October 4
1271	1854, September 24
1272	1855, September 13
1273	1856, September 1*
1274	1857, August 22
1275	1858, August 11
1276	1859, July 31
1277	1860, July 20*
1278	1861, July 9
1279	1862, June 29
1280	1863, June 18
1281	1864, June 6*
1282	1865, May 27
1283	1866, May 16
1284	1867, May 5
1285	1868, April 24*
1286	1869, April 13
1287	1870, April 3
1288	1871, March 23
1289	1872, March 11*
1290	1873, March 1
1291	1874, February 18
1292	1875, Febuary 7
1293	1876, January 28*
1294	1877, January 16
1295	1878, January 5
1296	1878, December 26
1297	1879, December 15
1298	1880, December 4*
1299	1881, November 23
1300	1882, November 12
1301	1883, November 2
1302	1884, October 21*
1303	1885, October 10
1304	1886, September 30
1305	1887, September 19
1306	1888, September 7*
1307	1889, August 28
1308	1890, August 17
1309	1891, August 7
1310	1892, July 26*
1311	1893, July 15
1312	1894, July 5
1313	1895, June 24
1314	1896, June 12*
1315	1897, June 2
1316	1898, May 22
1317	1899, May 12
1318	1900, May 1
1319	1901, April 20
1320	1902, april 10
1321	1903, March 30
1322	1904, March 18*
1323	1905, March 8
1324	1906, February 25
1325	1907, February 14
1326	1908, February 4*
1327	1909, January 23
1328	1910, January 13
1329	1911, January 2
1330	1911, December 22
1332	1913, November 30
1333	1914, November 19
1334	1915, November 9
1335	1916, October 28*
1336	1917, October 17
1337	1918, October 7
1338	1919, September 26
1339	1920, September 15*
1340	1921, September 4
1341	1922, August 24
1342	1923, August 14
1343	1924, August 2*
1344	1925, July 22
1345	1926, July 12
1346	1927, July 1
1347	1928, June 20*
1348	1929, June 9
1349	1930, May 29
1350	1931, May 19
1351	1932, May 7*
1352	1933, April 26
1353	1934, April 16
1354	1935, April 5
1355	1936, March 24*
1356	1937, March 14
1357	1938, March 3
1358	1939, February 21
1359	1940, February 10*

AH Hejira	AD Christian Date
1360	1941, January 29
1361	1942, January 19
1362	1943, January 8
1363	1943, December 28
1364	1944, December 17*
1365	1945, December 6
1366	1946, November 25
1367	1947, November 15
1368	1948, November 3*
1369	1949, October 24
1370	1950, October 13
1371	1951, October 2
1372	1952, September 21*
1373	1953, September 10
1374	1954, August 30
1375	1955, August 20
1376	1956, August 8*
1377	1957, July 29
1378	1958, July 18
1379	1959, July 7
1380	1960, June 25*
1381	1961, June 14
1382	1962, June 4
1383	1963, May 25
1384	1964, May 13*
1385	1965, May 2
1386	1966, April 22
1387	1967, April 11
1388	1968, March 31*
1389	1969, march 20
1390	1970, March 9
1391	1971, February 27
1392	1972, February 16*
1393	1973, February 4
1394	1974, January 25
1395	1975, January 14
1396	1976, January 3*
1397	1976, December 23*
1398	1977, December 12
1399	1978, December 2
1400	1979, November 21
1401	1980, November 9*
1402	1981, October 30
1403	1982, October 19
1404	1984, October 8
1405	1984, September 27*
1406	1985, September 16
1407	1986, September 6
1409	1987, August 26
1409	1988, August 14*
1410	1989, August 3
1411	1990, July 24
1412	1991, July 13
1413	1992, July 2*
1414	1993, June 21
1415	1994, June 10
1416	1995, May 31
1417	1996, May 19*
1418	1997, May 9
1419	1998, April 28
1420	1999, April 17
1421	2000, April 6*
1422	2001, March 26
1423	2002, March 15
1424	2003, March 5
1425	2004, February 22*
1426	2005, February 10
1427	2006, January 31
1428	2007, January 20
1429	2008, January 10*
1430	2008, December 29
1431	2009, December 18
1432	2010, December 8
1433	2011, November 27*
1434	2012, November 15
1435	2013, November 5
1436	2014, October 25
1437	2015, October 15*
1438	2016, October 3
1439	2017, September 22
1440	2018, September 12
1441	2019, September 11*
1442	2020, August 20
1443	2021, August 10
1444	2022, July 30
1445	2023, July 19*
1446	2024, July 8
1447	2025, June 27
1448	2026, June 17
1449	2027, June 6*
1450	2028, May25

FOREIGN EXCHANGE TABLE

The latest foreign exchange rates below apply to trade with banks in the country of origin. The left column shows the number of units per U.S. dollar at the official rate. The right column shows the number of units per dollar at the free market rate.

Country	Official #/$	Market #/$
Afghanistan (New Afghani)	49.6	–
Albania (Lek)	93	–
Algeria (Dinar)	69	–
Andorra uses Euro	.757	–
Angola (Readjust Kwanza)	80	–
Anguilla uses E.C. Dollar	2.7	–
Antigua uses E.C. Dollar	2.7	–
Argentina (Peso)	3.06	–
Armenia (Dram)	365	–
Aruba (Florin)	1.79	–
Australia (Dollar)	1.273	–
Austria (Euro)	.757	–
Azerbaijan (Manat)	4,600	–
Bahamas (Dollar)	1.0	–
Bahrain Is. (Dinar)	.377	–
Bangladesh (Taka)	70	–
Barbados (Dollar)	2.0	–
Belarus (Ruble)	2,140	–
Belgium (Euro)	.757	–
Belize (Dollar)	1.97	–
Benin uses CFA Franc West	490	–
Bermuda (Dollar)	1.0	–
Bhutan (Ngultrum)	45	–
Bolivia (Boliviano)	7.99	–
Bosnia-Herzegovina (Conv. marka)	1.47	–
Botswana (Pula)	6.05	–
British Virgin Islands uses U.S. Dollar	1.00	–
Brazil (Real)	2.14	–
Brunei (Dollar)	1.54	–
Bulgaria (Lev)	1.47	–
Burkina Faso uses CFA Fr.West	490	–
Burma (Kyat)	6.42	1,250
Burundi (Franc)	1,040	–
Cambodia (Riel)	4,050	–
Cameroon uses CFA Franc Central	490	–
Canada (Dollar)	1.149	–
Cape Verde (Escudo)	83.1	–
Cayman Is.(Dollar)	0.82	–
Central African Rep.	490	–
CFA Franc Central	490	–
CFA Franc West	490	–
CFP Franc	90	–
Chad uses CFA Franc Central	490	–
Chile (Peso)	525	–
China, P.R. (Renminbi Yuan)	7.825	–
Colombia (Peso)	2,280	–
Comoros (Franc)	370	–
Congo uses CFA Franc Central	490	–
Congo-Dem.Rep. (Congolese Franc)	490	–
Cook Islands (Dollar)	1.73	–
Costa Rica (Colon)	517	–
Croatia (Kuna)	5.74	–
Cuba (Peso)	1.00	27.00
Cyprus (Pound)	.43	–
Czech Republic (Koruna)	21.1	–
Denmark (Danish Krone)	5.65	–
Djibouti (Franc)	178	–
Dominica uses E.C. Dollar	2.7	–
Dominican Republic (Peso)	32.8	–
East Caribbean (Dollar)	2.7	–
Ecuador uses U.S. Dollar		
Egypt (Pound)	5.72	–
El Salvador (U.S. Dollar)	1.00	–
England (Sterling Pound)	.512	–
Equatorial Guinea uses CFA Franc Central	490	–
Eritrea (Nafka)	15	–
Estonia (Kroon)	11.9	–
Ethiopia (Birr)	8.75	–
Euro	.757	–
Falkland Is. (Pound)	.512	–
Faroe Islands (Krona)	5.65	–
Fiji Islands (Dollar)	1.67	–
Finland (Euro)	.757	–
France (Euro)	.757	–
French Polynesia uses CFP Franc	90	–
Gabon (CFA Franc)	490	–
Gambia (Dalasi)	28	–
Georgia (Lari)	1.73	–
Germany (Euro)	.757	–
Ghana (Cedi)	9,200	–
Gibraltar (Pound)	.512	–
Greece (Euro)	.757	–
Greenland uses Danish Krone	5.65	–
Grenada uses E.C. Dollar	2.7	–
Guatemala (Quetzal)	7.63	–
Guernsey uses Sterling Pound	.512	–
Guinea Bissau (CFA Franc)	490	–
Guinea Conakry (Franc)	5,550	–
Guyana (Dollar)	200	–
Haiti (Gourde)	38.9	–
Honduras (Lempira)	18.9	–
Hong Kong (Dollar)	7.773	–
Hungary (Forint)	195	–
Iceland (Krona)	69.5	–
India (Rupee)	44.7	–
Indonesia (Rupiah)	9,075	–
Iran (Rial)	9,230	–
Iraq (Dinar)	1,425	–
Ireland (Euro)	.757	–
Isle of Man uses Sterling Pound	.512	–
Israel (New Sheqalim)	4.19	–
Italy (Euro)	.757	–
Ivory Coast uses CFA Franc West	490	–
Jamaica (Dollar)	67	–
Japan (Yen)	116.3	–
Jersey uses Sterling Pound	.512	–
Jordan (Dinar)	.71	–
Kazakhstan (Tenge)	130	–
Kenya (Shilling)	70	–
Kiribati uses Australian Dollar	1.273	–
Korea-PDR (Won)	2.2	500
Korea-Rep. (Won)	920	–
Kuwait (Dinar)	.289	–
Kyrgyzstan (Som)	39	–
Laos (Kip)	9720	–
Latvia (Lats)	.53	–
Lebanon (Pound)	1,510	–
Lesotho (Maloti)	7.09	–
Liberia (Dollar)	53.3	–
Libya (Dinar)	1.27	–
Liechtenstein uses Swiss Franc	1.205	–
Lithuania (Litas)	2.62	–
Luxembourg (Euro)	.757	–
Macao (Pataca)	8.0	–
Macedonia (New Denar)	46	–
Madagascar (Franc)	2,040	–
Malawi (Kwacha)	140	–
Malaysia (Ringgit)	3.55	–
Maldives (Rufiya)	12.8	–
Mali uses CFA Franc West	490	–
Malta (Lira)	3.1	–
Marshall Islands uses U.S.Dollar		
Mauritania (Ouguiya)	270	–
Mauritius (Rupee)	32.5	–
Mexico (Peso)	10.82	–
Moldova (Leu)	13.1	–
Monaco uses Euro	.757	–
Mongolia (Tugrik)	1,165	–
Montenegro uses Euro	.757	–
Montserrat uses E.C. Dollar	2.7	–
Morocco (Dirham)	8.44	–
Mozambique (New Metical)	26.3	–
Myanmar (Burma) (Kyat)	6.42	1,250
Namibia (Rand)	7.09	–
Nauru uses Australian Dollar	1.456	–
Nepal (Rupee)	71.6	–
Netherlands (Euro)	.757	–
Netherlands Antilles (Gulden)	1.79	–
New Caledonia uses CFP Franc	90	–
New Zealand (Dollar)	1.493	–
Nicaragua (Cordoba Oro)	17.9	–
Niger uses CFA Franc West	490	–
Nigeria (Naira)	128	–
Northern Ireland uses Sterling Pound	.512	–
Norway (Krone)	6.16	–
Oman (Rial)	.385	–
Pakistan (Rupee)	60.9	–
Palau uses U.S.Dollar		
Panama (Balboa) uses U.S.Dollar		
Papua New Guinea (Kina)	3.02	–
Paraguay (Guarani)	5,400	–
Peru (Nuevo Sol)	3.21	–
Philippines (Peso)	50	–
Poland (Zloty)	2.9	–
Portugal (Euro)	.757	–
Qatar (Riyal)	3.64	–
Romania (New Leu)	2.6	–
Russia (New Ruble)	26.3	–
Rwanda (Franc)	550	–
St. Helena (Pound)	.512	–
St. Kitts uses E.C. Dollar	2.7	–
St. Lucia uses E.C. Dollar	2.7	–
St. Vincent uses E.C. Dollar	2.7	–
San Marino uses Euro	.757	–
Sao Tome e Principe (Dobra)	6,780	–
Saudi Arabia (Riyal)	3.75	–
Scotland uses Sterling Pound	.512	–
Senegal uses CFA Franc West	490	–
Serbia (Dinar)	59.9	–
Seychelles (Rupee)	5.59	6.40
Sierra Leone (Leone)	2,990	–
Singapore (Dollar)	1.55	–
Slovakia (Sk. Koruna)	26.8	–
Slovenia (Tolar)	180	–
Solomon Is.(Dollar)	7.63	–
Somalia (Shilling)	1,370	–
Somaliland (Somali Shilling)	1,800	4,000
South Africa (Rand)	7.09	–
Spain (Euro)	.757	–
Sri Lanka (Rupee)	110	–
Sudan (Dinar)	200	300
Surinam (Dollar)	2.75	–
Swaziland (Lilangeni)	7.09	–
Sweden (Krona)	6.87	–
Switzerland (Franc)	1.205	–
Syria (Pound)	52.2	–
Taiwan (NT Dollar)	32.4	–
Tajikistan (Somoni)	3.40	–
Tanzania (Shilling)	1,280	–
Thailand (Baht)	35.5	–
Togo uses CFA Franc West	490	–
Tonga (Pa'anga)	1.99	–
Transdniestra (Ruble)	6.51	–
Trinidad & Tobago (Dollar)	6.28	–
Tunisia (Dinar)	1.3	–
Turkey (New Lira)	1.43	–
Turkmenistan (Manat)	5,200	–
Turks & Caicos uses U.S. Dollar		
Tuvalu uses Australian Dollar	1.273	–
Uganda (Shilling)	1,800	–
Ukraine (Hryvnia)	5.03	–
United Arab Emirates (Dirham)	3.673	–
Uruguay (Peso Uruguayo)	24.3	–
Uzbekistan (Sum)	1,235	–
Vanuatu (Vatu)	106	–
Vatican City uses Euro	.757	–
Venezuela (Bolivar)	2,150	2,300
Vietnam (Dong)	16,050	–
Western Samoa (Tala)	2.66	–
Yemen (Rial)	198	–
Zambia (Kwacha)	4,050	–
Zimbabwe (revalued Dollar)	250	–

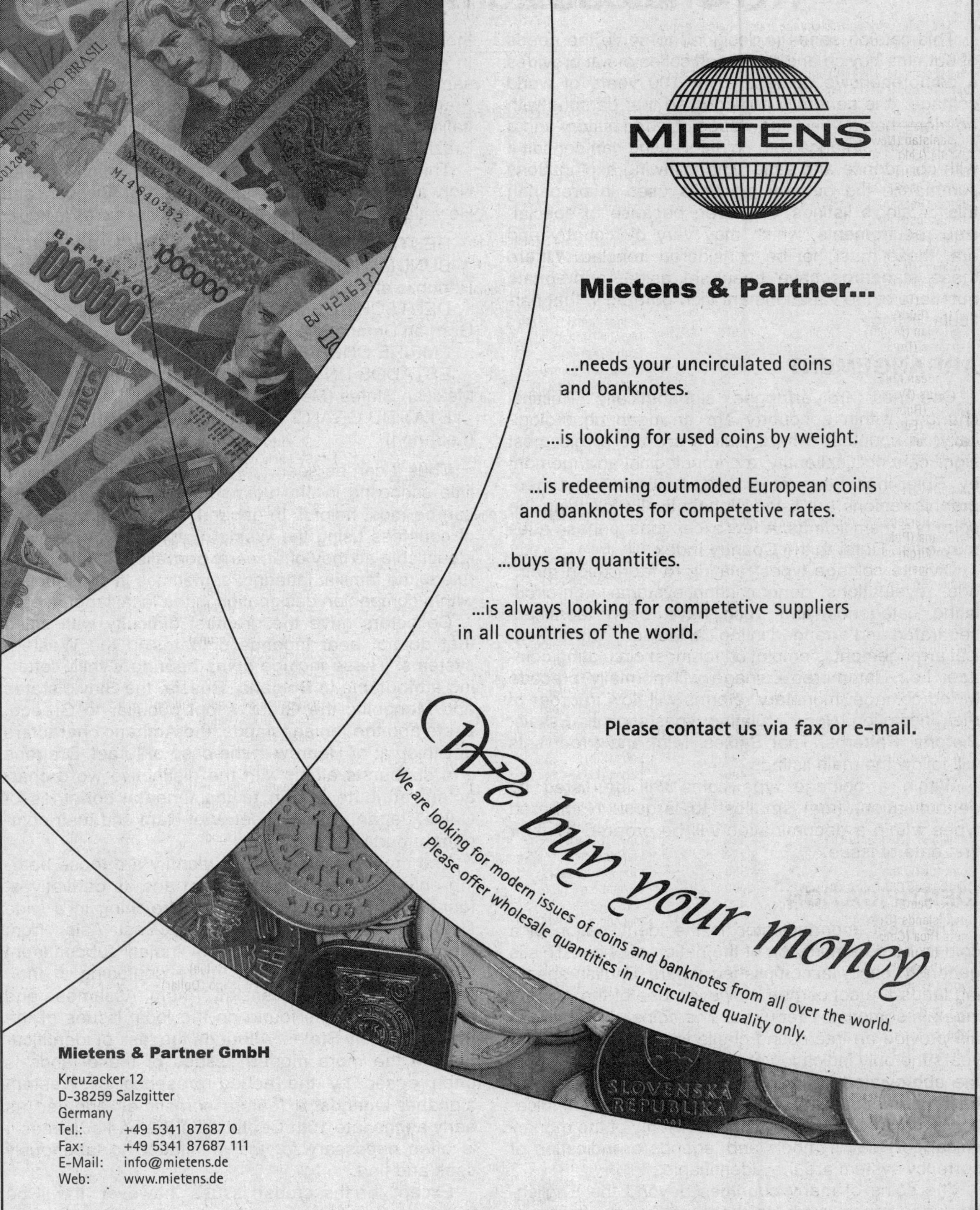
MIETENS
Mietens & Partner...
...needs your uncirculated coins
and banknotes.
...is looking for used coins by weight.
...is redeeming outmoded European coins
and banknotes for competetive rates.
...buys any quantities.
...is always looking for competetive suppliers
in all countries of the world.
Please contact us via fax or e-mail.
We buy your money
We are looking for modern issues of coins and banknotes from all over the world.
Please offer wholesale quantities in uncirculated quality only.
Mietens & Partner GmbH
Kreuzacker 12
D-38259 Salzgitter
Germany
Tel.: +49 5341 87687 0
Fax: +49 5341 87687 111
E-Mail: info@mietens.de
Web: www.mietens.de

HOW TO USE THIS CATALOG

This catalog series is designed to serve the needs of both the novice and advanced collectors. It provides a comprehensive guide to over 100 years of world coinage. It is generally arranged so that persons with no more than a basic knowledge of world history and a casual acquaintance with coin collecting can consult it with confidence and ease. The following explanations summarize the general practices used in preparing this catalog's listings. However, because of specialized requirements, which may vary by country and era, these must not be considered ironclad. Where these standards have been set aside, appropriate notations of the variations are incorporated in that particular listing.

ARRANGEMENT

Countries are arranged alphabetically. Political changes within a country are arranged chronologically. In countries where Rulers are the single most significant political entity, a chronological arrangement by Ruler has been employed. Distinctive sub-geographic regions are listed alphabetically following the country's main listings. A few exceptions to these rules may exist. Refer to the Country Index.

Diverse coinage types relating to fabrication methods, revaluations, denomination systems, non-circulating categories and such have been identified, separated and arranged in logical fashion. Chronological arrangement is employed for most circulating coinage, i.e., Hammered coinage will normally precede Milled coinage, monetary reforms will flow in order of their institution. Non-circulating types such as Essais, Pieforts, Patterns, Trial Strikes, Mint and Proof sets will follow the main listings.

Within a coinage type coins will be listed by denomination, from smallest to largest. Numbered types within a denomination will be ordered by their first date of issue.

IDENTIFICATION

The most important step in the identification of a coin is the determination of the nation of origin. This is generally easily accomplished where English-speaking lands are concerned, however, use of the country index is sometimes required. The coins of Great Britain provide an interesting challenge. For hundreds of years the only indication of the country of origin was in the abbreviated Latin legends. In recent times there have been occasions when there has been no indication of origin. Only through the familiarity of the monarchical portraits, symbols and legends or indication of currency system are they identifiable.

The coins of many countries beyond the English-language realm, such as those of French, Italian or Spanish heritage, are also quite easy to identify through reference to their legends, which appear in the national languages based on Western alphabets. In many instances the name is spelled exactly the same in English as in the national language, such as France; while in other cases it varies only slightly, like Italia for Italy, Belgique or Belgie for Belgium, Brasil for Brazil and Danmark for Denmark.

This is not always the case, however, as in Norge for Norway, Espana for Spain, Sverige for Sweden and Helvetia for Switzerland. Some other examples include:

DEUTSCHES REICH - Germany 1873-1945

BUNDESREPUBLIC DEUTSCHLAND - Federal Republic of Germany.

DEUTSCHE DEMOKRATISCHE REPUBLIK - German Democratic Republic.

EMPIRE CHERIFIEN MAROC - Morocco.

ESTADOS UNIDOS MEXICANOS - United Mexican States (Mexico).

ETAT DU GRAND LIBAN - State of Great Lebanon (Lebanon).

Thus it can be seen there are instances in which a little schooling in the rudiments of foreign languages can be most helpful. In general, colonial possessions of countries using the Western alphabet are similarly identifiable as they often carry portraits of their current rulers, the familiar lettering, sometimes in combination with a companion designation in the local language.

Collectors have the greatest difficulty with coins that do not bear legends or dates in the Western systems. These include coins bearing Cyrillic lettering attributable to Bulgaria, Russia, the Slavic states and Mongolia; the Greek script peculiar to Greece, Crete and the Ionian Islands; the Amharic characters of Ethiopia; or Hebrew in the case of Israel. Dragons and sunbursts along with the distinctive word characters attribute a coin to the Oriental countries of China, Japan, Korea, Tibet, Viet Nam and their component parts.

The most difficult coins to identify are those bearing only Persian or Arabic script and its derivatives, found on the issues of nations stretching in a wide swath across North Africa and East Asia, from Morocco to Indonesia, and the Indian subcontinent coinages which surely are more confusing in their vast array of Nagari, Sanskrit, Ahom, Assamese and other local dialects found on the local issues of the Indian Princely States. Although the task of identification on the more modern issues of these lands is often eased by the added presence of Western alphabet legends, a feature sometimes adopted as early as the late 19th Century, for the earlier pieces it is often necessary for the uninitiated to laboriously seek and find.

Except for the cruder issues, however, it will be found that certain characteristics and symbols featured in addition to the predominant legends are typical on coins from a given country or group of countries. The toughra monogram, for instance, occurs on some of the coins of Afghanistan, Egypt, the Sudan, Pakistan, Turkey and other areas of the late Ottoman Empire. A predominant design feature on the coins of Nepal is the trident; while neighboring Tibet features a lotus blossom or lion on many of their issues.

To assist in identification of the more difficult coins, we have assembled the Instant Identifier and Monogram sections presented on the following pages. They are designed to provide a point of beginning for collectors by allowing them to compare unidentified coins with photographic details from typical issues.

We also suggest reference to the Index of Coin Denominations presented here and also the comprehensive Country Index, where the inscription will be found listed just as it appears on the coin for nations using the Western alphabet.

DATING

Coin dating is the final basic attribution consideration. Here, the problem can be more difficult because the reading of a coin date is subject not only to the vagaries of numeric styling, but to calendar variations caused by the observance of various religious eras or regal periods from country to country, or even within a country. Here again, with the exception of the sphere from North Africa through the Orient, it will be found that most countries rely on Western date numerals and Christian (AD) era reckoning, although in a few instances, coin dating has been tied to the year of a reign or government. The Vatican, for example dates its coinage according to the year of reign of the current pope, in addition to the Christian-era date.

Countries in the Arabic sphere generally date their coins to the Muslim era (AH), which commenced on July 16, 622 AD (Julian calendar), when the prophet Mohammed fled from Mecca to Medina. As their calendar is reckoned by the lunar year of 354 days, which is about three percent (precisely 2.98%) shorter than the Christian year, a formula is required to convert AH dating to its Western equivalent. To convert an AH date to the approximate AD date, subtract three percent of the AH date (round to the closest whole number) from the AH date and add 622. A chart converting all AH years from 1010 (July 2, 1601) to 1450 (May 25, 2028) may be found elsewhere in the catalog under the name Hejira Date Chart.

The Muslim calendar is not always based on the lunar year (AH), however, causing some confusion, particularly in Afghanistan and Iran, where a calendar based on the solar year (SH) was introduced around 1920. These dates can be converted to AD by simply adding 621. In 1976 the government of Iran implemented a new solar calendar based on the foundation of the Iranian monarchy in 559 BC. The first year observed on the new calendar was 2535 (MS), which commenced March 20, 1976. A reversion to the traditional SH dating standard occurred a few years later.

Several different eras of reckoning, including Christian and Muslim (AH), have been used to date coins of the Indian subcontinent. The two basic systems are the Vikrama Samvat (VS), which dates from Oct. 18, 58 BC, and the Saka era, the origin of which is reckoned from March 3, 78 AD. Dating according to both eras appears on various coins of the area.

Coins of Thailand (Siam) are found dated by three different eras. The most predominant is the Buddhist era (BE), which originated in 543 BC. Next is the Bangkok or Ratanakosindsok (RS) era, dating from 1781 AD; followed by the Chula-Sakarat (CS) era, dating from 638 AD. The latter era originated in Burma and is used on that country's coins.

Other calendars include that of the Ethiopian era (EE), which commenced seven years, eight months after AD dating; and that of the Jewish people, which commenced on Oct. 7, 3761 BC. Korea claims a legendary dating from 2333 BC, which is acknowledged in some of its coin dating. Some coin issues of the Indonesian area carry dates determined by the Javanese Aji Saka era (AS), a calendar of 354 days (100 Javanese years equal 97 Christian or Gregorian calendar years), which can be matched to AD dating by comparing it to AH dating.

The following table indicates the year dating for the various eras, which correspond to 2007 in Christian calendar reckoning, but it must be remembered that there are overlaps between the eras in some instances.

Christian era (AD)	-2007
Muslim era (AH)	-AH1428
Solar year (SH)	-SH1385
Monarchic Solar era (MS)	-MS2566
Vikrama Samvat (VS)	-VS2064
Saka era (SE)	-SE1929
Buddhist era (BE)	-BE2550
Bangkok era (RS)	-RS226
Chula-Sakarat era (CS)	-CS1369
Ethiopian era (EE)	-EE2000
Korean era	-4340
Javanese Aji Saka era (AS)	-AS1940
Fasli era (FE)	-FE1417
Jewish era (JE)	-JE5767
Roman	-MMVII

Coins of Asian origin - principally Japan, Korea, China, Turkestan and Tibet and some modern gold issues of Turkey - are generally dated to the year of the government, dynasty, reign or cyclic eras, with the dates indicated in Asian characters which usually read from right to left. In recent years, however, some dating has been according to the Christian calendar and in Western numerals. In Japan, Asian character dating was reversed to read from left to right in Showa year 23 (1948 AD).

More detailed guides to less prevalent coin dating systems, which are strictly local in nature, are presented with the appropriate listings.

Some coins carry dates according to both locally observed and Christian eras. This is particularly true in the Arabic world, where the Hejira date may be indicated in Arabic numerals and the Christian date in Western numerals, or both dates in either form.

The date actually carried on a given coin is generally cataloged here in the first column (Date) to the right of the catalog number. If this date is by a non-Christian dating system, such as 'AH' (Muslim), the Christian equivalent date will appear in parentheses(), for example AH1336(1917). Dates listed alone in the date column which do not actually appear on a given coin, or dates which are known, but do not appear on the coin, are generally enclosed by parentheses with 'ND' at the left, for example ND(1926).

Timing differentials between some era of reckoning, particularly the 354-day Mohammedan and 365-day Christian years, cause situations whereby coins which carry dates for both eras exist bearing two year dates from one calendar combined with a single date from another.

Countermarked Coinage is presented with both 'Countermark Date' and 'Host Coin' date for each type. Actual date representation follows the rules outlined above.

NUMBERING SYSTEM

Some catalog numbers assigned in this volume are based on established references. This practice has been observed for two reasons: First, when world coins are listed chronologically they are basically self-cataloging; second, there was no need to confuse collectors with totally new numeric designations where appropriate systems already existed. As time progressed we found many of these established systems incomplete and inadequate and have now replaced many with new KM numbers. When numbers change appropriate cross-referencing has been provided.

Some of the coins listed in this catalog are identified or cross-referenced by numbers assigned by R.S. Yeoman (Y#), or slight adaptations thereof, in his Modern World Coins, and Current Coins of the World. For the pre-Yeoman dated issues, the numbers assigned by William D. Craig (C#) in his Coins of the World (1750-1850 period), 3rd edition, have generally been applied.

In some countries, listings are cross-referenced to Robert Friedberg's (FR#) Gold Coins of the World or Coins of the British World. Major Fred Pridmore's (P#) studies of British colonial coinage are also referenced, as are W.H. Valentine's (V#) references on the Modern Copper Coins of the Mohammedan States. Coins issued under the Chinese sphere of influence are assigned numbers from E. Kann's (K#) Illustrated Catalog of Chinese Coins and T.K. Hsu's (Su) work of similar title. In most cases, these cross-reference numbers are presented in the descriptive text for each type.

DENOMINATIONS

The second basic consideration to be met in the attribution of a coin is the determination of denomination. Since denominations are usually expressed in numeric rather than word form on a coin, this is usually quite easily accomplished on coins from nations which use Western numerals, except in those instances where issues are devoid of any mention of face value, and denomination must be attributed by size, metallic composition or weight. Coins listed in this volume are generally illustrated in actual size. Where size is critical to proper attribution, the coin's millimeter size is indicated.

The sphere of countries stretching from North Africa through the Orient, on which numeric symbols generally unfamiliar to Westerners are employed, often provide the collector with a much greater challenge. This is particularly true on nearly all pre-20th Century issues. On some of the more modern issues and increasingly so as the years progress, Western-style numerals usually presented in combination with the local numeric system are becoming more commonplace on these coins.

Determination of a coin's currency system can also be valuable in attributing the issue to its country of origin. A comprehensive alphabetical index of currency names, applicable to the countries as cataloged in this volume, with all individual nations of use for each, is presented in this section.

The included table of Standard International Numeral Systems presents charts of the basic numeric designations found on coins of non-Western origin. Although denomination numerals are generally prominently displayed on coins, it must be remembered that these are general representations of characters, which individual coin engravers may have rendered in widely varying styles. Where numeric or script denominations designation forms peculiar to a given coin or country apply, such as the script used on some Persian (Iranian) issues. They are so indicated or illustrated in conjunction with the appropriate listings.

MINTAGES

Quantities minted of each date are indicated where that information is available, generally stated in millions or rounded off to the nearest 10,000 pieces when more exact figures are not available. On quantities of a few thousand or less, actual mintages are generally indicated. For combined mintage figures the abbreviation "Inc. Above" means Included Above, while "Inc. Below" means Included Below. "Est." beside a mintage figure indicates the number given is an estimate or mintage limit.

MINT AND PRIVY MARKS

The presence of distinctive, but frequently inconspicuously placed, mintmarks indicates the mint of issue for many of the coins listed in this catalog. An appropriate designation in the date listings notes the presence, if any, of a mint mark on a particular coin type by incorporating the letter or letters of the mint mark adjoining the date, i.e., 1950D or 1927R.

The presence of mint and/or mintmaster's privy marks on a coin in non-letter form is indicated by incorporating the mint letter in lower case within parentheses adjoining the date; i.e. 1927(a). The corresponding mark is illustrated or identified in the introduction of the country.

In countries such as France and Mexico, where many mints may be producing like coinage in the same denomination during the same time period, divisions by mint have been employed. In these cases the mint mark may appear next to the individual date listings and/or the mint name or mint mark may be listed in the Note field of the type description.

Where listings incorporate mintmaster initials, they are always presented in capital letters separated from the date by one character space; i.e., 1850 MF. The different mintmark and mintmaster letters found on the coins of any country, state or city of issue are always shown at the beginning of listings.

METALS

Each numbered type listing will contain a description of the coins metallic content. The traditional coinage metals and their symbolic chemical abbreviations sometimes used in this catalog are:

Platinum - (PT)	Copper - (Cu)
Gold - (Au)	Brass -
Silver - (Ag)	Copper-nickel- (CN)
Billion -	Lead - (Pb)
Nickel - (Ni)	Steel -
Zinc - (Zn)	Tin - (Sn)
Bronze - (Ae)	Aluminum - (Al)

During the 18th and 19th centuries, most of the world's coins were struck of copper or bronze, silver and gold. Commencing in the early years of the 20th century, however, numerous new coinage metals, primarily non-precious metal alloys, were introduced. Gold has not been widely used for circulation coinages since World War I, although silver remained a popular coinage metal in most parts of the world until after World War II. With the disappearance of silver for circulation coinage, numerous additional compositions were introduced to coinage applications.

Most recent is the development of clad or plated planchets in order to maintain circulation life and extend the life of a set of production dies as used in the production of the copper-nickel clad copper 50 centesimos of Panama or in the latter case to reduce production costs of the planchets and yet provide a coin quite similar in appearance to its predecessor as in the case of the copper plated zinc core United States 1983 cent.

Modern commemorative coins have employed still more unusual methods such as bimetallic coins, color applications and precious metal or gem inlays.

OFF-METAL STRIKES

Off-metal strikes previously designated by "(OMS)" which also included the wide range of error coinage struck in other than their officially authorized compositions have been incorporated into Pattern listings along with special issues, which were struck for presentation or other reasons.

Collectors of Germanic coinage may be familiar with the term "Abschlag" which quickly identifies similar types of coinage.

PRECIOUS METAL WEIGHTS

Listings of weight, fineness and actual silver (ASW), gold (AGW), platinum or palladium (APW) content of most machine-struck silver, gold, platinum and palladium coins are provided in this edition. This information will be found incorporated in each separate type listing, along with other data related to the coin.

The ASW, AGW and APW figures were determined by multiplying the gross weight of a given coin by its known or tested fineness and converting the resulting gram or grain weight to troy ounces, rounded to the nearest ten-thousandth of an ounce. A silver coin with a 24.25-gram weight and .875 fineness for example, would have a fine weight of approximately 21.2188 grams, or a .6822 ASW, a factor that can be used to accurately determine the intrinsic value for multiple examples.

The ASW, AGW or APW figure can be multiplied by the spot price of each precious metal to determine the current intrinsic value of any coin accompanied by these designations.

Coin weights are indicated in grams (abbreviated "g") along with fineness where the information is of value in differentiating between types. These weights are based on 31.103 grams per troy (scientific) ounce, as opposed to the avoirdupois (commercial) standard of 28.35 grams. Actual coin weights are generally shown in hundredths or thousands of a gram; i.e., 0.500 SILVER 2.9200g.WEIGHTS AND FINENESSES

As the silver and gold bullion markets have advanced and declined sharply over the years, the fineness and total precious metal content of coins has become especially significant where bullion coins - issues which trade on the basis of their intrinsic metallic content rather than numismatic value - are concerned. In many instances, such issues have become worth more in bullion form than their nominal collector values or denominations indicate.

Establishing the weight of a coin can also be valuable for determining its denomination. Actual weight is also necessary to ascertain the specific gravity of the coin's metallic content, an important factor in determining authenticity.

TROY WEIGHT STANDARDS

24 Grains = 1 Pennyweight
480 Grains = 1 Ounce
31.103 Grams = 1 Ounce

UNIFORM WEIGHTS

15.432 Grains = 1 Gram
0.0648 Gram = 1 Grain

AVOIRDUPOIS STANDARDS

27-11/32 Grains = 11 Dram
437-1/2 Grains = 1 Ounce
28.350 Grams = 1 Ounce

BULLION VALUE

The simplest method for determining the bullion value of a precious metal coin is to multiply the actual precious metal weight by the current spot price for that metal. Using the example above, a silver coin with a .6822 actual silver weight (ASW) would have an intrinsic value of $6.65 when the spot price of silver is $9.75. If the spot price of silver rose to $11.00 that same coins intrinsic value would rise to $7.50.

Valuations for most of the silver, gold, platinum and palladium coins listed in this edition are based on assumed market values of **$9.75** per troy ounce for silver, **$550** for gold, **$1000** for platinum, and **$285** for palladium. To arrive at accurate current market indications for these issues, increase or decrease the valuations appropriately based on any variations in these indicated levels.

HOMELAND TYPES

Hòmeland types are coins which colonial powers used in a colony, but do not bear that location's name. In some cases they were legal tender in the homeland, in others not. They are listed under the homeland and cross-referenced at the colony listing.

COUNTERMARKS/COUNTERSTAMPS

There is some confusion among collectors over the terms "countermark" and "counterstamp" when applied to a coin bearing an additional mark or change of design and/or denomination.

To clarify, a countermark might be considered similar to the "hall mark" applied to a piece of silverware, by which a silversmith assured the quality of the piece. In the same way, a countermark assures the quality of the coin on which it is placed, as, for example, when the royal crown of England was countermarked (punched into) on segmented Spanish reales, allowing them to circulate in commerce in the British West Indies. An additional countermark indicating the new denomination may also be encountered on these coins.

Countermarks are generally applied singularly and in most cases indiscriminately on either side of the "host" coin.

Counterstamped coins are more extensively altered. The counterstamping is done with a set of dies, rather than a hand punch. The coin being counterstamped is placed between the new dies and struck as if it were a blank planchet as found with the Manila 8 reales issue of the Philippines. A more unusual application where the counterstamp dies were smaller than the host coin in the revalidated 50 centimos and 1 colon of Costa Rica issued in 1923.

Coin Alignment

Medal Alignment

COIN vs MEDAL ALIGNMENT

Some coins are struck with obverse and reverse aligned at a rotation of 180 degrees from each other. When a coin is held for vertical viewing with the obverse design aligned upright and the index finger and thumb at the top and bottom, upon rotation from left to right for viewing the reverse, the latter will be upside down. Such alignment is called "coin rotation." Other coins are struck with the obverse and reverse designs mated on an alignment of zero or 360 degrees. If such an example is held and rotated as described, the reverse will appear upright. This is the alignment, which is generally observed in the striking of medals, and for that reason coins produced in this manner are considered struck in "medal rotation". In some instances, often through error, certain coin issues have been struck to both alignment standards, creating interesting collectible varieties, which will be found noted in some listings. In addition, some countries are now producing coins with other designated obverse to reverse alignments which are considered standard for this type.

PHOTOGRAPHS

To assist the reader in coin identification, every effort has been made to present actual size photographs of every coinage type listed. Obverse and reverse are illustrated, except when a change in design is restricted to one side, and the coin has a diameter of 39mm or larger, in which case only the side required for identification of the type is generally illustrated. All coins up to 60mm are illustrated actual size, to the nearest 1/2mm up to 25mm, and to the nearest 1mm thereafter. Coins larger than 60mm diameter are illustrated in reduced size, with the actual size noted in the descriptive text block. Where slight change in size is important to coin type identification, actual millimeter measurements are stated.

TRADE COINS

From approximately 1750-1940, a number of nations, particularly European colonial powers and commercial traders, minted trade coins to facilitate commerce with the local populace of Africa, the Arab countries, the Indian subcontinental, Southeast Asia and the Far East. Such coins generally circulated at a value based on the weight and fineness of their silver or gold content, rather than their stated denomination. Examples include the sovereigns of Great Britain and the gold ducat issues of Austria, Hungary and the Netherlands. Trade coinage will sometimes be found listed at the end of the domestic issues.

VALUATIONS

Values quoted in this catalog represent the current market and are compiled from recommendations provided and verified through various source documents and specialized consultants. It should be stressed, however, that this book is intended to serve only as an aid for evaluating coins, actual market conditions are constantly changing and additional influences, such as particularly strong local demand for certain coin series, fluctuation of international exchange rates, changes in spot price of precious metals and worldwide collection patterns must also be considered. Publication of this catalog is not intended as a solicitation by the publisher, editors or contributors to buy or sell the coins listed at the prices indicated.

All valuations are stated in U.S. dollars, based on careful assessment of the varied international collector market. Valuations for coins priced below $100.00 are generally stated in full amounts - i.e. 37.50 or 95.00 - while valuations at or above that figure are rounded off in even dollars - i.e. $125.00 is expressed 125. A comma is added to indicate thousands of dollars in value.

For the convenience of overseas collectors and for U.S. collectors doing business with overseas dealers, the base exchange rate for the national currencies of approximately 180 countries are presented in the Foreign Exchange Table.

It should be noted that when particularly select uncirculated or proof-like examples of uncirculated coins become available they can be expected to command proportionately high premiums. Such examples in reference to choice Germanic Thalers are referred to as "erst schlage" or first strikes.

MEDALLIC ISSUES

Medallic issues are similar to coin-type issues and can generally be identified as commemoratives produced to the country's established coinage standards but without the usual indicator of denomination. These pieces sometimes feature designs adapted from the country's regular issue or commemorative coinage, and occassionally have been issued in conjunction with related coinage issues. Medallic issues, though bearing these similarites to coinage issues, are not coins and therefore are **not** listed in this catalog, but can be found in the companion catalog Unusual World Coins.

RESTRIKES, COUNTERFEITS

Deceptive restrike and counterfeit (both contemporary and modern) examples exist of some coin issues. Where possible, the existence of restrikes is noted. Warnings are also incorporated in instances where particularly deceptive counterfeits are known to exist. Collectors who are uncertain about the authenticity of a coin held in their collection, or being offered for sale, should take the precaution of having it authenticated by the American Numismatic Association Authentication Bureau, 818 N. Cascade, Colorado Springs, CO 80903. Their reasonably priced certification tests are widely accepted by collectors and dealers alike.

NON-CIRCULATING LEGAL TENDER COINS

Coins of non-circulating legal tender (NCLT) origin are individually listed and integrated by denomination into the regular listings for each country. These coins fall outside the customary definitions of coin-of-the-realm issues, but where created and sold by, or under authorization of, agencies of sovereign governments expressly for collectors. These are primarily individual coins and sets of a commemorative nature, marketed at prices substantially in excess of face value, and usually do not have counterparts released for circulation.

EDGE VARIETIES

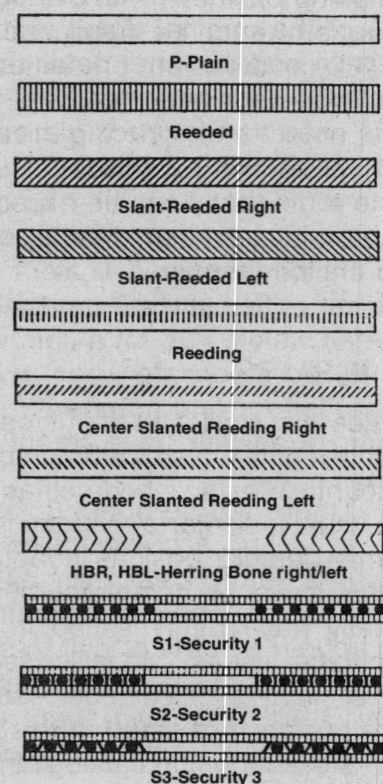

NEW ISSUES

All newly released coins dated up to the year 2000 that have been physically observed by our staff or identified by reliable sources and have been confirmed by press time have been incorporated in this edition. Exceptions exist in some countries where current date coin production lags far behind or information on current issues is less accessible.

SETS

Listings in this catalog for specimen, proof and mint sets are for official, government-produced sets. In many instances privately packaged sets also exist.

Mint Sets/Fleur de Coin Sets: Specially prepared by worldwide mints to provide banks, collectors and government dignitaries with examples of current coinage. Usually subjected to rigorous inspection to insure that top quality specimens of selected business strikes are provided. One of the most popular mint set is that given out by the monarch of Great Britain each year on Maunday Thursday. This set contains four special coins in denominations of 1, 2, 3 and 4 pence, struck in silver and contained in a little pouch. They have been given away in a special ceremony for the poor for more than two centuries.

The Paris Mint introduced polyvinyl plastic cases packed within a cardboard box for homeland and colonial Fleur de Coin sets of the 1960s. British colonial sets were issued in velvet-lined metal cases similar to those used for proof sets. For its client nations, the Franklin Mint introduced a sealed composition of cardboard and specially molded hard clear plastic protective container inserted in a soft plastic wallet. Recent discovery that soft polyvinyl packaging has proved hazardous to coins has resulted in a change to the use of hard, inert plastics for virtually all mint sets.

Some of the highest quality mint sets ever produced were those struck by the Franklin Mint during 1972-74. In many cases matte finish dies were used to strike a polished proof planchet. Later on, from 1975, sets contained highly polished, glassy-looking coins (similar to those struck by the Bombay Mint) for collectors over a period of 12 years.

Specimen Sets: Forerunners of today's proof sets. In most cases the coins were specially struck, perhaps even double struck, to produce a very soft or matte finish on the effigies and fields, along with high, sharp, "wire" rims. The finish is rather dull to the naked eye.

The original purpose of these sets was to provide VIPs, monarchs and mintmasters around the world with samples of the highest quality workmanship of a particular mint. These were usually housed in elaborate velvet-lined leather and metal cases.

Proof-like Sets are relatively new to the field of numismatics. During the mid 1950s the Royal Canadian Mint furnished the hobby with specially selected early business strike coins that exhibited some qualities similar to proof coinage. However, the "proof-like" fields are generally flawed and the edges are rounded. These pieces are not double struck. These are commonly encountered in cardboard holders, later in soft plastic or pliofilm packaging. Of late, the Royal Canadian Mint packages such sets in rigid plastic cases.

Many worldwide officially issued proof sets would in reality fall into this category upon careful examination of the quality of the coin's finish.

Another term encountered in this category is "Special Select," used to describe the crowns of the Union of South Africa and 100-schilling coins produced for collectors in the late 1970s by the Austrian Mint.

Proof Sets: This is undoubtedly among the most misused terms in the hobby, not only by collectors and dealers, but also by many of the world mints.

A true proof set must be at least double-struck on specially prepared polished planchets and struck using dies (often themselves polished) of the highest quality.

Modern-day proof quality consists of frosted effigies surrounded by absolute mirror-like fields.

Listings for proof sets in this catalog are for officially issued proof sets so designated by the issuing authority, and may or may not possess what are considered modern proof quality standards.

It is necessary for collectors to acquire the knowledge to allow them to differentiate true proof sets from would-be proof sets and proof-like sets which may be encountered.

CONDITIONS/GRADING

Wherever possible, coin valuations are given in four or five grades of preservation. For modern commemoratives, which do not circulate, only uncirculated values are usually sufficient. Proof issues are indicated by the word "Proof" next to the date, with valuation proceeded by the word "value" following the mintage. For very recent circulating coins and coins of limited value, one, two or three grade values are presented.

There are almost no grading guides for world coins. What follows is an attempt to help bridge that gap until a detailed, illustrated guide becomes available.

In grading world coins, there are two elements to look for: 1) Overall wear, and 2) loss of design details, such as strands of hair, feathers on eagles, designs on coats of arms, etc.

The age, rarity or type of a coin should not be a consideration in grading.

Grade each coin by the weaker of the two sides. This method appears to give results most nearly consistent with conservative American Numismatic Association standards for U.S. coins. Split grades, i.e., F/VF for obverse and reverse, respectively, are normally no more than one grade apart. If the two sides are more than one grade apart, the series of coins probably wears differently on each side and should then be graded by the weaker side alone.

Grade by the amount of overall wear and loss of design detail evident on each side of the coin. On coins with a moderately small design element which is prone to early wear, grade by that design alone. For example, the 5-ore (KM#554) of Sweden has a crown above the monogram on which the beads on the arches show wear most clearly. So, grade by the crown alone.

For **Brilliant Uncirculated** (BU) grades there will be no visible signs of wear or handling, even under a 30-power microscope. Full mint luster will be present. Ideally no bags marks will be evident.

For **Uncirculated** (Unc.) grades there will be no visible signs of wear or handling, even under a 30-power microscope. Bag marks may be present.

For **Almost Uncirculated** (AU), all detail will be visible. There will be wear only on the highest point of the coin. There will often be half or more of the original mint luster present.

On the **Extremely Fine** (XF or EF) coin, there will be about 95% of the original detail visible. Or, on a coin with a design with no inner detail to wear down, there will be a light wear over nearly all the coin. If a small design is used as the grading area, about 90% of the original detail will be visible. This latter rule stems from the logic that a smaller amount of detail needs to be present because a small area is being used to grade the whole coin.

The **Very Fine** (VF) coin will have about 75% of the original detail visible. Or, on a coin with no inner detail, there will be moderate wear over the entire coin. Corners of letters and numbers may be weak. A small grading area will have about 66% of the original detail.

For **Fine** (F), there will be about 50% of the original detail visible. Or, on a coin with no inner detail, there will be fairly heavy wear over all of the coin. Sides of letters will be weak. A typically uncleaned coin will often appear as dirty or dull. A small grading area will have just under 50% of the original detail.

On the **Very Good** (VG) coin, there will be about 25% of the original detail visible. There will be heavy wear on all of the coin.

The **Good** (G) coin's design will be clearly outlined but with substantial wear. Some of the larger detail may be visible. The rim may have a few weak spots of wear.

On the **About Good** (AG) coin, there will typically be only a silhouette of a large design. The rim will be worn down into the letters if any.

Strong or weak strikes, partially weak strikes, damage, corrosion, attractive or unattractive toning, dipping or cleaning should be described along with the above grades. These factors affect the quality of the coin just as do wear and loss of detail, but are easier to describe.

In the case of countermarked/counterstamped coins, the condition of the host coin will have a bearing on the end valuation. The important factor in determining the grade is the condition, clarity and completeness of the countermark itself. This is in reference to countermarks/counterstamps having raised design while being struck in a depression.

Incuse countermarks cannot be graded for wear. They are graded by the clarity and completeness including the condition of the host coin which will also have more bearing on the final grade/valuation determined.

STANDARD INTERNATIONAL GRADING TERMINOLOGY AND ABBREVIATIONS

	PROOF	UNCIRCULATED	EXTREMELY FINE	VERY FINE	FINE	VERY GOOD	GOOD	POOR
U.S. and ENGLISH SPEAKING LANDS	PRF	UNC	EF or XF	VF	F	VG	G	PR
BRAZIL	—	(1)FDC or FC	(3) S	(5) MBC	(7) BC	(8) BC/R	(9) R	UT GeG
DENMARK	M	0	01	1 +	1	1 ÷	2	3
FINLAND	00	0	01	1 +	1	1?	2	3
FRANCE	FB Flan Bruni	FDC Fleur de Coin	SUP Superbe	TTB Très très beau	TB Très beau	B Beau	TBC Très Bien Conservée	BC Bien Conservée
GERMANY	PP Polierte Platte	STG Stempelglanz	VZ Vorzüglich	SS Sehr schön	S Schön	S.G.E. Sehr gut erhalten	G.E. Gut erhalten	Gering erhalten
ITALY	FS Fondo Specchio	FDC Fior di Conio	SPL Splendido	BB Bellissimo	MB Molto Bello	B Bello	M	—
JAPAN	—	未使用	極美品	美品	並品	—	—	—
NETHERLANDS	— Proef	FDC Fleur de Coin	Pr. Prachtig	Z.f. Zeer fraai	Fr. Fraai	Z.g. Zeer goed	G	—
NORWAY	M	0	01	1 +	1	1 ÷	2	3
PORTUGAL	—	Soberba	Bela	MBC	BC	MREG	REG	MC
SPAIN	Prueba	SC	EBC	MBC	BC +	BC	RC	MC
SWEDEN	Polerad	0	01	1 +	1	1?	2	—

Sending Scanned Images by Email

We have been receiving an ever-increasing flow of scanned images from sources worldwide. Unfortunately, many of these scans could not be used due to the type of scan, or simple incompatability with our systems. We appreciate the effort it takes to produce these images and accuracy they add to the catalog listings.

Here are a few simple instructions to follow when producing these scans. We encourage you to continue sending new images or upgrades to those currently illustrated and please do not hesitate to ask questions about this process.

- Scan all images within a resolution range of 200 dpi to 300 dpi
- Size setting should be at 100%
- Scan in true 4-color
- Save images as 'jpeg' or 'tiff' and name in such a way, which clearly identifies the country of origin
- Please email with a request to confirm receipt of the attachment
- Please send images to Randy.Thern@fwpubs.com

UNITED STATES OF
FIVE CENT

LIBERTY
IN GOD WE TRUST
1954
UNITED STATES

A GUIDE TO INTERNATIONAL NUMERICS

	ENGLISH	CZECH	DANISH	DUTCH	ESPERANTO	FRENCH
1/4	one-quarter	jeden-ctvrt	én kvart	een-kwart	unu-kvar'ono	un-quart
1/2	one-half	jeden-polovieni or pul	én halv	een-half	unu-du'one	un-demi
1	one	jeden	én	een	unu	un
2	two	dve	to	twee	du	deux
3	three	tri	tre	drie	tri	trois
4	four	ctyri	fire	vier	kvar	quatre
5	five	pet	fem	vijf	kvin	cinq
6	six	sest	seks	zes	ses	six
7	seven	sedm	syv	zeven	sep	sept
8	eight	osm	otte	acht	ok	huit
9	nine	devet	ni	negen	nau	neuf
10	ten	deset	ti	tien	dek	dix
12	twelve	dvanáct	tolv	twaalf	dek du	douze
15	fifteen	patnáct	femten	vijftien	dek kvin	quinze
20	twenty	dvacet	tyve	twintig	du'dek	vingt
24	twenty-four	dvacet-ctyri	fire og tyve	twintig-vier	du'dek kvar	vingt-quatre
25	twenty-five	dvacet-pet	fem og tyve	twintig-vijf	du'dek kvin	vingt-cinq
30	thirty	tricet	tredive	dertig	tri'dek	trente
40	forty	ctyricet	fyrre	veertig	kvar'dek	quarante
50	fifty	padesát	halvtreds	vijftig	kvin'dek	cinquante
60	sixty	sedesát	tres	zestig	ses'dek	soixante
70	seventy	sedmdesát	halvfjerds	zeventig	sep'dek	soixante dix
80	eighty	osemdesát	firs	tachtig	ok'dek	quatre-vingt
90	ninety	devadesát	halvfems	negentig	nau'dek	quatre-vingt-dix
100	one hundred	jedno sto	et hundrede	een-honderd	unu-cento	un-cent
1000	thousand	tisíc	tusind	duizend	mil	mille

	GERMAN	HUNGARIAN	INDONESIAN	ITALIAN	NORWEGIAN	POLISH
1/4	ein viertel	egy-negyed	satu-suku	uno-guarto	en-fjeerdedel	jeden-c weirc
1/2	einhalb	egy-fél	satu-setengah	uno-mezzo	en-halv	jeden-polowa
1	ein	egy	satu	uno	en	jeden
2	zwei	kettö	dud	due	to	dwa
3	drei	három	tiga	tre	tre	trzy
4	vier	négy	empot	quattro	fire	cztery
5	fünf	öt	lima	cinque	fem	piec'
6	sechs	hat	enam	sei	seks	szes'c'
7	sieben	hét	tudjuh	sette	sju	siedem
8	acht	nyolc	delapan	otto	atte	osiem
9	neun	kilenc	sembilan	nove	ni	dziewiec'
10	zehn	tí z	sepuluh	dieci	ti	dziesiec'
12	zwölf	tizenketto	duabelas	dodici	tolv	dwanas' cie
15	fünfzehn	tizenöt	lima belas	quindici	femten	pietnas'cie
20	zwanzig	húsz	dua pulah	venti	tjue or tyve	dwadzies'cia
24	vierundzwanzig	húsz-négy	dua pulah-empot	venti-quattro	tjue-fire or tyve-fire	dwadzies'cia-cztery
25	fünfundzwanzig	húsz-öt	dua-pulah-lima	venti-cinque	tjue-fem or tyve-fem	dwadzies'cia-piec
30	dreissig	harminc	tigapulah	trenta	tredve	trydzies'ci
40	vierzig	negyven	empat pulah	quaranta	forti	czterdries'ci
50	fünfzig	otven	lima pulah	cinquanta	femti	piec'dziesiat
60	sechzig	hatvan	enam pulah	sessanta	seksti	szes'c'dziesiat
70	siebzig	hetven	tudjuh pulu	settanta	sytti	siedemdziesiat
80	achtzig	nyolvan	delapan puluh	ottonta	atti	osiemdziesiat
90	neunzig	kilencven	sembilan puluh	novanta	nitty	dziewiec'dziesiat
100	ein hundert	egy-száz	satu-seratus	uno-cento	en-hundre	jeden-sto
1000	tausend	ezer	seribu	mille	tusen	tysiac

	PORTUGUESE	ROMANIAN	SERBO-CROATIAN	SPANISH	SWEDISH	TURKISH
1/4	um-quarto	un-sfert	jedan-ceturtina	un-cuarto	en-fjärdedel	bir-ceyrek
1/2	un-meio	o-jumatate	jedan-polovina	un-medio	en-hälft	bir-yarim
1	um	un	jedan	uno	en	bir
2	dois	doi	dva	dos	tva	iki
3	trés	trei	tri	tres	tre	üc
4	quatro	patru	cetiri	cuatro	fyra	dört
5	cinco	cinci	pet	cinco	fem	bes
6	seis	sase	sest	seis	sex	alti
7	sete	sapte	sedam	siete	sju	yedi
8	oito	opt	osam	ocho	atta	sekiz
9	nove	noua	devet	nueve	io	dokuz
10	dez	zece	deset	diez	tio	on
12	doze	doisprezece	dvanaest	doce	tolv	on iki
15	quinze	cincisprezece	petnaest	quince	femton	on bes
20	vinte	douazeci	dvadset	veintę	tjugu	yirmi
24	vinte-quatro	douazeci-patru	dvadesel-citiri	veinticuatro	tjugu-fyra	yirmi-dört
25	vinte-cinco	douazeci-cinci	dvadeset-pet	veinticinco	tjugu-fem	yirmi-bes
30	trinta	treizeci	trideset	treinta	trettio	otuz
40	quarenta	patruzeci	cetrdeset	cuarenta	fyrtio	kirk
50	cinqüenta	cincizeci	padeset	cincuenta	femtio	elli
60	sessenta	saizeci	sezdeset	sesenta	sextio	altmis
70	setenta	saptezeci	sedamdeset	setenta	sjuttio	yetmis
80	oitenta	optzeci	osamdeset	ochenta	attio	seksen
90	noventa	novazeci	devedeset	noventa	nittio	doksan
100	un-cem	o-suta	jedan-sto	cien	en-hundra	bir-yüz

AFGHANISTAN

The Islamic State of Afghanistan, which occupies a mountainous region of Southwest Asia, has an area of 251,825 sq. mi. (652,090 sq. km.) and a population of 25.59 million. Presently, about a fifth of the total population lives in exile as refugees, (mostly in Pakistan). Capital: Kabul. It is bordered by Iran, Pakistan, Turkmenistan, Uzbekistan, Tajikistan, and China's Sinkiang Province. Agriculture and herding are the principal industries; textile mills and cement factories add to the industrial sector. Cotton, wool, fruits, nuts, oil, sheepskin coats and hand-woven carpets are normally exported but foreign trade has been interrupted since 1979.

Because of its strategic position astride the ancient land route to India, Afghanistan (formerly known as Aryana and Khorasan) was invaded by Darius I, Alexander the Great, various Scythian tribes, the White Huns, the Arabs, the Turks, Genghis Khan, Tamerlane, the Mughals, the Persians, and in more recent times by Great Britain. It was a powerful empire under the Kushans, Hephthalites, Ghaznavids and Ghorids. The name Afghanistan, "Land of the Afghans," came into use in the eighteenth and nineteenth centuries to describe the realm of the Afghan kings. For a short period, this mountainous region was the easternmost frontier of the Iranian world, with strong cultural influences from the Turks and Mongols to the north and India to the south.

Previous to 1747, Afghan Kings ruled not only in Afghanistan, but also in India, of which Sher Shah Suri was one. Ahmad Shah Abdali, founder of the Durrani dynasty, established his rule at Qandahar in 1747. His clan was known as Saddozai. He conquered large territories in India and eastern Iran, which were lost by his grandson Shah Zaman. A new family, the Barakzai, drove the Durrani king out of Kabul, the capital, in 1819, but the Durranis were not eliminated completely until 1858. Further conflicts among the Barakzai prevented full unity until the reign of Abdur Rahman in 1880. In 1929, King Amanullah, grandson of Abdul Rahman, was driven out of the country by a commoner known as Baccha-i-Saqao, "Son of the Water-Carrier", who ruled as Habibullah for less than a year before he was defeated by Muhammad Nadir Shah, a relative of the Barakzai. The last king, Muhammad Zahir Shah, became a constitutional though still autocratic monarch in 1964. In 1973 a coup d'etat displaced him and created the Republic of Afghanistan. A subsequent military coup established the pro-Soviet Democratic Republic of Afghanistan in 1978. Mounting resistance in the countryside and violence within the government led to the Soviet invasion of late 1979 and the installation of Babrak Karmal as prime minister. A brutal civil war ensued, which continues to the present, even after Soviet forces withdrew in 1989 and Karmal's government was defeated. An unstable coalition of former *Mujahideen* (Freedom Fighters) factions attempted to govern for several years but have been gradually overcome by the Taliban, a Muslim fundamentalist force supported from Pakistan.

On September 11, 2001, a terrorist attack on the United States, supported by the Taliban, led to retaliatory strikes by the U.S. Military and subsequent dismantling of the Taliban regime. During a UN-sponsored conference on Afghanistan that was held in Bonn, Germany, in early November 2001, an agreement was reached for an Interim Authority, under the leadership of Hamid Karzai, to be instated in Afghanistan on December 22, 2001 and to hold power for the following four to six months. During that time a "loya jirga" (Grand Council) is scheduled to decide on the follow-on Transitional Authority.

Afghanistan's traditional coinage was much like that of its neighbors Iran and India. There were four major mints: Kabul, Qandahar, Balkh and Herat. The early Durranis also controlled mints in Iran and India. On gold and silver coins, the inscriptions in Persian (called *Dari* in Afghanistan) included the name of the mint city and, normally, of the ruler recognized there, but some issues are anonymous. The arrangement of the inscriptions, and frequently the name of the ruler, was different at each mint. Copper coins were controlled locally and usually did not name any ruler. For these reasons the coinage of each mint is treated separately. The relative values of gold, silver, and copper coins were not fixed but were determined in the marketplace.

In 1890 Abdur Rahman had a modern mint set up in Kabul using British minting machinery and the help of British advisors. The other mints were closed down, except for the issue of local coppers. The new system had 60 paisa equal one rupee; intermediate denominations also had special names. In 1901 the name Afghanistan appeared on coins for the first time. A decimal system, 100 puls to the afghani, was introduced in 1925. The gold amani, rated at 20 afghanis, was a bullion coin.

The national symbol on most coins of the kingdom is a stylized mosque, within which is seen the *mihrab*, a niche indicating the direction of Mecca, and the *minbar*, the pulpit, with a flight of steps leading up to it. Inscriptions in Pashtu were first used under the rebel Habibullah, but did not become standard until 1950.

Until 1919, coins were dated by the lunar Islamic Hejira calendar (AH), often with the king's regnal year as a second date. The solar Hejira (SH) calendar was introduced in 1919 (1337 AH, 1298 SH). The rebel Habibullah reinstated lunar Hejira dating (AH 1347-50), but the solar calendar was used thereafter. The solar Hejira year begins on the first day of spring, about March 21. Adding 621 to the SH year yields the AD year in which it begins.

RULERS

Names of rulers are shown in Perso-Arabic script in the style usually found on their coins; they are not always in a straight line.

BARAKZAI DYNASTY

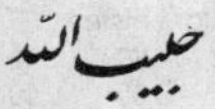

Habibullah,
AH1319-337/1901-1919AD

امان الله

Amanullah,
AH1337, SH1298-1307/1919-1929AD

حبیب الله
۱۳۴۷(ه۴۸)

Habibullah (rebel, known as Baccha-i-Saqao),
AH1347-1348/1929AD

محمد نادر شاه

Muhammed Nadir Shah, AH1348-1350,
SH1310-1312/1929-1933AD

محمد ظاهر شاه

Muhammad Zahir Shah,
SH1312-1352/1933-1973AD

Republic, SH1352-1358/1973-1979AD
Democratic Republic, SH1358-1373/1979-1994 AD
Islamic Republic, SH1373-1381/1994-2002AD

MINT NAMES

Coins were struck at numerous mints in Afghanistan and adjacent lands. These are listed below, together with their honorific titles, and shown in the style ordinarily found on the coins.

افغانستان
Afghanistan

غزني
Ghazni

هراة هرات
Herat

كابل
Kabul

قندهار
Qandahar

MINT EPITHETS

دار الملك
"Dar al-Mulk"
Abode of the King

دار النصرات
"Dar al-Nusrat"

KINGDOM

Habibullah
AH1319-1337 / 1901-1919AD

LOCAL COINAGE

KM# 957 PAISA
Copper **Mint:** Herat **Note:** Counterstruck over Iran, 50 Dinars, Y#4.

Date	Mintage	Good	VG	F	VF	XF
AH1322	—	4.00	6.50	12.50	18.00	—
AH1328	—	3.00	5.00	10.00	16.00	—

KM# 956.1 PAISA
Copper **Mint:** Herat **Note:** Round or irregular flan.

Date	Mintage	Good	VG	F	VF	XF
AH1322	—	2.50	4.00	7.50	12.50	—
AH1328	—	2.50	4.00	7.50	12.50	—
AH1329	—	2.50	4.00	7.50	12.50	—
AH1330	—	2.50	4.00	7.50	12.50	—
AH1331	—	2.50	4.00	7.50	12.50	—
AH1332	—	2.50	4.00	7.50	12.50	—
ND Date off flan	—	1.50	2.50	5.00	8.00	—

KM# 956.2 PAISA
Copper **Reverse:** In a rayed circle **Mint:** Herat

Date	Mintage	Good	VG	F	VF	XF
AH1332	—	3.00	5.00	8.50	15.00	—

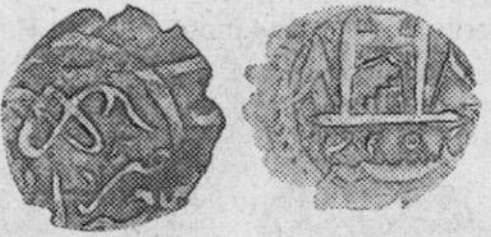

KM# 956.3 PAISA
Copper **Obverse:** Scroll symbol **Mint:** Herat

Date	Mintage	Good	VG	F	VF	XF
AH1325	—	3.00	5.00	8.50	15.00	—

KM# 960.1 PAISA
Copper **Mint:** Qandahar **Note:** Dump.

Date	Mintage	Good	VG	F	VF	XF
AH1322	—	4.50	7.50	12.50	17.50	—

KM# 960.4 PAISA
Copper **Mint:** Qandahar **Note:** Counterstruck on British East India Co., 1/4 Anna.

Date	Mintage	Good	VG	F	VF	XF
AH1322	—	4.00	7.50	12.50	20.00	—
AH1330	—	4.00	7.50	12.50	20.00	—

KM# 960.2 PAISA
Copper **Mint:** Qandahar **Note:** Counterstruck on Iran 50 dinars, Y#4.

Date	Mintage	Good	VG	F	VF	XF
AH1321	—	3.00	5.00	8.00	15.00	—
AH1322	—	3.00	5.00	8.00	15.00	—

KM# 960.3 PAISA
Copper **Mint:** Qandahar **Note:** Counterstruck on Muscat and Oman, 1/4 Anna, KM#4.

Date	Mintage	Good	VG	F	VF	XF
AH1322	—	3.75	6.50	10.00	16.00	—

KM# 960.5 PAISA
Copper **Mint:** Qandahar **Note:** Overstruck on Oman, 1/4 Anna, KM#3.1.

Date	Mintage	Good	VG	F	VF	XF
AH1322	—	3.75	6.50	10.00	16.00	—

KM# 963 PAISA
Copper **Mint:** Ghazni **Note:** Struck over British East India Co., 1/4 Anna.

Date	Mintage	Good	VG	F	VF	XF
AH1322	—	10.00	20.00	35.00	75.00	—

KM# 958.1 PAISA
Copper **Obverse:** "Dar al-Nusrat" added above date **Mint:** Herat

Date	Mintage	Good	VG	F	VF	XF
AH1331	—	2.50	4.00	7.50	12.50	—

KM# 958.2 PAISA
Copper **Reverse:** Date below mosque **Mint:** Herat

Date	Mintage	Good	VG	F	VF	XF
AH1331	—	3.50	5.00	8.50	15.00	—

KM# 964 PAISA
Copper **Mint:** Qandahar

Date	Mintage	Good	VG	F	VF	XF
AH1333	—	2.00	3.50	6.00	10.00	—
AH1334	—	2.00	3.50	6.00	10.00	—

KM# 973 PAISA
Copper **Mint:** Kabul

Date	Mintage	Good	VG	F	VF	XF
ND	—	—	—	—	—	—

KM# 959 2 PAISE
Copper **Mint:** Without Mint Name **Note:** Similar to Paisa, KM#965 but inscribed "Do Paisa" below mosque.

Date	Mintage	Good	VG	F	VF	XF
AH1329	—	3.00	5.00	8.50	15.00	—

MILLED COINAGE

10 Dinar = 1 Paisa; 5 Paise = 1 Shahi; 2 Shahi = 1 Sanar; 2 Sanar = 1 Abbasi; 1-1/2 Abbasi = 1 Qiran; 2 Qiran = 1 Kabuli Rupee; 1 Tilla = 10 Rupees

KM# 848 PAISA
Bronze Or Brass **Mint:** Afghanistan

Date	Mintage	VG	F	VF	XF	Unc
AH1329	—	6.00	12.00	25.00	45.00	—
AH1329/17	—	8.00	16.00	35.00	60.00	—

Note: On KM#828 obverse die

KM# 849 PAISA
Brass, 21 mm. **Mint:** Afghanistan

Date	Mintage	VG	F	VF	XF	Unc
AH1329	—	2.00	4.00	7.50	15.00	—
AH1331	—	2.00	4.00	7.50	15.00	—

KM# 849a PAISA
Bronze, 21 mm. **Mint:** Afghanistan

Date	Mintage	VG	F	VF	XF	Unc
AH1334	—	3.00	6.00	11.50	20.00	—

KM# 854 PAISA
Bronze Or Brass, 19 mm. **Mint:** Afghanistan **Note:** Thick flan, reduced size.

Date	Mintage	VG	F	VF	XF	Unc
AH1336	—	3.00	6.00	12.00	25.00	—

KM# 855 PAISA
Bronze Or Brass **Mint:** Afghanistan **Note:** Thin flan.

Date	Mintage	VG	F	VF	XF	Unc
AH1336	—	6.50	10.00	20.00	35.00	—
AH1337	—	2.00	4.00	8.00	16.00	—

KM# 857 PAISA
Bronze Or Brass, 20 mm. **Mint:** Afghanistan **Note:** Thin flan.

Date	Mintage	VG	F	VF	XF	Unc
AH1337	—	6.50	10.00	20.00	35.00	—

KM# 858 PAISA
Bronze Or Brass, 19-20 mm. **Mint:** Afghanistan **Note:** Thin flan. Size varies.

Date	Mintage	VG	F	VF	XF	Unc
AH1337 (1918)	—	3.00	6.00	10.00	20.00	—
Note: Three varieties are known dated AH1337						
SH1298 (1919)	—	4.50	8.00	15.00	32.50	—

KM# 846 SANAR (10 Paisa)
1.5500 g., 0.5000 Silver .0249 oz. ASW **Mint:** Afghanistan

Date	Mintage	VG	F	VF	XF	Unc
AH1325	—	10.00	20.00	35.00	60.00	—
AH1326	—	5.00	7.50	12.50	22.50	—
AH1328	—	5.00	7.50	12.50	22.50	—
AH1329	—	5.75	8.50	14.00	25.00	—

KM# 850 SANAR (10 Paisa)
1.5500 g., 0.5000 Silver .0249 oz. ASW **Mint:** Afghanistan **Note:** Coins dated AH1333 and 1337 are known in two varieties.

Date	Mintage	VG	F	VF	XF	Unc
AH1329	—	4.00	7.00	12.00	22.00	—
AH1330	—	3.00	6.00	10.00	20.00	—
AH1331	—	3.00	6.00	10.00	20.00	—
AH1332	—	3.00	6.00	10.00	20.00	—
AH1333	—	3.00	5.00	9.00	16.00	—
AH1335	—	3.00	5.00	9.00	16.00	—
AH1337	—	3.00	6.00	10.00	20.00	—

KM# 863 3 SHAHI (15 Paisa)
Copper, 32-33 mm. **Obverse:** Without "Al-Ghazi" **Reverse:** Mosque in eight-pointed star **Mint:** Afghanistan **Note:** Size varies.

Date	Mintage	VG	F	VF	XF	Unc
AH1337 (1918)	—	5.00	12.00	22.00	40.00	—

Note: Three varieties are known

KM# 869 3 SHAHI (15 Paisa)
Copper **Obverse:** "Shamsi" left and below date **Mint:** Afghanistan

Date	Mintage	VG	F	VF	XF	Unc
SH1298 (1919)	—	2.00	4.00	10.00	20.00	—

Note: Shamsi (Solar) is an additional word written on some of the coins dated SH1298, to show the change from a lunar to solar calendar

KM# 837 ABBASI (20 Paisa)
3.1100 g., 0.5000 Silver .0499 oz. ASW **Mint:** Afghanistan

Date	Mintage	VG	F	VF	XF	Unc
AH1320	—	30.00	60.00	100	225	—

KM# 845 ABBASI (20 Paisa)
3.1100 g., 0.5000 Silver .0499 oz. ASW **Mint:** Afghanistan

Date	Mintage	VG	F	VF	XF	Unc
AH1324	—	35.00	70.00	125	250	—
AH1328	—	35.00	70.00	125	250	—
AH1329	—	50.00	100	175	300	—

KM# 851 ABBASI (20 Paisa)
3.1100 g., 0.5000 Silver .0499 oz. ASW **Mint:** Afghanistan

Date	Mintage	VG	F	VF	XF	Unc
AH1329	—	6.00	11.00	16.00	24.00	—
AH1330	—	6.00	11.00	16.00	24.00	—
AH1333	—	5.00	10.00	15.00	22.50	—
AH1334	—	5.00	10.00	15.00	22.50	—
AH1335	—	5.00	10.00	15.00	22.50	—
AH1337	—	5.00	10.00	15.00	22.50	—

KM# 831 1/2 RUPEE (Qiran)
4.6500 g., 0.5000 Silver .0747 oz. ASW **Obverse:** Toughra **Reverse:** Crossed cannons below mosque **Mint:** Afghanistan

Date	Mintage	VG	F	VF	XF	Unc
AH1319	—	20.00	40.00	75.00	125	—

KM# 838 1/2 RUPEE (Qiran)
4.6500 g., 0.5000 Silver .0747 oz. ASW **Obverse:** Toughra divides date **Mint:** Afghanistan

Date	Mintage	VG	F	VF	XF	Unc
AH1320	—	25.00	45.00	85.00	140	—
AH1325	—	20.00	40.00	75.00	125	—

KM# 841 1/2 RUPEE (Qiran)
4.6500 g., 0.5000 Silver .0747 oz. ASW **Obverse:** Date at upper right of toughra **Reverse:** Dated AH1320 **Mint:** Afghanistan

Date	Mintage	VG	F	VF	XF	Unc
AH1321	—	25.00	45.00	85.00	140	—
AH1323	—	30.00	55.00	100	170	—

KM# 844.1 1/2 RUPEE (Qiran)

4.6500 g., 0.5000 Silver .0747 oz. ASW **Obverse:** Inscription and date **Reverse:** Frozen date AH1320 split above mosque **Mint:** Afghanistan

Date	Mintage	VG	F	VF	XF	Unc
AH1323	—	6.00	9.00	16.00	28.00	—
AH1324	—	6.00	9.00	15.00	25.00	—
AH1326	—	6.00	9.00	15.00	25.00	—
AH1327/6	—	6.00	9.00	15.00	25.00	—
AH1327	—	6.00	9.00	15.00	25.00	—

KM# 844.2 1/2 RUPEE (Qiran)

4.6500 g., 0.5000 Silver .0747 oz. ASW **Obverse:** Inscription and date **Reverse:** Actual date at top **Mint:** Afghanistan

Date	Mintage	VG	F	VF	XF	Unc
AH1326/3	—	25.00	45.00	75.00	135	—

Note: AH1326/0 for actual date on reverse

Date	Mintage	VG	F	VF	XF	Unc
AH1328	—	25.00	45.00	75.00	135	—
AH1329	—	25.00	45.00	75.00	135	—

KM# 852 1/2 RUPEE (Qiran)

4.6000 g., 0.5000 Silver .0739 oz. ASW **Mint:** Afghanistan

Date	Mintage	VG	F	VF	XF	Unc
AH1329	—	3.50	5.50	8.50	16.00	—
AH1333	—	3.50	5.50	8.50	16.00	—
AH1334	—	4.50	7.50	12.50	22.50	—
AH1335	—	4.50	7.50	12.50	22.50	—
AH1337	—	3.50	5.50	8.50	16.00	—

KM# 864 1/2 RUPEE (Qiran)

5.0000 g., Silver **Obv. Legend:** "Habibullah" **Reverse:** Star of Solomon **Mint:** Afghanistan

Date	Mintage	VG	F	VF	XF	Unc
AH1335	—	—	300	500	—	—

KM# 865 1/2 RUPEE (Qiran)

Silver **Obverse:** Uncircled inscription **Mint:** Afghanistan

Date	Mintage	VG	F	VF	XF	Unc
AH1337 (1918)	—	4.00	9.00	15.00	25.00	—

Note: Five varieties are known

KM# 832 RUPEE

9.2000 g., 0.5000 Silver .0755 oz. ASW **Obverse:** Toughra of Habibullah in wreath, star above **Mint:** Afghanistan

Date	Mintage	VG	F	VF	XF	Unc
AH1319	—	8.00	12.00	25.00	70.00	—

Note: Two varieties are known

KM# 833.1 RUPEE

9.2000 g., 0.5000 Silver .0755 oz. ASW **Obverse:** "Afghanistan" above small toughra, star at right **Reverse:** Large inverted pyramid dome **Mint:** Afghanistan

Date	Mintage	VG	F	VF	XF	Unc
AH1319	—	4.00	5.50	10.00	25.00	—
AH1320	—	4.00	5.50	8.50	20.00	—
AH1325	—	7.00	15.00	25.00	50.00	—

KM# 833.2 RUPEE

9.2000 g., 0.5000 Silver .0755 oz. ASW **Obverse:** Without star **Mint:** Afghanistan

Date	Mintage	VG	F	VF	XF	Unc
AH1319	—	4.00	5.50	10.00	25.00	—
AH1325	—	7.00	15.00	25.00	50.00	—

KM# 839 RUPEE

9.2000 g., 0.5000 Silver .0755 oz. ASW **Obverse:** "Afghanistan" divided by a star above large toughra **Mint:** Afghanistan

Date	Mintage	VG	F	VF	XF	Unc
AH1320	—	4.00	6.00	10.00	20.00	—

KM# 840.1 RUPEE

9.2000 g., 0.5000 Silver .0755 oz. ASW **Reverse:** Small dome mosque **Mint:** Afghanistan

Date	Mintage	VG	F	VF	XF	Unc
AH1320	—	5.00	8.00	15.00	35.00	—

KM# 840.2 RUPEE

9.2000 g., 0.5000 Silver .0755 oz. ASW **Obverse:** Date in loop of toughra **Mint:** Afghanistan

Date	Mintage	VG	F	VF	XF	Unc
AH1321	—	10.00	15.00	25.00	50.00	—

KM# 842.1 RUPEE

9.2000 g., 0.5000 Silver .0755 oz. ASW **Reverse:** "Afghanistan" above mosque, crossed swords and cannons **Mint:** Afghanistan

Date	Mintage	VG	F	VF	XF	Unc
AH1321	—	4.00	7.00	11.00	22.50	—

Note: Two varieties exist for AH1321 date

Date	Mintage	VG	F	VF	XF	Unc
AH1322	—	4.00	7.00	11.00	22.50	—

KM# 842.2 RUPEE

9.2000 g., 0.5000 Silver .0755 oz. ASW **Reverse:** Crossed cannons **Mint:** Afghanistan

Date	Mintage	VG	F	VF	XF	Unc
AH1322	—	4.00	5.00	9.00	20.00	—
AH1324	—	4.00	5.00	9.00	20.00	—
AH1325	—	5.00	8.00	12.00	25.00	—
AH1326	—	4.00	6.00	10.00	20.00	—
AH1327/6	—	6.00	8.00	15.00	30.00	—
AH1327	—	4.00	6.00	10.00	20.00	—

Date	Mintage	VG	F	VF	XF	Unc
AH1328	—	6.00	8.00	15.00	30.00	—

Note: Two varieties exist for AH1328 date.

Date	Mintage	VG	F	VF	XF	Unc
AH1329	—	6.00	8.00	15.00	30.00	—

KM# 847.1 RUPEE

9.2000 g., 0.5000 Silver .0755 oz. ASW **Obverse:** Date divided 13 Arabic "j" 28 **Reverse:** Large dome mosque without "Afghanistan" **Mint:** Afghanistan

Date	Mintage	VG	F	VF	XF	Unc
AH1328	—	7.00	15.00	25.00	50.00	—

KM# 847.2 RUPEE

9.2000 g., 0.5000 Silver .0755 oz. ASW **Obverse:** Date divided 132 Arabic "j" 8 **Mint:** Afghanistan

Date	Mintage	VG	F	VF	XF	Unc
AH1328	—	10.00	20.00	30.00	60.00	—

KM# 853 RUPEE

9.2000 g., 0.5000 Silver .0755 oz. ASW, 25-26 mm. **Obverse:** Name and titles of Habibullah in sprays **Reverse:** Mosque within sunburst **Mint:** Afghanistan **Note:** Size varies. Two varieties exist for AH1330, 1331, and 1337 and three varieties exist for AH1333; thickness of obverse inscription and size of mosque dome on reverse vary.

Date	Mintage	VG	F	VF	XF	Unc
AH1329	—	4.00	6.00	10.00	20.00	—
AH1330	—	4.00	6.00	9.00	18.50	—
AH1331	—	4.00	6.00	9.00	18.50	—
AH1332	—	4.00	6.00	9.00	18.50	—
AH1333	—	4.00	6.00	9.00	18.50	—
AH1334	—	4.00	6.00	9.00	18.50	—
AH1335	—	4.00	6.00	9.00	18.50	—
AH1337	—	4.00	6.00	10.00	20.00	—

KM# 853a RUPEE

10.0500 g., 0.9000 Gold 0.2908 oz. AGW, 26 mm. **Obverse:** Name and titles in sprays **Reverse:** Mosque in sunburst

Date	Mintage	F	VF	XF	Unc
AH1334	—	—	—	1,625	—

KM# 835 TILLA (10 Rupees)

4.6000 g., 0.9000 Gold .1331 oz. AGW, 19 mm. **Obverse:** Star above toughra **Mint:** Afghanistan

Date	Mintage	VG	F	VF	XF	Unc
AH1319	—	90.00	115	170	240	—

KM# 836.1 TILLA (10 Rupees)

4.6000 g., 0.9000 Gold .1331 oz. AGW **Obverse:** Legend divided by star above toughra **Obv. Legend:** "Afghanistan" **Mint:** Afghanistan

Date	Mintage	VG	F	VF	XF	Unc
AH1319	—	95.00	125	180	250	—

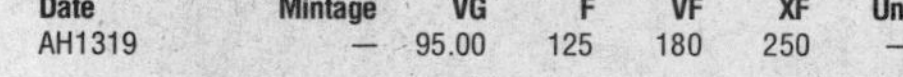

KM# 836.2 TILLA (10 Rupees)
4.6000 g., 0.9000 Gold .1331 oz. AGW **Obverse:** Legend above toughra with star to right **Obv. Legend:** "Afghanistan" **Mint:** Afghanistan

Date	Mintage	VG	F	VF	XF	Unc
AH1320	—	95.00	125	180	250	—

KM# A856 TILLA (10 Rupees)
4.6000 g., 0.9000 Gold .1331 oz. AGW **Obverse:** Date divided **Mint:** Afghanistan

Date	Mintage	VG	F	VF	XF	Unc
AH1325	—	—	450	650	900	—

KM# 856 TILLA (10 Rupees)
4.6000 g., 0.9000 Gold .1331 oz. AGW **Obv. Legend:** Habibullah... **Mint:** Afghanistan

Date	Mintage	VG	F	VF	XF	Unc
AH1335	—	170	200	260	330	—
AH1336	—	100	120	175	240	—
AH1337	—	110	130	180	220	—

KM# 879 2 TILLAS (20 Rupees)
9.2000 g., 0.9000 Gold .2661 oz. AGW, 22 mm. **Mint:** Afghanistan

Date	Mintage	F	VF	XF	Unc
SH1298 (1919)	—	BV	185	250	400

KM# 903 4 TILLAS (40 Rupees)
18.5300 g., 0.9000 Gold .1997 oz. AGW **Mint:** Afghanistan

Date	Mintage	VG	F	VF	XF	Unc
AH1337 Rare	—	—	—	—	—	—

KM# 889 5 AMANI (50 Rupees)
23.0000 g., 0.9000 Gold .6656 oz. AGW **Obverse:** Persian "5" above toughra; "Al Ghazi" at right **Reverse:** Legend above mosque **Rev. Legend:** "Amaniya" **Mint:** Afghanistan

Date	Mintage	VG	F	VF	XF	Unc
SH1299 (1920)	—	BV	450	675	1,500	—

KM# 890 5 AMANI (50 Rupees)
23.0000 g., 0.9000 Gold .6656 oz. AGW **Obverse:** Star above toughra **Reverse:** Persian "5" above mosque **Mint:** Afghanistan

Date	Mintage	VG	F	VF	XF	Unc
SH1299	—	BV	450	675	1,500	—

Amanullah
AH1337-1348 / 1919-1929AD

LOCAL COINAGE

KM# 965 PAISA
Copper **Obverse:** Denomination "Yek Paisa" **Mint:** Without Mint Name **Note:** Crudely struck. Without mint name, believed to be struck at Kabul.

Date	Mintage	Good	VG	F	VF	XF
SH1298 (1919)	—	4.50	7.50	12.50	22.00	—
SH1299 (1920)	—	4.50	7.50	12.50	22.00	—

KM# 966 PAISA
Copper **Mint:** Without Mint Name **Note:** Crudely struck; without mint name, believed to be struck at Kabul.

Date	Mintage	Good	VG	F	VF	XF
SH1299 (1920)	—	6.00	10.00	16.50	27.50	—

KM# 967 SHAHI (5 Paise)
Copper **Reverse:** Both denominations **Mint:** Without Mint Name **Note:** Crudely struck; without mint name, believed to be struck at Kabul.

Date	Mintage	Good	VG	F	VF	XF
AH1338 - SH1298 (1919)	—	6.00	10.00	16.50	27.50	—
AH1338 - SH1299 (1920)	—	7.50	12.50	20.00	35.00	—
AH1339 - SH1299 (1920)	—	6.00	10.00	16.50	27.50	—

KM# A846 10 PAISE
Copper **Mint:** Without Mint Name **Note:** Crudely struck; believed to be struck at Kabul.

Date	Mintage	Good	VG	F	VF	XF
SH1299 (1920)	—	7.50	12.50	20.00	35.00	—

MILLED COINAGE

10 Dinar = 1 Paisa; 5 Paise = 1 Shahi; 2 Shahi = 1 Sanar; 2 Sanar = 1 Abbasi; 1-1/2 Abbasi = 1 Qiran; 2 Qiran = 1 Kabuli Rupee; 1 Tilla = 10 Rupees

KM# 906 5 PUL
3.0000 g., Bronze Or Brass **Mint:** Afghanistan

Date	Mintage	F	VF	XF	Unc
SH1304 (1925)	—	1.75	3.50	6.00	14.00
SH1305 (1926)	—	1.50	3.00	5.50	14.00

KM# 907 10 PUL
6.0000 g., Copper **Mint:** Afghanistan

Date	Mintage	F	VF	XF	Unc
SH1304 (1925)	—	2.00	4.00	6.00	15.00
SH1305 (1926)	—	2.50	4.50	7.00	20.00
SH1306 (1927)	—	2.50	4.50	7.00	20.00

KM# 908 20 PUL
2.0000 g., Billon **Mint:** Afghanistan **Note:** Varieties exist.

Date	Mintage	F	VF	XF	Unc
SH1304 (1925)	—	50.00	75.00	100	170
SH134 (1925) Error	—	—	—	—	—
ND(ca.1926)	—	35.00	60.00	90.00	160

KM# 880 PAISA
Bronze Or Brass **Mint:** Afghanistan

Date	Mintage	VG	F	VF	XF	Unc
SH1299 (1920)	—	2.50	5.50	12.00	22.50	—
SH1300 (1921)	—	3.50	7.00	15.00	25.00	—
SH1301 (1922)	—	3.50	7.00	15.00	25.00	—
Note: Two varieties are known dated SH1301						
SH1302 (1923)	—	2.50	5.50	12.00	22.50	—
SH1303 (1924)	—	2.50	5.50	12.00	22.50	—

KM# 909 1/2 AFGHANI (50 Pul)
5.0000 g., 0.5000 Silver .0803 oz. ASW **Obverse:** Date below toughra **Mint:** Afghanistan

Date	Mintage	F	VF	XF	Unc
SH1304/7 (1925)	—	2.00	3.50	6.50	18.50
Note: Two varieties are known dated SH1304					
SH1305/8 (1926)	—	2.00	3.50	6.50	18.50
SH1306/9 (1927)	—	2.00	3.50	6.50	18.50

KM# 915 1/2 AFGHANI (50 Pul)
5.0000 g., 0.5000 Silver .0803 oz. ASW **Obverse:** Date below mosque **Mint:** Afghanistan

Date	Mintage	F	VF	XF	Unc
SH1307/10 (1928)	—	3.00	6.00	12.00	35.00

KM# 910 AFGHANI (100 Pul)
10.0000 g., 0.9000 Silver .2893 oz. ASW **Obverse:** Date below toughra **Mint:** Afghanistan **Note:** Two varieties each are known for dates SH1305-06.

Date	Mintage	F	VF	XF	Unc
SH1304/7 (1925)	—	4.50	6.50	12.50	28.00
Note: Three varieties are known for date SH1304					
SH1305/8 (1926)	—	4.50	6.50	12.50	28.00
SH1305/9 (1926)	—	4.50	6.50	12.50	28.00
SH1306/9 (1927)	—	4.50	6.50	12.50	28.00

KM# 859 SHAHI (5 Paise)
Copper Or Brass **Mint:** Afghanistan **Note:** Thick flan.

Date	Mintage	VG	F	VF	XF	Unc
AH1337	—	12.00	22.00	40.00	70.00	—

KM# 860 SHAHI (5 Paise)
Copper Or Brass **Mint:** Afghanistan **Note:** Thin flan.

Date	Mintage	VG	F	VF	XF	Unc
AH1337	—	10.00	20.00	35.00	55.00	—

KM# 861 SANAR (10 Paisa)
Copper Or Brass **Mint:** Afghanistan **Note:** Thick flan.

Date	Mintage	VG	F	VF	XF	Unc
AH1337	—	10.00	17.50	30.00	55.00	—

KM# 862 SANAR (10 Paisa)
Copper Or Brass **Mint:** Afghanistan **Note:** Thin flan.

Date	Mintage	VG	F	VF	XF	Unc
AH1337	—	9.00	14.00	20.00	35.00	—

KM# 881 3 SHAHI (15 Paisa)
Copper **Obverse:** Without "Shamsi" **Mint:** Afghanistan **Note:** Four varieties for date SH1299 and three varieties for date SH1300 are known.

Date	Mintage	VG	F	VF	XF	Unc
SH1298 (1919)	—	4.00	15.00	22.00	40.00	—
AH1299 (1920)	—	1.50	3.50	8.00	17.00	—
AH1300 (1921)	—	1.50	3.50	8.00	17.00	—

KM# 870 3 SHAHI (15 Paisa)
Copper, 32-33 mm. **Obverse:** "Al-Ghazi", without "Shamsi" by date **Reverse:** Mosque in eight-pointed star **Mint:** Afghanistan **Note:** Size varies.

Date	Mintage	VG	F	VF	XF	Unc
SH1298 (1919)	—	3.00	5.00	10.00	20.00	—
SH1299 (1920)	—	3.00	5.00	10.00	20.00	—

Note: 2 varieties of SH1299 exist

KM# 871.1 3 SHAHI (15 Paisa)
11.5000 g., Copper **Obverse:** "Al-Ghazi, Shamsi" **Mint:** Afghanistan **Note:** Thick flan.

Date	Mintage	VG	F	VF	XF	Unc
SH1298 (1919)	—	10.00	15.00	22.00	40.00	—

KM# 871.2 3 SHAHI (15 Paisa)
9.0000 g., Copper **Mint:** Afghanistan **Note:** Thin flan.

Date	Mintage	VG	F	VF	XF	Unc
SH1298 (1919)	—	2.00	4.00	9.00	18.00	—

Note: Two reverse varieties with 10 or 11 circular stars exist

KM# 872 3 SHAHI (15 Paisa)
Copper **Obverse:** "Shamsi" **Reverse:** Mosque in seven-pointed star **Mint:** Afghanistan

Date	Mintage	VG	F	VF	XF	Unc
SH1298 (1919)	—	2.00	4.00	9.00	18.00	—

KM# 881a 3 SHAHI (15 Paisa)
Brass **Mint:** Afghanistan **Note:** Prev. KM#892.

Date	Mintage	VG	F	VF	XF	Unc
SH1300 (1921)	—	4.00	8.00	15.00	30.00	—

KM# 893 3 SHAHI (15 Paisa)
Copper **Reverse:** Mosque in seven-pointed star **Mint:** Afghanistan

Date	Mintage	VG	F	VF	XF	Unc
SH1300 (1921)	—	1.50	3.50	8.00	17.00	—
SH1301 (1922)	—	1.50	3.50	8.00	17.00	—
Note: 2 varieties of SH1301 exist						
SH130x (1923) (error)	—	—	—	—	—	—
SH1303 (1924)	—	1.50	3.50	8.00	17.00	—

KM# 891 3 SHAHI (15 Paisa)
Brass **Obverse:** Eight stars around perimeter **Reverse:** Eight stars around perimeter **Mint:** Afghanistan

Date	Mintage	VG	F	VF	XF	Unc
SH1300 (1921)	—	—	—	—	—	—

KM# 874 ABBASI (20 Paisa)
Copper Or Billon **Mint:** Afghanistan

Date	Mintage	VG	F	VF	XF	Unc
SH1298 (1919)	—	50.00	75.00	90.00	150	—

KM# 882 ABBASI (20 Paisa)
Copper Or Billon, 25 mm. **Mint:** Afghanistan

Date	Mintage	VG	F	VF	XF	Unc
SH1299 (1920)	—	15.00	30.00	50.00	75.00	—

KM# 883 ABBASI (20 Paisa)
Copper Or Billon **Mint:** Afghanistan

Date	Mintage	VG	F	VF	XF	Unc
SH1299 (1920)	—	2.00	6.00	15.00	30.00	—
SH1300 (1921)	—	2.00	6.00	15.00	30.00	—
SH1301 (1922)	—	2.00	6.00	15.00	30.00	—
Note: Two varieties for date SH1301 exist						
SH1302 (1923)	—	2.00	6.00	15.00	30.00	—
SH2031 (1923) Error	—	7.00	15.00	30.00	50.00	—
SH1303 (1924)	—	2.00	6.00	15.00	30.00	—

KM# 866 1/2 RUPEE (Qiran)
Silver **Obverse:** Legend within circle and wreath **Mint:** Afghanistan

Date	Mintage	VG	F	VF	XF	Unc
AH1337 (1918)	—	150	300	500	725	—

KM# 875 1/2 RUPEE (Qiran)
4.7500 g., 0.5000 Silver .0763 oz. ASW **Obverse:** Star above inscription, "Shamsi" **Mint:** Afghanistan

Date	Mintage	VG	F	VF	XF	Unc
SH1298 (1919)	—	3.00	6.00	10.00	20.00	—

Note: Two varieties are known

KM# 876 1/2 RUPEE (Qiran)
4.7500 g., 0.5000 Silver .0763 oz. ASW **Obverse:** "Al-Ghazi" above inscription, "Shamsi" **Mint:** Afghanistan

Date	Mintage	VG	F	VF	XF	Unc
SH1298 (1919)	—	15.00	30.00	50.00	75.00	—

KM# 884 1/2 RUPEE (Qiran)
4.7500 g., 0.5000 Silver .0763 oz. ASW **Obverse:** Without "Shamsi" **Mint:** Afghanistan

Date	Mintage	VG	F	VF	XF	Unc
SH1299 (1920)	—	3.00	4.00	7.00	15.00	—
Note: Two varieties are known dated 1299						
SH1300 (1921)	—	3.00	4.00	7.00	15.00	—

KM# 894 1/2 RUPEE (Qiran)
4.7500 g., 0.5000 Silver .0763 oz. ASW **Mint:** Afghanistan

Date	Mintage	VG	F	VF	XF	Unc
SH1300 (1921)	—	2.00	4.00	7.00	12.00	—
SH1301 (1922)	—	2.00	4.00	7.00	12.00	—
SH1302 (1923)	—	2.00	4.00	7.00	12.00	—
SH1303 (1924)	—	2.00	4.00	7.00	12.00	—

KM# 867 RUPEE
9.2000 g., 0.5000 Silver .0755 oz. ASW **Obverse:** Name and titles of Amanullah, star above inscription **Mint:** Afghanistan

Date	Mintage	VG	F	VF	XF	Unc
AH1337 (1918)	—	6.00	10.00	18.00	30.00	—

Note: Seven varieties are known

KM# 877 RUPEE
9.0000 g., 0.9000 Silver .2604 oz. ASW **Obverse:** "Al-Ghazi" above inscription **Mint:** Afghanistan

Date	Mintage	VG	F	VF	XF	Unc
SH1298 (1919)	—	4.50	6.50	10.00	18.50	—
Note: Four varieties are known for date SH1298						
SH1299 (1920)	—	4.50	6.50	10.00	18.50	—
Note: Two varieties are known for date SH1299						

KM# 885 RUPEE
9.2500 g., 0.9000 Silver .2676 oz. ASW **Obverse:** Toughra of Amanullah **Mint:** Afghanistan

Date	Mintage	VG	F	VF	XF	Unc
SH1299 (1920)	—	4.25	5.50	8.00	16.50	—
SH1300 (1921)	—	4.25	5.50	8.00	16.50	—
SH1301 (1922)	—	4.25	5.50	8.00	16.50	—
SH1302/1 (1923)	—	4.25	5.50	8.00	16.50	—
SH1302 (1923)	—	4.25	5.50	8.00	16.50	—
SH1303 (1924)	—	4.25	5.50	8.00	16.50	—

KM# 878 2-1/2 RUPEES
22.9200 g., 0.9000 Silver .6632 oz. ASW **Mint:** Afghanistan **Note:** Two varieties each are known for dates SH1298-1300.

Date	Mintage	VG	F	VF	XF	Unc
SH1298 (1919)	—	12.50	16.50	20.00	45.00	—
SH1299 (1920)	—	9.50	12.50	17.50	40.00	—
SH1300 (1921)	—	9.50	12.50	17.50	40.00	—
SH1301 (1922)	—	9.50	12.50	15.00	35.00	—
SH1302 (1923)	—	9.50	12.50	15.00	35.00	—
SH1303 (1924)	—	9.50	12.50	15.00	35.00	—

KM# 834.1 5 RUPEES
45.6000 g., 0.9000 Silver 1.3194 oz. ASW **Reverse:** Similar to KM#826 **Mint:** Afghanistan

Date	Mintage	VG	F	VF	XF	Unc
AH1319	—	28.00	45.00	90.00	175	—

KM# 834.2 5 RUPEES
45.6000 g., 0.9000 Silver 1.3194 oz. ASW **Obverse:** Date at left of toughra **Mint:** Afghanistan

Date	Mintage	VG	F	VF	XF	Unc
AH1319	—	28.00	45.00	90.00	175	—

KM# 843 5 RUPEES
45.6000 g., 0.9000 Silver 1.3194 oz. ASW **Mint:** Afghanistan
Note: Most dates are recut dies. Two varieties are known for each date, AH1324 and 1327.

Date	Mintage	VG	F	VF	XF	Unc
AH1322	—	20.00	30.00	50.00	100	—
AH1324	—	18.50	22.50	45.00	90.00	—
AH1326	—	18.50	22.50	45.00	90.00	—
AH1327/6	—	18.50	22.50	45.00	90.00	—
AH1328	—	22.50	32.50	55.00	120	—
AH1329	—	25.00	40.00	70.00	145	—

KM# 886 1/2 AMANI (5 Rupees)
2.3000 g., 0.9000 Gold .0665 oz. AGW **Mint:** Afghanistan

Date	Mintage	VG	F	VF	XF	Unc
SH1299 (1920)	—	55.00	70.00	95.00	135	—

KM# 911 1/2 AMANI (5 Rupees)
3.0000 g., 0.9000 Gold .0868 oz. AGW **Mint:** Afghanistan

Date	Mintage	VG	F	VF	XF	Unc
SH1304/7 (1925)	—	—	65.00	90.00	115	160
SH1305/8 (1926)	—	—	65.00	90.00	115	160
SH1306/9 (1927)	—	—	65.00	90.00	115	160

KM# 868.1 TILLA (10 Rupees)
4.6000 g., 0.9000 Gold .1331 oz. AGW **Obv. Legend:** "Amanullah..." **Reverse:** Crossed swords below mosque **Mint:** Afghanistan

Date	Mintage	VG	F	VF	XF	Unc
AH1337 (1918)	—	100	125	160	225	—

KM# 868.2 TILLA (10 Rupees)
4.6000 g., 0.9000 Gold .1331 oz. AGW, 21 mm. **Reverse:** 6-pointed star below mosque **Mint:** Afghanistan

Date	Mintage	VG	F	VF	XF	Unc
AH1337 (1918)	—	100	135	175	250	—

KM# 887 AMANI (10 Rupees)
4.6000 g., 0.9000 Gold .1331 oz. AGW, 22.5 mm. **Mint:** Afghanistan

Date	Mintage	VG	F	VF	XF	Unc
SH1299 (1920)	—	BV	100	130	175	—

KM# 912 AMANI
6.0000 g., 0.9000 Gold .1736 oz. AGW **Mint:** Afghanistan

Date	Mintage	F	VF	XF	Unc
SH1304/7 (1925)	—	BV	120	130	180
SH1305/8 (1926)	—	BV	120	150	220
SH1306/9 (1927)	—	BV	120	130	180

KM# 888 2 AMANI (20 Rupees)
9.2000 g., 0.9000 Gold .2662 oz. AGW **Mint:** Afghanistan

Date	Mintage	VG	F	VF	XF	Unc
SH1299 (1920)	—	BV	175	200	275	300
SH1300 (1921)	—	BV	175	200	275	300
SH1301 (1922)	—	BV	175	200	275	300
SH1302 (1923)	—	BV	175	200	275	300
SH1303 (1924)	—	BV	175	200	275	300

KM# 914 2-1/2 AMANI
15.0000 g., 0.9000 Gold .4340 oz. AGW **Mint:** Afghanistan

Date	Mintage	F	VF	XF	Unc
SH1306/9 (1927)	—	—	—	5,000	7,000

KM# 900 HABIBI (30 Rupees)
4.6000 g., 0.9000 Gold .1331 oz. AGW **Obverse:** Small star replaces "30 Rupees" in legend

Date	Mintage	VG	F	VF	XF	Unc
AH1347	—	90.00	130	200	325	—

DECIMAL COINAGE

100 Pul = 1 Afghani; 20 Afghani = 1 Amani

KM# 905 2 PUL
2.0000 g., Bronze Or Brass **Mint:** Afghanistan

Date	Mintage	F	VF	XF	Unc
SH1304 (1925)	—	3.00	5.00	9.00	15.00
SH1305 (1926)	—	3.00	5.00	9.00	15.00

KM# 916 AFGHANI (100 Pul)
10.0000 g., 0.9000 Silver .2893 oz. ASW **Obverse:** Date below mosque **Mint:** Afghanistan

KM# 913 2-1/2 AFGHANIS
25.0000 g., 0.9000 Silver .7234 oz. ASW **Mint:** Afghanistan
Note: Two varieties are known for each date.

Date	Mintage	F	VF	XF	Unc
SH1305/8 (1926)	—	15.00	25.00	50.00	125
SH1306/9 (1927)	—	15.00	20.00	40.00	90.00

Habibullah Ghazi

Rebel ; AH1347-1348 / 1929AD; Struck in the name of Baccha-i-Saqao

LOCAL COINAGE

KM# 969 5 PAISE
Brass **Mint:** Herat

Date	Mintage	Good	VG	F	VF	XF
AH1347	—	5.00	8.50	15.00	25.00	—

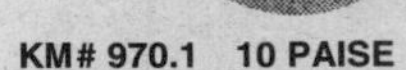

KM# 970.1 10 PAISE
Brass **Reverse:** Denomination "Dah" written above "Paisa" **Mint:** Herat

Date	Mintage	Good	VG	F	VF	XF
AH1347	—	6.00	10.00	16.50	27.50	—

KM# 970.2 10 PAISE
Brass **Reverse:** Denomination "Dah" written at right of "Paisa" **Mint:** Herat

Date	Mintage	Good	VG	F	VF	XF
AH1347	—	7.50	12.50	20.00	35.00	—

KM# 972 20 PAISE
Brass **Mint:** Herat

Date	Mintage	Good	VG	F	VF	XF
AH1347	—	7.50	12.50	20.00	35.00	—
AH1348	—	10.00	15.00	25.00	40.00	—

Muhammed Nadir Shah

AH1348-1350 / 1929-1933AD

MILLED COINAGE

10 Dinar = 1 Paisa; 5 Paise = 1 Shahi; 2 Shahi = 1 Sanar; 2 Sanar = 1 Abbasi; 1-1/2 Abbasi = 1 Qiran; 2 Qiran = 1 Kabuli Rupee; 1 Tilla = 10 Rupees

KM# 901 10 PAISE
Copper **Mint:** Afghanistan

Date	Mintage	VG	F	VF	XF	Unc
AH1348	—	6.00	12.00	20.00	40.00	—

KM# 895 20 PAISE
Bronze Or Brass **Mint:** Afghanistan

Date	Mintage	VG	F	VF	XF	Unc
AH1347	—	3.00	5.00	7.50	18.00	—

KM# 896 1/2 RUPEE (Qiran)
4.7000 g., 0.5000 Silver .0755 oz. ASW **Mint:** Afghanistan

Date	Mintage	VG	F	VF	XF	Unc
AH1347	—	4.00	7.00	12.00	20.00	—

KM# 902 1/2 RUPEE (Qiran)
4.7000 g., 0.5000 Silver .0755 oz. ASW **Mint:** Afghanistan

Date	Mintage	VG	F	VF	XF	Unc
AH1348	—	12.00	20.00	32.00	50.00	—

KM# 897 RUPEE
9.1000 g., 0.9000 Silver .2633 oz. ASW **Obverse:** Name and titles of Amir Habibullah (The Usurper) **Mint:** Afghanistan

Date	Mintage	VG	F	VF	XF	Unc
AH1347	—	5.00	9.00	15.00	25.00	—

KM# 898 RUPEE
9.1000 g., 0.9000 Silver .2633 oz. ASW **Obverse:** Title in circle **Mint:** Afghanistan

Date	Mintage	VG	F	VF	XF	Unc
AH1347	—	25.00	35.00	55.00	90.00	—

KM# 899 HABIBI (30 Rupees)
4.6000 g., 0.9000 Gold .1331 oz. AGW, 21 mm. **Mint:** Afghanistan

Date	Mintage	VG	F	VF	XF	Unc
AH1347	—	90.00	130	200	325	—

DECIMAL COINAGE

100 Pul = 1 Afghani; 20 Afghani = 1 Amani

KM# A922 PUL
Bronze Or Brass, 15 mm. **Mint:** Afghanistan

Date	Mintage	F	VF	XF	Unc
AH1349 (1930)	—	0.75	1.25	1.75	2.50

KM# 922 PUL
Bronze Or Brass, 15 mm. **Obverse:** Toughra **Mint:** Afghanistan

Date	Mintage	F	VF	XF	Unc
AH1349 (1930)	—	100	250	300	400

KM# 917 2 PUL
2.0000 g., Bronze Or Brass, 18 mm. **Mint:** Afghanistan

Date	Mintage	F	VF	XF	Unc
AH1348 (1929)	—	1.25	2.50	3.50	8.00
AH1349/8 (1930)	—	1.25	2.50	3.50	8.00

KM# 923 5 PUL
3.0000 g., Bronze Or Brass, 22 mm. **Mint:** Afghanistan

Date	Mintage	F	VF	XF	Unc
AH1349 (1930)	—	1.75	2.75	4.50	12.50
AH1350 (1931)	—	1.25	2.25	3.50	12.50

Note: Two varieties are known dated AH1350

KM# 929 5 PUL
3.0000 g., Bronze Or Brass, 21 mm. **Mint:** Afghanistan

Date	Mintage	F	VF	XF	Unc
SH1311 (1932)	—	2.50	5.50	9.00	20.00
SH1312 (1933)	—	2.50	5.50	9.00	20.00
SH1313 (1934)	—	2.50	5.50	9.00	20.00
SH1314 (1935)	—	2.50	5.50	9.00	20.00

KM# 918 10 PUL
Copper Or Brass, 25 mm. **Mint:** Afghanistan **Note:** Illustration shows an example struck off-center; prices are for properly struck specimens.

Date	Mintage	F	VF	XF	Unc
AH1348 (1929)	—	2.00	3.50	5.00	15.00
AH1349 (1930) 2 varieties	—	2.25	4.00	5.50	15.00

KM# 930 10 PUL
Bronze Or Brass, 23 mm. **Mint:** Afghanistan

Date	Mintage	F	VF	XF	Unc
SH1311 (1932)	—	1.50	2.50	4.00	15.00
SH1312 (1933)	—	1.50	2.50	4.00	15.00
SH1313 (1934)	—	1.50	2.50	4.00	15.00
SH1314 (1935)	—	1.50	2.50	4.00	15.00

KM# 919 20 PUL
Copper Or Brass, 25 mm. **Mint:** Afghanistan

Date	Mintage	F	VF	XF	Unc
AH1348 (1929)	—	2.00	4.00	10.00	22.00
AH1349 (1930)	—	3.00	5.00	12.00	25.00

KM# 924 25 PUL
Copper Or Brass, 25 mm. **Mint:** Afghanistan

Date	Mintage	F	VF	XF	Unc
AH1349	—	2.50	5.00	10.00	20.00

Note: Two varieties are known dated AH1349.

KM# 920 1/2 AFGHANI (50 Pul)
5.0000 g., 0.5000 Silver .0803 oz. ASW, 24 mm. **Obverse:** Date below mosque **Mint:** Afghanistan **Note:** Prev. KM#919.

Date	Mintage	F	VF	XF	Unc
AH1348/1 (1929)	—	1.75	2.50	5.00	14.00
AH1349/2 (1930)	—	1.75	2.50	5.00	14.00
AH1350/3 (1931)	—	1.75	2.50	5.00	14.00

KM# 926 1/2 AFGHANI (50 Pul)
4.7500 g., 0.5000 Silver .0763 oz. ASW, 24 mm. **Mint:** Afghanistan

Date	Mintage	F	VF	XF	Unc
SH1310 (1931)	—	2.00	3.00	5.50	15.00
SH1311 (1932)	—	1.75	2.25	4.50	12.50
Note: Two die varieties exist					
SH1312 (1933)	—	2.00	3.00	5.50	15.00

Note: With and without diamond-shaped dot beneath the wreath on the obverse

KM# 921 AFGHANI (100 Pul)
9.9500 g., 0.9000 Silver .2879 oz. ASW, 30 mm. **Mint:** Afghanistan

Date	Mintage	F	VF	XF	Unc
AH1348 (1929)	—	4.50	6.00	9.00	16.50
AH1349 (1930)	—	4.50	6.00	9.00	16.50
AH1350 (1931)	—	4.50	6.00	9.00	16.50

KM# 927.1 AFGHANI (100 Pul)
10.0000 g., 0.9000 Silver .2893 oz. ASW, 27 mm. **Mint:** Afghanistan

Date	Mintage	F	VF	XF	Unc
SH1310 (1931)	—	40.00	55.00	70.00	100
SH1311 (1932)	—	110	160	180	260

KM# 927.2 AFGHANI (100 Pul)
10.0000 g., 0.9000 Silver .2893 oz. ASW **Mint:** Afghanistan **Note:** Thick flan.

Date	Mintage	F	VF	XF	Unc
SH1310 (1931)	—	250	375	500	700

KM# 925 20 AFGHANIS
6.0000 g., 0.9000 Gold .1736 oz. AGW, 22 mm. **Mint:** Afghanistan

Date	Mintage	F	VF	XF	Unc
AH1348	—	130	175	200	300
AH1349	—	BV	120	165	240
AH1350	—	BV	120	165	240

Muhammed Zahir Shah

SH1312-1352 / 1933-1973AD

DECIMAL COINAGE

100 Pul = 1 Afghani; 20 Afghani = 1 Amani

KM# 928 2 PUL

2.0000 g., Bronze Or Brass **Mint:** Afghanistan

Date	Mintage	F	VF	XF	Unc
SH1311 (1932)	—	2.00	3.00	4.00	12.00
SH1312 (1933)	—	1.50	2.25	3.00	10.00
SH1313 (1934)	—	1.75	2.75	3.75	10.00
SH1314 (1935)	—	2.00	3.00	4.00	12.00

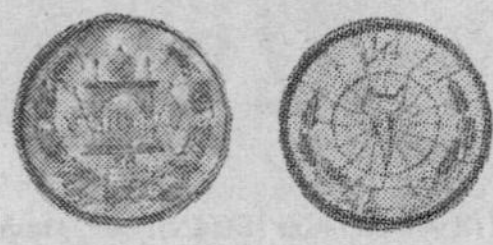

KM# 936 2 PUL

2.0000 g., Bronze, 15 mm. **Mint:** Afghanistan

Date	Mintage	F	VF	XF	Unc
SH1316 (1937)	—	0.15	0.20	0.35	1.00

KM# 937 3 PUL

Bronze, 16 mm. **Mint:** Afghanistan

Date	Mintage	F	VF	XF	Unc
SH1316 (1937)	—	0.35	0.50	0.75	2.00

KM# 938 5 PUL

3.0000 g., Bronze, 17 mm. **Mint:** Afghanistan

Date	Mintage	F	VF	XF	Unc
SH1316 (1937)	—	0.35	0.50	0.75	2.00

KM# 939 10 PUL

2.5000 g., Copper-Nickel, 17.9 mm. **Mint:** Afghanistan

Date	Mintage	F	VF	XF	Unc
SH1316 (1937)	—	0.40	0.65	1.00	3.00

KM# 931 25 PUL

Bronze Or Brass **Mint:** Afghanistan

Date	Mintage	F	VF	XF	Unc
SH1312 (1933)	—	2.00	4.00	12.00	25.00
SH1313 (1934)	—	2.00	4.00	12.00	25.00
SH1314 (1935)	—	2.00	4.50	14.00	28.00
SH1316 (1937)	—	2.00	4.50	14.00	28.00

KM# 940 25 PUL

2.9000 g., Copper-Nickel, 20.1 mm. **Mint:** Afghanistan

Date	Mintage	F	VF	XF	Unc
SH1316 (1937)	—	0.60	0.75	1.50	3.50

KM# 941 25 PUL

Bronze, 20 mm. **Mint:** Afghanistan

Date	Mintage	F	VF	XF	Unc
SH1330 (1951)	—	0.30	0.50	0.75	2.50
SH1331 (1952)	—	0.30	0.50	0.75	2.50
SH1332 (1953)	—	0.30	0.50	0.75	2.50
SH1333 (1954)	—	1.00	2.00	3.50	6.00

KM# 943 25 PUL

Nickel Clad Steel **Edge:** Reeded **Mint:** Afghanistan

Date	Mintage	F	VF	XF	Unc
SH1331 (1952)	—	1.00	2.00	3.50	7.00
SH1332 (1953)	—	1.50	3.00	5.00	9.00

KM# 944 25 PUL

Nickel Clad Steel **Edge:** Plain **Mint:** Afghanistan

Date	Mintage	F	VF	XF	Unc
SH1331 (1952)	—	0.35	0.65	1.00	3.00
SH1332 (1953)	—	0.35	0.65	1.00	3.00
SH1333 (1954)	—	0.35	0.65	1.00	3.00
SH1334/2 (1955)	—	1.50	3.00	5.00	9.00
SH1334 (1955)	—	0.35	0.65	1.00	3.00

KM# 945 25 PUL

Aluminum, 24 mm. **Mint:** Afghanistan **Note:** Struck on oversize 2 Afghani KM#949 planchets in 1970.

Date	Mintage	F	VF	XF	Unc
SH1331 (1952)	—	0.50	1.00	3.00	10.00

KM# 932.1 1/2 AFGHANI (50 Pul)

4.7500 g., 0.5000 Silver .0763 oz. ASW, 24 mm. **Obverse:** Smaller dotted circle **Mint:** Afghanistan

Date	Mintage	F	VF	XF	Unc
SH1312 (1933)	—	1.75	3.00	6.00	16.00

KM# 932.2 1/2 AFGHANI (50 Pul)

4.7500 g., 0.5000 Silver .0763 oz. ASW, 24 mm. **Obverse:** Larger dotted circle **Mint:** Afghanistan

Date	Mintage	F	VF	XF	Unc
SH1313 (1934)	—	1.75	3.00	6.00	16.00
SH1314 (1935)	—	1.75	3.00	6.00	16.00
SH1315 (1936)	—	1.50	2.50	5.50	15.00
SH1316 (1937)	—	1.50	2.50	5.50	15.00

KM# 947 1/2 AFGHANI (50 Pul)

5.0000 g., Nickel Clad Steel, 22.3 mm. **Obverse:** Denomination in words **Mint:** Afghanistan

Date	Mintage	F	VF	XF	Unc
SH1331 (1952)	—	0.50	1.00	2.00	4.00
SH133x (1953)	—	5.00	7.50	12.50	20.00

KM# 942.1 50 PUL

Bronze, 22.5 mm. **Obverse:** Denomination in numerals **Mint:** Afghanistan

Date	Mintage	F	VF	XF	Unc
SH1330 (1951)	—	0.50	1.00	2.00	4.00
SH133x (1951)	—	1.50	3.00	5.00	9.00

KM# 942.2 50 PUL

Bronze, 24 mm. **Mint:** Afghanistan

Date	Mintage	F	VF	XF	Unc
SH1330 (1951)	—	20.00	30.00	40.00	50.00

KM# 946 50 PUL

Nickel Clad Steel **Mint:** Afghanistan

Date	Mintage	F	VF	XF	Unc
SH1331 (1952)	—	0.20	0.35	0.65	2.00
SH1332 (1953)	—	0.20	0.35	0.65	2.00
SH1333 (1954)	—	1.00	2.00	3.50	6.00
SH1334/2 (1955)	—	0.40	0.65	1.00	2.50
SH1334 (1955)	—	0.20	0.35	0.65	2.00

KM# 953 AFGHANI (100 Pul)

Nickel Clad Steel **Edge:** Reeded **Mint:** Afghanistan

Date	Mintage	F	VF	XF	Unc
SH1340 (1961)	—	0.20	0.35	0.60	1.25

KM# 949 2 AFGHANIS

Aluminum **Mint:** Afghanistan **Note:** This issue was withdrawn and demonetized due to extensive counterfeiting.

Date	Mintage	F	VF	XF	Unc
SH1337 (1958)	—	0.60	1.00	1.50	2.50

KM# 954.1 2 AFGHANIS

Nickel Clad Steel **Edge:** Plain **Mint:** Afghanistan **Note:** Coin turn.

Date	Mintage	F	VF	XF	Unc
SH1340 (1961)	—	0.25	0.45	0.85	2.00

KM# 954.2 2 AFGHANIS

Nickel Clad Steel **Mint:** Afghanistan **Note:** Medallic die orientation.

Date	Mintage	F	VF	XF	Unc
SH1340 (1961)	—	0.75	1.25	2.25	5.00

Note: Some evidence indicates that this variety was the first Republican issue struck in 1973

KM# 950 5 AFGHANIS

Aluminum **Mint:** Afghanistan **Note:** This issue was withdrawn and demonetized due to extensive counterfeiting.

Date	Mintage	F	VF	XF	Unc
SH1337 (1958)	—	1.00	2.00	3.50	5.00

KM# 955 5 AFGHANIS

Nickel Clad Steel **Edge:** Reeded **Mint:** Afghanistan **Note:** Mohammed Sahir Shah

Date	Mintage	F	VF	XF	Unc
SH1340 (1961)	—	0.35	0.75	1.50	3.00

KM# 948 10 AFGHANIS
Aluminum **Mint:** Afghanistan

Date	Mintage	F	VF	XF	Unc
SH1336 (1957)	—	—	—	—	900

KM# 935 4 GRAMS
4.0000 g., 0.9000 Gold .1157 oz. AGW **Mint:** Afghanistan

Date	Mintage	F	VF	XF	Unc
SH1315 (1936)	—	BV	90.00	125	165
SH1317 (1938)	—	BV	90.00	125	165

KM# 933 TILLA
6.0000 g., 0.9000 Gold .1736 oz. AGW **Mint:** Afghanistan

Date	Mintage	F	VF	XF	Unc
SH1313 (1934)	—	125	150	185	275

KM# 934 8 GRAMS
8.0000 g., 0.9000 Gold .2314 oz. AGW **Mint:** Afghanistan

Date	Mintage	F	VF	XF	Unc
SH1314 (1935)	—	BV	155	175	250
SH1315 (1936)	—	BV	155	175	250
SH1317 (1938)	—	BV	155	175	250

KM# 952 8 GRAMS
8.0000 g., 0.9000 Gold .2314 oz. AGW **Mint:** Afghanistan

Date	Mintage	F	VF	XF	Unc
SH1339 (1960)	200	—	—	325	800

Note: Struck for royal presentation purposes. Specimens struck with the same dies (including the "8 grams", the "8" having been effaced after striking), but on thin planchets weighing 3.9-4.0 grams, exist, they are regarded as "mint sports". Market value $250.00 in Unc

REPUBLIC
SH1352-1357 / 1973-1978AD
STANDARD COINAGE

KM# 975 25 PUL
Brass Clad Steel

Date	Mintage	F	VF	XF	Unc
SH1352(1973)	45,950,000	0.25	0.50	1.00	2.00

KM# 976 50 PUL
Copper Clad Steel **Edge:** Plain

Date	Mintage	F	VF	XF	Unc
SH1352(1973)	24,750,000	0.50	1.00	2.00	4.00

KM# 977 5 AFGHANIS
Copper-Nickel Clad Steel

Date	Mintage	F	VF	XF	Unc
SH1352(1973)	34,750,000	1.75	3.50	5.00	10.00

KM# 978 250 AFGHANIS
28.5700 g., 0.9250 Silver .8496 oz. ASW **Subject:** Conservation **Obverse:** National arms **Reverse:** Snow Leopard

Date	Mintage	F	VF	XF	Unc
1978	4,370	—	—	—	30.00

KM# 979 250 AFGHANIS
28.2800 g., 0.9250 Silver .8410 oz. ASW **Subject:** Conservation **Obverse:** National arms **Reverse:** Snow Leopard

Date	Mintage	F	VF	XF	Unc
1978 Proof	4,387	Value: 40.00			

KM# 980 500 AFGHANIS
35.3000 g., 0.9250 Silver 1.0498 oz. ASW **Subject:** Conservation **Obverse:** National arms **Reverse:** Siberian Crane

Date	Mintage	F	VF	XF	Unc
1978	4,374	—	—	—	25.00

KM# 981 500 AFGHANIS
35.0000 g., 0.9250 Silver 1.0408 oz. ASW **Series:** Conservation **Subject:** Siberian Crane

Date	Mintage	F	VF	XF	Unc
1978 Proof	4,218	Value: 35.00			

KM# 982 10000 AFGHANIS
33.4370 g., 0.9000 Gold .9676 oz. AGW **Subject:** Conservation **Obverse:** National arms **Reverse:** Marco Polo Sheep

Date	Mintage	F	VF	XF	Unc
1978	694	—	—	—	650
1978 Proof	181	Value: 1,100			

DEMOCRATIC REPUBLIC
SH1358-1371 / 1979-1992AD
STANDARD COINAGE

KM# 990 25 PUL
Aluminum-Bronze **Obverse:** National arms **Reverse:** Value at center

Date	Mintage	F	VF	XF	Unc
SH1357 (1978)	—	0.25	0.50	1.00	2.00

KM# 996 25 PUL
Aluminum-Bronze **Obverse:** National arms **Reverse:** Value at center

Date	Mintage	F	VF	XF	Unc
SH1359 (1980)	—	0.20	0.35	0.70	1.50

KM# 992 50 PUL
3.0000 g., Aluminum-Bronze **Obverse:** National arms **Reverse:** Value at center

Date	Mintage	F	VF	XF	Unc
SH1357 (1978)	—	0.50	0.80	1.50	2.50

KM# 997 50 PUL
Aluminum-Bronze **Obverse:** National arms **Reverse:** Value at center

Date	Mintage	F	VF	XF	Unc
SH1359 (1980)	—	0.25	0.50	1.00	2.00

KM# 993 AFGHANI
Copper-Nickel **Obverse:** National arms **Reverse:** Value at center

Date	Mintage	F	VF	XF	Unc
SH1357 (1978)	—	0.60	1.00	2.00	4.00

KM# 998 AFGHANI
Copper-Nickel **Obverse:** National arms **Reverse:** Value at center

Date	Mintage	F	VF	XF	Unc
SH1359 (1980)	—	0.50	0.80	1.50	2.50

KM# 994 2 AFGHANIS
Copper-Nickel **Obverse:** National arms **Reverse:** Value at center

Date	Mintage	F	VF	XF	Unc
SH1357 (1978)	—	1.00	1.50	2.00	4.00
SH1358 (1979)	—	1.00	1.50	2.00	4.00

KM# 999 2 AFGHANIS
Copper-Nickel **Obverse:** Similar to 1 Afghani, KM#998

Date	Mintage	F	VF	XF	Unc
SH1359 (1980)	—	0.60	1.00	1.50	3.00

KM# 995 5 AFGHANIS
7.4000 g., Copper-Nickel **Obverse:** National arms **Reverse:** Value at center

Date	Mintage	F	VF	XF	Unc
SH1357 (1978)	—	1.00	2.00	4.00	6.50

KM# 1000 5 AFGHANIS
7.4000 g., Copper-Nickel

Date	Mintage	F	VF	XF	Unc
SH1359 (1980)	—	1.00	1.50	2.00	4.00

KM# 1001 5 AFGHANIS
Brass **Series:** F.A.O. **Subject:** World Food Day **Obverse:** National arms **Reverse:** FAO logo

Date	Mintage	F	VF	XF	Unc
SH1360 (1981)	—	0.25	0.50	1.00	1.75

KM# 1015 10 AFGHANIS
Brass **Subject:** 70th Anniversary of Independence **Obverse:** Arch **Reverse:** Bank logo

Date	Mintage	F	VF	XF	Unc
1989	—	—	—	—	3.50

KM# 1016 50 AFGHANIS
Copper-Nickel **Subject:** 100 Years of the Automobile **Obverse:** National arms **Reverse:** Ferrari

Date	Mintage	F	VF	XF	Unc
ND(1986)	—	—	—	—	14.00

KM# 1006 50 AFGHANIS
Copper-Nickel **Subject:** World Wildlife Fund **Obverse:** National arms **Reverse:** Leopard

Date	Mintage	F	VF	XF	Unc
1987	28,000	—	—	—	15.00

KM# 1024 50 AFGHANIS
Copper **Subject:** Prehistoric Animals **Obverse:** National arms **Reverse:** Deinotherium-Elephant

Date	Mintage	F	VF	XF	Unc
1993	—	—	—	—	20.00

KM# 1032 50 AFGHANIS
Copper **Subject:** Prehistoric Animals **Obverse:** National arms **Reverse:** Ankylosaurus

Date	Mintage	F	VF	XF	Unc
1995 Proof	100	Value: 65.00			

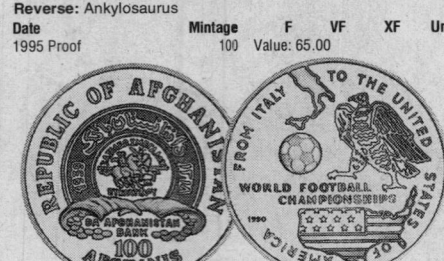

KM# 1014 100 AFGHANIS
Copper-Nickel **Series:** World Soccer Championship **Subject:** Italy to U.S.A. **Obverse:** Bank logo **Reverse:** World Football Championship

Date	Mintage	F	VF	XF	Unc
1990 Proof	10,000	Value: 14.00			

KM# 1017 250 AFGHANIS
20.3100 g., 0.9250 Silver .8716 oz. ASW **Subject:** Conservation **Obverse:** National arms **Reverse:** Snow Leopard

Date	Mintage	F	VF	XF	Unc
1978 4 known	—	—	—	—	500

KM# 1018 500 AFGHANIS
35.4400 g., 0.9250 Silver 1.0539 oz. ASW **Subject:** Conservation **Obverse:** National arms **Reverse:** Siberian Crane

Date	Mintage	F	VF	XF	Unc
1978 4 known	—	—	—	—	500

KM# 1002 500 AFGHANIS
9.0600 g., 0.9000 Silver .2622 oz. ASW **Series:** F.A.O. **Subject:** World Food Day **Obverse:** National arms **Reverse:** FAO

Date	Mintage	F	VF	XF	Unc
SH1360(1981) Proof	—	Value: 25.00			

KM# 1003 500 AFGHANIS
12.0000 g., 0.9990 Silver .3855 oz. ASW **Series:** 100th Anniversary of the Automobile **Reverse:** Ferrari

Date	Mintage	F	VF	XF	Unc
ND(1986)	2,000	—	—	—	40.00

KM# 1004 500 AFGHANIS
12.0000 g., 0.9990 Silver .3855 oz. ASW **Subject:** 1988 Winter Games,Calgary **Obverse:** National arms **Reverse:** Ice dancers

Date	Mintage	F	VF	XF	Unc
ND(1986)	10,000	—	—	—	35.00

KM# 1005 500 AFGHANIS

12.0000 g., 0.9990 Silver .3855 oz. ASW **Subject:** Wildlife Preservation **Obverse:** National arms **Reverse:** Leopard

Date	Mintage	F	VF	XF	Unc
1986	5,000	—	—	—	35.00

KM# 1010 500 AFGHANIS

12.0000 g., 0.9990 Silver .3855 oz. ASW **Series:** 1988 Summer Olympics **Subject:** Volleyball **Mint:** Havana, Cuba

Date	Mintage	F	VF	XF	Unc
1987 (k)	10,000	—	—	—	25.00

KM# 1007 500 AFGHANIS

12.0000 g., 0.9990 Silver .3855 oz. ASW **Subject:** European Soccer Championship - West Germany **Obverse:** National Arms **Reverse:** European Football Championship **Mint:** Havana, Cuba

Date	Mintage	F	VF	XF	Unc
1988 (k)	Est. 5,000	—	—	—	37.50

KM# 1009 500 AFGHANIS

16.0000 g., 0.9990 Silver .5145 oz. ASW **Series:** 1986 World Soccer Championship - Mexico **Obverse:** National Arms **Reverse:** World Football Championship-Mexico 86

Date	Mintage	F	VF	XF	Unc
ND(1988)	5,000	—	—	—	32.00

KM# 1008.1 500 AFGHANIS

16.0000 g., 0.9990 Silver .5145 oz. ASW **Series:** 1992 Winter Olympics **Subject:** Bobsledding **Obverse:** Short thick letters **Reverse:** XVI Winter Olympic Games-Bobsled; 1989 in center-Albertville, 1992 at bottom

Date	Mintage	F	VF	XF	Unc
1989 Proof	Est. 10,000	Value: 30.00			

KM# 1008.2 500 AFGHANIS

16.0000 g., 0.9990 Silver .5145 oz. ASW **Series:** 1992 Winter Olympics **Subject:** Bobsledding **Obverse:** Tall thin letters

Date	Mintage	F	VF	XF	Unc
1989 Proof	Inc. above	Value: 35.00			

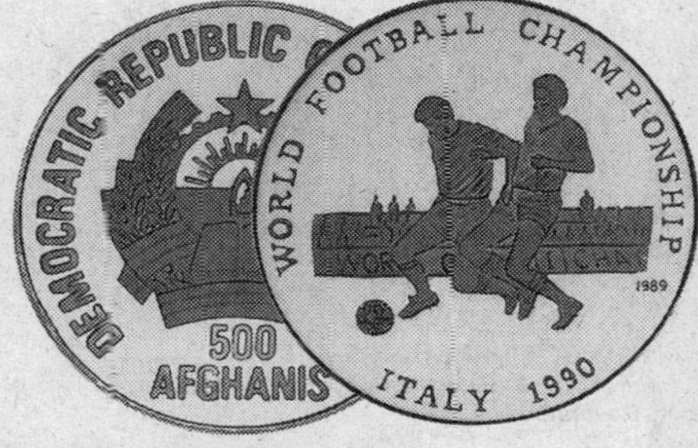

KM# 1011 500 AFGHANIS

16.0000 g., 0.9990 Silver .5145 oz. ASW **Series:** 1990 World Soccer Championship **Obverse:** National Arms **Reverse:** World Football Championship-Italy 1990

Date	Mintage	F	VF	XF	Unc
1989 Proof	10,000	Value: 30.00			

KM# 1012 500 AFGHANIS

16.0000 g., 0.9990 Silver .5145 oz. ASW **Series:** 1992 Summer Olympics **Subject:** Field Hockey **Obverse:** National Arms **Reverse:** XXV Olympic Games-Barcelona-Date, field hockey players between dates

Date	Mintage	F	VF	XF	Unc
1989 Proof	10,000	Value: 30.00			

KM# 1013 500 AFGHANIS

12.0000 g., 0.9990 Silver .3855 oz. ASW **Series:** 1994 World Cup Soccer Games U.S.A. **Obverse:** National Arms **Reverse:** XV World Cup across top - United States of America; date across bottom

Date	Mintage	F	VF	XF	Unc
1991	—	—	—	—	30.00

KM# 1022 500 AFGHANIS

20.0000 g., 0.9990 Silver .6430 oz. ASW **Series:** 1994 World Cup Soccer Games - U.S.A. **Obverse:** National Arms **Reverse:** XV World Cup across top - soccer player with date, USA in center

Date	Mintage	F	VF	XF	Unc
1992 Proof	—	Value: 45.00			

KM# 1020 500 AFGHANIS

16.0000 g., 0.9990 Silver .5145 oz. ASW **Subject:** Prehistoric Animals **Obverse:** National Arms **Reverse:** Deinotherium-Elephant

Date	Mintage	F	VF	XF	Unc
1993 Proof	—	Value: 45.00			

KM# 1021 500 AFGHANIS

16.0000 g., 0.9990 Silver .5145 oz. ASW **Subject:** Prehistoric Animals **Obverse:** National Arms **Reverse:** Styracosaurus

Date	Mintage	F	VF	XF	Unc
1994 Proof	—	Value: 45.00			

KM# 1035 500 AFGHANIS

16.0000 g., 0.9990 Silver .5145 oz. ASW **Subject:** Prehistoric Animals **Obverse:** National Arms **Reverse:** Ankylosaurus

Date	Mintage	F	VF	XF	Unc
1995 Proof	—	Value: 50.00			

KM# 1023 500 AFGHANIS

20.0000 g., 0.9990 Silver .6430 oz. ASW **Series:** 1996 Olympics **Obverse:** National Arms **Reverse:** Three runners and building, small date under building, large date under runners **Rev. Legend:** FROM ATHENS TO ATLANTA

Date	Mintage	F	VF	XF	Unc
1995 Proof	15,000	Value: 22.50			

KM# 1019 10000 AFGHANIS
33.6600 g., 0.9000 Gold .9739 oz. AGW **Subject:** Conservation **Obverse:** National Arms **Reverse:** Marco Polo Sheep

Date	Mintage	F	VF	XF	Unc
1978 4 known	—	—	—	—	2,000

ISLAMIC STATE
SH1373-1381 / 1994-2002AD
STANDARD COINAGE

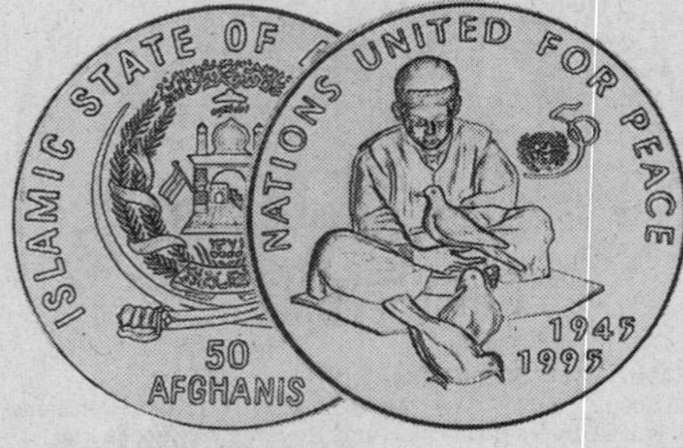

KM# 1026 50 AFGHANIS
Copper-Nickel **Series:** 50th Anniversary - United Nations **Obverse:** State emblem **Reverse:** Meditating figure with three doves

Date	Mintage	F	VF	XF	Unc
ND(1995)	—	—	—	—	8.50

KM# 1030 50 AFGHANIS
Copper-Nickel **Series:** World Food Summit **Obverse:** State emblem **Reverse:** Gate of Zafar

Date	Mintage	F	VF	XF	Unc
1996	—	—	—	—	8.50

KM# 1037 50 AFGHANIS
Copper-Nickel **Series:** Sydney Olympics 2000 **Obverse:** State emblem **Reverse:** Equestrian event

Date	Mintage	F	VF	XF	Unc
1999	10,000	—	—	—	7.50

KM# 1031 500 AFGHANIS
28.4300 g., 0.9250 Silver .8455 oz. ASW **Series:** 50th Anniversary United Nations **Obverse:** State emblem **Reverse:** Meditating figure with three doves

Date	Mintage	F	VF	XF	Unc
ND(1995) Proof	—	Value: 35.00			

KM# 1025 500 AFGHANIS
20.0000 g., 0.9990 Silver .6430 oz. ASW **Subject:** Multicolor Lynx **Obverse:** State emblem **Reverse:** Multicolor Lynx

Date	Mintage	F	VF	XF	Unc
1996 Proof	—	Value: 50.00			

KM# 1027 500 AFGHANIS
20.0000 g., 0.9990 Silver .6430 oz. ASW **Subject:** XVI World Cup Soccer - France **Obverse:** State emblem **Reverse:** Soccer player going for goal

Date	Mintage	F	VF	XF	Unc
1996	100	—	—	—	100
1996 Proof	—	Value: 45.00			

KM# 1028 500 AFGHANIS
20.1300 g., 0.9990 Silver .6465 oz. ASW **Subject:** World Food Summit - Rome **Obverse:** State emblem **Reverse:** Zafar Gate, F.A.O. logo, dates

Date	Mintage	F	VF	XF	Unc
1996 Proof	—	Value: 45.00			

KM# 1036 500 AFGHANIS
20.3100 g., 0.9990 Silver .6465 oz. ASW **Series:** Sydney Olympics 2000 **Obverse:** National emblem **Reverse:** Winged goddess bearing torch, Greek temples behind

Date	Mintage	F	VF	XF	Unc
1996 Proof	500	Value: 40.00			

KM# 1036a 500 AFGHANIS
15.0000 g., 0.9990 Silver .4818 oz. ASW **Series:** Sydney Olympics 2000 **Obverse:** State Emblem **Reverse:** Winged Goddess bearing torch, Greek temples behind

Date	Mintage	F	VF	XF	Unc
1998 Proof	7,500	Value: 27.50			

KM# 1040 500 AFGHANIS
20.0000 g., 0.9990 Silver 0.6424 oz. ASW, 38 mm. **Subject:** World Cup Soccer **Obverse:** State Emblem **Reverse:** Multicolor soccer players, flags and ball **Edge:** Reeded **Mint:** Havana, Cuba

Date	Mintage	F	VF	XF	Unc
1996 Proof	—	Value: 35.00			

KM# 1029 500 AFGHANIS
14.9500 g., 0.9990 Silver .4802 oz. ASW **Series:** World of Adventure **Obverse:** State emblem **Reverse:** Multicolor enamel airplane and statue, cameo portrait

Date	Mintage	F	VF	XF	Unc
1996 Proof	—	Value: 45.00			

KM# 1039 500 AFGHANIS
15.0000 g., 0.9990 Silver .4818 oz. ASW **Subject:** 16th World Cup - Soccer **Obverse:** State Emblem **Reverse:** Soccer player superimposed on ball **Edge:** Plain

Date	Mintage	F	VF	XF	Unc
1997 Proof	—	Value: 37.50			

KM# 1033 500 AFGHANIS
20.0000 g., 0.9990 Silver .6430 oz. ASW **Series:** Sydney Olympics 2000 **Obverse:** State Emblem **Reverse:** Javelin thrower

Date	Mintage	F	VF	XF	Unc
1998 Proof	5,000	Value: 37.50			

KM# 1034 500 AFGHANIS
20.0000 g., 0.9990 Silver .6430 oz. ASW **Subject:** Fauna of Asia **Obverse:** State Emblem **Reverse:** Marco Polo Sheep

Date	Mintage	F	VF	XF	Unc
1998	100	—	—	—	75.00

KM# 1038 500 AFGHANIS
20.0000 g., 0.9990 Silver .6430 oz. ASW **Subject:** Sydney Olympics - 2000 - XXVII Olympiad **Obverse:** State Emblem **Reverse:** Equestrian event

Date	Mintage	F	VF	XF	Unc
1999 Proof	5,000	Value: 30.00			

KM# 1041 500 AFGHANIS
14.9000 g., 0.9990 Silver 0.4786 oz. ASW, 35 mm. **Subject:** Third Millennium **Obverse:** State Emblem **Reverse:** Millennium change design **Edge:** Plain

Date	Mintage	F	VF	XF	Unc
ND(1999) Proof	—	Value: 30.00			

KM# 1042 500 AFGHANIS
15.0000 g., 0.9990 Silver 0.4818 oz. ASW, 35 mm. **Obverse:** State Emblem **Reverse:** Snow Leopard **Edge:** Plain

Date	Mintage	F	VF	XF	Unc
2000 Proof	—	Value: 35.00			

PATTERNS

Including off metal strikes

KM#	Date	Mintage	Identification	Mkt Val
Pn1	SH1310	—	1/2 Afghani. Silver. 4.7500 g.	—
Pn2	SH1336	—	5 Afghanis. Silver. Legend within off-center circle, denomination. National emblem with wreath, date	350
Pn3	SH1336	—	10 Afghanis. Silver. Toughra within off-center circle, denomination. National emblem with wreath, date	350

PIEFORTS

KM#	Date	Mintage	Identification	Mkt Val
P1.1	1989	110	500 Afghanis. 0.9990 Silver. National Arms. XVI Winter Olympic Games, bobsled 1989 in center, Albertville date at bottom. KM#1008.2	85.00
P1.2	1989	—	500 Afghanis. 0.9990 Silver. KM#1008.2, pine tree without needles	125
P1.3	1989	—	500 Afghanis. 0.9990 Silver. KM#1008.2, pine tree with sagging branches	85.00
P1.4	1989	—	500 Afghanis. 0.9990 Silver. KM#1008.2, pine tree with uplifted branches	85.00
P2	1996	—	500 Afghanis. Silver. KM#1029	65.00
P3	1998	—	500 Afghanis. Silver. KM#1033	120
P4	1999	—	500 Afghanis. Silver. KM#1038	80.00

Ajman is the smallest and poorest of the emirates in the United Arab Emirates. It has an estimated area of 100sq. mi. (250 sq. km.) and a population of 6,000. Ajman's first act as an autonomous entity was entering into a treaty with Great Britain in 1820. On December 2, 1971 Ajman became one of the 6 original members of the United Arab Emirates.

TITLE

عجمان

Ajman

RULERS

Abdul Aziz Bin Humaid al-Naimi, 1900-1908
Humaid Bin Abdul Aziz al-Naimi, 1908-1928
Rashid Bin Hamad al-Naimi, 1928-1981
Humaid Bin Rashid al-Naimi, 1981--

MONETARY SYSTEM

100 Dirhams = 1 Riyal

UNITED ARAB EMIRATE

NON-CIRCULATING LEGAL TENDER COINAGE

KM# 1.1 RIYAL
3.9500 g., 0.6400 Silver .0812 oz. ASW **Obv:** Value in circle **Rev:** Two dates

Date	Mintage	F	VF	XF	Unc	BU
AH1389 - 1969	20,000	—	—	—	8.00	10.00
AH1389 - 1969 Proof	1,200	Value: 45.00				

KM# 1.2 RIYAL
3.9500 g., 0.6400 Silver .0812 oz. ASW **Rev:** Three dates

Date	Mintage	F	VF	XF	Unc	BU
AH1390 - 1970	—	—	—	—	20.00	22.50

KM# 2.1 2 RIYALS
6.4500 g., 0.8350 Silver .1731 oz. ASW **Obv:** Value in circle **Rev:** Two dates

Date	Mintage	F	VF	XF	Unc	BU
AH1389-1969	20,000	—	—	—	17.50	20.00
AH1389-1969 Proof	1,200	Value: 55.00				

KM# 2.2 2 RIYALS
6.4500 g., 0.8350 Silver .1731 oz. ASW **Rev:** Three dates

Date	Mintage	F	VF	XF	Unc	BU
AH1390-1970	—	—	—	—	30.00	32.50

KM# 3.1 5 RIYALS
15.0000 g., 0.8350 Silver .4027 oz. ASW **Rev:** Two dates

Date	Mintage	F	VF	XF	Unc	BU
AH1389-1969	10,000	—	—	—	22.50	25.00
AH1389-1969 Proof	1,200	Value: 60.00				

KM# 3.2 5 RIYALS
15.0000 g., 0.8350 Silver .4027 oz. ASW **Obv:** Value in circle **Rev:** Three dates

Date	Mintage	F	VF	XF	Unc	BU
AH1390-1970	—	—	—	—	50.00	55.00
AH1390-1970 Proof	—	Value: 90.00				

KM# 12 5 RIYALS
15.0000 g., 0.9250 Silver .4460 oz. ASW **Subject:** Death of Gamal Abdel Nassar **Obv:** National Arms **Rev:** Gamal Abdel Nassar

Date	Mintage	F	VF	XF	Unc	BU
AH1390-1970 Proof	5,000	Value: 30.00				

KM# 17 5 RIYALS
15.0000 g., 0.9250 Silver .4460 oz. ASW **Obv:** National Arms **Rev:** Dag Hammarskjold

Date	Mintage	F	VF	XF	Unc	BU
ND(1970) Proof	1,175	Value: 75.00				

KM# 18 5 RIYALS
15.0000 g., 0.9250 Silver .4460 oz. ASW **Obv:** National Arms **Rev:** Mahatma Gandhi

Date	Mintage	F	VF	XF	Unc	BU
ND(1970) Proof	1,175	Value: 75.00				

KM# 19 5 RIYALS
15.0000 g., 0.9250 Silver .4460 oz. ASW **Obv:** National Arms **Rev:** Martin Luther King

Date	Mintage	F	VF	XF	Unc	BU
ND(1970) Proof	1,175	Value: 75.00				

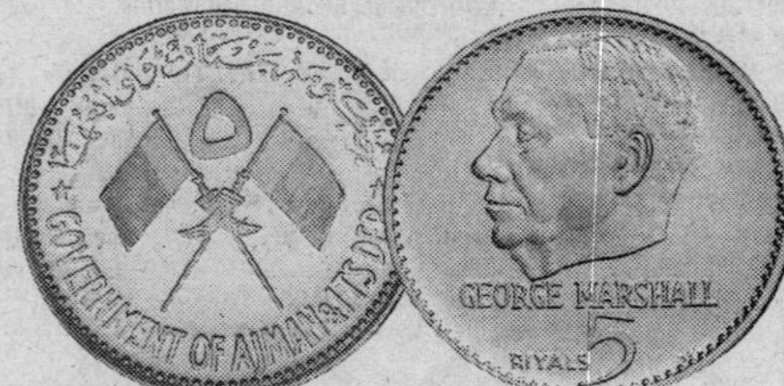

KM# 20 5 RIYALS
15.0000 g., 0.9250 Silver .4460 oz. ASW **Obv:** National Arms **Rev:** George C. Marshall

Date	Mintage	F	VF	XF	Unc	BU
ND(1970) Proof	1,175	Value: 75.00				

KM# 21 5 RIYALS
15.0000 g., 0.9250 Silver .4460 oz. ASW **Obv:** National Arms **Rev:** Bertrand A. Russell

Date	Mintage	F	VF	XF	Unc	BU
ND(1970) Proof	1,175	Value: 75.00				

KM# 22 5 RIYALS
15.0000 g., 0.9250 Silver .4460 oz. ASW **Obv:** National Arms **Rev:** Albert Schweitzer

Date	Mintage	F	VF	XF	Unc	BU
ND(1970) Proof	1,175	Value: 75.00				

KM# 23 5 RIYALS
15.0000 g., 0.9250 Silver .4460 oz. ASW **Obv:** National Arms **Rev:** Jan Palach

Date	Mintage	F	VF	XF	Unc	BU
ND(1970) Proof	1,175	Value: 75.00				

KM# 24 5 RIYALS
15.0000 g., 0.9250 Silver .4460 oz. ASW **Obv:** National Arms **Rev:** Albert J. Luthuli

Date	Mintage	F	VF	XF	Unc	BU
ND(1970) Proof	1,175	Value: 75.00				

KM# 26 5 RIYALS
15.0000 g., 0.9250 Silver .4460 oz. ASW **Series:** F.A.O. **Obv:** National Arms **Rev:** Open hands holding grain, F.A.O. below

Date	Mintage	F	VF	XF	Unc	BU
AH1390-1970 Proof	2,000	Value: 85.00				

Note: This issue is not recognized by the F.A.O.

KM# 27 5 RIYALS
15.0000 g., 0.9250 Silver .4460 oz. ASW **Subject:** Save Venice **Obv:** National arms above bust **Rev:** Save Venice,value

Date	Mintage	F	VF	XF	Unc	BU
ND(1971) Proof	4,800	Value: 135				

KM# 5 7-1/2 RIYALS
23.0000 g., 0.9250 Silver .6840 oz. ASW **Subject:** Rashid bin Humaid al-Naimi **Obv:** National arms above bust **Rev:** Bonefish

Date	Mintage	F	VF	XF	Unc	BU
AH1389-1970	4,350	—	—	—	55.00	60.00
AH1389-1970 Proof	650	Value: 90.00				

KM# 6 7-1/2 RIYALS
23.0000 g., 0.9250 Silver .6840 oz. ASW **Obv:** Head of Rashid bin Humaid al-Naimi in circle **Rev:** Barbary Falcon

Date	Mintage	F	VF	XF	Unc	BU
AH1389-1970	4,350	—	—	—	55.00	60.00
AH1389-1970 Proof	650	Value: 90.00				

KM# 7 7-1/2 RIYALS
23.0000 g., 0.9250 Silver .6840 oz. ASW **Obv:** Head of Rashid bin Humaid al-Naimi in circle **Rev:** Gazelle

Date	Mintage	F	VF	XF	Unc	BU
AH1389-1970	4,350	—	—	—	60.00	65.00
AH1389-1970 Proof	650	Value: 95.00				

KM# 13 7-1/2 RIYALS
23.0000 g., 0.8350 Silver .6175 oz. ASW **Subject:** Death of Gamal Abdel Nassar **Obv:** National Arms;value at bottom **Rev:** Gamal Abdel Nassar

Date	Mintage	F	VF	XF	Unc	BU
AH1390-1970 Proof	6,000	Value: 50.00				

KM# 9.1 10 RIYALS
30.0000 g., 0.9250 Silver .8923 oz. ASW **Obv:** National Arms **Rev:** Vladimir Lenin

Date	Mintage	F	VF	XF	Unc	BU
ND(1970) Proof	—	Value: 175				
ND(1970) Matte	—	—	—	—	—	175

KM# 9.2 10 RIYALS
30.0000 g., 0.9250 Silver .8923 oz. ASW **Obv:** PROOF added

Date	Mintage	F	VF	XF	Unc	BU
ND(1970) Proof	3,200	Value: 50.00				

KM# 28 25 RIYALS
5.1750 g., 0.9000 Gold .1497 oz. AGW **Rev:** Dag Hammarskjold

Date	Mintage	F	VF	XF	Unc	BU
ND(1970) Proof	—	Value: 165				

KM# 29 25 RIYALS
5.1750 g., 0.9000 Gold .1497 oz. AGW **Rev:** Mahatma Gandhi

Date	Mintage	F	VF	XF	Unc	BU
ND(1970) Proof	—	Value: 165				

KM# 30 25 RIYALS
5.1750 g., 0.9000 Gold .1497 oz. AGW **Rev:** Martin Luther King

Date	Mintage	F	VF	XF	Unc	BU
ND(1970) Proof	—	Value: 165				

KM# 31 25 RIYALS
5.1750 g., 0.9000 Gold .1497 oz. AGW **Rev:** George C. Marshall

Date	Mintage	F	VF	XF	Unc	BU
ND(1970) Proof	—	Value: 165				

KM# 32 25 RIYALS
5.1750 g., 0.9000 Gold .1497 oz. AGW **Rev:** Bertrand A. Russell

Date	Mintage	F	VF	XF	Unc	BU
ND(1970) Proof	—	Value: 165				

KM# 33 25 RIYALS
5.1750 g., 0.9000 Gold .1497 oz. AGW **Rev:** Albert Schweitzer

Date	Mintage	F	VF	XF	Unc	BU
ND(1970) Proof	—	Value: 165				

KM# 34 25 RIYALS
5.1750 g., 0.9000 Gold .1497 oz. AGW **Rev:** Jan Palach

Date	Mintage	F	VF	XF	Unc	BU
ND(1970) Proof	—	Value: 165				

KM# 35 25 RIYALS
5.1750 g., 0.9000 Gold .1497 oz. AGW **Rev:** Albert J. Luthuli

Date	Mintage	F	VF	XF	Unc	BU
ND(1970) Proof	—	Value: 165				

KM# 15 25 RIYALS
5.1750 g., 0.9000 Gold .1497 oz. AGW **Subject:** Death of Gamal Abdel Nassar **Obv:** National arms, value below **Rev:** Gamal Abdel Nassar **Note:** Some examples have a serial number on the obverse below the bust.

Date	Mintage	F	VF	XF	Unc	BU
AH1390 Proof	1,100	Value: 145				

KM# 36 25 RIYALS
5.1750 g., 0.9000 Gold .1497 oz. AGW **Rev:** Two men ringing large bell **Rev. Legend:** Save Venice

Date	Mintage	F	VF	XF	Unc	BU
ND(1971) Proof	—	Value: 200				

KM# 16 50 RIYALS
10.3500 g., 0.9000 Gold .2995 oz. AGW **Subject:** Death of Gamal Abdel Nassar **Obv:** Arms **Rev:** Gamal Abdel Nassar **Note:** Similar to 7.5 Riyals, KM#13. Some examples have a serial number below the bust on the obverse.

Date	Mintage	F	VF	XF	Unc	BU
AH1390 Proof	700	Value: 250				

KM# 39 50 RIYALS
10.3500 g., 0.9000 Gold .2995 oz. AGW **Subject:** Save Venice **Obv:** National arms above bust of Rashid bin Humaid al-Naimi **Rev:** Stallion, value

Date	Mintage	F	VF	XF	Unc	BU
ND(1971) Proof	—	Value: 365				

KM# 41 75 RIYALS
15.5300 g., 0.9000 Gold .4494 oz. AGW **Series:** F.A.O. **Obv:** Fish

Date	Mintage	F	VF	XF	Unc	BU
AH1389-1969 Proof	—	Value: 425				

KM# 10 100 RIYALS
20.7000 g., 0.9000 Gold .5990 oz. AGW **Rev:** Vladimir Lenin

Date	Mintage	F	VF	XF	Unc	BU
ND(1970) Proof	1,000	Value: 475				

KM# 40 100 RIYALS
20.7000 g., 0.9000 Gold .5990 oz. AGW **Subject:** Save Venice **Obv:** National arms above bust of Rashid bin Humaid al-Naimi **Rev:** Save Venice;courthouse, value at bottom left

Date	Mintage	F	VF	XF	Unc	BU
ND(1971) Proof	—	Value: 500				

ESSAIS

With Assay or Proof

KM#	Date	Mintage	Identification	Mkt Val
E1	1969	1,250	Riyal. Silver. Value in circle. Two dates. KM#1.1	40.00

KM#	Date	Mintage	Identification	Mkt Val
E2	1969	1,250	2 Riyals. Silver. Value in circle. Two dates. KM#2.1	50.00

KM#	Date	Mintage	Identification	Mkt Val
E3	1969	1,250	5 Riyals. Silver. Value in circle. Two dates. KM#3.1	55.00

KM#	Date	Mintage	Identification	Mkt Val
E4	1970	100	Riyal. Value in circle. Three dates. KM#1.2	50.00

KM#	Date	Mintage	Identification	Mkt Val
E5	1970	100	2 Riyals. KM#2.2	60.00

KM#	Date	Mintage	Identification	Mkt Val
E6	1970	100	5 Riyals. Value in circle. Three dates. KM#3.2	80.00
E7	1970	—	5 Riyals. Aluminum. KM#12	40.00

KM#	Date	Mintage	Identification	Mkt Val
E8	1970	—	7-1/2 Riyals. Silver. Bust of Rashid bin Humaid al-Naimi below arms. Fish with value in circle. KM#5	100

KM#	Date	Mintage	Identification	Mkt Val
E9	1970	—	7-1/2 Riyals. Silver. Head of Rashid bin Humaid al-Naimi in circle. Barbary Falcon,value in circle. KM#6	100
E10	1970	—	7-1/2 Riyals. Aluminum. KM#7	120
E11	1970	—	7-1/2 Riyals. Aluminum. KM#13	55.00
E12	ND(1970)	800	10 Riyals. KM#9.2	80.00

PATTERNS

Including off metal strikes

KM#	Date	Mintage	Identification	Mkt Val
Pn1	1970	—	100 Dirhams. Copper-Nickel.	—

MINT SETS

KM#	Date	Mintage	Identification	Issue Price	Mkt Val
MS1	1969 (3)	—	KM#1.1-3.1	—	55.00
MS2	1970 (3)	4,350	KM#5-7	—	185

PROOF SETS

KM#	Date	Mintage	Identification	Issue Price	Mkt Val
PS1	1969 (3)	1,200	KM#1.1-3.1	11.22	160
PS2	1970 (8)	1,175	KM#17-24	—	600
PS3	1970 (8)	—	KM#28-35	—	1,320
PS4	1970 (4)	—	KM#12, 13, 15, 16	—	475
PS5	1970 (3)	100	KM#E4-6	—	190
PS6	1970 (3)	650	KM#5-7	19.50	275
PS7	1970 (3)	—	KM#E9, E7, 10	—	620
PS8	1970 (2)	800	KM#E7, 10	—	520
PS9	1970 (2)	5,000	KM#12, 13	9.50	80.00
PS10	1970 (3)	—	KM#12, 13, 15	—	225
PS11	1970 (3)	—	KM#9.1, 9.2, 10	—	700
PS12	1971 (4)	—	KM#27, 36, 39, 40	—	1,200

The Republic of Albania, a Balkan republic bounded by Macedonia, Greece, Montenegro, and the Adriatic Sea, has an area of 11,100 sq. mi. (28,748 sq. km.) and a population of 3.49 million. Capital: Tirane. The country is predominantly agricultural, although recent progress has been made in the manufacturing and mining sectors. Petroleum, chrome, iron, copper, cotton textiles, tobacco and wood products are exported.

Since it had been part of the Greek and Roman empires little is known of the early history of Albania. After the disintegration of the Roman Empire Albania was overrun by Goths, Byzantines, Venetians and Turks. Skanderbeg, the national hero, resisted the Turks and established an independent Albania in 1443, but in 1468 the country again fell to the Turks and remained part of the Ottoman Empire for more than 400 years.

Independence was re-established by revolt in 1912, and the present borders established in 1913 by a conference of European powers, which, in 1914, placed Prince William of Wied on the throne; popular discontent forced his abdication within months. In 1920, following World War I occupancy by several nations, a republic was set up. Ahmed Zogu seized the presidency in 1925, and in 1928 he proclaimed himself king with the title of Zog I. King Zog fled when Italy occupied Albania in 1939 and enthroned King Victor Emanuel of Italy. Upon the surrender of Italy to the Allies in 1943, German troops occupied the country. They withdrew in 1944, and communist partisans seized power, naming Gen. Enver Hoxha provisional president. In 1946, following a victory by the communist front in the 1945 elections, a new constitution modeled on that of the USSR was adopted. In accordance with the constitution of Dec. 28, 1976, the official name of Albania was changed from the Peoples Republic of Albania to the Peoples Socialist Republic of Albania.

Albania's former communists were routed in elections. March 1992, amid economic collapse and social unrest, Sali Berisha was elected as the first non-communist president since World War II. Rexhep Mejdani, elected president in 1997, succeeds him.

RULERS

Ahmed Bey Zogu - King Zog I, 1928-1939
Vittorio Emanuele III, 1939-1943

MINT MARKS

L – London
R - Rome
V – Vienna

MONETARY SYSTEM

100 Qindar Leku = 1 Lek
100 Qindar Ari = 1 Frang Ar = 5 Lek

KINGDOM

STANDARD COINAGE

KM# 1 5 QINDAR LEKU

Bronze **Obv:** Lion head left **Rev:** Value above oak branch **Designer:** Giuseppe Romagnoli

Date	Mintage	F	VF	XF	Unc	BU
1926R	512,000	22.00	60.00	90.00	200	—

KM# 2 10 QINDAR LEKU

Bronze **Obv:** Eagle's head right **Rev:** Value between olive branches **Designer:** Giuseppe Romagnoli

Date	Mintage	F	VF	XF	Unc	BU
1926R	511,000	16.00	50.00	80.00	160	—

KM# 14 QINDAR AR

Bronze **Obv:** Two headed Eagle **Rev:** Value above oak leaves and acorn

Date	Mintage	F	VF	XF	Unc	BU
1935R	2,000,000	2.50	6.00	14.00	32.00	—

KM# 15 2 QINDAR ARI

Bronze **Obv:** Two headed Eagle **Rev:** Value above oak leaves

Date	Mintage	F	VF	XF	Unc	BU
1935R	1,500,000	3.50	10.00	18.00	38.00	—

KM# 3 1/4 LEKU

Nickel **Obv:** Lion advancing left **Rev:** Oak branch above value **Designer:** Giuseppe Romagnoli

Date	Mintage	F	VF	XF	Unc	BU
1926R	506,000	3.50	8.00	22.00	48.00	—
1927R	756,000	3.50	8.00	16.00	38.00	—

KM# 4 1/2 LEK

Nickel **Obv:** Two headed Eagle **Rev:** Hercules wrestling Nemean lion **Designer:** Giuseppe Romagnoli

Date	Mintage	F	VF	XF	Unc	BU
1926R	1,002,000	3.00	6.00	14.00	28.00	—

KM# 13 1/2 LEK

Nickel **Obv:** Kings arms **Rev:** Hercules wrestling Nemean lion **Designer:** Giuseppe Romagnoli

Date	Mintage	F	VF	XF	Unc	BU
1930V	500,000	3.00	5.50	12.00	26.00	—
1931L	500,000	3.00	5.50	12.00	26.00	—
1931L Proof	—	Value: 200				

KM# 5 LEK

8.0000 g., Nickel, 26.7 mm. **Obv:** Man facing right **Rev:** Caped man on horse, facing right **Designer:** Giuseppe Romagnoli

Date	Mintage	F	VF	XF	Unc	BU
1926R	1,004,000	2.00	4.00	10.00	25.00	—
1927R	506,000	3.00	7.00	16.00	36.00	—
1930V	1,250,000	1.50	3.00	7.00	22.00	—
1931L	1,000,000	2.00	4.00	10.00	25.00	—
1931L Proof	—	Value: 220				

KM# 6 FRANG AR

5.0000 g., 0.8350 Silver .1342 oz. ASW, 23 mm. **Obv:** Helmeted head facing right **Rev:** Prow of ancient ship **Designer:** Giuseppe Romagnoli

Date	Mintage	F	VF	XF	Unc	BU
1927R	100,000	70.00	130	200	380	—
1928R	60,000	70.00	140	220	400	—

KM# 16 FRANG AR

5.0000 g., 0.8350 Silver .1342 oz. ASW, 23.20 mm. **Obv:** Head of King Zog facing right, date below **Rev:** Kings Arms

Date	Mintage	F	VF	XF	Unc	BU
1935R	700,000	5.00	10.00	22.00	60.00	—
1937R	600,000	5.00	12.00	27.50	70.00	—

KM# 18 FRANG AR

5.0000 g., 0.8350 Silver .1342 oz. ASW, 23 mm. **Subject:** 25th Anniversary of Independence **Obv:** Head of King Zog facing right, date below **Rev:** Kings Arms **Designer:** Romagnoli

Date	Mintage	F	VF	XF	Unc	BU
1937R	50,000	8.00	16.00	36.00	90.00	—

KM# 7 2 FRANGA ARI

10.0000 g., 0.8350 Silver .2684 oz. ASW, 28 mm. **Obv:** Eagle facing left **Rev:** Sower **Designer:** Romagnoli

Date	Mintage	F	VF	XF	Unc	BU
1926R	50,000	60.00	130	250	400	—
1927R	50,000	70.00	150	270	400	—
1928R	60,000	60.00	130	250	400	—

KM# 17 2 FRANGA ARI

10.0000 g., 0.8350 Silver .2684 oz. ASW **Obv:** Head of King Zog facing right, date below **Rev:** Kings Arms

Date	Mintage	F	VF	XF	Unc	BU
1935R	150,000	10.00	30.00	75.00	130	—

KM# 19 2 FRANGA ARI

10.0000 g., 0.8350 Silver .2684 oz. ASW **Subject:** 25th Anniversary of Independence **Obv:** Head of King Zog facing right,date below **Rev:** Kings arms

Date	Mintage	F	VF	XF	Unc	BU
1937R	25,000	15.00	30.00	80.00	150	—

KM# 8.1 5 FRANGA ARI

25.0000 g., 0.9000 Silver .7234 oz. ASW **Obv:** Head of Amet Zogu facing right **Rev:** Man with plow facing left, value **Designer:** Giuseppe Romagnoli

Date	Mintage	F	VF	XF	Unc	BU
1926R	60,000	100	220	450	700	—
1927V	Est. 40,000	—	—	—	—	—

Note: Only exist as provas

KM# 8.2 5 FRANGA ARI

25.0000 g., 0.9000 Silver .7234 oz. ASW **Obv:** Star below bust **Rev:** Kings arms with date below **Designer:** Giuseppe Romagnoli

Date	Mintage	F	VF	XF	Unc	BU
1926R	Inc. above	130	300	490	750	—

KM# 9 10 FRANGA ARI

3.2258 g., 0.9000 Gold .0933 oz. AGW **Obv:** Head of Amet Zogu facing left **Rev:** Kings arms **Designer:** Romagnoli

Date	Mintage	F	VF	XF	Unc	BU
1927R	6,000	120	150	250	360	—

KM# 10 20 FRANGA ARI

6.4516 g., 0.9000 Gold .1867 oz. AGW, 21 mm. **Obv:** Head of Amet Zogu facing left **Rev:** Lion of St. Mark **Designer:** Romagnoli

Date	Mintage	F	VF	XF	Unc	BU
1926R	—	BV	155	260	360	—
1927R	6,000	BV	150	250	375	—

KM# 12 20 FRANGA ARI

6.4516 g., 0.9000 Gold .1867 oz. AGW, 21 mm. **Subject:** George Kastrioti "Skanderbeg" **Obv:** Lion of St. Mark facing right, date below **Rev:** Bust facing right **Designer:** Romagnoli

Date	Mintage	F	VF	XF	Unc	BU
1926R	5,900	140	180	330	440	—
1926 Fasces	100	—	—	4,200	6,500	—

Note: 90 pieces were reported melted

Date	Mintage	F	VF	XF	Unc	BU
1927V	5,453	120	160	290	390	—

KM# 20 20 FRANGA ARI

6.4516 g., 0.9000 Gold .1867 oz. AGW, 21 mm. **Subject:** 25th Anniversary of Independence **Obv:** King Zog facing right, date below **Rev:** Kings arms

Date	Mintage	F	VF	XF	Unc	BU
1937R	2,500	—	200	300	450	—

KM# 22 20 FRANGA ARI

6.4516 g., 0.9000 Gold .1867 oz. AGW, 21 mm. **Subject:** Marriage of King Zog to Countess Geraldine Apponyi, April 27, 1938 **Obv:** King Zog facing right, date below **Rev:** Kings arms

Date	Mintage	F	VF	XF	Unc	BU
1938R	2,500	—	200	300	450	—

KM# 24 20 FRANGA ARI

6.4516 g., 0.9000 Gold .1867 oz. AGW, 21 mm. **Subject:** 10th Anniversary - Reign of King Zog **Obv:** King Zog facing right, date below **Rev:** Kings arms

Date	Mintage	F	VF	XF	Unc	BU
1938R	1,000	—	200	350	520	—

Note: Pieces struck in 1969 from new dies

KM# 25 50 FRANGA ARI

16.1290 g., 0.9000 Gold .4667 oz. AGW **Subject:** 10th Anniversary - Reign of King Zog **Obv:** King Zog facing right, date below **Rev:** Kings Arms

Date	Mintage	F	VF	XF	Unc	BU
1938R	600	—	550	850	1,600	—

Note: Pieces struck in 1969 from new dies

KM# 11.1 100 FRANGA ARI

32.2580 g., 0.9000 Gold .9335 oz. AGW, 35 mm. **Designer:** Giuseppe Romagnoli

Date	Mintage	F	VF	XF	Unc	BU
1926R	6,614	—	650	900	1,500	—

Note: Mintage figures includes provas, Pr7-9

KM# 11.2 100 FRANGA ARI

32.2580 g., 0.9000 Gold .9335 oz. AGW, 35 mm. **Obv:** Amet Zogu with star below **Rev:** Two horse chariot, value below **Designer:** Giuseppe Romagnoli

Date	Mintage	F	VF	XF	Unc	BU
1926R	Inc. above	—	650	1,000	1,600	—

KM# 11.3 100 FRANGA ARI

32.2580 g., 0.9000 Gold .9335 oz. AGW, 35 mm. **Obv:** 2 stars below bust **Rev:** Two horse chariot, value below **Designer:** Romagnoli

Date	Mintage	F	VF	XF	Unc	BU
1926R	Inc. above	—	650	1,000	1,600	—

KM# 11a.1 100 FRANGA ARI

32.2580 g., 0.9000 Gold .9335 oz. AGW, 35 mm. **Obv:** Amet Zogu facing left **Rev:** Two horse chariot, value below **Designer:** Romagnoli

Date	Mintage	F	VF	XF	Unc	BU
1927R	5,000	—	600	800	1,300	—

Note: Mintage figure includes provas, Pr17-19

KM# 11a.2 100 FRANGA ARI

32.2580 g., 0.9000 Gold .9335 oz. AGW **Obv:** Star below bust

Date	Mintage	F	VF	XF	Unc	BU
1927R	Inc. above	—	650	1,000	1,700	—

KM# 11a.3 100 FRANGA ARI

32.2580 g., 0.9000 Gold .9335 oz. AGW **Obv:** 2 stars below bust

Date	Mintage	F	VF	XF	Unc	BU
1927R	Inc. above	—	650	1,000	1,700	—

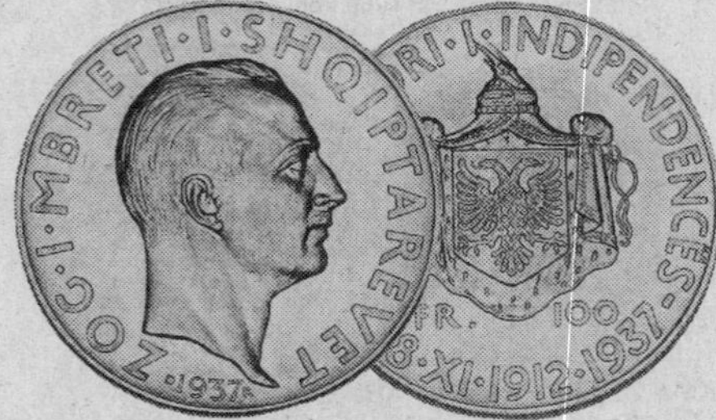

KM# 21 100 FRANGA ARI

32.2580 g., 0.9000 Gold .9335 oz. AGW, 35 mm. **Subject:** 25th Anniversary of Independence **Obv:** King Zog facing right, date below **Rev:** Kings arms

Date	Mintage	F	VF	XF	Unc	BU
1937R	500	—	900	1,500	2,200	—

KM# 23 100 FRANGA ARI

32.2580 g., 0.9000 Gold .9335 oz. AGW, 35 mm. **Subject:** Marriage of King Zog to Countess Geraldine Apponyi, April 27, 1938 **Obv:** King Zog facing right, date below **Rev:** Kings Arms

Date	Mintage	F	VF	XF	Unc	BU
1938R	500	—	900	1,500	2,200	—

KM# 26 100 FRANGA ARI

32.2580 g., 0.9000 Gold .9335 oz. AGW, 35 mm. **Subject:** 10th Anniversary - Reign of King Zog **Obv:** King Zog facing right, date below **Rev:** Kings arms

Date	Mintage	F	VF	XF	Unc	BU
1938R	500	—	900	1,500	2,200	—

Note: Pieces restruck in 1969 from new dies

ITALIAN OCCUPATION WWII

STANDARD COINAGE

KM# 27 0.05 LEK

Aluminum-Bronze **Obv:** King Vittorio Emmanuel III facing right **Rev:** Value below oak branch **Designer:** Romagnoli

Date	Mintage	F	VF	XF	Unc	BU
1940R	1,400,000	3.00	6.00	16.00	32.00	—
1941R Rare	200,000	100	150	330	550	—

KM# 28 0.10 LEK

Aluminum-Bronze **Obv:** King Vitterio Emmanuel III facing left **Rev:** Value below olive branch **Designer:** Romagnoli

Date	Mintage	F	VF	XF	Unc	BU
1940R	550,000	4.00	8.00	20.00	35.00	—
1941R	250,000	18.00	50.00	100	170	—

KM# 29 0.20 LEK

4.0000 g., Stainless Steel, 21.7 mm. **Obv:** King Vittorio Emmanuel III helmeted facing right **Rev:** Two headed Eagle between columns, value below **Designer:** Romagnoli

Date	Mintage	F	VF	XF	Unc	BU
1939R	900,000	1.00	4.00	8.00	14.00	—
Note: 1939 dated coins exist in 2 varieties, magnetic and non-magnetic						
1940R	700,000	1.00	2.00	6.00	16.00	—
1941R	1,400,000	1.00	2.00	4.00	12.00	—

KM# 30 0.50 LEK

Stainless Steel **Obv:** King Vittorio Emmanuel III helmeted facing left **Rev:** Two headed Eagle between columns, value below **Designer:** Romagnoli

Date	Mintage	F	VF	XF	Unc	BU
1939R	100,000	1.50	4.00	10.00	28.00	—
Note: 1939 dated coins exist in two varieties, magnetic and non-magnetic						
1940R	500,000	1.50	3.00	6.00	16.00	—
1941R	—	1.50	3.00	7.00	18.00	—

KM# 31 LEK

Stainless Steel **Obv:** King Vittorio Emmanuel III helmeted facing right **Rev:** Two headed Eagle between columns,value below **Designer:** Romagnoli **Note:** Coins dated after 1939 were not struck for circulation.

Date	Mintage	F	VF	XF	Unc	BU
1939R	2,100,000	1.50	2.50	5.00	15.00	—
Note: 1939 dated coins exist in two varieties, magnetic and non-magnetic						
1940R Rare	1,500,000	—	—	—	—	—
Note: The official mintage figure is large, but few examples are known						
1941R Rare	1,000,000	—	—	—	—	—
Note: The official mintage figure is large, but few examples are known						

KM# 32 2 LEK

Stainless Steel **Obv:** King Vittorio Emmanuel III helmeted facing left **Rev:** Two headed Eagle between columns,value below **Designer:** Romagnoli **Note:** Coins dated after 1939 were not struck for circulation.

Date	Mintage	F	VF	XF	Unc	BU
1939R	1,300,000	2.00	4.00	8.00	18.00	—
Note: 1939 dated coins exist in 2 varieties, magnetic and non-magnetic						
1940R Rare	—	—	—	—	—	—
1941R Rare	—	—	—	—	—	—

KM# 33 5 LEK

5.0000 g., 0.8350 Silver .1342 oz. ASW **Obv:** king Vittori oEmmanuel III facing left **Rev:** Two headed Eagle between columns,value

Date	Mintage	F	VF	XF	Unc	BU
1939R	1,350,000	6.00	12.00	35.00	75.00	—

KM# 34 10 LEK

10.0000 g., 0.8350 Silver .2684 oz. ASW **Obv:** King Vittorio Emmanuel III facing right **Rev:** Two headed Eagle between columns, value

Date	Mintage	F	VF	XF	Unc	BU
1939R	175,000	40.00	70.00	120	220	—

PEOPLE'S SOCIALIST REPUBLIC

1945 - 1990

STANDARD COINAGE

KM# 39 5 QINDARKA

Aluminum **Obv:** National Arms **Rev:** Five stars across top, value in center of wheat

Date	Mintage	F	VF	XF	Unc	BU
1964	—	0.10	0.25	0.50	1.25	1.50

KM# 44 5 QINDARKA

0.8000 g., Aluminum, 18 mm. **Subject:** 25th Anniversary of Liberation **Obv:** National Arms, two dates below **Rev:** Five stars across top, value in center of wheat

Date	Mintage	F	VF	XF	Unc	BU
ND (1969)	—	0.10	0.20	0.30	0.85	1.25

KM# 71 5 QINDARKA
Aluminum **Obv:** National Arms **Rev:** Value between wheat **Edge:** Plain

Date	Mintage	F	VF	XF	Unc	BU
1988	—	—	—	0.20	0.65	1.00

KM# 40 10 QINDARKA
Aluminum **Obv:** National Arms **Rev:** Five stars across top,value at center between wheat

Date	Mintage	F	VF	XF	Unc	BU
1964	—	0.15	0.30	0.60	1.50	1.75

KM# 45 10 QINDARKA
1.2000 g., Aluminum, 20 mm. **Subject:** 25th Anniversary of Liberation **Obv:** National Arms, two dates **Rev:** Five stars across top, value at center between wheat

Date	Mintage	F	VF	XF	Unc	BU
ND (1969)	—	0.10	0.20	0.35	1.00	1.25

KM# 60 10 QINDARKA
Aluminum, 20 mm. **Obv:** National Arms **Rev:** Value at center between wheat **Edge:** Plain

Date	Mintage	F	VF	XF	Unc	BU
1988	—	—	—	0.30	0.80	1.25

KM# 41 20 QINDARKA
1.5000 g., Aluminum, 22 mm. **Obv:** National Arms **Rev:** Five stars across top, value at center between wheat

Date	Mintage	F	VF	XF	Unc	BU
1964	—	0.20	0.40	0.60	1.75	2.00

KM# 46 20 QINDARKA
1.6000 g., Aluminum, 22 mm. **Subject:** 25th Anniversary of Liberation **Obv:** National Arms, two dates **Rev:** Five stars across top,value at center between wheat

Date	Mintage	F	VF	XF	Unc	BU
ND (1969)	—	0.15	0.30	0.50	1.25	1.50

KM# 65 20 QINDARKA
Aluminum **Obv:** National Arms **Rev:** Value at center between wheat

Date	Mintage	F	VF	XF	Unc	BU
1988	—	—	—	0.20	0.80	1.25

KM# 42 50 QINDARKA
Aluminum **Obv:** National Arms **Rev:** Five stars across top, value at center between wheat

Date	Mintage	F	VF	XF	Unc	BU
1964	—	0.50	0.75	2.00	4.00	6.00

KM# 47 50 QINDARKA
2.0000 g., Aluminum, 24.4 mm. **Subject:** 25th Anniversary of Liberation **Rev:** Two half-length figures holding torch aloft, value below

Date	Mintage	F	VF	XF	Unc	BU
ND (1969)	—	0.30	0.50	1.00	2.00	3.00

KM# 72 50 QINDARKA
2.0000 g., Aluminum, 24.1 mm. **Obv:** National Arms **Rev:** Value at center between wheat, inside beaded circle **Edge:** Plain

Date	Mintage	F	VF	XF	Unc	BU
1988	—	—	—	0.50	1.40	2.25

KM# 35 1/2 LEKU
Zinc **Obv:** National Arms inside 3/4 circle of stars **Rev:** Value inside circle of stars, date at bottom

Date	Mintage	F	VF	XF	Unc	BU
1947	—	0.40	0.80	2.00	5.00	7.00
1957	—	0.25	0.50	1.00	2.00	3.00

KM# 36 LEK
Zinc **Obv:** National Arms inside 3/4 circle of stars **Rev:** Value inside circle of stars, date at bottom

Date	Mintage	F	VF	XF	Unc	BU
1947	—	0.60	1.00	3.00	6.00	8.00
1957	—	0.35	0.75	1.50	3.00	4.00

KM# 43 LEK
2.3000 g., Aluminum, 26.5 mm. **Obv:** National Arms between stars, date at bottom **Rev:** Five stars across top, value at center of wheat

Date	Mintage	F	VF	XF	Unc	BU
1964	—	0.50	1.00	2.00	4.00	5.50

KM# 48 LEK
2.3000 g., Aluminum, 26.5 mm. **Subject:** 25th Anniversary of Liberation **Obv:** National Arms between stars,two dates at bottom **Rev:** Armed man with knee on man on ground, value below

Date	Mintage	F	VF	XF	Unc	BU
ND (1969)	—	0.35	0.75	1.25	3.00	4.50

KM# 66 LEK
Aluminum-Bronze **Obv:** National Arms inside legend, date below **Rev:** Large value above wheat inside beaded circle

Date	Mintage	F	VF	XF	Unc	BU
1988	—	—	—	0.50	1.80	2.25

KM# 74 LEK
2.0000 g., Aluminum, 24.2 mm. **Obv:** National Arms **Rev:** Large value above wheat inside beaded circle

Date	Mintage	F	VF	XF	Unc	BU
1988	—	—	—	0.40	1.60	2.00

KM# 37 2 LEKE
Zinc **Obv:** National Arms inside 3/4/circle of stars, beaded edge **Rev:** Large value at center of circle stars, date below, beaded edge

Date	Mintage	F	VF	XF	Unc	BU
1947	—	0.50	1.25	3.00	6.00	8.00
1957	—	0.35	0.75	1.50	3.00	4.00

KM# 67 2 LEKE
7.6000 g., Copper-Nickel, 26 mm. **Subject:** 45th Anniversary - WWII **Obv:** National Arms inside legend, date below **Rev:** Armed man standing inside star, right arm raised, value to right

Date	Mintage	F	VF	XF	Unc	BU
1989	—	—	—	1.00	3.75	5.50

KM# 73 2 LEKE
Copper-Nickel **Obv:** National Arms inside legend, date below **Rev:** Large value above wheat inside beaded circle

Date	Mintage	F	VF	XF	Unc	BU
1989	—	—	—	1.20	4.00	5.50

KM# 38 5 LEKE

Zinc **Obv:** National Arms inside 3/4 circle of stars **Rev:** Large value inside circle of stars, date below

Date	Mintage	F	VF	XF	Unc	BU
1947	—	1.00	1.75	4.50	8.00	10.00
1957	—	0.50	1.00	2.00	3.50	5.00

KM# 49.1 5 LEKE

16.6600 g., 0.9990 Silver .5165 oz. ASW **Subject:** 500th Anniversary - Liga Lissi Skanderbeg's Victory Over the Turks **Obv:** Arms on shield, swords behind, flanking sides, cap on top, two dates below shield **Rev:** Without date below arms, oval fineness countermark punched in

Date	Mintage	F	VF	XF	Unc	BU
ND (1969) Proof	8,540	Value: 28.00				

Note: Countermarks for 1968 and 1969 coins were hand positioned, then punched. The result is a variety of countermark positions, to the left and right of LEKE

KM# 49.2 5 LEKE

16.6600 g., 0.9990 Silver .5165 oz. ASW **Obv:** Arms on shield, cap above shield, swords behind, flanking sides, two dates below shield **Rev:** Date below arms

Date	Mintage	F	VF	XF	Unc	BU
1969 Proof	1,500	Value: 26.00				

Note: Countermarks for 1968 and 1969 coins were hand positioned, then punched. The result is a variety of countermark positions, to the left and right of LEKE

KM# 49.3 5 LEKE

16.6600 g., 0.9990 Silver .5165 oz. ASW **Obv:** Arms on shield, cap above shield, swords behind flanking sides, two dates below **Rev:** Date below arms, oval fineness in relief

Date	Mintage	F	VF	XF	Unc	BU
1970 Proof	500	Value: 40.00				

Note: For the 1970 issue the fineness marking has been incorporated in the dies

KM# 57 5 LEKE

28.2000 g., Copper-Nickel, 38.7 mm. **Subject:** Seaport of Durazzo **Obv:** National Arms, outer beaded circle, date below arms **Rev:** Ship on water at right, seaport to the left, value at bottom

Date	Mintage	F	VF	XF	Unc	BU
1987	Est. 50,000	—	—	6.00	12.50	15.00

KM# 57a 5 LEKE

50.0000 g., 0.9000 Gold 1.4470 oz. AGW **Subject:** Seaport of Durazzo

Date	Mintage	F	VF	XF	Unc	BU
1987 Proof	5	Value: 2,500				

KM# 61 5 LEKE

28.2000 g., Copper-Nickel, 38.7 mm. **Subject:** 42nd Anniversary of First Railroad **Obv:** Train engine emerging from tunnel, left side, circle surrounding, legend outside circle with date at bottom **Rev:** Caboose in tunnel, right side, date on tracks, lower left, circle surrounding all, value below circle **Edge:** Reeded

Date	Mintage	F	VF	XF	Unc	BU
1988	20,000	—	—	6.50	18.00	24.00

KM# 50.1 10 LEKE

33.3300 g., 0.9990 Silver 1.0354 oz. ASW **Subject:** 500th Anniversary - Death of Prince Skanderbeg **Obv:** Man on horse facing right, between dates **Rev:** Oval fineness countermark punched in, no date below; value below arms

Date	Mintage	F	VF	XF	Unc	BU
ND Proof	8,540	Value: 40.00				

Note: Countermark for 1968 and 1969 coins were hand positioned, then punched. The result is a variety of countermark positions, to the left and right of LEKE

KM# 50.2 10 LEKE

33.3300 g., 0.9990 Silver 1.0354 oz. ASW **Rev:** Date below arms

Date	Mintage	F	VF	XF	Unc	BU
1969 Proof	1,500	Value: 45.00				

Note: Countermark for 1968 and 1969 coins were hand positioned, then punched. The result is a variety of countermark positions, to the left and right of LEKE

KM# 50.3 10 LEKE

33.3300 g., 0.9990 Silver 1.0354 oz. ASW **Obv:** Man on horse facing right, between dates **Rev:** Oval fineness is in relief, date below arms, value below date

Date	Mintage	F	VF	XF	Unc	BU
1970 Proof	500	Value: 52.00				

Note: For the 1970 issues the fineness marking has been incorporated in the dies

KM# 50.4 10 LEKE

33.3300 g., 0.9990 Silver 1.0354 oz. ASW **Obv:** Man on horse facing right, between dates **Rev:** Hallmark countermark left of LEKE, oval fineness countermark in relief, date below arms, value below date

Date	Mintage	F	VF	XF	Unc	BU
1970 Proof	Inc. above	Value: 52.00				

Note: For the 1970 issues the fineness marking has been incorporated in the dies

KM# 51.1 20 LEKE

3.9500 g., 0.9000 Gold .1143 oz. AGW **Subject:** 500th Anniversary - Death of Prince Skanderbeg **Obv:** Skanderberg helmet within wreath, scythe at left of helmet **Rev:** Oval fineness countermark punched in

Date	Mintage	F	VF	XF	Unc	BU
1968	2,920	Value: 95.00				

Note: Countermark for 1968 and 1969 coins were hand positioned, then punched. The result is a variety of countermark positions, to the left and right of LEKE

KM# 51.2 20 LEKE

3.9500 g., 0.9000 Gold .1143 oz. AGW **Obv:** Skanderberg helmet within wreath, scythe at left of helmet **Rev:** Without fineness countermark (error)

Date	Mintage	F	VF	XF	Unc	BU
1968 Proof	Inc. above	Value: 95.00				

KM# 51.3 20 LEKE

3.9500 g., 0.9000 Gold .1143 oz. AGW **Obv:** Skanderberg helmet within wreath, scythe at left of helmet **Rev:** Cornucopia countermark at right of LEKE **Note:** Variety of countermark positions.

Date	Mintage	F	VF	XF	Unc	BU
1968 Paris	24	—	—	350	420	450

KM# 51.4 20 LEKE
3.9500 g., 0.9000 Gold .1143 oz. AGW **Rev:** Date added below arms **Note:** Variety of countermark positions.

Date	Mintage	F	VF	XF	Unc	BU
1969 Proof	650	Value: 140				

KM# 51.5 20 LEKE
3.9500 g., 0.9000 Gold .1143 oz. AGW **Obv:** Skanderberg helmet within wreath, scythe to left of helmet **Rev:** Date below arms, oval fineness in relief, incorporated in dies

Date	Mintage	F	VF	XF	Unc	BU
1970 Proof	500	Value: 150				

KM# 51.6 20 LEKE
3.9500 g., 0.9000 Gold .1143 oz. AGW **Obv:** Skanderberg helmet within wreath, scythe to left of helmet **Rev:** Sunken countermark 1 AR left of LEKE and raised oval fineness countermark on right incorporated into the dies

Date	Mintage	F	VF	XF	Unc	BU
1970 Proof	—	Value: 200				

KM# 52.1 25 LEKE
83.3300 g., 0.9990 Silver 2.5887 oz. ASW **Obv:** Dance with swords **Rev:** Date below arms, oval fineness countermark

Date	Mintage	F	VF	XF	Unc	BU
1968 Proof	8,540	Value: 54.00				

Note: Countermarks for 1968 and 1969 coins were hand positioned, then punched; the result is a variety of countermark positions, to the left and the right of LEKE

KM# 52.2 25 LEKE
83.3300 g., 0.9990 Silver 2.5887 oz. ASW **Obv:** Date below scene **Rev:** Date below arms, oval fineness countermark

Date	Mintage	F	VF	XF	Unc	BU
1969 Proof	—	Value: 65.00				

KM# 52.3 25 LEKE
83.3300 g., 0.9990 Silver 2.5887 oz. ASW, 60 mm. **Obv:** Without date **Rev:** Oval fineness countermark in relief **Note:** Photo reduced.

Date	Mintage	F	VF	XF	Unc	BU
1970 Proof	500	Value: 90.00				

Note: For the 1970 issue the fineness marking has been incorporated in the dies

KM# 53.1 50 LEKE
9.8700 g., 0.9000 Gold .2856 oz. AGW **Obv:** Argirocastrum Ruins, date below **Rev:** Oval fineness countermark

Date	Mintage	F	VF	XF	Unc	BU
1968 Proof	3,120	Value: 185				

KM# 53.2 50 LEKE
9.8700 g., 0.9000 Gold .2856 oz. AGW **Obv:** Argirocastrum ruins, date below **Rev:** Date below arms, oval fineness countermark, value below date

Date	Mintage	F	VF	XF	Unc	BU
1969 Proof	500	Value: 275				

KM# 53.3 50 LEKE
9.8700 g., 0.9000 Gold .2856 oz. AGW **Obv:** Without date **Rev:** Oval fineness countermark in relief

Date	Mintage	F	VF	XF	Unc	BU
1970 Proof	100	Value: 420				

Note: For the 1970 issue the fineness marking has been incorporated in the dies

KM# 58a 50 LEKE
155.5000 g., 0.9990 Gold 4.9950 oz. AGW **Subject:** Seaport of Durazzo

Date	Mintage	F	VF	XF	Unc	BU
1987 Proof	5	Value: 6,500				

KM# 58 50 LEKE
168.1500 g., 0.9250 Silver 5.0012 oz. ASW, 65 mm. **Subject:** Seaport of Durazzo **Obv:** Similar to 5 Leke, KM#57 **Rev:** Similar to KM#57 **Note:** Photo reduced.

Date	Mintage	F	VF	XF	Unc	BU
1987 Proof	Est. 15,000	Value: 140				

KM# 62 50 LEKE
168.1500 g., 0.9250 Silver 5.0012 oz. ASW, 65 mm. **Subject:** 42nd Anniversary - First Railroad **Obv:** Train engine in tunnel, left side, inside circle, legend surrounding circle, two dates at bottom **Rev:** Caboose in tunnel, right side, date on tracks, bottom left, circle surrounding all, value below circle **Note:** Photo reduced.

Date	Mintage	F	VF	XF	Unc	BU
1988 Proof	7,500	Value: 320				

KM# 54.1 100 LEKE
19.7500 g., 0.9000 Gold .5715 oz. AGW **Obv:** Peasant girl in national dress, date below **Rev:** Oval fineness countermark

Date	Mintage	F	VF	XF	Unc	BU
1968 Proof	3,470	Value: 385				

KM# 54.2 100 LEKE
19.7500 g., 0.9000 Gold .5715 oz. AGW **Obv:** Date below scene **Rev:** Date below arms, oval fineness countermark

Date	Mintage	F	VF	XF	Unc	BU
1969 Proof	450	Value: 480				

KM# 54.3 100 LEKE
19.7500 g., 0.9000 Gold .5715 oz. AGW **Obv:** Without date **Rev:** Oval fineness countermark in relief incorporated into the dies

Date	Mintage	F	VF	XF	Unc	BU
1970 Proof	Inc. above	Value: 500				

KM# 59 100 LEKE
6.4500 g., 0.9000 Gold .1866 oz. AGW **Subject:** Seaport of Durazzo **Obv:** Arms **Rev:** Ship in harbor **Note:** Similar to 5 Leke, KM#57.

Date	Mintage	F	VF	XF	Unc	BU
1987 Proof	5,000	Value: 185				

KM# 63 100 LEKE
6.4500 g., 0.9000 Gold .1866 oz. AGW **Subject:** 42nd Anniversary - First Railroad **Obv:** Train engine emerging from tunnel **Rev:** Caboose leaving tunnel **Note:** Similar to 50 Leke, KM#62, but without hole in coin

Date	Mintage	F	VF	XF	Unc	BU
1988 Proof	2,000	Value: 280				

KM# 55.1 200 LEKE
39.4900 g., 0.9000 Gold 1.1427 oz. AGW **Subject:** Buthrotum Ruins **Obv:** Head in front of Buthrotum Ruins, facing right **Rev:** Similar to 100 Leke, KM#54.1, value below arms

Date	Mintage	F	VF	XF	Unc	BU
1968 Proof	2,170	Value: 750				

KM# 55.2 200 LEKE
39.4900 g., 0.9000 Gold 1.1427 oz. AGW **Rev:** Date below arms, oval fineness countermark in a variety of positions

Date	Mintage	F	VF	XF	Unc	BU
1969 Proof	200	Value: 820				

KM# 55.3 200 LEKE
39.4900 g., 0.9000 Gold 1.1427 oz. AGW **Obv:** Without date **Rev:** Oval fineness countermark in relief incorporated into the die

Date	Mintage	F	VF	XF	Unc	BU
1970 Proof	Inc. above	Value: 850				

KM# 56.1 500 LEKE
98.7400 g., 0.9000 Gold 2.8574 oz. AGW **Subject:** 500th Anniversary - Death of Prince Skanderbeg **Rev:** Similar to 100 Leke, KM#54.1

Date	Mintage	F	VF	XF	Unc	BU
1968 Proof	1,520	Value: 1,875				

KM# 56.2 500 LEKE
98.7400 g., 0.9000 Gold 2.8574 oz. AGW **Rev:** Date below arms, oval fineness countermark in a variety of positions

Date	Mintage	F	VF	XF	Unc	BU
1969 Proof	200	Value: 1,950				

KM# 56.3 500 LEKE
98.7400 g., 0.9000 Gold 2.8574 oz. AGW **Obv:** Without date **Rev:** Oval fineness countermark in relief incorporated into the die

Date	Mintage	F	VF	XF	Unc	BU
1970 Proof	Inc. above	Value: 2,000				

KM# 64 7500 LEKE
483.7500 g., 0.9000 Gold 13.9992 oz. AGW **Subject:** 42nd Anniversary - First Railroad **Obv:** Train engine emerging from tunnel **Rev:** Caboose leaving tunnel **Note:** Similar to 50 Leke, KM#62.

Date	Mintage	F	VF	XF	Unc	BU
1988 Proof	50	Value: 10,000				

REPUBLIC

STANDARD COINAGE

KM# 75 LEK
3.0000 g., Bronze, 18.1 mm. **Obv:** Pelican **Rev:** Denomination

Date	Mintage	F	VF	XF	Unc	BU
1996	—	—	—	0.40	1.50	2.00

KM# 76 5 LEKE
3.1000 g., Steel, 20 mm. **Obv:** Imperial eagle **Rev:** Olive branch, denomination

Date	Mintage	F	VF	XF	Unc	BU
1995	—	—	—	—	1.00	1.25
2000	—	—	—	—	1.00	1.25

KM# 68 10 LEKE
52.5000 g., 0.9250 Silver 1.5613 oz. ASW **Subject:** 1992 Summer Olympics - Equestrian **Rev:** Horse and rider right, incuse design

Date	Mintage	F	VF	XF	Unc	BU
1991	980	—	—	150	200	220

KM# 69 10 LEKE
52.5000 g., 0.9250 Silver 1.5613 oz. ASW **Subject:** 1992 Summer Olympics - Equestrian **Obv:** National Arms, value below, date at bottom **Rev:** Horse and rider left, relief design

Date	Mintage	F	VF	XF	Unc	BU
1991	980	—	—	150	200	220

KM# 70 10 LEKE
28.4600 g., 0.9250 Silver .8464 oz. ASW **Subject:** 1992 Summer Olympics - Boxing **Obv:** National Arms dividing date **Rev:** Boxers left, value right center **Rev. Designer:** Willem Vis

Date	Mintage	F	VF	XF	Unc	BU
1992 Proof	20,000	Value: 48.00				

KM# 77 10 LEKE
3.6000 g., Brass, 21.1 mm. **Obv:** Fortress **Rev:** Denomination, sprig with berries

Date	Mintage	F	VF	XF	Unc	BU
1996	—	—	—	—	1.25	1.50
2000	—	—	—	—	1.25	1.50

KM# 78 20 LEKE
4.9000 g., Brass, 23.5 mm. **Obv:** Ancient sailing vessel **Rev:** Denomination

Date	Mintage	F	VF	XF	Unc	BU
1996	—	—	—	—	1.60	2.00
2000	—	—	—	—	1.60	2.00

KM# 79 50 LEKE
5.5000 g., Copper-Nickel, 24.5 mm. **Obv:** Ancient equestrian **Rev:** Denomination, tied oak sprigs

Date	Mintage	F	VF	XF	Unc	BU
1996	—	—	—	—	2.00	3.00
2000	—	—	—	—	2.00	3.00

KM# 80 100 LEKE
6.7000 g., Bi-Metallic Aluminum-Bronze center in Copper-Nickel ring, 24.7 mm. **Obv:** Teuta, Illyrian queen, stateswoman, reigned 231 BC **Rev:** Denomination in wreath. **Edge:** Reeded

Date	Mintage	F	VF	XF	Unc	BU
2000	—	—	—	—	4.00	5.00

TRIAL STRIKES

KM#	Date	Mintage	Identification	Issue Price	Mkt Val
TS1	1969	—	500 Leke. Goldine-Brass. 56.3200 g. 55 mm. Blank with MET countermark. Like KM56.2.	—	175

PATTERNS

Including off metal strikes

KM#	Date	Mintage	Identification	Mkt Val
Pn1	1927	—	Frang Ar. Silver. Plain edge. Prev. KM#Pn7.	500
Pn2	1927	—	5 Franga Ari. Copper. Prev. KM#Pn9.	—
Pn3	1928	—	2 Lek. Copper-Nickel. Prev. KM#Pn11.	—
Pn4	1968	—	10 Leke. 0.9990 Silver. 31.6000 g. Like 10 Leke, KM#50. Blank except for MET in rectangle at 6 o'clock. Reeded edge.	—

ESSAIS

KM#	Date	Mintage	Identification	Mkt Val
E1	1926	—	5 Qindar Leku. Bronze.	—
E2	1926	—	10 Qindar Ari. Bronze. Prev. KM#Pn2.	—
E3	1926	—	1/2 Lek. Nickel. Prev. KM#Pn3.	—
E4	1926	50	2 Franga Ari. Silver. Prev. KM#Pn4.	500
E5	1927	—	Lek. Nickel. Prev. KM#Pn5.	—
E6	1927	—	Frang Ar. Silver. Prev. KM#Pn6.	500
E7	1927	50	2 Franga Ari. Silver. Prev. KM#Pn8.	650
E8	1927	—	100 Franga Ari. Silver. Prev. KM#Pn10.	—
E9	1928	—	2 Lek. Nickel. Prev. KM#Pn12.	—
E10	1928	50	Frang Ar. Silver. Prev. KM#Pn13.	500
E11	1928	50	2 Franga Ari. Silver. Prev. KM#Pn14.	650
E12	1938	—	100 Franga Ari. Gold. Without signature. Prev. KM#Pn15.	—
E13	1986	10	5 Leke. Copper-Nickel. 27.7900 g.	200

PIEFORTS

KM#	Date	Mintage	Identification	Mkt Val
P1	1988	250	50 Leke. 0.9250 Silver. KM#62 without tunnel hole.	500

PROVAS

Standard metals unless otherwise stated

KM#	Date	Mintage	Identification	Mkt Val
Pr1	1926R	50	5 Qindar Leku. Bronze. KM#1.	400
Pr2	1926R	50	10 Qindar Leku. Bronze. KM#2.	400
Pr3	1926R	50	1/4 Leku. Nickel. Male lion left. Oak leaf across top, value below. KM#3.	500
Pr4	1926	—	1/2 Lek. Nickel.	400
Pr5	1926R	—	1/2 Lek. Nickel. KM#4.	400
Pr6	1926R	50	Lek. Nickel. KM#5.	500
Pr7	1926R	—	2 Franga Ari. Silver. KM#7.	500
Pr8	1926R	—	5 Franga Ari. Silver. KM#8. Modern copy of 5 Franga Ari exist in copper and bronze.	750
Pr9	1926R	—	5 Franga Ari. Copper. KM#8. Modern copy of 5 Franga Ari exist in copper and bronze.	450
Pr10	1926R	—	5 Franga Ari. Silver. KM#8. Modern copy of 5 Franga Ari exist in copper and bronze.	500
Pr11	1926R	—	5 Franga Ari. Copper. KM#8. Modern copy of 5 Franga Ari exist in copper and bronze.	450
Pr12	1926R	50	20 Franga Ari. Gold. KM#12.	650
Pr13	1926	—	20 Franga Ari. Gold. KM#12.	5,000
Pr14	1926R	—	100 Franga Ari. Gold. KM#11.1.	2,000
Pr15	1926R	—	100 Franga Ari. Gold. Biga, right. Star, KM#11.2.	2,000
Pr16	1926R	—	100 Franga Ari. Gold. King Zog, left. Biga, right. 2 stars, KM#11.3.	2,000
Pr17	1927R	—	1/4 Leku. Nickel. KM#3.	500
Pr18	1927R	—	Lek. Nickel. KM#5.	500
Pr19	1927R	50	Frang Ar. Silver. KM#6.	300
Pr20	1927V	—	Frang Ar. Silver. KM#6.	350
Pr21	1927R	—	2 Franga Ari. Silver. KM#7.	300
Pr22	1927V	—	5 Franga Ari. Silver.	450
Pr23	1927V	—	5 Franga Ari. Silver. Matte proof.	—
Pr24	1927	—	10 Franga Ari. Gold. KM#9.	850
PrA25	1927R	—	Frang Ar. Silver. King, right. Double eagle, date at bottom. Similar to KM#9.	—
Pr25	1927R	50	10 Franga Ari. Gold. KM#9.	700
Pr26	1927	—	20 Franga Ari. Gold. KM#10.	800
Pr27	1927V	—	20 Franga Ari. Gold. KM#12.	600
Pr28	1927R	50	20 Franga Ari. Gold. KM#10.	600
Pr29	1927R	—	100 Franga Ari. KM#11a.	2,200
Pr30	1927R	—	100 Franga Ari. Gold. Star, KM#11a.1.	2,200
Pr31	1927R	—	100 Franga Ari. Gold. 2 stars, KM#11a.2.	2,200
PrA32	1927V	—	100 Franga Ari. Silver. King Zog, right. Man with oxen pulling plow, left. Similar to 5 Franga Ari, KM#8.1.	2,200
Pr32	1928R	—	2 Lek. Copper-Nickel. KM#28.	200
Pr33	1928R	—	2 Lek. Nickel. KM#28.	—
PrA34	1928R	—	2 Lek. Nickel. 9.7800 g. Portrait, right. Double eagle.	300
Pr34	1928R	—	Frang Ar. Silver. KM#6.	200
Pr35	1928R	—	2 Franga Ari. Silver. KM#7.	250
PrA36	1928R	—	2 Franga Ari. Silver. 10.0400 g. Portrait. Double eagle.	350
Pr36	1928R	50	100 Franga Ari. Gold. Portrait, left. Double eagle, cap on top, date bottom left. Bare head.	3,000
Pr37	1928R	50	100 Franga Ari. Gold. Portrait in wreath, left. Double eagle, cap on top, date at bottom left. Bare head, wreath.	3,000
Pr38	1928R	50	100 Franga Ari. Gold. Uniformed bust,right,laureated circle surrounding. Double eagle, cap on top, date bottom left, laureated circle surrounding. Uniformed bust.	3,750

KM#	Date	Mintage	Identification	Mkt Val

KM#	Date	Mintage	Identification	Mkt Val
Pr39	1929R	50	100 Franga Ari. Gold. Portrait in wreath, left. Double eagle, cap on top, date below tail. Bare head, wreath.	3,000
Pr40	1935R	50	Qindar Ar. Bronze. KM#14.	300
Pr41	1935R	50	2 Qindar Ari. Bronze. KM#15.	300
Pr42	1935	50	Frang Ar. Silver.	400
Pr43	1935	50	2 Franga Ari. Silver.	500
Pr44	1935	—	5 Franga Ari. Silver. Pattern.	—
Pr45	1937R	50	Frang Ar. Silver. KM#16.	450
Pr46	1937R	50	Frang Ar. Silver.	500
Pr47	1937R	50	2 Franga Ari. Silver.	525
Pr48	1937R	—	10 Franga Ari. Gold. Reported, not confirmed	—
Pr49	1937R	50	20 Franga Ari. Gold. KM#20.	850

KM#	Date	Mintage	Identification	Mkt Val
Pr50	1937R	50	100 Franga Ari. Gold. Portrait,bare head,right. Arms on ornate shield. KM#21.	2,400
Pr51	1938R	50	20 Franga Ari. Gold. KM#22.	800
Pr52	1938R	50	20 Franga Ari. Gold. KM#24.	800
Pr53	1938R	50	50 Franga Ari.	2,200

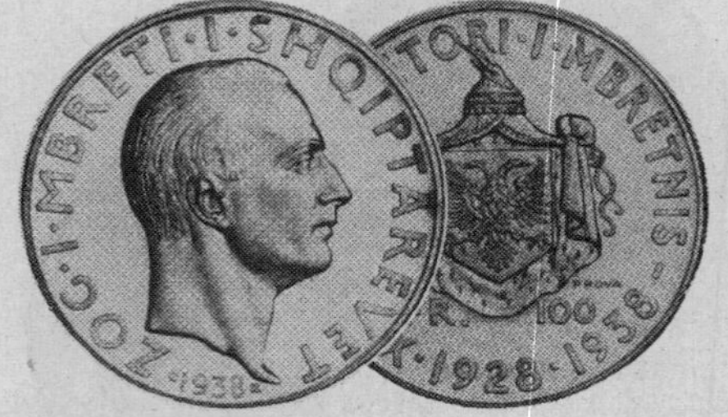

KM#	Date	Mintage	Identification	Mkt Val
Pr54	1938R	50	100 Franga Ari. Gold. KM#26.	2,400
Pr55	1938R	50	100 Franga Ari. Gold. KM#23.	2,400
Pr56	1939	—	0.05 Lek. Proof.	400
Pr57	1939	—	0.10 Lek. Proof.	400
Pr58	1939	—	0.20 Lek. Proof.	500
Pr59	1939	—	0.50 Lek. Proof.	500
Pr60	1939	—	Lek. Proof.	500
Pr61	1939	—	2 Lek. Proof.	525
Pr62	1939	—	5 Lek. Proof.	500
Pr63	1939	—	10 Lek. Silver. Proof.	625
Pr64	1947	—	10 Qindar Leku. Aluminum.	—
Pr65	1947	—	5 Qindar Leku. Tombac.	—
Pr66	1947	—	10 Qindar Leku. Aluminum.	—
Pr67	1947	—	10 Qindar Leku. Tombac.	—
Pr68	1947	—	20 Qindar Leku. Aluminum.	—
Pr69	1947	—	20 Qindar Leku. Tombac.	—
Pr70	1947	—	50 Qindar Leku. Aluminum.	—
Pr71	1947	—	50 Qindar Leku. Tombac.	—

MINT SETS

KM#	Date	Mintage	Identification	Issue Price	Mkt Val
MS1	1969 (5)	—	KM#44-48	5.00	25.00

PROOF SETS

KM#	Date	Mintage	Identification	Issue Price	Mkt Val
PS1	1968 (5)	1,500	KM#51.1, 53.1-56	470	3,000
PS2	1968 (8)	1,540	KM#49-56	—	3,200
PSA2	1968 (3)	8,540	KM#49, 50, 52	44.00	110
PS3	1969 (5)	—	KM#51, 53-56	470	3,385
PS4	1969 (8)	—	KM#49-56	—	3,525
PSA4	1969 (3)	1,500	KM#49, 50, 52	45.00	135
PS5	1970 (5)	—	KM#51.5, 53-56	516	3,525
PS6	1970 (3)	500	KM#49-50, 52	45.00	170
PS7	1991 (2)	980	KM#68-69	—	400

ALDERNEY

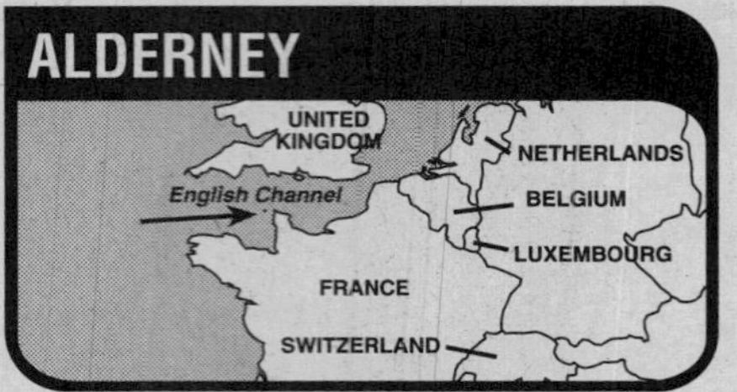

Alderney, the northernmost and third largest of the Channel Islands, separated from the coast of France by the dangerous 8-mile-wide tidal channel, has an area of 3 sq. mi. (8 km.) and a population of 1,686. It is a dependency of the British island of Guernsey, to the southwest. Capital: St. Anne. Principal industries are agriculture and raising cattle.

There is evidence of settlement in prehistoric times and Roman coins have been discovered on the island along with evidence of their buildings. Toward the close of the reign of Henry VIII, France began making plans to seize the Island of Sark. The English, realizing its strategic importance, began to build a defensive fort, which was abandoned some years later when Edward VI died. France constructed a large naval base at its northern tip, which incited the English into making Alderney the "Gibraltar of the Channel." Most of the Islanders were evacuated before the German occupation in 1940 but returned in 1945 when the Germans surrendered.

The Channel Islands have never been subject to the British Parliament and are self-governing units under the direct rule of the Crown acting through the Privy Council. Alderney is within the Bailiwick of Guernsey (q.v.). It is one of the nine Channel Islands, the only part of the Duchy of Normandy still belonging to the British Crown, and has been a British possession since the Norman Conquest of 1066. Legislation was only recently introduced for the issue of its own coinage, a right it now shares with Jersey and Guernsey.

RULERS
British

MONETARY SYSTEM
100 Pence = 1 Pound Sterling

DEPENDENCY

STANDARD COINAGE

KM# 4 POUND

9.5000 g., 0.9250 Silver .2826 oz. ASW, 22.5 mm. **Ruler:** Elizabeth II **Subject:** 40th Anniversary - Coronation **Obv:** Crowned bust, right, date below **Rev:** Royal carriage **Designer:** Raphael Maklouf

Date	Mintage	F	VF	XF	Unc	BU
1993 Proof	Est. 20,000	Value: 30.00				

KM# 12 POUND

9.5000 g., 0.9250 Silver .2826 oz. ASW, 22.5 mm. **Ruler:** Elizabeth II **Subject:** VE Day **Obv:** crowned bust, right **Rev:** VE Monogram and dove **Designer:** Raphael Maklouf

Date	Mintage	F	VF	XF	Unc	BU
ND(1995) Proof	Est. 20,000	Value: 30.00				

KM# 12a POUND

15.8000 g., 0.9160 Gold .4653 oz. AGW, 22.5 mm. **Ruler:** Elizabeth II **Subject:** VE Day **Rev:** VE Monogram and dove

Date	Mintage	F	VF	XF	Unc	BU
ND(1995) Proof	500	Value: 345				

KM# 1 2 POUNDS

28.2800 g., Copper-Nickel, 38.5 mm. **Ruler:** Elizabeth II **Subject:** Royal Visit **Obv:** Crowned bust, right, date below **Obv. Designer:** Raphael Maklouf **Rev:** Arms surrounded by thrift plant

Date	Mintage	F	VF	XF	Unc	BU
1989	—	—	—	—	9.00	10.00

KM# 1a 2 POUNDS

28.2800 g., 0.9250 Silver .8411 oz. ASW **Ruler:** Elizabeth II **Subject:** Royal Visit

Date	Mintage	F	VF	XF	Unc	BU
1989 Proof	5,000	Value: 50.00				

KM# 1b 2 POUNDS

47.5400 g., 0.9170 Gold 1.4011 oz. AGW **Ruler:** Elizabeth II **Subject:** Royal Visit

Date	Mintage	F	VF	XF	Unc	BU
1989 Proof	100	Value: 1,000				

KM# 2 2 POUNDS

28.2800 g., Copper-Nickel, 38.5 mm. **Ruler:** Elizabeth II **Subject:** Queen Mother's 90th Birthday **Obv. Designer:** Raphael Maklouf **Rev:** Queen Mother in cameo facing left, Glamis rose sprays flanking **Rev. Designer:** Michael Rizzello

Date	Mintage	F	VF	XF	Unc	BU
1990	—	—	—	—	8.50	9.50

KM# 2a 2 POUNDS

28.2800 g., 0.9250 Silver .8411 oz. ASW **Ruler:** Elizabeth II **Subject:** Royal Visit

Date	Mintage	F	VF	XF	Unc	BU
1990 Proof	5,000	Value: 50.00				

KM# 2b 2 POUNDS

47.5400 g., 0.9170 Gold 1.4011 oz. AGW **Ruler:** Elizabeth II **Subject:** Queen Mother's 90th Birthday

Date	Mintage	F	VF	XF	Unc	BU
1990 Proof	90	Value: 1,100				

KM# 3 2 POUNDS

28.2800 g., Copper-Nickel, 38.5 mm. **Ruler:** Elizabeth II **Subject:** 40th Anniversary - Queen's Reign **Obv. Designer:** Raphael Maklouf **Rev:** Sailing ship on water, Crowned initials below within wreath **Rev. Designer:** Willem Vis

Date	Mintage	F	VF	XF	Unc	BU
1992	—	—	—	—	8.50	9.50

KM# 3a 2 POUNDS

28.2800 g., 0.9250 Silver .8411 oz. ASW **Ruler:** Elizabeth II **Subject:** 40th Anniversary - Queen's Reign

Date	Mintage	F	VF	XF	Unc	BU
1992 Proof	5,000	Value: 40.00				

KM# 3b 2 POUNDS

47.5400 g., 0.9170 Gold 1.4011 oz. AGW **Ruler:** Elizabeth II **Subject:** 40th Anniversary - Queen's Reign

Date	Mintage	F	VF	XF	Unc	BU
1992 Proof	150	Value: 985				

KM# 5 2 POUNDS

28.2800 g., Copper-Nickel, 38.8 mm. **Ruler:** Elizabeth II **Subject:** 40th Anniversary - Coronation **Obv. Designer:** Raphael Maklouf **Rev:** Coronation coach, flags of the Union, Alderney of May 24 1989 **Rev. Designer:** John Savage

Date	Mintage	F	VF	XF	Unc	BU
1993	—	—	—	—	8.00	9.00

KM# 5a 2 POUNDS

28.2800 g., 0.9250 Silver .8411 oz. ASW **Ruler:** Elizabeth II **Subject:** 40th Anniversary - Coronation

Date	Mintage	F	VF	XF	Unc	BU
1993 Proof	Est. 5,000	Value: 45.00				

KM# 7 2 POUNDS

28.2800 g., Copper-Nickel, 38.5 mm. **Ruler:** Elizabeth II **Subject:** Normandy Invasion **Obv. Designer:** Raphael Maklouf **Rev:** Normandy beach landing scene **Rev. Designer:** John Savage

Date	Mintage	F	VF	XF	Unc	BU
1994	Est. 5,000,000	—	—	—	9.00	10.00

KM# 7a 2 POUNDS

28.2800 g., 0.9250 Silver .8411 oz. ASW **Ruler:** Elizabeth II **Subject:** Normandy Invasion **Rev:** Normandy beach landing scene

Date	Mintage	F	VF	XF	Unc	BU
1994 Proof	—	Value: 45.00				

KM# 13 2 POUNDS

28.2800 g., Copper-Nickel, 38.5 mm. **Ruler:** Elizabeth II **Subject:** Islander's Return **Obv. Designer:** Raphael Maklouf **Rev:** Steamship Autocarrier **Rev. Designer:** Willem Vis

Date	Mintage	F	VF	XF	Unc	BU
ND(1995)	—	—	—	—	10.00	12.00

KM# 13a 2 POUNDS

28.2800 g., 0.9250 Silver .8411 oz. ASW **Ruler:** Elizabeth II **Subject:** Islander's Return **Rev:** Steamship

Date	Mintage	F	VF	XF	Unc	BU
ND(1995) Proof	10,000	Value: 45.00				

KM# 13b 2 POUNDS

47.5400 g., 0.9160 Gold 1.4011 oz. AGW **Ruler:** Elizabeth II **Subject:** Islander's Return **Rev:** Steamship

Date	Mintage	F	VF	XF	Unc	BU
ND(1995) Proof	250	Value: 945				

KM# 16 2 POUNDS

28.2800 g., Copper-Nickel, 38.5 mm. **Ruler:** Elizabeth II **Subject:** World Wildlife Fund **Obv:** Queen's portrait **Obv. Designer:** Raphael Maklouf **Rev:** 2 Puffin birds

Date	Mintage	F	VF	XF	Unc	BU
1997	—	—	—	—	11.00	12.50

KM# 16a 2 POUNDS

28.2800 g. 0.9250 Silver .8410 oz. ASW **Ruler:** Elizabeth II **Subject:** World Wildlife Fund **Rev:** 2 Puffin birds

Date	Mintage	F	VF	XF	Unc	BU
1997 Proof	—	Value: 47.50				

KM# 17 2 POUNDS

28.2800 g., Silver, 38.5 mm. **Ruler:** Elizabeth II **Subject:** Queen's Golden Wedding Anniversary **Obv:** Queen's portrait **Obv. Designer:** Raphael Maklouf **Rev:** Queen crowning Prince Charles

Date	Mintage	F	VF	XF	Unc	BU
ND(1997)	—	—	—	—	8.50	9.50

KM# 18 2 POUNDS

28.2800 g., Silver, 38.5 mm. **Ruler:** Elizabeth II **Subject:** Total Eclipse of the Sun **Obv:** Queen's portrait **Obv. Designer:** Raphael Maklouf **Rev:** 2 sea birds and church **Rev. Designer:** Willem Vis

Date	Mintage	F	VF	XF	Unc	BU
1999	—	—	—	—	14.00	16.00

KM# 18a 2 POUNDS

28.2800 g., 0.9250 Silver .8410 oz. ASW **Ruler:** Elizabeth II **Subject:** Total Eclipse of the Sun **Obv:** Queen's portrait **Rev:** 2 sea birds and church

Date	Mintage	F	VF	XF	Unc	BU
1999 Proof	Est. 10,000	Value: 47.50				

KM# 18b 2 POUNDS

47.5400 g., 0.9170 Gold 1.4011 oz. AGW **Ruler:** Elizabeth II **Subject:** Total Eclipse of the Sun **Obv:** Queen's portrait **Rev:** 2 sea birds and church

Date	Mintage	F	VF	XF	Unc	BU
1999 Proof	Est. 100	Value: 1,300				

KM# 56 5 POUNDS

28.2800 g., Copper-Nickel, 38.5 mm. **Ruler:** Elizabeth II **Subject:** Queen Mother - Children

Date	Mintage	F	VF	XF	Unc	BU
1995	—	—	—	—	15.00	16.50

KM# 14 5 POUNDS

28.2800 g., Copper-Nickel, 38.5 mm. **Ruler:** Elizabeth II **Subject:** Queen Mother - Children **Obv. Designer:** Raphael Maklouf **Rev:** Queen Mother with children within circle

Date	Mintage	F	VF	XF	Unc	BU
1995	—	—	—	—	15.00	16.50

KM# 14a 5 POUNDS

28.2800 g., 0.9250 Silver .8411 oz. ASW **Ruler:** Elizabeth II **Subject:** Queen Mother - Children

Date	Mintage	F	VF	XF	Unc	BU
1995 Proof	10,000	Value: 50.00				

KM# 14b 5 POUNDS

47.5400 g., 0.9160 Gold 1.4011 oz. AGW **Ruler:** Elizabeth II **Subject:** Queen Mother - Children

Date	Mintage	F	VF	XF	Unc	BU
1995 Proof	150	Value: 965				

KM# 15 5 POUNDS

28.2800 g., Copper-Nickel, 38.5 mm. **Ruler:** Elizabeth II **Subject:** Queen Elizabeth's 70th Birthday - Flowers **Obv:** Crowned bust, right **Obv. Designer:** Raphael Maklouf **Rev:** Rose, thistle, daffodil, clover representing the UK **Rev. Designer:** John Savage

Date	Mintage	F	VF	XF	Unc	BU
1996	—	—	—	—	16.00	17.50

KM# 15a 5 POUNDS

28.2800 g., 0.9250 Silver .8411 oz. ASW **Ruler:** Elizabeth II **Subject:** Queen Elizabeth's 70th Birthday - Flowers

Date	Mintage	F	VF	XF	Unc	BU
1996 Proof	Est. 10,000	Value: 50.00				

KM# 15b 5 POUNDS

47.5400 g., 0.9170 Gold 1.4012 oz. AGW **Ruler:** Elizabeth II **Subject:** Queen Elizabeth's 70th Birthday - Flowers

Date	Mintage	F	VF	XF	Unc	BU
1996 Proof	250	Value: 1,225				

KM# 19 5 POUNDS

Copper-Nickel **Ruler:** Elizabeth II **Subject:** Total Eclipse of the Sun **Obv:** Portrait of Queen **Obv. Designer:** Raphael Maklouf **Rev:** Map of Alderney, pre, post and actual phases of eclipse

Date	Mintage	F	VF	XF	Unc	BU
1999	—	—	—	—	18.00	20.00

KM# 19a 5 POUNDS

28.2800 g., 0.9250 Silver .8410 oz. ASW **Ruler:** Elizabeth II

Date	Mintage	F	VF	XF	Unc	BU
1999 Proof	Est. 10,000	Value: 55.00				

KM# 20 5 POUNDS
28.2800 g., 0.9250 Silver 0.841 oz. ASW **Ruler:** Elizabeth II
Subject: Winston Churchill **Obv:** Queen's portrait **Rev:** Winston Churchill wearing hat **Rev. Designer:** Tony Hansard **Edge Lettering:** And our dear Channel Islands are also to be freed today

Date	Mintage	F	VF	XF	Unc	BU
1999	—	—	—	—	15.00	17.50

KM# 20a 5 POUNDS
47.5400 g., 0.9166 Gold 1.4011 oz. AGW **Ruler:** Elizabeth II
Subject: Winston Churchill **Obv:** Queen's portrait **Rev:** Winston Churchill wearing hat **Edge Lettering:** And our dear Channel Islands are also to be freed today

Date	Mintage	F	VF	XF	Unc	BU
1999 Proof	125	Value: 950				

KM# 21 5 POUNDS
28.2800 g., Copper-Nickel **Ruler:** Elizabeth II **Subject:** 60th Anniversary - Battle of Britain **Obv:** Queen Elizabeth's head right **Rev:** Spitfires and Hurricane, pilot at bottom center **Rev. Designer:** Tony Hansard **Edge:** Reeded

Date	Mintage	F	VF	XF	Unc	BU
2000	—	—	—	—	18.00	20.00

KM# 52 5 POUNDS
28.2800 g., 0.9250 Silver 0.841 oz. ASW, 38.6 mm. **Ruler:** Elizabeth II **Subject:** Queen Mother's 100th Birthday **Obv:** Queen Elizabeth II **Obv. Designer:** Raphael Maklouf **Rev:** Queen Mother above value **Edge:** Reeded

Date	Mintage	F	VF	XF	Unc	BU
2000	—	Value: 55.00				

KM# 21a 5 POUNDS
28.2800 g., 0.9250 Silver .8410 oz. ASW **Ruler:** Elizabeth II
Subject: 60th Anniversary - Battle of Britain **Obv:** Queen Elizabeth's head right **Rev:** Two spitfires in flight, pilot at bottom center **Edge:** Reeded

Date	Mintage	F	VF	XF	Unc	BU
2000 Proof	—	Value: 55.00				

KM# 8 10 POUNDS
3.1300 g., 0.9990 Gold .1005 oz. AGW **Ruler:** Elizabeth II
Subject: Normandy Invasion **Obv. Designer:** Raphael Maklouf
Rev: Paratroopers and Transport Plane

Date	Mintage	F	VF	XF	Unc	BU
1994 Proof	Est. 1,000	Value: 95.00				

KM# 6 25 POUNDS
8.5130 g., 0.9170 Gold .2507 oz. AGW **Ruler:** Elizabeth II
Subject: 40th Anniversary - Coronation **Obv. Designer:** Raphael Maklouf **Rev:** Royal carriage **Rev. Designer:** John Savage

Date	Mintage	F	VF	XF	Unc	BU
1993 Proof	Est. 1,000	Value: 210				

KM# 9 25 POUNDS
7.8100 g., 0.9990 Gold .2509 oz. AGW **Ruler:** Elizabeth II
Subject: Normandy Invasion **Obv. Designer:** Raphael Maklouf
Rev: Fighter planes and tank

Date	Mintage	F	VF	XF	Unc	BU
1994 Proof	Est. 1,000	Value: 210				

KM# 57 25 POUNDS
7.8100 g., 0.9990 Gold 0.2508 oz. AGW **Ruler:** Elizabeth II
Subject: Normandy Invasion **Rev:** Fighter planes and tank

Date	Mintage	F	VF	XF	Unc	BU
1994 Proof	—	Value: 200				

KM# 23 25 POUNDS
28.0000 g., Copper-Nickel **Ruler:** Elizabeth II **Subject:** Golden Wedding Anniversary - Elizabeth and Philip **Obv:** Queen Elizabeth's head right **Rev:** Queen Elizabeth crowning Charles as Prince of Wales, date (1947-1997) in legend

Date	Mintage	F	VF	XF	Unc	BU
ND(1997)	—	—	—	—	18.00	20.00

KM# 23a 25 POUNDS
28.2800 g., 0.9250 Silver .8410 oz. ASW **Ruler:** Elizabeth II
Subject: Golden Wedding Anniversary - Elizabeth and Philip
Obv: Queen Elizabeth's head right **Rev:** Queen Elizabeth crowning Charles as Prince of Wales, date (1947-1997) in legend

Date	Mintage	F	VF	XF	Unc	BU
ND(1997) Proof	—	Value: 22.50				

KM# 23b 25 POUNDS
8.4300 g., 0.9160 Gold .2483 oz. AGW **Ruler:** Elizabeth II
Subject: Golden Wedding Anniversary - Elizabeth and Philip
Obv: Queen Elizabeth's head right **Rev:** Queen Elizabeth crowning Charles as Prince of Wales, date (1947-1997) in legend

Date	Mintage	F	VF	XF	Unc	BU
ND(1997) Proof	—	Value: 200				

KM# 22 25 POUNDS
7.8100 g., 0.9160 Gold .2302 oz. AGW **Ruler:** Elizabeth II **Subject:** 60th Anniversary - Battle of Britain **Obv:** Queen Elizabeth's head right **Rev:** Two spitfires in flight, pilot at bottom center **Edge:** Reeded

Date	Mintage	F	VF	XF	Unc	BU
2000	—	Value: 275				

KM# 10 50 POUNDS
15.6000 g., 0.9990 Gold .5014 oz. AGW **Ruler:** Elizabeth II
Subject: Normandy Invasion **Obv. Designer:** Raphael Maklouf
Rev: British gliders

Date	Mintage	F	VF	XF	Unc	BU
1994	Est. 1,000	Value: 450				

Note: In Proof sets only

KM# 11 100 POUNDS
31.2100 g., 0.9990 Gold 1.0025 oz. AGW **Ruler:** Elizabeth II
Subject: Normandy Invasion **Obv:** Crowned bust, right, date below **Obv. Designer:** Raphael Maklouf **Rev:** Normandy beach landing scene

Date	Mintage	F	VF	XF	Unc	BU
1994 Proof	Est. 500	Value: 825				

PIEFORTS

KM#	Date	Mintage	Identification	Mkt Val
P1	1989	500	2 Pounds. 0.9250 Silver. KM#1a.	100
P2	1990	500	2 Pounds. 0.9250 Silver. KM#2a.	100
P3	1992	750	2 Pounds. 0.9250 Silver. KM#3a.	70.00
P4	1993	500	2 Pounds. 0.9250 Silver. KM#5a.	80.00
P5	1994	500	2 Pounds. 0.9250 Silver. KM#7a.	80.00
P6	ND(1995)	500	2 Pounds. 0.9250 Silver. KM#13a.	90.00
P7	1995	500	5 Pounds. 0.9250 Silver. KM#14a.	85.00
P8	1996	500	5 Pounds. 0.9250 Silver. KM#15a.	90.00

PROOF SETS

KM#	Date	Mintage	Identification	Issue Price	Mkt Val
PS1	1994 (5)	500	KM#7a, 8-11	—	1,650
PS2	1994 (4)	I.A.	KM#8-11	—	1,600
PS3	1994 (4)	500	KM#7a, 8-10	—	800
PS4	1994 (3)	I.A.	KM#8-10	—	750

ALGERIA

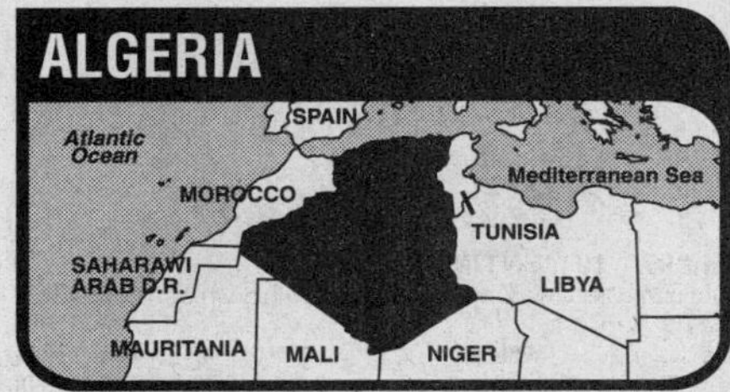

The Democratic and Popular Republic of Algeria, a North African country fronting on the Mediterranean Sea between Tunisia and Morocco, has an area of 919,595 sq. mi. (2,381,740 sq. km.) and a population of 31.6 million. Capital: Algiers (Alger). Most of the country's working population is engaged in agriculture although a recent industrial diversification, financed by oil revenues, is making steady progress. Wines, fruits, iron and zinc ores, phosphates, tobacco products, liquified natural gas, and petroleum are exported.

Algiers, the capital and chief seaport of Algeria, was the site of Phoenician and Roman settlements before the present Moslem city was founded about 950. Nominally part of the sultanate of Tilimsan, Algiers had a large measure of independence under the amirs of its own. In 1492 the Jews and Moors who had been expelled from Spain settled in Algiers and enjoyed an increasing influence until the imposition of Turkish control in 1518. For the following three centuries, Algiers was the headquarters of the notorious Barbary pirates as Turkish control became more and more nominal. The French took Algiers in 1830, and after a long and wearisome war completed the conquest of Algeria and annexed it to France, 1848. Following the armistice signed by France and Nazi Germany on June 22, 1940, Algeria fell under Vichy Government control until liberated by the Allied invasion forces under the command of Gen. D. D. Eisenhower on Nov. 8, 1942. The inability to obtain equal rights with Frenchmen led to an organized revolt which began on Nov. 1, 1954 and lasted until a ceasefire was signed on July l, 1962. Independence was proclaimed on July 5, 1962, following a self-determination referendum, and the Republic was declared on September 25, 1962.

MINT MARKS
Paris – Privy marks only

MONETARY SYSTEMS
100 Centimes = 1 Franc

FRENCH OCCUPATION

COLONIAL COINAGE

KM# 91 20 FRANCS
Copper-Nickel **Obv:** Head with laureled hood, right **Rev:** Value between columns of wheat, date at center **Designer:** P. Turin

Date	Mintage	F	VF	XF	Unc	BU
1949(a)	25,556,000	1.00	2.00	5.00	10.00	—
1956(a)	7,500,000	1.00	2.50	6.00	12.50	—

KM# 92 50 FRANCS
Copper-Nickel **Obv:** Man with laureled hood, right **Rev:** Value between columns of wheat, date below **Designer:** P. Turin

Date	Mintage	F	VF	XF	Unc	BU
1949(a)	18,000,000	1.50	3.00	9.00	18.00	—

KM# 93 100 FRANCS
Copper-Nickel, 29.8 mm. **Obv:** Man with laureled hood. right **Rev:** Value between wheat columns, date below **Edge:** Reeded

Designer: P. Turin **Note:** During World War II homeland coins were struck at the Paris Mint and the French 2 Francs, Y#89 were struck at the Philadelphia Mint for use in French African Territories.

Date	Mintage	F	VF	XF	Unc	BU
1950(a)	22,189,000	1.50	3.00	10.00	20.00	—
1952(a)	12,000,000	2.00	4.00	12.00	25.00	—

TOKEN COINAGE

Alger

KM# TnA1 5 CENTIMES
Aluminum **Issuer:** Alger Chamber of Commerce **Obv:** Symbol between palm trees, beaded circle surrounding all **Rev:** Value above sprigs,with J. Bory

Date	Mintage	F	VF	XF	Unc	BU
1916	—	5.00	10.00	20.00	35.00	—
1917	—	—	175	250	500	—

Note: The year 1917 is not a regular issue

Date	Mintage	F	VF	XF	Unc	BU
1919	—	4.00	6.00	12.00	18.00	35.00
1921	—	5.00	10.00	20.00	35.00	—

KM# TnA2 5 CENTIMES
Iron **Issuer:** Alger Chamber of Commerce

Date	Mintage	F	VF	XF	Unc	BU
1916	—	30.00	50.00	100	200	—

KM# TnA3 5 CENTIMES
Zinc **Issuer:** Alger Chamber of Commerce

Date	Mintage	F	VF	XF	Unc	BU
1917	—	3.50	10.00	20.00	40.00	—
1919	—	—	35.00	70.00	150	—

Note: The year 1919 is not a regular issue

KM# TnA4 5 CENTIMES
Brass **Issuer:** Alger Chamber of Commerce

Date	Mintage	F	VF	XF	Unc	BU
1921	—	—	35.00	70.00	150	—

Note: Not a regular issue

KM# TnA5 10 CENTIMES
Aluminum **Issuer:** Alger Chamber of Commerce **Obv:** Symbol between palm trees, beaded circle surrounding all **Rev:** Value above sprigs,without J. Bory

Date	Mintage	F	VF	XF	Unc	BU
1916 Without J. Bory	—	6.00	10.00	20.00	45.00	85.00
1918 with J. Bory	—	6.00	10.00	20.00	45.00	85.00
1918 Without J. Bory	—	6.00	10.00	15.00	32.00	85.00
1919 With J. Bory	—	4.00	6.00	12.00	25.00	75.00
1921 With J. Bory	—	3.00	6.00	12.00	25.00	75.00
1921 Without J. Bory	—	6.00	10.00	20.00	45.00	85.00

KM# TnA6 10 CENTIMES
Iron **Issuer:** Alger Chamber of Commerce **Rev:** Without J. Bory

Date	Mintage	F	VF	XF	Unc	BU
1916	—	10.00	22.00	50.00	100	—

KM# TnA7 10 CENTIMES
Zinc **Issuer:** Alger Chamber of Commerce

Date	Mintage	F	VF	XF	Unc	BU
1917	—	5.00	12.50	30.00	60.00	—
1918	—	—	40.00	100	160	—

Note: 1918 is not a regular issue

Date	Mintage	F	VF	XF	Unc	BU
1919	—	—	40.00	100	160	—

Note: 1919 is not a regular issue

KM# TnA8 10 CENTIMES
Brass **Issuer:** Alger Chamber of Commerce **Note:** Not a regular issue.

Date	Mintage	F	VF	XF	Unc	BU
1919	—	—	50.00	110	225	375
1921	—	—	65.00	125	245	—

Bone

KM# TnB1 5 CENTIMES
Aluminum **Issuer:** Bone Chamber of Commerce

Date	Mintage	F	VF	XF	Unc	BU
1915	—	6.00	10.00	15.00	30.00	75.00
ND(1915)	—	5.00	9.00	13.00	25.00	65.00

KM# TnB2 5 CENTIMES
Brass **Issuer:** Bone Chamber of Commerce **Note:** Not a regular issue.

Date	Mintage	F	VF	XF	Unc	BU
ND(1915)	—	—	30.00	80.00	120	—

KM# TnB3 10 CENTIMES
Aluminum **Issuer:** Bone Chamber of Commerce

Date	Mintage	F	VF	XF	Unc	BU
1915	—	4.00	10.00	22.00	40.00	90.00
ND(1915)	—	4.00	9.00	20.00	35.00	85.00

KM# TnB4 10 CENTIMES
Brass **Issuer:** Bone Chamber of Commerce **Note:** Not a regular issue.

Date	Mintage	F	VF	XF	Unc	BU
ND(1915)	—	—	32.50	65.00	130	—

KM# TnB5 50 CENTIMES
Brass **Issuer:** Bone Chamber of Commerce **Obv:** Head left, within wreath **Rev:** Value at center

Date	Mintage	F	VF	XF	Unc	BU
ND(1915)	—	15.00	30.00	50.00	75.00	150

KM# TnB6 50 CENTIMES
Copper-Nickel **Issuer:** Bone Chamber of Commerce **Note:** Not a regular issue.

Date	Mintage	F	VF	XF	Unc	BU
ND(1915)	—	—	40.00	90.00	185	350

KM# TnB7 FRANC
Brass **Issuer:** Bone Chamber of Commerce **Obv:** Head left, within wreath **Rev:** Value at center

Date	Mintage	F	VF	XF	Unc	BU
ND(1915)	—	25.00	40.00	65.00	120	—

KM# TnB8 FRANC
Copper-Nickel **Issuer:** Bone Chamber of Commerce **Note:** Not a regular issue.

Date	Mintage	F	VF	XF	Unc	BU
ND(1915)	—	—	60.00	120	225	—

KM# TnB9 FRANC
Copper **Issuer:** Bone Chamber of Commerce **Note:** Not a regular issue.

Date	Mintage	F	VF	XF	Unc	BU
ND(1915)	—	—	90.00	150	300	—

Bougie

KM# TnC1 5 CENTIMES
Aluminum **Issuer:** Bougie Chamber of Commerce **Obv:** Name of issuer, dots flank date **Rev:** Large value at center

Date	Mintage	F	VF	XF	Unc	BU
1915	—	5.00	10.00	25.00	50.00	100

KM# TnC2.1 10 CENTIMES
Aluminum **Issuer:** Bougie Chamber of Commerce **Obv:** Name of issuer, dots flank date **Rev:** Large value at center

Date	Mintage	F	VF	XF	Unc	BU
1915	—	6.00	12.00	28.00	60.00	120

KM# TnC2.2 10 CENTIMES
Aluminum **Issuer:** Bougie Chamber of Commerce **Obv:** Dot and triangle at right of date

Date	Mintage	F	VF	XF	Unc	BU
1915	—	5.00	10.00	20.00	45.00	—

KM# TnC2a 10 CENTIMES
Zinc **Issuer:** Bougie Chamber of Commerce

Date	Mintage	F	VF	XF	Unc	BU
1915	—	30.00	50.00	120	250	—

Constantine

KM# TnD1 5 CENTIMES

Aluminum **Issuer:** Constantine Chamber of Commerce

Date	Mintage	F	VF	XF	Unc	BU
1922	—	25.00	35.00	60.00	120	—

KM# TnD2 10 CENTIMES

Aluminum **Issuer:** Constantine Chamber of Commerce

Date	Mintage	F	VF	XF	Unc	BU
1922	—	20.00	30.00	50.00	100	200

Oran

KM# TnE1 5 CENTIMES

Aluminum **Issuer:** Oran Chamber of Commerce **Obv:** Small crowned shield, date below flanked by dots **Rev:** Large value left of spray

Date	Mintage	F	VF	XF	Unc	BU
1921	—	4.50	9.00	25.00	50.00	100

KM# TnE2 10 CENTIMES

Aluminum **Issuer:** Oran Chamber of Commerce **Obv:** Small crowned shield, date below flanked by dots **Rev:** Large value left of tree

Date	Mintage	F	VF	XF	Unc	BU
1921	—	3.00	7.00	25.00	45.00	—

KM# TnE2a 10 CENTIMES

Brass **Issuer:** Oran Chamber of Commerce

Date	Mintage	F	VF	XF	Unc	BU
1921	—	—	75.00	150	300	—

KM# TnE3 25 CENTIMES

Aluminum **Issuer:** Oran Chamber of Commerce **Obv:** Similar to 10 Centimes, KM#TnE2 **Rev:** Similar to 25 Centimes, KM#TnE4

Date	Mintage	F	VF	XF	Unc	BU
1921	—	4.00	8.50	25.00	50.00	—

KM# TnE4 25 CENTIMES

Aluminum **Issuer:** Oran Chamber of Commerce **Obv:** Small crowned shield, chains **Rev:** Large value within wreath

Date	Mintage	F	VF	XF	Unc	BU
1921	—	5.00	10.00	30.00	60.00	—

KM# TnE5 25 CENTIMES

Aluminum **Issuer:** Oran Chamber of Commerce **Note:** For further listings of private token issues refer to the catalogue of "French Emergency Tokens of 1914-1922" by Robert Lamb.

Date	Mintage	F	VF	XF	Unc	BU
1922	—	5.00	10.00	30.00	60.00	115

REPUBLIC

MONETARY SYSTEM

100 Centimes = 1 Dinar

STANDARD COINAGE

KM# 94 CENTIME

Aluminum, 11.5 mm. **Obv:** Small arms within wreath **Rev:** Value at center of scalloped circle **Edge:** Plain

Date	Mintage	F	VF	XF	Unc	BU
AH1383-1964	35,000,000	—	0.20	0.40	1.00	2.00

KM# 95 2 CENTIMES

Aluminum, 18.3 mm. **Obv:** Arms within wreath **Rev:** Value at center of scalloped circle **Edge:** Plain

Date	Mintage	F	VF	XF	Unc	BU
AH1383-1964	50,000,000	—	0.20	0.40	1.00	2.00

KM# 96 5 CENTIMES

Aluminum **Obv:** Arms within wreath **Rev:** Value at center of scalloped circle

Date	Mintage	F	VF	XF	Unc	BU
AH1383-1964	40,000,000	—	0.25	0.45	1.25	2.50

KM# 101 5 CENTIMES

Aluminum **Series:** F.A.O. **Subject:** 1st Four Year Plan **Obv:** Value at center **Rev:** Two dates center of circle, circle consists of gear teeth on left, sprays of grain on right **Note:** Varieties exist.

Date	Mintage	F	VF	XF	Unc	BU
ND(1970)	50,000,000	—	0.15	0.30	0.75	—

KM# 106 5 CENTIMES

Aluminum **Series:** F.A.O. **Subject:** 2nd Four Year Plan **Obv:** Large value at center **Rev:** Two dates at center of circle, circle consists of gear teeth on left, sprays of grain on right

Date	Mintage	F	VF	XF	Unc	BU
ND(1974)	10,000,000	—	0.15	0.30	0.75	1.50

KM# 113 5 CENTIMES

Aluminum **Series:** F.A.O. **Subject:** 1st Five Year Plan **Obv:** Large value at center **Rev:** Inscription within circle of gear teeth on left, grain spray on right

Date	Mintage	F	VF	XF	Unc	BU
ND(1980)	—	2.00	5.00	12.00	25.00	—

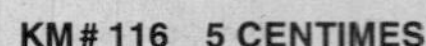

KM# 116 5 CENTIMES

Aluminum **Series:** F.A.O. **Subject:** 2nd Five Year Plan **Obv:** Large value at center **Rev:** Two dates center of circle, circle consists of geared teeth on right, sprays of grain on left **Note:** Varieties exist in planchet thickness.

Date	Mintage	F	VF	XF	Unc	BU
ND(1985)	—	—	0.10	0.25	0.70	1.50

KM# 97 10 CENTIMES

Aluminum-Bronze **Obv:** Small arms within wreath **Rev:** Value in circle

Date	Mintage	F	VF	XF	Unc	BU
AH1383-1964	—	—	0.25	0.75	2.00	3.00

KM# 115 10 CENTIMES

Aluminum **Obv:** Large value in circle **Rev:** Palm tree flanked by rosettes, date below tree **Note:** Varieties exist.

Date	Mintage	F	VF	XF	Unc	BU
1984	—	0.15	0.25	0.75	3.00	4.00

KM# 98 20 CENTIMES

Aluminum-Bronze **Obv:** Arms within wreath **Rev:** Value in circle

Date	Mintage	F	VF	XF	Unc	BU
AH1383-1964	—	—	0.25	0.75	2.00	3.00

KM# 103 20 CENTIMES

Brass **Series:** F.A.O. **Subject:** Agricultural Revolution **Obv:** Value in circle **Rev:** Cornucopeia, date above **Designer:** Mohamed Temmam

Date	Mintage	F	VF	XF	Unc	BU
1972	20,000,000	—	0.10	0.25	0.75	1.25

KM# 107.1 20 CENTIMES

Aluminum-Bronze **Series:** F.A.O. **Obv:** Value at center of circle **Rev:** Rams head left, date below

Date	Mintage	F	VF	XF	Unc	BU
1975	50,000,000	—	0.20	0.45	1.75	—

KM# 107.2 20 CENTIMES

Aluminum-Bronze **Series:** F.A.O. **Obv:** Small flower above 20 **Rev:** Rams head left, date below

Date	Mintage	F	VF	XF	Unc	BU
1975	Inc. above	—	0.15	0.30	1.50	—

KM# 118 20 CENTIMES

Aluminum-Bronze **Series:** F.A.O. **Obv:** Value in circle **Rev:** Rams head left, date below

Date	Mintage	F	VF	XF	Unc	BU
1987	60,000,000	0.50	1.00	2.00	8.00	—

KM# 99 50 CENTIMES

Aluminum-Bronze **Obv:** Arms within wreath **Rev:** Value in circle

Date	Mintage	F	VF	XF	Unc	BU
AH1383-1964	—	—	0.25	0.75	2.00	3.50

KM# 102 50 CENTIMES

Copper-Nickel-Zinc **Obv:** Book, divider on top, bottle at bottom **Rev:** Value in circle **Edge:** Reeded

Date	Mintage	F	VF	XF	Unc	BU
AH1391-1971(a)	10,000,000	0.25	0.50	1.50	6.00	—
AH1393-1973	10,000,000	0.25	0.50	1.50	6.00	—

KM# 109 50 CENTIMES

Brass **Subject:** 30th Anniversary French-Algerian Clash **Obv:** Value in circle **Rev:** Inscription

Date	Mintage	F	VF	XF	Unc	BU
ND(1975)	18,000,000	—	0.20	0.50	2.00	—

KM# 111 50 CENTIMES

Aluminum-Bronze **Subject:** 1400th Anniversary of Mohammad's Flight **Obv:** Value in circle **Rev:** Value, outline of Mosque

Date	Mintage	F	VF	XF	Unc	BU
AH1400-1980	—	0.15	0.25	0.50	2.50	4.50

KM# 119 50 CENTIMES

Aluminum-Bronze **Subject:** 25th Anniversary of Constitution **Obv:** Value in circle **Rev:** Stylized design

Date	Mintage	F	VF	XF	Unc	BU
1988	40,000,000	0.15	0.25	0.75	3.00	6.00

KM# 127 1/4 DINAR

1.1500 g., Aluminum **Subject:** Fennec Fox **Obv:** Value in small circle **Rev:** Fennec Fox head, facing

Date	Mintage	F	VF	XF	Unc	BU
1992-AH1413	—	—	0.65	1.25	2.50	—
1992-AH1413 Proof	—	Value: 12.00				
1998-AH1418	—	—	0.65	1.25	2.50	—

KM# 128 1/2 DINAR

Steel **Subject:** Barbary Horse **Obv:** Value in small circle **Rev:** Encirled Barbary horse head dividing date at top, facing 3/4 left

Date	Mintage	F	VF	XF	Unc	BU
AH1413-1992	—	—	0.65	1.25	2.75	—
AH1413-1992 Proof	—	Value: 12.00				

KM# 100 DINAR

Copper-Nickel **Obv:** Large arms within wreath **Rev:** Large value in circle

Date	Mintage	F	VF	XF	Unc	BU
AH1383-1964	15,000,000	0.25	0.50	1.00	4.00	—
AH1383-1964 Proof	—	Value: 40.00				

KM# 104.1 DINAR

Copper-Nickel **Series:** F.A.O. **Obv:** Large value in circle **Rev:** Hands grasped at top, man on tractor facing flanked by sprigs, date below **Designer:** Mohamed Temmam

Date	Mintage	F	VF	XF	Unc	BU
1972	20,000,000	0.25	0.50	1.00	2.50	3.50

KM# 104.2 DINAR

Copper-Nickel **Obv:** Legend touches inner circle **Designer:** Mohamed Temmam

Date	Mintage	F	VF	XF	Unc	BU
1972	Inc. above	0.20	0.45	0.85	2.00	3.00

KM# 112 DINAR

Copper-Nickel **Subject:** 20th Anniversary of Independence **Obv:** Large value in circle **Rev:** Circle of hands

Date	Mintage	F	VF	XF	Unc	BU
ND(1983)	—	0.35	0.75	1.50	4.50	6.50

KM# 117 DINAR

Copper-Nickel **Subject:** 25th Anniversary of Independence - Monument **Obv:** Large value in circle **Rev:** Monument within grain wreath

Date	Mintage	F	VF	XF	Unc	BU
1987	—	0.35	0.75	1.50	4.00	6.00

KM# 120 DINAR

3.2200 g., 0.9200 Gold .0953 oz. AGW **Subject:** Historical Coin - 5 Aspers of Abd-el-Kader **Obv:** Old Islamic coin at center **Rev:** Old Islamic coin

Date	Mintage	F	VF	XF	Unc	BU
AH1411	—	—	—	—	125	150

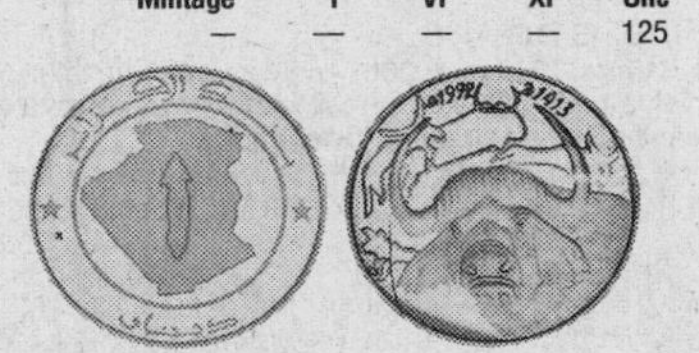

KM# 129 DINAR

Steel **Subject:** Buffalo **Obv:** Value on silhouette of country, within circle **Rev:** Prehistoric buffalo 3/4 facing, buffalo drawings in back of horns

Date	Mintage	F	VF	XF	Unc	BU
AH1413-1992	—	—	1.00	2.00	4.00	—
AH1413-1992 Proof	—	Value: 15.00				
AH1417-1997	—	—	—	2.00	4.00	—
AH1419-1999	—	—	1.00	2.00	4.00	—
AH1420-2000	—	—	1.00	2.00	4.00	—

KM# 121 2 DINARS

6.4500 g., 0.9200 Gold .1908 oz. AGW **Subject:** Historical Coin - Dinar of 762 A.D. Rostomiden Dynasty

Date	Mintage	F	VF	XF	Unc	BU
AH1411	—	—	—	—	250	300

KM# 130 2 DINARS

Steel **Subject:** Camel's Head **Obv:** Value on silhouette of country **Rev:** Camel head, right

Date	Mintage	F	VF	XF	Unc	BU
AH1413-1992	—	—	1.00	2.50	5.00	—
AH1413-1992 Proof	—	Value: 18.00				
AH1414-1993	—	—	1.00	2.50	5.00	—
AH1417-1996	—	—	—	—	—	—
AH1417-1997	—	—	1.00	2.50	5.00	—
AH1419-1999	—	—	1.00	2.50	5.00	—

KM# 133 2 DINARS

Gold **Subject:** Historical Coin - 2 Dinar of Abd Al-Qadir, AH1222-1300

Date	Mintage	F	VF	XF	Unc	BU
AH1417	—	—	—	—	275	325

KM# 105 5 DINARS

12.0000 g., 0.7500 Silver .2893 oz. ASW, 31 mm. **Series:** F.A.O. **Subject:** 10th Anniversary **Obv:** Large value flanked by small flowers within circle **Rev:** Tower with grain head at base dividing dates at bottom, Five stars flanking **Note:** Privy mark: owl.

Date	Mintage	F	VF	XF	Unc	BU
ND(1972)(a)	5,000,000	—	6.00	10.00	16.50	—

KM# 105a.1 5 DINARS

Nickel, 31 mm. **Edge:** Reeded

Date	Mintage	F	VF	XF	Unc	BU
ND(1972)(a)	10,000,000	—	4.00	8.00	14.50	—

KM# 105a.2 5 DINARS

Nickel, 31 mm. **Note:** Privy mark: dolphin.

Date	Mintage	F	VF	XF	Unc	BU
ND(1972)(a)	10,000,000	—	4.00	8.00	14.50	—

KM# 108 5 DINARS
Nickel, 31 mm. **Subject:** 20th Anniversary of Revolution **Obv:** Large value in circle flanked by rosettes **Rev:** Armed revolutionary man leaning, right, two dates lower right

Date	Mintage	F	VF	XF	Unc	BU
ND(1974)(a)	—	—	3.50	7.00	12.50	—

KM# 114 5 DINARS
Nickel **Subject:** 30th Anniversary of Revolution **Obv:** Value flanked by small rosettes in circle **Rev:** Hands holding symbol, flanked by dates divided by stars

Date	Mintage	F	VF	XF	Unc	BU
ND(1984)	—	—	2.50	5.00	10.00	—

KM# 122 5 DINARS
16.1200 g., 0.9200 Gold .4768 oz. AGW **Subject:** Historical Coin - Denar of Numidian King Massinissa, 238-148 B.C. **Obv:** Standing elephant left, within circle flanked by value **Rev:** King, left within beaded circle

Date	Mintage	F	VF	XF	Unc	BU
AH1411-1991	—	—	—	—	550	650

KM# 123 5 DINARS
Steel **Obv:** Denomination **Rev:** Large value in circle, date above

Date	Mintage	F	VF	XF	Unc	BU
AH1413-1992	—	—	1.50	3.50	7.00	—
AH1413-1992 Proof	—	Value: 20.00				
AH1414-1993	—	—	1.50	3.50	7.00	—
AH1418-1997	—	—	1.50	3.50	7.00	—
AH1417-1997	—	—	1.50	3.50	7.00	—
AH1418-1998	—	—	1.50	3.50	7.00	—
AH1419-1998	—	—	1.50	3.50	7.00	—
AH1420-1999	—	—	1.50	3.50	7.00	—
AH1420-2000	—	—	1.50	3.50	7.00	—

KM# 110 10 DINARS
11.3700 g., Aluminum-Bronze **Obv:** Inscription within circle, wreath surrounds **Rev:** Large value within circle, date above **Shape:** 10-sided

Date	Mintage	F	VF	XF	Unc	BU
1979	25,001,000	—	2.00	4.00	8.00	—
1981(a)	40,000,000	—	2.00	4.00	8.00	—

KM# 110a 10 DINARS
14.6000 g., 0.9250 Silver .4342 oz. ASW

Date	Mintage	F	VF	XF	Unc	BU
1979	1,000	—	—	—	35.00	—

KM# 110b 10 DINARS
24.5000 g., 0.9000 Gold .7090 oz. AGW

Date	Mintage	F	VF	XF	Unc	BU
1979	100	—	—	—	1,000	1,250

KM# 124 10 DINARS
4.9500 g., Bi-Metallic Aluminum center in Steel ring, 26.5 mm. **Obv:** Denomination **Rev:** Falcon

Date	Mintage	F	VF	XF	Unc	BU
AH1413-1992	—	—	2.00	4.50	10.00	—
AH1413-1992 Proof	—	—	—	—	—	—
AH1414-1993	—	—	2.00	4.50	10.00	—
AH1418-1997	—	—	2.00	4.50	10.00	—

KM# 134 10 DINARS
14.6000 g., 0.8350 Silver 0.3919 oz. ASW, 31.5 mm. **Subject:** Jugurtha, King of Numidia (154-104BC) **Obv:** Denomination **Rev:** Head of Jugurtha left **Edge:** Reeded

Date	Mintage	F	VF	XF	Unc	BU
AH1415 (1994)	—	—	—	—	75.00	—

KM# 135 10 DINARS
14.6000 g., 0.8350 Silver 0.3919 oz. ASW, 31.5 mm. **Subject:** Abdelhamid Benbadis (1889-1940) **Obv:** Denomination **Rev:** 1/2 bust of Benbadis half left **Edge:** Reeded

Date	Mintage	F	VF	XF	Unc	BU
AH1415 (1994)	—	—	—	—	75.00	—

KM# 136 10 DINARS
14.6000 g., 0.8350 Silver 0.3919 oz. ASW, 31.5 mm. **Subject:** Houari Boumediene (1922-1978) **Obv:** Denomination **Rev:** Bust of Boumediene half left **Edge:** Reeded

Date	Mintage	F	VF	XF	Unc	BU
AH1415 (1994)	—	—	—	—	75.00	—

KM# 125 20 DINARS
8.6200 g., Bi-Metallic Brass center in Steel ring, 27.5 mm. **Obv:** Denomination **Rev:** Lion head, left

Date	Mintage	F	VF	XF	Unc	BU
AH1413-1992	—	—	3.00	6.00	12.50	—
AH1413-1992 Proof	—	—	—	—	—	—
AH1414-1993	—	—	3.00	6.00	12.50	—
AH1416-1996	—	—	3.00	6.00	12.50	—
AH1417-1996	—	—	3.00	6.00	12.50	—
AH1417-1997	—	—	3.00	6.00	12.50	—
AH1418-1997	—	—	3.00	6.00	12.50	—
AH1420-1999	—	—	3.00	6.00	12.50	—
AH1421-2000	—	—	3.00	6.00	12.50	—

KM# 126 50 DINARS
9.2700 g., Bi-Metallic Steel center in Brass ring, 28.5 mm. **Obv:** Denomination **Rev:** Gazelle head, left

Date	Mintage	F	VF	XF	Unc	BU
AH1413-1996	—	—	4.00	8.00	15.00	—
AH1413-1992 Proof	—	Value: 35.00				
AH1414-1993	—	—	4.00	8.00	15.00	—
AH1416-1996	—	—	4.00	8.00	15.00	—
AH1417-1996	—	—	4.00	8.00	15.00	—
AH1414-1996	—	—	4.00	8.00	15.00	—
AH1418-1998	—	—	4.00	8.00	15.00	—
AH1419-1999	—	—	4.00	8.00	15.00	—
AH1420-1999	—	—	4.00	8.00	15.00	—

KM# 131 50 DINARS
Bi-Metallic Steel center in Brass ring, 28.5 mm. **Subject:** 40th Anniversary - Start of the Revolution **Obv:** Large value in circle **Rev:** Star dividing dates at right in circle

Date	Mintage	F	VF	XF	Unc	BU
ND(1994)	—	—	6.00	10.00	17.50	—
ND(1994) Proof	—	Value: 37.50				

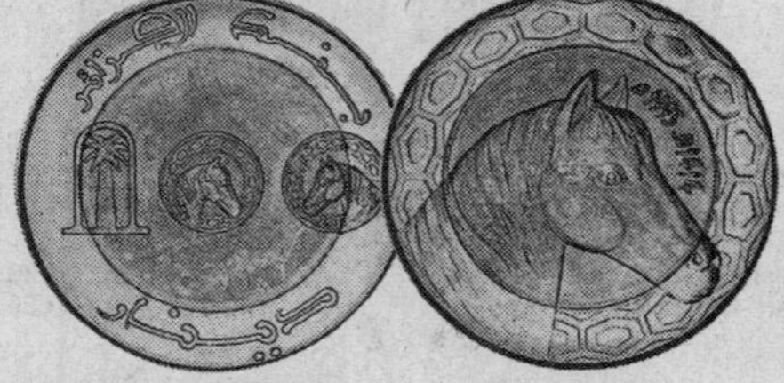

KM# 132 100 DINARS
11.0000 g., Bi-Metallic Aluminum-Bronze center in Stainless Steel ring, 29.5 mm. **Obv:** Denomination stylized with reverse design **Rev:** Horse head, right

Date	Mintage	F	VF	XF	Unc	BU
AH1413-1992	—	—	6.00	12.00	20.00	—
AH1414-1993	—	—	6.00	12.00	20.00	—
AH1415-1994	—	—	6.00	12.00	20.00	—
AH1417-1997	—	—	6.00	12.00	20.00	—
AH1418-1998	—	—	6.00	12.00	20.00	—
AH1421-2000	—	—	6.00	12.00	20.00	—

ESSAIS

Standard metals unless otherwise noted

KM#	Date	Mintage	Identification	Issue Price	Mkt Val
E1	1949(a)	1,500	20 Francs. Copper-Nickel. KM#91.	—	35.00
E2	1949(a)	1,500	50 Francs. Copper-Nickel. KM#92.	—	45.00
E3	1950(a)	1,500	100 Francs. Copper-Nickel. KM#93.	—	50.00

KM#	Date	Mintage	Identification	Issue Price	Mkt Val

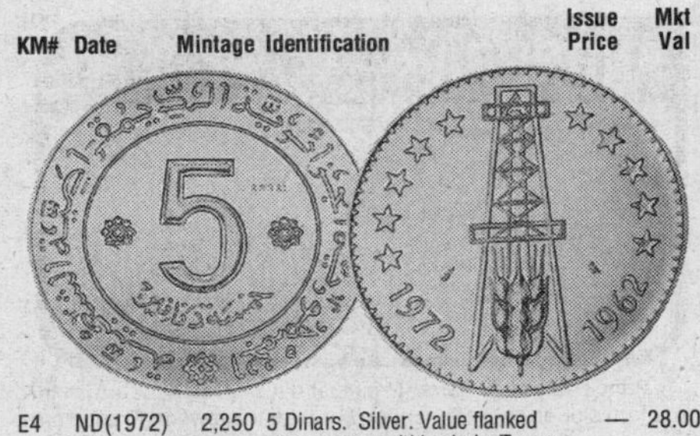

KM#	Date	Mintage	Identification	Issue Price	Mkt Val
E4	ND(1972) (a)	2,250	5 Dinars. Silver. Value flanked by rosettes within circle. Tower with grain head at base dividing dates below, five stars flanking tower. KM#105.	—	28.00
E5	ND(1972) (a)	1,000	5 Dinars. Nickel. KM#105a.	—	35.00

KM#	Date	Mintage	Identification	Issue Price	Mkt Val
E6	ND(1974) (a)	3,300	5 Dinars. Nickel. Large value flanked by rosettes within circle. Armed revolutionary man leaning, right,two dates bottom right. KM#108.	—	20.00
E7	1981	2,670	10 Dinars. Aluminum-Bronze. KM#110.	—	25.00

PIEFORTS WITH ESSAI

Double thickness - Standard metals unless otherwise noted

KM#	Date	Mintage	Identification	Issue Price	Mkt Val

KM#	Date	Mintage	Identification	Issue Price	Mkt Val
PE1	1949(a)	104	20 Francs. Copper-Nickel. Head with laureated hood, right. Value, with date below, between columns of grain. KM#91.	—	90.00

KM#	Date	Mintage	Identification	Issue Price	Mkt Val
PE2	1949(a)	104	50 Francs. Copper-Nickel. Head with laureated hood, right. Value, with date below, between columns of grain. KM#92.	—	95.00

KM#	Date	Mintage	Identification	Issue Price	Mkt Val
PE3	1950(a)	104	100 Francs. Copper-Nickel. Head with laureated hood, right. Value, with date below, between columns of grain. KM#93.	—	100

PROOF SETS

KM#	Date	Mintage	Identification	Issue Price	Mkt Val
PS1	AH1413 (1992) (8)	—	KM#123-130	—	160

AMERICAN SAMOA

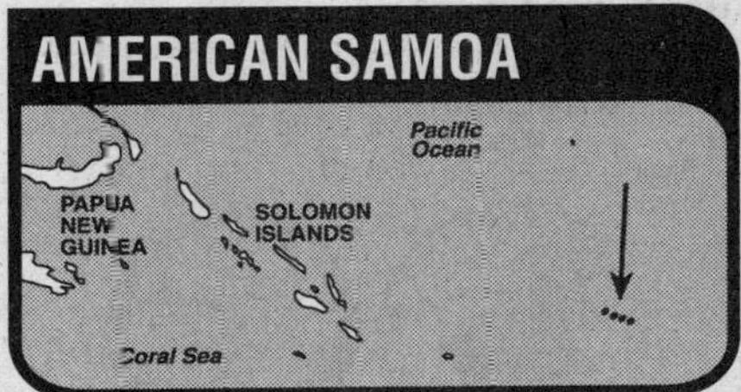

The Territory of American Samoa, with a population of 41,000, consists of seven major islands with a total land area of 76 sq. mi. (199 sq. km.) which are located about 2300 miles south-southwest of Hawaii. American Samoa was settled by the Polynesians around 600 BC. The capital is Pago Pago.

Samoa's long isolation from the western world ended in 1722 when the Dutch explorer, Jacob Roggeveen, came upon the islands. However, it wasn't until 1831 that European influence had any real impact. In that year, John Williams of the London Missionary Society arrived with eight Tahitian missionaries.

By 1900 the Samoan islands were being claimed by both Germany and the United States. Germany annexed several islands, which now comprise Western Samoa; the U.S. took Tutuila to use Pago Pago Bay as a coaling station for naval ships.

As Japan began emerging as an international power in the mid-1930's, the U.S. Naval station on Tutuila began to acquire new strategic importance; and in 1940 the Samoan Islands became a training and staging area for the U.S. Marine Corps.

A. P. Lutali, Governor of American Samoa, signed a historic proclamation on May 23, 1988 that authorized the minting of the first numismatic issue for this unincorporated territory administered by the United States Department of the Interior.

MONETARY SYSTEM

100 Cents = 1 Dollar

U.S. TERRITORY

MILLED COINAGE

KM# 1.1 DOLLAR

31.1000 g., Bronze 2mm Thick **Subject:** America's Cup **Obv:** Americas Cup **Rev:** No ornamentation at sides in legend gaps **Edge:** Reeded

Date	Mintage	F	VF	XF	Unc	BU
1988 Proof	100,000	Value: 30.00				

Note: Mintage limit of 100,000

KM# 1.2 DOLLAR

31.1000 g., Bronze 3mm Thick, Lighter in color than KM-1.1, 39 mm. **Obv:** Americas Cup **Rev:** 2 sailboats with crossed sails; Rope-like ornamentation at sides in legend gaps **Edge:** Plain **Note:** Currently being minted under the 100,000 mintage limit authorization of KM-1.1

Date	Mintage	F	VF	XF	Unc	BU
1988 Proof	Inc. above	Value: 28.00				

KM# 2 5 DOLLARS

31.1000 g., 0.9990 Silver 1.0000 oz. ASW **Subject:** America's Cup **Obv:** Americas Cup

Date	Mintage	F	VF	XF	Unc	BU
1988 Proof	1,000	Value: 60.00				

KM# 6.1 5 DOLLARS

31.1000 g., 0.9990 Silver 1.0000 oz. ASW **Subject:** XXIV Olympics **Obv:** Olympic logo above crossed symbol within circle, date below circle **Rev:** Olympic rings above Chamshil Stadium, value below **Note:** Coin die alignment.

Date	Mintage	F	VF	XF	Unc	BU
1988 Proof	1,000	Value: 65.00				

KM# 6.2 5 DOLLARS

31.1000 g., 0.9990 Silver 1.0000 oz. ASW **Note:** Medallic die alignment.

Date	Mintage	F	VF	XF	Unc	BU
1988 Proof	—	Value: 225				

KM# 3 25 DOLLARS

155.5150 g., 0.9990 Silver 5.0000 oz. ASW, 63 mm. **Subject:** America's Cup '88 **Obv:** America's Cup **Rev:** Sailboat **Note:** Photo reduced.

Date	Mintage	F	VF	XF	Unc	BU
1988 Proof	100	Value: 245				

KM# 7 25 DOLLARS

155.5150 g., 0.9990 Silver 5.0000 oz. ASW, 63 mm. **Subject:** XXIV Olympics **Obv:** Bust of Gov. Lutali left **Rev:** Chamshil Stadium, large value below, five olympic rings above **Note:** Photo reduced.

Date	Mintage	F	VF	XF	Unc	BU
ND(1988) Proof	100	Value: 475				

KM# 9 25 DOLLARS

155.5150 g., 0.9990 Silver 5.0000 oz. ASW, 63 mm. **Subject:** Olympics **Obv:** Olympic logo above symbol within circle, date below circle **Rev:** Olympic logo above Chamshil Stadium, value at bottom **Note:** Photo reduced.

Date	Mintage	F	VF	XF	Unc	BU
1988 Proof	100	Value: 245				

KM# 10 25 DOLLARS

155.5150 g., 0.9990 Silver 5.0000 oz. ASW **Subject:** XXIV Olympics **Rev:** Chamshil Stadium **Note:** Similar to KM#7 but denomination: TWENTY-FIVE.

Date	Mintage	F	VF	XF	Unc	BU
1988 Proof	—	Value: 550				

KM# 4 50 DOLLARS

8.6397 g., 0.9000 Gold .2500 oz. AGW **Subject:** America's Cup **Obv:** Olympic symbols **Rev:** Americas Cup

Date	Mintage	F	VF	XF	Unc	BU
1988 Proof	100	Value: 300				

KM# 5 100 DOLLARS

31.1000 g., 0.9990 Gold 1.0000 oz. AGW **Subject:** America's Cup **Obv:** State seal **Rev:** USA's yacht passing New Zealand's yacht

Date	Mintage	F	VF	XF	Unc	BU
1988 Proof	50	Value: 975				

KM# 8 100 DOLLARS

31.1000 g., 0.9990 Gold 1.0000 oz. AGW **Subject:** XXIV Olympics **Obv:** State seal **Rev:** Olympic rings and Chamshil Stadium above denomination

Date	Mintage	F	VF	XF	Unc	BU
1988 Proof	50	Value: 1,250				

KM# 11 100 DOLLARS

31.1000 g., 0.9990 Gold 1.0000 oz. AGW **Obv:** USA's yacht passing New Zealand's yacht **Rev:** Olympic rings and Chamshil Stadium above denomination **Note:** Mule.

Date	Mintage	F	VF	XF	Unc	BU
1988 Proof	5	Value: 2,250				

PROOF SETS

KM#	Date	Mintage	Identification	Issue Price	Mkt Val
PS1	1988 (3)	—	KM#2-4	315	575

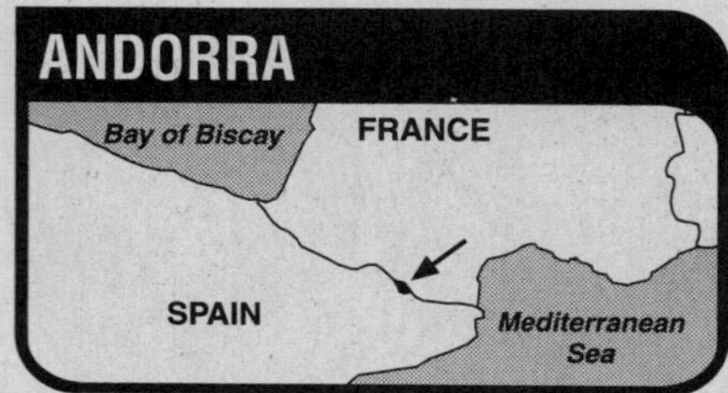

Principality of Andorra (Principat d'Andorra), situated on the southern slopes of the Pyrenees Mountains between France and Spain, has an area of 181 sq. mi. (453 sq. km.) and a population of 80,000. Capital: Andorra la Vella. Tourism is the chief source of income. Timber, cattle and derivatives, and furniture are exported.

According to tradition, the independence of Andorra derives from a charter Charlemagne granted the people of Andorra in 806 in recognition of their help in battling the Moors. An agreement between the Count of Foix (France) and the Bishop of Seo de Urgel (Spanish) in 1278 to recognize each other as Co-Princes of Andorra gave the state what has been its political form and territorial extent continuously to the present day. Over the years, the title on the French side passed to the Kings of Navarre, then to the Kings of France, and is now held by the President of France.

RULER

Joan D.M. Bisbe D'Urgell I

MONETARY SYSTEM

100 Centims = 1 Diner
100 Pesetas = 1 Diner, 1983-85
125 Pesetas = 1 Diner, 1986-

NOTE: The Diners have been struck for collectors while the Euro is used in everyday commerce.

MINT MARK

Crowned M = Madrid

PRINCIPALITY

DECIMAL COINAGE

KM# 171 CENTIM

1.2500 g., Aluminum, 22 mm. **Subject:** F.A.O. **Obv:** Denomination **Rev:** Winged figure carrying wheat **Edge:** Plain

Date	Mintage	F	VF	XF	Unc	BU
1999	—	—	—	—	1.50	2.00

KM# 164 10 CENTIMS

6.8100 g., Brass **Obv:** National arms **Rev:** Building and arms **Edge:** Plain

Date	Mintage	F	VF	XF	Unc	BU
1997	—	—	—	—	4.00	5.00

KM# 33 25 CENTIMS

Bronze, 22 mm. **Obv:** Joan D. M. Bisbe D'Urgell I **Rev:** Crowned value within wreath **Edge:** Plain

Date	Mintage	F	VF	XF	Unc	BU
1986	10,000	—	—	—	5.00	5.50

KM# 109 25 CENTIMS
Copper-Nickel, 30 mm. **Subject:** 50th Anniversary - F.A.O. **Obv:** Crowned arms to left of five line inscription, value below, date at bottom **Rev:** People on globe adoring F.A.O. logo

Date	Mintage	F	VF	XF	Unc	BU
1995	50,000	—	—	—	7.00	8.00

KM# 134 50 CENTIMS
0.6221 g., 0.9990 Gold .0100 oz. AGW **Obv:** Fleury cross **Rev:** Portrait of Queen Isabella I **Note:** Similar to 20 Diners, KM#137.

Date	Mintage	F	VF	XF	Unc	BU
1997 Proof	Est. 50,000	Value: 35.00				

KM# 14 DINER
Brass **Obv:** Joan D.M. Bisbe D'Urgell I **Rev:** Arms within circle,lower circle divides value, date at bottom

Date	Mintage	F	VF	XF	Unc	BU
1983	28,000	—	—	—	8.50	11.50

KM# 15 DINER
Cast Copper-Zinc **Obv:** Joan D.M.Bisbe D'Urgell I, left **Rev:** Crowned oval arms flanked by cherubs, value below

Date	Mintage	F	VF	XF	Unc	BU
1984	7,500	—	—	—	9.00	12.00

KM# 35 DINER
Brass **Obv:** Crowned value within wreath **Rev:** Bust of Joan D.M.Bisbe D'Urgell I, right

Date	Mintage	F	VF	XF	Unc	BU
1986	10,000	—	—	—	8.50	11.50

KM# 49 DINER
Copper-Nickel **Subject:** Pont de la Margineda **Obv:** Bridge **Rev:** Large value, date to left

Date	Mintage	F	VF	XF	Unc	BU
1988	5,000	—	—	—	10.00	12.00

KM# 66 DINER
10.3000 g., 0.9990 Silver .3312 oz. ASW **Obv:** Eagle with wings open, value below **Rev:** Arms within circle

Date	Mintage	F	VF	XF	Unc	BU
1990	6,000	—	—	—	25.00	27.50

KM# 127 DINER
10.0000 g., 0.5000 Silver .1607 oz. ASW **Subject:** Treaty of Rome **Obv:** Crowned arms **Rev:** Seated Europa placing laurel wreath on her head

Date	Mintage	F	VF	XF	Unc	BU
1997 Proof	30,000	Value: 20.00				

KM# 135 DINER
1.2441 g., 0.9990 Gold .0400 oz. AGW **Obv:** Fleury cross **Rev:** Portrait of Queen Isabella I **Note:** Similar to 20 Diners, KM#137.

Date	Mintage	F	VF	XF	Unc	BU
1997 Proof	Est. 10,000	Value: 55.00				

KM# 19 2 DINERS
Bi-Metallic Bronze center in Copper-Nickel ring **Subject:** Wildlife **Obv:** Crowned shielded arms divide value **Rev:** Bear,left

Date	Mintage	F	VF	XF	Unc	BU
1984	5,000	—	—	—	27.50	30.00

KM# 20 2 DINERS
Bi-Metallic Bronze center in Copper-Nickel ring **Subject:** Wildlife **Obv:** Crowned shielded arms divide value **Rev:** Red squirrel, facing

Date	Mintage	F	VF	XF	Unc	BU
1984	5,000	—	—	—	27.50	30.00

KM# 21 2 DINERS
Bi-Metallic Bronze center in Copper-Nickel ring **Subject:** Wildlife **Obv:** Crowned shielded arms divide value **Rev:** Ibex, facing

Date	Mintage	F	VF	XF	Unc	BU
1984	5,000	—	—	—	27.50	30.00

KM# 27 2 DINERS
Bi-Metallic Bronze center in Copper-Nickel ring **Subject:** 1988 Winter Olympics **Obv:** Arms in circle **Rev:** Skier, facing

Date	Mintage	F	VF	XF	Unc	BU
1985	11,000	—	—	—	22.50	25.00

KM# 28 2 DINERS
Bi-Metallic Bronze center in Copper-Nickel ring **Subject:** 1988 Summer Olympics **Obv:** Arms within circle **Rev:** High jumper

Date	Mintage	F	VF	XF	Unc	BU
1985	11,000	—	—	—	22.50	25.00

KM# 36 2 DINERS
Brass **Obv:** Joan D.M. Bisbe D'Urgell I, right **Rev:** Crowned value, date below within wreath

Date	Mintage	F	VF	XF	Unc	BU
1986	10,000	—	—	—	12.50	14.50

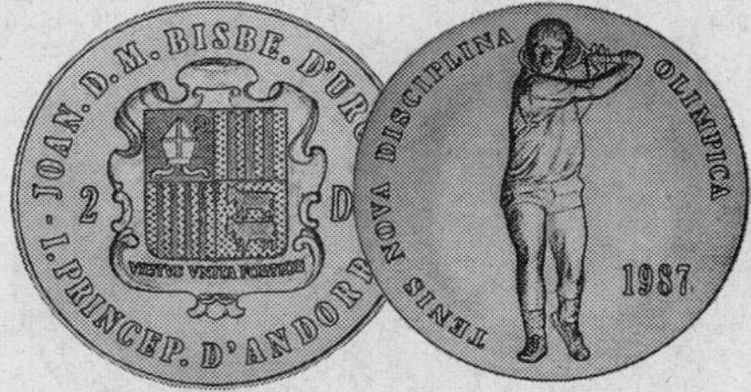

KM# 40 2 DINERS
Copper-Nickel **Subject:** 1988 Summer Olympics **Obv:** Arms on ornate shield divide value **Rev:** Tennis player facing, date bottom right

Date	Mintage	F	VF	XF	Unc	BU
1987	20,000	—	—	—	14.50	16.50

KM# 46.2 2 DINERS
Copper-Nickel **Subject:** 1992 Winter & Summer Olympics **Rev:** Kayaker and skier **Note:** Medallic die rotation.

Date	Mintage	F	VF	XF	Unc	BU
1987	Inc. above	—	—	—	13.50	15.00

KM# 46.1 2 DINERS
Copper-Nickel **Subject:** 1992 Winter & Summer Olympics **Obv:** Small arms on shield, upper right, value at center, left **Rev:** Kayaker and skier **Note:** Prev. KM#46. Coin die rotation.

Date	Mintage	F	VF	XF	Unc	BU
1987	Est. 24,000	—	—	—	13.50	15.00

KM# 50 2 DINERS
Copper-Nickel **Obv:** Church of Santa Coloma **Rev:** Large value, date to bottom right

Date	Mintage	F	VF	XF	Unc	BU
1988	5,000	—	—	—	15.00	17.50

KM# 140 2 DINERS
20.0000 g., 0.9250 Silver .5948 oz. ASW **Subject:** 1998 Winter Olympics **Obv:** Crowned arms to left of five line inscription, value below, date at bottom **Rev:** Bobsled

Date	Mintage	F	VF	XF	Unc	BU
1997 (1998) Proof	30,000	Value: 22.50				

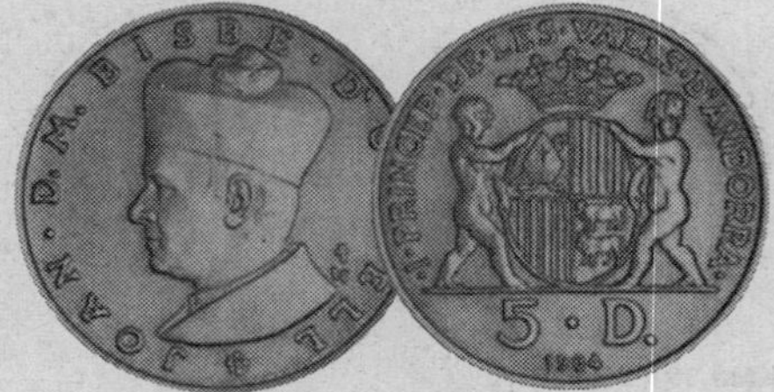

KM# 16 5 DINERS
Cast Copper **Obv:** Joan D.M. Bisbe D'Urgell I, left **Rev:** Crowned arms in oval flanked by cherubs, value below, date at bottom

Date	Mintage	F	VF	XF	Unc	BU
1984	7,500	—	—	—	13.50	15.00

KM# 29 5 DINERS
Cast Copper **Subject:** 2nd Congress of the Catalan Language **Obv:** Ornate arms **Rev:** Standing armored figure holding shield, rose stem below shield, figure divides value, date in legend

Date	Mintage	F	VF	XF	Unc	BU
1986	6,000	—	—	—	15.00	16.50

KM# 37 5 DINERS
Bronze **Obv:** Bust of Joan D.M. Bisbe D'Urgell I, right **Rev:** Crowned value, date below within wreath

Date	Mintage	F	VF	XF	Unc	BU
1986	10,000	—	—	—	17.50	20.00

KM# 51 5 DINERS
Copper-Nickel **Obv:** Church of St. Climent de Pal **Rev:** Large value, date

Date	Mintage	F	VF	XF	Unc	BU
1988	5,000	—	—	—	17.50	20.00

KM# 80 5 DINERS
10.0000 g., 0.5000 Silver .1608 oz. ASW **Subject:** 1994 Winter Olympics **Obv:** Crowned arms to left of five line inscription, value below, date at bottom **Rev:** Cross-country skier

Date	Mintage	F	VF	XF	Unc	BU
1993 Proof	50,000	Value: 13.50				

KM# 102 5 DINERS
15.0000 g., 0.9250 Silver .4461 oz. ASW **Subject:** Andorran Circle of the Arts - 25th Anniversary **Obv:** Crowned arms to left of five line inscription, value below, date at bottom **Rev:** 3/4 Statue standing, left, tablet with quill on left of statue, figures in doorway on right

Date	Mintage	F	VF	XF	Unc	BU
1993 Proof	3,000	Value: 25.00				

KM# 111 5 DINERS
1.2500 g., 0.9990 Gold .0401 oz. AGW **Subject:** Wildlife **Obv:** Crowned arms to left of five line inscription, value below, date at bottom **Rev:** Red squirrel, left

Date	Mintage	F	VF	XF	Unc	BU
1994 Proof	—	Value: 70.00				

KM# 112 5 DINERS
1.5552 g., 0.9990 Gold .0500 oz. AGW **Obv:** Defiant eagle **Rev:** Crowned denomination within wreath

Date	Mintage	F	VF	XF	Unc	BU
1995 Proof	—	Value: 60.00				

KM# 116 5 DINERS
15.0000 g., 0.9250 Silver .4461 oz. ASW **Subject:** XXIII Photographers Federation Congress **Rev:** Hand on camera

Date	Mintage	F	VF	XF	Unc	BU
1995 Proof	3,000	Value: 25.00				

KM# 117 5 DINERS
1.2441 g., 0.9990 Gold .0400 oz. AGW **Subject:** Wildlife **Obv:** Crowned arms to left of five line inscription, value below, date at bottom **Rev:** Chamois, left

Date	Mintage	F	VF	XF	Unc	BU
1996 Proof	Est. 100,000	Value: 55.00				

KM# 118 5 DINERS
1.2441 g., 0.9990 Gold .0400 oz. AGW **Subject:** Wildlife **Rev:** Brown bear and cub

Date	Mintage	F	VF	XF	Unc	BU
1996 Proof	Est. 100,000	Value: 55.00				

KM# 141 5 DINERS
3.1103 g., 0.5850 Gold .0585 oz. AGW **Subject:** 1998 Winter Olympics **Obv:** Crowned arms to left of five line inscription, value below, date at bottom **Rev:** Downhill skier

Date	Mintage	F	VF	XF	Unc	BU
1997 (1998) Proof	5,000	Value: 65.00				

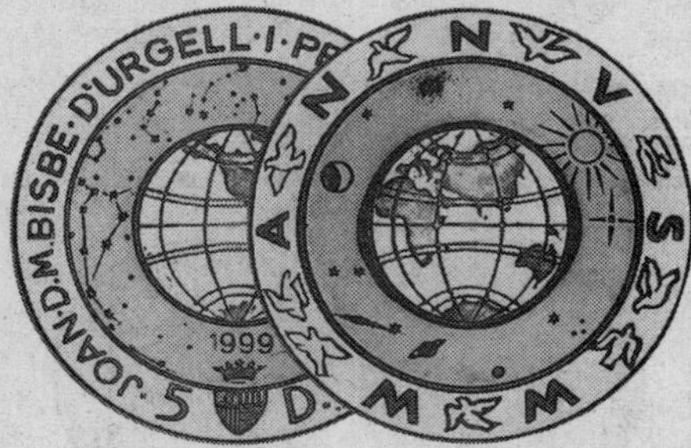

KM# 155 5 DINERS
27.0000 g., Bi-Metallic Silver center in Brass ring, 38.3 mm. **Obv:** World globe amid stars **Rev:** World globe with sun, planets and stars **Note:** Silver center and brass ring are within a silver ring.

Date	Mintage	F	VF	XF	Unc	BU
1999 Proof	—	Value: 30.00				

KM# 187 5 DINERS
15.5500 g., 0.9250 Silver 0.4624 oz. ASW **Obv:** National arms in wreath **Rev:** Nativity scene

Date	Mintage	F	VF	XF	Unc	BU
2000 Proof	25,000	Value: 22.50				

KM# 17 10 DINERS
8.0000 g., 0.9000 Cast Silver .2315 oz. **Obv:** Joan D.M. Bisbe D'Urgell I, left **Rev:** Crowned arms on oval shield flanked by cherubs, value below, date at bottom

Date	Mintage	F	VF	XF	Unc	BU
1984	7,500	—	—	—	22.50	25.00

KM# 34 10 DINERS
8.0000 g., 0.9000 Cast Silver .2315 oz. **Subject:** 1988 World Cup Soccer Games **Obv:** Arms on shield within legend **Rev:** Soccer ball below, world globe above, ball and globe divide value, date in legend, bottom

Date	Mintage	F	VF	XF	Unc	BU
1986 Prooflike	10,000	—	—	—	22.50	24.00

KM# 38 10 DINERS
8.0000 g., 0.9250 Silver .2379 oz. ASW **Obv:** Joan D.M. Bisbe D'Urgell I, right **Rev:** Crowned value, date below within wreath

Date	Mintage	F	VF	XF	Unc	BU
1986	10,000	—	—	—	22.50	25.00

KM# 52 10 DINERS
8.0000 g., 0.9250 Silver .2379 oz. ASW **Obv:** Church of St. Joan de Caselles **Rev:** Large value, small vertical date to left

Date	Mintage	F	VF	XF	Unc	BU
1988	5,000	—	—	—	22.50	25.00

KM# 53 10 DINERS
12.0000 g., 0.9250 Silver .3569 oz. ASW **Subject:** 1990 World Cup Soccer Games **Obv:** Crowned arms to left of five line inscription, value below, date at bottom **Rev:** Figures on soccer field

Date	Mintage	F	VF	XF	Unc	BU
1989 Proof	20,000	Value: 13.50				

KM# 55 10 DINERS
12.0000 g., 0.9250 Silver .3569 oz. ASW **Subject:** 1992 Winter Olympics **Obv:** Crowned arms to left of five line inscription, value below, date at bottom **Rev:** Downhill skier

Date	Mintage	F	VF	XF	Unc	BU
1989 Proof	15,000	Value: 13.50				

KM# 56 10 DINERS
12.0000 g., 0.9250 Silver .3569 oz. ASW **Subject:** 1992 Summer Olympics **Obv:** Crowned arms to left of five line inscription, value below, date at bottom **Rev:** Soccer

Date	Mintage	F	VF	XF	Unc	BU
1989 Proof	15,000	Value: 13.50				

KM# 60 10 DINERS
12.0000 g., 0.9250 Silver .3569 oz. ASW **Subject:** 1990 World Cup Soccer Games **Obv:** Crowned arms to left of five line inscription, value below, date at bottom **Rev:** Map of Italy and soccer ball

Date	Mintage	F	VF	XF	Unc	BU
1989 Proof	20,000	Value: 13.50				

KM# 71 10 DINERS
12.0000 g., 0.9250 Silver .3569 oz. ASW **Subject:** ECU Customs Union **Obv:** Arms above "ECU", within circle of stars/beads **Rev:** Charlemagne

Date	Mintage	F	VF	XF	Unc	BU
ND(1992) Proof	15,000	Value: 35.00				

KM# 74 10 DINERS
31.1035 g., 0.9250 Silver .9250 oz. ASW **Subject:** Wildlife **Obv:** Crowned arms to left of five line inscription, value below, date at bottom **Rev:** Red squirrel, left

Date	Mintage	F	VF	XF	Unc	BU
1992 Proof	15,000	Value: 35.00				

KM# 75 10 DINERS
31.1035 g., 0.9250 Silver .9250 oz. ASW **Subject:** Wildlife **Obv:** Crowned arms to left of five line inscription, value below, date at bottom **Rev:** Chamois

Date	Mintage	F	VF	XF	Unc	BU
1992 Proof	15,000	Value: 30.00				

KM# 76 10 DINERS
31.1035 g., 0.9250 Silver .9250 oz. ASW **Subject:** Wildlife **Obv:** Crowned arms to left of five line inscription, value below, date at bottom **Rev:** Brown bear and cub

Date	Mintage	F	VF	XF	Unc	BU
1992 Proof	15,000	Value: 35.00				

KM# 78 10 DINERS
31.1035 g., 0.9250 Silver .9250 oz. ASW **Subject:** Discovery of the New World **Obv:** Crowned arms to left of five line inscription, value below, date at bottom **Rev:** Stylized ship on globe

Date	Mintage	F	VF	XF	Unc	BU
1992 Proof	15,000	Value: 28.00				

KM# 84 10 DINERS
31.4700 g., 0.9250 Silver .9359 oz. ASW **Obv:** Crowned arms above denomination and date **Rev:** Stylized tree and birds

Date	Mintage	F	VF	XF	Unc	BU
1993 Proof	15,000	Value: 30.00				

KM# 85 10 DINERS
31.4700 g., 0.9250 Silver .9359 oz. ASW **Subject:** Space Exploration **Obv:** Crowned arms to left of five line inscription, value below, date at bottom **Rev:** Tethered space walker Edward White

Date	Mintage	F	VF	XF	Unc	BU
1993 Proof	15,000	Value: 50.00				

KM# 86 10 DINERS
31.4700 g., 0.9250 Silver .9359 oz. ASW **Subject:** 1994 World Cup Soccer **Obv:** Crowned arms to left of five line inscription, value below, date at bottom **Rev:** Player before world map

Date	Mintage	F	VF	XF	Unc	BU
1993 Proof	20,000	Value: 28.00				

KM# 89 10 DINERS
31.4700 g., 0.9250 Silver .9359 oz. ASW **Subject:** ECU Customs Union **Obv:** Arms within circle of stars/beads **Rev:** St. George divides value,rose stem below feet

Date	Mintage	F	VF	XF	Unc	BU
1993 Proof	25,000	Value: 30.00				

KM# 95 10 DINERS
31.4700 g., 0.9250 Silver .9359 oz. ASW **Subject:** 1996 Summer Olympic Games **Rev:** Cyclists

Date	Mintage	F	VF	XF	Unc	BU
1994 Proof	50,000	Value: 22.50				

KM# 97 10 DINERS
31.4700 g., 0.9250 Silver .9359 oz. ASW **Subject:** Andorra U.N. Membership **Obv:** Crowned arms above "ECU" **Rev:** Woman kneeling, left hand on globe, globe symbol in wreath behind

Date	Mintage	F	VF	XF	Unc	BU
1994 Proof	25,000	Value: 37.50				

KM# 98 10 DINERS
31.4700 g., 0.9250 Silver .9359 oz. ASW **Subject:** Discovery of the New World **Obv:** Crowned arms to left of five line legend, value below, date at bottom **Rev:** Sailing ship, small bust of cherub, top left, eight pointed star to right of ship

Date	Mintage	F	VF	XF	Unc	BU
1994 Proof	20,000	Value: 42.50				

KM# 99 10 DINERS
31.4700 g., 0.9250 Silver .9359 oz. ASW **Subject:** ECU Customs Union **Obv:** Arms above "ECU", within circle of stars/beads **Rev:** Peter III of Catalonia and Aragon divides date, cross flanked by dots below feet

Date	Mintage	F	VF	XF	Unc	BU
1994 Proof	25,000	Value: 40.00				

KM# 105 10 DINERS
31.4700 g., 0.9250 Silver .9359 oz. ASW **Subject:** ECU Customs Union **Rev:** Ramon Berenguer III

Date	Mintage	F	VF	XF	Unc	BU
1995 Proof	30,000	Value: 42.50				

KM# 108 10 DINERS
31.6000 g., 0.9250 Silver .9308 oz. ASW **Subject:** Admission to the Council of Europe **Obv:** Arms above "ECU" **Rev:** Woman, left, walking through starred arch, arms forward, container in right hand

Date	Mintage	F	VF	XF	Unc	BU
1995 Proof	35,000	Value: 37.50				

KM# 110 10 DINERS
31.1035 g., 0.9250 Silver .9250 oz. ASW **Subject:** 50th Anniversary - F.A.O. **Obv:** Crowned arms to left of five line inscription, value below, date at bottom **Rev:** Ceres holding grain

Date	Mintage	F	VF	XF	Unc	BU
1995 Proof	10,000	Value: 35.00				

KM# 113 10 DINERS
31.1035 g., 0.9250 Silver .9250 oz. ASW **Subject:** Wildlife **Obv:** Crowned arms to left of five line inscription, value below, date at bottom **Rev:** Wolf, facing

Date	Mintage	F	VF	XF	Unc	BU
1995 Proof	20,000	Value: 55.00				

KM# 114 10 DINERS
31.1035 g., 0.9250 Silver .9250 oz. ASW **Subject:** Agnus Dei **Obv:** Crowned arms above "ECU" **Rev:** Lamb of God within circle, circle of stars surrounding

Date	Mintage	F	VF	XF	Unc	BU
1995 Proof	Est. 35,000	Value: 35.00				

KM# 119 10 DINERS
31.4700 g., 0.9250 Silver .9359 oz. ASW **Obv:** Arms above "ECU" **Rev:** Frederic II on throne

Date	Mintage	F	VF	XF	Unc	BU
1996 Proof	Est. 30,000	Value: 35.00				

KM# A127 10 DINERS
31.4700 g., 0.9250 Silver .9359 oz. ASW **Subject:** Wildlife Protection **Obv:** Crowned arms **Rev:** Diving sea otter

Date	Mintage	F	VF	XF	Unc	BU
1996 Proof	15,000	Value: 42.50				

KM# 120 10 DINERS
31.4700 g., 0.9250 Silver .9359 oz. ASW **Obv:** Crowned Arms, date below **Rev:** Sailing ship

Date	Mintage	F	VF	XF	Unc	BU
1996 Proof	Est. 20,000	Value: 40.00				

KM# 121 10 DINERS
31.4700 g., 0.9250 Silver .9359 oz. ASW **Obv:** Crowned Arms above date **Rev:** Pope crowning Charlemagne

Date	Mintage	F	VF	XF	Unc	BU
1996 Proof	Est. 30,000	Value: 32.50				

KM# 125 10 DINERS
31.4700 g., 0.9250 Silver .9359 oz. ASW **Subject:** 25th Anniversary - Msgr. Alanis, Co-prince and Bishop of Andorra **Obv:** Crowned arms above "EURO" **Rev:** Enthroned prince, date

Date	Mintage	F	VF	XF	Unc	BU
1996 Proof	30,000	Value: 32.50				

KM# 130 10 DINERS
31.4700 g., 0.9250 Silver .9359 oz. ASW **Subject:** Treaty of Rome **Obv:** Crowned arms above "EURO" **Rev:** Seated Europa with olive branch and "EURO" shield, dates

Date	Mintage	F	VF	XF	Unc	BU
1997 Proof	25,000	Value: 40.00				

KM# 166 10 DINERS
31.5500 g., 0.9250 Silver .9383 oz. ASW **Subject:** Palau del Princep **Obv:** Crowned arms above "EURO" **Rev:** Crowned arms on house corner **Edge:** Reeded

Date	Mintage	F	VF	XF	Unc	BU
1997 Proof	—	Value: 35.00				

KM# 131 10 DINERS
31.4700 g., 0.9250 Silver .9359 oz. ASW **Subject:** Wildlife **Obv:** Crowned arms, date below **Rev:** Vixen with kit

Date	Mintage	F	VF	XF	Unc	BU
1997 Proof	15,000	Value: 60.00				

KM# 132 10 DINERS
31.4700 g., 0.9250 Silver .9359 oz. ASW **Obv:** Crowned arms above "ECU" **Rev:** Johan Sebastian Bach portrait, facing 3/4 right, dates

Date	Mintage	F	VF	XF	Unc	BU
1997 Proof	Est. 25,000	Value: 27.50				

KM# 133 10 DINERS
31.4700 g., 0.9250 Silver .9359 oz. ASW **Obv:** Crowned arms above "ECU" **Rev:** Antonio Vivaldi portrait, 3/4 left, dates

Date	Mintage	F	VF	XF	Unc	BU
1997 Proof	Est. 25,000	Value: 27.50				

KM# 136 10 DINERS
3.1103 g., 0.9990 Gold .1000 oz. AGW **Obv:** Fleury cross **Rev:** Portrait of Isabella I **Note:** Similar to 20 Diners, KM#137

Date	Mintage	F	VF	XF	Unc	BU
1997 Proof	Est. 5,000	Value: 100				

KM# 142 10 DINERS
31.4700 g., 0.9250 Silver .9359 oz. ASW **Subject:** 1998 World Cup Soccer **Obv:** Crowned arms and denomination **Rev:** Eiffel Tower and soccer ball

Date	Mintage	F	VF	XF	Unc	BU
1997 Proof	15,000	Value: 45.00				

KM# 143 10 DINERS
31.4700 g., 0.9250 Silver .9359 oz. ASW **Subject:** Human Rights **Obv:** Crowned arms above "EURO" **Rev:** Allegorical figure of Justice

Date	Mintage	F	VF	XF	Unc	BU
1998 Proof	25,000	Value: 42.50				

KM# 165 10 DINERS
31.1100 g., 0.9990 Silver 1 oz. ASW **Subject:** Year of the Tiger **Obv:** Multicolored cartoon tiger and Chinese legend **Rev:** Crowned value within wreath **Edge:** Reeded

Date	Mintage	F	VF	XF	Unc	BU
1998 Proof	—	Value: 50.00				

KM# 146 10 DINERS
31.4700 g., 0.9250 Silver .9359 oz. ASW **Obv:** Crowned arms above "ECU" **Rev:** Portrait of Claudio Monteverdi,3/4 right, dates

Date	Mintage	F	VF	XF	Unc	BU
1998 Proof	25,000	Value: 27.50				

KM# 147 10 DINERS
31.4700 g., 0.9250 Silver .9359 oz. ASW **Subject:** George Friedrich Handel **Obv:** Crowned arms above "ECU" **Rev:** Portrait, dates

Date	Mintage	F	VF	XF	Unc	BU
1998 Proof	25,000	Value: 27.50				

KM# 150 10 DINERS
31.4700 g., 0.9250 Silver .9359 oz. ASW **Subject:** Europa **Obv:** Crowned arms above "EURO" **Rev:** Seated Europa

Date	Mintage	F	VF	XF	Unc	BU
1998 Proof	25,000	Value: 35.00				

KM# 151 10 DINERS
31.4700 g., 0.9250 Silver .9359 oz. ASW **Subject:** Europa **Obv:** Crowned arms above "EURO" **Rev:** Europa driving quadriga

Date	Mintage	F	VF	XF	Unc	BU
1998 Proof	25,000	Value: 35.00				

KM# 153 10 DINERS
31.4700 g., 0.9250 Silver .9359 oz. ASW **Subject:** 50th Anniversary - European Council **Obv:** Crowned arms above "EURO" **Rev:** Statue of Democracy

Date	Mintage	F	VF	XF	Unc	BU
1999 Proof	15,000	Value: 37.50				

KM# 156 10 DINERS
31.4700 g., 0.9250 Silver .9359 oz. ASW, 38.6 mm. **Subject:** Jubilee 2000 **Obv:** National arms **Rev:** Birth of Jesus **Edge:** Reeded

Date	Mintage	F	VF	XF	Unc	BU
1999 Proof	15,000	Value: 40.00				

KM# 157 10 DINERS
31.4700 g., 0.9250 Silver .9359 oz. ASW **Subject:** Jubilee 2000 **Obv:** National arms **Rev:** Slaughter of the Innocents - Man with sword killing children

Date	Mintage	F	VF	XF	Unc	BU
1999 Proof	15,000	Value: 40.00				

KM# 158 10 DINERS
31.4700 g., 0.9250 Silver .9359 oz. ASW **Subject:** Jubilee 2000 **Obv:** National arms **Rev:** John the Baptist baptizing Jesus

Date	Mintage	F	VF	XF	Unc	BU
1999 Proof	15,000	Value: 40.00				

KM# 154 10 DINERS
31.4700 g., 0.9250 Silver .9359 oz. ASW **Subject:** 50th Anniversary - European Council **Obv:** Crowned arms above "EURO" **Rev:** Statue of Human Rights

Date	Mintage	F	VF	XF	Unc	BU
1999 Proof	15,000	Value: 37.50				

KM# 159 10 DINERS
31.4700 g., 0.9250 Silver .9359 oz. ASW **Subject:** Jubilee 2000 **Obv:** National arms **Rev:** Prodigal Son - Son kneeling before his father

Date	Mintage	F	VF	XF	Unc	BU
1999 Proof	15,000	Value: 40.00				

KM# 160 10 DINERS
31.4700 g., 0.9250 Silver .9359 oz. ASW **Subject:** Jubilee 2000 **Obv:** National arms **Rev:** Jesus' entry into Jerusalem

Date	Mintage	F	VF	XF	Unc	BU
1999 Proof	15,000	Value: 40.00				

KM# 161 10 DINERS
31.4700 g., 0.9250 Silver .9359 oz. ASW **Subject:** Jubilee 2000 **Obv:** National arms **Rev:** Last Supper scene

Date	Mintage	F	VF	XF	Unc	BU
1999 Proof	15,000	Value: 40.00				

KM# 162 10 DINERS
31.4700 g., 0.9250 Silver .9359 oz. ASW **Subject:** Jubilee 2000 **Obv:** National arms **Rev:** Jesus on the cross

Date	Mintage	F	VF	XF	Unc	BU
1999 Proof	15,000	Value: 40.00				

KM# 163 10 DINERS
31.4700 g., 0.9250 Silver .9359 oz. ASW **Subject:** Jubilee 2000 **Obv:** National arms **Rev:** Jesus standing in boat

Date	Mintage	F	VF	XF	Unc	BU
1999 Proof	15,000	Value: 40.00				

KM# 22 20 DINERS
16.0000 g., 0.8350 Silver .4296 oz. ASW **Subject:** Wildlife **Obv:** Crowned arms **Rev:** Bear with cub

Date	Mintage	F	VF	XF	Unc	BU
1984 Proof	5,000	Value: 37.50				

KM# 23 20 DINERS
16.0000 g., 0.8350 Silver .4296 oz. ASW **Subject:** Wildlife **Obv:** Crowned arms **Rev:** Red squirrel

Date	Mintage	F	VF	XF	Unc	BU
1984 Proof	5,000	Value: 37.50				

KM# 24 20 DINERS
16.0000 g., 0.8350 Silver .4296 oz. ASW **Subject:** Wildlife **Obv:** Crowned arms **Rev:** Ibex

Date	Mintage	F	VF	XF	Unc	BU
1984 Proof	5,000	Value: 35.00				

KM# 25 20 DINERS
16.0000 g., 0.9000 Silver .4630 oz. ASW **Subject:** 1984 Summer Olympics **Obv:** Crowned arms **Rev:** Shooter

Date	Mintage	F	VF	XF	Unc	BU
1984 Proof	10,000	Value: 25.00				

KM# 26 20 DINERS
16.0000 g., 0.9000 Silver .4630 oz. ASW **Subject:** Christmas **Obv:** Ornate arms **Rev:** Madonna and child

Date	Mintage	F	VF	XF	Unc	BU
1985 Proof	7,000	Value: 27.50				

KM# 39 20 DINERS
16.0000 g., 0.9000 Silver .4630 oz. ASW **Subject:** Olympic Tennis **Rev:** Tennis player, date lower right

Date	Mintage	F	VF	XF	Unc	BU
1987	10,000	—	—	—	50.00	55.00

KM# 43 20 DINERS
16.0000 g., 0.9000 Silver .4630 oz. ASW **Subject:** 1988 Summer Olympics **Obv:** Crowned arms **Rev:** Chamshil Stadium

Date	Mintage	F	VF	XF	Unc	BU
1988	12,000	—	—	—	50.00	55.00

KM# 47 20 DINERS
16.0000 g., 0.9250 Silver .4759 oz. ASW **Subject:** 1992 Winter Olympics, Albertville **Obv:** Crowned arms to left of five line inscription, value below, date at bottom **Rev:** Pair of figure skaters

Date	Mintage	F	VF	XF	Unc	BU
1988 Proof	15,000	Value: 25.00				

KM# 48 20 DINERS
16.0000 g., 0.9250 Silver .4759 oz. ASW **Subject:** 1992 Summer Olympics **Obv:** Crowned arms to left of five line inscription, value below, date at bottom **Rev:** Gymnast on rings

Date	Mintage	F	VF	XF	Unc	BU
1988 Proof	15,000	Value: 28.00				

KM# 54 20 DINERS
16.0000 g., 0.9250 Silver .4759 oz. ASW **Subject:** 1992 Summer Olympics **Obv:** Crowned arms to left of five line inscription, value below, date at bottom **Rev:** Wind surfer

Date	Mintage	F	VF	XF	Unc	BU
1989 Proof	15,000	Value: 35.00				

KM# 57 20 DINERS
16.0000 g., 0.9250 Silver .4759 oz. ASW **Subject:** 1992 Summer Olympics **Obv:** Crowned arms to left of five line inscription, value below, date at bottom **Rev:** Kayaker

Date	Mintage	F	VF	XF	Unc	BU
1989 Proof	15,000	Value: 35.00				

KM# 58 20 DINERS
16.0000 g., 0.9250 Silver .4759 oz. ASW **Subject:** 1992 Summer Olympics, Barcelona **Obv:** Crowned arms to left of five line inscription, value below, date at bottom **Rev:** Hurdler

Date	Mintage	F	VF	XF	Unc	BU
1990 Proof	15,000	Value: 35.00				

KM# 59 20 DINERS
16.0000 g., 0.9250 Silver .4759 oz. ASW **Subject:** 1992 Summer Olympics **Obv:** Crowned arms to left of five line inscription, value below, date at bottom **Rev:** Equestrian

Date	Mintage	F	VF	XF	Unc	BU
1990 Proof	15,000	Value: 35.00				

KM# 67 20 DINERS
21.0000 g., 0.9250 Silver .6246 oz. ASW **Subject:** European Small States Games **Obv:** Crowned arms to left of five line inscription, value below, date at bottom **Rev:** Cyclist

Date	Mintage	F	VF	XF	Unc	BU
1991 Proof	5,000	Value: 40.00				

KM# 72 20 DINERS
26.5000 g., 0.9250 Silver .7435 oz. ASW **Subject:** ECU Customs Union **Obv:** Similar to 10 Diners, KM#71 **Rev:** Charlemagne **Note:** With 1.5 g. 0.917 gold inlay, 0.0442 oz. AGW.

Date	Mintage	F	VF	XF	Unc	BU
ND(1992)	5,000	—	—	—	110	115

KM# 90 20 DINERS
26.5000 g., 0.9250 Silver .7435 oz. ASW **Subject:** ECU Customs Union **Rev:** St. George **Note:** With 1.5 g. 0.917 gold inlay, 0.0442 oz. AGW.

Date	Mintage	F	VF	XF	Unc	BU
1993 Matte	5,000	—	—	—	120	125

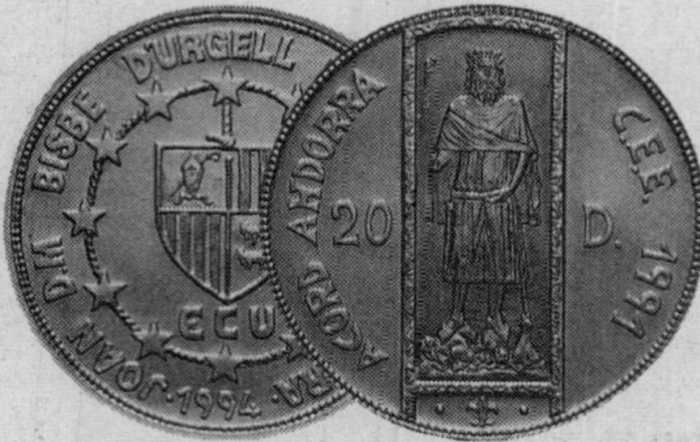

KM# 100 20 DINERS
26.5000 g., 0.9250 Silver .7435 oz. ASW **Subject:** ECU Customs Union **Obv:** Arms above "ECU",within wreath of stars on rope **Rev:** Peter III of Catalonia and Aragon **Note:** With 1.5 g. 0.917 gold inlay, 0.0442 oz. AGW.

Date	Mintage	F	VF	XF	Unc	BU
1994	5,000	—	—	—	85.00	90.00

KM# 106 20 DINERS
25.0000 g., 0.9250 Silver .7435 oz. ASW **Subject:** ECU Customs Union **Obv:** Arms above "ECU", within wreath of stars on rope **Rev:** Ramon Berenger III, three pointed crown flanked by dots below horse hooves **Note:** With 1.6 g. 0.917 gold inlay, 0.0442 oz. AGW.

Date	Mintage	F	VF	XF	Unc	BU
1995	6,000	—	—	—	85.00	90.00

KM# 122 20 DINERS
25.0000 g., 0.9250 Silver .7435 oz. ASW **Obv:** Crowned arms and "ECU", date below arms **Rev:** Charlemagne being crowned **Note:** With 1.6 g. 0.917 gold inlay, 0.0442 oz. AGW.

Date	Mintage	F	VF	XF	Unc	BU
1996	Est. 5,000	—	—	—	170	175

KM# 128 20 DINERS
25.0000 g., 0.9250 Silver .7435 oz. ASW **Subject:** Treaty at Rome **Obv:** Crowned arms above "EURO" **Rev:** Seated Europa with child holding "EURO" shield **Note:** With 1.6 g. 0.917 gold inlay, 0.0442 oz. AGW.

Date	Mintage	F	VF	XF	Unc	BU
1997	5,000	—	—	—	85.00	90.00

KM# 137 20 DINERS
6.2207 g., 0.9990 Gold .2000 oz. AGW **Obv:** Fleury cross **Rev:** Portrait of Isabella I, right

Date	Mintage	F	VF	XF	Unc	BU
1997 Proof	Est. 3,500	Value: 185				

KM# 144 20 DINERS
25.0000 g., 0.9250 Silver .7435 oz. ASW **Subject:** Human Rights **Obv:** Crowned arms above "EURO" **Rev:** Young family and broken chain **Note:** With 1.5 g. 0.917 gold inlay, 0.0442 oz. AGW.

Date	Mintage	F	VF	XF	Unc	BU
1998	5,000	—	—	—	80.00	85.00

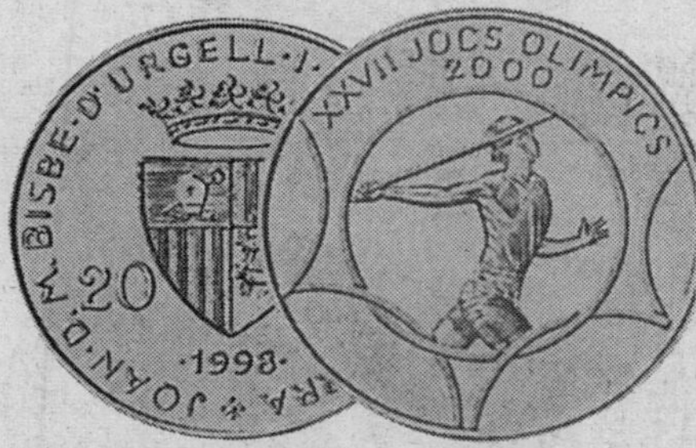

KM# 148 20 DINERS
25.0000 g., 0.9250 Silver .7435 oz. ASW **Subject:** Olympics 2000 **Obv:** Crowned arms above date **Rev:** Javelin thrower **Note:** With 1.5 g. 0.917 gold inlay, 0.0442 oz. AGW.

Date	Mintage	F	VF	XF	Unc	BU
1998	5,000	—	—	—	70.00	75.00

KM# 149 20 DINERS
25.0000 g., 0.9250 Silver .7435 oz. ASW **Subject:** Olympics 2000 **Obv:** Crowned arms above date **Rev:** Discus thrower

Date	Mintage	F	VF	XF	Unc	BU
1998	5,000	—	—	—	70.00	75.00

KM# 167 20 DINERS
25.0000 g., 0.9250 Silver .7435 oz. ASW **Subject:** XXVII JOCS 2000 Olympics **Obv:** Crowned arms, date and denomination **Rev:** Hurdler on gold inlay **Edge:** Plain

Date	Mintage	F	VF	XF	Unc	BU
2000	6,000	—	—	—	70.00	75.00

KM# 168 20 DINERS

25.0000 g., 0.9250 Silver .7435 oz. ASW **Subject:** XXVII JOCS 2000 Olympics **Obv:** Crowned arms, date and denomination **Rev:** Runner on gold inlay **Edge:** Plain

Date	Mintage	F	VF	XF	Unc	BU
2000	6,000	—	—	—	70.00	75.00

KM# 169 20 DINERS

25.0000 g., 0.9250 Silver .7435 oz. ASW **Subject:** XXVII JOCS 2000 Olympics **Obv:** Crowned arms, date and denomination **Rev:** Long jumper on gold inlay **Edge:** Plain

Date	Mintage	F	VF	XF	Unc	BU
2000	6,000	—	—	—	70.00	75.00

KM# 170 20 DINERS

25.0000 g., 0.9250 Silver .7435 oz. ASW **Subject:** XXVII JOCS 2000 Olympics **Obv:** Crowned arms, date and denomination **Rev:** Pole vaulter on gold inlay **Edge:** Plain

Date	Mintage	F	VF	XF	Unc	BU
2000	6,000	—	—	—	70.00	75.00

KM# 18 25 DINERS

20.0000 g., 0.9000 Silver .5787 oz. ASW **Obv:** Joan D.M. Bisbe D'Urgell I, left **Rev:** Crowned oval arms flanked by cherubs, value below, date at bottom

Date	Mintage	F	VF	XF	Unc	BU
1984	4,450	—	—	—	35.00	45.00
1984 Proof	550	Value: 120				

KM# 44.1 25 DINERS

20.0000 g., 0.9000 Silver .5787 oz. ASW **Subject:** 700th Anniversary - Andorra's Governing Charter **Obv:** Fleury cross **Rev:** Grasped hands, right hand armored, left hand marked on back **Note:** Medallic die rotation.

Date	Mintage	F	VF	XF	Unc	BU
ND(1988)	20,000	—	—	—	32.50	40.00

KM# 44.2 25 DINERS

20.0000 g., 0.9000 Silver .5787 oz. ASW **Subject:** 700th Anniversary - Andorra's Governing Charter **Note:** Medallic die rotation.

Date	Mintage	F	VF	XF	Unc	BU
ND(1988) Proof	10,000	Value: 45.00				

KM# 61 25 DINERS

20.0000 g., 0.9000 Silver .5787 oz. ASW **Subject:** Millenary of the Bishop of Sala **Obv:** Building within circle **Rev:** Bishop on horseback, value below

Date	Mintage	F	VF	XF	Unc	BU
1989	Est. 5,000	—	—	—	50.00	60.00

KM# 65 25 DINERS

28.2800 g., 0.9250 Silver .8411 oz. ASW **Subject:** Red Cross **Obv:** Crowned arms to left of five line inscription, value below **Rev:** Cross on dove, date below

Date	Mintage	F	VF	XF	Unc	BU
1991 Proof	3,000	Value: 57.50				

KM# 69 25 DINERS

25.0000 g., 0.9250 Silver .7435 oz. ASW **Subject:** 20th Anniversary - Episcopal Co-prince **Note:** With 0.917 gold inlay, 0.0442 oz. AGW.

Date	Mintage	F	VF	XF	Unc	BU
1991	2,500	—	—	—	85.00	95.00

KM# 73 25 DINERS

7.7700 g., 0.5830 Gold .1456 oz. AGW **Subject:** ECU Customs Union **Obv:** Arms with "ECU" below within circle of stars/beads **Rev:** St. Ermengol

Date	Mintage	F	VF	XF	Unc	BU
1992 Proof	3,000	Value: 115				

KM# 81 25 DINERS

7.7700 g., 0.5830 Gold .1456 oz. AGW **Subject:** 1994 Winter Olympic Games, Lillehammer **Obv:** Crowned arms to left of five line inscription, value below, date at bottom **Rev:** Downhill skier

Date	Mintage	F	VF	XF	Unc	BU
1993 Proof	6,000	Value: 125				

KM# 91 25 DINERS

7.7700 g., 0.5830 Gold .1456 oz. AGW **Subject:** ECU Customs Union **Obv:** Arms above "ECU" within circle of stars/beads **Rev:** Bishop riding a horse

Date	Mintage	F	VF	XF	Unc	BU
1993 Proof	5,000	Value: 115				

KM# 92 25 DINERS

7.7700 g., 0.5830 Gold .1456 oz. AGW **Subject:** 1994 World Cup Soccer **Obv:** Crowned arms to left of five line inscription, value below, date at bottom **Rev:** Soccer player on right, outline of bird on top left

Date	Mintage	F	VF	XF	Unc	BU
1993 Proof	5,000	Value: 125				

KM# 96 25 DINERS

7.7700 g., 0.5830 Gold .1456 oz. AGW **Subject:** 1994 Summer Olympic Games **Rev:** Tennis

Date	Mintage	F	VF	XF	Unc	BU
1994 Proof	5,000	Value: 125				

KM# 101 25 DINERS

7.7700 g., 0.5830 Gold .1456 oz. AGW **Subject:** ECU Customs Union **Obv:** Coat of arms **Rev:** Bishop Pere D'Urg standing

Date	Mintage	F	VF	XF	Unc	BU
1994 Proof	5,000	Value: 115				

KM# 107 25 DINERS

7.7700 g., 0.5830 Gold .1456 oz. AGW **Subject:** ECU Customs Union **Obv:** Coat of arms **Rev:** Bishop Pere D'Urg seated

Date	Mintage	F	VF	XF	Unc	BU
1995 Proof	5,000	Value: 115				

KM# 123 25 DINERS
7.7700 g., 0.5830 Gold .1456 oz. AGW **Obv:** Arms and "ECU" **Rev:** Seated Europa

Date	Mintage	F	VF	XF	Unc	BU
1996 Proof	Est. 5,000	Value: 115				

KM# 129 25 DINERS
7.7700 g., 0.5830 Gold .1456 oz. AGW **Subject:** Treaty of Rome **Obv:** Crowned arms **Rev:** Europa on knee, holding large "EURO" shield

Date	Mintage	F	VF	XF	Unc	BU
1997 Proof	5,000	Value: 115				

KM# 139 25 DINERS
Bi-Metallic Gold center in Platinum ring **Obv:** Fleury cross **Rev:** Swan in water

Date	Mintage	F	VF	XF	Unc	BU
1997 Proof	10,000	Value: 250				

KM# 145 25 DINERS
7.7700 g., 0.5850 Gold .1461 oz. AGW **Subject:** Human Rights **Obv:** Crowned arms **Rev:** Seated woman with quill

Date	Mintage	F	VF	XF	Unc	BU
1998 Proof	5,000	Value: 115				

KM# 63 50 DINERS
15.5500 g., 0.9990 Gold .5000 oz. AGW **Obv:** Defiant eagle **Rev:** Arms within circle **Note:** There is a similar 1988 half-ounce without the denomination.

Date	Mintage	F	VF	XF	Unc	BU
1989	3,000	—	—	—	—	345
1989 Proof	—	Value: 375				

KM# 62 50 DINERS
17.0250 g., 0.9170 Gold .5000 oz. AGW **Obv:** Arms within circle outlined with dots, value below **Rev:** Castle, Antoni Gaudi to left, two dates to right

Date	Mintage	F	VF	XF	Unc	BU
1990 Proof	3,000	Value: 350				

KM# 64 50 DINERS
15.5500 g., 0.9990 Gold .5000 oz. AGW **Subject:** Wildlife **Rev:** Red squirrel

Date	Mintage	F	VF	XF	Unc	BU
1990 Proof	2,500	Value: 350				

KM# 68 50 DINERS
15.5500 g., 0.9990 Gold .5000 oz. AGW **Subject:** Wildlife **Obv:** Crowned arms to left of five line inscription, value below, date below **Rev:** Chamois

Date	Mintage	F	VF	XF	Unc	BU
1991 Proof	Est. 2,500	Value: 350				

KM# 70 50 DINERS
13.3400 g., 0.5850 Gold .2509 oz. AGW **Subject:** 1992 Summer Olympic Games **Obv:** Crowned arms to left of five line inscription, value below, date at bottom **Rev:** Gymnast on rings

Date	Mintage	F	VF	XF	Unc	BU
1991 Proof	3,000	Value: 225				

KM# 93 50 DINERS
13.3400 g., 0.5850 Gold .2509 oz. AGW **Obv:** Defiant eagle **Rev:** Crowned value within wreath

Date	Mintage	F	VF	XF	Unc	BU
1992	—	—	—	—	225	250

KM# 77 50 DINERS
15.5520 g., 0.9999 Gold .4995 oz. AGW **Subject:** Wildlife **Obv:** Crowned arms to left of five line inscription, value below, date at bottom **Rev:** Bears

Date	Mintage	F	VF	XF	Unc	BU
1992 Proof	2,500	Value: 350				

KM# 82 50 DINERS
16.9650 g., 0.9160 Gold .4996 oz. AGW **Obv:** Crowned arms to left of five line inscription, value below, date at bottom **Rev:** Musician Pau Casals

Date	Mintage	F	VF	XF	Unc	BU
1993 Proof	5,000	Value: 345				

KM# 104 50 DINERS
155.5100 g., 0.9250 Silver 4.6253 oz. ASW, 65 mm. **Subject:** 1st Anniversary - Andorran Constitution **Obv:** Arms above "ECU" **Rev:** Seated woman with open scroll, within large letter "C", date below, value to right **Note:** Photo reduced.

Date	Mintage	F	VF	XF	Unc	BU
1994	5,000	—	—	—	150	165

KM# 115 50 DINERS
155.5100 g., 0.9250 Silver 4.5058 oz. ASW, 65.8 mm. **Subject:** 1996 Olympic Games **Obv:** Arms above date **Rev:** Angel lighting Olympic flame **Note:** Photo reduced.

Date	Mintage	F	VF	XF	Unc	BU
1995	5,000	—	—	—	185	200

KM# 124 50 DINERS
155.5100 g., 0.9250 Silver 4.6253 oz. ASW, 65 mm. **Subject:** Our Lady of Maritxell - Patroness of Andorra **Obv:** Crowned arms in inner circle **Rev:** Enthroned Madonna and child **Note:** With insert of 2.5 g. 0.917 gold, 0.0737 AGW. Photo reduced.

Date	Mintage	F	VF	XF	Unc	BU
1996	5,000	—	—	—	225	240

KM# 152 50 DINERS
15.5520 g., 0.9160 Gold .4583 oz. AGW **Subject:** 250th Anniversary - Synod Constitution **Obv:** Clerical arms **Rev:** Madonna and child

Date	Mintage	F	VF	XF	Unc	BU
1998 Proof	1,998	Value: 350				

KM# 41 100 DINERS
5.0000 g., 0.9990 Gold .1607 oz. AGW **Obv:** Joan D.M. Bisbe D'Urgell I, left **Rev:** Value, date below, within crowned wreath

Date	Mintage	F	VF	XF	Unc	BU
1987	2,000	—	—	—	165	195

KM# 42 100 DINERS
5.0000 g., 0.9990 Gold .1607 oz. AGW **Obv:** Arms within circle **Rev:** Flying bird, mountains in background, date below

Date	Mintage	F	VF	XF	Unc	BU
1988	2,000	—	—	—	250	275

KM# 79 100 DINERS
31.1035 g., 0.9990 Gold 1 oz. AGW **Obv:** Defiant eagle above value **Note:** There is a similar 1988 one-ounce without the denomination.

Date	Mintage	F	VF	XF	Unc	BU
1989	3,000	—	—	—	675	700

KM# 94 100 DINERS
31.1035 g., 0.9990 Gold 1 oz. AGW **Obv:** Defiant eagle, date below **Rev:** Value within crowned wreath

Date	Mintage	F	VF	XF	Unc	BU
1992	—	—	—	—	675	700

KM# 45 250 DINERS
12.0000 g., 0.9990 Gold .3858 oz. AGW **Subject:** 700th Anniversary - Andorra's Governing Charter **Obv:** Fleury cross, value at bottom **Rev:** Grasped hands, right hand armored, left hand has mark on back

Date	Mintage	F	VF	XF	Unc	BU
ND(1988)	3,000	—	—	—	310	335

KM# 30 SOVEREIGN
8.0000 g., 0.9180 Gold .2361 oz. AGW **Obv:** Joan D.M. Bisbe D'Urgell I, left **Rev:** Divided arms, value at top **Note:** Latin legend.

Date	Mintage	F	VF	XF	Unc	BU
1982	1,500	—	—	—	185	210

KM# 31 SOVEREIGN
8.0000 g., 0.9180 Gold .2361 oz. AGW **Obv:** Joan D.M. Bisbe D'Urgell I, left **Rev:** Divided arms, value at top **Note:** Catalan legend.

Date	Mintage	F	VF	XF	Unc	BU
1982	1,500	—	—	—	185	210

KM# 32 SOVEREIGN
8.0000 g., 0.9180 Gold .2361 oz. AGW **Obv:** Joan D.M. Bisbe D'Urgell I, right **Rev:** Crowned arms flanked by cherubs, value below **Note:** Latin legends.

Date	Mintage	F	VF	XF	Unc	BU
1983	1,500	—	—	—	185	210

PATTERNS

KM#	Date	Mintage	Identification	Mkt Val
Pn1	1987	—	2 Diners. Nickel Plated Bronze. KM#46.	140

MINT SETS

KM#	Date	Mintage	Identification	Issue Price	Mkt Val
MS1	1986 (5)	—	KM#33, 35-38	31.00	75.00

PROOF SETS

KM#	Date	Mintage	Identification	Issue Price	Mkt Val
PS1	1963 (2)	1,000	KM#M3, M4	51.00	60.00
PS2	1964 (2)	—	M5, M6	51.00	60.00
PS3	1964 (2)	4	X#M5a, M6a	—	1,700
PS4	1965 (2)	—	M7, M8	80.00	65.00
PS5	1965 (2)	—	X#M7a, M8a	—	1,700

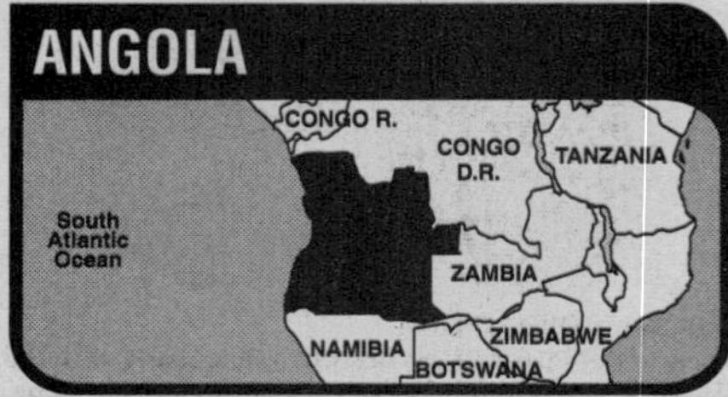

The Republic of Angola, a country on the west coast of southern Africa bounded by Congo Democratic Republic, Zambia, and Namibia (Southwest Africa), has an area of 481,351 sq. mi. (1,246,700 sq. km.) and a population of 12.78 million, predominantly Bantu in origin. Capital: Luanda. Most of the people are engaged in subsistence agriculture. However, important oil and mineral deposits make Angola potentially one of the richest countries in Africa. Iron and diamonds are exported.

The Portuguese navigator, Diogo Cao, discovered Angola in 1482 Angola. Portuguese settlers arrived in 1491, and established Angola as a major slaving center, which sent about 3 million slaves to the New World.

A revolt, characterized by guerrilla warfare, against Portuguese rule began in 1961 and continued until 1974, when a new regime in Portugal offered independence. The independence movement was actively supported by three groups; the National Front, based in Zaire, the Soviet-backed Popular Movement, and the moderate National Union. Independence was proclaimed on Nov. 11, 1975, and the Portuguese departed, leaving the Angolan people to work out their own political destiny. Within hours, each of the independence groups proclaimed itself Angola's sole ruler. A bloody intertribal civil war erupted in which the Communist Popular Movement, assisted by Soviet arms and Cuban mercenaries, was the eventual victor.

RULER

Portuguese until 1975

MINT MARK

KN - King's Norton

PORTUGUESE COLONY

DECIMAL COINAGE

Commencing 1910

100 Centavos = 20 Macutas = 1 Escudo

100 Centavos = 1 Escudo

KM# 60 CENTAVO

Bronze **Obv:** Value **Rev:** Arms, date below

Date	Mintage	F	VF	XF	Unc	BU
1921	1,360,000	7.50	20.00	60.00	125	170

KM# 61 2 CENTAVOS

Bronze **Obv:** Value **Rev:** Arms, date below

Date	Mintage	F	VF	XF	Unc	BU
1921	530,000	10.00	15.00	60.00	135	—

KM# 62 5 CENTAVOS

Bronze **Obv:** Value **Rev:** Arms, date below

Date	Mintage	F	VF	XF	Unc	BU
1921	720,000	5.00	18.00	45.00	80.00	—
1922	5,680,000	4.00	14.00	30.00	55.00	90.00
1923	5,840,000	4.00	14.00	30.00	55.00	90.00
1924	—	12.00	35.00	70.00	140	—

KM# 66 5 CENTAVOS (1 Macuta)

Nickel-Bronze **Obv:** Head left **Rev:** Arms, value below

Date	Mintage	F	VF	XF	Unc	BU
1927	2,001,999	2.50	6.00	15.00	27.50	—

KM# 63 10 CENTAVOS

Copper-Nickel **Obv:** Value **Rev:** Head, left

Date	Mintage	F	VF	XF	Unc	BU
1921	160,000	10.00	30.00	65.00	120	—
1922	340,000	7.50	15.00	45.00	85.00	175
1923	2,960,000	3.50	8.00	20.00	45.00	115

KM# 70 10 CENTAVOS

Bronze, 17.8 mm. **Subject:** 300th Anniversary - Revolution of 1648 **Obv:** Value **Rev:** Five crowns above arms, date below **Edge:** Plain

Date	Mintage	F	VF	XF	Unc	BU
1948	10,000,000	0.50	1.00	3.50	7.50	10.00
1949	10,000,000	0.35	0.75	3.00	6.50	9.00

KM# 82 10 CENTAVOS

Aluminum **Obv:** Value **Rev:** Five crowns above arms, date below

Date	Mintage	F	VF	XF	Unc	BU
1974	4,000,000	—	—	—	17.50	22.00

Note: Not released for circulation, but relatively available

KM# 67 10 CENTAVOS (2 Macutas)

Copper-Nickel **Obv:** Head, left **Rev:** Arms, value below

Date	Mintage	F	VF	XF	Unc	BU
1927	2,003,000	2.00	4.00	16.00	32.00	—
1928	1,000,000	2.00	4.00	16.00	32.00	45.00

KM# 64 20 CENTAVOS

Copper-Nickel **Obv:** Value **Rev:** Head left

Date	Mintage	F	VF	XF	Unc	BU
1921	2,115,000	4.00	9.00	22.00	40.00	100
1922	1,730,000	6.50	14.50	35.00	65.00	—

KM# 71 20 CENTAVOS

Bronze, 20.5 mm. **Subject:** 300th Anniversary - Revolution of 1648 **Obv:** Value **Rev:** Five crowns above arms, date below **Edge:** Plain

Date	Mintage	F	VF	XF	Unc	BU
1948	7,850,000	0.50	1.00	2.00	4.50	25.00
1949	2,150,000	10.00	30.00	60.00	100	140

KM# 78 20 CENTAVOS

Bronze, 18.2 mm. **Obv:** Value **Rev:** Five crowns above arms, date below **Edge:** Plain

Date	Mintage	F	VF	XF	Unc	BU
1962	3,000,000	—	0.25	0.65	1.75	—

KM# 68 20 CENTAVOS (4 Macutas)

Copper-Nickel **Obv:** Laureled head, left **Rev:** Arms, value below

Date	Mintage	F	VF	XF	Unc	BU
1927	2,001,000	2.50	4.00	8.00	25.00	—
1928	500,000	3.50	6.00	15.00	35.00	50.00

KM# 65 50 CENTAVOS

Nickel **Obv:** Head left, date below **Rev:** Arms, value in legend

Date	Mintage	F	VF	XF	Unc	BU
1922	6,000,000	3.00	10.00	20.00	40.00	—
1923 KN	6,000,000	—	—	225	375	—
1923	Inc. above	3.00	10.00	20.00	40.00	—

KM# 69 50 CENTAVOS

Nickel-Bronze **Obv:** Laureled, hooded bust with long hair, left **Rev:** Arms, value below

Date	Mintage	F	VF	XF	Unc	BU
1927	1,608,000	5.00	18.00	35.00	70.00	—
1928/7	1,600,000	5.00	18.00	40.00	75.00	—
1928	Inc. above	3.50	12.50	30.00	65.00	—

KM# 72 50 CENTAVOS

Nickel-Bronze **Subject:** 300th Anniversary - Revolution of 1648 **Obv:** Value **Rev:** Five crowns above arms, date below

Date	Mintage	F	VF	XF	Unc	BU
1948	4,000,000	0.50	1.00	3.50	8.00	27.50
1950	4,000,000	0.50	1.00	3.50	8.00	27.50

KM# 75 50 CENTAVOS

Bronze, 20 mm. **Obv:** Value **Rev:** Five crowns above arms, date below **Edge:** Plain

Date	Mintage	F	VF	XF	Unc	BU
1953	5,000,000	—	0.25	0.65	2.50	6.00
1954	11,731,000	—	0.20	0.40	1.75	4.50
1955 Rare	1,126,000	—	3.00	10.00	40.00	85.00

Date	Mintage	F	VF	XF	Unc	BU
1957	8,873,000	—	0.20	0.45	2.00	4.50
1958	17,520,000	—	0.15	0.35	1.50	4.00
1961	8,750,000	—	0.20	0.45	2.00	4.50

KM# 75a 50 CENTAVOS

Copper-Nickel

Date	Mintage	F	VF	XF	Unc	BU
1974	150	—	—	125	250	—

Note: Not released for circulation

KM# 76 ESCUDO

Bronze, 26 mm. **Obv:** Value **Rev:** Five crowns above arms, date below

Date	Mintage	F	VF	XF	Unc	BU
1953	2,001,000	—	1.50	6.00	15.00	—
1956	2,989,000	—	1.00	4.00	10.00	—
1963	5,000,000	—	1.00	2.00	7.00	18.00
1965	5,000,000	—	1.00	2.00	7.00	18.00
1972	10,000,000	—	0.75	1.50	4.50	10.00
1974	6,214,000	—	0.75	1.50	4.50	15.00

KM# 76a ESCUDO

Copper-Nickel **Note:** Not released for circulation.

Date	Mintage	F	VF	XF	Unc	BU
1972 Rare	—	—	—	—	—	—
1974 Rare	—	—	—	—	—	—

KM# 77 2-1/2 ESCUDOS

Copper-Nickel, 20 mm. **Obv:** Arms, date below **Rev:** Five crowns above arms, value below **Edge:** Reeded

Date	Mintage	F	VF	XF	Unc	BU
1953	6,008,000	—	1.00	4.00	10.00	27.50
1956	9,992,000	—	0.35	2.00	4.00	9.50
1967	6,000,000	—	0.35	2.00	4.00	9.50
1968	5,000,000	—	0.35	2.00	4.00	9.50
1969	5,000,000	—	0.35	2.00	4.00	9.50
1974	19,999,000	—	0.25	1.00	3.00	9.00

KM# 81 5 ESCUDOS

Copper-Nickel **Obv:** Arms, date below **Rev:** Five crowns above arms, value below

Date	Mintage	F	VF	XF	Unc	BU
1972	8,000,000	—	10.00	20.00	45.00	80.00
1974	Est. 3,343,000	—	—	250	450	—

Note: Not released for circulation

KM# 73 10 ESCUDOS

5.0000 g., 0.7200 Silver .1157 oz. ASW **Obv:** Arms, date below **Rev:** Five crowns above arms, value below

Date	Mintage	F	VF	XF	Unc	BU
1952	2,023,000	—	2.50	5.00	10.00	20.00
1955	1,977,000	—	2.50	5.00	10.00	20.00

KM# 79 10 ESCUDOS

Copper-Nickel **Obv:** Arms, date below **Rev:** Five crowns above arms, value below

Date	Mintage	F	VF	XF	Unc	BU
1969	3,022,000	—	1.50	3.00	6.00	14.50
1970	978,000	—	2.00	4.00	7.00	18.00

KM# 74 20 ESCUDOS

10.0000 g., 0.7200 Silver .2315 oz. ASW **Obv:** Arms, date below **Rev:** Five crowns above arms, value below

Date	Mintage	F	VF	XF	Unc	BU
1952	1,002,999	—	3.50	7.00	14.00	32.50
1955	997,000	—	3.50	6.00	12.00	28.00

KM# 80 20 ESCUDOS

Nickel **Obv:** Arms on ornate shield, date below **Rev:** Arms, value below

Date	Mintage	F	VF	XF	Unc	BU
1971	1,572,000	—	0.75	2.00	4.00	7.50
1972	428,000	—	2.50	5.00	10.00	30.00

PEOPLES REPUBLIC

DECIMAL COINAGE

1975 - 1998

100 Lwei = 1 Kwanza

KM# 90 50 LWEI

Copper-Nickel **Obv:** National arms **Rev:** Large value, dots near rim

Date	Mintage	F	VF	XF	Unc	BU
ND(1977)	—	—	0.15	0.35	1.25	2.50
1979	—	—	0.10	0.30	1.00	1.50

KM# 83 KWANZA

Copper-Nickel **Obv:** National arms **Rev:** Large value, dots near rim

Date	Mintage	F	VF	XF	Unc	BU
ND(1977)	—	—	0.30	0.50	1.50	—
1978	—	—	0.25	0.40	1.50	—
1979	—	—	0.25	0.40	1.50	—

KM# 84 2 KWANZAS

Copper-Nickel **Obv:** National arms **Rev:** Large value, dots near rim

Date	Mintage	F	VF	XF	Unc	BU
ND(1977)	—	—	0.40	0.60	1.75	—

KM# 85 5 KWANZAS

Copper-Nickel **Obv:** National arms **Rev:** Large value, dots near rim

Date	Mintage	F	VF	XF	Unc	BU
ND(1977)	—	—	0.65	1.25	3.00	—

KM# 86.1 10 KWANZAS

Copper-Nickel **Obv:** National arms **Rev:** Small date, dots near rim, Large value

Date	Mintage	F	VF	XF	Unc	BU
ND(1977)	—	—	1.25	2.00	3.50	—
1978	—	—	1.50	2.50	4.50	—

KM# 86.2 10 KWANZAS

Copper-Nickel **Rev:** Large date, dots away from rim

Date	Mintage	F	VF	XF	Unc	BU
1978	—	—	1.50	2.50	4.50	—

KM# 87 20 KWANZAS

Copper-Nickel **Obv:** National arms **Rev:** Large value, dots near rim

Date	Mintage	F	VF	XF	Unc	BU
1978	—	—	2.00	3.00	6.00	—

KM# 91 50 KWANZAS

Copper **Obv:** National arms **Rev:** Large value, dots near rim

Date	Mintage	F	VF	XF	Unc	BU
ND(1991)	—	—	2.50	4.50	9.00	—

KM# 101 50 KWANZAS

Copper Clad Steel, 23.3 mm. **Subject:** 15th Anniversary of the Angolan Kwanza Currency **Obv:** National arms within legend **Rev:** Value above anniversary date "8 Jan. 92" **Edge:** Reeded

Date	Mintage	F	VF	XF	Unc	BU
ND(1992)	—	—	55.00	90.00	—	—

KM# 92 100 KWANZAS
Copper **Obv:** National arms **Rev:** Large value, dots near rim

Date	Mintage	F	VF	XF	Unc	BU
ND(1991)	—	—	3.50	6.50	14.00	—

REFORM COINAGE

1999 -

KM# 95 10 CENTIMOS
1.5000 g., Copper Plated Steel, 15 mm. **Obv:** National arms, country name and date **Rev:** Denomination **Edge:** Plain

Date	Mintage	F	VF	XF	Unc	BU
1999	—	—	—	—	0.50	—

KM# 96 50 CENTIMOS
3.0000 g., Copper Plated Steel, 18 mm. **Obv:** National arms, country name and date **Rev:** Denomination **Edge:** Plain

Date	Mintage	F	VF	XF	Unc	BU
1999	—	—	—	—	1.00	—

KM# 97 KWANZA
4.5000 g., Nickel Plated Steel, 21 mm. **Obv:** National arms, country name and date **Rev:** Denomination **Edge:** Reeded

Date	Mintage	F	VF	XF	Unc	BU
1999	—	—	—	—	1.50	—

KM# 98 2 KWANZAS
5.0000 g., Nickel Plated Steel, 22 mm. **Obv:** National arms, country name and date **Rev:** Denomination **Edge:** Reeded

Date	Mintage	F	VF	XF	Unc	BU
1999	—	—	—	—	2.00	—

KM# 99 5 KWANZAS
7.0000 g., Nickel Plated Steel, 26 mm. **Obv:** National arms, country name and date **Rev:** Denomination **Edge:** Reeded

Date	Mintage	F	VF	XF	Unc	BU
1999	—	—	—	—	3.50	—

KM# 93 10 KWANZAS
24.2250 g., Copper-Nickel **Subject:** Olympics **Obv:** National arms **Rev:** Olympic logo and allegory **Edge:** Reeded

Date	Mintage	F	VF	XF	Unc	BU
1999 Proof	—	Value: 13.50				

KM# 100 10 KWANZAS
23.0500 g., Copper-Nickel **Subject:** Prince Henry the Navigator **Obv:** National arms **Rev:** Prince Henry in armour half facing left **Edge:** Reeded

Date	Mintage	F	VF	XF	Unc	BU
1999 Proof	—	Value: 15.00				

KM# 94 100 KWANZAS
25.0000 g., 0.9250 Silver .7435 oz. ASW **Subject:** Olympics **Obv:** National arms **Rev:** Olympic logo and Allegory

Date	Mintage	F	VF	XF	Unc	BU
1999 Proof	—	Value: 30.00				

PATTERNS

Including off metal strikes

KM#	Date	Mintage	Identification	Mkt Val
Pn7	1972	—	50 Escudos. Silver. Shield within circle. Cross with winged arms and waves on top.	1,500

PROVAS

KM#	Date	Mintage	Identification	Issue Price	Mkt Val
Pr1	1921	—	Centavo. Bronze. KM#60.	—	95.00
Pr2	1921	—	2 Centavos. Bronze center. KM#61.	—	135
Pr3	1921	—	5 Centavos. Bronze. KM#62.	—	80.00
Pr4	1921	—	10 Centavos. Copper-Nickel. KM#63.	—	110
Pr5	1921	—	20 Centavos. Copper-Nickel. KM#64.	—	40.00
Pr6	1922	—	5 Centavos. Bronze. KM#62.	—	55.00
Pr7	1922	—	10 Centavos. Copper-Nickel. KM#63.	—	80.00
Pr8	1922	—	20 Centavos. Copper-Nickel. KM#64.	—	65.00
Pr9	1923	—	5 Centavos. Bronze. KM#62.	—	55.00
Pr10	1923	—	10 Centavos. Copper-Nickel. KM#63.	—	45.00
Pr12	1924	—	5 Centavos. Bronze. KM#62.	—	135
Pr13	1927	—	5 Centavos. Nickel-Bronze. KM#66.	—	35.00
Pr14	1927	—	10 Centavos. Copper-Nickel. KM#67.	—	35.00
Pr15	1927	—	20 Centavos. Copper-Nickel. KM#68.	—	30.00
Pr16	1927	—	50 Centavos. Nickel-Bronze. KM#69.	—	65.00
Pr17	1928	—	10 Centavos. Copper-Nickel. KM#67.	—	40.00
Pr18	1928	—	20 Centavos. Copper-Nickel. KM#68.	—	40.00
Pr19	1928	—	50 Centavos. Nickel-Bronze. KM#69.	—	65.00
Pr20	1948	—	10 Centavos. Bronze. KM#70.	—	22.50
Pr21	1948	—	20 Centavos. Bronze. KM#71.	—	22.50
Pr22	1948	—	50 Centavos. Nickel-Bronze. KM#72.	—	22.50
Pr23	1949	—	10 Centavos. Bronze. KM#70.	—	22.50
Pr24	1949	—	20 Centavos. Bronze. KM#71.	—	22.50
Pr25	1949	—	50 Centavos. Nickel-Bronze. KM#72.	—	22.50
Pr26	1950	—	50 Centavos. Nickel-Bronze. KM#72.	—	20.00
Pr27	1952	—	10 Escudos. Silver. KM#73.	—	30.00
Pr28	1952	—	20 Escudos. Silver. KM#74.	—	45.00
Pr29	1953	—	50 Centavos. Bronze. KM#75.	—	20.00
Pr30	1953	—	Escudo. Bronze. KM#76.	—	22.50
Pr31	1953	—	2-1/2 Escudos. Copper-Nickel. KM#77.	—	32.00
Pr32	1954	—	50 Centavos. Bronze. KM#75.	—	20.00
Pr33	1954	—	Escudo. Bronze. KM#76.	—	22.50
Pr34	1954	—	2-1/2 Escudos. Copper-Nickel. KM#77.	—	32.00
Pr35	1955	—	50 Centavos. Bronze. KM#75.	—	20.00
Pr36	1955	—	Escudo. Bronze. KM#76.	—	22.50
Pr37	1955	—	2-1/2 Escudos. Copper-Nickel. KM#77.	—	32.00
Pr38	1955	—	10 Escudos. Silver. KM#73.	—	32.00
Pr39	1955	—	20 Escudos. Silver. KM#74.	—	45.00
Pr40	1956	—	50 Centavos. Bronze. KM#75.	—	15.00
Pr41	1956	—	Escudo. Bronze. KM#76.	—	15.00
Pr42	1956	—	2-1/2 Escudos. Copper-Nickel. KM#77.	—	15.00
Pr43	1957	—	50 Centavos. Bronze. KM#75.	—	15.00
Pr44	1957	—	Escudo. Bronze center. KM#76.	—	15.00
Pr45	1957	—	2-1/2 Escudos. Copper-Nickel. KM#77.	—	15.00
Pr46	1958	—	50 Centavos. Bronze center. KM#75.	—	15.00
Pr47	1958	—	Escudo. Bronze. KM#76.	—	15.00
Pr48	1958	—	2-1/2 Escudos. Copper-Nickel. KM#77.	—	15.00
Pr49	1959	—	50 Centavos. Bronze. KM#75.	—	15.00
Pr50	1959	—	Escudo. Bronze. KM#76.	—	15.00
Pr51	1959	—	2-1/2 Escudos. Copper-Nickel. KM#77.	—	15.00
Pr52	1960	—	50 Centavos. Bronze. KM#75.	—	15.00
Pr53	1960	—	Escudo. Bronze. KM#76.	—	15.00
Pr54	1960	—	2-1/2 Escudos. Copper-Nickel. KM#77.	—	15.00
Pr55	1961	—	50 Centavos. Bronze. KM#75.	—	15.00
Pr56	1961	—	Escudo. Bronze. KM#76.	—	15.00
Pr57	1961	—	2-1/2 Escudos. Copper-Nickel. KM#77.	—	15.00
Pr58	1962	—	20 Centavos. Bronze. KM#78.	—	15.00
Pr59	1962	—	Escudo. Bronze. KM#76.	—	15.00
Pr60	1962	—	2-1/2 Escudos. Copper-Nickel. KM#77.	—	15.00
Pr61	1963	—	Escudo. Bronze. KM#76.	—	15.00
Pr62	1963	—	2-1/2 Escudos. Copper-Nickel. KM#77.	—	15.00
Pr63	1964	—	Escudo. Bronze. KM#76.	—	15.00
Pr64	1964	—	2-1/2 Escudos. Copper-Nickel. KM#77.	—	15.00
Pr65	1965	—	Escudo. Bronze. KM#76.	—	15.00
Pr66	1965	—	2-1/2 Escudos. Copper-Nickel. KM#77.	—	15.00
Pr67	1966	—	Escudo. Bronze. KM#76.	—	15.00
Pr68	1966	—	2-1/2 Escudos. Copper-Nickel. KM#77.	—	15.00
Pr69	1967	—	Escudo. Bronze. KM#76.	—	15.00
Pr70	1967	—	2-1/2 Escudos. Copper-Nickel. KM#77.	—	15.00
Pr71	1968	—	Escudo. Bronze. KM#76.	—	15.00
Pr72	1968	—	2-1/2 Escudos. Copper-Nickel. KM#77.	—	15.00
Pr73	1969	—	Escudo. Bronze. KM#76.	—	15.00
Pr74	1969	—	2-1/2 Escudos. Copper-Nickel. KM#77.	—	15.00
Pr75	1969	—	10 Escudos. Copper-Nickel. KM#79.	—	15.00
Pr76	1970	—	Escudo. Bronze. KM#76.	—	15.00
Pr77	1970	—	2-1/2 Escudos. Copper-Nickel. KM#77.	—	15.00
Pr78	1970	—	10 Escudos. Copper-Nickel. KM#79.	—	15.00
Pr79	1971	—	Escudo. Bronze. KM#76.	—	15.00
Pr80	1971	—	2-1/2 Escudos. Copper-Nickel. KM#77.	—	15.00
Pr81	1971	—	20 Escudos. Nickel. KM#80.	—	15.00
Pr82	1972	—	Escudo. Bronze. KM#76.	—	15.00
Pr83	1972	—	2-1/2 Escudos. Copper-Nickel. KM#77.	—	15.00
Pr84	1972	—	5 Escudos. Copper-Nickel. KM#81.	—	15.00
Pr85	1972	—	20 Escudos. Nickel. KM#80.	—	15.00
Pr86	1974	—	Escudo. Bronze. KM#76.	—	15.00

MINT SETS

KM#	Date	Mintage	Identification	Issue Price	Mkt Val
MS1	ND (1979) (6)	—	KM#83, 84, 85, 86.2, 87, 90 This set was assembled by the National Bank of Angola in a folder which presents a brief monetary history of Angola including some banknote pictures.	20.00	20.00

ANGUILLA

The British dependency of Anguilla, a self-governing British territory situated in the east Caribbean Sea about 60 miles (100 km.) northwest of St. Kitts, has an area of 35 sq. mi. (91 sq. km.) and an approximate population of 12,000. Capital: The Valley. In recent years, tourism has replaced the traditional fishing, stock raising and salt production as the main industry.

Anguilla was discovered by Columbus in 1493 and became a British colony in 1650. As the other British areas in the West Indies did, Anguilla officially adapted to sterling beginning in 1825. From 1950 to 1965, Anguilla was a member of the British Caribbean Territories (Eastern Group) Currency Board, whose coinage it used. In March 1967, Anguilla was joined politically with St. Christopher (St. Kitts), as it had been for much of its colonial history, and Nevis to form a British associated state.

On June 16, 1967, the Provisional Government of Anguilla unilaterally declared its independence and seceded from the Federation. Later, on July 11, 1967, a vote of confidence was taken and the results favored independence. Britain refused to accept the declaration (nor did any other country recognize it) and appointed a British administrator whom Anguilla accepted. However, in Feb. 1969 Anguilla ousted the British emissary, voted to sever all ties with Britain, and established the Republic of Anguilla. The following month Britain landed a force of paratroopers and policemen. This bloodless counteraction ended the self-proclaimed republic and resulted in the installation of a governing commissioner. The troops were withdrawn in Sept. 1969, and the Anguilla Act of July 1971 placed Anguilla directly under British control. A new constitution in 1976 established Anguilla as a self-governing British dependant territory. Britain retains power over defense, police and civil service, and foreign affairs. Since 1981, Anguilla has employed the coinage of the East Caribbean States.

NOTE: There is no evidence that the issues of the self-proclaimed Provisional Government ever actually circulated. The c/s series most likely served as souvenirs of the "revolution".

RULERS
British

BRITISH COLONY

DECIMAL COINAGE

KM# 15 1/2 DOLLAR
3.6100 g., 0.9990 Silver .1160 oz. ASW **Obv:** St. Mary's Church **Rev:** State arms

Date	Mintage	F	VF	XF	Unc	BU
ND Proof	4,200	Value: 25.00				
1969 Proof	—	Value: 25.00				
1970 Proof	Inc. above	Value: 25.00				

KM# 16 DOLLAR
7.1800 g., 0.9990 Silver .2308 oz. ASW **Obv:** Map - Seahorse, Caribbean Silver Lobster, Shell **Rev:** State arms

Date	Mintage	F	VF	XF	Unc	BU
ND Proof	4,450	Value: 30.00				
1969 Proof	—	Value: 30.00				
1970 Proof	Inc. above	Value: 30.00				

KM# 17 2 DOLLARS
14.1400 g., 0.9990 Silver .4546 oz. ASW **Obv:** National flag and map **Rev:** State arms

Date	Mintage	F	VF	XF	Unc	BU
ND Proof	4,150	Value: 40.00				
1969 Proof	—	Value: 40.00				
1970 Proof	Inc. above	Value: 40.00				

KM# 18.1 4 DOLLARS
28.4800 g., 0.9990 Silver .9156 oz. ASW **Obv:** Ship - Atlantic Star **Rev:** State arms, value at bottom

Date	Mintage	F	VF	XF	Unc	BU
ND Proof	5,100	Value: 70.00				
1969 Proof	—	Value: 70.00				
1970 Proof	Inc. above	Value: 70.00				

KM# 18.2 4 DOLLARS
28.4800 g., 0.9990 Silver .9156 oz. ASW **Obv:** Ship- Atlantic Star **Rev:** 2 hallmarks at 4 o'clock, state arms, value at bottom

Date	Mintage	F	VF	XF	Unc	BU
1970 Proof	—	Value: 100				

KM# 20 5 DOLLARS
2.4600 g., 0.9000 Gold .0711 oz. AGW **Obv:** Methodist Church of West End

Date	Mintage	F	VF	XF	Unc	BU
ND Proof	1,925	Value: 85.00				
1969 Proof	Inc. above	Value: 85.00				
1970 Proof	Inc. above	Value: 85.00				

KM# 21 10 DOLLARS
4.9300 g., 0.9000 Gold .1426 oz. AGW **Obv:** Dolphin, Caribbean Silver Lobster, Starfish

Date	Mintage	F	VF	XF	Unc	BU
ND Proof	1,615	Value: 125				
1969 Proof	Inc. above	Value: 125				
1970 Proof	Inc. above	Value: 125				

KM# 22 20 DOLLARS
9.8700 g., 0.9000 Gold .2856 oz. AGW **Obv:** Mermaids

Date	Mintage	F	VF	XF	Unc	BU
ND Proof	1,395	Value: 285				
1969 Proof	Inc. above	Value: 285				
1970 Proof	Inc. above	Value: 285				

KM# 26 25 DOLLARS
31.0000 g., 0.9990 Silver 0.9957 oz. ASW **Subject:** 1st Year of Independence **Obv:** Three intertwined dolphins form circle **Rev:** President Ronald Webster bust left

Date	Mintage	F	VF	XF	Unc	BU
1968 Proof	—	Value: 70.00				

KM# 23 100 DOLLARS
49.3700 g., 0.9000 Gold 1.4287 oz. AGW **Subject:** Demonstrating Population **Obv:** People of Anguilla within beaded circle, grain spray below circle

Date	Mintage	F	VF	XF	Unc	BU
ND Proof	710	Value: 1,000				
1969 Proof	—	Value: 1,000				
1970 Proof	Inc. above	Value: 1,000				

KM# 27 200 DOLLARS
38.0000 g., 0.9170 Gold 1.1203 oz. AGW **Subject:** 1st Year of Independence **Obv:** Three intertwined dolphins form circle **Rev:** President Ronald Webster bust left

Date	Mintage	F	VF	XF	Unc	BU
1968 Proof	—	Value: 800				

KM# 28 1500 DOLLARS

62.0000 g., 0.9990 Platinum 1.9914 oz. APW **Subject:** 1st Year of Independence **Obv:** Three intertwined dolphins form circle **Rev:** President Ronald Wester bust facing left

Date	Mintage	F	VF	XF	Unc	BU
1968 Proof	—	Value: 2,500				

TRIAL STRIKES

KM#	Date	Mintage	Identification	Mkt Val
TS1	ND (1969)	—	5 Dollars. Goldine-Brass. 1.5100 g. 50 mm. Design of KM-20. Blank with MET countermark. Reeded edge. Uniface.	75.00

KM#	Date	Mintage	Identification	Mkt Val
TS2	1969	—	100 Dollars. Goldine. 50 mm.	—

KM#	Date	Mintage	Identification	Mkt Val
TS3	ND (1969)	—	5 Dollars. Goldine-Brass. 29.2100 g. 14 mm. Design of KM-23. Blank with MET countermark. Reeded edge.	200

PROOF SETS

KM#	Date	Mintage	Identification	Issue Price	Mkt Val
PS1	1969 (8)	—	KM#15-18.1, 20-23	226	1,650
PS2	1969 (4)	—	KM#15-18.1	25.50	165
PS3	1969 (4)	—	KM#20-23	200	1,500
PS4	1970 (8)	—	KM#15-18.1, 20-23	226	1,650
PS5	1970 (4)	—	KM#15-18.1	25.50	165
PS6	1970 (4)	—	KM#20-23	200	1,500

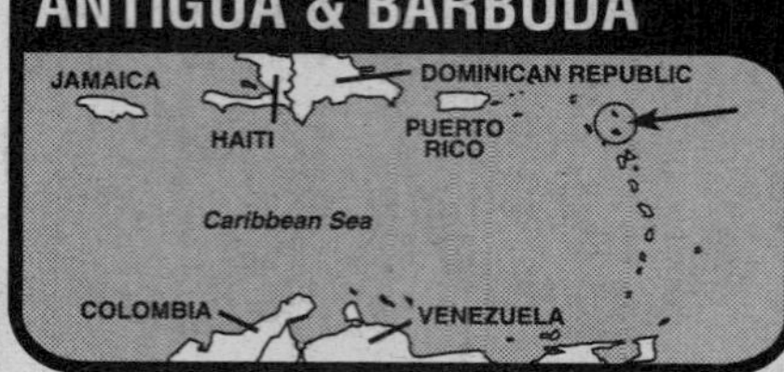

Antigua and Barbuda are located on the eastern edge of the Leeward Islands in the Caribbean Sea, have an area of 170 sq. mi. (440 sq. km.) and an estimated population of 68,000. Capital: St. John's. Prior to 1967, Antigua and its dependencies Barbuda and Redonda, comprised a presidency of the Leeward Islands. The mountainous island produces sugar, molasses, rum, cotton and fruit. Tourism is making an increasingly valuable contribution to the economy.

Antigua was discovered by Columbus in 1493, settled by British colonists from St. Kitts in 1632, occupied by the French in 1666, and ceded to Britain in 1667. It became an associated state with internal self-government on February 27, 1967. On November 1, 1981 it became independent as Antigua and Barbuda. As a constitutional monarchy, Elizabeth II is Queen of Antigua and Barbuda and Head of State.

Spanish silver coinage and French colonial "Black Dogs" were used throughout the islands' early history; however, late in the seventeenth century the introduction of British tin farthings was attempted with complete lack of success. In 1822, British colonial Anchor Money was introduced.

From 1825 to 1955, Antigua was on the sterling standard and used British coins. Coins of the British Caribbean Territories (Eastern Group) and East Caribbean States circulated from 1955, and banknotes of East Caribbean Currency Authority are now used on the island. The early coinage was augmented by that of the East Caribbean States in 1981.

RULERS

British

ANTIGUA

BRITISH ADMINISTRATION

DECIMAL COINAGE

100 Cents = 1 Dollar

KM# 1 4 DOLLARS

28.3000 g., Copper-Nickel, 38.5 mm. **Ruler:** Elizabeth II **Series:** F.A.O. **Obv:** Helmeted arms with supporters, date below **Rev:** Value at bottom divides sugar cane and banana tree branch **Edge:** Reeded

Date	Mintage	F	VF	XF	Unc	BU
1970	14,000	—	6.00	10.00	20.00	30.00
1970 Proof	2,000	Value: 35.00				

Note: For similar issues see Barbados, Dominica, Grenada, Montserrat, St. Kitts, St. Lucia and St. Vincent.

ANTIGUA & BARBUDA

BRITISH ADMINISTRATION

DECIMAL COINAGE

KM# 5 10 DOLLARS

Copper-Nickel, 38.8 mm. **Ruler:** Elizabeth II **Subject:** Royal Visit **Obv:** Crowned bust of Queen Elizabeth II right **Obv. Designer:** Raphael Maklouf **Rev:** Arms in circle with country name above, date in legend, value below

Date	Mintage	F	VF	XF	Unc	BU
1985	100,000	—	—	—	25.00	35.00

KM# 5a 10 DOLLARS

28.2800 g., 0.9250 Silver .8409 oz. ASW **Ruler:** Elizabeth II

Date	Mintage	F	VF	XF	Unc	BU
1985 Proof	5,000	Value: 50.00				

KM# 5b 10 DOLLARS

47.5400 g., 0.9170 Gold 1.4013 oz. AGW **Ruler:** Elizabeth II

Date	Mintage	F	VF	XF	Unc	BU
1985 Proof	250	Value: 1,250				

KM# 2 30 DOLLARS

31.1000 g., 0.5000 Silver .5 oz. ASW **Ruler:** Elizabeth II **Subject:** George Washington - Yorktown, 1781 **Obv:** Helmeted arms, date below, value at bottom **Rev:** George Washington between two figures, lighting cannon

Date	Mintage	F	VF	XF	Unc	BU
1982 Proof	1,200	Value: 60.00				

KM# 3 30 DOLLARS

31.1000 g., 0.5000 Silver .5 oz. ASW **Ruler:** Elizabeth II **Subject:** George Washington - Inauguration, 1789 **Obv:** Helmeted arms, date below, value at bottom **Rev:** George Washington and men rowing across the Delaware

Date	Mintage	F	VF	XF	Unc	BU
1982 Proof	1,125	Value: 60.00				

KM# 4 30 DOLLARS

31.3000 g., 0.5000 Silver .5 oz. ASW **Ruler:** Elizabeth II **Subject:** George Washington - Verplanck's Point, 1790 **Obv:** Helmeted arms, date below, value at bottom **Rev:** George Washington standing next to horse, left

Date	Mintage	F	VF	XF	Unc	BU
1982 Proof	675	Value: 70.00				

KM# 6 100 DOLLARS

Silver **Ruler:** Elizabeth II **Subject:** Tropical Birds **Obv:** Arms in circle, country name above, date below **Rev:** Cattle Egret

Date	Mintage	F	VF	XF	Unc	BU
1988 Proof	10,000	Value: 125				

ARGENTINA

The Argentine Republic, located in southern South America, has an area of 1,073,518 sq. mi. (3,761,274 sq. km.) and an estimated population of 37.03 million. Capital: Buenos Aires. Its varied topography ranges from the subtropical lowlands of the north to the towering Andean Mountains in the west and the windswept Patagonian steppe in the south. The rolling, fertile pampas of central Argentina are ideal for agriculture and grazing, and support most of the republic's population. Meatpacking, flour milling, textiles, sugar refining and dairy products are the principal industries. Oil is found in Patagonia, but most mineral requirements must be imported.

Argentina was discovered in 1516 by the Spanish navigator Juan de Solis. A permanent Spanish colony was established at Buenos Aires in 1580, but the colony developed slowly. When Napoleon conquered Spain, the Argentines set up their own government on May 25, 1810. Independence was formally declared on July 9, 1816. A strong tendency toward local autonomy, fostered by difficult transportation, resulted in a federalized union with much authority left to the states or provinces, which resulted in the coinage of 1817-1867.

Internal conflict through the first half century of Argentine independence resulted in a provisional national coinage, chiefly of crown-sized silver. Provincial issues mainly of minor denominations supplemented this.

MINT MARKS

A = Korea
B = Great Britain
BA = Buenos Aires
CORDOBA, CORDOVA
C = France
PTS = Potosi monogram (Bolivia)
R, RA, RIOJA, RIOXA
SE = Santiago del Estero
T, TM = Tucuman
TIERRA DEL FUEGO

MONETARY SYSTEM

8 Reales = 8 Soles = 1/2 Escudo
16 Reales or Soles = 1 Escudo
10 Decimos = 1 Real
100 Centavos = 1 Peso
10 Pesos = 1 Argentino
(Commencing 1970)
100 Old Pesos = 1 New Peso
(Commencing June 1983)
10,000 New Pesos = 1 Peso Argentino
1,000 Pesos Argentino = 1 Austral
(Commencing 1985)
1,000 Pesos Argentinos = 1 Austral
100 Centavos = 1 Austral
(Commencing 1992)
10,000 Australs = 1 Peso

REPUBLIC

DECIMAL COINAGE

KM# 37 CENTAVO

Bronze **Obv:** Argentine arms **Rev:** Value within wreath **Note:** Prev. KM#12.

Date	Mintage	F	VF	XF	Unc	BU
1939	3,488,000	0.25	0.50	1.50	4.00	—
1940	3,140,000	0.15	0.35	1.00	2.00	—
1941	4,572,000	0.15	0.35	1.00	2.00	—
1942	495,000	0.30	0.75	1.50	7.50	—
1943	1,293,500	0.10	0.25	0.55	1.50	—
1944	3,102,743	0.20	0.50	1.00	2.75	—

KM# 37a CENTAVO

Copper **Obv:** Argentine arms **Rev:** Value within wreath **Note:** Cruder diework. Prev. KM#12a.

Date	Mintage	F	VF	XF	Unc	BU
1945	420,000	0.20	0.50	1.00	4.00	—
1946/6	4,450,000	0.15	0.35	0.50	2.00	3.00
1947	5,630,000	0.15	0.35	0.50	2.00	3.00
1948	4,419,545	0.15	0.35	0.50	2.00	3.00

KM# 38 2 CENTAVOS

Bronze **Obv:** Argentine arms **Rev:** Value within wreath **Note:** Prev. KM#13.

Date	Mintage	F	VF	XF	Unc	BU
1939	5,490,000	0.15	0.35	1.00	4.50	—
1940	4,625,000	0.15	0.35	1.00	5.00	—
1941	4,566,805	0.15	0.35	1.00	5.00	—
1942	2,082,492	0.15	0.35	1.00	5.50	—
1944	387,072	0.25	0.50	1.25	7.50	—
1945	4,585,000	0.15	0.35	1.00	5.00	—
1946/1946	3,395,000	0.15	0.35	1.00	5.00	—
1947	4,395,000	0.15	0.35	1.00	5.00	—

KM# 38a 2 CENTAVOS

Copper **Obv:** Argentine arms **Rev:** Value within wreath **Note:** Cruder diework. Prev. KM#13a.

Date	Mintage	F	VF	XF	Unc	BU
1947	Inc. above	0.15	0.35	1.00	5.50	—
1948	3,645,000	0.15	0.35	1.00	5.50	—
1949/9	7,290,000	0.15	0.35	1.00	3.50	5.00
1950	903,070	0.25	0.65	1.25	6.50	—

KM# 34 5 CENTAVOS

Copper-Nickel **Obv:** Capped liberty head, left **Rev:** Value within wreath **Note:** Prev. KM#9.

Date	Mintage	F	VF	XF	Unc	BU
1903	2,502,000	0.25	0.50	3.00	18.00	—
1904	2,518,000	0.25	0.50	3.00	18.00	—
1905	4,359,000	0.25	0.50	3.00	18.00	—
1906	3,939,000	0.25	0.50	3.00	18.00	—
1907	1,682,000	0.50	1.00	5.00	20.00	—
1908	1,693,000	0.50	1.00	5.00	20.00	—
1909	4,650,000	0.25	0.50	3.50	20.00	—
1910	1,469,000	0.75	2.00	6.00	24.00	—
1911	1,431,000	0.25	0.75	4.00	20.00	—
1912	2,377,000	0.25	0.75	4.00	20.00	—
1913	1,477,000	0.25	0.75	4.00	20.00	—
1914	1,097,000	0.50	1.00	5.00	22.00	—
1915	1,310,000	0.30	0.75	3.50	20.00	—
1916	1,310,000	0.30	0.75	3.50	18.00	—
1917	1,009,000	0.75	1.50	4.00	20.00	—
1918	2,287,000	0.25	0.50	3.00	15.00	—
1919	2,476,000	0.25	0.50	3.00	10.00	—
1920	5,235,000	0.25	0.50	3.00	10.00	—
1921	7,040,000	0.20	0.35	2.00	8.00	—
1922	9,427,000	0.20	0.35	2.00	10.00	—
1923	6,256,000	0.20	0.35	2.00	10.00	—
1924	6,355,000	0.20	0.35	2.00	10.00	—
1925	3,955,000	0.20	0.35	2.00	10.00	—
1926	3,560,000	0.20	0.35	2.00	10.00	—
1927	5,650,000	0.20	0.35	2.00	10.00	—
1928	6,380,000	0.20	0.35	2.00	10.00	—
1929	11,831,000	0.20	0.35	2.00	10.00	—
1930 round top 3	7,110,000	0.20	0.35	2.00	10.00	—
1931 flat top 3	506,000	2.00	4.00	9.00	25.00	—
1933 round top 3	5,537,000	0.10	0.25	1.00	4.00	—
1934 round top 3	1,288,000	0.25	0.50	3.00	8.00	—
1935	3,052,000	0.10	0.25	1.00	4.00	—
1936	7,175,000	0.10	0.25	1.00	4.00	—
1937	7,063,000	0.10	0.25	1.00	4.00	—
1938	10,252,000	0.10	0.25	1.00	3.50	—
1939	7,171,000	0.10	0.25	1.00	4.00	—
1940	10,191,000	0.10	0.25	1.00	3.50	—

Date	Mintage	F	VF	XF	Unc	BU
1941	951,000	0.50	1.00	3.00	12.00	—
1942	8,692,000	0.10	0.25	1.00	3.50	—

KM# 40 5 CENTAVOS

Aluminum-Bronze **Obv:** Value at center, grain spray on left, head of cow on right **Rev:** Grain sprig behind capped head, right **Note:** Prev. KM#15.

Date	Mintage	F	VF	XF	Unc	BU
1942	2,130,000	0.25	0.50	1.50	5.00	—
1943 round top 3	15,778,000	0.10	0.25	0.75	3.00	4.00
1944	21,081,000	0.10	0.25	0.75	3.00	4.00
1945	21,600,000	0.10	0.25	0.75	3.00	4.00
1946	20,460,000	0.10	0.25	0.75	3.00	4.00
1947	22,520,000	0.10	0.25	0.75	3.00	4.00
1948	42,790,000	0.10	0.25	0.50	2.00	3.00
1949	35,470,000	0.10	0.25	0.75	3.00	4.00
1950	13,500,000	0.10	0.25	0.75	3.00	4.00

KM# 43 5 CENTAVOS

Copper-Nickel, 17 mm. **Obv:** Value **Rev:** Jose de San Martin bust facing right **Edge:** Reeded **Designer:** Mario Baiardi **Note:** Prev. KM#18.

Date	Mintage	F	VF	XF	Unc	BU
1950	3,460,000	0.20	0.40	0.60	2.00	3.00

KM# 46 5 CENTAVOS

Copper-Nickel, 17 mm. **Obv:** Value **Rev:** Jose de San Martin bust facing right **Edge:** Reeded **Designer:** Mario Baiardi **Note:** Prev. KM#21.

Date	Mintage	F	VF	XF	Unc	BU
1951	34,994,000	—	0.20	0.30	0.50	0.75
1952	33,110,000	—	0.20	0.30	0.50	0.75
1953	20,129,000	—	0.20	0.30	0.50	0.75

KM# 46a 5 CENTAVOS

Copper-Nickel Clad Steel, 17 mm. **Rev:** Jose de San Martin bust facing right **Edge:** Plain **Designer:** Mario Baiardi **Note:** Prev. KM#21a.

Date	Mintage	F	VF	XF	Unc	BU
1953	36,300,000	—	0.15	0.20	0.35	0.50

KM# 50 5 CENTAVOS

Copper-Nickel Clad Steel, 17.2 mm. **Obv:** Value **Rev:** Jose de San Martin bust facing right **Edge:** Plain **Designer:** Mario Baiardi **Note:** Prev. KM#25.

Date	Mintage	F	VF	XF	Unc	BU
1954	50,640,000	—	0.15	0.20	0.35	0.50
1955	42,200,000	—	0.15	0.20	0.35	0.50
1956	36,870,000	—	0.15	0.20	0.35	0.50

KM# 53 5 CENTAVOS

Copper-Nickel Clad Steel **Obv:** Capped liberty head, left **Rev:** Value within wreath **Edge:** Plain **Note:** Prev. KM#28.

Date	Mintage	F	VF	XF	Unc	BU
1957	26,930,000	—	0.15	0.20	0.35	0.50
1958	13,108,000	—	0.15	0.20	0.35	0.50
1959	14,971,000	—	0.15	0.20	0.35	0.50

KM# 35 10 CENTAVOS

Copper-Nickel **Obv:** Capped liberty head **Rev:** Denomination **Edge:** Reeded **Note:** Prev. KM#10.

Date	Mintage	F	VF	XF	Unc	BU
1905	3,785,000	0.50	1.00	3.50	20.00	—
1906	3,854,000	0.50	1.00	3.50	20.00	—
1907	2,355,000	0.50	1.00	4.50	22.00	—
1908	2,280,000	0.50	1.00	4.50	22.00	—
1909	3,738,000	0.50	1.00	3.50	20.00	—
1910	3,026,000	0.50	1.00	3.50	20.00	—
1911	2,142,000	0.75	2.00	5.00	24.00	—
1912	2,993,000	0.75	2.00	5.00	24.00	—
1913 round top 3	1,828,000	1.00	2.50	5.50	25.00	—
1914	751,000	1.00	2.50	5.50	25.00	—
1915	2,607,000	0.50	1.00	3.50	20.00	—
1916	835,000	1.00	2.50	5.50	25.00	—
1918	3,897,000	0.50	1.00	3.50	20.00	—
1919	2,517,000	0.50	1.00	3.50	25.00	—
1920	7,509,000	0.25	0.75	2.50	20.00	—
1921	11,564,000	0.25	0.60	2.00	15.00	—
1922	6,542,000	0.20	0.50	2.00	20.00	—
1923	5,301,000	0.20	0.50	2.00	15.00	—
1924	3,489,000	0.20	0.50	1.75	10.00	—
1925	5,415,000	0.20	0.50	1.75	10.00	—
1926	5,055,000	0.15	0.35	1.50	9.00	—
1927	5,205,000	0.15	0.35	1.50	9.00	—
1928	8,255,000	0.15	0.35	1.50	9.00	—
1929	2,501,000	0.15	0.35	1.50	9.00	—
1930 round top 3	14,586,000	0.15	0.35	1.00	6.00	—
1931 flat top 3	893,000	0.50	1.00	2.50	20.00	—
1933	5,394,000	0.15	0.35	1.50	8.00	—
1934	3,319,000	0.15	0.35	1.50	8.00	—
1935	1,018,000	0.30	0.75	2.00	15.00	—
1936	3,000,000	0.15	0.35	1.50	12.00	—
1937	11,766,000	0.15	0.35	1.00	4.00	—
1938	10,494,000	0.15	0.35	1.00	4.00	—
1939	5,585,000	0.15	0.35	1.00	5.00	—
1940	3,955,000	0.15	0.35	1.00	5.00	—
1941	4,101,000	0.15	0.35	1.00	5.00	—
1942	2,962,000	0.15	0.25	1.00	5.00	—

KM# 41 10 CENTAVOS

Aluminum-Bronze **Obv:** Value center, grain sprig on left, head of cow on right **Rev:** Grain sprig behind capped head facing right **Note:** Prev. KM#16.

Date	Mintage	F	VF	XF	Unc	BU
1942	15,541,000	0.15	0.25	1.00	4.00	—
1943	13,916,000	0.15	0.35	1.25	6.00	—
1944	16,411,000	0.15	0.25	1.00	4.00	—
1945	12,500,000	0.25	0.50	2.00	7.00	—
1946	15,790,000	0.15	0.25	1.00	4.00	—
1947	36,430,000	0.15	0.25	1.00	2.50	3.50
1948	54,685,000	0.15	0.25	1.00	2.50	3.50
1949	57,740,000	0.15	0.25	1.00	2.50	3.50
1950	42,825,000	0.15	0.25	1.00	2.50	3.50

KM# 44 10 CENTAVOS

Copper-Nickel, 19 mm. **Obv:** Value **Rev:** Jose de San Martin bust facing right **Edge:** Reeded **Designer:** Mario Baiardi **Note:** Prev. KM#19.

Date	Mintage	F	VF	XF	Unc	BU
1950	17,505,000	0.20	0.40	0.60	1.75	2.50

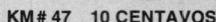

KM# 47 10 CENTAVOS

Copper-Nickel, 19 mm. **Obv:** Value **Rev:** Jose de San Martín bust right **Edge:** Reeded **Designer:** Mario Baiardi **Note:** Prev. KM#22.

Date	Mintage	F	VF	XF	Unc	BU
1951	98,521,000	—	0.20	0.30	0.50	0.75
1952	67,328,000	—	0.20	0.30	0.50	0.75

KM# 47a 10 CENTAVOS

Nickel Clad Steel, 19 mm. **Edge:** Plain **Designer:** Mario Baiardi **Note:** Prev. KM#22a.

Date	Mintage	F	VF	XF	Unc	BU
1952	33,240,000	—	0.10	0.15	0.25	0.50
1953	106,685,000	—	0.10	0.15	0.25	0.50

KM# 51 10 CENTAVOS

Nickel Clad Steel, 19 mm. **Obv:** Value **Rev:** Jose de San Martin facing right **Edge:** Plain **Designer:** Mario Baiardi **Note:** Prev. KM#26.

Date	Mintage	F	VF	XF	Unc	BU
1954	117,200,000	—	0.10	0.15	0.25	0.50
1955	97,045,000	—	0.10	0.15	0.25	0.50
1956	122,630,000	—	0.10	0.15	0.25	0.50

KM# 54 10 CENTAVOS

Nickel Clad Steel **Obv:** Capped liberty head facing left **Rev:** Value within wreath **Edge:** Plain **Note:** Prev. KM#29.

Date	Mintage	F	VF	XF	Unc	BU
1957	52,810,000	—	0.10	0.15	0.25	0.50
1958	41,916,000	—	0.10	0.15	0.25	0.50
1959	29,183,000	—	0.10	0.15	0.25	0.50

KM# 36 20 CENTAVOS

Copper-Nickel **Obv:** Capped liberty head, left **Rev:** Value within wreath **Note:** Prev. KM#11.

Date	Mintage	F	VF	XF	Unc	BU
1905	4,455,000	0.75	2.00	5.00	38.00	—
1906	4,331,000	0.75	2.00	5.00	38.00	—
1907	3,730,000	1.00	3.00	7.00	40.00	—
1908	719,000	2.25	5.00	10.00	45.00	—
1909	1,329,000	0.50	1.50	4.00	35.00	—
1910	1,845,000	0.50	1.50	4.00	35.00	—
1911	1,110,000	0.50	1.50	4.00	35.00	—
1912	2,402,000	0.50	1.50	4.00	35.00	—
1913	1,579,000	0.50	1.00	3.00	30.00	—
1914	527,000	2.25	5.00	12.00	50.00	—
1915	1,921,000	0.50	1.00	3.00	30.00	—
1916	985,000	0.50	1.25	4.00	35.00	—
1918	1,638,000	0.40	0.75	3.00	30.00	—
1919	2,280,000	0.40	0.75	3.00	30.00	—
1920	7,572,000	0.40	0.75	2.50	20.00	—
1921	5,286,000	0.25	0.60	2.50	30.00	—
1922	2,324,000	0.25	0.60	2.50	30.00	—
1923	4,416,000	0.25	0.60	2.50	30.00	—
1924	3,676,000	0.25	0.60	2.00	30.00	—
1925	3,799,000	0.25	0.60	2.00	30.00	—
1926	3,250,000	0.25	0.50	2.00	25.00	—
1927	2,880,000	0.25	0.50	2.00	25.00	—
1928	2,886,000	0.25	0.50	2.00	25.00	—
1929	8,361,000	0.25	0.50	1.25	12.00	—
1930	8,281,000	0.25	0.50	1.25	12.00	—
1931	315,000	2.25	5.00	10.00	35.00	—
1935	1,127,000	0.25	0.60	1.75	12.50	—
1936	855,000	0.50	1.25	2.50	15.00	—
1937	3,314,000	0.25	0.50	1.50	9.00	—
1938	6,449,000	0.25	0.50	1.25	9.00	—
1939	3,555,000	0.25	0.50	1.25	9.00	—
1940	4,465,000	0.25	0.50	1.25	9.00	—
1941	600,000	0.50	1.00	2.00	12.50	—
1942	4,844,000	0.25	0.50	1.25	9.00	—

KM# 42 20 CENTAVOS

Aluminum-Bronze **Obv:** Value at center, grain sprig to left, head of cow to right **Rev:** Grain sprig behind capped head facing right **Note:** Prev. KM#17.

Date	Mintage	F	VF	XF	Unc	BU
1942	10,255,000	0.25	0.50	2.00	10.00	—
1943	13,775,000	0.15	0.35	1.50	7.00	—
1944	12,225,000	0.15	0.35	1.75	8.00	—
1945	13,340,000	0.15	0.35	1.50	7.00	—
1946	14,625,000	0.15	0.35	1.50	7.00	—
1947	23,165,000	0.15	0.25	1.25	6.00	7.50
1948	32,245,000	0.15	0.25	1.25	6.00	7.50
1949	67,115,000	0.15	0.25	1.25	6.00	7.50
1950	40,071,000	0.15	0.25	1.25	6.00	7.50

KM# 45 20 CENTAVOS

Copper-Nickel, 21 mm. **Obv:** Value **Rev:** Jose de San Martín portrait right **Edge:** Reeded **Designer:** Mario Baiardi **Note:** Prev. KM#20.

Date	Mintage	F	VF	XF	Unc	BU
1950	86,770,000	0.15	0.25	0.60	1.50	2.00

KM# 48 20 CENTAVOS

Copper-Nickel, 21 mm. **Obv:** Value **Rev:** Jose de San Martín bust right **Edge:** Reeded **Designer:** Mario Baiardi **Note:** Prev. KM#23.

Date	Mintage	F	VF	XF	Unc	BU
1951	85,782,000	0.10	0.20	0.30	0.50	0.75
1952	69,796,000	0.10	0.20	0.30	0.50	0.75

KM# 48a 20 CENTAVOS

Nickel Clad Steel, 21 mm. **Rev:** Jose de San Martín portrait right **Edge:** Plain **Designer:** Mario Baiardi **Note:** Prev. KM#23a.

Date	Mintage	F	VF	XF	Unc	BU
1952	12,863,000	—	0.15	0.25	0.50	0.75
1953	36,893,000	—	0.15	0.40	1.00	1.50

KM# 52 20 CENTAVOS

Nickel Clad Steel, 21 mm. **Obv:** Value **Rev:** Jose de San Martin bust facing right **Designer:** Mario Baiardi **Note:** Head size reduced slightly. Prev. KM#27.

Date	Mintage	F	VF	XF	Unc	BU
1954	52,563,000	—	0.15	0.20	0.25	0.50
1955	46,952,000	—	0.15	0.20	0.25	0.50
1956	35,995,000	—	0.15	0.20	0.25	0.50

KM# 55 20 CENTAVOS

Nickel Clad Steel **Obv:** Capped liberty head left **Rev:** Value within wreath **Note:** Prev. KM#30.

Date	Mintage	F	VF	XF	Unc	BU
1957	89,365,000	—	0.15	0.20	0.25	0.50
1958	52,710,000	—	0.15	0.20	0.25	0.50
1959	56,585,000	—	0.15	0.20	0.25	0.50
1960	21,254,000	—	0.15	0.20	0.25	0.50
1961	2,083,000	—	0.25	0.50	1.50	2.00

KM# 39 50 CENTAVOS

Nickel **Obv:** Capped liberty head, left **Rev:** Value within wreath **Edge:** Reeded **Note:** Prev. KM#14.

Date	Mintage	F	VF	XF	Unc	BU
1941	1,000,000	0.40	1.00	2.00	6.00	—

KM# 49 50 CENTAVOS

Nickel Clad Steel **Obv:** Value **Rev:** Jose de San Martín bust right **Edge:** Plain **Designer:** Mario Baiardi **Note:** Prev. KM#24.

Date	Mintage	F	VF	XF	Unc	BU
1952	29,736,000	0.10	0.20	0.35	1.25	2.00
1953	62,814,000	0.10	0.20	0.35	1.25	2.00
1954	132,224,000	0.10	0.20	0.35	1.00	1.50
1955	75,490,000	0.10	0.20	0.35	1.25	2.00
1956	19,120,000	0.10	0.20	0.50	2.00	3.00

KM# 56 50 CENTAVOS

Nickel Clad Steel, 23.2 mm. **Obv:** Capped liberty head, left **Rev:** Value within wreath **Edge:** Plain **Note:** Prev. KM#31.

Date	Mintage	F	VF	XF	Unc	BU
1957	18,139,000	0.10	0.20	0.45	1.25	2.00
1958	51,750,000	0.10	0.20	0.35	1.00	1.50
1959	13,997,000	0.10	0.20	0.45	1.25	2.00
1960	26,038,000	0.10	0.20	0.35	1.00	1.50
1961	11,106,000	0.10	0.20	0.45	1.25	2.00

KM# 57 PESO

Nickel Clad Steel **Obv:** Capped liberty head, left **Rev:** Value within wreath **Note:** Prev. KM#32.

Date	Mintage	F	VF	XF	Unc	BU
1957	118,118,000	0.10	0.20	0.40	2.00	3.00
1958	118,151,000	0.10	0.20	0.40	2.00	3.00
1959	237,733,000	0.10	0.20	0.30	1.50	2.50
1960	75,048,000	0.10	0.30	0.50	2.50	3.50
1961	76,897,000	0.10	0.30	0.50	2.50	3.50
1962	30,006,000	0.10	0.30	0.50	3.00	4.00

KM# 58 PESO

Nickel Clad Steel, 25.5 mm. **Subject:** 150th Anniversary - Removal of Spanish Viceroy **Obv:** Argentine arms, value at bottom **Rev:** Building, two dates below **Edge:** Reeded **Note:** Prev. KM#33.

Date	Mintage	F	VF	XF	Unc	BU
ND(1960)	98,751,000	0.20	0.50	0.75	2.00	3.00

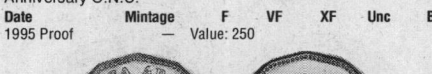

KM# 59 5 PESOS

Nickel Clad Steel, 21.5 mm. **Obv:** Sailing ship-Fragata Sarmiento **Rev:** Value above date flanked by sprays **Edge:** Plain **Note:** Prev. KM#34.

Date	Mintage	F	VF	XF	Unc	BU
1961	37,423,000	0.15	0.25	0.50	3.00	3.50
1962	42,362,000	0.15	0.25	0.50	3.00	3.50
1963	71,769,000	0.15	0.25	0.40	2.00	2.50
1964	12,302,000	0.20	0.35	0.60	3.50	4.00
1965	19,450,000	0.15	0.25	0.50	3.00	3.50
1966	17,259,000	0.15	0.25	0.50	3.00	3.50
1967	17,805,000	0.15	0.25	0.50	3.00	3.50
1968	12,634,000	0.20	0.35	0.60	3.50	4.00

KM# 136 5 PESOS

8.0640 g., 0.9000 Gold 0.2333 oz. AGW **Subject:** 50th Anniversary O.N.U.

Date	Mintage	F	VF	XF	Unc	BU
1995 Proof	—	Value: 250				

KM# 60 10 PESOS

Nickel Clad Steel, 23.6 mm. **Obv:** Gaucho **Edge:** Plain **Note:** Prev. KM#35.

Date	Mintage	F	VF	XF	Unc	BU
1962	57,401,000	0.15	0.25	0.50	3.00	3.50
1963	136,792,000	0.15	0.20	0.35	2.00	2.50
1964	46,576,000	0.15	0.25	0.50	3.00	3.50
1965	40,640,000	0.15	0.25	0.50	3.00	3.50
1966	50,733,000	0.15	0.20	0.40	2.50	3.00
1967	43,050,000	0.15	0.25	0.50	3.00	3.50
1968	36,588,000	0.15	0.25	0.50	3.00	3.50

KM# 62 10 PESOS

Nickel Clad Steel **Subject:** 150th Anniversary - Declaration of Independence. **Rev:** Building facing right, two dates below **Note:** Prev. KM#37.

Date	Mintage	F	VF	XF	Unc	BU
ND(1966)	29,336,000	0.15	0.25	0.50	3.00	3.50

KM# 61 25 PESOS

Nickel Clad Steel, 26 mm. **Subject:** 1st issue of National Coinage in 1813. **Obv:** Radiant sunface within circle **Rev:** Argentine arms within circle **Edge:** Plain **Note:** Prev. KM#36.

Date	Mintage	F	VF	XF	Unc	BU
1964	20,485,000	0.15	0.25	0.50	3.00	3.75
1965	14,884,000	0.15	0.25	0.50	3.00	3.75
1966	16,426,000	0.15	0.25	0.50	3.00	3.75
1967	15,734,000	0.15	0.25	0.50	3.00	3.75
1968	4,446,000	0.15	0.25	0.75	3.50	4.50

KM# 63 25 PESOS

Nickel Clad Steel, 26 mm. **Subject:** 80th Anniversary - Death of D. Faustino Sarmiento **Rev:** Head of Domingo Faustino Samiento, left, date below **Note:** Prev. KM#38.

Date	Mintage	F	VF	XF	Unc	BU
1968	15,804,000	0.25	0.60	0.85	1.65	2.00

REFORM COINAGE

1970-1983; 100 Old Pesos = 1 New Peso

KM# 64 CENTAVO

Aluminum **Obv:** Capped Liberty head, left **Rev:** Value to left of grain sprig, date below **Note:** Prev. KM#39.

Date	Mintage	F	VF	XF	Unc	BU
1970	54,568,115	—	—	0.10	0.30	0.50
1971	44,644,000	—	—	0.10	0.30	0.50
1972	92,430,000	—	—	0.10	0.30	0.50
1973	29,515,000	—	—	0.10	0.30	0.50
1974	5,162,000	—	—	0.15	0.35	0.60
1975	3,840,000	—	0.10	0.20	0.50	0.75

KM# 65 5 CENTAVOS

Aluminum, 18 mm. **Obv:** Capped liberty head, left **Rev:** Value with grain sprig to left **Note:** Prev. KM#40.

Date	Mintage	F	VF	XF	Unc	BU
1970	56,174,000	—	0.10	0.15	0.40	0.60
1971	3,798,000	0.10	0.20	0.35	0.65	0.90
1972	84,250,000	—	0.10	0.15	0.40	0.60
1973	113,912,000	—	0.10	0.15	0.40	0.60
1974	18,150,000	—	0.10	0.15	0.40	0.60
1975	6,940,000	0.10	0.20	0.35	0.65	0.90

KM# 66 10 CENTAVOS

Brass **Obv:** Capped liberty head, left **Rev:** Value with grain sprig to left **Note:** Prev. KM#41.

Date	Mintage	F	VF	XF	Unc	BU
1970	64,585,300	—	0.10	0.15	0.35	0.55
1971	135,623,000	—	0.10	0.15	0.35	0.55
1973	19,930,000	—	0.10	0.15	0.35	0.55
1974	79,156,000	—	0.10	0.15	0.35	0.55
1975	31,270,000	—	0.10	0.15	0.35	0.55
1976	730,000	0.10	0.20	0.35	1.00	1.75

KM# 67 20 CENTAVOS

Brass, 18.5 mm. **Obv:** Capped liberty head, left **Rev:** Value with grain sprig to left **Note:** Prev. KM#42.

Date	Mintage	F	VF	XF	Unc	BU
1970	27,029,000	—	0.10	0.15	0.35	0.55
1971	33,211,000	—	0.10	0.15	0.35	0.55
1972	220,000	1.00	2.00	4.00	8.00	10.00
1973	9,676,000	—	0.10	0.15	0.35	0.55
1974	41,024,000	—	0.10	0.15	0.35	0.55
1975	26,540,000	—	0.10	0.15	0.35	0.55
1976	960,000	—	0.10	0.15	0.35	0.55

KM# 68 50 CENTAVOS

Brass **Obv:** Capped liberty head, left **Rev:** Value with grain sprig to left **Note:** Prev. KM#43.

Date	Mintage	F	VF	XF	Unc	BU
1970	56,103,729	0.10	0.15	0.30	0.60	0.80
1971	34,947,000	0.10	0.15	0.30	0.60	0.80
1972	40,960,000	0.10	0.15	0.30	0.60	0.80
1973	59,472,124	0.10	0.15	0.30	0.60	0.80
1974	64,063,000	0.10	0.15	0.30	0.60	0.80
1975	64,859,000	0.10	0.15	0.30	0.60	0.80
1976	9,768,000	0.10	0.15	0.30	0.60	0.80

KM# 69 PESO

Aluminum-Brass, 22 mm. **Obv:** Radiant sunface, grain sprays below **Rev:** Value with grain sprig to left **Note:** Wide and narrow rim varieties exist. Prev. KM#44.

Date	Mintage	F	VF	XF	Unc	BU
1974	77,292,000	—	0.10	0.25	0.75	1.00
1975	423,000,000	—	0.10	0.20	0.50	0.75
1976	100,075,000	—	0.10	0.20	0.50	0.75

KM# 71 5 PESOS

Aluminum-Bronze **Obv:** Radiant sunface, grain sprays below **Rev:** Value with grain sprig to left **Note:** Prev. KM#46.

Date	Mintage	F	VF	XF	Unc	BU
1976	118,353,000	—	0.10	0.20	0.65	0.90
1977	66,765,684	—	0.10	0.20	0.65	0.90

KM# 73 5 PESOS

Aluminum-Bronze **Subject:** Admiral G. Brown Bicentennial **Note:** Prev. KM#48.

Date	Mintage	F	VF	XF	Unc	BU
1977	11,297,808	0.10	0.15	0.30	0.75	1.00

KM# 72 10 PESOS

Aluminum-Bronze **Obv:** Radiant sunface, grain sprays below **Rev:** Value with grain sprig to left **Note:** Prev. KM#47.

Date	Mintage	F	VF	XF	Unc	BU
1976	130,216,724	0.10	0.15	0.35	1.00	1.25
1977	191,520,382	0.10	0.15	0.35	1.00	1.25
1978	259,424,310	0.10	0.15	0.35	1.00	1.25

KM# 74 10 PESOS

Aluminum-Bronze **Subject:** Admiral G. Brown Bicentennial **Obv:** Armored bust of Admiral G. Brown right dividing dates **Rev:** Value with grain sprigs to left, date below **Note:** Prev. KM#49.

Date	Mintage	F	VF	XF	Unc	BU
1977	60,008,179	0.10	0.20	0.50	1.25	1.50

KM# 75 20 PESOS

Aluminum-Bronze **Subject:** 1978 World Soccer Championship **Obv:** Two soccer players, country above with two numbered year below country to right **Rev:** Soccer ball within symbol, top right, small mark to left, value below, date at bottom **Note:** Prev. KM#50.

Date	Mintage	F	VF	XF	Unc	BU
1977	1,506,000	0.10	0.20	0.40	1.00	1.25
1978	2,000,000	0.10	0.20	0.40	1.00	1.25

KM# 76 50 PESOS

Aluminum-Bronze **Subject:** 1978 World Soccer Championship **Obv:** Soccer player on lined globe, country name above with two numbered year below at right **Rev:** Soccer ball within symbol, top right, value below, date at bottom, small mark to left of symbol **Note:** Prev. KM#51.

Date	Mintage	F	VF	XF	Unc	BU
1977	1,506,000	0.10	0.20	0.40	1.00	1.25
1978	2,000,000	0.10	0.20	0.40	1.00	1.25

KM# 81 50 PESOS

Aluminum-Bronze **Subject:** 200th Anniversary - Birth of Jose de San Martín **Obv:** Value, date below flanked by stars **Rev:** Armored bust of Jose de San Martin left, two dates at right **Note:** Prev. KM#56.

Date	Mintage	F	VF	XF	Unc	BU
1978	40,601,000	0.20	0.50	1.00	2.00	2.50

KM# 83 50 PESOS

Aluminum-Bronze **Obv:** Value, date below **Rev:** Bust of Jose de San Martin left **Note:** Prev. KM#58.

Date	Mintage	F	VF	XF	Unc	BU
1979	21,728,900	0.10	0.25	0.65	1.50	2.00
1980	—	0.10	0.25	0.65	1.50	2.00

Note: Mintage included with 1980 date of KM#83a

KM# 83a 50 PESOS

Brass Clad Steel **Rev:** Jose de San Martín portrait right **Note:** Prev. KM#58a.

Date	Mintage	F	VF	XF	Unc	BU
1980	94,730,000	0.10	0.25	0.65	1.25	1.50
1981	26,507,500	0.10	0.25	0.65	1.25	1.50

KM# 84 50 PESOS

Aluminum-Bronze **Subject:** Conquest of Patagonia Centennial **Obv:** Value, date below **Rev:** Man on horse, lance in right hand, facing left **Note:** Prev. KM#59.

Date	Mintage	F	VF	XF	Unc	BU
1979	34,761,829	0.10	0.25	0.65	2.50	3.00

KM# 77 100 PESOS

Aluminum-Bronze **Subject:** 1978 World Soccer Championship **Obv:** Stadium on lined globe, country name above with two numbered year below at right **Rev:** Soccer ball within symbol, top right, value below, date at bottom, small mark at left of symbol **Note:** Prev. KM#52.

Date	Mintage	F	VF	XF	Unc	BU
1977	1,506,000	0.15	0.30	0.75	1.50	2.00
1978	2,000,000	0.15	0.30	0.75	1.50	2.00

KM# 82 100 PESOS

Aluminum-Bronze **Subject:** 200th Anniversary - Birth of Jose de San Martín **Obv:** Value at center, small mark at top, date at bottom **Rev:** Armored bust of Jose de San Martin, left **Note:** Prev. KM#57.

Date	Mintage	F	VF	XF	Unc	BU
1978	113,826,000	—	0.50	1.00	2.00	2.50
1979	—	—	—	—	—	800

KM# 85 100 PESOS

Aluminum-Bronze, 27.4 mm. **Obv:** Value at center, small mark at top, date at bottom **Rev:** Jose de San Martín portrait left **Note:** Prev. KM#60.

Date	Mintage	F	VF	XF	Unc	BU
1978	—	—	—	—	—	300
1979	43,389,383	0.15	0.30	0.75	1.25	1.50
1980	154,260,000	0.15	0.30	0.75	1.25	1.50

KM# 85a 100 PESOS

Brass Clad Steel **Rev:** Jose de San Martín portrait left **Note:** Prev. KM#60a.

Date	Mintage	F	VF	XF	Unc	BU
1980	Inc. above	0.15	0.30	0.75	1.50	1.75
1981	99,512,000	0.15	0.30	0.75	1.25	1.50

KM# 86 100 PESOS

Aluminum-Bronze **Subject:** Conquest of Patagonia Centennial **Obv:** Value center, small mark at top, date below **Rev:** Man on horse holding lance in right, facing left **Note:** Prev. KM#61.

Date	Mintage	F	VF	XF	Unc	BU
1979	34,132,135	0.15	0.30	0.75	2.50	3.00

KM# 78 1000 PESOS

10.0000 g., 0.9000 Silver .2893 oz. ASW **Subject:** 1978 World Soccer Championship **Obv:** Country name at top with two numbered year, below right, small radiant sunface to left of five line inscription **Note:** Prev. KM#53.

Date	Mintage	F	VF	XF	Unc	BU
1977	98,837	—	—	4.50	6.00	7.50
1977 Proof	1,000	Value: 17.50				
1978 Proof	1,750	Value: 17.50				
1978	187,383	—	—	4.50	6.00	7.50

KM# 79 2000 PESOS

15.0000 g., 0.9000 Silver .4340 oz. ASW **Subject:** 1978 World Soccer Championship **Obv:** Argentine arms beneath five sets of small arms, country name, year at bottom **Rev:** Soccer ball within symbol, top right, value below, date at bottom **Note:** Prev. KM#54.

Date	Mintage	F	VF	XF	Unc	BU
1977	98,837	—	—	6.50	10.00	12.00
1977 Proof	1,000	Value: 22.50				
1978	187,383	—	—	6.50	9.50	11.50
1978 Proof	1,750	Value: 22.50				

KM# 80 3000 PESOS

25.0000 g., 0.9000 Silver .7234 oz. ASW **Subject:** 1978 World Soccer Championship **Obv:** Map of country on lined globe, grain sprigs below, country at top **Rev:** Soccer ball within symbol, top right, value below, date at bottom **Note:** Prev. KM#55.

Date	Mintage	F	VF	XF	Unc	BU
1977	98,837	—	—	10.50	15.50	17.50
1977 Proof	1,000	Value: 35.00				
1978 Proof	1,750	Value: 35.00				
1978	187,383	—	—	10.50	14.50	16.50

REFORM COINAGE

1983-1985; 10,000 Pesos = 1 Peso Argentino; 100 Centavos = 1 Peso Argentino

KM# 87 CENTAVO

Aluminum **Obv:** Capped liberty head, left **Rev:** Value, date below **Note:** Prev. KM#62.

Date	Mintage	F	VF	XF	Unc	BU
1983	19,959,000	—	—	—	0.20	0.35

KM# 88 5 CENTAVOS

Aluminurn **Obv:** Capped liberty head, left **Rev:** Value, daate below **Note:** Prev. KM#63.

Date	Mintage	F	VF	XF	Unc	BU
1983	59,870,000	—	—	—	0.25	0.40

KM# 89 10 CENTAVOS

Aluminum **Obv:** Capped liberty head, left **Rev:** Value, date below **Note:** Prev. KM#64. Struck at the British Royal Mint.

Date	Mintage	F	VF	XF	Unc	BU
1983	307,513,000	—	—	—	0.25	0.40

KM# 90 50 CENTAVOS

Aluminum **Obv:** Capped liberty head, left **Rev:** Value, date below **Note:** Prev. KM#65.

Date	Mintage	F	VF	XF	Unc	BU
1983	243,909,000	—	—	—	0.45	0.60

KM# 91 PESO

Aluminum **Obv:** Capitol building **Rev:** Value, date below **Note:** National Congress. Prev. KM#66.

Date	Mintage	F	VF	XF	Unc	BU
1984	184,691,379	—	—	—	0.50	0.65

KM# 92 5 PESOS

Brass **Obv:** Buenos Aires City Hall **Rev:** Valtue, date at bottom **Note:** Prev. KM#67.

Date	Mintage	F	VF	XF	Unc	BU
1984	11,206,000	—	—	—	0.65	0.80
1985	14,168,000	—	—	—	0.65	0.80

KM# 93 10 PESOS

Brass **Obv:** Independence Hall at Tucuman **Rev:** Value, date at bottom **Note:** Prev. KM#68.

Date	Mintage	F	VF	XF	Unc	BU
1984	16,528,000	—	—	—	0.85	1.00
1985	9,898,717	—	—	—	0.85	1.00

KM# 94 50 PESOS

Aluminum-Bronze **Subject:** 50th Anniversary of Central Bank **Obv:** Value, date at bottom **Rev:** Small capped liberty head within wreath, circle surrounding **Note:** Prev. KM#69.

Date	Mintage	F	VF	XF	Unc	BU
1985	3,300,000	—	—	—	1.25	1.50

REFORM COINAGE

1985-1992; 1,000 Pesos Argentinos = 1 Austral; 100 Centavos = 1 Austral

KM# 95 1/2 CENTAVO

Brass **Obv:** Rufous Hornero Bird **Rev:** Value, date below **Note:** Prev. KM#70.

Date	Mintage	F	VF	XF	Unc	BU
1985	7,490,000	—	—	—	0.45	1.00

KM# 96.1 CENTAVO

Brass, 20 mm. **Obv:** Common Rhea **Rev:** Value, date below **Note:** Thick flan. Prev. KM#71.1.

Date	Mintage	F	VF	XF	Unc	BU
1985	76,082,000	—	—	—	0.75	1.00

KM# 96.2 CENTAVO

Brass, 20 mm. **Obv:** Common Rhea **Note:** Thin flan. Prev. KM#71.2.

Date	Mintage	F	VF	XF	Unc	BU
1986	118,934,000	—	—	—	0.75	1.00
1987	87,315,000	—	—	—	0.75	1.00

KM# 97.1 5 CENTAVOS

Brass, 23 mm. **Obv:** Pampas Cat **Rev:** Value, date below **Edge:** Plain **Note:** Thick flan. Prev. KM#72.1.

Date	Mintage	F	VF	XF	Unc	BU
1985	36,924,000	—	—	—	1.60	2.50

KM# 97.2 5 CENTAVOS

Brass, 23 mm. **Obv:** Pampas Cat **Edge:** Plain **Note:** Thin flan. Prev. KM#72.2.

Date	Mintage	F	VF	XF	Unc	BU
1986	66,414,000	—	—	—	1.50	2.00
1987	56,181,000	—	—	—	1.50	2.00
1988	23,895,000	—	—	—	1.50	2.00

KM# 98 10 CENTAVOS

4.4500 g., Brass, 21.5 mm. **Obv:** Argentine arms **Rev:** Value, date below **Note:** Prev. KM#73.

Date	Mintage	F	VF	XF	Unc	BU
1985	23,268,000	—	—	—	0.65	0.85
1986	158,427,000	—	—	—	0.65	0.85
1987	184,330,000	—	—	—	0.65	0.85
1988	174,003,000	—	—	—	0.65	0.85

KM# 99 50 CENTAVOS
5.4000 g., Brass, 24.5 mm. **Obv:** Capped liberty head, left **Rev:** Value, date below **Note:** Varieties exist. Previous KM#74.

Date	Mintage	F	VF	XF	Unc	BU
1985	13,884,000	—	—	—	1.50	2.00
1986	59,074,000	—	—	—	1.45	1.85
1987	64,525,000	—	—	—	1.45	1.85
1988	62,388,000	—	—	—	1.45	1.85

KM# 100 AUSTRAL
Aluminum **Obv:** Buenos Aires City Hall **Rev:** Large value in box at right, double lined "A" at top left, date below "A" **Note:** Prev. KM#75.

Date	Mintage	F	VF	XF	Unc	BU
1989	57,400,000	—	—	—	0.15	0.30

KM# 101 5 AUSTRALES
Aluminum, 21.6 mm. **Obv:** Independence Hall at Tucuman **Rev:** Large value in box at right, double lined "A" at left top, date below "A" **Edge:** Plain **Note:** Prev. KM#76.

Date	Mintage	F	VF	XF	Unc	BU
1989	46,894,977	—	—	—	0.25	0.40

KM# 102 10 AUSTRALES
Aluminum, 23.2 mm. **Obv:** Casa del Acuerdo **Rev:** Large value in box at right, double lined "A" at top left, date below "A" **Edge:** Plain **Note:** Prev. KM#77.

Date	Mintage	F	VF	XF	Unc	BU
1989	99,600,000	—	—	—	0.35	0.50

KM# 103 100 AUSTRALES
Aluminum **Obv:** Argentine arms **Rev:** Large value in box, small double lined "A" at top, date below box **Note:** Prev. KM#78.

Date	Mintage	F	VF	XF	Unc	BU
1990	18,003,500	—	—	—	0.25	0.40
1991	31,996,500	—	—	—	0.25	0.40

KM# 104 500 AUSTRALES
Aluminum **Obv:** Argentine arms **Rev:** Large value in box, small double lined "A" at top, date below box **Note:** Prev. KM#79.

Date	Mintage	F	VF	XF	Unc	BU
1990	29,312,000	—	—	—	0.35	0.50
1991	50,087,100	—	—	—	0.35	0.50

KM# 105 1000 AUSTRALES
Aluminum, 24.5 mm. **Obv:** Argentine arms **Rev:** Large value in box, small double lined "A" at top, date below box **Edge:** Plain **Note:** Prev. KM#80.

Date	Mintage	F	VF	XF	Unc	BU
1990	8,282,000	—	—	—	0.60	0.75
1991	41,618,000	—	—	—	0.60	0.75

KM# 106 1000 AUSTRALES
27.0000 g., 0.9250 Silver .8029 oz. ASW **Subject:** Ibero - American Series **Obv:** Argentine arms within legend and circle of arms **Rev:** Two globes, rising radiant sun above with four crowns above, flanked by columns within inner circle surrounded by legend **Note:** Prev. KM#81.

Date	Mintage	F	VF	XF	Unc	BU
1991 Proof	5,000	Value: 47.50				

REFORM COINAGE

1992; 10,000 Australes = 1 Peso

KM# 108 CENTAVO
Brass **Obv:** Five line inscription within wreath **Rev:** Large value, date below **Edge:** Plain **Shape:** Octagonal **Note:** Prev. KM#83.

Date	Mintage	F	VF	XF	Unc	BU
1992	30,000,000	—	—	—	0.25	0.40

KM# 113 CENTAVO
Brass **Edge:** Reeded **Shape:** Round **Note:** Prev. KM#88.

Date	Mintage	F	VF	XF	Unc	BU
1992	30,000,000	—	—	—	0.25	0.40
1993	79,000,000	—	—	—	0.25	0.40

KM# 113a CENTAVO
Bronze, 11.2 mm. **Edge:** Reeded **Shape:** Round **Note:** Prev. KM#88a.

Date	Mintage	F	VF	XF	Unc	BU
1993	48,000,000	—	—	—	0.25	0.40
1997	50,000,000	—	—	—	0.25	0.40
1998	50,000,000	—	—	—	0.25	0.40
1999	70,000,000	—	—	—	0.25	0.40
2000	37,000,000	—	—	—	0.25	0.40

KM# 109 5 CENTAVOS
Brass **Obv:** Radiant sunface **Rev:** Large value, date below **Note:** Prev. KM#84.

Date	Mintage	F	VF	XF	Unc	BU
1992	230,000,000	—	—	—	0.45	0.60
1993	20,000,000	—	—	—	0.45	0.60

KM# 109a.1 5 CENTAVOS
Copper-Nickel **Obv:** Radiant sunface, Fine lettering **Rev:** Value, date below **Note:** Prev. KM#84a.1.

Date	Mintage	F	VF	XF	Unc	BU
1993	245,500,000	—	—	—	0.45	0.65

KM# 109a.2 5 CENTAVOS
Copper-Nickel **Obv:** Radiant sunface. Bold lettering **Note:** Prev. KM#84a.2.

Date	Mintage	F	VF	XF	Unc	BU
1994	5,000,000	—	—	—	0.45	0.65
1995	25,000,000	—	—	—	0.45	0.60

KM# 107 10 CENTAVOS
Aluminum-Bronze **Obv:** Argentine arms **Rev:** Value, date below **Edge:** Reeded **Note:** Prev. KM#82.

Date	Mintage	F	VF	XF	Unc	BU
1992	805,000,000	—	—	—	0.65	0.85
1993	500,000,000	—	—	—	0.65	0.85
1994	80,000,000	—	—	—	0.65	0.85

KM# 110.1 25 CENTAVOS
Brass **Obv:** Towered building, fine lettering **Rev:** Large value, date below **Note:** Prev. KM#85.1.

Date	Mintage	F	VF	XF	Unc	BU
1992	150,000,000	—	—	—	1.25	1.50

KM# 110.2 25 CENTAVOS
Brass **Obv:** Towered building, bold lettering **Note:** Prev. KM#85.2.

Date	Mintage	F	VF	XF	Unc	BU
1993	80,000,000	—	—	—	1.25	1.50

KM# 110a 25 CENTAVOS
Copper-Nickel **Obv:** Towered building, bold lettering **Note:** Prev. KM#85a.

Date	Mintage	F	VF	XF	Unc	BU
1993	390,000,000	—	—	—	1.25	1.50
1994	200,000,000	—	—	—	1.25	1.50
1996	96,000,000	—	—	—	1.25	1.50

KM# 111.1 50 CENTAVOS
Brass **Obv:** Tucuman Province Capital Building; fine lettering **Rev:** Large value, date below **Note:** Prev. KM#86.1.

Date	Mintage	F	VF	XF	Unc	BU
1992	290,000,000	—	—	—	1.75	2.00
1993	—	—	—	—	1.75	2.00
1994	—	—	—	—	1.75	2.00

KM# 111.2 50 CENTAVOS
Copper-Nickel **Obv:** Tucuman Province Capital Building; bold lettering. **Note:** Prev. KM#86.2.

Date	Mintage	F	VF	XF	Unc	BU
1993	120,000,000	—	—	—	1.75	2.00
1994	304,000,000	—	—	—	1.75	2.00

KM# 119 50 CENTAVOS
Copper-Aluminum **Subject:** 50th Anniversary - UNICEF **Obv:** Girl with rag doll **Rev:** UNICEF logo above denomination **Note:** Prev. KM#94.

Date	Mintage	F	VF	XF	Unc	BU
1996	1,000,000	—	—	—	2.00	2.25

KM# 121 50 CENTAVOS

Copper-Aluminum **Subject:** 50th Anniversary - Women's Right to Vote **Obv:** Bust of Eva Peron right **Rev:** Value with two dates above in circle, legend across top, date at bottom divides wreath **Designer:** Mario Baiardi **Note:** Prev. KM#96.

Date	Mintage	F	VF	XF	Unc	BU
1997	2,000,000	—	—	—	2.25	2.50

KM# 124 50 CENTAVOS

Copper-Aluminum **Subject:** Mercosur **Obv:** Southern Cross constellation **Rev:** Value in circle, date below circle **Note:** Prev. KM#99.

Date	Mintage	F	VF	XF	Unc	BU
1998	1,000,000	—	—	—	2.25	2.50

KM# 129.1 50 CENTAVOS

5.9200 g., Brass, 25.1 mm. **Subject:** General Guemes **Obv:** Bearded portrait, right **Rev:** Value in circle **Edge:** Plain **Note:** Prev. KM#129

Date	Mintage	F	VF	XF	Unc	BU
2000	1,695,000	—	—	—	2.25	2.50

KM# 129.2 50 CENTAVOS

5.9200 g., Brass, 25.1 mm. **Subject:** General Guemes **Obv:** Bearded portrait **Rev:** Denomination **Edge:** Reeded

Date	Mintage	F	VF	XF	Unc	BU
2000	5,000	—	—	—	4.50	6.00

KM# 130.1 50 CENTAVOS

5.9200 g., Brass, 25.1 mm. **Subject:** General San Martin **Obv:** Stylized portrait, facing **Rev:** Value to right of building **Edge:** Reeded **Note:** Previous KM#130

Date	Mintage	F	VF	XF	Unc	BU
2000	995,000	—	—	—	2.25	2.50

KM# 130.2 50 CENTAVOS

5.9200 g., Brass, 25.1 mm. **Subject:** General San Martin **Obv:** Stylized portrait **Rev:** Denomination and building **Edge:** Plain

Date	Mintage	F	VF	XF	Unc	BU
2000	5,000	—	—	—	4.50	6.00

KM# 112.1 PESO

Bi-Metallic Brass center in Copper-Nickel ring **Subject:** First Argentine Coin Design **Obv:** Large legend, Argentine arms in circle **Rev:** Large legend; pointed 9s, radiant sun at center **Note:** Prev. KM#87.1.

Date	Mintage	F	VF	XF	Unc	BU
1994A	75,000,000	—	—	—	4.50	5.00
Note: Medal rotation						
1995A	185,000,000	—	—	—	4.50	5.00
Note: Medal rotation						

Date	Mintage	F	VF	XF	Unc	BU
1995B	14,000,000	—	—	—	4.50	5.00
1996A	30,000,000	—	—	—	4.50	5.00

KM# 112.2 PESO

Bi-Metallic Brass center in Copper-Nickel ring **Subject:** First Argentine Coin Design **Obv:** Small legend, Argentine arms in circle **Rev:** Small legend; rounded 9, date divides wreath, radiant sun at center **Note:** Prev. KM#87.2.

Date	Mintage	F	VF	XF	Unc	BU
1995C	90,000,000	—	—	—	4.50	5.00

KM# 112.3 PESO

Bi-Metallic Brass center in Copper-Nickel ring **Subject:** First Argentine Coin Design **Obv:** Small legend, Argentine arms in circle **Rev:** Error, PROVINGIAS, radiant sun, legend in circle, value at top date at bottom divides wreath **Note:** Prev. KM#87.3.

Date	Mintage	F	VF	XF	Unc	BU
1995B	56,000,000	—	—	—	7.50	8.00

KM# 126 PESO

25.0000 g., 0.9000 Silver .7234 oz. ASW **Subject:** 50th Anniversary - United Nations **Obv:** Dove over national arms **Rev:** UN logo, denomination, dates **Note:** Prev KM#101.

Date	Mintage	F	VF	XF	Unc	BU
1995 Proof	500	Value: 35.00				

KM# 120 PESO

Bi-Metallic Brass center in Copper-Nickel ring, 23 mm. **Subject:** 50th Anniversary - UNICEF **Obv:** Girl with rag doll **Rev:** UNICEF logo above denomination **Note:** Prev. KM#95. Medal rotation.

Date	Mintage	F	VF	XF	Unc	BU
1996	1,000,000	—	—	—	4.50	5.00

KM# 122 PESO

Bi-Metallic Brass center in Copper-Nickel ring, 23 mm. **Subject:** 50th Anniversary - Women's Suffrage Law **Obv:** Bust of Eva Duarte de Peron right (social reformer) **Rev:** Denomination **Edge:** Reeded **Designer:** Mario Baiardi **Note:** Prev. KM#97. Medal rotation.

Date	Mintage	F	VF	XF	Unc	BU
1997	1,000,000	—	—	—	5.00	5.50

KM# 125 PESO

Bi-Metallic Brass center in Copper-Nickel ring, 23 mm. **Subject:** Mercosur **Obv:** Southern Cross constellation **Rev:** Denomination **Note:** Prev. KM#100. Medal rotation.

Date	Mintage	F	VF	XF	Unc	BU
1998	496,715	—	—	—	4.00	5.00

KM# 127 PESO

25.0000 g., 0.9000 Silver .7234 oz. ASW **Subject:** 100th Anniversary - Birth of Jorge Luis Borges **Obv:** Profile of Borges left, dates **Rev:** Labyrinth, sundial, denomination and date **Note:** Prev. KM#102.

Date	Mintage	F	VF	XF	Unc	BU
1999 Proof	5,000	Value: 37.50				

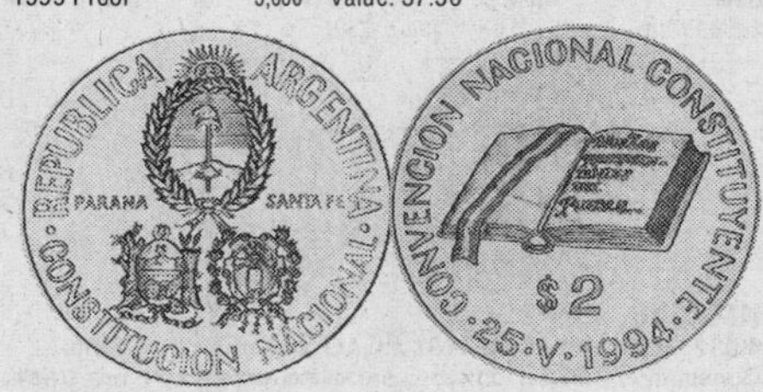

KM# 114 2 PESOS

Nickel **Subject:** National Constitution Convention **Obv:** Argentine arms above two small arms **Rev:** Open book, ribbon across left page, five line inscription on right page, value below book **Note:** Prev. KM#89.

Date	Mintage	F	VF	XF	Unc	BU
ND(1994)	1,000,000	—	—	—	8.00	9.00
ND(1994) Proof	1,000	Value: 16.00				

KM# 114a 2 PESOS

12.4800 g., 0.9000 Silver .3612 oz. ASW **Subject:** National Constitution Convention **Note:** Prev. KM#89a.

Date	Mintage	F	VF	XF	Unc	BU
ND (1994)	5,000	—	—	—	12.50	14.50
ND (1994) Proof	1,500	Value: 25.00				

KM# 128 2 PESOS

Copper-Nickel **Subject:** 100th Anniversary - Birth of Jorge Luis Borges **Obv:** Profile head of Borges left **Rev:** Labyrinth, sundial, denomination and date **Note:** Prev. KM#103.

Date	Mintage	F	VF	XF	Unc	BU
1999	1,000,000	—	—	—	8.00	9.00

KM# 115 5 PESOS
Nickel **Subject:** National Constitution Convention **Obv:** Argentine arms above two smaller arms **Rev:** Open book, ribbon across left page, five line inscription on right page, value below **Note:** Prev. KM#90.

Date	Mintage	F	VF	XF	Unc	BU
ND (1994)	1,000,000	—	—	—	15.00	16.50
ND (1994) Proof	1,000	Value: 25.00				

KM# 115a 5 PESOS
24.8000 g., 0.9000 Silver .7177 oz. ASW **Subject:** National Constitution Convention **Note:** Prev. KM#90a.

Date	Mintage	F	VF	XF	Unc	BU
ND(1994)	5,000	—	—	—	25.00	30.00
ND(1994) Proof	1,500	Value: 60.00				

KM# 134 5 PESOS
8.0640 g., 0.9000 Gold 0.2333 oz. AGW, 22 mm. **Obv:** Writer Jorge Luis Borges, left, (1899-1986) **Rev:** Sundial within labyrinth **Edge:** Reeded

Date	Mintage	F	VF	XF	Unc	BU
1999 Proof	2,000	Value: 185				

KM# 137 5 PESOS
8.0640 g., 0.9000 Gold 0.2333 oz. AGW, 22 mm. **Obv:** San Martin **Rev:** Building and value **Edge:** Reeded

Date	Mintage	F	VF	XF	Unc	BU
2000 Proof	1,000	Value: 250				

KM# 116 25 PESOS
4.0320 g., 0.9000 Gold .1167 oz. AGW **Subject:** National Constitution Convention **Obv:** Argentine arms above two small arms **Rev:** Open book, ribbon across left page, five line inscription on right page **Note:** Prev. KM#91.

Date	Mintage	F	VF	XF	Unc	BU
ND(1994)	5,000	—	—	—	90.00	100
ND(1994) Proof	1,000	Value: 135				

KM# 118 25 PESOS
27.0000 g., 0.9250 Silver .8030 oz. ASW **Subject:** Environmental Protection **Rev:** Giant Armadillo **Note:** Prev. KM#93.

Date	Mintage	F	VF	XF	Unc	BU
1997 Proof	5,000	Value: 45.00				

KM# 123 25 PESOS
27.0000 g., 0.9250 Silver .8030 oz. ASW **Subject:** Ibero-American Series - LaZamba **Obv:** Argentine arms within legend and circle of arms **Rev:** Zamba dancers **Note:** Prev. KM#98.

Date	Mintage	F	VF	XF	Unc	BU
1997 Proof	5,000	Value: 55.00				

KM# 131 25 PESOS
26.9000 g., 0.9250 Silver 0.8 oz. ASW, 40 mm. **Subject:** Ibero-America Series **Obv:** Argentine arms within legend and circle of arms **Rev:** Bronco busting scene **Edge:** Reeded

Date	Mintage	F	VF	XF	Unc	BU
2000 Proof	5,000	Value: 60.00				

KM# 117 50 PESOS
8.0640 g., 0.9000 Gold .2334 oz. AGW **Subject:** National Constitution Convention **Obv:** Argentine arms above two small arms **Rev:** Open book, ribbon across left page, five line inscription on right page **Note:** Prev. KM#92.

Date	Mintage	F	VF	XF	Unc	BU
ND (1994)	5,000	—	—	—	165	180
ND (1994) Proof	1,000	Value: 225				

PATTERNS

Including off metal strikes

KM#	Date	Mintage	Identification	Mkt Val
Pn35	19xx	—	Centavo. Copper.	—
Pn36	19xx	—	2 Centavos. Copper.	—
Pn37	1925	—	2 Centavos. Copper.	—
Pn38	1925	—	2 Centavos. Bronze.	—
Pn39	1932	—	Argentino. Copper.	—
Pn40	1932	—	Argentino. Bronze.	—
Pn41	1933	—	Argentino. Bronze.	—
Pn42	1934	—	Argentino. Copper.	—
Pn43	1935	—	Centavo. Copper.	400
Pn44	1935	—	2 Centavos. Copper.	400
Pn45	1936	—	50 Centavos. Bronze.	—
Pn46	1936	—	50 Centavos. Copper-Nickel.	700
Pn47	1936	—	Peso. Bronze.	—
Pn48	1936	—	Peso. Copper-Nickel.	475
Pn49	1937	—	Centavo. Copper. Argentine arms within wreath. Blank, post horn mint mark.	—
Pn50	1938	—	Centavo. Copper.	250
Pn51	1938	—	2 Centavos. Copper.	275
Pn52	1940	—	50 Centavos. Bronze.	225
Pn53	1940	—	50 Centavos. Copper-Nickel. Head by Oudine.	375
Pn54	1940	—	50 Centavos. Nickel. Head by L. Bazor.	—
Pn55	1941	—	50 Centavos. Nickel.	—
Pn56	1943	—	Peso. Bronze.	—
Pn57	1943	—	Peso. Nickel.	—
Pn58	1943	—	Peso. Bronze. Condor.	—
Pn59	1945	—	Peso. Bronze.	—
Pn60	1945	—	Peso. Copper-Nickel.	—
Pn61	1946	—	Peso. Bronze.	—
Pn62	1946	—	Peso. Copper-Nickel.	550
Pn63	1971	—	50 Centavos. Silverish Aluminum. KM#43	75.00
Pn64	1975	—	Peso. Aluminum-Brass. KM#45	125
Pn65	1976	—	5 Pesos. Silverish Aluminum. KM#46	—
Pn66	1977	—	10 Pesos. Silverish Aluminum-Brass. KM#47	—

MINT SETS

KM#	Date	Mintage	Identification	Issue Price	Mkt Val
MS2	1970 (5)	—	KM#64-68	—	2.00
MS3	1977 (6)	—	KM#75-80	—	32.00
MS4	1977 (3)	—	KM#75-77	—	4.00
MS5	1978 (6)	—	KM#75-80	—	30.00
MS6	1983 (4)	—	KM#87-90	—	2.00

PROOF SETS

KM#	Date	Mintage	Identification	Issue Price	Mkt Val
PS1	1977 (3)	1,000	KM#78-80	—	75.00
PS2	1978 (3)	1,750	KM#78-80	153	75.00
PS3	ND(1994) (2)	5,500	KM#114, 115	—	40.00
PS4	ND(1994) (2)	1,000	KM#114a, 115a	79.50	85.00
PS5	ND(1994) (2)	1,000	KM#116, 117	375	360

CATAMARCA

A province located in northwest Argentina having an area of 38,540 sq. mi. and a population of 309,130. Capital: Catamarca. Agriculture and mining are the main industries.

PROVINCE

TOKEN COINAGE

Stabilization Currency Unit

KM# Tn1 100000 AUSTRALES
15.0000 g., 0.9000 Silver .4341 oz. ASW **Subject:** Fray Mamerto Esquiu **Obv:** Double headed figure **Rev:** Head, 3/4 left, date below

Date	Mintage	F	VF	XF	Unc	BU
1990	200,000	—	—	—	28.50	32.50

KM# Tn3 100000 AUSTRALES
14.8500 g., 0.9000 Silver .4297 oz. ASW **Subject:** 100th Anniversary - Coronation of Our Lady of the Valley **Obv:** Double headed figure **Rev:** Imperial crown with cross on top dividing dates

Date	Mintage	F	VF	XF	Unc	BU
1991	—	—	—	—	28.50	32.50

KM# Tn2 4000000 AUSTRALES
20.0000 g., 0.7500 Gold .4823 oz. AGW **Subject:** Fray Mamerto Esquiu **Note:** Denomination determined upon release.

Date	Mintage	F	VF	XF	Unc	BU
1990	200	—	—	—	920	940

LA RIOJA

La Rioja (Rioxa), a city and province in northwest Argentina, directly to the south of Catamarca. More than one third of its population of 270,702 resides in the capital city of La Rioja. Total area of the province is 35,649 sq. mi. and the main industries are centered around agriculture and include olive trees, grapes and wine production.

PROVINCE

TOKEN COINAGE

Stabilization Currency Unit

KM# Tn1 100000 AUSTRALES
15.0000 g., 0.9000 Silver .4341 oz. ASW **Subject:** 400th Anniversary - Foundation of La Rioja **Obv:** Mountains in oval within wreath, 1/2 radiant sunface at top **Rev:** Statue standing, divides dates

Date	Mintage	F	VF	XF	Unc	BU
1991	200,000	—	—	—	28.50	32.50

KM# Tn2 4000000 AUSTRALES
20.0000 g., 0.7500 Gold .4823 oz. AGW **Subject:** 400th Anniversary - Foundation of La Rioja

Date	Mintage	F	VF	XF	Unc	BU
1991	1,000	—	—	—	900	920

The Republic of Armenia, formerly Armenian S.S.R., is bordered to the north by Georgia, the east by Azerbaijan and the south and west by Turkey and Iran. It has an area of 11,506 sq. mi. (29,800 sq. km) and an estimated population of 3.66 million. Capital: Yerevan. Agriculture including cotton, vineyards and orchards, hydroelectricity, chemicals - primarily synthetic rubber and fertilizers, vast mineral deposits of copper, zinc and aluminum, and production of steel and paper are major industries.

Russia occupied Armenia in 1801 until the Russo-Turkish war of 1878. British intervention excluded either side from remaining although the Armenians remained more loyal to the Ottoman Turks, but in 1894 the Ottoman Turks sent in an expeditionary force of Kurds fearing a revolutionary movement. Large massacres were followed by retaliations, then amnesty was proclaimed which led right into WW I and once again occupation by Russian forces in 1916. After the Russian revolution the Georgians, Armenians and Azerbaijanis formed the short-lived Transcaucasian Federal Republic on Sept. 20, 1917, which broke up into three independent republics on May 26, 1918. Communism developed and in Sept. 1920 the Turks attacked the Armenian Republic; the Russians soon followed suit from Azerbaijan routing the Turks. On Nov. 29, 1920 Armenia was proclaimed a Soviet Socialist Republic. On March 12, 1922, Armenia, Georgia and Azerbaijan were combined to form the Transcaucasian Soviet Federated Socialist Republic, which on Dec. 30, 1922, became a part of U.S.S.R. On Dec. 5, 1936, the Transcaucasian federation was dissolved and Armenia became a constituent Republic of the U.S.S.R. A new constitution was adopted in April 1978. Elections took place on May 20, 1990. The Supreme Soviet adopted a declaration of sovereignty in Aug. 1991, voting to unite Armenia with Nagorno - Karabakh. This newly constituted "Republic of Armenia" became fully independent by popular vote in Sept. 1991. It became a member of the CIS in Dec. 1991.

Fighting between Christians in Armenia and Muslim forces of Azerbaijan escalated in 1992 and continued through early 1994. Each country claimed the Nagorno-Karabakh, an Armenian ethnic enclave, in Azerbaijan. A temporary cease-fire was announced in May 1994.

MONETARY SYSTEM

100 Luma = 1 Dram

MINT NAME

Revan, (Erevan, now Yerevan)

REPUBLIC

STANDARD COINAGE

KM# 51 10 LUMA

0.6000 g., Aluminum, 16 mm. **Obv:** National arms **Rev:** Value over date **Edge:** Plain

Date	Mintage	F	VF	XF	Unc	BU
1994	—	—	—	—	0.40	0.50

KM# 52 20 LUMA

0.7500 g., Aluminum, 18 mm. **Obv:** National arms **Rev:** Value over date **Edge:** Plain

Date	Mintage	F	VF	XF	Unc	BU
1994	—	—	—	—	0.50	0.65

KM# 53 50 LUMA

0.9500 g., Aluminum, 20 mm. **Obv:** National arms **Rev:** Value over date **Edge:** Plain

Date	Mintage	F	VF	XF	Unc	BU
1994	—	—	—	—	0.60	0.75

KM# 54 DRAM

1.4500 g., Aluminum, 22 mm. **Obv:** National arms **Rev:** Value over date in sprays **Edge:** Plain

Date	Mintage	F	VF	XF	Unc	BU
1994	—	—	—	—	0.75	1.00

KM# 55 3 DRAM

1.6500 g., Aluminum, 24 mm. **Obv:** National arms **Rev:** Value over date within sprays **Edge:** Plain

Date	Mintage	F	VF	XF	Unc	BU
1994	—	—	—	—	1.00	1.25

KM# 56 5 DRAM

2.0000 g., Aluminum, 26 mm. **Obv:** National arms **Rev:** Value over date within sprays **Edge:** Plain

Date	Mintage	F	VF	XF	Unc	BU
1994	—	—	—	—	1.50	1.75

KM# 81 5 DRAM

31.3700 g., 0.9990 Silver 1.0076 oz. ASW, 38 mm. **Subject:** 5th Anniversary - Dram Currency, introduced on November 22, 1993 **Obv:** National arms **Rev:** 6 banknote designs **Designer:** Arachya Aslanjan and Ashont Maroukyan

Date	Mintage	F	VF	XF	Unc	BU
1998 Proof	500	Value: 70.00				

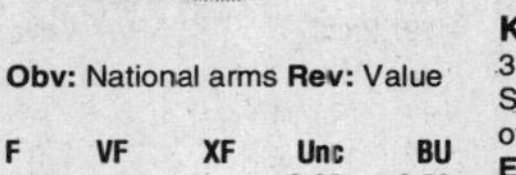

KM# 58 10 DRAM

2.3000 g., Aluminum, 28 mm. **Obv:** National arms **Rev:** Value over date within sprays

Date	Mintage	F	VF	XF	Unc	BU
1994	—	—	—	—	2.00	2.50

KM# 82 10 DRAM

31.0000 g., 0.9990 Silver 1.0130 oz. ASW, 38 mm. **Subject:** 10th Anniversary - Earthquake, December 7, 1988 **Obv:** National arms **Rev:** Map and building

Date	Mintage	F	VF	XF	Unc	BU
1998 Proof	1,000	Value: 70.00				

KM# 57 25 DRAM

31.1035 g., 0.9990 Silver 1.0000 oz. ASW, 38 mm. **Subject:** 1918 Battle of Sardarapat **Obv:** National arms **Rev:** Symbolic design **Edge:** Numbered

Date	Mintage	F	VF	XF	Unc	BU
1994 Proof	3,000	Value: 60.00				

KM# 59 25 DRAM

28.2800 g., 0.9250 Silver .8411 oz. ASW, 38.61 mm. **Obv:** National arms above value **Rev:** Apricot **Designer:** Hirachia Aslanian

Date	Mintage	F	VF	XF	Unc	BU
1994 Proof	10,000	Value: 60.00				

KM# 60 25 DRAM

31.1035 g., 0.9990 Silver 1.0000 oz. ASW **Subject:** David of Sasun **Obv:** National arms above denomination **Rev:** Monument of David mounted on rearing horse with sword held with two hands **Edge:** Numbered

Date	Mintage	F	VF	XF	Unc	BU
1994 Proof	5,000	Value: 50.00				

KM# 61 25 DRAM
31.1035 g., 0.9990 Silver 1.0000 oz. ASW, 38 mm.
Subject: Temple of Garni **Obv:** National arms over value and date **Rev:** Temple building **Edge:** Numbered

Date	Mintage	F	VF	XF	Unc	BU
1994 Proof	5,000	Value: 50.00				

KM# 62 25 DRAM
31.1035 g., 0.9990 Silver 1.0000 oz. ASW **Subject:** Jakharak **Obv:** National arms above denomination **Rev:** Woman spinning

Date	Mintage	F	VF	XF	Unc	BU
1994 Proof	5,000	Value: 50.00				

KM# 63 25 DRAM
31.1035 g., 0.9990 Silver 1.0000 oz. ASW **Subject:** Artsakh **Obv:** National arms above denomination **Rev:** Symbolic artifacts, sword, eagle, church....

Date	Mintage	F	VF	XF	Unc	BU
1994 Proof	5,000	Value: 50.00				

KM# 72 100 DRAM
28.2800 g., 0.9250 Silver .8411 oz. ASW, 38.6 mm.
Subject: 50th Anniversary - United Nations **Obv:** National arms **Rev:** Seated Madonna and child

Date	Mintage	F	VF	XF	Unc	BU
1995 Proof	100,000	Value: 50.00				

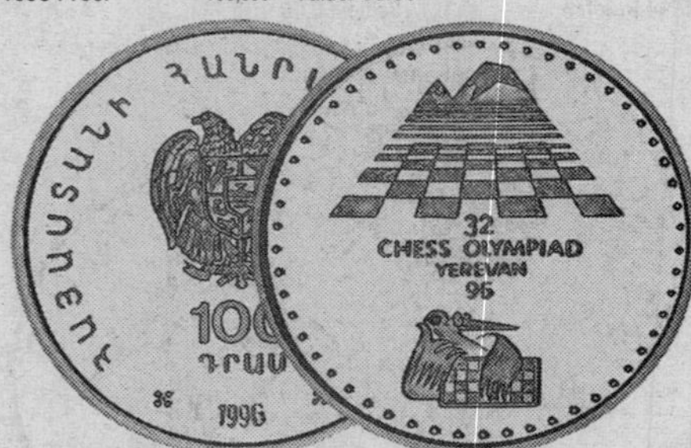

KM# 64 100 DRAM
31.1035 g., 0.9990 Silver 1.0000 oz. ASW, 38 mm.
Subject: Chess Olympics in Yerevan **Obv:** National arms above value **Rev:** Symbolic chess board

Date	Mintage	F	VF	XF	Unc	BU
1996 Proof	2,000	Value: 50.00				

KM# 70 100 DRAM
28.2800 g., 0.9250 Silver .8411 oz. ASW, 38.61 mm. **Subject:** XXXII Chess Olympiad **Obv:** Eagle and lion support arms **Rev:** Stylized stork and chessboard **Designer:** Hrachya Aslanian

Date	Mintage	F	VF	XF	Unc	BU
1996 Proof	10,000	Value: 55.00				

KM# 77 100 DRAM
31.1500 g., 0.9990 Silver 1.0005 oz. ASW, 38 mm.
Subject: Marshal Bagramian, Centennial **Obv:** National arms **Rev:** Uniformed portrait

Date	Mintage	F	VF	XF	Unc	BU
1996 Proof	—	Value: 300				
1997 Proof	1,200	Value: 50.00				

KM# 69 100 DRAM
10.8000 g., Copper-Nickel, 29.5 mm. **Subject:** XXXII Chess Olympiad in Yerevan **Obv:** Eagle and lion support arms **Rev:** Stylized stork and chessboard in inner circle **Designer:** Hrachya Aslanian

Date	Mintage	F	VF	XF	Unc	BU
1996	—	—	—	—	7.00	9.00
1996 Proof	2,000	Value: 12.50				

KM# 71 100 DRAM
28.2800 g., Copper-Nickel, 38.61 mm. **Subject:** WWF Conserving Nature 1997 **Obv:** National emblem **Rev:** Caucasian otter

Date	Mintage	F	VF	XF	Unc	BU
1997	—	—	—	—	12.00	14.00

KM# 71a 100 DRAM
28.2800 g., 0.9250 Silver .8410 oz. ASW, 38.61 mm. **Subject:** WWF Conserving Nature **Obv:** National emblem **Rev:** Caucasian otter

Date	Mintage	F	VF	XF	Unc	BU
1997 Proof	15,000	Value: 50.00				

KM# 76 100 DRAM
10.8000 g., Copper-Nickel, 28.5 mm. **Subject:** Charents **Obv:** National emblem **Rev:** Facial portrait of poet, Yogishe Charents, Centennial **Designer:** Hrochya Aslanyan

Date	Mintage	F	VF	XF	Unc	BU
1997	—	—	—	—	6.00	8.00

KM# 78 100 DRAM
Copper-Nickel, 38.61 mm. **Subject:** WWF Conserving Nature **Obv:** National arms **Rev:** Armenian silver seagull

Date	Mintage	F	VF	XF	Unc	BU
1998	—	—	—	—	12.00	14.00

KM# 78a 100 DRAM
28.2800 g., 0.9250 Silver 0.841 oz. ASW, 38.61 mm. **Subject:** WWF Conserving Nature **Obv:** National arms **Rev:** Armenian silver seagull

Date	Mintage	F	VF	XF	Unc	BU
1998 Proof	15,000	Value: 50.00				

KM# 79 100 DRAM
28.2800 g., 0.9250 Silver .8410 oz. ASW, 38.61 mm. **Subject:** XVIII Olympic Winter Games **Obv:** Arms **Rev:** Downhill skiers

Date	Mintage	F	VF	XF	Unc	BU
1998 Proof	10,000	Value: 65.00				

KM# 80 100 DRAM
28.2800 g., 0.9250 Silver .8410 oz. ASW, 38.61 mm. **Subject:** 1998 World Cup Soccer **Obv:** Arms **Rev:** Soccer players, map of France

Date	Mintage	F	VF	XF	Unc	BU
1998 Proof	10,000	Value: 50.00				

KM# 100 200 DRAM
31.1000 g., 0.9990 Silver 0.9989 oz. ASW, 38 mm. **Obv:** National arms **Rev:** A.S. Pushkin left, 200th Anniversary of birth June 6, 1799

Date	Mintage	F	VF	XF	Unc	BU
1999 Proof	500	Value: 65.00				

KM# 65 500 DRAM
155.5175 g., 0.9990 Silver 5.000 oz. ASW, 63 mm. **Subject:** National Assembly Building **Obv:** National arms above value **Rev:** View of building **Edge:** 5TO .999 AG and serial number **Note:** Photo reduced.

Date	Mintage	F	VF	XF	Unc	BU
1995 Proof	300	Value: 200				

KM# 66 500 DRAM
155.5175 g., 0.9990 Silver 5.000 oz. ASW, 63 mm. **Subject:** Historical Armenian Coat of Arms Series **Obv:** National arms **Rev:** Arms of the Kingdom of Cilicia **Note:** Photo reduced.

Date	Mintage	F	VF	XF	Unc	BU
1995 Proof	300	Value: 200				

KM# 67 500 DRAM
155.5175 g., 0.9990 Silver 5.000 oz. ASW, 63 mm. **Subject:** Historical Armenian Coat of Arms Series **Obv:** National arms **Rev:** Arms of Arshakonni dynasty 66-428 AD **Note:** Photo reduced.

Date	Mintage	F	VF	XF	Unc	BU
1995 Proof	300	Value: 200				

KM# 74 500 DRAM
155.5175 g., 0.9990 Silver 5.000 oz. ASW, 63 mm. **Subject:** Historical Armenian Coat of Arms - Double Eagle **Obv:** National arms **Rev:** Arms of the Artashesyan Dynasty 189 BC to 1 AD **Note:** Photo reduced.

Date	Mintage	F	VF	XF	Unc	BU
1995 Proof	300	Value: 200				

KM# 73 500 DRAM
155.5175 g., 0.9990 Silver 5.000 oz. ASW, 63 mm. **Subject:** Historical Armenian Coat of Arms - Lion **Obv:** National arms **Rev:** Arms of the Bagratourni dynasty **Edge:** With 5T0 .999 AG and serial number **Note:** Photo reduced.

Date	Mintage	F	VF	XF	Unc	BU
1995 Proof	300	Value: 200				

KM# 68 1000 DRAM
31.1035 g., 0.9990 Silver 1.0000 oz. ASW **Subject:** Early Armenian Currency - Vignette from 100 Rouble Note **Obv:** National arms above value **Rev:** Vignette from 100 Rouble note

Date	Mintage	F	VF	XF	Unc	BU
1994 Proof	5,000	Value: 50.00				

KM# 83 1000 DRAM
31.3100 g., 0.9990 Silver 1.0056 oz. ASW, 38 mm. **Subject:** 1700th Anniversary of the Adoption of Christianity in Armenia **Obv:** National arms **Rev:** Etchmiadzin church

Date	Mintage	F	VF	XF	Unc	BU
1998 Proof	1,700	Value: 120				

KM# 84 1000 DRAM
31.3100 g., 0.9990 Silver 1.0056 oz. ASW, 38 mm. **Subject:** 1700th Anniversary of the Adoption of Christianity in Armenia **Obv:** National arms **Rev:** Ani church tower

Date	Mintage	F	VF	XF	Unc	BU
1998 Proof	1,700	Value: 65.00				

KM# 85 1000 DRAM
31.3100 g., 0.9990 Silver 1.0056 oz. ASW, 38 mm. **Subject:** 1700th Anniversary of the Adoption of Christianity in Armenia **Obv:** National arms **Rev:** Haghpat carved stone cross, khachkar

Date	Mintage	F	VF	XF	Unc	BU
1998 Proof	1,700	Value: 65.00				

KM# 88 2000 DRAMS
28.2800 g., 0.9250 Silver 0.8476 oz. ASW, 38.6 mm. **Subject:** Millennium **Obv:** National arms **Rev:** Mounted St. George slaying a dragon **Edge:** Plain **Shape:** Octagonal

Date	Mintage	F	VF	XF	Unc	BU
2000 Proof	30,000	Value: 75.00				

KM# 89 5000 DRAMS
31.1000 g., 0.9990 Silver 1.004 oz. ASW, 38 mm. **Subject:** 1700th Anniversary of the adoption of Christianity in Armenia **Obv:** National arms **Rev:** Holy Cross Church (915) Aghtamer Island in Lake Van **Edge:** Plain with serial number

Date	Mintage	F	VF	XF	Unc	BU
1999 Proof	1,700	Value: 65.00				

KM# 101 5000 DRAMS
31.1000 g., 0.9990 Silver 0.9989 oz. ASW, 38 mm. **Obv:** National arms **Rev:** Chess Grand Master Tigran Petrosyan

Date	Mintage	F	VF	XF	Unc	BU
1999 Proof	500	Value: 70.00				

KM# 103 5000 DRAMS
31.1000 g., 0.9990 Silver 0.9989 oz. ASW, 38 mm. **Obv:** National arms **Rev:** First Pan-Armenian Games logo in Yerevan August 28 to September 15 1999

Date	Mintage	F	VF	XF	Unc	BU
1999 Proof	500	Value: 65.00				

KM# 104 5000 DRAMS
31.1000 g., 0.9990 Silver 0.9989 oz. ASW, 38 mm. **Obv:** National arms **Rev:** Large tree logo of the First Pan-Armenian Congress of the Armenian Diaspora September 22-23, 1999

Date	Mintage	F	VF	XF	Unc	BU
1999 Proof	500	Value: 65.00				

KM# 90 10000 DRAMS
8.6400 g., 0.9000 Gold 0.25 oz. AGW, 22 mm. **Subject:** Christian Armenia - Ani **Obv:** National arms **Rev:** Church tower **Edge:** Plain with serial number

Date	Mintage	F	VF	XF	Unc	BU
1998 Proof	1,700	Value: 250				

KM# 91 10000 DRAMS
8.6400 g., 0.9000 Gold 0.25 oz. AGW, 22 mm. **Subject:** 1700th Anniversary of the adoption of Christianity in Armenia **Obv:** National arms **Rev:** Multi-towered church **Edge:** Plain with serial number

Date	Mintage	F	VF	XF	Unc	BU
1998 Proof	1,700	Value: 250				

KM# 75.1 25000 DRAM
4.3000 g., 0.9000 Gold .1244 oz. AGW, 18 mm. **Obv:** National arms **Rev:** Portrait of goddess Anahit **Edge:** Reeded

Date	Mintage	F	VF	XF	Unc	BU
1997 Proof	—	Value: 160				

KM# 75.2 25000 DRAM
4.3000 g., 0.9000 Gold .1244 oz. AGW, 18 mm. **Obv:** National arms **Rev:** Portrait of goddess Anahit left **Edge:** Plain

Date	Mintage	F	VF	XF	Unc	BU
1997 Proof	—	Value: 160				

KM# 92 50000 DRAMS
8.6400 g., 0.9000 Gold 0.25 oz. AGW, 22 mm. **Subject:** 1700th Anniversary of the Adoption of Christianity in Armenia **Obv:** National arms **Rev:** Holy Cross Church (915) Aghtamer Island in Lake Van **Edge:** Plain with serial number

Date	Mintage	F	VF	XF	Unc	BU
1999 Proof	1,700	Value: 250				

KM# 105 50000 DRAMS
8.6000 g., 0.9000 Gold 0.2488 oz. AGW, 22 mm. **Obv:** National arms on an ancient coin design **Rev:** Ancient Armenian King Tigran the Great 95-55 BC

Date	Mintage	F	VF	XF	Unc	BU
1999 Proof	500	Value: 265				

KM# 102 100000 DRAMS
17.2000 g., 0.9000 Gold 0.4977 oz. AGW, 30 mm. **Obv:** National arms **Rev:** Noah's descent from Mt. Ararat

Date	Mintage	F	VF	XF	Unc	BU
1999 Proof	1,000	Value: 425				

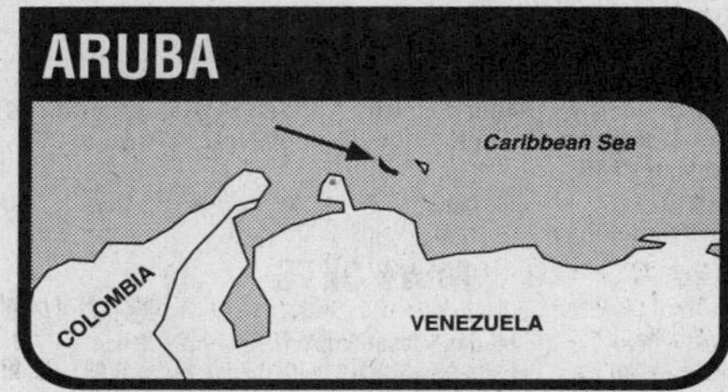

Aruba, formerly a part of the Netherlands Antilles, achieved on Jan. 1, 1986 a special status, "status aparte" as the third state under the Dutch crown, together with the Netherlands and the remaining five islands of the Netherlands Antilles. On Dec. 15, 1954 the Netherlands Antilles were given complete domestic autonomy and granted equality within the Kingdom of the Netherlands. The separate constitution put in place for Aruba in 1986 established it as an autonomous government within the Kingdom of the Netherlands. In 1990 Aruba opted to remain a part of the Kingdom without the promise of future independence.

The second largest island of the Netherlands Antilles, Aruba is situated near the Venezuelan coast. The island has an area of 74-1/2 sq. mi. (193 sq. km.) and a population of 65,974. Capital: Oranjestad, named after the Dutch royal family. Aruba was important in the processing and transportation of petroleum products in the first part of the twentieth century, but today the chief industry is tourism.

For earlier issues see Curacao and the Netherlands Antilles.

RULERS
Dutch

MINT MARKS
(u) Utrecht - Privy marks only
Anvil, 1986-1988
Bow and Arrow, 1989-1999
Bow and Arrow w/star, 2000-

MONETARY SYSTEM
100 Cents = 1 Florin

DUTCH STATE
"Status Aparte"
REGULAR COINAGE

KM# 1 5 CENTS
2.0000 g., Nickel Bonded Steel, 16 mm. **Obv:** National arms **Rev:** Geometric design with value **Edge:** Plain

Date	Mintage	F	VF	XF	Unc	BU
1986(u)	776,000	—	0.10	0.15	0.20	0.50
1987(u)	461,651	—	0.10	0.15	0.20	0.50
1988(u)	656,500	—	—	0.20	0.50	0.60
1989(u)	770,000	—	—	0.20	0.50	0.60
1990(u)	612,000	—	—	0.20	0.50	0.60
1991(u)	412,000	—	—	0.20	0.50	1.00
1992(u)	810,500	—	—	—	0.20	0.50
1993(u)	709,100	—	—	—	0.20	0.50
1994(u)	709,100	—	—	—	0.20	0.50
1995(u)	808,500	—	—	—	0.20	0.50
1996(u)	587,500	—	—	—	0.20	0.50
1997(u)	535,500	—	—	—	0.20	0.50
1998(u)	920,000	—	—	—	0.20	0.50
1999(u)	823,000	—	—	—	0.20	0.50
2000(u)	886,500	—	—	—	0.20	0.50

KM# 2 10 CENTS
3.0000 g., Nickel Bonded Steel, 18 mm. **Obv:** National arms **Rev:** Geometric design with value **Edge:** Reeded

Date	Mintage	F	VF	XF	Unc	BU
1986(u)	856,200	—	0.20	0.35	0.60	0.75
1987(u)	371,651	—	0.20	0.35	0.60	0.75
1988(u)	986,500	—	—	0.10	0.35	0.50
1989(u)	610,000	—	—	0.10	0.35	0.50
1990(u)	762,000	—	—	0.10	0.35	0.50
1991(u)	512,000	—	—	0.10	0.35	0.50
1992(u)	610,500	—	—	0.10	0.35	0.50
1993(u)	1,009,100	—	—	—	0.30	0.50
1994(u)	409,100	—	—	—	0.30	0.50
1995(u)	918,500	—	—	—	0.30	0.50
1996(u)	457,500	—	—	—	0.30	0.50
1997(u)	423,500	—	—	—	0.30	0.50
1998(u)	954,000	—	—	—	0.30	0.50
1999(u)	1,004,000	—	—	—	0.30	0.50
2000(u)	759,500	—	—	—	0.30	0.50

KM# 3 25 CENTS
3.5000 g., Nickel Bonded Steel, 20 mm. **Obv:** National arms **Rev:** Geometric design with value **Edge:** Plain

Date	Mintage	F	VF	XF	Unc	BU
1986(u)	856,200	—	0.20	0.40	0.75	1.50
1987(u)	331,651	—	0.20	0.40	0.75	1.50
1988(u)	116,500	—	0.20	0.40	0.75	1.50
1989(u)	360,000	—	—	0.30	0.60	1.20
1990(u)	512,000	—	—	—	0.40	0.80
1991(u)	612,000	—	—	—	0.40	0.80
1992(u)	460,500	—	—	—	0.40	0.80
1993(u)	609,100	—	—	—	0.40	0.80
1994(u)	109,100	—	—	—	0.40	0.80
1995(u)	608,500	—	—	—	0.40	0.80
1996(u)	287,500	—	—	—	0.60	1.00
1997(u)	467,500	—	—	—	0.50	0.90
1998(u)	541,000	—	—	—	0.40	0.80
1999(u)	332,000	—	—	—	0.40	0.80
2000(u)	330,500	—	—	—	0.40	0.80

KM# 4 50 CENTS
5.0000 g., Nickel Bonded Steel, 20 mm. **Obv:** National arms **Rev:** Geometric design with value **Edge:** Plain **Shape:** 4-sided

Date	Mintage	F	VF	XF	Unc	BU
1986(u)	486,200	—	0.30	0.50	1.00	1.50
1987(u)	121,651	—	0.30	0.50	1.00	1.50
1988(u)	216,500	—	—	0.35	1.00	1.50
1989(u)	110,000	—	—	0.75	1.50	2.25
1990(u)	262,000	—	—	0.50	1.00	1.50
1991(u)	312,000	—	—	0.40	0.90	1.10
1992(u)	310,500	—	—	0.40	0.90	1.10
1993(u)	459,100	—	—	0.35	0.65	0.80
1994(u)	309,100	—	—	0.35	0.65	0.80
1995(u)	258,500	—	—	0.40	0.90	1.10
1996(u)	392,500	—	—	0.35	0.65	0.80
1997(u)	27,500	—	—	0.60	1.25	2.00
1998(u)	197,000	—	—	0.35	0.65	0.80
1999(u)	445,000	—	—	0.35	0.65	0.80
2000(u)	54,500	—	—	0.50	1.00	1.20

KM# 5 FLORIN
8.5000 Nickel Bonded Steel, 26 mm. **Obv:** Head left **Rev:** National arms **Edge:** Lettered **Edge Lettering:** GOD * ZiJ * MET * ONS

Date	Mintage	F	VF	XF	Unc	BU
1986(u)	536,200	—	0.60	1.00	2.00	3.00
1987(u)	221,651	—	0.60	1.00	2.00	3.00
1988(u)	566,500	—	—	0.65	1.25	2.25
1989(u)	410,000	—	—	0.65	1.25	2.25
1990(u)	412,000	—	—	0.65	1.25	2.25
1991(u)	162,000	—	—	1.00	2.00	3.00
1992(u)	510,500	—	—	0.65	1.25	2.25
1993(u)	409,100	—	—	0.65	1.25	2.25
1994(u)	109,100	—	—	0.65	1.25	2.25
1995(u)	208,500	—	—	0.65	1.25	2.25
1996(u)	132,500	—	—	1.00	2.00	3.00
1997(u)	415,500	—	—	0.65	1.25	2.25
1998(u)	300,000	—	—	0.65	1.25	2.25
1999(u)	430,000	—	—	0.65	1.25	2.25
2000(u)	295,500	—	—	0.65	1.25	2.25

KM# 6 2-1/2 FLORIN
10.3000 g., Nickel Bonded Steel, 30 mm. **Obv:** Head left **Rev:** National arms **Edge:** Lettered **Edge Lettering:** GOD * ZiJ * MET * ONS

Date	Mintage	F	VF	XF	Unc	BU
1986(u)	106,200	—	—	1.75	2.50	3.75
1987(u)	31,651	—	—	1.75	3.50	5.00
1988(u)	26,500	—	—	1.75	3.50	5.00
1989(u)	15,000	—	—	2.00	4.00	6.00
1990(u)	17,000	—	—	2.00	4.00	6.00
1991(u)	17,000	—	—	2.00	4.00	6.00
1992(u)	12,500	—	—	2.00	4.00	6.00
1993(u)	11,100	—	—	2.00	4.00	6.00
1994(u)	11,100	—	—	2.00	4.00	6.00
1995(u)	10,500	—	—	2.00	4.00	6.00
1996(u)	7,500	—	—	1.75	3.50	6.00
Note: In sets only						
1997(u)	7,500	—	—	1.75	3.50	6.00
Note: In sets only						
1998(u)	8,000	—	—	1.75	3.50	6.00
Note: In sets only						
1999(u)	7,500	—	—	1.75	3.50	6.00
Note: In sets only						
2000(u)	7,500	—	—	1.75	3.50	6.00
Note: In sets only						

KM# 12 5 FLORIN
8.6400 g., Nickel Bonded Steel, 26 mm. **Obv:** Head left **Rev:** National arms **Edge:** Plain **Shape:** 4-sided

Date	Mintage	F	VF	XF	Unc	BU
1995(u)	200,500	—	—	2.00	4.50	6.00
1996(u)	357,500	—	—	2.00	4.50	6.00
1997(u)	27,500	—	—	2.25	5.50	7.00
1998(u)	162,000	—	—	2.00	4.50	6.00
1999(u)	86,200	—	—	2.25	5.50	7.00
2000(u)	7,500	—	—	3.00	6.00	7.50
Note: In sets only						

KM# 7 25 FLORIN
25.0000 g., 0.9250 Silver .7435 oz. ASW, 38 mm. **Subject:** Independence **Obv:** Head of Queen Beatrix left **Rev:** Arms, treaty name, date, and value **Edge Lettering:** GOD * ZiJ * MET * ONS **Designer:** E. Fingal

Date	Mintage	F	VF	XF	Unc	BU
ND(1986)(u)	5,000	—	—	—	30.00	—
ND(1986)(u) Proof	10,250	Value: 25.00				

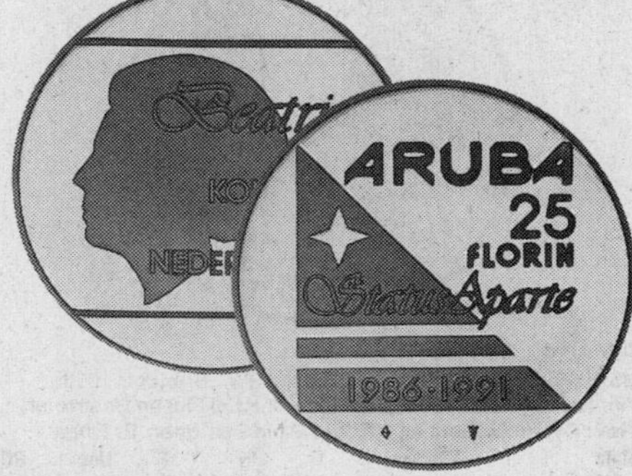

KM# 8 25 FLORIN
25.0000 g., 0.9250 Silver .7435 oz. ASW, 38 mm. **Subject:** Independence **Obv:** Head of Queen Beatrix left **Rev:** Triangular portion of flag, treaty name, date, value **Edge Lettering:** GOD * ZiJ * MET * ONS **Designer:** E. Fingal

Date	Mintage	F	VF	XF	Unc	BU
ND(1991)(u)	2,500	—	—	—	25.00	—
ND(1991)(u) Proof	4,600	Value: 40.00				

KM# 10 25 FLORIN
25.0000 g., 0.9250 Silver .7435 oz. ASW, 38 mm. **Series:** 1992 Olympics **Subject:** Windsurfing **Obv:** Head of Queen Beatrix left **Obv. Designer:** E. Fingal **Rev:** Windsurfer **Rev. Designer:** D. J. Hegeman **Edge:** Plain

Date	Mintage	F	VF	XF	Unc	BU
1992(u)	2,000	—	—	—	35.00	—
1992(u) Proof	16,000	Value: 37.50				

KM# 11 25 FLORIN
25.0000 g., 0.9250 Silver .7435 oz. ASW, 38 mm. **Subject:** Oil for Peace (WWII) **Obv:** Head of Queen Beatrix left **Obv. Designer:** E. Fingal **Rev:** Freighter, tankers and refinery **Rev. Designer:** Elles Klosterman **Edge:** Plain

Date	Mintage	F	VF	XF	Unc	BU
1994(u)	1,500	—	—	—	37.50	—
1994(u) Proof	4,000	Value: 40.00				

KM# 13 25 FLORIN
25.0000 g., 0.9250 Silver .7435 oz. ASW, 38 mm. **Subject:** 100th Anniversary of the Olympics **Obv:** Head of Queen Beatrix left **Rev:** Cyclist and logo **Edge:** Plain **Designer:** E. Fingal

Date	Mintage	F	VF	XF	Unc	BU
1995(u)	1,000	—	—	—	35.00	—
1995(u) Proof	2,100	Value: 42.50				

KM# 14 25 FLORIN
25.0000 g., 0.9250 Silver .7435 oz. ASW **Subject:** 100th Anniversary of the Olympics **Obv:** Head of Queen Beatrix left **Rev:** Cyclist, without logo **Edge:** Plain **Designer:** E. Fingal

Date	Mintage	F	VF	XF	Unc	BU
1995(u) Proof	1,700	Value: 50.00				

KM# 15 25 FLORIN
25.0000 g., 0.9250 Silver .7435 oz. ASW, 38 mm. **Obv:** Head of Queen Beatrix left **Obv. Designer:** E. Fingal **Rev:** Sea turtles with pre-Columbian design **Rev. Designer:** J. Lobban **Edge:** Plain

Date	Mintage	F	VF	XF	Unc	BU
1995(u)	3,500	—	—	—	40.00	45.00
1995(u) Proof	2,100	Value: 55.00				

KM# 18 25 FLORIN
25.0000 g., 0.9250 Silver .7435 oz. ASW, 38 mm. **Subject:** Tradition With Vision - Discovery 1499 **Obv:** Portrait of Vespucci, sailing vessel, map **Rev:** Spanish fan and aboriginal design, dates **Rev. Designer:** E. Fingal **Edge:** Plain

Date	Mintage	F	VF	XF	Unc	BU
ND(1999)(u) Proof	1,850	Value: 50.00				

KM# 21 25 FLORIN
25.0000 g., 0.9250 Silver 0.7435 oz. ASW, 38 mm. **Subject:** Olympics **Obv:** Head of Queen Beatrix left **Rev:** Catamaran sailboat **Edge:** Plain

Date	Mintage	F	VF	XF	Unc	BU
2000(u) Proof	3,500	Value: 45.00				

KM# 9 50 FLORIN
6.7200 g., 0.9000 Gold .1945 oz. AGW, 22.5 mm. **Subject:** Independence **Obv:** Head of Queen Beatrix left **Rev:** Triangular portion of flag, treaty name and date **Edge:** Grained **Designer:** E. Fingal

Date	Mintage	F	VF	XF	Unc	BU
ND(1991)(u) Proof	2,600	Value: 200				

KM# 16 50 FLORIN
25.0000 g., 0.9250 Silver .7435 oz. ASW, 38 mm. **Subject:** 10th Anniversary of Autonomy **Obv:** Head of Queen Beatrix left **Rev:** Portions of national flag and anthem score **Designer:** E. Fingal **Note:** Similar to 100 Florin, KM#17

Date	Mintage	F	VF	XF	Unc	BU
ND(1996)(u)	500	—	—	—	47.50	—
ND(1996)(u) Proof	2,000	Value: 42.50				

KM# 17 100 FLORIN
6.7200 g., 0.9000 Gold .1945 oz. AGW, 22.5 mm. **Subject:** 10th Anniversary of Autonomy **Obv:** Head of Queen Beatrix left **Rev:** Portions of national flag and anthem score **Edge:** Grained **Designer:** E. Fingal

Date	Mintage	F	VF	XF	Unc	BU
ND(1996)(u) Proof	535	Value: 275				

KM# 19 100 FLORIN
6.7200 g., 0.9000 Gold .1945 oz. AGW, 22.5 mm. **Subject:** Tradition With Vision - Discovery 1499 **Obv:** Portrait of Vespucci, sailing vessel, map **Rev:** Spanish fan and aboriginal design, dates **Rev. Designer:** E. Fingal **Edge:** Grained **Note:** Similar to 25 Florin, KM#18.

Date	Mintage	F	VF	XF	Unc	BU
ND(1999)(u) Proof	1,100	Value: 260				

MINT SETS

KM#	Date	Mintage	Identification	Issue Price	Mkt Val
MS1	1986 (6)	36,200	KM#1-6, with medal	8.95	10.00
MS2	1987 (6)	21,650	KM#1-6, with medal	9.95	12.00
MS3	1988 (6)	16,500	KM#1-6, with medal	12.95	12.00
MS4	1989 (6)	10,000	KM#1-6, with medal	12.00	12.00
MS5	1990 (6)	12,000	KM#1-6, with medal	—	13.00
MS6	1991 (6)	12,000	KM#1-6, with medal	14.50	13.00
MS7	1992 (6)	10,500	KM#1-6, with medal	—	13.00
MS8	1993 (6)	9,100	KM#1-6, with medal	—	14.50
MS9	1994 (6)	9,100	KM#1-6, with medal	14.50	15.50
MS10	1995 (1)	1,000	KM#12	—	20.00
MS11	1995 (6)	8,500	KM#1-6, with medal	17.50	13.50
MS12	1995 (2)	2,500	KM#15, 5 Florin banknote, with medal	56.50	50.00
MS13	1996 (7)	7,500	KM#1-6, 12, with medal	17.50	15.00
MS14	1997 (7)	7,500	KM#1-6, 12, with medal	17.50	15.00
MS15	1998 (7)	8,000	KM#1-6, 12, with medal	17.50	15.00
MS16	1999 (7)	7,000	KM#1-6, 12, with medal	17.50	15.00
MS17	2000 (7)	7,500	KM#1-6, 12	15.00	15.00

PROOF SETS

KM#	Date	Mintage	Identification	Issue Price	Mkt Val
PS1	1999 (5)	—	KM#18-19, with Netherlands Antilles KM#45-47 Tradition with Vision 1499-1999	580	850

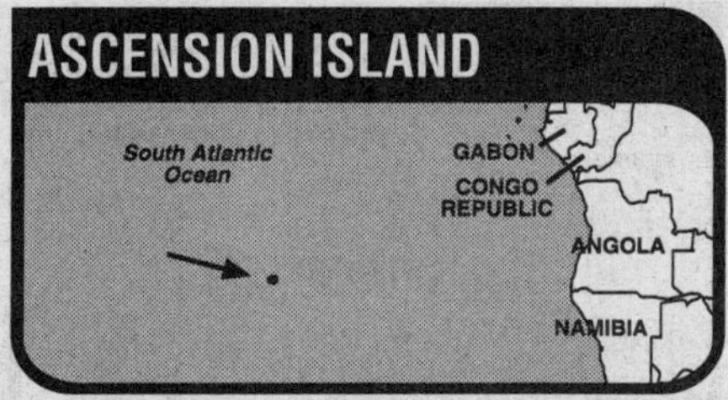

An island of volcanic origin, Ascension Island lies in the South Atlantic, 700 miles (1,100 km.) northwest of St. Helena. It has an area of 34 sq. mi. (88 sq. km.) on an island 9 miles (14 km.) long and 6 miles (10 km.) wide. Approximate population: 1,146. Although having little vegetation and scant rainfall, the island has a very healthy climate. The island is the nesting place for a large number of sea turtles and sooty terns. Phosphates and guano are the chief natural sources of income.

The island was discovered on Ascension Day, 1501, by Joao da Nova, a Portuguese navigator. It lay unoccupied until 1815, when occupied by the British. It was under Admiralty rule until 1922 when it was annexed as a dependency of St. Helena. During World War II an airfield was built that has been used as a fueling stop for Trans-atlantic flights to Southern Europe, North Africa and the Near-East.

RULERS
British

MINT MARK
PM - Pobjoy Mint

BRITISH ADMINISTRATION

STANDARD COINAGE

KM# 1 25 PENCE (Crown)
Copper-Nickel, 38.5 mm. **Subject:** 25th Anniversary of Coronation **Obv:** Young bust of Queen Elizabeth right **Obv. Designer:** Arnold Machin **Rev:** Lion left above sea turtle

Date	Mintage	F	VF	XF	Unc	BU
1978PM	—	—	—	—	7.50	10.00

KM# 1a 25 PENCE (Crown)
28.2800 g., 0.9250 Silver .8411 oz. ASW **Subject:** 25th Anniversary of Coronation **Obv:** Young bust of Queen Elizabeth II right **Rev:** Lion left above sea turtle

Date	Mintage	F	VF	XF	Unc	BU
1978PM	70,000	—	—	—	15.00	16.50
1978PM Proof	25,000	Value: 22.50				

KM# 2 25 PENCE (Crown)
28.2800 g., 0.9250 Silver .8411 oz. ASW, 38.5 mm. **Subject:** 25th Anniversary of the Coronation **Obv:** Isle of Man, bust of young Elizabeth wearing crown, right **Obv. Designer:** Arnold Machin **Rev:** Lion left above sea turtle **Note:** Error; mule.

Date	Mintage	F	VF	XF	Unc	BU
ND(1978)PM	367	—	—	150	200	—

KM# 3 25 PENCE (Crown)
Copper-Nickel, 38.5 mm. **Subject:** Wedding of Prince Charles and Lady Diana **Obv:** Young bust of Queen Elizabeth II right **Obv. Designer:** Arnold Machin **Rev:** 2 coats of arms

Date	Mintage	F	VF	XF	Unc	BU
1981PM	50,000	—	—	—	4.50	6.00

KM# 3a 25 PENCE (Crown)
28.2800 g., 0.5000 Silver .4546 oz. ASW **Subject:** Wedding of Prince Charles and Lady Diana **Obv:** Young bust of Queen Elizabeth II right **Rev:** 2 coats of arms

Date	Mintage	F	VF	XF	Unc	BU
1981	500	—	—	—	50.00	55.00

KM# 3b 25 PENCE (Crown)
28.2800 g , 0.9250 Silver .8411 oz. ASW **Subject:** Wedding of Prince Charles and Lady Diana **Obv:** Young bust of Queen Elizabeth II right **Rev:** 2 coats of arms

Date	Mintage	F	VF	XF	Unc	BU
1981 Proof	30,000	Value: 22.50				

KM# 4 25 PENCE (Crown)
28.2800 g., 0.9250 Silver .8411 oz. ASW **Series:** International Year of the Scout **Obv:** Bust of Queen Elizabeth II right **Obv. Designer:** Arnold Machin **Rev:** Scoutmaster, 3/4 left

Date	Mintage	F	VF	XF	Unc	BU
ND(1983)	10,000	—	—	—	30.00	32.50
ND(1983) Proof	10,000	Value: 42.50				

KM# 6 50 PENCE
Copper-Nickel, 38.5 mm. **Subject:** Royal Visit of Prince Andrew **Obv:** Young bust of Queen Elizabeth II, right **Obv. Designer:** Arnold Machin **Rev:** Bust of Prince Andrew left

Date	Mintage	F	VF	XF	Unc	BU
1984	125,000	—	—	—	4.00	5.50

KM# 6a 50 PENCE
28.2800 g., 0.9250 Silver .8411 oz. ASW **Subject:** Royal Visit of Prince Andrew **Obv:** Bust of young Queen Elizabeth II right **Rev:** Bust of Prince Andrew left

Date	Mintage	F	VF	XF	Unc	BU
1984 Proof	5,000	Value: 22.50				

KM# 7 50 PENCE
Copper-Nickel, 38.5 mm. **Obv:** Bust of crowned Queen Elizabeth II, right **Obv. Designer:** Raphael Maklouf **Rev:** Queen Mother fishing with waders and hat

Date	Mintage	F	VF	XF	Unc	BU
1995	—	—	—	—	4.00	5.50

KM# 7a 50 PENCE
28.2800 g., 0.9250 Silver .841 oz. ASW **Obv:** Crowned bust of Queen Elizabeth II right **Rev:** Queen Mother fishing in waders and hat

Date	Mintage	F	VF	XF	Unc	BU
1995 Proof	—	Value: 32.50				

KM# 7b 50 PENCE
47.5400 g., 0.9160 Gold 1.4001 oz. AGW **Obv:** Crowned bust of Queen Elizabeth II right **Rev:** Queen Mother fishing with waders and hat

Date	Mintage	F	VF	XF	Unc	BU
1995 Proof	150	Value: 950				

KM# 8 50 PENCE
Copper-Nickel, 38.5 mm. **Subject:** 70th Birthday - Queen Elizabeth II **Obv:** Crowned bust of Queen Elizabeth II, right **Obv. Designer:** Raphael Maklouf **Rev:** 2 soldiers with standard **Rev. Designer:** Willem Vis

Date	Mintage	F	VF	XF	Unc	BU
1996	—	—	—	—	6.50	8.00

KM# 8a 50 PENCE
28.2800 g., 0.9250 Silver .8411 oz. ASW **Subject:** 70th Birthday - Queen Elizabeth II **Obv:** Crowned bust of Queen Elizabeth II right **Rev:** 2 soldiers holding the standard

Date	Mintage	F	VF	XF	Unc	BU
1996 Proof	5,000	Value: 50.00				

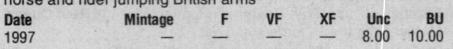

KM# 11 50 PENCE
Copper-Nickel, 38.5 mm. **Series:** Montreal Olympics **Subject:** Queen's portrait **Obv:** Bust of Queen Elizabeth II right **Obv. Designer:** Raphael Maklouf **Rev:** Royal couple behind horse and rider jumping British arms

Date	Mintage	F	VF	XF	Unc	BU
1997	—	—	—	—	8.00	10.00

KM# 9 50 PENCE
Copper-Nickel, 38.5 mm. **Subject:** World Wildlife Fund - Conserving Nature **Obv:** Crowned bust of Queen Elizabeth I, right **Obv. Designer:** Raphael Maklouf **Rev:** Frigate birds

Date	Mintage	F	VF	XF	Unc	BU
1998	—	—	—	—	10.00	12.50

KM# 9a 50 PENCE
28.2800 g., 0.9250 Silver 0.841 oz. ASW, 38.5 mm. **Subject:** World Wildlife Fund - Conserving Nature **Obv:** Crowned bust of Queen Elizabeth II right **Rev:** Frigate birds

Date	Mintage	F	VF	XF	Unc	BU
1998 Proof	—	Value: 45.00				

KM# 10 50 PENCE
Copper-Nickel **Subject:** World Wildlife Fund - Conserving Nature **Obv:** Crowned bust of Queen Elizabeth II, right **Obv. Designer:** Raphael Maklouf **Rev:** Long-tailed birds

Date	Mintage	F	VF	XF	Unc	BU
1998	—	—	—	—	10.00	12.50

KM# 10a 50 PENCE
28.2800 g., 0.9250 Silver 0.841 oz. ASW **Subject:** World Wildlife Fund - Conserving Nature **Obv:** Crowned bust of Queen Elizabeth II right **Rev:** Long-tailed birds

Date	Mintage	F	VF	XF	Unc	BU
1998 Proof	—	Value: 45.00				

KM# 12 50 PENCE
28.7600 g., Copper-Nickel, 38.5 mm. **Subject:** 100th Birthday of the Queen Mother **Obv:** Crowned bust of Queen Elizabeth II, right **Obv. Designer:** Raphael Maklouf **Rev:** Queen Mother's bust 3/4 facing half left **Edge:** Reeded

Date	Mintage	F	VF	XF	Unc	BU
ND(2000)	—	—	—	—	8.50	10.00

KM# 12a 50 PENCE
28.2800 g., 0.9250 Silver 0.841 oz. ASW, 38.6 mm. **Subject:** Queen Mother's 100th Birthday **Obv:** Crowned bust of Queen Elizabeth II right **Rev:** Queen Mother above dates 1900-2000 **Edge:** Reeded

Date	Mintage	F	VF	XF	Unc	BU
ND(2000) Proof	10,000	Value: 40.00				

KM# 12b 50 PENCE
47.5400 g., 0.9166 Gold 1.401 oz. AGW, 38.6 mm. **Subject:** Queen Mother's 100th Birthday **Obv:** Crowned bust of Queen Elizabeth II, right **Obv. Designer:** Raphael Maklouf **Rev:** Queen Mother above dates 1900-2000 **Edge:** Reeded

Date	Mintage	F	VF	XF	Unc	BU
ND(2000) Proof	100	Value: 1,150				

KM# 5 2 POUNDS
15.9800 g., 0.9170 Gold .4712 oz. AGW **Series:** International Year of the Scout **Rev:** Boy Scout

Date	Mintage	F	VF	XF	Unc	BU
1983	2,000	—	—	—	450	475
1983 Proof	2,000	Value: 500				

PIEFORTS

KM#	Date	Mintage	Identification	Mkt Val
P1	1995	500	50 Pence. Silver. KM7a.	55.00

AUSTRALIA

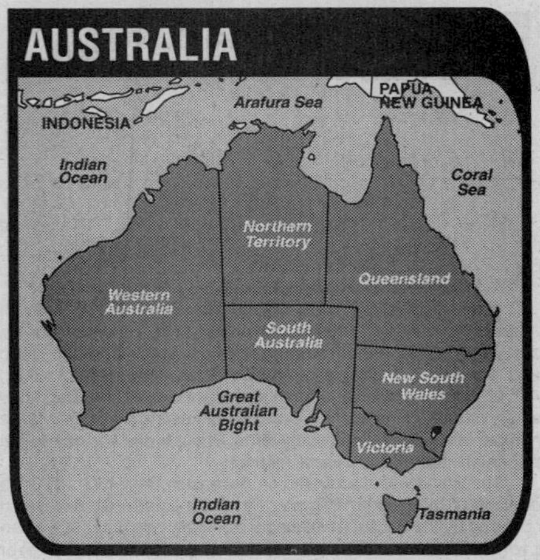

The Commonwealth of Australia, the smallest continent in the world, is located south of Indonesia between the Indian and Pacific oceans. It has an area of 2,967,893 sq. mi. (7,686,850 sq. km.) and an estimated population of 18.84 million. Capital: Canberra. Due to its early and sustained isolation, Australia is the habitat of such curious and unique fauna as the kangaroo, koala, platypus, wombat, echidna and frilled-necked lizard. The continent possesses extensive mineral deposits, the most important of which are iron ore, coal, gold, silver, nickel, uranium, lead and zinc. Raising livestock, mining and manufacturing are the principal industries. Chief exports are wool, meat, wheat, iron ore, coal and nonferrous metals.

The first Caucasians to see Australia probably were Portuguese and Spanish navigators of the late 16th century. In 1770, Captain James Cook explored the east coast and annexed it for Great Britain. New South Wales was founded as a penal colony, following the loss of British North America, by Captain Arthur Phillip on January 26, 1788, a date now celebrated as Australia Day. Dates of creation of the six colonies that now comprise the states of the Australian Commonwealth are: New South Wales, 1823; Tasmania, 1825; Western Australia, 1838; South Australia, 1842; Victoria, 1851; Queensland, 1859. The British Parliament approved a constitution providing for the federation of the colonies in 1900. The Commonwealth of Australia came into being in 1901. Australia passed the Statute of Westminster Adoption Act on October 9, 1942, which officially established Australia's complete autonomy in external and internal affairs, thereby formalizing a situation that had existed for years. Australia is a member of the Commonwealth of Nations. Elizabeth II is Head of State as Queen of Australia.

Australia's currency system was changed from Pounds-Shillings-Pence to a decimal system of Dollars and Cents on Feb. 14, 1966.

RULER
British until 1942

MINT MARKS

Abbr.	Mint	Mint Marks
A	Adelaide	-
(b)	Bombay	I below bust; dots before and after HALF PENNY, 1942-43
(b)	Bombay	I below bust dots before and after PENNY, 1942-43
B	Brisbane	-
(c)	Calcutta	I above date, 1916-18
(c)	Canberra	None, 1966 to date
C	Canberra	-
D	Denver	D above date 1/-& 2/-, below date on 3d
D	Denver	D below date on 6d
H	Heaton	H below date on silvere coins, 1914-15
H	Heaton	H above date on bronze coins
(L)	London	1910-1915 (no marks), 1966
M	Melbourne	M below date on silver coins, 1916-20
M	Melbourne	M above date on the ground on gold coins w/St. George
M	Melbourne	-
(m)	Melbourne	Dot below scroll on penny, 1919-20
(m)	Melbourne	Two dots; below lower scroll and above upper, 1919-20
(m)	Melbourne	None, 1921-1964, 1966
P	Perth	P above date on the ground on gold coins w/St. George
(p)	Perth	Dot between KG (designer's initials), 1940-41
(p)	Perth	Dot after PENNY, 1941-51, 1954-64
(p)	Perth	Dot after AUSTRALIA, 1952-53
(p)	Perth	Dot before SHILLING, 1946
(p)	Perth	None, 1922 penny, 1966
P	Perth	Nuggets, 1986
PL	London	PL after PENNY in 1951
PL	London	PL on bottom folds of ribbon, 1951 threepence
PL	London	PL above date on sixpence
PL		1951
S	San Francisco	S above or below date, 1942-44, mm exists w/ and w/o bulbous serifs
S	Sydney	S above date on the ground on gold coins w/St. George
S	Sydney	-
(sy)	Sydney	Dot above bottom scroll on penny 1920
(sy)	Sydney	None, 1919-1926

Mint designations are shown in ( ). Ex. 1978(m).
Mint marks are shown after date. Ex. 1978M.

PRIVY MARKS

- (ae) - American Eagle
- (aa) - Adelaide Assay
- (ba) - Basler Stab
- (bg) - Brandenburg Gate
- (d) – Ducat
- (dp) – Dump
- (e) – Emu
- (ev) - Edward V
- (f) – Fok
- (f1) - Rev. 1 Florin, KM#31
- (f3) - Rev. 1 Florin, KM#33
- (f7) - Rev. 1 Florin, KM#47
- (ge) - Golden Eagle
- (gv) - George V, small head
- (gV) - George V, large head
- (h) – Hague
- (hd) - Holey Dollar
- (j) – Johanna
- (jw) - Japanese Royal Wedding
- (l) – Luk
- (lh) - Liberty Head
- (p) – Prospector
- (qv) - Queen Victoria
- (rv) - Royal Visit Florin, Rev. 1 Florin, KM#55
- (s) – Shu
- (sg) - Spade Guinea
- (sm) - Sydney Mint Sovereign
- (so) - Sydney Opera House
- (sp) - Star Pagoda
- (sq) – State Quarter
- (sr) - Swan River/Rottnest Island Tercentenary
- (ta) - Team Australia (Commonwealth Games)
- (hd) - Holey Dollar
- (w) – Whales
- (ww) - 50 Years Beyond WWII

MONETARY SYSTEM

Sterling Coinage (Until 1966)
12 Pence = 1 Shilling
2 Shillings = 1 Florin
5 Shillings = 1 Crown
20 Shillings = 1 Pound
1 Sovereign = 1 Pound

Decimal Coinage (Commencing 1966)
100 Cents = 1 Dollar

BRITISH COLONY

TRADE COINAGE

KM# 12 1/2 SOVEREIGN

3.9940 g., 0.9170 Gold .1177 oz. AGW **Ruler:** Victoria
Obv: Veiled head left **Obv. Designer:** Thomas Brock **Rev:** St. George slaying dragon, mint mark above date

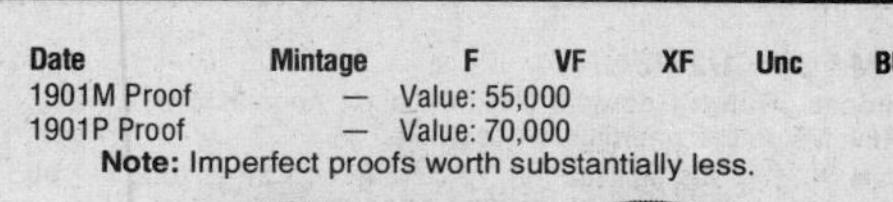

Date	Mintage	F	VF	XF	Unc	BU
1901M Proof	—	Value: 55,000				
1901P Proof	—	Value: 70,000				

Note: Imperfect proofs worth substantially less.

KM# 13 SOVEREIGN

7.9881 g., 0.9170 Gold .2354 oz. AGW **Ruler:** Victoria
Obv: Older veiled head **Rev:** St. George on horseback with sword slaying the dragon

Date	Mintage	F	VF	XF	Unc	BU
1901S	3,012,000	—	BV	155	220	—
1901M	3,987,000	—	BV	155	220	—
1901M Proof	—	Value: 45,000				
1901P	2,889,000	—	BV	155	220	—
1901P Proof	—	Value: 45,000				

COMMONWEALTH OF AUSTRALIA

MINT MARKS
M – Melbourne
P – Perth
S – Sydney
(sy) - Sydney

STERLING COINAGE

KM# 22 1/2 PENNY

Bronze **Ruler:** George V **Obv:** Crowned bust left **Obv. Designer:** E. B. MacKennal **Rev:** Denomination within circle **Edge:** Plain

Date	Mintage	F	VF	XF	Unc	BU
1911(L)	2,832,000	1.00	3.00	15.00	215	—
1911(L) Proof	—	Value: 14,000				
1912H	2,400,000	1.00	4.00	18.00	285	—
1912H Proof	—	Value: 14,000				
1913(L) Wide date	2,160,000	1.00	4.00	32.00	500	—
1913(L) Narrow date	Inc. above	1.00	4.00	32.00	500	—
1914(L)	1,440,000	2.00	10.00	50.00	825	—
1914H	1,200,000	2.00	9.00	45.00	650	—
1915H	720,000	15.00	50.00	250	3,000	—
1916(c) I	3,600,000	1.00	2.00	14.00	225	—
1916(c) I Proof	—	Value: 15,000				
1917(c) I	5,760,000	1.00	2.00	15.00	225	—
1918(c) I	1,440,000	5.00	20.00	125	2,350	—
1919(sy)	3,326,000	0.50	2.00	15.00	315	—
1919(sy) Proof	—	Value: 16,500				
1920(sy)	4,114,000	1.00	5.00	30.00	320	—
1920(m) Proof	—	Value: 20,000				
1921(sy)	5,280,000	0.50	2.00	17.50	225	—
1922(sy)	6,924,000	0.50	2.00	22.00	250	—
1923(sy)	Est. 1,113,000	1,200	4,000	25,000	50,000	—

Note: Dies dated 1922 were used for the majority of the calendar year 1923, leaving only a small portion of this mintage figure as 1923 dated coins.

Date	Mintage	F	VF	XF	Unc	BU
1923(sy) Proof; Rare	—	—	—	—	—	—

Note: Noble Numismatics sale No. 62, 11-99, nearly FDC proof realized $56,745.

Date	Mintage	F	VF	XF	Unc	BU
1924(m)	682,000	2.00	6.00	65.00	1,275	—
1924(m) Proof	—	Value: 14,000				
1925(m)	1,147,000	1.00	5.00	30.00	1,200	—
1925(m) Proof	—	Value: 36,000				
1926(m & sy)	4,139,000	0.50	1.00	15.00	420	—
1926(m) Proof	—	Value: 14,000				
1927(m)	3,072,000	0.50	1.00	15.00	300	—
1927(m) Proof	50	Value: 15,500				
1928(m)	2,318,000	1.00	4.00	25.00	625	—
1928(m) Proof	—	Value: 15,500				
1929(m)	2,635,000	0.20	0.65	18.00	320	—
1929(m) Proof	—	Value: 14,000				
1930(m)	638,000	1.50	3.00	35.00	900	—
1930(m) Proof	—	Value: 45,000				
1931(m)	370,000	1.50	3.00	35.00	900	—
1931(m) Proof	—	Value: 16,000				
1932(m)	2,554,000	0.50	1.00	10.00	150	—
1932(m) Proof	—	Value: 16,000				
1933(m)	4,608,000	0.50	1.00	10.00	125	—
1933(m) Proof	—	Value: 15,500				
1934(m)	3,816,000	0.50	1.00	10.00	125	—
1934(m) Proof	100	Value: 11,500				
1935(m)	2,916,000	0.50	1.00	10.00	125	—
1935(m) Proof	100	Value: 11,500				
1936(m)	2,562,000	0.50	0.75	5.00	75.00	—
1936(m) Proof	—	Value: 14,750				

KM# 30 1/2 PENNY

Bronze **Ruler:** George V **Obv:** India 1/4 Anna, KM#511 **Rev:** Value in inner circle **Note:** Mule.

Date	Mintage	F	VF	XF	Unc	BU
1916(c) I	Est. 10	55,000	85,000	—	—	—

KM# 35 1/2 PENNY

Bronze **Ruler:** George VI **Obv:** Head left **Obv. Designer:** T.H. Paget **Rev:** Value in inner circle **Edge:** Plain

Date	Mintage	F	VF	XF	Unc	BU
1938(m)	3,014,000	0.25	0.50	3.00	35.00	—
1938(m) Proof	250	Value: 5,000				
1939(m)	4,382,000	0.25	0.50	3.50	60.00	—
1939(m) Proof	—	Value: 8,000				

KM# 41 1/2 PENNY

Bronze **Ruler:** George VI **Obv:** Head left **Obv. Designer:** T. H. Paget **Rev:** Kangaroo leaping right above value **Rev. Designer:** George Kruger Gray

Date	Mintage	F	VF	XF	Unc	BU
1939(m)	504,000	3.75	6.50	45.00	525	—
1939(m) Proof	100	Value: 7,500				
1940(m)	2,294,000	0.20	0.75	5.00	100	—
1940(m) Proof	—	Value: 10,500				
1941(m)	5,011,000	0.20	0.65	4.00	60.00	—
1941(m) Proof	—	Value: 10,500				
1942(m)	720,000	1.50	3.75	18.00	145	—
1942(m) Proof	—	Value: 7,500				
1942(p)	4,334,000	0.25	1.00	5.00	75.00	—
1942(p) Proof	—	Value: 7,000				
1942(b) I Wide date	6,000,000	0.25	0.50	3.00	40.00	—
1942(b) I Narrow date	Inc. above	0.25	0.50	3.00	40.00	—
1942(b) I Proof	—	Value: 6,500				
1943(m)	33,989,000	0.15	0.25	2.00	17.50	—
1943(p) Proof	—	Value: 7,000				
1943(b) I	6,000,000	0.20	0.35	3.00	35.00	—
1943(b) I Proof	—	Value: 6,500				
1944(m)	720,000	1.50	5.00	27.50	165	—
1945(p)	3,033,000	0.75	2.00	12.50	75.00	—
1945(p) Proof	—	Value: 7,500				
1945(p) Without dot	Inc. above	1.25	2.50	12.50	75.00	—
1946(p)	13,747,000	0.15	0.25	2.00	20.00	—
1946(p) Proof	—	Value: 7,500				
1947(p)	9,293,000	0.15	0.25	2.50	35.00	—
1947(p) Proof	—	Value: 8,000				
1948(m)	4,608,000	0.25	0.50	2.75	22.50	—
1948(m) Proof	—	Value: 8,000				
1948(p)	25,553,000	0.15	0.25	2.00	20.00	—
1948(p) Proof	—	Value: 7,800				

KM# 42 1/2 PENNY

Bronze **Ruler:** George VI **Obv:** Head left **Obv. Legend:** IND: IMP: dropped **Obv. Designer:** T.H. Paget **Rev:** Kangaroo leaping right **Rev. Designer:** George Kruger Gray

Date	Mintage	F	VF	XF	Unc	BU
1949(m) Proof	—	Value: 9,000				
1949(p)	22,310,000	0.15	0.25	2.00	15.00	—
1949(p) Proof	—	Value: 9,000				
1950(p)	12,014,000	0.15	0.50	2.00	20.00	—
1950(p) Proof	—	Value: 10,000				
1951(p) With dot, Proof	—	Value: 11,000				
1951(p) With dot	—	0.15	0.35	2.00	15.00	—
1951(p) Without dot	29,422,000	0.15	0.35	2.50	15.00	—
1951(p) Without dot; Proof	—	Value: 11,000				
1951PL	17,040,000	0.15	0.25	1.25	6.00	—
Note: 5,040,000 struck at the Birmingham Mint.						
1951PL Proof	—	Value: 6,500				
1952(p)	1,832,000	0.50	2.00	4.00	45.00	—
1952(p) Proof	—	Value: 6,500				

KM# 49 1/2 PENNY

Bronze **Ruler:** Elizabeth II **Obv:** Laureate bust right **Obv. Legend:** DEI • GRATIA • REGINA + ELIZABETH • II • **Obv. Designer:** Mary Gillick **Rev:** Kangaroo leaping right **Rev. Designer:** George Kruger Gray

Date	Mintage	F	VF	XF	Unc	BU
1953(p)	23,967,000	0.15	0.25	0.50	10.00	—
1953(p) Proof	16	Value: 6,000				
1954(p)	21,963,000	0.15	0.25	0.50	10.00	—
1954(p) Proof	—	Value: 6,000				
1955(p) Without dot	9,343,000	0.15	0.25	0.50	10.00	—
1955(p) Without dot; Proof	301	Value: 5,000				

KM# 61 1/2 PENNY

Bronze **Ruler:** Elizabeth II **Obv:** Laureate bust right **Obv. Legend:** DEI • GRATIA • REGINA • F:D: + ELIZABETH • II • **Obv. Designer:** Mary Gillick **Rev:** Kangaroo leaping right **Rev. Designer:** George Kruger Gray

Date	Mintage	F	VF	XF	Unc	BU
1959(m)	10,166,000	0.10	0.15	0.25	1.50	2.50
1959(m) Proof	1,506	Value: 350				
1960(p)	17,812,000	0.10	0.15	0.25	1.00	1.50
1960(p) Proof	1,030	Value: 300				
1961(p)	20,183,000	0.10	0.15	0.25	1.00	1.50
1961(p) Proof	1,040	Value: 300				
1962(p)	10,259,000	0.10	0.15	0.25	2.00	2.50
1962(p) Proof	1,064	Value: 300				
1963(p)	16,410,000	0.10	0.15	0.25	1.00	2.00
1963(p) Proof	1,060	Value: 300				
1964(p)	18,230,000	0.10	0.15	0.25	1.00	2.00
1964(p) Proof; 1 known	—	Value: 16,500				

KM# 23 PENNY

Bronze, 30.5 mm. **Ruler:** George V **Obv:** Crowned bust left **Obv. Legend:** GEORGIVS V D.G. BRITT: OMN: REX F.D: IND: IMP **Obv. Designer:** E.B. MacKennal **Rev:** Value in inner circle **Edge:** Plain

Date	Mintage	F	VF	XF	Unc	BU
1911(L)	3,768,000	1.00	4.00	22.50	450	750
1911(L) Proof	—	Value: 20,000				
1912H	3,600,000	1.00	4.00	27.50	500	950
1912H Proof	—	Value: 3,000				
1913(L) Narrow date	2,520,000	1.25	5.00	32.50	700	—
1913(L) Wide date	Inc. above	1.25	5.00	32.50	700	—
1914(L)	720,000	3.00	12.50	175	1,600	—
1915(L)	960,000	2.25	10.00	200	2,000	—
1915H	1,320,000	2.00	8.50	150	1,500	—
1916(c) I	3,324,000	1.00	2.00	22.50	400	—
1916(c) I Proof	—	Value: 35,000				
1917(c) I	6,240,000	1.00	2.00	22.50	325	—
1918(c) I	1,200,000	3.00	10.00	225	2,250	—
1919(m)	5,810,000	1.00	2.00	35.00	450	950
Note: Without dots						
1919(m)	Inc. above	1.00	2.00	35.00	400	900
Note: Dot below bottom scroll						
1919(m)	—	40.00	125	1,000	3,500	—
Note: Dots below bottom scroll and above upper						
1919(m) Proof	—	Value: 37,500				
1920(m & sy)	9,041,000	45.00	300	1,100	7,500	—
Note: Without dots						
1920(m)	Inc. above	2.00	10.00	125	1,350	—
Note: Dot below bottom scroll						
1920(m) Proof	—	Value: 25,000				
1920(sy)	Inc. above	2.00	10.00	125	1,350	—
Note: Dot above bottom scroll						
1920	Inc. above	15.00	80.00	725	4,500	—

Date	Mintage	F	VF	XF	Unc	BU
Note: Dots below bottom scroll and above upper						
1921(m & sy)	7,438,000	1.00	6.00	80.00	750	—
1922(m & p)	12,697,000	1.00	6.00	100	825	—
1923(m)	5,654,000	1.00	6.00	75.00	700	—
1923(m) Proof	—	Value: 25,000				
1924(m & sy)	4,656,000	1.00	5.00	60.00	600	—
1924(m) Proof	—	Value: 18,000				
1925(m)	1,639,000	75.00	200	1,100	9,500	—
1925(m) Proof	—	Value: 90,000				
1926(m & sy)	1,859,000	2.00	8.00	150	1,400	—
1926(m) Proof	—	Value: 18,000				
1927(m)	4,922,000	0.50	2.25	50.00	350	—
1927(m) Proof	50	Value: 25,000				
1928(m)	3,038,000	0.50	3.00	55.00	950	—
1928(m) Proof	—	Value: 16,000				
1929(m)	2,599,000	0.50	3.00	60.00	1,100	—
1929(m) Proof	—	Value: 16,000				
1930(m)	Est. 3,000	8,000	12,500	30,000	60,000	—
1930(m) Proof; Rare	—	—	—	—	—	—
Note: Noble Numismatics sale No. 52, 7-97, nearly FDC proof realized $126,500. Noble Numismatics sale No. 62, 11-99, FDC proof realized $162,665.						
1931(m) Normal date alignment	494,000	2.00	7.50	125	1,450	—
1931(m) Fallen 1 in date	Inc. above	2.00	7.50	125	1,450	—
1931(m) Proof	—	Value: 35,000				
1932(m)	2,117,000	0.50	3.00	45.00	300	—
1933/2(m)	5,818,000	15.00	30.00	185	1,350	—
1933(m)	Inc. above	0.25	2.00	20.00	125	—
1933(m) Proof	—	Value: 15,000				
1934(m)	5,808,000	0.25	2.00	20.00	125	—
1934(m) Proof	100	Value: 11,000				
1935(m)	3,725,000	0.25	2.00	20.00	115	—
1935(m) Proof	100	Value: 7,500				
1936(m)	9,890,000	0.25	1.00	15.00	100	—
1936(m) Proof	—	Value: 12,500				

KM# 36 PENNY

Bronze, 30.5 mm. **Ruler:** George VI **Obv:** Head left **Obv. Legend:** GEORGIVS VI D:G:BR: OMN: REX F.D: IND: IMP **Obv. Designer:** T. H. Paget **Rev:** Kangaroo leaping left **Rev. Designer:** George Kruger Gray **Edge:** Plain

Date	Mintage	F	VF	XF	Unc	BU
1938(m)	5,552,000	0.25	1.00	12.00	45.00	—
1938(m) Proof	250	Value: 7,500				
1939(m)	6,240,000	0.25	1.00	12.00	50.00	—
1939(m) Proof	—	Value: 11,500				
1940(m)	4,075,000	0.50	2.00	20.00	100	—
1940(p) K.G.	1,114,000	1.50	5.00	50.00	475	—
1941(m)	1,588,000	0.30	2.00	15.00	80.00	—
1941(p) K.G.	12,794,000	0.75	2.00	40.00	180	—
1941(p) Proof	—	Value: 10,000				
1941(p)	Inc. above	0.25	2.00	15.00	70.00	—
1941(p) K.G. high dot after Y	Inc. above	0.50	2.00	70.00	90.00	—
1942(p)	12,245,000	0.15	1.50	10.00	35.00	—
1942(p) Proof	—	Value: 8,500				
1942(b) I	9,000,000	0.15	0.50	8.00	35.00	—
1942(b) Without I	Inc. above	3.00	6.00	40.00	200	—
1942(b) Proof	—	Value: 8,000				
1943(m)	11,112,000	0.20	0.50	10.00	40.00	—
1943(p)	33,086,000	0.15	0.50	10.00	40.00	—
1943(p) Proof	—	Value: 10,000				
1943(b) I	9,000,000	0.20	0.50	8.00	40.00	—
Note: Small and large denticle varieties exist.						
1943(b) I Without I	Inc. above	1.75	3.75	20.00	110	—
1943(b) Proof	—	Value: 11,500				
1944(m)	2,112,000	0.50	3.75	25.00	145	—
1944(p)	27,830,000	0.15	0.50	7.00	45.00	—
1944(p) Proof	—	Value: 9,000				
1945(p)	15,173,000	0.20	0.75	8.00	60.00	—
Note: With and without a large dot after the KG.						
1945(p) Proof	—	Value: 9,000				
1945(b) I Rare	6	—	—	—	—	—
1945(m) Rare	—	—	—	—	—	—
Note: Considered by many to be a pattern						
1946(m)	240,000	42.50	75.00	265	1,500	—
1947(m)	6,864,000	0.15	0.40	4.50	25.00	—
1947(p)	4,490,000	0.50	2.00	40.00	275	—
1947(p) Proof	—	Value: 8,750				
1948(m)	26,616,000	0.15	0.40	3.50	20.00	—
1948(p)	1,534,000	0.75	4.00	60.00	450	—
1948(p) Proof	—	Value: 11,500				

KM# 43 PENNY

Bronze, 30.5 mm. **Ruler:** George VI **Obv:** Head left **Obv. Legend:** IND: IMP. dropped **Obv. Designer:** T. H. Paget **Rev:** Kangaroo leaping left **Rev. Designer:** George Kruger Gray **Edge:** Plain

Date	Mintage	F	VF	XF	Unc	BU
1949(m)	27,065,000	0.15	0.25	2.00	16.00	—
1949(m) Proof	—	Value: 10,000				
1950(m)	36,359,000	0.15	0.25	2.50	18.00	—
1950(m) Proof	—	Value: 9,500				
1950(p)	21,488,000	0.20	1.00	12.50	60.00	—
1950(p) Proof	—	Value: 9,500				
1951(m)	21,240,000	0.15	0.20	1.00	15.00	—
1951(p)	12,888,000	0.20	1.00	9.00	45.00	—
1951(p) Proof	—	Value: 9,500				
1951PL	18,000,000	0.15	0.25	0.85	10.00	—
1951PL Proof	—	Value: 9,000				
1952(m)	12,408,000	0.15	0.30	1.00	12.00	—
1952(m) Proof	—	Value: 8,000				
1952(p)	45,514,000	0.15	0.30	1.00	10.00	—
Note: Two varieties of the 2 in the date.						
1952(p) Proof	—	Value: 8,000				

KM# 50 PENNY

Bronze, 30.5 mm. **Ruler:** Elizabeth II **Obv:** Laureate bust, right **Obv. Legend:** DEI • GRATIA • REGINA + ELIZABETH • II • **Obv. Designer:** Mary Gillick **Rev:** Kangaroo leaping left **Rev. Designer:** George Kruger Gray **Edge:** Plain

Date	Mintage	F	VF	XF	Unc	BU
1953(m)	6,936,000	0.20	0.50	2.00	20.00	—
Note: Two varieties to the numeral 5.						
1953(m) Proof	—	Value: 7,500				
1953(p)	6,203,000	0.20	0.65	2.50	20.00	—
1953(p) Proof	16	Value: 7,500				

KM# 56 PENNY

Bronze, 30.5 mm. **Ruler:** Elizabeth II **Obv:** Laureate bust right **Obv. Legend:** F:D: added **Obv. Designer:** Mary Gillick **Rev:** Kangaroo leaping left **Rev. Designer:** George Kruger Gray **Edge:** Plain

Date	Mintage	F	VF	XF	Unc	BU
1955(m)	6,336,000	0.50	1.00	2.50	15.00	20.00
1955(m) Proof	1,200	Value: 400				
1955(p)	11,110,000	0.10	0.20	0.85	10.00	25.00
1955(p) Proof	301	Value: 3,000				
1956(m)	13,872,000	0.10	0.20	0.85	8.00	17.50
1956(m) Proof	1,500	Value: 400				
1956(p)	12,121,000	0.10	0.20	0.85	8.00	18.50
1956(p) Proof	417	Value: 2,800				
1957(p)	15,978,000	0.10	0.20	0.85	5.00	10.00
1957(p) Proof	1,112	Value: 400				
1958(m)	10,012,000	0.10	0.20	0.85	5.00	10.00
1958(m) Proof	1,506	Value: 400				
1958(p)	14,428,000	0.10	0.20	0.85	6.00	12.50
1958(p) Proof	1,028	Value: 500				
1959(m)	1,617,000	0.50	1.25	8.50	50.00	90.00
1959(m) Proof	1,506	Value: 500				
1959(p)	14,428,000	0.10	0.20	0.85	5.00	10.00
1959(p) Proof	1,030	Value: 500				
1960(p)	20,515,000	0.10	0.20	0.85	2.50	3.50
1960(p) Proof	1,030	Value: 500				
1961(p)	30,607,000	0.10	0.20	0.40	1.25	2.50
1961(p) Proof	1,040	Value: 500				
1962(p)	34,851,000	0.10	0.20	0.40	1.25	2.50
1962(p) Proof	1,064	Value: 500				
1963(p)	10,258,000	0.10	0.20	0.40	1.25	2.50
1963(p) Proof	1,100	Value: 550				
1964(m)	49,130,000	0.10	0.20	0.50	1.25	1.75
1964(p)	54,590,000	0.10	0.20	0.50	1.25	1.75
1964(p) Proof; 1 known	—	Value: 10,000				

KM# 18 THREEPENCE

1.4100 g., 0.9250 Silver .0419 oz. ASW, 16 mm. **Ruler:** Edward VII **Obv:** Bust right **Obv. Designer:** G. W. de Saulles **Rev:** Arms **Rev. Designer:** W. H. J. Blakemore **Edge:** Plain

Date	Mintage	F	VF	XF	Unc	BU
1910(L)	4,000,000	1.75	5.00	18.50	60.00	—
1910(L) Proof	—	Value: 6,500				

KM# 24 THREEPENCE

1.4100 g. 0.9250 Silver .0419 oz. ASW, 16 mm. **Ruler:** George V **Obv:** Crowned bust left **Obv. Designer:** E. B. MacKennal **Rev:** Arms **Rev. Designer:** W. H. J. Blakemore **Edge:** Plain

Date	Mintage	F	VF	XF	Unc	BU
1911(L)	2,000,000	5.00	15.00	75.00	300	—
1911(L) Proof	—	Value: 12,000				
1911(L) Proof	—	Value: 40,000				
Note: Reeded edge						
1912(L)	2,400,000	10.00	50.00	200	1,250	—
1914(L)	1,600,000	10.00	27.50	200	750	—
1915(L)	800,000	25.00	85.00	300	1,550	—
1916M	1,913,000	5.00	15.00	110	575	—
1916M Proof	25	Value: 7,500				
1917M	3,808,000	1.75	6.00	35.00	200	—
1918M	3,119,000	1.75	6.00	35.00	200	—
1918M Proof	—	Value: 30,000				
1919M	3,201,000	2.50	6.00	40.00	220	—
1919M Proof	—	Value: 11,500				
1920M	4,196,000	7.50	25.00	100	675	—
1920M Proof	—	Value: 12,000				
1921M	7,378,000	1.75	4.25	35.00	145	—
1921(m)	Inc. above	8.00	35.00	150	725	—
1921M Proof	—	Value: 12,500				
1922/1(m)	900	10,000	22,500	—	—	—
1922(m)	5,531,000	1.75	7.50	50.00	250	—
1922(m) Proof	—	Value: 11,500				
1923(m)	815,000	20.00	65.00	225	1,250	—
1924(m & sy)	2,013,999	5.50	20.00	90.00	550	—
1924(m) Proof	—	Value: 8,500				
1925(m & sy) Proof	4,347,000	0.65	5.00	45.00	200	—
1925(m) Proof	—	Value: 10,000				
1926(m & sy)	6,158,000	0.65	3.00	27.50	150	—
1926(m) Proof	—	Value: 9,500				
1927(m)	6,720,000	0.65	3.00	27.50	150	—
1927(m) Proof	50	Value: 9,500				
1928(m)	5,000,000	0.75	3.50	30.00	175	—
1928(m) Proof	—	Value: 9,500				
1934(m) Proof	100	Value: 4,500				
1934/3(m)	1,616,000	25.00	85.00	250	1,150	—
1934(m)	Inc. above	0.65	2.00	25.00	145	—
1935(m) Proof	—	Value: 3,500				
1935(m)	2,800,000	0.65	2.00	22.50	150	—
1936(m) Proof	—	Value: 4,000				
1936(m)	3,600,000	0.50	1.25	15.00	75.00	—

KM# 37 THREEPENCE

1.4100 g., 0.9250 Silver .0419 oz. ASW, 16 mm. **Ruler:** George VI **Obv:** Head left **Obv. Designer:** T. H. Paget **Rev:** Three wheat stalks divide date **Rev. Designer:** George Kruger Gray

Date	Mintage	F	VF	XF	Unc	BU
1938(m)	4,560,000	0.50	1.25	6.50	27.50	—
1938(m) Proof	250	Value: 4,000				
1939(m)	3,856,000	0.50	1.50	9.50	50.00	—
1939(m) Proof	—	—	—	—	—	—
1940(m)	3,840,000	0.50	1.50	9.50	55.00	—
1941(m)	7,584,000	0.50	1.00	6.00	30.00	—
1942(m)	528,000	12.50	35.00	225	1,250	—
1942D	16,000,000	BV	0.55	1.00	11.50	—
1942S	8,000,000	BV	0.65	1.25	11.50	—
1943(m)	24,912,000	BV	0.55	0.85	11.50	—
1943D	16,000,000	BV	0.55	1.00	13.50	—
1943S	8,000,000	BV	0.65	1.25	14.50	—
1944S	32,000,000	BV	0.55	0.85	5.50	—
Note: Two varieties to the "S" mintmark.						

KM# 37a THREEPENCE

1.4100 g., 0.5000 Silver .0226 oz. ASW, 16 mm. **Ruler:** George VI **Obv:** Head left **Obv. Designer:** T. H. Paget **Rev:** 3 wheat stalks divide date **Rev. Designer:** George Kruger Gray

Date	Mintage	F	VF	XF	Unc	BU
1947(m)	4,176,000	0.85	2.00	9.50	55.00	—
1948(m)	26,208,000	—	BV	1.75	6.00	10.00

KM# 44 THREEPENCE

1.4100 g., 0.5000 Silver .0226 oz. ASW, 16 mm. **Ruler:** George VI **Obv:** Head left **Obv. Legend:** IND: IMP. dropped **Obv. Designer:** T. H. Paget **Rev:** Three wheat stalks divide date **Rev. Designer:** George Kruger Gray

Date	Mintage	F	VF	XF	Unc	BU
1949(m)	26,400,000	—	BV	1.75	3.00	—
1949(m) Proof	—	—	—	—	—	—
1950(m)	35,456,000	—	BV	1.75	7.00	12.00
1951(m)	15,856,000	—	0.50	2.50	12.00	25.00
1951PL	40,000,000	—	BV	1.00	4.00	6.50
1951PL Proof	—	Value: 8,000				
1952(m)	21,560,000	—	BV	1.25	8.00	15.00

KM# 51 THREEPENCE

1.4100 g., 0.5000 Silver .0226 oz. ASW, 16 mm. **Ruler:** Elizabeth II **Obv:** Laureate bust, right **Obv. Designer:** Mary Gillick **Rev:** Three wheat stalks divide date **Rev. Designer:** George Kruger Gray **Edge:** Plain

Date	Mintage	F	VF	XF	Unc	BU
1953(m)	7,664,000	BV	1.75	4.00	20.00	—
1953(m) Proof	—	Value: 8,000				
1954(m)	2,672,000	0.85	2.50	4.50	30.00	—
1954(m) Proof	—	Value: 8,000				

KM# 57 THREEPENCE

1.4100 g., 0.5000 Silver .0226 oz. ASW, 16 mm. **Ruler:** Elizabeth II **Obv:** Laureate bust right **Obv. Legend:** F:D: added **Obv. Designer:** Mary Gillick **Rev:** Three wheat stalks divide date **Rev. Designer:** George Kruger Gray **Edge:** Plain

Date	Mintage	F	VF	XF	Unc	BU
1955(m)	27,088,000	—	BV	1.25	6.00	—
1955(m) Proof	1,040	Value: 225				
1956(m)	14,088,000	—	BV	1.25	6.00	—
1956(m) Proof	1,500	Value: 65.00				
1957(m)	26,704,000	—	BV	0.85	3.00	—
1957(m) Proof	1,256	Value: 65.00				
1958(m)	11,248,000	—	BV	1.75	6.50	—
1958(m) Proof	1,506	Value: 65.00				
1959(m)	19,888,000	—	BV	0.85	3.00	—
1959(m) Proof	1,506	Value: 65.00				
1960(m)	19,600,000	—	BV	0.60	1.50	—
1960(m) Proof	1,509	Value: 65.00				
1961(m)	33,840,000	—	BV	0.60	1.50	—
1961(m) Proof	1,506	Value: 65.00				
1962(m)	15,968,000	—	BV	0.60	1.50	—
1962(m) Proof	2,016	Value: 60.00				
1963(m)	44,016,000	—	BV	0.50	1.50	—
1963(m) Proof	5,042	Value: 50.00				
1964(m)	20,320,000	—	BV	0.50	1.75	—

KM# 19 SIXPENCE

2.8200 g., 0.9250 Silver .0838 oz. ASW, 19.5 mm. **Ruler:** Edward VII **Obv:** Crowned bust right **Obv. Designer:** G. W. de Salles **Rev:** Arms **Rev. Designer:** W. H. J. Blakemore **Edge:** Reeded

Date	Mintage	F	VF	XF	Unc	BU
1910(L)	3,046,000	5.00	16.50	60.00	200	325
1910(L) Proof	—	Value: 10,000				

KM# 25 SIXPENCE

2.8200 g., 0.9250 Silver .0838 oz. ASW, 19.5 mm. **Ruler:** George V **Obv:** Crowned bust left **Obv. Designer:** E. B. MacKennal **Rev:** Arms **Rev. Designer:** W. H. J. Blakemore **Edge:** Reeded

Date	Mintage	F	VF	XF	Unc	BU
1911(L)	1,000,000	7.00	24.00	125	875	2,250
1911(L) Proof	—	Value: 17,500				
1912(L)	1,600,000	30.00	85.00	450	1,500	3,200
1914(L)	1,800,000	5.50	20.00	125	750	1,750
1916M	1,769,000	20.00	70.00	225	1,200	2,500
1916M Proof	25	Value: 12,000				
1917M	1,632,000	15.00	55.00	185	875	1,750
1917M Proof	—	Value: 16,500				
1918M	915,000	40.00	150	400	2,250	4,750
1918M Proof	—	Value: 50,000				
1919M	1,521,000	12.00	35.00	120	850	1,400
1919M Proof	—	Value: 17,500				
1920M	1,476,000	15.00	60.00	185	1,150	2,500
1920M Proof	—	Value: 17,500				
1921(m) Proof	—	Value: 16,500				
1921(m & sy)	3,795,000	7.00	16.80	150	400	1,250
1922(sy)	1,488,000	20.00	95.00	400	2,000	2,750
1922(sy) Proof	—	Value: 28,500				
1923(m & sy)	1,458,000	10.00	37.50	250	1,000	1,850
1924(m) Proof	—	Value: 15,000				
1924(m & sy)	1,038,000	15.00	65.00	250	1,500	2,500
1925(m) Proof	—	Value: 13,500				
1925(m & sy)	3,266,000	2.00	25.00	85.00	375	1,000
1926(m) Proof	—	Value: 14,500				
1926(m & sy)	3,609,000	2.00	7.00	27.50	165	325
1927(m)	3,592,000	2.00	6.00	20.00	150	325
1927(m) Proof	50	Value: 14,500				
1928(m)	2,721,000	2.00	6.00	20.00	175	400
1928(m) Proof	—	Value: 14,500				
1934(m)	1,024,000	2.50	7.00	35.00	350	1,100
1934(m) Proof	100	Value: 6,000				
1935(m)	392,000	5.00	12.00	100	950	1,400
1935(m) Proof	—	Value: 13,500				
1936(m)	1,800,000	1.50	3.00	10.00	125	275
1936(m) Proof	—	Value: 12,500				

KM# 38 SIXPENCE

2.8200 g., 0.9250 Silver .0838 oz. ASW, 19.5 mm. **Ruler:** George VI **Obv:** Head left **Obv. Designer:** T. H. Paget **Rev:** Arms **Rev. Designer:** W. H. J. Blakemore **Edge:** Reeded

Date	Mintage	F	VF	XF	Unc	BU
1938(m)	2,864,000	1.25	2.25	7.00	40.00	—
1938(m) Proof	250	Value: 4,700				
1939(m)	1,600,000	1.25	2.50	13.50	150	—
1939(m) Proof	—	—	—	—	—	—
1940(m)	1,600,000	1.25	2.50	10.00	75.00	—
1941(m)	2,912,000	1.25	2.25	5.50	45.00	—
1942(m)	8,968,000	—	BV	4.00	32.00	—
1942D	12,000,000	—	BV	2.25	14.00	—
1942S	4,000,000	—	BV	2.25	20.00	—
1943D	8,000,000	—	BV	3.50	12.50	—
1943S	4,000,000	—	BV	2.25	20.00	—
1944S	4,000,000	—	BV	2.50	15.00	—
1945(m)	10,096,000	—	BV	2.50	14.00	—

KM# 38a SIXPENCE

2.8200 g., 0.5000 Silver .0453 oz. ASW **Ruler:** George VI **Obv:** Head left **Obv. Designer:** T. H. Paget **Rev:** Arms **Rev. Designer:** W. H. J. Blakemore **Edge:** Reeded

Date	Mintage	F	VF	XF	Unc	BU
1946(m)	10,024,000	—	BV	4.00	25.00	—
1946(m) Proof	—	Value: 9,500				
1948(m)	1,584,000	—	BV	4.00	35.00	—

KM# 45 SIXPENCE

2.8200 g., 0.5000 Silver .0453 oz. ASW, 19.5 mm. **Ruler:** George VI **Obv:** Head left **Obv. Legend:** IND: IMP. dropped **Obv. Designer:** T. H. Paget **Rev:** Arms **Rev. Designer:** W. H. J. Blakemore **Edge:** Plain

Date	Mintage	F	VF	XF	Unc	BU
1950(m)	10,272,000	BV	2.50	4.00	35.00	—
1950(m) Proof	—	Value: 8,000				
1951(m)	13,760,000	BV	1.75	3.00	22.50	—
1951PL	20,024,000	—	BV	2.00	8.50	—
1951PL Proof	—	Value: 8,500				
1952(m)	2,112,000	2.00	5.00	30.00	200	—

KM# 52 SIXPENCE

2.8200 g., 0.5000 Silver .0453 oz. ASW, 19.5 mm. **Ruler:** Elizabeth II **Obv:** Laureate bust right **Obv. Designer:** Mary Gillick **Rev:** Arms **Rev. Designer:** W. H. J. Blakemore **Edge:** Reeded

Date	Mintage	F	VF	XF	Unc	BU
1953(m)	1,152,000	2.00	5.00	20.00	150	—
1953(m) Proof	—	Value: 7,000				
1954(m)	7,672,000	—	BV	1.75	5.00	—
1954(m) Proof	—	Value: 7,500				

KM# 58 SIXPENCE

2.8200 g., 0.5000 Silver .0453 oz. ASW, 19.5 mm. **Ruler:** Elizabeth II **Obv:** Laureate bust right **Obv. Legend:** F:D: added **Obv. Designer:** Mary Gillick **Rev:** Arms **Rev. Designer:** W. H. J. Blakemore **Edge:** Reeded

Date	Mintage	F	VF	XF	Unc	BU
1955(m)	14,248,000	—	BV	2.00	12.50	—
1955(m) Proof	1,200	Value: 150				
1956(m)	7,904,000	—	2.50	5.00	28.00	—
1956(m) Proof	1,500	Value: 90.00				
1957(m)	13,752,000	—	BV	1.25	4.00	—
1957(m) Proof	1,256	Value: 100				
1958(m)	17,944,000	—	BV	1.25	4.00	—
1958(m) Proof	1,506	Value: 95.00				
1959(m)	11,728,000	—	BV	1.25	6.00	—
1959(m) Proof	1,506	Value: 85.00				
1960(m)	18,592,000	—	BV	1.25	5.00	—
1960(m) Proof	1,509	Value: 85.00				
1961(m)	9,152,000	—	BV	1.25	3.00	—
1961(m) Proof	1,506	Value: 85.00				
1962(m)	44,816,000	—	BV	1.25	2.00	—
1962(m) Proof	2,016	Value: 75.00				
1963(m)	25,056,000	—	BV	1.25	2.00	—
1963(m) Proof	5,042	Value: 65.00				

KM# 20 SHILLING

5.6500 g., 0.9250 Silver .1680 oz. ASW, 23.5 mm. **Ruler:** Edward VII **Obv:** Crowned bust right **Obv. Designer:** G. W. de Saulles **Rev:** Arms **Rev. Designer:** W. H. J. Blakemore **Edge:** Reeded

Date	Mintage	F	VF	XF	Unc	BU
1910(L)	2,536,000	5.00	25.00	75.00	250	—
1910(L) Proof	—	Value: 18,500				

KM# 26 SHILLING

5.6500 g., 0.9250 Silver .1680 oz. ASW, 23.5 mm. **Ruler:** George V **Obv:** Crowned bust left **Obv. Designer:** E. B. MacKennal **Rev:** Arms **Rev. Designer:** W. H. J. Blakemore **Edge:** Reeded

Date	Mintage	F	VF	XF	Unc	BU
1911(L)	1,700,000	12.00	27.50	200	1,200	2,000
1911(L) Proof	—	Value: 35,000				
1912(L)	1,000,000	20.00	60.00	250	3,500	—
1913(L)	1,200,000	16.00	45.00	200	3,000	—
1914(L)	3,300,000	6.50	17.50	95.00	850	1,500
1915(L)	800,000	30.00	100	600	3,500	—
1915H Proof	—	Value: 50,000				
1915H	500,000	55.00	175	900	6,500	—
1916M	5,141,000	3.00	12.00	45.00	250	—
1916M Proof	25	Value: 13,500				
1917M	5,274,000	3.00	12.00	45.00	250	—
1918M	3,761,000	4.00	15.00	65.00	350	—
1919M Proof	—	—	—	—	—	—
1920M	520,000	7.50	50.00	225	1,500	—
1920M Proof	—	Value: 45,000				
Note: Considered by many to be a pattern						
1921(sy) Star	1,641,000	20.00	115	550	3,500	—
1921(m) Star; Proof	—	Value: 35,000				
1922(m)	2,040,000	7.50	20.00	125	650	—
1922(m) Proof	—	Value: 15,000				
1924(m & sy)	674,000	16.00	75.00	245	1,750	—
1924(m) Proof	—	Value: 25,000				
1925/3(m & sy)	1,448,000	2.50	10.00	70.00	375	—
1925(m) Proof	—	Value: 20,000				
1926(m & sy)	2,352,000	2.50	10.00	85.00	425	—
1926(m) Proof	—	Value: 18,500				
1927(m)	1,146,000	3.00	10.00	55.00	325	—
1927(m) Proof	50	Value: 18,500				
1928(m)	664,000	15.00	40.00	225	1,500	—
1928(m) Proof	—	Value: 20,000				
1931(m)	1,000,000	3.00	10.00	55.00	325	—
1931(m) Proof	—	Value: 18,000				
1933(m)	220,000	80.00	200	250	4,000	—
1933(m) Proof	—	Value: 40,000				
1934(m)	480,000	7.50	20.00	90.00	500	—
1934(m) Proof	100	Value: 7,000				
1935(m)	500,000	3.00	8.00	40.00	275	—
1935(m) Proof	—	Value: 8,000				
1936(m)	2,000,000	2.00	6.00	30.00	265	—
1936(m) Proof	—	Value: 15,000				

KM# 39 SHILLING

5.6500 g., 0.9250 Silver .1680 oz. ASW, 23.5 mm. **Ruler:** George VI **Obv:** Head left **Obv. Designer:** T. H. Paget **Rev:** Rams head left above value and date **Rev. Designer:** George Kruger Gray **Edge:** Reeded

Date	Mintage	F	VF	XF	Unc	BU
1938(m)	1,484,000	2.50	4.00	10.00	60.00	—
1938(m) Proof	250	Value: 4,500				
1939(m)	1,520,000	2.25	4.50	18.00	120	—
1939(m) Proof	—	Value: 15,000				
1940(m)	760,000	4.00	11.50	40.00	250	—
1941(m)	3,040,000	BV	3.75	7.00	50.00	—
1942(m)	1,380,000	BV	3.00	7.00	45.00	—
1942S	4,000,000	BV	2.50	4.00	25.00	—
1943(m)	2,720,000	2.50	5.00	15.00	90.00	—
1943S	16,000,000	BV	2.50	3.50	15.00	—
1944(m)	14,576,000	BV	2.75	7.00	55.00	—
1944S	8,000,000	BV	2.50	3.50	15.00	—

KM# 39a SHILLING

5.6500 g., 0.5000 Silver .0908 oz. ASW, 23.5 mm. **Ruler:** George VI **Obv:** Head left **Obv. Designer:** T. H. Paget **Rev:** Ram's head left above value **Rev. Designer:** George Kruger-Grey **Edge:** Reeded

Date	Mintage	F	VF	XF	Unc	BU
1946(m)	10,072,000	BV	2.75	5.00	25.00	—
1946(p)	1,316,000	3.00	9.00	30.00	150	—
1948(m)	4,131,999	BV	3.00	6.00	28.00	—

KM# 46 SHILLING

5.6500 g., 0.5000 Silver .0908 oz. ASW, 23.5 mm. **Ruler:** George VI **Obv:** Head left **Obv. Legend:** IND: IMP. dropped **Obv. Designer:** T. H. Paget **Rev:** Ram's head left above value, date **Rev. Designer:** George Kruger Gray **Edge:** Reeded

Date	Mintage	F	VF	XF	Unc	BU
1950(m)	7,188,000	BV	2.75	4.50	22.50	—
1952(m)	19,644,000	BV	2.50	3.50	15.00	—

KM# 53 SHILLING

5.5600 g., 0.5000 Silver .0908 oz. ASW, 23.5 mm. **Ruler:** Elizabeth II **Obv:** Laureate bust right **Obv. Designer:** Mary Gillick **Rev:** Ram's head left above value, date **Rev. Designer:** George Kruger Gray **Edge:** Reeded

Date	Mintage	F	VF	XF	Unc	BU
1953(m)	12,204,000	BV	2.00	4.00	14.50	—
1953(m) Proof	—	Value: 6,000				

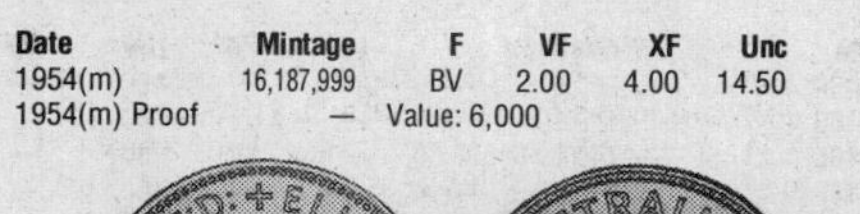

Date	Mintage	F	VF	XF	Unc	BU
1954(m)	16,187,999	BV	2.00	4.00	14.50	—
1954(m) Proof	—	Value: 6,000				

KM# 59 SHILLING

5.5600 g., 0.5000 Silver .0908 oz. ASW, 23.5 mm. **Ruler:** Elizabeth II **Obv:** Laureate bust right **Obv. Legend:** F:D: added **Obv. Designer:** Mary Gillick **Rev:** Ram's head left above value, date **Rev. Designer:** George Kruger Gray **Edge:** Reeded

Date	Mintage	F	VF	XF	Unc	BU
1955(m)	7,492,000	BV	1.75	3.50	25.00	—
1955(m) Proof	1,200	Value: 125				
1956(m)	6,064,000	BV	1.50	4.50	40.00	—
1956(m) Proof	1,500	Value: 115				
1957(m)	12,668,000	—	BV	1.50	6.00	—
1957(m) Proof	1,256	Value: 140				
1958(m)	7,412,000	—	BV	1.50	6.00	—
1958(m) Proof	1,506	Value: 115				
1959(m)	10,876,000	—	BV	1.00	5.00	—
1959(m) Proof	1,506	Value: 100				
1960(m)	14,512,000	—	—	BV	3.00	—
1960(m) Proof	1,509	Value: 100				
1961(m)	31,864,000	—	—	BV	2.25	—
1961(m) Proof	1,506	Value: 100				
1962(m)	6,592,000	—	—	BV	2.25	—
1962(m) Proof	2,016	Value: 100				
1963(m)	10,072,000	—	—	BV	2.25	—
1963(m) Proof	5,042	Value: 90.00				

KM# 21 FLORIN

11.3100 g., 0.9250 Silver .3363 oz. ASW, 28.5 mm. **Ruler:** Edward VII **Obv:** Crowned bust right **Obv. Designer:** G. W. de Saulles **Rev:** Arms **Rev. Designer:** W. H. J. Blakemore **Edge:** Reeded

Date	Mintage	F	VF	XF	Unc	BU
1910(L)	1,259,000	25.00	145	350	1,450	—
1910(L) Proof	—	Value: 75,000				

KM# 27 FLORIN

11.3100 g., 0.9250 Silver .3363 oz. ASW, 28.5 mm. **Ruler:** George V **Obv:** Crowned bust left **Obv. Designer:** E. B. MacKennal **Rev:** Arms **Rev. Designer:** W. H. J. Blakemore **Edge:** Reeded

Date	Mintage	F	VF	XF	Unc	BU
1911(L)	950,000	40.00	250	1,250	5,000	—
1911(L) Proof	—	Value: 85,000				
1912(L)	1,000,000	30.00	300	1,500	6,000	—
1913(L)	1,200,000	20.00	135	685	4,000	—
1913(L) Proof	—	Value: 65,000				
1914(L)	2,300,000	10.00	35.00	350	2,000	—
1914H	500,000	50.00	200	850	5,000	—
1914H Proof	—	Value: 85,000				
1915(L)	500,000	50.00	210	950	7,500	15,000
1915H	750,000	30.00	125	800	7,000	—
1915H Proof	—	Value: 80,000				
1916M	2,752,000	7.50	30.00	650	2,000	—
1916M Proof	25	Value: 35,000				
1917M	4,305,000	7.50	28.00	650	1,500	—
1917M Proof	—	Value: 35,000				
1918M	2,095,000	10.00	30.00	125	1,650	—
1918M Proof	—	Value: 35,000				
1919M	1,677,000	20.00	120	750	2,500	—
1919M Proof	—	Value: 75,000				
1920M Star; Proof	—	Value: 95,000				
1921(m)	1,247,000	20.00	120	750	4,000	6,500
1921(m) Proof	—	Value: 80,000				
1922(m)	2,057,999	18.00	90.00	550	2,250	5,000
1922(m) Proof	—	Value: 70,000				
1923(m)	1,038,000	12.50	75.00	350	2,800	3,750
1924(m) Proof	—	Value: 35,000				
1924(m & sy)	1,582,000	8.50	60.00	325	2,000	3,250
1925(m & sy)	2,960,000	7.50	25.00	200	1,500	2,750
1925(m) Proof	—	Value: 25,000				
1926(m & sy)	2,487,000	7.50	25.00	300	1,600	4,000
1926(m) Proof	—	Value: 25,000				
1927(m)	3,420,000	6.00	15.00	70.00	425	—
1927(m) Proof	50	Value: 25,000				
1928(m)	1,962,000	7.00	15.00	80.00	550	—
1928(m) Proof	—	Value: 30,000				
1931(m)	3,129,000	4.75	10.00	37.50	165	—
1931(m) Proof	—	Value: 25,000				
1932(m)	188,000	100	350	1,100	6,750	—
1933(m)	488,000	25.00	300	850	4,250	—
1934(m)	1,674,000	4.75	12.50	55.00	350	—
1934(m) Proof	100	Value: 20,000				
1935(m)	915,000	4.75	10.00	65.00	425	—
1935(m) Proof	—	Value: 30,000				
1936(m)	2,382,000	BV	5.00	17.50	180	—
1936(m) Proof	—	Value: 25,000				

KM# 31 FLORIN

11.3100 g., 0.9250 Silver .3363 oz. ASW, 28.5 mm. **Ruler:** George V **Subject:** Opening of Parliament House, Canberra **Obv:** Crowned head left **Rev. Designer:** George Kruger Gray **Edge:** Reeded

Date	Mintage	F	VF	XF	Unc	BU
1927(m)	2,000,000	BV	6.50	22.50	120	200
1927(m) Proof	400	Value: 15,000				

KM# 33 FLORIN

11.3100 g., 0.9250 Silver .3363 oz. ASW, 28.5 mm. **Ruler:** George V **Subject:** Centennial of Victoria and Melbourne **Obv:** Crowned bust left **Rev:** Horse prancing left with rider holding torch **Rev. Designer:** George Kruger Gray

Date	Mintage	F	VF	XF	Unc	BU
ND(1934)	Est. 54,000	70.00	95.00	165	320	625

Note: 21,000 pieces were melted

Date	Mintage	F	VF	XF	Unc	BU
ND(1934) Proof	—	Value: 16,500				

KM# 40 FLORIN

11.3100 g., 0.9250 Silver .3363 oz. ASW, 28.5 mm. **Ruler:** George VI **Obv:** Head left **Obv. Designer:** T. H. Paget **Rev:** Arms **Rev. Designer:** George Kruger Gray **Edge:** Reeded

Date	Mintage	F	VF	XF	Unc	BU
1938(m)	2,990,000	BV	4.50	15.00	45.00	—
1938(m) Proof	—	Value: 6,500				
1939(m)	630,000	10.00	35.00	125	600	—
1939(m) Proof	—	Value: 8,500				
1940(m)	3,410,000	—	BV	8.50	35.00	—
1941(m)	7,614,000	—	BV	7.50	30.00	—
1942(m)	17,986,000	—	BV	5.00	25.00	—
1942S	6,000,000	—	BV	5.00	20.00	—
1943(m)	12,762,000	—	BV	5.00	18.00	—
1943S	11,000,000	—	BV	5.00	18.00	—
1944(m)	22,440,000	—	BV	5.00	18.00	—
1944S	11,000,000	—	BV	5.00	18.00	—
1945(m)	11,970,000	—	BV	12.00	45.00	—

KM# 40a FLORIN

11.3100 g., 0.5000 Silver .1818 oz. ASW, 28.5 mm. **Ruler:** George VI **Obv:** Head left **Obv. Designer:** T. H. Paget **Rev:** Arms **Rev. Designer:** George Kruger-Grey

Date	Mintage	F	VF	XF	Unc	BU
1946(m)	22,154,000	—	BV	3.50	18.50	—
1946(m) Proof	—	Value: 13,000				
1947(m)	39,2[illegible]2,000	—	BV	3.50	18.50	—
1947(m) Proof	—	Value: 13,000				

KM# 47 FLORIN

11.3100 g., 0.5000 Silver .1818 oz. ASW, 28.5 mm. **Ruler:** George VI **Subject:** 50th Year Jubilee **Obv:** Head left **Obv. Designer:** T. H. Paget **Rev:** Crowned crossed scepter and sword divide Jubilee dates **Rev. Designer:** Leslie Bowles **Edge:** Reeded

Date	Mintage	F	VF	XF	Unc	BU
1951(m)	2,000,000	—	BV	4.00	15.00	25.00

KM# 47a FLORIN

Copper-Nickel, 28.5 mm. **Ruler:** George VI **Subject:** 50th Year - Jubilee **Obv:** Head left **Obv. Designer:** T. H. Paget **Rev:** Crowned crossed scepter and sword divide Jubilee dates **Rev. Designer:** Leslie Bowles **Edge:** Reeded

Date	Mintage	F	VF	XF	Unc	BU
1951(L) Proof	—	Value: 15,000				

Note: Thought by many to be a trial strike or pattern

KM# 48 FLORIN

11.3100 g., 0.5000 Silver .1818 oz. ASW, 28.5 mm. **Ruler:** George VI **Obv:** Head left **Obv. Legend:** IND: IMP. dropped **Obv. Designer:** T. H. Paget **Rev:** Arms **Rev. Designer:** George Kruger Gray **Edge:** Reeded

Date	Mintage	F	VF	XF	Unc	BU
1951(m)	10,068,000	BV	3.50	12.50	45.00	100
1952(m)	10,044,000	BV	3.50	12.50	45.00	100

KM# 54 FLORIN

11.3100 g., 0.5000 Silver .1818 oz. ASW, 28.5 mm. **Ruler:** Elizabeth II **Obv:** Laureate bust right **Obv. Designer:** Mary Gillick **Rev:** Arms **Rev. Designer:** George Kruger Gray **Edge:** Reeded

Date	Mintage	F	VF	XF	Unc	BU
1953(m)	12,658,000	—	BV	3.50	20.00	50.00

Note: Normal and large beads on the reverse.

Date	Mintage	F	VF	XF	Unc	BU
1953(m) Proof	—	Value: 7,500				
1954(m)	15,366,000	—	BV	4.50	25.00	65.00
1954(m) Proof	—	Value: 20,000				

KM# 55 FLORIN

11.3100 g., 0.5000 Silver .1818 oz. ASW, 28.5 mm. **Ruler:** Elizabeth II **Subject:** Royal Visit **Obv:** Laureate bust right **Obv. Designer:** Mary Gillick **Rev:** Lion and kangaroo facing right **Rev. Designer:** Leslie Bowles

Date	Mintage	F	VF	XF	Unc	BU
1954(m)	4,000,000	BV	2.75	4.50	22.50	—
1954(m) Proof	—	Value: 13,500				

KM# 60 FLORIN

11.3100 g., 0.5000 Silver .1818 oz. ASW, 28.5 mm.
Ruler: Elizabeth II **Obv:** Laureate bust right **Obv. Legend:** F:D: added **Obv. Designer:** Mary Gillick **Rev:** Arms **Rev. Designer:** George Kruger Gray **Edge:** Reeded

Date	Mintage	F	VF	XF	Unc	BU
1956(m)	8,090,000	BV	3.50	8.00	55.00	—
1956(m) Proof	1,500	Value: 75.00				
1957(m)	9,278,000	—	BV	2.75	8.00	—
1957(m) Proof	1,256	Value: 100				
1958(m)	8,972,000	—	BV	3.00	7.00	—
1958(m) Proof	1,506	Value: 75.00				
1959(m)	3,500,000	—	BV	3.00	6.00	—
1959(m) Proof	1,506	Value: 100				
1960(m)	15,760,000	—	BV	2.50	5.00	—
1960(m) Proof	1,509	Value: 75.00				
1961(m)	9,452,000	—	BV	2.75	6.00	—
1961(m) Proof	1,506	Value: 65.00				
1962(m)	13,748,000	—	BV	2.50	5.00	—
1962(m) Proof	2,016	Value: 65.00				
1963(m)	12,002,000	—	BV	2.50	5.00	—
1963(m) Proof	5,042	Value: 60.00				

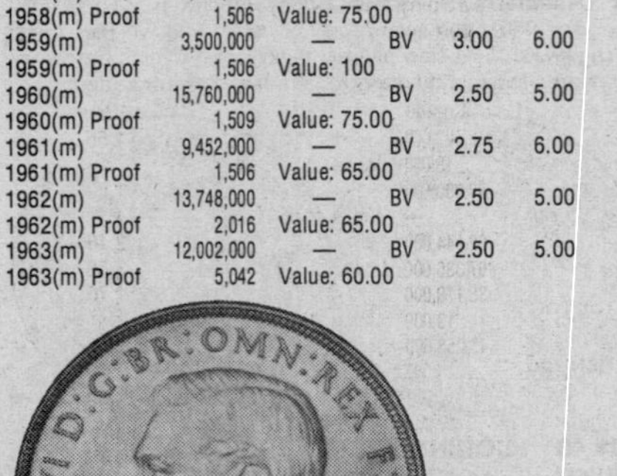

KM# 34 CROWN

28.2800 g., 0.9250 Silver .8411 oz. ASW, 38 mm.
Ruler: George VI **Obv:** Head left **Obv. Designer:** T. H. Paget **Rev:** Crown above date and value **Rev. Designer:** George Kruger Gray **Edge:** Reeded

Date	Mintage	F	VF	XF	Unc	BU
1937(m)	1,008,000	12.50	16.50	22.50	75.00	225
1937(m) Proof	100	Value: 15,000				
1938(m)	102,000	20.00	35.00	90.00	350	950
1938(m) Proof	250	Value: 25,000				

TRADE COINAGE

KM# 14 1/2 SOVEREIGN

3.9940 g., 0.9170 Gold .1177 oz. AGW **Ruler:** Edward VII
Obv: Head right **Obv. Designer:** G.W. DeSaulles **Rev:** St. George slaying dragon

Date	Mintage	F	VF	XF	Unc	BU
1902S	84,000	BV	100	150	500	
1902S Proof	—	Value: 60,000				
1902S Frosted, Proof	—	Value: 55,000				
1903S	231,000	BV	100	150	550	—
1904P	60,000	100	250	750	2,000	—
1906S	308,000	BV	100	125	400	—
1906M	82,000	100	175	400	1,500	—
1907M	400,000	BV	100	125	475	—
1908S	538,000	BV	100	125	450	—
1908M	—	BV	100	125	550	—
1908P	25,000	120	250	700	2,000	—
1909M	186,000	BV	100	125	375	—
1909P	44,000	100	225	425	1,500	—
1910S	474,000	BV	100	125	375	—

KM# 28 1/2 SOVEREIGN

3.9940 g., 0.9170 Gold .1177 oz. AGW **Ruler:** George V
Obv: Head left **Rev:** St. George slaying dragon

Date	Mintage	F	VF	XF	Unc	BU
1911S	252,000	BV	90.00	100	160	—
1911S Matte Proof	—	Value: 47,500				
1911P	130,000	80.00	110	165	300	—
1912S	278,000	BV	90.00	100	150	—
1914S	322,000	BV	90.00	100	150	—
1915P	138,000	BV	90.00	125	250	—
1915S	892,000	BV	80.00	100	150	—
1915M	125,000	BV	90.00	100	160	—
1916S	448,000	BV	85.00	100	150	—
1918P	—	300	500	1,100	2,000	—

Note: Estimated 200-250 pieces minted

KM# 15 SOVEREIGN

7.9881 g., 0.9170 Gold .2354 oz. AGW **Ruler:** Edward VII
Obv: Head right **Obv. Designer:** G.W. DeSaulles **Rev:** St. George on horseback with sword slaying the dragon

Date	Mintage	F	VF	XF	Unc	BU
1902S	2,813,000	—	—	BV	165	—
1902S Proof	—	Value: 50,000				
1902S Frosted proof	—	Value: 60,000				
1902M	4,267,000	—	—	BV	165	—
1902P	4,289,000	—	—	BV	170	—
1903S	2,806,000	—	—	BV	165	—
1903M	3,521,000	—	—	BV	165	—
1903P	4,674,000	—	—	BV	180	—
1904S	2,986,000	—	—	BV	165	—
1904M	3,743,000	—	—	BV	165	—
1904M Proof	—	Value: 50,000				
1904P	4,506,000	—	—	BV	180	—
1905S	2,778,000	—	—	BV	165	—
1905M	3,633,000	—	—	BV	165	—
1905P	4,876,000	—	—	BV	180	—
1906S	2,792,000	—	—	BV	165	—
1906M	3,657,000	—	—	BV	165	—
1906P	4,829,000	—	—	BV	180	—
1907S	2,539,000	—	—	BV	165	—
1907M	3,332,000	—	—	BV	165	—
1907P	4,972,000	—	—	BV	175	—
1908S	2,017,000	—	—	BV	165	—
1908M	3,080,000	—	—	BV	165	—
1908P	4,875,000	—	—	BV	165	—
1909S	2,057,000	—	—	BV	165	—
1909M	3,029,000	—	—	BV	165	—
1909P	4,524,000	—	—	BV	165	—
1910S	2,135,000	—	—	BV	165	—
1910M	3,054,000	—	—	BV	165	—
1910M Proof	—	Value: 50,000				
1910P	4,690,000	—	—	BV	165	—

KM# 29 SOVEREIGN

7.9881 g., 0.9170 Gold .2354 oz. AGW **Ruler:** George V
Obv: Head left **Rev:** St. George on horseback with sword slaying the dragon

Date	Mintage	F	VF	XF	Unc	BU
1911S	2,519,000	—	—	BV	160	—
1911S Proof	—	Value: 50,000				
1911M	2,851,000	—	—	BV	160	—
1911M Proof	—	Value: 50,000				
1911P	4,373,000	—	—	BV	160	—
1912S	2,227,000	—	—	BV	160	—
1912M	2,467,000	—	—	BV	160	—
1912P	4,278,000	—	—	BV	160	—
1913S	2,249,000	—	—	BV	160	—
1913M	2,323,000	—	—	BV	160	—
1913P	4,635,000	—	—	BV	160	—
1914S	1,774,000	—	—	BV	160	—
1914S Proof	—	Value: 47,500				
1914M	2,012,000	—	—	BV	160	—
1914P	4,815,000	—	—	BV	160	—
1915S	1,346,000	—	—	BV	160	—
1915M	1,637,000	—	—	BV	160	—
1915P	4,373,000	—	—	BV	160	—
1916S	1,242,000	—	—	BV	160	—
1916M	1,277,000	—	—	BV	160	—
1916P	4,906,000	—	—	BV	160	—
1917S	1,666,000	—	—	BV	160	—
1917M	934,000	—	—	BV	160	—
1917P	4,110,000	—	—	BV	160	—
1918S	3,716,000	—	—	BV	160	—
1918M	4,969,000	—	—	BV	160	—
1918P	3,812,000	—	—	BV	160	—
1919S	1,835,000	—	—	BV	160	—
1919M	514,000	—	BV	160	200	—
1919P	2,995,000	—	—	BV	160	—
1920S	360,000	20,000	30,000	50,000	120,000	—
1920M	530,000	1,100	1,750	2,500	3,000	—
1920P	2,421,000	—	—	BV	160	—
1921S	839,000	400	850	1,300	2,000	—
1921M	240,000	2,000	4,500	6,000	8,500	—
1921P	2,314,000	—	—	BV	160	—
1922S	578,000	3,000	6,000	9,500	14,000	—
1922S Proof	—	Value: 55,000				
1922M	608,000	1,250	3,000	5,250	7,500	—
1922P	2,298,000	—	—	BV	160	—
1923S	416,000	1,500	3,500	5,500	9,500	—
1923S Proof	—	Value: 50,000				
1923M	510,000	—	—	BV	200	—
1923P	2,124,000	—	—	BV	160	—
1924S	394,000	275	625	900	1,600	—
1924M	278,000	—	BV	160	200	—
1924P	1,464,000	BV	155	175	250	—
1925S	5,632,000	—	—	BV	160	—
1925M	3,311,000	—	—	BV	160	—
1925P	1,837,000	—	BV	160	200	—
1926S	1,030,999	5,000	8,000	12,000	15,000	—
1926S Proof	—	Value: 60,000				
1926M	211,000	—	BV	155	200	—
1926P	1,131,000	400	1,100	1,500	2,000	—
1927M	310,000	—	—	—	—	—

Note: None known.

Date	Mintage	F	VF	XF	Unc	BU
1927P	1,383,000	BV	175	250	400	—
1928M	413,000	800	1,250	1,800	2,250	—
1928P	1,333,000	BV	160	175	225	—

KM# 32 SOVEREIGN

7.9881 g., 0.9170 Gold .2354 oz. AGW **Ruler:** George V
Obv: Head left **Rev:** St. George on horseback with sword slaying the dragon

Date	Mintage	F	VF	XF	Unc	BU
1929M	436,000	600	1,000	1,750	2,750	—
1929M Proof	—	Value: 40,000				
1929P	1,606,000	—	—	BV	185	—
1930M	77,000	BV	160	200	275	—
1930M Proof	—	Value: 40,000				
1930P	1,915,000	—	—	BV	185	—
1931M	57,000	185	250	350	500	—
1931M Proof	—	Value: 45,000				
1931P	1,173,000	—	—	BV	185	—

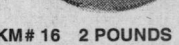

KM# 16 2 POUNDS

15.9761 g., 0.9170 Gold .4707 oz. AGW **Ruler:** Edward VII **Obv:** Head right **Obv. Designer:** G.W. DeSaulles **Rev:** St. George on horseback with sword slaying the dragon **Note:** Gilt lead electrotypes exist.

Date	Mintage	F	VF	XF	Unc	BU
1902S Matte Proof Rare	4	—	—	—	—	—

KM# 17 5 POUNDS
39.9403 g., 0.9170 Gold 1.1771 oz. AGW **Ruler:** Edward VII **Obv:** Head right **Obv. Designer:** G.W. DeSaulles **Rev:** St. George on horseback with sword slaying the dragon **Note:** Gilt lead electrotypes exist.

Date	Mintage	F	VF	XF	Unc	BU
1902S Proof; Rare	Est. 3	—	—	—	—	—
1902S Matte Proof; Rare	Inc. above	—	—	—	—	—

Note: Spink Australia Sale #30 11-89 nearly FDC realized $38,500

DECIMAL COINAGE

KM# 62 CENT
2.6000 g., Bronze, 17.51 mm. **Ruler:** Elizabeth II **Obv:** Young bust right **Obv. Designer:** Arnold Machin **Rev:** Ring-tailed opossum **Rev. Designer:** Stuart Devlin **Edge:** Plain

Date	Mintage	F	VF	XF	Unc	BU
1966(c)	146,457,000	—	—	0.15	0.65	1.50
1966(c) Proof	18,000	Value: 2.50				
1966(m)	238,990,000	—	0.15	0.25	1.25	2.00
Note: Blunted whisker on right						
1966(p)	26,620,000	0.15	0.30	1.25	7.00	12.00
Note: Blunted 2nd whisker from right						
1967	110,055,000	—	0.15	0.25	1.75	3.50
1968	19,930,000	0.15	0.30	1.25	9.00	18.00
1969	87,680,000	—	—	0.15	0.50	0.85
1969 Proof	13,000	Value: 2.50				
1970	72,560,000	—	—	0.15	0.50	0.85
1970 Proof	15,000	Value: 2.50				
1971	102,455,000	—	—	0.15	0.35	0.60
1971 Proof	10,000	Value: 2.50				
1972	82,400,000	—	—	0.10	0.35	0.60
1972 Proof	10,000	Value: 2.50				
1973	140,710,000	—	—	0.10	0.25	0.60
1973 Proof	10,000	Value: 2.50				
1974	131,720,000	—	—	0.10	0.25	0.60
1974 Proof	11,000	Value: 2.50				
1975	134,775,000	—	—	—	0.20	0.60
1975 Proof	23,000	Value: 0.65				
1976	172,935,000	—	—	—	0.20	0.60
1976 Proof	21,000	Value: 1.50				
1977	153,430,000	—	—	—	0.20	0.60
1977 Proof	55,000	Value: 0.65				
1978	97,253,000	—	—	—	0.20	0.60
1978 Proof	39,000	Value: 0.65				
1979	130,339,000	—	—	—	0.20	0.60
1979 Proof	36,000	Value: 0.65				
1980	137,892,000	—	—	—	0.20	0.60
1980 Proof	68,000	Value: 0.65				
1981	223,900,000	—	—	—	0.20	0.60
1981 Proof	86,000	Value: 0.65				
1982	134,290,000	—	—	—	0.20	0.60
1982 Proof	100,000	Value: 0.65				
1983	205,625,000	—	—	—	0.20	0.60
1983 Proof	80,000	Value: 0.65				
1984	74,735,000	—	—	—	0.20	0.60
1984 Proof	61,000	Value: 0.65				

KM# 78 CENT
2.6000 g., Bronze, 17.51 mm. **Ruler:** Elizabeth II **Obv:** Crowned head right **Obv. Designer:** Raphael Maklouf **Rev:** Ring-tailed opossum **Rev. Designer:** Stuart Devlin

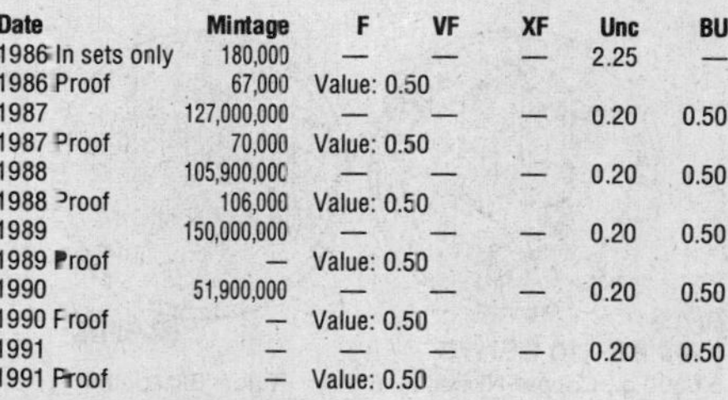

Date	Mintage	F	VF	XF	Unc	BU
1985	38,300,000	—	—	—	0.20	0.50
1985 Proof	75,000	Value: 0.50				
1986 In sets only	180,000	—	—	—	2.25	—
1986 Proof	67,000	Value: 0.50				
1987	127,000,000	—	—	—	0.20	0.50
1987 Proof	70,000	Value: 0.50				
1988	105,900,000	—	—	—	0.20	0.50
1988 Proof	106,000	Value: 0.50				
1989	150,000,000	—	—	—	0.20	0.50
1989 Proof	—	Value: 0.50				
1990	51,900,000	—	—	—	0.20	0.50
1990 Proof	—	Value: 0.50				
1991	—	—	—	—	0.20	0.50
1991 Proof	—	Value: 0.50				

KM# 78a CENT
3.0100 g., 0.9250 Silver .0895 oz. ASW, 17.51 mm. **Ruler:** Elizabeth II **Obv:** Crowned head right **Rev:** Ring-tailed opossum **Rev. Designer:** Stuart Devlin

Date	Mintage	F	VF	XF	Unc	BU
1991 Proof	23,000	Value: 10.00				

Note: In Proof sets only

KM# 63 2 CENTS
5.2000 g., Bronze, 21.6 mm. **Ruler:** Elizabeth II **Obv:** Young bust right **Obv. Designer:** Arnold Machin **Rev:** Frilled Lizard **Rev. Designer:** Stuart Devlin

Date	Mintage	F	VF	XF	Unc	BU
1966(c)	145,226,000	—	—	0.10	0.35	0.75
1966(c) Proof	18,000	Value: 5.00				
1966(m)	66,575,000	—	0.15	0.35	2.25	4.00
Note: Blunted 3rd left claw						
1966(p)	217,735,000	—	0.15	0.25	1.25	2.00
Note: Blunted 1st right claw						
1967	73,250,000	—	0.15	0.30	3.50	6.00
1967	Inc. above	—	—	—	65.00	75.00
Note: Without designer's initials on reverse						
1968	17,000,000	—	0.15	0.55	5.00	12.50
1969	12,940,000	—	0.15	0.30	2.25	4.00
1969 Proof	13,000	Value: 4.75				
1970	39,872,000	—	—	0.15	0.60	0.75
1970 Proof	15,000	Value: 4.75				
1971	60,735,000	—	—	0.15	0.60	0.75
1971 Proof	10,000	Value: 4.75				
1972	77,570,000	—	—	0.10	0.60	0.75
1972 Proof	10,000	Value: 4.25				
1973	94,058,000	—	—	0.10	0.60	0.75
1973 Proof	10,000	Value: 4.25				
1974	177,723,000	—	—	0.10	0.50	0.75
1974 Proof	11,000	Value: 4.25				
1975	100,045,000	—	—	0.10	0.60	0.75
1975 Proof	23,000	Value: 0.75				
1976	121,882,000	—	—	0.10	0.35	0.75
1976 Proof	21,000	Value: 2.25				
1977	102,000,000	—	—	0.10	0.35	0.75
1977 Proof	55,000	Value: 0.75				
1978	128,700,000	—	—	0.10	0.35	0.75
1978 Proof	39,000	Value: 0.75				
1979	69,705,000	—	—	0.10	0.35	0.75
1979 Proof	36,000	Value: 0.75				
1980	145,603,000	—	—	0.10	0.35	0.75
1980 Proof	68,000	Value: 0.75				
1981	247,300,000	—	—	0.10	0.35	0.75
1981 Proof	86,000	Value: 0.75				
1982	121,770,000	—	—	0.10	0.35	0.75
1982 Proof	100,000	Value: 0.75				
1983	177,227,000	—	—	0.10	0.35	0.75
1983 Proof	80,000	Value: 0.75				
1984	57,963,000	—	—	0.10	0.35	0.75
1984 Proof	61,000	Value: 0.75				

KM# 79 2 CENTS
5.2000 g., Bronze, 21.6 mm. **Ruler:** Elizabeth II **Obv:** Crowned head right **Obv. Designer:** Raphael Maklouf **Rev:** Frilled Lizard **Rev. Designer:** Stuart Devlin **Edge:** Plain

Date	Mintage	F	VF	XF	Unc	BU
1985	34,700,000	—	—	0.10	0.20	0.75
1985 Proof	75,000	Value: 0.75				
1986 In sets only	180,000	—	—	—	0.75	1.25
1986 Proof	67,000	Value: 0.75				
1987 In sets only	200,000	—	—	—	0.75	1.25
1987 Proof	70,000	Value: 0.75				
1988	23,905,000	—	—	0.10	0.50	0.75
1988 Proof	106,000	Value: 0.75				
1989	11[illegible],000,000	—	—	0.10	0.50	0.75
1989 Proof	—	Value: 0.75				
1990	—	—	—	0.10	0.50	0.75
1990 Proof	—	Value: 0.75				
1991	—	—	—	0.10	0.50	0.75
1991 Proof	—	Value: 0.75				

KM# 79a 2 CENTS
6.0600 g., 0.9250 Silver .1802 oz. ASW, 21.6 mm. **Ruler:** Elizabeth II **Obv:** Crowned head right **Rev:** Frilled lizard **Rev. Designer:** Stuart Devlin

Date	Mintage	F	VF	XF	Unc	BU
1991 Proof	23,000	Value: 10.00				

Note: In Proof sets only

KM# 64 5 CENTS
2.8000 g., Copper-Nickel, 19.4 mm. **Ruler:** Elizabeth II **Obv:** Young bust right **Obv. Designer:** Arnold Machin **Rev:** Short-beaked Spiny Anteater **Rev. Designer:** Stuart Devlin **Note:** For 1966 dated examples, the length of the whisker on top of the forward-most claw at left will indicate the mint: Canberra (less than .5mm) or London (greater than .6mm).

Date	Mintage	F	VF	XF	Unc	BU
1966(c)	45,427,000	—	0.15	0.25	1.50	—
1966(c) Proof	18,000	Value: 7.50				
1966(L)	30,000,000	—	0.15	0.25	1.50	—
1966(L) Proof	—	Value: 12.50				
1967	62,144,000	—	0.15	0.35	2.75	—
1968	67,336,000	—	0.15	0.40	3.50	—
1969	38,170,000	—	0.15	0.20	1.75	—
1969 Proof	13,000	Value: 10.00				
1970	46,058,000	—	—	0.15	2.25	—
1970 Proof	15,000	Value: 10.00				
1971	39,516,000	—	0.15	0.25	2.50	—
1971 Proof	10,000	Value: 10.00				
1972	8,256,000	0.15	0.30	1.50	12.50	—
1972 Proof	10,000	Value: 8.50				
1973	48,816,000	—	0.15	0.20	0.75	—
1973 Proof	10,000	Value: 8.50				
1974	64,248,000	—	0.15	0.20	0.75	—
1974 Proof	11,000	Value: 8.50				
1975	44,256,000	—	—	0.10	0.50	—
1975 Proof	23,000	Value: 1.75				
1976	113,180,000	—	—	0.10	0.50	—
1976 Proof	21,000	Value: 3.75				
1977	108,800,000	—	—	0.10	0.50	—
1977 Proof	55,000	Value: 1.75				
1978	25,210,000	—	—	0.10	0.50	—
1978 Proof	39,000	Value: 1.75				
1979	44,533,000	—	—	0.10	0.50	—
1979 Proof	36,000	Value: 1.75				
1980	115,042,000	—	—	0.10	0.50	—
1980 Proof	68,000	Value: 1.25				
1981	162,264,000	—	—	0.10	0.50	—
1981 Proof	86,000	Value: 1.25				
1982	139,468,000	—	—	0.10	0.50	—
1982 Proof	100,000	Value: 1.25				
1983	131,568,000	—	—	0.10	0.50	—
1983 Proof	80,000	Value: 1.75				
1984	35,436,000	—	—	0.10	0.50	—
1984 Proof	61,000	Value: 1.75				

KM# 80 5 CENTS
2.8000 g., Copper-Nickel, 19.4 mm. **Ruler:** Elizabeth II **Obv:** Crowned head right **Obv. Designer:** Raphael Maklouf **Rev:** Short-beaked Spiny Anteater **Rev. Designer:** Stuart Devlin

Date	Mintage	F	VF	XF	Unc	BU
1985	170,000	—	—	—	3.50	—
Note: In Mint sets only						
1985 Proof	75,000	Value: 2.50				
1986	180,000	—	—	—	0.75	—
Note: In Mint sets only						
1986 Proof	67,000	Value: 0.75				
1987	73,500,000	—	—	—	0.50	—
1987 Proof	70,000	Value: 0.75				
1988	106,100,000	—	—	—	0.50	—
1988 Proof	106,000	Value: 0.75				
1989	75,000,000	—	—	—	0.50	—
1989 Proof	—	Value: 0.75				
1990	33,200,000	—	—	—	0.50	—
1990 Proof	—	Value: 0.75				
1991	18,400,000	—	—	—	0.50	—
1991 Proof	—	Value: 0.75				
1992	36,200,000	—	—	—	0.50	0.75
1992 Proof	47,000	Value: 0.75				
1993	93,840,000	—	—	—	0.50	0.75
1993 Proof	—	Value: 0.75				
1994	146,669,000	—	—	—	0.50	0.75
1994 Proof	—	Value: 0.75				

Date	Mintage	F	VF	XF	Unc	BU
1995	84,987,000	—	—	—	0.50	0.75
1995 Proof	—	Value: 0.75				
1996	79,210,000	—	—	—	0.50	0.75
1996 Proof	—	Value: 0.75				
1997	100,680,000	—	—	—	0.50	0.75
1997 Proof	—	Value: 0.75				
1998	88,532,000	—	—	—	0.50	0.75
1998 Proof	—	Value: 0.75				

KM# 80a 5 CENTS

3.2700 g., 0.9250 Silver .0972 oz. ASW, 19.4 mm. **Ruler:** Elizabeth II **Obv:** Crowned head right **Rev:** Short-beaked Spiny Anteater **Rev. Designer:** Stuart Devlin

Date	Mintage	F	VF	XF	Unc	BU
1991 Proof	23,000	Value: 15.00				

Note: In Proof sets only

KM# 401 5 CENTS

2.8300 g., Copper-Nickel, 19.4 mm. **Ruler:** Elizabeth II **Obv:** Rank-Broadley portrait **Rev:** Short-beaked Spiny Anteater **Rev. Designer:** Stuart Devlin

Date	Mintage	F	VF	XF	Unc	BU
1999	179,016,000	—	—	—	0.20	0.50
1999 Proof	—	Value: 0.75				
2000	97,422,000	—	—	—	0.20	0.50
2000 Proof	—	Value: 0.75				

KM# 481 5 CENTS

5.5300 g., 0.9990 Silver .1776 oz. ASW, 25 mm. **Ruler:** Elizabeth II **Series:** Masterpieces in Silver **Rev:** Half penny reverse design of KM#41 **Edge:** Reeded

Date	Mintage	F	VF	XF	Unc	BU
1999 Proof	15,000	Value: 8.00				

KM# 65 10 CENTS

5.6500 g., Copper-Nickel, 23.6 mm. **Ruler:** Elizabeth II **Obv:** Young bust right **Obv. Designer:** Arnold Machin **Rev:** Superb Lyre-bird **Rev. Designer:** Stuart Devlin **Note:** For 1966 dated examples, 11 spikes on the left Lyre-bird indicates a strike from Canberra, 12 spikes indicate a London strike.

Date	Mintage	F	VF	XF	Unc	BU
1966(c)	10,984,000	—	0.15	0.35	3.50	—
1966(c) Proof	18,000	Value: 8.00				
1966(L)	30,000,000	—	0.15	0.35	3.00	—
1966(L) Proof	—	Value: 12.00				
1967	51,032,000	—	0.15	0.55	6.50	—
1968	57,194,000	—	0.15	0.45	7.50	—
1969	22,146,000	—	0.15	0.25	2.75	—
1969 Proof	13,000	Value: 8.50				
1970	22,306,000	—	0.15	0.25	2.25	—
1970 Proof	15,000	Value: 8.50				
1971	20,726,000	—	0.10	0.30	5.00	—
1971 Proof	10,000	Value: 8.00				
1972	12,502,000	—	0.10	0.50	8.00	—
1972 Proof	10,000	Value: 7.00				
1973	27,320,000	—	0.10	0.15	2.00	—
1973 Proof	10,000	Value: 7.00				
1974	46,550,000	—	0.10	0.15	2.00	—
1974 Proof	11,000	Value: 7.00				
1975	50,900,000	—	0.10	0.15	0.75	—
1975 Proof	23,000	Value: 1.75				
1976	57,060,000	—	0.10	0.15	0.75	—
1976 Proof	21,000	Value: 3.75				
1977	10,940,000	—	0.10	0.15	0.85	—
1977 Proof	55,000	Value: 1.75				
1978	48,400,000	—	0.10	0.15	0.50	—
1978 Proof	39,000	Value: 1.75				
1979	36,950,000	—	0.10	0.15	0.50	—
1979 Proof	36,000	Value: 1.75				
1980	55,084,000	—	0.10	0.15	0.50	—
1980 Proof	68,000	Value: 1.50				
1981	116,060,000	—	0.10	0.15	0.50	—

Note: One 1981 coin was struck on a Sri Lanka 50 cents planchet, KM#135.1. It carries an approximate value of $600

Date	Mintage	F	VF	XF	Unc	BU
1981 Proof	86,000	Value: 1.50				
1982	61,492,000	—	0.10	0.15	0.50	—
1982 Proof	100,000	Value: 1.50				
1983	82,318,000	—	0.10	0.15	0.50	—
1983 Proof	80,000	Value: 1.75				
1984	25,728,000	—	0.10	0.15	0.50	—
1984 Proof	61,000	Value: 1.75				

KM# 81 10 CENTS

5.6500 g., Copper-Nickel, 23.6 mm. **Ruler:** Elizabeth II **Obv:** Crowned head right **Obv. Designer:** Raphael Maklouf **Rev:** Superb Lyre-bird **Rev. Designer:** Stuart Devlin

Date	Mintage	F	VF	XF	Unc	BU
1985	2,100,000	—	—	0.10	0.20	—
1985 Proof	75,000	Value: 1.00				
1986	180,000	—	—	—	1.00	—

Note: In mint sets only

Date	Mintage	F	VF	XF	Unc	BU
1986 Proof	67,000	Value: 1.00				
1987	200,000	—	—	—	1.00	—

Note: In mint sets only

Date	Mintage	F	VF	XF	Unc	BU
1987 Proof	70,000	Value: 1.00				
1988	46,900,000	—	—	—	0.50	0.80
1988 Proof	106,000	Value: 1.00				
1989	45,000,000	—	—	—	0.50	0.80
1989 Proof	—	Value: 1.00				
1990	17,000,000	—	—	—	0.50	0.80
1990 Proof	—	Value: 1.00				
1991	3,174,000	—	—	—	0.50	0.80
1991 Proof	—	Value: 1.00				
1992	29,800,000	—	—	—	0.50	0.80
1992 Proof	47,000	Value: 1.00				
1993	23,100,000	—	—	—	0.50	0.80
1993 Proof	—	Value: 1.00				
1994	43,726,000	—	—	—	0.50	0.80
1994 Proof	—	Value: 1.00				
1995	—	—	—	—	0.50	0.80
1995 Proof	—	Value: 1.00				
1996	—	—	—	—	0.50	0.80
1996 Proof	—	Value: 1.00				
1997	5,700,000	—	—	—	0.50	0.80
1997 Proof	—	Value: 2.00				
1998	47,989,000	—	—	—	0.50	0.80
1998 Proof	—	Value: 2.00				

KM# 81a 10 CENTS

6.5200 g., 0.9250 Silver .1939 oz. ASW, 23.6 mm. **Ruler:** Elizabeth II **Obv:** Crowned head right **Rev:** Superb Lyre-bird **Rev. Designer:** Stuart Devlin

Date	Mintage	F	VF	XF	Unc	BU
1991 Proof	23,000	Value: 15.00				

Note: In Proof sets only

KM# 402 10 CENTS

5.6500 g., Copper-Nickel, 23.6 mm. **Ruler:** Elizabeth II **Obv:** Head right by Rank-Broadley **Rev:** Superb Lyre-bird **Rev. Designer:** Stuart Devlin

Date	Mintage	F	VF	XF	Unc	BU
1999	94,889,000	—	—	—	0.50	0.80
1999 Proof	—	Value: 1.00				
2000	51,117,000	—	—	—	0.50	0.80
2000 Proof	—	Value: 1.00				

KM# 482 10 CENTS

8.3600 g., 0.9990 Silver .2685 oz. ASW, 30 mm. **Ruler:** Elizabeth II **Series:** Masterpieces in Silver **Obv:** Head right **Rev:** Penny reverse design of KM#23 **Edge:** Reeded

Date	Mintage	F	VF	XF	Unc	BU
1999 Proof	15,000	Value: 12.00				

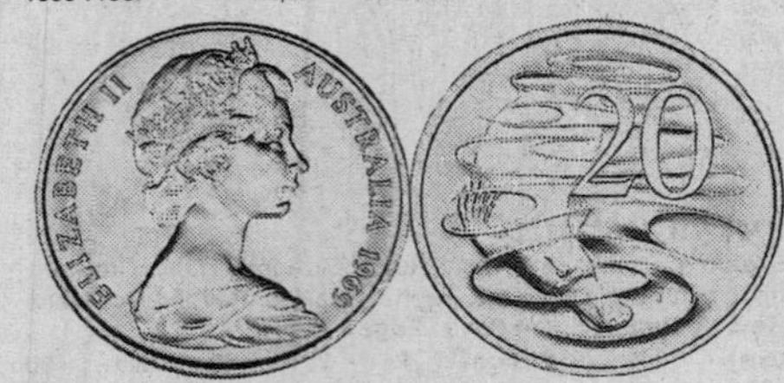

KM# 66 20 CENTS

11.3000 g., Copper-Nickel, 28.5 mm. **Ruler:** Elizabeth II **Obv:** Young bust right **Obv. Designer:** Arnold Machin **Rev:** Duckbill Platypus **Rev. Designer:** Stuart Devlin **Note:** For 1966 dated examples, strikes from Canberra show a gap between sea line and right face of platypus

Date	Mintage	F	VF	XF	Unc	BU
1966(c)	28,223,000	—	0.20	1.00	18.00	—
1966(c) Proof	18,000	Value: 10.00				
1966(L)	—	—	—	—	650	850

Note: Wave on base of 2

Date	Mintage	F	VF	XF	Unc	BU
1966(L)	30,000,000	—	0.20	1.00	16.50	—
1966(L) Proof	—	Value: 12.50				
1967	83,848,000	—	0.20	1.15	13.50	—
1968	40,537,000	—	0.20	1.00	20.00	—
1969	16,501,999	—	0.20	1.00	15.00	—
1969 Proof	13,000	Value: 13.50				
1970	23,271,000	—	0.20	0.50	7.00	—
1970 Proof	15,000	Value: 11.50				
1971	8,947,000	—	0.20	1.00	25.00	—
1971 Proof	10,000	Value: 11.50				
1972	16,643,000	—	0.15	0.50	8.00	—
1972 Proof	10,000	Value: 10.00				
1973	23,356,000	—	0.15	0.45	9.00	—
1973 Proof	10,000	Value: 10.00				
1974	33,548,000	—	0.15	0.45	8.50	—
1974 Proof	11,000	Value: 10.00				
1975	53,300,000	—	0.15	0.20	1.75	—
1975 Proof	23,000	Value: 2.25				
1976	59,774,000	—	0.15	0.20	0.75	—
1976 Proof	21,000	Value: 3.75				
1977	41,272,000	—	0.15	0.20	0.75	—
1977 Proof	55,000	Value: 1.75				
1978	37,400,000	—	0.15	0.20	0.75	—
1978 Proof	39,000	Value: 1.75				
1979	22,300,000	—	0.15	0.20	0.75	—
1979 Proof	36,000	Value: 1.75				
1980	84,400,000	—	0.15	0.20	0.60	—
1980 Proof	68,000	Value: 1.25				
1981	165,500,000	—	0.15	0.20	0.60	—

Note: Some 1981 dated coins were struck on a Hong Kong 2 Dollar planchet, KM#37. 6 pieces are reported. Each carries an approximate value of $800

Date	Mintage	F	VF	XF	Unc	BU
1981 Proof	86,000	Value: 1.25				
1982	76,600,000	—	0.15	0.20	0.60	—
1982 Proof	100,000	Value: 1.25				
1983	55,113,000	—	0.15	0.20	0.60	—
1983 Proof	80,000	Value: 1.75				
1984	27,820,000	—	0.15	0.20	0.60	—
1984 Proof	61,000	Value: 1.75				

KM# 82 20 CENTS

11.3000 g., Copper-Nickel, 28.5 mm. **Ruler:** Elizabeth II **Obv:** Crowned head right **Obv. Designer:** Raphael Maklouf **Rev:** Duckbill Platypus **Rev. Designer:** Stuart Devlin

Date	Mintage	F	VF	XF	Unc	BU
1985	2,700,000	—	0.15	0.20	0.30	—
1985 Proof	75,000	Value: 1.75				
1986	180,000	—	—	—	0.85	—

Note: In mint sets only

Date	Mintage	F	VF	XF	Unc	BU
1986 Proof	67,000	Value: 2.50				
1987	200,000	—	—	—	0.85	—

Note: In mint sets only

Date	Mintage	F	VF	XF	Unc	BU
1987 Proof	70,000	Value: 1.25				
1988	240,000	—	—	—	0.85	—

Note: In mint sets only

Date	Mintage	F	VF	XF	Unc	BU
1988 Proof	106,000	Value: 1.25				
1989	—	—	—	—	0.60	1.00
1989 Proof	—	Value: 1.25				
1990	—	—	—	—	0.60	1.00
1990 Proof	—	Value: 1.25				
1991	—	—	—	—	0.60	1.00
1991 Proof	—	Value: 1.25				
1992	—	—	—	—	0.60	1.00
1992 Proof	47,000	Value: 1.25				
1993	—	—	—	—	0.60	1.00
1993 Proof	—	Value: 1.25				
1994	14,330,000	—	—	—	0.60	1.00
1994 Proof	—	Value: 1.25				
1995	4,840,000	—	—	—	0.60	1.00
1995 Proof	—	Value: 1.25				
1996	20,596,000	—	—	—	0.60	1.00
1996 Proof	—	Value: 1.25				
1997	16,730,000	—	—	—	0.60	1.00
1997 Proof	—	Value: 1.25				
1998	28,830,000	—	—	—	0.60	1.00
1998 Proof	—	Value: 1.25				

KM# 82a 20 CENTS

13.0900 g., 0.9250 Silver .3893 oz. ASW, 28.5 mm. **Ruler:** Elizabeth II **Obv:** Head right **Rev:** Duckbill Platypus **Rev. Designer:** Stuart Devlin

Date	Mintage	F	VF	XF	Unc	BU
1991 Proof	23,000	Value: 20.00				

Note: In Proof sets only

KM# 295 20 CENTS
11.3000 g., Copper-Nickel, 28.5 mm. **Ruler:** Elizabeth II **Subject:** 50th Anniversary - United Nations **Obv:** Crowned head right **Rev:** UN logo over value **Rev. Legend:** UNITED NATIONS FIFTIETH ANNIVERSARY **Rev. Designer:** Horst Hahne

Date	Mintage	F	VF	XF	Unc	BU
1995	4,800,000	—	—	—	4.00	5.00

KM# 410 20 CENTS
13.3600 g., 0.9990 Silver .4291 oz. ASW **Ruler:** Elizabeth II **Subject:** Masterpieces in Silver **Obv:** Queens head right **Rev:** 1927 Florin design

Date	Mintage	F	VF	XF	Unc	BU
1998 Proof	—	Value: 20.00				

KM# 403 20 CENTS
11.3000 g., Copper-Nickel, 28.5 mm. **Ruler:** Elizabeth II **Obv:** Rank-Broadley portrait **Rev:** Duckbill Platypus **Rev. Designer:** Stuart Devlin

Date	Mintage	F	VF	XF	Unc	BU
1999	64,181,000	—	—	—	0.60	1.00
1999 Proof	—	Value: 2.50				
2000	35,584,000	—	—	—	0.60	1.00
2000 Proof	—	Value: 2.50				

KM# 483 20 CENTS
2.9900 g., 0.9990 Silver .0960 oz. ASW, 17.5 mm. **Ruler:** Elizabeth II **Series:** Masterpieces in Silver **Obv:** Head right **Rev:** Threepence reverse design of KM#37 **Edge:** Reeded

Date	Mintage	F	VF	XF	Unc	BU
1999 Proof	15,000	Value: 8.00				

KM# 496 20 CENTS
13.3600 g., 0.9990 Silver .4291 oz. ASW, 28.5 mm. **Ruler:** Elizabeth II **Series:** Masterpieces in Silver - 2000 Set **Obv:** Head with tiara right **Obv. Designer:** Ian Rank-Broadley **Rev:** Crowned bust right **Rev. Designer:** G.W. DeSaulles **Edge:** Reeded

Date	Mintage	F	VF	XF	Unc	BU
2000 Proof	15,000	Value: 25.00				

KM# 497 20 CENTS
13.3600 g., 0.9990 Silver .4291 oz. ASW, 28.5 mm. **Ruler:** Elizabeth II **Series:** Masterpieces in Silver - 2000 Set **Obv:** Rank-Broadley head with tiara right **Rev:** Crowned bust left **Rev. Designer:** E.B. MacKennal **Edge:** Reeded

Date	Mintage	F	VF	XF	Unc	BU
2000 Proof	15,000	Value: 25.00				

KM# 498 20 CENTS
13.3600 g., 0.9990 Silver .4291 oz. ASW, 28.5 mm. **Ruler:** Elizabeth II **Series:** Masterpieces in Silver - 2000 Set **Obv:** Rank-Broadley head with tiara right **Obv. Designer:** Ian Rank-Broadley **Rev:** Laureate bust right **Rev. Designer:** Mary Billick **Edge:** Reeded

Date	Mintage	F	VF	XF	Unc	BU
2000 Proof	15,000	Value: 25.00				

KM# 113 25 CENTS (The Dump)
7.7750 g., 0.9990 Silver .2500 oz. ASW **Ruler:** Elizabeth II **Obv:** Crowned head right **Obv. Designer:** Raphael Maklouf **Rev:** Aboriginal Culture **Rev. Designer:** Stuart Devlin

Date	Mintage	F	VF	XF	Unc	BU
1988 Proof	100,000	Value: 15.00				

KM# 132 25 CENTS (The Dump)
7.7750 g., 0.9990 Silver .2500 oz. ASW **Ruler:** Elizabeth II **Obv:** Crowned head right **Obv. Designer:** Raphael Maklouf **Rev:** Wandjina of Aboriginal Mythology **Rev. Designer:** Stuart Devlin

Date	Mintage	F	VF	XF	Unc	BU
1989 Proof	45,000	Value: 16.00				

KM# 155 25 CENTS (The Dump)
7.7750 g., 0.9990 Silver .2500 oz. ASW **Ruler:** Elizabeth II **Obv:** Crowned head right **Obv. Designer:** Raphael Maklouf **Rev:** 3 Mythological Creatures **Rev. Designer:** Stuart Devlin

Date	Mintage	F	VF	XF	Unc	BU
1990 Proof	30,000	Value: 17.50				

KM# 67 50 CENTS
13.2800 g., 0.8000 Silver .3416 oz. ASW, 31.5 mm. **Ruler:** Elizabeth II **Obv:** Young bust right **Obv. Designer:** Arnold Machin **Rev:** Coat of arms with kangaroo and emu supporters **Rev. Designer:** Stuart Devlin

Date	Mintage	F	VF	XF	Unc	BU
1966	36,454,000	—	—	BV	6.50	9.00
Note: On reverse, two parallel horizontal bars behind Emu's head.						
1966 Proof	18,000	Value: 75.00				

KM# 68 50 CENTS
15.5500 g., Copper-Nickel, 31.5 mm. **Ruler:** Elizabeth II **Obv:** Young bust right **Obv. Designer:** Arnold Machin **Rev:** Coat of arms with kangaroo and emu supporters **Rev. Designer:** Stuart Devlin **Edge:** 12-sided

Date	Mintage	F	VF	XF	Unc	BU
1969	14,015,000	—	0.45	1.00	12.50	—
1969 Proof	13,000	Value: 55.00				
1971	21,056,000	—	0.45	1.75	13.50	—
1971 Proof	10,000	Value: 35.00				
1972	5,586,000	—	0.45	2.50	20.00	—
1972 Proof	10,000	Value: 35.00				
1973	4,009,000	—	0.45	3.00	25.00	—
1973 Proof	10,000	Value: 35.00				
1974	8,962,000	—	0.45	2.00	16.50	—
1974 Proof	11,000	Value: 30.00				
1975	19,025,000	—	0.40	0.75	6.00	—
1975 Proof	23,000	Value: 10.00				
1976	27,280,000	—	0.40	0.75	6.00	—
1976 Proof	21,000	Value: 20.00				
1978	25,765,000	—	0.40	0.50	2.00	—
1978 Proof	39,000	Value: 6.75				
1979	24,886,000	—	0.40	0.50	2.00	—
1979 Proof	36,000	Value: 7.75				
1979	Inc. above	—	0.40	0.75	6.00	—
Note: On reverse, two parallel horizontal bars behind Emu's head.						
1980	38,681,000	—	0.40	0.50	2.00	—
1980	Inc. above	—	0.40	0.75	5.00	—
Note: On reverse, two parallel horizontal bars behind Emu's head.						
1980 Proof	68,000	Value: 5.50				
1981	24,168,000	—	0.40	0.50	1.50	—
1981 Proof	86,000	Value: 5.50				
1983	48,923,000	—	—	0.40	1.00	—
1983 Proof	80,000	Value: 7.75				
1984	26,281,000	—	—	0.40	1.00	—
1984 Proof	61,000	Value: 7.75				

KM# 69 50 CENTS
15.5500 g., Copper-Nickel, 31.5 mm. **Ruler:** Elizabeth II **Subject:** 200th Anniversary - Cook's Australian Voyage **Obv:** Young bust right **Obv. Designer:** Arnold Machin **Rev:** Bust of Captain Cook at left, map of Australia at right **Rev. Designer:** Stuart Devlin **Shape:** 12-sided

Date	Mintage	F	VF	XF	Unc	BU
1970	16,540,000	—	0.40	1.25	3.50	—
1970 Proof	15,000	Value: 50.00				

KM# 70 50 CENTS
15.5500 g., Copper-Nickel, 31.5 mm. **Ruler:** Elizabeth II **Subject:** Queen's Silver Jubilee **Obv:** Young bust right **Obv. Designer:** Arnold Machin **Rev:** Circular geometric design **Shape:** 12-sided

Date	Mintage	F	VF	XF	Unc	BU
1977	25,076,000	—	0.40	0.65	1.75	—
1977 Proof	55,000	Value: 7.50				

KM# A72 50 CENTS
Copper-Nickel, 31.5 mm. **Ruler:** Elizabeth II **Subject:** Mule **Obv:** Young bust right **Obv. Designer:** Arnold Machin **Rev:** Sailing canoe-Takia, denomination below

Date	Mintage	F	VF	XF	Unc	BU
1978	—	—	—	—	—	—

KM# 72 50 CENTS
15.5500 g., Copper-Nickel, 31.5 mm. **Ruler:** Elizabeth II **Subject:** Wedding of Prince Charles and Lady Diana

Obv. Designer: Arnold Machin **Rev:** Conjoined heads of Prince Charles and Lady Diana, left **Rev. Designer:** Stuart Devlin

Date	Mintage	F	VF	XF	Unc	BU
1981	44,100,000	—	0.40	0.50	1.25	—

KM# 74 50 CENTS

15.5500 g., Copper-Nickel, 31.5 mm. **Ruler:** Elizabeth II **Subject:** XII Commonwealth Games - Brisbane **Obv:** Young bust right **Obv. Designer:** Arnold Machin **Rev:** Circle of images representing different sporting events **Rev. Designer:** Stuart Devlin **Shape:** 12-sided

Date	Mintage	F	VF	XF	Unc	BU
1982	49,500,000	—	0.40	0.50	1.25	—
1982 Proof	100,000	Value: 5.50				

KM# 83 50 CENTS

15.5500 g., Copper-Nickel, 31.5 mm. **Ruler:** Elizabeth II **Obv:** Young bust with tiara right **Obv. Designer:** Raphael Maklouf **Rev:** Coat of arms with kangaroo and emu supporters **Rev. Designer:** Stuart Devlin **Shape:** 12-sided

Date	Mintage	F	VF	XF	Unc	BU
1985	1,000,000	—	—	0.40	0.60	—
1985 Proof	75,000	Value: 3.50				
1986 In sets only	180,000	—	—	—	3.00	—
1986 Proof	67,000	Value: 3.50				
1987 In sets only	200,000	—	—	—	3.00	—
1987 Proof	70,000	Value: 3.50				
1989	—	—	—	—	2.25	—
1989 Proof	—	Value: 3.50				
1990	—	—	—	—	2.25	—
1990 Proof	—	Value: 3.50				
1992	—	—	—	—	2.25	—
1992 Proof	47,000	Value: 3.50				
1993	980,000	—	—	—	2.25	—
1993 Proof	—	Value: 3.50				
1996	19,297,000	—	—	—	2.25	—
1996 Proof	—	Value: 3.50				
1997	4,340,000	—	—	—	2.25	—
1997 Proof	—	Value: 3.50				

KM# 99 50 CENTS

15.5500 g., Copper-Nickel, 31.5 mm. **Ruler:** Elizabeth II **Subject:** Australian Bicentennial **Obv:** Crowned head right **Obv. Designer:** Raphael Maklouf **Rev:** Captain Cook's ship sailing towards gridmarked map of Australia, compass at upper center **Rev. Legend:** AUSTRALIA - 1788-1988 **Rev. Designer:** Michael Tracey **Shape:** 12-sided

Date	Mintage	F	VF	XF	Unc	BU
1988	8,100,000	—	—	—	2.25	—
1988 Proof	106,000	Value: 3.50				

KM# 99a 50 CENTS

18.0000 g., 0.9250 Silver .5353 oz. ASW, 31.5 mm. **Ruler:** Elizabeth II **Subject:** Australian Bicentennial **Obv:** Crowned head right **Rev:** Captain Cook's ship sailing towards gridmarked map of Australia, compass at upper center

Date	Mintage	F	VF	XF	Unc	BU
1988 Proof	25,000	Value: 17.50				
1989 Proof	25,000	Value: 17.50				

KM# 127 50 CENTS

18.0000 g., 0.9250 Silver .5353 oz. ASW, 31.5 mm. **Ruler:** Elizabeth II **Subject:** Cook Commemorative **Obv:** Crowned head right **Rev:** Bust of Captain Cook at left, map of Australia at right

Date	Mintage	F	VF	XF	Unc	BU
1989 Proof	25,000	Value: 17.50				

KM# 128 50 CENTS

18.0000 g., 0.9250 Silver .5353 oz. ASW, 31.5 mm. **Ruler:** Elizabeth II **Subject:** Queen's Silver Jubilee **Obv:** Crowned head right **Rev:** Circular geometric design

Date	Mintage	F	VF	XF	Unc	BU
1989 Proof	25,000	Value: 17.50				

KM# 129 50 CENTS

18.0000 g., 0.9250 Silver .5353 oz. ASW, 31.5 mm. **Ruler:** Elizabeth II **Subject:** Wedding of Prince Charles and Lady Diana **Obv:** Crowned head right **Rev:** Conjoined heads of Prince Charles and Lady Diana left

Date	Mintage	F	VF	XF	Unc	BU
1989 Proof	25,000	Value: 17.50				

KM# 130 50 CENTS

18.0000 g., 0.9250 Silver .5353 oz. ASW, 31.5 mm. **Ruler:** Elizabeth II **Subject:** XII Commonwealth Games - Brisbane **Obv:** Crowned head right **Rev:** Circle of images representing different sporting events

Date	Mintage	F	VF	XF	Unc	BU
1989 Proof	25,000	Value: 17.50				

KM# 139 50 CENTS

15.5500 g., Copper-Nickel, 31.5 mm. **Ruler:** Elizabeth II **Subject:** 25th Anniversary of Decimal Currency **Obv:** Crowned head right **Obv. Designer:** Raphael Maklouf **Rev:** Head of Merino ram **Rev. Designer:** George Kruger-Grey

Date	Mintage	F	VF	XF	Unc	BU
1991	4,364,000	—	—	1.25	6.00	7.50
1991 Proof	—	Value: 12.50				

KM# 139a 50 CENTS

18.0000 g., 0.9250 Silver .5353 oz. ASW **Ruler:** Elizabeth II **Subject:** 25th Anniversary of Decimal Currency **Obv:** Crowned head right **Rev:** Head of Merino ram

Date	Mintage	F	VF	XF	Unc	BU
1991 Proof	23,000	Value: 18.00				

Note: In Proof sets only

KM# 257 50 CENTS

15.5000 g., Copper-Nickel, 31.5 mm. **Ruler:** Elizabeth II **Subject:** International Year of the Family **Obv:** Crowned head right **Obv. Designer:** Raphael Maklouf **Rev:** Crude drawings depicting a family **Rev. Designer:** Carolyn Rossier

Date	Mintage	F	VF	XF	Unc	BU
1994	21,200,000	—	—	1.00	3.00	—
1994 Proof	—	Value: 11.50				

KM# 294 50 CENTS

15.5000 g., Copper-Nickel, 31.5 mm. **Ruler:** Elizabeth II **Subject:** Weary Dunlop **Obv:** Crowned head right **Obv. Designer:** Raphael Maklouf **Rev:** Bust of Dunlop at center, value below **Rev. Designer:** Louis Laumen & Horst Hahne

Date	Mintage	F	VF	XF	Unc	BU
1995	15,860,000	—	—	0.85	2.75	—
1995 Proof	—	Value: 11.50				

KM# 364 50 CENTS

15.5500 g., Copper-Nickel, 31.5 mm. **Ruler:** Elizabeth II **Subject:** Discovery of Bass Strait **Obv:** Crowned head right **Obv. Designer:** Raphael Maklouf **Rev:** Busts of Bass and Flinders, map of Australia at lower left

Date	Mintage	F	VF	XF	Unc	BU
1998	22,390,000	—	—	0.85	3.50	—
1998 Proof	—	Value: 11.50				

KM# 411 50 CENTS

36.3100 g., 0.9990 Silver 1.1662 oz. ASW **Ruler:** Elizabeth II **Subject:** Masterpieces in Silver **Obv:** Crowned head right **Rev:** 1937 crown design

Date	Mintage	F	VF	XF	Unc	BU
1998 Proof	15,000	Value: 25.00				

KM# 404 50 CENTS

15.5500 g., Copper-Nickel, 31.5 mm. **Ruler:** Elizabeth II **Obv:** Head right **Obv. Designer:** Rank-Broadley **Rev:** Coat of arms with kangaroo and emu supporters

Date	Mintage	F	VF	XF	Unc	BU
1999	20,318,000	—	—	0.85	2.75	3.00
1999 Proof	—	Value: 6.50				

KM# 484 50 CENTS

3.2400 g., 0.9990 Silver .1041 oz. ASW, 19.4 mm. **Ruler:** Elizabeth II **Series:** Masterpieces in Silver **Obv:** Bust right **Rev:** Coat of arms with kangaroo and emu supporters **Edge:** Reeded

Date	Mintage	F	VF	XF	Unc	BU
1999 Proof	15,000	Value: 10.00				

KM# 437 50 CENTS

15.5500 g., Copper-Nickel, 31.5 mm. **Ruler:** Elizabeth II **Subject:** Royal Visit **Obv:** Head with tiara right **Rev:** Australian flag above Canberra Parliament House, British crown at right **Rev. Designer:** Vladimir Gottwald **Edge:** Plain **Shape:** 12-sided

Date	Mintage	F	VF	XF	Unc	BU
2000 Proof	5,000	Value: 2.50				

KM# 437a 50 CENTS

18.2400 g., 0.9990 Silver .5858 oz. ASW, 31.5 mm. **Ruler:** Elizabeth II **Subject:** Royal Visit **Obv:** Head with tiara right **Rev:** Australian flag above Canberra Parliament House, British crown at right

Date	Mintage	F	VF	XF	Unc	BU
2000 Proof	25,000	Value: 27.50				

KM# 488.1 50 CENTS

15.5500 g., Copper-Nickel, 31.5 mm. **Ruler:** Elizabeth II **Subject:** Millennium **Obv:** Head with tiara right **Rev:** Australian flag **Rev. Designer:** Vladimir Gottwald **Edge:** Plain **Shape:** 12-sided **Note:** Prev. KM#488.

Date	Mintage	F	VF	XF	Unc	BU
2000	16,600,000	—	—	—	3.00	—

KM# 488.2 50 CENTS
15.5500 g., Copper-Nickel, 31.5 mm. **Ruler:** Elizabeth II **Subject:** Millennium **Obv:** Head with tiara right **Rev:** Multicolor Australian flag **Edge:** Plain **Shape:** 12-sided **Note:** Prev. KM#488.1.

Date	Mintage	F	VF	XF	Unc	BU
2000 Proof	—	Value: 12.50				

KM# 522 50 CENTS
16.8860 g., 0.9990 Silver .5424 oz. ASW, 32.1 mm.
Ruler: Elizabeth II **Series:** Dragons **Obv:** Head with tiara right **Rev:** Dragon **Edge:** Reeded

Date	Mintage	F	VF	XF	Unc	BU
2000 Proof	—	Value: 25.00				

KM# 499 50 CENTS
36.3100 g., 0.9990 Silver 1.1662 oz. ASW, 38.7 mm.
Ruler: Elizabeth II **Series:** Masterpieces in Silver - 2000 Set **Obv:** Rank-Broadley head with tiara right **Rev:** Head left **Rev. Designer:** T.H. Paget **Edge:** Reeded

Date	Mintage	F	VF	XF	Unc	BU
2000 Proof	15,000	Value: 30.00				

KM# 112 DOLLAR (Holey Dollar)
31.1000 g., 0.9990 Silver 1.0000 oz. ASW **Ruler:** Elizabeth II **Subject:** Aboriginal Culture **Obv:** Holey dollar with legend around **Rev:** Holey dollar with snake around eating its tail **Shape:** Round with hole in middle

Date	Mintage	F	VF	XF	Unc	BU
1988 Proof	100,000	Value: 30.00				

KM# 131 DOLLAR (Holey Dollar)
31.1000 g., 0.9990 Silver 1.0000 oz. ASW **Ruler:** Elizabeth II **Obv:** Holey dollar with small silhouette of crowned Queen at top dividing legend, value at bottom **Rev:** 2 crocodiles around hole **Shape:** Round with hole in middle

Date	Mintage	F	VF	XF	Unc	BU
1989 Proof	45,000	Value: 35.00				

KM# 154 DOLLAR (Holey Dollar)
31.1000 g., 0.9990 Silver 1.0000 oz. ASW **Ruler:** Elizabeth II **Rev:** Stylized Natives and Jungle

Date	Mintage	F	VF	XF	Unc	BU
1990 Proof	30,000	Value: 40.00				

KM# 77 DOLLAR
9.0000 g., Nickel-Aluminum-Copper, 25 mm. **Ruler:** Elizabeth II **Obv:** Young bust right **Obv. Designer:** Arnold Machin **Rev:** 5 kangaroos, denomination **Rev. Designer:** Stuart Devlin

Date	Mintage	F	VF	XF	Unc	BU
1984	185,985,000	—	—	1.00	2.00	5.00
1984 Proof	159,000	Value: 9.00				

KM# 84 DOLLAR
9.0000 g., Nickel-Aluminum-Copper, 25 mm. **Ruler:** Elizabeth II **Obv. Designer:** Crowned head right **Rev:** 5 kangaroos, value **Rev. Designer:** Stuart Devlin

Date	Mintage	F	VF	XF	Unc	BU
1985	91,400,000	—	—	1.00	4.00	5.00
1985 Proof	75,000	Value: 9.00				
1987 In sets only	200,000	—	—	—	5.00	6.00
1987 Proof	70,000	Value: 9.00				
1989	—	—	—	1.00	4.00	5.00
1989 Proof	—	Value: 9.00				
1990	—	—	—	1.00	9.00	11.00
1990 Proof	—	Value: 9.00				
1991	—	—	—	1.00	4.00	5.00
1991 Proof	—	Value: 9.00				
1994	47,639,000	—	—	1.00	6.00	9.00
1994 Proof	—	Value: 9.00				
1995	21,412,000	—	—	1.00	4.00	6.00
1995 Proof	—	Value: 9.00				
1998	16,248,000	—	—	1.00	4.00	6.00
1998 Proof	—	Value: 9.00				

KM# 84a DOLLAR
11.4900 g., 0.9250 Silver .3417 oz. ASW, 25 mm. **Ruler:** Elizabeth II **Subject:** Masterpieces in Silver **Obv:** Crowned head right **Rev:** 5 kangaroos, value

Date	Mintage	F	VF	XF	Unc	BU
1990 Proof	25,000	Value: 35.00				
1991 Proof	23,000	Value: 35.00				

Note: In Proof sets only

KM# 87 DOLLAR
9.0000 g., Nickel-Aluminum-Copper, 25 mm. **Ruler:** Elizabeth II **Subject:** International Year of Peace **Obv:** Crowned head right **Obv. Designer:** Raphael Maklouf **Rev:** Dove above hands within wreath, value and legend below **Rev. Legend:** INTERNATIONAL YEAR OF PEACE **Rev. Designer:** Horst Hahne

Date	Mintage	F	VF	XF	Unc	BU
1986	25,100,000	—	—	—	4.00	6.00
1986 Proof	67,000	Value: 20.00				

KM# 87a DOLLAR
11.4900 g., 0.9250 Silver .3417 oz. ASW, 25 mm.
Ruler: Elizabeth II **Subject:** Masterpieces in Silver
Obv: Crowned head right

Date	Mintage	F	VF	XF	Unc	BU
1990 Proof	25,000	Value: 35.00				

KM# 100 DOLLAR
9.0000 g., Aluminum-Bronze, 25 mm. **Ruler:** Elizabeth II **Subject:** Aboriginal Art **Obv:** Crowned head right **Obv. Designer:** Raphael Maklouf **Rev:** Kangaroo on artistic patterned background, denomination below **Rev. Designer:** Stuart Devlin

Date	Mintage	F	VF	XF	Unc	BU
1988	20,294,000	—	—	—	4.00	6.00
1988 Proof	106,000	Value: 18.50				

KM# 100a DOLLAR
11.4900 g., 0.9250 Silver .3417 oz. ASW, 25 mm.
Ruler: Elizabeth II **Subject:** Masterpieces in Silver
Obv: Crowned head right **Rev:** Kangaroo on artistic patterned background, denomination below

Date	Mintage	F	VF	XF	Unc	BU
1988 Proof	25,000	Value: 35.00				
1990 Proof	25,000	Value: 35.00				

KM# 175 DOLLAR
9.0000 g., Nickel-Aluminum-Copper, 25.12 mm.
Ruler: Elizabeth II **Subject:** Barcelona - 25th Olympics
Obv: Crowned head right **Obv. Designer:** Raphael Maklouf
Rev: Female javelin thrower **Rev. Designer:** Margaret Priest
Edge: Alternating reeded and plain sections

Date	Mintage	F	VF	XF	Unc	BU
1992	13,996	—	—	—	65.00	—
Note: RAM wallet						
1992	Inc. above	—	—	—	55.00	—
Note: Olympic wallet						
1992 Proof	2,940	Value: 165				
1992	23,500	—	—	—	70.00	—
Note: Olympic card						

KM# 175a.1 DOLLAR
11.4900 g., 0.9250 Silver .3412 oz. ASW, 25 mm.
Ruler: Elizabeth II **Subject:** Barcelona - 25th Olympiad
Obv: Crowned head right **Rev:** Female javelin thrower

Date	Mintage	F	VF	XF	Unc	BU
1992 Proof	12,500	Value: 145				
Note: In Proof sets only						

KM# 175a.2 DOLLAR
11.4900 g., 0.9250 Silver .3412 oz. ASW, 25 mm. **Ruler:** Elizabeth II **Subject:** XXV Olympiad - Barcelona **Obv:** Crowned head right **Rev:** Female javelin thrower **Edge:** Reeded

Date	Mintage	F	VF	XF	Unc	BU
1992 Proof	2,500	Value: 300				

KM# 208 DOLLAR
9.0000 g., Nickel-Aluminum-Copper, 25 mm. **Ruler:** Elizabeth II **Obv:** Crowned head right **Obv. Designer:** Raphael Maklouf **Rev:** Stylized tree above value, 2 hands above Landcare Australia **Rev. Designer:** Vladimir Gottwald **Note:** Visitors at mints and coin shows were allowed to strike a coin for a fee at the following C - Canberra, M - Hall of Manufacturers Pavilion Coin Show, Melbourne and S - Sydney International Coin Fair.

Date	Mintage	F	VF	XF	Unc	BU
1993	17,917,000	—	—	—	3.00	4.50
1993 Proof	—	Value: 16.50				
1993C	91,993	—	—	—	6.00	8.00
1993M	60,104	—	—	—	7.50	10.00
1993S	87,939	—	—	—	6.00	8.00

KM# 208a.1 DOLLAR
Silver, 25 mm. **Ruler:** Elizabeth II **Obv:** Crowned head right **Rev:** Stylized tree, value below, hands above Landcare Australia **Edge:** Alternating reeded and plain sections

Date	Mintage	F	VF	XF	Unc	BU
1993 Proof	20,000	Value: 42.50				

KM# 208a.2 DOLLAR
Silver, 25 mm. **Ruler:** Elizabeth II **Obv:** Crowned head right **Rev:** Stylized tree, value below, hands above Landcare Australia **Edge:** Reeded

Date	Mintage	F	VF	XF	Unc	BU
1993 Proof	5,000	Value: 110				

KM# 258 DOLLAR
9.0000 g., Nickel-Aluminum-Copper, 25 mm. **Ruler:** Elizabeth II **Subject:** 10th Anniversary - Introduction of Dollar Coin **Obv. Designer:** Raphael Maklouf **Rev:** Paper money with coin design at left divides dates **Rev. Designer:** Vladimir Gottwald

Date	Mintage	F	VF	XF	Unc	BU
1994C	123,318	—	—	—	15.00	17.50
1994M	65,440	—	—	—	17.50	20.00
1994S	74,426	—	—	—	17.50	20.00

KM# 258a.1 DOLLAR
14.4900 g., 0.9250 Silver .3417 oz. ASW, 25 mm. **Ruler:** Elizabeth II **Subject:** 10th Anniversary - Introduction of Dollar Coin **Rev:** Paper money with coin design at left divides dates **Edge:** Reeded and plain sections

Date	Mintage	F	VF	XF	Unc	BU
1994 Proof	20,000	Value: 52.50				

KM# 258a.2 DOLLAR
14.4900 g., 0.9250 Silver .3417 oz. ASW, 25 mm. **Ruler:** Elizabeth II **Subject:** 10th Anniversary - Introduction of Dollar Coin **Rev:** Paper money with coin design at left divides dates **Edge:** Reeded

Date	Mintage	F	VF	XF	Unc	BU
1994 Proof	5,000	Value: 125				

KM# 269 DOLLAR
9.0000 g., Nickel-Aluminum-Copper, 25 mm. **Ruler:** Elizabeth II **Subject:** A.B. Banjo Paterson - Waltzing Matilda **Obv:** Crowned head right **Obv. Designer:** Raphael Maklouf **Rev:** 3/4-length figure of Banjo Paterson on a walkabout with walking stick

Date	Mintage	F	VF	XF	Unc	BU
1995B	74,353	—	—	—	35.00	45.00
1995C	156,453	—	—	—	28.00	30.00
1995M	74,255	—	—	—	35.00	40.00
1995S	82,810	—	—	—	30.00	35.00

KM# 269a.1 DOLLAR
14.4900 g., 0.9250 Silver .3417 oz. ASW, 25 mm. **Ruler:** Elizabeth II **Subject:** A.B. Banjo Paterson - Waltzing Matilda **Obv:** Crowned head right **Rev:** 3/4-length figure of Banjo Paterson on a walkabout with walking stick **Edge:** Alternating reeded and plain sections

Date	Mintage	F	VF	XF	Unc	BU
1995 Proof	20,000	Value: 70.00				

KM# 269a.2 DOLLAR
14.4900 g., 0.9250 Silver .3417 oz. ASW, 25 mm. **Ruler:** Elizabeth II **Subject:** A.B. Banjo Paterson - Waltzing Matilda **Obv:** Crowned head right **Rev:** 3/4-length figure of Banjo Paterson on a walkabout with walking stick **Edge:** Reeded

Date	Mintage	F	VF	XF	Unc	BU
1995 Proof	2,500	Value: 120				

KM# 310 DOLLAR
9.0000 g., Nickel-Aluminum-Copper, 25 mm. **Ruler:** Elizabeth II **Subject:** Sir Henry Parkes **Obv:** Crowned head right **Obv. Designer:** Raphael Maklouf **Rev:** Large head of Sir Henry Parkes half facing right, legend around **Rev. Legend:** SIR HENRY PARKES 1815-1896, FATHER OF FEDERATION

Date	Mintage	F	VF	XF	Unc	BU
1996	26,200,000	—	—	—	5.00	6.00
1996 Proof	—	—	—	—	—	—
1996A	29,127	—	—	—	11.50	13.50
1996B	41,128	—	—	—	7.50	10.00
1996C	272,980	—	—	—	6.00	8.00
1996M	38,030	—	—	—	11.50	13.50
1996S	72,186	—	—	—	7.50	10.00

KM# 310a DOLLAR
11.4900 g., 0.9250 Silver .3417 oz. ASW, 25 mm. **Ruler:** Elizabeth II **Subject:** Sir Henry Parkes **Obv:** Crowned head right **Rev:** Large head of Sir Henry Parkes half facing right, legend around **Rev. Legend:** SIR HENRY PARKES 1815-1896, FATHER OF FEDERATION

Date	Mintage	F	VF	XF	Unc	BU
1996 Proof	20,000	Value: 50.00				

KM# 326 DOLLAR
31.1035 g., 0.9990 Silver 1.0000 oz. ASW **Ruler:** Elizabeth II **Subject:** 30th Anniversary - Decimal Coinage **Obv:** Crowned head right **Obv. Designer:** Raphael Maklouf **Rev:** Map and seven different coin designs **Rev. Designer:** Horst Hahne

Date	Mintage	F	VF	XF	Unc	BU
1996 Proof	19,927	Value: 100				

KM# 327 DOLLAR
9.0000 g., Nickel-Aluminum-Copper, 25 mm. **Ruler:** Elizabeth II **Subject:** Sir Charles Kingsford Smith **Obv:** Crowned head right **Obv. Designer:** Raphael Maklouf **Rev:** Pilot above airplane, dates

Date	Mintage	F	VF	XF	Unc	BU
1997	24,381,000	—	—	—	20.00	22.50

KM# 721 DOLLAR
31.6300 g., 0.9990 Silver 1.0159 oz. ASW, 39.9 mm. **Ruler:** Elizabeth II **Obv:** Crowned head right **Rev:** Old Parliament building above 1927 one florin KM #31 coin design **Edge:** Reeded

Date	Mintage	F	VF	XF	Unc	BU
1997 Proof	—	Value: 65.00				

KM# 355 DOLLAR
9.0000 g., Nickel-Aluminum-Copper, 25 mm. **Ruler:** Elizabeth II **Subject:** Sir Charles Kingsford Smith **Obv:** Crowned head right **Obv. Designer:** Raphael Maklouf **Rev:** Head of Sir Smith over airplane over world map

Date	Mintage	F	VF	XF	Unc	BU
1997A	33,060	—	—	—	22.50	25.00
1997B	40,800	—	—	—	22.50	25.00
1997C	244,450	—	—	—	18.50	20.00
1997M	48,120	—	—	—	22.50	25.00
1997S	89,800	—	—	—	20.00	22.50

KM# 355a DOLLAR
11.6600 g., 0.9990 Silver .3752 oz. ASW, 25 mm. **Ruler:** Elizabeth II **Subject:** Sir Charles Kingsford Smith **Obv:** Crowned head right **Rev:** Head of Sir Smith over airplane over world map

Date	Mintage	F	VF	XF	Unc	BU
1997 Proof	20,000	Value: 55.00				

KM# 366 DOLLAR
9.0000 g., Nickel-Aluminum-Copper, 25 mm. **Ruler:** Elizabeth II **Obv:** Crowned head right **Obv. Designer:** Raphael Maklouf **Rev:** Bust of Howard Florey facing **Rev. Designer:** Horst Hahne

Date	Mintage	F	VF	XF	Unc	BU
1998A	21,120	—	—	—	11.50	13.50
1998B	29,914	—	—	—	11.50	13.50
1998C	82,035	—	—	—	9.00	11.50
1998M	21,309	—	—	—	11.50	13.50
1998S	58,514	—	—	—	9.00	11.50

KM# 366a DOLLAR
11.6600 g., 0.9990 Silver .3745 oz. ASW, 25 mm. **Ruler:** Elizabeth II **Obv:** Crowned head right **Rev:** Bust of Howard Florey facing

Date	Mintage	F	VF	XF	Unc	BU
1998 Proof	20,000	Value: 55.00				

KM# 412 DOLLAR
31.1035 g., 0.9990 Silver 1.0000 oz. ASW **Ruler:** Elizabeth II **Subject:** 10th Anniversary - New Parliament House **Obv:** Crowned head right **Rev:** Parliament building

Date	Mintage	F	VF	XF	Unc	BU
1998 Proof	17,096	Value: 50.00				

KM# 722 DOLLAR
31.5100 g., 0.9990 Silver 1.0121 oz. ASW, 39.9 mm. **Ruler:** Elizabeth II **Obv:** Crowned head right **Rev:** Old Parliament building above 1988 5 dollar KM #102 coin design **Edge:** Reeded

Date	Mintage	F	VF	XF	Unc	BU
1998 Proof	21,791	Value: 50.00				

KM# 485 DOLLAR
6.5700 g., 0.9990 Silver .2110 oz. ASW, 23.6 mm. **Ruler:** Elizabeth II **Series:** Masterpieces in Silver **Obv:** Head right **Rev:** Ram left above denomination and date **Edge:** Reeded

Date	Mintage	F	VF	XF	Unc	BU
1999 Proof	15,000	Value: 18.00				

KM# 400 DOLLAR
9.0000 g., Nickel-Aluminum-Copper, 25 mm. **Ruler:** Elizabeth II **Obv:** Rank-Broadley head with tiara right **Obv. Designer:** Ian Rank-Broadley **Rev:** Anzac soldier wearing bush hat, 3/4 left **Rev. Designer:** Wojciech Pietranik

Date	Mintage	F	VF	XF	Unc	BU
1999A	28,681	—	—	—	25.00	28.00
1999C	126,161	—	—	—	22.50	25.00
1999M	49,841	—	—	—	22.50	25.00
1999S	53,286	—	—	—	22.50	25.00
1999B	33,634	—	—	—	25.00	28.00
2000	47,830	—	—	—	85.00	95.00

KM# 400a DOLLAR
11.6600 g., 0.9990 Silver .3745 oz. ASW, 25 mm. **Ruler:** Elizabeth II **Subject:** The Last of the Anzacs **Obv:** Rank-Broadley head with tiara right **Rev:** Anzac soldier wearing bush hat **Edge:** Reeded and plain sections on edge

Date	Mintage	F	VF	XF	Unc	BU
1999 Proof	25,000	Value: 70.00				

KM# 405 DOLLAR
9.0000 g., Nickel-Aluminum-Copper, 25 mm. **Ruler:** Elizabeth II **Subject:** International Year of Older People **Obv:** Crowned head right **Obv. Designer:** Ian Rank-Broadley **Rev:** IYOP logo **Rev. Legend:** TOWARDS A SOCIETY FOR ALL AGES - INTERNATIONAL YEAR OF OLDER PERSONS

Date	Mintage	F	VF	XF	Unc	BU
1999	29,218,000	—	—	—	4.50	5.50
1999 Proof	—	Value: 18.50				

KM# 476 DOLLAR
31.1035 g., 0.9990 Silver 1.0000 oz. ASW **Ruler:** Elizabeth II **Subject:** Majestic Images **Obv:** Rank-Broadley head with tiara right **Rev:** Conjoined busts of Queen Elizabeth II by Mary Gillick, Arnold Machin and Raphael Maklouf **Edge:** Reeded

Date	Mintage	F	VF	XF	Unc	BU
1999 Proof	17,000	Value: 55.00				

KM# 422 DOLLAR

9.0000 g., Nickel-Aluminum-Copper, 25 mm. **Ruler:** Elizabeth II **Subject:** HMAS Sydney II **Obv:** Head with tiara right **Obv. Designer:** Ian Rank-Broadley **Rev:** Ship above denomination **Rev. Designer:** Vladimir Gottwald **Edge:** Reeded

Date	Mintage	F	VF	XF	Unc	BU
2000C	71,367	—	—	—	18.00	20.00
2000S	34,277	—	—	—	18.00	20.00

KM# 422a DOLLAR

11.6600 g., 0.9990 Silver .3754 oz. ASW, 25 mm. **Ruler:** Elizabeth II **Obv:** Head with tiara right **Rev:** HMAS Sydney II above value

Date	Mintage	F	VF	XF	Unc	BU
2000 Proof	20,000	Value: 55.00				

KM# 489 DOLLAR

9.0000 g., Nickel-Aluminum-Copper, 25 mm. **Ruler:** Elizabeth II **Subject:** Kangaroos **Obv:** Rank-Broadley head with tiara right **Rev:** Circle of 5 kangaroos **Rev. Designer:** Stuart Devlin **Edge:** Reeded and plain sections

Date	Mintage	F	VF	XF	Unc	BU
2000	7,592,000	—	—	—	18.00	20.00

KM# 493 DOLLAR

9.0000 g., Nickel-Aluminum-Copper, 24.9 mm. **Ruler:** Elizabeth II **Subject:** Victoria Cross **Obv:** Head with tiara right **Obv. Designer:** Ian Rank-Broadley **Rev:** The Victoria Cross **Edge:** Reeded and plain sections

Date	Mintage	F	VF	XF	Unc	BU
2000	49,877	—	—	—	165	175

KM# 509 DOLLAR

31.1035 g., 0.9990 Silver 1. oz. ASW, 40 mm. **Ruler:** Elizabeth II **Subject:** Proclamation Coins of Australia **Obv:** Head with tiara right **Obv. Designer:** Ian Rank-Broadley **Rev:** The Cartwell Penny of 1797 **Edge:** Reeded

Date	Mintage	F	VF	XF	Unc	BU
2000 Proof	—	Value: 45.00				

KM# 514 DOLLAR

31.1035 g., 0.9990 Silver 1. oz. ASW, 40.4 mm. **Ruler:** Elizabeth II **Subject:** Millennium **Obv:** Head with tiara right **Rev:** Gold inlay earth and radiant sun as seen from the moon's surface **Edge:** Reeded

Date	Mintage	F	VF	XF	Unc	BU
2000 Prooflike	30,000	—	—	—	—	37.50

KM# 529.1 DOLLAR

9.0000 g., Nickel-Aluminum-Copper, 24.9 mm. **Ruler:** Elizabeth II **Subject:** Olymphilex Exhibition **Obv:** Head with tiara right **Obv. Designer:** Ian Rank-Broadley **Rev:** Denomination and Olympic logo **Edge:** Plain **Edge Lettering:** Incuse SYDNEY

Date	Mintage	F	VF	XF	Unc	BU
2000	98,567	—	—	—	15.00	17.50

KM# 529.2 DOLLAR

9.0000 g., Nickel-Aluminum-Copper, 24.9 mm. **Ruler:** Elizabeth II **Obv:** Head with tiara right **Obv. Designer:** Ian Rank-Broadley **Rev:** Denomination and Olympic logo **Edge:** Plain **Edge Lettering:** Incuse CANBERRA

Date	Mintage	F	VF	XF	Unc	BU
2000	72,573	—	—	—	15.00	17.50

KM# 101 2 DOLLARS

6.6000 g., Aluminum-Bronze, 20.62 mm. **Ruler:** Elizabeth II **Subject:** Aboriginal Man **Obv:** Crowned head right **Obv. Designer:** Raphael Maklouf **Rev:** 1/2-length figure of Aborigine man at left, 5 stars above value **Rev. Designer:** Horst Hahne

Date	Mintage	F	VF	XF	Unc	BU
1988	160,700,000	—	—	—	4.25	5.00
1988 Proof	106,000	Value: 7.50				
1989	30,000,000	—	—	—	4.25	5.00
1989 Proof	—	Value: 7.50				
1990	8,700,000	—	—	—	4.25	5.00
1990 Proof	—	Value: 7.50				
1991	—	—	—	—	4.25	5.00
1991 Proof	—	Value: 7.50				
1992	11,500,000	—	—	—	4.25	5.00
1992 Proof	47,000	Value: 7.50				
1993	4,870,000	—	—	—	6.00	9.00
1993 Proof	—	Value: 7.50				
1994	22,143,000	—	—	—	4.50	6.00
1994 Proof	—	Value: 10.00				
1995	13,929,000	—	—	—	4.25	5.00
1995 Proof	—	Value: 10.00				
1996	13,909,000	—	—	—	4.25	5.00
1996 Proof	—	Value: 10.00				
1997	19,039,000	—	—	—	4.50	6.00
1997 Proof	—	Value: 10.00				
1998	8,719,000	—	—	—	4.25	5.00
1998 Proof	—	Value: 10.00				

KM# 101a 2 DOLLARS

8.4300 g., 0.9250 Silver .2507 oz. ASW, 20.62 mm. **Ruler:** Elizabeth II **Obv:** Crowned head right **Rev:** Aborigine man at left, 5 stars above value at right **Rev. Designer:** Horst Hahne

Date	Mintage	F	VF	XF	Unc	BU
1988 Proof	25,000	Value: 14.50				
1991 Proof	23,000	Value: 14.50				

Note: In Proof sets only

KM# 406 2 DOLLARS

6.6000 g., Aluminum-Bronze, 20.62 mm. **Ruler:** Elizabeth II **Obv:** Rank-Broadley head right **Rev:** Aboriginal man at left, stars above at right

Date	Mintage	F	VF	XF	Unc	BU
1999	0,494,000	—	—	—	6.00	10.00
1999 Proof	—	Value: 11.50				
2000	5,706,000	—	—	—	7.50	12.50
2000 Proof	—	Value: 20.00				

KM# 486 2 DOLLARS

13.3600 g., 0.9990 Silver .4291 oz. ASW, 28.5 mm. **Ruler:** Elizabeth II **Series:** Masterpieces in Silver **Obv:** Crowned head right **Rev:** St. George on horseback slaying the dragon **Edge:** Reeded

Date	Mintage	F	VF	XF	Unc	BU
1999 Proof	15,000	Value: 22.00				

KM# 500 2 DOLLARS

8.5500 g., 0.9990 Silver .2746 oz. ASW, 20.5 mm. **Ruler:** Elizabeth II **Series:** Masterpieces in Silver - 2000 Set **Obv:** Head with tiara right **Obv. Designer:** Ian Rank-Broadley **Rev:** Queen Victoria's bust, older with veiled head, left **Edge:** Reeded

Date	Mintage	F	VF	XF	Unc	BU
2000 Proof	15,000	Value: 27.50				

KM# 102 5 DOLLARS

Aluminum-Bronze, 38.74 mm. **Ruler:** Elizabeth II **Obv:** Crowned head right **Obv. Designer:** Raphael Maklouf **Rev:** Parliament House, Value below **Rev. Designer:** Stuart Devlin

Date	Mintage	F	VF	XF	Unc	BU
1988	3,000,000	—	—	—	5.00	6.50
1988 Proof	80,000	Value: 15.00				

KM# 102a 5 DOLLARS

35.7900 g., 0.9250 Silver 1.0645 oz. ASW, 38.74 mm. **Ruler:** Elizabeth II **Obv:** Crowned head right **Rev:** Parliament House **Rev. Designer:** Stuart Devlin

Date	Mintage	F	VF	XF	Unc	BU
1988 Proof	25,000	Value: 18.50				

KM# 134 5 DOLLARS

Aluminum-Bronze, 38.74 mm. **Ruler:** Elizabeth II **Subject:** ANZAC Memorial **Obv:** Crowned head right **Obv. Designer:** Raphael Maklouf **Rev:** Simpson and his donkey, value at top left

Date	Mintage	F	VF	XF	Unc	BU
1990	774,349	—	—	—	5.50	7.00
1990 Proof	33,752	Value: 37.50				

KM# 190 5 DOLLARS

Aluminum-Bronze, 38.74 mm. **Ruler:** Elizabeth II **Subject:** Australian Role in Space Industry, value at bottom **Obv:** Crowned head right **Obv. Designer:** Raphael Maklouf

Date	Mintage	F	VF	XF	Unc	BU
1992	238,979	—	—	—	6.00	7.50
1992 Proof	25,006	Value: 20.00				

KM# 213 5 DOLLARS
35.7900 g., 0.9250 Silver 1.0645 oz. ASW **Ruler:** Elizabeth II **Subject:** Aboriginal Exploration, value bottom left **Obv:** Crowned head right **Obv. Designer:** Raphael Maklouf **Rev:** Aborigine with spear in front of Australian geophysical map

Date	Mintage	F	VF	XF	Unc	BU
1993 Proof	20,000	Value: 24.00				

KM# 214 5 DOLLARS
35.7900 g., 0.9250 Silver 1.0645 oz. ASW **Ruler:** Elizabeth II **Obv:** Crowned head right **Obv. Designer:** Raphael Maklouf **Rev:** Bust of Abel Tasman in front of Australian map, value at top right

Date	Mintage	F	VF	XF	Unc	BU
1993 Proof	20,000	Value: 24.00				

KM# 215 5 DOLLARS
35.7900 g., 0.9250 Silver 1.0645 oz. ASW **Ruler:** Elizabeth II **Obv:** Crowned head right **Obv. Designer:** Raphael Maklouf **Rev:** Bust left in front of Australian map, large value to right of head

Date	Mintage	F	VF	XF	Unc	BU
1993 Proof	20,000	Value: 24.00				

KM# 216 5 DOLLARS
35.7900 g., 0.9250 Silver 1.0645 oz. ASW **Ruler:** Elizabeth II **Obv:** Crowned head right **Obv. Designer:** Raphael Maklouf **Rev:** Bust left in front of Australian map with value upper right

Date	Mintage	F	VF	XF	Unc	BU
1993 Proof	20,000	Value: 24.00				

KM# 217 5 DOLLARS
35.7900 g., 0.9250 Silver 1.0645 oz. ASW **Ruler:** Elizabeth II **Obv:** Crowned head right **Obv. Designer:** Raphael Maklouf **Rev:** Heads at left in front of Australian map with value upper right

Date	Mintage	F	VF	XF	Unc	BU
1993 Proof	20,000	Value: 22.50				

KM# 224 5 DOLLARS
Bi-Metallic Aluminum-Bronze center in Stainless Steel ring, 28.12 mm. **Ruler:** Elizabeth II **Subject:** Women's Enfranchisement - 100 - Year Anniversary of Women's Vote in South Australia **Obv:** Crowned head right within inner circle **Obv. Designer:** Raphael Maklouf **Rev:** Head of Irish-born suffragist Mary Lee facing, within inner circle, value below circle **Note:** Non-magnetic.

Date	Mintage	F	VF	XF	Unc	BU
1994 Proof	22,500	Value: 25.00				
1994	250,121	—	—	—	11.00	12.50

KM# 224a 5 DOLLARS
Aluminum-Bronze **Ruler:** Elizabeth II **Subject:** Women's Enfranchisement - 100 Year Anniversary of Women's Vote in South Australia **Obv:** Crowned head right within inner circle **Rev:** Head of Mary Lee facing, Irish-born suffragist

Date	Mintage	F	VF	XF	Unc	BU
1994 Proof	2,500	Value: 35.00				

KM# 264 5 DOLLARS
31.1040 g., 0.9250 Silver 1.0870 oz. ASW **Ruler:** Elizabeth II **Subject:** Australian Explorers **Obv:** Crowned head right **Obv. Designer:** Raphael Maklouf **Rev:** Bust of Ludwig Leichhardt in front of route he explored, value bottom right

Date	Mintage	F	VF	XF	Unc	BU
1994 Proof	Est. 20,000	Value: 20.00				

KM# 265 5 DOLLARS
31.1040 g., 0.9250 Silver 1.0870 oz. ASW **Ruler:** Elizabeth II **Subject:** Australian Explorers **Obv:** Crowned head right **Obv. Designer:** Raphael Maklouf **Rev:** Bust 3/4 left, in front of route he explored on Australian map, value left of bust

Date	Mintage	F	VF	XF	Unc	BU
1994 Proof	Est. 20,000	Value: 20.00				

KM# 266 5 DOLLARS
31.1040 g., 0.9250 Silver 1.0870 oz. ASW **Ruler:** Elizabeth II **Subject:** Australian Explorers **Obv:** Crowned head right **Obv. Designer:** Raphael Maklouf **Rev:** Bust 3/4 right, to right of route he explored on map, value above map

Date	Mintage	F	VF	XF	Unc	BU
1994 Proof	Est. 20,000	Value: 20.00				

KM# 267 5 DOLLARS
31.1040 g., 0.9250 Silver 1.0870 oz. ASW **Ruler:** Elizabeth II **Subject:** Australian Explorers **Obv:** Crowned head right **Obv. Designer:** Raphael Maklouf **Rev:** Head 3/4 right, to right of map of exploration route at left, value right of beard

Date	Mintage	F	VF	XF	Unc	BU
1994 Proof	Est. 20,000	Value: 20.00				

KM# 268 5 DOLLARS
31.1040 g., 0.9250 Silver 1.0870 oz. ASW **Ruler:** Elizabeth II **Subject:** Australian Explorers **Obv:** Crowned head right **Obv. Designer:** Raphael Maklouf **Rev:** Bust left of route explored on map at right, value above map

Date	Mintage	F	VF	XF	Unc	BU
1994 Proof	Est. 20,000	Value: 20.00				

KM# 303 5 DOLLARS
35.7900 g., 0.9250 Silver 1.0645 oz. ASW **Ruler:** Elizabeth II **Subject:** The Gold Rush Era **Obv:** Crowned head right **Obv. Designer:** Raphael Maklouf **Rev:** Two miners with supplies in front of mine, value at right **Rev. Designer:** Wojciech Pietranik

Date	Mintage	F	VF	XF	Unc	BU
1995 Proof	20,000	Value: 20.00				

KM# 304 5 DOLLARS
35.7900 g., 0.9250 Silver 1.0645 oz. ASW **Ruler:** Elizabeth II **Subject:** Cobb and Co. 1853 **Obv:** Crowned head right **Obv. Designer:** Raphael Maklouf **Rev:** Cobb & Co. Company stagecoach, value above **Rev. Designer:** Wojciech Pietranik

Date	Mintage	F	VF	XF	Unc	BU
1995 Proof	20,000	Value: 20.00				

KM# 305 5 DOLLARS
35.7900 g., 0.9250 Silver 1.0645 oz. ASW **Ruler:** Elizabeth II **Subject:** Elizabeth MacArthur, 1766-1850 - Wool Merchant **Obv:** Crowned head right **Obv. Designer:** Raphael Maklouf **Rev:** Head facing at lower right, flock of sheep above left, value below **Rev. Designer:** Wojciech Pietranik

Date	Mintage	F	VF	XF	Unc	BU
1995 Proof	20,000	Value: 20.00				

KM# 306 5 DOLLARS
35.7900 g., 0.9250 Silver 1.0645 oz. ASW **Ruler:** Elizabeth II **Subject:** Col. William Light, 1786-1839 - City Plan **Obv:** Crowned head right **Obv. Designer:** Raphael Maklouf **Rev:** Head of Col. Light at lower right half right, city plan at left, value below **Rev. Designer:** Wojciech Pietranik

Date	Mintage	F	VF	XF	Unc	BU
1995 Proof	20,000	Value: 20.00				

KM# 307 5 DOLLARS
35.7900 g., 0.9250 Silver 1.0645 oz. ASW **Ruler:** Elizabeth II **Subject:** Charles Todd, 1827-1910 - Telegraph Line **Obv:** Crowned head right **Obv. Designer:** Raphael Maklouf **Rev:** Head of Todd at lower right, telegraph line in background, value at lower left **Rev. Designer:** Wojciech Pietranik

Date	Mintage	F	VF	XF	Unc	BU
1995 Proof	20,000	Value: 20.00				

KM# 311 5 DOLLARS
Bi-Metallic Aluminum-Bronze center in Stainless Steel ring, 28.12 mm. **Ruler:** Elizabeth II **Subject:** Sir Donald Bradman - Cricket Player **Obv:** Crowned head right **Obv. Designer:** Raphael Maklouf **Rev:** 1/2-length figure holding bat within inner circle, value below, subject name above **Rev. Designer:** Wojciech Pietranik **Shape:** 24-sided **Note:** Non-magnetic.

Date	Mintage	F	VF	XF	Unc	BU
1996	500,000	—	—	—	11.00	12.50
1997	—	—	—	—	11.00	12.50

KM# 312 5 DOLLARS
Aluminum-Bronze, 38.74 mm. **Ruler:** Elizabeth II **Subject:** Sir Donald Bradman, Cricket player, **Obv:** Crowned head right **Obv. Designer:** Raphael Maklouf **Rev:** Standing figure in uniform within inner circle, value below **Rev. Designer:** Wojciech Pietranik

Date	Mintage	F	VF	XF	Unc	BU
1996 Proof	22,500	Value: 40.00				

KM# 328 5 DOLLARS
35.7900 g., 0.9250 Silver 1.0645 oz. ASW **Ruler:** Elizabeth II **Subject:** Stockman **Obv:** Crowned head right **Rev:** Cowboy with whip, value top left

Date	Mintage	F	VF	XF	Unc	BU
1996 Proof	20,000	Value: 20.00				

KM# 329 5 DOLLARS
35.7900 g., 0.9250 Silver 1.0645 oz. ASW **Ruler:** Elizabeth II **Subject:** Horse Racing **Obv:** Crowned head right **Rev:** Horse racing scene, denomination below

Date	Mintage	F	VF	XF	Unc	BU
1996 Proof	20,000	Value: 20.00				

KM# 330 5 DOLLARS
35.7900 g., 0.9250 Silver 1.0645 oz. ASW **Ruler:** Elizabeth II **Obv:** Crowned head right **Rev:** Bust of soprano Dame Nellie Melba, with large hat, 3/4 facing, at right, drape, inscription and value at left

Date	Mintage	F	VF	XF	Unc	BU
1996 Proof	20,000	Value: 20.00				

KM# 331 5 DOLLARS
35.7900 g., 0.9250 Silver 1.0645 oz. ASW **Ruler:** Elizabeth II **Subject:** Tom Roberts **Obv:** Crowned head right **Rev:** Half-length figure 3/4 facing, in front of painting, value at lower right

Date	Mintage	F	VF	XF	Unc	BU
1996 Proof	20,000	Value: 20.00				

KM# 332 5 DOLLARS
35.7900 g., 0.9250 Silver 1.0645 oz. ASW **Ruler:** Elizabeth II **Subject:** Henry Lawson **Obv:** Crowned head right **Rev:** Author's portrait and letter to friends, value bottom left

Date	Mintage	F	VF	XF	Unc	BU
1996 Proof	20,000	Value: 20.00				

KM# 356 5 DOLLARS
20.0000 g., Aluminum-Bronze, 38.74 mm. **Ruler:** Elizabeth II **Subject:** Sydney 2000 **Obv:** Crowned head right **Obv. Designer:** Raphael Maklouf **Rev:** Runner,left, Olympic logo below right elbow, value lower left

Date	Mintage	F	VF	XF	Unc	BU
2000 (1997)	—	—	—	—	9.00	10.00

KM# 357 5 DOLLARS
20.0000 g., Aluminum-Bronze, 38.74 mm. **Ruler:** Elizabeth II **Series:** Sydney 2000 Olympics **Obv:** Bust right **Obv. Designer:** Raphael Maklouf **Rev:** Gymnast, value at right, Olympic logo bottom right

Date	Mintage	F	VF	XF	Unc	BU
2000 (1997)	—	—	—	—	8.00	9.00

KM# 358 5 DOLLARS
20.0000 g., Aluminum-Bronze, 38.74 mm. **Ruler:** Elizabeth II **Series:** Sydney 2000 Olympics **Obv:** Crowned head right **Obv. Designer:** Raphael Maklouf **Rev:** Sailors, Olympic logo, upper right, value above rings

Date	Mintage	F	VF	XF	Unc	BU
2000 (1997)	—	—	—	—	9.00	10.00

KM# 359 5 DOLLARS
20.0000 g., Aluminum-Bronze **Ruler:** Elizabeth II **Subject:** Sydney 2000 **Obv:** Crowned head right **Obv. Designer:** Raphael Maklouf **Rev:** Archer on left, Olympic logo at right, value above head

Date	Mintage	F	VF	XF	Unc	BU
2000 (1997)	—	—	—	—	9.00	10.00

KM# 360 5 DOLLARS
20.0000 g., Aluminum-Bronze, 38.74 mm. **Ruler:** Elizabeth II **Series:** Sydney 2000 Olympics **Obv:** Crowned head right **Obv. Designer:** Raphael Maklouf **Rev:** Field hockey player Olympic logo lower right, value at upper right

Date	Mintage	F	VF	XF	Unc	BU
2000 (1997)	—	—	—	—	8.00	9.00

KM# 361 5 DOLLARS
20.0000 g., Aluminum-Bronze, 38.74 mm. **Ruler:** Elizabeth II **Series:** Sydney 2000 Olympics **Obv:** Crowned head right **Obv. Designer:** Raphael Maklouf **Rev:** Power lifter, Olympic logo at lower right, value upper right

Date	Mintage	F	VF	XF	Unc	BU
2000 (1997)	—	—	—	—	8.00	9.00

KM# 544 5 DOLLARS
35.7900 g., 0.9250 Silver 1.0644 oz. ASW, 38.9 mm. **Ruler:** Elizabeth II **Series:** Masterpieces of Transportation **Obv:** Crowned head right **Rev:** Camel pack train, value upper right **Edge:** Reeded

Date	Mintage	F	VF	XF	Unc	BU
1997 Proof	10,000	Value: 25.00				

KM# 545 5 DOLLARS
35.7900 g., 0.9250 Silver 1.0644 oz. ASW, 38.9 mm. **Ruler:** Elizabeth II **Series:** Masterpieces of Transportation **Obv:** Crowned head right **Rev:** Riverboat, value below **Edge:** Reeded

Date	Mintage	F	VF	XF	Unc	BU
1997 Proof	10,000	Value: 25.00				

KM# 546 5 DOLLARS
35.7900 g., 0.9250 Silver 1.0644 oz. ASW, 38.9 mm. **Ruler:** Elizabeth II **Series:** Masterpieces of Transportation **Obv:** Crowned head right **Rev:** Steam locomotive, value at top **Edge:** Reeded

Date	Mintage	F	VF	XF	Unc	BU
1997 Proof	10,000	Value: 25.00				

KM# 547 5 DOLLARS
35.7900 g., 0.9250 Silver 1.0644 oz. ASW, 38.9 mm. **Ruler:** Elizabeth II **Series:** Masterpieces of Transportation **Obv:** Crowned head right **Rev:** Ox-drawn wagons, value below **Edge:** Reeded

Date	Mintage	F	VF	XF	Unc	BU
1997 Proof	10,000	Value: 25.00				

KM# 548 5 DOLLARS
35.7900 g., 0.9250 Silver 1.0644 oz. ASW, 38.9 mm. **Ruler:** Elizabeth II **Series:** Masterpieces of Transportation **Obv:** Crowned head right **Rev:** Steam tractor, value below **Edge:** Reeded

Date	Mintage	F	VF	XF	Unc	BU
1997 Proof	10,000	Value: 25.00				

KM# 386 5 DOLLARS
20.0000 g., Aluminum-Bronze, 38.74 mm. **Ruler:** Elizabeth II **Subject:** 70th Anniversary - Royal Flying Doctor **Obv:** Crowned head right **Rev:** Radio dispatcher and airplane divides legend, value at right

Date	Mintage	F	VF	XF	Unc	BU
1998 Proof	Est. 20,000	Value: 18.50				

KM# 368 5 DOLLARS
20.0000 g., Aluminum-Bronze, 38.74 mm. **Ruler:** Elizabeth II **Series:** Sydney 2000 Olympics **Obv:** Crowned head right **Obv. Designer:** Raphael Maklouf **Rev:** Cyclist, Olympic logo to right of head, value behind cyclist

Date	Mintage	F	VF	XF	Unc	BU
2000 (1998)	—	—	—	—	9.00	10.00

KM# 369 5 DOLLARS
20.0000 g., Aluminum-Bronze, 38.74 mm. **Ruler:** Elizabeth II **Series:** Sydney 2000 Olympics **Obv:** Crowned head right **Obv. Designer:** Raphael Maklouf **Rev:** Soccer player, Olympic logo on right, value at left

Date	Mintage	F	VF	XF	Unc	BU
2000 (1998)	—	—	—	—	9.00	10.00

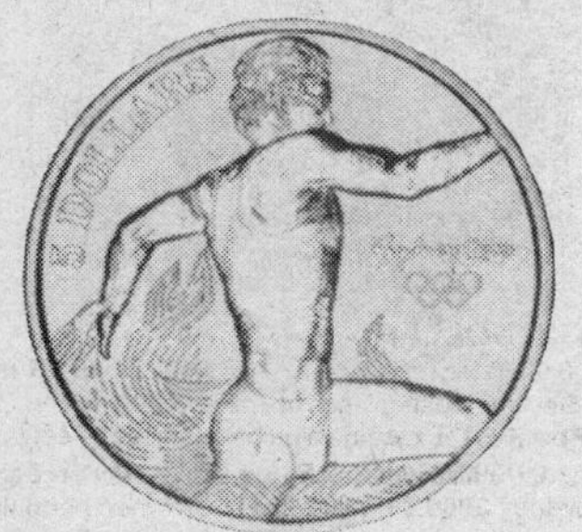

KM# 370 5 DOLLARS
20.0000 g., Aluminum-Bronze, 38.74 mm. **Ruler:** Elizabeth II **Series:** Sydney 2000 Olympics **Obv:** Crowned head right **Obv. Designer:** Raphael Maklouf **Rev:** Triathlon swimmer, Olympic logo on right, value upper left

Date	Mintage	F	VF	XF	Unc	BU
2000 (1998)	—	—	—	—	9.00	10.00

KM# 371 5 DOLLARS
31.6350 g., 0.9990 Silver 1.0161 oz. ASW **Ruler:** Elizabeth II **Series:** Sydney 2000 Olympics **Obv:** Crowned head right **Rev:** Australian map above multicolor logo, Olympic logo at bottom **Rev. Designer:** Stuart Devlin and Nova Peris-Kneebone

Date	Mintage	F	VF	XF	Unc	BU
2000 (1998) Proof	Est. 100,000	Value: 45.00				

KM# 372 5 DOLLARS
31.6350 g., 0.9990 Silver 1.0161 oz. ASW **Ruler:** Elizabeth II **Series:** Sydney 2000 Olympics **Obv:** Crowned head right **Rev:** Two Great White sharks within wreath, Olympic logo at bottom **Rev. Designer:** Stuart Devlin

Date	Mintage	F	VF	XF	Unc	BU
2000 (1998) Proof	Est. 100,000	Value: 50.00				

KM# 374 5 DOLLARS
Bi-Metallic Aluminum-Bronze center in Stainless Steel ring, 28.12 mm. **Ruler:** Elizabeth II **Subject:** 70 Years - Royal Flying Doctor Service **Obv:** Head with tiara right within inner circle **Obv. Designer:** Ian Rank-Broadley **Rev:** Insignia above bi-plane, two dates below, within circle, value below circle

Date	Mintage	F	VF	XF	Unc	BU
1998	—	—	—	—	10.00	12.00

KM# 375 5 DOLLARS
20.0000 g., Aluminum-Bronze, 38.74 mm. **Ruler:** Elizabeth II **Series:** Sydney 2000 Summer Olympics **Obv:** Crowned head right **Obv. Designer:** Ian Rank-Broadley **Rev:** Two netball players, Olympic logo at right, value on left

Date	Mintage	F	VF	XF	Unc	BU
2000 (1998)	—	—	—	—	9.00	10.00

KM# 376 5 DOLLARS
20.0000 g., Aluminum-Bronze, 38.74 mm. **Ruler:** Elizabeth II **Series:** Sydney 2000 Olympics **Obv:** Crowned head right **Obv. Designer:** Ian Rank-Broadley **Rev:** Two wrestlers, Olympic logo to left, value at upper right

Date	Mintage	F	VF	XF	Unc	BU
2000 (1998)	—	—	—	—	9.00	10.00

KM# 377 5 DOLLARS
20.0000 g., Aluminum-Bronze, 38.74 mm. **Ruler:** Elizabeth II **Series:** Sydney 2000 Summer Olympics **Obv:** Crowned head right **Obv. Designer:** Ian Rank-Broadley **Rev:** Canoeing event, Olympic logo at left, value at top

Date	Mintage	F	VF	XF	Unc	BU
2000 (1998)	—	—	—	—	9.00	10.00

KM# 378 5 DOLLARS
20.0000 g., Aluminum-Bronze, 38.74 mm. **Ruler:** Elizabeth II **Series:** Sydney 2000 Olympics **Obv:** Crowned head right **Obv. Designer:** Ian Rank-Broadley **Rev:** Softball player swinging bat, Olympic logo at right, value at left

Date	Mintage	F	VF	XF	Unc	BU
2000 (1998)	—	—	—	—	9.00	10.00

KM# 379 5 DOLLARS
31.6350 g., 0.9990 Silver 1.0161 oz. ASW **Ruler:** Elizabeth II **Series:** Sydney 2000 Olympics **Obv:** Crowned head right **Obv. Designer:** Ian Rank-Broadley **Rev:** Frill-necked lizard within wreath, Olympic logo below **Rev. Designer:** Stuart Devlin

Date	Mintage	F	VF	XF	Unc	BU
2000 (1998) Proof	Est. 100,000	Value: 55.00				

KM# 380 5 DOLLARS
31.6350 g., 0.9990 Silver 1.0161 oz. ASW **Ruler:** Elizabeth II **Series:** Sydney 2000 Olympics **Obv:** Crowned head right **Obv. Designer:** Ian Rank-Broadley **Rev:** 9 Australian faces of different races, Olympic logo at bottom **Rev. Designer:** Stuart Devlin

Date	Mintage	F	VF	XF	Unc	BU
2000 (1998) Proof	Est. 100,000	Value: 40.00				

KM# 381 5 DOLLARS
31.6350 g., 0.9990 Silver 1.0161 oz. ASW **Ruler:** Elizabeth II **Series:** Sydney 2000 Olympics **Obv:** Crowned head right **Obv. Designer:** Raphael Maklouf **Rev:** Two dancing figures in dream circle, within circle of aquatic life, wreath encircling all, Olympic logo at bottom **Rev. Designer:** Stuart Devlin and Nova Peris-Kneebone

Date	Mintage	F	VF	XF	Unc	BU
2000 (1998) Proof	Est. 100,000	Value: 45.00				

KM# 382 5 DOLLARS
31.6350 g., 0.9990 Silver 1.0161 oz. ASW **Ruler:** Elizabeth II **Series:** Sydney 2000 Olympics **Obv:** Crowned head right **Rev:** Kangaroo in circle of grass trees, Olympic logo below, legend encircling all **Rev. Inscription:** Stuart Devlin

Date	Mintage	F	VF	XF	Unc	BU
2000 (1998) Proof	Est. 100,000	Value: 60.00				

KM# 407 5 DOLLARS
20.0000 g., Brass, 38.74 mm. **Ruler:** Elizabeth II **Series:** Sydney 2000 Olympics **Obv:** Crowned head right **Obv. Designer:** Ian Rank-Broadley **Rev:** Two basketball players, value upper right, Olympic logo lower left

Date	Mintage	F	VF	XF	Unc	BU
2000 (1999)	—	—	—	—	8.00	9.00

KM# 408 5 DOLLARS
20.0000 g., Brass, 38.74 mm. **Ruler:** Elizabeth II **Series:** Sydney 2000 Summer Olympics **Obv:** Crowned head right **Obv. Designer:** Ian Rank-Broadley **Rev:** Tae Kwon Do competitor, Olympic logo at top, value on right

Date	Mintage	F	VF	XF	Unc	BU
2000 (1999)	—	—	—	—	8.00	9.00

KM# 409 5 DOLLARS
20.0000 g., Brass, 38.74 mm. **Ruler:** Elizabeth II **Series:** Sydney 2000 Olympics **Obv:** Crowned head right **Obv. Designer:** Ian Rank-Broadley **Rev:** Tennis player, value at left, Olympic logo below tennis ball

Date	Mintage	F	VF	XF	Unc	BU
2000 (1999)	—	—	—	—	8.00	9.00

KM# 418 5 DOLLARS
20.0000 g., Brass, 38.74 mm. **Ruler:** Elizabeth II **Series:** Sydney 2000 Olympics **Obv:** Crowned head right **Obv. Designer:** Ian Rank-Broadley **Rev:** Shooter with shotgun, Olympic logo above, value on right

Date	Mintage	F	VF	XF	Unc	BU
2000 (1999)	—	—	—	—	8.00	9.00

KM# 419 5 DOLLARS
20.0000 g., Brass, 38.74 mm. **Ruler:** Elizabeth II **Series:** Sydney 2000 Olympics **Obv:** Crowned head right **Obv. Designer:** Ian Rank-Broadley **Rev:** Table tennis player, Olympic logo upper left, value at top

Date	Mintage	F	VF	XF	Unc	BU
2000 (1999)	—	—	—	—	8.00	9.00

KM# 420 5 DOLLARS
20.0000 g., Brass, 38.74 mm. **Ruler:** Elizabeth II **Series:** Sydney 2000 Olympics **Obv:** Crowned head right **Obv. Designer:** Ian Rank-Broadley **Rev:** Fencer in action, Olympic logo below right arm, value at left

Date	Mintage	F	VF	XF	Unc	BU
2000 (1999)	—	—	—	—	8.00	9.00

KM# 421 5 DOLLARS
20.0000 g., Brass, 38.74 mm. **Ruler:** Elizabeth II **Series:** Sydney 2000 Olympics **Obv:** Crowned head right **Obv. Designer:** Ian Rank-Broadley **Rev:** Badminton player, Olympic logo above, value top right

Date	Mintage	F	VF	XF	Unc	BU
2000 (1999)	—	—	—	—	9.00	10.00

KM# 438 5 DOLLARS
31.6350 g., 0.9990 Silver 1.0161 oz. ASW **Ruler:** Elizabeth II **Series:** Sydney 2000 Olympics **Obv:** Crowned head right **Rev:** Two emus with eggs and chicks within wreath, Olympic logo at bottom **Rev. Designer:** Stuart Devlin **Edge:** Reeded

Date	Mintage	F	VF	XF	Unc	BU
2000 (1999) Proof	100,000	Value: 50.00				

KM# 439 5 DOLLARS
31.6350 g., 0.9990 Silver 1.0161 oz. ASW **Ruler:** Elizabeth II **Series:** Sydney 2000 Olympics **Obv:** Crowned head right **Rev:** Koala in tree within wreath, Olympic logo below **Rev. Designer:** Stuart Devlin

Date	Mintage	F	VF	XF	Unc	BU
2000 (1999) Proof	100,000	Value: 40.00				

KM# 440 5 DOLLARS
31.6350 g., 0.9990 Silver 1.0161 oz. ASW **Ruler:** Elizabeth II **Series:** Sydney 2000 Olympics **Obv:** Crowned head right **Rev:** Three radiant circular views within circle of round maps Olympic logo at bottom **Rev. Designer:** Stuart Devlin

Date	Mintage	F	VF	XF	Unc	BU
2000 Proof	100,000	Value: 37.50				

KM# 441 5 DOLLARS
31.6350 g., 0.9990 Silver 1.0161 oz. ASW **Ruler:** Elizabeth II **Series:** Sydney 2000 Olympics **Obv:** Crowned head right **Rev:** 7 figures positioned like spokes in a wheel, Olympic logo at bottom **Rev. Designer:** Stuart Devlin

Date	Mintage	F	VF	XF	Unc	BU
2000 Proof	100,000	Value: 37.50				

KM# 478 5 DOLLARS
10.5200 g., Bi-Metallic Aluminum-Bronze center in Stainless Steel ring, 28.12 mm. **Ruler:** Elizabeth II **Subject:** Phar Lap **Obv:** Head with tiara right within inner circle **Rev:** Jockey atop Phar Lap racing, right, within circle, divides date, value below circle **Edge:** Plain **Shape:** 24-sided

Date	Mintage	F	VF	XF	Unc	BU
2000	—	—	—	—	10.00	12.00

KM# 510 5 DOLLARS
28.0000 g., Aluminum-Bronze, 38.7 mm. **Ruler:** Elizabeth II **Subject:** Phar Lap **Obv:** Head with tiara right within inner circle **Rev:** Phar Lap and jockey facing right within horseshoe turned to left, value on bottom of shoe, subject name and date on top of shoe **Edge:** Reeded

Date	Mintage	F	VF	XF	Unc	BU
2000 Proof	20,000	Value: 25.00				

KM# 515 5 DOLLARS
31.6350 g., 0.9990 Silver 1.0161 oz. ASW, 40.5 mm. **Ruler:** Elizabeth II **Series:** Olympics - Sydney Harbor Bridge **Obv:** Crowned head right **Rev:** Sydney suspension bridge within harbor wreath, Olympic logo at bottom **Rev. Designer:** Stuart Devlin **Edge Lettering:** GAMES OF THE XXVII OLYMPIAD twice

Date	Mintage	F	VF	XF	Unc	BU
2000 Prooflike	100,000	—	—	—	40.00	—

KM# 516 5 DOLLARS
31.6350 g., 0.9990 Silver 1.0161 oz. ASW, 40.5 mm. **Ruler:** Elizabeth II **Series:** Olympics - Kookaburra **Obv:** Crowned head right **Rev:** Kookaburra with Waratah leaves, within wreath, Olympic logo at bottom **Rev. Designer:** Stuart Devlin

Date	Mintage	F	VF	XF	Unc	BU
2000 Prooflike	100,000	—	—	—	45.00	—

KM# 517 5 DOLLARS
Aluminum-Bronze, 38.6 mm. **Ruler:** Elizabeth II **Subject:** Paralympics **Obv:** Crowned head right **Rev:** Wheelchair racer and multicolor logo, small value to right of chair **Rev. Designer:** Wojciech Pietranik **Edge:** Reeded

Date	Mintage	F	VF	XF	Unc	BU
2000	Est. 30,000	—	—	—	12.50	15.00

KM# 429 5 DOLLARS
20.0000 g., Brass, 38.74 mm. **Ruler:** Elizabeth II **Series:** Sydney 2000 Olympics **Obv:** Crowned head right **Obv. Designer:** Ian Rank-Broadley **Rev:** Pentathlon events portrayed by 5 participants, Olympic logo at lower left, value at bottom

Date	Mintage	F	VF	XF	Unc	BU
2000	—	—	—	—	9.00	10.00

KM# 430 5 DOLLARS
20.0000 g., Brass, 38.74 mm. **Ruler:** Elizabeth II **Obv:** Crowned head right **Obv. Designer:** Ian Rank-Broadley **Rev:** Judo match, Olympic logo lower right, value at top

Date	Mintage	F	VF	XF	Unc	BU
2000	—	—	—	—	8.00	9.00

KM# 431 5 DOLLARS
20.0000 g., Brass, 38.74 mm. **Ruler:** Elizabeth II **Series:** Sydney 2000 Olympics **Obv:** Crowned head right **Obv. Designer:** Ian Rank-Broadley **Rev:** Rower, Olympic logo upper left, value upper right

Date	Mintage	F	VF	XF	Unc	BU
2000	—	—	—	—	9.00	10.00

KM# 432 5 DOLLARS
20.0000 g., Brass, 38.74 mm. **Ruler:** Elizabeth II **Series:** Sydney 2000 Olympics **Obv:** Crowned head right **Obv. Designer:** Ian Rank-Broadley **Rev:** Two men boxing, value upper left, Olympic logo divides boxers at bottom

Date	Mintage	F	VF	XF	Unc	BU
2000	—	—	—	—	9.00	10.00

KM# 433 5 DOLLARS
20.0000 g., Brass, 38.74 mm. **Ruler:** Elizabeth II **Series:** Sydney 2000 Olympics **Obv:** Crowned head right **Obv. Designer:** Ian Rank-Broadley **Rev:** Volleyball player, Olympic logo below ball, value at left

Date	Mintage	F	VF	XF	Unc	BU
2000	—	—	—	—	9.00	10.00

KM# 434 5 DOLLARS
20.0000 g., Brass, 38.74 mm. **Ruler:** Elizabeth II **Series:** Sydney 2000 Olympics **Obv:** Crowned head right **Obv. Designer:** Ian Rank-Broadley **Rev:** Equestrian putting horse through jumps

Date	Mintage	F	VF	XF	Unc	BU
2000	—	—	—	—	9.00	10.00

KM# 435 5 DOLLARS
20.0000 g., Brass, 38.74 mm. **Ruler:** Elizabeth II **Series:** Sydney 2000 Olympics **Obv:** Crowned head right **Obv. Designer:** Ian Rank-Broadley **Rev:** Pitcher winding up

Date	Mintage	F	VF	XF	Unc	BU
2000	—	—	—	—	9.00	10.00

KM# 436 5 DOLLARS
20.0000 g., Brass, 38.74 mm. **Ruler:** Elizabeth II **Series:** Sydney 2000 Olympics **Obv:** Crowned head right **Obv. Designer:** Ian Rank-Broadley **Rev:** Swimmer, Olympic logo below, value above

Date	Mintage	F	VF	XF	Unc	BU
2000	—	—	—	—	9.00	10.00

KM# 75 10 DOLLARS
20.0000 g., 0.9250 Silver .5949 oz. ASW **Ruler:** Elizabeth II **Subject:** XII Commonwealth Games - Brisbane **Obv:** Young bust right **Obv. Designer:** Arnold Machin **Rev:** Outline of country with hurdles on top at center of shield of athletes, legend surrounds all **Rev. Designer:** Stuart Devlin

Date	Mintage	F	VF	XF	Unc	BU
1982	125,700	—	—	—	9.50	11.50
1982 Proof	85,142	Value: 14.50				

KM# 85 10 DOLLARS
20.0000 g., 0.9250 Silver .5949 oz. ASW **Ruler:** Elizabeth II **Subject:** 150th Anniversary - State of Victoria **Obv:** Crowned head right **Obv. Designer:** Raphael Maklouf **Rev:** Arms of Victoria, value at bottom, state name divides dates at top

Date	Mintage	F	VF	XF	Unc	BU
1985	81,751	—	—	—	10.00	12.00
1985 Proof	55,806	Value: 17.50				

KM# 88 10 DOLLARS
20.0000 g., 0.9250 Silver .5949 oz. ASW **Ruler:** Elizabeth II **Subject:** 150th Anniversary - South Australia **Obv:** Crowned head right **Obv. Designer:** Raphael Maklouf **Rev:** Arms of South Australia, value below, name divides dates at top

Date	Mintage	F	VF	XF	Unc	BU
1986	78,100	—	—	—	10.00	12.00
1986 Proof	52,150	Value: 17.50				

KM# 93 10 DOLLARS
20.0000 g., 0.9250 Silver .5949 oz. ASW **Ruler:** Elizabeth II **Subject:** New South Wales **Obv:** Crowned head right **Obv. Designer:** Raphael Maklouf **Rev:** Arms of New South Wales, value below **Rev. Designer:** Horst Hahne

Date	Mintage	F	VF	XF	Unc	BU
1987	55,000	—	—	—	10.00	12.00
1987 Proof	50,500	Value: 17.50				

KM# 103 10 DOLLARS
20.0000 g., 0.9250 Silver .5949 oz. ASW **Ruler:** Elizabeth II **Subject:** Landing of Governor Philip **Obv:** Crowned head right **Obv. Designer:** Raphael Maklouf **Rev:** Large sailing ship to right, smaller ships behind and left, canoe with rowers in foreground, value at top left **Rev. Designer:** Stuart Devlin

Date	Mintage	F	VF	XF	Unc	BU
1988	111,497	—	—	—	12.00	14.00
1988 Proof	80,099	Value: 20.00				

KM# 114 10 DOLLARS
20.0000 g., 0.9250 Silver .5949 oz. ASW **Ruler:** Elizabeth II **Subject:** Queensland **Obv:** Crowned head right **Obv. Designer:** Raphael Maklouf **Rev:** Arms of Queensland, name of subject at top, value below arms **Rev. Designer:** Horst Hahne

Date	Mintage	F	VF	XF	Unc	BU
1989	48,929	—	—	—	10.00	12.00
1989 Proof	48,573	Value: 17.50				

KM# 133 10 DOLLARS
20.0000 g., 0.9250 Silver .5949 oz. ASW **Ruler:** Elizabeth II **Obv:** Crowned head right **Obv. Designer:** Raphael Maklouf **Rev:** Kookaburras, value above

Date	Mintage	F	VF	XF	Unc	BU
1989 Proof	50,000	Value: 45.00				

KM# 137 10 DOLLARS
20.0000 g., 0.9250 Silver .5949 oz. ASW **Ruler:** Elizabeth II **Subject:** Western Australia **Obv:** Crowned head right **Obv. Designer:** Raphael Maklouf **Rev:** Western Australia coat of arms, value below

Date	Mintage	F	VF	XF	Unc	BU
1990	28,133	—	—	—	12.00	14.00
1990 Proof	29,089	Value: 25.00				

KM# 136 10 DOLLARS
20.0000 g., 0.9250 Silver .5949 oz. ASW **Ruler:** Elizabeth II **Obv:** Crowned head right **Obv. Designer:** Raphael Maklouf **Rev:** Sulpher-crested cockatoo, value above

Date	Mintage	F	VF	XF	Unc	BU
1990 Proof	49,801	Value: 45.00				

KM# 153 10 DOLLARS
20.0000 g., 0.9250 Silver .5949 oz. ASW **Ruler:** Elizabeth II **Subject:** Tasmania **Obv:** Crowned head right **Obv. Designer:** Raphael Maklouf **Rev:** Arms of Tasmania, value below, subject name above

Date	Mintage	F	VF	XF	Unc	BU
1991	26,150	—	—	—	12.00	14.00
1991 Proof	27,664	Value: 30.00				

KM# 156 10 DOLLARS
20.0000 g., 0.9250 Silver .5949 oz. ASW **Ruler:** Elizabeth II **Obv:** Crowned head right **Obv. Designer:** Raphael Maklouf **Rev:** Jabiru Stork,right, value above

Date	Mintage	F	VF	XF	Unc	BU
1991 Proof	32,446	Value: 35.00				

KM# 188 10 DOLLARS
20.0000 g., 0.9250 Silver .5949 oz. ASW **Ruler:** Elizabeth II **Obv:** Crowned head right **Obv. Designer:** Raphael Maklouf **Rev:** Northern Territory state arms, value below, subject name above

Date	Mintage	F	VF	XF	Unc	BU
1992	24,164	—	—	—	10.00	12.00
1992 Proof	24,404	Value: 20.00				

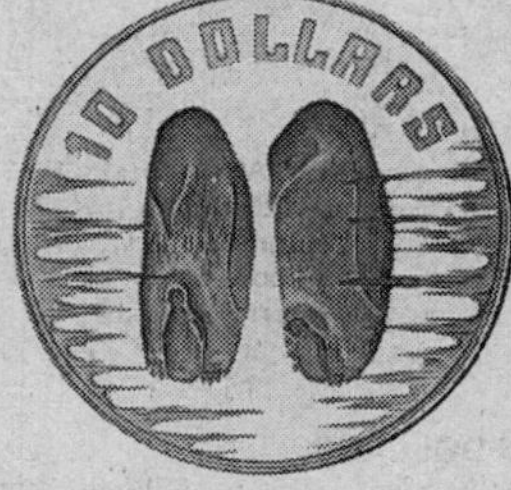

KM# 199 10 DOLLARS
20.0000 g., 0.9250 Silver .5949 oz. ASW **Ruler:** Elizabeth II **Obv:** Crowned head right **Obv. Designer:** Raphael Maklouf **Rev:** Emperor Penguins with chicks, value above

Date	Mintage	F	VF	XF	Unc	BU
1992 Proof	Est. 25,319	Value: 55.00				

KM# 210 10 DOLLARS
20.0000 g., 0.9250 Silver .5949 oz. ASW **Ruler:** Elizabeth II **Obv:** Crowned head right **Obv. Designer:** Raphael Maklouf **Rev:** Australian Capital Territory state arms, value below

Date	Mintage	F	VF	XF	Unc	BU
1993	19,288	—	—	—	12.00	14.00
1993 Proof	21,183	Value: 22.50				

KM# 317 10 DOLLARS
20.0000 g., 0.9250 Silver .5949 oz. ASW **Ruler:** Elizabeth II **Subject:** UNEP - Palm Cockatoo **Obv:** Crowned head right **Obv. Designer:** Raphael Maklouf **Rev:** Palm cockatoo with UNEP logo at left, value at right

Date	Mintage	F	VF	XF	Unc	BU
1993 Proof	Est. 55,000	Value: 40.00				

KM# 221 10 DOLLARS
20.0000 g., 0.9250 Silver .5949 oz. ASW **Ruler:** Elizabeth II **Obv:** Crowned head right **Obv. Designer:** Raphael Maklouf **Rev:** Palm cockatoo, value at right

Date	Mintage	F	VF	XF	Unc	BU
1993 Proof	22,172	Value: 40.00				

KM# 225 10 DOLLARS
20.7700 g., 0.9990 Silver .6678 oz. ASW **Ruler:** Elizabeth II **Series:** Olympic Gold Medalists - Edwin Flack 1896 **Obv:** Crowned head right within circle **Obv. Designer:** Raphael Maklouf **Rev:** Edwin Flack with Olympic Flame above wreath within circle, legend above, value below **Rev. Designer:** Horst Hahne

Date	Mintage	F	VF	XF	Unc	BU
1994 Matte Proof	21,484	Value: 18.50				

KM# 226 10 DOLLARS
20.7700 g., 0.9990 Silver .6678 oz. ASW **Ruler:** Elizabeth II **Series:** Olympic Gold Medalists - Sarah Durack 1912 **Obv:** Crowned head right within circle **Obv. Designer:** Raphael Maklouf **Rev:** Circle surrounds swimmer within wreath above gold medal, cenomination below **Rev. Designer:** Horst Hahne

Date	Mintage	F	VF	XF	Unc	BU
1994 Matte Proof	21,484	Value: 18.50				

KM# 223 10 DOLLARS
20.0000 g., 0.9250 Silver .5949 oz. ASW **Ruler:** Elizabeth II **Obv:** Crowned head right **Rev:** Wedge-tailed eagle, left, value at left **Rev. Designer:** Horst Hahne

Date	Mintage	F	VF	XF	Unc	BU
1994 Proof	23,326	Value: 35.00				

KM# 296 10 DOLLARS
20.7700 g., 0.9990 Silver .6678 oz. ASW **Ruler:** Elizabeth II **Obv:** Crowned head right **Obv. Designer:** Raphael Maklouf **Rev:** Numbat right, value at left **Rev. Designer:** Vladimir Gottwald

Date	Mintage	F	VF	XF	Unc	BU
1995 Proof	25,000	Value: 35.00				

KM# 301 10 DOLLARS
20.7700 g., 0.9990 Silver .6678 oz. ASW **Ruler:** Elizabeth II **Series:** Olympic Gold Medalists - Dawn Fraser **Obv:** Crowned head right **Rev:** Half-length portrait

Date	Mintage	F	VF	XF	Unc	BU
1995 Matte Proof	Est. 30,000	Value: 27.50				

KM# 302 10 DOLLARS
20.7700 g., 0.9990 Silver .6678 oz. ASW **Ruler:** Elizabeth II **Series:** Olympic Gold Medalists - Murray Rose **Obv:** Crowned head right **Rev:** Murray Rose

Date	Mintage	F	VF	XF	Unc	BU
1995 Matte Proof	Est. 30,000	Value: 27.50				

KM# 314 10 DOLLARS
20.0000 g., 0.9250 Silver .5949 oz. ASW **Ruler:** Elizabeth II **Rev:** Southern right whale with baby, value below **Rev. Designer:** Vladimir Gottwald

Date	Mintage	F	VF	XF	Unc	BU
1996 Proof	24,000	Value: 45.00				

KM# 315 10 DOLLARS
20.7700 g., 0.9990 Silver .6678 oz. ASW **Ruler:** Elizabeth II **Series:** Australia's Greatest Olympics - 1956 **Obv:** Crowned head right **Rev:** Betty Cuthbert, sprint champion 1956, born 1938 within circle, value below circle **Rev. Designer:** Horst Hahne

Date	Mintage	F	VF	XF	Unc	BU
1996 Matte Unc	15,300	—	—	—	60.00	—

KM# 316 10 DOLLARS
20.7700 g., 0.9990 Silver .6678 oz. ASW **Ruler:** Elizabeth II **Series:** Australia's Greatest Olympics - 1956 **Obv:** Crowned head right **Rev:** Shirley Strickland, hurdling champion, 1952 and 1956 within circle, value below circle **Rev. Designer:** Horst Hahne

Date	Mintage	F	VF	XF	Unc	BU
1996 Matte Unc	15,300	—	—	—	60.00	—

KM# 353 10 DOLLARS
20.7700 g., 0.9990 Silver .6678 oz. ASW **Ruler:** Elizabeth II **Subject:** Sydney Opera House **Obv:** Crowned head right **Obv. Designer:** Raphael Maklouf **Rev:** Opera house and Sydney shoreline within circle, legend above circle, value below **Rev. Designer:** Horst Hahne

Date	Mintage	F	VF	XF	Unc	BU
1997 Matte Proof	20,000	Value: 32.50				

KM# 354 10 DOLLARS
20.7700 g., 0.9990 Silver .6678 oz. ASW **Ruler:** Elizabeth II **Subject:** Sydney Harbour Bridge **Obv:** Crowned head right **Obv. Designer:** Raphael Maklouf **Rev:** Bridge over harbour within circle, value below circle, legend above **Rev. Designer:** Horst Hahne

Date	Mintage	F	VF	XF	Unc	BU
1997 Matte Proof	20,000	Value: 32.50				

KM# 367.1 10 DOLLARS
20.0000 g., 0.9990 Silver .6678 oz. ASW **Ruler:** Elizabeth II **Subject:** Red-tailed Black Cockatoo **Obv:** Crowned head right **Obv. Designer:** Raphael Maklouf **Rev:** Cockatoo perched in dead tree, left, value to left

Date	Mintage	F	VF	XF	Unc	BU
1997 Proof	24,000	Value: 40.00				

KM# 367.2 10 DOLLARS
40.0000 g., 0.9250 Silver 1.1896 oz. ASW **Ruler:** Elizabeth II **Subject:** Red-tailed Black Cockatoo **Obv:** Crowned head right **Rev:** Cockatoo perched in dead tree

Date	Mintage	F	VF	XF	Unc	BU
1997 Proof	14,000	Value: 50.00				

KM# 387 10 DOLLARS
20.7700 g., 0.9990 Silver .6671 oz. ASW **Ruler:** Elizabeth II **Subject:** Melbourne **Obv:** Crowned head right **Rev:** Melbourne cricket grounds

Date	Mintage	F	VF	XF	Unc	BU
1998 Matte Proof	20,000	Value: 32.50				

KM# 388 10 DOLLARS
20.7700 g., 0.9990 Silver .6671 oz. ASW **Ruler:** Elizabeth II **Subject:** Melbourne **Obv:** Crowned head right **Rev:** Street car

Date	Mintage	F	VF	XF	Unc	BU
1998 Matte Proof	20,000	Value: 32.50				

KM# 397 10 DOLLARS
20.0000 g., 0.9250 Silver .5948 oz. ASW **Ruler:** Elizabeth II **Subject:** Northern Hairy-nosed Wombat **Obv:** Head with tiara right **Obv. Designer:** Ian Rank-Broadley **Rev:** Wombat above denomination

Date	Mintage	F	VF	XF	Unc	BU
1998 Proof	24,000	Value: 35.00				

KM# 414 10 DOLLARS
20.7700 g., 0.9990 Silver .6671 oz. ASW **Ruler:** Elizabeth II **Subject:** The Snowy Mountains Scheme **Obv:** Head with tiara right within inner circle **Obv. Designer:** Ian Rank-Broadley **Rev:** Tunnel building scene within circle, value below, legend above **Rev. Designer:** Vladimir Gottwald

Date	Mintage	F	VF	XF	Unc	BU
1999	20,000	—	—	—	27.50	—

KM# 415 10 DOLLARS
20.7700 g., 0.9990 Silver .6671 oz. ASW **Ruler:** Elizabeth II **Subject:** The Snowy Mountains Scheme **Obv:** Head with tiara right within inner circle **Obv. Designer:** Ian Rank-Broadley **Rev:** Dam building scene within circle, value below, legend above **Rev. Designer:** Vladimir Gottwald

Date	Mintage	F	VF	XF	Unc	BU
1999	20,000	—	—	—	27.50	—

KM# 423 10 DOLLARS
33.5300 g., Bi-Metallic Copper center in .999 Silver ring **Ruler:** Elizabeth II **Subject:** Millennium Series, The Past **Obv:** Head with tiara right within circle **Obv. Designer:** Ian Rank-Broadley **Rev:** Seedling on Australian map above denomination with rising sun background **Rev. Designer:** Peter Soobik **Edge:** Reeded

Date	Mintage	F	VF	XF	Unc	BU
1999 Proof	20,000	Value: 650				

KM# 511 10 DOLLARS
36.0100 g., 0.9990 Silver 1.1566 oz. ASW, 38.7 mm. **Ruler:** Elizabeth II **Series:** Millennium - The Present **Obv:** Head with tiara right within circle **Rev:** Australian map behind young tree, value at base of tree, all within circle, surrounded by circle of stick figures and ovals **Edge:** Reeded

Date	Mintage	F	VF	XF	Unc	BU
2000 Proof	20,000	Value: 225				

KM# 518 10 DOLLARS
311.0350 g., 0.9990 Silver 10.0000 oz. ASW, 75 mm. **Ruler:** Elizabeth II **Subject:** Paralympics **Obv:** Head with tiara right, denomination below **Obv. Designer:** Ian Rank-Broadley **Rev:** Sydney Opera House and harbor bridge **Edge:** Lettering with logo **Edge Lettering:** GAMES OF THE XI PARALYMPIAD **Note:** Photo reduced.

Date	Mintage	F	VF	XF	Unc	BU
2000 Prooflike	3,000	—	—	—	400	—

KM# 218 20 DOLLARS
33.6200 g., 0.9250 Silver 1.0000 oz. ASW **Ruler:** Elizabeth II **Series:** Olympics **Subject:** Track Winners **Obv:** Crowned head right, denomination below **Obv. Designer:** Raphael Maklouf **Rev:** Three athletes on podium, Olympic logo uppper right with two dates below **Edge Lettering:** CITIUS ALTIUS FORTIUS

Date	Mintage	F	VF	XF	Unc	BU
1993 Proof	100,000	Value: 35.00				

KM# 219 20 DOLLARS
33.6200 g., 0.9250 Silver 1.0000 oz. ASW **Ruler:** Elizabeth II **Series:** Olympics **Subject:** Swimmers **Obv:** Crowned bust right, denomination below **Obv. Designer:** Raphael Maklouf **Rev:** Four swimmers, Olympic logo upper right with two dates below **Rev. Designer:** CITIUS ALTIUS FORTIUS

Date	Mintage	F	VF	XF	Unc	BU
1993 Proof	100,000	Value: 35.00				

KM# 519 20 DOLLARS
Bi-Metallic Gold center in Silver ring, 32 mm. **Ruler:** Elizabeth II **Subject:** Millennium **Obv:** Head with tiara right within circle, denomination below **Obv. Designer:** Ian Rank-Broadley **Rev:** Earth view from space **Edge:** Reeded

Date	Mintage	F	VF	XF	Unc	BU
2000 Prooflike	Est. 7,500	—	—	—	—	550

KM# 200 25 DOLLARS
33.6300 g., 0.9250 Silver 1.0001 oz. ASW **Ruler:** Elizabeth II **Subject:** 40th Anniversary - Reign of Queen Elizabeth II - Queen Mother **Obv:** Queens portrait **Rev:** Bust of Queen Mother with tiara right, value below, within wreath of crowns **Rev. Designer:** Stuart Devlin

Date	Mintage	F	VF	XF	Unc	BU
1992 Proof	—	Value: 30.00				

KM# 201 25 DOLLARS
33.6300 g., 0.9250 Silver 1.0001 oz. ASW **Ruler:** Elizabeth II **Subject:** 40th Anniversary - Reign of Queen Elizabeth II - Princess Diana **Obv:** Queens portrait **Rev:** Bust of Princess Diana with tiara right, value below, within wreath of crowns **Rev. Designer:** Stuart Devlin

Date	Mintage	F	VF	XF	Unc	BU
1992 Proof	—	Value: 30.00				

KM# 202 25 DOLLARS
33.6300 g., 0.9250 Silver 1.0001 oz. ASW **Ruler:** Elizabeth II **Subject:** 40th Anniversary - Reign of Queen Elizabeth II - Princess Anne **Obv:** Queens portrait **Rev:** Bust of Princess Anne with tiara right, value below, within wreath of crowns **Rev. Designer:** Stuart Devlin

Date	Mintage	F	VF	XF	Unc	BU
1992 Proof	—	Value: 30.00				

KM# 203 25 DOLLARS
33.6300 g., 0.9250 Silver 1.0001 oz. ASW **Ruler:** Elizabeth II **Subject:** 40th Anniversary - Reign of Queen Elizabeth II - Princess Margaret **Obv:** Queens portrait **Rev:** Bust of Princess Margaret with tiara left, value below, within wreath of crowns **Rev. Designer:** Stuart Devlin

Date	Mintage	F	VF	XF	Unc	BU
1992 Proof	—	Value: 30.00				

KM# 520 30 DOLLARS
1002.5020 g., 0.9990 Silver 32.2312 oz. ASW, 100 mm. **Ruler:** Elizabeth II **Series:** Olympics **Obv:** Head with tiara right, denomination below **Obv. Designer:** Ian Rank-Broadley **Rev:** Multicolor logo in center **Rev. Designer:** Stuart Devlin **Edge Lettering:** GAMES OF THE XXVII OLYMPIAD (logo) 1 KILO .999 SILVER **Note:** Photo reduced.

Date	Mintage	F	VF	XF	Unc	BU
2000 Proof	20,000	Value: 650				

KM# 313 40 DOLLARS
31.1850 g., 0.9995 Palladium 1.0021 oz. **Ruler:** Elizabeth II **Obv:** Crowned head right, denomination below **Obv. Designer:** Raphael Maklouf **Rev:** The Australian emu, left, date below

Date	Mintage	F	VF	XF	Unc	BU
1995	—	—	—	—	500	—
1995 Proof	Est. 2,500	Value: 550				

KM# 343 40 DOLLARS
31.1850 g., 0.9995 Palladium 1.0021 oz. **Ruler:** Elizabeth II **Obv:** Crowned head right, denomination below **Rev:** Emu and chicks

Date	Mintage	F	VF	XF	Unc	BU
1996 Proof	Est. 2,500	Value: 550				

KM# 308 100 DOLLARS
10.3678 g., 0.9160 Gold .3053 oz. AGW **Ruler:** Elizabeth II **Obv:** Queens portrait **Rev:** The Waratah Flower, value below **Rev. Designer:** Horst Hahne

Date	Mintage	F	VF	XF	Unc	BU
1995	3,000	—	—	—	210	—

KM# 308a 100 DOLLARS
10.3678 g., 0.9999 Gold .3333 oz. AGW **Ruler:** Elizabeth II **Obv:** Queens portrait **Rev:** The Waratah flower **Rev. Designer:** Horst Hahne

Date	Mintage	F	VF	XF	Unc	BU
1995 Proof	2,500	Value: 300				

KM# 333 100 DOLLARS
10.3678 g., 0.9160 Gold .3053 oz. AGW **Ruler:** Elizabeth II **Subject:** Tasmanial Blue Gum Flower **Obv:** Queens portrait **Rev:** Flowering plant with long, droopy leaves

Date	Mintage	F	VF	XF	Unc	BU
1996	—	—	—	—	210	—

KM# 333a 100 DOLLARS
10.3678 g., 0.9999 Gold .3333 oz. AGW **Ruler:** Elizabeth II **Subject:** Tasmanial Blue Gum flower **Obv:** Queens portrait **Rev:** Flowering plant with long, droopy leaves

Date	Mintage	F	VF	XF	Unc	BU
1996 Proof	—	Value: 300				

KM# 384 100 DOLLARS
10.3678 g., 0.9167 Gold .3053 oz. AGW **Ruler:** Elizabeth II **Subject:** Mangles' Kangaroo Paw Flower, value below **Obv:** Queens portrait **Rev:** Flower

Date	Mintage	F	VF	XF	Unc	BU
1997	3,000	—	—	—	210	—

KM# 373 100 DOLLARS
10.0210 g., 0.9999 Gold .3222 oz. AGW **Ruler:** Elizabeth II **Series:** Sydney Olympics 2000 **Obv:** Crowned head right, denomination below **Obv. Designer:** Raphael Maklouf **Rev:** Runner training in rain, Olympic logo above right foot **Rev. Designer:** Stuart Devlin

Date	Mintage	F	VF	XF	Unc	BU
2000 (1998) Proof	—	Value: 265				

KM# 383 100 DOLLARS
10.0210 g., 0.9999 Gold .3222 oz. AGW **Ruler:** Elizabeth II **Series:** Sydney Olympics 2000 **Obv:** Crowned head right, denomination below **Obv. Designer:** Raphael Maklouf **Rev:** Multicolor games logo within wreath **Rev. Designer:** Stuart Devlin

Date	Mintage	F	VF	XF	Unc	BU
2000 (1998) Proof	Est. 30,000	Value: 265				

KM# 480 100 DOLLARS
10.3678 g., 0.9160 Gold .3056 oz. AGW, 25 mm. **Ruler:** Elizabeth II **Subject:** Stuart's Desert Pea **Obv:** Queens portrait **Rev:** Plant with pods **Edge:** Reeded

Date	Mintage	F	VF	XF	Unc	BU
1998	3,000	—	—	—	210	—

KM# 480a 100 DOLLARS
10.3678 g., 0.9990 Gold .3333 oz. AGW, 25 mm. **Ruler:** Elizabeth II **Subject:** Stuart's Desert Pea **Obv:** Queens portrait **Rev:** Plant with pods **Edge:** Reeded

Date	Mintage	F	VF	XF	Unc	BU
1998 Proof	2,500	Value: 275				

KM# 487 100 DOLLARS
10.3678 g., 0.9160 Gold .3056 oz. AGW, 25 mm. **Ruler:** Elizabeth II **Obv:** Queens portrait **Rev:** Common Heath flowers, value below **Rev. Designer:** Horst Hahne **Edge:** Reeded

Date	Mintage	F	VF	XF	Unc	BU
1999	3,000	—	—	—	210	—

KM# 487a 100 DOLLARS
10.3678 g., 0.9990 Gold .3333 oz. AGW, 25 mm. **Ruler:** Elizabeth II **Obv:** Queens portrait **Rev:** Common Heath flowers **Edge:** Reeded

Date	Mintage	F	VF	XF	Unc	BU
1999 Proof	2,500	Value: 275				

KM# 442 100 DOLLARS
10.0000 g., 0.9990 Gold .3215 oz. AGW **Ruler:** Elizabeth II **Series:** Sydney Olympics 2000 **Obv:** Crowned head right **Rev:** 3 athletic workout scenes, Olympic logo at bottom **Rev. Designer:** Stuart Devlin **Edge:** Reeded

Date	Mintage	F	VF	XF	Unc	BU
2000 (1999) Proof	30,000	Value: 265				

KM# 443 100 DOLLARS
10.0000 g., 0.9990 Gold .3215 oz. AGW **Ruler:** Elizabeth II **Series:** Sydney Olympics 2000 **Obv:** Crowned head right **Rev:** Shot putter teaching seated children, Olympic logo below **Rev. Designer:** Stuart Devlin **Edge:** Reeded

Date	Mintage	F	VF	XF	Unc	BU
2000 (1999) Proof	30,000	Value: 265				

KM# 444 100 DOLLARS
10.0000 g., 0.9990 Gold .3215 oz. AGW **Ruler:** Elizabeth II **Series:** Sydney Olympics 2000 **Obv:** Crowned head right **Rev:** Sprinter being coached, Olympic logo at bottom **Rev. Designer:** Stuart Devlin **Edge:** Reeded

Date	Mintage	F	VF	XF	Unc	BU
2000 (1999) Proof	30,000	Value: 265				

KM# 474 100 DOLLARS
Bi-Metallic Gold center in Silver ring .2354 oz. **Ruler:** Elizabeth II **Subject:** Perth Mint Centennial Sovereign **Obv:** Head with tiara right within inner circle **Obv. Designer:** Ian Rank-Broadley **Rev:** St. George with sword on horseback slaying dragon, circle surrounds all, dates below **Edge:** Reeded

Date	Mintage	F	VF	XF	Unc	BU
ND(1999) Proof	7,500	Value: 500				

KM# 512 100 DOLLARS
10.3678 g., 0.9160 Gold .3056 oz. AGW, 25 mm. **Ruler:** Elizabeth II **Subject:** Cooktown Orchid **Obv:** Queens portrait **Rev:** Orchid and denomination **Edge:** Reeded

Date	Mintage	F	VF	XF	Unc	BU
2000	3,000	—	—	—	210	—

KM# 512a 100 DOLLARS
10.3678 g., 0.9990 Gold .3333 oz. AGW, 25 mm. **Ruler:** Elizabeth II **Subject:** Cooktown Orchid **Obv:** Queens portrait **Rev:** Orchid and denomination **Edge:** Reeded

Date	Mintage	F	VF	XF	Unc	BU
2000 Proof	2,500	Value: 275				

KM# 521 100 DOLLARS
10.0000 g., 0.9990 Gold .3215 oz. AGW, 25 mm. **Ruler:** Elizabeth II **Series:** Olympics **Obv:** Head with tiara right, denomination below **Obv. Designer:** Ian Rank-Broadley **Rev:** Multicolor torch flames within circle of figures **Rev. Designer:** Stuart Devlin **Edge:** Reeded

Date	Mintage	F	VF	XF	Unc	BU
2000 Proof	20,000	Value: 385				

KM# 309 150 DOLLARS
15.5517 g., 0.9999 Gold .5000 oz. AGW **Ruler:** Elizabeth II **Obv:** Queens portrait **Rev:** The Waratah Flower above value

Date	Mintage	F	VF	XF	Unc	BU
1995 Proof	1,500	Value: 600				

KM# 334 150 DOLLARS
15.5517 g., 0.9999 Gold .5000 oz. AGW **Ruler:** Elizabeth II **Subject:** Tasmanian Blue Gum Flower **Obv:** Queens portrait **Rev:** Tasmanian Blue Gum Flower above value **Rev. Designer:** Horst Hahne

Date	Mintage	F	VF	XF	Unc	BU
1996 Proof	—	Value: 500				

KM# 413 150 DOLLARS
15.5517 g., 0.9999 Gold .5000 oz. AGW **Ruler:** Elizabeth II **Obv:** Queens portrait **Rev:** Stuart's desert pea

Date	Mintage	F	VF	XF	Unc	BU
1998 Proof	1,500	Value: 450				

KM# 475 150 DOLLARS
15.5517 g., 0.9999 Gold .5000 oz. AGW **Ruler:** Elizabeth II **Subject:** Common Heath Flower **Obv:** Queens portrait **Rev:** Heath flowers above value **Rev. Designer:** Horst Hahne **Edge:** Reeded

Date	Mintage	F	VF	XF	Unc	BU
1999 Proof	1,500	Value: 450				

KM# 513 150 DOLLARS
15.5518 g., 0.9990 Gold .5000 oz. AGW, 30 mm. **Ruler:** Elizabeth II **Subject:** Cooktown Orchid **Obv:** Queens portrait **Rev:** Orchid above value **Rev. Designer:** Horst Hahne **Edge:** Reeded

Date	Mintage	F	VF	XF	Unc	BU
2000 Proof	1,500	Value: 500				

KM# 71 200 DOLLARS
10.0000 g., 0.9170 Gold .2948 oz. AGW **Ruler:** Elizabeth II **Obv:** Young bust right **Obv. Designer:** Arnold Machin **Rev:** Koala in tree, value below **Rev. Designer:** Stuart Devlin

Date	Mintage	F	VF	XF	Unc	BU
1980	207,500	—	—	—	200	—
1980 Proof	50,077	Value: 220				
1983	88,000	—	—	—	200	—
1983 Proof	15,889	Value: 220				
1984	49,200	—	—	—	200	—
1984 Proof	12,559	Value: 220				

KM# 73 200 DOLLARS
10.0000 g., 0.9170 Gold .2948 oz. AGW **Ruler:** Elizabeth II **Subject:** Wedding of Prince Charles and Lady Diana **Obv:** Young bust right **Obv. Designer:** Arnold Machin **Rev:** Conjoined heads of Prince Charles and Lady Diana left **Rev. Designer:** Stuart Devlin

Date	Mintage	F	VF	XF	Unc	BU
1981	77,890	—	—	—	200	—

KM# 76 200 DOLLARS
10.0000 g., 0.9170 Gold .2948 oz. AGW **Ruler:** Elizabeth II **Subject:** XII Commonwealth Games - Brisbane **Obv:** Young bust right **Obv. Designer:** Arnold Machin **Rev:** Athlete running over hurdles, value below hurdler **Rev. Designer:** Margaret Priest

Date	Mintage	F	VF	XF	Unc	BU
1982	77,206	—	—	—	200	—
1982 Proof	30,032	Value: 220				

KM# 86 200 DOLLARS
10.0000 g., 0.9170 Gold .2948 oz. AGW **Ruler:** Elizabeth II **Obv:** Crowned head right **Obv. Designer:** Raphael Maklouf **Rev:** Koala in tree, value below **Rev. Designer:** Stuart Devlin

Date	Mintage	F	VF	XF	Unc	BU
1985	29,186	—	—	—	200	—
1985 Proof	16,691	Value: 220				
1986	15,298	—	—	—	200	—
1986 Proof	16,654	Value: 220				

KM# 94 200 DOLLARS
10.0000 g., 0.9170 Gold .2948 oz. AGW **Ruler:** Elizabeth II **Obv:** Crowned head right **Obv. Designer:** Raphael Maklouf **Rev:** 1/2-length bust right, value below, 1787 above right shoulder **Rev. Designer:** Horst Hahne

Date	Mintage	F	VF	XF	Unc	BU
1987	20,800	—	—	—	200	—
1987 Proof	20,000	Value: 220				

KM# 115 200 DOLLARS
10.0000 g., 0.9170 Gold .2948 oz. AGW **Ruler:** Elizabeth II **Subject:** Bicentennial of Australia **Obv:** Crowned head right **Obv. Designer:** Raphael Maklouf **Rev:** Early colonist standing in front of water in Sydney Cove, ship in background at right, value below

Date	Mintage	F	VF	XF	Unc	BU
1988	11,000	—	—	—	200	—
1988 Proof	20,000	Value: 220				

KM# 116 200 DOLLARS
10.0000 g., 0.9170 Gold .2948 oz. AGW **Ruler:** Elizabeth II **Subject:** Pride of Australia **Obv:** Crowned head right **Obv. Designer:** Raphael Maklouf **Rev:** Frilled-neck lizard, value below

Date	Mintage	F	VF	XF	Unc	BU
1989	10,020	—	—	—	200	—
1989 Proof	24,736	Value: 220				

KM# 135 200 DOLLARS
10.0000 g., 0.9170 Gold .2948 oz. AGW **Ruler:** Elizabeth II **Subject:** Pride of Australia **Obv:** Crowned head right **Obv. Designer:** Raphael Maklouf **Rev:** Platypus above value **Rev. Designer:** Horst Hahne

Date	Mintage	F	VF	XF	Unc	BU
1990	8,340	—	—	—	200	—
1990 Proof	14,616	Value: 220				

KM# 160 200 DOLLARS
10.0000 g., 0.9170 Gold .2948 oz. AGW **Ruler:** Elizabeth II **Subject:** Pride of Australia **Obv:** Crowned head right **Obv. Designer:** Raphael Maklouf **Rev:** Standing emu between tall grass, value below

Date	Mintage	F	VF	XF	Unc	BU
1991	6,879	—	—	—	200	—
1991 Proof	9,560	Value: 220				

KM# 259 200 DOLLARS
10.0000 g., 0.9170 Gold .2948 oz. AGW **Ruler:** Elizabeth II **Subject:** Pride of Australia **Obv:** Crowned head right **Obv. Designer:** Raphael Maklouf **Rev:** Echidna above value

Date	Mintage	F	VF	XF	Unc	BU
1992	3,935	—	—	—	210	—
1992 Proof	5,921	Value: 225				

KM# 220 200 DOLLARS
16.8200 g., 0.9170 Gold .4958 oz. AGW **Ruler:** Elizabeth II **Series:** Olympic Centenary - 1896-1996 **Obv:** Crowned head right **Obv. Designer:** Raphael Maklouf **Rev:** Gymnast in flight, Olympic logo top right **Edge Lettering:** CITIUS ALTIUS FORTIUS

Date	Mintage	F	VF	XF	Unc	BU
1993 Proof	60,000	Value: 350				

KM# 222 200 DOLLARS
10.0000 g., 0.9170 Gold .2948 oz. AGW **Ruler:** Elizabeth II **Subject:** Pride of Australia **Obv:** Crowned head right **Obv. Designer:** Raphael Maklouf **Rev:** Squirrel glider possum, value below

Date	Mintage	F	VF	XF	Unc	BU
1993	3,014	—	—	—	210	—
1993 Proof	5,000	Value: 225				

KM# 262 200 DOLLARS
10.0000 g., 0.9170 Gold .2948 oz. AGW **Ruler:** Elizabeth II **Subject:** Pride of Australia **Obv:** Crowned head right **Obv. Designer:** Raphael Maklouf **Rev:** Tasmanian devil, value below **Rev. Designer:** Horst Hahne

Date	Mintage	F	VF	XF	Unc	BU
1994	4,000	—	—	—	210	—
1994 Proof	5,000	Value: 225				

KM# 385 200 DOLLARS
15.5517 g., 0.9999 Gold .5000 oz. AGW **Ruler:** Elizabeth II **Subject:** Mangles' Kangaroo Paw Flower **Obv:** Queens portrait **Rev:** Flower

Date	Mintage	F	VF	XF	Unc	BU
1997 Proof	—	Value: 400				

KM# 204 250 DOLLARS
16.9500 g., 0.9170 Gold .4995 oz. AGW **Ruler:** Elizabeth II **Subject:** 40th Anniversary - Reign of Queen Elizabeth II - Queen Mother **Obv:** Queens portrait **Rev:** Portrait of Queen Mother right, within circle of crowns **Rev. Designer:** Stuart Devlin

Date	Mintage	F	VF	XF	Unc	BU
1992 Proof	Est. 5,000	Value: 345				

KM# 205 250 DOLLARS
16.9500 g., 0.9170 Gold .4995 oz. AGW **Ruler:** Elizabeth II **Subject:** 40th Anniversary - Reign of Queen Elizabeth II - Princess Diana **Obv:** Queens portrait **Rev:** Portrait of Princess Diana right, within circle of crowns **Rev. Designer:** Stuart Devlin

Date	Mintage	F	VF	XF	Unc	BU
1992 Proof	Est. 5,000	Value: 350				

KM# 206 250 DOLLARS
16.9500 g., 0.9170 Gold .4995 oz. AGW **Ruler:** Elizabeth II **Subject:** 40th Anniversary - Reign of Queen Elizabeth II - Princess Anne **Obv:** Queens portrait **Rev:** Portrait of Princess Anne right, within circle of crowns **Rev. Designer:** Stuart Devlin

Date	Mintage	F	VF	XF	Unc	BU
1992 Proof	Est. 5,000	Value: 345				

KM# 207 250 DOLLARS
16.9500 g., 0.9170 Gold .4995 oz. AGW **Ruler:** Elizabeth II **Subject:** 40th Anniversary - Reign of Queen Elizabeth II - Princess Margaret **Obv:** Queens portrait **Rev:** Bust of Princess Margaret left, within circle of crowns **Rev. Designer:** Stuart Devlin

Date	Mintage	F	VF	XF	Unc	BU
1992 Proof	Est. 5,000	Value: 345				

SILVER BULLION - KANGAROO

KM# 211.1 DOLLAR
31.5700 g., 0.9990 Silver 1.0140 oz. ASW **Ruler:** Elizabeth II **Obv:** Crowned head right **Obv. Designer:** Raphael Maklouf **Rev:** Kangaroo leaping right, value above **Rev. Designer:** Horst Hahne **Edge:** Reeded

Date	Mintage	F	VF	XF	Unc	BU
1993C	73,000	—	—	—	23.50	—

KM# 211.2 DOLLAR
31.5700 g., 0.9990 Silver 1.0140 oz. ASW **Ruler:** Elizabeth II **Obv:** Crowned head right **Rev:** Kangaroo leaping right **Rev. Designer:** Horst Hahne **Edge:** Reeded and plain sections

Date	Mintage	F	VF	XF	Unc	BU
1993C	5,000	—	—	—	50.00	—

KM# 263.1 DOLLAR
31.6350 g., 0.9990 Silver 1.0161 oz. ASW **Ruler:** Elizabeth II **Obv:** Crowned head right **Rev:** Kangaroo leaping right, value above **Rev. Designer:** Horst Hahne **Edge:** Reeded

Date	Mintage	F	VF	XF	Unc	BU
1994C	45,000	—	—	—	30.00	—

KM# 263.2 DOLLAR
31.6350 g., 0.9990 Silver 1.0161 oz. ASW **Ruler:** Elizabeth II **Obv:** Crowned head right **Rev:** Kangaroo leaping right **Rev. Designer:** Horst Hahne **Edge:** Reeded and plain sections

Date	Mintage	F	VF	XF	Unc	BU
1994C	2,500	—	—	—	120	—

KM# 293.1 DOLLAR
31.6350 g., 0.9990 Silver 1.0161 oz. ASW **Ruler:** Elizabeth II **Obv:** Crowned head right **Rev:** Kangaroo head facing half left, value above **Rev. Designer:** Horst Hahne **Edge:** Reeded

Date	Mintage	F	VF	XF	Unc	BU
1995C	73,000	—	—	—	27.50	—

KM# 293.2 DOLLAR
31.6350 g., 0.9990 Silver 1.0161 oz. ASW **Ruler:** Elizabeth II **Obv:** Crowned head right **Rev:** Kangaroo head facing half left **Rev. Designer:** Horst Hahne **Edge:** Reeded and plain sections

Date	Mintage	F	VF	XF	Unc	BU
1995C	2,500	—	—	—	110	—

KM# 297 DOLLAR
31.6350 g., 0.9990 Silver 1.0161 oz. ASW **Ruler:** Elizabeth II **Obv:** Crowned head right **Rev:** Mother and baby kangaroo, value above **Rev. Designer:** Horst Hahne

Date	Mintage	F	VF	XF	Unc	BU
1996	—	—	—	—	25.00	—

KM# 325 DOLLAR
31.5600 g., 0.9990 Silver 1.0136 oz. ASW **Ruler:** Elizabeth II **Obv:** Crowned head right **Rev:** Kangaroo drinking water, reflection, value at bottom **Rev. Designer:** Horst Hahne

Date	Mintage	F	VF	XF	Unc	BU
1997C	—	—	—	—	23.50	—

KM# 365 DOLLAR
32.0000 g., 0.9990 Silver 1.0278 oz. ASW **Ruler:** Elizabeth II **Obv:** Crowned head right **Rev:** Kangaroo bounding left, value above **Rev. Designer:** Horst Hahne

Date	Mintage	F	VF	XF	Unc	BU
1998C	—	—	—	—	23.50	—

KM# 398 DOLLAR
32.2500 g., 0.9990 Silver 1.0358 oz. ASW **Ruler:** Elizabeth II **Obv:** Rank-Broadley crowned head right **Rev:** Pair of kangaroos, value at right **Rev. Designer:** Horst Hahne

Date	Mintage	F	VF	XF	Unc	BU
1999	—	—	—	—	25.00	—
1999 Proof	—	Value: 75.00				

KM# 490.1 DOLLAR
31.1035 g., 0.9990 Silver 1. oz. ASW, 40 mm. **Ruler:** Elizabeth II **Obv:** Rank-Broadley crowned head right **Rev:** Kangaroo with Australian map background, value top right **Rev. Designer:** Vladimir Gottwald **Edge:** Reeded

Date	Mintage	F	VF	XF	Unc	BU
2000 Proof	—	Value: 65.00				
2000	—	—	—	—	25.00	—

KM# 490.2 DOLLAR
32.1500 g., 0.9990 Silver 1.0326 oz. ASW, 39.9 mm. **Ruler:** Elizabeth II **Obv:** Crowned head right **Rev:** Multicolor kangaroo on dark red map and green value **Rev. Designer:** Vladimir Gottwald **Edge:** Reeded

Date	Mintage	F	VF	XF	Unc	BU
2000	—	—	—	—	27.50	32.50

SILVER BULLION - KOOKABURRA

KM# 164 DOLLAR
31.1000 g., 0.9990 Silver 1.0000 oz. ASW **Ruler:** Elizabeth II **Obv:** Crowned head right, denomination below **Obv. Designer:** Raphael Maklouf **Rev:** Australian Kookaburra in tree left, date below

Date	Mintage	F	VF	XF	Unc	BU
1992	300,000	—	—	—	25.00	—

KM# 209 DOLLAR
31.1000 g., 0.9990 Silver 1.0000 oz. ASW **Ruler:** Elizabeth II **Obv:** Crowned head right **Rev:** Australian kookaburra feeding nestlings in tree, date below

Date	Mintage	F	VF	XF	Unc	BU
1992 Proof	—	Value: 40.00				
1992 (ae) Proof	750	Value: 185				
1993	Est. 300,000	—	—	—	25.00	—

KM# 212.1 DOLLAR
31.1035 g., 0.9990 Silver 1.0000 oz. ASW **Ruler:** Elizabeth II **Obv:** Crowned head right, denomination below **Obv. Designer:** Raphael Maklouf **Rev:** Pair of Kookaburras, date below

Date	Mintage	F	VF	XF	Unc	BU
1993 AE Proof	—	Value: 30.00				
1993 AE Proof	—	Value: 30.00				
1993 (ge) Proof	500	Value: 75.00				
1993 (so) Proof	13,000	Value: 45.00				
1994(p) BU	—	—	—	—	25.00	—
1994 Proof	2,500	Value: 32.10				
1994 (ta) Specimen	15,000	—	—	—	27.50	—

KM# 212.2 DOLLAR
31.1035 g., 0.9990 Silver 1.0000 oz. ASW **Ruler:** Elizabeth II **Obv:** Crowned head right, denomination below **Obv. Designer:** Raphael Maklouf **Rev:** American Eagle privy mark above date below 2 kookaburras on tree branch

Date	Mintage	F	VF	XF	Unc	BU
1993 AE Proof	500	Value: 65.00				

Date	Mintage	F	VF	XF	Unc	BU
1993 AE Proof	500	Value: 75.00				

KM# 260 DOLLAR

31.1035 g., 0.9990 Silver 1.0000 oz. ASW **Ruler:** Elizabeth II **Obv:** Crowned head right, denomination below **Obv. Designer:** Raphael Maklouf **Rev:** Kookaburra on branch left, denmination below **Rev. Designer:** Stuart Devlin

Date	Mintage	F	VF	XF	Unc	BU
1994 Proof	2,500	Value: 45.00				
1995	300,000	—	—	—	25.00	—

KM# 289.1 DOLLAR

31.6350 g., 0.9990 Silver 1.0161 oz. ASW **Ruler:** Elizabeth II **Obv:** Crowned head right **Rev:** Kookaburra in flight, date below

Date	Mintage	F	VF	XF	Unc	BU
1995P Proof	4,900	Value: 30.00				
1996	300,000	—	—	—	25.00	—
1996 (bg)	5,000	—	—	—	40.00	—
1996 (ba)	2,500	—	—	—	42.00	—
1996 (sr)	5,000	—	—	—	40.00	—

KM# 289.2 DOLLAR

31.1035 g., 0.9990 Silver 1.0000 oz. ASW **Ruler:** Elizabeth II **Obv:** Crowned head right **Rev:** Kookaburra in flight, date below **Edge:** Reeded and inscribed with date and serial

Date	Mintage	F	VF	XF	Unc	BU
1996	1,500	—	—	—	45.00	—

KM# 701 DOLLAR

31.1035 g., 0.9990 Silver 0.999 oz. ASW **Ruler:** Elizabeth II **Obv:** Crowned head right **Rev:** Kookaburra

Date	Mintage	F	VF	XF	Unc	BU
1996 Proof	—	Value: 35.00				
1997	—	—	—	—	—	—

KM# 318 DOLLAR

31.1035 g., 0.9990 Silver 1.0000 oz. ASW **Ruler:** Elizabeth II **Obv:** Crowned head right within circle, denomination below **Obv. Designer:** Raphael Maklouf **Rev:** Kookaburra and nestlings, mark at right of bird, date below **Note:** With Utrecht Coat of Arms privy mark.

Date	Mintage	F	VF	XF	Unc	BU
1997	—	—	—	—	25.00	—
1997 (u)	300,000	—	—	—	25.00	—

KM# 362 DOLLAR

31.1035 g., 0.9990 Silver 1.0000 oz. ASW **Ruler:** Elizabeth II **Obv:** Crowned head right, denomination below **Obv. Designer:** Raphael Maklouf **Rev:** Kookaburra on fence right, date below

Date	Mintage	F	VF	XF	Unc	BU
1997 Proof	2,000	Value: 35.00				
1998 (1997)	—	—	—	—	27.50	—

KM# 399 DOLLAR

32.2500 g., 0.9990 Silver 1.0358 oz. ASW **Ruler:** Elizabeth II **Obv:** Head with tiara right within circle, denomination below **Obv. Designer:** Ian Rank-Broadley **Rev:** Adult and chick kookaburras on branch left, date below

Date	Mintage	F	VF	XF	Unc	BU
1999	—	—	—	—	27.00	—
1999	5,000	—	—	—	24.00	—
Note: Belgian 50 frank coin design privy mark						
1999	5,000	—	—	—	24.00	—
Note: German 1 mark coin design privy mark						
1999	5,000	—	—	—	24.00	—
Note: Irish 1 punt coin design privy mark						
1999	5,000	—	—	—	24.00	—
Note: Luxembourg 50 francs coin design privy mark						
1999	5,000	—	—	—	24.00	—
Note: Netherlands 1 gulden coin design privy mark						
1999	5,000	—	—	—	24.00	—
Note: Spanish 100 pesetas coin design privy mark						
1999	5,000	—	—	—	24.00	—
Note: Austrian 20 schilling coin design privy mark						
1999	5,000	—	—	—	24.00	—
Note: Finnish 1 markka coin design privy mark						
1999	5,000	—	—	—	24.00	—
Note: French 5 francs coin design privy mark						
1999	5,000	—	—	—	24.00	—
Note: Italian 1000 lire coin design privy mark						
1999	5,000	—	—	—	24.00	—
Note: Portuguese 50 escudo coin design privy mark						

KM# 604 DOLLAR

31.1035 g., 0.9990 Silver 0.999 oz. ASW, 40.4 mm. **Ruler:** Elizabeth II **Subject:** U.S. State Quarter - Delaware

Date	Mintage	F	VF	XF	Unc	BU
1999	75,000	—	—	—	27.50	—

KM# 605 DOLLAR

31.1035 g., 0.9990 Silver 0.999 oz. ASW, 40.4 mm. **Ruler:** Elizabeth II **Subject:** U.S. State Quarter - Pennsylvania

Date	Mintage	F	VF	XF	Unc	BU
1999	75,000	—	—	—	27.50	—

KM# 606 DOLLAR

31.1035 g., 0.9990 Silver 0.999 oz. ASW, 40.4 mm. **Ruler:** Elizabeth II **Subject:** U.S. State Quarter - New Jersey

Date	Mintage	F	VF	XF	Unc	BU
1999	75,000	—	—	—	27.50	—

KM# 607 DOLLAR

31.1035 g., 0.9990 Silver 0.999 oz. ASW, 40.4 mm. **Ruler:** Elizabeth II **Subject:** U.S. State Quarter - Georgia

Date	Mintage	F	VF	XF	Unc	BU
1999	75,000	—	—	—	27.50	—

KM# 608 DOLLAR

31.1035 g., 0.9990 Silver 0.999 oz. ASW, 40.4 mm. **Ruler:** Elizabeth II **Subject:** U.S. State Quarter - Connecticut

Date	Mintage	F	VF	XF	Unc	BU
1999	75,000	—	—	—	27.50	—

KM# 416 DOLLAR

31.7700 g., 0.9990 Silver 1.0204 oz. ASW **Obv:** Queen's head with tiara, right, within circle, value below circle **Obv. Designer:** Ian Rank-Broadley **Rev:** Kookaburra on branch, left, silver weight and date in legend

Date	Mintage	F	VF	XF	Unc	BU
2000 (1999)	—	—	—	—	25.00	—

KM# 611 DOLLAR

31.1035 g., 0.9990 Silver 0.999 oz. ASW, 40.4 mm. **Ruler:** Elizabeth II **Subject:** U.S. State Quarter - Massachusetts

Date	Mintage	F	VF	XF	Unc	BU
2000	75,000	—	—	—	27.50	—

KM# 612 DOLLAR

31.1035 g., 0.9990 Silver 0.999 oz. ASW, 40.4 mm. **Ruler:** Elizabeth II **Subject:** U.S. State Quarter - Maryland

Date	Mintage	F	VF	XF	Unc	BU
2000	75,000	—	—	—	27.50	—

KM# 613 DOLLAR

31.1035 g., 0.9990 Silver 0.999 oz. ASW, 40.4 mm. **Ruler:** Elizabeth II **Subject:** U.S. State Quarter - South Carolina

Date	Mintage	F	VF	XF	Unc	BU
2000	75,000	—	—	—	27.50	—

KM# 614 DOLLAR

31.1035 g., 0.9990 Silver 0.999 oz. ASW, 40.4 mm. **Ruler:** Elizabeth II **Subject:** U.S. State Quarter - New Hampshire

Date	Mintage	F	VF	XF	Unc	BU
2000	75,000	—	—	—	27.50	—

KM# 615 DOLLAR

31.1035 g., 0.9990 Silver 0.999 oz. ASW, 40.4 mm. **Ruler:** Elizabeth II **Subject:** U.S. State Quarter - Virginia

Date	Mintage	F	VF	XF	Unc	BU
2000	75,000	—	—	—	27.50	—

KM# 179 2 DOLLARS

62.2070 g., 0.9990 Silver 2.0000 oz. ASW **Ruler:** Elizabeth II **Obv:** Crowned head right within inner circle, denomination below **Obv. Designer:** Raphael Maklouf **Rev:** Australian Kookaburra on stump right within circle, date below **Rev. Designer:** Stuart Devlin

Date	Mintage	F	VF	XF	Unc	BU
1992	—	—	—	—	42.50	—
1992 Proof	5,000	Value: 85.00				

Date	Mintage	F	VF	XF	Unc	BU
1992 (gv) Proof	500	Value: 165				
1992 (hd) Specimen	1,000	—	—	—	125	—
1993 (dp) Specimen	1,000	—	—	—	125	—
1993	—	—	—	—	115	—
1993 (w) Specimen	1,000	—	—	—	135	—
1993 (e) Specimen	1,000	—	—	—	115	—
1993 (ta) Specimen	1,000	—	—	—	115	—

KM# 227 2 DOLLARS
62.2070 g., 0.9990 Silver 2.0000 oz. ASW **Ruler:** Elizabeth II **Obv:** Crowned head right, denomination below **Rev:** Kookaburra feeding nestling right, date below

Date	Mintage	F	VF	XF	Unc	BU
1992 Proof	—	Value: 85.00				
1992 (aa) Proof	500	Value: 375				
1993	—	—	—	—	42.50	—
1993 Proof	—	Value: 85.00				

KM# 176 2 DOLLARS
62.2070 g., 0.9990 Silver 1.998 oz. ASW, 50 mm. **Subject:** Kookaburra **Obv:** Elizabeth II **Rev:** Kookaburra on branch next to tree trunk **Edge:** Segmented reeding

Date	Mintage	F	VF	XF	Unc	BU
1992P	—	—	—	—	37.50	40.00

KM# 230 2 DOLLARS
62.2070 g., 0.9990 Silver 2.0000 oz. ASW **Ruler:** Elizabeth II **Obv:** Crowned head right, denomination below **Rev:** Pair of Kookaburras on branch, date below

Date	Mintage	F	VF	XF	Unc	BU
1993	—	—	—	—	42.50	—
1993 Proof	—	Value: 85.00				
1993 (sm) Proof	750	Value: 200				
1993 (ae) Proof	500	Value: 300				
1994 (ev) Proof	1,500	Value: 200				
1994	—	—	—	—	42.50	—
1994 Proof	—	Value: 85.00				
1994 (gv) Specimen	1,000	—	—	—	275	—
1994 (gv) Specimen	1,500	—	—	—	180	—

KM# 261 2 DOLLARS
62.2070 g., 0.9990 Silver 2.0000 oz. ASW **Ruler:** Elizabeth II **Obv:** Crowned head right, denomination below **Rev:** Kookaburra on branch right, within circle, date below

Date	Mintage	F	VF	XF	Unc	BU
1994P Proof	—	Value: 100				
1995	—	—	—	—	42.50	—
1995 (f1) Proof	1,500	Value: 120				
1995 (f3) Proof	1,500	Value: 135				
1995 (f7) Proof	1,500	Value: 100				
1995 (rv) Proof	1,500	Value: 90.00				

KM# 290 2 DOLLARS
62.2070 g., 0.9990 Silver 2.0000 oz. ASW **Ruler:** Elizabeth II **Obv:** Crowned head right, denomination below **Rev:** Kookaburra in flight, date below

Date	Mintage	F	VF	XF	Unc	BU
1995P Proof	650	Value: 65.00				
1995P (ww) Proof	1,300	Value: 135				
1995 (ge) Proof	800	Value: 135				
Note: Privy marks on gold insert						
1996	—	—	—	—	42.50	—
1996 (h) Proof	1,500	Value: 70.00				
1996 (d) Proof	1,500	Value: 115				
Note: Privy marks on gold insert						
1996 (j) Proof	1,500	Value: 120				
Note: Privy marks on gold insert						
1996 (sg) Proof	1,500	Value: 130				
Note: Privy marks on gold insert						
1996 (sp) Proof	1,500	Value: 135				
Note: Privy marks on gold insert						

KM# 319 2 DOLLARS
62.2070 g., 0.9990 Silver 2.0000 oz. ASW **Ruler:** Elizabeth II **Obv:** Crowned head right, denomination below **Rev:** Kookaburra and nestling within circle, date below

Date	Mintage	F	VF	XF	Unc	BU
1997	—	—	—	—	42.50	—

KM# 363 2 DOLLARS
62.2070 g., 0.9990 Silver 2.0000 oz. ASW **Ruler:** Elizabeth II **Obv:** Crowned head right, denomination below **Rev:** Kookaburra on fence, right, within circle, date below

Date	Mintage	F	VF	XF	Unc	BU
1998 (1997)	—	—	—	—	42.50	—
1997 Proof	2,000	Value: 110				

KM# 445 2 DOLLARS
62.7700 g., 0.9990 Silver 2.0000 oz. ASW **Ruler:** Elizabeth II **Obv:** Crowned head right, denomination below **Rev:** 2 Kookaburras on branch **Edge:** Interrupted reeding on edge

Date	Mintage	F	VF	XF	Unc	BU
1999	—	—	—	—	42.50	47.50
2000 Proof	—	Value: 100				

KM# 417.1 2 DOLLARS
62.8500 g., 0.9990 Silver 2.0187 oz. ASW **Ruler:** Elizabeth II **Obv:** Crowned head right, denomination below **Rev:** Kookaburra on branch left, within circle, date below

Date	Mintage	F	VF	XF	Unc	BU
1999 Proof	—	—	—	—	—	—
2000(1999)	—	—	—	—	40.00	—

KM# 417.3 2 DOLLARS
62.8500 g., 0.9990 Silver 2.0187 oz. ASW **Ruler:** Elizabeth II **Subject:** USA State Quarters - 2000 **Obv:** Crowned head right, denomination below **Rev:** Kookaburra on branch with five state quarter designs added below **Edge:** Reeded and plain sections **Note:** Rev. with 1933 Shilling obv. & rev. design copper inserts.

Date	Mintage	F	VF	XF	Unc	BU
1999	1,500	—	—	—	70.00	—

KM# 417.4 2 DOLLARS
62.8500 g., 0.9999 Silver 2.0205 oz. ASW **Ruler:** Elizabeth II **Subject:** USA State Quarters - 2000 **Obv:** Crowned head right, denomination below **Rev:** Kookaburra on branch with five state quarter designs added below **Edge:** Reeded and plain sections **Note:** Reverse with 1930 Penny obverse and reverse design copper inserts.

Date	Mintage	F	VF	XF	Unc	BU
1999 Proof	—	Value: 95.00				

KM# 417.5 2 DOLLARS
62.8500 g., 0.9990 Silver 2.0187 oz. ASW **Ruler:** Elizabeth II **Subject:** USA State Quarters - 2000 **Obv:** Crowned head right, denomination below **Rev:** Kookaburra on branch with five state quarter designs added below **Edge:** Reeded and plain sections **Note:** Reverse with 1932 Florin obverse and reverse design copper inserts.

Date	Mintage	F	VF	XF	Unc	BU
1999 Proof	—	Value: 95.00				

KM# 417.6 2 DOLLARS
62.8500 g., 0.9990 Silver 2.0187 oz. ASW **Ruler:** Elizabeth II **Subject:** USA State Quarters - 2000 **Obv:** Crowned head right, denomination below **Rev:** Kookaburra on branch with five state quarter designs and date below **Edge:** Reeded and plain sections

Date	Mintage	F	VF	XF	Unc	BU
2000 (1999)	—	—	—	—	150	—

KM# 609 2 DOLLARS
62.2070 g., 0.9990 Silver 1.998 oz. ASW **Ruler:** Elizabeth II **Subject:** USA State Quarters - 1999 **Obv:** Crowned head right, denomination below **Rev:** Kookaburra on branch with five state quarter designs added below **Edge:** Reeded and plain sections

Date	Mintage	F	VF	XF	Unc	BU
1999	10,000	—	—	—	47.50	—

KM# 616 2 DOLLARS
62.2070 g., 0.9990 Silver 1.998 oz. ASW **Ruler:** Elizabeth II **Subject:** USA State Quarters - 2000 **Obv:** Crowned head right, denomination below **Rev:** Kookaburra on branch with five state quarter designs added below **Edge:** Reeded and plain sections **Note:** Prev. KM#417.2.

Date	Mintage	F	VF	XF	Unc	BU
2000	10,000	—	—	—	47.50	—

KM# 189 5 DOLLARS
31.1030 g., 0.9990 Silver 1.0000 oz. ASW **Ruler:** Elizabeth II **Obv:** Crowned head right, denomination below **Obv. Designer:** Raphael Maklouf **Rev:** Australian Kookaburra sitting on stump right, date below **Rev. Designer:** Stuart Devlin

Date	Mintage	F	VF	XF	Unc	BU
1990	300,000	—	—	—	25.00	—

KM# 138 5 DOLLARS
31.1030 g., 0.9990 Silver 1.0000 oz. ASW **Ruler:** Elizabeth II **Obv:** Crowned head right, denomination below **Obv. Designer:** Raphael Maklouf **Rev:** Australian Kookaburra sitting on branch facing right, date below **Rev. Designer:** Stuart Devlin **Note:** Special coin fair issues exist.

Date	Mintage	F	VF	XF	Unc	BU
1990 Proof	22,000	Value: 27.50				
1991	300,000	—	—	—	22.50	—
1991 Proof	—	Value: 27.50				

KM# 161 10 DOLLARS
62.2140 g., 0.9990 Silver 2.0000 oz. ASW **Ruler:** Elizabeth II **Obv:** Crowned head right, denomination below **Obv. Designer:** Raphael Maklouf **Rev:** Australian Kookaburra sitting on stump facing right, date below **Rev. Designer:** Stuart Devlin **Note:** Photo reduced.

Date	Mintage	F	VF	XF	Unc	BU
1991	—	—	—	—	42.50	—
1991 Proof	5,000	Value: 60.00				

KM# 177 10 DOLLARS
311.0350 g., 0.9990 Silver 9.99 oz. ASW, 75 mm. **Subject:** Kookaburra **Obv:** Elizabeth II **Rev:** Kookaburra on branch next to tree **Edge** Segmented reeding **Note:** Photo reduced.

Date	Mintage	F	VF	XF	Unc	BU
1992P	—	—	—	—	175	200
1992P Proof	—	Value: 325				

KM# 180 10 DOLLARS
311.0670 g., 0.9990 Silver 10.0000 oz. ASW **Ruler:** Elizabeth II **Obv:** Crowned head right, denomination below **Rev:** Australian kookaburra sitting on branch facing right, date below

Date	Mintage	F	VF	XF	Unc	BU
1992	—	—	—	—	155	—
1992 Proof	2,500	Value: 325				

KM# 228 10 DOLLARS
311.0670 g., 0.9990 Silver 10.0000 oz. ASW **Ruler:** Elizabeth II **Obv:** Crowned head right, denomination below **Rev:** Kookaburra feeding nestling

Date	Mintage	F	VF	XF	Unc	BU
1993	—	—	—	—	165	—
1993 Proof	—	Value: 200				

KM# 231 10 DOLLARS
311.0350 g., 0.9990 Silver 10.0000 oz. ASW, 75 mm. **Ruler:** Elizabeth II **Subject:** The Australian Kookaburra **Obv:** Crowned head right, denomination below **Rev:** Pair of Kookaburras on branch, square mark above date below **Note:** Photo reduced.

Date	Mintage	F	VF	XF	Unc	BU
1993 (ae) Proof	500	Value: 550				
1994	—	—	—	—	165	—
1994 Proof	—	Value: 200				

KM# 270 10 DOLLARS
311.0670 g., 0.9990 Silver 10.0000 oz. ASW **Ruler:** Elizabeth II **Obv:** Crowned head right, denomination below **Rev:** Kookaburra on branch looking left, date below **Note:** Photo reduced.

Date	Mintage	F	VF	XF	Unc	BU
1994P Proof	—	Value: 300				
1995	—	—	—	—	165	—
1995 Proof	—	Value: 300				

KM# 291 10 DOLLARS
311.0670 g., 0.9990 Silver 10.0000 oz. ASW, 75.5 mm. **Ruler:** Elizabeth II **Obv:** Crowned head right, denomination below **Rev:** Kookaburra in flight right, date below, small "p" above bird's tail **Note:** Photo reduced.

Date	Mintage	F	VF	XF	Unc	BU
1995P Proof	1,300	Value: 275				
1995 (ge) Proof	800	Value: 300				
Note: Privy mark on gold insert						
1996	—	—	—	—	165	—

KM# 351 10 DOLLARS
311.0670 g., 0.9990 Silver 10.0000 oz. ASW **Ruler:** Elizabeth II **Subject:** Kookaburra and Nestling **Obv:** Crowned head right, denomination below **Rev:** Kookaburra looking right, nestling

Date	Mintage	F	VF	XF	Unc	BU
1997	—	—	—	—	165	—

KM# 494 10 DOLLARS
311.0350 g., 0.9990 Silver 10.0000 oz. ASW, 75 mm. **Ruler:** Elizabeth II **Subject:** Kookaburra Bullion **Obv:** Crowned head right, denomination below **Rev:** Kookaburra on fence right, date below **Edge:** Reeded and plain sections **Note:** Photo reduced.

Date	Mintage	F	VF	XF	Unc	BU
1997P Proof	—	Value: 325				

KM# 446 10 DOLLARS
312.3470 g., 0.9990 Silver 10.0000 oz. ASW **Ruler:** Elizabeth II **Obv:** Crowned head right, denomination below **Rev:** Two kookaburras on branch **Edge:** Interrupted reeding **Note:** Photo reduced.

Date	Mintage	F	VF	XF	Unc	BU
2000	—	—	—	—	165	—

KM# 181 30 DOLLARS
1100.1000 g., 0.9990 Silver 35.3376 oz. ASW, 100 mm. **Ruler:** Elizabeth II **Obv:** Crowned head right within inner circle, denomination below **Obv. Designer:** Raphael Maklouf **Rev:** Australian Kookaburra on stump facing right within circle, date below **Note:** Photo reduced.

Date	Mintage	F	VF	XF	Unc	BU
1992	—	—	—	—	525	—
1992 Proof	1,000	Value: 600				
1993	—	—	—	—	525	—
1993 (jw) Proof	210	Value: 550				

KM# 178 30 DOLLARS
1000.0000 g., 0.9990 Silver 32.1186 oz. ASW, 100 mm. **Subject:** Kookaburra **Obv:** Elizabeth II **Rev:** Kookaburra on branch next to tree trunk **Edge:** Segmented reeding

Date	Mintage	F	VF	XF	Unc	BU
1992P	—	—	—	—	525	—
1992P Proof	—	Value: 650				

KM# 229 30 DOLLARS
1000.2108 g., 0.9990 Silver 32.1575 oz. ASW **Ruler:** Elizabeth II **Obv:** Crowned head right, denomination below **Rev:** Kookaburra feeding nestling **Note:** Similar to 1 Dollar, KM#209.

Date	Mintage	F	VF	XF	Unc	BU
1993	—	—	—	—	500	—
1993 Proof	—	Value: 475				

KM# 232 30 DOLLARS
1000.2108 g., 0.9990 Silver 32.1575 oz. ASW, 100 mm. **Obv:** Bust of Queen Elizabeth II, right **Rev:** Pair of kookaburras on branch within circle, silver weight and date in legend **Note:** Photo reduced.

Date	Mintage	F	VF	XF	Unc	BU
1994	—	—	—	—	500	—
1994 Proof	—	Value: 475				

KM# 271 30 DOLLARS
1000.2108 g., 0.9990 Silver 32.1575 oz. ASW **Ruler:** Elizabeth II **Obv:** Crowned head right, denomination below **Rev:** Kookaburra on branch looking left, date below **Note:** Photo reduced.

Date	Mintage	F	VF	XF	Unc	BU
1994P Proof	—	Value: 535				
1995	—	—	—	—	500	—
1995 Proof	—	Value: 535				

KM# 292 30 DOLLARS
1000.2108 g., 0.9990 Silver 32.1575 oz. ASW, 101 mm. **Ruler:** Elizabeth II **Obv:** Crowned head right, denomination below **Rev:** Kookaburra in flight, date below **Note:** Photo reduced.

Date	Mintage	F	VF	XF	Unc	BU
1995 (lh) Proof	500	Value: 525				
1995P Proof	1,000	Value: 550				
1996	—	—	—	—	500	—

KM# 495 30 DOLLARS
1100.1000 g., 0.9990 Silver 35.3376 oz. ASW, 100 mm. **Ruler:** Elizabeth II **Subject:** Kookaburra Bullion **Obv:** Crowned head right, denomination below **Rev:** Kookaburra on fence facing right, date below **Edge:** Reeded and plain sections with serial number **Note:** Photo reduced.

Date	Mintage	F	VF	XF	Unc	BU
1997P Proof	—	Value: 550				
1998P	—	—	—	—	525	—

KM# 610 30 DOLLARS
1002.5020 g., 0.9990 Silver 32.1989 oz. ASW **Ruler:** Elizabeth II **Subject:** USA State Quarters - 1999 **Obv:** Crowned head right, denomination below **Rev:** Kookaburra on branch with five state quarter designs added below **Edge:** Reeded and plain sections

Date	Mintage	F	VF	XF	Unc	BU
1999	1,000	—	—	—	485	—

KM# 447 30 DOLLARS
1002.5020 g., 0.9990 Silver 32.1989 oz. ASW **Ruler:** Elizabeth II **Obv:** Crowned head right, denomination below **Rev:** Two kookaburras on branch, date below **Edge:** Reeded **Note:** Photo reduced.

Date	Mintage	F	VF	XF	Unc	BU
1999	—	—	—	—	525	—
2000 Proof	—	Value: 600				

KM# 617 30 DOLLARS
1002.5020 g., 0.9990 Silver 32.1989 oz. ASW **Ruler:** Elizabeth II **Subject:** USA State Quarters - 2000 **Obv:** Crowned head right, denomination below **Rev:** Kookaburra on branch with five state quarter designs added below **Edge:** Reeded and plain sections **Note:** Photo reduced.

Date	Mintage	F	VF	XF	Unc	BU
2000	1,000	—	—	—	485	—

KM# 162 50 DOLLARS
311.0670 g., 0.9990 Silver 10.0000 oz. ASW **Ruler:** Elizabeth II **Subject:** Australian Kookaburra **Obv:** Crowned head right, denomination below **Rev:** Kookaburra bird

Date	Mintage	F	VF	XF	Unc	BU
1991	—	—	—	—	150	—
1991 Proof	2,500	Value: 250				

KM# 163 150 DOLLARS
1000.1000 g., 0.9990 Silver 32.1575 oz. ASW **Ruler:** Elizabeth II **Subject:** Australian Kookaburra **Obv:** Crowned head right, denomination below **Rev:** Kookaburra bird **Note:** Kilo

Date	Mintage	F	VF	XF	Unc	BU
1991	—	—	—	—	475	—
1991 Proof	1,000	Value: 600				

BULLION - LUNAR YEAR

KM# 501 50 CENTS
16.8860 g., 0.9990 Silver .5424 oz. ASW, 32.1 mm. **Ruler:** Elizabeth II **Subject:** Year of the Rabbit **Obv:** Head with tiara right, denomination below **Obv. Designer:** Ian Rank-Broadley **Rev:** Rabbit right, date at left **Edge:** Reeded

Date	Mintage	F	VF	XF	Unc	BU
1999	—	—	—	—	15.00	17.50
1999 Proof	5,000	Value: 28.00				

KM# 502 DOLLAR
31.6350 g., 0.9990 Silver 1.0161 oz. ASW, 40.6 mm. **Ruler:** Elizabeth II **Subject:** Year of the Rabbit **Obv:** Head with tiara right, denomination below **Obv. Designer:** Ian Rank-Broadley **Rev:** Rabbit right, date at left **Edge:** Reeded

Date	Mintage	F	VF	XF	Unc	BU
1999	—	—	—	—	25.00	27.50
1999 Proof	2,500	Value: 45.00				

KM# 502a DOLLAR
31.6350 g., 0.9990 Silver 1.0161 oz. ASW, 40.6 mm. **Ruler:** Elizabeth II **Subject:** Year of the Rabbit **Obv:** Head with tiara right, denomination below **Rev:** Rabbit right, date at left **Edge:** Reeded

Date	Mintage	F	VF	XF	Unc	BU
1999	50,000	—	—	—	50.00	55.00

KM# 424 DOLLAR
31.1035 g., 0.9990 Silver 1.0000 oz. ASW **Ruler:** Elizabeth II **Subject:** Year of the Dragon **Obv:** Head with tiara right within circle, denomination below **Obv. Designer:** Ian Rank-Broadley **Rev:** Dragon, date at left

Date	Mintage	F	VF	XF	Unc	BU
2000	—	—	—	—	25.00	27.50
2000 Proof	—	Value: 45.00				

KM# 424a DOLLAR
31.6350 g., 0.9990 Silver, 40.6 mm. **Ruler:** Elizabeth II **Subject:** Year of the Dragon **Obv:** Head with tiara right, denomination below **Rev:** Gold-plated dragon, date at left **Edge:** Reeded

Date	Mintage	F	VF	XF	Unc	BU
2000	50,000	—	—	—	50.00	55.00

KM# 503 2 DOLLARS
62.7700 g., 0.9990 Silver 2.0161 oz. ASW, 49.9 mm. **Ruler:** Elizabeth II **Subject:** Year of the Rabbit **Obv:** Head with tiara right, denomination below **Obv. Designer:** Ian Rank-Broadley **Rev:** Rabbit right, date at left **Edge:** Reeded and plain sections

Date	Mintage	F	VF	XF	Unc	BU
1999	—	—	—	—	35.00	—
1999 Proof	2,500	Value: 95.00				

KM# 523 2 DOLLARS
62.2070 g., 0.9990 Silver 2. oz. ASW, 50.3 mm. **Ruler:** Elizabeth II **Series:** Dragons **Subject:** Year of the Dragon **Obv:** Head with tiara right, denomination below **Rev:** Dragon, date at left **Edge:** Segmented reeding

Date	Mintage	F	VF	XF	Unc	BU
2000 Proof	—	Value: 110				

KM# 566 5 DOLLARS
1.5552 g., 0.9990 Gold 0.05 oz. AGW, 14.1 mm. **Ruler:** Elizabeth II **Subject:** Year of the Rat **Obv:** Crowned head right, denomination below **Rev:** Rat, right **Edge:** Reeded

Date	Mintage	F	VF	XF	Unc	BU
1996P	100,000	—	—	—	—	45.00

KM# 567 5 DOLLARS
1.5552 g., 0.9990 Gold 0.05 oz. AGW, 14.1 mm. **Ruler:** Elizabeth II **Subject:** Year of the Ox **Obv:** Crowned head right, denomination below **Rev:** Ox, left **Edge:** Reeded

Date	Mintage	F	VF	XF	Unc	BU
1997P	100,000	—	—	—	—	45.00

KM# 568 5 DOLLARS
1.5552 g., 0.9990 Gold 0.05 oz. AGW, 14.1 mm. **Ruler:** Elizabeth II **Subject:** Year of the Tiger **Obv:** Crowned head right, denomination below **Rev:** Tiger springing right **Edge:** Reeded

Date	Mintage	F	VF	XF	Unc	BU
1998P	100,000	—	—	—	—	45.00

KM# 425 5 DOLLARS
1.5710 g., 0.9999 Gold .0500 oz. AGW **Ruler:** Elizabeth II **Subject:** Year of the Rabbit **Obv:** Crowned head right, denomination below **Rev:** Rabbit **Note:** Similar to 100 Dollars, KM#428.

Date	Mintage	F	VF	XF	Unc	BU
1999	Est. 100,000	—	—	—	—	45.00

KM# 569 5 DOLLARS
1.5552 g., 0.9990 Gold 0.05 oz. AGW, 14.1 mm. **Ruler:** Elizabeth II **Subject:** Year of the Dragon **Obv:** Crowned head right, denomination below **Rev:** Dragon **Edge:** Reeded

Date	Mintage	F	VF	XF	Unc	BU
2000P	100,000	—	—	—	—	40.00

KM# 504 10 DOLLARS
312.3470 g., 0.9990 Silver 10.0321 oz. ASW, 75.5 mm. **Ruler:** Elizabeth II **Subject:** Year of the Rabbit **Obv:** Head with tiara right, denomination below **Obv. Designer:** Ian Rank-Broadley **Rev:** Rabbit right, date at left **Edge:** Reeded and plain sections **Note:** Photo reduced.

Date	Mintage	F	VF	XF	Unc	BU
1999	—	—	—	—	160	170
1999 Proof	2,500	Value: 350				

KM# 524 10 DOLLARS
311.0350 g., 0.9990 Silver 10.0000 oz. ASW, 75.5 mm. **Ruler:** Elizabeth II **Series:** Dragons **Subject:** Year of the Dragon **Obv:** Head with tiara right, denomination below **Rev:** Dragon **Edge:** Segmented reeding

Date	Mintage	F	VF	XF	Unc	BU
2000	—	—	—	—	165	185
2000 Proof	—	Value: 285				

KM# 298 15 DOLLARS
3.1103 g., 0.9990 Gold .1000 oz. AGW **Ruler:** Elizabeth II **Subject:** Year of the Rat **Obv:** Crowned head right, denomination below **Rev:** Rat facing right

Date	Mintage	F	VF	XF	Unc	BU
1996	—	—	—	—	—	80.00
1996 Proof	—	Value: 75.00				

KM# 335 15 DOLLARS
3.1103 g., 0.9990 Gold .1000 oz. AGW **Ruler:** Elizabeth II **Subject:** Year of the Ox **Obv:** Crowned head right, denomination below **Rev:** Bull ox looking right

Date	Mintage	F	VF	XF	Unc	BU
1997	—	—	—	—	—	75.00
1997 Proof	—	Value: 95.00				

KM# 506 15 DOLLARS
3.1103 g., 0.9990 Gold 0.0999 oz. AGW, 16.1 mm. **Ruler:** Elizabeth II **Subject:** Year of the Tiger **Obv:** Crowned head right, denomination below **Rev:** Tiger springing right **Edge:** Reeded

Date	Mintage	F	VF	XF	Unc	BU
1998	—	—	—	—	—	75.00
1998P	—	—	—	—	—	95.00

KM# 426 15 DOLLARS
3.1130 g., 0.9999 Gold .1000 oz. AGW **Ruler:** Elizabeth II **Subject:** Year of the Rabbit **Obv:** Crowned head right, denomination below **Rev:** Rabbit facing right **Note:** Similar to 100 Dollars, KM#428.

Date	Mintage	F	VF	XF	Unc	BU
1999 Proof	—	Value: 95.00				
1999	Est. 80,000	—	—	—	—	75.00

KM# 526 15 DOLLARS
3.1103 g., 0.9990 Gold .1000 oz. AGW, 16.1 mm. **Ruler:** Elizabeth II **Subject:** Year of the Dragon **Obv:** Crowned head right, denomination below **Rev:** Dragon **Edge:** Reeded

Date	Mintage	F	VF	XF	Unc	BU
2000	—	—	—	—	—	85.00
2000 Proof	—	Value: 100				

KM# 299 25 DOLLARS
7.7508 g., 0.9990 Gold .2500 oz. AGW **Ruler:** Elizabeth II **Subject:** Year of the Rat **Obv:** Crowned head right, denomination below **Rev:** Rat facing right

Date	Mintage	F	VF	XF	Unc	BU
1996	—	—	—	—	—	170
1996 Proof	—	Value: 225				

KM# 336 25 DOLLARS
7.7508 g., 0.9990 Gold .2500 oz. AGW **Ruler:** Elizabeth II **Subject:** Year of the Ox **Obv:** Crowned head right, denomination below **Rev:** Bull ox looking right

Date	Mintage	F	VF	XF	Unc	BU
1997	—	—	—	—	—	170
1997 Proof	8,888	Value: 225				

KM# 507 25 DOLLARS
7.7759 g., 0.9990 Gold 0.2498 oz. AGW, 20.1 mm. **Ruler:** Elizabeth II **Subject:** Year of the Tiger **Obv:** Crowned head right, denomination below **Rev:** Tiger springing right **Edge:** Reeded

Date	Mintage	F	VF	XF	Unc	BU
1998P	—	—	—	—	—	170
1998P Proof	—	Value: 225				

KM# 427 25 DOLLARS
7.8070 g., 0.9999 Gold .2510 oz. AGW **Ruler:** Elizabeth II **Subject:** Year of the Rabbit **Obv:** Crowned head right, denomination below **Rev:** Rabbit facing right **Edge:** Reeded

Date	Mintage	F	VF	XF	Unc	BU
1999	Est. 60,000	—	—	—	—	170
1999 Proof	—	Value: 200				

KM# 527 25 DOLLARS
7.7508 g., 0.9990 Gold .2500 oz. AGW, 20.1 mm. **Ruler:** Elizabeth II **Subject:** Year of the Dragon **Obv:** Crowned head right, denomination below **Rev:** Dragon **Edge:** Reeded

Date	Mintage	F	VF	XF	Unc	BU
2000	—	—	—	—	—	185
2000 Proof	—	Value: 225				

KM# 505 30 DOLLARS
1002.5020 g., 0.9990 Silver 32.1989 oz. ASW, 101 mm. **Ruler:** Elizabeth II **Subject:** Year of the Rabbit **Obv:** Head with tiara right, denomination below **Rev:** Rabbit right, date at left **Edge:** Reeded and plain sections **Note:** Photo reduced.

Date	Mintage	F	VF	XF	Unc	BU
1999 Proof	2,500	Value: 525				
1999	—	—	—	—	475	—

KM# 525.1 30 DOLLARS
1002.5020 g., 0.9990 Silver 32.2312 oz. ASW, 101 mm. **Ruler:** Elizabeth II **Subject:** Year of the Dragon **Obv:** Head with tiara right, denomination below **Rev:** Dragon **Edge:** Segmented reeding **Note:** Prev. KM#525.

Date	Mintage	F	VF	XF	Unc	BU
2000	—	—	—	—	500	—
2000 Proof	—	Value: 550				

KM# 525.2 30 DOLLARS
0.9990 Silver **Ruler:** Elizabeth II **Subject:** Year of the Dragon **Obv:** Head with tiara right, denomination below **Rev:** Dragon with diamonds for eyes and multicolor ornamentation

Date	Mintage	F	VF	XF	Unc	BU
2000 Proof	5,000	Value: 485				

KM# 300 100 DOLLARS
31.1035 g., 0.9990 Gold 1.0000 oz. AGW **Ruler:** Elizabeth II **Subject:** Year of the Rat **Obv:** Crowned head right, denomination below **Obv. Designer:** Raphael Maklouf **Rev:** Rat facing right, date at left

Date	Mintage	F	VF	XF	Unc	BU
1996	—	—	—	—	—	675
1996 Proof	—	Value: 725				

KM# 337 100 DOLLARS
31.1035 g., 0.9990 Gold 1.0000 oz. AGW **Ruler:** Elizabeth II **Subject:** Year of the Ox **Obv:** Crowned head right, denomination below **Obv. Designer:** Raphael Maklouf **Rev:** Ox left, looking right, date at left

Date	Mintage	F	VF	XF	Unc	BU
1997	—	—	—	—	—	675
1997 Proof	8,888	Value: 725				

KM# 508 100 DOLLARS
31.1035 g., 0.9990 Gold 0.999 oz. AGW, 32.1 mm. **Ruler:** Elizabeth II **Subject:** Year of the Tiger **Obv:** Crowned head right, denomination below **Rev:** Tiger springing right, date at left **Edge:** Reeded

Date	Mintage	F	VF	XF	Unc	BU
1998	—	—	—	—	—	675
1998P Proof	—	Value: 750				

KM# 428 100 DOLLARS
31.1620 g., 0.9999 Gold 1.0529 oz. AGW **Ruler:** Elizabeth II **Subject:** Year of the Rabbit **Obv:** Crowned head right, denomination below **Rev:** Seated rabbit left, date at left **Edge:** Reeded

Date	Mintage	F	VF	XF	Unc	BU
1999 Proof	—	Value: 725				
1999	Est. 30,000	—	—	—	—	675

KM# 528 100 DOLLARS
31.1035 g., 0.9990 Gold 1. oz. AGW, 32.1 mm. **Ruler:** Elizabeth II **Subject:** Year of the Dragon **Obv:** Crowned head right, denomination below **Rev:** Dragon **Edge:** Reeded

Date	Mintage	F	VF	XF	Unc	BU
2000	—	—	—	—	—	750
2000 Proof	—	Value: 800				

KM# 667 200 DOLLARS
62.2140 g., 0.9990 Gold 1.9982 oz. AGW, 40.6 mm. **Ruler:** Elizabeth II **Subject:** Year of the Dragon **Obv:** Crowned head right, denomination below **Rev:** Dragon **Edge:** Reeded

Date	Mintage	F	VF	XF	Unc	BU
2000	—	—	—	—	—	1,350

KM# 702 1000 DOLLARS
311.0480 g., 0.9999 Gold 10.0000 oz. AGW **Ruler:** Elizabeth II **Subject:** Year of the Dragon **Obv:** Crowned head right, denomination below **Rev:** Dragon

Date	Mintage	F	VF	XF	Unc	BU
2000	—	—	—	—	—	7,500

KM# 703 3000 DOLLARS
1000.0000 g., 0.9999 Gold 32.1475 oz. AGW **Ruler:** Elizabeth II **Subject:** Year of the Dragon **Obv:** Crowned head right, denomination below **Rev:** Dragon

Date	Mintage	F	VF	XF	Unc	BU
2000	—	—	—	—	BV+10%	—

GOLD BULLION - KANGAROO

KM# 117 5 DOLLARS
1.5710 g., 0.9990 Gold .0500 oz. AGW **Ruler:** Elizabeth II **Subject:** Red Kangaroo **Obv:** Crowned head right, denomination below **Rev:** Kangaroo leaping left, date below **Rev. Designer:** Stuart Devlin

Date	Mintage	F	VF	XF	Unc	BU
1989 Proof	2,200	Value: 50.00				
1990	Est. 200,000	—	—	—	BV+ 35%	—

KM# 140 5 DOLLARS
1.5710 g., 0.9990 Gold .0500 oz. AGW **Ruler:** Elizabeth II **Obv:** Crowned head right, denomination below **Rev:** Gray Kangaroo right, date below **Rev. Designer:** Stuart Devlin

Date	Mintage	F	VF	XF	Unc	BU
1990 Proof	7,000	Value: 50.00				
1991	200,000	—	—	—	BV+35%	—

KM# 165 5 DOLLARS
1.5710 g., 0.9990 Gold .0500 oz. AGW **Ruler:** Elizabeth II **Subject:** Common Wallaroo **Obv:** Crowned head right, denomination below **Rev:** Kangaroo bounding left, date below **Note:** 1992 (ae) previously listed here is now KM#389.

Date	Mintage	F	VF	XF	Unc	BU
1991 Proof	3,525	Value: 48.00				
1992	200,000	—	—	—	BV+ 35%	—

KM# 389 5 DOLLARS
1.5710 g., 0.9990 Gold .0500 oz. AGW **Ruler:** Elizabeth II **Obv:** Crowned head right, denomination below **Rev:** Nail-tailed Wallaby

Date	Mintage	F	VF	XF	Unc	BU
1992 (ae) Proof	500	Value: 60.00				

KM# 233 5 DOLLARS
1.5710 g., 0.9990 Gold .0500 oz. AGW **Ruler:** Elizabeth II **Obv:** Crowned head right, denomination below **Rev:** Whiptail Wallaby

Date	Mintage	F	VF	XF	Unc	BU
1993 Proof	—	Value: 55.00				
1994	—	—	—	—	BV+ 35%	—

KM# 241 5 DOLLARS
1.5710 g., 0.9990 Gold .0500 oz. AGW **Ruler:** Elizabeth II **Obv. Legend:** Crowned head right, denomination below **Rev:** Red Kangaroo facing front, date below **Rev. Designer:** Stuart Devlin

Date	Mintage	F	VF	XF	Unc	BU
1994 Proof	—	Value: 50.00				
1995	200,000	—	—	—	BV+35%	—

KM# 272 5 DOLLARS
1.5710 g., 0.9990 Gold .0500 oz. AGW **Ruler:** Elizabeth II **Obv:** Crowned head right, denomination below **Rev:** Two kangaroos standing, date below **Rev. Designer:** Stuart Devlin

Date	Mintage	F	VF	XF	Unc	BU
1995 Proof	300	Value: 55.00				
1996	200,000	—	—	—	BV+35%	—

KM# 320 5 DOLLARS
1.5710 g., 0.9990 Gold .0500 oz. AGW **Ruler:** Elizabeth II **Obv:** Crowned head right, denomination below **Rev:** Kangaroo bounding right

Date	Mintage	F	VF	XF	Unc	BU
1996P Proof	—	Value: 60.00				

Note: In proof sets only

KM# 338 5 DOLLARS
1.5710 g., 0.9999 Gold .0500 oz. AGW **Ruler:** Elizabeth II **Obv:** Crowned head right, denomination below **Rev:** Kangaroo bounding right

Date	Mintage	F	VF	XF	Unc	BU
1997	200,000	—	—	—	BV+ 35%	—
1997 Proof	—	Value: 50.00				

KM# 448 5 DOLLARS
1.5710 g., 0.9990 Gold .0505 oz. AGW **Ruler:** Elizabeth II **Obv:** Crowned head right, denomination below **Rev:** Kangaroo facing left **Edge:** Reeded

Date	Mintage	F	VF	XF	Unc	BU
1999	200,000	—	—	—	—	50.00

KM# 464 5 DOLLARS
1.5710 g., 0.9990 Gold .0505 oz. AGW **Ruler:** Elizabeth II **Obv:** Crowned head right, denomination below **Rev:** Two kangaroos bounding left

Date	Mintage	F	VF	XF	Unc	BU
2000	—	—	—	—	—	50.00

KM# 118 15 DOLLARS
3.1103 g., 0.9990 Gold .1000 oz. AGW **Ruler:** Elizabeth II **Obv:** Crowned head right, denomination below **Rev:** Red kangaroo leaping left, date below **Rev. Designer:** Stuart Devlin

Date	Mintage	F	VF	XF	Unc	BU
1989 Proof	2,200	Value: 80.00				
1990	200,000	—	—	—	BV+12%	—

KM# 141 15 DOLLARS
3.1103 g., 0.9990 Gold .1000 oz. AGW **Ruler:** Elizabeth II **Obv:** Crowned head right, denomination below **Rev:** Gray kangaroo standing facing left, date below **Rev. Designer:** Stuart Devlin

Date	Mintage	F	VF	XF	Unc	BU
1990 Proof	7,000	Value: 80.00				
1991	150,000	—	—	—	BV+12%	—

KM# 166 15 DOLLARS
3.1103 g., 0.9990 Gold .1000 oz. AGW **Ruler:** Elizabeth II **Subject:** Common Wallaroo **Obv:** Crowned head right, denomination below **Rev:** Radiant common walleroo facing right

Date	Mintage	F	VF	XF	Unc	BU
1991 Proof	1,975	Value: 80.00				
1992	150,000	—	—	—	BV+12%	—

KM# 390 15 DOLLARS
3.1103 g., 0.9990 Gold .1000 oz. AGW **Ruler:** Elizabeth II **Obv:** Crowned head right, denomination below **Rev:** Nail-tailed wallaby

Date	Mintage	F	VF	XF	Unc	BU
1992 (ae) Proof	500	Value: 110				

KM# 234 15 DOLLARS
3.1103 g., 0.9990 Gold .1000 oz. AGW **Ruler:** Elizabeth II **Obv:** Crowned head right, denomination below **Rev:** Whiptail wallaby

Date	Mintage	F	VF	XF	Unc	BU
1993 Proof	—	Value: 85.00				
1994	—	—	—	—	BV+12%	—

KM# 242 15 DOLLARS
3.1103 g., 0.9990 Gold .1000 oz. AGW **Ruler:** Elizabeth II **Obv:** Crowned head right, denomination below **Rev:** Red kangaroo standing facing forward, date below **Rev. Designer:** Stuart Devlin

Date	Mintage	F	VF	XF	Unc	BU
1994 Proof	—	Value: 85.00				
1995	200,000	—	—	—	BV+12%	—

KM# 273 15 DOLLARS
3.1103 g., 0.9990 Gold .1000 oz. AGW **Ruler:** Elizabeth II **Obv:** Crowned head right, denomination below **Rev:** Two kangaroos, date below **Rev. Designer:** Stuart Devlin

Date	Mintage	F	VF	XF	Unc	BU
1995 Proof	900	Value: 85.00				
1996	200,000	—	—	—	BV+12%	—

KM# 321 15 DOLLARS
3.1103 g., 0.9990 Gold .1000 oz. AGW **Ruler:** Elizabeth II **Obv:** Crowned head right, denomination below **Rev:** Kangaroo bounding right

Date	Mintage	F	VF	XF	Unc	BU
1996P Proof	400	Value: 200				

Note: In Proof sets only

KM# 339 15 DOLLARS
3.1103 g., 0.9990 Gold .1000 oz. AGW **Ruler:** Elizabeth II **Obv:** Crowned head right, denomination below **Rev:** Kangaroo bounding right

Date	Mintage	F	VF	XF	Unc	BU
1997	200,000	—	—	—	70.00	—
1997 Proof	—	Value: 80.00				

KM# 449 15 DOLLARS
3.1330 g., 0.9990 Gold .1000 oz. AGW **Ruler:** Elizabeth II **Obv:** Crowned head right, denomination below **Rev:** Kangaroo facing left **Edge:** Reeded

Date	Mintage	F	VF	XF	Unc	BU
1999	200,000	—	—	—	70.00	—

KM# 465 15 DOLLARS
3.1330 g., 0.9990 Gold .1000 oz. AGW **Ruler:** Elizabeth II **Obv:** Crowned head right, denomination below **Rev:** Two kangaroos bounding left **Edge:** Reeded

Date	Mintage	F	VF	XF	Unc	BU
2000	—	—	—	—	70.00	—

KM# 119 25 DOLLARS
7.7508 g., 0.9990 Gold .2500 oz. AGW **Ruler:** Elizabeth II **Obv:** Crowned head right, denomination below **Rev:** Red kangaroo **Rev. Designer:** Stuart Devlin

Date	Mintage	F	VF	XF	Unc	BU
1989 Proof	2,200	Value: 185				
1990	Est. 200,000	—	—	—	BV+10%	—

KM# 142 25 DOLLARS
7.7508 g., 0.9990 Gold .2500 oz. AGW **Ruler:** Elizabeth II **Obv:** Crowned head right, denomination below **Rev:** Gray kangaroo standing right, date below **Rev. Designer:** Stuart Devlin

Date	Mintage	F	VF	XF	Unc	BU
1990 Proof	7,000	Value: 185				
1991	100,000	—	—	—	BV+10%	—

KM# 167 25 DOLLARS
7.7508 g., 0.9990 Gold .2500 oz. AGW **Ruler:** Elizabeth II **Subject:** Common Wallaroo **Obv:** Crowned head right, denomination below **Rev:** Radiant walleroo facing right

Date	Mintage	F	VF	XF	Unc	BU
1991 Proof	1,991	Value: 185				
1992	100,000	—	—	—	BV+10%	—

KM# 391 25 DOLLARS
7.7508 g., 0.9990 Gold .2500 oz. AGW **Ruler:** Elizabeth II **Obv:** Crowned head right, denomination below **Obv. Designer:** Raphael Maklouf **Rev:** Nail-tailed wallaby standing right, date below **Rev. Designer:** Stuart Devlin

Date	Mintage	F	VF	XF	Unc	BU
1992 (ae) Proof	500	Value: 225				

KM# 235 25 DOLLARS
7.7508 g., 0.9990 Gold .2500 oz. AGW **Ruler:** Elizabeth II **Obv:** Crowned head right, denomination below **Rev:** Whiptail wallaby

Date	Mintage	F	VF	XF	Unc	BU
1993 (f) Proof	200	—	—	—	—	—
1993 Proof	—	Value: 190				
1994	—	—	—	—	BV+10%	—

KM# 243 25 DOLLARS
7.7508 g., 0.9990 Gold .2500 oz. AGW **Ruler:** Elizabeth II **Obv:** Crowned head right, denomination below **Rev:** Red kangaroo standing facing, date below **Rev. Designer:** Stuart Devlin

Date	Mintage	F	VF	XF	Unc	BU
1994 Proof	—	Value: 190				
1995	150,000	—	—	—	BV+10%	—

KM# 274 25 DOLLARS
7.7508 g., 0.9990 Gold .2500 oz. AGW **Ruler:** Elizabeth II **Obv:** Crowned head right, denomination below **Rev:** Two kangaroos, date below **Rev. Designer:** Stuart Devlin

Date	Mintage	F	VF	XF	Unc	BU
1995 Proof	650	Value: 190				
1996	150,000	—	—	—	BV+10%	—

KM# 322 25 DOLLARS
7.7508 g., 0.9990 Gold .2500 oz. AGW **Ruler:** Elizabeth II **Obv:** Crowned head right, denomination below **Rev:** Kangaroo bounding right

Date	Mintage	F	VF	XF	Unc	BU
1996(p) Proof	400	Value: 350				

Note: In sets only

KM# 340 25 DOLLARS
7.7508 g., 0.9990 Gold .2500 oz. AGW **Ruler:** Elizabeth II **Obv:** Crowned head right, denomination below **Rev:** Kangaroo bounding right

Date	Mintage	F	VF	XF	Unc	BU
1997	200,000	—	—	—	BV+10%	—
1997 Proof	—	Value: 190				

KM# 450 25 DOLLARS
7.8070 g., 0.9990 Gold .2500 oz. AGW **Ruler:** Elizabeth II **Obv:** Crowned head right, denomination below **Rev:** Kangaroo facing left **Edge:** Reeded

Date	Mintage	F	VF	XF	Unc	BU
1999	150,000	—	—	—	BV+10%	—

KM# 466 25 DOLLARS
7.8070 g., 0.9990 Gold .2500 oz. AGW **Ruler:** Elizabeth II **Obv:** Crowned head right, denomination below **Rev:** Two kangaroos bounding left **Edge:** Reeded

Date	Mintage	F	VF	XF	Unc	BU
2000	—	—	—	—	BV+10%	—

KM# 120 50 DOLLARS
15.5017 g., 0.9990 Gold .5000 oz. AGW **Ruler:** Elizabeth II **Obv:** Crowned head right, denomination below **Rev:** Red kangaroo leaping left, date below

Date	Mintage	F	VF	XF	Unc	BU
1989 Proof	2,200	Value: 350				
1990	Est. 240,000	—	—	—	BV+7%	—

KM# 143 50 DOLLARS
15.5017 g., 0.9990 Gold .5000 oz. AGW **Ruler:** Elizabeth II **Obv:** Crowned head right, denomination below **Rev:** Gray kangaroo facing right looking left, date below **Rev. Designer:** Stuart Devlin

Date	Mintage	F	VF	XF	Unc	BU
1990 Proof	5,000	Value: 350				
1991	100,000	—	—	—	BV+7%	—

KM# 168 50 DOLLARS
15.5017 g., 0.9990 Gold .5000 oz. AGW **Ruler:** Elizabeth II **Subject:** Common wallaroo **Obv:** Crowned head right, denomination below **Rev:** Radiant common wallaroo facing right

Date	Mintage	F	VF	XF	Unc	BU
1991 Proof	1,096	Value: 365				
1992	100,000	—	—	—	BV+7%	—

KM# 392 50 DOLLARS
15.5017 g., 0.9990 Gold .5000 oz. AGW **Ruler:** Elizabeth II **Obv:** Crowned head right, denomination below **Rev:** Nail-tailed wallaby

Date	Mintage	F	VF	XF	Unc	BU
1992 (ae) Proof	500	Value: 500				

KM# 236 50 DOLLARS
15.5017 g., 0.9990 Gold .5000 oz. AGW **Ruler:** Elizabeth II **Obv:** Crowned head right, denomination below **Rev:** Whiptail wallaby

Date	Mintage	F	VF	XF	Unc	BU
1993 Proof	—	Value: 380				
1994	—	—	—	—	BV+7%	—

KM# 244 50 DOLLARS
15.5017 g., 0.9990 Gold .5000 oz. AGW **Ruler:** Elizabeth II **Obv:** Crowned head right, denomination below **Rev:** Red kangaroo standing facing front, date below **Rev. Designer:** Stuart Devlin

Date	Mintage	F	VF	XF	Unc	BU
1994 Proof	—	Value: 380				
1995	30,000	—	—	—	BV+10%	—
1995 (f) Proof	10,000	Value: 350				

KM# 275.1 50 DOLLARS
15.5017 g., 0.9990 Gold .5000 oz. AGW **Ruler:** Elizabeth II **Obv:** Crowned head right, denomination below **Rev:** Two kangaroos, date below **Rev. Designer:** Stuart Devlin

Date	Mintage	F	VF	XF	Unc	BU
1995 Proof	300	Value: 380				
1996	100,000	—	—	—	BV+7%	—
1996 (s) Proof	13,000	Value: 350				
1996 (l) Proof	3,000	Value: 350				
Note: In Proof sets only						
1996 (f) Proof	13,000	Value: 350				

KM# 275.2 50 DOLLARS
15.5017 g., 0.9990 Gold .5000 oz. AGW **Ruler:** Elizabeth II **Obv:** Crowned head right, denomination below **Rev:** Two kangaroos, date below **Edge:** Reeded and inscribed with date and serial number

Date	Mintage	F	VF	XF	Unc	BU
1996 Proof	500	Value: 360				

KM# 341 50 DOLLARS
15.5017 g., 0.9990 Gold .5000 oz. AGW **Ruler:** Elizabeth II **Obv:** Crowned head right, denomination below **Rev:** Kangaroo bounding right

Date	Mintage	F	VF	XF	Unc	BU
1996 (p) Proof	400	Value: 600				
Note: In Proof sets only						
1997	100,000	—	—	—	—	340
1997 Proof	—	Value: 350				
1997 (f) Proof	13,000	Value: 350				
1997 (l) Proof	10,000	Value: 350				
Note: In Proof sets only						
1997 (s) Proof	13,000	Value: 350				

KM# 451 50 DOLLARS
15.5940 g., 0.9990 Gold .5000 oz. AGW **Ruler:** Elizabeth II **Obv:** Crowned head right, denomination below **Rev:** Kangaroo facing left **Edge:** Reeded

Date	Mintage	F	VF	XF	Unc	BU
1999	100,000	—	—	—	—	340

KM# 467 50 DOLLARS
15.5940 g., 0.9990 Gold .5000 oz. AGW **Obv:** Crowned head right, denomination below **Rev:** Two kangaroos bounding left **Edge:** Reeded

Date	Mintage	F	VF	XF	Unc	BU
2000	—	—	—	—	—	340

KM# 121 100 DOLLARS
31.1035 g., 0.9990 Gold 1.0000 oz. AGW **Ruler:** Elizabeth II **Obv:** Crowned head right, denomination below **Rev:** Red kangaroo bounding left, date below **Rev. Designer:** Stuart Devlin

Date	Mintage	F	VF	XF	Unc	BU
1989 Proof	2,200	Value: 690				
1990	—	—	—	—	BV+4%	—

KM# 144 100 DOLLARS
31.1035 g., 0.9990 Gold 1.0000 oz. AGW **Ruler:** Elizabeth II **Obv. Designer:** Crowned head right, denomination below **Rev:** Gray kangaroo standing looking left, date below **Rev. Designer:** Stuart Devlin

Date	Mintage	F	VF	XF	Unc	BU
1990 Proof	8,000	Value: 690				
1991	250,000	—	—	—	BV+4%	—

KM# 169 100 DOLLARS
31.1035 g., 0.9990 Gold 1.0000 oz. AGW **Ruler:** Elizabeth II **Obv:** Crowned head right, denomination below **Rev:** Common wallaroo on all fours facing right, date below **Rev. Designer:** Stuart Devlin

Date	Mintage	F	VF	XF	Unc	BU
1991 Proof	3,000	Value: 690				
1992	250,000	—	—	—	BV+4%	—

KM# 393 100 DOLLARS
31.1035 g., 0.9990 Gold 1.0000 oz. AGW **Ruler:** Elizabeth II **Obv:** Crowned head right, denomination below **Rev:** Nail-tailed wallaby

Date	Mintage	F	VF	XF	Unc	BU
1992 Proof	784	Value: 690				
1993	—	—	—	—	BV+4%	—

KM# 237 100 DOLLARS
31.1035 g., 0.9990 Gold 1.0000 oz. AGW **Ruler:** Elizabeth II **Obv:** Crowned head right, denomination below **Rev:** Whiptail wallaby

Date	Mintage	F	VF	XF	Unc	BU
1993 Proof	—	Value: 700				
1993 (f) Proof	150	Value: 750				
1994	—	—	—	—	BV+4%	—

KM# 245 100 DOLLARS
31.1035 g., 0.9990 Gold 1.0000 oz. AGW **Ruler:** Elizabeth II **Obv:** Crowned head right, denomination below **Obv. Designer:** Raphael Maklouf **Rev:** Red kangaroo facing forward, date below **Rev. Designer:** Stuart Devlin

Date	Mintage	F	VF	XF	Unc	BU
1994 Proof	—	Value: 690				
1995	350,000	—	—	—	BV+4%	—

KM# 276 100 DOLLARS
31.1035 g., 0.9990 Gold 1.0000 oz. AGW **Ruler:** Elizabeth II **Obv:** Crowned head right, denomination below **Rev:** Two kangaroos **Rev. Designer:** Stuart Devlin

Date	Mintage	F	VF	XF	Unc	BU
1995 (ww) Proof	600	Value: 700				
1995 Proof	300	Value: 725				
1996	350,000	—	—	—	BV+4%	—

KM# 342 100 DOLLARS
31.1035 g., 0.9990 Gold 1.0000 oz. AGW **Ruler:** Elizabeth II **Obv:** Crowned head right, denomination below **Rev:** Kangaroo bounding right

Date	Mintage	F	VF	XF	Unc	BU
1996 (p) Proof	—	Value: 695				
Note: In Proof sets only						
1997	350,000	—	—	—	BV+4%	—
1997 Proof	—	Value: 690				

KM# 452 100 DOLLARS
31.1620 g., 0.9990 Gold 1.0000 oz. AGW **Ruler:** Elizabeth II **Obv:** Crowned head right, denomination below **Rev:** Kangaroo facing left **Edge:** Reeded

Date	Mintage	F	VF	XF	Unc	BU
1999	350,000	—	—	—	BV+4%	—

KM# 468 100 DOLLARS
31.1620 g., 0.9990 Gold 1.0000 oz. AGW **Ruler:** Elizabeth II **Obv:** Crowned head right, denomination below **Rev:** Two kangaroos bounding left, date below **Edge:** Reeded

Date	Mintage	F	VF	XF	Unc	BU
2000	—	—	—	—	—	BV+4%

KM# 182 200 DOLLARS
62.2140 g., 0.9990 Gold 2.0000 oz. AGW **Ruler:** Elizabeth II **Obv:** Crowned head right, denomination below **Rev:** Red kangaroo leaping left, date below **Rev. Designer:** Stuart Devlin

Date	Mintage	F	VF	XF	Unc	BU
1992	—	—	—	—	BV+4%	—
1994 Prooflike	—	—	—	—	BV+4%	—

Date	Mintage	F	VF	XF	Unc	BU
1995	—	—	—	—	BV+4%	—
1996	—	—	—	—	BV+4%	—
1997	—	—	—	—	BV+4%	—

KM# 394 200 DOLLARS
62.2140 g., 0.9990 Gold 2.0000 oz. AGW **Ruler:** Elizabeth II **Obv:** Crowned head right, denomination below **Rev:** Nail-tailed wallaby

Date	Mintage	F	VF	XF	Unc	BU
1992 Proof	152	Value: 1,450				

KM# 238 200 DOLLARS
62.2140 g., 0.9999 Gold 2.0000 oz. AGW **Ruler:** Elizabeth II **Obv:** Crowned head right, denomination below **Rev:** Whiptail wallaby

Date	Mintage	F	VF	XF	Unc	BU
1993 Proof	—	Value: 1,650				

KM# 246 200 DOLLARS
62.2140 g., 0.9999 Gold 2.0000 oz. AGW **Ruler:** Elizabeth II **Obv:** Crowned head right, denomination below **Rev:** Red kangaroo

Date	Mintage	F	VF	XF	Unc	BU
1994 Proof	325	Value: 1,700				

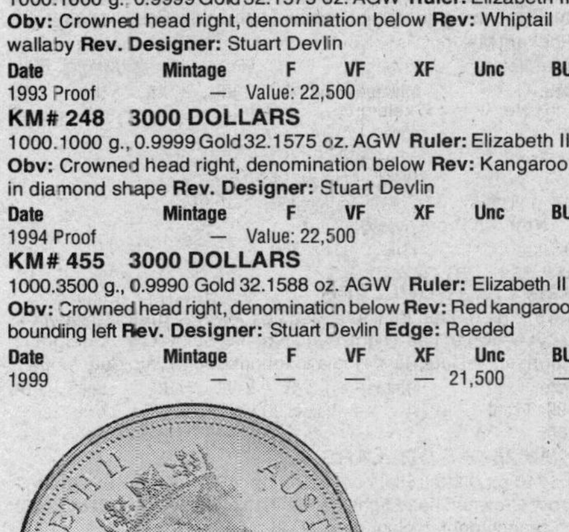

KM# 277 200 DOLLARS
62.2140 g., 0.9999 Gold 2.0000 oz. AGW **Ruler:** Elizabeth II **Obv:** Crowned head right, denomination below **Rev:** Two kangaroos, date below **Rev. Designer:** Stuart Devlin

Date	Mintage	F	VF	XF	Unc	BU
1995 Proof	100	Value: 1,800				

KM# 150 500 DOLLARS
62.2140 g., 0.9990 Gold 2.0000 oz. AGW **Ruler:** Elizabeth II **Obv:** Crowned head right, denomination below **Rev:** Red kangaroo facing left

Date	Mintage	F	VF	XF	Unc	BU
1991	—	—	—	—	BV+4%	—
1991 Proof	491	Value: 1,650				

KM# 395 1000 DOLLARS
311.0670 g., 0.9990 Gold 10.0000 oz. AGW **Ruler:** Elizabeth II **Obv:** Crowned head right, denomination below **Rev:** Nail-tailed wallaby

Date	Mintage	F	VF	XF	Unc	BU
1992 Proof	40	Value: 8,000				

KM# 239 1000 DOLLARS
311.0670 g., 0.9999 Gold 10.0000 oz. AGW **Ruler:** Elizabeth II **Obv:** Crowned head right, denomination below **Rev:** Red kangaroo

Date	Mintage	F	VF	XF	Unc	BU
1993 Proof	—	Value: 7,500				

KM# 247 1000 DOLLARS
311.0670 g., 0.9999 Gold 10.0000 oz. AGW **Ruler:** Elizabeth II **Obv:** Crowned head right, denomination below **Rev:** Kangaroo in diamond shape

Date	Mintage	F	VF	XF	Unc	BU
1994 Proof	—	Value: 7,500				

KM# 183 1000 DOLLARS
311.0670 g., 0.9999 Gold 10.0000 oz. AGW **Ruler:** Elizabeth II **Obv:** Crowned head right, denomination below **Rev:** Red kangaroo

Date	Mintage	F	VF	XF	Unc	BU
1995	—	—	—	—	BV+3%	—
1996	—	—	—	—	BV+3%	—
1997	—	—	—	—	BV+3%	—

KM# 454 1000 DOLLARS
311.3170 g., 0.9990 Gold 10.0000 oz. AGW **Ruler:** Elizabeth II **Obv:** Crowned head right, denomination below **Rev:** Red kangaroo bounding left **Edge:** Reeded

Date	Mintage	F	VF	XF	Unc	BU
1999	—	—	—	—	7,000	—

KM# 151 2500 DOLLARS
311.0670 g., 0.9990 Gold 10.0000 oz. AGW **Ruler:** Elizabeth II **Obv:** Crowned head right, denomination below **Rev:** Red kangaroo

Date	Mintage	F	VF	XF	Unc	BU
1991	—	—	—	—	BV+3%	—
1991 Proof	124	Value: 7,500				

KM# 184 3000 DOLLARS
1000.1000 g., 0.9999 Gold 32.1575 oz. AGW **Ruler:** Elizabeth II **Obv:** Crowned head right, denomination below **Rev:** Red kangaroo

Date	Mintage	F	VF	XF	Unc	BU
1992	—	—	—	—	BV+3%	—
1992 Proof	25	Value: 24,500				
1995	—	—	—	—	BV+4%	—
1996	—	—	—	—	BV+3%	—
1997	—	—	—	—	BV+3%	—

KM# 396 3000 DOLLARS
1000.1000 g., 0.9999 Platinum 32.1575 oz. APW **Ruler:** Elizabeth II **Obv:** Crowned head right, denomination below **Rev:** Nail-tailed wallaby

Date	Mintage	F	VF	XF	Unc	BU
1992 Proof	25	Value: 42,500				

KM# 240 3000 DOLLARS
1000.1000 g., 0.9999 Gold 32.1575 oz. AGW **Ruler:** Elizabeth II **Obv:** Crowned head right, denomination below **Rev:** Whiptail wallaby **Rev. Designer:** Stuart Devlin

Date	Mintage	F	VF	XF	Unc	BU
1993 Proof	—	Value: 22,500				

KM# 248 3000 DOLLARS
1000.1000 g., 0.9999 Gold 32.1575 oz. AGW **Ruler:** Elizabeth II **Obv:** Crowned head right, denomination below **Rev:** Kangaroo in diamond shape **Rev. Designer:** Stuart Devlin

Date	Mintage	F	VF	XF	Unc	BU
1994 Proof	—	Value: 22,500				

KM# 455 3000 DOLLARS
1000.3500 g., 0.9990 Gold 32.1588 oz. AGW **Ruler:** Elizabeth II **Obv:** Crowned head right, denomination below **Rev:** Red kangaroo bounding left **Rev. Designer:** Stuart Devlin **Edge:** Reeded

Date	Mintage	F	VF	XF	Unc	BU
1999	—	—	—	—	21,500	—

KM# 152 10000 DOLLARS
1000.1000 g., 0.9990 Gold 32.1575 oz. AGW **Ruler:** Elizabeth II **Obv:** Crowned head right, denomination below **Obv. Designer:** Raphael Maklouf **Rev:** Red kangaroo leaping left, date below **Rev. Designer:** Stuart Devlin

Date	Mintage	F	VF	XF	Unc	BU
1991	—	—	—	—	BV+3%	—
1991 Proof	95	Value: 22,500				

GOLD BULLION - NUGGET

KM# 89 15 DOLLARS
3.1103 g., 0.9990 Gold .1000 oz. AGW **Ruler:** Elizabeth II **Obv:** Crowned head right, denomination below **Rev:** Little Hero, date below **Rev. Designer:** Stuart Devlin

Date	Mintage	F	VF	XF	Unc	BU
1986P Proof	15,000	Value: 85.00				
1987	266,000	—	—	—	BV+12%	—
1988	104,000	—	—	—	BV+12%	—
1989	—	—	—	—	BV+12%	—

KM# 95 15 DOLLARS
3.1103 g., 0.9990 Gold .1000 oz. AGW **Ruler:** Elizabeth II **Obv:** Crowned head right, denomination below **Rev:** Golden Aussie, date below **Rev. Designer:** Stuart Devlin

Date	Mintage	F	VF	XF	Unc	BU
1987P Proof	15,000	Value: 80.00				

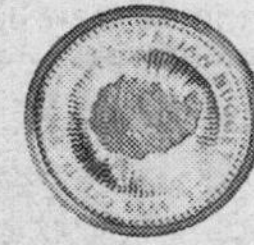

KM# 104 15 DOLLARS
3.1103 g., 0.9990 Gold .1000 oz. AGW **Ruler:** Elizabeth II **Obv:** Crowned head right, denomination below **Rev:** Jubilee Nugget, date below **Rev. Designer:** Stuart Devlin

Date	Mintage	F	VF	XF	Unc	BU
1988P Proof	Est. 10,000	Value: 80.00				

KM# 90 25 DOLLARS
7.7508 g., 0.9990 Gold .2500 oz. AGW **Ruler:** Elizabeth II **Obv:** Crowned head right, denomination below **Rev:** Golden Eagle, date below **Rev. Designer:** Stuart Devlin

Date	Mintage	F	VF	XF	Unc	BU
1986P Proof	15,000	Value: 180				
1987	233,000	—	—	—	BV+10%	—
1988	75,000	—	—	—	BV+10%	—
1989	—	—	—	—	BV+10%	—

KM# 96 25 DOLLARS
7.7508 g., 0.9990 Gold .2500 oz. AGW **Ruler:** Elizabeth II **Obv:** Crowned head right, denomination below **Rev:** Father's Day, date below **Rev. Designer:** Stuart Devlin

Date	Mintage	F	VF	XF	Unc	BU
1987P Proof	15,000	Value: 180				

KM# 105 25 DOLLARS
7.7508 g., 0.9990 Gold .2500 oz. AGW **Ruler:** Elizabeth II **Obv:** Crowned head right, denomination below **Rev:** Ruby Well Nugget, date below **Rev. Designer:** Stuart Devlin

Date	Mintage	F	VF	XF	Unc	BU
1988P Proof	Est. 10,000	Value: 180				

KM# 124 25 DOLLARS
7.7508 g., 0.9990 Gold .2500 oz. AGW **Ruler:** Elizabeth II **Obv:** Crowned head right, denomination below **Rev:** Koala bear with cub on its back sitting on branch

Date	Mintage	F	VF	XF	Unc	BU
1989 Proof	2,400	Value: 200				
1990 Proof	—	Value: 200				

KM# 91 50 DOLLARS
15.5017 g., 0.9990 Gold .5000 oz. AGW **Ruler:** Elizabeth II **Obv:** Crowned head right, denomination below **Rev:** Hand of Faith, date below **Rev. Designer:** Stuart Devlin

Date	Mintage	F	VF	XF	Unc	BU
1986P Proof	15,000	Value: 360				
1987	188,000	—	—	—	BV+7%	—
1988	75,000	—	—	—	BV+7%	—
1989	100,000	—	—	—	BV+7%	—

KM# 97 50 DOLLARS
15.5017 g., 0.9990 Gold .5000 oz. AGW **Ruler:** Elizabeth II **Obv:** Crowned head right, denomination below **Obv. Designer:** Raphael Maklouf **Rev:** Bobby Dazzler, date below **Rev. Designer:** Stuart Devlin

Date	Mintage	F	VF	XF	Unc	BU
1987P Proof	15,000	Value: 360				

KM# 106 50 DOLLARS
15.5017 g., 0.9990 Gold .5000 oz. AGW **Ruler:** Elizabeth II **Obv:** Crowned head right, denomination below **Rev:** Welcome nugget, date below **Rev. Designer:** Stuart Devlin

Date	Mintage	F	VF	XF	Unc	BU
1988P Proof	Est. 10,000	Value: 360				

KM# 92 100 DOLLARS
31.1035 g., 0.9990 Gold 1.0000 oz. AGW **Ruler:** Elizabeth II **Obv:** Crowned head right, denomination below **Obv. Designer:** Raphael Maklouf **Rev:** Welcome Stranger, date below **Rev. Designer:** Stuart Devlin

Date	Mintage	F	VF	XF	Unc	BU
1986P Proof	15,000	Value: 690				
1987	259,000	—	—	—	BV+4%	—
1988	116,000	—	—	—	BV+4%	—
1989	—	—	—	—	BV+4%	—

KM# 98 100 DOLLARS
31.1035 g., 0.9990 Gold 1.0000 oz. AGW **Ruler:** Elizabeth II **Obv:** Crowned head right, denomination below **Rev:** Poseidon, date below **Rev. Designer:** Stuart Devlin

Date	Mintage	F	VF	XF	Unc	BU
1987P Proof	15,000	Value: 690				

KM# 107 100 DOLLARS
31.1035 g., 0.9990 Gold 1.0000 oz. AGW **Ruler:** Elizabeth II **Obv:** Crowned head right, denomination below **Obv. Designer:** Raphael Maklouf **Rev:** Pride of Australia nugget **Rev. Designer:** Stuart Devlin

Date	Mintage	F	VF	XF	Unc	BU
1988P Proof	Est. 10,000	Value: 690				

PLATINUM BULLION

Koala

KM# 122 5 DOLLARS
1.5710 g., 0.9990 Platinum .0500 oz. APW **Ruler:** Elizabeth II **Obv:** Crowned head right, denomination below **Rev:** Koala

Date	Mintage	F	VF	XF	Unc	BU
1989 Proof	2,400	Value: 85.00				
1990 Proof	—	Value: 85.00				

KM# 145 5 DOLLARS
1.5710 g., 0.9990 Platinum .0500 oz. APW **Ruler:** Elizabeth II **Obv:** Crowned head right, denomination below **Rev:** Koala on tree limb facing right, date below

Date	Mintage	F	VF	XF	Unc	BU
1990 Proof	2,500	Value: 90.00				
1991	20,000	—	—	—	BV+ 35%	—
1991 Proof	1,000	Value: 90.00				

KM# 170 5 DOLLARS
1.5710 g., 0.9990 Platinum .0500 oz. APW **Ruler:** Elizabeth II **Subject:** Koala **Obv:** Crowned head right, denomination below **Rev:** Koala sitting facing in crook of tree

Date	Mintage	F	VF	XF	Unc	BU
1992	20,000	—	—	—	BV+ 35%	—

KM# 191 5 DOLLARS
1.5710 g., 0.9990 Platinum .0500 oz. APW **Ruler:** Elizabeth II **Obv:** Crowned head right, denomination below **Rev:** Koala facing left, sitting on branch, date below

Date	Mintage	F	VF	XF	Unc	BU
1993	Est. 20,000	—	—	—	BV+ 35%	—

KM# 249 5 DOLLARS
1.5710 g., 0.9990 Platinum .0500 oz. APW **Ruler:** Elizabeth II **Obv:** Crowned head right, denomination below **Obv. Designer:** Raphael Maklouf **Rev:** Koala mother and baby on branch facing, date below

Date	Mintage	F	VF	XF	Unc	BU
1994	20,000	—	—	—	BV+35%	—

KM# 278 5 DOLLARS
1.5710 g., 0.9990 Platinum .0500 oz. APW **Ruler:** Elizabeth II **Obv:** Crowned head right, denomination below **Obv. Designer:** Raphael Maklouf **Rev:** Koala in fork of tree facing, date below

Date	Mintage	F	VF	XF	Unc	BU
1994 Proof	—	Value: 90.00				
1995	—	—	—	—	BV+35%	—

KM# 283 5 DOLLARS
1.5710 g., 0.9990 Platinum .0500 oz. APW **Ruler:** Elizabeth II **Obv:** Crowned head right, denomination below **Rev:** Baby koala on branch right, facing, date below

Date	Mintage	F	VF	XF	Unc	BU
1995 Proof	200	Value: 90.00				
1996	20,000	—	—	—	BV+35%	—

KM# 344 5 DOLLARS
1.5710 g., 0.9995 Platinum .0500 oz. APW **Ruler:** Elizabeth II **Subject:** Koala Bullion **Obv:** Crowned head right, denomination below **Rev:** Cuddling koalas

Date	Mintage	F	VF	XF	Unc	BU
1997	20,000	—	—	—	BV+ 35%	—
1997 Proof	—	Value: 90.00				

KM# 456 5 DOLLARS
1.5710 g., 0.9990 Platinum .0500 oz. APW **Ruler:** Elizabeth II **Obv:** Crowned head right, denomination below **Rev:** Koala on log

Date	Mintage	F	VF	XF	Unc	BU
1999	20,000	—	—	—	—	BV+4%

KM# 469 5 DOLLARS
1.5710 g., 0.9990 Platinum .0500 oz. APW **Ruler:** Elizabeth II **Obv:** Crowned head right, denomination below **Rev:** Seated koala

Date	Mintage	F	VF	XF	Unc	BU
2000	—	—	—	—	—	BV+4%

KM# 108 15 DOLLARS
3.1370 g., 0.9990 Platinum .1000 oz. APW **Ruler:** Elizabeth II **Obv:** Crowned head right, denomination below **Rev:** Koala sitting facing

Date	Mintage	F	VF	XF	Unc	BU
1988	—	—	—	—	BV+15%	
1989 Proof	—	Value: 150				

KM# 123 15 DOLLARS
3.1370 g., 0.9990 Platinum .1000 oz. APW **Ruler:** Elizabeth II **Obv:** Crowned head right, denomination below **Rev:** Koala on tree branch with cub on her back

Date	Mintage	F	VF	XF	Unc	BU
1989 Proof	2,400	Value: 150				
1990 Proof	—	Value: 150				

KM# 146 15 DOLLARS
3.1370 g., 0.9990 Platinum .1000 oz. APW **Ruler:** Elizabeth II **Subject:** Koala **Obv:** Crowned head right, denomination below **Rev:** Koala on branch facing left, looking right, date below

Date	Mintage	F	VF	XF	Unc	BU
1990 Proof	2,500	Value: 150				
1991	20,000	—	—	—	BV+15%	—
1991 Proof	1,000	Value: 150				

KM# 171 15 DOLLARS
3.1370 g., 0.9990 Platinum .1000 oz. APW **Ruler:** Elizabeth II **Subject:** Koala Bullion **Obv:** Crowned head right, denomination below **Rev:** Koala in crook of tree facing

Date	Mintage	F	VF	XF	Unc	BU
1992	20,000	—	—	—	BV+ 15%	—

KM# 192 15 DOLLARS
3.1370 g., 0.9990 Platinum .1000 oz. APW **Ruler:** Elizabeth II **Obv:** Crowned head right, denomination below **Rev:** Koala climbing tree

Date	Mintage	F	VF	XF	Unc	BU
1993	Est. 20,000	—	—	—	BV+15%	—

KM# 250 15 DOLLARS
3.1370 g., 0.9990 Platinum .1000 oz. APW **Ruler:** Elizabeth II **Obv:** Crowned head right, denomination below **Obv. Designer:** Raphael Maklouf **Rev:** Koala mother and baby facing forward, date below

Date	Mintage	F	VF	XF	Unc	BU
1994	20,000	—	—	—	BV+15%	—

KM# 279 15 DOLLARS
3.1370 g., 0.9990 Platinum .1000 oz. APW **Ruler:** Elizabeth II **Obv:** Crowned head right, denomination below **Rev:** Koala in fork of tree facing forward, date below

Date	Mintage	F	VF	XF	Unc	BU
1994 Proof	—	Value: 150				
1995	—	—	—	—	BV+15%	—

KM# 284 15 DOLLARS
3.1370 g., 0.9990 Platinum .1000 oz. APW **Ruler:** Elizabeth II **Obv:** Crowned head right, denomination below **Rev:** Baby koala on branch, right facing forward, date below

Date	Mintage	F	VF	XF	Unc	BU
1995 Proof	800	Value: 150				
1996	20,000	—	—	—	BV+15%	—

KM# 345 15 DOLLARS
3.1103 g., 0.9995 Platinum .1000 oz. APW **Ruler:** Elizabeth II **Subject:** Koalas **Obv:** Crowned head right, denomination below **Rev:** Cuddling koalas

Date	Mintage	F	VF	XF	Unc	BU
1997	20,000	—	—	—	BV+15%	—
1997 Proof	—	Value: 150				

KM# 457 15 DOLLARS
3.1370 g., 0.9990 Platinum .1000 oz. APW **Ruler:** Elizabeth II **Obv:** Crowned head right, denomination below **Rev:** Koala on log facing forward, date below **Edge:** Reeded

Date	Mintage	F	VF	XF	Unc	BU
1999	20,000	—	—	—	BV+15%	—

KM# 470 15 DOLLARS
3.1370 g., 0.9990 Platinum .1000 oz. APW **Ruler:** Elizabeth II **Obv:** Crowned head right, denomination below **Rev:** Seated koala **Edge:** Reeded

Date	Mintage	F	VF	XF	Unc	BU
2000	—	—	—	—	BV+15%	—

KM# 109 25 DOLLARS
7.8150 g., 0.9990 Platinum .2500 oz. APW **Ruler:** Elizabeth II **Obv:** Crowned head right, denomination below **Rev:** Seated koala facing

Date	Mintage	F	VF	XF	Unc	BU
1988	—	—	—	—	BV+10%	—
1989 Proof	—	Value: 360				

KM# 147 25 DOLLARS
7.8150 g., 0.9990 Platinum .2500 oz. APW **Ruler:** Elizabeth II **Obv:** Crowned head right, denomination below **Rev:** Koala on branch left facing right, date below

Date	Mintage	F	VF	XF	Unc	BU
1990 Proof	2,500	Value: 350				
1991	20,000	—	—	—	BV+10%	—
1991 Proof	1,000	Value: 350				

KM# 172 25 DOLLARS
7.8150 g., 0.9990 Platinum .2500 oz. APW **Ruler:** Elizabeth II **Subject:** Koala **Obv:** Crowned head right, denomination below **Rev:** Koala seated crook of tree

Date	Mintage	F	VF	XF	Unc	BU
1992	20,000	—	—	—	BV+10%	—

KM# 193 25 DOLLARS
7.8150 g., 0.9990 Platinum .2500 oz. APW **Ruler:** Elizabeth II **Obv:** Crowned head right, denomination below **Obv. Designer:** Raphael Maklouf **Rev:** Koala sitting in tree right facing left, date below

Date	Mintage	F	VF	XF	Unc	BU
1992 (ae) Proof	750	Value: 350				
1993	Est. 20,000	—	—	—	BV+10%	—

KM# 251 25 DOLLARS
7.8150 g., 0.9990 Platinum .2500 oz. APW **Ruler:** Elizabeth II **Obv:** Crowned head right, denomination below **Obv. Designer:** Raphael Maklouf **Rev:** Koala mother and baby on branch facing forward, date below

Date	Mintage	F	VF	XF	Unc	BU
1994	20,000	—	—	—	BV+10%	—

KM# 280 25 DOLLARS
7.8150 g., 0.9990 Platinum .2500 oz. APW **Ruler:** Elizabeth II **Obv:** Crowned head right, denomination below **Rev:** Koala in fork of tree facing forward, date below

Date	Mintage	F	VF	XF	Unc	BU
1994 Proof	—	Value: 350				
1995	—	—	—	—	BV+10%	—

KM# 285 25 DOLLARS
7.8150 g., 0.9990 Platinum .2500 oz. APW **Ruler:** Elizabeth II **Obv:** Crowned head right, denomination below **Rev:** Baby koala on branch right facing forward, date below

Date	Mintage	F	VF	XF	Unc	BU
1995 Proof	200	Value: 360				
1996	20,000	—	—	—	BV+10%	—

KM# 346 25 DOLLARS
7.7508 g., 0.9995 Platinum .2500 oz. APW **Ruler:** Elizabeth II **Subject:** Koala Bullion **Obv:** Crowned head right, denomination below **Rev:** Cuddling koalas

Date	Mintage	F	VF	XF	Unc	BU
1997	20,000	—	—	—	BV+10%	—
1997 Proof	—	Value: 360				

KM# 458 25 DOLLARS
7.8150 g., 0.9990 Platinum .2500 oz. APW **Ruler:** Elizabeth II **Obv:** Crowned head right, denomination below **Rev:** Koala on log facing forward, date below **Edge:** Reeded

Date	Mintage	F	VF	XF	Unc	BU
1999	20,000	—	—	—	BV+10%	—

KM# 471 25 DOLLARS
7.8150 g., 0.9990 Platinum .2500 oz. APW **Ruler:** Elizabeth II **Obv:** Crowned head right, denomination below **Rev:** Seated koala **Edge:** Reeded

Date	Mintage	F	VF	XF	Unc	BU
2000	—	—	—	—	BV+10%	—

KM# 110 50 DOLLARS
15.6050 g., 0.9990 Platinum .5000 oz. APW **Ruler:** Elizabeth II **Obv:** Crowned head right, denomination below **Obv. Designer:** Raphael Maklouf **Rev:** Koala bear on log facing forward, date below **Rev. Designer:** Michael Tracey

Date	Mintage	F	VF	XF	Unc	BU
1988	—	—	—	—	BV+7%	—
1988 Proof	12,000	Value: 690				
1989 Proof	—	Value: 690				

KM# 125 50 DOLLARS
15.6050 g., 0.9990 Platinum .5000 oz. APW **Ruler:** Elizabeth II **Obv:** Crowned head right, denomination below **Rev:** Koala bear on tree branch with cub on back

Date	Mintage	F	VF	XF	Unc	BU
1989 Proof	2,400	Value: 690				
1990 Proof	8,000	Value: 690				

KM# 148 50 DOLLARS
15.6050 g., 0.9990 Platinum .5000 oz. APW **Ruler:** Elizabeth II **Obv:** Crowned head right, denomination below **Obv. Designer:** Raphael Maklouf **Rev:** Koala bear in tree left facing right, date below

Date	Mintage	F	VF	XF	Unc	BU
1990 Proof	5,500	Value: 690				
1991	20,000	—	—	—	BV+7%	—
1991 Proof	2,000	Value: 690				

KM# 173 50 DOLLARS
15.6050 g., 0.9990 Platinum .5000 oz. APW **Ruler:** Elizabeth II **Subject:** Koala **Obv:** Crowned head right, denomination below **Rev:** Koala in crook of tree facing

Date	Mintage	F	VF	XF	Unc	BU
1992	20,000	—	—	—	BV+7%	—

KM# 194 50 DOLLARS
15.6050 g. 0.9990 Platinum .5000 oz. APW **Ruler:** Elizabeth II **Obv:** Crowned head right, denomination below **Rev:** Koala sitting in tree right, facing left, date below

Date	Mintage	F	VF	XF	Unc	BU
1993	Est. 20,000	—	—	—	BV+7%	—

KM# 252 50 DOLLARS
15.6050 g., 0.9990 Platinum .5000 oz. APW **Ruler:** Elizabeth II **Obv:** Crowned head right, denomination below **Obv. Designer:** Raphael Maklouf **Rev:** Koala mother and baby in tree facing forward, date below

Date	Mintage	F	VF	XF	Unc	BU
1994	5,000	—	—	—	BV+7%	—

KM# 281 50 DOLLARS
15.6050 g., 0.9990 Platinum .5000 oz. APW **Ruler:** Elizabeth II **Obv:** Crowned head right, denomination below **Rev:** Koala in fork of tree left, facing forward

Date	Mintage	F	VF	XF	Unc	BU
1994 Proof	—	Value: 690				
1995	—	—	—	—	BV+7%	—

KM# 286 50 DOLLARS
15.6050 g., 0.9990 Platinum .5000 oz. APW **Ruler:** Elizabeth II **Obv:** Crowned head right, denomination below **Rev:** Baby koala on branch right, facing forward, date below

Date	Mintage	F	VF	XF	Unc	BU
1995 (ww) Proof	300	Value: 690				

Note: In Proof sets only

Date	Mintage	F	VF	XF	Unc	BU
1995 Proof	450	Value: 690				
1996	5,000	—	—	—	BV+7%	—

KM# 347 50 DOLLARS
15.5518 g., 0.9995 Platinum .5000 oz. APW **Ruler:** Elizabeth II **Subject:** Koala Bullion **Obv:** Crowned head right, denomination below **Rev:** Cuddling koalas

Date	Mintage	F	VF	XF	Unc	BU
1997	5,000	—	—	—	BV+7%	—
1997 Proof	—	Value: 690				

KM# 459 50 DOLLARS
15.6050 g., 0.9990 Platinum .5000 oz. APW **Ruler:** Elizabeth II **Obv:** Crowned head right, denomination below **Rev:** Koala on log left, facing forward **Edge:** Reeded

Date	Mintage	F	VF	XF	Unc	BU
1999	5,000	—	—	—	—	BV+7%

KM# 472 50 DOLLARS
15.6050 g., 0.9990 Platinum .5000 oz. APW **Ruler:** Elizabeth II **Obv:** Crowned head right, denomination below **Rev:** Seated koala **Edge:** Reeded

Date	Mintage	F	VF	XF	Unc	BU
2000	—	—	—	—	—	BV+7%

KM# 111 100 DOLLARS
31.1850 g., 0.9990 Platinum 1.0000 oz. APW **Ruler:** Elizabeth II **Obv:** Crowned head right, denomination below **Obv. Designer:** Raphael Maklouf **Rev:** Seated Koala facing forward, date below

Date	Mintage	F	VF	XF	Unc	BU
1988	—	—	—	—	BV+4%	—
1989 Proof	—	Value: 1,350				

KM# 126 100 DOLLARS
31.1850 g., 0.9990 Platinum 1.0000 oz. APW **Ruler:** Elizabeth II **Obv:** Crowned head right, denomination below **Obv. Designer:** Raphael Maklouf **Rev:** Koala with baby on branch left, facing right

Date	Mintage	F	VF	XF	Unc	BU
1989 Proof	2,400	Value: 1,350				
1990 Proof	—	Value: 1,350				

KM# 149 100 DOLLARS

31.1850 g., 0.9990 Platinum 1.0000 oz. APW **Ruler:** Elizabeth II **Obv:** Crowned head right, denomination below **Rev:** Koala bear in tree left, facing right

Date	Mintage	F	VF	XF	Unc	BU
1990 Proof	3,500	Value: 1,350				
1991	75,000	—	—	—	BV+4%	—
1991 Proof	1,000	Value: 1,350				

KM# 174 100 DOLLARS

31.1850 g., 0.9990 Platinum 1.0000 oz. APW **Ruler:** Elizabeth II **Obv:** Crowned head right, denomination below **Rev:** Koala in fork of tree facing, date below

Date	Mintage	F	VF	XF	Unc	BU
1992	75,000	—	—	—	BV+4%	—

KM# 195 100 DOLLARS

31.1850 g., 0.9990 Platinum 1.0000 oz. APW **Ruler:** Elizabeth II **Obv:** Crowned head right, denomination below **Obv. Designer:** Raphael Maklouf **Rev:** Koala in fork of tree right, facing left, date below

Date	Mintage	F	VF	XF	Unc	BU
1993	Est. 80,000	—	—	—	BV+4%	—

KM# 253 100 DOLLARS

31.1850 g., 0.9990 Platinum 1.0000 oz. APW **Ruler:** Elizabeth II **Obv:** Crowned head right, denomination below **Obv. Designer:** Raphael Maklouf **Rev:** Koala mother and baby on branch facing forward. date below

Date	Mintage	F	VF	XF	Unc	BU
1994 Prooflike	100,000	—	—	—	BV+4%	—

KM# 282 100 DOLLARS

31.1850 g., 0.9990 Platinum 1.0000 oz. APW **Ruler:** Elizabeth II **Obv:** Crowned head of Queen Elizabeth II, right **Obv. Designer:** Raphael Maklouf **Rev:** Koala in fork of tree left, facing forward, date below

Date	Mintage	F	VF	XF	Unc	BU
1994 Proof	—	Value: 1,350				
1995	—	—	—	—	BV+4%	—

KM# 287 100 DOLLARS

31.1850 g., 0.9990 Platinum 1.0000 oz. APW **Ruler:** Elizabeth II **Obv:** Crowned head right, denomination below **Obv. Designer:** Raphael Maklouf **Rev:** Baby koala on branch right, date below

Date	Mintage	F	VF	XF	Unc	BU
1995 Proof	200	Value: 1,350				
1996	100,000	—	—	—	BV+4%	—

KM# 348 100 DOLLARS

31.1850 g., 0.9990 Platinum 1.0000 oz. APW **Ruler:** Elizabeth II **Subject:** Koala Bullion **Obv:** Crowned head right, denomination below **Rev:** Cuddling koalas

Date	Mintage	F	VF	XF	Unc	BU
1997	100,000	—	—	—	BV+4%	—
1997 Proof	—	Value: 1,350				

KM# 460 100 DOLLARS

31.1850 g., 0.9990 Platinum 1.0000 oz. APW **Ruler:** Elizabeth II **Obv:** Crowned head right, denomination below **Rev:** Koala on log left, date below **Edge:** Reeded

Date	Mintage	F	VF	XF	Unc	BU
1999	100,000	—	—	—	BV+4%	—

KM# 473 100 DOLLARS

31.1850 g., 0.9990 Platinum 1.0000 oz. APW **Ruler:** Elizabeth II **Obv:** Crowned head right, denomination below **Rev:** Seated koala with branches left, date below **Edge:** Reeded

Date	Mintage	F	VF	XF	Unc	BU
2000	—	—	—	—	BV+4%	—

KM# 185 200 DOLLARS

62.2140 g., 0.9995 Platinum 2.0000 oz. APW **Ruler:** Elizabeth II **Obv:** Crowned head right, denomination below **Rev:** Koala bear in tree left, looking right, date below

Date	Mintage	F	VF	XF	Unc	BU
1992	—	—	—	—	BV+4%	—
1992 Proof	—	Value: 2,650				
1996	—	—	—	—	BV+4%	—

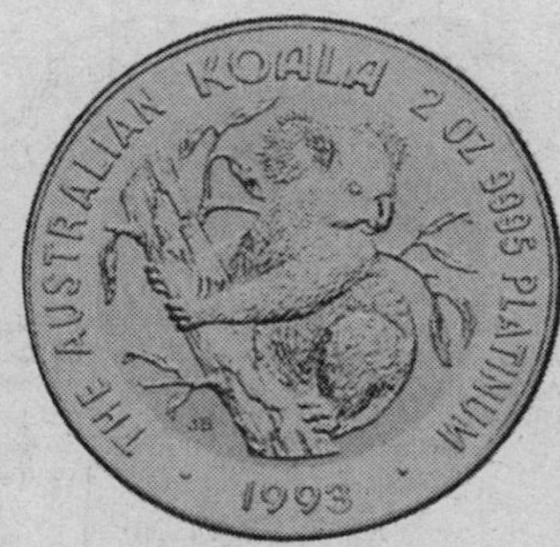

KM# 196 200 DOLLARS

62.2140 g., 0.9995 Platinum 2.0000 oz. APW **Ruler:** Elizabeth II **Obv:** Crowned head right, denomination below **Rev:** Koala bear in tree left, looking right, date below

Date	Mintage	F	VF	XF	Unc	BU
1993	—	—	—	—	BV+4%	—
1994	—	—	—	—	BV+4%	—
1995	—	—	—	—	BV+4%	—
1997	—	—	—	—	BV+4%	—

KM# 254 200 DOLLARS

62.2140 g., 0.9995 Platinum 2.0000 oz. APW **Ruler:** Elizabeth II **Obv:** Crowned head right, denomination below **Rev:** Koala with cub

Date	Mintage	F	VF	XF	Unc	BU
1994 Proof	—	Value: 2,650				

KM# 288 200 DOLLARS

62.2140 g., 0.9995 Platinum 2.0000 oz. APW **Ruler:** Elizabeth II **Obv:** Crowned head right, denomination below **Rev:** Baby koala on branch right, date below

Date	Mintage	F	VF	XF	Unc	BU
1995 Proof	100	Value: 2,650				

KM# 461 200 DOLLARS

62.3130 g., 0.9990 Platinum 2.0000 oz. APW **Ruler:** Elizabeth II **Obv:** Crowned head right, denomination below **Rev:** Koala in tree left, looking right, date below **Edge:** Reeded

Date	Mintage	F	VF	XF	Unc	BU
1999	—	—	—	—	BV+4%	—

KM# 157 500 DOLLARS

62.2140 g., 0.9990 Platinum 2.0000 oz. APW **Ruler:** Elizabeth II **Subject:** Koala Bullion **Obv:** Crowned head right, denomination below **Rev:** Koala in tree

Date	Mintage	F	VF	XF	Unc	BU
1991	—	—	—	—	BV+4%	—
1991 Proof	250	Value: 2,650				

KM# 186 1000 DOLLARS

311.0670 g., 0.9995 Platinum 10.0000 oz. APW **Ruler:** Elizabeth II **Obv:** Crowned head right, denomination below **Rev:** Koala

Date	Mintage	F	VF	XF	Unc	BU
1992	—	—	—	—	BV+4%	—
1992 Proof	—	Value: 13,250				
1996	—	—	—	—	BV+4%	—

KM# 197 1000 DOLLARS
311.0670 g., 0.9995 Platinum 10.0000 oz. APW, 60.3 mm. **Ruler:** Elizabeth II **Obv:** Crowned head right, denomination below **Rev:** Koala on branch left, looking right, date below **Note:** Photo reduced.

Date	Mintage	F	VF	XF	Unc	BU
1993	—	—	—	—	BV+4%	—
1994	—	—	—	—	BV+4%	—
1995	—	—	—	—	BV+4%	—
1997	—	—	—	—	BV+4%	—

KM# 255 1000 DOLLARS
311.0670 g., 0.9995 Platinum 10.0000 oz. APW **Ruler:** Elizabeth II **Obv:** Crowned head right, denomination below **Rev:** Koala with cub

Date	Mintage	F	VF	XF	Unc	BU
1994	—	—	—	—	BV+4%	—

KM# 462 1000 DOLLARS
311.6910 g., 0.9990 Platinum 10.0000 oz. APW **Ruler:** Elizabeth II **Obv:** Crowned head right, denomination below **Rev:** Koala in tree **Edge:** Reeded **Note:** Photo reduced.

Date	Mintage	F	VF	XF	Unc	BU
1999	—	—	—	—	BV+4%	—

KM# 158 2500 DOLLARS
311.0670 g., 0.9990 Platinum 10.0000 oz. APW **Ruler:** Elizabeth II **Subject:** Koala Bullion **Obv:** Crowned head right, denomination below **Rev:** Koala in tree

Date	Mintage	F	VF	XF	Unc	BU
1991	—	—	—	—	BV+4%	—
1991 Proof	100	Value: 13,250				

KM# 187 3000 DOLLARS
1000.1000 g., 0.9999 Platinum 32.1575 oz. APW **Ruler:** Elizabeth II **Obv:** Crowned head right, denomination below **Rev:** Koala in tree, date below

Date	Mintage	F	VF	XF	Unc	BU
1992	—	—	—	—	BV+3.5%	—
1992 Proof	—	Value: 42,250				
1996	—	—	—	—	BV+3.5%	—

KM# 198 3000 DOLLARS
1000.1000 g., 0.9999 Platinum 32.1575 oz. APW, 75.3 mm. **Ruler:** Elizabeth II **Obv:** Crowned head right, denomination below **Rev:** Koala on tree branch left, looking right, date below **Note:** Photo reduced.

Date	Mintage	F	VF	XF	Unc	BU
1993	—	—	—	—	BV+3.5%	—
1994	—	—	—	—	BV+3.5%	—
1995	—	—	—	—	BV+3.5%	—
1997	—	—	—	—	BV+3.5%	—

KM# 256 3000 DOLLARS
1000.1000 g., 0.9995 Platinum 32.1575 oz. APW **Ruler:** Elizabeth II **Obv:** Crowned head right, denomination below **Rev:** Koala with cub

Date	Mintage	F	VF	XF	Unc	BU
1994	—	—	—	—	BV+3.5%	—

KM# 463 3000 DOLLARS
1001.0000 g., 0.9990 Platinum 32.1668 oz. APW **Ruler:** Elizabeth II **Obv:** Crowned head right, denomination below **Rev:** Koala in tree **Edge:** Reeded **Note:** Photo reduced.

Date	Mintage	F	VF	XF	Unc	BU
1999	—	—	—	—	BV+3.5%	—

KM# 159 10000 DOLLARS
1000.1000 g., 0.9990 Platinum 32.1575 oz. APW **Ruler:** Elizabeth II **Subject:** Koala Bullion **Obv:** Crowned head right, denomination below **Rev:** Koala

Date	Mintage	F	VF	XF	Unc	BU
1991	—	—	—	—	BV+3.5%	—
1991 Proof	50	Value: 42,250				

TOKEN COINAGE

P.O.W.

WWI Liverpool (NSW)

KM# Tn1.3 PENNY
Brass **Issuer:** WWII Internment Camp **Note:** No hole (error).

Date	Mintage	F	VF	XF	Unc	BU
ND(1943)	—	—	—	175	200	—

KM# Tn-A1 THREEPENCE
Aluminum **Issuer:** WWI Liverpool (NSW) **Obv:** Double-headed eagle **Rev:** Large 3d **Shape:** Square

Date	Mintage	F	VF	XF	Unc	BU
ND	—	—	350	550	1,250	—

KM# Tn-B1 THREEPENCE
Aluminum **Issuer:** WWI Liverpool (NSW) **Obv:** Crown divides D - K **Rev:** Small 3d **Shape:** Oval

Date	Mintage	F	VF	XF	Unc	BU
ND	—	—	450	750	1,500	—

WWII Internment Camp

KM# Tn1.1 PENNY
Brass **Issuer:** WWII Internment Camp **Obv:** Center hole with beads and wreath around, legend above and below **Obv. Legend:** INTERNMENT / CAMPS **Rev:** Center hole with beads and wreath around, legend above and below **Rev. Legend:** ONE / PENNY

Date	Mintage	F	VF	XF	Unc	BU
ND(1943)	—	40.00	50.00	75.00	125	—

KM# Tn1.1a PENNY
Copper-Nickel **Issuer:** WWII Internment Camp **Obv:** Center hole with beads and wreath around, legend above and below **Obv. Legend:** INTERNMENT / CAMPS **Rev:** Center hole with beads and wreath around, legend above and below **Rev. Legend:** ONE / PENNY **Note:** Spink Australia Sale Nov. 1981. Lot 666A $600.

Date	Mintage	F	VF	XF	Unc	BU
ND(1943)	—	—	—	—	4,500	—

KM# Tn1.2 PENNY
Brass **Issuer:** WWII Internment Camp **Note:** Center hole misplaced (error).

Date	Mintage	F	VF	XF	Unc	BU
ND(1943)	—	75.00	90.00	120	—	—

KM# Tn2.1 THREEPENCE
Bronze **Issuer:** WWII Internment Camp **Obv:** Center hole with wreath around **Obv. Legend:** INTERNMENT CAMPS **Rev:** Center hole with wreath around **Rev. Legend:** THREE PENCE

Date	Mintage	F	VF	XF	Unc	BU
ND(1943)	—	40.00	55.00	80.00	135	—

KM# Tn2.2 THREEPENCE
Bronze **Issuer:** WWII Internment Camp **Obv:** Center hole with wreath around **Obv. Legend:** INTERNMENT CAMP **Rev. Legend:** THREE PENCE

Date	Mintage	F	VF	XF	Unc	BU
ND(1943) Rare	—	—	—	—	—	—

KM# Tn3 SHILLING
Bronze **Issuer:** WWII Internment Camp **Obv:** Center hole with wreath around **Obv. Legend:** INTERNMENT CAMPS **Rev:** Center hole with wreath around **Rev. Legend:** ONE SHILLING

Date	Mintage	F	VF	XF	Unc	BU
ND(1943)	—	150	175	250	350	—

KM# Tn4.1 2 SHILLING
Bronze **Issuer:** WWII Internment Camp **Obv:** Center hole with beads and wreath around **Obv. Legend:** INTERNMENT CAMPS **Rev:** Center hole with beads and wreath around **Rev. Legend:** TWO SHILLINGS

Date	Mintage	F	VF	XF	Unc	BU
ND(1943)	—	200	300	500	750	—

KM# Tn4.2 2 SHILLING

Bronze **Issuer:** WWII Internment Camp **Obv:** Beaded circle at center, wreath around **Obv. Legend:** INTERNMENT CAMPS **Rev:** Beaded circle at center, wreath around **Rev. Legend:** TWO SHILLINGS **Note:** Without center hole.

Date	Mintage	F	VF	XF	Unc	BU
ND(1943)	—	325	450	650	—	—

KM# Tn4.3 2 SHILLING

Bronze **Issuer:** WWII Internment Camp **Obv:** Off center hole partially within beaded circle, wreath surrounding **Obv. Legend:** Internment Camps **Rev:** Off center hole partially within beaded circle, wreath surrounding **Rev. Legend:** Two shillings **Note:** Center hole misplaced.

Date	Mintage	F	VF	XF	Unc	BU
ND(1943)	—	275	400	600	900	—

KM# Tn5.1 5 SHILLING

Bronze **Obv:** Center hole with beads and wreath around **Obv. Legend:** INTERNMENT CAMPS **Rev:** Center hole with beads and wreath around **Rev. Legend:** FIVE SHILLINGS

Date	Mintage	F	VF	XF	Unc	BU
ND(1943)	—	—	600	750	1,000	—

KM# Tn5.2 5 SHILLING

Bronze **Obv:** Center circle with beads and wreath around **Obv. Legend:** INTERNMENT CAMPS **Rev:** Center circle with beads and wreath around **Rev. Legend:** FIVE SHILLINGS **Note:** Without center hole.

Date	Mintage	F	VF	XF	Unc	BU
ND(1943)	—	—	750	1,000	1,750	—

KM# Tn5.3 5 SHILLING

Bronze **Obv:** Center circle with beads and wreath around **Obv. Legend:** INTERNMENT CAMPS **Rev:** Center circle with beads and wreath around **Rev. Legend:** FIVE SHILLINGS **Note:** Center hole misplaced,(hole at top of coin)

Date	Mintage	F	VF	XF	Unc	BU
ND(1943)	—	—	650	850	1,350	—

PATTERNS

Including off metal strikes

KM#	Date	Mintage	Identification	Mkt Val
Pn7	1909	—	Florin.	—
Pn8	1919	—	Penny. Copper-Nickel. 3.8900 g. T.3.	4,500
Pn8a	1919	—	Penny. Copper-Nickel. 4.2100 g. T.3.	4,500
Pn8b	1919	—	Penny. Copper-Nickel. 4.5400 g. T.3.	4,500
Pn9	1919	—	Penny. Copper-Nickel. 3.8900 g. T.4.	4,500
Pn9a	1919	—	Penny. 0.9170 Silver. 4.6700 g. T.4.	12,500
Pn10	1919	—	Penny. Copper-Nickel. 3.8900 g. T.5.	5,000
Pn10a	1919	—	Penny. 0.9170 Silver. 4.6700 g. T.5.	12,500
Pn11	1919	—	Penny. Copper-Nickel. 3.8900 g. T.6.	4,500
Pn11a	1919	—	Penny. 0.9170 Silver. 4.4100 g. T.6.	12,500
Pn12	1919	—	Shilling. 0.6250 Silver. KM#26.	50,000
Pn13	1920	—	1/2 Penny. Copper-Nickel. 1.8100 g. T.1.	4,000
Pn13a	1920	—	1/2 Penny. 0.9170 Silver. T.1.	20,000
Pn14	1920	—	Penny. Copper-Nickel. 3.8900 g. T.7.	4,000
Pn14a	1920	—	Penny. Lead. T.7.	3,500
Pn15	1920	—	Penny. Copper-Nickel. 3.8900 g. T.8.	6,000
Pn16	1920	—	Penny. Copper-Nickel. 3.8900 g. T.9.	6,500
Pn17	1920	—	Penny. Copper-Nickel. 3.8900 g. T.10.	8,500
PnA18	1920	—	Shilling. Silver. KM#26, star above date.	12,000
Pn18	1920	—	Florin. Silver. KM#27, star above date.	15,000
Pn19	1921	—	1/2 Penny. Copper-Nickel. 1.8100 g. T.2.	6,000
Pn20	1921	—	Penny. Copper-Nickel. 3.8900 g. T.11.	35,000
Pn20a	1921	—	Penny. Copper-Nickel. 4.2100 g. T.11.	3,000
Pn20b	1921	—	Penny. Copper-Nickel. 4.5400 g. T.11.	3,000
Pn20c	1921	—	Penny. Nickel. T.11.	3,000
Pn21	1921	—	Penny. Copper-Nickel. 3.8900 g. T.12.	30,000
Pn21a	1921	—	Penny. Copper-Nickel. 4.2100 g. T.12.	3,000
Pn21b	1921	—	Penny. Copper-Nickel. 4.5400 g. T.12.	3,000
Pn22	1921	—	Penny. T.13.	—

KM#	Date	Mintage	Identification	Mkt Val
Pn24	1937	12	Penny. Bronze. King's head, left. Kangaroo hopping, left, date below tail, value at bottom.	28,000
Pn25	1937	7	Threepence. Silver.	30,000
Pn26	1937	6	Shilling. Silver.	—
Pn28	1951	—	2 Shilling. Copper-Nickel. Jubilee	5,000
Pn29	1967	—	50 Cents. Silver. KM#67.	—
Pn30	1968	—	50 Cents. Copper-Nickel. KM#68.	—

PIEFORTS

KM#	Date	Mintage	Identification	Mkt Val
P1	1989	15,000	10 Dollars. 0.9250 Silver. Kookaburra, KM#133.	100
P2	1990	15,000	10 Dollars. 0.9250 Silver. Cockatoo, KM#136.	115
P3	1991	17,000	10 Dollars. 0.9250 Silver. Jabiru Stork, Proof, KM#156.	70.00
P4	1992	15,000	10 Dollars. 0.9250 Silver. Penguins.	85.00
P5	1993	—	10 Dollars. 0.9250 Silver. Palm cockatoo, KM#221.	100
P6	1994	15,000	10 Dollars. 0.9250 Silver. Wedge tailed eagle, Proof, KM#223.	75.00
P7	1995	15,000	10 Dollars. 0.9250 Silver. Numbat, KM#296.	75.00
P8	1996	14,000	10 Dollars. Silver. Whales, Proof, KM#314.	75.00
P9	1997	14,000	10 Dollars. Silver. Cockatoo, Proof, KM#367.	75.00
P10	1998	14,000	10 Dollars. Silver. Wombat, Proof, KM#397.	75.00

TRIAL STRIKES

KM#	Date	Mintage	Identification	Mkt Val
TS1	ND(1927)	—	Shilling. Silver. Crowned King's head, left. Uniface.	5,500

KM#	Date	Mintage	Identification	Mkt Val
TS2	ND(1927)	—	Florin. Silver. Crowned King's head, left. Uniface. KM7.	6,500

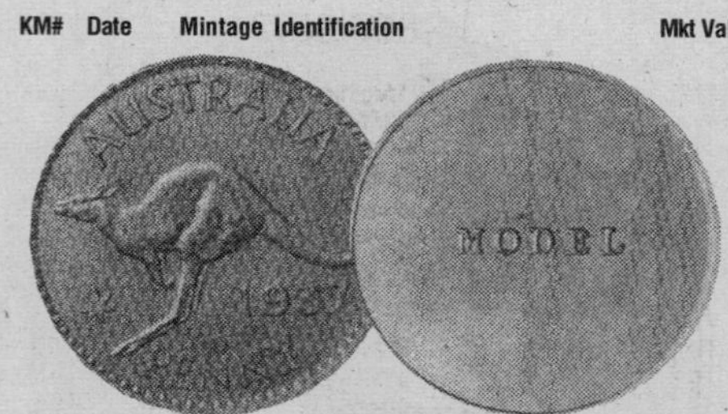

KM#	Date	Mintage	Identification	Mkt Val
TS3	1937	8	Penny. Bronze. Kangaroo hopping, left, date below tail, value at bottom. Uniface, reverse.	9,000
TS4	1937	15	Threepence. Silver. Uniface, reverse.	7,000
TSA5	1937	—	Sixpence. Silver. Uniface, reverse.	—

KM#	Date	Mintage	Identification	Mkt Val
TS5	1937	20	Shilling. Silver. Uniface, reverse.	5,500
TS6	1937	15	Florin. Silver. Uniface, reverse. Spink Remick Sale 9-06.	75,000
TS7	1937(L)	—	Crown. Uniface, reverse. Spink Remick Sale 9-06.	—

MINT SETS

KM#	Date	Mintage	Identification	Issue Price	Mkt Val
MS1	1966 (6)	16,359	KM62-67 (Card)	2.00	18.00
MS2	1969 (6)	31,176	KM62-66,68	2.50	25.00
MS3	1970 (6)	40,230	KM62-66, 69	2.50	10.00
MS4	1971 (6)	28,572	KM62-66,68	2.50	20.00
MS5	1972 (6)	39,068	KM62-66,68	2.75	20.00
MS6	1973 (6)	30,928	KM62-66,68	3.40	20.00
MS7	1974 (6)	25,948	KM62-66,68	3.60	18.00
MS8	1975 (6)	30,121	KM62-66,68	3.30	8.00
MS9	1976 (6)	40,004	KM62-66,68	3.80	8.00
MS10	1977 (6)	128,000	KM62-66, 70	4.20	5.00
MS11	1978 (6)	70,000	KM62-66,68	4.20	5.00
MS12	1979 (6)	70,000	KM62-66,68	4.50	4.50
MS13	1980 (6)	100,000	KM62-66,68	5.75	4.00
MS14	1981 (6)	120,010	KM62-66,68	6.50	4.50
MS15	1982 (6)	195,950	KM62-66,74	6.50	4.00
MS16	1983 (6)	155,700	KM62-66,68	5.00	7.50
MS17	1984 (6)	150,014	KM62-66,68	7.00	7.50
MS18	1985 (7)	170,000	KM78-84	4.00	8.50
MS19	1986 (7)	180,000	KM78-83,87	5.50	5.00
MS20	1987 (7)	200,000	KM78-84	8.00	4.00
MS21	1988 (8)	240,000	KM78-82,99-101	12.00	4.00
MS22	1989 (8)	—	KM78-84,101	12.00	4.00
MS23	1990 (8)	—	KM78-84, 101	12.00	45.00
MS24	1991 (8)	25,000	KM78-82,84,101,139	13.00	7.50
MS25	1992 (6)	104,000	KM80-83,101,175a.1	10.00	15.00
MS26	1993 (6)	—	KM80-83,101,208	10.00	5.00
MS27	1994 (6)	90,000	KM80-82,84,101,257	11.25	5.00
MS28	1994 (6)	—	KM80-82,84,101,257 birth year holder	11.25	20.00
MS29	1995 (6)	—	KM80-82,84,101,294	—	16.00
MS30	1996 (6)	—	KM80-83,101,310 Baby Set	14.80	15.00
MS31	1996 (6)	—	KM80-83,101,310 plus Bronze Gumnut Baby medal	19.35	30.00
MS32	1997 (6)	—	KM80-83,101,327	—	17.50
MSA32	1997 (2)	—	KM327, 355	—	7.00
MS33	1998 (6)	—	KM80-82,83,101,364	12.75	12.75
MS34	1998 (6)	—	KM80-82,84,101,364	16.60	17.50
MS35	1999 (6)	—	KM401-406	16.95	16.95
MSA36	1999 (6)	—	KM401-406 plus Copper medal, Baby set	20.50	20.50
MS37	1999 (2)	—	KM400,405	—	10.00
MS38	2000 (6)	—	KM401-403, 406, 488-489	10.60	18.00

PROOF SETS

KM#	Date	Mintage	Identification	Issue Price	Mkt Val
PS1	1902S (4)	—	KM14-17 Rare	—	—
PS2	1911(L) (4)	—	KM24-27	—	25,000
PS3	1916M (4)	25	KM24-27	—	7,000
PS4	1925(m) (5)	—	KM22-26	—	13,650
PS5	1926(m) (6)	—	KM22-27	—	9,400
PS6	1927(m) (6)	50	KM22-27	—	7,150
PS7	1928(m) (6)	—	KM22-27	—	9,550
PS8	1929(m) (2)	—	KM22-23	—	3,250
PSA9	1930(m) (2)	—	KM22-23	—	85.00
PS9	1931(m) (4)	—	KM22-27	—	7,000
PS10	1933(m) (2)	—	KM22-23	—	2,000
PS11	1934(m) (6)	100	KM22-27	—	7,500
PS12	1935(m) (6)	100	KM22-27	—	4,800
PS13	1936(m) (6)	—	KM22-27	—	6,350
PS14	1938(m) (6)	250	KM35-40	—	5,500
PS15	1953(p) (2)	—	KM49-50	—	3,500
PS16	1955(m) (4)	1,200	KM56-59	—	250
PS17	1955(p) (2)	301	KM49,56	—	2,000
PS18	1956(m) (5)	1,500	KM56-60	—	325
PS19	1957(m) (4)	1,256	KM57-60	—	225
PS20	1958(m) (5)	1,506	KM56-60	—	250
PS21	1959(m) (6)	1,506	KM56-61	—	325
PS22	1960(m) (4)	1,509	KM57-60	—	175
PS23	1960(p) (2)	1,030	KM56,61	—	225
PS24	1961(m) (4)	1,506	KM57-60	—	175
PS25	1961(p) (2)	1,040	KM56,61	—	225
PS25a	1961(p) (2)	1,040	KM56,61	—	225
PS26	1962(m) (4)	2,016	KM57-60	—	150
PS27	1962(p) (2)	1,064	KM56,61	—	200
PS28	1963(m) (4)	5,042	KM57-60	—	125
PS29	1963(p) (2)	1,064	KM56,61	—	225
PS30	1966 (6)	18,110	KM62-67	15.70	120
PS31	1969 (6)	12,696	KM62-66,68	11.25	110
PS32	1970 (6)	15,112	KM62-66,69	11.30	55.00
PS33	1971 (6)	10,066	KM62-66,68	11.30	50.00
PS34	1972 (6)	10,272	KM62-66,68	14.00	55.00
PS35	1973 (6)	10,090	KM62-66,68	15.50	70.00
PS36	1974 (6)	11,103	KM62-66,68	18.00	45.00
PS37	1975 (6)	23,021	KM62-66,68	17.00	15.00
PS38	1976 (6)	21,200	KM62-66,68	20.20	20.00
PS39	1977 (6)	55,000	KM62-66,70	20.20	12.00
PS40	1978 (6)	38,513	KM62-66,68	—	10.00
PS41	1979 (6)	36,000	KM62-66,68	—	10.00
PS42	1980 (6)	68,000	KM62-66,68	—	8.00
PS43	1981 (6)	86,008	KM62-66,68	48.00	8.00
PS44	1982 (6)	100,000	KM62-66,74	50.00	8.00
PS45	1983 (6)	80,000	KM62-66,68	39.00	10.00
PS46	1984 (6)	61,398	62-66,68	39.00	10.00
PS47	1985 (7)	74,809	KM78-84	27.50	20.00
PS48	1986 (7)	67,000	KM78-83,87	40.00	15.00
PS49	1986P (4)	12,000	KM89-92	1,445	1,350
PS50	1986P (2)	3,000	KM89,90	305	325
PS51	1987 (7)	69,684	KM78-84	40.00	12.00
PS52	1987 (4)	12,000	KM95-98	1,440	1,300
PS53	1987 (2)	3,000	KM95, 96	305	350
PS54	1988 (8)	101,000	KM78-82, 99-101	—	15.00
PS55	1988 (8)	5,000	KM78-82, 99-101, Coin Fair	—	80.00
PS56	1988 (4)	25,000	KM99a-102a	85.00	130
PS57	1988	9,000	KM104-107	—	1,300
PS58	1988 (2)	1,000	KM104-105	—	235
PS59	1988 (2)	—	KM112-113	50.00	42.50
PS60	1989 (8)	2,500	KM78-84,101	—	15.00
PS61	1989 (8)	—	KM78-84, 101 Coin Fair	—	70.00
PS62	1989 (5)	2,200	KM117-121	1,595	1,300
PS63	1989 (5)	2,400	KM122-126	1,995	1,300
PS64	1989 (5)	25,000	KM99a,127-130	—	130
PS65	1989 (2)	—	KM131-132	—	42.50
PS66	1990 (8)	—	KM78-84,101	55.00	20.00
PS67	1990 (8)	—	KM78-84, 101 Coin Fair	—	80.00
PS68	1990 (5)	5,000	KM140-144	—	1,300
PS69	1990 (5)	2,500	KM145-149	—	1,300
PS70	1990 (3)	2,000	KM140-142	464	300
PS71	1990 (3)	1,000	KM138,144,149	1,900	1,800
PS72	1990 (2)	—	KM154-155	—	42.50
PS73	1990 (3)	25,000	KM84a, 87a, 100a. Sydney Coin Fair.	135	110
PS74	1991 (3)	1,000	KM140-142	—	300
PS75	1991 (8)	24,000	KM78-82,84,101,139	55.00	30.00
PS76	1991 (8)	1,000	KM78-82,84,101a,139	—	70.00
PS77	1991 (8)	23,000	KM78a-82a,84a, 101a, 139a	—	140
PS78	1991 (5)	2,000	KM140-144	—	1,100
PS79	1991 (5)	1,000	PS145-149	—	2,750
PS80	1992 (6)	47,000	KM80-83, 101, 175.1	40.00	25.00
PS81	1992 (4)	500	KM165-168	—	750
PS82	1992 (4)	—	KM200-203, plus medal	120	120
PS83	1992 (4)	5,000	KM204-207 plus medal	1,520	1,600
PSA84	1992 (3)	264	KM389-391	252	375
PSB84	1992 (5)	628	KM389-393	1,058	1,600
PSC84	1992 (4)	500	KM389-392 plus medal	759	1,000
PSD84	1992(ae) (3)	750	KM193, 209, 391	—	800
PSE84	1993 (4)	500	KM212, 230, 231 plus silver bar	—	300
PS84	1993 (6)	—	KM80-83, 101, 208	—	20.00
PS85	1993 (5)	20,000	KM213-217	94.50	100
PS86	1994 (6)	45,000	KM80-82, 84, 101, 257	—	20.00
PS87	1994 (5)	20,000	KM264-268	101	125
PS88	1994 (4)	20,000	KM182, 232 (2), 253	—	2,000
PSA89	1994 (4)	—	KM#260, 261, 270, 271	—	850
PS89	1994 (3)	25	KM241, 260, 278	304	350
PSA90	1995 (6)	—	KM80-82, 84, 101, 294	—	35.00
PS90	1995 (5)	300	KM272-276	—	1,300
PSA91	1995 (3)	600	KM#289, 272, 283	—	350
PS91	1995 (5)	200	KM283-287	—	1,300
PSA92	1995 (3)	300	KM276, 286, 290	—	1,300
PS92	1995 (4)	1,000	KM289-292	—	1,290
PS93	1995 (3)	300	KM289-291	—	390
PS94	1995 (2)	600	KM289-290	—	42.00
PSA95	1995 (2)	800	KM290-291	—	395
PS95	1996 (3)	3,000	KM275 (f), (l), (s) privy marks	—	800
PS96	1996 (6)	45,000	KM80-83, 101, 310. Baby set.	47.40	18.00
PS97	1996 (7)	—	KM80-83, 101, 310, plus silver gumnut baby medal	59.25	75.00
PSA98	1996 (3)	400	KM321-322, 341	1,500	1,350
PSB98	1996 (6)	—	KM80-83, 101, 310	—	20.00
PS98	1997 (3)	3,888	KM335-337	914	975
PSA99	1997 (2)	20,000	KM#353, 354	—	56.00
PS99	1997 (3)	3,000	KM341 (f), (l), (s) privy marks	782	900
PS100	1998 (6)	—	KM80-82, 84, 101, 364	40.60	30.00
PS101	1998 (6)	—	KM80-82, 84, 101, 364. Baby set.	50.75	52.50
PS102	1999 (6)	—	KM401-406	—	35.00
PS103	1999 (3)	1,000	KM501-503	—	170
PS104	1999 (6)	15,000	KM481-486	66.25	75.00
PS105	2000 (5)	—	KM496-500 plus 20.5-gram silver ingot	—	135
PS106	2000 (6)	—	KM401-403, 406, 488.1, 489	34.35	40.00

AUSTRIA

The Republic of Austria, a parliamentary democracy located in mountainous central Europe, has an area of 32,374 sq. mi. (83,850 sq. km.) and a population of 8.08 million. Capital: Wien (Vienna). Austria is primarily an industrial country. Machinery, iron, steel, textiles, yarns and timber are exported.

The territories later to be known as Austria were overrun in pre-Roman times by various tribes, including the Celts. Upon the fall of the Roman Empire, the country became a margravate of Charlemagne's Empire. Premysl II of Otakar, King of Bohemia, gained possession in 1252, only to lose the territory to Rudolf of Habsburg in 1276. Thereafter, until World War I, the story of Austria was conducted by the ruling Habsburgs.

During the 17th century, Austrian coinage reflected the geo-political strife of three wars. From 1618-1648, the Thirty Years' War between northern Protestants and southern Catholics produced low quality, "kipperwhipper" strikes of 12, 24, 30, 60, 75 and 150 Kreuzer. Later, during the Austrian-Turkish War, 1660-1664, coinages used to maintain soldier's salaries also reported the steady division of Hungarian territories. Finally, between 1683 and 1699, during the second Austrian-Turkish conflict, new issues of 3, 6 and 15 Kreuzers were struck, being necessary to help defray mounting expenses of the war effort.

During World War I, the Austro-Hungarian Empire was one of the Central Powers with Germany, Bulgaria and Turkey. At the end of the war, the Empire was dismembered and Austria established as an independent republic. In March 1938, Austria was incorporated into Hitler's short-lived Greater German Reich. Allied forces of both East and West occupied Austria in April 1945, and subsequently divided it into 4 zones of military occupation. On May 15, 1955, the 4 powers formally recognized Austria as a sovereign independent democratic state.

NOTE: During the **GERMAN OCCUPATION** (1938-1945), the German Reichsmark coins and banknotes were circulated.

MONETARY SYSTEM

150 Schillings = 100 Reichsmark

RULERS

Franz Joseph I, 1848-1916

Karl I, 1916-1918

EMPIRE

REFORM COINAGE

100 Heller = 1 Corona

KM# 2800 HELLER

Bronze **Ruler:** Franz Joseph I **Designer:**

Date	Mintage	F	VF	XF	Unc	BU
1901	52,096,000	0.20	0.35	1.00	3.00	—
1902	20,553,000	0.20	0.50	1.25	3.00	—
1903	13,779,000	0.20	0.35	0.50	2.50	—
1909	12,668,000	0.20	0.35	0.50	2.50	—
1910	21,941,000	0.20	0.35	0.50	2.50	—
1911	18,387,000	0.20	0.35	0.50	2.50	—
1912	27,053,000	0.20	0.35	0.50	2.50	—
1913	8,782,000	0.20	0.35	0.50	2.50	—
1914	9,906,000	0.20	0.35	0.50	2.50	—
1915	5,673,000	0.20	0.35	0.75	2.50	—
1916	12,484,000	0.35	0.75	1.50	4.00	—

KM# 2823 HELLER

Bronze, 17 mm. **Ruler:** Franz Joseph I **Obv:** Austrian shield on crowned double eagle's breast **Rev:** Value above sprays, date below, within shield

Date	Mintage	F	VF	XF	Unc	BU
1916	Inc. above	4.00	6.00	14.00	20.00	—

KM# 2801 2 HELLER

Bronze, 19 mm. **Ruler:** Franz Joseph I **Obv:** Shield on crowned double eagle's breast **Rev:** Value above sprays, date below, within shield

Date	Mintage	F	VF	XF	Unc	BU
1901	12,157,000	2.50	5.00	15.00	35.00	—
1902	18,760,000	0.15	0.50	1.50	3.00	—
1903	26,983,000	0.50	1.50	3.00	8.00	—
1904	12,863,000	0.15	0.50	4.00	14.00	—
1905	6,679,000	0.75	2.75	5.50	15.00	—
1906	20,104,000	0.50	1.50	3.00	8.00	—
1907	23,804,000	0.15	0.25	0.75	3.00	—

Date	Mintage	F	VF	XF	Unc	BU
1908	21,984,000	0.15	0.25	0.75	3.00	—
1909	25,975,000	0.15	0.25	0.75	3.00	—
1910	28,406,000	0.50	1.50	3.00	8.00	—
1911	50,007,058	0.15	0.25	0.50	2.00	—
1912	74,234,000	0.15	0.20	0.35	2.00	—
1913	27,432,000	0.35	0.75	2.25	6.00	—
1914	60,674,000	0.15	0.20	0.35	2.00	—
1915	7,871,000	0.15	0.20	0.35	2.00	—

KM# 2824 2 HELLER

Iron **Ruler:** Karl I **Obv:** Austrian shield on crowned double eagle's breast **Rev:** Value above date, within wreath

Date	Mintage	F	VF	XF	Unc	BU
1916	61,909,000	0.50	1.00	2.00	7.50	—
1917	81,186,000	0.25	0.50	1.00	5.00	—
1918	66,352,999	0.25	0.50	1.00	4.00	—

KM# 2802 10 HELLER

Nickel **Ruler:** Franz Joseph I **Rev:** Value above date within decorative shield

Date	Mintage	F	VF	XF	Unc	BU
1907	8,662,000	0.25	0.50	1.00	4.00	—
1908	7,772,000	0.75	1.50	2.50	6.00	—
1909	20,462,000	0.15	0.25	0.75	2.50	—
1910	10,164,000	0.15	0.25	0.75	2.50	—
1911	3,634,000	1.00	2.00	3.50	8.00	—

KM# 2822 10 HELLER

Copper-Nickel-Zinc **Ruler:** Franz Joseph I **Obv:** Shield on crowned double eagle's breast **Rev:** Value within wreath, date below

Date	Mintage	F	VF	XF	Unc	BU
1915	18,366,000	0.15	0.25	0.50	2.00	—
1916	27,487,000	0.15	0.25	0.50	2.00	—

KM# 2825 10 HELLER

Copper-Nickel-Zinc **Ruler:** Franz Joseph I **Obv:** Austrian shield on crowned double eagle's breast **Rev:** Value within wreath, date below

Date	Mintage	F	VF	XF	Unc	BU
1916	14,804,000	0.75	1.50	3.00	5.00	—

KM# 2803 20 HELLER

Nickel, 21 mm. **Ruler:** Franz Joseph I **Obv:** Shield on crowned double eagle's breast **Rev:** Value above date at center of ornate shield

Date	Mintage	F	VF	XF	Unc	BU
1907	7,650,000	0.75	1.50	3.00	12.00	—
1908	7,469,000	0.75	1.25	2.50	9.00	—
1909	7,592,000	3.00	6.00	12.00	20.00	—
1911	19,560,000	0.25	0.35	1.00	5.00	—
1914	2,342,000	5.00	10.00	15.00	25.00	—

KM# 2826 20 HELLER

Iron **Ruler:** Karl I **Obv:** Austrian shield on crowned double eagle's breast **Rev:** Value within wreath, date below

Date	Mintage	F	VF	XF	Unc	BU
1916	130,770,000	0.50	1.25	2.00	6.50	—
1917	127,420,000	0.50	1.25	2.00	5.50	—
1918	48,985,000	0.25	0.65	1.25	4.50	—

KM# 2804 CORONA

5.0000 g., 0.8350 Silver .1342 oz. ASW **Ruler:** Franz Joseph I **Obv:** Laureate bust

Date	Mintage	F	VF	XF	Unc	BU
1901	10,387,000	2.00	3.00	5.00	10.00	—
1902	2,947,000	2.00	4.25	7.50	15.00	—
1903	2,198,000	2.00	4.25	8.00	29.00	—
1904	993,000	4.00	8.50	17.50	50.00	—
1905	505,000	10.00	25.00	45.00	70.00	—
1906	164,500	80.00	125	200	450	—
1907	244,000	30.00	60.00	100	300	—

KM# 2808 CORONA

5.0000 g., 0.8350 Silver .1342 oz. ASW **Ruler:** Franz Joseph I **Subject:** 60th Anniversary of Reign **Obv:** Head right **Rev:** Crown at top divides dates, FII on spray at center, value at bottom **Designer:** R. Marshall & R. Neuberger

Date	Mintage	F	VF	XF	Unc	BU
ND(1908)	4,784,992	2.50	3.50	6.00	12.00	—

KM# 2820 CORONA

5.0000 g., 0.8350 Silver .1342 oz. ASW **Ruler:** Franz Joseph I **Obv:** Head right **Rev:** Crown above value, date at bottom, sprays flanking

Date	Mintage	F	VF	XF	Unc	BU
1912	8,457,000	1.85	2.25	3.50	8.00	—
1913	9,345,000	1.85	2.25	3.50	7.00	—
1914	37,897,000	1.85	2.25	3.00	6.00	—
1915	23,000,134	1.85	2.25	3.00	6.00	—
1916	12,415,404	1.85	2.25	3.00	6.00	—

KM# 2821 2 CORONA

10.0000 g., 0.8350 Silver .2684 oz. ASW **Ruler:** Franz Joseph I **Obv:** Head right **Rev:** Crowned double eagle above date

Date	Mintage	F	VF	XF	Unc	BU
1912	10,244,500	3.75	5.00	7.00	10.00	—
1913	7,256,002	3.75	5.00	7.00	10.00	—

KM# 2807 5 CORONA

24.0000 g., 0.9000 Silver .6945 oz. ASW **Ruler:** Franz Joseph I **Obv:** Laureate head right **Rev:** Crowned double eagle within circle surrounded by wreath of crowns in circles and leaves, date divides value at bottom

Date	Mintage	F	VF	XF	Unc	BU
1907	1,539,000	12.00	16.50	45.00	145	—
1907 Proof	—	Value: 650				

KM# 2809 5 CORONA

24.0000 g., 0.9000 Silver .6945 oz. ASW, 35 mm. **Ruler:** Franz Joseph I **Subject:** 60th Anniversary of Reign **Obv:** Head right **Rev:** Running figure of Fame **Designer:** R. Marshall & R. Neuberger

Date	Mintage	F	VF	XF	Unc	BU
ND(1908)	5,089,700	10.00	14.00	28.00	65.00	—
ND(1908) Proof	—	Value: 650				

KM# 2813 5 CORONA

24.0000 g., 0.9000 Silver .6945 oz. ASW **Ruler:** Franz Joseph I **Obv:** Large head, right, continuous legend **Rev:** Crowned double eagle with shield on breast within circle, five crowns in circles and leaf sprays surrounding, date divides value at bottom

Date	Mintage	F	VF	XF	Unc	BU
1909	1,708,800	11.00	16.00	40.00	125	—

KM# 2814 5 CORONA

24.0000 g., 0.9000 Silver .6945 oz. ASW **Ruler:** Franz Joseph I **Obv:** Head right **Rev:** National arms, date below divides denomination

Date	Mintage	F	VF	XF	Unc	BU
1909	1,775,787	11.00	15.00	35.00	90.00	—

KM# 2805 10 CORONA

3.3875 g., 0.9000 Gold .0980 oz. AGW, 19 mm. **Ruler:** Franz Joseph I **Obv:** Laureate head right **Rev:** Crowned double eagle with value and date below

Date	Mintage	F	VF	XF	Unc	BU
1905 - MDCCCCV	1,933,230	—	BV	70.00	90.00	—
1906 - MDCCCCVI	1,081,161	—	BV	70.00	90.00	—

KM# 2810 10 CORONA

3.3875 g., 0.9000 Gold .0980 oz. AGW, 19 mm. **Ruler:** Franz Joseph I **Subject:** 60th Anniversary of Reign **Obv:** Small plain head right **Rev:** Crowned double eagle, tail divides two dates, value at bottom **Designer:** R. Marshall & R. Neuberger

Date	Mintage	F	VF	XF	Unc	BU
ND(1908)	654,022	—	BV	70.00	100	—

KM# 2815 10 CORONA
3.3875 g., 0.9000 Gold .0980 oz. AGW, 19 mm. **Ruler:** Franz Joseph I **Obv:** Head right **Rev:** Crowned double eagle, date and value at bottom

Date	Mintage	F	VF	XF	Unc	BU
1909 - MDCCCCIX	2,319,872	—	BV	65.00	85.00	—

KM# 2816 10 CORONA
3.3875 g., 0.9000 Gold .0980 oz. AGW, 19 mm. **Ruler:** Franz Joseph I **Obv:** Large right **Rev:** Crowned double eagle, date and value at bottom

Date	Mintage	F	VF	XF	Unc	BU
1909 - MDCCCCIX	192,135	—	65.00	80.00	100	—
1910 - MDCCCCX	1,055,387	—	BV	65.00	80.00	—
1911 - MDCCCCXI	1,285,667	—	BV	65.00	80.00	—
1912 - MDCCCCXII Restrike	—	—	—	—	BV+ 10%	—

KM# 2806 20 CORONA
6.7751 g., 0.9000 Gold .1960 oz. AGW, 21 mm. **Ruler:** Franz Joseph I **Obv:** Laureate head right **Rev:** Crowned double eagle, value and date at bottom

Date	Mintage	F	VF	XF	Unc	BU
1901 - MDCCCCI	48,677	200	400	600	800	—
1902 - MDCCCCII	440,751	—	BV	130	160	—
1903 - MDCCCCIII	322,679	—	BV	130	160	—
1904 - MDCCCCIV	494,356	—	BV	130	160	—
1905 - MDCCCCV	146,097	BV	130	150	170	—

KM# 2811 20 CORONA
6.7751 g., 0.9000 Gold .1960 oz. AGW, 21 mm. **Ruler:** Franz Joseph I **Subject:** 60th Anniversary of Reign **Obv:** Head right **Rev:** Crowned double eagle, crown divides two dates, value at bottom **Designer:** R. Marshall & R. Neuberger

Date	Mintage	F	VF	XF	Unc	BU
1908	188,000	BV	195	285	380	—

KM# 2817 20 CORONA
6.7751 g., 0.9000 Gold .1960 oz. AGW, 21 mm. **Ruler:** Franz Joseph I **Rev:** Crowned double eagle, value and date at bottom **Designer:** Rudolf Marschall

Date	Mintage	F	VF	XF	Unc	BU
1909 - MDCCCCIX	227,754	450	750	1,400	1,800	—

KM# 2818 20 CORONA
6.7751 g., 0.9000 Gold .1960 oz. AGW, 21 mm. **Ruler:** Franz Joseph I **Obv:** Head of Franz Joseph I, right

Date	Mintage	F	VF	XF	Unc	BU
MDCCCCIX (1909)	102,404	575	1,150	2,000	2,800	—
MDCCCCX (1910)	386,031	BV	150	250	350	—
MDCCCCXI (1911)	59,313	135	550	800	975	—
MDCCCCXII (1912)	4,460	250	550	1,350	2,000	—
MDCCCCXIII (1913)	28,058	350	900	1,800	3,000	—
MDCCCCXIV (1914)	82,104	135	550	800	1,000	—
MDCCCCXV (1915) Restrike	—	—	—	—	BV+ 5%	—
MDCCCCXVI (1916)	71,763	2,500	3,500	5,500	7,500	—

KM# 2827 20 CORONA
6.7751 g., 0.9000 Gold .1960 oz. AGW, 21 mm. **Ruler:** Franz Joseph I **Obv:** Head right **Rev:** Austrian shield on crowned double eagle, value and date at bottom

Date	Mintage	F	VF	XF	Unc	BU
1916 - MDCCCCXVI	Inc. above	450	750	900	1,200	—

KM# 2828 20 CORONA
6.7751 g., 0.9000 Gold .1960 oz. AGW, 21 mm. **Ruler:** Karl I **Obv:** Head right **Rev:** Crowned national arms, date below divides denomination **Note:** 2000 pieces struck, all but one specimen were remelted.

Date	Mintage	F	VF	XF	Unc	BU
1918 - MDCCCCXVIII Unique	Est. 2,000	—	—	—	—	—

KM# 2812 100 CORONA
33.8753 g., 0.9000 Gold .9803 oz. AGW, 37 mm. **Ruler:** Franz Joseph I **Subject:** 60th Anniversary of Reign **Obv:** Head right **Rev:** Resting figure of Fame **Designer:** Rudolf Marschall

Date	Mintage	F	VF	XF	Unc	BU
ND(1908)	16,000	BV	950	1,200	1,700	—
ND(1908) Proof	—	Value: 1,850				

KM# 2819 100 CORONA
33.8753 g., 0.9000 Gold .9803 oz. AGW, 37 mm. **Ruler:** Franz Joseph I **Obv:** Head right **Obv. Designer:** Stefan Schwartz **Rev:** Crowned double eagle, tail dividing value, date at bottom

Date	Mintage	F	VF	XF	Unc	BU
1909	3,203	BV	650	950	1,500	—
1910	3,074	BV	650	950	1,500	—
1911	11,165	BV	650	950	1,500	—
1912	3,591	640	850	1,150	2,000	—
1913	2,696	BV	800	1,200	1,700	—
1914	1,195	BV	650	1,000	1,600	—
1915 Restrike	—	—	—	—	BV+ 2%	—
1915 Restrike, Proof	—	—	—	—	—	—

TRADE COINAGE

KM# 2267 DUCAT
3.4909 g., 0.9860 Gold .1106 oz. AGW **Ruler:** Franz Joseph I **Obv:** Laureat head of Franz Joseph I, right **Rev:** Crowned double eagle, date in legend **Note:** 996,721 pieces were struck from 1920-1936.

Date	Mintage	F	VF	XF	Unc	BU
1901	348,621	BV	100	125	175	—
1902	311,471	BV	100	125	175	—
1903	380,014	BV	100	125	175	—
1904	517,118	BV	100	125	175	—
1905	391,534	BV	125	150	200	—
1906	491,574	BV	125	150	200	—
1907	554,205	BV	125	175	250	—
1908	408,832	BV	80.00	125	175	—
1909	366,318	BV	80.00	100	150	—
1910	440,424	BV	80.00	100	150	—
1911	590,826	BV	80.00	100	125	—
1912	494,991	BV	80.00	100	125	—
1913	319,926	BV	80.00	100	125	—
1914	378,241	BV	80.00	100	125	—
1915 Restrike	—	—	—	—	BV+ 10%	—
1951 Error for 1915	—	75.00	125	150	225	—

KM# 2276 4 DUCAT
13.9636 g., 0.9860 Gold .4430 oz. AGW **Ruler:** Franz Joseph I **Obv:** Laureate, armored bust of Franz Joseph I right **Rev:** Crowned double eagle, value at bottom **Note:** Similar to KM#2272, but without mint

Date	Mintage	F	VF	XF	Unc	BU
1901	51,597	290	450	800	1,100	—
1902	69,380	290	450	800	1,100	—
1903	72,658	290	450	800	1,100	—
1904	80,086	290	450	800	1,100	—
1905	90,906	290	450	800	1,100	—
1906	123,443	290	350	500	800	—
1907	104,295	290	350	500	800	—
1908	80,428	290	350	550	870	—
1909	83,852	285	300	450	680	—
1910	101,000	285	300	350	580	—
1911	141,857	285	300	325	450	—
1912	150,691	285	300	325	450	—
1913	119,133	285	300	325	450	—
1914	102,712	285	300	325	450	—
1915 (- 1936) Restrike	—	—	—	—	BV+ 8%	—

Note: 496,501 pieces were struck from 1920-1936

TRADE COINAGE

Restrikes

KM# T1 THALER
28.0668 g., 0.8330 Silver .7517 oz. ASW, 41 mm. **Obv:** Bust of Mother Theresa, right **Rev:** Imperial Eagle

Date	Mintage	F	VF	XF	Unc	BU
1780 SF Proof	—	Value: 12.00				

Note: Restrike - 1853 to present

Date	Mintage	F	VF	XF	Unc	BU
1780 SF	—	—	—	—	10.00	—

Note: Restrike; 1853 to present

KM# T2 20 DUCAT
72.7500 g., Gold **Obv:** Bust of Maria Theresa, right **Rev:** Imperial Eagle **Note:** Struck for Haile Selassie.

Date	Mintage	F	VF	XF	Unc	BU
1780 SF	—	—	—	—	1,750	—

Note: Restrike - 1950s

REPUBLIC

REFORM COINAGE

10,000 Kronen = 1 Schilling

KM# 2830 20 KRONEN
6.7751 g., 0.9000 Gold .1960 oz. AGW **Obv:** Imperial Eagle, date below **Rev:** Value within wreath **Designer:** Richard Placht

Date	Mintage	F	VF	XF	Unc	BU
1923	6,988	650	1,400	1,850	2,500	—
1924	10,337	650	1,400	1,850	2,500	—

KM# 2831 100 KRONEN
33.8753 g., 0.9000 Gold .9802 oz. AGW **Obv:** Imperial Eagle, date below **Rev:** Value within wreath **Designer:** Richard Placht

Date	Mintage	F	VF	XF	Unc	BU
1923	617	750	1,550	2,250	3,500	—
1923 Proof	—	Value: 4,000				
1924	2,851	750	1,550	2,250	3,500	—

KM# 2832 100 KRONEN
Bronze **Obv:** Eagle's head, right **Rev:** Value to right of leaf, date below **Designer:** Heinrich Zita

Date	Mintage	F	VF	XF	Unc	BU
1923	6,403,680	4.00	8.00	15.00	30.00	—
1924	43,013,920	0.25	0.50	1.50	4.50	—

KM# 2833 200 KRONEN
Bronze **Obv:** Thick cross, date below **Rev:** Large value **Designer:** Filip Häuslerr

Date	Mintage	F	VF	XF	Unc	BU
1924	57,160,000	0.50	1.00	2.00	6.50	—

KM# 2834 1000 KRONEN
Copper-Nickel **Obv:** Woman of Tyrol, right **Rev:** Value within wreath **Designer:** Heinrich Zita

Date	Mintage	F	VF	XF	Unc	BU
1924	72,353,000	0.75	1.50	3.00	8.00	—

PRE WWII DECIMAL COINAGE

100 Groschen - 1 Schilling

KM# 2836 GROSCHEN
Bronze **Obv:** Eagle's head, right **Rev:** Large value, date below **Designer:** Heinrich Zita

Date	Mintage	F	VF	XF	Unc	BU
1925	30,465,000	0.10	0.20	0.50	2.00	—
1926	15,487,000	0.10	0.30	0.75	2.00	—
1927	9,318,000	0.10	0.30	0.75	2.50	—
1928	17,189,000	0.10	0.30	0.75	2.50	—
1929	11,400,000	0.10	0.30	0.75	2.50	—
1930	8,893,000	0.10	0.30	0.75	2.50	—
1931	971,000	10.00	20.00	30.00	60.00	—
1932	3,040,000	1.00	2.50	5.00	7.50	—
1933	3,940,000	0.50	1.00	2.00	6.00	—
1934	4,232,000	0.15	0.50	1.00	4.00	—
1935	3,740,000	0.15	0.50	1.00	4.00	—
1936	6,020,000	0.50	1.00	3.00	9.00	—
1937	5,830,000	0.50	1.00	2.00	7.50	—
1938	1,650,000	2.00	3.00	6.00	15.00	—

KM# 2837 2 GROSCHEN
Bronze **Obv:** Thick cross, date below **Rev:** Large value

Date	Mintage	F	VF	XF	Unc	BU
1925	29,892,000	0.10	0.25	0.50	1.50	—
1926	17,700,000	0.10	0.30	0.75	2.00	—
1927	7,757,000	0.20	0.75	2.00	5.00	—
1928	19,478,000	0.10	0.30	0.75	2.00	—
1929	16,184,000	0.10	0.30	0.75	2.00	—
1930	5,709,000	0.20	0.60	1.50	4.00	—
1934	812,000	7.00	12.00	15.00	25.00	—
1935	3,148,000	0.20	0.60	1.50	4.00	—
1936	4,410,000	0.15	0.30	1.00	3.00	—
1937	3,790,000	0.20	0.40	1.25	3.50	—
1938	860,000	2.50	4.00	6.50	12.50	—

KM# 2846 5 GROSCHEN
Copper-Nickel **Obv:** Thick cross, date below **Obv. Designer:** Adolf Hofmann **Rev:** Large value **Rev. Designer:** Philipp Häusler

Date	Mintage	F	VF	XF	Unc	BU
1931	16,631,000	0.15	0.40	0.80	2.00	—
1932	4,700,000	0.25	1.00	2.00	5.00	—
1934	3,210,000	0.30	1.00	2.50	6.00	—
1936	1,240,000	2.00	4.00	7.50	15.00	—
1937	1,540,000	20.00	30.00	45.00	80.00	—
1938	870,000	125	175	250	425	—

KM# 2838 10 GROSCHEN
Copper-Nickel, 22 mm. **Obv:** Woman of Tyrol, right **Rev:** Value above date within wreath **Designer:** Heinrich Zita

Date	Mintage	F	VF	XF	Unc	BU
1925	66,199,000	0.10	0.25	0.50	3.00	—
1928	11,468,000	0.50	1.00	4.00	12.00	—
1929	12,000,000	0.40	0.75	1.50	4.50	—

KM# 2850 50 GROSCHEN
Copper-Nickel **Obv:** Numeric value in box within circle, value at bottom **Obv. Designer:** G. Baudisch **Rev:** Austrian shield on haloed double eagle's breast, tail dividing date **Rev. Designer:** Michael Powolny

Date	Mintage	F	VF	XF	Unc	BU
1934	8,224,822	20.00	35.00	50.00	90.00	—
1934 Proof	Inc. above	Value: 125				

KM# 2854 50 GROSCHEN
Copper-Nickel **Obv:** Austrian shield on haloed double eagle's breast, value at bottom **Rev:** Large value above date

Date	Mintage	F	VF	XF	Unc	BU
1935	11,435,000	0.75	1.25	2.50	5.00	—
1935 Proof	Inc. above	Value: 80.00				
1936	1,000,000	30.00	40.00	60.00	115	—
1936 Proof	Inc. above	Value: 140				

KM# 2839 1/2 SCHILLING
3.0000 g., 0.6400 Silver .0617 oz. ASW **Obv:** Austrian shield at center **Rev:** Numeric value in diamond at center **Designer:** Philipp Häusler

Date	Mintage	F	VF	XF	Unc	BU
1925	18,370,000	1.25	2.50	4.00	8.00	—
1926	12,943,000	2.00	4.00	7.00	12.50	—

KM# 2835 SCHILLING
7.0000 g., 0.8000 Silver .1800 oz. ASW **Obv:** Parliament building in Vienna, date below **Rev:** Coat of arms on spray of edelweiss, value

Date	Mintage	F	VF	XF	Unc	BU
1924	11,086,000	2.50	3.50	6.00	10.00	—

KM# 2840 SCHILLING
6.0000 g., 0.6400 Silver .1235 oz. ASW **Obv:** Parliament building in Vienna, date below **Rev:** Coat of arms on spray of edelweiss, value

Date	Mintage	F	VF	XF	Unc	BU
1925	38,209,000	1.75	2.25	3.50	7.00	—
1926	20,157,000	1.75	2.50	4.00	8.00	—
1932	700,000	30.00	65.00	90.00	150	—

KM# 2851 SCHILLING

Copper-Nickel **Obv:** Two sprigs of grain in center with large numeric value on top **Rev:** Austrian shield on haloed double eagles breast, tail dividing date

Date	Mintage	F	VF	XF	Unc	BU
1934	30,641,000	1.00	2.00	3.50	7.50	—
1934 Proof	—	Value: 150				
1935	11,987,000	3.00	6.00	12.50	30.00	—

KM# 2843 2 SCHILLING

12.0000 g., 0.6400 Silver .2469 oz. ASW **Subject:** Centennial - Death of Franz Schubert **Obv:** Value within circle of shields **Rev:** Head of Franz Schubert, left, date at bottom left **Rev. Designer:** Edwin Grienauer

Date	Mintage	F	VF	XF	Unc	BU
1928	6,900,000	3.75	5.00	8.00	16.00	—

KM# 2844 2 SCHILLING

12.0000 g., 0.6400 Silver .2469 oz. ASW **Subject:** 100th Anniversary - Birth of Dr. Theodor Billroth, Surgeon **Obv:** Value within circle of shields **Rev:** Head of Dr. Theodor Billroth, left, date below **Rev. Designer:** Edwin Grienauer

Date	Mintage	F	VF	XF	Unc	BU
1929	2,000,000	6.00	9.00	18.00	32.50	—

KM# 2845 2 SCHILLING

12.0000 g., 0.6400 Silver .2469 oz. ASW **Subject:** 7th Centennial - Death of Walther von der Vogelweide, Minstrel **Obv:** Value within circle of shields **Rev:** Figure of Walther von der Vogelweide sitting, left, with doves, harp on lower left. date at bottom **Rev. Designer:** Edwin Grienauer

Date	Mintage	F	VF	XF	Unc	BU
1930	500,000	5.00	6.00	9.00	18.00	—
1930 Proof	Inc. above	Value: 125				

KM# 2847 2 SCHILLING

12.0000 g., 0.6400 Silver .2469 oz. ASW **Subject:** 175th Anniversary - Birth of Wolfgang Mozart, Composer **Obv:** Value within circle of shields **Rev:** Head of Wolfgang Mozart, right, two dates at bottom **Rev. Designer:** Edwin Grienauer

Date	Mintage	F	VF	XF	Unc	BU
1931	500,000	9.00	18.00	28.00	50.00	—
1931 Proof	Inc. above	Value: 300				

KM# 2848 2 SCHILLING

12.0000 g., 0.6400 Silver .2469 oz. ASW **Subject:** 200th Anniversary - Birth of Joseph Haydn, Composer **Obv:** Value within circle of shields **Rev:** Head of Joseph Haydn, left, date below **Rev. Designer:** Edwin Grienauer

Date	Mintage	F	VF	XF	Unc	BU
1932	300,000	25.00	50.00	100	175	—
1932 Proof	Inc. above	Value: 550				

KM# 2849 2 SCHILLING

12.0000 g., 0.6400 Silver .2469 oz. ASW **Subject:** Death of Dr. Ignaz Seipel, Chancellor **Obv:** Value within circle of shields **Rev:** Head of Dr. Ignaz Seipel, right, two dates at bottom **Rev. Designer:** Hanisch and Concée

Date	Mintage	F	VF	XF	Unc	BU
ND(1933) Proof	Inc. above	Value: 400				
ND(1933)	400,000	10.00	20.00	35.00	60.00	—

KM# 2852 2 SCHILLING

12.0000 g., 0.6400 Silver .2469 oz. ASW **Subject:** Death of Dr. Engelbert Dollfuss, Chancellor **Obv:** Value within circle of shields **Rev:** Head of Dr. Engelbert Dollfuss, right, two dates at bottom **Rev. Designer:** Edwin Grienauer

Date	Mintage	F	VF	XF	Unc	BU
1934	1,500,000	7.00	12.00	20.00	32.50	—
1934 Proof	Inc. above	Value: 275				

KM# 2855 2 SCHILLING

12.0000 g., 0.6400 Silver .2469 oz. ASW **Subject:** 25th Anniversary - Death of Dr. Karl Lueger, Politician, Social reformer **Obv:** Haloed double eagle with Austrian shield, date divides value at bottom **Rev:** Head of Dr. Karl Lueger, right **Rev. Designer:** Rudolf Marschall

Date	Mintage	F	VF	XF	Unc	BU
1935	500,000	8.00	16.00	25.00	45.00	—
1935 Proof	Inc. above	Value: 285				

KM# 2858 2 SCHILLING

12.0000 g., 0.6400 Silver .2469 oz. ASW **Subject:** Bicentennial - Death of Prince Eugen of Savoy, Imperial Austrian Field Marshal **Obv:** Haloed double eagle with Austrian shield, date divides value below **Rev:** Head of Prince Eugen of Savoy, left **Rev. Designer:** Edwin Grienauer

Date	Mintage	F	VF	XF	Unc	BU
1936	500,000	6.00	9.00	18.00	30.00	—
1936 Proof	Inc. above	Value: 225				

KM# 2859 2 SCHILLING

12.0000 g., 0.6400 Silver .2469 oz. ASW **Subject:** Bicentennial - Completion of St. Charles Church 1737 **Obv:** Haloed double eagle with Austrian shield, date divides value below **Rev:** St. Charles Church, date at bottom **Rev. Designer:** Edwin Grienauer

Date	Mintage	F	VF	XF	Unc	BU
1937	500,000	6.00	9.00	18.00	30.00	—
1937 Proof	Inc. above	Value: 185				

KM# 2853 5 SCHILLING

15.0000 g., 0.8350 Silver .4027 oz. ASW **Obv:** Haloed double eagle with Austrian shield, value **Rev:** Standing figure of Madonna of Mariazell, date below

Date	Mintage	F	VF	XF	Unc	BU
1934	3,066,000	11.50	17.50	32.50	60.00	—
1934 Proof	—	Value: 220				
1935	5,377,000	11.50	17.50	32.50	60.00	—
1936	1,557,000	45.00	85.00	125	185	—

KM# 2841 25 SCHILLING

5.8810 g., 0.9000 Gold .1702 oz. AGW **Obv:** Imperial Eagle with Austrian shield on breast, holding hammer and sickle, **Rev:** Value at top flanked by edelweiss sprays, date divided by sprigs at bottom **Designer:** Arnold Hartig

Date	Mintage	F	VF	XF	Unc	BU
1926 Prooflike	276,705	—	—	—	125	—
1927 Prooflike	72,672	—	—	—	135	—
1928 Prooflike	134,041	—	—	—	125	—
1929 Prooflike	243,269	—	—	—	125	—
1930 Prooflike	129,535	—	—	—	135	—
1931 Prooflike	169,002	—	—	—	125	—
1933 Prooflike	4,944	—	—	—	1,850	—
1934 Prooflike	11,000	—	—	—	600	—

KM# 2856 25 SCHILLING

5.8810 g., 0.9000 Gold .1702 oz. AGW **Obv:** Haloed double eagle with Austrian shield on breast, value below **Obv. Designer:** Joseph Prinz **Rev:** Half figure of St. Leopold, facing 3/4 forward, date at bottom **Rev. Designer:** Edwin Grienauer

Date	Mintage	F	VF	XF	Unc	BU
1935 Prooflike	2,880	—	—	—	1,000	—
1936 Prooflike	7,260	—	—	—	850	—
1937 Prooflike	7,660	—	—	—	850	—
1938 Prooflike	1,360	—	—	—	25,000	—

KM# 2842 100 SCHILLING

23.5245 g., 0.9000 Gold .6806 oz. AGW **Obv:** Imperial Eagle with Austrian shield on breast holding hammer and sickle **Rev:** Value at top flanked by edelweiss sprays, date below, one star on either side **Designer:** Arnold Hartig

Date	Mintage	F	VF	XF	Unc	BU
1926 Prooflike	63,795	—	—	—	455	—
1927 Prooflike	68,746	—	—	—	455	—
1928 Prooflike	40,188	—	—	—	550	—
1929 Prooflike	74,849	—	—	—	455	—
1930 Prooflike	24,849	—	—	—	455	—
1931 Prooflike	101,935	—	—	—	455	—
1933 Prooflike	4,727	—	—	—	1,550	—
1934 Prooflike	9,383	—	—	—	600	—

KM# 2857 100 SCHILLING

23.5245 g., 0.9000 Gold .6806 oz. AGW **Obv:** Haloed eagle with Austrian shield on breast, value below **Rev:** Standing figure of Madonna of Mariazell, facing, date below

Date	Mintage	F	VF	XF	Unc	BU
1935 Prooflike	951	—	—	—	5,500	—
1936 Prooflike	12,000	—	—	—	1,650	—
1937 Prooflike	2,900	—	—	—	2,250	—
1938 Prooflike	1,400	—	—	—	25,000	—

POST WWII DECIMAL COINAGE

100 Groschen - 1 Schilling

KM# 2873 GROSCHEN

Zinc **Obv:** Imperial Eagle with Austrian shield on breast **Rev:** Large value above date, spray of leaves below

Date	Mintage	F	VF	XF	Unc	BU
1947	23,758,000	0.15	0.25	0.75	2.50	—

KM# 2876 2 GROSCHEN

0.9000 g., Aluminum, 18 mm. **Obv:** Imperial Eagle with Austrian shield on breast, holding hammer and sickle **Obv. Designer:** Michael Powolny **Rev:** Large value in circle, date below circle **Rev. Designer:** Benno Rost **Edge:** Plain

Date	Mintage	F	VF	XF	Unc	BU
1950	21,652,000	—	0.15	0.60	4.00	—
1950 Proof	—	Value: 28.00				
1951	7,377,000	—	0.25	1.00	4.50	—
1951 Proof	—	Value: 300				
1952	37,851,000	—	0.15	0.50	2.50	—
1952 Proof	—	Value: 25.00				
1954	46,167,000	—	0.15	0.50	2.50	—
1954 Proof	—	Value: 50.00				
1957	26,923,000	—	0.15	0.50	3.00	—
1957 Proof	—	Value: 45.00				
1962	6,692,000	—	0.15	0.50	2.50	—
1962 Proof	—	Value: 28.00				
1964 Proof	173,000	Value: 6.50				
1965	14,475,000	—	0.10	0.30	1.50	—
1965 Proof	—	Value: 2.50				
1966	7,454,000	—	0.10	0.30	1.50	—
1966 Proof	—	Value: 7.50				
1967 Proof	13,000	Value: 100				
1968	1,803,400	—	0.10	0.30	1.50	—
1968 Proof	21,600	Value: 10.00				
1969 Proof	57,000	Value: 6.00				
1970 Proof	260,000	Value: 2.50				
1971 Proof	145,000	Value: 2.50				
1972	2,763,000	—	—	0.20	0.50	—
1972 Proof	132,000	Value: 1.00				
1973	5,883,000	—	—	0.20	0.50	—
1973 Proof	149,000	Value: 1.00				
1974	1,387,000	—	—	0.20	0.50	—
1974 Proof	93,000	Value: 1.00				
1975	1,096,000	—	—	0.20	0.50	—
1975 Proof	52,000	Value: 1.00				
1976	2,755,000	—	—	0.20	0.50	—
1976 Proof	45,000	Value: 1.00				
1977	1,837,000	—	—	0.20	0.50	—
1977 Proof	47,000	Value: 1.00				
1978	1,527,000	—	—	0.20	0.50	—
1978 Proof	44,000	Value: 1.00				
1979	2,434,000	—	—	0.20	0.50	—
1979 Proof	44,000	Value: 1.00				
1980	1,893,000	—	—	0.20	0.50	—
1980 Proof	48,000	Value: 10.00				
1981	950,000	—	—	0.20	0.50	—
1981 Proof	49,000	Value: 10.00				
1982	3,950,000	—	—	0.20	0.50	—
1982 Proof	50,000	Value: 3.00				
1983	2,665,000	—	—	0.20	0.50	—
1983 Proof	65,000	Value: 2.00				
1984	500,000	—	—	0.20	0.50	—
1984 Proof	65,000	Value: 2.00				
1985	1,060,000	—	—	0.20	0.50	—
1985 Proof	45,000	Value: 5.00				
1986	1,798,000	—	—	0.20	0.50	—
1986 Proof	42,000	Value: 10.00				
1987	958,000	—	—	0.20	0.50	—
1987 Proof	42,000	Value: 6.00				
1988	1,061,000	—	—	0.20	0.50	—
1988 Proof	39,000	Value: 2.00				
1989	950,000	—	—	0.20	0.50	—
1989 Proof	38,000	Value: 2.00				
1990 Proof	35,000	Value: 22.00				
1991	2,600,000	—	—	0.20	0.50	—
1991 Proof	27,000	Value: 5.00				
1992	25,000	—	—	—	20.00	—
Note: In sets only						
1992 Proof	25,000	Value: 15.00				
1993	35,000	—	—	—	20.00	—
Note: In sets only						
1993 Proof	28,000	Value: 7.00				
1994	25,000	—	—	—	25.00	—
Note: In sets only						
1994 Proof	25,000	Value: 30.00				

KM# 2875 5 GROSCHEN

2.5000 g., Zinc, 19 mm. **Obv:** Imperial Eagle with Austrian shield on breast, holding hammer and sickle **Obv. Designer:** Michael Powolny **Rev. Designer:** Adolf Hofmann **Edge:** Reeded

Date	Mintage	F	VF	XF	Unc	BU
1948	17,269,000	—	0.20	0.75	12.00	—
1950	19,426,431	—	0.20	0.75	8.00	—
1950 Proof	—	Value: 200				
1951	12,454,569	—	0.20	0.75	12.00	—
1951 Proof	—	Value: 35.00				
1953	14,931,000	—	0.15	0.75	8.00	—
1955	12,288,000	—	0.15	0.75	12.00	—
1957	26,809,000	—	0.15	0.75	6.00	—
1957 Proof	—	Value: 50.00				
1961	3,429,000	—	0.20	0.75	8.00	—
1961 Proof	—	Value: 25.00				
1962	5,999,000	—	0.20	0.75	8.00	—
1963	13,293,000	—	0.15	0.75	8.00	—
1963 Proof	—	Value: 40.00				
1964	4,659,000	—	0.15	0.75	4.00	—
1964 Proof	—	Value: 2.50				
1965	13,704,000	—	0.10	0.50	3.00	—
1965 Proof	—	Value: 2.50				
1966	9,348,000	—	0.10	0.50	3.00	—
1966 Proof	—	Value: 8.00				
1967	4,404,000	—	0.10	0.50	3.00	—
1967 Proof	—	Value: 10.00				
1968	31,418,400	—	0.10	0.50	3.00	—
1968 Proof	15,600	Value: 8.00				
1969 Proof	44,000	Value: 10.00				
1970 Proof	144,000	Value: 2.50				
1971 Proof	125,000	Value: 2.50				
1972	10,979,000	—	—	0.20	0.75	—
1972 Proof	116,000	Value: 1.00				
1973	10,336,000	—	—	0.20	0.75	—
1973 Proof	120,000	Value: 1.00				
1974	2,911,000	—	—	0.20	0.75	—
1974 Proof	87,000	Value: 1.00				
1975	7,102,000	—	—	0.20	0.75	—
1975 Proof	51,000	Value: 1.00				
1976	8,079,000	—	—	0.20	0.75	—
1976 Proof	45,000	Value: 1.00				
1977	1,600,000	—	—	0.20	0.75	—
1977 Proof	45,000	Value: 1.00				
1978	2,657,000	—	—	0.20	0.75	—
1978 Proof	44,000	Value: 1.00				
1979	4,927,000	—	—	0.20	0.75	—
1979 Proof	44,000	Value: 1.00				
1980	3,100,000	—	—	0.20	0.75	—
1980 Proof	48,000	Value: 8.00				
1981	450,000	—	—	0.20	0.75	—
1981 Proof	49,000	Value: 8.00				
1982	3,950,000	—	—	0.20	0.75	—
1982 Proof	50,000	Value: 2.50				
1983	501,000	—	—	0.20	0.75	—
1983 Proof	65,000	Value: 2.50				
1984	988,000	—	—	0.20	0.75	—
1984 Proof	65,000	Value: 2.50				
1985	1,914,000	—	—	0.20	0.75	—
1985 Proof	45,000	Value: 4.00				
1986	1,008,000	—	—	0.20	0.75	—
1986 Proof	42,000	Value: 7.00				
1987	1,458,000	—	—	0.20	0.75	—
1987 Proof	42,000	Value: 4.00				
1988	1,261,000	—	—	0.20	0.75	—
1988 Proof	39,000	Value: 3.00				
1989	2,604,000	—	—	0.20	0.75	—
1989 Proof	38,000	Value: 2.00				
1990	2,608,000	—	—	0.20	0.75	—
1990 Proof	35,000	Value: 6.00				
1991	2,400,000	—	—	0.20	0.75	—
1991 Proof	27,000	Value: 6.00				
1992	671,000	—	—	0.20	0.75	—
1992 Proof	25,000	Value: 10.00				
1993	35,000	—	—	—	12.00	—
Note: In sets only						
1993 Proof	28,000	Value: 7.00				
1994	25,000	—	—	—	15.00	—
Note: In sets only						
1994 Proof	25,000	Value: 20.00				

KM# 2874 10 GROSCHEN

Zinc, 21 mm. **Obv:** Imperial Eagle with Austrian shield on breast, holding hammer and sickle **Rev:** Large value above date, trumpet flower spray below **Edge:** Plain

Date	Mintage	F	VF	XF	Unc	BU
1947	6,845,000	0.75	2.00	4.00	22.00	—
1947 Proof	—	Value: 55.00				
1948	66,205,000	0.20	0.50	1.00	3.50	—
1948 Proof	—	Value: 65.00				
1949	51,202,000	0.20	0.50	1.00	3.50	—
1949 Proof	—	Value: 75.00				

KM# 2878 10 GROSCHEN

1.1000 g., Aluminum, 20 mm. **Obv:** Small Imperial Eagle with Austrian shield on breast, at top between numbers, scalloped rim, stylized inscription below **Rev:** Large value above date, scalloped rim **Edge:** Plain **Designer:** Hans Köttenstorfer

Date	Mintage	F	VF	XF	Unc	BU
1951	9,573,000	—	0.20	0.75	8.00	—
1951 Proof	—	Value: 85.00				
1952	45,911,400	—	0.10	0.50	4.00	—
1952 Proof	—	Value: 50.00				
1953	22,577,600	—	0.10	0.50	4.00	—
1953 Proof	—	Value: 175				
1955	51,707,000	—	0.10	0.50	4.00	—
1955 Proof	—	Value: 28.00				
1957	33,509,000	—	0.10	0.50	4.00	—
1957 Proof	—	Value: 150				
1959	80,719,000	—	0.10	0.35	3.50	—

Date	Mintage	F	VF	XF	Unc	BU
1959 Proof	—	Value: 45.00				
1961	11,283,000	—	0.20	0.75	8.00	—
1961 Proof	—	—	—	—	—	—
1962	24,635,000	—	0.10	0.35	3.50	—
1962 Proof	—	Value: 40.00				
1963	38,062,000	—	0.10	0.35	3.50	—
1963 Proof	—	Value: 45.00				
1964	34,928,000	—	0.10	0.20	2.00	—
1964 Proof	—	Value: 1.50				
1965	40,615,000	—	0.10	0.20	2.00	—
1965 Proof	—	Value: 1.50				
1966	24,991,000	—	0.10	0.20	2.00	—
1966 Proof	—	Value: 6.00				
1967	32,552,999	—	0.10	0.20	2.00	—
1967 Proof	—	Value: 12.00				
1968	42,395,800	—	0.10	0.20	2.00	—
1968 Proof	16,000	Value: 8.00				
1969	19,953,000	—	0.10	0.20	2.00	—
1969 Proof	27,000	Value: 5.00				
1970	36,997,500	—	—	0.10	0.45	—
1970 Proof	102,000	Value: 1.00				
1971	57,450,000	—	—	0.10	0.45	—
1971 Proof	82,000	Value: 1.00				
1972	75,661,000	—	—	0.10	0.45	—
1972 Proof	81,000	Value: 1.00				
1973	60,244,000	—	—	0.10	0.45	—
1973 Proof	97,000	Value: 0.75				
1974	55,924,000	—	—	0.10	0.45	—
1974 Proof	78,000	Value: 0.75				
1975	60,576,000	—	—	0.10	0.45	—
1975 Proof	49,000	Value: 0.75				
1976	39,357,000	—	—	0.10	0.45	—
1976 Proof	44,000	Value: 0.75				
1977	53,610,000	—	—	0.10	0.45	—
1977 Proof	44,000	Value: 0.75				
1978	57,857,000	—	—	0.10	0.45	—
1978 Proof	43,000	Value: 0.75				
1979	103,686,000	—	—	—	0.45	—
1979 Proof	44,000	Value: 0.75				
1980	79,848,000	—	—	—	0.45	—
1980 Proof	48,000	Value: 2.00				
1981	92,268,000	—	—	—	0.45	—
1981 Proof	49,000	Value: 2.00				
1982	99,950,000	—	—	—	0.45	—
1982 Proof	50,000	Value: 0.75				
1983	93,768,000	—	—	—	0.45	—
1983 Proof	65,000	Value: 0.75				
1984	86,603,000	—	—	—	0.45	—
1984 Proof	65,000	Value: 0.75				
1985	86,304,000	—	—	—	0.45	—
1985 Proof	45,000	Value: 0.75				
1986	108,912,000	—	—	—	0.45	—
1986 Proof	42,000	Value: 1.50				
1987	114,058,000	—	—	—	0.45	—
1987 Proof	42,000	Value: 0.75				
1988	114,461,000	—	—	—	0.45	—
1988 Proof	39,000	Value: 0.75				
1989	127,784,000	—	—	—	0.45	—
1989 Proof	38,000	Value: 0.75				
1990	182,050,000	—	—	—	0.45	—
1990 Proof	35,000	Value: 1.50				
1991	145,000,000	—	—	—	0.45	—
1991 Proof	27,000	Value: 1.50				
1992	125,000,000	—	—	—	0.45	—
1992 Proof	25,000	Value: 1.50				
1993	120,000,000	—	—	—	0.45	—
1993 Proof	28,000	Value: 1.50				
1994	110,000,000	—	—	—	0.45	—
1994 Proof	25,000	Value: 2.00				
1995	80,000,000	—	—	—	0.45	—
1995 Proof	27,000	Value: 1.50				
1996	100,000,000	—	—	—	0.45	—
1996 Proof	25,000	Value: 2.50				
1997	—	—	—	—	0.45	—
1997 Proof	25,000	Value: 2.50				
1998	32,000,000	—	—	—	0.45	—
1998 Proof	25,000	Value: 3.00				
1999	—	—	—	—	0.45	—
1999 Proof	50,000	Value: 1.50				
2000	—	—	—	—	0.45	—
2000 Proof	75,000	Value: 1.50				

KM# 2877 20 GROSCHEN

Aluminum-Bronze **Obv:** Imperial Eagle with Austrian shield on breast, holding hammer and sickle **Rev:** Value at center above date

Date	Mintage	F	VF	XF	Unc	BU
1950	1,610,000	0.20	0.50	2.00	13.50	—
1950 Proof	—	Value: 40.00				
1951	7,781,000	0.10	0.25	0.75	2.75	—
1951 Proof	—	Value: 25.00				
1954	5,343,000	0.10	0.25	0.75	2.75	—
1954 Proof	—	Value: 275				

KM# 2870 50 GROSCHEN

Aluminum **Obv:** Imperial Eagle with Austrian shield on breast holding hammer and sickle **Rev:** Numeric value on Austrian shield at center, date divided below shield

Date	Mintage	F	VF	XF	Unc	BU
1946	13,058,000	0.20	0.50	1.75	10.00	—
1946 Proof	—	Value: 75.00				
1947	26,990,000	0.15	0.35	1.25	6.50	—
1947 Proof	—	Value: 35.00				
1952	7,455,000	0.40	1.00	2.50	8.50	—
1952 Proof	—	Value: 55.00				
1955	16,919,000	0.20	0.40	1.25	4.50	—
1955 Proof	—	Value: 55.00				

KM# 2885 50 GROSCHEN

3.0000 g., Aluminum-Bronze, 19.5 mm. **Obv:** Austrian shield **Obv. Designer:** Hans Köttenstorfer **Rev:** Large value above date **Rev. Designer:** Ferdinand Welz

Date	Mintage	F	VF	XF	Unc	BU
1959	14,122,000	—	0.50	2.00	15.00	—
1959 Proof	—	Value: 25.00				
1960	22,404,000	—	0.20	1.50	12.00	—
1960 Proof	—	Value: 100				
1961	19,891,000	—	0.50	2.00	15.00	—
1961 Proof	—	Value: 75.00				
1962	10,008,000	—	0.40	1.75	15.00	—
1962 Proof	—	Value: 40.00				
1963	9,483,000	—	0.50	2.00	18.00	—
1963 Proof	—	Value: 40.00				
1964	5,331,000	—	0.15	0.75	3.00	—
1964 Proof	—	Value: 1.50				
1965	1,500,700	—	0.15	0.75	3.00	—
1965 Proof	—	Value: 1.50				
1966	7,322,000	—	0.15	0.75	3.00	—
1966 Proof	—	Value: 10.00				
1967	8,237,000	—	0.15	0.75	3.00	—
1967 Proof	—	Value: 15.00				
1968	7,741,600	—	0.15	0.75	3.00	—
1968 Proof	15,400	Value: 10.00				
1969	7,070,000	—	0.15	0.75	3.00	—
1969 Proof	26,000	Value: 5.00				
1970	29,941,000	—	0.10	0.50	2.00	—
1970 Proof	128,000	Value: 3.00				
1971	14,217,000	—	—	0.25	1.50	—
1971 Proof	84,000	Value: 2.50				
1972	17,367,000	—	—	0.25	1.50	—
1972 Proof	80,000	Value: 2.00				
1973	17,902,000	—	—	0.25	1.50	—
1973 Proof	90,000	Value: 2.00				
1974	15,852,000	—	—	0.25	1.50	—
1974 Proof	76,000	Value: 2.00				
1975	7,726,000	—	—	0.15	1.00	—
1975 Proof	49,000	Value: 1.50				
1976	11,150,000	—	—	0.15	1.00	—
1976 Proof	44,000	Value: 1.50				
1977	7,258,000	—	—	0.15	1.00	—
1977 Proof	44,000	Value: 1.50				
1978	12,407,000	—	—	0.15	1.00	—
1978 Proof	43,000	Value: 1.50				
1979	16,351,000	—	—	0.15	1.00	—
1979 Proof	44,000	Value: 1.50				
1980	29,884,000	—	—	0.15	1.25	—
1980 Proof	48,000	Value: 3.50				
1981	12,993,000	—	—	0.15	1.25	—
1981 Proof	49,000	Value: 3.50				
1982	9,950,000	—	—	0.15	1.00	—
1982 Proof	50,000	Value: 1.50				
1983	15,182,000	—	—	0.15	1.00	—
1983 Proof	65,000	Value: 1.50				
1984	20,742,000	—	—	0.15	1.00	—
1984 Proof	65,000	Value: 2.00				
1985	15,654,000	—	—	0.15	1.00	—
1985 Proof	45,000	Value: 2.00				
1986	17,016,000	—	—	0.15	0.75	—
1986 Proof	42,000	Value: 2.00				
1987	7,258,000	—	—	0.15	0.75	—
1987 Proof	42,000	Value: 2.00				
1988	16,267,000	—	—	0.15	0.75	—
1988 Proof	39,000	Value: 2.00				
1989	17,353,000	—	—	0.15	0.75	—
1989 Proof	38,000	Value: 2.00				
1990	29,653,000	—	—	0.15	0.75	—
1990 Proof	35,000	Value: 2.00				
1991	44,990,000	—	—	0.15	0.75	—
1991 Proof	27,000	Value: 2.00				
1992	20,000,000	—	—	—	0.45	—
1992 Proof	25,000	Value: 2.00				
1993	15,000,000	—	—	—	0.45	—
1993 Proof	28,000	Value: 2.00				
1994	10,000,000	—	—	—	0.45	—
1994 Proof	25,000	Value: 2.50				
1995	20,000,000	—	—	—	0.45	—
1995 Proof	27,000	Value: 2.00				
1996	15,000,000	—	—	—	0.45	—
1996 Proof	25,000	Value: 2.50				
1997	10,000,000	—	—	—	0.45	—
1997 Proof	25,000	Value: 2.50				
1998	—	—	—	—	0.45	—
1998 Proof	25,000	Value: 3.00				
Note: In sets only						
1999	—	—	—	—	0.45	—
1999 Proof	50,000	Value: 2.00				
Note: In sets only						
2000	4,300,000	—	—	—	0.45	—
2000 Proof	75,000	Value: 2.00				
Note: In sets only						

KM# 2871 SCHILLING

Aluminum **Obv:** Full figure with seedbag on left hip, dropping seed from right hand, divides value **Rev:** Imperial Eagle with Austrian shield, tail dividing date

Date	Mintage	F	VF	XF	Unc	BU
1946	27,336,000	0.30	1.00	2.50	20.00	—
1946 Proof	—	Value: 500				
1947	35,838,000	0.20	0.50	1.50	6.00	—
1947 Proof	—	Value: 35.00				
1952	23,231,000	0.25	0.75	1.65	7.00	—
1952 Proof	—	Value: 50.00				
1957	28,649,000	0.25	0.75	1.65	7.00	—
1957 Proof	—	Value: 145				

KM# 2886 SCHILLING

4.2000 g., Aluminum-Bronze, 22.5 mm. **Obv:** Large value above date **Obv. Designer:** Edwin Grienauer **Rev:** Edelweiss flower **Rev. Designer:** Ferdinand Welz **Edge:** Plain

Date	Mintage	F	VF	XF	Unc	BU
1959	46,726,000	—	0.25	0.75	12.00	—
1959 Proof	—	Value: 15.00				
1960	46,111,000	—	0.25	1.50	20.00	—
1960 Proof	—	Value: 200				
1961	51,115,000	—	0.25	1.50	15.00	—
1961 Proof	—	Value: 400				
1962	9,303,000	—	0.25	1.50	15.00	—
1962 Proof	—	Value: 65.00				
1963	24,845,000	—	0.25	1.50	20.00	—
1963 Proof	—	Value: 45.00				
1964	11,709,000	—	0.25	1.25	3.50	—
1964 Proof	—	Value: 2.00				
1965	9,155,100	—	0.25	0.75	3.50	—
1965 Proof	27,900	Value: 8.00				
1966	18,688,000	—	0.25	0.75	3.50	—
1966 Proof	—	Value: 8.00				
1967	22,214,000	—	0.25	0.75	3.50	—
1967 Proof	—	Value: 12.00				
1968	30,860,000	—	0.25	0.75	3.50	—
1968 Proof	17,000	Value: 8.00				
1969	10,285,000	—	0.25	0.75	3.50	—
1969 Proof	28,000	Value: 4.00				
1970	10,678,600	—	0.20	0.50	2.50	—
1970 Proof	100,400	Value: 1.75				
1971	27,974,000	—	0.20	0.50	2.50	—
1971 Proof	82,000	Value: 1.75				
1972	54,577,000	—	0.15	0.30	1.50	—
1972 Proof	78,000	Value: 1.25				
1973	41,332,000	—	0.15	0.30	1.50	—
1973 Proof	90,000	Value: 1.25				
1974	43,712,000	—	0.15	0.30	1.50	—
1974 Proof	77,000	Value: 1.25				
1975	13,989,000	—	0.15	0.30	1.50	—
1975 Proof	49,000	Value: 1.25				
1976	28,748,000	—	0.15	0.30	1.50	—
1976 Proof	44,000	Value: 1.25				
1977	19,584,000	—	0.15	0.30	1.50	—
1977 Proof	44,000	Value: 1.25				
1978	35,632,000	—	0.15	0.30	1.50	—
1978 Proof	43,000	Value: 1.25				
1979	64,802,000	—	0.15	0.30	1.50	—
1979 Proof	44,000	Value: 1.25				

Date	Mintage	F	VF	XF	Unc	BU
1980	49,855,000	—	—	0.15	0.75	—
1980 Proof	48,000	Value: 2.50				
1981	37,502,000	—	—	0.15	0.75	—
1981 Proof	49,000	Value: 2.50				
1982	29,950,000	—	—	0.15	0.75	—
1982 Proof	50,000	Value: 1.50				
1983	38,186,000	—	—	0.15	0.75	—
1983 Proof	65,000	Value: 1.50				
1984	31,891,000	—	—	0.15	0.75	—
1984 Proof	65,000	Value: 1.50				
1985	49,154,000	—	—	0.15	0.75	—
1985 Proof	45,000	Value: 1.50				
1986	57,618,000	—	—	—	0.65	—
1986 Proof	42,000	Value: 1.50				
1987	44,158,000	—	—	—	0.65	—
1987 Proof	42,000	Value: 1.50				
1988	51,561,000	—	—	—	0.65	—
1988 Proof	39,000	Value: 1.50				
1989	62,821,000	—	—	—	0.65	—
1989 Proof	38,000	Value: 1.50				
1990	103,710,000	—	—	—	0.50	—
1990 Proof	35,000	Value: 1.50				
1991	117,700,000	—	—	—	0.50	—
1991 Proof	27,000	Value: 1.50				
1992	55,000,000	—	—	—	1.25	—
1992 Proof	25,000	Value: 2.00				
1993	60,000,000	—	—	—	1.25	—
1993 Proof	28,000	Value: 2.00				
1994	50,000,000	—	—	—	1.25	—
1994 Proof	25,000	Value: 3.00				
1995	70,000,000	—	—	—	1.25	—
1995 Proof	27,000	Value: 2.50				
1996	65,000,000	—	—	—	1.25	—
1996 Proof	25,000	Value: 3.50				
1997	50,000,000	—	—	—	1.25	—
1997 Proof	25,000	Value: 4.00				
1998	60,000,000	—	—	—	1.25	—
1998 Proof	25,000	Value: 4.50				
1999	—	—	—	—	1.25	—
1999 Proof	50,000	Value: 2.00				
Note: In sets only						
2000	42,200,000	—	—	—	1.25	—
2000 Proof	75,000	Value: 2.00				
Note: In sets only						

KM# 2872 2 SCHILLING

Aluminum **Obv:** Imperial Eagle with Austrian shield on breast, holding hammer and sickle **Rev:** Thick value above spray of leaves and berries, grain sprigs at top

Date	Mintage	F	VF	XF	Unc	BU
1946	10,082,000	0.45	1.25	2.75	25.00	—
1946 Proof	—	Value: 700				
1947	20,140,000	0.45	1.25	2.50	20.00	—
1947 Proof	—	Value: 40.00				
1952	149,000	55.00	100	200	350	—
1952 Proof	—	Value: 900				

KM# 2879 5 SCHILLING

Aluminum **Obv:** Large value at center, geared rim **Rev:** Imperial Eagle with Austrian shield on breast, holding hammer and sickle

Date	Mintage	F	VF	XF	Unc	BU
1952	29,873,000	1.00	2.00	5.00	12.50	—
1952 Proof	—	Value: 45.00				
1957	240,000	100	380	540	900	—
1957 Proof	—	Value: 700				

KM# 2889 5 SCHILLING

5.2000 g., 0.6400 Silver .1070 oz. ASW, 23.5 mm. **Obv:** Lippizaner stallion with rider, rearing, left **Obv. Designer:** Hans Köttenstorfer **Rev:** Austrian shield divides date, value above, sprays below **Rev. Designer:** Josef Köblinger **Edge:** Reeded

Date	Mintage	F	VF	XF	Unc	BU
1960	12,618,000	—	BV	2.50	5.50	—
1960 Proof	1,000	Value: 65.00				
1961	17,902,000	—	BV	2.50	4.50	—
1961 Proof	—	Value: 25.00				
1962	6,771,000	—	BV	2.50	4.50	—
1962 Proof	—	Value: 50.00				
1963	1,811,000	BV	2.00	4.00	14.50	—
1963 Proof	—	Value: 120				
1964	4,030,000	—	BV	2.00	3.50	—
1964 Proof	—	Value: 3.50				
1965	4,759,000	—	BV	2.00	3.50	—
1965 Proof	—	Value: 3.50				
1966	4,481,000	—	BV	2.00	3.50	—
1966 Proof	—	Value: 8.00				
1967	1,900,000	BV	2.00	4.00	6.00	—
1967 Proof	—	Value: 15.00				
1968	4,792,300	—	BV	2.00	3.50	—
1968 Proof	19,700	Value: 8.00				

KM# 2889a 5 SCHILLING

4.8000 g., Copper-Nickel, 23.5 mm. **Obv:** Lippizaner stallion with rider, rearing left **Obv. Designer:** Hans Köttenstorfer **Rev:** Austrian shield divides date, value above, sprays below **Rev. Designer:** Josef Köblinger **Edge:** Plain

Date	Mintage	F	VF	XF	Unc	BU
1968	2,075,000	—	1.00	2.50	5.00	—
1969	41,222,000	—	0.75	1.50	4.00	—
1969 Proof	21,000	Value: 6.00				
1970	15,770,700	—	—	1.00	4.00	—
1970 Proof	92,300	Value: 2.50				
1971	21,422,000	—	—	1.00	4.00	—
1971 Proof	84,000	Value: 2.50				
1972	5,430,000	—	—	1.00	4.00	—
1972 Proof	75,000	Value: 2.50				
1973	8,259,000	—	—	1.00	4.00	—
1973 Proof	87,000	Value: 2.50				
1974	17,956,000	—	—	1.00	4.00	—
1974 Proof	76,000	Value: 2.50				
1975	6,849,000	—	—	0.75	4.00	—
1975 Proof	49,000	Value: 2.50				
1976	1,458,000	—	—	1.00	5.00	—
1976 Proof	44,000	Value: 4.00				
1977	6,423,000	—	—	0.65	2.50	—
1977 Proof	44,000	Value: 2.75				
1978	9,907,000	—	—	0.65	2.50	—
1978 Proof	43,000	Value: 2.75				
1979	11,607,000	—	—	0.65	2.50	—
1979 Proof	44,000	Value: 2.75				
1980	14,898,000	—	—	0.65	2.50	—
1980 Proof	48,000	Value: 3.50				
1981	13,837,000	—	—	0.65	2.50	—
1981 Proof	49,000	Value: 3.50				
1982	4,950,000	—	—	0.65	2.00	—
1982 Proof	50,000	Value: 2.50				
1983	9,268,000	—	—	0.65	2.00	—
1983 Proof	65,000	Value: 2.50				
1984	13,763,000	—	—	0.65	2.00	—
1984 Proof	65,000	Value: 2.50				
1985	12,754,000	—	—	0.60	2.00	—
1985 Proof	45,000	Value: 3.00				
1986	16,558,000	—	—	0.60	2.00	—
1986 Proof	42,000	Value: 3.00				
1987	9,758,000	—	—	0.60	2.00	—
1987 Proof	42,000	Value: 3.00				
1988	10,161,000	—	—	0.60	2.00	—
1988 Proof	39,000	Value: 3.00				
1989	24,043,000	—	—	0.60	2.00	—
1989 Proof	38,000	Value: 3.00				
1990	36,512,000	—	—	0.60	2.00	—
1990 Proof	35,000	Value: 2.50				
1991	24,000,000	—	—	0.60	2.00	—
1991 Proof	27,000	Value: 2.50				
1992	20,000,000	—	—	—	2.00	—
1992 Proof	25,000	Value: 2.50				
1993	20,000,000	—	—	—	2.00	—
1993 Proof	28,000	Value: 2.50				

Date	Mintage	F	VF	XF	Unc	BU
1994	10,000,000	—	—	—	2.00	—
1994 Proof	25,000	Value: 3.50				
1995	20,000,000	—	—	—	2.00	—
1995 Proof	27,000	Value: 2.50				
1996	10,000,000	—	—	—	2.00	—
1996 Proof	25,000	Value: 3.50				
1997	10,000,000	—	—	—	2.00	—
1997 Proof	25,000	Value: 4.00				
1998	10,000,000	—	—	—	2.00	—
1998 Proof	25,000	Value: 4.50				
1999	—	—	—	—	2.00	—
1999 Proof	50,000	Value: 2.50				
Note: In sets only						
2000	1,500,000	—	—	—	2.00	—
2000 Proof	75,000	Value: 2.50				
Note: In sets only						

KM# 2882 10 SCHILLING

7.5000 g., 0.6400 Silver .1543 oz. ASW **Obv:** Austrian shield **Obv. Designer:** Kurt Bodlak **Rev:** Woman of Wachau, left, value at lower right, date to right of hat **Rev. Designer:** Ferdinand Welz

Date	Mintage	F	VF	XF	Unc	BU
1957	15,635,500	BV	2.25	3.00	7.50	—
1957 Proof	—	Value: 80.00				
1958	27,280,000	BV	2.25	3.00	7.50	—
1958 Proof	—	Value: 700				
1959	4,739,500	BV	2.25	3.50	11.50	—
1959 Proof	—	Value: 40.00				
1964	187,000	7.00	10.00	25.00	45.00	—
1964 Proof	27,000	Value: 15.00				
1965	1,721,000	BV	2.25	3.50	11.50	—
1965 Proof	—	Value: 8.00				
1966	3,430,500	BV	2.25	3.50	9.00	—
1966 Proof	—	Value: 12.00				
1967	1,393,500	BV	2.25	3.50	11.50	—
1967 Proof	—	Value: 15.00				
1968	1,525,000	BV	2.25	3.50	10.00	—
1968 Proof	15,000	Value: 9.00				
1969	1,317,500	BV	2.25	3.50	11.50	—
1969 Proof	20,000	Value: 12.00				
1970	4,493,900	—	BV	2.75	6.50	—
1970 Proof	89,100	Value: 5.00				
1971	7,320,500	—	BV	2.75	5.50	—
1971 Proof	80,000	Value: 5.00				
1972	14,210,500	—	BV	2.75	4.50	—
1972 Proof	75,000	Value: 5.00				
1973	14,559,000	—	BV	2.75	4.50	—
1973 Proof	80,000	Value: 5.00				

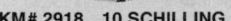

KM# 2918 10 SCHILLING

6.2000 g., Copper-Nickel Plated Nickel, 26 mm. **Obv:** Imperial Eagle with Austrian shield on breast, holding hammer and sickle **Obv. Designer:** Kurt Bodlak **Rev:** Woman of Wachau left, value and date right of hat **Rev. Designer:** Ferdinand Welz

Date	Mintage	F	VF	XF	Unc	BU
1974	59,877,000	—	—	2.00	6.00	—
1974 Proof	75,500	Value: 4.00				
1975	16,869,500	—	—	2.00	6.00	—
1975 Proof	49,000	Value: 3.00				
1976	13,459,500	—	—	2.00	6.00	—
1976 Proof	44,000	Value: 3.00				
1977	3,804,000	—	—	2.00	6.00	—
1977 Proof	44,000	Value: 3.00				
1978	6,813,000	—	—	2.00	6.00	—
1978 Proof	43,000	Value: 3.00				
1979	11,702,000	—	—	2.00	6.00	—
1979 Proof	44,000	Value: 2.50				
1980	10,884,000	—	—	2.00	6.00	—
1980 Proof	48,000	Value: 6.50				
1981	9,470,000	—	—	2.00	6.00	—
1981 Proof	49,000	Value: 6.50				
1982	4,950,000	—	—	2.00	5.00	—
1982 Proof	50,000	Value: 2.50				
1983	8,993,000	—	—	1.50	4.00	—
1983 Proof	65,000	Value: 2.50				
1984	7,936,000	—	—	1.50	4.00	—
1984 Proof	65,000	Value: 2.50				
1985	9,009,000	—	—	1.50	4.00	—
1985 Proof	45,000	Value: 2.50				
1986	8,189,000	—	—	1.50	4.00	—

Date	Mintage	F	VF	XF	Unc	BU
1986 Proof	42,000	Value: 2.50				
1987	9,258,000	—	—	1.50	4.00	—
1987 Proof	42,000	Value: 2.50				
1988	9,011,000	—	—	1.50	4.00	—
1988 Proof	39,000	Value: 4.50				
1989	16,233,000	—	—	1.25	3.00	—
1989 Proof	38,000	Value: 2.50				
1990	27,150,000	—	—	1.25	3.00	—
1990 Proof	35,000	Value: 2.50				
1991	18,000,000	—	—	1.25	3.00	—
1991 Proof	27,000	Value: 2.50				
1992	10,952,000	—	—	—	2.00	—
1992 Proof	25,000	Value: 2.50				
1993	12,500,000	—	—	—	2.00	—
1993 Proof	28,000	Value: 2.50				
1994	15,000,000	—	—	—	2.00	—
1994 Proof	25,000	Value: 3.50				
1995	12,500,000	—	—	—	2.00	—
1995 Proof	27,000	Value: 2.50				
1996	12,500,000	—	—	—	2.00	—
1996 Proof	25,000	Value: 4.00				
1997	11,000,000	—	—	—	2.00	—
1997 Proof	25,000	Value: 4.50				
1998	5,000,000	—	—	—	2.00	—
1998 Proof	25,000	Value: 5.00				
1999	—	—	—	—	2.00	—
1999 Proof	50,000	Value: 2.50				
Note: In sets only						
2000	1,175,000	—	—	—	2.00	—
2000 Proof	75,000	Value: 2.50				
Note: In sets only						

KM# 2946.1 20 SCHILLING

8.0000 g., Copper-Aluminum-Nickel, 27.8 mm. **Obv:** Nine people standing (representing the nine Austrian provinces), center figure holding Austrian shield aloft **Rev:** Numeric value within shaded box within circle, date below box **Edge:** Edge with incuse dots **Designer:** Helmut Zobol

Date	Mintage	F	VF	XF	Unc	BU
1980	9,851,500	—	—	2.50	3.50	—
1980 Proof	48,000	Value: 20.00				
1981	450,500	—	—	4.50	7.50	—
1981 Proof	49,000	Value: 22.50				
1991	140,000	—	—	2.25	5.00	—

KM# 2955.1 20 SCHILLING

8.0000 g., Copper-Aluminum-Nickel, 27.8 mm. **Subject:** 250th Anniversary - Birth of Joseph Haydn **Obv:** Value within box, small Austrian shield divides date below **Obv. Designer:** Kurt Bodlak **Rev:** Bust of Joseph Haydn, 3/4 right, two dates to his left, his name to his right **Rev. Designer:** Thomas Pesendorfer **Edge:** With incuse dots

Date	Mintage	F	VF	XF	Unc	BU
1982	3,100,000	—	—	2.25	3.50	—
1982 Proof	50,000	Value: 9.00				
1991	140,000	—	—	2.25	5.00	—

KM# 2955.2 20 SCHILLING

8.0000 g., Copper-Aluminum-Nickel, 27.8 mm. **Edge:** Plain

Date	Mintage	F	VF	XF	Unc	BU
1992	100,000	—	—	2.25	6.00	—
1993	180,000	—	—	2.25	5.00	—

KM# 2960.1 20 SCHILLING

8.0000 g., Copper-Aluminum-Nickel, 27.8 mm. **Obv:** Value within box, Austrian shield divides date below **Rev:** Hochosterwitz Castle, small double shield lower right, date at bottom **Edge:** With incuse dots **Designer:** Kurt Bodlak

Date	Mintage	F	VF	XF	Unc	BU
1983	1,002,000	—	—	2.25	3.50	—
1983 Proof	65,000	Value: 7.50				
1991	140,000	—	—	2.25	4.50	—

KM# 2965.1 20 SCHILLING

8.0000 g., Copper-Aluminum-Nickel, 27.8 mm. **Obv:** Value within box, Austrian shield divides date below **Obv. Designer:** Kurt Bodlak **Rev:** Grafenegg Palace, date at upper left **Rev. Designer:** Josef Kaiser **Edge:** With incuse dots

Date	Mintage	F	VF	XF	Unc	BU
1984	1,203,000	—	—	2.25	3.50	—
1984 Proof	65,000	Value: 7.50				
1991	140,000	—	—	2.25	4.50	—

KM# 2970.1 20 SCHILLING

8.0000 g., Copper-Aluminum-Nickel, 27.8 mm. **Subject:** 200th Anniversary - Diocese of Linz **Obv:** Value within box, Austrian shield divides date below **Obv. Designer:** Kurt Bodlak **Rev:** Two shields on decorative background within circle, two dates below circle **Rev. Designer:** Josef Fösleiter **Edge:** With incuse dots

Date	Mintage	F	VF	XF	Unc	BU
1985	814,000	—	—	2.25	4.50	—
1985 Proof	45,000	Value: 11.50				
1991	140,000	—	—	2.25	4.50	—

KM# 2975.1 20 SCHILLING

8.0000 g., Copper-Aluminum-Nickel, 27.8 mm. **Subject:** 800th Anniversary - Georgenberger Treaty **Obv:** Value within box, Austrian shield divides date below **Obv. Designer:** Kurt Bodlak **Rev:** Ottakar IV of Steyr and Leopold V of Austria holding the secret treaty **Rev. Designer:** Thomas Pesendorfer **Edge:** With incuse dots

Date	Mintage	F	VF	XF	Unc	BU
1986	801,000	—	—	2.25	4.50	—
1986 Proof	42,000	Value: 16.50				
1991	140,000	—	—	2.25	4.50	—

KM# 2975.2 20 SCHILLING

8.0000 g., Copper-Aluminum-Nickel, 27.8 mm. **Edge:** Plain

Date	Mintage	F	VF	XF	Unc	BU
1992	100,000	—	—	2.25	5.00	—
1993	180,000	—	—	2.25	4.50	—

KM# 2980.1 20 SCHILLING

8.0000 g., Copper-Aluminum-Nickel, 27.8 mm. **Subject:** 300th Anniversary - Birth of Salzburg's Archbishop Thun **Obv:** Value within box, Austrian shield divides date below **Obv. Designer:** Kurt Bodlak **Rev:** Bishop's hat above supported arms, dates below supporters, subject name at bottom with date below **Rev. Designer:** Josef Kaiser **Edge:** With incuse dots

Date	Mintage	F	VF	XF	Unc	BU
1987	508,000	—	—	2.25	4.50	—
1987 Proof	42,000	Value: 11.50				
1991	140,000	—	—	2.25	4.50	—

KM# 2980.2 20 SCHILLING

8.0000 g., Copper-Aluminum-Nickel, 27.8 mm. **Edge:** Plain

Date	Mintage	F	VF	XF	Unc	BU
1992	100,000	—	—	2.25	5.00	—
1993	180,000	—	—	2.25	4.50	—

KM# 2988.1 20 SCHILLING

8.0000 g., Copper-Aluminum-Nickel, 27.8 mm. **Obv:** Value within box, Austrian shield divides date below **Obv. Designer:** Kurt Bodlak **Rev:** Crowned eagle - Tyrol **Rev. Designer:** Thomas Pesendorfer **Edge:** With incuse dots

Date	Mintage	F	VF	XF	Unc	BU
1989	252,000	—	—	2.25	4.50	—
1989 Proof	38,000	Value: 8.00				
1991	140,000	—	—	2.25	4.50	—

KM# 2988.2 20 SCHILLING

8.0000 g., Copper-Aluminum-Nickel, 27.8 mm. **Edge:** Plain

Date	Mintage	F	VF	XF	Unc	BU
1992	100,000	—	—	2.25	5.00	—
1993	180,000	—	—	2.25	4.50	—

KM# 2993.1 20 SCHILLING

8.0000 g., Copper-Aluminum-Nickel, 27.8 mm. **Obv:** Value within box, Austrian shield divides date below **Obv. Designer:** Kurt Bodlak **Rev:** Martinsturm in Bregenz, small shield at upper left **Rev. Designer:** Herbert Wähner **Edge:** With incuse dots

Date	Mintage	F	VF	XF	Unc	BU
1990	250,000	—	—	2.25	4.50	—
1990 Proof	35,000	Value: 10.00				
1991	—	—	—	—	—	—
1991	140,000	—	—	2.25	4.50	—

KM# 2993.2 20 SCHILLING

8.0000 g., Copper-Aluminum-Nickel, 27.8 mm. **Edge:** Plain

Date	Mintage	F	VF	XF	Unc	BU
1992	100,000	—	—	2.25	5.00	—
1993	180,000	—	—	2.25	4.50	—

KM# 2995.1 20 SCHILLING

8.0000 g., Copper-Aluminum-Nickel, 27.8 mm. **Subject:** 200th Anniversary - Birth of Franz Grillparzer **Obv:** Value within shield, Austrian shield divides date below **Obv. Designer:** Kurt Bodlak **Rev:** Bust of Franz Grillparzer on left, looking right, theater building on the right **Rev. Designer:** Alfred Zierler **Edge:** With incuse dots

Date	Mintage	F	VF	XF	Unc	BU
1991	1,860,000	—	—	2.25	4.50	—
1991 Proof	27,000	Value: 10.00				

KM# 2995.2 20 SCHILLING

8.0000 g., Copper-Aluminum-Nickel, 27.8 mm. **Edge:** Plain

Date	Mintage	F	VF	XF	Unc	BU
1992	1,000,000	—	—	2.25	5.00	—
1992 Proof	25,000	Value: 12.50				
1993	1,800,000	—	—	2.25	4.50	—
1993 Proof	28,000	Value: 10.00				

KM# 2965.2 20 SCHILLING

8.0000 g., Copper-Aluminum-Nickel, 27.8 mm. **Edge:** Plain

Date	Mintage	F	VF	XF	Unc	BU
1992	100,000	—	—	2.25	5.00	—
1993	180,000	—	—	2.25	4.50	—

KM# 2960.2 20 SCHILLING

8.0000 g., Copper-Aluminum-Nickel, 27.8 mm. **Edge:** Plain

Date	Mintage	F	VF	XF	Unc	BU
1992	100,000	—	—	2.25	5.00	—
1993	180,000	—	—	2.25	4.50	—

KM# 2946.2 20 SCHILLING

8.0000 g., Copper-Aluminum-Nickel, 27.8 mm. **Edge:** Plain

Date	Mintage	F	VF	XF	Unc	BU
1992	.100,000	—	—	2.25	6.00	—
1992 Proof	25,000	Value: 10.00				
1993	180,000	—	—	2.25	5.00	—
1993 Proof	28,000	Value: 10.00				

KM# 2970.2 20 SCHILLING

8.0000 g., Copper-Aluminum-Nickel, 27.8 mm. **Edge:** Plain

Date	Mintage	F	VF	XF	Unc	BU
1992	100,000	—	—	2.25	5.00	—
1993	180,000	—	—	2.25	4.50	—

KM# 3016 20 SCHILLING

8.0000 g., Copper-Aluminum-Nickel, 27.8 mm. **Subject:** 800th Anniversary - Vienna Mint **Obv:** Value within box, Austrian shield divides date below **Obv. Designer:** Kurt Bodlak **Rev:** Vienna Mint, two dates below **Rev. Designer:** Thomas Pesendorfer

Date	Mintage	F	VF	XF	Unc	BU
1994	2,000,000	—	—	—	4.50	—
1994 Proof	25,000	Value: 12.50				

KM# 3022 20 SCHILLING

8.0000 g., Copper-Aluminum-Nickel, 27.8 mm. **Subject:** 1000th Anniversary - Krems **Obv:** Value within box, Austrian shield below **Obv. Designer:** Kurt Bodlak **Rev:** Krems within box, dates flanking, legend at top **Rev. Designer:** Thomas Pesendorfer and Christa Reiter

Date	Mintage	F	VF	XF	Unc	BU
1995	2,000,000	—	—	—	4.50	—
1995 Proof	27,000	Value: 10.00				

KM# 3033 20 SCHILLING

8.0000 g., Copper-Aluminum-Nickel, 27.8 mm. **Obv:** Value within box, Austrian shield divides date at bottom **Obv. Designer:** Kurt Bodlak **Rev:** Bust of Anton Bruckner, 3/4 facing, two dates below, name on the left, building on the right **Rev. Designer:** Christa Reiter

Date	Mintage	F	VF	XF	Unc	BU
1996	—	—	—	—	4.50	—
1996 Proof	25,000	Value: 15.00				

KM# 3041 20 SCHILLING

8.0000 g., Copper-Aluminum-Nickel, 27.8 mm. **Subject:** 850th Anniversary of St. Stephen's Cathedral **Obv:** Value within box, Austrian shield divides date below **Obv. Designer:** Kurt Bodlak **Rev:** St. Stephen's Cathedral, two dates above **Rev. Designer:** Thomas Pesendorfer

Date	Mintage	F	VF	XF	Unc	BU
1997	700,000	—	—	—	4.50	—
1997 Proof	25,000	Value: 16.50				

KM# 3048 20 SCHILLING

8.0000 g., Copper-Aluminum-Nickel, 27.8 mm. **Subject:** 500th Anniversary of Michael Pacher's Death **Obv:** Value within box, Austrian shield divides date below **Rev:** Pacher's altar at St. Wolfgang **Designer:** Herbert Wähner

Date	Mintage	F	VF	XF	Unc	BU
1998	200,000	—	—	—	5.00	—
1998 Proof	25,000	Value: 17.50				

KM# 3056 20 SCHILLING

8.0000 g., Copper-Aluminum-Nickel, 27.8 mm. **Obv:** Value within box, Austrian shield divides date below **Rev:** Hugo Von Hofmannsthal **Designer:** Herbert Wähner

Date	Mintage	F	VF	XF	Unc	BU
1999	400,000	—	—	—	4.50	—
1999 Proof	50,000	Value: 12.50				

KM# 3064 20 SCHILLING

8.0000 g., Brass, 27.8 mm. **Subject:** 150th Anniversary - First Austrian Postage Stamp **Obv:** Value within box, Austrian shield divides date below **Rev:** Canceled stamp design **Edge:** Plain **Designer:** Andreas Zanaschka

Date	Mintage	F	VF	XF	Unc	BU
2000	400,000	—	—	—	4.50	—
2000 Proof	75,000	Value: 12.50				

KM# 2880 25 SCHILLING

13.0000 g., 0.8000 Silver .3344 oz. ASW, 30.5 mm. **Subject:** Reopening of the National Theater in Vienna **Obv:** Dragon within 3/4 circle of shields, larger Austrian shield at lower left, value to right of this **Rev:** Muse with mask and lyre

Date	Mintage	F	VF	XF	Unc	BU
1955	1,499,000	5.00	7.50	10.00	20.00	—
1955 Proof	Est. 5,000	Value: 100				

KM# 2881 25 SCHILLING

13.0000 g., 0.8000 Silver .3344 oz. ASW, 30.5 mm. **Subject:** 200th Anniversary - Birth of Wolfgang Mozart **Obv:** Value within beaded circle, small spray of leaves below, surrounded by 3/4 circle of shields, **Rev:** Full length statue of Wolfgang Mozart, two dates below **Rev. Designer:** Grienauer

Date	Mintage	F	VF	XF	Unc	BU
1956	4,999,000	—	—	4.50	5.50	—
1956 Proof	Est. 1,500	Value: 350				

KM# 2883 25 SCHILLING

13.0000 g., 0.8000 Silver .3344 oz. ASW, 30.5 mm. **Subject:** 8th Centennial - Mariazell Basilica **Obv:** Value within beaded circle, small spray of leaves below, 3/4 circle of shields surrounding **Rev:** Mariazell Basilica, name below, two dates at bottom **Rev. Designer:** Grienauer **Designer:** Edwin Grienauer

Date	Mintage	F	VF	XF	Unc	BU
1957	4,999,000	—	—	4.50	5.50	—
1957 Proof	Est. 1,500	Value: 300				

KM# 2884 25 SCHILLING

13.0000 g., 0.8000 Silver .3344 oz. ASW, 30.5 mm. **Subject:** 100th Anniversary - Birth of Auer von Welsbach, Chemist **Obv:** Value within beaded circle, small spray below, 3/4 circle of shields surrounds **Rev:** Head of Auer von Welsbach, right, date below **Rev. Designer:** Ludwig Jujer

Date	Mintage	F	VF	XF	Unc	BU
1958	4,999,000	—	—	4.50	5.50	—
1958 Proof	Est. 500	Value: 1,500				

KM# 2887 25 SCHILLING

13.0000 g., 0.8000 Silver .3344 oz. ASW, 30.5 mm. **Subject:** Centennial - Death of Archduke Johann, military leader in the trench wars **Obv:** Dragon within 3/4 circle of shields, larger Austrian shield lower left, value to right of this **Rev:** Collared head of Archduke Johann, right, collar divides date **Rev. Designer:** Norz

Date	Mintage	F	VF	XF	Unc	BU
1959	1,899,000	—	—	4.75	6.00	—
1959 Proof	Est. 1,000	Value: 300				

KM# 2890 25 SCHILLING

13.0000 g., 0.8000 Silver .3344 oz. ASW, 30.5 mm. **Subject:** 40th Anniversary - Carinthian Plebescite **Obv:** Value within beaded circle above small spray of leaves, 3/4 circle of shields surrounds **Rev:** Large urn dividing two standing figures, shield below urn divides date **Rev. Designer:** Kottenstorfer

Date	Mintage	F	VF	XF	Unc	BU
1960	1,599,000	—	—	4.75	6.00	—
1960 Proof	Est. 900	Value: 350				

KM# 2891 25 SCHILLING
13.0000 g., 0.8000 Silver .3344 oz. ASW, 30.5 mm. **Subject:** 40th Anniversary - Burgenland, Haydenkirche in Eisenstadt **Obv:** Value within beaded circle, small sprays below, 3/4 circle of shields surrounding **Rev:** Building, two dates lower left

Date	Mintage	F	VF	XF	Unc	BU
1961	1,399,000	—	—	4.75	6.00	—
1961 Proof	Est. 1,200	Value: 175				

KM# 2892 25 SCHILLING
13.0000 g., 0.8000 Silver .3344 oz. ASW, 30.5 mm. **Obv:** Value within beaded circle, small spray of leaves below, 3/4 circle of shields surrounding **Rev:** Head of Anton Bruckner, right, Composer, date below **Rev. Designer:** Grienauer

Date	Mintage	F	VF	XF	Unc	BU
1962	2,399,000	—	—	4.50	5.50	—
1962 Proof	Est. 3,000	Value: 150				

KM# 2893 25 SCHILLING
13.0000 g., 0.8000 Silver .3344 oz. ASW, 30.5 mm. **Subject:** 300th Anniversary - Birth of Prince Eugen **Obv:** Value within beaded circle, small spray of leaves below, 3/4 circle of shields surrounding **Rev:** Half-length figure of Prince Eugen pointing, left, facing right, date below **Rev. Designer:** Grienauer

Date	Mintage	F	VF	XF	Unc	BU
1963	1,994,000	—	—	4.50	5.50	—
1963 Proof	5,931	Value: 80.00				

KM# 2895.1 25 SCHILLING
13.0000 g., 0.8000 Silver .3344 oz. ASW, 30.5 mm. **Obv:** Value within circle of shields **Rev:** Head of Franz Grillparzer, Poet, right, date below **Rev. Designer:** Grienauer **Designer:** Edwin Grienauer

Date	Mintage	F	VF	XF	Unc	BU
1964	1,664,000	—	—	4.75	6.00	—
1964 Proof	36,000	Value: 8.00				

KM# 2895.2 25 SCHILLING
13.0000 g., 0.8000 Silver .3344 oz. ASW, 30.5 mm. **Obv:** Value within beaded circle, small spray of leaves below, surrounded by 3/4 circle of shields **Rev:** Head of Franz Grillparzer, right, date below **Rev. Designer:** Grienauer **Note:** Obverse; Nine shields, (error)

Date	Mintage	F	VF	XF	Unc	BU
1964 Proof	3,660	Value: 300				

KM# 2897 25 SCHILLING
13.0000 g., 0.8000 Silver .3344 oz. ASW, 30.5 mm. **Subject:** 150th Anniversary - Vienna Technical High School **Obv:** Value within circle of shields **Rev:** J.J. Ritter von Prechtl, technologist, director

Date	Mintage	F	VF	XF	Unc	BU
1965	1,563,000	—	—	4.75	6.00	—
1965 Proof	37,000	Value: 15.00				

KM# 2899 25 SCHILLING
13.0000 g., 0.8000 Silver .3344 oz. ASW, 30.5 mm. **Subject:** 130th Anniversary - Death of Ferdinand Raimund **Obv:** Value within circle of shields **Rev:** Half-length figure of Ferdinand Raimund, arms crossed, 3/4 right, date on right **Rev. Designer:** F. Welz

Date	Mintage	F	VF	XF	Unc	BU
1966	1,388,000	—	—	4.75	6.00	—
1966 Proof	11,800	Value: 50.00				

KM# 2901 25 SCHILLING
13.0000 g., 0.8000 Silver .3344 oz. ASW, 30.5 mm. **Subject:** 250th Anniversary - Birth of Maria Theresa, Empress **Obv:** Value within circle of shields **Rev:** Bust of Maria Theresa, right, divides dates, date below right shoulder

Date	Mintage	F	VF	XF	Unc	BU
1967	2,472,000	—	—	4.50	5.50	—
1967 Proof	28,000	Value: 25.00				

KM# 2903 25 SCHILLING
13.0000 g., 0.8000 Silver .3344 oz. ASW, 30.5 mm. **Subject:** 300th Anniversary - Birth of Von Hildebrandt **Obv:** Value within circle of shields **Rev:** Main gateway to Belvedere Castle

Date	Mintage	F	VF	XF	Unc	BU
1968	1,258,000	—	—	5.00	8.50	—
1968 Proof	42,000	Value: 18.00				

KM# 2905 25 SCHILLING
13.0000 g., 0.8000 Silver .3344 oz. ASW, 30.5 mm. **Obv:** Value within circle of shields **Rev:** Head of Peter Rosegger, poet, writer left, date below

Date	Mintage	F	VF	XF	Unc	BU
1969	1,356,000	—	—	4.75	6.00	—
1969 Proof	44,000	Value: 18.00				

KM# 2907 25 SCHILLING
13.0000 g., 0.8000 Silver .3344 oz. ASW, 30.5 mm. **Subject:** 100th Anniversary - Birth of Franz Lehar, Composer **Obv:** Value within circle of shields **Rev:** Head of Franz Lehar,3/4 left, date to the left, two dates below **Rev. Designer:** F. Welz

Date	Mintage	F	VF	XF	Unc	BU
1970	1,661,000	—	—	4.50	5.50	—
1970 Proof	139,000	Value: 7.50				

KM# 2910 25 SCHILLING
13.0000 g., 0.8000 Silver .3344 oz. ASW, 30.5 mm. **Subject:** 200th Anniversary - Vienna Bourse **Obv:** Value within circle of shields **Rev:** City building, two dates below, Austrian shield lower right

Date	Mintage	F	VF	XF	Unc	BU
1971	1,804,000	—	—	4.50	5.00	—
1971 Proof	196,000	Value: 6.00				

KM# 2912 25 SCHILLING
13.0000 g., 0.8000 Silver .3344 oz. ASW, 30.5 mm. **Subject:** 50th Anniversary - Death of Carl M. Ziehrer, Composer **Obv:** Value within circle of shields **Rev:** Head of Carl M. Ziehrer, facing, three dates below

Date	Mintage	F	VF	XF	Unc	BU
ND(1972)	1,955,000	—	—	4.50	5.00	—
ND(1972) Proof	145,000	Value: 6.00				

KM# 2915 25 SCHILLING
13.0000 g., 0.8000 Silver .3344 oz. ASW, 30.5 mm. **Subject:** 100th Anniversary - Birth of Max Reinhardt, Producer, Theatrical manager **Obv:** Value within circle of shields **Rev:** Head of Max Reinhardt, left, three dates below

Date	Mintage	F	VF	XF	Unc	BU
ND(1973)	2,323,000	—	—	4.50	5.00	—
ND(1973) Proof	177,000	Value: 6.00				

KM# 2888 50 SCHILLING

20.0000 g., 0.9000 Silver .5787 oz. ASW, 34 mm. **Subject:** 150th Anniversary - Liberation of Tyrol **Obv:** Imperial Eagle within 3/4 circle of shields, wreath encircling head **Obv. Designer:** Michael Norz **Rev:** Andreas Hofer facing forward, two dates below **Rev. Designer:** Edwin Grienauer

Date	Mintage	F	VF	XF	Unc	BU
ND(1959)	2,999,000	—	BV	8.00	10.00	—
ND(1959) Proof	Est. 800	Value: 425				

KM# 2894 50 SCHILLING

20.0000 g., 0.9000 Silver .5787 oz. ASW, 34 mm. **Subject:** 600th Anniversary - Union with Tirol **Obv:** Value within beaded circle, small spray below, 3/4 circle of shields surrounding **Obv. Designer:** Arnold Hartig **Rev:** Arms of Tyrol and Austria above two dates **Rev. Designer:** Ferdinand Welz

Date	Mintage	F	VF	XF	Unc	BU
ND(1963)	2,989,600	—	BV	8.00	9.00	—
ND(1963) Proof	10,400	Value: 75.00				

KM# 2896 50 SCHILLING

20.0000 g., 0.9000 Silver .5787 oz. ASW, 34 mm. **Series:** Winter Olympics **Obv:** Value within beaded circle, small spray of leaves below, 3/4 circle of shields surrounding **Obv. Designer:** Arnold Hartig **Rev:** Innsbruck - Ski jumper, left, Olympic logo above **Rev. Designer:** Edwin Grienauer

Date	Mintage	F	VF	XF	Unc	BU
1964	2,832,050	—	BV	8.00	10.00	—
1964 Proof	67,950	Value: 20.00				

KM# 2898 50 SCHILLING

20.0000 g., 0.9000 Silver .5787 oz. ASW, 34 mm. **Subject:** 600th Anniversary - Vienna University **Obv:** Value within circle of shields **Obv. Designer:** Edwin Grienauer **Rev:** Crowned head, 3/4 right **Rev. Designer:** Ferdinand Welz

Date	Mintage	F	VF	XF	Unc	BU
ND(1965)	2,163,000	—	BV	8.00	9.00	—
ND(1965) Proof	37,000	Value: 30.00				

KM# 2900 50 SCHILLING

20.0000 g., 0.9000 Silver .5787 oz. ASW, 34 mm. **Subject:** 150th Anniversary - National Bank **Obv:** Value within circle of shields **Obv. Designer:** Edwin Grienauer **Rev:** National Bank building above two line inscription, two dates below **Rev. Designer:** Michael Norz

Date	Mintage	F	VF	XF	Unc	BU
ND(1966)	1,782,600	—	BV	8.00	9.00	—
ND(1966) Proof	17,400	Value: 60.00				

KM# 2902 50 SCHILLING

20.0000 g., 0.9000 Silver .5787 oz. ASW, 34 mm. **Subject:** Centennial of the Blue Danube Waltz **Obv. Designer:** Edwin Grienauer **Rev:** Johann Strauss the Younger, playing the violin, date below **Rev. Designer:** Kurt Bodlak

Date	Mintage	F	VF	XF	Unc	BU
1967	2,973,900	—	BV	8.00	9.00	—
1967 Proof	26,100	Value: 60.00				

KM# 2904.1 50 SCHILLING

20.0000 g., 0.9000 Silver .5787 oz. ASW, 34 mm. **Subject:** 50th Anniversary - The Republic **Obv:** Value within circle of shields **Obv. Designer:** Edwin Grienauer **Rev:** Parliament building in Vienna, matte surface between pillars, dates divided at bottom **Rev. Designer:** Fritz Tiefenthaler

Date	Mintage	F	VF	XF	Unc	BU
ND(1968)	1,660,200	—	BV	8.00	9.00	—
ND(1968) Proof	39,800	Value: 22.50				

KM# 2904.2 50 SCHILLING

20.0000 g., 0.9000 Silver .5787 oz. ASW, 34 mm. **Rev:** Parliament building in Vienna, proof surface between pillars

Date	Mintage	F	VF	XF	Unc	BU
1968 Proof	—	Value: 150				

KM# 2906 50 SCHILLING

20.0000 g., 0.9000 Silver .5787 oz. ASW, 34 mm. **Subject:** 450th Anniversary - Death of Maximilian I **Obv:** Value within circle of shields **Obv. Designer:** Edwin Grienauer **Rev:** Bust of Maximillian I with hat, right, dates in legend **Rev. Designer:** Hans Köttenstorfer

Date	Mintage	F	VF	XF	Unc	BU
1969	2,045,000	—	BV	8.00	9.00	—
1969 Proof	55,000	Value: 22.50				

KM# 2908 50 SCHILLING

20.0000 g., 0.9000 Silver .5787 oz. ASW, 34 mm. **Subject:** 300th Anniversary - Innsbruck University **Obv:** Value within circle of shields **Obv. Designer:** Edwin Grienauer **Rev:** 1673 University seal, date at bottom **Rev. Designer:** Fritz Tiefenthaler

Date	Mintage	F	VF	XF	Unc	BU
1970	2,087,300	—	BV	8.00	9.00	—
1970 Proof	11,700	Value: 9.00				

KM# 2909 50 SCHILLING

20.0000 g., 0.9000 Silver .5787 oz. ASW, 34 mm. **Subject:** 100th Anniversary - Birth of Dr. Karl Renner, president **Obv:** Value within circle of shields **Rev:** Head of Dr. Karl Renner, right, date on left collar, two dates at left

Date	Mintage	F	VF	XF	Unc	BU
1970	2,213,800	—	BV	8.00	9.00	—
1970 Proof	286,200	Value: 8.00				

KM# 2911 50 SCHILLING

20.0000 g., 0.9000 Silver .5787 oz. ASW, 34 mm. **Subject:** 80th Anniversary - Birth of Julius Raab, chancellor **Obv:** Value within circle of shields **Obv. Designer:** Edwin Grienauer **Rev:** Head of Julius Raab, right, date below, two dates at left **Rev. Designer:** Hans Köttenstorfer

Date	Mintage	F	VF	XF	Unc	BU
1971	2,317,000	—	BV	8.00	9.00	—
1971 Proof	183,000	Value: 8.00				

KM# 2913 50 SCHILLING

20.0000 g., 0.9000 Silver .5787 oz. ASW, 34 mm. **Subject:** 350th Anniversary - Salzburg University **Obv:** Value within circle of shields **Obv. Designer:** Edwin Grienauer **Rev:** Great seal of the University within circle, three dates below **Rev. Designer:** Kurt Bodlak

Date	Mintage	F	VF	XF	Unc	BU
ND(1972)	2,864,000	—	BV	8.00	9.00	—
ND(1972) Proof	136,000	Value: 8.00				

KM# 2914 50 SCHILLING
20.0000 g., 0.9000 Silver .5787 oz. ASW, 34 mm. **Subject:** 100th Anniversary - Institute of Agriculture **Obv:** Value within circle of shields **Obv. Designer:** Edwin Grienauer **Rev:** Institute of Agriculture, shields flank inscription and dates below **Rev. Designer:** Fritz Tiefenthaler

Date	Mintage	F	VF	XF	Unc	BU
ND(1972)	1,891,000	—	BV	8.00	9.00	—
ND(1972) Proof	109,000	Value: 8.00				

KM# 2916 50 SCHILLING
20.0000 g., 0.9000 Silver .5787 oz. ASW, 34 mm. **Subject:** 500th Anniversary - Bummerl House **Obv:** Value within circle of shields **Obv. Designer:** Edwin Grienauer **Rev:** Bummerl House within circle, two shields flank date at top **Rev. Designer:** Fritz Tiefenthaler

Date	Mintage	F	VF	XF	Unc	BU
1973	2,841,800	—	BV	8.00	9.00	—
1973 Proof	158,200	Value: 8.00				

KM# 2917 50 SCHILLING
20.0000 g., 0.9000 Silver .5787 oz. ASW, 34 mm. **Subject:** 100th Anniversary - Birth of Dr. Theodor Korner, President **Obv:** Value within circle of shields **Obv. Designer:** Edwin Grienauer **Rev:** Head of Dr. Theodor Korner, right, three dates below **Rev. Designer:** Rudolf Schmidt

Date	Mintage	F	VF	XF	Unc	BU
ND(1973)	2,868,000	—	BV	8.00	9.00	—
ND(1973) Proof	131,600	Value: 8.00				

KM# 2919 50 SCHILLING
20.0000 g., 0.6400 Silver .4115 oz. ASW **Subject:** Vienna International Flower show **Obv:** Value within circle of shields **Obv. Designer:** Edwin Grienauer **Rev:** International Flower Show, date at bottom **Rev. Designer:** Helmut Zobl

Date	Mintage	F	VF	XF	Unc	BU
1974	2,279,000	—	—	5.50	6.50	—
1974 Proof	221,000	Value: 7.50				

KM# 2920 50 SCHILLING
20.0000 g., 0.6400 Silver .4115 oz. ASW **Subject:** 125th Anniversary - Austrian Police Force **Obv:** Value within circle of shields **Obv. Designer:** Edwin Grienauer **Rev:** Imperial Eagle on shield, within wreath, within circle **Rev. Designer:** Fritz Tiefenthaler

Date	Mintage	F	VF	XF	Unc	BU
ND(1974)	2,258,600	—	—	5.50	6.50	—
ND(1974) Proof	241,400	Value: 7.50				

KM# 2921 50 SCHILLING
20.0000 g., 0.6400 Silver .4115 oz. ASW **Subject:** 1200th Anniversary - Salzburg Cathedral **Obv:** Value within circle of shields **Obv. Designer:** Edwin Grienauer **Rev:** St. Rupert and St. Vincent holding cathedral, date below **Rev. Designer:** Hans Köttenstorfer

Date	Mintage	F	VF	XF	Unc	BU
1974	2,292,600	—	—	5.50	6.50	—
1974 Proof	207,400	Value: 7.50				

KM# 2922 50 SCHILLING
20.0000 g., 0.6400 Silver 04115 oz. ASW **Subject:** 50th Anniversary - Austrian Broadcasting **Obv:** Value within circle of shields **Obv. Designer:** Edwin Grienauer **Rev:** Broadcasting symbol, two dates at top **Rev. Designer:** Helga Wenisch

Date	Mintage	F	VF	XF	Unc	BU
1974	2,290,000	—	—	5.50	6.50	—
1974 Proof	210,000	Value: 7.50				

KM# 2937 50 SCHILLING
20.0000 g., 0.6400 Silver 04115 oz. ASW **Subject:** 150th Anniversary - Death of Franz Schubert, Composer **Obv:** Value within circle of shields **Obv. Designer:** Edwin Grienauer **Rev:** Bust of Franz Schubert, looking left, date below **Rev. Designer:** Alfred Zierler

Date	Mintage	F	VF	XF	Unc	BU
1978	1,868,000	—	—	5.50	6.50	—
1978 Proof	132,000	Value: 7.50				

KM# 3038 50 SCHILLING
Bi-Metallic Copper-Nickel Clad Nickel center in Aluminum-Bronze ring, 26.5 mm. **Subject:** Austrian Millennium **Obv:** Circle of provincial arms around denomination **Obv. Designer:** Herbert Wähner **Rev:** Arms below Heinrich I as knight on horse back, within circle, two dates at right **Rev. Designer:** Andreas Zanaschka

Date	Mintage	F	VF	XF	Unc	BU
ND(1996)	900,000	—	—	—	14.00	—
ND(1996) BU	100,000	—	—	—	25.00	—

KM# 3044 50 SCHILLING
Bi-Metallic Copper-Nickel Clad Nickel center in Aluminum-Bronze ring, 26.5 mm. **Subject:** 100th Anniversary - Wiener Secession **Obv:** Value within circle of provincial arms **Obv. Designer:** Herbert Wähner **Rev:** Vienna Secession building portal within circle, two dates at bottom, divided **Rev. Designer:** Andreas Zanaschka

Date	Mintage	F	VF	XF	Unc	BU
ND(1997)	1,500,000	—	—	—	8.00	—
ND(1997) BU	100,000	—	—	—	11.50	—

KM# 3050 50 SCHILLING
Bi-Metallic Copper-Nickel Clad Nickel center in Aluminum-Bronze ring, 26.5 mm. **Subject:** Austrian Presidency of the European Union **Obv:** Value within circle of provincial arms **Obv. Designer:** Herbert Wähner **Rev:** New Hofburg palace with logo, within circle, date at bottom **Rev. Designer:** Thomas Pesendorfer

Date	Mintage	F	VF	XF	Unc	BU
1998	1,200,000	—	—	—	8.00	—
1998 BU	100,000	—	—	—	11.50	—

KM# 3053 50 SCHILLING
Bi-Metallic Copper-Nickel Clad Nickel center in Aluminum-Bronze ring, 26.5 mm. **Obv:** Value within circle of provincial arms **Obv. Designer:** Herbert Wähner **Rev:** Head of Konrad Lorenz, looking right, with three Greylag geese on the right, within circle, two dates below circle **Rev. Designer:** Thomas Pesendorfer

Date	Mintage	F	VF	XF	Unc	BU
1998	1,200,000	—	—	—	7.00	—
1998 Special Unc	100,000	—	—	—	9.00	—

KM# 3057 50 SCHILLING
Bi-Metallic Copper-Nickel Clad Nickel center in Aluminum-Bronze ring, 26.5 mm. **Subject:** Euro Currency **Obv:** Value within circle of provincial arms **Obv. Designer:** Herbert Wähner **Rev:** Euro currency designs within circle, date below **Rev. Designer:** Thomas Pesendorfer

Date	Mintage	F	VF	XF	Unc	BU
1999	1,200,000	—	—	—	7.00	—
1999 Special Unc	100,000	—	—	—	9.00	—

KM# 3061 50 SCHILLING
Bi-Metallic Copper-Nickel clad Nickel center in Aluminum-Bronze ring, 26.5 mm. **Subject:** Centenary - Death of Johann Strauss **Obv:** Value within circle of provincial arms **Obv. Designer:** Herbert Wähner **Rev:** Bust of Johann Strauss, facing right, two dates to his right, two figures to his left, all within circle, music notes below circle **Rev. Designer:** Helmut Andexlinger

Date	Mintage	F	VF	XF	Unc	BU
ND(1999)	600,000	—	—	—	7.00	—
ND(1999) Special Unc	100,000	—	—	—	9.00	—

KM# 3066 50 SCHILLING
Bi-Metallic Copper-Nickel clad Nickel center in Aluminum-Bronze ring, 26.5 mm. **Obv:** Value within circle of provincial arms **Obv. Designer:** Herbert Wähner **Rev:** Bust of Sigmund Freud facing 1/4 left, two dates at upper right, all within circle **Rev. Designer:** Thomas Pesendorfer and Gustav Klimt **Edge:** Plain

Date	Mintage	F	VF	XF	Unc	BU
ND(2000)	600,000	—	—	—	7.00	—
ND(2000) Special Unc	90,000	—	—	—	9.00	—

KM# 3070 50 SCHILLING
Bi-Metallic Copper-Nickel clad Nickel center in Aluminum-Bronze ring, 26.5 mm. **Obv:** Value within circle of provincial arms **Obv. Designer:** Herbert Wähner **Rev:** Antique automobile on left and portrait of Ferdinand Porsche, facing, on right within circle, two dates lower right of circle **Rev. Designer:** Thomas Pesendorfer **Edge:** Plain **Note:** 100,000 of the Unc. coins are in blister-packs, with a value of $8.00 each.

Date	Mintage	F	VF	XF	Unc	BU
2000	700,000	—	—	—	7.00	—

KM# 2926 100 SCHILLING
23.9300 g., 0.6400 Silver .4924 oz. ASW **Series:** Winter Olympics - Innsbruck **Obv:** Value within circle of shields **Rev:** Emblem, Olympic logo above **Rev. Designer:** Ferdinand Welz

Date	Mintage	F	VF	XF	Unc	BU
ND(1974)	2,826,000	—	—	—	9.00	—
ND(1974) Proof	374,000	Value: 10.00				

KM# 2927 100 SCHILLING
23.9300 g., 0.6400 Silver .4924 oz. ASW **Series:** Winter Olympics - Innsbruck **Obv:** Box surrounds stylized Imperial Eagle, Austrian shield on breast, holding hammer and sickle above value, small shield below box **Obv. Designer:** Helmuth Gsollpointner **Rev:** Buildings and Olympic logo **Rev. Designer:** Arthur Zelger

Date	Mintage	F	VF	XF	Unc	BU
ND(1974)(h)	2,692,000	—	—	—	9.00	—
ND(1974)(v) Select	Inc. above	—	—	—	12.50	—
ND(1974)(h) Proof	223,000	Value: 10.00				
ND(1974)(v)	2,718,000	—	—	—	9.00	—
ND(1974)(h) Select	Inc. above	—	—	—	12.50	—
ND(1974)(v) Proof	232,000	Value: 10.00				

KM# 2928 100 SCHILLING
23.9300 g., 0.6400 Silver .4924 oz. ASW **Series:** Winter Olympics - Innsbruck **Obv:** Box surrounds stylized Imperial Eagle, Austrian shield on breast, holding hammer and sickle above value, small shield below box **Rev:** Skier

Date	Mintage	F	VF	XF	Unc	BU
ND(1974)(h)	2,636,000	—	—	—	9.00	—
ND(1974)(v) Select	Inc. above	—	—	—	12.50	—
ND(1974)(h) Proof	179,000	Value: 10.00				
ND(1974)(v)	2,641,000	—	—	—	9.00	—
ND(1974)(h) Select	Inc. above	—	—	—	12.50	—
ND(1974)(v) Proof	184,000	Value: 10.00				

KM# 2929 100 SCHILLING
23.9300 g., 0.6400 Silver .4924 oz. ASW **Series:** Winter Olympics - Innsbruck **Obv:** Box surrounds stylized Imperial Eagle, Austrian shield on breast, above value, small shield below box **Rev:** Ski jump, Olympic logo upper left, circle surrounds, date lower right

Date	Mintage	F	VF	XF	Unc	BU
ND(1974)(h)	2,611,000	—	—	—	9.00	—
ND(1974)(h) Select	Inc. above	—	—	—	12.50	—
ND(1974)(h) Proof	179,000	Value: 10.00				
ND(1974)(v)	2,627,000	—	—	—	9.00	—
ND(1974)(v) Select	Inc. above	—	—	—	12.50	—
ND(1974)(v) Proof	188,000	Value: 10.00				

KM# 2923 100 SCHILLING
23.9300 g., 0.6400 Silver .4924 oz. ASW **Subject:** 150th Anniversary - Birth of Johann Strauss the Younger, Composer **Obv:** Value within circle of shields **Rev:** Monument with standing statue of Strauss with violin, date below

Date	Mintage	F	VF	XF	Unc	BU
1975	2,646,000	—	—	—	9.00	—
1975 Select	Inc. above	—	—	—	12.00	—
1975 Proof	209,000	Value: 10.00				

KM# 2924 100 SCHILLING
23.9300 g., 0.6400 Silver .4924 oz. ASW **Subject:** 20th Anniversary - State Treaty **Obv:** Box surrounds stylized Imperial Eagle, Austrian shield on breast, holding hammer and sickle, value below **Rev:** Round Austrian shield at center, date below **Designer:** Helmuth Gsollpointner

Date	Mintage	F	VF	XF	Unc	BU
1975	3,215,000	—	—	—	9.00	—
1975 Select	Inc. above	—	—	—	10.00	—
1975 Proof	225,000	Value: 10.00				

KM# 2925 100 SCHILLING
23.9300 g., 0.6400 Silver .4924 oz. ASW **Subject:** 50th Anniversary - Schilling **Obv:** Box surrounds stylized Imperial Eagle, Austrian shield on breast, holding hammer and sickle, value below **Obv. Designer:** Helmuth Gsollpointer **Rev:** Sower, a plowed field **Rev. Designer:** Helmut Zobl

Date	Mintage	F	VF	XF	Unc	BU
1975	3,234,000	—	—	—	9.00	—
1975 Select	Inc. above	—	—	—	10.00	—
1975 Proof	201,000	Value: 10.00				

KM# 2930 100 SCHILLING
23.9300 g., 0.6400 Silver .4924 oz. ASW **Subject:** 200th Anniversary - Burgtheater **Obv:** Value within circle of shields **Rev:** Burgtheater, small crowned double eagle divides dates at top

Date	Mintage	F	VF	XF	Unc	BU
ND(1976)	1,630,000	—	—	—	9.50	—
ND(1976) Select	Inc. above	—	—	—	11.50	—
ND(1976) Proof	220,000	Value: 11.50				

KM# 2931 100 SCHILLING
23.9300 g., 0.6400 Silver .4924 oz. ASW **Subject:** 1000th Anniversary - Carinthia **Obv:** Box surrounds stylized Imperial Eagle, Austrian shield on breast, value below **Rev:** Monument, shield at lower right, two dates at bottom

Date	Mintage	F	VF	XF	Unc	BU
ND(1976)	1,632,000	—	—	—	9.50	—

Date	Mintage	F	VF	XF	Unc	BU
ND(1976) Select	Inc. above	—	—	—	11.50	—
ND(1976) Proof	168,000	Value: 11.50				

KM# 2932 100 SCHILLING
23.9300 g., 0.6400 Silver .4924 oz. ASW **Subject:** 175th Anniversary - Birth of Johann Nestroy, Singer **Obv:** Value surrounds Imperial Eagle with Austrian shield on breast **Rev:** Head of Johann Nestroy, 3/4 left, two dates on the right, one date on left

Date	Mintage	F	VF	XF	Unc	BU
1976	1,761,000	—	—	—	9.50	—
1976 Select	—	—	—	—	11.50	—
1976 Proof	139,000	Value: 11.50				

KM# 2934 100 SCHILLING
23.9300 g., 0.6400 Silver .4924 oz. ASW **Subject:** 1200th Anniversary - Kremsmunster Monastery **Obv:** Value within circle of shields **Rev:** Chalice, divides dates at top

Date	Mintage	F	VF	XF	Unc	BU
ND(1977)	1,865,000	—	—	—	9.50	—
ND(1977) Select	Inc. above	—	—	—	11.50	—
ND(1977) Proof	135,000	Value: 12.50				

KM# 2935 100 SCHILLING
23.9300 g., 0.6400 Silver .4924 oz. ASW **Subject:** 900th Anniversary - Hohensalzburg Fortress **Obv:** Box surrounds stylized Imperial Eagle, Austrian shield on breast, value below **Rev:** Hohensalzburg Fortress on right, dates divided by four line inscription on left

Date	Mintage	F	VF	XF	Unc	BU
1977	1,878,000	—	—	—	9.50	—
1977 Select	Inc. above	—	—	—	11.50	—
1977 Proof	122,000	Value: 12.50				

KM# 2936 100 SCHILLING
23.9300 g., 0.6400 Silver .4924 oz. ASW **Subject:** 500th Anniversary - Hall Mint **Obv:** Value and three rows of shields within circle, two dates below circle **Rev:** Knight in full armor on armored horseback, right,and four shields, within circle,date in legend, two shields below circle

Date	Mintage	F	VF	XF	Unc	BU
1977	1,868,000	—	—	—	9.50	—

Date	Mintage	F	VF	XF	Unc	BU
1977 Select	Inc. above	—	—	—	11.50	—
1977 Proof	132,000	Value: 16.50				

KM# 2938 100 SCHILLING
23.9300 g., 0.6400 Silver .4924 oz. ASW **Subject:** 700th Anniversary - Gmunden **Obv:** Box surrounds stylized Imperial Eagle, Austrian shield on breast,holding hammer and sickle, value below **Rev:** Gmunden, building within circle, two dates at upper left

Date	Mintage	F	VF	XF	Unc	BU
1978	1,870,000	—	—	—	9.50	—
1978 Select	Inc. above	—	—	—	11.50	—
1978 Proof	130,000	Value: 12.50				

KM# 2939 100 SCHILLING
23.9300 g., 0.6400 Silver .4924 oz. ASW **Subject:** 700th Anniversary - Battle of Durnkrut and Jedenspeigen **Obv:** Standing figures holding hands form a circle with an Austrian shield at center, value below, beaded circle surrounds all **Rev:** Bust of Rudolf I

Date	Mintage	F	VF	XF	Unc	BU
1978	1,677,000	—	—	—	9.50	—
1978 Select	Inc. above	—	—	—	11.50	—
1978 Proof	123,000	Value: 12.50				

KM# 2940 100 SCHILLING
23.9300 g., 0.6400 Silver .4924 oz. ASW **Subject:** 1100th Anniversary - Founding of Villach **Obv:** Box surrounds stylized Imperial Eagle, Austrian shield on breast, holding hammer and sickle, value below **Rev:** Village divides shields with dates above

Date	Mintage	F	VF	XF	Unc	BU
ND(1978)	1,569,000	—	—	—	9.50	—
ND(1978) Select	Inc. above	—	—	—	11.50	—
ND(1978) Proof	131,000	Value: 12.50				

KM# 2941 100 SCHILLING
23.9300 g., 0.6400 Silver .4924 oz. ASW **Subject:** Opening of Arlberg Tunnel **Obv:** Value and three rows of shields within circle, date below circle divided by small hammer and sickle emblem **Rev:** Sun above banner, mountains below, hands in front of mountains, circle surrounds all, two dates in legend, two shields below circle

Date	Mintage	F	VF	XF	Unc	BU
1978	1,764 000	—	—	—	9.50	—
1978 Select	80,000	—	—	—	11.50	—
1978 Proof	156,000	Value: 12.50				

KM# 2942 100 SCHILLING
23.9300 g., 0.6400 Silver .4924 oz. ASW **Subject:** 700th Anniversary - Cathedral of Wiener Neustadt **Obv:** Imperial Eagle with Austrian shield on breast, holding hammer and sickle, value below **Rev:** Cathedral, date at bottom

Date	Mintage	F	VF	XF	Unc	BU
1979	1,796,000	—	—	—	9.50	—
1979 Select	70,000	—	—	—	11.50	—
1979 Proof	134,000	Value: 12.50				

KM# 2943 100 SCHILLING
23.9300 g., 0.6400 Silver .4924 oz. ASW **Subject:** 200th Anniversary - Inn District

Date	Mintage	F	VF	XF	Unc	BU
1979	1,795,000	—	—	—	9.50	—
1979 Select	75,000	—	—	—	11.50	—
1979 Proof	130,000	Value: 12.50				

KM# 2944 100 SCHILLING
23.9300 g., 0.6400 Silver .4924 oz. ASW **Obv:** Value within circle of shields **Rev:** Vienna International center, date bottom right

Date	Mintage	F	VF	XF	Unc	BU
1979	1,780,000	—	—	—	9.50	—
1979 Select	75,000	—	—	—	11.50	—
1979 Proof	145,000	Value: 12.50				

KM# 2945 100 SCHILLING
23.9300 g., 0.6400 Silver .4924 oz. ASW **Obv:** Value within circle of shields **Rev:** Festival and Congress Hall at Bregenz, date lower right

Date	Mintage	F	VF	XF	Unc	BU
1979	1,498,000	—	—	—	9.50	—
1979 Select	75,000	—	—	—	11.50	—
1979 Proof	161,000	Value: 12.50				

KM# 2996 100 SCHILLING
20.0000 g., 0.9000 Silver .5209 oz. ASW, 34 mm. **Obv:** Mozart-Salzburg, value below **Rev:** Mozart with violin and piano, right, two dates at left **Designer:** Thomas Pesenforfer

Date	Mintage	F	VF	XF	Unc	BU
1991 Proof	100,000	Value: 32.50				

KM# 2998 100 SCHILLING
20.0000 g., 0.9000 Silver .5209 oz. ASW, 34 mm. **Obv:** Mozart's Vienna Years- Burgtheater, value below **Rev:** Mozart seated at piano, left, two dates at right **Designer:** Thomas Pesenforfer

Date	Mintage	F	VF	XF	Unc	BU
1991 Proof	100,000	Value: 32.50				

KM# 3001 100 SCHILLING
20.0000 g., 0.9000 Silver .5209 oz. ASW, 34 mm. **Obv:** Rudolph I seated on throne flanked by figures kneeling, value at bottom **Rev:** Half-length figure of Rudolph I, facing **Designer:** Alfred Zierler

Date	Mintage	F	VF	XF	Unc	BU
1991 Proof	75,000	Value: 135				

KM# 3003 100 SCHILLING
20.0000 g., 0.9000 Silver .5209 oz. ASW, 34 mm. **Obv:** Two seated figures facing each other, ribbon between heads, value at bottom **Rev:** Half-length figure of Maximillian I, with crown and armor, right **Designer:** Thomas Pesendorfer

Date	Mintage	F	VF	XF	Unc	BU
1992 Proof	75,000	Value: 75.00				

KM# 3005 100 SCHILLING
20.0000 g., 0.9000 Silver .5788 oz. ASW, 34 mm. **Obv:** Theater building, value below **Rev:** Bust of Otto Nicolai, 3/4 right **Designer:** Thomas Pesendorfer

Date	Mintage	F	VF	XF	Unc	BU
1992 Proof	75,000	Value: 35.00				

KM# 3007 100 SCHILLING
18.0000 g., 0.9000 Silver .5209 oz. ASW, 34 mm. **Obv:** Two half-length figures, 3/4 left, above inscription, value at bottom **Rev:** 3/4 length figure of Karl V in armor,facing 1/4 left, shield above each shoulder **Designer:** Herbert Wähner

Date	Mintage	F	VF	XF	Unc	BU
1992 Proof	75,000	Value: 50.00				

KM# 3009 100 SCHILLING
20.0000 g., 0.9000 Silver .5209 oz. ASW, 34 mm. **Obv:** Armed figures on kneeling horses outside of city, value at bottom **Rev:** Kaiser Leopold I, in armor and robe, facing 1/4 right **Designer:** Thomas Pesendorfer

Date	Mintage	F	VF	XF	Unc	BU
1993 Proof	75,000	Value: 35.00				

KM# 3019 100 SCHILLING
20.0000 g., 0.9000 Silver .5209 oz. ASW, 34 mm. **Obv:** City buildings with water in foreground, date below, value at bottom **Rev:** Half-length figure of Franz Joseph I in uniform, 3/4 facing, two small crowns at left **Designer:** Thomas Pesendorfer

Date	Mintage	F	VF	XF	Unc	BU
1994 Proof	75,000	Value: 35.00				

KM# 3020 100 SCHILLING
20.0000 g., 0.9000 Silver .5209 oz. ASW, 34 mm. **Subject:** 1848 Revolution **Obv:** Armed figures and Bishop in front of church, value at bottom **Rev:** Seated half-length figure of Archduke Johann, 3/4 facing, looking right, two dates to right of left hand **Designer:** Thomas Pesendorfer

Date	Mintage	F	VF	XF	Unc	BU
1994 Proof	75,000	Value: 35.00				

KM# 3034 100 SCHILLING
20.0000 g., 0.9000 Silver .5209 oz. ASW, 34 mm. **Subject:** First Republic **Obv:** Columned buildings, statue at right, people in foreground, date below, value at bottom **Obv. Designer:** Thomas Pesendorfer **Rev:** Coin, buildings and symbols, two dates lower right **Rev. Designer:** Herbert Wähner

Date	Mintage	F	VF	XF	Unc	BU
1995 Proof	75,000	Value: 35.00				

KM# 3036 100 SCHILLING
20.0000 g., 0.9000 Silver .5209 oz. ASW, 34 mm. **Obv:** Four armored figures divide date, value at bottom **Obv. Designer:** Thomas Pesendorfer **Rev:** Crowned half-length figure of Leopold III, facing, Austrian shield in left hand **Rev. Designer:** Herbert Wähner

Date	Mintage	F	VF	XF	Unc	BU
1996 Proof	75,000	Value: 35.00				

KM# 3046 100 SCHILLING
20.0000 g., 0.9000 Silver .5209 oz. ASW, 34 mm. **Series:** Habsburg Tragedies **Obv:** Standing portrait in uniform of Emperor Maximilian of Mexico **Obv. Designer:** Herbert Wähner **Rev:** Miramar palace and the SMS Novard **Rev. Designer:** Andreas Zanaschka

Date	Mintage	F	VF	XF	Unc	BU
1997 Proof	45,000	Value: 40.00				

KM# 3051 100 SCHILLING
20.0000 g., 0.9000 Silver .5209 oz. ASW, 34 mm. **Series:** Habsburg Tragedies **Obv:** Standing portrait in uniform of Crown Prince Rudolf, 3/4 left **Obv. Designer:** Herbert Wähner **Rev:** Hearse with military honor guard **Rev. Designer:** Andreas Zanaschka

Date	Mintage	F	VF	XF	Unc	BU
1998 Proof	Est. 40,000	Value: 40.00				

KM# 3059 100 SCHILLING
20.0000 g., 0.9000 Silver .5209 oz. ASW, 34 mm. **Series:** Habsburg Tragedies **Obv:** Archduke Franz Ferdinand and Sophie, 3/4 right **Rev:** The Royal couple getting into the car **Designer:** Thomas Pesendorfer

Date	Mintage	F	VF	XF	Unc	BU
1999 Proof	50,000	Value: 40.00				

KM# 3063 100 SCHILLING
Bi-Metallic Titanium center in Silver ring, 34 mm. **Subject:** Communications **Obv:** Computer chip design **Obv. Designer:** Herbert Wähner **Rev:** World map at center in ring **Rev. Designer:** Andreas Zanaschka **Edge:** Plain

Date	Mintage	F	VF	XF	Unc	BU
2000 Proof	50,000	Value: 45.00				

KM# 3068 100 SCHILLING
20.0000 g., 0.9000 Silver .5209 oz. ASW, 34 mm. **Obv:** Celtic salt miner **Rev:** Celtic coin design with mounted warrior **Edge:** Reeded **Designer:** Thomas Pesendorfer

Date	Mintage	F	VF	XF	Unc	BU
2000 Proof	30,000	Value: 40.00				

KM# 3069 100 SCHILLING
20.0000 g., 0.9000 Silver .5209 oz. ASW, 34 mm. **Obv:** Ancient Roman troops crossing pontoon bridge **Rev:** Bust of Marcus Aurelius right **Edge:** Reeded **Designer:** Thomas Pesendorfer

Date	Mintage	F	VF	XF	Unc	BU
2000 Proof	30,000	Value: 40.00				

KM# 3026 200 SCHILLING
33.6300 g., 0.9250 Silver 1.0000 oz. ASW **Series:** Olympic Centenary, 1896-1996 **Obv:** Male and Female figures standing with outstretched arms joined form a circle around Austrian shield, value and date at bottom **Rev:** Ribbon dancer on knees, left, looking up, Olympic logo upper right **Edge Lettering:** CITIUS ALTIUS FORTIUS

Date	Mintage	F	VF	XF	Unc	BU
1995 Proof	Est. 100,000	Value: 32.50				

KM# 3027 200 SCHILLING
33.6300 g., 0.9250 Silver 1.0000 oz. ASW **Series:** Olympics **Rev:** Skier **Edge Lettering:** CITIUS ALTIUS FORTIUS

Date	Mintage	F	VF	XF	Unc	BU
1995 Proof	Est. 100,000	Value: 32.50				

KM# 2947 500 SCHILLING
24.0000 g., 0.6400 Silver .4930 oz. ASW **Subject:** Millennium **Obv:** Value within circle of shields **Obv. Designer:** Edwin Grienauer **Rev:** City of Steyr **Rev. Designer:** H. Köttenstorfer

Date	Mintage	F	VF	XF	Unc	BU
1980	825,800	—	—	—	50.00	—
1980 Select	63,000	—	—	—	52.00	—
1980 Proof	111,200	Value: 58.00				

KM# 2948 500 SCHILLING
24.0000 g., 0.6400 Silver .4930 oz. ASW **Subject:** 25th Anniversary - State Treaty **Obv:** Value within circle of shields **Obv. Designer:** Edwin Grienauer **Rev:** Belvedere Castle, two dates below **Rev. Designer:** A. Zemann

Date	Mintage	F	VF	XF	Unc	BU
ND(1980)	787,000	—	—	—	50.00	—
ND(1980) Select	79,000	—	—	—	52.00	—
ND(1980) Proof	134,000	Value: 58.00				

KM# 2949 500 SCHILLING
24.0000 g., 0.6400 Silver .4930 oz. ASW **Subject:** Bicentennial - Death of Maria Theresa **Obv:** Value within circle of shields **Obv. Designer:** Edwin Grienauer **Rev:** Bust of Maria Theresa, right, date at right **Rev. Designer:** Kurt Bodlak

Date	Mintage	F	VF	XF	Unc	BU
1980	842,000	—	—	—	50.00	—
1980 Select	86,400	—	—	—	50.00	—
1980 Proof	171,600	Value: 55.00				

KM# 2950 500 SCHILLING
24.0000 g., 0.6400 Silver .4930 oz. ASW **Subject:** Centennial - Austrian Red Cross **Obv:** Value within circle of shields **Obv. Designer:** Edwin Grienauer **Rev:** Henri Dunant, Philanthropist, two dates at right **Rev. Designer:** Kurt Bodlak

Date	Mintage	F	VF	XF	Unc	BU
ND(1980)	860,000	—	—	—	50.00	—
ND(1980) Select	90,000	—	—	—	50.00	—
ND(1980) Proof	200,000	Value: 55.00				

KM# 2951 500 SCHILLING
24.0000 g., 0.6400 Silver .4930 oz. ASW **Subject:** 800th Anniversary - Verdun Altar **Obv:** Value within circle of shields **Obv. Designer:** Edwin Grienauer **Rev:** Man fighting lion in doorway divides dates, within circle **Rev. Designer:** Kurt Bodlak

Date	Mintage	F	VF	XF	Unc	BU
ND(1981)	865,000	—	—	—	50.00	—
ND(1981) Select	85,000	—	—	—	50.00	—
ND(1981) Proof	200,000	Value: 58.00				

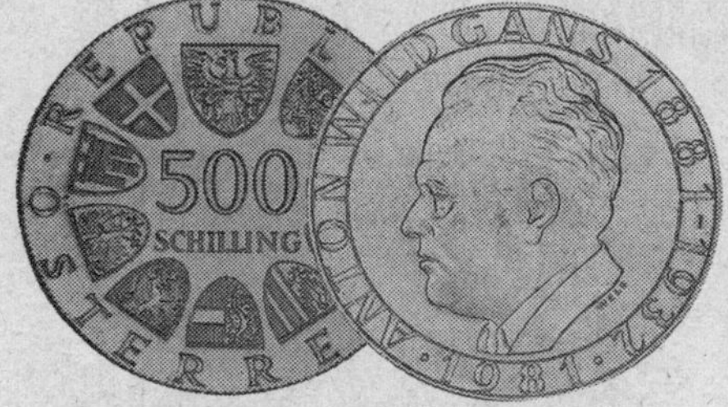

KM# 2952 500 SCHILLING
24.0000 g., 0.6400 Silver .4930 oz. ASW **Subject:** 100th Anniversary - Birth of Anton Wildgans, Writer **Obv:** Value within circle of shields **Obv. Designer:** Edwin Grienauer **Rev:** Head of Anton Wildgans, left, within circle, three dates outside circle **Rev. Designer:** Ferdinand Welz

Date	Mintage	F	VF	XF	Unc	BU
1981	911,200	—	—	—	50.00	—
1981 Select	72,000	—	—	—	50.00	—
1981 Proof	166,800	Value: 55.00				

KM# 2953 500 SCHILLING
24.0000 g., 0.6400 Silver .4930 oz. ASW **Subject:** 100th Anniversary - Birth of Otto Bauer, Politician **Obv:** Value within circle of shields **Obv. Designer:** Edwin Grienauer **Rev:** Head of Otto Bauer, 3/4 left, two dates at right **Rev. Designer:** Alfred Zierler

Date	Mintage	F	VF	XF	Unc	BU
ND(1981)	929,000	—	—	—	50.00	—
ND(1981) Select	65,000	—	—	—	50.00	—
ND(1981) Proof	156,000	Value: 55.00				

KM# 2954 500 SCHILLING
24.0000 g., 0.6400 Silver .4930 oz. ASW **Subject:** 200th Anniversary - Religious Tolerance **Obv:** Value within circle of shields **Obv. Designer:** Edwin Grienauer **Rev:** Cross with religious symbols below, dates above, within circle **Rev. Designer:** Wolfgang Pichl

Date	Mintage	F	VF	XF	Unc	BU
ND(1981)	792,000	—	—	—	50.00	—
ND(1981) Select	60,000	—	—	—	50.00	—
ND(1981) Proof	148,000	Value: 55.00				

KM# 2956 500 SCHILLING
24.0000 g., 0.6400 Silver .4930 oz. ASW **Subject:** 1500th Anniversary - Death of St. Severin **Obv:** Value within circle of shields **Obv. Designer:** Edwin Grienauer **Rev:** Standing figure of St. Severin divides dates, urns lower left, pillars at lower right **Rev. Designer:** F. Mayr

Date	Mintage	F	VF	XF	Unc	BU
ND(1982)	837,400	—	—	—	50.00	—
ND(1982) Select	42,600	—	—	—	50.00	—
ND(1982) Proof	120,000	Value: 55.00				

KM# 2957 500 SCHILLING
24.0000 g., 0.6400 Silver .4930 oz. ASW **Subject:** 500 Years of Austrian Printing **Obv:** Value within circle of shields **Obv. Designer:** Edwin Grienauer **Rev:** Ancient printing system, date at bottom **Rev. Designer:** Kurt Bodlak

Date	Mintage	F	VF	XF	Unc	BU
1982	589,600	—	—	—	50.00	—
1982 Select	42,200	—	—	—	50.00	—
1982 Proof	118,200	Value: 55.00				

KM# 2958 500 SCHILLING
24.0000 g., 0.6400 Silver .4930 oz. ASW **Subject:** 825 Years of the Mariazell Shrine **Obv:** Value within circle of shields **Obv. Designer:** Edwin Grienauer **Rev:** Standing figure of enshrined Madonna of Mariazell holding child, date below in leaves **Rev. Designer:** Fritz Tiefenthaler

Date	Mintage	F	VF	XF	Unc	BU
1982	589,600	—	—	—	50.00	—

Date	Mintage	F	VF	XF	Unc	BU
1982 Select	41,600	—	—	—	50.00	—
1982 Proof	118,800	Value: 55.00				

KM# 2959 500 SCHILLING
24.0000 g., 0.6400 Silver .4930 oz. ASW **Subject:** 80th Anniversary - Birth of Leopold Figl **Obv:** Value within circle of shields **Obv. Designer:** Edwin Grienauer **Rev:** Bust of Leopold Figl, left **Rev. Designer:** Alfred Zierler

Date	Mintage	F	VF	XF	Unc	BU
1982	344,000	—	—	—	50.00	—
1982 Select	39,600	—	—	—	50.00	—
1982 Proof	116,400	Value: 60.00				

KM# 2961 500 SCHILLING
24.0000 g., 0.9250 Silver .7125 oz. ASW **Subject:** World Cup Horse Jumping Championship **Obv:** Value within circle of shields **Obv. Designer:** Edwin Grienauer **Rev:** Horse Jumper **Rev. Designer:** Thomas Pesendorfer

Date	Mintage	F	VF	XF	Unc	BU
1983	367,600	—	—	—	50.00	—
1983 Proof	132,400	Value: 55.00				

KM# 2962 500 SCHILLING
24.0000 g., 0.9250 Silver .7125 oz. ASW **Subject:** Centennial - Vienna City Hall **Obv:** Value within circle of shields **Rev:** Vienna City Hall, dates below

Date	Mintage	F	VF	XF	Unc	BU
ND(1983)	466,200	—	—	—	50.00	—
ND(1973) Proof	133,800	Value: 55.00				

KM# 2963 500 SCHILLING
24.0000 g., 0.9250 Silver .7125 oz. ASW **Subject:** Catholic Day - Pope's Visit **Obv:** Value within circle of shields **Obv. Designer:** Edwin Grienauer **Rev:** Pope Johannes Paul II, left, arms raised, cross with Jesus in left hand, cross dividing date behind head **Rev. Designer:** Fritz Tiefenthaler

Date	Mintage	F	VF	XF	Unc	BU
1983	600,000	—	—	—	50.00	—
1983 Select	60,000	—	—	—	50.00	—
1983 Proof	140,000	Value: 55.00				

KM# 2964 500 SCHILLING
24.0000 g., 0.9250 Silver .7125 oz. ASW **Subject:** Centennial - Parliament Building **Obv:** Value within circle of shields **Obv. Designer:** Edwin Grienauer **Rev:** Parliament Building, date upper left **Rev. Designer:** Werner Kugler

Date	Mintage	F	VF	XF	Unc	BU
1983	522,600	—	—	—	50.00	—
1983 Proof	137,000	Value: 55.00				

KM# 2966 500 SCHILLING
24.0000 g., 0.9250 Silver .7125 oz. ASW **Subject:** 175th Anniversary - Tirolean Revolution **Obv:** Value within circle of shields **Obv. Designer:** Edwin Grienauer **Rev:** Atatue of Tirolean Man standing, two dates lower left **Rev. Designer:** Alfred Zierler

Date	Mintage	F	VF	XF	Unc	BU
ND(1984)	455,400	—	—	—	50.00	—
ND(1984) Proof	144,600	Value: 55.00				

KM# 2967 500 SCHILLING
24.0000 g., 0.9250 Silver .7125 oz. ASW **Subject:** 100th Anniversary - Commercial Shipping on Lake Constance **Obv:** Value within circle of shields **Obv. Designer:** Edwin Grienauer **Rev:** Commercial ship on water, within 3/4 circle, date below, left of small shield **Rev. Designer:** Kurt Bodlak

Date	Mintage	F	VF	XF	Unc	BU
1984	457,800	—	—	—	50.00	—
1984 Proof	142,200	Value: 55.00				

KM# 2968 500 SCHILLING
24.0000 g., 0.9250 Silver .7125 oz. ASW **Subject:** 700th Anniversary - Stams Stift in Tirol **Obv:** Value within circle of shields **Obv. Designer:** Edwin Grienauer **Rev:** Building, small shield below **Rev. Designer:** Alfred Zierler

Date	Mintage	F	VF	XF	Unc	BU
1984	462,000	—	—	—	50.00	—
1984 Proof	138,000	Value: 55.00				

KM# 2969 500 SCHILLING

24.0000 g., 0.9250 Silver .7125 oz. ASW **Subject:** Centennial - Death of Fanny Elssler **Obv:** Value within circle of shields **Obv. Designer:** Edwin Grienauer **Rev:** Full-length view of Fanny Elssler, 1810-1884, in inner circle **Rev. Designer:** Fritz Tiefenthaler

Date	Mintage	F	VF	XF	Unc	BU
1984	464,800	—	—	—	50.00	—
1984 Proof	135,200	Value: 55.00				

KM# 2971 500 SCHILLING

24.0000 g., 0.9250 Silver .7125 oz. ASW **Subject:** 400th Anniversary - Graz University **Obv:** Value within circle of shields **Obv. Designer:** Edwin Grienauer **Rev:** Bust of Archduke with ruffled collar, right, date below, within circle **Rev. Designer:** Kurt Bodlak

Date	Mintage	F	VF	XF	Unc	BU
1985	481,000	—	—	—	50.00	—
1985 Proof	119,000	Value: 55.00				

KM# 2972 500 SCHILLING

24.0000 g., 0.9250 Silver .7125 oz. ASW **Subject:** 40 Years of Peace in Austria **Obv:** Value within circle of shields **Obv. Designer:** Edwin Grienauer **Rev:** Woman standing in front of Austrian map holding branch of leaves **Rev. Designer:** Alfred Zierler

Date	Mintage	F	VF	XF	Unc	BU
ND(1985)	384,000	—	—	—	50.00	—
ND(1985) Proof	116,000	Value: 55.00				

KM# 2973 500 SCHILLING

24.0000 g., 0.9250 Silver .7125 oz. ASW **Subject:** 500th Anniversary - Canonization of Leopold III **Obv:** Value within circle of shields **Obv. Designer:** Edwin Grienauer **Rev:** Crowned standing figure of Leopold III, facing, holding model of church in left hand, divides dates **Rev. Designer:** Christa Reiter

Date	Mintage	F	VF	XF	Unc	BU
ND(1985)	388,000	—	—	—	50.00	—
ND(1985) Proof	112,000	Value: 55.00				

KM# 2974 500 SCHILLING

24.0000 g., 0.9250 Silver .7125 oz. ASW **Subject:** 2000th Anniversary - Bregenz **Obv:** Value within circle of shields **Obv. Designer:** Edwin Grienauer **Rev:** Two coins on coin, left one with laureate head right, right one with shield of arms, date at bottom **Rev. Designer:** Kurt Bodlak

Date	Mintage	F	VF	XF	Unc	BU
1985	387,800	—	—	—	50.00	—
1985 Proof	112,200	Value: 55.00				

KM# 2976 500 SCHILLING

24.0000 g., 0.9250 Silver .7125 oz. ASW **Subject:** 300th Anniversary - St. Florian's Abbey **Obv:** Value within circle of shields **Rev:** St. Florian's Abbey, two dates below, small shield lower left

Date	Mintage	F	VF	XF	Unc	BU
ND(1986)	303,200	—	—	—	50.00	—
ND(1986) Proof	96,800	Value: 55.00				

KM# 2977 500 SCHILLING

24.0000 g., 0.9250 Silver .7125 oz. ASW **Subject:** 500th Anniversary - First Thaler Coin Struck at Hall Mint **Obv:** Value within circle of shields **Obv. Designer:** Edwin Grienauer **Rev:** Crowned figure with scepter, center, small eagle with shield at left, within inner circle, two dates below circle **Rev. Designer:** Kurt Bodlak

Date	Mintage	F	VF	XF	Unc	BU
ND(1986)	302,000	—	—	—	50.00	—
ND(1986) Proof	99,000	Value: 58.00				

KM# 2978 500 SCHILLING

24.0000 g., 0.9250 Silver .7125 oz. ASW **Subject:** 250th Anniversary - Birth of Prince Eugene of Savoy **Obv:** Value within circle of shields **Obv. Designer:** Edwin Grienauer **Rev:** Man on rearing horse, three dates at bottom **Rev. Designer:** Thomas Pesendorfer

Date	Mintage	F	VF	XF	Unc	BU
1986	300,400	—	—	—	50.00	—
1986 Proof	99 600	Value: 55.00				

KM# 2979 500 SCHILLING

24.0000 g., 0.9250 Silver .7125 oz. ASW **Subject:** European Conference on Security and Cooperation **Obv:** Value within circle of shields **Obv. Designer:** Edwin Grienauer **Rev:** Globe with map at top, inscription below, small shield at bottom with date to right **Rev. Designer:** Josef Kaiser

Date	Mintage	F	VF	XF	Unc	BU
1986	202,600	—	—	—	50.00	—
1986 Proof	97,400	Value: 55.00				

KM# 2981 500 SCHILLING

24.0000 g., 0.9250 Silver .7125 oz. ASW **Subject:** 150th Anniversary - Austrian Railroad **Obv:** Value within circle of shields **Obv. Designer:** Edwin Grienauer **Rev:** Trains, two dates to lower right **Rev. Designer:** Alfred Zierler

Date	Mintage	F	VF	XF	Unc	BU
ND(1987)	206,000	—	—	—	50.00	—
ND(1987) Proof	94,800	Value: 60.00				

KM# 2982 500 SCHILLING

24.0000 g., 0.9250 Silver .7125 oz. ASW **Subject:** 400th Anniversary - Birth of Salzburg's Archbishop von Raitenau **Obv:** Value within circle of shields **Obv. Designer:** Edwin Grienauer **Rev:** Bust of Archbishop von Raitenau, 3/4 left, two dates at left **Rev. Designer:** Josef Fösleitner

Date	Mintage	F	VF	XF	Unc	BU
ND(1987)	206,400	—	—	—	50.00	—
ND(1987) Proof	93,600	Value: 55.00				

KM# 2983 500 SCHILLING

24.0000 g., 0.9250 Silver .7125 oz. ASW **Subject:** 800th Anniversary - Holy Cross Church **Obv:** Value within circle of shields **Obv. Designer:** Edwin Grienauer **Rev:** Holy Cross Church, date at upper left **Rev. Designer:** Werner Kogler

Date	Mintage	F	VF	XF	Unc	BU
1987	205,200	—	—	—	50.00	—
1987 Proof	94,800	Value: 55.00				

KM# 2984 500 SCHILLING
24.0000 g., 0.9250 Silver .7125 oz. ASW **Subject:** 850th Anniversary - St. Georgenberg Abbey **Obv:** Value within circle of shields **Obv. Designer:** Edwin Grienauer **Rev:** St. Georgenberg Abbey, two dates at bottom **Rev. Designer:** Alfred Zierler

Date	Mintage	F	VF	XF	Unc	BU
ND(1988)	211,800	—	—	—	50.00	—
ND(1988) Proof	88,200	Value: 58.00				

KM# 2985 500 SCHILLING
24.0000 g., 0.9250 Silver .7125 oz. ASW **Subject:** Pope's Visit to Austria **Obv:** Value within circle of shields **Obv. Designer:** Edwin Grienauer **Rev:** Pope Johannes Paul II, with high collar, right, date at bottom **Rev. Designer:** Ferdinand Welz

Date	Mintage	F	VF	XF	Unc	BU
1988	211,200	—	—	—	50.00	—
1988 Proof	88,800	Value: 58.00				

KM# 2986 500 SCHILLING
24.0000 g., 0.9250 Silver .7125 oz. ASW **Subject:** 100th Anniversary - Victor Adler and Christian Social Party **Obv:** Value within circle of shields **Rev:** Head of Victor Adler, facing, date below name at lower right **Rev. Designer:** Werner Kugler

Date	Mintage	F	VF	XF	Unc	BU
1988	213,200	—	—	—	50.00	—
1988 Proof	86,800	Value: 58.00				

KM# 2987 500 SCHILLING
24.0000 g., 0.9250 Silver .7125 oz. ASW **Obv:** Bust of Gustav Klimt, facing, value below **Rev:** Art Nouveau bust of woman facing forward **Designer:** Alfred Zierler

Date	Mintage	F	VF	XF	Unc	BU
1989	236,600	—	—	—	50.00	—
1989 Proof	88,000	Value: 58.00				

KM# 2991 500 SCHILLING
24.0000 g., 0.9250 Silver .7125 oz. ASW **Obv:** Head of Koloman Moser, facing 3/4 left, value below **Rev:** Stained glass, winged figure standing at center **Designer:** Herbert Wähner

Date	Mintage	F	VF	XF	Unc	BU
1989	228,000	—	—	—	50.00	—
1989 Proof	83,200	Value: 55.00				

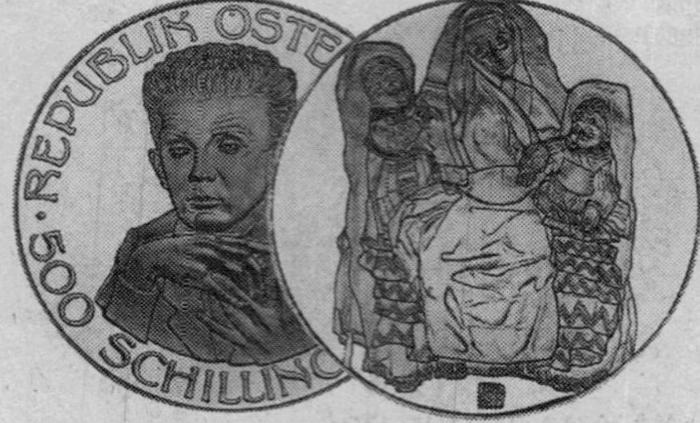

KM# 2992 500 SCHILLING
24.0000 g., 0.9250 Silver .7125 oz. ASW **Obv:** Bust of Egon Schiele, 3/4 facing, value below **Rev:** Expressionism, mother with two children **Designer:** Thomas Pesendorfer

Date	Mintage	F	VF	XF	Unc	BU
1990	246,600	—	—	—	50.00	—
1990 Proof	81,800	Value: 55.00				

KM# 2994 500 SCHILLING
24.0000 g., 0.9250 Silver .7125 oz. ASW **Obv:** Head of Oskar Kokoschka, 3/4 left, value below **Rev:** Expressionism, woman figure facing right

Date	Mintage	F	VF	XF	Unc	BU
1990	245,200	—	—	—	50.00	—
1990 Proof	81,000	Value: 55.00				

KM# 2997 500 SCHILLING
8.1130 g., 0.9860 Gold .2578 oz. AGW **Obv:** Bust of Mozart, 3/4 right, value at lower right **Rev:** Half-length figure of Don Giovanni playing instrument, facing, looking right **Designer:** Herbert Wähner

Date	Mintage	F	VF	XF	Unc	BU
1991 Proof	50,000	Value: 245				

KM# 3000 500 SCHILLING
24.0000 g., 0.9250 Silver .7125 oz. ASW **Obv:** Head of Herbert von Karajan facing left, right of artistic inscription **Rev:** Salzburg Festspielhaus **Designer:** Herbert Wähner

Date	Mintage	F	VF	XF	Unc	BU
1991	240,000	—	—	—	47.50	—
1991 Proof	74,400	Value: 55.00				

KM# 3002 500 SCHILLING
24.0000 g., 0.9250 Silver .7125 oz. ASW **Obv:** Head of Karl Bohm facing at right, inscription at left **Obv. Designer:** Herbert Waehner **Rev:** Building, inscription below **Designer:** Herbert Wähner

Date	Mintage	F	VF	XF	Unc	BU
1991	240,000	—	—	—	47.50	—
1991 Proof	72,400	Value: 55.00				

KM# 3006 500 SCHILLING
8.1130 g., 0.9860 Gold .2578 oz. AGW **Subject:** 150th Anniversary - Vienna Philharmonic **Obv:** Vienna Philharmonic Hall, date below, value at bottom **Rev:** Orchestra instruments, five violins facing

Date	Mintage	F	VF	XF	Unc	BU
1992 Proof	43,000	Value: 185				

KM# 3010 500 SCHILLING
24.0000 g., 0.9250 Silver .7125 oz. ASW **Obv:** Head of Gustav Mahler facing left at right, inscription at left **Rev:** Nude figure standing in center with harp at top, inscription below feet **Designer:** Herbert Wähner

Date	Mintage	F	VF	XF	Unc	BU
1992	237,000	—	—	—	47.50	—
1992 Proof	64,000	Value: 60.00				

KM# 3021 500 SCHILLING
24.0000 g., 0.9250 Silver .7125 oz. ASW **Obv:** Head of Richard Strauss facing forward at right, inscription at left **Rev:** Man and woman standing, man slightly bent at waist **Designer:** Herbert Wähner

Date	Mintage	F	VF	XF	Unc	BU
1992	236,000	—	—	—	47.50	—
1992 Proof	62,900	Value: 60.00				

KM# 3011 500 SCHILLING
24.0000 g., 0.9250 Silver .7125 oz. ASW **Obv:** Hallstatt and the Lakes Region, value below **Rev:** Boats on water **Designer:** Thomas Pesendorfer

Date	Mintage	F	VF	XF	Unc	BU
1993	211,200	—	—	—	47.50	—
1993 Proof	60,000	Value: 60.00				

KM# 3012 500 SCHILLING
8.1130 g., 0.9860 Gold .2578 oz. AGW **Obv:** City building, date at right, value at bottom **Rev:** Aligned heads of Emperors Rudolf II, Ferdinand II, and Archduke Leopold Wilhelm, right

Date	Mintage	F	VF	XF	Unc	BU
1993 Proof	50,000	Value: 650				

KM# 3014 500 SCHILLING
24.0000 g., 0.9250 Silver .7125 oz. ASW **Obv:** Alpine Region, value at bottom **Rev:** Two Alpine dancers **Designer:** Herbert Wähner

Date	Mintage	F	VF	XF	Unc	BU
1993	211,600	—	—	—	47.50	—
1993 Proof	60,000	Value: 60.00				

KM# 3015 500 SCHILLING
8.1130 g., 0.9860 Gold .2578 oz. AGW **Obv:** Congress of Vienna, value below **Rev:** Armored bust of Franz I, facing, looking left, small crown at left, two dates on right

Date	Mintage	F	VF	XF	Unc	BU
1994 Proof	50,000	Value: 225				

KM# 3017 500 SCHILLING
24.0000 g., 0.9250 Silver .7125 oz. ASW **Obv:** Pannonian Region, value below **Rev:** Dancers

Date	Mintage	F	VF	XF	Unc	BU
1994	188,600	—	—	—	47.50	—
1994 Proof	55,000	Value: 60.00				

KM# 3024 500 SCHILLING
24.0000 g., 0.9250 Silver .7125 oz. ASW **Obv:** River Region, value below, date at bottom **Rev:** Folk paraders **Designer:** Thomas Pesendorfer

Date	Mintage	F	VF	XF	Unc	BU
1994	187,800	—	—	—	47.50	—
1994 Proof	55,000	Value: 60.00				

KM# 3025 500 SCHILLING
24.0000 g., 0.9250 Silver .7125 oz. ASW **Obv:** Austrian Hill Country, value below, date at bottom **Rev:** Farm couple **Designer:** Herbert Wähner

Date	Mintage	F	VF	XF	Unc	BU
1995	185,000	—	—	—	47.50	—
1995 Proof	55,000	Value: 60.00				

KM# 3029 500 SCHILLING
24.0000 g., 0.9250 Silver .7125 oz. ASW **Obv:** Alpine foothills, value below, date at bottom **Rev:** Lumberjack **Designer:** Thomas Pesendorfer

Date	Mintage	F	VF	XF	Unc	BU
1995	Est. 184,000	—	—	—	47.50	—
1995 Proof	Est. 50,000	Value: 60.00				

KM# 3023 500 SCHILLING
Bi-Metallic Silver center in Gold ring **Subject:** European Union - Austrian Membership **Obv:** Symbol with Austrian shield at right, value below, within circle **Rev:** Scene of city within circle **Note:** Stars in outer ring are completely punched through.

Date	Mintage	F	VF	XF	Unc	BU
1995 Proof	40,000	Value: 185				

KM# 3032 500 SCHILLING
8.1130 g., 0.9860 Gold .2578 oz. AGW **Obv:** Men on horseback, value below, date at lower right **Rev:** Half-length figure of Heinrich II Jasomirgott, sword in right hand, 3/4 facing

Date	Mintage	F	VF	XF	Unc	BU
1996 Proof	Est. 50,000	Value: 255				

KM# 3035 500 SCHILLING
24.0000 g., 0.9250 Silver .7125 oz. ASW **Obv:** The Mill Region, value below, date at bottom **Rev:** Man and woman with grain **Designer:** Thomas Pesendorfer

Date	Mintage	F	VF	XF	Unc	BU
1996	185,000	—	—	—	47.50	—
1996 Proof	50,000	Value: 60.00				

KM# 3039 500 SCHILLING
24.0000 g., 0.9250 Silver .7125 oz. ASW **Series:** Town Series - Innsbruck Square **Obv:** View of town square, value below, date at bottom **Rev:** Outdoor market scene **Designer:** Herbert Wähner

Date	Mintage	F	VF	XF	Unc	BU
1996	160,000	—	—	—	47.50	—
1996 BU	25,000	—	—	—	50.00	—
1996 Proof	50,000	Value: 60.00				

KM# 3040 500 SCHILLING
8.0400 g., 0.9950 Gold .2578 oz. AGW **Obv:** Franz Schubert at piano, S. M. Vogl in foreground, form a sepia sketch by Moritz von Schwind **Rev:** Bust of Franz Schubert, facing, two dates at left, line of musical score **Designer:** Leopold Kupel Wieser

Date	Mintage	F	VF	XF	Unc	BU
1997 Proof	Est. 50,000	Value: 240				

KM# 3042 500 SCHILLING

24.0000 g., 0.9250 Silver .7125 oz. ASW **Series:** Town Series - Bruck an der Mur **Obv:** Ornate pavilion on cobblestone street, value below, date at bottom **Rev:** Ironsmith at work **Designer:** Thomas Pesendorfer

Date	Mintage	F	VF	XF	Unc	BU
1997	125,000	—	—	—	42.00	—
1997 Special Unc	25,000	—	—	—	50.00	—
1997 Proof	45,000	Value: 60.00				

KM# 3045 500 SCHILLING

24.0000 g., 0.9250 Silver .7125 oz. ASW **Obv:** Stone pulpit of St. Stephen's cathedral, value below **Rev:** Stone mason at work **Designer:** Thomas Pesendorfer

Date	Mintage	F	VF	XF	Unc	BU
1997	125,000	—	—	—	42.00	—
1997 Special Unc	25,000	—	—	—	50.00	—
1997 Proof	45,000	Value: 60.00				

KM# 3047 500 SCHILLING

8.0400 g., 0.9950 Gold .2559 oz. AGW, 22 mm. **Obv:** New York and Kyoto views, value at bottom **Rev:** Vienna Boy's Choir **Designer:** Thomas Pesendorfer

Date	Mintage	F	VF	XF	Unc	BU
ND(1998) Proof	Est. 50,000	Value: 250				

KM# 3049 500 SCHILLING

22.2000 g., 0.9250 Silver .6602 oz. ASW, 37 mm. **Obv:** Interior view of Adimont Abbey Library, value below legend, date at bottom **Obv. Designer:** Thomas Pesendorfer **Rev:** Printers at work **Rev. Designer:** Herbert Wähner **Note:** Book printing.

Date	Mintage	F	VF	XF	Unc	BU
1998	125,000	—	—	—	42.00	—
1998 BU	25,000	—	—	—	50.00	—
1998 Proof	50,000	Value: 60.00				

KM# 3054 500 SCHILLING

22.2000 g., 0.9250 Silver .6602 oz. ASW, 37 mm. **Obv:** Gold chalice and church, value left of chalice, date at bottom **Obv. Designer:** Herbert Wähner **Rev:** Goldsmith at work **Rev. Designer:** Andreas Zamaschka

Date	Mintage	F	VF	XF	Unc	BU
1998	125,000	—	—	—	42.00	—
1998 Special Unc	17,000	—	—	—	50.00	—
1998 Proof	35,000	Value: 60.00				

KM# 3055 500 SCHILLING

8.0400 g., 0.9250 Gold .2559 oz. AGW, 22 mm. **Obv:** Waltzing couple and Strauss monument, value below **Obv. Designer:** Thomas Pesendorfer **Rev:** Busts of Johann Strauss and son, Johann, 3/4 left, dates to left and right of busts **Rev. Designer:** Herbert Wähner

Date	Mintage	F	VF	XF	Unc	BU
1999 Proof	Est. 50,000	Value: 250				

KM# 3058 500 SCHILLING

24.0000 g., 0.9250 Silver .7137 oz. ASW **Obv:** Rosenburg Castle, falcon on perch in castle jousting court, value and date at bottom **Obv. Designer:** Thomas Pesendorfer **Rev:** Jousting knights **Rev. Designer:** Andreas Zamaschka

Date	Mintage	F	VF	XF	Unc	BU
1999	Est. 125,000	—	—	—	42.00	—
1999 Special Unc	25,000	—	—	—	50.00	—
1999 Proof	50,000	Value: 60.00				

KM# 3060 500 SCHILLING

24.0000 g., 0.9250 Silver .7137 oz. ASW **Obv:** Burg Lockenhaus, value and date at bottom **Rev:** Two Templar knights on horseback, left **Designer:** Thomas Pesendorfer

Date	Mintage	F	VF	XF	Unc	BU
1999	Est. 125,000	—	—	—	42.00	—
1999 Special Unc	25,000	—	—	—	50.00	—
1999 Proof	50,000	Value: 60.00				

KM# 3065 500 SCHILLING

10.1400 g., 0.9860 Gold .3170 oz. AGW, 22 mm. **Subject:** 2000th Birthday of Jesus Christ **Obv:** Three wise men presenting gifts within circle, value below circle **Rev:** Portrait of Jesus, facing **Designer:** Thomas Pesendorfer

Date	Mintage	F	VF	XF	Unc	BU
2000 Proof	Est. 50,000	Value: 265				

KM# 3067 500 SCHILLING

24.0000 g., 0.9250 Silver .7137 oz. ASW, 37 mm. **Obv:** Hochosterwitz Castle, value lower left **Obv. Designer:** Andreas Zanaschka **Rev:** Walter von der Vogelweide and royal couple **Rev. Designer:** Thomas Pesendorfer **Edge:** Lettered

Date	Mintage	F	VF	XF	Unc	BU
2000	95,000	—	—	—	42.00	—
2000 Special Unc	50,000	—	—	—	50.00	—
2000 Proof	25,000	Value: 55.00				

KM# 3071 500 SCHILLING

24.0000 g., 0.9250 Silver .7137 oz. ASW, 37 mm. **Obv:** Burg Hohenwerfen Castle, value at bottom **Obv. Designer:** Thomas Pesendorfer **Rev:** Medieval falcon training scene **Rev. Designer:** Herbert Wähner **Edge:** Lettered

Date	Mintage	F	VF	XF	Unc	BU
2000	600,000	—	—	—	42.00	—
2000 Special Unc	100,000	—	—	—	50.00	—
2000 Proof	30,000	Value: 55.00				

KM# 2933 1000 SCHILLING

13.5000 g., 0.9000 Gold .3906 oz. AGW **Subject:** Babenberg Dynasty Millennium **Obv:** Imperial Eagle with Austrian shield on breast, holding hammer and sickle, value below **Rev:** Seal of Duke Friedrich II within circle, dates above circle **Note:** Exists in shades of red to yellow gold.

Date	Mintage	F	VF	XF	Unc	BU
ND(1976)	1,800,000	—	—	—	—	265

KM# 2999 1000 SCHILLING
16.2250 g., 0.9860 Gold .5155 oz. AGW **Obv:** Head of Mozart with high collar, left, date below collar, violin on right **Rev:** The Magic Flute Opera from a 1789 drawing by Dora Stode **Designer:** Alfred Zieger

Date	Mintage	F	VF	XF	Unc	BU
1991 Proof	30,000	Value: 485				

KM# 3008 1000 SCHILLING
16.2250 g., 0.9860 Gold .5155 oz. AGW **Obv:** City building, value below, date upper right **Rev:** 1/2-length figure of Johann Strauss playing violin looking forward

Date	Mintage	F	VF	XF	Unc	BU
1992 Proof	42,000	Value: 345				

KM# 3013 1000 SCHILLING
16.2250 g., 0.9860 Gold .5155 oz. AGW **Obv:** Buildings, date below, value at bottom **Rev:** 3/4 length torso of Maria Theresa holding scepter in right hand, half facing right

Date	Mintage	F	VF	XF	Unc	BU
1993 Proof	50,000	Value: 350				

KM# 3018 1000 SCHILLING
Bi-Metallic Gold center in Silver ring **Subject:** 800th Anniversary of the Vienna Mint **Obv:** Symbol at center of three circles, two dates above **Rev:** Crowned figure on horseback in center of three circles surrounded by circle of laborers **Designer:** Alfred Ziegler

Date	Mintage	F	VF	XF	Unc	BU
ND(1994) Proof	50,000	Value: 330				

KM# 3028 1000 SCHILLING
16.9700 g., 0.9170 Gold .5014 oz. AGW **Series:** Olympics **Obv:** Building, statue on right, date at base, shield on left, value above **Rev:** Head of Zeus on left, facing, Olympic logo, flame to the right **Edge Lettering:** CITIUS ALTIUS FORTIUS

Date	Mintage	F	VF	XF	Unc	BU
1995 Proof	Est. 60,000	Value: 335				

KM# 3030 1000 SCHILLING
16.2250 g., 0.9860 Gold .5155 oz. AGW **Subject:** 50th Anniversary - Second Republic **Obv:** Five men aligned behind railing, center man holding book, date below railing, value at bottom **Rev:** Stylized design

Date	Mintage	F	VF	XF	Unc	BU
1995 Proof	49,000	Value: 350				

KM# 3037 1000 SCHILLING
16.2250 g., 0.9860 Gold .5155 oz. AGW **Subject:** Millennium of the Name Osterreich **Obv:** Land grant within circle, dates at bottom, value below circle **Rev:** Seated, crowned figure of Otto III, facing

Date	Mintage	F	VF	XF	Unc	BU
ND(1996) Proof	50,000	Value: 340				

KM# 3043 1000 SCHILLING
16.0800 g., 0.9950 Gold .5118 oz. AGW **Subject:** Habsburg Tragedies - Marie Antoinette **Obv:** Half-length figure of Marie holding flowers, 3/4 right, value and date lower left **Rev:** Marie on trial

Date	Mintage	F	VF	XF	Unc	BU
1997 Proof	Est. 50,000	Value: 335				

KM# 3052 1000 SCHILLING
16.0800 g., 0.9950 Gold .5155 oz. AGW 30 mm. **Subject:** 100th Anniversary of Queen Elisabeth's Assassination by Luigi Luccheni in Geneva **Obv:** Bust of Empress Elisabeth, Queen of Hungary, 3/4 right **Rev:** Scene of Elizabeth's final moment

Date	Mintage	F	VF	XF	Unc	BU
1998 Proof	Est. 50,000	Value: 340				

KM# 3062 1000 SCHILLING
16.0800 g., 0.9950 Gold .5118 oz. AGW, 30 mm. **Obv:** Emperor Karl I bust facing **Rev:** Interior view Habsburg crypt

Date	Mintage	F	VF	XF	Unc	BU
1999 Proof	Est. 50,000	Value: 335				

KM# 3072 1000 SCHILLING
16.2200 g., 0.9860 Gold .5027 oz. AGW **Obv:** Heidentor ancient gate and statue **Rev:** Constantius II portrait **Edge:** Reeded **Designer:** Herbert Wähner

Date	Mintage	F	VF	XF	Unc	BU
2000	30,000	—	—	—	—	330

BULLION COINAGE

Philharmonic Issues

KM# 3004 200 SCHILLING
3.1100 g., 0.9999 Gold .1000 oz. AGW **Series:** Vienna Philharmonic Orchestra **Obv:** The Golden Hall organ **Rev:** Instruments **Designer:** Thomas Pesendorfer

Date	Mintage	F	VF	XF	Unc	BU
1991	93,000	—	—	—	BV+13%	—
1992	102,000	—	—	—	BV+13%	—
1993	107,500	—	—	—	BV+13%	—
1994	94,500	—	—	—	BV+13%	—
1995	169,500	—	—	—	BV+13%	—
1996	170,000	—	—	—	BV+13%	—
1997	59,000	—	—	—	BV+13%	—
1998	88,500	—	—	—	BV+13%	—
1999	101,500	—	—	—	BV+13%	—
2000	85,500	—	—	—	BV+13%	—

KM# 2989 500 SCHILLING
7.7760 g., 0.9999 Gold .2505 oz. AGW **Series:** Vienna Philharmonic Orchestra **Obv:** The Golden Hall organ **Rev:** Orchestra instruments, five violins facing **Designer:** Thomas Pesendorfer

Date	Mintage	F	VF	XF	Unc	BU
1989	586,000	—	—	—	BV+10%	—
1990	46,000	—	—	—	BV+10%	—
1991	24,000	—	—	—	BV+10%	—
1992	186,000	—	—	—	BV+10%	—
1993	166,000	—	—	—	BV+10%	—
1994	12,000	—	—	—	BV+10%	—
1995	174,000	—	—	—	BV+10%	—
1996	184,000	—	—	—	BV+10%	—
1997	66,000	—	—	—	BV+10%	—
1998	38,000	—	—	—	BV+10%	—
1999	81,600	—	—	—	BV+10%	—
2000	38,000	—	—	—	BV+10%	—

KM# 3031 1000 SCHILLING
15.5500 g., 0.9999 Gold .5000 oz. AGW **Series:** Vienna Philharmonic Orchestra **Obv:** The Golden Hall organ **Rev:** Orchestra instruments, five violins facing **Designer:** Thomas Pesendorfer

Date	Mintage	F	VF	XF	Unc	BU
1994	79,000	—	—	—	BV+8%	—
1995	105,500	—	—	—	BV+8%	—
1996	82,500	—	—	—	BV+8%	—
1997	65,500	—	—	—	BV+8%	—

Date	Mintage	F	VF	XF	Unc	BU
1998	34,000	—	—	—	BV+8%	—
1999	10,000	—	—	—	BV+8%	—
2000	38,500	—	—	—	BV+8%	—

KM# 2990 2000 SCHILLING

31.1035 g., 0.9999 Gold 1.0002 oz. AGW **Series:** Vienna Philharmonic Orchestra **Obv:** The Golden Hall organ **Rev:** Orchestra instruments, five violins facing **Designer:** Thomas Pesendorfer

Date	Mintage	F	VF	XF	Unc	BU
1989	484,000	—	—	—	BV+4%	—
1990	406,500	—	—	—	BV+4%	—
1991	341,000	—	—	—	BV+4%	—
1992	444,500	—	—	—	BV+4%	—
1993	339,500	—	—	—	BV+4%	—
1994	68,000	—	—	—	BV+4%	—
1995	650,000	—	—	—	BV+4%	—
1996	400,500	—	—	—	BV+4%	—
1997	381,500	—	—	—	BV+4%	—
1998	294,000	—	—	—	BV+4%	—
1999	275,000	—	—	—	BV+4%	—
2000	125,500	—	—	—	BV+4%	—

PATTERNS

Including off metal strikes

KM#	Date	Mintage	Identification	Mkt Val
Pn68	1908	—	100 Kronen. Without mint mark.	—
Pn69	1909	—	100 Kronen. Without mint mark.	—
Pn70	1910	—	2 Kronen. Silver. Similar to KM#2821.	2,350
Pn71	1913	—	Krone. Aluminum. KM#2820.	—
Pn72	1913	—	2 Corona. Aluminum. KM#2821.	200
Pn73	ND	—	50 Heller. Iron.	235
Pn74	1914	—	Heller. Copper. Privately produced by Karl Goetz in Munich, Germany.	150
Pn75	1914	—	Heller. Silver. Privately produced by Karl Goetz in Munich, Germany.	275
Pn76	1915	—	2 Heller. Bronze. KM#2801.	—
Pn77	1915	—	2 Heller. Iron. KM#2801.	—
Pn78	1915	—	20 Heller. Iron. KM#2826.	450
Pn79	1915	—	1/2 Krone. Silver. 2.5200 g.	—
Pn80	1915	—	Ducat. Aluminum. Plain edge.	100
Pn81	1915	—	Ducat. Copper. Reeded edge.	400
Pn82	1916	—	Heller. Iron. KM#2823.	275
Pn83	1916	—	2 Heller. Iron.	—
Pn84	1916	—	10 Heller. Aluminum. KM#2825.	275
Pn85	1916	—	Krone. Aluminum. KM#2820.	145
Pn86	1917	—	10 Heller. Steel. Plain edge. 10 in square, thick planchet.	—
Pn87	1917	—	10 Heller. Steel. Plain edge. 10 in square, thin planchet.	250
Pn88	1917	—	10 Heller. Steel. Milled edge.	—
Pn89	1918	—	20 Heller. Aluminum. 20 in square.	—
Pn90	1918	—	20 Heller. Aluminum. KM#2826.	250
Pn91	1918	—	5 Kronen. Brass.	—
Pn92	1918	—	20 Kronen. Copper.	—
Pn93	1918	—	20 Kronen. Gold.	—
Pn94	ND	—	10 Schilling. Nickel.	180
Pn95	ND	—	20 Schilling. Nickel.	400
Pn96	1924	—	1/2 Schilling. Silver. KM#2839.	1,250
Pn97	1924	—	Schilling. Silver. KM#2835.	825
Pn98	1924	—	Schilling. Silver. KM#2835. KM#2835. Octagonal planchets, 1 pair.	700
Pn99	1924	—	20 Kronen. Copper. Reeded edge. KM#2830.	1,500
Pn100	1924	—	20 Kronen. Silver. Reeded edge. Uniface, KM#2830.	700
Pn101	1930	—	100 Schilling. Silver. Plain edge. KM#2842.	2,000
Pn102	1931	—	5 Groschen. Copper-Nickel.	—
Pn103	1931	—	5 Groschen. Gold. KM#2846.	1,200
Pn104	1931	—	100 Schilling. Copper. KM#2842.	1,000
Pn105	1934	—	50 Groschen. Copper-Nickel. Uniface.	—
Pn106	1934	—	50 Groschen. Copper-Nickel. Uniface.	—
Pn107	1934	—	Schilling. Copper-Nickel. Uniface.	1,750
Pn108	1934	—	Schilling. Copper-Nickel. Uniface.	1,750
Pn109	1934	—	2 Schilling. Zinc. KM#2852.	1,000
Pn110	1934	—	2 Schilling. Zinc. One side struck on octagonal planchet, KM#2852.	600
Pn111	1935	—	25 Schilling. Gold. J. Prinz.	—
Pn112	1935	—	100 Schilling. Gold. J. Prinz.	—
Pn113	1937	—	2 Schilling. Copper. KM#2859.	200
Pn114	1938	—	5 Groschen. Gold. KM#2846.	1,200
Pn115	1947	—	Schilling. Copper-Nickel. KM#2871.	500
Pn116	1959	—	Schilling. Aluminum-Bronze. Similar to KM#2886.	850

TRIAL STRIKES

KM#	Date	Mintage	Identification	Mkt Val
TS1	1934	—	50 Groschen. Uniface.	—
TS2	1934	—	50 Groschen. Uniface.	—
TS3	ND(1973)	—	5 Schilling. Nickel.	275
TS5	ND(1973)	—	20 Schilling. Nickel.	350
TS4	ND(1973)	—	10 Schilling. Nickel.	200
TS6	ND(1984)	—	5 Groschen. Aluminum. Plain edge.	175

MINT SETS

KM#	Date	Mintage	Identification	Issue Price	Mkt Val
MS1	1992 (8)	25,000	KM#2875-2876, 2878, 2885-2886, 2889a, 2918	—	50.00
MS2	1993 (8)	35,000	KM#2875-2876, 2878, 2885-2886, 2889a, 2918, 2946.2	—	40.00
MS3	1994 (8)	25,000	KM#2875-2876, 2878, 2885-2886, 2889a, 2918, 3016	—	70.00
MS4	1995 (6)	27,000	KM#2878, 2885-2886, 2889a, 2918, 3022	—	50.00
MS5	1996 (6)	25,000	KM#2878, 2885-2886, 2889a, 2918, 3033	—	35.00
MS6	1997 (6)	25,000	KM#2878, 2885-2886, 2889a, 2918, 3041	—	30.00
MS7	1998 (6)	—	KM#2878, 2885-2886, 2889a, 2918, 3048	—	22.50
MS8	1999 (6)	—	KM#2878, 2885-2886, 2889a, 2918, 3056	22.00	22.50
MS9	2000 (6)	—	KM#2878, 2885-2886, 2889a, 2918, 3064	—	22.50

PROOF SETS

KM#	Date	Mintage	Identification	Issue Price	Mkt Val
PS1	1959 (2)	1,000	KM#2887-2888	—	725
PS2	1964 (9)	69,731	KM#2875-2876, 2878, 2882, 2885-2886, 2889, 2895.1, 2896	—	55.00
PS3	1964 (9)	2,700	KM#2875-2876, 2878, 2882, 2885-2886, 2889, 2895.2, 2896 (error set)	—	365
PS4	1964 (7)	—	KM#2875-2876, 2878, 2882, 2885-2886, 2889	—	22.50
PS5	1965 (7)	83,000	KM#2875-2876, 2878, 2882, 2885-2886, 2889	—	10.00
PS6	1965 (4)	38,000	KM#2882, 2889, 2897-2898	5.00	42.50
PS7	1966 (9)	1,765	KM#2875-2876, 2878, 2882, 2885-2886, 2889, 2899-2900	—	180
PS8	1966 (7)	—	KM#2875-2876, 2878, 2882, 2885-2886, 2889	—	60.00
PS9	1967 (9)	1,163	KM#2875-2876, 2878, 2882, 2885-2886, 2889, 2901-2902	5.50	300
PS10	1967 (7)	—	KM#2875-2876, 2878, 2882, 2885-2886, 2889	—	200
PS11	1968 (9)	15,200	KM#2875-2876, 2878, 2882, 2885-2886, 2889, 2903, 2904.1	5.75	110
PS12	1968 (7)	20,000	KM#2875-2876, 2878, 2882, 2885-2886, 2889	—	65.00
PS13	1969 (9)	20,000	KM#2875-2876, 2878, 2882, 2885-2886, 2889a, 2905-2906	7.50	90.00
PS14	1969 (7)	21,000	KM#2875-2876, 2878, 2882, 2885-2886, 2889a	—	50.00
PS15	1970 (9)	—	KM#2875-2876, 2878, 2882, 2885-2886, 2889a, 2907-2908	8.25	35.00
PS16	1970 (9)	—	KM#2875-2876, 2878, 2882, 2885-2886, 2889a, 2907, 2909	8.25	35.00
PS17	1970 (7)	92,000	KM#2875-2876, 2878, 2882, 2885-2886, 2889a	—	8.50
PS18	1970 (3)	—	KM#2907-2909	7.00	25.00
PS19	1971 (9)	—	KM#2875-2876, 2878, 2882, 2885-2886, 2889a, 2910-2911	8.25	28.00
PS20	1971 (7)	84,000	KM#2875-2876, 2878, 2882, 2885-2886, 2889a	—	8.50
PS21	1972 (9)	—	KM#2875-2876, 2878, 2882, 2885-2886, 2889a, 2912-2913	8.50	25.00
PS22	1972 (9)	—	KM#2875-2876, 2878, 2882, 2885-2886, 2889a, 2912, 2914	8.50	25.00
PS23	1972 (7)	75,000	KM#2875-2876, 2878, 2882, 2885-2886, 2889a	—	8.50
PS24	1972 (3)	—	KM#2912-2914	7.50	22.50
PS25	1972 (3)	—	KM#2912-2914	—	22.50
PS26	1973 (9)	—	KM#2875-2876, 2878, 2882, 2885-2886, 289a, 2915-2916	—	25.00
PS27	1973 (7)	87,000	KM#2875-2876, 2878, 2882, 2885-2886, 2889a	—	10.00
PS28	1974 (12)	—	KM#2875-2876, 2878, 2885-2886, 2889a, 2918-2922, 2926	29.70	55.00
PS29	1974 (8)	—	KM#2875-2876, 2878, 2885-2886, 2889a, 2918, 2921	—	20.00
PS30	1974 (7)	76,000	KM#2875-2876, 2878, 2885-2886, 2889a, 2918	—	8.50
PS31	1974 (5)	—	KM#2919-2922, 2926	27.00	42.00
PS32	1975 (10)	—	KM#2875-2876, 2878, 2885-2886, 289a, 2918, 2923-2925	30.00	45.00
PS33	1975 (7)	49,000	KM#2875-2876, 2878, 2885-2886, 2889a, 2918	—	8.50
PS34	1975 (3)	—	KM#2923-2925	27.00	35.00
PS35	1976 (7)	44,000	KM#2875-2876, 2878, 2885-2886, 2889a, 2918	3.00	9.50
PS36	1976-1977 (6)	—	KM#2930-2932, 2934-2936	27.00	85.00
PS37	1977 (7)	44,000	KM#2875-2876, 2878, 2885-2886, 2889a, 2918	3.15	8.50
PS38	1978 (7)	43,000	KM#2875-2876, 2878, 2885-2886, 2889a, 2918	—	9.50
PS39	1979 (7)	44,000	KM#2875-2876, 2878, 2885-2886, 2889a, 2918	—	9.50
PS40	1980 (8)	48,000	KM#2875-2876, 2878, 2885-2886, 2889a, 2918, 2946	—	28.00
PS42	1981 (8)	49,000	KM#2875-2876, 2878, 2885-2886, 2889a, 2918, 2946.1	—	28.00
PS43	1982 (8)	50,000	KM#2875-2876, 2878, 2885-2886, 2889a, 2918, 2955.1	—	14.00
PS44	1983 (8)	65,000	KM#2875-2876, 2878, 2885-2886, 2889a, 2918, 2960.1	—	12.50
PS45	1984 (8)	65,000	KM#2875-2876, 2878, 2885-2886, 2889a, 2918, 2965.1	—	12.50
PS46	1985 (8)	45,000	KM#2875-2876, 2878, 2885-2886, 2889a, 2918, 2970.1	—	20.00
PS47	1986 (8)	42,000	KM#2875-2876, 2878, 2885-2886, 2889a, 2918, 2975.1	—	30.00
PS48	1987 (8)	42,000	KM#2875-2876, 2878, 2885-2886, 2889a, 2918, 2980.1	—	22.00
PS49	1988 (7)	39,000	KM#2875-2876, 2878, 2885-2886, 2889a, 2918	—	12.50
PS50	1989 (8)	38,000	KM#2875-2876, 2878, 2885-2886, 2889a, 2918, 2988.1	—	17.50
PS51	1990 (8)	35,000	KM#2875-2876, 2878, 2885-2886, 2889a, 2918, 2993.1	—	42.50
PS52	1991 (8)	27,000	KM#2875-2876, 2878, 2885-2886, 2889a, 2918, 2995.1	—	22.00
PS53	1992 (8)	25,000	KM#2875-2876, 2878, 2885-2886, 2889a, 2918	—	45.00
PS54	1993 (8)	28,000	KM#2875-2876, 2878, 2885-2886, 2889a, 2918, 2946.2	—	35.00
PS55	1994 (8)	25,000	KM#2875-2876, 2878, 2885-2886, 2889a, 2918, 3016	—	75.00
PS56	1995 (6)	27,000	KM#2878, 2885, 2886, 2889a, 2918, 3022	—	37.50
PS57	1996 (6)	25,000	KM#2878, 2885, 2886, 2889a, 2918, 3033	—	45.00
PS58	1997 (6)	25,000	KM#2878, 2885, 2886, 2889a, 2918, 3041	—	50.00
PS59	1998 (6)	25,000	KM#2878, 2885, 2886, 2889a, 2918, 3048	—	60.00
PS60	1999 (6)	25,000	KM#2878, 2885, 2886, 2889a, 2918, 3056	—	27.50
PS61	2000 (6)	—	KM#2878, 2885, 2886, 2889a, 2918, 3064	—	27.50

AZERBAIJAN

The Republic of Azerbaijan (formerly Azerbaijan S.S.R.) includes the Nakhichevan Autonomous Republic. Situated in the eastern area of Transcaucasia, it is bordered in the west by Armenia, in the north by Georgia and Dagestan, to the east by the Caspian Sea and to the south by Iran. It has an area of 33,430 sq. mi. (86,600 sq. km.) and a population of 7.8 million. Capital: Baku. The area is rich in mineral deposits of aluminum, copper, iron, lead, salt and zinc, with oil as its leading industry. Agriculture and livestock follow in importance.

In 1990 it adopted a declaration of republican sovereignty and in Aug. 1991 declared itself formally independent. This action was approved by a vote of referendum in Jan. 1992. It announced its intention of joining the CIS in Dec. 1991, but a parliamentary resolution of Oct. 1992 declined to confirm its involvement. On Sept. 20, 1993, Azerbaijan became a member of the CIS. Communist President Mutaibov was relieved of his office in May 1992. On June 7, in the first democratic election in the country's history, a National Council replaced Mutaibov with Abulfez Elchibey. Surat Huseynov led a military coup against Elchibey and seized power on June 30, 1993. Huseynov became prime minister with former communist Geidar Aliyev, president.

Fighting commenced between Muslim forces of Azerbaijan and Christian forces of Armenia in 1992 and continued through early 1994. Each faction claimed the Nagorno-Karabakh, an Armenian ethnic enclave, in Azerbaijan. A cease-fire was declared in May 1994.

MONETARY SYSTEM
100 Qapik = 1 Manat

REPUBLIC

DECIMAL COINAGE

KM# 1 5 QAPIK
Brass **Obv:** Value **Rev:** Three symbols above date at center of sun

Date	Mintage	F	VF	XF	Unc	BU
1992	—	—	—	2.00	4.00	5.00

KM# 1a 5 QAPIK
0.8500 g., Aluminum, 17.1 mm. **Obv:** Value **Rev:** Three symbols above date at center of sun **Edge:** Plain

Date	Mintage	F	VF	XF	Unc	BU
1993	—	—	—	—	1.00	1.50

KM# 2 10 QAPIK
Copper Nickel **Obv:** Denomination **Rev:** Star with date **Edge:** Plain

Date	Mintage	F	VF	XF	Unc	BU
1992	—	—	—	1.00	2.00	2.50

KM# 2a 10 QAPIK
1.0500 g., Aluminum, 18.6 mm. **Obv:** Denomination **Rev:** Star with date **Edge:** Plain

Date	Mintage	F	VF	XF	Unc	BU
1992	—	—	—	—	0.50	0.75

KM# 3 20 QAPIK
Brass **Obv:** Moon and star at center **Rev:** Value above date within star **Edge:** Plain

Date	Mintage	F	VF	XF	Unc	BU
1992	—	—	—	1.00	2.00	2.50
1993	—	—	—	1.00	2.00	2.50

KM# 3a 20 QAPIK
1.1500 g., Aluminum, 20.1 mm. **Edge:** Plain **Note:** Varieties in spelling of Respublikas exist.

Date	Mintage	F	VF	XF	Unc	BU
1992	—	—	—	—	0.75	1.00
1993	—	—	—	—	0.75	1.00

Note: Two die varieties exist

KM# 4 50 QAPIK
Copper-Nickel **Obv:** Maiden tower ruins **Rev:** Value above date within ornate circle **Edge:** Plain

Date	Mintage	F	VF	XF	Unc	BU
1992	—	—	—	1.50	3.50	4.50
1994	—	—	—	1.50	3.50	4.50

KM# 4a 50 QAPIK
1.4500 g., Aluminum, 23 mm. **Edge:** Plain

Date	Mintage	F	VF	XF	Unc	BU
1992	—	—	—	—	1.25	1.50
1993	—	—	—	—	0.75	1.00

KM# 5 50 MANAT
28.2800 g., 0.9250 Silver .8411 oz. ASW **Subject:** 500th Anniversary Mehemmed Fuzuli **Obv:** Deer by man comforting fallen comrade within circle, date below circle **Rev:** Portrait of Fuzuli bust looking left

Date	Mintage	F	VF	XF	Unc	BU
1996	—	—	—	—	40.00	45.00
1996 Proof	5,000	Value: 65.00				

KM# 38 50 MANAT
33.9200 g., 0.9250 Silver 1.0088 oz. ASW, 38.6 mm. **Obv:** Musician riding horse within circle, date below circle **Rev:** Four line inscription within circle **Edge:** Reeded

Date	Mintage	F	VF	XF	Unc	BU
1999 Proof	1,000	Value: 70.00				

KM# 6 100 MANAT
7.9800 g., 0.9167 Gold .2354 oz. AGW **Subject:** 500th Anniversary Mehemmed Fuzuli **Obv:** Deer by man comforting fallen comrade **Rev:** Portrait of Fuzuli

Date	Mintage	F	VF	XF	Unc	BU
1996 Proof	500	Value: 325				

AZORES

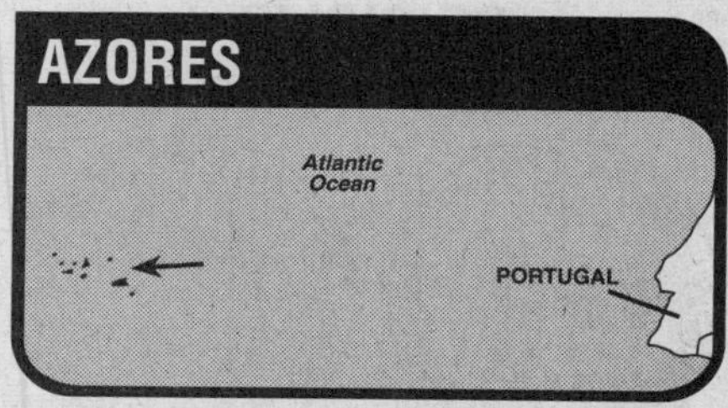

The Azores, an archipelago of nine islands of volcanic origin, are located in the Atlantic Ocean 740 miles (1,190 km.) west of Cape de Roca, Portugal. They are the westernmost region of Europe under the administration of Portugal and have an area of 902 sq. mi. (2,305 sq. km.) and a population of 236,000. Principal city: Ponta Delgada. The natives are mainly of Portuguese descent and earn their livelihood by fishing, wine making, basket weaving and the growing of fruit, grains and sugar cane. Pineapples are the chief item of export. The climate is particularly temperate, making the islands a favorite winter resort.

The Azores were discovered about 1427 by the Portuguese navigator Diogo de Sevill. Portugal secured the islands in the 15th century and established the first settlement on Santa Maria about 1439. From 1580 to 1640 the Azores were subject to Spain.

The Azores' first provincial coinage was ordered by law of August 19, 1750. Copper coins were struck for circulation in both the Azores and Madeira Islands, keeping the same technical specifications but with different designs. In 1795 a second provincial coinage was introduced but the weight was reduced by 50 percent.

Angra on Terceira Island became the capital of the captaincy-general of the Azores in 1766 and it was here in 1826 that the constitutionalists set up a pro-Pedro government in opposition to King Miguel in Lisbon. The whole Portuguese fleet attacked Terceira and was repelled at Praia, after which Azoreans, Brazilians and British mercenaries defeated Miguel in Portugal. Maria de Gloria, Pedro's daughter, was proclaimed queen of Portugal on Terceira in 1828.

A U.S. naval base was established at Ponta Delgada in 1917.

After World War II, the islands acquired a renewed importance as a refueling stop for transatlantic air transport. The United States maintains defense bases in the Azores as part of the collective security program of NATO.

In 1976 the archipelago became the Autonomous Region of Azores.

Note: Portuguese 50 Centavos and 1 Escudo pieces dated 1935 were issued for circulation in Azores. These are found under the appropriate listing in Portugal.

RULERS
Portuguese

MONETARY SYSTEM
1000 Reis (Insulanos) = 1 Milreis

PORTUGUESE ADMINISTRATION

PROVINCIAL COINAGE

KM# 16 5 REIS
Copper **Subject:** Carlos I **Obv:** Crowned arms **Rev:** Value within wreath, date below

Date	Mintage	F	VF	XF	Unc	BU
1901	800,000	1.75	3.50	9.00	25.00	—

KM# 17 10 REIS
Copper **Subject:** Carlos I **Obv:** Crowned arms **Rev:** Value within wreath, date below

Date	Mintage	F	VF	XF	Unc	BU
1901	600,000	2.00	4.00	10.00	28.00	—

REPUBLIC

DECIMAL COINAGE

KM# 43 25 ESCUDOS
Copper-Nickel, 28.5 mm. **Subject:** Regional Autonomy **Obv:** Shields above denomination, stars below **Rev:** Supported arms **Edge:** Reeded

Date	Mintage	F	VF	XF	Unc	BU
1980	770,000	—	—	2.50	5.00	7.50

KM# 43a 25 ESCUDOS
11.0000 g., 0.9250 Silver .3272 oz. ASW **Subject:** Regional Autonomy **Obv:** Shields above denomination, stars below **Rev:** Supported arms

Date	Mintage	F	VF	XF	Unc	BU
1980 Proof	12,000	Value: 22.00				

KM# 44 100 ESCUDOS
Copper-Nickel **Subject:** Regional Autonomy **Obv:** Shields above denomination, stars below **Rev:** Supported arms

Date	Mintage	F	VF	XF	Unc	BU
1980	270,000	—	—	4.50	10.00	12.50

KM# 44a 100 ESCUDOS
16.5000 g., 0.9250 Silver .4908 oz. ASW **Subject:** Regional Autonomy **Obv:** Shields above denomination, stars below **Rev:** Supported arms

Date	Mintage	F	VF	XF	Unc	BU
1980 Proof	12,000	Value: 42.50				

KM# 45 100 ESCUDOS
Copper-Nickel **Subject:** 10th Anniversary of Regional Autonomy **Obv:** Supported arms, value below **Rev:** Hydrangea plant, date below **Designer:** Isabel and F. Branca

Date	Mintage	F	VF	XF	Unc	BU
1986	750,000	—	—	—	6.50	8.50

KM# 45a 100 ESCUDOS
16.5000 g., 0.9250 Silver .4908 oz. ASW **Subject:** 10th Anniversary of Regional Autonomy **Obv:** Supported arms **Rev:** Flower

Date	Mintage	F	VF	XF	Unc	BU
1986	20,000	—	—	—	25.00	28.00
1986 Proof	10,000	Value: 35.00				

KM# 46 100 ESCUDOS
Copper-Nickel **Subject:** 100th Anniversary - Death of Poet Antero de Quental **Obv:** Offered hand with radiant sun behind, shield of arms below left, value at right **Rev:** Bust of Antero de Quental, facing, two dates at left

Date	Mintage	F	VF	XF	Unc	BU
1991	750,000	—	—	—	5.00	7.50

KM# 46a 100 ESCUDOS
18.5000 g., 0.9250 Silver .5503 oz. ASW, 36 mm.
Subject: 100th Anniversary - Death of Poet Antero de Quental **Obv:** Offered hand with radiant sun behind, shield of arms below left **Rev:** Bust of Antero de Quental facing

Date	Mintage	F	VF	XF	Unc	BU
1991	20,000	—	—	—	30.00	32.50
1991 Proof	30,000	Value: 40.00				

KM# 47 100 ESCUDOS
Copper-Nickel **Subject:** Centennial of Azorean Autonomy **Obv:** Sun with star at center, over water, shield of arms below, value at bottom **Rev:** Goshawk with wings spread below dates, 1895 above 1995

Date	Mintage	F	VF	XF	Unc	BU
ND(1995)	500,000	—	—	—	7.50	10.00

KM# 47a 100 ESCUDOS
18.5000 g., 0.9250 Silver .5502 oz. ASW **Subject:** Centennial of Azorean Autonomy **Rev:** Goshawk with wings spread below dates, 1895 over 1995

Date	Mintage	F	VF	XF	Unc	BU
ND(1995)	5,000	—	—	—	35.00	40.00
ND(1995) Proof	10,000	Value: 50.00				

PATTERNS

Including off metal strikes

KM#	Date	Mintage	Identification	Mkt Val
Pn5	1901	—	5 Reis. Aluminum.	725
Pn6	1901	—	10 Reis. Aluminum.	725

PROVAS

KM#	Date	Mintage	Identification	Mkt Val
Pr1	1980	—	25 Escudos. Copper-Nickel. Incuse PROVA.	150

KM#	Date	Mintage	Identification	Mkt Val
Pr2	1980	—	100 Escudos. Copper-Nickel. Shields above value, stars below. Supported arms. Incuse PROVA.	175
Pr3	1986	—	100 Escudos. Copper-Nickel. Incuse PROVA.	175

PROOF SETS

KM#	Date	Mintage	Identification	Issue Price	Mkt Val
PS1	1980 (2)	12,000	KM43a-44a	40.00	70.00

BAHAMAS

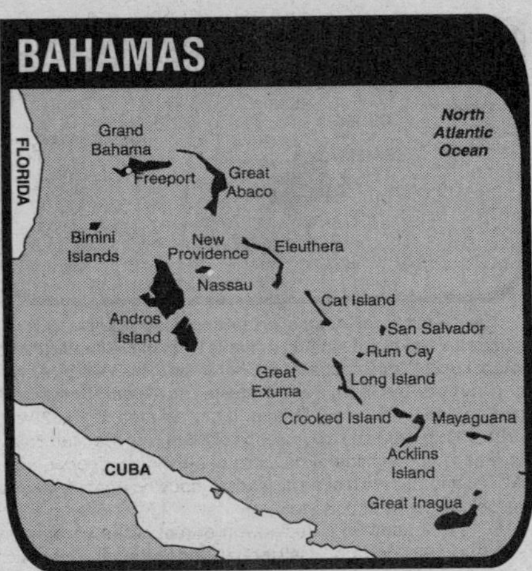

The Commonwealth of the Bahamas is an archipelago of about 3,000 islands, cays and rocks located in the Atlantic Ocean east of Florida and north of Cuba. The total land area of the 800 mile (1,287 km.) long chain of islands is 5,382 sq. mi. (13,935 sq. km.). They have a population of 302,000. Capital: Nassau. The Bahamas import most of their food and manufactured products and export cement, refined oil, pulpwood and lobsters. Tourism is the principal industry.

The Bahamas were discovered by Columbus October, 1492, upon his sighting of the island of San Salvador, but Spain made no attempt to settle them. British influence began in 1626 when Charles I granted them to the lord proprietors of Carolina, with settlements in 1629 at New Providence by colonists from the northern territory. Although the Bahamas were temporarily under Spanish control in 1641 and 1703, they continued under British proprietors until 1717, when, as the result of political and economic mismanagement, the civil and military governments were surrendered to the King and the islands designated a British Crown Colony. Full international agreement on British possession of the islands resulted from the Treaty of Versailles in 1783. The Bahamas obtained complete internal self-government under the constitution of Jan. 7, 1964. Full independence was achieved on July 10, 1973. The Bahamas is a member of the Caribbean community and the common market. Elizabeth II is Head of State, as Queen of the United Kingdom and is represented by a governor general.

The coinage of Great Britain was legal tender in the Bahamas from 1825 to the issuing of a definitive coinage in 1966.

RULERS
British

MINT MARKS
Through 1969 all decimal coinage of the Bahamas was executed at the Royal Mint in England. Since that time issues have been struck at both the Royal Mint and at the Franklin Mint (FM) in the U.S.A. While the mint mark of the latter appears on coins dated 1971 and subsequently, it is missing from the 1970 issues.
JP – John Pinches, London
None - Royal Mint
(t) - Tower of London
FM - Franklin Mint, U.S.A.

***NOTE**: From 1975-1985 the Franklin Mint produced coinage in up to 3 different qualities. Qualities of issue are designated in ( ) after each date and are defined as follows:

(M) MATTE - Normal circulation strike or a dull finish produced by sandblasting special uncirculated (polish finish) or proof quality dies.

(U) SPECIAL UNCIRCULATED - Polished or proof-like in appearance without any frosted features.

(P) PROOF - The highest quality obtainable having mirror-like fields and frosted features.

MONETARY SYSTEM
12 Pence = 1 Shilling

COMMONWEALTH

DECIMAL COINAGE

100 Cents = 1 Dollar

KM# 2 CENT
Nickel-Brass, 22.5 mm. **Obv:** Queen Elizabeth II right **Obv. Designer:** Arnold Machin **Rev:** Starfish above date, value at top

Date	Mintage	F	VF	XF	Unc	BU
1966	7,312,000	—	—	0.10	0.50	1.50
1968	800,000	—	—	0.25	0.75	2.25
1969	4,036,000	—	—	0.10	0.50	1.50
1969 Proof	10,000	Value: 1.00				

KM# 15 CENT

Bronze **Obv:** Bust of Queen Elizabeth II right with tiara **Obv. Designer:** Arnold Machin **Rev:** Starfish above date, value at top **Note:** Proof specimens of this date are struck in "special brass" which looks like a pale bronze.

Date	Mintage	F	VF	XF	Unc	BU
1970	125,000	—	0.10	0.25	0.50	1.50
1970 Proof	23,000	Value: 1.00				

KM# 16 CENT

Brass **Obv:** Bust of Queen Elizabeth II right with tiara **Obv. Designer:** Arnold Machin **Rev:** Starfish above date, value at top

Date	Mintage	F	VF	XF	Unc	BU
1971FM	1,007,000	—	—	0.10	0.50	1.50
1971FM (P)	31,000	Value: 1.00				
1972FM	1,037,000	—	—	0.10	0.50	1.50
1972FM (P)	35,000	Value: 1.00				
1973	7,000,000	—	—	0.10	0.50	1.50
1973FM	1,040,000	—	—	0.10	0.50	1.50
1973FM (P)	35,000	Value: 1.00				

KM# 59 CENT

Brass, 19 mm. **Obv:** National arms above date **Rev:** Starfish, value at top

Date	Mintage	F	VF	XF	Unc	BU
1974	11,000	—	—	0.20	0.50	1.50
1974FM	71,000	—	—	0.10	0.25	0.75
1974FM (P)	94,000	Value: 1.00				
1975FM (M)	60,000	—	—	0.10	0.25	0.75
1975FM (U)	3,845	—	—	0.10	0.50	1.50
1975FM (P)	29,000	Value: 1.00				
1976FM (M)	60,000	—	—	0.10	0.25	0.75
1976FM (U)	1,453	—	—	0.10	0.50	1.50
1976FM (P)	23,000	Value: 1.00				
1977	3,000,000	—	—	0.10	0.25	0.75
1977FM (M)	60,000	—	—	0.10	0.25	0.75
1977FM (U)	713	—	—	0.50	1.50	4.50
1977FM (P)	11,000	Value: 1.00				
1978FM (M)	60,000	—	—	0.10	0.25	0.75
1978FM (U)	767	—	—	0.50	1.50	4.50
1978FM (P)	6,931	Value: 1.50				
1979	—	—	—	0.10	0.25	0.75
1979FM (P)	2,053	Value: 2.00				
1980	4,000,000	—	—	0.10	0.25	0.75
1980FM (P)	2,084	Value: 2.00				
1981	5,000,000	—	—	0.10	0.25	0.75
1981FM (M)	—	—	—	0.10	0.25	0.75
1981FM (P)	1,980	Value: 2.00				
1982	5,000,000	—	—	0.10	0.25	0.75
1982FM (M)	—	—	—	0.10	0.25	0.75
1982FM (P)	1,217	Value: 2.00				
1983	8,000,000	—	—	0.10	0.25	0.75
1983FM (P)	1,020	Value: 2.00				
1984	—	—	—	0.10	0.25	0.75
1984FM (P)	7,500	Value: 1.50				
1985	12,000,000	—	—	0.10	0.25	0.75
1985FM (P)	7,500	Value: 1.00				

KM# 59a CENT

Copper Plated Zinc **Obv:** National arms above date **Rev:** Starfish, value at top

Date	Mintage	F	VF	XF	Unc	BU
1985	—	—	—	0.10	0.25	0.75
1987	12,000,000	—	—	0.10	0.25	0.75
1989	12,000,000	—	—	0.10	0.25	0.75
1989 Proof	—	Value: 2.00				
1990	—	—	—	0.10	0.25	0.75
1991	—	—	—	0.10	0.25	0.75
1992	—	—	—	0.10	0.25	0.75
1995	—	—	—	0.10	0.25	0.75
1997	—	—	—	0.10	0.25	0.75
1998	—	—	—	0.10	0.25	0.75
1999	—	—	—	0.10	0.25	0.75

KM# 3 5 CENTS

Copper-Nickel, 21 mm. **Obv:** Bust of Queen Elizabeth II right with tiara **Rev:** Pineapple above garland divides date and value **Note:** The obverse of this coin also comes muled with the reverse of a New Zealand 2-cent piece, KM#32. The undated 1967 error is listed as New Zealand KM#33.

Date	Mintage	F	VF	XF	Unc	BU
1966	2,571,000	—	—	0.10	0.25	0.75
1968	600,000	—	—	0.30	1.25	3.00
1969	2,026,000	—	—	0.10	0.25	0.75
1969 Proof	75,000	Value: 1.00				
1970	26,000	—	—	0.30	0.60	1.80
1970 Proof	23,000	Value: 1.50				

KM# 17 5 CENTS

Copper-Nickel, 21 mm. **Obv:** Bust of Queen Elizabeth II right with tiara **Rev:** Pineapple above garland divides date and value

Date	Mintage	F	VF	XF	Unc	BU
1971FM	13,000	—	—	0.15	0.40	1.20
1971FM (P)	31,000	Value: 1.00				
1972FM	11,000	—	—	0.15	0.40	1.20
1972FM (P)	35,000	Value: 1.00				
1973FM	21,000	—	—	0.15	0.40	1.20
1973FM (P)	35,000	Value: 1.00				

KM# 38 5 CENTS

Copper-Nickel, 21 mm. **Obv. Legend:** THE COMMONWEALTH OF THE BAHAMAS

Date	Mintage	F	VF	XF	Unc	BU
1973	1,000,000	—	—	0.10	0.65	1.75

KM# 60 5 CENTS

Copper-Nickel, 21 mm. **Obv:** National arms above date **Rev:** Pineapple above garland divides value at top

Date	Mintage	F	VF	XF	Unc	BU
1974FM	23,000	—	—	0.10	0.50	1.50
1974FM (P)	94,000	Value: 1.00				
1975	—	—	—	0.10	0.30	0.90
1975FM (M)	12,000	—	—	0.10	0.50	1.50
1975FM (U)	3,845	—	—	0.15	0.75	2.25
1975FM (P)	29,000	Value: 1.00				
1976FM (M)	12,000	—	—	0.10	0.25	0.75
1976FM (U)	1,453	—	—	0.50	1.00	3.00
1976FM (P)	23,000	Value: 1.00				
1977FM (M)	12,000	—	—	0.10	0.35	1.00
1977FM (U)	713	—	—	0.50	1.50	4.50
1977FM (P)	11,000	Value: 1.00				
1978FM (M)	12,000	—	—	0.10	0.35	1.00
1978FM (U)	767	—	—	0.50	1.50	4.50
1978FM (P)	6,931	Value: 1.00				
1979FM (P)	2,053	Value: 1.50				
1980FM (P)	2,084	Value: 1.50				
1981	—	—	—	0.10	0.25	0.75
1981FM (P)	1,980	Value: 1.50				
1982FM (P)	1,217	Value: 1.50				
1983	2,000,000	—	—	0.10	0.25	0.75
1983FM (P)	1,020	Value: 1.50				
1984	—	—	—	0.10	0.25	0.75
1984FM (P)	1,036	Value: 1.50				
1985FM (P)	7,500	Value: 1.50				
1987	4,000,000	—	—	0.10	0.25	0.75
1989	—	—	—	0.10	0.25	0.75
1989 (P)	—	Value: 1.50				
1991	—	—	—	0.10	0.25	0.75
1992	—	—	—	0.10	0.25	0.75
1998	—	—	—	0.10	0.25	0.75
1999	—	—	—	0.10	0.25	0.75
2000	—	—	—	0.10	0.25	0.75

KM# 4 10 CENTS

Copper-Nickel, 23.5 mm. **Obv:** Bust of Queen Elizabeth II right with tiara, within beaded circle **Rev:** Bone Fish, value below, date above

Date	Mintage	F	VF	XF	Unc	BU
1966	2,198,000	—	—	0.10	0.50	1.50
1968	550,000	—	—	0.50	4.00	8.00
1969	2,026,000	—	—	0.10	0.50	1.50
1969 Proof	10,000	Value: 1.00				
1970	27,000	—	—	0.15	0.60	1.80
1970 Proof	23,000	Value: 1.00				

KM# 18 10 CENTS

Copper-Nickel, 23.5 mm. **Obv:** Bust of Queen Elizabeth II right with tiara, within beaded circle **Rev:** Bone Fish, value below, date above

Date	Mintage	F	VF	XF	Unc	BU
1971FM	13,000	—	—	0.15	0.50	1.50
1971FM (P)	31,000	Value: 1.00				
1972FM	11,000	—	—	0.15	0.50	1.50
1972FM (P)	35,000	Value: 1.00				
1973FM	15,000	—	—	0.15	0.50	1.50
1973FM (P)	35,000	Value: 1.00				

KM# 39 10 CENTS

Copper-Nickel, 23.5 mm. **Obv. Legend:** THE COMMONWEALTH OF THE BAHAMAS

Date	Mintage	F	VF	XF	Unc	BU
1973	1,000,000	—	—	0.15	1.00	2.00

KM# 61 10 CENTS

Copper-Nickel, 23.5 mm. **Obv:** National arms, date below, within beaded circle **Rev:** Bone Fish, value below, within beaded circle

Date	Mintage	F	VF	XF	Unc	BU
1974FM	17,000	—	—	0.10	0.50	1.50
1974FM (P)	94,000	Value: 1.50				
1975	3,000,000	—	—	0.10	0.50	1.50
1975FM (M)	6,000	—	—	0.15	0.50	1.50
1975FM (U)	3,845	—	—	0.15	0.50	1.50
1975FM (P)	29,000	Value: 1.50				
1976FM (M)	6,000	—	—	0.15	0.50	1.50
1976FM (U)	1,453	—	—	0.25	1.00	3.00
1976FM (P)	23,000	Value: 1.50				
1977FM (M)	6,000	—	—	0.15	0.50	1.50
1977FM (U)	713	—	—	0.50	1.50	3.00
1977FM (P)	11,000	Value: 1.50				
1978FM (M)	6,000	—	—	0.15	0.50	1.50
1978FM (U)	767	—	—	0.50	1.50	3.00
1978FM (P)	6,931	Value: 2.00				
1979FM (P)	2,053	Value: 2.50				
1980	2,500,000	—	—	0.10	0.50	1.50
1980FM (P)	2,084	Value: 2.50				
1981FM (P)	1,980	Value: 2.50				
1982	2,000,000	—	—	0.10	0.50	1.50
1982FM (P)	1,217	Value: 2.50				
1983FM (P)	1,020	Value: 2.50				
1984FM (P)	1,036	Value: 2.50				
1985	2,000,000	—	—	0.10	0.50	1.50
1985FM (M)	—	—	—	0.15	0.50	1.50
1985FM (P)	7,500	Value: 2.00				
1987	3,000,000	—	—	0.15	0.50	1.50
1989	—	—	—	0.15	0.50	1.50
1989	—	Value: 2.00				
1991	—	—	—	0.15	0.50	1.50
1992	—	—	—	0.15	0.50	1.50
1998	—	—	—	0.15	0.50	1.50

KM# 5 15 CENTS

Copper-Nickel, 25 mm. **Obv:** Bust of Queen Elizabeth II right with tiara **Rev:** Hibiscus, date divides value at bottom **Shape:** 4-sided

Date	Mintage	F	VF	XF	Unc	BU
1966	930,000	—	—	0.20	0.75	2.25
1969	1,026,000	—	—	0.20	0.75	2.25
1969 Proof	10,000	Value: 2.00				
1970	28,000	—	—	0.25	0.75	2.25
1970 Proof	23,000	Value: 1.50				

KM# 19 15 CENTS

Copper-Nickel, 25 mm. **Obv:** Bust of Queen Elizabeth II right with tiara **Rev:** Hibiscus, date divides value below **Shape:** 4-sided

Date	Mintage	F	VF	XF	Unc	BU
1971FM	13,000	—	—	0.20	0.50	1.50
1971FM Proof	31,000	Value: 1.50				
1972FM	11,000	—	—	0.20	0.50	1.50
1972FM Proof	35,000	Value: 1.50				
1973FM	14,000	—	—	0.20	0.50	1.50
1973FM Proof	35,000	Value: 1.50				

KM# 62 15 CENTS

Copper-Nickel, 25 mm. **Obv:** National arms above date **Rev:** Hibiscus, value divided at bottom **Shape:** 4-sided

Date	Mintage	F	VF	XF	Unc	BU
1974FM	15,000	—	—	0.20	0.50	1.50
1974FM (P)	94,000	Value: 1.50				
1975FM (M)	3,500	—	—	0.25	1.00	3.00
1975FM (U)	3,845	—	—	0.25	1.00	3.00
1975FM (P)	29,000	Value: 1.50				
1976FM (M)	3,500	—	—	0.25	1.00	3.00
1976FM (U)	1,453	—	—	0.30	1.50	4.50
1976FM (P)	23,000	Value: 1.50				
1977FM (M)	3,500	—	—	0.25	1.00	3.00
1977FM (U)	713	—	—	0.50	2.00	6.00
1977FM (P)	11,000	Value: 1.00				
1978FM (M)	3,500	—	—	0.25	1.00	3.00
1978FM (U)	767	—	—	0.50	2.00	6.00
1978FM (P)	6,931	Value: 1.50				
1979FM (P)	2,053	Value: 2.00				
1980FM (P)	2,084	Value: 2.00				
1981FM (P)	1,980	Value: 2.00				
1982FM (P)	1,217	Value: 2.50				
1983FM (P)	1,020	Value: 3.00				
1984FM (P)	1,036	Value: 3.00				
1985FM (P)	7,500	Value: 2.25				
1989	—	—	—	0.20	0.50	1.50
1989 (P)	—	Value: 3.00				
1991	—	—	—	0.20	0.50	1.50
1992	—	—	—	0.20	0.50	1.50

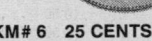

KM# 6 25 CENTS

Nickel, 24 mm. **Obv:** Bust of Queen Elizabeth II right with tiara **Rev:** Bahaminian sloop, value, date

Date	Mintage	F	VF	XF	Unc	BU
1966	3,685,000	—	—	0.30	0.50	1.50
1969	1,026,000	—	—	0.30	0.50	1.50
1969	10,000	Value: 1.50				
1970	26,000	—	—	0.35	0.75	2.25
1970FM (P)	23,000	Value: 2.00				
1970FM (M)	—	—	—	—	—	—

KM# 20 25 CENTS

Nickel, 24 mm. **Obv:** Bust of Queen Elizabeth II right with tiara **Rev:** Bahaminian Sloop, value, date

Date	Mintage	F	VF	XF	Unc	BU
1971FM	13,000	—	—	0.30	0.50	1.50
1971FM (P)	31,000	Value: 1.50				
1972FM	11,000	—	—	0.30	0.50	1.50
1972FM (M)	—	—	—	0.30	0.50	1.50
1972FM (P)	35,000	Value: 1.50				
1973FM	12,000	—	—	0.30	0.50	1.50
1973FM (P)	35,000	Value: 1.50				

KM# 63.1 25 CENTS

6.9000 g., Copper-Nickel, 24 mm. **Obv:** National arms above date, beaded rim **Rev:** Bahaminian Sloop, value above

Date	Mintage	F	VF	XF	Unc	BU
1974FM	13,000	—	—	0.30	0.50	1.50
1974FM (P)	94,000	Value: 1.50				
1975FM (M)	2,400	—	—	0.35	1.00	3.00
1975FM (U)	3,845	—	—	0.35	1.00	3.00
1975FM (P)	29,000	Value: 1.50				
1976FM (M)	2,400	—	—	0.35	1.00	3.00
1976FM (U)	1,453	—	—	0.35	1.25	3.75
1976FM (P)	23,000	Value: 1.50				
1977	—	—	—	0.30	0.50	1.50
1977FM (M)	2,400	—	—	0.35	1.00	3.00
1977FM (U)	713	—	—	0.50	3.00	9.00
1977FM (P)	11,000	Value: 1.50				
1978FM	2,400	—	—	0.35	1.00	3.00
1978FM (U)	767	—	—	0.50	3.00	9.00
1978FM (P)	6,931	Value: 2.00				
1979	—	—	—	0.30	0.50	1.50
1979FM (P)	2,053	Value: 3.00				
1980FM (P)	2,084	Value: 3.00				
1981	1,600,000	—	—	0.30	0.50	1.50
1981FM (P)	1,980	Value: 3.00				
1982FM (P)	1,217	Value: 4.00				
1983FM (P)	1,020	Value: 4.00				
1984FM (P)	1,036	Value: 4.00				
1985	2,000,000	—	—	0.30	0.50	1.50
1985FM (P)	7,500	Value: 2.00				
1987	—	—	—	0.30	0.50	1.50
1989	—	—	—	0.30	0.50	1.50
1989 (P)	—	Value: 3.00				

KM# 63.2 25 CENTS

5.7000 g., Copper-Nickel, 24 mm.

Date	Mintage	F	VF	XF	Unc	BU
1991	—	—	—	0.30	0.50	1.50
1992	—	—	—	0.30	0.50	1.50
1998	—	—	—	0.30	0.50	1.50
2000	—	—	—	0.30	0.50	1.50

KM# 7 50 CENTS

10.3700 g., 0.8000 Silver .2667 oz. ASW, 29 mm. **Obv:** Bust of Queen Elizabeth II right with tiara **Rev:** Blue Marlin, value and date at right

Date	Mintage	F	VF	XF	Unc	BU
1966	701,000	—	—	BV	3.75	5.00
1969	26,000	—	—	BV	3.75	5.00
1969 Proof	10,000	Value: 6.00				
1970	25,000	—	—	BV	3.75	5.00
1970 Proof	23,000	Value: 6.00				

KM# 21 50 CENTS

10.3700 g., 0.8000 Silver .2667 oz. ASW, 29 mm. **Obv:** Bust of Queen Elizabeth II right with tiara **Rev:** Blue Marlin, value and date at right

Date	Mintage	F	VF	XF	Unc	BU
1971FM	14,000	—	—	BV	3.75	5.00
1971FM (P)	31,000	Value: 6.00				
1972FM	12,000	—	—	BV	3.75	5.00
1972FM (P)	35,000	Value: 6.00				
1973FM	11,000	—	—	BV	3.75	5.00
1973FM (P)	35,000	Value: 6.00				

KM# 64 50 CENTS

Copper-Nickel, 29 mm. **Obv:** National arms, date below **Rev:** Blue Marlin, value at right

Date	Mintage	F	VF	XF	Unc	BU
1974FM	12,000	—	—	0.60	2.00	4.00
1975FM (M)	1,200	—	—	1.00	6.00	12.00
1975FM (U)	3,828	—	—	0.65	4.00	8.00
1976FM (M)	1,200	—	—	0.75	5.00	10.00
1976FM (U)	1,453	—	—	0.65	4.00	8.00
1977FM (M)	1,200	—	—	0.75	5.00	10.00
1977FM (U)	713	—	—	1.25	10.00	15.00
1978FM (M)	1,200	—	—	1.00	8.00	12.00
1978FM (U)	767	—	—	1.25	10.00	15.00
1981FM (P)	1,980	Value: 6.00				
1982FM (P)	1,217	Value: 7.00				
1983FM (P)	1,020	Value: 7.00				
1984FM (P)	1,036	Value: 7.00				
1985FM (P)	7,500	Value: 5.00				
1989	—	—	—	0.75	2.25	3.00
1989 Proof	—	Value: 5.00				
1991	—	—	—	0.75	2.25	3.00
1992	—	—	—	0.75	2.25	3.00

KM# 64a 50 CENTS

10.3700 g., 0.8000 Silver .2667 oz. ASW, 29 mm.

Date	Mintage	F	VF	XF	Unc	BU
1974FM (P)	94,000	Value: 8.00				
1975FM (P)	29,000	Value: 8.00				
1976FM (P)	23,000	Value: 8.00				
1977FM (P)	11,000	Value: 8.00				
1978FM (P)	6,931	Value: 8.00				
1979FM (P)	2,053	Value: 15.00				
1980FM (P)	2,084	Value: 15.00				

KM# 8 DOLLAR

18.1400 g., 0.8000 Silver .4666 oz. ASW, 34 mm. **Obv:** Bust of Queen Elizabeth II right with tiara **Rev:** Conch shell above garland, within 3/4 beaded circle, value and date above circle

Date	Mintage	F	VF	XF	Unc	BU
1966	406,000	—	—	BV	6.50	10.00
1969	26,000	—	—	BV	5.00	10.00
1969 Proof	10,000	Value: 8.00				
1970	27,000	—	—	BV	6.50	10.00
1970 Proof	23,000	Value: 8.00				

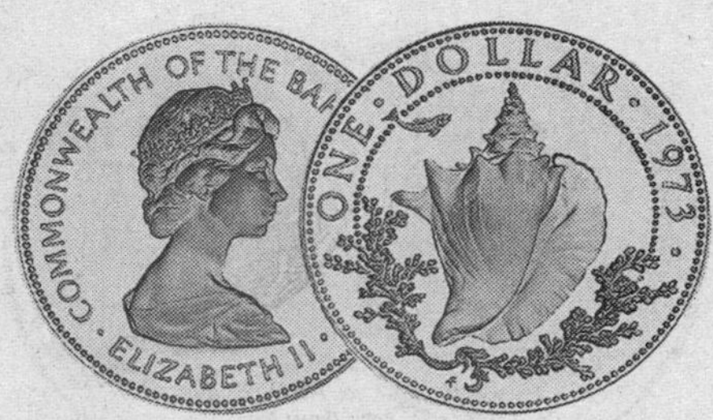

KM# 22 DOLLAR

18.1400 g., 0.8000 Silver .4666 oz. ASW, 34 mm. **Obv:** Bust of Queen Elizabeth II right with tiara **Rev:** Conch shell above garland within 3/4 beaded circle, value and date above

Date	Mintage	F	VF	XF	Unc	BU
1971FM	15,000	—	—	BV	6.50	10.00
1971FM (P)	31,000	Value: 8.00				
1972FM	18,000	—	—	BV	6.50	10.00
1972FM (P)	35,000	Value: 8.00				
1973FM	10,000	—	—	BV	6.50	10.00
1973FM (P)	35,000	Value: 8.00				

KM# 65 DOLLAR

Copper-Nickel, 34 mm. **Obv:** National arms above daate **Rev:** Conch shell above garland within 3/4 beaded circle, value at top

Date	Mintage	F	VF	XF	Unc	BU
1974FM	12,000	—	—	1.25	4.00	6.00
1975FM (M)	600	—	—	7.50	25.00	—
1975FM (U)	3,845	—	—	1.50	9.00	12.00
1976FM (M)	600	—	—	7.50	25.00	—
1976FM (U)	1,453	—	—	1.75	10.00	13.50
1977FM (M)	600	—	—	7.50	25.00	—
1977FM (U)	713	—	—	5.00	25.00	—
1978FM (U)	1,367	—	—	2.00	10.00	13.50

KM# 65a DOLLAR

18.1400 g., 0.8000 Silver .4666 oz. ASW, 34 mm.

Date	Mintage	F	VF	XF	Unc	BU
1974FM (P)	94,000	Value: 8.00				
1975FM (P)	29,000	Value: 8.00				
1976FM (P)	23,000	Value: 10.00				
1977FM (P)	11,000	Value: 10.00				
1978FM (P)	6,931	Value: 12.00				
1979FM (P)	2,053	Value: 17.00				
1980FM (P)	2,084	Value: 17.00				

KM# 65b DOLLAR

Copper-Nickel, 32 mm.

Date	Mintage	F	VF	XF	Unc	BU
1981FM (P)	1,980	Value: 17.00				
1989	—	—	—	1.50	4.00	6.00
1989 (P)	Est. 2,000	Value: 17.00				
1991	—	—	—	1.50	4.00	6.00
1992	—	—	—	1.50	4.00	6.00

KM# 89 DOLLAR

Copper-Nickel **Obv:** National arms, date below **Rev:** Poinciana flower, value above

Date	Mintage	F	VF	XF	Unc	BU
1982FM (P)	1,217	Value: 20.00				

KM# 93 DOLLAR

Copper-Nickel **Subject:** 10th Anniversary of Independence **Rev:** Allamanda flower, value above

Date	Mintage	F	VF	XF	Unc	BU
1983FM (P)	1,020	Value: 20.00				

KM# 104 DOLLAR

Copper-Nickel **Rev:** Bougainvillea flower, value above

Date	Mintage	F	VF	XF	Unc	BU
1984FM (P)	1,036	Value: 20.00				
1985FM (P)	7,500	Value: 10.00				

KM# 154 DOLLAR

Copper-Nickel **Designer:** **Note:** Golf - Hole in One. Similar to 5 Dollars, KM#155.

Date	Mintage	F	VF	XF	Unc	BU
1994	20,000	—	—	—	15.00	—

KM# 186 DOLLAR

1.2442 g., 0.9999 Gold .0400 oz. AGW **Rev:** Two flamingos **Note:** Similar to 5 Dollars, KM#188.

Date	Mintage	F	VF	XF	Unc	BU
1995 Proof	—	Value: 50.00				

KM# 176 DOLLAR

31.1800 g., 0.9990 Silver 1.0015 oz. ASW **Subject:** Third Millennium - Year 2000 **Obv:** Crowned bust of Queen Elizabeth II right, date below **Rev:** Artistic map, value below

Date	Mintage	F	VF	XF	Unc	BU
1996 Proof	50,000	Value: 35.00				

KM# 9 2 DOLLARS

29.8000 g., 0.9250 Silver .8863 oz. ASW, 40 mm. **Obv:** Bust of Queen Elizabeth II right with tiara **Obv. Designer:** Arnold Machin **Rev:** National bird - two flamingos, value and date at top

Date	Mintage	F	VF	XF	Unc	BU
1966	104,000	—	—	BV	12.00	14.00
1969	26,000	—	—	BV	12.00	14.50
1969 Proof	10,000	Value: 12.00				
1970	32,000	—	—	BV	12.00	14.50
1970 Proof	23,000	Value: 12.00				

KM# 23 2 DOLLARS

29.8000 g., 0.9250 Silver .8863 oz. ASW, 40 mm. **Obv:** Bust of Queen Elizabeth II right with tiara **Rev:** National bird-two flamingos, value and date at top

Date	Mintage	F	VF	XF	Unc	BU
1971FM	88,000	—	—	BV	12.00	14.50
1971FM (P)	60,000	Value: 12.00				
1972FM	65,000	—	—	BV	12.00	14.50
1972FM (P)	59,000	Value: 12.00				
1973FM	43,000	—	—	BV	12.50	14.00
1973FM (P)	50,000	Value: 13.00				

KM# 66 2 DOLLARS

Copper-Nickel, 40 mm. **Obv:** National arms, date below **Rev:** National bird-two flamingos, value above

Date	Mintage	F	VF	XF	Unc	BU
1974FM	37,000	—	—	2.25	6.00	8.00
1975FM (M)	300	—	—	9.00	25.00	—
1975FM (U)	8,810	—	—	2.25	7.00	9.00
1976FM (M)	300	—	—	9.00	25.00	—

Date	Mintage	F	VF	XF	Unc	BU
1976FM (U)	4,381	—	—	2.50	10.00	12.00
1977FM (M)	300	—	—	9.00	25.00	—
1977FM (U)	946	—	—	3.00	20.00	—
1978FM (U)	1,067	—	—	3.00	15.00	—
1979FM (U)	300	—	—	7.50	25.00	—
1980FM (U)	—	—	—	—	75.00	—

KM# 66a 2 DOLLARS

29.8000 g., 0.9250 Silver .8863 oz. ASW, 40 mm.

Date	Mintage	F	VF	XF	Unc	BU
1974FM (P)	129,000	Value: 12.00				
1975FM (P)	45,000	Value: 12.00				
1976FM (P)	35,000	Value: 12.00				
1977FM (P)	15,000	Value: 13.50				
1978FM (P)	11,000	Value: 16.50				
1979FM (P)	2,053	Value: 27.50				
1980FM (P)	2,084	Value: 27.50				

KM# 66b 2 DOLLARS

Copper-Nickel, 40 mm.

Date	Mintage	F	VF	XF	Unc	BU
1981FM (P)	1,980	Value: 25.00				
1989	—	—	—	2.25	6.00	8.00

KM# 66c 2 DOLLARS

16.8500 g., 0.9250 Silver .5012 oz. ASW **Obv:** National arms, date below **Rev:** National bird-two flamingos, value above

Date	Mintage	F	VF	XF	Unc	BU
1989	Est. 4,000	Value: 30.00				
1991	600	—	—	—	80.00	—

KM# 90 2 DOLLARS

Copper-Nickel **Obv:** National arms, date below **Rev:** Bahama swallows, value at top

Date	Mintage	F	VF	XF	Unc	BU
1982FM (P)	1,217	Value: 30.00				

KM# 94 2 DOLLARS

Copper-Nickel **Subject:** 10th Anniversary of Independence **Rev:** Honeycreepers, value at top

Date	Mintage	F	VF	XF	Unc	BU
1983FM (P)	1,020	Value: 30.00				

KM# 105 2 DOLLARS

Copper-Nickel **Rev:** Flamingos in flight, value at top

Date	Mintage	F	VF	XF	Unc	BU
1984FM (P)	1,036	Value: 30.00				
1985FM (P)	7,500	Value: 25.00				

KM# 158 2 DOLLARS

28.2800 g., 0.9250 Silver .8411 oz. ASW **Subject:** Royal Visit **Rev:** Portraits and yacht, date at right

Date	Mintage	F	VF	XF	Unc	BU
1994 Proof	10,000	Value: 40.00				

KM# 164 2 DOLLARS

30.0800 g., 0.9990 Silver .9982 oz. ASW **Series:** Flora and Fauna **Obv:** National arms, date below **Rev:** Hibiscus flower and value within square, coin value below **Note:** "Applique"

Date	Mintage	F	VF	XF	Unc	BU
1995 Proof	25,000	Value: 40.00				

KM# 165 2 DOLLARS

31.4000 g., 0.9990 Silver 1.0085 oz. ASW **Series:** Flora and Fauna **Rev:** Bahama Amazon Parrot on branch, value below **Note:** "Applique"

Date	Mintage	F	VF	XF	Unc	BU
1995 Proof	10,000	Value: 45.00				

KM# 166 2 DOLLARS

31.4000 g., 0.9990 Silver 1.0085 oz. ASW **Series:** Flora and Fauna **Rev:** Caribbean Monk Seal, value below **Note:** "Applique"

Date	Mintage	F	VF	XF	Unc	BU
1995 Proof	10,000	Value: 45.00				

KM# 183.1 2 DOLLARS

23.3300 g., 0.9250 Silver 0.6938 oz. ASW **Series:** Olympics **Subject:** Catamaran Sailing **Obv:** Crowned bust of Queen Elizabeth II right, date below **Rev:** Two figures on catamaran, sailing, value below **Rev. Legend:** OLIMPIC GAMES...

Date	Mintage	F	VF	XF	Unc	BU
1995 Proof	30,000	Value: 35.00				

KM# 183.2 2 DOLLARS

23.3300 g., 0.9250 Silver .6938 oz. ASW **Series:** Olympics **Subject:** Catamaran Sailing **Rev:** Two figures on catamaran, sailing, value below **Rev. Legend:** OLYMPIC GAMES...

Date	Mintage	F	VF	XF	Unc	BU
1995	—	—	—	—	150	—

KM# 187 2 DOLLARS

3.1103 g., 0.9999 Gold .1000 oz. AGW **Rev:** Two flamingos **Note:** Similar to 5 Dollars, KM#188.

Date	Mintage	F	VF	XF	Unc	BU
1995 Proof	—	Value: 85.00				

KM# 203 2 DOLLARS

23.3300 g., 0.9250 Silver .6938 oz. ASW, 38.6 mm. **Subject:** Protect Our World **Obv:** Queen's head right **Rev:** Flamingo and map, value below **Edge:** Reeded

Date	Mintage	F	VF	XF	Unc	BU
1996 Proof	—	Value: 50.00				

KM# 177 2 DOLLARS

3.1103 g., 0.9999 Gold .1000 oz. AGW **Subject:** Third Millennium - Year 2000 **Obv:** Queen's portrait **Rev:** Sea shell shaped map **Note:** Similar to 1 Dollar, KM#176.

Date	Mintage	F	VF	XF	Unc	BU
1996 Proof	10,000	Value: 80.00				

KM# 206 2 DOLLARS

23.2300 g., 0.9250 Silver 0.6908 oz. ASW, 38.6 mm. **Subject:** UNICEF **Obv:** Bust of Queen Elizabeth II, right **Rev:** Two boys and a dolphin, value below **Edge:** Reeded

Date	Mintage	F	VF	XF	Unc	BU
1997 Proof	25,000	Value: 30.00				

KM# 204 2 DOLLARS

23.3200 g., 0.9250 Silver 0.6935 oz. ASW, 38.5 mm. **Subject:** Queen Mother **Obv:** Crowned bust of Queen Elizabeth II right, date below **Rev:** Queen Mother's portrait circa 1908, within beaded circle, value below circle **Edge:** Reeded

Date	Mintage	F	VF	XF	Unc	BU
1997 Proof	—	Value: 50.00				

KM# 198 2 DOLLARS

28.2800 g., 0.9250 Silver .8410 oz. ASW **Subject:** WWF Conserving Nature **Obv:** Queen's portrait **Rev:** Spotfin Butterfly Fish and a Queen Angelfish, value below

Date	Mintage	F	VF	XF	Unc	BU
1997 Proof	Est. 15,000	Value: 45.00				

KM# 207 2 DOLLARS

28.2000 g., 0.9250 Silver with gilt outer ring 0.8387 oz. ASW, 38.5 mm. **Subject:** Queen Mother **Obv:** Queen's portrait **Rev:** Queen Mother with dog **Edge:** Reeded

Date	Mintage	F	VF	XF	Unc	BU
2000 Proof	—	Value: 50.00				

KM# 10 5 DOLLARS

42.1200 g., 0.9250 Silver 1.2527 oz. ASW, 45 mm. **Obv:** Bust of Queen Elizabeth II right with tiara **Obv. Designer:** Arnold Machin **Rev:** Shield with crown at top, sailing ships below, banner below shield, garland above, date at right, value above

Date	Mintage	F	VF	XF	Unc	BU
1966	100,000	—	—	BV	17.50	18.50
1969	36,000	—	—	BV	17.50	18.50
1969 Proof	10,000	Value: 17.50				
1970	43,000	—	—	BV	17.50	18.50
1970 Proof	23,000	Value: 17.50				

KM# 24 5 DOLLARS

42.1200 g., 0.9250 Silver 1.2527 oz. ASW, 45 mm. **Obv:** Young bust of Queen Elizabeth II right **Obv. Designer:** Arnold Machin **Rev:** National arms, date and value

Date	Mintage	F	VF	XF	Unc	BU
1971FM	29,000	—	—	BV	16.50	17.50
1971FM (P)	31,000	Value: 16.50				

KM# 33 5 DOLLARS

42.1200 g., 0.9250 Silver 1.2527 oz. ASW, 45 mm. **Obv:** Young Queen Elizabeth II right **Rev:** National arms, value, date

Date	Mintage	F	VF	XF	Unc	BU
1972FM	32,000	—	—	BV	16.50	17.50
1972FM (P)	35,000	Value: 16.50				
1973FM	32,000	—	—	BV	16.50	17.50
1973FM (P)	35,000	Value: 16.50				

KM# 67 5 DOLLARS

Copper-Nickel, 45 mm. **Obv:** National arms **Rev:** National flag, value above

Date	Mintage	F	VF	XF	Unc	BU
1974FM	32,000	—	—	—	8.00	—
1975FM (M)	200	—	—	—	40.00	—
1975FM (U)	7,058	—	—	—	10.00	—
1976FM (M)	200	—	—	—	40.00	—
1976FM (U)	2,591	—	—	—	15.00	—
1977FM (M)	200	—	—	—	40.00	—
1977FM (U)	801	—	—	—	20.00	—
1978FM (U)	1,244	—	—	—	15.00	—

KM# 67a 5 DOLLARS

42.1200 g., 0.9250 Silver 1.2527 oz. ASW **Designer:**

Date	Mintage	F	VF	XF	Unc	BU
1974FM (P)	94,000	Value: 16.50				
1975FM (P)	29,000	Value: 17.50				
1976FM (P)	23,000	Value: 17.50				
1977FM (P)	11,000	Value: 25.00				
1978FM (P)	6,931	Value: 30.00				
1979FM (P)	2,053	Value: 35.00				
1980FM (P)	2,084	Value: 35.00				

KM# 67b 5 DOLLARS

42.1200 g., 0.5000 Silver .6771 oz. ASW **Designer:** **Note:** Reduced diameter.

Date	Mintage	F	VF	XF	Unc	BU
1981FM (P)	1,980	Value: 35.00				

KM# 91 5 DOLLARS

42.1200 g., 0.5000 Silver .6771 oz. ASW **Obv:** National arms **Rev:** Flag below globe, value at bottom

Date	Mintage	F	VF	XF	Unc	BU
1982FM (P)	1,217	Value: 40.00				

KM# 95 5 DOLLARS

42.1200 g., 0.5000 Silver .6771 oz. ASW **Subject:** 10th Anniversary of Independence **Rev:** Flamingo

Date	Mintage	F	VF	XF	Unc	BU
1983FM (P)	1,020	Value: 40.00				

KM# 106 5 DOLLARS

42.1200 g., 0.5000 Silver .6771 oz. ASW **Rev:** Historical map, value above

Date	Mintage	F	VF	XF	Unc	BU
1984FM (P)	1,036	Value: 40.00				

KM# 107 5 DOLLARS

42.1200 g., 0.5000 Silver .6771 oz. ASW **Obv:** National arms, date below **Rev:** Half-length Christopher Columbus looking left, value above

Date	Mintage	F	VF	XF	Unc	BU
1985FM (P)	7,847	Value: 25.00				

KM# 132 5 DOLLARS

19.4400 g., 0.9250 Silver .5782 oz. ASW **Obv:** National arms, date below **Rev:** Standing Christopher Columbus with sword and flag before radiant sun, value lower left, date below

Date	Mintage	F	VF	XF	Unc	BU
1989 Proof	Est. 4,000	Value: 35.00				
1991	750	—	—	—	—	85.00
1991 Proof	7,000	Value: 40.00				

KM# 139 5 DOLLARS

19.4400 g., 0.9250 Silver .5782 oz. ASW **Series:** 500th Anniversary of the Americas **Rev:** Bust of Columbus at left, standing Ferdinand and Isabella at right, value below

Date	Mintage	F	VF	XF	Unc	BU
1991 Proof	Est. 25,000	Value: 25.00				

KM# 140 5 DOLLARS
19.4400 g., 0.9250 Silver .5782 oz. ASW **Series:** 500th Anniversary of the Americas **Subject:** Columbus sighting land **Rev:** Columbus on ship, inset of picture at right, "1492" below inset, value at bottom

Date	Mintage	F	VF	XF	Unc	BU
1991 Proof	Est. 25,000	Value: 25.00				

KM# 141 5 DOLLARS
19.4400 g., 0.9250 Silver .5782 oz. ASW **Series:** 500th Anniversary of the Americas **Subject:** Columbus claiming the land **Rev:** Columbus claiming the land, value at bottom

Date	Mintage	F	VF	XF	Unc	BU
1991 Proof	Est. 25,000	Value: 25.00				

KM# 142 5 DOLLARS
19.4400 g., 0.9250 Silver .5782 oz. ASW **Series:** 500th Anniversary of the Americas **Rev:** Bust of Jacques Cartier, 3/4 right, and map, value at bottom

Date	Mintage	F	VF	XF	Unc	BU
1991 Proof	Est. 25,000	Value: 25.00				

KM# 143 5 DOLLARS
19.4400 g., 0.9250 Silver .5782 oz. ASW **Series:** 500th Anniversary of the Americas **Rev:** Bust of President Thomas Jefferson, facing, looking left, Independence Hall at left with date below, value at bottom

Date	Mintage	F	VF	XF	Unc	BU
1991 Proof	Est. 25,000	Value: 25.00				

KM# 144 5 DOLLARS
19.4400 g., 0.9250 Silver .5782 oz. ASW **Series:** 500th Anniversary of the Americas **Rev:** Heads of Simon Bolivar and Jose San Martin on right, looking left, small statue of man on horseback at left, names at left, value at bottom

Date	Mintage	F	VF	XF	Unc	BU
1991 Proof	Est. 25,000	Value: 25.00				

KM# 146 5 DOLLARS
19.4400 g., 0.9250 Silver .5782 oz. ASW **Series:** 500th Anniversary of the Americas **Subject:** Electric light demonstration **Rev:** Bust of Thomas Edison with arms crossed, facing, light bulbs and inscription over left shoulder, people and name at right shoulder, value at bottom

Date	Mintage	F	VF	XF	Unc	BU
1991 Proof	Est. 25,000	Value: 25.00				

KM# 145 5 DOLLARS
19.4400 g., 0.9250 Silver .5782 oz. ASW **Series:** 500th Anniversary of the Americas **Subject:** Abolition of slavery **Rev:** Bust of President Abraham Lincoln, 3/4 right, two figures at right, date at left, value at bottom

Date	Mintage	F	VF	XF	Unc	BU
1991 Proof	Est. 25,000	Value: 25.00				

KM# 147 5 DOLLARS
19.4400 g., 0.9250 Silver .5782 oz. ASW **Series:** 500th Anniversary of the Americas **Subject:** Wright brothers' first airplane flight **Rev:** Two standing figures below plane, small date at right, words on lower left, value at bottom

Date	Mintage	F	VF	XF	Unc	BU
1991 Proof	Est. 25,000	Value: 25.00				

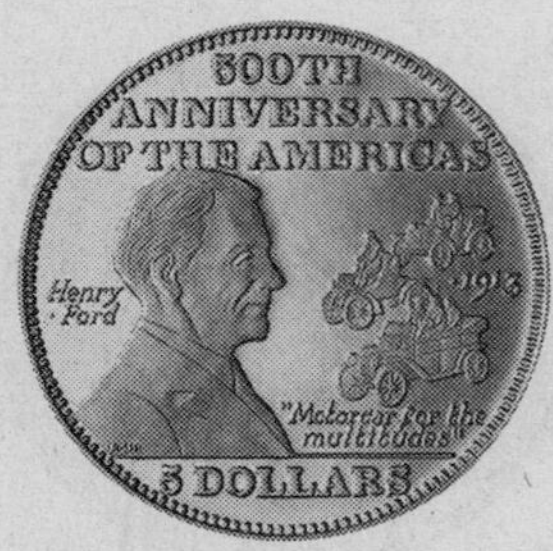

KM# 148 5 DOLLARS
19.4400 g., 0.9250 Silver .5782 oz. ASW **Series:** 500th Anniversary of the Americas **Rev:** Bust of Henry Ford on left facing right, automobiles at right with date and inscription, value at bottom

Date	Mintage	F	VF	XF	Unc	BU
1991 Proof	Est. 25,000	Value: 25.00				

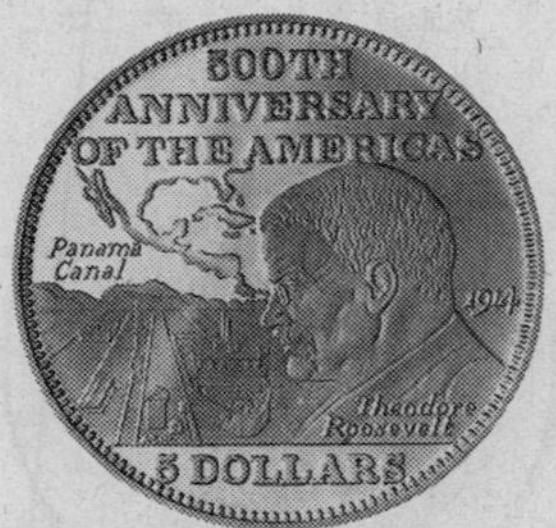

KM# 149 5 DOLLARS
19.4400 g., 0.9250 Silver .5782 oz. ASW **Series:** 500th Anniversary of the Americas **Rev:** Bust of President Roosevelt on right looking left, Panama Canal on left, value at bottom

Date	Mintage	F	VF	XF	Unc	BU
1991 Proof	Est. 25,000	Value: 25.00				

KM# 150 5 DOLLARS
19.4400 g., 0.9250 Silver .5782 oz. ASW **Series:** 500th Anniversary of the Americas **Subject:** First manned moonlanding **Rev:** Astronaut on moon on left, planets in orbit and inscription on right, value at bottom

Date	Mintage	F	VF	XF	Unc	BU
1991 Proof	Est. 25,000	Value: 25.00				

KM# 138 5 DOLLARS
19.4400 g., 0.9250 Silver .5782 oz. ASW **Series:** Discovery of the New World **Obv:** Coat of arms **Rev:** Columbus' ships within circle, value below circle

Date	Mintage	F	VF	XF	Unc	BU
1992 Proof	Est. 25,000	Value: 25.00				

KM# 192 5 DOLLARS
1.5550 g., 0.5000 Gold .0250 oz. AGW **Obv:** Crowned bust of Queen Elizabeth II right, date below **Obv. Designer:** Raphael Maklouf **Rev:** Facing pair of flamingos, value above

Date	Mintage	F	VF	XF	Unc	BU
1992 Proof	Est. 750	Value: 70.00				

KM# 159 5 DOLLARS
23.3300 g., 0.9250 Silver .6939 oz. ASW **Obv:** Crowned bust of Queen Elizabeth II right, date below **Rev:** Pirate Captain Howell Davis, value below, within circle

Date	Mintage	F	VF	XF	Unc	BU
1993 Proof	Est. 5,000	Value: 35.00				

KM# 160 5 DOLLARS
23.3300 g., 0.9250 Silver .6939 oz. ASW **Obv:** Crowned bust of Queen Elizabeth II right, date below **Rev:** Pirate Captain Charles Vane, value at left foot, within circle

Date	Mintage	F	VF	XF	Unc	BU
1993 Proof	Est. 5,000	Value: 35.00				

KM# 161 5 DOLLARS
23.3300 g., 0.9250 Silver .6939 oz. ASW **Rev:** Pirate Captain Edward Teach, value lower left, within circle

Date	Mintage	F	VF	XF	Unc	BU
1993 Proof	Est. 5,000	Value: 35.00				

KM# 169 5 DOLLARS
23.3300 g., 0.9250 Silver .6939 oz. ASW **Subject:** World Soccer Championship **Rev:** Soccer player kicking soccer ball value at lower left

Date	Mintage	F	VF	XF	Unc	BU
1993 Proof	Est. 15,000	Value: 35.00				

KM# 170 5 DOLLARS
23.3300 g., 0.9250 Silver .6939 oz. ASW **Rev:** Sailing ship, flamingo on right, Marlin on left, value at bottom

Date	Mintage	F	VF	XF	Unc	BU
1993 Proof	Est. 20,000	Value: 35.00				

KM# 201 5 DOLLARS
3.1103 g., 0.9990 Gold .1000 oz. AGW **Subject:** Golf - Hole in One **Obv:** National arms within 3/4 circle, legend around, date below **Obv. Legend:** COMMONWEALTH OF THE BAHAMAS **Rev:** Golf ball rolling towards cup, value lower right

Date	Mintage	F	VF	XF	Unc	BU
1994 Proof	250,000	Value: 120				

KM# 171 5 DOLLARS
31.1035 g., 0.9990 Silver 1.000 oz. ASW **Rev:** Space shuttle and satellite, value at upper left

Date	Mintage	F	VF	XF	Unc	BU
1994 Proof	Est. 10,000	Value: 60.00				

KM# 172 5 DOLLARS
31.1035 g., 0.9990 Silver 1.000 oz. ASW **Obv:** Crowned bust of Queen Elizabeth II right, date below **Rev:** Two Whistling Swans in flight, value at bottom

Date	Mintage	F	VF	XF	Unc	BU
1994 Proof	Est. 15,000	Value: 55.00				

KM# 173 5 DOLLARS
31.4700 g., 0.9250 Silver .9359 oz. ASW **Rev:** Ponce De Leon on horseback at right, small building at left, value below

Date	Mintage	F	VF	XF	Unc	BU
1994 Proof	Est. 10,000	Value: 40.00				

KM# 155 5 DOLLARS
31.1035 g., 0.9990 Silver 1.0000 oz. ASW **Subject:** Golf - Hole in One **Obv:** National arms within 3/4 circle, legend around, date below **Obv. Legend:** COMMONWEALTH OF THE BAHAMAS **Rev:** Golf ball rolling towards cup **Note:** The cup is an actual hole in the coin.

Date	Mintage	F	VF	XF	Unc	BU
1994 Proof	Est. 50,000	Value: 45.00				

KM# 188 5 DOLLARS
6.2207 g., 0.9999 Gold .2000 oz. AGW **Obv:** Crowned bust of Queen Elizabeth II right, date below **Rev:** Two flamingos facing, value below

Date	Mintage	F	VF	XF	Unc	BU
1995 Proof	—	Value: 185				

KM# 178 5 DOLLARS
7.7758 g., 0.9999 Gold .2500 oz. AGW **Subject:** Third Millennium - Year 2000 **Obv:** Bust of Queen Elizabeth II right **Rev:** Seashell-shaped world map

Date	Mintage	F	VF	XF	Unc	BU
1996 Proof	5,000	Value: 180				

KM# 11 10 DOLLARS
3.9943 g., 0.9170 Gold .1177 oz. AGW **Subject:** Adoption of New Constitution **Obv:** Bust of Queen Elizabeth II right with tiara **Rev:** Fortress, date below, value above

Date	Mintage	F	VF	XF	Unc	BU
1967	6,200	—	—	—	85.00	—
1967 Proof	850	Value: 100				

KM# 25 10 DOLLARS
3.9943 g., 0.9170 Gold .1177 oz. AGW **Obv:** Bust of Queen Elizabeth II right with tiara **Rev:** Fortress, date below, value above

Date	Mintage	F	VF	XF	Unc	BU
1971	23,000	—	—	—	80.00	—
1971(t) Proof	1,250	Value: 90.00				

KM# 26.1 10 DOLLARS
3.9943 g., 0.9170 Gold .1177 oz. AGW **Obv:** Bust of Queen Elizabeth II right with tiara **Rev:** Fortress, date below, value above, hallmark and fineness stamped right of date **Note:** Struck by the Gori and Zucchi Mint, Italy. Prev. KM#26.

Date	Mintage	F	VF	XF	Unc	BU
1971	—	—	—	—	80.00	—

KM# 26.2 10 DOLLARS
3.9943 g., 0.9170 Gold 0.1177 oz. AGW **Rev:** Hallmark and finess stamped left of date **Note:** Struck by the Gori and Zucchi Mint, Italy.

Date	Mintage	F	VF	XF	Unc	BU
1971	—	—	—	—	80.00	—

KM# 34 10 DOLLARS
3.1950 g., 0.9170 Gold .0940 oz. AGW **Obv:** Bust of Queen Elizabeth II right **Rev:** Fortress, date below, value above

Date	Mintage	F	VF	XF	Unc	BU
1972	11,000	—	—	—	65.00	—
1972 Proof	1,250	Value: 75.00				

KM# 40.1 10 DOLLARS
1.4500 g., 0.7500 Gold .0349 oz. AGW **Subject:** Independence Day - July 10 **Obv:** Bust of Queen Elizabeth II right with tiara, date below **Rev:** Tobacco Dove, value, without fineness and date

Date	Mintage	F	VF	XF	Unc	BU
1973	—	—	—	—	30.00	—
1973 Proof	—	Value: 35.00				

KM# 40.2 10 DOLLARS
1.4500 g., 0.7500 Gold .0349 oz. AGW **Obv:** Bust of Queen Elizabeth II right with tiara, date below **Rev:** Tobacco Dove divides value, date at right, date without fineness

Date	Mintage	F	VF	XF	Unc	BU
1973	—	—	—	—	30.00	—

KM# 41 10 DOLLARS
1.4500 g., 0.5850 Gold .0272 oz. AGW **Obv:** Bust of Queen Elizabeth II right with tiara, date below **Rev:** Tobacco Dove divides value, date at right, .585 fineness and date

Date	Mintage	F	VF	XF	Unc	BU
1973	9,960	—	—	—	32.00	—
1973 Proof	1,260	Value: 35.00				

KM# 42 10 DOLLARS
49.7500 g., 0.9250 Silver 1.4795 oz. ASW, 50 mm.
Subject: Independence Day - July 10 **Obv:** Legend around queen's portrait **Rev:** Santa Maria with full sails, value below

Date	Mintage	F	VF	XF	Unc	BU
1973FM	28,000	—	—	—	22.50	—
1973FM Proof	63,000	Value: 22.50				

KM# 68 10 DOLLARS
Copper-Nickel, 50 mm. **Subject:** 1st Anniversary of Independence **Obv:** National arms, date below **Rev:** Head of Sir Milo B. Butler, Governor-General right, value above, legend below

Date	Mintage	F	VF	XF	Unc	BU
1974FM Proof	4,825	—	—	—	12.00	—

KM# 68a 10 DOLLARS
50.4200 g., 0.9250 Silver 1.4994 oz. ASW, 50 mm.
Subject: 1st Anniversary of Independence **Obv:** National arms, date below **Rev:** Head of Sir Milo B. Butler, Governor-General right, value above, legend below

Date	Mintage	F	VF	XF	Unc	BU
1974FM Proof	43,000	Value: 22.50				

KM# 76 10 DOLLARS
Copper-Nickel, 50 mm. **Subject:** Anniversary of Independence **Obv:** National arms with supporters, date below **Rev:** Yellow Elder, value at top

Date	Mintage	F	VF	XF	Unc	BU
1975FM (M)	100	—	—	—	90.00	—
1975FM (U)	5,325	—	—	—	12.50	—
1976FM (M)	100	—	—	—	90.00	—
1976FM (U)	100	—	—	—	90.00	—
1977FM (M)	100	—	—	—	90.00	—
1977FM (U)	369	—	—	—	60.00	—

KM# 76a 10 DOLLARS
49.1000 g., 0.9250 Silver 1.4602 oz. ASW **Designer:**

Date	Mintage	F	VF	XF	Unc	BU
1975FM (P)	63,000	Value: 20.00				
1976FM (P)	10,000	Value: 22.50				
1977FM (P)	4,424	Value: 25.00				

KM# 78.1 10 DOLLARS
45.3600 g., 0.5000 Silver .7291 oz. ASW, 50 mm. **Subject:** 5th Anniversary of Independence **Obv:** National arms, date below **Rev:** Head of Prince Charles, right, value at bottom

Date	Mintage	F	VF	XF	Unc	BU
1978 Proof	50,000	Value: 25.00				

KM# 78.2 10 DOLLARS
45.3600 g., 0.5000 Silver .7291 oz. ASW, 50 mm. **Obv:** National arms, date below **Rev:** Head of Prince Charles, right, tower mint mark after DOLLARS

Date	Mintage	F	VF	XF	Unc	BU
1978(t) Proof	—	Value: 25.00				

KM# 79 10 DOLLARS
45.3600 g., 0.5000 Silver .7291 oz. ASW, 50 mm. **Subject:** 5th Anniversary of Independence **Obv:** National arms, date below **Rev:** Head of Sir Milo B. Butler, 3/4 left, value at bottom

Date	Mintage	F	VF	XF	Unc	BU
1978 Proof	50,000	Value: 20.00				

KM# 84 10 DOLLARS
30.2800 g., 0.5000 Silver .4868 oz. ASW **Subject:** 10th Anniversary Caribbean Development Bank **Obv:** National arms **Rev:** Flag below globe, value at bottom

Date	Mintage	F	VF	XF	Unc	BU
1980FM Proof	1,001	Value: 25.00				

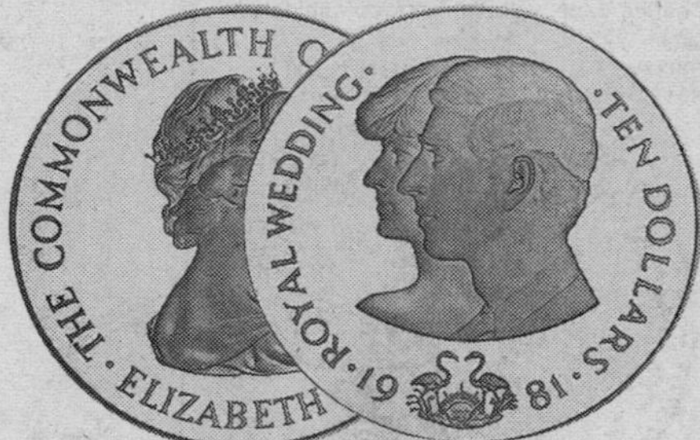

KM# 85 10 DOLLARS
28.2800 g., 0.9250 Silver .8410 oz. ASW **Subject:** Wedding of Prince Charles and Lady Diana **Obv:** Bust of Queen Elizabeth II right with tiara **Obv. Designer:** Arnold Machin **Rev:** Conjoined busts of royal couple left

Date	Mintage	F	VF	XF	Unc	BU
1981 Proof	39,000	Value: 30.00				

KM# 96 10 DOLLARS
30.2800 g., 0.5000 Silver .4867 oz. ASW **Subject:** 30th Anniversary - Coronation of Queen Elizabeth **Obv:** National arms, date below **Rev:** Royal symbols divided by sceptres, dates at either side, value at bottom

Date	Mintage	F	VF	XF	Unc	BU
1983FM Proof	3,374	Value: 25.00				

KM# 97 10 DOLLARS
23.3300 g., 0.9250 Silver .6939 oz. ASW **Subject:** 10th Anniversary of Independence **Rev:** Standing figure in front of flag, value below

Date	Mintage	F	VF	XF	Unc	BU
1983 Proof	800	Value: 37.50				

KM# 114 10 DOLLARS
23.3300 g., 0.9250 Silver .6939 oz. ASW **Subject:** Los Angeles Olympics **Obv:** National arms **Rev:** Sprinter, symbol at right, value at bottom

Date	Mintage	F	VF	XF	Unc	BU
1984 Proof	2,100	Value: 40.00				

KM# 127 10 DOLLARS
29.1700 g., 0.5000 Silver .4690 oz. ASW **Subject:** 10th Anniversary of Central Bank **Obv:** National arms **Rev:** Sand dollar, value at top

Date	Mintage	F	VF	XF	Unc	BU
1984 Proof	1,001	Value: 45.00				

KM# 109 10 DOLLARS
28.2800 g., 0.9250 Silver .8411 oz. ASW **Subject:** Royal Visit **Obv:** Bust of Queen Elizabeth II right **Rev:** National arms, value below

Date	Mintage	F	VF	XF	Unc	BU
1985 Proof	1,060	Value: 40.00				

KM# 109a 10 DOLLARS
47.5400 g., 0.9170 Gold 1.4013 oz. AGW **Subject:** Royal Visit

Date	Mintage	F	VF	XF	Unc	BU
1985 Proof	Est. 250	Value: 925				

KM# 113 10 DOLLARS
28.2800 g., 0.5000 Silver .4546 oz. ASW **Subject:** Commonwealth Games **Obv:** National arms, date below **Rev:** Competitor running left, value at right

Date	Mintage	F	VF	XF	Unc	BU
1986	899	—	—	—	30.00	—

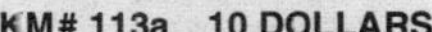

KM# 113a 10 DOLLARS
28.2800 g., 0.9250 Silver .8411 oz. ASW **Subject:** Commonwealth Games **Obv:** National arms, date below **Rev:** Competitor running left, value at right

Date	Mintage	F	VF	XF	Unc	BU
1986 Proof	1,343	Value: 32.00				

KM# 120 10 DOLLARS
28.2800 g., 0.9250 Silver .8411 oz. ASW **Rev:** Queen Isabella receiving Columbus

Date	Mintage	F	VF	XF	Unc	BU
1987 Proof	1,800	Value: 32.00				

KM# 123 10 DOLLARS
28.2800 g., 0.9250 Silver .8411 oz. ASW **Subject:** Columbus discovering America **Obv:** Queen Elizabeth **Rev:** Columbus sighting America, date below

Date	Mintage	F	VF	XF	Unc	BU
1988 Proof	1,704	Value: 32.00				

KM# 128 10 DOLLARS
28.2800 g., 0.9250 Silver .8411 oz. ASW **Obv:** Queen Elizabeth **Rev:** Columbus with flag and sword

Date	Mintage	F	VF	XF	Unc	BU
1989 Proof	Est. 10,000	Value: 25.00				

KM# 133 10 DOLLARS
28.2800 g., 0.9250 Silver .8411 oz. ASW **Series:** Discovery of the New World **Obv:** Queen Elizabeth **Rev:** Bust of Columbus, left, within circle, value below

Date	Mintage	F	VF	XF	Unc	BU
1990	550	—	—	—	110	—
1990 Proof	10,000	Value: 25.00				

KM# 196 10 DOLLARS
28.2800 g., 0.9250 Silver .8411 oz. ASW **Series:** Discovery of the New World **Obv:** Queen's portrait **Rev:** 5 men rowing boat, Columbus' ships in background, all in inner circle, value below

Date	Mintage	F	VF	XF	Unc	BU
1991 Proof	—	Value: 25.00				

KM# 193 10 DOLLARS
3.1450 g., 0.5000 Gold .0505 oz. AGW **Obv:** Bust of Queen Elizabeth II right, date below **Rev:** Two flamingos facing, value above

Date	Mintage	F	VF	XF	Unc	BU
1992 Proof	Est. 750	Value: 100				

KM# 197 10 DOLLARS
28.2800 g., 0.9250 Silver .8411 oz. ASW **Series:** Discovery of the New World **Obv:** Crowned bust of Queen Elizabeth II right, date below **Obv. Designer:** Raphael Maklouf **Rev:** Nina, Pinta, Santa Maria ships within circle, value below

Date	Mintage	F	VF	XF	Unc	BU
1992 Proof	—	Value: 25.00				

KM# 162 10 DOLLARS
136.0800 g., 0.9250 Silver 4.074 oz. ASW **Subject:** Expulsion of pirates **Obv:** Queen's portrait, legend around, date below **Obv. Legend:** • COMMONWEALTH OF THE BAHAMAS • **Rev:** Pirate ship, value below **Rev. Legend:** • EXPULSIS PIRATIS • RESTITUTA COMMERCIA •

Date	Mintage	F	VF	XF	Unc	BU
1993 Proof	Est. 2,000	Value: 120				

KM# 156 10 DOLLARS
7.7759 g., 0.9990 Gold .2500 oz. AGW **Subject:** Golf - Hole-in-One **Obv:** National arms **Rev:** Golfer making hole-in-one

Date	Mintage	F	VF	XF	Unc	BU
1994 Proof	2,500	Value: 225				

KM# 167 10 DOLLARS
155.5175 g., 0.9990 Silver 5.0000 oz. ASW **Obv:** Multicolor National arms **Rev:** Multicolor Bahama parrot on branch, value at bottom

Date	Mintage	F	VF	XF	Unc	BU
1995 Proof	2,500	Value: 175				

KM# 168 10 DOLLARS
15.5518 g., 0.9990 Gold .5000 oz. AGW **Obv:** Queen's portrait **Rev:** Bahama Parrot

Date	Mintage	F	VF	XF	Unc	BU
1995 Proof	2,000	Value: 345				

KM# 174 10 DOLLARS
28.2800 g., 0.9250 Silver .8411 oz. ASW **Subject:** 25th Anniversary - Caribbean Development Bank **Obv:** National arms **Rev:** Globe within inscription, butterflies flanking, birds and flowers below

Date	Mintage	F	VF	XF	Unc	BU
ND(1995) Proof	1,000	Value: 40.00				

KM# 189 10 DOLLARS
15.5517 g., 0.9999 Gold .5000 oz. AGW **Obv:** Queen's portrait **Rev:** Two flamingos facing

Date	Mintage	F	VF	XF	Unc	BU
1995 Proof	—	Value: 345				

KM# 179 10 DOLLARS
15.5517 g., 0.9999 Gold .5000 oz. AGW **Subject:** Third Millennium - Year 2000 **Obv:** Queen's portrait **Rev:** Seashell-shaped world map

Date	Mintage	F	VF	XF	Unc	BU
1996 Proof	5,000	Value: 345				

KM# 200 10 DOLLARS
31.1035 g., 0.9990 Silver 1.0000 oz. ASW **Subject:** 50th Anniversary of the University of the West Indies **Obv:** National arms **Rev:** University arms, dates

Date	Mintage	F	VF	XF	Unc	BU
1998 Proof	1,000	Value: 50.00				

KM# 12 20 DOLLARS
7.9880 g., 0.9170 Gold .2355 oz. AGW **Subject:** Adoption of New Constitution **Obv:** Bust of Queen Elizabeth II right **Rev:** Lighthouse, date below

Date	Mintage	F	VF	XF	Unc	BU
1967	6,200	—	—	—	160	—
1967 Proof	850	Value: 175				

KM# 27 20 DOLLARS
7.9880 g., 0.9170 Gold .2355 oz. AGW **Obv:** Bust of Queen Elizabeth II with tiara right **Rev:** Lighthouse, value at top, date at bottom

Date	Mintage	F	VF	XF	Unc	BU
1971	22,000	—	—	—	160	—
1971(t) Proof	1,250	Value: 170				

KM# 28 20 DOLLARS
7.9880 g., 0.9170 Gold .2355 oz. AGW **Obv:** Bust of Queen Elizabeth II right with tiara **Rev:** Lighthouse above date, value at top, hallmark and fineness stamped at bottom **Note:** Struck by the Gori and Zucchi Mint, Italy.

Date	Mintage	F	VF	XF	Unc	BU
1971 Proof	—	—	—	—	160	—

KM# 35 20 DOLLARS
6.4800 g., 0.9170 Gold .1880 oz. AGW **Obv:** Bust of Queen Elizabeth II right **Rev:** Lighthouse above date, value at top

Date	Mintage	F	VF	XF	Unc	BU
1972	10,000	—	—	—	125	—
1972 Proof	1,250	Value: 135				

KM# 43.1 20 DOLLARS
2.9000 g., 0.7500 Gold .0699 oz. AGW **Subject:** Independence Day - July 10 **Obv:** Bust of Queen Elizabeth II right with tiara, date below **Rev:** Flamingos, without fineness and date, value at bottom

Date	Mintage	F	VF	XF	Unc	BU
1973	—	—	—	—	50.00	—
1973 Proof	—	Value: 60.00				

KM# 43.2 20 DOLLARS
2.9000 g., 0.7500 Gold .0699 oz. AGW **Subject:** Independence Day - July 10 **Obv:** Bust of Queen Elizabeth II right with tiara **Rev:** Flamingos, without fineness, high date

Date	Mintage	F	VF	XF	Unc	BU
1973	—	—	—	—	50.00	—
1973 Proof	—	Value: 60.00				

KM# 44 20 DOLLARS
2.9000 g., 0.5850 Gold .0545 oz. AGW **Obv:** Bust of Queen Elizabeth II right with tiara, date below **Rev:** Flamingos, .585 fineness, low date, value at bottom

Date	Mintage	F	VF	XF	Unc	BU
1973	8,660	—	—	—	45.00	—
1973 Proof	1,260	Value: 50.00				

KM# 157 20 DOLLARS
15.5517 g., 0.9990 Gold .5000 oz. AGW **Obv:** Arms **Rev:** Golfer making hole-in-one

Date	Mintage	F	VF	XF	Unc	BU
1994 Proof	2,500	Value: 345				

KM# 82 25 DOLLARS
37.3800 g., 0.9250 Silver 1.1117 oz. ASW **Subject:** 250th Anniversary of Parliament **Obv:** National arms, date below **Rev:** Royal sceptre divides dates, value at bottom

Date	Mintage	F	VF	XF	Unc	BU
1979 Proof	3,002	Value: 40.00				

KM# 110 25 DOLLARS
120.0000 g., 0.9250 Silver 3.5687 oz. ASW, 63 mm. **Subject:** Columbus' Discovery of America **Obv:** National arms **Rev:** Columbus claiming the land by planting flag, crew with clergy holding cross behind, value above, date below

Date	Mintage	F	VF	XF	Unc	BU
1985 Proof	1,950	Value: 70.00				

KM# 115 25 DOLLARS
129.6000 g., 0.9250 Silver 3.8547 oz. ASW, 63 mm. **Subject:** Bird Conservation **Obv:** National arms **Rev:** Flamingos, value at top **Rev. Designer:** Michael Rizzello

Date	Mintage	F	VF	XF	Unc	BU
1985 Proof	1,060	Value: 75.00				

KM# 118 25 DOLLARS
129.6000 g., 0.9250 Silver 3.8547 oz. ASW **Obv:** Queen's portrait **Rev:** Queen Isabella receiving Columbus

Date	Mintage	F	VF	XF	Unc	BU
1987 Proof	1,750	Value: 70.00				

KM# 124 25 DOLLARS
136.0000 g., 0.9250 Silver 4.0446 oz. ASW **Subject:** Columbus Discovering New World **Obv:** Queen's portrait **Rev:** Columbus on deck pointing towards land, date at bottom

Date	Mintage	F	VF	XF	Unc	BU
1988 Proof	954	Value: 120				

KM# 129 25 DOLLARS
136.0000 g., 0.9250 Silver 4.0446 oz. ASW **Obv:** Queen Elizabeth **Rev:** Christopher Columbus, radiant sun and ocean in background, value below right hand, circle surrounds, date below circle

Date	Mintage	F	VF	XF	Unc	BU
1989 Proof	1,572	Value: 100				

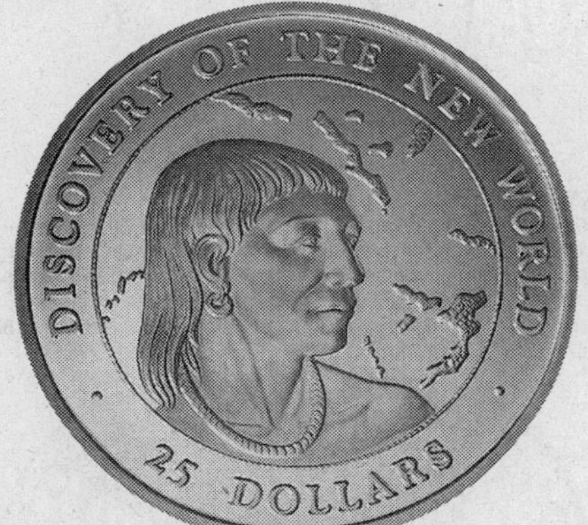

KM# 134 25 DOLLARS
136.0000 g., 0.9250 Silver 4.0446 oz. ASW **Series:** Discovery of the New World **Obv:** Queen Elizabeth **Rev:** Aborigine looking right, within circle, value below circle

Date	Mintage	F	VF	XF	Unc	BU
1990 Proof	5,000	Value: 75.00				

KM# 153 25 DOLLARS
136.0000 g., 0.9250 Silver 4.0446 oz. ASW **Series:** Discovery of the New World **Obv:** Queen Elizabeth **Rev:** Facing half bust of Columbus holding map, ship at left, circle surrounds, value below circle

Date	Mintage	F	VF	XF	Unc	BU
1991 Proof	Est. 500	Value: 175				

KM# 194 25 DOLLARS
7.8300 g., 0.5000 Gold .1258 oz. AGW **Obv:** Bust of Queen Elizabeth II right, date below **Rev:** Pair of flamingos, value above

Date	Mintage	F	VF	XF	Unc	BU
1992 Proof	Est. 750	Value: 175				

KM# 191 25 DOLLARS
136.0000 g., 0.9250 Silver 4.0446 oz. ASW, 63 mm. **Series:** Discovery of the New World **Obv:** Bust of Queen Elizabeth II right, date below **Rev:** Columbus meeting native Americans, within circle, value below circle **Note:** Photo reduced.

Date	Mintage	F	VF	XF	Unc	BU
1992 Proof	—	Value: 175				

KM# 202 25 DOLLARS
31.1035 g., 0.9999 Gold 1.0000 oz. AGW **Subject:** Golf - Hole-in-One **Obv:** National arms **Rev:** Golf ball rolling towards hole

Date	Mintage	F	VF	XF	Unc	BU
1994 Proof	—	Value: 675				

KM# 190 25 DOLLARS
31.1035 g., 0.9999 Gold 1.0000 oz. AGW **Obv:** Bust of Queen Elizabeth II right, date below **Rev:** Two flamingos, value at bottom

Date	Mintage	F	VF	XF	Unc	BU
1995 Proof	—	Value: 650				

KM# 180 25 DOLLARS
31.1035 g., 0.9999 Gold 1.0000 oz. AGW **Subject:** Third Millennium - Year 2000 **Obv:** Bust of Queen Elizabeth II right **Rev:** Seashell-shaped world map

Date	Mintage	F	VF	XF	Unc	BU
1996 Proof	5,000	Value: 650				

KM# 13 50 DOLLARS
19.9710 g., 0.9170 Gold .5888 oz. AGW **Subject:** Adoption of New Constitution **Obv:** Bust of Queen Elizabeth II right with tiara **Rev:** Santa Maria in full sail, value and date above

Date	Mintage	F	VF	XF	Unc	BU
1967	1,200	—	—	—	385	—
1967 Proof	850	Value: 400				

KM# 29 50 DOLLARS
19.9710 g., 0.9170 Gold .5888 oz. AGW **Obv:** Bust of Queen Elizabeth II right with tiara **Rev:** Santa Maria in full sail, value and date above

Date	Mintage	F	VF	XF	Unc	BU
1971	6,800	—	—	—	385	—
1971(t) Proof	1,250	Value: 400				

KM# 30 50 DOLLARS
19.9710 g., 0.9170 Gold .5888 oz. AGW **Obv:** Bust of Queen Elizabeth II right with tiara **Rev:** Santa Maria in full sail, value and above, hallmark and fineness stamped at bottom **Note:** Struck by the Gori and Zucchi Mint, Italy.

Date	Mintage	F	VF	XF	Unc	BU
1971	—	—	—	—	385	—

KM# 36 50 DOLLARS
15.9700 g., 0.9170 Gold .4708 oz. AGW **Obv:** Bust of Queen Elizabeth II right

Date	Mintage	F	VF	XF	Unc	BU
1972	2,250	—	—	—	325	—
1972 Proof	1,250	Value: 350				

KM# 45 50 DOLLARS
7.2700 g., 0.7500 Gold .1753 oz. AGW **Subject:** Independence Day - July 10 **Obv:** Bust of Queen Elizabeth II right, date below **Rev:** Spiny lobster, date below, value at bottom; without fineness

Date	Mintage	F	VF	XF	Unc	BU
1973	—	—	—	—	120	—
1973 Proof	—	Value: 130				

KM# 46 50 DOLLARS
7.2700 g., 0.5850 Gold .1367 oz. AGW **Obv:** Bust of Queen Elizabeth II right with tiara, date below **Rev:** Spiny lobster, .585 fineness to left, date to right, value at bottom

Date	Mintage	F	VF	XF	Unc	BU
1973	5,160	—	—	—	95.00	—
1973 Proof	1,260	Value: 110				

KM# 47 50 DOLLARS
7.3000 g., 0.7500 Gold .1760 oz. AGW **Obv:** Bust of Queen Elizabeth II right with tiara, date below **Rev:** Spiny lobster, without date or fineness, value at bottom

Date	Mintage	F	VF	XF	Unc	BU
1973	—	—	—	—	135	—

KM# 48 50 DOLLARS

15.6448 g., 0.5000 Gold .2515 oz. AGW **Subject:** Independence Day - July 10 **Obv:** Bust of Queen Elizabeth II right with tiara **Rev:** Two flamingos, value below

Date	Mintage	F	VF	XF	Unc	BU
1973JP	23,000	—	—	—	165	—
1973JP	18,000	Value: 175				

KM# 69 50 DOLLARS

2.7300 g., 0.9170 Gold .0804 oz. AGW **Subject:** 1st Anniversary of Independence **Obv:** Bust of Queen Elizabeth II right with tiara, date below **Rev:** Tobacco Dove, value, date, without fineness

Date	Mintage	F	VF	XF	Unc	BU
1974	34,000	—	—	—	55.00	—
1974 Proof	20,000	Value: 60.00				
1975	26,000	—	—	—	60.00	—
1975 Proof	15,000	Value: 65.00				
1976	2,207	—	—	—	70.00	—
1976 Proof	Inc. above	Value: 65.00				
1977	1,090	—	—	—	70.00	—
1977 Proof	—	Value: 85.00				

KM# 70 50 DOLLARS

2.7300 g., 0.9170 Gold .0804 oz. AGW **Obv:** Bust of Queen Elizabeth II right with tiara, date below **Rev:** Tobacco Dove, value date, .917 fineness

Date	Mintage	F	VF	XF	Unc	BU
1974	—	—	—	—	60.00	—

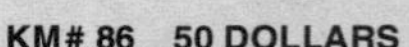

KM# 86 50 DOLLARS

2.6800 g., 0.5000 Gold .0430 oz. AGW **Obv:** National arms, date below **Rev:** Flamingos in flight

Date	Mintage	F	VF	XF	Unc	BU
1981FM Proof	2,050	Value: 65.00				

KM# 92 50 DOLLARS

2.6800 g., 0.5000 Gold .0430 oz. AGW **Obv:** National arms, date below **Rev:** Marlin (Swordfish), value above

Date	Mintage	F	VF	XF	Unc	BU
1982FM Proof	841	Value: 125				

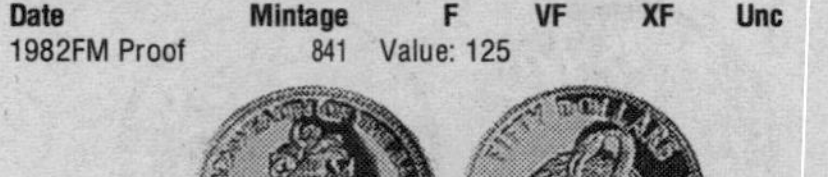

KM# 98 50 DOLLARS

2.6800 g., 0.5000 Gold .0430 oz. AGW **Subject:** 10th Anniversary of Independence **Obv:** National arms, date below **Rev:** Flamingo, value above

Date	Mintage	F	VF	XF	Unc	BU
1983FM Proof	962	Value: 100				

KM# 103 50 DOLLARS

2.6800 g., 0.5000 Gold .0430 oz. AGW **Obv:** National arms, date below **Rev:** Golden Allamanda, value above

Date	Mintage	F	VF	XF	Unc	BU
1984FM Proof	3,716	Value: 50.00				

KM# 108 50 DOLLARS

2.6800 g., 0.5000 Gold .0430 oz. AGW **Obv:** National arms, date below **Rev:** Santa Maria, value above

Date	Mintage	F	VF	XF	Unc	BU
1985FM Proof	1,575	Value: 70.00				

KM# 199 50 DOLLARS

6.4800 g., 0.9167 Gold .1875 oz. AGW **Subject:** Junkanoo Festival **Obv:** Crowned bust of Queen Elizabeth II right, date below **Rev:** Three costumed musicians, value below

Date	Mintage	F	VF	XF	Unc	BU
1994 Proof	—	Value: 150				

KM# 181 50 DOLLARS

2000.0000 g., 0.9990 Silver 64.2371 oz. ASW **Subject:** Third Millennium - Year 2000 **Obv:** Bust of Queen Elizabeth II right **Rev:** Seashell-shaped world map

Date	Mintage	F	VF	XF	Unc	BU
1996 Proof	2,000	Value: 875				

KM# 14 100 DOLLARS

39.9400 g., 0.9170 Gold 1.1776 oz. AGW **Subject:** Adoption of New Constitution **Obv:** Bust of Queen Elizabeth II right with tiara **Rev:** Columbus, date divides value at bottom

Date	Mintage	F	VF	XF	Unc	BU
1967	1,200	—	—	—	775	—
1967 Proof	850	Value: 820				

KM# 31 100 DOLLARS

39.9400 g., 0.9170 Gold 1.1776 oz. AGW **Obv:** Bust of Queen Elizabeth II right with tiara **Rev:** Shield with crown at top, sailing ship at bottom, ribbon below shield, garland above, value, date

Date	Mintage	F	VF	XF	Unc	BU
1971	6,800	—	—	—	775	—
1971(t) Proof	1,250	Value: 820				

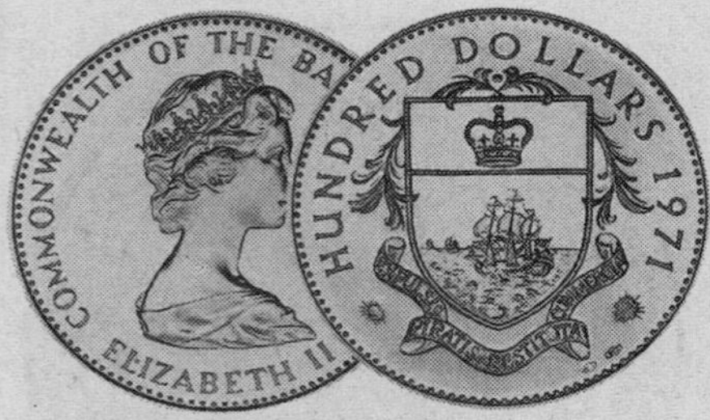

KM# 32.1 100 DOLLARS

39.9400 g., 0.9170 Gold 1.1776 oz. AGW **Obv:** Bust of Queen Elizabeth II right with tiara **Rev:** Shield with crown at top, sailing ship at bottom, ribbon below shield, garland above, value, date; hallmark and fineness at bottom right

Date	Mintage	F	VF	XF	Unc	BU
1971	—	—	—	—	775	—

KM# 32.2 100 DOLLARS

39.9400 g., 0.9170 Gold 1.1776 oz. AGW **Obv:** Bust of Queen Elizabeth II right with tiara **Rev:** Shield with crown at top, sailing ship at bottom, ribbon below shield, garland on top, value, date; hallmark at bottom right, without fineness

Date	Mintage	F	VF	XF	Unc	BU
1971	—	—	—	—	775	—

KM# 32.3 100 DOLLARS

39.9400 g., 0.9170 Gold 1.1776 oz. AGW **Obv:** Bust of Queen Elizabeth II right with tiara **Rev:** Shield with crown at top, sailing ship at bottom, ribbon below shield, garland above, value, date; fineness at bottom right without hallmark **Note:** Struck by the Gori and Zucchi Mint, Italy.

Date	Mintage	F	VF	XF	Unc	BU
1971	—	—	—	—	775	—

KM# 37 100 DOLLARS

31.9500 g., 0.9170 Gold .9420 oz. AGW **Obv:** Bust of Queen Elizabeth II right **Note:** The 1972 proof $100 is serially numbered on the edge.

Date	Mintage	F	VF	XF	Unc	BU
1972	2,250	—	—	—	620	—
1972 Proof	1,250	Value: 640				

KM# 49.1 100 DOLLARS

14.5400 g., 0.7500 Gold .3506 oz. AGW **Subject:** Independence Day - July 10 **Obv:** Bust of Queen Elizabeth II right with tiara, date below **Rev:** National arms, value above, date below; without fineness

Date	Mintage	F	VF	XF	Unc	BU
1973	—	—	—	—	235	—

KM# 49.2 100 DOLLARS

14.5400 g., 0.7500 Gold .3506 oz. AGW **Subject:** Independence Day - July 10 **Obv:** Bust of Queen Elizabeth II right with tiara, date below **Rev:** National arms, value above; without date or fineness

Date	Mintage	F	VF	XF	Unc	BU
1973 Proof	—	Value: 235				

KM# 50.1 100 DOLLARS

14.5400 g., 0.5850 Gold .2735 oz. AGW **Obv:** Bust of Queen Elizabeth II right with tiara, date below **Rev:** National arms, value above, .585 fineness to left, date to right

Date	Mintage	F	VF	XF	Unc	BU
1973	4,660	—	—	—	185	—
1973 Proof	1,260	Value: 200				

Note: Serial number on reverse

KM# 50.2 100 DOLLARS

14.5400 g., 0.5850 Gold .2735 oz. AGW **Obv:** Bust of Queen Elizabeth II right, date below **Rev:** National arms, value above, date and fineness at right, serial number at left

Date	Mintage	F	VF	XF	Unc	BU
1973	—	—	—	—	185	—

KM# 50.3 100 DOLLARS

14.5400 g., 0.5850 Gold .2735 oz. AGW **Obv:** Bust of Queen Elizabeth II right with tiara, date below **Rev:** National arms, value above, serial number at left, fineness below, date at right

Date	Mintage	F	VF	XF	Unc	BU
1973	—	—	—	—	185	—

KM# 71 100 DOLLARS

18.0145 g., 0.5000 Gold .2896 oz. AGW **Subject:** 1st Anniversary of Independence **Obv:** National arms, date below **Rev:** Two flamingos, value at bottom, date at right

Date	Mintage	F	VF	XF	Unc	BU
1974	4,486	—	—	—	190	—
1974 Proof	4,153	Value: 200				

KM# 72 100 DOLLARS

5.4600 g., 0.9170 Gold .1609 oz. AGW **Obv:** Bust of Queen Elizabeth II right with tiara, date below **Rev:** Broken waves behind flamingos' legs, value at bottom

Date	Mintage	F	VF	XF	Unc	BU
1974	29,000	—	—	—	110	—
1975	—	—	—	—	125	—

KM# 73 100 DOLLARS

5.4600 g., 0.9170 Gold .1609 oz. AGW **Obv:** Bust of Queen Elizabeth II right with tiara, date below **Rev:** Unbroken waves behind flamingos' legs, value at bottom

Date	Mintage	F	VF	XF	Unc	BU
1974 Proof	17,000	Value: 110				
1975 Proof	—	Value: 120				
1976	—	—	—	—	110	—
1976 Proof	—	Value: 120				
1977	—	—	—	—	120	—
1977 Proof	—	Value: 130				

KM# 74 100 DOLLARS

5.4600 g., 0.9170 Gold .1609 oz. AGW **Obv:** Bust of Queen Elizabeth II right with tiara, date below **Rev:** Unbroken waves behind flamingos legs, date at right, value at bottom; .917 fineness in oval

Date	Mintage	F	VF	XF	Unc	BU
1974	—	—	—	—	110	—

KM# 77 100 DOLLARS

18.0145 g., 0.5000 Gold .2896 oz. AGW **Subject:** 2nd Anniversary of Independence **Obv:** National arms, date below **Rev:** Bahama Amazon Parrot, value at bottom

Date	Mintage	F	VF	XF	Unc	BU
1975	3,694	—	—	—	190	—
1975 Proof	3,145	Value: 200				
1976 Proof	761	Value: 210				
1977 Proof	2,023	Value: 200				

KM# 80 100 DOLLARS

13.6000 g., 0.9630 Gold .4211 oz. AGW **Subject:** 5th Anniversary of Independence **Obv:** National arms, date below **Rev:** Bust of H.R.H Prince Charles, right, value below

Date	Mintage	F	VF	XF	Unc	BU
1978 Proof	3,275	Value: 285				

KM# 81 100 DOLLARS

13.6000 g., 0.9630 Gold .4211 oz. AGW **Subject:** 5th Anniversary of Independence **Obv:** National arms, date below **Rev:** Head of Sir Milo B. Butler, 1/2 left, value at bottom

Date	Mintage	F	VF	XF	Unc	BU
1978 Proof	25,000	Value: 285				

KM# 87 100 DOLLARS

6.4800 g., 0.9000 Gold .1875 oz. AGW **Subject:** Wedding of Prince Charles and Lady Diana **Obv:** Bust of Queen Elizabeth II right with tiara **Rev:** Conjoined busts of royal couple left

Date	Mintage	F	VF	XF	Unc	BU
1981 Proof	10,000	Value: 180				

KM# 99 100 DOLLARS

6.4800 g., 0.9000 Gold .1875 oz. AGW **Subject:** 10th Anniversary of Independence **Obv:** National arms, date below **Rev:** Bust of soldier left within unfurled flag, value at bottom

Date	Mintage	F	VF	XF	Unc	BU
1983 Proof	400	Value: 200				

KM# 111 100 DOLLARS

6.4800 g., 0.9000 Gold .1875 oz. AGW **Subject:** Columbus' Discovery of America **Obv:** National arms **Rev:** Columbus with group of people, date at bottom, value at top

Date	Mintage	F	VF	XF	Unc	BU
1985 Proof	450	Value: 200				

KM# 119 100 DOLLARS

6.4800 g., 0.9000 Gold .1875 oz. AGW **Obv:** Crowned bust of Queen Elizabeth II right **Rev:** Queen Isabella receiving Christopher Columbus, date below, value at top

Date	Mintage	F	VF	XF	Unc	BU
1987 Proof	849	Value: 185				

KM# 125 100 DOLLARS

6.4800 g., 0.9000 Gold .1875 oz. AGW **Subject:** Columbus Discovering America **Obv:** Bust of Queen Elizabeth II right **Rev:** Columbus sighting America

Date	Mintage	F	VF	XF	Unc	BU
1988 Proof	854	Value: 185				

KM# 130 100 DOLLARS

6.4800 g., 0.9000 Gold .1875 oz. AGW **Obv:** Queen Elizabeth **Rev:** Christopher Columbus, radiant sun and ocean in background within circle, date below, and at right of circle

Date	Mintage	F	VF	XF	Unc	BU
1989 Proof	Est. 5,000	Value: 180				

KM# 135 100 DOLLARS
6.4800 g., 0.9000 Gold .1875 oz. AGW **Subject:** Discovery of New World **Obv:** Queen Elizabeth II, date below **Rev:** Bust of Columbus left, value below circle

Date	Mintage	F	VF	XF	Unc	BU
1990	500	—	—	—	250	—
1990 Proof	5,000	Value: 175				

KM# 151 100 DOLLARS
6.4800 g., 0.9000 Gold .1875 oz. AGW **Subject:** Discovery of New World **Obv:** Crowned bust of Queen Elizabeth II right, date below **Rev:** 5 men rowing boat, ships in background within inner circle, legend above, value below

Date	Mintage	F	VF	XF	Unc	BU
1991	500	—	—	—	250	—

KM# 152 100 DOLLARS
6.4800 g., 0.9000 Gold .1875 oz. AGW **Subject:** Discovery of New World **Obv:** Crowned bust of Queen Elizabeth II right, date below **Rev:** Columbus' ships within circle, value below circle

Date	Mintage	F	VF	XF	Unc	BU
1992 Proof	Est. 5,000,000	Value: 170				
1992 Matte	—	Value: 250				

KM# 195 100 DOLLARS
999.9775 g., 0.9990 Silver 32.1500 oz. ASW **Subject:** Discovery of New World **Obv:** Bust of Queen Elizabeth II right, date below **Obv. Designer:** Raphael Maklouf **Rev:** Columbus' three ships - the Niña, the Pinta, the Santa Maria, within circle, value below circle

Date	Mintage	F	VF	XF	Unc	BU
1992 Proof	Est. 1,500	Value: 600				

KM# 163 100 DOLLARS
999.9775 g., 0.9990 Silver 32.1500 oz. ASW **Series:** Whales of the World **Obv:** Bust of Queen Elizabeth II right, date below **Rev:** Blue Whale with baby, within circle, value below circle

Date	Mintage	F	VF	XF	Unc	BU
1993	750	—	—	—	500	—

KM# 184 100 DOLLARS
999.9775 g., 0.9990 Silver 32.1500 oz. ASW **Series:** Whales of the World **Obv:** Bust of Queen Elizabeth II right, date below **Rev:** Killer Whales in inner circle, value below

Date	Mintage	F	VF	XF	Unc	BU
1994 Proof	750	Value: 550				

KM# 185 100 DOLLARS
999.9775 g., 0.9990 Silver 32.1500 oz. ASW **Series:** Whales of the World **Obv:** Bust of Queen Elizabeth II right, date below **Rev:** Humpback Whales within inner circle, value below

Date	Mintage	F	VF	XF	Unc	BU
1995 Proof	750	Value: 600				

KM# 51 150 DOLLARS
8.1900 g., 0.9170 Gold .2414 oz. AGW **Subject:** Independence Day - July 10 **Obv:** Bust of Queen Elizabeth II right with tiara, date below **Rev:** Spiny Lobster, value, small date at right

Date	Mintage	F	VF	XF	Unc	BU
1973	—	—	—	—	160	—
1973 Proof	—	Value: 170				
1974	7,128	—	—	—	165	—
1974 Proof	4,787	Value: 170				
1975	3,141	—	—	—	165	—
1975 Proof	2,770	Value: 180				
1976 Proof	168	Value: 300				
1977 Proof	327	Value: 240				

KM# 52 150 DOLLARS
8.1900 g., 0.9170 Gold .2414 oz. AGW **Obv:** Bust of Queen Elizabeth II right with tiara, date below **Rev:** Spiny Lobster, value, small date at right

Date	Mintage	F	VF	XF	Unc	BU
1974 Proof	—	Value: 170				

KM# 53 150 DOLLARS
8.1900 g., 0.9170 Gold .2414 oz. AGW **Obv:** Bust of Queen Elizabeth II right with tiara, date below **Rev:** Spiny Lobster, value, small date at right; .917 fineness in oval

Date	Mintage	F	VF	XF	Unc	BU
1974	—	—	—	—	170	—

KM# 54 200 DOLLARS
10.9200 g., 0.9170 Gold .3219 oz. AGW **Subject:** Independence Day - July 10 **Obv:** Bust of Queen Elizabeth II right with tiara, date below **Rev:** National arms, value above small date at right

Date	Mintage	F	VF	XF	Unc	BU
1973	—	—	—	—	210	—
1973 Proof	—	Value: 225				
1974	5,528	—	—	—	210	—
1974 Proof	3,587	Value: 225				
1975	1,545	—	—	—	215	—
1975 Proof	1,570	Value: 235				
1976 Proof	168	Value: 300				
1977 Proof	321	Value: 280				

KM# 56 200 DOLLARS
10.9200 g., 0.9170 Gold .3219 oz. AGW **Obv:** Bust of Queen Elizabeth II right with tiara, date below **Rev:** National arms, value above, small date at right; .917 fineness in oval

Date	Mintage	F	VF	XF	Unc	BU
1974	—	—	—	—	210	—

KM# 57 200 DOLLARS
10.9200 g., 0.9170 Gold .3219 oz. AGW **Obv:** Bust of Queen Elizabeth II right **Rev:** .916 fineness at left, serial number stamped below arms

Date	Mintage	F	VF	XF	Unc	BU
1974	—	—	—	—	210	—

KM# 83 250 DOLLARS
10.5800 g., 0.9000 Gold .3061 oz. AGW **Subject:** 250th Anniversary of Parliament **Obv:** Princess Anne's bust 1/2 left in inner circle, value below **Rev:** National arms, date below

Date	Mintage	F	VF	XF	Unc	BU
1979 Proof	1,835	Value: 225				

KM# 117 250 DOLLARS
47.5400 g., 0.9170 Gold 1.4017 oz. AGW **Subject:** Commonwealth Games **Obv:** National arms **Rev:** Competitor running left, value at right, logo below

Date	Mintage	F	VF	XF	Unc	BU
1985 Proof	101	Value: 1,000				

KM# 137 250 DOLLARS
47.5400 g., 0.9170 Gold 1.4017 oz. AGW **Subject:** Royal Visit **Obv:** Crowned bust of Queen Elizabeth II, right **Obv. Designer:** Raphael Maklouf **Rev:** National arms, value below

Date	Mintage	F	VF	XF	Unc	BU
1985 Proof	100	Value: 1,000				

KM# 121 250 DOLLARS
47.5400 g., 0.9170 Gold 1.4017 oz. AGW **Obv:** Bust of Queen Elizabeth II right **Rev:** Queen Isabella receiving Columbus, date at bottom, value at top

Date	Mintage	F	VF	XF	Unc	BU
1987 Proof	100	Value: 1,000				

KM# 126 250 DOLLARS
47.5400 g., 0.9170 Gold 1.4017 oz. AGW **Subject:** Columbus Discovers the New World **Obv:** Bust of Queen Elizabeth II right **Rev:** Columbus sighting land, date at bottom, value at top

Date	Mintage	F	VF	XF	Unc	BU
1988 Proof	53	Value: 1,100				

KM# 131 250 DOLLARS
47.5400 g., 0.9170 Gold 1.4017 oz. AGW **Obv:** Bust of Queen Elizabeth II right **Rev:** Christopher Columbus

Date	Mintage	F	VF	XF	Unc	BU
1989 Proof	Est. 250	Value: 950				

KM# 136 250 DOLLARS
47.5400 g., 0.9170 Gold 1.4017 oz. AGW **Subject:** Discovery of New World **Obv:** Bust of Queen Elizabeth II right **Rev:** Native American facing right, within circle, value at bottom

Date	Mintage	F	VF	XF	Unc	BU
1990 Proof	500	Value: 925				

KM# 175 250 DOLLARS
47.5400 g., 0.9170 Gold 1.4017 oz. AGW **Subject:** Discovery of the New World **Rev:** Columbus meeting native Americans, within circle, value below circle

Date	Mintage	F	VF	XF	Unc	BU
1992 Proof	Est. 500	Value: 925				

KM# 182 250 DOLLARS
47.5400 g., 0.9170 Gold 1.4017 oz. AGW **Subject:** Royal Visit **Note:** Similar to 2 Dollars, KM#158.

Date	Mintage	F	VF	XF	Unc	BU
1994 Proof	100	Value: 1,200				

KM# 88 500 DOLLARS
25.9200 g., 0.9000 Gold .7500 oz. AGW **Subject:** Wedding of Prince Charles and Lady Diana **Obv:** Bust of Queen Elizabeth II right with tiara **Obv. Designer:** Arnold Machin **Rev:** Conjoined busts of royal couple left

Date	Mintage	F	VF	XF	Unc	BU
1981 Proof	5,000	Value: 520				

KM# 100 1000 DOLLARS
41.4700 g., 0.9000 Gold 1.2001 oz. AGW **Subject:** America's Cup Challenge **Obv:** Bust of Queen Elizabeth II right with tiara, date below **Obv. Designer:** Arnold Machin **Rev:** Sailboat, value at left

Date	Mintage	F	VF	XF	Unc	BU
1983 Proof	300	Value: 820				

KM# 75 2500 DOLLARS
407.2600 g., 0.9170 Gold 12.0082 oz. AGW, 72 mm. **Obv:** National arms **Rev:** Two flamingos, value above, date below
Note: Photo reduced.

Date	Mintage	F	VF	XF	Unc	BU
1974 Proof	204	Value: 8,000				
1977 Proof	168	Value: 9,000				

KM# 101 2500 DOLLARS
407.2600 g., 0.9170 Gold 12.0082 oz. AGW, 72 mm. **Subject:** 10th Anniversary of Independence **Obv:** Bust of young Queen Elizabeth II right **Rev:** National arms, value below

Date	Mintage	F	VF	XF	Unc	BU
1983 Proof	55	Value: 9,500				

KM# 112 2500 DOLLARS
407.2600 g., 0.9170 Gold 12.0082 oz. AGW, 72 mm. **Subject:** Columbus' Discovery of America **Obv:** Bust of Queen Elizabeth II right **Rev:** Columbus with crew claiming land for Spain, planting flag, date below

Date	Mintage	F	VF	XF	Unc	BU
1985 Proof	37	Value: 10,000				

KM# 116 2500 DOLLARS
407.2600 g., 0.9170 Gold 12.0082 oz. AGW, 72 mm.
Rev: Kneeling Columbus and Queen Isabella, date at bottom
Rev. Designer: Frank Gasparro

Date	Mintage	F	VF	XF	Unc	BU
1987 Proof	20	Value: 10,250				

KM# 122 2500 DOLLARS
407.2600 g., 0.9170 Gold 12.0082 oz. AGW **Obv:** Bust of Queen Elizabeth II right **Rev:** Columbus sighting "New World"

Date	Mintage	F	VF	XF	Unc	BU
1988 Proof	32	Value: 10,000				

MINT SETS

KM#	Date	Mintage	Identification	Issue Price	Mkt Val
MS1	1966 (9)	75,050	KM#2-10	16.00	18.00

KM#	Date	Mintage	Identification	Issue Price	Mkt Val
MS2	1966 (7)	500,000	KM#2-8	5.25	9.00
MS3	1967 (4)	1,200	KM#11-14	180	1,350
MS4	1969	26,221	KM#2-10	20.25	20.00
MS5	1970 (9)	25,135	KM#3-10, 15	20.25	25.00
MS6	1971 (9)	12,895	KM#16-24	20.25	25.00
MS7	1971 (4)	6,800	KM#25, 27, 29, 31	185	1,100
MS8	1972 (9)	10,128	KM#16-23, 33	22.75	25.00
MS9	1972 (4)	2,250	KM#34-37	185	900
MS10	1973 (9)	9,853	KM#16-23, 33	23.75	30.00
MS11	1973 (4)	4,660	KM#40, 43, 47, 49.1	—	460
MS12	1973 (2)	—	KM#40, 43	—	100
MS13	1974 (9)	11,004	KM#59-67	22.50	32.00
MS14	1974 (4)	5,528	KM#51, 54, 69, 72	—	575
MS15	1974 (2)	—	KM#68, 71	—	200
MS16	1975 (9)	3,845	KM#59-67	27.00	35.00
MS17	1975 (4)	1,545	KM#51, 54, 69, 72	—	650
MS18	1976 (9)	1,453	KM#59-67	27.00	40.00
MS19	1977 (9)	731	KM#59-67	27.00	75.00
MS20	1978 (9)	767	KM#59-67	27.00	75.00
MS21	1989 (7)	—	KM#59a, 60-64, 65b	—	30.00
MS22	1991 (7)	5,000	KM#59a, 60-64, 65b	—	30.00
MS23	1992 (7)	—	KM#59a, 60-64, 65b	24.00	30.00

PROOF SETS

KM#	Date	Mintage	Identification	Issue Price	Mkt Val
PS1	1967 (4)	850	KM#11-14	252	1,300
PS2	1969 (9)	10,381	KM#2-10	35.00	30.00
PS3	1970 (9)	22,827	KM#3-10, 15	35.00	30.00
PS4	1971 (9)	30,507	KM#16-24	35.00	30.00
PS5A	1971 (4)	1,250	KM#25, 27, 29, 31	298	1,200
PS5B	1971 (4)	—	KM#26, 28, 30, 32.1	—	1,000
PS6	1972 (9)	34,789	KM#16-23, 33	35.00	30.00
PS7	1972 (4)	1,250	KM#34-37	565	1,200
PS8	1973 (9)	34,815	KM#16-23, 33	35.00	35.00
PS9	1973 (4)	1,260	KM#41, 44, 46, 50	402	500
PS10	1974 (9)	93,776	KM#59-63, 64a-67a	45.00	35.00
PS11	1974 (4)	3,587	KM#51, 54, 69, 73	1,000	600
PS12	1975 (9)	29,095	KM#59-63, 64a-67a	59.00	40.00
PS13	1975 (4)	1,570	KM#51, 54, 69, 73	1,000	650
PS14	1976 (9)	22,570	KM#59-63, 64a-67a	59.00	42.50
PS15	1976 (4)	—	KM#51, 54, 69, 73	1,000	750
PS16	1977 (9)	10,812	KM#59-63, 64a-67a	59.00	50.00
PS17	1977 (4)	—	KM#51, 54, 69, 73	—	700
PS18	1978 (9)	6,931	KM#59-63, 64a-67a	59.00	55.00
PS19	1979 (9)	2,053	KM#59-63, 64a-67a	115	75.00
PS20	1979 (2)	—	KM#82-83	445	375
PS21	1980 (9)	2,084	KM#59-63, 64a-67a	145	75.00
PS22	1981 (9)	1,980	KM#59-64, 65b-67b	62.00	60.00
PS23	1982 (9)	—	KM#59-64, 89-91	67.00	75.00
PS24	1983 (9)	1,009	KM#59-64, 93-95	67.00	75.00
PS25	1984 (9)	7,500	KM#59-64, 104-106	72.00	60.00
PS26	1985 (9)	1,576	KM#59-64, 104, 105, 107	—	65.00
PS27	1989 (9)	2,000	KM#59a, 60-64, 65b, 66c, 132	107	100
PS28	1991 (12)	25,000	KM#139-150	425	400
PS29	1992 (3)	750	KM#192-194 + gold-plated silver ingot	—	400

BAHRAIN

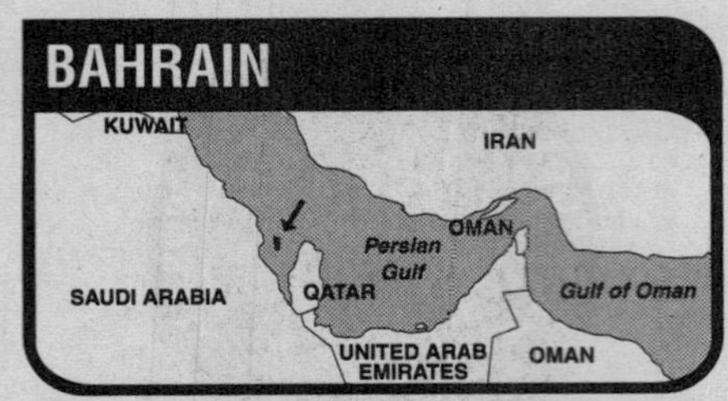

The State of Bahrain, a group of islands in the Persian Gulf off Saudi Arabia, has an area of 268 sq. mi. (622 sq. km.) and a population of 618,000. Capital: Manama. Prior to the depression of the 1930's, the economy was based on pearl fishing. Petroleum and aluminum industries and transit trade are the vital factors in the economy today.

The Portuguese occupied the islands in 1507 but were driven out in 1602 by Arab subjects of Persia. They in turn were ejected by Arabs of the Atalba tribe from the Arabian mainland who have maintained possession up to the present time. The ruling sheikh of Bahrain entered into relations with Great Britain in 1805 and concluded a binding treaty of protection in 1861. In 1968 Great Britain decided to terminate treaty relations with the Persian Gulf sheikhdoms. Unable to agree on terms of union with the other sheikhdoms, Bahrain decided to seek independence as a separate entity and became fully independent on August 14, 1971.

Bahrain took part in the Arab oil embargo against the U.S. and other nations. The government bought controlling interest in the oil industry in 1975.

The coinage of the State of Bahrain was struck at the Royal Mint, London, England.

RULERS

Al Khalifa Dynasty
Isa Bin Ali, 1869-1932
Hamad Bin Isa, 1932-1942
Salman Bin Hamad, 1942-1961
Isa Bin Salman, 1961-1999
Hamed Bin Isa, 1999-

MINT MARKS

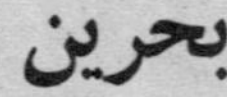

Bahrain

البحرين

al-Bahrain = of the two seas

MONETARY SYSTEM

Falus, Fulus — Fals, Fils — Falsan

1000 Fils = 1 Dinar

KINGDOM OF BAHRAIN

STANDARD COINAGE

KM# 1 FILS
Bronze, 1.5 mm. **Obv:** Date palm within circle, dates below **Rev:** Denomination

Date	Mintage	F	VF	XF	Unc	BU
AH1385-1965	1,500,000	—	0.10	0.20	0.40	0.60
AH1385-1965 Proof	12,000	Value: 1.00				
AH1386-1966	1,500,000	—	0.10	0.20	0.40	0.60
AH1386-1966 Proof	—	Value: 2.00				

KM# 1a FILS
1.5000 g., 0.9250 Silver .0446 oz. ASW, 1.5 mm. **Obv:** Date palm within circle, dates below **Rev:** Denomination

Date	Mintage	F	VF	XF	Unc	BU
AH1403-1983 Proof	Est. 15,000	Value: 4.00				

KM# 2 5 FILS
2.0000 g., Bronze, 18.5 mm. **Obv:** Palm tree within circle **Rev:** Denomination

Date	Mintage	F	VF	XF	Unc	BU
AH1385-1965	8,000,000	—	0.10	0.20	0.40	0.60
AH1385-1965 Proof	12,000	Value: 1.00				

KM# 2a 5 FILS
2.0000 g., 0.9250 Silver .0595 oz. ASW, 18.5 mm. **Obv:** Palm tree within **Rev:** Denomination

Date	Mintage	F	VF	XF	Unc	BU
AH1403-1983 Proof	Est. 15,000	Value: 4.00				

KM# 16 5 FILS
Brass **Obv:** Palm tree within circle, dates below circle **Rev:** Inner circle holds value behind box with denomination inside, outer circle of chain surrounds

Date	Mintage	F	VF	XF	Unc	BU
AH1412-1992	—	—	—	—	0.50	0.75
AH1412-1992	—	—	—	—	0.50	0.75

KM# 3 10 FILS
4.7500 g., Bronze, 23.5 mm. **Obv:** Palm tree within circle, dates below **Rev:** Denomination

Date	Mintage	F	VF	XF	Unc	BU
AH1385-1965	8,500,000	—	0.10	0.25	0.50	0.75
AH1385-1965 Proof	12,000	Value: 1.50				

KM# 3a 10 FILS
4.7500 g., 0.9250 Silver .1413 oz. ASW, 23.5 mm. **Obv:** Palm tree within circle, dates below **Rev:** Denomination

Date	Mintage	F	VF	XF	Unc	BU
AH1403-1983 Proof	Est. 15,000	Value: 5.00				

KM# 17 10 FILS
Brass **Obv:** Palm tree within circle, dates below circle **Rev:** Inner circle holds value behind box with denomination inside, outer cirlce of chain surrounds

Date	Mintage	F	VF	XF	Unc	BU
AH1412-1991	—	—	—	—	0.75	1.00
AH1412-1992	—	—	—	—	0.75	1.00
AH1420-2000	—	—	—	—	0.75	1.00

KM# 4 25 FILS
1.7500 g., Copper-Nickel, 16.5 mm. **Obv:** Palm tree within circle, dates below circle **Rev:** Denomination **Edge:** Reeded

Date	Mintage	F	VF	XF	Unc	BU
AH1385-1965	11,250,000	—	0.20	0.35	0.75	1.25
AH1385-1965 Proof	12,000	Value: 2.00				

KM# 4a 25 FILS
1.7500 g., 0.9250 Silver .0521 oz. ASW, 16.5 mm. **Obv:** Palm tree within circle, dates below circle **Rev:** Denomination **Edge:** Reeded

Date	Mintage	F	VF	XF	Unc	BU
AH1403-1983 Proof	Est. 15,000	Value: 5.00				

KM# 18 25 FILS
Copper-Nickel **Obv:** Ancient painting within circle, dates on opposite sides **Rev:** Numeric denomination back of boxed denomination within circle, chain surrounds

Date	Mintage	F	VF	XF	Unc	BU
AH1412-1992	—	—	—	—	1.25	1.50
AH1420-2000	—	—	—	—	1.25	1.50

KM# 5 50 FILS
3.1000 g., Copper-Nickel, 20 mm. **Obv:** Palm tree within circle, dates below circle **Rev:** Denomination

Date	Mintage	F	VF	XF	Unc	BU
AH1385-1965	6,909,000	—	0.25	0.55	1.25	1.65
AH1385-1965 Proof	12,000	Value: 2.50				

KM# 5a 50 FILS
3.1000 g., 0.9250 Silver .0922 oz. ASW, 20 mm. **Obv:** Palm tree within circle, dates below circle **Rev:** Denomination

Date	Mintage	F	VF	XF	Unc	BU
AH1403-1983 Proof	Est. 15,000	Value: 6.00				

KM# 19 50 FILS
Copper-Nickel **Obv:** Stylized sailboats within circle, dates at either side **Rev:** Numeric denomination back of boxed denomination within circle, chain surrounds

Date	Mintage	F	VF	XF	Unc	BU
AH1412-1992	—	—	—	—	1.50	1.75
AH1420-2000	—	—	—	—	1.50	1.75

KM# 6 100 FILS
6.5000 g., Copper-Nickel, 25 mm. **Obv:** Palm tree within circle, dates below circle **Rev:** Denomination **Edge:** Reeded

Date	Mintage	F	VF	XF	Unc	BU
AH1385-1965	8,300,000	—	0.35	0.75	1.50	2.00
AH1385-1965 Proof	12,000	Value: 3.50				

KM# 6a 100 FILS
6.5000 g., 0.9250 Silver .1933 oz. ASW, 25 mm. **Obv:** Palm tree within circle, dates below circle **Rev:** Denomination **Edge:** Reeded

Date	Mintage	F	VF	XF	Unc	BU
AH1403-1983 Proof	Est. 15,000	Value: 7.00				

KM# 20 100 FILS
Bi-Metallic Copper-Nickel center in Brass ring, 24 mm. **Obv:** Coat of arms within circle, dates at opposite sides **Rev:** Numeric denomination back of boxed denomination within circle, chain surrounds **Edge:** Reeded

Date	Mintage	F	VF	XF	Unc	BU
AH1412-1991	—	—	—	—	3.50	4.00
AH1412-1992	—	—	—	—	3.50	4.00
AH1415-1994	—	—	—	—	3.50	4.00
AH1416-1995	—	—	—	—	3.50	4.00
AH1417-1997	—	—	—	—	3.50	4.00
AH1420-2000	—	—	—	—	3.50	4.00

KM# 7 250 FILS
Copper-Nickel **Series:** F.A.O. **Obv:** Boat, palm tree at right **Rev:** F.A.O., divided by lines in center circle, head of grain at center below "A", value at lower left

Date	Mintage	F	VF	XF	Unc	BU
AH1389-1969	50,000	—	1.50	2.50	5.00	6.50

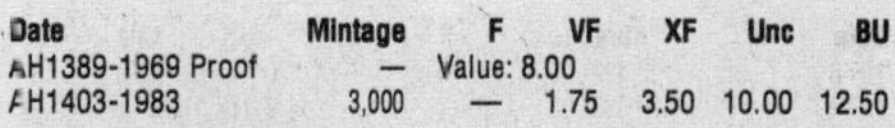

Date	Mintage	F	VF	XF	Unc	BU
AH1389-1969 Proof	—	Value: 8.00				
AH1403-1983	3,000	—	1.75	3.50	10.00	12.50

KM# 7a 250 FILS
15.0000 g., 0.9250 Silver .4461 oz. ASW **Series:** F.A.O. **Obv:** Boat, palm tree **Rev:** F.A.O., divided by lines in center circle, head of grain at center below "A", value at lower left

Date	Mintage	F	VF	XF	Unc	BU
AH1403-1983 Proof	Est. 15,000	Value: 14.50				

KM# 8 500 FILS
18.3000 g., 0.8000 Silver .4707 oz. ASW **Obv:** Sheik Isa facing left **Rev:** Opening of Isa Town, crowned arms at center of octagon, circle surrounds

Date	Mintage	F	VF	XF	Unc	BU
AH1385-1965 Proof	12,000	Value: 17.50				
AH1388-1968	50,000	—	6.50	7.50	12.50	15.00
AH1388-1968 Proof	—	Value: 17.50				

KM# 8a 500 FILS
18.0600 g., 0.9250 Silver .5372 oz. ASW **Obv:** Sheik Isa facing **Rev:** Opening of Isa Town, crowned arms at center of octagon, circle surrounds

Date	Mintage	F	VF	XF	Unc	BU
AH1403-1983 Proof	Est. 15,000	Value: 35.00				

KM# 22 500 FILS
Bi-Metallic Brass center in Copper-Nickel ring, 27 mm. **Obv:** Monument and inscription **Obv. Inscription:** STATE OF BAHRAIN **Rev:** Denomination **Edge:** Reeded **Note:** Total weight: 9.05 grams.

Date	Mintage	F	VF	XF	Unc	BU
2000	—	—	—	—	6.00	7.50

KM# 13 5 DINARS
19.4400 g., 0.9250 Silver .5782 oz. ASW **Obv:** Sheik Isa facing left **Rev:** Gazelle running, left, within circle, date below **Edge Lettering:** World Wildlife Fund

Date	Mintage	F	VF	XF	Unc	BU
AH1406-1986 Proof	Est. 25,000	Value: 40.00				

KM# 14 5 DINARS
19.4400 g., 0.9250 Silver .5782 oz. ASW **Subject:** Save The Children **Obv:** Sheik Isa facing left **Rev:** Children playing, date at bottom

Date	Mintage	F	VF	XF	Unc	BU
AH1410-1990 Proof	Est. 20,000	Value: 36.50				

KM# 21 5 DINARS
28.2300 g., 0.9250 Silver .8395 oz. ASW **Subject:** 50th Anniversary - United Nations **Obv:** Sheik Isa facing left **Rev:** UN building, value at bottom divides dates

Date	Mintage	F	VF	XF	Unc	BU
ND(1995) Proof	—	Value: 37.50				

KM# 23 5 DINARS
19.4000 g., 0.9250 Silver 0.5769 oz. ASW, 35.9 mm. **Subject:** UNICEF **Obv:** Sheik Isa facing left **Rev:** Children within circle, date below circle **Edge:** Reeded

Date	Mintage	F	VF	XF	Unc	BU
AH1419-1998 Proof	—	Value: 40.00				

KM# 11 50 DINARS
15.9800 g., 0.9170 Gold .4712 oz. AGW **Subject:** 50th Anniversary of Bahrain Monetary Agency

Date	Mintage	F	VF	XF	Unc	BU
AH1398-1978 Proof	5,000	Value: 350				

KM# 12 100 DINARS
31.9600 g., 0.9170 Gold .9424 oz. AGW **Subject:** 50th Anniversary of Bahrain Monetary Agency **Obv:** Sheik Isa facing left **Rev:** Coat of arms divides dates, circle surrounds, value at lower left

Date	Mintage	F	VF	XF	Unc	BU
AH1398-1978 Proof	5,000	Value: 675				

MINT SETS

KM#	Date	Mintage	Identification	Issue Price	Mkt Val
MS1	1992 (5)	—	KM#16-20	—	10.00

PROOF SETS

KM#	Date	Mintage	Identification	Issue Price	Mkt Val
PS1	1965 (7)	12,000	KM#1-6, 8	—	30.00
PS2	1965, 1968, 1969 (8)	20,000	KM#1-6 1965; KM7 1969; KM8 1968	32.00	35.00
PS3	1983 (7)	15,000	KM#1a-8a	99.00	80.00

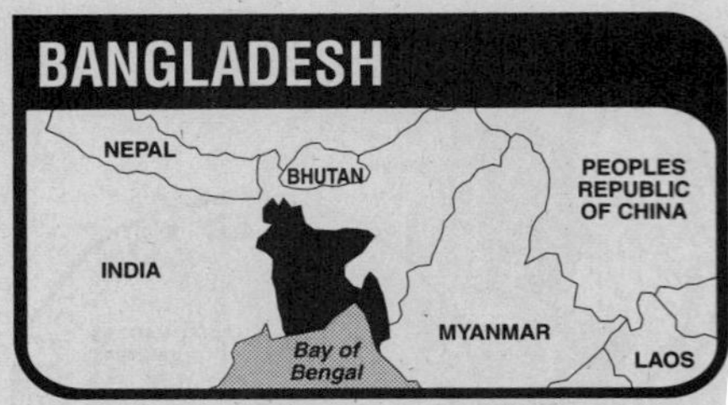

The Peoples Republic of Bangladesh (formerly East Pakistan), a parliamentary democracy located on the Bay of Bengal bordered by India and Burma, has an area of 55,598 sq. mi. (143,998 sq. km.) and a population of 128.1 million. Capital: Dhaka. The economy is predominantly agricultural. Jute products, jute and tea are exported.

British rule over the vast Indian sub-continent ended in 1947 when British India attained independence and was partitioned into the two successor states of India and Pakistan. Pakistan consisted of East and West Pakistan, two areas united by the Moslem religion but separated by culture and 1,000 miles of Indian territory. Restive under the de facto rule of the militant but fewer West Pakistanis, the East Pakistanis unsuccessfully demanded greater economic benefits and political reforms. The inability of the leaders of East and West Pakistan to resolve a political breakdown occasioned by the East Pakistan success in the general elections of 1970 precipitated massive civil disobedience in East Pakistan which West Pakistan sought to suppress militarily. East Pakistan seceded from Pakistan, March 26, 1971, and with the support of India declared an independent Peoples Republic of Bangladesh.

Bangladesh is a member of the Commonwealth of Nations. The president is the Head of State and the Government.

MONETARY SYSTEM

100 Poisha = 1 Taka

DATING

Christian era using Bengali numerals.

PEOPLES REPUBLIC

STANDARD COINAGE

KM# 5 POISHA

Aluminum **Obv:** Value within decorative circle **Rev:** Shapla flower on waves, within wreath

Date	Mintage	F	VF	XF	Unc	BU
1974	300,000,000	—	—	0.10	0.15	—

KM# 1 5 POISHA

Aluminum **Obv:** Value and symbol within toothed circle **Rev:** Shapla flower on waves, within wreath **Shape:** 4-sided

Date	Mintage	F	VF	XF	Unc	BU
1973	Est. 47,088,000	—	—	0.10	0.20	—
1974	—	—	—	0.10	0.20	—

KM# 6 5 POISHA

Aluminum **Series:** F.A.O. **Obv:** Value and symbol within toothed circle **Rev:** Shapla flower on waves, within wreath **Shape:** 4-sided

Date	Mintage	F	VF	XF	Unc	BU
1974	5,000,000	—	—	0.10	0.20	—
1975	3,000,000	—	—	0.10	0.20	—
1976	3,000,000	—	—	0.10	0.20	—
1977	—	—	—	0.10	0.20	—

KM# 10 5 POISHA

Aluminum **Series:** F.A.O. **Obv:** Value at right, 2/3 toothed circle at left, symbol within **Rev:** Shapla flower on waves, within wreath **Shape:** 4-sided

Date	Mintage	F	VF	XF	Unc	BU
1977	90,000,000	—	—	0.10	0.15	—
1978	52,432,000	—	—	0.10	0.25	—
1979	120,096,000	—	—	0.10	0.15	—
1980	127,008,000	—	—	0.10	0.15	—
1981	72,992,000	—	—	0.10	0.15	—

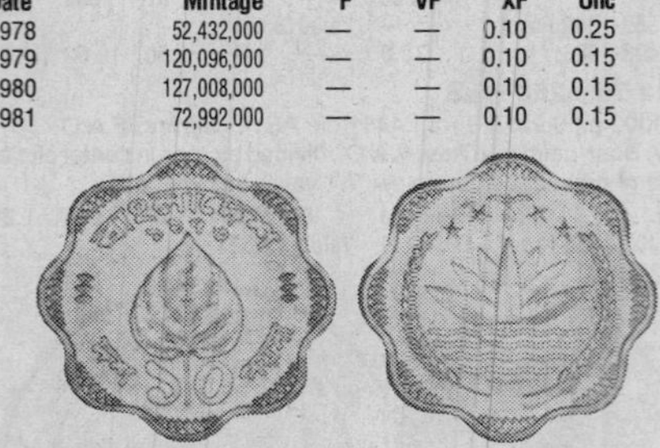

KM# 2 10 POISHA

Aluminum, 24 mm. **Obv:** Large leaf at center, stem divides value **Rev:** Shapla flower on waves, within wreath **Shape:** Scalloped

Date	Mintage	F	VF	XF	Unc	BU
1973	Est. 21,500,000	—	—	0.10	0.35	—
1974	—	—	—	0.10	0.35	—

KM# 7 10 POISHA

Aluminum, 24 mm. **Series:** F.A.O. **Obv:** Value at bottom, vehicle and plant at center **Rev:** Shapla flower on waves, within wreath **Shape:** Scalloped

Date	Mintage	F	VF	XF	Unc	BU
1974	5,000,000	—	—	0.15	0.35	—
1975	4,000,000	—	—	0.15	0.35	—
1976	4,000,000	—	—	0.15	0.35	—
1977	4,000,000	—	—	0.15	0.35	—
1978	141,744,000	—	—	0.15	0.30	—
1979	—	—	—	0.15	0.40	—

KM# 11.1 10 POISHA

1.9800 g., Aluminum, 24 mm. **Series:** F.A.O. **Obv:** Family above value **Rev:** Shapla flower on waves, within wreath **Shape:** Scalloped

Date	Mintage	F	VF	XF	Unc	BU
1977	48,000,000	—	—	0.15	0.30	—
1978	77,518,000	—	—	0.15	0.30	—
1979	170,112,000	—	—	0.15	0.30	—
1980	200,000,000	—	—	0.15	0.30	—

KM# 11.2 10 POISHA

1.3900 g., Aluminum, 22 mm. **Series:** F.A.O. **Rev:** Shapla flower **Shape:** Scalloped **Note:** Reduced size.

Date	Mintage	F	VF	XF	Unc	BU
1981	—	—	—	0.25	0.50	—
1983	142,848,000	—	—	0.15	0.30	—
1984	57,152,000	—	—	0.15	0.30	—

KM# 3 25 POISHA

Steel, 19 mm. **Obv:** Rohu, right, value below **Rev:** Shapla flower on waves, within wreath

Date	Mintage	F	VF	XF	Unc	BU
1973	Est. 25,072,000	—	—	0.25	0.75	1.00

KM# 8 25 POISHA

Steel, 19 mm. **Series:** F.A.O. **Obv:** Carp, egg, banana, squash, value at bottom **Rev:** Shapla flower on waves, within wreath

Date	Mintage	F	VF	XF	Unc	BU
1974	5,000,000	—	—	0.20	0.50	—
1975	6,000,000	—	—	0.20	0.50	—
1976	6,000,000	—	—	0.20	0.50	—
1977	51,300,000	—	—	0.15	0.50	—
1978	66,750,000	—	—	0.15	0.50	—
1979	—	—	—	0.15	0.50	—

KM# 12 25 POISHA

Steel, 19 mm. **Obv:** Tiger head, left, within circle **Rev:** Shapla flower on waves, within wreath

Date	Mintage	F	VF	XF	Unc	BU
1977	45,300,000	—	—	0.20	0.75	—
1978	66,750,000	—	—	0.20	0.75	—
1979	56,704,000	—	—	0.20	0.75	—
1980	228,992,000	—	—	0.20	0.75	—
1981	45,072,000	—	—	0.20	0.75	—
1983	96,128,000	—	—	0.20	0.75	—
1984	203,872,000	—	—	0.20	0.75	—
1991	50,002,000	—	—	0.20	0.75	—

KM# 4 50 POISHA

Steel **Obv:** Bird, left, value below **Rev:** Shapla flower on waves, within wreath

Date	Mintage	F	VF	XF	Unc	BU
1973	18,000,000	—	0.25	0.75	2.50	3.50

KM# 13 50 POISHA

Steel **Series:** F.A.O. **Obv:** Symbols within circle, value at bottom **Rev:** Shapla flower on waves, within wreath

Date	Mintage	F	VF	XF	Unc	BU
1977	12,700,000	—	—	0.20	0.75	—
1978	37,300,000	—	—	0.20	0.75	—
1979	2,208,000	—	—	0.20	0.75	—
1980	124,512,000	—	—	0.20	0.50	—
1981	36,680,000	—	—	0.20	0.75	—
1983	31,392,000	—	—	0.20	0.75	—
1984	168,608,000	—	—	0.20	0.50	—
1994	—	—	—	0.20	0.50	—

KM# 9.1 TAKA

Copper-Nickel **Series:** F.A.O. **Obv:** Stylized family, value at right **Rev:** Shapla flower on waves, within wreath

Date	Mintage	F	VF	XF	Unc	BU
1975	4,000,000	—	0.15	0.45	1.00	—
1976	—	—	0.15	0.45	1.00	—
1977	—	—	0.15	0.45	1.00	—

KM# 9.2 TAKA

Steel **Obv:** Stylized family, value at right **Rev:** Shapla flower on waves, within wreath **Note:** Magnetic. Varieties exist.

Date	Mintage	F	VF	XF	Unc	BU
1992	—	—	0.15	0.45	1.00	—
1993	—	—	0.15	0.45	1.00	—
1995	—	—	0.15	0.45	1.00	—

KM# 9.3 TAKA

3.9800 g., Brass **Obv:** Stylized family, value at right **Rev:** Shapla flower on waves, within wreath

Date	Mintage	F	VF	XF	Unc	BU
1996	—	—	0.20	0.65	1.85	—

Date	Mintage	F	VF	XF	Unc	BU
1997	—	—	0.20	0.65	1.85	—
1999	—	—	0.20	0.65	1.85	—

KM# 14 TAKA

31.3500 g., 0.9250 Silver .9323 oz. ASW **Subject:** Barcelona 1992 - 25th Summer Olympics **Obv:** Shapla flower **Rev:** Torch runner

Date	Mintage	F	VF	XF	Unc	BU
1992 Proof	Est. 40,000	Value: 32.50				

KM# 15 TAKA

31.3500 g., 0.9250 Silver .9323 oz. ASW **Subject:** Endangered Wildlife **Obv:** Shapla flower **Rev:** Deer

Date	Mintage	F	VF	XF	Unc	BU
1993 Proof	Est. 15,000	Value: 40.00				

KM# 16 TAKA

31.3500 g., 0.9250 Silver .9323 oz. ASW **Subject:** World Cup Soccer, 1994 **Obv:** Shapla flower

Date	Mintage	F	VF	XF	Unc	BU
1993 Proof	40,000	Value: 35.00				

KM# 17 TAKA

31.3500 g., 0.9250 Silver .9323 oz. ASW **Subject:** 20th Victory Day **Obv:** Seven portraits within circle **Rev:** National memorial, value divides date below

Date	Mintage	F	VF	XF	Unc	BU
1991 Proof	—	Value: 32.50				

KM# 9.4 TAKA

Brass **Obv:** Stylized family, value at right **Rev:** Shapla flower on waves, within wreath

Date	Mintage	F	VF	XF	Unc	BU
1998	—	—	—	0.50	1.25	—
1999	—	—	—	0.50	1.25	—

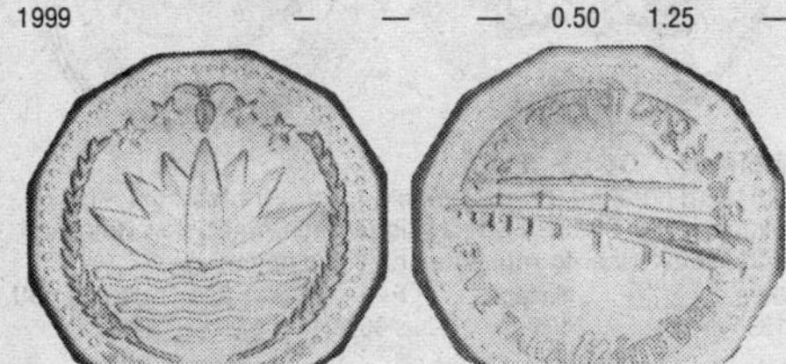

KM# 18.1 5 TAKA

7.8700 g., Steel **Obv:** Shapla flower on waves, within wreath **Rev:** Bridge

Date	Mintage	F	VF	XF	Unc	BU
1994	—	—	—	—	1.75	—

KM# 18.2 5 TAKA

8.1700 g., Steel **Obv:** Shapla flower on waves, within wreath, thicker design **Rev:** Bridge, value, denomination at bottom

Date	Mintage	F	VF	XF	Unc	BU
1996	—	—	—	—	2.25	—

BARBADOS

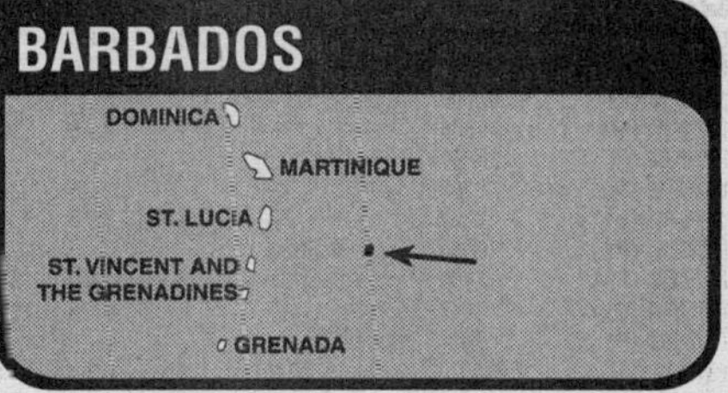

Barbados, an independent state within the British Commonwealth, is located in the Windward Islands of the West Indies east of St. Vincent. The coral island has an area of 166 sq. mi. (430 sq. km.) and a population of 269,000. Capital: Bridgetown. The economy is based on sugar and tourism. Sugar, petroleum products, molasses, and rum are exported.

Barbados was named by the Portuguese who achieved the first landing on the island in 1563. British sailors landed at the site of present-day Holetown in 1624. Barbados was under uninterrupted British control from the time of the first British settlement in 1627 until it obtained independence on Nov. 30, 1966. It is a member of the Commonwealth of Nations. Elizabeth II is Head of State as Queen of Barbados.

Unmarked side cut pieces of Spanish and Spanish Colonial 1, 2 and 8 reales were the principal coinage medium of 18th-century Barbados. The "Neptune" tokens issued by Sir Phillip Gibbs, a local plantation owner, circulated freely but were never established as legal coinage. The coinage and banknotes of the British Caribbean Territories (Eastern Group) were employed prior to 1973 when Barbados issued a decimal coinage.

RULERS

British, until 1966

MINT MARKS

FM - Franklin Mint, U.S.A.*

None - Royal Mint

***NOTE**: From 1975-1985 the Franklin Mint produced coinage in up to 3 different qualities. Qualities of issue are designated in ( ) after each date and are defined as follows:

(M) MATTE - Normal circulation strike or a dull finish produced by sandblasting special uncirculated (polish finish) or proof quality dies.

(U) SPECIAL UNCIRCULATED - Polished or proof-like in appearance without any frosted features.

(P) PROOF - The highest quality obtainable having mirror-like fields and frosted features.

MONETARY SYSTEM

100 Cents = 1 Dollar

INDEPENDENT SOVEREIGN STATE

within the British Commonwealth

DECIMAL COINAGE

KM# 10 CENT

Bronze, 19 mm. **Obv:** National arms divide date **Rev:** Neptune symbol above value **Edge:** Plain **Designer:** Philip Nathan

Date	Mintage	F	VF	XF	Unc	BU
1973	5,000,000	—	—	0.10	0.25	0.75
1973FM (M)	7,500	—	—	0.50	1.00	3.00
1973FM (P)	97,000	Value: 1.00				
1974FM (M)	8,708	—	—	0.50	1.00	3.00
1974FM (P)	36,000	Value: 1.00				
1975FM (M)	5,000	—	—	0.35	0.75	2.25
1975FM (U)	1,360	—	—	0.50	1.00	3.00
1975FM (P)	20,000	Value: 1.00				
1977FM (M)	2,102	—	—	—	0.75	1.50
1977FM (U)	468	—	—	1.50	3.00	6.00
1977FM (P)	5,014	Value: 1.00				
1978	4,[illegible]07,000	—	—	0.10	0.25	0.75
1978FM (M)	2,000	—	—	0.50	1.00	3.00
1978FM (U)	2,517	—	—	0.60	1.50	4.50
1978FM (P)	4,436	Value: 1.50				
1979	5,6[illegible]6,000	—	—	0.10	0.25	0.75
1979FM (M)	1,500	—	—	—	1.00	3.00
1979FM (U)	523	—	—	1.00	2.50	6.00
1979FM (P)	4,126	Value: 1.50				
1980	14,400,000	—	—	0.10	0.25	0.75
1980FM (M)	1,500	—	—	0.50	1.00	3.00
1980FM (U)	649	—	—	1.00	2.00	6.00
1980FM (P)	2,111	Value: 3.00				
1981	10,160,000	—	—	0.10	0.25	0.75
1981FM (M)	1,500	—	—	—	1.00	3.00
1981FM (U)	327	—	—	1.00	2.00	6.00
1981FM (P)	943	Value: 4.50				
1982	5,040,000	—	—	0.10	0.25	0.75
1982FM (U)	1,500	—	—	—	1.25	3.75
1982FM (P)	843	Value: 4.50				
1983FM (M)	1,500	—	—	—	1.00	4.50
1983FM (U)	—	—	—	—	1.25	3.75
1983FM (P)	459	Value: 4.50				
1984	5,008,000	—	—	0.10	0.25	0.75
1984FM (M)	868	—	—	—	1.25	4.50
1984FM (P)	—	Value: 3.00				
1985	—	—	—	0.10	0.25	0.75
1986	—	—	—	0.10	0.25	0.75
1987	10,000,000	—	—	0.10	0.25	0.75
1988	12,136,000	—	—	0.10	0.25	0.75
1989	—	—	—	0.10	0.25	0.75
1990	—	—	—	0.10	0.25	0.75
1991	—	—	—	0.10	0.25	0.75

KM# 10a CENT

Copper Plated Zinc, 19 mm. **Obv:** National arms divide date **Rev:** Trident above value **Edge:** Plain

Date	Mintage	F	VF	XF	Unc	BU
1992	—	—	—	0.10	0.25	0.75
1993	—	—	—	0.10	0.25	0.75
1995	—	—	—	0.10	0.25	0.75
1996	—	—	—	0.10	0.25	0.75
1997	—	—	—	0.10	0.25	0.75
1998	—	—	—	0.10	0.25	0.75
1999	—	—	—	0.10	0.25	0.75
2000	—	—	—	0.10	0.25	0.75

KM# 19 CENT

Copper Plated Zinc, 19 mm. **Subject:** 10th Anniversary of Independence **Obv:** National arms divide dates **Rev:** Neptune symbol above value **Edge:** Plain **Designer:** Philip Nathan

Date	Mintage	F	VF	XF	Unc	BU
ND(1976)	6,406,000	—	—	0.10	0.20	0.60
ND(1976)FM (M)	5,000	—	—	—	0.50	1.50
ND(1976)FM (U)	996	—	—	—	1.00	3.00
ND(1976)FM (P)	12,000	Value: 1.00				

KM# 11 5 CENTS

Brass, 21 mm. **Obv:** National arms divide dates **Rev:** South Point Lighthouse above value **Edge:** Plain **Designer:** Philip Nathan

Date	Mintage	F	VF	XF	Unc	BU
1973FM (M)	7,500	—	—	—	1.25	3.75
1973	3,000,000	—	0.10	0.15	0.35	1.00
1973FM (P)	97,000	Value: 1.50				
1974FM (M)	8,708	—	—	—	1.25	3.75
1974FM (P)	36,000	Value: 1.50				
1975FM (M)	5,000	—	—	—	1.00	3.00
1975FM (U)	1,360	—	—	—	1.25	3.75
1975FM (P)	20,000	Value: 1.50				
1977FM (M)	2,100	—	—	1.00	2.00	5.00
1977FM (U)	468	—	—	1.50	3.00	6.00
1977FM (P)	5,014	Value: 1.50				
1978FM (M)	2,000	—	—	—	0.75	1.25
1978FM (U)	2,517	—	—	1.25	2.75	5.00
1978FM (P)	4,436	Value: 3.75				
1979	4,800,000	—	0.10	0.15	0.35	1.00
1979FM (M)	1,500	—	—	—	0.75	1.50
1979FM (U)	523	—	—	—	2.75	5.00
1979FM (P)	4,126	Value: 3.75				
1980FM (M)	1,500	—	—	—	1.00	3.00
1980FM (U)	649	—	—	1.00	2.25	6.75
1980FM (P)	2,111	Value: 4.25				
1981FM (M)	1,500	—	—	—	1.00	3.00
1981FM (U)	327	—	—	1.00	2.25	6.75
1981FM (P)	943	Value: 4.25				
1982	2,100,000	—	0.10	0.15	0.35	1.00
1982FM (U)	1,500	—	—	0.75	1.50	4.50
1982FM (P)	843	Value: 4.25				
1983FM (M)	1,500	—	—	0.75	1.50	4.50
1983FM (U)	—	—	—	0.75	1.50	4.50
1983FM (P)	459	Value: 4.25				
1984FM	1,737	—	—	0.75	1.50	4.50
1984FM (P)	—	Value: 4.25				
1985	—	—	—	—	0.25	0.75
1986	—	—	—	—	0.25	0.75
1988	4,200,000	—	—	—	0.25	0.75
1989	—	—	—	—	0.25	0.75
1991	—	—	—	—	0.25	0.75
1994	—	—	—	—	0.25	0.75
1995	—	—	—	—	0.25	0.75
1996	—	—	—	—	0.25	0.75
1997	—	—	—	—	0.25	0.75
1998	—	—	—	—	0.25	0.75
1999	—	—	—	—	0.25	0.75
2000	—	—	—	—	0.25	0.75

KM# 20 5 CENTS

Brass, 21 mm. **Subject:** 10th Anniversary of Independence **Obv:** National arms divide dates **Rev:** Lighthouse above value **Edge:** Plain **Designer:** Philip Nathan

Date	Mintage	F	VF	XF	Unc	BU
ND(1976)FM (M)	5,000	—	—	—	1.00	3.00
ND(1976)FM (U)	12,000	—	—	—	1.00	2.00
ND(1976)FM (P)	—	Value: 1.50				

KM# 12 10 CENTS

Copper-Nickel, 17.5 mm. **Obv:** National arms divide dates **Rev:** Laughing Gull above value **Edge:** Reeded **Designer:** Philip Nathan

Date	Mintage	F	VF	XF	Unc	BU
1973	4,000,000	—	0.10	0.15	0.50	1.50
1973FM (M)	5,000	—	—	—	1.50	3.00
1973FM (P)	97,000	Value: 2.00				
1974FM (M)	6,208	—	—	—	1.50	3.00
1974FM (P)	36,000	Value: 2.00				
1975FM (M)	2,500	—	—	—	1.00	3.00
1975FM (U)	1,360	—	—	—	1.50	3.00
1975FM (P)	20,000	Value: 2.00				
1977FM (M)	2,100	—	—	—	1.00	3.00
1977FM (U)	468	—	—	2.50	4.00	8.00
1977FM (P)	5,014	Value: 2.00				
1978FM (M)	2,000	—	—	—	1.00	3.00
1978FM (U)	2,517	—	—	—	3.00	6.00
1978FM (P)	4,436	Value: 3.00				
1979	2,500,000	—	0.10	0.20	0.60	1.25
1979FM (M)	1,500	—	—	1.00	2.50	5.00
1979FM (U)	523	—	—	1.50	3.00	8.00
1979FM (P)	4,126	Value: 3.00				
1980	3,500,000	—	0.10	0.15	0.50	1.25
1980FM (M)	1,500	—	—	—	1.00	3.00
1980FM (U)	649	—	—	1.00	2.50	7.00
1980FM (P)	2,111	Value: 4.00				
1981FM (M)	1,500	—	—	—	1.00	3.00
1981FM (U)	327	—	—	—	2.50	7.00
1981FM (P)	943	Value: 4.00				
1982FM (U)	1,500	—	—	—	1.75	4.25
1982FM (P)	843	Value: 4.00				
1983FM (M)	1,500	—	—	—	1.75	4.25
1983FM (U)	—	—	—	—	1.75	4.25
1983FM (P)	459	Value: 4.00				
1984	3,400,000	—	0.10	0.15	0.50	1.50
1984FM (P)	—	Value: 4.50				
1985	—	—	0.10	0.15	0.50	1.50
1986	—	—	0.10	0.15	0.50	1.50
1987	3,500,000	—	0.10	0.15	0.50	1.50
1988	—	—	0.10	0.15	0.50	1.50
1989	—	—	0.10	0.15	0.50	1.50
1990	—	—	0.10	0.15	0.50	1.50
1992	—	—	0.10	0.15	0.50	1.50
1995	—	—	0.10	0.15	0.50	1.50
1996	—	—	0.10	0.15	0.50	1.50
1998	—	—	0.10	0.15	0.50	1.50
2000	—	—	0.10	0.15	0.50	1.50

KM# 21 10 CENTS

Copper-Nickel, 17.5 mm. **Subject:** 10th Anniversary of Independence **Obv:** National arms divide dates **Rev:** Gull above value **Edge:** Reeded **Designer:** Philip Nathan

Date	Mintage	F	VF	XF	Unc	BU
ND(1976)FM (M)	2,500	—	—	—	0.75	2.25
ND(1976)FM (U)	996	—	—	—	1.75	5.00
ND(1976)FM (P)	12,000	Value: 3.00				

KM# 13 25 CENTS

Copper-Nickel, 23.6 mm. **Obv:** National arms divide dates **Rev:** Morgan Lewis Sugar Mill, value above **Edge:** Reeded **Designer:** Philip Nathan

Date	Mintage	F	VF	XF	Unc	BU
1973	6,000,000	—	0.15	0.30	0.60	1.20
1973FM (M)	4,300	—	—	—	1.75	3.50
1973FM (P)	97,000	Value: 2.50				
1974FM (M)	5,508	—	—	—	1.75	3.50
1974FM (P)	36,000	Value: 2.50				
1975FM (M)	1,800	—	—	—	1.25	3.00
1975FM (U)	1,360	—	—	—	1.75	3.50
1975FM (P)	20,000	Value: 2.50				
1977FM (M)	2,100	—	—	—	1.00	3.00
1977FM (U)	468	—	—	—	4.25	10.00
1977FM (P)	5,014	Value: 2.50				
1978	2,407,000	—	0.20	0.40	0.80	1.60
1978FM (M)	2,000	—	—	—	1.00	3.00
1978FM (U)	2,517	—	—	—	3.25	9.00
1978FM (P)	4,436	Value: 3.50				
1979	1,200,000	—	0.20	0.40	0.80	1.60
1979FM (M)	1,500	—	—	—	1.00	3.00
1979FM (U)	523	—	—	—	3.00	9.00
1979FM (P)	4,126,000	Value: 3.50				
1980	2,700,000	—	0.15	0.30	0.60	1.60
1980FM (M)	1,500	—	—	0.75	3.00	8.00
1980FM (U)	649	—	—	—	2.75	10.00
1980FM (P)	2,111	Value: 3.50				
1981	4,365,000	—	0.15	0.30	0.60	1.60
1981FM (M)	1,500	—	—	0.75	3.00	8.00
1981FM (U)	327	—	—	—	2.75	10.00
1981FM (P)	943	Value: 4.50				
1982FM (U)	1,500	—	—	—	2.00	4.50
1982FM (P)	843	Value: 4.50				
1983FM (M)	1,500	—	—	—	2.00	4.50
1983FM (U)	—	—	—	—	2.00	4.50
1983FM (P)	459	Value: 4.50				
1984FM	868	—	—	—	2.00	4.50
1984FM (P)	—	Value: 5.00				
1985	—	—	0.15	0.30	0.60	1.60
1986	—	—	0.15	0.30	0.60	1.60
1987	3,150,000	—	—	—	2.00	3.00
1988	—	—	0.15	0.30	0.60	1.60
1989	—	—	0.15	0.30	0.60	1.60
1990	—	—	0.15	0.30	0.60	1.60
1994	—	—	0.15	0.30	0.60	1.60
1996	—	—	0.15	0.30	0.60	1.60
1998	—	—	0.15	0.30	0.60	1.60
2000	—	—	0.15	0.30	0.60	1.60

KM# 22 25 CENTS

Copper-Nickel, 23.6 mm. **Subject:** 10th Anniversary of Independence **Obv:** National arms divide dates **Rev:** Morgan Lewis Sugar Mill, value above **Edge:** Reeded **Designer:** Philip Nathan

Date	Mintage	F	VF	XF	Unc	BU
ND(1976)FM (M)	1,800	—	—	—	1.25	3.75
ND(1976)FM (U)	996	—	—	1.00	2.00	6.00
ND(1976)FM (P)	12,000	Value: 2.00				

KM# 14.1 DOLLAR

Copper-Nickel, 28 mm. **Obv:** National arms divide dates **Rev:** Flying fish, value below **Edge:** Plain **Shape:** Seven sided coin **Designer:** Philip Nathan

Date	Mintage	F	VF	XF	Unc	BU
1973FM (M)	3,000	—	—	—	2.00	6.00
1973FM (P)	97,000	Value: 2.00				
1973	3,955,000	—	0.60	0.75	1.50	3.00
1974FM (M)	4,208	—	—	—	2.00	6.00
1974FM (P)	36,000	Value: 3.00				
1975FM (P)	20,000	Value: 3.00				
1975FM (M)	500	—	—	1.25	3.50	9.00
1975FM (U)	1,360	—	—	—	2.00	6.00
1977FM (U)	468	—	—	1.50	4.50	10.00
1977FM (P)	5,014	Value: 6.00				
1977FM (M)	600	—	—	1.75	5.00	9.00
1978FM (U)	1,017	—	—	1.25	3.50	6.00
1978FM (P)	4,436	Value: 6.00				
1979FM (U)	523	—	—	1.25	3.50	9.00
1979FM (P)	4,126	Value: 6.00				
1979	2,000,000	—	0.75	1.25	1.75	2.50
1979FM (M)	600	—	—	1.50	3.00	9.00
1980FM (M)	600	—	—	1.50	3.50	9.00
1980FM (U)	649	—	—	1.50	3.50	9.00
1980FM (P)	2,111	Value: 6.00				
1981FM (M)	600	—	—	1.25	3.00	9.00
1981FM (U)	327	—	—	1.50	3.50	9.00
1981FM (P)	943	Value: 6.00				
1982FM (U)	600	—	—	1.25	3.00	9.00
1982FM (P)	843	Value: 6.00				
1983FM (P)	459	Value: 7.50				
1983FM (M)	600	—	—	1.25	3.00	9.00
1983FM (U)	—	—	—	1.25	3.00	9.00
1984FM (P)	—	Value: 4.50				
1984FM	469	—	—	—	3.50	9.00
1985	—	—	—	—	1.50	3.00
1986	—	—	—	—	1.50	3.00

KM# 14.2 DOLLAR

Copper-Nickel, 28 mm. **Obv:** National arms divide date **Rev:** Flying fish, denomination below

Date	Mintage	F	VF	XF	Unc	BU
1988	3,145,000	—	—	0.75	2.25	3.00
1989	—	—	—	0.75	2.25	3.00
1994	—	—	—	0.75	2.25	3.00
1998	—	—	—	0.75	2.25	3.00

KM# 23 DOLLAR

Copper-Nickel, 28 mm. **Subject:** 10th Anniversary of Independence **Obv:** National arms divide dates **Rev:** Flying fish above value **Edge:** Plain **Shape:** Seven sided coin. **Designer:** Philip Nathan

Date	Mintage	F	VF	XF	Unc	BU
ND(1976)FM (M)	500	—	—	1.50	4.00	9.00
ND(1976)FM (U)	996	—	—	1.25	3.50	9.00
ND(1976)FM (P)	12,000	Value: 4.00				

KM# 57 DOLLAR

10.0000 g., 0.5000 Silver .1607 oz. ASW **Obv:** National arms, date at bottom **Rev:** Bust of Queen Mother facing, date and value below

Date	Mintage	F	VF	XF	Unc	BU
1994 Proof	Est. 50,000	Value: 28.00				

KM# 65 DOLLAR

9.9400 g., 0.9250 Silver .2956 oz. ASW **Subject:** Queen Mother's 95th Birthday **Obv:** National arms, date below **Rev:** Bust of Queen Mother facing, date and value below

Date	Mintage	F	VF	XF	Unc	BU
1995 Proof	Est. 50,000	Value: 35.00				

KM# 64 DOLLAR

10.2400 g., 0.9250 Silver 0.3045 oz. ASW, 30 mm. **Obv:** National arms **Rev:** Royal couple below gold inset monogrammed shield **Edge:** Reeded

Date	Mintage	F	VF	XF	Unc	BU
1997 Proof	—	Value: 30.00				

KM# 15 2 DOLLARS
Copper-Nickel, 37 mm. **Rev:** Staghorn coral, large value at bottom **Edge:** Reeded **Designer:** Philip Nathan

Date	Mintage	F	VF	XF	Unc	BU
1973FM (M)	3,000	—	—	1.25	5.00	9.00
1973FM (P)	97,000	Value: 6.00				
1974FM (M)	4,208	—	—	1.25	5.00	9.00
1974FM (P)	36,000	Value: 6.00				
1975FM (M)	500	—	—	1.25	5.00	9.00
1975FM (U)	1,360	—	—	1.25	5.00	9.00
1975FM (P)	20,000	Value: 6.00				
1977FM (M)	600	—	—	1.25	5.00	9.00
1977FM (U)	468	—	—	1.50	5.50	10.00
1977FM (P)	5,014	Value: 9.00				
1978FM (U)	1,017	—	—	1.25	5.00	9.00
1978FM (P)	4,436	Value: 9.00				
1979FM (M)	600	—	—	1.25	5.00	10.00
1979FM (U)	523	—	—	1.25	5.00	10.00
1979FM (P)	4,126	Value: 9.00				
1980FM (M)	600	—	—	1.25	5.00	10.00
1980FM (U)	649	—	—	1.25	5.00	10.00
1980FM (P)	2,111	Value: 9.00				
1981FM (M)	600	—	—	1.25	5.00	10.00
1981FM (U)	327	—	—	1.25	5.00	10.00
1981FM (P)	943	Value: 9.00				
1982FM (U)	600	—	—	1.25	5.00	10.00
1982FM (P)	843	Value: 9.00				
1983FM (U)	—	—	—	1.25	5.00	10.00
1983FM (P)	459	Value: 9.00				
1984FM (U)	473	—	—	1.25	5.00	10.00
1984FM (P)	—	Value: 9.00				

KM# 24 2 DOLLARS
Copper-Nickel, 37 mm. **Subject:** 10th Anniversary of Independence **Rev:** Staghorn coral, large value at bottom **Edge:** Reeded **Designer:** Philip Nathan

Date	Mintage	F	VF	XF	Unc	BU
ND(1976)FM (M)	500	—	—	2.00	6.00	10.00
ND(1976)FM (U)	996	—	—	2.00	6.00	9.00
ND(1976)FM (P)	12,000	Value: 10.00				

KM# A9 4 DOLLARS
Copper-Nickel, 38.5 mm. **Series:** F.A.O. **Obv:** National arms **Rev:** Value at bottom divides sugarcane and banana tree branch **Edge:** Reeded

Date	Mintage	F	VF	XF	Unc	BU
1970	30,000	—	4.00	7.00	15.00	20.00
1970 Proof	2,000	Value: 25.00				

KM# 16 5 DOLLARS
Copper-Nickel, 40 mm. **Obv:** National arms divide date **Rev:** Shell Fountain in Bridgetown's Trafalgar Square, value above **Edge:** Reeded **Designer:** Philip Nathan

Date	Mintage	F	VF	XF	Unc	BU
1974FM (M)	3,958	—	—	1.25	5.00	7.50
1975FM (M)	250	—	—	1.25	8.00	9.50
1975FM (U)	1,360	—	—	1.25	5.00	7.50
1977FM (M)	600	—	—	1.25	5.00	7.50
1977FM (U)	468	—	—	1.25	5.00	7.50
1978FM (U)	1,017	—	—	1.25	5.00	7.50
1979FM (M)	600	—	—	1.25	5.00	7.50
1979FM (U)	523	—	—	1.25	5.00	7.50
1980FM (M)	600	—	—	1.25	5.00	7.50
1980FM (U)	649	—	—	1.25	5.00	7.50
1981FM (M)	600	—	—	1.25	5.00	7.50
1981FM (U)	1,156	—	—	1.25	5.00	7.50
1982FM (U)	600	—	—	1.25	5.00	7.50
1982FM (P)	843	—	—	1.25	5.00	7.50
1983FM (M)	600	—	—	1.25	5.00	7.50
1983FM (U)	261	—	—	1.25	5.00	7.50
1984FM	470	—	—	1.25	5.00	7.50

KM# 16a 5 DOLLARS
31.1000 g., 0.8000 Silver .7999 oz. ASW, 40 mm. **Obv:** National arms **Rev:** Shell Fountain in Bridgetown's Trafalgar Square, value above **Edge:** Reeded

Date	Mintage	F	VF	XF	Unc	BU
1973FM (P)	97,000	Value: 11.50				
1973FM (M)	2,750	—	—	—	14.50	16.50
1974FM (P)	36,000	Value: 12.50				
1975FM (P)	20,000	Value: 13.50				
1977FM (P)	5,014	Value: 15.00				
1978FM (P)	4,436	Value: 15.00				
1979FM (P)	4,126	Value: 15.00				
1980FM (P)	2,111	Value: 17.50				
1981FM (P)	835	Value: 22.00				
1982FM (P)	658	Value: 22.00				
1983FM (P)	130	Value: 32.00				
1984FM (P)	—	Value: 32.00				

KM# 25 5 DOLLARS
Copper-Nickel, 40 mm. **Subject:** 10th Anniversary of Independence **Obv:** National arms divide dates **Rev:** Shell Fountain, value above **Edge:** Reeded **Designer:** Philip Nathan

Date	Mintage	F	VF	XF	Unc	BU
ND(1976)FM (M)	250	—	—	7.50	25.00	—
ND(1976)FM (U)	996	—	—	7.50	12.50	—

KM# 25a 5 DOLLARS
31.1000 g., 0.8000 Silver .7999 oz. ASW, 40 mm. **Subject:** 10th Anniversary of Independence **Obv:** National arms divide dates **Rev:** Shell Fountain, value above **Edge:** Reeded

Date	Mintage	F	VF	XF	Unc	BU
ND(1976)FM (P)	12,000	Value: 16.50				

KM# 54 5 DOLLARS
28.5500 g., 0.9250 Silver .8492 oz. ASW **Subject:** World Cup Soccer **Obv:** National arms, date below **Rev:** Head of Native American with headdress, left, soccer player in foreground on right, value lower right

Date	Mintage	F	VF	XF	Unc	BU
1994 Proof	Est. 10,000	Value: 37.50				

KM# 55 5 DOLLARS
28.2800 g., 0.9250 Silver .8411 oz. ASW **Subject:** UN Global SIDS Conference **Obv:** National arms **Rev:** Stylized tropical island view

Date	Mintage	F	VF	XF	Unc	BU
1994 Proof	2,000	Value: 40.00				

KM# 58 5 DOLLARS
31.4700 g., 0.9250 Silver .9359 oz. ASW **Obv:** National arms **Rev:** Queen Mother's engagement portrait right, date below, within beaded circle, value below circle

Date	Mintage	F	VF	XF	Unc	BU
1994 Proof	Est. 20,000	Value: 50.00				

KM# 59 5 DOLLARS
28.2800 g., 0.9250 Silver .8411 oz. ASW **Obv:** National arms **Rev:** Pedro A. Campo, seated at left, looking right, value at lower right

Date	Mintage	F	VF	XF	Unc	BU
1994 Proof	Est. 10,000	Value: 50.00				

KM# 62 5 DOLLARS
Copper-Nickel **Subject:** 50th Anniversary - United Nations **Obv:** National arms **Rev:** Military figure raising flag, numbers at right signify years, two dates at right, value at bottom

Date	Mintage	F	VF	XF	Unc	BU
1995	—	—	—	—	8.00	—

KM# 62a 5 DOLLARS
28.2800 g., 0.9250 Silver .8411 oz. ASW **Subject:** 50th Anniversary - United Nations **Obv:** National arms **Rev:** Military figure raising flag, numbers at right signify years, two dates at right, value at bottom

Date	Mintage	F	VF	XF	Unc	BU
1995 Proof	Est. 105,000	Value: 32.50				

KM# 63 5 DOLLARS
28.2800 g., 0.9250 Silver .8411 oz. ASW **Obv:** National arms **Rev:** First European settlers, 1625, value at bottom

Date	Mintage	F	VF	XF	Unc	BU
1995 Proof	Est. 15,000	Value: 40.00				

KM# 68 5 DOLLARS
28.5000 g., 0.9250 Silver 0.8476 oz. ASW, 38.5 mm. **Subject:** Queen's 70th Birthday **Obv:** National arms **Rev:** Royal couple, waving, two dates below, value at bottom **Edge:** Reeded

Date	Mintage	F	VF	XF	Unc	BU
1996 Proof	—	Value: 40.00				

KM# 67 5 DOLLARS
28.1000 g., 0.9250 Silver .8357 oz. ASW, 38.6 mm. **Subject:** Eternal Flame **Obv:** National arms, two dates below **Rev:** Denomination and eternal flame **Edge:** Reeded **Shape:** Octagonal

Date	Mintage	F	VF	XF	Unc	BU
1999-2000 Proof	—	Value: 60.00				

KM# 17 10 DOLLARS
Copper-Nickel **Subject:** Neptune, God of the Sea **Obv:** National arms divide date **Rev:** Neptune at left, looking right, whale under right hand, value at bottom **Edge:** Reeded **Designer:** Philip Nathan

Date	Mintage	F	VF	XF	Unc	BU
1974FM (M)	3,958	—	—	3.00	10.00	12.00
1975FM (M)	250	—	—	3.00	20.00	25.00
1975FM (U)	1,360	—	—	3.00	12.50	14.00
1977FM (M)	600	—	—	3.00	12.50	14.50
1977FM (U)	468	—	—	3.00	12.50	14.50
1978FM (U)	1,017	—	—	3.00	12.50	14.00
1979FM (M)	600	—	—	3.00	12.50	14.50
1979FM (U)	523	—	—	3.00	12.50	14.50
1980FM (M)	600	—	—	3.00	12.50	14.50
1980FM (U)	649	—	—	3.00	12.50	14.50
1981FM (M)	600	—	—	3.00	12.50	14.50
1981FM (U)	1,156	—	—	3.00	12.50	14.00

KM# 17a 10 DOLLARS
37.9000 g., 0.9250 Silver 1.1271 oz. ASW **Subject:** Neptune, God of the Sea **Obv:** National arms divide date **Rev:** Neptune at left, looking right, whale under right hand, value at bottom **Edge:** Reeded

Date	Mintage	F	VF	XF	Unc	BU
1973FM (M)	2,750	—	—	—	16.50	18.50
1973FM (P)	97,000	Value: 15.50				
1974FM (P)	57,000	Value: 15.50				
1975FM (P)	29,000	Value: 15.50				
1977FM (P)	7,212	Value: 17.50				
1978FM (P)	7,079	Value: 17.50				
1979FM (P)	6,534	Value: 17.50				
1980FM (P)	3,618	Value: 20.00				
1981FM (P)	835	Value: 45.00				

KM# 26 10 DOLLARS
Copper-Nickel **Subject:** 10th Anniversary of Independence **Obv:** National arms divide dates **Rev:** Neptune at left, looking right, whale under right hand, value at bottom **Edge:** Reeded **Designer:** Philip Nathan

Date	Mintage	F	VF	XF	Unc	BU
ND(1976)FM (M)	250	—	—	10.00	30.00	35.00
ND(1976)FM (U)	996	—	—	7.50	15.00	17.50

KM# 26a 10 DOLLARS
37.9000 g., 0.9250 Silver 1.1271 oz. ASW **Subject:** 10th Anniversary of Independence **Obv:** National arms divide dates **Rev:** Neptune at left, looking right, whale under right hand, value at bottom **Edge:** Reeded

Date	Mintage	F	VF	XF	Unc	BU
ND(1976)FM (P)	16,000	Value: 17.50				

KM# 34 10 DOLLARS
Copper-Nickel **Subject:** 10th Anniversary of the Central Bank of Barbados **Obv:** Similar to KM#26 **Rev:** Upright Blue Marlin within inner circle divides date, legend surrounds, value below **Edge:** Reeded

Date	Mintage	F	VF	XF	Unc	BU
1982FM (U)	600	—	—	—	55.00	—

KM# 34a 10 DOLLARS
35.5200 g., 0.9250 Silver 1.0564 oz. ASW **Designer:**

Date	Mintage	F	VF	XF	Unc	BU
1982FM (P)	851	Value: 45.00				

KM# 36 10 DOLLARS
Copper-Nickel **Subject:** Summer Olympics **Obv:** National arms divide date **Rev:** Pelican with wings raised, right, value below

Date	Mintage	F	VF	XF	Unc	BU
1983FM (M)	600	—	—	—	100	—
1983FM (U)	141	—	—	—	145	—

KM# 36a 10 DOLLARS
35.5200 g., 0.9250 Silver 1.0564 oz. ASW **Subject:** Summer Olympics **Obv:** National arms divide date **Rev:** Pelican with wings raised, right, value below

Date	Mintage	F	VF	XF	Unc	BU
1983FM (P)	679	Value: 125				

KM# 40 10 DOLLARS
35.5200 g., 0.9250 Silver 1.0564 oz. ASW **Subject:** Dolphins **Obv:** National arms divide date **Rev:** Three dolphins, left, value below

Date	Mintage	F	VF	XF	Unc	BU
1984FM (M)	—	—	—	—	—	—
1984FM (P)	469	Value: 175				

KM# 50 10 DOLLARS
28.2800 g., 0.9250 Silver .8411 oz. ASW **Subject:** International Cricket Belt Buckle **Obv:** National arms, date below **Rev:** Buckle, value below

Date	Mintage	F	VF	XF	Unc	BU
1991 Proof	5,000	Value: 55.00				

KM# 52 10 DOLLARS
23.3300 g., 0.9250 Silver .6938 oz. ASW **Subject:** Discovery of America **Obv:** Crowned bust of Queen Elizabeth II right **Obv. Designer:** Raphael Maklouf **Rev:** Columbus and Native American, ship and scroll, value at bottom

Date	Mintage	F	VF	XF	Unc	BU
1991 Matte	750	Value: 65.00				
1991 Proof	Est. 25,000	Value: 35.00				

KM# 53 10 DOLLARS
23.3300 g., 0.9250 Silver .6938 oz. ASW **Subject:** Discovery of America **Obv:** Crowned bust of Queen Elizabeth II right **Obv. Designer:** Raphael Maklouf **Rev:** Columbus and Tribal Chief, scroll between, value below

Date	Mintage	F	VF	XF	Unc	BU
1992 Matte	500	Value: 65.00				
1992 Proof	Est. 25,000	Value: 35.00				

KM# 61 10 DOLLARS
23.3300 g., 0.9250 Silver .6938 oz. ASW **Subject:** 1992 Summer Olympics **Obv:** Crowned bust of Queen Elizabeth II right **Obv. Designer:** Raphael Maklouf **Rev:** Sailboards, value at bottom

Date	Mintage	F	VF	XF	Unc	BU
1992 Proof	10,000	Value: 50.00				

KM# 60 10 DOLLARS
7.7800 g., 0.5830 Gold .1458 oz. AGW **Subject:** Queen Mother's Engagement **Obv:** National arms, date below **Rev:** Queen Mother's engagement portrait right within beaded circle, value below circle

Date	Mintage	F	VF	XF	Unc	BU
1995 Proof	Est. 5,000	Value: 150				

KM# 66 10 DOLLARS
28.2800 g., 0.9250 Silver .8410 oz. ASW **Subject:** 50th Anniversary of the University of the West Indies **Obv:** National arms, date below **Rev:** University arms, dates below

Date	Mintage	F	VF	XF	Unc	BU
1998 Proof	1,000	Value: 55.00				

KM# 46 20 DOLLARS
23.3300 g., 0.9250 Silver .6938 oz. ASW **Subject:** Decade For Women **Obv:** National arms, date below **Rev:** Teacher with class, value at bottom

Date	Mintage	F	VF	XF	Unc	BU
1985 Proof	1,633	Value: 45.00				

KM# 49 20 DOLLARS
23.3300 g., 0.9250 Silver .6938 oz. ASW **Subject:** Summer Olympics **Obv:** National arms, value below **Rev:** Men running hurdles

Date	Mintage	F	VF	XF	Unc	BU
1988	15,000	—	—	—	28.00	—

KM# 27 25 DOLLARS
28.2800 g., 0.9250 Silver .8410 oz. ASW **Subject:** Coronation Jubilee **Obv:** Portrait of Queen Elizabeth II **Rev:** Imperial Crown with supporters, two dates below, value at bottom

Date	Mintage	F	VF	XF	Unc	BU
1978FM (M)	300	—	—	—	90.00	—
1978FM (U)	69	—	—	—	250	—
1978FM (P)	8,728	Value: 18.00				

KM# 30 25 DOLLARS
30.2800 g., 0.5000 Silver .4868 oz. ASW **Subject:** 10th Anniversary of Caribbean Development Bank **Obv:** National arms **Rev:** Globe above flag divides dates, value at bottom

Date	Mintage	F	VF	XF	Unc	BU
ND(1980)FM (P)	2,345	Value: 25.00				

KM# 31 25 DOLLARS
30.2800 g., 0.5000 Silver .4868 oz. ASW **Subject:** Caribbean Festival of Arts **Obv:** Similar to KM#30 **Rev:** Artistic design, value at right

Date	Mintage	F	VF	XF	Unc	BU
1981FM (P)	1,008	Value: 30.00				

KM# 37 25 DOLLARS
30.2800 g., 0.5000 Silver .4868 oz. ASW **Subject:** 30th Anniversary Coronation of Queen Elizabeth II **Obv:** National arms, divide date **Rev:** Crossed sceptres divide royal symbols-top and bottom; and dates at sides, value at bottom

Date	Mintage	F	VF	XF	Unc	BU
1983FM (P)	2,951	Value: 22.50				

KM# 43 25 DOLLARS
28.2800 g., 0.9250 Silver .8410 oz. ASW **Subject:** Royal Visit **Obv:** Crowned bust of Queen Elizabeth II right **Obv. Designer:** Raphael Maklouf **Rev:** National arms, value below

Date	Mintage	F	VF	XF	Unc	BU
1985	Est. 5,000	—	—	—	32.50	—

KM# 43a 25 DOLLARS
47.5400 g., 0.9170 Gold 1.4013 oz. AGW **Subject:** Royal Visit **Obv:** Crowned bust of Queen Elizabeth II right **Rev:** National arms, value below

Date	Mintage	F	VF	XF	Unc	BU
1985	Est. 250	Value: 965				

KM# 44 25 DOLLARS
28.2800 g., 0.5000 Silver .4546 oz. ASW **Subject:** Commonwealth Games **Obv:** National arms, date below **Rev:** Discus thrower, two large circles behind, value below

Date	Mintage	F	VF	XF	Unc	BU
1986	Est. 50,000	—	—	—	25.00	—

KM# 44a 25 DOLLARS
28.2800 g., 0.9250 Silver .8410 oz. ASW **Subject:** Commonwealth Games **Obv:** National arms, date below **Rev:** Discus thrower, two large circles behind, value below

Date	Mintage	F	VF	XF	Unc	BU
1986	Est. 20,000	Value: 30.00				

KM# 70 25 DOLLARS
31.4400 g., 0.9990 Silver 1.0098 oz. ASW, 37.85 mm. **Subject:** 25th Anniversary of the Central Bank **Obv:** National arms **Rev:** Upright Blue Marlin, right, divides dates, within circle **Edge:** Reeded

Date	Mintage	F	VF	XF	Unc	BU
ND (1997) Proof	—	Value: 75.00				

KM# 32 50 DOLLARS
27.3500 g., 0.5000 Silver .4397 oz. ASW **Subject:** World Food Day **Obv:** F.A.O. divided by lines, grain sprig below "A", date at bottom, circle surrounds all **Rev:** Black Belly Sheep right, value below

Date	Mintage	F	VF	XF	Unc	BU
1981FM (U)	6,012	—	—	—	40.00	—

KM# 42 50 DOLLARS
16.8500 g., 0.5000 Silver .2709 oz. ASW **Series:** F.A.O. **Obv:** F.A.O. divided by lines, grain sprig below "A", all within circle, date below circle **Rev:** Fourwing flying fish, value below **Edge:** Reeded

Date	Mintage	F	VF	XF	Unc	BU
1984	3,600	—	—	—	35.00	—

KM# 47 50 DOLLARS
33.6250 g., 0.9250 Silver 1.0000 oz. ASW **Subject:** 350th Anniversary of Parliament **Obv:** National arms, value below **Rev:** Parliament Building within circle, two dates below

Date	Mintage	F	VF	XF	Unc	BU
ND(1989) Proof	Est. 5,000	Value: 35.00				

KM# 51 50 DOLLARS
15.9800 g., 0.9170 Gold .4709 oz. AGW **Subject:** International Cricket Belt Buckle **Rev:** Cricket player on belt buckle
Note: Similar to 10 Dollars, KM#50.

Date	Mintage	F	VF	XF	Unc	BU
1991 Proof	500	Value: 530				

KM# 56 50 DOLLARS
15.9800 g., 0.9170 Gold .4709 oz. AGW **Subject:** UN Global SIDS Conference **Obv:** National arms, date below **Rev:** Large artistic hand, small house and tree within, value at bottom
Designer: Robert Elderton

Date	Mintage	F	VF	XF	Unc	BU
1994 Proof	100	Value: 550				

KM# 18 100 DOLLARS
6.2100 g., 0.5000 Gold .0998 oz. AGW **Subject:** 350th Anniversary - The English Ship - Olive Blossom **Obv:** National arms divide dates **Rev:** Olive Blossom with full sails, value below

Date	Mintage	F	VF	XF	Unc	BU
ND(1975)FM (M)	50	—	—	—	250	—
ND(1975)FM (U)	16,000	—	—	—	75.00	—
ND(1975)FM (P)	23,000	Value: 85.00				

KM# 28 100 DOLLARS
4.0600 g., 0.9000 Gold .1174 oz. AGW **Subject:** Human Rights **Obv:** National arms **Rev:** Praying hands beneath rolled scroll divide date

Date	Mintage	F	VF	XF	Unc	BU
1978	1,114	—	—	—	125	—

KM# 28a 100 DOLLARS
5.0500 g., 0.9000 Gold .1461 oz. AGW **Subject:** Human Rights **Obv:** National arms **Rev:** Praying hands beneath rolled scroll divide date

Date	Mintage	F	VF	XF	Unc	BU
1978 Proof	Inc. above	Value: 150				

KM# 38 100 DOLLARS
6.2100 g., 0.5000 Gold .0998 oz. AGW **Subject:** Neptune, God of the Sea **Obv:** National arms divide date **Rev:** Standing figure of Neptune looking right, value above

Date	Mintage	F	VF	XF	Unc	BU
1983FM (U)	3	—	—	—	—	—
1983FM (P)	484	Value: 225				

KM# 39 100 DOLLARS
6.2100 g., 0.5000 Gold .0998 oz. AGW **Subject:** Triton, Son of Neptune **Obv:** National arms divide date **Rev:** Full figure of Triton blowing horn left, value above

Date	Mintage	F	VF	XF	Unc	BU
1984FM (P)	1,103	Value: 170				

KM# 41 100 DOLLARS
6.2100 g., 0.5000 Gold .0998 oz. AGW **Subject:** Amphitrite, Wife of Neptune **Obv:** National arms divide date **Rev:** Full figure of Amphitrite looking left, value above

Date	Mintage	F	VF	XF	Unc	BU
1985FM (P)	1,276	Value: 185				

KM# 48 100 DOLLARS
15.9760 g., 0.9170 Gold .4709 oz. AGW **Subject:** 350th Anniversary of Parliament **Obv:** Crowned bust of Queen Elizabeth II right, value below **Rev:** Parliament Building within circle, two dates below

Date	Mintage	F	VF	XF	Unc	BU
ND(1989)FM	Est. 500	Value: 350				

KM# 33 150 DOLLARS
7.1300 g., 0.5000 Gold .1146 oz. AGW **Subject:** National Flower - Poinciana **Obv:** National arms divide date **Rev:** Flower and map, value surrounds

Date	Mintage	F	VF	XF	Unc	BU
1981FM (U)	7	—	—	—	—	—
1981FM (P)	1,140	Value: 125				

KM# 29 200 DOLLARS
8.1200 g., 0.9000 Gold .2349 oz. AGW **Subject:** Year of the Child **Obv:** National arms **Rev:** Artistic design , date at bottom

Date	Mintage	F	VF	XF	Unc	BU
1979	1,121	—	—	—	225	—

KM# 29a 200 DOLLARS
10.1000 g., 0.9000 Gold .2922 oz. AGW **Subject:** Year of the Child **Obv:** National arms **Rev:** Artistic design , date at bottom

Date	Mintage	F	VF	XF	Unc	BU
1979 Proof	Inc. above	Value: 275				

KM# 35 250 DOLLARS
6.6000 g., 0.9000 Gold .1910 oz. AGW **Subject:** 250th Anniversary of Birth of George Washington **Obv:** National arms divide date **Rev:** Small bust of George Washington below building, value above

Date	Mintage	F	VF	XF	Unc	BU
1982FM (P)	802	Value: 185				

KM# 45 250 DOLLARS
47.5400 g., 0.9170 Gold 1.4017 oz. AGW **Subject:** Commonwealth Games **Note:** Similar to 25 Dollars, KM#44.

Date	Mintage	F	VF	XF	Unc	BU
1986 Proof	150	Value: 985				

MINT SETS

KM#	Date	Mintage	Identification	Issue Price	Mkt Val
MS1	1973 (8)	2,500	KM#10-15, 16a, 17a	25.00	25.00
MS2	1974 (8)	3,708	KM#10-17	25.00	20.00
MS3	1975 (8)	1,360	KM#10-17	27.50	22.50
MS4	1976 (8)	996	KM#19-26	27.50	30.00
MS5	1977 (8)	468	KM#10-17	27.50	30.00
MS6	1978 (8)	517	KM#10-17	29.00	30.00
MS7	1979 (8)	523	KM#10-17	29.00	30.00
MS8	1980 (8)	649	KM#10-17	30.00	30.00
MS9	1981 (8)	327	KM#10-17	30.00	35.00
MS10	1982 (8)	—	KM#10-16, 34	35.00	45.00
MS11	1983 (8)	141	KM#10-16, 36	35.50	100
MS12	1989 (5)	—	KM#10-14.1	17.00	17.00

PROOF SETS

KM#	Date	Mintage	Identification	Issue Price	Mkt Val
PS1	1973 (8)	97,454	KM#109-15, 16a, 17a	37.50	30.00
PS2	1974 (8)	35,600	KM#10-15, 16a, 17a	50.00	30.00
PS3	1975 (8)	20,458	KM#10-15, 16a, 17a	55.00	30.00
PS4	1976 (8)	11,929	KM#19-24, 25a, 26a	55.00	40.00
PS5	1977 (8)	5,014	KM#10-15, 16a, 17a	55.00	35.00
PS6	1978 (8)	4,436	KM#10-15, 16a, 17a	58.00	37.50
PS7	1979 (8)	4,126	KM#10-15, 16a, 17a	60.00	37.50
PS8	1980 (8)	2,011	KM#10-15, 16a, 17a	117	45.00
PS9	1980 (2)	—	KM#16a, 17a	115	32.50
PS10	1981 (8)	—	KM#10-15, 16a, 17a	117	80.00
PS11	1982 (8)	—	KM#10-15, 16a, 34a	117	80.00
PS12	1983 (8)	—	KM#10-15, 16a, 36a	—	170
PS13	1984 (8)	—	KM#10-15, 16a, 40	132	200

Belarus (Byelorussia, Belorussia, or White Russia- formerly the Belorussian S.S.R.) is situated along the western Dvina and Dnieper Rivers, bounded in the west by Poland, to the north by Latvia and Lithuania, to the east by Russia and the south by the Ukraine. It has an area of 80,154 sq. mi. (207,600 sq. km.) and a population of 4.8 million. Capital: Minsk. Chief products: peat, salt, and agricultural products including flax, fodder and grasses for cattle breeding and dairy products.

There never existed an independent state of Byelorussia. Until the partitions of Poland at the end of the 18th century, the history of Byelorussia is identical with that of Lithuania.

When Russia incorporated the whole of Byelorussia into its territories in 1795, it claimed to be recovering old Russian lands and denied that the Byelorussians were a separate nation. Significant efforts for independence did not occur until 1918 and were met by external antagonism from German, Polish, and Russian influences.

Soviet and anti-Communist sympathies continued to reflect the political and social unrest of the U.S.S.R. for Byelorussia. Finally, on August 25, 1991, following an unsuccessful coup, the Supreme Soviet adopted a declaration of independence, and the "Republic of Belarus" was proclaimed in September. In December, it became a founder member of the CIS.

MONETARY SYSTEM
100 Kapeek = 1 Rouble

REPUBLIC

STANDARD COINAGE

KM# 6 ROUBLE

Copper-Nickel, 38.61 mm. **Subject:** 50th Anniversary - United Nations **Obv:** National arms, date at bottom **Rev:** Crane flying over map and UN logo **Designer:** A.I. Zimenko and D.G. Belitsky

Date	Mintage	F	VF	XF	Unc	BU
1996	—	—	—	—	20.00	—

KM# 6a ROUBLE

28.5100 g., 0.9250 Silver .8479 oz. ASW, 38.61 mm. **Rev:** Crane flying over map and UN logo **Designer:** A.I. Zimenko and D.G. Belitsky

Date	Mintage	F	VF	XF	Unc	BU
1996 Proof	20,000	Value: 225				

KM# 7 ROUBLE

Copper-Nickel, 32 mm. **Subject:** Olympics **Obv:** National arms and denomination **Rev:** Gymnast on the rings **Designer:** A.I. Zimenko and D.G. Belitsky

Date	Mintage	F	VF	XF	Unc	BU
1996	5,000	—	—	—	17.50	—

KM# 8 ROUBLE

Copper-Nickel, 32 mm **Subject:** Olympics **Obv:** National arms **Rev:** Ribbon dancer **Designer:** A.I. Zimenko and D.g. Belitsky

Date	Mintage	F	VF	XF	Unc	BU
1996 Prooflike	5,000	—	—	—	17.50	—

KM# 31 ROUBLE

7.9800 g., 0.9167 Gold .2532 oz. AGW, 22.85 mm. **Subject:** United Nations 50th Anniversary **Obv:** National arms, date at bottom **Rev:** Crane flying over map and U.N. logo **Designer:** A.I. Zimenko and D.G. Belitsky

Date	Mintage	F	VF	XF	Unc	BU
1996 Proof	5,000	Value: 1,500				

KM# 9 ROUBLE

Copper-Nickel, 33 mm. **Subject:** Third Anniversary of Independence **Obv:** National arms, date below, circle surrounds **Rev:** Monument July 3 **Designer:** T.S. Radivilko

Date	Mintage	F	VF	XF	Unc	BU
1997 Prooflike	5,000	—	—	—	17.50	—

KM# 34 ROUBLE

Copper-Nickel, 32 mm. **Subject:** Olympics **Obv:** National arms and denomination **Obv. Designer:** A.I. Zimenko and D.G. Belitsky **Rev:** Biathalon skier with rifle **Rev. Designer:** T.S. Radivilko

Date	Mintage	F	VF	XF	Unc	BU
1997 Prooflike	5,000	—	—	—	15.00	—

KM# 36 ROUBLE

Copper-Nickel, 32 mm. **Subject:** Olympics **Obv:** National arms and denomination **Obv. Designer:** A.I. Zimenko and D.G. Belitsky **Rev:** Two hockey players **Rev. Designer:** T.S. Radivilko

Date	Mintage	F	VF	XF	Unc	BU
1997 Prooflike	5,000	—	—	—	15.00	—

KM# 18 ROUBLE

Copper-Nickel, 32 mm. **Subject:** Architecture of Belarus **Obv:** National arms **Rev:** Castle at Mir **Rev. Designer:** T.S. Radivilko

Date	Mintage	F	VF	XF	Unc	BU
1998 Proof	2,000	Value: 75.00				

KM# 19 ROUBLE
Copper-Nickel, 32 mm. **Subject:** Cities of Belarus **Obv:** National arms **Rev:** Walled city of Polatsk with city arms

Date	Mintage	F	VF	XF	Unc	BU
1998 Proof	2,000	Value: 65.00				

KM# 20 ROUBLE
Copper-Nickel, 33 mm. **Subject:** 200th Anniversary - Birth of A. Mitskevich - Poet **Obv:** National arms **Rev:** Mitskevich portrait, dates 1798-1855 **Designer:** T.S. Radivilko

Date	Mintage	F	VF	XF	Unc	BU
1998 Proof	2,000	Value: 75.00				

KM# 21 ROUBLE
Copper-Nickel **Subject:** Olympics **Obv:** National arms and denomination **Rev:** Hurdlers, Olympic crest

Date	Mintage	F	VF	XF	Unc	BU
1998 Proof	5,000	Value: 11.50				

KM# 22 ROUBLE
Copper-Nickel, 33 mm. **Subject:** Cities of Belarus **Obv:** National arms, date below, within circle **Obv. Designer:** A.I. Zimenko and D.G. Belitsky **Rev:** Minsk view with city arms, within circle **Rev. Designer:** T.S. Radivilko

Date	Mintage	F	VF	XF	Unc	BU
1999 Proof	2,000	Value: 75.00				

KM# 23 ROUBLE
Copper-Nickel, 33 mm. **Subject:** 100th Anniversary - Birth of Mikhas Lynkou **Obv:** National arms **Rev:** Head of Lynkou facing right **Designer:** T.S. Radivilko

Date	Mintage	F	VF	XF	Unc	BU
1999 Proof	1,000	Value: 250				

KM# 40 ROUBLE
14.5000 g., Copper-Nickel, 33 mm. **Subject:** G.P. Glebov **Obv:** National arms **Rev:** Glebats portrait with two smaller portraits, dates 1899-1967 **Edge:** Reeded **Designer:** T.S. Radivilko

Date	Mintage	F	VF	XF	Unc	BU
1999 Proof	1,000	Value: 300				

KM# 41 ROUBLE
Copper-Nickel, 33 mm. **Subject:** 2000 Years **Obv:** National arms **Obv. Designer:** T.S. Radivilko **Rev:** Bethlehem view **Rev. Designer:** V.V. Lemachko

Date	Mintage	F	VF	XF	Unc	BU
1999 Proof	10,000	Value: 35.00				

KM# 63 ROUBLE
14.3600 g., Copper-Nickel, 33 mm. **Subject:** Jubilee 2000 **Obv:** National arms **Rev:** Logo and three churches of Pinsk, Grodna and Minsk **Edge:** Reeded **Designer:** T.S. Radivilko

Date	Mintage	F	VF	XF	Unc	BU
1999 Proof	10,000	Value: 37.50				

KM# 48 ROUBLE
13.2000 g., Copper-Nickel, 31.9 mm. **Subject:** Architecture **Obv:** National arms **Obv. Designer:** T.S. Radivilko **Rev:** St. Boris and St. Gleb Church **Rev. Designer:** R. Kotovich **Edge:** Reeded

Date	Mintage	F	VF	XF	Unc	BU
2000 Proof	2,000	Value: 50.00				

KM# 24 10 ROUBLES
16.9600 g., 0.9250 Silver .5044 oz. ASW, 33 mm. **Subject:** 200th Anniversary - Birth of A. Mitskevich **Obv:** National arms **Rev:** Portrait Mitskevich facing left, dates 1798-1855 **Designer:** T.S. Radivilko

Date	Mintage	F	VF	XF	Unc	BU
1998 Proof	2,000	Value: 50.00				

KM# 25 10 ROUBLES
16.9600 g., 0.9250 Silver .5044 oz. ASW, 33 mm. **Subject:** G.P. Glebov - Theatre Artist **Obv:** National arms **Rev:** Glebats portrait with two smaller portraits, dates 1899-1967 **Designer:** T.S. Radivilko

Date	Mintage	F	VF	XF	Unc	BU
1999 Proof	1,200	Value: 50.00				

KM# 26 10 ROUBLES
16.9600 g., 0.9250 Silver .5044 oz. ASW, 33 mm. **Subject:** 100th Anniversary - Birth of Mikhas Lynkou **Obv:** National arms **Rev:** Head of Lynkou facing right, dates 1899-1975 **Designer:** T.S. Radivilko

Date	Mintage	F	VF	XF	Unc	BU
1999 Proof	1,200	Value: 75.00				

KM# 13 20 ROUBLES
33.8400 g., 0.9250 Silver 1.0064 oz. ASW, 39 mm. **Subject:** Olympics **Obv:** National arms and denomination **Rev:** Olympic crest, gymnast on rings **Designer:** A.I. Zimenko and D.G. Belitsky

Date	Mintage	F	VF	XF	Unc	BU
1996 Proof	1,000	Value: 225				

KM# 14 20 ROUBLES
33.8400 g., 0.9250 Silver 1.0064 oz. ASW, 39 mm. **Subject:** Olympics **Obv:** National arms and denomination **Rev:** Ribbon dancer **Designer:** A.I. Zimenko and D.G. Belitsky

Date	Mintage	F	VF	XF	Unc	BU
1996 Proof	1,000	Value: 225				

KM# 10 20 ROUBLES
34.7400 g., 0.9000 Silver 1.0052 oz. ASW, 39 mm. **Subject:** Monument of Independence **Obv:** National arms and denomination **Rev:** Date July 3 **Designer:** T.S. Radivilko

Date	Mintage	F	VF	XF	Unc	BU
1997 Proof	3,000	Value: 50.00				

KM# 11 20 ROUBLES
34.7400 g., 0.9000 Silver 1.0052 oz. ASW, 39 mm. **Subject:** Russia-Belarus State Treaty **Obv:** National arms **Obv. Designer:** T.S. Radivilko **Rev:** 2 city views with respective national emblems and the date April 2 1996 at bottom **Rev. Designer:** A.V. Baklanov

Date	Mintage	F	VF	XF	Unc	BU
1997 Proof	5,000	Value: 50.00				

KM# 12 20 ROUBLES
31.4800 g., 0.9990 Silver 1.0110 oz. ASW, 39 mm. **Subject:** 75th Anniversary - Banking System **Obv:** National arms **Rev:** Bank building **Designer:** T.S. Radivilko

Date	Mintage	F	VF	XF	Unc	BU
1997 Proof	2,000	Value: 175				

KM# 15 20 ROUBLES
31.0300 g., 0.9250 Silver .9228 oz. ASW, 39 mm. **Subject:** Olympics **Obv:** National arms and denomination **Obv. Designer:** A.I. Zimenko and D.G. Belitsky **Rev:** Biathlon skier **Rev. Designer:** T.S. Radivilko

Date	Mintage	F	VF	XF	Unc	BU
1997 Proof	Est. 1,000	Value: 200				

KM# 16 20 ROUBLES
31.1500 g., 0.9250 Silver .9264 oz. ASW, 39 mm. **Subject:** Olympics **Obv:** National arms **Obv. Designer:** A.I. Zimenko and B.G. Belitsky **Rev:** Two hockey players **Rev. Designer:** T.S. Radivilko

Date	Mintage	F	VF	XF	Unc	BU
1997 Proof	Est. 1,000	Value: 200				

KM# 27 20 ROUBLES
33.5200 g., 0.9250 Silver .9969 oz. ASW, 38.61 mm. **Subject:** Architecture of Belarus **Obv:** National arms, date below, within circle **Rev:** Castle and Mir and seal **Rev. Designer:** T.S. Radivilko

Date	Mintage	F	VF	XF	Unc	BU
1998 Proof	2,000	Value: 175				

KM# 28 20 ROUBLES
33.5200 g., 0.9250 Silver .9969 oz. ASW **Subject:** Cities of Belarus **Obv:** National arms **Rev:** Polatsk with city arms above

Date	Mintage	F	VF	XF	Unc	BU
1998 Proof	2,000	Value: 125				

KM# 29 20 ROUBLES
33.5200 g., 0.9250 Silver .9969 oz. ASW **Subject:** Olympics **Obv:** National arms and denomination **Obv. Designer:** A.I. Zimenko and D.G. Belitsky **Rev:** Hurdlers, Olympic crest

Date	Mintage	F	VF	XF	Unc	BU
1998 Proof	1,000	Value: 175				

KM# 17 20 ROUBLES
33.9000 g., 0.9250 Silver 1.0082 oz. ASW, 39 mm. **Subject:** 80th Anniversary - Financial System **Obv:** National arms, date below, within circle **Rev:** Anniversary logo **Rev. Designer:** T.S. Radivilko

Date	Mintage	F	VF	XF	Unc	BU
1999 Proof	1,000	Value: 500				

KM# 30 20 ROUBLES
33.5200 g., 0.9250 Silver .9969 oz. ASW, 39 mm. **Subject:** Cities of Belarus **Obv:** National arms, date below, within circle **Rev:** Minsk view with city arms **Rev. Designer:** T.S. Radivilko

Date	Mintage	F	VF	XF	Unc	BU
1999 Proof	2,000	Value: 180				

KM# 42 20 ROUBLES
33.8600 g., 0.9250 Silver 1.0070 oz. ASW **Subject:** 2000 Years of Christianity **Obv:** National arms, date below, within circle **Obv. Designer:** T.S. Radivilko **Rev:** Bethlehem view **Rev. Designer:** V.V. Lemachko **Edge:** Reeded

Date	Mintage	F	VF	XF	Unc	BU
1999 Proof	5,000	Value: 250				

KM# 43 20 ROUBLES
33.8600 g., 0.9250 Silver 1.0070 oz. ASW **Subject:** Jubilee 2000 **Obv:** National arms **Rev:** Three churches of Pinsk, Grodno and Minsk **Designer:** T.S. Radivilko

Date	Mintage	F	VF	XF	Unc	BU
1999 Proof	5,000	Value: 400				

KM# 66 20 ROUBLES
33.8500 g., 0.9250 Silver 1.0067 oz. ASW, 38.5 mm. **Obv:** National arms **Rev:** Borisoglebsk church in Grodno **Edge:** Reeded

Date	Mintage	F	VF	XF	Unc	BU
1999 Proof	2,000	Value: 150				

KM# 68 20 ROUBLES
33.8500 g., 0.9250 Silver 1.0067 oz. ASW, 38.5 mm. **Obv:** National arms **Obv. Designer:** T.S. Radivilko **Rev:** Synkovichi church **Rev. Designer:** R. Kotovich **Edge:** Reeded

Date	Mintage	F	VF	XF	Unc	BU
2000 Proof	2,000	Value: 75.00				

KM# 52 20 ROUBLES
31.4500 g., 0.9250 Silver 0.9353 oz. ASW, 38.6 mm. **Subject:** 2002 Winter Olympics **Obv:** National arms, date below, within circle **Rev:** Discus thrower **Edge:** Reeded **Designer:** T.S. Radivilko

Date	Mintage	F	VF	XF	Unc	BU
2000 Proof	20,000	Value: 150				

KM# 32 50 ROUBLES
7.7800 g., 0.9990 Gold .2499 oz. AGW, 22 mm. **Subject:** Olympics **Obv:** National arms and denomination **Rev:** Ribbon dancer **Designer:** A.I. Zimenko and D.G. Belitsky

Date	Mintage	F	VF	XF	Unc	BU
1996 Proof	500	Value: 600				

KM# 33 50 ROUBLES
7.7800 g., 0.9990 Gold .2499 oz. AGW, 22 mm. **Obv:** National arms and denomination **Rev:** Gymnast on rings **Designer:** A.I. Zimenko and D.G. Belitsky

Date	Mintage	F	VF	XF	Unc	BU
1996 Proof	500	Value: 600				

KM# 35 50 ROUBLES
7.7800 g., 0.9990 Gold .2499 oz. AGW, 22 mm. **Obv:** National arms and denomination **Obv. Designer:** A.I. Zimenko and D.G. Belitsky **Rev:** Biathalow skier with rifle **Rev. Designer:** T.S. Radivilko

Date	Mintage	F	VF	XF	Unc	BU
1997 Proof	500	Value: 550				

KM# 37 50 ROUBLES
7.7800 g., 0.9990 Gold .2499 oz. AGW, 22 mm. **Obv:** National arms and denomination **Obv. Designer:** A.I. Zimenko and D.G. Belitsky **Rev:** Two hockey players **Rev. Designer:** T.S. Radivilko

Date	Mintage	F	VF	XF	Unc	BU
1997 Proof	500	Value: 600				

KM# 38 50 ROUBLES
7.7800 g., 0.9990 Gold .2499 oz. AGW **Obv:** National arms and denomination **Obv. Designer:** A.I. Zimenko and D.G. Belitsky **Rev:** Two hurdlers

Date	Mintage	F	VF	XF	Unc	BU
1997 Proof	500	Value: 550				

BELGIAN CONGO

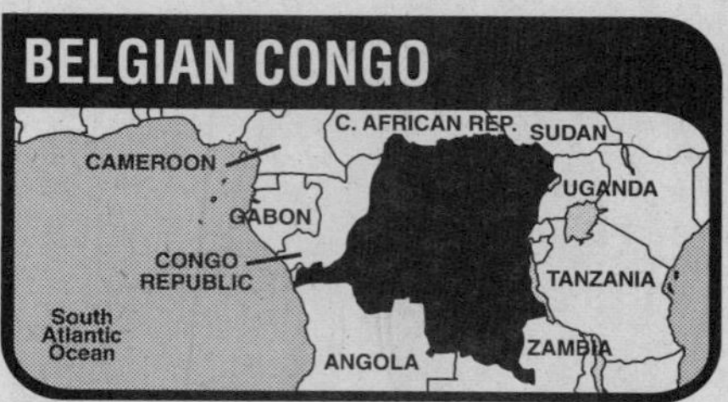

The Belgian Congo and Ruanda-Urundi were united administratively from 1925 to 1960. Ruanda-Urundi was made a U.N. Trust territory in 1946. Coins for these 2 areas were made jointly between 1952 and 1960. Ruanda-Urundi became the Republic of Rwanda on June 1, 1962.

MONETARY SYSTEM
100 Centimes = 1 Franc

RULERS
Belgium

COLONY

DECIMAL COINAGE

KM# 15 CENTIME
Copper **Obv:** Hole at center of crowned "A"s, circle surrounds **Rev:** Center hole within star, date below star, value above

Date	Mintage	F	VF	XF	Unc	BU
1910	2,000,000	1.00	2.00	3.00	10.00	25.00
1919	500,000	1.00	2.00	3.00	15.00	40.00

KM# 16 2 CENTIMES
Copper **Obv:** Hole at center of crowned "A"s, circle surrounds **Rev:** Hole at center of star, date below star, value above

Date	Mintage	F	VF	XF	Unc	BU
1910	1,500,000	1.00	3.00	7.00	30.00	60.00
1919	500,000	1.50	3.50	10.00	35.00	75.00

KM# 12 5 CENTIMES
Copper-Nickel **Obv:** Hole at cente of crowned"JL", circle surrounds **Rev:** Hole at center of star, date below star, value above

Date	Mintage	F	VF	XF	Unc	BU
1909	1,800,000	5.00	12.50	40.00	125	210

KM# 17 5 CENTIMES
Copper-Nickel **Obv:** Hole at center of crowned "A"s, within circle **Rev:** Hole at center of star, date below star, value above

Date	Mintage	F	VF	XF	Unc	BU
1910(H)	6,000,000	0.75	1.50	3.50	16.00	60.00
1911(H)	5,000,000	0.75	1.50	3.50	16.00	50.00
1917(H)	1,000,000	3.00	7.00	18.00	55.00	100
1917(H) Proof	—	Value: 175				
1919(H)	3,000,000	1.50	3.00	7.00	25.00	—
1919	6,850,000	0.50	1.00	2.50	16.00	—
1920	2,740,000	0.50	1.00	3.50	18.00	—
1920/10(H)	—	—	—	—	—	—
1921	17,260,000	0.25	0.75	1.50	10.00	—
1921(H)	3,000,000	1.00	2.00	6.00	20.00	—
1925	11,000,000	0.25	0.75	2.00	10.00	—
1926/5	5,770,000	2.25	4.50	—	—	—
1926	Inc. above	0.25	1.00	2.00	9.00	—
1927	2,000,000	0.50	1.00	2.50	10.00	—
1928/6	1,500,000	2.00	4.00	8.00	20.00	—
1928	Inc. above	0.75	1.25	3.00	10.00	—

KM# 10 10 CENTIMES
Copper-Nickel **Designer:**

Date	Mintage	F	VF	XF	Unc	BU
1906	100,000	4.00	10.00	25.00	60.00	—
1908	800,000	3.00	7.50	20.00	50.00	—

KM# 13 10 CENTIMES
Copper-Nickel **Obv:** Hole at center of crowned "L"s, backs touching, within circle **Rev:** Hole at center of star, date below star, value above

Date	Mintage	F	VF	XF	Unc	BU
1909	1,500,000	8.00	20.00	70.00	200	300

KM# 18 10 CENTIMES
Copper-Nickel **Obv:** Hole at center of crowned "A"s, within circle **Rev:** Hole at center of star, date below star, value above

Date	Mintage	F	VF	XF	Unc	BU
1910	5,000,000	0.50	1.00	3.00	15.00	50.00
1911	5,000,000	0.50	1.00	3.00	15.00	50.00
1917(H)	500,000	5.00	10.00	25.00	75.00	—
1919(H)	1,500,000	0.75	1.25	4.00	18.00	—
1919	3,430,000	0.50	1.00	3.50	16.50	—
1920	1,510,000	0.75	1.25	4.00	18.00	—
1921	13,540,000	0.25	0.75	2.00	10.00	—
1921(H)	3,000,000	0.75	1.50	3.50	16.50	—
1922	14,950,000	0.25	1.00	2.50	10.00	—
1924	3,600,000	0.50	1.50	3.00	15.00	—
1925/4	4,800,000	2.00	4.00	8.00	50.00	—
1925	Inc. above	0.25	1.00	3.00	15.00	—
1927	2,020,000	0.25	1.00	3.00	12.00	—
1928/7	5,600,000	1.00	3.00	8.00	40.00	—
1928	Inc. above	0.25	1.00	3.00	12.00	—
1928/3	—	—	—	—	—	—
1928/5	—	—	—	—	—	—

KM# 11 20 CENTIMES
Copper-Nickel **Designer:**

Date	Mintage	F	VF	XF	Unc	BU
1906	100,000	5.00	12.50	25.00	70.00	—
1908	400,000	4.00	7.50	15.00	50.00	—

KM# 14 20 CENTIMES
Copper-Nickel **Obv:** Hole at center of crowned "L"s, backs touching, within circle **Rev:** Hole at center of star, date below star, value above

Date	Mintage	F	VF	XF	Unc	BU
1909	300,000	10.00	25.00	65.00	180	—

KM# 19 20 CENTIMES
Copper-Nickel **Obv:** Hole at center of crowned "A"s, within circle **Rev:** Hole at center of star, date below star, value above

Date	Mintage	F	VF	XF	Unc	BU
1910	1,000,000	2.00	5.00	12.00	40.00	120
1911	1,250,000	1.50	4.00	10.00	35.00	120

KM# 22 50 CENTIMES
Copper-Nickel, 23.8 mm. **Obv:** Laureate head, left, French legend **Rev:** Oil palm divides denomination and date **Rev. Legend:** CONGO BELGE **Edge:** Reeded

Date	Mintage	F	VF	XF	Unc	BU
1921	4,000,000	0.60	2.00	8.00	35.00	80.00
1922	6,000,000	0.60	2.00	8.00	30.00	80.00
1923	7,200,000	0.60	2.00	8.00	30.00	80.00
1924	1,096,000	0.75	3.00	10.00	45.00	—
1925	16,104,000	0.60	2.00	7.00	30.00	80.00
1926/5	16,000,000	1.00	4.00	12.00	50.00	—
1926	Inc. above	0.60	2.00	8.00	30.00	80.00
1927	10,000,000	0.60	2.00	8.00	30.00	80.00
1929/7	7,504,000	0.60	2.00	9.00	50.00	—
1929/8	Inc. above	1.00	4.00	15.00	90.00	—
1929	Inc. above	0.60	2.00	7.00	30.00	80.00

KM# 23 50 CENTIMES
Copper-Nickel **Obv:** Lareate head, left **Rev:** Oil palm divides denomination and date, Flemish legend **Rev. Legend:** BELGISCH CONGO

Date	Mintage	F	VF	XF	Unc	BU
1921	4,000,000	0.60	2.00	8.00	32.00	—
1922	5,592,000	0.60	2.00	7.00	30.00	—
1923	7,208,000	0.60	2.00	7.00	30.00	—
1924	7,000,000	0.60	2.00	8.00	32.00	—
1925/4	10,600,000	1.50	7.00	20.00	90.00	—
1925	Inc. above	0.60	2.00	7.00	30.00	—
1926	25,200,000	0.60	2.00	7.00	27.50	—
1927	4,800,000	0.60	2.00	8.00	30.00	—
1928	7,484,000	0.60	2.00	7.00	30.00	—
1929/8	116,000	25.00	50.00	75.00	120	—
1929	Inc. above	20.00	40.00	70.00	100	—

KM# 20 FRANC
Copper-Nickel **Obv:** Laureate head, left **Rev:** Oil palm divides denomination and date, French legend **Rev. Legend:** CONGO BELGE

Date	Mintage	F	VF	XF	Unc	BU
1920	4,000,000	0.85	2.75	10.00	37.50	—
1922	5,000,000	0.85	2.75	9.00	32.00	—
1923/2	5,000,000	2.00	7.00	16.00	45.00	—
1923	Inc. above	0.85	2.75	9.00	32.00	—
1924	6,[illegible]30,000	0.85	2.75	9.00	35.00	—
1925	10,470,000	0.85	2.75	9.00	32.00	—
1926/5	12,500,000	2.00	7.00	16.50	50.00	—
1926	Inc above	0.85	2.75	8.00	30.00	—
1927	15,250,000	0.85	2.75	8.00	30.00	—
1929	5,763,000	0.85	2.75	9.00	32.00	—
1930	5,000,000	0.85	2.75	10.00	40.00	—

KM# 21 FRANC
Copper-Nickel **Obv:** Laureate head, left **Rev:** Oil palm divides denomination and date, Flemish legend **Rev. Legend:** BELGISCH CONGO

Date	Mintage	F	VF	XF	Unc	BU
1920	475,000	2.00	5.00	16.50	50.00	—
1921	3,525,000	0.85	3.00	9.00	37.50	—

Date	Mintage	F	VF	XF	Unc	BU
1922	5,000,000	0.85	3.00	9.00	37.50	—
1923/2	7,362,000	2.00	5.00	17.00	55.00	—
1923	Inc. above	0.85	2.75	9.00	32.00	—
1924	4,608,000	0.85	3.00	10.00	37.50	—
1925	9,530,000	0.85	2.75	9.00	32.00	—
1925/3	—	—	—	—	—	—
1926/5	17,000,000	2.00	5.00	17.00	55.00	—
1926	Inc. above	0.85	2.75	9.00	32.00	—
1928	9,250,000	0.85	2.75	9.00	32.00	—
1929	4,250,000	0.85	3.00	10.00	37.50	—

KM# 26 FRANC
Brass **Obv:** Denomination, legend at top and bottom **Rev:** African elephant, date below

Date	Mintage	F	VF	XF	Unc	BU
1944	25,000,000	0.50	1.00	3.00	10.00	12.50
1946	15,000,000	0.75	1.50	3.50	11.00	13.50
1949	15,000,000	0.75	1.50	3.00	11.00	13.50

KM# 25 2 FRANCS
Brass **Obv:** Denomination, stars flanking **Rev:** African elephant, left, date below **Shape:** 6-sided

Date	Mintage	F	VF	XF	Unc	BU
1943	25,000,000	2.50	6.00	15.00	50.00	75.00

KM# 28 2 FRANCS
Brass **Obv:** Denomination, stars flanking, legend at top and bottom **Rev:** African elephant left, date below

Date	Mintage	F	VF	XF	Unc	BU
1946	13,000,000	1.00	2.00	3.50	22.00	—
1947	12,000,000	1.00	2.00	4.00	25.00	—

KM# 24 5 FRANCS
Nickel-Bronze **Obv:** Head of Leopold III, left **Rev:** Lion above denomination, star at left of denomination, legend surrounds

Date	Mintage	F	VF	XF	Unc	BU
1936	2,600,000	5.00	10.00	30.00	125	150
1937	11,400,000	4.00	12.00	35.00	140	170

KM# 29 5 FRANCS
Brass **Obv:** Denomination at center, stars flanking, legend at top and bottom **Rev:** African elephant left, date below

Date	Mintage	F	VF	XF	Unc	BU
1947	10,000,000	3.00	7.00	15.00	50.00	90.00

KM# 27 50 FRANCS
17.5000 g., 0.5000 Silver .2814 oz. ASW **Obv:** Denomination at center, stars flanking, legend at top and bottom **Rev:** African elephant left, date below

Date	Mintage	F	VF	XF	Unc	BU
1944	1,000,000	20.00	50.00	75.00	175	425

RUANDA-URUNDI

PROVINCE

DECIMAL COINAGE

KM# 2 50 CENTIMES
Aluminum **Obv:** Crowned arms divide date **Rev:** Oil palm divides denomination

Date	Mintage	F	VF	XF	Unc	BU
1954 DB	4,700,000	—	0.35	0.75	2.00	3.00
1955 DB	20,300,000	—	0.15	0.60	1.50	2.50

KM# 4 FRANC
Aluminum **Obv:** Crowned arms divide date **Rev:** Oil palm divides denomination

Date	Mintage	F	VF	XF	Unc	BU
1957	10,000,000	—	0.50	1.00	2.00	3.50
1958	20,000,000	—	0.50	1.00	2.00	3.00
1959	20,000,000	—	0.50	1.00	2.00	3.00
1960	20,000,000	—	0.50	1.00	2.00	3.00

KM# 1 5 FRANCS
Brass **Designer:**

Date	Mintage	F	VF	XF	Unc	BU
1952	10,000,000	—	2.50	5.00	10.00	15.00

KM# 3 5 FRANCS
Aluminum, 31 mm. **Obv:** Crowned arms divide date **Rev:** Oil palm divides denomination **Edge:** Reeded

Date	Mintage	F	VF	XF	Unc	BU
1956 DB	10,000,000	—	1.00	2.00	4.00	6.00
1958 DB	26,110,000	—	0.75	1.75	3.50	5.00
1959 DB	3,890,000	—	1.00	2.50	5.00	7.00

ESSAIS

KM#	Date	Mintage	Identification	Mkt Val
E1	1952	—	5 Francs. Value at center of star. Tree divides denomination and date.	35.00
E1a	1952	—	5 Francs. Silver.	235
E2	1954	—	50 Centimes.	25.00
E3	1954	—	50 Centimes. Silver.	140

KM#	Date	Mintage	Identification	Mkt Val
E4	1956 DB	—	5 Francs. Crowned arms divide date. Tree divides denomination.	30.00
E5	1957	—	Franc. Crowned arms divides date. Tree divides denomination.	20.00
E6	1960	—	Franc. Bronze.	90.00

BELGIUM

The Kingdom of Belgium, a constitutional monarchy in northwest Europe, has an area of 11,780 sq. mi. (30,519 sq. km.) and a population of 10.1 million, chiefly Dutch-speaking Flemish and French-speaking Walloons. Capital: Brussels. Agriculture, dairy farming, and the processing of raw materials for re-export are the principal industries. Beurs voor Diamant in Antwerp is the world's largest diamond trading center. Iron and steel, machinery motor vehicles, chemicals, textile yarns and fabrics comprise the principal exports.

At the Congress of Vienna in 1815 the area was reunited with the Netherlands, but in 1830 independence was gained and the constitutional monarchy of Belgium was established. A large part of the Duchy of Luxembourg was incorporated into Belgium and the first king was Leopold I of Saxe-Coburg-Gotha. It was invaded by the German Army in August, 1914 and the German forces carried on a devastating occupation of most of the territory until the Armistice. Belgium joined the League of Nations. On May 10, 1940 it was invaded again by the German army. The Belgian and Allied forces were quickly overwhelmed and were evacuated through Dunkirk. Allied troops reached Belgium again in Sept. 1944. Prince Charles, Count of Flanders, assumed King Leopold's responsibilities until liberation by the U.S. Army in Austria on May 8, 1945. As of January 1, 1989, Belgium became a federal kingdom.

RULERS
Leopold II, 1865-1909
Albert I, 1909-1934
Leopold III, 1934-1950
Baudouin I, 1951-1993
Albert II, 1993-

MINT MARKS
Angel head - Brussels

MINTMASTERS' INITIALS & PRIVY MARKS
(b) - bird - Vogelier
Lamb head – Lambret

NOTE: Beginning in 1987, the letters "qp" appear on the coins - (quality proof)

MONETARY SYSTEM
100 Centimes = 1 Franc
1 Euro = 100 Cents

LEGENDS

Belgian coins are usually inscribed either in Dutch, French or both. However some modern coins are being inscribed in Latin or German. The language used is best told by noting the spelling of the name of the country.

(Fr) French: BELGIQUE or BELGES
(Du) Dutch: BELGIE or BELGEN
(La) Latin: BELGICA
(Ge) German: BELGIEN

Many Belgian coins are collected by what is known as Position A and Position B edges. Some dates command a premium depending on the position which are as follows:

Position A: Coins with portrait side down having upright edge lettering.

Position B: Coins with portrait side up having upright edge lettering.

KINGDOM

DECIMAL COINAGE

KM# 33.1 CENTIME
Copper, 18 mm. **Obv:** Crowned design, date below, legend in French **Obv. Legend:** DES BELGES **Rev:** Tablet to left of seated lion looking right, denomination below

Date	Mintage	F	VF	XF	Unc	BU
1901/801 Near 1	3,743,000	0.50	2.50	5.00	18.00	—
1901/801 Far 1	Inc. above	0.50	2.50	5.00	18.00	—
1901	Inc. above	0.25	0.50	1.50	5.00	—
1902/802 Near 2	2,847,000	1.00	2.00	4.00	10.00	—
1902/802 Far 2	Inc. above	1.00	2.00	4.00	10.00	—
1902/801	Inc. above	1.00	2.00	4.00	10.00	—
1902/1	Inc. above	1.00	2.00	4.00	10.00	—
1902	Inc. above	0.20	0.50	1.50	5.00	—
1907	3,967,000	0.20	0.50	1.50	4.00	—

KM# 33.2 CENTIME
Copper **Designer:** **Note:** Thin flan.

Date	Mintage	F	VF	XF	Unc	BU
1901	Inc. above	1.00	1.50	4.00	12.50	—
1902	Inc. above	1.00	1.50	6.00	15.00	—

KM# 33.3 CENTIME

Copper **Rev:** Additional stop in signature... BRAEMT.F.

Date	Mintage	F	VF	XF	Unc	BU
1902	Inc. above	1.00	2.00	10.00	30.00	—

KM# 34.1 CENTIME

Copper **Obv:** Crowned design, date below, legend in Dutch **Obv. Legend:** DER BELGEN **Rev:** Tablet at left of seated lion looking right, denomination below

Date	Mintage	F	VF	XF	Unc	BU
1901/899	Inc. above	0.75	2.25	4.50	18.00	—
1901	Inc. above	0.25	0.50	1.50	5.00	—
1902/1	2,482,000	1.25	3.50	9.00	10.00	—
1902	Inc. above	0.25	0.50	1.50	5.00	—
1907	3,966,000	0.25	0.50	1.50	4.00	—

KM# 34.2 CENTIME

Copper **Designer:** **Note:** Thin flan.

Date	Mintage	F	VF	XF	Unc	BU
1901	Inc. above	1.00	1.50	8.00	25.00	—
1902	Inc. above	1.00	1.50	8.00	25.00	—

KM# 76 CENTIME

Copper, 11 mm. **Obv:** Crowned letter "A", date below, legend in French **Obv. Legend:** DES BELGES **Rev:** Tablet at left of seated lion looking right, denomination below **Edge:** Reeded

Date	Mintage	F	VF	XF	Unc	BU
1912	2,540,000	0.20	0.50	2.50	7.00	—
1914	870,000	0.25	0.75	3.50	10.00	—

KM# 77 CENTIME

Copper, 11 mm. **Obv:** Crowned letter "A", date below, legend in Dutch **Obv. Legend:** DER BELGEN **Rev:** Tablet to left of seated lion looking right, denomination below **Edge:** Reeded

Date	Mintage	F	VF	XF	Unc	BU
1912	2,542,000	0.20	0.50	1.50	4.00	—

KM# 35.1 2 CENTIMES

Copper **Obv:** Legend in French **Obv. Legend:** DES BELGES

Date	Mintage	F	VF	XF	Unc	BU
1902	2,490,000	0.15	0.50	4.00	15.00	—
1905	4,981,000	0.15	0.50	4.00	10.00	—
1909	Inc. above	0.15	0.50	4.00	10.00	—
1909/5	4,983,000	0.75	3.00	15.00	50.00	—
1909/1809	Inc. above	1.00	5.00	30.00	85.00	—

KM# 35.2 2 CENTIMES

Copper **Designer:** **Note:** Thin flan.

Date	Mintage	F	VF	XF	Unc	BU
1902	Inc. above	3.00	5.00	35.00	75.00	125

KM# 36 2 CENTIMES

Copper **Obv:** Crowned design, date below, legend in Dutch **Obv. Legend:** DER BELGEN **Rev:** Tablet to left of seated lion looking right, denomination below

Date	Mintage	F	VF	XF	Unc	BU
1902	2,488,000	0.15	1.50	4.00	15.00	—
1905/2	4,986,000	1.50	3.00	15.00	50.00	—
1905	Inc. above	0.15	1.00	4.00	10.00	—
1909	565,000	0.50	2.00	12.00	50.00	—

KM# 65 2 CENTIMES

Copper **Obv:** Crowned letter "A", date below, legend in Dutch **Obv. Legend:** DER BELGEN **Rev:** Tablet to left of seated lion looking right, denomination below

Date	Mintage	F	VF	XF	Unc	BU
1910	1,248,000	0.25	0.50	3.00	10.00	—
1911 Large date	6,441,000	0.15	0.35	1.50	5.00	—
1911 Small date	Inc. above	0.15	0.35	1.50	5.00	—
1912	1,602,000	0.35	1.00	3.00	8.00	—
1919	4,998,000	0.15	0.35	0.75	3.00	—

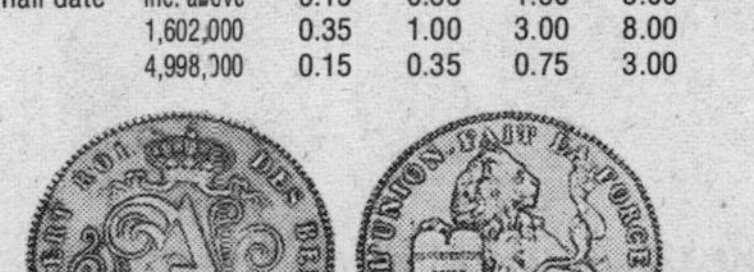

KM# 64 2 CENTIMES

Copper **Obv:** Crowned letter "A", date below, legend in French **Obv. Legend:** DES BELGES **Rev:** Tablet to left of seated lion looking right, denomination below

Date	Mintage	F	VF	XF	Unc	BU
1911	645,000	1.50	3.00	14.00	40.00	—
1912/1	4,928,000	1.00	3.00	10.00	25.00	—
1912	Inc. above	0.15	0.50	2.00	5.00	—
1914	491,000	1.00	2.50	12.00	30.00	—
1919/4	5,000,000	0.75	1.00	3.00	7.00	—
1919	Inc. above	0.15	0.25	1.00	3.00	—

KM# 40 5 CENTIMES

Copper-Nickel **Obv:** Legend in French **Obv. Legend:** DES BELGES

Date	Mintage	F	VF	XF	Unc	BU
1901	—	10.00	30.00	65.00	140	—

KM# 44 5 CENTIMES

Copper-Nickel **Obv:** Denomination above star, circle surrounds **Rev:** Rampant lion left within circle, date below

Date	Mintage	F	VF	XF	Unc	BU
1901	2,494,000	3.00	20.00	35.00	70.00	—

KM# 45 5 CENTIMES

Copper-Nickel **Obv:** Denomination above star, circle surrounds, legend in Dutch **Obv. Legend:** DER BELGEN **Rev:** Rampant lion left within circle, date below

Date	Mintage	F	VF	XF	Unc	BU
1901	2,491,000	3.00	20.00	35.00	70.00	—

KM# 46 5 CENTIMES

Copper-Nickel **Obv:** Hole at center of crowned design, small date below, legend in French **Obv. Legend:** BELGIQUE **Rev:** Spray of leaves to left of hole, denomination at right **Designer:** A. Michaux

Date	Mintage	F	VF	XF	Unc	BU
1901	202,000	15.00	50.00	90.00	175	—
1902/1	1,416,000	0.50	8.00	15.00	45.00	—
1902	Inc. above	0.25	3.00	7.00	22.00	—
1903	654,000	1.00	8.00	15.00	45.00	—

KM# 47 5 CENTIMES

Copper-Nickel **Obv:** Hole at center of crowned design, small date below, legend in Dutch **Obv. Legend:** BELGIE **Rev:** Spray of leaves to left of center hole, denomination to right **Designer:** A. Michaux

Date	Mintage	F	VF	XF	Unc	BU
1902/1	1,485,000	1.75	5.50	22.50	45.00	—
1902	Inc. above	0.15	3.00	7.00	22.00	—
1903	1,002,000	1.00	8.00	25.00	50.00	—

KM# 54 5 CENTIMES

Copper-Nickel **Obv:** Hole at center of crowned design, large date below, legend in French **Obv. Legend:** BELGIQUE **Rev:** Spray of leaves to left of center hole, denomination to right **Designer:** A. Michaux

Date	Mintage	F	VF	XF	Unc	BU
1904	5,814,000	0.15	0.35	2.00	7.00	—
1905/4	9,575,000	0.30	1.00	3.00	15.00	—
1905	Inc. above	0.15	0.35	2.00	7.00	—
1905 WICHAUX (error)	Inc. above	2.00	15.00	25.00	60.00	—
1905 A. MICHAUX	Inc. above	1.00	3.50	15.00	40.00	—
1906/5	8,463,000	0.30	1.50	3.00	12.00	—
1906	Inc. above	0.15	0.35	2.00	6.00	—
1907	993,000	1.00	6.00	12.00	30.00	—

KM# 55 5 CENTIMES

Copper-Nickel **Obv:** Hole at center of crowned design, large date below, legend in Dutch **Obv. Legend:** BELGIE **Rev:** Spray of leaves to left of center hole, denomination to right **Designer:** A. Michaux

Date	Mintage	F	VF	XF	Unc	BU
1904	5,812,000	0.15	0.35	2.00	7.00	—
1905/3	7,002,000	0.35	2.50	15.00	30.00	—
1905/4	Inc. above	0.30	1.50	4.00	15.00	—
1905	Inc. above	0.15	0.35	2.00	7.00	—
1905 Without cross	Inc. above	—	1.50	6.00	20.00	—
1906	11,016,000	0.15	0.35	2.00	7.00	—
1906 Without cross	Inc. above	0.30	1.50	4.00	15.00	—
1907	998,000	1.00	3.00	15.00	30.00	—

KM# 66 5 CENTIMES

Copper-Nickel **Obv:** Hole at center of crowned design, date below,legend in French **Obv. Legend:** BELGIQUE **Rev:** Spray of leaves to left of center hole, denomination to right **Designer:** A. Michaux

Date	Mintage	F	VF	XF	Unc	BU
1910	8,011,000	0.10	0.35	1.25	4.00	—
1913/0	5,005,000	0.20	0.75	2.25	10.00	—
1913	Inc. above	0.10	0.40	1.50	7.00	—
1914	1,004,000	1.00	3.00	8.00	25.00	—
1920/10	10,040,000	0.10	1.00	3.00	7.00	—
1920	Inc. above	0.10	0.35	1.25	4.00	—
1922/0	12,640,000	0.10	1.50	4.00	9.00	—
1922/1	Inc. above	0.10	1.50	3.50	9.00	—
1922	Inc. above	0.10	0.35	1.25	4.00	—
1923/13	9,000,000	0.10	0.75	2.50	8.00	—
1923	Inc. above	0.10	0.35	1.25	4.00	—
1925/13	15,860,000	0.10	0.50	2.00	8.00	—
1925/23	Inc. above	0.10	0.50	2.00	8.00	—
1925	Inc. above	0.10	0.35	1.25	4.00	—
1926/5	7,000,000	0.10	1.00	2.50	8.00	—
1926	Inc. above	0.10	0.35	1.25	4.00	—
1927	2,000,000	0.10	1.00	2.50	9.00	—
1927 5 Cen	—	5.00	15.00	30.00	100	—
Note: Obverse of KM#66 paired with the reverse of KM#67						
1928	12,507,000	0.10	0.35	1.25	4.00	—

KM# 67 5 CENTIMES

Copper-Nickel **Obv:** Hole in center of crowned design, date below, legend in Dutch **Obv. Legend:** BELGIE **Rev:** Spray of leaves to left of center hole, denomination to right, plain field above 5 **Designer:** A. Michaux

Date	Mintage	F	VF	XF	Unc	BU
1910	8,033,000	0.10	0.35	1.25	4.00	—
1914	6,040,000	0.10	0.35	1.25	4.00	—
1920/10	10,030,000	0.10	0.35	1.25	6.00	—
1920	Inc. above	0.10	0.50	3.00	12.00	—
1921/11	4,200,000	0.10	1.00	2.50	12.00	—
1921	Inc. above	0.10	1.00	2.00	9.00	—
1922/12	13,180,000	0.10	1.00	2.50	8.00	—
1922/0	Inc. above	0.10	1.00	3.00	9.00	—

Date	Mintage	F	VF	XF	Unc	BU
1922	Inc. above	0.10	0.35	1.25	4.00	—
1923/13	3,530,000	0.10	1.00	3.00	10.00	—
1923	Inc. above	0.10	0.75	2.00	9.00	—
1924/11	5,260,000	0.10	1.00	2.50	9.00	—
1924/14	Inc. above	0.10	0.50	1.75	9.00	—
1924	Inc. above	0.10	0.35	1.25	4.00	—
1925/13	13,000,000	0.10	1.00	2.50	8.00	—
1925/15 High 2	Inc. above	0.10	1.00	2.00	9.00	—
1925/15 Level 2	Inc. above	0.10	1.00	2.00	9.00	—
1925/3	Inc. above	0.10	0.60	2.00	9.00	—
1925	Inc. above	0.10	0.35	1.25	4.00	—
1927	6,938,000	0.10	0.35	1.25	4.00	—
1928/3	6,252,000	0.10	0.75	2.50	9.00	—
1928	Inc. above	0.10	0.35	1.25	4.00	—

KM# 80 5 CENTIMES

Zinc **Obv:** Denomination within circle, date below circle, legend in French **Obv. Legend:** BELGIQUE-BELGIE **Rev:** Rampant lion, left, within circle **Note:** German Occupation WW I

Date	Mintage	F	VF	XF	Unc	BU
1915	10,199,000	0.15	2.00	4.00	15.00	25.00
1916	45,464,000	0.10	0.60	2.00	7.00	10.00

KM# 94 5 CENTIMES

Nickel-Brass **Obv:** Hole at center of crowned design, date below, legend in Dutch **Obv. Legend:** BELGIE **Rev:** Spray of leaves to left of center hole, denomination at right, star added above 5

Date	Mintage	F	VF	XF	Unc	BU
1930	3,000,000	0.10	0.20	0.35	3.00	—
1931	7,430,000	0.10	0.20	0.35	3.00	—

KM# 93 5 CENTIMES

Nickel-Brass **Obv:** Legend in French **Obv. Legend:** BELGIQUE **Rev:** Star added above 5

Date	Mintage	F	VF	XF	Unc	BU
1932	5,520,000	0.10	0.20	0.35	3.00	—

KM# 110.1 5 CENTIMES

Nickel-Brass **Obv:** Three shields above denomination, legend in French, hole at center **Obv. Legend:** BELGIQUE-BELGIE **Rev:** Hole at center of crowned design, date below

Date	Mintage	F	VF	XF	Unc	BU
1938	4,970,000	0.10	0.20	0.75	2.00	—
1939	—	—	—	—	—	—

Note: Struck at a later date

KM# 110.2 5 CENTIMES

Nickel-Brass **Designer:** **Note:** Medal alignment.

Date	Mintage	F	VF	XF	Unc	BU
1938	Inc. above	1.25	3.00	8.00	30.00	—

KM# 111 5 CENTIMES

Nickel-Brass **Obv:** Three shields above denomination, hole at center, legend in Dutch **Obv. Legend:** BELGIE-BELGIQUE **Rev:** Crowned design above date, hole at center

Date	Mintage	F	VF	XF	Unc	BU
1939	3,000,000	0.10	0.20	0.75	3.00	—
1940	1,970,000	0.20	0.50	1.50	5.00	—

KM# 124 5 CENTIMES

Zinc **Obv:** Legend in Dutch **Obv. Legend:** BELGIE-BELGIQUE

Date	Mintage	F	VF	XF	Unc	BU
1941	4,000,000	0.15	0.75	2.50	15.00	—
1942	18,430,000	0.10	0.20	1.00	4.00	—

KM# 123 5 CENTIMES

Zinc **Obv:** Three shields above denomination, dots flank denomination, hole at center, legend in French **Obv. Legend:** BELGIQUE-BELGIE **Rev:** Crowned design above date, hole at center **Note:** German Occupation WW II

Date	Mintage	F	VF	XF	Unc	BU
1941	10,000,000	0.10	0.20	1.00	4.00	—
1943	7,606,000	0.10	0.20	1.50	6.00	—

KM# 42 10 CENTIMES

Copper-Nickel **Obv:** Denomination above star, within circle, legend in French **Obv. Legend:** DES BELGES **Rev:** Rampant lion left within circle, date below, stars flanking

Date	Mintage	F	VF	XF	Unc	BU
1901	551,000	30.00	140	200	325	350

KM# 43 10 CENTIMES

Copper-Nickel **Obv:** Denomination above star, within circle, legend in Dutch **Obv. Legend:** DER BELGEN **Rev:** Rampant lion left within circle, stars flank date below

Date	Mintage	F	VF	XF	Unc	BU
1901	556,000	30.00	175	225	350	400

KM# 48 10 CENTIMES

Copper-Nickel, 22 mm. **Obv:** Crowned design above small date, hole at center, legend in French **Obv. Legend:** BELGIQUE **Rev:** Spray of leaves to left of center hole, denomination to right **Designer:** A. Michaux

Date	Mintage	F	VF	XF	Unc	BU
1901	582,000	6.00	15.00	40.00	130	—
1902/1	5,866,000	0.50	3.00	15.00	30.00	—
1902	Inc. above	0.15	1.00	3.00	7.00	—
1903	763,000	1.00	4.00	15.00	35.00	—

KM# 49 10 CENTIMES

Copper-Nickel, 22 mm. **Obv:** Crowned design above small date, hole at center, legend in Dutch, **Obv. Legend:** BELGIE **Rev:** Spray of leaves to left of center hole, denomination to right **Designer:** A. Michaux

Date	Mintage	F	VF	XF	Unc	BU
1902	1,560,000	0.20	2.00	8.00	15.00	—
1903/2	—	0.50	1.25	7.00	20.00	—
1903	5,658,000	0.20	1.00	2.50	7.00	—

KM# 52 10 CENTIMES

Copper-Nickel, 22 mm. **Obv:** Crowned design above large date, hole at center, legend in French **Obv. Legend:** BELGIQUE **Rev:** Spray of leaves to left center hole, denomination to right **Designer:** A. Michaux

Date	Mintage	F	VF	XF	Unc	BU
1903	Inc. above	2.00	15.00	30.00	55.00	—
1904	16,354,000	0.15	1.00	3.00	7.00	—
1905/4	14,392,000	0.25	1.00	5.00	15.00	—
1905	Inc. above	0.15	0.60	2.00	7.00	—
1906/5	1,483,000	0.50	1.50	5.00	18.00	—
1906	Inc. above	0.25	0.75	5.00	15.00	—

KM# 53 10 CENTIMES

Copper-Nickel, 22 mm. **Obv:** Crowned design above large date, hole at center, legend in Dutch **Obv. Legend:** BELGIE **Rev:** Spray of leaves to left of center hole, denomination to right **Designer:** A. Michaux

Date	Mintage	F	VF	XF	Unc	BU
1903	Inc. above	1.00	4.00	15.00	35.00	—
1904	16,834,000	0.20	0.50	2.00	7.00	—
1905/3	13,758,000	0.35	1.00	3.00	15.00	—
1905/4	Inc. above	0.30	1.00	3.00	15.00	—
1905	Inc. above	0.20	0.50	2.00	7.00	—
1906/5	2,017,000	0.50	1.25	4.00	15.00	—
Note: Point above center of 6						
1906/5	Inc. above	0.50	1.25	4.00	15.00	—
Note: Point above right side of 6						
1906	Inc. above	0.10	0.75	5.00	18.00	—

KM# 81 10 CENTIMES

Zinc **Obv:** Denomination within circle, date below, legend in French **Obv. Legend:** BELGIQUE-BELGIE **Rev:** Rampant lion, left, within circle **Note:** German Occupation. All of KM#81 have dots after the date. The 1916 is distinguished by a period after the date.

Date	Mintage	F	VF	XF	Unc	BU
1915	9,681,000	0.25	1.50	4.00	15.00	30.00
1916/15	37,382,000	20.00	30.00	100	175	—
.1916.	Inc. above	0.15	0.75	3.00	10.00	20.00
Note: With dots before and after date						
.1916	Inc. above	7.00	15.00	50.00	100	—
Note: With dot before date						
1916.	Inc. above	10.00	25.00	100	200	—
Note: With dot after date						
1917	1,447,000	17.50	25.00	85.00	200	—

KM# 85.1 10 CENTIMES

Copper-Nickel, 22 mm. **Obv:** Crowned design above date, hole at center, legend in French **Obv. Legend:** BELGIQUE **Rev:** Spray of leaves to left of center hole, denomination to right **Designer:** A. Michaux

Date	Mintage	F	VF	XF	Unc	BU
1920	6,520,000	0.15	0.40	1.50	4.50	—
1911	—	—	—	—	—	—
Note: Struck at a later date						
1921	7,215,000	0.15	0.20	1.00	4.00	—
1923	20,625,000	0.10	0.20	1.00	4.00	—
1926/3	6,916,000	0.20	0.75	3.00	12.00	—
1926	Inc. above	0.15	0.20	1.00	4.00	—
1926/5	Inc. above	0.20	0.75	3.00	12.00	—
1927	8,125,000	0.15	0.20	1.00	4.00	—
1928/3	6,895,000	0.20	1.00	4.00	10.00	—
1928/5	Inc. above	0.20	1.00	4.00	10.00	—
1928	Inc. above	0.15	0.20	1.00	4.00	—
1929	12,260,000	0.15	0.20	1.00	4.00	—

KM# 85.2 10 CENTIMES

Copper-Nickel, 22 mm. **Rev:** Single line below ES of CES **Designer:** A. Michaux

Date	Mintage	F	VF	XF	Unc	BU
1920	Inc. above	0.50	3.00	10.00	20.00	—
1921	Inc. above	1.50	10.00	18.00	45.00	—

KM# 86 10 CENTIMES

Copper-Nickel, 22 mm. **Obv:** Crowned design above date, hole at center, legend in Dutch **Obv. Legend:** BELGIE **Rev:** Spray of leaves to left of center hole, denomination to right, plain field above 10 **Edge:** Plain **Designer:** A. Michaux

Date	Mintage	F	VF	XF	Unc	BU
1920	5,050,000	0.15	0.20	1.00	5.00	—
1921	7,580,000	0.15	0.20	1.00	4.00	—
1922	6,250,000	0.15	0.20	1.00	4.00	—
1924	5,825,000	0.15	0.20	1.00	6.00	—
1925/4	8,160,000	0.20	0.40	2.00	10.00	—
1925/3	Inc. above	0.20	0.40	2.00	10.00	—
1925	Inc. above	0.10	0.20	1.00	4.00	—
1926/5	6,250,000	0.20	0.40	2.00	10.00	—
1926/3	Inc. above	0.20	0.40	2.00	10.00	—
1926	Inc. above	0.15	0.20	1.00	4.00	—
1927	10,625,000	0.15	0.20	1.00	4.00	—
1928/5	6,750,000	0.20	0.40	2.00	10.00	—
1928/3	Inc. above	0.20	0.40	2.00	10.00	—
1928	Inc. above	0.15	0.20	1.00	4.00	—
1929	4,668,000	0.15	0.20	1.00	4.00	—
1930	—	15.00	30.00	100	250	—

KM# 95.1 10 CENTIMES

Nickel-Brass, 22 mm. **Obv:** Legend in French **Obv. Legend:** BELGIQUE **Rev:** Star added above 10

Date	Mintage	F	VF	XF	Unc	BU
1930/20	2,000,000	50.00	120	275	450	—
1930	Inc. above	20.00	100	250	400	—
1931	6,270,000	5.00	10.00	20.00	50.00	—
1932	1,270,000	35.00	200	300	450	—
1932	Inc. above	50.00	220	350	500	—

Note: A instead of signature

KM# 95.2 10 CENTIMES

Nickel-Brass, 22 mm. **Rev:** Single line below ES of CES

Date	Mintage	F	VF	XF	Unc	BU
1931	Inc. above	2.00	8.00	20.00	50.00	—
1932	Inc. above	45.00	200	350	500	—

KM# 96 10 CENTIMES

Nickel-Brass, 22 mm. **Obv:** Crowned design above date, hole at center, legend in Dutch **Obv. Legend:** BELGIE **Rev:** Spray of leaves to left of center hole, denomination to right, star added above 10 **Designer:** A. Michaux

Date	Mintage	F	VF	XF	Unc	BU
1930	1,581,000	0.30	0.75	3.00	10.00	—
1931	5,000,000	25.00	100	200	350	—

KM# 112 10 CENTIMES

Nickel-Brass, 22 mm. **Obv:** Three shields above denomination, hole at center, legend in French **Obv. Legend:** BELGIQUE-BELGIE **Rev:** Crowned design above date, hole at center

Date	Mintage	F	VF	XF	Unc	BU
1938	6,000,000	0.10	0.25	0.50	1.50	—
1939	7,000,000	0.50	1.00	3.00	15.00	—

KM# 113.1 10 CENTIMES

Nickel-Brass, 22 mm. **Obv:** Three shields above denomination, hole at center, legend in Dutch **Obv. Legend:** BELGIE-BELGIQUE **Rev:** Crowned design above date, hole at center

Date	Mintage	F	VF	XF	Unc	BU
1939	8,425,000	0.10	0.25	0.50	1.50	—

KM# 113.2 10 CENTIMES

Nickel-Brass, 22 mm. **Note:** Thin flan.

Date	Mintage	F	VF	XF	Unc	BU
1939	Inc. above	1.25	3.00	10.00	35.00	—

KM# 126 10 CENTIMES

Zinc, 22 mm. **Obv:** Three shields above denomination, hole at center, legend in Dutch **Obv. Legend:** BELGIE-BELGIQUE **Rev:** Crowned design above date, hole at center **Edge:** Plain

Date	Mintage	F	VF	XF	Unc	BU
1941	7,000,000	0.15	2.00	5.00	10.00	—
1942	21,000,000	0.15	0.25	1.50	4.00	—
1943	22,000,000	0.15	0.25	1.50	4.00	—
1944	28,140,000	0.15	0.25	1.50	4.00	—
1945	8,000,000	0.15	2.00	5.00	10.00	—
1946	5,370,000	0.15	1.00	2.00	8.00	—

KM# 125 10 CENTIMES

Zinc, 22 mm. **Obv:** Three shields above denomination, hole at center, legend in French **Obv. Legend:** BELGIQUE-BELGIE **Rev:** Crowned design above date, hole at center **Edge:** Plain **Note:** German Occupation WW II.

Date	Mintage	F	VF	XF	Unc	BU
1941	10,000,000	0.15	0.25	1.50	4.00	—
1942	17,000,000	0.15	0.25	1.50	4.00	—
1943	22,500,000	0.15	0.25	1.50	4.00	—
1945	—	—	—	—	—	—
Note: Struck at a later date						
1946	Est. 10,370,000	—	—	—	—	—
Note: Not released for circulation						

KM# 146 20 CENTIMES

Bronze, 17 mm. **Obv:** Crowned denomination divides date, legend in French **Obv. Legend:** BELGIQUE **Rev:** Helmeted head, left, small miner's lamp at right **Edge:** Plain

Date	Mintage	F	VF	XF	Unc	BU
1953	14,150,000	—	0.10	0.20	0.50	—
1953	—	—	0.10	0.75	2.50	—
Note: CENTIMES not touching rim						
1954	—	—	400	600	800	—
Note: Considered by some to be an Essai						
1957	13,300,000	—	—	0.10	0.50	—
1958	8,700,000	—	—	0.10	0.50	—
1959	19,670,000	—	—	0.10	0.50	—
1962	410,000	—	6.00	10.00	18.00	—
1963	2,550,000	0.10	0.20	0.50	1.00	—

KM# 147.1 20 CENTIMES

Bronze, 17 mm **Obv:** Crowned denomination divides date, legend in Dutch **Obv. Legend:** BELGIE **Rev:** Helmeted head, left, small miner's lamp at right **Edge:** Plain

Date	Mintage	F	VF	XF	Unc	BU
1954	50,130,000	—	—	0.10	0.50	—
1960	7,530,000	—	—	0.10	0.50	—

KM# 147.2 20 CENTIMES

Bronze, 17 mm. **Obv:** CENTIMES touching rim **Edge:** Plain

Date	Mintage	F	VF	XF	Unc	BU
1954	Inc. above	—	0.15	0.75	2.50	—
1960	Inc. above	—	0.15	0.75	2.50	—

KM# 62 25 CENTIMES

Copper-Nickel **Obv:** Crowned design above date, hole at center, legend in French **Obv. Legend:** BELGIQUE **Rev:** Spray of leaves to left of center hole, denomination to right **Designer:** A. Michaux

Date	Mintage	F	VF	XF	Unc	BU
1908	4,007,000	0.50	4.00	20.00	50.00	—
1909/8	1,998,000	4.00	40.00	150	275	—
1909	Inc. above	1.00	8.00	30.00	70.00	—

KM# 63 25 CENTIMES

Copper-Nickel **Obv:** Crowned design above date, hole at center, legend in Dutch **Obv. Legend:** BELGIE **Rev:** Spray of leaves to left of center hole, denomination to right **Designer:** A. Michaux

Date	Mintage	F	VF	XF	Unc	BU
1908	4,011,000	0.50	4.00	20.00	50.00	—

KM# 69 25 CENTIMES

Copper-Nickel **Obv:** Crowned design above date, hole at center, legend in Dutch **Obv. Legend:** BELGIE **Rev:** Sprays to left of center circle, denomination to right **Designer:** A. Michaux

Date	Mintage	F	VF	XF	Unc	BU
1910	2,006,000	0.15	1.00	8.00	20.00	—
1911	—	—	—	—	—	—
Note: Struck at a later date						
1913	2,010,000	0.15	3.00	8.00	20.00	—
1921	11,173,000	0.15	0.25	2.00	6.00	—
1922/1	14,200,000	1.00	10.00	20.00	45.00	—
1922	Inc. above	0.15	0.25	2.00	6.00	—
1926/3	6,400,000	0.35	6.00	12.00	25.00	—
1926	Inc. above	0.10	0.40	2.00	6.00	—
1927/3	3,799,000	0.35	5.00	10.00	25.00	—
1927	Inc. above	0.10	0.25	2.00	8.00	—
1928	9,200,000	0.10	0.25	2.00	6.00	—
1929	8,980,000	0.10	0.25	2.00	6.00	—

KM# 68.1 25 CENTIMES

Copper-Nickel **Obv:** Crowned design above date, hole at center, legend in French **Obv. Legend:** BELGIQUE **Rev:** Spray of leaves to left of center circle, denomination to right **Designer:** A. Michaux

Date	Mintage	F	VF	XF	Unc	BU
1913	2,011,000	0.15	3.00	8.00	20.00	—
1920	2,844,000	0.15	2.00	7.00	18.00	—
1921	7,464,000	0.10	0.25	2.00	6.00	—
1922	7,600,000	0.10	0.25	2.00	6.00	—
1923	11,356,000	0.15	0.25	2.00	6.00	—
1926/3	1,300,000	1.00	5.00	12.00	30.00	—
1926	Inc. above	0.50	5.00	12.00	30.00	—
1927/3	8,800,000	1.00	10.00	20.00	45.00	—
1927	Inc. above	0.10	0.25	2.00	6.00	—
1928	4,351,000	0.10	1.00	2.00	8.00	—
1929	9,600,000	0.10	0.25	2.00	6.00	—

KM# 68.2 25 CENTIMES

Copper-Nickel **Rev:** Single line below ES of CES

Date	Mintage	F	VF	XF	Unc	BU
1920	Inc. above	0.50	2.00	8.00	25.00	—
1921	Inc. above	0.35	1.50	6.00	15.00	—

KM# 82 25 CENTIMES

Zinc **Obv:** Denomination within beaded circle, stars flank date below, legend in French **Obv. Legend:** BELGIQUE-BELGIE **Rev:** Rampant lion, left, within beaded circle **Note:** German Occupation WW I

Date	Mintage	F	VF	XF	Unc	BU
1915	8,080,000	0.50	4.00	9.00	22.00	—
1916	10,671,000	0.50	3.00	7.00	15.00	—
1917	3,555,000	2.00	10.00	18.00	40.00	—
1918	5,489,000	1.00	8.00	12.00	30.00	—

KM# 114.1 25 CENTIMES
Nickel-Brass **Obv:** Three shields above denomination, hole in center, legend in French **Obv. Legend:** BELGIQUE-BELGIE **Rev:** Crowned design above date, hole in center

Date	Mintage	F	VF	XF	Unc	BU
1938	7,200,000	—	0.25	1.00	4.00	—
1939	7,732,000	—	0.25	1.00	4.00	—

KM# 114.2 25 CENTIMES
Nickel-Brass **Designer:** **Note:** Medal alignment.

Date	Mintage	F	VF	XF	Unc	BU
1939	Inc. above	1.75	3.00	10.00	30.00	—

KM# 115.1 25 CENTIMES
Nickel-Brass **Obv:** Three shields above denomination, hole at center, legend in Dutch **Obv. Legend:** BELGIE-BELGIQUE **Rev:** Crowned design above date, hole at center

Date	Mintage	F	VF	XF	Unc	BU
1938	14,932,000	—	0.25	1.00	3.00	—

KM# 115.2 25 CENTIMES
Nickel-Brass **Designer:** **Note:** Medal alignment.

Date	Mintage	F	VF	XF	Unc	BU
1938	Inc. above	5.00	10.00	20.00	30.00	—

KM# 131 25 CENTIMES
Zinc **Obv:** Three shields above denomination, hole at center, legend in French **Obv. Legend:** BELGIQUE-BELGIE **Rev:** Crowned design above date, hole at center **Note:** German Occupation WW II.

Date	Mintage	F	VF	XF	Unc	BU
1941 Rare	—	—	—	—	—	—
1942	14,400,000	—	0.20	0.75	3.00	10.00
1943	21,600,000	—	0.20	0.75	3.00	10.00
1945	—	—	—	—	—	—
Note: Struck at a later date						
1946	21,428,000	—	0.20	0.75	3.00	10.00
1947	Est. 300,000	—	—	—	—	—
Note: Not released for circulation						

KM# 132 25 CENTIMES
Zinc **Obv:** Three shields above denomination, hole at center, legend in Dutch **Obv. Legend:** BELGIE-BELGIQUE **Rev:** Crowned design above date, hole at center

Date	Mintage	F	VF	XF	Unc	BU
1942	14,400,000	—	1.00	2.00	6.00	18.00
1943	21,600,000	—	0.20	0.75	3.00	10.00
1944	25,960,000	—	0.20	0.75	3.00	10.00
1945	8,200,000	—	0.50	2.50	8.00	22.00
1946	11,652,000	—	0.50	2.50	10.00	30.00
1947	Est. 316,000	—	—	—	—	—
Note: Not released for circulation						

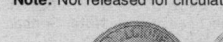

KM# 153.1 25 CENTIMES
Copper-Nickel, 16 mm. **Obv:** Large denomination between mint marks, legend in French **Obv. Legend:** BELGIQUE **Rev:** Crowned "B" divides date **Note:** Mint mark - Angel Head. Mintmaster Vogeleer's privy mark - Bird.

Date	Mintage	F	VF	XF	Unc	BU
1964	21,770,000	—	—	0.10	0.15	—
1965	11,440,000	—	—	0.10	0.15	—
1966	19,990,000	—	—	0.10	0.15	—
1967	6,820,000	—	—	0.10	0.50	—
1968	25,250,000	—	—	0.10	0.15	—
1969	7,670,000	—	—	0.10	0.30	—
1970	27,000,000	—	—	0.10	0.15	—
1971	16,000,000	—	—	0.10	0.15	—
1972	20,000,000	—	—	0.10	0.15	—
1973	12,500,000	—	—	0.10	0.15	—
1974	20,000,000	—	—	0.10	0.15	—
1975	12,000,000	—	—	0.10	0.15	—

KM# 153.2 25 CENTIMES
Copper-Nickel, 16 mm. **Note:** Medal alignment. Mint mark - Angel Head. Mintmaster Vogeleer's privy mark - Bird.

Date	Mintage	F	VF	XF	Unc	BU
1964	Inc. above	—	—	5.00	12.00	—
1965	Inc. above	—	—	10.00	25.00	—
1967	Inc. above	—	—	10.00	25.00	—
1970	Inc. above	—	—	5.00	12.00	—
1971	Inc. above	—	—	5.00	12.00	—
1974	Inc. above	—	—	10.00	25.00	—

KM# 154.1 25 CENTIMES
Copper-Nickel, 16 mm. **Obv:** Large denomination between mint marks, legend in Dutch **Obv. Legend:** BELGIE **Rev:** Crowned "B" divides date **Edge:** Plain **Note:** Mint mark - Angel Head. Mintmaster Vogeleer's privy mark - Bird.

Date	Mintage	F	VF	XF	Unc	BU
1964	21,300,000	—	—	0.10	0.15	—
1965	7,900,000	—	—	0.10	0.30	—
1966	23,420,000	—	—	0.10	0.15	—
1967	7,720,000	—	—	0.10	0.30	—
1968	22,750,000	—	—	0.10	0.15	—
1969	25,190,000	—	—	0.10	0.15	—
1970	12,000,000	—	—	0.10	0.15	—
1971	16,000,000	—	—	0.10	0.15	—
1972	20,000,000	—	—	0.10	0.15	—
1973	12,500,000	—	—	0.10	0.15	—
1974	20,000,000	—	—	0.10	0.15	—
1975	12,000,000	—	—	0.10	0.15	—

KM# 154.2 25 CENTIMES
Copper-Nickel, 16 mm. **Edge:** Plain **Note:** Medal alignment. Mint mark - Angel Head. Mintmaster Vogeleer's privy mark - Bird.

Date	Mintage	F	VF	XF	Unc	BU
1964	Inc. above	—	—	5.00	12.00	—
1965	Inc. above	—	—	5.00	15.00	—
1966	Inc. above	—	—	5.00	12.00	—
1967	Inc. above	—	—	6.00	15.00	—
1969	Inc. above	—	—	5.00	12.00	—
1971	Inc. above	—	—	6.00	15.00	—
1972	Inc. above	—	—	5.00	12.00	—

KM# 50 50 CENTIMES
2.5000 g., 0.8350 Silver .0671 oz. ASW **Obv:** Bearded head of Leopold II, left, legend in French **Obv. Legend:** DES BELGES **Rev:** Tablet to right of seated lion, looking left, denomination below, date to left of lion

Date	Mintage	F	VF	XF	Unc	BU
1901	3,000,000	2.00	8.00	30.00	75.00	—

KM# 51 50 CENTIMES
2.5000 g., 0.8350 Silver .0671 oz. ASW **Obv:** Legend in Dutch **Obv. Legend:** DER BELGEN

Date	Mintage	F	VF	XF	Unc	BU
1901	3,000,000	2.00	8.00	30.00	75.00	150

KM# 60.1 50 CENTIMES
2.5000 g., 0.8350 Silver .0671 oz. ASW **Obv:** Bearded head of Leopold II, left, legend in French **Obv. Legend:** DES BELGES **Rev:** Denomination above date within wreath

Date	Mintage	F	VF	XF	Unc	BU
1907	545,000	3.00	8.00	18.00	70.00	140
1909	2,503,000	1.00	4.00	12.00	35.00	—

KM# 60.2 50 CENTIMES
2.5000 g., 0.8350 Silver .0671 oz. ASW **Obv:** Without period in signature

Date	Mintage	F	VF	XF	Unc	BU
1907	Inc. above	4.00	10.00	25.00	100	140
1909	Inc. above	2.00	5.00	12.00	35.00	—

KM# 61.1 50 CENTIMES
2.5000 g., 0.8350 Silver .0671 oz. ASW **Obv:** Bearded head of Leopold II, left, legend in Dutch **Obv. Legend:** DER BELGEN **Rev:** Denomination above date within wreath

Date	Mintage	F	VF	XF	Unc	BU
1907	545,000	3.00	10.00	25.00	70.00	140
1909	2,510,000	1.00	5.00	12.00	35.00	—

KM# 61.2 50 CENTIMES
2.5000 g., 0.8350 Silver .0671 oz. ASW **Obv:** Bearded head of Leopold II, left, legend in Dutch **Obv. Legend:** DER BELGEN **Note:** Medal alignment

Date	Mintage	F	VF	XF	Unc	BU
1909	Inc. above	12.50	15.00	45.00	135	180

KM# 61.3 50 CENTIMES
2.5000 g., 0.8350 Silver .0671 oz. ASW **Obv:** Bearded head of Leopold II, left, legend in Dutch, without periods in signature **Obv. Legend:** DER BELGEN **Rev:** Denomination above date within wreath

Date	Mintage	F	VF	XF	Unc	BU
1909	Inc. above	2.00	5.00	12.00	35.00	—

KM# 70 50 CENTIMES
2.5000 g., 0.8350 Silver .0671 oz. ASW **Obv:** Head of Albert, left, legend in French **Obv. Legend:** DES BELGES **Rev:** Denomination above date within wreath

Date	Mintage	F	VF	XF	Unc	BU
1910	1,900,000	1.00	5.00	12.00	30.00	—
1911	2,063,000	3.00	10.00	15.00	60.00	—
1912	1,000,000	0.85	1.25	2.00	6.00	—
1914	240,000	2.50	9.00	15.00	40.00	—

KM# 71 50 CENTIMES
2.5000 g., 0.8350 Silver .0671 oz. ASW **Obv:** Head of Albert, left, legend in Dutch **Obv. Legend:** DER BELGEN **Rev:** Denomination above date within wreath

Date	Mintage	F	VF	XF	Unc	BU
1910	1,900,000	3.00	10.00	15.00	60.00	—
1911	2,063,000	0.85	1.25	2.00	6.00	—
1912	1,000,000	0.85	1.25	2.00	6.00	—
1914	—	35.00	70.00	200	500	—

KM# 83 50 CENTIMES
Zinc **Obv:** Hole at center of star, tiny stars flank date below, legend in Dutch **Obv. Legend:** BELGIE-BELGIQUE **Rev:** Spray of leaves to left of center hole, denomination to right, small shield with rampant lion on spray **Note:** German Occupation WW I

Date	Mintage	F	VF	XF	Unc	BU
1918	7,394,000	0.50	6.00	10.00	25.00	50.00

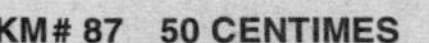

KM# 87 50 CENTIMES
Nickel **Obv:** Allegorically female figure of Belgium kneeling, wounded but recovering **Obv. Legend:** BELGIQUE **Rev:** Caduceus divides denomination and dates

Date	Mintage	F	VF	XF	Unc	BU
1922	6,180,000	0.15	0.25	0.50	3.00	—
1923	8,820,000	0.15	0.25	0.50	3.00	—

Date	Mintage	F	VF	XF	Unc	BU
1927	1,750,000	0.15	0.30	0.50	3.00	—
1928	3,000,000	0.15	0.35	1.00	4.00	—
1929	1,000,000	0.25	0.50	3.00	12.00	—
1930	1,000,000	0.25	0.50	3.00	10.00	—
1932/23	2,530,000	1.00	3.00	10.00	25.00	—
1932	Inc. above	0.15	0.50	1.00	4.00	—
1933	2,861,000	0.15	0.25	0.75	4.00	—

KM# 88 50 CENTIMES

Nickel **Obv:** Allegorically female figure of Belgium kneeling, wounded but recovering **Obv. Legend:** BELGIE **Rev:** Caduceus divides denomination and date

Date	Mintage	F	VF	XF	Unc	BU
1922	—	—	—	—	—	—
Note: Struck at a later date						
1923	15,000,000	0.20	0.25	0.50	3.00	—
1928/3	10,000,000	0.25	0.50	3.00	10.00	—
1928	Inc. above	0.20	0.25	0.50	3.00	—
1930/20	2,252,000	0.50	2.00	3.50	16.00	—
1930	Inc. above	0.20	0.75	2.50	6.00	—
1932/22	—	0.25	3.00	3.00	15.00	—
1932	2,000,000	0.20	0.50	1.00	4.00	—
1933	1,189,000	1.00	5.00	9.00	16.50	—
1934	935,000	75.00	175	225	300	—

KM# 118 50 CENTIMES

Nickel **Obv:** Legend in French **Obv. Legend:** BELGIQUE-BELGIE **Note:** Striking interrupted by the war. Very few coins have been officially released into circulation.

Date	Mintage	F	VF	XF	Unc	BU
1939	15,500,000	200	400	800	1,300	—

KM# 144 50 CENTIMES

2.7500 g., Bronze, 19 mm. **Obv:** Crowned denomination divides date, legend in French **Obv. Legend:** BELGIQUE **Rev:** Helmeted mine worker left, miner's lamp at right, large head, tip of neck 1/2 mm from rim **Edge:** Plain

Date	Mintage	F	VF	XF	Unc	BU
1952	3,520,000	—	0.10	0.50	2.50	—
1953	22,620,000	—	—	0.10	0.35	—
1955	29,160,000	—	—	0.10	0.35	—

KM# 145 50 CENTIMES

2.7500 g., Bronze, 19 mm. **Obv:** Crowned denomination divides date, legend in Dutch **Obv. Legend:** BELGIE **Rev:** Helmeted mine worker left, miner's lamp at right, large head **Edge:** Plain

Date	Mintage	F	VF	XF	Unc	BU
1952	5,830,000	—	0.10	0.50	2.00	—
1953	22,930,000	—	—	0.10	0.35	—
1954	15,730,000	—	—	0.10	0.35	—

KM# 149.1 50 CENTIMES

2.7500 g., Bronze, 19 mm. **Ruler:** Baudouin I **Obv:** Crowned denomination divides date **Rev:** Helmeted miner left, miners lamp at right, smaller head, legend in Dutch **Rev. Legend:** BELGIE **Edge:** Plain

Date	Mintage	F	VF	XF	Unc	BU
1956	5,640,000	—	—	0.10	0.75	—
1957	13,800,000	—	—	0.10	0.25	—
1958	19,480,000	—	—	0.10	0.20	—
1962	4,150,000	—	—	0.10	2.00	—
1963	1,110,000	—	—	0.10	3.00	—
1964	19,340,000	—	—	0.10	0.15	—
1965	9,590,000	—	—	0.10	0.15	—
1966	6,930,000	—	—	0.10	0.15	—
1967	6,970,000	—	—	0.10	0.15	—
1968	2,000,000	—	—	0.10	1.00	—
1969	10,000,000	—	—	0.10	0.15	—
1970	12,000,000	—	—	0.10	0.15	—
1971	1,250,000	—	—	0.10	1.00	—
1972	7,000,000	—	—	0.10	0.15	—
1973	3,000,000	—	—	0.10	0.15	—
1974	5,000,000	—	—	0.10	0.15	—
1975	7,000,000	—	—	0.10	0.15	—
1976	8,000,000	—	—	0.10	0.15	—
1977	13,000,000	—	—	0.10	0.15	—
1978	2,500,000	—	—	0.10	1.00	—
1979	40,000,000	—	—	0.10	0.15	—
1980	20,000,000	—	—	0.10	0.15	—
1981	2,000,000	—	—	0.10	1.00	—
1982	7,000,000	—	—	0.10	0.15	—
1983	14,100,000	—	—	0.10	0.15	—
1985	6,000,000	—	—	0.10	0.15	—
1987	9,000,000	—	—	0.10	0.15	—
1988	9,000,000	—	—	0.10	0.15	—
1989	60,000	—	—	—	3.00	—
Note: In sets only						
1990	60,000	—	—	—	3.00	—
Note: In sets only						
1991	6,000,000	—	—	—	0.50	—
1992	7,060,000	—	—	0.10	0.15	—
1993	10,000,000	—	—	0.10	0.15	—
1994	10,000,000	—	—	0.10	0.15	—
1995	60,000	—	—	—	2.00	—
Note: In sets only						
1996	11,000,000	—	—	—	0.50	—
1997	60,000	—	—	—	2.00	—
Note: In sets only						
1998	30,000,000	—	—	—	0.10	—
1999	60,000	—	—	—	2.00	—
Note: In sets only						
1999	Inc. above	—	—	—	25.00	—
Note: Medal alignment						
2000	60,000	—	—	—	2.00	—
Note: In sets only						
2000	Inc. above	—	—	—	25.00	—
Note: Medal alignment						

KM# 149.2 50 CENTIMES

2.7500 g., Bronze, 19 mm. **Edge:** Plain **Note:** Medal alignment.

Date	Mintage	F	VF	XF	Unc	BU
1953	Inc. above	—	—	15.00	30.00	—
1958	Inc. above	—	—	15.00	30.00	—
1967	Inc. above	—	—	15.00	30.00	—
1969	Inc. above	—	—	15.00	30.00	—
1977	Inc. above	—	—	15.00	30.00	—
1979	Inc. above	—	—	15.00	30.00	—
1981	Inc. above	—	—	15.00	30.00	—

KM# 148.1 50 CENTIMES

2.7500 g., Bronze, 19 mm. **Ruler:** Baudouin I **Obv:** Crowned denomination divides date, legend in French **Obv. Legend:** BELGIQUE **Rev:** Helmeted miner left, miners lamp at right, smaller head, tip of neck 1mm from rim **Edge:** Plain

Date	Mintage	F	VF	XF	Unc	BU
1958	9,750,000	—	—	0.10	0.25	—
1959	17,350,000	—	—	0.10	0.20	—
1962	6,160,000	—	—	0.10	2.00	—
1964	5,860,000	—	—	0.10	2.00	—
1965	10,320,000	—	—	0.10	0.15	—
1966	11,040,000	—	—	0.10	0.15	—
1967	7,200,000	—	—	0.10	0.15	—
1968	2,000,000	—	—	0.10	2.00	—
1969	10,000,000	—	—	0.10	0.15	—
1970	16,000,000	—	—	0.10	0.15	—
1971	1,250,000	—	—	0.10	2.00	—
1972	3,000,000	—	—	0.10	0.15	—
1973	3,000,000	—	—	0.10	0.15	—
1974	5,000,000	—	—	0.10	0.15	—
1974 Wide rim	Inc. above	—	—	0.10	0.15	—
1975	7,000,000	—	—	0.10	0.15	—
1976	8,000,000	—	—	0.10	0.15	—
1977	13,000,000	—	—	0.10	0.15	—
1978	2,500,000	—	—	0.10	1.00	—
1979	20,000,000	—	—	0.10	0.15	—
1980	20,000,000	—	—	0.10	0.15	—
1981	2,000,000	—	—	0.10	1.00	—
1982	7,000,000	—	—	0.10	0.15	—
1983	14,100,000	—	—	0.10	0.15	—
1985	6,000,000	—	—	0.10	0.15	—
1987	9,000,000	—	—	0.10	0.15	—
1988	4,500,000	—	—	0.10	0.15	—
1989	60,000	—	—	—	3.00	—
Note: In sets only						
1990	60,000	—	—	—	3.00	—
Note: In sets only						
1991	6,000,000	—	—	—	0.10	—
1992	7,060,000	—	—	0.10	0.15	—
1993	10,000,000	—	—	0.10	0.15	—
1994	10,000,000	—	—	0.10	0.15	—
1995	60,000	—	—	—	2.00	—
Note: In sets only						
1996	11,000,000	—	—	0.10	0.15	—
1997	60,000	—	—	—	2.00	—
Note: In sets only						
1998	30,000,000	—	—	—	0.10	—
1999	60,000	—	—	—	2.00	—
Note: In sets only						
1999	Inc. above	—	—	—	25.00	—
Note: Medal alignment						
2000	60,000	—	—	—	2.00	—
Note: In sets only						
2000	Inc. above	—	—	—	25.00	—
Note: Medal alignment						

KM# 148.2 50 CENTIMES

2.7500 g., Bronze, 19 mm. **Edge:** Plain **Note:** Medal alignment.

Date	Mintage	F	VF	XF	Unc	BU
1953	Inc. above	—	—	15.00	30.00	—
1959	Inc. above	—	—	15.00	30.00	—
1965	Inc. above	—	—	15.00	30.00	—
1966	Inc. above	—	—	15.00	30.00	—
1967	Inc. above	—	—	15.00	30.00	—
1969	Inc. above	—	—	15.00	30.00	—
1974	Inc. above	—	—	15.00	30.00	—
1976	Inc. above	—	—	15.00	30.00	—
1980	—	—	—	15.00	30.00	—

KM# 56.1 FRANC

5.0000 g., 0.8350 Silver .1342 oz. ASW **Obv:** Legend in French **Obv. Legend:** DES BELGES

Date	Mintage	F	VF	XF	Unc	BU
1904	803,000	3.00	14.00	40.00	75.00	160
1909	2,250,000	1.50	10.00	30.00	45.00	—

KM# 56.2 FRANC

5.0000 g., 0.8350 Silver .1342 oz. ASW **Obv:** Without period in signature

Date	Mintage	F	VF	XF	Unc	BU
1904	Inc. above	5.00	35.00	60.00	140	—
1909	Inc. above	1.50	10.00	30.00	45.00	—

KM# 57.1 FRANC

5.0000 g., 0.8350 Silver .1342 oz. ASW **Obv:** Bearded head of Leopold II, left, legend in Dutch **Obv. Legend:** DER BELGEN **Rev:** Denomination above date within wreath

Date	Mintage	F	VF	XF	Unc	BU
1904	803,000	3.00	14.00	40.00	75.00	—
1909	2,250,000	2.50	10.00	30.00	50.00	—

KM# 57.2 FRANC

5.0000 g., 0.8350 Silver .1342 oz. ASW **Obv:** Without period in signature

Date	Mintage	F	VF	XF	Unc	BU
1909	Inc. above	1.50	8.00	30.00	45.00	—

KM# 72.1 FRANC

5.0000 g., 0.8350 Silver .1342 oz. ASW **Obv:** Legend in French **Obv. Legend:** DES BELGES

Date	Mintage	F	VF	XF	Unc	BU
1910	2,190,000	1.75	5.00	18.00	35.00	—
1911	2,810,000	BV	2.00	5.00	12.00	—
1912	3,250,000	BV	1.50	2.50	5.00	—
1913	3,000,000	BV	1.50	2.50	5.00	—
1914	10,563,000	BV	1.50	2.50	5.00	—
1917	8,540,000	350	700	1,500	2,000	—
1918	1,469,000	300	600	1,400	2,000	—

KM# 72.2 FRANC

5.0000 g., 0.8350 Silver .1342 oz. ASW **Designer:** **Note:** Medal alignment.

Date	Mintage	F	VF	XF	Unc	BU
1914	Inc. above	4.50	12.50	50.00	125	275

KM# 73.1 FRANC

5.0000 g., 0.8350 Silver .1342 oz. ASW **Obv:** Head of Albert, left, legend in Dutch **Obv. Legend:** DER BELGEN **Rev:** Denomination above date within wreath

Date	Mintage	F	VF	XF	Unc	BU
1910	2,750,000	2.00	15.00	35.00	65.00	145
1911	2,250,000	BV	2.00	5.00	12.00	—
1912	3,250,000	BV	1.50	2.50	5.00	—
1913	3,000,000	BV	1.50	2.50	5.00	—
1914	10,222,000	BV	1.50	2.50	5.00	—
1918	—	300	600	1,400	2,000	—

KM# 73.2 FRANC

5.0000 g., 0.8350 Silver .1342 oz. ASW **Designer:** **Note:** Medal alignment.

Date	Mintage	F	VF	XF	Unc	BU
1914	Inc. above	4.50	12.50	50.00	125	275

KM# 89 FRANC
Nickel, 22.5 mm. **Obv:** Kneeling figure, legend in French **Obv. Legend:** BELGIQUE **Rev:** Caduceus divides denomination and date **Edge:** Reeded

Date	Mintage	F	VF	XF	Unc	BU
1922	14,000,000	0.15	0.25	1.00	3.00	—
1923	22,500,000	0.15	0.25	1.00	3.00	—
1928/3	5,000,000	0.25	1.50	5.00	12.00	—
1928/7	Inc. above	0.25	1.50	5.00	12.00	—
1928	Inc. above	0.15	0.25	1.00	4.00	—
1929	7,415,000	0.15	0.25	1.00	3.50	—
1930	5,365,000	0.15	0.25	1.00	5.00	—
1931	—	250	700	1,000	1,800	—
1933	1,998,000	0.25	1.50	5.00	15.00	—
1934/24	10,263,000	0.25	1.50	6.00	12.00	—
1934	Inc. above	0.15	0.25	1.00	3.00	—

KM# 90 FRANC
Nickel, 22.5 mm. **Obv:** Kneeling figure, legend in Dutch **Obv. Legend:** BELGIE **Rev:** Caduceus divides denomination and date **Edge:** Reeded

Date	Mintage	F	VF	XF	Unc	BU
1922	19,000,000	0.15	0.25	1.00	3.00	—
1923/2	17,500,000	0.20	1.50	4.00	12.00	—
1923	Inc. above	0.15	0.25	1.00	3.00	—
1928/3	4,975,000	0.20	2.00	5.00	12.00	—
1928/7	Inc. above	0.20	2.00	5.00	12.00	—
1928	Inc. above	0.15	0.50	2.00	6.00	—
1929	10,365,000	0.15	0.25	1.00	3.00	—
1933	786,000	200	900	1,200	2,000	—
1933/23	—	—	—	—	—	—
1934/24	8,025,000	0.35	2.50	7.00	15.00	—
1934	Inc. above	0.15	0.50	1.00	3.00	—
1935/23	2,238,000	1.50	4.00	12.00	35.00	—
1935	Inc. above	0.25	0.75	2.00	6.00	—

KM# 119 FRANC
Nickel, 21.5 mm. **Obv:** Three shields, legend in French **Obv. Legend:** BELGIQUE-BELGIE **Rev:** Seated lion, right, facing left above date, denomination to right

Date	Mintage	F	VF	XF	Unc	BU
1939	46,865,000	0.15	0.25	0.50	1.50	—
1940	—	—	—	—	—	—

Note: Struck at a later date

KM# 120 FRANC
Nickel, 21.5 mm. **Obv:** Three shields, legend in Dutch **Obv. Legend:** BELGIE-BELGIQUE **Rev:** Seated lion, right, facing left above date, denomination at right

Date	Mintage	F	VF	XF	Unc	BU
1939	36,000,000	0.15	0.25	0.50	1.50	—
1940	10,865,000	0.20	0.40	0.75	2.50	—

KM# 127 FRANC
Zinc, 21.5 mm. **Obv:** Rampant lion, left on shield, legend in French **Obv. Legend:** BELGIQUE-BELGIE **Rev:** Crowned letter "L"s, backs touching, divide denomination, date below
Note: German Occupation WW II.

Date	Mintage	F	VF	XF	Unc	BU
1941	16,000,000	0.20	0.75	1.50	12.00	25.00
1942	25,000,000	0.20	0.75	1.50	5.00	10.00
1943	28,000,000	0.20	0.75	1.50	5.00	10.00
1947	3,175,000	60.00	125	400	700	1,000

KM# 128 FRANC
Zinc, 21.5 mm. **Obv:** Rampant lion, left, on shield, legend in Dutch **Obv. Legend:** BELGIE-BELGIQUE **Rev:** Crowned "L"s, backs touching, divide denomination, date below

Date	Mintage	F	VF	XF	Unc	BU
1942	42,000,000	0.20	0.75	1.50	5.00	10.00
1943	28,000,000	0.20	0.75	1.50	5.00	10.00
1944	24,190,000	0.20	0.75	1.50	5.00	10.00
1945	15,930,000	0.20	1.00	4.00	12.00	25.00
1946	36,000,000	0.20	0.75	1.50	6.00	18.00
1947	3,000,000	25.00	40.00	100	200	350

KM# 142.1 FRANC
4.0000 g., Copper-Nickel, 21 mm. **Obv:** Plant divides denomination , crown at top, legend in French **Obv. Legend:** BELGIQUE **Rev:** Laureate bust, left, small symbol at right, date at left **Rev. Designer:** Rau **Edge:** Reeded

Date	Mintage	F	VF	XF	Unc	BU
1950	13,630,000	—	—	0.10	8.00	—
1951	51,025,000	—	—	0.10	3.00	—
1952	53,205,000	—	—	0.10	5.00	—
1954	4,980,000	—	0.10	0.25	4.00	—
1955	3,960,000	—	0.10	0.25	3.00	—
1956	10,000,000	—	—	0.10	1.00	—
1958	31,750,000	—	—	0.10	1.00	—
1959	9,000,000	—	—	0.10	1.00	—
1960	10,000,000	—	—	0.10	1.00	—
1961	5,030,000	—	—	0.10	2.00	—
1962	12,250,000	—	—	0.10	0.50	—
1963	18,700,000	—	—	0.10	0.50	—
1964	10,110,000	—	—	0.10	0.50	—
1965	10,185,000	—	—	0.10	0.50	—
1966	16,430,000	—	—	0.10	0.50	—
1967	32,945,000	—	—	0.10	0.50	—
1968	8,000,000	—	—	0.10	0.50	—
1969	21,950,000	—	—	0.10	0.50	—
1970	35,500,000	—	—	0.10	0.50	—
1971	10,000,000	—	—	0.10	0.30	—
1972	35,000,000	—	—	0.10	0.30	—
1973	42,500,000	—	—	0.10	0.30	—
1974	30,000,000	—	—	0.10	0.30	—
1975	80,000,000	—	—	0.10	0.30	—
1976	18,000,000	—	—	0.10	0.30	—
1977	68,500,000	—	—	0.10	0.30	—
1978	47,500,000	—	—	0.10	0.30	—
1979	25,000,000	—	—	0.10	0.30	—
1980	66,500,000	—	—	0.10	0.30	—
1981	2,000,000	0.10	0.20	0.50	3.00	—
1988	17,500,000	—	—	0.10	0.30	—

KM# 142.2 FRANC
4.0000 g., Copper-Nickel, 21 mm. **Edge:** Reeded **Note:** Medal alignment.

Date	Mintage	F	VF	XF	Unc	BU
1952	Inc. above	—	10.00	30.00	60.00	—
1956	Inc. above	—	10.00	30.00	60.00	—
1958	Inc. above	—	10.00	30.00	60.00	—
1959	Inc. above	—	10.00	30.00	60.00	—
1963	Inc. above	—	10.00	30.00	60.00	—
1965	Inc. above	—	10.00	30.00	60.00	—
1966	Inc. above	—	10.00	30.00	60.00	—
1969	Inc. above	—	10.00	30.00	60.00	—
1970	Inc. above	—	10.00	30.00	60.00	—
1974	Inc. above	—	10.00	30.00	60.00	—
1975	Inc. above	—	10.00	30.00	60.00	—
1977	Inc. above	—	10.00	30.00	60.00	—
1978	Inc. above	—	10.00	30.00	60.00	—
1979	Inc. above	—	10.00	30.00	60.00	—
1988	Inc. above	—	10.00	30.00	60.00	—

KM# 143.1 FRANC
4.0000 g., Copper-Nickel, 21 mm. **Obv:** Plant divides denomination, crown at top, legend in Dutch **Obv. Legend:** BELGIE **Rev:** Laureate bust, left, date at left, small symbol at right **Rev. Designer:** Rau **Edge:** Reeded

Date	Mintage	F	VF	XF	Unc	BU
1950	10,000,000	—	—	0.10	8.00	—
1951	53,750,000	—	—	0.10	3.00	—
1952	49,145,000	—	—	0.10	5.00	—
1953	9,915,000	—	—	0.10	3.00	—
1954	4,940,000	—	0.10	0.25	4.00	—
1955	3,960,000	—	0.10	0.25	4.00	—
1956	10,040,000	—	—	0.10	1.00	—
1957	18,315,000	—	—	0.10	1.00	—
1958	17,365,000	—	—	0.10	1.00	—
1959	5,830,000	—	—	0.10	2.00	—
1960	5,555,000	—	—	0.10	2.00	—
1961	9,350,000	—	—	0.10	1.00	—
1962	10,720,000	—	—	0.10	0.50	—
1963	23,460,000	—	—	0.10	0.50	—
1964	7,430,000	—	—	0.10	0.50	—
1965	11,190,000	—	—	0.10	0.50	—
1966	20,990,000	—	—	0.10	0.50	—
1967	27,470,000	—	—	0.10	0.50	—
1968	8,170,000	—	—	0.10	0.30	—
1969	21,730,000	—	—	0.10	0.30	—
1970	35,730,000	—	—	0.10	0.30	—
1971	10,000,000	—	—	0.10	0.30	—
1972	35,000,000	—	—	0.10	0.30	—
1973	42,500,000	—	—	0.10	0.30	—
1974	30,000,000	—	—	0.10	0.30	—
1975	80,000,000	—	—	0.10	0.30	—
1976	18,000,000	—	—	0.10	0.30	—
1977	68,500,000	—	—	0.10	0.30	—
1978	47,500,000	—	—	0.10	0.30	—
1979	50,000,000	—	—	0.10	0.30	—
1980	66,500,000	—	—	0.10	0.30	—
1981	2,000,000	—	—	0.10	3.00	—
1988	17,500,000	—	—	0.10	0.30	—

KM# 143.2 FRANC
4.0000 g., Copper-Nickel, 21 mm. **Edge:** Reeded **Note:** Medal alignment.

Date	Mintage	F	VF	XF	Unc	BU
1951	Inc. above	—	10.00	30.00	60.00	—
1952	Inc. above	—	10.00	30.00	60.00	—
1956	Inc. above	—	10.00	30.00	60.00	—
1957	Inc. above	—	10.00	30.00	60.00	—
1958	Inc. above	—	10.00	30.00	60.00	—
1964	Inc. above	—	10.00	30.00	60.00	—
1970	Inc. above	—	10.00	30.00	60.00	—
1971	Inc. above	—	10.00	30.00	60.00	—
1973	Inc. above	—	10.00	30.00	60.00	—
1976	Inc. above	—	10.00	30.00	60.00	—
1977	Inc. above	—	10.00	30.00	60.00	—
1979	Inc. above	—	10.00	30.00	60.00	—
1981	Inc. above	—	10.00	30.00	60.00	—

KM# 171 FRANC
Nickel Plated Iron, 18 mm. **Obv:** Head, left, small mark lower right, dutch legend **Obv. Legend:** BOUDEWIJN I **Rev:** Center symbol divides Crown at left from denomination at right and dates, legend in Dutch **Rev. Legend:** BELGIE

Date	Mintage	F	VF	XF	Unc	BU
1989	200,060,000	—	—	—	0.35	—
1989 medal alignment	—	—	10.00	30.00	60.00	—
1990	200,060,000	—	—	—	0.35	—
1991	200,060,000	—	—	—	0.35	—
1992 In sets only	60,000	—	—	—	18.00	—
1993	15,060,000	—	—	—	0.35	—

KM# 170 FRANC
Nickel Plated Iron, 18 mm. **Obv:** Head left, French legend **Obv. Legend:** BAUDOUIN I **Rev:** Center symbol divides Crown on left from denomination on right and dates, legend in French **Rev. Legend:** BELGIQUE

Date	Mintage	F	VF	XF	Unc	BU
1989	200,060,000	—	—	—	0.35	—

Date	Mintage	F	VF	XF	Unc	BU
1989 medal alignment	—	—	10.00	30.00	60.00	—
1990	200,060,000	—	—	—	0.35	—
1991	200,060,000	—	—	—	0.35	—
1992 In sets only	60,000	—	—	—	18.00	—
1993	15,060,000	—	—	—	0.35	—

KM# 188 FRANC

Nickel Plated Iron, 18 mm. **Ruler:** Albert II **Obv:** Head left, outline around back of head **Rev:** Vertical line divides date and large denomination, legend in Dutch **Rev. Legend:** BELGIE

Date	Mintage	F	VF	XF	Unc	BU
1994	75,060,000	—	—	—	0.30	—
1995	75,060,000	—	—	—	0.30	—
1996	95,060,000	—	—	—	0.30	—
1997	95,060,000	—	—	—	0.30	—
1998	75,060,000	—	—	—	0.30	—
1999	60,000	—	—	—	3.00	—
Note: In sets only						
1999	Inc. above	—	—	—	25.00	—
Note: Medal alignment						
2000	60,000	—	—	—	3.00	—
Note: In sets only						
2000	Inc. above	—	—	—	25.00	—
Note: Medal alignment						

KM# 187 FRANC

Nickel Plated Iron, 18 mm. **Ruler:** Albert II **Obv:** Head left, outline around back of head **Rev:** Vertical line divides date and large denomination, legend in French **Rev. Legend:** BELGIQUE **Note:** Mint mark - Angel Head. Unknown mintmaster's privy mark - scales.

Date	Mintage	F	VF	XF	Unc	BU
1994	75,060,000	—	—	—	0.30	—
1995	75,060,000	—	—	—	0.30	—
1996	75,060,000	—	—	—	0.30	—
1997	95,060,000	—	—	—	0.30	—
1998	75,060,000	—	—	—	0.30	—
1999	60,000	—	—	—	3.00	—
Note: In sets only						
1999	Inc. above	—	—	—	25.00	—
Note: Medal alignment						
2000	60,000	—	—	—	3.00	—
Note: In sets only						
2000	Inc. above	—	—	—	25.00	—
Note: Medal alignment						

KM# 58.1 2 FRANCS (2 Frank)

10.0000 g., 0.8350 Silver .2685 oz. ASW **Obv:** Legend in French **Obv. Legend:** DES BELGES

Date	Mintage	F	VF	XF	Unc	BU
1904	400,000	6.00	20.00	55.00	100	250
1909	1,088,000	3.50	10.00	30.00	50.00	—

KM# 58.2 2 FRANCS (2 Frank)

10.0000 g., 0.8350 Silver .2685 oz. ASW **Obv:** Without period in signature

Date	Mintage	F	VF	XF	Unc	BU
1904	Inc. above	9.00	50.00	120	225	500

KM# 59 2 FRANCS (2 Frank)

10.0000 g., 0.8350 Silver .2685 oz. ASW **Obv:** Bearded head of Leopold II, left, legend in Dutch **Obv. Legend:** DER BELGEN **Rev:** Denomination above date within wreath

Date	Mintage	F	VF	XF	Unc	BU
1904	400,000	6.00	20.00	55.00	100	—
1909	1,088,000	3.50	10.00	30.00	50.00	—

KM# 74 2 FRANCS (2 Frank)

10.0000 g., 0.8350 Silver .2685 oz. ASW **Obv:** Head of Albert, left, legend in French **Obv. Legend:** DES BELGES **Rev:** Denomination above date within wreath

Date	Mintage	F	VF	XF	Unc	BU
1910	800,000	BV	10.00	25.00	50.00	—
1911	1,000,000	BV	7.00	15.00	30.00	—
1912	375,000	3.50	15.00	30.00	55.00	—

KM# 75 2 FRANCS (2 Frank)

10.0000 g., 0.8350 Silver .2685 oz. ASW **Obv:** Head of Albert, left, legend in Dutch **Obv. Legend:** DER BELGEN **Rev:** Denomination above date within wreath

Date	Mintage	F	VF	XF	Unc	BU
1911	1,775,000	BV	4.00	10.00	25.00	—
1912	375,000	BV	10.00	20.00	50.00	—

KM# 91.1 2 FRANCS (2 Frank)

Nickel **Obv:** Kneeling figure, legend in French **Obv. Legend:** BELGIQUE **Rev:** Caduceus divides denomination and date

Date	Mintage	F	VF	XF	Unc	BU
1923	7,500,000	0.50	2.00	8.00	20.00	—
1930/20	1,250,000	12.00	60.00	140	250	—
1930	Inc. above	10.00	50.00	100	200	—

KM# 91.2 2 FRANCS (2 Frank)

Nickel **Designer:** **Note:** Medal alignment

Date	Mintage	F	VF	XF	Unc	BU
1923	Inc. above	5.00	8.00	45.00	110	—

KM# 92 2 FRANCS (2 Frank)

Nickel **Obv:** Kneeling figure, legend in Dutch **Obv. Legend:** BELGIE **Rev:** Caduceus divides denomination and date

Date	Mintage	F	VF	XF	Unc	BU
1923	6,500,000	0.25	3.00	10.00	25.00	—
1924	1,000,000	5.00	20.00	45.00	100	—
1930/20	1,252,000	15.00	55.00	125	250	—
1930	Inc. above	8.00	45.00	100	200	—

KM# 133 2 FRANCS (2 Frank)

Zinc Coated Steel, 19 mm. **Obv:** Sprays below legend, small star at top, legend in French **Obv. Legend:** BELGIQUE-BELGIE **Rev:** Denomination flanked by sprays, date below **Edge:** Plain **Note:** Allied Occupation issue. Made in U.S.A. on blanks for 1943 cents.

Date	Mintage	F	VF	XF	Unc	BU
1944	25,000,000	0.25	0.50	1.50	5.00	10.00

KM# 133a 2 FRANCS (2 Frank)

Silver **Designer:** **Note:** Made in error in U.S.A. on blanks for Netherlands 25 cents.

Date	Mintage	F	VF	XF	Unc	BU
1944	—	200	300	325	450	700

KM# 97.1 5 FRANCS - 5 FRANK (Un / Een Belga)

Nickel **Obv:** Head of Albert, left **Obv. Legend:** DES BELGES **Rev:** Wreath surrounds denomination and date, crown at top, value: UN BELGA **Note:** All dates exist in position A and B, values are the same.

Date	Mintage	F	VF	XF	Unc	BU
1930	1,600,000	1.50	6.00	12.00	25.00	—
1931	9,032,000	1.00	4.00	10.00	20.00	—
1932	3,600,000	1.50	7.00	14.00	30.00	—
1933	1,387,000	6.00	15.00	35.00	80.00	—
1934	1,000,000	30.00	75.00	160	350	—

KM# 97.2 5 FRANCS - 5 FRANK (Un / Een Belga)

Nickel **Designer:** **Note:** Medal alignment. Edge varieties exist.

Date	Mintage	F	VF	XF	Unc	BU
1930	Inc. above	17.50	50.00	150	350	—

KM# 98 5 FRANCS - 5 FRANK (Un / Een Belga)

Nickel **Obv:** Head of Albert, legend in Dutch **Obv. Legend:** DER BELGEN **Rev:** Denomination and date within wreath, Crown at top, value: EEN BELGA **Note:** All dates exist in position A and B, values are the same.

Date	Mintage	F	VF	XF	Unc	BU
1930	5,086,000	2.00	8.00	16.00	40.00	—
1931	5,336,000	1.50	6.00	12.00	25.00	—
1932	3,683,000	1.50	7.00	14.00	30.00	—
1933	2,514,000	8.00	20.00	40.00	80.00	—

KM# 108.1 5 FRANCS - 5 FRANK (Un / Een Belga)

Nickel, 31 mm. **Obv. Designer:** Rau **Rev:** Head of Leopold III, left, date at lower right, legend in French **Rev. Legend:** BELGIQUE **Note:** Both dates exist in position A and B, values are the same.

Date	Mintage	F	VF	XF	Unc	BU
1936	650,000	6.00	25.00	50.00	85.00	—
1937	1,848,000	6.00	20.00	40.00	70.00	—

KM# 108.2 5 FRANCS - 5 FRANK (Un / Een Belga)

Nickel, 31 mm. **Note:** Medal alignment.

Date	Mintage	F	VF	XF	Unc	BU
1936	Inc. above	17.50	55.00	150	350	—

KM# 109.1 5 FRANCS - 5 FRANK (Un / Een Belga)

Nickel, 31 mm. **Obv:** Head of Leopold III, left, small date, lower right **Obv. Designer:** Rau **Rev:** Crown above denomination, sprays below, legend in Dutch **Rev. Legend:** BELGIE **Note:** Both dates exist in position A and B, values are the same.

Date	Mintage	F	VF	XF	Unc	BU
1936	2,498,000	4.00	15.00	35.00	50.00	—
1937	—	—	—	—	—	—

KM# 109.2 5 FRANCS - 5 FRANK (Un / Een Belga)

Nickel **Designer:** **Note:** Medal alignment. Edge varieties exist.

Date	Mintage	F	VF	XF	Unc	BU
1936	Inc. above	15.00	50.00	150	325	—

KM# 117.1 5 FRANCS - 5 FRANK (Un / Een Belga)
Nickel **Obv:** Three shields, legend in Dutch **Obv. Legend:** BELGIE-BELGIQUE **Rev:** Seated lion, right, looking left, date below, denomination at right **Note:** Milled edge, lettering with crown.

Date	Mintage	F	VF	XF	Unc	BU
1938 Position A	3,200,000	20.00	50.00	80.00	125	—
1938 Position B	Inc. above	20.00	50.00	80.00	125	—
1939 Position A	8,219,000	20.00	50.00	80.00	125	—
1939 Position B	Inc. above	20.00	50.00	80.00	125	—

KM# 117.2 5 FRANCS - 5 FRANK (Un / Een Belga)
Nickel **Designer: Note:** Milled edge, lettering with star.

Date	Mintage	F	VF	XF	Unc	BU
1938 Position B	Inc. above	25.00	60.00	90.00	160	—
1938 Position B	Inc. above	25.00	60.00	90.00	160	—
1939 Position A	Inc. above	0.15	2.00	3.00	5.00	—
1939 Position B	Inc. above	0.15	2.00	3.00	5.00	—

KM# 116.1 5 FRANCS - 5 FRANK (Un / Een Belga)
Nickel **Obv:** Three shields, legend in French **Obv. Legend:** BELGIQUE-BELGIE **Rev:** Seated lion, right, looking left, denomination at right, date below **Note:** Milled edge, lettering with crown.

Date	Mintage	F	VF	XF	Unc	BU
1938 Position A	11,419,000	0.20	4.00	7.00	10.00	—
1938 Position B	Inc. above	0.30	4.00	7.00	10.00	—

KM# 116.2 5 FRANCS - 5 FRANK (Un / Een Belga)
Nickel **Designer: Note:** Milled edge, lettering with star.

Date	Mintage	F	VF	XF	Unc	BU
1939 Position A	Inc. above	500	1,200	2,000	3,000	—
1939 Position B	Inc. above	500	1,200	2,000	3,000	—

KM# 116.3 5 FRANCS - 5 FRANK (Un / Een Belga)
Nickel **Designer: Note:** Milled edge, without lettering (error).

Date	Mintage	F	VF	XF	Unc	BU
1938	Inc. above	40.00	70.00	135	300	—

KM# 117.3 5 FRANCS - 5 FRANK (Un / Een Belga)
Nickel **Designer: Note:** Milled edge, without lettering (error).

Date	Mintage	F	VF	XF	Unc	BU
1939	Inc. above	30.00	60.00	175	350	—

KM# 129.1 5 FRANCS - 5 FRANK (Un / Een Belga)
Zinc, 24.8 mm. **Obv:** Head of Leopold III, right, legend in French **Obv. Legend:** DES BELGES **Obv. Designer:** Rau **Rev:** Crown above large decorated denomination, flanked by symbols, date at bottom **Edge:** Reeded **Note:** German Occupation WW II.

Date	Mintage	F	VF	XF	Unc	BU
1941	15,200,000	1.00	2.50	5.00	12.00	—
1943	16,236,000	1.00	2.50	5.00	12.00	—
1944	1,868,000	6.00	17.00	35.00	65.00	—
1945	3,200,000	2.00	5.00	10.00	25.00	—
1946	4,452,000	5.00	12.00	20.00	35.00	—
1947	3,100,000	30.00	80.00	150	240	—

KM# 129.2 5 FRANCS - 5 FRANK (Un / Een Belga)
Zinc, 24.8 mm. **Note:** Medal alignment.

Date	Mintage	F	VF	XF	Unc	BU
1943	Inc. above	5.00	15.00	50.00	130	—

KM# 130 5 FRANCS - 5 FRANK (Un / Een Belga)
Zinc, 24.8 mm. **Obv:** Head of Leopold III, right, legend in Dutch **Obv. Legend:** DER BELGEN **Obv. Designer:** Rau **Rev:** Crown above large decorated denomination flanked by symbols, date at bottom

Date	Mintage	F	VF	XF	Unc	BU
1941	27,544,000	0.75	2.00	4.00	10.00	—
1945	3,200,000	30.00	80.00	125	200	—
1946 Rare	4,000,000	—	—	—	—	—
1947	36,000	175	650	900	1,500	—

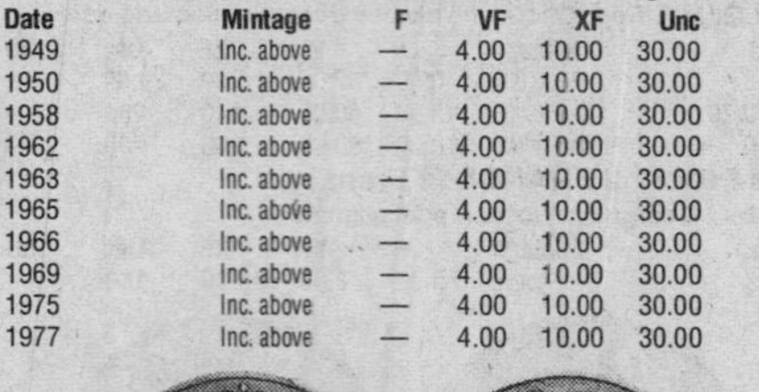

KM# 134.1 5 FRANCS - 5 FRANK (Un / Een Belga)
6.0000 g., Copper-Nickel, 24 mm. **Obv:** Plant divides denomination, Crown at top, legend in French **Obv. Legend:** BELGIQUE **Obv. Designer:** Rau **Rev:** Laureate head, left, small diamonds flank date at left, symbol at right **Edge:** Reeded

Date	Mintage	F	VF	XF	Unc	BU
1948	5,304,000	—	4.00	10.00	25.00	—
1949	38,752,000	—	—	1.00	6.00	—
1950	23,948,000	—	—	1.00	6.00	—
1958	9,088,000	—	—	1.00	3.00	—
1961	6,000,000	—	—	1.00	3.00	—
1962	6,576,000	—	—	1.00	3.00	—
1963	11,144,000	—	—	1.00	3.00	—
1964	3,520,000	—	1.00	2.00	5.00	—
1965	11,988,000	—	—	1.00	3.00	—
1966	6,772,000	—	—	1.00	3.00	—
1967	13,268,000	—	—	1.00	3.00	—
1968	5,192,000	—	1.00	2.00	4.00	—
1969	22,235,000	—	—	1.00	3.00	—
1969	Inc. above	3.00	5.00	10.00	20.00	—
Note: Without engraver's name						
1970	2,000,000	—	1.00	2.00	5.00	—
1971	15,000,000	—	—	0.20	0.50	—
1972	17,500,000	—	—	0.20	0.50	—
1973	10,000,000	—	—	0.20	0.50	—
1974	25,000,000	—	—	0.20	0.50	—
1975	34,000,000	—	—	0.20	0.50	—
1975	—	1.00	5.00	8.00	15.00	—
Note: Without engraver's name						
1976	7,500,000	—	—	0.20	0.75	—
1977	22,500,000	—	—	0.20	0.50	—
1978	27,500,000	—	—	0.20	0.50	—
1979	5,000,000	—	—	0.50	1.00	—
1980	11,000,000	—	—	0.20	0.35	—
1981	2,000,000	—	—	1.00	2.00	—

KM# 134.2 5 FRANCS - 5 FRANK (Un / Een Belga)
6.0000 g., Copper-Nickel, 24 mm. **Note:** Medal alignment.

Date	Mintage	F	VF	XF	Unc	BU
1949	Inc. above	—	4.00	10.00	30.00	—
1950	Inc. above	—	4.00	10.00	30.00	—
1958	Inc. above	—	4.00	10.00	30.00	—
1962	Inc. above	—	4.00	10.00	30.00	—
1963	Inc. above	—	4.00	10.00	30.00	—
1965	Inc. above	—	4.00	10.00	30.00	—
1966	Inc. above	—	4.00	10.00	30.00	—
1969	Inc. above	—	4.00	10.00	30.00	—
1975	Inc. above	—	4.00	10.00	30.00	—
1977	Inc. above	—	4.00	10.00	30.00	—

KM# 135.1 5 FRANCS - 5 FRANK (Un / Een Belga)
6.0000 g., Copper-Nickel, 24 mm. **Obv:** Plant divides denomination, Crown at top, legend in Dutch **Obv. Legend:** BELGIE **Obv. Designer:** Rau **Rev:** Laureate head, left, small diamonds flank date at left, symbol at right **Edge:** Reeded

Date	Mintage	F	VF	XF	Unc	BU
1948	4,800,000	—	4.00	10.00	25.00	—
1949	31,500,000	—	—	1.00	6.00	—
1950	34,728,000	—	—	1.00	6.00	—
1958	2,672,000	—	1.00	2.00	6.00	—
1960	5,896,000	—	—	1.00	3.00	—
1961	4,120,000	—	1.00	2.00	5.00	—
1962	7,624,000	—	—	1.00	3.00	—
1963	6,136,000	—	—	1.00	3.00	—
1964	8,128,000	—	—	1.00	3.00	—
1965	9,956,000	—	—	1.00	3.00	—
1966	7,136,000	—	—	1.00	3.00	—
1966	—	3.00	5.00	10.00	20.00	—
Note: Without engraver's name						
1967	16,132,000	—	—	1.00	3.00	—
1968	3,200,000	—	1.00	2.00	5.00	—
1969	21,500,000	—	—	1.00	3.00	—
1970	2,000,000	—	1.00	2.00	5.00	—
1971	15,000,000	—	—	0.20	0.50	—
1972	17,500,000	—	—	0.20	0.50	—
1972	Inc. above	1.00	5.00	8.00	15.00	—
Note: Without engraver's name						
1973	10,000,000	—	—	0.20	0.50	—
1974	25,000,000	—	—	0.20	0.50	—
1974	—	1.00	5.00	8.00	15.00	—
Note: Without engraver's name						
1975	34,000,000	—	—	0.20	0.50	—
1976	7,500,000	—	—	0.20	0.75	—
1977	22,500,000	—	—	0.20	0.50	—
1978	27,500,000	—	—	0.20	0.50	—
1979	10,000,000	—	—	0.50	1.00	—
1980	11,000,000	—	—	0.20	0.50	—
1981	2,000,000	—	—	1.00	2.00	—

KM# 135.2 5 FRANCS - 5 FRANK (Un / Een Belga)
6.0000 g., Copper-Nickel, 24 mm. **Note:** Medal alignment.

Date	Mintage	F	VF	XF	Unc	BU
1950	Inc. above	—	4.00	10.00	30.00	—
1962	Inc. above	—	4.00	10.00	30.00	—
1963	Inc. above	—	4.00	10.00	30.00	—
1965	Inc. above	—	4.00	10.00	30.00	—
1966	Inc. above	—	4.00	10.00	30.00	—
1969	Inc. above	—	4.00	10.00	30.00	—
1974	Inc. above	—	4.00	10.00	30.00	—

KM# 163 5 FRANCS - 5 FRANK (Un / Een Belga)
Brass Or Aluminum-Bronze, 24 mm. **Obv:** Face, left, on divided coin **Rev:** Stylized denomination, date at bottom, legend in French **Rev. Legend:** BELGIQUE

Date	Mintage	F	VF	XF	Unc	BU
1986	208,400,000	—	—	0.35	0.65	—
1987	22,500,000	—	—	0.35	1.00	—
1988	26,500,000	—	—	0.35	1.00	—
1989 In sets only	60,000	—	—	—	4.00	—
1990 In sets only	60,000	—	—	—	4.00	—
1991 In sets only	60,000	—	—	—	4.00	—
1992	5,060,000	—	—	0.35	2.00	—
1993	15,060,000	—	—	0.35	1.00	—

KM# 164 5 FRANCS - 5 FRANK (Un / Een Belga)
Brass Or Aluminum-Bronze, 24 mm. **Obv:** Face, left, on divided coin **Rev:** Stylized denomination, date at bottom, legend in Dutch **Rev. Legend:** BELGIE

Date	Mintage	F	VF	XF	Unc	BU
1986	208,400,000	—	—	0.35	0.65	—
1987	22,500,000	—	—	0.35	1.00	—
1988	26,500,000	—	—	0.35	1.00	—
1989 In sets only	60,000	—	—	—	4.00	—
1990 In sets only	60,000	—	—	—	4.00	—
1991 In sets only	60,000	—	—	—	4.00	—
1992	5,060,000	—	—	0.35	2.00	—
1993	15,060,000	—	—	0.35	1.00	—

KM# 190 5 FRANCS - 5 FRANK (Un / Een Belga)
Aluminum-Bronze, 24 mm. **Ruler:** Albert II **Obv:** Head left, outline around back of head **Rev:** Vertical line divides date and large denomination, legend in Dutch **Rev. Legend:** BELGIE **Note:** Mint mark - Angel head. Mintmaster R. Coenen's privy mark - Scale.

Date	Mintage	F	VF	XF	Unc	BU
1994	30,060,000	—	—	—	0.50	—
1995	60,000	—	—	—	2.00	—
Note: In sets only						
1996	3,133,000	—	—	—	1.00	—
1997	60,000	—	—	—	5.00	—
Note: In sets only						
1998	6,500,000	—	—	—	0.50	—
1999	60,000	—	—	—	4.00	—
Note: In sets only						
1999 Medal alignment	5,000	—	—	—	20.00	—
2000	60,000	—	—	—	4.00	—
Note: In sets only						
2000 Medal alignment	5,000	—	—	—	20.00	—

KM# 189 5 FRANCS - 5 FRANK (Un / Een Belga)
Aluminum-Bronze, 24 mm. **Ruler:** Albert II **Obv:** Head left, outline around back of head **Rev:** Vertical line divides date and denomination, legend in French **Rev. Legend:** BELGIQUE **Note:** Struck at Brussels Mint. Mint mark - Angel head. Mintmaster R. Coenen's privy mark - Scale.

Date	Mintage	F	VF	XF	Unc	BU
1994	15,060,000	—	—	—	0.50	—
1995	60,000	—	—	—	4.00	—
Note: In sets only						
1996	6,860,000	—	—	—	1.00	—
1997	60,000	—	—	—	5.00	—
Note: In sets only						
1998	32,560,000	—	—	—	0.50	—
1999	60,000	—	—	—	4.00	—
Note: In sets only						
1999 Medal alignment	5,000	—	—	—	20.00	—
2000	60,000	—	—	—	4.00	—
Note: In sets only						
2000 Medal alignment	5,000	—	—	—	20.00	—

KM# 99 10 FRANCS - 10 FRANK
(Deux / Twee Belgas)
Nickel **Subject:** Independence Centennial **Rev:** Legend in French **Rev. Legend:** BELGIQUE **Note:** Exists in position A or B, values are the same.

Date	Mintage	F	VF	XF	Unc	BU
1930	2,699,000	25.00	70.00	130	200	—

KM# 100 10 FRANCS - 10 FRANK
(Deux / Twee Belgas)
Nickel **Obv:** Conjoined heads of Leopold I, Leopold II and Albert I, left, two dates at bottom **Rev:** Denomination flanked by sprays, legend in Dutch **Rev. Legend:** BELGIE **Note:** Exists in position A or B, values are the same.

Date	Mintage	F	VF	XF	Unc	BU
1930	3,000,000	30.00	75.00	140	250	500

KM# 155.1 10 FRANCS - 10 FRANK
(Deux / Twee Belgas)
8.0000 g., Nickel, 27 mm. **Obv:** Head, left **Obv. Designer:** Harry Elstrom **Rev:** Crowned arms divide denomination, date at bottom, legend in French **Rev. Legend:** BELGIQUE **Rev. Designer:** J. DeBast **Edge:** Plain **Note:** Mint mark - Angel head. Mintmaster Vogeleer's privy mark - Bird.

Date	Mintage	F	VF	XF	Unc	BU
1969	22,235,000	—	—	0.40	0.70	—
1970	9,500,000	—	—	0.40	0.70	—
1971	15,000,000	—	—	0.40	0.70	—
1972	10,000,000	—	—	0.40	0.70	—
1973	10,000,000	—	—	0.40	0.70	—
1974	5,000,000	—	—	0.50	1.00	—
1975	5,000,000	—	—	0.50	1.00	—
1976	7,500,000	—	—	0.50	1.00	—
1977	7,000,000	—	—	0.50	1.00	—
1978	2,500,000	—	—	1.00	2.50	—
1979	5,000,000	—	—	0.60	1.50	—

KM# 155.2 10 FRANCS - 10 FRANK
(Deux / Twee Belgas)
8.0000 g., Nickel, 27 mm. **Note:** Medal alignment. Struck at Brussels Mint. Mint mark - Angel head. Mintmaster Vogeleer's privy mark - Bird.

Date	Mintage	F	VF	XF	Unc	BU
1969	Inc. above	—	6.00	12.00	35.00	—
1974	Inc. above	—	6.00	12.00	35.00	—
1977	Inc. above	—	6.00	12.00	35.00	—
1978	Inc. above	—	6.00	12.00	30.00	—

KM# 156.1 10 FRANCS - 10 FRANK
(Deux / Twee Belgas)
8.0000 g., Nickel, 27 mm. **Obv:** Head, left **Obv. Designer:** Harry Elstrom **Rev:** Crowned arms divide denomination, date at bottom, legend in Dutch **Rev. Legend:** BELGIE **Rev. Designer:** J. DeBast **Edge:** Plain **Note:** Mint mark - Angel head. Mintmaster Vogeleer's privy mark - Bird.

Date	Mintage	F	VF	XF	Unc	BU
1969	21,500,000	—	—	0.40	0.70	—
1970	10,000,000	—	—	0.40	0.70	—
1971	15,000,000	—	—	0.40	0.70	—
1972	10,000,000	—	—	0.40	0.70	—
1973	10,000,000	—	—	0.40	0.70	—
1974	5,000,000	—	—	0.50	1.00	—
1975	5,000,000	—	—	0.50	1.00	—
1976	7,500,000	—	—	0.50	1.00	—
1977	7,000,000	—	—	0.50	1.00	—
1978	2,500,000	—	—	1.00	2.50	—
1979	10,000,000	—	—	0.60	1.50	—

KM# 156.2 10 FRANCS - 10 FRANK
(Deux / Twee Belgas)
8.0000 g., Nickel, 27 mm. **Note:** Medal alignment. Struck at Brussels Mint. Mint mark - Angel head. Mintmaster Vogeleer's privy mark - Bird.

Date	Mintage	F	VF	XF	Unc	BU
1971	Inc. above	—	6.00	12.00	35.00	—
1976	Inc. above	—	6.00	12.00	35.00	—

KM# 78 20 FRANCS (20 Frank)
6.4516 g., 0.9000 Gold .1867 oz. AGW **Obv:** Armored bust of Albert, left, legend in French **Obv. Legend:** DES BELGES **Rev:** Crowned arms divide denomination and date

Date	Mintage	F	VF	XF	Unc	BU
1914 Position A	125,000	—	—	BV	150	250
1914 Position B	Inc. above	300	600	800	1,000	—

KM# 79 20 FRANCS (20 Frank)
6.4516 g., 0.9000 Gold .1867 oz. AGW **Obv:** Armored bust of Albert, left, legend in Dutch **Obv. Legend:** DER BELGEN **Rev:** Crowned arms divide denomination and date

Date	Mintage	F	VF	XF	Unc	BU
1914 Position A	125,000	—	—	BV	125	160
1914 Position B	Inc. above	—	BV	125	140	185

KM# 101.1 20 FRANCS - 20 FRANK
(Vier / Quatre Belgas)
Nickel **Obv:** Head of Albert, left, legend in French **Obv. Legend:** DES BELGES **Rev:** Crowned arms divide denomination and date **Note:** All dates exist in position A and B, values are the same.

Date	Mintage	F	VF	XF	Unc	BU
1931	3,957,000	20.00	50.00	110	160	175
1932	5,472,000	20.00	50.00	110	160	175
1934	—	—	—	—	—	—
Note: Struck at a later date						

KM# 101.2 20 FRANCS - 20 FRANK
(Vier / Quatre Belgas)
Nickel **Designer:** **Note:** Medal alignment. Edge varieties exist.

Date	Mintage	F	VF	XF	Unc	BU
1932	Inc. above	65.00	175	400	600	—

KM# 102 20 FRANCS - 20 FRANK
(Vier / Quatre Belgas)
Nickel **Obv:** Legend in Dutch **Obv. Legend:** DER BELGEN **Note:** All dates exist in position A and B, values are the same.

Date	Mintage	F	VF	XF	Unc	BU
1931	2,600,000	25.00	55.00	120	175	200
1932	6,950,000	15.00	45.00	100	140	175
1934	—	—	—	—	—	—
Note: Struck at a later date						

KM# 103.1 20 FRANCS - 20 FRANK
(Vier / Quatre Belgas)
11.0000 g., 0.6800 Silver .2405 oz. ASW **Obv:** Head of Albert, left, legend in French **Obv. Legend:** DES BELGES **Rev:** Crowned arms divide denomination and date

Date	Mintage	F	VF	XF	Unc	BU
1933 Position A	200,000	20.00	60.00	100	150	—
1933 Position B	Inc. above	25.00	75.00	120	175	—
1934 Position A	12,300,000	—	4.00	8.00	12.00	—
1934 Position B	Inc. above	—	4.00	8.00	12.00	—

KM# 104.1 20 FRANCS - 20 FRANK
(Vier / Quatre Belgas)
11.0000 g., 0.6800 Silver .2405 oz. ASW **Obv:** Head of Albert, left, legend in Dutch **Obv. Legend:** DER BELGEN **Rev:** Crowned arms divide denomination and date

Date	Mintage	F	VF	XF	Unc	BU
1933 Position B	Inc. above	16.00	40.00	65.00	125	—
1933 Position A	200,000	14.00	30.00	60.00	110	—
1934 Position A	12,300,000	—	2.00	4.00	7.00	—
1934 Position B	Inc. above	—	2.00	4.00	7.00	—

KM# 103.2 20 FRANCS - 20 FRANK
(Vier / Quatre Belgas)
11.0000 g., 0.6800 Silver .2405 oz. ASW **Designer:** **Note:** Medal alignment.

Date	Mintage	F	VF	XF	Unc	BU
1934	Inc. above	35.00	80.00	190	400	—

KM# 104.2 20 FRANCS - 20 FRANK
(Vier / Quatre Belgas)
11.0000 g., 0.6800 Silver .2405 oz. ASW **Designer:** **Note:** Medal alignment.

Date	Mintage	F	VF	XF	Unc	BU
1934	Inc. above	30.00	70.00	170	350	—

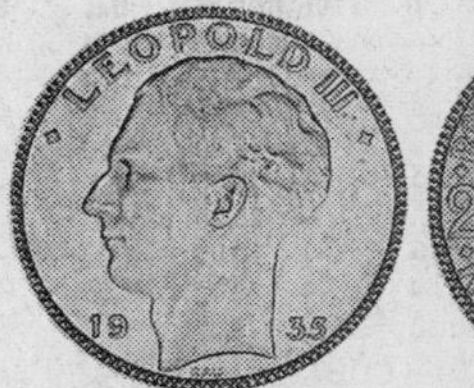

KM# 105 20 FRANCS - 20 FRANK
(Vier / Quatre Belgas)
11.0000 g., 0.6800 Silver .2405 oz. ASW **Obv:** Head of Leopold III, left, neck divides date **Obv. Designer:** Rau **Rev:** Crown above sprig divides denomination **Note:** Both dates exist in position A and B, values are the same. Coins dated 1934 exist with and without umlauts above E in BELGIE.

Date	Mintage	F	VF	XF	Unc	BU
1934	1,250,000	3.00	8.00	12.00	20.00	—
1935	10,760,000	BV	3.50	5.50	8.00	—

KM# 140.2 20 FRANCS - 20 FRANK
(Vier / Quatre Belgas)
8.0000 g., 0.8350 Silver .2148 oz. ASW, 27 mm. **Edge:** Plain **Note:** Medal alignment.

Date	Mintage	F	VF	XF	Unc	BU
1949	Inc. above	15.00	35.00	75.00	125	—
1950	Inc. above	15.00	35.00	75.00	125	—

KM# 141.2 20 FRANCS - 20 FRANK
(Vier / Quatre Belgas)

8.0000 g., 0.8350 Silver .2148 oz. ASW **Edge:** Reeded **Note:** Medal alignment.

Date	Mintage	F	VF	XF	Unc	BU
1949	Inc. above	20.00	35.00	85.00	135	—
1951	Inc. above	15.00	40.00	95.00	160	—

KM# 140.1 20 FRANCS - 20 FRANK
(Vier / Quatre Belgas)

8.0000 g., 0.8350 Silver .2148 oz. ASW, 27 mm. **Obv:** Rampant lion, left, with shield, denomination below, legend in French **Obv. Legend:** BELGIQUE **Rev:** Helmeted head, right, small caduceus divides date at left **Rev. Designer:** Rau **Edge:** Reeded

Date	Mintage	F	VF	XF	Unc	BU
1949	4,600,000	—	3.50	6.00	10.00	—
1950	12,957,000	—	2.50	4.00	7.00	—
1951	—	—	—	—	—	—
1953	3,953,000	—	6.00	9.00	15.00	—
1954	4,835,000	15.00	45.00	80.00	120	—
1955	1,730,000	200	650	900	1,400	—

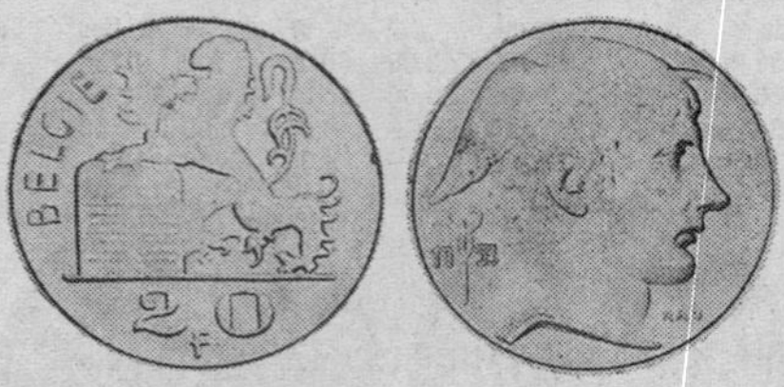

KM# 141.1 20 FRANCS - 20 FRANK
(Vier / Quatre Belgas)

8.0000 g., 0.8350 Silver .2148 oz. ASW, 27 mm. **Obv:** Rampant lion, left, with shield, denomination below, legend in Dutch **Obv. Legend:** BELGIE **Rev:** Helmeted head, right, small caduceus divides date at left **Rev. Designer:** Rau **Edge:** Reeded

Date	Mintage	F	VF	XF	Unc	BU
1949	5,545,000	—	3.00	5.00	9.00	—
1950	—	150	500	800	1,200	—
1951	7,885,000	—	2.50	4.00	7.00	—
1953	6,625,000	—	2.50	4.50	8.00	—
1954	5,323,000	12.00	35.00	60.00	100	—
1955	3,760,000	50.00	125	200	275	—

KM# 159 20 FRANCS - 20 FRANK
(Vier / Quatre Belgas)

8.5000 g., Nickel-Bronze, 25.65 mm. **Obv:** Head, left **Rev:** Denomination at right above stylized spray, legend in French **Rev. Legend:** BELGIQUE **Designer:** Harry Elstrom

Date	Mintage	F	VF	XF	Unc	BU
1980	60,000,000	—	—	0.70	2.00	—
1981	60,000,000	—	—	0.70	2.00	—
1982	54,000,000	—	—	0.70	2.00	—
1989 In sets only	60,000	—	—	—	6.00	—
1990 In sets only	60,000	—	—	—	6.00	—
1991 In sets only	60,000	—	—	—	6.00	—
1992	2,610,000	—	—	0.70	4.00	—
1993	7,540,000	—	—	0.70	3.00	—

KM# 160 20 FRANCS - 20 FRANK
(Vier / Quatre Belgas)

8.5000 g., Nickel-Bronze, 25.65 mm. **Obv:** Head, left **Rev:** Denomination at right above stylized spray, legend in Dutch **Rev. Legend:** BELGIE **Designer:** Harry Elstrom

Date	Mintage	F	VF	XF	Unc	BU
1980	60,000,000	—	—	0.70	2.00	—
1981	60,000,000	—	—	0.70	2.00	—
1982	54,000,000	—	—	0.70	2.00	—
1989 In sets only	60,000	—	—	—	6.00	—
1990 In sets only	60,000	—	—	—	6.00	—
1991 In sets only	60,000	—	—	—	6.00	—
1992	2,610,000	—	—	0.70	4.00	—
1993	7,540,000	—	—	0.70	3.00	—

KM# 191 20 FRANCS - 20 FRANK
(Vier / Quatre Belgas)

8.5000 g., Nickel-Bronze, 25.65 mm. **Ruler:** Albert II **Obv:** Head left, outline around back of head **Rev:** Vertical line divides date and large denomination, legend in French **Rev. Legend:** BELGIQUE **Note:** Mint mark - Angel head. Mintmaster R. Coenen's privy mark - Scale.

Date	Mintage	F	VF	XF	Unc	BU
1994	12,560,000	—	—	0.70	1.00	—
1995	60,000	—	—	—	5.00	—
Note: In sets only						
1996	14,485,000	—	—	—	1.00	—
Note: In sets only						
1997	60,000	—	—	—	5.00	—
Note: In sets only						
1998	6,500,000	—	—	—	3.00	—
1999	60,000	—	—	—	5.00	—
Note: In sets only						
1999 Medal alignment	5,000	—	—	—	20.00	—
2000	60,000	—	—	—	5.00	—
Note: In sets only						
2000 Medal alignment	5,000	—	—	—	20.00	—

KM# 192 20 FRANCS - 20 FRANK
(Vier / Quatre Belgas)

8.5000 g., Nickel-Bronze, 25.65 mm. **Ruler:** Albert II **Obv:** Head left, outline around back of head **Rev:** Vertical line divides date and large denomination, legend in Dutch **Rev. Legend:** BELGIE **Note:** Mint mark - Angel head. Mintmaster R. Coenen's privy mark - Scale.

Date	Mintage	F	VF	XF	Unc	BU
1994	12,560,000	—	—	0.70	1.00	—
1995	60,000	—	—	—	5.00	—
Note: In sets only						
1996	3,133,000	—	—	—	3.00	—
1997	60,000	—	—	—	5.00	—
Note: In sets only						
1998	6,500,000	—	—	—	3.00	—
1999	60,000	—	—	—	5.00	—
Note: In sets only						
1999 Medal alignment	5,000	—	—	—	20.00	—
2000	60,000	—	—	—	5.00	—
Note: In sets only						
2000 Medal alignment	5,000	—	—	—	20.00	—

KM# 106.1 50 FRANCS (50 Frank)

22.0000 g., 0.6800 Silver .4810 oz. ASW, 35 mm. **Subject:** Brussels Exposition and Railway Centennial **Obv:** St. Michael slaying dragon (Brussels' patron saint) **Obv. Legend:** DE BELGIQUE **Rev:** Brussels train station, two dates above, legend in French **Rev. Legend:** DE FER BELGES **Designer:** Paul Wissgert **Note:** Exists in positions A and B, values are the same.

Date	Mintage	F	VF	XF	Unc	BU
1935	140,000	50.00	90.00	125	200	400

KM# 106.2 50 FRANCS (50 Frank)

22.0000 g., 0.6800 Silver .4810 oz. ASW, 35 mm. **Note:** Medal alignment. Exists in positions A and B, values are the same.

Date	Mintage	F	VF	XF	Unc	BU
1935	Inc. above	200	450	600	825	—

KM# 107.1 50 FRANCS (50 Frank)

22.0000 g., 0.6800 Silver .4810 oz. ASW, 35 mm. **Obv:** St. Michael slaying dragon (Brussels' patron saint) **Obv. Legend:** BELGIE **Rev:** Brussels railway station, two dates above, legend in Dutch **Rev. Legend:** DER BELGISCHE **Designer:** Paul Wissaert **Note:** Exists in positions A and B, values are the same.

Date	Mintage	F	VF	XF	Unc	BU
1935	140,000	60.00	125	150	225	450

KM# 107.2 50 FRANCS (50 Frank)

22.0000 g., 0.6800 Silver .4810 oz. ASW, 35 mm. **Note:** Medal alignment. Exists in positions A and B, values are the same.

Date	Mintage	F	VF	XF	Unc	BU
1935	Inc. above	300	700	900	1,500	—

KM# 121 50 FRANCS (50 Frank)

20.0000 g., 0.8350 Silver .5369 oz. ASW **Obv:** Head of Leopold III, left, date below **Rev:** Crown above nine shields dividing denomination, legend in French **Rev. Legend:** BELGIQUE: BELGIE **Note:** Both dates exist in positions A and B, values are the same.

Date	Mintage	F	VF	XF	Unc	BU
1939	1,000,000	BV	8.00	12.00	18.00	—
1940	631,000	7.00	15.00	25.00	35.00	—

KM# 122.1 50 FRANCS (50 Frank)

20.0000 g., 0.8350 Silver .5369 oz. ASW **Obv:** Head of Leopold III, left, date below **Rev:** Crown above nine shields dividing denomination, legend in Dutch **Rev. Legend:** BELGIE: BELGIQUE **Note:** Both dates exist in positions A and B, values are the same.

Date	Mintage	F	VF	XF	Unc	BU
1939	1,000,000	BV	8.00	12.00	18.00	—
1940	631,000	7.00	15.00	25.00	35.00	—

KM# 122.2 50 FRANCS (50 Frank)

20.0000 g., 0.8350 Silver .5369 oz. ASW **Rev:** Without cross on crown **Note:** Both dates exist in positions A and B, values are the same.

Date	Mintage	F	VF	XF	Unc	BU
1939	Inc. above	8.00	30.00	40.00	55.00	—
1940	Inc. above	8.00	30.00	40.00	55.00	—

KM# 122.3 50 FRANCS (50 Frank)

20.0000 g., 0.8350 Silver .5369 oz. ASW **Rev:** Triangle in third arms from left, cross on crown **Note:** Both dates exist in positions A and B, values are the same.

Date	Mintage	F	VF	XF	Unc	BU
1940	Inc. above	15.00	35.00	60.00	85.00	—

KM# 122.4 50 FRANCS (50 Frank)

20.0000 g., 0.8350 Silver .5369 oz. ASW **Rev:** Without cross on crown **Note:** Both dates exist in positions A and B, values are the same.

Date	Mintage	F	VF	XF	Unc	BU
1940	Inc. above	30.00	90.00	140	200	—

KM# 136.1 50 FRANCS (50 Frank)
12.5000 g., 0.8350 Silver .3356 oz. ASW, 30 mm. **Obv:** Rampant lion with shield, left, denomination below, legend in French **Obv. Legend:** BELGIQUE **Rev:** Helmeted head, right, small caduceus divides date at left **Rev. Designer:** Rau

Date	Mintage	F	VF	XF	Unc	BU
1948	2,000,000	—	BV	4.50	7.00	—
Note: Exists in position A and B, values are the same						
1949	4,354,000	—	BV	4.50	6.00	—
1950	—	200	600	1,000	1,750	—
1951	2,904,000	—	BV	4.50	6.50	—
1954	3,232,000	5.00	12.00	20.00	30.00	—

KM# 136.2 50 FRANCS (50 Frank)
12.5000 g., 0.8350 Silver .3356 oz. ASW, 30 mm. **Note:** Medal alignment.

Date	Mintage	F	VF	XF	Unc	BU
1949	Inc. above	10.00	30.00	90.00	175	250

KM# 137 50 FRANCS (50 Frank)
12.5000 g., 0.8350 Silver .3356 oz. ASW, 30 mm. **Obv:** Rampant lion with shield, left, denomination below, legend in Dutch **Obv. Legend:** BELGIE **Rev:** Helmeted head, right, small caduceus divides date at left **Rev. Designer:** Rau

Date	Mintage	F	VF	XF	Unc	BU
1948	3,000,000	—	BV	4.50	7.00	—
1950	4,110,000	—	BV	4.50	6.00	—
1951	1,698,000	—	BV	4.50	8.00	—
1954	2,978,000	—	BV	4.50	6.50	—

KM# 150.1 50 FRANCS (50 Frank)
12.5000 g., 0.8350 Silver .3356 oz. ASW, 29 mm. **Subject:** Brussels World Fair **Obv:** Head of Baudouin, left, within circle, legend in French **Obv. Legend:** DES BELGES **Rev:** World's Fair, Steeple divides date from denomination **Designer:** Reeded

Date	Mintage	F	VF	XF	Unc	BU
1958	476,000	—	BV	6.50	10.00	—

KM# 150.2 50 FRANCS (50 Frank)
12.5000 g., 0.8350 Silver .3356 oz. ASW, 29 mm. **Note:** Medal alignment.

Date	Mintage	F	VF	XF	Unc	BU
1958	Inc. above	18.00	45.00	100	180	250

KM# 151.1 50 FRANCS (50 Frank)
12.5000 g., 0.8350 Silver .3356 oz. ASW, 29 mm. **Obv:** Head of Baudouin, left, within circle, legend in Dutch **Obv. Legend:** DER BELGEN **Rev:** World's Fair, Steeple divides date from denomination **Edge:** Reeded **Designer:** Carlos van Dionant

Date	Mintage	F	VF	XF	Unc	BU
1958	382,000	BV	5.00	7.50	10.00	—

KM# 151.2 50 FRANCS (50 Frank)
12.5000 g., 0.8350 Silver .3356 oz. ASW, 29 mm. **Note:** Medal alignment.

Date	Mintage	F	VF	XF	Unc	BU
1958	Inc. above	15.00	35.00	75.00	125	—

KM# 152.1 50 FRANCS (50 Frank)
12.5000 g., 0.8350 Silver .3356 oz. ASW, 29 mm. **Subject:** King Baudouin's marriage to Doña Fabiola de Mora y Aragon **Obv:** Conjoined heads of King Baudoin and Dona Fabiola de Mora y Aragon, left **Rev:** Arms flanked by sprays divide Crown and denomination

Date	Mintage	F	VF	XF	Unc	BU
1960	500,000	BV	4.50	6.00	9.00	15.00

KM# 152.2 50 FRANCS (50 Frank)
12.5000 g., 0.8350 Silver .3356 oz. ASW, 29 mm. **Note:** Medal alignment.

Date	Mintage	F	VF	XF	Unc	BU
1960	Inc. above	12.50	30.00	60.00	120	200

KM# 168 50 FRANCS (50 Frank)
Nickel, 22.5 mm. **Obv:** Face, left, on divided coin **Rev:** Denomination, date at bottom, legend in French **Rev. Legend:** BELGIQUE

Date	Mintage	F	VF	XF	Unc	BU
1987	30,000,000	—	—	2.00	3.00	—
1988	3,500,000	—	—	2.00	6.00	—
1989	15,060,000	—	—	2.00	4.00	—
1990	15,060,000	—	—	2.00	4.00	—
1991	3,500,000	—	—	2.00	5.00	—
1992	15,060,000	—	—	2.00	4.00	—
1993	15,060,000	—	—	2.00	4.00	—

KM# 169 50 FRANCS (50 Frank)
Nickel, 22.5 mm. **Obv:** Face, left, on divided coin **Rev:** Denomination, date at bottom **Rev. Legend:** BELGIE

Date	Mintage	F	VF	XF	Unc	BU
1987	30,000,000	—	—	2.00	3.00	—
1988	3,500,000	—	—	2.00	6.00	—
1989	15 060,000	—	—	2.00	4.00	—
1990	15,060,000	—	—	2.00	4.00	—
1991	3,500,000	—	—	2.00	5.00	—
1992	15,060,000	—	—	2.00	4.00	—
1993	15,060,000	—	—	2.00	4.00	—

KM# 193 50 FRANCS (50 Frank)
Nickel, 22.5 mm. **Ruler:** Albert II **Obv:** Head left, outline around back of head **Rev:** Vertical line divides large denomination and date, legend in French **Rev. Legend:** BELGIQUE **Note:** Mint mark - Angel head. Mintmaster R. Coenen's privy mark - Scale.

Date	Mintage	F	VF	XF	Unc	BU
1994	5,060,000	—	—	2.00	3.00	—
1995	60,000	—	—	5.00	8.00	—
Note: In sets only						
1996	60,000	—	—	5.00	8.00	—
Note: In sets only						
1997	60,000	—	—	5.00	8.00	—
Note: In sets only						
1998	3,060,000	—	—	3.00	4.50	—
1999	60,000	—	—	5.00	8.00	—
Note: In sets only						
1999 Medal alignment	5,000	Value: 20.00				
2000	60,000	—	—	5.00	8.00	—
Note: In sets only						
2000 Medal alignment	5,000	Value: 20.00				

KM# 194 50 FRANCS (50 Frank)
Nickel, 22.5 mm. **Ruler:** Albert II **Obv:** Head left, outline around back of head **Rev:** Vertical line divides large denomination and date, legend in Dutch **Rev. Legend:** BELGIE **Note:** Mint mark - Angel head. Mintmaster R. Coenen's privy mark - Scale.

Date	Mintage	F	VF	XF	Unc	BU
1994	5,060,000	—	—	2.00	3.00	—
1995	60,000	—	—	5.00	8.00	—
Note: In sets only						
1996	60,000	—	—	5.00	8.00	—
Note: In sets only						
1997	60,000	—	—	5.00	8.00	—
Note: In sets only						
1998	3,060,000	—	—	3.00	4.50	—
1999	60,000	—	—	3.00	8.00	—
Note: In sets only						
1999 Medal alignment	5,000	Value: 20.00				
2000	60,000	—	—	5.00	8.00	—
Note: In sets only						
2000 Medal alignment	5,000	Value: 20.00				

KM# 213.1 50 FRANCS (50 Frank)
Nickel, 22.5 mm. **Subject:** European Soccer Championship **Obv:** Head of Albert II, left **Rev:** Soccer ball, legend in French **Rev. Legend:** BELGIQUE **Edge:** Reeded

Date	Mintage	F	VF	XF	Unc	BU
2000	500,000	—	—	—	6.00	—

KM# 213.2 50 FRANCS (50 Frank)
Nickel, 22.5 mm. **Note:** Medal alignment.

Date	Mintage	F	VF	XF	Unc	BU
2000	20,000	Value: 22.00				

KM# 214.1 50 FRANCS (50 Frank)
Nickel, 22.5 mm. **Subject:** European Soccer Championship **Obv:** Head of Albert II, left, rear of head outlined **Rev:** Soccer ball, legend in Dutch **Rev. Legend:** BELGIE **Edge:** Reeded

Date	Mintage	F	VF	XF	Unc	BU
2000	500,000	—	—	4.00	6.00	—

KM# 214.2 50 FRANCS (50 Frank)
Nickel, 22.5 mm. **Note:** Medal alignment.

Date	Mintage	F	VF	XF	Unc	BU
2000	20,000	Value: 22.00				

KM# 138.1 100 FRANCS (100 Frank)
18.0000 g., 0.8350 Silver .4832 oz. ASW **Obv:** Crowned arms within wreath divide denomination, legend in French **Obv. Legend:** BELGIQUE **Rev:** Conjoined heads left of Leopold I, Leopold II, Albert I and Leopold III, left, Crown divides date at top, star at bottom

Date	Mintage	F	VF	XF	Unc	BU
1948	1,000,000	—	BV	5.00	10.00	—
1949	106,000	7.50	15.00	25.00	45.00	—
1950	2,807,000	—	BV	5.00	9.00	—
1954	2,517,000	—	BV	5.00	10.00	—

KM# 138.2 100 FRANCS (100 Frank)
18.0000 g., 0.8350 Silver .4832 oz. ASW **Designer:** **Note:** Medal alignment.

Date	Mintage	F	VF	XF	Unc	BU
1948	Inc. above	10.00	40.00	90.00	220	—
1950	Inc. above	10.00	40.00	90.00	200	—

KM# 139.1 100 FRANCS (100 Frank)
18.0000 g., 0.8350 Silver .4832 oz. ASW **Obv:** Crowned arms within wreath divide denomination, legend in Dutch **Obv. Legend:** BELGIE **Rev:** Conjoined heads left of Leopold I, Leopold II, Albert I and Leopold III, left, Crown divides date at top, star at bottom

Date	Mintage	F	VF	XF	Unc	BU
1948	1,000,000	—	BV	5.00	10.00	—
1949	2,271,000	—	BV	5.00	9.00	—
1950	—	300	500	850	1,200	—
1951	4,691,000	—	BV	5.00	9.00	—

KM# 139.2 100 FRANCS (100 Frank)
18.0000 g., 0.8350 Silver .4832 oz. ASW **Designer:** **Note:** Medal alignment.

Date	Mintage	F	VF	XF	Unc	BU
1948	Inc. above	10.00	40.00	90.00	200	—
1949	Inc. above	7.50	30.00	75.00	160	—
1951	Inc. above	10.00	40.00	90.00	200	—

KM# 215 200 FRANCS (200 Frank)
Silver **Subject:** The Universe **Obv:** Legend in French **Obv. Legend:** BELGIQUE

Date	Mintage	F	VF	XF	Unc	BU
2000	50,000	—	—	—	15.00	—
2000 (qp)	10,000	Value: 45.00				

KM# 216 200 FRANCS (200 Frank)
Silver **Subject:** Nature **Obv:** Legend in Dutch **Obv. Legend:** BELGIE

Date	Mintage	F	VF	XF	Unc	BU
2000	50,000	—	—	—	15.00	—
2000 (qp)	10,000	Value: 45.00				

KM# 217 200 FRANCS (200 Frank)
Silver **Subject:** The City **Obv:** Legend in German **Obv. Legend:** BELGIEN

Date	Mintage	F	VF	XF	Unc	BU
2000	50,000	—	—	—	15.00	—
2000 (qp)	10,000	—	—	—	45.00	—

KM# 157.1 250 FRANCS (250 Frank)
25.0000 g., 0.8350 Silver .6711 oz. ASW, 36.5 mm. **Subject:** Silver Jubilee of King Baudouin **Obv:** Head of Baudouin, left, legend in French **Obv. Legend:** ROI DES BELGES **Rev:** Crowned large "B", denomination below **Edge:** Reeded **Note:** Mint mark - Angel head. Mintmaster Vogeleer's privy mark - Bird.

Date	Mintage	F	VF	XF	Unc	BU
ND(1976)	1,000,000	—	—	BV	9.50	—
Note: Large B, slant 5						
ND(1976)	Inc. above	—	BV	12.00	20.00	—
Note: Small B, upright 5						

KM# 157.2 250 FRANCS (250 Frank)
25.0000 g., 0.8350 Silver .6711 oz. ASW, 36.5 mm. **Edge:** Stars **Note:** Mint mark - Angel head. Mintmaster Vogeleer's privy mark - Bird.

Date	Mintage	F	VF	XF	Unc	BU
ND(1976) Prooflike	100,000	—	—	—	15.00	—

KM# 158.1 250 FRANCS (250 Frank)
25.0000 g., 0.8350 Silver .6711 oz. ASW, 36.5 mm. **Obv:** Head of Baudouin, left, legend in Dutch **Obv. Legend:** KONING DER BELGEN **Rev:** Crowned large "B", denomination below **Edge:** Reeded **Note:** Mint mark - Angel head. Mintmaster Vogeleer's privy mark - Bird.

Date	Mintage	F	VF	XF	Unc	BU
ND(1976)	1,000,000	—	—	BV	9.50	—
Note: Large B, slant 5						
ND(1976)	Inc. above	BV	15.00	20.00	30.00	—
Note: Small B, upright 5						

KM# 158.2 250 FRANCS (250 Frank)
25.0000 g., 0.8350 Silver .6711 oz. ASW, 36.5 mm. **Edge:** Stars **Note:** Mint mark - Angel head. Mintmaster Vogeleer's privy mark - Bird.

Date	Mintage	F	VF	XF	Unc	BU
ND(1976) Prooflike	100,000	—	—	—	15.00	—

KM# 195 250 FRANCS (250 Frank)
18.7500 g., 0.9250 Silver .5571 oz. ASW **Subject:** BE-NE-LUX Treaty **Obv:** Head of Albert II, 3/4 facing **Rev:** Three buildings, three sets of arms below, divide denomination and dates, legend on left **Note:** Mint mark - Angel head. Mintmaster R. Coenen's privy mark - Scale.

Date	Mintage	F	VF	XF	Unc	BU
ND(1994)	90,000	—	—	—	15.00	—
ND(1994) Proof	1,800	Value: 50.00				

KM# 199 250 FRANCS (250 Frank)
18.7500 g., 0.9250 Silver .5571 oz. ASW **Subject:** 60th Anniversary - Death of Queen Astrid (car death) **Obv:** Crown above two sets of arms, denomination at bottom **Rev:** Bust of crowned Queen Astrid 1/4 facing right **Note:** Mint mark - Angel head. Mintmaster R. Coenen's privy mark - Scale.

Date	Mintage	F	VF	XF	Unc	BU
ND(1995)	177,000	—	—	—	10.00	—
ND(1995) Proof	25,000	Value: 50.00				

KM# 202 250 FRANCS (250 Frank)
18.7500 g., 0.9250 Silver .5571 oz. ASW **Subject:** 20th Anniversary - King Baudouin Foundation **Obv:** Royal couple and monogram **Rev:** Denomination, stylized design and royal monogram

Date	Mintage	F	VF	XF	Unc	BU
ND(1996)	100,000	—	—	—	15.00	—
ND(1996) Proof	25,000	Value: 35.00				

KM# 207 250 FRANCS (250 Frank)
18.7500 g., 0.9250 Silver .5571 oz. ASW **Subject:** 60th Birthday - Queen Paola **Obv:** Denomination **Rev:** Portrait, left **Designer:** Gretha Jonker **Note:** Mint mark - Angel head. Mintmaster R. Coenen's privy mark - Scale.

Date	Mintage	F	VF	XF	Unc	BU
1997	—	—	—	—	15.00	—
1997 Proof	25,000	Value: 35.00				

KM# 208 250 FRANCS (250 Frank)
18.7500 g., 0.9250 Silver .5571 oz. ASW **Subject:** King Boudewijn - Queen Fabiola **Obv:** Heads of King and Queen, queen in profile facing left, king 1/4 facing left **Rev:** Pelican with nestlings, above denomination, at right, "F" dividing dates at center

Date	Mintage	F	VF	XF	Unc	BU
ND(1998)	—	—	—	—	15.00	—
ND(1998) Proof	25,000	Value: 35.00				

KM# 209 250 FRANCS (250 Frank)
18.7500 g., 0.9250 Silver .5571 oz. ASW **Subject:** 40th Wedding Anniversary - King Albert and Queen Paola **Obv:** King and Queen's conjoining busts left **Rev:** St. Gudule Cathedral and city hall, dates at right, denomination at bottom **Edge:** Reeded

Date	Mintage	F	VF	XF	Unc	BU
ND(1999)	100,000	—	—	—	15.00	—
ND(1999) Proof	25,000	Value: 35.00				

KM# 218 250 FRANCS (250 Frank)
18.7500 g., 0.9250 Silver .5571 oz. ASW **Subject:** Marriage of Prince Philip and Princess Mathilde **Rev:** Two hands joined on a rose

Date	Mintage	F	VF	XF	Unc	BU
1999	200,000	—	—	—	15.00	—
1999 Proof	25,000	Value: 35.00				

KM# 161 500 FRANCS (500 Frank)
Silver Clad Copper-Nickel **Subject:** 150th Anniversary of Independence **Obv:** Five heads within circles, legend and crown divide dates, French legend **Rev:** Legend on map of country, denomination below, French legend **Note:** Mint mark - Angel head. Mintmaster Vogeleer's privy mark - Bird.

Date	Mintage	F	VF	XF	Unc	BU
ND(1980)	1,000,000	—	—	—	9.00	—

KM# 161a 500 FRANCS (500 Frank)
25.0000 g., 0.5100 Silver .4099 oz. ASW **Obv:** French legend **Rev:** French legend **Note:** Mint mark - Angel head. Mintmaster Vogeleer's privy mark - Bird.

Date	Mintage	F	VF	XF	Unc	BU
ND(1980) Proof	53,000	Value: 20.00				

KM# 162 500 FRANCS (500 Frank)
Silver Clad Copper-Nickel **Obv:** Five heads within circles, legend with crown divides dates, Dutch legend **Rev:** Legend on map of country, denomination below, Dutch legend **Note:** Mint mark - Angel head. Mintmaster Vogeleer's privy mark - Bird.

Date	Mintage	F	VF	XF	Unc	BU
ND(1980)	1,000,000	—	—	—	9.00	—

KM# 162a 500 FRANCS (500 Frank)
25.0000 g., 0.5100 Silver .4099 oz. ASW **Rev:** Dutch legend **Note:** Mint mark - Angel Head. Mintmaster Vogeleer's privy mark - Bird.

Date	Mintage	F	VF	XF	Unc	BU
ND(1980) Proof	52,000	Value: 20.00				

KM# 165 500 FRANCS (500 Frank)
25.0000 g., 0.5100 Silver .4099 oz. ASW **Obv:** Five heads within circles, legend with crown divides dates, Dutch legend **Rev:** Legend on map of country, denomination below, Dutch legend **Note:** Mule. Mint mark - Angel head. Mintmaster Vogeleer's privy mark - Bird.

Date	Mintage	F	VF	XF	Unc	BU
1980	—	—	—	—	1,000	—

KM# 178 500 FRANCS (500 Frank)
22.8500 g., 0.8330 Silver .6120 oz. ASW **Subject:** 60th Birthday of King Baudouin **Obv:** Head of King Baudouin, left, two dates below **Rev:** Denomination divides crown and date, Dutch legends

Date	Mintage	F	VF	XF	Unc	BU
1990	475,000	—	—	—	20.00	—
1990 Proof	10,000	Value: 45.00				

KM# 179 500 FRANCS (500 Frank)
22.8500 g., 0.8330 Silver .6120 oz. ASW **Subject:** 60th Birthday of King Baudouin **Obv:** Head of King Boudouin, left, two dates below **Rev:** Denomination divides crown and date, French legends

Date	Mintage	F	VF	XF	Unc	BU
1990	475,000	—	—	—	20.00	—
1990 Proof	10,000	Value: 45.00				

KM# 180 500 FRANCS (500 Frank)
22.8500 g., 0.8330 Silver .6120 oz. ASW **Subject:** 60th Birthday of King Baudouin **Obv:** Head of King Baudouin, left, two dates below **Rev:** Denomination divides crown and date, German legends

Date	Mintage	F	VF	XF	Unc	BU
1990	50,000	—	—	—	20.00	—
1990 Proof	10,000	Value: 45.00				

KM# 196 500 FRANCS (500 Frank)
22.8500 g., 0.8330 Silver .6120 oz. ASW **Subject:** 40th Year of Reign **Obv:** Stylized design around **Rev:** Crown above, denomination, year below, Dutch legend

Date	Mintage	F	VF	XF	Unc	BU
1991	250,000	—	—	—	30.00	—
1991 Proof	10,000	Value: 25.00				

KM# 197 500 FRANCS (500 Frank)
22.8500 g., 0.8330 Silver .6120 oz. ASW **Subject:** 40th Year of Reign **Obv:** Stylized design around **Rev:** Crown above, denomination, year below, French legend

Date	Mintage	F	VF	XF	Unc	BU
1991	250,000	—	—	—	30.00	—
1991 Proof	10,000	Value: 25.00				

KM# 198 500 FRANCS (500 Frank)
22.8500 g., 0.8330 Silver .6120 oz. ASW **Subject:** 40th Year of Reign **Obv:** Stylized design around **Rev:** Crown above, denomination, year below, German legend

Date	Mintage	F	VF	XF	Unc	BU
1991	250,000	—	—	—	30.00	—
1991 Proof	10,000	Value: 25.00				

KM# 186 500 FRANCS (500 Frank)
22.8500 g., 0.8330 Silver .6120 oz. ASW **Subject:** Europalaia - Mexico Exposition **Obv:** Design, legend and denomination within circle **Rev:** Mexico Exposition designs **Note:** Mint mark - Angel head. Mintmaster R. Coenen's privy mark - Scale.

Date	Mintage	F	VF	XF	Unc	BU
ND(1993)	52,000	—	—	—	25.00	—
ND(1993) Proof	8,000	Value: 30.00				

KM# 212 500 FRANCS (500 Frank)
22.8500 g., 0.9250 Silver .6975 oz. ASW **Subject:** Brussels - European Culture Capital **Obv:** Denomination and European map **Rev:** Portraits of Albert and Elizabeth in ruffled collars **Edge:** Plain

Date	Mintage	F	VF	XF	Unc	BU
ND(1999)	200,000	—	—	—	30.00	—
ND(1999) (qp)	30,000	Value: 45.00				

KM# 219 500 FRANCS (500 Frank)
22.8500 g., 0.9250 Silver .6975 oz. ASW, 37 mm. **Subject:** Europe: Charles V **Obv:** Map and denomination **Rev:** Charles V of Spain and building **Edge:** Plain

Date	Mintage	F	VF	XF	Unc	BU
2000 (qp)	40,000	Value: 45.00				
ND(2000)	100,000	—	—	—	30.00	—

KM# 210 5000 FRANCS
15.5500 g., 0.9990 Gold .4994 oz. AGW **Subject:** Brussels - European Culture Capital **Obv:** Denomination and European map **Rev:** Portraits of Albert and Elizabeth in ruffled collars **Edge:** Plain

Date	Mintage	F	VF	XF	Unc	BU
ND(1999) (qp)	2,000	Value: 500				

KM# 220 5000 FRANCS
15.5500 g., 0.9990 Gold .4994 oz. AGW, 29 mm. **Subject:** Europe: Charles V **Obv:** Map and denomination **Rev:** Charles V of Spain with building **Edge:** Plain

Date	Mintage	F	VF	XF	Unc	BU
ND(2000) (qp)	2,000	Value: 500				

TRADE COINAGE

European Currency Units

KM# 166 5 ECU
22.8500 g., 0.8330 Silver .6120 oz. ASW **Subject:** 30th Anniversary - Treaties of Rome **Obv:** Denomination, date and stars within circle **Rev:** Bust of Charles V, right

Date	Mintage	F	VF	XF	Unc	BU
1987	985,000	—	—	—	12.00	—
1987 (qp)	15,000	Value: 70.00				
1988 (qp)	15,000	Value: 70.00				

KM# 183 5 ECU
22.8500 g., 0.8330 Silver .6120 oz. ASW **Obv:** Denomination, date and stars within circle **Rev:** Laureate head of Charlemagne, right

Date	Mintage	F	VF	XF	Unc	BU
1991 (qp)	10,000	Value: 55.00				

KM# 185 5 ECU
22.8500 g., 0.9250 Silver .6796 oz. ASW **Subject:** Belgian Presidency of the E.C. **Obv:** Head of King Baudouin, left **Rev:** Denomination, date and stars within circle

Date	Mintage	F	VF	XF	Unc	BU
1993 (qp)	25,000	Value: 45.00				

KM# 200 5 ECU
22.8500 g., 0.9250 Silver .6796 oz. ASW **Subject:** 50th Anniversary - United Nations

Date	Mintage	F	VF	XF	Unc	BU
1995 (qp)	125,000	Value: 35.00				

KM# 203 5 ECU
22.8500 g., 0.9250 Silver .6796 oz. ASW **Subject:** 50th Anniversary - UNICEF **Obv:** Royal couple, left **Rev:** UNICEF logo

Date	Mintage	F	VF	XF	Unc	BU
1996 (qp)	Est. 40,000	Value: 45.00				

KM# 205 5 ECU
22.8500 g., 0.9250 Silver .6796 oz. ASW **Subject:** 40th Anniversary - Treaty of Rome **Obv:** Portraits of Albert II and Baudouin, left, date at bottom **Rev:** European Union map

Date	Mintage	F	VF	XF	Unc	BU
1997 (qp)	Est. 30,000	Value: 45.00				

KM# 221 5 ECU
22.8500 g., 0.9250 Silver .6796 oz. ASW **Subject:** 50th Anniversary - Human Rights Declaration

Date	Mintage	F	VF	XF	Unc	BU
1998 (qp)	30,000	Value: 45.00				

KM# 172 10 ECU
3.1100 g., 0.9990 Gold .1000 oz. AGW **Rev:** Charles V bust right

Date	Mintage	F	VF	XF	Unc	BU
1989 (qp)	2,000	Value: 200				
1990 (qp)	5,000	Value: 140				

KM# 176 10 ECU
Bi-Metallic 5.30g .900 Gold center in 3.11g .833 Silver ring **Subject:** 60th Birthday of King Baudouin **Rev:** Denomination, date and stars within circle

Date	Mintage	F	VF	XF	Unc	BU
1990 (qp)	42,000	Value: 75.00				

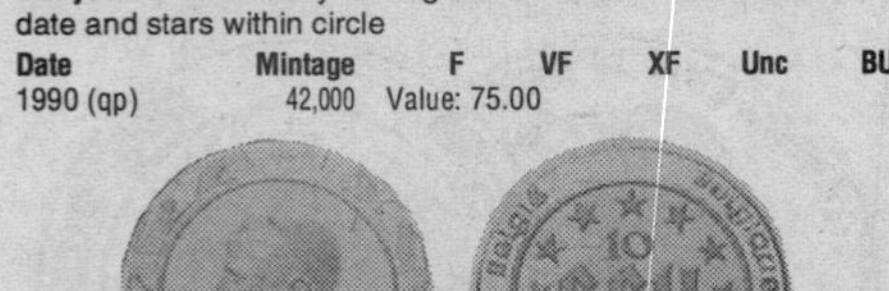

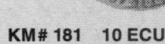

KM# 181 10 ECU
Bi-Metallic 5.30g .900 Gold center in 3.11g .833 Silver ring **Subject:** 40th Year of Reign of King Baudouin **Obv:** Head of King Baudouin, left within circle, two dates below circle **Rev:** Denomination, date and stars within circle

Date	Mintage	F	VF	XF	Unc	BU
1991 (qp)	16,000	Value: 90.00				

KM# 177 20 ECU
Bi-Metallic 10.50g .900 Gold center in 6.22g .833 Silver ring **Subject:** 60th Birthday of King Baudouin **Obv:** Head of King Baudouin, left, within circle, two dates below circle **Rev:** Denomination, date and stars within circle

Date	Mintage	F	VF	XF	Unc	BU
1990 (qp)	35,000	Value: 160				

KM# 182 20 ECU
Bi-Metallic Gold center in Silver ring **Subject:** 40th Year of Reign of King Baudouin

Date	Mintage	F	VF	XF	Unc	BU
1991 (qp)	13,000	Value: 185				

KM# 173 25 ECU
7.7750 g., 0.9990 Gold .2500 oz. AGW **Obv:** Denomination, date and stars within circle **Rev:** Laureate Diocletian bust, right

Date	Mintage	F	VF	XF	Unc	BU
1989	30,000	—	—	BV	170	—
1989 (qp)	2,000	Value: 225				
1990 (qp)	5,000	Value: 180				

KM# 167 50 ECU
17.2800 g., 0.9000 Gold .5000 oz. AGW **Subject:** 30th Anniversary - Treaties of Rome **Obv:** Denomination, date and stars within circle

Date	Mintage	F	VF	XF	Unc	BU
1987	1,502,000	—	—	BV	340	—
1987 (qp)	15,000	Value: 350				
1988 (qp)	15,000	Value: 350				

KM# 174 50 ECU
15.5550 g., 0.9990 Gold .5000 oz. AGW **Obv:** Denomination, date and stars within circle **Rev:** Charlemagne seated on dais, facing

Date	Mintage	F	VF	XF	Unc	BU
1989	60,000	—	—	BV	340	—
1989 (qp)	2,000	Value: 400				
1990 (qp)	5,000	Value: 350				

KM# 184 50 ECU
15.5550 g., 0.9990 Gold .5000 oz. AGW **Rev:** Charlemagne bust right

Date	Mintage	F	VF	XF	Unc	BU
1991 (qp)	4,000	Value: 450				

KM# 213 50 ECU
15.5550 g., 0.9990 Gold .5000 oz. AGW **Subject:** Belgian Presidency of the E.C.

Date	Mintage	F	VF	XF	Unc	BU
1993 (qp)	10,000	Value: 375				

KM# 201 50 ECU
15.5550 g., 0.9990 Gold .5000 oz. AGW **Subject:** 50th Anniversary - United Nations

Date	Mintage	F	VF	XF	Unc	BU
1995 (qp)	2,500	Value: 400				

KM# 204 50 ECU
15.5550 g., 0.9990 Gold .5000 oz. AGW **Subject:** 50th Anniversary - UNICEF **Obv:** Conjoined busts of Royal couple, left, denomination above date at right **Rev:** UNICEF logo

Date	Mintage	F	VF	XF	Unc	BU
1996 (qp)	2,500	Value: 450				

KM# 206 50 ECU
15.5550 g., 0.9990 Gold .5000 oz. AGW **Subject:** 40th Anniversary - Treaty of Rome **Obv:** Conjoined heads of Albert II and Baudouin, left, date below, denomination at right **Rev:** European Union map

Date	Mintage	F	VF	XF	Unc	BU
1997 (qp)	2,500	Value: 500				

KM# 211 50 ECU
15.5550 g., 0.9990 Gold .5000 oz. AGW **Subject:** 50th Anniversary - Human Rights Declaration

Date	Mintage	F	VF	XF	Unc	BU
1998 (qp)	2,500	Value: 500				

KM# 175 100 ECU
31.1030 g., 0.9990 Gold 1.0000 oz. AGW **Obv:** Denomination, date and stars within circle **Rev:** Bust of Maria Theresa, stateswoman, right

Date	Mintage	F	VF	XF	Unc	BU
1989	50,000	—	—	BV	675	—
1989 (qp)	2,000	Value: 800				
1990 (qp)	5,000	Value: 700				

EURO COINAGE

European Union Issues

KM# 224 EURO CENT
2.2700 g., Copper Plated Steel, 16.2 mm. **Ruler:** Albert II **Obv:** Head left within inner circle, stars 3/4 surround, date below **Obv. Designer:** Jan Alfons Keustermans **Rev:** Denomination and globe **Rev. Designer:** Luc Luycx **Edge:** Plain

Date	Mintage	F	VF	XF	Unc	BU
1999	235,240,000	—	—	—	0.35	0.75
1999 Proof	15,000	Value: 12.00				
2000	40,000	—	—	—	37.50	42.50
2000 Proof	15,000	Value: 15.00				

KM# 225 2 EURO CENTS
3.0300 g., Copper Plated Steel, 18.7 mm. **Ruler:** Albert II **Obv:** Head left within circle, stars 3/4 surround, date below **Obv. Designer:** Jan Alfons Keustermans **Rev:** Denomination and globe **Rev. Designer:** Luc Luycx **Edge:** Grooved

Date	Mintage	F	VF	XF	Unc	BU
1999 Proof	15,000	Value: 15.00				

Date	Mintage	F	VF	XF	Unc	BU
1999	40,000	—	—	—	10.00	12.50
2000 Proof	15,000	Value: 12.00				
2000	373,040,000	—	—	—	0.50	1.00

KM# 226 5 EURO CENTS

3.8600 g., Copper Plated Steel, 21.2 mm. **Ruler:** Albert II **Obv:** Head left within circle, stars 3/4 surround, date below **Obv. Designer:** Jan Alfons Keustermans **Rev:** Denomination and globe **Rev. Designer:** Luc Luycx **Edge:** Plain

Date	Mintage	F	VF	XF	Unc	BU
1999 Proof	15,000	Value: 12.00				
1999	300,040,000	—	—	—	0.75	1.25
2000	40,000	—	—	—	10.00	12.50
2000 Proof	15,000	Value: 15.00				

KM# 227 10 EURO CENTS

4.0700 g., Brass, 19.7 mm. **Ruler:** Albert II **Obv:** Head left within inner circle, stars 3/4 surround, date below **Obv. Designer:** Jan Alfons Keustermans **Rev:** Denomination and map **Rev. Designer:** Luc Luycx **Edge:** Reeded

Date	Mintage	F	VF	XF	Unc	BU
1999	180,990,000	—	—	—	0.75	1.25
1999 Proof	15,000	Value: 12.00				
2000	40,000	—	—	—	10.00	12.50
2000 Proof	15,000	Value: 15.00				

KM# 228 20 EURO CENTS

5.7300 g., Brass, 22.1 mm. **Ruler:** Albert II **Obv:** Head left within circle, stars 3/4 surround, date below **Obv. Designer:** Jan Alfons Keustermans **Rev:** Denomination and map **Rev. Designer:** Luc Luycx **Edge:** Notched

Date	Mintage	F	VF	XF	Unc	BU
1999 Proof	15,000	Value: 15.00				
1999	40,000	—	—	—	10.00	12.50
2000	181,040,000	—	—	—	0.75	1.25
2000 Proof	15,000	Value: 12.00				

KM# 229 50 EURO CENTS

7.8100 g., Brass, 24.2 mm. **Ruler:** Albert II **Obv:** Head left within circle, stars 3/4 surround, date below **Obv. Designer:** Jan Alfons Keustermans **Rev:** Denomination and map **Rev. Designer:** Luc Luycx **Edge:** Reeded

Date	Mintage	F	VF	XF	Unc	BU
1999	197,040,000	—	—	—	0.75	1.25
1999 Proof	15,000	Value: 12.00				
2000	40,000	—	—	—	10.00	12.50
2000 Proof	15,000	Value: 15.00				

KM# 230 EURO

7.5000 g., Bi-Metallic Copper-Nickel center in Brass ring, 23.2 mm. **Ruler:** Albert II **Obv:** Head left within circle, stars 3/4 surround, date below **Obv. Designer:** Jan Alfons Keustermans **Rev:** Denomination and map **Rev. Designer:** Luc Luycx **Edge:** Reeded and plain sections

Date	Mintage	F	VF	XF	Unc	BU
1999	160,040,000	—	—	—	2.50	4.50
1999 Proof	15,000	Value: 15.00				
2000	40,000	—	—	—	12.50	15.00
2000 Proof	15,000	Value: 18.00				

KM# 231 2 EURO

8.5200 g., Bi-Metallic Brass center in Copper-Nickel ring, 25.7 mm. **Ruler:** Albert II **Obv:** Head left within circle, stars 3/4 surround, date below **Obv. Designer:** Jan Alfons Keustermans **Rev:** Denomination and map **Rev. Designer:** Luc Luycx **Edge:** Reeded with 2's and stars

Date	Mintage	F	VF	XF	Unc	BU
1999	40,000	—	—	—	12.50	15.00
1999 Proof	15,000	Value: 20.00				
2000 Proof	15,000	Value: 18.00				
2000	120,040,000	—	—	—	3.50	5.50

PATTERNS

Including off metal strikes

KM#	Date	Mintage	Identification	Mkt Val
Pn91	1901	—	Centime. Copper. KM#33.3	250
Pn92	1901	—	5 Centimes. Pewter.	200
Pn93	1901	—	5 Centimes. Brass Plated Nickel.	250
Pn94	1901	—	5 Centimes. Copper-Iron Alloy. KM#45	250
Pn95	1901	—	5 Centimes. Copper. Designer's initials as A.M.; KM#46	275
Pn96	1901	—	5 Centimes. Copper. Thin flan, KM#46	250
Pn97	1901	—	10 Centimes. Nickel. KM#48	260
Pn98	1901	—	10 Centimes. Copper-Nickel.	275
Pn99	1901	—	50 Centimes. Copper. KM#50	250
Pn100	1901	—	50 Centimes. Silver.	450
Pn101	1901	—	Franc. Silver.	500
Pn102	1901	—	Franc. Silver. Head left. Lion with constitution.	600
Pn103	1901	—	2 Francs. Silver.	800
Pn104	1901	—	2 Francs. Silver. Head left. Lion with constitution. Reeded edge.	950
Pn105	1902	—	5 Centimes. Nickel.	100
Pn106	1902	—	5 Centimes. Copper-Nickel. Without center hole; KM#47.	200
Pn107	19xx	—	Franc. Nickel-Brass.	400
Pn108	1902	—	Franc. Silver. Reeded edge. Small portrait, KM#56.1	350
Pn109	1902	—	Franc. Silver. Plain edge. Small portrait, KM#56.1	350
Pn110	1903	—	Franc. Silver. Reeded edge. Small portrait, KM#56.1	350
Pn111	1903	—	Franc. Silver. Plain edge. Small portrait, KM#56.1	350
Pn112	1903	—	Franc. Silver.	—
Pn113	1903	—	Franc. Silver.	—
Pn114	1903	—	Franc. Silver.	—
Pn115	1903	—	Franc. Silver.	—
Pn116	1903	—	Franc. Silver.	—
Pn117	1903	—	Franc. Silver.	—
Pn118	1903	—	Franc. Silver.	—
Pn119	1903	—	Franc. Silver.	—
Pn136	1904	—	50 Centimes. Silver. Plain edge. KM#60.1	—
Pn137	1904	—	50 Centimes. Silver. Reeded edge. KM#60.1	—
Pn138	1904	—	50 Centimes. Silver. Smaller designs, KM#60.1	—
Pn139	1904	—	Franc. Silver. Reeded edge. Thin flan, KM#56.1.	—
Pn140	1904	—	Franc. Silver. Plain edge. Thick flan, KM#56.1.	500
Pn141	1904	—	2 Francs. Silver. Plain edge. KM#58.1.	—
Pn142	1904	—	2 Francs. Silver. Reeded edge. Thin flan, KM#58.1.	—
Pn143	1904	—	2 Francs. Silver. Plain edge. Thick flan, KM#58.1.	600
Pn144	1904	—	2 Francs. Silver. Plain edge. KM#59.1.	—
Pn145	1904	—	2 Francs. Silver. Reeded edge. Thin flan, KM#59.1.	—
Pn146	1904	—	2 Francs. Silver. Plain edge. Thick flan, KM#59.1.	600
Pn147	1906	—	5 Centimes. Nickel-Brass. Restrike, KM#93.	—
Pn148	1907	—	Centime. Copper. Reeded edge. Thick flan, KM#34.1.	—
Pn149	1907	—	25 Centimes. Copper-Nickel.	—
Pn150	1909	—	Franc. Silver. Reeded edge. KM#73.1	400
Pn151	1910	—	5 Centimes. Gold. Not holed, KM#67	1,000
Pn152	1910	—	5 Centimes. Silver. Not holed, KM#67	450
Pn153	1910	—	5 Centimes. Bronze. Not holed, KM#67	175
Pn154	1910	—	5 Centimes. Aluminum. Not holed, KM#67	150
Pn155	1910	—	Franc. Silver. Reeded edge. KM#72.	350
Pn156	1910	—	Franc. Silver. Reeded edge. Thick planchet, KM#72.	450
Pn157	1910	—	Franc. Silver. Reeded edge. Thin planchet, KM#72.	—
Pn158	1910	—	Franc. Silver. Designer's name as Devreese, KM#72.	—
Pn159	1910	—	Franc. Silver. Plain edge. KM#73.1	—
Pn160	1910	—	2 Francs. Silver. Plain edge. KM#74.	425
Pn161	1911	—	Centime. Copper. Restrike.	—
Pn162	1911	—	10 Centimes. Copper. Not holed.	—
Pn163	1911	—	10 Centimes. Brass. Holed.	—
Pn164	1911	—	10 Centimes. Copper-Nickel. Not holed.	—
Pn165	1911	—	10 Centimes. Gold. KM#85.1.	1,600
Pn166	1911	—	10 Centimes. Silver. KM#85.1.	490
Pn167	1911	—	10 Centimes. Bronze. KM#85.1.	—
Pn168	1911	—	10 Centimes. Copper. KM#85.1.	—
Pn169	1911	—	10 Centimes. Aluminum. KM#85.1.	—
Pn170	1911	—	10 Centimes. Gold. KM#86	—
Pn171	1911	—	10 Centimes. Silver. KM#86.	—
Pn172	1911	—	10 Centimes. Bronze. KM#86.	—
Pn173	1911	—	10 Centimes. Copper. KM#86.	—
Pn174	1911	—	10 Centimes. Aluminum. KM#86.	—
Pn175	1911	—	Franc. Silver. Reeded edge. Designer's name as Devreese, KM#73.	—
Pn176	1911	—	Franc. Silver. Plain edge. Designer's name as Devreese, KM#73.	—
Pn177	1911	—	2 Francs. Copper. KM#74.	350
Pn178	1911	—	2 Francs. Gold.	1,500
Pn179	1911	—	10 Francs. Gold. Dutch legend.	2,000
Pn180	1911	—	10 Francs. Gold. French legend.	2,000
Pn181	1911	—	20 Francs. Brass Plated Copper.	—
Pn182	1911	—	20 Francs. Nickel.	—
Pn183	1911	—	20 Francs. Gold. Dutch legend.	2,250
Pn184	1911	—	20 Francs. Gold. French legend.	2,500
Pn185	1911	—	20 Francs. Pewter.	—
Pn186	1911	—	100 Francs. Aluminum-Nickel. Dutch legend.	—
Pn187	1911	—	100 Francs. Aluminum-Nickel. French legend.	—
Pn188	1911	—	100 Francs. Silver. Reeded edge.	—
Pn189	1912/1	—	Centime. Copper. Restrike, ESSAI.	400
Pn190	1912	—	10 Francs. Gold. Dutch legend.	2,000
Pn191	1912	—	10 Francs. Gold. French legend.	2,000
Pn192	1912	—	10 Francs. Gold. Reeded edge.	—
Pn193	1912	3	100 Francs. Gold. Dutch legend.	16,000
Pn194	1912	6	100 Francs. Gold. French legend.	12,500
Pn195	1914	—	2 Francs. Silver. Unadopted portrait. ESSAI/ MONETAIRE/ 1914.	4,000
Pn196	ND(1915)	—	Centime. Zinc.	—
Pn197	1915	—	5 Centimes. Copper-Iron Bi-Metal. Reeded edge. KM#66.	—
Pn198	1915	—	10 Centimes. Copper-Iron Bi-Metal. KM#681.	—
Pn199	1915	—	25 Centimes. Pot Metal.	—
Pn200	1916	—	10 Centimes. Copper-Iron Bi-Metal. KM#81.	—
Pn201	1917	—	10 Centimes. Silver. Plain edge. KM#81.	—
Pn202	1918	—	25 Centimes. Silver. Plain edge. KM#82.	—
Pn203	ND(1918)	—	25 Centimes. Copper-Iron Bi-Metal. 2 branches around legend. ESSAI MONETAIRE. Legend around 25 CES.	400
Pn204	ND(1918)	—	25 Centimes. Zinc. Legend around 25 CENT. Lion, ESSAI.	350
Pn205	ND(1918)	—	25 Centimes. Silver. 16 sided.	—
Pn206	1918	—	50 Centimes. Gold. KM#83.	1,500
Pn207	1918	—	50 Centimes. Silver. KM#83.	—
Pn208	1918	—	50 Centimes. Tan Bronze. KM#83.	—
Pn209	1918	—	50 Centimes. Red Bronze. KM#83.	—
Pn210	1918	—	50 Centimes. Aluminum. KM#83.	—
Pn211	1918	—	50 Centimes. Silver. Not holed.	—
Pn212	1918	—	50 Centimes. Nickel. Not holed.	—
Pn213	1918	—	50 Centimes. Copper-Nickel. Not holed.	—
PnA215	1920	—	20 Francs. Silver. Victory and Peace.	500
Pn214	1920	—	5 Centimes. Nickel. Reeded edge. Not holed, KM#66.	400
Pn215	1920	—	20 Francs. 0.6000 Silver. Victory.	400
Pn216	1921	—	5 Centimes. Nickel. KM#69	—
Pn218	1922	—	50 Centimes. Bronze.	—
Pn226	1922	—	50 Centimes. Bronze. Reeded edge. KM#87	—
Pn217	1922	—	5 Centimes. Nickel-Brass. Restrike, KM#94	—
Pn219	1922	—	50 Centimes. Silver. Plain edge. KM#87	—
Pn220	1922	—	50 Centimes. Bronze. Plain edge. KM#87	—
Pn221	1922	—	50 Centimes. Aluminum. Plain edge. KM#87	—
Pn222	1922	—	50 Centimes. Nickel. Plain edge. KM#87	—
Pn223	1922	—	50 Centimes. Copper. Plain edge. KM#87	—
Pn224	1922	—	50 Centimes. Copper-Tin Alloy. Plain edge. KM#87	—
Pn225	1922	—	50 Centimes. Silver. Reeded edge. KM#87	—
Pn227	1922	—	50 Centimes. Aluminum. Reeded edge. KM#87	—
Pn228	1922	—	50 Centimes. Nickel. Reeded edge. KM#87	—
Pn229	1922	—	50 Centimes. Copper. Reeded edge. KM#87	—
Pn230	1922	—	50 Centimes. Copper-Tin Alloy. Reeded edge. KM#87	—
Pn231	1922	—	50 Centimes. Silver. Plain edge. KM#88	—
Pn232	1922	—	50 Centimes. Bronze. Plain edge. KM#88	—
Pn233	1922	—	50 Centimes. Aluminum. Plain edge. KM#88	—
Pn234	1922	—	50 Centimes. Copper. Plain edge. KM#88	—

KM#	Date	Mintage	Identification	Mkt Val
Pn235	1922	—	50 Centimes. Copper-Tin Alloy. Plain edge. KM#88	—
Pn236	1922	—	50 Centimes. Silver. Reeded edge. KM#88	—
Pn237	1922	—	50 Centimes. Bronze. Reeded edge. KM#88	—
Pn238	1922	—	50 Centimes. Aluminum. Reeded edge. KM#88	—
Pn239	1922	—	50 Centimes. Copper. Reeded edge. KM#88	—
Pn240	1922	—	50 Centimes. Copper-Tin Alloy. Reeded edge. KM#88	—
Pn241	1922	—	Franc. Silver. Plain edge. KM#89	800
Pn242	1922	—	Franc. Bronze. Plain edge. KM#89	—
Pn243	1922	—	Franc. Aluminum. Plain edge. KM#89	—
Pn244	1922	—	Franc. Copper. Plain edge. KM#89	—
Pn245	1922	—	Franc. Copper-Tin Alloy. Plain edge. KM#89	—
Pn246	1922	—	Franc. Silver. Reeded edge. KM#89	750
Pn247	1922	—	Franc. Bronze. Reeded edge. KM#89	—
Pn248	1922	—	Franc. Aluminum. Reeded edge. KM#89	—
Pn249	1922	—	Franc. Copper. Reeded edge. KM#89	—
Pn250	1922	—	Franc. Copper-Tin Alloy. Reeded edge. KM#89	—
Pn251	1922	—	Franc. Silver. Plain edge. KM#90	—
Pn252	1922	—	Franc. Bronze. Plain edge. KM#90	—
Pn253	1922	—	Franc. Aluminum. Plain edge. KM#90	—
Pn254	1922	—	Franc. Nickel. Plain edge. Irregular flan, KM#90.	—
Pn255	1922	—	Franc. Copper. Plain edge. KM#90.	—
Pn256	1922	—	Franc. Copper-Tin Alloy. Plain edge. KM#90.	—
Pn257	1922	—	Franc. Silver. Reeded edge. KM#90.	—
Pn258	1922	—	Franc. Bronze. Reeded edge. KM#90.	—
Pn259	1922	—	Franc. Aluminum. Reeded edge. KM#90.	—
Pn260	1922	—	Franc. Copper. Reeded edge. KM#90.	—
Pn261	1922	—	Franc. Copper-Tin Alloy. Reeded edge. KM#90.	—
Pn262	1922	—	Franc. Nickel. KM#89. KM#90.	—
Pn263	1923	—	2 Francs. Silver. ESSAI, KM#91.1.	—
Pn264	1923	—	2 Francs. Bronze. ESSAI, KM#91.1.	—
Pn265	1923	—	2 Francs. Aluminum. ESSAI, KM#91.1.	—
Pn266	1923	—	2 Francs. Copper-Tin Alloy. ESSAI, KM#91.1.	—
Pn267	1926	—	5 Francs. Red Bronze. ESSAI	—
Pn268	1926	—	5 Francs. Silver. Head left. Wreath with 5 FR within.	—
Pn269	1926	—	5 Francs. Bronze. Head left. Wreath with 5 FR within.	—
Pn270	1926	—	5 Francs. Nickel. Head left. Wreath with 5 FR within.	—
Pn271	1926	—	5 Francs. Copper-Tin Alloy. Head left. Wreath with 5 FR within.	—
Pn272	1926	—	5 Francs. Silver. Crown above 5 Francs.	—
Pn273	1926	—	5 Francs. Bronze. Crown above 5 Francs.	—
Pn274	1926	—	5 Francs. Nickel. Crown above 5 Francs.	—
Pn275	1926	—	5 Francs. Copper-Tin Alloy. Crown above 5 Francs.	—
Pn276	1926	—	5 Francs. Silver. Crown above oak wreath, 5 Francs within.	—
Pn277	1926	—	5 Francs. Bronze. Crown above oak wreath, 5 Francs within.	—
Pn278	1926	—	5 Francs. Copper-Tin Alloy. Crown above oak wreath, 5 Francs within.	—
Pn279	1926	—	5 Francs. Gold. Wreath, UN BELGA CINQ FRANCS.	1,750
Pn280	1926	—	5 Francs. Silver. Wreath, UN BELGA CINQ FRANCS.	—
Pn281	1926	—	5 Francs. Bronze. Wreath, UN BELGA CINQ FRANCS.	—
Pn282	1926	—	5 Francs. Nickel. Wreath, UN BELGA CINQ FRANCS.	—
Pn283	1926	—	5 Francs. Copper-Tin Alloy. Wreath, UN BELGA CINQ FRANCS.	—
Pn284	1926	—	5 Francs. Gold. Lion in shield, SF flanking.	1,750
Pn285	1926	—	5 Francs. Silver. Lion in shield, SF flanking.	—
Pn286	1926	—	5 Francs. Bronze. Lion in shield, SF flanking.	—
Pn287	1926	—	5 Francs. Nickel. Lion in shield, SF flanking.	—
Pn288	1926	—	5 Francs. Copper-Tin Alloy. Lion in shield, SF flanking.	—
Pn289	1927	—	5 Francs. Silver. Head by Bonnetain. 2 laurel branches, UN BELGA/OU/5 FRANCS/ESSAI.	425
Pn290	1927	—	5 Francs. Copper. Head by Bonnetain. 2 laurel branches, UN BELGA/OU/5 FRANCS/ESSAI.	425
Pn291	1927	—	5 Francs. Copper-Tin Alloy. Head by Bonnetain. 2 laurel branches, UN BELGA/OU/5 FRANCS/ESSAI.	425
Pn292	1927	—	5 Francs. Nickel.	—
Pn293	1929	—	5 Centimes. Copper-Nickel. Not holed, KM#67.	—
Pn294	1929	—	10 Centimes. Nickel. Not holed, ESSAI, KM#85.1.	—
Pn295	1929	—	10 Centimes. Gold. KM#85.1.	1,000
Pn296	1929	—	10 Centimes. Silver. KM#85.1.	—
Pn297	1929	—	10 Centimes. Bronze. KM#85.1.	—
Pn298	1929	—	10 Centimes. Copper. KM#85.1.	—
Pn299	1929	—	10 Centimes. Aluminum. KM#85.1.	—
Pn300	1929	—	25 Centimes. Gold. ESSAI, KM#68.1.	1,200
Pn301	1929	—	25 Centimes. Silver. ESSAI, KM#68.1.	—
Pn302	1929	—	25 Centimes. Bronze. ESSAI, KM#68.1.	—
Pn303	1929	—	25 Centimes. Copper. ESSAI, KM#68.1.	—
Pn304	1929	—	25 Centimes. Aluminum. ESSAI, KM#68.1.	—
Pn305	1929	—	25 Centimes. Gold. ESSAI, KM#69.	1,200
Pn306	1929	—	25 Centimes. Silver. ESSAI, KM#69.	—
Pn307	1929	—	25 Centimes. Bronze. ESSAI, KM#69.	—
Pn308	1929	—	25 Centimes. Copper. ESSAI, KM#69.	—
Pn309	1929	—	25 Centimes. Aluminum. ESSAI, KM#69.	—
Pn310	1929	—	5 Francs. Nickel.	—
Pn311	1929	—	5 Francs. Bronze.	—
Pn312	1930	—	2 Francs. Copper. KM#92.	—
Pn313	1930	—	2 Francs. Matte Bronze. KM#92.	—
Pn314	1930	—	10 Francs. Brass.	250
Pn315	1930	—	20 Francs. Silver.	—
Pn316	1931	—	Franc. Nickel.	—
Pn317	1931	—	20 Francs. Bronze. French legend.	250
Pn318	1931	—	20 Francs. Bronze. Dutch legend.	250
Pn319	1932	—	5 Centimes. Copper-Nickel.	—
Pn320	1932	—	5 Centimes. Dupriez's design.	—
Pn321	1932	—	5 Centimes. Copper. Not holed, KM#93.	—
Pn322	1932	—	50 Centimes. Nickel. KM#87. KM#88. Reeded edge.	—
Pn323	1932	—	50 Centimes. Nickel. KM#87. KM#88. Plain edge.	—
Pn324	1933	—	5 Francs. Silver.	—
Pn325	1933	—	10 Francs. Nickel.	—
Pn326	1933	—	10 Francs. Nickel. DEUX BELGAS/OU/10 FRANCS.	—
Pn327	1933	—	50 Francs. Silver. 10/BELGAS/50/ FRANCS within 2 oak branches. Plain edge.	—
Pn328	1933	—	50 Francs. Silver. Cross ornaments on edge.	—
Pn329	1933	—	50 Francs. Silver. Reeded edge.	—
Pn330	1933	—	50 Francs. Silver. Small head of Albert within pellet circle. Value within 2 laurel branches.	—
Pn331	1933	—	50 Francs. Silver. Bust by Bonnetain. Value within laurel branches.	—
Pn332	1933	—	100 Francs. Silver. Bust by Bonnetain. 20/BELGAS/100/ FRANCS within 2 laurel branches.	—
Pn333	1933	—	100 Francs. By Devreese	—
Pn334	1933	—	100 Francs. L'UNION FAIT LA FORCE/100 FRS. By Devreese	—
Pn335	1933	—	100 Francs. Bronze. 20/BELGAS/100 FRANCS between 2 branches.	—
Pn336	1933	—	500 Francs. Bronze. 20/BELGAS/500/FRANCS between laurel and oak branches.	250
Pn337	1933	—	500 Francs. Nickel.	—
Pn338	1934	—	5 Francs. Bronze.	100
Pn339	1934	—	20 Francs. Bronze.	125
Pn340	1935	—	Franc. Copper-Tin Alloy. Reeded edge.	—
Pn341	1935	—	Franc. Nickel. Reeded edge.	—
Pn342	1935	—	Franc. Silver. Allegory of Belgium kneeling left; BELGIQUE \ BELGIE at sides. Caduceus between IF and date. Plain edge.	—
Pn343	1935	—	Franc. Silver. Allegory of Belgium kneeling left. Plain edge.	—
Pn344	1935	—	Franc. Copper. Allegory of Belgium kneeling left. Plain edge.	—
Pn345	1935	—	Franc. Nickel. Allegory of Belgium kneeling left. Plain edge.	—
Pn346	1935	—	40 Francs. 0.6800 Silver. Lettered edge.	14,000
Pn347	1935	—	40 Francs. Silver. Plain edge. Restrike.	—
Pn348	1935	—	40 Francs. Copper-Tin Alloy. Lettered edge. Expo commemorative.	—
Pn349	1935	—	40 Francs. Gold. Reeded edge. Expo commemorative.	—
Pn350	1935	—	40 Francs. Silver. Reeded edge. Expo commemorative.	—
Pn351	1935	—	40 Francs. Bronze. Reeded edge. Expo commemorative.	—
Pn352	1935	—	40 Francs. Copper. Reeded edge. Expo commemorative.	—
Pn353	1935	—	40 Francs. Copper-Tin Alloy. Reeded edge. Expo commemorative.	—
Pn354	1935	—	40 Francs. Nickel. Reeded edge. Expo commemorative.	—
Pn355	1935	—	40 Francs. Aluminum. Reeded edge. Expo commemorative.	—
Pn356	1935	—	40 Francs. Gold. Expo commemorative, thin planchet	2,000
Pn357	1935	—	40 Francs. Silver. Expo commemorative, thin planchet	800
Pn358	1935	—	40 Francs. Bronze. Expo commemorative, thin planchet	400
Pn359	1935	—	40 Francs. Copper. Expo commemorative, thin planchet	400
Pn360	1935	—	40 Francs. Copper-Tin Alloy. Expo commemorative.	400
Pn361	1935	—	40 Francs. Nickel. Expo commemorative, thin planchet	450
Pn362	1935	—	40 Francs. Aluminum. Expo commemorative, thin planchet	400
Pn363	1935	—	50 Francs. 0.6800 Silver. Plain edge.	600
Pn364	1935	—	50 Francs. Silver. Plain edge. KM#106.1.	—
Pn365	1935	—	50 Francs. Copper. Plain edge. KM#106.1.	—
Pn366	1935	—	50 Francs. Copper-Tin Alloy. Plain edge. KM#106.1.	—
Pn367	1935	—	50 Francs. Copper-Tin Alloy. Edge inscription. KM#106.1.	—
Pn368	1935	—	50 Francs. Gold. Reeded edge. KM#106.1.	—
Pn369	1935	—	50 Francs. Silver. Reeded edge. KM#106.1.	—
Pn370	1935	—	50 Francs. Bronze. Reeded edge. KM#106.1.	—
Pn371	1935	—	50 Francs. Copper. Reeded edge. KM#106.1.	—
Pn372	1935	—	50 Francs. Copper-Tin Alloy. Reeded edge. KM#106.1.	—
Pn373	1935	—	50 Francs. Aluminum. Reeded edge. KM#106.1.	—
Pn374	1935	—	50 Francs. Silver. Plain edge. KM#107.1.	—
Pn375	1935	—	50 Francs. Copper-Tin Alloy. Plain edge. KM#107.1.	—
Pn376	1935	—	50 Francs. Bronze. Edge inscription, KM#107.1.	—
Pn377	1935	—	50 Francs. Copper-Tin Alloy. Reeded edge. KM#107.1.	—
Pn378	1936	—	5 Francs. Nickel.	—
Pn379	1938	—	5 Centimes. Copper-Tin Alloy. KM#110.1	—
Pn380	1938	—	5 Centimes. Bronze. KM#110.1	—
Pn381	1938	—	5 Centimes. Tin. Not holed, KM#110.1	—
Pn382	1938	—	10 Centimes. Copper-Tin Alloy. Thin planchet, KM#112.	—
Pn383	1938	—	10 Centimes. Copper-Tin Alloy. Thick planchet, KM#112.	—
Pn384	1938	—	10 Centimes. Bronze. KM#112.	—
Pn385	1938	—	10 Centimes. Copper-Tin Alloy. Large letters, not holed.	—
Pn386	1938	—	25 Centimes. Nickel. Large shields.	—
Pn387	1938	—	25 Centimes. Copper-Tin Alloy. Not holed.	—
Pn388	1938	—	20 Francs. Silver.	—
Pn389	1938	—	20 Francs. Silver. Similar to KM#121.	—
Pn390	1938	—	20 Francs. Bronze. Similar to KM#121.	—
Pn391	1938	—	20 Francs. Copper. Similar to KM#121.	—
Pn392	1938	—	20 Francs. Copper-Tin Alloy. Similar to KM#121.	—
Pn393	1938	—	20 Francs. Nickel. Similar to KM#121.	—
Pn394	1938	—	20 Francs. Silver.	—
Pn395	1938	—	20 Francs. Copper-Tin Alloy.	—
Pn396	1938	—	20 Francs. Tin.	—
Pn397	1938	—	20 Francs. Silver. Thick planchet.	1,000
Pn398	1938	—	20 Francs. Copper-Tin Alloy. Thick planchet.	500
Pn399	1938	—	20 Francs. Tin. Thick planchet.	—
Pn400	1938	—	20 Francs. Silver. Small portrait.	—
Pn401	1938	—	20 Francs. Bronze. Small portrait.	—
Pn402	1938	—	20 Francs. Copper-Tin Alloy. Small portrait.	—
Pn403	1938	—	20 Francs. Tin. Small portrait.	—
Pn404	1938	—	50 Francs. Silver. Plain edge. KM#121.1.	—
Pn405	1938	—	50 Francs. Copper-Tin Alloy. Plain edge. KM#121.1.	—
Pn406	1938	—	50 Francs. Copper. Plain edge.	—
Pn407	1938	—	50 Francs. Copper. Plain edge. ESSAI	—
Pn408	1939	—	25 Centimes. Copper-Tin Alloy. Not holed, KM#114.1.	—
Pn409	1939	—	25 Centimes. Bronze. KM#114.1.	—
Pn410	1939	—	Franc. Nickel. KM#120.	—
Pn411	1939	—	Franc. Bronze. Reeded edge. KM#120.	—
Pn412	1939	—	Franc. Copper-Tin Alloy. Reeded edge. KM#120.	—
Pn413	1939	—	50 Francs. Copper-Tin Alloy. Lettered edge. KM#121.1.	—
Pn414	1939	—	50 Francs. Bronze. Lettered edge. KM#121.1.	—
Pn415	1940	—	Franc. Nickel. Restrike, KM#119.	—
Pn416	1940	—	5 Francs. Copper-Tin Alloy. Portrait by Rau, Leopold III ROI DE BELGES. 5/FRANCS/1940 between oak and laurel branches.	—
Pn417	1940	—	5 Francs. Copper-Tin Alloy. Portrait by Rau. Thick planchet.	400
Pn418	1940	—	5 Francs. Copper-Tin Alloy. Portrait by Rau. KM#108.1.	—
Pn419	1940	—	5 Francs. Copper-Tin Alloy. Portrait by Rau. KM#108.1. Thick planchet.	400
Pn420	1940	—	5 Francs. Copper-Tin Alloy. Leopold III.	—
Pn421	1940	—	5 Francs. Copper-Tin Alloy. Leopold III. Thick planchet.	400
Pn422	1940	—	5 Francs. Nickel. Leopold III. Reeded edge.	—
Pn423	1940	—	5 Francs. Nickel. Leopold III. Reeded edge. Thick planchet.	400
Pn424	1940	—	5 Francs. Silver. Leopold III. KM#108.1.	—
Pn425	1940	—	5 Francs. Silver. Leopold III. KM#108.1. Thick planchet.	400
Pn426	1940	—	5 Francs. Copper-Tin Alloy. Leopold III, ROI DES BELGES. KM#108.1. Thick planchet.	400

KM#	Date	Mintage	Identification	Mkt Val
Pn427	1941	—	10 Centimes. Silver. Reeded edge. KM#130.	—
Pn428	1941	—	5 Francs. Silver. Reeded edge. KM#130.	—
Pn429	1944	—	2 Francs. Silver. KM#133.	—
Pn430	1948	—	100 Francs. Copper. ESSAI, KM#138.	—
Pn431	1948	—	100 Francs. Copper. ESSAI, KM#139.1.	—
Pn432	1949	—	5 Francs. Copper. KM#134.1.	—
Pn433	1949	—	5 Francs. Copper. KM#135.1.	—
Pn434	1949	—	50 Francs. Bronze.	—
Pn435	1949	—	100 Francs. Silver.	—
Pn436	1949	—	100 Francs. Silver.	—
Pn437	1949	—	1000 Francs. Bronze. Plain edge.	—
Pn438	1949	—	1000 Francs. Silver.	900
Pn439	1949	—	1000 Francs. Gold. ESSAI	10,920
Pn440	ND	—	1000 Francs. Bronze.	—
Pn441	1949	—	1000 Francs. Bronze. Milled edge.	—
Pn442	1951	—	20 Francs. Copper. ESSAI, KM#140.1	—
Pn443	1951	—	20 Francs. Copper. ESSAI, KM#141.1	—
Pn444	1951	—	20 Francs. Copper. ESSAI, KM#136.1.	—
Pn445	1951	—	50 Francs. Copper. ESSAI, KM#137	—
Pn446	1952	—	Franc. Copper. KM#142.1	—
Pn447	1952	—	Franc. Copper. KM#143.1	—

PIEFORTS

KM#	Date	Mintage	Identification	Mkt Val
P4	1912	—	10 Francs. Gold. Plain edge.	2,500
P5	1912	—	10 Francs. Silver. Plain edge.	850
P6	1918	—	50 Centimes. Zinc. Plain edge. Not holed, KM#83.	900
P7	1920	—	25 Centimes. Nickel. Plain edge. KM#68.1.	—
P8	1926	—	5 Centimes. Copper. Plain edge. Not holed, KM#66.	—
P9	1935	—	Franc. Silver.	1,000
P10	1935	—	Franc. Copper.	400
P11	1935	—	Franc. Nickel.	250
P12	1989	—	100 Ecu. Gold. KM#175	1,000

TRIAL STRIKES

KM#	Date	Mintage	Identification	Mkt Val
TS5	1903	—	Franc. Pewter. Uniface. Rectangle planchet.	1,000
TS6	1904	—	Franc. Pewter. Uniface. Rectangle planchet.	1,000
TS7	ND(1904)	—	2 Francs. Lead. Uniface.	50.00
TS8	1910	—	2 Francs. Portrait, uniface.	—
TS9	1910	—	2 Francs. KM#74. Uniface.	—
TS10	1911	—	20 Francs. Gold. Error obverse.	1,250
TS11	1911	—	20 Francs. Aluminum. Error obverse.	600
TS12	1918	—	50 Centimes. Klippe.	1,000
TS13	1926	—	5 Francs. Nickel. Klippe.	1,000
TS14	1933	—	10 Francs. Silver. Legend within 2 branches.	—
TS15	1933	—	50 Francs. Silver. Irregular flan.	—
TS16	1949	—	1000 Francs. Red Copper. Klippe.	400
TS17	1949	—	1000 Francs. Yellow Copper. Klippe.	400
TS18	1949	—	1000 Francs. Red Copper. Klippe.	400
TS19	1949	—	1000 Francs. Yellow Copper. Klippe.	400
TS20	1949	—	1000 Francs. Silver. Klippe.	800

"FDC" SETS

KM#	Date	Mintage	Identification	Issue Price	Mkt Val
SS1	1970 (5)	5,000	KM#135.1, 143.1, 149.1, 154.1, 156.1 DU	0.60	225
SS2	1970 (5)	5,000	KM#134.1, 142.1, 148.1, 153.1, 155.1 FR	0.60	225
SS3	1971 (5)	10,000	KM#135.1, 143.1, 149.1, 154.1, 156.1 DU	0.63	75.00
SS4	1971 (5)	10,000	KM#134.1, 142.1, 148.1, 153.1, 155.1 FR	0.63	75.00
SS5	1972 (5)	10,000	KM#135.1, 143.1, 149.1, 154.1, 156.1 DU	0.70	85.00
SS6	1972 (5)	10,000	KM#134.1, 142.1, 148.1, 153.1, 155.1 FR	0.70	85.00
SS7	1973 (5)	16,778	KM#135.1, 143.1, 149.1, 154.1, 156.1 DU	0.80	40.00
SS8	1973 (5)	15,000	KM#134.1, 142.1, 148.1, 153.1, 155.1 FR	0.80	40.00
SS9	1974 (5)	20,608	KM#135.1, 143.1, 149,.1 154.1, 156.1 DU	1.10	22.00
SS10	1974 (5)	19,000	KM#134.1, 142.1, 148.1, 153.1, 155.1 FR	1.10	22.00
SS11	1975 (10)	45,752	KM#135.1, 143.1, 149.1, 154.1, 156.1 DU, 134.1, 142.1, 148.1, 153.1, 155.1 FR	2.50	10.00
SS12	1976 (10)	15,000	KM#135, 143, 149, 156, 158.1 DU, 134, 142, 148, 155, 157.1 FR	20.75	60.00
SS13	1977 (8)	45,938	KM#135, 143, 149, 156 DU, 134, 142, 148, 155 FR	2.65	6.00
SS14	1978 (8)	46,237	KM#135, 143, 149, 156 DU, 134, 142, 148, 155 FR	4.00	8.00
SS15	1979 (8)	49,997	KM#135, 143, 149, 156 DU, 134, 142, 148, 155 FR	4.00	6.00
SS16	1980 (8)	60,000	KM#135, 143, 149, 160 DU, 134, 142, 148, 159 FR	4.00	5.00
SS17	1981 (8)	54,331	KM#135, 143, 149, 160 DU, 134, 142, 148, 159 FR	3.25	8.00

MINT SETS

KM#	Date	Mintage	Identification	Issue Price	Mkt Val
MS1	1989 (10)	60,000	KM#149, 160, 164, 169, 171 DU; 148, 159, 163, 168, 170 FR	11.00	35.00
MS2	1990 (10)	60,000	KM#149, 160, 164, 169, 171 DU; 148, 159, 163, 168, 170 FR	13.00	30.00
MS3	1991 (10)	60,000	KM#149, 160, 164, 169, 171 DU; 148, 159, 163, 168, 170 FR	13.00	25.00
MS4	1991 (3)	—	KM#196-198	—	30.00
MS5	1992 (10)	60,000	KM#149, 160, 164, 169, 171 DU; 148, 159,	15.00	40.00
MS6	1993 (10)	40,000	KM#149, 160, 164, 169, 171 DU; 148, 159, 163, 168, 170 FR	15.00	15.00
MS7	1994 (10)	60,000	KM#148 1, 149.1, 187-194, medal	15.00	15.00
MS8	1995 (10)	60,000	KM#148.1, 149.1, 187-194, medal	15.00	25.00
MS9	1996 (10)	60,000	KM#148.1, 149.1, 187-194, medal	15.00	17.00
MS10	1997 (10)	60,000	KM#148.1, 149.1, 187-194, medal	—	25.00
MS11	1998 (10)	60,000	KM#148.1, 149.1, 187-194	15.00	20.00
MS12	1999 (10)	60,000	KM#148.1, 149.1, 187-194	15.00	30.00
MS13	2000 (10)	60,000	KM#148.1, 149.1, 187-194	15.00	30.00
MS14	2001 (10)	60,000	KM#148.1, 149.1, 187-194	15.00	30.00

PROOF SETS

KM#	Date	Mintage	Identification	Issue Price	Mkt Val
PS1	1987 (2)	15,000	KM#166-167	395	350
PS2	1988 (2)	15,000	KM#166-167	395	350
PS3	1989 (4)	2,000	KM#172-175	1,300	1,650
PS4	1990 (4)	5,000	KM#172-175	1,300	900
PS5	1990 (3)	10,000	KM#178-180	100	120
PS6	1991 (3)	10,000	KM#196-198	100	85.00
PS7	2000 (3)	10,000	KM#215-217	75.00	140
PS8	1999 (8)	15,000	KM#224-231	80.00	85.00
PS9	2000 (3)	15,000	KM#224-231	80.00	85.00

GHENT

GERMAN OCCUPATION WWI

TOKEN COINAGE

KM# Tn1 50 CENTIMES

Brass-Plated Iron **Obv:** Rampant lion, left, within inner circle **Rev:** Denomination within inner circle, box surrounds **Shape:** Square **Note:** Similar to KM#Tn1a, thin "5C".

Date	Mintage	F	VF	XF	Unc	BU
1915	512,000	7.00	15.00	25.00	40.00	125

KM# Tn1a 50 CENTIMES

Brass-Plated Iron **Rev:** Thick "50"

Date	Mintage	F	VF	XF	Unc	BU
1915	Inc. above	7.00	15.00	25.00	40 00	125

KM# Tn2 FRANKEN

Brass-Plated Iron **Obv:** Rampant lion, left, within inner circle **Rev:** Denomination within inner circle, box surrounds

Date	Mintage	F	VF	XF	Unc	BU
1915	370,000	7.00	15.00	25.00	40.00	125

KM# Tn2a FRANKEN

Brass-Plated Iron **Rev:** 11. 1919 instead of 1.1. 1919

Date	Mintage	F	VF	XF	Unc	BU
1915	Inc. above	8.00	17.00	26.00	45.00	150

KM# Tn3 FRANKEN

Gilt Copper **Obv:** Lion in circle, STAD GENT VILLE DE GAND around **Rev:** 1915 1 FR in circle, UIT BETAALBAAR 1 JANUARI 1918 REMBOURSABLE 1 JANVIER 1920 along sides of square **Shape:** Square **Note:** This token was struck in 1920 for the benefit of charity.

Date	Mintage	F	VF	XF	Unc	BU
1915	—	50.00	200	350	600	1,100

KM# Tn4 2 FRANKEN

Brass-Plated Iron **Obv:** Rampant lion, left, within inner circle **Rev:** Denomination within inner circle, box surrounds **Shape:** Square

Date	Mintage	F	VF	XF	Unc	BU
1915	314,000	10.00	25.00	40.00	60.00	150

KM# Tn5 2 FRANKEN

Gilt Copper **Obv:** Arms in circle, STAD GENT FIDES ET AMOR around **Rev:** 1928 2 FRANK in circle, UIT BETAAL BAAR JANUARI 1922 PAX ET LABOR around **Note:** This token was struck in 1920 for the benefit of charity.

Date	Mintage	F	VF	XF	Unc	BU
1918	—	45.00	175	300	550	900

KM# Tn6 5 FRANKEN

Brass-Plated Iron **Obv:** Crowned shield within circle **Rev:** Denomination within inner circle, box surrounds

Date	Mintage	F	VF	XF	Unc	BU
1917	108,000	17.50	30.00	45.00	100	175

KM# Tn7 5 FRANKEN

Brass-Plated Iron **Obv:** Crowned arms within circle **Rev:** Denomination below date, within circle

Date	Mintage	F	VF	XF	Unc	BU
1918	339,000	15.00	27.00	40.00	90.00	160

BELIZE (British Honduras)

Belize, formerly British Honduras, but now an independent member of the Commonwealth of Nations, is situated in Central America south of Mexico and east and north of Guatemala, with an area of 8,867 sq. mi. (22,960 sq. km.) and a population of *242,000. Capital: Belmopan. Tourism now augments Belize's economy, in addition to sugar, citrus fruits, chicle and hardwoods which are exported.

The area, site of the ancient Mayan civilization, was sighted by Columbus in 1502, and settled by shipwrecked English seamen in 1638. British buccaneers settled the former capital of Belize in the 17th century. Britain claimed administrative right over the area after the emancipation of Central America from Spain. In 1825, Imperial coins were introduced into the colony and were rated against the Spanish dollar and Honduran currency. It was declared a colony subordinate to Jamaica in 1862 and was established as the separate Crown Colony of British Honduras in 1884. In May, 1885 an order in Council authorized coins for the colony, with the first shipment arriving in July. While the Guatemalan peso was originally the standard of value, in 1894 the colony changed to the gold standard, based on the U.S. gold dollar. The anti-British Peoples United Party, which attained power in 1954, won a constitution, effective in 1964 which established self-government under a British appointed governor. British Honduras became Belize on June 1, 1973, following the passage of a surprise bill by the Peoples United Party, but the constitutional relationship with Britain remained unchanged.

In Dec. 1975, the U.N. General Assembly adopted a resolution supporting the right of the people of Belize to self-determination, and asking Britain and Guatemala to renew their negotiations on the future of Belize. Independence was obtained on Sept. 21, 1981. Elizabeth II is Head of State as Queen of Belize.

RULERS

British, until 1981

MINT MARKS

H - Birmingham Mint

No mm - Royal Mint

***NOTE**: From 1975-1985 the Franklin Mint produced coinage in up to 3 different qualities. Qualities of issue are designated in ( ) after each date and are defined as follows:

(M) MATTE - Normal circulation strike or a dull finish produced by sandblasting special uncirculated (polish finish) or proof quality dies.

(U) SPECIAL UNCIRCULATED - Polished or proof-like in appearance without any frosted features.

(P) PROOF - The highest quality obtainable having mirror-like fields and frosted features.

MONETARY SYSTEM

Commencing 1864

100 Cents = 1 Dollar

BRITISH COLONIAL & CONSTITUTIONAL

DECIMAL COINAGE

KM# 33 CENT

Bronze, 19.5 mm. **Obv:** Bust of Queen Elizabeth, right **Obv. Designer:** Cecil Thomas **Rev:** Denomination within circle, date lower right of circle **Shape:** Scalloped

Date	Mintage	F	VF	XF	Unc	BU
1973	400,000	—	—	0.10	0.25	0.60
1974	2,000,000	—	—	0.10	0.20	0.50
1975	Inc. above	—	—	0.10	0.15	0.45
1976	3,000,000	—	—	0.10	0.15	0.45

KM# 33a CENT

0.8000 g., Aluminum, 19.5 mm. **Obv:** Bust of Queen Elizabeth right **Rev:** Denomination within circle **Shape:** Scalloped

Date	Mintage	F	VF	XF	Unc	BU
1976	2,049,999	—	—	0.10	0.25	0.60
1979	2,505,000	—	—	0.10	0.25	0.60
1980	1,505,000	—	—	0.10	0.25	0.60
1982	—	—	—	0.10	0.25	0.60
1983	—	—	—	0.10	0.25	0.60
1986	—	—	—	0.10	0.25	0.60
1987	—	—	—	0.10	0.25	0.60
1989	—	—	—	0.10	0.25	0.60
1991	—	—	—	0.10	0.25	0.60
1992	—	—	—	0.10	0.25	0.60

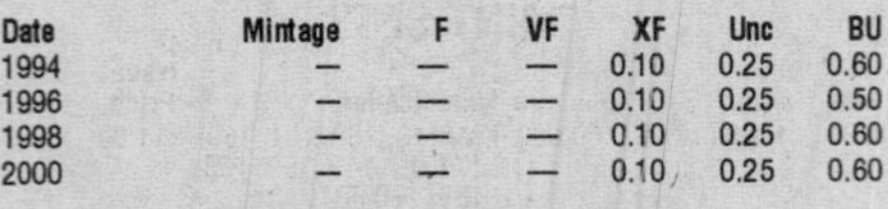

Date	Mintage	F	VF	XF	Unc	BU
1994	—	—	—	0.10	0.25	0.60
1996	—	—	—	0.10	0.25	0.50
1998	—	—	—	0.10	0.25	0.60
2000	—	—	—	0.10	0.25	0.60

KM# 38 CENT

Bronze **Obv:** National arms, date below, within wreath **Rev:** Swallow-tailed kite right, denomination above **Designer:** Michael Rizzello

Date	Mintage	F	VF	XF	Unc	BU
1974FM (M)	225,000	—	—	0.40	0.75	1.50
1974FM (P)	21,000	Value: 1.25				

KM# 38a CENT

3.0200 g., 0.9250 Silver .0898 oz. ASW **Rev:** Swallow-tailed kite

Date	Mintage	F	VF	XF	Unc	BU
1974FM (P)	31,000	Value: 3.50				

KM# 46 CENT

Bronze **Obv:** National arms, date below, within wreath **Rev:** Swallow-tailed kite right, denomination above **Shape:** Scalloped **Designer:** Michael Rizzello

Date	Mintage	F	VF	XF	Unc	BU
1975FM (M)	118,000	—	—	0.10	0.75	1.50
1975FM (U)	1,095	—	—	0.20	1.00	2.00
1975FM (P)	8,794	Value: 2.00				
1976FM (M)	126,000	—	—	0.10	0.75	1.50
1976FM (U)	759	—	—	0.20	1.00	2.00
1976FM (P)	4,893	Value: 2.00				

KM# 46a CENT

3.0200 g., 0.9250 Silver .0898 oz. ASW **Rev:** Swallow-tailed kite **Shape:** Scalloped **Designer:** Michael Rizzello

Date	Mintage	F	VF	XF	Unc	BU
1975FM (P)	13,000	Value: 3.00				
1976FM (P)	5,897	Value: 3.00				
1977FM (P)	3,197	Value: 3.00				
1978FM (P)	3,342	Value: 3.00				
1979FM (P)	2,445	Value: 3.00				
1980FM (P)	1,826	Value: 3.00				
1981FM (P)	615	Value: 3.50				

KM# 46b CENT

Aluminum **Obv:** National arms, date below, within wreath **Rev:** Swallow-tailed kite right, denomination above **Shape:** Scalloped **Designer:** Michael Rizzello

Date	Mintage	F	VF	XF	Unc	BU
1977FM (U)	126,000	—	—	0.10	0.75	1.30
1977FM (P)	2,107	Value: 2.00				
1978FM (U)	125,000	—	—	0.10	0.75	1.30
1978FM (P)	1,671	Value: 2.00				
1979FM (U)	808	—	—	0.15	0.75	1.00
1979FM (P)	1,287	Value: 2.00				
1980FM (U)	761	—	—	0.15	0.75	1.00
1980FM (P)	920	Value: 2.00				
1981FM (U)	297	—	—	0.15	0.75	1.00
1981FM (P)	643	Value: 2.00				

KM# 83 CENT

Aluminum **Rev:** Swallow-tailed kite **Shape:** Scalloped **Designer:** Michael Rizzello

Date	Mintage	F	VF	XF	Unc	BU
1982FM (U)	—	—	0.15	0.25	1.50	1.75
1982FM (P)	—	Value. 3.00				
1983FM (U)	—	—	0.15	0.25	1.50	1.75
1983FM (P)	—	Value: 3.00				

KM# 83a CENT

3.0200 g., 0.9250 Silver .0898 oz. ASW **Rev:** Swallow-tailed kite **Shape:** Scalloped **Designer:** Michael Rizzello

Date	Mintage	F	VF	XF	Unc	BU
1982FM (P)	381	Value: 7.50				
1983FM (P)	336	Value: 7.50				

KM# 90 CENT

Aluminum **Rev:** Swallow-tailed kite right, denomination above **Rev. Designer:** Michael Rizzello **Shape:** Scalloped

Date	Mintage	F	VF	XF	Unc	BU
1984FM (U)	—	—	0.15	0.25	1.50	1.75
1984FM (P)	—	Value: 3.00				

KM# 90a CENT

3.0200 g., 0.9250 Silver .0898 oz. ASW **Rev:** Swallow-tailed kite **Shape:** Scalloped

Date	Mintage	F	VF	XF	Unc	BU
1984FM (P)	—	Value: 7.50				
1985 Proof	212	Value: 10.00				

KM# 34 5 CENTS

Nickel-Brass, 20.15 mm. **Obv:** Crowned bust of Queen Elizabeth II, right **Obv. Designer:** Cecil Thomas **Rev:** Denomination within circle, date below circle

Date	Mintage	F	VF	XF	Unc	BU
1973	210,000	—	—	0.50	1.00	2.00
1974	210,000	—	—	0.50	1.00	2.00
1975	420,000	—	—	0.15	0.40	1.00
1976	570,000	—	—	0.15	0.40	1.00
1979	—	—	—	0.15	0.40	1.00

KM# 34a 5 CENTS

1.0000 g., Aluminum, 20.15 mm. **Obv:** Bust of Queen Elizabeth II right **Obv. Designer:** Cecil Thomas **Rev:** Denomination within circle

Date	Mintage	F	VF	XF	Unc	BU
1976	1,000,000	—	—	0.10	0.25	0.60
1979	960,000	—	—	0.10	0.25	0.75
1980	1,040,000	—	—	0.10	0.25	0.60
1986	—	—	—	0.10	0.25	0.60
1987	—	—	—	0.10	0.25	0.60
1989	—	—	—	0.10	0.25	0.60
1991	—	—	—	0.10	0.25	0.60
1992	—	—	—	0.10	0.25	0.60
1993	—	—	—	0.10	0.25	0.60
1994	—	—	—	0.10	0.25	0.60
2000	—	—	—	0.10	0.25	0.60

KM# 39 5 CENTS

Nickel-Brass, 20 mm. **Obv:** National arms, date below, within wreath **Rev:** Fork-tailed flycatchers, denomination above **Designer:** Michael Rizzello

Date	Mintage	F	VF	XF	Unc	BU
1974FM (M)	50,000	—	—	0.25	1.25	2.50
1974FM (P)	21,000	Value: 2.00				

KM# 39a 5 CENTS

4.3500 g., 0.9250 Silver .1293 oz. ASW, 20 mm. **Rev:** Fork-tailed flycatcher

Date	Mintage	F	VF	XF	Unc	BU
1974FM (P)	31,000	Value: 3.00				

KM# 47 5 CENTS

Nickel-Brass, 20 mm. **Obv:** National arms, date below, within wreath **Rev:** Fork-tailed flycatchers, denomination above **Designer:** Michael Rizzello

Date	Mintage	F	VF	XF	Unc	BU
1975FM (M)	24,000	—	—	0.25	1.50	2.50
1975FM (U)	1,095	—	—	0.25	1.50	2.50
1975FM (P)	8,794	Value: 1.25				
1976FM (M)	25,000	—	—	0.25	1.50	2.50
1976FM (U)	759	—	—	0.25	1.50	2.50
1976FM (P)	4,893	Value: 1.25				

KM# 47a 5 CENTS

4.3500 g., 0.9250 Silver .1293 oz. ASW, 20 mm. **Rev:** Fork-tailed flycatcher

Date	Mintage	F	VF	XF	Unc	BU
1975FM (P)	13,000	Value: 2.75				
1976FM (P)	5,897	Value: 2.75				
1977FM (P)	3,197	Value: 2.75				
1978FM (P)	3,342	Value: 2.75				
1979FM (P)	2,445	Value: 2.75				
1980FM (P)	1,826	Value: 2.75				
1981FM (P)	615	Value: 3.50				

KM# 47b 5 CENTS

Aluminum **Rev:** Fork-tailed flycatcher

Date	Mintage	F	VF	XF	Unc	BU
1977FM (U)	26,000	—	—	0.10	0.50	0.75
1977FM (P)	2,107	Value: 2.00				
1978FM (U)	25,000	—	—	0.10	0.50	0.75
1978FM (P)	1,671	Value: 2.00				
1979FM (U)	808	—	—	0.15	0.75	1.00
1979FM (P)	1,287	—	—	0.25	1.00	1.50
1980FM (U)	761	—	—	0.15	0.75	1.00
1980FM (P)	920	Value: 2.00				
1981FM (U)	297	—	—	0.15	0.75	1.00
1981FM (P)	643	Value: 2.00				

KM# 64 5 CENTS

1.0000 g., Aluminum, 20.15 mm. **Series:** World Food Day **Obv:** Crowned bust of Queen Elizabeth II right **Obv. Designer:** Cecil Thomas **Rev:** Denomination, date upper right

Date	Mintage	F	VF	XF	Unc	BU
1981	—	—	—	0.10	0.35	0.70

KM# 84 5 CENTS

Aluminum **Obv:** National arms within wreath, date below **Rev:** Fork-tailed flycatchers, denomination above **Designer:** Michael Rizzello

Date	Mintage	F	VF	XF	Unc	BU
1982FM (U)	—	—	0.15	0.35	1.50	2.00
1982FM (P)	—	Value: 3.00				
1983FM (U)	—	—	0.15	0.35	1.50	2.00
1983FM (P)	—	Value: 3.00				

KM# 84a 5 CENTS

4.3500 g., 0.9250 Silver .1293 oz. ASW **Rev:** Fork-tailed flycatcher

Date	Mintage	F	VF	XF	Unc	BU
1982FM (P)	381	Value: 12.00				
1983FM (P)	479	Value: 12.00				

KM# 91 5 CENTS

Aluminum **Designer:** Michael Rizzello

Date	Mintage	F	VF	XF	Unc	BU
1984FM (U)	—	—	0.25	0.50	1.75	2.25
1984FM (P)	—	Value: 3.00				

KM# 91a 5 CENTS

4.3500 g., 0.9250 Silver .1293 oz. ASW **Obv:** National arms within wreath, date below **Rev:** Fork-tailed flycatchers, denomination above

Date	Mintage	F	VF	XF	Unc	BU
1984FM (P)	—	Value: 12.00				
1985 Proof	212	Value: 13.50				

KM# 35 10 CENTS

2.4000 g., Copper-Nickel, 16.95 mm. **Obv:** Crowned bust of Queen Elizabeth, right **Rev:** Denomination within circle, date below

Date	Mintage	F	VF	XF	Unc	BU
1974	100,000	—	0.15	0.35	0.60	1.25
1975	200,000	—	0.10	0.25	0.50	1.00
1976	700,000	—	0.10	0.20	0.45	0.75
1979	800,000	—	0.10	0.20	0.40	0.75
1980	—	—	0.10	0.20	0.40	0.75
1981	—	—	0.10	0.20	0.40	0.75
1992	—	—	0.10	0.20	0.40	0.75
2000	—	—	—	0.15	0.40	0.60

KM# 40 10 CENTS

2.4000 g., Copper-Nickel, 16.95 mm. **Obv:** National arms, date below, within wreath **Rev:** Long-tailed hermit right, denomination above **Designer:** Michael Rizzello

Date	Mintage	F	VF	XF	Unc	BU
1974FM (M)	27,000	—	—	0.50	2.00	4.00
1974FM (P)	21,000	Value: 1.75				

KM# 40a 10 CENTS

2.7900 g., 0.9250 Silver .0829 oz. ASW, 16.95 mm. **Rev:** Long-tailed hermit

Date	Mintage	F	VF	XF	Unc	BU
1974FM (P)	31,000	Value: 3.50				

KM# 48 10 CENTS

2.4000 g., Copper-Nickel, 16.95 mm. **Obv:** National arms, date below, within wreath **Rev:** Long-tailed hermit right, denomination above **Designer:** Michael Rizzello

Date	Mintage	F	VF	XF	Unc	BU
1975FM (M)	12,000	—	—	0.25	1.50	2.00
1975FM (L)	1,095	—	—	0.30	2.00	4.00
1975FM (P)	8,794	Value: 1.50				
1976FM (M)	13,000	—	—	0.25	1.50	2.00
1976FM (U)	759	—	—	0.35	2.50	4.00
1976FM (P)	4,893	Value: 1.50				
1977FM (U)	14,000	—	—	0.25	1.50	2.00
1977FM (P)	2,107	Value: 2.00				
1978FM (U)	13,000	—	—	0.25	1.50	1.75
1978FM (P)	1,671	Value: 3.00				
1979FM (U)	808	—	—	1.00	3.00	6.00
1979FM (P)	1,287	Value: 3.00				
1980FM (U)	761	—	—	1.00	3.00	6.00
1980FM (P)	920	Value: 3.00				
1981FM (U)	297	—	—	1.00	3.00	6.00
1981FM (P)	643	Value: 4.00				

KM# 48a 10 CENTS

2.7900 g., 0.9250 Silver .0829 oz. ASW, 16.95 mm. **Rev:** Long-tailed hermit

Date	Mintage	F	VF	XF	Unc	BU
1975FM (P)	13,000	Value: 3.00				
1976FM (P)	5,897	Value: 3.00				
1977FM (P)	3,197	Value: 3.00				
1978FM (P)	3,342	Value: 3.00				
1979FM (P)	2,445	Value: 3.00				
1980FM (P)	1,826	Value: 3.00				
1981FM (P)	615	Value: 4.00				

KM# 85 10 CENTS

2.4000 g., Copper-Nickel, 16.95 mm. **Rev:** Long-tailed hermit **Designer:** Michael Rizzello

Date	Mintage	F	VF	XF	Unc	BU
1982FM (U)	—	—	0.25	0.50	2.50	3.50
1982FM (P)	—	Value: 3.50				
1983FM (U)	—	—	0.25	0.50	2.50	3.50
1983FM (P)	—	Value: 3.50				

KM# 85a 10 CENTS

2.7900 g., 0.9250 Silver .0829 oz. ASW **Rev:** Long-tailed hermit

Date	Mintage	F	VF	XF	Unc	BU
1982FM (P)	381	Value: 13.50				
1983FM (P)	3 2	Value: 13.50				

KM# 92 10 CENTS

2.4000 g., Copper-Nickel, 16.95 mm. **Obv:** National arms within wreath, date below **Rev:** Michael Rizzello

Date	Mintage	F	VF	XF	Unc	BU
1984FM (U)	—	—	0.25	0.50	2.50	3.50
1984FM (P)	—	Value: 3.50				

KM# 92a 10 CENTS

2.7900 g., 0.9250 Silver .0829 oz. ASW, 16.95 mm. **Obv:** National arms within wreath, date below **Rev:** Long-tailed hermit right, denomination above **Rev. Designer:** Michael Rizzello

Date	Mintage	F	VF	XF	Unc	BU
1984FM (P)	—	Value: 13.50				
1985 Proof	212	Value: 15.50				

KM# 36 25 CENTS

5.6000 g., Copper-Nickel, 23.6 mm. **Obv:** Crowned bust of Queen Elizabeth II right **Obv. Designer:** Cecil Thomas **Rev:** Denomination within circle, date below

Date	Mintage	F	VF	XF	Unc	BU
1974	100,000	—	0.35	0.65	1.25	2.50
1975	200,000	—	0.20	0.35	0.75	1.00
1976	790,000	—	0.20	0.35	0.75	1.00
1979	500,000	—	0.20	0.35	0.75	1.00
1980	—	—	0.20	0.35	0.75	1.00
1981	—	—	0.20	0.35	0.75	1.00
1986	—	—	0.20	0.35	0.75	1.00
1987	—	—	0.20	0.35	0.75	1.00
1988	—	—	0.20	0.35	0.75	1.00
1989	—	—	0.20	0.35	0.75	1.00
1991	—	—	0.20	0.35	0.75	1.00
1992	—	—	0.20	0.35	0.75	1.00
1993	—	—	0.20	0.35	0.75	1.00
1994	—	—	0.20	0.35	0.75	1.00
2000	—	—	0.20	0.35	0.75	1.50

KM# 41 25 CENTS

Copper-Nickel, 23.6 mm. **Obv:** National arms, date below, within wreath **Rev:** Blue-crowned motmot left, denomination above **Designer:** Michael Rizzello

Date	Mintage	F	VF	XF	Unc	BU
1974FM (M)	13,000	—	—	1.00	3.50	5.00
1974FM (P)	21,000	Value: 3.00				

KM# 41a 25 CENTS

6.6000 g., 0.9250 Silver .1962 oz. ASW **Rev:** Blue-crowned motmot

Date	Mintage	F	VF	XF	Unc	BU
1974FM (P)	31,000	Value: 5.00				

KM# 49 25 CENTS

Copper-Nickel, 23.6 mm. **Obv:** National arms above date within wreath **Rev:** Blue-crowned motmot left, denomination below **Designer:** Michael Rizzello

Date	Mintage	F	VF	XF	Unc	BU
1975FM (M)	4,716	—	—	0.40	3.00	4.00
1975FM (U)	1,095	—	—	0.40	3.00	4.00
1975FM (P)	8,794	Value: 2.50				
1976FM (M)	5,000	—	—	0.50	4.00	5.00
1976FM (U)	759	—	—	0.45	3.50	4.50
1976FM (P)	4,893	Value: 2.50				
1977FM (U)	5,520	—	—	0.30	3.00	4.00
1977FM (P)	2,107	Value: 2.75				
1978FM (U)	5,458	—	—	0.30	3.00	4.50
1978FM (P)	1,671	Value: 2.75				
1979FM (U)	808	—	—	0.40	3.00	4.50
1979FM (P)	1,287	Value: 3.00				
1980FM (U)	761	—	—	0.40	3.00	4.50
1980FM (P)	920	Value: 3.00				
1981FM (U)	297	—	—	0.40	3.00	6.00
1981FM (P)	643	Value: 3.00				

KM# 49a 25 CENTS

6.6000 g., 0.9250 Silver .1962 oz. ASW **Obv:** National arms above date within wreath **Rev:** Blue-crowned motmot

Date	Mintage	F	VF	XF	Unc	BU
1975FM (P)	13,000	Value: 3.75				
1976FM (P)	5,897	Value: 3.75				
1977FM (P)	3,197	Value: 3.75				
1978FM (P)	3,342	Value: 3.75				
1979FM (P)	2,445	Value: 3.75				
1980FM (P)	1,826	Value: 3.75				
1981FM (P)	615	Value: 5.50				

KM# 86 25 CENTS

Copper-Nickel, 23.6 mm. **Obv:** National arms within wreath, date below **Rev:** Blue-crowned motmot right, denomination below **Rev. Designer:** Michael Rizzello

Date	Mintage	F	VF	XF	Unc	BU
1982FM (U)	—	—	0.50	1.00	4.00	5.00
1982FM (P)	—	Value: 5.00				
1983FM (U)	—	—	0.50	1.00	4.00	5.00
1983FM (P)	—	Value: 5.00				

KM# 86a 25 CENTS

6.6000 g., 0.9250 Silver .1962 oz. ASW **Obv:** National arms within wreath, date below **Rev:** Blue-crowned motmot

Date	Mintage	F	VF	XF	Unc	BU
1982FM (P)	381	Value: 18.50				
1983FM (P)	314	Value: 18.50				

KM# 93 25 CENTS

Copper-Nickel, 23.6 mm. **Obv:** National arms within wreath, date below **Rev:** Blue-crowned motmot right, denomination below **Rev. Designer:** Michael Rizzello

Date	Mintage	F	VF	XF	Unc	BU
1984FM (U)	—	—	0.50	1.00	4.00	5.00
1984FM (P)	—	Value: 5.00				

KM# 93a 25 CENTS

6.6000 g., 0.9250 Silver .1962 oz. ASW **Obv:** National arms within wreath, date below **Rev:** Blue-crowned motmot

Date	Mintage	F	VF	XF	Unc	BU
1984FM (P)	—	Value: 18.50				
1985 Proof	212	Value: 22.50				

KM# 77 25 CENTS

5.6000 g., Copper-Nickel, 23.6 mm. **Subject:** World Forestry Congress **Obv:** Crowned bust of Queen Elizabeth right **Obv. Designer:** Cecil Thomas **Rev:** Denomination within circle, date below

Date	Mintage	F	VF	XF	Unc	BU
1985	—	—	0.25	0.40	0.85	1.10

KM# 37 50 CENTS

9.0000 g., Copper-Nickel, 27.7 mm. **Obv:** Crowned bust of Queen Elizabeth right **Obv. Designer:** Cecil Thomas **Rev:** Denomination within circle, date below

Date	Mintage	F	VF	XF	Unc	BU
1974	123,000	—	0.50	1.50	3.00	4.50
1975	Inc. above	—	0.40	0.75	2.00	3.00
1976	312,000	—	0.40	0.75	2.00	3.00
1979	125,000	—	0.50	1.50	3.00	4.50
1980	—	—	0.40	0.75	1.75	2.75
1989	—	—	0.40	0.75	1.75	2.75
1991	—	—	0.50	1.00	2.00	3.00
1992	—	—	0.50	1.00	2.00	3.00
1993	—	—	0.50	1.00	2.00	3.00

KM# 42 50 CENTS

Copper-Nickel, 27.7 mm. **Rev:** Frigate bird

Date	Mintage	F	VF	XF	Unc	BU
1974FM (M)	8,806	—	—	0.40	4.50	—
1974FM (P)	21,000	Value: 3.50				

KM# 42a 50 CENTS

9.9400 g., 0.9250 Silver .3197 oz. ASW, 27.7 mm. **Rev:** Frigate bird

Date	Mintage	F	VF	XF	Unc	BU
1974FM (P)	31,000	Value: 8.00				

KM# 50 50 CENTS

Copper-Nickel, 27.7 mm. **Obv:** National arms above date within wreath **Rev:** Frigate birds, denomination above **Designer:** Michael Rizzello

Date	Mintage	F	VF	XF	Unc	BU
1975FM (M)	2,358	—	—	0.65	6.00	7.00
1975FM (U)	1,095	—	—	0.45	4.50	6.00
1975FM (P)	8,794	Value: 4.00				
1976FM (M)	3,259	—	—	0.55	5.00	6.00
1976FM (U)	759	—	—	0.55	5.00	6.00
1976FM (P)	4,893	Value: 6.00				
1977FM (U)	3,540	—	—	0.45	4.50	6.00
1977FM (P)	2,107	Value: 6.00				
1978FM (U)	2,958	—	—	0.45	4.50	6.00
1978FM (P)	1,671	Value: 6.00				
1979FM (U)	808	—	—	0.55	5.00	7.50
1979FM (P)	1,287	Value: 6.00				
1980FM (U)	761	—	—	0.55	5.00	7.50
1980FM (P)	920	Value: 6.50				
1981FM (U)	297	—	—	0.55	5.00	7.50
1981FM (P)	643	Value: 6.50				

KM# 50a 50 CENTS

9.9400 g., 0.9250 Silver .3197 oz. ASW, 27.7 mm. **Obv:** National arms above date within wreath **Rev:** Frigate bird

Date	Mintage	F	VF	XF	Unc	BU
1975FM (P)	13,000	Value: 6.75				
1976FM (P)	5,897	Value: 6.75				
1977FM (P)	3,197	Value: 6.75				
1978FM (P)	3,342	Value: 6.75				
1979FM (P)	2,445	Value: 6.75				
1980FM (P)	1,826	Value: 6.75				
1981FM (P)	615	Value: 9.00				

KM# 87 50 CENTS

Copper-Nickel, 27.7 mm. **Obv:** National arms within wreath, date below **Rev:** Frigate birds, denomination above **Rev. Designer:** Michael Rizzello

Date	Mintage	F	VF	XF	Unc	BU
1982FM (U)	—	—	0.75	1.50	6.50	7.00
1982FM (P)	—	Value: 7.50				
1983FM (U)	—	—	0.75	1.50	6.50	7.00
1983FM (P)	—	Value: 7.50				

KM# 87a 50 CENTS

9.9400 g., 0.9250 Silver .3197 oz. ASW, 27.7 mm. **Obv:** National arms within wreath, date below **Rev:** Frigate bird

Date	Mintage	F	VF	XF	Unc	BU
1982FM (P)	381	Value: 27.50				
1983FM (P)	312	Value: 27.50				

KM# 94 50 CENTS

Copper-Nickel, 27.7 mm. **Obv:** National arms within wreath, date below **Rev:** Frigate birds, denomination above **Rev. Designer:** Michael Rizzello

Date	Mintage	F	VF	XF	Unc	BU
1984FM (U)	—	—	0.75	1.50	6.50	7.00
1984FM (P)	—	Value: 7.50				

KM# 94a 50 CENTS

9.9400 g., 0.9250 Silver .3197 oz. ASW, 27.7 mm. **Obv:** National arms within wreath, date below **Rev:** Frigate bird

Date	Mintage	F	VF	XF	Unc	BU
1984FM (P)	—	Value: 27.50				
1985 Proof	212	Value: 32.50				

KM# 118 50 CENTS

Copper-Nickel **Obv:** New portrait of Queen Elizabeth II **Rev:** Denomination within circle, date below

Date	Mintage	F	VF	XF	Unc	BU
1992	—	—	0.50	1.00	2.00	3.50
1993	—	—	0.50	1.00	2.00	3.50

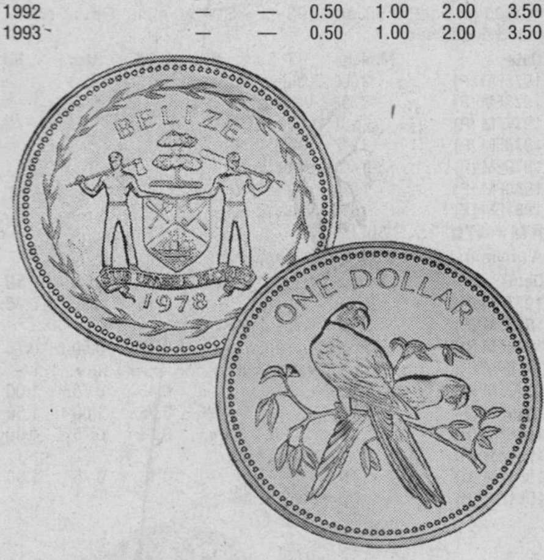

KM# 43 DOLLAR

Copper-Nickel, 35 mm. **Obv:** National arms above date within wreath **Rev:** Scarlet macaws, denomination above **Designer:** Michael Rizzello

Date	Mintage	F	VF	XF	Unc	BU
1974FM (M)	6,656	—	—	1.00	9.00	10.00
1974FM (P)	21,000	Value: 6.00				
1975FM (M)	1,182	—	—	1.50	10.00	12.50
1975FM (U)	1,095	—	—	0.75	9.00	10.00
1975FM (P)	8,794	Value: 6.00				
1976FM (M)	1,250	—	—	1.50	10.00	12.50
1976FM (U)	759	—	—	1.25	9.00	12.50
1976FM (P)	4,893	Value: 6.00				
1977FM (U)	1,770	—	—	1.00	9.00	10.00
1977FM (P)	2,107	Value: 6.00				
1978FM (U)	1,708	—	—	1.00	9.00	10.00
1978FM (P)	1,671	Value: 6.00				
1979FM (U)	808	—	—	1.25	9.00	10.00
1979FM (P)	1,287	Value: 6.00				
1980FM (U)	761	—	—	1.25	9.00	10.00
1980FM (P)	920	Value: 6.00				
1981FM (U)	297	—	—	1.50	10.00	12.50
1981FM (P)	643	Value: 8.50				

KM# 43a DOLLAR

19.8900 g., 0.9250 Silver .5915 oz. ASW, 35 mm. **Obv:** National arms above date within wreath **Rev:** Scarlet macaw

Date	Mintage	F	VF	XF	Unc	BU
1974FM (P)	31,000	Value: 10.00				
1975FM (P)	13,000	Value: 12.50				
1976FM (P)	5,897	Value: 12.50				
1977FM (P)	3,197	Value: 12.50				
1978FM (P)	3,342	Value: 12.50				
1979FM (P)	2,445	Value: 12.50				
1980FM (P)	1,826	Value: 12.50				
1981FM (P)	615	Value: 13.50				

KM# 88 DOLLAR

Copper-Nickel, 35 mm. **Obv:** National arms within wreath, date below **Rev:** Scarlet macaws, denomination above **Rev. Designer:** Michael Rizzello

Date	Mintage	F	VF	XF	Unc	BU
1982FM (U)	—	—	1.50	3.00	10.00	12.50
1982FM (P)	—	Value: 8.50				
1983FM (U)	—	—	1.50	3.00	10.00	12.50
1983FM (P)	—	Value: 8.50				

KM# 88a DOLLAR

19.8900 g., 0.9250 Silver .5915 oz. ASW, 35 mm. **Obv:** National arms within wreath, date below **Rev:** Scarlet macaw

Date	Mintage	F	VF	XF	Unc	BU
1982FM (P)	381	Value: 37.50				
1983FM (P)	1,589	Value: 37.50				

KM# 95 DOLLAR

Copper-Nickel, 35 mm. **Obv:** National arms within wreath, date below **Rev:** Scarlet macaws, denomination above **Rev. Designer:** Michael Rizzello

Date	Mintage	F	VF	XF	Unc	BU
1984FM (U)	—	—	1.50	3.00	10.00	12.50
1984FM (P)	—	Value: 8.50				

KM# 95a DOLLAR

19.8900 g., 0.9250 Silver .5915 oz. ASW, 35 mm. **Obv:** National arms within wreath, date below **Rev:** Scarlet macaws, denomination above

Date	Mintage	F	VF	XF	Unc	BU
1984FM (P)	—	Value: 37.50				
1985 Proof	212	Value: 45.00				

KM# 99 DOLLAR

Nickel-Brass, 27 mm. **Obv:** Crowned bust of Queen Elizabeth II right **Obv. Designer:** Raphael Maklouf **Rev:** Columbus' three ships, denomination above, date below **Rev. Designer:** Robert Elderton **Edge:** Alternating reeded and plain **Shape:** 10-sided

Date	Mintage	F	VF	XF	Unc	BU
1990	—	—	—	—	2.25	3.00
1991	—	—	—	—	2.25	3.00
1992	—	—	—	—	2.25	3.00
2000	—	—	—	—	2.25	3.00

KM# 99a DOLLAR

9.0000 g., 0.9250 Silver .2676 oz. ASW, 27 mm. **Obv:** Crowned Queen's portrait, right **Rev:** Columbus' three ships

Date	Mintage	F	VF	XF	Unc	BU
1990 Proof	Est. 5,000	Value: 32.50				

KM# 135 DOLLAR

15.9500 g., Silver, 28.2 mm. **Subject:** Queen Elizabeth II - The Queen Mother - Summer in Balmoral Castle **Obv:** National arms **Rev:** Balmoral Castle **Edge:** Reeded

Date	Mintage	F	VF	XF	Unc	BU
1997	—	—	—	—	—	—

KM# 100 2 DOLLARS

Copper-Nickel **Subject:** Queen Mother's 90th Birthday **Obv:** Crowned bust of Queen Elizabeth II right **Obv. Designer:** Raphael Maklouf **Rev:** Crowned ornate "E"s, backs intertwined, sprays flanking, two dates below **Rev. Designer:** Robert Elderton

Date	Mintage	F	VF	XF	Unc	BU
ND(1990)	—	—	—	—	6.00	7.50

KM# 100a 2 DOLLARS

28.2800 g., 0.9250 Silver .8411 oz. ASW **Subject:** Queen Mother's 90th Birthday **Obv:** Crowned Queen's portrait, right **Rev:** Crowned ornate "E"s, backs intertwined, sprays flanking, two dates below

Date	Mintage	F	VF	XF	Unc	BU
ND(1990) Proof	Est. 10,000	Value: 45.00				

KM# 119 2 DOLLARS

28.2800 g., 0.9250 Silver .8411 oz. ASW **Subject:** 40th Anniversary - Coronation of Queen Elizabeth II **Obv:** Crowned Queen's portrait, right **Obv. Designer:** Raphael Maklouf **Rev:** Facing Queen Elizabeth II on horseback saluting, two dates at bottom

Date	Mintage	F	VF	XF	Unc	BU
ND(1993) Proof	Est. 10,000	Value: 45.00				

KM# 131 2 DOLLARS

Copper-Nickel, 28 mm. **Subject:** Battle of St. George's Caye **Obv:** National arms within wreath, denomination below **Rev:** Oar-powered landing craft shorebound, within circle, two dates below

Date	Mintage	F	VF	XF	Unc	BU
ND(1998)	—	—	—	—	7.00	10.00

KM# 132 2 DOLLARS

28.2800 g., 0.9250 Silver .8410 oz. ASW, 38.6 mm. **Subject:** Heritage Protection **Obv:** National arms **Rev:** Large building, people, jaguar and arms, denomination below **Edge:** Reeded

Date	Mintage	F	VF	XF	Unc	BU
1998 Proof	5,000	Value: 55.00				

KM# 44 5 DOLLARS

Copper-Nickel, 37.8 mm. **Obv:** National arms above date within wreath **Rev:** Keel-billed toucan, right, denomination above **Designer:** Michael Rizzello

Date	Mintage	F	VF	XF	Unc	BU
1974FM (M)	4,936	—	—	2.75	7.50	—
1974FM (P)	21,000	Value: 6.50				
1975FM (M)	237	—	—	5.00	22.50	—
1975FM (U)	1,095	—	—	2.75	7.50	—
1975FM (P)	8,794	Value: 6.50				
1976FM (M)	250	—	—	5.00	20.00	—
1976FM (U)	759	—	—	2.75	7.50	—
1976FM (P)	4,893	Value: 6.50				
1977FM (U)	720	—	—	2.75	7.50	—
1977FM (P)	2,107	Value: 7.50				
1978FM (U)	708	—	—	2.75	7.50	—
1978FM (P)	1,671	Value: 7.50				
1979FM (U)	808	—	—	2.75	7.50	—
1979FM (P)	1,287	Value: 7.50				
1980FM (U)	761	—	—	2.75	7.50	—
1980FM (P)	920	Value: 7.50				
1981FM (U)	297	—	—	2.75	7.50	—
1981FM (P)	643	Value: 8.50				

KM# 44a 5 DOLLARS

26.4000 g., 0.9250 Silver .7851 oz. ASW, 37.8 mm. **Obv:** National arms above date within wreath **Rev:** Keel-billed toucan

Date	Mintage	F	VF	XF	Unc	BU
1974FM (P)	31,000	Value: 11.00				
1975FM (P)	13,000	Value: 11.50				
1976FM (P)	5,897	Value: 12.50				
1977FM (P)	3,197	Value: 12.50				
1978FM (P)	3,342	Value: 12.50				
1979FM (P)	2,445	Value: 12.50				
1980FM (P)	1,826	Value: 12.50				
1981FM (P)	615	Value: 16.50				

KM# 89 5 DOLLARS

Copper-Nickel, 37.8 mm. **Obv:** National arms above date within wreath **Rev:** Keel-billed toucan

Date	Mintage	F	VF	XF	Unc	BU
1982FM (U)	—	—	2.00	4.00	12.00	15.00
1982FM (P)	—	Value: 15.00				
1983FM (U)	—	—	2.00	4.00	12.00	15.00
1983FM (P)	—	Value: 15.00				

KM# 89a 5 DOLLARS

26.4000 g., 0.9250 Silver .7851 oz. ASW, 37.8 mm. **Obv:** National arms above date within wreath **Rev:** Keel-billed toucan

Date	Mintage	F	VF	XF	Unc	BU
1982FM (P)	381	Value: 50.00				
1983FM (P)	311	Value: 50.00				

KM# 96 5 DOLLARS

Copper-Nickel, 37.8 mm. **Obv:** National arms within wreath, date below **Rev:** Keel-billed toucan, right, denomination above **Rev. Designer:** Michael Rizzello

Date	Mintage	F	VF	XF	Unc	BU
1984FM (U)	—	—	2.00	4.00	12.00	15.00
1984FM (P)	—	Value: 17.50				

KM# 96a 5 DOLLARS
26.4000 g., 0.9250 Silver .7851 oz. ASW, 37.8 mm. **Obv:** National arms within wreath, date below **Rev:** Keel-billed toucan, right, denomination above **Rev. Designer:** Michael Rizzello

Date	Mintage	F	VF	XF	Unc	BU
1984FM (P)	—	Value: 50.00				
1985 Proof	212	Value: 60.00				

KM# 107 5 DOLLARS
28.2800 g., 0.9250 Silver .8411 oz. ASW **Subject:** 50th Anniversary - Battle of El Alamein - Field Marshall Rommel **Obv:** Bust of Queen Elizabeth II right **Rev:** Field Marshall Rommel, right, in uniform, denomination lower right

Date	Mintage	F	VF	XF	Unc	BU
1992 Proof	Est. 5,000	Value: 45.00				

KM# 108 5 DOLLARS
28.2800 g., 0.9250 Silver .8411 oz. ASW **Subject:** 50th Anniversary - Battle of El Alamein - Lt. Gen. Montgomery **Obv:** Bust of Queen Elizabeth II right **Rev:** Lt. Gen. Montgomery, denomination at bottom

Date	Mintage	F	VF	XF	Unc	BU
1992 Proof	Est. 5,000	Value: 45.00				

KM# 126 5 DOLLARS
28.2800 g., 0.9250 Silver .8411 oz. ASW **Subject:** Queen Mother - Balmoral Castle **Obv:** National arms within wreath, date below **Rev:** Balmoral Castle above date, denomination at bottom

Date	Mintage	F	VF	XF	Unc	BU
1995 Proof	Est. 40,000	Value: 35.00				

KM# 133 5 DOLLARS
28.5000 g., 0.9250 Silver 0.8476 oz. ASW, 38.5 mm. **Subject:** Queen Elizabeth II's Golden Wedding Anniversary **Obv:** National arms within wreath, date below **Rev:** Royal couple below gold inset shield, denomination at bottom **Edge:** Reeded

Date	Mintage	F	VF	XF	Unc	BU
1997 Proof	—	Value: 45.00				

KM# 45 10 DOLLARS
Copper-Nickel, 40 mm. **Obv:** National arms above date within wreath **Rev:** Great curassow, right, denomination above

Date	Mintage	F	VF	XF	Unc	BU
1974FM (M)	4,726	—	—	3.50	9.00	11.00
1974FM (P)	21,000	Value: 8.00				
1975FM (M)	117	—	—	12.50	45.00	55.00
1975FM (U)	1,095	—	—	3.50	10.00	12.50
1975FM (P)	8,794	Value: 9.00				
1976FM (M)	125	—	—	10.00	35.00	55.00
1976FM (U)	759	—	—	3.50	10.00	12.50
1976FM (P)	4,893	Value: 10.00				
1977FM (U)	645	—	—	4.00	12.00	15.00
1977FM (P)	2,107	Value: 12.50				
1978FM (U)	583	—	—	5.00	12.00	15.00
1978FM (P)	1,671	Value: 12.50				

KM# 45a 10 DOLLARS
29.8000 g., 0.9250 Silver .8863 oz. ASW, 40 mm. **Obv:** National arms above date within wreath **Rev:** Great curassow

Date	Mintage	F	VF	XF	Unc	BU
1974FM (P)	31,000	Value: 12.50				
1975FM (P)	13,000	Value: 13.50				
1976FM (P)	5,897	Value: 14.00				
1977FM (P)	3,197	Value: 16.00				
1978FM (P)	3,342	Value: 16.00				

KM# 57 10 DOLLARS
Copper-Nickel, 40 mm. **Obv:** National arms above date within wreath **Rev:** Flying jabirus, denomination above

Date	Mintage	F	VF	XF	Unc	BU
1979FM (U)	808	—	—	5.00	25.00	35.00
1979FM (P)	1,287	Value: 30.00				

KM# 57a 10 DOLLARS
29.8000 g., 0.9250 Silver .8863 oz. ASW, 40 mm. **Obv:** National arms above date within wreath **Rev:** Flying jabirus

Date	Mintage	F	VF	XF	Unc	BU
1979FM (P)	2,445	Value: 40.00				

KM# 60 10 DOLLARS
Copper-Nickel, 40 mm. **Obv:** National arms above date within wreath **Rev:** Two Scarlet ibis, denomination above

Date	Mintage	F	VF	XF	Unc	BU
1980FM (U)	761	—	—	5.00	25.00	35.00
1980FM (P)	920	Value: 28.00				

KM# 60a 10 DOLLARS
25.5000 g., 0.9250 Silver .7583 oz. ASW, 40 mm. **Obv:** National arms above date within wreath **Rev:** Scarlet ibis

Date	Mintage	F	VF	XF	Unc	BU
1980FM (P)	1,826	Value: 50.00				

KM# 65 10 DOLLARS
Copper-Nickel, 40 mm. **Obv:** National arms above date within wreath **Rev:** Roseate spoonbill, left, denomination above

Date	Mintage	F	VF	XF	Unc	BU
1981FM (U)	297	—	7.50	15.00	40.00	50.00
1981FM (P)	643	Value: 50.00				

KM# 65a 10 DOLLARS
25.5000 g., 0.9250 Silver .7583 oz. ASW, 40 mm. **Obv:** National arms above date within wreath **Rev:** Roseate spoonbill

Date	Mintage	F	VF	XF	Unc	BU
1981FM (P)	615	Value: 75.00				

KM# 69 10 DOLLARS
Copper-Nickel, 40 mm. **Obv:** National arms above date within wreath **Rev:** Yellow-crowned Amazon parrot, right, denomination at bottom

Date	Mintage	F	VF	XF	Unc	BU
1982FM (U)	—	—	10.00	20.00	45.00	50.00
1982FM (P)	—	Value: 65.00				

KM# 69a 10 DOLLARS
25.5000 g., 0.9250 Silver .7583 oz. ASW, 40 mm. **Obv:** National arms above date within wreath **Rev:** Yellow-crowned Amazon parrot

Date	Mintage	F	VF	XF	Unc	BU
1982FM (P)	381	Value: 120				

KM# 80 10 DOLLARS
Copper-Nickel, 40 mm. **Obv:** National arms within wreath, date below **Rev:** Great Curassow, right, denomination above **Rev. Designer:** Michael Rizzello **Note:** Mule.

Date	Mintage	F	VF	XF	Unc	BU
1982FM (U)	—	—	—	—	25.00	35.00

KM# 71 10 DOLLARS

Copper-Nickel, 40 mm. **Obv:** National arms above date within wreath **Rev:** Ringed Kingfisher, right, denomination above

Date	Mintage	F	VF	XF	Unc	BU
1983FM (U)	—	—	10.00	20.00	50.00	60.00
1983FM (P)	—	Value: 65.00				

KM# 71a 10 DOLLARS

25.5000 g., 0.9250 Silver .7583 oz. ASW, 40 mm. **Obv:** National arms above date within wreath **Rev:** Ringed kingfisher

Date	Mintage	F	VF	XF	Unc	BU
1983FM (P)	334	Value: 135				

KM# 75 10 DOLLARS

Copper-Nickel, 40 mm. **Obv:** National arms within wreath, date below **Rev:** Laughing falcon, left, head divides denomination at top

Date	Mintage	F	VF	XF	Unc	BU
1984FM (U)	—	—	—	—	50.00	55.00
1984FM (P)	—	Value: 60.00				

KM# 75a 10 DOLLARS

25.5000 g., 0.9250 Silver .7583 oz. ASW, 40 mm. **Obv:** National arms within wreath, date below **Rev:** Laughing falcon

Date	Mintage	F	VF	XF	Unc	BU
1984FM (P)	—	Value: 115				
1985 Proof	212	Value: 135				

KM# 102 10 DOLLARS

Copper-Nickel **Subject:** 10th Anniversary of Independence **Obv:** National arms within wreath, denomination below **Rev:** Building within circle, dates below

Date	Mintage	F	VF	XF	Unc	BU
ND(1991)	1,000,000	—	—	—	8.50	10.00

KM# 102a 10 DOLLARS

28.2800 g., 0.9250 Silver .8411 oz. ASW **Subject:** 10th Anniversary of Independence **Obv:** National arms within wreath, denomination below **Rev:** Building within circle, dates below

Date	Mintage	F	VF	XF	Unc	BU
ND(1991) Proof	Est. 1,000	Value: 37.50				

KM# 104 10 DOLLARS

28.2800 g., 0.9250 Silver .8411 oz. ASW **Subject:** 10th Anniversary of Central Bank **Obv:** National arms within wreath, denomination below **Rev:** Jabiru stork, left, within circle, two dates at bottom

Date	Mintage	F	VF	XF	Unc	BU
1992 Proof	Est. 1,000	Value: 40.00				

KM# 109 10 DOLLARS

155.6000 g., 0.9990 Silver 5.0032 oz. ASW **Subject:** 50th Anniversary - Battle of El Alamein - Lt. Gen. Montgomery **Obv:** Portrait of Queen Elizabeth II **Rev:** Similar to 250 Dollars, KM#113

Date	Mintage	F	VF	XF	Unc	BU
1992 Proof	Est. 2,500	Value: 150				

KM# 121 10 DOLLARS

28.2800 g., 0.9250 Silver .8411 oz. ASW **Subject:** Royal visit **Obv:** Queen's portrait **Rev:** Cameo portraits above flowers

Date	Mintage	F	VF	XF	Unc	BU
1994 Proof	—	Value: 42.50				

KM# 123 10 DOLLARS

28.2800 g., 0.9250 Silver .8411 oz. ASW **Subject:** World Cup Soccer **Obv:** National arms within wreath, date below **Rev:** Soccer net and ball, denomination at bottom

Date	Mintage	F	VF	XF	Unc	BU
1994 Proof	Est. 10,000	Value: 45.00				

KM# 124 10 DOLLARS

28.2800 g., 0.9250 Silver .8411 oz. ASW **Obv:** National arms within wreath, date at below **Rev:** Carrack sailing ship, denomination at bottom

Date	Mintage	F	VF	XF	Unc	BU
1995 Proof	Est. 15,000	Value: 40.00				

KM# 125 10 DOLLARS

28.2800 g., 0.9250 Silver .8411 oz. ASW **Series:** Endangered Wildlife **Obv:** National arms within wreath, date below **Rev:** Howler monkey on branch, left, denomination below

Date	Mintage	F	VF	XF	Unc	BU
1995 Proof	Est. 10,000	Value: 45.00				

KM# 127 10 DOLLARS

28.2800 g., 0.9250 Silver .8411 oz. ASW **Series:** Atlanta 1996 - 26th Summer Olympics **Obv:** National arms within wreath, date below **Rev:** Female softball player, denomination below

Date	Mintage	F	VF	XF	Unc	BU
1996 Proof	Est. 10,000	Value: 45.00				

KM# 128 10 DOLLARS

28.2800 g., 0.9250 Silver .8411 oz. ASW **Subject:** Battle of St. George's Caye **Obv:** National arms within wreath, denomination below **Rev:** Oar-powered gunboats within circle, two dates below

Date	Mintage	F	VF	XF	Unc	BU
ND(1998) Proof	—	Value: 55.00				

KM# 130 10 DOLLARS

28.2800 g., 0.9250 Silver .8411 oz. ASW **Subject:** 50th Anniversary - University of the West Indies **Obv:** National arms within wreath, denomination below **Rev:** University arms, two dates below

Date	Mintage	F	VF	XF	Unc	BU
ND(1999) Proof	1,000	Value: 55.00				

KM# 79 20 DOLLARS

23.3300 g., 0.9250 Silver .6938 oz. ASW **Series:** Los Angeles Olympics **Obv:** National arms within wreath, date below **Rev:** Bicyclist, Olympic torch at right, denomination lower left

Date	Mintage	F	VF	XF	Unc	BU
1984 Proof	1,050	Value: 45.00				

KM# 82 20 DOLLARS
23.3300 g., 0.9250 Silver .6938 oz. ASW **Series:** Decade for Women **Obv:** National arms within wreath, date below **Rev:** Figures of women and trees, 3/4 surround legend and symbol at center, denomination at bottom

Date	Mintage	F	VF	XF	Unc	BU
1985 Proof	Est. 20,000	Value: 27.50				

KM# 54 25 DOLLARS
27.8100 g., 0.9250 Silver .8270 oz. ASW **Subject:** 25th Anniversary of Coronation **Obv:** Bust of Queen Elizabeth II, right, date below **Obv. Designer:** Arnold Machin **Rev:** Crown with supporters, two dates below, denomination at bottom

Date	Mintage	F	VF	XF	Unc	BU
1978FM (U)	352	—	—	22.00	50.00	60.00
1978FM (P)	8,438	Value: 17.50				

KM# 61 25 DOLLARS
30.2800 g., 0.5000 Silver .4686 oz. ASW **Subject:** 10th Anniversary - Caribbean Development Bank **Obv:** National arms **Rev:** Globe above flag, denomination below

Date	Mintage	F	VF	XF	Unc	BU
ND(1980)FM (P)	2,647	Value: 25.00				

KM# 72 25 DOLLARS
30.2800 g., 0.5000 Silver .4686 oz. ASW **Subject:** 30th Anniversary of Coronation **Obv:** National arms within wreath, date below **Rev:** Crossed sceptres divide dates and royal symbols, denomination at bottom

Date	Mintage	F	VF	XF	Unc	BU
1983FM (P)	2,944	Value: 20.00				

KM# 78 25 DOLLARS
28.2800 g., 0.9250 Silver .8411 oz. ASW **Subject:** Royal visit

Date	Mintage	F	VF	XF	Unc	BU
1985 Proof	Est. 5,000	Value: 25.00				

KM# 97 25 DOLLARS
28.2800 g., 0.9250 Silver .8411 oz. ASW **Subject:** 500th Anniversary - Columbus Discovery of New World **Obv:** Crowned bust of Queen Elizabeth II right **Obv. Designer:** Raphael Maklouf **Rev:** Ship in full sail, denomination at bottom

Date	Mintage	F	VF	XF	Unc	BU
1989 Proof	Est. 5,000	Value: 35.00				

KM# 106 25 DOLLARS
28.2800 g., 0.9250 Silver .8411 oz. ASW **Series:** Barcelona 1992 - 25th Summer Olympics **Obv:** National arms within wreath, denomination below **Rev:** Hurdlers jumping large date

Date	Mintage	F	VF	XF	Unc	BU
1992 Proof	30,000	Value: 27.50				

KM# 110 25 DOLLARS
3.1300 g., 0.9990 Gold .1000 oz. AGW **Subject:** 50th Anniversary - Battle of El Alamein **Obv:** Bust of Queen Elizabeth II right **Rev:** 4 tanks, denomination at bottom **Rev. Designer:** Willem Vis

Date	Mintage	F	VF	XF	Unc	BU
1992 Proof	Est. 500	Value: 85.00				

KM# 66 50 DOLLARS
1.5000 g., 0.5000 Gold .0241 oz. AGW **Obv:** National arms, date below, 3/4 wreath surrounds **Rev:** White-necked Jacobin hummingbird, right, drinking from flower, date below

Date	Mintage	F	VF	XF	Unc	BU
1981FM (U)	200	—	—	—	65.00	70.00
1981FM (P)	2,873	Value: 50.00				

KM# 81 50 DOLLARS
129.6000 g., 0.9250 Silver 3.8547 oz. ASW, 63 mm. **Subject:** Bird Conservation **Obv:** National arms within wreath, date below **Rev:** Red-footed booby, left, denomination above **Rev. Designer:** Michael Rizzello

Date	Mintage	F	VF	XF	Unc	BU
1985 Proof	Est. 10,000	Value: 110				

KM# 111 50 DOLLARS
7.8100 g., 0.9990 Gold .2511 oz. AGW **Subject:** 50th Anniversary - Battle of El Alamein **Obv:** Bust of Queen Elizabeth II right **Rev:** Field Marshall Rommel, right, in uniform, denomination lower right **Rev. Designer:** Willem Vis

Date	Mintage	F	VF	XF	Unc	BU
1992 Proof	Est. 500	Value: 225				

KM# 51 100 DOLLARS
6.2100 g., 0.5000 Gold .0998 oz. AGW **Subject:** 30th Anniversary of United Nations **Obv:** National arms above date within wreath **Rev:** Buildings, design above, denomination at top

Date	Mintage	F	VF	XF	Unc	BU
1975FM (M)	100	—	—	—	200	—
1975FM (U)	2,028	—	—	—	75.00	—
1975FM (P)	8,126	Value: 70.00				

KM# 52 100 DOLLARS
6.2100 g., 0.5000 Gold .0998 oz. AGW **Obv:** National arms above date, denomination below **Rev:** Ancient Mayan symbols representing numbers and days

Date	Mintage	F	VF	XF	Unc	BU
1976FM (M)	216	—	—	—	175	—
1976FM (P)	11,000	Value: 70.00				

KM# 53 100 DOLLARS
6.2100 g., 0.5000 Gold .0998 oz. AGW **Obv:** National arms above date, denomination at bottom **Rev:** Kinich Ahau, Mayan sun god

Date	Mintage	F	VF	XF	Unc	BU
1977FM (M)	200	—	—	—	135	—

Date	Mintage	F	VF	XF	Unc	BU
1977FM (U)	51	—	—	—	350	—
1977FM (P)	7,859	Value: 70.00				

KM# 55 100 DOLLARS
6.2100 g., 0.5000 Gold .0998 oz. AGW **Obv:** National arms above date, denomination below **Rev:** Itzamna Lord of Heaven, Ruler of the Gods

Date	Mintage	F	VF	XF	Unc	BU
1978FM (U)	351	—	—	—	150	—
1978FM (P)	7,178	Value: 70.00				

KM# 58 100 DOLLARS
6.2100 g., 0.5000 Gold .0998 oz. AGW **Obv:** National arms, denomination below **Rev:** Queen angelfish, left, date below

Date	Mintage	F	VF	XF	Unc	BU
1979FM (U)	400	—	—	—	125	—
1979FM (P)	4,465	Value: 90.00				

KM# 59 100 DOLLARS
6.4700 g., 0.5000 Gold .1040 oz. AGW **Obv:** National arms, denomination below **Rev:** Star of Bethlehem, date below

Date	Mintage	F	VF	XF	Unc	BU
1979FM (U)	—	—	—	—	120	—
1979FM (P)	—	Value: 80.00				

KM# 62 100 DOLLARS
6.2100 g., 0.5000 Gold .0998 oz. AGW **Obv:** National arms, denomination below **Rev:** Moorish idol reef fish, date below

Date	Mintage	F	VF	XF	Unc	BU
1980FM (U)	400	—	—	—	150	—
1980FM (P)	3,993	Value: 100				

KM# 63 100 DOLLARS
6.2100 g., 0.5000 Gold .0998 oz. AGW **Obv:** National arms, denomination below **Rev:** Orchids, date below

Date	Mintage	F	VF	XF	Unc	BU
1980FM (U)	250	—	—	—	140	—
1980FM (P)	2,454	Value: 95.00				

KM# 67 100 DOLLARS
6.2100 g., 0.5000 Gold .0998 oz. AGW **Obv:** National arms above denomination within circle **Rev:** Yellow swallowtail butterfly within circle, date below **Shape:** Five-sided coin

Date	Mintage	F	VF	XF	Unc	BU
1981FM (U)	200	—	—	—	200	—
1981FM (P)	1,658	Value: 250				

KM# 68 100 DOLLARS
6.2100 g., 0.5000 Gold .0998 oz. AGW **Subject:** National independence **Rev:** Vertical date to left of map

Date	Mintage	F	VF	XF	Unc	BU
1981FM (U)	50	—	—	—	325	—
1981FM (P)	1,401	Value: 125				

KM# 70 100 DOLLARS
6.2100 g., 0.5000 Gold .0998 oz. AGW **Obv:** National arms within wreath, denomination below **Rev:** Kinkajou, left, date below

Date	Mintage	F	VF	XF	Unc	BU
1982FM (U)	10	—	—	—	500	—
1982FM (P)	586	Value: 200				

KM# 73 100 DOLLARS
6.2100 g., 0.5000 Gold .0998 oz. AGW **Obv:** National arms within wreath, denomination below **Rev:** Margay jungle cat, right, date below

Date	Mintage	F	VF	XF	Unc	BU
1983FM (U)	20	—	—	—	400	—
1983FM (P)	494	Value: 250				

KM# 74 100 DOLLARS
6.2100 g., 0.5000 Gold .0998 oz. AGW **Obv:** National arms within wreath, denomination below **Rev:** White-tailed deer, facing, date lower right

Date	Mintage	F	VF	XF	Unc	BU
1984FM (P)	965	Value: 150				

KM# 76 100 DOLLARS
6.2100 g., 0.5000 Gold .0998 oz. AGW **Obv:** national arms within wreath, denomination below **Rev:** Ocelot, facing, date below

Date	Mintage	F	VF	XF	Unc	BU
1985FM (P) Proof	899	Value: 250				

KM# 103 100 DOLLARS
15.9760 g., 0.9170 Gold .4708 oz. AGW **Subject:** 10th Anniversary of Independence **Note:** Similar to 10 Dollars, KM#102.

Date	Mintage	F	VF	XF	Unc	BU
1991 Proof	Est. 500	Value: 550				

KM# 112 100 DOLLARS
15.6000 g., 0.9990 Gold .5016 oz. AGW **Subject:** 50th Anniversary - Battle of El Alamein **Obv:** Bust of Queen Elizabeth II right **Rev:** Infantry advancing, denomination below **Rev. Designer:** Willem Vis

Date	Mintage	F	VF	XF	Unc	BU
1992 Proof	Est. 500	Value: 450				

KM# 129 100 DOLLARS
15.9700 g., 0.9170 Gold .4707 oz. AGW **Subject:** Battle of St. George's Caye **Note:** Similar to KM#128.

Date	Mintage	F	VF	XF	Unc	BU
ND(1998) Proof	—	Value: 675				

KM# 56 250 DOLLARS
8.8100 g., 0.9000 Gold .2549 oz. AGW **Obv:** National arms above date, denomination below **Rev:** Jaguar, date at right **Rev. Designer:** Gilroy Roberts

Date	Mintage	F	VF	XF	Unc	BU
1978FM (U)	200	—	—	—	210	225
1978FM (P)	Est. 3,399	Value: 220				

Note: 1,712 pieces were used in first-day covers

KM# 98 250 DOLLARS
15.9800 g., 0.9170 Gold .4708 oz. AGW **Subject:** 500th Anniversary of Columbus' Discovery of America

Date	Mintage	F	VF	XF	Unc	BU
1989 Proof	Est. 500	Value: 375				

KM# 105 250 DOLLARS
15.9800 g., 0.9170 Gold .4708 oz. AGW **Subject:** 10th Anniversary of Central Bank **Rev:** Jabiru stork **Note:** Similar to KM#104.

Date	Mintage	F	VF	XF	Unc	BU
1992	Est. 500	Value: 350				

KM# 113 250 DOLLARS
31.2100 g., 0.9990 Gold 1.0035 oz. AGW **Subject:** 50th Anniversary - Battle of El Alamein **Obv:** Bust of Queen Elizabeth II right **Rev:** Lt. Gen. Montgomery, denomination at bottom **Rev. Designer:** Willem Vis

Date	Mintage	F	VF	XF	Unc	BU
1992 Proof	Est. 500	Value: 700				

KM# 101 500 DOLLARS
47.5400 g., 0.9170 Gold 1.4018 oz. AGW **Subject:** Royal Visit
Note: Similar to KM#78.

Date	Mintage	F	VF	XF	Unc	BU
1985 Proof	Est. 250	Value: 1,000				

KM# 120 500 DOLLARS
47.5400 g., 0.9170 Gold 1.4018 oz. AGW **Subject:** 40th Anniversary - Coronation of Queen Elizabeth II

Date	Mintage	F	VF	XF	Unc	BU
1993 Proof	Est. 100	Value: 1,150				

KM# 122 500 DOLLARS
47.5400 g., 0.9170 Gold 1.4018 oz. AGW **Subject:** Royal Visit
Rev: Cameo portraits, flanked by roses, flowers above denomination

Date	Mintage	F	VF	XF	Unc	BU
1994 Proof	—	Value: 1,150				

PIEFORTS

KM#	Date	Mintage	Identification	Mkt Val
P1	1990	1,000	Dollar. 0.9250 Silver. KM99a.	60.00

MINT SETS

KM#	Date	Mintage	Identification	Issue Price	Mkt Val
MS1	1974 (8)	4,506	KM38-45	20.00	20.00
MS2	1975 (8)	1,095	KM43-50	27.50	30.00
MS3	1976 (8)	759	KM43-50	27.50	32.00
MS4	1977 (8)	—	KM43-45, 46b -47b, 48-50	27.50	30.00
MS5	1978 (8)	458	KM43-45, 46b-47b, 48-50	28.50	32.00
MS6	1979 (8)	808	KM43-44, 46b-47b, 48-50, 57	28.50	32.00
MS7	1980 (8)	761	KM43-44, 46b-47b, 48-50, 60	29.50	40.00
MS8	1981 (8)	297	KM43-44, 46b-47b, 48-50, 65	29.50	60.00
MS9	1982 (8)	—	KM69, 83-89	29.50	60.00
MS10	1983 (8)	—	KM71, 83-89	29.50	65.00
MS11	1984 (8)	—	KM75, 90-96	—	75.00
MS12	1992 (6)	—	KM33a, 34a, 35-37, 99	24.00	24.00

PROOF SETS

KM#	Date	Mintage	Identification	Issue Price	Mkt Val
PS1	1974 (8)	21,470	KM38-45	35.00	18.00
PS2	1974 (8)	31,368	KM38a-45a	100	40.00
PS3	1975 (8)	8,794	KM43-50	37.50	22.00
PS4	1975 (8)	13,275	KM43a-50a	110	40.00
PS5	1976 (8)	4,893	KM43-50	37.50	25.00
PS6	1976 (8)	5,897	KM43a-50a	110	45.00
PS7	1977 (8)	2,107	KM43-45, 46b-47b, 48-50	37.50	30.00
PS8	1977 (8)	3,197	KM43a-50a	110	47.50
PS9	1978 (8)	1,671	KM43-45, 46b, 47b, 48-50	39.50	30.00
PS10	1978 (8)	3,342	KM43a-50a	110	47.50
PS11	1979 (8)	1,287	KM43-44, 46b-47b, 48-50, 57	41.50	35.00
PS12	1979 (8)	2,445	KM43a-44a, 46a-50a, 57a	112	70.00
PS13	1980 (8)	920	KM43-44, 46b-47b, 48-50, 60	41.50	40.00
PS14	1980 (8)	1,826	KM43a-44a, 46a-50a, 60a	222	80.00
PS15	1981 (8)	643	KM43-44, 46b-47b, 48-50, 65	41.50	60.00
PS16	1981 (8)	615	KM43a-44a, 46a-50a, 65a	—	115
PS17	1982 (8)	—	KM69, 83-89	49.50	75.00
PS18	1982 (8)	381	KM69a, 83a-89a	222	285
PS19	1983 (8)	306	KM71, 83-89	37.00	70.00
PS20	1983 (8)	241	KM71a, 83a-89a	197	300
PS21	1984 (8)	—	KM75, 90-96	37.00	65.00
PS22	1984 (8)	397	KM75a, 90a-96a	197	280
PS23	1985 (8)	212	KM75a, 90a-96a	—	325
PS24	1992 (4)	500	KM110-113	1,600	1,450
PS25	1992 (2)	—	KM107-108	100	100

BENIN (Dahomey)

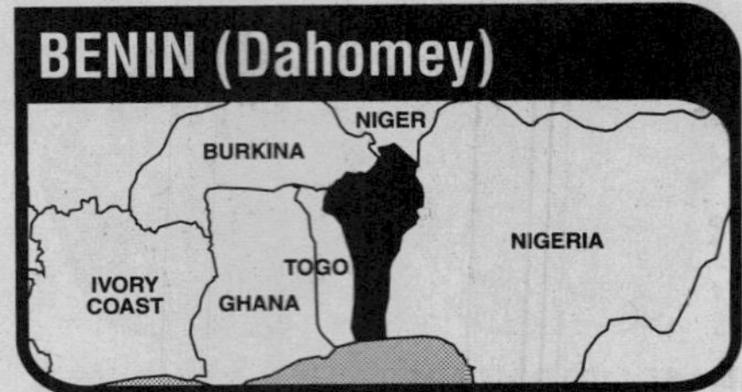

The Republic of Benin (formerly the Republic of Dahomey), located on the south side of the African bulge between Togo and Nigeria, has an area of 43,500 sq. mi. (112,620 sq. km.) and a population of 5.5 million. Capital: Porto-Novo. The principal industry of Benin, one of the poorest countries of West Africa, is the processing of palm oil products. Palm kernel oil, peanuts, cotton, and coffee are exported.

PEOPLES REPUBLIC

STANDARD COINAGE

KM# 10 200 FRANCS
Copper **Obv:** National arms, denomination below **Rev:** Sailing ship - Preussen, date below

Date	Mintage	F	VF	XF	Unc	BU
1993	—	—	—	—	7.50	—
1993 Proof	100	Value: 85.00				

KM# 8 200 FRANCS
Copper-Nickel **Series:** Prehistoric Animals **Obv:** National arms, denomination below **Rev:** Dinosaurs - Acanthopholis, right, date lower right

Date	Mintage	F	VF	XF	Unc	BU
1994	—	—	—	—	25.00	—

KM# 15 200 FRANCS
Copper **Series:** Prehistoric Animals **Obv:** National arms, denomination below **Rev:** Dinosaurs - Tyrannosaurus Rex, left, date lower right

Date	Mintage	F	VF	XF	Unc	BU
1994	—	—	—	—	20.00	—
1994 Proof	100	Value: 85.00				

KM# 16 200 FRANCS
Copper-Nickel **Subject:** United Nations - 50 Years **Obv:** National arms, denomination below **Rev:** Family in boat, building in background, two dates at bottom

Date	Mintage	F	VF	XF	Unc	BU
ND(1995)	—	—	—	—	8.50	—

KM# 17 200 FRANCS
Nickel-Bonded Steel And Enamel **Rev:** WWI Austrian Hansa - Brandenburg D. I

Date	Mintage	F	VF	XF	Unc	BU
1995	25,000	—	—	—	30.00	—

KM# 23 200 FRANCS
Copper **Series:** Prehistoric Animals **Obv:** National arms, denomination below **Rev:** Iguanodon, looking left, date at lower left

Date	Mintage	F	VF	XF	Unc	BU
1995 Proof	100	Value: 85.00				

KM# 25 200 FRANCS
Copper-Nickel **Series:** Sydney 2000 **Obv:** National arms, denomination below **Rev:** Classic sculpture and racing scullcraft, date below

Date	Mintage	F	VF	XF	Unc	BU
1999	10,000	—	—	—	7.50	—

KM# 3 500 FRANCS
12.0000 g., 0.9990 Silver .3858 oz. ASW **Subject:** 1992 World Cup Soccer **Obv:** National arms, denomination below **Rev:** Soccer goalie, large date in legend, small date at bottom

Date	Mintage	F	VF	XF	Unc	BU
1992	Est. 10,000	—	—	—	45.00	—

KM# 14 500 FRANCS
8.2500 g., 0.9990 Silver .2650 oz. ASW **Rev:** Soccer - Eifel Tower, flag and ball, date below **Edge Lettering:** 1995 World Cup Soccer

Date	Mintage	F	VF	XF	Unc	BU
1995 Proof	30,000	Value: 22.50				

KM# 31 500 FRANCS
8.2500 g., 0.9990 Silver .2650 oz. ASW, 30.1 mm. **Obv:** National arms, denomination below **Rev:** Sailing ship, Gorch Fock **Edge:** Plain

Date	Mintage	F	VF	XF	Unc	BU
1996 Proof	10,000	Value: 22.50				

KM# 1 1000 FRANCS
19.9100 g., 0.9990 Silver .6402 oz. ASW **Obv:** National arms, denomination below **Rev:** Five hands holding jar **Note:** Five hands holding jar

Date	Mintage	F	VF	XF	Unc	BU
ND(1992) Proof	1,000	Value: 38.00				

KM# 2 1000 FRANCS
19.9100 g., 0.9990 Silver .6402 oz. ASW **Obv:** National arms, denomination below **Rev:** National map in radiant sun

Date	Mintage	F	VF	XF	Unc	BU
ND(1992) Proof	1,000	Value: 37.50				

KM# 4 1000 FRANCS
20.0000 g., 0.9990 Silver .6430 oz. ASW **Series:** Barcelona 1992 - 25th Summer Olympics **Rev:** Gymnast, date at right

Date	Mintage	F	VF	XF	Unc	BU
1992 Proof	Est. 5,000	Value: 28.00				

KM# 5 1000 FRANCS
20.0000 g., 0.9990 Silver .6430 oz. ASW **Subject:** 1992 World Cup Soccer **Obv:** National arms, denomination below **Rev:** Player kicking ball, date at rght

Date	Mintage	F	VF	XF	Unc	BU
1992 Proof	Est. 10,000	Value: 35.00				

KM# 6 1000 FRANCS
20.0000 g., 0.9990 Silver .6430 oz. ASW **Subject:** Protection of Nature **Rev:** Elephant, within inner circle, elephants, (trunk to tail), form outer circle

Date	Mintage	F	VF	XF	Unc	BU
1993 Proof	—	Value: 60.00				

KM# 7 1000 FRANCS
20.0000 g., 0.9990 Silver .6430 oz. ASW **Rev:** Sailing ship - Preussen, date below

Date	Mintage	F	VF	XF	Unc	BU
1993	100	—	—	—	150	—
1993 Proof	10,000	Value: 32.50				

KM# 27 1000 FRANCS
20.0000 g., 0.9990 Silver .6430 oz. ASW **Series:** Protection of Nature **Rev:** Elephant, people, tree, map

Date	Mintage	F	VF	XF	Unc	BU
1993 Proof	—	Value: 37.50				

KM# 9 1000 FRANCS
15.8600 g., 0.9940 Silver .5095 oz. ASW **Series:** Dinosaurs **Obv:** National arms, denomination below **Rev:** Tyrannosaurus Rex, left, date below tail

Date	Mintage	F	VF	XF	Unc	BU
1994 Proof	—	Value: 50.00				

KM# 12 1000 FRANCS
20.0000 g., 0.9990 Silver .6424 oz. ASW **Series:** 1996 Olympics **Rev:** Three runners, large date below, small date at left

Date	Mintage	F	VF	XF	Unc	BU
1995 Proof	15,000	Value: 28.00				

KM# 13 1000 FRANCS
20.0000 g., 0.9990 Silver .6424 oz. ASW **Subject:** 35 Years of Independence **Rev:** Woman stirring pot, hut at back left

Date	Mintage	F	VF	XF	Unc	BU
1995 Proof	2,000	Value: 35.00				

KM# 18 1000 FRANCS
20.0000 g., 0.9990 Silver .6424 oz. ASW **Rev:** WWI Austrian Hansa - Brandenburg D. I, date lower right

Date	Mintage	F	VF	XF	Unc	BU
1995 Proof	15,000	Value: 45.00				

KM# 28 1000 FRANCS
20.0000 g., 0.9990 Silver .6424 oz. ASW **Series:** Prehistoric Animals **Rev:** Iguanodon, looking left, date below tail **Edge:** Plain

Date	Mintage	F	VF	XF	Unc	BU
1995 Proof	—	Value: 35.00				

KM# 19 1000 FRANCS
20.0000 g., 0.9990 Silver .6424 oz. ASW **Rev:** Head of Multicolor panther, 3/4 facing, date above

Date	Mintage	F	VF	XF	Unc	BU
1996 Proof	—	Value: 60.00				

KM# 20 1000 FRANCS
15.0000 g., 0.9990 Silver .4817 oz. ASW **Subject:** 1996 World Cup Soccer **Obv:** National arms, denomination below **Rev:** Two multicolor soccer players, small date at left

Date	Mintage	F	VF	XF	Unc	BU
1996 Proof	—	Value: 45.00				

KM# 50 1000 FRANCS
Silver, 35 mm. **Subject:** Sports **Rev:** 16th World Series Soccer

Date	Mintage	F	VF	XF	Unc	BU
1996	—	Value: 35.00				

KM# 43 1000 FRANCS
15.0000 g., 0.9990 Silver 0.4818 oz. ASW, 35 mm. **Obv:** National arms, denomination below **Rev:** Multicolor zebra **Edge:** Plain

Date	Mintage	F	VF	XF	Unc	BU
1997 Proof	—	Value: 55.00				

KM# 48 1000 FRANCS
15.0000 g., 0.9990 Silver 0.4818 oz. ASW, 34 mm. **Subject:** Soccer **Obv:** National arms **Rev:** Multicolor Eiffel Tower and ball **Edge:** Plain

Date	Mintage	F	VF	XF	Unc	BU
1997 Proof	—	Value: 25.00				

KM# 21 1000 FRANCS
15.0000 g., 0.9990 Silver .4817 oz. ASW **Series:** 2000 Summer Olympics **Obv:** National arms, denomination below **Rev:** Multicolored shot-putter and Olympic torch, date at right

Date	Mintage	F	VF	XF	Unc	BU
1997	100	—	—	—	150	—
1997 Proof	—	Value: 40.00				

KM# 24 1000 FRANCS
20.0000 g., 0.9990 Silver .6430 oz. ASW **Series:** 2000 Summer Olympics **Obv:** National arms, denomination below **Rev:** Two runners and statue

Date	Mintage	F	VF	XF	Unc	BU
1997	100	—	—	—	100	—
1997 Proof	7,500	Value: 32.50				

KM# 26 1000 FRANCS
20.1300 g., 0.9990 Silver .6465 oz. ASW **Series:** 2000 Summer Olympics **Obv:** National arms, denomination below **Rev:** Classic statue and racing scullcraft, date below

Date	Mintage	F	VF	XF	Unc	BU
1999 Proof	5,000	Value: 35.00				

KM# 51 1000 FRANCS
Silver, 23 mm. **Subject:** Wildlife **Rev:** Elephant with calf

Date	Mintage	F	VF	XF	Unc	BU
1999	—	Value: 40.00				

KM# 39 1000 FRANCS
14.9600 g., 0.9990 Silver 0.4805 oz. ASW, 34.9 mm. **Subject:** Gutenberg **Obv:** National arms, denomination below **Rev:** Portrait and printing press, two dates lower right **Edge:** Plain

Date	Mintage	F	VF	XF	Unc	BU
1999 Proof	7,000	Value: 30.00				

KM# 47 1000 FRANCS
14.9600 g., 0.9990 Silver 0.4805 oz. ASW, 35 mm. **Obv:** National arms **Rev:** Calipers, radiant sun and grid **Edge:** Plain

Date	Mintage	F	VF	XF	Unc	BU
2000 Proof	—	Value: 35.00				

KM# 11 6000 FRANCS
20.1300 g., 0.9990 Silver .6465 oz. ASW **Series:** Protection of Nature **Obv:** National arms, denomination below **Rev:** Elephant within inner circle, elephants, (trunk to tail), form outer circle

Date	Mintage	F	VF	XF	Unc	BU
1993 Proof	5,000	Value: 60.00				

KM# 22 6000 FRANCS
28.3400 g., 0.9250 Silver .8248 oz. ASW **Subject:** 50th Anniversary U.N. **Obv:** National arms, denomination below **Rev:** Family in boat, two dates at bottom

Date	Mintage	F	VF	XF	Unc	BU
ND(1995) Proof	—	Value: 42.50				

KM# 34 15000 FRANCS
500.0000 g., 0.9990 Silver 16.0593 oz. ASW, 84.8 mm. **Subject:** Wildlife Protection **Obv:** National arms, denomination below **Rev:** Multicolor crocodile, date at right **Edge:** Reeded **Note:** Photo reduced.

Date	Mintage	F	VF	XF	Unc	BU
1996 Proof	300	Value: 350				
1997 Proof	—	Value: 300				

KM# 36 20000 FRANCS
846.0152 g., 0.9990 Silver 27.2 oz. ASW, 90.4 mm. **Subject:** African Fauna **Obv:** National arms, denomination below **Rev:** Multicolor zebra, date upper right **Edge:** Plain **Note:** Photo reduced.

Date	Mintage	F	VF	XF	Unc	BU
1997 Proof	—	Value: 600				

KM# 29 30000 FRANCS
15.5500 g., 0.9990 Gold .4494 oz. AGW **Obv:** National arms **Rev:** Map in radiant sun **Edge:** Reeded

Date	Mintage	F	VF	XF	Unc	BU
ND(1992) Proof	Est. 100	Value: 600				

KM# 30 100000 FRANCS
31.1035 g., 0.9990 Gold 1.0000 oz. AGW **Obv:** National arms **Rev:** President **Edge:** Reeded

Date	Mintage	F	VF	XF	Unc	BU
1992 Rare	Est. 10	Value: 1,500				

PIEFORTS

KM#	Date	Mintage	Identification	Mkt Val
P1	1997	—	1000 Francs. Silver. KM#21	200
P2	1997	—	1000 Francs. Silver. KM#24.	175
P3	1999	—	1000 Francs. Silver. KM#26.	135

The Parliamentary British Colony of Bermuda, situated in the western Atlantic Ocean 660 miles (1,062 km.) east of North Carolina, has an area of 20.6 sq. mi. (53 sq. km.) and a population of 61,600. Capital: Hamilton. Concentrated essences, beauty preparations, and cut flowers are exported. Most Bermudians derive their livelihood from tourism. The British monarch is the head of state and is represented by a governor.

Bermuda was discovered by Juan de Bermudez, a Spanish navigator, in about 1503. British influence dates from 1609 when a group of Virginia-bound British colonists under the command of Sir George Somers was shipwrecked on the islands for 10 months. The islands were settled in 1612 by 60 British colonists from the Virginia Colony and became a crown colony in 1684. The earliest coins issued for the island were the "Hogge Money" series of 2, 3, 6 and 12 pence, the name derived from the pig in the obverse design, a recognition of the quantity of such animals then found there. The next issue for Bermuda was the Birmingham coppers of 1793; all locally circulating coinage was demonetized in 1842, when the currency of the United Kingdom became standard. Internal autonomy was obtained by the constitution of June 8, 1968.

In February, 1970, Bermuda converted from its former currency, which was sterling, to a decimal currency, the dollar unit which is equal to one U.S. dollar. On July 31, 1972, Bermuda severed its monetary link with the British pound sterling and pegged its dollar to be the same value as the U.S. dollar.

RULERS
British

MINT MARKS
CHI - Valcambi, Switzerland
FM - Franklin Mint, U.S.A.*

***NOTE**: From 1975-1985 the Franklin Mint produced coinage in up to 3 different qualities. Qualities of issue are designated in ( ) after each date and are defined as follows:

(M) MATTE - Normal circulation strike or a dull finish produced by sandblasting special uncirculated (polish finish) or proof quality dies.

(U) SPECIAL UNCIRCULATED - Polished or proof-like in appearance without any frosted features.

(P) PROOF - The highest quality obtainable having mirror-like fields and frosted features.

MONETARY SYSTEM
12 Pence = 1 Shilling
20 Shillings = 1 Pound

BRITISH ADMINISTRATION

POUND STERLING COINAGE

KM# 13 CROWN
28.2800 g., 0.9250 Silver .8411 oz. ASW, 38 mm. **Subject:** 350th Anniversary - Colony Founding **Obv:** Crowned bust of Queen Elizabeth II right **Obv. Designer:** Cecil Thomas **Rev:** Ships circling land, dates flank, denomination below, **Rev. Designer:** N. Silliman

Date	Mintage	F	VF	XF	Unc	BU
1959	100,000	—	BV	12.00	15.00	—
1959 Matte proof	—	Value: 1,000				

Note: Mintage: 6-10

KM# 14 CROWN
22.3200 g., 0.5000 Silver .3636 oz. ASW, 36 mm. **Obv:** Bust of Queen Elizabeth II right **Obv. Designer:** Cecil Thomas **Rev:** Lion holding shield divides date **Rev. Designer:** George Kruger-Gray

Date	Mintage	F	VF	XF	Unc	BU
1964	470,000	—	—	BV	6.50	—
1964 Proof	30,000	Value: 8.50				

DECIMAL COINAGE

100 Cents = 1 Dollar

KM# 15 CENT
Bronze, 19 mm. **Obv:** Queen's bust, right **Rev:** Wild boar, left, date below, denomination above

Date	Mintage	F	VF	XF	Unc	BU
1970	5,500,000	—	—	0.10	0.30	0.50
1970 Proof	11,000	Value: 0.50				
1971	4,256,000	—	—	0.10	0.30	0.50
1973	2,144,000	—	—	0.10	0.30	0.50
1974	856,000	—	—	0.10	0.35	0.60
1975	1,000,000	—	—	0.10	0.30	0.50
1976	1,000,000	—	—	0.10	0.30	0.50
1977	2,000,000	—	—	0.10	0.30	0.50
1978	3,160,000	—	—	0.10	0.30	0.50
1980	3,520,000	—	—	0.10	0.30	0.50
1981	3,200,000	—	—	0.10	0.30	0.50
1982	320,000	—	—	0.10	0.30	0.50
1983	800,000	—	—	0.10	0.30	0.50
1983 Proof	6,474	Value: 1.00				
1984	800,000	—	—	0.10	0.30	0.50
1985	800,000	—	—	0.10	0.30	0.50

KM# 44 CENT
Bronze, 19 mm. **Obv:** Crowned Queen's bust, right **Rev:** Wild boar, left date below, denomination above

Date	Mintage	F	VF	XF	Unc	BU
1986	1,360,000	—	—	0.10	0.30	0.50
1986 Proof	Inc. above	Value: 2.00				
1987	2,048,000	—	—	0.10	0.30	0.50
1990	1,500,000	—	—	0.10	0.30	0.50

KM# 44a CENT
Steel, 19 mm. **Obv:** Crowned Queen's bust, right **Rev:** Wild boar, left, date below, denomination above **Note:** Copper coated.

Date	Mintage	F	VF	XF	Unc	BU
1988	2,500,000	—	—	—	2.50	3.50

KM# 44b CENT
Copper Plated Zinc, 19 mm. **Obv:** Crowned Queen's bust, right **Rev:** Wild boar, left, date below, denomination above

Date	Mintage	F	VF	XF	Unc	BU
1991	2,400,000	—	—	0.10	0.25	0.50
1993	1,600,000	—	—	0.10	0.25	0.50
1994	1,440,000	—	—	0.10	0.25	0.50
1995	1,920,000	—	—	0.10	0.25	0.50
1996	3,200,000	—	—	0.10	0.25	0.50
1997	3,400,000	—	—	0.10	0.25	0.50

KM# 44c CENT
3.7000 g., 0.9250 Silver .11 oz. ASW, 19 mm. **Obv:** Crowned Queen's bust, right **Rev:** Wild boar, left, date below, denomination above **Note:** In sets only.

Date	Mintage	F	VF	XF	Unc	BU
1995 Proof	2,000	Value: 5.00				

KM# 44d CENT
6.2000 g., 0.9170 Gold .1827 oz. AGW, 19 mm. **Obv:** Crowned Queen's bust, right **Rev:** Wild boar, left, date below, denomination above **Note:** In sets only.

Date	Mintage	F	VF	XF	Unc	BU
1995 Proof	500	Value: 145				

KM# 107 CENT
Copper Plated Zinc, 19 mm. **Obv:** Head with tiara right **Obv. Designer:** Rank-Broadley **Rev:** Wild boar left, divides date and denomination

Date	Mintage	F	VF	XF	Unc	BU
1999	2,400,000	—	—	—	0.50	0.75
1999 Proof	2,500	Value: 2.50				
2000	—	—	—	—	0.50	0.75
2000 Proof	—	Value: 2.50				

KM# 16 5 CENTS
Copper-Nickel, 21 mm. **Obv:** Queen's bust, right **Rev:** Queen angel fish, left, date below, denomination above

Date	Mintage	F	VF	XF	Unc	BU
1970	2,190,000	—	0.10	0.15	0.50	0.75
1970 Proof	11,000	Value: 0.50				
1974	310,000	—	0.10	0.15	0.50	0.75
1975	500,000	—	0.10	0.15	0.50	0.75
1977	500,000	—	0.10	0.15	0.50	0.75
1979	500,000	—	0.10	0.15	0.50	0.75
1980	1,100,000	—	0.10	0.15	0.50	0.75
1981	900,000	—	0.10	0.15	0.50	0.75
1982	200,000	—	0.10	0.15	0.50	0.75
1983	800,000	—	0.10	0.15	0.50	0.75
1983 Proof	6,474	Value: 1.50				
1984	500,000	—	0.10	0.15	0.50	0.75
1985	—	—	0.10	0.15	0.50	0.75

KM# 45 5 CENTS
Copper-Nickel, 21 mm. **Obv:** Crowned Queen's bust, right **Rev:** Queen angel fish, left, date below, denomination above

Date	Mintage	F	VF	XF	Unc	BU
1986	1,400,000	—	0.10	0.15	0.50	0.75
1986 Proof	Inc. above	Value: 2.50				
1987	1,050,000	—	0.10	0.15	0.50	0.75
1988	700,000	—	0.10	0.15	0.50	0.75
1990	700,000	—	0.10	0.15	0.50	0.75
1993	600,000	—	0.10	0.15	0.50	0.75
1994	1,100,000	—	0.10	0.15	0.50	0.75
1995	700,000	—	0.10	0.15	0.50	0.75
1996	1,500,000	—	0.10	0.15	0.50	0.75
1997	300,000	—	0.10	0.15	0.50	0.75

KM# 45a 5 CENTS
5.7000 g., 0.9250 Silver .1695 oz. ASW, 21 mm. **Obv:** Crowned Queen's bust, right **Rev:** Queen angel fish, left, date below, denomination above **Note:** In sets only.

Date	Mintage	F	VF	XF	Unc	BU
1995 Proof	2,000	Value: 9.00				

KM# 45b 5 CENTS
5.7000 g., 0.9170 Gold .2859 oz. AGW, 21 mm. **Obv:** Crowned Queen's bust, right **Rev:** Queen angel fish, left, date below, denomination above **Note:** In sets only.

Date	Mintage	F	VF	XF	Unc	BU
1995 Proof	500	Value: 215				

KM# 108 5 CENTS
Copper-Nickel, 21 mm. **Obv:** Head with tiara right **Obv. Designer:** Rank-Broadley **Rev:** Queen angel fish left, divides date and denomination

Date	Mintage	F	VF	XF	Unc	BU
1999	900,000	—	—	—	0.75	1.00
1999 Proof	2,500	Value: 3.50				

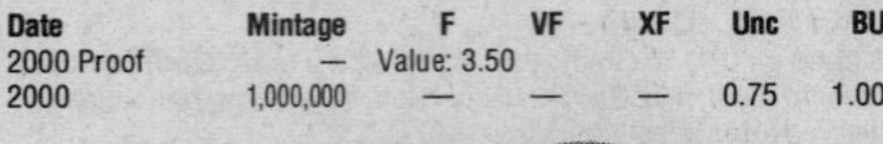

Date	Mintage	F	VF	XF	Unc	BU
2000 Proof	—	Value: 3.50				
2000	1,000,000	—	—	—	0.75	1.00

KM# 17 10 CENTS

Copper-Nickel, 17.8 mm. **Obv:** Queen's bust, right **Rev:** Bermuda lily, date above, stems divide denomination at bottom,

Date	Mintage	F	VF	XF	Unc	BU
1970	2,500,000	—	0.10	0.15	0.35	0.50
1970 Proof	11,000	Value: 0.50				
1971	2,000,000	—	0.10	0.15	0.35	0.50
1978	500,000	—	0.10	0.15	0.40	0.60
1979	800,000	—	0.10	0.15	0.40	0.60
1980	1,100,000	—	0.10	0.15	0.35	0.50
1981	1,300,000	—	0.10	0.15	0.35	0.50
1982	400,000	—	0.10	0.15	0.40	0.60
1983	1,000,000	—	0.10	0.15	0.35	0.50
1983 Proof	6,474	Value: 2.00				
1984	500,000	—	0.10	0.15	0.40	0.60
1985	—	—	0.10	0.15	0.40	0.60

KM# 46 10 CENTS

Copper-Nickel, 17.8 mm. **Obv:** Crowned Queen's bust, right **Rev:** Bermuda lily, date above, stems divide denomination below

Date	Mintage	F	VF	XF	Unc	BU
1986	750,000	—	0.10	0.15	0.40	0.60
1986 Proof	Inc. above	Value: 3.50				
1987	2,000,000	—	0.10	0.15	0.40	0.60
1988	720,000	—	0.10	0.15	0.40	0.60
1990	1,500,000	—	0.10	0.15	0.40	0.60
1993	15,000	—	0.10	0.15	0.40	0.60
1994	1,400,000	—	0.10	0.15	0.40	0.60
1995	1,400,000	—	0.10	0.15	0.40	0.60
1996	1,000,000	—	0.10	0.15	0.40	0.60
1997	800,000	—	0.10	0.15	0.40	0.60

KM# 46a 10 CENTS

2.8000 g., 0.9250 Silver .0833 oz. ASW, 17.8 mm. **Obv:** Crowned Queen's bust, right **Rev:** Bermuda lily, date above, stems divide denomination below **Note:** In sets only.

Date	Mintage	F	VF	XF	Unc	BU
1995 Proof	2,000	Value: 12.00				

KM# 46b 10 CENTS

4.7500 g., 0.9170 Gold .1400 oz. AGW, 17.8 mm. **Obv:** Crowned Queen's bust, right **Rev:** Bermuda lily, date above, stems divide denomination below **Note:** In sets only.

Date	Mintage	F	VF	XF	Unc	BU
1995 Proof	500	Value: 140				

KM# 109 10 CENTS

Copper-Nickel, 17.8 mm. **Obv:** Head with tiara right **Obv. Designer:** Rank-Broadley **Rev:** Bermuda lily divides date and denomination

Date	Mintage	F	VF	XF	Unc	BU
1999 Proof	2,500	Value: 6.00				
1999	1,400,000	—	—	—	0.85	1.00
2000	—	—	—	—	0.85	1.00
2000 Proof	—	Value: 6.00				

KM# 18 25 CENTS

Copper-Nickel, 24 mm. **Obv:** Queen's bust, right **Rev:** Yellow-billed tropical bird, right, date below, denomination above

Date	Mintage	F	VF	XF	Unc	BU
1970	1,500,000	—	0.30	0.50	1.25	1.50
1970 Proof	11,000	Value: 2.00				
1973	1,000,000	—	0.30	0.50	1.25	1.50
1979	570,000	—	0.30	0.50	1.25	1.50
1980	1,120,000	—	0.30	0.50	1.25	1.50
1981	2,200,000	—	0.30	0.50	1.25	1.50
1982	160,000	—	0.30	0.50	1.50	1.75
1983	600,000	—	0.30	0.50	1.25	1.50
1983 Proof	6,474	Value: 2.50				
1984	400,000	—	0.30	0.50	1.25	1.50
1985	—	—	0.30	0.50	1.25	1.50

KM# 32 25 CENTS

Copper-Nickel, 24 mm. **Subject:** 375th Anniversary of Bermuda **Obv:** Queen's bust, right **Rev:** Arms of the Bermudas, date below, denomination above

Date	Mintage	F	VF	XF	Unc	BU
1984	36,850	—	—	1.50	4.50	—

KM# 32a 25 CENTS

5.9600 g., 0.9250 Silver .1772 oz. ASW, 24 mm. **Subject:** 375th Anniversary of Bermuda **Obv:** Queen's bust, right **Rev:** Arms of the Bermudas

Date	Mintage	F	VF	XF	Unc	BU
1984 Proof	19,250	Value: 15.00				

KM# 33 25 CENTS

Copper-Nickel, 24 mm. **Subject:** 375th Anniversary of Bermuda **Obv:** Queen's bust, right **Rev:** City of Hamilton arms, date below, denomination above

Date	Mintage	F	VF	XF	Unc	BU
1984	36,850	—	—	1.50	4.50	—

KM# 33a 25 CENTS

5.9600 g., 0.9250 Silver .1772 oz. ASW, 24 mm. **Subject:** 375th Anniversary of Bermuda **Obv:** Queen's bust, right **Rev:** City of Hamilton arms

Date	Mintage	F	VF	XF	Unc	BU
1984 Proof	19,250	Value: 15.00				

KM# 34 25 CENTS

Copper-Nickel, 24 mm. **Subject:** 375th Anniversary of Bermuda **Obv:** Queen's bust, right **Rev:** Town of St. George arms, date below, denomination above

Date	Mintage	F	VF	XF	Unc	BU
1984	36,850	—	—	1.50	4.50	—

KM# 34a 25 CENTS

5.9600 g., 0.9250 Silver .1772 oz. ASW, 24 mm. **Subject:** 375th Anniversary of Bermuda **Obv:** Queen's bust, right **Rev:** Town of St. George arms

Date	Mintage	F	VF	XF	Unc	BU
1984 Proof	19,250	Value: 15.00				

KM# 35 25 CENTS

Copper-Nickel, 24 mm. **Subject:** 375th Anniversary of Bermuda **Obv:** Queen's bust, right **Rev:** Warwick Parish arms, date below, denomination above

Date	Mintage	F	VF	XF	Unc	BU
1984	36,850	—	—	1.50	4.50	—

KM# 35a 25 CENTS

5.9600 g., 0.9250 Silver .1772 oz. ASW, 24 mm. **Subject:** 375th Anniversary of Bermuda **Obv:** Queen's bust, right **Rev:** Warwick Parish arms

Date	Mintage	F	VF	XF	Unc	BU
1984 Proof	19,250	Value: 15.00				

KM# 36 25 CENTS

Copper-Nickel, 24 mm. **Subject:** 375th Anniversary of Bermuda **Obv:** Queen's bust, right **Rev:** Smith's Parish arms, date below, denomination above

Date	Mintage	F	VF	XF	Unc	BU
1984	36,850	—	—	1.50	4.50	—

KM# 36a 25 CENTS

5.9600 g., 0.9250 Silver .1772 oz. ASW, 24 mm. **Subject:** 375th Anniversary of Bermuda **Obv:** Queen's bust, right **Rev:** Smith's Parish arms

Date	Mintage	F	VF	XF	Unc	BU
1984 Proof	19,250	Value: 15.00				

KM# 37 25 CENTS

Copper-Nickel, 24 mm. **Subject:** 375th Anniversary of Bermuda **Obv:** Queen's bust, right **Rev:** Devonshire Parish arms, date below, denomination above

Date	Mintage	F	VF	XF	Unc	BU
1984	36,850	—	—	1.50	4.50	—

KM# 37a 25 CENTS

5.9600 g., 0.9250 Silver .1772 oz. ASW, 24 mm. **Subject:** 375th Anniversary of Bermuda **Obv:** Queen's bust, right **Rev:** Devonshire Parish arms

Date	Mintage	F	VF	XF	Unc	BU
1984 Proof	19,250	Value: 15.00				

KM# 38 25 CENTS

Copper-Nickel, 24 mm. **Subject:** 375th Anniversary of Bermuda **Obv:** Queen's bust, right **Rev:** Sandy's Parish arms, date below, denomination above

Date	Mintage	F	VF	XF	Unc	BU
1984	36,850	—	—	1.50	4.50	—

KM# 38a 25 CENTS

5.9600 g., 0.9250 Silver .1772 oz. ASW, 24 mm. **Subject:** 375th Anniversary of Bermuda **Obv:** Queen's bust, right **Rev:** Sandy's Parish arms

Date	Mintage	F	VF	XF	Unc	BU
1984 Proof	19,250	Value: 15.00				

KM# 39 25 CENTS

Copper-Nickel, 24 mm. **Subject:** 375th Anniversary of Bermuda **Obv:** Queen's bust, right **Rev:** Hamilton Parish arms, date below, denomination above

Date	Mintage	F	VF	XF	Unc	BU
1984	36,850	—	—	1.50	4.50	—

KM# 39a 25 CENTS

5.9600 g., 0.9250 Silver .1772 oz. ASW, 24 mm. **Subject:** 375th Anniversary of Bermuda **Obv:** Queen's bust, right **Rev:** Hamilton Parish arms

Date	Mintage	F	VF	XF	Unc	BU
1984 Proof	19,250	Value: 15.00				

KM# 40 25 CENTS
Copper-Nickel, 24 mm. **Subject:** 375th Anniversary of Bermuda **Obv:** Queen's bust, right **Rev:** Southampton Parish arms, date below, denomination above

Date	Mintage	F	VF	XF	Unc	BU
1984	36,850	—	—	1.50	4.50	—

KM# 40a 25 CENTS
5.9600 g., 0.9250 Silver .1772 oz. ASW, 24 mm. **Subject:** 375th Anniversary of Bermuda **Obv:** Queen's bust, right **Rev:** Southampton Parish arms

Date	Mintage	F	VF	XF	Unc	BU
1984 Proof	19,250	Value: 15.00				

KM# 41 25 CENTS
Copper-Nickel, 24 mm. **Subject:** 375th Anniversary of Bermuda **Obv:** Queen's bust, right **Rev:** Pembroke Parish arms, date below, denomination above

Date	Mintage	F	VF	XF	Unc	BU
1984	36,850	—	—	1.50	4.50	—

KM# 41a 25 CENTS
5.9600 g., 0.9250 Silver .1772 oz. ASW, 24 mm. **Subject:** 375th Anniversary of Bermuda **Obv:** Queen's bust, right **Rev:** Pembroke Parish arms

Date	Mintage	F	VF	XF	Unc	BU
1984 Proof	19,250	Value: 15.00				

KM# 42 25 CENTS
Copper-Nickel, 24 mm. **Subject:** 375th Anniversary of Bermuda **Obv:** Queen's bust, right **Rev:** Paget Parish arms, date below, denomination above

Date	Mintage	F	VF	XF	Unc	BU
1984	36,850	—	—	1.50	4.50	—

KM# 42a 25 CENTS
5.9600 g., 0.9250 Silver .1772 oz. ASW, 24 mm. **Subject:** 375th Anniversary of Bermuda **Obv:** Queen's bust, right **Rev:** Paget Parish arms

Date	Mintage	F	VF	XF	Unc	BU
1984 Proof	19,250	Value: 15.00				

KM# 47 25 CENTS
Copper-Nickel, 24 mm. **Subject:** Yellow-billed tropical bird, right, date below, denomination above **Obv:** Crowned Queen's bust, right

Date	Mintage	F	VF	XF	Unc	BU
1986	560,000	—	0.30	0.50	1.00	1.50
1986 Proof	2,500	Value: 6.00				
1987	600,000	—	0.30	0.50	1.00	1.50
1988	600,000	—	0.30	0.50	1.00	1.50
1993	480,000	—	0.30	0.50	1.00	1.50
1994	1,040,000	—	0.30	0.50	1.00	1.50
1995	960,000	—	0.30	0.50	1.00	1.50
1996	1,200,000	—	0.30	0.50	1.00	1.50
1997	—	—	0.30	0.50	1.00	1.50
1998	—	—	0.30	0.50	1.00	1.50

KM# 47a 25 CENTS
7.0000 g., 0.9250 Silver .2082 oz. ASW, 24 mm. **Subject:** Yellow-billed tropical bird **Obv:** Queen's bust, right **Note:** In sets only.

Date	Mintage	F	VF	XF	Unc	BU
1995 Proof	2,000	Value: 18.00				

KM# 47b 25 CENTS
11.7000 g., 0.9170 Gold .3448 oz. AGW, 24 mm. **Subject:** Yellow-billed tropical bird **Obv:** Queen's bust, right **Note:** In sets only.

Date	Mintage	F	VF	XF	Unc	BU
1995 Proof	500	Value: 250				

KM# 110 25 CENTS
Copper-Nickel, 24 mm. **Obv:** Head with tiara right **Obv. Designer:** Rank-Broadley **Rev:** Yellow-billed tropical bird right, divides date and denomination

Date	Mintage	F	VF	XF	Unc	BU
1999	800,000	—	—	—	1.50	2.00
1999 Proof	2,500	Value: 10.00				
2000	800,000	—	—	—	1.50	2.00
2000 Proof	—	Value: 9.00				

KM# 19 50 CENTS
Copper-Nickel, 30.5 mm. **Obv:** Bust of Queen Elizabeth II, right **Rev:** Arms, date below, denomination divided at top

Date	Mintage	F	VF	XF	Unc	BU
1970	1,000,000	—	0.60	0.75	1.00	1.50
1970 Proof	11,000	Value: 2.00				
1978	200,000	—	0.60	0.85	1.25	1.75
1980	60,000	—	0.60	0.85	1.50	2.00
1981	100,000	—	0.60	0.85	1.25	1.75
1982	80,000	—	0.60	0.85	1.50	2.00
1983	60,000	—	0.60	0.85	1.50	2.00
1983 Proof	6,474	Value: 4.50				
1984	40,000	—	0.60	0.85	1.50	2.00
1985	40,000	—	0.60	0.85	1.50	2.00

KM# 48 50 CENTS
Copper-Nickel, 30.5 mm. **Obv:** Bust of Queen Elizabeth II, right **Rev:** National arms, date below, denomination divided at top

Date	Mintage	F	VF	XF	Unc	BU
1986	60,000	—	0.60	0.85	1.50	2.00
1986 Proof	Inc. above	Value: 6.00				
1988	60,000	—	0.60	0.85	1.50	2.00

KM# 20 DOLLAR
28.2800 g., 0.8000 Silver .7273 oz. ASW **Obv:** Bust of Queen Elizabeth II right **Rev:** Map, fish above and below

Date	Mintage	F	VF	XF	Unc	BU
1970 Proof	11,000	Value: 16.00				

KM# 22 DOLLAR
28.2800 g., 0.5000 Silver .4546 oz. ASW **Subject:** Silver Wedding Anniversary **Obv:** Queen's bust, right **Rev:** Royal monograms divided by map, denomination and date below

Date	Mintage	F	VF	XF	Unc	BU
1972	65,074	—	—	—	9.00	—

KM# 22a DOLLAR
28.2800 g., 0.9250 Silver .8411 oz. ASW **Subject:** Silver Wedding Anniversary **Obv:** Queen's bust, right **Rev:** Royal monograms divided by map, denomination and date below

Date	Mintage	F	VF	XF	Unc	BU
1972 Proof	14,708	Value: 13.50				

KM# 28 DOLLAR
Copper-Nickel, 38.5 mm. **Subject:** Wedding of Prince Charles and Lady Diana **Obv:** Bust of Queen Elizabeth II, right **Rev:** Conjoined busts of the wedding couple

Date	Mintage	F	VF	XF	Unc	BU
1981	65,004	—	—	—	7.00	—

KM# 28a DOLLAR
28.2800 g., 0.9250 Silver .8411 oz. ASW **Subject:** Wedding of Prince Charles and Lady Diana **Obv:** Bust of Queen Elizabeth II, right **Rev:** Conjoined busts of the wedding couple

Date	Mintage	F	VF	XF	Unc	BU
1981 Proof	16,296	Value: 16.00				

KM# 30 DOLLAR
Nickel-Brass **Subject:** Cahow over Bermuda **Obv:** Queen's bust, right **Rev:** Bird flying over map, date below, denomination above

Date	Mintage	F	VF	XF	Unc	BU
1983	250,000	—	—	—	4.00	5.00
1983 Proof	6,474	Value: 7.00				

KM# 43 DOLLAR
Copper-Nickel, 38.5 mm. **Subject:** Cruise Ship Tourism **Obv:** Bust of Queen Elizabeth II, right **Rev:** The Bermuda Buttery, an early refrigeration building and a cruise ship in the distance

Date	Mintage	F	VF	XF	Unc	BU
1985	11,000	—	—	—	5.00	—

KM# 43a DOLLAR
28.2800 g., 0.9250 Silver .8411 oz. ASW **Subject:** Cruise Ship Tourism **Obv:** Bust of Queen Elizabeth II, right **Rev:** The Bermuda Buttery, an early refrigeration building and a cruise ship in the distance

Date	Mintage	F	VF	XF	Unc	BU
1985	2,500	—	—	—	25.00	—
1985 Proof	4,000	Value: 25.00				

KM# 49 DOLLAR
Copper-Nickel, 38.5 mm. **Series:** World Wildlife Fund **Obv:** Crowned Queen's bust, right **Rev:** Sea turtle, chelonia mydas, within circle, date below, denomination above

Date	Mintage	F	VF	XF	Unc	BU
1986	33,320	—	—	—	17.50	—

KM# 49a DOLLAR
28.2800 g., 0.9250 Silver .8411 oz. ASW **Series:** World Wildlife Fund **Obv:** Crowned Queen's bust, right **Rev:** Sea turtle within circle, denomination above

Date	Mintage	F	VF	XF	Unc	BU
1986	10,000	—	—	—	25.00	—
1986 Proof	Est. 21,872	Value: 35.00				

KM# 50 DOLLAR
Nickel-Brass **Obv:** Bust of Queen Elizabeth II, right **Rev:** Cahow over Bermuda

Date	Mintage	F	VF	XF	Unc	BU
1986 Proof	—	Value: 12.50				

KM# 52 DOLLAR
Copper-Nickel, 38.5 mm. **Subject:** 50th Anniversary of Commercial Aviation **Obv:** Crowned Queen's bust, right **Rev:** Amphibious plane, denomination below, date above

Date	Mintage	F	VF	XF	Unc	BU
1987	9,000	—	—	—	7.00	—

KM# 52a DOLLAR
28.2800 g., 0.6250 Silver .8411 oz. ASW **Subject:** 50th Anniversary of Commercial Aviation **Obv:** Crowned Queen's bust, right **Rev:** Amphibious plane, denomination below, date above

Date	Mintage	F	VF	XF	Unc	BU
1987	5,000	—	—	—	20.00	—
1987 Proof	5,000	Value: 20.00				

KM# 56 DOLLAR
Nickel-Brass, 26 mm. **Obv:** Crowned Queen's bust, right **Rev:** Boat with full sails, date below, denomination above **Rev. Designer:** Eldon Trimingham III **Edge:** Alternating reeded and plain **Note:** Circulation type.

Date	Mintage	F	VF	XF	Unc	BU
1988	2,000,000	—	—	—	3.00	4.00
1993	15,000	—	—	—	4.00	5.00
Note: In sets only.						
1996	—	—	—	—	3.00	4.00
1997	—	—	—	—	3.00	4.00

KM# 56a DOLLAR
9.2000 g., 0.9250 Silver .2736 oz. ASW **Obv:** C
bust, right **Rev:** Boat with full sails, date below, de

Date	Mintage	F	VF
1988 Proof	Est. 3,000	Value: 25.00	
1995 Proof	2,000	Value: 32.00	

Note: In sets only.

KM# 55 DOLLAR
Copper-Nickel, 38.5 mm. **Subject:** Railroad
Queen's bust, right **Rev:** Train, date below, de

Date	Mintage	F	VF
1988	2,000,000	—	—

KM# 55a DOLLAR
28.2800 g., 0.9250 Silver .8411 oz. ASW **Su**
Obv: Crowned Queen's bust, right **Rev:** Train
denomination above

Date	Mintage	F	VF
1988	5,000	—	—
1988 Proof	5,000	Value: 25.00	

KM# 56b DOLLAR
15.5000 g., 0.9170 Gold .4568 oz. AGW **Obv:**
bust, right **Rev:** Train, date below, denomina

Date	Mintage	F	VF
1995 Proof	500	Value: 400	

Note: In sets only.

KM# 61 DOLLAR
Copper-Nickel, 38.5 mm. **Subject:** Monar
Project **Obv:** Crowned Queen's bust, right **R**
Butterflies within flower chain, denomination
Rev. Designer: Frederick Mogford

Date	Mintage	F	VF
1989	5,000	—	—

KM# 61a DOLLAR
28.2800 g., 0.9250 Silver .8411 oz. ASW S
Conservation Project **Obv:** Crowned Queen
Monarch butterflies within flower chain, denom
above

Date	Mintage	F	VF
1989	5,000	—	—
1989 Proof	5,000	Value: 35.00	

KM# 67 DOLLAR
Copper-Nickel, 38.5 mm. **Subject:** Queen
birthday **Obv:** Crowned Queen's bust, right,
Rev: Crowned decorative "E"s, backs joined
two dates below **Rev. Designer:** Robert E

Date	Mintage	F	VF
1990	5,000	—	—

KM# 94 DOLLAR
Copper-Nickel, 38.5 mm. **Subject:** Queen Elizabeth II's 70th Birthday **Obv:** Queen's portrait **Rev:** Horse-drawn carriage, denomination divides dates below

Date	Mintage	F	VF	XF	Unc	BU
ND(1996)	5,000	—	—	—	12.00	—

KM# 105 DOLLAR
28.2800 g., 0.9250 Silver .8416 oz. ASW **Series:** Olympic Games **Obv:** Crowned Queen's bust, right **Rev:** Horse with rider, jumping right, denomination below

Date	Mintage	F	VF	XF	Unc	BU
1996 Proof	30,000	Value: 30.00				

KM# 95 DOLLAR
Copper-Nickel, 35 mm. **Subject:** Wreck of the Sea Venture **Obv:** Crowned Queen's portrait, right, within triangle, date below, denomination at left **Rev:** Shipwreck from Bermudan arms, within triangle **Shape:** 3-sided

Date	Mintage	F	VF	XF	Unc	BU
1997	—	—	—	—	12.00	—

KM# 126 DOLLAR
16.0000 g., 0.9250 Silver 0.4758 oz. ASW, 28.3 mm. **Subject:** Queen Mother **Obv:** Queen Elizabeth II **Rev:** 1937 Coronation portrait **Edge:** Reeded

Date	Mintage	F	VF	XF	Unc	BU
1997 Proof	—	Value: 20.00				

KM# 119 DOLLAR
28.2800 g., 0.9250 Silver .8410 oz. ASW, 39 mm. **Subject:** World Wildlife Fund - Conserving Nature **Obv:** Crowned Queen's bust, right, denomination below **Rev:** Bermuda Rock Skink (Eumeces longirostris) on rock, date below **Edge:** Reeded

Date	Mintage	F	VF	XF	Unc	BU
1997 Proof	—	Value: 35.00				

KM# 104 DOLLAR
Copper-Nickel, 35 mm. **Obv:** Crowned Queen's portrait, right, date below, denomination at left **Rev:** Sailing ship Deliverance and map **Rev. Designer:** John Warwick **Shape:** Triangular

Date	Mintage	F	VF	XF	Unc	BU
1998	—	—	—	—	12.00	—

KM# 104a DOLLAR
20.0000 g., 0.9250 Silver 0.5948 oz. ASW, 35 mm. **Obv:** Queen Elizabeth II **Rev:** Ship on map **Edge:** Plain **Shape:** Triangular

Date	Mintage	F	VF	XF	Unc	BU
1998 Proof	6,500	Value: 50.00				

KM# 125 DOLLAR
28.2800 g., Copper-Nickel, 38.6 mm. **Subject:** Millennium **Obv:** Queen's portrait **Rev:** Radiant sun behind sailing ship **Shape:** Scalloped

Date	Mintage	F	VF	XF	Unc	BU
1999-2000	—	—	—	—	22.00	—

KM# 111 DOLLAR
Nickel-Brass, 26 mm. **Obv:** Head with tiara right **Obv. Designer:** Rank-Broadley **Rev:** Sailboat divides date and denomination **Rev. Designer:** Eldron Trimingham III

Date	Mintage	F	VF	XF	Unc	BU
1999	12,000	—	—	—	3.00	3.50
1999 Proof	2,500	Value: 22.00				
2000	—	—	—	—	3.00	3.50
2000 Proof	—	Value: 22.00				

KM# 117 DOLLAR
28.2800 g., Copper-Nickel, 38.6 mm. **Subject:** Tall Ships **Obv:** Queen's head, right **Rev:** Three-masted sailing ship **Edge:** Reeded

Date	Mintage	F	VF	XF	Unc	BU
2000	10,000	—	—	—	12.00	—

KM# 117a DOLLAR
28.2800 g., 0.9250 Silver .8410 oz. ASW, 38.6 mm. **Subject:** Tall Ships **Obv:** Queen's head right **Rev:** Three-masted sailing ship **Edge:** Reeded

Date	Mintage	F	VF	XF	Unc	BU
2000 Proof	10,000	Value: 100				

KM# 122 DOLLAR
28.3000 g., 0.9250 Silver 0.8416 oz. ASW, 38.5 mm. **Subject:** Queen Mother **Obv:** Queen's portrait, right, within circle **Rev:** 1937 Coronation portrait, date below, within circle, denomination below circle **Edge:** Reeded

Date	Mintage	F	VF	XF	Unc	BU
2000 Proof	—	Value: 40.00				

KM# 64 2 DOLLARS
28.2800 g., 0.9250 Silver .8411 oz. ASW **Obv:** Crowned Queen's bust right **Rev:** Cicada insects, date below, denomination above

Date	Mintage	F	VF	XF	Unc	BU
1990 Proof	3,000	Value: 32.50				

KM# 65 2 DOLLARS
28.2800 g., 0.9250 Silver .8411 oz. ASW **Subject:** Wildlife **Obv:** Crowned Queen's bust, right **Rev:** Tree frog, left, date below, denomination above

Date	Mintage	F	VF	XF	Unc	BU
1990 Proof	3,000	Value: 32.50				

KM# 68 2 DOLLARS
28.2800 g., 0.9250 Silver .8411 oz. ASW **Obv:** Crowned Queen's bust, right **Rev:** Yellow-crowned night heron, left, denomination below, date above

Date	Mintage	F	VF	XF	Unc	BU
1991 Proof	3,000	Value: 30.00				

KM# 69 2 DOLLARS
28.2800 g., 0.9250 Silver .8411 oz. ASW **Obv:** Crowned Queen's bust, right **Rev:** Spiny lobster, date above, denomination below

Date	Mintage	F	VF	XF	Unc	BU
1991 Proof	3,000	Value: 30.00				

KM# 71 2 DOLLARS
28.2800 g., 0.9250 Silver .8411 oz. ASW **Obv:** Crowned Queen's bust, right **Rev:** Bluebird feeding nestling, denomination above, date below

Date	Mintage	F	VF	XF	Unc	BU
1992 Proof	2,500	Value: 30.00				

KM# 72 2 DOLLARS
28.2800 g., 0.9250 Silver .8411 oz. ASW **Obv:** Crowned Queen's bust, right **Rev:** Cedar tree, date below, denomination above

Date	Mintage	F	VF	XF	Unc	BU
1992 Proof	2,500	Value: 30.00				

KM# 81 2 DOLLARS
23.0000 g., 0.9250 Silver .684 oz. ASW **Subject:** 200 Years of Bermudan Coinage

Date	Mintage	F	VF	XF	Unc	BU
1993 Proof	5,000	Value: 28.00				

KM# 83 2 DOLLARS
28.2800 g., 0.9250 Silver .8411 oz. ASW **Obv:** Crowned Queen's bust, right **Rev:** Humpback whale, leaping right, date above, denomination below

Date	Mintage	F	VF	XF	Unc	BU
1993 Proof	2,000	Value: 35.00				

KM# 84 2 DOLLARS
28.2800 g., 0.9250 Silver .8411 oz. ASW **Obv:** Crowned Queen's bust, right **Rev:** Bermuda longtail bird, date above, denomination below

Date	Mintage	F	VF	XF	Unc	BU
1993 Proof	2,000	Value: 35.00				

KM# 89 2 DOLLARS
28.2800 g., 0.9250 Silver .8411 oz. ASW **Subject:** City of Hamilton's 200th Anniversary **Obv:** Crowned Queen's bust, right **Rev:** Ship at dock within circle

Date	Mintage	F	VF	XF	Unc	BU
1993 Proof	250	Value: 70.00				

KM# 86 2 DOLLARS
27.2800 g., 0.9250 Silver .8411 oz. ASW **Subject:** Royal visit **Obv:** Crowned Queen's bust, right **Rev:** Map divides conjoined heads of royal couple and royal emblem, circle surrounds all **Rev. Designer:** Robert Elderton

Date	Mintage	F	VF	XF	Unc	BU
1994 Proof	10,000	Value: 35.00				

KM# 87 2 DOLLARS
28.2800 g., 0.9250 Silver .8411 oz. ASW **Obv:** Crowned Queen's bust, right **Rev:** Long-snout seahorse, date below, denomination above

Date	Mintage	F	VF	XF	Unc	BU
1994 Proof	1,500	Value: 35.00				

KM# 88 2 DOLLARS
28.2800 g., 0.9250 Silver .8411 oz. ASW **Obv:** Crowned Queen's bust, right **Rev:** Lightbourn's fusinus (seashell), date below, denomination above

Date	Mintage	F	VF	XF	Unc	BU
1994 Proof	1,500	Value: 35.00				

KM# 123 2 DOLLARS
28.2000 g., 0.9250 Silver 0.8387 oz. ASW, 38.6 mm. **Subject:** Queen's 70th Birthday **Obv:** Crowned Queen's portrait, right **Rev:** Carriage and tree , denomination divides dates at bottom **Edge:** Reeded

Date	Mintage	F	VF	XF	Unc	BU
1996 Proof	12,500	Value: 35.00				

KM# 136 2 DOLLARS
28.1400 g., 0.9250 Silver 0.8369 oz. ASW, 38.6 mm. **Subject:** Town of St. George 200th Anniversary **Obv:** Elizabeth II **Rev:** St. George killing the dragon **Edge:** Reeded

Date	Mintage	F	VF	XF	Unc	BU
1997 Proof	250	Value: 150				

KM# 121 2 DOLLARS
28.1300 g., 0.9250 Silver 0.8366 oz. ASW, 38.5 mm. **Subject:** Queen's Golden Wedding Anniversary **Obv:** Crowned Queen's portrait, right **Rev:** Royal couple descending stairs with gold insert shield at right, denomination below, two dates at right **Edge:** Reeded

Date	Mintage	F	VF	XF	Unc	BU
ND(1997) Proof	—	Value: 45.00				

KM# 116 2 DOLLARS

28.2800 g., 0.9250 Silver .8410 oz. ASW, 38.6 mm. **Subject:** Millennium **Obv:** Queen's head right **Rev:** Radiant sun behind sailing ship dividing dates 1999-2000 above map **Shape:** Scalloped

Date	Mintage	F	VF	XF	Unc	BU
1999-2000 Proof	30,000	Value: 55.00				

KM# 92 3 DOLLARS

20.0000 g., 0.9250 Silver .5948 oz. ASW **Subject:** Bermuda Triangle **Obv:** Crowned Queen's portrait, right, within triangle, date below, denomination at left **Rev:** Map, compass, and capsizing ship, within triangle **Shape:** Three-sided coin **Note:** Similar to 60 Dollars, KM#93.

Date	Mintage	F	VF	XF	Unc	BU
1996 Proof	5,000	Value: 55.00				

KM# 99 3 DOLLARS

20.2500 g., 0.9250 Silver .6022 oz. ASW **Subject:** Wreck of the Sea Venture **Obv:** Queen's portrait **Rev:** Shipwreck scene

Date	Mintage	F	VF	XF	Unc	BU
1997 Proof	6,000	Value: 50.00				

KM# 106 3 DOLLARS

20.0000 g., 0.9250 Silver .5948 oz. ASW **Obv:** Crowned Queen's portrait, right, date below, denomination at left **Rev:** Sailing ship Deliverance and map within triangle **Rev. Designer:** John Warwick **Shape:** Three-sided

Date	Mintage	F	VF	XF	Unc	BU
1998 Proof	6,500	Value: 50.00				

KM# 106a 3 DOLLARS

31.4890 g., 0.9990 Gold 1.0114 oz. AGW, 35 mm. **Obv:** Queen Elizabeth II **Rev:** Ship on map **Edge:** Plain **Shape:** Triangular

Date	Mintage	F	VF	XF	Unc	BU
1998	—	—	—	—	—	1,400

KM# 31 5 DOLLARS

Nickel-Brass **Obv:** Queen's bust, right **Rev:** Onion superimposed over map, date below, denomination above

Date	Mintage	F	VF	XF	Unc	BU
1983	100,000	—	—	—	6.00	—
1983 Proof	6,474	Value: 10.00				

KM# 51 5 DOLLARS

Brass **Obv:** Bust of Queen Elizabeth II, right **Rev:** Onion superimposed over Bermuda map

Date	Mintage	F	VF	XF	Unc	BU
1986 Proof	2,500	Value: 12.50				

KM# 54 5 DOLLARS

155.5150 g., 0.9990 Silver 5 oz. ASW, 65 mm. **Subject:** Sea Venture Wreck **Obv:** Bust of Queen Elizabeth II, right **Rev:** Sailing ship, date and denomination below **Note:** Photo reduced.

Date	Mintage	F	VF	XF	Unc	BU
1987 Proof	6,800	Value: 85.00				

KM# 62 5 DOLLARS

155.5150 g., 0.9990 Silver 5 oz. ASW, 65 mm. **Subject:** San Antonio **Obv:** Portrait of Queen Elizabeth **Rev:** Sailing ship, date and denomination at upper right **Note:** Photo reduced.

Date	Mintage	F	VF	XF	Unc	BU
1988 Proof	1,500	Value: 125				

KM# 79 5 DOLLARS

155.5150 g., 0.9990 Silver 5 oz. ASW, 65 mm. **Series:** Olympics **Obv:** Portrait of Queen Elizabeth **Rev:** Olympic rings, within circle, value below **Note:** Photo reduced.

Date	Mintage	F	VF	XF	Unc	BU
1992 Proof	Est. 1,250	Value: 125				

KM# 90 5 DOLLARS

56.5600 g., 0.9250 Silver 1.6822 oz. ASW **Subject:** 375th Anniversary of Bermudan Parliament

Date	Mintage	F	VF	XF	Unc	BU
1995 Proof	375	Value: 130				

KM# 96 9 DOLLARS

155.5175 g., 0.9990 Silver 5 oz. ASW **Subject:** Bermuda Triangle **Obv:** Queen's portrait **Rev:** Map, compass, capsizing ship

Date	Mintage	F	VF	XF	Unc	BU
1996 Proof	Est. 1,000	Value: 180				

KM# 100 9 DOLLARS

155.5175 g., 0.9990 Silver 5 oz. ASW **Subject:** Wreck of the Sea Venture **Obv:** Queen's portrait **Rev:** Shipwreck scene

Date	Mintage	F	VF	XF	Unc	BU
1997 Proof	1,000	Value: 180				

KM# 112 9 DOLLARS

155.5200 g., 0.9990 Silver 4.9951 oz. ASW **Subject:** Bermuda Triangle **Obv:** Queen's portrait **Rev:** Sailing ship Deliverance and map **Rev. Designer:** John Warwick **Shape:** Triangular

Date	Mintage	F	VF	XF	Unc	BU
1998 Proof	1,000	Value: 180				

KM# 57 10 DOLLARS

3.1340 g., 0.9990 Gold .1007 oz. AGW **Subject:** Hogge money **Obv:** Queen's portrait **Rev:** Wild pig

Date	Mintage	F	VF	XF	Unc	BU
1989 Proof	500	Value: 100				

KM# 74 10 DOLLARS

3.1340 g., 0.9990 Gold .1007 oz. AGW **Subject:** Hogge money **Obv:** Crowned Queen's bust, right **Rev:** Ship within circle, denomination and date below circle

Date	Mintage	F	VF	XF	Unc	BU
1990 Proof	500	Value: 100				

KM# 66 10 DOLLARS

3.1340 g., 0.9990 Gold .1007 oz. AGW **Subject:** Wildlife **Obv:** Crowned Queen's bust, right **Rev:** Tree frog

Date	Mintage	F	VF	XF	Unc	BU
1990 Proof	500	Value: 85.00				

KM# 70 10 DOLLARS

3.1340 g., 0.9990 Gold .1007 oz. AGW **Obv:** Queen Elizabeth II **Rev:** Yellow-crowned night heron, left, date above, denomination below

Date	Mintage	F	VF	XF	Unc	BU
1991	2,500	—	—	—	80.00	—

KM# 73 10 DOLLARS

3.1340 g., 0.9990 Gold .1007 oz. AGW **Obv:** Crowned Queen's bust, right **Rev:** Bluebird feeding nestling

Date	Mintage	F	VF	XF	Unc	BU
1992	2,500	—	—	—	80.00	—

KM# 132 10 DOLLARS

3.1340 g., 0.9990 Gold 0.1007 oz. AGW, 17 mm. **Obv:** Queen Elizabeth II **Rev:** White-tailed Tropic Bird **Edge:** Reeded

Date	Mintage	F	VF	XF	Unc	BU
1993	1,501	—	—	—	80.00	—

KM# 133 10 DOLLARS

3.1340 g., 0.9990 Gold 0.1007 oz. AGW, 17 mm. **Obv:** Queen Elizabeth II **Rev:** Sea Horse **Edge:** Reeded

Date	Mintage	F	VF	XF	Unc	BU
1994	1,000	—	—	—	80.00	—

KM# 138 10 DOLLARS

7.7760 g., 0.5830 Gold Alloyed with .417 Silver 0.1458 oz. AGW, 25 mm. **Obv:** Queen Elizabeth II **Rev:** 1937 Coronation portrait **Edge:** Reeded

Date	Mintage	F	VF	XF	Unc	BU
1996 Proof	5,000	Value: 175				

KM# 118 15 DOLLARS
15.9700 g., 0.9990 Gold .5129 oz. AGW, 28.4 mm. **Subject:** Tall Ships **Obv:** Queen's head right, denomination below **Rev:** Three-masted sailing ship **Edge:** Reeded

Date	Mintage	F	VF	XF	Unc	BU
2000 Proof	1,500	Value: 385				

KM# 21 20 DOLLARS
7.9881 g., 0.9170 Gold .2355 oz. AGW **Obv:** Queen's bust, right **Rev:** Cahow in flight left, denomination below, date above

Date	Mintage	F	VF	XF	Unc	BU
1970 Proof	1,000	Value: 250				

KM# 137 20 DOLLARS
7.9800 g., 0.9990 Gold 0.2563 oz. AGW, 22 mm. **Obv:** Queen Elizabeth II **Rev:** New Millennium dawning over a ship at sea **Edge:** Plain **Shape:** Scalloped

Date	Mintage	F	VF	XF	Unc	BU
2000 Proof	2,000	Value: 185				

KM# 23 25 DOLLARS
Copper-Nickel **Subject:** Royal Visit **Obv:** Queen's bust, right, date upper left **Rev:** Scepter divides royal monograms, denomimation below

Date	Mintage	F	VF	XF	Unc	BU
1975FM (M)	100	—	—	—	45.00	—
1975FM (U)	1,193	—	—	—	60.00	—

KM# 23a 25 DOLLARS
48.7000 g., 0.9250 Silver 1.4483 oz. ASW **Subject:** Royal Visit **Obv:** Queen's bust, right, date upper left **Rev:** Scepter divides royal monograms, denomimation below

Date	Mintage	F	VF	XF	Unc	BU
1975FM (P) Proof	14,708	Value: 27.50				

KM# 25 25 DOLLARS
54.7500 g., 0.9250 Silver 1.6283 oz. ASW **Subject:** Queen's Silver Jubilee **Obv:** Queen's bust, right **Rev:** Sailing ship, date above, denomination below

Date	Mintage	F	VF	XF	Unc	BU
1977Chi	6,225	—	—	—	35.00	—
1977Chi Proof	5,613	Value: 35.00				
1977	Est. 2,312	—	—	—	80.00	—
Note: Struck at the Royal Canadian Mint						
1977 Proof	Est. 1,887	Value: 100				
Note: Struck at the Royal Canadian Mint						

KM# 53 25 DOLLARS
31.1000 g., 0.9990 Palladium 1 oz. **Subject:** Sea Venture **Obv:** Crowned Queen's bust, right **Rev:** Ship, date below, denomination upper left

Date	Mintage	F	VF	XF	Unc	BU
1987 Proof	15,800	Value: 400				

KM# 63 25 DOLLARS
31.1000 g., 0.9990 Palladium 1 oz. **Subject:** Shipwreck of San Antonio **Obv:** Portrait of Queen Elizabeth **Rev:** Capsizing ship, denomination and date above

Date	Mintage	F	VF	XF	Unc	BU
1988 Proof	2,000	Value: 425				

KM# 58 25 DOLLARS
7.8140 g., 0.9990 Gold .2512 oz. AGW **Subject:** Hogge Money **Obv:** Queen's portrait **Rev:** Ship

Date	Mintage	F	VF	XF	Unc	BU
1989 Proof	500	Value: 225				

KM# 75 25 DOLLARS
7.8140 g., 0.9990 Gold .2512 oz. AGW **Subject:** Hogge Money **Obv:** Queen's bust, right **Rev:** Wild pig

Date	Mintage	F	VF	XF	Unc	BU
1990 Proof	500	Value: 225				

KM# 97 30 DOLLARS
15.5518 g., 0.9990 Gold .5 oz. AGW **Subject:** Bermuda Triangle **Obv:** Queen's portrait **Rev:** Map, compass, capsizing ship

Date	Mintage	F	VF	XF	Unc	BU
1996 Proof	Est. 1,500	Value: 385				

KM# 101 30 DOLLARS
15.5518 g., 0.9990 Gold .5 oz. AGW **Subject:** Wreck of the Sea Venture **Obv:** Queen's portrait **Rev:** Shipwreck scene

Date	Mintage	F	VF	XF	Unc	BU
1997 Proof	1,500	Value: 385				

KM# 113 30 DOLLARS
15.5500 g., 0.9990 Gold .4994 oz. AGW **Obv:** Queen's portrait **Rev:** Sailing ship Deliverance and map **Rev. Designer:** John Warwick

Date	Mintage	F	VF	XF	Unc	BU
1998 Proof	1,500	Value: 385				

KM# 26 50 DOLLARS
4.0500 g., 0.9000 Gold .1172 oz. AGW **Subject:** Queen's Silver Jubilee **Obv:** Queen's bust, right **Rev:** Sailboat, denomination below, date upper left

Date	Mintage	F	VF	XF	Unc	BU
1977Chi	3,950	—	—	—	90.00	—
1977Chi Proof	4,070	Value: 110				
1977	Est. 520	—	—	—	235	—
Note: Struck at the Royal Canadian Mint						
1977 Proof	Est. 580	Value: 240				
Note: Struck at the Royal Canadian Mint						

KM# 59 50 DOLLARS
15.6080 g., 0.9990 Gold .5018 oz. AGW **Subject:** Hogge Money **Obv:** Queen's bust, right **Rev:** Wild pig within inner circle, denomination and date at bottom

Date	Mintage	F	VF	XF	Unc	BU
1989 Proof	500	Value: 350				

KM# 76 50 DOLLARS
15.6080 g., 0.9990 Gold .5018 oz. AGW **Subject:** Hogge Money **Obv:** Crowned Queen's bust, right **Rev:** Ship within circle, date and denomination below

Date	Mintage	F	VF	XF	Unc	BU
1990 Proof	500	Value: 350				

KM# 93 60 DOLLARS
31.4890 g., 0.9990 Gold 1.0124 oz. AGW **Subject:** Bermuda Triangle **Obv:** Crowned Queen's portrait, right, within triangle, date below, denomination at left **Rev:** Map, compass and capsizing ship, within triangle **Shape:** Triangular

Date	Mintage	F	VF	XF	Unc	BU
1996 Proof	1,500	Value: 785				

KM# 102 60 DOLLARS
31.4890 g., 0.9990 Gold 1.0124 oz. AGW **Subject:** Wreck of the Sea Venture **Obv:** Crowned Queen's portrait, right, within triangle, date below, denomination at left **Rev:** Shipwreck scene within triangle **Shape:** Triangular

Date	Mintage	F	VF	XF	Unc	BU
1997 Proof	1,500	Value: 785				

KM# 114 60 DOLLARS
31.4800 g., 0.9990 Gold 1.0111 oz. AGW **Obv:** Crowned Queen's portrait, right, within triangle, date below, denomination at left **Rev:** Sailing ship Deliverance and map within triangle **Rev. Designer:** John Warwick **Shape:** Triangular

Date	Mintage	F	VF	XF	Unc	BU
1998 Proof	1,500	Value: 785				

KM# 24 100 DOLLARS
7.0300 g., 0.9000 Gold .2034 oz. AGW **Subject:** Royal Visit **Obv:** Queen's bust, right, date upper left **Rev:** Sceptre divides royal emblems, denomination at bottom

Date	Mintage	F	VF	XF	Unc	BU
1975FM (M) Trial pieces	25	—	—	—	350	—
1975FM (M)	18,852	—	—	—	140	—
1975FM (M) Proof	27,270	Value: 145				

KM# 27 100 DOLLARS
8.1000 g., 0.9000 Gold .2344 oz. AGW **Subject:** Queen's Silver Jubilee **Rev:** Sailing ship Deliverance

Date	Mintage	F	VF	XF	Unc	BU
1977Chi	6,225	—	—	—	160	—
1977Chi Proof	5,613	Value: 175				
1977	Est. 2,312	—	—	—	225	—

Note: Struck at the Royal Canadian Mint

Date	Mintage	F	VF	XF	Unc	BU
1977 Proof	Est. 1,887	Value: 265				

Note: Struck at the Royal Canadian Mint

KM# 60 100 DOLLARS
31.2100 g., 0.9990 Gold 1.0035 oz. AGW **Subject:** Hogge Money **Obv:** Queen's bust, right **Rev:** Ship within circle, denomination and date below

Date	Mintage	F	VF	XF	Unc	BU
1989 Proof	500	Value: 675				

KM# 77 100 DOLLARS
31.2100 g., 0.9990 Gold 1.0035 oz. AGW **Subject:** Hogge Money **Obv:** Crowned Queen's portrait, right **Rev:** Wild pig within inner circle, denomination and date at bottom

Date	Mintage	F	VF	XF	Unc	BU
1990 Proof	500	Value: 675				

KM# 80 100 DOLLARS
47.5400 g., 0.9170 Gold 1.4017 oz. AGW **Series:** Olympics **Subject:** Portrait of Queen Elizabeth II **Rev:** Olympic rings, within circle, value below

Date	Mintage	F	VF	XF	Unc	BU
1992 Proof	Est. 250	Value: 950				

KM# 134 100 DOLLARS
47.5400 g., 0.9170 Gold 1.4016 oz. AGW, 38.6 mm. **Subject:** Royal Visit **Obv:** Queen Elizabeth II **Rev:** Royal couple above map **Edge:** Reeded

Date	Mintage	F	VF	XF	Unc	BU
1994 Proof	250	Value: 950				

KM# 98 180 DOLLARS
155.5175 g., 0.9990 Gold 5 oz. AGW **Subject:** Bermuda Triangle **Obv:** Queen's portrait **Rev:** Map, compass, capsizing ship

Date	Mintage	F	VF	XF	Unc	BU
1996 Proof	Est. 1,500	Value: 3,350				

KM# 103 180 DOLLARS
155.5175 g., 0.9990 Gold 5 oz. AGW **Subject:** Wreck of the Sea Venture **Obv:** Queen's portrait **Rev:** Shipwreck scene

Date	Mintage	F	VF	XF	Unc	BU
1997 Proof	99	Value: 4,000				

KM# 115 180 DOLLARS
155.5200 g., 0.9990 Gold 4.9951 oz. AGW **Obv:** Queen's portrait **Rev:** Sailing ship Deliverance and map **Shape:** Triangular

Date	Mintage	F	VF	XF	Unc	BU
1998 Proof	99	Value: 4,000				

KM# 82 200 DOLLARS
28.5000 g., 0.9990 Gold .9154 oz. AGW **Subject:** 200 Years - Bermudan Coinage **Obv:** Crowned Queen's portrait, right, denomination below, date at bottom **Rev:** Sailing ship, date below

Date	Mintage	F	VF	XF	Unc	BU
1993 Proof	200	Value: 625				

KM# 29 250 DOLLARS
15.9760 g., 0.9170 Gold .471 oz. AGW **Subject:** Wedding of Prince Charles and Lady Diana **Obv:** Queen's bust, right **Rev:** Conjoined heads of the royal couple, right, within circle, denomination below

Date	Mintage	F	VF	XF	Unc	BU
1981	217	—	—	—	475	525
1981 Proof	790	Value: 375				

PIEFORTS

KM#	Date	Mintage	Identification	Mkt Val
P1	1981	690	250 Dollars. 31.9520 g. KM29.	650
P2	1988	500	Dollar. 0.9250 Silver. 16.8000 g. KM56a.	185

MINT SETS

KM#	Date	Mintage	Identification	Issue Price	Mkt Val
MS1	1970 (5)	360,000	KM15-19	3.25	4.00
MS2	1977Chi (3)	—	KM25-27	175	250
MSA2	1977 (3)	—	KM25-27	—	750
MS3	1977Chi (2)	—	KM26-27	150	225
MS4	1984 (11)	3,350	KM32-42	24.95	27.50
MS5	1993 (5)	15,000	KM44b, 45-47, 56	—	10.00
MS7	1999 (5)	5,000	KM107-111	15.00	20.00

PROOF SETS

KM#	Date	Mintage	Identification	Issue Price	Mkt Val
PS1	1970 (6)	10,000	KM15-20	24.00	20.00
PS2	1970 (7)	1,000	KM15-21	216	280
PS3	1977Chi (3)	—	KM25-27	245	350
PSA3	1977 (3)	—	KM25-27	—	800
PS4	1977Chi (2)	—	KM26-27	210	265
PS5	1981 (3)	500	KM28a, 29, (P1), numbered set	1,500	1,350
PS6	1983 (7)	6,474	KM15-19, 30, 31	30.00	30.00
PS7	1984 (11)	1,750	KM32a-42a	250	200
PS8	1986 (7)	2,500	KM44-48, 50-51	50.00	50.00
PS10	1989 (4)	500	KM57-60	1,495	1,250
PS11	1990 (4)	500	KM74-77	—	1,250
PS12	1992 (3)	250	KM78-80	1,075	1,050
PS13	1992 (2)	500	KM71-72	75.00	110
PS14	1995 (5)	500	KM44d, 45b-47b, 56b	1,100	1,350
PSA14	1995 (5)	2,000	KM#44c, 45a, 46a, 47a, 56a	—	60.00
PS15	1996 (2)	1,000	KM96-97	—	600
PS16	1999 (5)	2,500	KM107-111	50.00	50.00

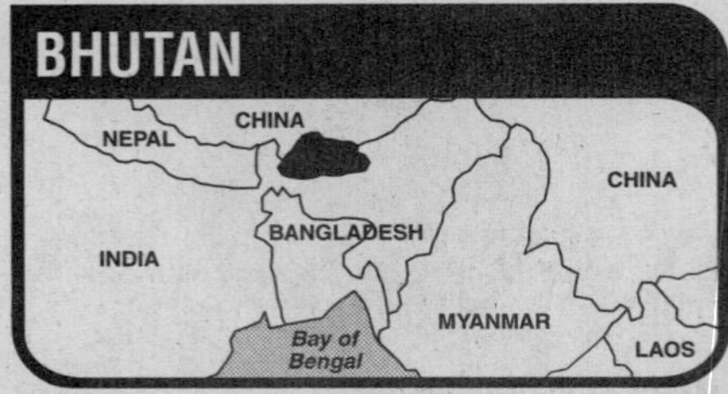

The Kingdom of Bhutan, a landlocked Himalayan country bordered by Tibet and India, has an area of 18,150 sq. mi. (47,000 sq. km.) and a population of *2.03 million. Capital: Thimphu. Virtually the entire population is engaged in agricultural and pastoral activities. Rice, wheat, barley, and yak butter are produced in sufficient quantity to make the country self-sufficient in food. The economy of Bhutan is primitive and many transactions are conducted on a barter basis.

Bhutan's early history is obscure, but is thought to have resembled that of rural medieval Europe. The country was conquered by Tibet in the 9th century, and a dual temporal and spiritual rule developed which operated until the mid-19th century, when the southern part of the country was occupied by the British and annexed to British India. Bhutan was established as a hereditary monarchy in 1907, and in 1910 agreed to British control of its external affairs. In 1949, India and Bhutan concluded a treaty whereby India assumed Britain's role in subsidizing Bhutan and guiding its foreign affairs. In 1971 Bhutan became a full member of the United Nations.

RULERS

Ugyen Wangchuk, 1907-1926
Jigme Wangchuk, 1926-1952
Jigme Dorji Wangchuk, 1952-1972
Jigme Singye Wangchuk, 1972-

CYCLICAL DATES

Earth-Dragon

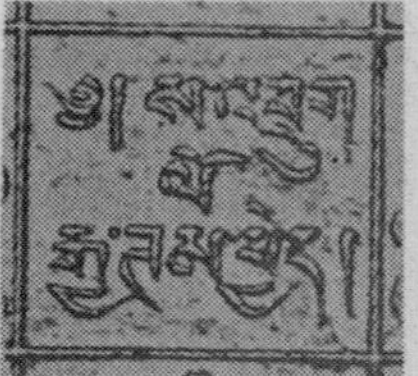

(1928)

Iron-Tiger

(1950)

OBVERSE LEGENDS

Normal

Modified

KINGDOM

HAMMERED COINAGE

Period IV, 1910-1927AD

KM# 16 1/2 RUPEE (Deb)

Copper

Date	Mintage	Good	VG	F	VF	XF
ND(1910-27)	—	—	—	—	—	—

KM# 17 1/2 RUPEE (Deb)

Silver

Date	Mintage	Good	VG	F	VF	XF
ND(1910-27)	—	10.00	15.00	25.00	35.00	—

KM# 17a 1/2 RUPEE (Deb)

Copper **Note:** Obverse is similar to KM#17, but symbols on reverse are arranged differently.

Date	Mintage	Good	VG	F	VF	XF
ND(1910-1927)	—	2.00	3.50	5.00	9.00	—

KM# 18 1/2 RUPEE (Deb)

Silver

Date	Mintage	Good	VG	F	VF	XF
ND(1910-27)	—	10.00	15.00	25.00	35.00	—

KM# 18a 1/2 RUPEE (Deb)

Copper **Note:** Obverse is similar to KM#18, but symbols on reverse are arranged differently.

Date	Mintage	Good	VG	F	VF	XF
ND(1910-1927)	—	2.00	3.50	5.00	9.00	—

KM# 18b 1/2 RUPEE (Deb)

Brass **Note:** Different reverse than KM#18, this was heretofore an unpublished variety.

Date	Mintage	Good	VG	F	VF	XF
ND(1910-1927)	—	2.00	3.50	5.00	9.00	—

KM# 19 1/2 RUPEE (Deb)

Silver

Date	Mintage	Good	VG	F	VF	XF
ND(1910-27)	—	10.00	15.00	25.00	35.00	—

KM# 19a 1/2 RUPEE (Deb)

Copper **Note:** Obverse is similar to KM#19, but symbols on reverse are arranged differently.

Date	Mintage	Good	VG	F	VF	XF
ND(1910-1927)	—	2.00	3.50	5.00	9.00	—

KM# 20 1/2 RUPEE (Deb)

Silver

Date	Mintage	Good	VG	F	VF	XF
ND(1910-27)	—	10.00	15.00	25.00	35.00	—

KM# 20a 1/2 RUPEE (Deb)

Copper **Note:** Obverse is similar to KM#20, but symbols on reverse are arranged differently.

Date	Mintage	Good	VG	F	VF	XF
ND(1910-27)	—	3.00	4.50	6.00	10.00	—

KM# 21 1/2 RUPEE (Deb)

Copper

Date	Mintage	Good	VG	F	VF	XF
ND(1910-27)	—	1.50	2.50	3.50	6.00	—

KM# 22 1/2 RUPEE (Deb)

Copper **Obv:** Interlacing opposite of KM#21 **Rev:** Interlacing opposite of KM#21 **Note:** Varieties exist.

Date	Mintage	Good	VG	F	VF	XF
ND(1910-27)	—	1.50	2.50	3.50	6.00	—

DECIMAL COINAGE

KM# 23.1 PICE

7.0000 g., Bronze, 26.5 mm. **Note:** Similar to KM#23.2.

Date	Mintage	F	VF	XF	Unc	BU
1928	—	22.50	40.00	65.00	100	—

KM# 23.2 PICE

4.9000 g., Bronze, 25.1 mm. **Obv:** Crowned bust, left **Rev:** Coin divided into nine sections, symbol on each section **Note:** Actually struck in 1931.

Date	Mintage	F	VF	XF	Unc	BU
1928	10,000	20.00	35.00	60.00	90.00	—
1928 Proof	—	Value: 100				

KM# A27 PICE

3.3000 g., Bronze **Rev:** Coin divided into nine sections, symbol in each section

Date	Mintage	F	VF	XF	Unc	BU
ND	—	—	—	—	—	—

KM# 27 PICE

2.9000 g., Bronze **Obv:** Square at center, four sections, one symbol in each **Rev:** Coin divided into nine sections, one symbol in each section **Note:** Actually struck in 1951 and 1955. Later strikes of 1955 dates differ in detail because of recut dies.

Date	Mintage	F	VF	XF	Unc	BU
ND	Est. 1,260,000	0.75	1.00	1.50	2.25	—

KM# 29 25 NAYA PAISA

Copper-Nickel **Subject:** 40th Anniversary - Accession of Jigme Wangchuk **Obv:** Crowned bust, left, two dates below **Rev:** Emblem within circle, denomination below

Date	Mintage	F	VF	XF	Unc	BU
1966	10,000	—	0.25	0.50	1.00	2.00
1966 Proof	6,000	Value: 1.50				

KM# 30 50 NAYA PAISA

Copper-Nickel **Subject:** 40th Anniversary - Accession of Jigme Wangchuk **Obv:** Crowned bust, left, dates below **Rev:** Emblem withn circle, denomination below

Date	Mintage	F	VF	XF	Unc	BU
1966	10,000	—	0.35	0.75	1.50	3.00
1966 Proof	6,000	Value: 2.50				

KM# 26 1/2 RUPEE

Nickel **Obv:** Crowned bust, left, normal legend **Rev:** Coin divided into nine sections, one symbol in each section **Note:** Weight varies: 5.78-5.90 grams.

Date	Mintage	F	VF	XF	Unc	BU
ND(1928)	20,000	2.00	3.00	4.50	7.00	—
Note: Actually struck in 1951						
ND(1950)	202,000	1.50	2.50	3.00	4.50	—
Note: Actually struck in 1955						

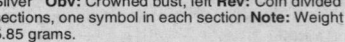

KM# 24 1/2 RUPEE

Silver **Obv:** Crowned bust, left **Rev:** Coin divided into nine sections, one symbol in each section **Note:** Weight varies: 5.83-5.85 grams.

Date	Mintage	F	VF	XF	Unc	BU
ND(1928)	50,000	10.00	15.00	22.50	35.00	—

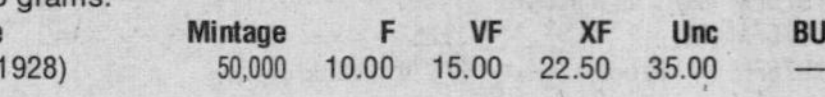

Date	Mintage	F	VF	XF	Unc	BU

Note: Actually struck in 1929

Date	Mintage	F	VF	XF	Unc	BU
ND(1928) Proof	—	Value: 100				

KM# 25 1/2 RUPEE

Silver **Obv:** Legend modified

Date	Mintage	F	VF	XF	Unc	BU
ND(1928)	Inc. above	10.00	15.00	22.50	35.00	—

Note: Actually struck in 1930

KM# 28 1/2 RUPEE

5.0800 g., Nickel **Obv:** Legend normal

Date	Mintage	F	VF	XF	Unc	BU
ND(1950)	10,000,000	0.75	1.00	1.50	2.25	—

Note: Actually struck in 1967-68

KM# 31 RUPEE

Copper-Nickel **Subject:** 40th Anniversary - Accession of Jigme Wangchuk **Obv:** Crowned bust, left, dates below **Rev:** Emblem divides date, denomination below

Date	Mintage	F	VF	XF	Unc	BU
1966	10,000	—	0.50	1.00	2.00	4.00
1966 Proof	6,000	Value: 3.50				

KM# 32 3 RUPEE

Copper-Nickel **Subject:** 40th Anniversary - Accession of Jigme Wangchuk **Obv:** Crowned bust, left, dates below **Rev:** Emblem divides date, denomination below

Date	Mintage	F	VF	XF	Unc	BU
1966	5,826	—	—	—	6.00	9.00
1966 Proof	6,000	Value: 7.50				

KM# 32a 3 RUPEE

28.2800 g., 0.9250 Silver .8411 oz. ASW **Subject:** 40th Anniversary - Accession of Jigme Wangchuk

Date	Mintage	F	VF	XF	Unc	BU
1966	—	—	—	—	375	—
1966 Proof	2,000	Value: 25.00				
1966 Matte proof	—	Value: 375				

KM# 33 SERTUM

7.9800 g., 0.9170 Gold .2352 oz. AGW **Subject:** 40th Anniversary - Accession of Jigme Wangchuk **Obv:** Crowned bust left, dates below **Rev:** Emblem divides date, denomination below

Date	Mintage	F	VF	XF	Unc	BU
1966	2,300	—	—	—	170	—
1966 Proof	598	Value: 200				

KM# 33a SERTUM

9.8400 g., 0.9500 Platinum .3005 oz. APW **Subject:** 40th Anniversary - Accession of Jigme Wangchuk

Date	Mintage	F	VF	XF	Unc	BU
1966 Proof	72	Value: 425				

KM# 36 SERTUM

7.9800 g., 0.9170 Gold .2352 oz. AGW **Obv:** Bust, right, date below

Date	Mintage	F	VF	XF	Unc	BU
1970	3,111	—	—	—	165	180

KM# 34 2 SERTUMS

15.9800 g., 0.9170 Gold .4711 oz. AGW **Subject:** 40th Anniversary - Accession of Jigme Wangchuk **Obv:** Crowned bust, left, dates below **Rev:** Emblem divides date, denomination below

Date	Mintage	F	VF	XF	Unc	BU
1966	800	—	—	—	335	—
1966 Proof	598	Value: 385				

KM# 34a 2 SERTUMS

19.6700 g., 0.9500 Platinum .6008 oz. APW **Subject:** 40th Anniversary - Accession of Jigme Wangchuk

Date	Mintage	F	VF	XF	Unc	BU
1966 Proof	72	Value: 825				

KM# 35 5 SERTUMS

39.9400 g., 0.9170 Gold 1.1776 oz. AGW **Subject:** 40th Anniversary - Accession of Jigme Wangchuk **Obv:** Crowned bust, left, dates below **Rev:** Emblem divides date, denomination below

Date	Mintage	F	VF	XF	Unc	BU
1966	800	—	—	—	825	—
1966 Proof	598	Value: 875				

KM# 35a 5 SERTUMS

49.1800 g., 0.9500 Platinum 1.5022 oz. APW **Subject:** 40th Anniversary - Accession of Jigme Wangchuk **Obv:** Crowned bust, left, dates below **Rev:** Emblem divides date, denomination below

Date	Mintage	F	VF	XF	Unc	BU
1966 Proof	72	Value: 1,950				

REFORM COINAGE

Commencing 1974; 100 Chetrums (Paisa) = 1 Ngultrum (Rupee); 100 Ngultrums = 1 Sertum

KM# 37 5 CHETRUMS

Aluminum, 22 mm. **Obv:** Crowned bust, left, date at left **Rev:** Emblem above denomination **Edge:** Plain **Shape:** 4-sided

Date	Mintage	F	VF	XF	Unc	BU
1974	—	—	0.10	0.20	0.50	0.75
1974 Proof	1,000	Value: 1.25				
1975	—	—	0.10	0.15	0.20	0.50
1975 Proof	—	Value: 1.25				

KM# 45 5 CHHERTUM

1.9000 g., Bronze, 17.15 mm. **Obv:** Symbols within circle, date below **Rev:** Symbols within circle, denomination below

Date	Mintage	F	VF	XF	Unc	BU
1979	—	—	0.10	0.20	0.50	0.75
1979 Proof	—	Value: 1.00				

KM# 38 10 CHETRUMS

Aluminum **Obv:** Crowned bust, left, date at left **Rev:** Denomination below design **Shape:** Scalloped

Date	Mintage	F	VF	XF	Unc	BU
1974	—	—	0.15	0.25	0.50	1.00
1974 Proof	1,000	Value: 1.50				

KM# 43 10 CHETRUMS

Aluminum **Series:** F.A.O. and International Women's Year **Obv:** Emblem above denomination **Rev:** Half figure facing left, grain sprig on left, date below **Shape:** Scalloped

Date	Mintage	F	VF	XF	Unc	BU
1975	4,000,000	—	0.15	0.25	0.65	1.25
1975 Proof	—	Value: 2.50				

KM# 46 10 CHHERTUM

3.6000 g., Bronze, 20.35 mm. **Obv:** Shell and design within circle, date below **Rev:** Coin divided into nine sections, within circle, symbol in each section, denomination below

Date	Mintage	F	VF	XF	Unc	BU
1979	—	—	0.15	0.30	1.00	1.50
1979 Proof	—	Value: 2.00				

KM# 39 20 CHETRUMS

Aluminum-Bronze, 22 mm. **Series:** F.A.O. **Obv:** Emblem above denomination **Rev:** Rice cultivation **Edge:** Plain

Date	Mintage	F	VF	XF	Unc	BU
1974	1,194,000	—	0.15	0.25	0.50	0.75
1974 Prooflike	—	—	—	—	1.50	—

Note: In mint sets only

Date	Mintage	F	VF	XF	Unc	BU
1974 Proof	1,000	Value: 2.00				

KM# 40.1 25 CHETRUMS

Copper-Nickel **Obv:** Crowned bust, left, date at left **Rev:** Fish above denomination, type I

Date	Mintage	F	VF	XF	Unc	BU
1974	—	—	0.10	0.20	0.75	1.25
1974 Proof	1,000	Value: 3.00				

KM# 40.2 25 CHETRUMS
Copper-Nickel **Obv:** Crowned bust, left, date at left **Rev:** Fish above denomination, type II

Date	Mintage	F	VF	XF	Unc	BU
1974	—	—	0.10	0.20	0.75	1.25
1975	—	—	0.10	0.20	0.75	1.25
1975 Proof	—	Value: 3.00				

KM# 47 25 CHHERTUM
4.6000 g., Copper-Nickel, 21.95 mm. **Obv:** Fish within circle, date below **Rev:** Emblem within circle, denomination below

Date	Mintage	F	VF	XF	Unc	BU
1979	—	—	0.25	0.50	1.25	1.75
1979 Proof	—	Value: 4.00				

KM# 47a 25 CHHERTUM
Steel **Obv:** Fish within circle, date below **Rev:** Emblem within circle, denomination below **Note:** Aluminum-bronze clad.

Date	Mintage	F	VF	XF	Unc	BU
1979	—	—	—	—	2.50	3.00

KM# 48 50 CHHERTUM
6.9000 g., Copper-Nickel, 25.85 mm. **Obv:** Emblem within circle, date below **Rev:** Coin divided into nine sections within circle, symbol in each section, denomination below

Date	Mintage	F	VF	XF	Unc	BU
1979	—	—	0.25	0.65	1.50	2.00
1979 Proof	—	Value: 5.00				

KM# 41 NGULTRUM
Copper-Nickel, 28 mm. **Obv:** Crowned bust, left, date at left **Rev:** Emblem above denomination **Edge:** Reeded security edge

Date	Mintage	F	VF	XF	Unc	BU
1974	—	—	0.20	0.50	1.25	1.75
1974 Proof	1,000	Value: 5.00				
1975	—	—	0.20	0.50	1.25	1.75
1975 Proof	—	Value: 5.00				

KM# 49 NGULTRUM
8.2000 g., Copper-Nickel, 27.95 mm. **Obv:** Emblem within circle, date below **Rev:** Coin divided into nine sections within circle, each has symbol, denomination below

Date	Mintage	F	VF	XF	Unc	BU
1979	—	—	0.30	0.75	2.00	2.75
1979 Proof	—	Value: 5.50				

KM# 49a NGULTRUM
Copper-Nickel Clad Steel **Obv:** Emblem within circle, date below **Rev:** Coin divided into nine sections within circle, each has symbol, denomination below

Date	Mintage	F	VF	XF	Unc	BU
1979	—	—	—	—	3.00	3.50

KM# 50 3 NGULTRUMS
Copper-Nickel, 38.5 mm. **Obv:** Crowned head, left, date below **Rev:** National emblem within circle, denomination at right **Edge:** Reeded

Date	Mintage	F	VF	XF	Unc	BU
1979	—	—	1.25	2.50	5.50	—
1979 Proof	—	Value: 8.50				

KM# 50a 3 NGULTRUMS
28.2800 g., 0.9250 Silver .8411 oz. ASW **Obv:** Crowned head, left, date below **Rev:** National emblem within circle, denomination at right

Date	Mintage	F	VF	XF	Unc	BU
1979 Proof	Est. 10,000	Value: 32.50				

KM# 42 15 NGULTRUMS
22.3000 g., 0.5000 Silver .3584 oz. ASW **Series:** F.A.O. **Obv:** Emblem above denomination **Rev:** Rice cultivation

Date	Mintage	F	VF	XF	Unc	BU
1974	30,000	—	—	—	8.50	—
1974 Prooflike	—	—	—	—	10.00	—
Note: In mint sets only						
1974 Proof	1,000	Value: 42.50				

KM# 44 30 NGULTRUMS
25.0000 g., 0.5000 Silver .4018 oz. ASW **Series:** F.A.O. and International Women's Year **Obv:** Emblem above denomination **Rev:** Half figure looking left, grain sprig on left, date at bottom

Date	Mintage	F	VF	XF	Unc	BU
1975	14,000	—	—	—	10.00	—
1975 Proof	—	Value: 20.00				

KM# 54 50 NGULTRUMS
28.2800 g., 0.9250 Silver .8411 oz. ASW **Series:** World Food Day **Obv:** Buffalo, right, within circle, denomination below

Date	Mintage	F	VF	XF	Unc	BU
1981	15,000	—	—	—	35.00	—
1981 Proof	5,000	Value: 45.00				

KM# 83 50 NGULTRUMS
Copper-Nickel **Subject:** 50 Years - United Nations **Obv:** National emblem within circle divides dates **Rev:** Bust, 3/4 right, symbol and dates at right, denomination below

Date	Mintage	F	VF	XF	Unc	BU
1995	—	—	—	—	8.00	—

KM# 104 50 NGULTRUMS
16.0000 g., 0.9250 Silver 0.4758 oz. ASW, 28.3 mm. **Subject:** British Queen Mother **Obv:** National emblem within circle divides dates **Rev:** Home at St. Paul's Walden Bury, date and denomination below **Edge:** Reeded

Date	Mintage	F	VF	XF	Unc	BU
1997 Proof	—	Value: 20.00				

KM# 58 100 NGULTRUMS
23.3300 g., 0.9250 Silver .6938 oz. ASW **Series:** Decade for Women **Obv:** National emblem within circle, date above, denomination below **Rev:** Women working

Date	Mintage	F	VF	XF	Unc	BU
1984 Proof	1,050	Value: 28.00				

KM# 84 100 NGULTRUMS
Copper-Nickel **Subject:** St. Paul's Walden Bury Palace **Obv:** National emblem within circle divides dates **Rev:** Palace within circle, date and denomination below

Date	Mintage	F	VF	XF	Unc	BU
1995	Est. 35,000	—	—	—	12.50	—

KM# 103 100 NGULTRUMS
20.0000 g., 0.9250 Silver .5948 oz. ASW, 34 mm. **Subject:** Olympic Games 2000 **Obv:** National arms within circle divides dates **Rev:** Archer at left sighting in on target at right, denomination below **Edge:** Reeded

Date	Mintage	F	VF	XF	Unc	BU
1998 Proof	—	Value: 18.50				

KM# 57 200 NGULTRUMS
28.2800 g., 0.9250 Silver .8411 oz. ASW **Series:** International Year of Disabled Persons **Obv:** Elephant carrying animals, tree and hills, date and denomination below **Rev:** Typist

Date	Mintage	F	VF	XF	Unc	BU
1981	10,000	—	—	—	40.00	—
1981 Proof	10,000	Value: 45.00				

KM# 55 200 NGULTRUMS
28.2800 g., 0.9250 Silver .8411 oz. ASW **Subject:** 75th Anniversary of Monarchy **Obv:** Crowned bust, facing, date below **Rev:** National emblem within circle **Note:** Issued in 1983.

Date	Mintage	F	VF	XF	Unc	BU
1982	10,000	—	—	—	30.00	—
1982 Proof	5,000	Value: 40.00				

KM# 86 200 NGULTRUMS
10.0000 g., 0.5000 Silver .1607 oz. ASW **Series:** Olympics **Obv:** National emblem within circle divides dates **Rev:** Two basketball players, denomination below

Date	Mintage	F	VF	XF	Unc	BU
1996 Proof	Est. 10,000	—	—	—	20.00	—

KM# 87 200 NGULTRUMS
10.0000 g., 0.5000 Silver .1607 oz. ASW **Series:** Olympics **Obv:** National emblem divides dates **Rev:** Skiing scene, denomination at right

Date	Mintage	F	VF	XF	Unc	BU
1996 Proof	Est. 50,000	—	—	—	15.00	—

KM# 61 300 NGULTRUMS
28.2800 g., 0.9250 Silver .8411 oz. ASW **Subject:** World Championship Soccer, denomination below **Obv:** Crowned head, left, date below

Date	Mintage	F	VF	XF	Unc	BU
1990 Proof	20,000	Value: 35.00				

KM# 65 300 NGULTRUMS
31.4700 g., 0.9250 Silver .9359 oz. ASW **Series:** Endangered wildlife **Rev:** Snow leopard, denomination below

Date	Mintage	F	VF	XF	Unc	BU
1991 Proof	Est. 25,000	Value: 35.00				

KM# 63 300 NGULTRUMS
28.2800 g., 0.9250 Silver .8411 oz. ASW **Obv:** National emblem divides dates **Rev:** Solar system scene, denomination below

Date	Mintage	F	VF	XF	Unc	BU
1992 Proof	—	Value: 32.50				

KM# 72 300 NGULTRUMS
31.4700 g., 0.9250 Silver .9359 oz. ASW **Subject:** World Cup Soccer **Obv:** National emblem within circle divides dates **Rev:** Two soccer players, radiant sunset behind, denomination below

Date	Mintage	F	VF	XF	Unc	BU
1992 Proof	20,000	Value: 27.50				

KM# 74 300 NGULTRUMS
31.4700 g., 0.9250 Silver .9359 oz. ASW **Series:** Lillehammer 1994 - 17th Winter Olympic Games **Obv:** National emblem within circle divides dates **Rev:** Speed skating, denomination below

Date	Mintage	F	VF	XF	Unc	BU
1992 Proof	40,000	Value: 22.50				

KM# 75 300 NGULTRUMS
31.4700 g., 0.9250 Silver .9359 oz. ASW **Series:** Endangered Wildlife **Obv:** National emblem within circle divides dates **Rev:** Golden langur monkey, denomination below

Date	Mintage	F	VF	XF	Unc	BU
1992 Proof	—	Value: 35.00				

KM# 76 300 NGULTRUMS
31.4700 g., 0.9250 Silver .9359 oz. ASW **Series:** Barcelona 1992 - 25th Summer Olympics **Obv:** National emblem within circle divides dates **Rev:** Archery scene, denomination below

Date	Mintage	F	VF	XF	Unc	BU
1992 Proof	20,000	Value: 20.00				

KM# 77 300 NGULTRUMS
31.4700 g., 0.9250 Silver .9359 oz. ASW **Series:** 1992 Olympic Games **Obv:** National emblem within circle divides dates **Rev:** Boxer, denomination below

Date	Mintage	F	VF	XF	Unc	BU
1992 Proof	20,000	Value: 22.00				

KM# 66 300 NGULTRUMS
31.4700 g., 0.9250 Silver .9359 oz. ASW **Subject:** 40th Anniversary - Coronation of Queen Elizabeth II **Obv:** National emblem within circle divides dates **Rev:** Royal Guard, palace in background, denomination and dates below

Date	Mintage	F	VF	XF	Unc	BU
1993 Proof	Est. 10,000	Value: 32.50				

KM# 67 300 NGULTRUMS
31.4700 g., 0.9250 Silver .9359 oz. ASW **Series:** Endangered Wildlife **Obv:** National emblem within circle divides dates **Rev:** Takin, denomination below

Date	Mintage	F	VF	XF	Unc	BU
1993 Proof	Est. 10,000	Value: 35.00				

KM# 68 300 NGULTRUMS
31.4700 g., 0.9250 Silver .9359 oz. ASW **Subject:** Protect Our World **Obv:** National emblem within circle divides dates **Rev:** Elephant, rhino, tree, and tiger, denomination below

Date	Mintage	F	VF	XF	Unc	BU
1993 Proof	Est. 10,000	Value: 50.00				

KM# 78 300 NGULTRUMS
31.3200 g., 0.9250 Silver .9314 oz. ASW **Subject:** World Championship Soccer **Obv:** National emblem within circle divides dates **Rev:** Ball in flight, denomination below

Date	Mintage	F	VF	XF	Unc	BU
1993 Proof	30,000	Value: 40.00				

KM# 79 300 NGULTRUMS
31.3200 g., 0.9250 Silver .9314 oz. ASW **Series:** Olympic Games **Rev:** Soccer, denomination below

Date	Mintage	F	VF	XF	Unc	BU
1993 Proof	30,000	Value: 25.00				

KM# 89 300 NGULTRUMS
31.3200 g., 0.9250 Silver .9314 oz. ASW **Subject:** Maurice Ravel **Obv:** National emblem **Rev:** Portrait, musician, dancer, and dates, denomination below

Date	Mintage	F	VF	XF	Unc	BU
1993 Proof	—	Value: 42.50				

KM# 69 300 NGULTRUMS
31.3200 g., 0.9250 Silver .9314 oz. ASW **Subject:** Protect Our World **Rev:** Rain forest, denomination below

Date	Mintage	F	VF	XF	Unc	BU
1994 Proof	Est. 10,000	Value: 45.00				

KM# 73 300 NGULTRUMS
31.3200 g., 0.9250 Silver .9314 oz. ASW **Series:** 1996 Olympic Games **Rev:** Basketball, denomination below

Date	Mintage	F	VF	XF	Unc	BU
1994 Proof	30,000	Value: 25.00				

KM# 88 300 NGULTRUMS
31.4500 g., 0.9250 Silver .9353 oz. ASW **Series:** Endangered Wildlife **Rev:** Kalij pheasant, denomination below

Date	Mintage	F	VF	XF	Unc	BU
1994 Proof	—	Value: 37.50				

KM# 81 300 NGULTRUMS
31.4500 g., 0.9250 Silver .9353 oz. ASW **Subject:** Joao Cabral **Obv:** National emblem **Rev:** Two explorers, denomination below

Date	Mintage	F	VF	XF	Unc	BU
1994 Proof	Est. 10,000	Value: 32.50				

KM# 80 300 NGULTRUMS
28.2800 g., 0.9250 Silver .8411 oz. ASW **Subject:** 50th Anniversary - United Nations **Obv:** National emblem within circle divides dates **Rev:** Bust, 3/4 right, symbol and dates at right, denomination below

Date	Mintage	F	VF	XF	Unc	BU
1995 Proof	Est. 100,000	Value: 32.50				

KM# 90 300 NGULTRUMS
31.5000 g., 0.9250 Silver .9368 oz. ASW **Subject:** Chinese Lunar Year **Obv:** National emblem within circle divides dates **Rev:** Seated monkey within circle, denomination below

Date	Mintage	F	VF	XF	Unc	BU
1996 Proof	—	Value: 28.50				

KM# 98 300 NGULTRUMS
31.5000 g., 0.9250 Silver .9368 oz. ASW **Subject:** Chinese Lunar Year **Obv:** National emblem **Rev:** Stylized dragon within circle, denomination below

Date	Mintage	F	VF	XF	Unc	BU
1996 Proof	—	Value: 30.00				

KM# 91 300 NGULTRUMS
31.5000 g., 0.9250 Silver .9368 oz. ASW **Subject:** Chinese Lunar Year **Obv:** National emblem **Rev:** Stylized rooster within circle, denomination below

Date	Mintage	F	VF	XF	Unc	BU
1996 Proof	—	Value: 28.50				

KM# 92 300 NGULTRUMS
31.5000 g., 0.9250 Silver .9368 oz. ASW **Subject:** Chinese Lunar Year **Obv:** National emblem **Rev:** Stylized dog within circle, denomination below

Date	Mintage	F	VF	XF	Unc	BU
1996 Proof	—	Value: 28.50				

KM# 93 300 NGULTRUMS
31.5000 g., 0.9250 Silver .9368 oz. ASW **Subject:** Chinese Lunar Year **Obv:** National emblem **Rev:** Stylized pig within circle, denomination below

Date	Mintage	F	VF	XF	Unc	BU
1996 Proof	—	Value: 28.50				

KM# 94 300 NGULTRUMS
31.5000 g., 0.9250 Silver .9368 oz. ASW **Subject:** Chinese Lunar Year **Obv:** National emblem **Rev:** Stylized rat within circle, denomination below

Date	Mintage	F	VF	XF	Unc	BU
1996 Proof	—	Value: 30.00				

KM# 95 300 NGULTRUMS
31.5000 g., 0.9250 Silver .9368 oz. ASW **Subject:** Chinese Lunar Year **Obv:** National emblem **Rev:** Stylized ox within circle, denomination below

Date	Mintage	F	VF	XF	Unc	BU
1996 Proof	—	Value: 28.50				

KM# 96 300 NGULTRUMS
31.5000 g., 0.9250 Silver .9368 oz. ASW **Subject:** Chinese Lunar Year **Obv:** National emblem within circle divides dates **Rev:** Stylized tiger within circle, denomination below

Date	Mintage	F	VF	XF	Unc	BU
1996 Proof	—	Value: 30.00				

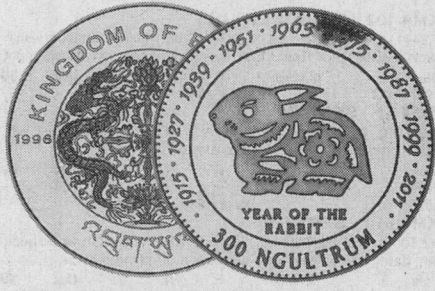

KM# 97 300 NGULTRUMS
31.5000 g., 0.9250 Silver .9368 oz. ASW **Subject:** Chinese Lunar Year **Obv:** National emblem **Rev:** Stylized rabbit within circle, denomination below

Date	Mintage	F	VF	XF	Unc	BU
1996 Proof	—	Value: 28.50				

KM# 99 300 NGULTRUMS
31.5000 g., 0.9250 Silver .9368 oz. ASW **Subject:** Chinese Lunar Year **Obv:** National emblem **Rev:** Stylized snake within circle, denomination below

Date	Mintage	F	VF	XF	Unc	BU
1996 Proof	—	Value: 30.00				

KM# 100 300 NGULTRUMS
31.5000 g., 0.9250 Silver .9368 oz. ASW **Subject:** Chinese Lunar Year **Obv:** National emblem **Rev:** Stylized horse within circle, denomination below

Date	Mintage	F	VF	XF	Unc	BU
1996 Proof	—	Value: 28.50				

KM# 101 300 NGULTRUMS
31.5000 g., 0.9250 Silver .9368 oz. ASW **Subject:** Chinese Lunar Year **Obv:** National emblem **Rev:** Stylized ram within circle, denomination below

Date	Mintage	F	VF	XF	Unc	BU
1996 Proof	—	Value: 28.50				

KM# 102 300 NGULTRUMS
1.2441 g., 0.9990 Gold .04 oz. AGW **Obv:** National emblem within circle divides dates **Rev:** Mask, facing, denomination at lower right

Date	Mintage	F	VF	XF	Unc	BU
1997 Proof	—	Value: 45.00				

KM# 51 SERTUM
7.9800 g., 0.9170 Gold .2352 oz. AGW **Obv:** Crowned bust, left, dates below **Rev:** Two dragons around inner circle

Date	Mintage	F	VF	XF	Unc	BU
1979	1,000	—	—	—	165	—
1979 Proof	1,000	Value: 185				

KM# 51a SERTUM
9.8500 g., 0.9500 Platinum .3008 oz. APW **Obv:** Crowned bust, left, dates below **Rev:** Two dragons around inner circle

Date	Mintage	F	VF	XF	Unc	BU
1979 Proof	—	Value: 400				

KM# 56 SERTUM
7.9900 g., 0.9170 Gold .2356 oz. AGW **Subject:** 75th Anniversary of Monarchy

Date	Mintage	F	VF	XF	Unc	BU
1982(1983)	1,000	—	—	—	165	—
1982(1983) Proof	1,000	Value: 185				

KM# 85 SERTUM
1.2442 g., 0.9999 Gold .04 oz. AGW **Subject:** 40th Anniversary - Queen Elizabeth II's Coronation **Obv:** National emblem within circle divides dates **Rev:** Royal Guard, palace in background, denomination and dates below

Date	Mintage	F	VF	XF	Unc	BU
1995	Est. 250,000	—	—	—	50.00	—

KM# 52 2 SERTUMS
15.9800 g., 0.9170 Gold .4711 oz. AGW **Obv:** Crowned bust, left, dates below **Rev:** Two dragons around inner circle

Date	Mintage	F	VF	XF	Unc	BU
1979	1,000	—	—	—	325	—
1979 Proof	1,000	Value: 350				

KM# 52a 2 SERTUMS
19.7000 g., 0.9500 Platinum .6017 oz. APW **Obv:** Crowned bust, left, dates below **Rev:** Two dragons around inner circle

Date	Mintage	F	VF	XF	Unc	BU
1979 Proof	—	Value: 775				

KM# 60 2 SERTUMS
15.9800 g., 0.9170 Gold .4711 oz. AGW **Series:** International Year of Disabled Persons **Obv:** Dragon, date below, denomination at right **Rev:** Typist

Date	Mintage	F	VF	XF	Unc	BU
1981	—	—	—	—	700	—
1981 Proof	—	Value: 900				

KM# 53 5 SERTUMS
39.9400 g., 0.9170 Gold 1.1776 oz. AGW **Obv:** Crowned bust, left, dates below **Rev:** Two dragons around inner circle

Date	Mintage	F	VF	XF	Unc	BU
1979	1,000	—	—	—	825	—
1979 Proof	1,000	Value: 850				

KM# 53a 5 SERTUMS
49.2000 g., 0.9500 Platinum 1.5022 oz. APW **Obv:** Crowned bust, left, dates below **Rev:** Two dragons around inner circle

Date	Mintage	F	VF	XF	Unc	BU
1979 Proof	—	Value: 1,950				

KM# 64 5 SERTRUMS
7.7760 g., 0.5833 Gold .1458 oz. AGW **Series:** Endangered Wildlife **Obv:** National emblem within circle divides dates **Rev:** Black-necked crane, denomination below

Date	Mintage	F	VF	XF	Unc	BU
1992 Proof	2,000	Value: 145				

KM# 70 5 SERTRUMS
7.7760 g., 0.5833 Gold .1458 oz. AGW **Series:** 1992 Olympics **Obv:** National emblem within circle divides dates **Rev:** Archer, denomination below

Date	Mintage	F	VF	XF	Unc	BU
1993 Proof	Est. 3,000	Value: 165				

KM# 71 5 SERTRUMS
7.7760 g., 0.5833 Gold .1458 oz. AGW **Subject:** World Cup '94 Soccer **Obv:** National emblem within circle divides dates **Rev:** Soccer players, denomination below

Date	Mintage	F	VF	XF	Unc	BU
1993 Proof	Est. 2,000	Value: 165				

KM# 82 5 SERTRUMS
7.7760 g., 0.5833 Gold .1458 oz. AGW **Series:** Olympics **Subject:** Tae kwon do **Obv:** National emblem within circle divides dates **Rev:** Karate practitioner, denomination below

Date	Mintage	F	VF	XF	Unc	BU
1994 Proof	Est. 3,000	Value: 165				

PIEFORTS

KM#	Date	Mintage	Identification	Mkt Val
P1	1981	—	2 Sertums. Gold. KM60.	1,500
P2	1981	—	200 Ngultrums. Silver. KM57.	300

MINT SETS

KM#	Date	Mintage	Identification	Issue Price	Mkt Val
MS1	1966 (3)	300	KM33-35	175	900
MS2	1974 (2)	—	KM39, 42	4.00	11.50
MS3	1974 (4)	—	KM37-38, 40-41	6.00	3.00
MS4	1979 (3)	1,000	KM51-53	1,575	900

PROOF SETS

KM#	Date	Mintage	Identification	Issue Price	Mkt Val
PS1	1966 (4)	6,000	KM29-32	11.50	15.00
PS2	1966 (3)	598	KM33-35	300	1,250
PS3	1966 (3)	72	KM33a-35a	685	2,250
PS4	1974 (6)	1,000	KM37-42	18.00	65.00
PS5	1975 (5)	—	KM37, 40-41, 43-44; rare	—	—
PS6	1979 (5)	20,000	KM45-49	30.00	15.00
PS7	1979 (3)	1,000	KM51-53	2,100	1,125
PS8	1979 (3)	—	KM51a-53a	2,400	2,250

BIAFRA

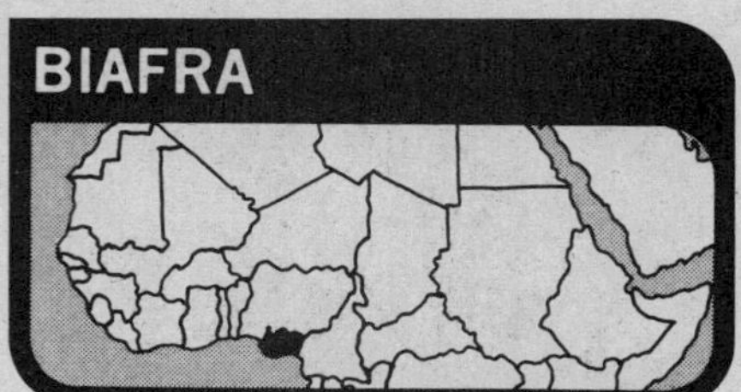

On May 30, 1967, the Eastern Region of the Republic of Nigeria, an area occupied principally by the proud and resourceful Ibo tribe, seceded from Nigeria and proclaimed itself the independent Republic of Biafra with Odumegwu Ojukwu as Chief of State. Civil war erupted and raged for 31 months. Casualties, including civilian, were about two million, the majority succumbing to malnutrition and disease. Biafra surrendered to the federal government on January 15, 1970.

MONETARY SYSTEM
12 Pence = 1 Shilling
20 Shillings = 1 Pound

INDEPENDENT REPUBLIC OF BIAFRA

STANDARD COINAGE

KM# 1 3 PENCE
Aluminum

Date	Mintage	F	VF	XF	Unc	BU
1969	—	—	15.00	22.50	35.00	—

KM# 12 6 PENCE
Aluminum **Obv:** Denomination, date above **Rev:** Radiant sun rising behind tree, legend below horseshoe design

Date	Mintage	F	VF	XF	Unc	BU
1969 5-10 pieces known	—	—	500	1,000	2,000	—

KM# 2 SHILLING
Aluminum, 23.5 mm. **Obv:** Eagle divides denomination and date **Rev:** Radiant sun rising behind tree, legend below horseshoe design **Edge:** Reeded

Date	Mintage	F	VF	XF	Unc	BU
1969	—	—	8.00	14.00	25.00	—

KM# 3 SHILLING
Aluminum, 23.5 mm. **Obv:** Eagle divides date and denomination **Rev:** Radiant sun rising behind tree, legend below horseshoe design

Date	Mintage	F	VF	XF	Unc	BU
1969	—	—	—	350	550	—

KM# 4 2-1/2 SHILLING
Aluminum **Obv:** Date and denomination below large cat **Rev:** Rising radiant sun behind tree, legend below horseshoe design

Date	Mintage	F	VF	XF	Unc	BU
1969	—	—	8.00	18.00	40.00	—

KM# 5 CROWN
28.0000 g., Silver **Subject:** Independence and Liberty **Obv:** Head, right, within circle **Rev:** Tree within circle, denomination below circle **Edge:** Plain

Date	Mintage	F	VF	XF	Unc	BU
1969 Rare	—	—	—	—	—	—

KM# 6 POUND
19.7600 g., 0.7500 Silver .4765 oz. ASW **Obv:** National arms, date below **Rev:** Defiant eagle with scroll, wreathed shield at back, denomination below

Date	Mintage	F	VF	XF	Unc	BU
1969	—	—	—	75.00	125	—

KM# 7 POUND
3.9940 g., 0.9170 Gold .1177 oz. AGW **Subject:** 2nd Anniversary of Independence **Obv:** Similar to 25 Pounds, KM#11, (national arms) **Rev:** Defiant eagle with scroll, wreathed shield at back, denomination below

Date	Mintage	F	VF	XF	Unc	BU
1969 Proof	3,000	Value: 175				

KM# 8 2 POUNDS
7.9881 g., 0.9170 Gold .2354 oz. AGW **Subject:** 2nd Anniversary of Independence **Obv:** Similar to 25 Pounds, KM#11, (national arms) **Rev:** Defiant eagle with scroll, wreathed shield at back, denomination below

Date	Mintage	F	VF	XF	Unc	BU
1969 Proof	3,000	Value: 250				

KM# 9 5 POUNDS
15.9761 g., 0.9170 Gold .4710 oz. AGW **Subject:** 2nd Ann versary of Independence **Obv:** Similar to 25 Pounds, KM#11, (national arms) **Rev:** Defiant eagle with scroll, wreathed shield at back, denomination below

Date	Mintage	F	VF	XF	Unc	BU
1969 Proof	3,000	Value: 500				

KM# 10 10 POUNDS
39.9403 g., 0.9170 Gold 1.1776 oz. AGW **Subject:** 2nd Anniversary of Independence **Obv:** Similar to 25 Pounds, KM#11, (national arms) **Rev:** Defiant eagle with scroll, wreathed shield at back, denomination below

Date	Mintage	F	VF	XF	Unc	BU
1969 Proof	3,000	Value: 845				

KM# 11 25 POUNDS
79.8805 g., 0.9170 Gold 2.3553 oz. AGW **Subject:** 2nd Anniversary of Independence **Obv:** National arms **Rev:** Defiant eagle with scroll, wreathed shield at back, denomination below

Date	Mintage	F	VF	XF	Unc	BU
1969 Proof	3,000	Value: 1,600				

PATTERNS

KM#	Date	Mintage	Identification	Mkt Val
Pn1	1968	—	Shilling. Aluminum. 29 mm. Similar to KM#3, without rope between eagle and denomination. Similar to KM#3, with textured palm trunk. Plain edge. Similar to KM#3, without rope below eagle, with textured palm trunk	1,500

PROOF SETS

KM#	Date	Mintage	Identification	Issue Price	Mkt Val
PS1	1969 (5)	3,000	KM7-11	464	3,375

BOHEMIA & MORAVIA

Bohemia, a western province in the Czech Republic, was combined with the majority of Moravia in central Czechoslovakia (excluding parts of north and south Moravia which were joined with Silesia in 1938) to form the German protectorate in March, 1939, after the German invasion. Toward the end of war in 1945 the protectorate was dissolved and Bohemia and Moravia once again became part of Czechoslovakia.

MONETARY SYSTEM
100 Haleru = 1 Koruna

GERMAN PROTECTORATE

STANDARD COINAGE

KM# 1 10 HALERU
1.8800 g., Zinc, 17 mm. **Obv:** Czech lion crowned, left **Obv. Designer:** Jaroslav Eder **Rev:** Charles bridge in Prague, denomination below **Rev. Designer:** O. Spaniel **Edge:** Plain

Date	Mintage	F	VF	XF	Unc	BU
1940	82,114,000	0.35	0.75	1.50	10.00	13.50
1941	Inc. above	0.25	0.50	1.25	9.00	12.00
1942	Inc. above	0.25	0.50	1.25	9.00	12.00
1943	Inc. above	0.35	0.75	1.50	10.00	13.50
1944	Inc. above	0.75	1.50	3.00	14.00	17.50

KM# 2 20 HALERU
2.6300 g., Zinc, 20 mm. **Obv:** Czech lion crowned, left **Obv. Designer:** Jaroslav Eder **Rev:** Wheat ears with sickle, denomination on left **Rev. Designer:** O. Spaniel **Edge:** Plain

Date	Mintage	F	VF	XF	Unc	BU
1940	106,526,000	0.25	0.50	1.25	9.00	12.00
1941	Inc. above	0.25	0.50	1.25	9.00	12.00
1942	Inc. above	0.25	0.50	1.25	9.00	12.00
1943	Inc. above	0.50	0.75	1.50	10.00	13.50
1944	Inc. above	0.50	1.00	2.00	12.00	16.50

KM# 3 50 HALERU
3.7000 g., Zinc, 22 mm. **Obv:** Czech lion crowned **Obv. Designer:** Jaroslav Eder **Rev:** Value within linden branches, wheat ears below **Rev. Designer:** O. Spaniel **Edge:** Milled

Date	Mintage	F	VF	XF	Unc	BU
1940	53,270,000	0.35	0.75	1.50	10.00	13.50
1941	Inc. above	0.35	0.75	1.50	10.00	13.50
1942	Inc. above	0.35	0.75	1.50	10.00	13.50
1943	Inc. above	0.75	1.50	3.00	15.00	20.00
1944	Inc. above	0.75	1.50	3.00	15.00	20.00

KM# 4 KORUNA
4.5000 g., Zinc, 23 mm. **Obv:** Czech lion crowned, left **Obv. Designer:** Jaroslav Eder **Rev:** Linden branches divide denomination and date **Rev. Designer:** O. Spaniel **Edge:** Milled

Date	Mintage	F	VF	XF	Unc	BU
1941	102,817,000	0.50	0.75	1.75	12.50	16.50
1942	Inc. above	0.50	0.75	1.75	12.50	16.50
1943	Inc. above	0.50	0.75	1.75	12.50	16.50
1944	Inc. above	0.50	0.75	1.75	12.50	16.50

PATTERNS

Including off metal strikes

KM#	Date	Mintage	Identification	Mkt Val
Pn1	1940	—	20 Haleru. Zinc. 2.6600 g. 19 mm. KM#2.	—
Pn2	1940	—	20 Haleru. Aluminum. 1.7800 g. 20.03 mm. KM#2.	—
Pn3	1940	—	50 Haleru. Aluminum. KM#3.	—
Pn4	1940	—	Koruna. Aluminum. KM#4.	—

The Republic of Bolivia, a landlocked country in west central South America, has an area of 424,165 sq. mi. (1,098,580 sq. km.) and a population of *8.33 million. Its capitals are: La Paz (administrative) and Sucre (constitutional). Principal exports are tin, zinc, antimony, tungsten, petroleum, natural gas, cotton and coffee.

Much of present day Bolivia was first dominated by the Tiahuanaco Culture ca.400 BC. It had in turn been incorporated into the Inca Empire by 1440AD prior to the arrival of the Spanish, in 1535, who reduced the Indian population to virtual slavery. When Joseph Napoleon was placed upon the throne of occupied Spain in 1809, a fervor of revolutionary activity quickened throughout Alto Peru - culminating in the 1809 Proclamation of Liberty. Sixteen bloody years of struggle ensued before the republic, named for the famed liberator Simon Bolivar, was established on August 6, 1825. Since then Bolivia has survived more than 16 constitutions, 78 Presidents, 3 military juntas and over 160 revolutions.

MINT MARKS

A - Paris
(a) - Paris, privy marks only
CHI - Valcambia
H - Heaton
KN - Kings' Norton

REPUBLIC

REFORM COINAGE

1870 - 1951

KM# 173.3 5 CENTAVOS

Copper-Nickel **Obv:** State arms within circle, stars below **Rev:** Caduceus divides denomination, sprays below, date at bottom

Date	Mintage	F	VF	XF	Unc	BU
1902	2,000,000	1.00	6.00	15.00	35.00	—
1907(a)	2,000,000	1.00	6.00	15.00	35.00	—
1908	3,000,000	2.00	8.00	20.00	35.00	—
1909	—	3.00	10.00	30.00	60.00	—

KM# 173.1 5 CENTAVOS

Copper-Nickel **Note:** Coins dated 1893, 1918 and 1919 medal rotation were struck at the Heaton Mint.

Date	Mintage	F	VF	XF	Unc	BU
1909	4,000,000	1.00	6.00	12.00	20.00	—
1918	530,000	6.00	15.00	40.00	75.00	—
1919	4,370,000	5.00	10.00	20.00	45.00	—

KM# 178 5 CENTAVOS

Copper-Nickel **Obv:** State emblem within circle, stars below **Rev:** Caduceus divides denomination, sprays below, date at bottom

Date	Mintage	F	VF	XF	Unc	BU
1935	5,000,000	1.00	2.00	5.00	12.00	—

KM# 174.3 10 CENTAVOS

Copper-Nickel **Obv:** State emblem within circle, stars below **Rev:** Caduceus divides denomination, sprays below, date at bottom

Date	Mintage	F	VF	XF	Unc	BU
1901	—	20.00	30.00	60.00	100	—
1902	8,500,000	2.00	5.00	12.00	30.00	—
1907/2	4,000,000	6.00	10.00	25.00	50.00	—
1907	Inc. above	2.00	5.00	12.00	30.00	—
1908	6,000,000	2.00	5.00	12.00	30.00	—
1909	8,000,000	2.00	5.00	12.00	30.00	—

KM# 174.1 10 CENTAVOS

Copper-Nickel **Rev:** Without privy marks **Note:** Coins dated 1893, 1918 and 1919 medal rotation were struck at the Heaton Mint.

Date	Mintage	F	VF	XF	Unc	BU
1918	1,335,000	3.00	8.00	20.00	45.00	—
1919	6,165,000	2.00	6.00	15.00	35.00	—

KM# 179.1 10 CENTAVOS

Copper-Nickel **Obv:** State emblem within circle, stars below **Rev:** Caduceus divides denomination, sprays below, date at bottom

Date	Mintage	F	VF	XF	Unc	BU
1935	10,000,000	0.50	1.00	2.50	10.00	—
1936	10,000,000	0.50	1.00	2.50	10.00	—

KM# 179.2 10 CENTAVOS

Copper-Nickel **Obv:** State emblem within circle, stars below **Rev:** Caduceus divides denomination, sprays below, date at bottom

Date	Mintage	F	VF	XF	Unc	BU
1939	—	0.50	1.00	2.50	10.00	—

KM# 179a 10 CENTAVOS

Zinc **Obv:** State emblem within circle, stars below **Rev:** Caduceus divides denomination, sprays below, date at bottom

Date	Mintage	F	VF	XF	Unc	BU
1942 (p)	10,000,000	0.50	1.00	2.50	10.00	—

KM# 180 10 CENTAVOS

Copper-Nickel, 22.5 mm. **Obv:** State emblem within circle, stars below **Rev:** Caduceus divides denomination, sprays below, date at bottom **Edge:** Reeded

Date	Mintage	F	VF	XF	Unc	BU
1937	20,000,000	0.50	1.00	2.50	10.00	—

KM# 159.2 20 CENTAVOS

4.6000 g., 0.9000 Silver .1331 oz. ASW **Obv:** National arms, stars below **Rev:** Denomination within wreath, date below **Note:** Reduced size dates and lettering, bar below CENTS. The small bar usually found below "S" in "9DS" is missing in the 1886-1888 and 1902 dates. Mint mark in monogram.

Date	Mintage	VG	F	VF	XF	Unc
1901PTS MM	40,000	2.50	5.00	13.50	28.00	60.00
1901PTS MM/.WM	—	2.50	5.00	16.50	35.00	75.00
1902PTS MM	—	6.50	10.00	20.00	50.00	100
1903PTS MM	10,000	10.00	15.00	30.00	75.00	125
1904PTS MM	—	7.00	12.00	20.00	75.00	150
1907PTS MM	—	45.00	90.00	150	275	475

KM# 176 20 CENTAVOS

4.0000 g., 0.8330 Silver .1071 oz. ASW **Obv:** National arms, stars below **Rev:** Denomination within wreath, date below

Date	Mintage	F	VF	XF	Unc	BU
1909H	1,500,000	2.50	5.00	15.00	30.00	—
1909H Proof	—	Value: 500				

KM# 183 20 CENTAVOS

Zinc **Obv:** State emblem within circle, stars below **Rev:** Caduceus divides denomination, sprays below, date at bottom **Note:** Medal rotation strike.

Date	Mintage	F	VF	XF	Unc	BU
1942 (p)	10,000,000	1.00	2.00	6.00	20.00	—

KM# 175.1 50 CENTAVOS (1/2 Boliviano)

11.5000 g., 0.9000 Silver .3328 oz. ASW **Obv:** National arms, stars below **Rev:** Denomination within wreath, date below **Note:** Mint mark in monogram.

Date	Mintage	VG	F	VF	XF	Unc
1901/0PTS MM	—	BV	7.50	18.50	37.50	60.00
1901PTS MM	Inc. above	BV	5.00	8.00	20.00	45.00
1902PTS MM	1,530,000	BV	5.00	8.00	20.00	45.00
1903/2PTS MM	690,000	BV	6.50	16.00	37.50	60.00
1903PTS MM	Inc. above	BV	5.00	8.00	20.00	45.00
1904PTS MM	1,290,000	BV	5.00	8.00	20.00	45.00
1905PTS MM	1,690,000	BV	5.00	8.00	20.00	45.00
1905PTS AB	Inc. above	BV	5.00	8.00	20.00	45.00
1906PTS MM	630,000	BV	5.00	10.00	30.00	55.00
1906PTS AB	5,500,000	BV	5.00	8.00	20.00	45.00
1907PTS MM	50,000	BV	6.00	10.00	30.00	55.00
1908PTS MM	—	BV	5.00	8.00	20.00	45.00
1908PTS MM Inverted 8	—	BV	12.00	25.00	50.00	75.00

KM# 177 50 CENTAVOS (1/2 Boliviano)

10.0000 g., 0.8330 Silver .2678 oz. ASW **Obv:** National arms, stars below **Rev:** Denomination within wreath, date below

Date	Mintage	VG	F	VF	XF	Unc
1909H	1,400,000	BV	5.00	10.00	25.00	40.00
1909H	—	Value: 350				

KM# 181 50 CENTAVOS (1/2 Boliviano)

Copper-Nickel **Obv:** State emblem within circle, stars below **Rev:** Hand holding torch divides date and denomination **Note:** Most melted upon receipt in Bolivia. Medal rotation strike.

Date	Mintage	F	VF	XF	Unc	BU
1937	8,000,000	10.00	25.00	45.00	75.00	—

KM# 182 50 CENTAVOS (1/2 Boliviano)
Copper-Nickel **Obv:** State emblem within circle, stars below **Rev:** Caduceus divides denomination, sprays below, date at bottom **Note:** Medal rotation strike.

Date	Mintage	F	VF	XF	Unc	BU
1939	—	0.25	0.50	1.00	5.00	—

KM# 182a.1 50 CENTAVOS (1/2 Boliviano)
Bronze, 24 mm. **Obv:** State emblem within circle, stars below **Rev:** Caduceus divides denomination, sprays below, date at bottom **Note:** Medal rotation strike.

Date	Mintage	F	VF	XF	Unc	BU
1942 (p)	10,000,000	0.35	0.60	1.25	5.00	—

KM# 182a.2 50 CENTAVOS (1/2 Boliviano)
Bronze, 24 mm. **Obv:** State emblem within circle, stars below **Rev:** Caduceus divides denomination, sprays below, date at bottom **Edge:** Reeded **Note:** Restrike - poor detail. Medal rotation strike.

Date	Mintage	F	VF	XF	Unc	BU
1942	5,310,000	0.25	0.50	1.00	4.00	—

KM# 184 BOLIVIANO
Bronze **Obv:** State emblem within circle, stars below **Rev:** Denomination within wreath, date below **Note:** Medal rotation strike. Mint mark in monogram.

Date	Mintage	F	VF	XF	Unc	BU
1951PTS	10,000,000	0.10	0.20	1.00	3.00	5.00
1951PTS Proof	10	Value: 200				
1951PTS H	15,000,000	0.10	0.20	1.00	3.00	5.00
1951PTS KN	15,000,000	0.25	0.50	1.50	4.00	6.00

KM# 185 5 BOLIVIANOS
Bronze **Obv:** National arms, stars below **Rev:** Denomination within wreath, date below **Note:** Medal rotation strike.

Date	Mintage	F	VF	XF	Unc	BU
1951	7,000,000	0.25	0.50	1.00	3.50	5.50
1951 Proof	—	Value: 200				
1951 H	15,000,000	0.25	0.50	1.00	3.50	5.50
1951 KN	15,000,000	0.60	0.90	1.50	4.00	6.00

KM# 186 10 BOLIVIANOS (1 Bolivar)
Bronze **Obv:** Armored bust, right **Rev:** Denomination within wreath, date below **Note:** Medal rotation strike.

Date	Mintage	F	VF	XF	Unc	BU
1951	40,000,000	0.60	1.00	2.00	4.50	6.50
1951 Proof	—	Value: 200				

REFORM COINAGE

1965-1979; 100 Centavos = 1 Peso Boliviano

KM# 187 5 CENTAVOS
Copper Clad Steel **Obv:** State emblem within circle, stars below **Rev:** Denomination, date below **Note:** Medal rotation.

Date	Mintage	F	VF	XF	Unc	BU
1965	10,000,000	0.20	0.30	0.65	1.50	2.00
1970	100,000	0.20	0.30	0.65	2.00	2.50

KM# 188 10 CENTAVOS
Copper Clad Steel **Obv:** State emblem within circle, stars below **Rev:** Denomination, date below **Note:** Medal rotation.

Date	Mintage	F	VF	XF	Unc	BU
1965	10,000,000	0.10	0.25	0.50	1.50	2.00
1967	—	0.10	0.20	0.40	1.00	1.50
1969	5,700,000	0.10	0.20	0.40	1.00	1.50
1971	200,000	0.15	0.25	0.50	1.00	1.50
1972	100,000	0.20	0.40	0.80	1.50	2.00
1973	6,000,000	0.10	0.20	0.40	1.00	1.50

KM# 189 20 CENTAVOS
Nickel Clad Steel **Obv:** State emblem within circle, stars below **Rev:** Denomination, date below **Note:** Medal rotation.

Date	Mintage	F	VF	XF	Unc	BU
1965	5,000,000	0.20	0.40	0.70	2.00	2.50
1967	—	0.20	0.40	0.65	1.75	2.25
1970	400,000	0.20	0.40	0.80	2.50	3.50
1971	400,000	0.20	0.40	0.80	2.50	3.50
1973	5,000,000	0.20	0.40	0.60	1.50	2.00

KM# 193 25 CENTAVOS
Nickel Clad Steel **Obv:** State emblem within circle, stars below **Rev:** Denomination, date below **Note:** Medal rotation.

Date	Mintage	F	VF	XF	Unc	BU
1971	—	0.15	0.30	0.60	1.00	1.50
1972	9,998,000	0.15	0.30	0.60	1.00	1.50

KM# 190 50 CENTAVOS
4.0000 g., Nickel Clad Steel, 24 mm. **Obv:** State emblem within circle, stars below **Rev:** Denomination, date at bottom **Note:** Medal rotation.

Date	Mintage	F	VF	XF	Unc	BU
1965	10,000,000	0.15	0.30	0.65	1.75	2.25
1967	—	0.15	0.30	0.65	1.25	1.75
1972	—	0.15	0.30	0.65	1.25	1.75
1973	5,000,000	0.15	0.30	0.65	1.25	1.75
1974	15,000,000	0.15	0.30	0.65	1.25	1.75
1978	5,000,000	0.15	0.30	0.65	1.25	1.75
1980	3,600,000	0.15	0.30	0.65	1.25	1.75

KM# 191 PESO BOLIVIANOS
6.0000 g., Nickel Clad Steel, 27 mm. **Series:** F.A.O. **Obv:** State emblem within circle, stars below **Rev:** Denomination **Note:** Medal rotation.

Date	Mintage	F	VF	XF	Unc	BU
ND(1968)	40,000	1.50	2.50	3.50	6.50	9.00

KM# 192 PESO BOLIVIANOS
6.0000 g., Nickel Clad Steel, 27 mm. **Series:** F.A.O. **Obv:** State emblem within circle, stars below **Rev:** Denomination, date below **Edge:** Reeded **Note:** Medal rotation.

Date	Mintage	F	VF	XF	Unc	BU
1968	10,000,000	0.20	0.40	0.80	1.75	2.50
1969	—	0.20	0.40	0.80	1.75	2.50
1970	10,000,000	0.20	0.40	0.80	1.75	2.50
1972	—	0.20	0.40	0.80	1.75	2.50
1973	5,000,000	0.20	0.40	0.80	1.75	2.50
1974 small date	15,000,000	0.20	0.40	0.80	1.75	2.50
1978	10,000,000	0.20	0.40	0.80	1.75	2.50
1980 large date	2,993,000	0.20	0.40	0.80	1.75	2.50

KM# 197 5 PESOS BOLIVIANOS
8.5000 g., Nickel Clad Steel, 30 mm. **Obv:** State arms within circle, stars below **Rev:** Denomination, date below **Note:** Medal rotation.

Date	Mintage	F	VF	XF	Unc	BU
1976	20,000,000	0.65	1.25	2.50	5.00	6.50
1978	10,000,000	0.65	1.25	2.50	5.00	6.50
1980	5,231,000	0.65	1.25	2.50	5.00	6.50

KM# 194 100 PESOS BOLIVIANOS
10.0000 g., 0.9330 Silver .3000 oz. ASW **Subject:** 150th Anniversary of Independence **Obv:** National arms divide dates **Rev:** Simon Bolivar and Hugo Banzer Suarez left, denomination below **Note:** Medal rotation.

Date	Mintage	F	VF	XF	Unc	BU
ND(1975)	160,000	BV	4.00	6.00	9.00	—

KM# 198 200 PESOS BOLIVIANOS
23.3300 g., 0.9250 Silver .6938 oz. ASW **Subject:** International Year of the Child **Obv:** State emblem within circle, eagle at top, stars below **Rev:** Children divide small symbols, date at bottom, denomination at top **Note:** Medal rotation.

Date	Mintage	F	VF	XF	Unc	BU
1979	15,000	Value: 16.50				

KM# 195 250 PESOS BOLIVIANOS
15.0000 g., 0.9330 Silver .4500 oz. ASW **Subject:** 150th Anniversary of Independence **Obv:** National arms divide dates **Rev:** Conjoined heads left with armored collars, denomination below **Note:** Medal rotation.

Date	Mintage	F	VF	XF	Unc	BU
ND(1975)	140,000	BV	6.00	8.00	13.50	—

KM# 196 500 PESOS BOLIVIANOS
22.0000 g., 0.9330 Silver .6600 oz. ASW **Subject:** 150th Anniversary of Independence

Date	Mintage	F	VF	XF	Unc	BU
ND(1975)	100,000	BV	9.00	15.00	22.00	—

KM# 199 4000 PESOS BOLIVIANOS
17.1700 g., 0.9000 Gold .4968 oz. AGW **Subject:** International Year of the Child **Obv:** State emblem within circle, eagle at top, stars below **Rev:** Child playing flute divides symbols, date below, denomination above

Date	Mintage	F	VF	XF	Unc	BU
1979 Proof	6,315	Value: 345				

REFORM COINAGE

1987-; 1,000,000 Peso Bolivianos = 1 Boliviano; 100 Centavos = 1 Boliviano

KM# 200 2 CENTAVOS
Stainless Steel **Obv:** National arms, star below **Rev:** Denomination within circle, date below

Date	Mintage	F	VF	XF	Unc	BU
1987	20,000,000	—	—	—	0.35	0.50

KM# 201 5 CENTAVOS
Stainless Steel **Obv:** National arms, star below **Rev:** Denomination within circle, date below

Date	Mintage	F	VF	XF	Unc	BU
1987	20,000,000	—	—	—	0.50	0.65

KM# 202 10 CENTAVOS
Stainless Steel **Obv:** National arms, star below **Rev:** Denomination within circle, date below

Date	Mintage	F	VF	XF	Unc	BU
1987	20,000,000	—	—	—	0.65	0.85
1991	23,000,000	—	—	—	0.50	0.65
1995	14,000,000	—	—	—	0.50	0.65
1997	33,000,000	—	—	—	0.50	0.65

KM# 202a 10 CENTAVOS
Copper Clad Steel

Date	Mintage	F	VF	XF	Unc	BU
1997	—	—	—	—	0.50	0.65

KM# 203 20 CENTAVOS
Stainless Steel, 22 mm. **Obv:** National arms, star below **Rev:** Denomination within circle, date below **Edge:** Plain

Date	Mintage	F	VF	XF	Unc	BU
1987	20,000,000	—	—	—	0.75	1.00
1991	20,000,000	—	—	—	0.65	0.85
1995	14,000,000	—	—	—	0.65	0.85
1997	19,000,000	—	—	—	0.65	0.85

KM# 204 50 CENTAVOS
Stainless Steel, 24 mm. **Obv:** National arms, star below **Rev:** Denomination within circle, date below **Edge:** Plain

Date	Mintage	F	VF	XF	Unc	BU
1987	15,000,000	—	—	—	1.00	1.25
1991	20,000,000	—	—	—	0.75	1.00
1995	14,000,000	—	—	—	0.75	1.00
1997	15,000,000	—	—	—	0.75	1.00

KM# 205 BOLIVIANO
Stainless Steel **Obv:** National arms, star below **Rev:** Denomination within circle, date below

Date	Mintage	F	VF	XF	Unc	BU
1987	10,000,000	—	—	—	1.75	2.00
1991	20,000,000	—	—	—	1.00	1.25
1995	9,000,000	—	—	—	1.00	1.25
1997	17,000,000	—	—	—	1.00	1.25

KM# 210 BOLIVIANO
27.0000 g., 0.9250 Silver .8030 oz. ASW **Subject:** 70th Anniversary - Bolivian Central Bank **Obv:** National arms above date, stars below **Rev:** Denomination above bank emblem, two dates below sprays

Date	Mintage	F	VF	XF	Unc	BU
1998 Proof	1,000	Value: 70.00				

KM# 206.1 2 BOLIVIANOS
Stainless Steel **Obv:** National arms, star below **Rev:** Denomination within circle, date below **Shape:** 11-sided

Date	Mintage	F	VF	XF	Unc	BU
1991	18,000,000	—	—	—	2.00	3.00

KM# 206.2 2 BOLIVIANOS
Stainless Steel, 29 mm. **Obv:** National arms, star below **Rev:** Denomination within circle, date below **Shape:** 11-sided **Note:** Increased size.

Date	Mintage	F	VF	XF	Unc	BU
1995	11,000,000	—	—	—	2.00	3.00
1997	—	—	—	—	2.00	3.00

KM# 207 10 BOLIVIANOS
27.0000 g., 0.9250 Silver .8029 oz. ASW **Series:** Ibero - American **Obv:** National arms within legend, arms surrounding **Rev:** Radiant sun behind mountains, denomination, within circle, two dates below

Date	Mintage	F	VF	XF	Unc	BU
1991 Proof	Est. 50,000	Value: 65.00				

KM# 209 10 BOLIVIANOS
27.1300 g., 0.9250 Silver .8068 oz. ASW **Series:** Ibero - American **Obv:** Bolivian arms within legend, arms surrounding **Rev:** Folk dancer, denomination within circle, date below

Date	Mintage	F	VF	XF	Unc	BU
1997 Proof	33,000	Value: 65.00				

KM# 211 50 BOLIVIANOS
27.0000 g., 0.9250 Silver .8030 oz. ASW **Subject:** 450th Anniversary of La Paz **Obv:** National arms, date below, stars at bottom **Rev:** City arms above church building, denomination, within circle, two dates below

Date	Mintage	F	VF	XF	Unc	BU
1998 Proof	2,000	Value: 70.00				

PATTERNS

Including off metal strikes

KM#	Date	Mintage	Identification	Mkt Val
Pn54	1902 MM	—	20 Centavos. Brass. Struck at La Paz.	100
Pn55	1902 MM	—	20 Centavos. Brass. Struck at La Paz. 1/2 Medio Boliviano/20 Centavos error.	75.00
Pn56	1902 MM	—	50 Centavos. Brass.	100
Pn57	1942	—	50 Centavos. Silver. Struck at La Paz. KM#182a.1.	300
Pn58	1952	—	35 Gramos. Brass. Struck at La Paz. KM MB4.	—

PIEFORTS

KM#	Date	Mintage	Identification	Issue Price	Mkt Val
P9	1979	90	200 Pesos. Silver. KM#198.	—	200
P10	1979	47	4000 Pesos. Gold. KM#199.	—	1,000

TRIAL STRIKES

KM#	Date	Mintage	Identification	Issue Price	Mkt Val
TS1	ND(1909)	—	20 Centavos. Silver. 23.2 mm. Uniface.	—	—
TS2	1942	—	10 Centavos. Lead. KM179a, uniface	—	150

BOSNIA AND HERZEGOVINA

The Republic of Bosnia and Herzegovina borders Croatia to the north and west, Serbia to the east and Montenegro in the southeast with only 12.4 mi. of coastline. The total land area is 19,735 sq. mi. (51,129 sq. km.). They have a population of *4.34 million. Capital: Sarajevo. Electricity, mining and agriculture are leading industries.

After the defeat of Germany in WWII, during which Bosnia was under the control of Pavelic of Croatia, a new Socialist Republic was formed under Marshall Tito having six constituent republics, all subservient, quite similar to the constitution of the U.S.S.R. Military and civil loyalty was with Tito, not with Moscow. In Jan. 1990, the Yugoslav Government announced a rewriting of the Constitution, abolishing the Communist Party's monopoly of power. Opposition parties were legalized in July 1990. On Oct. 15, 1991 the National Assembly adopted a "Memorandum on Sovereignty", the envisaged Bosnian autonomy within a Yugoslav federation. In March 1992, an agreement was reached under EC auspices by Moslems, Serbs and Croats to set up 3 autonomous ethnic communities under a central Bosnian authority. Independence was declared on April 5, 1992. The 2 Serbian members of government resigned and fighting broke out between all 3 ethnic communities. The Dayton (Ohio) Peace Accord was signed in 1995, which recognized the Federation of Bosnia and Herzegovina and the Srpska (Serbian) Republic. Both governments maintain separate military forces, school systems, etc. The United Nations is currently providing humanitarian aid while a recent peace treaty allowed NATO "Peace Keeping" forces to be deployed in Dec. 1995 replacing the United Nations troops previously acting in a similar role.

MINT MARKS
PM - Pobjoy Mint

MONETARY SYSTEM
1 Dinara = 100 Para, 1992-1998
1 Convertible Marka = 100 Convertible Feniga =
1 Deutschemark 1998-

NOTE: German Euros circulate freely.

REPUBLIC

STANDARD COINAGE

KM# 115 10 FENINGA
Copper-Plated-Steel **Obv:** Denomination on map within circle **Rev:** Triangle and stars, date at left, within circle

Date	Mintage	F	VF	XF	Unc	BU
1998	—	—	—	—	0.50	0.75
2000 In mint sets only	—	—	—	—	—	1.00

KM# 116 20 FENINGA
Copper-Plated-Steel **Obv:** Denomination on map within circle **Rev:** Triangle and stars, date at left, within circle

Date	Mintage	F	VF	XF	Unc	BU
1998	—	—	—	—	1.00	1.25
2000 In mint sets only	—	—	—	—	—	1.50

KM# 117 50 FENINGA
Copper-Plated-Steel **Obv:** Denomination on map within circle **Rev:** Triangle and stars, date at left, within circle

Date	Mintage	F	VF	XF	Unc	BU
1998	—	—	—	—	2.25	2.50
2000 In mint sets only	—	—	—	—	—	3.00

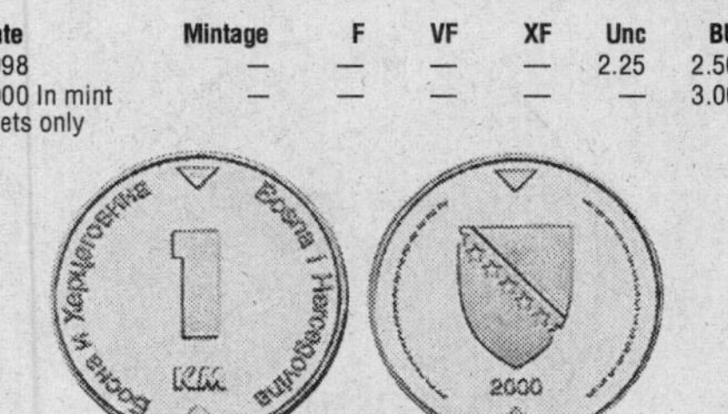

KM# 118 KONVERTIBLE MARKA
4.9000 g., Nickel Plated Steel, 23.23 mm. **Obv:** Denomination **Rev:** Coat of arms above date **Edge:** Reeded and plain sections

Date	Mintage	F	VF	XF	Unc	BU
2000	—	—	—	—	5.50	6.00

KM# 119 2 KONVERTIBLE MARKA
6.9000 g., Bi-Metallic Copper-Nickel center in Nickel-Brass ring, 25.75 mm. **Obv:** Denomination within circle **Rev:** Dove of peace, date at right, within circle **Edge:** Reeded and plain sections

Date	Mintage	F	VF	XF	Unc	BU
2000	—	—	—	—	13.50	15.00

DINARA COINAGE

KM# 1 500 DINARA
Copper-Nickel **Series:** Preserve Planet Earth **Obv:** National arms above bridge, date at bottom **Rev:** Brontosaurus, facing back, looking left, denomination below

Date	Mintage	F	VF	XF	Unc	BU
1993 Prooflike	—	—	—	—	—	12.00

KM# 4 500 DINARA
Copper-Nickel **Series:** Preserve Planet Earth **Obv:** National arms above bridge, date below **Rev:** Tyrannosaurus Rex, facing right, looking left, denomination below

Date	Mintage	F	VF	XF	Unc	BU
1993 Prooflike	—	—	—	—	—	12.00

KM# 20 500 DINARA
Copper-Nickel **Series:** Preserve Planet Earth **Obv:** National arms above bridge, date below **Rev:** Eohippus

Date	Mintage	F	VF	XF	Unc	BU
1994 Proof	—	—	—	—	9.00	12.00

KM# 23 500 DINARA
Copper-Nickel **Series:** Preserve Planet Earth **Obv:** National arms above bridge, date below **Rev:** Gray Wolf, right, above denomination

Date	Mintage	F	VF	XF	Unc	BU
1994 Prooflike	—	—	—	—	—	12.00

KM# 24 500 DINARA
Copper-Nickel **Series:** Preserve Planet Earth **Obv:** National arms above bridge, date below **Rev:** Black Bear, left, with cub facing, denomination below

Date	Mintage	F	VF	XF	Unc	BU
1994 Prooflike	—	—	—	—	—	12.00

KM# 25 500 DINARA
Copper-Nickel **Series:** Preserve Planet Earth **Obv:** National arms above bridge, date below **Rev:** River Kingfisher, left, fish in beak, denomination below

Date	Mintage	F	VF	XF	Unc	BU
1994	—	—	—	—	10.00	12.00

KM# 39 500 DINARA
Copper-Nickel **Series:** Preserve Planet Earth **Obv:** National arms above bridge, date below **Rev:** Przewalskii Horses

Date	Mintage	F	VF	XF	Unc	BU
1995	—	—	—	—	12.00	14.00

KM# 42 500 DINARA
Copper-Nickel **Series:** Preserve Planet Earth **Obv:** National arms above bridge, date below **Rev:** Hedgehogs

Date	Mintage	F	VF	XF	Unc	BU
1995	—	—	—	—	12.00	14.00

KM# 64 500 DINARA
Copper-Nickel **Series:** European Youth Olympics **Obv:** National arms above bridge, date below **Rev:** Flame

Date	Mintage	F	VF	XF	Unc	BU
1995	—	—	—	—	8.50	—

KM# 65 500 DINARA
Copper-Nickel **Series:** European Youth Olympics **Obv:** National arms above bridge, date below **Rev:** Rings

Date	Mintage	F	VF	XF	Unc	BU
1995	—	—	—	—	8.50	—

KM# 52 500 DINARA
Copper-Nickel **Series:** Olympics **Obv:** National arms above bridge, date below **Rev:** Long jumper

Date	Mintage	F	VF	XF	Unc	BU
1996	—	—	—	—	8.50	—

KM# 53 500 DINARA
Copper-Nickel **Series:** Olympics **Obv:** National arms above bridge, date below **Rev:** Sprinter

Date	Mintage	F	VF	XF	Unc	BU
1996	—	—	—	—	8.50	—

KM# 54 500 DINARA
Copper-Nickel **Series:** Olympics **Obv:** National arms above bridge, date below **Rev:** Wrestlers

Date	Mintage	F	VF	XF	Unc	BU
1996	—	—	—	—	8.50	—

KM# 55 500 DINARA
Copper-Nickel **Series:** Olympics **Obv:** National arms above bridge, date below **Rev:** Fencers

Date	Mintage	F	VF	XF	Unc	BU
1996	—	—	—	—	8.50	—

KM# 76 500 DINARA
Copper-Nickel **Series:** Preserve Planet Earth **Obv:** National arms above bridge, date below **Rev:** Hoopoe Birds

Date	Mintage	F	VF	XF	Unc	BU
1996	—	—	—	—	10.00	—

KM# 79 500 DINARA
Copper-Nickel **Series:** Preserve Planet Earth **Obv:** National arms above bridge, date below **Rev:** Goosander Birds

Date	Mintage	F	VF	XF	Unc	BU
1996	—	—	—	—	10.00	—

KM# 95 500 DINARA
Copper-Nickel **Subject:** Jurassic Park **Obv:** National arms above bridge, date below **Rev:** Tyrannosaurus Rex, Jurassic Park logo

Date	Mintage	F	VF	XF	Unc	BU
1997	—	—	—	—	10.00	—

KM# 2 750 DINARA
28.2800 g., 0.9250 Silver .8411 oz. ASW **Series:** Preserve Planet Earth **Obv:** National arms above bridge, date below **Rev:** Brontosaurus facing back, looking left, denomination below

Date	Mintage	F	VF	XF	Unc	BU
1993 Proof	Est. 30,000	Value: 37.50				

KM# 5 750 DINARA
28.2800 g., 0.9250 Silver .8411 oz. ASW **Series:** Preserve Planet Earth **Obv:** National arms above bridge, date below **Rev:** Tyrannosaurus Rex, facing right, looking left, denomination below

Date	Mintage	F	VF	XF	Unc	BU
1993 Proof	Est. 30,000	Value: 37.50				

KM# 7 750 DINARA
28.2800 g., 0.9250 Silver .8411 oz. ASW **Series:** Olympics **Obv:** National arms above bridge, date below **Rev:** 2 Bobsledders with sled, denomination below, within circle

Date	Mintage	F	VF	XF	Unc	BU
1993 Proof	Est. 30,000	Value: 45.00				

KM# 9 750 DINARA
28.2800 g., 0.9250 Silver .8411 oz. ASW **Series:** Olympics **Obv:** National arms above bridge, date below **Rev:** Downhill skier above denomination, within circle

Date	Mintage	F	VF	XF	Unc	BU
1993 Proof	Est. 30,000	Value: 45.00				

KM# 11 750 DINARA
28.2800 g., 0.9250 Silver .8411 oz. ASW **Series:** Olympics **Obv:** National arms above bridge, date below **Rev:** Cross-country skier above denomination, within circle

Date	Mintage	F	VF	XF	Unc	BU
1993 Proof	Est. 30,000	Value: 45.00				

KM# 13 750 DINARA
28.2800 g., 0.9250 Silver .8411 oz. ASW **Series:** Lillehammer 1994 - 17th Winter Olympic Games **Obv:** National arms above bridge, date below **Rev:** Pairs Figure Skating above denomination, within circle

Date	Mintage	F	VF	XF	Unc	BU
1993 Proof	Est. 30,000	Value: 45.00				

KM# 21 750 DINARA
28.2800 g., 0.9250 Silver .8411 oz. ASW **Series:** Preserve Planet Earth **Obv:** National arms above bridge, date below **Rev:** Eohippu **Note:** Similar to 10,000 Dinara, KM#22.

Date	Mintage	F	VF	XF	Unc	BU
1994 Proof	Est. 30,000	Value: 37.50				

KM# 26 750 DINARA
28.2800 g., 0.9250 Silver .8411 oz. ASW **Series:** Preserve Planet Earth **Obv:** National arms above bridge, date below **Rev:** Wolf right, denomination below

Date	Mintage	F	VF	XF	Unc	BU
1994 Proof	Est. 30,000	Value: 40.00				

KM# 27 750 DINARA

28.2800 g., 0.9250 Silver .8411 oz. ASW **Series:** Preserve Planet Earth **Obv:** National arms above bridge, date below **Rev:** Black bear left with cub facing, denomination below

Date	Mintage	F	VF	XF	Unc	BU
1994 Proof	Est. 30,000	Value: 37.50				

KM# 28 750 DINARA

28.2800 g., 0.9250 Silver .8411 oz. ASW **Series:** Preserve Planet Earth **Obv:** National arms above bridge, date below **Rev:** River Kingfisher left, fish in beak, denomination below

Date	Mintage	F	VF	XF	Unc	BU
1994 Proof	Est. 30,000	Value: 35.00				

KM# 40 750 DINARA

28.2800 g., 0.9250 Silver .8411 oz. ASW **Series:** Preserve Planet Earth **Obv:** National arms above bridge, date below **Rev:** Przewalskii horses right, denomination below

Date	Mintage	F	VF	XF	Unc	BU
1995 Proof	Est. 30,000	Value: 37.50				

KM# 43 750 DINARA

28.2800 g., 0.9250 Silver .8411 oz. ASW **Series:** Preserve Planet Earth **Obv:** National arms above bridge, date below **Rev:** Hedgehog left with babies, denomination below

Date	Mintage	F	VF	XF	Unc	BU
1995 Proof	Est. 30,000	Value: 37.50				

KM# 66 750 DINARA

28.2800 g., 0.9250 Silver .8411 oz. ASW **Series:** European Youth Olympics **Obv:** National arms above bridge, date below **Rev:** Figures within small circles on flame, denomination below

Date	Mintage	F	VF	XF	Unc	BU
1995 Proof	Est. 30,000	Value: 37.50				

KM# 67 750 DINARA

28.2800 g., 0.9250 Silver .8411 oz. ASW **Series:** European Youth Olympics **Obv:** National arms above bridge, date below **Rev:** Man on rings event, denomination below

Date	Mintage	F	VF	XF	Unc	BU
1995 Proof	Est. 30,000	Value: 37.50				

KM# 56 750 DINARA

28.2800 g., 0.9250 Silver .8411 oz. ASW **Series:** Atlanta 1996 - 26th Summer Olympics **Obv:** National arms above bridge, date below **Rev:** Long jumper right, denomination below

Date	Mintage	F	VF	XF	Unc	BU
1996 Proof	Est. 30,000	Value: 35.00				

KM# 57 750 DINARA

28.2800 g., 0.9250 Silver .8411 oz. ASW **Series:** Olympics **Obv:** National arms above bridge, date below **Rev:** Sprinter, right, denomination below

Date	Mintage	F	VF	XF	Unc	BU
1996 Proof	Est. 30,000	Value: 35.00				

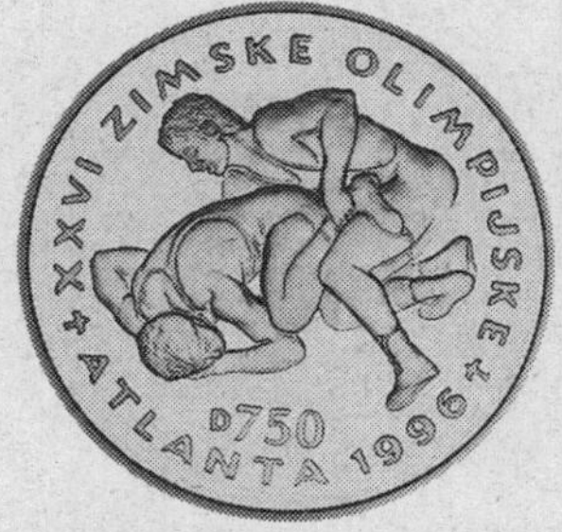

KM# 58 750 DINARA

28.2800 g., 0.9250 Silver .8411 oz. ASW **Series:** Olympics **Obv:** National arms above bridge, date below **Rev:** Wrestlers, denomination below

Date	Mintage	F	VF	XF	Unc	BU
1996 Proof	Est. 30,000	Value: 35.00				

KM# 59 750 DINARA

28.2800 g., 0.9250 Silver .8411 oz. ASW **Series:** Olympics **Obv:** National arms above bridge, date below **Rev:** Fencers, denomination below

Date	Mintage	F	VF	XF	Unc	BU
1996 Proof	Est. 30,000	Value: 35.00				

KM# 77 750 DINARA

28.2800 g., 0.9250 Silver .8411 oz. ASW **Series:** Preserve Planet Earth **Obv:** National arms above bridge, date below **Rev:** Hoopoe birds, denomination below

Date	Mintage	F	VF	XF	Unc	BU
1996 Proof	Est. 30,000	Value: 35.00				

KM# 80 750 DINARA

28.2800 g., 0.9250 Silver .8411 oz. ASW **Series:** Preserve Planet Earth **Obv:** National arms above bridge, date below **Rev:** Goosander birds, denomination below

Date	Mintage	F	VF	XF	Unc	BU
1996 Proof	Est. 30,000	Value: 35.00				

KM# 96 750 DINARA

28.2800 g., 0.9250 Silver .8411 oz. ASW **Subject:** Jurassic Park **Obv:** National arms above bridge, date below **Rev:** Tyrannosaurus Rex, left, Jurassic Park logo, denomination at bottom

Date	Mintage	F	VF	XF	Unc	BU
1997 Proof	Est. 10,000	Value: 45.00				

KM# 3 10000 DINARA

6.2200 g., 0.9990 Gold .1998 oz. AGW **Series:** Preserve Planet Earth **Obv:** National arms above bridge, date below **Rev:** Brontosaurus, facing back, looking left, denomination below

Date	Mintage	F	VF	XF	Unc	BU
1993 Proof	Est. 5,000	Value: 185				

KM# 6 10000 DINARA

6.2200 g., 0.9990 Gold .1998 oz. AGW **Series:** Preserve Planet Earth **Obv:** National arms above bridge, date below **Rev:** Tyrannosaurus Rex, facing right, looking left, denomination below

Date	Mintage	F	VF	XF	Unc	BU
1993 Proof	Est. 5,000	Value: 185				

KM# 8 10000 DINARA

6.2200 g., 0.9990 Gold .1998 oz. AGW **Series:** Olympics **Obv:** National arms above bridge, date below **Rev:** Two bobsledders starting race

Date	Mintage	F	VF	XF	Unc	BU
1993 Proof	Est. 5,000	Value: 190				

KM# 10 10000 DINARA

6.2200 g., 0.9990 Gold .1998 oz. AGW **Series:** Olympics **Obv:** National arms above bridge, date below **Rev:** Downhill skier

Date	Mintage	F	VF	XF	Unc	BU
1993	Est. 5,000	Value: 190				

KM# 12 10000 DINARA

6.2200 g., 0.9990 Gold .1998 oz. AGW **Series:** Olympics **Obv:** National arms above bridge, date below **Rev:** Cross-country skier

Date	Mintage	F	VF	XF	Unc	BU
1993 Proof	Est. 5,000	Value: 190				

KM# 14 10000 DINARA

6.2200 g., 0.9990 Gold .1998 oz. AGW **Series:** Olympics **Obv:** National arms above bridge, date below **Rev:** Pair skating

Date	Mintage	F	VF	XF	Unc	BU
1993 Proof	Est. 5,000	Value: 190				

KM# 22 10000 DINARA

6.2200 g., 0.9990 Gold .1998 oz. AGW **Series:** Preserve Planet Earth **Obv:** National arms above bridge, date below **Rev:** Eohippu, right, denomination below

Date	Mintage	F	VF	XF	Unc	BU
1994 Proof	Est. 5,000	Value: 185				

KM# 29 10000 DINARA

6.2200 g., 0.9990 Gold .1998 oz. AGW **Series:** Preserve Planet Earth **Obv:** National arms above bridge, date below **Rev:** Wolf walking right

Date	Mintage	F	VF	XF	Unc	BU
1994 Proof	5,000	Value: 185				

KM# 30 10000 DINARA

6.2200 g., 0.9990 Gold .1998 oz. AGW **Series:** Preserve Planet Earth **Obv:** National arms above bridge, date below **Rev:** Black bear and cub walking right

Date	Mintage	F	VF	XF	Unc	BU
1994 Proof	5,000	Value: 185				

KM# 31 10000 DINARA

6.2200 g., 0.9990 Gold .1998 oz. AGW **Series:** Preserve Planet Earth **Obv:** National arms above bridge, date below **Rev:** Kingfisher left with fish in bill

Date	Mintage	F	VF	XF	Unc	BU
1994 Proof	5,000	Value: 185				

KM# 41 10000 DINARA

6.2200 g., 0.9990 Gold .1998 oz. AGW **Series:** Preserve Planet Earth **Obv:** National arms above bridge, date below **Rev:** Przewalskii horses

Date	Mintage	F	VF	XF	Unc	BU
1995 Proof	Est. 5,000	Value: 185				

KM# 44 10000 DINARA

6.2200 g., 0.9990 Gold .1998 oz. AGW **Series:** Preserve Planet Earth **Obv:** National arms above bridge, date below **Rev:** Hedgehogs

Date	Mintage	F	VF	XF	Unc	BU
1995 Proof	Est. 5,000	Value: 185				

KM# 60 10000 DINARA

6.2200 g., 0.9990 Gold .1998 oz. AGW **Series:** Olympics **Obv:** National arms above bridge, date below **Rev:** Long jumper

Date	Mintage	F	VF	XF	Unc	BU
1996 Proof	Est. 5,000	Value: 200				

KM# 61 10000 DINARA

6.2200 g., 0.9990 Gold .1998 oz. AGW **Series:** Olympics **Obv:** National arms above bridge, date below **Rev:** Sprinter

Date	Mintage	F	VF	XF	Unc	BU
1996 Proof	Est. 5,000	Value: 200				

KM# 62 10000 DINARA

6.2200 g., 0.9990 Gold .1998 oz. AGW **Series:** Olympics **Obv:** National arms above bridge, date below **Rev:** Wrestlers

Date	Mintage	F	VF	XF	Unc	BU
1996 Proof	Est. 5,000	Value: 200				

KM# 63 10000 DINARA

6.2200 g., 0.9990 Gold .1998 oz. AGW **Series:** Olympics **Obv:** National arms above bridge, date below **Rev:** Fencers

Date	Mintage	F	VF	XF	Unc	BU
1996 Proof	Est. 5,000	Value: 200				

KM# 78 10000 DINARA

6.2200 g., 0.9990 Gold .1998 oz. AGW **Series:** Preserve Planet Earth **Obv:** National arms above bridge, date below **Rev:** Hoopoe birds

Date	Mintage	F	VF	XF	Unc	BU
1996 Proof	Est. 5,000	Value: 185				

KM# 81 10000 DINARA

6.2200 g., 0.9990 Gold .1998 oz. AGW **Series:** Preserve Planet Earth **Obv:** National arms above bridge, date below **Rev:** Goosander birds

Date	Mintage	F	VF	XF	Unc	BU
1996 Proof	Est. 5,000	Value: 185				

KM# 97 10000 DINARA

6.2200 g., 0.9990 Gold .1998 oz. AGW **Subject:** Jurassic Park **Obv:** National arms above bridge, date below **Rev:** Tyrannosaurus Rex, left, Jurassic Park logo above, denomination below

Date	Mintage	F	VF	XF	Unc	BU
1997 Proof	Est. 2,500	Value: 185				

MARKA / MARAKA COINAGE

KM# 98 5 MARKA

Copper-Nickel **Subject:** Princess Diana **Obv:** National arms above bridge, date below **Rev:** Portrait and map

Date	Mintage	F	VF	XF	Unc	BU
1998	—	—	—	—	9.50	—

KM# 111 5 MARKA

Copper-Nickel **Subject:** Sydney 2000 - 27th Summer Olympics **Obv:** National arms above bridge, date below **Rev:** Javelin thrower

Date	Mintage	F	VF	XF	Unc	BU
1998	—	—	—	—	8.50	—

KM# 99 10 MARKA

28.2800 g., 0.9250 Silver .8410 oz. ASW **Subject:** Princess Diana **Obv:** National arms above bridge, date below **Rev:** Portrait and map divide dates, denomination at bottom

Date	Mintage	F	VF	XF	Unc	BU
1998 Proof	Est. 10,000	Value: 55.00				

KM# 112 10 MARKA

28.2800 g., 0.9250 Silver .8410 oz. ASW **Subject:** Sydney 2000 - 27th Summer Olympics **Obv:** National arms above bridge, date below **Rev:** Javelin thrower, right, denomination lower left

Date	Mintage	F	VF	XF	Unc	BU
1998 Proof	Est. 10,000	Value: 50.00				

KM# 100 20 MARKA

1.2441 g., 0.9999 Gold .0400 oz. AGW **Subject:** Princess Diana **Obv:** National arms above bridge, date below **Rev:** Portrait and map

Date	Mintage	F	VF	XF	Unc	BU
1998 Proof	Est. 10,000	Value: 55.00				

KM# 101 50 MARKA

3.1103 g., 0.9999 Gold .1000 oz. AGW **Subject:** Princess Diana **Obv:** National arms above bridge, date below **Rev:** Portrait and map

Date	Mintage	F	VF	XF	Unc	BU
1998 Proof	Est. 7,500	Value: 110				

KM# 102 100 MARKA

6.2206 g., 0.9999 Gold .2000 oz. AGW **Subject:** Princess Diana **Obv:** National arms above bridge, date below **Rev:** Portrait and map

Date	Mintage	F	VF	XF	Unc	BU
1998 Proof	Est. 5,000	Value: 185				

KM# 113 100 MARKA

6.2206 g., 0.9999 Gold .2000 oz. AGW **Subject:** Sydney 2000 - 27th Summer Olympics **Obv:** National arms above bridge, date below **Rev:** Javelin thrower

Date	Mintage	F	VF	XF	Unc	BU
1998 Proof	Est. 5,000	Value: 185				

KM# 103 250 MARKA

15.5517 g., 0.9999 Gold .5000 oz. AGW **Subject:** Princess Diana **Obv:** National arms above bridge, date below **Rev:** Portrait and map

Date	Mintage	F	VF	XF	Unc	BU
1998 Proof	Est. 3,000	Value: 385				

TRADE COINAGE

KM# 15 1/25 DUKAT

1.2440 g., 0.9999 Gold .0400 oz. AGW **Subject:** Hajj - Kaaba in Mecca **Obv:** National arms above bridge, date below **Rev:** Building and denomination within circle

Date	Mintage	F	VF	XF	Unc	BU
1993 Proof	Est. 25,000	Value: 50.00				

KM# 16 1/10 DUKAT

3.1103 g., 0.9999 Gold .1000 oz. AGW **Subject:** Hajj - Kaaba in Mecca **Obv:** National arms above bridge, date below **Rev:** Building and denomination within circle

Date	Mintage	F	VF	XF	Unc	BU
1993 Proof	Est. 20,000	Value: 95.00				

KM# 17 1/5 DUKAT

6.2200 g., 0.9999 Gold .2000 oz. AGW **Subject:** Hajj - Kaaba in Mecca **Obv:** National arms above bridge, date below **Rev:** Building and denomination within circle

Date	Mintage	F	VF	XF	Unc	BU
1993 Proof	Est. 5,000	Value: 185				

KM# 18 1/2 DUKAT

15.5510 g., 0.9999 Gold .5000 oz. AGW **Subject:** Hajj - Kaaba in Mecca **Obv:** National arms above bridge, date below **Rev:** Building and denomination within circle

Date	Mintage	F	VF	XF	Unc	BU
1993 Proof	Est. 5,000	Value: 375				

KM# 19 DUKAT

31.1030 g., 0.9999 Gold 1.0000 oz. AGW **Subject:** Hajj - Kaaba in Mecca **Obv:** National arms above bridge, date below **Rev:** Building and denomination within circle

Date	Mintage	F	VF	XF	Unc	BU
1993 Proof	Est. 5,000	Value: 675				
1994 Proof	—	Value: 675				

KM# 32 1/25 SUVERENA
1.2441 g., 0.9999 Gold .0400 oz. AGW **Subject:** Lipizzaner Stallion **Obv:** National arms above bridge, date below **Rev:** Horse rearing right, denomination below

Date	Mintage	F	VF	XF	Unc	BU
1994 Proof	—	Value: 52.00				

KM# 45 1/25 SUVERENA
1.2441 g., 0.9999 Gold .0400 oz. AGW **Subject:** English Hack **Obv:** National arms above bridge, date below **Rev:** Horse running left, denomination below

Date	Mintage	F	VF	XF	Unc	BU
1995 Proof	Est. 15,000	Value: 52.00				

KM# 70 1/25 SUVERENA
1.2441 g., 0.9999 Gold .0400 oz. AGW **Subject:** Hanoverian Stallion **Obv:** National arms above bridge, date below **Rev:** Horse left, denomination below

Date	Mintage	F	VF	XF	Unc	BU
1996 Proof	Est. 15,000	Value: 52.00				

KM# 89 1/25 SUVERENA
1.2441 g., 0.9999 Gold .0400 oz. AGW **Subject:** The Arab **Obv:** National arms above bridge, date below **Rev:** Horse right, denomination below

Date	Mintage	F	VF	XF	Unc	BU
1997 Proof	Est. 15,000	Value: 52.00				

KM# 104 1/25 SUVERENA
1.2441 g., 0.9999 Gold .0400 oz. AGW **Subject:** Chinese Horse **Obv:** National arms above bridge, date below **Rev:** Horse, denomination below

Date	Mintage	F	VF	XF	Unc	BU
1998 Proof	Est. 15,000	Value: 52.00				

KM# 33 1/10 SUVERENA
3.1103 g., 0.9999 Gold .1000 oz. AGW **Subject:** Lipizzaner Stallion **Obv:** National arms above bridge, date below **Rev:** Horse rearing right, denomination below

Date	Mintage	F	VF	XF	Unc	BU
1994 Proof	—	Value: 100				

KM# 46 1/10 SUVERENA
3.1103 g., 0.9999 Gold .1000 oz. AGW **Subject:** English Hack **Obv:** National arms above bridge, date below **Rev:** Horse running left, denomination below

Date	Mintage	F	VF	XF	Unc	BU
1995 Proof	Est. 10,000	Value: 100				

KM# 71 1/10 SUVERENA
3.1103 g., 0.9999 Gold .1000 oz. AGW **Subject:** Hanoverian Stallion **Obv:** National arms above bridge, date below **Rev:** Horse left, denomination below

Date	Mintage	F	VF	XF	Unc	BU
1996 Proof	Est. 10,000	Value: 100				

KM# 90 1/10 SUVERENA
3.1103 g., 0.9999 Gold .1000 oz. AGW **Subject:** The Arab **Obv:** National arms above bridge, date below **Rev:** Horse right, denomination below

Date	Mintage	F	VF	XF	Unc	BU
1997 Proof	Est. 10,000	Value: 100				

KM# 105 1/10 SUVERENA
3.1103 g., 0.9999 Gold .1000 oz. AGW **Subject:** Chinese Horse **Obv:** National arms above bridge, date below **Rev:** Horse left, denomination below

Date	Mintage	F	VF	XF	Unc	BU
1998 Proof	Est. 10,000	Value: 100				

KM# 34 1/5 SUVERENA
6.2207 g., 0.9999 Gold .2000 oz. AGW **Subject:** Lipizzaner Stallion **Obv:** National arms above bridge, date below **Rev:** Horse rearing right, denomination below

Date	Mintage	F	VF	XF	Unc	BU
1994 Proof	—	Value: 185				

KM# 47 1/5 SUVERENA
6.2207 g., 0.9999 Gold .2000 oz. AGW **Subject:** English Hack **Obv:** National arms above bridge, date below **Rev:** Horse running left, denomination below

Date	Mintage	F	VF	XF	Unc	BU
1995 Proof	Est. 5,000	Value: 185				

KM# 72 1/5 SUVERENA
6.2207 g., 0.9999 Gold .2000 oz. AGW **Subject:** Hanoverian Stallion **Obv:** National arms above bridge, date below **Rev:** Horse left, denomination below

Date	Mintage	F	VF	XF	Unc	BU
1996 Proof	Est. 5,000	Value: 185				

KM# 91 1/5 SUVERENA
6.2207 g., 0.9999 Gold .2000 oz. AGW **Subject:** The Arab **Obv:** National arms above bridge, date below **Rev:** Horse right, denomination below

Date	Mintage	F	VF	XF	Unc	BU
1997 Proof	Est. 5,000	Value: 185				

KM# 106 1/5 SUVERENA
6.2207 g., 0.9999 Gold .2000 oz. AGW **Subject:** Chinese Horse **Obv:** National arms above bridge, date below **Rev:** Horse left, denomination below

Date	Mintage	F	VF	XF	Unc	BU
1998 Proof	Est. 5,000	Value: 185				

KM# 35 1/2 SUVERENA
15.5517 g., 0.9999 Gold .5000 oz. AGW **Subject:** Lipizzaner Stallion **Obv:** National arms above bridge, date below **Rev:** Horse rearing right, denomination below

Date	Mintage	F	VF	XF	Unc	BU
1994 Proof	—	Value: 375				

KM# 48 1/2 SUVERENA
15.5517 g., 0.9999 Gold .5000 oz. AGW **Subject:** English Hack **Obv:** National arms above bridge, date below **Rev:** Horse running left, denomination below

Date	Mintage	F	VF	XF	Unc	BU
1995 Proof	Est. 2,500	Value: 375				

KM# 73 1/2 SUVERENA
15.5517 g., 0.9999 Gold .5000 oz. AGW **Subject:** Hanoverian Stallion **Obv:** National arms above bridge, date below **Rev:** Horse left, denomination below

Date	Mintage	F	VF	XF	Unc	BU
1996 Proof	Est. 2,500	Value: 375				

KM# 92 1/2 SUVERENA
15.5517 g., 0.9999 Gold .5000 oz. AGW **Subject:** The Arab **Obv:** National arms above bridge, date below **Rev:** Horse right, denomination below

Date	Mintage	F	VF	XF	Unc	BU
1997 Proof	Est. 2,500	Value: 375				

KM# 107 1/2 SUVERENA
15.5517 g., 0.9999 Gold .5000 oz. AGW **Subject:** Chinese Horse **Obv:** National arms above bridge, date below **Rev:** Horse left, denomination below

Date	Mintage	F	VF	XF	Unc	BU
1998 Proof	Est. 2,500	Value: 375				

KM# 37 SUVERENA
31.1035 g., 0.9999 Silver 1.0000 oz. ASW **Subject:** Lipizzaner Stallion **Obv:** National arms above bridge, date below **Rev:** Horse rearing right, denomination below

Date	Mintage	F	VF	XF	Unc	BU
1994 Proof	—	Value: 50.00				

KM# 37a SUVERENA
31.1035 g. 0.9999 Gold 1.0000 oz. AGW **Subject:** Lipizzaner Stallion **Obv:** National arms above bridge, date below **Rev:** Horse rearing right, denomination below

Date	Mintage	F	VF	XF	Unc	BU
1994 Proof	—	Value: 700				

KM# 36 SUVERENA
Copper-Nickel **Subject:** Lipizzaner Stallion **Obv:** National arms above bridge, date below **Rev:** Horse rearing right, denomination below

Date	Mintage	F	VF	XF	Unc	BU
1994	—	—	—	—	10.00	12.00

KM# 49 SUVERENA
Copper-Nickel **Subject:** English Hack **Obv:** National arms above bridge, date below **Rev:** Horse running left, denomination below

Date	Mintage	F	VF	XF	Unc	BU
1995	—	—	—	—	10.00	12.00

KM# 50 SUVERENA
31.1035 g., 0.9999 Silver 1.0000 oz. ASW **Subject:** English Hack **Obv:** National arms above bridge, date below **Rev:** Horse running left, denomination below

Date	Mintage	F	VF	XF	Unc	BU
1995 Proof	Est. 30,000	Value: 50.00				

KM# 51 SUVERENA
31.1035 g., 0.9999 Gold 1.0000 oz. AGW **Subject:** English Hack **Obv:** National arms above bridge, date below **Rev:** Horse running left, denomination below

Date	Mintage	F	VF	XF	Unc	BU
1995 Proof	Est. 850	Value: 700				

KM# 74 SUVERENA
Copper-Nickel **Subject:** Hanoverian Stallion **Obv:** National arms above bridge, date below **Rev:** Horse left, denomination below

Date	Mintage	F	VF	XF	Unc	BU
1996	—	—	—	—	10.00	12.00

KM# 75 SUVERENA
31.1035 g., 0.9999 Silver 1.0000 oz. ASW **Subject:** Hanoverian Horse **Obv:** National arms above bridge, date below **Rev:** Horse left, denomination below

Date	Mintage	F	VF	XF	Unc	BU
1996 Proof	Est. 30,000	Value: 50.00				

KM# A76 SUVERENA
31.1035 g., 0.9999 Gold 1.0000 oz. AGW **Subject:** Hanoverian Horse **Obv:** National arms above bridge, date below **Rev:** Horse left, denomination below

Date	Mintage	F	VF	XF	Unc	BU
1996 Proof	850	Value: 700				

KM# 93 SUVERENA
Copper-Nickel **Subject:** The Arab **Obv:** National arms above bridge, date below **Rev:** Horse right, denomination below

Date	Mintage	F	VF	XF	Unc	BU
1997	—	—	—	—	12.00	15.00

KM# 93a SUVERENA
31.1035 g., 0.9999 Silver 1.0000 oz. ASW **Subject:** The Arab **Obv:** National arms above bridge, date below **Rev:** Horse right, denomination below

Date	Mintage	F	VF	XF	Unc	BU
1997 Proof	Est. 30,000	Value: 50.00				

KM# 93b SUVERENA
31.1035 g., 0.9999 Gold 1.0000 oz. AGW **Subject:** The Arab **Obv:** National arms above bridge, date below **Rev:** Horse right, denomination below

Date	Mintage	F	VF	XF	Unc	BU
1997 Proof	850	Value: 700				

KM# 108 SUVERENA
Copper-Nickel **Subject:** Chinese Horse **Obv:** National arms above bridge, date below **Rev:** Horse left, denomination below

Date	Mintage	F	VF	XF	Unc	BU
1998	—	—	—	—	10.00	12.00

KM# 108a SUVERENA
31.1035 g., 0.9999 Silver 1.0000 oz. ASW **Subject:** Chinese Horse **Obv:** National arms above bridge, date below **Rev:** Horse left, denomination below

Date	Mintage	F	VF	XF	Unc	BU
1998 Proof	Est. 30,000	Value: 50.00				

KM# 109 SUVERENA
31.1035 g., 0.9999 Gold 1.0000 oz. AGW **Subject:** Chinese Horse **Obv:** National arms above bridge, date below **Rev:** Horse left, denomination below

Date	Mintage	F	VF	XF	Unc	BU
1998 Proof	—	Value: 700				

KM# 82 14 ECUS
10.0000 g., 0.9250 Silver .8921 oz. ASW **Subject:** International Day of Peace **Obv:** National arms above bridge, date below **Rev:** Hands releasing bird of peace, symbol at center, denomination below

Date	Mintage	F	VF	XF	Unc	BU
1993 Proof	Est. 20,000	Value: 45.00				

KM# 83 14 ECUS
10.0000 g., 0.9250 Silver .8921 oz. ASW **Subject:** Peace - Teddy Bear **Obv:** National arms above bridge, date below **Rev:** Teddy bear above denomination

Date	Mintage	F	VF	XF	Unc	BU
1994 Proof	20,000	Value: 37.50				

KM# 84 14 ECUS
10.1000 g., 0.9250 Silver .3004 oz. ASW **Subject:** Peace - Allegorical Europa **Obv:** National arms above bridge, date below **Rev:** Allegorical Europa, denomination below

Date	Mintage	F	VF	XF	Unc	BU
1995 Proof	Est. 20,000	Value: 27.50				

KM# 85 14 ECUS + 2
9.9700 g., 0.9990 Silver .3205 oz. ASW **Subject:** War Relief Funding - Sarajevo Mosque **Obv:** National arms above bridge, date below **Rev:** Sarajevo Mosque, denomination below

Date	Mintage	F	VF	XF	Unc	BU
1993 Proof	20,000	Value: 30.00				

KM# 86 21 ECUS + 3
15.5600 g., 0.9990 Silver .5002 oz. ASW **Subject:** War Relief Funding - Sarajevo Mosque

Date	Mintage	F	VF	XF	Unc	BU
1993 Proof	Est. 15,000	Value: 60.00				

KM# 87 70 ECUS + 10
6.2200 g., 0.9990 Gold .2000 oz. AGW **Subject:** War Relief Funding - Sarajevo Mosque **Obv:** National arms above bridge, date below **Rev:** Dove of Peace above Sarajevo Mosque

Date	Mintage	F	VF	XF	Unc	BU
1993 Proof	Est. 5,000	Value: 185				

KM# 88 14 EURO
10.0000 g., 0.9250 Silver .2974 oz. ASW **Subject:** Peace **Obv:** National arms above bridge, date below **Rev:** Rose and the word PEACE in many languages, denomination below

Date	Mintage	F	VF	XF	Unc	BU
1996PM Proof	Est. 20,000	Value: 35.00				

KM# 110 14 EURO
10.0000 g., 0.9250 Silver .2974 oz. ASW **Subject:** Peace II **Obv:** National arms above bridge, date below **Rev:** Dove in flight with PEACE written in many different languages, denomination below

Date	Mintage	F	VF	XF	Unc	BU
1998PM Proof	Est. 20,000	Value: 40.00				

KM# 114 14 EURO
10.0000 g., 0.9250 Silver .2974 oz. ASW **Subject:** The Tree of Stability **Obv:** National arms above bridge, date below **Rev:** Woman planting oak tree, denomination below

Date	Mintage	F	VF	XF	Unc	BU
1999PM Proof	Est. 20,000	Value: 40.00				

MINT SETS

KM#	Date	Mintage	Identification	Issue Price	Mkt Val
MS1	2000 (5)	—	KM#115, 116, 117, 118, 119	20.00	25.00

PROOF SETS

KM#	Date	Mintage	Identification	Issue Price	Mkt Val
PS1	1996 (5)	500	KM#70-73, 76	—	1,400

BOTSWANA

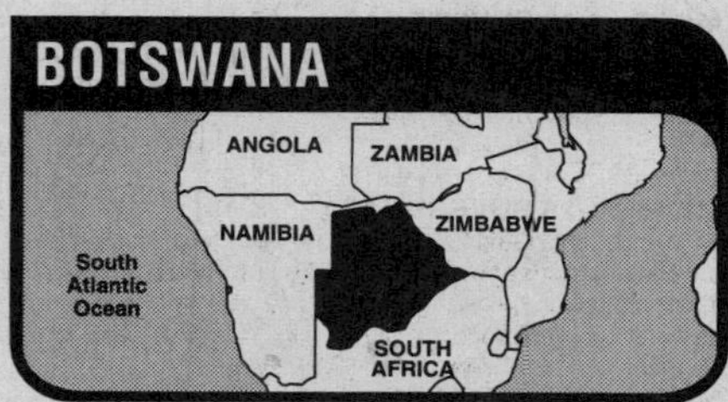

The Republic of Botswana (formerly Bechuanaland), located in south central Africa between Namibia and Zimbabwe, has an area of 224,607 sq. mi. (600,370 sq. km.) and a population of *1.62 million. Capital: Gaborone. Botswana is a member of a Customs Union with South Africa, Lesotho, and Swaziland. The economy is primarily pastoral with a rapidly developing mining industry, of which diamonds, copper and nickel are the chief elements. Meat products and diamonds comprise 85 percent of the exports.

Little is known of the origin of the peoples of Botswana. The early inhabitants, the Bushmen, did not develop a recorded history and are now dying out. The ancestors of the present Botswana residents probably arrived about 1600AD in Bantu migrations from the north and east. Bechuanaland was first united early in the 19th century under Chief Khama III to more effectively resist incursions by the Boer trekkers from Transvaal and by the neighboring Matabeles. As the Boer threat intensified, appeals for protection were made to the British Government, which proclaimed the whole of Bechuanaland a British protectorate in 1885. In 1895, the southern part of the protectorate was annexed to Cape Province. The northern part, known as the Bechuanaland Protectorate, remained under British administration until it became the independent Republic of Botswana on Sept. 30, 1966. Botswana is a member of the Commonwealth of Nations. The president is Chief of State and Head of government.

MINT MARKS
B - Berne

MONETARY SYSTEM
100 Cents = 1 Thebe

REPUBLIC

STANDARD COINAGE

KM# 1 50 CENTS
10.0000 g., 0.8000 Silver .2572 oz. ASW **Subject:** Independence Commemorative **Obv:** National arms with supporters, denomination below **Rev:** Sir Seretse Khama left **Designer:** J. H. Waser

Date	Mintage	F	VF	XF	Unc	BU
ND(1966)B	40,000	—	3.50	4.50	7.00	—
ND(1966)B Proof	10,000	Value: 12.00				

KM# 2 10 THEBE
11.2900 g., 0.9000 Gold .3270 oz. AGW **Subject:** Independence Commemorative **Obv:** National arms with supporters, denomination below **Rev:** Sir Seretse Khama left **Designer:** J. H. Waser

Date	Mintage	F	VF	XF	Unc	BU
ND(1966)B	5,100	—	—	—	235	—

REFORM COINAGE

100 Thebe = 1 Pula

KM# 3 THEBE
0.8000 g., Aluminum, 18.5 mm. **Obv:** National arms, date below **Rev:** Head of Turako, denomination upper right **Edge:** Reeded

Date	Mintage	F	VF	XF	Unc	BU
1976	15,000,000	—	0.10	0.15	0.40	0.75
1976 Proof	26,000	Value: 0.75				
1981 Proof	10,000	Value: 1.00				
1983	5,000,000	—	0.10	0.20	0.45	0.75

Date	Mintage	F	VF	XF	Unc	BU
1984	5,000,000	—	0.10	0.20	0.45	0.75
1985	—	—	0.10	0.20	0.45	0.75
1987	—	—	0.10	0.20	0.40	0.75
1988	—	—	0.10	0.20	0.40	0.75
1989	—	—	0.10	0.20	0.40	0.75
1991	—	—	0.10	0.20	0.40	0.75

KM# 14 2 THEBE

1.8000 g., Bronze, 17.4 mm. **Subject:** World Food Day **Obv:** National arms above date **Rev:** Millet, denomination at top **Shape:** 12-sided

Date	Mintage	F	VF	XF	Unc	BU
1981	9,990,000	—	0.15	0.25	0.50	0.75
1981 Proof	10,000	Value: 1.00				
1985	—	—	0.15	0.25	0.50	0.75

KM# 4 5 THEBE

2.8000 g., Bronze, 19.5 mm. **Obv:** National arms above date **Rev:** Toko left, denomination at top **Edge:** Reeded

Date	Mintage	F	VF	XF	Unc	BU
1976	3,000,000	—	0.15	0.25	0.50	1.00
1976 Proof	26,000	Value: 1.25				
1977	250,000	—	0.15	0.25	0.50	1.00
1979	200,000	—	0.15	0.25	0.50	1.00
1980	1,000,000	—	0.15	0.25	0.50	1.00
1981	4,990,000	—	0.15	0.25	0.50	1.00
1981 Proof	10,000	Value: 1.50				
1984	2,000,000	—	0.15	0.25	0.50	1.00
1985	—	—	0.15	0.25	0.50	1.00
1988	—	—	0.15	0.25	0.50	1.00
1989	—	—	0.15	0.25	0.50	1.00

KM# 4a.1 5 THEBE

Bronze Clad Steel, 19.5 mm. **Edge:** Plain

Date	Mintage	F	VF	XF	Unc	BU
1991	—	—	0.15	0.25	0.50	1.00

KM# 4a.2 5 THEBE

Bronze Clad Steel, 19.5 mm. **Edge:** Reeded **Note:** Modified design.

Date	Mintage	F	VF	XF	Unc	BU
1996	—	—	0.15	0.25	0.50	1.00

KM# 26 5 THEBE

Bronze Clad Steel **Obv:** National arms **Rev:** Toko bird **Shape:** 7-sided

Date	Mintage	F	VF	XF	Unc	BU
1998	—	—	0.15	0.25	0.50	1.00

KM# 5 10 THEBE

4.0000 g., Copper-Nickel, 22 mm. **Rev:** South African Oryx right, denomination above **Edge:** Reeded

Date	Mintage	F	VF	XF	Unc	BU
1976	1,500,000	—	0.25	0.40	0.75	1.25
1976 Proof	26,000	Value: 1.50				
1977	500,000	—	0.25	0.40	0.75	1.25
1979	750,000	—	0.25	0.40	0.75	1.25
1980	—	—	0.25	0.40	0.75	1.25
1981	2,590,000	—	0.25	0.40	0.75	1.25
1981 Proof	10,000	Value: 1.75				
1984	4,000,000	—	0.20	0.30	0.60	1.00
1985	—	—	0.20	0.30	0.60	1.00
1989	—	—	0.20	0.30	0.60	1.00

KM# 5a 10 THEBE

Nickel Clad Steel, 22 mm. **Edge:** Reeded

Date	Mintage	F	VF	XF	Unc	BU
1991	—	—	0.20	0.30	0.60	1.00

KM# 27 10 THEBE

Nickel Clad Steel **Obv:** National arms, date below **Rev:** South African Oryx right, denomination above

Date	Mintage	F	VF	XF	Unc	BU
1998	—	—	0.20	0.30	0.75	1.25

KM# 6 25 THEBE

5.8000 g., Copper-Nickel, 25 mm. **Obv:** National arms with supporters, date below **Rev:** Zebu left, denomination above **Edge:** Reeded

Date	Mintage	F	VF	XF	Unc	BU
1976	1,500,000	—	0.25	0.55	1.50	2.00
1976 Proof	26,000	Value: 2.50				
1977	265,000	—	0.25	0.60	1.75	2.25
1981	740,000	—	0.25	0.60	1.50	2.00
1981 Proof	10,000	Value: 2.50				
1982	400,000	—	0.25	0.60	1.75	2.25
1984	2,000,000	—	0.25	0.55	1.50	2.00
1985	—	—	0.30	0.60	1.50	2.00
1989	—	—	0.30	0.60	1.50	2.00

KM# 6a 25 THEBE

Nickel Clad Steel, 25 mm.

Date	Mintage	F	VF	XF	Unc	BU
1991	—	—	0.30	0.60	1.50	2.00

KM# 28 25 THEBE

Nickel Clad Steel **Obv:** National arms with supporters, date below **Rev:** Zebu bull, left, denomination above **Shape:** 7-sided

Date	Mintage	F	VF	XF	Unc	BU
1998	—	—	0.30	0.60	1.50	2.00
1999	—	—	0.30	0.60	1.50	2.00

KM# 7 50 THEBE

11.4000 g., Copper-Nickel, 28.5 mm. **Obv:** National arms with supporters, date below **Rev:** African Fish Eagle left, denomination above

Date	Mintage	F	VF	XF	Unc	BU
1976	266,000	—	0.65	1.35	2.25	2.75
1976 Proof	26,000	Value: 3.00				
1977	250,000	—	0.65	1.35	2.25	2.75
1980	—	—	0.65	1.35	2.25	2.75
1981 Proof	10,000	Value: 3.50				
1984	2,000,000	—	0.65	1.35	2.25	2.75
1985	—	—	0.65	1.35	2.25	2.75

KM# 7a 50 THEBE

Nickel Clad Steel, 28.5 mm.

Date	Mintage	F	VF	XF	Unc	BU
1991	—	—	0.65	1.35	2.25	2.75

KM# 29 50 THEBE

Nickel Clad Steel **Obv:** National arms with supporters, date below **Rev:** African Fish Eagle left, denomination above

Date	Mintage	F	VF	XF	Unc	BU
1996	—	—	0.50	1.00	2.00	2.50
1998	—	—	0.50	1.00	2.00	2.50

KM# 8 PULA

16.4000 g., Copper-Nickel, 29.5 mm. **Obv:** National arms with supporters, date below **Rev:** Zebra left, denomination above **Shape:** Scalloped

Date	Mintage	F	VF	XF	Unc	BU
1976	166,000	—	1.50	2.50	5.00	6.50
1976 Proof	26,000	Value: 7.00				
1977	500,000	—	1.50	2.50	5.00	6.50
1981	—	—	1.50	2.50	5.00	6.50
1981 Proof	10,000	Value: 7.50				
1985	—	—	1.50	2.50	5.00	6.50
1987	—	—	1.50	2.50	5.00	6.50

KM# 24 PULA

Nickel-Brass **Obv:** National arms with supporters, date below **Rev:** Zebra left, denomination above **Shape:** 7-sided

Date	Mintage	F	VF	XF	Unc	BU
1991	—	—	1.00	1.75	3.50	5.00
1997	—	—	1.00	1.75	3.50	5.00

KM# 17 2 PULA

28.2800 g., 0.5000 Silver .4546 oz. ASW, 38.61 mm. **Subject:** Commonwealth Games **Obv:** National arms with supporters, date below **Rev:** Sprinter with flag, denomination below

Date	Mintage	F	VF	XF	Unc	BU
1986	Est. 50,000	—	—	—	12.50	14.00

KM# 17a 2 PULA

28.2800 g., 0.9250 Silver .8411 oz. ASW **Obv:** National arms with supporters, date below **Rev:** Sprinter with flag, denomination below

Date	Mintage	F	VF	XF	Unc	BU
1986 Proof	Est. 20,000	Value: 25.00				

KM# 18 2 PULA

28.2800 g., 0.9250 Silver .8411 oz. ASW **Subject:** Wildlife **Rev:** Slaty Egret, egretta vinaceiguia

Date	Mintage	F	VF	XF	Unc	BU
1986 Proof	Est. 25,000	Value: 25.00				

KM# 22 2 PULA

28.2800 g., 0.9250 Silver .8411 oz. ASW **Subject:** Save The Children Fund **Obv:** National arms with supporters, date below **Rev:** Child milking goat, denomination below

Date	Mintage	F	VF	XF	Unc	BU
1989 Proof	Est. 20,000	Value: 32.00				

KM# 25 2 PULA
Nickel-Brass **Subject:** Wildlife **Obv:** National arms with suppporters, date below **Rev:** Rhinoceros, left, denomination above **Shape:** 7-sided

Date	Mintage	F	VF	XF	Unc	BU
1994	—	—	1.75	2.75	5.50	10.00

KM# 9 5 PULA
28.2800 g., 0.5000 Silver .4546 oz. ASW **Subject:** 10th Anniversary of Independence **Obv:** Bust left **Rev:** National Assembly Building, denomination above

Date	Mintage	F	VF	XF	Unc	BU
ND(1976)	31,000	—	—	—	15.00	16.50

KM# 9a 5 PULA
28.2800 g., 0.9250 Silver .8411 oz. ASW **Obv:** Bust left **Rev:** Buildings and flag, denomination above

Date	Mintage	F	VF	XF	Unc	BU
ND(1976) Proof	22,000	Value: 22.50				

KM# 11 5 PULA
28.5000 g., 0.5000 Silver .4582 oz. ASW **Subject:** Wildlife **Obv:** National arms with supporters, date below **Rev:** Gemsbok left, denomination above

Date	Mintage	F	VF	XF	Unc	BU
1978	4,026	—	—	—	24.00	26.00

KM# 11a 5 PULA
28.5000 g., 0.9250 Silver .8477 oz. ASW **Obv:** National arms with supporters, date below **Rev:** Gemsbok left, denomination below

Date	Mintage	F	VF	XF	Unc	BU
1978 Proof	4,172	Value: 35.00				

KM# 15 5 PULA
28.5000 g., 0.9250 Silver .8477 oz. ASW **Subject:** International Year of Disabled Persons **Obv:** National arms with supporters, date below **Rev:** Figures at table, hut in background, denomination lower left

Date	Mintage	F	VF	XF	Unc	BU
1981	13,000	—	—	—	25.00	30.00
1981 Proof	11,000	Value: 35.00				

KM# 19 5 PULA
15.9800 g., 0.9170 Gold .4711 oz. AGW **Subject:** Wildlife **Obv:** National arms with supporters, date below **Rev:** Red Lechwes (kobus leche leche) right, denomination above left

Date	Mintage	F	VF	XF	Unc	BU
1986 Proof	Est. 5,000	Value: 325				

KM# 20 5 PULA
Copper-Nickel **Subject:** Pope's Visit **Obv:** National arms with supporters, date below **Rev:** Bust left, denomination above

Date	Mintage	F	VF	XF	Unc	BU
1988	Est. 50,000	—	—	—	8.50	10.00

KM# 20a 5 PULA
28.2800 g., 0.9250 Silver .8411 oz. ASW **Obv:** Bust left **Rev:** National arms with supporters, date below

Date	Mintage	F	VF	XF	Unc	BU
1988 Proof	Est. 5,000	Value: 45.00				

KM# 21 5 PULA
28.2800 g., 0.9250 Silver .8411 oz. ASW **Subject:** 1988 Summer Olympics **Obv:** National arms with supporters, date below **Rev:** Runners

Date	Mintage	F	VF	XF	Unc	BU
1988 Proof	25,000	Value: 25.00				

Note: A copper-nickel strike variety of this coin does not exist

KM# 23 5 PULA
10.0000 g., 0.9170 Gold .2948 oz. AGW **Subject:** Save the Children Fund **Obv:** National arms with supporters, date below **Rev:** Woman with child left, denomination on left

Date	Mintage	F	VF	XF	Unc	BU
1989 Proof	Est. 3,000	Value: 350				

KM# 30 5 PULA
6.2000 g., Bi-Metallic Copper-Nickel center in Brass ring, 23.4 mm. **Obv:** National arms with supporters, date below, within circle **Rev:** Mophane worm on a mophane leaf, denomination below, within circle **Edge:** Reeded

Date	Mintage	F	VF	XF	Unc	BU
2000	—	—	—	—	6.50	9.00

KM# 12 10 PULA
35.0000 g., 0.5000 Silver .5627 oz. ASW **Subject:** Wildlife **Obv:** National arms with supporters, date below **Rev:** Klipspringer left, denomination above

Date	Mintage	F	VF	XF	Unc	BU
1978	4,088	—	—	—	32.00	40.00

KM# 12a 10 PULA
35.0000 g., 0.9250 Silver 1.0408 oz. ASW **Obv:** National arms with supporters, date below **Rev:** Klipspringer left, denomination above

Date	Mintage	F	VF	XF	Unc	BU
1978 Proof	3,989	Value: 42.00				

KM# 10 150 PULA
15.9800 g., 0.9170 Gold .4711 oz. AGW **Subject:** 10th Anniversary of Independence **Obv:** National arms with supporters, denomination above **Rev:** Bust left

Date	Mintage	F	VF	XF	Unc	BU
ND(1976)	2,520	—	—	—	320	340
ND(1976) Proof	2,000	Value: 365				

KM# 13 150 PULA

33.4370 g., 0.9000 Gold .9676 oz. AGW **Subject:** Wildlife **Obv:** National arms with supporters, date below **Rev:** Brown Hyena facing, denomination above left

Date	Mintage	F	VF	XF	Unc	BU
1978	664	—	—	—	675	750
1978 Proof	219	Value: 950				

KM# 16 150 PULA

15.9800 g., 0.9170 Gold .4711 oz. AGW **Subject:** International Year of Disabled Persons **Obv:** National arms with supporters, date below **Rev:** Figures with box, denomination lower right

Date	Mintage	F	VF	XF	Unc	BU
1981	4,158	—	—	—	320	340
1981 Proof	4,155	Value: 365				

PIEFORTS

KM#	Date	Mintage	Identification	Issue Price	Mkt Val
P1	1981	1,000	5 Pula. Silver. KM#15.	—	65.00
P2	1981	510	150 Pula. Gold. KM#16.	—	925

MINT SETS

KM#	Date	Mintage	Identification	Issue Price	Mkt Val
MS1	1978 (2)	—	KM#11, 12	—	55.00

PROOF SETS

KM#	Date	Mintage	Identification	Issue Price	Mkt Val
PS1	1976 (6)	20,000	KM#3-8	18.00	14.50
PS2	1978 (2)	—	KM#11a, 12a	—	65.00
PS3	1981 (7)	10,000	KM#3-8, 14	33.00	17.50

BRAZIL

The Federative Republic of Brazil, which comprises half the continent of South America and is the only Latin American country deriving its culture and language from Portugal, has an area of 3,286,488 sq. mi. (8,511,965 sq. km.) and a population of *169.2 million. Capital: Brasilia. The economy of Brazil is as varied and complex as any in the developing world. Agriculture is a mainstay of the economy, while only 4 percent of the area is under cultivation. Known mineral resources are almost unlimited in variety and size of reserves. A large, relatively sophisticated industry ranges from basic steel and chemical production to finished consumer goods. Coffee, cotton, iron ore and cocoa are the chief exports.

Brazil was discovered and claimed for Portugal by Admiral Pedro Alvares Cabral in 1500. Portugal established a settlement in 1532 and proclaimed the area a royal colony in 1549. During the Napoleonic Wars, Dom Joao VI established the seat of Portuguese government in Rio de Janeiro. When he returned to Portugal, his son Dom Pedro I declared Brazil's independence on Sept. 7, 1822, and became emperor of Brazil. The Empire of Brazil was maintained until 1889 when the federal republic was established. The Federative Republic was established in 1946 by terms of a constitution drawn up by a constituent assembly. Following a coup in 1964 the armed forces retained overall control under a dictatorship until civilian government was restored on March 15, 1985. The current constitution was adopted in 1988.

MINT MARKS

(a) - Paris, privy marks only
A - Berlin 1913
B - Bahia

MONETARY SYSTEM

(1833-1942)
1000 Reis = 1 Mil Reis

(1942-1967)
100 Centavos = 1 Cruzeiro

REPUBLIC

FIRST COINAGE - REIS

1889-1942

KM# 490 20 REIS

Bronze **Obv:** National arms, date below **Rev:** Denomination within beaded circle

Date	Mintage	F	VF	XF	Unc	BU
1901	713,000	1.00	4.50	9.50	20.00	—
1904	850,000	1.00	4.50	9.50	20.00	—
1905	1,075,000	3.50	7.00	14.50	48.00	—
1906	215,000	2.00	5.00	12.00	30.00	—
1908	4,558,000	1.00	4.50	9.50	20.00	—
1909	1,215,000	5.00	10.00	22.00	95.00	—
1910	828,000	1.00	4.50	9.50	20.00	—
1911	1,545,000	1.00	4.50	9.50	20.00	—
1912	480,000	1.00	4.50	9.50	25.00	—

KM# 516.1 20 REIS

Copper-Nickel **Rev:** No dot between "2" and "0" in denomination

Date	Mintage	F	VF	XF	Unc	BU
1918	—	0.25	0.50	2.00	5.00	—
1919	—	0.25	0.50	1.00	4.00	—
1920	—	0.25	0.50	1.25	5.00	—

KM# 516.2 20 REIS

Copper-Nickel **Obv:** Denomination at center, dot between "2" and "0" in denomination **Rev:** Bust with cap, right, within 3/4 circle of stars

Date	Mintage	F	VF	XF	Unc	BU
1919	2,870,000	0.25	0.50	1.00	4.00	—
1920	825,000	0.25	0.50	1.25	5.00	—
1921	1,020,000	0.25	0.50	1.25	5.00	—
1927	53,000	5.00	10.00	30.00	80.00	—
1935	100	200	450	900	1,500	—

KM# 491 40 REIS

Bronze **Obv:** Stars within inner circle, circle of stars surrounds, date at bottom **Rev:** Denomination within circle

Date	Mintage	F	VF	XF	Unc	BU
1901	525,000	0.75	2.00	3.00	15.00	—
1907	218,000	0.75	2.00	3.00	15.00	—
1908	4,639,000	0.75	2.00	3.00	15.00	—
1909	4,226,000	0.75	2.00	3.50	17.50	—
1910	848,000	0.75	2.00	4.00	20.00	—
1911	1,660,000	0.75	2.00	4.00	20.00	—
1912	819,000	1.00	2.50	4.50	22.50	—

KM# 517 50 REIS

Copper-Nickel **Obv:** Denomination within circle, date flanked by stars below **Rev:** Liberty head right

Date	Mintage	F	VF	XF	Unc	BU
1918	558,000	0.15	0.35	1.00	6.00	—
1919	558,000	0.15	0.35	1.00	6.00	—
1920	72,000	0.40	1.00	3.50	16.00	—
1921	682,000	0.15	0.35	1.00	6.00	—
1922	176,000	0.40	1.00	3.50	16.00	—
1925	128,000	0.40	1.50	4.00	20.00	—
1926	194,000	0.40	1.50	4.00	20.00	—
1931	20,000	2.00	10.00	40.00	85.00	—
1935	100	125	300	800	1,500	—

KM# 503 100 REIS

Copper-Nickel **Obv:** National arms, denomination above **Rev:** Liberty bust right **Note:** Roman numeral date.

Date	Mintage	F	VF	XF	Unc	BU
1901	15,775,000	0.40	1.50	3.50	20.00	—

KM# 518 100 REIS

Copper-Nickel, 21.3 mm. **Obv:** Denomination within circle, date below **Rev:** Liberty bust right

Date	Mintage	F	VF	XF	Unc	BU
1918	600,000	0.40	1.50	3.25	17.50	—
1919	1,219,000	0.40	1.50	3.25	17.50	—
1920	1,251,000	0.40	1.50	3.25	17.50	—
1921	853,000	0.40	1.50	3.25	17.50	—
1922	347,000	0.40	1.50	4.75	20.00	—
1923	956,000	0.40	1.50	4.75	20.00	—
1924	1,478,000	1.00	2.50	8.50	25.00	—
1925	2,502,000	0.30	1.25	2.75	17.00	—
1926	1,807,000	0.50	1.50	4.75	20.00	—
1927	1,451,000	0.30	1.25	2.75	17.00	—
1928	1,514,000	0.30	1.25	2.75	17.00	—
1929	2,503,000	0.30	1.25	2.75	17.00	—
1930	2,398,000	0.30	1.25	2.75	17.00	—
1931	2,500,000	0.25	1.00	2.25	17.00	—

Date	Mintage	F	VF	XF	Unc	BU
1932	948,000	0.25	1.00	2.25	17.00	—
1933	1,314,000	0.25	1.00	2.25	17.00	—
1934	3,614,000	0.25	1.00	2.25	17.00	—
1935	3,442,000	0.25	1.00	2.25	17.00	—

KM# 527 100 REIS

Copper-Nickel, 21 mm. **Subject:** 400th Anniversary of Colonization **Obv:** Cazique Tibirica **Obv. Designer:** Leopolds Campos **Rev:** Denomination below design **Rev. Designer:** Walter R. Toledo **Edge:** Reeded **Note:** Medal rotation.

Date	Mintage	F	VF	XF	Unc	BU
ND(1932)	1,012,000	0.50	1.00	2.25	6.50	—

KM# 536 100 REIS

Copper-Nickel, 19 mm. **Obv:** Anchor divides denomination **Obv. Designer:** Walter R. Toledo **Rev:** Admiral Marques Tamandare, founder of Brazilian Navy **Rev. Designer:** Calmon Barreto **Edge:** Plain **Note:** Medal rotation.

Date	Mintage	F	VF	XF	Unc	BU
1936	3,928,000	0.20	0.50	1.50	3.00	—
1937	7,905,000	0.10	0.35	1.00	2.50	—
1938	8,618,000	0.10	0.35	1.00	2.50	—

KM# 544 100 REIS

Copper-Nickel **Obv:** Denomination within wreath **Rev:** Head, left **Edge:** Fluted **Shape:** 16-sided

Date	Mintage	F	VF	XF	Unc	BU
1938	8,106,000	0.10	0.20	0.50	1.50	—
1940	8,797,000	0.10	0.20	0.50	1.50	—
1942	1,285,000	0.10	0.20	0.50	1.50	—

Note: The 1942 issue has a deeper yellow cast due to higher copper content

KM# 504 200 REIS

Copper-Nickel, 25 mm. **Obv:** National arms, denomination above **Rev:** Liberty bust right **Edge:** Plain **Note:** Roman numeral date.

Date	Mintage	F	VF	XF	Unc	BU
1901	12,625,000	0.35	1.00	2.50	15.00	—

KM# 519 200 REIS

Copper-Nickel, 25 mm. **Obv:** Denomination within circle, date below **Rev:** Liberty bust right

Date	Mintage	F	VF	XF	Unc	BU
1918	625,000	0.35	1.00	2.00	15.00	—
1919	882,000	0.35	1.00	2.00	15.00	—
1920	1,657,000	0.35	1.00	2.00	15.00	—
1921	1,135,000	0.35	1.00	2.00	15.00	—
1922	678,000	0.35	1.00	2.00	15.00	—
1923	1,655,000	0.35	1.00	2.00	15.00	—
1924	1,750,000	0.35	1.00	2.00	15.00	—
1925	2,081,999	0.35	1.00	2.00	15.00	—
1926	324,000	1.00	3.00	8.00	22.50	—
1927	1,806,000	0.35	1.00	2.00	15.00	—
1928	782,000	0.35	1.00	2.00	15.00	—
1929	2,440,000	0.25	1.00	2.00	15.00	—
1930	1,697,000	0.25	1.00	2.00	15.00	—
1931	1,830,000	0.25	1.00	2.00	15.00	—

Date	Mintage	F	VF	XF	Unc	BU
1932	761,000	0.25	1.00	2.00	15.00	—
1933	173,000	0.35	1.00	2.00	15.00	—
1934	612,000	0.25	1.00	2.00	15.00	—
1935	1,329,000	0.25	1.00	2.00	15.00	—

KM# 528 200 REIS

Copper-Nickel, 25 mm. **Subject:** 400th Anniversary of Colonization **Obv:** Globe with sash **Obv. Designer:** Calmon Barreto **Rev:** Ship, denomination below, two dates divided at top **Rev. Designer:** Arlindo Bastos **Note:** Medal rotation.

Date	Mintage	F	VF	XF	Unc	BU
ND(1932)	596,000	0.75	1.75	3.50	16.50	—

KM# 537 200 REIS

Copper-Nickel, 22 mm. **Obv:** Steam engine, date above, denomination below **Rev:** Viscount de Maua, railway builder facing **Edge:** Plain **Designer:** Leopolda Campos **Note:** Medal rotation.

Date	Mintage	F	VF	XF	Unc	BU
1936	2,256,000	0.30	0.75	2.00	8.50	—
1937	6,506,000	0.30	0.75	2.00	8.50	—
1938	5,787,000	0.30	0.75	2.00	8.50	—

KM# 545 200 REIS

Copper-Nickel **Obv:** Denomination, date below, within wreath **Rev:** Dr. Getulio Vargas left **Edge:** Fluted **Shape:** 18-sided

Date	Mintage	F	VF	XF	Unc	BU
1938	7,666,000	0.20	0.50	0.85	2.75	—
1940	10,161,000	0.15	0.40	0.60	2.25	—
1942	1,966,000	0.15	0.40	0.60	2.25	—

Note: The 1942 issue has a yellow cast due to higher copper content

KM# 538 300 REIS

Copper-Nickel, 25 mm. **Obv:** Harp divides denomination, date above **Obv. Designer:** Walter R. Toledo **Rev:** Composer Antonio Carlos Gomes facing **Rev. Designer:** Calmon Barreto **Edge:** Plain **Note:** Medal rotation.

Date	Mintage	F	VF	XF	Unc	BU
1936	3,029,000	0.30	1.25	4.00	11.50	—
1937	4,507,000	0.30	1.25	4.00	11.50	—
1938	3,753,000	0.30	1.25	4.00	11.50	—

KM# 546 300 REIS

Copper-Nickel **Obv:** Denomination above date within wreath **Rev:** Dr. Getulio Vargas left **Edge:** Fluted **Shape:** 20-sided

Date	Mintage	F	VF	XF	Unc	BU
1938	12,080,000	0.20	0.35	0.50	2.25	—
1940	8,124,000	0.20	0.35	0.50	2.25	—
1942	2,020,000	0.25	0.40	0.75	3.25	—

Note: The 1942 issue has a yellow cast due to higher copper content

KM# 505 400 REIS

Copper-Nickel, 30 mm. **Obv:** National arms, denomination above **Rev:** Liberty bust right, circle of stars surrounds **Edge:** Plain

Date	Mintage	F	VF	XF	Unc	BU
MCMI (1901)	5,531,000	1.50	3.00	8.00	30.00	—

KM# 515 400 REIS

Copper-Nickel **Obv:** National arms, denomination above within circle, date below **Rev:** Liberty bust left

Date	Mintage	F	VF	XF	Unc	BU
1914	646,000	15.00	35.00	75.00	150	—

Note: This is considered a pattern by many authorities

KM# 520 400 REIS

Copper-Nickel **Obv:** Denomination within circle, date below **Rev:** Liberty bust right

Date	Mintage	F	VF	XF	Unc	BU
1918	491,000	0.75	2.00	5.50	18.00	—
1919	891,000	0.75	2.00	5.50	18.00	—
1920	1,521,000	0.75	2.00	5.50	18.00	—
1921	871,000	0.50	1.75	5.50	18.00	—
1922	1,275,000	0.50	1.75	5.50	18.00	—
1923	764,000	0.50	1.75	5.50	18.00	—
1925	2,048,000	0.50	1.75	5.50	18.00	—
1926	1,034,000	0.50	1.75	5.50	18.00	—
1927	738,000	0.50	1.75	5.50	18.00	—
1929	869,000	0.50	1.75	5.50	18.00	—
1930	1,030,999	0.50	1.75	5.50	18.00	—
1931	1,431,000	0.50	1.75	5.50	18.00	—
1932	588,000	0.50	1.75	5.50	18.00	—
1935	225,000	0.50	1.75	5.50	18.00	—

KM# 529 400 REIS

Copper-Nickel, 30 mm. **Subject:** 400th Anniversary of Colonization **Obv:** Map divides dates within circle **Obv. Designer:** Walter R. Toledo **Rev:** Lusinian Cross **Rev. Designer:** Basilio Nunes Lusinian Cross **Note:** Medal rotation.

Date	Mintage	F	VF	XF	Unc	BU
ND(1932)	416,000	1.00	2.75	5.50	15.00	—

KM# 539 400 REIS
Copper-Nickel, 27 mm. **Obv:** Oil lamp, date above, denomination below **Obv. Designer:** Walter R. Toledo **Rev:** Bust of Oswaldo Cruz, Microbiologist, 3/4 left **Rev. Designer:** Calmon Barreto **Note:** Medal rotation.

Date	Mintage	F	VF	XF	Unc	BU
1936	2,079,000	0.50	1.00	2.75	8.50	—
1937	3,111,000	0.50	1.00	2.75	8.50	—
1938	2,681,000	0.50	1.00	2.75	8.50	—

KM# 547 400 REIS
Copper-Nickel, 23 mm. **Obv:** Denomination above date within wreath **Rev:** Bust of Dr. Getulio Vargas left **Edge:** Fluted **Shape:** 22-sided

Date	Mintage	F	VF	XF	Unc	BU
1938	10,620,000	0.25	0.50	1.00	2.25	—
1940	7,312,000	0.25	0.50	1.00	2.25	—
1942	1,496,000	0.25	0.50	1.50	3.25	—

Note: The 1942 issue has a yellow cast due to higher copper content

KM# 506 500 REIS
5.0000 g., 0.9000 Silver .1446 oz. ASW **Obv:** Liberty bust left, date below **Rev:** Denomination at center

Date	Mintage	F	VF	XF	Unc	BU
1906	352,000	BV	2.75	4.75	15.00	—
1907	1,282,000	BV	2.75	4.75	15.00	—
1908	498,000	BV	2.75	4.75	15.00	—
1911	8,000	20.00	35.00	70.00	150	—
1912	Est. 222,000	20.00	40.00	80.00	200	—

KM# 509 500 REIS
5.0000 g., 0.9000 Silver .1446 oz. ASW **Obv:** Liberty bust right within circle, date below **Rev:** Denomination within wreath, arms above

Date	Mintage	F	VF	XF	Unc	BU
1912	—	3.00	7.00	14.00	38.00	—

KM# 512 500 REIS
5.0000 g., 0.9000 Silver .1446 oz. ASW **Obv:** Liberty bust right within circle of stars, date below **Rev:** Denomination within wreath, arms above

Date	Mintage	F	VF	XF	Unc	BU
1913 A	—	BV	2.50	4.50	15.00	—

KM# 521.1 500 REIS
Aluminum-Bronze, 23 mm. **Subject:** Independence Centennial **Obv:** Dom Pedro and President Pessoa left **Obv. Designer:** Augusta G. Girardet **Rev:** Denomination at top, dates divided by centennial symbols **Rev. Designer:** Joao da Cruz Vargas

Date	Mintage	F	VF	XF	Unc	BU
ND(1922)	13,744,000	0.25	0.60	1.25	4.75	—

KM# 521.2 500 REIS
Aluminum-Bronze, 23 mm. **Obv:** Dom Pedro and President Pessoa left **Obv. Designer:** Augusta G. Girardet **Rev:** Denomination at top, dates divided by centennial symbols **Rev. Designer:** Joao da Cruz Vargas **Edge:** Reeded **Note:** Error: BBASIL instead of BRASIL.

Date	Mintage	F	VF	XF	Unc	BU
ND(1922)	Inc. above	17.50	35.00	55.00	120	—

KM# 524 500 REIS
Aluminum-Bronze **Obv:** Denomination within wreath, date below **Rev:** Kneeling liberty figure right

Date	Mintage	F	VF	XF	Unc	BU
1924	7,400,000	0.30	0.75	1.50	7.00	—
1927	2,725,000	0.30	0.75	1.50	7.00	—
1928	9,432,000	0.30	0.75	1.50	7.00	—
1930	146,000	1.00	2.00	3.75	9.00	—

KM# 530 500 REIS
Aluminum-Bronze, 23 mm. **Subject:** 400th Anniversary of Colonization **Obv:** Joao Ramalho, colonist, 3/4 right **Rev:** Clothing divides denomination **Edge:** Reeded **Designer:** Calmon Barreto **Note:** Medal rotation.

Date	Mintage	F	VF	XF	Unc	BU
ND(1932)	34,000	1.50	4.00	11.50	20.00	—

KM# 533 500 REIS
4.0000 g., Aluminum-Bronze, 22 mm. **Obv:** Column divides denomination, date below **Obv. Designer:** Walter R. Toledo **Rev:** Bust of Diego Antonio Feijo Regent of Brazil 1835-1837, 3/4 left **Rev. Designer:** Calmon Barreto **Note:** Medal rotation; wide rim.

Date	Mintage	F	VF	XF	Unc	BU
1935	14,000	2.00	9.00	20.00	40.00	—

KM# 540 500 REIS
5.0000 g., Aluminum-Bronze, 22 mm. **Obv:** Denomination divided by column, date below **Obv. Designer:** Walter R. Toledo **Rev:** Bust of Diego Antonio Feijo, 3/4 left **Rev. Designer:** Calmon Barreto **Note:** Medal rotation; thicker planchet.

Date	Mintage	F	VF	XF	Unc	BU
1936	1,326,000	0.60	1.25	4.75	9.00	—
1937	Inc. above	0.60	1.25	4.75	9.00	—
1938	—	0.60	1.25	4.75	9.00	—

KM# 549 500 REIS
5.0000 g., Aluminum-Bronze, 21 mm. **Obv:** Denomination above date within wreath **Rev:** Joaquim Machado de Assis, Author and Poet, 3/4 facing **Designer:** Benedito Ribeiro

Date	Mintage	F	VF	XF	Unc	BU
1939	5,928,000	0.50	1.00	3.00	8.00	—

KM# 507 1000 REIS
10.0000 g., 0.9000 Silver .2894 oz. ASW **Obv:** Laureate liberty head left, date below flanked by stars **Rev:** Denomination at center **Edge:** Reeded

Date	Mintage	F	VF	XF	Unc	BU
1906	420,000	BV	5.00	9.00	24.00	—
1907	1,282,000	BV	5.00	9.00	24.00	—
1908	1,624,000	BV	5.00	9.00	24.00	—
1909	816,000	BV	5.00	9.00	24.00	—
1910	2,354,000	BV	5.00	9.00	24.00	—
1911	2,810,000	BV	5.00	9.00	24.00	—
1912	Est. 1,570,000	BV	5.00	9.00	24.00	—

KM# 510 1000 REIS
10.0000 g., 0.9000 Silver .2894 oz. ASW **Obv:** Laureate head of Liberty right, circle surrounds, date below **Rev:** Denomination within wreath, arms above

Date	Mintage	F	VF	XF	Unc	BU
1912	Inc. above	BV	5.50	10.00	32.50	—
1913	2,525,000	BV	5.50	10.00	32.50	—

KM# 513 1000 REIS
10.0000 g., 0.9000 Silver .2894 oz. ASW, 26 mm. **Obv:** Laureate liberty head right, star circle surrounds, date below **Rev:** Denomination within wreath, arms above **Edge:** Reeded

Date	Mintage	F	VF	XF	Unc	BU
1913 A	—	—	BV	6.00	17.50	—

KM# 522.1 1000 REIS
Aluminum-Bronze, 26.8 mm. **Subject:** Independence Centennial **Obv:** Dom Pedro and President Pessoa **Obv. Designer:** Augusto G. Girardet **Rev:** Denomination at top, dates divided by centennial symbols **Rev. Designer:** Joao de Cruz Vargas **Edge:** Reeded

Date	Mintage	F	VF	XF	Unc	BU
ND(1922)	16,698,000	0.40	0.60	2.00	6.50	—

KM# 522.2 1000 REIS

Aluminum-Bronze, 25 mm. **Obv:** Dom Pedro and President Pessoa left **Obv. Designer:** Augusto G. Girardet **Rev:** Denomination at top, dates divided by centennial symbols at center **Rev. Designer:** Joao da Cruz Vargas **Edge:** Reeded **Note:** Error: BBASIL instead of BRASIL.

Date	Mintage	F	VF	XF	Unc	BU
ND(1922)	Inc. above	2.50	5.00	10.00	20.00	—

KM# 525 1000 REIS

Aluminum-Bronze **Obv:** Denomination within wreath, date below, monogram left of knot **Rev:** Kneeling liberty figure right

Date	Mintage	F	VF	XF	Unc	BU
1924	9,354,000	0.50	1.00	2.25	7.50	—
1925	6,205,000	0.50	1.00	2.25	7.50	—
1927	35,817,000	0.50	1.00	2.25	7.50	—
1928	1,899,000	0.50	1.00	2.25	7.50	—
1929	83,000	3.50	14.00	45.00	100	—
1930	45,000	3.50	14.00	45.00	100	—
1931	200,000	1.00	4.50	8.00	16.00	—

KM# 531 1000 REIS

7.0000 g., Aluminum-Bronze, 32 mm. **Subject:** 400th Anniversary of Colonization **Obv:** 3/4 figure of Martin Affonso da Sousa looking left **Obv. Designer:** Leopoldo Campos **Rev:** Denomination encircles arms **Rev. Designer:** Herminio Pereira **Edge:** Reeded **Note:** Medal rotation.

Date	Mintage	F	VF	XF	Unc	BU
ND(1932)	56,000	2.00	4.00	7.50	18.00	—

KM# 534 1000 REIS

8.0000 g., Aluminum-Bronze, 26 mm. **Obv:** Open bible, date above, denomination at top **Obv. Designer:** Walter R. Toledo **Rev:** Head of Jose de Anchieta left **Rev. Designer:** Calmon Barreto **Note:** Medal rotation.

Date	Mintage	F	VF	XF	Unc	BU
1935	138,000	1.00	2.00	4.00	9.00	—

KM# 541 1000 REIS

Aluminum-Bronze, 24.3 mm. **Obv:** Open bible, date above, denomination at top **Obv. Designer:** Walter R. Toledo **Rev:** Head of Jose de Anchieta left **Rev. Designer:** Calmon Barreto **Edge:** Reeded **Note:** Size reduced. Medal rotation.

Date	Mintage	F	VF	XF	Unc	BU
1936	926,000	0.50	1.00	2.50	7.00	—
1937	Inc. above	0.50	1.00	2.50	7.00	—
1938 LGCB under chin	—	0.50	1.00	2.50	7.00	—

KM# 550 1000 REIS

Aluminum-Bronze, 23 mm. **Obv:** Denomination above date within wreath **Rev:** Tobias Barreto de Menezes, Philosopher and Poet 3/4 right, BR monogram right of bust, two dates above right shoulder **Designer:** Benedito Ribeiro

Date	Mintage	F	VF	XF	Unc	BU
1939	9,586,000	0.25	0.75	2.00	6.50	—

KM# 508 2000 REIS

20.0000 g., 0.9000 Silver .5787 oz. ASW **Obv:** Liberty head left, date below flanked by stars **Rev:** Denomination at center

Date	Mintage	F	VF	XF	Unc	BU
1906	256,000	8.00	10.00	16.50	55.00	—
1907	2,863,000	BV	7.50	11.50	45.00	—
1908	1,707,000	BV	7.50	11.50	45.00	—
1910	585,000	8.00	10.00	16.50	55.00	—
1911	1,929,000	BV	7.50	11.50	45.00	—
1912	741,000	8.00	10.00	16.50	55.00	—

KM# 511 2000 REIS

20.0000 g., 0.9000 Silver .5787 oz. ASW **Obv:** Liberty head within circle, date below **Rev:** Denomination within wreath, national arms above

Date	Mintage	F	VF	XF	Unc	BU
1912	Inc. above	7.50	11.50	23.50	58.00	—
1913	395,000	7.50	11.50	23.50	62.00	—

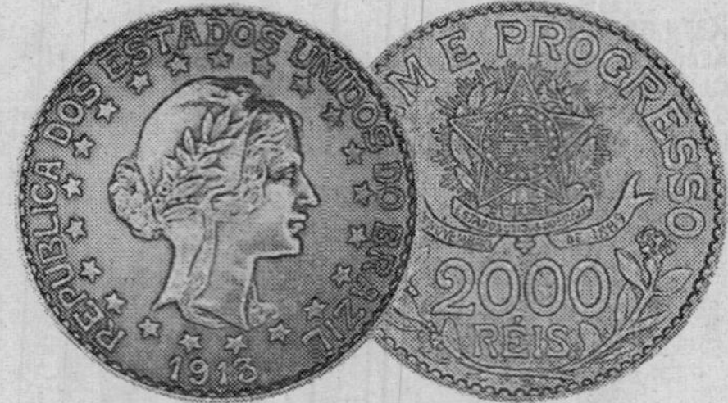

KM# 514 2000 REIS

20.0000 g., 0.9000 Silver .5787 oz. ASW **Obv:** Laureate liberty head right within circle, date below **Rev:** Denomination within wreath, national arms above, continuous legend

Date	Mintage	F	VF	XF	Unc	BU
1913 A	—	8.00	10.00	14.50	42.50	—

KM# 523 2000 REIS

7.9000 g., 0.9000 Silver .2285 oz. ASW, 26 mm. **Subject:** Independence Centennial **Obv:** Dom Pedro and President Pessoa left **Obv. Designer:** Augusto G. Girardet **Rev:** Two sets of arms, dates below, denomination at bottom **Rev. Designer:** Joao da Cruz Vargas **Edge:** Reeded

Date	Mintage	F	VF	XF	Unc	BU
ND(1922)	1,560,000	BV	3.25	4.50	9.00	—

KM# 523a 2000 REIS

7.9000 g., 0.5000 Silver .1269 oz. ASW, 26 mm. **Edge:** Reeded **Note:** Struck in both .900 and .500 fine silver, but can only be distinguished by analysis (and color), on worn specimens

Date	Mintage	F	VF	XF	Unc	BU
ND(1922)	Inc. above	BV	2.75	3.75	8.50	—

KM# 526 2000 REIS

7.9000 g., 0.5000 Silver .1269 oz. ASW **Obv:** Denomination within wreath, date below **Rev:** Laureate liberty head, right, within circle, stars surround

Date	Mintage	F	VF	XF	Unc	BU
1924	9,147,000	BV	2.00	3.75	12.00	—
1925	723,000	BV	2.00	3.75	12.00	—
1926	1,787,000	BV	2.00	3.75	12.00	—
1927	1,008,999	BV	2.50	4.75	14.00	—
1928	1,250,000	BV	2.00	3.75	12.00	—
1929	1,744,000	BV	2.00	3.75	12.00	—
1930	1,240,000	BV	2.00	3.75	12.00	—
1931	546,000	BV	2.00	3.75	12.00	—
1934	938,000	BV	2.00	3.75	12.00	—

KM# 532 2000 REIS

7.9000 g., 0.5000 Silver .1269 oz. ASW, 26 mm. **Subject:** 400th Anniversary of Colonization **Obv:** Bust of John III 3/4 right **Obv. Designer:** Leopoldo Campos **Rev:** Arms, denomination above **Rev. Designer:** Arlindo Bastos **Note:** Medal rotation.

Date	Mintage	F	VF	XF	Unc	BU
ND(1932)	695,000	2.00	3.00	5.00	15.00	—

KM# 535 2000 REIS

7.9000 g., 0.5000 Silver .1269 oz. ASW, 26 mm. **Obv:** Sword divides denomination, date lower right **Obv. Designer:** Walter R. Toledo **Rev:** Armored head of Duke of Caxias; left, CB below chin **Rev. Designer:** Leopoldo Campos **Edge:** Reeded **Note:** Medal rotation.

Date	Mintage	F	VF	XF	Unc	BU
1935	2,131,000	BV	2.00	3.75	12.50	—

KM# 542 2000 REIS

Aluminum-Bronze, 26 mm. **Obv:** Hilt divides denomination, date upper right **Obv. Designer:** Walter R. Toledo **Rev:** Armored bust of Duke of Caxias, right, crown at left **Rev. Designer:** Leopoldo Campos **Edge:** Plain **Shape:** Round **Note:** Medal rotation.

Date	Mintage	F	VF	XF	Unc	BU
1936	665,000	0.50	1.00	2.00	5.50	—
1937	Inc. above	0.50	1.00	2.00	5.50	—
1938	—	2.50	4.75	11.50	28.00	—

KM# 548 2000 REIS

Aluminum-Bronze, 26.3 mm. **Edge:** Plain **Note:** 24-sided planchet. Medal rotation.

Date	Mintage	F	VF	XF	Unc	BU
1937	—	25.00	50.00	125	300	—
1938	—	0.75	1.50	3.25	7.50	—

KM# 551 2000 REIS
Aluminum-Bronze, 26 mm. **Obv:** Denomination above date within wreath **Rev:** Bust of President Floriano Peixoto facing **Designer:** Orlando Moutinho

Date	Mintage	F	VF	XF	Unc	BU
1939	5,048,000	0.50	1.00	2.00	5.50	—

KM# 543 5000 REIS
10.0000 g., 0.6000 Silver .1929 oz. ASW, 26 mm. **Obv:** Wing above denomination **Obv. Designer:** Walter R. Toledo **Rev:** Head of aviation pioneer Alberto Santos Dumont left **Rev. Designer:** Calmon Barreto **Edge:** Reeded **Note:** Medal rotation.

Date	Mintage	F	VF	XF	Unc	BU
1936	1,986,000	BV	2.75	4.00	9.00	—
1937	414,000	BV	2.75	4.00	9.00	—
1938	994,000	BV	2.75	4.00	9.00	—

KM# 496 10000 REIS
8.9645 g., 0.9170 Gold .2643 oz. AGW **Obv:** Liberty bust left within circle, date below **Rev:** National arms, denomination below

Date	Mintage	F	VF	XF	Unc	BU
1901	111	185	250	700	1,150	—
1902 Unique	—	—	—	—	—	—
1903	391	185	250	700	1,150	—
1904	541	185	250	700	1,150	—
1906	572	185	250	700	1,150	—
1907	878	185	250	600	1,100	—
1908	689	185	250	600	1,100	1,500
1909	1,069	185	250	600	1,100	1,750
1911	137	220	350	800	1,350	—
1914	969	250	500	1,500	2,400	—
1915	4,314	250	500	1,400	2,000	—
1916	4,720	185	250	700	1,150	—
1919	526	185	250	700	1,150	—
1921	2,435	185	250	600	1,000	—
1922 Rare	6	—	—	—	—	—

KM# 497 20000 REIS
17.9290 g., 0.9170 Gold .5286 oz. AGW **Obv:** Liberty bust left, date below **Rev:** Stars within inner circle, stars surround

Date	Mintage	F	VF	XF	Unc	BU
1901	784	BV	375	700	1,350	1,850
1902	884	BV	375	700	1,350	—
1903	675	BV	375	700	1,350	—
1904	444	BV	375	700	1,350	—
1906	396	BV	500	900	1,600	—
1907	3,310	BV	360	550	1,100	—
1908	6,001,000	BV	360	550	1,100	—
1909	4,427	BV	360	550	1,100	—
1910	5,119	BV	360	550	1,100	1,350
1911	8,467	BV	360	550	1,100	—
1912	4,878	BV	360	550	1,100	—
1913	5,182	BV	360	600	1,200	—
1914	1,980	BV	375	700	1,400	—
1917	2,269	BV	400	800	1,550	—
1918	1,216	BV	400	800	1,550	—
1921	5,924	BV	360	600	1,200	—
1922	2,681	BV	400	800	1,550	—

REFORM COINAGE

1942-1967

100 Centavos = 1 Cruzeiro

KM# 555 10 CENTAVOS
Copper-Nickel **Obv:** Bust of Getulic Vargas 3/4 left **Rev:** Denomination above line, date below **Edge:** Plain **Note:** KM#555 has a very light yellowish appearance while KM#555a is a deeper yellow.

Date	Mintage	F	VF	XF	Unc	BU
1942	3,826,000	—	0.35	0.50	1.00	—
1943	13,565,000	—	0.25	0.35	0.75	—

KM# 555a.1 10 CENTAVOS
Aluminum-Bronze, 17.2 mm. **Obv:** Bust left, initial after "Brasil" **Rev:** Denomination above line, date below, initial at end of line above date **Edge:** Plain **Note:** KM#555 has a very light yellowish appearance while KM#555a is a deeper yellow.

Date	Mintage	F	VF	XF	Unc	BU
1943	Inc. above	—	0.25	0.35	0.75	—
1944	12,617,000	—	0.25	0.60	1.00	—
1945	24,674,000	—	0.25	0.60	1.00	—

KM# 555a.2 10 CENTAVOS
Aluminum-Bronze, 17.2 mm. **Obv:** Bust left **Rev:** Denomination above line, date below **Note:** Without initials.

Date	Mintage	F	VF	XF	Unc	BU
1944	—	—	0.25	0.60	1.00	—
1945	—	—	0.25	0.60	1.00	—
1946	35,159,000	—	0.25	0.60	1.00	—
1947	20,664,000	—	0.25	0.35	0.75	—

KM# 561 10 CENTAVOS
Aluminum-Bronze **Obv:** Jose Bonifacio de Andrada e Silva, Father of Independence left **Rev:** Denomination above line, date below

Date	Mintage	F	VF	XF	Unc	BU
1947	Inc. above	—	0.15	0.20	0.35	—
1948	45,041,000	—	0.15	0.20	0.35	—
1949	21,763,000	—	0.15	0.20	0.35	—
1950	16,329,999	—	0.15	0.20	0.35	—
1951	15,561,000	—	0.10	0.15	0.35	—
1952	10,966,000	—	0.10	0.20	0.50	—
1953	25,883,000	—	0.10	0.15	0.35	—
1954	17,031,000	—	0.10	0.15	0.35	—
1955	25,172,000	—	0.10	0.15	0.35	—

KM# 564 10 CENTAVOS
Aluminum **Obv:** National Arms **Rev:** Denomination above line, date below

Date	Mintage	F	VF	XF	Unc	BU
1956	741,000	—	0.10	0.15	0.50	—
1957	25,311,000	—	0.10	0.15	0.25	—
1958	5,813,000	—	0.10	0.15	0.25	—
1959	2,611,000	—	0.10	0.15	0.25	—
1960	624,000	—	0.10	0.15	0.50	—
1961	951,000	—	0.10	0.15	0.50	—

KM# 556 20 CENTAVOS
Copper-Nickel, 20 mm. **Obv:** Bust of Getulio Vargas 3/4 left **Rev:** Denomination above line, date below **Edge:** Plain **Note:** KM#556 has a very light yellowish appearance while KM#556a is a deeper yellow.

Date	Mintage	F	VF	XF	Unc	BU
1942	3,007,000	—	0.25	0.50	1.00	—
1943	13,392,000	—	0.15	0.40	0.75	—

KM# 556a 20 CENTAVOS
Aluminum-Bronze, 20 mm. **Obv:** Getulio Vargas bust left **Rev:** Denomination above line, date below **Edge:** Plain **Note:** KM#556 has a very light yellowish appearance while KM#556a is a deeper yellow.

Date	Mintage	F	VF	XF	Unc	BU
1943	Inc. above	—	0.15	0.35	0.75	—
1944	12,673,000	—	0.15	0.35	0.75	—
Note: Coins dated 1944 exist with and without designer's initials and straight or curved-back 9 in date						
1945	61,632,000	—	0.15	0.35	0.60	—
1946	31,526,000	—	0.15	0.35	0.60	—
1947	36,422,000	—	0.15	0.35	0.75	—
1948	39,671,000	—	0.15	0.35	0.75	—

KM# 562 20 CENTAVOS
Aluminum-Bronze **Obv:** Bust of author and lawyer Ruy Barbosa left **Rev:** Denomination above line, date below

Date	Mintage	F	VF	XF	Unc	BU
1948	Inc. above	—	0.15	0.25	0.50	—
1949	24,805,000	—	0.15	0.25	0.50	—
1950	15,145,000	—	0.15	0.25	0.50	—
1951	14,964,000	—	0.15	0.25	0.50	—
1952	10,942,000	—	0.15	0.25	0.50	—
1953	25,585,000	—	0.15	0.25	0.50	—
1954	16,477,000	—	0.15	0.25	0.50	—
1955	25,122,000	—	0.15	0.25	0.50	—
1956	6,716,000	—	0.15	0.25	0.50	—

KM# 565 20 CENTAVOS
Aluminum **Obv:** National arms **Rev:** Denomination above line, date below **Note:** Varieties exist in the thickness of the planchet for year 1956.

Date	Mintage	F	VF	XF	Unc	BU
1956	Inc. above	—	0.10	0.25	0.50	—
1957	27,110,000	—	0.10	0.20	0.40	—
1958	8,552,000	—	0.10	0.20	0.40	—
1959	4,810,000	—	0.10	0.20	0.40	—
1960	510,000	—	0.10	0.25	0.50	—
1961	2,332,000	—	0.10	0.20	0.40	—

KM# 557 50 CENTAVOS
Copper-Nickel, 21 mm. **Obv:** Bust of Getulio Vargas 3/4 left **Rev:** Denomination above line, date below **Note:** KM#557 has a very light yellowish appearance while KM#557a is a deeper yellow.

Date	Mintage	F	VF	XF	Unc	BU
1942	2,358,000	—	0.40	0.75	1.50	—
1943	13,392,000	—	0.35	0.50	1.00	—

KM# 557a 50 CENTAVOS
Aluminum-Bronze, 21 mm. **Obv:** Getulio Vargas bust left **Rev:** Denomination above line, date below **Edge:** Plain **Note:** KM#557 has a very light yellowish appearance while KM#557a is a deeper yellow.

Date	Mintage	F	VF	XF	Unc	BU
1943	Inc. above	—	0.30	0.50	1.00	—
1944	12,102,000	—	0.30	0.50	1.00	—
1945	73,222,000	—	0.30	0.50	1.00	—
1946	13,941,000	—	0.30	0.50	1.00	—
1947	23,588,000	—	0.20	0.50	1.00	—

KM# 563 50 CENTAVOS
Aluminum-Bronze **Obv:** Bust of General Eurico Gaspar Dutra left **Rev:** Denomination above line, date below

Date	Mintage	F	VF	XF	Unc	BU
1948	32,023,000	—	0.15	0.25	0.50	—
1949	11,392,000	—	0.15	0.25	0.50	—
1950	7,804,000	—	0.15	0.35	0.75	—
1951	7,523,000	—	0.15	0.35	0.75	—
1952	6,863,000	—	0.15	0.35	0.75	—
1953	17,372,000	—	0.15	0.25	0.50	—

Date	Mintage	F	VF	XF	Unc	BU
1954	11,353,000	—	0.15	0.25	0.50	—
1955	27,150,000	—	0.15	0.25	0.50	—
1956	32,130,000	—	0.15	0.25	0.50	—

KM# 566 50 CENTAVOS

Aluminum-Bronze **Obv:** National arms **Rev:** Denomination above line, date below

Date	Mintage	F	VF	XF	Unc	BU
1956	Inc. above	—	0.15	0.25	0.50	—

KM# 569 50 CENTAVOS

Aluminum **Obv:** National arms **Rev:** Denomination above line, date below

Date	Mintage	F	VF	XF	Unc	BU
1957	49,350,000	—	0.10	0.20	0.35	—
1958	59,815,000	—	0.10	0.20	0.35	—
1959	32,891,000	—	0.10	0.20	0.35	—
1960	15,997,000	—	0.10	0.20	0.35	—
1961	18,456,000	—	0.10	0.20	0.35	—

KM# 558 CRUZEIRO

Aluminum-Bronze **Obv:** Topographical map **Rev:** Denomination, date at left

Date	Mintage	F	VF	XF	Unc	BU
1942	381,000	—	0.50	1.00	3.50	—
1943	2,728,000	—	0.25	0.50	1.00	—
1944	3,820,000	—	0.25	0.50	1.00	—
1945	32,543,999	—	0.25	0.50	0.75	—
1946	49,794,000	—	0.25	0.50	1.00	—
1947	15,391,000	—	0.25	0.50	1.00	—
1949	7,889,000	—	0.25	0.50	1.00	—
1950	5,163,000	—	0.25	0.50	1.00	—
1951	3,757,000	—	0.25	0.50	1.00	—
1952	1,769,000	—	0.50	1.00	3.50	—
1953	5,195,000	—	0.25	0.50	1.00	—
1954	1,145,000	—	0.25	0.50	1.50	—
1955	1,758,000	—	0.25	0.50	1.00	—
1956	668,000	—	6.00	12.00	20.00	—

KM# 567 CRUZEIRO

Aluminum-Bronze **Obv:** National arms **Rev:** Denomination above line, date below

Date	Mintage	F	VF	XF	Unc	BU
1956	Inc. above	—	0.20	0.35	0.65	—

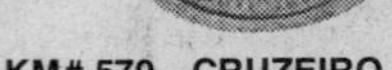

KM# 570 CRUZEIRO

Aluminum **Obv:** National arms **Rev:** Denomination above line, date below

Date	Mintage	F	VF	XF	Unc	BU
1957	11,849,000	—	0.20	0.75	2.50	—
1958	15,443,000	—	0.20	1.00	3.00	—
1959	25,010,000	—	0.20	0.75	2.50	—
1960	35,267,000	—	0.20	0.75	2.50	—
1961	22,181,000	—	0.20	1.00	3.00	—

KM# 559 2 CRUZEIROS

Aluminum-Bronze, 25 mm. **Obv:** Topographical map **Rev:** Denomination, date at left **Edge:** Reeded

Date	Mintage	F	VF	XF	Unc	BU
1942	276,000	—	0.75	1.50	4.00	—
1943	1,929,000	—	0.25	0.50	1.00	—
1944	3,820,000	—	0.25	0.50	1.00	—
1945	32,543,999	—	0.20	0.40	1.00	—
1946	33,650,000	—	0.20	0.40	1.00	—
1947	9,908,000	—	0.20	0.40	1.00	—
1949	11,252,000	—	0.20	0.40	1.00	—
1950	7,754,000	—	0.25	0.50	1.00	—
1951	390,000	—	0.40	1.00	3.00	—
1952	1,456,000	—	1.00	2.00	5.00	—
1953	3,582,000	—	0.20	0.40	1.00	—
1954	1,197,000	—	0.25	1.00	2.00	—
1955	1,838,000	—	0.20	0.50	1.00	—
1956	253,000	—	2.00	4.00	10.00	—

KM# 568 2 CRUZEIROS

Aluminum-Bronze **Obv:** National arms **Rev:** Denomination above line, date below

Date	Mintage	F	VF	XF	Unc	BU
1956	Inc. above	—	0.20	0.40	1.50	—

KM# 571 2 CRUZEIROS

Aluminum **Obv:** National arms **Rev:** Denomination above line, date below

Date	Mintage	F	VF	XF	Unc	BU
1957	194,000	—	0.25	0.50	1.50	—
1958	13,687,000	—	0.20	0.30	1.00	—
1959	20,894,000	—	0.20	0.30	1.00	—
1960	19,624,000	—	0.20	0.30	1.00	—
1961	24,924,000	—	0.20	0.30	1.00	—

KM# 560 5 CRUZEIROS

Aluminum-Bronze **Obv:** Topographical map **Rev:** Denomination, date at left

Date	Mintage	F	VF	XF	Unc	BU
1942	115,000	—	1.50	3.50	9.00	—
1943	222,000	—	1.00	2.50	7.00	—

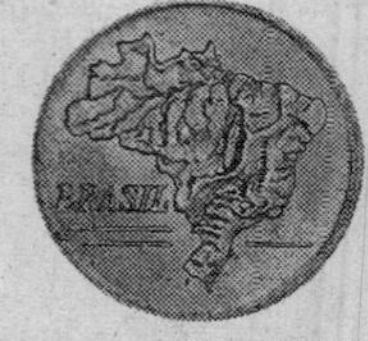

KM# 572 10 CRUZEIROS

Aluminum **Obv:** Topographical map **Rev:** Large denomination, date below

Date	Mintage	F	VF	XF	Unc	BU
1965	19,656,000	—	0.10	0.20	0.50	—

KM# 573 20 CRUZEIROS

Aluminum **Obv:** Topographical map **Rev:** Large denomination, date below

Date	Mintage	F	VF	XF	Unc	BU
1965	25,930,000	—	0.15	0.25	0.75	—

KM# 574 50 CRUZEIROS

Copper-Nickel **Obv:** Liberty head left **Rev:** Denomination above date

Date	Mintage	F	VF	XF	Unc	BU
1965	18,001,000	—	0.20	0.40	1.50	—

REFORM COINAGE

1967-1985

1000 Old Cruzeiros = 1 Cruzeiro Novo (New);
100 Centavos = 1 (New) Cruzeiro

KM# 575.1 CENTAVO

Stainless Steel **Obv:** Liberty head left **Rev:** Denomination above date

Date	Mintage	F	VF	XF	Unc	BU
1967	57,499,000	—	—	—	0.15	0.25

KM# 575.2 CENTAVO

Stainless Steel **Obv:** Liberty head left **Rev:** Denomination above date **Note:** Thinner planchet.

Date	Mintage	F	VF	XF	Unc	BU
1969	243,855,000	—	—	—	0.15	0.25
1975	—	—	—	0.15	0.30	0.50

KM# 585 CENTAVO

Stainless Steel **Series:** F.A.O. **Subject:** Sugar Cane **Obv:** Liberty head left **Rev:** Sugar cane, denomination and date to right

Date	Mintage	F	VF	XF	Unc	BU
1975	31,700,000	—	—	0.15	0.25	0.45
1976	18,355,000	—	—	—	0.20	0.45
1977	100,000	—	—	0.15	0.30	0.50
1978	50,000	—	—	0.15	0.30	0.50

KM# 589 CENTAVO

Stainless Steel **Series:** F.A.O. **Subject:** Soja **Obv:** Plants **Rev:** Denomination above date

Date	Mintage	F	VF	XF	Unc	BU
1979	100,000	—	0.15	0.35	1.00	1.25
1980	60,000	—	0.15	0.35	1.00	1.25
1981	100,000	—	0.15	0.35	1.00	1.25
1982	100,000	—	0.15	0.35	1.00	1.25
1983	—	—	0.15	0.35	1.00	1.25

KM# 576.1 2 CENTAVOS

Stainless Steel **Obv:** Liberty head left **Rev:** Denomination above date

Date	Mintage	F	VF	XF	Unc	BU
1967	65,226,000	—	—	—	0.25	0.50

KM# 576.2 2 CENTAVOS

Stainless Steel **Obv:** Liberty head left **Note:** Thinner planchet.

Date	Mintage	F	VF	XF	Unc	BU
1969	Est. 134,298,000	—	—	—	0.50	0.75

Note: Mintage figure includes coins struck through 1974 dated 1969

Date	Mintage	F	VF	XF	Unc	BU
1975	—	—	—	0.25	0.75	1.00

KM# 586 2 CENTAVOS

Stainless Steel **Series:** F.A.O. **Subject:** Soja **Obv:** Liberty head left **Rev:** Denomination above date, plant at left

Date	Mintage	F	VF	XF	Unc	BU
1975	31,400,000	—	—	0.15	0.25	0.45
1976	18,754,000	—	—	—	0.25	0.45
1977	100,000	—	—	0.20	0.50	0.75
1978	50,000	—	—	0.20	0.50	0.75

KM# 577.1 5 CENTAVOS

Stainless Steel **Obv:** Liberty head left **Rev:** Denomination above date

Date	Mintage	F	VF	XF	Unc	BU
1967	69,304,000	—	—	0.20	0.50	0.75

5 CENTAVOS 1969

KM# 577.2 5 CENTAVOS

Stainless Steel **Obv:** Liberty head left **Rev:** Denomination above date **Note:** Thinner planchet.

Date	Mintage	F	VF	XF	Unc	BU
1969	Est. 345,071,000	—	—	0.20	0.50	0.75

Note: Mintage figure includes coins struck through 1974 dated 1969

Date	Mintage	F	VF	XF	Unc	BU
1975	—	—	—	0.20	0.50	0.75

KM# 587.1 5 CENTAVOS

Stainless Steel, 21 mm. **Series:** F.A.O. **Subject:** Zebu **Obv:** Liberty head left **Rev:** Denomination and date to right of Zebu **Edge:** Plain

Date	Mintage	F	VF	XF	Unc	BU
1975	44,500,000	—	—	0.20	0.50	0.75
1976	134,267,000	—	—	0.20	0.50	0.75
1977	85,360	—	—	0.20	0.65	1.00
1978	34,090,000	—	—	0.20	0.65	1.00

KM# 587.2 5 CENTAVOS

Stainless Steel **Obv:** Liberty head left **Rev:** Denomination and date to right of Zebu, "5" over wavy lines

Date	Mintage	F	VF	XF	Unc	BU
1975	Inc. above	—	—	0.20	0.50	0.75
1976	Inc. above	—	—	0.20	0.50	0.75
1977	Inc. above	—	—	0.20	0.50	0.75
1978	Inc. above	—	—	0.20	0.65	1.00

KM# 578.1 10 CENTAVOS

Copper-Nickel **Obv:** Liberty head left **Rev:** Oil refinery, denomination and date at right

Date	Mintage	F	VF	XF	Unc	BU
1967	22,420,000	—	—	0.20	0.50	0.75

KM# 578.1a 10 CENTAVOS

Stainless Steel **Obv:** Liberty head left **Rev:** Oil refinery, denomination and date at right

Date	Mintage	F	VF	XF	Unc	BU
1974	114,598,000	—	—	0.20	0.40	0.60
1975	—	—	—	0.20	0.40	0.60
1976	—	—	—	0.20	0.40	0.60
1977	225,213,000	—	—	0.20	0.40	0.60
1978	225,000,000	—	—	0.20	0.40	0.60
1979	100,000	—	—	0.20	0.50	0.75

KM# 578.2 10 CENTAVOS

Copper-Nickel **Obv:** Liberty head left **Rev:** Oil refinery, denomination and date at right **Note:** Thinner planchet.

Date	Mintage	F	VF	XF	Unc	BU
1970	Est. 134,070,000	—	—	0.20	0.40	0.60

Note: Mintage figure includes coins struck through 1974 dated 1970

KM# 579.1a 20 CENTAVOS

Stainless Steel **Obv:** Liberty head left **Rev:** Denomination above date, oil derrick at left

Date	Mintage	F	VF	XF	Unc	BU
1975	102,367,000	—	—	0.20	0.50	0.75
1976	—	—	—	0.20	0.50	0.75
1977	240,001,000	—	—	0.20	0.50	0.75
1978	255,000,000	—	—	0.20	0.50	0.75
1979	116,000	—	—	0.25	0.65	1.00

KM# 579.1 20 CENTAVOS

Copper-Nickel **Obv:** Liberty head left **Rev:** Denomination above date, oil derrick at left **Note:** Thick planchet

Date	Mintage	F	VF	XF	Unc	BU
1967	123,610,000	—	—	0.20	0.50	0.75
1970	—	—	—	0.40	1.00	1.25

KM# 579.2 20 CENTAVOS

Copper-Nickel **Obv:** Liberty head left **Rev:** Denomination above date, oil derrick at left **Note:** Thinner planchet.

Date	Mintage	F	VF	XF	Unc	BU
1970	Est. 384,894,000	—	—	0.20	0.60	0.85

Note: Mintage figure includes coins struck through 1974 dated 1970

KM# 580 50 CENTAVOS

Nickel **Obv:** Liberty head left **Rev:** Freighter at pier divides date and denomination

Date	Mintage	F	VF	XF	Unc	BU
1967	12,987,000	—	0.25	0.50	1.25	1.50

KM# 580a 50 CENTAVOS

Copper-Nickel **Obv:** Liberty head left **Rev:** Freighter at pier divides date and denomination **Edge:** Reeded **Note:** Varieties of "7" in the date, with serif at top or bottom.

Date	Mintage	F	VF	XF	Unc	BU
1970	503,895,000	—	0.20	0.35	1.00	1.25
1975	—	—	0.20	0.35	1.00	1.25

KM# 580b 50 CENTAVOS

Stainless Steel, 27 mm. **Obv:** Liberty head left **Rev:** Freighter at pier divides denomination and date **Edge:** Plain **Note:** Varieties of "7" in the date, with serif at top or bottom.

Date	Mintage	F	VF	XF	Unc	BU
1975	79,062,000	—	0.20	0.35	1.00	1.25
1976	—	—	0.20	0.35	1.00	1.25
1977	160,019,000	—	0.20	0.35	1.00	1.25
1978	200,000,000	—	0.20	0.35	1.00	1.25
1979	104,000	—	0.25	0.45	1.25	1.50

KM# 581 CRUZEIRO

Nickel **Obv:** Liberty head left **Rev:** Denomination above date, spray at left

Date	Mintage	F	VF	XF	Unc	BU
1970	Est. 48,930,000	—	0.25	0.50	1.00	1.25

Note: Mintage figure includes coins struck through 1972 dated 1970

Date	Mintage	F	VF	XF	Unc	BU
1970 Proof	18,000	Value: 3.50				

KM# 581a CRUZEIRO

Copper-Nickel **Obv:** Liberty head left **Rev:** Denomination above date, spray at left

Date	Mintage	F	VF	XF	Unc	BU
1974	—	—	0.20	0.45	1.00	1.25
1975	21,613,000	—	0.20	0.45	1.00	1.25
1976	—	—	0.20	0.45	1.00	1.25
1977	98,000	—	0.25	0.50	1.25	1.50
1978	77,000	—	0.25	0.50	1.25	1.50

KM# 582 CRUZEIRO

Nickel, 29 mm. **Subject:** 150th Anniversary of Independence **Obv:** Pedro I and General Emilio Garrastazu Medici heads left, date below **Rev:** Map above denomination **Edge Lettering:** SESQUICENTENARIO DA INDEPENDENCIA

Date	Mintage	F	VF	XF	Unc	BU
1972	5,600,000	—	0.40	0.85	1.65	2.00

Note: Lettered edge

Date	Mintage	F	VF	XF	Unc	BU
1972	Inc. above	—	0.40	0.85	1.65	2.00

Note: Plain edge; Coins with plain edge are believed by some to be errors

Date	Mintage	F	VF	XF	Unc	BU
1972 Proof	—	Value: 3.50				

Note: Lettered edge

Date	Mintage	F	VF	XF	Unc	BU
1972 Proof	—	Value: 3.50				

Note: Plain edge; Coins with plain edge are believed by some to be errors

KM# 590 CRUZEIRO

Stainless Steel, 20 mm. **Obv:** Sugar cane **Rev:** Denomination above date, linear design **Edge:** Plain

Date	Mintage	F	VF	XF	Unc	BU
1979	596,000	—	0.15	0.25	0.75	1.00
1980	690,497,000	—	0.15	0.25	0.65	0.85
1981	560,000,000	—	0.15	0.25	0.65	0.85
1982	300,000,000	—	0.15	0.25	0.65	0.85
1983	100,000	—	0.15	0.25	0.75	1.00
1984	62,100,000	—	0.15	0.25	0.65	0.85

KM# 598 CRUZEIRO
3.1000 g., Stainless Steel, 19.9 mm. **Series:** F.A.O. **Obv:** Sugar cane **Rev:** Denomination above date, linear design

Date	Mintage	F	VF	XF	Unc	BU
1985	10,000,000	—	—	0.20	0.50	0.75

KM# 591 5 CRUZEIROS
Stainless Steel, 21.8 mm. **Obv:** Coffee plant **Rev:** Denomination above date, linear design **Edge:** Plain

Date	Mintage	F	VF	XF	Unc	BU
1980	288,200,000	—	0.20	0.35	0.75	1.00
1981	82,000,000	—	0.20	0.35	0.75	1.00
1982	108,000,000	—	0.20	0.35	0.75	1.00
1983	113,400,000	—	0.20	0.35	0.75	1.00
1984	243,000,000	—	0.20	0.35	0.75	1.00

KM# 599 5 CRUZEIROS
4.7000 g., Stainless Steel, 22 mm. **Series:** F.A.O. **Obv:** Coffee plant **Rev:** Denomination above date, linear design

Date	Mintage	F	VF	XF	Unc	BU
1985	10,000,000	—	0.20	0.40	0.85	1.25

KM# 588 10 CRUZEIROS
11.3000 g., 0.8000 Silver .2906 oz. ASW **Subject:** 10th Anniversary of Central Bank **Obv:** Bust of Humberto de Alencar Castelo Branco left **Rev:** Denomination, design at upper right **Note:** Medal rotation.

Date	Mintage	F	VF	XF	Unc	BU
1975	20,000	—	—	—	55.00	65.00

KM# 592.1 10 CRUZEIROS
Stainless Steel, 23.9 mm. **Obv:** Map of Brazil **Rev:** Denomination, value, date, linear design

Date	Mintage	F	VF	XF	Unc	BU
1980	100,010,000	—	—	0.50	0.75	1.00
1981	200,000,000	—	—	0.50	0.75	1.00
1982	331,000,000	—	—	0.50	0.75	1.00
1983	390,000,000	—	—	0.50	0.75	1.00
1984	390,000,000	—	—	0.50	0.75	1.00

KM# 592.2 10 CRUZEIROS
5.0000 g., Stainless Steel, 23.9 mm. **Obv:** Map of Brazil **Rev:** Value, date, linear design **Note:** Reduced weight.

Date	Mintage	F	VF	XF	Unc	BU
1985	201,000,000	—	—	0.50	0.75	1.00
1986	—	—	—	0.50	0.75	1.00

KM# 583 20 CRUZEIROS
18.0000 g., 0.9000 Silver .5208 oz. ASW **Subject:** 150th Anniversary of Independence **Obv:** Pedro I and General Emilio Garrastazu Medici heads left, date below **Rev:** Map above denomination **Edge Lettering:** SESQUICENTENARIO DA INDEPENDENCIA

Date	Mintage	F	VF	XF	Unc	BU
1972(a)	250,000	—	BV	8.00	11.50	13.50

KM# 593.1 20 CRUZEIROS
Stainless Steel, 26 mm. **Obv:** Francis of Assisi Church **Rev:** Denomination above date, linear design **Edge:** Plain

Date	Mintage	F	VF	XF	Unc	BU
1981	88,297,000	—	—	0.25	0.85	1.20
1982	158,200,000	—	—	0.20	0.65	0.85
1983	312,000,000	—	—	0.20	0.65	0.85
1984	226,000,000	—	—	0.20	0.65	0.85

KM# 593.2 20 CRUZEIROS
5.9000 g., Stainless Steel, 26 mm. **Obv:** Francis of Assisi Church **Rev:** Denomination above date, linear design **Edge:** Plain **Note:** Reduced weight.

Date	Mintage	F	VF	XF	Unc	BU
1985	205,000,000	—	—	0.20	0.65	0.85
1986	—	—	—	0.20	0.65	0.85

KM# 594.1 50 CRUZEIROS
Stainless Steel **Obv:** Map of Brasilia **Rev:** Denomination above date, linear design **Edge:** Plain

Date	Mintage	F	VF	XF	Unc	BU
1981	57,000,000	—	—	0.35	1.00	1.50
1982	134,000,000	—	—	0.20	0.65	0.85
1983	181,800,000	—	—	0.20	0.65	0.85
1984	292,418,000	—	—	0.20	0.65	0.85

KM# 594.2 50 CRUZEIROS
7.5000 g., Stainless Steel, 27.9 mm. **Obv:** Map **Rev:** Denomination above date, linear design **Note:** Reduced weight.

Date	Mintage	F	VF	XF	Unc	BU
1985	180,000,000	—	—	0.20	0.65	0.85
1986	—	—	—	0.20	0.65	0.85

KM# 595 100 CRUZEIROS
2.2000 g., Stainless Steel, 16.95 mm. **Obv:** National arms **Rev:** Denomination above date

Date	Mintage	F	VF	XF	Unc	BU
1985	162,000,000	—	—	0.20	0.40	0.65
1986	—	—	—	0.20	0.40	0.65

KM# 596 200 CRUZEIROS
2.7000 g., Stainless Steel, 18.9 mm. **Obv:** National arms **Rev:** Denomination above date

Date	Mintage	F	VF	XF	Unc	BU
1985	55,000,000	—	—	0.25	0.50	0.75
1986	—	—	—	0.25	0.50	0.75

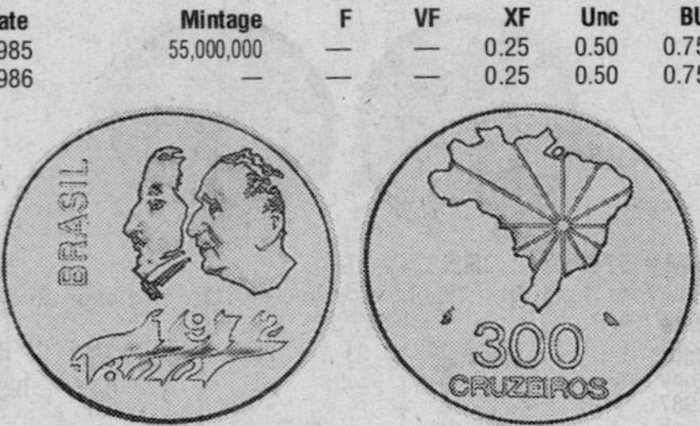

KM# 584 300 CRUZEIROS
16.6500 g., 0.9200 Gold .4925 oz. AGW **Subject:** 150th Anniversary of Independence **Obv:** Pedro I and general Emilio Garrastazu Medici heads left, date below **Rev:** Denomination below map **Edge Lettering:** SESQUICENTENARIO DA INDEPENDENCIA

Date	Mintage	F	VF	XF	Unc	BU
1972(a)	30,000	—	—	—	335	350

KM# 597 500 CRUZEIROS
3.7000 g., Stainless Steel, 20.95 mm. **Obv:** National arms **Rev:** Denomination above date

Date	Mintage	F	VF	XF	Unc	BU
1985	74,000,000	—	—	0.35	1.00	1.25
1986	—	—	—	0.35	1.00	1.25

REFORM COINAGE

1986-1989

1000 Cruzeiros Novos = 1 Cruzado; 100 Centavos = 1 Cruzado

KM# 600 CENTAVO
Stainless Steel **Obv:** National arms **Rev:** Denomination above date

Date	Mintage	F	VF	XF	Unc	BU
1986	100,000,000	—	—	—	0.15	0.25
1987	1,000,000	—	—	—	0.20	0.35
1988	1,000,000	—	—	—	0.20	0.35

KM# 601 5 CENTAVOS
Stainless Steel **Obv:** National arms **Rev:** Denomination above date

Date	Mintage	F	VF	XF	Unc	BU
1986	99,282,000	—	—	—	0.15	0.25
1987	1,000,000	—	—	—	0.20	0.35
1988	1,000,000	—	—	—	0.20	0.35

KM# 602 10 CENTAVOS
Stainless Steel **Obv:** National arms **Rev:** Denomination above date

Date	Mintage	F	VF	XF	Unc	BU
1986	200,000,000	—	—	—	0.15	0.25
1987	245,628,000	—	—	—	0.15	0.25
1988	21,293,000	—	—	—	0.20	0.35

KM# 603 20 CENTAVOS
Stainless Steel **Obv:** National arms **Rev:** Denomination above date

Date	Mintage	F	VF	XF	Unc	BU
1986	140,000,000	—	—	—	0.20	0.30
1987	157,500,000	—	—	—	0.20	0.30
1988	16,000,000	—	—	—	0.25	0.40

KM# 604 50 CENTAVOS
Stainless Steel **Obv:** National arms **Rev:** Denomination above date

Date	Mintage	F	VF	XF	Unc	BU
1986	200,000,000	—	—	—	0.35	0.50
1987	201,884,000	—	—	—	0.35	0.50
1988	131,255,000	—	—	—	0.35	0.50

KM# 605 CRUZADO
Stainless Steel **Obv:** National arms **Rev:** Date divides denomination

Date	Mintage	F	VF	XF	Unc	BU
1986	—	—	—	—	1.00	1.25
1987	383,087,000	—	—	—	0.45	0.65
1988	321,216,000	—	—	—	0.45	0.65

KM# 606 5 CRUZADOS
Stainless Steel, 25 mm. **Obv:** National arms **Rev:** Date divides denomination **Edge:** Plain

Date	Mintage	F	VF	XF	Unc	BU
1986	—	—	—	—	1.50	1.75
1987	141,000,000	—	—	—	0.65	0.85
1988	291,906,000	—	—	—	0.65	0.85

KM# 607 10 CRUZADOS
Stainless Steel **Obv:** National arms **Rev:** Date divides denomination

Date	Mintage	F	VF	XF	Unc	BU
1987	131,500,000	—	—	—	1.75	2.00
1988	457,977,000	—	—	—	0.85	1.00

KM# 608 100 CRUZADOS
Stainless Steel **Subject:** Abolition of Slavery Centennial - Male **Obv:** Denomination **Rev:** Outline divides dates on left from head on right

Date	Mintage	F	VF	XF	Unc	BU
ND	200,000	—	—	1.00	3.00	3.50

KM# 609 100 CRUZADOS
Stainless Steel **Subject:** Abolition of Slavery Centennial - Female **Obv:** Denomination **Rev:** Outline divides dates on left from head on right

Date	Mintage	F	VF	XF	Unc	BU
ND	200,000	—	—	1.00	3.00	3.50

KM# 610 100 CRUZADOS
Stainless Steel **Subject:** Abolition of Slavery Centennial - Child **Obv:** Denomination **Rev:** Outline divides dates on left from head on right

Date	Mintage	F	VF	XF	Unc	BU
ND	200,000	—	—	1.00	3.00	3.50

REFORM COINAGE

1989-1990

1000 Old Cruzados = 1 Cruzado Novo

KM# 611 CENTAVO
Stainless Steel **Obv:** Outlined denomination **Rev:** Farmer, date divides cows at bottom

Date	Mintage	F	VF	XF	Unc	BU
1989	—	—	—	—	0.35	0.50
1990	—	—	—	—	0.35	0.50

KM# 612 5 CENTAVOS
Stainless Steel **Obv:** Outlined denomination **Rev:** Fisherman, two fish above date at bottom

Date	Mintage	F	VF	XF	Unc	BU
1989	—	—	—	—	0.45	0.60
1990	—	—	—	—	0.45	0.60

KM# 613 10 CENTAVOS
Stainless Steel, 18.3 mm. **Obv:** Outlined denomination **Rev:** Miner, three diamonds above date at bottom **Edge:** Plain

Date	Mintage	F	VF	XF	Unc	BU
1989	—	—	—	—	0.60	0.75
1990	—	—	—	—	0.60	0.75

KM# 614 50 CENTAVOS
Stainless Steel **Obv:** Outlined denomination **Rev:** Figure above design, date at bottom

Date	Mintage	F	VF	XF	Unc	BU
1989	—	—	—	—	1.25	1.50
1990	—	—	—	—	1.25	1.50

KM# 615 NOVO CRUZADO
Stainless Steel **Subject:** Centennial of the Republic **Obv:** Denomination **Rev:** Laureate liberty bust 3/4 left divides dates

Date	Mintage	F	VF	XF	Unc	BU
ND(1989)	—	—	—	—	2.00	2.50

KM# 616 200 NOVOS CRUZADOS
13.4700 g., 0.9990 Silver .4331 oz. ASW **Subject:** Centennial of the Republic **Obv:** Denomination **Rev:** Laureate liberty bust 3/4 left divides dates

Date	Mintage	F	VF	XF	Unc	BU
ND(1989) Proof	30,000	Value: 35.00				
ND (1989) Proof	30,000	Value: 35.00				

REFORM COINAGE

1990-1993

100 Centavos = 1 Cruzeiro; 1 Cruzado Novo = 1 Cruzeiro

KM# 617 CRUZEIRO
Stainless Steel **Obv:** Outlined denomination **Rev:** Date lower right of design

Date	Mintage	F	VF	XF	Unc	BU
1990	—	—	—	—	0.35	0.50

KM# 618.1 5 CRUZEIROS
Stainless Steel, 21.5 mm. **Obv:** Outlined denomination **Rev:** Laborer, date at bottom **Edge:** Plain

Date	Mintage	F	VF	XF	Unc	BU
1990	—	—	—	—	0.45	0.60

KM# 618.2 5 CRUZEIROS
Stainless Steel, 21.5 mm. **Obv:** Outlined denomination **Rev:** Laborer at top, small village above date at bottom **Edge:** Plain **Note:** Thinner planchet.

Date	Mintage	F	VF	XF	Unc	BU
1991	—	—	—	—	0.45	0.60
1992	—	—	—	—	0.45	0.60

KM# 619.1 10 CRUZEIROS
Stainless Steel **Obv:** Outlined denomination **Rev:** Laborer at top, small village above date at bottom

Date	Mintage	F	VF	XF	Unc	BU
1990	—	—	—	—	0.50	0.75

KM# 619.2 10 CRUZEIROS
Stainless Steel **Note:** Thinner planchet.

Date	Mintage	F	VF	XF	Unc	BU
1991	—	—	—	—	0.50	0.75
1992	—	—	—	—	0.50	0.75

KM# 620.1 50 CRUZEIROS
Stainless Steel, 23.5 mm. **Obv:** Outlined denomination **Rev:** Farmer, fish above date below

Date	Mintage	F	VF	XF	Unc	BU
1990	—	—	—	—	0.65	0.85

KM# 620.2 50 CRUZEIROS
Stainless Steel, 23.5 mm. **Obv:** Outlined denomination **Rev:** Farmer, fish above date below **Edge:** Plain **Note:** Thinner planchet.

Date	Mintage	F	VF	XF	Unc	BU
1991	—	—	—	—	0.60	0.80
1992	—	—	—	—	0.60	0.80

KM# 623 100 CRUZEIROS
Stainless Steel, 18 mm. **Obv:** Date left of denomination **Rev:** Manatee **Edge:** Plain

Date	Mintage	F	VF	XF	Unc	BU
1992	—	—	—	—	1.50	2.50
1993	—	—	—	—	1.50	2.50

KM# 621 500 CRUZEIROS
27.0000 g., 0.9250 Silver .8029 oz. ASW **Obv:** National arms at center, denomination below, 13 sets of arms surround **Rev:** Ibero - American Series, two dates at bottom

Date	Mintage	F	VF	XF	Unc	BU
1991 Proof	40,025	Value: 60.00				

KM# 624 500 CRUZEIROS
Stainless Steel **Obv:** Date left of denomination **Rev:** Loggerhead Sea Turtle

Date	Mintage	F	VF	XF	Unc	BU
1992	—	—	—	—	1.50	2.50
1993	—	—	—	—	1.50	2.50

KM# 626 1000 CRUZEIROS
Stainless Steel, 20 mm. **Obv:** Date to left of denomination **Rev:** Fish - Acara **Edge:** Plain

Date	Mintage	F	VF	XF	Unc	BU
1992	—	—	—	—	1.50	2.50
1993	—	—	—	—	1.50	2.50

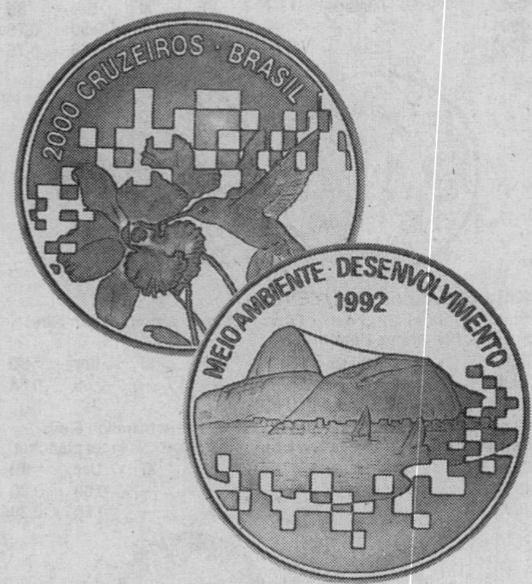

KM# 622 2000 CRUZEIROS
28.2000 g., 0.9250 Silver .7977 oz. ASW **Subject:** U.N. Conference on Environment and Development **Obv:** Hummingbird and flower, denomination above **Rev:** Ocean and mountains, date above

Date	Mintage	F	VF	XF	Unc	BU
1992 Proof	30,000	Value: 55.00				

KM# 625 5000 CRUZEIROS
Stainless Steel **Subject:** 200th Anniversary of Tiradentes' Death **Obv:** Denomination **Rev:** Bust left, two dates below

Date	Mintage	F	VF	XF	Unc	BU
ND	—	—	—	—	2.50	3.50

REFORM COINAGE

1993-1994

1000 Cruzeiros = 1 Cruzeiro Real

KM# 627 5 CRUZEIROS REAIS
Stainless Steel **Obv:** Date to left of denomination **Rev:** Macaw Parrots - Arara, left **Edge:** Plain

Date	Mintage	F	VF	XF	Unc	BU
1993	—	—	—	—	1.50	2.50
1994	—	—	—	—	1.50	2.50

KM# 628 10 CRUZEIROS REAL
Stainless Steel, 22 mm. **Obv:** Date to left of denomination **Rev:** Anteater - Tamandua, right **Edge:** Plain

Date	Mintage	F	VF	XF	Unc	BU
1993	—	—	—	—	1.50	2.50
1994	—	—	—	—	1.50	2.50

KM# 629 50 CRUZEIROS REAIS
Stainless Steel **Obv:** Date to left of denomination **Rev:** Mother jaguar and cub facing **Edge:** Plain

Date	Mintage	F	VF	XF	Unc	BU
1993	—	—	—	—	1.75	3.00
1994	—	—	—	—	1.75	3.00

KM# 630 100 CRUZEIROS REAIS
Stainless Steel **Obv:** Date to left of denomination **Rev:** Maned wolf right **Edge:** Plain

Date	Mintage	F	VF	XF	Unc	BU
1993	—	—	—	—	1.75	3.00
1994	—	—	—	—	1.75	3.00

REFORM COINAGE

1994-present

2750 Cruzeiros Reais = 1 Real; 100 Centavos = 1 Real

KM# 631 CENTAVO
Stainless Steel, 20 mm. **Obv:** Laureate liberty head left, linear design **Rev:** Denomination above date **Edge:** Plain

Date	Mintage	F	VF	XF	Unc	BU
1994	—	—	—	—	0.35	0.50
1995	—	—	—	—	0.35	0.50
1996	—	—	—	—	0.35	0.50
1997	—	—	—	—	0.35	0.50

KM# 647 CENTAVO
Copper Plated Steel, 17 mm. **Obv:** Cabral bust at right **Rev:** Denomination on linear design at left, 3/4 globe with sash on right, date below **Edge:** Plain

Date	Mintage	F	VF	XF	Unc	BU
1998	—	—	—	—	0.35	0.50
1999	—	—	—	—	0.10	0.20
2000	—	—	—	—	0.10	0.20

KM# 632 5 CENTAVOS
Stainless Steel, 21 mm. **Obv:** Laureate liberty head left, linear design **Rev:** Denomination above date **Edge:** Plain

Date	Mintage	F	VF	XF	Unc	BU
1994	—	—	—	—	0.45	0.65
1995	—	—	—	—	0.45	0.65
1996	—	—	—	—	0.45	0.65
1997	—	—	—	—	0.45	0.65

KM# 648 5 CENTAVOS
4.0500 g., Copper Plated Steel, 22 mm. **Obv:** Tiradente bust at right, dove at left **Rev:** Denomination on linear design at left, 3/4 globe with sash on right, date below **Edge:** Plain

Date	Mintage	F	VF	XF	Unc	BU
1998	—	—	—	—	0.45	0.65
1999	—	—	—	—	0.45	0.65
2000	—	—	—	—	0.45	0.65

KM# 633 10 CENTAVOS
Stainless Steel, 22 mm. **Obv:** Laureate liberty head, left, lined background **Rev:** Denomiation above date **Edge:** Plain

Date	Mintage	F	VF	XF	Unc	BU
1994	—	—	—	—	0.60	0.80
1995	—	—	—	—	0.60	0.80
1996	—	—	—	—	0.60	0.80
1997	—	—	—	—	0.60	0.80

KM# 641 10 CENTAVOS
Stainless Steel **Series:** F.A.O. **Obv:** Hands holding seedling **Rev:** Denomination above date

Date	Mintage	F	VF	XF	Unc	BU
1995	1,000,000	—	—	—	0.65	0.85

KM# 649.1 10 CENTAVOS
Brass Plated Steel, 20 mm. **Subject:** Pedro I **Obv:** Bust of Pedro, horseman with sword in left hand **Rev:** Denomination **Edge:** Plain **Note:** Majority of mintage recalled and melted.

Date	Mintage	F	VF	XF	Unc	BU
1997	—	—	—	—	—	—
1998	—	—	—	—	—	—

KM# 649.2 10 CENTAVOS

Brass Plated Steel, 20 mm. **Obv:** Bust of Pedro at right, horseman with sword in right hand at left **Rev:** Denomination on linear design at left, 3/4 globe with sash on right, date below **Edge:** Plain

Date	Mintage	F	VF	XF	Unc	BU
1998	—	—	—	—	0.60	0.80
1999	—	—	—	—	0.60	0.80
2000	—	—	—	—	0.60	0.80

KM# 634 25 CENTAVOS

Stainless Steel, 23.5 mm. **Obv:** Stylized laureate liberty head left, date below **Rev:** Outlined denomination, linear design **Edge:** Plain

Date	Mintage	F	VF	XF	Unc	BU
1994	—	—	—	—	0.75	1.00
1995	—	—	—	—	0.75	1.00

KM# 642 25 CENTAVOS

Stainless Steel **Series:** F.A.O. **Obv:** Farmer working **Rev:** Outlined denomination, linear design

Date	Mintage	F	VF	XF	Unc	BU
1995	1,000,000	—	—	—	0.80	1.20

KM# 650 25 CENTAVOS

Brass Plated Steel, 25 mm. **Obv:** Deodoro bust at right, national arms at left **Rev:** Denomination on linear design at left, 3/4 globe with sash on right, date below **Edge:** Reeded

Date	Mintage	F	VF	XF	Unc	BU
1998	—	—	—	—	0.75	1.00
1999	—	—	—	—	0.75	1.00
2000	—	—	—	—	0.75	1.00

KM# 635 50 CENTAVOS

Stainless Steel, 23 mm. **Obv:** Laureate liberty head left, linear design **Rev:** Denomination above date **Edge:** Plain

Date	Mintage	F	VF	XF	Unc	BU
1994	—	—	—	—	1.25	1.50
1995	—	—	—	—	1.25	1.50

KM# 651 50 CENTAVOS

Copper-Nickel, 23 mm. **Obv:** Rio Branco bust at right, map at left **Rev:** Denomination on linear design at left, 3/4 globe with sash on right, date below **Edge Lettering:** BRASIL ORDEM E PROGRESSO

Date	Mintage	F	VF	XF	Unc	BU
1998	—	—	—	—	1.25	1.50
1999	—	—	—	—	1.25	1.50

Date	Mintage	F	VF	XF	Unc	BU
1999 Proof	2,000	—	—	—	—	—
2000	—	—	—	—	1.25	1.50

KM# 636 REAL

Stainless Steel, 24 mm. **Obv:** Laureate liberty head left, linear design

Date	Mintage	F	VF	XF	Unc	BU
1994	—	—	—	—	2.50	2.75

KM# 652 REAL

Bi-Metallic Copper-Nickel center in Brass ring, 27 mm. **Obv:** Allegorical portrait left **Rev:** Denomination on linear design at left, 3/4 globe with sash on right, date below **Edge:** Segmented reeding **Note:** Total coin weight 7.8 grams.

Date	Mintage	F	VF	XF	Unc	BU
1998	—	—	—	—	2.75	3.50
1999	—	—	—	—	2.75	3.50
2000	—	—	—	—	3.00	4.50

KM# 653 REAL

Bi-Metallic Copper-Nickel center in Brass ring, 27 mm. **Subject:** Universal Declaration of Human Rights **Obv:** Globe **Rev:** Denomination left, globe with sash at right, date below, linear design

Date	Mintage	F	VF	XF	Unc	BU
1998	600,000	—	—	—	2.75	4.00

KM# 637 2 REAIS

27.0000 g., 0.9250 Silver .8029 oz. ASW **Subject:** 300th Anniversary - First Brazilian Mint **Obv:** Denomination to right of date, design in background **Rev:** 300th Anniversary year below inscription

Date	Mintage	F	VF	XF	Unc	BU
1994 Proof	7,000	Value: 65.00				

KM# 643 2 REAIS

27.0000 g., 0.9250 Silver .8029 oz. ASW **Subject:** Ayrton Senna - Race Driver

Date	Mintage	F	VF	XF	Unc	BU
1995 Proof	10,000	Value: 75.00				

KM# 640 3 REAIS

11.5000 g., 0.9250 Silver .3420 oz. ASW **Subject:** 30th Anniversary - Central Bank **Obv:** Bank logo **Rev:** Denomination, linear design

Date	Mintage	F	VF	XF	Unc	BU
ND Proof	Est. 5,000	Value: 40.00				

KM# 645 3 REAIS

11.5000 g., 0.9250 Silver .3420 oz. ASW **Subject:** Centennial of Belo Horizonte **Obv:** Denomination, date lower right **Rev:** Collage, name, dates

Date	Mintage	F	VF	XF	Unc	BU
1997 Proof	Est. 20,000	Value: 40.00				

KM# 638 4 REAIS

27.0000 g., 0.9250 Silver .8030 oz. ASW **Subject:** World Cup Soccer **Obv:** Hands lofting trophy divides date at bottom **Rev:** Denomination, background is soccer net

Date	Mintage	F	VF	XF	Unc	BU
1994 Proof	Est. 9,000	Value: 75.00				

KM# 654 5 REAIS

28.0000 g., 0.9990 Silver .8993 oz. ASW, 40 mm. **Subject:** 500 Years - Discovery of Brazil **Obv:** Partial compass face and feathers, anniversary inscription and dates at left **Rev:** Figure at left, ship at right, partial compass face and feathers at lower right **Edge:** Reeded

Date	Mintage	F	VF	XF	Unc	BU
ND(2000) Proof	20,000	Value: 65.00				

KM# 639 20 REAIS

8.0000 g., 0.9000 Gold .2315 oz. AGW **Subject:** World Cup Soccer **Obv:** Hand held trophy **Rev:** Denomination in net

Date	Mintage	F	VF	XF	Unc	BU
1994 Proof	Est. 2,000	Value: 245				

KM# 644 20 REAIS

8.0000 g., 0.9000 Gold .2315 oz. AGW **Subject:** Ayrton Senna - Race Driver

Date	Mintage	F	VF	XF	Unc	BU
1995 Proof	5,000	Value: 245				

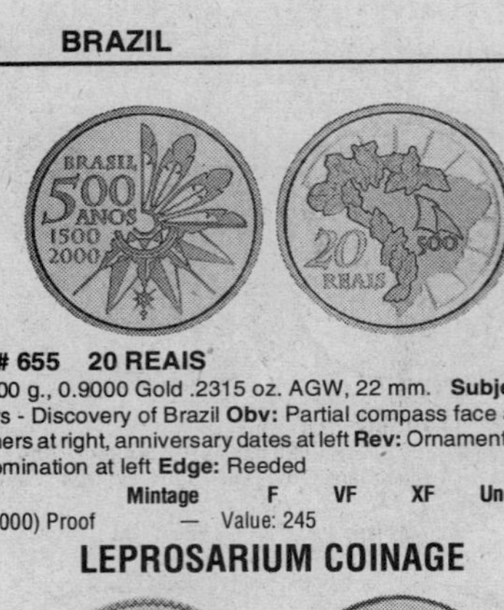

KM# 655 20 REAIS
8.0000 g., 0.9000 Gold .2315 oz. AGW, 22 mm. **Subject:** 500 Years - Discovery of Brazil **Obv:** Partial compass face and feathers at right, anniversary dates at left **Rev:** Ornamented map, denomination at left **Edge:** Reeded

Date	Mintage	F	VF	XF	Unc	BU
ND(2000) Proof	—	Value: 245				

LEPROSARIUM COINAGE

KM# L1 100 REIS
Brass **Issuer:** Colonia Santa Teresa **Obv:** Denomination **Rev:** C.S.I.

Date	Mintage	F	VF	XF	Unc	BU
ND(ca.1940)	—	—	—	150	250	350

KM# L2 200 REIS
Brass **Issuer:** Colonia Santa Teresa **Obv:** Denomination **Rev:** C.S.I.

Date	Mintage	F	VF	XF	Unc	BU
ND(ca.1940)	—	—	—	200	300	400

KM# L3 300 REIS
Brass **Issuer:** Colonia Santa Teresa **Obv:** Denomination **Rev:** C.S.I.

Date	Mintage	F	VF	XF	Unc	BU
ND(ca.1940)	—	—	—	250	350	450

KM# L4 500 REIS
Brass **Issuer:** Colonia Santa Teresa **Obv:** Denomination **Rev:** C.S.I.

Date	Mintage	F	VF	XF	Unc	BU
ND(ca.1940)	—	—	—	300	400	500

KM# L5 1000 REIS
Brass **Issuer:** Colonia Santa Teresa **Obv:** Denomination **Rev:** C.S.I.

Date	Mintage	F	VF	XF	Unc	BU
ND(ca.1940)	—	—	—	350	450	550

KM# L6 1.00 REIS
Brass **Issuer:** Santa Casa de Misericordia

Date	Mintage	F	VF	XF	Unc	BU
ND(ca.1920) Rare	—	—	—	—	—	—

KM# L7 2.00 REIS
Brass **Issuer:** Santa Casa de Misericordia **Obv:** Issuer name **Rev:** Denomination within circle

Date	Mintage	F	VF	XF	Unc	BU
ND(ca.1920)	—	—	250	450	—	—

KM# L8 5.00 REIS
Brass **Issuer:** Santa Casa de Misericordia

Date	Mintage	F	VF	XF	Unc	BU
ND(ca.1920) Rare	—	—	—	—	—	—

KM# L9 1.000 REIS
Brass **Issuer:** Santa Casa de Misericordia

Date	Mintage	F	VF	XF	Unc	BU
ND(ca.1920) Rare	—	—	—	—	—	—

KM# L10 5.000 REIS
Brass **Issuer:** Santa Casa de Misericordia

Date	Mintage	F	VF	XF	Unc	BU
ND(ca.1920)	—	—	550	750	—	—

PATTERNS

Including off metal strikes

KM#	Date	Mintage	Identification	Mkt Val
Pn179	1901	—	100 Reis. Nickel-Silver.	185
Pn180	1901	—	100 Reis. Nickel. Birmingham Mint	185
Pn181	1901	—	100 Reis. Nickel. Hamburg Mint	185
Pn182	1901	—	100 Reis. Silver.	285
Pn183	1901	—	100 Reis. Gold.	1,200
Pn184	1901	—	200 Reis. Nickel-Silver.	235
Pn185	1901	—	200 Reis. Nickel. Birmingham Mint	235
Pn186	1901	—	200 Reis. Nickel. Hamburg Mint	235
Pn187	1901	—	200 Reis. Silver.	300
Pn188	1901	—	200 Reis. Gold.	1,950
Pn189	1901	—	400 Reis. Nickel-Silver.	235
Pn190	1901	—	400 Reis. Nickel. Birmingham Mint	235
Pn191	1901	—	400 Reis. Nickel. Hamburg Mint	235
Pn192	1901	—	400 Reis. Silver.	600
Pn193	1901	—	400 Reis. Gold.	2,850
Pn194	1902	—	100 Reis. Nickel. MCMI. 1902.	375
Pn195	1907	—	100 Reis. Silver.	400
Pn196	1907	—	200 Reis. Silver.	600
Pn197	1907	—	500 Reis. Silver.	400
Pn198	1907	—	1000 Reis. Silver.	400
Pn199	1907	—	2000 Reis. Silver.	400
Pn200	1908	—	50 Reis. Silver.	400
Pn201	1908	—	500 Reis. Silver.	400
Pn202	1908	—	1000 Reis. Silver.	400
Pn203	1908	—	2000 Reis. Silver.	400
Pn204	1910	—	40 Reis. Silver.	400
Pn205	1910	—	1000 Reis. Silver.	400
Pn206	1910	—	2000 Reis. Silver.	450
Pn207	1912	—	2000 Reis. Copper.	325
Pn208	1913	—	1000 Reis. Copper.	325
Pn209	1914	—	50 Reis. Silver.	350
Pn210	1914	—	400 Reis. Nickel.	325
Pn211	1914	—	2000 Reis. Silver.	800
Pn212	1916	—	20 Reis. Silver.	300
Pn213	1916	—	200 Reis. Nickel.	285
Pn214	1916	—	200 Reis. Silver.	500
Pn215	1916	—	2000 Reis. Silver.	800
Pn216	1917	—	50 Reis. Nickel.	325
Pn217	1917	—	100 Reis. Nickel.	325
Pn218	1917	—	200 Reis. Nickel.	325
Pn219	1917	—	400 Reis. Nickel.	325
Pn220	1917	—	500 Reis. Nickel.	375
Pn221	1917	—	1000 Reis. Nickel.	325
Pn222	1917	—	2000 Reis. Nickel.	325
Pn223	1918	—	20 Reis. Nickel.	235
Pn224	1918	—	20 Reis. Nickel. Large planchet.	185
Pn225	1918	—	20 Reis. Silver.	350
Pn226	1918	—	2000 Reis. Nickel. Center hole.	285
Pn227	1921	—	1000 Reis.	200
Pn228	1921	—	2000 Reis.	400
Pn229	1921	—	10000 Reis. Gold.	1,100
Pn230	1921	—	20000 Reis. Gold.	1,100
Pn231	1922	—	50 Reis. Copper-Nickel.	285
Pn232	1922	—	50 Reis. Nickel-Silver.	185
Pn233	1922	—	500 Reis. Aluminum-Bronze.	185
Pn234	1922	—	500 Reis. Silver. Large planchet.	200
Pn235	1922	—	1000 Reis. Aluminum-Bronze.	185
Pn236	1922	—	2000 Reis. Silver.	300
Pn237	1922	—	2000 Reis. Silver.	275
Pn238	ND	—	2000 Reis. Silver.	275
Pn239	1922	—	2000 Reis. Silver.	275
Pn240	1922	—	2000 Reis. 0.6500 Silver.	275
Pn241	1922	—	2000 Reis. 0.8350 Silver.	275
Pn242	1922	—	2000 Reis. 0.9000 Silver.	275
Pn243	1923	—	1000 Reis. Silver.	400
Pn244	1923	—	2000 Reis. Silver.	285
Pn245	1923	—	2000 Reis. Silver.	285
Pn246	1923	—	2000 Reis. Silver.	285
Pn247	1923	—	2000 Reis. Silver.	285
Pn248	1923	—	2000 Reis. Silver.	285
Pn249	1923	—	2000 Reis. Silver.	285
Pn250	1924	—	100 Reis. Nickel.	185
Pn251	1924	—	400 Reis. Nickel.	185
Pn252	1924	—	500 Reis. Nickel.	185
Pn253	1924	—	500 Reis. Silver.	200
Pn254	1924	—	1000 Reis. Silver.	200
Pn255	1924	—	1000 Reis. Silver.	200
Pn256	1924	—	1000 Reis. Silver.	100
Pn257	1924	—	1000 Reis. Silver.	100
Pn258	1927	—	Cruzeiro. Copper.	185
Pn259	1927	—	Cruzeiro. Silver.	250
Pn260	1927	—	Cruzeiro. Gold.	285
Pn261	1927	—	2 Cruzeiros. Gold.	300
Pn262	1928	—	Cruzeiro. Nickel.	235
Pn263	1928	—	2 Cruzeiros. Nickel.	235
Pn264	1928	—	4 Cruzeiros. Nickel.	235
Pn265	1928	—	5 Cruzeiros. Nickel.	235
Pn266	1928	—	10 Cruzeiros. Nickel.	375
Pn267	1931	—	10 Reis. Silver.	185
Pn268	1932	—	100 Reis. Nickel-Silver. St. Vincent.	185
Pn269	1932	—	100 Reis. Silver. St. Vincent.	400
Pn270	1932	—	200 Reis. Nickel-Silver.	235
Pn271	1932	—	200 Reis. Copper-Nickel. St. Vincent.	235
Pn272	1932	—	200 Reis. Silver. St. Vincent.	250
Pn273	1932	—	400 Reis. Nickel-Silver.	265
Pn274	1932	—	400 Reis. Silver. St. Vincent.	285
Pn275	1932	—	500 Reis. Copper. Large planchet.	265
Pn276	1932	—	1000 Reis. Copper. St. Vincent.	285
Pn277	1932	—	1000 Reis. Aluminum-Bronze. Arms.	285
Pn278	1932	—	1000 Reis. Silver.	300
Pn279	1932	—	1000 Reis. Silver. Large planchet.	400
Pn280	1932	—	2000 Reis. Silver. St. Vincent.	285
Pn281	1935	—	200 Reis. Nickel. Large planchet.	185
Pn282	1935	—	400 Reis. Silver.	200
Pn283	1935	—	500 Reis. Nickel. 3.8500 g.	375
Pn284	1935	—	500 Reis. Nickel-Silver. 6.0000 g.	375
Pn285	1935	—	1000 Reis. Copper.	185
Pn286	1935	—	1000 Reis. Nickel.	185
Pn287	1935	—	1000 Reis. Nickel-Silver.	375
Pn288	1935	—	1000 Reis. Silver.	400
Pn289	1935	—	2000 Reis. Zinc.	285
Pn290	1935	—	2000 Reis. Bronze.	265
Pn291	1935	—	2000 Reis. Copper.	265
Pn292	1935	—	2000 Reis. Nickel-Silver.	375
Pn293	1935	—	2000 Reis. Silver.	350
Pn294	1936	—	100 Reis. Nickel-Silver.	185
Pn295	1936	—	100 Reis. Silver.	350
Pn296	1936	—	200 Reis. Nickel-Silver.	90.00
Pn297	1936	—	200 Reis. Silver.	100
Pn298	1936	—	300 Reis. Nickel-Silver.	90.00
Pn299	1936	—	400 Reis. Nickel-Silver.	90.00
Pn300	1936	—	400 Reis. Silver.	100
Pn301	1936	—	500 Reis. Nickel-Silver.	90.00
Pn302	1936	—	500 Reis. Silver.	100
Pn303	1936	—	1000 Reis. Nickel-Silver.	90.00
Pn304	1936	—	1000 Reis. Silver.	100
Pn305	1936	—	2000 Reis. Nickel-Silver.	90.00
Pn306	1936	—	5000 Reis. Zinc.	90.00
Pn307	1936	—	5000 Reis. Nickel-Silver.	90.00
Pn308	1936	—	5000 Reis. Silver.	100
Pn309	1937	—	100 Reis. Nickel.	90.00
Pn310	1937	—	300 Reis. Nickel-Silver.	90.00
Pn311	1937	—	300 Reis. Nickel.	90.00
Pn312	1938	—	200 Reis. Nickel.	90.00
Pn313	1938	—	2000 Reis. Copper.	90.00
Pn314	1939	—	500 Reis. Nickel.	90.00
Pn315	1939	—	1000 Reis.	90.00
Pn316	1939	—	2000 Reis. Aluminum-Bronze.	90.00
Pn317	1939	—	2000 Reis. Aluminum-Bronze. Peixoto.	90.00
Pn318	1940	—	10 Centavos. Silver.	90.00
Pn319	1940	—	100 Reis. Copper-Nickel.	90.00
Pn320	1940	—	100 Reis. Nickel.	90.00
Pn321	1940	—	200 Reis. Copper-Nickel.	90.00
Pn322	1940	—	200 Reis. Nickel.	90.00
Pn323	1940	—	300 Reis. Copper-Nickel.	90.00
Pn324	1940	—	300 Reis. Nickel.	90.00
Pn325	1940	—	400 Reis. Copper-Nickel.	90.00
Pn326	1940	—	400 Reis. Nickel.	90.00
Pn327	1941	—	10 Centavos. Nickel.	90.00
Pn328	1941	—	10 Centavos. Nickel-Silver.	90.00
Pn329	1941	—	50 Centavos. Brass.	90.00
Pn330	1941	—	50 Centavos. Nickel.	90.00
Pn331	1941	—	50 Centavos. Nickel-Silver.	90.00
Pn332	1941	—	50 Centavos. Nickel-Silver.	90.00
Pn333	1941	—	50 Centavos. Silver.	90.00
Pn334	1941	—	50 Centavos. Silver.	90.00
Pn335	1941	—	Cruzeiro. Nickel-Silver.	90.00
Pn336	1941	—	2 Cruzeiros. Nickel.	90.00
Pn337	1941	—	2 Cruzeiros. Nickel-Silver.	45.00
Pn338	1941	—	2 Cruzeiros. Silver.	75.00
Pn339	1942	—	100 Reis. Nickel.	45.00
Pn340	1942	—	200 Reis. Nickel.	45.00
Pn341	1942	—	300 Reis. Nickel.	45.00
Pn342	1942	—	400 Reis. Nickel.	45.00
Pn343	1942	—	2 Cruzeiros. Nickel.	45.00
Pn344	1942	—	2 Cruzeiros. Nickel-Silver.	45.00
Pn345	1943	—	10 Centavos. Nickel-Silver.	45.00
Pn346	1943	—	20 Centavos. Nickel-Silver.	45.00
Pn347	1943	—	20 Centavos. Silver.	45.00
Pn348	1943	—	50 Centavos. Nickel-Silver.	45.00
Pn349	1943	—	Cruzeiro. Silver.	50.00
Pn350	1945	—	10 Centavos. Nickel-Silver.	45.00

KM#	Date	Mintage	Identification	Mkt Val
Pn351	1945	—	10 Centavos. Silver.	45.00
Pn352	1945	—	50 Centavos. Nickel-Silver.	45.00
Pn353	1945	—	50 Centavos. Silver.	45.00
Pn354	1945	—	Cruzeiro. Nickel.	45.00
Pn355	1945	—	Cruzeiro. Nickel-Silver.	45.00
Pn356	1947	—	20 Centavos. Aluminum-Bronze.	150
Pn357	1947	—	50 Centavos. Aluminum-Bronze.	150
Pn358	1947	—	2 Cruzeiros. Aluminum-Bronze.	90.00
Pn360	1950	—	Cruzeiro. Silver.	60.00
Pn361	1950	—	Cruzeiro. Gold.	—
Pn362	1955	—	50 Centavos. Aluminum.	45.00
Pn363	1956	—	10 Centavos. Aluminum. Arms.	45.00
Pn364	1956	—	10 Centavos. Aluminum-Bronze. Arms.	45.00
Pn365	1956	—	10 Centavos. Aluminum-Bronze. Bonifacio.	45.00
Pn366	1956	—	20 Centavos. Aluminum-Bronze.	45.00
Pn367	1956	—	50 Centavos. Aluminum.	45.00
Pn368	1956	—	Cruzeiro. Aluminum.	45.00
Pn369	1961	—	2 Cruzeiros. Aluminum-Bronze.	90.00
Pn370	1962	—	5 Cruzeiros.	90.00
Pn371	1963	—	5 Cruzeiros. Aluminum. Map.	90.00
Pn372	1963	—	5 Cruzeiros. Aluminum. Arms.	90.00
Pn373	1963	—	5 Cruzeiros. Aluminum-Bronze. Arms.	90.00
Pn374	1964	—	5 Cruzeiros. Aluminum.	90.00
Pn375	1964	—	10 Cruzeiros. Aluminum.	90.00
Pn376	1964	—	20 Cruzeiros. Aluminum.	90.00
Pn377	1964	—	50 Cruzeiros. Nickel.	90.00
Pn378	1964	—	100 Cruzeiros. Nickel.	90.00
Pn379	1964	—	200 Cruzeiros. Nickel.	90.00
Pn380	1965	—	5 Cruzeiros. Aluminum. Map.	90.00
Pn381	1965	—	5 Cruzeiros. Aluminum. Arms.	90.00
Pn382	1966	—	Centavo. Stainless Steel.	90.00
Pn383	1966	—	2 Centavos. Stainless Steel.	90.00
Pn384	1966	—	5 Centavos. Stainless Steel.	90.00
Pn385	1966	—	5 Centavos. Nickel.	90.00
Pn386	1966	—	10 Centavos. Copper-Nickel.	90.00
Pn387	1966	—	20 Centavos. Copper-Nickel.	90.00
Pn388	1967	—	10 Centavos. Stainless Steel.	90.00
Pn389	1972	—	20 Cruzeiros. 0.9000 Silver. KM#583.	100

PROVAS

KM#	Date	Mintage	Identification	Mkt Val
Pr1	1967	—	Cruzeiro. Nickel. PROVA.	45.00
Pr2	1967	—	Cruzeiro. Nickel. PROVA.	45.00
Pr3	1970	—	20 Centavos. Stainless Steel. KM#579.1.	45.00
Pr4	1970	—	50 Centavos. Stainless Steel.	45.00
Pr5	1972	—	Cruzeiro. Nickel. Y#94.	150
Pr6	1972	—	20 Cruzeiros. Silver. Pedro I and General Emilio Garrastazu Medici heads, left, date below. Denomination below map. KM#583.	50.00
Pr7	1972	—	300 Cruzeiros. Brass. KM#584.	115
Pr8	1972	—	300 Cruzeiros. Gold. KM#584.	400
Pr9	1974	—	10 Centavos. Stainless Steel. KM#578.1a.	45.00
Pr10	1974	—	Cruzeiro. Nickel. KM#581.	45.00
Pr11	1975	—	Centavo. Stainless Steel. KM#585.	45.00
Pr12	1975	—	2 Centavos. Stainless Steel. KM#586.	45.00
Pr13	1975	—	5 Centavos. Stainless Steel. KM#587.1.	45.00
Pr14	1975	—	10 Centavos. Stainless Steel. KM#578.1a.	45.00
Pr15	1975	—	50 Centavos. Stainless Steel. KM#580b.	45.00
Pr16	1975	—	10 Cruzeiros. Silver. KM#588.	75.00
Pr17	1976	—	Centavo. Silver. KM#585.	75.00
Pr18	1976	—	2 Centavos. Stainless Steel. KM#586.	28.00
Pr19	1976	—	5 Centavos. Stainless Steel. KM#587.1.	45.00
Pr20	1980	5,000	Centavo. Steel. KM#589.	28.00
Pr21	1980	5,000	10 Centavos. Steel.	28.00
Pr22	1980	5,000	50 Centavos. Steel.	28.00
Pr23	1980	5,000	Cruzeiro. Steel. KM#590.	28.00
Pr24	1980	5,000	5 Cruzeiros. Steel. KM#591.	28.00
Pr25	1980	5,000	10 Cruzeiros. Steel. KM#592.	28.00
PrA26	1988	—	100 Cruzados. Stainless Steel. KM#608.	45.00
PrB26	1988	—	100 Cruzados. Stainless Steel. KM#609.	45.00
PrC26	1988	—	100 Cruzados. Stainless Steel. KM#610.	45.00
Pr26	1989	—	Centavo. Steel. KM#611.	38.00
Pr27	1989	—	5 Centavos. Steel. KM#612.	38.00
Pr28	1989	—	10 Centavos. Steel. KM#613.	42.00
Pr29	1989	—	50 Centavos. Steel. KM#614.	45.00
Pr30	ND	—	200 Novos Cruzados. 0.9990 Silver. KM#616.	100
Pr31	1990	—	Cruzeiro. Steel. KM#617.	38.00
Pr32	1990	—	5 Cruzeiros. Steel. KM#618.	38.00
Pr33	1990	—	10 Cruzeiros. Steel. KM#619.	42.00
Pr34	1990	—	50 Cruzeiros. Steel. KM#620.	45.00
Pr35	1991	—	500 Cruzeiros. 0.9250 Silver. KM#621.	120
Pr36	1992	—	2000 Cruzeiros. Silver. KM#622.	175
Pr37	ND	—	5000 Cruzeiros. Steel. KM#625.	80.00
Pr38	1994	—	4 Reais. 0.9250 Silver. KM#638.	185

TRIAL STRIKES

KM#	Date	Mintage	Identification	Mkt Val
TS4	1948	—	1000 Cruzeiros. Uniface.	750

MINT SETS

KM#	Date	Mintage	Identification	Issue Price	Mkt Val
MS1	1972 (2)	—	KM#582-583	—	12.50

This area, site of the ancient Mayan civilization, was sighted by Columbus in 1502, and settled by shipwrecked English seamen in 1638. British buccaneers settled the former capital of Belize in the 17th century. Britain claimed administrative right over the area after the emancipation of Central America from Spain. In 1825, Imperial coins were introduced into the colony and were rated against the Spanish dollar and Honduran currency. It was declared a colony subordinate to Jamaica in 1862 and was established as the separate Crown Colony of British Honduras in 1884. In May, 1885 an order in Council authorized coins for the colony, with the first shipment arriving in July. While the Guatemalan peso was originally the standard of value, in 1894 the colony changed to the gold standard, based on the U.S. gold dollar. The anti-British Peoples United Party, which attained power in 1954, won a constitution, effective in 1964 which established self-government under a British appointed governor. British Honduras became Belize on June 1, 1973, following the passage of a surprise bill by the Peoples United Party, but the constitutional relationship with Britain remained unchanged. Full independence was achieved in 1981.

MONETARY SYSTEM
100 Cents = 1 Dollar

MINT MARKS
H - Heaton

BRITISH COLONY

DECIMAL COINAGE

KM# 11 CENT

Bronze **Ruler:** Edward VII **Obv:** Bust of King Edward VII right **Obv. Designer:** G.W. DeSaulles **Rev:** Numeric denomination within circle, denomination and date below

Date	Mintage	F	VF	XF	Unc	BU
1904	50,000	6.00	15.00	50.00	90.00	—
1904 Proof	—	Value: 200				
1904 Matte Proof	—	Value: 1,550				
1906	50,000	12.00	27.50	65.00	225	—
1906 Matte Proof	—	Value: 1,050				
1909	25,000	35.00	80.00	150	300	—

KM# 15 CENT

Bronze **Ruler:** George V **Obv:** Bust of King George V left **Obv. Designer:** E.B. MacKennal **Rev:** Numeric denomination within circle, denomination and date below

Date	Mintage	F	VF	XF	Unc	BU
1911	50,000	60.00	100	200	500	—
1912H	50,000	85.00	160	250	600	—
1913	25,000	100	200	300	700	—

KM# 19 CENT

Bronze **Ruler:** George V **Obv:** Bust of King George V left **Obv. Designer:** E.B. MacKennal **Rev:** Numeric denomination within scalloped circle, denomination and date below

Date	Mintage	F	VF	XF	Unc	BU
1914	175,000	3.00	7.50	25.00	120	—
1916H	125,000	3.50	8.50	27.50	125	—
1918	40,000	7.00	15.00	40.00	150	—
1919	50,000	7.00	15.00	40.00	150	—
1924	50,000	7.00	15.00	40.00	125	—
1924 Proof	—	Value: 250				
1926	50,000	5.00	12.00	35.00	125	—
1926 Proof	—	Value: 225				
1936	40,000	2.00	5.00	20.00	65.00	—
1936 Proof	50	Value: 170				

KM# 21 CENT

Bronze **Ruler:** George VI **Obv:** Bust of King George VI left **Obv. Designer:** Percy Metcalf **Rev:** Numeric denomination within scalloped circle, denomination and date below

Date	Mintage	F	VF	XF	Unc	BU
1937	80,000	0.75	4.00	12.00	75.00	—
1937 Proof	—	Value: 170				
1939	50,000	2.00	7.00	20.00	150	—
1939 Proof	—	Value: 100				
1942	50,000	2.00	7.00	20.00	150	—
1942 Proof	—	Value: 125				
1943	100,000	1.00	5.00	15.00	125	—
1943 Proof	—	Value: 150				
1944	100,000	2.00	7.00	20.00	150	—
1944 Proof	—	Value: 200				
1945	130,000	0.75	2.00	7.50	50.00	—
1945 Proof	—	Value: 120				
1947	100,000	0.75	2.50	10.00	70.00	—
1947 Proof	—	Value: 150				

KM# 24 CENT

Bronze **Ruler:** George VI **Obv:** Bust of King George VI left **Obv. Legend:** Without EMPEROR OF INDIA **Obv. Designer:** Percy Metcalf **Rev:** Numeric denomination within scalloped circle, denomination and date below

Date	Mintage	F	VF	XF	Unc	BU
1949	100,000	0.60	1.50	4.00	16.50	—
1949 Proof	—	Value: 135				
1950	100,000	0.40	1.00	2.50	6.50	—
1950 Proof	—	Value: 135				
1951	100,000	0.60	1.50	4.00	16.50	—
1951 Proof	—	Value: 135				

KM# 27 CENT

Bronze **Ruler:** Elizabeth II **Obv:** Head right **Rev:** Numeric denomination within scalloped circle, date and denomination below **Edge:** Plain

Date	Mintage	F	VF	XF	Unc	BU
1954	200,000	0.50	0.75	1.00	5.00	—
1954 Proof	—	Value: 150				

KM# 30 CENT

Bronze, 19.5 mm. **Ruler:** Elizabeth II **Obv:** Bust of Queen Elizabeth II right **Obv. Designer:** Cecil Thomas **Rev:** Numeric denomination within scalloped circle, date and denomination below **Edge:** Plain **Shape:** Scalloped

Date	Mintage	F	VF	XF	Unc	BU
1956	200,000	0.10	0.25	0.50	3.50	—
1956 Proof	—	Value: 80.00				
1958	400,000	1.00	2.00	9.00	80.00	—
1958 Proof	—	Value: 80.00				
1959	200,000	1.00	2.50	10.00	100	—
1959 Proof	—	Value: 100				
1961	800,000	—	0.15	0.25	0.50	—
1961 Proof	—	Value: 80.00				
1964	300,000	—	0.10	0.30	0.90	—
1965	400,000	—	—	0.10	0.50	—
1966	100,000	—	—	0.10	0.50	—
1967	400,000	—	—	0.10	0.50	—
1968	200,000	—	—	0.10	0.50	—
1969	520,000	—	—	0.10	0.40	—
1970	120,000	—	—	0.10	0.40	—
1971	800,000	—	—	0.10	0.40	—
1972	800,000	—	—	0.10	0.40	—
1973	400,000	—	—	0.10	0.40	—

KM# 14 5 CENTS

Copper-Nickel **Ruler:** Edward VII **Obv:** Bust of King Edward VII right within circle, date below **Obv. Designer:** G.W. DeSaulles **Rev:** Denomination within circle **Edge:** Plain

Date	Mintage	F	VF	XF	Unc	BU
1907	10,000	25.00	50.00	100	250	—
1909	10,000	25.00	50.00	100	250	—

KM# 16 5 CENTS

Copper-Nickel **Ruler:** George V **Obv:** Bust of King George V left within circle, date below **Obv. Designer:** E.B. MacKennal **Rev:** Denomination within circle **Edge:** Plain

Date	Mintage	F	VF	XF	Unc	BU
1911	10,000	25.00	50.00	100	250	—
1912H	20,000	10.00	25.00	55.00	175	—
1912H Proof	—	Value: 550				
1916H	20,000	10.00	25.00	55.00	175	—
1918	20,000	10.00	25.00	55.00	175	—
1919	20,000	8.00	20.00	50.00	160	—
1936	60,000	2.50	5.00	20.00	75.00	—
1936 Proof	50	Value: 450				

KM# 22 5 CENTS

Copper-Nickel **Ruler:** George VI **Obv:** Head of King George VI left **Obv. Designer:** Percy Metcalf **Rev:** Denomination within circle, date below **Edge:** Plain

Date	Mintage	F	VF	XF	Unc	BU
1939	20,000	3.00	6.00	25.00	75.00	—
1939 Proof	—	Value: 275				

KM# 22a 5 CENTS

Nickel-Brass **Ruler:** George VI **Obv:** Head of King George VI left **Obv. Designer:** Percy Metcalf **Rev:** Denomination within circle, date below

Date	Mintage	F	VF	XF	Unc	BU
1942	30,000	5.00	15.00	65.00	200	—

Date	Mintage	F	VF	XF	Unc	BU
1942 Proof	—	Value: 300				
1943	40,000	2.00	12.00	60.00	190	—
1944	50,000	1.50	10.00	50.00	175	—
1944 Proof	—	Value: 275				
1945	65,000	1.00	5.00	15.00	75.00	—
1945 Proof	—	Value: 150				
1947	40,000	1.50	5.00	15.00	85.00	—
1947 Proof	—	Value: 185				

KM# 25 5 CENTS

Nickel-Brass, 20 mm. **Ruler:** George VI **Obv:** Head of King George VI left **Obv. Legend:** Legend without EMPEROR OF INDIA **Obv. Designer:** Percy Metcalf **Rev:** Denomination within circle, date below **Edge:** Plain

Date	Mintage	F	VF	XF	Unc	BU
1949	40,000	1.50	3.00	10.00	50.00	—
1949 Proof	—	Value: 150				
1950	225,000	0.40	1.00	4.00	30.00	—
1950 Proof	—	Value: 200				
1952	100,000	0.50	2.00	6.00	35.00	—
1952 Proof	—	Value: 250				

KM# 31 5 CENTS

Nickel-Brass **Ruler:** Elizabeth II **Obv:** Bust of Queen Elizabeth II right **Obv. Designer:** Cecil Thomas **Rev:** Denomination within circle, date below **Edge:** Plain

Date	Mintage	F	VF	XF	Unc	BU
1956	100,000	0.20	0.50	3.00	75.00	—
1956 Proof	—	Value: 125				
1957	100,000	0.30	0.75	1.50	10.00	—
1957 Proof	—	Value: 175				
1958	200,000	0.30	1.00	7.50	90.00	—
1958 Proof	—	Value: 125				
1959	100,000	0.40	2.00	10.00	100	—
1959 Proof	—	Value: 185				
1961	100,000	0.30	0.75	2.50	35.00	—
1961 Proof	—	Value: 120				
1962	200,000	0.15	0.35	0.65	2.00	—
1962 Proof	—	Value: 115				
1963	100,000	0.10	0.20	0.50	1.50	—
1963 Proof	—	Value: 175				
1964	100,000	0.10	0.15	0.35	1.00	—
1965	150,000	—	0.10	0.25	0.75	—
1966	150,000	—	0.10	0.20	0.60	—
1968	200,000	—	0.10	0.15	0.50	—
1969	540,000	—	0.10	0.15	0.50	—
1970	240,000	—	0.10	0.15	0.50	—
1971	450,000	—	0.10	0.15	0.50	—
1972	200,000	—	0.10	0.15	0.50	—
1973	210,000	—	0.10	0.15	0.75	—

KM# 20 10 CENTS

2.3240 g., 0.9250 Silver .0691 oz. ASW **Ruler:** George V **Obv:** Bust of King George V left **Obv. Designer:** E.B. MacKennal **Rev:** Denomination within circle, date below **Edge:** Reeded

Date	Mintage	F	VF	XF	Unc	BU
1918	10,000	15.00	25.00	100	350	—
1919	10,000	15.00	25.00	100	350	—
1936	30,000	6.00	12.00	25.00	100	—
1936 Proof	50	Value: 325				

KM# 23 10 CENTS

2.3240 g., 0.9250 Silver .0691 oz. ASW **Ruler:** George VI **Obv:** Head of King George VI left **Obv. Designer:** Percy Metcalf **Rev:** Denomination within circle, date below **Edge:** Plain

Date	Mintage	F	VF	XF	Unc	BU
1939	20,000	3.00	7.00	20.00	60.00	—
1939 Proof	—	Value: 300				
1942	10,000	10.00	20.00	60.00	250	—
1943	20,000	3.00	6.00	45.00	250	—

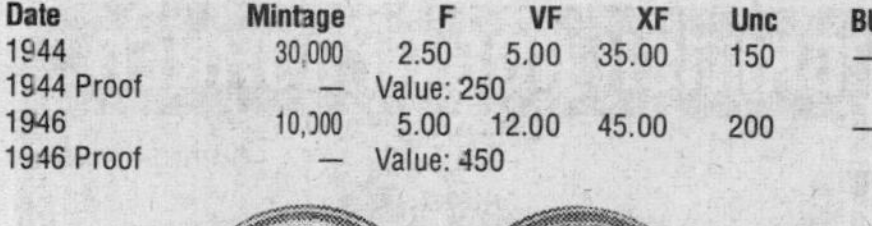

Date	Mintage	F	VF	XF	Unc	BU
1944	30,000	2.50	5.00	35.00	150	—
1944 Proof	—	Value: 250				
1946	10,000	5.00	12.00	45.00	200	—
1946 Proof	—	Value: 450				

KM# 32 10 CENTS

Copper-Nickel, 18 mm. **Ruler:** Elizabeth II **Obv:** Bust of Queen Elizabeth II right **Obv. Designer:** Cecil Thomas **Rev:** Denomination within circle, date below **Edge:** Plain

Date	Mintage	F	VF	XF	Unc	BU
1956	100,000	0.45	1.00	2.00	7.50	—
1956 Proof	—	Value: 200				
1959	100,000	0.65	1.50	2.00	37.50	—
1959 Proof	—	Value: 135				
1961	50,000	0.35	0.75	1.25	3.00	—
1961 Proof	—	Value: 135				
1963	50,000	0.20	0.50	0.75	2.00	—
1963 Proof	—	Value: 135				
1964	60,000	0.15	0.25	0.50	1.00	—
1965/6	200,000	5.00	10.00	20.00	40.00	—
1965	Inc. above	—	0.10	0.15	0.50	—
1970	—	—	0.10	0.15	0.75	—

KM# 9 25 CENTS

5.8100 g., 0.9250 Silver .1728 oz. ASW **Ruler:** Victoria **Obv:** Head of Queen Victoria left **Rev:** Denomination within circle, date below **Edge:** Plain

Date	Mintage	F	VF	XF	Unc	BU
1901	20,000	20.00	35.00	125	400	—
1901 Proof	30	Value: 650				

KM# 12 25 CENTS

5.8100 g., 0.9250 Silver .1728 oz. ASW **Ruler:** Edward VII **Obv:** Bust of King Edward VII right **Obv. Designer:** G.W. DeSaulles **Rev:** Denomination within circle, date below **Edge:** Reeded

Date	Mintage	F	VF	XF	Unc	BU
1906	30,000	15.00	30.00	110	375	—
1907	60,000	10.00	25.00	95.00	325	—

KM# 17 25 CENTS

5.8100 g., 0.9250 Silver .1728 oz. ASW **Ruler:** George V **Obv:** Bust of King George V left **Obv. Designer:** E.B. MacKennal **Rev:** Denomination within circle, date below **Edge:** Reeded

Date	Mintage	F	VF	XF	Unc	BU
1911	14,000	25.00	60.00	150	400	—
1919	40,000	8.00	17.50	75.00	250	—

KM# 26 25 CENTS

Copper-Nickel **Ruler:** George VI **Obv:** Head of King George VI left **Obv. Designer:** Percy Metcalf **Rev:** Denomination within circle, date below **Edge:** Reeded

Date	Mintage	F	VF	XF	Unc	BU
1952	75,000	2.00	5.00	50.00	200	—
1952 Proof	—	Value: 250				

KM# 29 25 CENTS

Copper-Nickel **Ruler:** Elizabeth II **Obv:** Bust of Queen Elizabeth II right **Obv. Designer:** Cecil Thomas **Edge:** Reeded

Date	Mintage	F	VF	XF	Unc	BU
1955	75,000	0.45	1.00	3.50	15.00	—
1955 Proof	—	Value: 150				
1960	75,000	0.45	1.00	5.00	100	—
1960 Proof	—	Value: 250				
1962	50,000	0.30	0.50	1.00	2.50	—
1962 Proof	—	Value: 150				
1963	50,000	0.30	0.50	2.00	7.50	—
1963 Proof	—	Value: 150				
1964	100,000	0.30	0.50	0.75	1.50	—
1965	75,000	—	0.50	1.00	2.00	—
1966	75,000	0.45	1.00	2.00	8.00	—
1968	125,000	0.25	0.50	1.00	2.00	—
1970	—	0.20	0.35	0.75	1.50	—
1971	150,000	0.20	0.30	0.50	1.50	—
1972	200,000	0.20	0.30	0.50	1.50	—
1973	100,000	0.20	0.30	0.60	1.75	—

KM# 10 50 CENTS

11.6200 g., 0.9250 Silver .3456 oz. ASW **Ruler:** Victoria **Obv:** Head of Queen Victoria left **Rev:** Denomination within circle, date below

Date	Mintage	F	VF	XF	Unc	BU
1901	10,000	35.00	80.00	400	1,000	—
1901 Proof	30	Value: 1,000				

KM# 13 50 CENTS

11.6200 g., 0.9250 Silver .3456 oz. ASW **Ruler:** Edward VII **Obv:** Bust of King Edward VII right **Obv. Designer:** G.W. DeSaulles **Rev:** Denomination within circle, date below

Date	Mintage	F	VF	XF	Unc	BU
1906	15,000	20.00	60.00	225	600	—
1907	19,000	18.00	55.00	170	500	—

KM# 18 50 CENTS

11.6200 g., 0.9250 Silver .3456 oz. ASW **Ruler:** George V **Obv:** Bust of King George V left **Obv. Designer:** E.B. MacKennal **Rev:** Denomination within circle, date below

Date	Mintage	F	VF	XF	Unc	BU
1911	12,000	30.00	75.00	250	850	—
1919	40,000	20.00	40.00	150	400	—
1919 Proof	—	Value: 1,250				

KM# 28 50 CENTS

Copper-Nickel **Ruler:** Elizabeth II **Obv:** Bust of Queen Elizabeth II right **Obv. Designer:** Cecil Thomas **Rev:** Denomination within circle, date below

Date	Mintage	F	VF	XF	Unc	BU
1954	75,000	0.30	0.50	1.00	4.00	—
1954 Proof	—	Value: 175				
1962	50,000	0.30	0.50	1.50	5.00	—
1962 Proof	—	Value: 200				
1964	50,000	0.30	0.50	1.50	3.50	—
1965	25,000	1.25	3.00	5.00	22.50	—
1966	25,000	1.00	2.00	4.00	15.00	—
1971	30,000	0.30	0.50	1.50	3.50	—

PROOF SETS

KM#	Date	Mintage	Identification	Issue Price	Mkt Val
PS1	1894 (5)	25	KM#6-10	—	3,000
PS2	1901 (2)	30	KM#9, 10	—	2,500
PS3	1936 (3)	50	KM#16, 19, 20	—	1,000
PS4	1939 (3)	—	KM#21-23	—	675
PS5	1949 (2)	—	KM#24, 25	—	300
PS6	1950 (2)	—	KM#24, 25	—	350
PS7	1954 (2)	—	KM#27, 28	—	300
PS8	1956 (3)	—	KM#30-32	—	400
PS9	1958 (2)	—	KM#30, 31	—	200

BRITISH NORTH BORNEO

British North Borneo (now known as *Sabah*), a former British protectorate and crown colony, occupies the northern tip of the island of Borneo. The island of Labuan, which lies 6 miles off the northwest coast of the island of Borneo, was attached to Singapore settlement in 1907. It became an independent settlement of the Straits Colony in 1912 and was incorporated with British North Borneo in 1946. In 1963 it became part of Malaysia.

RULERS

British

MINT MARKS

H - Heaton, Birmingham

MONETARY SYSTEM

100 Cents = 1 Straits Dollar

BRITISH PROTECTORATE

STANDARD COINAGE

KM# 1 1/2 CENT

Bronze **Obv:** Denomination within wreath **Rev:** National arms, date below

Date	Mintage	F	VF	XF	Unc	BU
1907H	1,000,000	50.00	135	195	390	—
1907H Proof	—	Value: 660				

KM# 3 CENT

Copper-Nickel **Obv:** Denomination within circle, date below **Rev:** National arms with supporters

Date	Mintage	F	VF	XF	Unc	BU
1904H	2,000,000	3.50	9.00	18.50	42.00	—
1921H	1,000,000	3.50	9.00	18.50	42.00	—
1935H	1,000,000	2.70	5.00	15.00	32.00	—
1938H	1,000,000	2.70	5.00	15.00	32.00	—
1941H	1,000,000	2.70	5.00	15.00	32.00	—

KM# 2 CENT

Bronze **Obv:** Denomination within wreath **Rev:** National arms with supporters, date below

Date	Mintage	F	VF	XF	Unc	BU
1907H	1,000,000	50.00	120	230	385	—
1907H Proof	—	Value: 780				

KM# 4 2-1/2 CENT

Copper-Nickel **Obv:** Denomination within circle, date below **Rev:** National arms with supporters

Date	Mintage	F	VF	XF	Unc	BU
1903H	2,000,000	4.60	14.00	35.00	125	—
1903H Proof	—	Value: 580				
1920H	280,000	11.00	33.00	80.00	180	—

KM# 5 5 CENTS

Copper-Nickel **Obv:** Denomination within circle, date below **Rev:** National arms with supporters

Date	Mintage	F	VF	XF	Unc	BU
1903H	1,000,000	7.00	14.00	26.00	65.00	—
1920H	100,000	11.00	22.00	60.00	110	—
1921H	500,000	5.00	11.00	22.00	65.00	—
1927H	150,000	5.00	11.00	22.00	65.00	—
1928H	150,000	3.00	6.00	16.00	55.00	—
1938H	500,000	2.00	4.00	10.00	27.00	—
1940H	500,000	2.00	4.00	10.00	27.00	—
1941H	1,000,000	2.00	4.00	10.00	27.00	—

KM# 6 25 CENTS

2.8300 g., 0.5000 Silver .0454 oz. ASW **Obv:** Denomination within circle, date below **Rev:** National arms with supporters

Date	Mintage	F	VF	XF	Unc	BU
1929H	400,000	35.00	55.00	110	200	—
1929H Proof	—	Value: 450				

BRITISH VIRGIN ISLANDS

The Colony of the Virgin Islands, a British colony situated in the Caribbean Sea northeast of Puerto Rico and west of the Leeward Islands, has an area of 59 sq. mi. (155 sq. km.) and a population of 13,000. Capital: Road Town. The principal islands of the 36-island group are Tortola, Virgin Gorda, Anegada, and Jost Van Dyke. The chief industries are fishing and stock raising. Fish, livestock and bananas are exported.

The Virgin Islands were discovered by Columbus in 1493, and named by him, Las Virgienes, in honor of St. Ursula and her companions. The British Virgin Islands were formerly part of the administration of the Leeward Islands but received a separate administration as a Crown Colony in 1950. A new constitution promulgated in 1967 provided for a ministerial form of government headed by the Governor.

The Government of the British Virgin Islands issued the first official coinage in its history on June 30, 1973, in honor of 300 years of constitutional government in the islands. U.S. coins and currency continue to be the primary medium of exchange, though the coinage of the British Virgin Islands is legal tender.

***NOTE**: From 1975-1985 the Franklin Mint produced coinage in up to 3 different qualities. Qualities of issue are designated in ( ) after each date and are defined as follows:

(M) MATTE - Normal circulation strike or a dull finish produced by sandblasting special uncirculated (polish finish) or proof quality dies.

(U) SPECIAL UNCIRCULATED - Polished or proof-like in appearance without any frosted features.

(P) PROOF - The highest quality obtainable having mirror-like fields and frosted features.

BRITISH COLONY

STANDARD COINAGE

KM# 1 CENT

Bronze **Obv:** Bust right, date below **Obv. Designer:** Arnold Machin **Rev:** Green-throated Carib and Antillean Crested Hummingbird, denomination in background **Rev. Designer:** Gilroy Roberts

Date	Mintage	F	VF	XF	Unc	BU
1973FM	53,000	—	—	0.10	0.50	1.00
1973FM (P)	181,000	Value: 1.00				
1974FM	22,000	—	—	0.10	0.50	1.00
1974FM (P)	94,000	Value: 1.00				
1975FM (M)	6,000	—	—	0.10	0.75	1.20
1975FM (U)	2,351	—	—	0.10	0.50	1.00
1975FM (P)	32,000	Value: 1.00				
1976FM (M)	12,000	—	—	0.10	0.50	1.00
1976FM (U)	996	—	—	0.10	0.50	1.00
1976FM (P)	15,000	Value: 1.00				
1977FM (M)	500	—	—	0.25	2.00	3.00
1977FM (U)	782	—	—	0.10	0.50	1.00
1977FM (P)	7,218	Value: 1.00				
1978FM (U)	1,443	—	—	0.10	0.50	1.00
1978FM (P)	7,059	Value: 1.00				
1979FM (U)	680	—	—	0.10	0.50	1.00
1979FM (P)	5,304	Value: 1.00				
1980FM (U)	1,007	—	—	0.10	0.50	1.00
1980FM (P)	3,421	Value: 1.00				
1981FM (U)	472	—	—	0.10	0.50	1.00
1981FM (P)	1,124	Value: 1.50				
1982FM (U)	—	—	—	0.10	0.50	1.00
1982FM (P)	—	Value: 1.50				
1983FM (U)	—	—	—	0.10	0.50	1.00
1983FM (P)	—	Value: 1.50				
1984FM (P)	—	Value: 1.50				

KM# 9 CENT

1.7500 g., 0.9250 Silver .0520 oz. ASW **Subject:** Queen's Silver Jubilee **Obv:** Bust right, date below **Obv. Designer:** Arnold Machin **Rev:** Green-throated Carib and Antillean Crested Hummingbird, denomination in background **Rev. Designer:** Gilroy Roberts

Date	Mintage	F	VF	XF	Unc	BU
1977FM (P)	17,000	Value: 2.50				

KM# 16 CENT

1.7500 g., 0.9250 Silver .0520 oz. ASW **Subject:** Coronation Jubilee **Obv:** Bust right, date below **Rev:** Hummingbird, denomination in background **Note:** Similar to KM#1.

Date	Mintage	F	VF	XF	Unc	BU
1978FM (P)	6,196	Value: 4.00				

KM# 42 CENT

Bronze **Obv:** Bust right, date below **Obv. Designer:** Raphael Maklouf **Rev:** Hawksbill Turtle, left, denomination uppper right

Date	Mintage	F	VF	XF	Unc	BU
1985FM (P)	—	Value: 4.50				

KM# 42a CENT

1.7500 g., 0.9250 Silver .0520 oz. ASW **Obv:** Bust right, date below **Rev:** Hawksbill turtle left, denomination below

Date	Mintage	F	VF	XF	Unc	BU
1985FM (P)	1,474	Value: 6.00				

KM# 2 5 CENTS

Copper-Nickel, 19.5 mm. **Obv:** Bust right, date below **Obv. Designer:** Arnold Machin **Rev:** Zenaida Doves, denomination in background **Rev. Designer:** Gilroy Roberts

Date	Mintage	F	VF	XF	Unc	BU
1973FM	26,000	—	—	0.15	0.75	1.00
1973FM (P)	181,000	Value: 1.25				
1974FM	18,000	—	—	0.15	0.75	1.00
1974FM (P)	94,000	Value: 1.25				
1975FM (M)	3,800	—	—	0.20	1.00	1.25
1975FM (U)	2,351	—	—	0.15	0.75	1.00
1975FM (P)	32,000	Value: 1.25				
1976FM (M)	4,800	—	—	0.20	1.00	1.25
1976FM (U)	996	—	—	0.15	1.25	1.50
1976FM (P)	15,000	Value: 1.25				
1977FM (M)	500	—	—	0.35	3.50	5.00
1977FM (U)	782	—	—	0.15	1.00	1.25
1977FM (P)	7,218	Value: 1.25				
1978FM (U)	1,443	—	—	0.15	1.00	1.25
1978FM (P)	7,059	Value: 1.25				
1979FM (U)	680	—	—	0.15	1.00	1.25
1979FM (P)	5,304	Value: 1.25				
1980FM (U)	1,007	—	—	0.15	1.00	1.25
1980FM (P)	3,421	Value: 1.25				
1981FM (U)	472	—	—	0.15	1.00	1.25
1981FM (P)	1,124	Value: 1.25				
1982FM (U)	—	—	—	0.15	1.00	1.25
1982FM (P)	—	Value: 1.25				
1983FM (U)	—	—	—	0.15	1.00	1.25
1983FM (P)	—	Value: 1.25				
1984FM (P)	—	Value: 1.25				

KM# 10 5 CENTS

3.5500 g., 0.9250 Silver .1055 oz. ASW, 19.5 mm. **Subject:** Queen's Silver Jubilee **Obv:** Bust right, date below **Obv. Designer:** Arnold Machin **Rev:** Zenaida Doves, denomination in background **Rev. Designer:** Gilroy Roberts

Date	Mintage	F	VF	XF	Unc	BU
1977FM (P)	17,000	Value: 3.00				

KM# 17 5 CENTS

3.5500 g., 0.9250 Silver .1055 oz. ASW, 19.5 mm. **Subject:** Coronation Jubilee **Obv:** Bust divides dates **Obv. Designer:** Arnold Machin **Rev:** Zenaida Doves, denomination in background **Rev. Designer:** Gilroy Roberts

Date	Mintage	F	VF	XF	Unc	BU
ND(1978)FM (P)	6,196	Value: 4.50				

KM# 43 5 CENTS

Copper-Nickel **Obv:** Bust right, date below **Obv. Designer:** Raphael Maklouf **Rev:** Bonito Fish, left, denomination above

Date	Mintage	F	VF	XF	Unc	BU
1985FM (P)	—	Value: 5.00				

KM# 43a 5 CENTS

3.5550 g., 0.9250 Silver .1055 oz. ASW **Obv:** Bust right, date below **Rev:** Bonito fish left, denomination above

Date	Mintage	F	VF	XF	Unc	BU
1985FM (P)	1,471	Value: 6.00				

KM# 3 10 CENTS

Copper-Nickel **Obv:** Bust right, date below **Obv. Designer:** Arnold Machin **Rev:** Ringed Kingfisher right, denomination in background **Rev. Designer:** Gilroy Roberts

Date	Mintage	F	VF	XF	Unc	BU
1973FM (U)	23,000	—	—	0.20	1.00	1.25
1973FM (P)	181,000	Value: 1.50				
1974FM (U)	13,000	—	—	0.20	1.00	1.25
1974FM (P)	94,000	Value: 1.50				
1975FM (M)	2,000	—	—	0.20	1.25	1.50
1975FM (U)	2,351	—	—	0.20	1.00	1.25
1975FM (P)	32,000	Value: 1.50				
1976FM (M)	3,000	—	—	0.20	1.00	1.25
1976FM (U)	996	—	—	0.20	1.25	1.50
1976FM (P)	15,000	Value: 1.50				
1977FM (M)	500	—	—	0.45	4.00	6.00
1977FM (U)	782	—	—	0.20	1.50	2.00
1977FM (P)	7,218	Value: 1.50				
1978FM (U)	1,443	—	—	0.20	1.25	1.50
1978FM (P)	7,059	Value: 1.50				
1979FM (U)	680	—	—	0.20	1.50	2.00
1979FM (P)	5,304	Value: 1.50				
1980FM (U)	1,007	—	—	0.20	1.50	2.00
1980FM (P)	3,421	Value: 1.50				
1981FM (U)	472	—	—	0.20	2.00	2.50
1981FM (P)	1,124	Value: 1.50				
1982FM (U)	—	—	—	0.20	2.00	2.50
1982FM (P)	—	Value: 1.50				
1983FM (U)	—	—	—	0.20	2.00	2.50
1983FM (P)	—	Value: 1.50				
1984FM (P)	—	Value: 1.50				

KM# 11 10 CENTS

6.4000 g., 0.9250 Silver .1903 oz. ASW **Subject:** Queen's Silver Jubilee **Obv:** Bust right, date below **Obv. Designer:** Arnold Machin **Rev:** Ringed Kingfisher left, denomination in background **Rev. Designer:** Gilroy Roberts

Date	Mintage	F	VF	XF	Unc	BU
1977FM (P)	17,000	Value: 5.00				

KM# 18 10 CENTS

6.4000 g., 0.9250 Silver .1903 oz. ASW **Subject:** Coronation Jubilee **Obv:** Bust divides dates **Obv. Designer:** Arnold Machin **Rev:** Ringed Kingfisher left, denomination in background **Rev. Designer:** Gilroy Roberts

Date	Mintage	F	VF	XF	Unc	BU
ND(1978)FM (P)	6,196	Value: 6.50				

KM# 44 10 CENTS

Copper-Nickel **Obv:** Bust right **Obv. Designer:** Raphael Maklouf **Rev:** Great Barracuda right, denomination above

Date	Mintage	F	VF	XF	Unc	BU
1985FM (P)	—	Value: 6.00				

KM# 44a 10 CENTS

6.4000 g., 0.9250 Silver .1903 oz. ASW **Obv:** Bust right **Rev:** Great Barracuda right, denomination above

Date	Mintage	F	VF	XF	Unc	BU
1985FM (P)	1,474	Value: 9.00				

KM# 4 25 CENTS

Copper-Nickel **Obv:** Bust right, date below **Obv. Designer:** Arnold Machin **Rev:** Mangrove Cuckoo, denomination in background **Rev. Designer:** Gilroy Roberts

Date	Mintage	F	VF	XF	Unc	BU
1973FM	21,000	—	—	0.30	1.50	1.75
1973FM (P)	181,000	Value: 1.50				
1974FM	12,000	—	—	0.30	1.50	1.75
1974FM (P)	94,000	Value: 2.00				
1975FM (M)	1,000	—	—	0.35	3.00	4.00
1975FM (U)	2,351	—	—	0.30	1.50	1.75
1975FM (P)	32,000	Value: 2.00				
1976FM (M)	2,000	—	—	0.30	2.00	3.00
1976FM (U)	996	—	—	0.30	2.50	3.50
1976FM (P)	15,000	Value: 2.00				
1977FM (M)	500	—	—	0.50	5.00	7.00
1977FM (U)	782	—	—	0.30	2.00	3.00
1977FM (P)	7,218	Value: 2.00				
1978FM (U)	1,443	—	—	0.30	1.75	2.25
1978FM (P)	7,059	Value: 2.00				
1979FM (U)	680	—	—	0.30	2.00	3.00
1979FM (P)	5,304	Value: 2.00				
1980FM (U)	1,007	—	—	0.30	2.00	3.00
1980FM (P)	3,421	Value: 2.00				
1981FM (U)	472	—	—	0.30	2.25	3.50
1981FM (P)	1,124	Value: 2.00				
1982FM (U)	—	—	—	0.30	2.25	3.50
1982FM (P)	—	Value: 2.00				
1983FM (U)	—	—	—	0.30	2.25	3.50
1983FM (P)	—	Value: 2.00				
1984FM (P)	—	Value: 2.00				

KM# 12 25 CENTS

8.8100 g., 0.9250 Silver .2620 oz. ASW **Subject:** Queen's Silver Jubilee **Obv. Designer:** Arnold Machin **Rev. Designer:** Gilroy Roberts

Date	Mintage	F	VF	XF	Unc	BU
1977FM (P)	17,000	Value: 7.00				

KM# 19 25 CENTS

8.8100 g., 0.9250 Silver .2620 oz. ASW **Subject:** Coronation Jubilee **Obv:** Bust divides dates **Obv. Designer:** Arnold Machin **Rev:** Mangrove Cuckoo, denomination in background **Rev. Designer:** Gilroy Roberts

Date	Mintage	F	VF	XF	Unc	BU
ND(1978)FM (P)	6,196	Value: 8.50				

KM# 45 25 CENTS

Copper-Nickel **Obv:** Bust right, date below **Obv. Designer:** Raphael Maklouf **Rev:** Blue Marlin jumping, denomination above

Date	Mintage	F	VF	XF	Unc	BU
1985FM (P)	—	Value: 8.00				

KM# 45a 25 CENTS

8.8100 g., 0.9250 Silver .2620 oz. ASW **Obv:** Bust right, date below **Rev:** Blue Marlin jumping, denomination above

Date	Mintage	F	VF	XF	Unc	BU
1985FM (P)	1,480	Value: 12.00				

KM# 5 50 CENTS

Copper-Nickel **Obv:** Bust right, date below **Obv. Designer:** Arnold Machin **Rev:** Brown Pelican, denomination in background **Rev. Designer:** Gilroy Roberts

Date	Mintage	F	VF	XF	Unc	BU
1973FM	20,000	—	—	0.75	2.00	3.00
1973FM (P)	181,000	Value: 2.50				
1974FM	12,000	—	—	0.75	2.00	3.00
1974FM (P)	94,000	Value: 2.50				
1975FM (M)	1,000	—	—	1.00	5.00	6.00
1975FM (U)	2,351	—	—	0.75	2.50	3.00
1975FM (P)	32,000	Value: 2.50				
1976FM (M)	2,000	—	—	0.75	3.00	4.00
1976FM (U)	996	—	—	0.75	3.50	4.50
1976FM (P)	15,000	Value: 2.50				
1977FM (M)	600	—	—	1.00	6.00	7.50
1977FM (U)	782	—	—	0.75	3.50	4.50
1977FM (P)	7,218	Value: 2.50				
1978FM (U)	1,543	—	—	0.75	2.50	3.00
1978FM (P)	7,059	Value: 2.50				
1979FM (U)	680	—	—	0.75	3.50	4.50
1979FM (P)	5,304	Value: 2.50				
1980FM (U)	1,007	—	—	0.75	3.00	4.00
1980FM (P)	3,421	Value: 2.50				
1981FM (U)	472	—	—	0.75	3.50	5.00
1981FM (P)	1,124	Value: 2.50				
1982FM (U)	—	—	—	0.75	3.50	5.00
1982FM (P)	—	Value: 2.50				
1983FM (U)	—	—	—	0.75	3.50	5.00
1983FM (P)	—	Value: 2.50				
1984FM (P)	—	Value: 2.50				

KM# 13 50 CENTS

16.7200 g., 0.9250 Silver .4972 oz. ASW **Subject:** Queen's Silver Jubilee **Obv:** Bust right, date below **Obv. Designer:** Arnold Machin **Rev:** Brown Pelican, denomination in background **Rev. Designer:** Gilroy Roberts

Date	Mintage	F	VF	XF	Unc	BU
1977FM (P)	17,000	Value: 11.50				

KM# 20 50 CENTS

16.7200 g., 0.9250 Silver .4972 oz. ASW **Subject:** Coronation Jubilee **Obv:** Bust right, divides dates **Obv. Designer:** Arnold Machin **Rev:** Brown Pelican, denomination in background **Rev. Designer:** Gilroy Roberts

Date	Mintage	F	VF	XF	Unc	BU
ND(1978)FM (P)	6,196	Value: 13.50				

KM# 46 50 CENTS

Copper-Nickel **Obv:** Bust right, date below **Obv. Designer:** Arnold Machin **Rev:** Dolphin fish, denomination lower left **Rev. Designer:** Gilroy Roberts

Date	Mintage	F	VF	XF	Unc	BU
1985FM (P)	—	Value: 12.00				

KM# 46a 50 CENTS

16.7200 g., 0.9250 Silver .4972 oz. ASW **Obv:** Bust right **Rev:** Dolphin fish, denomination lower left

Date	Mintage	F	VF	XF	Unc	BU
1985FM (P)	1,406	Value: 25.00				

KM# 6 DOLLAR

Copper-Nickel **Obv:** Bust right, date below **Obv. Designer:** Arnold Machin **Rev:** Magnificent Frigate, denomination below **Rev. Designer:** Gilroy Roberts

Date	Mintage	F	VF	XF	Unc	BU
1974FM (M)	12,000	—	—	2.00	5.50	7.00
1974FM (U)	—	—	—	—	—	—
1975FM (M)	800	—	—	2.50	8.00	9.00
1975FM (U)	2,351	—	—	2.50	6.50	7.00
1976FM (M)	1,800	—	—	2.50	6.50	7.00
1976FM (U)	996	—	—	2.50	8.00	9.00
1977FM (M)	800	—	—	2.50	8.00	9.00
1977FM (U)	782	—	—	2.50	8.00	9.00
1978FM (U)	1,743	—	—	2.50	6.50	7.00
1979FM (U)	680	—	—	2.50	8.00	9.00
1980FM (U)	1,007	—	—	2.50	6.50	7.00
1981FM (U)	472	—	—	2.50	10.00	11.50
1982FM (U)	—	—	—	2.50	10.00	11.50
1983FM (U)	—	—	—	2.50	10.00	11.50

KM# 6a DOLLAR

25.7000 g., 0.9250 Silver .7643 oz. ASW **Obv:** Bust right, date below **Rev:** Magnificent Frigate, denomination below

Date	Mintage	F	VF	XF	Unc	BU
1973FM (P)	181,000	Value: 11.00				
1973FM (M)	20,000	—	—	10.50	12.00	—
1974FM (P)	94,000	Value: 12.00				
1975FM (P)	32,000	Value: 13.00				
1976FM (P)	15,000	Value: 13.00				
1977FM (P)	7,218	Value: 14.00				
1978FM (P)	7,059	Value: 14.00				
1979FM (P)	5,304	Value: 15.00				
1980FM (P)	3,421	Value: 15.00				
1981FM (P)	1,124	Value: 16.00				

Date	Mintage	F	VF	XF	Unc	BU
1982FM (P)	1,865	Value: 16.00				
1983FM (P)	478	Value: 22.00				
1984FM (P)	—	Value: 16.00				

KM# 14 DOLLAR

25.7000 g., 0.9250 Silver .7643 oz. ASW **Subject:** Queen's Silver Jubilee **Obv:** Bust right, date below **Obv. Designer:** Arnold Machin **Rev:** Magnificent Frigate, denomination below **Rev. Designer:** Gilroy Roberts

Date	Mintage	F	VF	XF	Unc	BU
1977FM (P)	17,000	Value: 16.00				

KM# 21 DOLLAR

25.7000 g., 0.9250 Silver .7643 oz. ASW **Subject:** Coronation Jubilee **Obv:** Bust right, divides dates **Obv. Designer:** Arnold Machin **Rev:** Magnificent Frigate, denomination below **Rev. Designer:** Gilroy Roberts

Date	Mintage	F	VF	XF	Unc	BU
ND(1978)FM (P)	6,196	Value: 18.00				

KM# 47 DOLLAR

Copper-Nickel **Obv:** Bust right, date below **Obv. Designer:** Raphael Maklouf **Rev:** Butterfly Fish, denomination below

Date	Mintage	F	VF	XF	Unc	BU
1985FM (P)	—	Value: 30.00				

KM# 47a DOLLAR

24.7400 g., 0.9250 Silver .7358 oz. ASW **Obv:** Bust right, date below **Rev:** Butterfly fish, denomination below

Date	Mintage	F	VF	XF	Unc	BU
1985FM (P)	1,372	Value: 37.50				

KM# 169 DOLLAR

Copper-Nickel **Subject:** 500th Anniversary - Columbus' First Voyage to America **Obv:** Head right, two dates below **Rev:** VIGILATE on banner below shield with woman and twelve lamps, denomination above, wreath surrounds

Date	Mintage	F	VF	XF	Unc	BU
ND(1992)	—	Value: 20.00				

KM# 172 DOLLAR

Copper-Nickel, 38.6 mm. **Subject:** Queen Mother's 100th Birthday **Obv:** Queen's head right **Rev:** Queen Mother facing **Edge:** Reeded

Date	Mintage	F	VF	XF	Unc	BU
2000	100,000	—	—	—	6.50	8.50

KM# 175 DOLLAR

Copper-Nickel **Subject:** 1st Anniversary - Earl and Countess of Wessex **Obv:** Queen's head right **Rev:** Half figures of Earl and Countess of Wessex facing, date below **Edge:** Reeded

Date	Mintage	F	VF	XF	Unc	BU
2000	—	—	—	—	6.50	8.50

KM# 24 5 DOLLARS

Copper-Nickel **Obv:** Bust right, date below **Obv. Designer:** Arnold Machin **Rev:** Snowy Egret left, denomination below **Rev. Designer:** Gilroy Roberts

Date	Mintage	F	VF	XF	Unc	BU
1979FM (U)	680	—	—	—	50.00	—

KM# 24a 5 DOLLARS

40.5000 g., 0.9250 Silver 1.2044 oz. ASW **Obv:** Bust right, date below **Rev:** Snowy Egret left, denomination below

Date	Mintage	F	VF	XF	Unc	BU
1979FM (P)	5,304	Value: 35.00				

KM# 26 5 DOLLARS

Copper-Nickel **Obv:** Bust right, date below **Obv. Designer:** Arnold Machin **Rev:** Great Blue Heron right, denomination below **Rev. Designer:** Gilroy Roberts

Date	Mintage	F	VF	XF	Unc	BU
1980FM (U)	1,007	—	—	—	45.00	—

KM# 26a 5 DOLLARS

40.5000 g., 0.9250 Silver 1.2044 oz. ASW **Obv:** Bust right, date below **Rev:** Great Blue Heron right, denomination below

Date	Mintage	F	VF	XF	Unc	BU
1980FM (P)	3,421	Value: 35.00				

KM# 30 5 DOLLARS

Copper-Nickel **Subject:** Royal Tern left, denomination below **Obv:** Bust right, date below **Rev. Designer:** Gilroy Roberts

Date	Mintage	F	VF	XF	Unc	BU
1981FM (U)	472	—	—	—	45.00	—

KM# 30a 5 DOLLARS

40.5000 g., 0.9250 Silver 1.2044 oz. ASW **Obv:** Bust right, date below **Rev:** Royal Tern left, denomination below

Date	Mintage	F	VF	XF	Unc	BU
1981FM (P)	1,124	Value: 35.00				

KM# 33 5 DOLLARS

Copper-Nickel **Obv:** Bust right, date below **Rev:** White-tailed tropic birds, denomination below **Rev. Designer:** Gilroy Roberts

Date	Mintage	F	VF	XF	Unc	BU
1982FM (U)	—	—	—	—	50.00	—

KM# 33a 5 DOLLARS

40.5000 g., 0.9250 Silver 1.2044 oz. ASW **Obv:** Bust right, date below **Rev:** White-tailed tropic birds, denomination below

Date	Mintage	F	VF	XF	Unc	BU
1982FM (P)	1,865	Value: 35.00				

KM# 35 5 DOLLARS

Copper-Nickel **Subject:** Yellow Warblers **Obv:** Bust right, date below **Rev:** Yellow Warblers, denomination below **Rev. Designer:** Gilroy Roberts

Date	Mintage	F	VF	XF	Unc	BU
1983FM (U)	—	—	—	—	42.00	—

KM# 35a 5 DOLLARS

40.5000 g., 0.9250 Silver 1.2044 oz. ASW **Obv:** Bust right, date below **Rev:** Yellow Warblers, denomination below

Date	Mintage	F	VF	XF	Unc	BU
1983FM (P)	478	Value: 50.00				
1984FM (P)	—	Value: 50.00				

KM# 36 10 DOLLARS
30.2800 g., 0.5000 Silver .4868 oz. ASW **Subject:** 30th Anniversary - Coronation of Queen Elizabeth II **Obv:** Bust right, date below **Rev:** Sceptres divide dates and royal symbols

Date	Mintage	F	VF	XF	Unc	BU
1983FM (P)	2,957	Value: 17.50				

KM# 157 10 DOLLARS
Copper-Nickel **Subject:** Discovery of America - Columbus Landing **Obv:** Bust right, two dates below **Rev:** Columbus landing, denomination at upper left

Date	Mintage	F	VF	XF	Unc	BU
ND(1992)FM (P)	—	Value: 12.50				

KM# 173.1 10 DOLLARS
28.2800 g., 0.9250 Silver .8410 oz. ASW, 38.6 mm. **Obv:** Head right, date below **Rev:** Bust facing divides dates, denomination below **Edge:** Reeded

Date	Mintage	F	VF	XF	Unc	BU
2000 Proof	10,000	Value: 40.00				

KM# 173.2 10 DOLLARS
28.2800 g., 0.9250 Silver 0.841 oz. ASW, 38.6 mm. **Subject:** Queen Mother **Obv:** Head right, date below **Rev:** Queen Mother's portrait with a tiny sapphire mounted on her broach **Edge:** Reeded

Date	Mintage	F	VF	XF	Unc	BU
2000 Proof	1,000	Value: 45.00				

KM# 176 10 DOLLARS
28.2800 g., 0.9250 Silver .8410 oz. ASW **Subject:** 1st Anniversary - Earl and Countess of Wessex **Obv:** Head right **Rev:** Half figures of Earl and Countess of Wessex facing, date below, denomination at bottom **Edge:** Reeded

Date	Mintage	F	VF	XF	Unc	BU
2000 Proof	10,000	Value: 40.00				

KM# 48 20 DOLLARS
19.0900 g., 0.9250 Silver .5678 oz. ASW, 38 mm. **Obv:** Head right, date below **Rev:** Crossed cannons, denomination above

Date	Mintage	F	VF	XF	Unc	BU
1985FM (P)	—	Value: 15.00				

KM# 49 20 DOLLARS
19.0900 g., 0.9250 Silver .5678 oz. ASW, 38 mm. **Obv:** Head right, date below **Rev:** Porcelain cup divides denomination

Date	Mintage	F	VF	XF	Unc	BU
1985FM (P)	—	Value: 15.00				

KM# 50 20 DOLLARS
19.0900 g., 0.9250 Silver .5678 oz. ASW, 38 mm. **Obv:** Head right, date below **Rev:** Sextant divides denomination at top

Date	Mintage	F	VF	XF	Unc	BU
1985FM (P)	—	Value: 15.00				

KM# 51 20 DOLLARS
19.0900 g., 0.9250 Silver .5678 oz. ASW, 38 mm. **Obv:** Head right, date below **Rev:** Emerald and gold ring divides denomination

Date	Mintage	F	VF	XF	Unc	BU
1985FM (P)	—	Value: 15.00				

KM# 52 20 DOLLARS
19.0900 g., 0.9250 Silver .5678 oz. ASW, 38 mm. **Obv:** Head right, date below **Rev:** Gold doubloon of 1702 divides denomination

Date	Mintage	F	VF	XF	Unc	BU
1985FM (P)	—	Value: 15.00				

KM# 53 20 DOLLARS
19.0900 g., 0.9250 Silver .5678 oz. ASW, 38 mm. **Obv:** Head right, date below **Rev:** Anchor, denomination at top

Date	Mintage	F	VF	XF	Unc	BU
1985FM (P)	—	Value: 15.00				

KM# 54 20 DOLLARS
19.0900 g., 0.9250 Silver .5678 oz. ASW, 38 mm. **Obv:** Head right, date below **Rev:** Brass nocturnal, within square, divides denomination

Date	Mintage	F	VF	XF	Unc	BU
1985FM (P)	—	Value: 15.00				

KM# 55 20 DOLLARS
19.0900 g., 0.9250 Silver .5678 oz. ASW, 38 mm. **Obv:** Head right, date below **Rev:** Sword guillon, denomination above

Date	Mintage	F	VF	XF	Unc	BU
1985FM (P)	—	Value: 15.00				

KM# 56 20 DOLLARS

19.0900 g., 0.9250 Silver .5678 oz. ASW, 38 mm. **Obv:** Head right, date below **Rev:** Gold bar, divides denomination

Date	Mintage	F	VF	XF	Unc	BU
1985FM (P)	—	Value: 15.00				

KM# 57 20 DOLLARS

19.0900 g., 0.9250 Silver .5678 oz. ASW, 38 mm. **Subject:** Gold Escudo **Obv:** Head right, date below **Rev:** Obverse and reverse of gold escudo of 1733, denomination above

Date	Mintage	F	VF	XF	Unc	BU
1985FM (P)	—	Value: 15.00				

KM# 58 20 DOLLARS

19.0900 g., 0.9250 Silver .5678 oz. ASW, 38 mm. **Obv:** Similar to KM#48, (crowned Queen's bust, right, date below) **Rev:** Ivory sundial divides denomination

Date	Mintage	F	VF	XF	Unc	BU
1985FM (P)	—	Value: 15.00				

KM# 59 20 DOLLARS

19.0900 g., 0.9250 Silver .5678 oz. ASW, 38 mm. **Obv:** Head right, date below **Rev:** Gold monstrance, within square, divides denomination

Date	Mintage	F	VF	XF	Unc	BU
1985FM (P)	—	Value: 15.00				

KM# 60 20 DOLLARS

19.0900 g., 0.9250 Silver .5678 oz. ASW, 38 mm. **Obv:** Head right, date below **Rev:** Teapot within square, divides denomination

Date	Mintage	F	VF	XF	Unc	BU
1985FM (P)	—	Value: 15.00				

KM# 61 20 DOLLARS

19.0900 g., 0.9250 Silver .5678 oz. ASW, 38 mm. **Obv:** Similar to KM#48, (crowned Queen's bust, right, date below) **Rev:** Brass religious medallion divides denomination

Date	Mintage	F	VF	XF	Unc	BU
1985FM (P)	—	Value: 15.00				

KM# 62 20 DOLLARS

19.0900 g., 0.9250 Silver .5678 oz. ASW, 38 mm. **Obv:** Head right, date below **Rev:** Astrolable, divides denomination

Date	Mintage	F	VF	XF	Unc	BU
1985FM (P)	—	Value: 15.00				

KM# 64 20 DOLLARS

19.0900 g., 0.9250 Silver .5678 oz. ASW, 38 mm. **Obv:** Head right, date below **Rev:** Porcelain bottle within square divides denomination

Date	Mintage	F	VF	XF	Unc	BU
1985FM (P)	—	Value: 15.00				

KM# 65 20 DOLLARS

19.0900 g., 0.9250 Silver .5678 oz. ASW, 38 mm. **Obv:** Head right, date below **Rev:** Ship and Dutch cannons, within square, divides denomination

Date	Mintage	F	VF	XF	Unc	BU
1985FM (P)	—	Value: 15.00				

KM# 67 20 DOLLARS

19.0900 g., 0.9250 Silver .5678 oz. ASW, 38 mm. **Obv:** Head right, date below **Rev:** Ship's stern lantern, within square, divides denomination

Date	Mintage	F	VF	XF	Unc	BU
1985FM (P)	—	Value: 15.00				

KM# 68 20 DOLLARS

19.0900 g., 0.9250 Silver .5678 oz. ASW, 38 mm. **Obv:** Head right, date below **Rev:** Brass dividers, within square, divide denomination

Date	Mintage	F	VF	XF	Unc	BU
1985FM (P)	—	Value: 15.00				

KM# 69 20 DOLLARS

19.0900 g., 0.9250 Silver .5678 oz. ASW, 38 mm. **Obv:** Head right, date below **Rev:** Gold cross divides denomination

Date	Mintage	F	VF	XF	Unc	BU
1985FM (P)	—	Value: 15.00				

KM# 70 20 DOLLARS
19.0900 g., 0.9250 Silver .5678 oz. ASW, 38 mm. **Obv:** Head right, date below **Rev:** Perfume bottle divides denomination

Date	Mintage	F	VF	XF	Unc	BU
1985FM (P)	—	Value: 15.00				

KM# 71 20 DOLLARS
19.0900 g., 0.9250 Silver .5678 oz. ASW, 38 mm. **Obv:** Head right, date below **Rev:** Pocket watch, denomination above

Date	Mintage	F	VF	XF	Unc	BU
1985FM (P)	—	Value: 15.00				

KM# 72 20 DOLLARS
19.0900 g., 0.9250 Silver .5678 oz. ASW, 38 mm. **Obv:** Head right, date below **Rev:** Gold bracelet and button, denomination above

Date	Mintage	F	VF	XF	Unc	BU
1985FM (P)	—	Value: 15.00				

KM# 63.1 20 DOLLARS
19.0900 g., 0.9250 Silver .5678 oz. ASW, 38 mm. **Obv:** Head right, date below **Rev:** Bells, denomination above **Note:** FM mint mark at right.

Date	Mintage	F	VF	XF	Unc	BU
1985FM (P)	—	Value: 15.00				

KM# 63.2 20 DOLLARS
19.0900 g., 0.9250 Silver .5678 oz. ASW, 38 mm. **Obv:** Head right, date below **Rev:** Bells, denomination above **Note:** FM mint mark in center.

Date	Mintage	F	VF	XF	Unc	BU
1985FM (P)	—	Value: 15.00				

KM# 66 20 DOLLARS
19.0900 g., 0.9250 Silver .5678 oz. ASW, 38 mm. **Obv:** Head right, date below **Rev:** Ancient coin within square divides denomination **Note:** Spanish Colonial 8 Reales, Cob coin.

Date	Mintage	F	VF	XF	Unc	BU
1985FM (P)	—	Value: 15.00				

KM# 259 20 DOLLARS
19.1100 g., 0.9250 Silver 0.5683 oz. ASW, 37.9 mm. **Obv:** Queen Elizabeth II **Rev:** Ancient Egyptian reed sail boat **Edge:** Reeded

Date	Mintage	F	VF	XF	Unc	BU
2000FM Proof	—	Value: 22.50				

KM# 260 20 DOLLARS
19.6500 g., 0.9250 Silver 0.5844 oz. ASW, 37.9 mm. **Obv:** Queen Elizabeth II **Rev:** Hansa Cog trading ship, 14th Century **Edge:** Reeded

Date	Mintage	F	VF	XF	Unc	BU
2000FM Proof	—	Value: 22.50				

KM# 261 20 DOLLARS
18.9300 g., 0.9250 Silver 0.563 oz. ASW, 37.9 mm. **Obv:** Queen Elizabeth II **Rev:** Flag ship Santa Maria, 1492 **Edge:** Reeded

Date	Mintage	F	VF	XF	Unc	BU
2000FM Proof	—	Value: 22.50				

KM# 262 20 DOLLARS
19.2400 g., 0.9250 Silver 0.5722 oz. ASW, 37.9 mm. **Obv:** Queen Elizabeth II **Rev:** The Ark Royal, 1588 **Edge:** Reeded

Date	Mintage	F	VF	XF	Unc	BU
2000FM Proof	—	Value: 22.50				

KM# 263 20 DOLLARS
18.8000 g., 0.9250 Silver 0.5591 oz. ASW, 37.9 mm. **Obv:** Queen Elizabeth II **Rev:** Clipper ship Cutty Sark, 1869 **Edge:** Reeded

Date	Mintage	F	VF	XF	Unc	BU
2000FM Proof	—	Value: 22.50				

KM# 264 20 DOLLARS
19.2000 g., 0.9250 Silver 0.571 oz. ASW, 37.9 mm. **Obv:** Queen Elizabeth II **Rev:** Training ship SMS Preussen **Edge:** Reeded

Date	Mintage	F	VF	XF	Unc	BU
2000FM Proof	—	Value: 22.50				

KM# 22 25 DOLLARS
28.1000 g., 0.9250 Silver .8356 oz. ASW **Subject:** Coronation Jubilee **Obv:** Bust right, date below **Rev:** Imperial crown with supporters, two dates below, denomination at bottom

Date	Mintage	F	VF	XF	Unc	BU
1978FM (P)	8,438	Value: 25.00				

KM# 27 25 DOLLARS
1.5000 g., 0.5000 Gold .0241 oz. AGW **Obv:** Bust right, date below **Obv. Designer:** Arnold Machin **Rev:** Diving Osprey left, above denomination **Rev. Designer:** Gilroy Roberts

Date	Mintage	F	VF	XF	Unc	BU
1980FM (P)	11,000	Value: 40.00				

KM# 31.1 25 DOLLARS
1.5000 g., 0.5000 Gold .0241 oz. AGW **Obv:** Bust right, date below **Obv. Designer:** Arnold Machin **Rev:** Caribbean Sparrow Hawk right, above denomination **Rev. Designer:** Gilroy Roberts

Date	Mintage	F	VF	XF	Unc	BU
1981FM (P)	2,513	Value: 50.00				

KM# 31.2 25 DOLLARS
1.5000 g., 0.5000 Gold .0241 oz. AGW **Obv:** Bust right, date below, error, without FM mint mark **Rev:** Caribbean Sparrow Hawk right, denomination below

Date	Mintage	F	VF	XF	Unc	BU
1981 (P)	—	Value: 60.00				

KM# 41 25 DOLLARS
1.5000 g., 0.5000 Gold .0241 oz. AGW **Obv:** Bust right, date below **Obv. Designer:** Arnold Machin **Rev:** Hawk above denomination

Date	Mintage	F	VF	XF	Unc	BU
1982FM (P)	3,819	Value: 55.00				

KM# 37 25 DOLLARS
1.5000 g., 0.5000 Gold .0241 oz. AGW **Obv:** Bust right, date below **Obv. Designer:** Arnold Machin **Rev:** Merlin Hawk left, above denomination **Rev. Designer:** Gilroy Roberts

Date	Mintage	F	VF	XF	Unc	BU
1983FM (P)	5,949	Value: 50.00				

KM# 40 25 DOLLARS
1.5000 g., 0.5000 Gold .0241 oz. AGW **Obv:** Bust right, date below **Obv. Designer:** Arnold Machin **Rev:** Peregrine Falcon, above denomination

Date	Mintage	F	VF	XF	Unc	BU
1984FM (P)	97	Value: 115				

KM# 73 25 DOLLARS

1.5000 g., 0.5000 Gold .0241 oz. AGW **Obv:** Head right, date below **Obv. Designer:** Raphael Maklouf **Rev:** Marsh Hawk above denomination

Date	Mintage	F	VF	XF	Unc	BU
1985FM (P)	1,294	Value: 80.00				

KM# 90 25 DOLLARS

20.0900 g., 0.9250 Silver .5977 oz. ASW **Series:** Sunken Ship Treasures **Obv:** Head right, date below **Rev:** Ornamental lock plate divides denomination

Date	Mintage	F	VF	XF	Unc	BU
1988FM (P)	—	Value: 26.00				

KM# 91 25 DOLLARS

20.0900 g., 0.9250 Silver .5977 oz. ASW **Series:** Sunken Ship Treasures **Obv:** Head right, date below **Rev:** Royal coat of arms on bottle, within square, divides denomination

Date	Mintage	F	VF	XF	Unc	BU
1988FM (P)	—	Value: 26.00				

KM# 92 25 DOLLARS

20.0900 g., 0.9250 Silver .5977 oz. ASW **Series:** Sunken Ship Treasures **Obv:** Head right, date below **Rev:** Finger ring divides denomination

Date	Mintage	F	VF	XF	Unc	BU
1988FM (P)	—	Value: 26.00				

KM# 93 25 DOLLARS

20.0900 g., 0.9250 Silver .5977 oz. ASW **Series:** Sunken Ship Treasures **Obv:** Head right, date below **Rev:** Hour glass, within square, divides denomination

Date	Mintage	F	VF	XF	Unc	BU
1988FM (P)	—	Value: 26.00				

KM# 94 25 DOLLARS

20.0900 g., 0.9250 Silver .5977 oz. ASW **Series:** Sunken Ship Treasures **Obv:** Head right, date below **Rev:** Dagger and scabbard, within square, divide denomination

Date	Mintage	F	VF	XF	Unc	BU
1988FM (P)	—	Value: 26.00				

KM# 95 25 DOLLARS

20.0900 g., 0.9250 Silver .5977 oz. ASW **Series:** Sunken Ship Treasures **Obv:** Head right, date below **Rev:** Jewel-encrusted cross, denomination above

Date	Mintage	F	VF	XF	Unc	BU
1988FM (P)	—	Value: 26.00				

KM# 96 25 DOLLARS

20.0900 g., 0.9250 Silver .5977 oz. ASW **Series:** Sunken Ship Treasures **Rev:** Crossed keys, denomination above

Date	Mintage	F	VF	XF	Unc	BU
1988FM (P)	—	Value: 26.00				

KM# 97 25 DOLLARS

20.0900 g., 0.9250 Silver .5977 oz. ASW **Series:** Sunken Ship Treasures **Obv:** Head right, date below **Rev:** Belt buckle, denomination above

Date	Mintage	F	VF	XF	Unc	BU
1988FM (P)	—	Value: 26.00				

KM# 98 25 DOLLARS

20.0900 g., 0.9250 Silver .5977 oz. ASW **Series:** Sunken Ship Treasures **Obv:** Head right, date below **Rev:** American bottle, within square, divides denomination

Date	Mintage	F	VF	XF	Unc	BU
1988FM (P)	—	Value: 26.00				

KM# 99 25 DOLLARS

20.0900 g., 0.9250 Silver .5977 oz. ASW **Series:** Sunken Ship Treasures **Obv:** Head right, date below **Rev:** Religious medallion, within square, divides denomination

Date	Mintage	F	VF	XF	Unc	BU
1988FM (P)	—	Value: 26.00				

KM# 100 25 DOLLARS

20.0900 g., 0.9250 Silver .5977 oz. ASW **Series:** Sunken Ship Treasures **Obv:** Head right, date below **Rev:** Baby figurines, denomination above

Date	Mintage	F	VF	XF	Unc	BU
1988FM (P)	—	Value: 26.00				

KM# 101 25 DOLLARS
20.0900 g., 0.9250 Silver .5977 oz. ASW **Series:** Sunken Ship Treasures **Obv:** Head right, date below **Rev:** Insignia of the Royal French Marines, denomination above

Date	Mintage	F	VF	XF	Unc	BU
1988FM (P)	—	Value: 26.00				

KM# 102 25 DOLLARS
20.0900 g., 0.9250 Silver .5977 oz. ASW **Series:** Sunken Ship Treasures **Obv:** Head right, date below **Rev:** Engraved printing block, denomination above

Date	Mintage	F	VF	XF	Unc	BU
1988FM (P)	—	Value: 26.00				

KM# 103 25 DOLLARS
20.0900 g., 0.9250 Silver .5977 oz. ASW **Series:** Sunken Ship Treasures **Obv:** Head right, date below **Rev:** Antique clock, denomination above

Date	Mintage	F	VF	XF	Unc	BU
1988FM (P)	—	Value: 26.00				

KM# 132 25 DOLLARS
20.0900 g., 0.9250 Silver .5977 oz. ASW **Obv:** Head right, date below **Rev:** Flintlock pistol divides denomination

Date	Mintage	F	VF	XF	Unc	BU
1988FM (P)	—	Value: 26.00				

KM# 133 25 DOLLARS
20.0900 g., 0.9250 Silver .5977 oz. ASW **Obv:** Head right, date below **Rev:** Stylized fish statue, within square, divides denomination

Date	Mintage	F	VF	XF	Unc	BU
1988FM (P)	—	Value: 26.00				

KM# 134 25 DOLLARS
20.0900 g., 0.9250 Silver .5977 oz. ASW **Obv:** Head right, date below **Rev:** Mortar and pestle, denomination above

Date	Mintage	F	VF	XF	Unc	BU
1988FM (P)	—	Value: 26.00				

KM# 135 25 DOLLARS
20.0900 g., 0.9250 Silver .5977 oz. ASW **Obv:** Head right, date below **Rev:** Open-mouthed dragon head sculpture, within square, divides denomination

Date	Mintage	F	VF	XF	Unc	BU
1988FM (P)	—	Value: 26.00				

KM# 136 25 DOLLARS
20.0900 g., 0.9250 Silver .5977 oz. ASW **Obv:** Head right, date below **Rev:** Military mortar, within square, divides denomination

Date	Mintage	F	VF	XF	Unc	BU
1988FM (P)	—	Value: 26.00				

KM# 137 25 DOLLARS
20.0900 g., 0.9250 Silver .5977 oz. ASW **Obv:** Head right, date below **Rev:** Seated figure sculpture within square, divides denomination

Date	Mintage	F	VF	XF	Unc	BU
1988FM (P)	—	Value: 26.00				

KM# 138 25 DOLLARS
20.0900 g., 0.9250 Silver .5977 oz. ASW **Obv:** Head right, date below **Rev:** Lion sculpture within square divides denomination

Date	Mintage	F	VF	XF	Unc	BU
1988FM (P)	—	Value: 26.00				

KM# 139 25 DOLLARS
20.0900 g., 0.9250 Silver .5977 oz. ASW **Obv:** Head right, date below **Rev:** Violin divides denomination

Date	Mintage	F	VF	XF	Unc	BU
1988FM (P)	—	Value: 26.00				

KM# 140 25 DOLLARS
20.0900 g., 0.9250 Silver .5977 oz. ASW **Obv:** Head right, date below **Rev:** Chalice, denomination above

Date	Mintage	F	VF	XF	Unc	BU
1988FM (P)	—	Value: 26.00				

KM# 141 25 DOLLARS
20.0900 g., 0.9250 Silver .5977 oz. ASW **Obv:** Head right, date below **Rev:** Pitcher, denomination above

Date	Mintage	F	VF	XF	Unc	BU
1988FM (P)	—	Value: 26.00				

KM# 142 25 DOLLARS
20.0900 g., 0.9250 Silver .5977 oz. ASW **Obv:** Head right, date below **Rev:** Cannon, denomination below

Date	Mintage	F	VF	XF	Unc	BU
1988FM (P)	—	Value: 26.00				

KM# 104 25 DOLLARS
21.5400 g., 0.9250 Silver .6406 oz. ASW **Series:** Discovery of America **Obv:** Head right, date below **Rev:** Columbus planning voyage, denomination below

Date	Mintage	F	VF	XF	Unc	BU
ND(1992)FM (P)	—	Value: 30.00				

KM# 105 25 DOLLARS
21.5400 g., 0.9250 Silver .6406 oz. ASW **Series:** Discovery of America **Obv:** Head right, date below **Rev:** Columbus lecturing, denomination above

Date	Mintage	F	VF	XF	Unc	BU
ND(1992)FM (P)	—	Value: 30.00				

KM# 106 25 DOLLARS
21.5400 g., 0.9250 Silver .6406 oz. ASW **Series:** Discovery of America **Obv:** Head right, date below **Rev:** Queen Isabella offering jewels, denomination above

Date	Mintage	F	VF	XF	Unc	BU
ND 1992)FM (P)	—	Value: 30.00				

KM# 107 25 DOLLARS
21.5400 g., 0.9250 Silver .6406 oz. ASW **Series:** Discovery of America **Obv:** Head right, date below **Rev:** Columbus aboard ship denomination at left

Date	Mintage	F	VF	XF	Unc	BU
ND(1992)FM (P)	—	Value: 30.00				

KM# 108 25 DOLLARS
21.5400 g., 0.9250 Silver .6406 oz. ASW **Series:** Discovery of America **Obv:** Head right, date below **Rev:** Columbus on horseback, denomination above

Date	Mintage	F	VF	XF	Unc	BU
ND(1992)FM (P)	—	Value: 30.00				

KM# 109 25 DOLLARS
21.5400 g., 0.9250 Silver .6406 oz. ASW **Series:** Discovery of America **Obv:** Head right, date below **Rev:** Ship under full sail, denomination at right

Date	Mintage	F	VF	XF	Unc	BU
ND(1992)FM	—	Value: 30.00				

KM# 110 25 DOLLARS
21.5400 g., 0.9250 Silver .6406 oz. ASW **Series:** Discovery of America **Obv:** Head right, date below **Rev:** Ship at anchor, denomination upper left

Date	Mintage	F	VF	XF	Unc	BU
ND(1992)FM (P)	—	Value: 30.00				

KM# 111 25 DOLLARS
21.5400 g., 0.9250 Silver .6406 oz. ASW **Series:** Discovery of America **Obv:** Head right, date below **Rev:** Natives offering gifts, denomination above

Date	Mintage	F	VF	XF	Unc	BU
ND(1992)FM (P)	—	Value: 30.00				

KM# 112 25 DOLLARS
21.5400 g., 0.9250 Silver .6406 oz. ASW **Series:** Discovery of America **Obv:** Head right, date below **Rev:** Shipwreck, denomination above

Date	Mintage	F	VF	XF	Unc	BU
ND(1992)FM (P)	—	Value: 30.00				

KM# 113 25 DOLLARS
21.5400 g., 0.9250 Silver .6406 oz. ASW **Series:** Discovery of America **Obv:** Head right, date below **Rev:** Royal banquet, denomination upper left

Date	Mintage	F	VF	XF	Unc	BU
ND(1992)FM (P)	—	Value: 30.00				

KM# 114 25 DOLLARS
21.5400 g., 0.9250 Silver .6406 oz. ASW **Series:** Discovery of America **Obv:** Head right, date below **Rev:** Columbus predicting lunar eclipse to natives, denomination at left

Date	Mintage	F	VF	XF	Unc	BU
ND(1992)FM (P)	—	Value: 30.00				

KM# 115 25 DOLLARS
21.5400 g., 0.9250 Silver .6406 oz. ASW **Series:** Discovery of America **Obv:** Head right, date below **Rev:** Columbus on shore, denomination at left

Date	Mintage	F	VF	XF	Unc	BU
ND(1992)FM (P)	—	Value: 30.00				

KM# 116 25 DOLLARS
21.5400 g., 0.9250 Silver .6406 oz. ASW **Series:** Discovery of America **Obv:** Head right, date below **Rev:** Spanish figures, denomination upper right

Date	Mintage	F	VF	XF	Unc	BU
ND(1992)FM (P)	—	Value: 30.00				

KM# 117 25 DOLLARS
21.5400 g., 0.9250 Silver .6406 oz. ASW **Series:** Discovery of America **Obv:** Head right, date below **Rev:** Columbus with shore party, denomination above right

Date	Mintage	F	VF	XF	Unc	BU
ND(1992)FM (P)	—	Value: 30.00				

KM# 118 25 DOLLARS
21.5400 g., 0.9250 Silver .6406 oz. ASW **Series:** Discovery of America **Obv:** Head right, date below **Rev:** Columbus on death bed, denomination below

Date	Mintage	F	VF	XF	Unc	BU
ND(1992)FM (P)	—	Value: 30.00				

KM# 122 25 DOLLARS
21.5400 g., 0.9250 Silver .6406 oz. ASW **Series:** Discovery of America **Obv:** Head right, date below **Rev:** Columbus bowing before King Ferdinand, denomination,top left

Date	Mintage	F	VF	XF	Unc	BU
ND(1992)FM (P)	—	Value: 30.00				

KM# 123 25 DOLLARS
21.5400 g., 0.9250 Silver .6406 oz. ASW **Series:** Discovery of America **Obv:** Head right, two dates below **Rev:** Columbus before Queen Isabella, denomination; top right

Date	Mintage	F	VF	XF	Unc	BU
ND(1992)FM (P)	—	Value: 30.00				

KM# 124 25 DOLLARS
21.5400 g., 0.9250 Silver .6406 oz. ASW **Series:** Discovery of America **Obv:** Head right, two dates below **Rev:** Columbus before King Ferdinand and Queen Isabella, denomination above

Date	Mintage	F	VF	XF	Unc	BU
ND(1992)FM (P)	—	Value: 30.00				

KM# 125 25 DOLLARS
21.5400 g., 0.9250 Silver .6406 oz. ASW **Series:** Discovery of America **Obv:** Head right, two dates below **Rev:** Columbus getting provisions for his ships, denomination upper left

Date	Mintage	F	VF	XF	Unc	BU
ND(1992)FM (P)	—	Value: 30.00				

KM# 126 25 DOLLARS
21.5400 g., 0.9250 Silver .6406 oz. ASW **Series:** Discovery of America **Obv:** Head right, two dates below **Rev:** Four sailing ships, denomination lower left

Date	Mintage	F	VF	XF	Unc	BU
ND(1992)FM (P)	—	Value: 30.00				

KM# 127 25 DOLLARS
21.5400 g., 0.9250 Silver .6406 oz. ASW **Series:** Discovery of America **Obv:** Head right, two dates below **Rev:** Columbus navigating by stars

Date	Mintage	F	VF	XF	Unc	BU
ND(1992)FM (P)	—	Value: 30.00				

KM# 128 25 DOLLARS
21.5400 g., 0.9250 Silver .6406 oz. ASW **Series:** Discovery of America **Obv:** Head right, two dates below **Rev:** Sighting land, denomination upper left

Date	Mintage	F	VF	XF	Unc	BU
ND(1992)FM (P)	—	Value: 30.00				

KM# 129 25 DOLLARS
21.5400 g., 0.9250 Silver .6406 oz. ASW **Series:** Discovery of America **Obv:** Head right, two dates below **Rev:** Columbus claiming the newly discovered land, denomination upper left

Date	Mintage	F	VF	XF	Unc	BU
ND(1992)FM (P)	—	Value: 30.00				

KM# 130 25 DOLLARS
21.5400 g., 0.9250 Silver .6406 oz. ASW **Series:** Discovery of America **Obv:** Head right, two dates below **Rev:** Columbus seated on shore with shipwreck offshore, denomination upper right

Date	Mintage	F	VF	XF	Unc	BU
ND(1992)FM (P)	—	Value: 30.00				

KM# 131 25 DOLLARS
21.5400 g., 0.9250 Silver .6406 oz. ASW **Series:** Discovery of America **Obv:** Head right, two dates below **Rev:** Columbus as prisoner, denomination above

Date	Mintage	F	VF	XF	Unc	BU
ND(1992)FM (P)	—	Value: 30.00				

KM# 186 25 DOLLARS
20.0900 g., 0.9250 Silver 0.5975 oz. ASW, 40 mm. **Obv:** Bust right, date below, 1988 type of KM#90-103 **Rev:** Figure bowing to King, denomination upper left, type of KM#122 originally minted in 1992 **Edge:** Reeded **Note:** Mint error; muled dies.

Date	Mintage	F	VF	XF	Unc	BU
1988	—	—	—	—	800	—

KM# 178 25 DOLLARS
21.6000 g., 0.9250 Silver .6424 oz. ASW, 40 mm. **Series:** Endangered Wildlife **Obv:** Head right **Rev:** Three flamingos and four nests, denomination above **Edge:** Reeded

Date	Mintage	F	VF	XF	Unc	BU
1993 Proof	—	Value: 40.00				

KM# 179 25 DOLLARS
20.9000 g., 0.9250 Silver .5977 oz. ASW, 40 mm. **Subject:** Endangered Wildlife **Obv:** Head right **Rev:** Front half of tiger stalking left, denomination between legs **Edge:** Reeded

Date	Mintage	F	VF	XF	Unc	BU
1993FM (P)	—	Value: 40.00				

KM# 143 25 DOLLARS
20.0900 g., 0.9250 Silver .5977 oz. ASW **Series:** Endangered Wildlife **Obv:** Head right, date below **Rev:** African elephants right, trunks raised, denomination above

Date	Mintage	F	VF	XF	Unc	BU
1993FM (P)	—	Value: 40.00				

KM# 144 25 DOLLARS
20.0900 g., 0.9250 Silver .5977 oz. ASW **Series:** Endangered Wildlife **Obv:** Head right, date below **Rev:** Mountain gorilla left, denomination above

Date	Mintage	F	VF	XF	Unc	BU
1993FM (P)	—	Value: 40.00				

KM# 145 25 DOLLARS
20.0900 g., 0.9250 Silver .5977 oz. ASW **Series:** Endangered Wildlife **Obv:** Head right, date below **Rev:** Cape mountain zebra right, denomination top left

Date	Mintage	F	VF	XF	Unc	BU
1993FM (P)	—	Value: 40.00				

KM# 146 25 DOLLARS
20.0900 g., 0.9250 Silver .5977 oz. ASW **Series:** Endangered Wildlife **Obv:** Head right, date below **Rev:** Polar bear right, denomination below

Date	Mintage	F	VF	XF	Unc	BU
1993FM (P)	—	Value: 40.00				

KM# 147 25 DOLLARS
20.0900 g., 0.9250 Silver .5977 oz. ASW **Series:** Endangered Wildlife **Obv:** Head right, date below **Rev:** Bald Eagle, wings spread, denomination above

Date	Mintage	F	VF	XF	Unc	BU
1993FM (P)	—	Value: 40.00				

KM# 148 25 DOLLARS
20.0900 g., 0.9250 Silver .5977 oz. ASW **Series:** Endangered Wildlife **Obv:** Head right, date below **Rev:** Snow Leopard right, denomination top left

Date	Mintage	F	VF	XF	Unc	BU
1993FM (P)	—	Value: 40.00				

KM# 149 25 DOLLARS
20.0900 g., 0.9250 Silver .5977 oz. ASW **Series:** Endangered Wildlife **Obv:** Head right, date below **Rev:** Javan Rhinoceros left, denomination below

Date	Mintage	F	VF	XF	Unc	BU
1993FM (P)	—	Value: 40.00				

KM# 150 25 DOLLARS
20.0900 g., 0.9250 Silver .5977 oz. ASW **Series:** Endangered Wildlife **Obv:** Head right, date below **Rev:** Asian Lion left, denomination above

Date	Mintage	F	VF	XF	Unc	BU
1993FM (P)	—	Value: 40.00				

KM# 151 25 DOLLARS
20.0900 g., 0.9250 Silver .5977 oz. ASW **Series:** Endangered Wildlife **Obv:** Head right, date below **Rev:** Seated Giant Panda right, denomination at right

Date	Mintage	F	VF	XF	Unc	BU
1993FM (P)	—	Value: 40.00				

KM# 152 25 DOLLARS
20.0900 g., 0.9250 Silver .5977 oz. ASW **Series:** Endangered Wildlife **Obv:** Head right, date below **Rev:** Golden Lion Tamarin

Date	Mintage	F	VF	XF	Unc	BU
1993FM (P)	—	Value: 40.00				

KM# 153 25 DOLLARS
20.0900 g., 0.9250 Silver .5977 oz. ASW **Series:** Endangered Wildlife **Obv:** Head right, date below **Rev:** Pere David's deer, denomination upper left

Date	Mintage	F	VF	XF	Unc	BU
1993FM (P)	—	Value: 35.00				

KM# 154 25 DOLLARS
20.0900 g., 0.9250 Silver .5977 oz. ASW **Series:** Endangered Wildlife **Obv:** Head right, date below **Rev:** Spectacled bear standing, denomination upper right

Date	Mintage	F	VF	XF	Unc	BU
1993FM (P)	—	Value: 40.00				

KM# 155 25 DOLLARS
20.0900 g., 0.9250 Silver .5977 oz. ASW, 40 mm. **Series:** Endangered Wildlife **Obv:** Head right, date below **Rev:** Imperial Parrot on tree branch, denomination at left **Edge:** Reeded

Date	Mintage	F	VF	XF	Unc	BU
1993FM (P)	—	Value: 50.00				

KM# 158 25 DOLLARS
21.5900 g., 0.9250 Silver .6420 oz. ASW **Series:** Endangered Wildlife **Obv:** Head right, date below **Rev:** Pair of black-footed ferrets, one standing, right

Date	Mintage	F	VF	XF	Unc	BU
1993FM Proof	—	Value: 50.00				

KM# 159 25 DOLLARS
21.5900 g., 0.9250 Silver .6420 oz. ASW **Series:** Endangered Wildlife **Obv:** Head right, date below **Rev:** Large rock lizard right, denomination below

Date	Mintage	F	VF	XF	Unc	BU
1993FM Proof	—	Value: 50.00				

KM# 160 25 DOLLARS
21.5900 g., 0.9250 Silver .6420 oz. ASW **Series:** Endangered Wildlife **Obv:** Head right, date below **Rev:** Two Parma wallabies, one with offspring left, denomination above

Date	Mintage	F	VF	XF	Unc	BU
1993FM Proof	—	Value: 40.00				

KM# 161 25 DOLLARS
21.5900 g., 0.9250 Silver .6420 oz. ASW **Series:** Endangered Wildlife **Obv:** Head right, date below **Rev:** Pair of leatherback sea turtles and Portuguese Man-o-War jelly fish, denomination below

Date	Mintage	F	VF	XF	Unc	BU
1993FM Proof	—	Value: 45.00				

KM# 170 25 DOLLARS
21.3500 g., 0.9250 Silver .6349 oz. ASW **Series:** Endangered Wildlife **Obv:** Head right, date below **Rev:** Cheetah running left, denomination above

Date	Mintage	F	VF	XF	Unc	BU
1993FM (P)	—	Value: 40.00				

KM# 171 25 DOLLARS
21.3500 g., 0.9250 Silver .6349 oz. ASW **Series:** Endangered Wildlife **Obv:** Head right, date below **Rev:** European Bison in forest, left denomination below

Date	Mintage	F	VF	XF	Unc	BU
1993FM (P)	—	Value: 40.00				

KM# 165 25 DOLLARS
21.5900 g., 0.9250 Silver .6420 oz. ASW **Series:** Endangered Wildlife **Obv:** Head right, date below **Rev:** Two seals frolicking, denomination below

Date	Mintage	F	VF	XF	Unc	BU
1997	—	—	—	—	40.00	—

KM# 166 25 DOLLARS
21.5900 g., 0.9250 Silver .6420 oz. ASW **Series:** Endangered Wildlife **Obv:** Head right, date below **Rev:** Sea otter holding a sea urchin, denomination lower left

Date	Mintage	F	VF	XF	Unc	BU
1997	—	—	—	—	40.00	—

KM# 167 25 DOLLARS
21.5900 g., 0.9250 Silver .6420 oz. ASW **Series:** Endangered Wildlife **Obv:** Head right, date below **Rev:** Pair of sparring Arabian oryx, denomination above

Date	Mintage	F	VF	XF	Unc	BU
1997	—	—	—	—	35.00	—

KM# 168 25 DOLLARS
21.5900 g., 0.9250 Silver .6420 oz. ASW **Series:** Endangered Wildlife **Obv:** Head right, date below **Rev:** Diving humpback whale., denomination at left

Date	Mintage	F	VF	XF	Unc	BU
1997	—	—	—	—	40.00	—

KM# 28 50 DOLLARS
2.6800 g., 0.5000 Gold .0430 oz. AGW **Obv:** Bust right, date below **Rev:** Golden Dove of Christmas divides denomination

Date	Mintage	F	VF	XF	Unc	BU
1980 Proof	6,379	Value: 60.00				

KM# 75 50 DOLLARS
2.0687 g., 0.5000 Gold .0332 oz. AGW **Obv:** Bust right, date below **Rev:** Flute player, denomination below

Date	Mintage	F	VF	XF	Unc	BU
1988 Proof	—	Value: 55.00				

KM# 76 50 DOLLARS
2.0687 g., 0.5000 Gold .0332 oz. AGW **Obv:** Bust right, date below **Rev:** Bird's-head staff, denomination below

Date	Mintage	F	VF	XF	Unc	BU
1988 Proof	—	Value: 55.00				

KM# 77 50 DOLLARS
2.0687 g., 0.5000 Gold .0332 oz. AGW **Obv:** Bust right, date below **Rev** Double-spouted vessel, denomination above

Date	Mintage	F	VF	XF	Unc	BU
1988 Proof	—	Value: 55.00				

KM# 78 50 DOLLARS
2.0687 g., 0.5000 Gold .0332 oz. AGW **Obv:** Bust right, date below **Rev:** Deer-top bell divides denomination

Date	Mintage	F	VF	XF	Unc	BU
1988 Proof	—	Value: 55.00				

KM# 79 50 DOLLARS
2.0687 g., 0.5000 Gold .0332 oz. AGW **Obv:** Bust right, date below **Rev:** Two-headed animal, denomination above

Date	Mintage	F	VF	XF	Unc	BU
1988 Proof	—	Value: 55.00				

KM# 80 50 DOLLARS
2.0687 g., 0.5000 Gold .0332 oz. AGW **Obv:** Bust right, date below **Rev:** Turtle, denomination below

Date	Mintage	F	VF	XF	Unc	BU
1988 Proof	—	Value: 55.00				

KM# 81 50 DOLLARS
2.0687 g., 0.5000 Gold .0332 oz. AGW **Obv:** Bust right, date below **Rev:** Frog, denomination above

Date	Mintage	F	VF	XF	Unc	BU
1988 Proof	—	Value: 55.00				

KM# 82 50 DOLLARS
2.0687 g., 0.5000 Gold .0332 oz. AGW **Obv:** Bust right, date below **Rev:** Mixtec mask, denomination above

Date	Mintage	F	VF	XF	Unc	BU
1988 Proof	—	Value: 55.00				

KM# 83 50 DOLLARS
2.0687 g., 0.5000 Gold .0332 oz. AGW **Obv:** Bust right, date below **Rev:** Chimu gold beaker, denomination below

Date	Mintage	F	VF	XF	Unc	BU
1988 Proof	—	Value: 55.00				

KM# 84 50 DOLLARS
2.0687 g., 0.5000 Gold .0332 oz. AGW **Obv:** Bust right, date below **Rev:** Bird vessel, denomination above

Date	Mintage	F	VF	XF	Unc	BU
1988 Proof	—	Value: 55.00				

KM# 85 50 DOLLARS
2.0687 g., 0.5000 Gold .0332 oz. AGW **Obv:** Bust right, date below **Rev:** Ceremonial headdress, denomination below

Date	Mintage	F	VF	XF	Unc	BU
1988 Proof	—	Value: 55.00				

KM# 86 50 DOLLARS

2.0687 g., 0.5000 Gold .0332 oz. AGW **Obv:** Bust right, date below **Rev:** Sacrificial knife, denomination below

Date	Mintage	F	VF	XF	Unc	BU
1988 Proof	—	Value: 55.00				

KM# 87 50 DOLLARS

2.0687 g., 0.5000 Gold .0332 oz. AGW **Obv:** Bust right, date below **Rev:** Ceremonial dancer, denomination below

Date	Mintage	F	VF	XF	Unc	BU
1988 Proof	—	Value: 55.00				

KM# 88 50 DOLLARS

2.0687 g., 0.5000 Gold .0332 oz. AGW **Obv:** Bust right, date below **Rev:** Spanish Colonial gold coin, denomination below

Date	Mintage	F	VF	XF	Unc	BU
1988 Proof	—	Value: 55.00				

KM# 89 50 DOLLARS

2.0687 g., 0.5000 Gold .0332 oz. AGW **Obv:** Bust right, date below **Rev:** Crossed hands divide denomination

Date	Mintage	F	VF	XF	Unc	BU
1988 Proof	—	Value: 55.00				

KM# 7 100 DOLLARS

7.1000 g., 0.9000 Gold .2054 oz. AGW **Obv:** Bust right, date below **Obv. Designer:** Arnold Machin **Rev:** Royal Tern, denomination in background **Rev. Designer:** Gilroy Roberts

Date	Mintage	F	VF	XF	Unc	BU
1975FM (M) Rare	10	—	—	—	—	—
1975FM (U)	13,000	—	—	—	145	—
1975FM (P)	Est. 23,000	Value: 150				

Note: Includes 8,754 in First Day Covers

KM# 8 100 DOLLARS

7.1000 g., 0.9000 Gold .2054 oz. AGW **Subject:** 50th Birthday of Queen Elizabeth II **Obv:** Bust right, date below **Rev:** Crowned monogram above shield with woman and twelve lamps, VIGILATE on banner below, denomination above

Date	Mintage	F	VF	XF	Unc	BU
1976FM (M) Rare	10	—	—	—	—	—
1976FM (U)	1,752	—	—	—	145	—
1976FM (P)	12,000	Value: 150				

KM# 15 100 DOLLARS

7.1000 g., 0.9000 Gold .2054 oz. AGW **Subject:** Queen's Silver Jubilee **Obv:** Bust right, date below **Rev:** Imperial crown above two dates, denomination upper right

Date	Mintage	F	VF	XF	Unc	BU
1977FM (U) Rare	10	—	—	—	—	—
1977FM (P)	6,715	Value: 155				

KM# 23 100 DOLLARS

7.1000 g., 0.9000 Gold .2054 oz. AGW **Subject:** Coronation Jubilee **Obv:** Bust right, date below **Rev:** Crossed sceptres with royal orb, orb divides dates at top **Shape:** 25-sided

Date	Mintage	F	VF	XF	Unc	BU
1978FM (P)	5,772	Value: 160				

KM# 25 100 DOLLARS

7.1000 g., 0.9000 Gold .2054 oz. AGW **Obv:** Bust right, date below **Rev:** Bust of Sir Francis Drake with ruffed collar, right, denomination below

Date	Mintage	F	VF	XF	Unc	BU
1979FM (P)	3,216	Value: 170				

KM# 29 100 DOLLARS

7.1000 g., 0.9000 Gold .2054 oz. AGW **Subject:** 400th Anniversary of Drake's Voyage **Obv:** Bust right, date below **Rev:** The Golden Hind, denomination below

Date	Mintage	F	VF	XF	Unc	BU
1980 Proof	5,412	Value: 165				

KM# 32 100 DOLLARS

7.1000 g., 0.9000 Gold .2054 oz. AGW **Subject:** Knighting of Sir Francis Drake **Obv:** Bust right, date below **Rev:** Sir Francis Drake being knighted, denomination below

Date	Mintage	F	VF	XF	Unc	BU
1981FM (P)	1,321	Value: 185				

KM# 34 100 DOLLARS

7.1000 g., 0.9000 Gold .2054 oz. AGW **Subject:** 30th Anniversary - Reign of Queen Elizabeth II **Obv:** Bust right, date below **Rev:** Crowned monogram, denomination below **Shape:** 6-sided

Date	Mintage	F	VF	XF	Unc	BU
1982FM (P)	620	Value: 230				

KM# 38 100 DOLLARS

7.1000 g., 0.9000 Gold .2054 oz. AGW **Subject:** 30th Anniversary - Coronation of Queen Elizabeth II **Obv:** Bust right, date below **Rev:** Sceptres divide royal symbols and dates, denomination below **Shape:** 6-sided

Date	Mintage	F	VF	XF	Unc	BU
1983FM (P)	624	Value: 230				

KM# 39 100 DOLLARS

7.1000 g., 0.9000 Gold .2054 oz. AGW **Subject:** Flora - Ginger Thomas **Obv:** Bust right, date below **Rev:** Flower, denomination below

Date	Mintage	F	VF	XF	Unc	BU
1984FM (P)	25	Value: 475				

KM# 74 100 DOLLARS

7.1000 g., 0.9000 Gold .2054 oz. AGW **Subject:** Sir Francis Drake's West Indian Voyage **Obv:** Head right, date below **Rev:** Ship, denomination below **Shape:** 6-sided

Date	Mintage	F	VF	XF	Unc	BU
1985FM (P)	772	Value: 220				

KM# 119 100 DOLLARS

4.1180 g., 0.5000 Gold .0662 oz. AGW **Subject:** Discovery of America - King Ferdinand of Spain **Obv:** Head right, two dates below **Rev:** Bust, facing, denomination at right

Date	Mintage	F	VF	XF	Unc	BU
ND(1991)FM (P)	—	Value: 100				

KM# 162 100 DOLLARS

4.1180 g., 0.5000 Gold .0662 oz. AGW **Obv:** Head right, two dates below **Rev:** The Pinta, denomination upper right

Date	Mintage	F	VF	XF	Unc	BU
ND(1994) Proof	—	Value: 100				

KM# 256 100 DOLLARS

4.3100 g., 0.5000 Gold 0.0662 oz. AGW, 20.75 mm. **Obv:** Head right, date below **Rev:** Columbus' landing scene **Edge:** Reeded

Date	Mintage	F	VF	XF	Unc	BU
ND(1996?)FM Proof	—	Value: 100				

KM# 174.1 100 DOLLARS

6.2200 g., 0.9990 Gold .2000 oz. AGW **Subject:** Queen Mother's 100th Birthday **Obv:** Head right, date below **Rev:** 1/2 bust of Queen Mother facing **Edge:** Reeded

Date	Mintage	F	VF	XF	Unc	BU
2000 Proof	5,000	Value: 165				

KM# 174.2 100 DOLLARS
6.2200 g., 0.9999 Gold 0.2 oz. AGW, 22 mm. **Subject:** Queen Mother **Obv:** Head right, date below **Rev:** Queen Mother's portrait, facing, divides dates, a tiny black sapphire mounted on her broach, denomination below **Edge:** Reeded

Date	Mintage	F	VF	XF	Unc	BU
2000 Proof	1,000	Value: 195				

KM# 177 100 DOLLARS
6.2200 g., 0.9990 Gold .2000 oz. AGW **Subject:** 1st Anniversary - Earl and Countess of Wessex **Obv:** Head right, date below **Rev:** 1/2 figures of Earl and Countess of Wessex facing, date below **Edge:** Reeded

Date	Mintage	F	VF	XF	Unc	BU
2000 Proof	5,000	Value: 175				

KM# 120 250 DOLLARS
8.0494 g., 0.5000 Gold .1294 oz. AGW **Subject:** Quincentennial - Discovery of America **Obv:** Head right, two dates below **Rev:** Bust of young Queen Isabella, half left, denomination at left

Date	Mintage	F	VF	XF	Unc	BU
ND(1991)FM (P)	—	Value: 290				

KM# 163 250 DOLLARS
8.0494 g., 0.5000 Gold .1294 oz. AGW **Subject:** The Nina **Obv:** Head right, two dates below **Rev:** Ship, denomination above

Date	Mintage	F	VF	XF	Unc	BU
ND(1994) Proof	—	Value: 290				

KM# 257 250 DOLLARS
8.1700 g., 0.5000 Gold 0.1294 oz. AGW, 26 mm. **Obv:** Head right, two dates below **Rev:** Columbus' personal coat of arms **Edge:** Reeded

Date	Mintage	F	VF	XF	Unc	BU
ND(1996?)FM Proof	—	Value: 250				

KM# 121 500 DOLLARS
19.8126 g., 0.5000 Gold .3185 oz. AGW **Subject:** Discovery of America **Obv:** Bust right, two dates below **Rev:** Christopher Columbus, half right, denomination upper right

Date	Mintage	F	VF	XF	Unc	BU
ND(1991)FM (P)	—	Value: 500				

KM# 164 500 DOLLARS
19.8126 g., 0.5000 Gold .3185 oz. AGW **Subject:** The Santa Maria **Obv:** Head right, two dates below **Rev:** Ship sailing left, no gulls, denomination upper left

Date	Mintage	F	VF	XF	Unc	BU
ND(1994) Proof	—	Value: 500				

KM# 258 500 DOLLARS
20.2200 g., 0.5000 Gold 0.3185 oz. AGW, 35.75 mm. **Obv:** Head right, two dates below **Rev:** Columbus' three ships crossing the Atlantic to America **Edge:** Reeded

Date	Mintage	F	VF	XF	Unc	BU
ND(1996?)FM Proof	—	Value: 550				

KM# 156 1000 DOLLARS
14.8000 g., 0.9990 Platinum .4758 oz. APW **Subject:** Discovery of America **Obv:** Head right, two dates below **Rev:** Three ships sailing, denomination above, within circle,

Date	Mintage	F	VF	XF	Unc	BU
ND(1992) Proof	—	Value: 1,150				

MINT SETS

KM#	Date	Mintage	Identification	Issue Price	Mkt Val
MS1	1973 (6)	18,402	KM#1-5, 6a	11.50	8.00
MS2	1974 (6)	9,474	KM#1-6	10.00	8.00
MS3	1975 (6)	2,351	KM#1-6	12.50	10.00
MS4	1976 (6)	996	KM#1-6	13.50	12.00
MS5	1977 (6)	782	KM#1-6	12.50	12.00
MS6	1978 (6)	943	KM#1-6	13.00	12.00
MS7	1979 (7)	680	KM#1-6, 24	20.00	25.00
MS8	1980 (7)	1,007	KM#1-6, 26	21.00	25.00
MS9	1981 (9)	472	KM#1-6, 30	20.00	30.00
MS10	1982 (7)	—	KM#1-6, 33	28.50	35.00
MS11	1983 (7)	203	KM#1-6, 35	22.00	50.00

PROOF SETS

KM#	Date	Mintage	Identification	Issue Price	Mkt Val
PS1	1973 (6)	146,581	KM#1-5, 6a. Includes 34,418 proofs in First Day Covers	15.00	15.00
PS2	1974 (6)	93,555	KM#1-5, 6a	20.00	16.50
PS3	1975 (6)	32,244	KM#1-5, 6a	25.00	18.50
PS4	1976 (6)	15,003	KM#1-5, 6a	25.00	18.50
PS5	1977 (6)	7,218	KM#1-5, 6a	26.00	20.00
PS6	1977 (6)	17,366	KM#9-14	60.00	40.00
PS7	1978 (6)	7,059	KM#1-5, 6a	25.00	20.00
PS8	1978 (6)	6,196	KM#16-21	—	40.00
PS9	1979 (7)	5,304	KM#1-5, 6a, 24a	39.50	37.50
PS10	1980 (7)	3,421	KM#105, 6a, 26a	97.00	47.50
PS11	1981 (7)	1,124	KM#1-5, 6a, 30a	97.00	60.00
PS12	1982 (7)	—	KM#1-5, 6a, 33a	97.00	60.00
PS13	1983 (7)	478	KM#1-5, 6a, 35a	77.00	65.00
PS14	1984 (7)	5,000	KM#1-5, 6a, 35a	77.00	60.00
PS15	1985 (6)	—	KM#42-47	20.50	45.00
PS16	1985 (6)	—	KM#42a-47a	76.00	95.00
PS17	ND (1991) (3)	—	KM#119-121	975	1,050
PS18	ND (1994) (3)	—	KM#162-164	975	1,075
PS19	ND (1996) (3)	—	KM#256, 257, 258	—	1,025

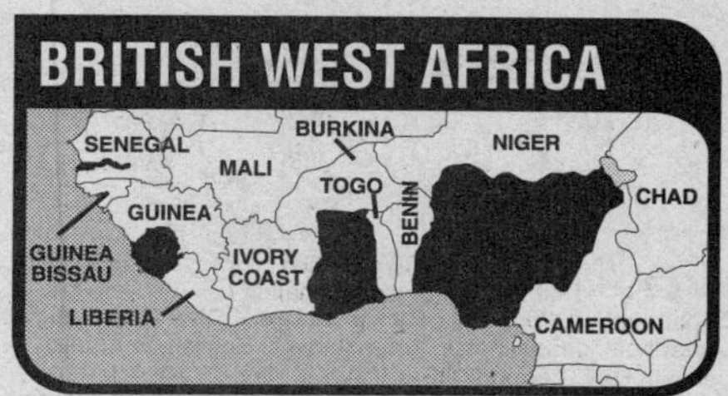

British West Africa was an administrative grouping of the four former British West African colonies of Gambia, Sierra Leone, Nigeria and Gold Coast (now Ghana). All are now independent republics and members of the British Commonwealth of Nations. See separate entries for individual statistics and history.

The Bank of British West Africa became the banker to the Colonial Government in 1894 and held this status until 1912. As such they were responsible for maintaining a proper supply of silver coinage for the colonies.

Through the subsidiary efforts of the Governor of Lagos, Nigeria a specific British West African coinage was put into use between 1907 and 1911. These coins bear the inscription, NIGERIA-BRITISH WEST AFRICA.

The four colonies were supplied with a common coinage and banknotes by the West African Currency Board from 1912 through 1958. This coinage bore the inscription BRITISH WEST AFRICA. The coinage, which includes three denominations of 1936 bearing the name of Edward VIII, is obsolete.

For later coinage see Gambia, Ghana, Sierra Leone and Nigeria.

RULERS
British, until 1958

MINT MARKS
G-J.R. Gaunt & Sons, Birmingham
H - Heaton Mint, Birmingham
K, KN - King's Norton, Birmingham
SA - Pretoria, South Africa
No mm - Royal Mint, London

MONETARY SYSTEM
12 Pence = 1 Shilling
20 Shillings = 1 Pound

BRITISH COLONIES

POUND COINAGE

KM# 1 1/10 PENNY
Aluminum **Ruler:** Edward VII **Obv:** Crown above center hole, denomination around hole in English, in Arabic beneath **Obv. Legend:** EDWARD VII KING & EMPEROR **Rev:** Hexagram divides date at bottom **Rev. Legend:** NIGERIA BRITISH WEST AFRICA

Date	Mintage	F	VF	XF	Unc	BU
1907	1,254,000	2.00	4.00	10.00	20.00	35.00
1908	8,363,000	1.00	3.00	6.00	15.00	25.00
1908 Proof	—	Value: 300				

KM# 3 1/10 PENNY
Copper-Nickel **Ruler:** Edward VII **Obv:** Crown above center hole, denomination around hole in English, in Arabic beneath **Obv. Legend:** EDWARD VII KING & EMPEROR **Rev:** Hexagram divides date at bottom **Rev. Legend:** NIGERIA BRITISH WEST AFRICA

Date	Mintage	F	VF	XF	Unc	BU
1908	9,600,000	0.30	0.50	1.00	2.00	3.50
1909	4,800,000	0.40	0.75	1.50	5.00	9.00
1910	7,200,000	0.50	1.00	2.00	7.50	12.50

KM# 4 1/10 PENNY
Copper-Nickel **Ruler:** George V **Obv:** Crown above center hole, denomination around hole in English, in Arabic beneath **Obv. Legend:** GEORGIVS V REX ET IND: IMP: **Rev:** Hexagram divides date at bottom **Rev. Legend:** NIGERIA BRITISH WEST AFRICA

Date	Mintage	F	VF	XF	Unc	BU
1911H	7,200,000	1.50	3.50	7.50	15.00	28.00

KM# 7 1/10 PENNY

Copper-Nickel, 20.5 mm. **Ruler:** George V **Obv:** Crown above center hole, denomination around hole in English, in Arabic beneath **Obv. Legend:** GEORGIVS V REX ET IND: IMP: **Rev:** Hexagram divides date at bottom **Rev. Legend:** BRITISH WEST AFRICA **Edge:** Plain

Date	Mintage	F	VF	XF	Unc	BU
1912H	10,800,000	0.30	0.75	1.50	3.50	7.00
1913	4,632,000	1.00	2.00	3.50	6.50	11.50
1913H	1,080,000	0.30	0.75	1.50	3.50	7.00
1914	1,200,000	3.00	5.00	10.00	22.50	40.00
1914H	20,088,000	0.50	1.25	2.00	5.00	9.00
1915H	10,032,000	0.30	0.75	1.50	5.00	9.00
1916H	480,000	25.00	50.00	75.00	150	175
1917H	9,384,000	2.00	3.00	5.00	15.00	25.00
1919H	912,000	1.25	2.00	4.00	7.50	13.50
1919KN	480,000	10.00	25.00	50.00	75.00	—
1920H	1,560,000	2.00	3.00	5.00	10.00	18.00
1920KN	12,996,000	0.40	1.00	3.00	5.00	9.00
1920KN Proof	—	Value: 125				
1922KN	7,265,000	1.00	1.75	4.50	12.00	20.00
1923KN	12,000,000	0.30	0.75	1.50	5.00	9.00
1925	2,400,000	5.00	10.00	20.00	40.00	70.00
1925H	12,000,000	2.00	3.00	5.00	12.00	20.00
1925KN	12,000,000	0.75	1.50	3.00	8.00	15.00
1926	12,000,000	0.75	1.50	2.50	6.00	10.00
1927	3,984,000	0.20	0.50	1.50	3.00	6.00
1927 Proof	—	Value: 150				
1928	11,760,000	0.20	0.50	1.50	3.00	6.00
1928 Proof	—	Value: 150				
1928H	2,964,000	0.20	0.50	1.50	3.00	6.00
1928KN	3,151,000	2.00	3.00	6.00	15.00	25.00
1930	9,600,000	2.00	3.00	6.00	15.00	25.00
1930 Proof	—	Value: 150				
1931	9,840,000	0.20	0.50	1.00	3.00	6.00
1931 Proof	—	Value: 150				
1932	3,600,000	0.20	0.50	1.50	5.00	9.00
1932 Proof	—	Value: 150				
1933	7,200,000	0.20	0.50	1.50	3.50	7.00
1933 Proof	—	Value: 150				
1934	4,800,000	0.75	1.50	3.00	6.00	10.00
1934 Proof	—	Value: 150				
1935	13,200,000	0.75	1.50	3.00	7.50	12.50
1935 Proof	—	Value: 150				
1936	9,720,000	0.20	0.50	1.00	3.00	6.00
1936 Proof	—	Value: 150				

KM# 14 1/10 PENNY

Copper-Nickel **Ruler:** Edward VIII **Obv:** Crown above center hole, denomination around hole in English, in Arabic beneath **Obv. Legend:** EDWARDVS VIII REX ET IND: IMP: **Rev:** Hexagram divides date at bottom **Rev. Legend:** BRITISH WEST AFRICA

Date	Mintage	F	VF	XF	Unc	BU
1936	5,880,000	0.25	0.50	1.00	2.50	4.50
1936 Proof	—	Value: 200				
1936H	1,404,000	50.00	75.00	125	250	—
1936H Proof	—	Value: 300				
1936KN	3,000,000	1.00	2.00	3.50	9.00	15.00
1936KN Proof	—	Value: 200				

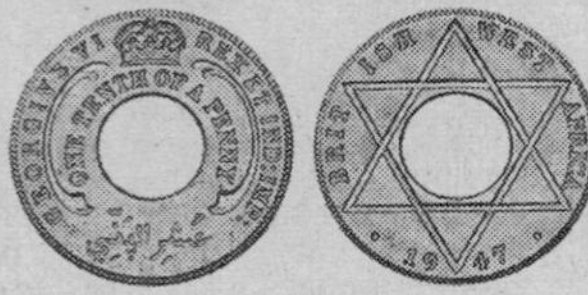

KM# 20 1/10 PENNY

Copper-Nickel **Ruler:** George VI **Obv:** Crown above center hole, denomination around hole in English, in Arabic beneath **Obv. Legend:** GEORGIVS VI REX ET IND: IMP: **Rev:** Hexagram divides date at bottom **Rev. Legend:** BRITISH WEST AFRICA

Date	Mintage	F	VF	XF	Unc	BU
1938	12,000,000	0.10	0.25	0.50	1.50	2.50
1938 Proof	—	Value: 125				
1938H	1,596,000	5.00	8.00	12.00	22.50	40.00
1938H Proof	—	Value: 100				
1939	9,840,000	0.25	0.50	1.00	3.50	6.00
1939 Proof	—	Value: 200				
1940	13,920,000	0.25	0.50	1.00	2.00	3.50
1940 Proof	—	Value: 125				
1941	16,560,000	1.00	2.00	4.00	8.00	14.00
1941 Proof	—	Value: 125				
1942	12,360,000	1.00	2.50	4.50	10.00	18.00
1942 Proof	—	Value: 125				
1943	22,560,000	1.00	2.50	5.00	10.00	18.00
1944	10,440,000	1.00	2.50	5.00	10.00	18.00
1944 Proof	—	Value: 150				
1945	25,706,000	0.50	1.00	1.75	6.00	10.00
1945 Proof	—	Value: 125				
1946	2,803,000	1.00	2.00	4.00	9.00	15.00
1946 Proof	—	Value: 125				
1946H	5,004,000	1.00	2.00	4.00	9.00	15.00
1946KN	1,152,000	0.25	0.50	1.00	3.00	5.50
1946KN Proof	—	Value: 125				
1947	4,202,000	0.50	1.00	2.00	5.00	9.00
1947 Proof	—	Value: 125				
1947KN	3,900,000	200	300	500	600	—

KM# 26 1/10 PENNY

Copper-Nickel, 20 mm. **Obv:** Crown above center hole, denomination around hole in English, in Arabic beneath **Obv. Legend:** GEORGIVS SEXTVS REX **Rev:** Hexagram divides date at bottom **Rev. Legend:** BRITISH WEST AFRICA

Date	Mintage	F	VF	XF	Unc	BU
1949H	3,700,000	1.00	2.00	3.00	6.00	10.00
1949KN	3,036,000	1.00	2.00	3.00	5.00	9.00
1950KN	13,200,000	0.25	0.50	1.00	2.50	4.50
1950KN Proof	—	Value: 150				

KM# 26a 1/10 PENNY

Bronze, 20 mm. **Obv:** Crown above center hole, denomination around hole in English, in Arabic beneath **Obv. Legend:** GEORGIVS SEXTVS REX **Rev:** Hexagram divides date at bottom **Rev. Legend:** BRITISH WEST AFRICA

Date	Mintage	F	VF	XF	Unc	BU
1952	15,060,000	0.50	1.00	2.00	6.00	10.00
1952 Proof	—	Value: 150				

KM# 32 1/10 PENNY

Bronze, 20 mm. **Ruler:** Elizabeth II **Obv:** Crown above center hole, denomination around hole in English, in Arabic beneath **Obv. Legend:** QUEEN ELIZABETH THE SECOND **Rev:** Hexagram divides date at bottom **Rev. Legend:** BRITISH WEST AFRICA

Date	Mintage	F	VF	XF	Unc	BU
1954	4,800,000	0.50	1.00	2.00	4.00	8.00
1954 Proof	—	Value: 150				
1956	2,400,000	100	200	400	700	—
1956 Proof	—	Value: 750				
1957	7,200,000	60.00	120	220	325	—
1957 Proof	—	Value: 600				

KM# 5 1/2 PENNY

Copper-Nickel **Ruler:** George V **Obv:** Crown above center hole, denomination around hole in English, in Arabic beneath **Obv. Legend:** GEORGIVS V REX ET IND: IMP: **Rev:** Hexagram divides date at bottom **Rev. Legend:** NIGERIA BRITISH WEST AFRICA

Date	Mintage	F	VF	XF	Unc	BU
1911H	3,360,000	4.50	12.00	25.00	40.00	75.00

KM# 8 1/2 PENNY

Copper-Nickel, 25.2 mm. **Ruler:** George V **Obv:** Crown above center hole, denomination around hole in English, in Arabic beneath **Obv. Legend:** GEORGIVS V REX ET IND: IMP: **Rev:** Hexagram divides date at bottom **Rev. Legend:** BRITISH WEST AFRICA **Edge:** Plain

Date	Mintage	F	VF	XF	Unc	BU
1912H	3,120,000	2.00	5.00	7.00	20.00	35.00
1913	1,382,000	150	250	325	500	—
1913H	216,000	5.00	10.00	17.50	30.00	55.00
1914	240,000	10.00	20.00	35.00	60.00	110
1914H	586,000	20.00	30.00	50.00	75.00	135
1914K	3,360,000	3.00	6.00	17.50	30.00	55.00
1914K Proof	—	Value: 225				
Note: Issued with East Africa KM#11 in a double (4 pc.) specimen set						
1915H	3,577,000	1.00	2.00	4.00	15.00	25.00
1916H	4,046,000	1.00	3.00	5.00	15.00	25.00
1917H	214,000	6.00	12.00	28.00	50.00	90.00
1918H	490,000	2.50	5.00	10.00	30.00	55.00
1919H	4,950,000	1.25	2.50	6.00	20.00	35.00
1919KN	3,861,000	1.25	2.50	7.50	25.00	45.00
1920H	26,285,000	1.50	3.00	7.50	15.00	25.00
1920KN	13,844,000	0.50	3.00	8.50	16.50	30.00
1922KN	5,817,000	300	500	750	1,200	—
1927	528,000	20.00	30.00	65.00	135	250
1927 Proof	—	Value: 225				
1929	336,000	6.00	22.00	47.50	95.00	165
1929 Proof	—	Value: 225				
1931	96,000	500	800	1,200	1,500	—
1931 Proof	—	Value: 225				
1932	960,000	2.50	15.00	35.00	55.00	100
1932 Proof	—	Value: 225				
1933	2,122,000	12.00	23.50	55.00	110	200
1933 Proof	—	Value: 225				
1934	1,694,000	2.50	15.00	35.00	75.00	135
1934 Proof	—	Value: 225				
1935	3,271,000	1.00	3.00	18.00	35.00	60.00
1935 Proof	—	Value: 225				
1936	5,400,000	2.50	5.00	18.00	32.00	55.00
1936 Proof	—	Value: 225				

KM# 15 1/2 PENNY

Copper-Nickel, 25.2 mm. **Ruler:** George VI **Obv:** Crown above center hole, denomination around hole in English, in Arabic beneath **Obv. Legend:** GEORGIVS VI REX • ET IND: IMP: **Rev:** Hexagram divides date at bottom **Rev. Legend:** BRITISH WEST AFRICA **Edge:** Plain

Date	Mintage	F	VF	XF	Unc	BU
1936	14,760,000	0.25	0.50	1.00	2.50	4.50
1936 Proof	—	Value: 200				
1936H	2,400,000	1.00	2.00	5.00	12.50	20.00
1936H Proof	—	Value: 200				
1936KN	2,298,000	0.65	1.25	2.25	4.00	7.00
1936KN Proof	—	Value: 200				

KM# 18 1/2 PENNY

Copper-Nickel **Ruler:** George VI **Obv:** Crown above center hole, denomination around hole in English, in Arabic beneath **Obv. Legend:** GEORGIVS VI REX • ET IND: IMP: **Rev:** Hexagram divides date at bottom **Rev. Legend:** BRITISH WEST AFRICA

Date	Mintage	F	VF	XF	Unc	BU
1937H	4,800,000	0.40	0.85	1.50	4.00	7.00
1937H Proof	—	Value: 125				
1937KN	5,577,000	0.40	0.85	3.00	5.00	9.00
1940KN	2,410,000	2.00	4.00	6.00	15.00	25.00
1940KN Proof	—	Value: 125				
1941H	2,400,000	0.40	2.00	6.00	12.00	20.00
1942	4,800,000	0.40	0.85	4.00	8.50	15.00
1943	3,360,000	0.50	1.00	5.00	10.00	18.00
1944	3,600,000	1.00	3.00	7.00	20.00	35.00

Date	Mintage	F	VF	XF	Unc	BU
1944 Proof	—	Value: 125				
1946	3,600,000	0.25	1.00	3.00	7.00	12.50
1946 Proof	—	Value: 125				
1947H	15,218,000	0.35	0.75	1.25	5.00	9.00
1947KN	12,000,000	0.40	0.85	2.00	6.00	10.00

KM# 27 1/2 PENNY

Copper-Nickel **Ruler:** Edward VII **Obv:** Crown above center hole, denomination around hole in English, in Arabic beneath **Obv. Legend:** GEORGIVS SEXTVS REX **Rev:** Hexagram divides date at bottom **Rev. Legend:** BRITISH WEST AFRICA

Date	Mintage	F	VF	XF	Unc	BU
1949H	5,909,000	1.50	3.50	12.00	22.00	40.00
1949KN	3,413,000	1.50	3.50	12.00	25.00	45.00
1951	3,468,000	1.50	3.50	12.00	25.00	45.00
1951 Proof	—	Value: 250				

KM# 27a 1/2 PENNY

Bronze **Obv:** Crown above center hole, denomination around hole in English, in Arabic beneath **Obv. Legend:** GEORGIVS SEXTVS REX **Rev:** Denomination around hole in English, in Arabic beneath **Rev. Legend:** BRITISH WEST AFRICA

Date	Mintage	F	VF	XF	Unc	BU
1952	11,332,000	0.25	0.50	2.50	5.50	9.50
1952 Proof	—	Value: 150				
1952H	27,603,000	0.20	0.35	0.75	2.00	3.50
1952KN	4,800,000	0.50	2.00	5.00	10.00	18.00

KM# 2 PENNY

Copper-Nickel, 30.5 mm. **Ruler:** Edward VII **Obv:** Crown above center hole, denomination around hole in English, in Arabic beneath **Obv. Legend:** EDWARD VII KING & EMPEROR **Rev:** Hexagram, date beneath **Rev. Legend:** NIGERIA BRITISH WEST AFRICA

Date	Mintage	F	VF	XF	Unc	BU
1907	863,000	2.00	5.00	9.00	20.00	35.00
1908	3,217,000	2.00	4.00	8.00	17.50	30.00
1909	960,000	3.50	9.00	28.00	45.00	80.00
1910	2,520,000	2.75	7.00	12.00	25.00	45.00

KM# 6 PENNY

Copper-Nickel, 30.5 mm. **Ruler:** George V **Obv:** Crown above center hole, denomination around hole in English, in Arabic beneath **Obv. Legend:** GEORGIVS V REX ET IND: IMP: **Rev:** Hexagram, date beneath **Rev. Legend:** NIGERIA BRITISH WEST AFRICA

Date	Mintage	F	VF	XF	Unc	BU
1911H	1,920,000	18.00	50.00	100	150	—

KM# 9 PENNY

Copper-Nickel, 30.5 mm. **Ruler:** George V **Obv:** Crown above center hole, denomination around hole in English, in Arabic beneath **Obv. Legend:** GEORGIVS V REX ET IND: IMP: **Rev:** Hexagram, date beneath **Rev. Legend:** BRITISH WEST AFRICA

Date	Mintage	F	VF	XF	Unc	BU
1912H	1,560,000	1.50	3.00	10.00	22.50	40.00
1913	1,680,000	7.50	25.00	45.00	75.00	135
1913H	144,000	5.00	10.00	17.50	35.00	60.00
1914	3,000,000	2.50	5.00	10.00	22.50	40.00
1914H	72,000	35.00	50.00	120	200	—
1915H	3,295,000	1.25	2.00	7.00	15.00	25.00
1916H	3,461,000	1.25	2.00	10.00	20.00	35.00
1917H	444,000	5.00	7.00	24.00	45.00	80.00
1918H	994,000	7.50	15.00	45.00	75.00	135
1919H	21,864,000	1.25	2.50	7.00	15.00	25.00
1919KN	264,000	7.50	25.00	35.00	50.00	90.00
1920H	37,870,000	1.00	1.75	5.50	12.50	22.50
1920KN	20,685,000	1.00	2.00	8.00	17.50	30.00
1922KN	3,971,000	400	750	1,000	1,500	—
1926	8,039,999	2.00	4.00	15.00	30.00	55.00
1927	792,000	25.00	45.00	125	200	—
1927 Proof	—	Value: 225				
1928	6,672,000	2.00	4.00	12.00	25.00	45.00
1928 Proof	—	Value: 225				
1929	636,000	20.00	35.00	65.00	100	—
1929 Proof	—	Value: 225				
1933	2,806,000	2.00	14.00	32.50	65.00	120
1933 Proof	—	Value: 225				
1934	2,640,000	3.50	15.00	35.00	75.00	135
1934 Proof	—	Value: 225				
1935	8,551,000	1.25	12.50	27.50	45.00	80.00
1935 Proof	—	Value: 225				
1936	7,368,000	1.25	3.50	12.00	25.00	45.00
1936 Proof	—	Value: 225				

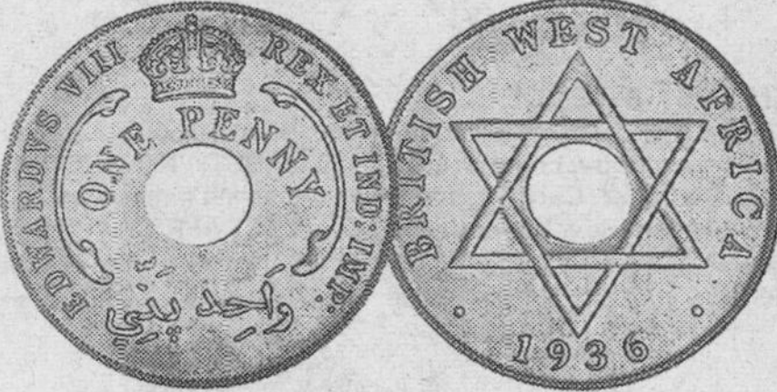

KM# 16 PENNY

Copper-Nickel, 30.5 mm. **Ruler:** Edward VIII **Obv:** Crown above center hole, denomination around hole in English, in Arabic beneath **Obv. Legend:** EDWARDVS VIII REX ET IND: IMP: **Rev:** Hexagram, date beneath **Rev. Legend:** BRITISH WEST AFRICA **Edge:** Plain

Date	Mintage	F	VF	XF	Unc	BU
1936	7,992,000	0.50	1.00	3.50	7.00	12.50
1936 Proof	—	Value: 250				
1936H	12,600,000	0.35	0.75	1.00	2.25	4.00
1936H Proof	—	Value: 250				
1936KN	12,512,000	0.35	0.75	1.00	2.25	4.00
1936KN Proof	—	Value: 250				

KM# 17 PENNY

Copper-Nickel, 30.5 mm. **Ruler:** Edward VIII **Obv:** Crown above center hole, denomination in English beneath **Obv. Legend:** EDWARDVS VIII REX ET IND: IMP: **Rev:** Hexagram, date beneath **Rev. Legend:** BRITISH WEST AFRICA **Note:** Mule.

Date	Mintage	F	VF	XF	Unc	BU
1936H	—	125	165	225	350	—

KM# 19 PENNY

Copper-Nickel, 30.5 mm. **Ruler:** George VI **Obv:** Crown above center hole, denomination around hole in English, in Arabic beneath **Obv. Legend:** GEORGIVS VI REX • ET IND: IMP: **Rev:** Hexagram, date beneath **Rev. Legend:** BRITISH WEST AFRICA **Edge:** Plain

Date	Mintage	F	VF	XF	Unc	BU
1937H	11,999,000	0.50	0.75	1.25	2.00	3.50
1937H Proof	—	Value: 200				
1937KN	11,999,000	0.50	0.75	1.25	2.00	3.50
1937KN Proof	—	Value: 200				
1940	3,840,000	0.50	0.75	1.25	2.00	3.50
1940 Proof	—	—	—	—	—	—
1940H	2,400,000	0.50	0.75	3.00	8.00	14.00
1940KN	2,400,000	0.75	1.50	4.50	10.00	18.00
1941	6,960,000	0.35	0.75	1.25	3.50	6.00
1941 Proof	—	—	—	—	—	—
1942	18,840,000	0.30	0.60	1.00	3.00	5.00
1943	28,920,000	0.30	0.60	1.00	3.00	5.00
1943H	7,140,000	2.00	5.00	10.00	20.00	35.00
1944	19,440,000	0.30	0.60	1.00	4.00	7.00
1945	6,072,000	0.45	0.90	1.75	5.00	9.00
1945 Proof	—	Value: 150				
1945H	9,000,000	1.00	2.00	4.50	10.00	18.00
1945KN	9,557,000	0.75	1.50	3.00	7.00	12.00
1946H	10,446,000	0.85	1.75	3.75	8.00	14.00
1946KN	11,976,000	0.30	0.60	1.00	5.00	9.00
1946SA	1,020,000	250	500	750	1,150	—
1947H	12,443,000	0.30	0.60	1.00	5.00	9.00
1947KN	9,829,000	0.30	0.60	1.00	5.00	9.00
1947SA	58,980,000	0.30	0.60	1.00	4.50	7.50

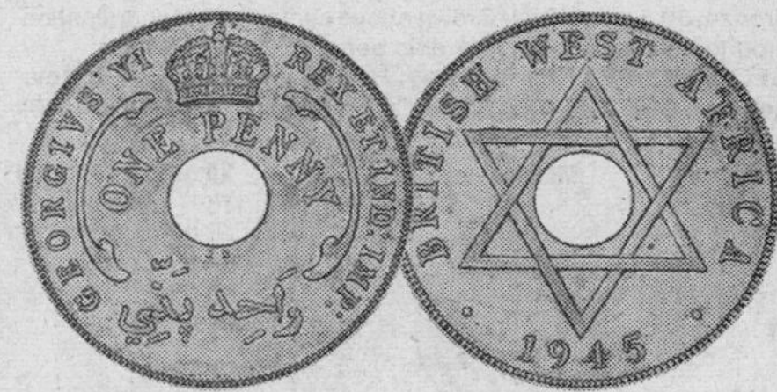

KM# 25 PENNY

Copper-Nickel, 30.5 mm. **Ruler:** George VI **Obv:** Crown above center hole, denomination around hole in English, in Arabic beneath **Obv. Legend:** GEORGIVS VI REX • ET IND: IMP: **Rev:** Hexagram, date beneath **Rev. Legend:** BRITISH WEST AFRICA **Note:** Mule, obverse KM#16, reverse KM#19.

Date	Mintage	F	VF	XF	Unc	BU
1945H	—	2,000	3,000	4,000	6,000	—

KM# 30 PENNY

Copper-Nickel, 30.5 mm. **Obv:** Crown above center hole, denomination around hole in English, in Arabic beneath **Obv. Legend:** GEORGIVS SEXTVS REX **Rev:** Hexagram, date beneath **Rev. Legend:** BRITISH WEST AFRICA

Date	Mintage	F	VF	XF	Unc	BU
1951	1,258,000	7.50	12.50	27.50	45.00	80.00
1951 Proof	—	Value: 250				
1951KN	2,692,000	6.00	10.00	20.00	35.00	60.00

KM# 30a PENNY

Bronze, 30.5 mm. **Obv:** Crown above center hole, denomination around hole in English, in Arabic beneath **Obv. Legend:** GEORGIVS SEXTVS REX **Rev:** Hexagram, date beneath **Rev. Legend:** BRITISH WEST AFRICA

Date	Mintage	F	VF	XF	Unc	BU
1952	10,542,000	0.75	1.50	3.00	8.50	15.00
1952 Proof	—	Value: 175				
1952H	30,794,000	0.20	0.40	0.60	3.00	5.00
1952KN	45,398,000	0.20	0.40	0.60	3.00	5.00
1952KN Proof	—	Value: 175				

KM# 33 PENNY
Bronze, 30.5 mm. **Ruler:** Elizabeth II **Obv:** Crown above center hole, denomination around hole in English, in Arabic beneath **Obv. Legend:** QUEEN ELIZABETH THE SECOND **Rev:** Hexagram, date beneath **Rev. Legend:** BRITISH WEST AFRICA

Date	Mintage	F	VF	XF	Unc	BU
1956H	13,503,000	0.75	1.50	3.50	9.00	16.00
1956KN	13,500,000	0.30	0.60	2.50	8.00	14.00
1957	9,000,000	0.75	1.50	6.00	13.50	25.00
1957 Proof	—	Value: 150				
1957H	5,340,000	1.00	2.50	10.00	20.00	35.00
1957KN	5,600,000	1.00	2.50	8.00	16.00	28.00
1957 N	Inc. above	125	175	250	—	—
Note: Error strike missing the K						
1958	12,200,000	0.75	1.50	6.00	13.50	25.00
1958 Proof	—	Value: 125				
1958KN	Inc. above	0.75	1.50	5.00	10.00	18.00

KM# 34 PENNY
Bronze, 30.5 mm. **Obv:** Crown above center hole, denomination around hole in English, in Arabic beneath **Obv. Legend:** GEORGIVS SEXTVS REX **Rev:** Hexagram, date beneath **Rev. Legend:** BRITISH WEST AFRICA **Note:** Mule, obverse KM#30, reverse KM#33.

Date	Mintage	F	VF	XF	Unc	BU
1956H	—	50.00	100	175	250	—

KM# 10 3 PENCE
1.1438 g., 0.9250 Silver .0420 oz. ASW **Ruler:** George V **Obv:** Bust of King George V left **Obv. Legend:** GEORGIVS V D.G.BRITT: OMN:REX F.D.IND:IMP: **Obv. Designer:** E.B. MacKennal **Rev:** Denomination in wreath, date beneath **Rev. Legend:** BRITISH WEST AFRICA

Date	Mintage	F	VF	XF	Unc	BU
1913	240,000	3.50	7.50	45.00	90.00	—
1913 Proof	—	Value: 250				
1913H	496,000	2.00	4.00	15.00	30.00	65.00
1914H	1,560,000	1.00	2.00	12.50	25.00	45.00
1915H	270,000	18.00	25.00	60.00	100	—
1916H	820,000	10.00	15.00	35.00	65.00	—
1917H	3,600,000	1.50	2.50	12.50	25.00	45.00
1918H	1,722,000	1.75	3.50	10.00	20.00	35.00
1919H	19,826,000	1.00	2.00	6.00	15.00	25.00
1919H Proof	—	Value: 200				

KM# 10a 3 PENCE
1.1438 g., 0.5000 Silver .0227 oz. ASW **Ruler:** George V **Obv:** Bust of George V facing left **Obv. Legend:** GEORGIVS V D.G.BRITT: OMN:REX F.D.IND:IMP: **Rev:** Denomination in wreath, date beneath **Rev. Legend:** BRITISH WEST AFRICA

Date	Mintage	F	VF	XF	Unc	BU
1920H	3,616,000	25.00	50.00	125	185	—

KM# 10b 3 PENCE
Tin-Brass **Ruler:** George V **Obv:** Bust of George V facing left **Obv. Legend:** GEORGIVS V D.G.BRITT: OMN:REX F.D.IND:IMP: **Rev:** Denomination in wreath, date beneath **Rev. Legend:** BRITISH WEST AFRICA

Date	Mintage	F	VF	XF	Unc	BU
1920KN	19,000,000	1.00	5.00	12.50	25.00	45.00
1920KN Proof	—	Value: 75.00				
1920KN Unique	—	—	—	—	—	—
Note: Mint mark on obverse below bust						
1925	8,800,000	1.50	5.00	20.00	40.00	70.00
1926	1,600,000	10.00	25.00	50.00	85.00	—
1927	800,000	20.00	40.00	100	200	—
1928	1,760,000	10.00	35.00	70.00	125	—
1928 Proof	—	Value: 175				
1933	2,800,000	2.00	4.50	28.00	50.00	70.00
1933 Proof	—	Value: 200				
1934	6,400,000	1.00	12.50	20.00	35.00	60.00
1934 Proof	—	Value: 200				
1935	11,560,000	1.00	12.50	20.00	35.00	60.00
1935 Proof	—	Value: 200				
1936	17,160,000	1.00	3.50	15.00	28.00	50.00
1936 Proof	—	Value: 200				
1936H	1,000,000	15.00	25.00	55.00	85.00	—
1936H Proof	—	Value: 200				
1936KN	2,037,999	10.00	15.00	35.00	65.00	110

KM# 21 3 PENCE
Copper-Nickel **Ruler:** George VI **Obv:** Bust of George VI facing left **Obv. Legend:** GEORGIVS VI D.G.BRITT: OMN:REX F.D.IND:IMP: **Obv. Designer:** Percy Metcalf **Rev:** Denomination in wreath, date beneath **Rev. Legend:** BRITISH WEST AFRICA

Date	Mintage	F	VF	XF	Unc	BU
1938H	7,000,000	0.30	0.60	2.50	7.50	12.50
1938H Proof	—	Value: 200				
1938KN	9,056,000	0.35	0.75	2.50	8.00	14.00
1938KN Proof	—	Value: 250				
1939H	16,500,000	0.30	0.60	2.00	5.00	9.00
1939H Proof	—	Value: 300				
1939KN	15,500,000	0.30	0.60	2.00	8.00	14.00
1939KN Proof	—	Value: 200				
1940H	3,862,000	0.50	1.00	2.50	7.50	13.50
1940KN	10,000,000	0.30	0.60	2.00	5.00	9.00
1941H	5,032,000	0.40	0.85	3.50	9.00	16.00
1943H	5,106,000	0.40	0.85	6.00	15.00	25.00
1943KN	9,502,000	0.40	0.85	3.50	9.00	16.00
1944KN	2,536,000	0.40	0.85	6.50	15.00	25.00
1945H	998,000	3.00	5.00	12.00	20.00	35.00
1945KN	3,000,000	0.40	0.85	5.00	12.50	22.00
1946KN	7,488,000	0.40	0.85	3.50	9.00	16.00
1947H	10,000,000	0.35	0.75	3.50	8.00	14.00
1947KN	11,248,000	0.40	0.85	3.50	8.00	14.00

KM# 35 3 PENCE
Copper-Nickel **Ruler:** Elizabeth II **Obv:** Bust of Queen Elizabeth II facing right **Obv. Legend:** QUEEN ELIZABETH THE SECOND **Obv. Designer:** Cecil Thomas **Rev:** Denomination in wreath, date beneath **Rev. Legend:** BRITISH WEST AFRICA

Date	Mintage	F	VF	XF	Unc	BU
1957H	800,000	35.00	60.00	180	300	—

KM# 11 6 PENCE
2.8276 g., 0.9250 Silver .0841 oz. ASW **Ruler:** George V **Obv:** Bust of King George V facing left **Obv. Legend:** GEORGIVS V D.G.BRITT: OMN:REX F.D.IND:IMP: **Obv. Designer:** E.B. MacKennal **Rev:** Denomination in wreath, date beneath **Rev. Legend:** BRITISH WEST AFRICA

Date	Mintage	F	VF	XF	Unc	BU
1913	560,000	3.00	5.00	20.00	35.00	60.00
1913 Proof	—	Value: 350				
1913H	400,000	3.00	5.00	20.00	37.50	65.00
1914H	952,000	2.75	5.00	25.00	40.00	70.00
1916H	400,000	5.00	10.00	40.00	60.00	—
1917H	2,400,000	3.00	5.00	20.00	37.50	65.00
1918H	1,160,000	2.00	5.00	20.00	37.50	65.00
1919H	8,676,000	2.00	3.50	11.50	22.00	40.00
1919H Proof	—	Value: 200				

KM# 11a 6 PENCE
2.8276 g., 0.5000 Silver .0454 oz. ASW **Ruler:** George V **Obv:** Bust of George V facing left **Obv. Legend:** GEORGIVS V D.G.BRITT: OMN:REX F.D.IND:IMP: **Rev:** Denomination in wreath, date beneath **Rev. Legend:** BRITISH WEST AFRICA

Date	Mintage	F	VF	XF	Unc	BU
1920H	2,948,000	12.50	30.00	100	185	—
1920H Proof	—	Value: 275				

KM# 11b 6 PENCE
Tin-Brass **Ruler:** George V **Obv:** Bust of George V facing left **Obv. Legend:** GEORGIVS V D.G.BRITT: OMN:REX F.D.IND:IMP: **Rev:** Denomination in wreath, date beneath **Rev. Legend:** BRITISH WEST AFRICA

Date	Mintage	F	VF	XF	Unc	BU
1920KN	12,000,000	1.00	5.00	20.00	37.50	65.00
1920KN Proof	—	Value: 125				
1923H	2,000,000	5.00	22.50	60.00	95.00	—
1924	1,000,000	15.00	30.00	100	165	—
1924H	1,000,000	15.00	30.00	100	165	—
1924KN	1,000,000	15.00	30.00	100	165	—
1925	2,800,000	3.50	7.00	35.00	60.00	100
1928	400,000	25.00	50.00	175	250	—
1928 Proof	—	Value: 200				
1933	1,000,000	20.00	40.00	125	185	—
1933 Proof	—	Value: 225				
1935	4,000,000	5.00	12.50	25.00	50.00	90.00
1935 Proof	—	Value: 225				
1936	10,400,000	7.50	15.00	25.00	50.00	90.00
1936 Proof	—	Value: 225				
1936H	480,000	25.00	50.00	125	200	—
1936H Proof	—	Value: 225				
1936KN	2,696,000	15.00	25.00	35.00	70.00	125
1936KN Proof	—	Value: 225				

KM# 22 6 PENCE
Nickel-Brass **Ruler:** George VI **Obv:** Bust of King George VI facing left **Obv. Legend:** GEORGIVS VI D.G.BRITT: OMN:REX F.D.IND:IMP: **Obv. Designer:** Percy Metcalf **Rev:** Denomination in wreath, date beneath **Rev. Legend:** BRITISH WEST AFRICA

Date	Mintage	F	VF	XF	Unc	BU
1938	12,114,000	0.50	1.00	2.00	8.00	14.00
1938 Proof	—	Value: 200				
1940	17,829,000	0.75	1.50	3.00	10.00	18.00
1940 Proof	—	Value: 200				
1942	1,600,000	2.50	4.00	10.00	20.00	35.00
1943	10,586,000	0.75	1.75	5.00	11.00	20.00
1944	1,814,000	2.00	3.00	15.00	30.00	55.00
1945	4,000,000	1.00	2.00	12.50	25.00	45.00
1945 Proof	—	Value: 200				
1946	4,000,000	2.50	5.00	25.00	50.00	90.00
1946 Proof	—	Value: 225				
1947	6,120,000	0.50	1.50	5.00	15.00	25.00
1947 Proof	—	Value: 175				

KM# 31 6 PENCE
Nickel-Brass **Ruler:** George VI **Obv:** Bust of King George VI facing left **Obv. Legend:** GEORGIVS VI DIE GRA. BRITT. OMN: REX FID: DEF: **Obv. Designer:** Percy Metcalf **Rev:** Denomination in wreath, date beneath **Rev. Legend:** BRITISH WEST AFRICA

Date	Mintage	F	VF	XF	Unc	BU
1952	2,544,000	—	—	—	250	—
1952 Proof	—	Value: 300				

Note: This type was never released into circulation and the majority of the mintage was melted down at Riverside Metal Company in New Jersey; Approximately 167 pieces avoided the furnace and found their way into the numismatic market

KM# 12 SHILLING
5.6552 g., 0.9250 Silver .1682 oz. ASW **Ruler:** George V **Obv:** Bust of King George V facing left **Obv. Legend:** GEORGIVS V D.G.BRITT: OMN:REX F.D.IND:IMP: **Obv. Designer:** E.B. MacKennal **Rev:** Palm tree divides date in circular frame **Rev. Legend:** BRITISH WEST AFRICA

Date	Mintage	F	VF	XF	Unc	BU
1913	8,800,000	2.75	4.50	12.50	22.50	45.00
1913 Proof	—	Value: 400				
1913H	3,540,000	10.00	20.00	55.00	100	—
1914	3,000,000	2.75	4.50	15.00	35.00	65.00
1914H	11,292,000	2.75	4.50	12.50	30.00	55.00
1915H	254,000	20.00	40.00	100	165	—
1916H	11,838,000	2.85	5.00	18.50	35.00	65.00
1917H	15,018,000	2.85	5.00	18.50	35.00	65.00
1918H	9,486,000	2.85	5.50	20.00	40.00	70.00
1918H Proof	—	Value: 200				
1919	2,000,000	10.00	15.00	30.00	55.00	95.00
1919H Proof	—	Value: 200				
1919H	992,000	15.00	30.00	65.00	100	—
1920	828,000	22.50	40.00	100	165	—

KM# 12a SHILLING

Tin-Brass **Ruler:** George V **Obv:** Bust of George V facing left **Obv. Legend:** GEORGIVS V D.G.BRITT: OMN:REX F.D.IND:IMP: **Rev:** Palm tree divides date in circular frame **Rev. Legend:** BRITISH WEST AFRICA

Date	Mintage	F	VF	XF	Unc	BU
1920G	16,000	1,000	2,000	2,500	3,000	—
1920KN	38,800,000	1.50	5.00	12.50	32.50	55.00
1920KN Proof	—	Value: 200				
1920KN Unique	—	—	—	—	—	—
Note: Mint mark on obverse below bust						
1922KN	32,324,000	2.00	6.50	35.00	70.00	—
1923H	24,384,000	4.00	7.50	25.00	45.00	80.00
1923KN	5,000,000	8.00	15.00	50.00	90.00	—
1924	17,000,000	2.00	6.50	35.00	60.00	110
1924H	9,567,000	10.00	20.00	70.00	125	—
1924KN	7,000,000	7.50	15.00	45.00	80.00	—
1925	19,800,000	4.00	8.00	22.00	45.00	80.00
1926	19,952,000	2.00	5.00	20.00	40.00	70.00
1927	22,248,000	1.50	4.00	18.50	35.00	60.00
1927 Proof	—	Value: 250				
1928	10,000,000	20.00	35.00	75.00	225	—
1928 Proof	—	Value: 300				
1936	70,200,000	3.00	6.50	18.00	32.50	55.00
1936 Proof	—	Value: 225				
1936H	10,920,000	12.50	22.50	45.00	75.00	—
1936KN	14,962,000	2.00	5.00	25.00	42.50	75.00
1936KN Proof	—	Value: 200				

KM# 23 SHILLING

Nickel-Brass **Ruler:** George VI **Obv:** Bust of King George VI facing left **Obv. Legend:** GEORGIVS VI D.G.BRITT: OMN:REX F.D.IND:IMP: **Obv. Designer:** Percy Metcalf **Rev:** Palm tree divides date in circular frame **Rev. Legend:** BRITISH WEST AFRICA

Date	Mintage	F	VF	XF	Unc	BU
1938	57,806,000	0.50	1.25	4.50	12.00	20.00
1938 Proof	—	Value: 200				
1939	55,472,000	0.50	1.25	6.50	18.00	30.00
1939 Proof	—	Value: 200				
1940	40,311,000	0.50	1.25	5.50	15.00	25.00
1940 Proof	—	Value: 200				
1942	42,000,000	0.50	1.25	6.50	18.00	30.00
1943	133,600,000	0.50	1.25	5.50	15.00	25.00
1945	8,010,000	1.00	1.50	12.00	25.00	42.00
1945 Proof	—	Value: 200				
1945H	12,864,000	2.00	3.50	18.00	35.00	60.00
1945KN	11,120,000	1.00	2.00	12.00	25.00	42.00
1946	37,350,000	1.00	2.00	18.00	35.00	60.00
1946 Proof	—	Value: 200				
1946H	—	750	1,000	2,000	4,000	—
1947	99,200,000	0.50	1.00	4.50	12.00	20.00
1947 Proof	—	Value: 200				
1947H	10,000,000	1.50	3.00	17.50	30.00	50.00
1947KN	10,384,000	0.50	1.00	6.50	16.50	28.00

KM# 28 SHILLING

Tin-Brass **Ruler:** George VI **Obv:** Bust of King George VI facing left **Obv. Legend:** GEORGIVS VI DEI GRA. BRITT. OMN. REX FID: DEF: **Obv. Designer:** Percy Metcalf **Rev:** Palm tree divides date in circular frame **Rev. Legend:** BRITISH WEST AFRICA

Date	Mintage	F	VF	XF	Unc	BU
1949	70,000,000	0.50	2.50	12.00	25.00	42.00
1949 Proof	—	Value: 175				
1949H	10,000,000	1.25	4.00	12.50	27.50	47.50
1949KN	10,016,000	1.25	4.00	12.50	27.50	47.50
1949KN Proof	—	Value: 200				
1951	35,346,000	1.25	5.00	15.00	30.00	50.00
1951 Proof	—	Value: 175				
1951H	10,000,000	1.25	5.00	15.00	30.00	50.00
1951KN	16,832,000	1.25	5.00	15.00	30.00	50.00
1952	98,654,000	0.50	1.00	3.00	9.00	15.00
1952 Proof	—	Value: 200				
1952KN	41,653,000	0.50	1.00	2.00	6.00	10.00
1952H	44,096,000	0.50	1.00	2.00	7.50	12.50
1952KN Proof	—	Value: 175				

KM# 13 2 SHILLING

11.3104 g., 0.9250 Silver .3364 oz. ASW **Ruler:** George V **Obv:** Bust of King George V facing left **Obv. Legend:** GEORGIVS V D.G.BRITT: OMN:REX F.D.IND:IMP: **Obv. Designer:** E.B. MacKennal **Rev:** Palm tree divides date in circular frame **Rev. Legend:** BRITISH WEST AFRICA

Date	Mintage	F	VF	XF	Unc	BU
1913	2,100,000	5.00	9.00	17.50	45.00	80.00
1913 Proof	—	Value: 500				
1913H	1,176,000	6.00	15.00	27.50	55.00	95.00
1914	330,000	15.00	50.00	125	200	—
1914H	637,000	10.00	25.00	45.00	75.00	135
1915H	66,000	25.00	60.00	125	185	—
1916H	9,824,000	5.00	15.00	30.00	60.00	110
1917H	1,059,000	15.00	40.00	100	165	—
1917H Proof	—	Value: 300				
1918H	7,294,000	5.00	12.00	30.00	55.00	95.00
1919	2,000,000	6.00	20.00	50.00	85.00	150
1919H	10,866,000	4.75	10.00	40.00	65.00	115
1919H Proof	—	Value: 200				
1920	683,000	30.00	60.00	175	250	—

KM# 13a 2 SHILLING

11.3104 g., 0.5000 Silver .1818 oz. ASW **Ruler:** George V **Obv:** Bust of George V facing left **Obv. Legend:** GEORGIVS V D.G.BRITT: OMN:REX F.D.IND:IMP: **Rev:** Palm tree divides date in circular frame **Rev. Legend:** BRITISH WEST AFRICA

Date	Mintage	F	VF	XF	Unc	BU
1920H	1,926,000	30.00	55.00	175	275	—

KM# 13b 2 SHILLING

Tin-Brass **Ruler:** George V **Obv:** Bust of George V facing left **Obv. Legend:** GEORGIVS V D.G.BRITT: OMN:REX F.D.IND:IMP: **Rev:** Palm tree divides date in circular frame **Rev. Legend:** BRITISH WEST AFRICA

Date	Mintage	F	VF	XF	Unc	BU
1920KN	15,856,000	2.50	5.00	20.00	40.00	70.00
1920KN Proof	—	Value: 250				
1922	10,000,000	3.00	9.00	27.50	55.00	95.00
1922KN	5,500,000	6.00	15.00	45.00	75.00	135
1922KN Proof	—	Value: 250				
1923H	12,696,000	4.00	12.00	37.50	65.00	115
1924	1,500,000	8.00	20.00	55.00	90.00	160
1925	3,700,000	4.00	12.00	40.00	70.00	125
1926	11,500,000	4.50	15.00	50.00	80.00	140
1927	11,100,000	6.00	20.00	65.00	100	185
1927 Proof	—	Value: 250				
1928	7,900,000	1,500	2,000	3,000	5,000	—
1928 Proof	—	Value: 3,000				
1936	32,939,999	5.00	12.00	35.00	60.00	100
1936 Proof	—	Value: 250				
1936H	8,703,000	6.00	18.00	45.00	75.00	130
1936KN	8,794,000	6.00	18.00	45.00	75.00	130

KM# 24 2 SHILLING

Nickel-Brass **Ruler:** George VI **Obv:** Bust of King George VI facing left **Obv. Legend:** GEORGIVS VI D.G.BRITT: OMN:REX F.D.IND:IMP: **Obv. Designer:** Percy Metcalf **Rev:** Palm tree divides date in circular frame **Rev. Legend:** BRITISH WEST AFRICA

Date	Mintage	F	VF	XF	Unc	BU
1938H	2,000,000	1.00	2.00	6.50	15.00	28.00
1938KN	27,852,000	1.00	2.00	6.50	15.00	28.00
Note: Grained edge variety exists, valued at $325						
1939H	5,750,000	2.00	5.00	20.00	35.00	65.00
1939KN	4,250,000	1.00	4.00	16.50	30.00	55.00
1939KN Proof	—	Value: 200				
1942KN	10,000,000	1.25	4.50	17.00	30.00	55.00
1946H	10,500,000	1.25	4.00	12.00	27.50	50.00
1946KN	4,800,000	1.25	7.00	27.00	42.50	80.00
1947H	5,055,000	1.00	6.00	25.00	40.00	75.00
1947KN	4,200,000	1.25	7.00	27.00	42.50	80.00

KM# 29 2 SHILLING

Nickel-Brass **Ruler:** George VI **Obv:** Bust of King George VI facing left **Obv. Legend:** GEORGIVS VI DIE GRA. BRITT. OMN: REX FID: DEF: **Obv. Designer:** Percy Metcalf **Rev:** Palm tree divides date in circular frame **Rev. Legend:** BRITISH WEST AFRICA

Date	Mintage	F	VF	XF	Unc	BU
1949H	7,500,000	1.25	7.00	22.00	40.00	75.00
1949KN	7,576,000	1.25	6.00	20.00	35.00	65.00
1951H	6,566,000	1.25	7.00	22.00	40.00	75.00
1951H Proof	—	Value: 250				
1952H	4,410,000	2.00	8.00	22.50	42.00	80.00
1952KN	1,236,000	8.00	20.00	50.00	75.00	145

PATTERNS

Including off metal strikes

KM#	Date	Mintage	Identification	Mkt Val
Pn1	1906	4	1/10 Penny. Aluminum. Crown above center hole, denomination around hole in English, in Arabic beneath. EDWARD VII KING & EMPEROR. Hexagram divides date at bottom. NIGERIA BRITISH WEST AFRICA.	3,000
Pn2	1906	—	Penny. Copper-Nickel. Two varieties known, thick and thin flan.	3,000
Pn3	1920G	—	Shilling. Silver. 6.2700 g.	1,500
Pn4	1920KN	—	2 Shilling. Silver. Uniface.	250
PnA4	1920	—	Penny. Brass. #KM9.	1,800
Pn5	1925	—	Shilling. Nickel-Brass. Bare headed. ROYAL MINT 1925 edge.	2,000
Pn6	1936H	—	Shilling. Nickel-Brass. King's bust, left. Palm tree divides date in circular frame. Security edge. Raised word SPECIMEN in field above date.	600
PnA6	1936	—	Shilling. Nickel-Brass. Security edge. Raised word SPECIMEN in field above date.	—
Pn7	1936KN	—	Shilling. Nickel-Brass. Fine reeded edge. Word SPECIMEN in field above date.	450
Pn8	1936KN	—	Shilling. Nickel-Brass. Security edge. Raised word SPECIMEN in field above date.	550
Pn9	1936KN	—	Shilling. Nickel-Brass. Coarser reeded edge. Without word SPECIMEN.	1,500
Pn10	1938KN	—	2 Shilling. Nickel-Brass. Security edge. Raised word SPECIMEN in field.	800
PnA10	1937H	—	Penny. Bronze. KM#19.	1,000
Pn11	1952KN	—	2 Shilling. Nickel-Brass. Raised word SPECIMEN in field below date.	450
PnA11	1949KN	—	2 Shilling. Copper Nickel.	140
Pn12	ND	—	Shilling. Nickel-Brass. KM#13b. Raised word MODEL.	1,000

TRIAL STRIKES

KM#	Date	Mintage	Identification	Mkt Val
TS1	1952	—	Shilling. Steel. King's head, left. Palm tree divides date within circular frame. Raised word TRIAL vertical in field on both sides.	165
TS2	1952	—	Shilling. Nickel. Raised word TRIAL vertical in field on both sides.	125
TS3	1952	—	Shilling. Steel. Palm tree divides date, raised word TRIAL vertical. King's head, raised word TRIAL horizontal.	175
TS4	1952	—	Shilling. Nickel. Raised word TRIAL vertical. Raised word TRIAL horizontal.	100

SPECIMEN SETS (SS)

KM#	Date	Mintage	Identification	Issue Price	Mkt Val
SS1	1913 (8)	14	KM10-13 Double set	—	1,250
SS2	1913 (4)	200	KM10-13	—	550
SS3	1919H (8)	2	KM10-13 Double set	—	1,500
SS4	1920KN (8)	36	KM10b-11b, 12a, 13b Double set	—	1,150
SSA5	1920KN (4)	4	KM10b-11b, 12a, 13b	—	—
SS5	1928 (4)	—	KM10b-11b, 12a, 13b	—	1,000
SS6	1936H (3)	—	KM14-16	—	450
SS7	1952 (4)	—	KM26a-27a, 30a, 31	—	750

BRUNEI

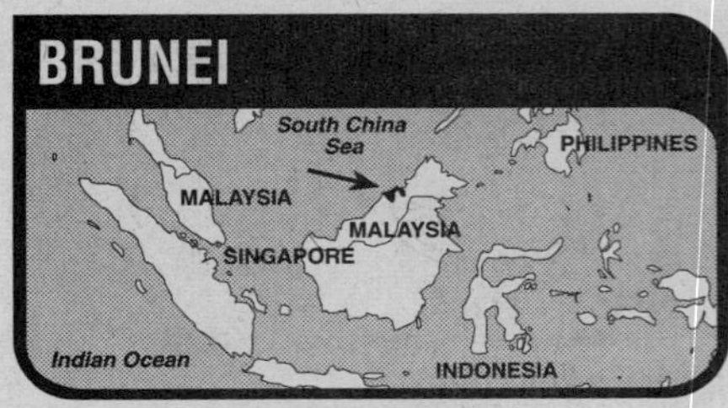

Negara Brunei Darussalam (State of Brunei), an independent sultanate on the northwest coast of the island of Borneo, has an area of 2,226 sq. mi. (5,765 sq. km.) and a population of *326,000. Capital: Bandar Seri Begawan. Crude oil and rubber are exported.

Magellan was the first European to visit Brunei in 1521. It was a powerful state, ruling over northern Borneo and adjacent islands from the 16th to the 19th century. Brunei became a British protectorate in 1888 and a British dependency in 1905. The Constitution of 1959 restored control over internal affairs to the sultan, while delegating responsibility for defense and foreign affairs to Britain. On January 1, 1984 it became independent and is a member of the Commonwealth of Nations.

TITLES

Negri Brunei

RULERS

Sultan Hashim Jalal, 1885-1906
British 1906-1950
Sultan Sir Omar Ali Saifuddin III, 1950-1967
Sultan Hassanal Bolkiah I, 1967-

MONETARY SYSTEM

100 Sen = 1 Dollar

SULTANATE

DECIMAL COINAGE

100 Sen = 1 Dollar (Ringgit)

KM# 4 SEN

Bronze **Ruler:** Sultan Sir Omar Ali Saifuddin III **Obv:** Uniformed head left **Rev:** Native design, denomination below, date at right

Date	Mintage	F	VF	XF	Unc	BU
1967	1,000,000	—	0.20	1.00	1.40	2.00

KM# 9 SEN

Bronze **Ruler:** Sultan Hassanal Bolkiah I **Obv:** Head right **Rev:** Native design, denomination below, date at right

Date	Mintage	F	VF	XF	Unc	BU
1968	60,000	—	0.30	1.70	3.50	4.00
1970	140,000	—	0.20	0.60	1.00	1.50
1970 Proof	4,000	Value: 4.00				
1971	400,000	—	0.10	0.25	0.80	1.25
1973	120,000	—	0.20	0.80	2.50	3.00
1974	640,000	—	—	0.25	0.80	1.25
1976	140,000	—	—	0.25	0.80	1.25
1977	140,000	—	—	0.25	0.80	1.25

KM# 15 SEN

Bronze **Ruler:** Sultan Hassanal Bolkiah I **Obv:** Head right **Rev:** Native design, denomination below, date at right, legend without numeral 'I' in title

Date	Mintage	F	VF	XF	Unc	BU
1977	280,000	—	—	0.25	0.70	1.00
1978	269,000	—	—	0.25	0.70	1.00
1979	250,000	—	0.10	0.50	1.00	1.50
1979 Proof	10,000	Value: 2.00				
1980	260,000	—	—	0.25	0.70	1.00
1981	540,000	—	—	0.25	0.70	1.00
1982	100,000	—	—	2.00	3.00	3.50
1983	500,000	—	—	0.25	0.50	0.75
1984	400,000	—	—	0.25	0.50	0.75
1984 Proof	3,000	Value: 2.00				
1985	200,000	—	—	0.20	0.50	0.75
1985 Proof	—	Value: 2.00				
1986	101,000	—	—	—	0.50	0.75
1986 Proof	7,000	Value: 2.00				

KM# 15a SEN

Copper Clad Steel **Ruler:** Sultan Hassanal Bolkiah I **Obv:** Head right **Rev:** Native design, denomination below, date at right, legend without numeral 'I' in title

Date	Mintage	F	VF	XF	Unc	BU
1986	102,000	—	—	—	0.40	0.65
1987	390,000	—	—	—	0.40	0.65
1988	500,000	—	—	—	0.40	0.65
1989	601,000	—	—	—	0.40	0.65
1990	680,000	—	—	—	0.40	0.65
1991	680,000	—	—	—	0.40	0.65
1992	887,000	—	—	—	0.40	0.65
1993	948,000	—	—	—	0.40	0.65

KM# 15b SEN

2.9200 g., 0.9250 Silver .0869 oz. ASW **Ruler:** Sultan Hassanal Bolkiah I **Obv:** Head right **Rev:** Native design, denomination below, date at right, legend without numeral 'I' in title

Date	Mintage	F	VF	XF	Unc	BU
1987 Proof	2,000	Value: 3.00				
1988 Proof	2,000	Value: 3.00				
1989 Proof	2,000	Value: 3.00				
1990 Proof	2,000	Value: 3.00				
1991 Proof	2,000	Value: 3.00				
1992 Proof	2,000	Value: 3.00				
1993 Proof	2,000	Value: 3.00				

KM# 42 SEN

3.1000 g., 0.9250 Silver .0922 oz. ASW **Subject:** 25 Years - Currency Board **Obv:** Sultan's portrait **Rev:** Mosque **Edge:** Reeded

Date	Mintage	F	VF	XF	Unc	BU
1992 Proof	2,000	—	—	—	5.00	—

KM# 34 SEN

Copper Clad Steel **Ruler:** Sultan Hassanal Bolkiah I **Obv:** Uniformed bust facing **Rev:** Native design denomination below, date at right

Date	Mintage	F	VF	XF	Unc	BU
1993	680,000	—	—	—	0.35	0.50
1994	1,900,000	—	—	—	0.15	0.25
1995	—	—	—	—	—	—
1996	3,044,000	—	—	—	0.15	0.25

KM# 34a SEN

2.9200 g., 0.9250 Silver 0.0868 oz. ASW, 17.7 mm. **Ruler:** Sultan Hassanal Bolkiah I **Obv:** Uniformed bust facing **Rev:** Native design denomination below, date at right **Edge:** Plain

Date	Mintage	F	VF	XF	Unc	BU
1993 Proof	—	Value: 4.00				
1994 Proof	—	Value: 4.00				

KM# 54 SEN

Copper Clad Steel **Ruler:** Sultan Hassanal Bolkiah I **Subject:** 10 Years of Independence **Obv:** Sultan's portrait **Rev:** National arms

Date	Mintage	F	VF	XF	Unc	BU
ND(1994)	—	—	—	—	1.00	1.50

KM# 54a SEN

3.1000 g., 0.9250 Silver .0922 oz. ASW **Ruler:** Sultan Hassanal Bolkiah I **Subject:** 10 Years of Independence **Obv:** Sultan's portrait **Rev:** National arms

Date	Mintage	F	VF	XF	Unc	BU
ND(1994) Proof	1,980	Value: 7.00				

KM# 5 5 SEN

Copper-Nickel **Ruler:** Sultan Sir Omar Ali Saifuddin III **Obv:** Uniformed head left **Rev:** Native design, denomination below, date at right

Date	Mintage	F	VF	XF	Unc	BU
1967	1,500,000	—	0.20	1.20	2.00	2.50

KM# 10 5 SEN

Copper-Nickel **Ruler:** Sultan Hassanal Bolkiah I **Obv:** Head right **Rev:** Native design, denomination below, date at right

Date	Mintage	F	VF	XF	Unc	BU
1968	320,000	—	0.15	0.75	1.50	2.00
1970	760,000	—	0.15	0.75	1.50	2.00
1970 Proof	4,000	Value: 4.00				
1971	320,000	—	0.15	0.75	1.50	2.00
1973	128,000	—	0.25	1.50	2.50	3.00
1974	576,000	—	0.15	0.50	1.25	2.00
1976	384,000	—	0.15	0.75	1.50	2.00
1977	384,000	—	0.15	0.75	1.50	2.00

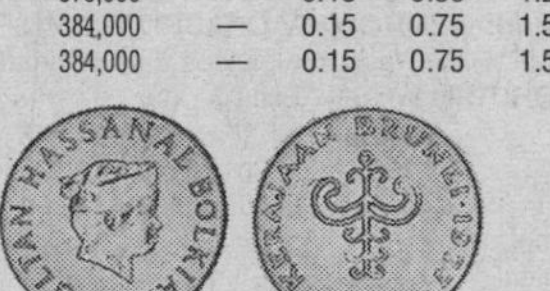

KM# 16 5 SEN

Copper-Nickel **Ruler:** Sultan Hassanal Bolkiah I **Obv:** Head right, legend without numeral 'I' in title **Rev:** Native design denomination below, date at right

Date	Mintage	F	VF	XF	Unc	BU
1977	920,000	—	0.10	0.30	0.60	1.00
1978	640,000	—	0.10	0.30	0.60	1.00
1979	650,000	—	0.15	0.45	0.80	1.25
1979 Proof	10,000	Value: 3.00				
1980	640,000	—	0.10	0.30	0.50	0.75
1981	960,000	—	0.10	0.30	0.50	0.75
1982	240,000	—	0.50	1.25	2.25	3.00
1983	1,280,000	—	—	0.10	0.30	0.50
1984 Proof	3,000	Value: 3.00				
1984	800,000	—	—	0.10	0.30	0.50
1985	800,000	—	—	0.10	0.30	0.50
1985 Proof	—	Value: 3.00				
1986 Proof	7,000	Value: 3.00				
1986	189,000	—	—	—	0.30	0.50
1987	960,000	—	—	—	0.30	0.50
1988	820,000	—	—	—	0.30	0.50
1989	1,504,000	—	—	—	0.30	0.50
1990	1,340,000	—	—	—	0.30	0.50
1991	1,340,000	—	—	—	0.30	0.50
1992	1,900,000	—	—	—	0.30	0.50
1993	1,951,000	—	—	—	0.30	0.50

KM# 16a 5 SEN

1.6500 g., 0.9250 Silver .0490 oz. ASW **Ruler:** Sultan Hassanal Bolkiah I **Obv:** Head right, legend without numeral "1" in title **Rev:** Native design denomination below, date at right

Date	Mintage	F	VF	XF	Unc	BU
1987 Proof	2,000	Value: 3.00				
1988 Proof	2,000	Value: 3.00				
1989 Proof	2,000	Value: 3.00				
1990 Proof	2,000	Value: 3.00				
1991 Proof	2,000	Value: 3.00				
1992 Proof	2,000	Value: 3.00				
1993 Proof	2,000	Value: 3.00				

KM# 43 5 SEN

1.9000 g., 0.9250 Silver .0565 oz. ASW **Subject:** 25 Years - Currency Board **Obv:** Sultan's portrait **Rev:** Mosque **Edge:** Reeded

Date	Mintage	F	VF	XF	Unc	BU
1992 Proof	2,000	Value: 7.00				

KM# 35 5 SEN

Copper-Nickel **Ruler:** Sultan Hassanal Bolkiah I **Obv:** Uniformed bust facing **Rev:** Native design, denomination below, date at right

Date	Mintage	F	VF	XF	Unc	BU
1993	1,340,000	—	—	—	0.50	0.75
1994	2,600,000	—	—	—	0.40	0.65
1996	3,571,000	—	—	—	0.40	0.65
2000	—	—	—	—	0.50	0.75

KM# 35a 5 SEN

1.6500 g., 0.9250 Silver 0.0491 oz. ASW, 16.26 mm. **Ruler:** Sultan Hassanal Bolkiah I **Obv:** Uniformed bust facing **Rev:** Native design **Edge:** Reeded

Date	Mintage	F	VF	XF	Unc	BU
1993 Proof	—	Value: 4.00				
1994 Proof	—	Value: 4.00				

KM# 55 5 SEN

Copper-Nickel .0565 oz. **Ruler:** Sultan Hassanal Bolkiah I **Subject:** 10 Years of Independence **Obv:** Sultan's portrait **Rev:** National arms

Date	Mintage	F	VF	XF	Unc	BU
ND(1994)	3,000	—	—	—	1.50	2.00

KM# 55a 5 SEN

1.9000 g., 0.9250 Silver .0565 oz. ASW **Ruler:** Sultan Hassanal Bolkiah I **Subject:** 10 Years of Independence **Obv:** Sultan's portrait **Rev:** National arms

Date	Mintage	F	VF	XF	Unc	BU
ND(1994) Proof	1,980	Value: 9.00				

KM# 6 10 SEN
Copper-Nickel **Ruler:** Sultan Sir Omar Ali Saifuddin III **Obv:** Uniformed head left **Rev:** Native design, denomination below, date at right

Date	Mintage	F	VF	XF	Unc	BU
1967	3,510,000	—	0.25	1.00	2.00	3.00

KM# 11 10 SEN
Copper-Nickel

Date	Mintage	F	VF	XF	Unc	BU
1968	580,000	—	0.25	0.75	1.50	2.00
1970 Proof	4,000	Value: 4.00				
1970	1,360,000	—	0.25	0.75	1.50	2.00
1971	420,000	—	0.25	0.75	1.30	2.00
1973	300,000	—	0.25	0.75	1.30	2.00
1974	1,410,000	—	0.15	0.55	1.00	1.50
1976	920,000	—	0.15	0.55	1.00	1.50
1977	920,000	—	0.15	0.55	1.00	1.50

KM# 17 10 SEN
Copper-Nickel **Ruler:** Sultan Hassanal Bolkiah I **Obv:** Head right, legend without numeral 'I' in title **Rev:** Native design, denomination below, date at right **Edge:** Reeded

Date	Mintage	F	VF	XF	Unc	BU
1977	1,800,000	—	0.10	0.30	0.80	1.25
1978	1,080,000	—	0.10	0.30	0.80	1.25
1979	2,050,000	—	0.10	0.30	0.80	1.25
1979 Proof	10,000	Value: 4.00				
1980	2,840,000	—	—	0.10	0.40	0.65
1981	976,000	—	—	0.10	0.40	0.65
1983	1,080,000	—	—	0.10	0.40	0.65
1984 Proof	3,000	Value: 4.25				
1984	1,400,000	—	—	0.10	0.40	0.65
1985	1,540,000	—	—	0.10	0.30	0.50
1985 Proof	—	Value: 4.25				
1986 Proof	7,000	Value: 4.25				
1986	2,181,000	—	—	—	0.30	0.50
1987	2,560,000	—	—	—	0.30	0.50
1988	960,000	—	—	—	0.30	0.50
1989	1,000,000	—	—	—	0.30	0.50
1990	1,800,000	—	—	—	0.30	0.50
1991	1,800,000	—	—	—	0.30	0.50
1992	3,839,000	—	—	—	0.30	0.50
1993	3,973,000	—	—	—	0.30	0.50

KM# 17a 10 SEN
3.3500 g., 0.9250 Silver .0996 oz. ASW **Ruler:** Sultan Hassanal Bolkiah I **Obv:** Head right, legend without numeral 'I' in title **Rev:** Native design, denomination below, date at right

Date	Mintage	F	VF	XF	Unc	BU
1987 Proof	2,000	Value: 6.00				
1988 Proof	2,000	Value: 6.00				
1989 Proof	2,000	Value: 6.00				
1990 Proof	2,000	Value: 6.00				
1991 Proof	2,000	Value: 6.00				
1992 Proof	2,000	Value: 6.00				
1993 Proof	2,000	Value: 6.00				

KM# 44 10 SEN
3.5000 g., 0.9250 Silver .1041 oz. ASW **Obv:** Sultan's portrait **Rev:** Mosque **Edge:** Reeded

Date	Mintage	F	VF	XF	Unc	BU
1992 Proof	2,000	Value: 10.00				

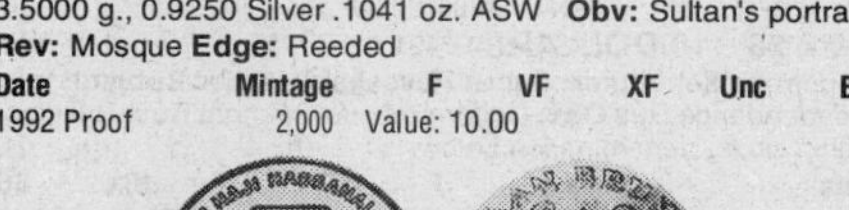

KM# 36 10 SEN
Copper-Nickel **Ruler:** Sultan Hassanal Bolkiah I **Obv:** Uniformed bust facing **Rev:** Native design, denomination below, date at right

Date	Mintage	F	VF	XF	Unc	BU
1993	1,800,000	—	—	—	0.55	0.85
1994	2,200,000	—	—	—	0.50	0.75
1996	3,618,000	—	—	—	0.50	0.75

KM# 36a 10 SEN
3.3500 g., 0.9250 Silver 0.0996 oz. ASW, 19.4 mm. **Ruler:** Sultan Hassanal Bolkiah I **Obv:** Uniformed portrait **Rev:** Native design **Edge:** Reeded

Date	Mintage	F	VF	XF	Unc	BU
1993 Proof	—	Value: 6.00				
1994 Proof	—	Value: 6.00				

KM# 56 10 SEN
Copper-Nickel **Subject:** 10 Years of Independence **Obv:** Sultan's portrait **Rev:** National arms

Date	Mintage	F	VF	XF	Unc	BU
ND(1994)	3,000	—	—	—	2.00	3.00

KM# 56a 10 SEN
3.5000 g., 0.9250 Silver .1041 oz. ASW **Subject:** 10 Years of Independence **Obv:** Sultan's portrait **Rev:** National arms

Date	Mintage	F	VF	XF	Unc	BU
ND(1994) Proof	1,980	Value: 12.00				

KM# 7 20 SEN
Copper-Lead Alloy **Ruler:** Sultan Sir Omar Ali Saifuddin III **Obv:** Uniformed head left **Rev:** Native design, denomination below, date at right

Date	Mintage	F	VF	XF	Unc	BU
1967	2,130,000	—	0.35	1.50	4.00	6.00

KM# 12 20 SEN
Copper-Nickel **Ruler:** Sultan Hassanal Bolkiah I **Obv:** Head right **Rev:** Native design, denomination below, date at right

Date	Mintage	F	VF	XF	Unc	BU
1968	510,000	—	0.20	1.00	3.00	3.50
1970 Proof	4,000	Value: 4.00				
1970	850,000	—	0.15	0.85	3.00	3.50
1971	450,000	—	0.20	1.00	2.00	2.50
1973	450,000	—	0.20	2.00	4.00	4.50
1974	700,000	—	0.15	1.00	2.00	2.50
1976	640,000	—	0.15	1.00	2.00	2.50
1977	640,000	—	0.15	1.00	2.00	2.50

KM# 18 20 SEN
Copper-Nickel **Ruler:** Sultan Hassanal Bolkiah I **Obv:** Head right, legend without numeral 'I' in title **Rev:** Native design, denomination below, date at right

Date	Mintage	F	VF	XF	Unc	BU
1977	1,200,000	—	0.15	0.65	2.00	2.50
1978	720,000	—	0.20	0.75	2.00	2.50
1979 Proof	10,000	Value: 4.50				
1979	1,060,000	—	0.20	0.75	2.00	2.50
1980	1,540,000	—	0.15	0.65	2.00	2.50
1981	2,140,000	—	0.10	0.60	2.00	2.50
1982	120,000	—	2.00	6.00	12.00	15.00
1983	1,350,000	—	0.10	0.35	1.00	1.50
1984	750,000	—	0.10	0.35	1.00	1.50
1984 Proof	3,000	Value: 4.75				
1985	1,000,000	—	0.10	0.35	1.00	1.50
1985 Proof	—	Value: 4.75				
1986	2,639,000	—	—	—	1.00	1.50
1986 Proof	7,000	Value: 4.75				
1987	2,400,000	—	—	—	1.00	1.50
1988	560,000	—	—	—	1.00	1.50
1989	500,000	—	—	—	1.00	1.50
1990	720,000	—	—	—	1.00	1.50
1991	725,000	—	—	—	1.00	1.50
1992	2,432,000	—	—	—	1.00	1.50
1993	2,521,000	—	—	—	1.00	1.50

KM# 18a 20 SEN
6.5100 g., 0.9250 Silver .1936 oz. ASW **Ruler:** Sultan Hassanal Bolkiah I **Obv:** Head right, legend without numeral 'I' in title **Rev:** Native design, denomination below, date at right

Date	Mintage	F	VF	XF	Unc	BU
1987 Proof	2,000	Value: 10.00				
1988 Proof	2,000	Value: 10.00				
1989 Proof	2,000	Value: 10.00				
1990 Proof	2,000	Value: 10.00				
1991 Proof	2,000	Value: 10.00				
1992 Proof	2,000	Value: 10.00				
1993 Proof	2,000	Value: 10.00				

KM# 45 20 SEN
6.7000 g., 0.9250 Silver .1993 oz. ASW **Subject:** 25 Years - Currency Board **Obv:** Sultan's portrait **Rev:** Mosque **Edge:** Reeded

Date	Mintage	F	VF	XF	Unc	BU
1992 Proof	2,000	Value: 12.00				

KM# 37 20 SEN
Copper-Nickel **Ruler:** Sultan Hassanal Bolkiah I **Obv:** Uniformed bust facing **Rev:** Native design, denomination below, date at right

Date	Mintage	F	VF	XF	Unc	BU
1993	720,000	—	—	—	1.00	1.50
1994	2,000,000	—	—	—	1.00	1.50
1996	2,767,000	—	—	—	0.75	1.25
2000	—	—	—	—	1.00	1.50

KM# 37a 20 SEN
6.5100 g., 0.9250 Silver 0.1936 oz. ASW, 23.5 mm. **Ruler:** Sultan Hassanal Bolkiah I **Obv:** Uniformed portrait **Rev:** Native design **Edge:** Reeded

Date	Mintage	F	VF	XF	Unc	BU
1993 Proof	—	Value: 10.00				
1994 Proof	—	Value: 10.00				

KM# 57 20 SEN
Copper-Nickel **Subject:** 10 Years of Independence **Obv:** Sultan's portrait **Rev:** National arms

Date	Mintage	F	VF	XF	Unc	BU
ND(1994)	3,000	—	—	—	2.50	3.50

KM# 57a 20 SEN
6.7000 g., 0.9250 Silver .1993 oz. ASW **Subject:** 10 Years of Independence **Obv:** Sultan's portrait **Rev:** National arms

Date	Mintage	F	VF	XF	Unc	BU
ND(1994) Proof	1,980	Value: 15.00				

KM# 8 50 SEN
Copper-Nickel **Ruler:** Sultan Sir Omar Ali Saifuddin III **Obv:** Uniformed head left within circle **Rev:** National arms, denomination below, date at right

Date	Mintage	F	VF	XF	Unc	BU
1967	788,000	—	0.75	2.00	5.00	7.00

KM# 13 50 SEN
Copper-Nickel **Ruler:** Sultan Hassanal Bolkiah I **Obv:** Head right **Rev:** National arms within circle, denomination below, date at right

Date	Mintage	F	VF	XF	Unc	BU
1968	212,000	—	0.50	2.00	3.00	3.50
1970	300,000	—	0.50	2.00	3.00	3.50
1970 Proof	4,000	Value: 6.50				
1971	320,000	—	0.45	2.00	3.00	3.50
1973	140,000	—	2.00	4.00	6.00	8.00
1974	244,000	—	0.45	2.00	3.00	3.50
1976	240,000	—	0.45	2.00	3.00	3.50
1977	240,000	—	0.45	2.00	3.00	3.50

KM# 19 50 SEN
Copper-Nickel **Ruler:** Sultan Hassanal Bolkiah I **Obv:** Head right, legend without numeral 'I' in title **Rev:** National arms within circle, denomination below, date at right

Date	Mintage	F	VF	XF	Unc	BU
1977	499,000	—	0.30	1.10	2.00	2.50
1978	264,000	—	0.30	1.10	2.00	2.50
1979	730,000	—	0.30	1.10	2.00	2.50
1979 Proof	10,000	Value: 6.50				
1980	536,000	—	0.30	1.10	2.00	2.50
1981	960,000	—	0.30	1.00	1.50	2.00

Date	Mintage	F	VF	XF	Unc	BU
1982	136,000	—	2.00	5.00	12.00	14.00
1983	408,000	—	0.30	0.80	1.50	2.00
1984	320,000	—	0.30	0.80	1.50	2.00
1984 Proof	3,000	Value: 6.75				
1985	450,000	—	0.30	0.80	1.50	2.00
1985 Proof	—	—	—	—	—	—
1986	1,067,000	—	—	—	1.50	2.00
1986 Proof	7,000	Value: 6.75				
1987	1,120,000	—	—	—	1.50	2.00
1988	250,000	—	—	—	1.50	2.00
1989	500,000	—	—	—	1.50	2.00
1990	472,000	—	—	—	1.50	2.00
1991	508,000	—	—	—	1.50	2.00
1992	1,072,000	—	—	—	1.50	2.00
1993	1,102,000	—	—	—	1.50	2.00

KM# 19a 50 SEN

10.8200 g., 0.9250 Silver .3218 oz. ASW **Ruler:** Sultan Hassanal Bolkiah I **Obv:** Head right, legend without numeral 'I' in title **Rev:** National arms within circle, denomination below, date at right

Date	Mintage	F	VF	XF	Unc	BU
1987 Proof	2,000	Value: 15.00				
1988 Proof	2,000	Value: 15.00				
1989 Proof	2,000	Value: 15.00				
1990 Proof	2,000	Value: 15.00				
1991 Proof	2,000	Value: 15.00				
1992 Proof	2,000	Value: 15.00				
1993 Proof	2,000	Value: 15.00				

KM# 46 50 SEN

11.1000 g., 0.9250 Silver .3301 oz. ASW **Subject:** 25 Years - Currency Board **Obv:** Sultan's portrait **Rev:** Mosque

Date	Mintage	F	VF	XF	Unc	BU
1992 Proof	2,000	Value: 20.00				

KM# 38 50 SEN

Copper-Nickel **Ruler:** Sultan Hassanal Bolkiah I **Obv:** Uniformed bust facing **Rev:** National arms within circle, denomination below, date at right **Edge:** Reeded and security edge

Date	Mintage	F	VF	XF	Unc	BU
1993	472,000	—	—	—	1.50	2.00
1994	600,000	—	—	—	1.50	2.00
1996	458,000	—	—	—	1.50	2.00

KM# 38a 50 SEN

10.8200 g., 0.9250 Silver 0.3218 oz. ASW, 27.7 mm. **Ruler:** Sultan Hassanal Bolkiah I **Obv:** Uniformed bust facing **Rev:** National arms within circle, denomination below, date at right **Edge:** Reeded

Date	Mintage	F	VF	XF	Unc	BU
1993 Proof	—	Value: 15.00				
1994 Proof	—	Value: 15.00				

KM# 58 50 SEN

Copper-Nickel **Subject:** 10 Years of Independence **Obv:** Sultan's portrait **Rev:** National arms

Date	Mintage	F	VF	XF	Unc	BU
ND(1994)	3,000	—	—	—	4.50	6.00

KM# 58a 50 SEN

11.1000 g., 0.9250 Silver .3301 oz. ASW **Subject:** 10 Years of Independence **Obv:** Sultan's portrait **Rev:** National arms

Date	Mintage	F	VF	XF	Unc	BU
ND(1994) Proof	1,980	Value: 20.00				

KM# 64 50 SEN

Copper-Nickel **Subject:** Sultan's 50th Birthday **Obv:** Sultan's portrait **Rev:** Waterfront building

Date	Mintage	F	VF	XF	Unc	BU
ND(1996) Proof	500	Value: 25.00				

KM# 14 DOLLAR

Copper-Nickel **Ruler:** Sultan Hassanal Bolkiah I **Obv:** Head right **Rev:** Antique cannon, date above, denomination below

Date	Mintage	F	VF	XF	Unc	BU
1970 Proof	5,000	Value: 80.00				

KM# 20 DOLLAR

Copper-Nickel **Obv:** Legend without numeral 'I' in title

Date	Mintage	F	VF	XF	Unc	BU
1979 Proof	10,000	Value: 20.00				
1984	5,000	—	—	—	10.00	12.00
1984 Proof	3,000	Value: 22.00				
1985	15,000	—	—	—	8.00	10.00
1985 Proof	10,000	Value: 20.00				
1986	10,000	—	—	—	8.00	10.00
1986 Proof	7,000	Value: 22.00				
1987	2,000	—	—	—	10.00	12.50
1988	2,000	—	—	—	10.00	12.50
1989	2,000	—	—	—	10.00	12.50
1990	3,000	—	—	—	10.00	12.50
1991	3,000	—	—	—	10.00	12.50
1992	—	—	—	—	10.00	12.50

KM# 20a DOLLAR

18.0500 g., 0.9250 Silver .5368 oz. ASW **Obv:** Legend without numeral 'I' in title

Date	Mintage	F	VF	XF	Unc	BU
1987 Proof	2,000	Value: 40.00				
1988 Proof	2,000	Value: 40.00				
1989 Proof	2,000	Value: 40.00				
1990 Proof	2,000	Value: 40.00				
1991 Proof	2,000	Value: 40.00				
1992 Proof	2,000	Value: 40.00				
1993 Proof	2,000	Value: 40.00				

KM# 47 DOLLAR

18.2000 g., 0.9250 Silver .5413 oz. ASW **Ruler:** Sultan Hassanal Bolkiah I **Subject:** 25th Anniversary of Brunei Currency Board **Obv:** Sultan Hassanal Bolkiah **Rev:** Mosque

Date	Mintage	F	VF	XF	Unc	BU
1992 Proof	2,000	Value: 40.00				

KM# 47a DOLLAR

0.9170 Gold **Ruler:** Sultan Hassanal Bolkiah I **Subject:** 25th Anniversary of Brunei Currency Board **Obv:** Sultan Hassanal Bolkiah **Rev:** Mosque

Date	Mintage	F	VF	XF	Unc	BU
1992 Proof	1,000	Value: 350				

KM# 76 DOLLAR

16.8000 g., Copper-Nickel, 33.3 mm. **Ruler:** Sultan Hassanal Bolkiah I **Obv:** Uniformed bust facing **Rev:** Antique cannon **Edge:** Reeded

Date	Mintage	F	VF	XF	Unc	BU
1993	—	—	—	—	10.00	12.50

KM# 76a DOLLAR

18.0500 g., 0.9250 Silver 0.5368 oz. ASW, 33.3 mm. **Ruler:** Sultan Hassanal Bolkiah I **Obv:** Uniformed bust facing **Rev:** Antique cannon **Edge:** Reeded

Date	Mintage	F	VF	XF	Unc	BU
1993 Proof	2,000	Value: 40.00				

KM# 59 DOLLAR

Copper-Nickel **Subject:** 10 Years of Independence **Obv:** Sultan's portrait **Rev:** National arms

Date	Mintage	F	VF	XF	Unc	BU
ND(1994)	3,000	—	—	—	8.00	10.00

KM# 59a DOLLAR

18.2000 g., 0.9250 Silver .5413 oz. ASW **Subject:** 10 Years of Independence **Obv:** Sultan's portrait **Rev:** National arms

Date	Mintage	F	VF	XF	Unc	BU
ND(1994) Proof	1,980	—	—	—	—	—

KM# 71 2 DOLLARS

9.3000 g., Copper-Nickel **Subject:** 20th SEA Games **Obv:** Sultan's multicolor portrait **Rev:** Multicolor logo above stadium **Edge:** Reeded

Date	Mintage	F	VF	XF	Unc	BU
1999 Proof	1,350	Value: 25.00				

KM# 74 2 DOLLARS

9.8000 g., Copper-Nickel, 27.3 mm. **Ruler:** Sultan Hassanal Bolkiah I **Subject:** APEC **Obv:** Multicolor bust of Sultan Haji Hassanal Bolkiah half facing **Rev:** Multicolor flower and APEC initials above date below world map, denomination at bottom **Rev. Legend:** ASIA PACIFIC ECONOMIC COOPERATION NEGARA BRUNEI DARUSSALAM **Edge:** Reeded

Date	Mintage	F	VF	XF	Unc	BU
2000 Proof	3,000	Value: 45.00				

KM# 68 3 DOLLARS

10.0000 g., Copper-Nickel **Subject:** 30 Years ASEAN **Obv:** Sultan's portrait **Rev:** Map and sailboat **Edge:** Reeded

Date	Mintage	F	VF	XF	Unc	BU
1997 Proof	750	Value: 35.00				

KM# 23 5 DOLLARS

Copper-Nickel **Ruler:** Sultan Hassanal Bolkiah I **Subject:** Year of Hejira 1400 **Obv:** Head right, legend without numeral 'I' in title **Rev:** Denomination below design

Date	Mintage	F	VF	XF	Unc	BU
AH1400 (1980)	10,000	—	5.00	15.00	30.00	35.00

KM# 48 5 DOLLARS

0.9170 Gold **Ruler:** Sultan Hassanal Bolkiah I **Subject:** 25th Anniversary of Brunei Currency Board **Obv:** Sultan Hassanal Bolkiah **Rev:** Mosque

Date	Mintage	F	VF	XF	Unc	BU
1992 Proof	1,000	Value: 365				

KM# 60 5 DOLLARS

Copper-Nickel **Subject:** 10 Years of Independence **Obv:** Sultan's portrait **Rev:** National arms

Date	Mintage	F	VF	XF	Unc	BU
ND(1994)	3,000	—	—	—	16.00	18.00

KM# 60a 5 DOLLARS

28.2800 g., 0.9250 Silver .8410 oz. ASW **Subject:** 10 Years of Independence **Obv:** Sultan's portrait **Rev:** National arms

Date	Mintage	F	VF	XF	Unc	BU
ND(1994) Proof	1,980	Value: 35.00				

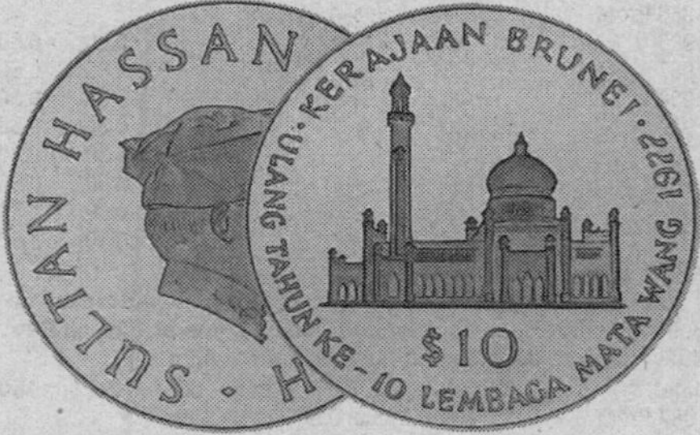

KM# 21 10 DOLLARS

28.2800 g., 0.9250 Silver .8411 oz. ASW **Ruler:** Sultan Hassanal Bolkiah I **Subject:** 10th Anniversary of Brunei Currency Board **Obv:** Head right, legend without numeral 'I' in title **Rev:** Mosque above denomination

Date	Mintage	F	VF	XF	Unc	BU
1977 Proof	10,000	Value: 90.00				

KM# 26 10 DOLLARS

Copper-Nickel **Ruler:** Sultan Hassanal Bolkiah I **Subject:** Independence Day **Obv:** Uniformed bust 3/4 right **Rev:** Building within circle, denomination below

Date	Mintage	F	VF	XF	Unc	BU
1984	15,000	—	—	—	25.00	30.00
1984 Proof	5,000	Value: 50.00				

KM# 49 10 DOLLARS

0.9170 Gold **Ruler:** Sultan Hassanal Bolkiah I **Subject:** 25th Anniversary of Brunei Currency Board **Obv:** Bust right **Rev:** Mosque

Date	Mintage	F	VF	XF	Unc	BU
1992 Proof	1,000	Value: 465				

KM# 61 10 DOLLARS

Copper-Nickel **Subject:** 10 Years of Independence **Obv:** Sultan's portrait **Rev:** National arms

Date	Mintage	F	VF	XF	Unc	BU
ND	3,000	—	—	—	18.00	20.00

KM# 61a 10 DOLLARS

30.7000 g., 0.9250 Silver .9130 oz. ASW **Subject:** 10 Years of Independence **Obv:** Sultan's portrait **Rev:** National arms

Date	Mintage	F	VF	XF	Unc	BU
ND(1994)	2,500	—	—	—	40.00	45.00
ND(1994) Proof	2,480	Value: 60.00				

KM# 32 20 DOLLARS
28.2800 g., 0.9250 Silver .8411 oz. ASW **Ruler:** Sultan Hassanal Bolkiah I **Subject:** 20th Anniversary of Brunei Currency Board **Obv:** Uniformed bust 3/4 right **Rev:** Mosque above denomination

Date	Mintage	F	VF	XF	Unc	BU
1987 Proof	3,000	Value: 70.00				

KM# 29 20 DOLLARS
28.2800 g., 0.9250 Silver .8411 oz. ASW **Ruler:** Sultan Hassanal Bolkiah I **Subject:** 20th Anniversary of Coronation **Obv:** Uniformed bust 3/4 right **Rev:** Arms within wreath divides dates at top, denomination below wreath

Date	Mintage	F	VF	XF	Unc	BU
ND(1988)	5,000	—	—	—	30.00	35.00
ND(1988) Proof	1,000	Value: 85.00				

KM# 72 20 DOLLARS
62.2000 g., 0.9990 Silver 2.0000 oz. ASW **Subject:** 20th SEA Games **Obv:** Sultan's multicolor portrait **Rev:** Multicolor logo above stadium **Edge:** Reeded

Date	Mintage	F	VF	XF	Unc	BU
1999 Proof	500	Value: 150				

KM# 39 25 DOLLARS
Copper-Nickel **Subject:** 25th Anniversary of Accession

Date	Mintage	F	VF	XF	Unc	BU
ND(1992) Proof	7,500	Value: 50.00				

KM# 39a 25 DOLLARS
0.9170 Gold **Subject:** 25th Anniversary of Accession

Date	Mintage	F	VF	XF	Unc	BU
ND(1992) Proof	—	Value: 585				

KM# 50 25 DOLLARS
31.1000 g., 0.9250 Silver .9249 oz. ASW, 38.7 mm. **Ruler:** Sultan Hassanal Bolkiah I **Subject:** 25th Anniversary of Brunei Currency Board **Obv:** Sultan Hassanal Bolkiah **Rev:** Mosque

Date	Mintage	F	VF	XF	Unc	BU
1992 Proof	2,000	Value: 75.00				

KM# 50a 25 DOLLARS
Gold **Ruler:** Sultan Hassanal Bolkiah I **Subject:** 25th Anniversary of Brunei Currency Board **Obv:** Sultan Hassanal Bolkiah. **Rev:** Mosque.

Date	Mintage	F	VF	XF	Unc	BU
1992 Proof	1,000	—	—	—	—	—

KM# 69 30 DOLLARS
62.2070 g., 0.9990 Silver 2.0000 oz. ASW **Ruler:** Sultan Hassanal Bolkiah I **Subject:** 30 Years - ASEAN **Obv:** Sultan Hassanal Bolkiah **Rev:** Seven multicolor flags

Date	Mintage	F	VF	XF	Unc	BU
1997 Proof	500	Value: 150				

KM# 70 30 DOLLARS
31.1000 g., 0.9170 Gold .9169 oz. AGW **Subject:** 30 Years - ASEAN **Obv:** Sultan Hassanal Bolkiah **Rev:** ASEAN logo

Date	Mintage	F	VF	XF	Unc	BU
1997 Proof	300	Value: 665				

KM# 24 50 DOLLARS
28.2800 g., 0.9250 Silver .8411 oz. ASW **Ruler:** Sultan Hassanal Bolkiah I **Subject:** Year of Hejira 1400 **Obv:** Head right, legend without numeral 'I' in title **Rev:** Design above denomination

Date	Mintage	F	VF	XF	Unc	BU
AH1400 (1980) Proof	3,000	Value: 145				

KM# 40 50 DOLLARS
30.7000 g., 0.9250 Silver .9130 oz. ASW, 42 mm. **Ruler:** Sultan Hassanal Bolkiah I **Subject:** 25th Anniversary of Accession **Obv:** Sultan Hassanal Bolkiah **Rev:** Royal procession **Edge:** Reeded

Date	Mintage	F	VF	XF	Unc	BU
ND(1992) Proof	3,500	Value: 140				

KM# 40a 50 DOLLARS
0.9170 Gold **Ruler:** Sultan Hassanal Bolkiah I **Subject:** 25th Anniversary of Accession **Obv:** Sultan Hassanal Bolkiah **Rev:** Royal procession

Date	Mintage	F	VF	XF	Unc	BU
ND(1992)	—	—	—	—	—	—

KM# 51 50 DOLLARS
0.9170 Gold **Ruler:** Sultan Hassanal Bolkiah I **Subject:** 25th Anniversary of Brunei Currency Board **Obv:** Sultan Hassanal Bolkiah **Rev:** Mosque

Date	Mintage	F	VF	XF	Unc	BU
1992 Proof	1,000	Value: 485				

KM# 65 50 DOLLARS
62.2070 g., 0.9990 Silver 2.0000 oz. ASW **Ruler:** Sultan Hassanal Bolkiah I **Subject:** 50th Birthday - Sultan Hassanal Bolkiah **Obv:** Sultan Hassanal Bolkiah's multicolor portrait **Rev:** Buildings on waterfront

Date	Mintage	F	VF	XF	Unc	BU
ND(1996) Proof	1,100	Value: 230				

KM# 66 50 DOLLARS
62.2070 g., 0.9990 Silver 2.0000 oz. ASW **Ruler:** Sultan Hassanal Bolkiah I **Subject:** 50th Birthday - Sultan Hassanal Bolkiah **Obv:** Sultan Bolkiah arms **Rev:** Building

Date	Mintage	F	VF	XF	Unc	BU
ND(1996) Proof	1,000	Value: 230				

KM# 67 50 DOLLARS
31.1035 g., 0.9170 Gold 1.0000 oz. AGW **Ruler:** Sultan Hassanal Bolkiah I **Subject:** 50th Birthday - Sultan Hassanal Bolkiah **Obv:** Sultan Hassanal Bolkiah **Rev:** Mosque

Date	Mintage	F	VF	XF	Unc	BU
ND(1996) Proof	500	Value: 685				

KM# 27 100 DOLLARS
28.2800 g., 0.9250 Silver .8411 oz. ASW **Ruler:** Sultan Hassanal Bolkiah I **Subject:** Independence Day **Obv:** Uniformed bust 3/4 right **Rev:** Mosque within circle, denomination below

Date	Mintage	F	VF	XF	Unc	BU
1984	5,000	—	—	—	140	150
1984 Proof	2,000	Value: 185				

KM# 33 100 DOLLARS
13.5000 g., 0.9170 Gold .3976 oz. AGW **Ruler:** Sultan Hassanal Bolkiah I **Subject:** 20th Anniversary of Brunei Currency Board **Obv:** Uniformed bust 3/4 right **Rev:** Mosque above denomination

Date	Mintage	F	VF	XF	Unc	BU
1987 Proof	1,000	Value: 500				

KM# 30 100 DOLLARS
31.1000 g., 0.9250 Silver .9250 oz. ASW **Ruler:** Sultan Hassanal Bolkiah I **Subject:** 20th Anniversary of Coronation **Obv:** Uniformed bust 3/4 right **Rev:** Arms within wreath divides dates at top, denomination below wreath

Date	Mintage	F	VF	XF	Unc	BU
ND(1988) Proof	2,000	Value: 175				

KM# 52 100 DOLLARS
0.9170 Gold **Ruler:** Sultan Hassanal Bolkiah I **Subject:** 25th Anniversary of Brunei Currency Board **Obv:** Sultan Hassanal Bolkiah **Rev:** Mosque

Date	Mintage	F	VF	XF	Unc	BU
1992 Proof	1,000	Value: 585				

KM# 62 100 DOLLARS
0.9170 White Gold **Ruler:** Sultan Hassanal Bolkiah I **Subject:** 10th Year of Independence **Obv:** Sultan Hassanal Bolkiah I **Rev:** National arms

Date	Mintage	F	VF	XF	Unc	BU
ND(1994)	1,480	—	—	—	525	545
ND(1994) Proof	1,500	Value: 565				

KM# 73 200 DOLLARS
31.1000 g., 0.9170 Gold .9169 oz. AGW **Ruler:** Sultan Hassanal Bolkiah I **Subject:** 20th SEA Games **Obv:** Sultan Hassanal Bolkiah I **Rev:** Multicolor logo above stadium

Date	Mintage	F	VF	XF	Unc	BU
1999 Proof	100	Value: 685				

KM# 53 250 DOLLARS
0.9170 Gold **Ruler:** Sultan Hassanal Bolkiah I **Subject:** 25th Anniversary of Brunei Currency Board **Obv:** Sultan Hassanal Bolkiah I **Rev:** Mosque

Date	Mintage	F	VF	XF	Unc	BU
1992 Proof	1,000	Value: 735				

KM# 41 500 DOLLARS
50.0000 g., 0.9170 Gold 1.4727 oz. AGW **Ruler:** Sultan Hassanal Bolkiah I **Subject:** 25th Anniversary of Accession **Obv:** Sultan's portrait **Rev:** Other portrait

Date	Mintage	F	VF	XF	Unc	BU
MS(1992) Proof	1,500	Value: 1,350				

KM# 25 750 DOLLARS
15.9800 g., 0.9170 Gold .4711 oz. AGW **Ruler:** Sultan Hassanal Bolkiah I **Subject:** Year of Hejira 1400 **Obv:** Head right **Rev:** Design above denomination

Date	Mintage	F	VF	XF	Unc	BU
AH1400 (1980) Proof	1,000	Value: 650				

KM# 22 1000 DOLLARS

50.0000 g., 0.9170 Gold 1.4742 oz. AGW **Ruler:** Sultan Hassanal Bolkiah I **Subject:** 10th Anniversary of Sultan's Coronation **Obv:** Head right **Rev:** Coronation design above denomination, date at right

Date	Mintage	F	VF	XF	Unc	BU
ND(1978) Proof	1,000	Value: 1,450				

KM# 28 1000 DOLLARS

50.0000 g., 0.9170 Gold 1.4742 oz. AGW **Ruler:** Sultan Hassanal Bolkiah I **Subject:** Independence Day **Obv:** Bust half right **Rev:** Off-shore oil rig, denomination below

Date	Mintage	F	VF	XF	Unc	BU
1984 Proof	1,000	Value: 1,300				
1984	4,000	—	—	—	1,050	1,150

KM# 31 1000 DOLLARS

50.0000 g., 0.9170 Gold 1.4742 oz. AGW **Ruler:** Sultan Hassanal Bolkiah I **Subject:** 20th Anniversary of Coronation **Obv:** Uniformed bust 3/4 right **Rev:** Arms within wreath divide dates at top, denomination below

Date	Mintage	F	VF	XF	Unc	BU
ND(1988) Proof	1,000	Value: 1,150				

KM# 63 1000 DOLLARS

0.9990 Gold **Ruler:** Sultan Hassanal Bolkiah I **Subject:** 10 Years of Independence **Obv:** Sultan Hassanal Bolkiah I **Rev:** National arms

Date	Mintage	F	VF	XF	Unc	BU
ND(1994)	500	—	—	—	1,275	1,350
ND(1994) Proof	480	Value: 1,450				

PROOF SETS

KM#	Date	Mintage	Identification	Issue Price	Mkt Val
PSA1	1970 (5)	—	KM9-13	—	30.00
PS1	1979 (6)	10,000	KM15-20	30.00	90.00
PS2	1984 (6)	3,000	MS15-20	—	80.00
PS3	1984 (3)	500	KM26-28	—	1,500
PS4	1985 (6)	10,000	KM15-20	30.00	80.00
PS5	1986 (6)	5,000	KM15-20	30.00	80.00
PS6	1987 (6)	2,000	KM15b, 16a-20a	52.00	80.00
PS7	1988 (6)	2,000	KM15b, 16a-20a	—	80.00
PS8	1989 (6)	2,000	KM15b, 16a-20a	—	80.00
PS9	1990 (6)	2,000	KM15b, 16a-20a	—	80.00
PS10	1991 (6)	2,000	KM15b, 16a-20a	—	80.00
PS11	1992 (6)	2,000	KM15b, 16a-20a	—	80.00
PS12	1992 (7)	2,000	KM42-47, 50	—	190
PS13	1992 (7)	1,000	KM47a, 48-53	—	3,000
PS14	1993 (6)	2,000	KM15b, 16a-20a	—	80.00
PS15	1994 (8)	1,980	KM54a-61a	—	200
PS16	1996 (4)	500	KM64-67	—	1,075
PS17	1997 (3)	500	KM68-70	—	740
PS18	1999 (3)	350	KM71-73	—	765

SPECIMEN SETS (SS)

KM#	Date	Mintage	Identification	Issue Price	Mkt Val
MS2	1984 (6)	5,000	KM15-20	—	15.00
MS3	1984 (3)	500	KM26-28	—	1,250
MS4	1985 (6)	15,000	KM15-20	10.00	30.00
MS5	1986 (6)	10,000	KM15-20	10.00	30.00
MS6	1987 (6)	3,000	KM15a, 16-20	15.60	30.00
MS7	1988 (6)	2,000	KM15a, 16-20	15.60	30.00
MS8	1989 (6)	2,000	KM15a, 16-20	—	30.00
MS9	1990 (6)	3,000	KM15a, 16-20	—	30.00
MS10	1991 (6)	3,000	KM15a, 16-20	—	30.00
MS11	1994 (8)	—	KM54-61	—	50.00

BULGARIA

The Republic of Bulgaria, formerly the Peoples Republic of Bulgaria, a Balkan country on the Black Sea in southeastern Europe, has an area of 42,855 sq. mi. (110,910 sq. km.) and a population of *8.31 million. Capital: Sofia. Agriculture remains a key component of the economy but industrialization, particularly heavy industry, has been emphasized since the late 1940s. Machinery, tobacco and cigarettes, wines and spirits, clothing and metals are the chief exports.

The area now occupied by Bulgaria was conquered by the Bulgars, an Asiatic tribe, in the 7th century. Bulgarian kingdoms continued to exist on the Bulgarian peninsula until it came under Turkish rule in 1395. In 1878, after nearly 500 years of Turkish rule, Bulgaria was made a principality under Turkish suzerainty. Union seven years later with Eastern Rumelia created a Balkan state with borders approximating those of present-day Bulgaria. A Bulgarian kingdom, fully independent of Turkey, was proclaimed Sept. 22, 1908. During WWI Bulgaria had been aligned with Germany. After the Armistice certain land concessions were given to Greece and Romania. In 1934 King Boris III suspended all political parties and established a dictatorial monarchy. In 1938 the military began rearming through the aide of the Anglo-French loan. As WW II developed, Bulgaria again supported the Germans but protected their Jewish community. Boris died mysteriously in 1943 and Simeon II became King at the age of six. The country was then ruled by a pro-Nazi regency until it was liberated by Soviet forces in 1944.

The monarchy was abolished and Simeon was ousted by plebiscite in 1946 and Bulgaria became a Peoples Republic on the Soviet pattern. After democratic reforms in 1989 the name was changed to the Republic of Bulgaria.

Coinage of the Peoples Republic features a number of politically oriented commemoratives.

RULERS

Ferdinand I, as Prince, 1887-1908
As King, 1908-1918
Boris III, 1918-1943

MINT MARKS

A - Berlin
(a) Cornucopia & torch - Paris
BP - Budapest
H - Heaton Mint, Birmingham
KB - Kormoczbanya
(p) Poissy - Thunderbolt

MONETARY SYSTEM

100 Stotinki = 1 Lev

PRINCIPALITY
Under Turkish Suzerainty
STANDARD COINAGE

KM# 22.1 STOTINKA

Bronze **Ruler:** Ferdinand I as Prince **Obv:** Crowned arms within circle **Rev:** Denomination above date, within wreath, privy marks and design name below denomination

Date	Mintage	F	VF	XF	Unc	BU
1901	20,000,000	1.25	2.50	7.50	17.50	—

KM# 22.2 STOTINKA

Bronze **Ruler:** Ferdinand I as Prince **Obv:** Crowned arms within circle **Rev:** Denomination above date within wreath, without privy marks and designer name

Date	Mintage	F	VF	XF	Unc	BU
1912	20,000,000	0.75	1.75	6.00	12.00	—

KM# 23.1 2 STOTINKI

Bronze **Ruler:** Ferdinand I **Obv:** Crowned arms within circle **Rev:** Denomination above date within wreath, privy marks and designer name below denomination

Date	Mintage	F	VF	XF	Unc	BU
1901(a)	40,000,000	1.00	2.00	5.00	10.00	—

KM# 23.2 2 STOTINKI

Bronze **Obv:** Crowned arms within circle **Rev:** Denomination above date within wreath, without privy marks and designer name

Date	Mintage	F	VF	XF	Unc	BU
1912	40,000,000	0.50	1.00	2.20	6.50	—

KM# 24 5 STOTINKI

Copper-Nickel **Obv:** Crowned arms within circle **Rev:** Denomination above date within wreath

Date	Mintage	F	VF	XF	Unc	BU
1906	14,000,000	0.20	0.60	2.00	6.00	—
1912	14,000,000	0.20	0.40	1.20	4.00	—
1913	20,000,000	0.20	0.40	1.50	4.00	—
1913 Proof	—	Value: 100				

KM# 24a 5 STOTINKI

Zinc **Obv:** Crowned arms within circle **Rev:** Denomination above date within wreath

Date	Mintage	F	VF	XF	Unc	BU
1917	53,200,000	0.60	1.00	2.50	6.00	—

KM# 25 10 STOTINKI

Copper-Nickel **Obv:** Crowned arms within circle **Rev:** Denomination above date within wreath

Date	Mintage	F	VF	XF	Unc	BU
1906	13,000,000	0.50	1.00	2.50	8.00	—
1912	13,000,000	0.20	0.40	1.75	4.50	—
1912 Proof	—	Value: 110				
1913	20,000,000	0.20	0.40	1.00	2.50	—

KM# 25a 10 STOTINKI

Zinc **Obv:** Crowned arms within circle **Rev:** Denomination above date within wreath

Date	Mintage	F	VF	XF	Unc	BU
1917	59,100,000	0.40	1.00	2.50	5.50	—
1917 Proof	—	Value: 130				

KM# 26 20 STOTINKI

Copper-Nickel **Obv:** Crowned arms within circle **Rev:** Denomination above date within wreath

Date	Mintage	F	VF	XF	Unc	BU
1906	10,000,000	0.50	1.50	3.50	10.00	—
1912	10,000,000	0.20	0.50	1.50	5.00	—
1913	5,000,000	0.20	1.00	2.00	6.00	—
1913	—	—	—	—	—	—

KM# 26a 20 STOTINKI

Zinc **Obv:** Crowned arms within circle **Rev:** Denomination above date within wreath

Date	Mintage	F	VF	XF	Unc	BU
1917	40,000,000	0.50	1.75	4.00	8.50	—
1917 Proof	—	Value: 125				

KINGDOM

STANDARD COINAGE

KM# 27 50 STOTINKI

2.5000 g., 0.8350 Silver .0671 oz. ASW **Obv:** Head right **Rev:** Denomination above date within wreath

Date	Mintage	F	VF	XF	Unc	BU
1910	400,000	1.75	4.00	9.00	20.00	—

KM# 30 50 STOTINKI

2.5000 g., 0.8350 Silver .0671 oz. ASW **Obv:** Head left **Rev:** Denomination above date within wreath

Date	Mintage	F	VF	XF	Unc	BU
1912	2,000,000	1.20	2.00	4.50	11.00	—
1913	3,000,000	1.20	2.00	3.50	8.00	—
1916	4,562,000	—	—	240	400	—

Note: Withdrawn from circulation and destroyed possibly only 100 pieces remain; Beware possible counterfeits

KM# 46 50 STOTINKI

Aluminum-Bronze **Obv:** Crowned arms with supporters **Rev:** Denomination above date within wreath

Date	Mintage	F	VF	XF	Unc	BU
1937	60,200,000	0.25	0.50	1.00	3.50	—

KM# 28 LEV

5.0000 g., 0.8350 Silver .1342 oz. ASW **Obv:** Head right **Rev:** Denomination above date within wreath

Date	Mintage	F	VF	XF	Unc	BU
1910	3,000,000	2.25	4.50	8.00	16.00	—

KM# 31 LEV

5.0000 g., 0.8350 Silver .1342 oz. ASW **Obv:** Head left **Rev:** Denomination above date within wreath

Date	Mintage	F	VF	XF	Unc	BU
1912	2,000,000	2.00	3.00	5.50	12.50	—
1913	3,500,000	2.00	3.00	5.00	10.00	—
1916	4,569,000	—	—	520	900	—

Note: Withdrawn from circulation and destroyed possibly only 50 pieces remain; Beware possible counterfeits

KM# 35 LEV

Aluminum **Obv:** Crowned arms with supporters on ornate shield **Rev:** Denomination above date within wreath

Date	Mintage	F	VF	XF	Unc	BU
1923	40,000,000	3.00	6.00	14.00	40.00	—

KM# 37 LEV

Copper-Nickel, 19.7 mm. **Obv:** Crowned arms with supporters on ornate shield **Rev:** Denomination above date within wreath **Edge:** Reeded

Date	Mintage	F	VF	XF	Unc	BU
1925	35,000,000	0.20	0.50	1.25	3.00	—
1925(p)	34,982,000	0.25	0.60	1.50	3.50	—

Note: The Poissy issue bears the thunderbolt mint mark

KM# 37a LEV

Iron **Obv:** Crowned arms with supporters on ornate shield **Rev:** Denomination above date within wreath

Date	Mintage	F	VF	XF	Unc	BU
1941	10,000,000	3.00	6.00	16.00	45.00	—

KM# 29 2 LEVA

10.0000 g., 0.8350 Silver .2685 oz. ASW **Obv:** Head right **Rev:** Denomination above date within wreath

Date	Mintage	F	VF	XF	Unc	BU
1910	400,000	4.50	7.50	16.00	45.00	—

KM# 32 2 LEVA

10.0000 g., 0.8350 Silver .2685 oz. ASW **Obv:** Head left **Rev:** Denomination above date within wreath

Date	Mintage	F	VF	XF	Unc	BU
1912	1,000,000	4.00	6.00	12.00	20.00	—
1913	500,000	4.00	6.00	14.00	20.00	—
1916	2,286,000	—	—	930	1,800	—

Note: Withdrawn from circulation and destroyed possibly only 30 pieces remain; Beware possible counterfeits

KM# 36 2 LEVA

Aluminum **Obv:** Crowned arms with supporters on ornate shield **Rev:** Denomination above date within wreath

Date	Mintage	F	VF	XF	Unc	BU
1923	20,000,000	3.50	7.00	18.00	55.00	—

KM# 38 2 LEVA

Copper-Nickel **Obv:** Crowned arms with supporters on ornate shield **Rev:** Denomination above date within wreath

Date	Mintage	F	VF	XF	Unc	BU
1925	20,000,000	0.40	0.80	1.50	3.00	—
1925(p)	20,000,000	0.50	1.00	2.25	5.00	—

Note: The Poissy issue bears the thunderbolt privy mark

KM# 38a 2 LEVA

Iron **Obv:** Crowned arms with supporters on ornate shield **Rev:** Denomination above date within wreath

Date	Mintage	F	VF	XF	Unc	BU
1941	15,000,000	0.75	1.50	8.50	24.00	—

KM# 49 2 LEVA
Iron **Obv:** Crowned arms with supporters **Rev:** Denomination above date within wreath

Date	Mintage	F	VF	XF	Unc	BU
1943	35,000,000	0.75	1.50	9.00	32.00	—

KM# 39 5 LEVA
Copper-Nickel **Obv:** Denomination above date within wreath **Rev:** Figure on horseback, animals below

Date	Mintage	F	VF	XF	Unc	BU
1930	20,001,000	0.60	1.25	3.50	10.00	—

KM# 39a 5 LEVA
Iron **Obv:** Denomination above date within wreath **Rev:** Figure on horseback, animals below

Date	Mintage	F	VF	XF	Unc	BU
1941	15,000,000	1.00	3.00	7.00	24.00	—

KM# 39b 5 LEVA
Nickel Clad Steel **Obv:** Denomination above date within wreath **Rev:** Figure on horseback, animals below

Date	Mintage	F	VF	XF	Unc	BU
1943	36,000,000	0.50	1.00	2.50	8.00	—

KM# 40 10 LEVA
Copper-Nickel, 30 mm. **Obv:** Denomination above date within wreath **Rev:** Figure on horseback, animals below **Edge:** Reeded

Date	Mintage	F	VF	XF	Unc	BU
1930	15,001,000	0.75	1.50	3.50	9.50	—

KM# 40a 10 LEVA
Iron **Obv:** Denomination above date within wreath **Rev:** Figure on horseback, animals below

Date	Mintage	F	VF	XF	Unc	BU
1941	2,200,000	6.00	12.00	26.00	68.00	—

KM# 40b 10 LEVA
Nickel Clad Steel **Obv:** Denomination above date within wreath **Rev:** Figure on horseback, animals below

Date	Mintage	F	VF	XF	Unc	BU
1943	25,000,000	0.60	1.25	3.00	8.00	—

KM# 33 20 LEVA
6.4516 g., 0.9000 Gold .1867 oz. AGW, 21 mm. **Subject:** Declaration of Independence **Obv:** Head left **Rev:** Crowned arms, denomination and date below

Date	Mintage	F	VF	XF	Unc	BU
1912	75,000	BV	175	275	460	—
1912 Proof	Inc. above	Value: 3,000				
1912 Proof; restrike	2,950	Value: 275				

Note: Official restrikes of this type were produced at the Bulgarian Mint in Sophia from 1967-68 and released prior to 2002; These pieces can be distinguished by their thicker more widely spaced edge legends

KM# 41 20 LEVA
4.0000 g., 0.5000 Silver .0643 oz. ASW **Obv:** Head left **Rev:** Denomination above date within wreath

Date	Mintage	F	VF	XF	Unc	BU
1930BP	10,016,000	1.25	2.50	4.00	9.00	—

KM# 47 20 LEVA
Copper-Nickel **Obv:** Head left **Rev:** Denomination above date within wreath

Date	Mintage	F	VF	XF	Unc	BU
1940A	6,650,000	0.50	1.00	2.00	6.00	—

KM# 42 50 LEVA
10.0000 g., 0.5000 Silver .1607 oz. ASW **Obv:** Head left **Rev:** Denomination above date within wreath

Date	Mintage	F	VF	XF	Unc	BU
1930BP	9,028,000	2.75	4.50	8.50	20.00	—

KM# 44 50 LEVA
10.0000 g., 0.5000 Silver .1607 oz. ASW **Obv:** Head left **Rev:** Denomination at top, date below, flower at bottom, grain sprigs flank

Date	Mintage	F	VF	XF	Unc	BU
1934	3,001,000	2.50	4.00	8.00	18.00	—
1934 Proof	—	—	—	—	—	—

KM# 48 50 LEVA
Copper-Nickel **Obv:** Head left **Rev:** Denomination above date within wreath

Date	Mintage	F	VF	XF	Unc	BU
1940A	12,340,000	0.75	1.50	3.00	8.00	—

KM# 48a 50 LEVA
Nickel Clad Steel **Obv:** Head left **Rev:** Denomination above date within wreath

Date	Mintage	F	VF	XF	Unc	BU
1943A	15,000,000	1.00	2.00	4.00	9.00	—

KM# 34 100 LEVA
32.2580 g., 0.9000 Gold .9334 oz. AGW, 35 mm. **Subject:** Declaration of Independence **Obv:** Head left **Rev:** Crowned arms divide denomination, date below

Date	Mintage	F	VF	XF	Unc	BU
1912	5,000	640	950	1,850	3,200	—
1912 Proof	Inc. above	Value: 6,000				
1912 Proof; restrike	1,000	Value: 1,000				

Note: Official restrikes of this type were produced at the Bulgarian Mint in Sophia from 1967-68 and released prior to 2002; These pieces can be distinguished by their thicker more widely spaced edge legends

KM# 43 100 LEVA
20.0000 g., 0.5000 Silver .3215 oz. ASW **Obv:** Head, left **Rev:** Denomination above date within wreath

Date	Mintage	F	VF	XF	Unc	BU
1930BP	1,556,000	BV	6.00	12.00	30.00	—

KM# 45 100 LEVA
20.0000 g., 0.5000 Silver .3215 oz. ASW **Obv:** Head left **Rev:** Denomination at top, date below, flower at bottom, grain sprigs flank

Date	Mintage	F	VF	XF	Unc	BU
1934	2,506,000	BV	5.00	8.00	15.00	—
1934 Proof	—	—	—	—	—	—
1937	2,207,000	BV	5.00	8.00	16.00	—

PEOPLES REPUBLIC

STANDARD COINAGE

KM# 50 STOTINKA
Brass **Obv:** National arms within circle **Rev:** Denomination above date at right, grain sprig at left

Date	Mintage	F	VF	XF	Unc	BU
1951	—	—	—	0.10	0.25	—

KM# 59 STOTINKA
Brass **Obv:** National arms within circle, date 9 / IX / 1944 on ribbon **Rev:** Denomination above date, grain sprigs flank

Date	Mintage	F	VF	XF	Unc	BU
1962	—	—	—	0.10	0.25	—
1970	—	—	0.30	0.80	3.00	—

KM# 84 STOTINKA

1.0000 g., Brass, 15.2 mm. **Obv:** National arms within circle, two dates on ribbon, '681-1944 **Rev:** Denomination above date, grain sprigs flank **Note:** Reeded and security edge varieties exist.

Date	Mintage	F	VF	XF	Unc	BU
1974	—	—	—	0.10	0.15	—
1979 Proof	2,000	Value: 1.50				
1980 Proof	2,000	Value: 1.50				
1981	137	—	—	—	20.00	—
1988	—	—	—	0.10	0.15	—
1989	—	—	—	0.10	0.15	—
1990	—	—	—	0.10	0.15	—

KM# 111 STOTINKA

Brass **Subject:** 1300th Anniversary of Bulgaria

Date	Mintage	F	VF	XF	Unc	BU
1981	—	—	0.10	0.20	0.50	—
1981 Proof	—	Value: 2.00				

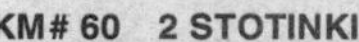

KM# 60 2 STOTINKI

Brass **Obv:** National arms within circle, date 9*IX*1944 on ribbon **Rev:** Denomination above date, grain sprigs flank

Date	Mintage	F	VF	XF	Unc	BU
1962	—	—	—	0.10	0.25	—

KM# 85 2 STOTINKI

2.0000 g., Brass, 18.1 mm. **Obv:** National arms within circle, two dates on ribbon, '681-1944 **Rev:** Denomination above date at right, grain sprig at left

Date	Mintage	F	VF	XF	Unc	BU
1974	—	—	—	0.10	0.25	—
1979 Proof	2,000	Value: 2.00				
1980 Proof	2,000	Value: 2.00				
1981 Rare	20	—	—	—	—	—
1988	—	—	—	0.10	0.25	—
1989	—	—	—	0.10	0.25	—
1990	—	—	—	0.10	0.25	—

KM# 112 2 STOTINKI

Brass **Subject:** 1300th Anniversary of Bulgaria **Obv:** National arms within circle **Rev:** Denomination above date at right, grain sprig at left

Date	Mintage	F	VF	XF	Unc	BU
1981	—	—	0.10	0.20	0.60	—
1981 Proof	—	Value: 2.50				

KM# 51 3 STOTINKI

Brass **Obv:** National arms within circle **Rev:** Denomination above date at right, grain sprig at left

Date	Mintage	F	VF	XF	Unc	BU
1951	—	—	0.10	0.25	0.75	—

KM# 52 5 STOTINKI

Brass **Obv:** National arms within circle **Rev:** Denomination above date at right, grain sprig at left

Date	Mintage	F	VF	XF	Unc	BU
1951	—	0.10	0.15	0.25	0.75	—

KM# 61 5 STOTINKI

Brass **Obv:** National arms within circle, date 9 • IX • 1944 on ribbon **Rev:** Denomination above date, grain sprigs flank

Date	Mintage	F	VF	XF	Unc	BU
1962	—	—	0.10	0.20	0.50	—

KM# 86 5 STOTINKI

3.1000 g., Brass, 22.35 mm. **Obv:** National arms within circle, two dates on ribbon '681-1944' **Rev:** Denomination above date, grain sprigs flank

Date	Mintage	F	VF	XF	Unc	BU
1974	—	—	0.10	0.15	0.25	—
1979 Proof	2,000	Value: 2.00				
1980 Proof	2,000	Value: 2.00				
1988	—	—	—	0.15	0.25	—
1989	—	—	—	0.15	0.25	—
1990	—	—	—	0.15	0.25	—

KM# 113 5 STOTINKI

Brass **Subject:** 1300th Anniversary of Bulgaria **Obv:** National arms within circle **Rev:** Denomination above date within wreath

Date	Mintage	F	VF	XF	Unc	BU
1981	—	—	0.10	0.25	0.75	—
1981 Proof	—	Value: 2.50				

KM# 53 10 STOTINKI

Copper-Nickel **Obv:** National arms within circle **Rev:** Denomination above date at right, grain sprig at left

Date	Mintage	F	VF	XF	Unc	BU
1951	—	—	0.10	0.20	0.40	—

KM# 62 10 STOTINKI

Nickel-Brass **Obv:** National arms within circle, date 9 • IX • 1944 on ribbon **Rev:** Denomination above date within wreath

Date	Mintage	F	VF	XF	Unc	BU
1962	—	—	0.10	0.20	0.40	—

KM# 87 10 STOTINKI

1.8000 g., Nickel-Brass, 17.1 mm. **Obv:** National arms within circle, two dates on arms, '681-1944' **Rev:** Denomination above date within wreath

Date	Mintage	F	VF	XF	Unc	BU
1974	—	—	0.10	0.15	0.25	—
1979 Proof	2,000	Value: 3.50				
1980 Proof	2,000	Value: 3.50				
1988	—	—	—	0.15	0.25	—
1989	—	—	—	0.15	0.25	—
1990	—	—	—	0.15	0.25	—

KM# 114 10 STOTINKI

Copper-Nickel **Subject:** 1300th Anniversary of Bulgaria **Obv:** National arms within circle **Rev:** Denomination above date within wreath

Date	Mintage	F	VF	XF	Unc	BU
1981	—	—	0.20	0.50	1.50	—
1981 Proof	—	Value: 3.50				

KM# 55 20 STOTINKI

Copper-Nickel, 21 mm. **Obv:** National arms within circle **Rev:** Denomination above date at right, grain sprig at left **Edge:** Reeded

Date	Mintage	F	VF	XF	Unc	BU
1952	—	1.00	2.50	7.50	20.00	—
1954	—	0.10	0.25	0.75	1.50	—

KM# 63 20 STOTINKI

Nickel-Brass **Obv:** Date 9 • IX • 1944 on ribbon

Date	Mintage	F	VF	XF	Unc	BU
1962	—	0.10	0.20	0.30	0.75	—

KM# 88 20 STOTINKI

2.9000 g., Nickel-Brass, 21.2 mm. **Obv:** National arms within circle, two dates on ribbon, '681-1944' **Rev:** Denomination above date within wreath

Date	Mintage	F	VF	XF	Unc	BU
1974	—	0.10	0.20	0.30	0.60	—
1979 Proof	2,000	Value: 3.50				
1980 Proof	2,000	Value: 3.50				
1988	—	—	—	0.30	0.60	—
Note: Large date (7mm) and small date (5mm) exist						
1989	—	—	—	0.30	0.60	—
1990	—	—	—	0.30	0.60	—

KM# 115 20 STOTINKI

Copper-Nickel **Subject:** 1300th Anniversary of Bulgaria **Obv:** National arms within circle **Rev:** Denomination above date within wreath

Date	Mintage	F	VF	XF	Unc	BU
1981	—	—	0.25	0.65	2.00	—
1981 Proof	—	Value: 4.00				

KM# 54 25 STOTINKI

Copper-Nickel **Obv:** National arms within circle **Rev:** Denomination above date at right, grain sprig at left

Date	Mintage	F	VF	XF	Unc	BU
1951	—	0.10	0.20	0.50	1.00	—

KM# 56 50 STOTINKI

Copper-Nickel **Obv:** National arms within circle **Rev:** Denomination above date at right, grain sprig at left

Date	Mintage	F	VF	XF	Unc	BU
1959	—	0.10	0.20	0.40	0.80	—

KM# 64 50 STOTINKI
Nickel-Brass **Obv:** National arms within circle, date 9 • IX • 1944 on ribbon **Rev:** Denomination above date within wreath

Date	Mintage	F	VF	XF	Unc	BU
1962	—	0.10	0.40	0.65	1.00	—

KM# 89 50 STOTINKI
4.2000 g., Nickel-Brass, 23.3 mm. **Obv:** Two dates on ribbon, '681-1944'

Date	Mintage	F	VF	XF	Unc	BU
1974	—	0.10	0.40	0.65	1.50	—
1979 Proof	2,000	Value: 4.00				
1980 Proof	2,000	Value: 4.00				
1988	—	—	—	0.50	1.00	—
1989	—	—	—	0.50	1.00	—
1990	—	—	—	0.50	1.00	—

KM# 98 50 STOTINKI
Copper-Nickel **Subject:** University Games at Sofia **Obv:** Runner with torch, left, date at lower left **Rev:** Denomination divides arms and date

Date	Mintage	F	VF	XF	Unc	BU
1977	2,000,000	0.20	0.40	0.75	1.50	—

KM# 116 50 STOTINKI
Copper-Nickel **Subject:** 1300th Anniversary of Bulgaria **Obv:** National arms within circle **Rev:** Denomination above date within wreath

Date	Mintage	F	VF	XF	Unc	BU
1981	—	—	0.30	0.60	1.80	—
1981 Proof	—	Value: 4.00				

KM# 57 LEV
Copper-Nickel **Obv:** National arms within circle, date 9 • IX • 1944 on ribbon **Rev:** Denomination above date within wreath

Date	Mintage	F	VF	XF	Unc	BU
1960	—	0.10	0.25	0.60	1.00	—

KM# 58 LEV
Nickel-Brass **Obv:** National arms within circle **Rev:** Denomination above date, grain sprigs flank

Date	Mintage	F	VF	XF	Unc	BU
1962	—	—	0.50	1.00	1.50	—

KM# 74 LEV
Nickel-Brass, 27 mm. **Subject:** 25th Anniversary of Socialist Revolution **Obv:** Wide denomination above date, grain sprigs flanking **Rev:** Monumont to the fighters of the resistance

Date	Mintage	F	VF	XF	Unc	BU
1969	2,410,196	0.35	0.60	1.25	2.50	—

KM# 76 LEV
Nickel-Brass, 27 mm. **Subject:** 90th Anniversary Liberation From Turks **Obv:** Denomination within wreath, date below **Rev:** Equestrian statue of Alexander II, Czar of Russia, dates flank

Date	Mintage	F	VF	XF	Unc	BU
1969	1,290,373	0.35	0.65	1.50	2.75	—

KM# 90 LEV
Nickel-Brass, 27 mm. **Obv:** Two dates '681-1944' on ribbon

Date	Mintage	F	VF	XF	Unc	BU
1974	—	—	0.50	1.00	2.00	—
1979 Proof	2,000	Value: 6.00				
1980 Proof	2,000	Value: 6.00				
1988	—	—	—	0.75	2.00	—
1989	—	—	—	0.75	2.00	—
1990	—	—	—	0.75	2.00	—

KM# 94 LEV
Bronze, 27 mm. **Subject:** 100th Anniversary of the "April Uprising" Against the Turks **Obv:** Lion above denomination, date at left, circle surrounds **Rev:** Weapons above date within circle

Date	Mintage	F	VF	XF	Unc	BU
1976	300,000	0.35	0.60	1.25	2.50	—
1976 Proof	—	Value: 4.00				

KM# 107 LEV
Copper-Nickel, 27 mm. **Subject:** World Cup Soccer Games in Spain **Obv:** Arms divide date above denomination **Rev:** World Cup trophy **Edge:** Plain

Date	Mintage	F	VF	XF	Unc	BU
1980	220,000	—	0.60	1.25	2.50	—
1980 Proof	30,000	Value: 3.50				

KM# 117 LEV
Copper-Nickel **Subject:** 1300th Anniversary of Bulgaria **Obv:** National arms within circle **Rev:** Denomination above date, grain sprigs flank

Date	Mintage	F	VF	XF	Unc	BU
1981	—	—	0.50	1.00	2.00	—
1981 Proof	—	—	—	—	—	—

KM# 118 LEV
Copper-Nickel, 27 mm. **Subject:** International Hunting Exposition **Obv:** Arms above denomination, grain sprigs flank, date at bottom left **Rev:** Antlered deer head, left, inscription at right

Date	Mintage	F	VF	XF	Unc	BU
1981	250,000	—	0.60	1.25	2.50	—
1981 Proof	50,000	Value: 3.50				

KM# 119 LEV
Copper-Nickel, 31 mm. **Subject:** Russo-Bulgarian Friendship **Obv:** Arms above denomination **Rev:** Flags at top, hands grasped at center, date at bottom **Note:** The same reverse die was used for both Bulgaria 1 Lev, KM#119 and Russia 1 Rouble, KM#189.

Date	Mintage	F	VF	XF	Unc	BU
1981	220,800	—	0.60	1.25	2.50	—
1981 Proof	50,000	Value: 3.50				

KM# 175 LEV
Copper-Nickel, 27 mm. **Series:** 1980 Winter Olympics **Obv:** National arms **Rev:** Hockey player, denomination and date at bottom **Edge:** Reeded

Date	Mintage	F	VF	XF	Unc	BU
1987	—	—	—	—	2.50	—
1987 Proof	300,000	Value: 3.50				

KM# 176 LEV
Copper-Nickel, 27 mm. **Series:** Summer Olympics **Obv:** National arms **Rev:** Sprinters, denomination and date below **Edge:** Reeded

Date	Mintage	F	VF	XF	Unc	BU
1988	—	—	—	—	2.50	—
1988 Proof	300,000	Value: 3.50				

KM# 65 2 LEVA
8.8889 g., 0.9000 Silver .2572 oz. ASW **Subject:** 1100th Anniversary - Slovanic Alphabet **Obv:** Denomination above shield **Rev:** St. Cyril and St. Methodias, dates at bottom

Date	Mintage	F	VF	XF	Unc	BU
ND(1963) Proof	10,000	Value: 15.00				

KM# 69 2 LEVA
8.8889 g., 0.9000 Silver .2572 oz. ASW **Subject:** 20th Anniversary Peoples Republic **Obv:** Flag above denomination, two dates at bottom **Rev:** Head left, two dates below

Date	Mintage	F	VF	XF	Unc	BU
ND(1964) Proof	20,000	Value: 15.00				

KM# 73 2 LEVA
Copper-Nickel, 30 mm. **Subject:** 1050th Anniversary - Death of Ochridsky, Founder of the First European University **Obv:** Denomination between columns **Rev:** Figure divides dates **Designer:** Krum Danjanov

Date	Mintage	F	VF	XF	Unc	BU
ND(1966)	506,000	—	1.00	2.00	4.00	—

KM# 75 2 LEVA
Copper-Nickel, 30 mm. **Subject:** 25th Anniversary of Socialist Revolution, September 9, 1944 **Obv:** Large denomination between grain sprigs, date at bottom **Rev:** Monument to the Soviet Soldiers in Plovdiv

Date	Mintage	F	VF	XF	Unc	BU
1969	1,082,210	—	0.75	1.75	3.50	—

KM# 77 2 LEVA
Copper-Nickel, 30 mm. **Subject:** 90th Anniversary - Liberation from Turks **Obv:** Denomination within wreath, date below **Rev:** The Battle on the Orlovo Enesdo (Eagle's nest) by the Russian painter Popov, two dates below

Date	Mintage	F	VF	XF	Unc	BU
1969	756,759	—	0.75	1.75	3.50	—

KM# 80 2 LEVA
Nickel-Brass, 30 mm. **Subject:** 150th Anniversary - Birth of Dobri Chintulov **Obv:** Denomination above date **Rev:** Head facing, two dates below **Designer:** Lubomic Prahof and Dimitar Donowski

Date	Mintage	F	VF	XF	Unc	BU
1972	100,000	—	1.25	2.50	4.50	—

KM# 95.1 2 LEVA
Copper-Nickel, 30 mm. **Subject:** 100th Anniversary of the "April Uprising" Against the Turks **Obv:** Wreath above denomination, date at left, circle surrounds **Rev:** Figure with cannon, date at left, within circle

Date	Mintage	F	VF	XF	Unc	BU
1976	224,800	—	0.75	1.50	3.00	—
1976 Proof	—	Value: 5.00				

KM# 95.2 2 LEVA
Copper-Nickel, 30 mm. **Obv:** Wreath above denomination, date at left, circle surrounds **Rev:** Figure with cannon, date at left, within circle **Edge:** Lettered

Date	Mintage	F	VF	XF	Unc	BU
1976	138	—	—	—	—	—

KM# 108 2 LEVA
Copper-Nickel, 30 mm. **Subject:** World Cup Soccer Games in Spain **Obv:** Soccer logo **Rev:** National arms within circle divides dates above denomination, grain sprigs flank **Edge:** Plain

Date	Mintage	F	VF	XF	Unc	BU
1980	220,000	—	0.60	1.20	2.50	—
1980 Proof	30,000	Value: 4.50				

KM# 110 2 LEVA
Copper-Nickel, 30 mm. **Subject:** 100th Anniversary - Birth of Yordan Yovkov, Writer **Obv:** Denomination above date **Rev:** Head facing, two dates below **Edge:** Plain

Date	Mintage	F	VF	XF	Unc	BU
1980	200,000	—	1.00	2.50	4.50	—

KM# 120 2 LEVA
Copper-Nickel, 30 mm. **Subject:** International Hunting Exposition **Obv:** National arms above denomination, date bottom left **Rev:** Half figure of hunter with hawk, left

Date	Mintage	F	VF	XF	Unc	BU
1981	250,000	—	0.75	1.50	3.00	—
1981 Proof	50,000	Value: 5.00				

KM# 121 2 LEVA
Copper-Nickel, 30 mm. **Subject:** 1300th Anniversary of Nationhood **Obv:** Line divides anniversary years and denomination, circle surrounds **Rev:** Equestrian figure, right, animal below **Edge:** Reeded

Date	Mintage	F	VF	XF	Unc	BU
1981	—	—	—	—	2.50	—
1981 Proof	—	Value: 4.00				

KM# 122 2 LEVA
Copper-Nickel, 30 mm. **Subject:** 1300th Anniversary of Nationhood **Obv:** Wreath divides arms and denomination, date at bottom left **Rev:** Mother and child, radiant sun in background **Edge:** Reeded

Date	Mintage	F	VF	XF	Unc	BU
1981 Proof	—	Value: 4.00				

KM# 123 2 LEVA
Copper-Nickel, 30 mm. **Subject:** 1300th Anniversary of Nationhood **Obv:** Line divides left facing head, date at right and denomination, circle surrounds **Rev:** Dimitrov **Edge:** Reeded

Date	Mintage	F	VF	XF	Unc	BU
1981	—	—	—	—	3.50	—
1981 Proof	—	Value: 5.00				

KM# 124 2 LEVA
Copper-Nickel, 30 mm. **Subject:** 1300th Anniversary of Nationhood **Obv:** Buildings above denomination, date lower right **Rev:** King and saint **Edge:** Reeded

Date	Mintage	F	VF	XF	Unc	BU
1981	—	—	—	—	2.50	—
1981 Proof	—	Value: 4.00				

KM# 125 2 LEVA
Copper-Nickel, 30 mm. **Subject:** 1300th Anniversary of Nationhood **Obv:** Line divides weapons on oak leaf, date at right and denomination within circle **Rev:** Soldier **Edge:** Reeded

Date	Mintage	F	VF	XF	Unc	BU
1981	—	—	—	—	2.50	—
1981 Proof	—	Value: 4.00				

KM# 126 2 LEVA
Copper-Nickel, 30 mm. **Subject:** 1300th Anniversary of Nationhood **Obv:** Line divides flower, date at right and denomination within circle **Rev:** Clandestine meeting **Edge:** Reeded

Date	Mintage	F	VF	XF	Unc	BU
1981 Proof	—	Value: 4.00				

KM# 127 2 LEVA
Copper-Nickel, 30 mm. **Subject:** 1300th Anniversary of Nationhood **Obv:** Decorative arms with supporters above denomination, date at left **Rev:** Cyrillic alphabet **Edge:** Reeded

Date	Mintage	F	VF	XF	Unc	BU
1981	—	—	—	—	2.50	—
1981 Proof	—	Value: 4.00				

KM# 128 2 LEVA
Copper-Nickel, 30 mm. **Subject:** 1300th Anniversary of Nationhood **Obv:** Arms within circle, denomination below flanked by symbols, date at lower left **Rev:** Rila Monastary **Edge:** Reeded

Date	Mintage	F	VF	XF	Unc	BU
1981	—	—	—	—	2.50	—
1981 Proof	—	Value: 4.00				

KM# 129 2 LEVA
Copper-Nickel, 30 mm. **Subject:** 1300th Anniversary of Nationhood **Obv:** Line divides weapons on shield flanked by flags, date at right and denomination below **Rev:** Russky monument **Edge:** Reeded

Date	Mintage	F	VF	XF	Unc	BU
1981 Proof	—	Value: 4.50				

KM# 130 2 LEVA
Copper-Nickel, 30 mm. **Subject:** 1300th Anniversary of Nationhood **Obv:** Sevastokratoritza Desislava - Founder of Bojana Church. denomination, date below **Rev:** Bojana church **Edge:** Reeded

Date	Mintage	F	VF	XF	Unc	BU
1981 Proof	300,000	Value: 4.50				

KM# 161 2 LEVA
Copper-Nickel, 30 mm. **Subject:** 1300th Anniversary of Nationhood - Oboriste Assembly **Obv:** National arms within circle at top, denomination below flanked by weapons, date at bottom left **Rev:** Inscription on monument within wreath **Edge:** Reeded

Date	Mintage	F	VF	XF	Unc	BU
1981 Proof	300,000	Value: 4.50				

KM# 162 2 LEVA
Copper-Nickel, 30 mm. **Subject:** 1300th Anniversary of Nationhood - Uprising of Assen and Peter **Obv:** Building above denomination and date **Rev:** Soldiers with weapons on horseback **Edge:** Reeded

Date	Mintage	F	VF	XF	Unc	BU
1981 Proof	300,000	Value: 4.50				

KM# 163 2 LEVA
Copper-Nickel, 30 mm. **Subject:** 1300th Anniversary of Nationhood - 100th Anniversary of Serbo-Bulgarian War **Obv:** Inscription within wreath above denomination and date **Rev:** Warrior women, facing, with shields and swords, rampant lion at left **Edge:** Reeded

Date	Mintage	F	VF	XF	Unc	BU
1981 Proof	—	Value: 4.50				

KM# 155 2 LEVA
Copper-Nickel, 30 mm. **Subject:** Soccer **Obv:** National arms **Rev:** Outstretched soccer figure, date at right, denomination below **Edge:** Reeded

Date	Mintage	F	VF	XF	Unc	BU
1986 Proof	100,000	Value: 4.00				

KM# 158 2 LEVA
Copper-Nickel, 30 mm. **Subject:** 13th World Eurythmic Championships - Varna 1987 **Obv:** Arena below map, denomination at bottom, date lower left **Rev:** Ribbon Dancer, left **Edge:** Reeded

Date	Mintage	F	VF	XF	Unc	BU
1987 Proof	300,000	Value: 3.50				

KM# 159 2 LEVA
Copper-Nickel, 30 mm. **Series:** Winter Olympics **Obv:** National arms **Rev:** Skier, denomination and date below **Edge:** Reeded

Date	Mintage	F	VF	XF	Unc	BU
1987	300,000	Value: 5.00				

KM# 165 2 LEVA
Copper-Nickel, 30 mm. **Subject:** 100th Anniversary of Sophia University **Obv:** University building, denomination and date at bottom **Rev:** Half figure with open book, two dates over left shoulder **Edge:** Reeded

Date	Mintage	F	VF	XF	Unc	BU
1988 Proof	—	Value: 4.00				

KM# 166 2 LEVA
Copper-Nickel, 30 mm. **Subject:** Soviet-Bulgarian Space Flight **Obv:** Denomination and date within wreath, arms above **Rev:** Space flight within diamond **Edge:** Reeded

Date	Mintage	F	VF	XF	Unc	BU
1988 Proof	300,000	Value: 3.00				

KM# 177 2 LEVA
Copper-Nickel, 30 mm. **Series:** Seoul 1988 - 24th Summer Olympic Games **Obv:** National arms **Rev:** High jumper, denomination and date below **Edge:** Reeded

Date	Mintage	F	VF	XF	Unc	BU
1988 Proof	300,000	Value: 3.50				

KM# 178 2 LEVA
Copper-Nickel, 30 mm. **Subject:** Sports **Obv:** National arms above denomination and date **Rev:** Rowers **Edge:** Reeded

Date	Mintage	F	VF	XF	Unc	BU
1989 Proof	300,000	Value: 3.00				

KM# 66 5 LEVA
16.6667 g., 0.9000 Silver .4823 oz. ASW **Subject:** 1100th Anniversary Slavic Alphabet **Obv:** Denomination above shield **Rev:** St. Cyril and St. Medhodius standing, two dates below

Date	Mintage	F	VF	XF	Unc	BU
ND(1963) Proof	5,000	Value: 27.50				

KM# 70 5 LEVA
16.6667 g., 0.9000 Silver .4823 oz. ASW **Subject:** 20th Anniversary Peoples Republic **Obv:** Flag above denomination, two dates below **Rev:** Head left, two dates below

Date	Mintage	F	VF	XF	Unc	BU
ND(1964) Proof	10,000	Value: 27.50				

KM# 78 5 LEVA
20.5000 g., 0.9000 Silver .5932 oz. ASW **Subject:** 120th Anniversary - Birth of Ivan Vazov, Poet **Obv:** National above date and denomination **Rev:** Head right, two dates at bottom

Date	Mintage	F	VF	XF	Unc	BU
1970	370,000	—	—	8.50	10.00	—
1970 Proof	109,700	Value: 11.50				

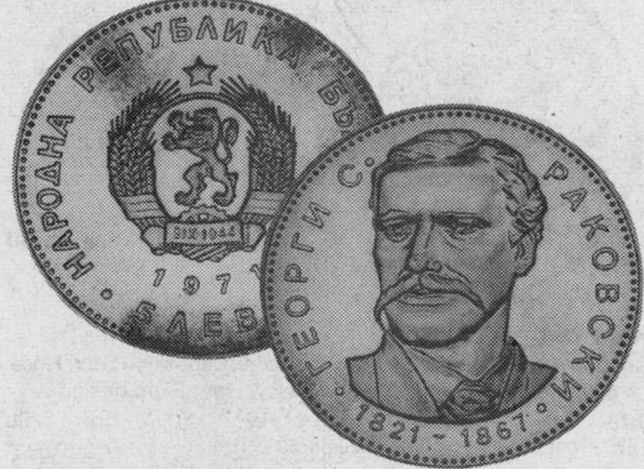

KM# 79 5 LEVA
20.5000 g., 0.9000 Silver .5932 oz. ASW **Subject:** 150th Anniversary - Birth of Georgi S. Rakovski, Constitution Author **Obv:** National arms above date, denomination below **Rev:** Bust 3/4 left, two dates below

Date	Mintage	F	VF	XF	Unc	BU
1971 Prooflike	300,000	—	—	—	11.50	—

KM# 81 5 LEVA
20.5000 g., 0.9000 Silver .5932 oz. ASW **Subject:** 250th Anniversary - Birth of Paisi Hilendarski, Historian **Obv:** National arms above denomination, date at left **Rev:** Figure with open book looking left, two dates below **Designer:** D. Prahov

Date	Mintage	F	VF	XF	Unc	BU
1972 Proof	200,000	Value: 11.50				

KM# 82 5 LEVA
20.5000 g., 0.9000 Silver .5932 oz. ASW **Subject:** Centennial - Death of Vasil Levski, Revolutionary **Obv:** National arms above denomination, date at left **Rev:** Head facing, divides dates

Date	Mintage	F	VF	XF	Unc	BU
1973 Proof	200,000	Value: 11.50				

KM# 83 5 LEVA
20.5000 g., 0.9000 Silver .5932 oz. ASW **Subject:** 50th Anniversary - Anti-fascist Uprising of September 9, 1923 **Obv:** National arms, date below **Rev:** Soldiers with flag, date below

Date	Mintage	F	VF	XF	Unc	BU
1973 Proof	200,000	Value: 11.50				

KM# 91 5 LEVA
20.5000 g., 0.9000 Silver .5932 oz. ASW **Subject:** 50th Anniversary - Death of Alexander Stamboliiski, Politician **Obv:** National arms, date and denomination below **Rev:** Head left, two dates below

Date	Mintage	F	VF	XF	Unc	BU
1974 Proof	200,000	Value: 11.50				

KM# 92 5 LEVA
20.5000 g., 0.9000 Silver .5932 oz. ASW **Subject:** 30th Anniversary - Liberation from Fascism September 9, 1944 **Obv:** National arms above denomination, date at left **Rev:** 2 soldiers and factory, two dates at right

Date	Mintage	F	VF	XF	Unc	BU
1974 Proof	200,000	Value: 12.00				

KM# 96 5 LEVA
20.5000 g., 0.9000 Silver .5932 oz. ASW **Subject:** Centennial - Death of Khristo Botev **Obv:** National arms above date and denomination **Rev:** Head 3/4 left, two dates upper right

Date	Mintage	F	VF	XF	Unc	BU
1976 Proof	196,660	Value: 11.50				

KM# 97 5 LEVA
20.5000 g., 0.5000 Silver .3295 oz. ASW **Subject:** 100th Anniversary of the "April Uprising" against the Turks **Obv:** Woman with sword divides dates, circle surrounds **Rev:** National arms above denomination, date at left

Date	Mintage	F	VF	XF	Unc	BU
1976 Proof	200,000	Value: 9.00				

KM# 99 5 LEVA
20.5000 g., 0.5000 Silver .3295 oz. ASW **Subject:** 150th Anniversary - Birth of Petko Slaveykov, Poet **Obv:** National arms above denomination, date at left **Rev:** Bust 3/4 left, two dates below

Date	Mintage	F	VF	XF	Unc	BU
1977 Proof	200,000	Value: 9.00				

KM# 100 5 LEVA
20.5000 g., 0.5000 Silver .3295 oz. ASW **Subject:** 100th Anniversary - Birth of Peio Javoroff, Poet and Actor **Obv:** National arms above denomination, date bottom left **Rev:** Bust left, looking forward, two dates at right

Date	Mintage	F	VF	XF	Unc	BU
1978 Proof	200,000	Value: 9.00				

KM# 101 5 LEVA

20.5000 g., 0.5000 Silver .3295 oz. ASW **Subject:** 100th Anniversary - National Library **Obv:** National arms, denomination below **Rev:** Statue in front of library, two dates above

Date	Mintage	F	VF	XF	Unc	BU
ND(1978) Proof	200,000	Value: 9.00				

KM# 103 5 LEVA

20.5000 g., 0.5000 Silver .3295 oz. ASW **Subject:** 100th Anniversary - Communication Systems **Obv:** National arms above denomination, date at left **Rev:** Radio tower within soundwaves, horn below divides dates

Date	Mintage	F	VF	XF	Unc	BU
1979	35,000	—	—	—	9.00	—
1979 Proof	15,000	Value: 12.50				

KM# 109 5 LEVA

Copper-Nickel, 34 mm. **Subject:** World Cup Soccer Games in Spain **Obv:** National arms divides date above denomination flanked by grain sprigs **Rev:** Soccer players, date at bottom right **Edge:** Plain

Date	Mintage	F	VF	XF	Unc	BU
1980	220,000	—	—	—	3.50	—
1980 Proof	30,000	Value: 6.00				

KM# 131 5 LEVA

Copper-Nickel **Subject:** International Hunting Exposition **Obv:** National arms above denomination, date at bottom left **Rev:** Antlered deer head, facing, date between antlers

Date	Mintage	F	VF	XF	Unc	BU
1981	250,000	—	—	—	4.50	—
1981 Proof	50,000	Value: 7.00				

KM# 132 5 LEVA

Copper-Nickel **Subject:** 1300th Anniversary of Nationhood - Friendship with Hungary **Obv:** National arms above denomination, date below, grain sprigs flank **Rev:** Quill and sword handle divide heads

Date	Mintage	F	VF	XF	Unc	BU
1981	140,000	—	—	—	3.50	—
1981 Proof	47,000	Value: 7.00				

KM# 140 5 LEVA

Copper-Nickel **Subject:** 100th Anniversary - Birth of Vladimir Dimitrov **Obv:** Denomination, date below **Rev:** Bust 3/4 left

Date	Mintage	F	VF	XF	Unc	BU
1982 Proof	283,050	Value: 5.00				

KM# 141 5 LEVA

Copper-Nickel, 34 mm. **Subject:** 40th Anniversary - Birth of Lyudmila Zhivkova **Obv:** Arms above denomination, date at lower left **Rev:** Head left, two dates at right

Date	Mintage	F	VF	XF	Unc	BU
1982 Proof	20,000	Value: 5.00				

KM# 142 5 LEVA

Copper-Nickel **Subject:** 2nd International Children's Assembly **Obv:** Assembly logo above denomination, bells encircle outer edge **Rev:** Tower within circle, bells encircle edge

Date	Mintage	F	VF	XF	Unc	BU
1982 Proof	200,000	Value: 4.00				

KM# 151 5 LEVA

Copper-Nickel, 34.5 mm. **Subject:** 3rd International Children's Assembly **Obv:** Assembly logo at top, denomination devides bells below, date lower left, child figures encircle edge **Rev:** Mosaic girl and boy with flowers, child figures encircle edge

Date	Mintage	F	VF	XF	Unc	BU
1985 Proof	100,000	Value: 4.00				

KM# 152 5 LEVA

Copper-Nickel **Subject:** 90th Anniversary of Tourism Movement - Konstantinov **Obv:** National arms above denomination, date lower left **Rev:** Head left within circle, two dates below

Date	Mintage	F	VF	XF	Unc	BU
1985 Proof	100,000	Value: 4.50				

KM# 153 5 LEVA

Copper-Nickel **Subject:** 4th Anniversary of UNESCO **Obv:** National arms above, bigas flank, denomination below, date lower left **Rev:** Logo above building

Date	Mintage	F	VF	XF	Unc	BU
1985 Proof	100,000	Value: 4.50				

KM# 154 5 LEVA

Copper-Nickel **Subject:** Young Inventors' Exposition **Obv:** Rose on globe, denomination and date below **Rev:** Expo design

Date	Mintage	F	VF	XF	Unc	BU
1985 Proof	100,000	Value: 4.50				

KM# 167.1 5 LEVA

Copper-Nickel **Subject:** Chiprovo Uprising **Obv:** National arms, date and denomination below **Rev:** Activists **Edge:** Plain

Date	Mintage	F	VF	XF	Unc	BU
1988 Proof	100,000	Value: 4.50				

KM# 167.2 5 LEVA

Copper-Nickel **Edge:** Reeded

Date	Mintage	F	VF	XF	Unc	BU
1988 Proof	—	Value: 5.00				

KM# 168 5 LEVA
Copper-Nickel **Subject:** 120th Anniversary - Dimitar and Karadzha **Obv:** National arms above denomination and date, oak leaves flank **Rev:** Conjoined busts above dates

Date	Mintage	F	VF	XF	Unc	BU
1988 Proof	100,000	Value: 4.00				

KM# 169 5 LEVA
Copper-Nickel **Obv:** National arms above denomination, date to left **Rev:** Bust of Kremikovski facing **Note:** Kremikovski

Date	Mintage	F	VF	XF	Unc	BU
1988 Proof	148,000	Value: 4.00				

KM# 170 5 LEVA
Copper-Nickel, 34 mm. **Subject:** Childrens' Assembly **Obv:** Denomination and date divides bell and logo within inner circle **Rev:** Child with birds within circle

Date	Mintage	F	VF	XF	Unc	BU
1988 Proof	100,000	Value: 4.00				

KM# 179 5 LEVA
Copper-Nickel **Subject:** 200th Birthday of Aprilov **Obv:** Building above denomination and date **Rev:** Bust 3/4 left, two dates below

Date	Mintage	F	VF	XF	Unc	BU
1989 Proof	100,000	Value: 4.00				

KM# 180 5 LEVA
Copper-Nickel **Subject:** 250th Anniversary - Birth of Vrachanski **Obv:** National arms within wreath, denomination below, date at bottom **Rev:** Half figure facing divides dates

Date	Mintage	F	VF	XF	Unc	BU
1989 Proof	100,000	Value: 4.00				

KM# 67 10 LEVA
8.4444 g., 0.9000 Gold .2443 oz. AGW **Subject:** 1100th Anniversary - Slavic Alphabet **Obv:** Denomination above shield **Rev:** Two figures above dates

Date	Mintage	F	VF	XF	Unc	BU
ND(1963) Proof	7,000	Value: 185				

KM# 71 10 LEVA
8.4444 g., 0.9000 Gold .2443 oz. AGW **Subject:** 20th Anniversary - Peoples Republic **Obv:** Flag above denomination, two dates below **Rev:** Head of Georgi Dimitrov, left, two dates below

Date	Mintage	F	VF	XF	Unc	BU
ND(1964) Proof	10,000	Value: 165				

KM# 93.1 10 LEVA
29.9500 g., 0.9000 Silver .8666 oz. ASW **Subject:** 10th Olympic Congress **Obv:** National arms above date and denomination **Rev:** Old coin above Olympic rings **Edge:** Inscription in Latin

Date	Mintage	F	VF	XF	Unc	BU
1975 Proof	50,000	Value: 17.50				

KM# 93.2 10 LEVA
29.9500 g., 0.9000 Silver .8666 oz. ASW **Obv:** National arms above date and denomination **Rev:** Old coin above Olympic rings **Edge:** Inscription in Cyrillic

Date	Mintage	F	VF	XF	Unc	BU
1975 Proof	50,000	Value: 17.50				

KM# 102 10 LEVA
29.8500 g., 0.5000 Silver .4798 oz. ASW **Subject:** 100th Anniversary - Liberation from Turks **Obv:** National arms **Rev:** Monument above dates

Date	Mintage	F	VF	XF	Unc	BU
ND(1978) Proof	200,000	Value: 13.50				

KM# 104 10 LEVA
23.3280 g., 0.9250 Silver .6938 oz. ASW **Series:** International Year of the Child **Obv:** Arms divide date above denomination **Rev:** Children divide symbols, date below

Date	Mintage	F	VF	XF	Unc	BU
1979 Proof	16,906	Value: 22.50				

KM# 105 10 LEVA
14.0000 g., 0.5000 Silver .2251 oz. ASW **Subject:** Bulgarian-Soviet Cosmonaut Flight **Obv:** National arms above denomination and date **Rev:** Cosmonaut flight; space shuttle

Date	Mintage	F	VF	XF	Unc	BU
1979 Proof	35,000	Value: 20.00				

KM# 105a 10 LEVA
23.8500 g., 0.9000 Silver .6901 oz. ASW **Obv:** National arms above denomination and date **Rev:** Cosmonaut flight; space shuttle

Date	Mintage	F	VF	XF	Unc	BU
1979 Proof	15,000	Value: 27.50				

KM# 143 10 LEVA
18.8800 g., 0.5000 Silver .3035 oz. ASW **Subject:** Soccer Games **Obv:** National arms divide date above denomination **Rev:** Ball and net

Date	Mintage	F	VF	XF	Unc	BU
1982 Proof	7,800	Value: 22.50				

KM# 144 10 LEVA
18.8800 g., 0.5000 Silver .3035 oz. ASW **Subject:** Soccer Games **Obv:** National arms within circle divide date, wreathed denomination below **Rev:** Soccer players

Date	Mintage	F	VF	XF	Unc	BU
1982 Proof	7,200	Value: 21.50				

KM# 146 10 LEVA
23.3300 g., 0.9250 Silver .6939 oz. ASW **Series:** Winter Olympics **Obv:** National arms above denomination, date at bottom left **Rev:** Downhill skier

Date	Mintage	F	VF	XF	Unc	BU
1984 Proof	8,464	Value: 16.00				

KM# 147 10 LEVA
Copper-Nickel **Subject:** Summer Olympics **Obv:** Arms over value **Rev:** Gymnast executing ribbon dance

Date	Mintage	F	VF	XF	Unc	BU
1984 Proof	2,000	Value: 14.50				

KM# 147a 10 LEVA
23.3300 g., 0.9250 Silver .6938 oz. ASW **Subject:** Summer Olympics **Obv:** Arms over value **Rev:** Gymnast executing the ribbon dance event

Date	Mintage	F	VF	XF	Unc	BU
1984 Proof	300	Value: 16.50				

KM# 149 10 LEVA
23.3300 g., 0.9250 Silver .6939 oz. ASW **Subject:** International Decade for Women **Obv:** National arms within wreath of roses, denomination and date below **Rev:** Woman carrying baskets of flowers, dates above

Date	Mintage	F	VF	XF	Unc	BU
1984 Proof	5,572	Value: 32.50				

KM# 157 10 LEVA
18.7500 g., 0.6400 Silver .3858 oz. ASW **Obv:** Design above denomination, date at left **Rev:** Cosmonauts

Date	Mintage	F	VF	XF	Unc	BU
1985 Proof	7,501	Value: 30.00				

KM# 184 10 LEVA
18.7500 g., 0.6400 Silver .3858 oz. ASW **Series:** 1988 Winter Olympics **Obv:** National arms **Rev:** Hockey player, denomination and date below

Date	Mintage	F	VF	XF	Unc	BU
1987 Proof	15,000	Value: 20.00				

KM# 185 10 LEVA
18.7500 g., 0.6400 Silver .3858 oz. ASW **Series:** Summer Olympics **Obv:** National arms **Rev:** Sprinters, denomination and date below

Date	Mintage	F	VF	XF	Unc	BU
1988 Proof	22,650	Value: 15.00				

KM# 68 20 LEVA
16.8889 g., 0.9000 Gold .4887 oz. AGW **Subject:** 100th Anniversary - Slavic Alphabet **Obv:** Denomination above shield **Rev:** Two figures above dates

Date	Mintage	F	VF	XF	Unc	BU
ND(1963) Proof	3,000	Value: 360				

KM# 72 20 LEVA
16.8889 g., 0.9000 Gold .4887 oz. AGW **Subject:** 20th Anniversary - Peoples Republic **Obv:** Flag above denomination, dates at bottom **Rev:** Head of Georgi Dimitrov, left, two dates below

Date	Mintage	F	VF	XF	Unc	BU
ND(1964) Proof	5,000	Value: 335				

KM# 106 20 LEVA
21.8000 g., 0.5000 Silver .3505 oz. ASW **Subject:** Centennial of Sofia as Capital **Obv:** National arms above ribbon, denomination and date at bottom **Rev:** Crowned head left, two dates bottom right

Date	Mintage	F	VF	XF	Unc	BU
1979	35,000	—	—	—	20.00	—

KM# 106a 20 LEVA
32.0000 g., 0.9000 Silver .9260 oz. ASW **Subject:** Centennial of Sofia as Capital **Obv:** National arms above ribbon, denomination and date at bottom **Rev:** Crowned head left, two dates lower right

Date	Mintage	F	VF	XF	Unc	BU
1979 Proof	15,000	Value: 32.50				

KM# 133.1 20 LEVA
14.0000 g., 0.5000 Silver .2250 oz. ASW **Subject:** 40th Anniversary - Birth of Lyudmila Zhivkova **Obv:** Denomination with date to left **Rev:** Head of Lyudmila Zhivkova left

Date	Mintage	F	VF	XF	Unc	BU
1982 Proof	10,000	Value: 20.00				

KM# 133.2 20 LEVA
14.0000 g., 0.5000 Silver 0.2251 oz. ASW **Obv:** Denomination between emblems of Children's Assembly and Year of the Child **Rev:** Head of Lyudmila Zhivkova, left, two dates at right

Date	Mintage	F	VF	XF	Unc	BU
1982 Proof	—	Value: 300				

KM# 164 20 LEVA
11.2200 g., 0.5000 Silver .1804 oz. ASW **Obv:** National arms, date and denomination below **Rev:** Bust of Vasil Levsky facing

Date	Mintage	F	VF	XF	Unc	BU
1987 Proof	100,000	Value: 12.50				

KM# 171 20 LEVA
11.3900 g., 0.5000 Silver .1830 oz. ASW **Subject:** Bulgarian Railways **Obv:** National arms within circle, denomination and date below **Rev:** Train engines, old and new, within circle

Date	Mintage	F	VF	XF	Unc	BU
1988 Proof	93,000	Value: 11.50				

KM# 172 20 LEVA
11.2200 g., 0.5000 Silver .1804 oz. ASW **Subject:** 110th Anniversary of Liberation **Obv:** Monument above denomination, date at right **Rev:** Liberation celebration, date below

Date	Mintage	F	VF	XF	Unc	BU
1988 Proof	100,000	Value: 11.50				

KM# 173 20 LEVA
11.5500 g., 0.5000 Silver .1855 oz. ASW **Subject:** 100th Anniversary of Sophia University **Obv:** University above spray, denomination and date below **Rev:** Man, moth and kite, dates at left

Date	Mintage	F	VF	XF	Unc	BU
1988 Proof	100,000	Value: 12.50				

KM# 174 20 LEVA
11.1900 g., 0.5000 Silver .1803 oz. ASW **Subject:** Soviet-Bulgarian Space Flight **Obv:** National arms above denomination, date at left **Rev:** Astronauts

Date	Mintage	F	VF	XF	Unc	BU
1988 Proof	100,000	Value: 12.50				

KM# 181 20 LEVA
Copper-Nickel-Zinc **Obv:** National arms within circle **Rev:** Denomination above date, grain sprigs flank

Date	Mintage	F	VF	XF	Unc	BU
1989 Proof	—	Value: 8.00				

KM# 183 20 LEVA
12.1300 g., 0.5000 Silver .2138 oz. ASW **Subject:** Academy of Science **Obv:** National arms within pegged circle **Rev:** Academy building, two dates above, denomination and date below within pegged circle

Date	Mintage	F	VF	XF	Unc	BU
1989 Proof	58,000	Value: 12.50				

KM# 134 25 LEVA
14.0000 g., 0.5000 Silver .2250 oz. ASW **Subject:** 1300th Anniversary of Nationhood **Obv:** National arms within wreath above denomination and date **Rev:** Woman and child, radiant sun in background

Date	Mintage	F	VF	XF	Unc	BU
1981 Proof	Est. 100,000	Value: 22.50				

KM# 145 25 LEVA
14.0000 g., 0.5000 Silver .2250 oz. ASW **Subject:** 100th Anniversary - Birth of Georgi Dimitrov **Obv:** National arms, denomination below, date at right **Rev:** Head left, two dates lower right

Date	Mintage	F	VF	XF	Unc	BU
1982 Proof	15,000	Value: 12.50				

KM# 148 25 LEVA
14.0000 g., 0.5000 Silver .2250 oz. ASW **Subject:** 40th Anniversary of Peoples Republic **Obv:** National arms at top, denomination below divides dates **Rev:** Flowers on design

Date	Mintage	F	VF	XF	Unc	BU
ND(1984) Proof	91,000	Value: 11.50				

KM# 156.1 25 LEVA
23.3300 g., 0.9250 Silver .6939 oz. ASW **Subject:** Soccer **Obv:** National arms **Rev:** Stylized eagle with soccer ball, denomination and date at left

Date	Mintage	F	VF	XF	Unc	BU
1986 Proof	12,902	Value: 25.00				

KM# 156.2 25 LEVA
23.3300 g., 0.9250 Silver .6939 oz. ASW **Obv:** National arms **Rev:** Stylized eagle with soccer ball, denomination at left, without date in field above eagle's head

Date	Mintage	F	VF	XF	Unc	BU
1986 Proof	Inc. above	Value: 30.00				

KM# 194 25 LEVA
23.3300 g., 0.9250 Silver .6939 oz. ASW **Subject:** Soccer **Obv:** National arms **Rev:** Soccer player, vertical date above, denomination at right

Date	Mintage	F	VF	XF	Unc	BU
1986 Proof	12,250	Value: 20.00				

KM# 160 25 LEVA
23.3300 g., 0.9250 Silver .6939 oz. ASW **Series:** Winter Olympics **Obv:** National arms **Rev:** Skier, date and denomination below

Date	Mintage	F	VF	XF	Unc	BU
1987 Proof	15,000	Value: 20.00				

KM# 186 25 LEVA
23.3300 g., 0.9250 Silver .6939 oz. ASW **Series:** Seoul 1988 - Summer Olympic Games **Subject:** High Jump **Obv:** National arms **Rev:** High jumper, date and denomination below

Date	Mintage	F	VF	XF	Unc	BU
1988 Proof	20,000	Value: 21.50				

KM# 187 25 LEVA
23.3300 g., 0.9250 Silver .6939 oz. ASW **Subject:** Soccer **Obv:** Denomination above date **Rev:** Two players, date below

Date	Mintage	F	VF	XF	Unc	BU
1989 Proof	17,600	Value: 25.00				

KM# 189 25 LEVA
23.3800 g., 0.9250 Silver .6954 oz. ASW **Series:** 1992 Summer Olympics **Obv:** National arms, date and denomination below **Rev:** Two rowers, date upper left

Date	Mintage	F	VF	XF	Unc	BU
1989 Proof	57,560	Value: 16.50				

KM# 190 25 LEVA
23.3800 g., 0.9250 Silver .6954 oz. ASW **Series:** Albertville 1992 - 16th Winter Olympic Games **Obv:** National arms, date and denomination below **Rev:** Figure skating pairs competition, date at right **Rev. Designer:** R. Alexandrova

Date	Mintage	F	VF	XF	Unc	BU
1989 Proof	48,449	Value: 17.50				

KM# 193 25 LEVA
23.3800 g., 0.9250 Silver .6954 oz. ASW **Subject:** Wildlife **Obv:** National arms, denomination and date below **Rev:** Mother bear and cubs

Date	Mintage	F	VF	XF	Unc	BU
1989 Proof	15,000	Value: 35.00				

KM# 191 25 LEVA
23.3800 g., 0.9250 Silver .6954 oz. ASW **Subject:** Soccer **Obv:** National arms, denomination and date below **Rev:** Globe, net, and shoe

Date	Mintage	F	VF	XF	Unc	BU
1990 Proof	15,600	Value: 22.50				

KM# 192 25 LEVA
23.3800 g., 0.9250 Silver .6954 oz. ASW **Subject:** Soccer **Obv:** National arms, date and denomination below **Rev:** Ball design, date

Date	Mintage	F	VF	XF	Unc	BU
1990 Proof	14,900	Value: 24.00				

KM# 195 25 LEVA
23.3800 g., 0.9250 Silver .6954 oz. ASW **Series:** Winter Olympics **Obv:** National arms, date and denomination below **Rev:** Cross-country skiers, date at right

Date	Mintage	F	VF	XF	Unc	BU
1990 Proof	46,400	Value: 16.50				

KM# 196 25 LEVA
23.3800 g., 0.9250 Silver .6954 oz. ASW **Series:** Summer Olympics **Obv:** National arms, date and denomination below **Rev:** Runners, date below

Date	Mintage	F	VF	XF	Unc	BU
1990 Proof	50,235	Value: 16.50				

KM# 197 25 LEVA
23.3800 g., 0.9250 Silver .6954 oz. ASW **Subject:** Wildlife **Obv:** National arms, date and denomination below **Rev:** Two lynx

Date	Mintage	F	VF	XF	Unc	BU
1990 Proof	14,840	Value: 35.00				

KM# 135 50 LEVA
20.5000 g., 0.9000 Silver .5932 oz. ASW **Subject:** 1300th Anniversary of Nationhood **Obv:** Dates above denomination **Rev:** Equestrian figure right, animal below

Date	Mintage	F	VF	XF	Unc	BU
1981 Proof	Est. 10,000	Value: 22.50				

KM# 136 50 LEVA
20.5000 g., 0.9000 Silver .5932 oz. ASW **Subject:** 1300th Anniversary of Nationhood **Obv:** Head of Georgi Dimitrov left, denomination below line **Rev:** Woman striding left

Date	Mintage	F	VF	XF	Unc	BU
1981 Proof	1,000	Value: 25.00				

KM# 137 50 LEVA
20.5000 g., 0.9000 Silver .5932 oz. ASW **Subject:** 1300th Anniversary of Nationhood **Obv:** National arms above sprays, date and denomination below **Rev:** Mother and child in front of radiant sun

Date	Mintage	F	VF	XF	Unc	BU
1981 Proof	1,000	Value: 30.00				

KM# 138 50 LEVA
20.5000 g., 0.9000 Silver .5932 oz. ASW **Subject:** 1300th Anniversary of Nationhood **Obv:** Buildings above date and denomination **Rev:** Warrior figures

Date	Mintage	F	VF	XF	Unc	BU
1981 Proof	Est. 10,000	Value: 23.50				

KM# 182 50 LEVA
Copper-Nickel-Zinc **Obv:** National arms within circle **Rev:** Denomination above date, grain sprays flank

Date	Mintage	F	VF	XF	Unc	BU
1989 Proof	—	Value: 12.00				

KM# 150 100 LEVA
8.4444 g., 0.9000 Gold .2443 oz. AGW **Subject:** International Womens Decade **Obv:** National arms within wreath, date and denomination below **Rev:** Woman with child divides dates **Note:** .076 Silver, .024 Copper

Date	Mintage	F	VF	XF	Unc	BU
1984 Proof	500	Value: 350				

KM# 150a 100 LEVA
8.4444 g., 0.9000 Gold .2443 oz. AGW **Subject:** International Womens Decade **Obv:** National arms within wreath, date and denomination below **Rev:** Woman with child divides date **Note:** .100 Copper

Date	Mintage	F	VF	XF	Unc	BU
1984	2,032	Value: 250				

KM# 139 1000 LEVA
16.8800 g., 0.9000 Gold .4885 oz. AGW **Subject:** 1300th Anniversary of Nationhood **Obv:** National arms above denomination and date **Rev:** Mother and child in front of radiant sun

Date	Mintage	F	VF	XF	Unc	BU
1981 Proof	2,000	Value: 385				

REPUBLIC

STANDARD COINAGE

KM# 199 10 STOTINKI
Nickel-Brass **Obv:** Ancient lion sculpture left within circle **Rev:** Denomination divides date

Date	Mintage	F	VF	XF	Unc	BU
1992	—	—	—	—	0.25	0.35

KM# 200 20 STOTINKI
Nickel-Brass **Obv:** Ancient lion sculpture left within circle **Rev:** Denomination divides date

Date	Mintage	F	VF	XF	Unc	BU
1992	—	—	—	—	0.35	0.50

KM# 201 50 STOTINKI
Nickel-Brass **Obv:** Ancient lion sculpture left within circle **Rev:** Denomination divides date

Date	Mintage	F	VF	XF	Unc	BU
1992	—	—	—	—	0.50	0.75

KM# 202 LEV
Nickel-Brass **Obv:** Madara horseman right within circle **Rev:** Denomination divides symbols, date below

Date	Mintage	F	VF	XF	Unc	BU
1992	—	—	—	—	0.75	1.00

KM# 203 2 LEVA
Nickel-Brass **Obv:** Madara horseman right within circle **Rev:** Denomination divides symbols, date below

Date	Mintage	F	VF	XF	Unc	BU
1992	—	—	—	—	1.25	1.50

KM# 204 5 LEVA
Nickel-Brass **Obv:** Madara horseman right within circle **Rev:** Denomination divides symbols, date below

Date	Mintage	F	VF	XF	Unc	BU
1992	—	—	—	—	1.75	2.00

KM# 205 10 LEVA
Copper-Nickel **Obv:** Madara horseman right within circle **Rev:** Denomination divides symbols, date below

Date	Mintage	F	VF	XF	Unc	BU
1992	—	—	—	—	2.50	3.00

KM# 224 10 LEVA
Brass **Obv:** Madara horseman right within circle **Rev:** Denomination divides symbols, date below **Note:** Reduced size and metal change.

Date	Mintage	F	VF	XF	Unc	BU
1997	—	—	—	—	1.25	1.50

KM# 228 20 LEVA
Brass **Obv:** Madara horseman right within circle **Rev:** Denomination divides symbols, date below

Date	Mintage	F	VF	XF	Unc	BU
1997	—	—	—	—	1.50	1.75

KM# 198 50 LEVA
10.0700 g., 0.9250 Silver .2995 oz. ASW **Series:** Olympics **Obv:** Denomination above date within wreath **Rev:** Downhill skier, date below

Date	Mintage	F	VF	XF	Unc	BU
1992 Proof	52,390	Value: 11.50				

KM# 213 50 LEVA
Copper-Nickel **Subject:** Centennial of Olympics in Bulgaria **Obv:** Denomination above date within wreath **Rev:** Gymnasts divide dates

Date	Mintage	F	VF	XF	Unc	BU
1994 Proof	19,2 0	Value: 5.00				

KM# 225 50 LEVA
Brass **Obv:** Madara horseman right within circle **Rev:** Denomination divides symbols, date below

Date	Mintage	F	VF	XF	Unc	BU
1997	—	—	—	—	1.75	2.00

KM# 212 100 LEVA
23.2300 g., 0.9250 Silver .6908 oz. ASW **Obv:** Denomination above date within wreath **Rev:** Old Ship Radetsky, date at right

Date	Mintage	F	VF	XF	Unc	BU
1992 Proof	28,765	Value: 25.00				

KM# 226 100 LEVA
23.2300 g., 0.9250 Silver .6908 oz. ASW **Obv:** Denomination above date within wreath **Rev:** Eagle descending on prey

Date	Mintage	F	VF	XF	Unc	BU
1992 Proof	27,651	Value: 30.00				

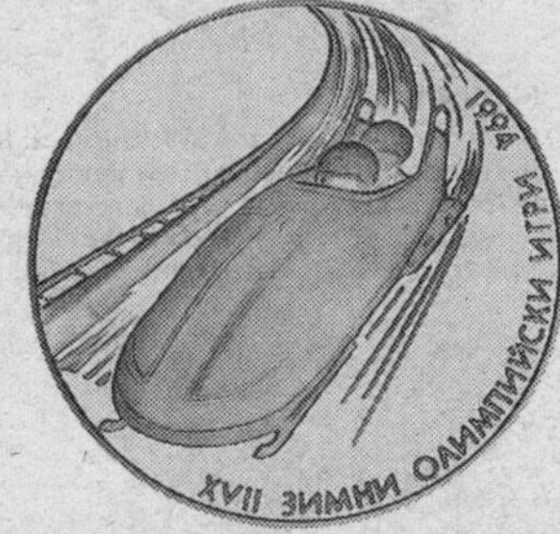

KM# 209 100 LEVA
23.3300 g., 0.9250 Silver .6939 oz. ASW **Series:** 1994 Olympics **Obv:** Denomination above date within wreath **Rev:** Bobsled, date upper right

Date	Mintage	F	VF	XF	Unc	BU
1993 Proof	33,690	Value: 22.50				

KM# 210 100 LEVA
23.3300 g., 0.9250 Silver .6939 oz. ASW **Subject:** 1994 World Cup Soccer **Obv:** Denomination above date within wreath **Rev:** Soccer player and buildings, within circle

Date	Mintage	F	VF	XF	Unc	BU
1993 Proof	27,840	Value: 28.50				

KM# 227 100 LEVA
23.3300 g., 0.9250 Silver .6939 oz. ASW **Obv:** Denomination above date within wreath **Rev:** Ibex, left

Date	Mintage	F	VF	XF	Unc	BU
1993 Proof	20,000	Value: 30.00				

KM# 231 100 LEVA
23.3300 g., 0.9250 Silver .6939 oz. ASW **Obv:** Denomination above date within wreath **Rev:** Parliament building

Date	Mintage	F	VF	XF	Unc	BU
1993 Proof	15,000	Value: 30.00				

KM# 206 500 LEVA
33.6250 g., 0.9250 Silver 1.0000 oz. ASW **Subject:** European Community - St. Theodor Stratilat **Obv:** ECU monogram and date in circle of stars **Rev:** Face within design, denomination at right

Date	Mintage	F	VF	XF	Unc	BU
1993 Proof	51,031	Value: 28.50				

KM# 211 500 LEVA
23.0000 g., 0.9250 Silver .6840 oz. ASW **Subject:** World Cup Soccer **Obv:** Denomination above date within wreath **Rev:** Soccer ball and net, date below

Date	Mintage	F	VF	XF	Unc	BU
1994 Proof	24,351	Value: 32.50				

KM# 219 500 LEVA
10.0000 g., 0.9250 Silver .2974 oz. ASW **Subject:** Soccer **Obv:** Denomination above date within wreath **Rev:** Two soccer players

Date	Mintage	F	VF	XF	Unc	BU
1996 Proof	60,000	Value: 25.00				

KM# 223 500 LEVA
10.0000 g., 0.9250 Silver 0.2974 oz. ASW, 30 mm. **Subject:** 100th Anniversary - National Art Academy **Obv:** Denomination above date within wreath **Rev:** Academy on paint palette **Edge:** Plain

Date	Mintage	F	VF	XF	Unc	BU
1996 Proof	30,000	Value: 50.00				

KM# 229 500 LEVA
Copper-Nickel-Zinc **Subject:** NATO **Obv:** Denomination above date within wreath **Rev:** City arms and NATO flag

Date	Mintage	F	VF	XF	Unc	BU
1997	30,000	—	—	—	5.00	—

KM# 214 1000 LEVA
23.3300 g., 0.9250 Silver .6939 oz. ASW **Series:** 50 Years - F.A.O. **Obv:** Denomination above date within wreath **Rev:** Wheat and globe within circle, two dates below

Date	Mintage	F	VF	XF	Unc	BU
1995 Proof	12,000	Value: 32.50				

KM# 215 1000 LEVA
23.3300 g., 0.9250 Silver .6939 oz. ASW **Subject:** 100 Years of Olympic Games **Obv:** Denomination above date within wreath **Rev:** Equestrian, left

Date	Mintage	F	VF	XF	Unc	BU
1995 Proof	28,713	Value: 30.00				

KM# 216 1000 LEVA
23.3300 g., 0.9250 Silver .6939 oz. ASW **Subject:** 110 Years - Union of Eastern Rumelia with the Bulgarian Principality **Obv:** Denomination above date within wreath **Rev:** Map behind figure with flag, two dates upper left

Date	Mintage	F	VF	XF	Unc	BU
1995 Proof	15,000	Value: 32.50				

KM# 217 1000 LEVA
33.6250 g., 0.9250 Silver 1.0000 oz. ASW **Subject:** Rozhen Peak Astronomical Observatory **Obv:** ECU monogram and date within circle of stars **Rev:** Observatory, circle of stars above, denomination below

Date	Mintage	F	VF	XF	Unc	BU
1995 Proof	32,796	Value: 32.50				

KM# 220 1000 LEVA
23.3300 g., 0.9250 Silver .6939 oz. ASW **Obv:** Denomination above date within wreath **Rev:** Sailing Ship Kaliakra

Date	Mintage	F	VF	XF	Unc	BU
1996 Proof	23,052	Value: 35.00				

KM# 221 1000 LEVA
23.3300 g., 0.9250 Silver .6939 oz. ASW **Series:** Olympics **Obv:** Denomination above date within wreath **Rev:** Speed skater

Date	Mintage	F	VF	XF	Unc	BU
1996 Proof	22,602	Value: 30.00				

KM# 222 1000 LEVA
33.6250 g., 0.9250 Silver 1.0000 oz. ASW **Subject:** St. Ivan of Rila **Obv:** ECU monogram and date within circle of stars **Rev:** Standing saint, church, and denomination

Date	Mintage	F	VF	XF	Unc	BU
1996 Proof	42,445	Value: 32.50				

KM# 232 1000 LEVA
23.3300 g., 0.9250 Silver .6938 oz. ASW **Subject:** UNICEF **Obv:** Denomination above date within wreath **Rev:** Singing child, UNICEF logo

Date	Mintage	F	VF	XF	Unc	BU
1997 Proof	6,001	Value: 30.00				

KM# 233 1000 LEVA
23.3300 g., 0.9250 Silver .6938 oz. ASW **Subject:** World Cup Soccer - France 1998 **Obv:** Denomination above date within wreath **Rev:** Three soccer players

Date	Mintage	F	VF	XF	Unc	BU
1997 Proof	22,606	Value: 35.00				

KM# 230 1000 LEVA
Copper-Nickel-Zinc **Subject:** Bulgarian Telegraphic Agency Centennial **Obv:** Crowned arms **Rev:** World map and logo **Note:** Prev. KM#239.

Date	Mintage	F	VF	XF	Unc	BU
1998 Proof	—	Value: 5.50				

KM# 207 5000 LEVA
8.6400 g., 0.9000 Gold .2500 oz. AGW **Subject:** European Community - Slavonic Alphabet **Obv:** ECU monogram and date within circle of stars **Rev:** Denomination to left of design

Date	Mintage	F	VF	XF	Unc	BU
1993 Proof	Est. 2,500	Value: 200				

KM# 243 5000 LEVA
10.0000 g., 0.9250 Silver .2974 oz. ASW **Obv:** National arms, date and denomination below **Rev:** Building above "EURO"

Date	Mintage	F	VF	XF	Unc	BU
1998 Proof	—	Value: 18.50				

KM# 208 10000 LEVA
15.5670 g., 0.9990 Platinum .4999 oz. APW **Rev:** Bust of Sevastokratoritza Desislava 1/2 right, founder of Boyana church, denomination at right

Date	Mintage	F	VF	XF	Unc	BU
1993 Proof	Est. 2,500	Value: 650				

KM# 218 10000 LEVA
8.6400 g., 0.9000 Gold .2500 oz. AGW **Obv:** Denomination above date within wreath **Rev:** St. Alexander Nevski Cathedral

Date	Mintage	F	VF	XF	Unc	BU
1994 Proof	30,000	Value: 200				

KM# 234 10000 LEVA
23.3300 g., 0.9250 Silver .6938 oz. ASW **Subject:** 120th Anniversary of Liberation **Obv:** National arms above date, denomination below **Rev:** Decorated soldier with flag

Date	Mintage	F	VF	XF	Unc	BU
1998 Proof	15,000	Value: 40.00				

KM# 235 10000 LEVA
23.3300 g., 0.9250 Silver .6938 oz. ASW **Subject:** United Europe **Obv:** Rider of Madara over dead lion **Rev:** Ancient cup and map

Date	Mintage	F	VF	XF	Unc	BU
1998 Proof	18,152	Value: 40.00				

KM# 236 20000 LEVA
1.5552 g., 0.9990 Gold .0500 oz. AGW **Subject:** Czar Ivan Alexander **Obv:** Stylized lion, left, date and denomination below **Rev:** Four human figure sculptures

Date	Mintage	F	VF	XF	Unc	BU
1998 Proof	—	Value: 75.00				

REFORM COINAGE

KM# 237 STOTINKA
Brass, 16 mm. **Obv:** Madara horseman right, animal below **Rev:** Denomination above date **Edge:** Plain

Date	Mintage	F	VF	XF	Unc	BU
1999	1,277,500	—	—	—	0.25	0.35
2000	—	—	—	—	0.25	0.35

KM# 238 2 STOTINKI
Brass, 18 mm. **Obv:** Madara horseman right, animal below **Rev:** Denomination above date **Edge:** Plain

Date	Mintage	F	VF	XF	Unc	BU
1999	2,048,900	—	—	—	0.35	0.50
2000	—	—	—	—	0.35	0.50

KM# 239 5 STOTINKI
Brass, 20 mm. **Obv:** Madara horseman right, animal below **Rev:** Denomination above date **Edge:** Plain **Note:** Prev. KM#A239.

Date	Mintage	F	VF	XF	Unc	BU
1999	3,453,025	—	—	—	0.50	0.65
2000	—	—	—	—	0.50	0.65

KM# 240 10 STOTINKI
Copper-Nickel, 18.5 mm. **Obv:** Madara horseman right, animal below **Rev:** Denomination above date **Edge:** Reeded

Date	Mintage	F	VF	XF	Unc	BU
1999	8,231,400	—	—	—	0.65	0.85

KM# 241 20 STOTINKI
Copper-Nickel, 20.5 mm. **Obv:** Madara horseman right, animal below **Rev:** Denomination above date **Edge:** Reeded

Date	Mintage	F	VF	XF	Unc	BU
1999	11,967,500	—	—	—	0.85	1.00

KM# 242 50 STOTINKI
Copper-Nickel, 22.5 mm. **Obv:** Madara horseman right, animal below **Rev:** Denomination above date **Edge:** Reeded

Date	Mintage	F	VF	XF	Unc	BU
1999	15,607,000	—	—	—	1.25	1.50

KM# 245 10 LEVA
23.3500 g., 0.9250 Silver 0.6944 oz. ASW, 38.5 mm. **Obv:** National arms **Rev:** Mediterranean Monk Seal, denomination above, date at left **Edge:** Plain

Date	Mintage	F	VF	XF	Unc	BU
1999 Proof	15,000	—	—	—	30.00	35.00

KM# 248 10 LEVA
23.3300 g., 0.9250 Silver 0.6938 oz. ASW, 38.5 mm. **Obv:** Bust of Theodor Burmov 3/4 left, denomination and date below **Rev:** "EURO" map in circle of stars **Edge:** Plain

Date	Mintage	F	VF	XF	Unc	BU
1999 Proof	20,000	Value: 35.00				

KM# 249 10 LEVA
23.3300 g., 0.9250 Silver 0.6938 oz. ASW, 38.5 mm. **Subject:** Euro Integration **Obv:** National arms, date and denomination below **Rev:** Plovdiv old town street view **Edge:** Plain

Date	Mintage	F	VF	XF	Unc	BU
1999 Proof	20,000	Value: 35.00				

KM# 250 10 LEVA
23.3300 g., 0.9250 Silver 0.6938 oz. ASW, 38.5 mm. **Subject:** Summer Olympic Games **Obv:** National arms **Rev:** High jumper divides date and denomination **Edge:** Plain

Date	Mintage	F	VF	XF	Unc	BU
1999 Proof	20,000	Value: 35.00				

KM# 251 10 LEVA
23.3300 g., 0.9250 Silver 0.6938 oz. ASW, 38.5 mm. **Subject:** Summer Olympics **Obv:** National arms, date and denomination below **Rev:** Weight lifter **Edge:** Plain

Date	Mintage	F	VF	XF	Unc	BU
2000 Proof	20,000	Value: 35.00				

KM# 252 10 LEVA
23.3300 g., 0.9250 Silver 0.6938 oz. ASW, 38.5 mm. **Subject:** Christianity **Obv:** National arms **Rev:** Church patriarch **Edge:** Plain

Date	Mintage	F	VF	XF	Unc	BU
2000 Proof	—	Value: 40.00				

KM# 253 10 LEVA
23.3300 g., 0.9250 Silver 0.6938 oz. ASW, 38.5 mm. **Subject:** Bulgarian Association with the European Union **Obv:** National arms, date and denomination below **Rev:** Bulgarian coin design of the Middle Ages featuring Czar Theodor Svetoslav **Edge:** Plain

Date	Mintage	F	VF	XF	Unc	BU
2000 Proof	20,000	Value: 40.00				

KM# 244 10 LEVA
10.3500 g., 0.8000 Silver .2662 oz. ASW, 33.9 mm. **Subject:** The Year 2000 **Obv:** National arms above date with pierced zeros, denomination below **Rev:** Bell above date with pierced zeros **Edge:** Plain

Date	Mintage	F	VF	XF	Unc	BU
2000 Proof	—	Value: 65.00				

KM# 255 100 LEVA
16.0000 g., 0.9000 Gold 0.4758 oz. AGW, 30 mm. **Subject:** Todor Burmov **Obv:** Bust 3/4 facing, date and denomination below **Rev:** "EURO" and map **Edge:** Plain

Date	Mintage	F	VF	XF	Unc	BU
1999 Proof	5,000	Value: 450				

KM# 256 20000 LEVA
1.5500 g., 0.9990 Gold 0.0498 oz. AGW **Obv:** National arms **Rev:** National Bank building, date and denomination below **Edge:** Plain

Date	Mintage	F	VF	XF	Unc	BU
1999 Proof	30,000	Value: 45.00				

ESSAIS

KM#	Date	Mintage	Identification	Mkt Val
E9	1925(a)	—	2 Leva. Copper-Nickel.	150

PIEFORTS

KM#	Date	Mintage	Identification	Mkt Val
P3	1979	2,000	10 Leva. Silver. KM#104	75.00

TRIAL STRIKES

KM#	Date	Mintage	Identification	Mkt Val
TS1	1901	—	2 Stotinki. Bronze. Uniface.	—
TS2	1901	—	2 Stotinki. Bronze. Uniface.	—

PATTERNS

Including off metal strikes

KM#	Date	Mintage	Identification	Mkt Val
PnA6	1923H	—	Lev. Aluminum. Similar to KM#35.	—
Pn6	1923H	—	Lev. Aluminum-Bronze.	—
Pn7	1923H	—	2 Leva. Aluminum.	275
PnA8	1923H	—	2 Leva. Aluminum. Similar to KM#36.	—
Pn8	1923H	—	2 Leva. Aluminum-Bronze.	—
Pn9	1928	2	5 Leva.	—
Pn10	1930	2	5 Leva.	—
Pn11	1930	2	10 Leva.	—
Pn12	1950	—	2 Leva. Nickel Alloy. 1.0800 g. 20.17 mm.	—
Pn13	1950	—	5 Leva. Nickel Alloy. 1.2400 g. 21.45 mm.	—
Pn14	1952	—	2 Stotinki. Copper-Nickel. 1.0000 g. 16mm.	—
Pn15	1952	—	20 Stotinki. Copper-Nickel. 3.0000 g. 21mm.	—
Pn16	1960	—	Lev. Copper-Nickel. 6.0000 g. 24mm.	—
Pn17	1960	—	Lev. Copper-Nickel. 5.0000 g. 24mm.	—
Pn18	1960	—	Lev. Aluminum. 2.3000 g. 25mm.	—
Pn19	1960	—	Lev. Aluminum. 1.3000 g. 20mm.	—
Pn20	1960	—	Lev. Copper. 3.6000 g. 20mm.	—
Pn21	1962	—	Lev. Copper-Nickel. 5.0000 g. 24mm.	—
Pn22	1962	—	Lev. Copper-Nickel. 5.0000 g. 24mm.	—
Pn23	1964	—	20 Leva. Copper. 8.6000 g. KM#72, 27mm.	—
Pn24	1966	—	Lev. Copper-Nickel. 4.8000 g. 24mm.	—
Pn25	1984	1,500	10 Leva. Copper-Nickel. Reeded edge. PROBA I; KM#146.	35.00
Pn26	1984	250	10 Leva. 0.6400 Silver. Plain edge. PROBA II; KM#146a.	100
Pn27	1984	50	10 Leva. 0.9250 Silver. Lettered edge. SPECIMEN; KM#146a.	200
Pn28	1984	2,000	10 Leva. Copper-Nickel. Reeded edge. PROBA I; KM#147.	55.00
Pn29	1984	300	10 Leva. 0.6400 Silver. Plain edge. PROBA II; KM#147a.	150
Pn30	1984	50	10 Leva. 0.9250 Silver. Lettered edge. SPECIMEN; KM#147a.	265

MINT SETS

KM#	Date	Mintage	Identification	Issue Price	Mkt Val
MS1	1981 (3)	—	KM#118, 120, 131	—	20.00
MS2	1992 (7)	—	KM#199-205	—	10.00
MS3	1999 (6)	—	KM#237-242, plus medal	—	12.00

PROOF SETS

KM#	Date	Mintage	Identification	Issue Price	Mkt Val
PS1	1912 (2)	—	KM#33-34. Official restrikes of these types were made in the 1960's.	—	7,500
PS2	1962/66 (9)	—	KM#58-64 (1962), 73 (1966) Issued after these types were demonetized in 1995 and 1997.	—	—
PS3	1963 (2)	5,000	KM#65-66	—	27.50
PS4	1963/73 (8)	—	KM#65-66, 69-70, 78-79, 80-81 mixed date set, REPUBLIQUE DE BULGARIE	—	155
PS5	1964 (2)	10,000	KM#69-70	—	27.50
PS6	1979 (7)	2,000	KM#84-90	—	22.50
PS7	1980 (7)	2,000	KM#84-90	—	22.50
PS8	2002 (7)	10,000	KM#237-242, 254	—	25.00

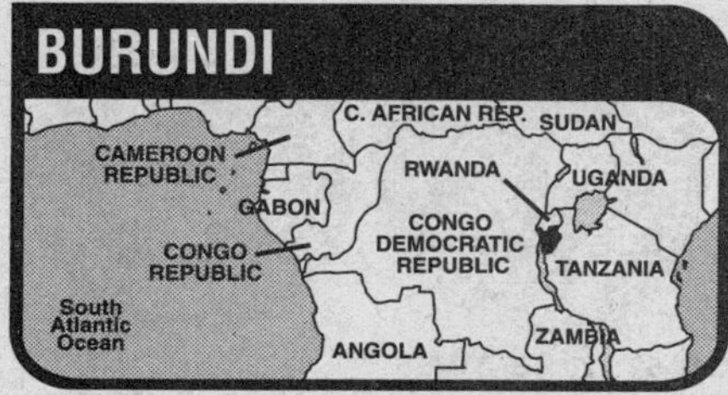

The Republic of Burundi, a landlocked country in central Africa, was a kingdom with a feudalistic society, caste system and Mwami (king) for more than 400 years before independence. It has an area of 10,740 sq. mi. (27,830 sq. km.) and a population of 6.3 million. Capital: Bujumbura. Plagued by poor soil, irregular rainfall and a single-crop economy, coffee, Burundi is barely able to feed itself. Coffee and tea are exported.

Although the area was visited by European explorers and missionaries in the latter half of the 19th century, it wasn't until the 1890s that it, together with Rwanda, fell under European domination as part of German East Africa. Following World War I, the territory was mandated to Belgium by the League of Nations and administered with the Belgian Congo. After World War II it became a U.N. Trust Territory. Limited self-government was established by U.N.-supervised elections in 1961. Burundi gained independence as a kingdom under Mwami Mwambutsa IV on July 1, 1962. The republic was established by military coup in 1966.

NOTE: For earlier coinage see Belgian Congo, and Rwanda and Burundi. For previously listed coinage dated 1966, coins of Mwambutsa IV and Ntare V, refer to *UNUSUAL WORLD COINS*, 3rd edition, Krause Publications, 1992.

RULERS
Mwambutsa IV, 1962-1966
Ntare V, 1966

MINT MARKS
PM - Pobjoy Mint
(b) - Privy Marks, Brussels

MONETARY SYSTEM
100 Centimes = 1 Franc

KINGDOM

STANDARD COINAGE

KM# 6 FRANC
Brass, 23 mm. **Obv:** Denomination within circle, circle with monogram below **Rev:** Arms above date **Edge:** Reeded

Date	Mintage	F	VF	XF	Unc	BU
1965	10,000,000	—	0.75	1.50	3.00	—

KM# 1 5 FRANCS
Copper Nickel **Ruler:** Mwambutsa IV **Subject:** Burundi Independence **Obv:** Uniformed bust left **Rev:** Arms, date and denomination below

Date	Mintage	F	VF	XF	Unc	BU
1962	—	—	—	—	—	—
1962 Proof	—	—	—	—	—	—

KM# 1a 5 FRANCS
24.1100 g., 0.9000 Silver .6976 oz. ASW **Ruler:** Mwambutsa IV **Subject:** Burundi Independence **Obv:** Uniformed bust left **Rev:** Arms, date and denomination below

Date	Mintage	F	VF	XF	Unc	BU
1962 Proof	—	—	—	—	—	—

KM# 2 10 FRANCS
3.2000 g., 0.9000 Gold .0926 oz. AGW **Ruler:** Mwambutsa IV **Subject:** Burundi Independence **Obv:** Uniformed bust left, beaded rim **Rev:** Arms, date and denomination below, beaded rim

Date	Mintage	F	VF	XF	Unc	BU
1962 Proof	7,500	Value: 75.00				

KM# 7 10 FRANCS
3.0000 g., 0.9000 Gold .0868 oz. AGW **Ruler:** Mwambutsa IV **Subject:** 50th Anniversary - Reign of Mwambutsa IV **Obv:** Uniformed bust 3/4 facing divides dates, beaded rim **Rev:** Arms, denomination below, beaded rim

Date	Mintage	F	VF	XF	Unc	BU
ND(1965)	—	—	—	—	60.00	—
ND(1965) Proof	5,000	Value: 75.00				

KM# 3 25 FRANCS
8.0000 g., 0.9000 Gold .2315 oz. AGW **Ruler:** Mwambutsa IV **Subject:** Burundi Independence **Obv:** Uniformed bust left, beaded rim **Rev:** Arms, denomination and date below, beaded rim

Date	Mintage	F	VF	XF	Unc	BU
1962 Proof	15,000	Value: 160				

KM# 8 25 FRANCS
7.5000 g., 0.9000 Gold .217 oz. AGW **Ruler:** Mwambutsa IV **Subject:** 50th Anniversary - Reign of Mwambutsa IV **Obv:** Uniformed bust 3/4 facing divides dates, beaded rim **Rev:** Arms, denomination below, beaded rim

Date	Mintage	F	VF	XF	Unc	BU
ND(1965)	—	—	—	—	155	—
ND(1965) Proof	5,000	Value: 170				

KM# 4 50 FRANCS
16.0000 g., 0.9000 Gold .4630 oz. AGW **Ruler:** Mwambutsa IV **Subject:** Burundi Independence **Obv:** Uniformed bust left, beaded rim **Rev:** Arms, denomination and date below, beaded rim

Date	Mintage	F	VF	XF	Unc	BU
1962 Proof	3,500	Value: 335				

KM# 9 50 FRANCS
15.0000 g., 0.9000 Gold .4340 oz. AGW **Ruler:** Mwambutsa IV **Subject:** 50th Anniversary - Reign of Mwambutsa IV **Obv:** Uniformed bust 3/4 facing divides dates, beaded rim **Rev:** Arms, denomination below, beaded rim

Date	Mintage	F	VF	XF	Unc	BU
ND(1965)	—	—	—	—	300	—
ND(1965) Proof	5,000	Value: 350				

KM# 5 100 FRANCS
32.0000 g., 0.9000 Gold .9260 oz. AGW **Ruler:** Mwambutsa IV **Subject:** Burundi Independence **Obv:** Uniformed bust left, beaded rim **Rev:** Arms, denomination and date below, beaded rim

Date	Mintage	F	VF	XF	Unc	BU
1962 Proof	2,500	Value: 685				

KM# 10 100 FRANCS
30.0000 g., 0.9000 Gold .8681 oz. AGW **Ruler:** Mwambutsa IV **Subject:** 50th Anniversary - Reign of Mwambutsa IV **Obv:** Uniformed bust 3/4 facing divides dates, beaded rim **Rev:** Arms, denomination below, beaded rim

Date	Mintage	F	VF	XF	Unc	BU
ND(1965)	—	—	—	—	600	—
ND(1965) Proof	5,000	Value: 650				

REPUBLIC

1966-

STANDARD COINAGE

KM# 18 FRANC
Aluminum **Obv:** Rising sun above date **Rev:** Denomination

Date	Mintage	F	VF	XF	Unc	BU
1970	10,000,000	2.00	4.50	7.50	17.50	20.00

KM# 19 FRANC
Aluminum **Obv:** Denomination **Rev:** Arms above date

Date	Mintage	F	VF	XF	Unc	BU
1976	5,000,000	—	0.30	0.75	1.75	2.50
1980	—	—	0.20	0.65	1.75	2.50
1990PM	—	—	0.15	0.50	1.50	2.00
1993PM	—	—	0.15	0.50	1.50	2.00

KM# 16 5 FRANCS
Aluminum **Obv:** Three stars at center, date below leaves **Rev:** Denomination within wreath

Date	Mintage	F	VF	XF	Unc	BU
1968(b)	2,000,000	—	0.25	0.85	2.00	2.75
1969(b)	2,000,000	—	0.25	0.85	2.00	2.75
1971(b)	2,000,000	—	0.25	0.85	2.00	2.75

KM# 20 5 FRANCS
Aluminum **Obv:** Arms above date **Rev:** Denomination

Date	Mintage	F	VF	XF	Unc	BU
1976	2,000,000	—	0.25	0.65	1.75	2.50
1980	—	—	0.25	0.65	1.75	2.50

KM# 11 10 FRANCS
3.2000 g., 0.9000 Gold .0926 oz. AGW **Subject:** First Anniversary of Republic

Date	Mintage	F	VF	XF	Unc	BU
1967 Proof	—	Value: 85.00				

KM# 17 10 FRANCS
Copper-Nickel, 28 mm. **Series:** F.A.O. **Subject:** First Anniversary of Republic **Obv:** Date at center **Rev:** Denomination at center **Edge:** Reeded

Date	Mintage	F	VF	XF	Unc	BU
1968	2,000,000	—	0.75	1.50	3.50	4.00
1971	2,000,000	—	0.75	1.50	3.50	4.00

KM# 12 20 FRANCS
6.4000 g., 0.9000 Gold .1852 oz. AGW **Subject:** First Anniversary of Republic

Date	Mintage	F	VF	XF	Unc	BU
ND(1967) Proof	—	Value: 135				

KM# 13 25 FRANCS
8.0000 g., 0.9000 Gold .2315 oz. AGW **Subject:** First Anniversary of Republic

Date	Mintage	F	VF	XF	Unc	BU
ND(1967) Proof	—	Value: 165				

KM# 14 50 FRANCS
16.0000 g., 0.9000 Gold .4630 oz. AGW **Subject:** First Anniversary of Republic **Obv:** Bust, facing **Rev:** Arms above denomination

Date	Mintage	F	VF	XF	Unc	BU
ND(1967) Proof	—	Value: 335				

KM# 15 100 FRANCS
32.0000 g., 0.9000 Gold .9261 oz. AGW **Subject:** First Anniversary of Republic

Date	Mintage	F	VF	XF	Unc	BU
ND(1967) Proof	—	Value: 665				

PROOF SETS

KM#	Date	Mintage	Identification	Issue Price	Mkt Val
PS1	1962 (4)	2,500	KM2-5	—	1,255
PS2	1965 (4)	5,000	KM7-10	—	1,245
PS3	1967 (5)	—	KM11-15	—	1,385

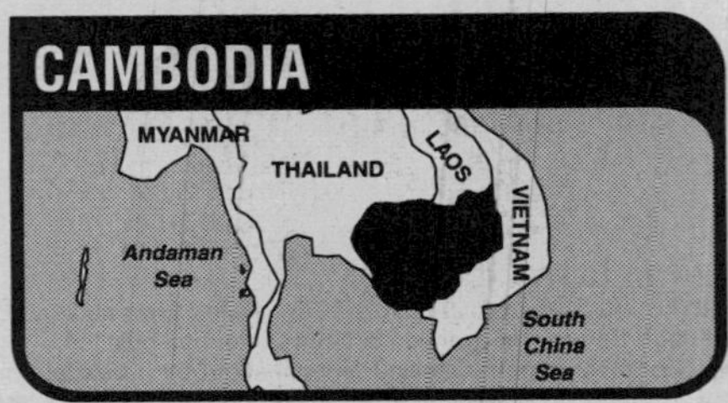

The State of Cambodia, formerly Democratic Kampuchea and the Khmer Republic, a land of paddy fields and forest-clad hills located on the Indo-Chinese peninsula, fronting on the Gulf of Thailand, has an area of 70,238 sq. mi. (181,040 sq. km.) and a population of *11.21 million. Capital: Phnom Penh. Agriculture is the basis of the economy, with rice the chief crop. Native industries include cattle breeding, weaving and rice milling. Rubber, cattle, corn, and timber are exported.

The region was the nucleus of the Khmer empire which flourished from the 5th to the 12th century and attained an excellence in art and architecture still evident in the magnificent ruins at Angkor. The Khmer empire once ruled over much of Southeast Asia, but began to decline in the 13th century as the Thai and Vietnamese invaded the region and attached its territories. At the request of the Cambodian king, a French protectorate attached to Cochin-China was established over the country in 1863, saving it from dissolution, and in 1885, Cambodia was included in the French Union of Indo-China.

France established a constitutional monarchy for Cambodia within the French Union in 1949. The 1954 Geneva Convention resulted in full independence for the Kingdom of Cambodia. King Sihanouk abdicated to his father and won the office of Prime Minister.

Prince Sihanouk was toppled by a bloodless coup led by Lon Nol in March of 1970. Sihanouk moved to Peking to head a government-in-exile. On Oct. 9, 1970, Cambodia became the Khmer Republic, and Lon Nol its President. The government of Lon Nol was in turn toppled, April 17, 1975, by the Khmer Rouge insurgents who took control of the government and renamed the country Democratic Kampuchea.

The Khmer Rouge completely eliminated the economy and created a state without money, exchange or barter while exterminating about 2 million Cambodians. These atrocities were finally halted at the beginning of 1979 when the Vietnamese regulars and Cambodian rebels launched an offensive that drove the Khmer Rouge out of Phnom Penh and the country acquired another new title - The Peoples Republic of Kampuchea.

In 1993 Prince Norodom Sihanouk returned to Kampuchea to lead the Supreme National Council.

RULERS

Kings of Cambodia

Norodom I, 1835-1904
Sisowath, 1904-1927
Sisowath Monivong, 1927-1941
Norodom Sihanouk, 1941-1955
Norodom Suramarit, 1955-1960
Heng Samrin, 1979-1985
Hun Sen, 1985-1991
Norodom Sihanouk, 1991-1993
Chairman, Supreme National Council
King, 1993-

MINT MARKS

(a) - Paris, privy marks only
(k) - Key, Havana, Cuba

MONETARY SYSTEM

(Commencing 1860)
100 Centimes = 1 Franc

INDEPENDENT KINGDOM

DECIMAL COINAGE

KM# 51 10 CENTIMES
Aluminum **Obv:** Bird statue left **Rev:** Denomination within wreath

Date	Mintage	F	VF	XF	Unc	BU
1953(a)	4,000,000	0.25	0.45	0.85	2.00	6.00

KM# 52 20 CENTIMES
Aluminum **Obv:** Two ceremonial bowls **Rev:** Denomination within wreath

Date	Mintage	F	VF	XF	Unc	BU
1953(a)	3,000,000	0.25	0.65	1.50	3.00	5.50

KM# 53 50 CENTIMES
Aluminum **Obv:** Royal emblem **Rev:** Denomination within wreath

Date	Mintage	F	VF	XF	Unc	BU
1953(a)	4,200,000	0.45	0.85	2.00	4.00	6.00

KM# 54 10 SEN
Aluminum, 23 mm. **Obv:** Bird statue left **Rev:** Denomination within wreath

Date	Mintage	F	VF	XF	Unc	BU
1959(a)	1,000,000	0.10	0.20	0.35	0.65	1.50

KM# 55 20 SEN
Aluminum, 27 mm. **Obv:** Two ceremonial bowls **Rev:** Denomination within wreath

Date	Mintage	F	VF	XF	Unc	BU
1959(a)	1,004,000	0.15	0.25	0.60	1.00	1.50

KM# 56 50 SEN
Aluminum **Obv:** Royal emblem **Rev:** Denomination within wreath

Date	Mintage	F	VF	XF	Unc	BU
1959(a)	3,399,000	0.20	0.35	0.75	1.50	2.50

KHMER REPUBLIC

1970 - 1975

DECIMAL COINAGE

KM# 59 RIEL
Copper-Nickel **Series:** F.A.O. **Obv:** Temple **Rev:** Grain bouquet, denomination

Date	Mintage	F	VF	XF	Unc	BU
1970	5,000,000	—	—	7.50	16.50	22.50

Note: According to the Royal Mint of Great Britain, this coin was minted at the Llantrissant Branch Mint in 1972 but dated 1969. According to the FAO, the coin was to have been dated 1971, but was "not minted" due to the fall of the Cambodian government in 1970. However, this coin was released in limited numbers in 1983. The photograph of the coin, supplied by the FAO, is dated 1970. This type is currently available from many sources in the numismatic market

KM# 60 5000 RIELS
19.0100 g., 0.9250 Silver .5654 oz. ASW **Obv:** Temple of Angkor Wat **Rev:** Royal emblem above denomination

Date	Mintage	F	VF	XF	Unc	BU
1974	500	—	—	—	65.00	70.00
1974 Proof	800	Value: 70.00				

KM# 61 5000 RIELS
19.0100 g., 0.9250 Silver .5654 oz. ASW **Obv:** Cambodian dancers **Rev:** Royal emblem above denomination

Date	Mintage	F	VF	XF	Unc	BU
1974	500	—	—	—	85.00	90.00
1974 Proof	800	Value: 90.00				

KM# 62 10000 RIELS
38.0300 g., 0.9250 Silver 1.1310 oz. ASW **Obv:** Bust of President Lon Nol left **Rev:** Royal emblem above denomination

Date	Mintage	F	VF	XF	Unc	BU
1974	500	—	—	—	110	115
1974 Proof	800	Value: 115				

KM# 63 10000 RIELS
38.0300 g., 0.9250 Silver 1.1310 oz. ASW **Obv:** Celestial dancer **Rev:** Royal emblem above denomination

Date	Mintage	F	VF	XF	Unc	BU
1974 Proof	800	Value: 150				
1974	500	—	—	—	140	150

KM# 64 50000 RIELS
6.7100 g., 0.9000 Gold .1941 oz. AGW **Obv:** Cambodian dancers **Rev:** Royal emblem above denomination

Date	Mintage	F	VF	XF	Unc	BU
1974	3,250	—	—	—	150	180
1974 Proof	2,300	Value: 225				

KM# 65 50000 RIELS
6.7100 g., 0.9000 Gold .1941 oz. AGW **Obv:** Celestial dancer **Rev:** Royal emblem above denomination

Date	Mintage	F	VF	XF	Unc	BU
1974	450	—	—	—	250	275
1974 Proof	300	Value: 375				

KM# 66 100000 RIELS
19.1700 g., 0.9000 Gold .5547 oz. AGW **Obv:** Bust of President Lon Nol left **Rev:** Royal emblem above denomination

Date	Mintage	F	VF	XF	Unc	BU
1974	250	—	—	—	450	475
1974 Proof	100	Value: 725				

PEOPLE'S REPUBLIC OF KAMPUCHEA

1979 - 1990

DECIMAL COINAGE

KM# 69 5 SEN
Aluminum **Obv:** Royal emblem **Rev:** Denomination, date at bottom

Date	Mintage	F	VF	XF	Unc	BU
1979	—	—	0.60	1.25	3.00	4.00

KM# 71 4 RIELS
Copper-Nickel **Subject:** Cambodian Transportation **Obv:** Royal emblem above denomination **Rev:** Old sailing ship, date at right

Date	Mintage	F	VF	XF	Unc	BU
1988(k)	1,500	—	—	—	12.50	14.50

KM# 75 4 RIELS
Copper-Nickel **Subject:** 700th Anniversary of Swiss Unity **Obv:** Royal emblem above denomination **Rev:** Standing figures of man and boy

Date	Mintage	F	VF	XF	Unc	BU
ND(1988)	15,000	—	—	—	10.00	12.00

KM# 91 4 RIELS
Copper **Rev:** Angkor Wat Temples

Date	Mintage	F	VF	XF	Unc	BU
ND(1988)	—	—	—	—	7.50	10.00

KM# 74 4 RIELS
Copper-Nickel **Subject:** World Championship Soccer - Italy **Obv:** Royal emblem above denomination **Rev:** Soccer ball with country names and dates, Italy at center

Date	Mintage	F	VF	XF	Unc	BU
1989	2,000	—	—	—	7.00	9.00

KM# 90 4 RIELS
Copper **Obv:** Royal emblem above denomination **Rev:** Angkor Wat Temples

Date	Mintage	F	VF	XF	Unc	BU
1989	—	—	—	—	8.50	11.50

KM# 70 20 RIELS
12.0600 g., 0.9990 Silver .3855 oz. ASW **Subject:** Cambodian Transportation **Obv:** Royal emblem above denomination **Rev:** Old sailing ship

Date	Mintage	F	VF	XF	Unc	BU
1988(k)	3,000	—	—	—	30.00	32.50

KM# 72 20 RIELS
12.0600 g., 0.9990 Silver .3855 oz. ASW **Subject:** World Championship Soccer - Mexico **Obv:** Royal emblem above denomination **Rev:** Soccer goalie, country name and date below

Date	Mintage	F	VF	XF	Unc	BU
1988	5,000	—	—	—	30.00	32.50

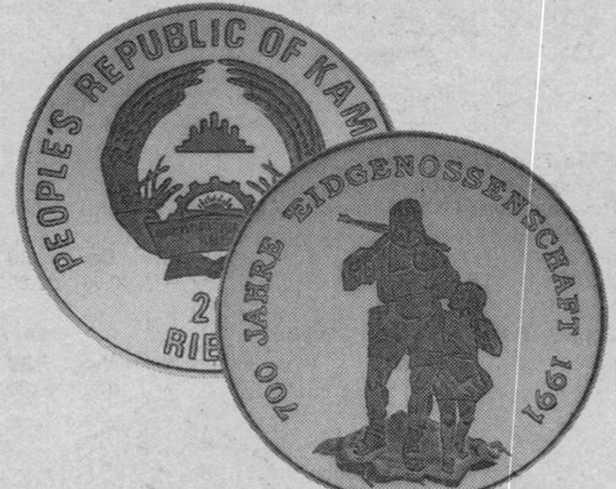

KM# 73 20 RIELS
16.0000 g., 0.9990 Silver .5145 oz. ASW **Subject:** 700th Anniversary of Swiss Unity - 1991 **Obv:** Royal emblem above denomination **Rev:** Standing figures of man and boy

Date	Mintage	F	VF	XF	Unc	BU
ND(1988) Proof	2,000	Value: 45.00				

KM# 78 20 RIELS
12.0000 g., 0.9990 Silver .3855 oz. ASW **Subject:** European Soccer Championship - Germany **Obv:** Royal emblem above denomination **Rev:** Soccer players, date below

Date	Mintage	F	VF	XF	Unc	BU
1988(k)	5,000	—	—	—	40.00	42.50

KM# 76 20 RIELS
16.0000 g., 0.9990 Silver .5145 oz. ASW **Obv:** Royal emblem above denomination **Rev:** Angkor Wat Temples

Date	Mintage	F	VF	XF	Unc	BU
1989 Proof	2,000	Value: 40.00				

KM# 79 20 RIELS
16.0000 g., 0.9990 Silver .5145 oz. ASW **Subject:** World Championship Soccer - Italy **Obv:** Royal emblem above denomination **Rev:** Soccer ball with country names and dates, Italy at center

Date	Mintage	F	VF	XF	Unc	BU
1989 Proof	10,000	Value: 28.00				

KM# 80 20 RIELS
16.0000 g., 0.9990 Silver .5145 oz. ASW **Subject:** Summer Olympics **Obv:** Royal emblem above denomination **Rev:** Fencers, date at right

Date	Mintage	F	VF	XF	Unc	BU
1989 Proof	10,000	Value: 32.50				

KM# 81 20 RIELS
16.0000 g., 0.9990 Silver .5145 oz. ASW **Subject:** Winter Olympics **Obv:** Royal emblem above denomination **Rev:** Skier, date at lower left

Date	Mintage	F	VF	XF	Unc	BU
1989 Proof	5,000	Value: 35.00				

KM# 77 40 RIELS
3.1500 g., 0.9990 Gold .1012 oz. AGW **Obv:** Royal emblem above denomination **Rev:** Angkor Wat Temples

Date	Mintage	F	VF	XF	Unc	BU
1989	500	—	—	—	145	—

KM# 82 40 RIELS
3.1500 g., 0.9990 Gold .1012 oz. AGW **Obv:** Royal emblem above denomination **Rev:** Folklore dance, date lower left

Date	Mintage	F	VF	XF	Unc	BU
1990	500	Value: 175				

STATE OF CAMBODIA

1990 - 1993

DECIMAL COINAGE

KM# 83 4 RIELS
Nickel Plated Steel **Subject:** Barcelona 1992 - 25th Summer Olympic Games **Obv:** National flag above denomination **Rev:** Tennis player, date below

Date	Mintage	F	VF	XF	Unc	BU
1991	5,000	—	—	—	13.50	15.00

KM# 86 4 RIELS
Copper-Nickel **Series:** Prehistoric animals, date at left **Obv:** National flag above denomination **Rev:** Cryptocleidus

Date	Mintage	F	VF	XF	Unc	BU
1993	—	—	—	—	25.00	30.00

KM# 89 4 RIELS
Copper-Nickel **Series:** Prehistoric Animals **Obv:** National flag above denomination **Rev:** Anatosaurus, date at right

Date	Mintage	F	VF	XF	Unc	BU
1994	—	—	—	—	25.00	30.00

KM# 84 20 RIELS
11.9600 g., 0.9990 Silver .3845 oz. ASW **Subject:** World Cup Soccer - 1994 **Obv:** National flag above denomination **Rev:** Player kicking ball, date at left

Date	Mintage	F	VF	XF	Unc	BU
1991	30,000	—	—	—	30.00	32.50

KM# 88 20 RIELS
11.9600 g., 0.9990 Silver .3845 oz. ASW **Subject:** World Cup Soccer - 1994 **Obv:** National flag above denomination **Rev:** 2 players kicking ball, date below

Date	Mintage	F	VF	XF	Unc	BU
1992 Proof	—	Value: 42.50				

KM# 85 20 RIELS
19.9500 g., 0.9990 Silver .6408 oz. ASW **Subject:** Protection of Nature **Obv:** National flag above denomination **Rev:** Asian elephants, date at right

Date	Mintage	F	VF	XF	Unc	BU
1993 Proof	—	Value: 50.00				

KM# 87 20 RIELS
16.0600 g., 0.9990 Silver .5145 oz. ASW **Series:** Prehistoric Animals **Obv:** National flag above denomination **Rev:** Indricotherium, date lower right

Date	Mintage	F	VF	XF	Unc	BU
1993	—	Value: 40.00				

KM# 96 20 RIELS
16.1000 g., 0.9990 Silver .5171 oz. ASW **Series:** Prehistoric Animals **Obv:** National flag above denomination **Rev:** Nothosaurus at water's edge, date lower right **Edge:** Plain

Date	Mintage	F	VF	XF	Unc	BU
1994 Proof	—	Value: 50.00				

KM# 97 20 RIELS
16.1000 g., 0.9990 Silver 0.5171 oz. ASW, 37.9 mm. **Subject:** Prehistoric Animals **Obv:** National flag above denomination **Rev:** Monoclonius, date lower left **Edge:** Plain

Date	Mintage	F	VF	XF	Unc	BU
1994 Proof	—	Value: 55.00				

KINGDOM OF CAMBODIA
1993 -
DECIMAL COINAGE

KM# 92 50 RIELS
1.6000 g., Steel, 15.9 mm. **Obv:** Single towered building **Rev:** Denomination within wreath

Date	Mintage	F	VF	XF	Unc	BU
BE2538-1994	—	—	—	—	0.25	0.45

KM# 93 100 RIELS
2.0000 g., Steel, 17.9 mm. **Obv:** Three-towered building **Rev:** Denomination within wreath

Date	Mintage	F	VF	XF	Unc	BU
BE2538-1994	—	—	—	—	0.50	0.85

KM# 94 200 RIELS
2.4000 g., Steel, 19.9 mm. **Obv:** 2 Ceremonial bowls **Rev:** Denomination within wreath

Date	Mintage	F	VF	XF	Unc	BU
BE2538-1994	—	—	—	—	1.00	1.50

KM# 95 500 RIELS
6.5000 g., Bi-Metallic Brass ring in Steel center, 25.8 mm. **Obv:** Royal emblem **Rev:** Denomination within wreath **Edge:** Plain and reeded sections

Date	Mintage	F	VF	XF	Unc	BU
BE2538-1994	—	—	—	—	4.50	6.00

ESSAIS

KM#	Date	Mintage	Identification	Issue Price	Mkt Val
E9	1953	1,200	10 Centimes.	—	20.00
E10	1953	1,200	20 Centimes.	—	22.00
E11	1953	1,200	50 Centimes.	—	25.00

PATTERNS

Including off metal strikes

KM#	Date	Mintage	Identification	Mkt Val
Pn15	1902	—	4 Francs. Silver. Palace at Phnom Penh	275
Pn16	1970	—	Riel. Copper-Nickel. KM59.	—

PIEFORTS WITH ESSAI

Double thickness
Standard metals unless otherwise noted

KM#	Date	Mintage	Identification	Issue Price	Mkt Val
PE9	1953	104	10 Centimes.	—	50.00
PE10	1953	104	20 Centimes.	—	65.00
PE11	1953	104	50 Centimes.	—	80.00

PIEFORTS

KM#	Date	Mintage	Identification	Mkt Val
P12	1989	110	20 Riels. 0.9990 Silver. KM80.	125
P13	1989	110	20 Riels. 0.9990 Silver. KM76.	125

MINT SETS

KM#	Date	Mintage	Identification	Issue Price	Mkt Val
MS1	1953 (3)	—	KM51,-53	—	10.00
MS2	1974 (7)	250	KM60-66	—	1,250
MS3	1974 (4)	500	KM60-63	—	400
MS4	BE2538 (1994) (4)	—	KM92-95 with 7 laminated banknotes	0.38	9.50

PROOF SETS

KM#	Date	Mintage	Identification	Issue Price	Mkt Val
PS1	1974 (7)	100	KM60-66	—	1,750
PS2	1974 (4)	800	KM60-63	—	425

CAMEROON

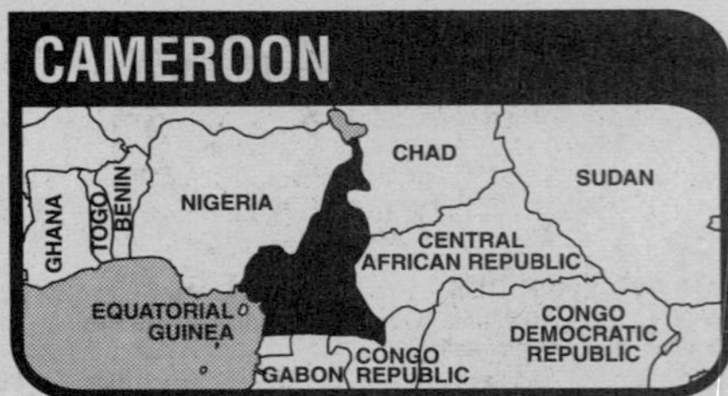

The Republic of Cameroon, located in west-central Africa on the Gulf of Guinea, has an area of 183,569 sq. mi. (475,445 sq. km.) and a population of *15.13 million. Capital: Yaounde. About 90 percent of the labor force is employed on the land; cash crops account for 80 percent of the country's export revenue. Cocoa, coffee, aluminum, cotton, rubber, and timber are exported.

European contact with what is now the United Republic of Cameroon began in the 16th century with the voyage of Portuguese navigator Fernando Po. The following three centuries saw continuous activity by Spanish, Dutch, and British traders and missionaries. The land was spared colonial rule until 1884, when treaties with tribal chiefs brought German domination. In 1919, the League of Nations divided the Cameroons between Great Britain and France, with the larger eastern area going to France. The French and British mandates were converted into United Nations trusteeships in 1946. French Cameroon became the independent Cameroon Republic on Jan. 1, 1960. The federation of East (French) and West (British) Cameroon was established in 1961 when the southern part of British Cameroon voted for reunification with the Cameroon Republic, and the northern part for union with Nigeria Cameroon joined the Commonwealth of Nations in November 1995.

Coins of French Equatorial Africa and of the monetary unions identified as the Equatorial African States and Central African States are also current in Cameroon.

MINT MARKS

(a) - Paris, privy marks only

SA - Pretoria, 1943

MONETARY SYSTEM

100 Centimes = 1 Franc

FRENCH MANDATE

STANDARD COINAGE

KM# 1 50 CENTIMES

Aluminum-Bronze **Obv:** Laureate head left, date below **Obv. Designer:** A. Patay **Rev:** Spray of branches below denomination

Date	Mintage	F	VF	XF	Unc	BU
1924(a)	4,000,000	1.50	3.50	22.00	100	250
1925(a)	2,500,000	2.00	5.00	25.00	110	275
1926(a)	7,800,000	1.00	2.00	15.00	75.00	200

KM# 4 50 CENTIMES

Bronze, 20.2 mm. **Obv:** Rooster left, monogramed shield top right **Rev:** Cross of Lorraine divides denomination below, date at bottom

Date	Mintage	F	VF	XF	Unc	BU
1943SA	4,000,000	2.00	3.50	7.00	28.00	38.00

KM# 6 50 CENTIMES

Bronze **Obv:** Rooster left, monogramed shield at top right, LIBRE added to legend **Rev:** Cross of Lorraine divides denomination below, date at bottom

Date	Mintage	F	VF	XF	Unc	BU
1943SA	4,000,000	2.50	5.50	12.00	22.00	30.00

KM# 2 FRANC

Aluminum-Bronze, 23 mm. **Obv:** Laureate head left, date below **Obv. Designer:** A. Patay **Rev:** Denomination above three branched spray **Edge:** Reeded

Date	Mintage	F	VF	XF	Unc	BU
1924(a)	3,000,000	2.00	4.00	20.00	100	250
1925(a)	1,722,000	3.00	6.00	30.00	125	285
1926(a)	12,928,000	1.00	2.00	12.00	60.00	150

KM# 5 FRANC

Bronze **Obv:** Rooster left, monogrammed shield top right **Rev:** Cross of Lorraine divides denomination below, date at bottom

Date	Mintage	F	VF	XF	Unc	BU
1943SA	3,000,000	2.50	4.50	17.50	32.00	42.00

KM# 7 FRANC

Bronze **Obv:** Rooster left, monogrammed shield at top right, LIBRE added to legend **Rev:** Cross of Lorraine divides denomination below, date at bottom

Date	Mintage	F	VF	XF	Unc	BU
1943SA	3,000,000	3.50	6.50	20.00	38.00	48.00

KM# 8 FRANC

Aluminum **Obv:** Winged bust left, date below **Obv. Designer:** G.B.L. Bazor **Rev:** Gazelle (gazella Leptoceros), antlers divide denomination

Date	Mintage	F	VF	XF	Unc	BU
1948(a)	8,000,000	0.15	0.35	0.85	1.50	2.50

KM# 3 2 FRANCS

Aluminum-Bronze **Obv:** Laureate head left, date below **Obv. Designer:** A. Patay **Rev:** Denomination above three branch spray

Date	Mintage	F	VF	XF	Unc	BU
1924(a)	500,000	5.00	15.00	65.00	185	300
1925(a)	100,000	8.00	25.00	100	300	500

KM# 9 2 FRANCS

Aluminum **Obv:** Winged bust left, date bilow **Obv. Designer:** G.G. L. Bazor **Rev:** Gazelle (gazella leptoceros), antlers divide denomination

Date	Mintage	F	VF	XF	Unc	BU
1948(a)	5,000,000	0.65	1.25	2.00	4.00	6.00

FRENCH EQUATORIAL AFRICA - CAMEROON

STANDARD COINAGE

KM# 10 5 FRANCS

Aluminum-Bronze **Obv:** Three giant eland **Obv. Designer:** G. B. L. Bazor **Rev:** Denomination

Date	Mintage	F	VF	XF	Unc	BU
1958(a)	30,000,000	0.25	0.50	1.00	3.00	5.00

KM# 11 10 FRANCS

Aluminum-Bronze **Obv:** Three giant eland left, date below **Obv. Designer:** G. B. L. Bazor **Rev:** Denomination within wreath

Date	Mintage	F	VF	XF	Unc	BU
1958(a)	25,000,000	0.25	0.50	1.50	4.00	6.00

KM# 12 25 FRANCS

Aluminum-Bronze **Obv:** Three giant eland left, date below **Obv. Designer:** G. B. L. Bazor **Rev:** Denomination within wreath

Date	Mintage	F	VF	XF	Unc	BU
1958(a)	12,000,000	0.50	1.00	2.00	6.00	8.00

REPUBLIC

STANDARD COINAGE

KM# 13 50 FRANCS

Copper-Nickel, 30 mm. **Subject:** Independence Commemorative **Obv:** Three giant eland left, date above **Obv. Designer:** G. B. L. Bazor **Rev:** Denomination within wreath

Date	Mintage	F	VF	XF	Unc	BU
1960(a)	9,000,000	2.00	3.50	5.50	10.00	12.50

KM# 14 100 FRANCS

Nickel **Obv:** Three giant eland left **Obv. Designer:** G. B. L. Bazor **Rev:** Denomination, date above **Note:** KM#14 was issued double thick and should not be considered a piefort.

Date	Mintage	F	VF	XF	Unc	BU
1966(a)	4,000,000	1.00	2.00	4.50	10.00	12.50
1967(a)	4,000,000	1.00	2.00	4.50	10.00	12.50
1968(a)	5,000,000	1.00	2.00	4.50	10.00	12.50

KM# 15 100 FRANCS

Nickel **Obv:** Three giant eland left **Obv. Designer:** G. B. L. Bazor **Rev:** Denomination within circle, date below **Note:** Refer also to Equatorial African States and Central African States.

Date	Mintage	F	VF	XF	Unc	BU
1971(a)	9,000,000	2.00	3.00	6.00	12.50	—
1972(a)	3,000,000	2.00	3.00	6.00	12.50	—

KM# 16 100 FRANCS

Nickel **Obv:** Three giant eland left **Obv. Designer:** G. B. L. Bazor **Rev:** Denomination within circle, date below **Note:** Mule

Date	Mintage	F	VF	XF	Unc	BU
1972(a)	4,000,000	6.50	12.50	22.50	45.00	—

KM# 17 100 FRANCS

Nickel **Obv:** Three giant eland left **Obv. Designer:** G. B. L. Bazor **Rev:** Denomination above date, within circle

Date	Mintage	F	VF	XF	Unc	BU
1975(a)	—	1.00	2.00	3.00	5.50	7.00
1980(a)	—	1.00	2.00	3.00	5.50	7.00
1982(a)	—	0.75	1.50	2.50	4.50	6.00
1983(a)	—	0.75	1.50	2.50	4.50	6.00
1984(a)	—	0.75	1.50	2.50	4.50	6.00
1986(a)	—	0.75	1.50	2.50	4.50	6.00

KM# 23 500 FRANCS

Copper-Nickel **Obv:** Plants divide denomination and date **Rev:** Head 3/4 left

Date	Mintage	F	VF	XF	Unc	BU
1985(a)	—	2.00	3.50	5.50	10.00	12.50
1986(a)	—	2.00	3.50	5.50	10.00	12.50
1988(a)	—	2.00	3.50	5.50	10.00	12.50

KM# 18 1000 FRANCS

3.5000 g., 0.9000 Gold .1012 oz. AGW **Subject:** 10th Anniversary of Independence **Obv:** Head of President El Hajj Ahmadou Ahidjo left **Rev:** Design at center, denomination below, arms above

Date	Mintage	F	VF	XF	Unc	BU
1970 Proof	4,000	Value: 95.00				

KM# 19 3000 FRANCS

10.5000 g., 0.9000 Gold .3038 oz. AGW **Subject:** 10th Anniversary of Independence **Obv:** Head of President El Hajj Ahmadou Ahidjo left **Rev:** Design at center, denomination below, arms above

Date	Mintage	F	VF	XF	Unc	BU
1970 Proof	4,000	Value: 220				

Note: With or without cornucopia mint mark on reverse

KM# 20 5000 FRANCS

17.5000 g., 0.9000 Gold .5064 oz. AGW **Subject:** 10th Anniversary of Independence **Obv:** Head of President El Hajj Ahmadou Ahidjo left **Rev:** Head, left, within center circle, denomination below, arms above

Date	Mintage	F	VF	XF	Unc	BU
1970 Proof	4,000	Value: 350				

KM# 21 10000 FRANCS

35.0000 g., 0.9000 Gold 1.0128 oz. AGW **Subject:** 10th Anniversary of Independence **Obv:** President El Hajj Ahmadou Ahidjo left **Rev:** Elands facing center, denomination below, arms above

Date	Mintage	F	VF	XF	Unc	BU
1970 Proof	4,000	Value: 700				

KM# 22 20000 FRANCS

70.0000 g., 0.9000 Gold 2.0257 oz. AGW **Subject:** 10th Anniversary of Independence **Obv:** Head of President El Hajj Ahmadou Ahidjo left **Rev:** Arms, denomination below

Date	Mintage	F	VF	XF	Unc	BU
1970 Proof	4,000	Value: 1,375				

ESSAIS

Standard metals unless otherwise noted

KM#	Date	Mintage	Identification	Issue Price	Mkt Val
E1	1924(a)	—	50 Centimes. Aluminum-Bronze. KM1.	—	100
E2	1924(a)	—	Franc. Aluminum-Bronze. KM2.	—	110

KM#	Date	Mintage	Identification	Issue Price	Mkt Val
E3	1924(a)	—	2 Francs. Aluminum-Bronze. Laureate head left, date below. Denomination above three branch spray. KM3.	—	140
E4	1943	—	1/2 Franc.	—	600
E5	1948(a)	2,000	Franc. Copper-Nickel. KM8.	—	25.00
E6	1948(a)	2,000	2 Francs. Copper-Nickel. KM9.	—	35.00
E7	1958(a)	2,030	5 Francs. Bi-Metallic. Copper-Nickel center. Brass ring. KM24.	—	15.00
E8	1958(a)	2,030	10 Francs. Iron-Blued. KM25.	—	17.50
E9	1958(a)	2,030	25 Francs. Nickel Plated Iron. KM26.	—	20.00

KM#	Date	Mintage	Identification	Issue Price	Mkt Val
E10	1960(a)	1,500	50 Francs. Copper-Nickel. Three giant eland left, date above. Denomina-tion within wreath. KM13.	—	27.50
E11	1966(a)	1,200	100 Francs. Nickel. KM14.	—	35.00
E12	1970(a)	—	1000 Francs. Bronze. KM18.	—	95.00
E13	1971(a)	1,550	100 Francs. Nickel. KM15.	—	22.50
E14	1971	6	100 Francs. Gold. KM15.	—	1,300
E15	1972(a)	1,550	100 Francs. Nickel. KM16.	—	30.00
E16	1975(a)	1,700	100 Francs. Nickel. KM17.	—	22.50

KM#	Date	Mintage	Identification	Issue Price	Mkt Val
E17	1985(a)	—	500 Francs. Copper-Nickel. Plants divide denomina-tion and date. KM23.	—	30.00

PIEFORTS WITH ESSAI

Double thickness - Standard metals unless otherwise noted

KM#	Date	Mintage	Identification	Issue Price	Mkt Val
PE1	1948(a)	104	Franc. Aluminum. KM8.	—	80.00
PE2	1948(a)	104	2 Francs. Aluminum. KM9.	—	85.00
PE3	1948(a)	—	2 Francs. Aluminum. KM9, double piefort.	—	475
PE4	1948(a)	—	2 Francs. Copper-Nickel. KM9.	—	250

PROOF SETS

KM#	Date	Mintage	Identification	Issue Price	Mkt Val
PS1	1970 (5)	4,000	KM18-22	—	2,750

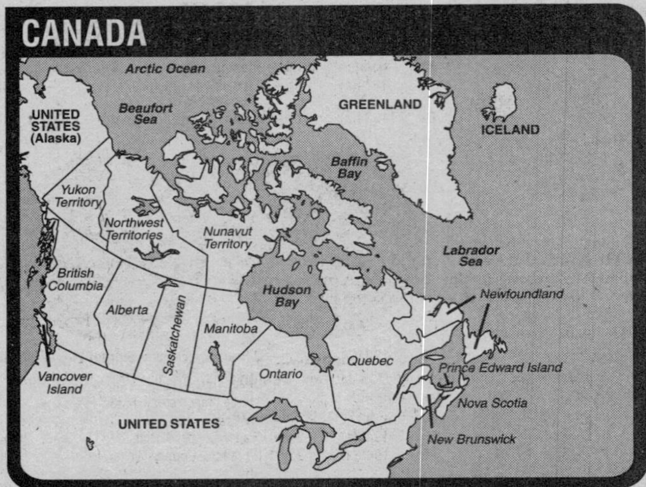

Canada is located to the north of the United States, and spans the full breadth of the northern portion of North America from Atlantic to Pacific oceans, except for the State of Alaska. It has a total area of 3,850,000 sq. mi. (9,971,550 sq. km.) and a population of 30.29 million. Capital: Ottawa.

Jacques Cartier, a French explorer, took possession of Canada for France in 1534, and for more than a century the history of Canada was that of a French colony. Samuel de Champlain helped to establish the first permanent colony in North America, in 1604 at Port Royal, Acadia – now Annapolis Royal, Nova Scotia. Four years later he founded the settlement in Quebec.

The British settled along the coast to the south while the French, motivated by a grand design, pushed into the interior. France's plan for a great American empire was to occupy the Mississippi heartland of the country, and from there to press in upon the narrow strip of English coastal settlements from the west. Inevitably, armed conflict erupted between the French and the British; consequently, Britain acquired Hudson Bay, Newfoundland and Nova Scotia from the French in 1713. British control of the rest of New France was secured in 1763, largely because of James Wolfe's great victory over Montcalm near Quebec in 1759.

During the American Revolution, Canada became a refuge for great numbers of American Royalists, most of whom settled in Ontario, thereby creating an English majority west of the Ottawa River. The ethnic imbalance contravened the effectiveness of the prevailing French type of government, and in 1791 the Constitutional act was passed by the British parliament, dividing Canada at the Ottawa River into two parts, each with its own government: Upper Canada, chiefly English and consisting of the southern section of what is now Ontario; and Lower Canada, chiefly French and consisting principally of the southern section of Quebec. Subsequent revolt by dissidents in both sections caused the British government to pass the Union Act, July 23, 1840, which united Lower and Upper Canada (as Canada East and Canada West) to form the Province of Canada, with one council and one assembly in which the two sections had equal numbers.

The union of the two provinces did not encourage political stability; the equal strength of the French and British made the task of government all but impossible. A further change was made with the passage of the British North American Act, which took effect on July 1, 1867, and established Canada as the first federal union in the British Empire. Four provinces entered the union at first: Upper Canada as Ontario, Lower Canada as Quebec, Nova Scotia and New Brunswick. The Hudson Bay Company's territories were acquired in 1869 out of which were formed the provinces of Manitoba, Saskatchewan and Alberta. British Columbia joined in 1871 and Prince Edward Island in 1873. Canada took over the Arctic Archipelago in 1895. In 1949 Newfoundland came into the confederation.

In the early years, Canada's coins were struck in England at the Royal Mint in London or at the Heaton Mint in Birmingham. Issues struck at the Royal Mint do not bear a mint mark, but those produced by Heaton carry an "H". All Canadian coins have been struck since January 2, 1908, at the Royal Canadian Mints at Ottawa and recently at Winnipeg except for some 1968 pure nickel dimes struck at the U.S. Mint in Philadelphia, and do not bear mint marks. Ottawa's mint mark (C) does not appear on some 20th Century Newfoundland issues, however, as it does on English type sovereigns struck there from 1908 through 1918.

Canada is a member of the Commonwealth of Nations. Elizabeth II is Head of State as Queen of Canada.

RULERS:
British 1763-

MONETARY SYSTEM
1 Dollar = 100 Cents

CONFEDERATION

CIRCULATION COINAGE

KM# 7 CENT **Weight:** 3.2400 g. **Composition:** Bronze **Ruler:** Victoria **Obverse:** Queen's head left within beaded circle **Obv. Designer:** Leonard C. Wyon **Reverse:** Denomination above date within beaded circle, chain of leaves surround **Edge:** Plain **Size:** 25.5 mm.

Date	Mintage	VG-8	F-12	VF-20	XF-40	MS-60	MS-63	Proof
1901	4,100,000	2.25	3.00	4.50	5.50	35.00	85.00	—

KM# 8 CENT **Weight:** 3.2400 g. **Composition:** Bronze **Ruler:** Edward VII **Obverse:** Kings bust right within beaded circle **Obv. Designer:** G. W. DeSaulles **Reverse:** Denomination above date within circle, chain of leaves surrounds **Edge:** Plain **Size:** 25.5 mm.

Date	Mintage	VG-8	F-12	VF-20	XF-40	MS-60	MS-63	Proof
1902	3,000,000	1.75	2.25	3.50	6.00	23.00	50.00	—
1903	4,000,000	1.75	2.25	3.00	6.00	25.00	55.00	—
1904	2,500,000	2.00	3.50	5.00	8.00	30.00	85.00	—
1905	2,000,000	3.50	4.00	7.50	12.00	40.00	100	—
1906	4,100,000	1.75	2.25	3.00	6.00	30.00	125	—
1907	2,400,000	2.00	2.25	4.50	9.00	30.00	125	—
1907H	800,000	8.00	16.00	20.00	35.00	150	350	—
1908	2,401,506	2.00	3.50	5.00	8.00	30.00	90.00	150
1909	3,973,339	1.25	1.75	3.00	6.00	25.00	70.00	—
1910	5,146,487	1.25	1.50	2.00	5.00	26.00	70.00	—

KM# 15 CENT **Weight:** 3.2400 g. **Composition:** Bronze **Ruler:** George V **Obverse:** King's bust left **Obv. Designer:** E. B. MacKennal **Reverse:** Denomination above date within beaded circle, chain of leaves surrounds **Edge:** Plain **Size:** 25.5 mm.

Date	Mintage	VG-8	F-12	VF-20	XF-40	MS-60	MS-63	Proof
1911	4,663,486	0.80	1.30	1.75	3.50	22.00	50.00	250

KM# 21 CENT **Weight:** 3.2400 g. **Composition:** Bronze **Ruler:** George V **Obverse:** King's bust left **Obv. Designer:** E. B. MacKennal **Reverse:** Denomination above date within beaded circle, chain of leaves surrounds **Edge:** Plain **Size:** 25.5 mm.

Date	Mintage	VG-8	F-12	VF-20	XF-40	MS-60	MS-63	Proof
1912	5,107,642	0.75	1.50	2.25	3.50	21.00	55.00	—
1913	5,735,405	0.75	1.50	2.25	4.00	23.00	80.00	—
1914	3,405,958	1.00	1.50	2.50	4.00	30.00	95.00	—
1915	4,932,134	0.75	1.50	2.25	4.00	25.00	70.00	—
1916	11,022,367	0.50	0.65	1.25	3.00	16.00	50.00	—
1917	11,899,254	0.50	0.65	0.90	2.25	13.00	45.00	—
1918	12,970,798	0.50	0.65	0.90	2.25	12.00	45.00	—
1919	11,279,634	0.50	0.65	0.90	2.25	12.00	45.00	—
1920	6,762,247	0.60	0.75	1.00	2.25	15.00	55.00	—

Dot

KM# 28 CENT **Weight:** 3.2400 g. **Composition:** Bronze **Ruler:** George V **Obverse:** King's bust left **Obv. Designer:** E. B. MacKennal **Reverse:** Denomination above date, leaves flank **Rev. Designer:** Fred Lewis **Edge:** Plain **Size:** 19.10 mm.

Date	Mintage	VG-8	F-12	VF-20	XF-40	MS-60	MS-63	Proof
1920	15,483,923	0.20	0.50	1.00	2.00	11.00	35.00	—
1921	7,601,627	0.50	0.75	1.75	5.00	30.00	125	—
1922	1,243,635	13.00	16.00	21.00	35.00	175	650	—
1923	1,019,002	19.00	21.00	30.00	45.00	275	1,200	—
1924	1,593,195	5.00	6.50	8.50	15.00	100	375	—
1925	1,000,622	18.00	21.00	27.00	40.00	175	550	—
1926	2,143,372	3.50	4.50	7.00	11.00	90.00	325	—
1927	3,553,928	0.90	1.25	2.25	6.00	35.00	125	—
1928	9,144,860	0.15	0.30	0.65	1.50	15.00	55.00	—
1929	12,159,840	0.15	0.30	0.65	1.50	15.00	55.00	—
1930	2,538,613	1.35	1.80	4.50	8.50	45.00	125	—
1931	3,842,776	0.65	1.00	1.75	5.50	35.00	125	—
1932	21,316,190	0.15	0.20	0.50	1.50	14.00	45.00	—
1933	12,079,310	0.15	0.20	0.50	1.50	14.00	45.00	—
1934	7,042,358	0.20	0.30	0.75	1.50	14.00	45.00	—
1935	7,526,400	0.20	0.30	0.75	1.50	14.00	40.00	—
1936	8,768,769	0.15	0.30	0.75	1.50	9.00	30.00	—
1936 dot below date; Rare	678,823	—	—	—	—	—	—	—

Note: Only one possible business strike is known to exist. No other examples (or possible business strikes) have ever surfaced.

Date	Mintage	VG-8	F-12	VF-20	XF-40	MS-60	MS-63	Proof
1936 dot below date, specimen, 3 known	—	—	—	—	—	—	—	—

Note: At the David Akers auction of the John Jay Pittman collection (Part 1, 10-97), a gem specimen realized $121,000. At the David Akers auction of the John Jay Pittman collection (Part 3, 10-99), a near choice specimen realized $115,000.

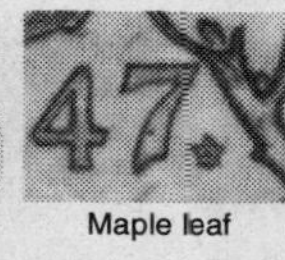
Maple leaf

KM# 32 CENT **Weight:** 3.2400 g. **Composition:** Bronze **Ruler:** George VI **Obverse:** Head left **Obv. Designer:** T. H. Paget **Reverse:** Maple leaf divides date and denomination **Rev. Designer:** George E. Kruger-Gray **Edge:** Plain **Size:** 19.10 mm.

Date	Mintage	VG-8	F-12	VF-20	XF-40	MS-60	MS-63	Proof
1937	10,040,231	0.40	0.50	0.75	1.00	3.00	9.00	—
1938	18,365,608	0.15	0.20	0.35	0.75	2.00	6.50	—
1939	21,600,319	0.15	0.20	0.35	0.70	1.75	5.00	—
1940	85,740,532	0.10	0.15	0.25	0.50	1.50	5.50	—
1941	56,336,011	0.10	0.15	0.25	0.50	6.00	50.00	—
1942	76,113,708	0.10	0.15	0.25	0.50	6.00	40.00	—
1943	89,111,969	0.10	0.15	0.25	0.45	3.50	25.00	—
1944	44,131,216	0.10	0.15	0.30	0.60	9.50	70.00	—
1945	77,268,591	0.10	0.15	0.20	0.30	2.25	14.00	—
1946	56,662,071	0.10	0.15	0.20	0.30	2.25	5.00	—
1947	31,093,901	0.10	0.15	0.20	0.30	2.25	6.00	—
1947 maple leaf	47,855,448	0.10	0.15	0.20	0.30	2.25	5.00	—

KM# 41 CENT **Weight:** 3.2400 g. **Composition:** Bronze **Ruler:** George VI **Obverse:** Modified legend **Obv. Designer:** T. H. Paget **Rev. Designer:** George E. Kruger-Gray **Edge:** Plain **Size:** 19.10 mm.

Date	Mintage	VG-8	F-12	VF-20	XF-40	MS-60	MS-63	Proof
1948	25,767,779	—	0.15	0.25	0.70	3.50	20.00	—
1949	33,128,933	—	0.10	0.15	0.25	2.00	6.00	—
1950	60,444,992	—	0.10	0.15	0.25	1.25	6.00	—
1951	80,430,379	—	0.10	0.15	0.20	1.25	8.00	—
1952	67,631,736	—	0.10	0.15	0.20	0.85	4.00	—

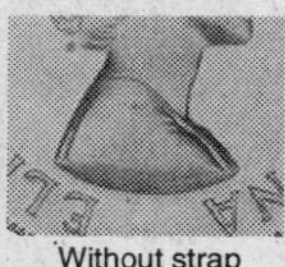
Without strap

With strap

KM# 49 CENT **Weight:** 3.2400 g. **Composition:** Bronze **Ruler:** Elizabeth II **Obverse:** Laureate bust right **Obv. Designer:** Mary Gillick **Reverse:** Maple leaf divides date and denomination **Rev. Designer:** George E. Kruger-Gray **Size:** 19.10 mm.

Date	Mintage	VG-8	F-12	VF-20	XF-40	MS-60	MS-63	Proof
1953	67,806,016	0.10	0.15	0.20	0.25	0.65	1.50	—
Note: Without strap								
1953	Inc. above	0.75	1.00	1.50	2.50	10.00	35.00	—
Note: With strap								
1954	22,181,760	0.10	0.15	0.25	0.40	1.50	4.00	—
Note: With strap								
1954 Prooflike only	Inc. above	—	—	—	—	150	300	—
Note: Without strap								
1955	56,403,193	—	0.10	0.15	0.20	0.35	1.00	—
Note: With strap								
1955	Inc. above	85.00	125	150	250	500	1,100	—
Note: Without strap								
1956	78,658,535	—	—	—	0.10	0.50	0.90	—
1957	100,601,792	—	—	—	0.10	0.15	0.25	—
1958	59,385,679	—	—	—	0.10	0.15	0.25	—
1959	83,615,343	—	—	—	0.10	0.15	0.25	—
1960	75,772,775	—	—	—	0.10	0.15	0.25	—
1961	139,598,404	—	—	—	—	0.15	0.20	—
1962	227,244,069	—	—	—	—	0.10	0.20	—
1963	279,076,334	—	—	—	—	0.10	0.20	—
1964	484,655,322	—	—	—	—	0.10	0.20	—

KM# 59.1 CENT **Weight:** 3.2400 g. **Composition:** Bronze **Ruler:** Elizabeth II **Obverse:** Queens bust right **Obv. Designer:** Arnold Machin **Reverse:** Maple leaf divides date and denomination **Rev. Designer:** George E. Kruger-Gray **Edge:** Plain **Size:** 19.10 mm.

Date	Mintage	VG-8	F-12	VF-20	XF-40	MS-60	MS-63	Proof
1965	304,441,082	—	—	—	0.40	1.00	4.00	—
Note: Small beads, pointed 5								
1965	Inc. above	—	—	—	—	0.15	0.20	—
Note: Small beads, blunt 5								
1965	Inc. above	—		3.00	5.00	12.00	35.00	—
Note: Large beads, pointed 5								
1965	Inc. above	—	—	—	0.10	0.15	0.20	—
Note: Large beads, blunt 5								
1966	184,151,087	—	—	—	—	0.10	0.20	—
1968	329,695,772	—	—	—	—	0.10	0.15	—
1969	335,240,929	—	—	—	—	0.10	0.15	—
1970	311,145,010	—	—	—	—	0.10	0.15	—
1971	298,228,936	—	—	—	—	0.10	0.15	—
1972	451,304,591	—	—	—	—	0.10	0.15	—
1973	457,059,852	—	—	—	—	0.10	0.15	—
1974	692,058,489	—	—	—	—	0.10	0.15	—
1975	642,318,000	—	—	—	—	0.10	0.15	—
1976	701,122,890	—	—	—	—	0.10	0.15	—
1977	453,762,670	—	—	—	—	0.10	0.15	—
1978	911,170,647	—	—	—	—	0.10	0.15	—

KM# 59.2 CENT **Weight:** 3.2400 g. **Composition:** Bronze **Ruler:** Elizabeth II **Obverse:** Queen's bust right **Obv. Designer:** Arnold Machin **Reverse:** Dove with wings spread, denomination above, dates below **Rev. Designer:** George E. Kruger-Gray **Edge:** Plain **Size:** 19.10 mm.

Date	Mintage	VG-8	F-12	VF-20	XF-40	MS-60	MS-63	Proof
1979	754,394,064	—	—	—	—	0.10	0.15	—

KM# 65 CENT **Composition:** Bronze **Ruler:** Elizabeth II **Subject:** Confederation Centennial **Obverse:** Queen's bust right **Obv. Designer:** Arnold Machin **Reverse:** Dove with wings spread, denomination above, two dates below **Rev. Designer:** Alex Coville **Size:** 19.10 mm.

Date	Mintage	VG-8	F-12	VF-20	XF-40	MS-60	MS-63	Proof
ND(1967)	345,140,645	—	—	—	—	0.10	0.20	1.00

KM# 127 CENT **Weight:** 2.8000 g. **Composition:** Bronze **Ruler:** Elizabeth II **Obverse:** Queen's bust right **Obv. Designer:** Arnold Machin **Rev. Designer:** George E. Kruger-Gray **Edge:** Plain **Size:** 19.10 mm. **Note:** Reduced weight.

Date	Mintage	VG-8	F-12	VF-20	XF-40	MS-60	MS-63	Proof
1980	912,052,318	—	—	—	—	0.10	0.15	—
1981	1,209,468,500	—	—	—	—	0.10	0.15	—
1981 Proof	199,000	—	—	—	—	—	—	1.50

KM# 132 CENT **Weight:** 2.5000 g. **Composition:** Bronze **Ruler:** Elizabeth II **Obverse:** Queen's bust right **Obv. Designer:** Arnold Machin **Reverse:** Maple leaf divides date and denomination **Rev. Designer:** George E. Kruger-Gray **Edge:** Plain **Shape:** Multi-sided **Size:** 19.10 mm. **Note:** Reduced weight.

Date	Mintage	VG-8	F-12	VF-20	XF-40	MS-60	MS-63	Proof
1982	911,001,000	—	—	—	—	0.10	0.15	—
1982 Proof	180,908	—	—	—	—	—	—	1.50
1983	975,510,000	—	—	—	—	0.10	0.15	—
1983 Proof	168,000	—	—	—	—	—	—	1.50
1984	838,225,000	—	—	—	—	0.10	0.15	—
1984 Proof	161,602	—	—	—	—	—	—	1.50
1985	771,772,500	—	—	—	3.00	10.00	19.00	—
Note: Pointed 5								
1985	Inc. above	—	—	—	—	0.10	0.15	—
Note: Blunt 5								
1985 Proof	157,037	—	—	—	—	—	—	1.50
Note: Blunt 5								
1986	740,335,000	—	—	—	—	0.10	0.15	—
1986 Proof	175,745	—	—	—	—	—	—	1.50
1987	774,549,000	—	—	—	—	0.10	0.15	—
1987 Proof	179,004	—	—	—	—	—	—	1.50
1988	482,676,752	—	—	—	—	0.10	0.15	—
1988 Proof	175,259	—	—	—	—	—	—	1.50
1989	1,077,347,200	—	—	—	—	0.10	0.15	—
1989 Proof	170,928	—	—	—	—	—	—	1.50

KM# 181 CENT **Weight:** 2.5000 g. **Composition:** Bronze **Ruler:** Elizabeth II **Obverse:** Crowned Queen's head right **Obv. Designer:** Dora dePedery-Hunt **Reverse:** Maple leaf divides date and denomination **Rev. Designer:** George E. Kruger-Gray **Edge:** Plain **Size:** 19.10 mm.

Date	Mintage	VG-8	F-12	VF-20	XF-40	MS-60	MS-63	Proof
1990	218,035,000	—	—	—	—	0.10	0.15	—
1990 Proof	140,649	—	—	—	—	—	—	2.50
1991	831,001,000	—	—	—	—	0.10	0.15	—
1991 Proof	131,888	—	—	—	—	—	—	3.50
1993	752,034,000	—	—	—	—	0.10	0.15	—
1993 Proof	145,065	—	—	—	—	—	—	2.00
1994	639,516,000	—	—	—	—	0.10	0.15	—
1994 Proof	146,424	—	—	—	—	—	—	2.50
1995	624,983,000	—	—	—	—	0.10	0.15	—
1996	445,746,000	—	—	—	—	0.10	0.15	—
1996 Proof	—	—	—	—	—	—	—	2.50

KM# 204 CENT **Composition:** Bronze **Ruler:** Elizabeth II **Subject:** Confederation 125 **Obverse:** Crowned Queen's head right **Obv. Designer:** Dora dePedery-Hunt **Reverse:** Maple leaf divides date and denomination **Rev. Designer:** George E. Kruger-Gray **Size:** 19.10 mm.

Date	Mintage	VG-8	F-12	VF-20	XF-40	MS-60	MS-63	Proof
ND(1992)	673,512,000	—	—	—	—	0.10	0.15	—
ND(1992) Proof	147,061	—	—	—	—	—	—	2.50

KM# 289 CENT **Composition:** Copper Plated Zinc **Ruler:** Elizabeth II **Obverse:** Crowned head right **Edge:** Round and plain **Size:** 19.10 mm.

Date	Mintage	VG-8	F-12	VF-20	XF-40	MS-60	MS-63	Proof
1997	549,868,000	—	—	—	—	0.10	0.15	—
1997 Proof	—	—	—	—	—	—	—	2.75
1998	999,578,000	—	—	—	—	0.10	0.15	—
1998 Proof	—	—	—	—	—	—	—	3.00
1998W	—	—	—	—	—	—	1.75	—
1999P	—	—	—	—	—	—	6.00	—
Note: Plated planchet, set only								
1999	1,089,625,000	—	—	—	—	0.10	0.15	—
1999W	—	—	—	—	—	—	—	—
1999 Proof	—	—	—	—	—	—	—	4.00
2000	771,908,206	—	—	—	—	0.10	0.15	—
2000 Proof	—	—	—	—	—	—	—	4.00
2000W	—	—	—	—	—	—	1.75	—

KM# 289a CENT **Composition:** Bronze **Size:** 19.10 mm.

Date	Mintage	VG-8	F-12	VF-20	XF-40	MS-60	MS-63	Proof
1998	—	—	—	—	—	—	0.75	—
Note: In Specimen sets only								

KM# 309 CENT **Weight:** 5.6700 g. **Composition:** 0.9250 Copper-Plated Silver 0.1677 oz. **Subject:** 90th Anniversary Royal Canadian Mint - 1908-1998 **Obv. Designer:** Dora dePedery-Hunt **Rev. Designer:** G. W. DeSaulles

Date	Mintage	VG-8	F-12	VF-20	XF-40	MS-60	MS-63	Proof
ND(1998)	25,000	—	—	—	—	—	16.00	—
Note: Antique finish								
ND(1998) Proof	—	—	—	—	—	—	—	—

KM# 332 CENT **Weight:** 5.6700 g. **Composition:** 0.9250 Silver .1677 oz. ASW **Ruler:** Elizabeth II **Subject:** 90th Anniversary Royal Canadian Mint - 1908-1998 **Obverse:** Crowned Queen's head right, with "Canada" added to head **Obv. Designer:** Dora dePedery-Hunt **Reverse:** Denomination above dates withn beaded circle, chain of leaves surrounds **Rev. Designer:** G. W. DeSaulles

Date	Mintage	VG-8	F-12	VF-20	XF-40	MS-60	MS-63	Proof
ND(2000) Proof	25,000	—	—	—	—	—	—	16.00
Note: Mirror finish								

KM# 2 5 CENTS **Weight:** 1.1620 g. **Composition:** 0.9250 Silver 0.0346 oz. ASW **Ruler:** Victoria **Obverse:** Head left **Reverse:** Denomination and date within wreath, crown above

Date	Mintage	VG-8	F-12	VF-20	XF-40	MS-60	MS-63	Proof
1901	2,000,000	4.50	6.50	12.00	35.00	150	400	—

KM# 9 5 CENTS **Weight:** 1.1620 g. **Composition:** 0.9250 Silver 0.0346 oz. ASW **Ruler:** Edward VII **Obv. Designer:** G. W. DeSaulles **Rev. Designer:** Leonard C. Wyon

Date	Mintage	VG-8	F-12	VF-20	XF-40	MS-60	MS-63	Proof
1902	2,120,000	2.25	3.00	4.00	7.00	35.00	55.00	—
1902	2,200,000	2.25	3.25	5.50	11.00	35.00	60.00	—
Note: Large broad H								
1902	Inc. above	7.50	13.00	24.00	40.00	100	175	—
Note: Small narrow H								

KM# 13 5 CENTS **Weight:** 1.1620 g. **Composition:** 0.9250 Silver 0.0346 oz. ASW **Ruler:** Edward VII **Obverse:** King's bust right **Reverse:** Denomination and date within wreath, crown at top

Date	Mintage	VG-8	F-12	VF-20	XF-40	MS-60	MS-63	Proof
1903	1,000,000	4.00	7.00	17.00	35.00	150	350	—
Note: 22 leaves								
1903H	2,640,000	1.75	3.00	7.00	16.00	100	300	—
Note: 21 leaves								
1904	2,400,000	2.75	4.50	7.00	23.00	175	500	—
1905	2,600,000	1.75	3.00	6.00	16.00	100	225	—
1906	3,100,000	2.25	3.00	6.00	13.00	85.00	225	—
1907	5,200,000	2.25	3.00	4.00	10.00	55.00	150	—
1908	1,220,524	6.00	10.00	23.00	35.00	100	175	—
1909	1,983,725	3.00	6.50	10.00	30.00	175	500	—
Note: Round leaves								
1909	Inc. above	12.00	18.00	35.00	95.00	550	1,300	—
Note: Pointed leaves								
1910	3,850,325	2.25	2.75	5.00	7.00	50.00	95.00	—
Note: Pointed leaves								
1910	Inc. above	10.00	17.00	30.00	85.00	400	1,300	—
Note: Round leaves								

KM# 16 5 CENTS **Weight:** 1.1620 g. **Composition:** 0.9250 Silver 0.0346 oz. ASW **Ruler:** George V **Obverse:** King's bust left **Obv. Designer:** E. B. MacKennal **Reverse:** Denomination and date within wreath, crown above **Rev. Designer:** Leonard C. Wyon

Date	Mintage	VG-8	F-12	VF-20	XF-40	MS-60	MS-63	Proof
1911	3,692,350	2.00	3.00	6.00	9.00	60.00	100	—

KM# 22 5 CENTS **Weight:** 1.1620 g. **Composition:** 0.9250 Silver 0.0346 oz. ASW **Ruler:** George V **Obverse:** King's bust left **Obv. Designer:** E. B. MacKennal **Reverse:** Denomination and date within wreath, crown above **Rev. Designer:** Leonard C. Wyon

Date	Mintage	VG-8	F-12	VF-20	XF-40	MS-60	MS-63	Proof
1912	5,863,170	2.00	3.00	5.00	9.00	50.00	150	—
1913	5,488,048	2.00	2.75	4.25	7.50	26.00	50.00	—
1914	4,202,179	2.00	3.00	5.00	9.00	50.00	125	—
1915	1,172,258	11.00	15.00	26.00	50.00	325	600	—
1916	2,481,675	2.75	5.00	9.00	22.00	100	250	—
1917	5,521,373	1.75	2.50	3.00	7.00	30.00	80.00	—
1918	6,052,298	1.75	2.50	3.00	6.50	30.00	65.00	—
1919	7,835,400	1.75	2.50	3.00	6.50	30.00	65.00	—

KM# 22a 5 CENTS **Weight:** 1.1664 g. **Composition:** 0.8000 Silver .0300 oz. ASW **Ruler:** George V **Obv. Designer:** E. B. MacKennal **Rev. Designer:** Leonard C. Wyon

Date	Mintage	VG-8	F-12	VF-20	XF-40	MS-60	MS-63	Proof
1920	10,649,851	1.75	2.50	3.00	6.50	26.00	50.00	—
1921	2,582,495	2,700	3,000	4,500	6,750	9,500	16,500	—
Note: Approximately 460 known; balance remelted. Stack's A.G. Carter Jr. Sale (12-89) choice BU, finest known, realized $57,200								

Near 6 Far 6

KM# 29 5 CENTS **Composition:** Nickel **Ruler:** George V **Obverse:** King's bust, left **Obv. Designer:** E. B. MacKennal **Reverse:** Maple leaves divide denomination and date **Rev. Designer:** W. H. J. Blakemore **Size:** 21.2 mm.

Date	Mintage	VG-8	F-12	VF-20	XF-40	MS-60	MS-63	Proof
1922	4,794,119	0.20	0.75	1.75	7.00	45.00	95.00	—
1923	2,502,279	0.40	1.25	5.50	16.00	100	275	—
1924	3,105,839	0.25	1.00	3.75	10.00	85.00	200	—
1925	201,921	55.00	70.00	100	200	1,200	3,600	—
1926 Near 6	938,162	2.25	4.00	16.00	60.00	375	1,300	—
1926 Far 6	Inc. above	100	150	300	600	1,500	4,300	—
1927	5,285,627	0.20	0.65	2.75	10.00	60.00	125	—
1928	4,577,712	0.20	0.65	2.75	10.00	55.00	100	—
1929	5,611,911	0.20	0.65	2.75	10.00	60.00	150	—
1930	3,704,673	0.20	1.00	2.75	11.00	90.00	200	—
1931	5,100,830	0.20	1.00	3.25	18.00	175	475	—
1932	3,198,566	0.20	1.00	3.25	16.00	150	350	—
1933	2,597,867	0.40	1.50	6.00	18.00	175	650	—
1934	3,827,304	0.20	1.00	3.00	16.00	150	375	—
1935	3,900,000	0.20	1.00	2.75	11.00	95.00	250	—
1936	4,400,450	0.20	0.65	1.75	9.00	50.00	100	—

KM# 33 5 CENTS **Composition:** Nickel **Ruler:** George VI **Obverse:** Head left **Obv. Designer:** T. H. Paget **Reverse:** Beaver on rock divides denomination and date **Rev. Designer:** George E. Kruger-Gray **Size:** 21.2 mm.

Date	Mintage	VG-8	F-12	VF-20	XF-40	MS-60	MS-63	Proof
1937 Dot	4,593,263	0.15	0.25	1.25	2.50	9.00	22.00	—
1938	3,898,974	0.20	0.90	2.00	7.00	75.00	150	—
1939	5,661,123	0.15	0.30	1.25	3.00	30.00	80.00	—
1940	13,920,197	0.15	0.20	0.75	2.25	18.00	55.00	—
1941	8,681,785	0.10	0.20	0.75	2.25	23.00	70.00	—
1942 Round	6,847,544	0.15	0.20	0.75	1.75	18.00	35.00	—

KM# 39 5 CENTS **Composition:** Tombac **Ruler:** George VI **Obverse:** Head left **Obv. Designer:** T. H. Paget **Reverse:** Beaver on rock divides denomination and date **Rev. Designer:** George E. Kruger-Gray **Shape:** 12-sided **Size:** 21.2 mm.

Date	Mintage	VG-8	F-12	VF-20	XF-40	MS-60	MS-63	Proof
1942	3,396,234	0.40	0.65	1.25	1.75	3.00	14.00	—

KM# 40 5 CENTS **Composition:** Tombac **Ruler:** George VI **Subject:** Victory **Obverse:** Head left **Obv. Designer:** T. H. Paget **Reverse:** Torch on "V" divides date **Rev. Designer:** Thomas Shingles **Size:** 21.2 mm.

Date	Mintage	VG-8	F-12	VF-20	XF-40	MS-60	MS-63	Proof
1943	24,760,256	0.20	0.30	0.40	0.80	3.00	9.00	—
1944	8,000	—	—	—	—	—	—	—
Note: 1 known								

KM# 40a 5 CENTS **Composition:** Chrome Plated Steel **Ruler:** George VI **Obverse:** Head left **Reverse:** Torch on "V" divides date **Size:** 21.2 mm.

Date	Mintage	VG-8	F-12	VF-20	XF-40	MS-60	MS-63	Proof
1944	11,532,784	0.15	0.20	0.40	0.90	2.00	4.00	—
1945	18,893,216	0.15	0.20	0.40	0.80	2.00	4.00	—

Dot Maple leaf

KM# 39a 5 CENTS **Composition:** Nickel **Ruler:** George VI **Obverse:** Head left **Obv. Designer:** T. H. Paget **Reverse:** Beaver on rock divides denomination and date **Rev. Designer:** George E. Kruger-Gray **Size:** 21.2 mm.

Date	Mintage	VG-8	F-12	VF-20	XF-40	MS-60	MS-63	Proof
1946	6,952,684	0.15	0.20	0.50	2.00	14.00	32.00	—
1947	7,603,724	0.15	0.20	0.50	1.25	10.00	25.00	—
1947 Dot	Inc. above	12.00	20.00	27.00	60.00	175	300	—
1947 Maple leaf	9,595,124	0.15	0.20	0.45	1.25	10.00	25.00	—

KM# 42 5 CENTS **Composition:** Nickel **Ruler:** George VI **Obverse:** Head left, modified legend **Obv. Designer:** T. H. Paget **Reverse:** Beaver on rock divides date and denomination **Rev. Designer:** George E. Kruger-Gray **Size:** 21.2 mm.

Date	Mintage	VG-8	F-12	VF-20	XF-40	MS-60	MS-63	Proof
1948	1,810,789	0.40	0.50	1.00	3.00	18.00	35.00	—
1949	13,037,090	0.15	0.20	0.35	0.75	6.00	12.00	—
1950	11,970,521	0.15	0.20	0.35	0.75	6.00	12.00	—

KM# 42a 5 CENTS **Composition:** Chromium And Nickel-Plated Steel **Ruler:** George VI **Obverse:** Head left **Obv. Designer:** T. H. Paget **Reverse:** Beaver on rock divides date and denomination **Rev. Designer:** George E. Kruger-Gray **Size:** 21.2 mm.

Date	Mintage	VG-8	F-12	VF-20	XF-40	MS-60	MS-63	Proof
1951	4,313,410	0.15	0.25	0.50	0.80	2.50	7.00	—
Note: Low relief; Second "A" in GRATIA points between denticles								
1951	Inc. above	400	525	700	1,000	1,900	3,100	—
Note: High relief; Second "A" in GRATIA points to a denticle								
1952	10,891,148	0.15	0.20	0.45	0.80	3.00	7.50	—

KM# 48 5 CENTS **Composition:** Nickel **Ruler:** George VI **Subject:** Nickel Bicentennial **Obverse:** Head left **Obv. Designer:** T. H. Paget **Reverse:** Buildings with center tower divide dates and denomination **Rev. Designer:** Stephen Trenka **Shape:** 12-sided **Size:** 21.2 mm.

Date	Mintage	VG-8	F-12	VF-20	XF-40	MS-60	MS-63	Proof
ND(1951)	9,028,507	0.15	0.20	0.25	0.45	1.75	5.50	—

KM# 50 5 CENTS **Composition:** Chromium And Nickel-Plated Steel **Ruler:** Elizabeth II **Obverse:** Laureate queen's bust, right **Obv. Designer:** Mary Gillick **Reverse:** Beaver on rock divides date and denomination **Rev. Designer:** George E. Kruger-Gray **Shape:** 12-sided **Size:** 21.2 mm.

Date	Mintage	VG-8	F-12	VF-20	XF-40	MS-60	MS-63	Proof
1953	16,635,552	0.15	0.20	0.40	0.90	3.00	4.50	—
Note: Without strap								
1953	Inc. above	200	350	500	750	1,300	2,300	—
Note: Without strap, near leaf								
1953	Inc. above	150	225	300	475	1,100	2,300	—
Note: With strap, far leaf								
1953	Inc. above	0.15	0.20	0.40	0.90	3.50	7.00	—
Note: With strap								
1954	6,998,662	0.15	0.25	0.50	1.00	4.00	8.00	—

KM# 50a 5 CENTS **Composition:** Nickel **Ruler:** Elizabeth II **Obverse:** Laureate queen's bust right **Obv. Designer:** Mary Gillick **Reverse:** Beaver on rock divides date and denomination **Rev. Designer:** George E. Kruger-Gray **Size:** 21.2 mm.

Date	Mintage	VG-8	F-12	VF-20	XF-40	MS-60	MS-63	Proof
1955	5,355,028	0.15	0.25	0.40	0.75	2.50	4.50	—
1956	9,399,854	—	0.20	0.30	0.45	2.25	3.50	—
1957	7,387,703	—	—	0.25	0.30	1.25	3.00	—
1958	7,607,521	—	—	0.25	0.30	1.25	3.00	—
1959	11,552,523	—	—	—	0.20	0.40	1.50	—
1960	37,157,433	—	—	—	0.15	0.50	1.50	—
1961	47,889,051	—	—	—	—	0.30	0.80	—
1962	46,307,305	—	—	—	—	0.30	0.80	—

KM# 57 5 CENTS **Composition:** Nickel **Ruler:** Elizabeth II **Obverse:** Laureate queen's bust right **Obv. Designer:** Mary Gillick **Reverse:** Beaver on rock divides date and denomination **Rev. Designer:** George E. Kruger-Gray **Shape:** Round **Size:** 21.2 mm.

Date	Mintage	VG-8	F-12	VF-20	XF-40	MS-60	MS-63	Proof
1963	43,970,320	—	—	—	—	0.20	0.50	—
1964	78,075,068	—	—	—	—	0.20	0.50	—
1964	—	8.00	10.00	12.00	17.00	30.00	60.00	—
Note: Extra water line								

KM# 60.1 5 CENTS **Weight:** 4.5400 g. **Composition:** Nickel **Ruler:** Elizabeth II **Obverse:** Queen's bust right **Obv. Designer:** Arnold Machin **Reverse:** Beaver on rock divides date and denomination **Rev. Designer:** George E. Kruger-Gray **Size:** 21.2 mm.

Date	Mintage	VG-8	F-12	VF-20	XF-40	MS-60	MS-63	Proof
1965	84,876,018	—	—	—	—	0.20	0.30	—
1966	27,976,648	—	—	—	—	0.20	0.30	—
1968	101,930,379	—	—	—	—	0.20	0.30	—
1969	27,830,229	—	—	—	—	0.20	0.30	—
1970	5,726,010	—	—	—	0.20	0.35	0.75	—
1971	27,312,609	—	—	—	—	0.20	0.30	—
1972	62,417,387	—	—	—	—	0.20	0.30	—
1973	53,507,435	—	—	—	—	0.20	0.30	—
1974	94,704,645	—	—	—	—	0.20	0.30	—
1975	138,882,000	—	—	—	—	0.20	0.30	—
1976	55,140,213	—	—	—	—	0.20	0.30	—
1977	89,120,791	—	—	—	—	0.20	0.30	—
1978	137,079,273	—	—	—	—	0.20	0.30	—

KM# 66 5 CENTS **Composition:** Nickel **Ruler:** Elizabeth II **Subject:** Confederation Centennial **Obverse:** Queen's bust right **Obv. Designer:** Arnold Machin **Reverse:** Snowshoe rabbit bounding left divides dates and denomination **Rev. Designer:** Alex Coville **Size:** 21.2 mm.

Date	Mintage	VG-8	F-12	VF-20	XF-40	MS-60	MS-63	Proof
ND(1967)	36,876,574	—	—	—	—	0.20	0.40	1.00

KM# 60.2 5 CENTS **Composition:** Nickel **Ruler:** Elizabeth II **Obverse:** Queen's bust right **Obv. Designer:** Arnold Machin **Reverse:** Beaver on rock divides date and denomination **Rev. Designer:** George E. Kruger-Gray **Size:** 21.2 mm.

Date	Mintage	VG-8	F-12	VF-20	XF-40	MS-60	MS-63	Proof
1979	186,295,825	—	—	—	—	0.20	0.30	—
1980	134,878,000	—	—	—	—	0.20	0.30	—
1981	99,107,900	—	—	—	—	0.20	0.30	—
1981 Proof	199,000	—	—	—	—	—	—	1.50

KM# 60.2a 5 CENTS **Weight:** 4.6000 g. **Composition:** Copper-Nickel **Ruler:** Elizabeth II **Obverse:** Queen's bust right **Obv. Designer:** Arnold Machin **Reverse:** Beaver on rock divides date and denomination **Rev. Designer:** George E. Kruger-Gray **Size:** 21.2 mm.

Date	Mintage	VG-8	F-12	VF-20	XF-40	MS-60	MS-63	Proof
1982	64,924,400	—	—	—	—	0.20	0.30	—
1982 Proof	180,908	—	—	—	—	—	—	1.50
1983	72,596,000	—	—	—	—	0.20	0.30	—
1983 Proof	168,000	—	—	—	—	—	—	1.50
1984	84,088,000	—	—	—	—	0.20	0.30	—
1984 Proof	161,602	—	—	—	—	—	—	1.50
1985	126,618,000	—	—	—	—	0.20	0.30	—
1985 Proof	157,037	—	—	—	—	—	—	1.50
1986	156,104,000	—	—	—	—	0.20	0.30	—
1986 Proof	175,745	—	—	—	—	—	—	1.50
1987	106,299,000	—	—	—	—	0.15	0.30	—
1987 Proof	179,004	—	—	—	—	—	—	1.50
1988	75,025,000	—	—	—	—	0.15	0.30	—
1988 Proof	175,259	—	—	—	—	—	—	1.50
1989	141,570,538	—	—	—	—	0.15	0.30	—
1989 Proof	170,928	—	—	—	—	—	—	1.50

KM# 182 5 CENTS **Weight:** 4.6000 g. **Composition:** Copper-Nickel **Ruler:** Elizabeth II **Obverse:** Crowned head right **Obv. Designer:** Dora dePedery-Hunt **Reverse:** Beaver on rock divides dates and denomination **Rev. Designer:** George E. Kruger-Gray **Size:** 21.2 mm.

Date	Mintage	VG-8	F-12	VF-20	XF-40	MS-60	MS-63	Proof
1990	42,537,000	—	—	—	—	0.15	0.30	—
1990 Proof	140,649	—	—	—	—	—	—	2.50
1991	10,931,000	—	—	—	—	0.30	0.55	—
1991 Proof	131,888	—	—	—	—	—	—	7.00
1993	86,877,000	—	—	—	—	0.15	0.30	—
1993 Proof	143,065	—	—	—	—	—	—	2.50
1994	99,352,000	—	—	—	—	0.15	0.30	—
1994 Proof	146,424	—	—	—	—	—	—	3.00
1995	78,528,000	—	—	—	—	0.15	0.30	—
1995 Proof	50,000	—	—	—	—	—	—	2.50
1996 Far 6	36,686,000	—	—	—	—	0.75	2.25	—
1996 Near 6	Inc. above	—	—	—	—	0.70	2.25	—
1996 Proof	—	—	—	—	—	—	—	6.00
1997	27,354,000	—	—	—	—	0.15	0.30	—
1997 Proof	—	—	—	—	—	—	—	5.00
1998	156,873,000	—	—	—	—	0.15	0.30	—
1998W	—	—	—	—	—	—	1.50	—
1998 Proof	—	—	—	—	—	—	—	5.00
1999	124,861,000	—	—	—	—	0.15	0.30	—
1999W	—	—	—	—	—	—	—	—
1999 Proof	—	—	—	—	—	—	—	5.00
2000	108,514,000	—	—	—	—	0.15	0.30	—
2000W	—	—	—	—	—	—	1.50	—
2000 Proof	—	—	—	—	—	—	—	5.00

KM# 205 5 CENTS **Composition:** Copper-Nickel **Ruler:** Elizabeth II **Subject:** Confederation 125 **Obverse:** Crowned Queen's head right **Obv. Designer:** Dora dePedery-Hunt **Reverse:** Beaver on rock divides date and denomination **Rev. Designer:** George E. Kruger-Gray **Size:** 21.2 mm.

Date	Mintage	VG-8	F-12	VF-20	XF-40	MS-60	MS-63	Proof
ND(1992)	53,732,000	—	—	—	—	0.15	0.30	—
ND(1992) Proof	147,061	—	—	—	—	—	—	4.00

KM# 182a 5 CENTS **Weight:** 5.3500 g. **Composition:** 0.9250 Silver 0.1591 oz. ASW **Ruler:** Elizabeth II **Obverse:** Crowned head right **Obv. Designer:** Dora dePedery-Hunt **Reverse:** Beaver on rock divides date and denomination **Rev. Designer:** George E. Kruger-Gray **Size:** 21.2 mm.

Date	Mintage	MS-63	Proof
1996 Proof	—	—	5.00
1997 Proof	—	—	5.00
1998 Proof	—	—	5.00
19980 Proof	—	—	5.00
1999 Proof	—	—	5.00
2000 Proof	—	—	5.00

KM# 182b 5 CENTS **Weight:** 3.9000 g. **Composition:** Nickel Plated Steel **Ruler:** Elizabeth II **Obverse:** Crowned head right **Obv. Designer:** Dora dePedery-Hunt **Reverse:** Beaver on rock divides date and denomination **Rev. Designer:** George E. Kruger-Gray **Edge:** Plain **Size:** 21.2 mm.

Date	Mintage	VG-8	F-12	VF-20	XF-40	MS-60	MS-63	Proof
1999 P	Est. 20,000	—	—	—	—	—	15.00	—
2000 P	Est. 2,300,000	—	—	—	—	1.50	3.50	—

KM# 310 5 CENTS **Weight:** 1.1670 g. **Composition:** 0.9250 Silver .0347 oz. ASW **Ruler:** Elizabeth II **Subject:** 90th Anniversary Royal Canadian Mint **Obverse:** Crowned Queen's head, right **Obv. Designer:** Dora dePedery-Hunt **Reverse:** Denomination and date within wreath, crown above **Rev. Designer:** W. H. J. Blackmore

Date	Mintage	MS-63	Proof
ND(1998)	25,000	12.00	—
ND(1998) Proof	25,000	—	12.00

KM# 400 5 CENTS **Composition:** 0.9250 Silver **Ruler:** Elizabeth II **Subject:** First French-Canadian Regiment **Obverse:** Crowned Queen's head right **Obv. Designer:** Dora dePedery-Hunt **Reverse:** Regimental drums, sash and baton, denomination above, date at right **Rev. Designer:** R. C. M. Staff **Edge:** Plain **Size:** 21.2 mm.

Date	Mintage	MS-63	Proof
2000 Proof	—	—	9.00

KM# 3 10 CENTS **Weight:** 2.3240 g. **Composition:** 0.9250 Silver 0.0691 oz. ASW **Ruler:** Victoria **Obverse:** Victoria head left **Reverse:** Denomination and date within wreath, crown above **Edge:** Reeded **Size:** 18.03 mm.

Date	Mintage	VG-8	F-12	VF-20	XF-40	MS-60	MS-63	Proof
1901	1,200,000	8.50	18.00	40.00	85.00	225	650	—

KM# 10 10 CENTS **Weight:** 2.3240 g. **Composition:** 0.9250 Silver 0.0691 oz. ASW **Ruler:** Edward VII **Obverse:** King's bust right **Obv. Designer:** G. W. DeSaulles **Reverse:** Denomination and date within wreath, crown above **Rev. Designer:** Leonard C. Wyon **Edge:** Reeded **Size:** 18.03 mm.

Date	Mintage	VG-8	F-12	VF-20	XF-40	MS-60	MS-63	Proof
1902	720,000	8.00	16.00	30.00	80.00	325	1,100	—
1902H	1,100,000	4.00	8.00	18.00	40.00	100	250	—
1903	500,000	14.00	30.00	75.00	200	1,000	2,100	—
1903H	1,320,000	7.00	16.00	30.00	65.00	250	550	—
1904	1,000,000	11.00	24.00	45.00	100	325	700	—
1905	1,000,000	6.50	24.00	55.00	100	475	1,100	—
1906	1,700,000	6.50	12.00	30.00	60.00	275	750	—
1907	2,620,000	4.25	11.00	23.00	40.00	200	425	—
1908	776,666	8.00	24.00	55.00	95.00	200	400	—
1909	1,697,200	6.00	18.00	40.00	95.00	375	1,000	—
Note: "Victorian" leaves, similar to 1902-08 coins								
1909	Inc. above	10.00	27.00	55.00	125	500	1,300	—
Note: Broad leaves, similar to 1910-12 coins								
1910	4,468,331	4.00	8.00	18.00	35.00	125	300	—

KM# 17 10 CENTS **Weight:** 2.3240 g. **Composition:** 0.9250 Silver 0.0691 oz. ASW **Ruler:** George V **Obverse:** King's bust left **Obv. Designer:** E. B. MacKennal **Reverse:** Denomination and date within wreath, crown above **Rev. Designer:** Leonard C. Wyon **Edge:** Reeded **Size:** 18.03 mm.

Date	Mintage	VG-8	F-12	VF-20	XF-40	MS-60	MS-63	Proof
1911	2,737,584	4.50	11.00	18.00	40.00	100	200	—

Small leaves

Broad leaves

KM# 23 10 CENTS **Weight:** 2.3240 g. **Composition:** 0.9250 Silver 0.0691 oz. ASW **Ruler:** George V **Obverse:** King's bust left **Obv. Designer:** E. B. MacKennal **Reverse:** Denomination and date within wreath, crown above **Rev. Designer:** Leonard C. Wyon **Edge:** Reeded **Size:** 18.03 mm.

Date	Mintage	VG-8	F-12	VF-20	XF-40	MS-60	MS-63	Proof
1912	3,235,557	1.75	4.25	9.00	30.00	175	500	—
1913	3,613,937	1.50	2.25	8.50	23.00	125	325	—
Note: Small leaves								
1913	Inc. above	95.00	175	350	900	5,600	20,000	—
Note: Large leaves								
1914	2,549,811	1.50	2.50	8.50	25.00	125	375	—
1915	688,057	6.00	15.00	30.00	100	325	650	—
1916	4,218,114	1.25	2.25	4.00	17.00	75.00	225	—
1917	5,011,988	1.00	1.50	3.00	10.00	50.00	95.00	—
1918	5,133,602	1.00	1.50	3.00	9.00	45.00	80.00	—
1919	7,877,722	1.00	1.50	3.00	9.00	45.00	80.00	—

KM# 23a 10 CENTS **Weight:** 2.3328 g. **Composition:** 0.8000 Silver 0.0600 oz. ASW **Ruler:** George V **Obverse:** King's bust left **Obv. Designer:** Leonard C. Wyon **Reverse:** Denomination and date within wreath, crown above **Edge:** Reeded **Size:** 18.03 mm.

Date	Mintage	VG-8	F-12	VF-20	XF-40	MS-60	MS-63	Proof
1920	6,305,345	1.00	1.50	3.00	12.00	50.00	125	—
1921	2,469,562	1.25	2.00	6.00	20.00	80.00	225	—
1928	2,458,602	1.00	1.75	4.00	12.00	55.00	125	—
1929	3,253,888	1.00	2.00	3.50	12.00	55.00	100	—
1930	1,831,043	1.00	2.50	4.50	14.00	60.00	125	—
1931	2,067,421	1.00	1.75	4.00	12.00	55.00	100	—
1932	1,154,317	1.50	2.50	9.00	23.00	90.00	225	—
1933	672,368	2.00	4.50	12.00	35.00	175	350	—
1934	409,067	3.00	6.00	22.00	60.00	250	500	—
1935	384,056	3.50	6.00	19.00	60.00	250	500	—
1936	2,460,871	1.00	1.25	3.00	9.00	45.00	80.00	—
1936 Dot on reverse	—	—	—	—	—	—	—	—

Note: Specimen, 4 known; David Akers sale of John Jay Pittman collection, Part 1, 10-97, a gem specimen realized $120,000

Maple leaf

KM# 34 10 CENTS **Weight:** 2.3328 g. **Composition:** 0.8000 Silver 0.0600 oz. ASW **Ruler:** George VI **Obverse:** Head left **Obv. Designer:** T. H. Paget **Reverse:** Sailboat, date at right, denomination below **Rev. Designer:** Emanuel Hahn **Edge:** Reeded **Size:** 18.03 mm.

Date	Mintage	VG-8	F-12	VF-20	XF-40	MS-60	MS-63	Proof
1937	2,500,095	BV	1.00	2.00	3.75	12.00	18.00	—
1938	4,197,323	0.85	1.75	3.25	6.50	40.00	90.00	—
1939	5,501,748	BV	1.25	2.50	5.00	45.00	95.00	—
1940	16,526,470	—	BV	1.50	3.00	15.00	30.00	—
1941	8,716,386	BV	1.25	2.50	6.00	35.00	90.00	—
1942	10,214,011	—	BV	1.25	4.00	30.00	50.00	—
1943	21,143,229	—	BV	1.25	4.00	18.00	35.00	—
1944	9,383,582	—	BV	1.50	4.50	25.00	45.00	—
1945	10,979,570	—	BV	1.25	4.00	18.00	27.00	—
1946	6,300,066	BV	1.00	2.00	4.50	30.00	50.00	—
1947	4,431,926	BV	1.25	2.50	6.00	30.00	50.00	—
1947	9,638,793	—	BV	1.50	3.00	10.00	15.00	—
Note: Maple leaf								

KM# 43 10 CENTS **Weight:** 2.3328 g. **Composition:** 0.8000 Silver 0.0600 oz. ASW **Ruler:** George VI **Obverse:** Head left, modified legend **Obv. Designer:** T. H. Paget **Reverse:** Sailboat, date at right, denomination below **Rev. Designer:** Emanuel Hahn **Size:** 18.03 mm.

Date	Mintage	VG-8	F-12	VF-20	XF-40	MS-60	MS-63	Proof
1948	422,741	2.00	3.50	7.50	13.00	45.00	70.00	—
1949	11,336,172	—	BV	0.85	2.00	9.00	13.00	—
1950	17,823,075	—	—	BV	1.50	8.00	12.00	—
1951	15,079,265	—	—	BV	1.50	6.00	11.00	—
1951	—	—	1.50	2.50	7.00	22.00	40.00	—
Note: Doubled die								
1952	10,474,455	—	—	BV	1.50	5.00	9.00	—

KM# 51 10 CENTS **Weight:** 2.3328 g. **Composition:** 0.8000 Silver 0.0600 oz. ASW **Ruler:** Elizabeth II **Obverse:** Laureate queen's bust right **Obv. Designer:** Mary Gillick **Reverse:** Sailboat, date at right, denomination below **Rev. Designer:** Emanuel Hahn **Size:** 18.03 mm.

Date	Mintage	VG-8	F-12	VF-20	XF-40	MS-60	MS-63	Proof
1953	17,706,395	—	BV	0.85	1.25	3.00	6.00	—
Note: Without straps								
1953	Inc. above	—	BV	0.85	1.25	5.00	8.00	—
Note: With straps								
1954	4,493,150	—	BV	1.00	2.25	10.00	18.00	—
1955	12,237,294	—	—	BV	0.85	3.00	7.00	—
1956	16,732,844	—	—	BV	0.85	3.00	6.00	—
1956	Inc. above	—	2.25	3.00	4.50	13.00	22.00	—
Note: Dot below date								
1957	16,110,229	—	—	—	BV	1.50	2.25	—
1958	10,621,236	—	—	—	BV	1.50	2.25	—
1959	19,691,433	—	—	—	BV	1.25	2.00	—
1960	45,446,835	—	—	—	BV	1.00	1.50	—
1961	26,850,859	—	—	—	BV	0.85	1.50	—
1962	41,864,335	—	—	—	BV	0.80	1.50	—
1963	41,916,208	—	—	—	BV	0.80	1.00	—
1964	49,518,549	—	—	—	BV	0.80	1.00	—

KM# 61 10 CENTS **Weight:** 2.3328 g. **Composition:** 0.8000 Silver 0.0600 oz. ASW **Ruler:** Elizabeth II **Obverse:** Queen's bust right **Obv. Designer:** Arnold Machin **Reverse:** Sailboat, date at right, denomination below **Size:** 18.03 mm.

Date	Mintage	VG-8	F-12	VF-20	XF-40	MS-60	MS-63	Proof
1965	56,965,392	—	—	—	BV	0.80	1.00	—
1966	34,567,898	—	—	—	BV	0.80	1.00	—

KM# 67 10 CENTS **Weight:** 2.3328 g. **Composition:** 0.8000 Silver 0.0600 oz. ASW **Ruler:** Elizabeth II **Subject:** Confederation Centennial **Obverse:** Bust right **Reverse:** Atlantic mackeral left, denomination above, dates below **Rev. Designer:** Alex Colville **Size:** 18.03 mm.

Date	Mintage	VG-8	F-12	VF-20	XF-40	MS-60	MS-63	Proof
ND(1967)	62,998,215	—	—	—	BV	0.60	1.20	2.00

KM# 67a 10 CENTS **Weight:** 2.3328 g. **Composition:** 0.5000 Silver 0.0372 oz. ASW **Ruler:** Elizabeth II **Subject:** Confederation Centennial **Obverse:** Bust right **Reverse:** Fish left, denomination above dates below **Size:** 18.03 mm.

Date	Mintage	VG-8	F-12	VF-20	XF-40	MS-60	MS-63	Proof
ND(1967)	Inc. above	—	—	—	BV	0.55	1.00	—

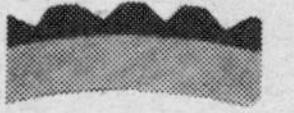

Ottawa reeding

KM# 72 10 CENTS **Weight:** 2.3328 g. **Composition:** 0.5000 Silver 0.0375 oz. ASW **Obv. Designer:** Arnold Machin **Rev. Designer:** Emanuel Hahn **Size:** 18.03 mm.

Date	Mintage	VG-8	F-12	VF-20	XF-40	MS-60	MS-63	Proof
1968	70,460,000	—	—	—	BV	0.50	0.90	—
Note: Ottawa reeding								

KM# 72a 10 CENTS **Composition:** Nickel **Obv. Designer:** Arnold Machin **Rev. Designer:** Emanuel Hahn **Size:** 18.03 mm.

Date	Mintage	VG-8	F-12	VF-20	XF-40	MS-60	MS-63	Proof
1968	87,412,930	—	—	—	0.15	0.20	0.35	—
Note: Ottawa reeding								

Philadelphia reeding

KM# 73 10 CENTS **Composition:** Nickel **Ruler:** Elizabeth II **Obverse:** Queen's bust right **Obv. Designer:** Arnold Machin **Reverse:** Sailboat, date at right, denomination below **Rev. Designer:** Emanuel Hahn **Size:** 18.03 mm.

Date	Mintage	VG-8	F-12	VF-20	XF-40	MS-60	MS-63	Proof
1968	85,170,000	—	—	—	0.15	0.25	0.35	—
Note: Philadelphia reeding								
1969	—	—	6,100	8,300	11,000	19,000	—	—
Note: Large date, large ship, 10-20 known								

KM# 77.1 10 CENTS **Weight:** 2.0700 g. **Composition:** Nickel **Ruler:** Elizabeth II **Obverse:** Bust right **Obv. Designer:** Arnold Machin **Reverse:** Redesigned smaller sailboat, date at right, denomination below **Rev. Designer:** Emanuel Hahn **Size:** 18.03 mm.

Date	Mintage	VG-8	F-12	VF-20	XF-40	MS-60	MS-63	Proof
1969	55,833,929	—	—	—	0.15	0.25	0.35	—
1970	5,249,296	—	—	—	0.25	0.40	0.90	—
1971	41,016,968	—	—	—	0.15	0.20	0.35	—
1972	60,169,387	—	—	—	0.15	0.20	0.35	—
1973	167,715,435	—	—	—	0.15	0.20	0.35	—
1974	201,566,565	—	—	—	0.15	0.20	0.35	—
1975	207,680,000	—	—	—	0.15	0.20	0.35	—
1976	95,018,533	—	—	—	0.15	0.20	0.35	—
1977	128,452,206	—	—	—	0.15	0.20	0.35	—
1978	170,366,431	—	—	—	0.15	0.20	0.35	—

KM# 77.2 10 CENTS **Weight:** 2.0700 g. **Composition:** Nickel **Ruler:** Elizabeth II **Obverse:** Smaller bust right **Obv. Designer:** Arnold Machin **Reverse:** Redesigned smaller sailboat, denomination below, date at right **Rev. Designer:** Emanuel Hahn **Size:** 18.03 mm.

Date	Mintage	VG-8	F-12	VF-20	XF-40	MS-60	MS-63	Proof
1979	237,321,321	—	—	—	0.15	0.20	0.35	—
1980	170,111,533	—	—	—	0.15	0.20	0.35	—
1981	123,912,900	—	—	—	0.15	0.20	0.35	—
1981 Proof	199,000	—	—	—	—	—	—	1.50
1982	93,475,000	—	—	—	0.15	0.20	0.35	—
1982 Proof	180,908	—	—	—	—	—	—	1.50
1983	111,065,000	—	—	—	0.15	0.20	0.35	—
1983 Proof	168,000	—	—	—	—	—	—	1.50
1984	121,690,000	—	—	—	0.15	0.20	0.35	—
1984 Proof	161,602	—	—	—	—	—	—	1.50
1985	143,025,000	—	—	—	0.15	0.20	0.35	—
1985 Proof	157,037	—	—	—	—	—	—	1.50
1986	168,620,000	—	—	—	0.15	0.20	0.35	—
1986 Proof	175,745	—	—	—	—	—	—	1.50
1987	147,309,000	—	—	—	0.15	0.20	0.35	—
1987 Proof	179,004	—	—	—	—	—	—	1.50
1988	162,998,558	—	—	—	0.15	0.20	0.35	—
1988 Proof	175,259	—	—	—	—	—	—	1.50
1989	199,104,414	—	—	—	0.15	0.20	0.35	—
1989 Proof	170,528	—	—	—	—	—	—	1.50

KM# 183 10 CENTS **Composition:** Nickel **Ruler:** Elizabeth II **Obverse:** Crowned head right **Obv. Designer:** Dora dePedery-Hunt **Reverse:** Sailboat, date at right, denomination below **Rev. Designer:** Emanuel Hahn **Size:** 18.03 mm.

Date	Mintage	VG-8	F-12	VF-20	XF-40	MS-60	MS-63	Proof
1990	65,023,000	—	—	—	0.15	0.20	0.35	—
1990 Proof	140,649	—	—	—	—	—	—	2.50
1991	50,397,000	—	—	—	0.15	0.30	0.45	—
1991 Proof	131,888	—	—	—	—	—	—	4.00
1993	135,569,000	—	—	—	0.15	0.20	0.35	—
1993 Proof	143,065	—	—	—	—	—	—	2.00
1994	145,800,000	—	—	—	0.15	0.20	0.35	—
1994 Proof	146,424	—	—	—	—	—	—	2.50
1995	123,875,000	—	—	—	0.15	0.20	0.35	—
1995 Proof	50,000	—	—	—	—	—	—	2.50
1996	51,814,000	—	—	—	0.15	0.20	0.35	—
1996 Proof	—	—	—	—	—	—	—	2.50
1997	43,126,000	—	—	—	0.15	0.20	0.35	—
1997 Proof	—	—	—	—	—	—	—	2.50
1998	203,514,000	—	—	—	0.15	0.20	0.35	—
1998W	—	—	—	—	—	—	1.50	—
1998 Proof	—	—	—	—	—	—	—	2.50
1999	258,462,000	—	—	—	0.15	0.20	0.35	—
1999 Proof	—	—	—	—	—	—	—	2.50
2000	159,125,000	—	—	—	0.15	0.20	0.35	—
2000 Proof	—	—	—	—	—	—	—	2.50
2000W	—	—	—	—	—	—	1.50	—

KM# 183a 10 CENTS **Weight:** 2.4000 g. **Composition:** 0.9250 Silver 0.0713 oz. ASW **Ruler:** Elizabeth II **Obverse:** Crowned head right **Reverse:** Sailboat, date at right, denomination below **Size:** 18.03 mm.

Date	Mintage	MS-63	Proof
1996 Proof	—	—	5.50
1997 Proof	—	—	5.50
1998 Proof	—	—	4.00
1998O Proof	—	—	4.00
1999 Proof	—	—	5.00
2000 Proof	—	—	5.00

KM# 183b 10 CENTS **Composition:** Nickel Plated Steel **Ruler:** Elizabeth II **Obverse:** Crowned head right **Obv. Designer:** Dora dePedery-Hunt **Reverse:** Sailboat, date at right, denomination below **Rev. Designer:** Emanuel Hahn **Edge:** Reeded **Size:** 18.03 mm.

Date	Mintage	MS-63	Proof
1999 P	Est. 20,000	15.00	—
2000 P	Est. 200	1,000	—

KM# 206 10 CENTS **Composition:** Nickel **Ruler:** Elizabeth II **Subject:** Confederation 125 **Obverse:** Crowned queen's head right **Reverse:** Sailboat, date at right, denomination below **Size:** 18.03 mm.

Date	Mintage	VG-8	F-12	VF-20	XF-40	MS-60	MS-63	Proof
ND(1992)	174,476,000	—	—	—	—	0.25	0.35	—
ND(1992) Proof	147,061	—	—	—	—	—	—	3.00

KM# 299 10 CENTS **Weight:** 2.4000 g. **Composition:** 0.9250 Silver .0714 oz. ASW **Ruler:** Elizabeth II **Subject:** John Cabot **Obverse:** Crowned queen's head right **Reverse:** Ship with full sails divides dates, denomination below **Rev. Designer:** Donald H. Curley **Size:** 18.03 mm.

Date	Mintage	MS-63	Proof
ND(1997) Proof	49,848	—	17.50

KM# 311 10 CENTS **Weight:** 2.3200 g. **Composition:** 0.9250 Silver .0690 oz. ASW **Ruler:** Elizabeth II **Subject:** 90th Anniversary Royal Canadian Mint **Obverse:** Crowned head right **Reverse:** Denomination and date within wreath, crown above **Size:** 18.03 mm.

Date	Mintage	MS-63	Proof
ND(1998) Matte	25,000	—	10.00
ND(1998) Proof	25,000	—	10.00

KM# 409 10 CENTS **Weight:** 2.4000 g. **Composition:** 0.9250 Silver .0714 oz. ASW **Subject:** First Canadian Credit Union **Obverse:** Crowned queen's head right **Reverse:** Alphonse Desjardins' house (founder of the first credit union in Canada), dates at right, denomination below **Edge:** Reeded **Size:** 18.03 mm.

Date	Mintage	MS-63	Proof
ND(2000) Proof	66,336	—	8.00

KM# 5 25 CENTS **Weight:** 5.8100 g. **Composition:** 0.9250 Silver 0.1728 oz. ASW **Ruler:** Victoria **Obverse:** Victoria's head left **Obv. Designer:** Leonard C. Wyon **Reverse:** Denomination above date within wreath, crown above **Size:** 23.88 mm.

Date	Mintage	VG-8	F-12	VF-20	XF-40	MS-60	MS-63	Proof
1901	640,000	12.00	22.00	50.00	150	550	1,200	—

KM# 11 25 CENTS **Weight:** 5.8100 g. **Composition:** 0.9250 Silver 0.1728 oz. ASW **Ruler:** Edward VII **Obverse:** King's bust right **Obv. Designer:** G. W. DeSaulles **Reverse:** Denomination and date within wreath, crown above **Size:** 23.4 mm.

Date	Mintage	VG-8	F-12	VF-20	XF-40	MS-60	MS-63	Proof
1902	464,000	10.00	27.00	65.00	175	750	1,900	—
1902H	800,000	6.50	16.00	45.00	100	250	500	—
1903	846,150	15.00	29.00	75.00	200	800	1,900	—
1904	400,000	20.00	55.00	150	350	1,600	5,000	—
1905	800,000	15.00	30.00	100	300	1,400	4,600	—
1906	1,237,843	8.00	21.00	55.00	225	750	1,700	—
Note: Large crown								
1906 Rare	Inc. above	2,500	3,900	6,000	8,000	—	16,000	—
Note: Small crown								
1907	2,088,000	6.50	16.00	55.00	125	425	1,200	—
1908	495,016	15.00	35.00	95.00	200	400	750	—
1909	1,335,929	13.00	26.00	70.00	175	600	1,700	—

KM# 11a 25 CENTS **Weight:** 5.8319 g. **Composition:** 0.9250 Silver 0.1734 oz. ASW
Ruler: Edward VII **Obverse:** Bust right **Reverse:** Denomination and date within wreath, crown above

Date	Mintage	VG-8	F-12	VF-20	XF-40	MS-60	MS-63	Proof
1910	3,577,569	5.50	16.00	40.00	85.00	275	600	—

KM# 18 25 CENTS **Weight:** 5.8319 g. **Composition:** 0.9250 Silver 0.1734 oz. ASW
Ruler: George V **Obverse:** King's bust left **Obv. Designer:** E. B. MacKennal **Reverse:** Denomination and date within wreath, crown above

Date	Mintage	VG-8	F-12	VF-20	XF-40	MS-60	MS-63	Proof
1911	1,721,341	6.50	18.00	35.00	85.00	250	425	—

KM# 24 25 CENTS **Weight:** 5.8319 g. **Composition:** 0.9250 Silver 0.1734 oz. ASW
Ruler: George V **Obverse:** King's bust left **Obv. Designer:** E. B. MacKennal **Reverse:** Denomination and date within wreath, crown above **Size:** 23.5 mm.

Date	Mintage	VG-8	F-12	VF-20	XF-40	MS-60	MS-63	Proof
1912	2,544,199	3.75	9.00	20.00	55.00	350	1,200	—
1913	2,213,595	3.25	8.50	17.00	50.00	300	950	—
1914	1,215,397	5.00	10.00	23.00	60.00	500	1,600	—
1915	242,382	16.00	45.00	150	425	2,200	6,100	—
1916	1,462,566	2.75	5.00	18.00	40.00	225	700	—
1917	3,365,644	2.25	4.50	11.00	30.00	125	225	—
1918	4,175,649	2.25	3.00	9.50	26.00	95.00	175	—
1919	5,852,262	2.25	3.00	9.50	25.00	95.00	175	—

Dot

KM# 24a 25 CENTS **Weight:** 5.8319 g. **Composition:** 0.8000 Silver 0.1500 oz. ASW
Ruler: George V **Obverse:** King's bust left **Obv. Designer:** E. B. MacKennal **Reverse:** Denomination and date within wreath, crown below

Date	Mintage	VG-8	F-12	VF-20	XF-40	MS-60	MS-63	Proof
1920	1,975,278	2.50	4.50	12.00	30.00	150	400	—
1921	597,337	11.00	24.00	80.00	225	1,100	2,700	—
1927	468,096	27.00	50.00	100	225	750	1,600	—
1928	2,114,178	2.75	4.50	13.00	35.00	125	325	—
1929	2,690,562	2.00	4.00	13.00	35.00	125	325	—
1930	968,748	2.50	5.00	18.00	40.00	200	500	—
1931	537,815	2.50	5.50	20.00	50.00	200	500	—
1932	537,994	2.50	6.00	25.00	50.00	200	500	—
1933	421,282	3.00	6.50	28.00	65.00	175	325	—
1934	384,350	3.50	9.00	30.00	70.00	225	500	—
1935	537,772	3.50	7.50	22.00	50.00	150	325	—
1936	972,094	2.00	3.50	8.00	21.00	95.00	175	—
1936 Dot	153,322	26.00	65.00	150	300	800	1,800	—

Note: David Akers John Jay Pittman sale Part Three, 10-99, nearly Choice Unc. realized $6,900; considered a possible specimen example

Maple leaf

KM# 35 25 CENTS **Weight:** 5.8319 g. **Composition:** 0.8000 Silver 0.1500 oz. ASW
Ruler: George VI **Obverse:** Head left **Obv. Designer:** T. H. Paget **Reverse:** Moose left, denomination above, date at right **Rev. Designer:** Emanuel Hahn **Size:** 23.5 mm.

Date	Mintage	VG-8	F-12	VF-20	XF-40	MS-60	MS-63	Proof
1937	2,690,176	2.50	2.00	4.00	6.00	16.00	25.00	—
1938	3,149,245	2.00	3.00	5.00	10.00	65.00	125	—
1939	3,532,495	2.00	2.75	5.00	7.00	50.00	75.00	—
1940	9,583,650	—	BV	2.00	2.50	15.00	30.00	—
1941	6,654,672	—	BV	2.00	2.50	16.00	30.00	—
1942	6,935,871	—	BV	2.00	2.50	17.00	45.00	—
1943	13,559,575	—	BV	2.00	2.50	16.00	30.00	—
1944	7,216,237	—	BV	2.00	2.50	26.00	50.00	—
1945	5,296,495	—	BV	2.00	2.50	16.00	30.00	—
1946	2,210,810	BV	2.00	4.00	8.00	45.00	75.00	—
1947	1,524,554	—	BV	4.00	8.00	50.00	95.00	—
1947	Inc. above	30.00	40.00	70.00	150	250	500	—
Note: Dot after 7								
1947	4,393,938	—	BV	2.00	3.00	16.00	32.00	—
Note: Maple leaf								

KM# 44 25 CENTS **Weight:** 5.8319 g. **Composition:** 0.8000 Silver 0.1500 oz. ASW
Ruler: George VI **Obverse:** Head left, modified legend **Obv. Designer:** T. H. Paget **Reverse:** Moose left, denomination above, date at right **Rev. Designer:** Emanuel Hahn **Size:** 23.5 mm.

Date	Mintage	VG-8	F-12	VF-20	XF-40	MS-60	MS-63	Proof
1948	2,564,424	BV	2.00	3.00	13.00	55.00	75.00	—
1949	7,988,830	—	BV	2.00	3.00	10.00	20.00	—
1950	9,673,335	—	—	BV	2.00	8.00	15.00	—
1951	8,290,719	—	—	BV	2.00	7.00	12.00	—
1952	8,859,642	—	—	BV	2.00	6.00	11.00	—

KM# 52 25 CENTS **Weight:** 5.8319 g. **Composition:** 0.8000 Silver 0.1500 oz. ASW
Ruler: Elizabeth II **Obverse:** Laureate Queen's bust, right **Obv. Designer:** Mary Gillick **Reverse:** Moose left, denomination above, date at right **Rev. Designer:** Emanuel Hahn **Size:** 23.8 mm.

Date	Mintage	VG-8	F-12	VF-20	XF-40	MS-60	MS-63	Proof
1953	10,546,769	—	—	BV	2.00	5.00	10.00	—
Note: Without strap								
1953	Inc. above	—	—	BV	2.00	6.50	18.00	—
Note: With strap								
1954	2,318,891	—	BV	2.00	7.00	25.00	40.00	—
1955	9,552,505	—	—	BV	2.00	6.00	15.00	—
1956	11,269,353	—	—	BV	2.00	3.25	6.50	—
1957	12,770,190	—	—	—	BV	2.50	5.00	—
1958	9,336,910	—	—	—	BV	2.50	5.00	—
1959	13,503,461	—	—	—	BV	2.00	3.00	—
1960	22,835,327	—	—	—	BV	2.00	3.00	—
1961	18,164,368	—	—	—	BV	2.00	3.00	—
1962	29,559,266	—	—	—	BV	2.00	2.50	—
1963	21,180,652	—	—	—	BV	2.00	2.25	—
1964	36,479,343	—	—	—	BV	2.00	2.25	—

KM# 62 25 CENTS **Weight:** 5.8319 g. **Composition:** 0.8000 Silver 0.1500 oz. ASW
Ruler: Elizabeth II **Obverse:** Bust right **Obv. Designer:** Arnold Machin **Reverse:** Moose left, denomination above, date at right **Rev. Designer:** Emanuel Hahn **Size:** 23.8 mm.

Date	Mintage	VG-8	F-12	VF-20	XF-40	MS-60	MS-63	Proof
1965	44,708,869	—	—	—	BV	2.00	2.25	—
1966	25,626,315	—	—	—	BV	2.00	2.25	—

KM# 62a 25 CENTS **Weight:** 5.8319 g. **Composition:** 0.5000 Silver 0.0937 oz. ASW
Obverse: Bust right **Obv. Designer:** Machin **Reverse:** Moose left, denomination above, date at right **Size:** 23.8 mm.

Date	Mintage	VG-8	F-12	VF-20	XF-40	MS-60	MS-63	Proof
1968	71,464,000	—	—	—	BV	1.25	1.50	—

KM# 62b 25 CENTS **Weight:** 5.0600 g. **Composition:** Nickel **Ruler:** Elizabeth II
Obverse: Bust right **Obv. Designer:** Machin **Reverse:** Moose left, denomination above, date at right **Size:** 23.8 mm.

Date	Mintage	VG-8	F-12	VF-20	XF-40	MS-60	MS-63	Proof
1968	88,686,931	—	—	—	0.30	0.45	0.75	—
1969	133,037,929	—	—	—	0.30	0.45	0.75	—
1970	10,302,010	—	—	—	0.30	1.00	2.00	—
1971	48,170,428	—	—	—	0.30	0.45	0.75	—
1972	43,743,387	—	—	—	0.30	0.45	0.75	—
1973	135,958,589	—	—	—	0.30	0.50	1.00	—
Note: Small bust								
1973	Inc. above	—	60.00	70.00	80.00	110	200	—
Note: Large bust								
1974	192,360,598	—	—	—	0.30	0.45	0.75	—
1975	141,148,000	—	—	—	0.30	0.45	0.75	—
1976	86,898,261	—	—	—	0.30	0.45	0.75	—
1977	99,634,555	—	—	—	0.30	0.45	0.75	—
1978	176,475,408	—	—	—	0.30	0.45	0.75	—

KM# 68 25 CENTS **Weight:** 5.8319 g. **Composition:** 0.8000 Silver 0.1500 oz. ASW **Ruler:** Elizabeth II **Subject:** Confederation Centennial **Obverse:** Bust right **Reverse:** Lynx striding left divides dates and denomination **Rev. Designer:** Alex Colville **Size:** 23.8 mm.

Date	Mintage	VG-8	F-12	VF-20	XF-40	MS-60	MS-63	Proof
ND(1967)	48,855,500	—	—	—	BV	2.00	2.25	—

KM# 68a 25 CENTS **Weight:** 5.8319 g. **Composition:** 0.5000 Silver 0.0937 oz. ASW **Ruler:** Elizabeth II **Subject:** Confederation Centennial **Obverse:** Bust right **Reverse:** Lynx striding left divides dates and denomination **Size:** 23.8 mm.

Date	Mintage	VG-8	F-12	VF-20	XF-40	MS-60	MS-63	Proof
ND(1967)	Inc. above	—	—	—	BV	1.50	1.75	—

KM# 81.1 25 CENTS **Composition:** Nickel **Ruler:** Elizabeth II **Subject:** Royal Candian Mounted Police Centennial **Obverse:** Bust right **Reverse:** Mountie divides dates, denomination above **Rev. Designer:** Paul Cedarberg **Size:** 23.8 mm. **Note:** 120 beads.

Date	Mintage	VG-8	F-12	VF-20	XF-40	MS-60	MS-63	Proof
ND(1973)	134,958,587	—	—	—	0.30	0.55	1.00	—

KM# 81.2 25 CENTS **Composition:** Nickel **Ruler:** Elizabeth II **Subject:** RCMP Centennial **Obverse:** Bust right **Reverse:** Mountie divides dates, denomination above **Size:** 23.8 mm. **Note:** 132 beads.

Date	Mintage	VG-8	F-12	VF-20	XF-40	MS-60	MS-63	Proof
ND(1973)	Inc. above	40.00	55.00	70.00	85.00	100	200	—

KM# 74 25 CENTS **Weight:** 5.0700 g. **Composition:** Nickel **Ruler:** Elizabeth II **Obverse:** Small bust right **Obv. Designer:** Machin **Rev. Designer:** Emanuel Hahn **Size:** 23.88 mm.

Date	Mintage	VG-8	F-12	VF-20	XF-40	MS-60	MS-63	Proof
1979	131,042,905	—	—	—	0.30	0.45	0.75	—
1980	76,178,000	—	—	—	0.30	0.45	0.75	—
1981	131,580,272	—	—	—	0.30	0.45	0.75	—
1981 Proof	199,000	—	—	—	—	—	—	2.00
1982	171,926,000	—	—	—	0.30	0.45	0.75	—
1982 Proof	180,908	—	—	—	—	—	—	2.00
1983	13,162,000	—	—	—	0.30	0.75	1.50	—
1983 Proof	168,000	—	—	—	—	—	—	3.00
1984	121,668,000	—	—	—	0.30	0.45	0.75	—
1984 Proof	161,602	—	—	—	—	—	—	2.00
1985	158,734,000	—	—	—	0.30	0.45	0.75	—
1985 Proof	157,037	—	—	—	—	—	—	2.00
1986	132,220,000	—	—	—	0.30	0.45	0.75	—
1986 Proof	175,745	—	—	—	—	—	—	2.00
1987	53,408,000	—	—	—	0.30	0.60	1.25	—
1987 Proof	179,004	—	—	—	—	—	—	2.00
1988	80,368,473	—	—	—	0.30	0.45	1.00	—
1988 Proof	175,259	—	—	—	—	—	—	2.00
1989	119,796,307	—	—	—	0.30	0.45	0.75	—
1989 Proof	170,928	—	—	—	—	—	—	2.00

KM# 184 25 CENTS **Weight:** 5.0700 g. **Composition:** Nickel **Ruler:** Elizabeth II **Obverse:** Crowned head right **Obv. Designer:** Dora dePedery-Hunt **Reverse:** Moose left, denomination above, date at right **Rev. Designer:** Emanuel Hahn **Size:** 23.88 mm.

Date	Mintage	VG-8	F-12	VF-20	XF-40	MS-60	MS-63	Proof
1990	31,258,000	—	—	—	0.30	0.45	0.90	—
1990 Proof	140,649	—	—	—	—	—	—	2.50
1991	459,000	—	—	2.00	3.50	6.00	12.00	—
1991 Proof	131,888	—	—	—	—	—	—	20.00
1993	73,758,000	—	—	—	0.25	0.35	0.70	—
1993 Proof	143,065	—	—	—	—	—	—	2.00
1994	77,670,000	—	—	—	0.25	0.35	0.70	—
1994 Proof	146,424	—	—	—	—	—	—	3.00
1995	89,210,000	—	—	—	0.25	0.35	0.70	—
1995 Proof	50,000	—	—	—	—	—	—	3.00
1996	28,106,000	—	—	—	—	—	0.70	—
1996 Proof	—	—	—	—	—	—	—	6.00
1997	—	—	—	—	—	—	0.70	—
1997 Proof	—	—	—	—	—	—	—	6.00
1998W	—	—	—	—	—	—	5.00	—
1999	258,888,000	—	—	—	—	—	0.75	—
1999 Proof	—	—	—	—	—	—	—	6.00
2000	434,087,000	—	—	—	—	—	0.75	—
2000 Proof	—	—	—	—	—	—	—	6.00
2000W	—	—	—	—	—	—	5.00	—

KM# 184a 25 CENTS **Weight:** 5.9000 g. **Composition:** 0.9250 Silver 0.1754 oz. ASW **Ruler:** Elizabeth II **Obverse:** Crowned head right **Reverse:** Moose left, denomination above, date at right **Size:** 23.88 mm.

Date	Mintage	VG-8	F-12	VF-20	XF-40	MS-60	MS-63	Proof
1996 Proof	—	—	—	—	—	—	—	6.50
1997 Proof	—	—	—	—	—	—	—	6.50
1998 Proof	—	—	—	—	—	—	—	5.50
19980 Proof	—	—	—	—	—	—	—	5.50
1999 Proof	—	—	—	—	—	—	—	5.50

KM# 184b 25 CENTS **Composition:** Nickel Plated Steel **Ruler:** Elizabeth II **Obverse:** Crowned head right **Reverse:** Moose left, denomination above, date at right **Size:** 23.8 mm.

Date	Mintage	VG-8	F-12	VF-20	XF-40	MS-60	MS-63	Proof
1999 P	Est. 20,000	—	—	—	—	—	20.00	—
2000 P	—	—	—	—	—	2,000	4,000	—

Note: 3-5 known

KM# 207 25 CENTS **Composition:** Nickel **Ruler:** Elizabeth II **Subject:** Confederation 125 **Obverse:** Crowned Queen's bust right **Obv. Designer:** Dora dePedery-Hunt **Reverse:** Moose left, denomination above, date at right **Rev. Designer:** Emanuel Hahn **Size:** 23.8 mm.

Date	Mintage	VG-8	F-12	VF-20	XF-40	MS-60	MS-63	Proof
ND(1992)	442,986	—	—	—	—	—	12.50	—
ND(1992) Proof	147,061	—	—	—	—	—	—	20.00

KM# 203 25 CENTS **Composition:** Nickel **Series:** 125th Anniversary of Confederation **Subject:** New Brunswick **Reverse:** Covered bridge in Newton, denomination below **Rev. Designer:** Ronald Lambert **Size:** 23.8 mm.

Date	Mintage	VG-8	F-12	VF-20	XF-40	MS-60	MS-63	Proof
ND(1992)	12,174,000	—	—	—	—	0.35	0.70	—

KM# 203a 25 CENTS **Weight:** 5.8319 g. **Composition:** 0.9250 Silver 0.1734 oz. ASW **Series:** 125th Anniversary of Confederation **Subject:** New Brunswick **Reverse:** Covered bridge in Newton, denomination below **Size:** 23.8 mm.

Date	Mintage	VG-8	F-12	VF-20	XF-40	MS-60	MS-63	Proof
ND(1992) Proof	149,579	—	—	—	—	—	—	5.50

KM# 212 25 CENTS **Composition:** Nickel **Series:** 125th Anniversary of Confederation **Subject:** Northwest Territories **Rev. Designer:** Beth McEachen **Size:** 23.8 mm.

Date	Mintage	VG-8	F-12	VF-20	XF-40	MS-60	MS-63	Proof
ND(1992)	12,582,000	—	—	—	—	0.35	0.70	—

KM# 212a 25 CENTS **Weight:** 5.8319 g. **Composition:** 0.9250 Silver 0.1734 oz. ASW **Series:** 125th Anniversary of Confederation **Subject:** Northwest Territories **Size:** 23.8 mm.

Date	Mintage	VG-8	F-12	VF-20	XF-40	MS-60	MS-63	Proof
ND(1992) Proof	149,579	—	—	—	—	—	—	5.50

KM# 213 25 CENTS **Composition:** Nickel **Series:** 125th Anniversary of Confederation **Subject:** Newfoundland **Reverse:** Fisherman rowing a dory, denomination below **Rev. Designer:** Christopher Newhook **Size:** 23.8 mm.

Date	Mintage	VG-8	F-12	VF-20	XF-40	MS-60	MS-63	Proof
ND(1992)	11,405,000	—	—	—	—	0.35	0.70	—

KM# 213a 25 CENTS **Weight:** 5.8319 g. **Composition:** 0.9250 Silver 0.1734 oz. ASW **Series:** 125th Anniversary of Confederation **Subject:** Newfoundland **Reverse:** Fisherman rowing a dory, denomination below **Size:** 23.8 mm.

Date	Mintage	VG-8	F-12	VF-20	XF-40	MS-60	MS-63	Proof
ND(1992) Proof	149,579	—	—	—	—	—	—	5.50

KM# 214 25 CENTS **Composition:** Nickel **Series:** 125th Anniversary of Confederation **Subject:** Manitoba **Rev. Designer:** Muriel Hope **Size:** 23.8 mm.

Date	Mintage	VG-8	F-12	VF-20	XF-40	MS-60	MS-63	Proof
ND(1992)	11,349,000	—	—	—	—	0.35	0.70	—

KM# 214a 25 CENTS **Weight:** 5.8319 g. **Composition:** 0.9250 Silver 0.1734 oz. ASW **Series:** 125th Anniversary of Confederation **Subject:** Manitoba **Size:** 23.8 mm.

Date	Mintage	VG-8	F-12	VF-20	XF-40	MS-60	MS-63	Proof
ND(1992) Proof	149,579	—	—	—	—	—	—	5.50

KM# 220 25 CENTS **Composition:** Nickel **Series:** 125th Anniversary of Confederation **Subject:** Yukon **Rev. Designer:** Libby Dulac **Size:** 23.8 mm.

Date	Mintage	VG-8	F-12	VF-20	XF-40	MS-60	MS-63	Proof
ND(1992)	10,388,000	—	—	—	—	0.35	0.70	—

KM# 220a 25 CENTS **Weight:** 5.8319 g. **Composition:** 0.9250 Silver 0.1734 oz. ASW **Series:** 125th Anniversary of Confederation **Subject:** Yukon **Size:** 23.8 mm.

Date	Mintage	VG-8	F-12	VF-20	XF-40	MS-60	MS-63	Proof
ND(1992) Proof	149,579	—	—	—	—	—	—	5.50

KM# 221 25 CENTS **Composition:** Nickel **Series:** 125th Anniversary of Confederation **Subject:** Alberta **Reverse:** Rock formations in the badlands near Drumhelter, denomination below **Rev. Designer:** Mel Heath **Size:** 23.8 mm.

Date	Mintage	VG-8	F-12	VF-20	XF-40	MS-60	MS-63	Proof
ND(1992)	12,133,000	—	—	—	—	0.35	0.70	—

KM# 221a 25 CENTS **Weight:** 5.8319 g. **Composition:** 0.9250 Silver 0.1734 oz. ASW **Series:** 125th Anniversary of Confederation **Subject:** Alberta **Reverse:** Rock formations in the badlands near Drumhelter, denomination below **Size:** 23.8 mm.

Date	Mintage	VG-8	F-12	VF-20	XF-40	MS-60	MS-63	Proof
ND(1992) Proof	—	—	—	—	—	—	—	5.50

KM# 222 25 CENTS **Composition:** Nickel **Series:** 125th Anniversary of Confederation **Subject:** Prince Edward Island **Rev. Designer:** Nigel Roe **Size:** 23.8 mm.

Date	Mintage	VG-8	F-12	VF-20	XF-40	MS-60	MS-63	Proof
ND(1992)	13,001,000	—	—	—	—	0.35	0.70	—

KM# 222a 25 CENTS **Weight:** 5.8319 g. **Composition:** 0.9250 Silver 0.1734 oz. ASW **Series:** 125th Anniversary of Confederation **Subject:** Prince Edward Island **Size:** 23.8 mm.

Date	Mintage	VG-8	F-12	VF-20	XF-40	MS-60	MS-63	Proof
ND(1992) Proof	149,579	—	—	—	—	—	—	5.50

KM# 223 25 CENTS **Composition:** Nickel **Series:** 125th Anniversary of Confederation **Subject:** Ontario **Reverse:** Jack pine, denomination below **Rev. Designer:** Greg Salmela **Size:** 23.8 mm.

Date	Mintage	VG-8	F-12	VF-20	XF-40	MS-60	MS-63	Proof
ND(1992)	14,263,000	—	—	—	—	0.35	0.70	—

KM# 223a 25 CENTS **Weight:** 5.8319 g. **Composition:** 0.9250 Silver 0.1734 oz. ASW **Series:** 125th Anniversary of Confederation **Subject:** Ontario **Reverse:** Jack pine, denomination below **Size:** 23.8 mm.

Date	Mintage	VG-8	F-12	VF-20	XF-40	MS-60	MS-63	Proof
ND(1992) Proof	149,579	—	—	—	—	—	—	5.50

KM# 231 25 CENTS **Composition:** Nickel **Series:** 125th Anniversary of Confederation **Subject:** Nova Scotia **Reverse:** Lighthouse, denomination below **Rev. Designer:** Bruce Wood **Size:** 23.8 mm.

Date	Mintage	VG-8	F-12	VF-20	XF-40	MS-60	MS-63	Proof
ND(1992)	13,600,000	—	—	—	—	0.35	0.70	—

KM# 231a 25 CENTS **Weight:** 5.8319 g. **Composition:** 0.9250 Silver 0.1734 oz. ASW **Series:** 125th Anniversary of Confederation **Subject:** Nova Scotia **Reverse:** Lighthouse, denomination below **Size:** 23.8 mm.

Date	Mintage	VG-8	F-12	VF-20	XF-40	MS-60	MS-63	Proof
ND(1992) Proof	149,579	—	—	—	—	—	—	5.50

KM# 232 25 CENTS **Composition:** Nickel **Ruler:** Elizabeth II **Series:** 125th Anniversary of Confederation **Subject:** British Columbia **Obverse:** Crowned head right, dates below **Reverse:** Large rock, whales, denomination below **Rev. Designer:** Carla Herrera Egan **Size:** 23.8 mm.

Date	Mintage	VG-8	F-12	VF-20	XF-40	MS-60	MS-63	Proof
ND(1992)	14,001,000	—	—	—	—	0.35	0.70	—

KM# 232a 25 CENTS **Weight:** 5.8319 g. **Composition:** 0.9250 Silver 0.1734 oz. ASW **Ruler:** Elizabeth II **Series:** 125th Anniversary of Confederation **Subject:** British Columbia **Obverse:** Crowned head right, dates below **Reverse:** Large rock, whales, denomination below **Size:** 23.8 mm.

Date	Mintage	VG-8	F-12	VF-20	XF-40	MS-60	MS-63	Proof
ND(1992) Proof	149,579	—	—	—	—	—	—	5.50

KM# 233 25 CENTS **Composition:** Nickel **Ruler:** Elizabeth II **Series:** 125th Anniversary of Confederation **Subject:** Saskatchewan **Reverse:** Buildings behind wall, grain stalks on right, denomination below **Rev. Designer:** Brian Cobb **Size:** 23.8 mm.

Date	Mintage	VG-8	F-12	VF-20	XF-40	MS-60	MS-63	Proof
ND(1992)	14,165,000	—	—	—	—	0.35	0.70	—

KM# 233a 25 CENTS **Weight:** 5.8319 g. **Composition:** 0.9250 Silver 0.1734 oz. ASW **Ruler:** Elizabeth II **Series:** 125th Anniversary of Confederation **Subject:** Saskatchewan **Reverse:** Buildings behind wall, grain stalks on right, denomination below **Size:** 23.8 mm.

Date	Mintage	VG-8	F-12	VF-20	XF-40	MS-60	MS-63	Proof
ND(1992) Proof	149,579	—	—	—	—	—	—	5.50

KM# 234 25 CENTS **Composition:** Nickel **Ruler:** Elizabeth II **Series:** 125th Anniversary of Confederation **Subject:** Quebec **Reverse:** Boats on water, large rocks in background, denomination below **Rev. Designer:** Romualdas Bukauskas **Size:** 23.8 mm.

Date	Mintage	VG-8	F-12	VF-20	XF-40	MS-60	MS-63	Proof
ND(1992)	13,607,000	—	—	—	—	0.35	0.70	—

KM# 234a 25 CENTS **Weight:** 5.8319 g. **Composition:** 0.9250 Silver 0.1734 oz. ASW **Ruler:** Elizabeth II **Series:** 125th Anniversary of Confederation **Subject:** Quebec **Reverse:** Boats on water, large rocks in background, denomination below **Size:** 23.8 mm.

Date	Mintage	VG-8	F-12	VF-20	XF-40	MS-60	MS-63	Proof
ND(1992) Proof	149,579	—	—	—	—	—	—	5.50

KM# 312 25 CENTS **Ruler:** Elizabeth II **Subject:** 90th Anniversary Royal Canadian Mint **Obverse:** Crowned Queen's head right **Reverse:** Denomination and date within wreath, crown above **Size:** 23.8 mm.

Date	Mintage	VG-8	F-12	VF-20	XF-40	MS-60	MS-63	Proof
ND(1998) Matte	25,000	—	—	—	—	—	—	15.00

KM# 342 25 CENTS **Composition:** Nickel **Series:** Millennium **Subject:** January - A Country Unfolds **Reverse:** Totem pole, portraits **Rev. Designer:** P. Ka-Kin Poon **Size:** 23.8 mm.

Date	Mintage	VG-8	F-12	VF-20	XF-40	MS-60	MS-63	Proof
1999	12,181,200	—	—	—	—	0.50	0.65	—

KM# 342a 25 CENTS **Weight:** 5.8319 g. **Composition:** 0.9250 Silver 0.1734 oz. ASW **Series:** Millennium **Subject:** January **Reverse:** Totem pole, portraits **Size:** 23.8 mm.

Date	Mintage	VG-8	F-12	VF-20	XF-40	MS-60	MS-63	Proof
1999 Proof	113,645	—	—	—	—	—	—	8.00

KM# 343 25 CENTS **Composition:** Nickel **Series:** Millennium **Subject:** February - Etched in Stone **Reverse:** Native petroglyphs **Rev. Designer:** L. Springer **Size:** 23.8 mm.

Date	Mintage	VG-8	F-12	VF-20	XF-40	MS-60	MS-63	Proof
1999	14,469,250	—	—	—	—	0.50	0.65	—

KM# 343a 25 CENTS **Weight:** 5.8319 g. **Composition:** 0.9250 Silver 0.1734 oz. ASW **Series:** Millennium **Subject:** February **Reverse:** Native petroglyphs **Size:** 23.8 mm.

Date	Mintage	VG-8	F-12	VF-20	XF-40	MS-60	MS-63	Proof
1999 Proof	113,645	—	—	—	—	—	—	8.00

KM# 344 25 CENTS **Composition:** Nickel **Series:** Millennium **Subject:** March - The Log Drive **Reverse:** Lumberjack **Rev. Designer:** M. Lavoie **Size:** 23.8 mm.

Date	Mintage	VG-8	F-12	VF-20	XF-40	MS-60	MS-63	Proof
1999	15,033,500	—	—	—	—	0.50	0.65	—

KM# 344a 25 CENTS **Weight:** 5.8319 g. **Composition:** 0.9250 Silver 0.1734 oz. ASW **Series:** Millennium **Subject:** March **Reverse:** Lumberjack **Size:** 23.8 mm.

Date	Mintage	VG-8	F-12	VF-20	XF-40	MS-60	MS-63	Proof
1999 Proof	113,645	—	—	—	—	—	—	8.00

KM# 345 25 CENTS **Composition:** Nickel **Series:** Millennium **Subject:** April - Our Northern Heritage **Reverse:** Owl, polar bear **Rev. Designer:** Ken Ojnak Ashevac **Size:** 23.8 mm.

Date	Mintage	VG-8	F-12	VF-20	XF-40	MS-60	MS-63	Proof
1999	15,446,000	—	—	—	—	0.50	0.65	—

KM# 345a 25 CENTS **Weight:** 5.8319 g. **Composition:** 0.9250 Silver 0.1734 oz. ASW **Series:** Millennium **Subject:** April **Reverse:** Owl, polar bear **Size:** 23.8 mm.

Date	Mintage	VG-8	F-12	VF-20	XF-40	MS-60	MS-63	Proof
1999 Proof	113,645	—	—	—	—	—	—	8.00

KM# 346 25 CENTS **Composition:** Nickel **Series:** Millennium **Subject:** May - The Voyageures **Reverse:** Voyageurs in canoe **Rev. Designer:** S. Mineok **Size:** 23.8 mm.

Date	Mintage	VG-8	F-12	VF-20	XF-40	MS-60	MS-63	Proof
1999	15,566,100	—	—	—	—	0.50	0.65	—

KM# 346a 25 CENTS **Weight:** 5.8319 g. **Composition:** 0.9250 Silver 0.1734 oz. ASW **Series:** Millennium **Subject:** May **Reverse:** Voyageurs in canoe **Size:** 23.8 mm.

Date	Mintage	VG-8	F-12	VF-20	XF-40	MS-60	MS-63	Proof
1999 Proof	113,645	—	—	—	—	—	—	8.00

KM# 347 25 CENTS **Composition:** Nickel **Series:** Millennium **Subject:** June - From Coast to Coast **Reverse:** 19th-century locomotive **Rev. Designer:** G. Ho **Size:** 23.8 mm.

Date	Mintage	VG-8	F-12	VF-20	XF-40	MS-60	MS-63	Proof
1999	20,432,750	—	—	—	—	0.50	0.65	—

KM# 347a 25 CENTS **Weight:** 5.8319 g. **Composition:** 0.9250 Silver 0.1734 oz. ASW **Series:** Millennium **Subject:** June **Reverse:** 19th-century locomotive **Size:** 23.8 mm.

Date	Mintage	VG-8	F-12	VF-20	XF-40	MS-60	MS-63	Proof
1999 Proof	113,645	—	—	—	—	—	—	8.00

KM# 348 25 CENTS **Composition:** Nickel **Series:** Millennium **Subject:** July - A Nation of People **Reverse:** 6 stylized portraits **Rev. Designer:** M. H. Sarkany **Size:** 23.8 mm.

Date	Mintage	VG-8	F-12	VF-20	XF-40	MS-60	MS-63	Proof
1999	17,321,000	—	—	—	—	0.50	0.65	—

KM# 348a 25 CENTS **Weight:** 5.8319 g. **Composition:** 0.9250 Silver 0.1734 oz. ASW **Series:** Millennium **Subject:** July **Reverse:** 6 stylized portraits **Size:** 23.8 mm.

Date	Mintage	VG-8	F-12	VF-20	XF-40	MS-60	MS-63	Proof
1999 Proof	113,645	—	—	—	—	—	—	8.00

KM# 349 25 CENTS **Composition:** Nickel **Series:** Millennium **Subject:** August - The Pioneer Spirit **Reverse:** Hay harvesting **Rev. Designer:** A. Botelho **Size:** 23.8 mm.

Date	Mintage	VG-8	F-12	VF-20	XF-40	MS-60	MS-63	Proof
1999	18,153,700	—	—	—	—	0.50	0.65	—

KM# 349a 25 CENTS **Weight:** 5.8319 g. **Composition:** 0.9250 Silver 0.1734 oz. ASW **Series:** Millennium **Subject:** August **Reverse:** Hay harvesting **Size:** 23.8 mm.

Date	Mintage	VG-8	F-12	VF-20	XF-40	MS-60	MS-63	Proof
1999 Proof	113,645	—	—	—	—	—	—	8.00

KM# 350 25 CENTS **Composition:** Nickel **Series:** Millennium **Subject:** September - Canada Through a Child's Eye **Reverse:** Childlike artwork **Rev. Designer:** Claudia Bertrand **Size:** 23.8 mm.

Date	Mintage	VG-8	F-12	VF-20	XF-40	MS-60	MS-63	Proof
1999	31,539,350	—	—	—	—	0.50	0.65	—

KM# 350a 25 CENTS **Weight:** 5.8319 g. **Composition:** 0.9250 Silver 0.1734 oz. ASW **Series:** Millennium **Subject:** September **Reverse:** Childlike artwork **Size:** 23.8 mm.

Date	Mintage	VG-8	F-12	VF-20	XF-40	MS-60	MS-63	Proof
1999 Proof	113,645	—	—	—	—	—	—	8.00

KM# 351 25 CENTS **Composition:** Nickel **Series:** Millennium **Subject:** October - Tribute to the First Nations **Reverse:** Aboriginal artwork **Rev. Designer:** J. E. Read **Size:** 23.8 mm.

Date	Mintage	VG-8	F-12	VF-20	XF-40	MS-60	MS-63	Proof
1999	32,136,650	—	—	—	—	0.50	0.65	—

KM# 351a 25 CENTS **Weight:** 5.8319 g. **Composition:** 0.9250 Silver 0.1734 oz. ASW **Series:** Millennium **Subject:** October **Reverse:** Aboriginal artwork **Size:** 23.8 mm.

Date	Mintage	VG-8	F-12	VF-20	XF-40	MS-60	MS-63	Proof
1999 Proof	113,645	—	—	—	—	—	—	8.00

KM# 352 25 CENTS **Composition:** Nickel **Series:** Millennium **Subject:** November - The Airplane Opens the North **Reverse:** Bush plane with landing skis **Rev. Designer:** B. R. Brown **Size:** 23.8 mm.

Date	Mintage	VG-8	F-12	VF-20	XF-40	MS-60	MS-63	Proof
1999	27,162,800	—	—	—	—	0.50	0.65	—

KM# 352a 25 CENTS **Weight:** 5.8319 g. **Composition:** 0.9250 Silver 0.1734 oz. ASW **Series:** Millennium **Subject:** November **Reverse:** Bush plane with landing skis **Size:** 23.8 mm.

Date	Mintage	VG-8	F-12	VF-20	XF-40	MS-60	MS-63	Proof
1999 Proof	113,645	—	—	—	—	—	—	8.00

KM# 353 25 CENTS **Composition:** Nickel **Series:** Millennium **Subject:** December - This is Canada **Reverse:** Eclectic geometric design **Rev. Designer:** J. L. P. Provencher **Size:** 23.8 mm.

Date	Mintage	VG-8	F-12	VF-20	XF-40	MS-60	MS-63	Proof
1999	43,339,200	—	—	—	—	0.50	0.70	—

KM# 353a 25 CENTS **Weight:** 5.8319 g. **Composition:** 0.9250 Silver 0.1734 oz. ASW **Series:** Millennium **Subject:** December **Reverse:** Eclectic geometric design **Size:** 23.8 mm.

Date	Mintage	VG-8	F-12	VF-20	XF-40	MS-60	MS-63	Proof
1999 Proof	113,645	—	—	—	—	—	—	8.00

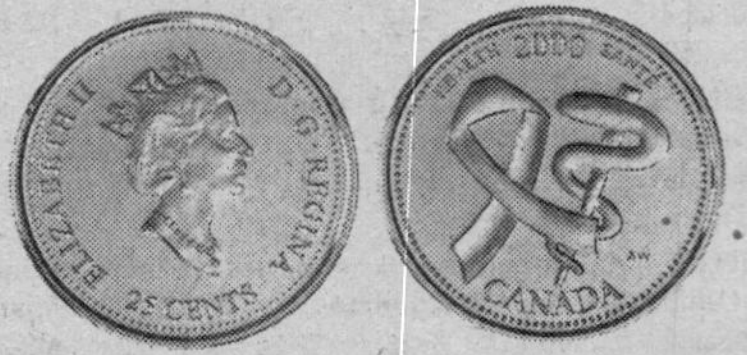

KM# 373 25 CENTS **Composition:** Nickel **Ruler:** Elizabeth II **Subject:** Health **Obverse:** Crowned head right, denomination below **Reverse:** Ribbon and caduceus, date above **Rev. Designer:** Anny Wassef **Size:** 23.8 mm.

Date	Mintage	VG-8	F-12	VF-20	XF-40	MS-60	MS-63	Proof
2000	35,470,900	—	—	—	—	0.50	0.65	—

KM# 373a 25 CENTS **Composition:** 0.9250 Silver **Ruler:** Elizabeth II **Subject:** Health **Obverse:** Crowned head right, denomination below **Reverse:** Ribbon and caduceus, date above **Size:** 23.8 mm.

Date	Mintage	VG-8	F-12	VF-20	XF-40	MS-60	MS-63	Proof
2000 Proof	76,956	—	—	—	—	—	—	8.00

KM# 374 25 CENTS **Composition:** Nickel **Ruler:** Elizabeth II **Subject:** Freedom **Obverse:** Crowned head right, denomination below **Reverse:** 2 children on maple leaf and rising sun, date above **Rev. Designer:** Kathy Vinish **Size:** 23.8 mm.

Date	Mintage	VG-8	F-12	VF-20	XF-40	MS-60	MS-63	Proof
2000	35,188,900	—	—	—	—	0.50	0.65	—

KM# 374a 25 CENTS **Composition:** 0.9250 Silver **Ruler:** Elizabeth II **Subject:** Freedom **Obverse:** Crowned head right, denomination below **Reverse:** 2 children on maple leaf and rising sun, date above **Size:** 23.8 mm.

Date	Mintage	VG-8	F-12	VF-20	XF-40	MS-60	MS-63	Proof
2000 Proof	76,956	—	—	—	—	—	—	6.00

KM# 375 25 CENTS **Composition:** Nickel **Ruler:** Elizabeth II **Subject:** Family **Obverse:** Crowned head right, denomination below **Reverse:** Wreath of native carvings, date above **Rev. Designer:** Wade Stephen Baker **Size:** 23.8 mm.

Date	Mintage	VG-8	F-12	VF-20	XF-40	MS-60	MS-63	Proof
2000	35,107,700	—	—	—	—	0.50	0.65	—

KM# 375a 25 CENTS **Composition:** 0.9250 Silver **Ruler:** Elizabeth II **Subject:** Family **Obverse:** Crowned head right, denomination below **Reverse:** Wreath of native carvings, date above **Size:** 23.8 mm.

Date	Mintage	VG-8	F-12	VF-20	XF-40	MS-60	MS-63	Proof
2000 Proof	76,956	—	—	—	—	—	—	6.00

KM# 376 25 CENTS **Composition:** Nickel **Ruler:** Elizabeth II **Subject:** Community **Obverse:** Crowned head right, denomination below **Reverse:** Map on globe, symbols surround, date above **Rev. Designer:** Michelle Thibodeau **Size:** 23.8 mm.

Date	Mintage	VG-8	F-12	VF-20	XF-40	MS-60	MS-63	Proof
2000	35,155,400	—	—	—	—	0.50	0.65	—

KM# 376a 25 CENTS **Composition:** 0.9250 Silver **Ruler:** Elizabeth II **Subject:** Community **Obverse:** Crowned head right, denomination below **Reverse:** Map on globe, symbols surround, date above **Size:** 23.8 mm.

Date	Mintage	VG-8	F-12	VF-20	XF-40	MS-60	MS-63	Proof
2000 Proof	76,956	—	—	—	—	—	—	6.00

KM# 377 25 CENTS **Composition:** Nickel **Ruler:** Elizabeth II **Subject:** Harmony **Obverse:** Crowned head right, denomination below **Reverse:** Maple leaf, date above **Rev. Designer:** Haver Demirer **Size:** 23.8 mm.

Date	Mintage	VG-8	F-12	VF-20	XF-40	MS-60	MS-63	Proof
2000	35,184,200	—	—	—	—	0.50	0.65	—

KM# 377a 25 CENTS **Composition:** 0.9250 Silver **Ruler:** Elizabeth II **Subject:** Harmony **Obverse:** Crowned head right, denomination below **Reverse:** Maple leaf **Size:** 23.8 mm.

Date	Mintage	VG-8	F-12	VF-20	XF-40	MS-60	MS-63	Proof
2000 Proof	76,956	—	—	—	—	—	—	6.00

KM# 378 25 CENTS **Composition:** Nickel **Ruler:** Elizabeth II **Subject:** Wisdom **Obverse:** Crowned head right, denomination below **Reverse:** Man with young child, date above **Rev. Designer:** Cezar Serbanescu **Size:** 23.8 mm.

Date	Mintage	VG-8	F-12	VF-20	XF-40	MS-60	MS-63	Proof
2000	35,123,950	—	—	—	—	0.50	0.65	—

KM# 378a 25 CENTS **Composition:** 0.9250 Silver **Ruler:** Elizabeth II **Subject:** Wisdom **Obverse:** Crowned head right, denomination below **Reverse:** Man with young child **Size:** 23.8 mm.

Date	Mintage	VG-8	F-12	VF-20	XF-40	MS-60	MS-63	Proof
2000 Proof	76,956	—	—	—	—	—	—	6.00

KM# 379 25 CENTS **Composition:** Nickel **Ruler:** Elizabeth I **Subject:** Creativity **Obverse:** Crowned head right, denomination below **Reverse:** Canoe full of children, date above **Rev. Designer:** Kong Tat Hui **Size:** 23.8 mm.

Date	Mintage	VG-8	F-12	VF-20	XF-40	MS-60	MS-63	Proof
2000	35,316,770	—	—	—	—	0.50	0.65	—

KM# 379a 25 CENTS **Composition:** 0.9250 Silver **Ruler:** Elizabeth II **Subject:** Creativity **Obverse:** Crowned head right, denomination below **Reverse:** Canoe full of children **Size:** 23.8 mm.

Date	Mintage	VG-8	F-12	VF-20	XF-40	MS-60	MS-63	Proof
2000 Proof	76,956	—	—	—	—	—	—	6.00

KM# 380 25 CENTS **Composition:** Nickel **Ruler:** Elizabeth II **Subject:** Ingenuity **Obverse:** Crowned head right, denomination below **Reverse:** Crescent-shaped city views, date above **Rev. Designer:** John Jaciw **Size:** 23.8 mm.

Date	Mintage	VG-8	F-12	VF-20	XF-40	MS-60	MS-63	Proof
2000	36,078,360	—	—	—	—	0.50	0.65	—

KM# 380a 25 CENTS **Composition:** 0.9250 Silver **Ruler:** Elizabeth II **Subject:** Ingenuity **Obverse:** Crowned head right, denomination below **Reverse:** Crescent-shaped city view **Size:** 23.8 mm.

Date	Mintage	VG-8	F-12	VF-20	XF-40	MS-60	MS-63	Proof
2000 Proof	76,956	—	—	—	—	—	—	6.00

KM# 381 25 CENTS **Composition:** Nickel **Ruler:** Elizabeth II **Subject:** Achievement **Obverse:** Crowned head right, denomination below **Reverse:** Rocket above jagged design, date above **Rev. Designer:** Daryl Dorosz **Size:** 23.8 mm.

Date	Mintage	VG-8	F-12	VF-20	XF-40	MS-60	MS-63	Proof
2000	35,312,750	—	—	—	—	0.50	0.65	—

KM# 381a 25 CENTS **Composition:** 0.9250 Silver **Ruler:** Elizabeth II **Subject:** Achievement **Obverse:** Crowned head right, denomination below **Reverse:** Rocket above jagged design **Size:** 23.8 mm.

Date	Mintage	VG-8	F-12	VF-20	XF-40	MS-60	MS-63	Proof
2000 Proof	76,956	—	—	—	—	—	—	6.00

KM# 382 25 CENTS **Composition:** Nickel **Ruler:** Elizabeth II **Subject:** Natural legacy **Obverse:** Crowned head right, denomination below **Reverse:** Environmental elements, date above **Rev. Designer:** Randy Trantau **Size:** 23.8 mm.

Date	Mintage	VG-8	F-12	VF-20	XF-40	MS-60	MS-63	Proof
2000	36,236,900	—	—	—	—	0.50	0.65	—

KM# 382a 25 CENTS **Composition:** 0.9250 Silver **Ruler:** Elizabeth II **Subject:** Natural legacy **Obverse:** Crowned head right, denomination below **Reverse:** Environmental elements **Size:** 23.8 mm.

Date	Mintage	VG-8	F-12	VF-20	XF-40	MS-60	MS-63	Proof
2000 Proof	76,956	—	—	—	—	—	—	6.00

KM# 383 25 CENTS **Composition:** Nickel **Ruler:** Elizabeth II **Subject:** Celebration **Obverse:** Crowned head right, denomination below **Reverse:** Fireworks, children behind flag, date above **Rev. Designer:** Laura Paxton **Size:** 23.8 mm.

Date	Mintage	VG-8	F-12	VF-20	XF-40	MS-60	MS-63	Proof
2000	35,144,100	—	—	—	—	0.50	0.65	—

KM# 383a 25 CENTS **Composition:** 0.9250 Silver **Ruler:** Elizabeth II **Subject:** Celebration **Obverse:** Crowned head right, denomination below **Reverse:** Fireworks, children behind flag **Size:** 23.8 mm.

Date	Mintage	VG-8	F-12	VF-20	XF-40	MS-60	MS-63	Proof
2000 Proof	76,956	—	—	—	—	—	—	6.00

KM# 384.1 25 CENTS **Composition:** Nickel **Ruler:** Elizabeth II **Subject:** Pride **Obverse:** Crowned Queen's head, right, denomination below **Reverse:** Large 2 in red with 3 small red maple leaves on large maple leaf, date above **Rev. Designer:** Donald F. Warkentin **Edge:** Reeded **Size:** 23.8 mm. **Note:** Colorized version.

Date	Mintage	VG-8	F-12	VF-20	XF-40	MS-60	MS-63	Proof
2000	49,399	—	—	—	—	—	6.50	—

KM# 384.2 25 CENTS **Composition:** Nickel **Ruler:** Elizabeth II **Subject:** Pride **Obverse:** Crowned Queen's head, right, denomination below **Reverse:** Large 2 with three small maple leaves on large maple leaf, date above **Rev. Designer:** Donald F. Warkentin **Size:** 23.8 mm.

Date	Mintage	VG-8	F-12	VF-20	XF-40	MS-60	MS-63	Proof
2000	50,666,800	—	—	—	—	0.50	0.65	—

KM# 384.2a 25 CENTS **Composition:** 0.9250 Silver **Ruler:** Elizabeth II **Subject:** Pride **Obverse:** Crowned head right, denomination below **Reverse:** 2 with 3 small maple leaves on large maple leaf **Size:** 23.8 mm.

Date	Mintage	VG-8	F-12	VF-20	XF-40	MS-60	MS-63	Proof
2000 Proof	76,956	—	—	—	—	—	—	6.00

KM# 6 50 CENTS **Weight:** 11.6200 g. **Composition:** 0.9250 Silver .3456 oz. ASW **Ruler:** Victoria **Obverse:** Victoria head left **Obv. Designer:** Leonard C. Wyon **Reverse:** Denomination and date within wreath, crown above

Date	Mintage	VG-8	F-12	VF-20	XF-40	MS-60	MS-63	Proof
1901	80,000	55.00	100	225	550	5,700	15,000	—

Victorian leaves

KM# 12 50 CENTS **Weight:** 11.6200 g. **Composition:** 0.9250 Silver .3456 oz. ASW **Ruler:** Edward VII **Obverse:** King's bust right **Obv. Designer:** G. W. DeSaulles **Reverse:** Denomination and date within wreath, crown above

Date	Mintage	VG-8	F-12	VF-20	XF-40	MS-60	MS-63	Proof
1902	120,000	15.00	35.00	100	250	1,300	3,500	—
1903H	140,000	22.00	45.00	175	450	1,500	3,700	—
1904	60,000	150	200	600	1,000	3,300	9,500	—
1905	40,000	150	275	600	1,400	6,000	15,000	—
1906	350,000	12.00	35.00	95.00	250	1,300	3,500	—
1907	300,000	12.00	35.00	95.00	250	1,400	3,900	—
1908	128,119	21.00	65.00	175	375	1,000	2,000	—
1909	302,118	17.00	60.00	175	475	2,400	7,600	—
1910	649,521	22.00	45.00	175	400	1,600	6,000	—

Note: Victorian leaves

Edwardian leaves

KM# 12a 50 CENTS **Weight:** 11.6638 g. **Composition:** 0.9250 Silver .3461 oz. ASW **Ruler:** Edward VII **Obverse:** Bust right **Obv. Designer:** G. W. DeSaulles **Reverse:** Denomination and date within wreath

Date	Mintage	VG-8	F-12	VF-20	XF-40	MS-60	MS-63	Proof
1910	Inc. above	8.00	29.00	85.00	250	1,200	3,300	—

Note: Edwardian leaves

KM# 19 50 CENTS **Weight:** 11.6638 g. **Composition:** 0.9250 Silver .3461 oz. ASW **Ruler:** George V **Obverse:** King's bust left **Obv. Designer:** E. B. MacKennal **Reverse:** Denomination and date within wreath, crown above

Date	Mintage	VG-8	F-12	VF-20	XF-40	MS-60	MS-63	Proof
1911	209,972	12.00	70.00	250	550	1,400	3,200	—

KM# 25 50 CENTS **Weight:** 11.6638 g. **Composition:** 0.9250 Silver .3461 oz. ASW **Ruler:** George V **Obverse:** King's bust left, modified legend **Obv. Designer:** E. B. MacKennal **Reverse:** Denomination and date within wreath, crown above

Date	Mintage	VG-8	F-12	VF-20	XF-40	MS-60	MS-63	Proof
1912	285,867	9.00	24.00	100	225	1,100	2,900	—
1913	265,889	9.00	24.00	150	300	1,400	4,800	—
1914	160,128	22.00	55.00	225	550	2,800	7,800	—
1916	459,070	6.00	14.00	55.00	175	650	2,100	—
1917	752,213	5.50	11.00	40.00	100	475	1,100	—
1918	754,989	5.00	10.00	30.00	90.00	400	1,000	—
1919	1,113,429	5.00	10.00	30.00	90.00	375	1,200	—

KM# 25a 50 CENTS **Weight:** 11.6638 g. **Composition:** 0.8000 Silver .3000 oz. ASW **Ruler:** George V **Obverse:** King's bust left **Obv. Designer:** E. B. MacKennal **Reverse:** Denomination and date within wreath, crown below

Date	Mintage	VG-8	F-12	VF-20	XF-40	MS-60	MS-63	Proof
1920	584,691	5.00	13.00	35.00	125	500	1,200	—
1921	—	22,000	24,000	28,000	32,000	50,000	90,000	
Note: 75 to 100 known; David Akers John Jay Pittman sale, Part Three, 10-99, Gem Unc. realized $63,250								
1929	228,328	5.00	13.00	35.00	100	475	1,100	—
1931	57,581	11.00	29.00	80.00	225	800	1,800	—
1932	19,213	150	185	375	800	3,600	8,300	—
1934	39,539	15.00	30.00	80.00	225	650	1,300	—
1936	38,550	15.00	29.00	70.00	175	500	1,000	—

KM# 36 50 CENTS **Weight:** 11.6638 g. **Composition:** 0.8000 Silver .3000 oz. ASW **Ruler:** George VI **Obverse:** Head left **Obv. Designer:** T. H. Paget **Reverse:** Crowned arms with supporters, denomination above, date below **Rev. Designer:** George E. Kruger-Gray **Size:** 30 mm.

Date	Mintage	VG-8	F-12	VF-20	XF-40	MS-60	MS-63	Proof
1937	192,016	BV	4.50	7.00	10.00	30.00	85.00	—
1938	192,018	BV	5.50	10.00	25.00	90.00	400	—
1939	287,976	BV	5.00	8.00	17.00	60.00	250	—
1940	1,996,566	—	—	BV	6.00	27.00	60.00	—
1941	1,714,874	—	—	BV	6.00	27.00	60.00	—
1942	1,974,164	—	—	BV	6.00	27.00	60.00	—
1943	3,109,583	—	—	BV	6.00	27.00	60.00	—
1944	2,460,205	—	—	BV	6.00	27.00	60.00	—
1945	1,959,528	—	—	BV	6.00	30.00	90.00	—
1946	950,235	—	BV	4.00	8.00	60.00	120	—
1946	Inc. above	15.00	28.00	45.00	150	1,100	2,800	—
Note: hoof in 6								
1947	424,885	—	BV	5.00	12.00	65.00	175	—
Note: straight 7								
1947	Inc. above	—	BV	6.00	15.00	100	300	—
Note: curved 7								
1947	38,433	18.00	23.00	45.00	70.00	160	275	—
Note: maple leaf, straight 7								
1947	Inc. above	1,000	1,300	1,700	2,200	3,900	7,000	—
Note: maple leaf, curved 7								

KM# 45 50 CENTS **Weight:** 11.6638 g. **Composition:** 0.8000 Silver .3000 oz. ASW **Ruler:** George VI **Obverse:** Head left, modified legend **Obv. Designer:** T. H. Paget **Reverse:** Crowned arms with supporters, denomination above, date below **Rev. Designer:** George E. Kruger-Gray

Date	Mintage	VG-8	F-12	VF-20	XF-40	MS-60	MS-63	Proof
1948	37,784	45.00	55.00	70.00	100	250	350	—
1949	858,991	—	—	BV	7.00	35.00	100	—
1949	Inc. above	7.00	12.00	25.00	60.00	325	750	—
Note: hoof over 9								
1950	2,384,179	4.25	7.00	11.00	35.00	125	225	—
Note: no lines								
1950	Inc. above	—	—	BV	4.50	9.00	30.00	—
Note: lines in 0								
1951	2,421,730	—	—	—	BV	9.00	26.00	—
1952	2,596,465	—	—	—	BV	6.00	18.00	—

KM# 53 50 CENTS **Weight:** 11.6638 g. **Composition:** 0.8000 Silver .3000 oz. ASW **Ruler:** Elizabeth II **Obverse:** Laureate Queen's bust right **Obv. Designer:** Mary Gillick **Reverse:** Crowned arms with supporters, denomination above, date below

Date	Mintage	VG-8	F-12	VF-20	XF-40	MS-60	MS-63	Proof
1953	1,630,429	—	—	—	BV	4.50	15.00	—
Note: small date								
1953	Inc. above	—	—	BV	4.50	15.00	35.00	—
Note: lg. date, straps								
1953	Inc. above	—	BV	5.00	14.00	75.00	150	—
Note: lg. date without straps								
1954	506,305	—	BV	4.25	7.00	18.00	35.00	—
1955	753,511	—	—	BV	5.00	15.00	30.00	—
1956	1,379,499	—	—	—	BV	6.00	14.00	—
1957	2,171,689	—	—	—	BV	5.00	10.00	—
1958	2,957,266	—	—	—	BV	4.25	8.50	—

KM# 56 50 CENTS **Weight:** 11.6638 g. **Composition:** 0.8000 Silver .3000 oz. ASW **Ruler:** Elizabeth II **Obverse:** Luareate Queen's bust right **Obv. Designer:** Mary Gillick **Reverse:** Crown divides date above arms with supporters, denomination at right **Rev. Designer:** Thomas Shingles **Size:** 30 mm.

Date	Mintage	VG-8	F-12	VF-20	XF-40	MS-60	MS-63	Proof
1959	3,095,535	—	—	—	BV	4.00	6.00	—
Note: horizontal shading								
1960	3,488,897	—	—	—	BV	4.00	5.00	—
1961	3,584,417	—	—	—	BV	4.00	5.00	—
1962	5,208,030	—	—	—	BV	4.00	5.00	—
1963	8,348,871	—	—	—	BV	4.00	5.00	—
1964	9,377,676	—	—	—	BV	4.00	5.00	—

KM# 63 50 CENTS **Weight:** 11.6638 g. **Composition:** 0.8000 Silver .3000 oz. ASW **Ruler:** Elizabeth II **Obverse:** Queen's bust right **Obv. Designer:** Arnold Machin **Reverse:** Crown divides date above arms with supporters, denomination at right **Rev. Designer:** Thomas Shingles

Date	Mintage	VG-8	F-12	VF-20	XF-40	MS-60	MS-63	Proof
1965	12,629,974	—	—	—	BV	4.00	5.00	—
1966	7,920,496	—	—	—	BV	4.00	5.00	—

KM# 69 50 CENTS **Weight:** 11.6638 g. **Composition:** 0.8000 Silver .3000 oz. ASW **Ruler:** Elizabeth II **Subject:** Confederation Centennial **Obverse:** Queen's bust right **Reverse:** Seated wolf howling divides denomination at top, dates at bottom **Rev. Designer:** Alex Colville **Size:** 29.5 mm.

Date	Mintage	VG-8	F-12	VF-20	XF-40	MS-60	MS-63	Proof
ND(1967)	4,211,392	—	—	—	BV	4.00	6.50	9.00

KM# 75.1 50 CENTS **Composition:** Nickel **Ruler:** Elizabeth II **Obverse:** Bust right **Obv. Designer:** Arnold Machin **Reverse:** Crown divides date above arms with supporters, denomination at right **Rev. Designer:** Thomas Shingles **Size:** 27.1 mm.

Date	Mintage	VG-8	F-12	VF-20	XF-40	MS-60	MS-63	Proof
1968	3,966,932	—	—	—	0.50	0.65	1.00	—
1969	7,113,929	—	—	—	0.50	0.65	1.00	—
1970	2,429,526	—	—	—	0.50	0.65	1.00	—
1971	2,166,444	—	—	—	0.50	0.65	1.00	—
1972	2,515,632	—	—	—	0.50	0.65	1.00	—
1973	2,546,096	—	—	—	0.50	0.65	1.00	—
1974	3,436,650	—	—	—	0.50	0.65	1.00	—
1975	3,710,000	—	—	—	0.50	0.65	1.00	—
1976	2,940,719	—	—	—	0.50	0.65	1.00	—

KM# 75.2 50 CENTS **Weight:** 8.1000 g. **Composition:** Nickel **Ruler:** Elizabeth II **Obverse:** Small bust of Queen right **Obv. Designer:** Arnold Machin **Reverse:** Crown divides date above arms with supporters, denomination at right **Rev. Designer:** Thomas Shingles **Size:** 27 mm.

Date	Mintage	VG-8	F-12	VF-20	XF-40	MS-60	MS-63	Proof
1977	709,839	—	—	0.50	0.75	1.35	2.00	—

KM# 75.3 50 CENTS **Weight:** 8.1000 g. **Composition:** Nickel **Ruler:** Elizabeth II **Obverse:** Queen's bust right **Obv. Designer:** Arnold Machin **Reverse:** Crown divides date above arms with supporters, denomination at right, redesigned arms **Rev. Designer:** Thomas Shingles **Size:** 27 mm.

Date	Mintage	VG-8	F-12	VF-20	XF-40	MS-60	MS-63	Proof
1978	3,341,892	—	—	—	0.50	0.65	1.00	—
Note: square jewels								
1978	Inc. above	—	—	1.00	2.50	3.00	6.00	—
Note: round jewels								
1979	3,425,000	—	—	—	0.50	0.65	1.00	—
1980	1,574,000	—	—	—	0.50	0.65	1.00	—
1981	2,690,272	—	—	—	0.50	0.65	1.00	—
1981 Proof	199,000	—	—	—	—	—	—	3.00
1982	2,236,674	—	—	—	30.00	40.00	60.00	—
Note: small beads								
1982 Proof	180,908	—	—	—	—	—	—	3.00
Note: small beads								
1982	Inc. above	—	—	—	0.50	0.65	1.00	—
Note: large beads								
1983	1,177,000	—	—	—	0.50	0.65	1.00	—
1983 Proof	168,000	—	—	—	—	—	—	3.00
1984	1,502,989	—	—	—	0.50	0.65	1.00	—
1984 Proof	161,602	—	—	—	—	—	—	3.00
1985	2,188,374	—	—	—	0.50	0.65	1.00	—
1985 Proof	157,037	—	—	—	—	—	—	3.00
1986	781,400	—	—	—	0.50	1.00	1.25	—
1986 Proof	175,745	—	—	—	—	—	—	3.00
1987	373,000	—	—	—	0.50	1.00	1.25	—
1987 Proof	179,004	—	—	—	—	—	—	3.50
1988	220,000	—	—	—	0.50	1.00	1.25	—
1988 Proof	175,259	—	—	—	—	—	—	3.00
1989	266,419	—	—	—	0.50	1.00	1.25	—
1989 Proof	170,928	—	—	—	—	—	—	3.00

KM# 185 50 CENTS **Composition:** Nickel **Ruler:** Elizabeth II **Obverse:** Crowned head right **Obv. Designer:** Dora dePedery-Hunt **Reverse:** Crown divides date above arms with supporters, denomination at right **Rev. Designer:** Thomas Shingles **Size:** 27 mm.

Date	Mintage	VG-8	F-12	VF-20	XF-40	MS-60	MS-63	Proof
1990	207,000	—	—	—	0.50	1.00	1.25	—
1990 Proof	140,649	—	—	—	—	—	—	5.00
1991	490,000	—	—	—	0.50	0.85	1.00	—
1991 Proof	131,888	—	—	—	—	—	—	7.00
1993	393,000	—	—	—	0.50	0.85	1.00	—
1993 Proof	143,065	—	—	—	—	—	—	3.00
1994	987,000	—	—	—	0.50	0.75	1.00	—
1994 Proof	146,424	—	—	—	—	—	—	4.00
1995	626,000	—	—	—	0.50	0.75	1.00	—
1995 Proof	50,000	—	—	—	—	—	—	4.00
1996	458,000	—	—	—	0.50	0.65	1.00	—
1996 Proof	—	—	—	—	—	—	—	—

KM# 185a 50 CENTS **Weight:** 11.6380 g. **Composition:** 0.9250 Silver .3461 oz. ASW **Ruler:** Elizabeth II **Obverse:** Crowned head right **Reverse:** Crown divides date above arms with supporters, denomination at right

Date	Mintage	MS-63	Proof
1996 Proof	—	—	9.00

KM# 208 50 CENTS **Composition:** Nickel **Ruler:** Elizabeth II **Subject:** Confederation 125 **Obverse:** Crowned Queen's head right **Obv. Designer:** Dora dePedery-Hunt **Reverse:** Crown divides date above arms with supporters, denomination at right **Rev. Designer:** Thomas Shingles **Size:** 27 mm.

Date	Mintage	VG-8	F-12	VF-20	XF-40	MS-60	MS-63	Proof
ND(1992)	445,000	—	—	—	0.50	0.75	1.00	—
ND(1992) Proof	147,061	—	—	—	—	—	—	5.00

KM# 261 50 CENTS **Weight:** 11.6638 g. **Composition:** 0.9250 Silver .3461 oz. ASW **Ruler:** Elizabeth II **Obverse:** Crowned head right **Reverse:** Atlantic Puffin, denomination and date at right **Rev. Designer:** Sheldon Beveridge

Date	Mintage	MS-63	Proof
1995 Proof	—	—	22.00

KM# 262 50 CENTS **Weight:** 11.6638 g. **Composition:** 0.9250 Silver .3461 oz. ASW **Ruler:** Elizabeth II **Obverse:** Crowned head right **Reverse:** Whooping crane left, denomination and date at right **Rev. Designer:** Stan Witten

Date	Mintage	MS-63	Proof
1995 Proof	—	—	22.00

KM# 263 50 CENTS **Weight:** 11.6638 g. **Composition:** 0.9250 Silver .3461 oz. ASW **Ruler:** Elizabeth II **Obverse:** Crowned head right **Reverse:** Gray Jays, denomination and date at right **Rev. Designer:** Sheldon Beveridge

Date	Mintage	MS-63	Proof
1995 Proof	—	—	22.00

KM# 264 50 CENTS **Weight:** 11.6638 g. **Composition:** 0.9250 Silver .3461 oz. ASW **Ruler:** Elizabeth II **Obverse:** Crowned head right **Reverse:** White-tailed ptarmigans, date and denomination at right **Rev. Designer:** Cosme Saffioti

Date	Mintage	MS-63	Proof
1995 Proof	—	—	22.00

KM# 283 50 CENTS **Weight:** 11.6638 g. **Composition:** 0.9250 Silver .3461 oz. ASW **Reverse:** Moose calf left, denomination and date at right **Rev. Designer:** Ago Aarand

Date	Mintage	MS-63	Proof
1996 Proof	—	—	20.00

KM# 284 50 CENTS **Weight:** 11.6638 g. **Composition:** 0.9250 Silver .3461 oz. ASW **Reverse:** Wood ducklings, date and denomination at right **Rev. Designer:** Sheldon Beveridge

Date	Mintage	MS-63	Proof
1996 Proof	—	—	20.00

KM# 285 50 CENTS **Weight:** 11.6638 g. **Composition:** 0.9250 Silver .3461 oz. ASW **Reverse:** Cougar kittens, date and denomination at right **Rev. Designer:** Stan Witten

Date	Mintage	MS-63	Proof
1996 Proof	—	—	20.00

KM# 286 50 CENTS **Weight:** 11.6638 g. **Composition:** 0.9250 Silver .3461 oz. ASW **Reverse:** Bear cubs standing, date and denomination at right **Rev. Designer:** Sheldon Beveridge

Date	Mintage	MS-63	Proof
1996 Proof	—	—	20.00

KM# 290 50 CENTS **Composition:** Nickel **Ruler:** Elizabeth II **Obv. Designer:** Dora dePedery-Hunt **Reverse:** Redesigned arms **Rev. Designer:** Cathy Bursey-Sabourin **Size:** 27.13 mm.

Date	Mintage	VG-8	F-12	VF-20	XF-40	MS-60	MS-63	Proof
1997	387,000	—	—	—	0.50	0.65	1.00	—
1997 Proof	—	—	—	—	—	—	—	—
1998	308,000	—	—	—	0.50	0.65	1.00	—
1998 Proof	—	—	—	—	—	—	—	—
1998W	—	—	—	—	—	—	2.00	—
1999	496,000	—	—	—	0.50	0.65	1.00	—
1999 Proof	—	—	—	—	—	—	—	—
2000	559,000	—	—	—	0.50	0.65	1.00	—
2000 Proof	—	—	—	—	—	—	—	—
2000W	—	—	—	—	—	—	1.50	—

KM# 290a 50 CENTS **Weight:** 11.6380 g. **Composition:** 0.9250 Silver .3461 oz. ASW **Ruler:** Elizabeth II **Obv. Designer:** Dora dePedery-Hunt **Reverse:** Redesigned arms **Rev. Designer:** Cathy Bursey-Sabourin

Date	Mintage	MS-63	Proof
1997 Proof	—	—	10.00
1998 Proof	—	—	10.00
1999 Proof	—	—	10.00
2000 Proof	—	—	10.00

KM# 292 50 CENTS **Weight:** 11.6638 g. **Composition:** 0.9250 Silver .3461 oz. ASW **Reverse:** Duck Toling Retriever, date and denomination at right **Rev. Designer:** Stan Witten

Date	Mintage	MS-63	Proof
1997 Proof	—	—	17.00

KM# 293 50 CENTS **Weight:** 11.6638 g. **Composition:** 0.9250 Silver .3461 oz. ASW **Reverse:** Labrador leaping left, date and denomination at right **Rev. Designer:** Sheldon Beveridge

Date	Mintage	MS-63	Proof
1997 Proof	—	—	17.00

KM# 294 50 CENTS **Weight:** 11.6638 g. **Composition:** 0.9250 Silver .3461 oz. ASW **Reverse:** Newfoundland right, date and denomination at right **Rev. Designer:** William Woodruff

Date	Mintage	MS-63	Proof
1997 Proof	—	—	17.00

KM# 295 50 CENTS **Weight:** 11.6638 g. **Composition:** 0.9250 Silver .3461 oz. ASW **Reverse:** Eskimo dog leaping forward, date and denomination at right **Rev. Designer:** Cosme Saffioti

Date	Mintage	MS-63	Proof
1997 Proof	—	—	17.00

KM# 313 50 CENTS **Weight:** 11.6638 g. **Composition:** 0.9250 Silver .3461 oz. ASW **Subject:** 90th Anniversary Royal Canadian Mint **Obverse:** Crowned Queen's head right **Reverse:** Denomination and date within wreath, crown above **Rev. Designer:** W. H. J. Blakemore

Date	Mintage	MS-63	Proof
ND(1998) Matte	25,000	—	15.00
ND(1998) Proof	25,000	—	15.00

KM# 314 50 CENTS **Weight:** 11.6638 g. **Composition:** 0.9250 Silver .3461 oz. ASW **Subject:** 110 Years Canadian Speed and Figure Skating **Reverse:** Speed skaters, dates below, denomination above **Rev. Designer:** Sheldon Beveridge

Date	Mintage	MS-63	Proof
ND(1998) Proof	—	—	9.00

KM# 315 50 CENTS **Weight:** 11.6638 g. **Composition:** 0.9250 Silver .3461 oz. ASW **Subject:** 100 Years Canadian Ski Racing **Reverse:** Skiers, dates below, denomination upper left **Rev. Designer:** Ago Aarand

Date	Mintage	MS-63	Proof
ND(1998) Proof	—	—	9.00

KM# 318 50 CENTS **Weight:** 11.6638 g. **Composition:** 0.9250 Silver .3461 oz. ASW **Reverse:** Killer Whales, date and denomination at right **Rev. Designer:** William Woodruff

Date	Mintage	MS-63	Proof
1998 Proof	—	—	15.00

KM# 319 50 CENTS **Weight:** 11.6638 g. **Composition:** 0.9250 Silver .3461 oz. ASW **Reverse:** Humpback whale, date and denomination at right **Rev. Designer:** Sheldon Beveridge

Date	Mintage	MS-63	Proof
1998 Proof	—	—	15.00

KM# 320 50 CENTS **Weight:** 11.6638 g. **Composition:** 0.9250 Silver .3461 oz. ASW **Reverse:** Beluga whales, date and denomination at right **Rev. Designer:** Cosme Saffioti

Date	Mintage	MS-63	Proof
1998 Proof	—	—	15.00

KM# 321 50 CENTS **Weight:** 11.6638 g. **Composition:** 0.9250 Silver .3461 oz. ASW **Reverse:** Blue whale, date and denomination at right **Rev. Designer:** Stan Witten

Date	Mintage	MS-63	Proof
1998 Proof	—	—	15.00

KM# 327 50 CENTS **Weight:** 11.6638 g. **Composition:** 0.9250 Silver .3461 oz. ASW **Ruler:** Elizabeth II **Subject:** 110 Years Canadian Soccer **Obverse:** Crowned Queen's head right **Reverse:** Soccer players, dates above, denomination at right **Rev. Designer:** Stan Witten

Date	Mintage	MS-63	Proof
ND(1998) Proof	—	—	9.00

KM# 328 50 CENTS **Weight:** 11.6638 g. **Composition:** 0.9250 Silver .3461 oz. ASW **Ruler:** Elizabeth II **Subject:** 20 Years Canadian Auto Racing **Obverse:** Crowned Queen's head, right **Reverse:** Race car divides date and denomination **Rev. Designer:** Cosme Saffioti

Date	Mintage	MS-63	Proof
ND(1998) Proof	—	—	9.00

KM# 333 50 CENTS **Weight:** 11.6638 g. **Composition:** 0.9250 Silver .3461 oz. ASW **Subject:** 1904 Canadian Open **Reverse:** Golfers, date at right, denomination below **Rev. Designer:** William Woodruff

Date	Mintage	MS-63	Proof
ND(1999) Proof	—	—	13.50

KM# 334 50 CENTS **Weight:** 11.6638 g. **Composition:** 0.9250 Silver .3461 oz. ASW **Subject:** First U.S.-Canadian Yacht Race **Reverse:** Yachts, dates at left, denomination below **Rev. Designer:** Stan Witten

Date	Mintage	MS-63	Proof
ND(1999) Proof	—	—	9.00

KM# 335 50 CENTS **Weight:** 11.6638 g. **Composition:** 0.9250 Silver .3461 oz. ASW **Series:** Canadian Cats **Reverse:** Cymric cat, date below, denomination at bottom **Rev. Designer:** Susan Taylor

Date	Mintage	MS-63	Proof
1999 Proof	—	—	17.50

KM# 336 50 CENTS **Weight:** 11.6638 g. **Composition:** 0.9250 Silver .3461 oz. ASW **Series:** Canadian Cats **Reverse:** Tonkinese cat, date below, denomination at bottom **Rev. Designer:** Susan Taylor

Date	Mintage	MS-63	Proof
1999 Proof	—	—	17.50

KM# 337 50 CENTS **Weight:** 11.6638 g. **Composition:** 0.9250 Silver .3461 oz. ASW **Series:** Canadian Cats **Reverse:** Cougar, date and denomination below **Rev. Designer:** Susan Taylor

Date	Mintage	MS-63	Proof
1999 Proof	—	—	17.00

KM# 338 50 CENTS **Weight:** 11.6638 g. **Composition:** 0.9250 Silver .3461 oz. ASW **Series:** Canadian Cats **Reverse:** Lynx, date and denomination below **Rev. Designer:** Susan Taylor

Date	Mintage	MS-63	Proof
1999 Proof	—	—	17.00

KM# 371 50 CENTS **Weight:** 9.3600 g. **Composition:** 0.9250 Silver 0.2784 oz. ASW **Subject:** Basketball **Obverse:** Queen's portrait **Reverse:** Basketball players **Rev. Designer:** Sheldon Beveridge **Edge:** Reeded **Size:** 27.1 mm.

Date	Mintage	MS-63	Proof
ND(1999) Proof	—	—	9.00

KM# 372 50 CENTS **Weight:** 9.3600 g. **Composition:** 0.9250 Silver 0.2784 oz. ASW **Obverse:** Queen's portrait **Reverse:** Football players **Rev. Designer:** Cosme Saffioti **Edge:** Reeded **Size:** 27.1 mm.

Date	Mintage	MS-63	Proof
ND(1999) Proof	—	—	9.00

KM# 290b 50 CENTS **Composition:** Nickel Plated Steel **Ruler:** Elizabeth II **Reverse:** Redesigned arms

Date	Mintage	MS-63	Proof
1999 P	Est. 20,000	15.00	—
2000 P	Est. 50	3,500	—

Note: Available only in RCM presentation coin clocks

KM# 385 50 CENTS **Composition:** 0.9250 Silver **Subject:** Ice Hockey **Reverse:** 4 hockey players **Rev. Designer:** Stanley Witten

Date	Mintage	MS-63	Proof
ND(2000) Proof	—	—	12.00

KM# 386 50 CENTS **Composition:** 0.9250 Silver **Subject:** Curling **Reverse:** Motion study of curlers, dates and denomination below **Rev. Designer:** Cosme Saffioti

Date	Mintage	MS-63	Proof
ND(2000) Proof	—	—	9.00

KM# 389 50 CENTS **Weight:** 9.3500 g. **Composition:** 0.9250 Silver **Ruler:** Elizabeth II **Obverse:** Crowned Queen's head right **Reverse:** Great horned owl, facing, date and denomination at right **Rev. Designer:** Susan Taylor

Date	Mintage	MS-63	Proof
2000 Proof	—	—	17.50

KM# 390 50 CENTS **Weight:** 9.3500 g. **Composition:** 0.9250 Silver **Ruler:** Elizabeth II **Obverse:** Crowned head right **Reverse:** Red-tailed hawk, dates and denomination at right

Date	Mintage	MS-63	Proof
2000 Proof	—	—	17.50

KM# 391 50 CENTS **Weight:** 9.3500 g. **Composition:** 0.9250 Silver **Ruler:** Elizabeth II **Obverse:** Crowned head right **Reverse:** Osprey, dates and denomination at right **Rev. Designer:** Susan Taylor

Date	Mintage	MS-63	Proof
2000 Proof	—	—	17.50

KM# 392 50 CENTS **Weight:** 9.3500 g. **Composition:** 0.9250 Silver **Ruler:** Elizabeth II **Obverse:** Crowned head right **Reverse:** Bald eagle, dates and denomination at right **Rev. Designer:** William Woodruff

Date	Mintage	MS-63	Proof
2000 Proof	—	—	17.50

KM# 393 50 CENTS **Composition:** 0.9250 Silver **Ruler:** Elizabeth II **Subject:** Steeplechase **Obverse:** Crowned Queen's head right **Reverse:** Steeplechase, dates and denomination below **Rev. Designer:** Susan Taylor

Date	Mintage	MS-63	Proof
2000 Proof	—	—	9.00

KM# 394 50 CENTS **Composition:** 0.9250 Silver **Ruler:** Elizabeth II **Subject:** Bowling **Rev. Designer:** William Woodruff

Date	Mintage	MS-63	Proof
2000 Proof	—	—	9.00

KM# 30 DOLLAR **Weight:** 23.3276 g. **Composition:** 0.8000 Silver 0.6000 oz. ASW **Ruler:** George V **Subject:** Silver Jubilee **Obverse:** Bust left **Obv. Designer:** Percy Metcalfe **Reverse:** Voyager, date and denomination below **Rev. Designer:** Emanuel Hahn

Date	Mintage	F-12	VF-20	XF-40	AU-50	MS-60	MS-63	Proof
1935	428,707	12.00	18.00	28.00	32.00	37.50	60.00	4,500

KM# 31 DOLLAR **Weight:** 23.3276 g. **Composition:** 0.8000 Silver 0.6000 oz. ASW **Ruler:** George V **Obverse:** King's bust left **Obv. Designer:** E. B. MacKennal **Reverse:** Voyageur, date and denomination below **Rev. Designer:** Emanuel Hahn

Date	Mintage	F-12	VF-20	XF-40	AU-50	MS-60	MS-63	Proof
1936	339,600	12.50	14.50	16.50	21.50	35.00	75.00	5,000

Pointed 7

Blunt 7

Maple leaf

KM# 37 DOLLAR **Weight:** 23.3276 g. **Composition:** 0.8000 Silver 0.6000 oz. ASW **Ruler:** George VI **Obverse:** Head left **Obv. Designer:** T. H. Paget **Reverse:** Voyageur, date and denomination below **Rev. Designer:** Emanuel Hahn

Date	Mintage	F-12	VF-20	XF-40	AU-50	MS-60	MS-63	Proof
1937	207,406	9.00	10.00	12.00	22.00	25.00	65.00	—
1937 Mirror Proof	1,295	—	—	—	—	—	—	650
1937 Matte Proof	Inc. above	—	—	—	—	—	—	250

Date	Mintage	F-12	VF-20	XF-40	AU-50	MS-60	MS-63	Proof
1938	90,304	25.00	35.00	45.00	55.00	70.00	175	6,000
1945	38,391	75.00	150	175	225	300	475	2,000
1946	93,055	15.00	25.00	35.00	45.00	95.00	225	1,800
1947		65.00	80.00	100	125	265	1,400	3,500
Note: Pointed 7								
1947	65,595	45.00	60.00	80.00	95.00	125	250	4,500
Note: Blunt 7								
1947	21,135	125	150	175	200	250	475	1,800
Note: Maple leaf								

KM# 38 DOLLAR **Weight:** 23.3276 g. **Composition:** 0.8000 Silver 0.6000 oz. ASW **Ruler:** George VI **Subject:** Royal Visit **Obverse:** Head left **Obv. Designer:** T. H. Paget **Reverse:** Tower at center of building, date and denomination below **Rev. Designer:** Emanuel Hahn

Date	Mintage	F-12	VF-20	XF-40	AU-50	MS-60	MS-63	Proof
1939	1,363,816	—	BV	9.00	10.00	12.00	20.00	—
1939	—	—	—	—	—	—	—	475
Note: Matte specimen								

KM# 46 DOLLAR **Weight:** 23.3276 g. **Composition:** 0.8000 Silver 0.6000 oz. ASW **Ruler:** George VI **Obverse:** Head left, modified left legend **Obv. Designer:** T. H. Paget **Reverse:** Voyageur, date and denomination below **Rev. Designer:** Emanuel Hahn

Date	Mintage	F-12	VF-20	XF-40	AU-50	MS-60	MS-63	Proof
1948	18,780	500	600	650	750	850	1,900	3,000
1950	261,002	BV	9.00	10.00	12.00	16.00	50.00	800
Note: With 3 water lines								
1950 Matte Proof	—	—	—	—	—	—	—	—
Note: With 4 water lines, 1 known								
1950	Inc. above	11.00	14.00	21.00	28.00	40.00	90.00	1,500
Note: Arnprior with 2-1/2 water lines								
1951	416,395	BV	9.00	10.00	11.00	13.00	23.00	650
Note: With 3 water lines								
1951	Inc. above	35.00	50.00	60.00	100	175	275	2,000
Note: Arnprior with 1-1/2 water lines								
1952	406,148	BV	9.00	10.00	11.00	12.00	23.00	1,000
Note: With 3 water lines								
1952	Inc. above	BV	12.00	15.00	18.00	40.00	60.00	1,250
Note: Short water lines, arnprior type								
1952	Inc. above	BV	9.00	10.00	11.00	16.50	45.00	—
Note: Without water lines								

KM# 47 DOLLAR **Weight:** 23.3276 g. **Composition:** 0.8000 Silver 0.6000 oz. ASW **Ruler:** George VI **Subject:** Newfoundland **Obverse:** Head left **Obv. Designer:** T. H. Paget **Reverse:** The Matthew, John Cabot's ship, date and denomination below **Rev. Designer:** Thomas Shingles

Date	Mintage	F-12	VF-20	XF-40	AU-50	MS-60	MS-63	Proof
1949	672,218	10.00	13.00	16.50	18.50	22.50	27.50	—
1949 Specimen proof	—	—	—	—	—	—	—	1,200

KM# 54 DOLLAR **Weight:** 23.3276 g. **Composition:** 0.8000 Silver 0.6000 oz. ASW **Ruler:** Elizabeth II **Obverse:** Laureate Queen's bust, right **Obv. Designer:** Mary Gillick **Reverse:** Voyageur, date and denomination below **Rev. Designer:** Emanuel Hahn **Note:** All genuine circulation strike 1955 Arnprior dollars have a die break running along the top of TI in the word GRATIA on the obverse.

Date	Mintage	F-12	VF-20	XF-40	AU-50	MS-60	MS-63	Proof
1953	1,074,578	—	—	BV	9.00	10.00	25.00	400
Note: Without strap, wire rim								
1953	Inc. above	—	—	BV	9.00	10.00	25.00	—
Note: With strap, flat rim								
1954	246,606	BV	9.00	10.00	11.00	16.00	35.00	—
1955	268,105	BV	9.00	10.00	11.00	15.00	29.00	—
Note: With 3 water lines								
1955	Inc. above	45.00	65.00	90.00	100	125	175	—
Note: Arnprior with 1-1/2 water lines* and die break								
1956	209,092	8.50	9.50	13.00	16.00	20.00	50.00	—
1957	496,389	—	—	—	BV	8.50	11.00	—
Note: With 3 water lines								
1957	Inc. above	—	BV	9.00	10.00	15.00	35.00	—
Note: With 1 water line								
1959	1,443,502	—	—	—	—		11.00	—
1960	1,420,486	—	—	—	—		11.00	—
1961	1,262,231	—	—	—	—		11.00	—
1962	1,884,789	—	—	—	—		11.00	—
1963	4,179,981	—	—	—	—		9.00	—

KM# 55 DOLLAR **Weight:** 23.3276 g. **Composition:** 0.8000 Silver 0.6000 oz. ASW **Ruler:** Elizabeth II **Subject:** British Columbia **Obverse:** Laureate Queen's bust right **Obv. Designer:** Mary Gillick **Reverse:** Totem Pole, dates at left, denomination below **Rev. Designer:** Stephan Trenka

Date	Mintage	F-12	VF-20	XF-40	AU-50	MS-60	MS-63	Proof
ND(1958)	3,039,630	—	—	BV	9.00	10.00	15.00	—

KM# 58 DOLLAR **Weight:** 23.3276 g. **Composition:** 0.8000 Silver 0.6000 oz. ASW **Ruler:** Elizabeth II **Subject:** Charlottetown **Obverse:** Laureate Queen's bust right **Reverse:** Design at center, dates at outer edges, denomination below **Rev. Designer:** Dinko Voldanovic **Size:** 36 mm.

Date	Mintage	F-12	VF-20	XF-40	AU-50	MS-60	MS-63	Proof
ND(1964)	7,296,832	—	—	—	—		9.00	—
ND(1964) Specimen proof	Inc. above	—	—	—	—	—	—	250

Small beads — Medium beads — Large beads

KM# 64.1 DOLLAR **Weight:** 23.3276 g. **Composition:** 0.8000 Silver 0.6000 oz. ASW **Ruler:** Elizabeth II **Obverse:** Queen's bust right **Obv. Designer:** Arnold Machin **Reverse:** Voyageur, date and denomination below **Rev. Designer:** Emanual Hahn **Size:** 36 mm.

Date	Mintage	F-12	VF-20	XF-40	AU-50	MS-60	MS-63	Proof
1965	10,768,569	—	—	—	—		9.00	—
Note: Small beads, pointed 5								
1965	Inc. above	—	—	—	—		9.00	—
Note: Small beads, blunt 5								
1965	Inc. above	—	—	—	—		9.00	—
Note: Large beads, blunt 5								
1965	Inc. above	—	—	—	—		11.00	—
Note: Large beads, pointed 5								
1965	Inc. above	—	BV	9.00	10.00	12.00	35.00	—
Note: Medium beads, pointed 5								
1966	9,912,178	—	—	—	—		9.00	—
Note: Large beads								
1966	485	—	—	1,200	1,500	1,800	2,200	—
Note: Small beads								

KM# 64.2a DOLLAR **Weight:** 23.3276 g. **Composition:** 0.5000 Silver 0.3750 oz. ASW **Ruler:** Elizabeth II **Obverse:** Smaller bust **Obv. Designer:** Arnold Machin **Reverse:** Voyageur **Rev. Designer:** Emanuel Hahn **Size:** 36 mm.

Date	Mintage	MS-63	P/L	Proof
1972 Proof	341,598	—	—	5.50
Note: Specimen $5.50.				

KM# 70 DOLLAR **Weight:** 23.3276 g. **Composition:** 0.8000 Silver 0.6000 oz. ASW **Ruler:** Elizabeth II **Subject:** Confederation Centennial **Obverse:** Queen's bust right **Obv. Designer:** Arnold Machin **Reverse:** Goose left, dates below, denomination above **Rev. Designer:** Alex Colville **Size:** 36 mm.

Date	Mintage	MS-63	Proof
ND(1967)	6,767,496	11.00	12.00

KM# 76.1 DOLLAR **Composition:** Nickel **Ruler:** Elizabeth II **Obverse:** Queen's bust right **Obv. Designer:** Arnold Machin **Reverse:** Voyageur, date and denomination below **Rev. Designer:** Emanuel Hahn **Size:** 32 mm.

Date	Mintage	MS-63	Proof
1968	5,579,714	1.25	—
1968	1,408,143	—	—
1968	—	5.00	—
Note: Small island			
1968	—	—	—
Note: No island			
1968	—	—	—
Note: Doubled die; exhibits extra water lines			
1969	4,809,313	1.25	—
1969	594,258	—	—
1972	2,676,041	1.50	—
1972	405,865	—	—

KM# 78 DOLLAR **Composition:** Nickel **Ruler:** Elizabeth II **Subject:** Manitoba **Obverse:** Queen's bust right **Reverse:** Pasque flower divides dates and denomination **Rev. Designer:** Raymond Taylor **Size:** 32 mm.

Date	Mintage	MS-63	Proof
1970	4,140,058	2.00	—
1970	645,869	—	—

KM# 79 DOLLAR **Composition:** Nickel **Ruler:** Elizabeth II **Subject:** British Columbia **Obverse:** Queen's bust right **Reverse:** Shield divides dates, denomination below, flowers above **Rev. Designer:** Thomas Shingles **Size:** 32 mm.

Date	Mintage	MS-63	Proof
1971	4,260,781	2.00	—
1971	468,729	—	—

KM# 80 DOLLAR **Weight:** 23.3276 g. **Composition:** 0.5000 Silver 0.3750 oz. ASW **Ruler:** Elizabeth II **Subject:** British Columbia **Obverse:** Queen's bust right **Reverse:** Crowned arms with supporters divide dates, maple at top divides denomination, crowned lion atop crown on shield **Rev. Designer:** Patrick Brindley **Size:** 36 mm.

Date	Mintage	MS-63	P/L	Spec.
1971	585,674	—	—	5.75

KM# 82 DOLLAR **Composition:** Nickel **Ruler:** Elizabeth II **Subject:** Prince Edward Island **Reverse:** Building, inscription below divides dates, denomination above **Rev. Designer:** Terry Manning **Size:** 32 mm.

Date	Mintage	MS-63	Proof
1973	3,196,452	2.00	—
1973 (c)	466,881	—	—

KM# 83 DOLLAR **Weight:** 23.3276 g. **Composition:** 0.5000 Silver 0.3750 oz. ASW **Ruler:** Elizabeth II **Obverse:** Queen's bust right **Reverse:** Mountie left, dates below, denomination at right **Rev. Designer:** Paul Cedarberg **Size:** 36 mm.

Date	Mintage	MS-63	P/L	Spec.
1973	1,031,271	—	—	6.50

KM# 83v DOLLAR **Note:** Mountie Dollar in blue case with R.C.M.P. crest.

Date	Mintage	MS-63	P/L	Spec.
1973	Inc. above	—	—	15.00

KM# 88a DOLLAR **Composition:** 0.5000 Silver **Ruler:** Elizabeth II **Subject:** Winnipeg Centennial **Obverse:** Queen's bust right **Reverse:** Zeros frame pictures, dates below, denomination at bottom **Rev. Designer:** Paul Pederson and Patrick Brindley **Size:** 36 mm.

Date	Mintage	MS-63	P/L	Spec.
1974	728,947	—	—	5.75

KM# 88 DOLLAR **Composition:** Nickel **Ruler:** Elizabeth II **Subject:** Winnipeg Centennial **Obverse:** Queen's bust right **Reverse:** Zeros frame pictures, dates below, denomination at bottom **Rev. Designer:** Paul Pederson and Patrick Brindley **Size:** 32 mm.

Date	Mintage	MS-63	Proof
1974	2,799,363	2.00	—
1974 (c)	363,786	—	—

KM# 97 DOLLAR **Weight:** 23.3276 g. **Composition:** 0.5000 Silver 0.3750 oz. ASW **Ruler:** Elizabeth II **Subject:** Calgary **Obverse:** Queen's bust right **Reverse:** Figure on bucking horse, dates divided below, denomination above **Rev. Designer:** Donald D. Paterson **Size:** 36 mm.

Date	Mintage	MS-63	P/L	Spec.
1975	930,956	—	—	5.75

KM# 76.3 DOLLAR **Composition:** Nickel **Ruler:** Elizabeth II **Obverse:** Bust right **Obv. Designer:** Arnold Machin **Reverse:** Voyageur **Rev. Designer:** Emanuel Hahn **Size:** 32 mm. **Note:** Only known in prooflike sets with 1976 obverse slightly modified.

Date	Mintage	MS-63	P/L	Proof
1975	Inc. above	—	3.00	—

Note: mule with 1976 obv.

KM# 76.2 DOLLAR **Composition:** Nickel **Ruler:** Elizabeth II **Obverse:** Smaller bust **Obv. Designer:** Arnold Machin **Reverse:** Voyageur **Rev. Designer:** Emanuel Hahn **Size:** 32 mm.

Date	Mintage	MS-63	Proof
1975	3,256,000	1.50	—
1975	322,325	—	—
1976	2,498,204	1.50	—
1976	274,106	—	—

KM# 106 DOLLAR **Weight:** 23.3276 g. **Composition:** 0.5000 Silver 0.3750 oz. ASW **Ruler:** Elizabeth II **Subject:** Parliament Library **Obverse:** Queen's bust right **Reverse:** Library building, dates below, denomination above **Rev. Designer:** Walter Ott and Patrick Brindley **Size:** 36 mm.

Date	Mintage	MS-63	P/L	Spec.
1976	578,708	—	—	6.50
1976	Inc. above	—	—	15.00

Note: Blue case VIP

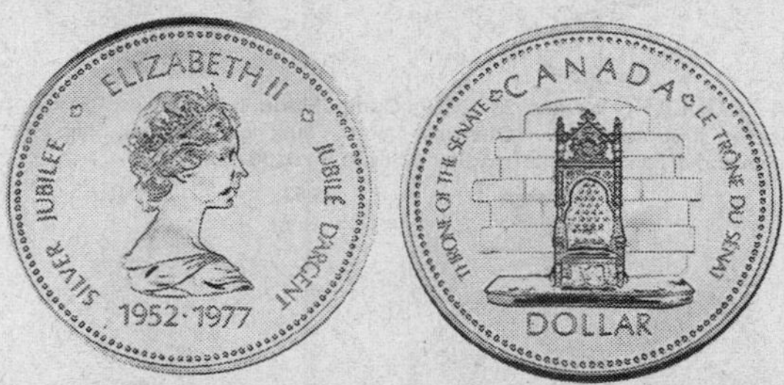

KM# 118 DOLLAR **Weight:** 23.3276 g. **Composition:** 0.5000 Silver 0.3750 oz. ASW **Ruler:** Elizabeth II **Subject:** Silver Jubilee **Obverse:** Queen's bust right, dates below **Reverse:** Throne, denomination below **Rev. Designer:** Raymond Lee **Size:** 36 mm.

Date	Mintage	MS-63	P/L	Spec.
1977	744,848	—	—	5.50
1977	Inc. above	—	—	25.00

Note: red case VIP

KM# 117 DOLLAR **Composition:** Nickel **Ruler:** Elizabeth II **Obverse:** Bust right **Obv. Designer:** Arnold Machin **Reverse:** Voyageur modified **Rev. Designer:** Emanuel Hahn **Size:** 32 mm.

Date	Mintage	MS-63	Proof
1977	1,393,745	2.25	—

KM# 120.1 DOLLAR **Weight:** 15.6200 g. **Composition:** Nickel **Ruler:** Elizabeth II **Obverse:** Queen's bust right **Obv. Designer:** Arnold Machin **Reverse:** Voyageur, date and denomination below **Rev. Designer:** Emanuel Hahn **Size:** 32.13 mm. **Note:** Modified design.

Date	Mintage	MS-63	Proof
1978	2,948,488	1.50	—
1979	2,954,842	1.50	—
1980	3,291,221	1.50	—
1981	2,778,900	1.50	—
1981 Proof	—	—	—
1982	1,098,500	1.50	—
1982 Proof	180,908	—	5.25
1983	2,267,525	1.50	—
1983 Proof	166,779	—	5.25
1984	1,223,486	1.50	—
1984 Proof	161,602	—	6.00
1985	3,104,092	1.50	—
1985 Proof	153,950	—	7.00
1986	3,089,225	2.00	—

Date	Mintage	MS-63	Proof
1986 Proof	176,224	—	7.50
1987	287,330	3.50	—
1987 Proof	175,686	—	7.50

KM# 120.2 DOLLAR **Composition:** Nickel **Ruler:** Elizabeth II **Obverse:** Bust right **Reverse:** Voyageur **Size:** 32.13 mm. **Note:** Modified design.

Date	Mintage	MS-63	P/L	Spec.
1985	—	1,900	—	—

Note: Mule with New Zealand 50 cent, KM-37 obverse

KM# 121 DOLLAR **Weight:** 23.3276 g. **Composition:** 0.5000 Silver 0.3750 oz. ASW **Ruler:** Elizabeth II **Subject:** XI Commonwealth Games **Obverse:** Queen's bust right **Reverse:** Commonwealth games, logo at center **Rev. Designer:** Raymond Taylor **Size:** 36 mm.

Date	Mintage	MS-63	P/L	Spec.
1978	709,602	—	—	5.50

KM# 124 DOLLAR **Weight:** 23.3276 g. **Composition:** 0.5000 Silver 0.3750 oz. ASW **Ruler:** Elizabeth II **Subject:** Griffon **Obverse:** Queen's bust right **Reverse:** Ship, dates below, denomination above **Rev. Designer:** Walter Schluep **Size:** 36 mm.

Date	Mintage	MS-63	P/L	Spec.
1979	826,695	—	—	8.50

KM# 128 DOLLAR **Weight:** 23.3276 g. **Composition:** 0.5000 Silver 0.3750 oz. ASW **Ruler:** Elizabeth II **Subject:** Arctic Territories **Obverse:** Queen's bust right **Reverse:** Bear right, date below, denomination above **Rev. Designer:** Donald D. Paterson **Size:** 36 mm.

Date	Mintage	MS-63	P/L	Spec.
1980	539,617	—	—	20.00

KM# 130 DOLLAR **Weight:** 23.3276 g. **Composition:** 0.5000 Silver 0.3750 oz. ASW **Ruler:** Elizabeth II **Subject:** Transcontinental Railroad **Obverse:** Queen's bust right **Reverse:** Train engine and map, date below, denomination above **Rev. Designer:** Christopher Gorey **Size:** 36 mm.

Date	Mintage	MS-63	P/L	Proof
1981	699,494	7.50	—	—
1981 Proof	—	—	—	13.50

KM# 133 DOLLAR **Weight:** 23.3276 g. **Composition:** 0.5000 Silver 0.3750 oz. ASW **Ruler:** Elizabeth II **Subject:** Regina **Obverse:** Queen's bust right **Reverse:** Cattle skull divides dates and denomination below **Rev. Designer:** Huntley Brown **Size:** 36 mm.

Date	Mintage	MS-63	P/L	Proof
1982	144,930	7.50	—	—
1982 Proof	758,958	—	—	7.00

KM# 134 DOLLAR **Composition:** Nickel **Ruler:** Elizabeth II **Subject:** Constitution **Obverse:** Queen's bust right **Reverse:** Meeting of Government **Rev. Designer:** Ago Aarand **Size:** 32 mm.

Date	Mintage	MS-63	P/L	Proof
1982	9,709,422	3.00	6.00	—

KM# 138 DOLLAR **Weight:** 23.3276 g. **Composition:** 0.5000 Silver 0.3750 oz. ASW **Ruler:** Elizabeth II **Subject:** Edmonton University Games **Obverse:** Queen's bust right **Reverse:** Athlete within game logo, date and denomination below **Rev. Designer:** Carola Tietz **Size:** 36 mm.

Date	Mintage	MS-63	P/L	Proof
1983	159,450	7.00	—	—
1983 Proof	506,847	—	—	6.00

KM# 140 DOLLAR **Weight:** 23.3276 g. **Composition:** 0.5000 Silver 0.3750 oz. ASW **Ruler:** Elizabeth II **Subject:** Toronto Sesquicentennial **Rev. Designer:** D. J. Craig **Size:** 36 mm.

Date	Mintage	MS-63	P/L	Proof
1984	133,610	7.50	—	—
1984 Proof	732,542	—	—	7.00

KM# 141 DOLLAR **Composition:** Nickel **Ruler:** Elizabeth II **Subject:** Jacques Cartier **Obverse:** Queen's bust right **Reverse:** Cross with shield above figures **Rev. Designer:** Hector Greville **Size:** 32 mm.

Date	Mintage	MS-63	P/L	Proof
1984	7,009,323	2.25	—	—
1984 Proof	87,760	—	—	6.00

KM# 143 DOLLAR **Weight:** 23.3276 g. **Composition:** 0.5000 Silver 0.3750 oz. ASW **Ruler:** Elizabeth II **Subject:** National Parks **Obverse:** Queen's bust right **Reverse:** Moose right, dates above, denomination below **Rev. Designer:** Karel Rohlicek **Size:** 36 mm.

Date	Mintage	MS-63	P/L	Proof
1985	163,314	7.50	—	—
1985 Proof	733,354	—	—	9.00

KM# 149 DOLLAR **Weight:** 23.3276 g. **Composition:** 0.5000 Silver 0.3750 oz. ASW **Ruler:** Elizabeth II **Subject:** Vancouver **Obverse:** Queen's bust right **Reverse:** Train left, dates divided below, denomination above **Rev. Designer:** Elliot John Morrison **Size:** 36 mm.

Date	Mintage	MS-63	P/L	Proof
1986	125,949	8.00	—	—
1986 Proof	680,004	—	—	7.50

KM# 154 DOLLAR **Weight:** 23.3276 g. **Composition:** 0.5000 Silver 0.3750 oz. ASW **Ruler:** Elizabeth II **Subject:** John Davis **Obverse:** Queen's bust right **Reverse:** Ship with masts, rock in background, dates below, denomination at bottom **Rev. Designer:** Christopher Gorey **Size:** 36 mm.

Date	Mintage	MS-63	P/L	Proof
1987	118,722	8.00	—	—
1987 Proof	602,374	—	—	9.00

KM# 157 DOLLAR **Weight:** 7.0000 g. **Composition:** Aureate-Bronze Plated Nickel **Ruler:** Elizabeth II **Obverse:** Queen's bust right **Obv. Designer:** Arnold Machin **Reverse:** Loon right, date and denomination below **Rev. Designer:** Robert R. Carmichael **Shape:** 11-sided **Size:** 26.5 mm.

Date	Mintage	MS-63	Proof
1987	205,405,000	2.25	—
1987 Proof	178,120	—	8.00
1988	138,893,539	2.25	—
1988 Proof	175,259	—	6.75
1989	184,773,902	3.00	—
1989 Proof	170,928	—	6.75

KM# 161 DOLLAR **Weight:** 23.3276 g. **Composition:** 0.5000 Silver 0.3750 oz. ASW **Subject:** Ironworks **Reverse:** Ironworkers, date and denomination below **Rev. Designer:** Robert R. Carmichael **Size:** 36 mm.

Date	Mintage	MS-63	P/L	Proof
1988	106,872	8.00	—	—
1988 Proof	255,013	—	—	16.00

KM# 168 DOLLAR **Weight:** 23.3276 g. **Composition:** 0.5000 Silver 0.3750 oz. ASW **Ruler:** Elizabeth II **Subject:** MacKenzie River **Obverse:** Queen's bust right **Reverse:** People in canoe, date above, denomination below **Rev. Designer:** John Mardon **Size:** 36 mm.

Date	Mintage	MS-63	P/L	Proof
1989	99,774	8.00	—	—
1989 Proof	244,062	—	—	16.00

KM# 170 DOLLAR **Weight:** 23.3276 g. **Composition:** 0.5000 Silver 0.3750 oz. ASW **Ruler:** Elizabeth II **Subject:** Henry Kelsey **Obverse:** Crowned Queen's head right **Reverse:** Kelsey with natives, dates below, denomination above **Rev. Designer:** D. J. Craig **Size:** 36 mm.

Date	Mintage	MS-63	P/L	Proof
1990	99,455	8.00	—	—
1990 Proof	254,959	—	—	18.00

KM# 186 DOLLAR **Weight:** 7.0000 g. **Composition:** Aureate-Bronze Plated Nickel **Ruler:** Elizabeth II **Obverse:** Crowned head right **Obv. Designer:** Dora dePedery-Hunt **Reverse:** Loon right, date and denomination **Rev. Designer:** Robert R. Carmichael **Shape:** 11-sided **Size:** 26.5 mm.

Date	Mintage	MS-63	Proof
1990	68,402,000	1.75	—
1990 Proof	140,649	—	7.00
1991	23,156,000	1.75	—
1991 Proof	—	—	13.00
1993	33,662,000	2.00	—
1993 Proof	—	—	6.00
1994	16,232,530	2.00	—
1994 Proof	—	—	7.00
1995	27,492,630	3.00	—
1995 Proof	—	—	7.00
1996	17,101,000	2.00	—
1996 Proof	—	—	7.50
1997	—	5.00	—
1997 Proof	—	—	8.00
1998	—	2.50	—
1998 Proof	—	—	10.00
1998W	—	—	—
1999	—	2.00	—
1999 Proof	—	—	8.00
2000	—	2.00	—
2000 Proof	—	—	8.00

KM# 179 DOLLAR **Weight:** 23.3276 g. **Composition:** 0.5000 Silver 0.3750 oz. ASW **Ruler:** Elizabeth II **Subject:** S.S. Frontenac **Obverse:** Crowned Queen's head right **Reverse:** Frontenac, date and denomination below **Rev. Designer:** D. J. Craig **Size:** 36 mm.

Date	Mintage	MS-63	P/L	Proof
1991	73,843	8.00	—	—
1991 Proof	195,424	—	—	24.00

KM# 210 DOLLAR **Weight:** 25.1750 g. **Composition:** 0.9250 Silver 0.7487 oz. ASW **Ruler:** Elizabeth II **Subject:** Stagecoach service **Obverse:** Crowned Queen's head right **Reverse:** Stagecoach, date and denomination below **Rev. Designer:** Karsten Smith **Size:** 36 mm.

Date	Mintage	MS-63	P/L	Proof
1992	78,160	11.00	—	—
1992 Proof	187,612	—	—	14.00

KM# 209 DOLLAR **Composition:** Aureate **Ruler:** Elizabeth II **Subject:** Loon right, dates and denomination **Obverse:** Crowned Queen's head right **Rev. Designer:** Robert R. Carmichael **Size:** 26.5 mm.

Date	Mintage	MS-63	Proof
ND(1992)	4,242,085	2.00	—
ND(1992) Proof	—	—	8.00

KM# 218 DOLLAR **Composition:** Aureate **Ruler:** Elizabeth II **Subject:** Parliament **Obverse:** Crowned Queen's head right, dates below **Reverse:** Backs of three seated figures in front of building, denomination below **Rev. Designer:** Rita Swanson **Size:** 26 mm.

Date	Mintage	MS-63	Proof
ND(1992)	23,915,000	2.25	—
ND(1992) Proof	24,227	—	9.00

KM# 235 DOLLAR **Weight:** 25.1750 g. **Composition:** 0.9250 Silver 0.7487 oz. ASW **Ruler:** Elizabeth II **Subject:** Stanley Cup hockey **Obverse:** Crowned Queen's head right **Reverse:** Hockey players between cups, dates below, denomination above **Rev. Designer:** Stewart Sherwood **Size:** 36 mm.

Date	Mintage	MS-63	P/L	Proof
1993	88,150	11.00	—	—
1993 Proof	294,314	—	—	14.00

KM# 251 DOLLAR **Weight:** 25.1750 g. **Composition:** 0.9250 Silver 0.7487 oz. ASW **Ruler:** Elizabeth II **Subject:** Last RCMP sled-dog patrol **Obverse:** Crowned Queen's head right **Reverse:** Dogsled, denomination divides dates below **Rev. Designer:** Ian Sparks **Size:** 36 mm.

Date	Mintage	MS-63	P/L	Proof
1994	61,561	12.00	—	—
1994 Proof	170,374	—	—	25.00

KM# 248 DOLLAR **Composition:** Aureate **Ruler:** Elizabeth II **Subject:** War Memorial **Obverse:** Crowned Queen's head right, date below **Reverse:** Memorial, denomination at right **Rev. Designer:** R. C. M. Staff **Size:** 26 mm.

Date	Mintage	MS-63	Proof
1994	20,004,830	2.25	—
1994 Proof	54,524	—	7.50

KM# 258 DOLLAR **Composition:** Aureate **Ruler:** Elizabeth II **Subject:** Peacekeeping Monument in Ottawa **Obverse:** Crowned Queen's head right, date below **Reverse:** Monument, denomination above right **Rev. Designer:** J. K. Harmon, R. G. Henriquez and C. H. Oberlander **Size:** 26 mm. **Note:** Mintage included with KM#186.

Date	Mintage	MS-63	Proof
1995	18,502,750	2.25	—
1995 Proof	43,293	—	7.50

KM# 259 DOLLAR **Weight:** 25.1750 g. **Composition:** 0.9250 Silver 0.7487 oz. ASW **Ruler:** Elizabeth II **Subject:** Hudson Bay Co. **Obverse:** Crowned Queen's head right **Reverse:** Explorers and ship, date and denomination below **Rev. Designer:** Vincent McIndoe **Size:** 36 mm.

Date	Mintage	MS-63	P/L	Proof
1995	61,819	12.00	—	—
1995 Proof	166,259	—	—	20.00

KM# 274 DOLLAR **Weight:** 25.1750 g. **Composition:** 0.9250 Silver 0.7487 oz. ASW **Subject:** McIntosh Apple **Reverse:** Apple, dates and denomination below **Rev. Designer:** Roger Hill **Size:** 36 mm.

Date	Mintage	MS-63	P/L	Proof
1996	58,834	12.00	—	—
1996 Proof	133,779	—	—	24.00

KM# 282 DOLLAR **Weight:** 25.1750 g. **Composition:** 0.9250 Silver 0.7487 oz. ASW **Ruler:** Elizabeth II **Subject:** 25th Anniversary Hockey Victory **Obverse:** Crowned Queen's head right **Reverse:** The winning goal by Paul Aenderson. Based on a painting by Andre l'Archeveque, dates at right, denomination at bottom **Rev. Designer:** Walter Burden **Size:** 36 mm.

Date	Mintage	MS-63	P/L	Proof
ND(1997)	155,252	11.50	—	—
ND(1997) Proof	184,965	—	—	24.00

KM# 291 DOLLAR **Composition:** Aureate **Ruler:** Elizabeth II **Subject:** Loon Dollar 10th Anniversary **Obverse:** Crowned Queen's head right **Reverse:** Loon in flight left, dates above, denomination below **Rev. Designer:** Jean-Luc Grondin **Size:** 26 mm.

Date	Mintage	MS-63	P/L	Proof
1997	—	—	20.00	—

KM# 296 DOLLAR **Weight:** 25.1750 g. **Composition:** 0.9250 Silver 0.7487 oz. ASW **Ruler:** Elizabeth II **Subject:** Loon Dollar 10th Anniversary **Obverse:** Crowned Queen's head right **Reverse:** Loon in flight left, dates above, denomination below **Rev. Designer:** Jean-Luc Grondin **Size:** 36 mm.

Date	Mintage	MS-63	P/L	Proof
1997 Proof	24,995	—	—	75.00

KM# 306 DOLLAR **Weight:** 25.1750 g. **Composition:** 0.9250 Silver 0.7487 oz. ASW **Ruler:** Elizabeth II **Subject:** 120th Anniversary Royal Canadian Mounted Police **Obverse:** Crowned Queen's head right **Reverse:** Mountie on horseback, dates at left, denomination above **Rev. Designer:** Adeline Halvorson **Size:** 36 mm. **Note:** Individually cased prooflikes, proofs or specimens are from broken-up prooflike or specimen sets.

Date	Mintage	MS-63	P/L	Proof
1998	79,777	—	11.50	—
1998 Proof	120,172	—	—	20.00

KM# 355 DOLLAR **Weight:** 25.1750 g. **Composition:** 0.9250 Silver 0.7487 oz. ASW **Subject:** International Year of Old Persons **Reverse:** Figures amid trees, date and denomination below **Rev. Designer:** S. Armstrong-Hodgson **Size:** 36 mm.

Date	Mintage	MS-63	P/L	Proof
1999 Proof	24,976	—	—	40.00

KM# 356 DOLLAR **Weight:** 25.1750 g. **Composition:** 0.9250 Silver 0.7487 oz. ASW **Ruler:** Elizabeth II **Subject:** Discovery of Queen Charlotte Isle **Obverse:** Crowned Queen's head right **Reverse:** Ship and three boats, dates at right, denomination below **Rev. Designer:** D. J. Craig **Size:** 36 mm.

Date	Mintage	MS-63	P/L	Proof
ND(1999)	67,655	—	11.50	—
ND(1999) Proof	126,435	—	—	22.50

KM# 401 DOLLAR **Weight:** 25.1750 g. **Composition:** 0.9250 Silver 0.7487 oz. ASW **Ruler:** Elizabeth II **Subject:** Voyage of Discovery **Obverse:** Crowned Queen's head right **Reverse:** Human and space shuttle, date above, denomination below **Rev. Designer:** D. F. Warkentine **Size:** 36 mm.

Date	Mintage	MS-63	P/L	Proof
2000	60,100	—	11.50	—
2000 Proof	114,130	—	—	22.50

KM# 443 DOLLAR **Weight:** 25.1750 g. **Composition:** 0.9250 Silver 0.7487 oz. ASW **Ruler:** Elizabeth II **Subject:** Queen's Golden Jubilee **Obverse:** Crowned head right, with anniversary date at left **Reverse:** Queen in her coach and a view of the coach, denomination below **Edge:** Reeded **Size:** 36 mm.

Date	Mintage	MS-63	P/L	Proof
ND(2000) Proof	125,000	—	—	20.00

KM# 270 2 DOLLARS **Weight:** 7.3000 g. **Composition:** Bi-Metallic **Ruler:** Elizabeth II **Obverse:** Crowned head right within circle, date below **Obv. Designer:** Dora dePedery-Hunt **Reverse:** Polar bear right within circle, denomination below **Rev. Designer:** Brent Townsend **Size:** 28 mm.

Date	Mintage	MS-63	Proof
1996	375,483,000	3.25	10.00
1997	16,942,000	3.25	—
1998	4,926,000	3.25	—
1998W	—	3.25	—
1999	25,130,000	3.25	—
2000	29,847,000	3.25	—
2000W	—	3.25	—

KM# 270a 2 DOLLARS **Weight:** 10.8414 g. **Composition:** Bi-Metallic **Ruler:** Elizabeth II **Obverse:** Head right within circle, date below **Reverse:** Polar bear right within circle, denomination below **Size:** 28 mm.

Date	Mintage	MS-63	P/L	Proof
1996 Proof	5,000	—	—	145

KM# 270b 2 DOLLARS **Weight:** 25.0000 g. **Composition:** Bi-Metallic Gold And Silver **Ruler:** Elizabeth II **Obverse:** Head right within circle, date below **Reverse:** Polar bear right within circle, denomination below **Edge:** 4.5mm thick **Size:** 28 mm.

Date	Mintage	MS-63	P/L	Proof
1996 Proof	10,000	—	—	55.00
1998 Proof	—	—	—	—

KM# 270c 2 DOLLARS **Weight:** 8.8300 g. **Composition:** 0.9250 Bi-Metallic Gold And Silver **Ruler:** Elizabeth II **Obverse:** Crowned head right within circle, date below **Reverse:** Polar bear right within circle, denomination below **Edge:** 1.8mm thickness **Size:** 28 mm. **Note:** Silver ring; Gold plated silver center. 8.83g., .925 silver, .2626 ASW.

Date	Mintage	MS-63	Proof
1996 Proof	10,000	—	12.00
1997 Proof	—	—	10.00
19980 Proof	—	—	12.00
1999 Proof	—	—	12.00
2000 Proof	—	—	12.00

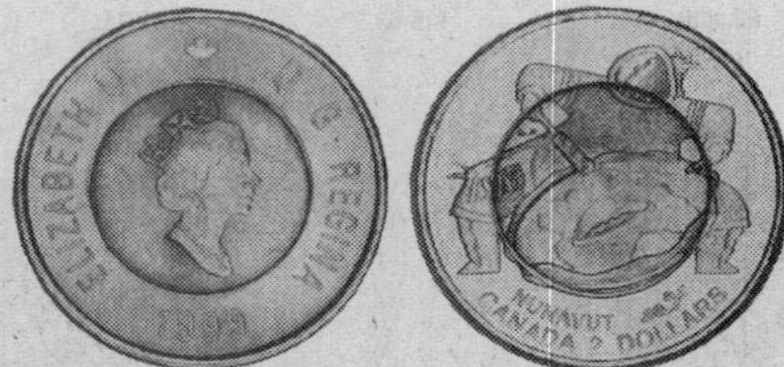

KM# 357 2 DOLLARS **Weight:** 7.3000 g. **Composition:** Bi-Metallic **Ruler:** Elizabeth II **Subject:** Nunavut **Obverse:** Crowned Queen's head right within circle, date below **Reverse:** Inuit person with drum, denomination below **Rev. Designer:** G. Arnaktavyok **Size:** 28 mm.

Date	Mintage	MS-63	P/L	Proof
1999	—	3.50	—	—

KM# 357a 2 DOLLARS **Weight:** 8.5200 g. **Composition:** 0.9250 Gold Plated Silver **Ruler:** Elizabeth II **Subject:** Nunavut **Obverse:** Queen's head right **Reverse:** Drum dancer **Edge:** Interrupted reeding **Size:** 28 mm.

Date	Mintage	MS-63	P/L	Proof
1999 Proof	—	—	—	15.00

KM# 357b 2 DOLLARS **Composition:** Gold **Ruler:** Elizabeth II **Subject:** Nunavut **Obverse:** Queen's head right **Reverse:** Drum dancer

Date	Mintage	MS-63	P/L	Proof
1999 Proof	10,000	—	—	175

KM# 399 2 DOLLARS **Weight:** 7.3000 g. **Composition:** Bi-Metallic **Ruler:** Elizabeth II **Subject:** Knowledge **Obverse:** Crowned head right within circle, denomination below **Reverse:** Polar bear and 2 cubs right within circle, date above **Rev. Designer:** Tony Bianco **Edge:** Reeded and plain sections **Size:** 28 mm.

Date	Mintage	MS-63	Proof
2000	—	3.50	—

KM# 399a 2 DOLLARS **Composition:** 0.9250 Gold Plated Silver **Ruler:** Elizabeth II **Subject:** Knowledge **Obverse:** Head right within circle, denomination below **Reverse:** Polar bear and 2 cubs within circle, date above

Date	Mintage	MS-63	P/L	Proof
2000 Proof	40,000	—	—	15.00

KM# 399b 2 DOLLARS **Weight:** 6.3100 g. **Composition:** 0.9160 Gold **Ruler:** Elizabeth II **Subject:** Knowledge **Obverse:** Head right within circle, denomination below **Reverse:** Polar bear and two cubs right within circle, date above

Date	Mintage	MS-63	P/L	Proof
2000 Proof	—	—	—	175

KM# 26 5 DOLLARS **Weight:** 8.3592 g. **Composition:** 0.9000 Gold 0.2419 oz. AGW **Ruler:** George V **Obverse:** King's bust left **Obv. Designer:** E. B. MacKennal **Reverse:** Arms within wreath, date and denomination below **Rev. Designer:** W. H. J. Blakemore

Date	Mintage	F-12	VF-20	XF-40	AU-50	MS-60	MS-63
1912	165,680	BV	160	175	200	250	550
1913	98,832	BV	160	175	200	250	600
1914	31,122	175	275	350	425	650	2,000

KM# 84 5 DOLLARS **Weight:** 24.3000 g. **Composition:** 0.9250 Silver 0.7227 oz. ASW **Ruler:** Elizabeth II **Subject:** 1976 Montreal Olympics **Obverse:** Queen's bust right, small maple below, date at right **Reverse:** Sailboat "Kingston", date at left, denomination below **Rev. Designer:** Georges Huel **Size:** 38 mm. **Note:** Series I.

Date	Mintage	MS-63	Proof
1973	—	9.75	—
1973 Proof	165,203	—	10.00

KM# 85 5 DOLLARS **Composition:** 0.9250 Silver 0.7227 oz. ASW **Ruler:** Elizabeth II **Subject:** 1976 Montreal Olympics **Obverse:** Bust right, small maple leaf below, date at right **Reverse:** North American map, denominaton below **Rev. Designer:** Georges Huel **Note:** Series I.

Date	Mintage	MS-63	Proof
1973	—	9.75	—
1973 Proof	165,203	—	10.00

KM# 89 5 DOLLARS **Weight:** 24.3000 g. **Composition:** 0.9250 Silver 0.7227 oz. ASW **Ruler:** Elizabeth II **Subject:** 1976 Montreal Olympics **Obverse:** Bust right, small maple leaf below, date at right **Reverse:** Olympic rings, denomination below **Rev. Designer:** Anthony Mann **Size:** 38 mm. **Note:** Series II.

Date	Mintage	MS-63	Proof
1974	—	9.75	—
1974 Proof	97,431	—	10.00

KM# 90 5 DOLLARS **Weight:** 24.3000 g. **Composition:** 0.9250 Silver 0.7227 oz. ASW **Ruler:** Elizabeth II **Subject:** 1976 Montreal Olympics **Obverse:** Bust right, small maple leaf below, date at right **Reverse:** Athlete with torch, denomination below **Rev. Designer:** Anthony Mann **Size:** 38 mm. **Note:** Series II.

Date	Mintage	MS-63	Proof
1974	—	9.75	—
1974 Proof	97,431	—	10.00

KM# 91 5 DOLLARS **Weight:** 24.3000 g. **Composition:** 0.9250 Silver 0.7227 oz. ASW **Ruler:** Elizabeth II **Subject:** 1976 Montreal Olympics **Obverse:** Bust right, small maple leaf below, date at right **Reverse:** Rower, denomination below **Rev. Designer:** Ken Danby **Size:** 38 mm. **Note:** Series III.

Date	Mintage	MS-63	Proof
1974	—	9.75	—
1974 Proof	104,684	—	10.00

KM# 92 5 DOLLARS **Weight:** 24.3000 g. **Composition:** 0.9250 Silver 0.7227 oz. ASW **Ruler:** Elizabeth II **Subject:** 1976 Montreal Olympics **Obverse:** Bust right, small maple leaf below, date at right **Reverse:** Canoeing, denomination below **Rev. Designer:** Ken Danby **Size:** 38 mm. **Note:** Series III.

Date	Mintage	MS-63	Proof
1974	—	9.75	—
1974 Proof	104,684	—	10.00

KM# 98 5 DOLLARS **Weight:** 24.3000 g. **Composition:** 0.9250 Silver 0.7227 oz. ASW **Ruler:** Elizabeth II **Subject:** 1976 Montreal Olympics **Obverse:** Bust right, small maple leaf below, date at right **Reverse:** Marathon, denomination below **Rev. Designer:** Leo Yerxa **Size:** 38 mm. **Note:** Series IV.

Date	Mintage	MS-63	Proof
1975	—	9.75	—
1975 Proof	89,155	—	10.00

KM# 99 5 DOLLARS **Weight:** 24.3000 g. **Composition:** 0.9250 Silver 0.7227 oz. ASW **Ruler:** Elizabeth II **Subject:** Montreal 1976 - 21st Summer Olympic Games **Obverse:** Bust right, small maple leaf below, date at right **Reverse:** Women's javelin event, denomination below **Rev. Designer:** Leo Yerxa **Size:** 38 mm. **Note:** Series IV.

Date	Mintage	MS-63	Proof
1975	—	9.75	—
1975 Proof	89,155	—	10.00

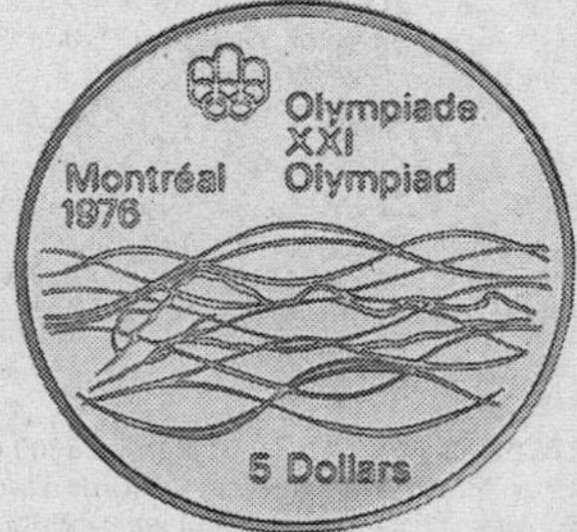

KM# 100 5 DOLLARS **Weight:** 24.3000 g. **Composition:** 0.9250 Silver 0.7227 oz. ASW **Ruler:** Elizabeth II **Subject:** 1976 Montreal Olympics **Obverse:** Bust right, small maple leaf below, date at right **Reverse:** Swimmer, denomination below **Rev. Designer:** Lynda Cooper **Size:** 38 mm. **Note:** Series V.

Date	Mintage	MS-63	Proof
1975	—	9.75	—
1975 Proof	89,155	—	10.00

KM# 101 5 DOLLARS **Weight:** 24.3000 g. **Composition:** 0.9250 Silver 0.7227 oz. ASW **Ruler:** Elizabeth II **Subject:** Montreal 1976 - 21st Summer Olympic Games **Obverse:** Bust right, small maple leaf below, date at right **Reverse:** Platform Diver, denomination below **Rev. Designer:** Lynda Cooper **Size:** 38 mm. **Note:** Series V.

Date	Mintage	MS-63	Proof
1975	—	9.75	—
1975 Proof	89,155	—	10.00

KM# 107 5 DOLLARS **Weight:** 24.3000 g. **Composition:** 0.9250 Silver 0.7227 oz. ASW **Ruler:** Elizabeth II **Subject:** 1976 Montreal Olympics **Obverse:** Bust right, small maple leaf below, date at right **Reverse:** Fencing, denomination below **Rev. Designer:** Shigeo Fukada **Size:** 38 mm. **Note:** Series VI.

Date	Mintage	MS-63	Proof
1976	—	9.75	—
1976 Proof	82,302	—	10.00

KM# 108 5 DOLLARS **Weight:** 24.3000 g. **Composition:** 0.9250 Silver 0.7227 oz. ASW **Ruler:** Elizabeth II **Subject:** 1976 Montreal Olympics **Obverse:** Bust right, small maple leaf below, date at right **Obv. Legend:** Boxing **Reverse:** Boxers, denomination below **Rev. Designer:** Shigeo Fukada **Size:** 38 mm. **Note:** Series VI.

Date	Mintage	MS-63	Proof
1976	—	9.75	—
1976 Proof	82,302	—	10.00

KM# 109 5 DOLLARS **Weight:** 24.3000 g. **Composition:** 0.9250 Silver 0.7227 oz. ASW **Ruler:** Elizabeth II **Subject:** 1976 Montreal Olympics **Obverse:** Bust right, small maple leaf below, date at right **Reverse:** Olympic village, denomination below **Rev. Designer:** Elliot John Morrison **Size:** 38 mm. **Note:** Series VII.

Date	Mintage	MS-63	Proof
1976	—	9.75	—
1976 Proof	76,908	—	10.00

KM# 110 5 DOLLARS **Weight:** 24.3000 g. **Composition:** 0.9250 Silver 0.7227 oz. ASW **Ruler:** Elizabeth II **Subject:** 1976 Montreal Olympics **Obverse:** Queen's bust, maple leaf below, date at right **Reverse:** Olympic flame, denomination below **Rev. Designer:** Elliott John Morrison **Size:** 38 mm. **Note:** Series VII.

Date	Mintage	MS-63	Proof
1976	—	9.75	—
1976 Proof	79,102	—	10.00

KM# 316 5 DOLLARS **Weight:** 31.3900 g. **Composition:** 0.9999 Silver 1.0091 oz. ASW **Subject:** Dr. Norman Bethune **Reverse:** Bethune and party, date at upper right **Rev. Designer:** Harvey Chan

Date	Mintage	MS-63	Proof
1998 Proof	61,000	—	35.00

KM# 398 5 DOLLARS **Composition:** Copper-Zinc-Nickel **Reverse:** Viking ship under sail **Rev. Designer:** Donald Curley **Note:** Sold in sets with Norway 20 kroner, KM#465.

Date	Mintage	MS-63	Proof
1999 Proof	—	—	18.50

KM# 27 10 DOLLARS **Weight:** 16.7185 g. **Composition:** 0.9000 Gold 0.4838 oz. AGW **Ruler:** George V **Obverse:** King's bust left **Obv. Designer:** E. B. MacKennal **Reverse:** Arms within wreath, date and denomination below **Rev. Designer:** W. H. J. Blackmore

Date	Mintage	F-12	VF-20	XF-40	AU-50	MS-60	MS-63
1912	74,759	BV	320	360	400	550	2,000
1913	149,232	BV	325	375	400	600	2,600
1914	140,068	BV	330	400	450	700	2,750

KM# 86.1 10 DOLLARS **Weight:** 48.6000 g. **Composition:** 0.9250 Silver 1.4454 oz. ASW **Ruler:** Elizabeth II **Subject:** 1976 Montreal Olympics **Obverse:** Queen's bust right, maple leaf below, date at right **Reverse:** World map, denomination below **Rev. Designer:** Georges Huel **Size:** 45 mm. **Note:** Series I.

Date	Mintage	MS-63	Proof
1973	103,426	19.50	—
1973 Proof	165,203	—	20.00

KM# 86.2 10 DOLLARS **Weight:** 48.6000 g. **Composition:** 0.9250 Silver 1.4454 oz. ASW **Ruler:** Elizabeth II **Subject:** 1976 Montreal Olympics **Obverse:** Bust right, small maple leaf below, date at right **Reverse:** World map **Rev. Designer:** Georges Huel **Size:** 45 mm. **Note:** Series I.

Date	Mintage	MS-63	Proof
1974	320	275	—

Note: Error: mule

KM# 87 10 DOLLARS **Weight:** 48.6000 g. **Composition:** 0.9250 Silver 1.4454 oz. ASW **Ruler:** Elizabeth II **Subject:** 1976 Montreal Olympics **Obverse:** Bust right, small maple leaf below, date at right **Reverse:** Montreal skyline, denomination below **Rev. Designer:** Georges Huel **Size:** 45 mm. **Note:** Series I.

Date	Mintage	MS-63	Proof
1973	—	19.50	—
1973 Proof	165,203	—	20.00

KM# 93 10 DOLLARS **Weight:** 48.6000 g. **Composition:** 0.9250 Silver 1.4454 oz. ASW **Ruler:** Elizabeth II **Subject:** 1976 Montreal Olympics **Obverse:** Bust right, small maple leaf below, date at right **Reverse:** Head of Zeus, denomination below **Rev. Designer:** Anthony Mann **Size:** 45 mm. **Note:** Series II.

Date	Mintage	MS-63	Proof
1974	—	19.50	—
1974 Proof	104,684	—	20.00

KM# 94 10 DOLLARS **Weight:** 48.6000 g. **Composition:** 0.9250 Silver 1.4454 oz. ASW **Ruler:** Elizabeth II **Subject:** 1976 Montreal Olympics **Obverse:** Bust right, small maple leaf below, date at right **Reverse:** Temple of Zeus, denomination below **Rev. Designer:** Anthony Mann **Size:** 45 mm. **Note:** Series II.

Date	Mintage	MS-63	Proof
1974	—	19.50	—
1974 Proof	104,684	—	20.00

KM# 95 10 DOLLARS **Weight:** 48.6000 g. **Composition:** 0.9250 Silver 1.4454 oz. ASW **Ruler:** Elizabeth II **Subject:** 1976 Montreal Olympics **Obverse:** Bust right, small maple leaf below, date at right **Reverse:** Cycling, denomination below **Rev. Designer:** Ken Danby **Size:** 45 mm. **Note:** Series III.

Date	Mintage	MS-63	Proof
1974	—	19.50	—
1974 Proof	97,431	—	20.00

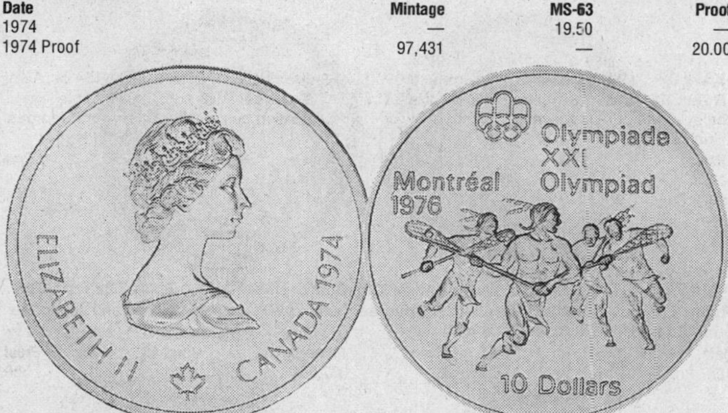

KM# 96 10 DOLLARS **Weight:** 48.6000 g. **Composition:** 0.9250 Silver 1.4454 oz. ASW **Ruler:** Elizabeth II **Subject:** 1976 Montreal Olympics **Obverse:** Bust right, small maple leaf below, date at right **Reverse:** Lacrosse, denomination below **Rev. Designer:** Ken Danby **Size:** 45 mm. **Note:** Series III.

Date	Mintage	MS-63	Proof
1974	—	19.50	—
1974 Proof	97,431	—	20.00

KM# 102 10 DOLLARS **Weight:** 48.6000 g. **Composition:** 0.9250 Silver 1.4454 oz. ASW **Ruler:** Elizabeth II **Subject:** 1976 Montreal Olympics **Obverse:** Bust right, small maple leaf below, date at right **Reverse:** Men's hurdles, denomination below **Rev. Designer:** Leo Yerxa **Size:** 45 mm. **Note:** Series IV.

Date	Mintage	MS-63	Proof
1975	—	19.50	—
1975 Proof	82,302	—	20.00

KM# 103 10 DOLLARS **Weight:** 48.6000 g. **Composition:** 0.9250 Silver 1.4454 oz. ASW **Ruler:** Elizabeth II **Subject:** Montreal 1976 - 21st Summer Olympic Games **Obverse:** Bust right, small maple leaf below, date at right **Reverse:** Women's shot put, denomination below **Rev. Designer:** Leo Yerxa **Size:** 45 mm. **Note:** Series IV.

Date	Mintage	MS-63	Proof
1975	—	19.50	—
1975 Proof	82,302	—	20.00

KM# 104 10 DOLLARS **Weight:** 48.6000 g. **Composition:** 0.9250 Silver 1.4454 oz. ASW **Ruler:** Elizabeth II **Subject:** 1976 Montreal Olympics **Obverse:** Bust right, small maple leaf below, date at right **Reverse:** Sailing, denomination below **Rev. Designer:** Lynda Cooper **Size:** 45 mm. **Note:** Series V.

Date	Mintage	MS-63	Proof
1975	—	19.50	—
1975 Proof	89,155	—	20.00

KM# 105 10 DOLLARS **Weight:** 48.6000 g. **Composition:** 0.9250 Silver 1.4454 oz. ASW **Ruler:** Elizabeth II **Subject:** 1976 Montreal Olympics **Obverse:** Bust right, small maple leaf below, date at right **Reverse:** Canoeing, denomination below **Rev. Designer:** Lynda Cooper **Size:** 45 mm. **Note:** Series V.

Date	Mintage	MS-63	Proof
1975	—	19.50	—
1975 Proof	89,155	—	20.00

KM# 111 10 DOLLARS **Weight:** 48.6000 g. **Composition:** 0.9250 Silver 1.4454 oz. ASW **Ruler:** Elizabeth II **Subject:** 1976 Montreal Olympics **Obverse:** Bust right, small maple leaf below, date at right **Reverse:** Football, denomination below **Rev. Designer:** Shigeo Fukada **Size:** 45 mm. **Note:** Series VI.

Date	Mintage	MS-63	Proof
1976	—	19.50	—
1976 Proof	76,908	—	20.00

KM# 112 10 DOLLARS **Weight:** 48.6000 g. **Composition:** 0.9250 Silver 1.4454 oz. ASW **Ruler:** Elizabeth II **Subject:** 1976 Montreal Olympics **Obverse:** Bust right, small maple leaf below, date at right **Reverse:** Field hockey **Rev. Designer:** Shigeo Fukada **Size:** 45 mm. **Note:** Series VI.

Date	Mintage	MS-63	Proof
1976	—	19.50	—
1976 Proof	76,908	—	20.00

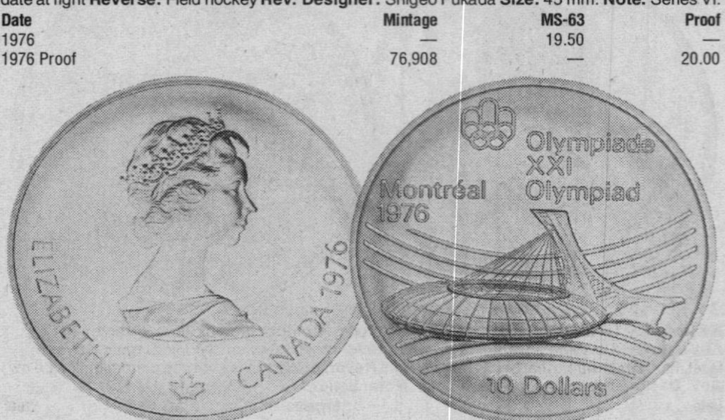

KM# 113 10 DOLLARS **Weight:** 48.6000 g. **Composition:** 0.9250 Silver 1.4454 oz. ASW **Ruler:** Elizabeth II **Subject:** 1976 Montreal Olympics **Obverse:** Bust right, small maple leaf below, date at right **Reverse:** Olympic Stadium, denomination below **Rev. Designer:** Elliott John Morrison **Size:** 45 mm. **Note:** Series VII.

Date	Mintage	MS-63	Proof
1976	—	19.50	—
1976 Proof	79,102	—	20.00

KM# 114 10 DOLLARS **Weight:** 48.6000 g. **Composition:** 0.9250 Silver 1.4454 oz. ASW **Ruler:** Elizabeth II **Subject:** 1976 Montreal Olympics **Obverse:** Bust right, small maple leaf below, date at right **Reverse:** Olympic Velodrome, denomination below **Rev. Designer:** Elliott John Morrison **Size:** 45 mm. **Note:** Series VII.

Date	Mintage	MS-63	Proof
1976	—	19.50	—
1976 Proof	79,102	—	20.00

KM# 215 15 DOLLARS **Weight:** 33.6300 g. **Composition:** 0.9250 Silver 1.0000 oz. ASW **Ruler:** Elizabeth II **Subject:** 1992 Olympics **Obverse:** Crowned Queen's head right, date at left, denomination below **Reverse:** Coaching track **Rev. Designer:** Stewart Sherwood **Size:** 39 mm.

Date	Mintage	MS-63	Proof
1992 Proof	275,000	—	28.00

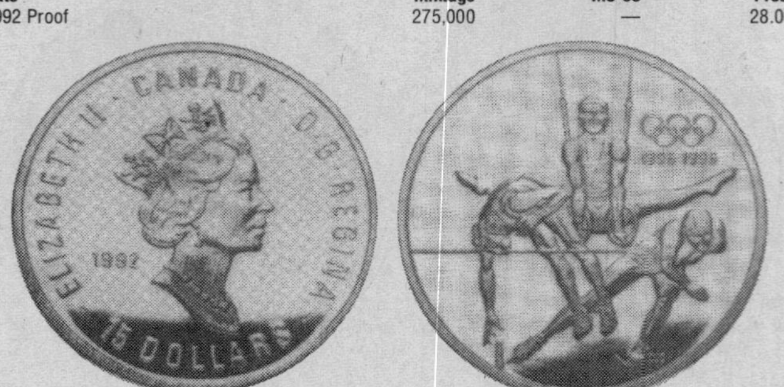

KM# 216 15 DOLLARS **Weight:** 33.6300 g. **Composition:** 0.9250 Silver 1.0000 oz. ASW **Ruler:** Elizabeth II **Subject:** 1992 Olympics **Obverse:** Crowned Queen's head right, date at left, denomination below **Reverse:** High jump, rings, speed skating **Rev. Designer:** David Craig

Date	Mintage	MS-63	Proof
1992 Proof	275,000	—	28.00

KM# 304 15 DOLLARS **Composition:** Bi-Metallic **Subject:** Year of the Tiger **Reverse:** Tiger within octagon at center, animal figures surround **Rev. Designer:** Harvey Chain **Size:** 40 mm.

Date	Mintage	MS-63	Proof
1998 Proof	68,888	—	275

KM# 331 15 DOLLARS **Composition:** Bi-Metallic **Subject:** Year of the Rabbitt **Reverse:** Rabbit within octagon at center, animal figures surround **Rev. Designer:** Harvey Chain

Date	Mintage	MS-63	Proof
1999 Proof	—	—	35.00

KM# 387 15 DOLLARS **Composition:** Bi-Metallic **Subject:** Year of the Dragon **Rev. Designer:** Harvey Chain

Date	Mintage	MS-63	Proof
2000 Proof	—	—	125

KM# 71 20 DOLLARS **Weight:** 18.2733 g. **Composition:** 0.9000 Gold 0.5288 oz. AGW **Ruler:** Elizabeth II **Subject:** Centennial **Obverse:** Bust right **Reverse:** Crowned and supported arms **Edge:** Reeded **Size:** 27.05 mm.

Date	Mintage	MS-63	Proof
1967 Proof	337,688	—	350

KM# 145 20 DOLLARS **Weight:** 33.6300 g. **Composition:** 0.9250 Silver 1.0000 oz. ASW **Ruler:** Elizabeth II **Subject:** 1988 Calgary Olympics **Obverse:** Queen's bust right, maple leaf below, date at right **Reverse:** Downhill skier, denomination below **Rev. Designer:** Ian Stewart **Edge:** Lettered **Size:** 40 mm.

Date	Mintage	MS-63	Proof
1985 Proof	406,360	—	21.50
1985 Proof	Inc. above	—	175

Note: Plain edge

KM# 146 20 DOLLARS **Weight:** 33.6300 g. **Composition:** 0.9250 Silver 1.0000 oz. ASW **Ruler:** Elizabeth II **Subject:** 1988 Calgary Olympics **Obverse:** Bust right, small maple leaf below, date at right **Reverse:** Speed skater, denomination below **Rev. Designer:** Friedrich Peter **Edge:** Lettered **Size:** 40 mm.

Date	Mintage	MS-63	Proof
1985 Proof	354,222	—	21.50
1985 Proof	Inc. above	—	175

Note: Plain edge

KM# 147 20 DOLLARS **Weight:** 33.6300 g. **Composition:** 0.9250 Silver 1.0000 oz. ASW **Ruler:** Elizabeth II **Subject:** 1988 Calgary Olympics **Obverse:** Bust right, small maple leaf below, date at right **Reverse:** Biathlon, denomination below **Rev. Designer:** John Mardon **Edge:** Lettered **Size:** 40 mm.

Date	Mintage	MS-63	Proof
1986 Proof	308,086	—	21.50
1986 Proof	Inc. above	—	175

Note: Plain edge

KM# 148 20 DOLLARS **Weight:** 33.6300 g. **Composition:** 0.9250 Silver 1.0000 oz. ASW **Ruler:** Elizabeth II **Subject:** 1988 Calgary Olympics **Obverse:** Bust right, small maple leaf below, date at right **Reverse:** Hockey, denomination below **Rev. Designer:** Ian Stewart **Edge:** Lettered **Size:** 40 mm.

Date	Mintage	MS-63	Proof
1986 Proof	396,602	—	21.50
1986 Proof	Inc. above	—	175

Note: Plain edge

KM# 150 20 DOLLARS **Weight:** 33.6300 g. **Composition:** 0.9250 Silver 1.0000 oz. ASW **Ruler:** Elizabeth II **Subject:** Calgary 1988 - 15th Winter Olympic Games **Obverse:** Bust right, small maple leaf below, date at right **Reverse:** Cross-country skier, denomination below **Rev. Designer:** Ian Stewart **Edge:** Lettered **Size:** 40 mm.

Date	Mintage	MS-63	Proof
1986 Proof	303,199	—	21.50

KM# 151 20 DOLLARS **Weight:** 33.6300 g. **Composition:** 0.9250 Silver 1.0000 oz. ASW **Ruler:** Elizabeth II **Subject:** 1988 Calgary Olympics **Obverse:** Bust right, small maple leaf below, date at right **Reverse:** Free-style skier, denomination below **Rev. Designer:** Walter Ott **Edge:** Lettered **Size:** 40 mm.

Date	Mintage	MS-63	Proof
1986 Proof	294,322	—	21.50
1986 Proof	Inc. above	—	175

Note: Plain edge

KM# 155 20 DOLLARS **Weight:** 34.1070 g. **Composition:** 0.9250 Silver 1.0000 oz. ASW **Ruler:** Elizabeth II **Subject:** Calgary 1988 - 15th Winter Olympic Games **Obverse:** Bust right, small maple leaf below, date at right **Reverse:** Figure skating pairs event, denomination below **Rev. Designer:** Raymond Taylor **Edge:** Lettered **Size:** 40 mm.

Date	Mintage	MS-63	Proof
1987 Proof	334,875	—	21.50

KM# 156 20 DOLLARS **Weight:** 34.1070 g. **Composition:** 0.9250 Silver 1.0000 oz. ASW **Ruler:** Elizabeth II **Subject:** 1988 Calgary Olympics **Obverse:** Bust right, small maple leaf below, date at right **Reverse:** Curling, denomination below **Rev. Designer:** Ian Stewart **Edge:** Lettered **Size:** 40 mm.

Date	Mintage	MS-63	Proof
1987 Proof	286,457	—	21.50

KM# 159 20 DOLLARS **Weight:** 34.1070 g. **Composition:** 0.9250 Silver 1.0000 oz. ASW **Ruler:** Elizabeth II **Subject:** 1988 Calgary Olympics **Obverse:** Bust right, small maple leaf below, date at right **Reverse:** Ski jumper, denomination below **Rev. Designer:** Raymond Taylor **Edge:** Lettered **Size:** 40 mm.

Date	Mintage	MS-63	Proof
1987 Proof	290,954	—	21.50

KM# 160 20 DOLLARS **Weight:** 34.1070 g. **Composition:** 0.9250 Silver 1.0000 oz. ASW **Ruler:** Elizabeth II **Subject:** 1988 Calgary Olympics **Obverse:** Queen's bust right, maple leaf below, date at right **Reverse:** Bobsled, denomination below **Rev. Designer:** John Mardon **Edge:** Lettered **Size:** 40 mm.

Date	Mintage	MS-63	Proof
1987 Proof	274,326	—	21.50

KM# 172 20 DOLLARS **Weight:** 31.1030 g. **Composition:** 0.9250 Silver 0.9743 oz. ASW **Ruler:** Elizabeth II **Subject:** Aviation **Obverse:** Crowned Queen's head right, date below **Reverse:** Lancaster, Fauquier in cameo, denomination below **Rev. Designer:** Robert R. Carmichael **Size:** 38 mm.

Date	Mintage	MS-63	Proof
1990 Proof	43,596	—	100

KM# 173 20 DOLLARS **Weight:** 31.1030 g. **Composition:** 0.9250 Silver 0.9743 oz. ASW **Ruler:** Elizabeth II **Subject:** Aviation **Obverse:** Crowned Queen's head right, date below **Reverse:** Anson and Harvard, Air Marshal Robert Leckie in cameo, denomination below **Rev. Designer:** Geoff Bennett **Size:** 38 mm.

Date	Mintage	MS-63	Proof
1990 Proof	41,844	—	35.00

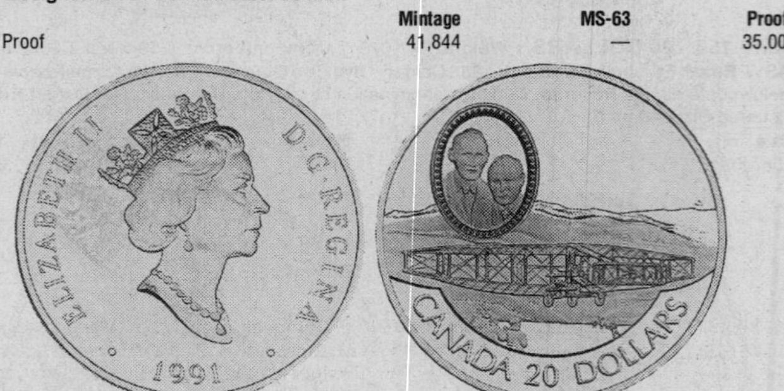

KM# 196 20 DOLLARS **Weight:** 31.1030 g. **Composition:** 0.9250 Silver 0.9743 oz. ASW **Ruler:** Elizabeth II **Subject:** Aviation **Obverse:** Crowned head right, date below **Reverse:** Silver Dart, John A. D. McCurdy and F. W. "Casey" Baldwin in cameo, denomination below **Rev. Designer:** George Velinger **Size:** 38 mm.

Date	Mintage	MS-63	Proof
1991 Proof	28,791	—	30.00

KM# 197 20 DOLLARS **Weight:** 31.1030 g. **Composition:** 0.9250 Silver 0.9742 oz. ASW **Ruler:** Elizabeth II **Subject:** Aviation **Obverse:** Crowned head right, date below **Reverse:** de Haviland Beaver, Philip C. Garratt in cameo, denomination below **Rev. Designer:** Peter Massman **Size:** 38 mm.

Date	Mintage	MS-63	Proof
1991 Proof	29,399	—	30.00

KM# 224 20 DOLLARS **Weight:** 31.1030 g. **Composition:** 0.9250 Silver 0.9743 oz. ASW **Ruler:** Elizabeth II **Subject:** Aviation **Obverse:** Crowned head right, date below **Reverse:** Curtiss JN-4 Canick ("Jenny"), Sir Frank W. Baillie in cameo, denomination below **Rev. Designer:** George Velinger **Size:** 38 mm.

Date	Mintage	MS-63	Proof
1992 Proof	33,105	—	30.00

KM# 225 20 DOLLARS **Weight:** 31.1030 g. **Composition:** 0.9250 Silver 0.9743 oz. ASW **Subject:** Aviation **Obverse:** Crowned head right, date below **Reverse:** de Haviland Gypsy Moth, Murton A. Seymour in cameo, denomination below **Rev. Designer:** John Mardon **Size:** 38 mm.

Date	Mintage	MS-63	Proof
1992 Proof	32,537	—	30.00

KM# 236 20 DOLLARS **Weight:** 31.1030 g. **Composition:** 0.9250 Silver 0.0257 oz. ASW **Ruler:** Elizabeth II **Subject:** Aviation **Obverse:** Crowned head right, date below **Reverse:** Fairchild 71C float plane, James A. Richardson, Sr. in cameo, denomination below **Rev. Designer:** Robert R. Carmichael **Size:** 38 mm.

Date	Mintage	MS-63	Proof
1993 Proof	32,199	—	30.00

KM# 237 20 DOLLARS **Weight:** 31.1030 g. **Composition:** 0.9250 Silver 0.9743 oz. ASW **Ruler:** Elizabeth II **Subject:** Aviation **Obverse:** Crowned head right, date below **Reverse:** Lockheed 14, Zebulon Lewis Leigh in cameo, denomination below **Rev. Designer:** Robert R. Carmichael **Size:** 38 mm.

Date	Mintage	MS-63	Proof
1993 Proof	32,550	—	30.00

KM# 246 20 DOLLARS **Weight:** 31.1030 g. **Composition:** 0.9250 Silver 0.9743 oz. ASW **Ruler:** Elizabeth II **Subject:** Aviation **Obverse:** Crowned head right, date below **Reverse:** Curtiss HS-2L seaplane, Stewart Graham in cameo, denomination below **Rev. Designer:** John Mardon **Size:** 38 mm.

Date	Mintage	MS-63	Proof
1994 Proof	31,242	—	30.00

KM# 247 20 DOLLARS **Weight:** 31.1030 g. **Composition:** 0.9250 Silver 0.9743 oz. ASW **Ruler:** Elizabeth II **Subject:** Aviation **Obverse:** Crowned head right, date below **Reverse:** Vickers Vedette, Wilfred T. Reid in cameo, denomination below **Rev. Designer:** Robert R. Carmichael **Size:** 38 mm.

Date	Mintage	MS-63	Proof
1994 Proof	30,880	—	30.00

KM# 271 20 DOLLARS **Weight:** 31.1030 g. **Composition:** 0.9250 Silver 0.9743 oz. ASW **Ruler:** Elizabeth II **Subject:** Aviation **Obverse:** Crowned head right, date below **Reverse:** C-FEA1 Fleet Cannuck, denomination below **Rev. Designer:** Robert Bradford **Size:** 38 mm.

Date	Mintage	MS-63	Proof
1995 Proof	17,438	—	30.00

KM# 272 20 DOLLARS **Weight:** 31.1030 g. **Composition:** 0.9250 Silver 0.9743 oz. ASW **Ruler:** Elizabeth II **Subject:** Aviation **Obverse:** Crowned head right, date below **Reverse:** DHC-1 Chipmunk, denomination below **Rev. Designer:** Robert Bradford **Size:** 38 mm.

Date	Mintage	MS-63	Proof
1995 Proof	17,722	—	30.00

KM# 276 20 DOLLARS **Weight:** 31.1030 g. **Composition:** 0.9250 Silver 0.9743 oz. ASW **Ruler:** Elizabeth II **Subject:** Aviation **Obverse:** Crowned head right, date below **Reverse:** CF-100 Cannuck, denomination below **Rev. Designer:** Jim Bruce **Size:** 38 mm.

Date	Mintage	MS-63	Proof
1996 Proof	18,508	—	32.50

KM# 277 20 DOLLARS **Weight:** 31.1030 g. **Composition:** 0.9250 Silver 0.9743 oz. ASW **Ruler:** Elizabeth II **Subject:** Aviation **Obverse:** Crowned head right, date below **Obv. Legend:** CF-105 Arrow, denomination below **Rev. Designer:** Jim Bruce **Size:** 38 mm.

Date	Mintage	MS-63	Proof
1996 Proof	27,163	—	65.00

KM# 297 20 DOLLARS **Weight:** 31.1030 g. **Composition:** 0.9250 Silver 0.9743 oz. ASW **Ruler:** Elizabeth II **Subject:** Aviation **Obverse:** Crowned head right, date below **Reverse:** Canadair F-86 Sabre, denomination below **Rev. Designer:** Ross Buckland **Size:** 38 mm.

Date	Mintage	MS-63	Proof
1997 Proof	14,389	—	30.00

KM# 298 20 DOLLARS Weight: 31.1030 g. **Composition:** 0.9250 Silver 0.9743 oz. ASW **Ruler:** Elizabeth II **Subject:** Aviation **Obverse:** Crowned head right, date below **Reverse:** Canadair CT-114 Tutor, denomination below **Rev. Designer:** Ross Buckland **Size:** 38 mm.

Date	Mintage	MS-63	Proof
1997 Proof	15,669	—	30.00

KM# 329 20 DOLLARS Weight: 31.1030 g. **Composition:** 0.9250 Silver 0.9743 oz. ASW **Ruler:** Elizabeth II **Subject:** Aviation **Obverse:** Crowned Queen's head, right, date below **Reverse:** CP-107 Argus, denomination below **Size:** 38 mm.

Date	Mintage	MS-63	Proof
1998 Proof	50,000,000	—	37.50

KM# 330 20 DOLLARS Weight: 31.1030 g. **Composition:** 0.9250 Silver 0.9743 oz. ASW **Ruler:** Elizabeth II **Subject:** Aviation **Obverse:** Crowned head right, date below **Reverse:** CP-215 Waterbomber, denomination below **Rev. Designer:** Peter Mossman **Size:** 38 mm.

Date	Mintage	MS-63	Proof
1998 Proof	50,000,000	—	37.50

KM# 339 20 DOLLARS Weight: 31.1030 g. **Composition:** 0.9250 Silver 0.9743 oz. ASW **Ruler:** Elizabeth II **Subject:** Aviation **Obverse:** Crowned head right, date below **Reverse:** DHC-6 Twin Otter, denomination below **Rev. Designer:** Neil Aird **Size:** 38 mm.

Date	Mintage	MS-63	Proof
1999 Proof	50,000,000	—	37.50

KM# 340 20 DOLLARS Weight: 31.1030 g. **Composition:** 0.9250 Silver 0.9743 oz. ASW **Ruler:** Elizabeth II **Subject:** Aviation **Obverse:** Crowned head right, date below **Reverse:** DHC-8 Dash 8, denomination below **Size:** 38 mm.

Date	Mintage	MS-63	Proof
1999 Proof	50,000,000	—	37.50

KM# 395 20 DOLLARS Composition: 0.9250 Silver **Ruler:** Elizabeth II **Subject:** First Canadian locomotive **Obverse:** Crowned head right, date below **Reverse:** Locomotive below multicolored cameo, denomination below **Size:** 38 mm.

Date	Mintage	MS-63	Proof
2000 Proof	—	—	40.00

KM# 396 20 DOLLARS Composition: 0.9250 Silver **Ruler:** Elizabeth II **Subject:** First Canadian self-propelled car **Obverse:** Crowned head right, date below **Reverse:** Car below multicolored cameo, denomination below **Size:** 38 mm.

Date	Mintage	MS-63	Proof
2000 Proof	—	—	40.00

KM# 397 20 DOLLARS Composition: 0.9250 Silver **Ruler:** Elizabeth II **Subject:** Bluenose sailboat **Obverse:** Crowned head right, date below **Reverse:** Boat below multicolored cameo, denomination below **Size:** 38 mm.

Date	Mintage	MS-63	Proof
2000 Proof	—	—	150

KM# 115 100 DOLLARS Weight: 13.3375 g. **Composition:** 0.5830 Gold 0.2500 oz. AGW **Ruler:** Elizabeth II **Subject:** 1976 Montreal Olympics **Obverse:** Queen's bust right, maple leaf below, date at right, beaded borders **Reverse:** Past and present Olympic figures, denomination at right **Rev. Designer:** Dora dePedery-Hunt **Size:** 27 mm.

Date	Mintage	MS-63	Proof
1976	650,000	175	—

KM# 116 100 DOLLARS **Weight:** 16.9655 g. **Composition:** 0.9170 Gold 0.5000 oz. AGW **Ruler:** Elizabeth II **Subject:** 1976 Montreal Olympics **Obverse:** Queen's bust right, maple leaf below, date at right, plain borders **Reverse:** Past and present Olympic figures, denomination at right **Rev. Designer:** Dora dePedery-Hunt **Size:** 25 mm.

Date	Mintage	MS-63	Proof
1976 Proof	337,342	—	340

KM# 119 100 DOLLARS **Weight:** 16.9655 g. **Composition:** 0.9170 Gold 0.5000 oz. AGW **Ruler:** Elizabeth II **Subject:** Queen's silver jubilee **Obverse:** Queen's bust, right **Reverse:** Bouquet of provincial flowers, denomination below **Rev. Designer:** Raymond Lee

Date	Mintage	MS-63	Proof
ND(1977) Proof	180,396	—	340

KM# 122 100 DOLLARS **Weight:** 16.9655 g. **Composition:** 0.9170 Gold 0.5000 oz. AGW **Ruler:** Elizabeth II **Subject:** Canadian unification **Obverse:** Queen's bust right, denomination at left, date upper right **Reverse:** Geese (representing the provinces) in flight formation **Rev. Designer:** Roger Savage

Date	Mintage	MS-63	Proof
1978 Proof	200,000	—	345

KM# 126 100 DOLLARS **Weight:** 16.9655 g. **Composition:** 0.9170 Gold 0.5000 oz. AGW **Ruler:** Elizabeth II **Subject:** International Year of the Child **Obverse:** Queen's bust right **Reverse:** Children with hands joined divide denomination and date **Rev. Designer:** Carola Tietz

Date	Mintage	MS-63	Proof
1979 Proof	250,000	—	340

KM# 129 100 DOLLARS **Weight:** 16.9655 g. **Composition:** 0.9170 Gold 0.5000 oz. AGW **Ruler:** Elizabeth II **Subject:** Arctic Territories **Obverse:** Queen's bust right, denomination at left, date above right **Reverse:** Kayaker **Rev. Designer:** Arnaldo Marchetti

Date	Mintage	MS-63	Proof
1980 Proof	300,000	—	340

KM# 131 100 DOLLARS **Weight:** 16.9655 g. **Comp.:** 0.9170 Gold 0.5000 oz. AGW **Ruler:** Elizabeth II **Subject:** National anthem **Obverse:** Queen's bust right, denomination at left, date above right **Reverse:** Music score on map **Rev. Designer:** Roger Savage

Date	Mintage	MS-63	Proof
1981 Proof	102,000	—	340

KM# 137 100 DOLLARS **Weight:** 16.9655 g. **Composition:** 0.9170 Gold 0.5000 oz. AGW **Ruler:** Elizabeth II **Subject:** New Constitution **Obverse:** Queen's bust right, denomination at left **Reverse:** Open book, maple leaf on right page, date below **Rev. Designer:** Friedrich Peter

Date	Mintage	MS-63	Proof
1982 Proof	121,708	—	340

KM# 139 100 DOLLARS **Weight:** 16.9655 g. **Composition:** 0.9170 Gold 0.5000 oz. AGW **Ruler:** Elizabeth II **Subject:** 400th Anniversary of St. John's, Newfoundland **Obverse:** Queen's bust right **Reverse:** Anchor divides building and ship, denomination below, dates above **Rev. Designer:** John Jaciw

Date	Mintage	MS-63	Proof
ND(1983) Proof	83,128	—	340

KM# 142 100 DOLLARS **Weight:** 16.9655 g. **Composition:** 0.9170 Gold 0.5000 oz. AGW **Ruler:** Elizabeth II **Subject:** Jacques Cartier **Obverse:** Queen's bust right **Reverse:** Cartier head on right facing left, ship on left, date lower right, denomination above **Rev. Designer:** Carola Tietz

Date	Mintage	MS-63	Proof
ND(1984) Proof	67,662	—	340

KM# 144 100 DOLLARS **Weight:** 16.9655 g. **Composition:** 0.9170 Gold 0.5000 oz. AGW **Ruler:** Elizabeth II **Subject:** National Parks **Obverse:** Queen's bust right **Reverse:** Big-horn sheep. denomination divides dates below **Rev. Designer:** Hector Greville

Date	Mintage	MS-63	Proof
ND(1985) Proof	61,332	—	340

KM# 152 100 DOLLARS **Weight:** 16.9655 g. **Composition:** 0.9170 Gold 0.5000 oz. AGW **Ruler:** Elizabeth II **Subject:** Peace **Obverse:** Queen's bust right **Reverse:** Maple leaves and letters intertwined, date at right, denomination below **Rev. Designer:** Dora dePedery-Hunt

Date	Mintage	MS-63	Proof
1986 Proof	76,409	—	340

KM# 158 100 DOLLARS **Weight:** 13.3375 g. **Composition:** 0.5830 Gold 0.2500 oz. AGW **Ruler:** Elizabeth II **Subject:** 1988 Calgary Olympics **Obverse:** Queen's bust right, maple leaf below, date at right **Reverse:** Torch and logo, denomination below **Rev. Designer:** Friedrich Peter **Edge:** Lettered in English and French

Date	Mintage	MS-63	Proof
1987 Proof	142,750	—	175
Note: lettered edge			
1987 Proof	Inc. above	—	350
Note: plain edge			

KM# 162 100 DOLLARS **Weight:** 13.3375 g. **Composition:** 0.5830 Gold 0.2500 oz. AGW **Subject:** Bowhead Whales, balaera mysticetus **Reverse:** Whales left, date below, within circle, denomination below **Rev. Designer:** Robert R. Carmichael

Date	Mintage	MS-63	Proof
1988 Proof	52,594	—	180

KM# 169 100 DOLLARS **Weight:** 13.3375 g. **Composition:** 0.5830 Gold 0.2500 oz. AGW **Ruler:** Elizabeth II **Subject:** Sainte-Marie **Obverse:** Queen's bust right **Reverse:** Huron Indian, Missionary and Mission building, denomination below, dates above **Rev. Designer:** D. J. Craig

Date	Mintage	MS-63	Proof
ND(1989) Proof	59,657	—	175

KM# 171 100 DOLLARS **Weight:** 13.3375 g. **Composition:** 0.5830 Gold 0.2500 oz. AGW **Ruler:** Elizabeth II **Subject:** International Literacy Year **Obverse:** Crowned Queen's head right, date below **Reverse:** Woman with children, denomination below **Rev. Designer:** John Mardon

Date	Mintage	MS-63	Proof
1990 Proof	49,940	—	175

KM# 180 100 DOLLARS **Weight:** 13.3375 g. **Composition:** 0.5830 Gold 0.2500 oz. AGW **Ruler:** Elizabeth II **Subject:** S.S. Empress of India **Obverse:** Crowned Queen's head right, date below **Reverse:** Ship, denomination below **Rev. Designer:** Karsten Smith

Date	Mintage	MS-63	Proof
1991 Proof	33,966	—	175

KM# 211 100 DOLLARS **Weight:** 13.3375 g. **Composition:** 0.5830 Gold 0.2500 oz. AGW **Subject:** Montreal **Obverse:** Crowned Queen's head right, date below **Reverse:** Half figure in foreground with paper, buildings in back, denomination below **Rev. Designer:** Stewart Sherwood

Date	Mintage	MS-63	Proof
1992 Proof	28,162	—	175

KM# 245 100 DOLLARS **Weight:** 13.3375 g. **Composition:** 0.5830 Gold 0.2500 oz. AGW **Ruler:** Elizabeth II **Subject:** Antique Automobiles **Obverse:** Crowned Queen's head right, date below **Reverse:** German Bene Victoria; Simmonds Steam Carriage; French Panhard-Levassor's Daimler; American Duryea; Canadian Featherston Haugh in center, denomination below **Rev. Designer:** John Mardon

Date	Mintage	MS-63	Proof
1993 Proof	25,971	—	180

KM# 249 100 DOLLARS **Weight:** 13.3375 g. **Composition:** 0.5830 Gold 0.2500 oz. AGW **Ruler:** Elizabeth II **Subject:** World War II Home Front **Obverse:** Crowned head right, date below **Reverse:** Kneeling figure working on plane, denomination below **Rev. Designer:** Paraskeva Clark

Date	Mintage	MS-63	Proof
1994 Proof	16,201	—	170

KM# 260 100 DOLLARS **Weight:** 13.3375 g. **Composition:** 0.5830 Gold 0.2500 oz. AGW **Subject:** Louisbourg **Obverse:** Crowned head right, date below **Reverse:** Ship and buildings, dates and denomination above **Rev. Designer:** Lewis Parker

Date	Mintage	MS-63	Proof
1995 Proof	16,916	—	180

KM# 273 100 DOLLARS **Weight:** 13.3375 g. **Composition:** 0.5830 Gold 0.2500 oz. AGW **Ruler:** Elizabeth II **Subject:** Klondike Gold Rush Centennial **Obverse:** Crowned head right, date below **Reverse:** Scene of Kate Carmack panning for gold, dates above, denomination lower left **Rev. Designer:** John Mantha

Date	Mintage	MS-63	Proof
ND(1996) Proof	17,973	—	180

KM# 287 100 DOLLARS **Weight:** 13.3375 g. **Composition:** 0.5830 Gold 0.2500 oz. AGW **Ruler:** Elizabeth II **Subject:** Alexander Graham Bell **Obverse:** Crowned head right, date below **Reverse:** A. G. Bell head right, globe and telephone, denomination upper right **Rev. Designer:** Donald H. Carley

Date	Mintage	MS-63	Proof
1997 Proof	14,775	—	180

KM# 307 100 DOLLARS **Weight:** 13.3375 g. **Composition:** 0.5830 Gold 0.2500 oz. AGW **Ruler:** Elizabeth II **Subject:** Discovery of Insulin **Obverse:** Crowned Queen's head right, date below **Reverse:** Nobel prize award figurine, dates at left, denomination at right **Rev. Designer:** Robert R. Carmichael

Date	Mintage	MS-63	Proof
1998 Proof	11,220	—	180

KM# 341 100 DOLLARS **Weight:** 13.3375 g. **Composition:** 0.5830 Gold 0.2500 oz. AGW **Ruler:** Elizabeth II **Subject:** 50th Anniversary Newfoundland Unity With Canada **Obverse:** Crowned head right, date below **Reverse:** Two designs at front, mountains in back, denomination below **Rev. Designer:** Jackie Gale-Vaillancourt

Date	Mintage	MS-63	Proof
1999 Proof	10,242	—	190

KM# 402 100 DOLLARS **Weight:** 13.3375 g. **Composition:** 0.5830 Gold 0.2500 oz. AGW **Ruler:** Elizabeth II **Subject:** McClure's Arctic expedition **Obverse:** Queen's portrait right, date below **Reverse:** Six men pulling supply sled to an icebound ship, denomination below **Rev. Designer:** John Mardon **Edge:** Reeded **Size:** 27 mm.

Date	Mintage	MS-63	Proof
2000 Proof	9,767	—	190

KM# 388 150 DOLLARS **Weight:** 13.6100 g. **Composition:** 0.7500 Gold .3282 oz. AGW **Subject:** Year of the Dragon **Rev. Designer:** Harvey Chan

Date	Mintage	MS-63	Proof
2000 Proof	8,851	—	650

KM# 217 175 DOLLARS **Weight:** 16.9700 g. **Composition:** 0.9170 Gold 0.5000 oz. AGW **Ruler:** Elizabeth II **Subject:** 1992 Olympics **Obverse:** Crowned Queen's head right, date at left, denomination below **Reverse:** Passing the torch **Rev. Designer:** Stewart Sherwood **Edge:** Lettered

Date	Mintage	MS-63	Proof
1992 Proof	22,092	—	340

KM# 178 200 DOLLARS **Weight:** 17.1350 g. **Composition:** 0.9170 Gold 0.5115 oz. AGW **Ruler:** Elizabeth II **Subject:** Canadian flag silver jubilee **Obverse:** Crowned Queen's head right, date below **Reverse:** People with flag, denomination above **Rev. Designer:** Stewart Sherwood **Size:** 29 mm.

Date	Mintage	MS-63	Proof
1990 Proof	20,980	—	350

KM# 202 200 DOLLARS **Weight:** 17.1350 g. **Composition:** 0.9170 Gold 0.5115 oz. AGW **Ruler:** Elizabeth II **Subject:** Hockey **Reverse:** Hockey players, denomination above **Rev. Designer:** Stewart Sherwood **Size:** 29 mm.

Date	Mintage	MS-63	Proof
1991 Proof	10,215	—	350

KM# 230 200 DOLLARS **Weight:** 17.1350 g. **Composition:** 0.9170 Gold 0.5115 oz. AGW **Subject:** Niagara Falls **Reverse:** Niagara Falls, denomination above **Rev. Designer:** John Marden **Size:** 29 mm.

Date	Mintage	MS-63	Proof
1992 Proof	9,465	—	350

KM# 244 200 DOLLARS **Weight:** 17.1350 g. **Composition:** 0.9170 Gold 0.5115 oz. AGW **Ruler:** Elizabeth II **Subject:** Mounted police **Obverse:** Crowned head right, date below **Reverse:** Mountie with children, denomination above **Rev. Designer:** Stewart Sherwood **Size:** 29 mm.

Date	Mintage	MS-63	Proof
1993 Proof	10,807	—	350

KM# 250 200 DOLLARS **Weight:** 17.1350 g. **Composition:** 0.9170 Gold 0.5115 oz. AGW **Subject:** Interpretation of 1908 novel by Lucy Maud Montgomery, 1874-1942, Anne of Green Gables **Reverse:** Figure sitting in window, denomination above **Rev. Designer:** Phoebe Gilman **Size:** 29 mm.

Date	Mintage	MS-63	Proof
1994 Proof	10,655	—	350

KM# 265 200 DOLLARS **Weight:** 17.1350 g. **Composition:** 0.9170 Gold 0.5115 oz. AGW **Ruler:** Elizabeth II **Subject:** Maple-syrup production **Obverse:** Crowned head right, date below **Reverse:** Maple syrup making, denomination at right **Rev. Designer:** J. D. Mantha **Size:** 29 mm.

Date	Mintage	MS-63	Proof
1995 Proof	6,579	—	350

KM# 275 200 DOLLARS **Weight:** 17.1350 g. **Composition:** 0.9170 Gold 0.5115 oz. AGW **Ruler:** Elizabeth II **Subject:** Transcontinental Canadian Railway **Obverse:** Crowned head right, date below **Reverse:** Train going through mountains, denomination below **Rev. Designer:** Suzanne Duranceau **Size:** 29 mm.

Date	Mintage	MS-63	Proof
1996 Proof	8,047	—	350

KM# 288 200 DOLLARS **Weight:** 17.1350 g. **Composition:** 0.9170 Gold 0.5115 oz. AGW **Ruler:** Elizabeth II **Subject:** Haida mask **Obverse:** Crowned head right, date below **Reverse:** Haida mask **Rev. Designer:** Robert Davidson **Size:** 29 mm.

Date	Mintage	MS-63	Proof
1997 Proof	11,610	—	450

KM# 317 200 DOLLARS **Weight:** 17.1350 g. **Composition:** 0.9170 Gold 0.5115 oz. AGW **Subject:** Legendary white buffalo **Obverse:** Crowned head right, date below **Reverse:** Buffalo **Rev. Designer:** Alex Janvler **Size:** 29 mm.

Date	Mintage	MS-63	Proof
1998 Proof	7,149	—	350

KM# 358 200 DOLLARS **Weight:** 17.1350 g. **Composition:** 0.9170 Gold 0.5115 oz. AGW **Subject:** Mikmaq butterfly **Reverse:** Butterfly within design **Rev. Designer:** Alan Syliboy **Size:** 29 mm.

Date	Mintage	MS-63	Proof
1999 Proof	6,510	—	350

KM# 403 200 DOLLARS **Weight:** 17.1350 g. **Composition:** 0.9170 Gold 0.5115 oz. AGW **Ruler:** Elizabeth II **Subject:** Motherhood **Obverse:** Crowned Queen's head right, date above, denomination at right **Reverse:** Inuit mother with infant **Rev. Designer:** Germaine Arnaktauyak **Edge:** Reeded **Size:** 29 mm.

Date	Mintage	MS-63	Proof
2000 Proof	6,284	—	350

KM# 308 350 DOLLARS **Weight:** 38.0500 g. **Composition:** 0.9999 Gold 1.2233 oz. AGW **Ruler:** Elizabeth II **Subject:** Flowers of Canada's Coat of Arms **Obverse:** Crowned Queen's head right, date behind, denomination at bottom **Reverse:** Flowers **Rev. Designer:** Pierre Leduc

Date	Mintage	MS-63	Proof
1998 Proof	664	—	875

KM# 370 350 DOLLARS **Weight:** 38.0500 g. **Composition:** 0.9999 Gold 1.2233 oz. AGW **Ruler:** Elizabeth II **Reverse:** Lady's slipper **Rev. Designer:** Henry Purdy

Date	Mintage	MS-63	Proof
1999 Proof	1,990	—	845

KM# 404 350 DOLLARS **Weight:** 38.0500 g. **Composition:** 0.9999 Gold 1.2233 oz. AGW **Ruler:** Elizabeth II **Obverse:** Queen's portrait **Reverse:** Three Pacific Dogwood flowers **Rev. Designer:** Caren Heine **Edge:** Reeded **Size:** 34 mm.

Date	Mintage	MS-63	Proof
2000 Proof	1,506	—	845

KM# 14 SOVEREIGN **Weight:** 7.9881 g. **Composition:** 0.9170 Gold .2354 oz. AGW **Ruler:** Edward VII **Reverse:** St. George slaying dragon, mint mark below horse's rear hooves

Date	Mintage	F-12	VF-20	XF-40	AU-50	MS-60	MS-63
1908C	636	1,250	1,850	2,350	2,600	2,850	4,000
1909C	16,273	160	200	245	285	500	1,600
1910C	28,012	BV	185	225	265	500	2,000

KM# 20 SOVEREIGN **Weight:** 7.9881 g. **Composition:** 0.9170 Gold 0.2354 oz. AGW **Ruler:** George V **Reverse:** St. George slaying dragon, mint mark below horse's rear hooves

Date	Mintage	F-12	VF-20	XF-40	AU-50	MS-60	MS-63
1911C	256,946	—	—	BV	155	160	180
1913C	3,715	550	700	950	1,200	1,500	3,000
1914C	14,871	175	225	350	450	600	950
1916C About 20 known	—	8,000	12,500	15,750	17,750	20,000	27,500
Note: Stacks' A.G. Carter Jr. Sale 12-89 Gem BU realized $82,500							
1917C	58,845	—	—	BV	160	175	500
1918C	106,514	—	—	BV	160	175	750
1919C	135,889	—	—	BV	160	175	650

SILVER BULLION COINAGE

KM# 163 5 DOLLARS **Weight:** 31.1000 g. **Composition:** 0.9999 Silver 1.0000 oz. ASW **Ruler:** Elizabeth II **Obverse:** Queen's bust right, denomination and date below **Obv. Designer:** Arnold Machin **Reverse:** Maple leaf flanked by 9999

Date	Mintage	MS-63	Proof
1988	1,155,931	15.00	—
1989	3,332,200	14.00	—
1989 Proof	29,999	—	30.00

KM# 187 5 DOLLARS **Weight:** 31.1000 g. **Composition:** 0.9999 Silver 1.0000 oz. ASW **Ruler:** Elizabeth II **Obverse:** Crowned head right, date and denomination below **Obv. Designer:** Dora de Pedery-Hunt **Reverse:** Maple leaf flanked by 9999

Date	Mintage	MS-63	Proof
1990	1,708,800	15.00	—
1991	644,300	16.50	—
1992	343,800	16.50	—
1993	889,946	15.00	—
1994	1,133,900	15.00	—
1995	326,244	16.00	—
1996	250,445	32.50	—
1997	100,970	17.50	—
1998 Tiger privy mark	25,000	18.50	—
1998 Titanic privy mark	26,000	75.00	—
1998 R.C.M.P. privy mark	25,000	32.50	—
1998 90th Anniversary R.C.M. privy mark	13,025	18.50	—
1998	591,359	16.50	—
1999 Rabbit privy mark	25,000	21.50	—
1999	1,229,442	16.00	—
1999 "Y2K" privy mark	9,999	27.50	—
2000 Dragon privy mark	25,000	22.50	—
2000 Expo Hanover privy mark	—	35.00	—
2000	403,652	16.00	—

KM# 363 5 DOLLARS **Weight:** 31.1000 g. **Composition:** 0.9999 Silver 1 oz. ASW **Ruler:** Elizabeth II **Obverse:** Crowned Queen's head right, date and denomination below **Reverse:** Maple leaf flanked by 9999

Date	Mintage	MS-63	Proof
1999/2000	298,775	17.50	—

Note: Fireworks privy mark

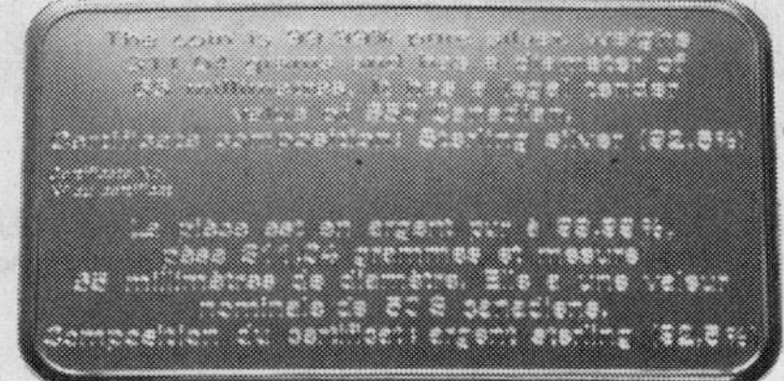

KM# 326 50 DOLLARS **Weight:** 311.0350 g. **Composition:** 0.9999 Silver 10.0000 oz. ASW **Subject:** 10th Anniversary Silver Maple Leaf **Reverse:** Maple leaf flanked by 9999 **Edge:** 10th ANNIVERSARY 10e ANNIVERSAIRE

Date	Mintage	MS-63	Proof
1998 Proof	25,000	—	165

GOLD BULLION COINAGE

KM# 238 DOLLAR **Weight:** 1.5551 g. **Composition:** 0.9999 Gold 0.05 oz. AGW **Ruler:** Elizabeth II **Obverse:** Crowned Queen's head right, denomination and date below **Reverse:** Maple leaf flanked by 9999

Date	Mintage	MS-63	Proof
1993	37,080	BV+37%	—
1994	78,860	BV+37%	—
1995	85,920	BV+37%	—
1996	56,520	BV+37%	—
1997	59,720	BV+37%	—
1998	44,260	BV+37%	—
1999	—	BV+46%	—
Note: Maple leaf with oval			
2000	—	—	—
Note: Maple leaf with oval			

KM# 365 DOLLAR **Weight:** 1.5551 g. **Composition:** 0.9999 Gold 0.05 oz. AGW **Reverse:** Maple leaf hologram

Date	Mintage	MS-63	Proof
1999	500	90.00	—

KM# 256 2 DOLLARS **Weight:** 2.0735 g. **Composition:** 0.9999 Gold 0.0666 oz. AGW **Ruler:** Elizabeth II **Obverse:** Crowned Queen's head right, denomination and date below **Reverse:** Maple leaf flanked by 9999

Date	Mintage	MS-63	Proof
1994	5,493	85.00	—

KM# 135 5 DOLLARS **Weight:** 3.1200 g. **Composition:** 0.9999 Gold .1000 oz. AGW **Ruler:** Elizabeth II **Obverse:** Queen's bust right, date and denomination below **Obv. Designer:** Arnold Machin **Reverse:** Maple leaf flanked by 9999

Date	Mintage	MS-63	Proof
1982	246,000	BV+14%	—
1983	304,000	BV+14%	—
1984	262,000	BV+14%	—
1985	398,000	BV+14%	—
1986	529,516	BV+14%	—
1987	459,000	BV+14%	—
1988	506,500	BV+14%	—
1989	539,000	BV+14%	—
1989 Proof	16,992	—	80.00

KM# 188 5 DOLLARS **Weight:** 3.1200 g. **Composition:** 0.9999 Gold 0.1000 oz. AGW **Ruler:** Elizabeth II **Obverse:** Elizabeth II effigy **Obv. Designer:** Dora dePedery-Hunt **Reverse:** Maple leaf

Date	Mintage	MS-63	Proof
1990	476,000	BV+14%	—
1991	322,000	BV+14%	—
1992	384,000	BV+14%	—
1993	248,630	BV+14%	—
1994	313,150	BV+14%	—
1995	294,890	BV+14%	—
1996	179,220	BV+14%	—
1997	188,540	BV+14%	—
1998	301,940	BV+14%	—
1999	—	BV+19%	—
Note: Maple leaf with oval "20 Years ANS" privy mark			
2000	—	BV+19%	—

KM# 366 5 DOLLARS **Weight:** 3.1200 g. **Composition:** 0.9999 Gold 0.1000 oz. AGW **Reverse:** Maple leaf hologram

Date	Mintage	MS-63	Proof
1999	500	160	—

KM# 136 10 DOLLARS **Weight:** 7.7850 g. **Composition:** 0.9999 Gold 0.2500 oz. AGW **Ruler:** Elizabeth II **Obverse:** Queen's bust right, date and denomination below **Obv. Designer:** Arnold Machin **Reverse:** Maple leaf flanked by 9999

Date	Mintage	MS-63	Proof
1982	184,000	BV+10%	—
1983	308,800	BV+10%	—
1984	242,400	BV+10%	—
1985	620,000	BV+10%	—
1986	915,200	BV+10%	—
1987	376,000	BV+10%	—
1988	436,000	BV+10%	—
1989	328,800	BV+10%	—
1989 Proof	6,998	—	185

KM# 189 10 DOLLARS **Weight:** 7.7850 g. **Composition:** 0.9999 Gold 0.2500 oz. AGW **Ruler:** Elizabeth II **Obverse:** Crowned Queen's head right, date and denomination below **Obv. Designer:** Dora dePedery-Hunt **Reverse:** Maple leaf flanked by 9999

Date	Mintage	MS-63	Proof
1990	253,600	BV+10%	—
1991	166,400	BV+10%	—
1992	179,600	BV+10%	—
1993	158,452	BV+10%	—
1994	148,792	BV+10%	—
1995	127,596	BV+10%	—
1996	89,148	BV+10%	—
1997	98,104	BV+10%	—
1998	85,472	BV+10%	—
1999	—	BV+15%	—
Note: Maple leaf with oval "20 Years ANS" privy mark			
2000	—	BV+15%	—
Note: Maple leaf with oval "2000" privy mark			

KM# 367 10 DOLLARS **Weight:** 7.7850 g. **Composition:** 0.9999 Gold 0.2500 oz. AGW **Reverse:** Maple leaf hologram

Date	Mintage	MS-63	Proof
1999	—	210	—

KM# 153 20 DOLLARS **Weight:** 15.5515 g. **Composition:** 0.9999 Gold 0.5000 oz. AGW **Ruler:** Elizabeth II **Obverse:** Queen's bust right, date and denomination below **Obv. Designer:** Arnold Machin **Reverse:** Maple leaf flanked by 9999 **Size:** 32 mm.

Date	Mintage	MS-63	Proof
1986	529,200	BV+7%	—
1987	332,800	BV+7%	—
1988	538,400	BV+7%	—
1989	259,200	BV+7%	—
1989 Proof	6,998	—	360

KM# 190 20 DOLLARS **Weight:** 15.5515 g. **Composition:** 0.9999 Gold 0.5000 oz. AGW **Ruler:** Elizabeth II **Obverse:** Crowned Queen's head right, date and denomination below **Obv. Designer:** Dora dePedery-Hunt **Reverse:** Maple leaf flanked by 9999

Date	Mintage	MS-63	Proof
1990	174,400	BV+7%	—
1991	96,200	BV+7%	—
1992	108,000	BV+7%	—
1993	99,492	BV+7%	—
1994	104,766	BV+7%	—
1995	103,162	BV+7%	—
1996	66,246	BV+7%	—
1997	63,354	BV+7%	—
1998	65,366	BV+7%	—
1999	—	BV+12%	—
Note: Maple leaf with oval "20 Years ANS" privy mark			
2000	—	BV+12%	—

KM# 368 20 DOLLARS **Weight:** 15.5515 g. **Composition:** 0.9999 Gold 0.5000 oz. AGW **Reverse:** Maple leaf hologram

Date	Mintage	MS-63	Proof
1999	500	700	—

KM# 125.1 50 DOLLARS **Weight:** 31.1030 g. **Composition:** 0.9990 Gold 1.0000 oz. AGW **Ruler:** Elizabeth II **Obverse:** Queen's bust right, denomination and date below **Reverse:** Maple leaf flanked by .999

Date	Mintage	MS-63	Proof
1979	1,000,000	BV+4%	—
1980	1,251,500	BV+4%	—
1981	863,000	BV+4%	—
1982	883,000	BV+4%	—

KM# 125.2 50 DOLLARS **Weight:** 31.1030 g. **Composition:** 0.9999 Gold 1.0000 oz. AGW **Ruler:** Elizabeth II **Obverse:** Queen's bust right, date and denomination below **Reverse:** Maple leaf flanked by .9999

Date	Mintage	MS-63	Proof
1983	843,000	BV+4%	—
1984	1,067,500	BV+4%	—
1985	1,908,000	BV+4%	—
1986	779,115	BV+4%	—
1987	978,000	BV+4%	—
1988	826,500	BV+4%	—
1989	856,000	BV+4%	—
1989 Proof	17,781	—	685

KM# 191 50 DOLLARS **Weight:** 31.1030 g. **Composition:** 0.9999 Gold 1.000 oz. AGW **Ruler:** Elizabeth II **Obverse:** Crowned Queen's head right, date and denomination below **Obv. Designer:** Dora dePedery-Hunt **Reverse:** Maple leaf flanked by .9999

Date	Mintage	MS-63	Proof
1990	815,000	BV+4%	—
1991	290,000	BV+4%	—
1992	368,900	BV+4%	—
1993	321,413	BV+4%	—
1994	180,357	BV+4%	—
1995	208,729	BV+4%	—
1996	143,682	BV+4%	—
1997	478,211	BV+4%	—
1998	593,704	BV+4%	—
1999	—	BV+7%	—
Note: Maple leaf with oval "20 Years ANS" privy mark			
2000	—	BV+7%	—
Note: Maple leaf with oval			

KM# 305 50 DOLLARS **Weight:** 31.1030 g. **Composition:** 0.9999 Gold 1 oz. AGW **Ruler:** Elizabeth II **Obverse:** Crowned Queen's head denomination below, within circle, dates below **Reverse:** Mountie at gallop right, within circle **Rev. Designer:** Ago Aarand **Shape:** 10-sided

Date	Mintage	MS-63	Proof
1997	12,913	685	—

KM# 369 50 DOLLARS **Weight:** 31.1030 g. **Composition:** 0.9999 Gold 1.0000 oz. AGW **Ruler:** Elizabeth II **Obverse:** Crowned Queen's head right, date and denomination below **Reverse:** Maple leaf hologram flanked by 9999, with fireworks privy mark

Date	Mintage	MS-63	Proof
2000	500	1,400	—

KM# 364 50 DOLLARS **Weight:** 31.1030 g. **Composition:** 0.9999 Gold 1.0000 oz. AGW **Ruler:** Elizabeth II **Obverse:** Crowned Queen's head right, denomination and date below **Reverse:** Maple leaf flanked by 9999, with fireworks privy mark

Date	Mintage	MS-63	Proof
2000	—	785	—

PLATINUM BULLION COINAGE

KM# 239 DOLLAR **Weight:** 1.5552 g. **Composition:** 0.9995 Platinum 0.0500 oz. APW **Ruler:** Elizabeth II **Obverse:** Crowned Queen's head right, date and denomination below **Reverse:** Maple leaf flanked by 9995

Date	Mintage	MS-63	Proof
1993	2,120	BV+35%	—
1994	4,260	BV+35%	—
1995	460	135	—
1996	1,640	BV+35%	—
1997	1,340	BV+35%	—
1998	2,000	BV+35%	—
1999	2,000	BV+35%	—

KM# 257 2 DOLLARS **Weight:** 2.0735 g. **Composition:** 0.9995 Platinum 0.0666 oz. APW **Ruler:** Elizabeth II **Obverse:** Crowned Queen's head right, date and denomination below **Reverse:** Maple leaf flanked by 9995

Date	Mintage	MS-63	Proof
1994	1,470	235	—

KM# 164 5 DOLLARS **Weight:** 3.1203 g. **Composition:** 0.9995 Platinum 0.1000 oz. APW **Ruler:** Elizabeth II **Obverse:** Queen's bust right, date and denomination below **Obv. Designer:** Arnold Machin **Reverse:** Maple leaf flanked by 9995

Date	Mintage	MS-63	Proof
1988	74,000	BV+18%	—
1989	18,000	BV+18%	—
1989 Proof	11,999	—	150

KM# 192 5 DOLLARS **Weight:** 3.1203 g. **Composition:** 0.9995 Platinum 0.1000 oz. APW **Obv. Designer:** dePedery-Hunt **Reverse:** Maple leaf

Date	Mintage	MS-63	Proof
1990	9,000	BV+18%	—
1991	13,000	BV+18%	—
1992	16,000	BV+18%	—
1993	14,020	BV+18%	—
1994	19,190	BV+18%	—
1995	8,940	BV+18%	—
1996	8,820	BV+18%	—
1997	7,050	BV+18%	—
1998	5,710	BV+18%	—
1999	2,000	BV+18%	—

KM# 165 10 DOLLARS **Weight:** 7.7857 g. **Composition:** 0.9995 Platinum 0.2500 oz. APW **Ruler:** Elizabeth II **Obverse:** Queen's bust right, date and denomination below **Obv. Designer:** Machin **Reverse:** Maple leaf flanked by 9995

Date	Mintage	MS-63	Proof
1988	93,600	BV+13%	—
1989	3,200	BV+13%	—
1989 Proof	1,999	—	360

KM# 193 10 DOLLARS **Weight:** 7.7857 g. **Composition:** 0.9995 Platinum 0.2500 oz. APW **Obv. Designer:** dePedery-Hunt **Reverse:** Maple leaf

Date	Mintage	MS-63	Proof
1990	1,600	BV+13%	—
1991	7,200	BV+13%	—
1992	11,600	BV+13%	—
1993	8,048	BV+13%	—
1994	9,456	BV+13%	—
1995	6,524	BV+13%	—
1996	6,160	BV+13%	—
1997	4,552	BV+13%	—
1998	3,816	BV+13%	—
1999	2,000	BV+13%	—

KM# 166 20 DOLLARS **Weight:** 15.5519 g. **Composition:** 0.9995 Platinum 0.5000 oz. APW **Ruler:** Elizabeth II **Obverse:** Queen's bust right, denomination and date below **Obv. Designer:** Machin **Reverse:** Maple leaf flanked by 9995

Date	Mintage	MS-63	Proof
1988	23,600	BV+9%	—
1989	4,800	BV+9%	—
1989 Proof	1,999	—	700

KM# 194 20 DOLLARS **Weight:** 15.5519 g. **Composition:** 0.9995 Platinum 0.5000 oz. APW **Obv. Designer:** dePedery-Hunt **Reverse:** Maple leaf

Date	Mintage	MS-63	Proof
1990	2,600	BV+9%	—
1991	5,600	BV+9%	—
1992	12,800	BV+9%	—
1993	6,022	BV+9%	—
1994	6,710	BV+9%	—
1995	6,308	BV+9%	—
1996	5,490	BV+9%	—
1997	3,990	BV+9%	—
1998	5,486	BV+9%	—
1999	500	BV+15%	—

KM# 174 30 DOLLARS **Weight:** 3.1100 g. **Composition:** 0.9990 Platinum 0.1000 oz. APW **Reverse:** Polar bear swimming, denomination below **Rev. Designer:** Robert Bateman

Date	Mintage	MS-63	Proof
1990 Proof	2,629	—	145

KM# 198 30 DOLLARS **Weight:** 3.1100 g. **Composition:** 0.9990 Platinum 0.1000 oz. APW **Reverse:** Snowy owl, denomination below **Rev. Designer:** Glen Loates

Date	Mintage	MS-63	Proof
1991 Proof	3,500	—	145

KM# 226 30 DOLLARS **Weight:** 3.1100 g. **Composition:** 0.9990 Platinum 0.1000 oz. APW **Reverse:** Cougar head and shoulders, denomination below **Rev. Designer:** George McLean

Date	Mintage	MS-63	Proof
1992 Proof	3,500	—	145

KM# 240 30 DOLLARS **Weight:** 3.1100 g. **Composition:** 0.9990 Platinum 0.1000 oz. APW **Reverse:** Arctic fox, denomination below **Rev. Designer:** Claude D'Angelo

Date	Mintage	MS-63	Proof
1993 Proof	3,500	—	150

KM# 252 30 DOLLARS **Weight:** 3.1100 g. **Composition:** 0.9990 Platinum 0.1000 oz. APW **Ruler:** Elizabeth II **Obverse:** Crowned Queen's head right, date below **Reverse:** Sea otter, denomination below **Rev. Designer:** Ron S. Parker

Date	Mintage	MS-63	Proof
1994 Proof	1,500	—	150

KM# 266 30 DOLLARS **Weight:** 3.1100 g. **Composition:** 0.9990 Platinum 0.1000 oz. APW **Ruler:** Elizabeth II **Obverse:** Crowned head right, date below **Reverse:** Canadian lynx, denomination below **Rev. Designer:** Michael Dumas

Date	Mintage	MS-63	Proof
1995 Proof	620	—	150

KM# 278 30 DOLLARS **Weight:** 3.1100 g. **Composition:** 0.9990 Platinum 0.1000 oz. APW **Ruler:** Elizabeth II **Obverse:** Crowned head right, date below **Reverse:** Falcon portrait, denomination below **Rev. Designer:** Dwayne Harty

Date	Mintage	MS-63	Proof
1996 Proof	489	—	150

KM# 300 30 DOLLARS **Weight:** 3.1100 g. **Composition:** 0.9995 Platinum 0.1000 oz. APW **Ruler:** Elizabeth II **Obverse:** Crowned head right, date below **Reverse:** Bison head, denomination below **Rev. Designer:** Chris Bacon

Date	Mintage	MS-63	Proof
1997 Proof	5,000	—	135

KM# 322 30 DOLLARS **Weight:** 3.1100 g. **Composition:** 0.9990 Platinum 0.1000 oz. APW **Ruler:** Elizabeth II **Obverse:** Crowned head right, date below **Reverse:** Grey wolf **Rev. Designer:** Kerr Burnett

Date	Mintage	MS-63	Proof
ND(1998) Proof	2,000	—	150

KM# 359 30 DOLLARS **Weight:** 3.1100 g. **Composition:** 0.9995 Platinum 0.1000 oz. APW **Ruler:** Elizabeth II **Obverse:** Crowned head right, date below **Reverse:** Musk ox **Rev. Designer:** Mark Hobson

Date	Mintage	MS-63	Proof
1999 Proof	1,500	—	150

KM# 405 30 DOLLARS **Weight:** 3.1100 g. **Composition:** 0.9995 Platinum .1000 oz. APW **Ruler:** Elizabeth II **Obverse:** Crowned head right, date below **Reverse:** Pronghorn antelope head, denomination below **Rev. Designer:** Mark Hobson **Edge:** Reeded **Size:** 16 mm.

Date	Mintage	MS-63	Proof
2000 Proof	600	—	150

KM# 167 50 DOLLARS **Weight:** 31.1030 g. **Composition:** 0.9995 Platinum 1.0000 oz. APW **Ruler:** Elizabeth II **Obverse:** Queen's bust right, denomination and date below **Obv. Designer:** Machin **Reverse:** Maple leaf flanked by 9995

Date	Mintage	MS-63	Proof
1988	37,500	BV+4%	—
1989	10,000	BV+4%	—
1989 Proof	5,965	—	1,325

KM# 195 50 DOLLARS **Weight:** 31.1030 g. **Composition:** 0.9995 Platinum 1.0000 oz. APW **Obv. Designer:** dePedery-Hunt **Reverse:** Maple leaf

Date	Mintage	MS-63	Proof
1990	15,100	BV+4%	—
1991	31,900	BV+4%	—
1992	40,500	BV+4%	—
1993	17,666	BV+4%	—
1994	36,245	BV+4%	—
1995	25,829	BV+4%	—
1996	62,273	BV+4%	—
1997	25,480	BV+4%	—
1998	10,403	BV+4%	—
1999	1,300	BV+10%	—

KM# 175 75 DOLLARS **Weight:** 7.7760 g. **Composition:** 0.9990 Platinum 0.2500 oz. APW **Reverse:** Polar bear resting, denomination below **Rev. Designer:** Robert Bateman

Date	Mintage	MS-63	Proof
1990 Proof	2,629	—	325

KM# 199 75 DOLLARS **Weight:** 7.7760 g. **Composition:** 0.9990 Platinum 0.2500 oz. APW **Reverse:** Snowy owls perched on branch, denomination below **Rev. Designer:** Glen Loates

Date	Mintage	MS-63	Proof
1991 Proof	3,500	—	325

KM# 227 75 DOLLARS **Weight:** 7.7760 g. **Composition:** 0.9990 Platinum 0.2500 oz. APW **Reverse:** Cougar prowling, denomination below **Rev. Designer:** George McLean

Date	Mintage	MS-63	Proof
1992 Proof	3,500	—	340

KM# 241 75 DOLLARS **Weight:** 7.7760 g. **Composition:** 0.9990 Platinum 0.2500 oz. APW **Reverse:** Two Arctic foxes, denomination below **Rev. Designer:** Claude D'Angelo

Date	Mintage	MS-63	Proof
1993 Proof	3,500	—	340

KM# 253 75 DOLLARS **Weight:** 7.7760 g. **Composition:** 0.9990 Platinum 0.2500 oz. APW **Ruler:** Elizabeth II **Obverse:** Crowned head right, date below **Reverse:** Sea otter eating urchin, denomination below **Rev. Designer:** Ron S. Parker

Date	Mintage	MS-63	Proof
1994 Proof	1,500	—	340

KM# 267 75 DOLLARS **Weight:** 7.7760 g. **Composition:** 0.9990 Platinum 0.2500 oz. APW **Ruler:** Elizabeth II **Obverse:** Crowned head right, date below **Reverse:** Two lynx kittens, denomination below **Rev. Designer:** Michael Dumas

Date	Mintage	MS-63	Proof
1995 Proof	1,500	—	340

KM# 279 75 DOLLARS **Weight:** 7.7760 g. **Composition:** 0.9990 Platinum 0.2500 oz. APW **Ruler:** Elizabeth II **Obverse:** Crowned head right, date below **Reverse:** Peregrine falcon, denomination below **Rev. Designer:** Dwayne Harty

Date	Mintage	MS-63	Proof
1996 Proof	1,500	—	340

KM# 301 75 DOLLARS **Weight:** 7.7760 g. **Composition:** 0.9990 Platinum 0.2500 oz. APW **Ruler:** Elizabeth II **Obverse:** Crowned head right, date below **Reverse:** Two bison calves, denomination below **Rev. Designer:** Chris Bacon

Date	Mintage	MS-63	Proof
1997 Proof	1,500	—	340

KM# 323 75 DOLLARS **Weight:** 7.7760 g. **Composition:** 0.9990 Platinum 0.2500 oz. APW **Ruler:** Elizabeth II **Obverse:** Crowned head right, date below **Reverse:** Gray wolf **Rev. Designer:** Kerr Burnett

Date	Mintage	MS-63	Proof
1998 Proof	1,000	—	340

KM# 360 75 DOLLARS **Weight:** 7.7760 g. **Composition:** 0.9990 Platinum 0.2500 oz. APW **Ruler:** Elizabeth II **Obverse:** Crowned head right, date below **Reverse:** Musk ox **Rev. Designer:** Mark Hobson

Date	Mintage	MS-63	Proof
1999 Proof	500	—	345

KM# 406 75 DOLLARS **Weight:** 7.7760 g. **Composition:** 0.9990 Platinum .2500 oz. APW **Obverse:** Queen's portrait **Reverse:** Standing pronghorn antelope, denomination below **Rev. Designer:** Mark Hobson **Edge:** Reeded **Size:** 20 mm.

Date	Mintage	MS-63	Proof
2000 Proof	600	—	345

KM# 176 150 DOLLARS **Weight:** 15.5520 g. **Composition:** 0.9990 Platinum 0.5000 oz. APW **Reverse:** Polar bear walking, denomination below **Rev. Designer:** Robert Bateman

Date	Mintage	MS-63	Proof
1990 Proof	2,629	—	675

KM# 200 150 DOLLARS **Weight:** 15.5520 g. **Composition:** 0.9990 Platinum 0.5000 oz. APW **Reverse:** Snowy owl flying, denomination below **Rev. Designer:** Glen Loates

Date	Mintage	MS-63	Proof
1991 Proof	3,500	—	675

KM# 228 150 DOLLARS **Weight:** 15.5520 g. **Composition:** 0.9990 Platinum 0.5000 oz. APW **Reverse:** Cougar mother and cub, denomination below **Rev. Designer:** George McLean

Date	Mintage	MS-63	Proof
1992 Proof	3,500	—	685

KM# 242 150 DOLLARS **Weight:** 15.5520 g. **Composition:** 0.9990 Platinum 0.5000 oz. APW **Reverse:** Arctic fox by lake, denomination below **Rev. Designer:** Claude D'Angelo

Date	Mintage	MS-63	Proof
1993 Proof	3,500	—	685

KM# 254 150 DOLLARS **Weight:** 15.5520 g. **Composition:** 0.9990 Platinum 0.5000 oz. APW **Ruler:** Elizabeth II **Obverse:** Crowned head right, date below **Reverse:** Sea otter mother carrying pup, denomination below **Rev. Designer:** Ron S. Parker

Date	Mintage	MS-63	Proof
1994 Proof	—	—	700

KM# 268 150 DOLLARS **Weight:** 15.5520 g. **Composition:** 0.9990 Platinum 0.5000 oz. APW **Ruler:** Elizabeth II **Obverse:** Crowned head right, date below **Reverse:** Prowling lynx, denomination below **Rev. Designer:** Michael Dumas

Date	Mintage	MS-63	Proof
1995 Proof	226	—	685

KM# 280 150 DOLLARS **Weight:** 15.5520 g. **Composition:** 0.9990 Platinum 0.5000 oz. APW **Ruler:** Elizabeth II **Obverse:** Crowned head right, date below **Reverse:** Peregrine falcon on branch, denomination below **Rev. Designer:** Dwayne Harty

Date	Mintage	MS-63	Proof
1996 Proof	100	—	685

KM# 302 150 DOLLARS **Weight:** 15.5520 g. **Composition:** 0.9990 Platinum 0.5000 oz. APW **Ruler:** Elizabeth II **Obverse:** Crowned head right, date below **Reverse:** Bison bull, denomination below **Rev. Designer:** Chris Bacon

Date	Mintage	MS-63	Proof
1997 Proof	4,000	—	685

KM# 324 150 DOLLARS **Weight:** 15.5520 g. **Composition:** 0.9990 Platinum 0.5000 oz. APW **Ruler:** Elizabeth II **Obverse:** Crowned head right, date below **Reverse:** Two gray wolf cubs, denomination below **Rev. Designer:** Kerr Burnett

Date	Mintage	MS-63	Proof
1998 Proof	2,000	—	685

KM# 361 150 DOLLARS **Weight:** 15.5520 g. **Composition:** 0.9990 Platinum 0.5000 oz. APW **Reverse:** Musk ox, denomination below **Rev. Designer:** Mark Hobson

Date	Mintage	MS-63	Proof
1999 Proof	500	—	700

KM# 407 150 DOLLARS **Weight:** 15.5500 g. **Composition:** 0.9990 Platinum .5000 oz. APW **Reverse:** Two pronghorn antelope, denomination below **Rev. Designer:** Mark Hobson **Edge:** Reeded **Size:** 25 mm.

Date	Mintage	MS-63	Proof
2000 Proof	600	—	700

KM# 177 300 DOLLARS **Weight:** 31.1035 g. **Composition:** 0.9990 Platinum 1.0000 oz. APW **Reverse:** Polar bear mother and cub, denomination below **Rev. Designer:** Robert Bateman

Date	Mintage	MS-63	Proof
1990 Proof	2,629	—	1,325

KM# 201 300 DOLLARS **Weight:** 31.1035 g. **Composition:** 0.9990 Platinum 1.0000 oz. APW **Reverse:** Snowy owl with chicks, denomination below **Rev. Designer:** Glen Loates

Date	Mintage	MS-63	Proof
1991 Proof	3,500	—	1,325

KM# 229 300 DOLLARS **Weight:** 31.1035 g. **Composition:** 0.9990 Platinum 1.0000 oz. APW **Reverse:** Cougar resting in tree, denomination below **Rev. Designer:** George McLean

Date	Mintage	MS-63	Proof
1992 Proof	3,500	—	1,325

KM# 243 300 DOLLARS **Weight:** 31.1035 g. **Composition:** 0.9990 Platinum 1.0000 oz. APW **Reverse:** Mother fox and three kits, denomination below **Rev. Designer:** Claude D'Angelo

Date	Mintage	MS-63	Proof
1993 Proof	3,500	—	1,325

KM# 255 300 DOLLARS **Weight:** 31.1035 g. **Composition:** 0.9990 Platinum 1.0000 oz. APW **Ruler:** Elizabeth II **Obverse:** Crowned head right, date below **Reverse:** Two otters swimming, denomination below **Rev. Designer:** Ron S. Parker

Date	Mintage	MS-63	Proof
1994 Proof	—	—	1,325

KM# 269 300 DOLLARS **Weight:** 31.1035 g. **Composition:** 0.9990 Platinum 1.0000 oz. APW **Ruler:** Elizabeth II **Obverse:** Crowned head right, date below **Reverse:** Female lynx and three kittens, denomination below **Rev. Designer:** Michael Dumas

Date	Mintage	MS-63	Proof
1995 Proof	1,500	—	1,325

KM# 281 300 DOLLARS **Weight:** 31.1035 g. **Composition:** 0.9990 Platinum 1.0000 oz. APW **Ruler:** Elizabeth II **Obverse:** Crowned head right, date below **Reverse:** Peregrine falcon feeding nestlings, denomination below **Rev. Designer:** Dwayne Harty

Date	Mintage	MS-63	Proof
1996 Proof	1,500	—	1,325

KM# 303 300 DOLLARS **Weight:** 31.1035 g. **Composition:** 0.9990 Platinum 1.0000 oz. APW **Ruler:** Elizabeth II **Obverse:** Crowned head right, date below **Reverse:** Bison family, denomination below **Rev. Designer:** Chris Bacon

Date	Mintage	MS-63	Proof
1997 Proof	1,500	—	1,325

KM# 325 300 DOLLARS **Weight:** 31.1035 g. **Composition:** 0.9990 Platinum 1.0000 oz. APW **Ruler:** Elizabeth II **Obverse:** Crowned head right, date below **Reverse:** Gray wolf and two cubs, denomination below **Rev. Designer:** Kerr Burnett

Date	Mintage	MS-63	Proof
1998 Proof	—	—	1,325

KM# 362 300 DOLLARS **Weight:** 31.1035 g. **Composition:** 0.9990 Platinum 1.0000 oz. APW **Ruler:** Elizabeth II **Obverse:** Crowned head right, date below **Reverse:** Musk ox **Rev. Designer:** Mark Hobson

Date	Mintage	MS-63	Proof
1999 Proof	500	—	1,325

KM# 408 300 DOLLARS **Weight:** 31.1035 g. **Composition:** 0.9990 Platinum 1.0000 oz. APW **Ruler:** Elizabeth II **Obverse:** Crowned head right, date below **Reverse:** Four pronghorn antelope, denomination below **Rev. Designer:** Mark Hobson **Edge:** Reeded **Size:** 30 mm.

Date	Mintage	MS-63	Proof
2000 Proof	600	—	1,325

PATTERNS

Including off metal strikes

KM	Date	Mintage	Identification	Mkt Val
Pn14	1911	—	Cent. Bronze.. Similar to 1912-1920.	10,000
Pn15	1911	—	Dollar. Silver..	650,000
Pn16	1911	—	Dollar. Lead..	—
Pn17	1911	—	5 Dollars. Gold..	—
Pn18	1911	—	10 Dollars. Gold..	—
Pn19	1928	—	5 Dollars. Bronze..	—
Pn20	1928	—	10 Dollars. Bronze..	—
Pn23	1964	—	Dollar. Tin.. Piefort	—
Pn24	1967	—	Dollar. Silver.. Unique.	—

TRIAL STRIKES

KM	Date	Mintage	Identification	Mkt Val
TS3	1928	—	5 Dollars. Bronze..	—
TS4	1928	—	10 Dollars. Bronze..	—
TS5	1937	—	Cent. Brass.. Thick planchet.	2,500
TS6	1937	—	5 Cents. Brass.. Thick planchet.	2,500
TS7	1937	—	10 Cents. Brass.. Thick planchet.	2,500
TS8	1937	—	25 Cents. Brass.. Thick planchet.	3,500
TS9	1937	—	25 Cents. Bronze..	3,500
TS10	1937	—	50 Cents. Brass.. Thick planchet.	5,000
TS11	1942	—	5 Cents. Nickel.. 12 sided.	—
TS12	1943	—	Cent. Copper Plated Steel..	—
TS13	1943	—	5 Cents. Steel..	—
TS14	1944	—	5 Cents. Tombac..	—
TS15	1951	—	5 Cents. Chrome Plated Steel..	—
TS16	1952	—	5 Cents..	—
TS17	1959	—	50 Cents. Tin..	—
TS18	1964	—	Dollar. Tin.. Piefort, unique.	—

CUSTOM PROOF-LIKE SETS (CPL)

KM	Date	Mintage	Identification	Issue Price	Mkt Val
CPL1	1971	33,517	KM59.1 (2 pcs.), 60.1, 62b-75.1, 77.1 ,79	6.50	6.00
CPL2	1971	38,198	KM59.1 (2 pcs.), 60.1, 62b, 75.1-77.1	6.50	6.00
CPL3	1973	35,676	KM59.1 (2 pcs.), 60.1, 75.1, 77.1, 81.1 obv. 120 beads, 82	6.50	7.00
CPL4	1973	I.A.	KM59.1 (2 pcs.), 60.1, 75.1, 77.1, 81.1 obv. 132 beads, 82	6.50	140
CPL5	1974	44,296	KM59.1 (2 pcs.), 60.1, 62b-75.1, 88	8.00	6.00
CPL6	1975	36,851	KM59.1 (2 pcs.), 60.1, 62b-75.1, 76.2, 77.1	8.00	6.00
CPL7	1976	28,162	KM59.1 (2 pcs.), 60.1, 62b-75.1, 76.2, 77.1	8.00	7.00
CPL8	1977	44,198	KM59.1 (2 pcs.), 60.1, 62b-75.2, 77.1, 117	8.15	5.50
CPL9	1978	41,000	KM59.1 (2 pcs.), 60.1, 62b-75.3, 77.1, 120.1	—	5.50
CPL10	1979	31,174	KM59.2 (2 pcs.), 60.2, 74, 75.3, 77.2, 120.1	10.75	5.50
CPL11	1980	41,447	KM60.2, 74, 75.3, 77.2, 120.1, 127 (2 pcs.)	10.75	6.00

MINT SETS

KM	Date	Mintage	Identification	Issue Price	Mkt Val
MS1	1973	I.A.	KM84-85, 86.1, 87; Olympic Commemoratives, Series I	45.00	40.00
MS2	1974	I.A.	KM89-90, 93-94; Olympic Commemoratives, Series II	48.00	40.00
MS3	1974	I.A.	KM91-92, 95-96; Olympic Commemorative, Series III	48.00	40.00
MS4	1975	I.A.	KM98-99, 102-103; Olympic Commemoratives, Series IV	48.00	40.00
MS5	1975	I.A.	KM100-101, 104-105; Olympic Commemoratives, Series V	60.00	40.00
MS6	1976	I.A.	KM107-108, 111-112; Olympic Commemoratives, Series VI	60.00	40.00
MS7	1976	I.A.	KM109-110, 113-114; Olympic Commemoratives, Series VII	60.00	40.00

OLYMPIC COMMEMORATIVES (OCP)

KM	Date	Mintage	Identification	Issue Price	Mkt Val
OCP1	1973	I.A.	KM84-87, Series I	78.50	45.00
OCP2	1974	I.A.	KM89-90, 93-94, Series II	88.50	45.00
OCP3	1974	I.A.	KM91-92, 95-96, Series III	88.50	45.00
OCP4	1975	I.A.	KM98-99, 102-103, Series IV	88.50	45.00
OCP5	1975	I.A.	KM100-101, 104-105, Series V	88.50	45.00
OCP6	1976	I.A.	KM107-108, 111-112, Series VI	88.50	45.00
OCP7	1976	I.A.	KM109-110, 113-114, Series VII	88.50	45.00

PROOF SETS

KM	Date	Mintage	Identification	Issue Price	Mkt Val
PS1	1981	199,000	KM60.2, 74, 75.3, 77.2, 120.1, 127, 130	36.00	17.50
PS2	1982	180,908	KM60.2a, 74, 75.3, 77.2, 120.1, 132-133	36.00	14.00
PS3	1983	166,779	KM60.2a, 74, 75.3, 77.2, 120.1, 132, 138	36.00	14.00
PS4	1984	161,602	KM60.2a, 74, 75.3, 77.2, 120.1, 132, 140	30.00	17.00
PS5	1985	157,037	KM60.2a, 74, 75.3, 77.2, 120.1, 132, 143	30.00	18.00
PS6	1986	175,745	KM60.2a, 74, 75.3, 77.2, 120.1, 132, 149	30.00	18.00
PS7	1987	179,004	KM60.2a, 74, 75.3, 77.2, 120.1, 132, 154	34.00	18.00
PS8	1988	175,259	KM60.2a, 74, 75.3, 77.2, 132, 157, 161	37.50	23.00
PS9	1989	170,928	KM60.2a, 74, 75.3, 77.2, 132, 157, 168	40.00	24.00
PS10	1989	6,823	KM125.2, 135-136, 153	1,190	1,100
PS11	1989	1,995	KM164-167	1,700	2,100
PS12	1989	2,550	KM125.2, 163, 167	1,530	1,775
PS13	1989	9,979	KM135, 163-164	165	225
PS14	1990	158,068	KM170, 181, 182, 183, 184, 185, 186	41.00	24.00
PS15	1990	2,629	KM174-177	1,720	2,475
PS16	1991	14,629	KM179, 181, 182, 183, 184, 185, 186	—	45.00
PS17	1991	873	KM198-201	1,760	2,475
PS18	1992	84,397	KM203a, 212a-214a, 218, 220a-223a, 231a-234a	—	60.00
PS19	1992	147,061	KM204-210	42.75	30.00
PS20	1992	3,500	KM226-229	1,680	2,500
PS21	1993	143,065	KM181, 182, 183, 184, 185, 186, 235	42.75	20.00
PS22	1993	3,500	KM240-243	1,329	2,500
PS23	1994	47,303	KM181-186, 248	47.50	28.00
PS24	1994	99,121	KM181, 182, 183, 184, 185, 186, 251	43.00	28.00
PS25	1994	1,500	KM252-255	915	2,520
PS26	1995	I.A.	KM181, 182, 183, 184, 185, 186, 259	37.45	25.00
PS27	1995	50,000	KM181, 182, 183, 184, 185, 258-259	49.45	22.00
PS28	1995	I.A.	KM261-264	42.00	60.00
PS29	1995	682	KM266-269	1,555	2,500
PS30	1995	I.A.	KM261-262	22.00	21.00
PS31	1995	I.A.	KM263-264	22.00	30.00
PS32	1996	423	KM278-281	1,555	2,500
PS33	1996	I.A.	KM181a, 182a, 183a, 184a, 185a, 186, 274	49.00	35.00
PS34	1996	I.A.	KM283-286	44.45	45.00
PS35	1997	I.A.	KM182a, 183a, 184a, 209, 270c, 282, 289,	60.00	30.00
PS36	1997	I.A.	KM292-295	44.45	35.00
PS37	1997	I.A.	KM300-303	1,530	2,485
PS38	1998	I.A.	KM182a, 183a, 184a, 186, 270b, 289, 290a, 306	59.45	50.00
PS39	1998	25,000	KM309-313	73.50	55.00
PS40	1998	61,000	KM316 w/China Y-727	72.50	30.00
PS41	1998	I.A.	KM318-321	44.45	38.00
PS42	1998	1,000	KM322-325	1,552	2,500
PS43	1998	25,000	KM310-313, 332	73.50	30.00
PS44	1999	I.A.	KM182a-184a, 186, 270c, 289, 290a,	59.45	60.00
PS45	1999	I.A.	KM335-338	39.95	40.00
PS46	1999	I.A.	KM342a-353a	99.45	75.00
PS47	1999	I.A.	KM359-362	1,425	2,520
PS48	2000	—	KM373a, 374a, 375a, 376a, 377a, 378a, 379a, 380a, 381a, 382a, 383a, 384.2a	101	90.00
PS49	2000	—	KM389-392	44.00	40.00
PS50	2000	600	KM405-408	1,416	2,520

PROOF-LIKE DOLLARS

KM	Date	Mintage	Identification	Issue Price	Mkt Val
D1.1	1951	I.A.	KM46, Canoe		175
D1.2	1951	I.A.	KM46, Arnprior		700
D2.1	1952	I.A.	KM46, water lines		1,200
D2.2	1952	I.A.	KM46, without water lines		175
D3	1953	1,200	KM54, Canoe w/shoulder fold	—	325
D4	1954	5,300	KM54, Canoe	1.25	150
D5	1955	7,950	KM54, Canoe	1.25	125
D5a	1955	I.A.	KM54, Arnprior	1.25	175
D6	1956	10,212	KM54, Canoe	1.25	70.00
D7	1957	16,241	KM54, Canoe	1.25	40.00
D8	1958	33,237	KM55, British Columbia	1.25	25.00
D9	1959	45,160	KM54, Canoe	1.25	15.00
D10	1960	82,728	KM54, Canoe	1.25	10.00
D11	1961	120,928	KM54, Canoe	1.25	7.50
D12	1962	248,901	KM54, Canoe	1.25	7.00
D13	1963	963,525	KM54, Canoe	1.25	6.00
D14	1964	2,862,441	KM58, Charlottetown	1.25	6.00
D15	1965	2,904,352	KM64.1, Canoe	—	6.00
D16	1966	672,514	KM64.1, Canoe	—	6.00
D17	1967	1,036,176	KM70, Confederation	—	7.50

PROOF-LIKE SETS (PL)

KM	Date	Mintage	Identification	Issue Price	Mkt Val
PL1	1953	1,200	KM49 w/o shoulder fold, 50-54	2.20	1,250
PL2	1953	I.A.	KM49-54	2.20	760
PL3	1954	3,000	KM49-54	2.50	450
PL4	1954	I.A.	KM49 w/o shoulder fold, 50-54	2.50	1,100
PL5	1955	6,300	KM49, 50a, 51-54	2.50	375
PL6	1955	I.A.	KM49, 50a, 51-54, Arnprior	2.50	500
PL7	1956	6,500	KM49, 50a, 51-54	2.50	225
PL8	1957	11,862	KM49, 50a, 51-54	2.50	150
PL9	1958	18,259	KM49, 50a, 51-53, 55	2.50	100
PL10	1959	31,577	KM49, 50a, 51, 52, 54, 56	2.50	45.00
PL11	1960	64,097	KM49, 50a, 51, 52, 54, 56	3.00	35.00
PL12	1961	98,373	KM49, 50a, 51, 52, 54, 56	3.00	16.00
PL13	1962	200,950	KM49, 50a, 51, 52, 54, 56	3.00	10.00
PL14	1963	673,006	KM49, 51, 52, 54, 56, 57	3.00	9.50
PL15	1964	1,653,162	KM49, 51, 52, 56-58	3.00	9.50
PL16	1965	2,904,352	KM59.1-60.1, 61-63, 64.1	4.00	9.50
PL17	1966	672,514	KM59.1-60.1, 61-63, 64.1	4.00	9.50
PL18	1967	961,887	KM65-70 (pliofilm flat pack)	4.00	12.00
PL18A	1967	70,583	KM65-70 and Silver Medal (red box)	12.00	16.00
PL18B	1967	337,688	KM65-71 (black box)	40.00	250
PL19	1968	521,641	KM59.1-60.1, 62b, 72a, 75.1-76.1	4.00	2.25
PL20	1969	326,203	KM59.1-60.1, 62b, 75.1-77.1	4.00	2.75
PL21	1970	349,120	KM59.1-60.1, 62b, 75.1, 77.1, 78	4.00	3.25
PL22	1971	253,311	KM59.1-60.1, 62b, 75.1, 77.1, 79	4.00	2.75
PL23	1972	224,275	KM59.1-60.1, 62b-77.1	4.00	2.75
PL24	1973	243,695	KM59.1-60.1, 62b-75.1 obv. 120 beads, 77.1, 81.1, 82	4.00	4.00
PL25	1973	I.A.	KM59.1-60.1, 62b-75.1 obv. 132 beads, 77.1, 81.2, 82	4.00	150
PL26	1974	213,589	KM59.1-60.1, 62b-75.1, 77.1, 88	5.00	3.00
PL27.1	1975	197,372	KM59.1, 60.1, 62b-75.1, 76.2, 77.1	5.00	2.50
PL27.2	1975	I.A.	KM59.1, 60.1, 62b-75.1, 76.3, 77.1	5.00	5.00
PL28	1976	171,737	KM59.1, 60.1, 62b-75.1, 76.2, 77.1	5.15	2.75
PL29	1977	225,307	KM59.1, 60.1, 62b, 75.2, 77.1, 117.1	5.15	2.75
PL30	1978	260,000	KM59.1-60.1, 62b, 75.3, 77.1, 120.1	5.25	2.75
PL31	1979	187,624	KM59.2-60.2, 74, 75.3, 77.2, 120.1	6.25	2.75
PL32	1980	410,842	KM60.2, 74, 75.3, 77.2, 120.1, 127	6.50	4.50
PL33	1981	186,250	KM60.2, 74, 75.3, 77.2, 120.1, 123	5.00	3.25
PL34	1982	203,287	KM60.2, 74, 75.3, 77.2, 120.1, 123	6.00	2.50
PL36	1983	190,838	KM60.2a, 74, 75.3, 77.2, 120.1, 132	5.00	5.00
PL36.1	1983	I.A.	KM60.2a, 74, 75.3, 77.2, 120.1, 132; set in folder packaged by British Royal Mint Coin Club	—	—
PL37	1984	181,249	KM60.2a, 74, 75.3, 77.2, 120.1, 132	5.25	5.00
PL38	1985	173,924	KM60.2a, 74, 75.3, 77.2, 120.1, 132	5.25	6.00
PL39	1986	167,338	KM60.2a, 74, 75.3, 77.2, 120.1, 132	5.25	6.50
PL40	1987	212,136	KM60.2a, 74, 75.3, 77.2, 120.1, 132	5.25	5.00
PL41	1988	182,048	KM60.2a, 74, 75.3, 77.2, 132, 157	6.05	5.00
PL42	1989	173,622	KM60.2a, 74, 75.3, 77.2, 132, 157	6.60	8.00
PL43	1990	170,791	KM181-186	7.40	8.00
PL44	1991	147,814	KM181-186	7.40	25.00
PL45	1992	217,597	KM204-209	8.25	11.00
PL46	1993	171,680	KM181-186	8.25	4.00
PL47	1994	141,676	KM181-185, 258	8.50	5.50
PL48	1994	18,794	KM181-185, 258 (Oh Canada holder)	—	8.50

KM	Date	Mintage	Identification	Issue Price	Mkt Val
PL49	1995	143,892	KM181-186	6.95	6.00
PL50	1995	50,927	KM181-186 (Oh Canada holder)	14.65	8.50
PL51	1995	36,443	KM181-186 (Baby Gift holder)	—	9.00
PL52	1996	116,736	KM181-186	—	14.00
PL53	1996	29,747	KM181-186 (Baby Gift holder)	—	14.00
PL54	1996	I.A.	KM181a-185a, 186	8.95	16.00
PL55	1996	I.A.	KM181a-185a, 186 (Oh Canada holder)	14.65	12.00
PL56	1996	I.A.	KM181a-185a, 186 (Baby Gift holder)	—	12.00
PL57	1997	I.A.	KM182a-184a, 209, 270, 289-290	10.45	8.00
PL58	1997	I.A.	KM182a-184a, 270, 289-291 (Oh Canada holder)	16.45	20.00
PL59	1997	I.A.	KM182a-184a, 209, 270, 289-290 (Baby Gift holder)	18.50	9.50
PL60	1998	I.A.	KM182-184, 186, 270, 289-290	10.45	10.00
PL61	1998	I.A.	KM182-184, 186, 270, 289-290 (Oh Canada holder)	16.45	12.00
PL62	1998	I.A.	KM182-184, 186, 270, 289-290 (Tiny Treasures holder)	16.45	12.00
PL63	1999	I.A.	KM342-353	16.95	10.00
PL64	2000	—	KM373-384	16.95	10.00

SPECIMEN SETS (SS)

KM	Date	Mintage	Identification	Issue Price	Mkt Val
SS12	1902	100	KM8-12	—	25,000
SS13	1902	I.A.	KM9 (Large H), 10, 11	—	6,500
SS14	1903	I.A.	KM10, 12, 13	—	7,000
SS15	1908	1,000	KM8, 10-13	—	2,200
SS16	1911	1,000	KM15-19	—	5,500
SS17	1911/12	5	KM15-20, 26-27	—	52,250
SS18	1921	I.A.	KM22-25, 28	—	120,000
SS19	1922	I.A.	KM28, 29	—	2,500
SS20	1923	I.A.	KM28, 29	—	5,000
SS21	1924	I.A.	KM28, 29	—	4,000
SS22	1925	I.A.	KM28, 29	—	7,000
SS23	1926	I.A.	KM28, 29 (Near 6)	—	5,000
SS24	1927	I.A.	KM24a, 28, 29	—	8,000
SS25	1928	I.A.	KM23a, 24a, 28, 29	—	12,000
SS26	1929	I.A.	KM23a,-25a, 28, 29	—	22,500
SS27	1930	I.A.	KM23a, 24a. 28, 29	—	16,000
SS28	1931	I.A.	KM23a-25a, 28, 29	—	26,500
SS29	1932	I.A.	KM23a-25a, 28, 29	—	20,000
SS30	1934	I.A.	KM23-25, 28, 29	—	23,000
SS31	1936	I.A.	KM23-25, 28, 29	—	12,000
SS32	1936	I.A.	KM23a(dot), 24a(dot), 25a, 28(dot), 29, 30	—	400,000
SS33	1937	1,025	KM32-37, Matte Finish	—	750
SS34	1937	I.A.	KM32-35, Mirror Fields	—	1,350
SS35	1937	75	KM32-37, Mirror Fields	—	3,900
SS36	1938	I.A.	KM32-37	—	18,250
SS-A36	1939	I.A.	KM32-35, 38, Matte Finish	—	—
SS-B36	1939	I.A.	KM32-35, 38, Mirror Fields	—	—
SS-C36	1942	I.A.	KM32, 33	—	1,000
SS-D36	1943	I.A.	KM32, 40	—	1,000
SS-A37	1944	I.A.	KM32, 40a	—	1,000
SS37	1944	3	KM32, 34-37, 40a	—	11,300
SS-A38	1945	I.A.	KM32, 40a	—	1,000
SS38	1945	6	KM32, 34-37, 40a	—	4,650
SS39	1946	15	KM32, 34-37, 39a	—	4,000
SS40	1947	I.A.	KM32, 34-37(7 curved), 37(7 pointed),	—	8,500
SS41	1947	I.A.	KM32, 34-36(7 curved), 37(blunt 7), 39a	—	6,200
SS42	1947	I.A.	KM32, 34-36(7 curved right), 37, 39a	—	4,250
SS43	1948	30	KM41-46	—	6,000
SS44	1949	20	KM41-45, 47	—	6,400
SS44A	1949	I.A.	KM47	—	1,550
SS45	1950	12	KM41-46	—	1,650
SS46	1950	I.A.	KM41-45, 46 (Arnprior)	—	3,175
SS47	1951	12	KM41, 48, 42a, 43-46 (w/water lines)	—	2,725
SS48	1952	2,317	KM41, 42a, 43-46 (water lines)	—	3,175
SS48A	1952	I.A.	KM41, 42a, 43-46 (w/o water lines)	—	3,175
SS49	1953	28	KM49 w/o straps, 50-54	—	1,850
SS50	1953	I.A.	KM49 w/ straps, 50-54	—	875
SS51	1964	I.A.	KM49, 51, 52, 56-58	—	850
SS52	1965	I.A.	KM59.1-60.1, 61-63, 64.1	—	850
SS56	1971	66,860	KM59.1-60.1, 62b-75.1, 77.1, 79 (2 pcs.); Double Dollar Prestige Sets	12.00	9.50
SS57	1972	36,349	KM59.1,-60.1, 62b-75.1, 76.1 (2 pcs.), 77; Double Dollar Prestige Sets	12.00	18.00
SS58	1973	119,819	KM59.1-60.1, 75.1, 77.1, 81.1, 82, 83; Double Dollar Prestige Sets	12.00	10.00
SS59	1973	I.A.	KM59.1-60.1, 75.1, 77.1, 81.2, 82, 83; Double Dollar Prestige Sets	—	150
SS60	1974	85,230	KM59.1-60.1, 62b-75.1, 77.1, 88, 88a; Double Dollar Prestige Sets	15.00	10.00
SS61	1975	97,263	KM59.1-60.1, 62b-75.1, 76.2, 77.1, 97; Double Dollar Prestige Sets	15.00	10.00
SS62	1976	87,744	KM59.1-60, 62b-75.1, 76.2, 77.1, 106; Double Dollar Prestige Sets	16.00	10.00
SS63	1977	142,577	KM59.1-60.1, 62b, 75.2, 77.1, 117.1, 118; Double Dollar Prestige Sets	16.50	10.00
SS64	1978	147,000	KM59.1-60.1, 62b, 75.3, 77.1, 120.1, 121; Double Dollar Prestige Sets	16.50	10.00
SS65	1979	155,698	KM59.2-60.2, 74, 75.3, 77.2, 120, 124; Double Dollar Prestige Sets	18.50	11.50
SS66	1980	162,875	KM60.2, 74-75.3, 77.2, 120, 127, 128; Double Dollar Prestige Sets	30.50	22.50
SS67	1981	71,300	KM60.2, 74, 75.3, 77.2, 120.1, 127; Regular Specimen Sets Resumed	10.00	5.50
SS68	1982	62,298	KM60.2a, 74, 75.3, 77.2, 120.1, 132; Regular Specimen Sets Resumed	11.50	5.50
SS69	1983	60,329	KM60.2a, 74, 75.3, 77.2, 120.1, 132; Regular Specimen Sets Resumed	12.75	5.50
SS70	1984	60,400	KM60.2a, 74, 75.3, 77.2, 120.1, 132; Regular Specimen Sets Resumed	10.00	5.50
SS71	1985	61,553	KM60.2a, 74, 75.3, 77.2, 120.1, 132; Regular Specimen Sets Resumed	10.00	6.00
SS72	1986	67,152	KM60.2a, 74, 75.3, 77.2, 120.1, 132; Regular Specimen Sets Resumed	10.00	6.00
SS72A	1987	75,194	KM60.2a, 74, 75.3, 77.2, 120.1, 132; Regular Specimen Sets Resumed	11.00	6.50
SS73	1988	70,205	KM60.2a, 74, 75.3, 77.2, 132, 157; Regular Specimen Sets Resumed	12.30	6.50
SS74	1989	75,306	KM60.2a, 74, 75.3, 77.2, 132, 157; Regular Specimen Sets Resumed	14.50	8.50
SS75	1990	76,611	KM181-186; Regular Specimen Sets Resumed	15.50	8.50
SS76	1991	68,552	KM181-186; Regular Specimen Sets Resumed	15.50	22.00
SS77	1992	78,328	KM204-209; Regular Specimen Sets Resumed	16.25	13.00
SS78	1993	77,351	KM181-186; Regular Specimen Sets Resumed	16.25	6.50
SS79	1994	77,349	KM181-186; Regular Specimen Sets Resumed	16.50	9.50
SS80	1995	I.A.	KM181-186; Regular Specimen Sets Resumed	13.95	9.50
SS82	1996	I.A.	KM181a-185a, 186; Regular Specimen Sets Resumed	18.95	12.00
SS83	1997	I.A.	KM182a-184a, 270, 289-291; Regular Specimen Sets Resumed	19.95	25.00
SS84	1998	I.A.	KM182-184, 186, 270, 289, 290; Regular Specimen Sets Resumed	19.95	11.00
SS85	1999	I.A.	KM182-184, 186, 270, 289a, 290; Regular Specimen Sets Resumed	19.95	11.00
SS90	2002	75,000	KM#444-449,462	30.00	22.50
SS91	2003	75,000	KM#182-184, 186, 270, 289, 290	30.00	27.50

V.I.P. SPECIMEN SETS (VS)

KM	Date	Mintage	Identification	Issue Price	Mkt Val
VS1	1969	4		—	2,000
VS2	1970	100	KM59.1-60.1, 74.1-75.1, 77.1, 78	—	525
VS3	1971	69	KM59.1-60.1, 74.1-75.1, 77.1, 79(2 pcs.)	—	525
VS4	1972	25	KM59.1-60.1, 74.1-75.1, 76.1, (2 pcs.), 77.1	—	650
VS5	1973	26	KM59.1-60.1, 75.1, 77.1, 81.1, 82, 83	—	650
VS6	1974	72	KM59.1-60.1, 74.1-75.1, 77.1, 88, 88a	—	525
VS7	1975	94	KM59.1-60.1, 74.1-75.1, 76.2, 77.1, 97	—	525
VS8	1976	I.A.	KM59.1-60.1, 74.1-75.1, 76.2, 77.1, 106	—	525

NEWFOUNDLAND

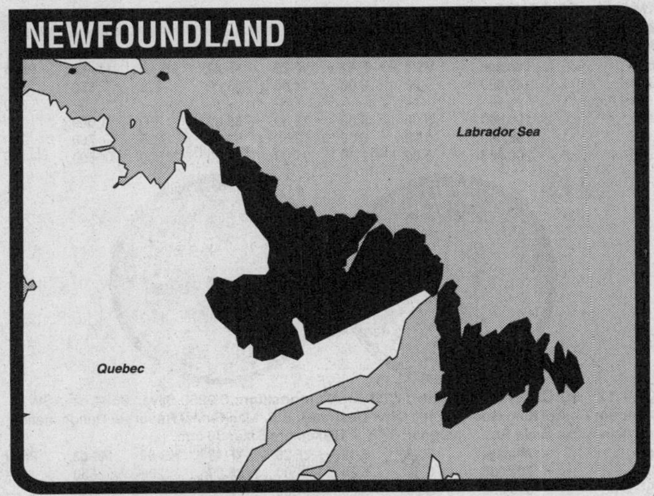

Island which along with Labrador became a province of Canada. Prehistoric inhabitants left evidence of an early presence on the island. Norsemen briefly settled on the island but officially discovered in 1497 by Italian explorer John Cabot. English settlements were sporadic and disputed by France. The English settled along the east coast and the French along the west coast of the island. With the treaty of Utrecht in 1713, it officially became English, but the fishing rights went to France. Controversies continued through the 19th century. Boundaries were set in 1927, colonial government reestablished 1934, became a province of Canada 1949.

PROVINCE

CIRCULATION COINAGE

KM# 9 CENT (Large) **Composition:** Bronze **Obverse:** Bust of King Edward VII right **Obv. Designer:** G.W. DeSaulles **Reverse:** Crown and date within center circle, wreath surrounds, denomination above **Rev. Designer:** Horace Morehen

Date	Mintage	VG-8	F-12	VF-20	XF-40	MS-60	MS-63	Proof
1904H	100,000	7.00	14.00	20.00	55.00	300	700	—
1904H Proof	—	—	—	—	—	—	—	4,000
1907	200,000	2.00	4.00	8.00	30.00	220	650	—
1909	200,000	2.00	4.00	7.00	19.00	100	150	—
1909 Proof	—	—	—	—	—	—	—	400

KM# 16 CENT (Large) **Composition:** Bronze **Obverse:** Bust of King George V left **Obv. Designer:** E.B. MacKennal **Reverse:** Crown and date within center circle, wreath surrounds, denomination above **Rev. Designer:** Horace Morehen

Date	Mintage	VG-8	F-12	VF-20	XF-40	MS-60	MS-63	Proof
1913	400,000	1.00	1.50	3.00	7.00	40.00	75.00	—
1917C	702,350	1.00	1.50	3.00	6.00	75.00	200	—
1917C Proof	—	—	—	—	—	—	—	800
1919C	300,000	1.00	2.00	3.00	10.00	175	300	—
1919C Proof	—	—	—	—	—	—	—	1,000
1920C	302,184	1.00	2.00	5.00	18.00	300	1,000	—
1929	300,000	1.00	1.50	3.00	6.00	55.00	100	—
1929C Proof	—	—	—	—	—	—	—	1,000
1936	300,000	1.00	1.25	1.75	4.00	28.00	75.00	—

KM# 18 CENT (Small) **Composition:** Bronze **Obverse:** Crowned bust of King George VI left **Obv. Designer:** Percy Metcalfe **Reverse:** Pitcher plant divides date, denomination below **Rev. Designer:** Walter J. Newman **Size:** 19 mm.

Date	Mintage	VG-8	F-12	VF-20	XF-40	MS-60	MS-63	Proof
1938	500,000	0.50	0.75	1.50	2.50	16.00	40.00	—
1938 Proof	—	—	—	—	—	—	—	1,000
1940	300,000	1.25	2.00	3.00	10.00	75.00	250	—
1940 Re-engraved date	—	30.00	40.00	125	70.00	500	900	—
1940 Proof	—	—	—	—	—	—	—	1,000
1941C	827,662	0.35	0.45	0.70	2.00	20.00	120	—
1941C Re-engraved date	—	9.00	13.00	30.00	65.00	250	700	—
1942	1,996,889	0.35	0.45	0.70	2.00	30.00	125	—
1943C	1,239,732	0.35	0.45	0.70	2.00	13.50	70.00	—
1944C	1,328,776	1.00	2.00	10.00	30.00	250	550	—
1947C	313,772	0.90	1.65	5.00	12.00	80.00	200	—
1947C Proof	—	—	—	—	—	—	—	2,000

KM# 7 5 CENTS **Weight:** 1.1782 g. **Composition:** 0.9250 Silver .0350 oz. ASW **Obverse:** Bust of King Edward VII right **Reverse:** Denomination and date within circle

Date	Mintage	VG-8	F-12	VF-20	XF-40	MS-60	MS-63	Proof
1903	100,000	4.00	9.00	18.00	45.00	435	1,350	—
1903 Proof	—	—	—	—	—	—	—	2,000
1904H	100,000	3.00	5.00	14.00	35.00	160	285	—
1904H Proof	—	—	—	—	—	—	—	1,200
1908	400,000	3.00	6.00	11.50	30.00	260	750	—

KM# 13 5 CENTS **Weight:** 1.1782 g. **Composition:** 0.9250 Silver .0350 oz. ASW **Obverse:** Bust of King George V left **Obv. Designer:** E.B. MacKennal **Reverse:** Denomination and date within circle **Rev. Designer:** G.W. DeSaulles

Date	Mintage	VG-8	F-12	VF-20	XF-40	MS-60	MS-63	Proof
1912	300,000	1.50	2.00	5.00	20.00	125	275	—
1912 Proof	—	—	—	—	—	—	—	2,000
1917C	300,319	1.50	3.00	7.00	25.00	250	650	—
1917C Proof	—	—	—	—	—	—	—	2,000
1919C	100,844	5.00	9.00	25.00	100	950	2,800	—
1919C Proof	—	—	—	—	—	—	—	2,000
1929	300,000	1.50	2.50	3.25	12.00	165	350	—

KM# 19 5 CENTS **Weight:** 1.1782 g. **Composition:** 0.9250 Silver .0350 oz. ASW **Obverse:** Crowned head of King George VI left **Obv. Designer:** Percy Metcalfe **Reverse:** Denomination and date within circle **Rev. Designer:** G.W. DeSaulles

Date	Mintage	VG-8	F-12	VF-20	XF-40	MS-60	MS-63	Proof
1938	100,000	0.85	1.50	2.00	7.00	70.00	225	—
1938 Proof	—	—	—	—	—	—	—	1,000
1940C	200,000	0.85	1.50	2.00	7.00	85.00	300	—
1940C Proof	—	—	—	—	—	—	—	2,000
1941C	621,641	0.65	1.50	2.00	4.00	15.00	35.00	—
1942C	298,348	0.85	1.50	2.00	4.00	17.50	40.00	—
1943C	351,666	0.65	1.00	2.00	4.00	15.00	30.00	—

KM# 19a 5 CENTS **Weight:** 1.1664 g. **Composition:** 0.8000 Silver .0300 oz. ASW **Obverse:** Crowned head of King George VI left **Obv. Designer:** Percy Metcalfe **Reverse:** Denomination and date within circle **Rev. Designer:** G.W. DeSaulles

Date	Mintage	VG-8	F-12	VF-20	XF-40	MS-60	MS-63	Proof
1944C	286,504	1.25	1.75	3.00	7.00	50.00	120	—
1945C	203,828	0.65	1.00	2.00	4.00	14.00	32.00	—
1946C	2,041	200	300	350	400	1,200	1,900	—
1946C Prooflike	—	—	—	—	—	—	2,500	—
1947C	38,400	2.00	3.00	5.00	17.00	65.00	200	—
1947C Prooflike	—	—	—	—	—	—	375	—

KM# 8 10 CENTS **Weight:** 2.3564 g. **Composition:** 0.9250 Silver .0701 oz. ASW **Obverse:** Bust of King Edward VII right **Reverse:** Denomination and date within circle

Date	Mintage	VG-8	F-12	VF-20	XF-40	MS-60	MS-63	Proof
1903	100,000	8.00	25.00	70.00	200	1,200	4,400	—
1903 Proof	—	—	—	—	—	—	—	2,500
1904H	100,000	4.00	10.00	30.00	90.00	200	350	—
1904H Proof	—	—	—	—	—	—	—	1,500

KM# 14 10 CENTS **Weight:** 2.3564 g. **Composition:** 0.9250 Silver .0701 oz. ASW
Obverse: Bust of King George V left **Obv. Designer:** E.B. MacKennal **Rev. Designer:** G.W. DeSaulles

Date	Mintage	VG-8	F-12	VF-20	XF-40	MS-60	MS-63	Proof
1912	150,000	1.20	3.00	10.00	40.00	165	300	—
1917C	250,805	1.20	3.00	11.00	40.00	400	1,500	—
1919C	54,342	2.00	6.00	18.00	55.00	175	350	—

KM# 20 10 CENTS **Weight:** 2.3564 g. **Composition:** 0.9250 Silver .0701 oz. ASW
Obverse: Crowned head of King George VI left **Obv. Designer:** Percy Metcalfe **Reverse:** Denomination and date within circle **Rev. Designer:** G.W. DeSaulles

Date	Mintage	VG-8	F-12	VF-20	XF-40	MS-60	MS-63	Proof
1938	100,000	1.10	1.75	3.00	11.00	80.00	300	—
1938 Proof	—	—	—	—	—	—	—	2,000
1940	100,000	1.10	1.50	3.00	10.00	80.00	300	—
1940 Proof	—	—	—	—	—	—	—	2,500
1941C	483,630	1.10	1.50	2.20	5.00	40.00	125	—
1942C	293,736	1.10	1.50	2.20	5.00	50.00	130	—
1943C	104,706	1.10	1.50	2.50	6.00	60.00	200	—
1944C	151,471	2.50	3.50	10.00	20.00	200	800	—

KM# 20a 10 CENTS **Weight:** 2.3328 g. **Composition:** 0.8000 Silver .0600 oz. ASW
Obverse: Crowned head of King George VI left **Obv. Designer:** Percy Metcalfe **Rev. Designer:** G.W. DeSaulles

Date	Mintage	VG-8	F-12	VF-20	XF-40	MS-60	MS-63	Proof
1945C	175,833	1.00	1.35	2.25	4.50	45.00	225	—
1946C	38,400	2.00	4.00	10.00	25.00	100	275	—
1946C Proof	—	—	—	—	—	—	—	750
1947C	61,988	1.50	3.00	4.50	14.00	65.00	275	—

KM# 10 20 CENTS **Weight:** 4.7127 g. **Composition:** 0.9250 Silver .1401 oz. ASW
Obverse: Bust of King Edward VII right **Obv. Designer:** G.W. DeSaulles **Reverse:** Denomination and date within circle **Rev. Designer:** W.H.J. Blakemore

Date	Mintage	VG-8	F-12	VF-20	XF-40	MS-60	MS-63	Proof
1904H	75,000	10.00	30.00	55.00	275	2,500	6,000	—
1904H Proof	—	—	—	—	—	—	—	1,850

KM# 15 20 CENTS **Weight:** 4.7127 g. **Composition:** 0.9250 Silver .1401 oz. ASW
Obverse: Bust of King George V left **Obv. Designer:** E.B. MacKennal **Reverse:** Denomination and date within circle **Rev. Designer:** W.H.J. Blakemore

Date	Mintage	VG-8	F-12	VF-20	XF-40	MS-60	MS-63	Proof
1912	350,000	2.50	5.00	14.00	55.00	325	850	—
1912 Proof	—	—	—	—	—	—	—	2,500

KM# 17 25 CENTS **Weight:** 5.8319 g. **Composition:** 0.9250 Silver .1734 oz. ASW
Obverse: Bust of King George V left **Obv. Designer:** E.B. MacKennal **Reverse:** Denomination and date within circle **Rev. Designer:** W.H.J. Blakemore

Date	Mintage	VG-8	F-12	VF-20	XF-40	MS-60	MS-63	Proof
1917C	464,779	3.00	4.00	7.00	17.00	145	300	—
1917C Proof	—	—	—	—	—	—	—	2,500
1919C	163,939	3.00	5.00	14.00	25.00	350	1,250	—
1919C Proof	—	—	—	—	—	—	—	2,500

KM# 11 50 CENTS **Weight:** 11.7800 g. **Composition:** 0.9250 Silver .3504 oz. ASW
Obverse: Bust of King Edward VII right **Obv. Designer:** G.W. DeSaulles **Rev. Designer:** W.H.J. Blakemore **Size:** 30 mm.

Date	Mintage	VG-8	F-12	VF-20	XF-40	MS-60	MS-63	Proof
1904H	140,000	5.00	6.00	14.00	55.00	275	850	—
1904H Proof	—	—	—	—	—	—	—	5,000
1907	100,000	5.00	6.00	22.00	65.00	350	1,000	—
1908	160,000	5.00	6.00	13.50	50.00	225	700	—
1909	200,000	5.00	12.00	21.00	55.00	300	800	—

KM# 12 50 CENTS **Weight:** 11.7800 g. **Composition:** 0.9250 Silver .3504 oz. ASW
Obverse: Bust of King George V left **Obv. Designer:** E.B. MacKennal **Reverse:** Denomination and date within circle **Rev. Designer:** W.H.J. Blakemore **Size:** 30 mm.

Date	Mintage	VG-8	F-12	VF-20	XF-40	MS-60	MS-63	Proof
1911	200,000	5.00	6.00	11.00	35.00	200	550	—
1917C	375,560	5.00	6.00	11.00	28.00	145	350	—
1917C Proof	—	—	—	—	—	—	—	2,500
1918C	294,824	5.00	6.00	11.00	28.00	145	350	—
1919C	306,267	5.00	6.00	11.00	30.00	325	1,150	—
1919C Proof	—	—	—	—	—	—	—	2,500

TRIAL STRIKES

KM	Date	Mintage	Identification	Mkt Val
TS3	1945	—	10 Cents. Nickel. .	—

CAPE VERDE

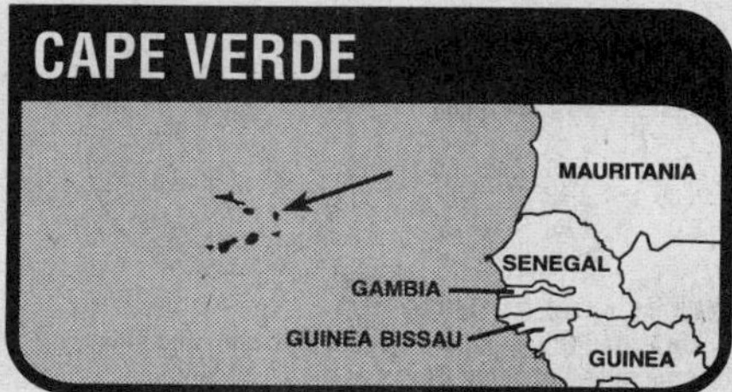

The Republic of Cape Verde, Africa's smallest republic, is located in the Atlantic Ocean, about 370 miles (595 km.) west of Dakar, Senegal, off the coast of Africa. The 14-island republic has an area of 1,557 sq. mi. (4,033 sq. km.) and a population of 435,983. Capital: Praia. The refueling of ships and aircraft is the chief economic function of the country. Fishing is important and agriculture is widely practiced, but the Cape Verdes are not self-sufficient in food. Fish products, salt, bananas, and shellfish are exported.

The date of discovery of the islands is uncertain. Possibly they were visited by Venetian captain Alvise Cadamosto in 1456. Portuguese navigator Diogo Gomes claimed them for Portugal in May of 1460. Settlement began two years later. The early importance and wealth of the islands, which caused them to be attacked by Sir Francis Drake and the Dutch, resulted from the monopoly of the Guinea slave trade granted the inhabitants in 1466. Poverty and famine occasioned by frequent periods of severe drought have marked the history of the country since abolition of the slave trade in 1876.

After 500 years of Portuguese rule, the Cape Verdes became independent on July 5, 1975. At the first general election, all seats of the new national assembly were won by the Party for the Independence of Guinea-Bissau and Cape Verde (PAIGC). The PAIGC linked the two former colonies into one state. Antonio Mascarenhas Monteiro won the first free presidential election in 1991.

RULERS

Portuguese, until 1975

MONETARY SYSTEM

100 Centavos = 1 Escudo

PORTUGUESE COLONY

COLONIAL COINAGE

KM# 1 5 CENTAVOS

Bronze **Obv:** Liberty head left **Rev:** Denmination at center, date below

Date	Mintage	F	VF	XF	Unc	BU
1930	1,000,000	0.75	1.50	3.50	10.00	—

KM# 2 10 CENTAVOS

Bronze **Obv:** Denomination at center, date below **Rev:** Liberty head left

Date	Mintage	F	VF	XF	Unc	BU
1930	1,500,000	0.75	1.50	4.00	12.00	—

KM# 3 20 CENTAVOS

Bronze **Obv:** Denomination at center, date below **Rev:** Liberty head left

Date	Mintage	F	VF	XF	Unc	BU
1930	1,500,000	1.00	2.00	5.00	15.00	—

KM# 4 50 CENTAVOS

Nickel-Bronze **Obv:** Liberty head right, long loose hair **Rev:** Encircled arms within wreath, denomination below

Date	Mintage	F	VF	XF	Unc	BU
1930	1,000,000	7.00	30.00	95.00	275	—

KM# 6 50 CENTAVOS

Nickel-Bronze **Obv:** Denomination **Rev:** Miniature crowns above encircled arms, date below

Date	Mintage	F	VF	XF	Unc	BU
1949	1,000,000	0.50	1.00	2.50	6.00	—

KM# 11 50 CENTAVOS

3.4000 g., Bronze, 20 mm. **Obv:** Denomination **Rev:** Miniature crowns above arms, date below

Date	Mintage	F	VF	XF	Unc	BU
1968	1,000,000	0.25	0.50	1.00	2.50	—

KM# 5 ESCUDO

Nickel-Bronze, 26 mm. **Obv:** Liberty head right, long loose hair **Rev:** Encircled arms within wreath, denomination below

Date	Mintage	F	VF	XF	Unc	BU
1930	50,000	15.00	65.00	125	350	—

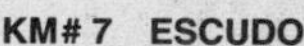

KM# 7 ESCUDO

Nickel-Bronze, 26 mm. **Obv:** Denomination **Rev:** Miniature crowns above encircled arms, date below

Date	Mintage	F	VF	XF	Unc	BU
1949	500,000	1.25	2.50	5.50	12.50	—

KM# 8 ESCUDO

8.0000 g., Bronze, 26 mm. **Obv:** Denomination **Rev:** Miniature crowns above encircled arms, date below

Date	Mintage	F	VF	XF	Unc	BU
1953	250,000	1.00	5.00	18.00	35.00	—
1968	500,000	0.50	1.00	2.00	5.00	—

KM# 9 2-1/2 ESCUDOS

3.5000 g., Nickel-Bronze, 20 mm. **Obv:** Arms on cross, date below **Rev:** Miniature crowns above arms, denomination below

Date	Mintage	F	VF	XF	Unc	BU
1953	500,000	1.50	8.00	35.00	85.00	—
1967	400,000	0.50	1.00	2.50	8.00	—

KM# 12 5 ESCUDOS

4.4100 g., Nickel-Bronze, 21 mm. **Obv:** Miniature crowns above arms, denomination below **Rev:** Arms on cross, date below

Date	Mintage	F	VF	XF	Unc	BU
1968	200,000	0.75	1.50	3.50	10.00	—

KM# 10 10 ESCUDOS

5.0000 g., 0.7200 Silver .1158 oz. ASW **Obv:** Arms on cross, date below **Rev:** Miniature crowns above arms, denomination below

Date	Mintage	F	VF	XF	Unc	BU
1953	400,000	2.00	3.50	6.50	18.00	—

REPUBLIC

DECIMAL COINAGE

KM# 15 20 CENTAVOS

1.3000 g., Aluminum, 21 mm. **Obv:** Emblem within wreath, date below **Rev:** Denomination above fish

Date	Mintage	F	VF	XF	Unc	BU
1977	—	0.10	0.20	0.30	0.65	—
1980	—	0.10	0.20	0.30	0.65	—

KM# 16 50 CENTAVOS

2.1000 g., Aluminum, 24.5 mm. **Obv:** Emblem within wreath, date below **Rev:** Denomination above fish

Date	Mintage	F	VF	XF	Unc	BU
1977	—	0.15	0.25	0.40	0.85	—
1980	—	0.15	0.25	0.40	0.85	—

KM# 17 ESCUDO

4.1000 g., Nickel-Bronze, 23.5 mm. **Series:** F.A.O. **Subject:** Education **Obv:** Emblem within wreath, denomination below, date at bottom **Rev:** Student at desk **Edge:** Reeded

Date	Mintage	F	VF	XF	Unc	BU
1977	1,000,000	0.25	0.50	0.85	1.75	3.00
1980	—	0.25	0.50	0.85	1.75	3.00

KM# 23 ESCUDO
Brass Plated Steel, 23.5 mm. **Subject:** 10th Anniversary of Independence **Obv:** Emblem within wreath below denomination and date **Rev:** Inscription below building **Edge:** Reeded

Date	Mintage	F	VF	XF	Unc	BU
1985	—	—	—	0.75	1.50	2.50
1985 Proof	—	—	—	—	—	—

KM# 23a ESCUDO
4.0000 g., 0.9250 Silver .1190 oz. ASW, 23.5 mm. **Subject:** 10th Anniversary of Indepencence **Obv:** Emblem within wreath below denomination and date **Rev:** Inscription below building

Date	Mintage	F	VF	XF	Unc	BU
1985 Proof	—	Value: 120				

KM# 23b ESCUDO
6.0000 g., 0.7500 Gold .1447 oz. AGW **Subject:** 10th Anniversary of Independence **Obv:** Emblem within wreath below denomination and date **Rev:** Inscription below building

Date	Mintage	F	VF	XF	Unc	BU
1985 Proof	50	Value: 250				

KM# 27 ESCUDO
Brass Plated Steel **Obv:** Denomination on National emblem, date below **Rev:** Tartaruga Sea Turtle

Date	Mintage	F	VF	XF	Unc	BU
1994	—	—	—	—	1.00	1.25

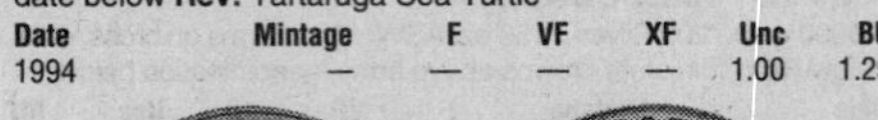

KM# 18 2-1/2 ESCUDOS
7.0000 g., Nickel-Bronze, 26 mm. **Series:** F.A.O. **Obv:** Emblem within wreath above denomination and date **Rev:** Coffee tree planting

Date	Mintage	F	VF	XF	Unc	BU
1977	1,200,000	0.25	0.50	0.85	1.75	—
1980	—	0.25	0.50	0.85	1.75	3.00
1982	—	0.25	0.50	0.85	1.75	—

KM# 28 5 ESCUDOS
Copper Plated Steel **Obv:** National emblem to right of denomination, date below **Rev:** Osprey

Date	Mintage	F	VF	XF	Unc	BU
1994	—	—	—	—	2.50	3.00

KM# 31 5 ESCUDOS
Copper Plated Steel **Obv:** National emblem to right of denomination, date below **Rev:** Flowers - Contra Bruxas

Date	Mintage	F	VF	XF	Unc	BU
1994	—	—	—	—	1.00	1.50

KM# 36 5 ESCUDOS
Copper Plated Steel **Obv:** National emblem to right of denomination, date below **Rev:** Sailboat - Belmira

Date	Mintage	F	VF	XF	Unc	BU
1994	—	—	—	—	1.00	1.50

KM# 19 10 ESCUDOS
9.0000 g., Copper-Nickel, 28.1 mm. **Obv:** Emblem within wreath above denomination and date **Rev:** Eduardo Mondlane

Date	Mintage	F	VF	XF	Unc	BU
1977	—	0.25	0.50	1.00	2.25	—
1980	—	0.25	0.50	1.00	2.25	—
1982	—	0.20	0.40	0.75	2.00	—

KM# 24 10 ESCUDOS
Copper-Nickel **Subject:** 10th Anniversary of Independence **Obv:** Emblem within wreath below denomination and date **Rev:** Letter design at center, star above

Date	Mintage	F	VF	XF	Unc	BU
1985	—	—	—	—	2.00	3.00
1985 Proof	—	—	—	—	—	—

KM# 24a 10 ESCUDOS
9.0000 g., 0.9250 Silver .2677 oz. ASW **Subject:** 10th Anniversary of Independence **Obv:** Emblem within wreath below denomination and date **Rev:** Letter design at center, star above

Date	Mintage	F	VF	XF	Unc	BU
1985 Proof	—	Value: 145				

KM# 24b 10 ESCUDOS
9.0000 g., 0.7500 Gold .2170 oz. AGW **Subject:** 10th Anniversary of Independence **Obv:** Emblem within wreath below denomination and date **Rev:** Letter design at center, star above

Date	Mintage	F	VF	XF	Unc	BU
1985 Proof	50	Value: 400				

KM# 29 10 ESCUDOS
Nickel Plated Steel **Obv:** National emblem, date at left, denomination upper left **Rev:** Brown-headed Kingfisher

Date	Mintage	F	VF	XF	Unc	BU
1994	—	—	—	—	4.00	5.00

KM# 32 10 ESCUDOS
Nickel Plated Steel **Obv:** National emblem, date at left, denomination upper left **Rev:** Flowers - Lingua De Vaca

Date	Mintage	F	VF	XF	Unc	BU
1994	—	—	—	—	1.50	2.00

KM# 41 10 ESCUDOS
Nickel Plated Steel **Obv:** National emblem, date at left, denomination upper left **Rev:** Sailship "Carvalho"

Date	Mintage	F	VF	XF	Unc	BU
1994	—	—	—	—	1.50	2.00

KM# 20 20 ESCUDOS
12.0000 g., Copper-Nickel, 31.1 mm. **Obv:** Emblem within wreath above denomination and date **Rev:** Domingos Ramos

Date	Mintage	F	VF	XF	Unc	BU
1977	—	0.35	0.65	1.25	2.75	—
1980	—	0.35	0.65	1.25	2.75	—
1982	—	0.25	0.50	1.00	2.50	—

KM# 30 20 ESCUDOS
Nickel Plated Steel **Obv:** National emblem, date divided below, denomination at bottom **Rev:** Brown Booby

Date	Mintage	F	VF	XF	Unc	BU
1994	—	—	—	—	4.00	5.00

KM# 33 20 ESCUDOS
Nickel Plated Steel **Obv:** National emblem, date divided below, denomination at bottom **Rev:** Flowers - Carqueja

Date	Mintage	F	VF	XF	Unc	BU
1994	—	—	—	—	2.00	3.00

KM# 42 20 ESCUDOS
Nickel Plated Steel **Obv:** National emblem, date divided below, denomination at bottom **Rev:** Sailship "Novas de Alegria"

Date	Mintage	F	VF	XF	Unc	BU
1994	—	—	—	—	2.00	3.00

KM# 21 50 ESCUDOS
16.3000 g., Copper-Nickel, 34.1 mm. **Obv:** Emblem within wreath above denomination and date **Rev:** Head of Amilcar Lopes Cabral left, two dates on right

Date	Mintage	F	VF	XF	Unc	BU
1977	—	1.00	1.50	2.50	4.50	—
1980	—	1.00	1.50	2.50	4.50	—

KM# 22 50 ESCUDOS
16.0000 g., Copper-Nickel, 34 mm. **Series:** F.A.O. **Subject:** World Fisheries Conference **Rev:** White sea bream fish left, two dates below **Rev. Designer:** Stuart Devtin

Date	Mintage	F	VF	XF	Unc	BU
1984	Est. 115,000	—	—	—	—	15.00

KM# 22a 50 ESCUDOS
16.0000 g., 0.9250 Silver .4759 oz. ASW **Series:** F.A.O. **Subject:** World Fisheries Conference **Rev:** White sea bream fish left, two dates below

Date	Mintage	F	VF	XF	Unc	BU
1984 Proof	Est. 20,000	Value: 50.00				

KM# 22b 50 ESCUDOS
27.0000 g., 0.9170 Gold .7958 oz. AGW **Series:** F.A.O. **Subject:** World Fisheries Conference **Rev:** White sea bream fish left, two dates below

Date	Mintage	F	VF	XF	Unc	BU
1984 Proof	Est. 100,000	Value: 1,500				

KM# 37 50 ESCUDOS
27.0000 g., Copper Nickel **Obv:** National emblem divides date, denomination above **Rev:** Cape Verde Sparrow left

Date	Mintage	F	VF	XF	Unc	BU
1994	—	—	—	—	12.00	14.00

KM# 43 50 ESCUDOS
Nickel Plated Steel 8 oz. **Obv:** National emblem divides date, denomination above **Rev:** Sailship "Senhor das Areias"

Date	Mintage	F	VF	XF	Unc	BU
1994	—	—	—	—	5.00	6.00

KM# 44 50 ESCUDOS
Nickel Plated Steel **Obv:** National emblem **Rev:** Macelina flowers

Date	Mintage	F	VF	XF	Unc	BU
1994	—	—	—	—	5.00	6.00

KM# 25 100 ESCUDOS
Copper-Nickel **Subject:** Papal Visit **Obv:** Emblem within wreath above denomination and date **Rev:** Half figure of Pope

Date	Mintage	F	VF	XF	Unc	BU
1990	—	—	—	—	7.50	9.50

KM# 25b 100 ESCUDOS
33.4000 g., 0.9000 Gold .9666 oz. AGW **Subject:** Papal Visit **Obv:** Emblem within wreath above denomination and date **Rev:** Half figure of Pope

Date	Mintage	F	VF	XF	Unc	BU
1990 Proof	—	—	—	—	—	—

KM# 25a 100 ESCUDOS
Silver **Subject:** Papal Visit **Obv:** Emblem within wreath above denomination and date **Rev:** Half figure of Pope

Date	Mintage	F	VF	XF	Unc	BU
1990 Proof	—	Value: 35.00				

KM# 38 100 ESCUDOS
Bi-Metallic Copper-Nickel center in Bronze ring **Obv:** National emblem divides date, denomination at top, value at bottom **Rev:** Saiao flowers

Date	Mintage	F	VF	XF	Unc	BU
1994	—	—	—	—	8.00	9.00

KM# 38a 100 ESCUDOS
Bi-Metallic Copper-Nickel center in Brass ring **Obv:** National emblem divides date, denomination at top, value at bottom **Rev:** Saiao flowers

Date	Mintage	F	VF	XF	Unc	BU
1994	—	—	—	—	8.00	9.00

KM# 39 100 ESCUDOS
Bi-Metallic Copper-Nickel center in Bronze ring **Obv:** National emblem divides date, denomination at top, value at bottom **Rev:** Raza Lark left within circle **Shape:** 10-sided

Date	Mintage	F	VF	XF	Unc	BU
1994	—	—	—	—	12.50	13.50

KM# 39a 100 ESCUDOS
Bi-Metallic Copper-Nickel center in Brass ring **Obv:** National emblem divides date, denomination at top, value at bottom **Rev:** Calhandra do Ilheu Raso bird

Date	Mintage	F	VF	XF	Unc	BU
1994	—	—	—	—	12.50	13.50

KM# 40 100 ESCUDOS
Bi-Metallic Copper-Nickel center in Bronze ring **Obv:** National emblem divides date, denomination at top, value at bottom **Rev:** Sailship Madalan

Date	Mintage	F	VF	XF	Unc	BU
1994	—	—	—	—	9.00	10.00

KM# 40a 100 ESCUDOS
Bi-Metallic Copper-Nickel center in Brass ring **Obv:** National emblem divides date, denomination at top, value at bottom **Rev.** **Designer:** Sailship Madalan

Date	Mintage	F	VF	XF	Unc	BU
1994	—	—	—	—	9.00	10.00

KM# 34 200 ESCUDOS
Copper-Nickel **Series:** F.A.O. **Obv:** National emblem above denomination **Rev:** Globe on water, date at right

Date	Mintage	F	VF	XF	Unc	BU
1995	—	—	—	—	8.00	9.50

KM# 35 200 ESCUDOS
Copper-Nickel **Subject:** 20th Year of Independence **Obv:** National emblem above denomination **Rev:** Two figures back to back, two dates below

Date	Mintage	F	VF	XF	Unc	BU
ND(1995)	—	—	—	—	8.00	9.50

KM# 13 250 ESCUDOS
16.4000 g., 0.9000 Silver .4745 oz. ASW, 33.5 mm. **Subject:** 1st Anniversary of Independence **Obv:** Denomination at right above fish, date below **Rev:** Date in center, star divides chain at bottom

Date	Mintage	F	VF	XF	Unc	BU
1976	13,000	—	—	—	16.50	18.50
1976 Proof	3,525	Value: 32.50				

KM# 26 1000 ESCUDOS
28.1100 g., 0.9250 Silver .8361 oz. ASW **Subject:** Tordesilhas Treaty **Obv:** National emblem at center, denomination below **Rev:** Ship between maps, two dates above **Rev. Designer:** A. Marinho

Date	Mintage	F	VF	XF	Unc	BU
ND(1994)	—	—	—	—	25.00	27.50
ND(1994) Proof	Est. 10,000	Value: 45.00				

KM# 14 2500 ESCUDOS
8.0000 g., 0.9000 Gold .2315 oz. AGW **Subject:** 1st Anniversary of Independence **Obv:** Emblem within wreath above denomination **Rev:** Head left, date below

Date	Mintage	F	VF	XF	Unc	BU
1976 Proof	3,409	Value: 245				

PIEFORTS

KM#	Date	Mintage	Identification	Issue Price	Mkt Val
P1	1984	520	50 Escudos. 0.9250 Silver. KM22a.	—	75.00

PROVAS

KM#	Date	Mintage	Identification	Issue Price	Mkt Val
Pr1	1930	—	5 Centavos. Bronze. Stamped "PROVA" in field. KM1.	—	35.00
Pr2	1930	—	10 Centavos. Bronze. Stamped "PROVA" in field. KM2.	—	35.00
Pr3	1930	—	20 Centavos. Bronze. Stamped "PROVA" in field. KM3.	—	35.00
Pr4	1930	—	50 Centavos. Nickel-Bronze. Stamped "PROVA" in field. KM4.	—	75.00
Pr5	1930	—	Escudo. Nickel-Bronze. Stamped "PROVA" in field. KM5.	—	100
Pr6	1949	—	50 Centavos. Nickel-Bronze. Stamped "PROVA" in field. KM6.	—	30.00
Pr7	1949	—	Escudo. Nickel-Bronze. Stamped "PROVA" in field. KM7.	—	35.00
Pr8	1953	—	Escudo. Bronze. Stamped "PROVA" in field. KM8.	—	35.00
Pr9	1953	—	2-1/2 Escudos. Nickel-Bronze. Stamped "PROVA" in field. KM9.	—	30.00
Pr10	1953	—	10 Escudos. Silver. Stamped "PROVA" in field. KM10.	—	35.00
Pr11	1954	—	Escudo. Stamped "PROVA" in field.	—	22.50
Pr12	1954	—	2-1/2 Escudos. Stamped "PROVA" in field.	—	30.00
Pr13	1955	—	Escudo. Stamped "PROVA" in field.	—	22.50
Pr14	1955	—	2-1/2 Escudos. Stamped "PROVA" in field.	—	30.00
Pr15	1956	—	Escudo. Stamped "PROVA" in field.	—	22.50
Pr16	1956	—	2-1/2 Escudos. Stamped "PROVA" in field.	—	30.00
Pr17	1957	—	Escudo. Stamped "PROVA" in field.	—	22.50
Pr18	1957	—	2-1/2 Escudos. Stamped "PROVA" in field.	—	30.00
Pr19	1958	—	Escudo. Stamped "PROVA" in field.	—	22.50
Pr20	1958	—	2-1/2 Escudos. Stamped "PROVA" in field.	—	30.00
Pr21	1959	—	Escudo. Stamped "PROVA" in field.	—	22.50
Pr22	1959	—	2-1/2 Escudos. Stamped "PROVA" in field.	—	30.00
Pr23	1960	—	Escudo. Stamped "PROVA" in field.	—	22.50
Pr24	1960	—	2-1/2 Escudos. Stamped "PROVA" in field.	—	30.00
Pr25	1961	—	Escudo. Stamped "PROVA" in field.	—	22.50
Pr26	1961	—	2-1/2 Escudos. Stamped "PROVA" in field.	—	30.00
Pr27	1962	—	Escudo. Stamped "PROVA" in field.	—	22.50
Pr28	1962	—	2-1/2 Escudos. Stamped "PROVA" in field.	—	30.00
Pr29	1963	—	Escudo. Stamped "PROVA" in field.	—	22.50
Pr30	1963	—	2-1/2 Escudos. Stamped "PROVA" in field.	—	30.00
Pr31	1964	—	Escudo. Stamped "PROVA" in field.	—	22.50
Pr32	1964	—	2-1/2 Escudos. Stamped "PROVA" in field.	—	30.00
Pr33	1965	—	Escudo. Stamped "PROVA" in field.	—	22.50
Pr34	1965	—	2-1/2 Escudos. Stamped "PROVA" in field.	—	30.00
Pr35	1966	—	Escudo. Stamped "PROVA" in field.	—	22.50
Pr36	1966	—	2-1/2 Escudos. Stamped "PROVA" in field.	—	30.00
Pr37	1967	—	Escudo. Stamped "PROVA" in field.	—	17.50
Pr38	1967	—	2-1/2 Escudos. Nickel-Bronze. Stamped "PROVA" in field. KM9.	—	22.50
Pr39	1968	—	50 Centavos. Bronze. Stamped "PROVA" in field. KM11.	—	17.50
Pr40	1968	—	Escudo. Bronze center. Stamped "PROVA" in field. KM8.	—	22.50
Pr41	1968	—	5 Escudos. Nickel-Bronze. Stamped "PROVA" in field. KM12.	—	25.00

PROOF SETS

KM#	Date	Mintage	Identification	Issue Price	Mkt Val
PS1	1976-77 (4)	—	KM13-14 1976, KM17-18 1977	—	300
PS2	1985 (2)	—	KM23a, 24a	—	265

CAYMAN ISLANDS

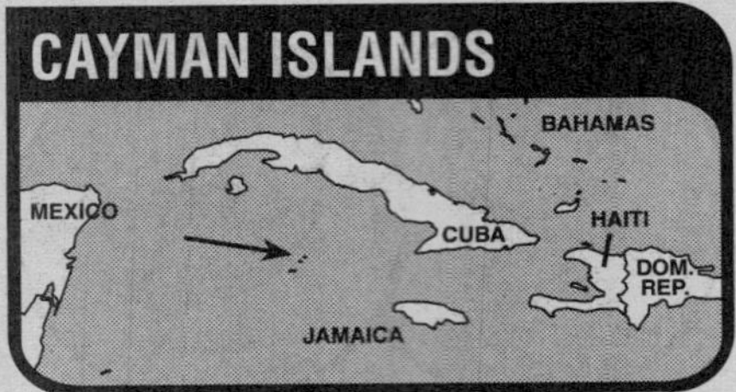

The Cayman Islands is a dependent territory of the United Kingdom with the British monarch as head of state. It is situated about 180 miles (290 km.) northwest of Jamaica, consists of three islands: Grand Cayman, Little Cayman, and Cayman Brac. The islands have an area of 102 sq. mi. (259 sq. km.) and a population of 33,200. Capital: George Town. Seafaring, commerce, banking, and tourism are the principal industries. Rope, turtle shells, and sharkskins are exported.

The islands were discovered by Columbus in 1503, and named by him Tortugas (Spanish for turtles') because of the great number of turtles in the nearby waters. Ceded to Britain in 1670, they were colonized from Jamaica by the British and remained dependencies of Jamaica until 1959, when they became a unit territory within the Federation of the West Indies. They became a separate colony when the Federation was dissolved in 1962. Since 1972 a form of self-government has existed, with the Governor responsible for defense and certain other affairs.

While the islands used Jamaican currency for much of their history, the Caymans issued its first national coinage in 1972. The $25 gold and silver commemorative coins issued in 1972 to celebrate the silver wedding anniversary of Queen Elizabeth II and Prince Philip are the first coins in 300 years of Commonwealth coinage to portray a member of the British royal family other than the reigning monarch.

RULERS

British

MINT MARKS

CHI - Valcambi

FM - Franklin Mint, U.S.A.*

MONETARY SYSTEM

100 Cents = 1 Dollar

BRITISH COLONY

DECIMAL COINAGE

KM# 1 CENT

Bronze, 17 mm. **Obv:** Young bust right, date below **Rev:** Great Caiman Thrush, denomination at right **Rev. Designer:** Stuart Devlin

Date	Mintage	F	VF	XF	Unc	BU
1972	2,155,000	—	—	0.10	0.25	0.75
1972 Proof	11,000	Value: 0.50				
1973 Proof	9,988	Value: 0.50				
1974 Proof	30,000	Value: 0.50				
1975 Proof	7,175	Value: 0.50				
1976 Proof	3,044	Value: 0.50				
1977	1,800,000	—	—	0.10	0.25	0.75
1977 Proof	1,970	Value: 1.00				
1979FM Proof	4,247	Value: 0.50				
1980FM	—	—	—	0.10	0.25	0.75
1980FM Proof	1,215	Value: 1.25				
1981FM Proof	865	Value: 1.50				
1982	—	—	—	0.10	0.25	0.75
1982FM Proof	589	Value: 1.50				
1983FM Proof	—	Value: 1.50				
1984FM Proof	—	Value: 1.50				
1986	1,000	Value: 1.50				

KM# 26 CENT

Bronze, 17 mm. **Subject:** 25th Anniversary of Coronation **Obv:** Young bust right, date below **Rev:** Great Caiman Thrush, denomination at right **Rev. Designer:** Stuart Devlin

Date	Mintage	F	VF	XF	Unc	BU
1978 Proof	1,303	Value: 2.00				

KM# 87 CENT

Bronze, 17 mm. **Obv:** Crowned bust right, date below **Rev:** Great Caiman Thrush, denomination at right **Rev. Designer:** Stuart Devlin

Date	Mintage	F	VF	XF	Unc	BU
1987	—	—	—	0.10	0.25	0.75
1987 Proof	317	Value: 3.00				
1988 Proof	318	Value: 3.00				
1990	—	—	—	0.10	0.25	0.75

KM# 87a CENT

2.5500 g., Bronze Clad Steel, 17 mm. **Obv:** Crowned bust right, date below **Rev:** Great Caiman Thrush, denomination at right **Rev. Designer:** Stuart Devlin

Date	Mintage	F	VF	XF	Unc	BU
1992	—	—	—	0.20	0.50	1.00
1996	—	—	—	0.15	0.35	0.75

KM# 131 CENT

2.5300 g., Bronze Plated Steel, 17 mm. **Obv:** Head with tiara right, date below **Rev:** Great Caiman thrush, denomination at right **Rev. Designer:** Stuart Devlin

Date	Mintage	F	VF	XF	Unc	BU
1999	—	—	—	0.20	0.50	1.00

KM# 2 5 CENTS

Copper-Nickel, 18 mm. **Obv:** Young bust right, date below **Rev:** Pink-spotted shrimp, denomination at right **Rev. Designer:** Stuart Devlin

Date	Mintage	F	VF	XF	Unc	BU
1972	300,000	—	—	0.10	0.50	1.00
1972 Proof	12,000	Value: 0.75				
1973	200,000	—	—	0.30	0.65	1.00

Note: 1973 Business strikes were not released to circulation

Date	Mintage	F	VF	XF	Unc	BU
1973 Proof	9,988	Value: 0.75				
1974 Proof	30,000	Value: 0.75				
1975 Proof	7,175	Value: 0.75				
1976 Proof	3,044	Value: 0.75				
1977	600,000	—	—	0.10	0.50	1.00
1977 Proof	1,980	Value: 0.75				
1979 Proof	4,247	Value: 0.75				
1980 Proof	—	Value: 2.00				
1981 Proof	—	Value: 2.50				
1982	—	—	—	0.10	0.50	1.00
1982 Proof	—	Value: 2.50				
1983 Proof	—	Value: 2.50				
1984 Proof	—	Value: 2.50				
1986	1,000	Value: 2.50				

KM# 27 5 CENTS

Copper-Nickel, 18 mm. **Subject:** 25th Anniversary of Coronation **Rev:** Pink-spotted shrimp **Rev. Designer:** Stuart Devlin

Date	Mintage	F	VF	XF	Unc	BU
1978 Proof	1,303	Value: 3.00				

KM# 88 5 CENTS

Copper-Nickel, 18 mm. **Obv:** Crowned bust right, date below **Rev:** Pink-spotted shrimp, denomination at right **Rev. Designer:** Stuart Devlin

Date	Mintage	F	VF	XF	Unc	BU
1987	—	—	—	0.10	0.35	1.00
1987 Proof	317	Value: 5.00				
1988 Proof	318	Value: 5.00				
1990	—	—	—	0.10	0.35	1.00

KM# 88a 5 CENTS

2.0000 g., Nickel Clad Steel, 18 mm. **Obv:** Crowned bust right, date below **Rev:** Pink-spotted shrimp, denomination at right **Rev. Designer:** Stuart Devlin

Date	Mintage	F	VF	XF	Unc	BU
1992	—	—	—	0.20	0.50	1.00
1996	—	—	—	0.10	0.35	1.00

KM# 132 5 CENTS
2.0000 g., Nickel Clad Steel, 18 mm. **Obv:** Head with tiara right, date below **Rev:** Pink-spotted shrimp, denomination at right **Rev. Designer:** Stuart Devlin **Edge:** Plain

Date	Mintage	F	VF	XF	Unc	BU
1999	—	—	—	—	0.50	1.00

KM# 3 10 CENTS
Copper-Nickel, 21 mm. **Obv:** Young bust right, date below **Rev:** Green Turtle, denomination at right **Rev. Designer:** Stuart Devlin

Date	Mintage	F	VF	XF	Unc	BU
1972	550,000	—	0.15	0.20	0.50	1.00
1972 Proof	11,000	Value: 1.00				
1973	200,000	—	0.25	0.50	1.00	1.25

Note: 1973 Business strikes were not released to circulation

Date	Mintage	F	VF	XF	Unc	BU
1973 Proof	9,988	Value: 1.00				
1974 Proof	30,000	Value: 1.00				
1975 Proof	7,175	Value: 1.00				
1976 Proof	3,044	Value: 1.00				
1977	960,000	—	0.15	0.20	0.50	1.00
1977 Proof	1,980	Value: 1.00				
1979FM Proof	4,247	Value: 1.00				
1980FM Proof	1,215	Value: 3.00				
1981FM Proof	865	Value: 3.00				
1982	—	—	0.15	0.20	0.50	1.00
1982FM Proof	589	Value: 3.00				
1983FM Proof	—	Value: 3.00				
1984FM Proof	—	Value: 3.00				
1986	1,000	Value: 3.00				

KM# 28 10 CENTS
Copper-Nickel, 21 mm. **Subject:** 25th Anniversary of Coronation **Rev:** Green Turtle **Rev. Designer:** Stuart Devlin

Date	Mintage	F	VF	XF	Unc	BU
1978 Proof	1,304	Value: 3.50				

KM# 89 10 CENTS
Copper-Nickel, 21 mm. **Obv:** Crowned bust right, date below **Rev:** Green turtle surfacing, denomination at right **Rev. Designer:** Stuart Devlin

Date	Mintage	F	VF	XF	Unc	BU
1987	—	—	0.15	0.20	0.50	1.00
1987 Proof	317	Value: 6.00				
1988 Proof	318	Value: 6.00				
1990	—	—	0.15	0.20	0.50	1.00

KM# 89a 10 CENTS
3.4500 g., Nickel Clad Steel, 21 mm. **Obv:** Crowned bust right, date below **Rev:** Green turtle surfacing, denomination at right **Rev. Designer:** Stuart Devlin

Date	Mintage	F	VF	XF	Unc	BU
1992	—	—	0.25	0.40	1.00	1.25
1996	—	—	0.20	0.30	0.75	1.00

KM# 133 10 CENTS
3.4300 g., Nickel Clad Steel, 21 mm. **Obv:** Head with tiara right, date below **Rev:** Green turtle, denomination at right **Rev. Designer:** Stuart Devlin **Edge:** Reeded

Date	Mintage	F	VF	XF	Unc	BU
1999	—	—	0.25	0.40	1.00	1.25

KM# 4 25 CENTS
Copper-Nickel, 24.2 mm. **Obv:** Young bust right, date below **Rev:** Schooner sailing right, denomination at right **Rev. Designer:** Stuart Devlin

Date	Mintage	F	VF	XF	Unc	BU
1972	350,000	—	0.35	0.50	1.00	1.25
1972 Proof	11,000	Value: 1.00				
1973	100,000	—	0.50	1.00	2.00	2.50

Note: 1973 Business strikes were not released to circulation

Date	Mintage	F	VF	XF	Unc	BU
1973 Proof	9,988	Value: 1.00				
1974 Proof	30,000	Value: 1.00				
1975 Proof	7,175	Value: 1.00				
1976 Proof	3,044	Value: 1.00				
1977	520,000	—	0.35	0.50	1.00	1.25
1977 Proof	1,980	Value: 1.00				
1979FM Proof	4,247	Value: 1.00				
1980FM Proof	1,215	Value: 3.50				
1981FM Proof	865	Value: 4.00				
1982	—	—	0.35	0.50	1.00	1.25
1982FM Proof	589	Value: 4.00				
1983FM Proof	—	Value: 4.00				
1984FM Proof	—	Value: 4.00				
1986 Proof	1,000	Value: 4.00				

KM# 29 25 CENTS
Copper-Nickel, 24.2 mm. **Subject:** 25th Anniversary of Coronation **Obv:** Young bust right, date below **Rev:** Schooner sailing right, denomination at right

Date	Mintage	F	VF	XF	Unc	BU
1978 Proof	1,303	Value: 4.00				

KM# 90 25 CENTS
Copper-Nickel, 24.2 mm. **Obv:** Crowned bust right, date below **Rev:** Schooner sailing right, denomination at right **Rev. Designer:** Stuart Devlin

Date	Mintage	F	VF	XF	Unc	BU
1987	—	—	0.35	0.50	1.00	1.25
1987 Proof	317	Value: 8.00				
1988 Proof	318	Value: 8.00				
1990	—	—	0.35	0.50	1.00	1.25

KM# 90a 25 CENTS
5.1000 g., Nickel Clad Steel, 24.2 mm. **Obv:** Crowned bust right, date below **Rev:** Schooner sailing right, denomination at right

Date	Mintage	F	VF	XF	Unc	BU
1992	—	—	0.45	0.75	1.50	1.75
1996	—	—	0.35	0.60	1.25	1.50

KM# 134 25 CENTS
5.0400 g., Nickel-Clad Steel, 24.2 mm. **Obv:** Head with tiara right, date below **Rev:** Schooner sailing right, denomination at right **Rev. Designer:** Stuart Devlin **Edge:** Reeded

Date	Mintage	F	VF	XF	Unc	BU
1999	—	—	—	0.75	1.50	1.75

KM# 5 50 CENTS
10.3000 g., 0.9250 Silver .3063 oz. ASW, 28.2 mm. **Obv:** Young bust right, date below **Rev:** Caribbean Emperor Fish, denomination at right

Date	Mintage	F	VF	XF	Unc	BU
1972	500	—	—	7.50	12.50	15.00
1972 Proof	11,000	Value: 8.00				
1973 Proof	9,988	Value: 8.00				
1974 Proof	30,000	Value: 8.00				
1975 Proof	7,175	Value: 8.00				
1976 Proof	3,044	Value: 8.00				
1977 Proof	1,980	Value: 8.00				
1979FM Proof	4,247	Value: 8.00				
1980FM Proof	1,215	Value: 8.00				
1981FM Proof	865	Value: 8.50				
1982FM Proof	589	Value: 8.50				

KM# 30 50 CENTS
10.3000 g., 0.9250 Silver, 28.2 mm. **Subject:** 25th Anniversary of Coronation **Obv:** Young bust right, date below **Rev:** Caribbean Emperor Fish, denomination at right

Date	Mintage	F	VF	XF	Unc	BU
1978 Proof	2,169	Value: 12.00				

KM# 73 50 CENTS
10.3000 g., 9.2500 Silver, 28.2 mm. **Obv:** Young bust right, date below **Rev:** Morning Glory, denomination at left

Date	Mintage	F	VF	XF	Unc	BU
1983FM Proof	—	Value: 15.00				
1984FM Proof	411	Value: 15.00				
1986 Proof	1,000	Value: 15.00				

KM# 91 50 CENTS
10.3000 g., 0.9250 Silver .3063 oz. ASW, 28.2 mm. **Obv:** Crowned bust right, date below

Date	Mintage	F	VF	XF	Unc	BU
1987 Proof	317	Value: 20.00				
1988 Proof	318	Value: 20.00				

KM# 6 DOLLAR
18.0000 g., 0.9250 Silver .5353 oz. ASW **Obv:** Young bust right, date below **Rev:** Poinciana flower, denomination within dollar symbol at left

Date	Mintage	F	VF	XF	Unc	BU
1972	500	—	—	8.50	15.00	—
1972 Proof	11,000	Value: 7.50				
1973 Proof	9,988	Value: 7.50				
1974 Proof	30,000	Value: 7.50				
1975 Proof	7,175	Value: 8.00				
1976 Proof	3,044	Value: 8.50				
1977 Proof	1,980	Value: 8.50				
1979FM Proof	4,247	Value: 8.50				
1980FM Proof	1,215	Value: 9.00				
1981FM Proof	865	Value: 10.00				
1982FM Proof	589	Value: 10.00				

KM# 31 DOLLAR
18.0000 g., 0.9250 Silver .5353 oz. ASW **Subject:** 25th Anniversary of Coronation **Obv:** Young bust right, date below **Rev:** Poinciana flower, denomination within dollar symbol at right

Date	Mintage	F	VF	XF	Unc	BU
1978 Proof	2,168	Value: 12.00				

KM# 74 DOLLAR
18.0000 g., 0.9250 Silver .5353 oz. ASW **Obv:** Young bust right, date below **Rev:** Pineapple, denomination within dollar symbol at left

Date	Mintage	F	VF	XF	Unc	BU
1983FM Proof	1,686	Value: 16.00				
1984FM Proof	456	Value: 16.00				
1986 Proof	1,000	Value: 16.00				

KM# 92 DOLLAR
18.0000 g., 0.9250 Silver .5353 oz. ASW **Obv:** Crowned bust right, date below

Date	Mintage	F	VF	XF	Unc	BU
1987 Proof	317	Value: 22.00				
1988 Proof	318	Value: 22.00				

KM# 103 DOLLAR
18.1400 g., 0.9250 Silver .5395 oz. ASW **Obv:** Crowned bust right **Rev:** Green Turtle divides date and denomination

Date	Mintage	F	VF	XF	Unc	BU
1990 Proof	Est. 5,000	Value: 75.00				

KM# 111 DOLLAR
18.1400 g., 0.9250 Silver .5395 oz. ASW **Obv:** Crowned bust right **Rev:** Rock Iquana divides date and denomination

Date	Mintage	F	VF	XF	Unc	BU
1992 Proof	Est. 5,000	Value: 50.00				

KM# 116 DOLLAR
18.1400 g., 0.9250 Silver .5395 oz. ASW **Obv:** Crowned bust right **Rev:** Cayman Ironwood Tree divides date and denomination **Rev. Designer:** Robert Elderton

Date	Mintage	F	VF	XF	Unc	BU
1994 Proof	Est. 10,000	Value: 37.50				

KM# 118 DOLLAR
28.2800 g., 0.9250 Silver .8411 oz. ASW **Subject:** Royal Visit **Rev:** Royal couple above yacht "Britannia"

Date	Mintage	F	VF	XF	Unc	BU
1994 Proof	Est. 10,000	Value: 50.00				

KM# 120 DOLLAR
28.2800 g., 0.9250 Silver .8411 oz. ASW **Obv:** Crowned bust right, date below **Rev:** Queen Mother's arms, date below, within beaded circle, denomination below

Date	Mintage	F	VF	XF	Unc	BU
1994 Proof	Est. 20,000	Value: 28.50				

KM# 121 DOLLAR
28.2800 g., 0.9250 Silver .8411 oz. ASW **Rev:** Sir Francis Drake at left, arms above denomination at right

Date	Mintage	F	VF	XF	Unc	BU
1994 Proof	Est. 10,000	Value: 30.00				

KM# 125 DOLLAR
28.2800 g., 0.9250 Silver .8411 oz. ASW **Obv:** Crowned bust right, date below **Rev:** Rock Iguana left, denomination below

Date	Mintage	F	VF	XF	Unc	BU
1995 Proof	Est. 10,000	Value: 55.00				

KM# 124 DOLLAR
28.2800 g., 0.9250 Silver .8411 oz. ASW **Subject:** Olympics **Obv:** Crowned bust right, date below **Rev:** Two sailboats, date above, denomination below

Date	Mintage	F	VF	XF	Unc	BU
1996 Proof	Est. 30,000	Value: 30.00				

KM# 122 DOLLAR
18.1400 g., 0.9250 Silver .5394 oz. ASW **Obv:** Crowned bust right **Rev:** Amazona Leucocephala Caymanesis - Parrot divides date and denomination **Rev. Designer:** Robert Elderton

Date	Mintage	F	VF	XF	Unc	BU
1996 Proof	Est. 10,000	Value: 50.00				

KM# 7 2 DOLLARS
29.4500 g., 0.9250 Silver .8758 oz. ASW **Obv:** Crowned bust right, date below **Rev:** Great Blue Heron, denomination above

Date	Mintage	F	VF	XF	Unc	BU
1972	500	—	—	—	20.00	25.00
1972 Proof	11,000	Value: 12.50				
1973 Proof	9,988	Value: 12.50				
1974 Proof	30,000	Value: 12.50				
1975 Proof	5,390	Value: 13.00				
1976 Proof	3,044	Value: 13.50				
1977 Proof	1,980	Value: 13.50				
1979FM Proof	4,247	Value: 13.50				

Date	Mintage	F	VF	XF	Unc	BU
1980FM Proof	1,215	Value: 18.00				
1981FM Proof	865	Value: 25.00				
1982FM Proof	589	Value: 25.00				
1986 Proof	1,000	Value: 18.00				

KM# 32 2 DOLLARS
29.4500 g., 0.9250 Silver .8758 oz. ASW **Subject:** 25th Anniversary of Coronation **Rev:** Great Blue Heron right, denomination above

Date	Mintage	F	VF	XF	Unc	BU
1978 Proof	2,169	Value: 22.50				

KM# 75 2 DOLLARS
29.4500 g., 0.9250 Silver .8758 oz. ASW **Rev:** Parrot, denomination at right

Date	Mintage	F	VF	XF	Unc	BU
1983FM Proof	409	Value: 45.00				
1984FM Proof	200	Value: 55.00				

KM# 93 2 DOLLARS
29.4500 g., 0.9250 Silver .8758 oz. ASW **Obv:** Crowned bust right, date below **Rev:** Great Blue Heron

Date	Mintage	F	VF	XF	Unc	BU
1987 Proof	317	Value: 45.00				
1988 Proof	318	Value: 45.00				

KM# 114 2 DOLLARS
28.2800 g., 0.9250 Silver .8411 oz. ASW **Obv:** Crowned bust right, denomination below **Rev:** Wreck of the "Ten Sails" **Rev. Designer:** John Savage

Date	Mintage	F	VF	XF	Unc	BU
1994 Proof	15,000	Value: 30.00				

KM# 127 2 DOLLARS
28.2800 g., 0.9250 Silver .8411 oz. ASW **Subject:** 25th Anniversary - Currency Board **Obv:** Crowned bust right, denomination below **Rev:** Coins and arms within circle, two dates below **Rev. Designer:** Robert Elderton and Stuart Devlin

Date	Mintage	F	VF	XF	Unc	BU
ND Proof	Est. 2,000	Value: 55.00				

KM# 128 2 DOLLARS
28.2800 g., 0.9250 Silver .8411 oz. ASW **Subject:** Queen's Golden Wedding Anniversary **Obv:** Queen's portrait **Rev:** Royal couple in carriage above gold-plated shield within circle, denomination below

Date	Mintage	F	VF	XF	Unc	BU
1997 Proof	Est. 30,000	Value: 57.00				

KM# 129 2 DOLLARS
28.2800 g., 0.9250 Silver .8411 oz. ASW **Obv:** Crowned bust right, date below **Rev:** Schooners "Arbutus I" and "Goldfield" under sail, denomination below **Rev. Designer:** Robert Elderton

Date	Mintage	F	VF	XF	Unc	BU
1997 Proof	Est. 5,000	Value: 60.00				

KM# 130 2 DOLLARS
15.5520 g., 0.9990 Silver .4995 oz. ASW **Subject:** Millennium **Obv:** Queen's portrait **Rev:** Ornate clock above denomination **Rev. Designer:** Christopher N. Lawrence **Shape:** Scalloped

Date	Mintage	F	VF	XF	Unc	BU
2000 Proof	30,000	Value: 47.50				

KM# 8 5 DOLLARS
35.5000 g., 0.9250 Silver 1.0557 oz. ASW **Obv:** Young bust right, date below **Rev:** Shield with turtle and pineapple above divides banner, denomination below

Date	Mintage	F	VF	XF	Unc	BU
1972	500	—	—	—	35.00	—
1972 Proof	11,000	Value: 14.50				
1973 Proof	17,000	Value: 14.50				
1974 Proof	26,000	Value: 14.50				
1975 Proof	7,753	Value: 15.00				
1976 Proof	5,177	Value: 15.00				
1977 Proof	3,525	Value: 16.00				
1979FM Proof	—	Value: 17.50				
1980FM Proof	—	Value: 20.00				
1981FM Proof	—	Value: 22.00				
1984FM Proof	—	Value: 22.00				
1986 Proof	1,000	Value: 22.00				

KM# 33 5 DOLLARS
35.5000 g., 0.9250 Silver 1.0557 oz. ASW **Subject:** 25th Anniversary of Coronation **Obv:** Young bust right, date below

Date	Mintage	F	VF	XF	Unc	BU
1978 Proof	2,168	Value: 28.50				

KM# 70 5 DOLLARS
35.5000 g., 0.9250 Silver 1.0557 oz. ASW **Subject:** 150th Anniversary of Parliamentary Government **Obv:** Young bust right, date below **Rev:** Shield with turtle and pineapple above divides banner, denomination below

Date	Mintage	F	VF	XF	Unc	BU
1982FM Proof	1,105	Value: 40.00				

KM# 76 5 DOLLARS
35.5000 g., 0.9250 Silver 1.0557 oz. ASW **Subject:** Royal Visit

Date	Mintage	F	VF	XF	Unc	BU
1983FM Proof	419	Value: 38.50				

KM# 81 5 DOLLARS
28.2800 g., 0.9250 Silver .8411 oz. ASW, 38.61 mm. **Subject:** 250th Anniversary of Royal Land Grant **Obv:** Crowned bust right, date below **Rev:** Map of islands divides dates and denomination

Date	Mintage	F	VF	XF	Unc	BU
1985 Proof	Est. 1,000	Value: 31.50				

KM# 80 5 DOLLARS
28.2800 g., 0.5000 Silver .4547 oz. ASW **Subject:** Commonwealth Games **Obv:** Crowned bust right, date below **Rev:** Long Jumper, denomination at right

Date	Mintage	F	VF	XF	Unc	BU
1986	50,000	—	—	—	12.50	—

KM# 80a 5 DOLLARS
28.2800 g., 0.9250 Silver .8411 oz. ASW **Subject:** Commonwealth Games **Obv:** Crowned bust right, date below **Rev:** Long Jumper

Date	Mintage	F	VF	XF	Unc	BU
1986 Proof	Est. 20,000	Value: 25.00				

KM# 85 5 DOLLARS
28.2800 g., 0.9250 Silver .8411 oz. ASW **Subject:** Queen Elizabeth II and Philip's 40th Wedding Anniversary **Obv:** Crowned bust right, denomination below **Rev:** Monogram above dates within wreath **Rev. Designer:** Norman Sillman

Date	Mintage	F	VF	XF	Unc	BU
ND(1987) Proof	Est. 2,000	Value: 30.00				

KM# 85a 5 DOLLARS
35.6400 g., 0.9250 Silver 1.0560 oz. ASW **Subject:** Queen Elizabeth II and Philip's 40th Wedding Anniversary **Obv:** Crowned bust right, denomination below **Rev:** Monogram above dates within wreath

Date	Mintage	F	VF	XF	Unc	BU
ND(1987) Proof	317	Value: 90.00				

KM# 95 5 DOLLARS
28.2800 g., 0.9250 Silver .8411 oz. ASW **Subject:** World Wildlife Fund **Obv:** Crowned bust right, denomination below **Rev:** Cuban Amazon, date below

Date	Mintage	F	VF	XF	Unc	BU
1987 Proof	—	Value: 35.00				

KM# 96 5 DOLLARS
28.2800 g., 0.9250 Silver .8411 oz. ASW **Subject:** 500th Anniversary of Columbus' Discovery of America **Obv:** Crowned bust right, date below **Rev:** Columbus in cameo above ships, denomination at bottom **Rev. Designer:** Robert Elderton

Date	Mintage	F	VF	XF	Unc	BU
1988 Proof	10,000	Value: 27.50				

KM# 98 5 DOLLARS
28.2800 g., 0.9250 Silver .8411 oz. ASW **Subject:** Visit of Princess Alexandra **Obv:** Crowned bust right, denomination below **Rev:** Arms of Princess Alexandria, date below **Note:** Similar to 250 Dollars, KM#99.

Date	Mintage	F	VF	XF	Unc	BU
1988 Proof	Est. 5,000	Value: 37.50				

KM# 94.1 5 DOLLARS
28.2800 g., 0.9250 Silver .8411 oz. ASW **Subject:** Seoul Olympics **Obv:** Crowned bust right, denomination below **Rev:** Sailboards **Rev. Designer:** Robert Elderton

Date	Mintage	F	VF	XF	Unc	BU
1988 Proof	20,000	Value: 27.50				

KM# 94.2 5 DOLLARS
35.6400 g., 0.9250 Silver 1.0560 oz. ASW **Subject:** Seoul Olympics **Obv:** Crowned bust right, date below **Rev:** Sailboards, denomination at left **Rev. Designer:** Robert Elderton

Date	Mintage	F	VF	XF	Unc	BU
1988 Proof	318	Value: 200				

KM# 100 5 DOLLARS
28.2800 g., 0.9250 Silver .8411 oz. ASW **Subject:** 100 Years of Postal Service **Rev:** Ship with small shield above, within circle, two dates below

Date	Mintage	F	VF	XF	Unc	BU
ND(1989) Proof	10,000	Value: 40.00				

KM# 102 5 DOLLARS
28.2800 g., 0.9250 Silver .8411 oz. ASW **Subject:** Save the Children Fund **Obv:** Crowned bust right, denomination below **Rev:** Two children sailing boats in water, within circle, date below

Date	Mintage	F	VF	XF	Unc	BU
1989 Proof	Est. 20,000	Value: 20.00				

KM# 108 5 DOLLARS
28.2800 g., 0.9250 Silver .8411 oz. ASW **Subject:** Queen Mother's Birth Centennial **Obv:** Crowned bust right, denomination below **Rev:** Crowned monogram within flowers, dates separate below **Rev. Designer:** Robert Elderton

Date	Mintage	F	VF	XF	Unc	BU
ND (1990) Proof	Est. 10,000	Value: 25.00				
ND(1990) Proof	Est. 10,000	Value: 25.00				

KM# 109 5 DOLLARS
28.2800 g., 0.9250 Silver .8411 oz. ASW **Subject:** 20th Anniversary of the Currency Board **Obv:** Crowned bust right, denomination below **Rev:** Islands and compass above ship within circle, dates below **Rev. Designer:** Robert Elderton

Date	Mintage	F	VF	XF	Unc	BU
ND(1991) Proof	Est. 2,500	Value: 40.00				

KM# 110 5 DOLLARS
28.2800 g., 0.9250 Silver .8411 oz. ASW **Subject:** 1992 Olympics - Barcelona **Obv:** Crowned bust right, date and denomination below **Rev:** Cycling, date at top **Rev. Designer:** Willem Vis

Date	Mintage	F	VF	XF	Unc	BU
1992 Proof	Est. 50,000	Value: 27.50				

KM# 112 5 DOLLARS
28.2800 g., 0.9250 Silver .8411 oz. ASW **Subject:** 40th Anniversary - Coronation of Queen Elizabeth **Obv:** Crowned bust right, denomination below **Rev:** Royal symbols, two dates below

Date	Mintage	F	VF	XF	Unc	BU
ND (1993) Proof	Est. 10,000	Value: 32.50				
ND(1993) Proof	Est. 13,000	Value: 45.00				

KM# 126 5 DOLLARS
28.2800 g., 0.9250 Silver .8411 oz. ASW **Subject:** 70th Birthday of Queen Elizabeth II **Obv:** Queen's portrait **Rev:** The Queen on horseback divides monogram, denomination divides dates below

Date	Mintage	F	VF	XF	Unc	BU
ND (1996) Proof	Est. 13,000	Value: 45.00				
ND(1996) Proof	13,000	Value: 45.00				

KM# 68 10 DOLLARS

Copper-Nickel **Subject:** Wedding of Prince Charles and Lady Diana **Obv:** Young bust right, date below **Rev:** Wedding couple below shield, date upper right, denomination below

Date	Mintage	F	VF	XF	Unc	BU
1981	—	—	—	—	7.50	—

KM# 68a 10 DOLLARS

28.2800 g., 0.9250 Silver .8411 oz. ASW **Subject:** Wedding of Prince Charles and Lady Diana **Obv:** Young bust right, date below **Rev:** Wedding couple below shield, date upper right, denomination below

Date	Mintage	F	VF	XF	Unc	BU
1981 Proof	40,000	Value: 17.50				

KM# 72 10 DOLLARS

27.8900 g., 0.9250 Silver .8295 oz. ASW **Subject:** International Year of the Child **Obv:** Young bust right, date below **Rev:** Two children following sea turtle, denomination above **Rev. Designer:** Michael Rizzello

Date	Mintage	F	VF	XF	Unc	BU
1982 Proof	6,616	Value: 22.50				

KM# 77 10 DOLLARS

23.4500 g., 0.9250 Silver .6975 oz. ASW **Subject:** Royal Visit **Obv:** Young bust right, date below **Rev:** Royal couple above shield within circle, denomination below

Date	Mintage	F	VF	XF	Unc	BU
1983FM Proof	10,000	Value: 30.00				

KM# 9 25 DOLLARS

51.3500 g., 0.9250 Silver 1.5271 oz. ASW, 45 mm. **Subject:** Queen Elizabeth II and Philip's 25th Wedding Anniversary **Rev:** Conjoined busts of royal couple facing right, denomination below

Date	Mintage	F	VF	XF	Unc	BU
1972	186,000	—	—	—	27.50	—
1972 Proof	26,000	Value: 32.50				

KM# 9a 25 DOLLARS

15.7500 g., 0.5000 Gold .2531 oz. AGW **Subject:** Queen Elizabeth II and Philip's 25th Wedding Anniversary **Rev:** Conjoined busts of royal couple facing right, denomination below

Date	Mintage	F	VF	XF	Unc	BU
1972	7,706	—	—	—	—	175
1972 Proof	21,000	Value: 170				

KM# 10 25 DOLLARS

51.3500 g., 0.9250 Silver 1.5271 oz. ASW, 45 mm. **Subject:** Churchill Centenary **Obv:** Shield divides banner, turtle and pineapple above, denomination below **Rev:** Bust facing, date at right **Rev. Designer:** Michael Rizzello

Date	Mintage	F	VF	XF	Unc	BU
1974	1,200	—	—	—	35.00	—
1974 Proof	12,000	Value: 32.50				

Note: 4300 sets were issued in proof containing KM#10 and Turks & Caicos Islands 20 Crowns KM#2 with an issue price of $80.00

KM# 14 25 DOLLARS

51.3500 g., 0.9250 Silver 1.5271 oz. ASW, 45 mm. **Subject:** Queen's Silver Jubliee **Obv:** Young bust right, date below **Rev:** Crowned arms with supporters above denomination

Date	Mintage	F	VF	XF	Unc	BU
1977	3,600	—	—	—	45.00	—
1977 Proof	7,854	Value: 45.00				

KM# 16 25 DOLLARS

51.3500 g., 0.9250 Silver 1.5271 oz. ASW, 45 mm. **Obv:** Young bust right, date below **Rev:** Queen Mary I facing 1/2 left in inner circle, denomination below **Rev. Designer:** Michael Rizzello

Date	Mintage	F	VF	XF	Unc	BU
1977 Proof	2,720	Value: 55.00				

KM# 17 25 DOLLARS

51.3500 g., 0.9250 Silver 1.5271 oz. ASW, 45 mm. **Obv:** Young bust right, date below **Rev:** Queen Elizabeth I half right with ruffed collar in inner circle, denomination below **Rev. Designer:** Michael Rizzello

Date	Mintage	F	VF	XF	Unc	BU
1977 Proof	2,677	Value: 55.00				

KM# 18 25 DOLLARS

51.3500 g., 0.9250 Silver 1.5271 oz. ASW, 45 mm. **Obv:** Young bust right, date below **Rev:** Queen Mary II half right in inner circle, denomination below **Rev. Designer:** Michael Rizzello

Date	Mintage	F	VF	XF	Unc	BU
1977 Proof	2,653	Value: 55.00				

KM# 19 25 DOLLARS

51.3500 g., 0.9250 Silver 1.5271 oz. ASW, 45 mm. **Obv:** Young bust right, date below **Rev:** Queen Anne half left in inner circle, denomination below **Rev. Designer:** Michael Rizzello

Date	Mintage	F	VF	XF	Unc	BU
1977 Proof	2,630	Value: 55.00				

KM# 20 25 DOLLARS

51.3500 g., 0.9250 Silver 1.5271 oz. ASW, 45 mm. **Obv:** Young bust right, date below **Rev:** Queen Victoria 3/4 left in inner circle, denomination below **Rev. Designer:** Michael Rizzello

Date	Mintage	F	VF	XF	Unc	BU
1977 Proof	2,623	Value: 55.00				

KM# 36 25 DOLLARS

51.3500 g., 0.9250 Silver 1.5271 oz. ASW, 45 mm. **Subject:** 25th Anniversary of Coronation **Obv:** Young bust right, date below **Rev:** Ampulla, denomination below

Date	Mintage	F	VF	XF	Unc	BU
1978 Proof	5,000	Value: 47.50				

KM# 37 25 DOLLARS

51.3500 g., 0.9250 Silver 1.5271 oz. ASW, 45 mm. **Subject:** 25th Anniversary of Coronation **Obv:** Young bust right, date below **Rev:** Orb, denomination below

Date	Mintage	F	VF	XF	Unc	BU
1978 Proof	5,000	Value: 47.50				

KM# 38 25 DOLLARS

51.3500 g., 0.9250 Silver 1.5271 oz. ASW, 45 mm. **Subject:** 25th Anniversary of Coronation **Obv:** Young bust right, date below **Rev:** St. Edward's crown, denomination below

Date	Mintage	F	VF	XF	Unc	BU
1978 Proof	5,000	Value: 47.50				

KM# 39 25 DOLLARS

51.3500 g., 0.9250 Silver 1.5271 oz. ASW, 45 mm. **Subject:** 25th Anniversary of Coronation **Obv:** Young bust right, date below **Rev:** Coronation chair, denomination below

Date	Mintage	F	VF	XF	Unc	BU
1978 Proof	5,000	Value: 47.50				

KM# 40 25 DOLLARS

51.3500 g., 0.9250 Silver 1.5271 oz. ASW, 45 mm. **Subject:** 25th Anniversary of Coronation **Obv:** Young bust right, date below **Rev:** Royal scepter, denomination below

Date	Mintage	F	VF	XF	Unc	BU
1978 Proof	5,000	Value: 47.50				

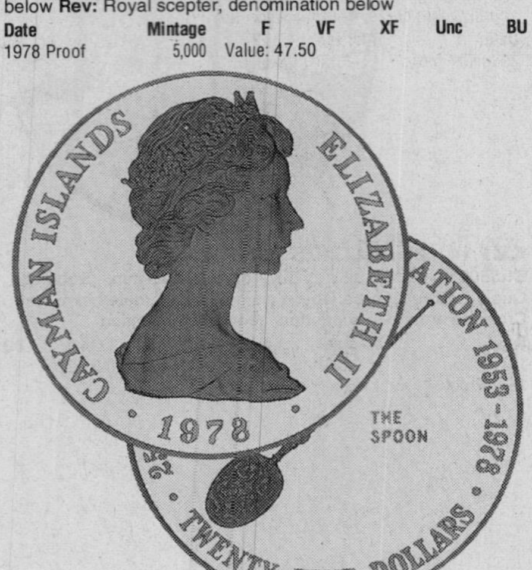

KM# 41 25 DOLLARS

51.3500 g., 0.9250 Silver 1.5271 oz. ASW, 45 mm. **Subject:** 25th Anniversary of Coronation **Obv:** Young bust right, date between dots **Rev:** Spoon, denomination below

Date	Mintage	F	VF	XF	Unc	BU
1978 Proof	5,000	Value: 47.50				

KM# 48 25 DOLLARS

35.6400 g., 0.5000 Silver .5729 oz. ASW **Obv:** Young bust right, date below **Rev:** Saxon Kings, denomination divides **Rev. Designer:** Michael Rizzello

Date	Mintage	F	VF	XF	Unc	BU
1980CHI Proof	12,000	Value: 35.00				

KM# 49 25 DOLLARS

35.6400 g., 0.5000 Silver .5729 oz. ASW **Obv:** Young bust right, date below **Rev:** Busts of Norman kings in a circle with names and dates, denomination in center **Rev. Designer:** Michael Rizzello

Date	Mintage	F	VF	XF	Unc	BU
1980CHI Proof	12,000	Value: 35.00				

KM# 50 25 DOLLARS

35.6400 g., 0.5000 Silver .5729 oz. ASW **Obv:** Young bust right, date below **Rev:** House of Plantagenet - I, denomination at center **Rev. Designer:** Michael Rizzello

Date	Mintage	F	VF	XF	Unc	BU
1980CHI Proof	12,000	Value: 35.00				

KM# 51 25 DOLLARS

35.6400 g., 0.5000 Silver .5729 oz. ASW **Obv:** Young bust right, date below **Rev:** House of Plantagenet - II, denomination at center **Rev. Designer:** Michael Rizzello

Date	Mintage	F	VF	XF	Unc	BU
1980CHI Proof	12,000	Value: 35.00				

KM# 52 25 DOLLARS
35.6400 g., 0.5000 Silver .5729 oz. ASW **Obv:** Young bust right, date below **Rev:** House of Lancaster, denomination at cente **Rev. Designer:** Michael Rizzello

Date	Mintage	F	VF	XF	Unc	BU
1980CHI Proof	12,000	Value: 35.00				

KM# 53 25 DOLLARS
35.6400 g., 0.5000 Silver .5729 oz. ASW **Obv:** Young bust right, date below **Rev:** House of York, denomination at center **Rev. Designer:** Michael Rizzello

Date	Mintage	F	VF	XF	Unc	BU
1980CHI Proof	12,000	Value: 35.00				

KM# 54 25 DOLLARS
35.6400 g., 0.5000 Silver .5729 oz. ASW **Obv:** Young bust right, date below **Rev:** House of Tudor, denomination at center **Rev. Designer:** Michael Rizzello

Date	Mintage	F	VF	XF	Unc	BU
1980CHI Proof	12,000	Value: 35.00				

KM# 55 25 DOLLARS
35.6400 g., 0.5000 Silver .5729 oz. ASW **Obv:** Young bust right, date below **Rev:** House of Stuart & Orange, denomination at center **Rev. Designer:** Michael Rizzello

Date	Mintage	F	VF	XF	Unc	BU
1980CHI Proof	12,000	Value: 35.00				

KM# 56 25 DOLLARS
35.6400 g., 0.5000 Silver .5729 oz. ASW **Obv:** Young bust right, date below **Rev:** House of Hanover, denomination at center **Rev. Designer:** Michael Rizzello

Date	Mintage	F	VF	XF	Unc	BU
1980CHI Proof	12,000	Value: 35.00				

KM# 57 25 DOLLARS
35.6400 g., 0.5000 Silver .5729 oz. ASW **Obv:** Young bust right, date below **Rev:** House of Saxe-Coburg and Windsor, denomination at center **Rev. Designer:** Michael Rizzello

Date	Mintage	F	VF	XF	Unc	BU
1980CHI Proof	12,000	Value: 35.00				

KM# 78 25 DOLLARS
64.8000 g., 0.9250 Silver 1.9273 oz. ASW **Subject:** Royal Visit **Obv:** Young bust right, date below **Rev:** Royal couple above shield within circle, denomination below

Date	Mintage	F	VF	XF	Unc	BU
1983FM Proof	5,000	Value: 50.00				

KM# 104 25 DOLLARS
3.1340 g., 0.9990 Gold .1006 oz. AGW **Subject:** Winston Churchill **Obv:** Young bust right, date below **Rev:** Evacuation of Dunkirk, denomination below **Rev. Designer:** Robert Elderton

Date	Mintage	F	VF	XF	Unc	BU
1990 Proof	Est. 500	Value: 95.00				

KM# 12 50 DOLLARS
64.9400 g., 0.9250 Silver 1.9314 oz. ASW **Subject:** Sovereign Queens of England **Obv:** Young bust right, date below **Rev:** Portraits of sovereign queens in circle with names and dates, denomination at center **Rev. Designer:** Michael Rizzello

Date	Mintage	F	VF	XF	Unc	BU
1975	33,000	—	—	—	50.00	—
1975 Proof	7,800	Value: 55.00				
1976	1,292	—	—	—	60.00	—
1976 Proof	2,843	Value: 60.00				
1977	2,400	—	—	—	60.00	—
1977 Proof	Inc. above	Value: 60.00				

KM# 21 50 DOLLARS
11.3400 g., 0.5000 Gold .1823 oz. AGW **Obv:** Young bust right, date below **Rev:** Bust half left, denomination below **Rev. Designer:** Michael Rizzello

Date	Mintage	F	VF	XF	Unc	BU
1977 Proof	1,999	Value: 135				

KM# 22 50 DOLLARS
11.3400 g., 0.5000 Gold .1823 oz. AGW **Obv:** Young bust right, date below **Rev:** Bust with high ruffled collar, 3/4 right within circle, denomination below **Rev. Designer:** Michael Rizzello

Date	Mintage	F	VF	XF	Unc	BU
1977 Proof	1,969	Value: 135				

KM# 23 50 DOLLARS
11.3400 g., 0.5000 Gold .1823 oz. AGW **Obv:** Young bust right, date below **Rev:** Bust 3/4 facing within circle, denomination below **Rev. Designer:** Michael Rizzello

Date	Mintage	F	VF	XF	Unc	BU
1977 Proof	1,961	Value: 135				

KM# 24 50 DOLLARS
11.3400 g., 0.5000 Gold .1823 oz. AGW **Obv:** Young bust right, date below **Rev:** Bust half left within circle, denomination below **Rev. Designer:** Michael Rizzello

Date	Mintage	F	VF	XF	Unc	BU
1977 Proof	1,938	Value: 135				

KM# 25 50 DOLLARS
11.3400 g., 0.5000 Gold .1823 oz. AGW **Obv:** Young bust right, date below **Rev:** Bust 3/4 left within circle, denomination below **Rev. Designer:** Michael Rizzello

Date	Mintage	F	VF	XF	Unc	BU
1977 Proof	1,932	Value: 135				

KM# 34 50 DOLLARS
64.9400 g., 0.9250 Silver 1.9314 oz. ASW **Obv:** Young bust right, date below **Rev:** Coronation Anniversary legend added to KM#12 **Rev. Designer:** Michael Rizzello

Date	Mintage	F	VF	XF	Unc	BU
1978 Proof	5,775	Value: 65.00				

KM# 42 50 DOLLARS
11.3400 g., 0.5000 Gold .1823 oz. AGW **Subject:** 25th Anniversary of Coronation **Obv:** Young bust right, date below **Rev:** Statue, denomination below

Date	Mintage	F	VF	XF	Unc	BU
1978 Proof	771	Value: 145				

KM# 43 50 DOLLARS
11.3400 g., 0.5000 Gold .1823 oz. AGW **Subject:** 25th Anniversary of Coronation **Obv:** Young bust right, date below **Rev:** Orb, denomination below

Date	Mintage	F	VF	XF	Unc	BU
1978 Proof	771	Value: 145				

KM# 44 50 DOLLARS
11.3400 g., 0.5000 Gold .1823 oz. AGW **Subject:** 25th Anniversary of Coronation **Obv:** Young bust right, date below **Rev:** St. Edward's Crown, denomination below

Date	Mintage	F	VF	XF	Unc	BU
1978 Proof	771	Value: 145				

KM# 45 50 DOLLARS
11.3400 g., 0.5000 Gold .1823 oz. AGW **Subject:** 25th Anniversary of Coronation **Obv:** Young bust right, date below **Rev:** Chair, denomination below

Date	Mintage	F	VF	XF	Unc	BU
1978 Proof	771	Value: 145				

KM# 46 50 DOLLARS
11.3400 g., 0.5000 Gold .1823 oz. AGW **Subject:** 25th Anniversary of Coronation **Obv:** Young bust right, date below **Rev:** Scepter, denomination below

Date	Mintage	F	VF	XF	Unc	BU
1978 Proof	771	Value: 145				

KM# 47 50 DOLLARS
11.3400 g., 0.5000 Gold .1823 oz. AGW **Subject:** 25th Anniversary of Coronation **Obv:** Young bust right, date below **Rev:** Spoon, denomination below

Date	Mintage	F	VF	XF	Unc	BU
1978 Proof	771	Value: 145				

KM# 58 50 DOLLARS
11.3400 g., 0.5000 Gold .1823 oz. AGW **Obv:** Young bust right, date below **Rev:** Saxon Kings, denomination at center **Rev. Designer:** Michael Rizzello

Date	Mintage	F	VF	XF	Unc	BU
1980 Proof	10,000	Value: 145				

KM# 59 50 DOLLARS
11.3400 g., 0.5000 Gold .1823 oz. AGW **Obv:** Young bust right, date below **Rev:** Norman Kings, denomination below **Rev. Designer:** Michael Rizzello

Date	Mintage	F	VF	XF	Unc	BU
1980 Proof	10,000	Value: 145				

KM# 60 50 DOLLARS
11.3400 g., 0.5000 Gold .1823 oz. AGW **Obv:** Young bust right, date below **Rev:** House of Plantagenet - I, denomination at center **Rev. Designer:** Michael Rizzello

Date	Mintage	F	VF	XF	Unc	BU
1980 Proof	11,000	Value: 145				

KM# 61 50 DOLLARS
11.3400 g., 0.5000 Gold .1823 oz. AGW **Obv:** Young bust right, date below **Rev:** House of Plantagenet - II, denomination at center **Rev. Designer:** Michael Rizzello

Date	Mintage	F	VF	XF	Unc	BU
1980 Proof	11,000	Value: 145				

KM# 62 50 DOLLARS
11.3400 g., 0.5000 Gold .1823 oz. AGW **Obv:** Young bust right, date below **Rev:** House of Lancaster, denomination at center **Rev. Designer:** Michael Rizzello

Date	Mintage	F	VF	XF	Unc	BU
1980 Proof	11,000	Value: 145				

KM# 63 50 DOLLARS
11.3400 g., 0.5000 Gold .1823 oz. AGW **Obv:** Young bust right, date below **Rev:** House of York, denomination at center **Rev. Designer:** Michael Rizzello

Date	Mintage	F	VF	XF	Unc	BU
1980 Proof	11,000	Value: 145				

KM# 64 50 DOLLARS
11.3400 g., 0.5000 Gold .1823 oz. AGW **Obv:** Young bust right, date below **Rev:** House of Tudor, denomination at center **Rev. Designer:** Michael Rizzello

Date	Mintage	F	VF	XF	Unc	BU
1980 Proof	11,000	Value: 145				

KM# 65 50 DOLLARS
11.3400 g., 0.5000 Gold .1823 oz. AGW **Obv:** Young bust right, date below **Rev:** House of Stuart and Oranage, enomination at center **Rev. Designer:** Michael Rizzello

Date	Mintage	F	VF	XF	Unc	BU
1980 Proof	11,000	Value: 145				

KM# 66 50 DOLLARS
11.3400 g., 0.5000 Gold .1823 oz. AGW **Obv:** Young bust right, date below **Rev:** House of Hanover, denomination at center **Rev. Designer:** Michael Rizzello

Date	Mintage	F	VF	XF	Unc	BU
1980 Proof	11,000	Value: 145				

KM# 67 50 DOLLARS
11.3400 g., 0.5000 Gold .1823 oz. AGW **Obv:** Young bust right, date below **Rev:** House of Saxe-Coburg and Windsor, denomination at center **Rev. Designer:** Michael Rizzello

Date	Mintage	F	VF	XF	Unc	BU
1980 Proof	11,000	Value: 145				

KM# 71 50 DOLLARS
5.0000 g., 0.9000 Gold .1447 oz. AGW **Subject:** 150th Anniversary of Parliamentary Government **Obv:** Young bust right, date below **Rev:** Shield divides banner, turtle and pineapple above, denomination below

Date	Mintage	F	VF	XF	Unc	BU
1982 Proof	585	Value: 135				

KM# 79 50 DOLLARS
5.1900 g., 0.9170 Gold .1530 oz. AGW **Subject:** Royal Visit **Obv:** Young bust right, date below **Rev:** Royal couple above shield within circle, denomination below

Date	Mintage	F	VF	XF	Unc	BU
1983	5,000	—	—	—	125	—

KM# 83 50 DOLLARS
129.6000 g., 0.9250 Silver 3.8547 oz. ASW, 63 mm. **Subject:** Bird Conservation **Obv:** Crowned bust right, date below **Rev:** Snowy Egret left, divides denomination above

Date	Mintage	F	VF	XF	Unc	BU
1985 Proof	10,000	Value: 95.00				

KM# 105 50 DOLLARS
7.8140 g., 0.9990 Gold .2509 oz. AGW **Rev:** Cameo Winston Churchill to center - Spitfires over Dover below **Rev. Designer:** Robert Elderton

Date	Mintage	F	VF	XF	Unc	BU
1990 Proof	Est. 500	Value: 190				

KM# 115 50 DOLLARS
15.9800 g., 0.9170 Gold .4708 oz. AGW **Obv:** Crowned bust right, date and denomination below **Rev:** Wreck of the Ten Sails **Rev. Designer:** John Savage

Date	Mintage	F	VF	XF	Unc	BU
1994 Proof	Est. 200	Value: 500				

KM# 11 100 DOLLARS
22.6801 g., 0.5000 Gold .3646 oz. AGW **Subject:** Churchill Centenary **Obv:** Shield divides banner, turtle and pineapple above, denomination below **Rev:** Bust facing **Rev. Designer:** Michael Rizzello

Date	Mintage	F	VF	XF	Unc	BU
1974	1,400	—	—	—	250	—
1974 Proof	6,300	Value: 245				

KM# 13 100 DOLLARS
22.6801 g., 0.5000 Gold .3646 oz. AGW **Obv:** Yooung bust right, date below **Rev:** Sovereign Queens of England within circles, denomination at center **Rev. Designer:** Michael Rizzello

Date	Mintage	F	VF	XF	Unc	BU
1975	8,053	—	—	—	245	—
1975 Proof	4,950	Value: 250				
1976	2,028	—	—	—	245	—
1976 Proof	3,560	Value: 250				
1977	—	—	—	—	245	—
1977 Proof	2,845	Value: 250				

KM# 15 100 DOLLARS
22.6801 g., 0.5000 Gold .3646 oz. AGW **Subject:** Queen's Silver Jubilee **Obv:** Young bust right, date below **Rev:** Crowned arms with supporters, denomination below

Date	Mintage	F	VF	XF	Unc	BU
1977	562	—	—	—	245	—
1977 Proof	4,386	Value: 250				

KM# 35 100 DOLLARS
22.6801 g., 0.5000 Gold .3646 oz. AGW **Obv:** Young bust right, date below **Rev:** Sovereign Queens of England within circles, denomination at center

Date	Mintage	F	VF	XF	Unc	BU
1978 Proof	1,973	Value: 260				

KM# 69 100 DOLLARS
8.0352 g., 0.9170 Gold .2369 oz. AGW **Subject:** Wedding of Prince Charles and Lady Diana **Obv:** Young bust right, date below **Rev:** Wedding couple within beaded circle, shield above divides date, denomination below

Date	Mintage	F	VF	XF	Unc	BU
1981 Proof	11,000	Value: 165				

KM# 97 100 DOLLARS
15.9800 g., 0.9170 Gold .4708 oz. AGW **Subject:** 500th Anniversary of Columbus' Discovery of America **Rev. Designer:** Robert Elderton

Date	Mintage	F	VF	XF	Unc	BU
1988 Proof	380	Value: 375				

KM# 101 100 DOLLARS
15.9800 g., 0.9170 Gold .4708 oz. AGW **Subject:** 100 Years of Postal Service **Obv:** Crowned bust right, denomination below **Rev:** Ship with small shield above, within circle, two dates below

Date	Mintage	F	VF	XF	Unc	BU
1989 Proof	93	Value: 475				

KM# 106 100 DOLLARS
15.6080 g., 0.9990 Gold .5013 oz. AGW **Subject:** Winston Churchill **Obv:** Crowned bust right, denomination below **Rev:** Evacuation of Dunkirk, denomination below **Rev. Designer:** Robert Elderton

Date	Mintage	F	VF	XF	Unc	BU
1990 Proof	500	Value: 360				

KM# 117 100 DOLLARS
30.5000 g., 0.9170 Gold .8974 oz. AGW **Obv:** Crowned bust right **Rev:** Cayman Ironwood Tree

Date	Mintage	F	VF	XF	Unc	BU
1994 Proof	Est. 15,000	Value: 635				

KM# 123 100 DOLLARS
15.9800 g., 0.9170 Gold .4708 oz. AGW **Obv:** Crowned bust right **Rev:** Amazona Leucocephala Caymanesis - Parrot

Date	Mintage	F	VF	XF	Unc	BU
1996 Proof	Est. 150	Value: 450				

KM# 82 250 DOLLARS
47.5400 g., 0.9170 Gold 1.4001 oz. AGW, 38.61 mm. **Subject:** 250th Anniversary of Royal Land Grant **Obv:** Crowned bust right, date below **Rev:** Map of islands divides dates and denomination

Date	Mintage	F	VF	XF	Unc	BU
1985 Proof	Est. 250	Value: 950				

KM# 84 250 DOLLARS
47.5400 g., 0.9170 Gold 1.4001 oz. AGW **Subject:** Commonwealth Games **Obv:** Crowned bust right, date below **Rev:** Long jumper, denomination at right

Date	Mintage	F	VF	XF	Unc	BU
1986 Proof	64	Value: 1,100				

KM# 86 250 DOLLARS
47.5400 g., 0.9170 Gold 1.4001 oz. AGW **Subject:** Queen Elizabeth II and Philip's 40th Wedding Anniversary **Obv:** Crowned bust right, denomination below **Rev:** E & P monogram **Rev. Designer:** Norman Sillman

Date	Mintage	F	VF	XF	Unc	BU
ND Proof	75	Value: 1,100				

KM# 99 250 DOLLARS
47.5400 g., 0.9170 Gold 1.4001 oz. AGW **Subject:** Visit of Princess Alexander **Obv:** Crowned bust right, denomination below **Rev:** Royal Arms of Princess Alexandria, date below

Date	Mintage	F	VF	XF	Unc	BU
1988 Proof	86	Value: 1,100				

KM# 107 250 DOLLARS
31.2100 g., 0.9990 Gold 1.0014 oz. AGW **Obv:** Crowned bust right **Rev:** Cameo Winston Churchill above Spitfires over Dover, denomination below **Rev. Designer:** Robert Elderton

Date	Mintage	F	VF	XF	Unc	BU
1990 Proof	Est. 500	Value: 775				

KM# 113 250 DOLLARS
47.5400 g., 0.9170 Gold 1.4013 oz. AGW **Subject:** 40th Anniversary - Coronation of Queen Elizabeth II

Date	Mintage	F	VF	XF	Unc	BU
1993 Proof	Est. 100	Value: 1,100				

KM# 119 250 DOLLARS
47.5400 g., 0.9170 Gold 1.4013 oz. AGW **Subject:** Royal Visit **Obv:** Portrait Queen Elizabeth **Rev:** Royal couple above yacht "Britannia"

Date	Mintage	F	VF	XF	Unc	BU
1994 Proof	200	Value: 1,100				

PIEFORTS

KM#	Date	Mintage	Identification	Issue Price	Mkt Val
P1	1982	74	10 Dollars. Silver. KM72.	250	120

MINT SETS

KM#	Date	Mintage	Identification	Issue Price	Mkt Val
MS1	1987 (4)	—	KM87-90	—	5.00
MS2	1992 (4)	—	KM87a-90a	8.00	8.00
MS3	1996 (4)	—	KM87a-90a	—	12.00

PROOF SETS

KM#	Date	Mintage	Identification	Issue Price	Mkt Val
PS1	1972 (8)	10,757	KM1-8	40.00	25.00
PS2	1973 (8)	9,988	KM1-8	40.00	25.00
PS3	1974 (8)	15,387	KM1-8	40.00	25.00
PS4	1974 (2)	2,400	KM10-11	245	255
PS5	1975 (8)	5,390	KM1-8	54.50	28.00
PS6	1975 (6)	1,785	KM1-6	31.50	10.00
PS7	1975 (2)	3,650	KM12-13	293	295
PS8	1976 (8)	3,044	KM1-8	54.50	30.00
PS9	1976 (2)	1,531	KM12-13	293	295
PS11	1977 (8)	1,970	KM1-8	52.50	35.00
PS12	1977 (6)	2,445	KM12, 16-20	315	310
PS13	1977 (6)	1,932	KM13, 21-25	651	775
PS14	1977 (2)	223	KM14-15	290	275
PS15	1978 (8)	1,303	KM26-33	79.50	60.00
PS16	1978 (6)	5,000	KM36-41	306	270
PS17	1978 (6)	771	KM42-47	600	850
PS18	1979 (8)	4,427	KM1-8	117	50.00
PS19	1980 (8)	1,215	KM1-8	147	45.00
PS20	1980 (10)	—	KM48-57	—	350
PS21	1981 (8)	865	KM1-8	147	50.00
PS22	1982 (8)	589	KM1-7, 70	147	65.00
PS23	1983 (8)	348	KM1-4, 73-76	157	125
PS24	1984 (8)	—	KM1-4, 8, 73-75	159	120
PS25	1986 (8)	330	KM1-4, 7-8, 73-74	150	85.00
PS26	1987 (8)	317	KM85a, 87-93	160	200
PS27	1988 (8)	318	KM87-93, 94.2	170	300
PS28	1990 (4)	500	KM104-107	1,650	1,400

CENTRAL AFRICAN REPUBLIC

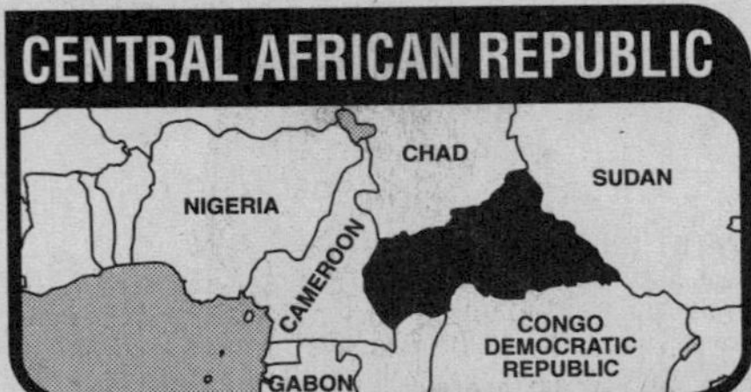

The Central African Republic, a landlocked country in Central Africa, bounded by Chad on the north, Cameroon on the west, Congo (Brazzaville) and Congo Democratic Republic, (formerly Zaire) on the south and the Sudan on the east, has an area of 240,324 sq. mi. (622,984 sq. km.) and a population of 3.2 million. Capital: Bangui. Deposits of uranium, iron ore, manganese and copper remain to be developed. Diamonds, cotton, timber and coffee are exported.

The area that is now the Central African Republic was constituted as the French territory of Ubangi-Shari in 1894. It was united with Chad in 1905 and joined with Middle Congo and Gabon in 1910, becoming one of the four territories of French Equatorial Africa. Upon dissolution of the federation on Dec. 1, 1958, the constituent territories became fully autonomous members of the French Community. Ubangi-Shari proclaimed its complete independence as the Central African Republic on Aug. 13, 1960.

On Jan. 1, 1966, Col. Jean-Bedel Bokassa, Chief of Staff of the Armed Forces, overthrew the government of President David Dacko and assumed power as president of the republic. President Bokassa abolished the constitution of 1959 and dissolved the National Assembly. In 1975 the Congress of the sole political party appointed Bokassa president for life. The republic became a constitutional monarchy on Dec. 4, 1976; President Bokassa was named Emperor Bokassa I. Bokassa was ousted as Central African emperor in a bloodless takeover of the government led by former president David Dacko on Sept. 20, 1979, and the African nation proclaimed once again a republic.

NOTE: For earlier coinage see French Equatorial Africa and Equatorial African States including later coinage as listed in Central African States.

RULERS
French, until 1960
Marshal Jean-Bedel Bokassa, 1976-1979

MINT MARKS
(a) - Paris, privy marks only

MONETARY SYSTEM
100 Centimes = 1 Franc

FIRST REPUBLIC

DECIMAL COINAGE

KM# 6 100 FRANCS
7.0000 g., Nickel, 25,5 mm. **Obv:** Three giant eland left **Obv. Designer:** G.B.L. Bazor **Rev:** Denomination within circle

Date	Mintage	F	VF	XF	Unc	BU
1971(a)	2,500,000	5.00	8.00	13.50	28.00	—
1972(a)	3,500,000	5.00	8.00	13.50	28.00	—

KM# 7 100 FRANCS
7.0000 g., Nickel, 25.5 mm. **Obv:** Three giant eland left **Obv. Designer:** G.B.L. Bazor **Rev:** Denomination, date below, within circle

Date	Mintage	F	VF	XF	Unc	BU
1975(a)	—	4.50	7.50	12.50	22.50	—
1976(a)	—	2.00	3.50	6.00	10.00	—
1979(a)	—	6.00	13.50	20.00	35.00	—
1982(a)	—	2.75	4.50	8.00	15.00	—
1983(a)	—	2.75	4.50	9.00	20.00	—
1984(a)	—	2.50	4.00	7.00	11.50	—
1985(a)	—	2.50	4.00	7.00	11.50	—
1988(a)	—	2.50	4.00	7.00	11.50	—
1990(a)	—	2.00	3.50	6.00	10.00	—
1996(a)	—	2.00	3.50	6.00	10.00	—
1998(a)	—	2.00	3.50	6.00	10.00	—

KM# 1 1000 FRANCS
3.5000 g., 0.9000 Gold .1012 oz. AGW **Subject:** 10th Anniversary of Independence **Obv:** Bust of President Jean Bedel Bokassa facing **Rev:** Three joined shields, radiant sun above center shield, denomination below

Date	Mintage	F	VF	XF	Unc	BU
1970 Proof	4,000	Value: 100				

KM# 2 3000 FRANCS
10.5000 g., 0.9000 Gold .3038 oz. AGW **Subject:** 10th Anniversary of Independence **Rev:** Bust with mortarboard facing, denomination below

Date	Mintage	F	VF	XF	Unc	BU
1970 Proof	4,000	Value: 225				

KM# 3 5000 FRANCS
17.5000 g., 0.9000 Gold .5064 oz. AGW **Subject:** 10th Anniversary of Independence; 1972 Munich Olympics **Obv:** Head left divides dates **Rev:** Wrestlers, date and denomination below

Date	Mintage	F	VF	XF	Unc	BU
1970 Proof	4,000	Value: 375				

KM# 4 10000 FRANCS
35.0000 g., 0.9000 Gold 1.0128 oz. AGW **Subject:** 10th Anniversary of Independence; ONU 24th Anniversary **Obv:** Head left divides dates **Rev:** Map at center, heads above, denomination below

Date	Mintage	F	VF	XF	Unc	BU
1970 Proof	4,000	Value: 745				

KM# 5 20000 FRANCS
70.0000 g., 0.9000 Gold 2.025728 oz. AGW **Subject:** 10th Anniversary of Independence; Operation Bohassa **Obv:** Head of Bokassa left, divides dates **Rev:** Symbols of independence, denomination below

Date	Mintage	F	VF	XF	Unc	BU
1970 Proof	4,000	Value: 1,550				

EMPIRE

DECIMAL COINAGE

KM# 8 100 FRANCS
7.0000 g., Nickel, 25.5 mm. **Obv:** Three giant eland left **Obv. Designer:** G.B.L. Bazor **Rev:** Denomination and date within circle **Rev. Legend:** EMPIRE CENTRAFRICAIN

Date	Mintage	F	VF	XF	Unc	BU
1978(a)	—	40.00	70.00	165	450	800

Note: Although KM8 was never officially released for circulation, examples of this type exhibiting mild to heavy wear have become available in the numismatic market

SECOND REPUBLIC

DECIMAL COINAGE

KM# 11 500 FRANCS
Copper-Nickel

Date	Mintage	F	VF	XF	Unc	BU
1985	—	7.50	15.00	30.00	55.00	—
1986	—	7.50	15.00	30.00	55.00	—

ESSAIS

KM#	Date	Mintage	Identification	Issue Price	Mkt Val
E1	1970	—	1000 Francs. Bronze. KM1.	—	125
E1a	1970	—	1000 Francs. Nickel.	—	125
E2	1971	1,450	100 Francs. Nickel. KM6.	—	25.00
E3	1971	4	100 Francs. Gold. KM6.	—	1,400
E4	1975	1,700	100 Francs. Nickel center. KM7.	—	22.00
E5	1978	1,900	100 Francs. Nickel. KM8.	—	250
E6	1985	1,700	500 Francs. Copper-Nickel. Plants divide date and denomination. Woman's head; 3/4 left. KM11.	—	45.00

PROOF SETS

KM#	Date	Mintage	Identification	Issue Price	Mkt Val
PS1	1970 (5)	40,000	KM1-5	375	3,000

CENTRAL AFRICAN STATES

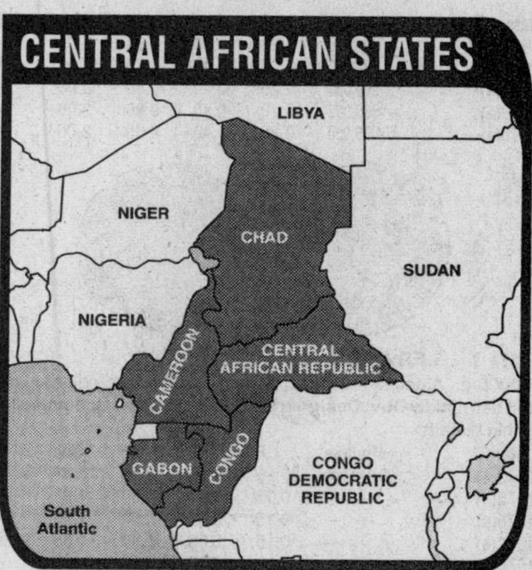

The Central African States, a monetary union comprised of Equatorial Guinea (a former Spanish possession), the former French possessions and now independent states of the Republic of Congo (Brazzaville), Gabon, Central African Republic, Chad and Cameroon, issues a common currency for the member states from a common central bank. The monetary unit, the African Financial Community franc, is tied to and supported by the French franc.

In 1960, an attempt was made to form a union of the newly independent republics of Chad, Congo, Central Africa and Gabon. The proposal was discarded when Chad refused to become a constituent member. The four countries then linked into an Equatorial Customs Unit, to which Cameroon became an associate member in 1961. A more extensive cooperation of the five republics, identified as the Central African Customs and Economic Union, was entered into force at the beginning of 1966.

In 1974 the Central Bank of the Equatorial African States, which had issued coins and paper currency in its own name and with the names of the constituent member nations, changed its name to the Bank of the Central African States. Equatorial Guinea converted to the CFA currency system issuing its first 100 Franc in 1985.

For earlier coinage see French Equatorial Africa.

Country Code Letters

To observe the movement of coinage throughout the states, the country of origin in which the coin is intended to circulate is designated by the following additional code letters:

A = Chad
B = Central African Republic
C = Congo
D = Gabon
E = Cameroon

By 1996 this practice was discontinued as the strategy had proved to be inconclusive.

MONETARY UNION

STANDARD COINAGE

KM# 13 100 FRANCS
Nickel **Obv:** Three giant eland **Rev:** Denomination

Date	Mintage	F	VF	XF	Unc	BU
1992(a)	—	—	—	—	4.50	6.00
1996(a)	—	—	—	—	4.50	6.00
1998(a)	—	—	—	—	4.50	6.00

KM# 8 FRANC
1.3000 g., Aluminum, 23 mm. **Obv:** Three giant eland left, date below **Obv. Designer:** G.B.L. Bazor **Rev:** Denomination within wreath

Date	Mintage	F	VF	XF	Unc	BU
1974(a)	3,000,000	0.30	0.60	1.00	2.50	—
1976(a)	4,000,000	0.30	0.60	1.00	2.50	—
1978(a)	1,100,000	0.20	0.40	0.80	2.00	—
1979(a)	250,000	0.20	0.40	0.80	2.00	—
1982(a)	400,000	0.20	0.40	0.80	2.00	—
1985(a)	300,000	0.20	0.40	0.80	2.00	—

Date	Mintage	F	VF	XF	Unc	BU
1986(a)	300,000	0.20	0.40	0.80	2.00	—
1988(a)	100,000	0.20	0.40	0.80	2.00	—
1990(a)	900,000	0.20	0.40	0.80	2.00	—
1992(a)	300,000	0.20	0.40	0.80	2.00	—
1998(a)	10,000,000	0.20	0.40	0.80	2.00	—

KM# 7 5 FRANCS

3.0000 g., Aluminum-Bronze, 20 mm. **Obv:** Three giant eland left, date below **Obv. Designer:** G.B.L. Bazor **Rev:** Denomination within wreath

Date	Mintage	F	VF	XF	Unc	BU
1973(a)	26,000,000	0.15	0.30	0.60	1.65	—
1975(a)	—	0.15	0.30	0.60	1.65	—
1976(a)	—	0.15	0.30	0.60	1.65	—
1977(a)	—	0.15	0.30	0.60	1.65	—
1978(a)	—	0.15	0.30	0.60	1.65	—
1979(a)	—	0.15	0.30	0.60	1.65	—
1980(a)	—	0.15	0.30	0.60	1.35	—
1981(a)	—	0.15	0.30	0.60	1.35	—
1982(a)	—	0.15	0.30	0.60	1.35	—
1983(a)	—	0.15	0.30	0.60	1.35	—
1984(a)	—	0.15	0.30	0.60	1.35	—
1985(a)	—	0.15	0.30	0.60	1.35	—
1992(a)	—	0.15	0.30	0.60	1.35	—
1996(a)	—	0.15	0.30	0.60	1.25	—
1998(a)	—	0.15	0.30	0.60	1.25	—

KM# 9 10 FRANCS

4.0000 g., Aluminum-Bronze, 23 mm. **Obv:** Three giant eland left, date below **Obv. Designer:** G.B.L. Bazor **Rev:** Denomination within wreath

Date	Mintage	F	VF	XF	Unc	BU
1974(a)	18,500,000	0.20	0.35	0.75	2.00	—
1975(a)	—	0.20	0.35	0.75	2.00	—
1976(a)	—	0.20	0.35	0.75	2.00	—
1977(a)	—	0.20	0.35	0.75	2.00	—
1978(a)	—	0.20	0.35	0.75	2.00	—
1979(a)	—	0.20	0.35	0.75	2.00	—
1980(a)	—	0.20	0.35	0.65	1.35	—
1981(a)	—	0.20	0.35	0.65	1.35	—
1982(a)	—	0.20	0.35	0.65	1.35	—
1983(a)	—	0.20	0.35	0.65	1.35	—
1984(a)	—	0.20	0.35	0.65	1.35	—
1985(a)	—	0.20	0.35	0.65	1.35	—
1992(a)	—	0.20	0.35	0.65	1.35	—
1996(a)	—	0.20	0.35	0.75	1.65	—
1998(a)	—	0.20	0.35	0.75	1.50	—

KM# 10 25 FRANCS

Aluminum-Bronze **Obv:** Three giant eland left, date below **Obv. Designer:** G.B.L. Bazor **Rev:** Denomination within wreath

Date	Mintage	F	VF	XF	Unc	BU
1975(a)	—	0.50	1.00	1.75	3.00	—
1976(a)	—	0.50	1.00	1.50	2.75	—
1978(a)	—	0.50	1.00	1.50	2.75	—
1982(a)	—	0.35	0.75	1.25	2.50	—
1983(a)	—	0.35	0.75	1.25	2.50	—
1984(a)	—	0.35	0.75	1.25	2.50	—
1985(a)	—	0.35	0.75	1.25	2.50	—
1986(a)	—	0.35	0.75	1.25	2.50	—
1988(a)	—	0.35	0.75	1.25	2.50	—
1990(a)	—	0.35	0.75	1.25	2.50	—
1991(a)	—	0.35	0.75	1.25	2.50	—
1992(a)	—	0.35	0.75	1.25	2.50	—
1996(a)	—	0.35	0.75	1.25	2.50	—
1998(a)	—	0.25	0.50	1.00	2.00	—

KM# 11 50 FRANCS

Nickel **Obv:** Three giant eland left, date below **Obv. Designer:** G.B.L. Bazor **Rev:** Denomination within flower design **Note:** Starting in 1996 an extra flora item was added where the mintmark was formerly located.

Date	Mintage	F	VF	XF	Unc	BU
1976(a) A	10,000,000	2.00	3.50	7.50	12.00	—
1976(a) B	Inc. above	2.00	3.50	7.50	12.00	—
1976(a) C	Inc. above	1.00	2.00	4.00	7.00	—
1976(a) D	Inc. above	1.00	2.00	4.00	7.00	—
1976(a) E	Inc. above	1.00	2.00	4.00	7.50	—
1977(a) A	—	2.00	3.50	7.50	12.00	—
1977(a) B	—	2.00	3.50	7.50	12.00	—
1977(a) C	—	1.00	2.00	4.00	7.00	—
1977(a) D	—	1.00	2.00	4.00	7.00	—
1977(a) E	—	1.00	2.00	4.00	7.50	—
1978(a) A	—	2.00	3.50	7.50	12.00	—
1978(a) B	—	2.00	3.50	7.50	12.00	—
1978(a) C	—	1.00	2.00	4.00	7.00	—
1978(a) D	—	1.00	2.00	4.00	7.00	—
1979(a) E	—	1.00	2.00	4.00	7.50	—
1979(a) B	—	1.00	2.00	4.00	7.50	—
1980(a) A	—	1.50	2.75	5.50	11.50	—
1980(a) C	—	0.75	1.50	3.50	6.00	—
1981(a) C	—	0.75	1.50	3.50	6.00	—
1981(a) D	—	0.85	1.75	3.75	6.50	—
1982(a) A	—	1.50	2.75	5.50	11.50	—
1983(a) B	—	0.75	1.50	3.50	6.00	—
1983(a) D	—	0.75	1.50	3.50	6.00	—
1983(a) E	—	0.75	1.50	3.50	6.00	—
1984(a) A	—	1.50	2.75	5.50	11.50	—
1984(a) B	—	1.50	2.75	5.50	11.50	—
1984(a) C	—	0.75	1.50	3.50	6.00	—
1984(a) D	—	0.75	1.50	3.50	6.00	—
1985(a) A	—	1.50	2.75	5.50	11.50	—
1985(a) B	—	1.50	2.75	5.50	11.50	—
1985(a) D	—	0.75	1.50	3.50	6.00	—
1986(a) B	—	1.50	2.75	5.50	11.50	—
1986(a) E	—	0.85	1.75	3.75	6.50	—
1988(a) B	—	1.50	2.75	5.50	11.50	—
1989(a) A	—	1.50	2.75	5.50	11.50	—
1990(a) B	—	1.50	2.75	5.50	11.50	—
1991(a) A	—	1.50	2.75	5.50	11.50	—
1996(a)	—	0.75	1.50	3.50	6.00	—
1998(a)	—	0.75	1.50	3.50	6.00	—

KM# 12 500 FRANCS

9.0000 g., Nickel, 28 mm. **Obv:** Half figure of woman within circle, date lower right **Rev:** Eland head left divides denomination above **Designer:** P. Lambert

Date	Mintage	F	VF	XF	Unc	BU
1976(a) A	4,000,000	5.50	8.50	13.50	22.00	—
1976(a) B	Inc. above	5.50	8.50	13.50	22.00	—
1976(a) C	Inc. above	4.50	8.00	12.50	20.00	—
1976(a) D	Inc. above	4.50	8.00	12.50	20.00	—
1976(a) E	Inc. above	4.50	8.00	12.50	20.00	—
1977(a) A	—	5.50	8.50	15.00	25.00	—
1977(a) B	—	5.50	8.50	15.00	25.00	—
1977(a) C	—	4.50	8.00	12.50	25.00	—
1977(a) D	—	4.50	8.00	12.50	20.00	—
1977(a) E	—	3.00	6.00	10.00	16.50	—
1979(a) D	—	3.50	7.00	12.00	18.50	—
1979(a) B	—	3.50	7.00	12.00	18.50	—
1979(a) E	—	3.50	7.00	12.00	18.50	—
1982(a) D	—	3.50	7.00	12.00	18.50	—
1984(a) A	—	3.50	7.00	12.00	18.50	—
1984(a) B	—	3.50	7.00	12.00	18.50	—
1984(a) C	—	3.50	7.00	12.00	18.50	—
1984(a) E	—	3.50	7.00	12.00	18.50	—

KM# 14 500 FRANCS

11.0000 g., Copper-Nickel, 30 mm. **Obv:** Native woman's head half left **Rev:** Plant divides denomination and date **Edge:** Plain

Date	Mintage	F	VF	XF	Unc	BU
1998(a)	—	—	—	—	16.00	18.00

ESSAIS

Standard metals unless otherwise noted

KM#	Date	Mintage	Identification	Issue Price	Mkt Val
E1	1973(a)	1,550	5 Francs. Aluminum-Bronze. KM7.	—	11.50

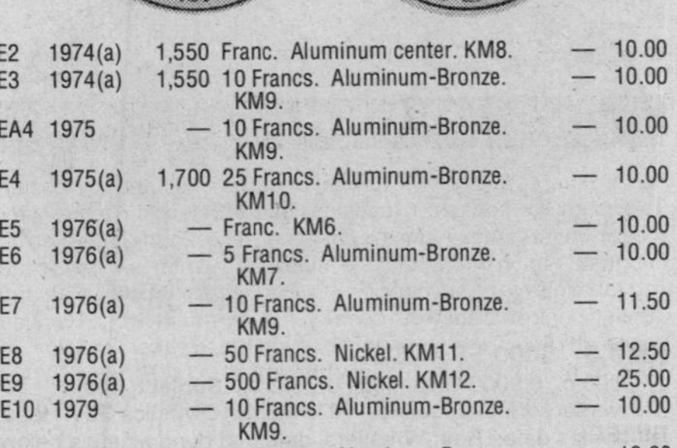

KM#	Date	Mintage	Identification	Issue Price	Mkt Val
E2	1974(a)	1,550	Franc. Aluminum center. KM8.	—	10.00
E3	1974(a)	1,550	10 Francs. Aluminum-Bronze. KM9.	—	10.00
EA4	1975	—	10 Francs. Aluminum-Bronze. KM9.	—	10.00
E4	1975(a)	1,700	25 Francs. Aluminum-Bronze. KM10.	—	10.00
E5	1976(a)	—	Franc. KM6.	—	10.00
E6	1976(a)	—	5 Francs. Aluminum-Bronze. KM7.	—	10.00
E7	1976(a)	—	10 Francs. Aluminum-Bronze. KM9.	—	11.50
E8	1976(a)	—	50 Francs. Nickel. KM11.	—	12.50
E9	1976(a)	—	500 Francs. Nickel. KM12.	—	25.00
E10	1979	—	10 Francs. Aluminum-Bronze. KM9.	—	10.00
E11	1983	—	10 Francs. Aluminum-Bronze. KM9.	—	10.00

PATTERNS

Including off metal strikes

KM#	Date	Mintage	Identification	Issue Price	Mkt Val
Pn1	1956	33	40 Francs. Aluminum-Bronze.	—	375
Pn2	1956	33	40 Francs. Aluminum-Bronze.	—	375
Pn3	1956	33	40 Francs. Aluminum-Bronze.	—	375
Pn4	1956	33	40 Francs. Aluminum-Bronze.	—	375
Pn5	1956	33	40 Francs. Aluminum-Bronze.	—	375
Pn6	1956	33	40 Francs. Aluminum-Bronze.	—	375

CENTRAL ASIA

In the several centuries prior to 1500 which witnessed the breakup of the Mongol Empire and the subsequent rise of smaller successor states, no single power or dynasty was able to control the vast expanses of Western and Central Asia. The region known previously as Transoxiana, the land beyond the Oxus River (modern Amu Darya), became the domain of the Shaybanids, then the Janids. The territory ruled by these dynasties had no set borders, which rather expanded and contracted as the fortunes of the rulers ebbed and flowed. At their greatest extent, the khanate took in parts of what are now northern Iran and Afghanistan, as well as part or all of modern Turkmenistan, Uzbekistan, Kazakhstan, Tadzhikistan and Kyrgyzstan. Coins are known to have been struck by virtually every ruler, but some are quite scarce owing to short reigns or the ever-changing political and economic situation.

MINTS

Asfarayin
Astarabad
Awbah
Badakhshan
Balkh
Bukhara
Heart
Hisar
Marw
Mashhad
Nimruz
Qarshi (copper only)
Qunduz
Samarqand
Tashkent (Tashkand)
Termez
Urdu (camp mint)

BUKHARA

Bukhara, a city and former emirate in southern Russian Turkestan, formed part (Sogdiana) of the Seleucid Empire after the conquest of Alexander the Great and incessantly remained an important region throughout the middle ages, often serving as the capital center for a succession of ruling dynasties of Iranian and Turkish origin until the 19th century. It became virtually a Russian vassal in1868 as a consequence of the Czarist invasion of 1866,following which it gradually became a part of Russian Turkestan and then part of Uzbekistan S.S.R., now Uzbekistan.

RULERS

Russian Vassal,
(since AH1284/1868AD)
Emir Abd al-Ahad,
AH1303-1328 / 1886-1910AD
Emir Sayyid Alim Khan,
AH1329-1339 / 1911-1920AD

MINT NAME

بخاراي شريف بخارا

Bukhara Bukhara-yi Sharif

MONETARY SYSTEM

Until AH1322/1905AD: 45 to 64 Pul (Fulus) = 4 Miri = 1 silver Tenga
19 to 21 Tenga = 1 Tilla (gold 4.55 g.)
Until AH1336-1338/1918-1920AD: copper Tenga or Tenga-fulus

Within the protectorate period, Russian currency of Roubles and Kopeks were officially in circulation: 1 silver Tenga = 20 Kopeks

Note: All copper, bronze and brass issues of Bukhara in the 20th century are anonymous. Some silver and gold issues traditionally bear the names of Emirs long since deceased.

Note: Denominations of 1/32 Tenga & Tilla are of very similar design under various rulers, but can be distinguished by date.

Note: Tilla coins are known with a date appearing as "134-", which is actually 1316 with the "1" and "6" stuck close together, appearing as a Persian "4".

Note: Most copper, bronze and brass AH1336-1338 dated coins of 2, 3, 10 and especially 20 Tenga exhibit considerable flat spots, die shifts and other defects. Well-struck specimens with fully struck design demand a considerable premium.

Note: The numerals "0" and "5" have variant forms in Bukhara, including an open "J" – type symbol for "5" instead of a closed symbol:

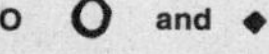 and

5 or instead of ٥ ٥

KHANATE

Emir Abd Al-Ahad
AH1303-1328/1886-1910AD

HAMMERED COINAGE

KM# 67.2 PUL (Fulus)

Copper **Obv:** Inscription and date **Obv. Inscription:** "Bukhara" **Rev:** Denomination and date

Date	Mintage	Good	VG	F	VF	XF
AH1319	—	—	—	—	—	—

KM# 87 1/32 TENGA (2 Fulus)

Copper **Obv:** Inscription and date **Obv. Inscription:** "zarb Bukhara-yi sharif" **Rev:** Inscription and date **Rev. Inscription:** "Fulus 32" **Note:** Large "32" above Fulus indicates the denomination (1/32 Tenga). Varieties exist. Prev. Y#1.

Date	Mintage	Good	VG	F	VF	XF
AH1322	—	10.00	15.00	20.00	30.00	40.00
AH1324	—	10.00	15.00	20.00	30.00	40.00

KM# 86 1/32 TENGA (2 Fulus)

Copper **Obv:** Inscription and date **Obv. Inscription:** "Fulus Bukhara" **Rev:** "32" in 6-petal ornate cartouche **Note:** Varieties exist on round or irregular flans. Size varies 14-17 mm. Large "32" above Fulus indicates the denomination (1/32 Tenga). Prev. #Y4.1.

Date	Mintage	Good	VG	F	VF	XF
AH1322	—	—	5.00	8.50	16.50	25.00
AH1323	—	—	4.00	7.00	12.00	20.00
Note: Coins exist with denomination error "23"						
AH1324	—	—	4.00	7.00	12.00	20.00
AH1327	—	—	6.00	10.00	18.00	30.00
AH1328	—	—	6.00	10.00	18.00	30.00

KM# 63 TENGA

Silver, 11-18 mm. **Note:** Varieties exist. Weight varies 3.06-3.25 grams; size varies. Die varieties exist with and without date on reverse. Struck in the name of late Emir Haydar. Prev. #Y2.

Date	Mintage	Good	VG	F	VF	XF
AH1319	—	—	10.00	15.00	25.00	60.00
AH1319//1308	—	—	30.00	50.00	75.00	100
AH1319//1311	—	—	30.00	50.00	75.00	100
AH1319 Recut 1311	—	—	10.00	20.00	35.00	60.00
AH1320//1319	—	—	10.00	20.00	35.00	60.00
AH1320//1320	—	—	17.50	30.00	50.00	80.00
AH1321//1320 1321 recut from 1320	—	—	10.00	20.00	35.00	60.00
AH1322	—	—	7.50	15.00	27.50	45.00
Note: Doubled flan errors dated AH1322/1322 consisting of two strikes forged together exist, weighing approximately 6.25 grams						

KM# 65 TILLA

4.5500 g., Gold **Note:** Struck in the name of late Ma'sum Ghazi (Emir Shah Murad). Die varieties exist with and without date on reverse. Prev. #Y3.

Date	Mintage	Good	VG	F	VF	XF
AH1319	—	—	95.00	110	135	185
AH1321	—	—	125	165	250	350
AH1322//1322	—	—	95.00	110	135	185
AH1324/1324	—	—	95.00	110	135	185
AH1324//1316	—	—	125	165	250	350
AH1324//1321	—	—	125	165	250	350
AH1325//1325	—	—	95.00	110	135	185
AH1325//1325	—	—	115	155	225	320
Note: Reverse date recut from 1324						
AH1327	—	—	100	135	200	300
AH1328	—	—	100	135	200	300
AH1328//1292	—	—	175	250	350	500
AH1328//1304	—	—	125	165	250	350
AH1328//1321	—	—	175	250	350	500

Emir Sayyid Alim Khan
AH1329-1339/1911-1920AD

HAMMERED COINAGE

KM# A63 1/32 TENGA (2 Fulus)

Copper **Obv. Inscription:** "Fulus Bukhara" **Rev:** "32" in a 6-petal ornate cartouche **Note:** Size varies 12-14 mm. Similar to KM#86. "32" indicates denomination (1/32 Tenga). Numerous die varieties exist including placement of date for 1332 with date inside or below Fulus.

Date	Mintage	Good	VG	F	VF	XF
AH1329	—	—	6.00	12.00	20.00	35.00
AH1330	—	—	4.00	7.00	15.00	22.50
Note: Date appearing as "1335" is actually "1330" with small circle instead of dot for zero						
AH1331	—	—	5.00	8.50	16.50	25.00
AH1332	—	—	4.00	7.00	15.00	22.50
AH1333	—	—	6.00	12.00	20.00	35.00
Note: Exists with denomination errors 21, 201, 22, 31, etc.						
AH13-33 Divided date	—	—	8.00	15.00	25.00	40.00
ND	—	—	12.50	25.00	40.00	75.00

KM# 42 2 FULUS

Copper **Obv:** Inscription and date **Obv. Inscription:** "Fulus Bukhara" **Rev:** "2" in 6-petal ornate cartouche **Note:** Many varieties exist, including placement of date for 1332 and 1333 with date inside or below Fulu. Size varies: 11-14mm. Prev. #Y4.

Date	Mintage	Good	VG	F	VF	XF
AH1330	—	—	15.00	27.50	45.00	70.00
AH1332	—	—	7.50	14.00	22.50	35.00
Note: This date exists with denomination error "6" and with "2" engraved above "32"						
AH1333	—	—	15.00	20.00	45.00	70.00
AH13-33 Divided date	—	—	20.00	35.00	50.00	75.00
ND	—	—	20.00	35.00	50.00	75.00
Note: With 2 above crescent in circle resembling an Arabic "4"						

KM# 44 4 FULUS

Copper **Obv:** Sanah and date, inscription below **Obv. Inscription:** "Bukhara" **Rev. Inscription:** "Chahar Fulus" **Note:** Size varies: 14-16 mm. Die varieties exist. Prev. #Y5.

Date	Mintage	Good	VG	F	VF	XF
AH1334	—	—	5.00	8.50	16.50	25.00
AH1335	—	—	30.00	50.00	80.00	125

KM# 45 8 FULUS

Copper **Obv:** Inscription, date below double line **Obv. Inscription:** "Bukhara" **Rev. Inscription:** "Hasht Fulus" **Note:** Size varies: 15-18mm. Die varieties exist. Prev. #YA5.

Date	Mintage	Good	VG	F	VF	XF
AH1335	—	—	5.00	8.50	16.50	25.00

KM# A6 1/2 TENGA

Copper, 14 mm. **Obv. Inscription:** Inscription and date in hextagonal frame **Rev:** "zarb Buhkhara" **Rev. Inscription:** "fulus nim tangah" **Note:** Prev. #Y6.

Date	Mintage	Good	VG	F	VF	XF
AH1336	—	—	15.00	30.00	50.00	100

KM# 46.1 TENGA

Copper, 13-16 mm. **Obv:** Inscription and date in dotted circle **Obv. Inscription:** "zarb Bukhara" **Rev. Inscription:** "fulus yak tangah" **Note:** Size varies. Small round or irregular flans, no border. Die varieties exist.

Date	Mintage	Good	VG	F	VF	XF
AH1336	—	—	20.00	35.00	55.00	80.00

KM# 46.2 TENGA

Copper, 17-20 mm. **Obv:** Inscription and date in beaded circle **Obv. Inscription:** "zarb Bukhara" **Rev. Inscription:** "fulus yak tangah" **Note:** Size varies. Large round or irregular flans, irregular flans are scarcer than round flans. Many varieties exist. Prev. #Y6a.

Date	Mintage	Good	VG	F	VF	XF
AH1336	—	—	6.00	12.00	20.00	35.00
AH1337	—	—	6.00	12.00	20.00	35.00
Note: This date exists with 5-rayed (outlined and full), and 6-rayed (outlined) star on obverse						
AH1337	—	—	10.00	17.50	30.00	50.00
Note: Overstruck on 8 Fulus KM#45						
AH1338	—	—	75.00	100	135	185

KM# 47 2 TENGA

Bronze, 22-23 mm. **Obv:** Inscription and date in dotted circle **Obv. Inscription:** "zarb bukhara" **Rev. Inscription:** "fulus du tangah" **Note:** Size varies. Varieties with upright and oblique milled edge exist, both years exist with 5-rayed (outlined and full), and 6-rayed (outlined) star on obverse. Prev. #Y7.

Date	Mintage	Good	VG	F	VF	XF
AH1336	—	—	6.00	12.00	25.00	55.00
AH1337	—	—	6.00	12.00	25.00	55.00

Note: Also exists without star (rare)

KM# 48 3 TENGA

Bronze, 24-26 mm. **Obv:** Inscription and date **Obv. Inscription:** "zarb Bukhara" **Rev. Inscription:** "fulus se tangah" **Note:** Greek meander circle both sides. Varieties with upright and oblique milled edge exist. Size varies. Prev. #Y8.

Date	Mintage	Good	VG	F	VF	XF
AH1336	—	—	6.00	12.00	25.00	50.00
AH1337	—	—	6.00	12.00	25.00	50.00

Note: Exists with 5-rayed outlined and full (whole or broken) star on obverse

Date	Mintage	Good	VG	F	VF	XF
AH1337	—	—	—	—	—	—

Note: Struck on small 23 mm and thin 2 Tenga flan

KM# 49 4 TENGA

Bronze **Obv:** Inscription and date **Obv. Inscription:** "zarb Bukhara" **Rev. Inscription:** "fulus chahar tangah" **Note:** Floral design circle on both sides. Prev. #Y9.

Date	Mintage	Good	VG	F	VF	XF
AH1336 Rare	—	—	—	—	—	—

Note: This denomination was officially announced for circulation, but its production in quantity was reduced as it was considered excessive and economically senseless

KM# 50 5 TENGA

Bronze, 28-30 mm. **Obv:** Inscription and date in almond-shaped inner border **Obv. Inscription:** "zarb Bukhara" **Rev. Inscription:** "fulus panj tangah" **Note:** Greek meander circle on both sides. Varieties exist with upright and oblique milled edge. Size varies. Prev. #Y10.

Date	Mintage	Good	VG	F	VF	XF
AH1336	—	—	25.00	40.00	65.00	100
AH1337	—	—	25.00	40.00	65.00	100

KM# 53 10 TENGA

Brass, 29 mm. **Obv:** Inscription and date **Obv. Inscription:** "zarb Bukhara" **Rev:** Inscription and date **Rev. Inscription:** "yakdah tangah" **Note:** Square frames on both sides vary in size, varieties exist with upright and oblique milled edge. Reverse date varies in position and arrangement (full or divided dates with different combinations). Prev. #Y11.

Date	Mintage	Good	VG	F	VF	XF
AH1337//1337	—	—	8.00	15.00	25.00	40.00

Note: With chain border on both sides

Date	Mintage	Good	VG	F	VF	XF
AH1337//1337	—	—	12.50	22.50	40.00	60.00

Note: With branch border (similar to 20 Tenga) on obverse

Date	Mintage	Good	VG	F	VF	XF
AH1337//1338	—	—	10.00	17.50	32.50	50.00
AH1338//1338	—	—	30.00	45.00	80.00	125

KM# 51.1 20 TENGA

Bronze Or Brass **Obv:** Inscription and date in crescent, 6-pointed circled star above **Obv. Inscription:** "zarb Bukharayi sharif" **Rev:** Inscription and date within 6-pointed star **Rev. Inscription:** "bist tangah" **Note:** Varieties exist with upright and oblique milled edge, obverse date varies in position and arrangement (full or divided dates with different combinations). Prev. KM#51 and #Y12.

Date	Mintage	Good	VG	F	VF	XF
AH1337	—	—	22.50	35.00	50.00	85.00

Note: Dated on both sides

Date	Mintage	Good	VG	F	VF	XF
AH1337	—	—	27.50	45.00	75.00	110

Note: Dated reverse only

KM# 51.2 20 TENGA

Brass, 33 mm. **Obv:** Inscription (mintname in error without second alif) and date in crescent, 6-pointed circled star above **Obv. Inscription:** "zarb Bukhari sharif" **Rev:** Inscription and date within 6-pointed star **Rev. Inscription:** "bist tangah"

Date	Mintage	Good	VG	F	VF	XF
AH1337	—	—	40.00	55.00	80.00	120

Note: Dated on both sides

KM# A65 TILLA

4.5500 g., Gold **Note:** Struck in the name of late Ma'sum Ghazi (Emir Shah Murad).

Date	Mintage	Good	VG	F	VF	XF
AH1329	—	—	95.00	110	135	185
AH1330	—	—	150	250	350	500
AH1331	—	—	120	180	250	350

KHIVA

Khwarezm (Khiva), a historical region, once a great kingdom under the names of Chorasmia, Khwarezm and Gurganj (Urgench), is located in the lower stream and the delta of the Amu Darya River, east of the Caspian Sea and south of the Aral Sea. Russia established relations with Khwarezm (Khiva Khanate) in the 17th century, occupied it in 1873, and annexed it in 1875. Revolution concentrated Russia's preoccupation elsewhere during 1917 and Khiva seized this opportunity to declare its independence. It was able to sustain this status for a scant two years. By 1919 the Soviet regime had reestablished control over the region and extinguished the independent state. In AH1338/1920AD it was proclaimed Khorezm People's Soviet Republic and later became part of the Uzbekistan S.S.R. (Qaraqalpaq Autonomous Republic), now Uzbekistan.

RULERS

Russian Vassals
(since AH1290 / 1873AD)
Sayyid Muhammad Rahim
AH1282-1328 / 1865-910AD
Isfandiyar
AH1328-1336 / 1910-1918AD
Sayyid Abdullah
Normally in AH1337-1338 / 1919-1920AD
Actual ruler – Muhammad Qurban Sardar (Junaid Khan)
AH1334-1338 / 1916-1920AD

MINT NAMES

خوارزم

Khwarezm

دار الاسلام خوارزم

Dar al-Islam Khwarezm

Note: All copper, bronze and brass issues of Khiva (Khorezm, Khwarezm) in the 20th century are anonymous, except the silver Tenga Y#8, which bears the name of a Khan, long since deceased.

MONETARY SYSTEM

24 to 32 Pul (Fulus) = 4 Shahi = 1 silver Tenga
about 20 Tenga = 1 Tilla (gold 4.55 g.)

AH1337-1338 / 1918-1920AD: copper Tenga or Tenga-fulus

Within the protectorate period, Russian currency of Rubles and Kopeks were officially in circulation: 1 silver Tenga was equivalent to 20 Kopeks.

Note: Denomination of Pul are of similar design under various rulers, but can be distinguished by date.
2 ½ & 5 Tenga: Ornamentation, size and design of borders and die rotation vary considerably. Crudely engraved dies with mostly simplified design are known struck on cast flans. Cast specimens exist.

Note: 50, 200 & 1000 Roubles coins with crude inscriptions are modern fantasies.

KHANATE

Sayyid Muhammad Rahim
AH1282-1328 / 1865-1910 AD

HAMMERED COINAGE

Y# 3.1 PUL (Fulus)

Copper **Obv:** Inscription in circle **Obv. Inscription:** "Khwarezm" **Rev:** Inscription, date appears as "3" above "1" or "2" above "2" **Rev. Inscription:** "fulus" **Note:** Oblong or irregular flans.

Date	Mintage	Good	VG	F	VF	XF
AH1322	—	5.00	8.00	20.00	35.00	—
AH1323	—	5.00	8.00	20.00	35.00	—
AH1324	—	5.00	8.00	20.00	35.00	—
AH1325	—	5.00	8.00	20.00	35.00	—
AH1326	—	5.00	8.00	20.00	35.00	—

Isfandiyar
AH1328-1336 / 1910-1918 AD

HAMMERED COINAGE

Y# 3.2 PUL (Fulus)

Copper **Obv:** Inscription in circle **Obv. Inscription:** "Khwarezm" **Rev:** Inscription, date appears as "3" above "1" or "2" above "2" **Rev. Inscription:** "fulus" **Note:** Oblong or irregular flans, similar to Y#3.1.

Date	Mintage	Good	VG	F	VF	XF
AH1328	—	5.00	8.00	20.00	35.00	—
AH1329	—	5.00	8.00	20.00	35.00	—

Sayyid Abdullah and Junaid Khan
AH1337-1338 / 1919-1920 AD

HAMMERED COINAGE

Y# A9.1 TENGA

Copper **Obv:** Inscription and date in dotted or reeded circle **Obv. Inscription:** "zarb Khwarezm" **Rev:** Rising sun and crescent, inscription below **Rev. Inscription:** "fulus bir tangah" **Note:** Size varies: 17-19 mm.

Date	Mintage	Good	VG	F	VF	XF
AH1337	—	—	75.00	120	200	400

Y# A9.2 TENGA

Copper **Obv:** Inscription and date in dotted or reeded circle **Obv. Inscription:** "zarb Khwarezm" **Rev:** No crescent above rising sun **Rev. Inscription:** "fulus bir tangah" **Note:** Die varieties exist with different border patterns and date above or below mint name. Crudely struck specimens with Tajik inscription "fulus yak tangah" (instead of the Uzbek "bir tangah") are modern forgeries. Size varies: 17-19mm.

Date	Mintage	Good	VG	F	VF	XF
AH1337	—	—	60.00	100	150	250

Y# 8 TENGA

2.2800 g., Silver **Note:** Struck in the name of Sayyid Muhammad Rahim; die varieties exist.

Date	Mintage	Good	VG	F	VF	XF
AH1337//1337	—	—	250	400	600	850

Note: The estimated number known to exist does not exceed 20 pieces

Y# 9.1 2-1/2 TENGA

Copper Or Bronze **Obv:** Inscription and date **Obv. Inscription:** "zarb Dar al-Islam Khwarezm" **Rev:** Rising sun and crescent, inscription below **Rev. Inscription:** "fulus iki yarim tangah" **Note:** Die varieties exist. Number of sun rays vary from 7 to 13. Date above mint name and strikes with additional date on reverse exist.

Date	Mintage	Good	VG	F	VF	XF
AH1337	—	—	30.00	45.00	75.00	120

Y# 9.2 2-1/2 TENGA

Bronze Or Brass, 20-22 mm. **Obv:** Inscription and date **Obv. Inscription:** "zarb Dar al-Islam Khwarezm" **Rev:** Full sun and crescent, inscription below **Rev. Inscription:** "fulus iki yarim tangah" **Note:** Many die varieties exist. Number of sun rays vary from 8 to 18, date above or below mintname. Strikes with additional date on reverse exist. Size varies.

Date	Mintage	Good	VG	F	VF	XF
AH1337	—	—	30.00	45.00	75.00	120

Note: Rare 1337 strikes over Russian Kopek Y#9.2 are known

Y# 9.3 2-1/2 TENGA

Bronze Or Brass, 20-22 mm. **Obv:** Inscription and date **Obv. Inscription:** "zarb Dar al-Islam Khwarezm" **Rev:** Full sun and crescent, modified inscription below **Rev. Inscription:** "iki yarim tangah fulus" **Note:** Many die varieties exist. Number of sun rays vary from 10-13. Size varies.

Date	Mintage	Good	VG	F	VF	XF
AH1337	—	—	25.00	40.00	70.00	—
Note: Date above or below mint name						
AH1338	—	—	150	250	400	—
Note: Date below mint name						

Y# 10.1 5 TENGA

Copper Or Bronze, 30 mm. **Obv:** Inscription and date **Obv. Inscription:** "zarb Dar al-Islam Khwarezm" **Rev:** Rising sun and crescent, inscription below **Rev. Inscription:** "fulus besh tangah"

Date	Mintage	Good	VG	F	VF	XF
AH1337 Rare	—	—	—	—	—	—

Y# 10.2 5 TENGA

Copper Or Bronze, 29-32 mm. **Obv:** Inscription and date **Obv. Inscription:** "zarb Dar al-Islam Khwarezm" **Rev:** Full sun and crescent, inscription below **Rev. Inscription:** "fulus besh tangah" **Note:** Many die varieties exist. Number of sun rays vary from 9-20, date above or below mint name. Strikes with additional date on reverse exist. Size varies.

Date	Mintage	Good	VG	F	VF	XF
AH1337	—	—	25.00	40.00	70.00	125

Y# 10.3 5 TENGA

Bronze Or Brass, 29-32 mm. **Obv:** Inscription and date **Obv. Inscription:** "zarb Dar al-Islam Khwarezm" **Rev:** Full sun and crescent, modified inscription below **Rev. Inscription:** "besh tangah fulus" **Note:** Many die varieties exist. Number of sun rays vary from 9-18, date appears above or below mint name. Strikes with additional date on reverse exist. Size varies.

Date	Mintage	Good	VG	F	VF	XF
AH1337	—	—	20.00	35.00	60.00	90.00
Note: Rare 1337 strikes over Russian 3 Kopek Y#11.2 are known						
AH1338	—	—	35.00	55.00	80.00	120

Y# 11.1 15 TENGA

Bronze, 28-31 mm. **Obv:** Inscription and date **Obv. Inscription:** "zarb Dar al-Islam Khwarezm" **Rev:** Inscription and date in crescent, 6-pointed circled star above **Rev. Inscription:** "on besh tangah fulus" **Note:** Size varies.

Date	Mintage	Good	VG	F	VF	XF
AH1338	—	—	120	200	350	600
Note: Struck on flans of 5 Tenga with obverse of 5 Tenga; In an attempt to replace 5 Tenga by 15 Tenga due to inflation, flans of 5 Tenga with obverse dies of 5 Tenga were used first; Confusion due to the similar size led to production and usage of special broader flans (see Y#11.2)						

Y# 11.2 15 TENGA

Bronze, 32-34 mm. **Obv. Inscription:** "zarb Dar al-Islam Khwarezm" **Rev:** Inscription and date in crescent, 6-pointed circled star above **Rev. Inscription:** "on besh tangah fulus" **Note:** Struck on broad flans. Strikes with or without date above mint name on obverse exist. Die varieties with different rim patterns on reverse exist. Size varies.

Date	Mintage	Good	VG	F	VF	XF
AH1338	—	—	100	175	250	400

KHOREZM PEOPLE'S SOVIET REPUBLIC

AH1338-1343 / 1920-1924 AD

HAMMERED COINAGE

Y# 15.1 20 ROUBLES

Copper Or Bronze, 25-26 mm. **Obv:** Inscription and date, star above, legend around **Obv. Legend:** "zarb fulus Khwarezm shuralar qarari ilan" **Obv. Inscription:** "yigirma manat" **Rev:** Divided arms above, inscription (in Russian) below **Note:** Die varieties exist. Both dates have 6 points in obverse star. Size varies.

Date	Mintage	Good	VG	F	VF	XF
AH1338	—	—	25.00	40.00	70.00	100
AH1339	—	—	40.00	70.00	100	150

Y# 15.2 20 ROUBLES

Copper Or Bronze, 25-26 mm. **Obv:** Inscription and date, star above, legend around **Obv. Legend:** "zarb fulus Khwarezm shuralar qarari ilan" **Obv. Inscription:** "yigirma manat" **Rev:** Crossed arms above, denomination "20 / RUB" (in Russian) below **Note:** Die varieties exist. Size varies.

Date	Mintage	Good	VG	F	VF	XF
AH1338	—	—	30.00	50.00	80.00	120
Note: 6 points in obverse star						
AH1339	—	—	20.00	35.00	50.00	80.00
Note: Varieties exist with 6 or 8 points in obverse star, with 8 stars much scarcer						

Y# 16.1 25 ROUBLES

Bronze Or Brass, 24-26 mm. **Obv:** Inscription and date above, legend below (starting on the right with "Khwarezm") **Obv. Legend:** "zarb fulus Khwarezm shuralar qarari ilan" **Obv. Inscription:** "yigirma besh manat" **Rev:** Arms in center, crescent and star above, denomination "25 RUBLES" (in Russian) around **Note:** Many die varieties exist with different arms design. Varieties exist with 8, 12, 16 or 18 points in reverse star. The strike with inverted "R" has 12 points in star. Size varies.

Date	Mintage	Good	VG	F	VF	XF
AH1339	—	—	17.50	30.00	40.00	75.00
AH1339	—	—	50.00	70.00	100	175
Note: With inverted Russian "R" in "Rubles"						

Y# 16.2 25 ROUBLES

Bronze Or Brass, 24-26 mm. **Obv:** Inscription and date above, legend below (starting on the right with "shuralar") **Obv. Legend:** "zarb fulus Khwarezm shuralar qarari ilan" **Obv. Inscription:** "yigirma besh manat" **Rev:** Arms in center, crescent and star above, denomination "25 Rubles" (in Russian) around **Note:** Many die varieties exist with different arms design. Varieties exist with 8, 12, 16 or 18 points in reverse star. The strike with inverted "R" has 12 points in star. Size varies.

Date	Mintage	Good	VG	F	VF	XF
AH1339	—	—	17.50	25.00	40.00	70.00
AH1339	—	—	50.00	70.00	100	175
Note: With inverted Russian "R" in "Rubles"						

Y# 17 100 ROUBLES

Bronze, 20-22 mm. **Obv:** Crescent and star in center, inscription and date above, legend below **Obv. Legend:** "zarb fulus Khwarezm shuralar qarari ilan" **Obv. Inscription:** "yuz manat" **Rev:** Denomination "100 Rubles" (in Russian), arms below **Note:** Die varieties exist. Varieties exist with 6 or 8 points in obverse star. Size varies.

Date	Mintage	Good	VG	F	VF	XF
AH1339	—	—	22.50	40.00	60.00	90.00

Y# 18 500 ROUBLES

Bronze, 24 mm. **Obv:** Inscription in center, 12-pointed star and date above, legend around **Obv. Legend:** "zarb fulus Khwarezmjumhuriyeti" **Obv. Inscription:** "500 / besh yuz manat / 500" **Rev:** Arms with two stars above, "Rubles" (in Russian) / "500" below **Note:** Genuine specimens appear like the pictured coin, no die varieties exist.

Date	Mintage	Good	VG	F	VF	XF
AH1339	—	—	100	175	250	350

Y# 19.1 500 ROUBLES

Bronze Or Brass, 18-20 mm. **Obv:** Inscription (in one word) in center, star and divided date above, legend around **Obv. Legend:** "zarb fulus jumhuriyeti Khwarezm" **Obv. Inscription:** "beshyuz manat" **Rev:** Arms with two stars above, "Rubles" (in Russian) / "500" below **Note:** Die varieties exist. Varieties exist with 8 or 17 points in obverse star, the later is much scarcer. Size varies.

Date	Mintage	Good	VG	F	VF	XF
AH1339	—	—	20.00	35.00	50.00	80.00

Y# 19.2 500 ROUBLES

Bronze Or Brass, 18-20 mm. **Obv:** Inscription (in 2 words) in center, star and divided date above, legend around **Obv. Legend:** "zarb fulus jumhuriyeti Khwarezm" **Obv. Inscription:** "besh yuz manat" **Rev:** Arms with two stars above, "Rubles" (in Russian) / "500" below **Note:** Die varieties exist. Two varieties of the arms design exist. Size varies.

Date	Mintage	Good	VG	F	VF	XF
AH1339	—	—	17.50	25.00	40.00	70.00
Note: Varieties exist with 5, 6, 8, 12 or 16 points in obverse star						
AH1340	—	—	22.50	40.00	60.00	90.00
Note: Varieties exist with 5 or 6 points in obverse star						

CEYLON

The earliest known inhabitants of Ceylon, the Veddahs, were subjugated by the Sinhalese from northern India in the 6th century B.C. Sinhalese rule was maintained until 1408, after which the island was controlled by China for 30 years. The Portuguese came to Ceylon in 1505 and maintained control of the coastal area for 150 years. The Dutch supplanted them in 1658, which were in turn supplanted by the British who seized the Dutch colonies in 1796, and made them a Crown Colony in 1802. In 1815, the British conquered the independent Kingdom of Kandy in the central part of the island. Constitutional changes in 1931 and 1946 granted the Ceylonese a measure of autonomy and a parliamentary form of government. Britain granted Ceylon independence as a self-governing state within the British Commonwealth on Feb. 4, 1948. On May 22, 1972, the Ceylonese adopted a new Constitution, which declared Ceylon to be the Republic of Sri Lanka –'Resplendent Island'

RULERS

British, 1796-1948

BRITISH COLONIAL

DECIMAL COINAGE

100 Cents = 1 Rupee

KM# 90 1/4 CENT

Copper **Ruler:** Victoria **Obv:** Head left within circle **Rev:** Tree within circle, date below, denomination above

Date	Mintage	F	VF	XF	Unc	BU
1901	216,000	1.50	3.00	5.00	12.00	—
1901 Proof	—	Value: 125				

KM# 100 1/4 CENT

Copper **Ruler:** Edward VII **Obv:** Crowned bust right **Rev:** Tree within circle, date below, denomination above

Date	Mintage	F	VF	XF	Unc	BU
1904	103,000	2.50	5.00	10.00	22.00	—
1904 Proof	—	Value: 150				

KM# 100a 1/4 CENT

Gold **Ruler:** Edward VII **Obv:** Crowned bust right **Rev:** Tree within circle, date below, denomination above

Date	Mintage	F	VF	XF	Unc	BU
1904	—	Value: 1,000				

KM# 91 1/2 CENT

2.3600 g., Copper, 18.3 mm. **Ruler:** Victoria **Obv:** Head left within circle **Rev:** Tree within circle, date below, denomination above

Date	Mintage	F	VF	XF	Unc	BU
1901	2,020,000	1.25	2.50	4.00	10.00	—

KM# 101 1/2 CENT

Copper **Ruler:** Edward VII **Obv:** Crowned bust right **Rev:** Tree within circle, date below, denomination above

Date	Mintage	F	VF	XF	Unc	BU
1904	2,012,000	1.00	2.00	5.00	12.00	—
1904 Proof	—	Value: 120				
1905	1,000,000	1.50	3.00	6.00	15.00	—
1905 Proof	—	Value: 120				
1906	3,056,000	1.00	2.00	5.00	12.00	—
1906 Proof	—	Value: 120				
1908	1,000,000	1.50	3.00	6.00	15.00	—
1908 Proof	—	Value: 200				

Date	Mintage	F	VF	XF	Unc	BU
1909	3,000,000	1.00	2.00	5.00	12.00	—
1909 Proof	—	Value: 120				

KM# 106 1/2 CENT

Copper **Ruler:** George V **Obv:** Crowned bust left **Rev:** Tree within circle, date below, denomination above

Date	Mintage	F	VF	XF	Unc	BU
1912	5,008,000	1.25	2.75	4.00	10.00	—
1912 Proof	—	Value: 120				
1914	2,000,000	1.25	2.75	6.00	12.00	—
1914 Proof	—	Value: 120				
1917	2,000,000	1.50	3.00	6.00	12.00	—
1917 Proof	—	Value: 120				
1926	5,000,000	0.50	1.00	2.00	5.00	—
1926 Proof	—	Value: 120				

KM# 110 1/2 CENT

Copper **Ruler:** George VI **Obv:** Crowned head left **Rev:** Tree within circle, date below, denomination above

Date	Mintage	F	VF	XF	Unc	BU
1937	3,026,000	0.30	0.85	1.50	3.50	—
1937 Proof	—	Value: 175				
1940	5,080,000	0.25	0.65	1.25	3.00	—

KM# 92 CENT

Copper **Ruler:** Victoria **Obv:** Head left within circle **Rev:** Tree within circle, date below, denomination above

Date	Mintage	F	VF	XF	Unc	BU
1901	1,014,000	2.50	5.00	10.00	22.00	—

KM# 102 CENT

Copper **Ruler:** Edward VII **Obv:** Crowned bust right **Rev:** Tree within circle, date below, denomination above

Date	Mintage	F	VF	XF	Unc	BU
1904	2,529,000	1.00	2.00	4.00	8.00	—
1904 Proof	—	Value: 125				
1905	1,509,000	1.25	2.25	5.00	10.00	—
1905 Proof	—	Value: 125				
1906	1,751,000	1.25	2.25	5.00	10.00	—
1906 Proof	—	Value: 125				
1908	—	1.00	2.00	4.00	8.00	—
1908 Proof	—	Value: 225				
1909	2,500,000	1.00	2.00	4.00	8.00	—
1909 Proof	—	Value: 125				
1910	8,236,000	0.50	1.00	2.50	5.00	—
1910 Proof	—	Value: 125				

KM# 107 CENT

Copper **Ruler:** George V **Obv:** Crowned bust left **Rev:** Tree within circle, date below, denomination above

Date	Mintage	F	VF	XF	Unc	BU
1912	5,855,000	0.50	1.00	2.00	4.00	—
1912 Proof	—	Value: 115				
1914	6,000,000	0.50	1.00	2.25	5.00	—
1914 Proof	—	Value: 115				
1917	1,000,000	1.00	1.75	3.00	8.00	—
1917 Proof	—	Value: 115				
1920	2,000,000	0.50	1.00	2,25	5.00	—
1920 Proof	—	Value: 115				

Date	Mintage	F	VF	XF	Unc	BU
1922	2,930,000	0.50	1.00	2.25	5.00	—
1922 Proof	—	Value: 115				
1923	2,500,000	0.50	1.00	2.25	5.00	—
1923 Proof	—	Value: 115				
1925	7,490,000	0.35	0.75	1.50	3.50	—
1925 Proof	—	Value: 115				
1926	3,750,000	0.35	0.75	1.50	3.50	—
1926 Proof	—	Value: 115				
1928	2,500,000	0.35	0.75	1.50	4.00	—
1928 Proof	—	Value: 115				
1929	5,000,000	0.35	0.75	1.50	3.50	—
1929 Proof	—	Value: 115				

KM# 111 CENT

Copper, 22 mm. **Ruler:** George VI **Obv:** Crowned head left, PM below neck at right **Rev:** Tree within circle, date below, denomination above **Note:** High relief.

Date	Mintage	F	VF	XF	Unc	BU
1937	4,538,000	0.25	0.50	1.25	3.00	—
1937 Proof	—	Value: 100				
1940	10,190,000	0.15	0.30	1.00	2.00	—
1940 Proof	—	Value: 75.00				
1942	20,780,000	0.15	0.30	1.00	2.00	—

KM# 111a CENT

Bronze **Ruler:** George VI **Obv:** Crowned head left **Rev:** Tree within circle, date below, denomination above **Note:** Low relief. Thin planchet.

Date	Mintage	F	VF	XF	Unc	BU
1942	Inc. above	0.15	0.30	0.75	1.75	—
1942 Proof	—	Value: 75.00				
1943	43,705,000	0.15	0.30	0.50	1.00	—
1945	34,100,000	0.15	0.35	0.60	1.20	—
1945 Proof	—	Value: 20.00				

Note: Frozen year 1945, restruck until 1962

KM# 117 2 CENTS

Nickel-Brass **Ruler:** George VI **Obv:** Crowned head left **Rev:** Denomination above date **Shape:** Scalloped

Date	Mintage	F	VF	XF	Unc	BU
1944	30,165,000	0.10	0.25	0.50	1.25	—

KM# 119 2 CENTS

Brass **Ruler:** George VI **Obv:** Crowned head left, legend without EMPEROR OF INDIA **Rev:** Denomination above date **Shape:** Scalloped

Date	Mintage	F	VF	XF	Unc	BU
1951	15,000,000	0.10	0.25	0.75	1.75	—
1951 Proof	150	Value: 20.00				

KM# 124 2 CENTS

Brass **Ruler:** Elizabeth II **Obv:** Laureate bust right **Rev:** Denomination above date **Shape:** Scalloped

Date	Mintage	F	VF	XF	Unc	BU
1955	37,131,000	0.10	0.15	0.25	0.65	—
1957	38,200,000	0.10	0.15	0.25	0.65	—
1957 Proof	—	Value: 75.00				

KM# 103 5 CENTS

Copper-Nickel, 18 mm. **Ruler:** Edward VII **Obv:** Crowned bust right **Rev:** Denomination above date **Shape:** Square

Date	Mintage	F	VF	XF	Unc	BU
1909	2,000,000	1.50	3.00	5.00	17.00	—
1910	4,000,000	1.00	2.00	3.50	12.00	—

KM# 108 5 CENTS

Copper-Nickel, 18 mm. **Ruler:** George V **Obv:** Crowned bust left **Rev:** Denomination above date **Shape:** 4-sided

Date	Mintage	F	VF	XF	Unc	BU
1912 H	4,000,000	0.75	1.50	3.00	10.00	—
1920	6,000,000	0.50	1.00	2.00	7.00	—
1926	3,000,000	0.75	1.50	4.00	12.50	—

KM# 113.1 5 CENTS

Nickel-Brass, 18 mm. **Ruler:** George VI **Obv:** Crowned head left **Rev:** Denomination above date **Shape:** Square

Date	Mintage	F	VF	XF	Unc	BU
1942	12,752,000	0.35	0.75	1.50	4.50	—
1942 Proof	—	Value: 50.00				
1943	Inc. above	0.35	0.75	1.50	4.50	—
1943 Proof	—	Value: 50.00				

KM# 113.2 5 CENTS

Nickel-Brass, 18 mm. **Ruler:** George VI **Obv:** Crowned head left **Rev:** Denomination above date **Note:** Thin planchet.

Date	Mintage	F	VF	XF	Unc	BU
1944	18,064,000	0.20	0.35	0.70	2.00	—
1945	31,192,000	0.15	0.30	0.60	1.75	—
1945 Proof	—	Value: 60.00				

Note: Varieties exist in bust, denomination and legend placement for 1945; The date was frozen at 1945 and these coins were struck until 1962

KM# 120 5 CENTS

Nickel-Brass, 18 mm. **Ruler:** George VI **Obv:** Crowned head left, legend without EMPEROR OF INDIA **Rev:** Denomination above date **Shape:** Square

Date	Mintage	F	VF	XF	Unc	BU
1951 Proof	150	Value: 20.00				
1951 Proof, restrike	—	Value: 12.00				

KM# 97 10 CENTS

1.1664 g., 0.8000 Silver .03 oz. ASW **Ruler:** Edward VII **Obv:** Crowned bust right **Rev:** Plant divides denomination above date

Date	Mintage	F	VF	XF	Unc	BU
1902	1,000,000	1.00	2.75	6.00	20.00	—
1902 Proof	—	Value: 150				
1903	1,000,000	1.00	2.75	6.00	20.00	—
1903 Proof	—	Value: 150				
1907	[illegible]00,000	2.50	5.00	15.00	25.00	—
1908	1,500,000	1.00	2.75	6.00	15.00	—
1909	1,000,000	1.00	2.75	6.00	15.00	—
1910	2,000,000	1.00	2.75	6.00	15.00	—

KM# 104 10 CENTS

1.1664 g., 0.8000 Silver .03 oz. ASW **Ruler:** George V **Obv:** Crowned bust left **Rev:** Plant divides denomination, date below

Date	Mintage	F	VF	XF	Unc	BU
1911	1,000,000	1.00	1.75	5.00	12.00	—
1912	1,000,000	1.25	2.00	6.00	15.00	—
1913	2,000,000	1.00	1.50	4.00	10.00	—
1914	2,000,000	1.00	1.50	4.00	10.00	—
1914 Proof	—	Value: 150				
1917	879,000	1.00	2.50	7.50	17.50	—
1917 Proof	—	Value: 150				

KM# 104a 10 CENTS

1.1664 g., 0.5500 Silver .0206 oz. ASW **Ruler:** George V **Obv:** Crowned bust left **Rev:** Plant divides denomination, date below

Date	Mintage	F	VF	XF	Unc	BU
1919 B	750,000	1.50	3.50	10.00	20.00	—
1919 B Proof	—	Value: 150				
1920 B	3,059,000	1.00	2.50	6.00	15.00	—
1920 B Proof	—	Value: 150				
1921 B	1,583,000	0.75	1.75	5.00	10.00	—
1921 Proof	—	Value: 150				
1922	282,000	1.75	3.50	10.00	25.00	—
1922 Proof	—	Value: 150				
1924	1,508,000	0.75	1.75	4.00	10.00	—
1924 Proof	—	Value: 150				
1925	1,500,000	0.75	1.75	4.00	10.00	—
1925 Proof	—	Value: 150				
1926	1,500,000	0.75	1.75	4.00	10.00	—
1926 Proof	—	Value: 150				
1927	1,500,000	0.75	1.75	4.00	10.00	—
1927 Proof	—	Value: 150				
1928	1,500,000	0.75	1.75	4.00	10.00	—
1928 Proof	—	Value: 150				

KM# 112 10 CENTS

1.1664 g., 0.8000 Silver .03 oz. ASW, 15.5 mm. **Ruler:** George VI **Obv:** Crowned head left **Rev:** Plant divides denomination, date below **Edge:** Reeded

Date	Mintage	F	VF	XF	Unc	BU
1941	16,271,000	0.65	1.00	2.50	6.00	—

KM# 118 10 CENTS

Nickel-Brass, 23 mm. **Ruler:** George VI **Obv:** Crowned head left **Rev:** Denomination above date **Shape:** Scalloped

Date	Mintage	F	VF	XF	Unc	BU
1944	30,500,000	0.25	0.50	1.00	3.00	—
1944 Proof	—	Value: 90.00				

KM# 121 10 CENTS

Nickel-Brass, 23 mm. **Ruler:** George VI **Obv:** Crowned head left, legend without EMPEROR OF INDIA **Rev:** Denomination above date **Shape:** Scalloped

Date	Mintage	F	VF	XF	Unc	BU
1951	34,760,000	0.10	0.20	0.40	1.25	—
1951 Proof	150	Value: 15.00				
1951 Proof, restrike	—	Value: 4.00				

Note: Frozen year 1951; restruck until 1962. Royal Mint strikes (1959-62) differ slightly in the formation of native inscriptions

KM# 98 25 CENTS

2.9160 g., 0.8000 Silver .075 oz. ASW **Ruler:** Edward VII **Obv:** Crowned bust right **Rev:** Plant divides denomination, date below

Date	Mintage	F	VF	XF	Unc	BU
1902	400,000	4.00	8.00	20.00	40.00	—
1902 Proof	—	Value: 150				
1903	400,000	4.00	8.00	20.00	40.00	—
1903 Proof	—	Value: 150				
1907	120,000	7.50	20.00	30.00	50.00	—
1908	400,000	4.00	8.00	15.00	35.00	—
1909	400,000	4.00	8.00	15.00	35.00	—
1910	800,000	2.00	5.00	10.00	20.00	—

KM# 105 25 CENTS

2.9160 g., 0.8000 Silver .075 oz. ASW **Ruler:** George V **Obv:** Crowned bust left **Rev:** Plant divides denomination, date below

Date	Mintage	F	VF	XF	Unc	BU
1911	400,000	3.00	6.00	12.00	30.00	—
1911 Proof	—	Value: 175				
1913	1,200,000	1.50	2.50	7.50	17.50	—
1913 Proof	—	Value: 175				
1914	400,000	3.00	6.00	12.00	25.00	—
1914 Proof	—	Value: 175				
1917	300,000	4.00	8.00	15.00	35.00	—
1917 Proof	—	Value: 175				

KM# 105a 25 CENTS

2.9160 g., 0.5500 Silver .0516 oz. ASW **Ruler:** George V **Obv:** Crowned bust left **Rev:** Plant divides denomination, date below

Date	Mintage	F	VF	XF	Unc	BU
1919 B	1,400,000	1.25	3.00	7.50	15.00	—
1919 B Proof	—	Value: 150				
1920 B	1,600,000	1.25	3.00	7.50	15.00	—
1920 B Proof	—	Value: 150				
1921 B	600,000	3.50	7.50	15.00	30.00	—
1921 B Proof	—	Value: 150				
1922	1,211,000	1.25	3.25	7.50	15.00	—
1922 Proof	—	Value: 150				
1925	1,004,000	1.25	3.50	7.50	15.00	—
1925 Proof	—	Value: 150				
1926	1,000,000	1.25	3.50	7.50	15.00	—
1926 Proof	—	Value: 150				

KM# 115 25 CENTS

Nickel-Brass **Ruler:** George VI **Obv:** Crowned head left **Rev:** Crown at top divides date, denomination below **Note:** Frozen date 1943, restruck until 1951.

Date	Mintage	F	VF	XF	Unc	BU
1943	13,920,000	0.25	0.50	1.00	2.50	—

KM# 122 25 CENTS

Nickel-Brass **Ruler:** George VI **Obv:** Legend without EMPEROR OF INDIA **Rev:** Crown divides date at top, denomination below

Date	Mintage	F	VF	XF	Unc	BU
1951	25,940,000	0.10	0.30	0.60	1.75	—
1951 Proof	150	Value: 20.00				
1951 Proof, restrike	—	Value: 4.00				

Note: Frozen year 1951; restruck until 1962. Royal Mint strikes (1959-62) differ in numerals 9 and 5

KM# 99 50 CENTS

5.8319 g., 0.8000 Silver .15 oz. ASW **Ruler:** Edward VII **Obv:** Crowned bust right **Rev:** Plant divides denomination, date below

Date	Mintage	F	VF	XF	Unc	BU
1902	200,000	5.00	10.00	30.00	70.00	—
1902 Proof	—	Value: 175				
1903	800,000	3.00	8.00	18.00	35.00	—
1903 Proof	—	Value: 175				
1910	200,000	7.00	13.00	30.00	60.00	—

KM# 109 50 CENTS

5.8319 g., 0.8000 Silver .15 oz. ASW **Ruler:** George V **Obv:** Crowned bust left **Rev:** Plant divides denomination, date below

Date	Mintage	F	VF	XF	Unc	BU
1913	400,000	7.00	13.00	30.00	60.00	—
1913 Proof	—	Value: 175				
1914	200,000	5.00	15.00	30.00	60.00	—
1914 Proof	—	Value: 175				
1917	1,073,000	2.50	5.00	10.00	20.00	—
1917 Proof	—	Value: 175				

KM# 109a 50 CENTS

5.8319 g., 0.5500 Silver .1031 oz. ASW **Ruler:** George V **Obv:** Crowned bust left **Rev:** Plant divides denomination, date below

Date	Mintage	F	VF	XF	Unc	BU
1919 B	750,000	1.65	3.50	7.00	16.00	—
1919 B Proof	—	Value: 120				
1920 B	800,000	1.65	3.50	7.00	16.00	—
1920 B Proof	—	Value: 120				
1921 B	800,000	1.65	3.50	7.00	16.00	—
1921 B Proof	—	Value: 120				
1922	1,040,000	1.65	3.50	7.00	16.00	—
1922 Proof	—	Value: 120				
1924	1,010,000	1.65	3.50	7.00	16.00	—
1924 Proof	—	Value: 120				
1925	500,000	2.00	5.00	10.00	20.00	—
1925 Proof	—	Value: 120				
1926	500,000	2.00	5.00	10.00	20.00	—
1926 Proof	—	Value: 120				
1927	500,000	2.00	5.00	10.00	20.00	—
1927 Proof	—	Value: 120				
1928	500,000	2.00	5.00	10.00	20.00	—
1928 Proof	—	Value: 120				
1929	500,000	2.00	5.00	10.00	20.00	—
1929 Proof	—	Value: 120				

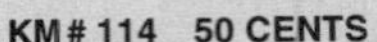

KM# 114 50 CENTS

5.8319 g., 0.8000 Silver .15 oz. ASW **Ruler:** George VI **Obv:** Crowned head left **Rev:** Plant divides denomination, date below

Date	Mintage	F	VF	XF	Unc	BU
1942	662,000	2.50	4.50	9.00	18.50	—

KM# 116 50 CENTS

Nickel-Brass **Ruler:** George VI **Obv:** Crowned head left **Rev:** Crown divides date above denomination **Note:** Frozen date 1943, restruck until 1951.

Date	Mintage	F	VF	XF	Unc	BU
1943	8,600,000	0.35	0.75	1.50	3.50	—

KM# 123 50 CENTS

Nickel-Brass **Ruler:** George VI **Obv:** Crowned head left, legend without EMPEROR OF INDIA **Rev:** Crown divides date above denomination

Date	Mintage	F	VF	XF	Unc	BU
1951	19,980,000	0.20	0.35	0.75	1.75	—
1951 Proof	150	Value: 20.00				
1951 Proof, restrike	—	Value: 5.00				

Note: Frozen year 1951; restruck until 1962. Royal Mint strikes (1959-62) differ slightly in the formation of native inscriptions

BRITISH COMMONWEALTH

DECIMAL COINAGE

100 Cents = 1 Rupee

KM# 125 RUPEE

Copper-Nickel, 28 mm. **Ruler:** Elizabeth II **Subject:** 2,500 Years of Buddhism **Obv:** Date and design at center, denomination at left **Rev:** Temple above 2500, design in background **Rev. Designer:** B. R. Sindall

Date	Mintage	F	VF	XF	Unc	BU
1957	2,000,000	0.50	1.00	2.00	3.00	—
1957 Proof	1,800	Value: 12.00				

KM# 126 5 RUPEES

28.2757 g., 0.9250 Silver .8409 oz. ASW, 39 mm. **Ruler:** Elizabeth II **Subject:** 2,500 Years of Buddhism **Obv:** Flowers and date at center, denomination at left **Rev:** 2500 within inner circle of flower, circle of animals surround, ducks encircle them **Rev. Designer:** B. R. Sindall

Date	Mintage	F	VF	XF	Unc	BU
1957	500,000	11.50	13.50	17.50	30.00	35.00

Note: 258,000 returned in 1962 to be melted at The Royal Mint

Date	Mintage	F	VF	XF	Unc	BU
1957 Proof	1,800	Value: 65.00				

DECIMAL COINAGE

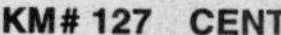

KM# 127 CENT

Aluminum, 16 mm. **Ruler:** Elizabeth II **Obv:** Denomination at center, date below **Rev:** Crowned arms

Date	Mintage	F	VF	XF	Unc	BU
1963	33,000,000	—	—	—	0.10	0.20
1965	12,000,000	—	—	0.10	0.15	0.25
1967	10,000,000	—	—	0.10	0.15	0.25
1968	22,505,000	—	—	—	0.10	0.20
1969	10,000,000	—	—	—	0.10	0.20
1970	15,000,000	—	—	—	0.10	0.20
1971	55,000,000	—	—	—	0.10	0.20
1971 Proof	20,000	Value: 0.50				

KM# 128 2 CENTS

Aluminum, 18.3 mm. **Ruler:** Elizabeth II **Obv:** Denomination at center, date below **Rev:** Crowned arms **Shape:** Scalloped

Date	Mintage	F	VF	XF	Unc	BU
1963	26,000,000	—	—	0.10	0.15	0.25
1965	7,000,000	—	—	0.10	0.15	0.25
1967	15,000,000	—	—	0.10	0.15	0.25
1968	15,000,000	—	—	0.10	0.15	0.25
1970	13,000,000	—	—	0.10	0.15	0.25
1971	45,000,000	—	—	0.10	0.15	0.25
1971 Proof	20,000	Value: 1.00				

KM# 129 5 CENTS

Nickel-Brass, 18 mm. **Ruler:** Elizabeth II **Obv:** Denomination at center, date below **Rev:** Crowned arms **Shape:** 4-sided

Date	Mintage	F	VF	XF	Unc	BU
1963	16,000,000	—	0.10	0.15	0.25	0.35
1965	9,000,000	—	0.10	0.15	0.25	0.35
1968	12,000,000	—	0.10	0.15	0.25	0.35
1969	2,500,000	—	0.10	0.20	0.40	0.60
1970	7,000,000	—	0.10	0.15	0.25	0.35
1971	32,000,000	—	0.10	0.15	0.25	0.35
1971 Proof	20,000	Value: 1.50				

KM# 130 10 CENTS

Nickel-Brass, 23 mm. **Ruler:** Elizabeth II **Obv:** Denomination at center, date below **Rev:** Crowned arms **Shape:** Scalloped

Date	Mintage	F	VF	XF	Unc	BU
1963	14,000,000	—	0.10	0.15	0.25	0.35
1965	3,000,000	—	0.10	0.15	0.35	0.50
1969	6,000,000	—	0.10	0.15	0.25	0.35
1971	29,000,000	—	0.10	0.15	0.20	0.30
1971 Proof	20,000	Value: 1.25				

KM# 131 25 CENTS

Copper-Nickel, 18 mm. **Ruler:** Elizabeth II **Obv:** Denomination at center, date below **Rev:** Crowned arms

Date	Mintage	F	VF	XF	Unc	BU
1963	30,000,000	—	0.10	0.20	0.40	0.55
1965	8,000,000	—	0.10	0.25	0.50	0.65
1971	24,000,000	—	0.10	0.15	0.30	0.45
1971 Proof	20,000	Value: 1.50				

KM# 132 50 CENTS

Copper-Nickel, 21.5 mm. **Ruler:** Elizabeth II **Obv:** Denomination at center, date below **Rev:** Crowned arms

Date	Mintage	F	VF	XF	Unc	BU
1963	15,000,000	0.10	0.20	0.35	0.75	1.00
1965	7,000,000	0.10	0.20	0.35	0.75	1.00
1971	4,000,000	0.25	0.50	0.75	1.50	1.75
1971 Proof	20,000	Value: 2.50				
1972	—	0.25	0.50	0.75	1.50	1.75

KM# 133 RUPEE

Copper-Nickel, 25.3 mm. **Ruler:** Elizabeth II **Obv:** Denomination above date **Rev:** Crowned arms

Date	Mintage	F	VF	XF	Unc	BU
1963	20,000,000	0.10	0.20	0.40	1.00	1.25
1965	5,000,000	0.15	0.25	0.50	1.25	1.50
1969	2,500,000	0.15	0.25	0.50	1.75	2.00
1971	5,000,000	0.15	0.25	0.50	1.50	1.75
1971 Proof	20,000	Value: 4.50				

KM# 134 2 RUPEES

Copper-Nickel **Ruler:** Elizabeth II **Series:** F.A.O. **Obv:** Large denomination above date **Rev:** King Parakramabahu I (1153-1186) between wheat stalks

Date	Mintage	F	VF	XF	Unc	BU
1968	500,000	0.50	1.50	2.25	3.50	5.00

PATTERNS

Including off metal strikes

KM#	Date	Mintage	Identification	Mkt Val
Pn8	1904	—	5 Cents. Copper.	3,500
Pn9	1942	—	Cent. Copper center. 22.4 mm. plain edge. KM#111 struck in Black Bakelite.	500
Pn10	1943	—	50 Cents.	—
Pn11	1965	—	10 Cents. Nickel-Brass. Similar to KM#130, with "TRIAL" in raised letters on obverse and reverse, struck at Birmingham Mint.	—
Pn12	1968	—	5 Cents. Nickel-Brass. Similar to KM#129, with "TRIAL" in raised letters on obverse and reverse, struck at Birmingham Mint.	—

PROOF SETS

KM#	Date	Mintage	Identification	Issue Price	Mkt Val
PS1	1951 (6)	150	KM111a (1945), 119-123 (1951). Restrikes exist.	—	40.00
PS2	1957 (2)	400	KM125-126	—	90.00
PS3	1957 (4)	700	KM125-126, 2 each	—	160
PS4	1971 (7)	20,000	KM127-133	—	12.50

CHAD

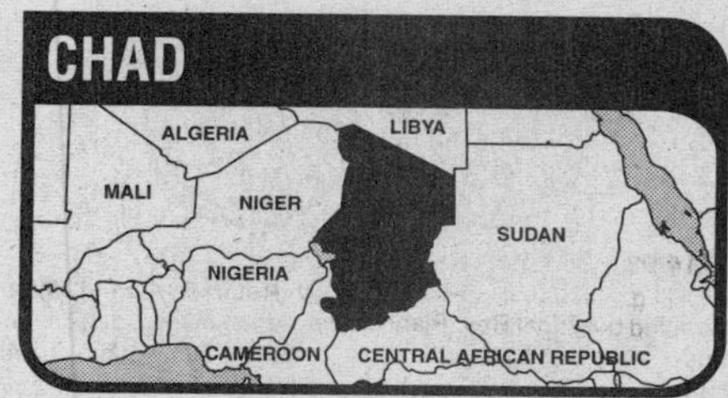

The Republic of Chad, a landlocked country of central Africa, is the largest country of former French Equatorial Africa. It has an area of 495,755 sq. mi. (1,284,000 sq. km.) and a population of *7.27 million. Capital: N'Djamena. An expanding livestock industry produces camels, cattle and sheep. Cotton (the chief product), ivory and palm oil are important exports.

Although supposedly known to Ptolemy, the Chad area was first visited by white men in 1823. Exaggerated estimates of its economic importance led to a race for its possession (1890-93), which resulted in the territory being divided by treaty between Great Britain, France and Germany. As a consequence of World War I, the German area was mandated to France in 1919. Chad was absorbed into the colony of French Equatorial Africa, as part of Ubangi-Shari, in 1910 and became a separate colony in 1920. Upon dissolution of French Equatorial Africa in 1959, the component states became autonomous members of the French Union. Chad became an independent republic on Aug. 11, 1960.

NOTE: For earlier and related coinage see French Equatorial Africa and the Equatorial African States. For later coinage see Central African States.

MINT MARKS

(a) - Paris, privy marks only
(b) = Brussels
NI - Numismatic Italiana, Arezzo, Italy

COMMEMORATIVE EDGE INSCRIPTIONS

1960 LIBERTE PROGRESS SOLIDARITE
1970/REPUBLIQUE DU TCHAD

REPUBLIC

DECIMAL COINAGE

KM# 1 100 FRANCS

5.0000 g., 0.9250 Silver .0957 oz. ASW **Subject:** 10th Anniversary of Independence **Obv:** Map of African continent **Rev:** Robert Francis Kennedy 3/4 right, denomination below

Date	Mintage	F	VF	XF	Unc	BU
1970(b) Proof	975	Value: 75.00				

KM# 2 100 FRANCS

7.0000 g., Nickel, 25.5 mm. **Obv:** Three Giant Eland left **Rev:** Denomination within circle, date below **Designer:** G.B.L. Bazor

Date	Mintage	F	VF	XF	Unc	BU
1971(a)	5,000,000	10.00	17.50	27.50	45.00	—
1972(a)	5,000,000	10.00	17.50	27.50	45.00	—

KM# 3 100 FRANCS

7.0000 g., Nickel, 25.5 mm. **Obv:** Three Giant Eland **Designer:** G.B.L. Bazor

Date	Mintage	F	VF	XF	Unc	BU
1975(a)	—	10.00	15.00	22.00	35.00	—
1978(a)	—	12.00	20.00	28.00	45.00	—
1980(a)	—	10.00	17.50	25.00	40.00	—
1982(a)	—	10.00	15.00	22.00	35.00	—
1984(a)	—	10.00	15.00	22.00	35.00	—
1985(a)	—	10.00	14.00	20.00	30.00	—
1988(a)	—	10.00	14.00	20.00	30.00	—
1990(a)	—	10.00	14.00	20.00	30.00	—
1991(a)	—	—	—	—	—	—

KM# 4 200 FRANCS

15.0000 g., 0.9250 Silver .4461 oz. ASW **Subject:** 10th Anniversary of Independence **Obv:** Map of African continent **Rev:** Martin Luther King Jr. facing divides dates, denomination below

Date	Mintage	F	VF	XF	Unc	BU
1970(b) Proof	952	Value: 150				

KM# 5 200 FRANCS

15.0000 g., 0.8000 Silver .3858 oz. ASW **Subject:** 10th Anniversary of Independence **Obv:** Map of African continent, denomination at left **Rev:** Charles de Gaulle 3/4 right divides dates

Date	Mintage	F	VF	XF	Unc	BU
1970(b) Proof	442	Value: 185				

KM# 6 200 FRANCS

15.0000 g., 0.8000 Silver .3858 oz. ASW **Subject:** 10th Anniversary of Independence **Rev:** Egypt's President Nasser 3/4 facing

Date	Mintage	F	VF	XF	Unc	BU
1970(b) Proof	435	Value: 150				

KM# 7 300 FRANCS

25.0000 g., 0.9250 Silver .8922 oz. ASW **Subject:** 10th Anniversary of Independence **Obv:** Map of African continent **Rev:** John Fitzgerald Kennedy left, Space Shuttle at left, denomination below

Date	Mintage	F	VF	XF	Unc	BU
1970(b) Proof	504	Value: 550				

KM# 13 500 FRANCS

Copper-Nickel **Obv:** Plants divide date and denomination **Rev:** Woman's head 3/4 left

Date	Mintage	F	VF	XF	Unc	BU
1985(a)	—	15.00	22.00	35.00	50.00	—

KM# 17 500 FRANCS

12.0000 g., Silver, 30 mm. **Subject:** Millennium **Obv:** Native portrait right within circle, denomination below **Rev:** Date atop radiant map of Africa

Date	Mintage	F	VF	XF	Unc	BU
2000 Proof	—	Value: 30.00				

KM# 8 1000 FRANCS

3.5000 g., 0.9000 Gold .1012 oz. AGW **Subject:** 10th Anniversary of Independence **Obv:** Nude half figure of woman right, shield of arms above, denomination at right **Rev:** Commandant Lamy 3/4 facing, date below

Date	Mintage	F	VF	XF	Unc	BU
ND(1970)(a)NI Proof	4,000	Value: 185				
ND(1970)NI Proof	Inc. above	Value: 185				

KM# 24 1000 FRANCS

Silver **Rev:** Okapi Johnston

Date	Mintage	F	VF	XF	Unc	BU
1999 Proof	—	Value: 45.00				

KM# 25 1000 FRANCS

Silver **Rev:** Bird of Paradise

Date	Mintage	F	VF	XF	Unc	BU
1999 Proof	—	Value: 45.00				

KM# 26 1000 FRANCS

Silver **Rev:** Giraffe

Date	Mintage	F	VF	XF	Unc	BU
1999 Proof	—	Value: 45.00				

KM# 27 1000 FRANCS

Silver **Rev:** Hippopotamus

Date	Mintage	F	VF	XF	Unc	BU
ND Proof	—	Value: 55.00				

KM# 16 1000 FRANCS

14.9700 g., 0.9850 Silver 0.4741 oz. ASW, 34 mm. **Obv:** Native portrait right within circle, denomination below **Rev:** Portrait of Galileo **Edge:** Plain

Date	Mintage	F	VF	XF	Unc	BU
1999 Proof	—	Value: 30.00				

KM# 9 3000 FRANCS

10.5000 g., 0.9000 Gold .3038 oz. AGW **Subject:** 10th Anniversary of Independence **Obv:** Shield of arms above map, denomination below, right **Rev:** Governor Eboue 3/4 left, date below

Date	Mintage	F	VF	XF	Unc	BU
ND(1970)(a)NI	4,000	Value: 240				
ND(1970)NI	Inc. above	Value: 240				

KM# 10 5000 FRANCS

17.5000 g., 0.9000 Gold .5064 oz. AGW **Subject:** 10th Anniversary of Independence **Obv:** Trees divide arch and arms, denomination below **Rev:** General Leclerc 3/4 facing, date below

Date	Mintage	F	VF	XF	Unc	BU
ND(1970)(a)NI Proof	4,000	Value: 350				
ND(1970)NI Proof	Inc. above	Value: 350				

KM# 11 10000 FRANCS

36.0000 g., 0.9000 Gold 1.0128 oz. AGW **Subject:** 10th Anniversary of Independence **Obv:** Arms above double cross, denomination below **Rev:** General Charles de Gaulle right, date below **Rev. Designer:** G. Simon

Date	Mintage	F	VF	XF	Unc	BU
ND(1970)(a)NI Proof	4,000	Value: 750				
ND (1970)NI Proof	Inc. above	Value: 750				

KM# 14 10000 FRANCS

36.0000 g., 0.9000 Gold 1.0128 oz. AGW **Subject:** 10th Anniversary of Independence **Obv:** Map of African continent, denomination at left **Rev:** Egypt's President Nasser facing

Date	Mintage	F	VF	XF	Unc	BU
1970(b) Proof	205	Value: 1,175				

KM# 15 10000 FRANCS

36.0000 g., 0.9000 Gold 1.0128 oz. AGW **Subject:** 10th Anniversary of Independence **Obv:** Map of Africa **Rev:** Charles de Gaulle facing

Date	Mintage	F	VF	XF	Unc	BU
1970 Proof	90	Value: 1,350				

KM# 12 20000 FRANCS

70.0000 g., 0.9000 Gold 2.0257 oz. AGW **Subject:** 10th Anniversary of Independence **Obv:** Francois Tombalbaye, left, date lower right **Rev. Designer:** G. Simon

Date	Mintage	F	VF	XF	Unc	BU
ND (1970)(a)NI Proof	Est. 4,000	Value: 1,600				
ND (1970)NI Proof	Inc. above	Value: 1,600				

ESSAIS

Standard metals unless otherwise noted

KM#	Date	Mintage	Identification	Issue Price	Mkt Val
E1	1970(a)	—	10000 Francs. Copper-Nickel-Aluminum. Arms above double cross, denomination below. Head of de Gaulle right, date below. KM#11.	—	150

KM#	Date	Mintage	Identification	Issue Price	Mkt Val
E3	1971(a)	1,400	100 Francs. Nickel. Three Giant Eland left. Denomination within circle, date below. KM#2.	—	23.50
E4	1971	4	100 Francs. Gold. KM#2.	—	1,500
E5	1975(a)	1,700	100 Francs. Nickel. KM#3.	—	22.50

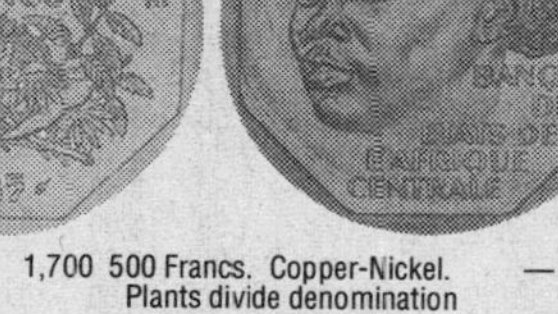

KM#	Date	Mintage	Identification	Issue Price	Mkt Val
E6	1985(a)	1,700	500 Francs. Copper-Nickel. Plants divide denomination and date. Woman's head 3/4 left. KM#13.	—	85.00

PROOF SETS

KM#	Date	Mintage	Identification	Issue Price	Mkt Val
PS1	1970 (5)	4,000	KM8-12	413	3,125
PS2	1970 (3)	—	KM1, 4, 7	33.00	775

CHILE

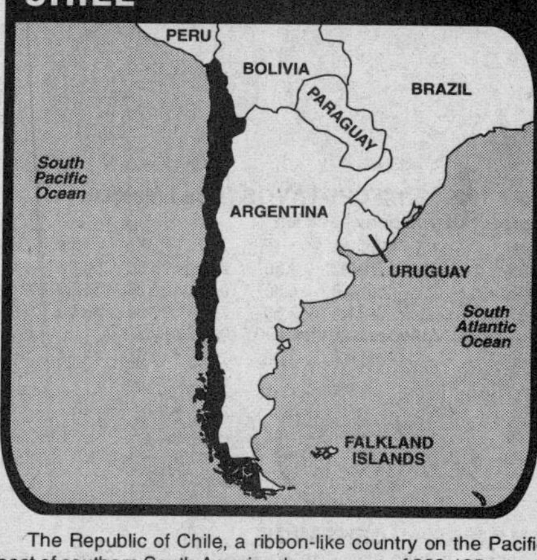

The Republic of Chile, a ribbon-like country on the Pacific coast of southern South America, has an area of 292,135 sq. mi. (756,950 sq. km.) and a population of *15.21 million. Capital: Santiago. Historically, the economic base of Chile has been the rich mineral deposits of its northern provinces. Copper has accounted for more than 75 percent of Chile's export earnings in recent years. Other important mineral exports are iron ore, iodine and nitrate of soda. Fresh fruits and vegetables, as well as wine are increasingly significant in inter-hemispheric trade.

Diego de Almargo was the first Spaniard to attempt to wrest Chile from the Incas and Araucanian tribes in 1536. He failed, and was followed by Pedro de Valdivia, a favorite of Pizarro, who founded Santiago in 1541. When the Napoleonic Wars involved Spain, leaving the constituent parts of the Spanish Empire to their own devices, Chilean patriots formed a national government and proclaimed the country's independence, Sept. 18, 1810. Independence however, was not secured until Feb. 12, 1818, after a bitter struggle led by Bernardo O'Higgins and San Martin. Despite a long steady history of monetary devaluation, reflected in declining weight and fineness in its currency, Chile developed a strong democracy. This was displaced when rampant inflation characterized chaotic and subsequently repressive governments in the mid to late 20th century.

RULERS

Spanish until 1818 .

MINT MARKS

So - Santiago

MONETARY SYSTEM

16 Reales = 1 Escudo

REPUBLIC

DECIMAL COINAGE

KM# 161 CENTAVO

Copper **Obv:** Liberty head left **Rev:** Denomination within wreath, date below

Date	Mintage	F	VF	XF	Unc	BU
1904	970,000	0.75	1.50	3.00	8.00	—
1908	174,000	1.50	3.00	9.00	16.00	—
1991 Rare	—	—	—	—	—	—
Note: Error for 1919						
1919	173,000	1.25	2.50	8.50	15.00	—

KM# 164 2 CENTAVOS

Copper **Obv:** Liberty head left **Rev:** Denomination within wreath, date below

Date	Mintage	F	VF	XF	Unc	BU
1919	147,000	1.50	3.00	6.00	17.50	—

KM# 162 2-1/2 CENTAVOS (Dos I Medio)

Copper **Obv:** Liberty head left

Date	Mintage	F	VF	XF	Unc	BU
1904	277,000	3.50	7.50	20.00	50.00	—
1906	161,000	4.50	10.00	22.00	55.00	—
1907	262,000	3.50	7.50	20.00	45.00	—

Note: Varieties exist for 1907 dated coins

Date	Mintage	F	VF	XF	Unc	BU
1908	201,000	3.00	7.00	19.00	45.00	—

KM# 155.2 5 CENTAVOS

1.0000 g., 0.5000 Silver .0160 oz. ASW, 14 mm. **Obv:** Defiant Condor on rock left, 0.5 below condor **Obv. Designer:** O. Roty **Rev:** Denomination above date within wreath **Note:** Varieties exist with 0.5, 0.5., 0/5.5., 0,5 or 05. below condor.

Date	Mintage	F	VF	XF	Unc	BU
1901/801	2,109,000	3.00	6.00	15.00	32.50	—

Note: With 05.

Date	Mintage	F	VF	XF	Unc	BU
1901/891	Inc. above	3.00	6.00	15.00	32.50	—
1901/896	Inc. above	3.00	6.00	15.00	32.50	—
1904/891/9	—	3.50	7.50	15.00	37.50	—
1904/894	2,527,000	3.50	7.50	15.00	37.50	—
1904/1	Inc. above	3.50	7.00	15.00	37.50	—

Note: With 0.5

Date	Mintage	F	VF	XF	Unc	BU
1904	Inc. above	2.00	5.00	10.00	27.50	—

Note: With 05.

Date	Mintage	F	VF	XF	Unc	BU
1906/4	713,000	5.00	10.00	25.00	45.00	—
1906	Inc. above	2.00	5.00	10.00	27.50	—
1907	2,791,000	2.00	3.00	8.00	22.50	—

Note: Exists with both 0.5 and 0.5. obverse varieties

Date	Mintage	F	VF	XF	Unc	BU
1907.	Inc. above	2.00	3.00	8.00	22.50	—
1909/899	—	2.50	5.00	12.00	27.50	—

KM# 155.2a 5 CENTAVOS

1.0000 g., 0.4000 Silver .0128 oz. ASW **Obv:** Defiant Condor on rock left **Obv. Designer:** O. Roty **Rev:** Denomination above date within wreath **Note:** Without fineness below condor.

Date	Mintage	F	VF	XF	Unc	BU
1908/1	—	2.50	5.00	10.00	22.50	—
1908/2	—	2.50	5.00	10.00	22.50	—
1908	3,642,000	2.00	3.00	7.00	18.00	—
1909/1	1,177,000	2.00	4.00	9.00	20.00	—
1909/2	—	2.00	4.00	9.00	20.00	—
1909/8	Inc. above	2.00	4.00	9.00	20.00	—
1909	Inc. above	2.00	5.00	9.00	20.00	—
1910/01	1,587,000	2.00	3.00	7.00	18.00	—
1910	Inc. above	2.00	3.00	7.00	18.00	—
1911	847,000	2.00	4.00	9.00	20.00	—
1913/1	—	2.50	5.00	10.00	22.50	—
1913/2	2,573,000	3.00	7.00	15.00	35.00	—

Note: Varieties exist with a dot below 1 in date for 1913

Date	Mintage	F	VF	XF	Unc	BU
1913	Inc. above	2.00	3.00	7.00	18.00	—

Note: Varieties exist with a dot below 1 in date for 1913

Date	Mintage	F	VF	XF	Unc	BU
1919	Inc. below	1.50	3.00	7.00	18.00	—

Note: With and without dash below second 9 in date

KM# 155.3 5 CENTAVOS

1.0000 g., 0.4500 Silver .0144 oz. ASW **Obv:** Defiant Condor on rock left, 0.45 below condor **Obv. Designer:** O. Roty **Rev:** Denomination above date within wreath

Date	Mintage	F	VF	XF	Unc	BU
1915/1	—	1.50	3.50	6.00	16.50	—
1915	2,250,000	1.50	3.00	5.00	15.00	—

Note: 1915 exists with flat and curved top on 5

Date	Mintage	F	VF	XF	Unc	BU
1916/1	4,337,000	1.50	3.50	6.00	16.50	—
1916/5	Inc. above	1.50	3.50	6.00	16.50	—
1916	Inc. above	1.50	3.00	5.00	15.00	—
1919/1	1,494,000	3.00	7.00	15.00	35.00	—

Note: With dash below second 9 in date

Date	Mintage	F	VF	XF	Unc	BU
1919/2	Inc. above	2.00	4.00	8.00	22.50	—
1919/5	Inc. above	2.00	4.00	8.00	22.50	—
1919	Inc. above	3.00	5.00	10.00	22.50	—

KM# 165 5 CENTAVOS

Copper-Nickel **Obv:** Defiant Condor on rock left, without designer's name O. ROTY at bottom **Obv. Designer:** O. Roty **Rev:** Denomination above date within wreath **Note:** Varieties exist.

Date	Mintage	F	VF	XF	Unc	BU
1920	718,000	1.00	1.50	3.00	12.00	—
1921	2,406,000	0.60	1.25	2.00	7.00	—
1922	3,872,000	0.60	1.25	2.00	7.00	—
1923	2,150,000	0.60	1.25	2.00	7.00	—
1925	994,000	0.60	1.25	2.00	7.00	—

Note: Obverse variety known with dot to left of right wing tip.

Date	Mintage	F	VF	XF	Unc	BU
1926	594,000	1.50	2.50	3.00	9.00	—
1927	1,276,000	0.50	1.00	2.00	6.00	—
1928	5,197,000	0.50	1.00	2.00	6.00	—
1933	3,000,000	5.00	10.00	25.00	55.00	—
1934	Inc. above	0.25	0.50	1.00	3.00	—
1936	2,000,000	0.25	0.50	1.00	3.00	—
1937	2,000,000	0.25	0.50	1.00	3.00	—
1938	2,000,000	0.25	0.50	1.00	3.00	—

KM# 156.2 10 CENTAVOS

2.0000 g., 0.5000 Silver .0321 oz. ASW, 17 mm. **Obv:** Defiant Condor on rock left, 0.5 below condor **Obv. Designer:** O. Roty **Rev:** Denomination above date within wreath **Note:** Obverse varieties exist with 0.5, 0,5, 0.5. or 0.5/9 below condor. Struck by law of January 19, 1899.

Date	Mintage	F	VF	XF	Unc	BU
1901/891	Inc. above	17.50	30.00	55.00	150	—
1901/896	—	17.50	30.00	55.00	150	—
1904/896	—	2.00	3.50	7.00	16.50	—
1904/899	779,000	2.00	3.50	7.00	16.50	—
1906	139,000	2.50	4.50	8.50	18.00	—
1907/807	—	2.50	4.50	8.50	18.00	—
1907/2	—	2.50	4.50	8.50	18.00	—
1907	3,151,000	2.00	3.50	7.00	16.50	—

Note: Exists with both 0.5 and 0.5. obverse varieties

KM# 156.2a 10 CENTAVOS

1.5000 g., 0.4000 Silver .0192 oz. ASW **Obv:** Defiant Condor on rock left **Obv. Designer:** O. Roty **Rev:** Denomination above date within wreath **Note:** Varities exist.

Date	Mintage	F	VF	XF	Unc	BU
1908/1	—	1.50	3.00	6.00	15.00	—
1908	4,149,000	1.00	2.00	4.50	12.00	—
1908/inverted 6	—	1.50	3.00	6.00	15.00	—
1909/8	2,964,000	1.50	3.00	6.00	15.00	—
1909	Inc. above	1.00	2.00	4.50	12.00	—
1913	1,269,000	1.50	3.00	6.00	15.00	—
1919/8	—	3.00	6.00	12.00	25.00	—
1919	883,000	2.50	5.00	10.00	20.00	—
1920/5	—	1.50	3.00	6.00	18.00	—
1920	2,109,000	1.00	2.00	4.50	12.00	—

KM# 156.3 10 CENTAVOS

1.5000 g., 0.4500 Silver .0217 oz. ASW **Obv:** Defiant Condor on rock left, 0.45 below condor **Obv. Designer:** O. Roty **Rev:** Denomination above date within wreath

Date	Mintage	F	VF	XF	Unc	BU
1915	1,620,000	1.00	1.50	3.00	7.50	—
1916	2,855,000	1.00	1.50	3.00	7.50	—
1917/1	—	2.00	3.50	7.00	18.00	—
1917	736,000	1.50	2.50	5.00	14.00	—
1918/5	—	2.00	3.50	7.00	18.00	—
1918	Inc. above	1.50	2.50	5.00	14.00	—
1919/3	—	2.00	3.50	7.00	18.00	—

KM# 166 10 CENTAVOS

Copper-Nickel **Obv:** Defiant Condor on rock left, without designer's name O. ROTY at bottom **Obv. Designer:** O. Roty **Rev:** Denomination above date within wreath **Edge:** Plain

Date	Mintage	F	VF	XF	Unc	BU
1920	451,000	1.50	3.50	7.00	15.00	—
1921	2,654,000	0.50	0.75	1.50	3.00	—
1922	4,017,000	0.50	0.75	1.50	3.00	—
1923	3,356,000	0.50	0.75	7.00	16.50	—
1924	1,445,000	0.50	0.75	1.50	3.00	—
1925	2,665,000	0.50	0.75	1.50	3.00	—
1927	523,000	1.00	2.00	3.50	7.00	—
1928	3,052,000	0.50	0.75	1.50	3.00	—
1932	1,500,000	1.00	2.00	3.50	7.00	—
1933/2	5,800,000	0.75	1.00	2.00	4.00	—
1933 Over reversed 3	—	0.50	1.00	2.00	5.00	—
1933	Inc. above	0.25	0.50	1.00	2.00	—
1934	900,000	0.50	0.75	1.50	3.00	—
1935	1,500,000	0.50	0.75	1.50	3.00	—
1936	3,300,000	0.25	0.50	1.00	2.00	—
1937 Over reversed 3	—	0.50	1.00	2.00	5.00	—
1937	2,000,000	0.25	0.50	1.00	2.00	—
1938 Over reversed 3	—	0.50	1.00	2.00	5.00	—
1938	5,000,000	0.25	0.50	1.00	2.00	—
1939 Over reversed 3	—	0.50	1.00	2.00	5.00	—
1939	1,200,000	0.25	0.50	1.00	2.00	—
1940	6,100,000	0.25	0.50	1.00	2.00	—
1941	900,000	1.00	2.00	3.00	6.00	—

KM# 151.2 20 CENTAVOS

4.0000 g., 0.5000 Silver .0643 oz. ASW, 21.5 mm. **Obv:** Defiant Condor on rock left, 0.5 below condor **Obv. Designer:** O. Roty **Rev:** Denomination above date within wreath **Note:** Obverse varieties with 0.5 or 0.5. exist. Issued by law of January 19, 1899.

Date	Mintage	F	VF	XF	Unc	BU
1906/806	—	2.50	6.00	12.00	25.00	—
1906/896	866,000	2.50	6.00	12.00	25.00	—
1906	Inc. above	2.00	5.00	10.00	20.00	—
1907/807	—	2.00	5.00	10.00	20.00	—
1907/895	7,625,000	2.00	5.00	10.00	20.00	—
1907	Inc. above	1.50	4.00	10.00	20.00	—

KM# 151.3 20 CENTAVOS

3.0000 g., 0.4000 Silver .0385 oz. ASW **Obv:** Defiant Condor on rock left, without 0.5 below condor **Obv. Designer:** O. Roty **Rev:** Denomination above date within wreath

Date	Mintage	F	VF	XF	Unc	BU
1907/807	—	1.50	3.50	8.00	16.50	—
1907	1,201,000	1.00	3.00	7.00	15.00	—
1908/808	—	1.50	3.50	8.00	16.50	—
1908	5,869,000	0.85	3.00	6.00	12.50	—
1909	1,080,000	0.85	3.00	6.00	12.50	—
1913/1	3,507,000	1.00	4.00	8.00	20.00	—
1913/50	Inc. above	1.00	4.00	8.00	20.00	—
1913	Inc. above	1.50	4.00	8.00	20.00	—
1919	3,749,000	0.85	3.00	6.00	12.50	—
1920	4,189,000	0.85	3.00	6.00	12.50	—

KM# 151.4 20 CENTAVOS

3.0000 g., 0.4500 Silver .0434 oz. ASW **Obv:** Defiant Condor on rock left, 0.45 below condors wing, O'Roty at bottom **Obv. Designer:** O. Roty **Rev:** Denomination above date within wreath

Date	Mintage	F	VF	XF	Unc	BU
1916	3,377,000	2.00	4.00	8.00	20.00	—

KM# 167.1 20 CENTAVOS
Copper-Nickel **Obv:** Without designer's name O. ROTY at bottom **Rev:** Denomination and date within wreath, large numeral **Edge:** Plain

Date	Mintage	F	VF	XF	Unc	BU
1920	499,000	1.00	2.50	5.50	15.00	—
1921	6,547,000	0.35	1.00	3.00	7.00	—
1922	8,261,000	0.35	1.00	3.00	7.00	—
1923	5,439,000	0.35	1.00	3.00	7.00	—
1924	6,096,000	0.35	1.00	3.00	7.00	—
1925	9,830,000	0.35	1.00	3.00	7.00	—
Note: Varieties exist with dot under 5 in date for 1925						
1929	9,685,000	0.35	1.00	3.00	7.00	—

KM# 167.3 20 CENTAVOS
Copper-Nickel **Obv:** Defiant Condor on rock left, with designer's name O. ROTY at bottom **Rev:** Denomination above date within wreath

Date	Mintage	F	VF	XF	Unc	BU
1932 Over reversed 3	—	0.50	1.00	2.00	6.50	—
1932	—	0.35	0.75	1.25	5.00	—
1933 Over reversed 3X	—	1.00	1.50	2.50	7.00	—
1933/ Reversed 33	1,000,000	1.00	1.50	2.50	7.00	—
1933	Inc. above	0.35	0.75	1.25	5.00	—
1937 Over reversed 3	—	1.00	1.50	2.50	7.00	—
1937	—	0.35	0.75	1.25	5.00	—
1938	3,043,000	0.35	0.75	1.25	5.00	—
1939 3/reversed 3	5,283,000	1.00	1.50	2.50	7.00	—
1939	Inc. above	0.35	0.75	1.25	3.50	—
1940	9,300,000	0.35	0.75	1.25	3.00	—
1941	3,000,000	0.35	0.75	1.25	3.50	—

KM# 167.4 20 CENTAVOS
Copper-Nickel **Obv:** With designer's name O. ROTY at bottom **Rev:** Denomination and date within wreath

Date	Mintage	F	VF	XF	Unc	BU
1929	Inc. above	1.00	2.50	5.00	10.00	—

KM# 167.2 20 CENTAVOS
Copper-Nickel **Obv:** Without designer's name **Rev:** Denomination and date within wreath, small numeral

Date	Mintage	F	VF	XF	Unc	BU
1932	—	0.50	1.00	2.00	6.00	—
1932 Over reversed 3	—	0.75	1.50	3.00	8.00	—
1933 Over reversed 3X	—	0.50	1.00	2.00	5.00	—
1933/ Reversed 33	59,000,000	0.50	1.00	2.00	5.00	—
1933	Inc. above	0.35	0.75	1.25	3.50	—

KM# 177 20 CENTAVOS
Copper **Obv:** Armored bust of General Bernardo O'Higgins, right, Thenot on truncation **Rev:** Denomination above date

Date	Mintage	F	VF	XF	Unc	BU
1942	30,000,000	0.15	0.25	1.00	4.00	—
1943	396,000,000	0.15	0.25	1.00	4.00	—
1944	29,100,000	0.15	0.25	1.00	4.00	—
1945	11,400,000	0.15	0.25	1.00	4.00	—
1946	13,800,000	0.15	0.25	1.00	4.00	—
1947	15,700,000	0.15	0.25	1.00	4.00	—
1948	15,200,000	0.15	0.25	1.00	4.00	—
1949	14,700,000	0.15	0.25	1.00	4.00	—
1950	15,200,000	0.15	0.25	1.00	4.00	—
1951	14,700,000	0.15	0.25	1.00	4.00	—
1952	15,500,000	0.15	0.25	1.00	4.00	—
1953	7,800,000	0.15	0.25	1.00	4.00	—

KM# 163 40 CENTAVOS
6.0000 g., 0.4000 Silver .0771 oz. ASW **Obv:** Defiant Condor on rock, left **Obv. Designer:** O. Roty **Rev:** Denomination above date within wreath

Date	Mintage	F	VF	XF	Unc	BU
1907	56,000	20.00	40.00	80.00	195	—
1908/6	—	7.00	14.00	28.00	55.00	—
1908	1,452,000	6.00	12.00	25.00	50.00	—

KM# 160 50 CENTAVOS
10.0000 g., 0.7000 Silver .2250 oz. ASW **Obv:** Defiant Condor on rock left **Obv. Designer:** O. Roty **Rev:** Denomination above date within wreath **Note:** Varieties with 0.7 or 0.7. exist.

Date	Mintage	F	VF	XF	Unc	BU
1902	2,022,000	6.00	12.00	22.50	50.00	—
1903	1,111,000	6.00	12.00	22.50	50.00	—
1905	1,075,000	6.00	12.00	22.50	50.00	—

KM# 178 50 CENTAVOS
Copper **Obv:** Bust of General Bernardo O'Higgins right, Thenot on truncation **Rev:** Denomination above date **Edge:** Plain

Date	Mintage	F	VF	XF	Unc	BU
1942	4,715,000	1.00	2.00	5.00	10.00	—

KM# 152.2 PESO
20.0000 g., 0.7000 Silver .4501 oz. ASW, 32 mm. **Obv:** Defiant Condor on rock, left, 0.7 below right wing **Obv. Designer:** O. Roty **Rev:** Denomination above date within wreath

Date	Mintage	F	VF	XF	Unc	BU
1902	178,000	12.00	25.00	60.00	125	—
1903	372,000	9.00	18.00	38.00	80.00	—
1905	429,000	9.00	18.00	38.00	80.00	—

KM# 152.3 PESO
12.0000 g., 0.9000 Silver .3472 oz. ASW, 31.5 mm. **Obv:** Defiant Condor on rock, left, 0.9 below right wing **Obv. Designer:** O. Roty **Rev:** Denomination above date within wreath

Date	Mintage	F	VF	XF	Unc	BU
1910	2,166,000	5.50	7.50	12.50	28.00	—

KM# 152.4 PESO
9.0000 g., 0.7200 Silver .2083 oz. ASW, 27.5 mm. **Obv:** Defiant Condor on rock, left, 0.72 below right wing **Obv. Designer:** O. Roty **Rev:** Denomination above date within wreath

Date	Mintage	F	VF	XF	Unc	BU
1915	6,032,000	3.75	5.50	8.00	18.00	—
1917	3,333,000	4.00	6.50	12.00	25.00	—

KM# 152.5 PESO
9.0000 g., 0.5000 Silver .1446 oz. ASW, 29 mm. **Obv:** Defiant Condor on rock, left, 0.5 below right wing **Obv. Designer:** O. Roty **Rev:** Denomination above date within wreath

Date	Mintage	F	VF	XF	Unc	BU
1921	2,287,000	2.75	3.75	7.50	16.00	—
1922	2,718,000	2.75	3.75	7.50	16.00	—

KM# 152.6 PESO
9.0000 g., 0.5000 Silver .1446 oz. ASW **Obv:** Defiant Condor on rock left, 0.5 below right wing **Rev:** Date and denomination within wreath **Note:** Struck with medal rotation.

Date	Mintage	F	VF	XF	Unc	BU
1924	1,748,000	2.75	3.75	7.50	16.00	—
1925	2,037,000	2.75	3.75	7.50	16.00	—

Note: Varieties of 1925 dated coins exist with flat and curved tops

KM# 142.2 PESO
25.0000 g., 0.9000 Silver .7234 oz. ASW **Obv:** Three plumes above shield within wreath, denomination below **Rev:** Defiant Condor above date, shield in right talon, flat top 3 **Note:** Medal alignment.

Date	Mintage	F	VF	XF	Unc	BU
1883(1925)	712,000	—	150	350	1,400	2,000

KM# 142.3 PESO
25.0000 g., 0.9000 Silver .7234 oz. ASW **Obv:** Three plumes above shield within wreath, denomination below **Rev:** Defiant Condor above date, shield in right talon, flat-top 3 **Note:** Coin alignment. Minted in 1925-26 and most coins were melted down in 1927.

Date	Mintage	F	VF	XF	Unc	BU
1883(1926)	149,000	—	150	300	850	1,250

KM# A171.1 PESO
9.0000 g., 0.5000 Silver .1446 oz. ASW **Obv:** Defiant Condor on rock left, 0.5 below right wing **Rev:** Date and denomination within wreath **Note:** A mule, with 0.5 and without mint mark on obverse.

Date	Mintage	F	VF	XF	Unc	BU
1927	—	15.00	30.00	45.00	90.00	—

KM# 171.1 PESO
9.0000 g., 0.5000 Silver .1446 oz. ASW **Obv:** Defiant Condor on rock left, 0.5 below right wing **Obv. Designer:** O. Roty **Rev:** Denomination above date within wreath

Date	Mintage	F	VF	XF	Unc	BU
1927So	3,890,000	4.00	6.00	10.00	20.00	—

KM# 171.2 PESO

9.0000 g., 0.5000 Silver .1446 oz. ASW **Obv:** Defiant Condor on rock left, 0.5 below right wing **Rev:** Date and denomination within wreath, thick numeral **Note:** Varieties 0.5 and 0,5 exist. Total of 2,431,608 pieces dated 1921-1927 were melted down in 1932.

Date	Mintage	F	VF	XF	Unc	BU
1927So	—	4.00	6.00	10.00	20.00	—

KM# 174 PESO

6.0000 g., 0.4000 Silver .0771 oz. ASW, 26 mm. **Obv:** Defiant Condor on rock left **Obv. Designer:** O. Roty **Rev:** Denomination above date within wreath

Date	Mintage	F	VF	XF	Unc	BU
1932	4,000,000	1.75	2.75	5.00	10.00	—

KM# 176.1 PESO

Copper-Nickel, 29 mm. **Obv:** Defiant Condor on rock left **Obv. Designer:** O. Roty **Rev:** Denomination above date within wreath

Date	Mintage	F	VF	XF	Unc	BU
1933	29,976,000	0.35	0.75	1.75	3.50	—

KM# 176.2 PESO

Copper-Nickel, 29 mm. **Obv:** Defiant Condor on rock left, O ROTY incuse on rock base **Obv. Designer:** O. Roty **Rev:** Denomination above date within wreath

Date	Mintage	F	VF	XF	Unc	BU
1940	150,000	2.00	3.00	6.00	12.00	—

KM# 179 PESO

Copper, 25 mm. **Obv:** Armored bust of General Bernardo O'Higgins right **Rev:** Denomination above date

Date	Mintage	F	VF	XF	Unc	BU
1942	15,150,000	0.10	0.35	2.00	9.00	—
1943	16,900,000	0.10	0.35	2.00	9.00	—
1944	12,050,000	0.10	0.35	2.00	9.00	—
1945	7,600,000	0.10	0.35	2.00	9.00	—
1946	2,050,000	0.10	0.35	5.00	15.00	—
1947	2,200,000	0.10	0.35	5.00	15.00	—
1948	5,900,000	0.10	0.25	2.00	5.00	—
1949	7,100,000	0.10	0.20	1.00	4.00	—
1950	7,250,000	0.10	0.20	1.00	4.00	—
1951	8,150,000	0.10	0.20	1.00	4.00	—
1952	10,400,000	0.10	0.20	1.00	4.00	—
1953 Short top 5	17,200,000	0.10	0.20	1.00	3.00	—
1953 Long top 5	Inc. above	0.10	0.20	1.00	3.00	—
1954	7,566,000	0.10	0.20	1.00	3.00	—

KM# 179a PESO

Aluminum, 25 mm. **Obv:** Armored bust, right **Rev:** Denomination above date

Date	Mintage	F	VF	XF	Unc	BU
1954	43,550,000	0.10	0.15	0.50	1.50	—
1954 Proof	—	Value: 25.00				
1955	69,050,000	0.10	0.15	0.50	1.50	—
1956	58,250,000	0.10	0.15	0.50	1.50	—
1956 Proof	—	Value: 25.00				
1957	49,250,000	0.10	0.15	0.50	1.50	—
1958	29,900	0.10	0.15	0.50	1.50	—

KM# 172 2 PESOS

18.0000 g., 0.5000 Silver .2893 oz. ASW **Obv:** Defiant Condor on rock left **Obv. Designer:** O. Roty **Rev:** Denomination above date within wreath **Note:** Obverse varieties 0.5 and 0,5 with curved top and flat top 5 exist. 459,510 pieces were melted down in 1932.

Date	Mintage	F	VF	XF	Unc	BU
1927	1,060,000	BV	4.50	9.00	20.00	—

KM# 159 5 PESOS

2.9955 g., 0.9170 Gold .0883 oz. AGW, 16.5 mm. **Obv:** Liberty head left **Rev:** Arms with supporters divide denomination and date

Date	Mintage	F	VF	XF	Unc	BU
1911	1,399	—	—	200	350	—

KM# 173.1 5 PESOS

25.0000 g., 0.9000 Silver .7234 oz. ASW **Obv:** Defiant Condor on rock, left, 0.9 below right wing **Obv. Designer:** O. Roty **Rev:** Denomination above date within wreath, narrow 5, width = 2.5mm

Date	Mintage	F	VF	XF	Unc	BU
1927	965,000	11.00	14.00	22.50	50.00	250

KM# 173.2 5 PESOS

25.0000 g., 0.9000 Silver .7234 oz. ASW **Obv:** Defiant Condor on rock left, 0.9 below right wing **Rev:** Denomination and date within wreath, wide numeral, width = 3mm **Note:** Varieties 0.9 and 0,9 exist. 436,510 pieces of KM#173.1 and #173.2 were melted down in 1932.

Date	Mintage	F	VF	XF	Unc	BU
1927	Inc. above	11.00	14.00	22.50	50.00	—

KM# 180 5 PESOS

Aluminum **Obv:** Condor in flight **Rev:** Denomination above date flanked by grain sprigs

Date	Mintage	F	VF	XF	Unc	BU
1956	1,600,000	0.15	0.35	0.50	1.25	—

KM# 182 5 PESOS

22.5000 g., 0.9990 Silver .7228 oz. ASW **Subject:** 150th Anniversary of Naval Academy **Obv:** Arms with supporters, date at left, denomination below **Rev:** Bust of Admiral Arturo Prat Chacon, 3/4 facing

Date	Mintage	F	VF	XF	Unc	BU
1968 Proof	1,200	Value: 28.50				

KM# 157 10 PESOS

5.9910 g., 0.9170 Gold .1766 oz. AGW, 21 mm. **Obv:** Head left **Rev:** Arms with supporters divide denomination and date

Date	Mintage	F	VF	XF	Unc	BU
1901	1,651,000	—	BV	130	200	—

KM# 181 10 PESOS

Aluminum **Obv:** Condor in flight **Rev:** Denomination above date, grain sprigs flank

Date	Mintage	F	VF	XF	Unc	BU
1956	13,100,000	0.15	0.35	0.50	0.75	1.50
1957	28,800,000	0.15	0.35	0.50	0.75	1.50
1958	44,500,000	0.15	0.35	0.50	0.75	1.50
1959	10,220,000	0.25	0.50	1.00	1.50	2.50

KM# 183 10 PESOS

45.0000 g., 0.9990 Silver 1.4455 oz. ASW **Subject:** Arrival of Liberation Fleet in 1820 under command of Lord Cochrane **Rev:** Liberation fleet, dates below

Date	Mintage	F	VF	XF	Unc	BU
1968 Proof	1,215	Value: 85.00				

KM# 158 20 PESOS

11.9821 g., 0.9170 Gold .3532 oz. AGW, 27 mm. **Obv:** Head left **Rev:** Arms with supporters divide denomination and date

Date	Mintage	F	VF	XF	Unc	BU
1906	41,000	—	BV	245	285	—
1907	12,000	—	BV	245	285	—
1908	26,000	—	BV	245	285	—
1910	28,000	—	BV	245	285	300

Date	Mintage	F	VF	XF	Unc	BU
1911	17,000	—	BV	245	285	300
1913/11	18,000	—	BV	245	285	300
1913	Inc. above	—	BV	245	285	300
1914	22,000	—	BV	245	285	300
1915	65,000	—	BV	245	285	300
1916	36,000	—	BV	245	285	300
1917	717,000	—	BV	245	285	300

KM# 168 20 PESOS
4.0679 g., 0.9000 Gold .1177 oz. AGW **Obv:** Head left, date below **Rev:** Arms with supporters, denomination above

Date	Mintage	F	VF	XF	Unc	BU
1926	85,000	—	BV	80.00	100	—
1958	500	BV	80.00	140	220	—
1959	25,000	—	—	BV	85.00	—
1961	20,000	—	—	BV	85.00	—
1964	—	—	—	BV	85.00	—
1976	99,000	—	—	BV	85.00	—
1977	38,000	—	—	BV	85.00	—
1979	30,000	—	—	BV	85.00	—
1980	30,000	—	—	BV	85.00	—

KM# 188 20 PESOS
4.0679 g., 0.9000 Gold .1177 oz. AGW **Obv:** Head left, date below **Rev:** Coat of arms on ornamental vines, denomination above

Date	Mintage	F	VF	XF	Unc	BU
1976	Inc. above	—	BV	80.00	100	—

KM# 169 50 PESOS
10.1698 g., 0.9000 Gold .2943 oz. AGW **Obv:** Head left, date below **Rev:** Coat of arms, denomination above

Date	Mintage	F	VF	XF	Unc	BU
1926	126,000	—	—	BV	195	220
1958	10,000	—	—	BV	195	220
1961	20,000	—	—	BV	195	220
1962	30,000	—	—	BV	195	220
1965	—	—	—	BV	195	220
1966	—	—	—	BV	195	220
1967	—	—	—	BV	195	220
1968	—	—	—	BV	195	220
1969	—	—	—	BV	195	220
1970	—	—	—	—	650	—
1974	—	—	—	BV	195	220

KM# 184 50 PESOS
10.1698 g., 0.9000 Gold .2943 oz. AGW **Subject:** 150th Anniversary of Military Academy **Obv:** Coat of arms above denomination **Rev:** Armored bust right of Bernardo O'Higgins, two dates below

Date	Mintage	F	VF	XF	Unc	BU
1968 Proof	2,515	Value: 225				

KM# 170 100 PESOS
20.3397 g., 0.9000 Gold .5886 oz. AGW **Obv:** Head left, date below **Rev:** Coat of arms, denomination above

Date	Mintage	F	VF	XF	Unc	BU
1926	678,000	—	—	BV	385	420

KM# 175 100 PESOS
20.3397 g., 0.9000 Gold .5886 oz. AGW **Obv:** Head left, date below, revised bust and legend style **Rev:** Coat of arms, denomination above, revised legend style

Date	Mintage	F	VF	XF	Unc	BU
1932	9,315	—	BV	390	450	—
1946	260,000	—	—	BV	385	410
1947	540,000	—	—	BV	385	410
1948	420,000	—	—	BV	385	410
1949	310,000	—	—	BV	385	410
1950	20,000	—	—	BV	385	410
1951	145,000	—	—	BV	385	410
1952	245,000	—	—	BV	385	410
1953	175,000	—	—	BV	385	410
1954	190,000	—	—	BV	385	410
1955	150,000	—	—	BV	385	410
1956	60,000	—	—	BV	385	410
1957	40,000	—	—	BV	385	410
1958	157,000	—	—	BV	385	410
1959	90,000	—	—	BV	385	410
1960	200,000	—	—	BV	385	410
1961	295,000	—	—	BV	385	410
1962	260,000	—	—	BV	385	410
1963	210,000	—	—	BV	385	410
1964	—	—	—	BV	385	410
1968	—	—	—	BV	385	410
1969	—	—	—	BV	385	410
1970	—	—	—	BV	385	410
1971	—	—	—	BV	385	410
1972	—	—	—	BV	385	410
1973	—	—	—	BV	385	410
1974	—	—	—	BV	385	410
1976	172,000	—	—	BV	385	410
1977	25,000	—	—	BV	385	410
1979	100,000	—	—	BV	385	410
1980	50,000	—	—	BV	385	410

KM# 185 100 PESOS
20.3397 g., 0.9000 Gold .5886 oz. AGW **Subject:** 150th Anniversary of National Coinage **Obv:** Coat of arms, date at left, denomination below **Rev:** Coinage press, liberty bust left

Date	Mintage	F	VF	XF	Unc	BU
1968 Proof	1,815	Value: 445				

KM# 186 200 PESOS
40.6794 g., 0.9000 Gold 1.1771 oz. AGW **Subject:** 150th Anniversary of San Martin's passage through Andes Mountains, from a painting by Vila Prades **Obv:** Coat of arms, date at left, denomination below **Rev:** Riders passing through mountains, two dates below

Date	Mintage	F	VF	XF	Unc	BU
1968 Proof	965	Value: 800				

KM# 187 500 PESOS
101.6985 g., 0.9000 Gold 2.9427 oz. AGW **Subject:** 150th Anniversary of National Flag **Rev:** Liberty bust left, waving flag in background, two dates below

Date	Mintage	F	VF	XF	Unc	BU
1968 Proof	—	Value: 2,000				

REFORM COINAGE

10 Pesos = 1 Centesimo; 100 Centesimos = 1 Escudo

KM# 192 1/2 CENTESIMO
Aluminum **Obv:** Condor in flight **Rev:** Denomination above date, grain sprigs flank

Date	Mintage	F	VF	XF	Unc	BU
1962	3,750,000	—	0.10	0.30	0.50	1.50
1962 Proof	—	Value: 10.00				
1963	8,100,000	—	0.10	0.30	0.50	1.50

KM# 189 CENTESIMO
Aluminum **Obv:** Condor in flight **Rev:** Denomination above date, grain sprigs flank

Date	Mintage	F	VF	XF	Unc	BU
1960	20,160,000	—	0.50	1.00	2.00	3.00
1960 Proof	—	Value: 45.00				
1961	Inc. above	—	0.50	1.00	2.00	3.00
1962	26,320,000	—	0.50	1.00	2.00	3.00
1963	27,100,000	—	0.50	1.00	2.00	3.00
1963 Proof	—	Value: 45.00				

KM# 193 2 CENTESIMOS

Aluminum-Bronze, 20 mm. **Obv:** Condor in flight **Rev:** Denomination above date, grain sprigs flank

Date	Mintage	F	VF	XF	Unc	BU
1960	2,050,000	—	—	—	50.00	—
Note: Not released for circulation						
1960 Proof	—	Value: 50.00				
1964	2,050,000	—	—	0.10	2.00	3.00
1965	32,550,000	—	—	0.10	2.00	3.00
1966	31,800,000	—	—	0.10	2.00	3.00
1967	34,750,000	—	—	0.10	2.00	3.00
1967 Proof	—	Value: 50.00				
1968	29,400,000	—	—	0.10	2.00	3.00
1969	—	—	—	—	3.00	5.00
1969 Proof	—	Value: 50.00				
1970	20,250,000	—	—	0.10	2.00	3.00

KM# 190 5 CENTESIMOS

Aluminum-Bronze **Obv:** Condor in flight **Rev:** Denomination above date, grain sprigs flank

Date	Mintage	F	VF	XF	Unc	BU
1960	—	—	—	—	75.00	—
Note: Not released for circulation						
1960 Proof	—	Value: 100				
1961	12,000	—	2.50	5.00	10.00	15.00
1962	—	—	2.00	4.00	10.00	15.00
1964	16,628,000	—	0.10	0.15	2.00	3.00
1965	27,680,000	—	0.10	0.15	2.00	3.00
1966	32,360,000	—	0.10	0.15	2.00	3.00
1966 Proof	—	Value: 50.00				
1967	19,680,000	—	0.10	0.15	2.00	3.00
1968	4,400,000	—	0.10	0.15	2.00	3.00
1968 Proof	—	Value: 50.00				
1969	13,200,000	—	—	—	5.00	7.00
1969 Proof	—	Value: 50.00				
1970	30,680,000	—	0.10	0.15	2.00	3.00
1971	16,080,000	—	0.10	0.15	2.00	3.00

KM# 191 10 CENTESIMOS

Aluminum-Bronze **Obv:** Condor in flight **Rev:** Denomination above date, grain sprigs flank

Date	Mintage	F	VF	XF	Unc	BU
1960	—	—	2.00	4.00	10.00	15.00
1960 Proof	—	Value: 70.00				
1961	1,915,000	—	0.10	1.00	4.00	6.00
1962	1,480,000	—	0.10	0.20	2.00	3.00
1963 Small date	10,980,000	—	0.10	0.20	2.00	3.00
1964	27,070,000	—	0.10	0.20	2.00	3.00
1965	49,480,000	—	0.10	0.20	2.00	3.00
1966	60,680,000	—	0.10	0.20	2.00	3.00
1967	27,520,000	—	0.10	0.25	2.00	3.00
1967 Proof	—	Value: 50.00				
1968	8,040,000	—	0.10	0.20	2.00	3.00
1969	15,660,000	—	—	—	5.00	7.00
1970 Large date	42,080,000	—	0.10	0.20	1.00	2.00

KM# 194 10 CENTESIMOS

Aluminum-Bronze, 18 mm. **Obv:** Armored bust of Bernardo O'Higgins, right **Rev:** Arms above denomination, date at left

Date	Mintage	F	VF	XF	Unc	BU
1971	99,700,000	—	—	0.10	0.15	0.25

KM# 195 20 CENTESIMOS

Aluminum-Bronze **Obv:** Bust of Jose Manuel Balmaceda left **Rev:** Arms above denomination, date at left

Date	Mintage	F	VF	XF	Unc	BU
1971	89,200,000	—	—	0.10	0.20	0.35
1972	—	—	0.10	0.20	1.00	1.50

KM# 196 50 CENTESIMOS

Aluminum-Bronze **Obv:** Bust of Manuel Rodriguez right **Rev:** Arms above denomination, date at left

Date	Mintage	F	VF	XF	Unc	BU
1971	58,300,000	—	0.10	0.15	0.25	0.45

KM# 197 ESCUDO

Copper-Nickel **Obv:** Bust of Jose Miguel Carrera 3/4 facing **Rev:** Arms above denomination, date at left

Date	Mintage	F	VF	XF	Unc	BU
1971	160,900,000	—	0.10	0.20	0.40	0.60
1972	Inc. above	—	0.10	0.20	0.40	0.60
1972 Proof	—	Value: 50.00				

KM# 198 2 ESCUDOS

Copper-Nickel **Obv:** Caupolican, Chief of Araucanian Indians **Rev:** Arms above denomination, date at left

Date	Mintage	F	VF	XF	Unc	BU
1971	106	—	—	—	150	—
Note: Not released for circulation						
1971 Proof	—	Value: 65.00				

KM# 199 5 ESCUDOS

Copper-Nickel **Obv:** Lautaro, Araucanian indian, upriser against Spain **Rev:** Arms above denomination, date at left

Date	Mintage	F	VF	XF	Unc	BU
1971	—	—	0.10	0.25	0.75	1.25
1972	—	—	0.10	0.25	0.75	1.25
1972 Proof	—	Value: 50.00				

KM# 199a 5 ESCUDOS

Aluminum **Obv:** Lautaro, Araucanian indian, upriser against Spain **Rev:** Arms above denomination, date at left

Date	Mintage	F	VF	XF	Unc	BU
1972	—	—	0.10	0.15	0.20	0.50

KM# 200 10 ESCUDOS

Aluminum **Obv:** Defiant Condor on rock left **Rev:** Denomination above date within wreath

Date	Mintage	F	VF	XF	Unc	BU
1974	33,750,000	—	0.10	0.15	0.35	0.50
1974 Proof	—	Value: 50.00				
1975	31,600,000	—	—	—	—	—
Note: Although recorded with mintage, no examples are known with this date						

KM# 201 50 ESCUDOS

Nickel-Brass **Obv:** Defiant Condor on rock left **Obv. Designer:** O. Roty **Rev:** Denomination above date within wreath **Shape:** 12-sided

Date	Mintage	F	VF	XF	Unc	BU
1974	5,700,000	—	0.15	0.25	0.60	0.85
1975	20,300,000	—	0.15	0.20	0.50	0.75

KM# 202 100 ESCUDOS

Nickel-Brass, 23.5 mm. **Obv:** Defiant Condor on rock left **Obv. Designer:** O. Roty **Rev:** Denomination above date within wreath **Shape:** 12-sided

Date	Mintage	F	VF	XF	Unc	BU
1974	32,100,000	—	0.20	0.35	0.75	1.00
1975	65,600,000	—	0.20	0.35	0.75	1.00

REFORM COINAGE

100 Centavos = 1 Peso; 1000 Old Escudos = 1 Peso

KM# 203 CENTAVO

Aluminum **Obv:** Defiant Condor on rock left **Obv. Designer:** O. Roty **Rev:** Denomination above date within wreath

Date	Mintage	F	VF	XF	Unc	BU
1975	2,000,000	—	0.10	0.15	0.50	0.75

KM# 204 5 CENTAVOS

Aluminum-Bronze **Obv:** Defiant Condor on rock left **Obv. Designer:** O. Roty **Rev:** Denomination above date within wreath **Shape:** 12-sided

Date	Mintage	F	VF	XF	Unc	BU
1975	5,400,000	—	—	0.10	0.25	0.75
1976	6,600,000	—	—	—	—	—
Note: Although recorded with mintage, no examples are known with this date						

KM# 204a 5 CENTAVOS

Aluminum **Obv:** Defiant Condor on rock left **Rev:** Date and denomination within wreath **Shape:** 12-sided

Date	Mintage	F	VF	XF	Unc	BU
1976	5,000,000	—	—	0.10	0.25	0.75

KM# 205 10 CENTAVOS

Aluminum-Bronze **Obv:** Defiant Condor on rock left **Obv. Designer:** O. Roty **Rev:** Denomination above date within wreath **Shape:** 12-sided

Date	Mintage	F	VF	XF	Unc	BU
1975	8,600,000	—	—	0.10	0.25	0.75
1976	9,000,000	—	—	—	—	—

Note: Although recorded with mintage, no examples are known with this date

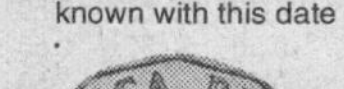

KM# 205a 10 CENTAVOS

Aluminum **Obv:** Defiant Condor on rock left **Obv. Designer:** O. Roty **Rev:** Denomination above date within wreath **Shape:** 12-sided

Date	Mintage	F	VF	XF	Unc	BU
1976	6,600,000	—	—	0.10	0.25	0.50
1977	57,800,000	—	—	0.10	0.25	0.50
1978	58,050,000	—	—	0.10	0.25	0.50
1979	101,950,000	—	—	0.10	0.25	0.50

KM# 206 50 CENTAVOS

Copper-Nickel **Obv:** Defiant Condor on rock left **Obv. Designer:** O. Roty **Rev:** Denomination above date within wreath

Date	Mintage	F	VF	XF	Unc	BU
1975	38,000,000	—	—	0.10	0.25	0.50
1976	1,000,000	—	0.50	1.00	2.00	3.00
1977	10,000,000	—	—	0.10	0.25	0.50

KM# 206a 50 CENTAVOS

Aluminum-Bronze **Obv:** Defiant Condor on rock left **Obv. Designer:** O. Roty **Rev:** Denomination above date within wreath

Date	Mintage	F	VF	XF	Unc	BU
1978	19,250,000	—	—	0.10	0.25	0.60
1979	28,000,000	—	—	0.10	0.25	0.60

KM# 207 PESO

Copper-Nickel, 24 mm. **Obv:** Armored bust of Bernardo O'Higgins right **Obv. Legend:** BERNARDO O'HIGGINS **Rev:** Denomination above date within wreath

Date	Mintage	F	VF	XF	Unc	BU
1975	51,000,000	—	0.10	0.15	0.25	0.35

KM# 208 PESO

Copper-Nickel, 24 mm. **Obv:** Armored bust of Bernardo O'Higgins right **Obv. Legend:** LIBERTADOR. B. O'HIGGINS **Rev:** Denomination above date within wreath

Date	Mintage	F	VF	XF	Unc	BU
1976	30,000,000	—	—	0.10	0.25	0.35
1977	20,000,000	—	—	0.10	0.25	0.35

KM# 208a PESO

Aluminum-Bronze, 24 mm. **Obv:** Armored bust of Bernardo O'Higgins right **Rev:** Denomination above date within wreath

Date	Mintage	F	VF	XF	Unc	BU
1978	39,706,000	—	—	0.10	0.25	0.35
1979	63,000,000	—	—	0.10	0.25	0.35

KM# 216.1 PESO

2.0000 g., Aluminum-Bronze, 17 mm. **Obv:** Armored bust right **Rev:** Denomination above date within wreath **Note:** Reduced size. Wide date.

Date	Mintage	F	VF	XF	Unc	BU
1981	40,000,000	—	—	0.10	0.20	0.30
1984	60,000,000	—	—	0.10	0.20	0.30
1985	20,000,000	—	—	0.10	0.20	0.30
1986	45,000,000	—	—	0.10	0.20	0.30
1987	80,000,000	—	—	0.10	0.20	0.30

KM# 216.2 PESO

Aluminum-Bronze **Obv:** Armored bust, right **Rev:** Denomination above date within wreath **Note:** Narrow date.

Date	Mintage	F	VF	XF	Unc	BU
1988	105,000,000	—	—	0.10	0.20	0.30
1989	205,000,000	—	—	0.10	0.20	0.30
1990	140,000,000	—	—	0.10	0.20	0.30
1991	140,000,000	—	—	0.10	0.20	0.30
1992	—	—	—	0.10	0.20	0.30

KM# 231 PESO

Aluminum **Obv:** Armored bust right **Rev:** Denomination above date within wreath **Shape:** 8-sided **Note:** Varieties exist.

Date	Mintage	F	VF	XF	Unc	BU
1992 Wide date	—	—	—	—	0.10	0.20
1993 Narrow date	—	—	—	—	0.10	0.20
1994	—	—	—	—	0.10	0.20
1995	—	—	—	—	0.10	0.20
1996	—	—	—	—	0.10	0.20
1997	—	—	—	—	0.10	0.20
1998	—	—	—	—	0.10	0.20
1999	—	—	—	—	0.10	0.20
2000	—	—	—	—	0.10	0.20

KM# 209 5 PESOS

Copper-Nickel, 25.8 mm. **Subject:** 3rd Anniversary of New Government **Obv:** Winged figure with upraised arms, broken chain on wrists **Rev:** Denomination above date within wreath

Date	Mintage	F	VF	XF	Unc	BU
1976	2,100,000	—	0.15	0.25	2.00	3.50
1977	28,300,000	—	0.15	0.25	2.00	3.00
1978	11,704,000	—	0.15	0.25	2.00	3.00
1980	8,200,000	—	0.15	0.25	2.00	3.00

KM# 217.1 5 PESOS

2.7000 g., Nickel-Brass, 19 mm. **Obv:** Winged figure with arms upraised, broken chain on wrists **Rev:** Denomination above date within wreath **Note:** Wide date.

Date	Mintage	F	VF	XF	Unc	BU
1981	17,000,000	—	—	0.10	0.50	0.75
1982	20,000,000	—	—	0.10	0.50	0.75
1984	12,000,000	—	—	0.10	0.50	0.75
1985	16,000,000	—	—	0.10	0.50	0.75
1986	16,000,000	—	—	0.10	0.50	0.75
1987	8,000,000	—	—	0.10	0.50	0.75

KM# 217.2 5 PESOS

Nickel-Brass **Obv:** Winged figure with arms upraised, broken chain on wrists **Rev:** Denomination above date within wreath **Note:** Narrow date.

Date	Mintage	F	VF	XF	Unc	BU
1988	27,000,000	—	—	0.10	0.50	0.75
1989	32,000,000	—	—	0.10	0.50	0.75
1990	23,000,000	—	—	0.10	0.50	0.75

KM# 229 5 PESOS

Nickel-Brass **Obv:** Armored bust of Bernardo O'Higgins right **Rev:** Denomination above date within wreath

Date	Mintage	F	VF	XF	Unc	BU
1990	8,000,000	—	—	0.10	0.50	0.75
1991	2,000,000	—	—	0.10	0.50	0.75
1992	—	—	—	0.10	0.50	0.75

KM# 232 5 PESOS

Aluminum-Bronze **Obv:** Armored bust right **Rev:** Denomination above date within wreath **Shape:** 8-sided **Note:** Varieties exist.

Date	Mintage	F	VF	XF	Unc	BU
1992 Wide date	—	—	—	0.10	0.35	0.60
1993 Narrow date	—	—	—	0.10	0.35	0.60
1994 Narrow date	—	—	—	0.10	0.35	0.60
1995 Narrow date	—	—	—	0.10	0.35	0.60
1996 Narrow date	—	—	—	0.10	0.35	0.60
1997 Narrow date	—	—	—	0.10	0.35	0.60
1998 Narrow date	—	—	—	0.10	0.35	0.60
1999 Narrow date	—	—	—	0.10	0.35	0.60
2000 Narrow date	—	—	—	0.10	0.35	0.60

KM# 210 10 PESOS

Copper-Nickel **Subject:** 3rd Anniversary of New Government **Obv:** Winged figure with arms upraised, broken chains on wrists **Rev:** Denomination above date within wreath

Date	Mintage	F	VF	XF	Unc	BU
1976	2,100,000	—	0.10	0.20	1.25	1.50
1977	30,000,000	—	0.10	0.20	1.00	1.25
1978	20,004,000	—	0.10	0.20	1.00	1.25
1979	7,000,000	—	0.10	0.20	1.00	1.25
1980	20,000,000	—	0.10	0.20	1.00	1.25

KM# 211 10 PESOS

44.8000 g., 0.9990 Silver 1.4390 oz. ASW **Subject:** 3rd Anniversary of New Government **Obv:** Coat of arms above denomination **Rev:** Winged figure with arms upraised, two dates above

Date	Mintage	F	VF	XF	Unc	BU
ND(1976) Proof	1,000	Value: 115				

KM# 218.1 10 PESOS

3.5000 g., Nickel-Brass, 21 mm. **Obv:** Winged figure with arms upraised, broken chain on wrists **Rev:** Denomination above date within wreath **Note:** Wide date, narrow rim.

Date	Mintage	F	VF	XF	Unc	BU
1981	55,000,000	—	0.10	0.20	0.50	0.75
1982	45,000,000	—	0.10	0.20	0.50	0.75
1984	30,000,000	—	0.10	0.20	0.50	0.75
1985	400,000	—	0.50	1.50	3.50	5.00
1986 Narrow date	25,000,000	—	0.10	0.20	0.50	0.75
1986 Wide date	Inc. above	—	0.10	0.20	0.50	0.75
1987	8,000,000	—	0.10	0.20	0.50	0.75

KM# 218.2 10 PESOS

Nickel-Brass **Obv:** Winged figure with arms upraised, broken chain on wrists **Rev:** Denomination above date within wreath **Note:** Narrow date.

Date	Mintage	F	VF	XF	Unc	BU
1988	45,000,000	—	0.10	0.20	0.50	0.75
1989	73,000,000	—	0.10	0.20	0.50	0.75

KM# 218.3 10 PESOS

Nickel-Brass **Obv:** Winged figure with arms upraised, broken chain on wrists **Rev:** Denomination above date within wreath **Note:** Wide rim.

Date	Mintage	F	VF	XF	Unc	BU
1990	10,000,000	—	0.10	0.20	0.50	0.75

KM# 228.1 10 PESOS

Nickel-Brass **Obv:** Small bust of Bernardo O'Higgins right, wide rim **Rev:** Denomination above date within wreath

Date	Mintage	F	VF	XF	Unc	BU
1990	5,000,000	—	0.10	0.20	0.50	0.75

KM# 228.2 10 PESOS

Nickel-Brass **Obv:** Armored bust of Bernardo O'Higgins right, normal rim **Rev:** Denomination above date within wreath **Note:** All 9's are curl tail 9's except for the 1999 date, these are straight tail 9's.

Date	Mintage	F	VF	XF	Unc	BU
1990	25,000,000	—	0.10	0.20	0.50	0.65
1991	—	—	0.10	0.20	0.50	0.65
1992	—	—	0.10	0.20	0.50	0.65
1993	—	—	0.10	0.20	0.50	0.65
1994	—	—	0.10	0.20	0.50	0.65
1995	—	—	0.10	0.20	0.50	0.65
1996	—	—	0.10	0.20	0.50	0.65
1997	—	—	0.10	0.20	0.50	0.65
1998	—	—	0.10	0.20	0.50	0.65
1999	—	—	0.10	0.20	0.50	0.65
2000	—	—	0.10	0.20	0.50	0.65

KM# 212 50 PESOS

10.1500 g., 0.9000 Gold .2937 oz. AGW **Subject:** 3rd Anniversary of New Government **Obv:** Coat of arms above denomination **Rev:** Winged figure with arms upraised, two dates above

Date	Mintage	F	VF	XF	Unc	BU
ND(1976)	1,900	—	—	—	220	275
ND(1976) Proof	Inc. above	Value: 325				

KM# 219.1 50 PESOS

7.0000 g., Aluminum-Bronze, 25.71 mm. **Obv:** Armored bust right **Rev:** Denomination above date within wreath **Shape:** 10-sided **Note:** Wide date.

Date	Mintage	F	VF	XF	Unc	BU
1981	12,000,000	—	0.25	0.50	1.25	1.50
1982	14,000,000	—	0.25	0.50	1.25	1.50
1985	400,000	—	0.60	1.50	3.50	5.00
1986	1,000,000	—	0.25	0.50	1.25	1.50
1987	4,000,000	—	0.25	0.50	1.25	1.50

KM# 219.2 50 PESOS

Aluminum-Bronze **Obv:** Armored bust right **Rev:** Denomination above date within wreath **Shape:** 10-sided **Note:** Narrow date.

Date	Mintage	F	VF	XF	Unc	BU
1988	4,800,000	—	0.25	0.50	1.25	1.50
1989	4,000,000	—	0.25	0.50	1.25	1.50
1991	10,845,000	—	0.25	0.50	1.25	1.50
1992	—	—	0.25	0.50	1.25	1.50
1993	—	—	0.25	0.50	1.25	1.50
1994	—	—	0.25	0.50	1.25	1.50
1995	—	—	0.25	0.50	1.25	1.50
1996	—	—	0.25	0.50	1.25	1.50
1997	—	—	0.25	0.50	1.25	1.50
1998	—	—	0.25	0.50	1.25	1.50
1999	—	—	0.25	0.50	1.25	1.50
2000	—	—	0.25	0.50	1.25	1.50

KM# 213 100 PESOS

20.3000 g., 0.9000 Gold .5874 oz. AGW **Subject:** 3rd Anniversary of New Government **Obv:** Coat of arms above date and denomination **Rev:** Winged figure with upraised arms, two dates above

Date	Mintage	F	VF	XF	Unc	BU
1976	2,900	—	—	—	420	450
1976 Proof	100	Value: 775				

KM# 226.1 100 PESOS

Aluminum-Bronze, 26.8 mm. **Obv:** Coat of arms **Rev:** Denomination above date within wreath **Edge:** POR LA RAZON O LA FUERZA **Note:** Wide date with pointed 9.

Date	Mintage	F	VF	XF	Unc	BU
1981	10,000,000	—	0.50	0.75	2.50	3.00
1984	8,000,000	—	0.50	0.75	2.50	3.00
1985	15,000,000	—	0.50	0.75	2.50	3.00
1986	11,000,000	—	0.50	0.75	2.50	3.00
1987	15,000,000	—	0.50	0.75	2.50	3.00

KM# 226.2 100 PESOS

Aluminum-Bronze, 26.8 mm. **Obv:** Coat of arms **Rev:** Denomination above date within wreath **Edge:** POR LA RAZON O LA FUERZA **Note:** Narrow date with curved 9.

Date	Mintage	F	VF	XF	Unc	BU
1989	20,000,000	—	0.50	0.75	2.50	3.00
1991	4,320,000	—	0.50	0.75	2.50	3.00
1992	—	—	0.50	0.75	2.50	3.00
1993	—	—	0.50	0.75	2.50	3.00
1994	—	—	0.50	0.75	2.50	3.00
1995	—	—	0.50	0.75	2.50	3.00
1996	—	—	0.50	0.75	2.50	3.00
1997	—	—	0.50	0.75	2.50	3.00
1998	—	—	0.50	0.75	2.50	3.00
1999	—	—	0.50	0.75	2.50	3.00
2000	—	—	0.50	0.75	2.50	3.00

KM# 214 500 PESOS

102.2700 g., 0.9000 Gold 2.9595 oz. AGW **Subject:** 3rd Anniversary of New Government **Obv:** Coat of arms, denomination below **Rev:** Winged figure with upraised arms, two dates above **Note:** Similar to 100 Pesos, KM#213.

Date	Mintage	F	VF	XF	Unc	BU
1976	500	—	—	—	2,000	2,150
1976 Proof	700	Value: 2,200				

KM# 235 500 PESOS

6.5000 g., Bi-Metallic Aluminum-bronze center in Copper-nickel ring, 25.9 mm. **Subject:** Cardinal Raul Silva Henriquez **Obv:** Bust of Henriquez within inner ring facing left **Rev:** Denomination above date within wreath **Edge:** Reeded

Date	Mintage	F	VF	XF	Unc	BU
2000	—	—	—	—	6.00	6.50
2000 Proof	—	—	—	—	—	—

KM# 233 2000 PESOS

8.2000 g., 0.5000 Silver .1318 oz. ASW **Subject:** 250th Anniversary of the Mint **Obv:** Building divides date and denomination **Rev:** Metal workers, two dates below

Date	Mintage	F	VF	XF	Unc	BU
1993	50,000	—	—	—	16.50	18.00

KM# 230 10000 PESOS

27.0000 g., 0.9250 Silver .8029 oz. ASW **Series:** Ibero - American **Obv:** Inner circle holds Coat of Arms, denomination within outer circle, 13 shields surround **Rev:** Three dates below three ships, globe in background

Date	Mintage	F	VF	XF	Unc	BU
1991 Proof	75,000	Value: 45.00				

PATTERNS

Including off metal strikes

KM#	Date	Mintage	Identification	Mkt Val
PnA26	1908	—	5 Centavos. Copper-Nickel.	250
PnB26	1908	—	10 Centavos. Brass.	—
PnC26	1914	—	50 Centavos. Silver.	—
Pn26	1914	—	Peso. Silver.	600
PnA27	1914	—	2 Pesos. Silver. Piefort, large flan.	500
Pn27	1914	—	2 Pesos. Silver. Piefort, small flan.	500
Pn28	1916	—	20 Centavos. Silver. 4.0000 g.	—
Pn29	1916	—	20 Centavos. Silver. 4.0400 g.	—
Pn30	1917	—	10 Centavos. Silver. 1.9000 g.	—
Pn31	1917	—	10 Centavos. Silver. 2.5200 g.	—
Pn32	1919	—	5 Centavos. Copper-Nickel.	—
Pn33	1919	—	5 Centavos. Silver. 1.4900 g.	—
Pn34	1919	—	5 Centavos. Silver. 1.5300 g.	—
Pn35	1919	—	10 Centavos. Copper-Nickel.	—
Pn36	1919	—	20 Centavos. Copper-Nickel.	—
Pn37	ND19xx	—	10 Centavos. Copper-Nickel. Center hole.	—
Pn38	1926	—	Peso. Silver. Indian, date below chin. Star within wreath divides denomination.	550
Pn39	1926	—	Peso. Silver. Fineness added.	550
Pn40	1926	—	Peso. Silver. Coat of arms. Without fineness.	600
Pn41	1926	—	2 Pesos. Silver. Condor. Coat of arms. Without fineness.	1,000
Pn42	1926	—	2 Pesos. Silver. Indian. Star in wreath. "5" fineness, Pn43.	600
Pn43	1926	—	2 Pesos. Silver. Indian. Star in wreath. "72" fineness, Pn44.	600
Pn44	1926	—	5 Pesos.	1,500
Pn45	1926	—	5 Pesos. Silver. Weak or no fineness (effaced from die).	1,500
Pn46	1926	—	5 Pesos. Silver.	1,250
Pn47	1927	—	Peso. Copper-Nickel.	250
Pn48	1927	—	Peso. Silver.	500
Pn49	1927	—	5 Pesos. Silver.	300
Pn50	1929	—	20 Centavos. Copper-Nickel. Center hole.	150
Pn51	1929	—	20 Centavos. Copper-Nickel. Pn49 but "CHILE" on reverse instead of "20".	125
Pn52	1929	—	Peso. Silver.	250
Pn53	ND(1929)	—	Peso. Silver. Without country, date or fineness.	250
Pn54	ND(1929)	—	Peso. Silver. Similar to Pn52, without mountains on obverse.	250
Pn55	1930	—	20 Centavos. Copper-Nickel. Center hole.	200
Pn56	1930	—	20 Centavos. Copper-Nickel. Pn54 but "20" instead of "CHILE" on obverse, with center hole.	200
Pn57	1930	—	Peso. Silver. Worker and factory. Value.	350
Pn58	1930	—	2 Pesos. Copper-Nickel. Condor. Value and date in wreath.	375
PnA59	1933	—	Peso. Nickel. KM#176.1.	—
Pn59	1933	—	Peso. Copper-Nickel. Condor. Value and date in wreath.	275
PnA60	1933	—	Peso. Copper-Nickel. Condor. Value and date in wreath. Mint punched cancelled.	275
Pn60	1938	—	5 Pesos. Brass.	500
Pn61	1938	—	5 Pesos. Copper-Nickel.	—
PnA62	ND(1938)	—	5 Pesos. Plain edge. Aluminum-Bronze or Silver.	400
Pn62	ND(1938)	—	5 Pesos. Silver. Without date.	300
PnA63	1941	—	20 Centavos. Bronze.	100
Pn63	1942	—	Peso. Copper. Like KM#179, but smaller diameter.	100
Pn64	1947	—	100 Pesos. Copper.	—
Pn65	1948	—	Onza. Silver.	75.00
Pn65a	1948	—	Onza. Copper.	25.00
PnA66	1951	—	10 Pesos. Aluminum-Bronze. Thick flan.	100
Pn66	1953	—	20 Centavos. Aluminum.	125
Pn67	1956	—	5 Pesos. Brass. KM#180.	—
Pn68	1959	—	10 Pesos. Brass. KM#181.	—
Pn69	1960	—	2 Centesimos. Brass. Uniface.	100
PnA70	1960	—	2 Centesimos. Aluminum-Bronze.	75.00
Pn70	1960	—	2 Centesimos. Copper-Nickel.	60.00
Pn71	1960	—	5 Centesimos. Copper. KM#190.	100
Pn72	1960	—	5 Centesimos. Copper-Nickel. Plain edge. KM#190.	90.00
Pn73	1960	—	5 Centesimos. Copper-Nickel. Milled edge. KM#190.	75.00
Pn74	1960	—	10 Centesimos. Copper. KM#191.	100
Pn75	1960	—	10 Centesimos. Copper-Nickel. KM#191.	40.00
Pn76	1960	—	10 Centesimos. Brass. KM#191.	—
Pn77	1960	—	10 Centesimos. Brass.	—
Pn78	1960	—	10 Centesimos. Aluminum-Bronze. Legend. Arms flanked by C-M.	65.00
Pn79	1960	—	10 Centesimos. Copper-Nickel. Legend. Arms flanked by C-M.	65.00
Pn80	1964	—	2 Centesimos. Copper-Nickel. KM#193.	75.00
Pn81	1968	—	100 Pesos. Copper. Center hole.	125
Pn82	1969	—	Peso. Copper-Nickel. Ten sided. Ten sided, arms with "C.M." below.	100
Pn83	1971	—	Peso. Nickel.	—
Pn84	ND	—	50 Pesos. Aluminum-Bronze. Equestrian statue of O'Higgins, left. Arms above denomiation within wreath.	—
Pn85	1971	—	2 Escudos. Silver. KM#198.	—
Pn86	1972	—	5 Escudos. Silver. KM#199.	—
Pn87	1972	—	Escudo. Silver. KM197.	—
Pn88	1974	—	10 Escudos. Aluminum.	—
Pn89	1979	5	100 Pesos. 0.5000 Silver. Equestrian statue of O'Higgins.	—

PIEFORTS

KM#	Date	Mintage	Identification	Mkt Val
P4	1951	—	10 Pesos. Aluminum-Bronze. KM#181.	125

TRIAL STRIKES

KM#	Date	Mintage	Identification	Mkt Val
TS7	ND(1960)	—	10 Centesimos. Copper-Nickel. Coat of arms flanked by C-M. Coat of arms flanked by C-M.	60.00
TS8	ND(1960)	—	10 Centesimos. Aluminum-Bronze. Coat of arms flanked by C-M. Coat of arms flanked by C-M.	50.00

PROOF SETS

KM#	Date	Mintage	Identification	Issue Price	Mkt Val
PS1	1968 (6)	—	KM#182-187. Total of 12,000 coins struck for each denomination including those available singly.	560	3,350
PS2	1968 (4)	—	KM#184-187. Total of 12,000 coins struck for each denomination including those available singly.	528	3,250
PS3	1968 (2)	—	KM#182, 183. Total of 12,000 coins struck for each denomination including those available singly.	31.50	100
PS4	1971/2 (3)	—	KM#197 (1972), KM#198 (1971), KM#199 (1972). Total of 12,000 coins struck for each denomination including those available singly.	—	150

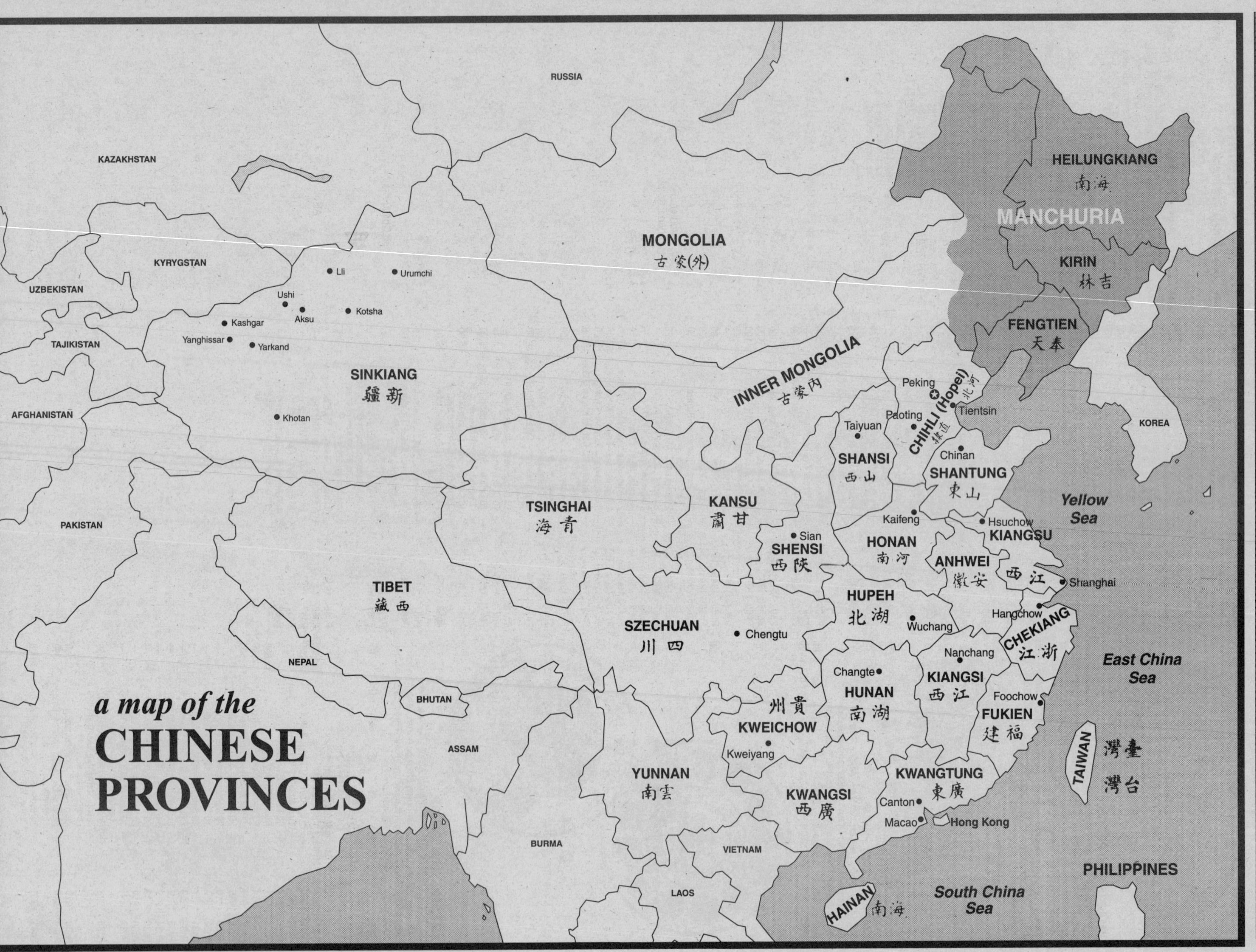

RUSSIA
KAZAKHSTAN
KYRYGSTAN
UZBEKISTAN
TAJIKISTAN
AFGHANISTAN
PAKISTAN
MONGOLIA
古蒙(外)
Lli
Urumchi
Ushi
Aksu
Kotsha
Kashgar
Yanghissar
Yarkand
SINKIANG
疆新
Khotan
INNER MONGOLIA
古蒙内
Peking
CHIHLI (Hopei)
Tientsin
Paoting
Taiyuan
SHANSI
西山
Chinan
SHANTUNG
東山
MANCHURIA
HEILUNGKIANG
南海
KIRIN
林吉
FENGTIEN
天奉
KOREA
Yellow Sea
TSINGHAI
海青
KANSU
肅甘
Kaifeng
Hsuchow
KIANGSU
Sian
SHENSI
西陜
HONAN
南河
ANHWEI
徽安
西江
Shanghai
TIBET
藏西
HUPEH
北湖
Wuchang
Hangchow
CHEKIANG
江浙
SZECHUAN
川四
Chengtu
East China Sea
NEPAL
BHUTAN
Nanchang
Changte
KIANGSI
西江
HUNAN
南湖
Foochow
FUKIEN
建福
州貴
KWEICHOW
Kweiyang
TAIWAN
灣臺
灣台
ASSAM
YUNNAN
南雲
KWANGTUNG
東廣
KWANGSI
西廣
Canton
Macao
Hong Kong
BURMA
VIETNAM
LAOS
PHILIPPINES
HAINAN
南海
South China Sea
a map of the
CHINESE
PROVINCES

CHINA

Before 1912, China was ruled by an imperial government. The republican administration which replaced it was itself supplanted on the Chinese mainland by a communist government in 1949, but it has remained in control of Taiwan and other offshore islands in the China Sea with a land area of approximately 14,000 square miles and a population of more than 14 million. The People's Republic of China administers some 3.7 million square miles and an estimated 1.19 billion people. This communist government, officially established on October 1, 1949, was admitted to the United Nations, replacing its nationalist predecessor, the Republic of China, in 1971.

Cast coins in base metals were used in China many centuries before the Christian era, but locally struck coinages of the western type in gold, silver, copper and other metals did not appear until 1888. In spite of the relatively short time that modern coins have been in use, the number of varieties is exceptionally large.

Both Nationalist and Communist China, as well as the prerevolutionary Imperial government and numerous provincial or other agencies, including some foreign-administered agencies and governments, have issued coins in China. Most of these have been in dollar (yuan) or dollar-fraction denominations, based on the internationally used dollar system, but coins in tael denominations were issued in the 1920's and earlier. The striking of coins nearly ceased in the late 1930's through the 1940's due to the war effort and a period of uncontrollable inflation while vast amounts of paper currency were issued by the Nationalist, Communist and Japanese occupation institutions.

EMPERORS

Obverse Types

光緒

KUANG-HSÜ

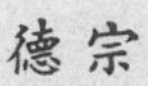

Te Tsung 1875-1908

Type A

光緒通寶

Kang-hsü T'ung-pao (Guangxu)

Type B

光緒重寶

Kuang-hsü Chung-pao

Type C

光緒元寶

Kuang-hsü Yuan-pao

Kuang-hsü - When the previous emperor died, his mother, the Empress Dowager Tz'u-hsi, chose her four-year-old nephew, born August 14, 1871, as emperor. She adopted the boy so that she could act as regent and on February 25, 1875, the young prince ascended the throne, taking the reign title of Kuang-hsü. In 1898 he tried to assert himself and collected a group of progressive officials around him. He issued a series of edicts for revamping of the military, abolition of civil service examinations, improvement of agriculture and restructuring of administrative procedures. During Kuang-hsü's reign (1875-1908) the Empress Dowager totally dominated the government. She confined the emperor to his palace and spread rumors that he was deathly ill. Foreign powers let it be known they would not take kindly to the Emperor's death. This saved his life but thereafter he had no power over the government. On November 15, 1908, Tz'u-hsi died under highly suspicious circumstances and the usually healthy emperor was announced as having died the previous day.

宣統

HSÜAN-T'UNG 1908-1911

Type A

宣統

Hsüan-t'ung T'ung-pao (Xuantong)

Hsuan-t'ung - The last emperor of the Ch'ing dynasty in China and Japan's puppet emperor, under the assumed name of K'ang-te, in Manchoukuo from 1934 to 1945, was born on February 7, 1906. He succeeded to the throne at the age of three on November 14, 1908. He reigned under a regency for three years but on February 12, 1912, was forced to abdicate the throne. He was permitted to continue living in the palace in Peking until he left secretly in 1924. On March 9, 1932, he was installed as president, and from 1934 to 1945 was emperor of Manchoukuo under the reign title of K'ang-te. He was taken prisoner by the Russians in August of 1945 and returned to China as a war criminal in 1950. He was pardoned in 1959 and went to live in Peking where he worked in the repair shop of a botanical garden. He died peacefully in Peking in 1967.

Although Hsüan-t'ung became Emperor in 1908, all the coins of his reign are based on an Accession year of 1909.

憲洪

HUNG-HSIEN

宣統通

(Yuan Shih-k'ai)
Dec. 15, 1915 - March 21, 1916

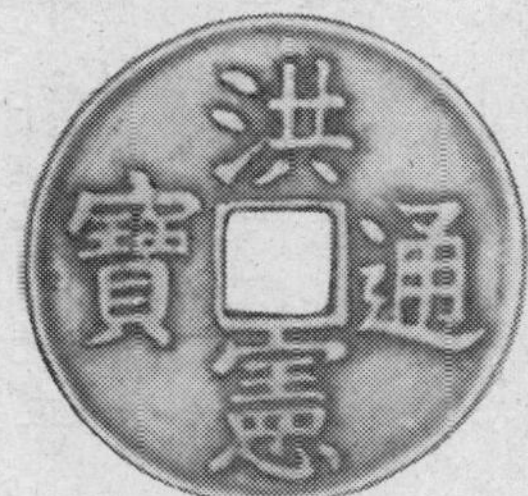

憲洪 通寶

Hung-hsien T'ung-pao

Hung-hsien (more popularly known as Yuan Shih-K'ai). Born in 1859 in Honan Province, he was the first Han Chinese to hold a viceroyalty and become a grand councillor without any academic qualifications. In 1885 he was made Chinese commissioner at Seoul. During the Boxer Rebellion of 1900, the division under his command was the only remnant of China's army to survive. He enjoyed the trust and support of the dowager empress, Tz'u-hsi, and at her death he was stripped of all his offices. However, when the tide of the revolution threatened to engulf the Manchus Yuan appeared as the only man who could lead the country to peace and unity. Both the Emperor and the provisional president recommended that Yuan be the first president of China. He contrived to make himself president for life and boldly tried to create a new imperial dynasty in 1915-1916. He died of uremia on June 6, 1916.

NOTE: For other legend types refer to Rebel Issues listed after Yunnan-Szechuan.

PROVINCIAL MINT NAMES

(and other source indicators)

Provincial names throughout the catalog are based on the Wade-Giles transliteration of the Chinese word. Current spellings, known as the "Pinyin" form, are widely adopted by the printed media. Example: Sinkiang = Xinjiang.

The column at left illustrates the full name as used on most provincial coinage while the column at right illustrates the abbreviated name that appears in the center of the obverse of the Tai-Ch'ing-Ti-Kuo copper coinage.

Full Name Right to Left reading	Single Character (1)
徽安 ANHWEI	皖 Huan
Also An-hwi, Anhui, now Anhui	
江浙 CHEKIANG	浙 Che
Also Cheh-kiang, now Zhejiang	
隸直 CHIHLI	直 Chih
Also Hopei (after 1928) now Hebei	
 CH'ING DYNASTY	
Tai Ch'ing, also Tsing Dynasty now Qing Dynasty	
江清 CHING-KIANG	淮 Huai
Also Tsing-kiang now Qingjiang	
天奉 FENGTIEN	奉 Feng
Also Fung-tien, Fun-tien Shengching Manchurian Provinces, now Liaoning	
建福 FUKIEN	閩 Min
Also Foo-kien, F.K., now Fujian	
江龍黑 HEILUNGKIANG	黑 Hei
Also Hei Lung Kiang, now Heilongjiang	
南河 HONAN	豫 Yu
Also Ho-nan, now Henan	
北河 HOPEH	冀 Chi
Also Chihli, Hopei, now Hebei	
南湖 HUNAN	湘 Hsiang
Also Hu-nan	
北湖 HUPEH	鄂 O
Also Hupei, Hu-peh, now Hubei	
部戶 HU PU (Board of Revenue)	戶 Hu
Also Hu Poo, Hoo Poo	
肅甘 KANSU	甘 Kan
Now Gansu	
南江 KIANGNAN	寗 Ning
Also Kiang Nan, now Jiangnan	

南江 寧
KIANGNAN Ning
Also Kiang Nan, now Jiangnan

西江 贛 or 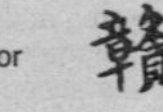
KIANGSI Kan
Also Kiang-si, Kiang-see, now Jiangxi

蘇江 蘇
KIANGSU Su
Also Kiang-soo, now Jiangsu

林吉 吉
KIRIN Chi
Also Chi-lin, now Jilin

西廣 桂
KWANGSI, KWANGSEA Kuei
Also Kwang-si, now Guangxi

東廣 粵
KWANGTUNG Yüeh
Also Kwang-tung, now Guangdong

州貴 黔
KWEICHOW Ch'ien
Also Kweichou, now Guizhou

洋北
PEIYANG MINT (Tientsin)
Also Pei Yang

西山 山
SHANSI Shan
Now Shanxi (Chin)

西陝 陝
SHENSI Shan
Also Shen-si, now Shaanxi

東山 東
SHANTUNG TUNG
Also Shang-tung, Shan-tung, now Shandong (Lu)

魯
SIKANG

疆新 新
SINKIANG Hsin
(Chinese Turkestan)
Also Sin-kiang, Hsin-kiang Sungarei, now Xinjiang

川四 川 蜀
SZECHUAN Ch'uan
Also Szechwan Szechuen, now Sichuan (Shu)

灣臺 
TAIWAN T'ai
Also Tai-wan, now Taiwan

灣台 
TAIWAN T'ai
(Alternate)

南雲 雲 滇
YÜNNAN Yün (Alternate) (Tien)
Also Yun-nan, now Yunnan

省三東
TUNG SAN SHENG
Manchuria

滇川
YUNNAN-SZECHUAN

GOVERNMENTAL NAMES

(and other source indicators)
Full Names (Right to left reading)

府政東冀
CHITUNG (Japanese puppet)

國和共埃維蘇華中
CHINESE SOVIET REPUBLIC

國洲滿大
MANCHOUKUO (Japanese puppet) (2)

行銀疆蒙
MENGCHIANG (Japanese puppet)

中華人民共和國
PEOPLES REPUBLIC OF CHINA (Communist) (3)

國民華中
REPUBLIC OF CHINA (Nationalist)

行銀備準合聯國中
NORTH CHINA (Japanese puppet)

(1) Single-character designators for provincial or regional mints are used primarily on copper coins of the Tai Ching Ti Kuo series.
(2) Vertical readings predominate.
(3) Reads left to right.
(4) For lists of mints in Sinkiang, see that section.

ADDITIONAL CHARACTERS

The additional characters illustrated and defined below are found on the reverse of cast bronze cash coins, usually above the square center hole. In the period covered by this catalog the following mints produced cash coins with these additional marks: Board of Revenue and Board of Works in Peking, Kweichow, Aksu and Ili in Sinkiang, Shantung, Szechuan, and all three mints listed in Yunnan.

CHARACTERS

一	I, YI	十一	Shih I	心	Hsin
二	Erh	合	Ho	宇	Yu
三	San	工	Kung	宙	Chou
四	Szu	主	Chu	來	Lai
五	Wu	川	Ch'uan	往	Wang
六	Liu	之	Chih	晋	Chin
七	Ch'i	正	Cheng	村	Ts'un
八	Pa	又	Yu	日	Jih
九	Chiu	山	Shan	列	Lieh
十	Shih	大 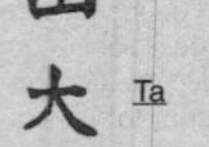	Ta	仁	Jen
主	Chung	中	Feng	手	Shang
順	Shun	云	Yun	手	Shou

天 T'ien 利 Li 穴 Kung
分 Fen

MINT MARK IDENTIFIER

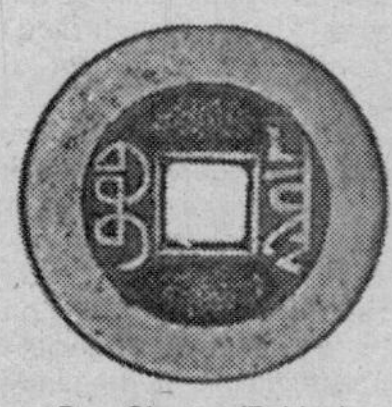
Boo-Clowan (Peking)
Hu-PU BOARD OF REVENUE

Boo-Yuwan (Peking)
Kung-Pu BOARD OZ
PUBLIC WORKS

Boo-an
An Mint
ANHWEI

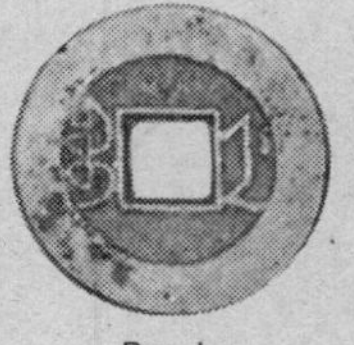
Boo-Je
Chê Mint
Hangchow
CHEKIANG

Boo-Ji
Chih Mint
Paoting
CHIHLI

Boo-GI
Chi Mint
Chichow
CHIHLI

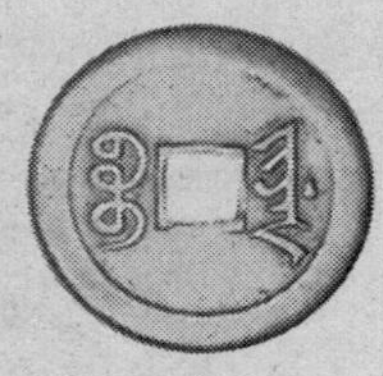
Boo-Jiyen
Ching Mint
Tientsin
CHIHLI

(Through Hsien-Feng era)

Boo-Fung
Fung Mint
FENGTIEN

Boo-Fu
Fu Mint
Fuchou
FUKIEN

Boo-Ho
Ho Mint
K'aifeng
HONAN

Boo-Nan
Nan Mint
Ch'ang-sha
HUNAN

Boo-Ji
Chi Mint
Chinan
SHANTUNG

Boo-Cuwan
Chuán Mint
Chengtu
SZECHUAN

Yarkand (Soche)
SINKIANG

Boo-Tai
Tai Mint
TAIWAN

Boo-De
Teh Mint
Chengte
CHIHLI

Boo-U
Wu Mint
Wuch'ang
HUPEH

Boo-San
Shan Mint
Sian
SHENSI

Boo-Yôn
Yûn Mint
Yûnnan Fu
YUNNAN

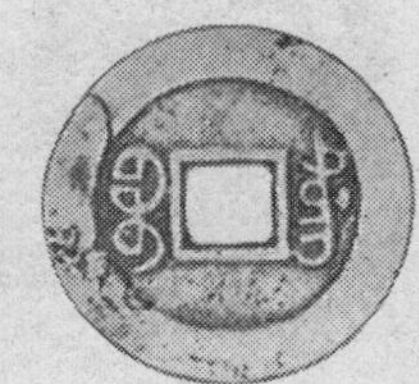

Boo-Dong
Tung Mint
Tungch'uan
YUNNAN

Boo-Gung
Kung Mint
Kungchang
KANSU

Boo-ch'ang
Ch'ang Mint
Nanchang
KIANGSI

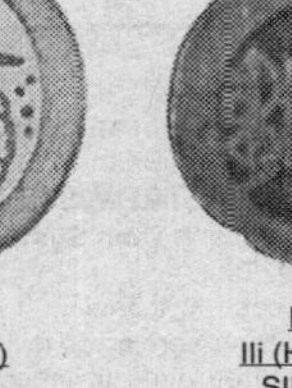

Aksu (Hocheng)
SINKIANG

Boo-Yi
Ili (Hweiyuan)
SINKIANG

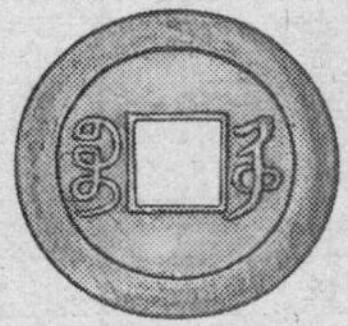

Boo-Gu
Ku Mint
Taku Arsenal
TIENTSIN, CHIHLI

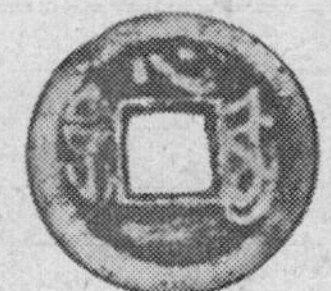

Boo-Fu
Fu Mint
Fuchow
YUNNAN

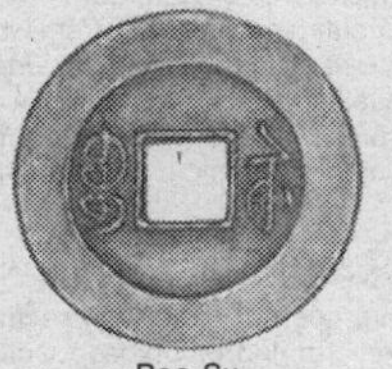

Boo-Su
Su Mint
Soohow
KIANGSU

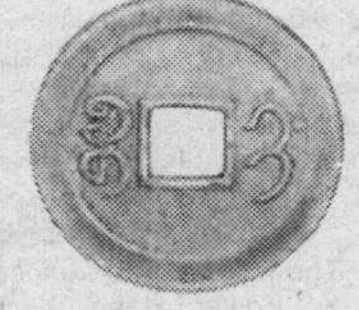

Boo-Gi
Chi Mint

KIRIN

(Kuang-hsu Era)

Kotsha (Kuche)
SINKIANG

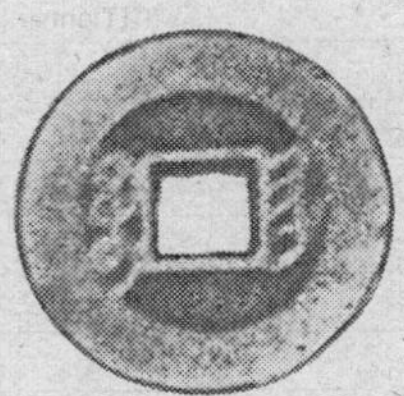

Boo-Jing
Ching Mint
Chingchow Fu
HUPEH

Boo-Gui
Kue Mint
Kuelin
KWANGSI

Boo-Guwang
Kuang Mint
Canton
KWANGTUNG

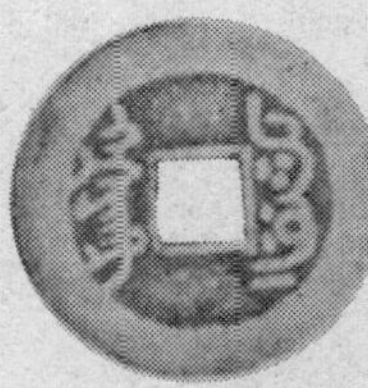

Kashgar (Shufu)
SINKIANG

Khotan (Hotien)
SINKIANG

Boo-Giyan
Kwei Mint
Kweiyang
KWEICHOW

Boo-Jin
Chin Mint
Taiyuan
SHANSI

Boo-Di
Di Mint
Urumchi (Tihwa)
SINKIANG

Ushi (Wushih)
SINKIANG

NON-CIRCULATING ISSUES:

Along with regular circulation coinage produced by the various mints certain cash types were cast in various sizes with the emperor's reign title on the obverse but with various characters and/or symbols not found in our mint identifiers. This listing is not complete but it will benefit the collector as an aid to proper identification.

PALACE ISSUES

(Palace Cash)

Usually 1-6 mace in weight, made of 60" copper and 40" zinc. Made for distribution in the palace during new year. Usually given to eunuchs and guards. Recipients hanged them under lamps - "lamp 'hanging' money."

Obv. ins: Kuang-hsü T'ung-pao
Rev. ins: T'ien-hsia T'ai-p'ing
"Peace under Heaven."

Note: The market value is about $60.00-100.00 in VF condition.

BIRTHDAY CASH

壽福

These issues have the normal reign title on the obverse but the reverse has two Chinese characters *Fu* in normal or seal script (happiness), at right and *Shou* (birthday) at left. The market value is about $60.00-100.00 in F/VF condition. Some are palace issues, but most are made by private sources as good luck amulets.

Kuang-hsü

NUMERALS

NUMBER	CONVENTIONAL	FORMAL	COMMERCIAL
1	一 元	壹 弌	〡
2	二	弍 貳	〢
3	三	叁 弎	〣
4	四	肆	〤
5	五	伍	〥
6	六	陸	〦
7	七	柒	〧
8	八	捌	〨
9	九	玖	〩
10	十	拾 什	十
20	十 二 or 廿	拾貳	〢十
25	五 十 二 or 五廿	伍拾貳	〢十〥
30	十 三 or 卅	拾叁	〣十
100	百 一	佰壹	〡百
1,000	千 一	仟壹	〡千
10,000	萬 一	萬壹	〡万
100,000	萬十 億 一	萬拾 億壹	十万
1,000,000	萬百一	萬佰壹	〡百万

NOTE: This table has been adapted from *Chinese Bank Notes* by Ward Smith and Brian Matravers.

MONETARY UNITS

Dollar Amounts		
DOLLAR *(Yuan)*	元 or 員	圓 or 圜
HALF DOLLAR *(Pan Yuan)*	圓 半	元中
50¢ *(Chiao/Hao)*	角伍	毫伍
10¢ *(Chiao/Hao)*	角壹	毫壹
1¢ *(Fen/Hsien)*	分壹	仙壹

COPPER AND CASH COIN AMOUNTS

COPPER *(Mei)*	枚	CASH *(Wen)*	文

Tael Amounts	
1 TAEL *(Liang)*	兩
HALF TAEL *(Pan Liang)*	兩半
5 MACE *(Wu Ch'ien)*	錢伍
1 MACE *(I Ch'ien)*	錢壹
1 CANDEREEN *(I Fen)*	分壹

COMMON PREFIXES

COPPER *(T'ung)*	銅	GOLD *(Chin)*	金
SILVER *(Yin)*	銀	Ku Ping *(Tael)**	平庫

NOTE: This table has been adapted from Chinese Bank Notes by Ward Smith and Brian Matravers.

MONETARY SYSTEM

Cash Coin System

800-1600 Cash = 1 Tael
400 Sinkiang 'red' cash = 1 Tael

In theory, 1000 cash were equal to a tael of silver, but in actuality the rate varied from time to time and place to place.

Dollar System

10 Cash (Wen, Ch'ien) = 1 Cent (Fen, Hsien)
10 Cents = 1 Chiao (Hao)
100 Cents = 1 Dollar (Yuan)
1 Dollar = 0.72 Tael

Imperial silver coins normally bore no denomination, but were inscribed with their weights as follows:
1 Dollar = 7 Mace and 2 Candareens
50 Cents = 3 Mace and 6 Candareens
20 Cents = 1 Mace and 4.4 Candareens
10 Cents = 7.2 Candareens
5 Cents = 3.6 Candareens

NOTE: *Candareen* is spelled *Candarin* and misspelled as *Caindarin* on Kirin Province Imperial coinage.

Tael System

10 Li = 1 Fen (Candareen)
10 Fen (Candareen) = 1 Ch'ien (Mace)
10 Ch'ien (Mace) = 1 Liang (Tael)

DATING

Most struck Chinese coins are dated by year within a given period, such as the regnal eras or the republican periods. A 1907 issue, for example, would be dated in the 33rd year of the Kuang Hsu era (1875 + 33 - 1 = 1907) or a 1926 issue is dated in the 15th year of the Republic (1912 + 15 - 1 = 1926). The mathematical discrepancy in both instances is accounted for by the fact that the first year is included in the elapsed time. Modern Chinese Communist coins are dated in western numerals using the western calendar, but earlier issues use conventional Chinese numerals. The coins of the Republic of China (Taiwan) are also dated in the year of the Republic, which is added to equal the calendar year. Still another method is a 60-year, repeating cycle, outlined in the table below.

The date is shown by the combination of two characters, the first from the top row and the second from the column at left. In this catalog, when a cyclical date is used, the abbreviation CD appears before the AD date.

Dates not in parentheses are those which appear on the coins. For undated coins, dates appearing in parentheses are the years in which the coin was actually minted. Undated coins for which the year of minting is unknown are listed with ND (No Date) in the date or year column.

CYCLICAL DATES

	庚	辛	壬	癸	甲	乙	丙	丁	戊	己
戌	1850 1910		1862 1922		1874 1934		1886 1946		1838 1898	
亥		1851 1911		1863 1923		1875 1935		1887 1947		1839 1899
子	1840 1900		1852 1912		1864 1924		1876 1936		1888 1948	
丑		1841 1901		1853 1913		1865 1925		1877 1937		1889 1949
寅	1830 1890		1842 1902		1854 1914		1866 1926		1878 1938	
卯		1831 1891		1843 1903		1855 1915		1867 1927		1879 1939
辰	1880 1940		1832 1892		1844 1904		1856 1916		1868 1928	
巳		1881 1941		1833 1893		1845 1905		1857 1917		1869 1929
午	1870 1930		1882 1942		1834 1894		1846 1906		1858 1918	
未		1871 1931		1883 1943		1835 1895		1847 1907		1859 1919
申	1860 1920		1872 1932		1884 1944		1836 1896		1848 1908	
酉		1861 1921		1873 1933		1885 1945		1837 1897		1849 1909

NOTE: This table has been adapted from *Chinese Bank Notes* by Ward Smith and Brian Matravers.

GRADING

Chinese coins should not be graded entirely by western standards. In addition to Fine, Very Fine, Extremely Fine (XF), and Uncirculated, the type of strike should be considered weak, medium or sharp strike. China had no rigid minting rules as we know them. For instance, Kirin (Jilin) and Sinkiang (Xinjiang) Provinces used some dies made of iron - hence, they wore out rapidly. Some communist army issues were apparently struck by crude hand methods on soft dies (it is hard to find two coins of the same die!). In general, especially for some minor coins, dies were used until they were worn well beyond western standards. Subsequently, one could have an uncirculated coin struck from worn dies with little of the design or letters still visible, but still uncirculated! All prices quoted are for well-struck (sharp struck), well-centered specimens. Most silver coins can be found from very fine to uncirculated. Some copper coins are difficult to find except in poorer grades.

REFERENCES

The following references have been used for this section:
K - Edward Kann - Illustrated Catalog of Chinese Coins.
Hsu - T.K. Hsu - Illustrated Catalog of Chinese Coins, 1981 edition.
W - A.M. Tracey Woodward - The Minted Ten-Cash Coins of China.

NOTE: The die struck 10 and 20 Cash coins are often found silver plated. This was not done at the mint. They were apparently plated to be passed to the unwary as silver coins.

IDENTIFICATION

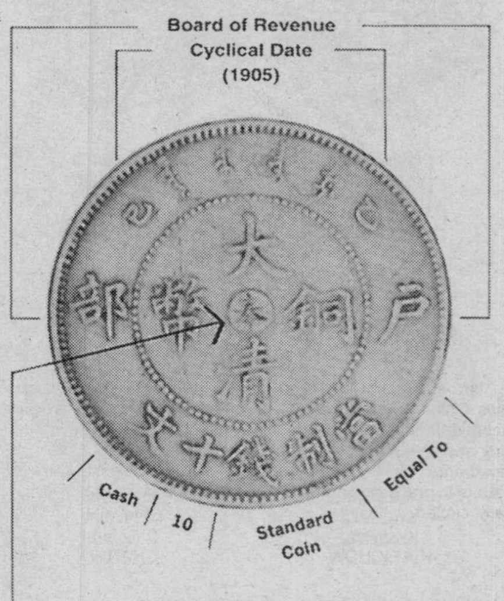

DRAGON TYPES
(Chinese Imperial Coins)

Side View Dragon-left (Silver Coins)

First used by the Kwangtung Mint in 1889. This was the standard (though not the only) dragon used on silver coins. Normally there is no circle around the dragon. Note the fireball beneath the dragon's chin. Normally there are seven flames on the fireball.

Side View Dragon-left (Copper Coins)

First used on copper coins in 1901 or 1902. The dragon may be circled or uncircled. Many varieties exist, with three to seven flames on the fireball.

Side View Dragon-right (Silver Coins)

First appears on the second series of Fukien. The dragon is redesigned with the dragon's body reversed.

Flying Dragon

Introduced in 1901. Copied from the dragon on Japanese coins. China used this dragon only on copper coins (with one rare exception). Note that the clouds around the dragon's body are curly and snake-like instead of puffy like those around the side view dragon. The fireball now appears as a pearl which the dragon is about to grasp, and normally has no flames. This dragon is normally circled.

Front View Dragon

Introduced about 1904, this type of dragon was not used by many mints. The dragon is usually uncircled and has few clouds around its body. Note the tiny mountain under the cloud beneath the fireball.

Tai Ch'ing Ti Kuo Dragon

In 1905 China carried out a coinage reform which standardized the designs of copper coins. All mints were ordered to use the same obverse and reverse designs, but to place a mint mark in the center of the obverse.

SYCEE (INGOTS)

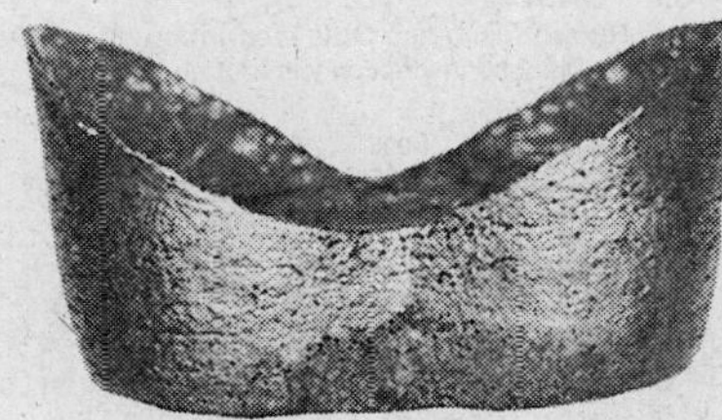

Prior to 1889 the general coinage issued by the Chinese government was the copper-alloy cash coin. Despite occasional short-lived experiments with silver and gold coinage, and disregarding paper money which tended to be unreliable, the government expected the people to get by solely with cash coins. This system worked well for individuals making purchases for themselves, but was unsatisfactory for trade and large business transactions, since a dollar's worth of cash coins weighed about four pounds. As a result, a private currency consisting of silver ingots, usually stamped by the firm which made them, came into use. These were the sycee ingots.

It is not known when these ingots first came into use. Some sources date them to the Yuan (Mongol) dynasty but they are certainly much older. Examples are known from as far back as the Han dynasty (206 BC - 220 AD) but prior to the Sung era (960 - 1280AD) they were used mainly for hoarding wealth. The development of commerce by the Sung dynasty, however, required the use of silver or gold to pay for large purchases. By the Mongol period (1280-1368) silver ingots and paper money had become the dominant currencies, especially for trade. The western explorers who traveled to China during this period (such as Marco Polo) mention both paper money and sycee but not a single one refers to cash coins.

During the Ming dynasty (1368-1644) trade fell off and the use of silver decreased. But toward the end of that dynasty, Dutch and British ships began a new China trade and sycee once again became common. During the 19th and early 20th centuries, the trade in sycee became enormous. Most of the sycee around today are from this period. In 1935 the Chinese government and in 1939 Sinkiang banned the use of sycee and it soon disappeared.

The word sycee (pronounced "sigh - see") is a western corruption of the Chinese word hsi-szu ("fine silk") or hsi yin ("fine silver") and is first known to have appeared in the English language in the late 1600's. By the early 1700's the word appeared regularly in the records of the British East India Company. Westerners also called these ingots "boat money" or "shoe money" owing to the fact that the most common type of ingot resembles a Chinese shoe. The Chinese, however, called the ingots by a variety of names, the most common of which were yuan pao, wen-yin (fine silver) and yin-ting (silver ingot).

The ingots were cast in molds (giving them their characteristic shapes) and while the metal was still semi-liquid, the inscription was impressed. It was due to this procedure that the sides of some sycee are higher than the center. The manufacturers were usually silver firms, often referred to as lu fang's, and after the sycee was finished it was occasionally tested and marked by the kung ku (public assayer).

Sycee were not circulated as we understand it. One didn't usually carry a sycee to market and spend it. Usually the ingots were used as a means of carrying a large amount of money on trips (as we would carry $100 bills instead of $5 bills) or for storing wealth. Large transactions between merchants or banks were paid by means of crates of sycee - each containing 60 fifty tael ingots.

Sycee are known in a variety of shapes the most common of which are the shoe or boat shaped, drum shaped, and loaf shaped (rectangular or hourglass-shaped, with a generally flat surface). Other shapes include one that resembles a double headed axe (this is the oldest type known), one that is square and flat, and others that are "fancy" (in the form of fish, butterflies, leaves, etc.).

Sycee have no denominations as they were simply ingots that passed by weight. Most are in more or less standard weights, however, the most common being 1, 5, 10 and 50 taels. Other weights known include 1/10, 1/5, 1/4, 1/3, 1/2, 2/3, 72/100 (this is the weight of a dollar), 3/4, 2, 3, 4, 6, 7, 8 and 25 taels. Most of the pieces weighing less than 5 taels were used as gifts or souvenirs.

The actual weight of any given value of sycee varied considerably due to the fact that the tael was not a single weight but a general term for a wide range of local weight standards. The weight of the tael varied depending upon location and type of tael in question. For example in one town, the weight of a tael of rice, of silver and of stones may each be different. In addition, the fineness of silver also varied depending upon location and type of tael in question. It was not true, as westerners often wrote, that sycee were made of pure silver. For most purposes, a weight of 37 grams may be used for the tael.

Weights and Current Market Value of Sycee

(Weights are approximate)

1/2 Tael	17-19 grams	26
72/100 Tael	25-27 grams	36
1 Tael	35-38 grams	46
2 Taels	70-75 grams	70
3 Taels	100-140 grams	85
5 Taels	175-190 grams	110
7 Taels	240-260 grams	125
10 Taels	350-380 grams	250
25 Taels	895-925 grams	3500
50 Taels	1790-1850 grams	2000
50 Taels, square	1790-1850 grams	1600

SZECHUAN WARLORD ISSUE

200 Cash

Obv: Mirror image of normal coin, Y#459.

NOTE: Certain coins found with degenerate or reversed English legends are usually considered to be local warlord issues while some authorities insist on referring to them as contemporary counterfeits.

EMPIRE

CH'ING DYNASTY

Manchu, 1644 - 1911

GENERAL CAST COINAGE

C# 1-16 CASH

Cast Brass **Ruler:** Kuang-hsü **Obv. Inscription:** Kuang-hsü T'ung-pao **Rev. Inscription:** Boo-ciowan

Date	Mintage	Good	VG	F	VF	XF
ND(1875-1908)	—	1.50	2.00	2.75	4.00	—

Note: For crude cast, red copper issues, see Sinkiang General coinage

C# 1-16.1 CASH

Cast Brass **Ruler:** Kuang-hsü **Series:** Thousand Character Classic **Obv. Inscription:** Kuang-hsü T'ung-pao **Rev:** Manchu inscription with "Chin" above **Rev. Inscription:** Boo-ciowan

Date	Mintage	Good	VG	F	VF	XF
ND(1875-1908)	—	6.00	9.00	13.50	20.00	—

C# 1-16.2 CASH

Cast Brass **Ruler:** Kuang-hsü **Series:** Thousand Character Classic **Obv. Inscription:** Kuang-hsü T'ung-pao **Rev:** Manchu inscription with "Chou" above **Rev. Inscription:** Boo-ciowan

Date	Mintage	Good	VG	F	VF	XF
ND(1875-1908)	—	6.00	9.00	13.50	20.00	—

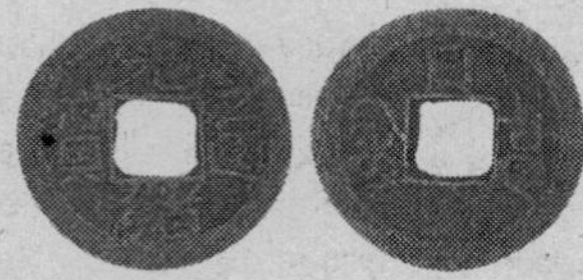

C# 1-16.3 CASH

Cast Brass **Ruler:** Kuang-hsü **Series:** Thousand Character Classic **Obv. Inscription:** Kuang-hsü T'ung-pao **Rev:** Manchu inscription with "Jih" above **Rev. Inscription:** Boo-ciowan

Date	Mintage	Good	VG	F	VF	XF
ND(1875-1908)	—	6.00	9.00	13.50	20.00	—

C# 1-16.4 CASH

Cast Brass **Ruler:** Kuang-hsü **Series:** Thousand Character Classic **Obv. Inscription:** Kuang-hsü T'ung-pao **Rev:** Manchu inscription with "Lai" above **Rev. Inscription:** Boo-ciowan

Date	Mintage	Good	VG	F	VF	XF
ND(1875-1908)	—	6.00	9.00	13.50	20.00	—

C# 1-16.5 CASH

Cast Brass **Ruler:** Kuang-hsü **Series:** Thousand Character Classic **Obv. Inscription:** Kuang-hsü T'ung-pao **Rev:** Manchu inscription with "Lieh" above **Rev. Inscription:** Boo-ciowan

Date	Mintage	Good	VG	F	VF	XF
ND(1875-1908)	—	6.00	9.00	13.50	20.00	—

C# 1-16.6 CASH

Cast Brass **Ruler:** Kuang-hsü **Series:** Thousand Character Classic **Obv. Inscription:** Kuang-hsü T'ung-pao **Rev:** Manchu inscription with "Wang" above **Rev. Inscription:** Boo-ciowan

Date	Mintage	Good	VG	F	VF	XF
ND(1875-1908)	—	6.00	9.00	13.50	20.00	—

C# 1-16.7 CASH

Cast Brass **Ruler:** Kuang-hsü **Series:** Thousand Character Classic **Obv. Inscription:** Kuang-hsü T'ung-pao **Rev:** Manchu inscription with "Yu" above **Rev. Inscription:** Boo-ciowan

Date	Mintage	Good	VG	F	VF	XF
ND(1875-1908)	—	6.00	9.00	13.50	20.00	—

C# 1-16.8 CASH

Cast Brass **Ruler:** Kuang-hsü **Obv. Inscription:** Kuang-hsü T'ung-pao **Rev:** Manchu inscription with dot below **Rev. Inscription:** Boo-ciowan

Date	Mintage	Good	VG	F	VF	XF
ND(1899-1901)	—	1.75	3.00	4.00	6.00	—

C# 1-16.9 CASH

Cast Brass **Ruler:** Kuang-hsü **Obv. Inscription:** Kuang-hsü T'ung-pao **Rev:** Manchu inscription with dot above **Rev. Inscription:** Boo-ciowan

Date	Mintage	Good	VG	F	VF	XF
ND(1899-1901)	—	1.75	3.00	4.00	6.00	—

C# 1-16.10 CASH

Cast Brass **Ruler:** Kuang-hsü **Series:** Thousand Character Classic **Obv. Inscription:** Kuang-hsü T'ung-pao **Rev:** Manchu inscription with "Shou" above **Rev. Inscription:** Boo-ciowan

Date	Mintage	Good	VG	F	VF	XF
ND(1875-1908)	—	6.00	9.00	13.50	20.00	—

C# 2-15 CASH

Cast Brass **Ruler:** Kuang-hsü **Obv. Inscription:** Kuang-hsü T'ung-pao **Rev:** Manchu inscription **Rev. Inscription:** Boo-yuwan **Note:** Size varies: 25-26mm.

Date	Mintage	Good	VG	F	VF	XF
ND(1875-1908)	—	1.50	3.00	6.00	7.00	—

Note: For crude cast copper strikes, see Sinkiang General Coinage

C# 2-15.1 CASH

Cast Brass **Ruler:** Kuang-hsü **Series:** Thousand Character Classic **Obv. Inscription:** Kuang-hsü T'ung-pao **Rev:** Manchu inscription with "Chou" above **Rev. Inscription:** Boo-yuwan **Note:** Size varies: 19-20mm.

Date	Mintage	Good	VG	F	VF	XF
ND(1899-1901)	—	6.00	10.00	15.00	20.00	—

C# 2-15.2 CASH

Cast Brass **Ruler:** Kuang-hsü **Series:** Thousand Character Classic **Obv. Inscription:** Kuang-hsü T'ung-pao **Rev:** Manchu inscription with "Lai" above **Rev. Inscription:** Boo-yuwan

Date	Mintage	Good	VG	F	VF	XF
ND(1899-1901)	—	6.00	10.00	15.00	20.00	—

C# 2-15.3 CASH

Cast Brass **Ruler:** Kuang-hsü **Series:** Thousand Character Classic **Obv. Inscription:** Kuang-hsü T'ung-pao **Rev:** Manchu inscription with "Lieh" above **Rev. Inscription:** Boo-yuwan

Date	Mintage	Good	VG	F	VF	XF
ND(1899-1901)	—	6.00	10.00	15.00	20.00	—

C# 2-15.4 CASH

Cast Brass **Ruler:** Kuang-hsü **Series:** Thousand Character Classic **Obv. Inscription:** Kuang-hsü T'ung-pao **Rev:** Manchu inscription with "Yu" above **Rev. Inscription:** Boo-yuwan

Date	Mintage	Good	VG	F	VF	XF
ND(1899-1901)	—	6.00	10.00	15.00	20.00	—

C# 2-15.5 CASH

Cast Brass, 20 mm. **Ruler:** Kuang-hsü **Series:** Thousand Character Classic **Obv. Inscription:** Kuang-hsü T'ung-pao **Rev:** Manchu inscription with "Jih" above **Rev. Inscription:** Boo-yuwan

Date	Mintage	Good	VG	F	VF	XF
ND(1899-1901)	—	6.00	10.00	15.00	20.00	—

C# 2-15.6 CASH

Cast Brass **Ruler:** Kuang-hsü **Series:** Thousand Character Classic **Obv. Inscription:** Kuang-hsü T'ung-pao **Rev:** Manchu inscription with "Wang" above **Rev. Inscription:** Boo-yuwan

Date	Mintage	Good	VG	F	VF	XF
ND(1899-1901)	—	6.00	10.00	15.00	20.00	—

C# 2-15.7 CASH

Cast Brass **Ruler:** Kuang-hsü **Series:** Thousand Character Classic **Obv. Inscription:** Kuang-hsü T'ung-pao **Rev:** Manchu inscription with "Jih" above, dot below **Rev. Inscription:** Boo-yuwan

Date	Mintage	Good	VG	F	VF	XF
ND(1899-1901)	—	6.00	10.00	15.00	20.00	—

C# 1-19.1 CASH

Cast Brass, 19 mm. **Ruler:** Hsüan-t'ung **Obv. Inscription:** Hsüan-t'ung T'ung-pao **Rev:** Manchu inscription **Rev. Inscription:** Boo-ciowan

Date	Mintage	Good	VG	F	VF	XF
ND(1909-11)	—	5.50	7.00	10.00	15.00	—

C# 1-19.2 CASH

Cast Brass, 24 mm. **Ruler:** Hsüan-t'ung **Obv. Inscription:** Hsüan-t'ung T'ung-pao **Rev:** Manchu inscription **Rev. Inscription:** Boo-ciowan

Date	Mintage	Good	VG	F	VF	XF
ND(1909-11)	—	10.00	15.00	25.00	30.00	—

C# 1-19a CASH

Iron, 23 mm. **Ruler:** Hsüan-t'ung **Obv. Inscription:** Hsüan-t'ung T'ung-pao **Rev:** Manchu inscription **Rev. Inscription:** Boo-ciowan

Date	Mintage	Good	VG	F	VF	XF
ND(1909-11)	—	12.00	20.00	30.00	50.00	—

C# 2-16 5 CASH

Cast Brass **Ruler:** Kuang-hsü **Obv. Inscription:** Kuang-hsü T'ung-pao **Rev:** Manchu inscription **Rev. Inscription:** Boo-yuwan

Date	Mintage	Good	VG	F	VF	XF
ND(1875-1908)	—	200	350	500	700	—

C# 1-17 10 CASH

Cast Brass, 30 mm. **Ruler:** Kuang-hsü **Obv. Inscription:** Kuang-hsü Chung-pao **Rev:** Manchu inscription with normal "Shih" for 10 below **Rev. Inscription:** Boo-ciowan

Date	Mintage	Good	VG	F	VF	XF
ND(1875-1908)	—	3.00	5.00	8.00	10.00	—

C# 1-18 10 CASH

Cast Brass, 28 mm. **Ruler:** Kuang-hsü **Obv. Inscription:** Kuang-hsü Chung-pao **Rev:** Manchu inscription with official "Shih" for 10 below **Rev. Inscription:** Boo-ciowan

Date	Mintage	Good	VG	F	VF	XF
ND(1875-1908)	—	4.50	7.50	10.00	15.00	—

C# 1-18.1 10 CASH

Cast Brass, 22 mm. **Ruler:** Kuang-hsü **Obv. Inscription:** Kuang-hsü Chung-pao **Rev:** Manchu inscription with official "Shih" for 10 below **Rev. Inscription:** Boo-ciowan

Date	Mintage	Good	VG	F	VF	XF
ND(1875-1908)	—	6.00	9.00	15.00	20.00	—

C# 2-17 10 CASH

Cast Brass **Ruler:** Kuang-hsü **Obv. Inscription:** Kuang-hsü Chung-pao **Rev:** Manchu inscription with normal Shih (10) below **Rev. Inscription:** Boo-yuwan **Note:** Size varies: 31-32mm.

Date	Mintage	Good	VG	F	VF	XF
ND(1875-1908)	—	4.50	7.50	10.00	25.00	—

C# 2-18 10 CASH

Cast Brass **Ruler:** Kuang-hsü **Obv. Inscription:** Kuang-hsü T'ung-pao **Rev:** Manchu inscription with official Shih (10) below **Rev. Inscription:** Boo-yuwan

Date	Mintage	Good	VG	F	VF	XF
ND(1880-1908)	—	6.00	10.00	15.00	35.00	—

STANDARD UNIFIED GENERAL COINAGE

A Central mint opened at Tientsin in 1905, was made responsible for producing most of the dies for the Tai Ch'ing Hu Poo coinage and for the 1910 and 1911 unified coinage. The mint was burned down in 1912 but resumed operations in 1914 with Yuan Shih-k'ai dollar issues. It continued producing dies for selected branch mints until 1921. It was superseded as the Central mint of China by Nanking in 1927 and by the new Nationalist Government mint at Shanghai in 1933.

Y# 7 CASH

Brass **Ruler:** Kuang-hsü **Obv. Legend:** "Kuang-hsü" **Rev:** Dragon **Note:** Struck.

Date	Mintage	VG	F	VF	XF	Unc
CD1908	—	1.00	3.00	6.00	12.00	—

Y# 18 CASH

Brass **Ruler:** Hsüan-t'ung **Obv. Legend:** "Hsüan-t'ung" **Rev:** Dragon **Note:** Struck.

Date	Mintage	VG	F	VF	XF	Unc
CD1909	—	25.00	50.00	85.00	135	—

Note: Inc. Y25

Y# 25 CASH

Brass **Obv. Inscription:** Tai-ch'ing T'ung-pi

Date	Mintage	VG	F	VF	XF	Unc
ND(1909)	92,126,000	1.00	1.50	2.00	3.00	—

Y# 8 2 CASH

Copper **Ruler:** Kuang-hsü **Obv. Inscription:** Tai-ch'ing T'ung-pi **Rev:** Dragon

Date	Mintage	VG	F	VF	XF	Unc
CD1905 Hu-pu	—	2.50	4.50	10.00	17.50	—
CD1906 Hu-pu	—	3.00	6.00	10.00	25.00	—

Y# 8.1 2 CASH

Copper **Ruler:** Kuang-hsü **Obv:** Four dots divide legend **Obv. Inscription** Tai-ch'ing T'ung-pi **Rev:** Dragon

Date	Mintage	VG	F	VF	XF	Unc
CD1907	—	7.00	18.00	25.00	40.00	—

Y# A18 2 CASH

Copper **Ruler:** Hsüan-t'ung **Obv. Inscription:** Hsüan-t'ung

Date	Mintage	VG	F	VF	XF	Unc
CD1909 Rare	13,353,000	—	—	—	—	—

Y# 3 5 CASH

Copper **Ruler:** Kuang-hsü **Obv. Inscription:** Kuang-hsü Yüan-pao **Rev:** Dragon **Rev. Legend:** HU POO

Date	Mintage	VG	F	VF	XF	Unc
ND(1903-05) Hu-pu	3,671,000	7.00	14.00	21.00	35.00	—

Y# 9 5 CASH

Copper **Ruler:** Kuang-hsü **Obv. Inscription:** Tai-ch'ing T'ung-pi **Rev:** Dragon; smaller legend **Rev. Legend:** Kuang-hsü

Date	Mintage	VG	F	VF	XF	Unc
CD1905	—	5.00	10.00	20.00	35.00	—
CD1906 Rare	—	—	—	—	—	—

Y# 9.1 5 CASH

Copper **Ruler:** Kuang-hsü **Obv:** Four dots divide legend **Obv. Legend:** Kuang-hsü **Obv. Inscription:** Tai-ch'ing T'ung-pi **Rev:** Dragon

Date	Mintage	VG	F	VF	XF	Unc
CD1907	—	16.50	40.00	75.00	125	—

Y# 19 5 CASH

Copper **Ruler:** Hsüan-t'ung **Obv. Legend:** Hsüan-t'ung

Date	Mintage	VG	F	VF	XF	Unc
CD1909	2,170,000	—	—	850	1,200	—

Y# 4 10 CASH

Copper **Ruler:** Kuang-hsü **Obv. Inscription:** Kuang-hsü Yüan-pao **Rev:** Side view dragon **Rev. Legend:** HU POO

Date	Mintage	VG	F	VF	XF	Unc
ND(1903-05)	281,171,000	0.65	2.00	3.50	6.00	25.00

Y# 4.1 10 CASH

Copper **Ruler:** Kuang-hsü **Rev:** Side view dragon; different rosettes; smaller legend **Rev. Legend:** HU POO

Date	Mintage	VG	F	VF	XF	Unc
ND(1903-05)	Inc. above	0.35	1.00	2.00	5.00	20.00

Y# 10 10 CASH

Copper **Ruler:** Kuang-hsü **Obv. Inscription:** Tai-ch'ing T'ung-pi **Rev:** Side view dragon **Rev. Legend:** Kuang-hsü Nien-tsao TAI-CHING-TI-KUO...

Date	Mintage	VG	F	VF	XF	Unc
CD1905	Inc. above	0.50	1.50	3.00	5.00	25.00

Y# 10.1 10 CASH

Copper **Ruler:** Kuang-hsü **Obv. Inscription:** Tai-ch'ing T'ung-pi **Rev:** Different dragon; larger legend **Rev. Legend:** TAI-CHING-TI-KUO...

Date	Mintage	VG	F	VF	XF	Unc
CD1905	—	10.00	25.00	65.00	110	200

Y# 10.2 10 CASH

Copper **Ruler:** Kuang-hsü **Obv. Inscription:** Tai-ch'ing T'ung-pi **Rev:** Dragon **Rev. Legend:** Kuang-hsü Nien-tsao TAI-CHING-TI-KUO

Date	Mintage	VG	F	VF	XF	Unc
CD1906	—	0.25	0.75	1.50	3.00	20.00

Y# 10.3 10 CASH

Copper **Ruler:** Kuang-hsü **Obv:** Without dots **Obv. Inscription:** Tai-ch'ing T'ung-pi **Rev:** Dragon; legend without dot after "KUO" **Rev. Legend:** Kuang-hsü Nien-tsao TAI-CHING-TI-KUO

Date	Mintage	VG	F	VF	XF	Unc
CD1907	—	0.35	1.00	2.00	4.50	18.00

Y# 10.4 10 CASH

Copper **Ruler:** Kuang-hsü **Obv. Inscription:** Tai-ch'ing T'ung-pi **Rev:** Dragon; legend with dot after "KUO" **Rev. Legend:** Kuang-hsü Nien-tsao TAI-CHING-TI-KUO.

Date	Mintage	VG	F	VF	XF	Unc
CD1907	—	0.35	1.00	2.00	4.50	18.00

Y# 10.4a 10 CASH

Brass **Ruler:** Kuang-hsü **Obv:** Without dots **Obv. Inscription:** Tai-ch'ing T'ung-pi **Rev:** Dragon **Rev. Legend:** Kuang-hsü Nien-tsao TAI-CHING-TI-KUO.

Date	Mintage	VG	F	VF	XF	Unc
CD1907	—	1.85	5.50	20.00	35.00	80.00

Y# 10.5 10 CASH

Copper **Ruler:** Kuang-hsü **Obv:** Four dots divide legend **Obv. Inscription:** Tai-ch'ing T'ung-pi **Rev:** Dragon **Rev. Legend:** Kuang-hsü Nien-tsao TAI-CHING-TI-KUO.

Date	Mintage	VG	F	VF	XF	Unc
CD1907	—	0.35	1.00	2.00	4.50	18.00

Y# 10.5a 10 CASH

Brass **Ruler:** Kuang-hsü **Obv. Inscription:** Tai-ch'ing T'ung-pi **Rev:** Dragon **Rev. Legend:** Kuang-hsü Nien-tsao TAI-CHING-TI-KUO.

Date	Mintage	VG	F	VF	XF	Unc
CD1907	—	1.85	5.50	15.00	30.00	85.00

Y# 20 10 CASH

Copper **Ruler:** Hsüan-t'ung **Obv. Inscription:** Tai-ch'ing T'ung-pi **Rev:** Waves below dragon **Rev. Legend:** Hsüan-t'ung Nien-tsao TAI-CHING-TI-KUO.

Date	Mintage	VG	F	VF	XF	Unc
CD1909	—	0.35	1.00	2.00	4.00	22.50

Y# 20.1 10 CASH

Copper **Ruler:** Hsüan-t'ung **Obv. Inscription:** Tai-ch'ing T'ung-pi **Rev:** Rosette below dragon, "U" of "KUO" inverted "A" **Rev. Legend:** Hsüan-t'ung Nien-tsao TAI-CHING-TI-KUO.

Date	Mintage	VG	F	VF	XF	Unc
CD1909	—	1.85	5.50	12.00	25.00	60.00

Note: Although this coin bears no indication of its origin, it was minted in the Manchurian Provinces ca.1922

Y# 20x 10 CASH

Copper **Ruler:** Hsüan-t'ung **Obv:** Rosette in center **Obv. Inscription:** Tai-ch'ing T'ung-pi **Rev:** Dragon **Rev. Legend:** Hsüan-t'ung Nien-tsao TAI-CHING-TI-KUO.

Date	Mintage	VG	F	VF	XF	Unc
CD1909	—	3.50	10.00	20.00	30.00	80.00

Note: Although this coin bears no indication of its origin, it was minted in Kirin Province

Y# 27 10 CASH

Bronze **Ruler:** Hsüan-t'ung **Obv:** Dragon **Obv. Inscription:** Tai-ch'ing T'ung-pi **Rev. Legend:** Hsüan-t'ung...

Date	Mintage	VG	F	VF	XF	Unc
3(1911)	95,585,000	0.85	2.50	4.00	8.00	40.00
3(1911) Proof; Rare	—	—	—	—	—	—

Y# 27a 10 CASH

Brass **Ruler:** Hsüan-t'ung **Obv:** Dragon **Obv. Inscription:** Tai-ch'ing T'ung-pi **Rev. Legend:** Hsüan-t'ung...

Date	Mintage	VG	F	VF	XF	Unc
3(1911)	—	12.00	30.00	45.00	95.00	150

Y# 5 20 CASH

Copper, 32 mm. **Ruler:** Kuang-hsü **Obv. Inscription:** Kuang-hsü Yüan-pao **Rev:** Dragon **Rev. Legend:** HU POO

Date	Mintage	VG	F	VF	XF	Unc
ND(1903) Restrike	—	0.50	1.00	2.00	3.00	—

Y# 5.1 20 CASH

Copper, 32 mm. **Ruler:** Kuang-hsü **Obv:** Four-point rosette in center **Obv. Inscription:** Kuang-hsü Yüan-pao **Rev:** Dragon **Rev. Legend:** HU POO

Date	Mintage	VG	F	VF	XF	Unc
ND(1903) Restrike	—	2.50	6.00	12.00	25.00	—

Y# 5.2 20 CASH

Copper, 32 mm. **Ruler:** Kuang-hsü **Obv. Inscription:** Kuang-hsü Yüan-pao **Rev:** Head of dragon and clouds redesigned **Rev. Legend:** HU POO

Date	Mintage	VG	F	VF	XF	Unc
ND(1903) Restrike	—	2.50	6.00	12.00	25.00	—

Note: Y#5-5.2 were struck at the Wuchang Mint in 1917 from unused dies prepared in 1903

Y# 5a 20 CASH

Copper, 32 mm. **Ruler:** Kuang-hsü **Obv. Inscription:** Kuang-hsü Yüan-pao **Rev:** Dragon in circle of dots **Rev. Legend:** HU POO

Date	Mintage	VG	F	VF	XF	Unc
ND(1903-05)	—	30.00	50.00	85.00	125	—

Y# 11 20 CASH

Copper, 32 mm. **Ruler:** Kuang-hsü **Obv. Inscription:** Tai-ch'ing T'ung-pi **Rev:** Dragon **Rev. Legend:** Kuang-hsü Nien-tsao, TAI-CHING-TI-KUO

Date	Mintage	VG	F	VF	XF	Unc
CD1905	—	12.50	30.00	50.00	75.00	—

Y# 11.1 20 CASH

Copper, 32 mm. **Ruler:** Kuang-hsü **Obv. Inscription:** Tai-ch'ing T'ung-pi **Rev:** Dragon **Rev. Legend:** Kuang-hsü Nien-tsao, TAI-CHING-TI-KUO

Date	Mintage	VG	F	VF	XF	Unc
CD1906	—	12.50	30.00	50.00	75.00	—

Y# 11.2 20 CASH

Copper, 32 mm. **Ruler:** Kuang-hsü **Obv:** Dots around date **Obv. Inscription:** Tai-ch'ing T'ung-pi **Rev:** Dragon **Rev. Legend:** Kuang-hsü Nien-tsao, TAI-CHING-TI-KUO **Note:** 1.2-1.7 mm. thick.

Date	Mintage	VG	F	VF	XF	Unc
CD1907	—	0.60	1.50	2.00	4.00	—

Y# 11.3 20 CASH

Copper, 32 mm. **Ruler:** Kuang-hsü **Obv. Inscription:** Tai-ch'ing T'ung-pi **Rev:** Dragon **Rev. Legend:** Kuang-hsü Nien-tsao, TAI-CHING-TI-KUO **Note:** 2.0-2.3 mm. thick.

Date	Mintage	VG	F	VF	XF	Unc
CD1907	—	2.50	6.00	12.00	25.00	—

Y# 11.3a 20 CASH

Brass, 32 mm. **Ruler:** Kuang-hsü **Obv. Inscription:** Tai-ch'ing T'ung-pi **Rev:** Dragon **Rev. Legend:** Kuang-hsü Nien-tsao, TAI-CHING-TI-KUO

Date	Mintage	VG	F	VF	XF	Unc
CD1907	—	3.50	8.00	15.00	30.00	—

Y# 21 20 CASH
Brass, 32 mm. **Ruler:** Hsüan-t'ung **Obv. Inscription:** Tai-ch'ing T'ung-pi **Rev:** With dot between "KUO" and COPPER; six waves beneath dragon **Rev. Legend:** Hsüan-t'ung Nien-tsao, TAI-CHING-TI-KUO...

Date	Mintage	VG	F	VF	XF	Unc
CD1909	—	1.00	2.50	5.00	10.00	—

Y# 21.1 20 CASH
Copper, 32 mm. **Ruler:** Hsüan-t'ung **Obv. Inscription:** Tai-ch'ing T'ung-pi **Rev:** Without dot between "KUO" and "COPPER"; six waves beneath dragon **Rev. Legend:** Hsüan-t'ung Nien-tsao, TAI-CHING-TI-KUO... **Note:** 1.2-1.7 mm. thick.

Date	Mintage	VG	F	VF	XF	Unc
CD1909	—	1.25	3.00	6.00	10.00	—

Y# 21.2 20 CASH
Copper, 32 mm. **Ruler:** Hsüan-t'ung **Obv. Inscription:** Tai-ch'ing T'ung-pi **Rev:** Without dot between "KUO" and "COPPER"; six waves beneath dragon **Rev. Legend:** Hsüan-t'ung Nien-tsao, TAI-CHING-TI-KUO... **Note:** 2.0-2.3 mm. thick.

Date	Mintage	VG	F	VF	XF	Unc
CD1909	—	1.25	3.00	6.00	10.00	—

Y# 21.3 20 CASH
Copper, 32 mm. **Ruler:** Hsüan-t'ung **Obv. Inscription:** Tai-ch'ing T'ung-pi **Rev:** Without dot between "KUO" and "COPPER"; rosette beneath dragon **Rev. Legend:** Hsüan-t'ung Nien-tsao, TAI-CHING-TI-KUO...

Date	Mintage	VG	F	VF	XF	Unc
CD1909 Restrike	—	6.00	15.00	40.00	70.00	—

Note: Although this coin bears no indication of its origin, it was minted in the Manchurian Provinces ca.1922

Y# 21.4 20 CASH
Copper, 32 mm. **Ruler:** Hsüan-t'ung **Obv. Inscription:** Tai-ch'ing T'ung-pi **Rev:** Without dot between "KUO" and "COPPER"; dot below dragon's chin **Rev. Legend:** Hsüan-t'ung Nien-tsao, TAI-CHING-TI-KUO...

Date	Mintage	VG	F	VF	XF	Unc
CD1909 Restrike	—	3.50	8.50	16.00	30.00	—

Note: Although this coin bears no indication of its origin, it was minted in the Manchurian Provinces ca.1922

Y# 21.5 20 CASH
Copper, 32 mm. **Ruler:** Hsüan-t'ung **Obv:** Inner circle of large dots **Obv. Inscription:** Tai-ch'ing T'ung-pi **Rev:** Without dot between "KUO" and "COPPER"; five crude waves beneath dragon with redesigned forehead; inner circle of large dots **Rev. Legend:** Hsüan-t'ung Nien-tsao, TAI-CHING-TI-KUO...

Date	Mintage	VG	F	VF	XF	Unc
CD1909	—	1.25	3.00	6.00	16.00	—

K# 215 10 CENTS
2.7000 g., 0.8200 Silver .0712 oz. ASW **Ruler:** Kuang-hsü **Obv. Inscription:** Tai-ch'ing Ti-kuo Yin-pi **Rev:** Dragon **Rev. Legend:** Kuang-hsü Nien-tsao, TAI-CHING-TI-KUO...

Date	Mintage	VG	F	VF	XF	Unc
CD1907	—	50.00	85.00	150	250	400

Y# 12 10 CENTS
2.7000 g., 0.8200 Silver .0712 oz. ASW **Ruler:** Kuang-hsü **Obv. Inscription:** Kuang-hsü Yüan-pao **Rev:** Dragon **Rev. Legend:** Kuang-hsü Nien-tsao, TAI-CHING-TI-KUO...

Date	Mintage	VG	F	VF	XF	Unc
ND(1908)	—	12.00	30.00	40.00	90.00	200

K# 222 10 CENTS
3.2000 g., 0.6500 Silver .0669 oz. ASW **Ruler:** Hsüan-t'ung **Obv. Inscription:** Tai-ch'ing Yin-pi **Rev:** Dragon **Rev. Legend:** Hsüan-t'ung Nien-tsao

Date	Mintage	VG	F	VF	XF	Unc
ND(1910)	—	50.00	85.00	150	250	500
ND(1910) Proof	—	Value: 750				

Y# 28 10 CENTS
2.7000 g., Silver **Ruler:** Hsüan-t'ung **Obv. Legend:** Hsüan-t'ung **Obv. Inscription:** Tai-ch'ing Yin-pi **Rev:** Dragon **Rev. Legend:** Hsüan-t'ung Nien-tsao

Date	Mintage	VG	F	VF	XF	Unc
3(1911)	—	5.00	15.00	30.00	75.00	180

Note: Refer to Hunan Republic 10 Cents, K#762

K# 214 20 CENTS
5.5000 g., 0.8200 Silver .1450 oz. ASW **Ruler:** Kuang-hsü **Obv. Inscription:** Tai-ch'ing Yin-pi **Rev:** Dragon **Rev. Legend:** Kuang-hsü Nien-tsao, TAI-CHING-TI-KUO...

Date	Mintage	VG	F	VF	XF	Unc
CD1907	—	50.00	100	150	250	450

Y# 13 20 CENTS
5.3000 g., 0.8200 Silver .1450 oz. ASW **Ruler:** Kuang-hsü **Obv. Inscription:** Kuang-hsü Yüan-pao **Rev:** Dragon **Rev. Legend:** Kuang-hsü Nien-tsao, TAI-CHING-TI-KUO...

Date	Mintage	VG	F	VF	XF	Unc
ND(1908)	—	20.00	60.00	100	150	260

K# 217w 20 CENTS
5.3000 g., 0.8200 Silver .1450 oz. ASW **Ruler:** Kuang-hsü **Obv. Inscription:** Kuang-hsü Yüan-pao **Rev:** Dragon **Rev. Legend:** Kuang-hsü Nien-tsao, TAI-CHING-TI-KUO... with "COPPER COIN" (error)

Date	Mintage	VG	F	VF	XF	Unc
ND(1908) Rare	—	—	—	—	—	—

Y# 29 20 CENTS
5.4000 g., 0.8200 Silver .1450 oz. ASW **Ruler:** Hsüan-t'ung **Obv. Legend:** Hsüan-t'ung **Obv. Inscription:** Tai-ch'ing Yin-pi **Rev:** Dragon

Date	Mintage	VG	F	VF	XF	Unc
3(1911)	—	25.00	60.00	125	200	350

K# 221 25 CENTS
6.7000 g., 0.8000 Silver .1724 oz. ASW **Ruler:** Hsüan-t'ung **Obv. Legend:** Hsüan-t'ung Nien-tsao **Obv. Inscription:** Tai-ch'ing Yin-pi **Rev:** Dragon

Date	Mintage	VG	F	VF	XF	Unc
ND(1910)	1,410,000	65.00	200	400	750	1,200
ND(1910) Proof	—	Value: 2,000				

K# 213 50 CENTS
13.6000 g., 0.8600 Silver .3761 oz. ASW **Ruler:** Kuang-hsü **Obv. Inscription:** Tai-ch'ing Yin-pi **Rev:** Dragon **Rev. Legend:** Kuang-hsü Nien-tsao, TAI-CHING-TI-KUO...

Date	Mintage	VG	F	VF	XF	Unc
CD1907	—	70.00	150	300	550	1,000

Y# 23 50 CENTS
13.4000 g., 0.8000 Silver .3447 oz. ASW **Ruler:** Hsüan-t'ung **Obv. Inscription:** Tai-ch'ing Yin-pi **Rev:** Dragon **Rev. Legend:** Hsüan-t'ung Nien-tsao

Date	Mintage	VG	F	VF	XF	Unc
ND(1910)	1,571,000	13.50	40.00	70.00	150	450
ND(1910) Proof	—	Value: 750				

Y# 30 50 CENTS
13.4000 g., 0.8000 Silver .3447 oz. ASW **Ruler:** Hsüan-t'ung
Obv. Legend: Hsüan-t'ung **Obv. Inscription:** Tai-ch'ing Yin-pi
Rev: Dragon

Date	Mintage	VG	F	VF	XF	Unc
3(1911)	Inc. above	100	300	650	1,000	2,000
3(1911) Proof	—	Value: 3,000				

K# 212 DOLLAR
26.9000 g., 0.9000 Silver .7785 oz. ASW **Ruler:** Kuang-hsü
Obv. Inscription: Tai-ch'ing Yin-pi **Rev:** Dragon **Rev. Legend:** Kuang-hsü Nien-tsao, TAI-CHING-TI-KOU...

Date	Mintage	VG	F	VF	XF	Unc
CD1907	—	250	500	1,000	1,750	2,500

Y# 14 DOLLAR
26.9000 g., 0.9000 Silver .7785 oz. ASW **Ruler:** Kuang-hsü
Obv. Inscription: Kuang-hsü Yüan-pao **Rev:** Dragon **Rev. Legend:** Kuang-hsü Nien-tsao, TAI-CHING-TI-KOU...

Date	Mintage	VG	F	VF	XF	Unc
ND(1908)	—	20.00	50.00	100	225	600

K# 219 DOLLAR
26.9000 g., 0.9000 Silver .7785 oz. ASW **Ruler:** Hsüan-t'ung
Obv. Inscription: Tai-ch'ing Yin-pi **Rev:** Dragon **Rev. Legend:** Hsüan-t'ung Nien-tsao

Date	Mintage	VG	F	VF	XF	Unc
ND(1910)	—	100	300	800	1,500	2,500
ND(1910) Proof	—	Value: 3,500				

Y# 31 DOLLAR
26.9000 g., 0.9000 Silver .7785 oz. ASW **Ruler:** Hsüan-t'ung
Obv. Legend: Hsüan-t'ung **Obv. Inscription:** Tai-ch'ing Yin-pi
Rev: Dragon

Date	Mintage	VG	F	VF	XF	Unc
3(1911)	77,153,000	15.00	25.00	37.50	75.00	450

Note: Struck at the Tientsin, Nanking, and Wuchang Mints without distinctive marks

Y# 31.1 DOLLAR
26.9000 g., 0.9000 Silver .7785 oz. ASW **Ruler:** Hsüan-t'ung
Obv. Legend: Hsüan-t'ung **Obv. Inscription:** Tai-ch'ing Yin-pi
Rev: Dragon; "dot" after "DOLLAR"

Date	Mintage	VG	F	VF	XF	Unc
3(1911)	Inc. above	20.00	40.00	60.00	100	500

PATTERNS

Standard Unified General

KM#	Date	Mintage	Identification	Mkt Val
Pn250	ND(1910)	—	10 Cents. Nickel. K222.	—
Pn251	ND(1910)	—	1/4 Dollar. Silver center. Plain edge. K221.	—
Pn264	ND	—	Cash. Brass. Hsu4a, square hole.	400
Pn265	ND	—	Cash. Brass. Hsu4b, without hole.	400
Pn266	ND	—	Cash. Copper. Y#7.	400
Pn267	ND	—	Cash. Brass. Y#25; without hole.	400
Pn268	CD1907	—	Dollar. Copper. K212.	—
Pn269	ND(1908)	—	20 Cents. Nickel. Milled edge. K217w.	—
Pn272	ND(1910)	—	Li. Copper. Hsu33.	400
Pn273	ND(1910)	—	5 Li. Copper. Hsu34.	550
Pn274	ND(1910)	—	5 Li. Bronze.	550
Pn275	ND(1910)	—	2 Cash. Copper. Hsu13.	400
Pn276	ND(1910)	—	2 Cash. Brass. With hole, Hsu13.	400
Pn277	ND(1910)	—	Fen. Copper. Hsu35.	600
Pn278	ND(1910)	—	Fen. Bronze.	600
Pn279	ND(1910)	—	2 Fen. Copper. Hsu36.	1,000
Pn280	ND(1910)	—	2 Fen. Bronze.	1,000
Pn281	3(1911)	—	5 Cash. Copper. Y26; Hsu30.	600
Pn282	3(1911)	—	5 Cash. Bronze. Y26a.	600
Pn283	3(1911)	—	20 Cash. Copper. Hsu32.	700
Pn284	3(1911)	—	20 Cash. Bronze.	700
Pn304	3(1911)	—	Dollar. Silver. K223.	15,000
Pn305	3(1911)	—	Dollar. Silver. K223a.	1,800
Pn306	3(1911)	—	Dollar. Silver. K223b.	—
Pn307	3(1911)	—	Dollar. Silver. K224.	35,000
Pn308	3(1911)	—	Dollar. Silver. K225.	22,000
Pn309	3(1911)	—	Dollar. Silver. K226.	15,000
Pn310	ND(1908)	—	20 Cents. Nickel. K217y.	—
Pn311	ND(1910)	—	10 Cents. Nickel. K222y.	125

PATTERNS

Peking Tael Series

KM#	Date	Mintage	Identification	Mkt Val
Pn290	29(1903)	—	5 Fen. Silver. K931.	2,500
Pn291	29(1903)	—	Ch'ien. Silver. K930.	2,800
Pn292	29(1903)	—	2 Ch'ien. Silver. K929.	3,800
Pn293	29(1903)	—	2 Ch'ien. Gold. K929v.	30,000
Pn294	29(1903)	—	5 Ch'ien. Silver. K928.	12,000
Pn295	29(1903)	—	Liang. Silver. K927.	48,000
Pn296	29(1903)	—	Liang. Gold. K927v.	80,000
Pn297	CD1906	—	Ch'ien. Silver. K937.	1,500
Pn298	CD1906	—	2 Ch'ien. Silver. 7.4800 g. K936.	1,800
Pn299	CD1906	—	5 Ch'ien. Silver. K935.	3,000
Pn300	CD1906	—	Liang. Silver. K934.	12,000
Pn301	CD1906	—	Liang. Gold. K1540. Tientsin Mint. 39.5mm, 37g. Large clouds, plain edge.	50,000
Pn302	CD1907	—	Liang. Gold. K1541. Tientsin Mint. 39.5mm, 37g. Small clouds, reeded edge.	50,000
PnA302	CD1906	—	Liang. Gold. Tientsin Mint. 39.5mm, 37g. Small clouds, reeded edge. Rare.	—
Pn303	CD1907	—	Liang. Silver. K1541v.	13,000
PnA303	CD1907	—	Liang. Gold. K1541a. Tientsin Mint. 39.5mm, 37g. Large clouds, plain edge. Rare.	—

TRIAL STRIKES

KM#	Date	Mintage	Identification	Mkt Val
TS3	1(1910)	—	Fen. White Metal. Hsu35, KM#Pn275. Uniface obverse.	125

PROOF SETS

KM#	Date	Mintage	Identification	Issue Price	Mkt Val
PS1	ND(1910) (4)	—	Y#23, K#219, 221, 222	—	—

ANHWEI PROVINCE

Anhui

A province located in eastern China. Made a separate province during the Manchu dynasty in the 17th century. Principally agricultural with some mining of coal and iron ore. Spanish-American 8 Reales saw wide circulation in this province until the end of World War I. The provincial mint at Anking began operations in 1897, closed in 1899, and later reopened in 1902. The primary production of the mint was cash coins but included a series of silver coinage.

EMPIRE

MILLED COINAGE

Y# 34 10 CASH
Copper **Ruler:** Kuang-hsü **Obv. Legend:** An-hui Sheng Tsao
Obv. Inscription: Kuang-hsü Yüan-pao **Rev:** Denomination: "ONE CEN" **Note:** May show various stages of recutting of "C" in "CEN."

Date	Mintage	VG	F	VF	XF	Unc
ND1902	—	35.00	50.00	85.00	150	—

Y# 34a 10 CASH
Copper **Ruler:** Kuang-hsü **Obv. Legend:** An-hui Sheng Tsao
Obv. Inscription: Kuang-hsü Yüan-pao **Rev:** Letter "A" inverted, denomination "ONE SEN"

Date	Mintage	VG	F	VF	XF	Unc
ND(1902)	—	50.00	80.00	125	350	—

Y# 34a.1 10 CASH
Copper **Ruler:** Kuang-hsü **Obv. Legend:** Kuang-hsü Yüan-pao
Rev: Letter "A" corrected, denomination "ONE SEN"

Date	Mintage	VG	F	VF	XF	Unc
ND(1902)	—	40.00	65.00	100	250	—

Y# 35 5 CASH
Copper **Ruler:** Kuang-hsü **Obv. Legend:** An-hui Sheng Tsao
Obv. Inscription: Kuang-hsü Yüan-pao **Rev:** Circled dragon
Rev. Legend: AN-HWEI

Date	Mintage	VG	F	VF	XF	Unc
ND(1902)	—	125	175	250	350	—

Y# 35.1 5 CASH
Copper **Ruler:** Kuang-hsü **Obv. Legend:** An-hui Sheng Tsao
Obv. Inscription: Kuang-hsü Yüan-pao **Rev:** Uncircled dragon
Rev. Legend: AN-HUI

Date	Mintage	VG	F	VF	XF	Unc
ND(c. 1902) Rare	—	—	—	—	—	—

Y# 36 10 CASH

Copper **Ruler:** Kuang-hsü **Obv. Legend:** An-hui Sheng Tsao **Obv. Inscription:** Kuang-hsü Yüan-pao **Rev:** Letter "N" backwards in "AN-HWEI" and in "TEN"

Date	Mintage	VG	F	VF	XF	Unc
ND(1902-06)	—	6.00	12.00	20.00	40.00	—

Y# 36.1 10 CASH

Copper **Ruler:** Kuang-hsü **Obv:** Small Manchu in center **Obv. Legend:** An-hui Sheng Tsao **Obv. Inscription:** Kuang-hsü Yüan-pao **Rev:** Rosettes close together, letter "N" corrected in "AN-HWEI" and in "TEN" **Edge:** Plain

Date	Mintage	VG	F	VF	XF	Unc
ND(1902-06)	—	1.00	2.50	5.00	10.00	—

Y# 36.1a 10 CASH

Copper **Ruler:** Kuang-hsü **Obv:** Small Manchu in center **Obv. Legend:** An-hui Sheng Tsao **Obv. Inscription:** Kuang-hsü Yüan-pao **Rev:** Rosettes close together, letter "N" corrected in AN-HWEI and in TEN **Edge:** Milled

Date	Mintage	VG	F	VF	XF	Unc
ND(1902-06) Rare	—	—	—	—	—	—

Y# 36.2 10 CASH

Copper **Ruler:** Kuang-hsü **Obv:** Smaller, redesigned rosettes, larger Manchu words in center **Obv. Legend:** An-hui Sheng Tsao **Obv. Inscription:** Kuang-hsü Yüan-pao **Rev:** Rosettes close together, larger clouds around redesigned dragon

Date	Mintage	VG	F	VF	XF	Unc
ND(1902-06)	—	1.50	4.00	6.00	10.00	—

Y# 36.3 10 CASH

Copper **Ruler:** Kuang-hsü **Obv:** Rosettes crude and heavy **Obv. Legend:** An-hui Sheng Tsao **Obv. Inscription:** Kuang-hsü Yüan-pao **Rev:** Rosettes close together, dragon's head redesigned

Date	Mintage	VG	F	VF	XF	Unc
ND(1902-08)	—	5.00	12.00	17.50	35.00	—

Y# 36.4 10 CASH

Copper **Ruler:** Kuang-hsü **Obv. Legend:** An-hui Sheng Tsao **Obv. Inscription:** Kuang-hsü Yüan-pao **Rev:** Rosettes far apart

Date	Mintage	VG	F	VF	XF	Unc
ND(1902-06)	—	1.00	2.50	5.00	10.00	—

Y# 36a 10 CASH

Copper **Ruler:** Kuang-hsü **Obv:** Small rosette at center, legend with 5 characters at bottom **Obv. Legend:** An-hui Sheng Tsao **Obv. Inscription:** Kuang-hsü Yüan-pao **Rev:** Large English legend above dragon, without "TEN CASH"

Date	Mintage	VG	F	VF	XF	Unc
ND(1902-06)	—	1.00	2.50	5.00	12.00	—

Y# 36a.1 10 CASH

Copper **Ruler:** Kuang-hsü **Obv:** Small rosette **Obv. Legend:** An-hui Sheng Tsao **Obv. Inscription:** Kuang-hsu Yüan-pao **Rev:** Small English legend above dragon

Date	Mintage	VG	F	VF	XF	Unc
ND(1902-06)	—	1.50	3.00	6.00	15.00	—

Y# 36a.2 10 CASH

Copper **Ruler:** Kuang-hsü **Obv. Legend:** An-hui Sheng Tsao **Obv. Inscription:** Kuang-hsü Yüan-pao **Rev:** Small English legend with larger clouds around dragon and only one cloud below dragon's tail

Date	Mintage	VG	F	VF	XF	Unc
ND(1902-06)	—	2.00	5.00	8.00	18.00	—

Y# 36a.3 10 CASH

Copper **Ruler:** Kuang-hsü **Obv:** Large rosette at center, legend with 2 characters at bottom **Obv. Legend:** An-hui Sheng Tsao **Obv. Inscription:** Kuang-hsü Yüan-pao

Date	Mintage	VG	F	VF	XF	Unc
ND(1902-06)	—	1.00	2.50	5.00	10.00	—

Y# 36a.4 10 CASH

Copper **Ruler:** Kuang-hsü **Obv:** Large rosette at center, legend with 5 characters at bottom **Obv. Legend:** An-hui Sheng Tsao **Obv. Inscription:** Kuang-hsü Yüan-pao

Date	Mintage	VG	F	VF	XF	Unc
ND(1902-06)	—	1.25	2.50	5.00	10.00	—

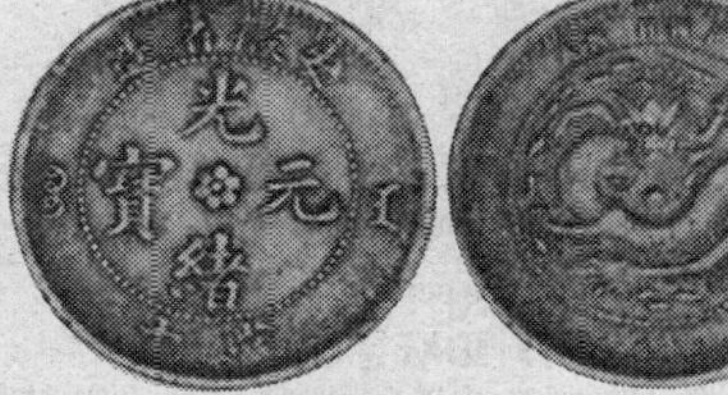

Y# 36a.5 10 CASH

Copper **Ruler:** Kuang-hsü **Obv:** Legend with 2 characters at bottom **Obv. Legend:** An-hui Sheng Tsao **Obv. Inscription:** Kuang-hsü Yüan-pao **Rev:** Small English legend above dragon

Date	Mintage	VG	F	VF	XF	Unc
ND(1902-06)	—	3.50	7.50	15.00	30.00	—

Y# 36a.6 10 CASH

Copper **Ruler:** Kuang-hsü **Obv:** Slightly smaller rosette at center with right Manchu word slightly higher than on Y#36a.5 **Obv. Legend:** An-hui Sheng Tsao **Obv. Inscription:** Kuang-hsü Yüan-pao **Rev:** Small English legend above dragon

Date	Mintage	VG	F	VF	XF	Unc
ND(1902-06)	—	1.00	2.50	5.00	10.00	—

Y# 38a 10 CASH

Copper **Ruler:** Kuang-hsü **Obv:** Legend with 2 characters at bottom **Obv. Legend:** An-hui Sheng Tsao **Obv. Inscription:** Kuang-hsü Yüan-pao **Rev:** "Ten" spelled "TOEN"

Date	Mintage	VG	F	VF	XF	Unc
ND(1902-06)	—	8.00	15.00	30.00	50.00	—

Y# 38a.1 10 CASH

Copper **Ruler:** Kuang-hsü **Obv:** Legend with 5 characters at bottom **Obv. Legend:** An-hui Sheng Tsao **Obv. Inscription:** Kuang-hsü Yüan-pao **Rev:** "Ten" spelled "TOEN"

Date	Mintage	VG	F	VF	XF	Unc
ND(1902-06)	—	35.00	70.00	150	250	—

Y# 38b 10 CASH

Copper **Ruler:** Kuang-hsü **Obv:** Legend with 2 characters at bottom **Obv. Legend:** An-hui Sheng Tsao **Obv. Inscription:** Kuang-hsü Yüan-pao **Rev:** Without "TEN CASH"

Date	Mintage	VG	F	VF	XF	Unc
ND(1902-06)	—	5.00	12.00	25.00	65.00	—

Y# 38b.1 10 CASH

Copper **Ruler:** Kuang-hsü **Obv:** Legend with 5 characters at bottom **Obv. Legend:** An-hui Sheng Tsao **Obv. Inscription:** Kuang-hsü Yüan-pao

Date	Mintage	VG	F	VF	XF	Unc
ND(1902-06)	—	15.00	35.00	50.00	140	—

Y# 39 10 CASH

Copper **Ruler:** Kuang-hsü **Obv:** Legend with 7 characters at bottom **Obv. Legend:** An-hui Sheng Tsao **Obv. Inscription:** Kuang-hsü Yüan-pao **Rev:** Rosettes at side and "AN-HUI" above dragon

Date	Mintage	VG	F	VF	XF	Unc
ND(1902-06) Rare	—	—	—	—	—	—

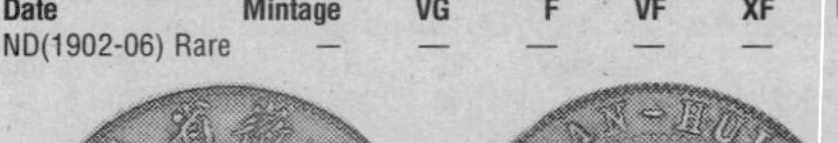

Y# 39.1 10 CASH

Copper **Ruler:** Kuang-hsü **Obv. Legend:** An-hui Sheng Tsao **Obv. Inscription:** Kuang-hsü Yüan-pao **Rev:** Stars at sides and "AN-HUI" above dragon

Date	Mintage	VG	F	VF	XF	Unc
ND(1902-06) Rare	—	—	—	—	—	—

Y# 39.2 10 CASH

Copper **Ruler:** Kuang-hsü **Obv. Legend:** An-hui Sheng Tsao **Obv. Inscription:** Kuang-hsü Yüan-pao **Rev:** "AN-HUI", upright dragon **Note:** Square-holed center.

Date	Mintage	VG	F	VF	XF	Unc
ND(1902-06) Rare	—	—	—	—	—	—

Y# 10a 10 CASH

Copper **Ruler:** Kuang-hsü **Obv:** Large mint mark at center **Obv. Inscription:** Tai-ch'ing T'ung-pi **Rev. Legend:** Kuang-hsü Nien-tsao, TAI-CHING-TI-KUO ...

Date	Mintage	VG	F	VF	XF	Unc
CD(1906)	—	1.00	2.50	5.00	10.00	—

Y# 10a.1 10 CASH

Copper **Ruler:** Kuang-hsü **Obv:** Small mint mark at center **Obv. Inscription:** Tai-ch'ing T'ung-pi **Rev. Legend:** Kuang-hsü Nien-tsao, TAI-CHING-TI-KUO ...

Date	Mintage	VG	F	VF	XF	Unc
CD(1906)	—	1.50	3.00	6.00	12.00	—

Y# 10a.2 10 CASH

Copper **Ruler:** Kuang-hsü **Obv:** More finely engraved, cloud near dragon's lower foot shaped like a 3 **Obv. Inscription:** Tai-ch'ing T'ung-pi **Rev:** More finely engraved **Rev. Legend:** Kuang-hsü Nien-tsao, TAI-CHING-TI-KUO ...

Date	Mintage	VG	F	VF	XF	Unc
CD1906	—	1.00	2.50	5.00	10.00	—

Y# 20a 10 CASH

Copper **Ruler:** Hsüan-t'ung **Obv. Inscription:** Tai-ch'ing T'ung-pi **Rev. Legend:** Hsüan-t'ung Nien-tsao, TAI-CHING-TI-KUO ...

Date	Mintage	VG	F	VF	XF	Unc
CD1909	—	12.50	25.00	50.00	125	—

Y# 20a.1 10 CASH

Copper **Ruler:** Hsüan-t'ung **Obv. Inscription:** Tai-ch'ing T'ung-pi **Rev:** Dot after "COIN" **Rev. Legend:** Hsüan-t'ung Nien-tsao, TAI-CHING-TI-KUO ...

Date	Mintage	VG	F	VF	XF	Unc
CD1909	—	35.00	65.00	130	225	—

Y# 37 20 CASH

Copper **Ruler:** Kuang-hsü **Obv. Legend:** An-hui Sheng Tsao **Obv. Inscription:** Kuang-hsü Yüan-pao

Date	Mintage	VG	F	VF	XF	Unc
ND(1902)	—	375	750	1,100	1,500	—

Y# 11a 20 CASH

Copper **Ruler:** Kuang-hsü **Obv. Inscription:** Tai-ch'ing T'ung-pi **Rev:** TAI-CHING-TI-KUO ... **Rev. Inscription:** Kuang-hsü Nien-tsao

Date	Mintage	VG	F	VF	XF	Unc
CD1906	—	37.50	75.00	150	300	—

Y# 43.5 20 CENTS

5.3000 g., 0.9200 Silver .1397 oz. ASW **Ruler:** Kuang-hsü **Obv. Inscription:** Kuang-hsü Yüan-pao **Rev:** Dragon

Date	Mintage	VG	F	VF	XF	Unc
27(1901) 1 known	—	—	—	—	—	—

Note: D.K.E. Ching Sale 6-91 VF++ realized $2,420

MILITARY TOKEN COINAGE

Given to An-hui Imperial troops by the Military Bureau for faithful and/or meritorious service.

KM# W45 10 CASH

Copper **Ruler:** Kuang-hsü **Issuer:** Anhwei Military Bureau **Obv:** Large central Chinese character "Cheang" (reward) **Obv. Legend:** An-hui Wu Dih Buh Yuen **Rev:** Legend around dragon **Rev. Legend:** AN-HWEI***TEN CASH***

Date	Mintage	VG	F	VF	XF	Unc
ND	—	125	225	375	550	—

KM# W46 10 CASH

Copper **Ruler:** Kuang-hsü **Issuer:** Anhwei Military Bureau **Obv. Legend:** An-hui Wu Dih Buh Yuen **Rev:** Legend around Dragon **Rev. Legend:** AN-HWEI***TEN CASH***

Date	Mintage	VG	F	VF	XF	Unc
ND	—	125	225	375	550	—

KM# W47 10 CASH

Copper **Ruler:** Kuang-hsü **Issuer:** Anhwei Military Bureau **Obv. Legend:** An-hui Wu Dih Buh Yuen **Rev:** Legend without "TEN CASH"

Date	Mintage	VG	F	VF	XF	Unc
ND	—	125	225	375	550	—

CHEKIANG PROVINCE

Zhejiang

A province located along the east coast of China. Although the smallest of the Chinese mainland provinces, it is one of the most densely populated. Economic interests are mostly agricultural with iron and coal mining and some fishing. A small mint opened in 1897. This was replaced by a larger mint which operated briefly 1898-99. Other mints opened in 1903 and 1905. These were merged with the Fukien Mint in 1906-07.

EMPIRE

PROVINCIAL CAST COINAGE

C# 4-19 CASH

Cast Brass **Ruler:** Kuang-hsü **Obv:** Type A **Obv. Inscription:** Kuang-hsü T'ung-pao **Rev. Inscription:** Boo-je **Note:** Size varies: 21-22mm.

Date	Mintage	Good	VG	F	VF	XF
ND(1875-1908)	—	3.00	4.50	6.50	10.00	12.00

C# 4-19.1 CASH

Cast Brass **Ruler:** Kuang-hsü **Obv. Inscription:** Kuang-hsü T'ung-pao **Rev:** More angular mint mark

Date	Mintage	Good	VG	F	VF	XF
ND(1875-1908)	—	2.00	3.00	4.00	6.00	8.00

MILLED COINAGE

Y# 8b 2 CASH

Copper **Ruler:** Kuang-hsü **Obv:** Inscription: Tai-ch'ing T'ung-pi **Rev:** Dragon

Date	Mintage	VG	F	VF	XF	Unc
CD1906	—	5.00	10.00	16.00	30.00	—

Y# 9b 5 CASH

Copper **Ruler:** Kuang-hsü **Obv:** Inscription: Tai-ch'ing T'ung-pi **Rev. Legend:** Kuang-hsü Nien-tsao, TAI-CHING-TI-KUO ...

Date	Mintage	VG	F	VF	XF	Unc
CD1906	—	5.00	10.00	16.00	30.00	—

Y# 49 10 CASH

Copper **Ruler:** Kuang-hsü **Obv:** Ball in circle in center, inscription: Kuang-hsü Yüan-pao **Obv. Legend:** Che-kiang Sheng Tsao **Rev:** Dragon

Date	Mintage	VG	F	VF	XF	Unc
ND(1903-06)	—	0.50	1.50	2.50	4.50	—

Y# 49a 10 CASH

Brass **Ruler:** Kuang-hsü **Obv:** Legend has 4 characters at bottom **Obv. Legend:** Che-kiang Sheng Tsao **Obv. Inscription:** Kuang-hsü Yüan-pao **Rev:** Dragon

Date	Mintage	VG	F	VF	XF	Unc
ND(1903-06)	—	3.00	6.00	11.00	20.00	—

Y# 49b 10 CASH

Copper **Ruler:** Kuang-hsü **Obv. Legend:** Che-kiang Sheng Tsao **Obv. Inscription:** Kuang-hsü Yüan-pao **Rev:** Dragon

Date	Mintage	VG	F	VF	XF	Unc
ND(1903-06)	—	6.00	12.00	25.00	45.00	—

Y# 49.1 10 CASH

Copper **Ruler:** Kuang-hsü **Obv:** Rosette at center and large Manchu "Boo" at left **Obv. Legend:** Che-kiang Sheng Tsao **Obv. Inscription:** Kuang-hsü Yüan-pao **Rev:** Dragon

Date	Mintage	VG	F	VF	XF	Unc
ND(1903-06)	—	0.50	1.50	2.50	4.50	—

Y# 49.1a 10 CASH

Brass **Ruler:** Kuang-hsü **Obv:** Rosette at center and large Manchu "Boo" at left **Obv. Legend:** Che-kiang Sheng Tsao **Obv. Inscription:** Kuang-hsü Yüan-pao **Rev:** Dragon

Date	Mintage	VG	F	VF	XF	Unc
ND(1903-06)	—	2.00	4.00	8.00	15.00	—

Y# 49.2 10 CASH

Copper **Ruler:** Kuang-hsü **Obv:** Small Manchu "Boo" at left **Obv. Legend:** Che-kiang Sheng Tsao **Obv. Inscription:** Kuang-hsü Yüan-pao **Rev:** Dragon **Note:** Similar to Y#49.1 but with coin die alignment

Date	Mintage	VG	F	VF	XF	Unc
ND(1903-06)	—	0.75	1.50	3.00	6.00	—

Y# 49.3 10 CASH

Copper **Ruler:** Kuang-hsü **Obv:** Rosette at center and small Manchu word at left **Obv. Legend:** Che-kiang Sheng Tsao **Obv. Inscription:** Kuang-hsü Yüan-pao **Rev:** Small, cramped dragon with few clouds around body

Date	Mintage	VG	F	VF	XF	Unc
ND(1903-06)	—	0.75	1.50	3.00	6.00	—

Y# 49.4 10 CASH

Copper **Ruler:** Kuang-hsü **Obv. Legend:** Che-kiang Sheng Tsao **Obv. Inscription:** Kuang-hsü Yüan-pao **Rev:** Dragon without ball in center circle

Date	Mintage	VG	F	VF	XF	Unc
ND(1903-06)	—	1.25	2.50	5.00	10.00	—

Y# 10b 10 CASH

Copper **Ruler:** Kuang-hsü **Obv. Inscription:** Tai-ch'ing T'ung-pi **Rev:** Dragon **Rev. Legend:** Kuang hsü Nien-tsao, TAI-CHING-TI-KUO with KUO spelled KIIO

Date	Mintage	VG	F	VF	XF	Unc
CD1906	—	1.00	2.00	4.00	8.00	—

Y# 10b.1 10 CASH

Copper **Ruler:** Kuang-hsü **Obv. Inscription:** Tai-ch'ing T'ung-pi **Rev:** Dragon **Rev. Legend:** Kuang hsü Nien-tsao, TAI-CHING-TI-KUO with KUO spelled KUO

Date	Mintage	VG	F	VF	XF	Unc
CD1906	—	2.50	5.00	10.00	20.00	—

Note: Chekiang and other 10 Cash coin types found struck over Korean 5 Fun coins are known; Why they were overstruck in China is unknown

Y# 50 20 CASH

Copper **Ruler:** Kuang-hsü **Obv. Legend:** Che-kiang Sheng Tsao **Obv. Inscription:** Kuang-hsü Yüan-pao **Rev:** Dragon **Note:** Two planchet sizes exist.

Date	Mintage	VG	F	VF	XF	Unc
ND(1903-04)	—	100	200	350	600	—

Y# 11b 20 CASH

Copper **Ruler:** Kuang-hsü **Obv. Inscription:** Tai-ch'ing T'ung-Pi **Rev. Legend:** Kuang-hsü Nien-tsao, TAI-CHING-TI-KUO ...

Date	Mintage	VG	F	VF	XF	Unc
CD1906	—	60.00	100	200	350	—

REPUBLIC

MILLED COINAGE

Y# 371 10 CENTS

2.6500 g., 0.6500 Silver .0554 oz. ASW **Obv:** Crossed flags **Rev. Legend:** CHE-KIANG PROVINCE

Date	Mintage	VG	F	VF	XF	Unc
13(1924)	4,464,000	1.50	4.00	7.00	10.00	25.00

Y# 373 20 CENTS

5.3000 g., Silver **Rev:** Large value "20" **Rev. Legend:** CHE-KIANG PROVINCE.

Date	Mintage	VG	F	VF	XF	Unc
13(1924)	—	100	300	500	700	1,500

PATTERNS

Including off metal strikes

KM#	Date	Mintage	Identification	Mkt Val
Pn4	ND(1902)	—	5 Cents. Silver. CHE-KIANG. K123-I.	2,100
Pn5	ND(1902)	—	10 Cents. Silver. CHE-KIANG. K122-I.	1,500
Pn6	ND(1902)	—	20 Cents. Silver. CHE-KIANG. K121-I.	1,500
Pn7	ND(1902)	—	Dollar. Silver. CHE-KIANG. K 119-I.	28,000
Pn8	ND(1902)	—	Dollar. Copper. CHE-KIANG. K 119-I.	6,000

KM#	Date	Mintage	Identification	Mkt Val
Pn9	ND(1903)	—	10 Cash. Copper. Y49.3a.	200
Pn10	ND(1903)	—	10 Cash. White Copper. Y49.3a. W132.	—
Pn11	13(1924)	—	20 Cents. Silver. Crossed flags. Y372.	1,200

CHIHLI PROVINCE

Hebei, Hopei

A province located in northeastern China which contains the eastern end of the Great Wall. An important producer of coal and some iron ore. In 1928 the provincial name was changed from Chihli to Hopei. The Paoting mint was established in 1745 and only produced cast cash coins.

A mint for struck cash was established in 1888 and the mint for the Peiyang silver coinage was added in 1896. This was destroyed during the Boxer Rebellion. A replacement mint was built in 1902 for the provincial coinage and merged with the Tientsin (Tianjin) Central mint in 1910.

EMPIRE

PROVINCIAL CAST COINAGE

C# 8-1.10 CASH

Brass, 22.1 mm. **Ruler:** Kuang-hsü **Obv. Inscription:** Kuang-hsü T'ung-pao **Rev:** Dot at upper left **Rev. Inscription:** Boo-jiyen

Date	Mintage	Good	VG	F	VF	XF
ND(1875-1908)	—	2.75	4.50	7.50	15.00	—

C# 8-1.9 CASH

Brass, 22.3 mm. **Ruler:** Kuang-hsü **Obv. Inscription:** Kuang-hsü T'ung-pao **Rev:** Dash above **Rev. Inscription:** Boo-jiyen

Date	Mintage	Good	VG	F	VF	XF
ND(1875-1908)	—	2.00	3.75	7.50	15.00	—

C# 3-1.1 CASH

Cast Brass, 23 mm. **Ruler:** Kuang-hsü **Obv. Inscription:** Kuang-hsü T'ung-pao **Rev:** Type 1 mint mark, Manchu inscription **Rev. Inscription:** Boo-gu

Date	Mintage	Good	VG	F	VF	XF
ND(1875-1908)	—	90.00	125	200	300	—

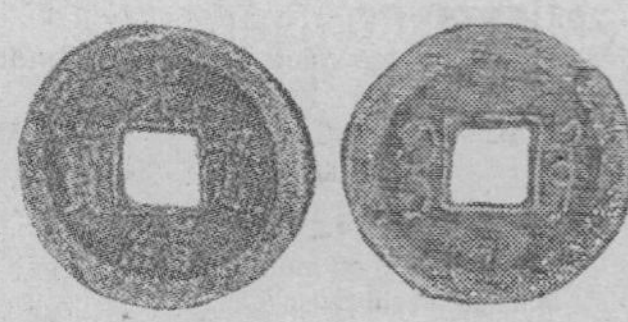

C# 3-1.2 CASH
Cast Brass, 22 mm. **Ruler:** Kuang-hsü **Obv. Inscription:** Kuang-hsü T'ung-pao **Rev:** Type 2 mint mark, Manchu inscription **Rev. Inscription:** Boo-gu

Date	Mintage	Good	VG	F	VF	XF
ND(1875-1908)	—	20.00	30.00	50.00	75.00	—

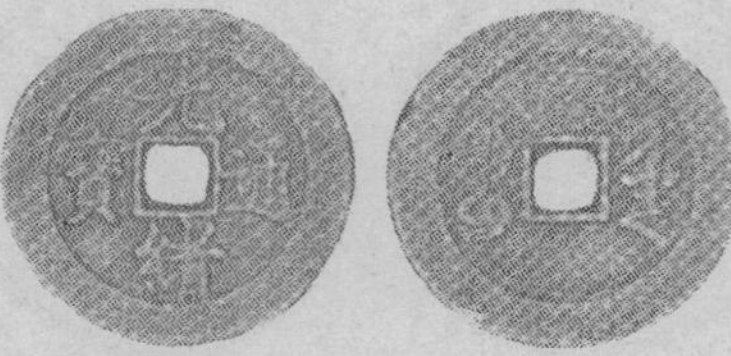

C# 8-1 CASH
Cast Brass, 23 mm. **Ruler:** Kuang-hsü **Obv. Inscription:** Kuang-hsü T'ung-pao **Rev:** Manchu inscription

Date	Mintage	Good	VG	F	VF	XF
ND(1875-1908)	—	2.50	4.50	7.50	12.00	—

C# 8-1.1 CASH
Cast Brass **Ruler:** Kuang-hsü **Obv. Inscription:** Kuang-hsü T'ung-pao **Rev:** Dot above, Manchu inscription **Rev. Inscription:** Boo-jiyen

Date	Mintage	Good	VG	F	VF	XF
ND(1875-1908)	—	2.75	4.50	7.50	15.00	—

C# 8-1.2 CASH
Cast Brass **Ruler:** Kuang-hsü **Obv. Inscription:** Kuang-hsü T'ung-pao **Rev:** Dot below, Manchu inscription **Rev. Inscription:** Boo-jiyen

Date	Mintage	Good	VG	F	VF	XF
ND(1875-1908)	—	2.00	3.50	6.00	10.00	—

C# 8-1.3 CASH
Cast Brass **Ruler:** Kuang-hsü **Obv. Inscription:** Kuang-hsü T'ung-pao **Rev:** 2 dots below, Manchu inscription **Rev. Inscription:** Boo-jiyen

Date	Mintage	Good	VG	F	VF	XF
ND(1875-1908)	—	3.50	5.50	9.00	15.00	—

C# 8-1.4 CASH
Cast Brass **Ruler:** Kuang-hsü **Obv. Inscription:** Kuang-hsü T'ung-pao **Rev:** Circle above Manchu inscription **Rev. Inscription:** Boo-jiyen

Date	Mintage	Good	VG	F	VF	XF
ND(1875-1908)	—	3.50	5.50	9.00	18.00	—

C# 8-1.5 CASH
Cast Brass **Ruler:** Kuang-hsü **Obv. Inscription:** Kuang-hsü T'ung-pao **Rev:** Circle below Manchu inscription **Rev. Inscription:** Boo-jiyen

Date	Mintage	Good	VG	F	VF	XF
ND(1875-1908)	—	3.50	5.50	9.00	18.00	—

C# 8-1.6 CASH
Cast Brass **Ruler:** Kuang-hsü **Obv. Inscription:** Kuang-hsü T'ung-pao **Rev:** Crescent above Manchu inscription **Rev. Inscription:** Boo-jiyen

Date	Mintage	Good	VG	F	VF	XF
ND(1875-1908)	—	3.50	5.50	9.00	18.00	—

C# 8-1.7 CASH
Cast Brass **Ruler:** Kuang-hsü **Obv. Inscription:** Kuang-hsü T'ung-pao **Rev:** Crescent below Manchu inscription **Rev. Inscription:** Boo-jiyen

Date	Mintage	Good	VG	F	VF	XF
ND(1875-1908)	—	2.00	3.75	7.50	17.00	—

C# 8-1.8 CASH
Cast Brass **Ruler:** Kuang-hsü **Obv. Inscription:** Kuang-hsü T'ung-pao **Rev:** Dash below Manchu inscription **Rev. Inscription:** Boo-jiyen

Date	Mintage	Good	VG	F	VF	XF
ND(1875-1908)	—	2.00	3.75	7.50	15.00	—

Note: Varieties exist with dots and crescents in different corners on reverse and also with incuse dots.

MILLED COINAGE

Y# 66 CASH
Brass **Ruler:** Kuang-hsü **Obv. Inscription:** Kuang-hsü T'ung-pao **Note:** Struck at Chin Mint (Peiyang Arsenal), Tientsin.

Date	Mintage	Good	VG	F	VF	XF
ND(1904-07)	—	1.50	4.00	6.00	12.00	25.00

Y# 7c CASH
Brass **Ruler:** Kuang-hsü **Obv. Legend:** Kuang-hsü **Rev:** Dragon **Note:** Struck at Chin Mint(Peiyang Arsenal), Tientsin.

Date	Mintage	Good	VG	F	VF	XF
CD1908	—	1.00	2.50	4.50	7.50	13.50

Y# 8c 2 CASH
Copper **Ruler:** Kuang-hsü **Note:** Struck at Chin Mint(Peiyang Arsenal), Tientsin.

Date	Mintage	VG	F	VF	XF	Unc
CD1906 Rare	—	—	—	—	—	—

Y# 9c 5 CASH
Copper **Ruler:** Kuang-hsü **Obv. Inscription:** Tai-ch'ing T'ung-pi **Rev. Legend:** Kuang-hsü Nien-tsao, TAI-CHING-TI-KUO ... **Note:** Struck at Chin Mint (Peiyang Arsenal), Tientsin.

Date	Mintage	Good	VG	F	VF	XF
CD1906	—	4.00	10.00	20.00	35.00	48.00

Y# 67 10 CASH
Copper **Ruler:** Kuang-hsü **Obv. Inscription:** Kuang-hsü Yüan-pao **Rev:** Side-view square-mouth dragon, hole in center of rosette **Rev. Legend:** PEI YANG **Note:** Struck at Chin Mint(Peiyang Arsenal), Tientsin.

Date	Mintage	Good	VG	F	VF	XF
ND(c.1906)	—	0.40	1.00	2.00	2.50	4.00

Note: Mulings exist with obverse of Kwangtung (Guangdong) Y#192 and reverse of Chihli Y#67; Refer to Kwangtung listings

Y# 67.1 10 CASH
Copper **Ruler:** Kuang-hsü **Obv. Inscription:** Kuang-hsü Yüan-pao **Rev:** Dragon with round mouth **Note:** Struck at Chin Mint (Peiyang Arsenal), Tientsin.

Date	Mintage	Good	VG	F	VF	XF
ND(c.1906)	—	0.40	1.00	2.00	2.50	4.00

Y# 67.2 10 CASH
Copper **Ruler:** Kuang-hsü **Obv. Inscription:** Kuang-hsü Yüan-pao **Rev:** Dot in center of rosettes, dragon with square mouth **Note:** Struck at Chin Mint (Peiyang Arsenal), Tientsin.

Date	Mintage	Good	VG	F	VF	XF
ND(c.1906)	—	0.40	1.00	2.00	2.50	4.00

Y# 67.3 10 CASH
Copper **Ruler:** Kuang-hsü **Obv. Inscription:** Kuang-hsü Yüan-pao **Rev:** Dot in center of rosettes, dragon with round mouth **Note:** Struck at Chin Mint (Peiyang Arsenal), Tientsin.

Date	Mintage	Good	VG	F	VF	XF
ND(c.1906)	—	0.40	1.00	2.00	2.50	4.00

Y# 67.4 10 CASH
Copper **Ruler:** Kuang-hsü **Obv. Inscription:** Kuang-hsü Yüan-pao **Rev:** Redesigned dragon with smaller body and smaller English legends **Note:** Struck at Chin Mint (Peiyang Arsenal), Tientsin.

Date	Mintage	Good	VG	F	VF	XF
ND(c.1906)	—	0.60	1.50	3.50	7.00	15.00

Y# 10c 10 CASH
Copper **Ruler:** Kuang-hsü **Obv. Inscription:** Tai-ch'ing T'ung-pi **Rev. Legend:** Kuang-hsü Nien-tsao, TAI-CHING-TI-KUO ... **Note:** Struck at Chin Mint (Peiyang Arsenal), Tientsin.

Date	Mintage	Good	VG	F	VF	XF
CD1906	—	0.40	1.00	2.00	3.00	5.00

Y# 68 20 CASH
Copper **Ruler:** Kuang-hsü **Note:** Struck at Chin Mint (Peiyang Arsenal), Tientsin.

Date	Mintage	Good	VG	F	VF	XF
ND(c. 1906)	—	10.00	20.00	30.00	40.00	100

Y# 68a 20 CASH
Brass **Ruler:** Kuang-hsü **Obv. Inscription:** Kuang-hsü Yüan-pao **Rev:** Side view dragon **Rev. Legend:** PEI YANG **Note:** Struck at Chin Mint (Peiyang Arsenal), Tientsin.

Date	Mintage	VG	F	VF	XF	Unc
ND(c.1906) Rare	—	—	—	—	—	—

Y# 68.1 20 CASH
Copper **Ruler:** Kuang-hsü **Obv. Inscription:** Kuang-hsü Yüan-pao **Rev:** Smaller lettering **Note:** Struck at Chin Mint (Peiyang Arsenal), Tientsin.

Date	Mintage	VG	F	VF	XF	Unc
ND(c.1906)	—	25.00	35.00	50.00	120	—

Y# 11c 20 CASH
Copper **Ruler:** Kuang-hsü **Obv. Inscription:** Tai-ch'ing T'ung-pi **Rev. Legend:** Kuang-hsü Nien-tsao, TAI-CHING-TI-KUO ... **Note:** Struck at Chin Mint (Peiyang Arsenal), Tientsin.

Date	Mintage	VG	F	VF	XF	Unc
CD1906	—	15.00	30.00	60.00	120	—

Y# 71a 20 CENTS
5.3000 g., 0.8200 Silver .1397 oz. ASW **Ruler:** Kuang-hsü **Obv. Inscription:** Kuang-hsü Yüan-pao **Rev:** Side view dragon, legend at bottom **Rev. Legend:** PEI YANG **Note:** Struck at Chin Mint (Peiyang Arsenal), Tientsin.

Date	Mintage	VG	F	VF	XF	Unc
31(1905)	161,000	15.00	37.50	75.00	150	350

Y# 73 DOLLAR
26.7000 g., 0.9000 Silver .7727 oz. ASW **Ruler:** Kuang-hsu **Obv. Inscription:** Kuang-hsü Yüan-pao **Rev:** Side view dragon, legend at bottom **Rev. Legend:** PEI YANG

Date	Mintage	VG	F	VF	XF	Unc
29(1903)	22,018,000	15.00	25.00	35.00	100	500

Y# 73.1 DOLLAR
26.7000 g., 0.9000 Silver .7727 oz. ASW **Ruler:** Kuang-hsü **Obv. Inscription:** Kuang-hsü Yüan-pao **Rev:** Side view dragon, legend at bottom, period after legend **Rev. Legend:** PEI YANG **Note:** Struck at Chin Mint (Peiyang Arsenal), Tientsin.

Date	Mintage	VG	F	VF	XF	Unc
29(1903)	Inc. above	15.00	25.00	35.00	100	700

Y# 73.2 DOLLAR
26.7000 g., 0.9000 Silver .7727 oz. ASW **Ruler:** Kuang-hsü **Obv. Inscription:** Kuang-hsü Yüan-pao **Rev:** Thinner side-view dragon, legend at bottom, year as "33rd" **Rev. Legend:** PEI YANG **Note:** Struck at Chin Mint (Peiyang Arsenal), Tientsin.

Date	Mintage	VG	F	VF	XF	Unc
33(1907)	2,341,000	17.50	30.00	55.00	120	1,100
34(1908)	—	12.00	22.00	30.00	60.00	350

Y# 73.3 DOLLAR
26.7000 g., 0.9000 Silver .7727 oz. ASW **Ruler:** Kuang-hsü **Obv. Inscription:** Kuang-hsü Yüan-pao **Rev:** Side view dragon, legend at bottom, short center spine to tail **Rev. Legend:** PEI YANG **Note:** Struck at Chin Mint (Peiyang Arsenal), Tientsin. Restruck during Republican times.

Date	Mintage	VG	F	VF	XF	Unc
34(1908)	—	12.00	22.00	30.00	60.00	350

Y# 73.4 DOLLAR
26.7000 g , 0.9000 Silver .7727 oz. ASW **Ruler:** Kuang-hsü **Obv. Inscription:** Kuang-hsü Yüan-pao **Rev:** Side view dragon, legend at bottom, crosslet 4 in date **Rev. Legend:** PEI YANG **Note:** Struck at Chin Mint (Peiyang Arsenal), Tientsin. Restruck during Republican times.

Date	Mintage	VG	F	VF	XF	Unc
34(1908)	—	30.00	50.00	125	250	1,100

Y# 74 TAEL
51.2000 g., Silver **Ruler:** Kuang-hsü **Obv. Inscription:** Kuang-hsü Yüan-pao **Rev:** Side view dragon, legend at bottom **Rev. Legend:** PEI YANG **Note:** Struck at Chin Mint (Peiyang Arsenal), Tientsin.

Date	Mintage	VG	F	VF	XF	Unc
33(1907)	—	—	6,000	8,000	15,000	35,000

Y# 74.1 TAEL
51.2000 g., Silver **Ruler:** Kuang-hsü **Obv. Inscription:** Kuang-hsü Yüan-pao **Rev:** Side view dragon, legend at bottom, 3 dots on pearl arranged horizontally **Rev. Legend:** PEI YANG **Note:** Struck at Chin Mint (Peiyang Arsenal), Tientsin.

Date	Mintage	VG	F	VF	XF	Unc
33(1907)	—	—	6,000	8,000	15,000	35,000

Y# 74.2 TAEL
51.2000 g., Silver **Ruler:** Kuang-hsü **Obv. Inscription:** Kuang-hsü Yüan-pao **Rev:** Side view dragon, legend at bottom, 3 dots on pearl arranged in arc **Rev. Legend:** PEI YANG **Note:** Struck at Chin Mint (Feiyang Arsenal), Tientsin.

Date	Mintage	VG	F	VF	XF	Unc
33(1907)	—	—	3,000	5,000	8,000	17,500

PATTERNS

Including off metal strikes

KM#	Date	Mintage	Identification	Mkt Val
Pn6	29(1903)	—	Dollar. Brass. Y73.	—
Pn7	33(1907)	—	Tael. Gold. Y74.	—

FENGTIEN PROVINCE

(Fungtien)
Liaoning

The southernmost province of the Three Eastern Provinces was known by a variety of names including Fengtien, Shengching, and Liaoning. The modern Mukden (Fengtien Province) Mint operated from 1897 to 1931.

EMPIRE

PROVINCIAL CAST COINAGE

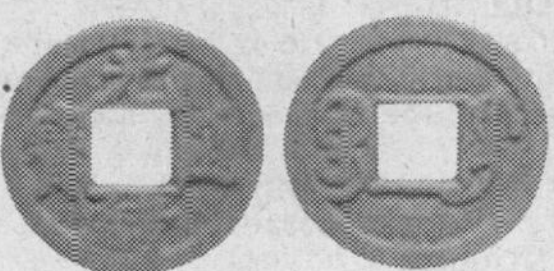

C# 9-1 CASH
Cast Brass **Ruler:** Kuang-hsü **Obv:** Type A **Obv. Inscription:** Kuang-hsü T'ung-pao **Rev:** Manchu inscription **Rev. Inscription:** Boo-fung

Date	Mintage	Good	VG	F	VF	XF
ND(1875-1908)	—	20.00	30.00	40.00	60.00	80.00

MILLED COINAGE

Y# 19e 5 CASH
Copper **Ruler:** Hsüan-t'ung **Obv. Inscription:** Tai-ching T'ung-pi **Rev. Legend:** Hsüan-t'ung Nien-tsao, TAI-CHING-TI-KUO ...

Date	Mintage	VG	F	VF	XF	Unc
CD1909	—	37.50	75.00	125	200	—

Y# 88 10 CASH
Brass **Ruler:** Kuang-hsü **Obv. Inscription:** Kuang-hsü Yüan-pao **Rev:** Province name spelled "FEN-TIEN"

Date	Mintage	VG	F	VF	XF	Unc
CD1903	—	50.00	90.00	135	225	—

Y# 89 10 CASH
Brass **Ruler:** Kuang-hsü **Obv. Inscription:** Kuang-hsü Yüan-pao **Rev. Legend:** FUNG-TIEN PROVINCE

Date	Mintage	VG	F	VF	XF	Unc
CD1903	—	3.75	7.50	25.00	40.00	—
CD1904	—	1.25	3.00	5.00	8.00	—
CD1905	—	1.50	4.50	10.00	12.00	—
CD1906	35,036,000	3.00	6.00	25.00	35.00	—

Y# 89.1 10 CASH
Brass **Ruler:** Kuang-hsü **Obv:** Manchu words in center reversed **Obv. Inscription:** Kuang-hsü Yüan-pao **Rev. Legend:** FUNG-TIEN PROVINCE

Date	Mintage	VG	F	VF	XF	Unc
CD1903	—	28.00	85.00	150	250	—

Y# 89.2 10 CASH
Brass **Ruler:** Kuang-hsü **Obv. Inscription:** Kuang-hsü Yüan-pao **Rev:** Large pearl **Rev. Legend:** FUNG-TIEN PROVINCE

Date	Mintage	VG	F	VF	XF	Unc
CD1905	—	1.25	4.00	8.00	15.00	—

Y# 10e 10 CASH
Copper **Ruler:** Kuang-hsü **Obv. Inscription:** Tai-ch'ing T'ung-pi **Rev:** Dragon, small pearl **Rev. Legend:** Kuang-hsü Nien-tsao, TAI-CHING TI KUO ....

Date	Mintage	VG	F	VF	XF	Unc
CD1905	—	1.25	4.00	8.00	15.00	—

Y# 10e.1 10 CASH
Copper **Ruler:** Kuang-hsü **Obv. Inscription:** Tai-ch'ing T'ung-pi **Rev:** Large pearl **Rev. Legend:** Kuang-hsü Nien-tsao, TAI-CHING-TI-KUO ...

Date	Mintage	VG	F	VF	XF	Unc
CD1905	—	1.25	4.00	8.00	15.00	—

Y# 10e.2 10 CASH
Copper **Ruler:** Kuang-hsü **Obv:** Mint mark on spherical disc in center **Obv. Inscription:** Tai-ch'ing T'ung-pi **Rev:** Large pearl **Rev. Legend:** Kuang-hsü Nien-tsao, TAI-CHING-TI KUO ...

Date	Mintage	VG	F	VF	XF	Unc
ND(1907)	130,000	1.00	3.00	6.00	20.00	—

Y# 10e.3 10 CASH
Copper **Ruler:** Kuang-hsü **Obv:** Mint mark on flat disc in center **Obv. Inscription:** Tai-ch'ing T'ung-pi **Rev. Legend:** Kuang-hsü Nien-tsao, TAI CHING TI KUO ...

Date	Mintage	VG	F	VF	XF	Unc
CD1907	Inc. above	0.50	1.50	3.00	6.00	—

Y# 20e 10 CASH
Copper **Ruler:** Hsüan-t'ung **Obv:** Mint mark on flat disc in center **Obv. Inscription:** Tai-ch'ing T'ung-pi **Rev. Legend:** Hsüan-T'ung Nien-tsao, TAI-CHING-TI-KUO ...

Date	Mintage	VG	F	VF	XF	Unc
CD1909	—	2.75	8.00	17.50	30.00	—

Y# 20e.1 10 CASH
Copper **Ruler:** Kuang-hsü **Obv. Inscription:** Tai-ch'ing T'ung-pi **Rev. Legend:** Kuang-hsü Nien-tsao, TAI CHING TI KUO ... **Note:** Mule, obverse Y#20e, reverse Y#10e. Prev. #W286.

Date	Mintage	VG	F	VF	XF	Unc
CD1909 6 known	—	—	—	—	—	—

Y# 90 20 CASH
Brass **Ruler:** Kuang-hsü **Obv. Legend:** Feng-tien Sheng Tsao **Obv. Inscription:** Kuang-hsü Yüan-pao **Rev. Legend:** FUNG TIEN PROVINCE

Date	Mintage	VG	F	VF	XF	Unc
CD1903	—	75.00	100	125	175	—
CD1904	—	5.50	11.00	22.50	55.00	—
CD1905	—	9.00	18.00	25.00	60.00	—

Y# 11e 20 CASH
Brass **Ruler:** Kuang-hsü **Obv. Inscription:** Tai-ching T'ung-pi **Rev. Legend:** Kuang-hsü Nien-tsao, TAI-CHING-TI-KUO ...

Date	Mintage	VG	F	VF	XF	Unc
CD1905	—	4.00	7.00	20.00	40.00	—
CD1907	—	6.00	12.00	25.00	50.00	—

Y# 11f 20 CASH
Copper **Ruler:** Kuang-hsü **Obv:** Inscription with "CD" at left and right **Obv. Inscription:** Tai-ching T'ung-pi **Rev. Legend:** Kuang-hsü Nien-tsao, TAI-CHING-TI-KUO...

Date	Mintage	VG	F	VF	XF	Unc
CD1907	—	—	—	—	—	—

Y# 11g 20 CASH
Copper **Ruler:** Kuang-hsü **Obv:** Inscription with Hu at right, Pu at left **Obv. Inscription:** Tai-ch'ing T'ung-pi **Rev:** Dragon **Rev. Legend:** Kuang-hsü Nien-tsao, TAI-CHING-TI-KUO...

Date	Mintage	VG	F	VF	XF	Unc
CD1905	—	—	—	—	—	—

Y# 21e 20 CASH
Brass **Ruler:** Hsüan-t'ung **Obv. Inscription:** Tai-ching T'ung-pi **Rev. Legend:** Hsüan-t'ung Nien-tsao, TAI-CHING-TI-KUO ...

Date	Mintage	VG	F	VF	XF	Unc
CD1909	—	25.00	60.00	110	175	—

Y# 91 20 CENTS
Silver, 24 mm. **Ruler:** Kuang-hsü **Obv. Legend:** Feng-tien Sheng Tsao **Obv. Inscription:** Kuang-hsü Yüan-pao **Rev:** Side view dragon, 8 rows of scales on dragon **Rev. Legend:** FUNG-TIEN PROVINCE

Date	Mintage	VG	F	VF	XF	Unc
CD1904	—	3.75	9.00	15.00	28.00	70.00

Y# 91.1 20 CENTS
Silver **Ruler:** Kuang-hsü **Obv. Legend:** Feng-tien Sheng Tsao **Obv. Inscription:** Kuang-hsü Yüan-pao **Rev:** Side view dragon, 5 rows of scales on dragon **Rev. Legend:** FUNG-TIEN PROVINCE

Date	Mintage	VG	F	VF	XF	Unc
CD1904	—	4.00	10.00	16.50	30.00	80.00

Y# 92 DOLLAR
26.4000 g., 0.8500 Silver .7215 oz. ASW **Ruler:** Kuang-hsü **Obv. Legend:** Feng-tien Sheng Tsao **Obv. Inscription:** Kuang-hsü Yüan-pao **Rev:** Side view dragon **Rev. Legend:** FUNG-TIEN PROVINCE

Date	Mintage	VG	F	VF	XF	Unc
CD1903	262,000	100	200	350	800	2,500

Y# 92.1 DOLLAR
26.4000 g., 0.8500 Silver .7215 oz. ASW **Ruler:** Kuang-hsü **Obv:** Manchu "Boo-funs" in center are reversed **Obv. Legend:** Feng-tien Sheng Tsao **Obv. Inscription:** Kuang-hsü Yüan-pao **Rev:** Side view dragon **Rev. Legend:** FUNG-TIEN PROVINCE

Date	Mintage	VG	F	VF	XF	Unc
CD1903	Inc. above	100	250	500	1,000	3,000

TOKEN COINAGE

KM# TnA1 10 CENTS
Copper **Ruler:** Kuang-hsü **Obv:** Dragon **Rev:** Tang-shih (10)

Date	Mintage	VG	F	VF	XF	Unc
ND(c.1904)	—	—	—	900	1,500	2,500

KM# Tn1 DOLLAR
Copper **Ruler:** Kuang-hsü **Obv:** Reverse of 10 Cash, Y#10e, small spiral on pearl **Rev. Inscription:** Tang-yüan(1 Dollar) **Note:** Woodward #242.

Date	Mintage	VG	F	VF	XF	Unc
ND(c.1904)	—	—	—	550	900	1,500

KM# Tn1a DOLLAR
Brass **Ruler:** Kuang-hsü **Obv:** Reverse of 10 Cash, Y#10e, small spiral on pearl **Rev. Inscription:** Tang-yüan(1 Dollar)

Date	Mintage	VG	F	VF	XF	Unc
ND(c.1904)	—	—	—	550	900	1,500

KM# Tn2 100 CENTS
Copper **Ruler:** Kuang-hsü **Obv:** Dragon, large spiral on pearl **Obv. Legend:** FUNG TIEN PROVINCE **Rev. Inscription:** Tang Pai **Note:** Silver forgeries exist. Woodward #243.

Date	Mintage	VG	F	VF	XF	Unc
ND(c.1904)	—	—	—	550	900	1,500

KM# Tn3 100 CENTS
Brass **Ruler:** Kuang-hsü **Obv. Legend:** FUNG-TIEN PROVINCE **Rev. Inscription:** Tang Pai **Note:** Silver forgeries exist.

Date	Mintage	VG	F	VF	XF	Unc
ND(c.1904)	—	—	—	—	—	—

PATTERNS

Including off metal strikes

KM#	Date	Mintage	Identification	Mkt Val
Pn2A	ND(c.1902)	—	10 Cents. Brass. Regular provincial design.	—
Pn3	ND(c.1902)	—	20 Cents. Brass. Regular provincial design.	—
Pn4	ND(c.1902)	—	20 Cents. Brass. Error, TENG-TIEN.	—
Pn5	ND(c.1902)	—	20 Cents. Silver. FENG-TIEN.	—
Pn6	ND(c.1902)	—	50 Cents. Brass. Error, TENG-TIEN.	—
Pn7	ND(c.1902)	—	Dollar. Aluminum. Error, TENG-TIEN.	50,000
Pn8	ND(c.1902)	—	Dollar. Silver. Error, TENG-TIEN.	—
Pn9	ND(c.1902)	—	Dollar. Brass. Error, TENG-TIEN.	—
Pn10	ND(c.1902)	—	10 Cash. Copper.	—
Pn11	CD1903	—	10 Cash. Copper. Y88.	—
Pn12	CD1903	—	10 Cash. Copper. Y89.	—
Pn13	CD1903	—	10 Cash. Copper. Y89.1.	—
Pn14	CD1903	—	20 Cash. Copper. Y90.	200
PnA15	CD1903	—	Tael. Silver. K931-I.	—

Note: Superior Goodman sale 6-91 about XF realized $187,000.

KM#	Date	Mintage	Identification	Mkt Val
Pn15	CD1904	—	10 Cash. Copper. Y89.	—
Pn16	CD1905	—	10 Cash. Copper. Y89.	—
Pn17	CD1905	—	20 Cash. Copper. Y90.	—

FUKIEN PROVINCE

Fujian

A province located on the southeastern coast of China, including the island of Taiwan until it became its own separate province in 1885. Although known mainly as an agricultural area, forestry and some mining, particularly iron ore and coal, are also important to the economy. The Foochow Mint operated throughout the Manchu dynasty. The Viceroy's or City mint was opened in 1896 for struck coinage. Two other mints were established in 1905, the Mamoi Arsenal Mint which struck the Custom-House issues until it closed in 1906, and the West Mint which later became the main Fukien (Fujian) Mint. It closed between 1914 and 1920. Various subsidiary mints were in operation from 1924 to 1925.

EMPIRE

PROVINCIAL CAST COINAGE

C# 10-25 CASH
Cast Brass **Ruler:** Kuang-hsü **Obv. Inscription:** Kuang hsü T'ung-pao **Rev:** Manchu inscription **Rev. Inscription:** Boo-fu **Note:** Schjöth #1581.

Date	Mintage	Good	VG	F	VF	XF
ND(1875-1908)	—	0.85	1.50	2.50	3.50	—

C# 10-25.1 CASH
Cast Brass **Ruler:** Kuang-hsü **Obv. Inscription:** Kuang hsü T'ung-pao **Rev:** Dot at top of hole, Manchu inscription **Rev. Inscription:** Boo-fu

Date	Mintage	Good	VG	F	VF	XF
ND(1875-1908)	—	2.50	4.00	6.50	10.00	—

C# 10-25.2 CASH
Cast Brass **Ruler:** Kuang-hsü **Obv. Inscription:** Kuang-hsü T'ung-pao **Rev:** Inverted Manchu inscription **Rev. Inscription:** Boo-fu

Date	Mintage	Good	VG	F	VF	XF
ND(1875-1908)	—	—	—	—	—	—

MILLED COINAGE

Y# 95 CASH
Brass **Ruler:** Kuang-hsü **Obv. Inscription:** Kuang hsü T'ung-pao **Rev. Inscription:** Manchu Boo-fu

Date	Mintage	VG	F	VF	XF	Unc
ND(1908)	—	6.00	10.00	15.00	30.00	—

Y# 7f CASH
Brass **Ruler:** Kuang-hsü **Obv:** Inscription: Kuang hsü **Rev:** Dragon

Date	Mintage	VG	F	VF	XF	Unc
CD1908	—	35.00	75.00	110	175	—

Y# 106 CASH
Brass **Ruler:** Hsüan-T'ung **Obv. Inscription:** Hsüan-t'ung T'ung-pao **Rev:** Manchu inscription **Rev. Inscription:** Manchu Boo-fu

Date	Mintage	VG	F	VF	XF	Unc
ND(1909)	—	15.00	25.00	50.00	80.00	—

Y# 8f 2 CASH
Brass **Obv. Inscription:** Tai-ching T'ung-pi **Rev:** Dragon

Date	Mintage	VG	F	VF	XF	Unc
CD1906	—	3.00	8.00	14.00	25.00	—

Y# 99 5 CASH
Copper **Ruler:** Kuang-hsü **Obv. Legend:** Fu-kien Kuan Chü Tsao **Obv. Inscription:** Kuang-hsü Yüan-pao **Rev:** Dragon **Rev. Legend:** FOO-KIEN

Date	Mintage	VG	F	VF	XF	Unc
ND(1901-03)	590,000	18.00	25.00	37.50	60.00	—

Y# 99a 5 CASH
Brass **Ruler:** Kuang-hsü **Obv. Legend:** Fu-kien Kuan Chü Tsao **Obv. Inscription:** Kuang-hsü Yüan-pao **Rev:** Dragon **Rev. Legend:** FOO-KIEN

Date	Mintage	VG	F	VF	XF	Unc
ND(1901-03)	—	12.00	25.00	50.00	75.00	—

Y# 97 10 CASH
Copper **Ruler:** Kuang-hsü **Obv:** Large characters at left and right **Obv. Legend:** Fu-kien Kuan Chü Tsao **Obv. Inscription:** Kuang-hsü Yüan-pao **Rev:** Dragon **Rev. Legend:** F.K. CUSTOM-HOUSE

Date	Mintage	VG	F	VF	XF	Unc
ND(1901-05)	417,031,000	0.50	1.50	2.50	8.00	25.00

Y# 97.1 10 CASH
Copper **Ruler:** Kuang-hsü **Obv:** Small characters at left and right sides **Obv. Legend:** Fu-kien Kuan Chü Tsao **Obv. Inscription:** Kuang-hsü Yüan-pao **Rev:** Dragon **Rev. Legend:** F.K. CUSTOM-HOUSE

Date	Mintage	VG	F	VF	XF	Unc
ND(1901-05)	Inc. above	0.65	2.00	4.00	10.00	30.00

Y# 98 10 CASH
Copper **Ruler:** Kuang-hsü **Obv. Legend:** Fu-kien Kuan Chü Tsao **Obv. Inscription:** Kuang-hsü Yüan-pao **Rev:** Dragon **Rev. Legend:** FOO-KIEN CUSTOM

Date	Mintage	VG	F	VF	XF	Unc
ND(1901-05)	Inc. above	35.00	100	150	250	—

Y# 100 10 CASH
Copper **Ruler:** Kuang-hsü **Obv. Legend:** Fu-kien Kuan Chü Tsao **Obv. Inscription:** Kuang-hsü Yüan-pao **Rev:** 1 cloud left of pearl, dragon **Rev. Legend:** FOO-KIEN

Date	Mintage	VG	F	VF	XF	Unc
ND(1901-05)	Inc. above	1.00	3.00	6.00	9.00	30.00

Y# 100.1 10 CASH
Copper **Ruler:** Kuang-hsü **Obv. Legend:** Fu-kien Kuan Chü Tsao **Obv. Inscription:** Kuang-hsü Yüan-pao **Rev:** 3 clouds left of pearl and without cloud above tip of dragon's tail, dragon **Rev. Legend:** FOO-KIEN

Date	Mintage	VG	F	VF	XF	Unc
ND(1901-05)	Inc. above	0.65	2.00	4.00	7.00	25.00

Y# 100.2 10 CASH
Copper **Ruler:** Kuang-hsü **Obv. Legend:** Fu-kien Kuan Chü Tsao **Obv. Inscription:** Kuang-hsü Yüan-pao **Rev:** 3 clouds left of pearl and a cloud above tip of dragon's tail, dragon **Rev. Legend:** FOO-KIEN

Date	Mintage	VG	F	VF	XF	Unc
ND(1901-05)	Inc. above	0.35	1.00	2.00	4.00	25.00

Y# 100.2a 10 CASH
Brass **Ruler:** Kuang-hsü **Obv. Legend:** Fu-kien Kuan Chü Tsao **Obv. Inscription:** Kuang-hsü Yüan-pao **Rev:** Dragon **Rev. Legend:** FOO-KIEN

Date	Mintage	VG	F	VF	XF	Unc
ND(1901-05)	Inc. above	—	—	—	—	—

Y# 100.3 10 CASH
Copper **Ruler:** Kuang-hsü **Obv. Legend:** Fu-kien Kuan Chü Tsao **Obv. Inscription:** Kuang-hsü Yüan-pao **Rev:** Dragon, denomination: 10 CASHES **Rev. Legend:** FOO-KIEN

Date	Mintage	VG	F	VF	XF	Unc
ND(1901-05)	Inc. above	4.00	12.00	20.00	45.00	—

Y# 10f 10 CASH
Copper **Ruler:** Kuang-hsü **Obv. Inscription:** Tai-ch'ing T'ung-pi **Rev:** Dragon, inscription, denomination 10 CASHES **Rev. Legend:** Kuang-hsü Nien-tsao, TAI-CHING-TI-KUO ...

Date	Mintage	VG	F	VF	XF	Unc
CD1906	—	0.25	0.75	1.50	3.00	20.00

Y# 20f 10 CASH
Copper **Ruler:** Hsüan-T'ung **Obv. Inscription:** Tai-ch'ing T'ung-pi **Rev:** Dragon **Rev. Legend:** Hsüan-tung Nien-tsao, TAI-CHING-TI-KUO ...

Date	Mintage	VG	F	VF	XF	Unc
CD1909	—	16.50	50.00	85.00	125	—

Y# 101.1 20 CASH
Copper **Ruler:** Kuang-hsü **Obv. Legend:** Fu-kien Kuan Chü Tsao **Obv. Inscription:** Kuang-hsü Yüan-pao **Rev:** Dragon **Rev. Legend:** FOO-KIEN

Date	Mintage	VG	F	VF	XF	Unc
ND(1901-02)	Inc. above	25.00	60.00	90.00	150	—

Y# 101 20 CASH
Copper **Ruler:** Kuang-hsü **Obv. Legend:** Fu-kien Kuan Chü Tsao **Obv. Inscription:** Kuang-hsü Yüan-pao **Rev:** Dragon **Rev. Legend:** FOO-KIEN

Date	Mintage	VG	F	VF	XF	Unc
ND(1901-02)	18,000	12.00	30.00	45.00	75.00	—

Y# 102 5 CENTS
1.3500 g., 0.8200 Silver .0356 oz. ASW **Ruler:** Kuang-hsü **Obv:** Legend with 5 characters at top, inscription **Obv. Legend:** Fu-kien Kuan Chü Tsao **Obv. Inscription:** Kuang-hsü Yüan-pao **Rev:** Side view dragon left

Date	Mintage	VG	F	VF	XF	Unc
ND(1896-1903)	—	2.50	7.00	13.00	22.50	60.00

Y# 102.1 5 CENTS
1.3500 g., 0.8200 Silver .0356 oz. ASW **Ruler:** Kuang-hsü **Obv:** Legend with four characters at top **Obv. Legend:** Fu-kien Kuan Chü Tsao **Obv. Inscription:** Kuang-hsü Yüan-pao **Rev:** Rosette at either side of side view dragon right

Date	Mintage	VG	F	VF	XF	Unc
ND(1903-08)	—	3.00	6.00	10.00	20.00	40.00

Y# 102.2 5 CENTS
1.3500 g., 0.8200 Silver .0356 oz. ASW **Ruler:** Kuang-hsü **Obv. Legend:** Fu-kien Kuan Chü Tsao **Obv. Inscription:** Kuang-hsü Yüan-pao **Rev:** Rosette above dragon's head

Date	Mintage	VG	F	VF	XF	Unc
ND(1903-08)	—	3.50	6.50	12.50	25.00	50.00

Y# 102.3 5 CENTS
1.3500 g., 0.8200 Silver .0356 oz. ASW **Ruler:** Kuang-hsü **Obv. Legend:** Fu-kien Kuan Chü Tsao **Obv. Inscription:** Kuang-hsü Yüan-pao **Rev. Legend:** PROVINCE FOO-KIEN

Date	Mintage	VG	F	VF	XF	Unc
ND(1903-08)	—	—	—	—	—	—

Y# 103 10 CENTS
2.7000 g., 0.8200 Silver .0712 oz. ASW **Ruler:** Kuang-hsü **Obv:** Legend with 5 characters at top, inscription **Obv. Legend:** Fu-kien Kuan Chü Tsao **Obv. Inscription:** Kuang-hsü Yüan-pao **Rev:** Rosette at either side of side view dragon left

Date	Mintage	VG	F	VF	XF	Unc
ND(1896-1903)	13,425,000	2.25	5.00	9.00	17.50	35.00

Y# 103.1 10 CENTS
2.7000 g., 0.8200 Silver .0712 oz. ASW **Ruler:** Kuang-hsü **Obv. Legend:** Fu-kien Kuan Chü Tsao **Obv. Inscription:** Kuang-hsü Yüan-pao **Rev:** Dot at either side of side view dragon left

Date	Mintage	VG	F	VF	XF	Unc
ND(1896-1903)	Inc. above	3.50	8.00	15.00	30.00	60.00

Y# 103.2 10 CENTS
2.7000 g., 0.8200 Silver .0712 oz. ASW **Ruler:** Kuang-hsü **Obv:** Legend has 4 characters at top **Obv. Legend:** Fu-kien Kuan Chü Tsao **Obv. Inscription:** Kuang-hsü Yüan-pao **Rev:** Small side view dragon right

Date	Mintage	VG	F	VF	XF	Unc
ND(1903-08)	Inc. above	1.50	3.00	6.00	12.00	30.00

Y# 103.3 10 CENTS
2.7000 g., 0.8200 Silver .0712 oz. ASW **Ruler:** Kuang-hsü **Obv:** Legend has 4 characters at top **Obv. Legend:** Fu-kien Kuan Chü Tsao **Obv. Inscription:** Kuang-hsü Yüan-pao **Rev:** Large side view dragon right

Date	Mintage	VG	F	VF	XF	Unc
ND(1903-08)	Inc. above	2.50	6.00	12.00	24.00	50.00

Y# 104 20 CENTS
5.4000 g., 0.8200 Silver .1424 oz. ASW **Ruler:** Kuang-hsü **Obv:** Legend has 5 characters at top, inscription **Obv. Legend:** Fu-kien Kuan Chü Tsao **Obv. Inscription:** Kuang-hsü Yüan-pao **Rev:** Dot at either side of side view dragon left

Date	Mintage	VG	F	VF	XF	Unc
ND(1896-1903)	31,772,000	2.25	4.50	7.00	12.50	30.00

Y# 104.1 20 CENTS
5.4000 g., 0.8200 Silver .1424 oz. ASW **Ruler:** Kuang-hsü **Obv. Legend:** Fu-kien Kuan Chü Tsao **Obv. Inscription:** Kuang-hsü Yüan-pao **Rev:** Rosette at either side of side view dragon left

Date	Mintage	VG	F	VF	XF	Unc
ND(1898-1903)	Inc. above	2.25	4.50	7.00	12.50	30.00

Y# 104.2 20 CENTS
5.4000 g., 0.8200 Silver .1424 oz. ASW **Ruler:** Kuang-hsü **Obv:** Legend has 4 characters at top **Obv. Legend:** Fu-kien Kuan Chü Tsao **Obv. Inscription:** Kuang-hsü Yüan-pao **Rev:** Side view dragon right **Note:** Variety with large side view dragon right on reverse exists.

Date	Mintage	VG	F	VF	XF	Unc
ND(1903-08)	Inc. above	2.25	4.50	7.00	12.50	30.00

REPUBLIC

PROVINCIAL CAST COINAGE

Y# 374 CASH
Cast Brass **Obv. Inscription:** Fu-chien T'ung-pao **Rev:** 6 stripes on right flag

Date	Mintage	VG	F	VF	XF	Unc
ND(c.1912)	—	50.00	80.00	125	165	—

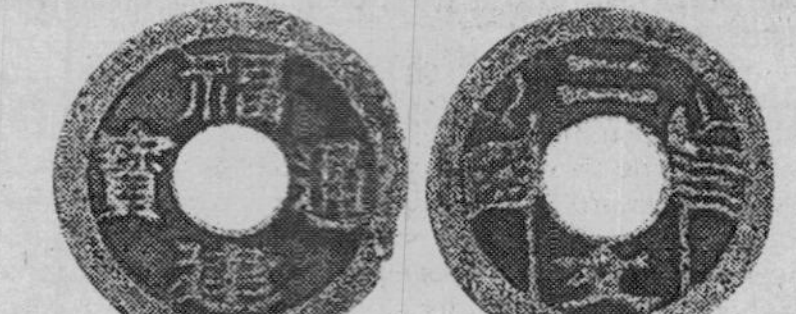

Y# 375 2 CASH
Cast Brass **Obv. Inscription:** Fu-chien T'ung-pao **Rev:** 5 stripes on right flag

Date	Mintage	VG	F	VF	XF	Unc
ND(c.1912)	—	12.50	17.50	22.50	30.00	—

Y# 375.1 2 CASH
Cast Brass **Obv. Inscription:** Fu-chien T'ung-pao **Rev:** 6 stripes on right flag

Date	Mintage	VG	F	VF	XF	Unc
ND(c.1912)	—	30.00	50.00	80.00	125	—

MILLED COINAGE

Y# 379 10 CASH
Copper **Obv. Legend:** Fu-Kien Túng Pien Tsang Tsao **Obv. Inscription:** Chung-hua Yüan-pao **Rev. Legend:** FOO-KIEN COPPER COIN

Date	Mintage	VG	F	VF	XF	Unc
ND(c.1912)	—	1.25	4.00	8.00	15.00	35.00

Y# 379a 10 CASH
Brass **Obv. Legend:** Fu-Kien Túng Pien Tsang Tsao **Obv. Inscription:** Chung-hua Yüan-pao **Rev. Legend:** FOO-KIEN COPPER COIN

Date	Mintage	VG	F	VF	XF	Unc
ND(c.1912)	—	18.50	37.50	50.00	87.50	125

Y# 380 10 CENTS
2.6000 g., Silver **Obv. Inscription:** Chung-hua Yüan-pao

Date	Mintage	VG	F	VF	XF	Unc
ND(c.1912)	—	25.00	37.50	100	200	350

Y# 382 10 CENTS
2.6000 g., Silver **Obv. Inscription:** Chung-hua Yüan-pao

Date	Mintage	VG	F	VF	XF	Unc
ND(c.1913)	—	1.25	2.50	5.00	9.00	20.00

Y# 380a 10 CENTS
2.6000 g., Silver **Obv:** Different legend in center **Obv. Inscription:** Chung-hua Yüan-pao **Note:** Similar to Y#380.

Date	Mintage	VG	F	VF	XF	Unc
CD1924	—	25.00	50.00	120	200	300

Y# 388 10 CENTS
2.6000 g., Silver, 18 mm. **Subject:** Canton martyrs

Date	Mintage	VG	F	VF	XF	Unc
17(1928)	—	2.50	7.50	15.00	30.00	50.00
20(1931)	—	3.50	10.00	25.00	50.00	75.00

Y# 390 10 CENTS
2.6000 g., Silver, 18 mm. **Subject:** Canton martyrs

Date	Mintage	VG	F	VF	XF	Unc
Yr. 21(1932)	—	40.00	100	150	200	375

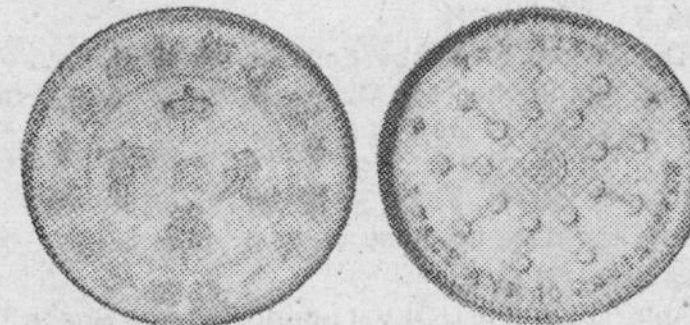

Y# 377 20 CENTS
5.0000 g., Silver **Obv. Inscription:** Chung-hua Yüan-pao

Date	Mintage	VG	F	VF	XF	Unc
CD1911	—	4.00	10.00	20.00	35.00	100

Y# A381 20 CENTS
5.4000 g., Silver **Obv. Inscription:** Chung-hua Yüan-pao

Date	Mintage	VG	F	VF	XF	Unc
ND(1912)	—	2.25	4.50	8.00	15.00	25.00

Y# 383 20 CENTS
5.2000 g., Silver

Date	Mintage	VG	F	VF	XF	Unc
ND(1923)	—	2.00	3.50	6.00	10.00	20.00

Note: Kann dates this coin 1913, but evidence suggests that it was struck in 1923

Y# 381 20 CENTS
5.3000 g., Silver **Obv:** Rosettes at sides, dot in middle of rosette center **Rev:** Rosettes at sides

Date	Mintage	VG	F	VF	XF	Unc
CD1923	—	2.25	4.00	7.50	12.00	28.00

Y# 381.1 20 CENTS
5.3000 g., Silver **Rev:** "MADE" spelled "MAIE" in legend

Date	Mintage	VG	F	VF	XF	Unc
CD1923	—	2.25	4.00	7.50	12.50	30.00

Y# 381.2 20 CENTS
5.3000 g., Silver **Rev. Legend:** MADEIN FOO-KIENMINT

Date	Mintage	VG	F	VF	XF	Unc
CD1923	—	2.25	4.00	7.50	12.50	30.00

Y# 381.3 20 CENTS
5.3000 g., Silver **Obv:** Without dot in middle of center rosette, 5-pointed star at sides in place of rosette

Date	Mintage	VG	F	VF	XF	Unc
CD1923	—	4.00	10.00	12.50	17.50	35.00

Y# 381.4 20 CENTS
5.0000 g., Silver **Obv:** Different legend in center

Date	Mintage	VG	F	VF	XF	Unc
CD1924	—	2.50	5.00	8.00	15.00	35.00

Y# 383a 20 CENTS
5.7000 g., Silver

Date	Mintage	VG	F	VF	XF	Unc
13(1924)	—	11.50	35.00	50.00	70.00	90.00

Y# 384 20 CENTS
5.0000 g., Silver **Subject:** Northern Expedition **Obv:** Crossed flags

Date	Mintage	VG	F	VF	XF	Unc
16(1927)	—	75.00	200	350	500	800

Y# 385 20 CENTS
5.3000 g., Silver **Subject:** Northern Expedition **Obv:** Crossed flags

Date	Mintage	VG	F	VF	XF	Unc
16(1927)	—	200	650	1,000	1,350	2,000

Y# 389.1 20 CENTS
5.3000 g., Silver, 23 mm. **Subject:** Canton martyrs **Obv:** Two rows of bricks at right of gate

Date	Mintage	VG	F	VF	XF	Unc
17(1928)	—	2.50	5.00	7.50	12.50	30.00
20(1931)	—	3.00	7.50	12.00	20.00	60.00

Y# 389.2 20 CENTS
5.5000 g., Silver, 23 mm. **Subject:** Canton martyrs **Obv:** Half brick in 3rd row of bricks at right of gate

Date	Mintage	VG	F	VF	XF	Unc
17(1928)	—	2.25	4.00	6.50	10.00	30.00
20(1931)	—	2.75	6.00	10.00	16.50	50.00

Y# 389.3 20 CENTS
5.5000 g., Silver, 23 mm. **Subject:** Canton martyrs **Rev:** 6-pointed star in legend

Date	Mintage	VG	F	VF	XF	Unc
20(1931)	—	—	—	—	—	—

Y# 391 20 CENTS
5.3000 g., Silver, 23 mm. **Subject:** Canton martyrs **Rev:** Crossed flags

Date	Mintage	VG	F	VF	XF	Unc
21(1932)	—	20.00	45.00	75.00	125	250

PATTERNS

Including off metal strikes

KM#	Date	Mintage	Identification	Mkt Val
Pn3	ND(c.1912)	—	2 Wen. Cast Brass. Obv. Ins: Fu-chien Sheng-tsao.	300
Pn4	ND(c.1912)	—	2 Wen. Cast Brass. Obv. Ins: Fu-chien T'ung-pao.	300
Pn5	ND(c.1912)	—	2 Wen. Cast Brass. Obv. Ins: Min-sheng T'ung-pao.	300
Pn6	16(1927)	—	20 Cents. Silver. 5.0000 g. Sun Yat-sen Memorial. K712.	600
Pn7	17(1928)	—	20 Cents. Brass. Y389.1.	—
Pn8	21(1932)	—	20 Cents. Brass. Y391	—

HEILUNGKIANG PROVINCE

Heilongjiang

The northwesternmost of the former Three Eastern Provinces, bordering on Siberia. Though very large in extent, it is only sparsely populated, for wide areas are desert land. Economically the district was always backward. Heilungkiang (Heilongjiang) Province had no mint of its own, and seemingly no silver money bearing its name was ever placed in circulation although Imperial patterns in the standard dragon design exist for at least the dollar and 50 cent denominations. During the beginning of the 20th century it was suggested to contract for silver coins from the Berlin Mint.

PATTERNS

Including off metal strikes

KM#	Date	Mintage	Identification	Mkt Val
Pn1	ND(1903)	—	50 Cents. Brass. KM584x.	20,000
Pn2	ND(1903)	—	Dollar. Silver. Rare.	—
Pn3	ND(1903)	—	Dollar. Brass.	50,000
Pn4	ND(1903)	—	Dollar. Silver Plated Brass.	—

HONAN PROVINCE

Henan

A province in east-central China. As well as being one of the most densely populated provinces it is also one of the most important agriculturally. It is the area of earliest settlement in China and has housed the capital during various dynasties. The Kaifeng Mint issued coins from its opening in 1647 through most of the rulers of the Manchu dynasty. In 1905 a modern mint opened at Kaifeng but closed in 1914. A mint in Loyang opened in 1924.

EMPIRE

PROVINCIAL CAST COINAGE

C# 3-1.1a CASH
Cast Zinc **Ruler:** Kuang-hsü **Obv. Inscription:** Kuang-hsü T'ung-pao **Rev:** Dot at upper left, Manchu inscription **Rev. Inscription:** Boo-ho

Date	Mintage	Good	VG	F	VF	XF
ND(1875-1908) Rare	—	—	—	—	—	—

C# 11-9 CASH
Cast Brass **Ruler:** Kuang-hsü **Obv. Inscription:** Kuang-hsü T'ung-pao **Rev:** Manchu inscription **Rev. Inscription:** Boo-ho

Date	Mintage	Good	VG	F	VF	XF
ND(1875-1908)	—	4.00	8.00	10.00	12.00	—

C# 11-9.1 CASH
Cast Brass **Ruler:** Kuang-hsü **Obv. Inscription:** Kuang-hsü T'ung-pao **Rev:** Circle above, Manchu inscription **Rev. Inscription:** Boo-ho

Date	Mintage	Good	VG	F	VF	XF
ND(1875-1908)	—	5.00	9.00	13.50	35.00	—

C# 11-9.2 CASH
Cast Brass **Ruler:** Kuang-hsü **Obv. Inscription:** Kuang-hsü T'ung-pao **Rev:** Circle below, Manchu inscription **Rev. Inscription:** Boo-ho

Date	Mintage	Good	VG	F	VF	XF
ND(1875-1908)	—	5.00	9.00	13.50	25.00	—

C# 11-9.3 CASH
Cast Brass **Ruler:** Kuang-hsü **Obv. Inscription:** Kuang-hsü T'ung-pao **Rev:** Crescent above, Manchu inscription **Rev. Inscription:** Boo-ho

Date	Mintage	Good	VG	F	VF	XF
ND(1875-1908)	—	5.00	9.00	13.50	25.00	—

C# 11-9.4 CASH
Cast Brass **Ruler:** Kuang-hsü **Obv. Inscription:** Kuang-hsü T'ung-pao **Rev:** Crescent below, Manchu inscription **Rev. Inscription:** Boo-ho

Date	Mintage	Good	VG	F	VF	XF
ND(1875-1908)	—	5.00	9.00	13.50	25.00	—

C# 11-9.5 CASH
Cast Brass **Ruler:** Kuang-hsü **Obv. Inscription:** Kuang-hsü T'ung-pao **Rev:** Crescent above, dot below, Manchu inscription **Rev. Inscription:** Boo-ho **Note:** Schjöth #1571.

Date	Mintage	Good	VG	F	VF	XF
ND(1875-1908)	—	5.00	9.00	13.50	25.00	—

C# 11-9.6 CASH

Cast Brass **Ruler:** Kuang-hsü **Obv. Inscription:** Kuang-hsü T'ung-pao **Rev:** Dot above, Manchu inscription **Rev. Inscription:** Boo-ho

Date	Mintage	Good	VG	F	VF	XF
ND(1875-1908)	—	5.00	9.00	13.50	20.00	—

C# 11-9.7 CASH

Cast Brass **Ruler:** Kuang-hsü **Obv. Inscription:** Kuang-hsü T'ung-pao **Rev:** Dot below, Manchu inscription **Rev. Inscription:** Boo-ho

Date	Mintage	Good	VG	F	VF	XF
ND(1875-1908)	—	5.00	9.00	13.50	20.00	—

C# 11-9.8 CASH

Cast Brass **Ruler:** Kuang-hsü **Obv. Inscription:** Kuang-hsü T'ung-pao **Rev:** Dot at upper left, Manchu inscription **Rev. Inscription:** Boo-ho **Note:** Crescent and dot varieties exist.

Date	Mintage	Good	VG	F	VF	XF
ND(1875-1908)	—	5.00	9.00	13.50	20.00	—

C# 11-9.9 CASH

Cast Brass **Ruler:** Kuang-hsü **Obv. Inscription:** Kuang-hsü T'ung-pao **Rev:** Crescent above, circle below

Date	Mintage	Good	VG	F	VF	XF
ND(1875-1908)	—	10.00	17.50	25.00	35.00	—

C# 11-9.10 CASH

Cast Brass **Ruler:** Kuang-hsü **Obv. Inscription:** Kuang-hsü T'ung-pao **Rev:** Dot in circle below

Date	Mintage	Good	VG	F	VF	XF
ND(1875-1908)	—	15.00	25.00	35.00	50.00	—

MILLED COINAGE

Y# 7g CASH

Brass **Ruler:** Kuang-hsü **Obv. Legend:** Kuang-hsü **Rev:** Side view dragon

Date	Mintage	VG	F	VF	XF	Unc
CD1908	—	10.00	25.00	42.50	75.00	—

Y# 7ga CASH

Copper **Ruler:** Kuang-hsü **Obv. Legend:** Kuang-hsü **Rev:** Side view dragon

Date	Mintage	VG	F	VF	XF	Unc
CD1908	—	20.00	50.00	85.00	150	—

Y# 108 10 CASH

Copper **Ruler:** Kuang-hsü **Obv. Legend:** Ho-nan Sheng Tsao **Obv. Inscription:** Kuang-hsü Yüan-pao **Rev:** Circled dragon without mountain below pearl with 3 flames

Date	Mintage	VG	F	VF	XF	Unc
ND(1905)	—	4.00	10.00	20.00	45.00	—

Y# 108a 10 CASH

Brass **Ruler:** Kuang-hsü **Obv:** Raised circled yin-yang in center **Obv. Legend:** Ho-nan Sheng Tsao **Obv. Inscription:** Kuang-hsü Yüan-pao **Rev:** Uncircled dragon, Honan spelled HOU-NAN **Note:** Dies made in Japan.

Date	Mintage	VG	F	VF	XF	Unc
ND(1905) Rare	—	—	—	—	—	—

Y# 108.1 10 CASH

Copper **Ruler:** Kuang-hsü **Obv. Legend:** Ho-nan Sheng Tsao **Obv. Inscription:** Kuang-hsü Yüan-pao **Rev:** Circled dragon without mountain below pearl with 5 flames

Date	Mintage	VG	F	VF	XF	Unc
ND(1905)	—	1.00	3.00	5.00	10.00	—

Y# 108.2 10 CASH

Copper **Ruler:** Kuang-hsü **Obv. Legend:** Ho-nan Sheng Tsao **Obv. Inscription:** Kuang-hsü Yüan-pao **Rev:** Circled dragon, mountain below pearl, very small English lettering

Date	Mintage	VG	F	VF	XF	Unc
ND(1905)	—	6.00	15.00	30.00	50.00	—

Y# 108.3 10 CASH

Copper **Ruler:** Kuang-hsü **Obv. Legend:** Ho-nan Sheng Tsao **Obv. Inscription:** Kuang-hsü Yüan-pao **Rev:** Circled dragon, large English legend

Date	Mintage	VG	F	VF	XF	Unc
ND(1905)	—	5.00	10.00	15.00	30.00	—

Y# 108a.1 10 CASH

Copper **Ruler:** Kuang-hsü **Obv:** Flat circled yin-yang **Obv. Legend:** Ho-nan Sheng Tsao **Obv. Inscription:** Kuang-hsü Yüan-pao **Rev:** Uncircled dragon

Date	Mintage	VG	F	VF	XF	Unc
ND(1905)	—	1.00	3.00	5.00	10.00	—

Y# 108a.2 10 CASH

Copper **Ruler:** Kuang-hsü **Obv:** Curved line on raised yin-yang slanted more **Obv. Legend:** Ho-nan Sheng Tsao **Obv. Inscription:** Kuang-hsü Yüan-pao **Rev:** Uncircled dragon

Date	Mintage	VG	F	VF	XF	Unc
ND(1905)	—	1.00	3.00	5.00	10.00	—

Y# 108a.3 10 CASH

Copper **Ruler:** Kuang-hsü **Obv:** Flat yin-yang slanted more **Obv. Legend:** Ho-nan Sheng Tsao **Obv. Inscription:** Kuang-hsü Yüan-pao **Rev:** Circled dragon, plain pearl

Date	Mintage	VG	F	VF	XF	Unc
ND(1905)	—	0.75	2.50	4.00	8.00	—

Note: Dies made in United States

Y# 108a.3a 10 CASH

Brass **Ruler:** Kuang-hsü **Obv. Legend:** Ho-nan Sheng Tsao **Obv. Inscription:** Kuang-hsü Yüan-pao **Rev:** Dragon

Date	Mintage	VG	F	VF	XF	Unc
ND(1905)	—	2.50	5.00	10.00	20.00	—

Y# 108a.4 10 CASH

Copper **Ruler:** Kuang-hsü **Obv. Legend:** Ho-nan Sheng Tsao **Obv. Inscription:** Kuang-hsü Yüan-pao **Rev:** Dragon, incuse swirl in pearl

Date	Mintage	VG	F	VF	XF	Unc
ND(1905)	—	1.00	3.00	5.00	12.00	—

Note: Dies made in United States

Y# 10g 10 CASH

Copper **Ruler:** Kuang-hsü **Obv. Inscription:** Tai-ch'ing T'ung-pi **Rev:** Dragon, period after COIN in legend **Rev. Legend:** Kuang-hsü Nien-tsao, TAI-CHING-TI-KUO ...

Date	Mintage	VG	F	VF	XF	Unc
CD1906	132,000,000	0.85	2.00	5.00	10.00	—

Y# 10g.1 10 CASH

Copper **Ruler:** Kuang-hsü **Obv. Inscription:** Tai-ch'ing T'ung-pi **Rev:** Dragon, period after COPPER in legend **Rev. Legend:** Kuang-hsü Nien-tsao, TAI-CHING-TI-KUO ...

Date	Mintage	VG	F	VF	XF	Unc
CD1906	—	1.25	3.00	6.00	10.00	—

Y# 10g.2 10 CASH

Copper **Ruler:** Kuang-hsü **Obv. Inscription:** Tai-ch'ing T'ung-pi **Rev:** Dragon **Rev. Legend:** Kuang-hsü Nien-tsao, TAI-CHING-TI-KUO ... **Note:** Cyclical dates at sides.

Date	Mintage	VG	F	VF	XF	Unc
CD1907 Rare	—	—	—	—	—	—

Y# 20g 10 CASH

Copper **Ruler:** Hsüan-t'ung **Obv. Inscription:** Tai-ch'ing T'ung-pi **Rev:** Dragon **Rev. Legend:** Hsüan-t'ung Nien-tsao, TAI-CHING-TI-KUO ... **Note:** Normally encountered with weak legends.

Date	Mintage	VG	F	VF	XF	Unc
CD1909	—	20.00	40.00	60.00	125	—
CD1911	—	5.00	15.00	25.00	50.00	—

REPUBLIC

MILLED COINAGE

Y# A392 10 CASH

Copper **Obv:** With lines above and below rosettes **Obv. Legend:** Chung Hua Min Kuo **Rev:** Crossed flags, florals at left and right **Rev. Legend:** HO-NAN

Date	Mintage	VG	F	VF	XF	Unc
ND(1913-14)	—	0.35	1.00	2.00	6.00	20.00

Y# A392.1 10 CASH

Copper **Obv:** Without lines above and below rosettes **Obv. Legend:** Chung Hua Min Kuo **Rev:** Crossed flags, florals at left and right **Rev. Legend:** HO-NAN

Date	Mintage	VG	F	VF	XF	Unc
ND(1913-14)	—	0.35	1.00	2.00	6.00	20.00

Y# A392.2 10 CASH

Copper **Obv. Legend:** Chung Hua Min Kuo **Rev:** Crossed flags, florals at left and right, letter "S" in "CASH" backwards **Rev. Legend:** HO-NAN

Date	Mintage	VG	F	VF	XF	Unc
ND(c.1920)	—	6.00	17.50	30.00	60.00	—

Y# 392.2 10 CASH

Copper **Obv:** Yüan at lower left with 3 horizontal strokes. **Obv. Legend:** Chung Hua Min Kuo **Rev:** Crossed flags, florals at left and right **Rev. Legend:** HO-NAN

Date	Mintage	VG	F	VF	XF	Unc
ND(ca.1920)	—	0.65	2.00	3.50	6.00	20.00

Y# 392 10 CASH

Copper **Obv:** Yüan at lower left with 2 horizontal strokes **Obv. Legend:** Chung Hua Min Kuo **Rev:** Value "TEN CASH" in larger letters at bottom **Rev. Legend:** HO-NAN

Date	Mintage	VG	F	VF	XF	Unc
ND(c.1920)	—	0.25	0.75	1.50	4.00	18.00

Y# 392.1 10 CASH

Copper **Obv:** Rosette in center higher in relation to heart-shaped leaves below, Yuan at lower left with 2 horizontal strokes **Obv. Legend:** Chung Hua Min Kuo **Rev:** Crossed flags, florals at left and right **Rev. Legend:** HO-NAN

Date	Mintage	VG	F	VF	XF	Unc
ND(c.1920)	—	0.65	2.00	3.50	6.00	20.00

Y# 393 20 CASH

Copper, 32 mm. **Obv:** Value in 6 characters at bottom **Obv. Legend:** Chung Hua Min Kuo **Rev:** Crossed flags, florals at left and right **Rev. Legend:** HO-NAN

Date	Mintage	Good	VG	F	VF	XF
ND(c.1920)	—	1.25	2.50	5.00	10.00	30.00

Y# 393.1 20 CASH

Copper, 32 mm. **Obv:** Value in 5 characters at bottom **Obv. Legend:** Chung Hua Min Kuo **Rev:** Crossed flags, florals at left and right **Rev. Legend:** HO-NAN

Date	Mintage	Good	VG	F	VF	XF
ND(c.1920)	—	1.00	2.00	4.00	6.00	20.00

Y# 393.2 20 CASH

Copper, 32 mm. **Obv:** Value in 6 characters below **Obv. Legend:** Chung Hua Min Kuo **Rev:** Crossed flags, florals at left and right **Rev. Legend:** CHINA

Date	Mintage	Good	VG	F	VF	XF
ND(c.1921)	—	12.50	25.00	45.00	175	—

Y# A397 20 CASH

Copper, 32 mm. **Obv:** Value in 6 characters below **Obv. Legend:** Chung Hua Min Kuo (year) Nien **Rev:** Star above crossed flags, florals at left and right

Date	Mintage	Good	VG	F	VF	XF
20(1931)	—	—	500	1,500	3,000	—

Y# 394 50 CASH

Copper **Obv. Legend:** Chung Hua Min Kuo **Rev:** Crossed flags, florals at left and right, short flag poles **Rev. Legend:** HO-NAN

Date	Mintage	Good	VG	F	VF	XF
ND(c.1920)	—	2.00	5.00	10.00	20.00	60.00

Y# 394.1 50 CASH

Copper **Obv. Legend:** Chung Hua Min Kuo **Rev:** Crossed flags, florals at left and right, long flag poles **Rev. Legend:** HO-NAN

Date	Mintage	Good	VG	F	VF	XF
ND(c.1920)	—	2.00	5.00	10.00	20.00	60.00

Y# 394b 50 CASH

Brass **Obv. Legend:** Chung Hua Min Kuo **Rev:** Crossed flags, florals at left and right **Rev. Legend:** HO-NAN

Date	Mintage	Good	VG	F	VF	XF
ND(c.1920)	—	10.00	20.00	40.00	80.00	225

Y# 394a 50 CASH

Brass **Obv. Legend:** Chung Hua Min Kuo **Rev:** Crossed flags, florals at left and right **Rev. Legend:** CHINA

Date	Mintage	Good	VG	F	VF	XF
ND(c.1921)	—	6.50	12.50	25.00	60.00	175

Y# 397 50 CASH

Brass **Obv:** National star at center **Obv. Legend:** Chung Hua Min Kuo (year) Nien **Rev:** Star above value in grain sprays

Date	Mintage	VG	F	VF	XF	Unc
20(1931)	—	120	200	330	—	—

Y# 395 100 CASH

Copper **Obv. Legend:** Chung Hua Min Kuo **Rev:** Crossed flags, florals at left and right, small star in right flag, tassels 4mm long **Rev. Legend:** HO-NAN

Date	Mintage	Good	VG	F	VF	XF
ND(c. 1928)	—	3.00	5.00	10.00	25.00	75.00

Y# 395.1 100 CASH

Copper **Rev:** Tassels 5mm long

Date	Mintage	Good	VG	F	VF	XF
ND(c. 1928)	—	3.75	6.50	12.50	30.00	90.00

Y# 395.2 100 CASH

Copper **Obv. Legend:** Chung Hua Min Kuo **Rev:** Crossed flags, florals at left and right, large star in right flag **Rev. Legend:** HO-NAN

Date	Mintage	Good	VG	F	VF	XF
ND(c. 1928)	—	—	—	—	—	—

Y# 398 100 CASH

Copper **Obv:** National star at center **Obv. Legend:** Chung Hua Min Kuo (year) Nien **Rev:** Star above value in grain sprays

Date	Mintage	VG	F	VF	XF	Unc
20(1931)	—	60.00	95.00	150	—	—

Y# 396 200 CASH

Copper **Obv. Legend:** Chung Hua Min Kuo **Rev:** Crossed flags, florals at left and right, large square inside right flag **Rev. Legend:** HO-NAN

Date	Mintage	Good	VG	F	VF	XF
ND(c.1928)	—	3.00	5.00	10.00	25.00	75.00

Y# 396.1 200 CASH

Copper **Obv. Legend:** Chung Hua Min Kuo **Rev:** Crossed flags, small panel with small star inside right flag, florals at left and right **Rev. Legend:** HO-NAN

Date	Mintage	Good	VG	F	VF	XF
ND(c.1928)	—	2.50	4.50	9.00	25.00	75.00

Y# 396.2 200 CASH

Copper **Obv. Legend:** Chung Hua Min Kuo **Rev:** Crossed flags, small panel with large star inside right flag, florals at left and right **Rev. Legend:** HO-NAN

Date	Mintage	Good	VG	F	VF	XF
ND(c.1928)	—	2.50	4.50	9.00	25.00	75.00

Y# 396a 200 CASH

Brass **Obv. Legend:** Chung Hua Min Kuo **Rev:** Crossed flags, small panel with large star inside right flag, florals at left and right **Rev. Legend:** HO-NAN

Date	Mintage	Good	VG	F	VF	XF
ND(c.1928)	—	6.00	15.00	22.50	45.00	135

PATTERNS

Including off metal strikes

KM#	Date	Mintage	Identification	Mkt Val
Pn1	CD1909	—	2 Cash. Brass.	—
Pn2	CD1909	—	5 Cash. Copper. Y19g.	—
Pn3	CD1909	—	20 Cash. Copper. Y21g.	—

HUNAN PROVINCE

A province in south-central China. Mining of coal, antimony, tungsten and tin is important as well as raising varied agricultural products. The Changsha Mint produced Cash coins from early in the Manchu dynasty. Its facility for struck coinage opened in 1897, and two further copper mints were added in 1905. All three mints were closed down in 1907, but one mint was reopened at a later date and produced vast quantities of republican copper coinage until 1926.

EMPIRE

PROVINCIAL CAST COINAGE

C# 12-7 CASH

Cast Brass **Ruler:** Kuang-hsü **Obv. Inscription:** Kuang-hsü T'ung-pao **Rev:** Manchu inscription **Rev. Inscription:** Boo-nan

Date	Mintage	Good	VG	F	VF	XF
ND(1875-1908)	—	7.50	15.00	21.50	30.00	—

MILLED COINAGE

Y# 112 10 CASH

Copper **Ruler:** Kuang-hsü **Obv:** Rosette in center with center of petals depressed; Manchu words at sides, "Tang Shih" at bottom **Obv. Legend:** Hu-nan Sheng Tsao **Obv. Inscription:** Kuang-hsü Yüan-pao **Rev:** Narrow spacing in HU-NAN above dragon **Rev. Legend:** HU-NAN

Date	Mintage	VG	F	VF	XF	Unc
ND(1902-06)	—	0.35	1.00	2.00	5.00	20.00

Y# 112.1 10 CASH

Copper **Ruler:** Kuang-hsü **Obv. Legend:** Hu-nan Sheng Tsao **Obv. Inscription:** Kuang-hsü Yüan-pao **Rev:** Dragon; wide spacing in HU-NAN **Rev. Legend:** HU-NAN

Date	Mintage	VG	F	VF	XF	Unc
ND(1902-06)	—	0.75	2.25	4.00	9.00	30.00

Y# 112.2 10 CASH

Copper **Ruler:** Kuang-hsü **Obv:** Petals of rosettes not depressed **Obv. Legend:** Hu-nan Sheng Tsao **Obv. Inscription:** Kuang-hsü Yüan-pao **Rev:** Dragon **Rev. Legend:** HU-NAN

Date	Mintage	VG	F	VF	XF	Unc
ND(1902-06)	—	0.50	1.50	2.50	6.00	20.00

Y# 112.3 10 CASH

Copper **Ruler:** Kuang-hsü **Obv:** Two Manchu words in center, "T'ung Yüan" at bottom **Obv. Legend:** Hu-nan Sheng Tsao **Obv. Inscription:** Kuang-hsü Yüan-pao **Rev:** Dragon **Rev. Legend:** HU-NAN

Date	Mintage	VG	F	VF	XF	Unc
ND(1902-06)	—	1.00	3.00	6.00	10.00	30.00

Y# 112.4 10 CASH

Copper **Ruler:** Kuang-hsü **Obv. Legend:** Hu-nan Sheng Tsao **Obv. Inscription:** Kuang-hsü Yüan-pao **Rev:** Dragon; narrow spacing in "HU-NAN" **Rev. Legend:** HU-NAN

Date	Mintage	VG	F	VF	XF	Unc
ND(1902-06)	—	0.50	1.50	2.50	6.00	20.00

Y# 112.5 10 CASH

Copper **Ruler:** Kuang-hsü **Obv:** Rosette in center, "Tang Shih" at bottom **Obv. Legend:** Hu-nan Sheng Tsao **Obv. Inscription:** Kuang-hsü Yüan-pao **Rev:** Dragon; ring around pearl **Rev. Legend:** HU-NAN

Date	Mintage	VG	F	VF	XF	Unc
ND(1902-06)	—	0.40	1.25	2.00	4.00	18.00

Y# 112.6 10 CASH

Copper **Ruler:** Kuang-hsü **Obv:** Centers of petals on rosette depressed **Obv. Legend:** Hu-nan Sheng Tsao **Obv. Inscription:** Kuang-hsü Yüan-pao **Rev:** Dragon **Rev. Legend:** HU-NAN

Date	Mintage	VG	F	VF	XF	Unc
ND(1902-06)	—	0.50	1.50	2.50	6.00	20.00

Y# 112.7 10 CASH

Copper **Ruler:** Kuang-hsü **Obv:** two Manchu words in center, "T'ung Yüan" at bottom **Obv. Legend:** Hu-nan Sheng Tsao **Obv. Inscription:** Kuang-hsü Yüan-pao **Rev:** Dragon; ring around pearl **Rev. Legend:** HU-NAN

Date	Mintage	VG	F	VF	XF	Unc
ND(1902-06)	—	0.50	1.50	2.50	6.00	20.00

Y# 112.8 10 CASH

Copper **Ruler:** Kuang-hsü **Obv:** Larger characters at left and right, and different characters below **Obv. Legend:** Hu-nan Sheng Tsao **Obv. Inscription:** Kuang-hsü Yüan-pao **Rev:** Dragon redesigned and small star at either side **Rev. Legend:** HU-NAN

Date	Mintage	VG	F	VF	XF	Unc
ND(1902-06)	—	1.75	5.00	10.00	17.50	40.00

Y# 112.9 10 CASH

Copper **Ruler:** Kuang-hsü **Obv:** Rosette in center; legend: four characters at bottom **Obv. Legend:** Hu-nan Sheng Tsao **Obv. Inscription:** Kuang-hsü Yüan-pao **Rev:** Redesigned dragon without pearl; rosette at either side **Rev. Legend:** HU-NAN

Date	Mintage	VG	F	VF	XF	Unc
ND(1902-06)	—	2.50	7.50	15.00	30.00	75.00

Y# 112.10 10 CASH

Copper **Ruler:** Kuang-hsü **Obv:** Two Manchu words in center with dot between; "T'ung Yüan" at bottom **Obv. Legend:** Hu-nan Sheng Tsao **Obv. Inscription:** Kuang-hsü Yüan-pao **Rev:** Dragon **Rev. Legend:** HU-NAN

Date	Mintage	VG	F	VF	XF	Unc
ND(1902-06)	—	0.35	1.00	2.00	4.00	18.00

Y# 112.11 10 CASH

Copper **Ruler:** Kuang-hsü **Obv:** Without dot between Manchu words, "T'ung Yüan" at bottom **Obv. Legend:** Hu-nan Sheng Tsao **Obv. Inscription:** Kuang-hsü Yüan-pao **Rev:** Dragon **Rev. Legend:** HU-NAN

Date	Mintage	VG	F	VF	XF	Unc
ND(1902-06)	—	0.35	1.00	2.00	4.00	18.00

Y# 112.12 10 CASH

Copper **Ruler:** Kuang-hsü **Obv:** Smaller 15.5 millimeter inner circle, with larger beads, "T'ung Yüan" at bottom **Obv. Legend:** Hu-nan Sheng Tsao **Obv. Inscription:** Kuang-hsü Yüan-pao **Rev:** Dragon **Rev. Legend:** HU-NAN

Date	Mintage	VG	F	VF	XF	Unc
ND(1902-06)	—	0.35	1.00	2.00	4.00	18.00

Y# 112.13 10 CASH

Copper **Ruler:** Kuang-hsü **Obv:** Two Manchu words in center, 18.4mm inner circle; "Huang T'ung" at bottom **Obv. Legend:** Hu-nan Sheng Tsao **Obv. Inscription:** Kuang-hsü Yüan-pao **Rev:** Dragon **Rev. Legend:** HU-NAN

Date	Mintage	VG	F	VF	XF	Unc
ND(1902-06)	—	8.50	25.00	45.00	80.00	—

Y# 112.14 10 CASH

Copper **Ruler:** Kuang-hsü **Obv:** Smaller 17.5mm inner circle; "Huang T'ung Yüan" at bottom **Obv. Legend:** Hu-nan Sheng Tsao **Obv. Inscription:** Kuang-hsü Yüan-pao **Rev:** Dragon **Rev. Legend:** HU-NAN

Date	Mintage	VG	F	VF	XF	Unc
ND(1902-06)	—	8.50	25.00	45.00	80.00	—

Y# 113 10 CASH

Copper **Ruler:** Kuang-hsü **Obv. Legend:** Hu-nan Sheng Tsao, six characters at bottom **Obv. Inscription:** Kuang-hsü Yüan-pao **Rev:** Flying dragon **Rev. Legend:** HU-NAN **Edge:** Reeded

Date	Mintage	VG	F	VF	XF	Unc
ND(1902-06)	—	1.25	4.00	8.00	15.00	40.00

Y# 113a 10 CASH

Brass, 28 mm. **Ruler:** Kuang-hsü **Obv. Legend:** Hu-nan Sheng Tsao, three characters at bottom **Obv. Inscription:** Kuang-hsü Yüan-pao **Rev:** Dragon **Rev. Legend:** HU-NAN

Date	Mintage	VG	F	VF	XF	Unc
ND(1902-06)	—	1.25	3.50	6.00	12.50	35.00

Y# 113.1 10 CASH

Copper **Ruler:** Kuang-hsü **Obv. Legend:** Hu-nan Sheng Tsao **Obv. Inscription:** Kuang-hsü Yüan-pao **Rev:** Dragon **Rev. Legend:** Inverted U in HU-NAN **Edge:** Reeded

Date	Mintage	VG	F	VF	XF	Unc
ND(1902-06)	—	4.50	12.50	25.00	45.00	—

Y# 10h 10 CASH

Copper **Ruler:** Kuang-hsü **Obv:** Upper and lower parts of character "Hu" connected **Obv. Inscription:** Tai-ch'ing T'ung-pi **Rev:** Dragon; dot between Chinese characters above dragon **Rev. Legend:** Kuang-hsü Nien-tsao, TAI-CHING-TI-KUO...

Date	Mintage	VG	F	VF	XF	Unc
CD1906	—	6.00	17.50	35.00	70.00	—

Y# 10h.1 10 CASH

Copper **Ruler:** Kuang-hsü **Obv:** Upper and lower parts of character "Hu' not connected **Obv. Inscription:** Tai-ch'ing T'ung-pi **Rev:** Dragon; dot between Chinese characters at top **Rev. Legend:** Kuang-hsü Nien-tsao, TAI-CHING-TI-KUO...

Date	Mintage	VG	F	VF	XF	Unc
CD1906	—	6.00	17.50	35.00	70.00	—

Y# 10h.2 10 CASH

Copper **Ruler:** Kuang-hsü **Obv. Inscription:** Tai-ch'ing T'ung-pi **Rev:** Dragon; seven flames on pearl **Rev. Legend:** Kuang-hsü Nien-tsao, TAI-CHING-TI-KUO...

Date	Mintage	VG	F	VF	XF	Unc
CD1906	—	0.65	2.00	4.00	8.00	22.00

Y# 10h.3 10 CASH

Copper **Ruler:** Kuang-hsü **Obv. Inscription:** Tai-ch'ing T'ung-pi **Rev:** Dragon; seven-flame pearl ornamented with toothlike projections **Rev. Legend:** Kuang-hsü Nien-tsao, TAI-CHING-TI-KUO...

Date	Mintage	VG	F	VF	XF	Unc
CD1906	—	0.65	2.00	3.50	6.00	18.00

Y# 10h.4 10 CASH

Copper **Ruler:** Kuang-hsü **Obv. Inscription:** Tai-ch'ing T'ung-pi **Rev:** Dragon; four flames on pearl **Rev. Legend:** Kuang-hsü Nien-tsao, TAI-CHING-TI-KUO...

Date	Mintage	VG	F	VF	XF	Unc
CD1906	—	1.00	3.00	6.00	10.00	22.00

Y# 10h.5 10 CASH

Copper **Ruler:** Kuang-hsü **Obv. Inscription:** Tai-ch'ing T'ung-pi **Rev:** Redesigned dragon with high waves beneath **Rev. Legend:** Kuang-hsü Nien-tsao, TAI-CHING-TI-KUO...

Date	Mintage	VG	F	VF	XF	Unc
CD1906	—	13.50	40.00	80.00	150	—

Y# 10h.6 10 CASH

Copper **Ruler:** Kuang-hsü **Obv:** Character "Hu" connected **Obv. Inscription:** Tai-ch'ing T'ung-pi **Rev:** Redesigned dragon, dot between COPPER COIN **Rev. Legend:** Kuang-hsü Nien-tsao, TAI-CHING-TI-KUO...

Date	Mintage	VG	F	VF	XF	Unc
CD1906	—	4.50	12.50	20.00	40.00	—

Y# 10h.7 10 CASH

Copper **Ruler:** Kuang-hsü **Obv:** Character "Hu" connected **Obv. Inscription:** Tai-ch'ing T'ung-pi **Rev:** Redesigned dragon with five flames on pearl **Rev. Legend:** Kuang-hsü Nien-tsao, TAI-CHING-TI-KUO... **Note:** Woodward #342 and #343

Date	Mintage	VG	F	VF	XF	Unc
CD1906	—	10.00	30.00	45.00	75.00	—

BULLION COINAGE

Mace/Tael Series

K# 961 CH'IEN (MACE)

3.6000 g., Silver **Obv:** Three lines of two characters each **Rev:** Two lines of two characters each

Date	Mintage	VG	F	VF	XF	Unc
ND(ca. 1906)	—	—	—	—	—	—

K# 951 CH'IEN (MACE)

3.7000 g., Silver **Issuer:** Fo-nau Official Bureau **Obv:** Two lines of two characters each **Rev:** Two lines of one character each

Date	Mintage	VG	F	VF	XF	Unc
ND(1906)	—	75.00	150	200	300	600

K# 971 CH'IEN (MACE)

3.7000 g., Silver **Issuer:** Ta Ching Gov't. Bank **Obv:** Two lines of two characters each **Rev:** Two lines of two characters each

Date	Mintage	VG	F	VF	XF	Unc
ND(ca.1908)	—	50.00	500	700	900	1,200

K# 984/5 CH'IEN (MACE)

3.7000 g., Silver **Issuer:** Chien-I, Changsha **Obv:** Two lines of three characters each **Rev:** Two lines of one character each

Date	Mintage	VG	F	VF	XF	Unc
ND(1908)	—	75.00	150	200	300	500

K# 950 2 CH'IEN (MACE)

7.3000 g., Silver **Issuer:** Fo-nan Official Bureau **Obv:** Two lines of two characters each **Rev:** Two lines of two characters each

Date	Mintage	VG	F	VF	XF	Unc
ND(1906)	—	75.00	150	200	300	600

K# 960 2 CH'IEN (MACE)

7.3000 g., Silver **Obv:** Three lines of two characters each **Rev:** Two lines of two characters each

Date	Mintage	VG	F	VF	XF	Unc
ND(1906)	—	—	—	—	—	—

K# 970 2 CH'IEN (MACE)

7.3000 g., Silver **Issuer:** Ta Ch'ing Gov't. Bank **Obv:** Three lines of two characters each **Rev:** Two lines of three characters each

Date	Mintage	VG	F	VF	XF	Unc
ND(1908)	—	250	500	700	900	1,200

K# 982/3 2 CH'IEN (MACE)

7.3000 g., Silver **Issuer:** Chien-I, Changsha **Obv:** Two lines of three characters each **Rev:** Two lines of two characters each

Date	Mintage	VG	F	VF	XF	Unc
ND(ca.1908)	—	75.00	150	200	300	500

K# 949 3 CH'IEN (MACE)

10.7000 g., Silver **Issuer:** Fo-nan Official Bureau **Obv:** Two lines of three characters each **Rev:** Two lines of three characters each

Date	Mintage	VG	F	VF	XF	Unc
ND(1906)	—	85.00	175	250	350	700

K# 959 3 CH'IEN (MACE)

10.7000 g., Silver **Obv:** Three lines of two characters each **Rev:** Two lines of three characters each

Date	Mintage	VG	F	VF	XF	Unc
ND(ca.1906)	—	85.00	175	250	350	700

K# 969 3 CH'IEN (MACE)

10.7000 g., Silver **Issuer:** Ta Ch'ing Gov't. Bank **Obv:** Three lines of two characters each **Rev:** Two lines of three characters each

Date	Mintage	VG	F	VF	XF	Unc
ND(ca.1908)	—	250	500	700	900	1,200

K# 981 3 CH'IEN (MACE)

10.7000 g., Silver **Issuer:** Chien-I, Changsha **Obv:** Two lines of three characters each **Rev:** Two lines of three characters each

Date	Mintage	VG	F	VF	XF	Unc
ND(ca.1908)	—	85.00	175	250	350	600

K# 981a 3 CH'IEN (MACE)

10.7000 g., Silver **Issuer:** Chien-I, Changsha **Obv:** Two lines of three characters each **Rev:** Two lines of three characters each **Note:** "official" character for three

Date	Mintage	VG	F	VF	XF	Unc
ND(ca.1908)	—	85.00	175	250	350	600

K# 948 4 CH'IEN (MACE)

14.3000 g., Silver **Issuer:** Fo-nan Official Bureau **Obv:** Two lines of three characters each **Rev:** Two lines of three characters each

Date	Mintage	VG	F	VF	XF	Unc
ND(1906)	—	85.00	175	250	350	700

K# 958 4 CH'IEN (MACE)

14.3000 g., Silver **Obv:** Three lines of two characters each **Rev:** Two lines of three characters each

Date	Mintage	VG	F	VF	XF	Unc
ND(ca.1906)	—	—	—	—	—	—

K# 968 4 CH'IEN (MACE)

14.3000 g., Silver **Issuer:** Ta Ch'ing Gov't. Bank **Obv:** Three lines of two characters each **Rev:** Two lines of three characters each

Date	Mintage	VG	F	VF	XF	Unc
ND(ca.1908)	—	300	600	800	1,000	1,200

K# 980 4 CH'IEN (MACE)

14.3000 g., Silver **Issuer:** Chien-I, Changsha **Obv:** Two lines of three characters each **Rev:** Two lines of three characters each

Date	Mintage	VG	F	VF	XF	Unc
ND(ca.1908)	—	85.00	175	250	350	600

K# 947 5 CH'IEN (MACE)

18.3000 g., Silver **Issuer:** Fo-nan Official Bureau **Obv:** Two lines of three characters each **Rev:** Two lines of three characters each

Date	Mintage	VG	F	VF	XF	Unc
ND(1906)	—	85.00	175	250	350	700

K# 957 5 CH'IEN (MACE)

18.3000 g., Silver **Obv:** Three lines of two characters each **Rev:** Two lines of three characters each

Date	Mintage	VG	F	VF	XF	Unc
ND(ca.1906)	—	70.00	—	—	—	—

K# 967 5 CH'IEN (MACE)

18.3000 g., Silver **Issuer:** Ta Ch'ing Gov't. Bank **Obv:** Three lines of two characters each **Rev:** Two lines of three characters each

Date	Mintage	VG	F	VF	XF	Unc
ND(ca.1908)	—	300	600	800	1,000	1,200

K# 979 5 CH'IEN (MACE)

18.3000 g., Silver **Issuer:** Chien-I, Changsha **Obv:** Two lines of three characters each **Rev:** Two lines of three characters each

Date	Mintage	VG	F	VF	XF	Unc
ND(ca.1908)	—	85.00	175	250	350	600

K# 946 6 CH'IEN (MACE)

21.4000 g., Silver **Issuer:** Fo-nan Official Bureau **Obv:** Two lines of three characters each **Rev:** Two lines of three characters each

Date	Mintage	VG	F	VF	XF	Unc
ND(1906)	—	175	350	425	550	800

K# 956 6 CH'IEN (MACE)

21.4000 g., Silver **Obv:** Three lines of two characters each **Rev:** Two lines of three characters each

Date	Mintage	VG	F	VF	XF	Unc
ND(ca.1906)	—	—	—	—	—	—

K# 966 6 CH'IEN (MACE)

21.4000 g., Silver **Issuer:** Ta Ch'ing Gov't. Bank **Obv:** Three lines of two characters each **Rev:** Two lines of three characters each

Date	Mintage	VG	F	VF	XF	Unc
ND(ca.1908)	—	300	600	800	1,000	1,200

K# 978 6 CH'IEN (MACE)

21.4000 g., Silver **Issuer:** Chien-I, Changsha **Obv:** Two lines of three characters each **Rev:** Two lines of three characters each

Date	Mintage	VG	F	VF	XF	Unc
ND(ca.1908)	—	110	225	300	400	700

K# 945 7 CH'IEN (MACE)

25.9000 g., Silver **Issuer:** Fo-nan Official Bureau **Obv:** Two lines of three characters each **Rev:** Two lines of three characters each

Date	Mintage	VG	F	VF	XF	Unc
ND(1906)	—	150	300	400	550	900

K# 955 7 CH'IEN (MACE)

25.9000 g., Silver **Obv:** Three lines of two characters each **Rev:** Two lines of three characters each

Date	Mintage	VG	F	VF	XF	Unc
ND(ca.1906)	—	—	—	—	—	—

K# 965 7 CH'IEN (MACE)

25.9000 g., Silver **Issuer:** Ta Ch'ing Gov't. Bank **Obv:** Three lines of two characters each **Rev:** Two lines of three characters each

Date	Mintage	VG	F	VF	XF	Unc
ND(ca.1908)	—	350	700	900	1,100	1,300

K# 977 7 CH'IEN (MACE)

25.9000 g., Silver **Issuer:** Chien-I, Changsha **Obv:** Two lines of three characters each **Rev:** Two lines of three characters each

Date	Mintage	VG	F	VF	XF	Unc
ND(ca.1908)	—	85.00	175	250	350	600

K# 944 8 CH'IEN (MACE)

29.2000 g., Silver **Issuer:** Fo-nan Official Bureau **Obv:** Two lines of three characters each **Rev:** Two lines of three characters each

Date	Mintage	VG	F	VF	XF	Unc
ND(1906)	—	150	300	400	550	900

K# 954 8 CH'IEN (MACE)

29.2000 g., Silver **Obv:** Three lines of two characters each **Rev:** Two lines of three characters each

Date	Mintage	VG	F	VF	XF	Unc
ND(ca.1906)	—	—	—	—	—	—

K# 964 8 CH'IEN (MACE)

29.2000 g., Silver **Issuer:** Ta Ch'ing Gov't. Bank **Obv:** Three lines of two characters each **Rev:** Two lines of three characters each

Date	Mintage	VG	F	VF	XF	Unc
ND(ca.1908)	—	275	700	900	1,100	1,300

K# 976 8 CH'IEN (MACE)

29.2000 g., Silver **Issuer:** Chien-I, Changsha **Obv:** Two lines of three characters each **Rev:** Two lines of three characters each

Date	Mintage	VG	F	VF	XF	Unc
ND(ca.1908)	—	175	350	425	550	900

K# 943 9 CH'IEN (MACE)

29.2000 g., Silver **Issuer:** Fo-nan Official Bureau **Obv:** Two lines of three characters each **Rev:** Two lines of three characters each

Date	Mintage	VG	F	VF	XF	Unc
ND(1906)	—	150	300	400	550	900

K# 953 9 CH'IEN (MACE)

29.2000 g., Silver **Obv:** Three lines of two characters each **Rev:** Two lines of three characters each

Date	Mintage	VG	F	VF	XF	Unc
ND(ca.1906)	—	—	—	—	—	—

K# 963 9 CH'IEN (MACE)

29.2000 g., Silver **Issuer:** Ta Ch'ing Gov't. Bank **Obv:** Three lines of two characters each **Rev:** Two lines of three characters each

Date	Mintage	VG	F	VF	XF	Unc
ND(ca.1908)	—	275	700	900	1,100	1,300

K# 975 9 CH'IEN (MACE)

29.2000 g., Silver **Issuer:** Chien-I, Changsha **Obv:** Two lines of three characters each **Rev:** Two lines of three characters each

Date	Mintage	VG	F	VF	XF	Unc
ND(ca.1908)	—	175	350	425	550	900

K# 942 LIANG (Tael)

35.9000 g., Silver **Issuer:** Fo-nan Official Bureau **Obv:** Two lines of three characters each **Rev:** Two lines of three characters each

Date	Mintage	VG	F	VF	XF	Unc
ND(1906)	—	110	225	300	450	800

K# 952 LIANG (Tael)

35.9000 g., Silver **Obv:** Three lines of two characters each **Rev:** Two lines of three characters each

Date	Mintage	VG	F	VF	XF	Unc
ND(ca.1906)	—	100	200	250	300	600

K# 962 LIANG (Tael)

35.9000 g., Silver **Issuer:** Ta Ch'ing Gov't. Bank **Obv:** Three lines of two characters each **Rev:** Two lines of three characters each

Date	Mintage	VG	F	VF	XF	Unc
ND(ca.1908)	—	250	600	800	1,000	1,200

K# 974 LIANG (Tael)

35.9000 g., Silver **Issuer:** Chien-I, Changsha **Obv:** Two lines of three characters each **Rev:** Two lines of three characters each

Date	Mintage	VG	F	VF	XF	Unc
ND(ca.1908)	—	125	250	325	450	700

K# 942r LIANG (Tael)

35.9000 g., Silver **Obv:** Three lines of four characters each

Date	Mintage	VG	F	VF	XF	Unc
ND(1908) Rare Uniface	—	200	400	500	600	1,000

TRANSITIONAL COINAGE

Y# 401.1 10 CASH

Copper **Ruler:** Hung-hsien **Obv. Legend:** THE FIRST YEAR OF HUNG SHUAN **Rev. Legend:** Hung-hsien Yüan-nien

Date	Mintage	VG	F	VF	XF	Unc
1(1915)	—	35.00	60.00	100	150	—

Y# 401.2 10 CASH

Copper **Ruler:** Hung-hsien **Obv:** Wider space in legend

Date	Mintage	VG	F	VF	XF	Unc
1(1915)	—	10.00	20.00	30.00	45.00	—

REPUBLIC

MILLED COINAGE

Y# 399 10 CASH

Copper **Obv:** Large rosette **Obv. Legend:** Chung Hua Min Kuo **Obv. Inscription:** Hu-nan T'ung-Tüan **Rev:** Center of star convex

Date	Mintage	VG	F	VF	XF	Unc
ND(1912)	—	0.65	2.00	4.00	7.50	24.00

Y# 399a 10 CASH

Brass **Obv. Legend:** Chung Hua Min Kuo **Obv. Inscription:** Hu-nan T'ung-Tüan

Date	Mintage	VG	F	VF	XF	Unc
ND(1912)	—	1.75	5.00	10.00	17.50	45.00

Y# 399.1 10 CASH

Copper **Obv:** Small rosette **Obv. Legend:** Chung Hua Min Kuo **Obv. Inscription:** Hu-nan T'ung-Tüan **Rev:** Center of star convex

Date	Mintage	VG	F	VF	XF	Unc
ND(1912)	—	0.67	2.00	4.00	7.00	24.00

Y# 399.2 10 CASH

Copper **Obv. Legend:** Chung Hua Min Kuo **Obv. Inscription:** Hu-nan T'ung-Tüan **Rev:** Center of star concave; star outlined

Date	Mintage	VG	F	VF	XF	Unc
ND(1912)	—	0.75	2.25	4.50	8.50	26.00

Y# 399.3 10 CASH

Copper **Obv. Legend:** Chung Hua Min Kuo **Obv. Inscription:** Hu-nan T'ung-Tüan **Rev:** Star not outlined

Date	Mintage	VG	F	VF	XF	Unc
ND(1912)	—	0.75	2.25	4.50	8.50	26.00

Y# 399.4 10 CASH

Copper **Obv:** Large rosette **Obv. Legend:** Chung Hua Min Kuo **Obv. Inscription:** Hu-nan T'ung-Tüan **Rev:** Center of star concave

Date	Mintage	VG	F	VF	XF	Unc
ND(1912)	—	0.75	2.25	4.50	8.50	26.00

Y# 399.5 10 CASH

Copper **Note:** Mule. General Issue, Y#306.

Date	Mintage	VG	F	VF	XF	Unc
ND(1912)	—	—	—	—	—	—

Y# 402 10 CASH

Copper **Subject:** Provincial Constitution **Obv:** Rosette above crossed flags **Obv. Legend:** THE REPUBLIC OF CHINA **Rev:** Trigram of the Pah Kwah in grain sprays

Date	Mintage	VG	F	VF	XF	Unc
11(1922)	—	15.00	25.00	38.00	60.00	—

Y# 402.1 10 CASH
Copper **Obv:** Star above crossed flags **Obv. Legend:** THE REPUBLIC OF CHINA **Rev:** Trigram of the Pah Kwah in grain sprays

Date	Mintage	VG	F	VF	XF	Unc
11(1922)	—	18.50	26.00	40.00	65.00	—

Y# 400 20 CASH
Copper **Obv. Legend:** THE REPUBLIC OF CHINA **Rev:** Rosette above crossed flags, florals at left and right, five characters at bottom in legend **Rev. Legend:** Hu Nan Shan Tsoh

Date	Mintage	VG	F	VF	XF	Unc
ND(1919)	—	1.25	3.00	7.50	15.00	—

Y# 400a 20 CASH
9.4700 g., Copper **Obv:** Denomination: "20 CASH" **Obv. Legend:** THE REPUBLIC OF CHINA **Rev. Legend:** Hu-Nan Shan Tsoh

Date	Mintage	VG	F	VF	XF	Unc
ND(1919)	—	50.00	75.00	100	150	—

Y# 400b 20 CASH
Brass **Obv:** Denomination: "20 CASH" **Obv. Legend:** THE REPUBLIC OF CHINA **Rev. Legend:** Hu-Nan Shan Tsoh

Date	Mintage	VG	F	VF	XF	Unc
ND(1919)	—	1.65	4.00	10.00	20.00	—

Y# 400.2 20 CASH
Copper

Date	Mintage	VG	F	VF	XF	Unc
ND(1919)	—	0.60	1.00	3.00	6.00	—

Y# 400.3 20 CASH
Copper **Obv:** 25 small curls in ribbon at base of plant **Obv. Legend:** THE REPUBLIC OF CHINA **Rev. Legend:** Hu-Nan Shan Tsoh

Date	Mintage	VG	F	VF	XF	Unc
ND(1919)	—	0.60	1.00	3.00	6.00	—

Y# 400.4 20 CASH
Copper **Obv:** Smaller rice grains **Obv. Legend:** THE REPUBLIC OF CHINA **Rev:** Crossed flags, floral ornament at left smaller **Rev. Legend:** Hu-Nan Shan Tsoh

Date	Mintage	VG	F	VF	XF	Unc
ND(1919)	—	0.60	1.00	3.00	6.00	—

Y# 400.5 20 CASH
Copper **Obv:** Thin ribbon at base of plant **Obv. Legend:** THE REPUBLIC OF CHINA **Rev. Legend:** Hu-Nan Shan Tsoh

Date	Mintage	VG	F	VF	XF	Unc
ND(1919)	—	0.60	1.00	3.00	6.00	—

Y# 400.6 20 CASH
Copper **Obv. Legend:** THE REPUBLIC OF CHINA **Rev:** Small pentagonal rosette above crossed flags **Rev. Legend:** Hu-Nan Shan Tsoh

Date	Mintage	VG	F	VF	XF	Unc
ND(1919)	—	0.60	1.00	3.00	6.00	—

Y# 400.7 20 CASH
Copper **Obv. Legend:** THE REPUBLIC OF CHINA **Rev:** Larger star-shaped rosette above crossed flags **Rev. Legend:** Hu-Nan Shan Tsoh

Date	Mintage	VG	F	VF	XF	Unc
ND(1919)	—	1.00	2.50	4.00	7.00	—

Y# 400.7b 20 CASH
Brass **Obv. Legend:** THE REPUBLIC OF CHINA **Rev. Legend:** Hu-Nan Shan Tsoh

Date	Mintage	VG	F	VF	XF	Unc
ND(1919)	—	1.65	4.00	8.00	15.00	—

Y# 400.8 20 CASH
Copper **Obv:** Larger star-shaped rosette above flags **Obv. Legend:** THE REPUBLIC OF CHINA **Rev. Legend:** Hu-Nan Shan Tsoh

Date	Mintage	VG	F	VF	XF	Unc
ND(1919)	—	1.00	2.50	4.00	7.00	—

Y# 400.9 20 CASH
Copper **Obv. Legend:** THE REPUBLIC OF CHINA **Rev:** Sharp pointed star above crossed flags, long inner ribbons **Rev. Legend:** Hu-Nan Shan Tsoh

Date	Mintage	VG	F	VF	XF	Unc
ND(1919)	—	1.00	2.50	4.00	7.00	—

Y# 400.10 20 CASH
Copper **Obv. Legend:** THE REPUBLIC OF CHINA **Rev:** Sharp 5-pointed star over crossed flags, short inner ribbons **Rev. Legend:** Hu-nan Sheng Tsao

Date	Mintage	VG	F	VF	XF	Unc
ND(1919)	—	20.00	25.00	30.00	35.00	—

Y# 400.11 20 CASH
Copper **Obv. Legend:** THE REPUBLIC OF CHINA **Rev:** Similar to Y#400.2; no dot in rosette above flags **Rev. Legend:** Hu-nan Sheng Tsao

Date	Mintage	VG	F	VF	XF	Unc
ND(1919)	—	—	—	—	—	—

Y# 403.1 20 CASH
Copper **Subject:** Provincial Constitution **Obv:** Rosette above crossed flags **Obv. Legend:** THE REPUBLIC OF CHINA **Rev:** Trigram of the Pah Kwah in large grain sprays

Date	Mintage	VG	F	VF	XF	Unc
11(1922)	—	22.50	35.00	65.00	90.00	—

Y# 403.2 20 CASH
Copper **Subject:** Provincial Constitution **Obv:** Rosette above crossed flags **Obv. Legend:** THE REPUBLIC OF CHINA **Rev:** Trigram of the Pah Kwah in smaller grain sprays

Date	Mintage	VG	F	VF	XF	Unc
11(1922)	—	35.00	75.00	100	150	—

Y# 404 DOLLAR
27.4000 g., Silver **Subject:** Provincial Constitution **Obv. Legend:** THE REPUBLIC OF CHINA **Rev:** Trigram of the Pah Kwah in grain sprays

Date	Mintage	VG	F	VF	XF	Unc
11(1922)	—	150	300	600	1,200	1,850

TRANSITIONAL COINAGE

K# 762 10 CENTS
Silver **Ruler:** Hung-hsien **Obv. Legend:** Hung-hsien Yüan-nien **Obv. Inscription:** Chung-hua Yin-pi **Rev:** "Flying" dragon

Date	Mintage	VG	F	VF	XF	Unc
ND(1915)	—	200	350	700	1,100	1,700

Note: Though Kann calls this coin as Essay, contemporary reports indicate that the coin actually circulated briefly in 1915. Not to be confused with Y#28, the obverse of which has a different legend in Chinese. (See General Issues - Empire.)

PATTERNS

Including off metal strikes

KM#	Date	Mintage	Identification	Mkt Val
Pn4	ND(1902)	—	10 Cash. Copper. Three characters at bottom, Y#112.10.	850
Pn5	ND(1902)	—	10 Cash. Copper. Three characters at bottom, Y#112.12.	350

Note: Two Heaton (Birmingham) proof patterns for a proposed brass coinage which wasn't adopted. Dies were recut with only 2 characters for issue.

KM#	Date	Mintage	Identification	Mkt Val
Pn6	ND(1915)	—	10 Cents. Nickel. Plain edge. K#762x	—
Pn7	ND(1915)	—	10 Cents. Copper. Plain edge. K#762y	450
Pn9	11(1922)	—	Dollar. Silver. General Chao Heng-ti	—
Pn10	11(1922)	—	Dollar. Copper. General Chao Heng-ti	—

HUPEH PROVINCE

Hubei

A province located in east-central China. Hilly, with some lakes and swamps, it has rich coal and iron deposits plus a varied agricultural program. The Wuchang Mint had been active from early in the Manchu dynasty and its modern equipment began operations in 1895. It probably closed in 1929.

EMPIRE

PROVINCIAL CAST COINAGE

C# 13-11 CASH
Cast Brass **Ruler:** Kuang-hsü **Obv. Inscription:** Kuang-hsü T'ung-pao **Rev. Inscription:** Manchu Boo-ching

Date	Mintage	Good	VG	F	VF	XF
ND(1875-1908)	—	12.50	20.00	30.00	45.00	—

C# 13-11.1 CASH
Cast Brass **Ruler:** Kuang-hsü **Obv. Inscription:** Kuang-hsü T'ung-pao **Rev. Inscription:** Manchu Boo-ching **Note:** Attribution of this mint mark to Chingchow is uncertain. Some authorities claim the Taku (Dagu) Mint in Tientsin struck this coin.

Date	Mintage	Good	VG	F	VF	XF
ND(1875-1908)	—	12.00	15.00	22.50	30.00	—

MILLED COINAGE

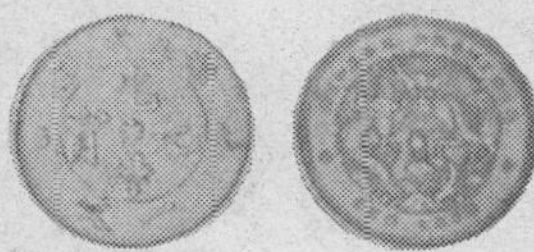

Y# 121 CASH
Brass **Ruler:** Kuang-hsü **Obv. Inscription:** Kuang-hsü Yüan-pao **Rev:** Dragon

Date	Mintage	VG	F	VF	XF	Unc
ND(1906)	66,474,000	8.00	12.00	18.00	25.00	—

Y# 7j CASH
Brass **Ruler:** Kuang-hsü **Obv:** Small m nt mark on small disc in center **Obv. Legend:** Kuang-hsü **Rev:** Dragon

Date	Mintage	VG	F	VF	XF	Unc
CD1908	Inc. above	3.50	8.00	15.00	25.00	—

Y# 7j.1 CASH
Brass **Ruler:** Kuang-hsü **Obv:** Large mint mark on small disc in center **Obv. Legend:** Kuang-hsü **Rev:** Dragon

Date	Mintage	VG	F	VF	XF	Unc
CD1908	Inc. above	3.50	8.00	15.00	25.00	—

Y# 8j 2 CASH
Copper **Ruler:** Kuang-hsü **Obv. Inscription:** Tai-ch'ing T'ung-pi **Rev:** Dragon

Date	Mintage	VG	F	VF	XF	Unc
CD(1906)	844,000	50.00	80.00	125	200	—

Y# 9j 5 CASH
Copper, 24 mm. **Ruler:** Kuang-hsü **Obv. Inscription:** Tai-ch'ing T'ung-pi **Rev. Legend:** Kuang-hsü Nien-tsao, TAI-CHING-TI-KUO ...

Date	Mintage	VG	F	VF	XF	Unc
CD1906	9,846,000	5.00	9.00	15.00	30.00	—

Y# 9j.1 5 CASH
Copper, 23 mm. **Ruler:** Kuang-hsü **Obv. Inscription:** Tai-ch'ing T'ung-pi **Rev:** Dragon redesigned **Rev. Legend:** Kuang-hsü Nien-tsao, TAI-CHING-TI-KUO ...

Date	Mintage	VG	F	VF	XF	Unc
CD1906	Inc. above	6.00	11.00	17.50	35.00	—

Y# 120 10 CASH
Copper **Ruler:** Kuang-hsü **Obv:** 8-petaled rosette **Obv. Legend:** Hu Peh Sheng Tsao **Obv. Inscription:** Kuang-hsü Yüan-pao **Rev:** Dragon surrounded by clouds

Date	Mintage	VG	F	VF	XF	Unc
ND(1902-05)	4,475,000	1.75	5.00	8.00	15.00	35.00

Y# 120a 10 CASH
Copper **Ruler:** Kuang-hsü **Obv. Legend:** Hu Peh Sheng Tsao **Obv. Inscription:** Kuang-hsü Yüan-pao **Rev:** Uncircled large dragon

Date	Mintage	VG	F	VF	XF	Unc
ND(1902-05)	Inc. above	1.00	3.50	7.00	13.50	30.00

Y# 120a.1 10 CASH
Copper **Ruler:** Kuang-hsü **Obv. Legend:** Hu Peh Sheng Tsao **Obv. Inscription:** Kuang-hsü Yüan-pao **Rev:** Slightly larger English letters, wide face on dragon

Date	Mintage	VG	F	VF	XF	Unc
ND(1902-05)	Inc. above	0.35	1.00	2.00	3.00	20.00

Y# 120a.2 10 CASH
Copper **Ruler:** Kuang-hsü **Obv. Legend:** Hu Peh Sheng Tsao **Obv. Inscription:** Kuang-hsü Yüan-pao **Rev:** Large pearl with many spines, narrower face on dragon

Date	Mintage	VG	F	VF	XF	Unc
ND(1902-05)	Inc. above	0.25	0.75	1.50	2.75	20.00

Y# 120a.3 10 CASH
Copper **Ruler:** Kuang-hsü **Obv. Legend:** Hu Peh Sheng Tsao **Obv. Inscription:** Kuang-hsü Yüan-pao **Rev:** Smaller pearl with fewer spines on dragon **Note:** Commonly found with medal alignment but also exists with coin alignment.

Date	Mintage	VG	F	VF	XF	Unc
ND(1902-05)	Inc. above	0.25	0.75	1.50	2.75	20.00

Y# 120a.3a 10 CASH
Brass **Ruler:** Kuang-hsü **Obv. Legend:** Hu Peh Sheng Tsao **Obv. Inscription:** Kuang-hsü Yüan-pao **Rev:** Dragon

Date	Mintage	VG	F	VF	XF	Unc
ND(1902-05)	Inc. above	—	—	—	—	—

Y# 120a.4 10 CASH
Copper **Ruler:** Kuang-hsü **Obv:** 5-petaled rosette, small Manchu word at right **Obv. Legend:** Hu Peh Sheng Tsao **Obv. Inscription:** Kuang-hsü Yüan-pao **Rev:** 4 dots in shape of cross at either side of dragon, PROVINCE spelled PHOVINCE, with "V" an inverted "A"

Date	Mintage	VG	F	VF	XF	Unc
ND(1902-05)	Inc. above	0.35	1.00	2.00	3.00	20.00

Y# 120a.5 10 CASH

Copper **Ruler:** Kuang-hsü **Obv:** Large Manchu at right **Obv. Legend:** Hu Peh Sheng Tsao **Obv. Inscription:** Kuang-hsü Yüan-pao **Rev:** "R" in PROVINCE inverted, "V" an inverted "A", dragon

Date	Mintage	VG	F	VF	XF	Unc
ND(1902-05)	Inc. above	0.35	1.00	2.00	3.00	20.00

Y# 120a.6 10 CASH

Copper **Ruler:** Kuang-hsü **Obv. Legend:** Hu Peh Sheng Tsao **Obv. Inscription:** Kuang-hsü Yüan-pao **Rev:** 6-pointed star at either side of dragon, hyphen in HU-PEH

Date	Mintage	VG	F	VF	XF	Unc
ND(1902-05)	Inc. above	0.35	1.00	2.00	3.00	20.00

Y# 120a.7 10 CASH

Copper **Ruler:** Kuang-hsü **Obv. Legend:** Hu Peh Sheng Tsao **Obv. Inscription:** Kuang-hsü Yüan-pao **Rev:** 6-pointed star at either side of dragon, without hyphen in HU-PEH

Date	Mintage	VG	F	VF	XF	Unc
ND(1902-05)	Inc. above	0.50	1.50	3.00	6.00	22.00

Y# 120a.8 10 CASH

Copper **Ruler:** Kuang-hsü **Obv:** 5-petaled rosette and small Manchu **Obv. Legend:** Hu Peh Sheng Tsao **Obv. Inscription:** Kuang-hsü Yüan-pao **Rev:** Dragon, very small pearl

Date	Mintage	VG	F	VF	XF	Unc
ND(1902-05)	Inc. above	1.00	3.50	6.00	12.00	25.00

Y# 120a.9 10 CASH

Copper **Ruler:** Kuang-hsü **Obv:** Square in circle **Obv. Legend:** Hu Peh Sheng Tsao **Obv. Inscription:** Kuang-hsü Yüan-pao **Rev:** Dragon, hyphen in HU-PEH

Date	Mintage	VG	F	VF	XF	Unc
ND(1902-05)	Inc. above	1.25	4.00	7.50	15.00	30.00

Y# 120a.10 10 CASH

Copper **Ruler:** Kuang-hsü **Obv:** Square in circle **Obv. Legend:** Hu Peh Sheng Tsao **Obv. Inscription:** Kuang-hsü Yüan-pao **Rev:** Dragon, without hyphen in HU-PEH

Date	Mintage	VG	F	VF	XF	Unc
ND(1902-05)	Inc. above	0.50	1.50	2.50	5.00	25.00

Y# 122 10 CASH

Copper **Ruler:** Kuang-hsü **Obv:** Second character from right at top is larger, 6-petalled rosette **Obv. Legend:** Hu-peh Sheng Tsao **Obv. Inscription:** Kuang-hsü Yüan-pao **Rev:** Front view dragon

Date	Mintage	VG	F	VF	XF	Unc
ND(1902-05)	Inc. above	0.20	0.60	1.50	3.00	20.00

Y# 122a 10 CASH

Copper **Ruler:** Kuang-hsü **Obv. Legend:** Hu-peh Sheng Tsao **Obv. Inscription:** Kuang-hsü Yüan-pao **Rev:** Circled front view of dragon

Date	Mintage	VG	F	VF	XF	Unc
ND(1902-05)	—	45.00	125	175	225	—

Y# 122.1 10 CASH

Copper **Ruler:** Kuang-hsü **Obv:** Second character from right "Pei" smaller **Obv. Legend:** Hu-peh Sheng Tsao **Obv. Inscription:** Kuang-hsü Yüan-pao **Rev:** Dragon

Date	Mintage	VG	F	VF	XF	Unc
ND(1902-05)	Inc. above	0.20	0.50	1.50	3.00	20.00

Y# 122.3 10 CASH

Copper **Ruler:** Kuang-hsü **Obv. Legend:** Hu-peh Sheng Tsao **Obv. Inscription:** Kuang-hsü Yüan-pao **Rev:** Clouds above dragon's head, 2 clouds below pearl instead of 1

Date	Mintage	VG	F	VF	XF	Unc
ND(1902-05)	Inc. above	0.65	2.00	5.00	10.00	35.00

Y# 122.4 10 CASH

Copper **Ruler:** Kuang-hsü **Obv. Legend:** Hu-peh Sheng Tsao **Obv. Inscription:** Kuang-hsü Yüan-pao **Rev:** Dragon, small circle around lower part of pearl, without dots on either side of mountain

Date	Mintage	VG	F	VF	XF	Unc
ND(1902-05)	Inc. above	0.65	2.00	5.00	10.00	35.00

Y# 122.5 10 CASH

Copper **Ruler:** Kuang-hsü **Obv. Legend:** Hu-peh Sheng Tsao **Obv. Inscription:** Kuang-hsü Yüan-pao **Rev:** Dragon, larger circle around larger pearl, larger English letters

Date	Mintage	VG	F	VF	XF	Unc
ND(1902-05)	Inc. above	0.65	2.00	5.00	10.00	25.00

Y# 10j 10 CASH

Copper **Ruler:** Kuang-hsü **Obv. Inscription:** Tai-ch'ing T'ung-pi **Rev:** Dragon, 7 flames on pearl **Rev. Legend:** Kuang hsü Nien-tsao, TAI-CHING-TI-KUO ...

Date	Mintage	VG	F	VF	XF	Unc
CD1906	1,865,558,000	0.25	0.75	1.00	2.00	20.00

Y# 10j.1 10 CASH

Copper, 28-29 mm. **Ruler:** Kuang-hsü **Obv. Inscription:** Tai-ch'ing T'ung-pi **Rev:** Redesigned dragon with wide lips, cloud-shaped bar below pearl with 5 flames **Rev. Legend:** Kuang hsü Nien-tsao, TAI-CHING-TI-KUO ...

Date	Mintage	VG	F	VF	XF	Unc
CD1906	Inc. above	0.65	2.00	5.00	10.00	25.00

Y# 10j.2 10 CASH

Copper, 30 mm. **Ruler:** Kuang-hsü **Obv. Inscription:** Tai-ch'ing T'ung-pi **Rev:** Dragon **Rev. Legend:** Kuang hsü Nien-tsao, TAI-CHING-TI-KUO ...

Date	Mintage	VG	F	VF	XF	Unc
CD1906	Inc. above	0.65	2.00	5.00	10.00	25.00

Y# 10j.3 10 CASH

Copper **Ruler:** Kuang-hsü **Obv. Inscription:** Tai-ch'ing T'ung-pi **Rev:** Different dragon with hook-shaped cloud beneath, pearl with 4 flames, large incuse swirl on pearl **Rev. Legend:** Kuang hsü Nien-tsao, TAI-CHING-TI-KUO ...

Date	Mintage	VG	F	VF	XF	Unc
CD1906	Inc. above	0.35	1.00	2.00	3.00	20.00

Y# 10j.4 10 CASH

Copper **Ruler:** Kuang-hsü **Obv. Inscription:** Tai-ch'ing T'ung-pi **Rev:** Dragon, small incuse swirl on pearl with 4 flames **Rev. Legend:** Kuang hsü Nien-tsao, TAI-CHING-TI-KUO ...

Date	Mintage	VG	F	VF	XF	Unc
CD1906	Inc. above	0.20	0.50	1.00	2.00	20.00

Y# 10j.5 10 CASH

Copper **Ruler:** Kuang-hsü **Obv. Inscription:** Tai-ch'ing T'ung-pi **Rev:** Dragon, swirl on pearl in relief with 4 flames **Rev. Legend:** Kuang hsü Nien-tsao, TAI-CHING-TI-KUO ...

Date	Mintage	VG	F	VF	XF	Unc
CD1906	Inc. above	0.25	0.75	1.00	2.00	20.00

Y# 20j 10 CASH

Copper **Ruler:** Hsüan-t'ung **Obv. Inscription:** Tai-ch'ing T'ung-pi **Rev:** Dragon, large incuse swirl on pearl **Rev. Legend:** Hsüan-t'ung Nien-tsao, TAI-CHING-TI-KUO ...

Date	Mintage	VG	F	VF	XF	Unc
CD1909	371,577,000	0.50	1.50	3.00	6.00	25.00

Y# 20j.1 10 CASH

Copper **Ruler:** Hsüan-t'ung **Obv. Inscription:** Tai-ch'ing T'ung-pi **Rev:** Dragon, small swirl in relief on pearl **Rev. Legend:** Hsüan-t'ung Nien-tsao, TAI-CHING-TI-KUO ...

Date	Mintage	VG	F	VF	XF	Unc
CD1909	Inc. above	0.50	1.50	3.00	6.00	25.00

Y# 20j.2 10 CASH

Copper **Ruler:** Hsüan-t'ung **Obv:** CD1909 over CD1906 **Obv. Inscription:** Tai-ch'ing T'ung-pi **Rev:** Dragon **Rev. Legend:** Hsüan-t'ung Nien-tsao, TAI-CHING-TI-KUO ...

Date	Mintage	VG	F	VF	XF	Unc
CD1909/1906	—	—	—	—	—	—

Y# 20j.3 10 CASH

Copper **Ruler:** Hsüan-t'ung **Obv:** Characters "Hsuan T'ung" re-engraved over characters "Kuang Hsu" **Obv. Inscription:** Tai-ch'ing T'ung-pi **Rev:** Dragon **Rev. Legend:** Hsüan-t'ung Nien-tsao, TAI-CHING-TI-KUO ...

Date	Mintage	VG	F	VF	XF	Unc
CD1909 Rare	—	—	—	—	—	—

Y# 11j 20 CASH

Copper **Ruler:** Kuang-hsü **Obv. Inscription:** Tai-ch'ing T'ung-pi **Rev:** Dragon **Rev. Legend:** Kuang-hsü Nien-tsao, TAI-CHING-TI-KUO ...

Date	Mintage	VG	F	VF	XF	Unc
CD1906	3,710,000	100	250	375	625	—

Y# 123 5 CENTS

1.3500 g., 0.8200 Silver .0356 oz. ASW **Ruler:** Kuang-hsü **Obv. Legend:** Hu-peh Sheng Tsao **Obv. Inscription:** Kuang-hsü Yüan-pao **Rev:** Dragon **Rev. Legend:** HU-PEH PROVINCE **Edge:** Reeded

Date	Mintage	VG	F	VF	XF	Unc
ND(1895-1905)	4,278,000	17.50	50.00	100	150	250

Y# 124.1 10 CENTS

2.7000 g., 0.8200 Silver .0712 oz. ASW, 18.6 mm. **Ruler:** Kuang-hsü **Obv. Legend:** Hu-peh Sheng Tsao **Obv. Inscription:** Kuang-hsü Yüan-pao **Rev:** Without characters beside dragon **Rev. Legend:** HU-PEH PROVINCE **Edge:** Reeded

Date	Mintage	VG	F	VF	XF	Unc
ND(1895-1907)	—	1.50	2.50	4.50	8.00	20.00

Note: 2 varieties of edge milling exist

Y# 129 10 CENTS

Silver **Ruler:** Hsüan-t'ung **Obv. Legend:** Hu-peh Sheng Tsao **Obv. Inscription:** Hsüan-t'ung Yüan-pao **Rev:** Dragon **Rev. Legend:** Kuang-hsü Nien-tsao, TAI-CHING-TI-KUO ...

Date	Mintage	VG	F	VF	XF	Unc
ND(1909)	—	100	200	400	600	800

Y# 125.1 20 CENTS

5.3000 g., 0.8200 Silver .1397 oz. ASW **Ruler:** Kuang-hsü **Obv. Legend:** Hu-peh Sheng Tsao **Obv. Inscription:** Kuang-hsü Yüan-pao **Rev:** Without characters beside dragon **Rev. Legend:** HU-PEH PROVINCE

Date	Mintage	VG	F	VF	XF	Unc
ND(1895-1907)	—	2.50	5.00	10.00	15.00	30.00

Y# 130 20 CENTS

Silver **Ruler:** Hsüan-t'ung **Obv. Legend:** Hu-peh Sheng Tsao **Obv. Inscription:** Hsüan-t'ung Yüan-pao **Rev:** Dragon **Rev. Legend:** HU-PEH PROVINCE

Date	Mintage	VG	F	VF	XF	Unc
ND(1909-11)	—	150	300	600	900	1,250

Y# 126 50 CENTS

13.5000 g., 0.8600 Silver .3733 oz. ASW **Ruler:** Kuang-hsü **Obv. Legend:** Hu-peh Sheng Tsao **Obv. Inscription:** Kuang-hsü Yüan-pao **Rev:** Dragon **Rev. Legend:** HU-PEH PROVINCE

Date	Mintage	VG	F	VF	XF	Unc
ND(1895-1905)	—	15.00	40.00	80.00	120	250

Y# 127.1 DOLLAR

26.7000 g., 0.9000 Silver .7727 oz. ASW **Ruler:** Kuang-hsü **Obv. Legend:** Hu-peh Sheng Tsao **Obv. Inscription:** Kuang-hsü Yüan-pao **Rev:** Without "Pen Sheng" at either side of dragon **Rev. Legend:** HU-PEH PROVINCE **Edge:** Reeded

Date	Mintage	VG	F	VF	XF	Unc
ND(1895-1907)	19,935,000	12.50	25.00	45.00	85.00	500

Y# 131 DOLLAR

27.0000 g., 0.9000 Silver .7814 oz. ASW **Ruler:** Hsüan-t'ung **Obv. Legend:** Hu-peh Sheng Tsao **Obv. Inscription:** Hsüan-t'ung Yüan-pao **Rev:** Dragon

Date	Mintage	VG	F	VF	XF	Unc
ND(1909-11)	2,703,000	11.50	22.00	35.00	65.00	400

BULLION COINAGE/TAEL SYSTEM

Y# 128.1 TAEL
37.7000 g., 0.8770 Silver 1.0631 oz. ASW **Ruler:** Kuang-hsü **Obv:** Large inscription **Obv. Inscription:** Kuang-hsü Yin-pi **Rev:** Two dragons forming circle **Rev. Legend:** HU-PEH PROVINCE

Date	Mintage	VG	F	VF	XF	Unc
30(1904)	648,000	165	525	1,000	3,000	4,500

Y# 128.2 TAEL
37.7000 g., 0.8770 Silver 1.0631 oz. ASW **Ruler:** Kuang-hsü **Obv:** Smaller inscription **Obv. Inscription:** Kuang-hsü Yin-pi **Rev:** Two dragons forming circle **Rev. Legend:** HU-PEH PROVINCE

Date	Mintage	VG	F	VF	XF	Unc
30(1904)	Inc. above	150	350	700	1,500	2,750

REPUBLIC

MILLED COINAGE

Y# A405 20 CASH
Brass **Note:** Attribution is uncertain. Probably minted in Szechuan (Sichuan).

Date	Mintage	VG	F	VF	XF	Unc
ND(c.1914)	—	40.00	85.00	115	165	—

Y# 405 50 CASH
Copper Or Brass **Obv. Legend:** Chung Hua Min Kuo (year) Nien **Note:** Crude strike. Similar coins dated Yr. 1 and Yr. 8 are known, but their status is uncertain.

Date	Mintage	VG	F	VF	XF	Unc
3(1914)	—	575	850	1,100	—	—
7(1918)	—	400	600	850	—	—

Y# 405.1 50 CASH
Copper Or Brass **Obv. Legend:** Chung Hua Min Kuo (year) Nien **Note:** Machine strike. Not to be confused with Szechuan (Sichuan) Y#449.

Date	Mintage	VG	F	VF	XF	Unc
7(1918)	—	575	850	1,100	—	—

Y# 406 20 CENTS
5.2000 g., Silver **Obv:** Characters "Tsao" at left and "Hu" at right of military bust of Yuan Shih-k'ai left **Note:** Do not confuse with Y#327 (see Republic-general issues).

Date	Mintage	VG	F	VF	XF	Unc
9(1920)	—	25.00	75.00	125	200	500

PATTERNS

Including off metal strikes

KM#	Date	Mintage	Identification	Mkt Val
PnA6	ND(1902)	—	10 Cash. White Copper. Y122.5. W518.	—
Pn6	ND(1902)	—	10 Cash. Brass. W480.	—
PnA7	3(1911)	—	10 Cents. Pewter. K48y.	—
Pn7	1(1916)	—	10 Cents. White Metal. K764x.	—

KANSU PROVINCE

Gansu

A province located in north-central China with a contrast of mountains and sandy plains. The west end of the Great Wall with its branches lies in Kansu (Gansu). Kansu (Gansu) was the eastern end of the "Silk Road" that led to central and western Asia. Two mints issued Cash coins. It has been reported, but not confirmed, that the Lanchow Mint operated as late as 1949.

REPUBLIC

MILLED COINAGE

Y# C407 20 CASH
Copper **Obv. Legend:** Chung Hua Min Kuo **Rev. Legend:** THE REPUBLIC OF CHINA

Date	Mintage	VG	F	VF	XF	Unc
ND(1920)	—	—	—	—	—	—

Y# D407 50 CASH
Copper **Obv. Legend:** Chung Hua Min Kuo **Rev. Legend:** THE REPUBLIC OF CHINA

Date	Mintage	VG	F	VF	XF	Unc
ND(1920)	—	70.00	150	250	—	—

Y# 408 50 CASH
Copper **Obv. Legend:** Chung Hua Min Kuo (year) Nien

Date	Mintage	VG	F	VF	XF	Unc
15(1926)	2,564,000	85.00	175	275	450	—

Y# A408 50 CASH
Copper **Obv:** National star **Obv. Legend:** Chung Hua Min Kuo (year) Nien **Rev:** Crossed flags

Date	Mintage	VG	F	VF	XF	Unc
ND(1927)	—	500	900	1,500	—	—

Y# 409 100 CASH
Copper **Obv. Legend:** Chung Hua Min Kuo (year) Nien **Rev:** Crossed flags

Date	Mintage	VG	F	VF	XF	Unc
15(1926)	—	35.00	50.00	100	150	—

Y# 407 DOLLAR
26.6000 g., Silver **Obv:** Military bust of Yüan Shih-kai left, "Su" at left, "Kan" at right **Obv. Legend:** Chung Hua Min Kuo (year) Nien **Rev:** Value in sprays

Date	Mintage	VG	F	VF	XF	Unc
3(1914)	—	100	275	450	800	2,000

Y# 410 DOLLAR
26.6000 g., Silver **Obv:** Facing bust of Sun Yat-sen **Obv. Legend:** Chung Hua Min Kuo (year) Nien **Rev:** National star

Date	Mintage	VG	F	VF	XF	Unc
17(1928)	—	125	385	700	1,200	2,200

PATTERNS

Including off metal strikes

KM#	Date	Mintage	Identification	Mkt Val
Pn1	ND(ca.1928)	—	5 Cash. Copper. Hsu#385.	650
Pn2	ND(ca.1928)	—	10 Cash. Copper.	—
Pn3	ND(1928)	—	5 Fen. Copper. Hsu#383.	300
Pn4	17(1928)	—	50 Cash. Copper.	—
Pn5	ND(ca.1928)	—	10 Fen. Copper. Hsu#384.	400

KIANGNAN

A district in eastern China made up of Anhwei (Anhui) and Kiangsu (Jiangsu) provinces. In 1667 the province of Kiangnan was divided into the present provinces of Anhwei (Anhui) and Kiangsu (Jiangsu). In 1723 Nanking, formerly the capital of Kiangnan, was made the capital of Liang-Chiang Chiang (an administrative area consisting of Anhwei (Anhui), Kiangsu (Jiangsu), and Kiangsi (Jiangxi) provinces).

Always highly regarded because of location, agriculture and manufacturing, Kiangnan has frequently been sought after by contending forces.

The Nanking Mint had been active during imperial times. Modern minting facilities began operations in 1897. A second mint was planned for the Kiangnan Arsenal in Shanghai in 1905. Mints for copper coins also operated in Chingkiang (Qingjiang) in central Kiangsu and at Soochow which is further south. A silver mint was planned for Shanghai in 1921. The Nanking Mint, the most important of the group, burned down in 1929. The Nationalist Government Central Mint was completed in Shanghai in 1930 and opened in 1933.

EMPIRE

MILLED COINAGE

The initials HAH, SY, CH and TH are those of mint officials and were placed on the coins as a guarantee of the coin's fineness. The 5-, 10-, and 20-cent coins are often found without a decimal point between the numbers on the reverse. The 1904 dated dollar was restruck during Republican times.

Y# 7k CASH
Brass **Ruler:** Kuang-hsü **Obv:** Bottom horizontal stroke in mint mark extends beyond outside vertical strokes **Obv. Legend:** Kuang-hsü **Rev:** Dragon

Date	Mintage	VG	F	VF	XF	Unc
CD(1908)	25,450,000	2.50	4.50	8.50	16.00	—

Y# 7k.1 CASH
Brass **Ruler:** Kuang-hsü **Obv:** Bottom horizontal stroke in mint mark does not extend beyond outside vertical strokes **Obv. Legend:** Kuang-hsü **Rev:** Dragon

Date	Mintage	VG	F	VF	XF	Unc
CD1908	Inc. above	3.50	6.50	12.50	21.50	—

Y# 9k.1 5 CASH
Copper **Ruler:** Kuang-hsü **Obv:** Mint mark incused on raised disk **Obv. Inscription:** Tai-ch'ing T'ung-pi **Rev:** Dragon **Rev. Legend:** Kuang-hsü Nien-tsao, TAI-CHING-TI-KUO...

Date	Mintage	VG	F	VF	XF	Unc
CD1906	—	35.00	65.00	100	150	—

Y# 9k.1a 5 CASH
Brass **Ruler:** Kuang-hsü **Obv. Inscription:** Tai-ch'ing T'ung-pi **Rev:** Dragon **Rev. Legend:** Kuang-hsü Nien-tsao, TAI-CHING-TI-KUO...

Date	Mintage	VG	F	VF	XF	Unc
CD1906	—	45.00	90.00	125	200	—

Y# 9k.2 5 CASH
Copper **Ruler:** Kuang-hsü **Obv:** Mint mark in relief at center without disk **Obv. Inscription:** Tai-ch'ing T'ung-pi **Rev:** Dragon **Rev. Legend:** Kuang-hsü Nien-tsao, TAI-CHING-TI-KUO...

Date	Mintage	VG	F	VF	XF	Unc
CD1906	—	45.00	90.00	125	200	—

Y# C140 10 CASH
Copper **Ruler:** Kuang-hsü **Obv:** Kiang-nan **Obv. Legend:** Chiang-nan Sheng Tsao **Obv. Inscription:** Kuang-hsü Yüan-pao **Rev:** Dragon **Rev. Legend:** KIANG-SOO **Note:** Mule; often confused with Y#162.

Date	Mintage	VG	F	VF	XF	Unc
CD1902	—	—	—	—	—	—
ND(ca.1902)	—	50.00	150	200	250	—

Y# 135 10 CASH
Copper **Ruler:** Kuang-hsü **Obv. Legend:** Chiang-nan Sheng Tsao **Obv. Inscription:** Kuang-hsü Yüan-pao **Rev:** Dragon **Edge:** Reeded

Date	Mintage	VG	F	VF	XF	Unc
ND(ca.1902)	—	10.00	30.00	60.00	100	—

Y# 135.1 10 CASH
Copper **Ruler:** Kuang-hsü **Obv. Legend:** Chiang-nan Sheng Tsao **Obv. Inscription:** Kuang-hsü Yüan-pao **Rev:** Dragon **Edge:** Plain

Date	Mintage	VG	F	VF	XF	Unc
ND(ca.1902)	—	10.00	30.00	60.00	100	—

Y# 135.2 10 CASH
Copper **Ruler:** Kuang-hsü **Obv:** Small Manchu words in center **Obv. Legend:** Chiang-nan Sheng Tsao **Obv. Inscription:** Kuang-hsü Yüan-pao **Rev:** Dragon

Date	Mintage	F	VF	XF	Unc	BU
CD1902	—	1.50	3.00	5.00	20.00	—

Y# 135.3 10 CASH
Copper **Ruler:** Kuang-hsü **Obv:** Large Manchu words in center **Obv. Legend:** Chiang-nan Sheng Tsao **Obv. Inscription:** Kuang-hsü Yüan-pao **Rev:** Dragon

Date	Mintage	VG	F	VF	XF	Unc
CD1902	—	2.00	6.50	12.50	25.00	45.00

Y# 135.4 10 CASH
Copper **Ruler:** Kuang-hsü **Obv. Legend:** Chiang-nan Sheng Tsao **Obv. Inscription:** Kuang-hsü Yüan-pao **Rev:** Dragon

Date	Mintage	VG	F	VF	XF	Unc
CD1903	—	1.25	4.00	5.00	7.00	24.00

Y# 135.5 10 CASH
Copper **Ruler:** Kuang-hsü **Obv. Legend:** Chiang-nan Sheng Tsao **Obv. Inscription:** Kuang-hsü Yüan-pao **Rev:** Dragon; cloud above letter "T" looks like number "3"

Date	Mintage	VG	F	VF	XF	Unc
CD1904	351,974,000	0.35	1.00	2.00	5.00	20.00

Y# 135.6 10 CASH
Copper **Ruler:** Kuang-hsü **Obv. Legend:** Chiang-nan Sheng Tsao **Obv. Inscription:** Kuang-hsü Yüan-pao **Rev:** Dragon; cloud above "T" redesigned; "CASH" spelled "GASH"

Date	Mintage	VG	F	VF	XF	Unc
CD1904	Inc. above	1.50	4.50	9.00	17.50	45.00

Y# 135.7 10 CASH
Copper **Ruler:** Kuang-hsü **Obv. Legend:** Chiang-nan Sheng Tsao **Obv. Inscription:** Kuang-hsü Yüan-pao **Rev:** Thin-tailed dragon; third design of cloud above letter "T"

Date	Mintage	VG	F	VF	XF	Unc
CD1904	Inc. above	0.50	1.50	3.00	5.00	20.00

Y# 135.8 10 CASH
Copper **Ruler:** Kuang-hsü **Obv. Legend:** Chiang-nan Sheng Tsao **Obv. Inscription:** Kuang-hsü Yüan-pao **Rev:** Fewer clouds around dragon; scales on dragon's body different, pearl smaller

Date	Mintage	VG	F	VF	XF	Unc
CD1904	Inc. above	1.50	4.50	9.00	17.50	45.00

Note: This coin is believed to be counterfeit

Y# 135.9 10 CASH

Copper **Ruler:** Kuang-hsü **Obv. Legend:** Chiang-nan Sheng Tsao **Obv. Inscription:** Kuang-hsü Yüan-pao **Rev:** Small rosette at either side of dragon

Date	Mintage	VG	F	VF	XF	Unc
CD1905	496,020,000	0.35	1.00	2.00	5.00	20.00

Y# 135.10 10 CASH

Copper **Ruler:** Kuang-hsü **Obv. Legend:** Chiang-nan Sheng Tsao **Obv. Inscription:** Kuang-hsü Yüan-pao **Rev:** Large oblong rosettes at either side of dragon

Date	Mintage	VG	F	VF	XF	Unc
CD1905	Inc. above	0.50	1.50	3.00	5.00	20.00

Y# 138 10 CASH

Copper **Ruler:** Kuang-hsü **Obv. Legend:** Chiang-nan Sheng Tsao **Obv. Inscription:** Kuang-hsü Yüan-pao **Rev:** Dragon; denomination: "TEN-CASH"

Date	Mintage	VG	F	VF	XF	Unc
CD1905	Inc. above	1.25	3.50	6.00	12.00	30.00

Y# 138.1 10 CASH

Copper **Ruler:** Kuang-hsü **Obv:** Rosette in center **Obv. Legend:** Chiang-nan Sheng Tsao **Obv. Inscription:** Kuang-hsü Yüan-pao **Rev:** Dragon; without hyphen in "TEN CASH"

Date	Mintage	VG	F	VF	XF	Unc
CD1905	Inc. above	0.25	0.75	1.50	5.00	20.00

Y# 10k 10 CASH

Copper **Ruler:** Kuang-hsü **Obv:** Mint mark in relief on raised disc **Obv. Inscription:** Tai-ch'ing T'ung-pi **Rev:** Dragon with wide face and incuse eyes **Rev. Legend:** Kuang-hsü Nien-tsao, TAI-CHING-TI-KUO...

Date	Mintage	VG	F	VF	XF	Unc
CD1906	504,800,000	0.45	1.25	2.50	5.00	20.00

Y# 10k.1 10 CASH

Copper **Ruler:** Kuang-hsü **Obv. Inscription:** Tai-ch'ing T'ung-pi **Rev:** Dragon with narrower face and raised dots for eyes **Rev. Legend:** Kuang-hsü Nien-tsao, TAI-CHING-TI-KUO...

Date	Mintage	VG	F	VF	XF	Unc
CD1906	Inc. above	0.45	1.25	2.50	5.00	20.00

Y# 10k.2 10 CASH

Copper **Ruler:** Kuang-hsü **Obv:** Mint mark in relief without raised disc **Obv. Inscription:** Tai-ch'ing T'ung-pi **Rev:** Dragon with wide face and incuse eyes **Rev. Legend:** Kuang-hsü Nien-tsao, TAI-CHING-TI-KUO...

Date	Mintage	VG	F	VF	XF	Unc
CD1906	Inc. above	0.35	1.00	2.50	5.00	20.00

Y# 10k.3 10 CASH

Copper **Ruler:** Kuang-hsü **Obv. Inscription:** Tai-ch'ing T'ung-pi **Rev:** Dragon with narrow face and raised dots for eyes **Rev. Legend:** Kuang-hsü Nien-tsao, TAI-CHING-TI-KUO...

Date	Mintage	VG	F	VF	XF	Unc
CD1906	Inc. above	0.35	1.00	2.50	5.00	20.00

Y# 10k.4 10 CASH

Copper **Ruler:** Kuang-hsü **Obv:** Mmint mark incuse on raised disc **Obv. Inscription:** Tai-ch'ing T'ung-pi **Rev:** Dragon **Rev. Legend:** Kuang-hsü Nien-tsao, TAI-CHING-TI-KUO...

Date	Mintage	VG	F	VF	XF	Unc
CD1906	Inc. above	4.50	12.50	25.00	45.00	—

Y# 10k.4a 10 CASH

Brass **Ruler:** Kuang-hsü **Obv. Inscription:** Tai-ch'ing T'ung-pi **Rev:** Dragon **Rev. Legend:** Kuang-hsü Nien-tsao, TAI-CHING-TI-KUO...

Date	Mintage	VG	F	VF	XF	Unc
CD1906	—	—	—	—	—	—

Y# A140 10 CASH

Copper **Ruler:** Kuang-hsü **Obv:** Y#10k.2 **Obv. Inscription:** Tai-ch'ing T'ung-Pi **Rev:** Dragon; Y#138 **Note:** Mule.

Date	Mintage	VG	F	VF	XF	Unc
CD1906	Inc. above	8.50	25.00	40.00	60.00	—

Y# B140 10 CASH

Copper **Ruler:** Kuang-hsü **Obv:** Y#138 **Obv. Legend:** Chiang-nan Sheng Tsao **Obv. Inscription:** Kuang-hsü Yüan-pao **Rev:** Dragon; Y#10k **Note:** Mule.

Date	Mintage	VG	F	VF	XF	Unc
CD1905	Inc. above	10.00	30.00	50.00	70.00	—

Y# D140 10 CASH

Copper **Ruler:** Kuang-hsü **Obv:** Y#138.1 **Obv. Legend:** Chiang-nan Sheng Tsao **Obv. Inscription:** Kuang-hsü Yüan-pao **Rev:** Dragon; Y#135 **Note:** Mule.

Date	Mintage	VG	F	VF	XF	Unc
CD1905	Inc. above	35.00	100	150	200	—

Note: Other Kiangnan mules exist, dated 1902 and 1903

Y# E140 10 CASH

Copper **Ruler:** Kuang-hsü **Obv:** Y#10.5 **Obv. Inscription:** Tai-ch'ing T'ung-pi **Rev:** Dragon; Kiangnan Y#138.1 **Note:** Mule.

Date	Mintage	VG	F	VF	XF	Unc
CD1907	—	35.00	100	225	300	—

Y# 140.1 10 CASH

Copper **Ruler:** Kuang-hsü **Obv:** Y#10k **Obv. Inscription:** Tai-ch'ing T'ung-Pi **Rev:** Dragon; Y#138 **Note:** Mule; raised or incused mint mark.

Date	Mintage	VG	F	VF	XF	Unc
CD1906	Inc. above	1.00	3.00	5.00	12.00	30.00

Y# 140.2 10 CASH

Copper **Ruler:** Kuang-hsü **Obv:** Y#10k **Obv. Inscription:** Tai-ch'ing T'ung-pi **Rev:** Dragon, Y#138 **Note:** Mule; mint mark incuse on raised disk.

Date	Mintage	VG	F	VF	XF	Unc
CD1906	Inc. above	1.00	3.00	5.00	12.00	30.00

Y# 10k.5 10 CASH

Copper **Ruler:** Kuang-hsü **Obv:** Mint mark incuse on raised disc **Obv. Inscription:** Tai-ch'ing T'ung-pi **Rev:** Dragon with wide face; seven flames on pearl **Rev. Legend:** Kuang-hsü Nien-tsao, TAI-CHING-TI-KUO...

Date	Mintage	VG	F	VF	XF	Unc
CD1907	552,000,000	0.50	1.50	3.00	5.00	20.00

Y# 10k.6 10 CASH

Copper **Ruler:** Kuang-hsü **Obv. Inscription:** Tai-ch'ing T'ung-pi **Rev:** Different dragon with narrow face an small mouth; five flames on pearl; dot after "COIN" **Rev. Legend:** Kuang-hsü Nien-tsao, TAI-CHING-TI-KUO...

Date	Mintage	VG	F	VF	XF	Unc
CD1907	Inc. above	0.35	1.00	2.00	4.50	20.00

Y# 10k.6a 10 CASH

Brass **Ruler:** Kuang-hsü **Obv. Inscription:** Tai-ch'ing T'ung-pi **Rev:** Dragon **Rev. Legend:** Kuang-hsü Nien-tsao, TAI-CHING-TI-KUO...

Date	Mintage	VG	F	VF	XF	Unc
CD1907	Inc. above	3.00	9.00	17.50	30.00	—

Y# 10k.7 10 CASH

Copper **Ruler:** Kuang-hsü **Obv. Inscription:** Tai-ch'ing T'ung-pi **Rev:** Dragon with large mouth and redesigned head; flame below pearl has long tail which touches dragon's body; "KUO" spelled "KIIO" **Rev. Legend:** Kuang-hsü Nien-tsao, TAI-CHING-TI-KUO...

Date	Mintage	VG	F	VF	XF	Unc
CD1907	Inc. above	0.35	1.00	2.50	5.00	20.00

Y# 10k.8 10 CASH

Copper **Ruler:** Kuang-hsü **Obv. Inscription:** Tai-ch'ing T'ung-pi **Rev:** Tail of flame below pearl does not touch dragon's body; dash after word "COIN"; "KUO" spelled "KUO" **Rev. Legend:** Kuang-hsü Nien-tsao, TAI-CHING-TI-KUO...

Date	Mintage	VG	F	VF	XF	Unc
CD1907	Inc. above	0.35	1.00	2.50	5.00	20.00

Y# 10k.9 10 CASH

Copper **Ruler:** Kuang-hsü **Obv. Inscription:** Tai-ch'ing T'ung-pi **Rev:** Dragon with square mouth; letter "K" in "KUO" larger than other letters; without dot or dash after "COIN" **Rev. Legend:** Kuang-hsü Nien-tsao, TAI-CHING-TI-KUO...

Date	Mintage	VG	F	VF	XF	Unc
CD1907	Inc. above	0.35	1.00	2.25	4.50	20.00

Y# 10k.9a 10 CASH

Copper **Ruler:** Kuang-hsü **Obv. Inscription:** Tai-ch'ing T'ung-pi **Rev:** Large flat-faced dragon **Rev. Legend:** Kuang-hsü Nien-tsao, TAI-CHING-TI-KUO...

Date	Mintage	VG	F	VF	XF	Unc
CD1907	—	—	—	—	—	—

Y# 10k.10 10 CASH

Copper **Ruler:** Kuang-hsü **Obv:** Mint mark incuse on raised disc **Obv. Inscription:** Tai-ch'ing T'ung-pi **Rev:** Dragon with small moutn; five flame pearl; dot after "COIN"; "KUO" spelled "KUO" **Rev. Legend:** Kuang-hsü Nien-tsao, TAI-CHING-TI-KUO...

Date	Mintage	VG	F	VF	XF	Unc
CD1908	442,750,000	0.35	1.00	2.50	5.00	20.00

Y# 10k.11 10 CASH

Copper **Ruler:** Kuang-hsü **Obv. Inscription:** Tai-ch'ing T'ung-pi **Rev:** Dragon has large mouth and redesigned head; tail on cloud beneath pearl touches dragon's body; "KUO" spelled "KIIO" **Rev. Legend:** Kuang-hsü Nien-tsao, TAI-CHING-TI-KUO...

Date	Mintage	VG	F	VF	XF	Unc
CD1908	Inc. above	0.35	1.00	2.00	4.00	20.00

Y# 10k.12 10 CASH

Copper **Ruler:** Kuang-hsü **Obv. Inscription:** Tai-ch'ing T'ung-pi **Rev:** Dragon; dash after "COIN"; "KUO" spelled "KUO" **Rev. Legend:** Kuang-hsü Nien-tsao, TAI-CHING-TI-KUO...

Date	Mintage	VG	F	VF	XF	Unc
CD1908	Inc. above	0.50	1.50	3.00	5.00	20.00

Y# 10k.13 10 CASH

Copper **Ruler:** Kuang-hsü **Obv. Inscription:** Tai-ch'ing T'ung-pi **Rev:** Dragon's head redesigned; without dot or dash after "COIN"; 'KUO" spelled "KIIO" **Rev. Legend:** Kuang-hsü Nien-tsao, TA -CHING-TI-KUO...

Date	Mintage	VG	F	VF	XF	Unc
CD1908	Inc. above	0.35	1.00	2.00	4.00	20.00

Note: Most of the 1907 and 1908 ten cash above have copper spelled GOPPER

Y# 10k.14 10 CASH

Copper **Ruler:** Kuang-hsü **Obv. Inscription:** Tai-ch'ing T'ung-pi **Rev:** Dragon's right mustache without hook **Rev. Legend:** TAI-GIIING-K IO GOPPER COIN

Date	Mintage	VG	F	VF	XF	Unc
CD1908	Inc. above	0.35	1.00	2.50	5.00	—

Y# 141a 5 CENTS

13.0000 g., 0.8200 Silver .0343 oz. ASW **Ruler:** Kuang-hsü **Obv. Legend:** Chiang-nan Sheng Tsao **Obv. Inscription:** Kuang-hsü Yüan-pao **Rev:** Without circle around dragon

Date	Mintage	VG	F	VF	XF	Unc
ND(1898)	Inc. above	2.50	10.00	15.00	30.00	50.00
CD1899	3,812	17.50	50.00	100	150	300
CD1900	618,000	3.00	10.00	15.00	30.00	50.00
CD1901	—	17.50	50.00	100	200	400

Y# 142a.5 10 CENTS

2.6000 g., 0.8200 Silver .0343 oz. ASW **Ruler:** Kuang-hsü **Obv:** Without initials **Obv. Legend:** Chiang-nan Sheng Tsao **Obv. Inscription:** Kuang-hsü Yüan-pao **Rev:** Large English letters

Date	Mintage	VG	F	VF	XF	Unc
CD1901	7,794,000	2.50	4.00	7.50	12.50	50.00

Y# 142a.6 10 CENTS

2.6000 g., 0.8200 Silver .0343 oz. ASW **Ruler:** Kuang-hsü **Obv:** Without initials **Obv. Legend:** Chiang-nan Sheng Tsao **Obv. Inscription:** Kuang-hsü Yüan-pao **Rev:** Small English letters

Date	Mintage	VG	F	VF	XF	Unc
CD1901	Inc. above	2.50	4.00	7.50	12.50	50.00

Y# 142a.7 10 CENTS

2.6000 g., 0.8200 Silver .0343 oz. ASW **Ruler:** Kuang-hsü **Obv:** Initials "HAH" **Obv. Legend:** Chiang-nan Sheng Tsao **Obv. Inscription:** Kuang-hsü Yüan-pao **Rev:** Large rosettes beside dragon

Date	Mintage	VG	F	VF	XF	Unc
CD1901	Inc. above	2.50	5.00	8.50	15.00	55.00

Y# 142a.8 10 CENTS

2.6000 g., 0.8200 Silver .0343 oz. ASW **Ruler:** Kuang-hsü **Obv. Legend:** Chiang-nan Sheng Tsao **Obv. Inscription:** Kuang-hsü Yüan-pao **Rev:** Small rosettes beside dragon

Date	Mintage	VG	F	VF	XF	Unc
CD1901	Inc. above	2.50	5.00	8.50	15.00	55.00

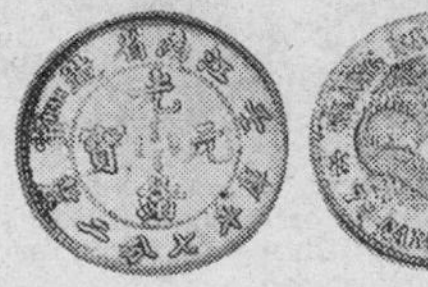

Y# 142a.9 10 CENTS

2.6000 g., 0.8200 Silver .0343 oz. ASW **Ruler:** Kuang-hsü **Obv. Legend:** Chiang-nan Sheng Tsao **Obv. Inscription:** Kuang-hsü Yüan-pao **Rev:** Large stars beside dragon

Date	Mintage	VG	F	VF	XF	Unc
CD1902	3,778,000	2.50	4.50	8.00	15.00	50.00

Y# 142a.10 10 CENTS

2.6000 g., 0.8200 Silver .0343 oz. ASW **Ruler:** Kuang-hsü **Obv. Legend:** Chiang-nan Sheng Tsao **Obv. Inscription:** Kuang-hsü Yüan-pao **Rev:** Small stars beside dragon

Date	Mintage	VG	F	VF	XF	Unc
CD1902	Inc. above	2.75	6.00	10.00	17.50	75.00

Y# 142a.11 10 CENTS

2.6000 g., 0.8200 Silver .0343 oz. ASW **Ruler:** Kuang-hsü **Obv:** Large rosette **Obv. Legend:** Chiang-nan Sheng Tsao **Obv. Inscription:** Kuang-hsü Yüan-pao

Date	Mintage	VG	F	VF	XF	Unc
CD1903	1,161,000	4.50	12.50	30.00	60.00	110

Y# 142a.12 10 CENTS

2.6000 g., 0.8200 Silver .0343 oz. ASW **Ruler:** Kuang-hsü **Obv:** Small rosette **Obv. Legend:** Chiang-nan Sheng Tsao **Obv. Inscription:** Kuang-hsü Yüan-pao

Date	Mintage	VG	F	VF	XF	Unc
CD1903	Inc. above	4.50	12.50	30.00	60.00	110

Y# 142a.13 10 CENTS

2.6000 g., 0.8200 Silver .0343 oz. ASW **Ruler:** Kuang-hsü **Obv:** Initials "HAH TH" **Obv. Legend:** Chiang-nan Sheng Tsao **Obv. Inscription:** Kuang-hsü Yüan-pao

Date	Mintage	VG	F	VF	XF	Unc
CD1904	897,000	3.25	6.00	12.50	30.00	90.00

Y# 142a.14 10 CENTS

2.6000 g., 0.8200 Silver .0343 oz. ASW **Ruler:** Kuang-hsü **Obv:** Initials "SY" upside down **Obv. Legend:** Chiang-nan Sheng Tsao **Obv. Inscription:** Kuang-hsü Yüan-pao

Date	Mintage	VG	F	VF	XF	Unc
CD1905	681,000	4.00	7.00	20.00	37.50	100

Y# 146 10 CENTS

2.6000 g., 0.8200 Silver .0343 oz. ASW **Ruler:** Hsüan-T'ung **Obv. Legend:** Chiang-nan Sheng Tsao **Obv. Inscription:** Hsüan-t'ung Yüan-pao **Rev:** Dragon

Date	Mintage	VG	F	VF	XF	Unc
ND(1911)	Est. 820,000	4.50	15.00	30.00	65.00	120

Note: Includes 590,000 pieces struck in debased silver in 1916

Y# 143a.6 20 CENTS
5.3000 g., 0.8200 Silver .1397 oz. ASW **Ruler:** Kuang-hsü **Obv:** Without initials **Obv. Legend:** Chiang-nan Sheng Tsao **Obv. Inscription:** Kuang-hsü Yüan-pao

Date	Mintage	VG	F	VF	XF	Unc
CD1901	47,114,000	4.00	6.50	10.00	16.50	55.00

Y# 143a.7 20 CENTS
5.3000 g., 0.8200 Silver .1397 oz. ASW **Ruler:** Kuang-hsü **Obv:** Initials "HAH" **Obv. Legend:** Chiang-nan Sheng Tsao **Obv. Inscription:** Kuang-hsü Yüan-pao

Date	Mintage	VG	F	VF	XF	Unc
CD1901	Inc. above	2.50	5.00	7.50	13.50	55.00

Y# 143a.8 20 CENTS
5.3000 g., 0.8200 Silver .1397 oz. ASW **Ruler:** Kuang-hsü **Obv. Legend:** Chiang-nan Sheng Tsao **Obv. Inscription:** Kuang-hsü Yüan-pao

Date	Mintage	VG	F	VF	XF	Unc
CD1902	15,754,000	2.75	5.00	7.50	13.50	55.00

Y# 143a.9 20 CENTS
5.3000 g., 0.8200 Silver .1397 oz. ASW **Ruler:** Kuang-hsü **Obv:** Rosette in outer legend **Obv. Legend:** Chiang-nan Sheng Tsao **Obv. Inscription:** Kuang-hsü Yüan-pao

Date	Mintage	VG	F	VF	XF	Unc
CD1903	2,432,000	4.00	12.50	25.00	55.00	120

Y# 143a.10 20 CENTS
5.3000 g., 0.8200 Silver .1397 oz. ASW **Ruler:** Kuang-hsü **Obv:** Without rosette **Obv. Legend:** Chiang-nan Sheng Tsao **Obv. Inscription:** Kuang-hsü Yüan-pao

Date	Mintage	VG	F	VF	XF	Unc
CD1903	Inc. above	5.00	15.00	35.00	70.00	200

Y# 143a.11 20 CENTS
5.3000 g., 0.8200 Silver .1397 oz. ASW **Ruler:** Kuang-hsü **Obv:** Initials "HAH TH" **Obv. Legend:** Chiang-nan Sheng Tsao **Obv. Inscription:** Kuang-hsü Yüan-pao

Date	Mintage	VG	F	VF	XF	Unc
CD1904	1,172,000	5.00	15.00	35.00	60.00	150

Y# 143a.12 20 CENTS
5.3000 g., 0.8200 Silver .1397 oz. ASW **Ruler:** Kuang-hsü **Obv:** Without initials **Obv. Legend:** Chiang-nan Sheng Tsao **Obv. Inscription:** Kuang-hsü Yüan-pao

Date	Mintage	VG	F	VF	XF	Unc
CD1905	828,000	4.00	12.50	30.00	50.00	130

Y# 143a.13 20 CENTS
5.3000 g., 0.8200 Silver .1397 oz. ASW **Ruler:** Kuang-hsü **Obv:** Initials "SY" **Obv. Legend:** Chiang-nan Sheng Tsao **Obv. Inscription:** Kuang-hsü Yüan-pao

Date	Mintage	VG	F	VF	XF	Unc
CD1905	Inc. above	4.00	12.50	25.00	40.00	110

Y# 143a.14 20 CENTS
5.3000 g., 0.8200 Silver .1397 oz. ASW **Ruler:** Kuang-hsü **Obv. Legend:** Chiang-nan Sheng Tsao **Obv. Inscription:** Kuang-hsü Yüan-pao **Rev. Legend:** ...MACI...

Date	Mintage	VG	F	VF	XF	Unc
CD1901	Inc. above	3.50	6.50	12.50	30.00	75.00

Y# 147 20 CENTS
5.3000 g., 0.8200 Silver .1397 oz. ASW **Ruler:** Hsüan-T'ung **Obv. Legend:** Chiang-nan Sheng Tsao **Obv. Inscription:** Hsüan-T'ung Yüan-pao **Rev:** Dragon

Date	Mintage	VG	F	VF	XF	Unc
ND(1911)	2,320,000	10.00	25.00	50.00	100	175

Note: Includes 2,005,000 pieces struck in debased silver in 1916

Y# 145a.5 DOLLAR
26.7000 g., 0.9000 Silver **Ruler:** Kuang-hsü **Obv:** Without initials **Obv. Legend:** Chiang-nan Sheng Tsao **Obv. Inscription:** Kuang-hsü Yüan-pao **Note:** Kann#86.

Date	Mintage	VG	F	VF	XF	Unc
CD1901	2,377,000	75.00	225	300	450	1,850

Y# 145a.6 DOLLAR
26.7000 g., 0.9000 Silver **Ruler:** Kuang-hsü **Obv:** Bold initials"HAH" without rosette **Obv. Legend:** Chiang-nan Sheng Tsao **Obv. Inscription:** Kuang-hsü Yüan-pao **Rev:** Petals of rosettes separated from each other

Date	Mintage	VG	F	VF	XF	Unc
CD1901	Inc. above	32.00	95.00	185	300	750

Y# 145a.7 DOLLAR
26.7000 g., 0.9000 Silver **Ruler:** Kuang-hsü **Obv:** Initials "HAH" and rosette **Obv. Legend:** Chiang-nan Sheng Tsao **Obv. Inscription:** Kuang-hsü Yüan-pao **Rev:** Petals of rosettes run together

Date	Mintage	VG	F	VF	XF	Unc
CD1901	Inc. above	15.00	30.00	50.00	125	450

Y# 145a.8 DOLLAR
25.7000 g., 0.9000 Silver **Ruler:** Kuang-hsü **Obv:** Small date, small "HAH" **Obv. Legend:** Chiang-nan Sheng Tsao **Obv. Inscription:** Kuang-hsü Yüan-pao **Rev:** Similar to Y#145a.4 **Note:** Kann#94.

Date	Mintage	VG	F	VF	XF	Unc
CD1902	3,562,000	15.00	35.00	75.00	150	500

Y# 145a.9 DOLLAR
27.0000 g., 0.9000 Silver **Ruler:** Kuang-hsü **Obv:** Larger date, larger "HAH" **Obv. Legend:** Chiang-nan Sheng Tsao **Obv. Inscription:** Kuang-hsü Yüan-pao

Date	Mintage	VG	F	VF	XF	Unc
CD1902	Inc. above	15.00	35.00	75.00	150	500

Y# 145a.10 DOLLAR
26.9000 g., 0.9000 Silver **Ruler:** Kuang-hsü **Obv:** "HAH" and rosettes in outer ring **Obv. Legend:** Chiang-nan Sheng Tsao **Obv. Inscription:** Kuang-hsü Yüan-pao **Note:** Kann#96.

Date	Mintage	VG	F	VF	XF	Unc
CD1903	1,489,000	20.00	60.00	125	275	700

Y# 145a.11 DOLLAR
27.0000 g., 0.9000 Silver **Ruler:** Kuang-hsü **Obv:** Without rosette in outer ring **Obv. Legend:** Chiang-nan Sheng Tsao **Obv. Inscription:** Kuang-hsü Yüan-pao **Note:** Kann#96c.

Date	Mintage	VG	F	VF	XF	Unc
CD1903	Inc. above	250	700	1,000	1,500	3,500

Y# 145a.12 DOLLAR
26.7000 g., 0.9000 Silver **Ruler:** Kuang-hsü **Obv:** Initials "HAH" and "CH" without dots or rosettes **Obv. Legend:** Chiang-nan Sheng Tsao **Obv. Inscription:** Kuang-hsü Yüan-pao **Rev:** Similar to Y#145a.4 **Note:** Kann#99.

Date	Mintage	VG	F	VF	XF	Unc
CD1904	44,725,000	15.00	25.00	40.00	60.00	300

Y# 145a.13 DOLLAR
27.0000 g., 0.9000 Silver **Ruler:** Kuang-hsü **Obv:** Dot at either side **Obv. Legend:** Chiang-nan Sheng Tsao **Obv. Inscription:** Kuang-hsü Yüan-pao

Date	Mintage	VG	F	VF	XF	Unc
CD1904	Inc. above	15.00	25.00	40.00	60.00	300

Y# 145a.14 DOLLAR
27.0000 g., 0.9000 Silver **Ruler:** Kuang-hsü **Obv. Inscription:** Kuang-hsü Yüan-pao **Rev:** Dot to left of numeral 7

Date	Mintage	VG	F	VF	XF	Unc
CD1904	Inc. above	15.00	25.00	40.00	60.00	250

Y# 145a.15 DOLLAR
27.0000 g., 0.9000 Silver **Ruler:** Kuang-hsü **Obv:** Four-petalled rosette at either side "HAH" and "CH" **Obv. Legend:** Chiang-nan Sheng Tsao **Obv. Inscription:** Kuang-hsü Yüan-pao

Date	Mintage	VG	F	VF	XF	Unc
CD1904	Inc. above	25.00	75.00	200	325	750

Y# 145a.16 DOLLAR
27.0000 g., 0.9000 Silver **Ruler:** Kuang-hsü **Obv:** Initials "HAH" and "TH" **Obv. Legend:** Chiang-nan Sheng Tsao **Obv. Inscription:** Kuang-hsü Yüan-pao

Date	Mintage	VG	F	VF	XF	Unc
CD1904	Inc. above	25.00	75.00	250	375	850

Y# 145a.17 DOLLAR
27.1000 g., 0.9000 Silver **Ruler:** Kuang-hsü **Obv:** Initials "SY" **Obv. Legend:** Chiang-nan Sheng Tsao **Obv. Inscription:** Kuang-hsü Yüan-pao **Rev:** Similar to Y#145a.10

Date	Mintage	VG	F	VF	XF	Unc
CD1905	634,000	25.00	55.00	110	325	1,000

Y# 145a.19 DOLLAR
27.0000 g., 0.9000 Silver **Ruler:** Kuang-hsü **Obv:** Dot at either side, without four central characters **Obv. Legend:** Chiang-nan Sheng Tsao **Obv. Inscription:** Kuang-hsü Yüan-pao

Date	Mintage	VG	F	VF	XF	Unc
CD1904	—	—	—	—	—	—

Y# 145a.21 DOLLAR
26.7000 g., 0.9000 Silver **Ruler:** Kuang-hsü **Obv:** Fine initials"HAH" without rosette **Obv. Legend:** Chiang-nan Sheng Tsao **Obv. Inscription:** Kuang-hsü Yüan-pao **Rev:** Similar to Y#145a.6 **Note:** Kann#90.

Date	Mintage	VG	F	VF	XF	Unc
CD1901	Inc. above	32.00	95.00	185	300	750

Y# 145a.22 DOLLAR
26.7000 g., 0.9000 Silver **Ruler:** Kuang-hsü **Obv:** Cross of six dots at upper right **Obv. Legend:** Chiang-nan Sheng Tsao **Obv. Inscription:** Kuang-hsü Yüan-pao **Rev:** Similar to Y#145a.6 **Note:** Kann#90b.

Date	Mintage	VG	F	VF	XF	Unc
CD1901	Inc. above	50.00	150	300	550	1,500

PATTERNS

Including off metal strikes

KM#	Date	Mintage	Identification	Mkt Val
Pn5	CD1906	—	2 Cash. Copper. Y#8k	2,000
Pn6	CD1906	—	20 Cash. Copper. Y#11k	—

KIANGSI PROVINCE

Jiangxi, Kiangsee

A province located in southeastern China. Mostly hilly with some mountains on the borders that produce coal and tungsten. Some of China's finest porcelain comes from this province. Kiangsi was visited by Marco Polo. A mint was opened in Nanchang in 1729, closed in 1733, reopened in 1736 and operated with reasonable continuity from that time. Modern machinery was introduced in 1901 although it only produced copper coins. The mint closed amidst internal problems in the 1920's.

EMPIRE

MILLED COINAGE

Horizontal rosette

Vertical rosette

Many Kiangsi (Jiangxi) coins have a six-petalled rosette in the center of the obverse, arranged so that two sides of the rosette are formed by two petals in line with each other. The remaining two sides have a single petal, standing out from the rest. The direction that these single petals point, determines whether the rosette is horizontal or vertical. A horizontal rosette has the single petals pointing left and right, while the single petals of the vertical rosette point up and down.

Y# 149 10 CASH
Copper **Ruler:** Kuang-hsü **Obv:** Vertical rosette at center **Obv. Legend:** Chiang-hsi Sheng Tsao **Obv. Inscription:** Kuang-hsü Yüan-pao **Rev:** Province name spelled "KIANG-SEE"

Date	Mintage	VG	F	VF	XF	Unc
ND(c. 1902)	—	5.00	10.00	15.00	30.00	—

Y# 149.1 10 CASH
Copper **Ruler:** Kuang-hsü **Obv:** Horizontal rosette at center **Obv. Legend:** Chiang-hsi Sheng Tsao **Obv. Inscription:** Kuang-hsü Yüan-pao

Date	Mintage	VG	F	VF	XF	Unc
ND(c.1902)	—	5.00	10.00	15.00	30.00	—

Y# 149.2 10 CASH
Copper **Ruler:** Kuang-hsü **Obv:** Different Manchu word at right **Obv Legend:** Chiang-hsi Sheng Tsao **Obv. Inscription:** Kuang-hsü Yüan-pao **Rev:** Circled dragon **Note:** May be a pattern.

Date	Mintage	VG	F	VF	XF	Unc
ND(c 1902) Rare	—	—	—	—	—	—

Y# 150 10 CASH
Copper **Ruler:** Kuang-hsü **Obv:** Manchu "Pao Yuan" at 3 and 9 o'clock **Obv. Legend:** Chiang-hsi Sheng Tsao **Obv. Inscription:** Kuang-hsü Yüan-pao **Rev:** Province name spelled "KIANG-SI", 2 stars at either side of dragon

Date	Mintage	VG	F	VF	XF	Unc
ND(c.1902)	—	2.00	6.00	11.00	17.50	35.00

Y# 150.1 10 CASH
Copper **Ruler:** Kuang-hsü **Obv:** Manchu "Pao Ch'ang" at center and Chinese reading "Ku P'ing" at 3 and 9 o'clock **Obv. Legend:** Chiang-hsi Sheng Tsao **Obv. Inscription:** Kuang-hsü Yüan-pao

Date	Mintage	VG	F	VF	XF	Unc
ND(c.1902)	—	1.00	3.00	6.00	12.00	25.00

Y# 150.2 10 CASH
Copper **Ruler:** Kuang-hsü **Obv:** Manchu "Pao Ch'ang" at 3 and 9 o'clock, horizontal rosette in center **Obv. Legend:** Chiang-hsi Sheng Tsao **Obv. Inscription:** Kuang-hsü Yüan-pao

Date	Mintage	VG	F	VF	XF	Unc
ND(c.1902)	—	0.35	1.00	2.00	5.00	20.00

Y# 150.2a 10 CASH
Brass **Ruler:** Kuang-hsü **Obv. Legend:** Chiang-hsi Sheng Tsao **Obv. Inscription:** Kuang-hsü Yüan-pao

Date	Mintage	VG	F	VF	XF	Unc
ND(c.1902)	—	1.75	5.00	10.00	20.00	40.00

Y# 150.3 10 CASH
Copper **Ruler:** Kuang-hsü **Obv:** Vertical rosette in center **Obv. Legend:** Chiang-hsi Sheng Tsao **Obv. Inscription:** Kuang-hsü Yüan-pao

Date	Mintage	VG	F	VF	XF	Unc
ND(c.1902)	—	0.35	1.00	2.00	5.00	20.00

Y# 150.4 10 CASH
Copper **Ruler:** Kuang-hsü **Obv:** Horizontal rosette **Obv. Legend:** Chiang-hsi Sheng Tsao **Obv. Inscription:** Kuang-hsü Yüan-pao **Rev:** 1 star at either side of dragon, large English lettering

Date	Mintage	VG	F	VF	XF	Unc
ND(c.1902)	—	0.35	1.00	2.00	5.00	20.00

Y# 150.4a 10 CASH
Brass **Ruler:** Kuang-hsü **Obv:** Horizontal rosette **Obv. Legend:** Chiang-hsi Sheng Tsao **Obv. Inscription:** Kuang-hsü Yüan-pao **Rev:** 1 star at either side of dragon, large English lettering

Date	Mintage	VG	F	VF	XF	Unc
ND(c.1902)	—	1.25	5.00	9.00	17.50	35.00

Y# 150.5 10 CASH
Copper **Ruler:** Kuang-hsü **Obv:** Vertical rosette **Obv. Legend:** Chiang-hsi Sheng Tsao **Obv. Inscription:** Kuang-hsü Yüan-pao

Date	Mintage	VG	F	VF	XF	Unc
ND(c.1902)	—	0.35	1.00	2.00	5.00	20.00

Y# 150.6 10 CASH
Copper **Ruler:** Kuang-hsü **Obv. Legend:** Chiang-hsi Sheng Tsao **Obv. Inscription:** Kuang-hsü Yüan-pao **Rev:** Smaller English lettering, 1 star at either side of dragon

Date	Mintage	VG	F	VF	XF	Unc
ND(c.1902)	—	0.35	1.00	2.00	5.00	20.00

Y# 150.7 10 CASH
Copper **Ruler:** Kuang-hsü **Obv:** Small rosette center **Obv. Legend:** Chiang-hsi Sheng Tsao **Obv. Inscription:** Kuang-hsü Yüan-pao **Rev:** 1 star at either side of dragon

Date	Mintage	VG	F	VF	XF	Unc
ND(c.1902)	—	2.00	6.00	11.00	17.50	35.00

Y# 150.8 10 CASH
Copper **Ruler:** Kuang-hsü **Obv. Legend:** Chiang-hsi Sheng Tsao **Obv. Inscription:** Kuang-hsü Yüan-pao **Rev:** 3 stars at either side of dragon

Date	Mintage	VG	F	VF	XF	Unc
ND(c.1902)	—	4.50	12.50	20.00	30.00	60.00

Y# 152 10 CASH
Copper **Ruler:** Kuang-hsü **Obv:** Manchu "Pao Ch'ang" at 3 and 9 o'clock **Obv. Legend:** Chiang-hsi Sheng Tsao **Obv. Inscription:** Kuang-hsü Yüan-pao **Rev:** Province name spelled "KIANG-SI", front view dragon, mountain below pearl

Date	Mintage	VG	F	VF	XF	Unc
ND(c.1902)	—	2.50	4.00	6.00	12.00	—

Y# 152.1 10 CASH
Copper **Ruler:** Kuang-hsü **Obv:** Horizontal rosette in center, Manchu "Pao Ch'ang" at 3 and 9 o'clock **Obv. Legend:** Chiang-hsi Sheng Tsao **Obv. Inscription:** Kuang-hsü Yüan-pao

Date	Mintage	VG	F	VF	XF	Unc
ND(c.1902)	—	2.50	4.00	6.00	12.00	—

Y# 152.2 10 CASH

Copper **Ruler:** Kuang-hsü **Obv:** Horizontal rosette in center, Manchu "Pao Ch'ang" at 3 and 9 o'clock, small character "10" **Obv. Legend:** Chiang-hsi Sheng Tsao **Obv. Inscription:** Kuang-hsü Yüan-pao

Date	Mintage	VG	F	VF	XF	Unc
ND(c.1902)	—	5.00	12.00	17.50	27.50	—

Y# 152.3 10 CASH

Copper **Ruler:** Kuang-hsü **Obv:** Horizontal rosette in center, Manchu "Pao Ch'ang" at 3 and 9 o'clock, large character "10" **Obv. Legend:** Chiang-hsi Sheng Tsao **Obv. Inscription:** Kuang-hsü Yüan-pao **Rev:** Without mountain below dragon

Date	Mintage	VG	F	VF	XF	Unc
ND(c.1902)	—	3.50	8.00	12.00	17.50	—

Y# 152.4 10 CASH

Copper **Ruler:** Kuang-hsü **Obv:** Horizontal rosette in center, small character "10" **Obv. Legend:** Chiang-hsi Sheng Tsao **Obv. Inscription:** Kuang-hsü Yüan-pao

Date	Mintage	VG	F	VF	XF	Unc
ND(c.1902)	—	3.50	8.00	12.00	17.50	—

Y# 152.5 10 CASH

Copper **Ruler:** Kuang-hsü **Obv:** Manchu "Pao Ch'ang" in center, Chinese "K'u P'ing" at 3 and 9 o'clock **Obv. Legend:** Chiang-hsi Sheng Tsao **Obv. Inscription:** Kuang-hsü Yüan-pao **Rev:** Without mountain below pearl, dragon's body repositioned

Date	Mintage	VG	F	VF	XF	Unc
ND(c.1902)	—	3.50	8.50	12.50	17.50	—

Y# 152.6 10 CASH

Copper **Ruler:** Kuang-hsü **Obv. Legend:** Chiang-hsi Sheng Tsao **Obv. Inscription:** Kuang-hsü Yüan-pao **Rev:** Mountain below dragon

Date	Mintage	VG	F	VF	XF	Unc
ND(c.1902)	—	3.25	7.50	11.00	16.00	—

Y# 152.7 10 CASH

Copper **Ruler:** Kuang-hsü **Obv:** Vertical rosette in center **Obv. Legend:** Chiang-hsi Sheng Tsao **Obv. Inscription:** Kuang-hsü Yüan-pao

Date	Mintage	VG	F	VF	XF	Unc
ND(c.1902)	—	—	—	—	—	—

Y# 153 10 CASH

Copper **Ruler:** Kuang-hsü **Obv. Legend:** Chiang-hsi Sheng Tsao **Obv. Inscription:** Kuang-hsü Yüan-pao **Rev:** Legend above front view dragon **Rev. Legend:** KIANG-SEE PROVINCE **Note:** Found with and without a swirl on the pearl below dragon's mouth.

Date	Mintage	VG	F	VF	XF	Unc
ND(c.1902)	—	2.00	4.50	7.00	11.00	—

Y# 153.1 10 CASH

Copper **Ruler:** Kuang-hsü **Obv:** Manchu "Pao Ch'ang" at center and Chinese "K'u P'ing" at 3 and 9 o'clock **Obv. Legend:** Chiang-hsi Sheng Tsao **Obv. Inscription:** Kuang-hsü Yüan-pao **Note:** Found with and without a swirl on the pearl below dragon's mouth.

Date	Mintage	VG	F	VF	XF	Unc
ND(c.1902)	—	0.80	2.00	3.50	7.00	—

Y# 153.2 10 CASH

Copper **Ruler:** Kuang-hsü **Obv:** Small Manchu "Pao Ch'ang" at 3 and 9 o'clock, small horizontal rosette in center **Obv. Legend:** Chiang-hsi Sheng Tsao **Obv. Inscription:** Kuang-hsü Yüan-pao **Note:** Found with and without a swirl on the pearl below dragon's mouth.

Date	Mintage	VG	F	VF	XF	Unc
ND(c. 1902)	—	0.80	2.00	3.50	7.00	—

Y# 153.3 10 CASH

Copper **Ruler:** Kuang-hsü **Obv:** Small vertical rosette in center **Obv. Legend:** Chiang-hsi Sheng Tsao **Obv. Inscription:** Kuang-hsü Yüan-pao **Note:** Found with and without a swirl on the pearl below dragon's mouth.

Date	Mintage	VG	F	VF	XF	Unc
ND(c.1902)	—	2.00	5.00	10.00	17.50	—

Y# 154 10 CASH

Copper **Ruler:** Kuang-hsü **Obv. Legend:** Chiang-hsi Sheng Tsao **Obv. Inscription:** Kuang-hsü Yüan-pao **Rev:** Legend above flying dragon **Rev. Legend:** KIANG SI

Date	Mintage	VG	F	VF	XF	Unc
ND(c.1902)	—	40.00	60.00	80.00	100	—

Y# 10m 10 CASH

Copper **Ruler:** Kuang-hsü **Obv. Inscription:** Tai-ch'ing T'ung-pi **Rev:** Dragon's eyes in relief **Rev. Legend:** Kuang-hsü Nien-tsao, TAI-CHING-TI-KUO ...

Date	Mintage	VG	F	VF	XF	Unc
CD1906	—	1.25	3.00	6.00	12.00	—

Y# 10m.1 10 CASH

Copper **Ruler:** Kuang-hsü **Obv. Inscription:** Tai-ch'ing T'ung-pi **Rev:** Dragon's eyes incuse **Rev. Legend:** Kuang-hsü Nien-tsao, TAI-CHING-TI-KUO ...

Date	Mintage	VG	F	VF	XF	Unc
CD1906	—	1.25	3.00	6.00	12.00	—

Y# 10m.2 10 CASH

Copper **Ruler:** Kuang-hsü **Obv. Inscription:** Tai-ch'ing T'ung-pi **Rev:** Dragon redesigned, small faint cloud beneath pearl **Rev. Legend:** Kuang-hsü Nien-tsao, TAI-CHING-TI-KUO ...

Date	Mintage	VG	F	VF	XF	Unc
CD1906	—	5.00	12.00	17.50	30.00	—

REPUBLIC

MILLED COINAGE

Horizontal rosette

Vertical rosette

Many Kiangsi (Jiangxi) coins have a six-petalled rosette in the center of the obverse, arranged so that two sides of the rosette are formed by two petals in line with each other. The remaining two sides have a single petal, standing out from the rest. The direction that these single petals point, determines whether the rosette is horizontal or vertical. A horizontal rosette has the single petals pointing left and right, while the single petals of the vertical rosette point up and down.

Y# 412 10 CASH

Copper **Obv:** Date appears at 3 and 9 o'clock, value in 5 characters in legend **Obv. Legend:** Chiang-hsi Sheng-tsao **Rev:** 9-pointed star inside circle and 5-petalled rosette at 3 and 9 o'clock, value in 5 characters below

Date	Mintage	VG	F	VF	XF	Unc
CD1912	—	200	300	450	650	—

Y# 412a 10 CASH

Copper **Obv:** Horizontal rosette in center with Chinese characters "Chiang Hsi" above and below; Value in 2 characters in legend **Obv. Legend:** Chung Hua Min Kuo **Rev:** 6-petalled rosette at either side, value in 2 characters below

Date	Mintage	VG	F	VF	XF	Unc
CD1912	—	1.25	3.00	5.00	9.00	—

Y# 412a.1 10 CASH
Copper **Obv:** Small, vertical rosette in center **Obv. Legend:** Chung Hua Min Kuo

Date	Mintage	VG	F	VF	XF	Unc
CD1912	—	1.25	3.00	5.00	9.00	—

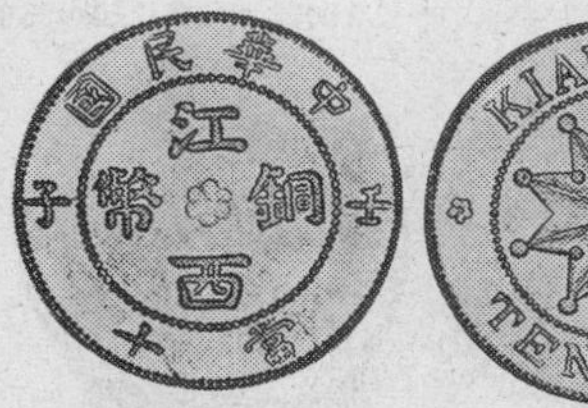

Y# 412a.2 10 CASH
Copper **Obv:** Large, vertical rosette in center; thick, large-center characters **Obv. Legend:** Chung Hua Min Kuo **Rev:** Small, 5-petalled rosettes at either side

Date	Mintage	VG	F	VF	XF	Unc
CD1912	—	6.00	12.00	17.50	27.50	—

Y# 412a.3 10 CASH
Copper **Obv:** Large, vertical rosette in center; thin-center characters **Obv. Legend:** Chung Hua Min Kuo

Date	Mintage	VG	F	VF	XF	Unc
CD1912	—	1.25	3.00	5.00	10.00	—

REBEL COINAGE

"Ta Han" was a rebel issue made before the revolution. Not only a symbol of defiance, this coin indicated secret membership. Ching law subjected those carrying these coins to execution.

Y# 411 10 CASH
Copper **Obv:** Mint mark incused on raised-disc center with Chinese characters on 4 sides, "Ta-Han T'ung-pi" character value in outer ring at bottom **Rev:** Ring of 9 balls without inscription

Date	Mintage	VG	F	VF	XF	Unc
CD1911 Rare	—	—	—	—	—	—

KIANGSU-CHINGKIANG PROVINCE

MILLED COINAGE

Y# 77 10 CASH
Copper **Ruler:** Kuang-hsü **Obv:** Large character at 3 o'clock **Obv. Inscription:** Kuang-hsü Yüan-pao **Rev. Legend:** * CHING * KIANG **Edge:** Reeded

Date	Mintage	VG	F	VF	XF	Unc
ND(1905)	—	0.85	2.50	4.00	7.50	25.00

Y# 77.1 10 CASH
Copper **Ruler:** Kuang-hsü **Obv:** Large character at 3 o'clock **Obv. Inscription:** Kuang-hsü Yüan-pao **Rev. Legend:** * CHING * KIANG **Edge:** Plain

Date	Mintage	VG	F	VF	XF	Unc
ND(1905)	—	0.85	2.50	4.00	7.50	25.00

Y# 77.2 (KM77.2) 10 CASH
Copper **Ruler:** Kuang-hsü **Obv:** Ring around center dot in rosette **Obv. Inscription:** Kuang-hsü Yüan-pao **Rev. Legend:** * CHING * KIANG **Edge:** Reeded

Date	Mintage	VG	F	VF	XF	Unc
ND(1905)	—	1.00	3.00	5.00	10.00	30.00
ND(1905)	—	1.00	3.00	5.00	10.00	30.00

Y# 77.3 10 CASH
Copper **Ruler:** Kuang-hsü **Obv:** Ring around center dot in rosette **Obv. Inscription:** Kuang-hsü Yüan-pao **Rev. Legend:** * CHING * KIANG **Edge:** Plain

Date	Mintage	VG	F	VF	XF	Unc
ND(1905)	—	3.00	9.00	12.00	15.00	35.00

Y# 77.4 10 CASH
Copper **Ruler:** Kuang-hsü **Obv:** Smaller character at 3 o'clock **Obv. Inscription:** Kuang-hsü Yüan-pao **Rev. Legend:** * CHING * KIANG **Edge:** Reeded

Date	Mintage	VG	F	VF	XF	Unc
ND(1905)	—	1.25	3.50	6.00	12.00	32.00

Y# 77.5 10 CASH
Copper **Ruler:** Kuang-hsü **Obv:** Smaller character at 3 o'clock **Obv. Inscription:** Kuang-hsü Yüan-pao **Rev. Legend:** * Ching * Kiang **Edge:** Plain

Date	Mintage	VG	F	VF	XF	Unc
ND(1905)	—	1.25	3.50	6.00	12.00	32.00

Y# 77.6 10 CASH
Copper **Ruler:** Kuang-hsü **Obv:** Without rosette **Obv. Inscription:** Kuang-hsü Yüan-pao **Rev. Legend:** * CHING * KIANG **Edge:** Reeded

Date	Mintage	VG	F	VF	XF	Unc
ND(1905)	—	1.00	3.00	5.00	10.00	30.00

Y# 77.7 10 CASH
Copper **Ruler:** Kuang-hsü **Obv:** Without rosette **Obv. Inscription:** YJuang-hsü Yüan-pao **Rev. Legend:** * CHING * KIANG **Edge:** Plain

Date	Mintage	VG	F	VF	XF	Unc
ND(1905)	—	2.75	8.00	10.00	15.00	35.00

Y# 78 10 CASH
Copper **Ruler:** Kuang-hsü **Obv:** Large character at 3 o'clock **Obv. Inscription:** Kuang-hsü Yüan-pao **Rev. Legend:** TSING-KIANG **Edge:** Reeded

Date	Mintage	VG	F	VF	XF	Unc
ND(1905)	—	0.50	1.50	3.00	5.00	20.00

Y# 78.1 10 CASH
Copper **Ruler:** Kuang-hsü **Obv:** Large character at 3 o'clock **Obv. Inscription:** Kuang-hsü Yüan-pao **Rev. Legend:** TSING-KIANG **Edge:** Plain

Date	Mintage	VG	F	VF	XF	Unc
ND(1905)	—	1.00	3.00	5.00	10.00	30.00

Y# 78.2 10 CASH
Copper **Ruler:** Kuang-hsü **Obv:** Small character at 3 o'clock **Obv. Inscription:** Kuang-hsü Yüan-pao **Rev. Legend:** TSING-KIANG **Edge:** Reeded

Date	Mintage	VG	F	VF	XF	Unc
ND(1905)	—	0.35	1.00	2.00	5.00	20.00

Y# 78.3 10 CASH
Copper **Ruler:** Kuang-hsü **Obv:** Small character at 3 o'clock **Obv. Inscription:** Kuang-hsü Yüan-pao **Rev. Legend:** TSING-KIANG **Edge:** Plain

Date	Mintage	VG	F	VF	XF	Unc
ND(1905)	—	0.35	1.00	2.00	5.00	20.00

Y# 78.4 10 CASH
Copper **Ruler:** Kuang-hsü **Obv:** Without rosette **Obv. Inscription:** Kuang-hsü Yüan-pao **Rev. Legend:** TSING-KIANG **Edge:** Reeded

Date	Mintage	VG	F	VF	XF	Unc
ND(1905)	—	1.25	3.50	6.00	15.00	35.00

Y# 10d 10 CASH
Copper **Ruler:** Kuang-hsü **Obv:** Small mint mark in center, without center raised disc **Obv. Inscription:** Tai-ch'ing T'ung-pi **Rev:** 5 flames on pearl **Rev. Legend:** Kuang-hsü Nien-tsao, TAI-CHING TI-KUO

Date	Mintage	VG	F	VF	XF	Unc
CD1906	—	8.50	25.00	50.00	100	—

Y# 10d.1 10 CASH
Copper **Ruler:** Kuang-hsü **Obv:** Small mint mark **Obv. Inscription:** Tai-ch'ing T'ung-pi **Rev:** 7 flames on pearl **Rev. Legend:** Kuang-hsü Nien-tsao, TAI-CHING-TI-KUO

Date	Mintage	VG	F	VF	XF	Unc
CD1906	—	0.50	1.50	2.50	5.00	20.00

Y# 10d.2 10 CASH
Copper **Ruler:** Kuang-hsü **Obv. Inscription:** Tai-ch'ing T'ung-pi **Rev:** 9 flames on pearl **Rev. Legend:** Kuang-hsü Nien-tsao, TAI-CHING - TI-KUO

Date	Mintage	VG	F	VF	XF	Unc
CD1906	—	0.35	1.00	2.00	5.00	20.00

Y# 10d.3 10 CASH
Copper **Ruler:** Kuang-hsü **Obv:** Large mint mark **Obv. Inscription:** Tai-ch'ing T'ung-pi **Rev:** 5 flames on pearl **Rev. Legend:** Kuang-hsü Nien-tsao, TAI-CHING TI-KUO

Date	Mintage	VG	F	VF	XF	Unc
CD1906	—	0.50	1.50	2.50	5.00	20.00

Y# 10d.4 10 CASH
Copper **Ruler:** Kuang-hsü **Obv. Inscription:** Tai-ch'ing T'ung-pi **Rev:** 7 flames on pearl **Rev. Legend:** Kuang-hsü Nien-tsao, TAI-CHING TI-KUO

Date	Mintage	VG	F	VF	XF	Unc
CD1906	—	0.50	1.50	2.50	5.00	20.00

Y# 10d.5 10 CASH

Copper **Ruler:** Kuang-hsü **Obv. Inscription:** Tai-ch'ing T'ung-pi **Rev:** 9 flames on pearl **Rev. Legend:** Kuang-hsü Nien-tsao, TAI-CHING TI-KUO

Date	Mintage	VG	F	VF	XF	Unc
CD1906	—	0.50	1.50	2.50	5.00	20.00

Y# 10d.6 10 CASH

Copper **Ruler:** Kuang-hsü **Obv:** Mint mark incused on raised disc **Obv. Inscription:** Tai-ch'ing T'ung-pi **Rev. Legend:** Kuang-hsü Nien-tsao, TAI-CHING TI-KUO... **Note:** Trial piece.

Date	Mintage	VG	F	VF	XF	Unc
CD1906	—	—	—	—	—	—

Note: 10 cash coins of Kiangsu (Jiangsu) and Chingkiang are often found plated with a silvery material. This was not done at the mint. Apparently they were plated so they could be passed to the unwary as silver coins.

KIANGSU-KIANGSOO PROVINCE

Jiangsu

A province located on the east coast of China. One of the smallest and most densely populated of all Chinese provinces. A mint opened in Soochow in 1667, but closed shortly after in 1670. A new mint opened in 1734 for producing cast coins and had continuous operation until about 1870. Modern equipment was introduced in 1898 and a second mint was opened in 1904. Both mints closed down production in 1906. Taels were produced in Shanghai by local silversmiths as early as 1856. These saw limited circulation in the immediate area.

EMPIRE

PROVINCIAL CAST COINAGE

C# 16-12 CASH

Cast Brass **Ruler:** Kuang-hsü **Obv. Inscription:** Kuang-hsü T'ung-pao **Rev:** Manchu inscription **Rev. Inscription:** Boo-su

Date	Mintage	Good	VG	F	VF	XF
ND(1875-1908)	—	2.25	4.50	8.00	13.00	—

C# 16-12.1 CASH

Cast Brass **Ruler:** Kuang-hsü **Obv. Inscription:** Kuang-hsü T'ung-pao **Rev:** Manchu inscription, circle above **Rev. Inscription:** Boo-su

Date	Mintage	Good	VG	F	VF	XF
ND(1875-1908)	—	3.00	6.00	10.00	16.00	—

C# 16-12.2 CASH

Cast Brass **Ruler:** Kuang-hsü **Obv. Inscription:** Kuang-hsü T'ung-pao **Rev:** Manchu inscription, crescent above **Rev. Inscription:** Boo-su

Date	Mintage	Good	VG	F	VF	XF
ND(1875-1908)	—	3.00	6.00	10.00	16.00	—

MILLED COINAGE

Y# 158 5 CASH

Copper **Ruler:** Kuang-hsü **Obv. Legend:** Chiang-hsü Sheng Tsao **Obv. Inscription:** Kuang-hsü Yüan-pao **Rev:** Side view dragon, "EIVE" for "FIVE"

Date	Mintage	VG	F	VF	XF	Unc
ND(1901)	—	12.00	32.50	55.00	100	—

Y# 9n 5 CASH

Brass **Ruler:** Kuang-hsü **Obv. Inscription:** Tai-ching T'ung-pi **Rev. Legend:** Kuang-hsü Nien-tsao, TAI-CHING-TI-KUO ...

Date	Mintage	VG	F	VF	XF	Unc
CD(1906)	—	25.00	75.00	125	200	—

Y# 162 10 CASH

Brass **Ruler:** Kuang-hsü **Obv:** Manchu words at center, without rosettes **Obv. Inscription:** Kuang-hsü Yüan-pao **Edge:** Reeded

Date	Mintage	VG	F	VF	XF	Unc
ND(c.1902)	—	1.25	3.75	6.00	12.00	32.00

Y# 162.1 10 CASH

Brass **Ruler:** Kuang-hsü **Obv:** Manchu in center, rosettes at 2 and 10 o'clock **Obv. Legend:** Chiang-hsü Sheng Tsao **Obv. Inscription:** Kuang-hsü Yüan-pao

Date	Mintage	VG	F	VF	XF	Unc
ND(c.1902)	—	0.35	1.00	2.00	5.00	20.00

Y# 162.2 10 CASH

Brass **Ruler:** Kuang-hsü **Obv. Legend:** Chiang-hsü Sheng Tsao **Obv. Inscription:** Kuang-hsü Yüan-pao **Edge:** Plain

Date	Mintage	VG	F	VF	XF	Unc
ND(c.1902)	—	0.35	1.00	2.00	5.00	20.00

Y# 162.3 10 CASH

Brass **Ruler:** Kuang-hsü **Obv:** Tiny rosettes **Obv. Legend:** Chiang-hsü Sheng Tsao **Obv. Inscription:** Kuang-hsü Yüan-pao **Rev:** Tiny rosettes **Edge:** Reeded

Date	Mintage	VG	F	VF	XF	Unc
ND(c.1902)	—	0.45	1.25	2.50	5.00	20.00

Y# 162.4 10 CASH

Brass **Ruler:** Kuang-hsü **Obv:** Rosette center, Manchu at 3 and 9 o'clock **Obv. Legend:** Chiang-hsü Sheng Tsao **Obv. Inscription:** Kuang-hsü Yüan-pao

Date	Mintage	VG	F	VF	XF	Unc
ND(c.1902)	—	0.35	1.00	2.00	5.00	20.00

Y# 162.5 10 CASH

Brass **Ruler:** Kuang-hsü **Obv. Legend:** Chiang-hsü Sheng Tsao **Obv. Inscription:** Kuang-hsü Yüan-pao **Edge:** Plain

Date	Mintage	VG	F	VF	XF	Unc
ND(c.1902)	—	0.35	1.00	2.00	5.00	20.00

Y# 162.6 10 CASH

Brass **Ruler:** Kuang-hsü **Obv:** Rosette center, large Manchu at 3 and 9 o'clock, higher than on Y#162.4 **Obv. Legend:** Chiang-hsü Sheng Tsao **Obv. Inscription:** Kuang-hsü Yüan-pao **Edge:** Reeded

Date	Mintage	VG	F	VF	XF	Unc
ND(c.1902)	—	0.50	1.50	2.50	5.00	20.00

Y# 162.7 10 CASH

Copper **Ruler:** Kuang-hsü **Obv. Legend:** Chiang-hsü Sheng Tsao **Obv. Inscription:** Kuang-hsü Yüan-pao **Edge:** Plain

Date	Mintage	VG	F	VF	XF	Unc
ND(c.1902)	—	0.50	1.50	2.50	5.00	25.00

Y# 162.7a 10 CASH

Brass **Ruler:** Kuang-hsü **Obv. Legend:** Chiang-hsü Sheng Tsao **Obv. Inscription:** Kuang-hsü Yüan-pao

Date	Mintage	VG	F	VF	XF	Unc
ND(c.1902) Rare	—	—	—	—	—	—

Y# 162.8 10 CASH

Copper **Ruler:** Kuang-hsü **Obv:** Manchu "Boo-su" at center **Obv. Legend:** Chiang-hsü Sheng Tsao **Obv. Inscription:** Kuang-hsü Yüan-pao **Edge:** Reeded

Date	Mintage	VG	F	VF	XF	Unc
CD(1902)	—	0.65	2.00	4.00	7.50	25.00

Y# 162.9 10 CASH

Copper **Ruler:** Kuang-hsü **Obv:** Manchu "Boo-su" at center **Obv. Legend:** Chiang-hsü Sheng Tsao **Obv. Inscription:** Kuang-hsü Yüan-pao **Edge:** Reeded

Date	Mintage	VG	F	VF	XF	Unc
CD(1903)	—	1.75	5.00	7.50	12.00	32.00

Y# 162.10 10 CASH

Copper **Ruler:** Kuang-hsü **Obv:** Rosette center, small Manchu "Boo-su" at 3 and 9 o'clock **Obv. Legend:** Chiang-hsü Sheng Tsao **Obv. Inscription:** Kuang-hsü Yüan-pao **Edge:** Plain

Date	Mintage	VG	F	VF	XF	Unc
CD(1905)	—	0.35	1.00	2.00	5.00	20.00

Y# 162.11 10 CASH

Copper **Ruler:** Kuang-hsü **Obv:** Larger Manchu "Boo-su" **Obv. Legend:** Chiang-hsü Sheng Tsao **Obv. Inscription:** Kuang-hsü Yüan-pao

Date	Mintage	VG	F	VF	XF	Unc
CD1905	—	0.85	2.50	5.00	8.00	25.00

Y# 162.12 10 CASH

Copper **Ruler:** Kuang-hsü **Obv. Legend:** Chiang-hsü Sheng Tsao **Obv. Inscription:** Kuang-hsü Yüan-pao **Rev:** Kiangsu spelled "KIANG-COO"

Date	Mintage	VG	F	VF	XF	Unc
CD1905	—	100	250	500	750	—

Note: Considered a contemporary counterfeit by some authorities

Y# 162.13 10 CASH

Copper **Ruler:** Kuang-hsü **Obv. Legend:** Chiang-hsü Sheng Tsao **Obv. Inscription:** Kuang-hsü Yüan-pao **Edge:** Plain

Date	Mintage	VG	F	VF	XF	Unc
CD(1902)	—	—	—	—	—	—

Y# A162 10 CASH

Copper **Ruler:** Kuang-hsü **Obv:** Kiangsu Y#162 **Obv. Legend:** Chiang-hsü Sheng Tsao **Obv. Inscription:** Kuang-hsü Yüan-pao **Rev:** Kiangnan Y#135 **Note:** Mule.

Date	Mintage	VG	F	VF	XF	Unc
ND(c.1905)	—	30.00	90.00	150	250	—

Y# B162 10 CASH

Copper **Ruler:** Kuang-hsü **Obv:** Kiangsu Y#162.8 **Obv. Legend:** Chiang-hsü Sheng Tsao **Obv. Inscription:** Kuang-hsü Yüan-pao **Rev:** Kiangnan Y#135 **Note:** Mule.

Date	Mintage	VG	F	VF	XF	Unc
CD(1902)	—	30.00	90.00	150	250	—

Y# C162 10 CASH

Copper **Ruler:** Kuang-hsü **Obv:** Kiangsu Y#162,9 **Obv. Legend:** Chiang-hsü Sheng Tsao **Obv. Inscription:** Kuang-hsü Yüan-pao **Rev:** Kiangnan Y#135 **Note:** Mule.

Date	Mintage	VG	F	VF	XF	Unc
CD(1903)	—	30.00	90.00	150	250	—

Y# 160 10 CASH

Brass **Ruler:** Kuang-hsü **Obv. Legend:** Chiang-hsü Sheng Tsao **Obv. Inscription:** Kuang-hsü Yüan-pao **Rev:** Cloud below all 3 letters of "SOO"

Date	Mintage	VG	F	VF	XF	Unc
ND(1904-05)	—	0.85	2.50	4.00	8.00	24.00

Y# 160.1 10 CASH

Brass **Ruler:** Kuang-hsü **Obv. Legend:** Chiang-hsü Sheng Tsao **Obv. Inscription:** Kuang-hsü Yüan-pao **Rev:** Cloud below first 2 letters of "SOO", Manchu "Boo" at 9 o'clock higher, dragon's body thinner

Date	Mintage	VG	F	VF	XF	Unc
ND(1904-05)	—	0.85	2.50	4.00	8.00	24.00

Y# 10n 10 CASH

Copper **Ruler:** Kuang-hsü **Obv:** Mint mark incused on raised disc **Obv. Inscription:** Tai-ch'ing T'ung-pi **Rev. Legend:** Kuang-hsü Nien-tsao, TAI-CHING-TI-KUO ... **Edge:** Plain

Date	Mintage	VG	F	VF	XF	Unc
CD1906	—	0.85	2.50	5.00	10.00	30.00

Y# 10n.1 10 CASH

Copper **Ruler:** Kuang-hsü **Obv:** Mint mark incused on raised disc **Obv. Inscription:** Tai-ch'ing T'ung-pi **Rev. Legend:** Kuang-hsü Nien-tsao, TAI-CHING-TI-KUO ... **Edge:** Reeded

Date	Mintage	VG	F	VF	XF	Unc
CD1906	—	2.00	6.00	11.00	17.50	40.00

Y# 10n.2 10 CASH

Copper **Ruler:** Kuang-hsü **Obv:** Mint mark in relief in field at center without raised disc **Obv. Inscription:** Tai-ch'ing T'ung-pi **Rev. Legend:** Kuang-hsü Nien-tsao, TAI-CHING-TI-KUO ... **Edge:** Plain

Date	Mintage	VG	F	VF	XF	Unc
CD1906	—	2.00	6.00	11.00	17.50	40.00

Y# 163 20 CASH

Copper **Ruler:** Kuang-hsü **Obv. Legend:** Chiang-hsü Sheng Tsao **Obv. Inscription:** Kuang-hsü Yüan-pao **Rev:** Dragon

Date	Mintage	VG	F	VF	XF	Unc
ND(c.1902)	—	17.50	32.50	45.00	65.00	—

Y# 163a 20 CASH

Brass **Ruler:** Kuang-hsü **Obv. Legend:** Chiang-hsü Sheng Tsao **Obv. Inscription:** Kuang-hsü Yüan-pao **Rev:** Dragon

Date	Mintage	VG	F	VF	XF	Unc
ND(c.1902)	—	30.00	45.00	70.00	110	—

Y# 11n.1 20 CASH

Copper **Ruler:** Kuang-hsü **Obv. Inscription:** Tai-ch'ing T'ung-pi **Rev. Legend:** Kuang-hsü Nien-tsao, TAI-CHING-TI-KUO ...

Date	Mintage	VG	F	VF	XF	Unc
CD1906	—	25.00	40.00	60.00	90.00	—

Y# 11n.1a 20 CASH

Brass **Ruler:** Kuang-hsü **Obv. Inscription:** Tai-ch'ing T'ung-pi **Rev. Legend:** Kuang-hsü Nien-tsao, TAI-CHING-TI-KUO ...

Date	Mintage	VG	F	VF	XF	Unc
CD1906	—	35.00	60.00	90.00	150	—

PATTERNS

Including off metal strikes

KM#	Date	Mintage	Identification	Mkt Val
Pn2	ND(c. 1901)	—	2 Cash. Brass. Y159.	200
Pn3	CD1905	—	2 Cash. Brass. Y8n.	200
Pn4	ND(c. 1906)	—	5 Cash. Brass. EIVE for FIVE. Y161.1.	300
Pn5	ND(c. 1906)	—	5 Cash. Copper. EIVE for FIVE. Y161.1a.	300
Pn6	ND(c. 1906)	—	10 Cash. White Copper. Y162.5, W826.	—
Pn7	CD(1906)	—	20 Cash. Copper. Character "Huai" in center. Y11d.	—

KIRIN PROVINCE

Jilin

A province of northeast China that was formed in 1945. Before that it was one of the three original provinces of Manchuria. Besides growing corn, wheat and tobacco, there is also coal mining. An arsenal in Kirin (Jilin) opened in 1881 and was chosen as a source for coinage attempts. In 1884 Tael trials were struck and regular coinage began in 1895. Modern equipment was installed in a new mint in Kirin (Jilin) in 1901. The issues of this mint were very prolific and many varieties exist due to the use of hand cut dies for the earlier issues. The mint burned down in 1911.

EMPIRE

PROVINCIAL CAST COINAGE

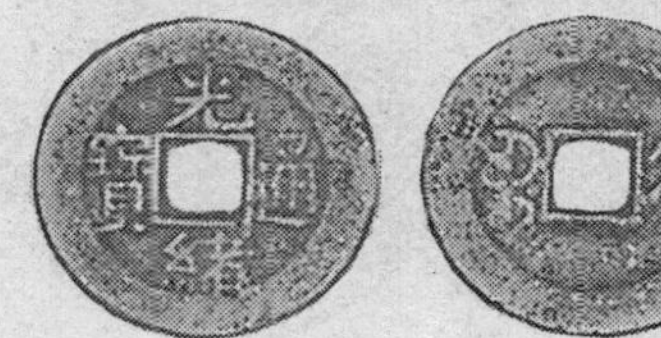

C# 17-1 CASH

Cast Brass **Ruler:** Kuang-hsü **Obv. Inscription:** Kuang-hsü T'ung-pao **Rev:** Manchu inscription **Rev. Inscription:** Boo-gi

Date	Mintage	Good	VG	F	VF	XF
ND(1875-80)	—	15.00	25.00	35.00	50.00	—

Note: This coin is sometimes erroneously attributed to Chi-chou (Chichow) in Chihli (Hebei) province, which used this mint mark in the Hsien-fêng and earlier reigns

MILLED COINAGE

Errors in the English legends are very common in the Kirin coinage. It has been estimated there are over 2500 die varieties of Kirin (Jilin) silver coins and more than 1000 varieties of copper 10 Cash. Listed here are basic types and major varieties only.

Y# 175 2 CASH

Bronze **Ruler:** Kuang-hsü **Obv. Inscription:** Kuang-hsü T'ung-pao **Note:** Mint mark: Manchu "Boo-gi".

Date	Mintage	VG	F	VF	XF	Unc
ND(ca.1905)	—	80.00	120	160	250	—

Y# 174 10 CASH

Bronze **Ruler:** Kuang-hsü **Obv. Inscription:** Kuang-hsü Yüan-pao **Note:** Mint mark: Manchu "Chi".

Date	Mintage	VG	F	VF	XF	Unc
ND(1901) Rare	—	—	—	—	—	—

Y# 176 10 CASH(ES)

Copper **Ruler:** Kuang-hsü **Obv. Legend:** Chi-lin Sheng Tsao **Obv. Inscription:** Kuang-hsü Yüan-pao **Rev:** Dragon

Date	Mintage	VG	F	VF	XF	Unc
ND(ca.1901)	—	35.00	60.00	90.00	125	—

Y# 176.1 10 CASH(ES)

Copper **Ruler:** Kuang-hsü **Obv. Legend:** Chi-lin Sheng Tsao **Obv. Inscription:** Kuang-hsü Yüan-pao **Rev:** Thinner dragon

Date	Mintage	VG	F	VF	XF	Unc
ND(ca.1901)	—	35.00	60.00	90.00	125	—

Y# 177 10 CASH(ES)

Copper **Ruler:** Kuang-hsü **Obv:** Small rosettes **Obv. Legend:** Chi-lin Sheng Tsao **Obv. Inscription:** Kuang-hsü Yüan-pao **Rev:** Dragon; large rosettes

Date	Mintage	VG	F	VF	XF	Unc
ND(ca.1903)	—	5.00	10.00	15.00	25.00	—

Y# 177.1 10 CASH(ES)
Copper **Ruler:** Kuang-hsü **Obv. Legend:** Chi-lin Sheng Tsao **Obv. Inscription:** Kuang-hsü Yüan-pao **Rev:** Dragon; small stars

Date	Mintage	VG	F	VF	XF	Unc
ND(ca.1903)	—	5.00	10.00	15.00	25.00	—

Y# 177.2 10 CASH(ES)
Copper **Ruler:** Kuang-hsü **Obv:** Small stars **Obv. Legend:** Chi-lin Sheng Tsao **Obv. Inscription:** Kuang-hsü Yüan-pao **Rev:** Dragon; large rosettes

Date	Mintage	VG	F	VF	XF	Unc
ND(ca.1903)	—	5.00	10.00	17.50	30.00	—

Y# 177.3 10 CASH(ES)
Copper **Ruler:** Kuang-hsü **Obv:** Small stars **Obv. Legend:** Chi-lin Sheng Tsao **Obv. Inscription:** Kuang-hsü Yüan-pao **Rev:** Dragon; small stars

Date	Mintage	VG	F	VF	XF	Unc
ND(ca.1903)	—	5.00	10.00	15.00	25.00	—

Y# 177.3a 10 CASH(ES)
Brass **Ruler:** Kuang-hsü **Obv. Legend:** Chi-lin Sheng Tsao **Obv. Inscription:** Kuang-hsü Yüan-pao **Rev:** Dragon

Date	Mintage	VG	F	VF	XF	Unc
ND(ca.1903)	—	5.00	10.00	17.50	30.00	—

Y# 177.4 10 CASH(ES)
Brass **Ruler:** Kuang-hsü **Obv:** Large stars **Obv. Legend:** Chi-lin Sheng Tsao **Obv. Inscription:** Kuang-hsü Yüan-pao **Rev:** Dragon; large stars

Date	Mintage	VG	F	VF	XF	Unc
ND(ca.1903)	—	4.00	7.00	12.00	17.50	—

Y# 177.5 10 CASH(ES)
Brass **Ruler:** Kuang-hsü **Obv:** Large stars **Obv. Legend:** Chi-lin Sheng Tsao **Obv. Inscription:** Kuang-hsü Yüan-pao **Rev:** Dragon; large rosettes

Date	Mintage	VG	F	VF	XF	Unc
ND(ca.1903)	—	4.00	7.00	12.00	17.50	—

Y# 177.6 10 CASH(ES)
Brass **Ruler:** Kuang-hsü **Obv:** Medium rosettes **Obv. Legend:** Chi-lin Sheng Tsao **Obv. Inscription:** Kuang-hsü Yüan-pao **Rev:** Dragon

Date	Mintage	VG	F	VF	XF	Unc
ND(ca.1903)	—	4.00	7.00	12.00	17.50	—

Y# 177.7 10 CASH(ES)
Brass **Ruler:** Kuang-hsü **Obv. Legend:** Chi-lin Sheng Tsao **Obv. Inscription:** Kuang-hsü Yüan-pao **Rev:** Dragon; "CASHES" spelled "CASHIS"

Date	Mintage	VG	F	VF	XF	Unc
ND(ca.1903)	—	60.00	100	160	250	—

Note: It is difficult to differentiate the stars and rosettes on worn coins; the rosettes have a raised dot in the center while the stars have a hole in the center; it has been estimated that 1000 varieties of Y#177 exist

Y# 20p 10 CASH(ES)
Copper **Ruler:** Hsüan-t'ung **Obv:** Very small mint mark **Obv. Inscription:** Tai-ch'ing T'ung-pi **Rev. Legend:** Hsüan-t'ung Nien-tsao, TAI-CHING-TI-KUO...

Date	Mintage	VG	F	VF	XF	Unc
CD1909	—	8.00	15.00	25.00	40.00	—

Y# 20p.1 10 CASH(ES)
Copper **Ruler:** Hsüan-t'ung **Obv:** Larger mint mark **Obv. Inscription:** Tai-ch'ing T'ung-pi **Rev:** Head of dragon, redesigned with more whiskers **Rev. Legend:** Hsüan-t'ung Nien-tsao, TAI-CHING-TI-KUO...

Date	Mintage	VG	F	VF	XF	Unc
CD1909	—	10.00	17.50	30.00	45.00	—

Y# 20p.2 10 CASH(ES)
Copper **Ruler:** Hsüan-t'ung **Obv:** Larger mint mark **Obv. Inscription:** Tai-ch'ing T'ung-pi **Rev:** Dragon similar to Y#20p **Rev. Legend:** Hsüan-t'ung Nien-tsao, TAI-CHING-TI-KUO...

Date	Mintage	VG	F	VF	XF	Unc
CD1909	—	10.00	17.50	30.00	45.00	—

Note: For Y#20x refer to General Issues-Empire

Y# 20p.3 10 CASH(ES)
Copper **Ruler:** Hsüan-t'ung **Obv:** Y#20p **Obv. Inscription:** Tai-ch'ing T'ung-pi **Rev:** General Issue - Empire Y#20.1 **Rev. Legend:** Hsüan-t'ung Nien-tsao, TAI-CHING-TI-KUO... **Note:** Mule.

Date	Mintage	VG	F	VF	XF	Unc
CD1909 2 known	—	—	—	—	3,500	—

Note: Though dated 1909, minted at Mukden ca.1922

Y# 178 20 CASH(ES)
Copper **Ruler:** Kuang-hsü **Obv. Legend:** Chi-lin Sheng Tsao **Obv. Inscription:** Kuang-hsü Yüan-pao **Rev:** Dragon

Date	Mintage	VG	F	VF	XF	Unc
ND(1903)	—	35.00	65.00	100	175	—

Y# 178.1 20 CASH(ES)
Copper **Ruler:** Kuang-hsü **Obv. Inscription:** Kuang-hsü Yüan-pao **Rev:** Dragon, "CASHES" spelled "CASHIS"

Date	Mintage	VG	F	VF	XF	Unc
ND(1903)	—	35.00	65.00	100	175	—

Y# A176 20 CASH(ES)
Copper **Ruler:** Kuang-hsü **Obv:** Manchu in center, eight characters below **Obv. Legend:** Chi-lin Sheng Tsao **Obv. Inscription:** Kuang-hsü Yüan-pao **Rev:** Dragon

Date	Mintage	VG	F	VF	XF	Unc
ND(1903)	—	80.00	200	400	700	—

Y# A176.1 20 CASH(ES)
Copper **Ruler:** Kuang-hsü **Obv:** Rosette in center, three characters below **Obv. Legend:** Chi-lin Sheng Tsao **Obv. Inscription:** Kuang-hsü Yüan-pao **Rev:** Dragon

Date	Mintage	VG	F	VF	XF	Unc
ND(1903)	—	80.00	225	425	725	—

Y# 21p 20 CASH(ES)
Copper **Ruler:** Kuang-hsü **Obv. Inscription:** Tai-ch'ing T'ung-pi **Rev:** Dragon **Rev. Legend:** Hsüan-t'ung Nien-tsao, TAI-CHING-TI-KUO...

Date	Mintage	VG	F	VF	XF	Unc
CD1909	—	120	250	450	750	—

Y# B176 50 CASHES
Brass **Ruler:** Kuang-hsü **Obv:** Chi-lin Sheng Tsao **Obv. Inscription:** Kuang-hsü Yüan-pao **Rev:** Side view dragon

Date	Mintage	Good	VG	F	VF	XF
CD1901 3 known	—	—	—	—	—	—

Note: D.K.E. Ching Sale 6-91 VG-F realized $3,410; a similar 20 Cashes and silver 50 Cent have been reported and are believed to be fantasies by some authorities

Y# C176 10 COPPERS
Brass **Ruler:** Kuang-hsü **Obv. Inscription:** Kuang-hsü Yüan-pao **Rev:** Dragon **Note:** Similar to 50 Cashes, Y#B176

Date	Mintage	VG	F	VF	XF	Unc
CD1901	—	—	—	—	—	—

Y# E176 30 CASHES
Brass **Ruler:** Kuang-hsü **Obv. Inscription:** Kuang-hsü Yüan-pao **Rev:** Side view dragon

Date	Mintage	VG	F	VF	XF	Unc
CD1901 Rare	—	—	—	—	—	—

Y# F176 100 CASHES
Brass **Ruler:** Kuang-hsü **Obv. Inscription:** Kuang-hsü Yüan-pao **Rev:** Side view dragon

Date	Mintage	VG	F	VF	XF	Unc
CD1901	—	—	—	—	—	—

Y# 179.1 5 CENTS
1.2700 g., Silver **Ruler:** Kuang-hsü **Obv. Inscription:** Kuang-hsü Yüan-pao **Rev:** Side view dragon; without crosses flanking weight **Note:** Kann #394, 416, 549

Date	Mintage	VG	F	VF	XF	Unc
CD1900	—	3.50	10.00	20.00	30.00	75.00
CD1906	—	2.75	6.50	12.50	30.00	70.00
CD1907	—	3.50	8.00	15.00	30.00	70.00
CD1908 Rare	—	—	—	—	—	—

Y# 179a 5 CENTS
1.2700 g., Silver **Ruler:** Kuang-hsü **Obv:** Yin-yang in center **Obv. Inscription:** Kuang-hsü Yüan-pao **Rev:** Side view dragon **Note:** Kann #444,465, 481, 510, 533.

Date	Mintage	VG	F	VF	XF	Unc
CD1900	—	2.50	7.50	15.00	30.00	60.00
CD1901	—	2.50	5.50	11.50	30.00	60.00
CD1902	—	3.00	6.50	12.50	30.00	70.00
CD1903	—	5.00	12.50	25.00	60.00	120
CD1904	—	4.00	10.00	15.00	40.00	85.00
CD1905	—	3.50	7.50	15.00	35.00	75.00

Y# 180a 10 CENTS
2.5500 g., Silver **Ruler:** Kuang-hsü **Obv:** Yin-yang in center **Obv. Legend:** Chi-lin Sheng Tsao **Obv. Inscription:** Kuang-hsü Yüan-pao **Rev:** Side view dragon **Note:** Kann #440, 464, 484.

Date	Mintage	VG	F	VF	XF	Unc
CD1900	—	2.50	7.50	15.00	30.00	75.00
CD1901	—	2.50	5.50	11.50	25.00	60.00
CD1902	—	3.00	7.50	15.00	35.00	75.00
CD1903	—	4.00	9.00	18.50	40.00	100
CD1904	—	15.00	35.00	60.00	150	400
CD1905	—	3.00	6.50	11.50	25.00	60.00

Y# 180.1 10 CENTS
2.5500 g., Silver **Ruler:** Kuang-hsü **Obv:** Large flower vase center **Obv. Legend:** Chi-lin Sheng Tsao **Obv. Inscription:** Kuang-hsü Yüan-pao **Rev:** Side view dragon; without crosses flanking weight **Note:** Kann #393, 416, 546.

Date	Mintage	VG	F	VF	XF	Unc
CD1906	—	3.00	6.50	12.50	30.00	70.00
CD1907	—	20.00	50.00	100	200	350

Y# 180c 10 CENTS
2.5500 g., Silver **Ruler:** Kuang-hsü **Obv:** Numeral 1 in center **Obv. Legend:** Chi-lin Tsao **Obv. Inscription:** Kuang-hsü Yüan-pao **Rev:** Side view dragon

Date	Mintage	VG	F	VF	XF	Unc
CD1908	—	30.00	80.00	150	225	500

Y# 181a 20 CENTS
5.1000 g., Silver **Ruler:** Kuang-hsü **Obv:** Yin-yang in center **Obv. Legend:** Chi-lin Sheng Tsao **Obv. Inscription:** Kuang-hsü Yüan-pao **Rev:** Side view dragon

Date	Mintage	VG	F	VF	XF	Unc
CD1901	22,508,000	3.50	6.50	15.00	25.00	60.00
CD1902	Inc. above	3.50	6.50	15.00	25.00	60.00
CD1903	Inc. above	3.50	6.50	15.00	25.00	60.00
CD1904	Inc. above	3.50	6.50	15.00	25.00	60.00
CD1905	Inc. above	3.50	6.50	15.00	25.00	60.00

Y# 181 20 CENTS
5.1000 g., Silver **Ruler:** Kuang-hsü **Obv:** Flower vase center **Obv. Legend:** Chi-lin Sheng Tsao **Obv. Inscription:** Kuang-hsü Yüan-pao **Rev:** Side view dragon

Date	Mintage	VG	F	VF	XF	Unc
CD1906	Inc. below	3.50	6.50	12.50	25.00	60.00
CD1907	Inc. below	3.50	6.50	12.50	25.00	60.00
CD1908	Inc. below	30.00	90.00	175	300	500

Y# 181b 20 CENTS
5.1000 g., Silver **Ruler:** Kuang-hsü **Obv:** Manchu words in center **Obv. Legend:** Chi-lin Tsao **Obv. Inscription:** Kuang-hsü Yüan-pao **Rev:** Side view dragon

Date	Mintage	VG	F	VF	XF	Unc
CD1908	Inc. above	17.50	50.00	100	150	275

Y# 181c 20 CENTS
5.1000 g., Silver **Ruler:** Kuang-hsü **Obv:** Numeral 2 center **Obv. Legend:** Chi-lin Tsao **Obv. Inscription:** Kuang-hsü Yüan-pao **Rev:** Side view dragon

Date	Mintage	VG	F	VF	XF	Unc
CD1908	Inc. above	8.50	25.00	50.00	85.00	150

Y# 22 20 CENTS
5.1000 g., Silver **Ruler:** Hsüan-t'ung **Obv:** Mint mark in relief on raised disc at center **Obv. Legend:** Chi-lin Sheng Tsao **Obv. Inscription:** Hsüan-t'ung Yüan-pao **Rev:** Side view dragon

Date	Mintage	VG	F	VF	XF	Unc
ND(1909)	—	12.00	35.00	70.00	125	225

Y# 22.2 20 CENTS
5.1000 g., Silver **Ruler:** Hsüan-t'ung **Obv:** Mint mark in circle at center **Obv. Inscription:** Hsüan-t'ung Yüan-pao **Rev:** Side view dragon

Date	Mintage	VG	F	VF	XF	Unc
ND(1909)	—	12.00	35.00	70.00	125	225

Y# 182a.1 50 CENTS
13.1000 g., Silver **Ruler:** Kuang-hsü **Obv:** Redesigned yin-yang in center **Obv. Legend:** Chi-lin Sheng Tsao **Obv. Inscription:** Kuang-hsü Yüan-pao **Rev:** Side view dragon

Date	Mintage	VG	F	VF	XF	Unc
CD1901	—	8.00	20.00	35.00	60.00	150
CD1902	—	8.00	20.00	35.00	60.00	150
CD1903	—	10.00	25.00	40.00	65.00	165
CD1904	—	8.00	20.00	35.00	60.00	150
CD1905	—	7.00	15.00	30.00	50.00	140

Y# 182b 50 CENTS
13.1000 g., Silver **Ruler:** Kuang-hsü **Obv:** Manchu words in center **Obv. Legend:** Chi-lin Tsao **Obv. Inscription:** Kuang-hsü Yüan-pao **Rev:** Side view dragon

Date	Mintage	VG	F	VF	XF	Unc
CD1908	—	25.00	75.00	150	275	450

Y# 182.3 50 CENTS
13.1000 g., Silver **Ruler:** Kuang-hsü **Obv. Legend:** Chi-lin Sheng Tsao **Obv. Inscription:** Kuang-hsü Yüan-pao **Rev:** Side view dragon

Date	Mintage	VG	F	VF	XF	Unc
CD1906	—	8.00	20.00	35.00	60.00	150
CD1907	—	8.00	20.00	35.00	60.00	150
CD1908	—	20.00	50.00	80.00	125	300

Y# 183.1 DOLLAR
26.1000 g., Silver **Ruler:** Kuang-hsü **Obv:** Large rosettes **Obv. Inscription:** Kuang-hsü Yüan-pao **Rev:** Side view dragon; without rosettes flanking weight

Date	Mintage	VG	F	VF	XF	Unc
ND(ca.1905)	—	375	1,200	2,250	4,000	7,500

Y# 183.2 DOLLAR
26.1000 g., Silver **Ruler:** Kuang-hsü **Obv. Inscription:** Kuang-hsü Yüan-pao **Rev:** Side view dragon **Rev. Legend:** 3.2 CAINDARINS 2 (error)

Date	Mintage	VG	F	VF	XF	Unc
CD1906	—	150	350	500	800	1,750

Y# 183.3 DOLLAR
26.1000 g., Silver **Ruler:** Kuang-hsü **Obv:** Small rosettes **Obv. Inscription:** "Kuang-hsü Yüan-pao" **Rev:** Side view dragon; small rosettes before and after weight "7 CANDARINS 2"

Date	Mintage	VG	F	VF	XF	Unc
ND(ca.1906)	—	75.00	160	250	400	1,000

Y# 183a.1 DOLLAR
26.1000 g., Silver **Ruler:** Kuang-hsü **Obv:** Redesigned Yin-yang in center **Obv. Legend:** Chi-lin Sheng Tsao **Obv. Inscription:** "Kuang-hsü Yüan-pao" **Rev:** Coarse-scaled, beady-eyed dragon

Date	Mintage	VG	F	VF	XF	Unc
CD1901	—	25.00	75.00	160	300	1,100
CD1902	—	25.00	75.00	160	300	1,100

Y# 183a.2 DOLLAR
26.1000 g., Silver **Ruler:** Kuang-hsü **Obv. Legend:** Chi-lin Sheng Tsao **Obv. Inscription:** "Kuang-hsü Yüan-pao" **Rev:** Fine dot-scaled, beady-eyed dragon

Date	Mintage	VG	F	VF	XF	Unc
CD1902	—	20.00	60.00	160	300	1,100
CD1903	—	25.00	75.00	160	300	800
CD1904	—	25.00	75.00	160	275	700
CD1905	—	25.00	75.00	160	275	700

Y# 183a.3 DOLLAR
26.1000 g., Silver **Ruler:** Kuang-hsü **Obv. Legend:** Chi-lin Sheng Tsao **Obv. Inscription:** "Kuang-hsü Yüan-pao" **Rev:** Fine oval-scaled, round-eyed dragon

Date	Mintage	VG	F	VF	XF	Unc
CD1905	—	20.00	50.00	160	275	800

Y# 183.4 DOLLAR
26.1000 g., Silver **Ruler:** Kuang-hsü **Obv:** Small leaves out of left basket **Obv. Legend:** Chi-lin Sheng Tsao **Obv. Inscription:** "Kuang-hsü Yüan-pao" **Rev:** Side view dragon; similar to Y#183.2

Date	Mintage	VG	F	VF	XF	Unc
ND(ca.1906)	—	30.00	90.00	200	300	800

Y# 183 DOLLAR
26.1000 g., Silver **Ruler:** Kuang-hsü **Obv:** Flower vase center **Obv. Legend:** Chi-lin Sheng Tsao **Obv. Inscription:** Kuang-hsü Yüan-pao **Rev:** Side view dragon; small rosettes before and after weight: "7 CANDARINS 2" or "7 CAINDARINS 2"

Date	Mintage	VG	F	VF	XF	Unc
CD1906	—	20.00	60.00	140	300	1,100
CD1907	—	45.00	125	200	400	1,500
CD1908	—	375	1,200	2,000	5,000	8,500

Y# 183b DOLLAR
26.1000 g., Silver **Ruler:** Kuang-hsü **Obv:** Manchu words in center **Obv. Legend:** Chi-lin Tsao **Obv. Inscription:** "Kuang-hsü Yüan-pao" **Rev:** Side view dragon

Date	Mintage	VG	F	VF	XF	Unc
CD1908	—	250	850	2,000	4,250	7,500

Y# 183c DOLLAR
26.1000 g., Silver **Ruler:** Kuang-hsü **Obv:** Numeral 11 in center **Obv. Legend:** Chi-lin Tsao **Obv. Inscription:** "Kuang-hsü Yüan-pao" **Rev:** Side view dragon

Date	Mintage	VG	F	VF	XF	Unc
CD1908	—	275	875	2,150	4,500	8,000

Note: The numeral 11 in center reflects the discount in subsidiary coinage; it took 11 dimes to equal the dollar

PATTERNS

Including off metal strikes

KM#	Date	Mintage	Identification	Mkt Val
Pn10	CD1902	—	50 Cents. Brass. Y#182a.1	—
Pn11	CD1908	—	20 Cents. Zinc. Y#181c	—
Pn12	ND(1909)	—	20 Cents. Silver. K#583, formerly Y#22.1	—

KWANGSI-KWANGSEA

Guangxi

A hilly region in southeast China with many forests. Large amounts of rice are grown adjacent to the many rivers. A mint opened in Kweilin in 1667, closed in 1670, reopened in 1679, closed again in 1681. It reopened in the mid-1700's and was a rather prolific issuer of Cash coins. In 1905 the government allowed modern mints to be established in Kwangsi (Guangxi) at Nanning (1905) and Kweilin (1905). The Nanning Mint began operation in 1919 and closed in 1923. In 1920 a new mint was opened at Wuchow and operated sporadically until 1929. In 1938 part of the Shanghai Central Mint was moved to Kweilin where it operated until at least 1945 and perhaps as late as 1949.

EMPIRE

PROVINCIAL CAST COINAGE

C# 18-9 CASH
Cast Brass **Ruler:** Kuang-hsü **Obv. Inscription:** Kuang-hsü T'ung-pao **Rev:** Manchu inscription **Rev. Inscription:** Boo-gui

Date	Mintage	Good	VG	F	VF	XF
ND(1875-1908)	—	5.50	8.50	13.50	25.00	—

REPUBLIC

MILLED COINAGE

Y# 413 CENT
Brass **Obv. Legend:** KWANG-SEA PROVINCE

Date	Mintage	VG	F	VF	XF	Unc
ND(1919)	—	50.00	150	250	400	—

Y# 413a CENT
Brass **Obv. Legend:** KWANG-SI

Date	Mintage	VG	F	VF	XF	Unc
8(1919)	—	15.00	40.00	75.00	150	—

Y# 347 CENT
Brass **Obv. Legend:** Chung Hua Min Kuo (year) Nien **Rev:** Large "Kuei" mint mark below Pu

Date	Mintage	VG	F	VF	XF	Unc
28(1939) Rare	—	—	—	—	—	—

Y# 347.1 CENT
Brass **Obv. Legend:** Chung Hua Min Kuo (year) Nien **Rev:** Small "Kuei" mint mark below Pu

Date	Mintage	VG	F	VF	XF	Unc
28(1939) Rare	—	—	—	—	—	—

Y# A415 5 CENTS
Copper-Nickel **Obv. Legend:** Chung Hua Min Kuo (year) Nien **Rev:** Large "5" in sprays

Date	Mintage	VG	F	VF	XF	Unc
12(1923)	—	50.00	150	250	400	600

Y# 414 10 CENTS
2.7000 g., Silver **Obv. Legend:** Chung Hua Min Kuo (year) Nien

Date	Mintage	VG	F	VF	XF	Unc
9(1920)	—	25.00	75.00	125	175	300

Y# 415 20 CENTS
5.3000 g., Silver **Obv. Legend:** Chung Hua Min Kuo (year) Nien **Rev. Legend:** KWANG-SEA PROVINCE

Date	Mintage	VG	F	VF	XF	Unc
8(1919)	—	25.00	60.00	85.00	135	200
9(1920)	—	30.00	80.00	125	175	300

Y# 415a 20 CENTS
5.3000 g., Silver **Obv. Legend:** Chung Hua Min Kuo (year) Nien **Rev. Legend:** KWANG-SI PROVINCE

Date	Mintage	VG	F	VF	XF	Unc
8(1919)	—	5.00	10.00	25.00	50.00	125
9(1920)	—	5.00	10.00	25.00	50.00	125
11(1922)	—	5.00	10.00	25.00	50.00	125
12(1923)	—	5.00	10.00	25.00	50.00	125
13(1924)	—	5.00	10.00	25.00	50.00	125
14(1925)	—	5.00	10.00	25.00	50.00	125

Y# 415a.1 20 CENTS
5.3000 g., Silver **Obv:** Character "Kuei" in center instead of dot **Obv. Legend:** Chung Hua Min Kuo (year) Nien

Date	Mintage	VG	F	VF	XF	Unc
13(1924)	—	35.00	80.00	100	150	250

Y# 415b 20 CENTS
5.3000 g., Silver **Obv:** Tiny character "Hsi" on dot center **Obv. Legend:** Chung Hua Min Kuo (year) Nien **Rev:** Wreath added around "20"

Date	Mintage	VG	F	VF	XF	Unc
15(1926)	—	2.00	3.50	6.50	10.00	20.00
15(1926)	—	2.00	3.50	6.50	10.00	20.00
Note: Without HSI						
16(1927)	—	2.00	3.50	6.50	10.00	20.00

Y# 416 20 CENTS

5.3000 g., Silver **Obv. Legend:** Chung Hua Min Kuo (year) Nien **Rev:** Elephant nose rock at Kueilin

Date	Mintage	VG	F	VF	XF	Unc
38(1949)	—	40.00	100	175	250	375

PIEFORTS

KM#	Date	Mintage	Identification	Mkt Val
P1	19(1921)	—	10 Cents. Bronze. Y414c. KM#Pn5.	250
P2	10(1921)	—	10 Cents. Brass. 3.2900 g. Y414b. KM#Pn4.	150

PATTERNS

Including off metal strikes

KM#	Date	Mintage	Identification	Mkt Val
Pn1	ND(1905)	—	10 Cash. Copper.	—
Pn2	CD1906	—	10 Cash. Copper.	—
Pn3	10(1921)	—	10 Cents. Copper. 2.11-2.22 grams. Y414a, K746-IIx.	110
Pn4	10(1921)	—	10 Cents. Brass. Y414b.	—
Pn5	10(1921)	—	10 Cents. Bronze. Y414c.	140
Pn6	10(1921)	—	10 Cents. Silver. Y414f.	—
Pn7	10(1921)	—	20 Cents. Copper. 4.68-4.97 grams. Y415c, K746-Ix.	100
Pn8	10(1921)	—	20 Cents. Bronze. Y415d.	—
Pn9	10(1921)	—	20 Cents. Brass. Y415e.	—
Pn10	10(1921)	—	20 Cents. Silver. 4.8700 g. Y415f.	750

KWANGTUNG PROVINCE

Guangdong

A province located on the southeast coast of China. Kwangtung (Guangdong) lies mostly in the tropics and has both mountains and plains. Its coastline is nearly 800 miles long and provides many good harbors. Because of the location of Guangzhou (Canton) in the province, Kwangtung (Guangdong) was the first to be visited by seaborne foreign traders. Hong Kong was ceded to Great Britain after the First Opium War in 1841. Kowloon was later ceded to Britain in 1860 and the New Territories (100 year lease) in 1898 and Macao to Portugal in 1887, Kwangchowwan was leased to France in 1898 (a property was restored in 1946). A modern mint opened in Guangzhou (Canton) in 1889 with Edward Wyon as superintendent. The mint was a large issuer of coins until it closed in 1931. The Nationalists reopened the mint briefly in 1949, striking a few silver dollars, before abandoning the mainland for their retreat to Taiwan.

The large island of Hainan was split off from Kwangtung (Guangdong) Province in 1988 and established as a separate province.

Hong Kong was returned to China by Britain on July 1, 1997 and established as a special administrative region, retaining its own coinage.

EMPIRE

PROVINCIAL CAST COINAGE

C# 19-7 CASH

Cast Brass **Ruler:** Kuang-hsü **Obv. Inscription:** Kuang-hsü T'ung-pao **Rev:** Manchu inscription **Rev. Inscription:** Boo-guwang

Date	Mintage	Good	VG	F	VF	XF
ND(1875-1908)	—	12.00	22.00	32.00	45.00	—

MILLED COINAGE

Y# 190 CASH

Brass **Ruler:** Kuang-hsü **Obv:** "Kuang" in a different style **Obv. Inscription:** Kuang-hsü T'ung-pao **Rev:** Manchu inscription **Rev. Inscription:** Boo-guwang

Date	Mintage	VG	F	VF	XF	Unc
ND(1890-1908)	1,059,253,000	—	0.10	0.25	1.00	2.00

Y# 191 CASH

Brass **Ruler:** Kuang-hsü **Obv. Inscription:** Kuang-hsü T'ung-pao **Rev:** Manchu inscription **Rev. Inscription:** Boo-guwang

Date	Mintage	VG	F	VF	XF	Unc
ND(1906-08)	—	—	0.10	0.25	1.00	3.00

Y# 204 CASH

Brass **Obv. Inscription:** Hsüan-t'ung T'uang pao **Rev:** Manchu inscription **Rev. Inscription:** Boo-guwang

Date	Mintage	VG	F	VF	XF	Unc
ND(1909-11)	—	0.20	0.50	1.00	2.00	5.00

Y# 20r 10 CASH

Copper **Ruler:** Hsuan-T'ung **Obv. Inscription:** Tai-ch'ing T'ung-pi **Rev:** Dragon **Rev. Legend:** Hsüan-t'ung Nien-tsao, TAI-CHING-TI KUO ...

Date	Mintage	VG	F	VF	XF	Unc
CD1909	—	0.50	1.50	3.00	5.00	25.00

Y# A192 CENT (10 Cash)

Copper **Ruler:** Kuang-hsü **Obv:** Y#192 **Obv. Inscription:** Kuang-hsü Yüan-pao **Rev:** Chihli 10 Cash, Y#67, dragon **Note:** Mule.

Date	Mintage	VG	F	VF	XF	Unc
ND(ca.1900)	—	8.50	25.00	35.00	50.00	125

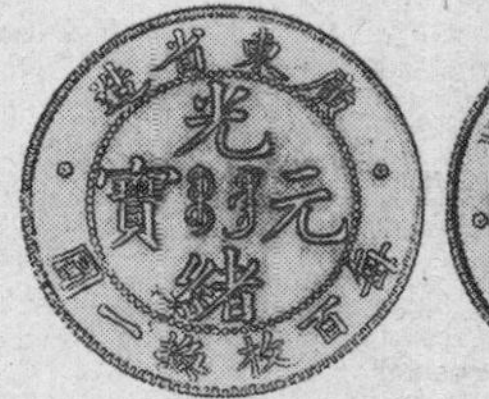

Y# 192 CENT (10 Cash)

Copper **Ruler:** Kuang-hsü **Obv. Legend:** Kuang-tung Sheng Tsao **Obv. Inscription:** Kuang-hsü Yüan-pao **Rev:** Dragon, ONE CENT

Date	Mintage	VG	F	VF	XF	Unc
ND(1900-06)	—	0.25	0.75	1.50	3.00	60.00

Y# 193 CENT (10 Cash)

Copper **Ruler:** Kuang-hsü **Obv. Legend:** Kuang-tung Sheng Tsao **Obv. Inscription:** Kuang-hsü Yüan-pao **Rev:** Dragon, TEN CASH

Date	Mintage	VG	F	VF	XF	Unc
ND(1900-06)	—	0.35	1.00	2.00	4.00	20.00

Note: Varieties in lettering exist, including spacing of characters.

Y# 10r CENT (10 Cash)

Copper **Ruler:** Kuang-hsü **Obv. Inscription:** Tai-ch'ing T'ung-pi **Rev:** Dragon **Rev. Legend:** Kuang-hsü Nien-tsao, TAI-CHING-TI KUO ...

Date	Mintage	VG	F	VF	XF	Unc
CD1906	79,000,000	0.35	1.00	2.00	4.00	20.00
CD1907	45,000,000	0.35	1.00	2.00	4.00	20.00
CD1908	62,736,000	0.35	1.00	2.00	4.00	20.00

Y# A193 CENT (10 Cash)

Copper **Ruler:** Kuang-hsü **Obv:** Y#192 **Obv. Legend:** Kuang-tung Sheng Tsao **Obv. Inscription:** Kuang-hsü Yuan-pao **Rev:** Y#193, dragon, "TEN CASH" **Note:** Mule.

Date	Mintage	VG	F	VF	XF	Unc
ND(c.1906)	—	6.50	20.00	28.50	40.00	100

Y# B193 CENT (10 Cash)

Copper **Ruler:** Kuang-hsü **Obv:** Y#193 **Obv. Legend:** Kuang-tung Sheng Tsao **Obv. Inscription:** Kuang-hsü Yuan-pao **Rev:** Y#192, dragon **Note:** Mule.

Date	Mintage	VG	F	VF	XF	Unc
ND(c.1906)	—	6.50	20.00	28.50	40.00	100

KM# B192 CENT

Copper **Ruler:** Kuang-hsü **Obv. Legend:** Kuang-hsü Yüan-pao **Obv. Inscription:** Kuang-hsü Yüan-pao **Note:** Prev. W#896.

Date	Mintage	VG	F	VF	XF	Unc
ND(ca.1906)	—	22.50	65.00	100	150	225

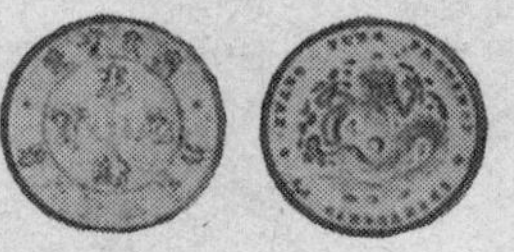

Y# 199 5 CENTS

1.3000 g., 0.8200 Silver .0343 oz. ASW **Ruler:** Kuang-hsü **Obv. Legend:** Kuang-tung Sheng Tsao **Obv. Inscription:** Kuang-hsü Yüan-pao **Rev:** English legend around dragon

Date	Mintage	VG	F	VF	XF	Unc
ND(1890-1905)	—	4.00	7.00	10.00	20.00	40.00

Y# 200 10 CENTS

2.7000 g., 0.8200 Silver .0712 oz. ASW **Ruler:** Kuang-hsü **Obv. Legend:** Kuang-tung Sheng Tsao **Obv. Inscription:** Kuang-hsü Yüan-pao **Rev:** English legends around dragon

Date	Mintage	VG	F	VF	XF	Unc
ND(1890-1908)	—	1.25	2.50	4.50	7.00	20.00

Y# 201 20 CENTS

5.5000 g., 0.8000 Silver .1415 oz. ASW **Ruler:** Kuang-hsü **Obv. Legend:** Kuang-tung Sheng Tsao **Obv. Inscription:** Kuang-hsü Yüan-pao **Rev:** Dragon

Date	Mintage	VG	F	VF	XF	Unc
ND(1890-1908)	—	2.25	3.00	4.00	6.00	12.50
ND(1890-1908) Proof, 10 known	—	Value: 400				

Y# 205 20 CENTS

5.5000 g., 0.8000 Silver .1415 oz. ASW **Ruler:** Hsuan-T'ung **Obv. Inscription:** Hsüan-t'ung Yüan-pao **Rev:** Dragon **Note:** Two varieties of edge reeding known.

Date	Mintage	VG	F	VF	XF	Unc
ND(1909-11)	94,774,000	2.50	4.50	6.00	9.00	20.00

Y# 202 50 CENTS

13.5000 g., 0.8600 Silver .3733 oz. ASW **Ruler:** Kuang-hsü **Obv. Legend:** Kuang-tung Sheng Tsao **Obv. Inscription:** Kuang-hsü Yüan-pao **Rev:** English legends around dragon

Date	Mintage	VG	F	VF	XF	Unc
ND(1890-1905)	—	7.00	20.00	40.00	75.00	250
ND(1890-1905) Proof	—	Value: 650				

Y# 203 DOLLAR

27.0000 g., 0.9000 Silver .7814 oz. ASW **Ruler:** Kuang-hsü **Obv. Legend:** Kuang-tung Sheng Tsao **Obv. Inscription:** Kuang-hsü Yüan-pao **Rev:** English legends around dragon

Date	Mintage	VG	F	VF	XF	Unc
ND(1890-1908)	—	15.00	30.00	45.00	75.00	650
ND(1890-1908) Proof	—	Value: 1,000				

Y# 206 DOLLAR

27.0000 g., 0.9000 Silver .7814 oz. ASW **Obv. Legend:** Kuang-tung Sheng Tsao **Obv. Inscription:** Hsüan-t'ung Yüan-pao **Rev:** Dragon

Date	Mintage	VG	F	VF	XF	Unc
ND(1909-11)	—	10.50	20.00	30.00	60.00	500

REPUBLIC

MILLED COINAGE

Y# 417 CENT

Bronze **Obv. Legend:** Chung Hua Min Kuo (year) Nien **Rev. Legend:** KWANG-TUNG PROVINCE

Date	Mintage	VG	F	VF	XF	Unc
1(1912)	18,836,000	0.50	1.50	2.25	5.00	22.00
3(1914)	14,750,000	0.50	1.50	2.25	5.00	22.00
4(1915)	6,350,000	1.25	4.00	6.00	15.00	35.00
5(1916)	18,388,000	0.65	2.00	3.00	7.50	30.00
7(1918)	—	2.50	7.50	12.50	20.00	45.00

Y# 417a CENT

Brass **Obv. Legend:** Chung Hua Min Kuo (year) Nien **Rev. Legend:** KWANG-TUNG PROVINCE

Date	Mintage	VG	F	VF	XF	Unc
1(1912)	Inc. above	—	—	—	—	—
3(1914)	Inc. above	0.65	2.00	5.00	10.00	25.00
4(1915)	Inc. above	1.00	3.00	7.50	15.00	30.00
5(1916)	Inc. above	0.45	1.25	3.00	6.00	20.00

Y# 418 2 CENTS

Brass **Obv. Legend:** Chung Hua Min Kuo (year) Nien **Rev. Legend:** KWANG-TUNG PROVINCE

Date	Mintage	VG	F	VF	XF	Unc
7(1918)	—	10.00	30.00	50.00	90.00	175

Y# 418a 2 CENTS

Copper **Obv. Legend:** Chung Hua Min Kuo (year) Nien **Rev. Legend:** KWANG-TUNG PROVINCE

Date	Mintage	VG	F	VF	XF	Unc
7(1918) Rare	—	—	—	—	—	—

Y# 420 5 CENTS

Copper-Nickel **Obv. Legend:** Chung Hua Min Kuo (year) Nien **Rev:** Large "5" in sprays **Rev. Legend:** KWANG-TUNG PROVINCE

Date	Mintage	VG	F	VF	XF	Unc
8(1919)	916,000	0.35	1.00	2.00	3.00	5.00

Y# 421 5 CENTS

Copper-Nickel **Obv. Legend:** Chung Hua Min Kuo (year) Nien **Rev:** Flag **Rev. Legend:** KWANG-TUNG PROVINCE

Date	Mintage	VG	F	VF	XF	Unc
10(1921)	666,000	0.45	1.25	3.00	6.50	12.50

Y# 420a 5 CENTS

Copper-Nickel **Obv. Legend:** Chung Hua Min Kuo (year) Nien **Rev:** Large "5" in sprays **Rev. Legend:** KWANG-TUNG PROVINCE

Date	Mintage	F	VF	XF	Unc	BU
12(1923)	480,000	1.00	2.00	3.00	5.00	—

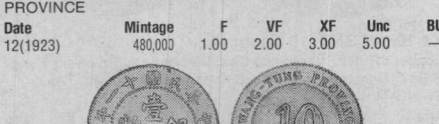

Y# 422 10 CENTS

2.7000 g., Silver **Obv. Legend:** Chung Hua Min Kuo (year) Nien **Rev:** Large "10" **Rev. Legend:** KWANG-TUNG PROVINCE

Date	Mintage	VG	F	VF	XF	Unc
2(1913)	8,798,000	1.50	2.50	4.00	5.00	10.00
3(1914)	Inc. above	1.75	2.75	4.50	6.00	12.00
11(1922)	—	2.25	4.00	7.00	10.00	25.00

Y# 425 10 CENTS

2.5000 g., Silver **Obv. Legend:** Chung Hua Min Kuo (year) Nien **Rev:** Bust of Sun Yat-sen **Rev. Legend:** KWANG-TUNG PROVINCE

Date	Mintage	VG	F	VF	XF	Unc
18(1929)	48,960,000	1.25	2.00	3.50	5.50	9.00

Y# 423 20 CENTS

5.4000 g., Silver **Obv. Legend:** Chung Hua Min Kuo (year) Nien **Rev. Legend:** KWANG-TUNG PROVINCE **Note:** The fineness of many of these 20-cent pieces, especially those dated Yr. 13 (1924), is as low as .500. In 1924 the Anhwei (Anhui) Mint secretly produced quantities of Kwangtung (Guangdong) 20-cent pieces that were only .400 fine. Standard issues were struck with a small dot in the center, 2 small rosettes at 4 and 8 o'clock; varieties exist with a large dot and large rosettes.

Date	Mintage	VG	F	VF	XF	Unc
1(1912)	88,000,000	2.25	2.75	3.75	6.50	12.00
2(1913)	109,974,000	2.25	2.75	3.75	6.50	12.00
3(1914)	41,691,000	2.25	2.75	3.75	6.50	12.00
4(1915)	22,332,000	3.00	6.00	12.00	25.00	100
7(1918)	—	2.25	2.75	3.75	6.00	10.00
8(1919)	195,000,000	2.00	2.50	3.50	4.50	7.00
9(1920)	197,000,000	2.00	2.50	3.50	4.50	7.00
10(1921)	402,250,000	2.00	2.50	3.50	4.50	7.00
11(1922)	350,000,000	2.00	2.50	3.50	4.50	7.00
12(1923)	4,400,000	2.50	3.50	5.50	8.50	20.00
13(1924)	55,109,000	2.50	3.50	5.50	8.50	20.00

Y# 424 20 CENTS

5.3000 g., Silver **Obv. Legend:** Chung Hua Min Kuo (year) Nien **Rev:** Bust of Sun Yat-sen **Rev. Legend:** KWANG-TUNG PROVINCE

Date	Mintage	VG	F	VF	XF	Unc
13(1924)	—	8.50	25.00	45.00	70.00	175

Y# 426 20 CENTS

5.3000 g., Silver **Obv:** Value in sprays **Obv. Legend:** Chung Hua Min Kuo (year) Nien **Rev:** Bust of Sun Yat-sen **Rev. Legend:** KWANG-TUNG PROVINCE

Date	Mintage	VG	F	VF	XF	Unc
17(1928)	28,530,000	8.50	25.00	40.00	60.00	150
18(1929)	779,738,000	2.50	3.50	5.50	7.00	12.50
19(1930) 1 known	—	—	—	—	—	3,500

PATTERNS

Including off metal strikes

KM#	Date	Mintage	Identification	Mkt Val
Pn16	ND(c. 1902)	—	1/2 Cent. Copper. Circled "flying" dragon.	—
Pn17	ND(1904)	—	Tael. Silver. K932.	—

Note: Superior Goodman sale 6-91 proof realized $41,800.

KM#	Date	Mintage	Identification	Mkt Val
PnA18	ND(1904)	—	Tael. Pewter. 6mm thick. K932x.	—
Pn18	ND(1904)	—	Tael. White Metal. K932y.	—
PnA19	ND(1906)	—	20 Cash. Copper. TCTK.	—
Pn19	3(1914)	—	10 Cents. Copper. Y422.	—
PnA20	4(1915)	—	Cent. Red Copper. Y417.	—
PnB20	5(1916)	—	Cent. Red Copper. Y417.	—
PnC20	7(1918)	—	Cent. Red Copper. Y417.	—
Pn20	8(1919)	—	20 Cents. Copper. Y423.	150
Pn21	9(1920)	—	20 Cents. Copper. Y423.	150
Pn22	10(1921)	—	20 Cents. Copper. Y423.	150

KM#	Date	Mintage	Identification	Mkt Val
PnA23	11(1922)	—	20 Cents. Copper. Y423.	150
Pn23	13(1924)	—	20 Cents. Gold. Y424.	—
Pn24	17(1928)	—	20 Cents. Copper. Y426.	—
Pn25	18(1929)	—	20 Cents. Copper. Y426.	—
Pn26	ND(ca. 1929)	—	20 Cents. Gold. Y426.	850
Pn27	25(1936)	—	Cent. Bronze. Sun Yat Sen.	3,000
Pn28	25(1936)	—	Cent. Copper.	700

KWEICHOW PROVINCE

Guizhou

A province located in southern China. It is basically a plateau region that is somewhat remote from the general traffic of China. The Kweichow Mint opened in 1730 and produced Cash coins until the end of the reign of Kuang Hsu. The Republic issues for this province are enigmatic as to their origin, as a mint supposedly did not exist in Kweichow (Guizhou) at this time.

EMPIRE

PROVINCIAL CAST COINAGE

C# 20-9 CASH

Cast Brass **Ruler:** Kuang-hsü **Obv. Inscription:** Kuang-hsü T'ung-pao **Rev:** Manchu inscription **Rev. Inscription:** Boo-jiyan

Date	Mintage	Good	VG	F	VF	XF
ND(1875-1908)	—	4.00	7.50	10.00	15.00	—

C# 20-9.1 CASH

Cast Brass **Ruler:** Kuang-hsü **Obv. Inscription:** Kuang-hsü T'ung-pao **Rev:** Manchu inscription **Rev. Inscription:** Boo-jiyan

Date	Mintage	Good	VG	F	VF	XF
ND(1875-1908)	—	5.00	9.00	12.50	18.50	—

C# 20-9.2 CASH

Cast Brass **Ruler:** Kuang-hsü **Obv. Inscription:** Kuang-hsü T'ung-pao **Rev:** Manchu inscription **Rev. Inscription:** Boo-jiyan

Date	Mintage	Good	VG	F	VF	XF
ND(1875-1905)	—	8.50	11.50	16.50	25.00	—

REPUBLIC

MILLED COINAGE

Y# 428 DOLLAR

25.8000 g., Silver, 39 mm. **Subject:** First Road in Kweichow **Obv. Legend:** Chung Hua Min Kuo (year) Nien

Date	Mintage	VG	F	VF	XF	Unc
17(1928)	648,000	200	400	750	1,750	7,000

Note: This coin is known as the "Auto Dollar" as it purports to portray the governor's automobile; minor varieties exist in Chinese legends and various automobile designs

Y# 433a DOLLAR

26.4000 g., Silver **Obv:** Square window in pavilion **Obv. Legend:** Chung Hua Min Kuo (year) Nien **Note:** Many conterfeits exist.

Date	Mintage	VG	F	VF	XF	Unc
38(1949) Rare	—	—	—	—	—	—

Note: This coin is known as the "Bamboo Dollar"

Y# 433 DOLLAR

26.4000 g., Silver **Obv:** Round window in pavilion **Obv. Legend:** Chung Hua Min Kuo (year) Nien **Rev:** Bamboo

Date	Mintage	VG	F	VF	XF	Unc
38(1949)	—	400	800	1,000	2,500	4,500

Note: This coin is known as the "Bamboo Dollar".

Y# A429 1/2 CENT

Copper **Obv. Legend:** Chung Hua Min Kuo (year) Nien

Date	Mintage	VG	F	VF	XF	Unc
38(1949)	—	450	750	—	—	—

Y# A429a 1/2 CENT

Brass **Obv. Legend:** Chung Hua Min Kuo (year) Nien

Date	Mintage	VG	F	VF	XF	Unc
38(1949)	—	300	450	—	—	—

Y# A429a.2 1/2 CENT

Brass **Obv:** Narrow, thick characters **Obv. Legend:** Chung Hua Min Kuo (year) Nien

Date	Mintage	VG	F	VF	XF	Unc
38(1949)	—	450	650	—	—	—

Y# 429 10 CENTS

Antimony **Obv. Legend:** Chung Hua Min Kuo (year) Nien

Date	Mintage	VG	F	VF	XF	Unc
20(1931)	—	250	450	650	900	—

Y# 430 20 CENTS

Silver **Obv. Legend:** Chung Hua Min Kuo (year) Nien

Date	Mintage	VG	F	VF	XF	Unc
38(1949)	—	45.00	125	200	300	425

Y# 431 20 CENTS

Silver **Obv. Legend:** Chung Hua Min Kuo (year) Nien

Date	Mintage	VG	F	VF	XF	Unc
38(1949)	—	—	—	—	—	3,750

Y# 432 50 CENTS

Silver **Obv. Legend:** Chung Hua Min Kuo (year) Nien

Date	Mintage	VG	F	VF	XF	Unc
38(1949)	—	—	—	1,750	3,000	5,300

MANCHURIAN PROVINCES

Since the 17th century, Manchuria has been divided into three provinces. The two northern provinces were called Heilungkiang and Kirin. Together the three provinces of Manchuria were known as the Manchurian Provinces in English or the Three Eastern Provinces in Chinese. Since the communist takeover in 1949, western Mongol-populated areas of Manchuria have been included in the Inner Mongolia Autonomous Region.

EMPIRE

MILLED COINAGE

Y# 209 10 CENTS

2.6000 g., 0.8900 Silver .0744 oz. ASW **Ruler:** Kuang-Hsü **Obv. Legend:** Tung-san Sheng Tsao **Obv. Inscription:** Kuang-hsü Yüan-pao **Rev:** Legend at bottom **Rev. Legend:** MANCHURIAN PROVINCES

Date	Mintage	VG	F	VF	XF	Unc
33(1907)	1,079,000	3.50	10.00	25.00	40.00	100

Y# 210 20 CENTS

5.2000 g., 0.8900 Silver .1488 oz. ASW **Ruler:** Kuang-Hsü **Obv:** One dot at either side **Obv. Legend:** Tung-san Sheng Tsao **Obv. Inscription:** Kuang-hsü Yüan-pao **Rev:** Legend at bottom **Rev. Legend:** MANCHURIAN PROVINCES

Date	Mintage	VG	F	VF	XF	Unc
33(1907)	—	6.50	20.00	30.00	60.00	120

Y# 210a.1 20 CENTS

5.2000 g., 0.8900 Silver .1388 oz. ASW **Ruler:** Kuang-Hsü **Obv:** Three rosettes at either side **Obv. Legend:** Tung-san Sheng Tsao **Obv. Inscription:** Kuang-hsü Yüan-pao **Rev:** Legend at bottom **Rev. Legend:** MANCHURIAN PROVINCES

Date	Mintage	VG	F	VF	XF	Unc
33(ca.1908)	249,219,000	3.50	9.00	17.50	35.00	70.00

Y# 210a.2 20 CENTS

5.2000 g., 0.8900 Silver .1388 oz. ASW **Ruler:** Kuang-Hsü **Obv:** One rosette at either side **Obv. Legend:** Tung-san Sheng Tsao **Obv. Inscription:** Kuang-hsü Yüan-pao **Rev:** Legend at bottom **Rev. Legend:** MANCHURIAN PROVINCES

Date	Mintage	VG	F	VF	XF	Unc
33(ca.1908)	Inc. above	2.75	6.00	12.00	20.00	60.00

Y# 213.2 20 CENTS

5.2000 g., 0.8900 Silver .1388 oz. ASW **Ruler:** Hsüan-t'ung **Obv:** One large-petaled rosette at either side **Obv. Legend:** Tung-san Sheng Tsao **Obv. Inscription:** Hsüan-t'ung Yüan-pao **Rev:** Legend at bottom; date as 1ST YEAR **Rev. Legend:** MANCHURIAN PROVINCES

Date	Mintage	VG	F	VF	XF	Unc
1(1909)	Inc. above	2.50	4.00	8.50	15.00	40.00

Y# 213 20 CENTS
5.2000 g., 0.8900 Silver .1388 oz. ASW **Ruler:** Hsüan-t'ung **Obv:** Two small stars flanking one large star at either side **Obv. Legend:** Tung-san Sheng Tsao **Obv. Inscription:** Hsüan-t'ung Yüan-pao **Rev:** Legend at bottom; date given as FIRST YEAR **Rev. Legend:** MANCHURIAN PROVINCES

Date	Mintage	VG	F	VF	XF	Unc
1(ca.1910)	Inc. above	2.50	4.00	7.50	12.50	30.00

Y# 213.1 20 CENTS
5.2000 g., 0.8900 Silver .1388 oz. ASW **Ruler:** Hsüan-t'ung **Obv:** One small star at either side **Obv. Legend:** Tung-san Sheng Tsao **Obv. Inscription:** Hsüan-t'ung Yüan-pao **Rev:** Legend at bottom **Rev. Legend:** MANCHURIAN PROVINCES

Date	Mintage	VG	F	VF	XF	Unc
1(ca.1910)	Inc. above	2.50	4.00	8.50	15.00	35.00

Y# 213.3 20 CENTS
5.2000 g., 0.8900 Silver .1388 oz. ASW **Ruler:** Hsüan-t'ung **Obv:** One large star between two dots **Obv. Legend:** Tung-san Sheng Tsao **Obv. Inscription:** Hsüan-t'ung Yüan-pao **Rev:** Legend at bottom **Rev. Legend:** MANCHURIAN PROVINCES

Date	Mintage	VG	F	VF	XF	Unc
1(ca.1910)	Inc. above	2.50	4.00	8.50	15.00	35.00

Y# 213a 20 CENTS
5.2000 g., 0.8900 Silver .1388 oz. ASW **Ruler:** Hsüan-t'ung **Obv:** Manchu "Boo-fu" at center **Obv. Legend:** Tung-san Sheng Tsao **Obv. Inscription:** Hsüan-t'ung Yüan-pao **Rev:** Error in legend **Rev. Legend:** MANCHURIAN PROVIENCES

Date	Mintage	VG	F	VF	XF	Unc
ND(ca.1911)	Inc. above	2.50	4.00	8.50	15.00	35.00

Y# 213a.6 20 CENTS
5.2000 g., 0.8900 Silver .1388 oz. ASW **Ruler:** Hsüan-t'ung **Obv:** Without Manchu "Boo-fu" at center **Obv. Legend:** Tung-san Sheng Tsao **Obv. Inscription:** Hsüan-t'ung Yüan-pao **Rev:** Error in legend **Rev. Legend:** MANCHURIAN PROVIENCES

Date	Mintage	VG	F	VF	XF	Unc
ND(ca.1912)	Inc. above	2.75	5.00	10.00	20.00	40.00

Y# 213a.4 20 CENTS
5.2000 g., 0.7000 Silver .1170 oz. ASW **Ruler:** Hsüan-t'ung **Obv:** Without Manchu "Boo-fu" at center **Obv. Legend:** Tung-san Sheng Tsao **Obv. Inscription:** Hsüan-t'ung Yüan-pao **Rev:** Legend at top **Rev. Legend:** MANCHURIAN PROVINCES

Date	Mintage	VG	F	VF	XF	Unc
ND(ca.1913)	Inc. above	2.50	5.00	10.00	20.00	40.00

Y# 213a.1 20 CENTS
5.2000 g., 0.7000 Silver .1170 oz. ASW **Ruler:** Hsüan-t'ung **Obv:** 5-petaled rosette in center with dot in center of rosette; dot below side rosettes **Obv. Legend:** Tung-san Sheng Tsao **Obv. Inscription:** Hsüan-t'ung Yüan-pao **Rev:** Legend at top **Rev. Legend:** MANCHURIAN PROVINCES

Date	Mintage	VG	F	VF	XF	Unc
ND(ca.1914-15)	Inc. above	2.25	4.00	8.50	15.00	30.00

Y# 213a.2 20 CENTS
5.2000 g., 0.7000 Silver .1170 oz. ASW **Ruler:** Hsüan-t'ung **Obv:** With dot below side rosettes **Obv. Legend:** Tung-san Sheng Tsao **Obv. Inscription:** Hsüan-t'ung Yüan-pao **Rev:** Legend at top **Rev. Legend:** MANCHURIAN PROVINCES

Date	Mintage	VG	F	VF	XF	Unc
ND(ca.1914-15)	Inc. above	2.25	4.00	8.50	15.00	30.00

Y# 213a.3 20 CENTS
5.2000 g., 0.7000 Silver .1170 oz. ASW **Ruler:** Hsüan-t'ung **Obv:** Without dot in center of 5-petaled rosette **Obv. Inscription:** Hsüan-t'ung Yüan-pao **Rev:** Legend at top **Rev. Legend:** MANCHURIAN PROVINCES

Date	Mintage	VG	F	VF	XF	Unc
ND(ca.1914-15)	Inc. above	2.25	4.00	8.50	15.00	30.00

Y# 211 50 CENTS
13.1000 g., 0.8900 Silver .3749 oz. ASW **Ruler:** Kuang-Hsü **Obv. Legend:** Tung-san Sheng Tsao **Obv. Inscription:** Kuang-Hsü Yüan-pao **Rev:** Legend at bottom **Rev. Legend:** MANCHURIAN PROVINCES

Date	Mintage	VG	F	VF	XF	Unc
33(1907)	—	65.00	175	350	650	1,200

Y# 212 DOLLAR
26.4000 g., 0.8900 Silver .7555 oz. ASW **Ruler:** Kuang-Hsü **Obv. Legend:** Tung-san Sheng Tsao **Obv. Inscription:** Kuang-Hsü Yüan-pao **Rev:** Legend at bottom **Rev. Legend:** MANCHURIAN PROVINCES

Date	Mintage	VG	F	VF	XF	Unc
33(1907)	—	150	400	800	1,500	4,000

REPUBLIC

MILLED COINAGE

Y# 434 CENT
Copper **Obv. Legend:** Chung Hua Min Kuo... **Rev:** Sunburst in floral sprays

Date	Mintage	VG	F	VF	XF	Unc
18(1929)	—	0.65	2.00	3.00	5.00	25.00

Y# 434a CENT
Brass **Obv. Legend:** Chung Hua Min Kuo... **Rev:** Sunburst in floral sprays

Date	Mintage	VG	F	VF	XF	Unc
18(1929)	—	—	—	—	—	—

PATTERNS

Including off metal strikes

KM#	Date	Mintage	Identification	Mkt Val
Pn1	18(1929)	—	Dollar. Silver.	—

Note: Superior Goodman sale 6-91 choice AU realized, $22,000

KM#	Date	Mintage	Identification	Mkt Val
Pn2	18(1929)	—	Fen. Copper. Y#434 with formal Chinese "One Fen"	—

SHANSI PROVINCE

Shanxi

A province located in northeastern China that has some of the richest coal deposits in the world. Parts of the Great Wall cross the province. Extensive agriculture of early China started here. Cited as a "model province" in the new Chinese Republic. Intermittently active mints from 1645. The modern mint was established in 1919. It operated until the mid-1920's and closed because of the public's resistance against the coins that were being produced.

EMPIRE

PROVINCIAL CAST COINAGE

C# 21-8 CASH
Cast Brass **Ruler:** Kuang-hsü **Obv:** Manchu inscription **Obv. Inscription:** Kuang-hsü T'ung-pao **Rev. Inscription:** Boo-Jin

Date	Mintage	Good	VG	F	VF	XF
ND(1875-1908)	—	6.50	11.50	17.50	35.00	—

REPUBLIC

MILLED COINAGE

Y# A435 10 CASH (1 Cent)
Copper **Obv:** Crossed flags **Obv. Legend:** Chung Hua Min Kuo **Rev:** Value in wheat sprays

Date	Mintage	VG	F	VF	XF	Unc
ND(ca.1912)	—	35.00	100	150	220	—

Y# 217 20 CENTS
4.8000 g., Silver **Ruler:** Hsuan-Tung **Obv. Legend:** Shan-hsi Sheng Tsao **Obv. Inscription:** Hsuan-t'ung Yuan-pao **Rev:** Side view dragon

Date	Mintage	VG	F	VF	XF	Unc
ND(ca.1911)	—	100	200	350	500	—

Note: Several varieties exist similar to Y#217, but struck more crudely in base metal and with different Chinese legends at the top of the obverse. English legends are usually blundered. These were struck about 1913 and thought to be warlord issues. Do not confuse these with coins of Fengtien (Liaoning), from which this was copied.

PATTERNS

Including off metal strikes

KM#	Date	Mintage	Identification	Mkt Val
Pn2	14(1925)	—	5 Cents. Nickel. K823.	—

SHANTUNG PROVINCE

Shandong

A province located on the northeastern coast of China. Confucius was born in this province. Parts of the province were leased to Great Britain and to Germany. Farming, fishing and mining are the chief occupations. A mint was opened at Tsinan in 1647 and was an intermittent producer for the empire. A modern mint was opened at Tsinan in 1905, but closed in 1906. Patterns were prepared between 1926-1933 in anticipation of a new coinage, but none were struck for circulation.

EMPIRE

PROVINCIAL CAST COINAGE

C# 22-6 CASH

Cast Brass **Ruler:** Kuang-hsü **Obv. Inscription:** Kuang-hsü T'ung-pao **Rev:** Type 1 mint mark **Rev. Inscription:** Boo-ji

Date	Mintage	Good	VG	F	VF	XF
ND(1875-1908)	—	10.00	18.50	27.50	40.00	—

Note: Refer to Tungch'uan, Yünnan Province, for one-cash C#27 series coins previously listed here.

MILLED COINAGE

Y# 8a 2 CASH

Copper **Ruler:** Kuang-hsü **Obv. Inscription:** Kuang-hsü T'ung-pao **Rev:** Dragon

Date	Mintage	VG	F	VF	XF	Unc
CD1906	—	12.00	25.00	35.00	70.00	—

Y# 220 10 CASH

Copper **Ruler:** Kuang-hsü **Obv. Inscription:** Kuang-hsü Yüan-pao **Rev:** Side view dragon

Date	Mintage	VG	F	VF	XF	Unc
ND(1904-05)	—	8.00	15.00	30.00	40.00	60.00

Y# 221 10 CASH

Copper **Ruler:** Kuang-hsü **Obv:** Thin Manchu words in center, flying dragon **Obv. Legend:** Shen-tung Sheng Tsao **Obv. Inscription:** Kuang-hsü Yüan-pao **Rev:** SHANTUNG

Date	Mintage	VG	F	VF	XF	Unc
ND(1904-05)	—	2.75	7.00	11.00	17.50	40.00

Y# 221a 10 CASH

Copper **Ruler:** Kuang-hsü **Obv:** Thick Manchu in center, flying dragon **Obv. Legend:** Shen-tung Sheng Tsao **Obv. Inscription:** Kuang-hsü Yüan-pao **Rev:** SHANG-TUNG

Date	Mintage	VG	F	VF	XF	Unc
ND(1904-05)	—	1.00	2.50	4.00	7.50	20.00

Y# 221a.1 10 CASH

Copper **Ruler:** Kuang-hsü **Obv:** Thin Manchu in center, flying dragon **Obv. Legend:** Shen-tung Sheng Tsao **Obv. Inscription:** Kuang-hsü Yüan-pao

Date	Mintage	VG	F	VF	XF	Unc
ND(1904-05)	—	2.00	5.00	10.00	17.50	40.00

Y# 221.1 10 CASH

Copper **Ruler:** Kuang-hsü **Obv:** Thick Manchu in center, flying dragon **Obv. Legend:** Shen-tung Sheng Tsao **Obv. Inscription:** Kuang-hsü Yüan-pao

Date	Mintage	VG	F	VF	XF	Unc
ND(1904-05)	—	1.50	3.50	7.00	14.00	30.00

Y# 221.2 10 CASH

Copper **Ruler:** Kuang-hsü **Obv:** Smaller stars, flying dragon **Obv. Legend:** Shen-tung Sheng Tsao **Obv. Inscription:** Kuang-hsü Yüan-pao

Date	Mintage	VG	F	VF	XF	Unc
ND(1904-05)	—	1.50	3.50	7.00	14.00	30.00

Y# 221.3 10 CASH

Copper **Ruler:** Kuang-hsü **Obv:** Similar to Y#220, flying dragon **Obv. Legend:** Shen-tung Sheng Tsao **Obv. Inscription:** Kuang-hsü Yüan-pao **Rev:** Similar to Y#221

Date	Mintage	VG	F	VF	XF	Unc
ND(1904-05)	—	62.50	125	200	300	—

Y# 10s 10 CASH

Brass **Ruler:** Kuang-hsü **Obv. Inscription:** Tai-ch'ing T'ung-pi **Rev:** 6 large waves below dragon **Rev. Legend:** Kuang-hsü Nien-tsao, TAI-CHING-TI-KUO ...

Date	Mintage	VG	F	VF	XF	Unc
CD1906	—	2.00	6.00	10.00	17.50	40.00

Y# 10s.1 10 CASH

Copper **Ruler:** Kuang-hsü **Obv. Inscription:** Tai-ch'ing T'ung-pi **Rev. Legend:** Kuang-hsü Nien-tsao, TAI-CHING-TI-KUO ...

Date	Mintage	VG	F	VF	XF	Unc
CD1906	—	2.50	7.50	12.50	25.00	50.00

Y# 10s.1a 10 CASH

Copper **Ruler:** Kuang-hsü **Obv. Inscription:** Tai-ch'ing T'ung-pi **Rev:** 5 small waves below dragon **Rev. Legend:** Kuang-hsü Nien-tsao, TAI-CHING-TI-KUO ...

Date	Mintage	VG	F	VF	XF	Unc
CD1906	—	1.75	5.00	10.00	17.50	40.00

Y# 10s.2a 10 CASH

Copper **Ruler:** Kuang-hsü **Obv. Inscription:** Tai-ch'ing T'ung-pi **Rev:** Dragon with larger forehead and narrower face, pearl redesigned **Rev. Legend:** Kuang-hsü Nien-tsao, TAI-CHING-TI-KUO ...

Date	Mintage	VG	F	VF	XF	Unc
CD1906	—	2.75	8.00	15.00	30.00	60.00

PATTERNS

Including off metal strikes

KM#	Date	Mintage	Identification	Mkt Val
Pn7	15(1926)	—	10 Dollars. Gold. K1536.	2,500
Pn8	15(1926)	—	10 Dollars. Pewter. K1536y.	—
Pn9	15(1926)	—	20 Dollars. Gold. K1535.	3,000
Pn10	15(1926)	—	20 Dollars. Pewter. K1535y.	—
Pn11	21(1932)	—	20 Cash. Copper. Wide flan.	—
Pn12	22(1933)	—	2 Cents. Nickel. K827.	—
Pn13	22(1933)	—	20 Cash. Copper.	—

SHENSI PROVINCE

Shaanxi

A province located in central China that is a rich agricultural area. A very important province in the early development of China. An active imperial mint was located at Sian (Xi'an).

EMPIRE

PROVINCIAL CAST COINAGE

C# 23-13 CASH

Cast Brass **Ruler:** Kuang-hsü **Obv:** Type A **Obv. Inscription:** Kuang-hsü T'ung-pao **Rev:** Manchu inscription **Rev. Inscription:** Boo-san

Date	Mintage	Good	VG	F	VF	XF
ND(1875-1908)	—	20.00	35.00	50.00	75.00	—

REPUBLIC

MILLED COINAGE

Y# 435 CENT

Copper **Obv:** Crossed flags **Obv. Legend:** IMTYPIF: "I Mei Ta Yuan Pi I (1) Fen" (One is 1/100 of Large Dollar Coin = 1 Cent) **Obv. Inscription:** Chung Hua Min Kuo **Rev:** Value above wheat sprays

Date	Mintage	VG	F	VF	XF	Unc
ND(c.1928)	—	25.00	40.00	70.00	150	—

Y# 436 2 CENTS

Copper **Obv:** Crossed flags, star between flags **Obv. Legend:** IMTYPEF: "I Mei Ta Yüan Pi Erh (2) Fen" **Obv. Inscription:** Chung Hua Min Kuo **Rev:** Value above wheat sprays **Note:** Dentilated borders.

Date	Mintage	VG	F	VF	XF	Unc
ND(c.1928)	—	35.00	60.00	90.00	150	—

Y# 436.1 2 CENTS
Copper **Obv:** Crossed flags, without star between flags **Obv. Legend:** IMTYPEF: "I Mei Ta Yüan Pi Erh (2) Fen" **Obv. Inscription:** Chung Hua Min Kuo **Rev:** Value above wheat sprays **Note:** Large Chinese legends.

Date	Mintage	VG	F	VF	XF	Unc
ND(c.1928)	—	15.00	25.00	40.00	75.00	—

Y# 436.2 2 CENTS
Copper **Obv:** Crossed flags, star in center **Obv. Legend:** IMTYPEF: "I Mei Ta Yüan Pi Erh (2) Fen" **Obv. Inscription:** Chung Hua Min Kuo **Rev:** Value above wheat sprays, star in center

Date	Mintage	VG	F	VF	XF	Unc
ND(c.1928)	—	40.00	75.00	120	225	—

Y# 436.3 2 CENTS
Copper **Obv:** Crossed flags, without star between flags **Obv. Legend:** IMTYPEF: "I Mei Ta Yüan Pi Erh (2) Fen" **Obv. Inscription:** Chung Hua Min Kuo **Rev:** Value above wheat sprays **Note:** Small Chinese legends.

Date	Mintage	VG	F	VF	XF	Unc
ND(c.1928)	—	25.00	50.00	80.00	125	—

Y# 436.4 2 CENTS
Copper **Obv:** Crossed flags **Obv. Legend:** IMTYPEF: "I Mei Ta Yüan Pi Erh (2) Fen" **Obv. Inscription:** Chung Hua Min Kuo **Rev:** Value above wheat sprays **Note:** Pearled borders.

Date	Mintage	VG	F	VF	XF	Unc
ND(c.1928)	—	50.00	80.00	120	200	—

Y# 436.5 2 CENTS
Copper **Obv:** Crossed flags, similar to Y#436.2 but with star between flags **Obv. Legend:** IMTYPEF: "I Mei Ta Yüan Pi Erh (2) Fen" **Obv. Inscription:** Chung Hua Min Kuo **Rev:** Value above wheat sprays **Note:** Large Chinese legends.

Date	Mintage	VG	F	VF	XF	Unc
ND(c.1928)	—	40.00	75.00	120	225	—

SINKIANG PROVINCE

Hsinkiang, Xinjiang
"New Dominion"

An autonomous region in western China, often referred to as Chinese Turkestan. High mountains surround 2000 ft. tableland on three sides with a large desert in center of this province. Many salt lakes, mining and some farming and oil. Inhabited by early man and was referred to as the "Silk Route" to the West. Sinkiang (Xinjiang) has been historically under the control of many factions, including Genghis Khan. It became a province in 1884. China has made claim to Sinkiang (Xinjiang) for many, many years. This rule has been more nominal than actual. Sinkiang (Xinjiang) had eight imperial mints, only three of which were in operation toward the end of the reign of Kuang Hsu. Only two mints operated during the early years of the republic. In 1949, due to a drastic coin shortage and lack of confidence in the inflated paper money, it was planned to mint some dollars in Sinkiang (Xinjiang). These did not see much circulation, however, due to the defeat of the nationalists, though they have recently appeared in considerable numbers in today's market.

PATTERNS

NOTE: A number of previously listed cast coins of Sinkiang Province are now known to be patterns - "mother" cash or "seed" cash for which no circulating issues are known. The following coins are, therefore, no longer listed. Most were probably manufactured in Beijing. They are generally made of brass rather than the purer copper usual to Sinkiang. The following coins are, therefore, no longer listed here: Craig #30-9, 30-11a, 30-12a, 30-14, 30-15a, 30-16, 30-17, 28-4.1, 28-8a, 28-9a, 28-9c, 28-10, 31-1a, 31-1v, 31-2, 32-4, 32-5, 33-12, 33-21, 34-2, 34-3, 35-5a and 35-6.

MONETARY SYSTEM

2 Pul = 1 Cash
2 Cash = 5 Li
4 Cash = 10 Li = 1 Fen
25 Cash = 10 Fen = 1 Miscal = 1 Ch'ien, Mace, Tanga
10 Miscals (Mace) = 1 Liang (Tael or Sar)
20 Miscals (Tangas) = 1 Tilla

LOCAL MINT NAMES AND MARKS

Mint	Chinese	Uyghur	Manchu
Aksu	城阿	اقصو	
Ili, now Yining	犁伊	الي	
Kashgar, now Kashi	什喀	كشقر	
Khotan, now Hotan	闐和	ختن	
Kuche, now Kuqa	車庫	كوچا	
Urumchi, now Urumqi	什烏	اورمچي	
Ushi, now Wushi (Uqturpan)	羌爾葉	اوش	
Yangihissar, now Yengisar		ينگى حصار	
Yarkand, now Shache (Yarkant)		ياركند	

EMPIRE

LOCAL CAST COINAGE

C# 30-18 10 CASH
Cast Copper **Ruler:** Kuang-hsü **Obv. Inscription:** Kuang-hsü Chung-pao **Rev:** Character "A" (for Aksu) above center hole, "Aksu" in Turki at right, in Manchu at left

Date	Mintage	Good	VG	F	VF	XF
ND(1875-1908)	—	1.50	2.50	4.00	8.00	—

C# 30-18.1 10 CASH
Cast Copper **Ruler:** Kuang-hsü **Rev:** "Asku" in Manchu at right, in Turki at left

Date	Mintage	Good	VG	F	VF	XF
ND(1875-1908)	—	7.50	12.50	19.00	35.00	—

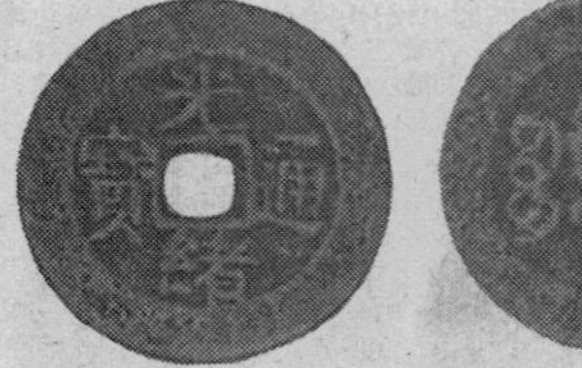

C# 30-19 10 CASH
Cast Copper **Ruler:** Kuang-hsü **Obv. Inscription:** Kuang-hsü T'ung-pao **Rev:** Character "K'a" (for Kashgar) above

Date	Mintage	Good	VG	F	VF	XF
ND(1886-1908)	—	2.00	4.50	6.50	13.50	—

Note: Cast in the Aksu Mint for the Kashgar Mint, beginning in 1886 during the reign of Kuang-Hsü

PROVINCIAL CAST COINAGE

KM# 10 CASH
Cast Copper **Ruler:** Kuang-hsü **Obv. Inscription:** Kuang-hsü T'ung-pao **Rev:** Manchu inscription for Hu-pu Board of Revenue **Rev. Inscription:** Boo Ciowan

Date	Mintage	Good	VG	F	VF	XF
ND(1875-1908)	—	1.50	3.50	6.00	9.50	—

KM# 11 CASH
Cast Copper **Ruler:** Kuang-hsü **Rev:** Similar to KM#10 but entire reverse is in inverted mirror image

Date	Mintage	Good	VG	F	VF	XF
ND(1875-1908)	—	3.50	6.00	9.00	13.50	—

KM# 12 CASH
Cast Copper **Ruler:** Kuang-hsü **Obv. Inscription:** Kuang-hsü T'ung-pao **Rev:** Similar to KM#11

Date	Mintage	Good	VG	F	VF	XF
ND(1875-1908)	—	1.50	3.50	6.00	9.50	—

KM# 13 CASH

Cast Copper **Ruler:** Kuang-hsü **Obv. Inscription:** Kuang-hsü T'ung-pao **Rev:** Illiterate Manchu inscription **Rev. Inscription:** Boo Chuan or Yuan

Date	Mintage	Good	VG	F	VF	XF
ND(1875-1908)	—	1.50	3.50	6.00	9.50	—

KM# 14 CASH

Cast Copper **Ruler:** Kuang-hsü **Obv. Inscription:** Kuang-hsü T'ung-pao **Rev:** Illiterate Manchu inscription **Rev. Inscription:** Boo-Chuan

Date	Mintage	Good	VG	F	VF	XF
ND(1875-1908)	—	1.50	3.00	5.00	8.50	—

Note: The five one-cash varieties listed above could be confused with Beijing issues C1-16 or C2-15, but they are much more crudely cast, and are made of red copper rather than brass; see Landon Ross, 1986, Numismatics International Bulletin 20(3) for a more detailed review

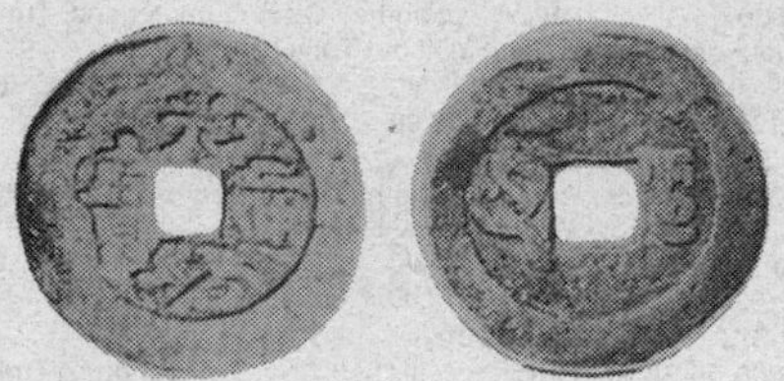

C# 33-23 CASH

Cast Copper **Ruler:** Kuang-hsü **Obv. Inscription:** Kuang-hsü T'ung-pao

Date	Mintage	Good	VG	F	VF	XF
ND(1875-1908)	—	6.00	8.00	12.00	20.00	—

C# 33-18.1 10 CASH

Cast Copper **Ruler:** Kuang-hsü **Rev:** Semi-circle at lower right

Date	Mintage	Good	VG	F	VF	XF
ND(1875-1908)	—	7.50	13.50	22.50	35.00	—

KM# 7.1 10 CASH

Cast Copper **Ruler:** Kuang-hsü **Obv. Inscription:** Kuang-hsü T'ung-pao **Rev:** "Pao Ku" with "K'u" (for Kuche) above

Date	Mintage	Good	VG	F	VF	XF
ND(1875-1908)	—	1.50	3.00	5.00	10.00	—

KM# 7.2 10 CASH

Cast Copper **Ruler:** Kuang-hsü **Obv. Inscription:** Kuang-hsü T'ung-pao **Rev:** "Pao" (for Kuche) at left reversed

Date	Mintage	Good	VG	F	VF	XF
ND(1875-1908)	—	7.50	13.50	22.50	35.00	—

KM# 8 10 CASH

Cast Copper **Ruler:** Kuang-hsü **Obv. Inscription:** Kuang-hsü T'ung-pao **Rev:** "Manchu Boo Hsin" with "Hsin" (new, but here standing for the Tihwa (now Urumqi) Mint) above

Date	Mintage	Good	VG	F	VF	XF
ND(1875-1908)	—	3.50	5.00	7.50	15.00	—

KM# 9 10 CASH

Cast Copper **Ruler:** Kuang-hsü **Obv. Inscription:** Kuang-hsü T'ung-pao **Rev;** "Manchu Boo Hsin" (for Tihwa Mint) with "Hsin" (new) above

Date	Mintage	Good	VG	F	VF	XF
ND(1875-1908)	—	3.00	4.50	7.00	15.00	—

C# 32-6 10 CASH

Cast Copper **Ruler:** Kuang-hsü **Obv. Inscription:** Kuang-hsü T'ung-pao **Rev:** "Kashgar" in Turki at left, in Manchu at right, "K'a" (Kashgar) above

Date	Mintage	Good	VG	F	VF	XF
ND(1875-1908)	—	5.00	9.50	15.00	25.00	—

C# 32-6.1 10 CASH

Cast Copper **Ruler:** Kuang-hsü **Obv. Inscription:** Kuang-hsü T'ung-pao **Rev:** Turki-Manchu inscription (right-left) **Rev. Inscription:** Boo-Kashgar

Date	Mintage	Good	VG	F	VF	XF
ND(1875-1908)	—	5.00	9.50	15.00	25.00	—

C# 33-16 10 CASH

Cast Copper **Ruler:** Kuang-hsü **Obv. Inscription:** Kuang-hsü T'ung-pao

Date	Mintage	Good	VG	F	VF	XF
ND(1875-1908)	—	10.00	20.00	30.00	50.00	—

C# 33-18 10 CASH

Cast Copper **Ruler:** Kuang-hsü **Obv. Inscription:** Kuang-hsü T'ung-pao **Rev:** Character "K'u" above

Date	Mintage	Good	VG	F	VF	XF
ND1875-1908)	—	7.50	12.00	17.50	35.00	—

C# 33-19 10 CASH

Cast Copper **Ruler:** Kuang-hsü **Obv. Inscription:** Kuang-hsü T'ung-pao **Rev:** Manchu inscription, "kuce" in simple style **Rev. Inscription:** Boo-kuce

Date	Mintage	Good	VG	F	VF	XF
ND(1875-1908)	—	2.00	3.00	10.00	18.00	—

C# 34-4 10 CASH

Cast Copper **Ruler:** Hsüan-t'ung **Rev:** "K'u" (Kuche) above, "Ushi" in Manchu and Turki right and left

Date	Mintage	Good	VG	F	VF	XF
ND(1909-1911)	—	50.00	80.00	150	—	—

Note: Cast in Ushi to the order of the Kuche Mint; it is the last of the "red" copper cash

GENERAL CAST COINAGE

KM# 16 10 CASH

Cast Copper **Ruler:** Kuang-hsü **Obv. Inscription:** Kuang-hsü Ting Wei **Rev:** "Boo-yuan?" with "Hsin" (new) above

Date	Mintage	Good	VG	F	VF	XF
CD1907	—	7.50	17.50	30.00	—	—

KM# 17 10 CASH

Cast Copper **Ruler:** Kuang-hsü **Obv. Inscription:** "Kuang-hsü Wu-shen"

Date	Mintage	Good	VG	F	VF	XF
CD1908	—	11.50	25.00	45.00	—	—

MILLED COINAGE

Y# 1 FEN, 5 LI

Copper **Ruler:** Kuang-hsü **Obv:** Large dots in circle, dentilated rims **Obv. Inscription:** Kuang-hsü Yüan-pao **Rev:** Front view dragon **Note:** Two varieties are reported.

Date	Mintage	Good	VG	F	VF	XF
ND(ca.1906)	—	150	200	350	550	—

Y# 1a FEN, 5 LI

Copper **Ruler:** Kuang-hsü **Obv:** Small dots in circle, dotted rims **Obv. Inscription:** Kuang-hsü Yüan-pao **Rev:** Front view dragon
Note: Modern copy.

Date	Mintage	F	VF	XF	Unc	BU
ND(ca.1906)	—	—	—	25.00	35.00	—

Note: The legend on this coin states that it is valued at 1 Fen 5 Li of silver (about 15 Cash); the coin is the size of a normal 10 Cash piece of Sinkiang (Xinjiang), but these pieces are usually larger than those of the other provinces; for this reason, it is assumed the coin was overvalued to benefit the government

Y# A1 2 FEN 5 LI

Copper **Ruler:** Kuang-hsü **Obv. Inscription:** Kuang-hsü Yüan-pao **Rev:** Front view dragon

Date	Mintage	Good	VG	F	VF	XF
ND(ca.1906) Rare	—	—	—	—	—	—

Note: This denomination was recalled shortly after issue and the dies re-engraved 1 Fen and 5 Li to produce Y#1; do not confuse poorly re-engraved Chinese numeral "172" examples of Y#1 for Y#A1; note the difference in spacing of the Chinese characters below the rosettes between Y#1 and Y#A1

Y# B1 2 FEN 5 LI

Copper **Ruler:** Kuang-hsü **Obv. Inscription:** Kuang-hsü Yüan-pao **Rev:** Side view dragon

Date	Mintage	Good	VG	F	VF	XF
ND(ca.1906) Rare	—	—	—	—	—	—

Note: Status unknown

Y# 2.1 10 CASH

Copper **Ruler:** Hsüan-t'ung **Obv. Inscription:** Hsüan-t'ung Yüan-pao **Rev:** Without Chinese legend above side-view dragon

Date	Mintage	Good	VG	F	VF	XF
ND(ca.1909)	—	25.00	42.50	75.00	175	—

Y# 2.2 10 CASH

Copper **Ruler:** Hsüan-t'ung **Obv. Inscription:** Hsüan-t'ung Yüan-pao **Rev:** Chinese legend with "Nien" (year) added above dragon

Date	Mintage	Good	VG	F	VF	XF
CD1910	—	25.00	42.50	75.00	175	—
CD1911	—	30.00	50.00	100	200	—

Y# 2.3 10 CASH

Copper **Ruler:** Hsüan-t'ung **Obv:** Double ring around star in center of inscription **Obv. Inscription:** Hsüan-t'ung Yüan-pao

Date	Mintage	Good	VG	F	VF	XF
CD1911	—	30.00	50.00	100	200	—

Y# 2a 10 CASH

Copper **Ruler:** Hsüan-t'ung **Obv:** Large characters within center circle **Obv. Inscription:** Hsüan-t'ung Yüan-pao

Date	Mintage	VG	F	VF	XF	Unc
CD1910	—	—	—	—	25.00	35.00

Note: Modern copy

Y# A38.1 10 CASH

Copper **Ruler:** Hung-hsien **Obv:** Chinese legend "Hung-hsien T'ung-pi" in inner dotted circle

Date	Mintage	Good	VG	F	VF	XF
AH1334	—	120	180	250	—	—

Y# A38.2 10 CASH

Copper **Ruler:** Hung-hsien

Date	Mintage	Good	VG	F	VF	XF
AH1334	—	120	180	250	—	—

Note: Y#A38.1 and A38.2 were issued for the brief reign of Yuan Shih-kai as Emperor Hung-hsien (1916)

Y# B16 MISCAL (Mace)

3.5000 g., Silver **Ruler:** Kuang-hsü **Obv:** "Kashgar" at right, value at left **Obv. Inscription:** Kuang-hsü Yin-yüan

Date	Mintage	VG	F	VF	XF	Unc
AH1331 Error for 1321	—	50.00	85.00	175	250	—
AH1322	—	50.00	85.00	175	250	—

Y# C16 MISCAL (Mace)

3.5000 g., Silver **Ruler:** Kuang-hsü **Obv:** "Kashgar" in Chinese at right and left of value **Rev:** Turki inscription in sprays

Date	Mintage	VG	F	VF	XF	Unc
AH1322	—	45.00	70.00	125	200	—

Y# 3 MISCAL (Mace)

3.5000 g., Silver **Ruler:** Kuang-hsü **Obv:** Outer legend: Turki without dot in center **Rev:** Without Turki legend

Date	Mintage	VG	F	VF	XF	Unc
ND(1905)	—	75.00	125	200	325	—

Y# 3.1 MISCAL (Mace)

3.5000 g., Silver **Ruler:** Kuang-hsü **Obv. Legend:** Turki with dot in center **Rev:** Without Turki legend

Date	Mintage	VG	F	VF	XF	Unc
ND(1905)	—	75.00	125	200	325	—

Y# 3.2 MISCAL (Mace)

3.5000 g., Silver **Ruler:** Kuang-hsü **Obv:** Without outer Turki legend **Rev:** Turki legend

Date	Mintage	VG	F	VF	XF	Unc
ND(1905)	—	325	550	900	1,500	—

Y# 3.3 MISCAL (Mace)

3.5000 g., Silver **Ruler:** Kuang-hsü **Obv:** Without outer Turki legend **Rev:** Without outer Turki legend

Date	Mintage	VG	F	VF	XF	Unc
ND(1905)	—	90.00	150	250	400	—

Y# A20.1 MISCAL (Mace)

3.5000 g., Silver **Ruler:** Kuang-hsü **Obv:** Turki at right and left of value, date at lower left **Rev:** Side view dragon

Date	Mintage	VG	F	VF	XF	Unc
AH1323	—	200	350	600	1,000	—

Y# A20.2 MISCAL (Mace)

3.5000 g., Silver **Ruler:** Kuang-hsü **Obv:** Turki at right and left of value, date at lower right **Rev:** Side view dragon

Date	Mintage	VG	F	VF	XF	Unc
AH1323	—	200	350	600	1,000	—

Y# A20.3 MISCAL (Mace)

3.5000 g., Silver **Ruler:** Kuang-hsü **Obv:** Inverted Turki legends at right and left of value

Date	Mintage	VG	F	VF	XF	Unc
AH1323	—	200	350	600	1,000	—

Y# 10 MISCAL (Mace)

3.5000 g., Silver **Ruler:** Kuang-hsü **Obv:** Without outer Turki legend **Rev:** Legend above dragon, 1 MACE below **Rev. Legend:** SUNGAREI

Date	Mintage	VG	F	VF	XF	Unc
ND(1906)	—	110	225	400	650	—

Y# A12 GOLD MISCAL (Mace)

7.8000 g., Gold **Ruler:** Kuang-hsü **Rev:** Legend above dragon, "2 MACE" below **Rev. Legend:** SUNGAREI **Note:** Similar to 2 Miscals (Silver) Y#11.

Date	Mintage	VG	F	VF	XF	Unc
ND(ca.1906)	—	—	—	—	—	—

Note: Reported, not confirmed

Y# 8 GOLD MISCAL (Mace)

3.9000 g., Gold **Ruler:** Kuang-hsü **Rev:** Turki legend around uncircled dragon

Date	Mintage	VG	F	VF	XF	Unc
ND(ca.1907)	—	145	400	650	950	1,350

Y# 8.1 GOLD MISCAL (Mace)

3.9000 g., Gold **Ruler:** Kuang-hsü **Rev:** Without Turki legend around uncircled dragon

Date	Mintage	VG	F	VF	XF	Unc
ND(ca.1907)	—	250	750	1,250	1,850	2,650

Y# 8.2 GOLD MISCAL (Mace)

3.9000 g., Gold **Ruler:** Kuang-hsü **Rev:** Turki legend at left differs

Date	Mintage	VG	F	VF	XF	Unc
ND(ca.1907)	—	160	450	750	1,150	1,650

Y# 8.3 GOLD MISCAL (Mace)

3.9000 g., Gold **Ruler:** Kuang-hsü **Rev:** Turki legend in outer circle

Date	Mintage	VG	F	VF	XF	Unc
ND(ca.1907)	—	185	550	950	1,350	2,000

Y# 9 GOLD 2 MISCALS

7.8000 g., Gold **Ruler:** Kuang-hsü **Obv:** Narrow-spaced Chinese "2" **Rev:** Turki legend around uncircled dragon

Date	Mintage	VG	F	VF	XF	Unc
ND(ca.1906)	—	250	750	1,350	2,000	2,800

Y# 9.1 GOLD 2 MISCALS

7.8000 g., Gold **Ruler:** Kuang-hsü **Obv:** Wide-spaced Chinese "2" **Rev:** Redesigned dragon

Date	Mintage	VG	F	VF	XF	Unc
ND(ca.1906)	—	250	750	1,350	2,000	2,800

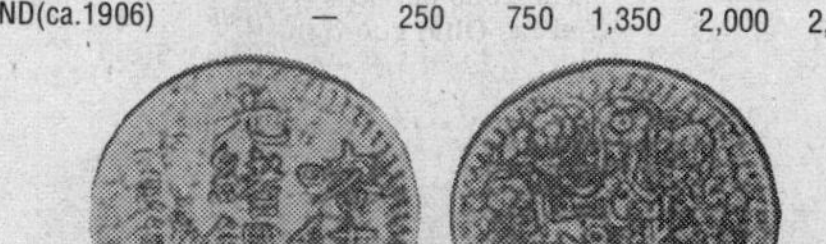

Y# 17a 2 MISCALS (2 Mace)

7.2000 g., Silver **Ruler:** Kuang-hsü **Obv:** Inscription between Kashgar and value **Obv. Inscription:** Kuang-hsü Yin-yüan

Date	Mintage	VG	F	VF	XF	Unc
AH1311	—	—	—	—	—	—
Note: Error						
AH1312	—	12.50	22.50	32.50	50.00	—
AH1313	—	12.50	22.50	32.50	50.00	—
AH1314	—	12.50	22.50	32.50	50.00	—
AH1315	—	12.50	22.50	32.50	50.00	—
AH1317	—	12.50	22.50	32.50	50.00	—
AH1319	—	12.50	22.50	32.50	50.00	—
AH1320	—	17.50	30.00	45.00	75.00	—

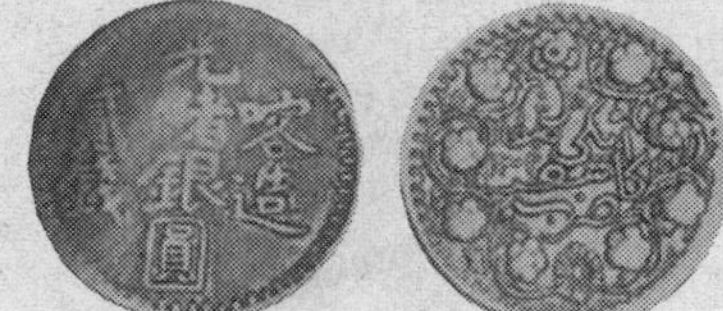

Y# 17a.1 2 MISCALS (2 Mace)

7.2000 g., Silver **Ruler:** Kuang-hsü **Obv:** Inscription between "K'a Tsao" at right, value at left **Obv. Inscription:** Kuang-hsü Yin-yüan

Date	Mintage	VG	F	VF	XF	Unc
AH1320 Rare	—	—	—	—	—	—

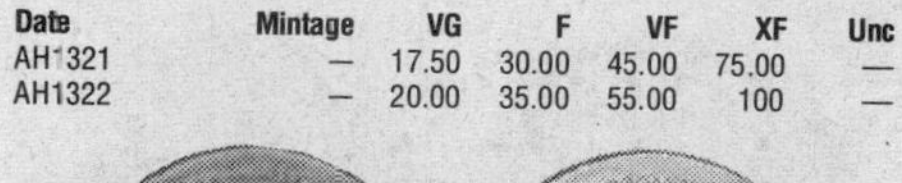

Date	Mintage	VG	F	VF	XF	Unc
AH1321	—	17.50	30.00	45.00	75.00	—
AH1322	—	20.00	35.00	55.00	100	—

Y# 33 2 MISCALS (2 Mace)

Silver **Ruler:** Kuang-hsü **Obv:** Inscription between "Tihwa" and value with normal Êrh (2) at left **Obv. Inscription:** "Kuang-hsü Yin-yüan" **Rev. Inscription:** Turki in floral wreath

Date	Mintage	VG	F	VF	XF	Unc
AH1321	—	15.00	22.00	55.00	90.00	—
AH1322	—	15.00	22.00	55.00	90.00	—
AH1323	—	17.50	30.00	55.00	90.00	—

Y# 33.1 2 MISCALS (2 Mace)

Silver **Ruler:** Kuang-hsü **Obv:** Inscription between "Tihwa" and value with official Êrh (2) at left **Obv. Inscription:** "Kuang-hsü Yin-yüan" **Rev. Inscription:** Turki in floral wreath

Date	Mintage	VG	F	VF	XF	Unc
AH1323	—	15.00	22.00	55.00	90.00	—
AH1324	—	15.00	22.00	55.00	90.00	—
AH1325	—	15.00	22.00	55.00	90.00	—

Y# B20.1 2 MISCALS (2 Mace)

7.2000 g., Silver **Obv. Legend:** Chinese and Turki around inscription Kuang-hsü Yüan-pao **Rev:** Dragon

Date	Mintage	VG	F	VF	XF	Unc
AH1323	—	175	300	500	850	—

Y# B20.2 2 MISCALS (2 Mace)

7.2000 g., Silver **Obv. Legend:** Chinese and Turki around inscription Kuang-hsü Yüan-pao **Rev:** Dragon

Date	Mintage	VG	F	VF	XF	Unc
AH1323	—	175	300	500	850	—

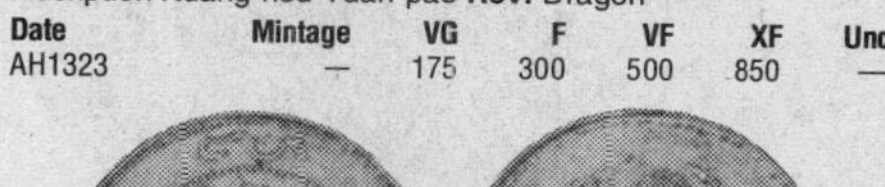

Y# 4 2 MISCALS (2 Mace)

7.2000 g., Silver **Ruler:** Kuang-hsü **Obv:** Turki outer legend **Rev:** Without Turki legend

Date	Mintage	VG	F	VF	XF	Unc
ND(1905)	—	50.00	75.00	150	400	—

Y# 4.1 2 MISCALS (2 Mace)

7.2000 g., Silver **Ruler:** Kuang-hsü **Obv:** Continuous Turki outer legend **Rev:** Without Turki legend

Date	Mintage	VG	F	VF	XF	Unc
ND(1905)	—	100	150	250	325	—

Y# 4.2 2 MISCALS (2 Mace)

7.2000 g., Silver **Ruler:** Kuang-hsü **Obv:** Without outer Turki legend **Rev:** Turki legend

Date	Mintage	VG	F	VF	XF	Unc
ND(1905)	—	150	250	400	650	—

Y# 4.3 2 MISCALS (2 Mace)

7.2000 g., Silver **Ruler:** Kuang-hsü **Rev:** Redesigned dragon without Turki legends

Date	Mintage	VG	F	VF	XF	Unc
ND(1905)	—	150	250	400	650	—

Y# 4.4 2 MISCALS (2 Mace)

7.2000 g., Silver **Ruler:** Kuang-hsü **Obv:** Turki outer legend **Rev:** Circled dragon without Turki legend

Date	Mintage	VG	F	VF	XF	Unc
ND(1905) Rare	—	—	—	—	—	—

Y# 11 2 MISCALS (2 Mace)

7.2000 g., Silver **Ruler:** Kuang-hsü **Rev:** Legend above dragon, "2 MACE" below **Rev. Legend:** SUNGAREI

Date	Mintage	VG	F	VF	XF	Unc
ND(1906)	—	200	425	850	1,350	—

Y# 23 2 MISCALS (2 Mace)

7.2000 g., Silver **Obv. Legend:** Chinese and Turki around inscription Ta-Ch'ing Yin-pi **Rev:** Dragon in circle surrounded by sprays

Date	Mintage	VG	F	VF	XF	Unc
AH1324 Rare	—	—	—	—	—	—
AH1325	—	20.00	40.00	65.00	110	—
AH1326	—	20.00	40.00	65.00	110	—
AH1327	—	25.00	50.00	80.00	150	—
AH1329	—	35.00	65.00	110	175	—

Y# 29 2 MISCALS (2 Mace)

7.2000 g., Silver **Obv:** Turki legend around Yin-Yüan Êrh-ch'ien within a beaded circle **Rev:** Double ring around small dragon, floral pattern outside without legend

Date	Mintage	VG	F	VF	XF	Unc
AH1329	—	55.00	90.00	150	250	—

Y# 29.1 2 MISCALS (2 Mace)

7.2000 g., Silver **Obv:** Yin-yüan Êrh-ch'ien **Rev:** Turki legend below larger dragon within single circle

Date	Mintage	VG	F	VF	XF	Unc
AH1329	—	75.00	125	200	325	—

Y# 18a 3 MISCALS

10.5000 g., Silver **Ruler:** Kuang-hsü **Obv:** Inscription between Kashgar and value **Obv. Inscription:** Kuang-hsü Yin-yüan **Rev:** Turki in floral wreath

Date	Mintage	VG	F	VF	XF	Unc
AH1319	—	10.00	20.00	32.50	65.00	—
AH1320	—	10.00	20.00	32.50	65.00	—

Y# 18a.1 3 MISCALS

10.5000 g., Silver **Ruler:** Kuang-hsü **Obv:** Inscription between "K'a Tsao" and value **Obv. Inscription:** "Kuang-hsü Yin-yüan" **Rev:** Turki in floral wreath

Date	Mintage	VG	F	VF	XF	Unc
AH1320	—	10.00	20.00	32.50	65.00	—
AH1321	—	10.00	20.00	32.50	65.00	—
AH1322	—	10.00	20.00	32.50	65.00	—

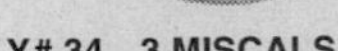

Y# 34 3 MISCALS
10.3000 g., Silver **Ruler:** Kuang-hsü **Obv:** Inscription between "Tihwa" and value with normal "San" (3) at left **Obv. Inscription:** "Kuang-hsü Yin-yüan" **Rev. Inscription:** Turki in floral wreath

Date	Mintage	VG	F	VF	XF	Unc
AH1321	—	17.50	30.00	75.00	110	—
AH1322	—	17.50	30.00	75.00	110	—
AH1323	—	17.50	30.00	75.00	110	—

Y# 34a 3 MISCALS
10.3000 g., Silver **Ruler:** Kuang-hsü **Obv:** Inscription between "Tihwa" and value with official "San" (3) at left **Obv. Inscription:** Kuang-hsü Yin-yüan **Rev. Inscription:** Turki in floral wreath

Date	Mintage	VG	F	VF	XF	Unc
AH1322	—	10.00	20.00	32.50	65.00	—
AH1323	—	10.00	20.00	32.50	65.00	—
AH1324	—	10.00	20.00	32.50	65.00	—
AH1325	—	10.00	20.00	32.50	65.00	—

Y# 35 3 MISCALS
17.9000 g., Silver **Ruler:** Kuang-hsü **Obv:** Inscription between "Tihwa" and value with normal "Wu" (5) at left **Obv. Inscription:** "Kuang-hsü Yin-yüan" **Rev. Inscription:** Turki in floral wreath

Date	Mintage	VG	F	VF	XF	Unc
AH1321	—	20.00	35.00	70.00	125	—
AH1322	—	20.00	35.00	70.00	125	—
AH1323	—	20.00	35.00	70.00	125	—

Y# 35a 3 MISCALS
17.9000 g., Silver **Ruler:** Kuang-hsü **Obv:** Inscription between "Tihwa" and value with official "Wu" (5) at left **Obv. Inscription:** "Kuang-hsü Yin-yüan" **Rev. Inscription:** Turki in floral wreath

Date	Mintage	VG	F	VF	XF	Unc
AH1323	—	20.00	40.00	70.00	125	—
AH1324	—	15.00	30.00	60.00	100	—
AH1325	—	15.00	30.00	60.00	100	—

Y# 20 3 MISCALS
10.5000 g., Silver **Ruler:** Kuang-hsü **Obv. Legend:** Turki and Chinese around inscription with normal "San"; (3) in Chinese at bottom **Obv. Inscription:** "Ta-ch'ing Yüan-pao"

Date	Mintage	VG	F	VF	XF	Unc
AH1323	—	85.00	175	275	450	—

Y# 20.1 3 MISCALS
10.5000 g., Silver **Ruler:** Kuang-hsü **Obv. Legend:** Turki and Chinese around inscription with official "San"; (3) in Chinese at bottom **Obv. Inscription:** "Ta-ch'ing Yüan-pao"

Date	Mintage	VG	F	VF	XF	Unc
AH1323	—	100	200	325	550	—

Y# 20.2 3 MISCALS
10.5000 g., Silver **Ruler:** Kuang-hsü **Obv. Legend:** Turki and Chinese around inscription with official "San", (3) in Chinese at bottom, date at lower right **Obv. Inscription:** "Ta-ch'ing Yüan-pao"

Date	Mintage	VG	F	VF	XF	Unc
AH1323	—	100	200	365	600	—

Y# 30 3 MISCALS
10.5000 g., Silver **Obv. Inscription:** "Yin-yüan San-ch'ien" **Rev:** Turki legend below small, side view dragon in circle

Date	Mintage	VG	F	VF	XF	Unc
AH1329	—	200	350	600	1,000	—

Y# 5 4 MISCALS (4 Mace)
14.2000 g., Silver **Ruler:** Kuang-hsü

Date	Mintage	VG	F	VF	XF	Unc
ND(1905)	—	85.00	125	200	400	—

Y# 19a.1 5 MISCALS
17.2000 g., Silver **Ruler:** Kuang-hsü **Obv:** Inscription between "K'a Tsao" at right, value at left **Obv. Inscription:** Kuang-hsü Yin-yüan

Date	Mintage	VG	F	VF	XF	Unc
AH1311 Error	—	—	—	—	—	—
AH1321	—	12.50	20.00	30.00	60.00	—
AH1322	—	12.50	20.00	30.00	60.00	—

Y# 19a 5 MISCALS
17.2000 g., Silver **Ruler:** Kuang-hsü **Obv:** Inscription between "Kashgar" and value; Chinese characters "K'a Shih" at right **Obv. Inscription:** Kuang-hsü Yin-yüan **Rev:** Turki inscription within sprays

Date	Mintage	VG	F	VF	XF	Unc
AH1311 Error	—	—	—	—	—	—
AH1313	—	17.50	25.00	40.00	70.00	—
AH1314	—	17.50	25.00	40.00	70.00	—
AH1315	—	17.50	25.00	40.00	70.00	—
AH1316	—	17.50	25.00	40.00	70.00	—
AH1317	—	17.50	25.00	40.00	70.00	—
AH1319	—	17.50	25.00	40.00	70.00	—
AH1320	—	17.50	25.00	40.00	70.00	—

Y# 21 5 MISCALS
17.2000 g., Silver **Ruler:** Kuang-hsü **Obv:** Chinese and Turki around inscription; date at upper left **Obv. Inscription:** "Ta-ch'ing Yüan-pao" **Rev:** Side view dragon's tail points to right **Note:** Kann #1110.

Date	Mintage	VG	F	VF	XF	Unc
AH1323	—	20.00	30.00	45.00	75.00	—

Y# 21.1 5 MISCALS
17.2000 g., Silver **Obv:** Simple 5 in Chinese, date at lower right **Rev:** Dragon's tail points to right

Date	Mintage	VG	F	VF	XF	Unc
AH1323	—	20.00	30.00	45.00	75.00	—

Y# 21.2 5 MISCALS
17.2000 g., Silver **Ruler:** Kuang-hsü **Obv:** Inverted Turki legend, date at lower right **Rev:** Dragon

Date	Mintage	VG	F	VF	XF	Unc
AH1323	—	22.50	35.00	60.00	100	—

Y# 21.3 5 MISCALS
17.2000 g., Silver **Ruler:** Kuang-hsü **Obv:** Normal "Wu" (5) at bottom, date at lower right **Rev:** Dragon

Date	Mintage	VG	F	VF	XF	Unc
AH1323 Rare	—	—	—	—	—	—

Y# 21.4 5 MISCALS
17.2000 g., Silver **Ruler:** Kuang-hsü **Obv:** Date at upper left **Rev:** Side view dragon's tail points to left

Date	Mintage	VG	F	VF	XF	Unc
AH1323	—	15.00	25.00	50.00	90.00	—

Y# 21.5 5 MISCALS
17.2000 g., Silver **Ruler:** Kuang-hsü **Obv:** Date at lower right **Rev:** Dragon

Date	Mintage	VG	F	VF	XF	Unc
AH1323	—	15.00	25.00	50.00	90.00	—

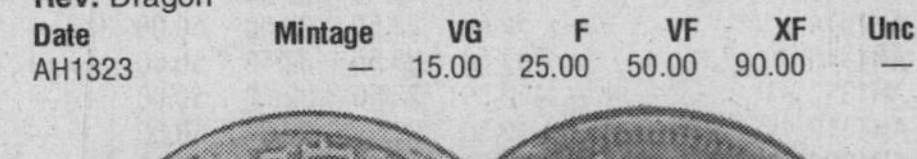

Y# 21.6 5 MISCALS
17.2000 g., Silver **Ruler:** Kuang-hsü **Obv:** Inverted Turki legend, date at lower right **Rev:** Dragon

Date	Mintage	VG	F	VF	XF	Unc
AH1323	—	20.00	35.00	80.00	135	—

Y# 21.7 5 MISCALS
17.2000 g., Silver **Ruler:** Kuang-hsü **Obv:** Date at upper right **Rev:** Dragon

Date	Mintage	VG	F	VF	XF	Unc
AH1323	—	20.00	30.00	45.00	75.00	—

Y# 25 5 MISCALS
17.2000 g., Silver **Ruler:** Kuang-hsü **Obv:** "Kashgar Tsao" at top between standard Turki legend; inscription: "Ta-ch'ing Yin-pi" **Rev:** Dragon

Date	Mintage	VG	F	VF	XF	Unc
ND(ca.1906)	—	22.50	40.00	85.00	150	—

Y# 25.1 5 MISCALS
17.2000 g., Silver **Obv:** Date at left or upper left **Rev:** Dragon

Date	Mintage	VG	F	VF	XF	Unc
AH1325	—	22.50	40.00	85.00	150	—
AH1326	—	22.50	40.00	85.00	150	—
AH1327	—	22.50	40.00	85.00	150	—

Y# 25.2 5 MISCALS
17.2000 g., Silver **Rev:** Dragon **Note:** Similar to Y#25.1. Varieties exist in date placement.

Date	Mintage	VG	F	VF	XF	Unc
AH1325	—	22.50	40.00	85.00	150	—
AH1326	—	22.50	40.00	85.00	150	—
AH1327	—	22.50	40.00	85.00	150	—

Y# 25.3 5 MISCALS
17.2000 g., Silver **Obv:** Inverted Turki legend, date at upper right, right, or lower right **Obv. Legend:** Dragon

Date	Mintage	VG	F	VF	XF	Unc
AH1325	—	17.50	25.00	75.00	110	—
AH1326	—	17.50	25.00	75.00	110	—

Date	Mintage	VG	F	VF	XF	Unc
AH1328	—	17.50	25.00	75.00	110	—

Note: Error for 1326

Y# 25.4 5 MISCALS
17.2000 g., Silver **Obv:** "Kashgar" at top between standard Turki legend with date at upper right **Rev:** Dragon

Date	Mintage	VG	F	VF	XF	Unc
AH1325	—	20.00	35.00	100	150	—

Y# 25.8 5 MISCALS
17.2000 g., Silver **Obv:** Date at upper left or left **Rev:** Dragon **Note:** Varieties exist.

Date	Mintage	VG	F	VF	XF	Unc
AH1325	—	17.50	25.00	75.00	110	—

Y# 25.9 5 MISCALS
17.2000 g., Silver **Obv:** Similar to Y#25.4 **Rev:** Dragon, floral sprays reversed

Date	Mintage	VG	F	VF	XF	Unc
AH1325	—	50.00	100	165	275	—

Y# 25.10 5 MISCALS
17.2000 g., Silver **Obv:** Date at upper left **Rev:** Dragon, standard florals

Date	Mintage	VG	F	VF	XF	Unc
AH1325	—	50.00	100	165	275	—

Y# 25.11 5 MISCALS
17.2000 g., Silver **Obv:** Date at upper left **Rev:** Dragon, three rosettes at top

Date	Mintage	VG	F	VF	XF	Unc
AH1325	—	600	800	1,000	1,200	—

Y# 27 5 MISCALS
17.2000 g., Silver **Ruler:** Hsüan-t'ung **Obv:** "Kashgar" at top, Turki below; star in center **Obv. Inscription:** "Hsüan-t'ung Yin-pi" **Rev:** Dragon

Date	Mintage	VG	F	VF	XF	Unc
AH1327	—	20.00	30.00	65.00	110	—
AH1328	—	25.00	50.00	90.00	150	—

Y# 27.1 5 MISCALS
17.2000 g., Silver **Ruler:** Hsüan-t'ung **Obv:** Official "Wu" (5) at right, dot in center **Rev:** Dragon

Date	Mintage	VG	F	VF	XF	Unc
AH1328	—	35.00	65.00	150	225	—

Y# 27.2 5 MISCALS
17.2000 g., Silver **Ruler:** Hsüan-t'ung **Obv:** Rosette in center

Date	Mintage	VG	F	VF	XF	Unc
AH1329	—	50.00	100	200	275	—

Y# 31 5 MISCALS
17.2000 g., Silver **Ruler:** Kuang-hsü **Obv. Legend:** Legend "Kashgar" at top, Turki below around side view dragon, star at center and at right **Rev:** Inscription between value **Rev. Inscription:** "Hsiang-yin" (soldier's pay) **Note:** Varieties with two and three tail spines on dragon exist.

Date	Mintage	VG	F	VF	XF	Unc
AH1330	—	20.00	40.00	100	150	—
AH1329	—	20.00	40.00	100	150	—
AH1321	—	20.00	40.00	100	150	—
Note: Error for 1331						
AH1331	—	20.00	40.00	100	150	—

Y# A28 5 MISCALS
17.2000 g., Silver **Ruler:** Hsüan-t'ung **Obv:** "Kashgar" at top, normal "Wu" (5) at right, star in center **Obv. Inscription:** "Hsüan-t'ung Yüan-pao" **Rev:** Side view dragon **Note:** Prev. Y#27.3.

Date	Mintage	VG	F	VF	XF	Unc
AH1329	—	17.50	25.00	75.00	110	—

Y# A28.1 5 MISCALS
17.2000 g., Silver **Ruler:** Hsüan-t'ung **Obv:** Dot in center **Rev:** Side view dragon **Note:** Prev. Y#27.4.

Date	Mintage	VG	F	VF	XF	Unc
AH1329	—	17.50	25.00	75.00	110	—

Y# A28.2 5 MISCALS
17.2000 g., Silver **Ruler:** Hsüan-t'ung **Obv:** Rosette in center **Rev:** Side view dragon **Note:** Prev. Y#27.5.

Date	Mintage	VG	F	VF	XF	Unc
AH1329	—	17.50	25.00	75.00	110	—

Y# A28.3 5 MISCALS
17.2000 g., Silver **Ruler:** Hsüan-t'ung **Obv:** Official "Wu" (5) at right, star in center **Rev:** Side view dragon **Note:** Prev. Y#27.6.

Date	Mintage	VG	F	VF	XF	Unc
AH1329	—	17.50	25.00	75.00	110	—

Y# 31.2 5 MISCALS

17.2000 g., Silver **Ruler:** Kuang-hsü **Obv:** Rosettes in outer field

Date	Mintage	VG	F	VF	XF	Unc
AH1329	—	50.00	100	165	275	—

Y# 31.3 5 MISCALS

17.2000 g., Silver **Ruler:** Kuang-hsü **Rev:** Rosettes in center

Date	Mintage	VG	F	VF	XF	Unc
AH1329	—	22.50	75.00	100	150	—

Y# 6 5 MISCALS (5 Mace)

17.9000 g., Silver **Ruler:** Kuang-hsü **Obv:** Without dot or rosette in center **Rev:** Uncircled dragon

Date	Mintage	VG	F	VF	XF	Unc
ND(1905)	—	15.00	25.00	60.00	175	—

Y# 6.1 5 MISCALS (5 Mace)

17.9000 g., Silver **Ruler:** Kuang-hsü **Rev:** Circled dragon, without rosettes

Date	Mintage	VG	F	VF	XF	Unc
ND(1905)	—	15.00	25.00	50.00	90.00	—

Y# 6.2 5 MISCALS (5 Mace)

17.9000 g., Silver **Ruler:** Kuang-hsü **Rev:** Large rosettes at sides of dragon

Date	Mintage	VG	F	VF	XF	Unc
ND(1905)	—	15.00	25.00	50.00	90.00	—

Y# 6.3 5 MISCALS (5 Mace)

17.9000 g., Silver **Ruler:** Kuang-hsü **Obv:** Dot in center **Rev:** Without rosettes, circled dragon

Date	Mintage	VG	F	VF	XF	Unc
ND(1905)	—	15.00	25.00	50.00	90.00	—

Y# 6.4 5 MISCALS (5 Mace)

17.9000 g., Silver **Ruler:** Kuang-hsü **Obv:** Cross in center

Date	Mintage	VG	F	VF	XF	Unc
ND(1905)	—	15.00	25.00	50.00	90.00	—

Y# 6.5 5 MISCALS (5 Mace)

17.9000 g., Silver **Ruler:** Kuang-hsü **Obv:** Large rosette in center, middle of which is depressed

Date	Mintage	VG	F	VF	XF	Unc
ND(1905)	—	15.00	25.00	50.00	90.00	—

Y# 6.6 5 MISCALS (5 Mace)

17.9000 g., Silver **Ruler:** Kuang-hsü **Obv:** Eight-petalled rosette in center, middle of which is raised **Rev:** Small rosettes at sides of dragon

Date	Mintage	VG	F	VF	XF	Unc
ND(1905)	—	15.00	25.00	50.00	90.00	—

Y# 6.7 5 MISCALS (5 Mace)

17.9000 g., Silver **Ruler:** Kuang-hsü **Rev:** Bat above uncircled dragon's head

Date	Mintage	VG	F	VF	XF	Unc
ND(1905)	—	175	300	450	700	—

Y# 6.8 5 MISCALS (5 Mace)

17.9000 g., Silver **Ruler:** Kuang-hsü **Rev:** Turki legend around uncircled dragon

Date	Mintage	VG	F	VF	XF	Unc
ND(1905)	—	400	600	—	—	—

Y# 6.9 5 MISCALS (5 Mace)

17.9000 g., Silver **Ruler:** Kuang-hsü **Rev:** Legend above uncircled dragon, "5 MACE" below **Rev. Legend:** SUNGAREI

Date	Mintage	VG	F	VF	XF	Unc
ND(1906) Rare	—	—	—	—	—	—

Note: Some authorities consider this coin a fantasy

Y# 6.10 5 MISCALS (5 Mace)

17.9000 g., Silver **Ruler:** Kuang-hsü **Rev:** Without SUNGREI, with four bats and many clouds around dragon

Date	Mintage	VG	F	VF	XF	Unc
ND(1906) Rare	—	—	—	—	—	—

Y# 6.11 5 MISCALS (5 Mace)

17.9000 g., Silver **Ruler:** Kuang-hsü **Obv:** Turki legend rotated **Rev:** Bat above dragon's head

Date	Mintage	VG	F	VF	XF	Unc
ND(1906) Rare	—	—	—	—	—	—

Y# 7 SAR (Tael)

35.5000 g., Silver **Ruler:** Kuang-hsü **Obv:** Without Turki legend **Rev:** Without Turki legend, rosettes at sides of uncircled dtagon

Date	Mintage	VG	F	VF	XF	Unc
ND(1905)	—	25.00	40.00	60.00	140	—

Y# 7.1 SAR (Tael)

35.5000 g., Silver **Ruler:** Kuang-hsü **Rev:** Turki legend around circled dragon, without rosettes

Date	Mintage	VG	F	VF	XF	Unc
ND(1905)	—	40.00	65.00	100	300	—

Y# 7.2 SAR (Tael)

35.5000 g., Silver **Ruler:** Kuang-hsü **Rev:** Turki legend around uncircled dragon

Date	Mintage	VG	F	VF	XF	Unc
ND(1905)	—	500	850	1,250	1,600	—

Y# 7.3 SAR (Tael)

35.5000 g., Silver **Ruler:** Kuang-hsü **Obv:** Outer Turki legend, rosette in center **Rev:** Without Turki legend, with rosettes at sides of uncircled dragon

Date	Mintage	VG	F	VF	XF	Unc
ND(1905)	—	35.00	50.00	70.00	150	—

Y# 26 SAR (Tael)

35.2000 g., Silver **Obv:** Chinese "Kashgar" at top wtih Turki "Kashgar" to left **Obv. Inscription:** "Ta-ch'ing Yin-pi" **Rev:** Side view dragon in sprays

Date	Mintage	VG	F	VF	XF	Unc
AH1325	—	200	300	500	850	—

Y# 26.1 SAR (Tael)

35.2000 g., Silver **Obv:** "Kashgar Tsao" at top

Date	Mintage	VG	F	VF	XF	Unc
AH1325	—	1,200	2,750	5,000	7,000	—

Y# 26.2 SAR (Tael)

35.2000 g., Silver **Obv:** Chinese "Kashgar" at top wtih Turki "Kashgar" to right

Date	Mintage	VG	F	VF	XF	Unc
AH1325	—	300	500	700	1,200	—

REPUBLIC

PROVINCIAL CAST COINAGE

Y# 37.1 10 CASH
Cast Copper, 32 mm. **Obv. Inscription:** Chung Hua Min Kuo **Rev:** Crossed flags

Date	Mintage	Good	VG	F	VF	XF
ND(ca.1912)	—	35.00	55.00	80.00	—	—

Y# 37.2 10 CASH
Cast Copper, 29 mm. **Obv. Inscription:** Chung Hua Min Kuo **Rev:** Crossed flags

Date	Mintage	Good	VG	F	VF	XF
ND(ca.1912)	—	35.00	55.00	80.00	—	—

MILLED COINAGE

Y# A36.1 5 CASH
Copper **Obv:** Large Chinese inscription **Obv. Inscription:** "Chung-hua Min-kuo" between "T'ung-pi" **Rev:** Flag **Rev. Legend:** Chinese outer, Turki inner, around flag

Date	Mintage	Good	VG	F	VF	XF
ND(ca.1912)	—	275	375	500	700	—

Y# A36.2 5 CASH
Copper **Obv:** Small Chinese inscription **Obv. Inscription:** "Chung-hua Min-kuo" between "T'ung-pi" **Rev:** Flag **Rev. Legend:** Chinese outer, Turki inner, around flag

Date	Mintage	Good	VG	F	VF	XF
ND(ca.1912)	—	275	375	500	700	—

Y# 36 5 CASH
Copper **Obv. Legend:** Chinese around inscription "Chung-hua Min-kuo" **Rev:** Crossed flags **Rev. Inscription:** Turki above and below crossed flags

Date	Mintage	Good	VG	F	VF	XF
AH1331	—	100	135	225	350	—

Y# B39.1 10 CASH
Copper **Obv:** Large character "Shih" (ten), normal "Pao" **Obv. Legend:** Chung Hua Min Kuo **Rev:** Crossed flags

Date	Mintage	Good	VG	F	VF	XF
ND	—	8.50	15.00	25.00	37.50	65.00

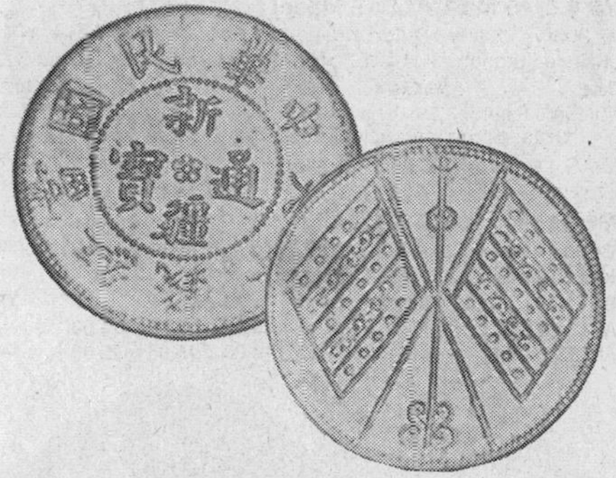

Y# B39.2 10 CASH
Copper **Obv:** Small character "Shih" (ten) **Obv. Legend:** Chung Hua Min Kuo **Rev:** Small crossed flags

Date	Mintage	Good	VG	F	VF	XF
ND	—	12.50	25.00	35.00	50.00	85.00

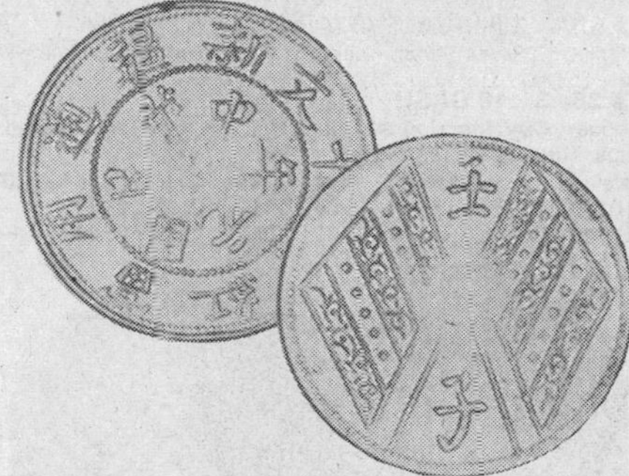

Y# A39.1 10 CASH
Copper **Obv. Legend:** Chung Hua Min Kuo **Rev:** Large crossed flags with vertical stirpes

Date	Mintage	Good	VG	F	VF	XF
CD1 (1912)	—	7.50	13.50	18.50	28.50	49.50

Y# B36.1 10 CASH
Copper **Obv:** Large Chinese inscription **Obv. Inscription:** "Chung-hua Min-kuo" between "T'ung-pi" **Rev:** Flag **Rev. Legend:** Chinese outer, Turki inner, around flag

Date	Mintage	Good	VG	F	VF	XF
ND(ca.1912)	—	25.00	37.50	50.00	85.00	—

Y# B36.2 10 CASH
Copper **Obv:** Small Chinese inscription **Obv. Inscription:** "Chung-hua Min-kuo" between "T'ung-pi" **Rev:** Flag **Rev. Legend:** Chinese outer, Turki inner, around flag

Date	Mintage	Good	VG	F	VF	XF
ND(ca.1912)	—	25.00	37.50	50.00	85.00	—

Y# 38.1 10 CASH
Copper **Obv:** Chinese legend: "Shih Wen" (10 Cash) at upper left **Rev:** Crossed flags, date at upper center

Date	Mintage	Good	VG	F	VF	XF
AH1332 (1913)	—	7.50	15.00	20.00	35.00	—
ND(ca.1913)	—	7.50	15.00	20.00	35.00	—
AH1333 (1914)	—	7.50	15.00	20.00	35.00	—
AH1334 (1915)	—	7.50	15.00	20.00	35.00	—

Y# 38.2 10 CASH
Copper **Rev:** Crossed flags, modified Turki legend with date at bottom

Date	Mintage	Good	VG	F	VF	XF
AH1331 (1912)	—	8.50	12.50	17.50	30.00	—
AH1332 (1913)	—	8.50	12.50	17.50	30.00	—
AH1334 (1915)	—	8.50	12.50	17.50	30.00	—
AH1335 (1916)	—	8.50	12.50	17.50	30.00	—

Y# A39.2 10 CASH
Copper **Rev:** Small crossed flags with vertical stirpes

Date	Mintage	Good	VG	F	VF	XF
1 (1912)	—	7.00	12.00	16.50	25.50	47.50

Note: This type exists with a great variety of the "Shih" (ten), and "Pao" characters

Y# F38 10 CASH

Copper **Ruler:** Kuang-hsü **Obv:** Chinese characters "Shih Wen" (10 Wen) at lower left **Rev:** Crossed flags, upper Turki legend inverted

Date	Mintage	Good	VG	F	VF	XF
AH1332 (1913)	—	35.00	65.00	85.00	125	—

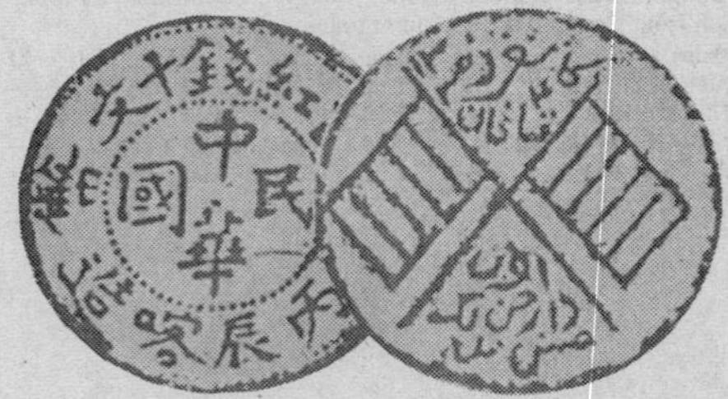

Y# 38.1 10 CASH

Copper **Obv:** Chinese legend: "Shih Wen" (10 Cash) at upper left **Rev:** Crossed flags, date at upper center

Date	Mintage	Good	VG	F	VF	XF
AH1332 (1913)	—	7.50	15.00	20.00	35.00	—
ND(ca.1913)	—	7.50	15.00	20.00	35.00	—
AH1333 (1914)	—	7.50	15.00	20.00	35.00	—
AH1334 (1915)	—	7.50	15.00	20.00	35.00	—

Y# 38.3 10 CASH

Copper **Obv:** Two lower right Chinese characters different **Obv. Inscription:** Chung Hua Min Kuo **Rev:** Crossed flags, AH date at top

Date	Mintage	Good	VG	F	VF	XF
AH133-4 (1915)	—	50.00	75.00	125	200	—

Y# 38.5 10 CASH

Copper **Obv:** Outer Chinese legend wtihout "Shih" of "Kashgar" at lower left **Obv. Inscription:** Chung Hua Min Kuo **Rev:** Crossed flags, Turki legend in florals with "Zarb Kashgar" at top **Note:** Rev: similar to Y#A38.2

Date	Mintage	Good	VG	F	VF	XF
AH1334 (1915)	—	37.50	60.00	100	150	—

Y# 38.6 10 CASH

Copper **Obv. Inscription:** Chung Hua Min Kuo **Rev:** Single flower in lower Turki legend

Date	Mintage	Good	VG	F	VF	XF
AH1334	—	—	—	—	—	—

Y# 38.7 10 CASH

Copper **Obv. Inscription:** Chung Hua Min Kuo **Rev:** Without flowers or florals in Turki legends

Date	Mintage	Good	VG	F	VF	XF
AH1334 (1915)	—	—	—	—	—	—

Y# C39 10 CASH

Copper **Obv. Inscription:** Chung Hua Min Kuo **Rev:** Turki legend around crossed flags

Date	Mintage	Good	VG	F	VF	XF
CD1921 Rare	—	—	—	—	—	—

Note: Status unknown

Y# 38a.1 10 CASH

Copper **Obv:** Chinese date at upper right with rosette **Obv. Inscription:** Chung Hua Min Kuo

Date	Mintage	Good	VG	F	VF	XF
AH1340 (1921)	—	5.00	10.00	15.00	25.00	—
AH1339 (1921)	—	5.00	10.00	15.00	25.00	—

Y# 38a.3 10 CASH

Copper **Obv. Inscription:** Chung Hua Min Kuo **Rev:** Crossed flags, Turki legend rearranged

Date	Mintage	Good	VG	F	VF	XF
AH1340 (1921)	—	5.00	10.00	15.00	25.00	—
AH1339 (1921)	—	5.00	10.00	15.00	25.00	—

Y# 38a.2 10 CASH

Copper **Obv:** Outer Chinese legend without "Shih" of "Kashgar" at upper left **Obv. Inscription:** Chung Hua Min Kuo **Rev:** Crossed flags

Date	Mintage	Good	VG	F	VF	XF
AH134x (1921)	—	5.00	10.00	15.00	25.00	—

Y# 38a.5 10 CASH

Copper **Obv:** Crowded Chinese year "11" **Obv. Inscription:** Chung Hua Min Kuo **Rev:** Crossed flags

Date	Mintage	Good	VG	F	VF	XF
AH1340 (1921)	—	25.00	40.00	65.00	100	—

Y# 38b.1 10 CASH

Copper **Obv:** Chinese legend "Min-kuo T'ung-yüan" in inner circle with "Kashgar" at right **Obv. Inscription:** Min Kuo T'ung Yüan **Rev:** Crossed flags

Date	Mintage	Good	VG	F	VF	XF
AH1340 (1921)	—	15.00	30.00	40.00	65.00	—

Y# 38b.2 10 CASH

Copper **Obv:** Outer Chinese legend rotated **Obv. Inscription:** Min Kuo T'ung Yüan **Rev:** Crossed flags

Date	Mintage	Good	VG	F	VF	XF
AH134x (1921)	—	15.00	30.00	40.00	65.00	—

Y# A44.1 10 CASH

Copper **Obv. Inscription:** Chung Hua Min Kuo **Rev:** Crossed flags

Date	Mintage	Good	VG	F	VF	XF
11(1922)	—	50.00	75.00	100	125	—

Y# A44.2 10 CASH

Copper **Obv. Inscription:** Chung Hua Min Kuo **Rev:** Crossed flags reversed

Date	Mintage	Good	VG	F	VF	XF
11(1922)	—	50.00	75.00	100	125	—

Y# B38.4 10 CASH

Copper **Obv:** Chinese date at left and right **Obv. Inscription:** Chung Hua Min Kuo **Rev:** Outlined sunburst **Rev. Inscription:** T'ung Yüan

Date	Mintage	Good	VG	F	VF	XF
CD1928	—	3.00	5.50	8.00	16.00	—
CD1929	—	5.00	7.50	15.00	25.00	—

Y# B38.1 10 CASH

Copper **Obv:** Chinese legend in inner circle; Chinese date at left and right of upper legend **Obv. Inscription:** Min Kuo T'ung Yüan **Rev:** Chinese characters "T'ung Yüan" in solid sunburst

Date	Mintage	Good	VG	F	VF	XF
CD1928	—	40.00	80.00	120	200	—

Y# B38.2 10 CASH

Copper **Obv:** Upper legend **Obv. Legend:** "Hsinchiang Kashgar Tsao" **Obv. Inscription:** Min Kuo T'ung Yüan **Rev:** Outlined sunburst **Rev. Inscription:** Small T'ung Yüan

Date	Mintage	Good	VG	F	VF	XF
CD1928	—	30.00	70.00	100	180	—

Note: A similar coin with same upper legend and cyclical date 1929 at sides is reported

Y# B38.3 10 CASH

Copper **Obv:** Upper legend **Obv. Legend:** "Hsinchiang K'a Tsao" **Obv. Inscription:** Min Kuo T'ung Yüan **Rev:** Outlined sunburst **Rev. Inscription:** Large T'ung Yüan

Date	Mintage	Good	VG	F	VF	XF
CD1928	—	15.00	23.00	30.00	50.00	—

Y# B38.5 10 CASH

Copper **Obv. Inscription:** Chung Hua Min Kuo **Rev:** Outlined finely rayed sunburst **Rev. Inscription:** T'ung Yüan

Date	Mintage	Good	VG	F	VF	XF
CD1928	—	60.00	90.00	140	200	—

Y# B38.7 10 CASH

Copper **Obv. Legend:** HSINCHIANG KASHGAR TSAO **Obv. Inscription:** Chung Hua Min Kuo **Rev:** Outlined sunburst (as Y#B38.3) **Rev. Inscription:** Large T'ung Yüan

Date	Mintage	Good	VG	F	VF	XF
CD1928	—	15.00	23.00	50.00	—	—

Y# B38b.1 10 CASH

Copper **Obv. Inscription:** Chung Hua Min Kuo **Rev:** Turki legend in solid sunburst

Date	Mintage	Good	VG	F	VF	XF
AH1346	—	125	175	300	400	—

Y# B38b.2 10 CASH

Copper **Obv:** Similar to Y#B838d **Obv. Inscription:** Chung Hua Min Kuo **Rev:** Turki legend in solid sunburst

Date	Mintage	Good	VG	F	VF	XF
AH1346	—	150	200	350	500	—

Y# B38c.1 10 CASH

Copper **Obv. Inscription:** Min Kuo T'ung Yüan **Rev:** Chinese character "Jih" in solid sunburst

Date	Mintage	Good	VG	F	VF	XF
CD1928	—	175	275	425	600	—

Y# B38c.2 10 CASH

Copper **Obv:** Like B38c.1 **Obv. Inscription:** Min Kuo T'ung Yüan **Rev:** Chinese character "Jih" in rayed sunburst

Date	Mintage	Good	VG	F	VF	XF
CD1928	—	175	275	425	600	—

Y# B38c.3 10 CASH

Copper **Obv:** Like Y#B38b.1 **Obv. Inscription:** Min Kuo T'ung Yüan **Rev:** Like Y#B38c.1

Date	Mintage	Good	VG	F	VF	XF
CD1928	—	175	275	425	600	—

Y# B38c.4 10 CASH

Copper **Obv. Legend:** Cyclic date at left and right like Y#B38.4 **Obv. Inscription:** Min Kuo T'ung Yüan

Date	Mintage	Good	VG	F	VF	XF
CD1928	—	175	275	425	600	—

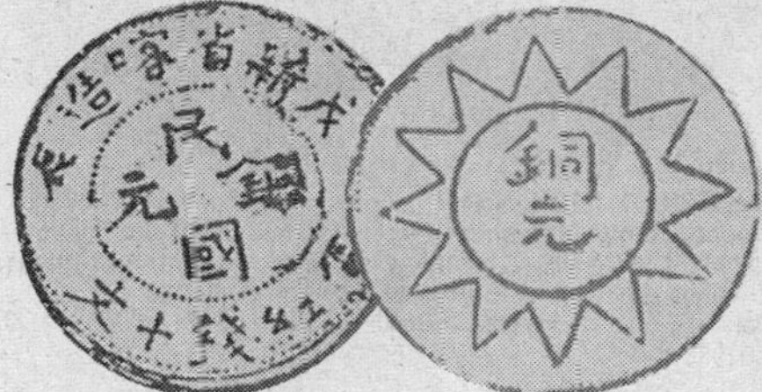

Y# B38d 10 CASH

Copper **Obv:** Chinese legend in inner circle **Obv. Inscription:** Min Kuo T'ung Yüan **Rev:** Chinese characters "T'ung Yüan" in solid sunburst

Date	Mintage	Good	VG	F	VF	XF
CD1928	—	125	175	300	400	—

Y# 44.2 10 CASH

Copper **Obv:** Small eight-petaled rosette in center **Obv. Inscription:** Chung Hua Min Kuo **Rev:** Flag at right without inner circle

Date	Mintage	Good	VG	F	VF	XF
CD1929	—	4.50	7.50	12.00	16.00	—
CD1930	—	4.50	7.50	12.00	16.00	—

Y# 40.1 10 CASH

Copper **Obv:** Chinese legend in inner circle with "Hsin Chiang" at upper right **Obv. Inscription:** Chung Hua Min Kuo **Rev:** Flags with solid sunbursts with inner circles

Date	Mintage	Good	VG	F	VF	XF
CD1929	—	7.00	12.00	16.50	25.00	40.00
CD1930 Rare	—	—	—	—	—	—

Note: The cyclical date character at left exists closed, which is rare, and open for CD1929

Y# 44.6 10 CASH

Copper **Obv. Inscription:** Chung Hua Min Kuo **Rev:** Reversed flags with large solid sunbursts

Date	Mintage	Good	VG	F	VF	XF
CD1929	—	3.00	7.00	13.00	18.00	—
CD1930	—	4.00	8.00	15.00	20.00	—

Y# 40.2 10 CASH

Copper **Obv:** Large starburst in center **Obv. Inscription:** Chung Hua Min Kuo **Rev:** Long streamers

Date	Mintage	Good	VG	F	VF	XF
CD1929 Rare	—	7.00	12.00	16.50	25.00	40.00

Note: Y#40 inscribed "Sheng Ch'eng" (provincial capital) in upper legend refers to Tihwa (Urumchi, now Ürümqi)

Y# 40.3 10 CASH

Copper **Obv:** Cyclical date at upper right in legend **Obv. Inscription:** Chung Hua Min Kuo

Date	Mintage	Good	VG	F	VF	XF
CD1930 Rare	—	—	—	—	—	—

Y# 44.1 10 CASH

Copper **Obv. Legend:** "Hsinchiang K'ashih Tsao" **Obv.**

Inscription: Chung Hua Min Kuo **Rev:** Crossed flags with wide outlined sunbursts; flags at right with inner circle

Date	Mintage	Good	VG	F	VF	XF
CD1929	—	5.00	8.50	17.50	32.50	—

Y# 44.3 10 CASH

Copper **Obv:** Star with rays in center **Obv. Inscription:** Chung Hua Min Kuo **Rev:** Crossed flags

Date	Mintage	Good	VG	F	VF	XF
CD1930	—	8.50	17.50	22.50	37.50	—

Y# 44.4 10 CASH

Copper **Obv:** Eight-petaled rosette in center **Obv. Inscription:** Chung Hua Min Kuo **Rev:** Crossed flags with narrow outlined sunbursts

Date	Mintage	Good	VG	F	VF	XF
CD1930	—	10.00	20.00	35.00	55.00	—

Y# 44.5 10 CASH

Copper **Obv. Inscription:** Chung Hua Min Kuo **Rev:** Crossed flags with solid sunbursts

Date	Mintage	Good	VG	F	VF	XF
CD1933	—	4.00	8.00	15.00	20.00	—

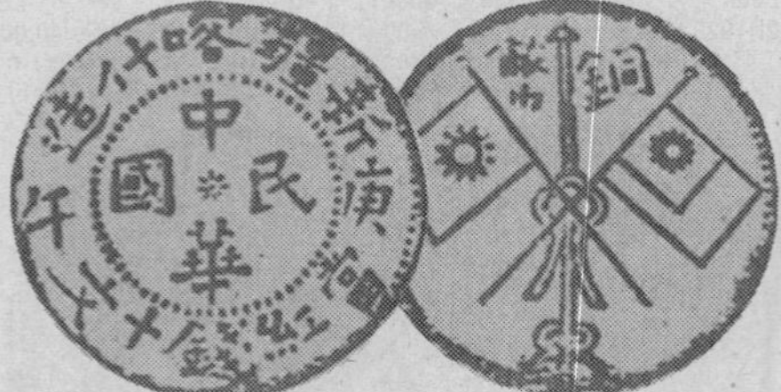

Y# 44.7 10 CASH

Copper **Obv. Inscription:** Chung Hua Min Kuo **Rev:** Reversed crossed flags with small solid sunbursts

Date	Mintage	Good	VG	F	VF	XF
CD1930	—	25.00	50.00	100	165	—

Y# 44.8 10 CASH

Copper **Obv:** Uper legend **Obv. Legend:** "Hsinchiang K'ashih Tsao" **Obv. Inscription:** Chung Hua Min Kuo **Rev:** Crossed flags

Date	Mintage	Good	VG	F	VF	XF
CD1929	—	75.00	100	125	150	—

Y# 44.9 10 CASH

Copper **Obv. Inscription:** Chung Hua Min Kuo **Rev:** Reversed crossed flags with large "flower petal" outlined sunbursts

Date	Mintage	Good	VG	F	VF	XF
CD1930	—	4.00	8.00	15.00	20.00	—

Y# 44.10 10 CASH

Copper **Obv. Inscription:** Chung Hua Min Kuo **Rev:** Crossed flags reversed

Date	Mintage	Good	VG	F	VF	XF
CD1930	—	—	—	—	—	—

Y# B38.6 10 CASH

Copper **Obv. Inscription:** Chung Hua Min Kuo **Rev:** Sunburst **Rev. Inscription:** T'ung Yüan

Date	Mintage	Good	VG	F	VF	XF
CD1929	—	40.00	60.00	100	170	—

Y# B38a.1 10 CASH

Copper **Obv:** Chinese characters for date to left and right of "Chung Hua Min Kuo" in inner circle **Obv. Inscription:** Chung Hua Min Kuo **Rev:** Turki legend in oulined sunburst

Date	Mintage	Good	VG	F	VF	XF
CD1929	—	100	165	250	350	—

Y# B38a.2 10 CASH

Copper **Obv. Legend:** "Hsinchiang K'ashih Tsao" **Obv. Inscription:** Chung Hua Min Kuo **Rev:** Sunburst

Date	Mintage	Good	VG	F	VF	XF
CD1929	—	75.00	100	125	150	—

Y# 48 20 CASH

Copper **Obv. Inscription:** Chung Hua Min Kuo **Rev:** Crossed flags

Date	Mintage	Good	VG	F	VF	XF
AH133x (1921) Rare	—	—	—	—	—	—

Y# A41.1 20 CASH

Copper **Obv:** Chinese legend in inner circle with "Hsin Chiang" at upper right **Obv. Inscription:** Chung Hua Min Kuo **Rev:** Crossed flags

Date	Mintage	Good	VG	F	VF	XF
CD1929	—	75.00	125	200	300	—
CD1930	—	85.00	140	225	335	—

Note: Y#A41.1 inscribed "Sheng Ch'eng" (provincial capital) in upper legend refers to Tihwa (Urumchi now Urumqi)

Y# A41.2 20 CASH

Copper **Obv:** Cyclical date at upper right **Obv. Inscription:** Chung Hua Min Kuo **Rev:** Crossed flags

Date	Mintage	Good	VG	F	VF	XF
CD1930 Rare	—	—	—	—	—	—

Y# 39.1 20 CASH

Copper **Obv:** 8-petaled rosette in center **Obv. Inscription:** Hsin Chiang T'ung Pao **Rev:** Two stripes in crossed flags have arabesques

Date	Mintage	VG	F	VF	XF	Unc
ND	—	10.00	16.50	20.00	27.50	—

Y# 39.2 20 CASH

Copper **Obv:** 5-petaled rosette in center **Obv. Inscription:** Hsin Chiang T'ung Pao **Rev:** Crossed flags

Date	Mintage	VG	F	VF	XF	Unc
ND	—	50.00	100	150	225	—

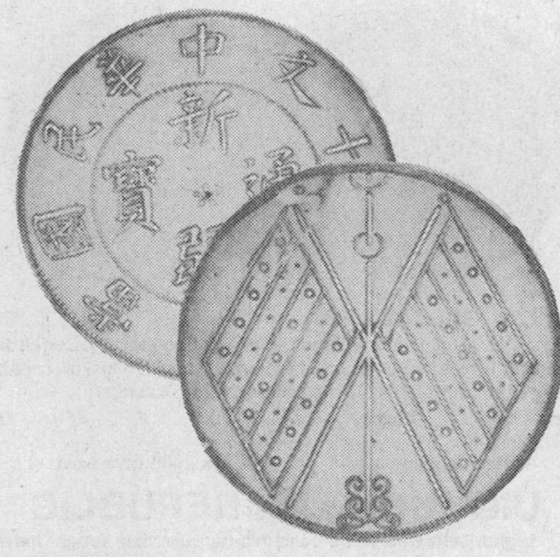

Y# 39.3 20 CASH

Copper **Obv. Inscription:** Hsin Chiang T'ung Pao **Rev:** Crossed flags without arabesques

Date	Mintage	VG	F	VF	XF	Unc
ND Restrike	—	—	—	—	50.00	75.00

Y# 43 5 MISCALS

17.3000 g., Silver **Obv:** Stars dividing Chinese legends **Obv. Inscription:** Chung Hua Min Kuo **Rev:** Crossed flags dividing Turki legend

Date	Mintage	VG	F	VF	XF	Unc
AH1331	—	40.00	75.00	160	275	—
AH1332	—	40.00	75.00	160	275	—

Y# 43.1 5 MISCALS

17.3000 g., Silver **Obv:** Rosettes dividing Chinese legend **Obv. Inscription:** Chung Hua Min Kuo **Rev:** Crossed flags **Note:** Varieties exist.

Date	Mintage	VG	F	VF	XF	Unc
AH1330	—	35.00	65.00	135	225	—
AH1331	—	35.00	65.00	135	225	—
AH1332	—	35.00	65.00	135	225	—
AH13-32	—	35.00	65.00	135	225	—

Y# 43.2 5 MISCALS

17.3000 g., Silver **Obv:** Rosettes dividing Chinese legend **Obv. Inscription:** Chung Hua Min Kuo **Rev:** Crossed flags

Date	Mintage	VG	F	VF	XF	Unc
AH1334	—	45.00	85.00	185	325	—
AH133-4	—	45.00	85.00	185	325	—

Note: Varieties exist

Y# 43.3 5 MISCALS

17.3000 g., Silver **Obv:** Rosette in center, floral arrangements dividing Chinese legend **Obv. Inscription:** Chung Hua Min Kuo **Rev:** Crossed flags **Note:** Varieties exist.

Date	Mintage	VG	F	VF	XF	Unc
AH13-32	—	40.00	75.00	160	275	—
AH133-4	—	45.00	85.00	185	325	—

Y# 43.4 5 MISCALS

17.3000 g., Silver **Obv:** Stars divide rotated outer Chinese legend **Obv. Inscription:** Chung Hua Min Kuo **Rev:** Crossed flags

Date	Mintage	VG	F	VF	XF	Unc
AHx13x(ca.1916)	—	—	—	—	—	—

Note: Considered contemporary forgeries by some experts

Y# 41 5 MISCALS (5 Mace)

17.9000 g., Silver **Obv. Legend:** Chung Hua Min Kuo (year) Nien **Rev:** Two stripes in crossed flags have arabesques

Date	Mintage	VG	F	VF	XF	Unc
1(1912)	—	40.00	65.00	150	200	—

Y# 41a 5 MISCALS (5 Mace)

17.9000 g., Silver **Obv. Legend:** Chung Hua Min Kuo (year) Nien **Rev:** Four stripes in crossed flags have arabesques

Date	Mintage	VG	F	VF	XF	Unc
1(1912)	—	40.00	65.00	150	200	—

Y# 42 SAR (Tael)

35.9000 g., Silver **Obv. Legend:** Chung Hua Min Kuo (year) Nien **Rev:** Two stripes in crossed flags have arabesques

Date	Mintage	VG	F	VF	XF	Unc
1(1912)	—	60.00	100	200	350	—

Y# 42a SAR (Tael)

35.9000 g., Silver **Obv:** Similar to Y#42 **Obv. Legend:** Chung Hua Min Kuo (year) Nien **Rev:** Four stripes in crossed flags have arabesques

Date	Mintage	VG	F	VF	XF	Unc
1(1912)	—	60.00	100	200	350	—

Y# 45 SAR (Tael)

35.0000 g., Silver **Obv:** Large characters **Rev:** Rosette at top between wheat ears

Date	Mintage	VG	F	VF	XF	Unc
6(1917)	—	17.50	22.50	32.50	50.00	—

Y# 45.1 SAR (Tael)

35.0000 g., Silver **Obv:** Similar to Y#45 but with small characters **Rev:** Without rosette at top

Date	Mintage	VG	F	VF	XF	Unc
6(1917)	—	17.50	22.50	32.50	50.00	—

Y# 45.2 SAR (Tael)
35.0000 g., Silver **Rev:** Rosette at top between more ornate branches

Date	Mintage	VG	F	VF	XF	Unc
7(1918)	—	20.00	25.00	42.50	75.00	—

Y# 46 DOLLAR (Yuan)
Silver **Obv:** Similar to Y#46.2 but with larger Chinese characters **Rev:** Think pointed base "1" **Note:** Kann #1267a reports a variety in the character "Kuo".

Date	Mintage	VG	F	VF	XF	Unc
38//1949	—	16.00	22.50	35.00	60.00	—

Y# 46.1 DOLLAR (Yuan)
Silver **Obv:** Similar to Y#46.2 but with larger Chinese characters **Rev:** Think pointed base "1" with large serif

Date	Mintage	VG	F	VF	XF	Unc
38//1949	—	16.00	22.50	35.00	60.00	—

Y# 46.2 DOLLAR (Yuan)
Silver **Obv:** Smaller Chinese characters **Rev:** Thin pointed base "1"

Date	Mintage	VG	F	VF	XF	Unc
38//1949	—	16.00	22.50	37.50	60.00	—

Y# 46.3 DOLLAR (Yuan)
Silver **Rev:** Square-based "1"

Date	Mintage	VG	F	VF	XF	Unc
38//1949	—	20.00	30.00	50.00	100	—

Y# 46.4 DOLLAR (Yuan)
Silver **Obv:** Outlined Chinese characters "Yüan" in center

Date	Mintage	VG	F	VF	XF	Unc
38//1949	—	22.50	35.00	75.00	150	—

Y# 46.5 DOLLAR (Yuan)
Silver **Note:** 9-4-9-1 (1949) at bottom.

Date	Mintage	VG	F	VF	XF	Unc
38//1949	—	75.00	150	200	250	—

ISLAMIC REPUBLIC OF EASTERN TURKESTAN

MILLED COINAGE

Y# E38.1 20 CASH
Copper, 32-34 mm. **Rev:** Crossed flags

Date	Mintage	Good	VG	F	VF	XF
AH1352	—	50.00	100	150	225	—

Y# E38.2 20 CASH
Copper **Rev:** Crossed flags reversed

Date	Mintage	Good	VG	F	VF	XF
AH1352	—	50.00	100	150	225	—

Y# E38.3 20 CASH
Copper, 32-34 mm. **Rev:** Crossed flags, sun in partial frame in left flag, denomination given as two wen (sic)

Date	Mintage	Good	VG	F	VF	XF
AH1352	—	60.00	120	200	300	—

Y# E38.4 20 CASH
Copper **Rev:** Crossed flags, large sun in national flag at left **Note:** Varieties exist.

Date	Mintage	Good	VG	F	VF	XF
AH1352	—	50.00	100	150	225	—

Note: Crudely cut Chinese denomination appears as 2 instead of 20; also encountered overstruck on 10 Cash, Y#44 varieties

Y# G38 20 CASH
Copper **Obv:** Similar to 20 Cash, Y#E38.3 **Rev:** Crossed flags, small flag at left

Date	Mintage	Good	VG	F	VF	XF
AH1352	—	50.00	100	150	225	—

Y# E39 MISCAL
Silver **Obv:** Turki legend around central Turki legend **Obv. Legend:** "Sharket Turkhestan Cumhuriyet Islamiyesi" around "Muskuk, sanah 1252" **Rev:** Turki legend **Rev. Legend:** "Zarb Kashgar"

Date	Mintage	Good	VG	F	VF	XF
AH1352 Rare	—	—	—	—	—	—

Note: Varieties of sun with eight and nine rays exist

UIGHURISTAN REPUBLIC

Uighuristan was a rebel Islamic republic that sought independence from China. The rebellion was quickly crushed. Coins of the Republic were all made by over-striking on Kashgar Republic 10 Cash coins.

MILLED COINAGE

Y# D38.1 10 CASH
Copper **Rev:** Crossed flags, flag at right without fringe

Date	Mintage	Good	VG	F	VF	XF
AH1352	—	50.00	100	160	250	—

Y# D38.2 10 CASH
Copper **Rev:** Crossed flags, flag at right with partial fringe

Date	Mintage	Good	VG	F	VF	XF
AH1352	—	50.00	100	160	250	—

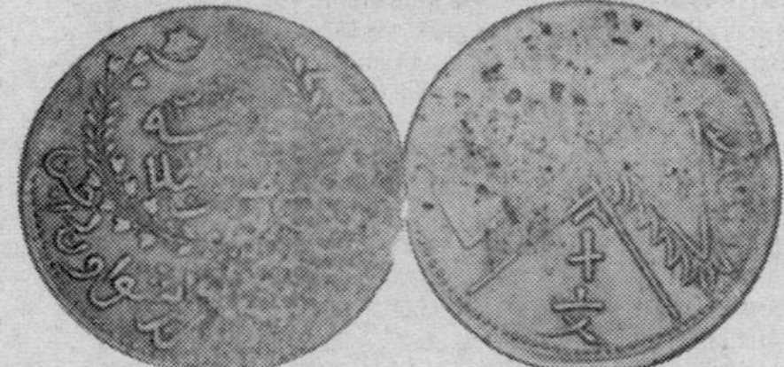

Y# D38.3 10 CASH
Copper **Rev:** Crossed flags, flag at right with full fringe

Date	Mintage	Good	VG	F	VF	XF
AH1352	—	50.00	100	160	250	—

Note: Encountered overstruck on various earlier Republican Series 10 Cash

PATTERNS

Including off metal strikes

KM#	Date	Mintage	Identification	Mkt Val
Pn40	AH1324	—	Tael. Silver.	—
Pn41	ND(ca.1906)	—	Mace. Copper. SUNGAREI. Y#10; Kann#1034.	1,600
Pn42	ND(ca.1906)	—	2 Mace. Silver. SUNGAREI. Y#11; Kann #1033.	3,000
Pn43	ND(ca.1906)	—	2 Mace. Copper. SUNGAREI. Kann #1033x.	1,200
Pn44	ND(ca.1906)	—	4 Mace. Silver. SUNGAREI.	8,000
Pn45	ND(ca.1906)	—	4 Mace. Brass. SUNGAREI.	1,250
Pn46	ND(ca.1906)	—	5 Mace. Silver. Kann #1032.	—
Pn47	ND(ca.1906)	—	7 Mace. Silver. SUNGAREI. 2 Candareens, Y#12. Kann #1031.	—

SUIYUAN PROVINCE

In November 1913, the central government grouped together 19 Mongolian and 12 Shansi districts to form the Suiyuan Special Administrative Zone. In 1928, the name was changed to Suiyuan Province. The province was joined with other Mongolian provinces to form Inner Mongolia after the communist takeover in 1949.

REPUBLIC

MILLED COINAGE

KM# 3 FEN

Shell Casing Brass **Obv:** White Tower **Rev:** Ancient spade coin between Yi and Fen

Date	Mintage	VG	F	VF	XF	Unc
38(1949)	—	175	250	350	550	—

KM# 5 5 FEN

Shell Casing Brass **Obv:** White Tower **Rev:** Ancient spade coin between Wu(5) and Fen

Date	Mintage	VG	F	VF	XF	Unc
38(1949)	—	600	750	1,000	1,350	—

SZECHUAN PROVINCE

Sichuan

A province located in south-central China. The largest of the traditional Chinese provinces, Szechuan (Sichuan) is a plateau region watered by many rivers. These rivers carry much trading traffic. Agriculture or mining are the occupational choices of most of the populace. In World War II the national capital was moved to Chungking in Szechuan (Sichuan). Chengtu was an active imperial mint that opened in 1732 and was in practically continuous operation until the advent of modern equipment. Modern minting was introduced in the province when Chengtu began milled coinage in 1898. A mint was authorized for Chungking in 1905 but it did not begin operations until 1913. The Chengtu Mint was looted by soldiers in 1925. The last republic issues from Szechuan (Sichuan) were dated 1932.

The machinery for the first Szechuan (Sichuan) Mint was produced in New Jersey and the dies were engraved in Philadelphia. The mint was opened in 1898, but closed within a few months and did not reopen until 1901. There is no doubt now that Y#234-238 (K#145-149) were the first issues of this mint, contrary to the Kann listings.

EMPIRE

PROVINCIAL CAST COINAGE

C# 24-9 CASH

Cast Brass **Ruler:** Kuang-hsü **Obv. Inscription:** Kuang-hsü T'ung-pao **Rev:** Manchu inscription **Rev. Inscription:** Boo-Cuwan

Date	Mintage	Good	VG	F	VF	XF
ND(1875-1908)	—	4.50	7.50	11.50	22.50	—

MILLED COINAGE

Y# 225 5 CASH

Copper **Ruler:** Kuang-hsü **Obv:** Manchu at center **Obv. Legend:** Szu-ch'uan Kuan Chü Tsao **Obv. Inscription:** Kuang-hsü Yüan-pao **Rev:** Side view dragon

Date	Mintage	VG	F	VF	XF	Unc
ND(1903-04)	85,000	50.00	70.00	100	150	—

Y# 225a 5 CASH

Brass **Ruler:** Kuang-hsü **Obv. Legend:** Szu-ch'uan Kuan Chü Tsao **Obv. Inscription:** Kuang-hsü Yüan-pao

Date	Mintage	VG	F	VF	XF	Unc
ND(1903-04) Rare	Inc. above	—	—	—	—	—

Y# 228 5 CASH

Brass **Ruler:** Kuang-hsü **Obv:** Flower at center **Obv. Legend:** Szu-ch'uan Sheng Tsao **Obv. Inscription:** Kuang-hsü Yüan-pao **Rev:** Flying dragon

Date	Mintage	VG	F	VF	XF	Unc
ND(1903-04)	Inc. above	350	500	750	—	—

Y# A229 5 CASH

Brass **Ruler:** Kuang-hsü **Obv:** Flower at center **Obv. Legend:** Szu-ch-uan Sheng Tsao **Obv. Inscription:** Kuang-hsü Yüan-pao **Rev:** Side view dragon **Note:** Prev. Y#A228.

Date	Mintage	VG	F	VF	XF	Unc
ND(1903-04)	Inc. above	100	140	200	300	—

Y# 226 10 CASH

Copper **Ruler:** Kuang-hsü **Obv:** Thick Manchu in center, large rosettes **Obv. Legend:** Szu-ch'uan Kuan Chü Tsao **Obv. Inscription:** Kuang-hsü Yüan-pao

Date	Mintage	VG	F	VF	XF	Unc
ND(1903-05)	95,960,000	12.50	25.00	35.00	60.00	—

Y# 226.1 10 CASH

Copper **Ruler:** Kuang-hsü **Obv:** Thin Manchu in center, small rosettes **Obv. Legend:** Szu-ch'uan Kuan Chü Tsao **Obv. Inscription:** Kuang-hsü Yüan-pao

Date	Mintage	VG	F	VF	XF	Unc
ND(1903-05)	Inc. above	22.50	45.00	70.00	125	—

Y# 226.2 10 CASH

Copper **Ruler:** Kuang-hsü **Obv:** Large rosettes **Obv. Legend:** Szu-ch'uan Kuan Chü Tsao **Obv. Inscription:** Kuang-hsü Yüan-pao

Date	Mintage	VG	F	VF	XF	Unc
ND(1903-05)	Inc. above	20.00	40.00	60.00	100	—

Y# 229 10 CASH

Copper **Ruler:** Kuang-hsü **Obv:** Legend with two characters at bottom, 6-9mm apart **Obv. Legend:** Szu-ch'uan Sheng Tsao **Obv. Inscription:** Kuang-hsü Yüan-pao **Rev:** Trident-shaped flame on dragon's body below letters CHU

Date	Mintage	VG	F	VF	XF	Unc
ND(1903-05)	Inc. above	4.00	6.50	10.00	17.50	—

Y# 229.1 10 CASH

Copper **Ruler:** Kuang-hsü **Obv:** Legend with characters at bottom, 4-5mm apart **Obv. Legend:** Szu-ch'uan Sheng Tsao **Obv. Inscription:** Kuang-hsü Yüan-pao

Date	Mintage	VG	F	VF	XF	Unc
ND(1903-05)	Inc. above	4.00	6.50	10.00	17.50	—

Y# 229.2 10 CASH

Copper **Ruler:** Kuang-hsü **Obv:** Manchu at 3 o'clock is lower in relation to center characters **Obv. Legend:** Szu-ch'uan Sheng Tsao **Obv. Inscription:** Kuang-hsü Yüan-pao

Date	Mintage	VG	F	VF	XF	Unc
ND(1903-05)	Inc. above	4.00	6.50	10.00	17.50	—

Y# 229.3 10 CASH

Copper **Ruler:** Kuang-hsü **Obv:** Characters 6-9mm apart **Obv. Legend:** Szu-ch'uan Sheng Tsao **Obv. Inscription:** Kuang-hsü Yüan-pao **Rev:** Trident-shaped flame below letters HUE

Date	Mintage	VG	F	VF	XF	Unc
ND(1903-05)	Inc. above	4.00	6.50	10.00	17.50	—

Y# 229.3a 10 CASH

Brass **Ruler:** Kuang-hsü **Obv. Legend:** Szu-ch'uan Sheng Tsao **Obv. Inscription:** Kuang-hsü Yüan-pao

Date	Mintage	VG	F	VF	XF	Unc
ND(1903-05)	Inc. above	4.00	6.50	10.00	17.50	—

Y# 229.4 10 CASH

Brass **Ruler:** Kuang-hsü **Obv:** Characters 4-5mm apart **Obv. Legend:** Szu-ch'uan Sheng Tsao **Obv. Inscription:** Kuang-hsü Yüan-pao

Date	Mintage	VG	F	VF	XF	Unc
ND(1903-05)	Inc. above	4.00	6.50	10.00	17.50	—

Y# 229.5 10 CASH

Brass **Ruler:** Kuang-hsü **Obv:** Bottom characters 6-9mm apart **Obv. Legend:** Szu-ch'uan Sheng Tsao **Obv. Inscription:** Kuang-hsü Yüan-pao **Rev:** Without trident-shaped flame, instead a cloud pointing to the letter U

Date	Mintage	VG	F	VF	XF	Unc
ND(1903-05)	Inc. above	2.50	4.00	7.50	12.00	—

Y# 229.5a 10 CASH

Copper **Ruler:** Kuang-hsü **Obv. Legend:** Szu-ch'uan Sheng Tsao **Obv. Inscription:** Kuang-hsü Yüan-pao

Date	Mintage	VG	F	VF	XF	Unc
ND(1903-05)	Inc. above	3.00	5.00	10.00	15.00	—

Y# 229.6 10 CASH

Brass **Ruler:** Kuang-hsü **Obv:** Characters 4-5mm apart **Obv. Legend:** Szu-ch'uan Sheng Tsao **Obv. Inscription:** Kuang-hsü Yüan-pao

Date	Mintage	VG	F	VF	XF	Unc
ND(1903-05)	Inc. above	4.00	6.00	10.00	17.50	—

Y# 229.6a 10 CASH

Copper **Ruler:** Kuang-hsü **Obv. Legend:** Szu-ch'uan Sheng Tsao **Obv. Inscription:** Kuang-hsü Yüan-pao

Date	Mintage	VG	F	VF	XF	Unc
ND(1903-05)	Inc. above	2.00	3.00	5.50	10.00	—

Y# 229.7 10 CASH

Brass **Ruler:** Kuang-hsü **Obv:** Manchu at 3 o'clock is lower **Obv. Legend:** Szu-ch'uan Sheng Tsao **Obv. Inscription:** Kuang-hsü Yüan-pao

Date	Mintage	VG	F	VF	XF	Unc
ND(1903-05)	Inc. above	3.75	6.00	10.00	17.50	—

Y# 229.7a 10 CASH

Copper **Ruler:** Kuang-hsü **Obv. Legend:** Szu-ch'uan Sheng Tsao **Obv. Inscription:** Kuang-hsü Yüan-pao

Date	Mintage	VG	F	VF	XF	Unc
ND(1903-05)	Inc. above	2.00	3.50	6.00	9.00	—

Y# 229.8 10 CASH

Brass **Ruler:** Kuang-hsü **Obv:** Characters 4-5mm apart **Obv. Legend:** Szu-ch'uan Sheng Tsao **Obv. Inscription:** Kuang-hsü Yüan-pao **Rev:** Without cloud below CHU, high point of dragon's body below letter "C", tail joins body above "S" in "CASH"

Date	Mintage	VG	F	VF	XF	Unc
ND(1903-05)	Inc. above	4.00	6.00	9.00	17.50	—

Y# 229.8a 10 CASH

Copper **Ruler:** Kuang-hsü **Obv. Legend:** Szu-ch'uan Sheng Tsao **Obv. Inscription:** Kuang-hsü Yüan-pao

Date	Mintage	VG	F	VF	XF	Unc
ND(1903-05)	Inc. above	2.00	3.50	6.00	9.00	—

Y# 229.9 10 CASH

Copper **Ruler:** Kuang-hsü **Obv. Legend:** Szu-ch'uan Sheng Tsao **Obv. Inscription:** Kuang-hsü Yüan-pao **Rev:** High point of dragon's body below letter H, tail joins body above letter "C" in "CASH"

Date	Mintage	VG	F	VF	XF	Unc
ND(1903-05)	Inc. above	2.00	3.50	6.00	9.00	—

Y# 231 10 CASH

Copper **Ruler:** Kuang-hsü **Obv. Legend:** Szu-ch'uan Sheng Tsao **Obv. Inscription:** Kuang-hsü Yüan-pao

Date	Mintage	VG	F	VF	XF	Unc
ND(1903-05)	Inc. above	150	200	225	275	—

Y# 10t 10 CASH

Copper **Ruler:** Kuang-hsü **Obv. Inscription:** Ta-ch'ing T'ung-pi **Rev. Legend:** Kuang-hsü Nien-tsao, TAI-CHING-TI-KUO...

Date	Mintage	VG	F	VF	XF	Unc
CD(1906)	337,748,000	1.00	1.50	3.00	6.00	—

Y# 20t.1 10 CASH

Copper **Ruler:** Hsüan-t'ung **Obv:** Bottom of Manchu word at 11 o'clock curls to left **Obv. Inscription:** Ta-ch'ing T'ung-pi **Rev. Legend:** Hsüan-t'ung Nien-tsao, TAI-CHING-TI-KUO...

Date	Mintage	VG	F	VF	XF	Unc
CD(1909)	231,930,000	1.00	1.50	3.00	6.00	—

Y# 20t.1a 10 CASH

Brass **Ruler:** Hsüan-t'ung **Obv. Inscription:** Ta-ch'ing T'ung-pi **Rev. Legend:** Hsüan-t'ung Nien-tsao, TAI-CHING-TI-KUO...

Date	Mintage	VG	F	VF	XF	Unc
CD(1909)	Inc. above	3.00	5.00	10.00	15.00	—

Y# 20t.2 10 CASH

Copper **Ruler:** Hsüan-t'ung **Obv:** Bottom of Manchu word at 11 o'clock curls to right **Obv. Inscription:** Ta-ch'ing T'ung-pi **Rev. Legend:** Hsüan-t'ung Nien-tsao, TAI-CHING-TI-KUO...

Date	Mintage	VG	F	VF	XF	Unc
CD1909	Inc. above	5.00	9.00	12.00	17.50	—

Y# 227 20 CASH

Copper **Ruler:** Kuang-hsü **Obv. Inscription:** Kuang-hsü Yüan-pao

Date	Mintage	VG	F	VF	XF	Unc
ND(1903-05)	25,319,000	100	125	175	250	—

Y# 230 20 CASH

Copper **Ruler:** Kuang-hsü **Obv:** Small Manchu at 3 and 9 o'clock **Obv. Legend:** Szu-ch'uan Sheng Tsao **Obv. Inscription:** Kuang-hsü Yüan-pao **Rev:** Trident flame points to "E" of "SZE"

Date	Mintage	VG	F	VF	XF	Unc
ND(1903-05)	Inc. above	10.00	15.00	30.00	50.00	—

Y# 230.1 20 CASH

Copper **Ruler:** Kuang-hsü **Obv:** Large Manchu at 3 and 9 o'clock **Obv. Legend:** Szu-ch'uan Sheng Tsao **Obv. Inscription:** Kuang-hsü Yüan-pao **Rev:** Large trident flame points to "C" of "CHUEN" **Note:** Varieties exist.

Date	Mintage	VG	F	VF	XF	Unc
ND(1903-05)	Inc. above	30.00	50.00	80.00	150	—

Y# 230.3 20 CASH

Copper **Ruler:** Kuang-hsü **Obv:** Large Manchu **Obv. Legend:** Szu-ch'uan Sheng Tsao **Obv. Inscription:** Kuang-hsü Yüan-pao **Rev:** Trident flame below "ZE"

Date	Mintage	VG	F	VF	XF	Unc
ND(1903-05)	Inc. above	15.00	30.00	50.00	80.00	—

Y# 230.4 20 CASH

Copper **Ruler:** Kuang-hsü **Obv. Legend:** Szu-ch'uan Sheng Tsao **Obv. Inscription:** Kuang-hsü Yüan-pao **Rev:** Trident flame below "CHU" of "CHUEN", large letters

Date	Mintage	VG	F	VF	XF	Unc
ND(1903-05)	—	30.00	60.00	100	160	—

Y# 230.5 20 CASH

Copper **Ruler:** Kuang-hsü **Obv. Legend:** Szu-ch'uan Sheng Tsao **Obv. Inscription:** Kuang-hsü Yüan-pao **Rev:** Trident flame points to "E" of "CHUEN", small letters

Date	Mintage	VG	F	VF	XF	Unc
ND(1903-05)	Inc. above	—	—	—	—	—

Y# 230.6 20 CASH

Copper **Ruler:** Kuang-hsü **Obv:** Different small Manchu **Obv. Legend:** Szu-ch'uan Sheng Tsao **Obv. Inscription:** Kuang-hsü Yüan-pao **Rev:** Large 5-petaled rosettes, dragon differs

Date	Mintage	VG	F	VF	XF	Unc
ND(1903-05)	Inc. above	12.50	20.00	35.00	60.00	—

Y# 230.7a 20 CASH

Brass **Ruler:** Kuang-hsü **Obv:** Small Manchu **Obv. Legend:** Szu-ch'uan Sheng Tsao **Obv. Inscription:** Kuang-hsü Yüan-pao **Rev:** Larger cloud below "CHUEN"

Date	Mintage	VG	F	VF	XF	Unc
ND(1903-05)	Inc. above	15.00	25.00	40.00	70.00	—

Y# 11t 20 CASH
Copper **Obv. Inscription:** Ta-ch'ing T'ung-pi

Date	Mintage	VG	F	VF	XF	Unc
CD1906	51,028,000	10.00	22.50	35.00	60.00	—

Y# 21t.1 20 CASH
Copper **Obv:** Bottom of Manchu word at 11 o'clock curls right **Obv. Inscription:** Ta-ch'ing T'ung-pi

Date	Mintage	VG	F	VF	XF	Unc
CD1909	33,414,000	15.00	27.50	40.00	70.00	—

Y# 21t.1a 20 CASH
Brass **Obv. Inscription:** Ta-ch'ing T'ung-pi

Date	Mintage	VG	F	VF	XF	Unc
CD1909	Inc. above	25.00	35.00	65.00	100	—

Y# 21t.2 20 CASH
Copper **Obv:** Bottom of Manchu word at 11 o'clock curls left **Obv. Inscription:** Ta-ch'ing T'ung-pi

Date	Mintage	VG	F	VF	XF	Unc
CD1909	—	15.00	27.50	40.00	70.00	—

Y# 234 5 CENTS
1.3000 g., 0.8200 Silver .0343 oz. ASW, 15.82 mm. **Ruler:** Kuang-hsü **Obv. Legend:** Szu-ch'uan Sheng Tsao **Obv. Inscription:** Kuang-hsü Yüan-pao **Edge:** Reeded

Date	Mintage	VG	F	VF	XF	Unc
ND(1898; 1901-08)	671,000	4.50	12.50	17.50	30.00	80.00

Y# 234.1 5 CENTS
1.3000 g., 0.8200 Silver .0343 oz. ASW, 15.82 mm. **Ruler:** Kuang-hsü **Obv. Legend:** Szu-ch'uan Sheng Tsao **Obv. Inscription:** Kuang-hsü Yüan-pao **Rev:** With errors in the English legend **Rev. Legend:** 8ZECHUEN PROVIN(D inverted) EI? (errors) **Edge:** Reeded

Date	Mintage	VG	F	VF	XF	Unc
ND(1901-08)	Inc. above	5.00	15.00	25.00	50.00	110

Y# 239 5 CENTS
1.3000 g., 0.8200 Silver .0343 oz. ASW **Ruler:** Hsüan-t'ung **Obv. Legend:** Szu-ch'uan Sheng Tsao **Obv. Inscription:** Hsüan-t'ung Yüan-pao

Date	Mintage	VG	F	VF	XF	Unc
ND(1910)	566,000	10.00	25.00	40.00	70.00	170

Y# 235 10 CENTS
2.6000 g., 0.8200 Silver .0686 oz. ASW **Ruler:** Kuang-hsü **Obv. Legend:** Szu-ch'uan Sheng Tsao **Obv. Inscription:** Kuang-hsü Yüan-pao

Date	Mintage	VG	F	VF	XF	Unc
ND(1898; 1901-08)	1,274,000	3.50	10.00	20.00	30.00	90.00

Y# 240 10 CENTS
2.6000 g., 0.8200 Silver .0686 oz. ASW **Ruler:** Hsüan-t'ung **Obv. Legend:** Szu-ch'uan Sheng Tsao **Obv. Inscription:** Hsüan-t'ung Yüan-pao

Date	Mintage	VG	F	VF	XF	Unc
ND(1909-11)	278,000	8.50	25.00	30.00	55.00	120

Y# 236 20 CENTS
5.3000 g., 0.8200 Silver .1397 oz. ASW **Ruler:** Kuang-hsü **Obv. Legend:** Szu-ch'uan Sheng Tsao **Obv. Inscription:** Kuang-hsü Yüan-pao **Rev:** Five flames on pearl

Date	Mintage	VG	F	VF	XF	Unc
ND(1898; 1901-08)	897,000	3.50	10.00	20.00	40.00	100

Y# 236.1 20 CENTS
5.3000 g., 0.8200 Silver .1397 oz. ASW **Ruler:** Kuang-hsü **Obv. Legend:** Szu-ch'uan Sheng Tsao **Obv. Inscription:** Kuang-hsü Yüan-pao **Rev:** Six flames on pearl

Date	Mintage	VG	F	VF	XF	Unc
ND(1898; 1901-08)	Inc. above	3.50	10.00	20.00	40.00	100

Y# 236.2 20 CENTS
5.3000 g., 0.8200 Silver .1397 oz. ASW **Ruler:** Kuang-hsü **Obv. Legend:** Szu-ch'uan Sheng Tsao **Obv. Inscription:** Kuang-hsü Yüan-pao **Rev:** Seven flames on pearl

Date	Mintage	VG	F	VF	XF	Unc
ND(1898; 1901-08)	Inc. above	3.50	10.00	20.00	40.00	100

Y# 236.3 20 CENTS
5.3000 g., 0.8200 Silver .1397 oz. ASW **Ruler:** Kuang-hsü **Obv. Legend:** Szu-ch'uan Sheng Tsao **Obv. Inscription:** Kuang-hsü Yüan-pao **Rev:** Various errors in English legend

Date	Mintage	VG	F	VF	XF	Unc
ND(1901-08)	Inc. above	5.00	15.00	25.00	50.00	125

Y# 241 20 CENTS
5.3000 g., 0.8200 Silver .1397 oz. ASW **Ruler:** Hsüan-t'ung **Obv. Legend:** Szu-ch'uan Sheng Tsao **Obv. Inscription:** Hsüan-t'ung Yüan-pao

Date	Mintage	VG	F	VF	XF	Unc
ND(1909-11) Rare	41,000	—	—	—	—	—

Y# 237 50 CENTS
13.2000 g., 0.8600 Silver .3650 oz. ASW **Ruler:** Kuang-hsü **Obv. Legend:** Szu-ch'uan Sheng Tsao **Obv. Inscription:** Kuang-hsü Yüan-pao **Rev:** Dragon with narrow face, small cross at either side, large fireball

Date	Mintage	VG	F	VF	XF	Unc
ND(1898; 1901-08)	474,000	10.00	22.50	40.00	100	300

Y# 237.1 50 CENTS
13.2000 g., 0.8600 Silver .3650 oz. ASW **Ruler:** Kuang-hsü **Obv. Legend:** Szu-ch'uan Sheng Tsao **Obv. Inscription:** Kuang-hsü Yüan-pao **Rev:** Various errors in English legend

Date	Mintage	VG	F	VF	XF	Unc
ND(1901-08)	Inc. above	15.00	30.00	75.00	150	300

Y# 237.2 50 CENTS
13.2000 g., 0.8600 Silver .3650 oz. ASW **Ruler:** Kuang-hsü **Obv. Legend:** Szu-ch'uan Sheng Tsao **Obv. Inscription:** Kuang-hsü Yüan-pao **Rev:** Dragon with tapering face and small chin, small fireball, small cross at either side of dragon

Date	Mintage	VG	F	VF	XF	Unc
ND(1901-08)	Inc. above	12.50	25.00	50.00	135	275

Y# 237.3 50 CENTS
13.2000 g., 0.8600 Silver .3650 oz. ASW **Ruler:** Kuang-hsü **Obv. Legend:** Szu-ch'uan Sheng Tsao **Obv. Inscription:** Kuang-hsü Yüan-pao **Rev:** Dragon with wide face and smaller fireball, thicker spines on top of dragon's head, small cross at either side of dragon

Date	Mintage	VG	F	VF	XF	Unc
ND(1901-08)	Inc. above	12.50	25.00	50.00	135	275

Y# 242 50 CENTS
13.2000 g., 0.8600 Silver **Ruler:** Hsüan-t'ung **Obv. Legend:** Szu-ch'uan Sheng Tsao **Obv. Inscription:** Hsüan-t'ung Yüan-pao

Date	Mintage	VG	F	VF	XF	Unc
ND(1909-11)	38,000	30.00	85.00	150	200	350

Y# 242.1 50 CENTS
13.2000 g., 0.8600 Silver **Ruler:** Hsüan-t'ung **Obv. Legend:** Szu-ch'uan Sheng Tsao **Obv. Inscription:** Hsüan-t'ung Yüan-pao **Rev:** Inverted "A" in place of "V" in "PROVINCE" in legend

Date	Mintage	VG	F	VF	XF	Unc
ND(1901-11)	Inc. above	30.00	85.00	150	200	350

Y# 238 DOLLAR
26.8000 g., 0.9000 Silver .7756 oz. ASW **Ruler:** Kuang-hsü **Obv. Legend:** Szu-ch'uan Sheng Tsao **Obv. Inscription:** Kuang-hsü Yüan-pao **Rev:** Dragon with narrow face and large fireball, small cross at either side of dragon

Date	Mintage	VG	F	VF	XF	Unc
ND(1901-08)	6,487,000	15.00	25.00	37.50	85.00	1,100

Y# 238.1 DOLLAR
26.8000 g., 0.9000 Silver .7756 oz. ASW **Ruler:** Kuang-hsü **Obv. Legend:** Szu-ch'uan Sheng Tsao **Obv. Inscription:** Kuang-hsü Yüan-pao **Rev:** Inverted "A" instead of "V" in "PROVINCE" in legend

Date	Mintage	VG	F	VF	XF	Unc
ND(1901-08)	Inc. above	15.00	25.00	35.00	80.00	1,100

Y# 238.2 DOLLAR
26.8000 g., 0.9000 Silver .7756 oz. ASW **Ruler:** Kuang-hsü
Obv. Inscription: Kuang-hsü Yüan-pao **Rev:** Dragon with wider face and flatter pearl, small cross at either side of dragon

Date	Mintage	VG	F	VF	XF	Unc
ND(1901-08)	Inc. above	15.00	20.00	30.00	80.00	1,100

Y# 238.3 DOLLAR
26.8000 g., 0.9000 Silver .7756 oz. ASW **Ruler:** Kuang-hsü
Obv. Legend: Szu-ch'uan Sheng Tsao **Obv. Inscription:** Kuang-hsü Yüan-pao **Rev:** "7 MACE" and "3 CANDAREENS" instead of "2 CANDAREENS"

Date	Mintage	VG	F	VF	XF	Unc
ND(1901-08)	Inc. above	20.00	40.00	80.00	175	1,600

Y# 243 DOLLAR
26.8000 g., 0.9000 Silver .7756 oz. ASW **Ruler:** Hsüan-t'ung
Obv. Legend: Szu-ch'uan Sheng Tsao **Obv. Inscription:** Hsüan-t'ung Yüan-pao **Rev:** Large spines on dragon's body

Date	Mintage	VG	F	VF	XF	Unc
ND(1909-11)	2,846,000	15.00	20.00	30.00	75.00	1,100

Y# 243.1 DOLLAR
26.8000 g., 0.9000 Silver .7756 oz. ASW **Ruler:** Hsüan-t'ung **Obv. Legend:** Szu-ch'uan Sheng Tsao **Obv. Inscription:** Hsüan-t'ung Yüan-pao **Rev:** Inverted "A" instead of "V" in "PROVINCE"

Date	Mintage	VG	F	VF	XF	Unc
ND(1909-11)	Inc. above	15.00	20.00	35.00	80.00	1,150

Y# 243.2 DOLLAR
26.8000 g., 0.9000 Silver .7756 oz. ASW **Ruler:** Hsüan-t'ung
Obv. Legend: Szu-ch'uan Sheng Tsao **Obv. Inscription:** Hsüan-t'ung Yüan-pao **Rev:** Small spines on dragon's body

Date	Mintage	VG	F	VF	XF	Unc
ND(1909-11)	Inc. above	25.00	65.00	100	200	1,250

REPUBLIC

CUT MILLED COINAGE

Y# 459y 50 CASH
Brass **Note:** 200 Cash, Y#459 cut into quarters.

Date	Mintage	VG	F	VF	XF	Unc
2(1913)	—	30.00	35.00	40.00	50.00	—

Y# 459x 100 CASH
Copper Or Brass **Note:** 200 Cash, Y#459 cut in half.

Date	Mintage	VG	F	VF	XF	Unc
2(1913)	—	3.50	9.50	17.00	45.00	—

MILLED COINAGE

Y# 466 100 CASH
Copper **Obv. Legend:** CHUNG HUA MIN KUO NIEN (Years)
Obv. Inscription: Ch'uan **Rev:** Manchu "Boo-yuan" with Chinese "K'a" (for Kashgar) above

Date	Mintage	VG	F	VF	XF	Unc
15 (1926)	—	150	225	300	400	—
19 (1930)	—	125	150	200	300	—

Y# 466a 100 CASH
Brass **Obv. Legend:** CHUNG HUA MIN KUO NIEN (Years)
Obv. Inscription: Ch'uan **Rev:** Manchu "Boo-yuan" with Chinese "K'u" (for Kuche) above

Date	Mintage	VG	F	VF	XF	Unc
19 (1930)	—	125	150	225	375	—

DECIMAL COINAGE

Y# 441a 5 CASH
Brass **Obv:** Crossed flags **Obv. Legend:** Chung Hua Min Kuo (year) Nien **Rev:** Lion standing left

Date	Mintage	VG	F	VF	XF	Unc
1(1912)	Inc. above	—	—	—	—	—

Y# 441b 5 CASH
Silver **Obv:** Crossed flags **Obv. Legend:** Chung Hua Min Kuo (year) Nien **Rev:** Lion standing left

Date	Mintage	VG	F	VF	XF	Unc
1(1912)	—	—	—	1,000	1,500	—

Note: Modern forgeries of Y#441 in copper and of Y#441b in silver exist

Y# 443 5 CASH
Copper **Obv. Legend:** Chung Hua Min Kuo (year) Nien

Date	Mintage	VG	F	VF	XF	Unc
1(1912)	Inc. above	35.00	70.00	110	150	—

Y# 443a 5 CASH
Brass **Obv. Legend:** Chung Hua Min Kuo (year) Nien

Date	Mintage	VG	F	VF	XF	Unc
1(1912) Rare	—	—	—	—	—	—

Y# 446 5 CASH
Copper **Obv. Legend:** Chung Hua Min Kuo (year) Nien

Date	Mintage	VG	F	VF	XF	Unc
1(1912) Rare	Inc. above	—	—	—	—	—

Y# 446a 5 CASH
Brass **Obv:** Chung Hua Min Kuo (year) Nien

Date	Mintage	VG	F	VF	XF	Unc
1(1912) Rare	Inc. above	—	—	—	—	—

Y# 441 5 CASH
Copper **Obv:** Crossed flags **Obv. Legend:** Chung Hua Min Kuo (year) Nien **Rev:** Lion standing left **Note:** Varieties exist.

Date	Mintage	VG	F	VF	XF	Unc
1(1912)	471,000	40.00	80.00	130	250	—

Y# 447 10 CASH
Copper **Obv:** Two rosettes **Obv. Legend:** Chung Hua Min Kuo (year) Nien

Date	Mintage	VG	F	VF	XF	Unc
1(1912)	108,618,000	1.75	3.00	10.00	20.00	—
2(1913)	Inc. above	6.00	15.00	25.00	50.00	—

Y# 447a 10 CASH
Brass **Obv. Legend:** Chung Hua Min Kuo (year) Nien

Date	Mintage	VG	F	VF	XF	Unc
1(1912)	Inc. above	0.80	1.50	2.50	5.00	—
2(1913)	Inc. above	1.65	4.00	8.00	20.00	—

Y# 447.1a 10 CASH
Brass **Obv:** Three rosettes **Obv. Legend:** Chung Hua Min Kuo (year) Nien

Date	Mintage	VG	F	VF	XF	Unc
2(1913) Rare	Inc. above	—	—	—	—	—

Y# 475 10 CASH
Red Copper **Obv:** Characters in five-petaled flower **Obv. Legend:** Chung Hua Min Kuo (year) Nien **Rev:** Denomination above sun

Date	Mintage	VG	F	VF	XF	Unc
19(1930) Rare	—	—	—	—	—	—

Y# 448 20 CASH
Copper **Obv:** Two rosettes **Obv. Legend:** Chung Hua Min Kuo (year) Nien

Date	Mintage	VG	F	VF	XF	Unc
1(1912)	115,061,000	1.00	2.50	5.00	15.00	—

Note: Character for "first" instead of number one in date

Y# 448a 20 CASH
Brass **Obv. Legend:** Chung Hua Min Kuo (year) Nien

Date	Mintage	VG	F	VF	XF	Unc
1(1912)	Inc. above	0.75	1.50	2.50	6.00	—
2(1913)	Inc. above	1.00	2.00	3.50	7.00	—

Note: Character for "first" instead of number one in date

Y# 448.1 20 CASH
Copper **Obv:** Three rosettes

Date	Mintage	VG	F	VF	XF	Unc
2(1913)	Inc. above	250	350	450	800	—
3(1914)	Inc. above	250	350	450	800	—

Y# 448.1a 20 CASH
Brass **Obv. Legend:** Chung Hua Min Kuo (year) Nien

Date	Mintage	VG	F	VF	XF	Unc
2(1913)	Inc. above	2.50	6.00	12.00	25.00	—
3(1914)	Inc. above	2.50	6.00	12.00	25.00	—

Note: There are many varieties of this 20 Cash; small and large rosettes; open and closed size characters and exaggerated size character with horns

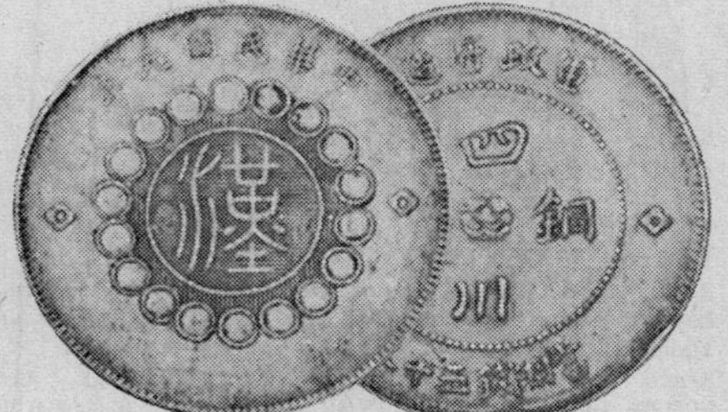

Y# 449 50 CASH
Copper **Obv. Legend:** Chung Hua Min Kuo (year) Nien **Rev:** Small flower in center

Date	Mintage	VG	F	VF	XF	Unc
1(1912)	489,382,000	2.00	4.00	7.00	15.00	—

Y# 449a 50 CASH
Brass **Obv. Legend:** Chung Hua Min Kuo (year) Nien

Date	Mintage	VG	F	VF	XF	Unc
1(1912)	Inc. above	1.50	3.50	6.00	10.00	—

Y# 449.1 50 CASH
Copper **Obv. Legend:** Chung Hua Min Kuo (year) Nien **Rev:** Larger flower in center

Date	Mintage	VG	F	VF	XF	Unc
1(1912)	Inc. above	2.00	5.00	10.00	20.00	—

Y# 449.1a 50 CASH
Brass **Obv. Legend:** Chung Hua Min Kuo (year) Nien

Date	Mintage	VG	F	VF	XF	Unc
1(1912)	Inc. above	2.50	6.00	12.50	25.00	—

Note: A Yr. 7 is reported, but its authenticity is not verified

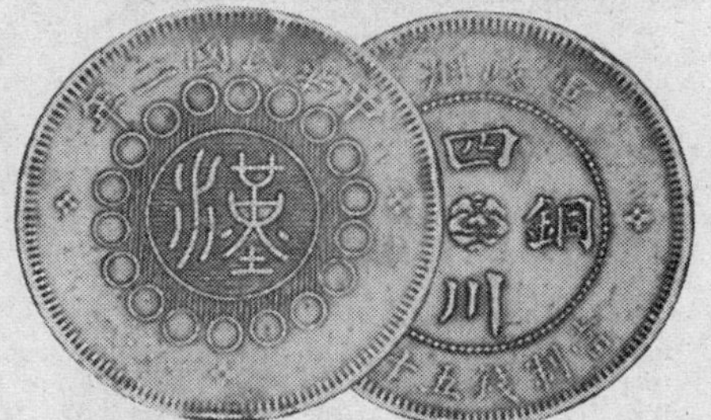

Y# 449.2 50 CASH
Copper **Obv:** Three rosettes **Obv. Legend:** Chung Hua Min Kuo (year) Nien **Rev:** Small flower in center

Date	Mintage	VG	F	VF	XF	Unc
2(1913)	Inc. above	2.25	5.50	11.00	22.00	—

Y# 449.2a 50 CASH
Brass **Obv. Legend:** Chung Hua Min Kuo (year) Nien

Date	Mintage	VG	F	VF	XF	Unc
2(1913)	Inc. above	2.25	5.50	11.00	22.00	—
3(1914)	Inc. above	2.25	5.50	11.00	22.00	—

Y# 462 50 CASH
Copper **Obv. Legend:** Chung Hua Min Kuo (year) Nien

Date	Mintage	VG	F	VF	XF	Unc
15(1926)	90,000	18.50	35.00	65.00	100	—

Y# 462a 50 CASH
Brass **Obv. Legend:** Chung Hua Min Kuo (year) Nien

Date	Mintage	VG	F	VF	XF	Unc
15(1926)	Inc. above	16.50	32.50	55.00	80.00	—

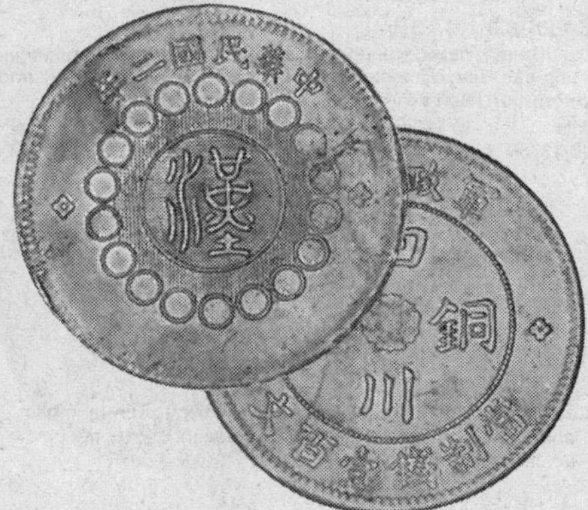

Y# 450 100 CASH
Copper **Obv:** Two rosettes **Obv. Legend:** Chung Hua Min Kuo (year) Nien **Rev:** Large flower in center

Date	Mintage	VG	F	VF	XF	Unc
2(1913)	399,212,000	2.50	6.00	8.50	17.50	—
3(1914)	—	30.00	40.00	50.00	60.00	—

Y# 450a 100 CASH
Brass **Obv. Legend:** Chung Hua Min Kuo (year) Nien

Date	Mintage	VG	F	VF	XF	Unc
2(1913)	Inc. above	1.50	3.00	6.00	10.00	—

Y# 450.1 100 CASH
Copper **Obv:** Three rosettes **Obv. Legend:** Chung Hua Min Kuo (year) Nien **Rev:** Small flower in center

Date	Mintage	VG	F	VF	XF	Unc
2(1913)	Inc. above	3.50	9.00	15.00	25.00	—
3(1914)	—	—	—	—	—	—

Y# 463.1 100 CASH
Copper **Obv. Legend:** Chung Hua Min Kuo (year) Nien **Rev:** Large value "100", large leaves

Date	Mintage	VG	F	VF	XF	Unc
15(1926)	7,055,000	3.50	9.00	15.00	25.00	—

Y# 463a.1 100 CASH
Brass **Obv. Legend:** Chung Hua Min Kuo (year) Nien **Rev:** Large value "100", large leaves

Date	Mintage	VG	F	VF	XF	Unc
15(1926)	Inc. above	3.25	8.00	12.50	20.00	—

Y# 463.2 100 CASH
Copper **Obv. Legend:** Chung Hua Min Kuo (year) Nien **Rev:** Small value "100", small leaves

Date	Mintage	VG	F	VF	XF	Unc
15(1926)	Inc. above	3.50	9.00	15.00	25.00	—

Y# 463a.2 100 CASH
Brass **Obv. Legend:** Chung Hua Min Kuo (year) Nien **Rev:** Small value "100", small leaves

Date	Mintage	VG	F	VF	XF	Unc
15(1926)	Inc. above	3.25	8.00	12.50	20.00	—

Y# 459a 200 CASH
Brass **Obv:** Flowers **Obv. Legend:** Chung Hua Min Kuo (year) Nien **Rev:** Crossed flags **Rev. Legend:** THE REPUBLIC OF CHINA

Date	Mintage	VG	F	VF	XF	Unc
2(1913)	—	20.00	40.00	80.00	125	—

Y# 459.1 200 CASH
Copper **Obv:** Flowers **Obv. Legend:** Chung Hua Min Kuo (year) Nien **Rev:** Crossed flags **Rev. Legend:** THE REPUBLIC OF CHINA

Date	Mintage	VG	F	VF	XF	Unc
2(1913)	Inc. above	6.00	10.00	25.00	40.00	—

Y# 459.1a 200 CASH
Brass **Obv:** Flowers **Obv. Legend:** Chung Hua Min Kuo (year) Nien **Rev:** Crossed flags **Rev. Legend:** THE REPUBLIC OF CHINA

Date	Mintage	VG	F	VF	XF	Unc
2(1913)	—	4.50	8.00	20.00	35.00	—

Y# 459.2 200 CASH
Copper **Obv:** Flowers **Obv. Legend:** Chung Hua Min Kuo (year) Nien **Rev:** Crossed flags **Rev. Legend:** THE REPUBLIC OF CHINA

Date	Mintage	VG	F	VF	XF	Unc
2(1913)	Inc. above	5.00	9.00	22.50	37.50	—

Note: For cut segments refer to 50 Cash, Y#459y and 100 Cash, Y#459x

Y# 459 200 CASH
Copper **Obv:** Flowers **Obv. Legend:** Chung Hua Min Kuo (year) Nien **Rev:** Crossed flags **Rev. Legend:** THE REPUBLIC OF CHINA

Date	Mintage	VG	F	VF	XF	Unc
2(1913) Rare	—	—	—	—	—	—

Y# 464.2 200 CASH
Brass **Obv:** Similar to Y#464 **Obv. Legend:** Chung Hua Min Kuo (year) Nien **Obv. Inscription:** Ch'uan **Rev:** Dot within first 0 of 200

Date	Mintage	VG	F	VF	XF	Unc
15(1926)	Inc. above	—	—	—	—	—

Note: Many varieties: open and closed buds; overstruck on earlier pieces and on virgin flans; different sizes and thicknesses

Y# 464 200 CASH
Copper **Obv. Legend:** Chung Hua Min Kuo (year) Nien **Obv. Inscription:** Ch'uan **Edge:** Plain

Date	Mintage	VG	F	VF	XF	Unc
15(1926)	404,644,000	4.00	12.00	17.00	35.00	—

Y# 464a 200 CASH
Brass **Obv. Legend:** Chung Hua Min Kuo (year) Nien **Obv. Inscription:** Ch'uan **Edge:** Plain

Date	Mintage	VG	F	VF	XF	Unc
15(1926)	Inc. above	4.50	12.00	17.00	35.00	—

Y# 464.1 200 CASH
Copper **Obv. Legend:** Chung Hua Min Kuo (year) Nien **Obv. Inscription:** Ch'uan **Edge:** Reeded

Date	Mintage	VG	F	VF	XF	Unc
15(1926)	Inc. above	6.00	15.00	25.00	45.00	—

Y# 464.1a 200 CASH
Brass **Obv. Legend:** Chung Hua Min Kuo (year) Nien **Obv. Inscription:** Ch'uan **Edge:** Reeded

Date	Mintage	VG	F	VF	XF	Unc
15(1926)	Inc. above	—	—	—	—	—

Y# 476 2 CENTS
Copper **Obv. Legend:** Chung Hua Min Kuo (year) Nien

Date	Mintage	VG	F	VF	XF	Unc
19(1930) Rare	—	—	—	—	—	—

Y# 476a 2 CENTS
Brass **Obv. Legend:** Chung Hua Min Kuo (year) Nien

Date	Mintage	VG	F	VF	XF	Unc
19(1930)	—	—	—	—	—	—

Y# 453 10 CENTS

2.6000 g., Silver **Obv. Legend:** Chung Hua Min Kuo (year) Nien

Date	Mintage	VG	F	VF	XF	Unc
1(1912)	370,000	8.50	25.00	40.00	75.00	150

Y# 468 10 CENTS

Copper-Nickel **Obv. Legend:** Chung Hua Min Kuo (year) Nien

Date	Mintage	VG	F	VF	XF	Unc
ND(ca.1926)	—	4.50	12.50	20.00	45.00	70.00

Y# 468a 10 CENTS

Silver **Obv. Legend:** Chung Hua Min Kuo (year) Nien

Date	Mintage	VG	F	VF	XF	Unc
ND(ca.1926)	—	12.00	35.00	75.00	125	200

Y# 468b 10 CENTS

Iron **Obv. Legend:** Chung Hua Min Kuo (year) Nien

Date	Mintage	VG	F	VF	XF	Unc
ND(ca.1926)	—	6.50	20.00	50.00	70.00	125

Y# 454 20 CENTS

5.2000 g., Silver **Obv. Legend:** Chung Hua Min Kuo (year) Nien

Date	Mintage	VG	F	VF	XF	Unc
1(1912)	95,000	17.00	50.00	85.00	150	300

K# 795 20 CENTS

5.2000 g., Silver, 25 mm. **Subject:** Sikang Szechuan Army in the Tibetan War **Obv:** Bust of governor Liu Wen-hwei of Szechuan facing **Obv. Legend:** Chung Hua Min Kuo (year) Nien **Rev:** Crossed flags

Date	Mintage	VG	F	VF	XF	Unc
1932	—	3,000	5,000	6,000	7,500	18,000

Y# 455 50 CENTS

12.9000 g., Silver **Obv. Legend:** Chung Hua Min Kuo (year) Nien

Date	Mintage	VG	F	VF	XF	Unc
1(1912)	37,942,000	7.50	15.00	25.00	50.00	125
2(1913) Rare	Inc. above	—	—	—	—	—

Y# 473 50 CENTS

10.5000 g., Silver **Subject:** Sun Yat-sen **Obv. Legend:** Chung Hua Min Kuo (year) Nien

Date	Mintage	VG	F	VF	XF	Unc
17(1928)	Inc. above	—	—	—	—	—

Y# 456 DOLLAR

25.6000 g., Silver **Obv. Legend:** Chung Hua Min Kuo (year) Nien

Date	Mintage	VG	F	VF	XF	Unc
1(1912)	55,670,000	10.00	14.00	22.00	55.00	350
2(1913) Rare	Inc. above	—	—	—	—	—

Y# 456.1 DOLLAR

25.6000 g., Silver **Obv. Legend:** Chung Hua Min Kuo (year) Nien **Rev:** Right hand character with two dots instead of horizontal stroke

Date	Mintage	VG	F	VF	XF	Unc
1(1912)	Inc. above	12.00	25.00	50.00	100	550

Note: Silver content ranged from 0.880 to 0.500 fine

Y# 474 DOLLAR

25.5000 g., Silver **Subject:** Sun Yat-sen **Obv. Legend:** Chung Hua Min Kuo (year) Nien

Date	Mintage	VG	F	VF	XF	Unc
17(1928)	Inc. above	—	—	—	—	—

PATTERNS

Including off metal strikes

KM#	Date	Mintage	Identification	Mkt Val
Pn16	ND(ca.1901)	—	20 Cents. Aluminum. Dragon type.	—
Pn17	ND(1902)	—	5 Cents. Brass. K#149y	200
Pn18	ND(1902)	—	10 Cents. Brass. K#148y	250
Pn19	ND(1902)	—	20 Cents. Brass. K#147y	300
Pn20	ND(1902)	—	50 Cents. Brass. K#146y	400
Pn21	ND(1902)	—	Dollar. Brass. K#145y	800
Pn22	CD1906	—	2 Cash. Copper. Y#8t	—
Pn23	CD1906	—	5 Cash. Copper. Y#9t	—
Pn24	CD1908	—	Cash. Brass. Y#7t	300
Pn25	CD1908	—	5 Cash. Brass.	—
Pn26	ND(ca.1912)	—	10 Cents. Copper.	—
Pn27	1(1912)	—	50 Cents. Copper. Y#455	—
Pn28	ND(ca.1926)	—	10 Cents. Brass. Y#468	—
Pn29	17(1928)	—	Dollar. Copper. Y#474	—
Pn30	ND(1941)	—	50 Cents. Temple. Spade. World War II	—

YUNNAN PROVINCE

A province located in south China bordering Burma, Laos and Vietnam. It is very mountainous with many lakes. Yunnan was the home of various active imperial mints. A modern mint was established at Kunming in 1905 and the first struck copper coins were issued in 1906 and the first struck silver coins in 1908. General Tang Chi-yao issued coins in gold, silver and copper with his portrait in 1919. The last Republican coins were struck here in 1949.

EMPIRE

PROVINCIAL CAST COINAGE

C# 27-6 CASH

Cast Brass **Ruler:** Kuang-hsü **Obv. Inscription:** Kuang-hsü T'ung-pao **Rev:** Manchu inscription **Rev. Inscription:** Boo-dong

Date	Mintage	Good	VG	F	VF	XF
ND(1875-1908)	—	4.00	6.50	9.00	15.00	—

C# 26-9 CASH

Cast Brass **Ruler:** Kuang-hsü **Obv. Inscription:** Kuang-hsü T'ung-pao **Rev:** Manchu inscription **Rev. Inscription:** Boo-yôn

Date	Mintage	Good	VG	F	VF	XF
ND(1875-1908)	—	2.00	4.00	6.50	9.00	—

C# 26-9.1 CASH

Cast Brass **Ruler:** Kuang-hsü **Obv. Inscription:** Kuang-hsü T'ung-pao **Rev:** Manchu inscription, "Kung" above **Rev. Inscription:** Boo-yôn

Date	Mintage	Good	VG	F	VF	XF
ND(1875-1908)	—	2.00	5.00	7.50	10.00	—

C# 26-9.2 CASH

Cast Brass **Ruler:** Kuang-hsü **Obv. Inscription:** Kuang-hsü T'ung-pao **Rev:** Manchu inscription, "Szu" (four) above **Rev. Inscription:** Boo-yôn

Date	Mintage	Good	VG	F	VF	XF
ND(1875-1908)	—	2.50	5.00	7.50	10.00	—

C# 26-9.3 CASH

Cast Brass **Ruler:** Kuang-hsü **Obv. Inscription:** Kuang-hsü T'ung-pao **Rev:** Manchu inscription, "Chin" above **Rev. Inscription:** Boo-yôn

Date	Mintage	Good	VG	F	VF	XF
ND(1875-1908)	—	2.50	5.00	7.50	10.00	—

C# 26-9.4 CASH

Cast Brass **Ruler:** Kuang-hsü **Obv. Inscription:** Kuang-hsü T'ung-pao **Rev:** Manchu inscription, crescent above, dot below **Rev. Inscription:** Boo-yôn

Date	Mintage	Good	VG	F	VF	XF
ND(1875-1908)	—	2.50	5.00	7.50	12.00	—

C# 26-9.5 CASH

Cast Brass **Ruler:** Kuang-hsü **Obv. Inscription:** Kuang-hsü T'ung-pao **Rev:** Manchu inscription, dot above hole **Rev. Inscription:** Boo-yôn

Date	Mintage	Good	VG	F	VF	XF
ND(1875-1908)	—	2.50	5.00	7.50	12.00	—

C# 27-6.1 CASH

Cast Brass **Ruler:** Kuang-hsü **Obv. Inscription:** Kuang-hsü T'ung-pao **Rev:** Manchu inscription, "Chin" above **Rev. Inscription:** Boo-dong

Date	Mintage	Good	VG	F	VF	XF
ND(1875-1908)	—	5.00	7.50	10.00	15.00	—

C# 27-6.2 CASH

Cast Brass **Ruler:** Kuang-hsü **Obv. Inscription:** Kuang-hsü T'ung-pao **Rev:** Manchu inscription, "Ts'un" below **Rev. Inscription:** Boo-dong

Date	Mintage	Good	VG	F	VF	XF
ND(1875-1908)	—	5.00	7.50	10.00	15.00	—

C# 27-7 CASH

Cast Brass **Ruler:** Hsüan-t'ung **Obv. Inscription:** Hsuan-t'ung T'ung-pao **Rev:** "Ts'un" below inscription **Rev. Inscription:** Manchu Boo-dong

Date	Mintage	Good	VG	F	VF	XF
ND(1909-11) Rare	—	—	—	—	—	—

C# 26-11 CASH

Cast Brass **Ruler:** Hsüan-t'ung **Obv. Inscription:** Hsuan-t'ung T'ung-pao **Rev:** "Kung" above hole **Rev. Inscription:** Manchu Boo-yôn **Note:** Struck at Yün Mint (Yünnanfu).

Date	Mintage	Good	VG	F	VF	XF
ND(1909-11)	—	75.00	100	150	220	—

C# 26-12 CASH

Cast Brass **Ruler:** Hsüan-t'ung **Obv. Inscription:** Hsuan-t'ung T'ung-pao **Rev:** "Shan" above hole **Rev. Inscription:** Manchu Boo-yôn

Date	Mintage	Good	VG	F	VF	XF
ND(1909-11)	—	30.00	40.00	50.00	100	—

C# 26-13 CASH

Cast Brass **Ruler:** Hsüan-t'ung **Obv. Inscription:** Hsuan-t'ung T'ung-pao **Rev:** Without character above hole **Rev. Inscription:** Manchu Boo-yôn

Date	Mintage	Good	VG	F	VF	XF
ND(1909-11)	—	35.00	45.00	55.00	100	—

MILLED COINAGE

Y# 10u 10 CASH

Copper **Obv:** Inscription: Tai-ching T'ung-pi with large mint mark "Yun" in center **Rev:** Side view dragon

Date	Mintage	VG	F	VF	XF	Unc
CD1906	36,701,000	10.00	22.00	35.00	60.00	—

Y# 10u.1 10 CASH

Copper **Obv:** Inscription with small mint mark "Yun" in center **Obv. Inscription:** Tai-ching T'ung-pi **Rev:** Side view dragon

Date	Mintage	VG	F	VF	XF	Unc
CD1906	Inc. above	25.00	55.00	85.00	125	—

Y# 10v 10 CASH

Copper **Obv:** Inscription with mint mark "Tien" in center **Obv. Inscription:** Tai-ching T'ung-pi **Rev:** Side view dragon

Date	Mintage	VG	F	VF	XF	Unc
CD1906	Inc. above	12.50	30.00	40.00	65.00	—

Y# 11u 20 CASH

Copper **Obv:** Inscription with large mint mark "Yun" in center **Obv. Inscription:** Tai-ching T'ung-pi **Rev:** Side view dragon

Date	Mintage	VG	F	VF	XF	Unc
CD1906	645,000	125	175	225	275	—

Y# 11u.1 20 CASH

Copper **Obv:** Inscription with small mint mark "Yun" in center **Obv. Inscription:** Tai-ching T'ung-pi **Rev:** Side view dragon

Date	Mintage	VG	F	VF	XF	Unc
CD1906	—	150	275	400	550	—

Y# 11v.1 20 CASH

Copper **Obv:** Inscription with mint mark "Tien" in center **Obv. Inscription:** Tai-ching T'ung-pi **Rev:** Side view dragon

Date	Mintage	VG	F	VF	XF	Unc
CD1906	Inc. above	150	275	400	550	—

Y# 11v.1a 20 CASH

Brass **Obv. Inscription:** Tai-ching T'ung-pi **Rev:** Side view dragon

Date	Mintage	VG	F	VF	XF	Unc
CD1906	Inc. above	175	350	450	600	—

Y# 252 20 CENTS

Brass **Ruler:** Kuang-hsü **Obv. Legend:** Yün-nan Sheng Tsao **Obv. Inscription:** Kuang-hsü Yuan-pao **Rev:** Side view dragon **Note:** Many minor varieties.

Date	Mintage	VG	F	VF	XF	Unc
ND(1908)	532,000	6.00	18.50	35.00	60.00	125

Y# 253 50 CENTS

13.2000 g., 0.8000 Silver .3395 oz. ASW **Ruler:** Kuang-hsü **Obv. Legend:** Yün-nan Sheng Tsao **Obv. Inscription:** Kuang-hsü Yuan-pao **Rev:** Side view dragon

Date	Mintage	VG	F	VF	XF	Unc
ND(1908)	—	5.50	8.50	16.00	25.00	110

Y# 259 50 CENTS

13.2000 g., 0.8000 Silver .3395 oz. ASW **Ruler:** Hsüan-t'ung **Obv. Legend:** Yün-nan Sheng Tsao **Obv. Inscription:** Hsüan-t'ung-pao **Rev:** Side view dragon; seven flames on pearl

Date	Mintage	VG	F	VF	XF	Unc
ND(1909-11)	—	5.50	8.50	16.50	27.50	120

Y# 259.1 50 CENTS

13.2000 g., 0.8000 Silver .3395 oz. ASW **Ruler:** Hsüan-t'ung **Obv. Legend:** Yün-nan Sheng Tsao **Obv. Inscription:** Hsüan-t'ung-pao **Rev:** Side view dragon; nine flames on pearl

Date	Mintage	VG	F	VF	XF	Unc
ND(1909-11)	—	5.50	8.50	16.50	27.50	120

Y# 254 DOLLAR

26.8000 g., 0.9000 Silver .7755 oz. ASW **Ruler:** Kuang-hsü **Obv. Legend:** Yün-nan Sheng Tsao **Obv. Inscription:** Kuang-hsü Yüan-pao **Rev:** Side view dragon

Date	Mintage	VG	F	VF	XF	Unc
ND(1908)	—	15.00	25.00	37.50	75.00	550

Y# 260 DOLLAR

26.8000 g., 0.9000 Silver .7755 oz. ASW **Ruler:** Hsüan-t'ung **Obv. Legend:** Yün-nan Sheng Tsao **Obv. Inscription:** Hsüan-t'ung T'ung-pao **Rev:** Side view dragon

Date	Mintage	VG	F	VF	XF	Unc
ND(1909-11)	—	15.00	25.00	35.00	85.00	550

Y# 260.1 DOLLAR
26.8000 g., 0.9000 Silver .7755 oz. ASW **Ruler:** Hsüan-t'ung
Obv. Legend: Yün-nan Sheng Tsao **Obv. Inscription:** Hsüan-t'ung T'ung-pao **Rev:** Side view dragon

Date	Mintage	VG	F	VF	XF	Unc
CD1910 Rare	—	—	—	—	—	—

REPUBLIC

TRANSITIONAL COINAGE

In the name of the Republic

KM# 5 CASH
Cast Copper Or Brass **Obv. Inscription:** Min-kuo T'ung-pao **Rev:** Inscription **Rev. Inscription:** Tung-ch'uan

Date	Mintage	Good	VG	F	VF	XF
ND(1912)	—	10.00	20.00	50.00	100	—

KM# 5a CASH
Cast Copper Or Brass **Obv. Inscription:** Min-kuo T'ung-pao **Rev:** Inscription **Rev. Inscription:** Boo-yôn

Date	Mintage	Good	VG	F	VF	XF
ND(1912)	—	100	125	180	—	—

KM# 4 10 CASH
Brass **Obv. Inscription:** Min-kuo T'ung-pao

Date	Mintage	Good	VG	F	VF	XF
ND(1912)	—	15.00	25.00	55.00	100	—

RESTRUCK IMPERIAL COINAGE

The following imperial coins are reign-dated 1875-1908. These coins were apparently restruck from previously unused dies at intervals from 1911 through to 1949, and with a progressively reduced silver content. The dates and silver content shown are approximate.

Y# 255 10 CENTS
2.6500 g., 0.6500 Silver .0554 oz. ASW **Obv. Legend:** Yün-nan Sheng Tsao **Obv. Inscription:** Kuang-hsü Yüan-pao **Rev:** Side view dragon with two circles beneath pearl

Date	Mintage	VG	F	VF	XF	Unc
ND(1911-15)	902,000	5.00	15.00	30.00	45.00	120

Y# 256 20 CENTS
5.3000 g., 0.8000 Silver .1363 oz. ASW **Obv. Legend:** Yün-nan Sheng Tsao **Obv. Inscription:** Kuang-hsü Yüan-pao **Rev:** Side view dragon with two circles beneath pearl

Date	Mintage	VG	F	VF	XF	Unc
ND(1911-15)	—	4.50	12.50	17.50	32.50	75.00

Y# 256a 20 CENTS
5.3000 g., 0.6500 Silver .1108 oz. ASW **Obv. Legend:** Yün-nan Sheng Tsao **Obv. Inscription:** Kuang-hsü Yüan-pao **Rev:** Side view dragon with three circles beneath pearl

Date	Mintage	VG	F	VF	XF	Unc
ND(1911-15)	—	4.50	12.50	22.50	37.50	75.00

Y# 256b 20 CENTS
5.3000 g., 0.4000 Silver .0682 oz. ASW **Obv. Legend:** Yün-nan Sheng Tsao **Obv. Inscription:** Kuang-hsü Yüan-pao **Rev:** Side view dragon with two or three circles beneath pearl

Date	Mintage	VG	F	VF	XF	Unc
ND(1920-31)	—	—	—	—	—	—

Y# 257 50 CENTS
13.2000 g., 0.8000 Silver .3395 oz. ASW **Obv. Legend:** Yün-nan Sheng Tsao **Obv. Inscription:** Kuang-hsü Yüan-pao **Rev:** Side view dragon with two circles below pearl

Date	Mintage	VG	F	VF	XF	Unc
ND(1911-15)	—	5.00	7.00	12.00	20.00	35.00

Y# 257.1 50 CENTS
13.2000 g., 0.8000 Silver .3395 oz. ASW **Obv. Legend:** Yün-nan Sheng Tsao **Obv. Inscription:** Kuang-hsü Yüan-pao **Rev:** Side view dragon with three circles below pearl

Date	Mintage	VG	F	VF	XF	Unc
ND(1911-15)	—	4.75	6.50	10.00	16.00	28.00

Y# 257.2 50 CENTS
13.2000 g., 0.5000 Silver .2122 oz. ASW **Obv. Legend:** Yün-nan Sheng Tsao **Obv. Inscription:** Kuang-hsü Yüan-pao **Rev:** Side view dragon with four circles below pearl

Date	Mintage	VG	F	VF	XF	Unc
ND(1920-31)	—	4.75	6.50	10.00	16.00	28.00

Note: There are more than 30 minor varieties of Y#257

Y# 257.3 50 CENTS
13.2000 g., 0.5000 Silver - Billon **Obv. Legend:** Yün-nan Sheng Tsao **Obv. Inscription:** Kuang-hsü Yuan-pao **Rev:** Side view dragon with two circles beneath pearl, large circle around center circle of rosettes

Date	Mintage	VG	F	VF	XF	Unc
ND(1949)	—	—	—	—	—	—

Y# 258 DOLLAR
26.8000 g., 0.9000 Silver .7755 oz. ASW **Obv. Legend:** Yün-nan Sheng Tsao **Obv. Inscription:** Kuang-hsü Yüan-pao **Rev:** Side view dragon with one circle below pearl

Date	Mintage	VG	F	VF	XF	Unc
ND(1911-15)	—	15.00	22.50	30.00	45.00	500

Y# 258.1 DOLLAR
26.8000 g., 0.9000 Silver .7755 oz. ASW **Obv. Legend:** Yün-nan Sheng Tsao **Obv. Inscription:** Kuang-hsü Yüan-pao **Rev:** Side view dragon with four circles below pearl

Date	Mintage	VG	F	VF	XF	Unc
ND(1920-22)	—	15.00	22.50	30.00	45.00	500

STANDARD COINAGE

Y# 488 CENT
Brass **Obv:** Crossed flags **Obv. Legend:** Chung Hua Min Kuo

Date	Mintage	VG	F	VF	XF	Unc
21 (1932) Rare	—	—	—	—	—	—

Y# 489 2 CENTS
Brass **Obv:** Crossed flags **Obv. Legend:** Chung Hua Min Kuo

Date	Mintage	VG	F	VF	XF	Unc
21 (1932)	—	175	325	500	750	—

Y# 478 50 CASH
Brass **Obv:** Crossed flags **Obv. Legend:** Yün-nan Sheng Tsao **Rev:** Bust of General T'ang Chi-yao facing

Date	Mintage	VG	F	VF	XF	Unc
ND(ca.1919)	—	10.00	20.00	40.00	70.00	—

Y# 478a 50 CASH
Copper **Obv:** Crossed flags **Obv. Legend:** Yün-nan Sheng Tsao **Rev:** Bust of General T'ang Chi-yao facing

Date	Mintage	VG	F	VF	XF	Unc
ND(ca.1919)	—	20.00	40.00	80.00	125	—

Y# 485 5 CENTS
Copper-Nickel **Obv. Legend:** Chung Hua Min Kuo (year) Nien **Rev:** Flag

Date	Mintage	VG	F	VF	XF	Unc
12(1923)	—	22.50	32.50	47.50	75.00	—

Y# 490 5 CENTS
Copper **Obv:** Crossed flags **Obv. Legend:** Chung Hua Min Kuo

Date	Mintage	VG	F	VF	XF	Unc
21(1932)	—	125	175	250	350	—

Y# 486 10 CENTS
Copper-Nickel **Obv. Legend:** Chung Hua Min Kuo (year) Nien **Rev:** Flag **Edge:** Reeded

Date	Mintage	VG	F	VF	XF	Unc
12(1923)	—	1.75	2.50	3.75	7.50	—

Y# 486.1 10 CENTS
Copper-Nickel **Obv. Legend:** Chung Hua Min Kuo (year) Nien **Rev:** Flag **Edge:** Plain

Date	Mintage	VG	F	VF	XF	Unc
12(1923)	—	2.50	4.00	6.50	12.50	—

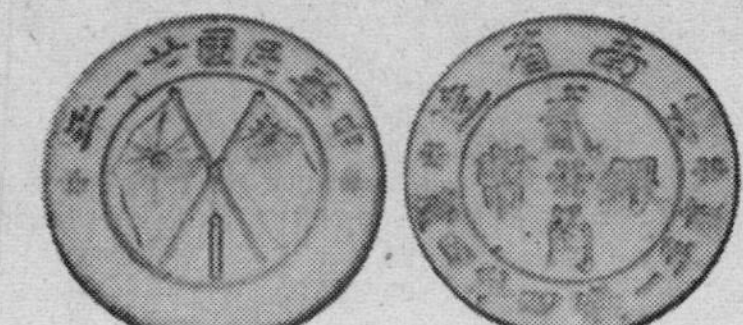

Y# 491 20 CENTS
5.6000 g., Silver **Obv:** Crossed flags **Obv. Legend:** Chung Hua Min Kuo (year) Nien

Date	Mintage	VG	F	VF	XF	Unc
21(1932)	—	2.50	4.00	6.00	9.00	20.00

Y# 493 20 CENTS
5.6000 g., Silver **Rev:** Provincial capitol

Date	Mintage	VG	F	VF	XF	Unc
38(1949)	—	2.75	5.00	7.50	12.50	40.00

Y# 480 50 CENTS
13.1000 g., 0.8500 Silver **Obv:** Bust of General T'ang Chi-yao right **Rev:** Crossed flags

Date	Mintage	VG	F	VF	XF	Unc
ND(ca.1916)	—	6.00	12.00	22.00	50.00	250

Y# 479 50 CENTS
13.1000 g., 0.8500 Silver, 33 mm. **Obv:** Bust of General T'ang Chi-yao facing **Rev:** Crossed flags

Date	Mintage	VG	F	VF	XF	Unc
ND(ca.1917)	—	5.50	9.00	18.00	30.00	95.00

Y# 479.1 50 CENTS
13.1000 g., 0.8500 Silver, 33 mm. **Obv:** Bust of General T'ang Chi-yao facing **Rev:** Crossed flags with circle in center of flag at left

Date	Mintage	VG	F	VF	XF	Unc
ND(ca.1917)	—	5.50	9.00	18.00	30.00	95.00

Y# 492 50 CENTS
13.1000 g., 0.5000 Silver **Obv:** Crossed flags **Obv. Legend:** Chung Hua Min Kuo (year) Nien

Date	Mintage	VG	F	VF	XF	Unc
21	—	3.50	6.00	9.00	15.00	50.00

K# 1521 5 DOLLARS
Gold **Obv. Inscription:** "Equal to 5 (silver) Dollars" **Note:** Uniface; Similar to 10 Dollars, K#1520.

Date	Mintage	VG	F	VF	XF	Unc
ND(1917) Rare	—	—	—	—	—	—

Y# 481 5 DOLLARS
4.5000 g., 0.7500 Gold .1085 oz. AGW, 18 mm. **Obv:** Bust of General T'ang Chi-yao facing **Rev:** With numeral 2 below flag tassels

Date	Mintage	VG	F	VF	XF	Unc
ND(1919)	Est. 60,000	75.00	220	500	800	1,250

K# 1529 5 DOLLARS
4.5000 g., 0.7500 Gold .1085 oz. AGW **Obv. Inscription:** Wu(5)-Yüan Chin-pi **Rev:** Tien in wheat sprays **Edge:** Plain

Date	Mintage	VG	F	VF	XF	Unc
ND(1925)	—	—	—	1,500	2,200	3,000

K# 1520 10 DOLLARS
Gold **Obv. Inscription:** "Equal to 10 Silver Dollars" **Note:** Uniface.

Date	Mintage	VG	F	VF	XF	Unc
ND Rare	—	—	—	—	—	—

Y# 482 10 DOLLARS
8.5000 g., 0.7500 Gold .2050 oz. AGW, 23 mm. **Obv:** Bust of General T'ang Chi-yao facing **Rev:** With numeral 1 below flag tassels

Date	Mintage	VG	F	VF	XF	Unc
ND(1919)	900,000	135	275	650	1,000	1,400

Y# 482.1 10 DOLLARS
8.5000 g., 0.7500 Gold .2050 oz. AGW, 23 mm. **Obv:** Bust of General T'ang Chi-yao facing **Rev:** Without numeral 1 below flag tassels

Date	Mintage	VG	F	VF	XF	Unc
ND(1919)	Inc. above	135	275	900	1,200	1,800

K# 1528 10 DOLLARS
8.5000 g., 0.7500 Gold .2050 oz. AGW **Obv. Inscription:** Shih(10)-yüan Chin-pi **Rev:** Tien in wheat sprays **Edge:** Plain

Date	Mintage	VG	F	VF	XF	Unc
ND(1925)	—	—	—	1,500	2,200	3,000

PATTERNS

Including off metal strikes

KM#	Date	Mintage	Identification	Mkt Val
Pn1	ND(ca.1902)	—	Cash. Brass. Tungch'uwan	—
Pn2	ND(1908)	—	10 Cash. Copper.	250
Pn3	ND(1908)	—	50 Cents. Copper. Y#253.	200
Pn4	ND(1908)	—	50 Cents. Brass. Y#253.	250
Pn5	ND(1908)	—	50 Cents. Copper. Y#257.	200
Pn6	ND(1908)	—	Dollar. Copper. Y#254.	350
Pn7	ND(1925)	—	5 Dollars. Silver.	200
Pn8	ND(1925)	—	10 Dollars. Silver.	300
Pn9	ND(1925)	—	10 Dollars. Pewter. K#1528y.	—

YUNNAN-SZECHUAN

Yunnan-Sichuan

These two coins have a 2-character mint mark in the center of the obverse, indicating the provinces of Yunnan and Szechuan (Sichuan).

EMPIRE

PROVINCIAL CAST COINAGE

Y# 10w 10 CASH
Copper **Ruler:** Kuang-hsü **Obv. Inscription:** Ta-ching T'ung-pi **Rev. Legend:** Kuang-hsu Nien Tsao, TAI-CHING-TI-KUO...

Date	Mintage	VG	F	VF	XF	Unc
CD 1906	—	20.00	40.00	60.00	110	—

Y# 11w 20 CASH
Copper **Ruler:** Kuang-hsü **Obv. Inscription:** Ta-ch'ing T'ung-pi **Rev. Legend:** Kuang-hsü Nien Tsao, TAI-CHING-TI-KUO...

Date	Mintage	VG	F	VF	XF	Unc
CD 1906	—	100	150	200	250	—

CHINA, REPUBLIC OF

On December 15, 1915 Yuan Shih-K'ai had himself formally chosen and proclaimed emperor. Opposition developed within China and among various foreign powers. A rebellion broke out in Yünnan and spread to other southern provinces. Opposition was so great that Yuan rescinded the monarchy on March 21, 1916. On June 6th he died.

EMPIRE

TRANSITIONAL COINAGE

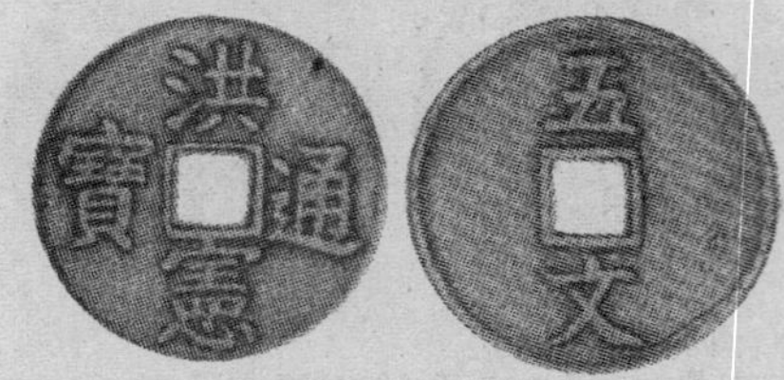

KM# 1 5 CASH (5 Wen)
Copper **Ruler:** Hung-hsien **Obverse:** Inscription: Hung-hsien T'ung-pao

Date	Mintage	VG	F	VF	XF	Unc
ND(1916) Rare	—	—	—	—	—	—

Note: Questionable, believed to be a fantasy by some authorities

X# 1320 10 CASH (10 Wen)
Bronze **Ruler:** Hung-hsien **Obv. Inscription:** Hung-hsien T'ung-pao **Note:** Prev. KM#2. Uniface. Believed to be a fantasy by some authorities.

Date	Mintage	Good	VG	F	VF	XF
ND(1916) Rare	—	—	—	—	—	—

REPUBLIC

STANDARD COINAGE

Y# 301 10 CASH (10 Wen)
Copper **Mint:** Nanking **Obverse:** Crossed flags, florals at left and right **Reverse:** Double circle with small rosettes separating legend

Date	Mintage	VG	F	VF	XF	Unc
ND(ca.1912)	—	0.20	0.50	0.75	1.50	15.00

Y# 301a 10 CASH (10 Wen)
Brass **Obverse:** Crossed flags, florals at left and right **Reverse:** Double circle with small rosettes separating legend

Date	Mintage	VG	F	VF	XF	Unc
ND(ca.1912)	—	—	—	—	—	—

Y# 301.1 10 CASH (10 Wen)
Copper **Obverse:** Second character from right in bottom legend is rounded **Reverse:** Double circle with three dots separating legend

Date	Mintage	VG	F	VF	XF	Unc
ND(ca.1912)	—	0.35	1.00	2.00	5.00	22.00

Y# 301.2 10 CASH (10 Wen)
Copper **Obverse:** Second character from right in bottom legend is rounded **Reverse:** Double circle with two dots separating legend

Date	Mintage	VG	F	VF	XF	Unc
ND(ca.1912)	—	0.20	0.50	1.00	2.50	16.00

Y# 301.3 10 CASH (10 Wen)
Copper **Mint:** Nanking **Obverse:** Small star on flag **Reverse:** Double circle with six-pointed stars separating legend

Date	Mintage	VG	F	VF	XF	Unc
ND(ca.1912)	—	0.25	0.75	1.50	3.00	18.00

Y# 301.4 10 CASH (10 Wen)
Copper **Obverse:** Large star on flag extending to edges of flag **Reverse:** Double circle with six-pointed stars separating legend

Date	Mintage	VG	F	VF	XF	Unc
ND(ca.1912)	—	3.50	10.00	15.00	25.00	65.00

Y# 301.4a 10 CASH (10 Wen)
Brass **Obverse:** Large star on flag extending to edges of flag **Reverse:** Double circle with six-pointed stars separating legend

Date	Mintage	VG	F	VF	XF	Unc
ND(ca.1912)	—	—	—	—	—	—

Y# 301.5 10 CASH (10 Wen)
Copper **Obverse:** Flower wtih many stems **Reverse:** Single circle

Date	Mintage	VG	F	VF	XF	Unc
ND(ca.1912)	—	0.25	0.75	1.50	3.00	20.00

Y# 301.6 10 CASH (10 Wen)
Copper **Obverse:** Flower wtih fewer stems **Reverse:** Single circle

Date	Mintage	VG	F	VF	XF	Unc
ND(ca.1912)	—	0.25	0.75	1.50	3.00	20.00

Y# 309 10 CASH (10 Wen)
Copper **Mint:** Tientsin

Date	Mintage	VG	F	VF	XF	Unc
ND(1914-17)	—	3.50	10.00	20.00	40.00	120

Note: Pieces with L. GIORGI near rim are patterns

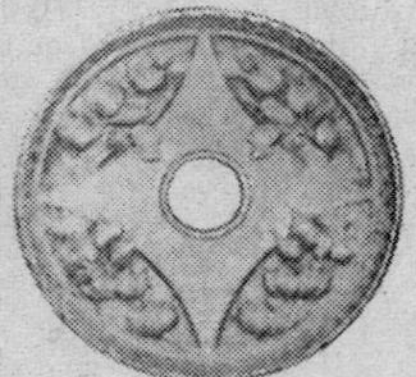

Y# 324 10 CASH (10 Wen)
Bronze **Mint:** Tientsin

Date	Mintage	VG	F	VF	XF	Unc
5(1916)	—	1.75	5.00	10.00	20.00	50.00

Note: Pieces with "L. GIORGI" near rim are patterns

Y# 307 10 CASH (10 Wen)
Copper **Mint:** Taiyüan **Obverse:** One large rosette on either side **Reverse:** Slender leaves and short ribbon

Date	Mintage	VG	F	VF	XF	Unc
ND(1919)	421,138,000	0.20	0.50	1.00	3.00	14.00

Y# 307a 10 CASH (10 Wen)
Copper **Obverse:** Crossed flags, three rosettes on either side, ornate right flag **Reverse:** Long ribbon

Date	Mintage	VG	F	VF	XF	Unc
ND(1919)	Inc. above	0.40	1.00	2.00	4.00	12.50

Y# 307a.1 10 CASH (10 Wen)
Copper **Obverse:** Crossed flags, three rosettes on either side, ornate right flag **Reverse:** Short ribbon and smaller wheat ears

Date	Mintage	VG	F	VF	XF	Unc
ND(1919)	Inc. above	3.50	10.00	20.00	40.00	100

Y# 307b 10 CASH (10 Wen)
Brass **Obverse:** Crossed flags, three rosettes at either side, ornate right flag **Reverse:** Long ribbon

Date	Mintage	VG	F	VF	XF	Unc
ND(1919)	—	—	—	—	—	—

Y# 307.1 10 CASH (10 Wen)
Copper **Reverse:** Larger leaves and longer ribbon

Date	Mintage	VG	F	VF	XF	Unc
ND(1919)	Inc. above	3.50	10.00	20.00	40.00	100

Y# 302 10 CASH (10 Wen)
Copper **Mint:** Anhwei **Reverse:** Vine above leaf at 12-o'clock; wreath tied at bottom; M-shaped leaves at base of wheat ears

Date	Mintage	VG	F	VF	XF	Unc
ND(ca.1920)	—	0.20	0.60	1.50	3.00	18.00

Y# 302a 10 CASH (10 Wen)
Brass **Obverse:** Crossed flags, florals at left and right **Reverse:** Vine above leaf at 12-o'clock; wreath tied at bottom; M-shaped leaves at base of wheat ears

Date	Mintage	VG	F	VF	XF	Unc
ND(ca.1920)	—	—	—	—	—	—

Y# 302.1 10 CASH (10 Wen)
Copper **Obverse:** Crossed flags, florals at left and right **Reverse:** Vine above leaf at 12-o'clock, wreath tied at bottom; M-shaped leaves at base of larger wheat ears

Date	Mintage	VG	F	VF	XF	Unc
ND(ca.1920)	—	0.35	1.00	3.50	6.50	20.00

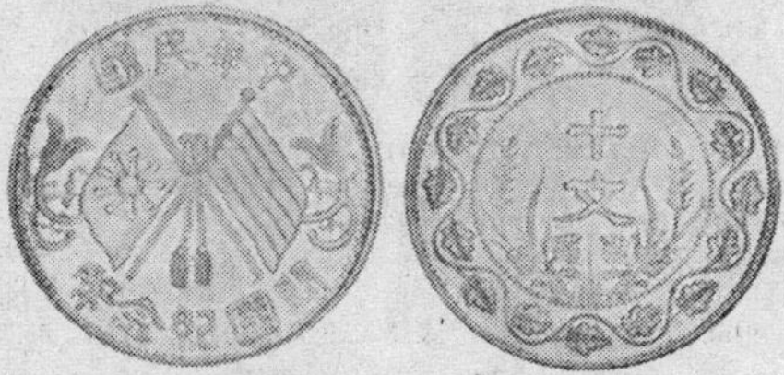

Y# 302.2 10 CASH (10 Wen)
Copper **Reverse:** Vine beneath leaf at 12-o'clock; wreath not tied at bottom; without M-shaped leaves at base of wheat ears

Date	Mintage	VG	F	VF	XF	Unc
ND(ca.1920)	—	0.50	1.50	4.00	8.00	22.00

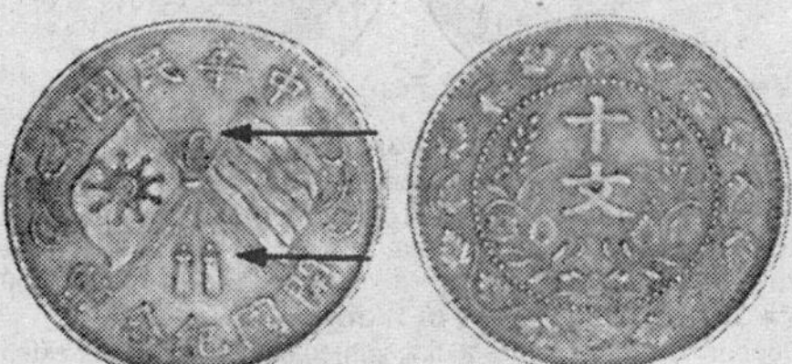

Y# 302.3 10 CASH (10 Wen)
Copper **Reverse:** Leaves pointing clockwise

Date	Mintage	VG	F	VF	XF	Unc
ND(ca.1920)	—	10.00	30.00	40.00	60.00	115

Y# 303 10 CASH (10 Wen)
Copper **Obverse:** Crossed flags, small star-shaped rosettes at left and right **Reverse:** Small 4-petaled rosettes separating legend

Date	Mintage	VG	F	VF	XF	Unc
ND(ca.1920)	—	0.20	0.50	1.00	2.00	15.00

Y# 303a 10 CASH (10 Wen)
Brass **Obverse:** Crossed flags, stars replace rosettes at left and right **Reverse:** Small 4-petaled rosettes separating legend

Date	Mintage	VG	F	VF	XF	Unc
ND(ca.1920)	—	0.50	1.50	4.00	10.00	22.50

Y# 303.1 10 CASH (10 Wen)
Copper **Obverse:** Crossed flags, left flag's star in relief, small star-shaped rosettes at left and right **Reverse:** Small 4-petaled rosettes separating legend

Date	Mintage	VG	F	VF	XF	Unc
ND(ca.1920)	—	0.20	0.50	1.00	2.00	15.00

Y# 303.3 10 CASH (10 Wen)
Copper **Obverse:** Large rosettes replace stars **Reverse:** Stars separating legend

Date	Mintage	VG	F	VF	XF	Unc
ND(ca.1920)	—	1.00	3.00	6.25	12.50	25.00

Y# 303.4 10 CASH (10 Wen)
Copper **Obverse:** Crossed flags, very small pentagonal rosettes at left and right

Date	Mintage	VG	F	VF	XF	Unc
ND(ca.1920)	—	0.25	0.75	1.50	3.00	15.00

Y# 303.4a 10 CASH (10 Wen)
Brass **Obverse:** Crossed flags, very small pentagonal rosettes at left and right **Reverse:** Stars separating legend

Date	Mintage	VG	F	VF	XF	Unc
ND(ca.1920)	—	1.00	3.00	6.25	12.50	25.00

Y# 303.5 10 CASH (10 Wen)
Brass **Obverse:** Crossed flags, three large rosettes at left and right **Reverse:** Stars separate legend

Date	Mintage	VG	F	VF	XF	Unc
ND(ca.1920)	—	—	—	—	—	—

Y# 304 10 CASH (10 Wen)
Copper **Mint:** Anhwei **Obverse:** Circled flags flanked by pentagonal rosettes

Date	Mintage	VG	F	VF	XF	Unc
ND(ca,1920)	—	3.75	11.50	21.50	42.50	85.00

Y# 305 10 CASH (10 Wen)
Copper **Mint:** Changsha **Reverse:** Chrysanthemum

Date	Mintage	VG	F	VF	XF	Unc
ND(ca.1920)	—	5.00	15.00	25.00	50.00	115

Y# 306a 10 CASH (10 Wen)
Copper **Obverse:** Crossed flags, five characters in lower legend

Date	Mintage	VG	F	VF	XF	Unc
ND(ca.1920)	—	1.75	5.00	12.00	25.00	65.00

Y# 306b 10 CASH (10 Wen)
Brass **Obverse:** Crossed flags, five characters in lower legend

Date	Mintage	VG	F	VF	XF	Unc
ND(ca.1920)	—	0.35	1.00	2.50	5.00	18.00

Y# 306.1 10 CASH (10 Wen)
Copper **Mint:** Changsha **Obverse:** Crossed flags, florals at left and right **Reverse:** Wheat ear design within circle

Date	Mintage	VG	F	VF	XF	Unc
ND(ca.1920)	—	0.20	0.50	1.25	3.00	14.00

Y# 306.1b 10 CASH (10 Wen)
Copper **Obverse:** Crossed flags, florals at left and right **Reverse:** Thin leaf blade between lower wheat ears

Date	Mintage	VG	F	VF	XF	Unc
ND(ca.1920)	—	1.75	5.00	7.50	14.00	30.00

Y# 306.2 10 CASH (10 Wen)
Copper **Obverse:** Crossed flags, florals at left and right, dot on either side of upper legend **Reverse:** Wheat ear design within circle

Date	Mintage	VG	F	VF	XF	Unc
ND(ca.1920)	—	0.35	1.00	2.00	3.50	15.00

Y# 306.2b 10 CASH (10 Wen)

Brass **Obverse:** Crossed flags, florals at left and right, dot on either side of upper legend **Reverse:** Thin leaf blade between lower wheat ears

Date	Mintage	VG	F	VF	XF	Unc
ND(ca.1920)	—	0.45	1.25	3.00	5.00	15.00

Y# 306.3 10 CASH (10 Wen)

Copper **Obverse:** Star between flags **Reverse:** Wheat ear design within circle

Date	Mintage	VG	F	VF	XF	Unc
ND(ca.1920)	—	6.50	20.00	40.00	75.00	—

Y# 306.4 10 CASH (10 Wen)

Copper **Obverse:** Elongated rosettes, different characters in bottom legend **Reverse:** Thin leaf blade between lower wheat ears

Date	Mintage	VG	F	VF	XF	Unc
ND(ca.1920)	—	9.00	27.50	55.00	85.00	215

Y# 311 10 CASH (10 Wen)

Copper **Mint:** Kalgan

Date	Mintage	VG	F	VF	XF	Unc
13(1924)	—	65.00	175	350	500	850

Y# 308 20 CASH (20 Wen)

Copper, 32.3 mm. **Mint:** Taiyüan **Obverse:** Crossed flags **Reverse:** Value in sprays

Date	Mintage	VG	F	VF	XF	Unc
8(1919)	200,861,000	0.50	1.50	3.00	7.50	30.00

Y# 308b 20 CASH (20 Wen)

Cast Brass **Obverse:** Crossed flags **Reverse:** Value in sprays

Date	Mintage	Good	VG	F	VF	XF
8(1919)	—	10.00	15.00	18.50	27.50	—

Note: A "warlord" issue; refer to note under Szechuan - Republic

Y# 308a 20 CASH (20 Wen)

Copper **Obverse:** Crossed flags **Reverse:** Value in sprays

Date	Mintage	VG	F	VF	XF	Unc
10(1921)	Inc. above	0.35	1.00	2.50	6.00	30.00

Y# 310 20 CASH (20 Wen)

Copper **Mint:** Tientsin **Obverse:** Crossed flags **Reverse:** Value in sprays

Date	Mintage	VG	F	VF	XF	Unc
ND(ca.1921)	—	5.00	15.00	30.00	70.00	135

Note: Some sources date these 20 Cash pieces bearing crossed flags ca.1912, but many were not struck until the 1920s; this coin is usually found weakly struck and lightweight

Y# 312 20 CASH (20 Wen)

Copper **Mint:** Kalgan **Obverse:** Crossed flags **Reverse:** Value in sprays

Date	Mintage	VG	F	VF	XF	Unc
13 (1924)	—	3.50	10.00	30.00	70.00	135

Note: This coin is usually found weakly struck

HSU# 9 20 CASH (20 Wen)

Copper **Obverse:** Crossed flags **Reverse:** Value in sprays **Note:** Nationalist commemorative.

Date	Mintage	VG	F	VF	XF	Unc
ND(1927-28)	—	75.00	225	400	650	900

HSU# 445a 500 CASH (500 Wen)

Copper **Subject:** Nationalist Commemorative **Obverse:** Crossed flags **Reverse:** Value in sprays

Date	Mintage	VG	F	VF	XF	Unc
ND(1927/8) Rare	12	—	—	—	—	—

Y# 323 1/2 CENT (1/2 Fen)

Bronze **Mint:** Tientsin

Date	Mintage	VG	F	VF	XF	Unc
5(1916)	1,789,000	1.75	5.00	10.00	20.00	45.00

Y# 346 1/2 CENT (1/2 Fen)

Bronze

Date	Mintage	VG	F	VF	XF	Unc
25(1936)	64,720,000	0.25	0.75	1.50	3.00	7.50
28(1939) Rare	—	—	—	—	—	—

Y# 353 CENT (1 Fen)

Brass **Note:** Shi Kwan Cent.

Date	Mintage	VG	F	VF	XF	Unc
28(1939)	—	13.50	40.00	60.00	120	200

Y# 355 CENT (1 Fen)

Aluminum

Date	Mintage	VG	F	VF	XF	Unc
29(1940)	150,000,000	—	0.10	0.25	0.50	1.50

Y# 357 CENT (1 Fen)

Brass

Date	Mintage	VG	F	VF	XF	Unc
29(1940)	50,000,000	0.25	0.75	1.00	2.00	4.00

Y# 363 CENT (1 Fen)
Bronze

Date	Mintage	VG	F	VF	XF	Unc
37(1948)	—	1.50	4.00	10.00	15.00	20.00

Y# 325a 2 CENTS (2 Fen)
Bronze

Date	Mintage	VG	F	VF	XF	Unc
22(1933)	—	13.50	40.00	60.00	95.00	150

Y# 354 2 CENTS (2 Fen)
Brass

Date	Mintage	VG	F	VF	XF	Unc
28(1939)	300,000,000	3.50	10.00	15.00	25.00	50.00

Y# 358 2 CENTS (2 Fen)
Brass

Date	Mintage	VG	F	VF	XF	Unc
29(1940)	—	0.20	0.50	1.00	1.50	2.00
30(1941) Rare	—	—	—	—	—	—

Y# 348 5 CENTS (5 Fen)
Nickel, 18.5 mm.

Date	Mintage	VG	F	VF	XF	Unc
25(1936)	72,844,000	0.35	1.00	1.50	3.00	6.00
27(1938)	34,325,000	0.75	2.50	4.50	8.00	15.00
28(1939)	6,000,000	3.50	10.00	15.00	25.00	50.00

Y# 348.1 5 CENTS (5 Fen)
Nickel **Reverse:** A mint mark below spade (Vienna)

Date	Mintage	VG	F	VF	XF	Unc
25(1936)	20,000,000	0.35	1.00	2.00	3.50	15.00

Y# 348.2 5 CENTS (5 Fen)
Nickel **Obverse:** Character "P'ing" on both sides of portrait

Date	Mintage	VG	F	VF	XF	Unc
25(1936)	—	17.50	50.00	80.00	125	175

Y# 348.3 5 CENTS (5 Fen)
Nickel **Obverse:** Character "Ch'ing" on both sides of portrait

Date	Mintage	VG	F	VF	XF	Unc
25(1936)	—	17.50	50.00	80.00	125	175

Y# 356 5 CENTS (5 Fen)
Aluminum

Date	Mintage	VG	F	VF	XF	Unc
29(1940)	350,000,000	0.20	0.50	1.00	2.50	4.00

Y# 359 5 CENTS (5 Fen)
Copper-Nickel

Date	Mintage	VG	F	VF	XF	Unc
29(1940)	57,000,000	0.10	0.25	1.50	2.50	5.00
30(1941)	96,000,000	0.10	0.25	1.50	2.50	6.00

Y# 347 10 CENTS
Copper

Date	Mintage	VG	F	VF	XF	Unc
25(1936)	311,780,000	0.15	0.40	0.75	1.75	2.50
26(1937)	307,198,000	0.15	0.45	1.00	1.50	3.00
27(1938)	12,000,000	1.00	3.00	5.00	8.00	16.00
28(1939)	75,000,000	0.65	2.00	4.00	7.00	15.00

K# 602 10 CENTS (1 Chiao)
2.3000 g., Silver, 18 mm. **Subject:** Sun Yat-sen Founding of the Republic **Obverse:** Bust left within circle **Reverse:** Two 5-pointed stars dividing legend at top **Note:** vertical reeding

Date	Mintage	VG	F	VF	XF	Unc
ND(1912)	—	65.00	200	500	700	1,250

K# 602b 10 CENTS (1 Chiao)
2.3000 g., Silver, 18 mm. **Subject:** Sun Yat-sen Founding of the Republic **Obverse:** Bust left within circle **Reverse:** Two 5-pointed stars dividing legend at top **Edge:** Engrailed with circles

Date	Mintage	VG	F	VF	XF	Unc
ND(1912)	—	—	—	700	850	1,500

Y# 326 10 CENTS (1 Chiao)
2.7000 g., 0.7000 Silver .0607 oz. ASW

Date	Mintage	VG	F	VF	XF	Unc
3(1914)	—	2.00	5.00	10.00	20.00	70.00
3 Specimen	—	Value: 500				
5(1916)	—	6.50	20.00	35.00	60.00	125
5 Specimen	—	Value: 750				

Y# 334 10 CENTS (1 Chiao)
Silver **Subject:** Pu Yi wedding

Date	Mintage	VG	F	VF	XF	Unc
15(1926)	—	2.00	5.00	12.00	25.00	60.00

Y# 339 10 CENTS (1 Chiao)
2.5000 g., Silver, 18 mm. **Subject:** Death of Sun Yat-sen

Date	Mintage	VG	F	VF	XF	Unc
16(1927)	—	10.00	25.00	40.00	70.00	145

Y# 349 10 CENTS (1 Chiao)
Nickel, 21 mm.

Date	Mintage	VG	F	VF	XF	Unc
25(1936)	73,866,000	0.20	0.60	1.00	3.00	7.50
27(1938)	110,203,000	0.65	2.00	4.25	8.00	20.00
28(1939)	68,000,000	0.50	1.50	3.50	10.00	27.50

Y# 349a 10 CENTS (1 Chiao)
Non-Magnetic Nickel Alloy

Date	Mintage	VG	F	VF	XF	Unc
25(1936)	1,000,000	6.00	18.00	30.00	40.00	65.00

Note: All of the Y#349 coins were supposed to have been minted in pure nickel at the Shanghai Mint; However, in 1936 a warlord had the Tientsin Mint produce about one million 10 Cent pieces of heavily alloyed nickel; The result is that the Shanghai pieces are attracted to a magnet while the Tientsin pieces are not

Y# 349.1 10 CENTS (1 Chiao)
Nickel **Reverse:** Mint mark A below spade (Vienna Mint)

Date	Mintage	VG	F	VF	XF	Unc
25(1936)A	60,000,000	0.35	1.00	2.00	8.00	25.00

Y# 360 10 CENTS (1 Chiao)
Copper-Nickel, 21 mm. **Edge:** Reeded

Date	Mintage	VG	F	VF	XF	Unc
29(1940)	68,000,000	0.20	0.50	2.50	8.00	15.00
30(1941)	254,000,000	0.20	0.50	1.50	2.50	5.00
31(1942)	10,000,000	8.50	25.00	60.00	80.00	120

Y# 360.1 10 CENTS (1 Chiao)
Copper-Nickel **Edge:** Plain

Date	Mintage	VG	F	VF	XF	Unc
29(1940) Rare	Inc. above	—	—	—	—	—
30(1941)	Inc. above	0.65	2.00	7.50	10.00	15.00

Y# 317 20 CENTS (2 Chiao)
5.2000 g., Silver, 23 mm. **Subject:** Founding of the Republic

Date	Mintage	VG	F	VF	XF	Unc
ND(1912)	155,000	6.50	15.00	20.00	38.00	85.00

Y# 327 20 CENTS (2 Chiao)
5.4000 g., 0.7000 Silver .1215 oz. ASW

Date	Mintage	VG	F	VF	XF	Unc
3(1914)	—	2.25	3.50	6.00	12.00	70.00
3 Specimen	—	Value: 250				
5(1916)	—	2.25	3.50	6.00	15.00	90.00
5 Specimen	—	Value: 500				
9(1920)	—	45.00	100	275	500	1,000

Y# 335 20 CENTS (2 Chiao)
5.2000 g., Silver **Subject:** Pu Yi Wedding

Date	Mintage	VG	F	VF	XF	Unc
15(1926)	—	3.50	10.00	15.00	30.00	80.00

Y# 340 20 CENTS (2 Chiao)
5.3000 g., Silver, 23 mm. **Subject:** Death of Sun Yat-sen

Date	Mintage	VG	F	VF	XF	Unc
16(1927)	—	6.50	15.00	25.00	40.00	100

Y# 350 20 CENTS (20 Fen)
Nickel

Date	Mintage	VG	F	VF	XF	Unc
25(1936)	49,620,000	0.20	0.50	2.50	6.00	10.00
27(1938)	61,248,000	0.35	1.00	2.00	7.00	12.00
28(1939)	38,000,000	0.65	2.00	5.00	10.00	15.00

Y# 350.1 20 CENTS (20 Fen)
Nickel **Reverse:** Mint mark A below spade (Vienna Mint)

Date	Mintage	VG	F	VF	XF	Unc
25(1936)A	40,000,000	0.35	1.00	2.00	3.50	6.00

Y# 361 20 CENTS (20 Fen)
Copper-Nickel

Date	Mintage	VG	F	VF	XF	Unc
31(1942)	32,300,000	0.15	0.40	1.00	2.25	4.00

Y# 328 50 CENTS (1/2 Yuan)
13.6000 g., 0.7000 Silver .3060 oz. ASW

Date	Mintage	VG	F	VF	XF	Unc
3(1914)	—	8.50	25.00	45.00	75.00	250
3 Specimen	—	Value: 1,000				

Y# 362 50 CENTS (1/2 Yuan)
Copper-Nickel, 28 mm. **Edge:** Reeded

Date	Mintage	VG	F	VF	XF	Unc
31(1942)	57,000,000	0.50	1.50	3.00	7.50	15.00
32(1943)	4,000,000	1.25	3.50	9.50	17.50	30.00

Y# 318 DOLLAR (Yuan)
26.9000 g., 0.9000 Silver .7785 oz. ASW, 39 mm. **Subject:** Sun Yat-sen Founding of the Republic **Obverse:** Sun Yat-sen facing left **Reverse:** Two five-pointed stars dividing legend at top

Date	Mintage	VG	F	VF	XF	Unc
ND(1912)	—	50.00	150	300	450	850

Y# 318.1 DOLLAR (Yuan)
26.9000 g., 0.9000 Silver .7785 oz. ASW, 39 mm. **Obverse:** Dot below ear

Date	Mintage	VG	F	VF	XF	Unc
ND(1912)	—	—	—	—	—	—

Note: For similar issue with rosettes see Y#318a.1 (1927)

Y# 319 DOLLAR (Yuan)
27.3000 g., 0.9000 Silver .7900 oz. ASW, 39 mm. **Obverse:** Sun Yat-sent facing left

Date	Mintage	VG	F	VF	XF	Unc
ND(1912)	—	35.00	100	285	400	650

Y# 320 DOLLAR (Yuan)
26.5000 g., Silver, 39 mm. **Subject:** Li Yüan-hung Founding of Republic Rev. Designer: Chu Tse-fang

Date	Mintage	VG	F	VF	XF	Unc
ND(1912)	—	150	450	900	1,500	2,000

Y# 320.1 DOLLAR (Yuan)
26.5000 g., Silver, 39 mm. **Rev. Legend:** OE for OF

Date	Mintage	VG	F	VF	XF	Unc
ND(1912)	—	175	550	1,100	1,800	—

Y# 320.2 DOLLAR (Yuan)
26.5000 g., Silver **Rev. Legend:** CIIINA for CHINA

Date	Mintage	VG	F	VF	XF	Unc
ND(1912)	—	175	550	1,100	1,800	—

Y# 321 DOLLAR (Yuan)
26.5000 g., Silver, 39 mm. **Subject:** Li Yüan-hung Founding of Republic

Date	Mintage	VG	F	VF	XF	Unc
ND(1912)	—	20.00	60.00	120	200	400

Y# 321.1 DOLLAR (Yuan)
26.5000 g., Silver, 39 mm. **Reverse:** H of "THE" in legend engraved as I I

Date	Mintage	VG	F	VF	XF	Unc
ND(1912)	—	25.00	70.00	150	225	425

Y# 322 DOLLAR (Yuan)
26.7000 g., 0.9000 Silver .7474 oz. ASW, 39 mm. **Subject:** Yüan Shih-kai Founding of Republic **Designer:** Luigi Giorgi **Note:** 2.8mm thickness.

Date	Mintage	VG	F	VF	XF	Unc
ND(1914)	20,000	100	175	300	450	600

Y# 322.1 DOLLAR (Yuan)
26.7000 g., 0.9000 Silver .7474 oz. ASW, 39 mm. **Subject:** Yüan Shih-kai Founding of Republic **Note:** 3.25mm thickness.

Date	Mintage	VG	F	VF	XF	Unc
ND(ca.1918)	—	100	175	300	450	600

Note: A restrike made about 1918 for collectors

Y# 329 DOLLAR (Yuan)
26.4000 g., 0.8900 Silver .7555 oz. ASW **Subject:** Yüan Shih-kai **Obverse:** Six characters above head **Note:** Vertical reeding.

Date	Mintage	VG	F	VF	XF	Unc
3(1914)	—	10.00	12.50	16.00	25.00	50.00

Y# 329.1 DOLLAR (Yuan)
26.4000 g., 0.8900 Silver .7555 oz. ASW **Note:** Edge engrailed with circles.

Date	Mintage	VG	F	VF	XF	Unc
3(1914)	—	15.00	60.00	150	1,000	2,200

Y# 329.2 DOLLAR (Yuan)
26.4000 g., 0.8900 Silver .7555 oz. ASW **Edge:** Ornamented with alternating T's

Date	Mintage	VG	F	VF	XF	Unc
3	—	15.00	60.00	150	1,000	2,200

Y# 329.3 DOLLAR (Yuan)
26.4000 g., 0.8900 Silver .7555 oz. ASW **Edge:** Plain

Date	Mintage	VG	F	VF	XF	Unc
3(1914)	—	15.00	40.00	75.00	500	800

Y# 329.4 DOLLAR (Yuan)
26.4000 g., 0.8900 Silver .7555 oz. ASW **Note:** Tiny circle in ribbon bow. This is a mint mark, but it is not clear what mint is indicated.

Date	Mintage	VG	F	VF	XF	Unc
3(1914)	—	12.00	20.00	40.00	85.00	200

Y# 332 DOLLAR (Yuan)
26.8000 g., Silver, 39 mm. **Ruler:** Hung-hsien **Subject:** Inauguration of Hung-hsien Regime **Obverse:** Bust of Hung-hsien in military uniform with plumed hat facing **Reverse:** Winged dragon left **Designer:** Luigi Giorgi **Note:** K#663.

Date	Mintage	VG	F	VF	XF	Unc
ND(1916)	—	100	400	700	1,000	1,500

Y# 329.6 DOLLAR (Yuan)
26.4000 g., 0.8900 Silver .7555 oz. ASW **Obverse:** Seven characters above head

Date	Mintage	VG	F	VF	XF	Unc
8(1919)	—	11.00	13.00	18.50	45.00	135
9(1920)	—	10.00	12.00	14.50	22.50	50.00
10(1921)	—	10.00	12.00	14.50	22.50	50.00

Y# 329.5 DOLLAR (Yuan)
26.4000 g., 0.8900 Silver .7555 oz. ASW **Edge:** Oblique reeding

Date	Mintage	VG	F	VF	XF	Unc
10(1921)	—	12.00	20.00	32.50	45.00	75.00

K# 676 DOLLAR (Yuan)
26.5000 g., Silver, 39 mm. **Subject:** President Hsu Shih-chang **Edge:** Reeded

Date	Mintage	VG	F	VF	XF	Unc
10(1921)	—	125	250	500	900	1,650

K# 676.1 DOLLAR (Yuan)
26.5000 g., Silver, 39 mm. **Edge:** Plain

Date	Mintage	VG	F	VF	XF	Unc
10(1921)	—	200	500	800	1,500	2,500

K# 677 DOLLAR (Yuan)
26.7000 g., Silver, 39 mm. **Obverse:** Bust of President Tsao Kun facing

Date	Mintage	VG	F	VF	XF	Unc
ND(1923)	50,000	125	250	500	850	1,500

K# 678 DOLLAR (Yuan)
26.7000 g., Silver, 39 mm. **Obverse:** Bust of President Tsao Kun in military uniform facing

Date	Mintage	VG	F	VF	XF	Unc
ND(1923)	—	—	—	500	850	1,500

Y# 336 DOLLAR (Yuan)
26.8000 g., Silver **Subject:** Pu Yi Wedding **Reverse:** Value in small characters

Date	Mintage	VG	F	VF	XF	Unc
12(1923)	—	200	500	900	1,500	2,500

Y# 336.1 DOLLAR (Yuan)
26.8000 g., Silver **Subject:** Pu Yi Wedding **Reverse:** Value in large characters

Date	Mintage	VG	F	VF	XF	Unc
12(1923)	—	250	500	1,000	2,750	4,500

K# 683 DOLLAR (Yuan)
Silver, 39 mm. **Obverse:** Bust of President Tuan Chi-jui facing

Date	Mintage	VG	F	VF	XF	Unc
ND(1924)	—	125	200	450	800	1,500

K# 690 DOLLAR (Yuan)

26.5000 g., Silver, 39 mm. **Obverse:** Bust of General Chu Yu-pu facing

Date	Mintage	VG	F	VF	XF	Unc
ND(1927)	—	—	—	5,000	9,000	16,000

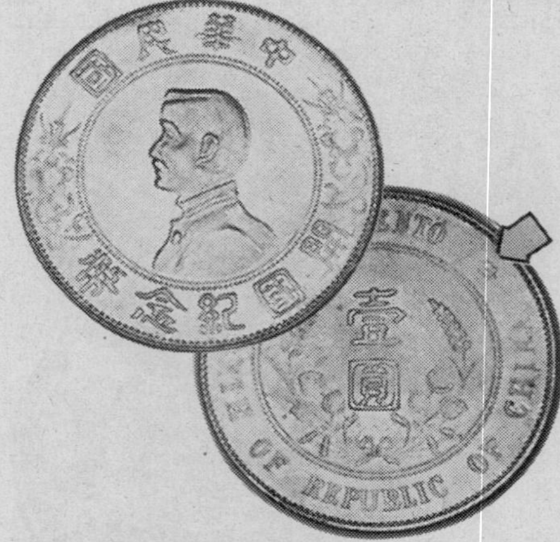

Y# 318a.1 DOLLAR (Yuan)

27.0000 g., 0.8900 Silver .7727 oz. ASW **Obverse:** Bust of Sun Yat-sen left **Reverse:** Two rosettes dividing legend at top **Edge:** Incuse reeding

Date	Mintage	VG	F	VF	XF	Unc
ND(1927)	—	10.00	12.00	14.00	17.50	35.00

Y# 318a.2 DOLLAR (Yuan)

27.0000 g., 0.8900 Silver .7727 oz. ASW **Edge:** Reeding in relief

Date	Mintage	VG	F	VF	XF	Unc
ND(1927)	—	10.00	12.00	14.00	17.50	35.00

Note: Varieties exist with errors in the English legend. For similar coins with 5-pointed stars dividing legends, see Y#318 (1912). In 1949 the Canton Mint restruck Memento dollars. There are modern restrikes in red copper and brass.

K# 609 DOLLAR (Yuan)

27.0000 g., Silver **Obverse:** Bust of Sun Yat-sen **Reverse:** Sun Yat-sen Memorial

Date	Mintage	VG	F	VF	XF	Unc
16(1927)	480	750	1,500	3,000	5,000	9,500

Y# 344 DOLLAR (Yuan)

26.7000 g., 0.8800 Silver .7555 oz. ASW **Obverse:** Bust of Sun Yat-sen left **Reverse:** 3 wild geese flying above junk, rising sun

Date	Mintage	VG	F	VF	XF	Unc
21(1932)	2,260,000	100	175	300	400	600

Y# 345 DOLLAR (Yuan)

26.7000 g., 0.8800 Silver .7555 oz. ASW **Reverse:** Without birds above junk or rising sun

Date	Mintage	VG	F	VF	XF	Unc
22(1933)(1933)	46,400,000	4.00	12.50	15.00	20.00	45.00
22(1933)	46,400,000	10.00	12.50	15.00	20.00	50.00
23(1934)(1934)	128,740,000	3.00	9.00	12.50	15.00	25.00

Note: In 1949, three U.S. mints restruck a total of 30 million "Junk Dollars" dated Year 23

Date	Mintage	VG	F	VF	XF	Unc
23(1934)	128,740,000	10.00	12.00	14.00	16.00	30.00

Note: In 1949, three U.S. mints restruck a total of 30 million "Junk Dollars" dated Year 23.

Y# 333a 10 DOLLARS

7.0500 g., Yellow Gold **Ruler:** Hung-hsien

Date	Mintage	VG	F	VF	XF	Unc
1(1916)	—	—	—	2,500	4,000	5,500

Y# 333 10 DOLLARS

7.0500 g., Red Gold **Ruler:** Hung-hsien **Obverse:** Bust of Hung-hsien left **Reverse:** Winged dragon left **Note:** K#1515.

Date	Mintage	VG	F	VF	XF	Unc
1(1916)	—	—	—	2,500	4,000	5,500

Y# 330 10 DOLLARS

8.1500 g., 0.8500 Gold .2227 oz. AGW **Ruler:** Hung-hsien **Note:** K#1531.

Date	Mintage	VG	F	VF	XF	Unc
8(1919)	—	—	—	2,000	2,850	4,000

Y# 331 20 DOLLARS

16.3000 g., 0.8500 Gold .4456 oz. AGW **Ruler:** Hung-hsien **Note:** K#1530.

Date	Mintage	VG	F	VF	XF	Unc
8(1919)	—	—	—	—	5,500	8,500

Y# 324a FEN

Bronze

Date	Mintage	VG	F	VF	XF	Unc
22(1933)	—	2.75	8.00	15.00	30.00	100

TOKEN COINAGE

KM# Tn1 FEN

Brass **Mint:** Shansi Arsenal

Date	Mintage	F	VF	XF	Unc
17(1928)	—	75.00	125	175	300

Note: This token is usually found with small punch marks near center on obverse and reverse

KM# Tn2 2 FEN

Brass **Mint:** Shansi Arsenal

Date	Mintage	F	VF	XF	Unc
17(1928)	—	150	250	400	650

Note: This token has always been found with small punch marks near center on obverse and reverse

KM# Tn3 5 FEN

Brass **Mint:** Shansi Arsenal **Note:** Similar to 2 Fen, KM#Tn2.

Date	Mintage	F	VF	XF	Unc
17(1928)	—	450	750	1,250	—

Note: This token has always been found with small punch marks near center on obverse and reverse

KM# Tn4 10 FEN

Brass **Mint:** Shansi Arsenal **Note:** Similar to 2 Fen, KM#Tn2.

Date	Mintage	F	VF	XF	Unc
17(1928)	—	450	.750	1,250	—

Note: This token has always been found with small punch marks near center on obverse and reverse

PATTERNS

Including off metal strikes

KM#	Date	Mintage	Identification	Mkt Val
Pn2	ND(1912)	—	Cash. Copper Or Brass.	—
Pn3	ND(1912)	—	Cash. Zinc.	—
Pn4	ND(1912)	—	Cash. Iron.	—
Pn5	ND(1912)	—	10 Cash. Copper. Hsu13	1,000
PnA6	ND(1912)	—	10 Cash. Copper. Similar to Pn5 but larger bust; W972.	—
Pn6	ND(1912)	—	10 Cash. Gold.	—
Pn7	ND(1912)	—	20 Cents. Gold. Y#317	3,500
Pn8	ND(1912)	—	Dollar. Gold. Y#318	—
Pn9	ND(1912)	—	Dollar. Gold. Y#318 - K#1550	20,000
PnA10	ND(1912)	—	Dollar. Silver. Li Yuan-hung	—
Pn10	ND(1912)	—	Dollar. Silver. Chin Teh-chuen, K#672. Many counterfeits exist.	50,000
Pn11	ND(1912)	—	Dollar. Eyes in relief. Chin Teh-chuen, K#672a.	—

Note: All known examples are counterfeit.

KM#	Date	Mintage	Identification	Mkt Val
Pn12	ND(1912)	—	Dollar. Bronze. K#672x	—

Note: All known examples are counterfeit.

KM#	Date	Mintage	Identification	Mkt Val
PnA13	ND(1914)	—	10 Cash. Copper. With L. GEORGI; Y#309.	800
Pn13	ND3(1914)	—	5 Cents. Nickel. K#815	—
Pn14	ND3(1914)	—	5 Cents. Nickel. Plain edge. Essay, K#815a	—
Pn15	ND3(1914)	—	5 Cents. Nickel. Milled edge. Essay, K#815b; with G. L.	—
Pn16	ND3(1914)	—	5 Cents. Silver. Milled edge. Essay, K#815c; with G. L.	350

KM#	Date	Mintage	Identification	Mkt Val
Pn17	ND3(1914)	—	5 Cents. Copper. Essay, K#815x	225
Pn18	ND3(1914)	—	5 Cents. Pewter. Plain edge. Essay, K#815y	—
Pn19	ND3(1914)	—	5 Cents. Copper. With G. L., essay, K#815z	—
Pn20	ND3(1914)	—	10 Cents. Silver. With G. L., K#659a	700
Pn21	ND3(1914)	—	10 Cents. Copper. Y#326	45.00
Pn22	ND3(1914)	—	10 Cents. Nickel. Y#326	350
Pn23	ND3(1914)	—	20 Cents. Silver. With G. L.; K#657a	900
Pn24	ND3(1914)	—	20 Cents. Copper. . Y#327	65.00
Pn25	ND3(1914)	—	20 Cents. Nickel. . Y#327	375
Pn26	ND3(1914)	—	20 Cents. Pewter. . Y#327	300
Pn27	ND3(1914)	—	50 Cents. Silver. With L. GIORGI; Yuan Shih-kai, K#655a.	1,150
Pn28	ND(1914)	—	Dollar. Silver. With L. GIORGI; Yuan Shih-kai, K#642a.	9,500
Pn29	ND(1914)	—	Dollar. Gold. With L. GIORGI, Yuan Shih-kai; K#1558	25,000
Pn30	ND(1914)	—	Dollar. Silver. Yuan Shih-kai, plumes of hat touch rim; K#644.	10,500
Pn31	ND(1914)	—	Dollar. Silver. With L. GIORGI; Yuan Shih-kai, K#645	15,000
Pn32	ND3(1914)	—	Dollar. Silver. K#643	7,000
Pn33	ND3(1914)	—	Dollar. Silver. 26.1400 g.. With L. GIORGI; K#643a	7,000
Pn34	ND(1914)	—	Dollar. Copper. Y#322	500
Pn35	ND(1914)	—	Dollar. Brass. Y#322	600
Pn36	ND(1914)	—	Dollar. Gold. Y#329	25,000
Pn37	ND(1914)	—	Dollar. Copper. Y#329	450
Pn38	ND(1914)	—	Dollar. Brass. Y#329	400
PnA39	ND(1914)	—	5 Dollars. Gold. K#1517	6,000
Pn39	ND5(1916)	—	1/2 Cent. Copper. Without center hole; Y#323	350
Pn40	ND5(1916)	—	10 Cash. Copper. Without center hole; Y#324	400
Pn41	ND5(1916)	—	10 Cash. Copper. With L. GIORGI; Y#324.3	—
Pn42	ND5(1916)	—	20 Cash. Copper. Hsu44	650
Pn43	ND5(1916)	—	20 Cents. Copper. Y#327	—
Pn44	ND(1916)	—	Dollar. Gold. Y#332. It has been verified that the San Francisco Mint actually struck 2 pieces in gold in 1928.	14,000
Pn45	ND(1916)	—	Dollar. White Metal. Y#332	—
Pn47	ND(1916)	—	Dollar. Silver. With L. GIORGI; plumes don't touch rim; K#663a.	25,000
Pn48	ND(1916)	—	Dollar. Silver. With L. GIORGI; K#663d	15,000
Pn50	ND1(1916)	—	10 Dollars. Gold. with L. G. Hung-hsien, near shoulder; K#1515a	—
Pn51	ND1(1916)	—	10 Dollars. Copper. with L. G. Hung-hsien, near shoulder; K#1515y	—
Pn52	ND(1916)	—	Dollar. Silver. Plumes of hat touch rim; K#664	10,500
Pn53	ND(1916)	—	Dollar. Gold. With L. GIORGI; K#1560	50,000
Pn54	ND1(1916)	—	10 Dollars. Silver. Y#333	—
Pn55	ND1(1916)	—	10 Dollars. Copper. Y#333	375
Pn56	ND8(1919)	—	10 Cash. Copper. Hsu29	1,000
Pn57	ND8(1919)	—	10 Cash. Copper. Hsu30	1,000
Pn59	ND8(1919)	—	10 Dollars. Copper. Y#330	325
Pn60	ND8(1919)	—	10 Dollars. Brass. Y#330	325
Pn61	ND8(1919)	—	20 Dollars. Copper. Y#331	485
Pn62	ND10(1921)	—	Dollar. Gold. K#1570	24,000
Pn63	ND10(1921)	—	Dollar. Silver. Reeded edge. K#676a.1	2,500
Pn64	ND10(1921)	—	Dollar. Silver. Plain edge. K#676a.2	2,500
Pn65	ND10(1921)	—	Dollar. Gold. Reeded edge. K#1570	25,000
Pn66	ND10(1921)	—	Dollar. Gold. Plain edge. K#1570a	25,000
Pn67	ND(1923)	—	Dollar. Gold. K#1572	17,500
Pn68	ND(1923)	—	Dollar. Copper. K#677x	450
Pn69	ND(1923)	—	Dollar. Brass. K#677y	450
Pn70	ND12(1923)	—	Dollar. Gold. Y#336	25,000
Pn71	ND12(1923)	—	Dollar. Copper. Y#336	—
Pn72	ND12(1923)	—	Dollar. Gold. Y#336.1	—
Pn73	ND(1924)	—	Dollar. Gold. K#1577	20,000
Pn74	ND(1924)	—	Dollar. Copper. K#683x	700
Pn75	ND(1924)	—	Dollar. Pewter. K#683y	700
Pn76	ND15(1926)	—	10 Cents. Copper. Y#334	125
Pn77	ND15(1926)	—	10 Cents. Lead. Y#334	90.00
Pn78	ND15(1926)	—	20 Cents. Copper. Y#335	65.00
PnA79	ND15(1926)	—	Dollar. Silver. K#604	150,000
Pn79	ND15(1926)	—	Dollar. Silver. K#685	27,500
Pn80	ND16(1927)	—	10 Cents. Copper. Y#339	—
Pn81	ND16(1927)	—	10 Cents. Gold. Y#339	—
Pn82	ND(1927)	—	Dollar. Gold. Y#318	—
Pn83	ND(1927)	—	Dollar. Copper. Y#318	225
Pn84	ND(1927)	—	Dollar. Silver. K#687	60,000
Pn85	ND16(1927)	—	Dollar. Silver. K#686	65,000
Pn86	ND(1928)	—	20 Cash. Copper. Y#337	—
Pn87	ND(1928)	—	20 Cash. Copper. Similar to 1 Chiao.	—
Pn90	ND17(1928)	—	Dollar. Silver. K#688	20,000
Pn91	ND17(1928)	—	Dollar. Copper. K#688x	3,500
PnA92	ND17(1928)	—	Dollar. Gold. K#688z	—
Pn92	ND17(1928)	—	Dollar. Pewter. K#688y	6,500
Pn93	ND18(1929)	—	20 Cents. Silver. K#611	—
Pn94	ND18(1929)	—	10 Cents. Copper-Nickel. Vienna; K#617yVI	850
Pn95	ND18(1929)	—	20 Cents. Copper-Nickel. Vienna; K#617yV	—
Pn96	ND18(1929)	—	50 Cents. Copper-Nickel. Vienna; K#617yIV	—
Pn97	ND18(1929)	—	Dollar. Silver. Italian; K#614	4,000
Pn98	ND18(1929)	—	Dollar. Silver. With designer's name. K#614a	6,000
Pn99	ND18(1929)	—	Dollar. Silver. English; K#615	2,750
Pn100	ND18(1929)	—	Dollar. Silver. American; K#616	2,750
Pn101	ND18(1929)	—	Dollar. Silver. Austrian; K#61	2,200
Pn102	ND18(1929)	—	Dollar. Silver. Japanese; K#618	900

Note: In 1929 China invited several mints to submit designs for a new Sun Yat-sen Dollar, with his bust on one side and a junk on the other. All designs were very much alike, differing mainly in details of the portrait, the waves, and the junk.

KM#	Date	Mintage	Identification	Mkt Val
Pn103	ND18(1929)	—	10 Cents. Silver. K#617yIII	850
Pn104	ND18(1929)	—	20 Cents. Silver. K#617yII	850
Pn105	ND18(1929)	—	50 Cents. Silver. K#617yI	850
Pn106	ND18(1929)	—	Dollar. Silver. K#610	50,000
Pn107	ND18(1929)	—	20 Cents. Silver. K#611	5,000
Pn108	ND18(1929)	—	Dollar. Silver. Wreath. K#612	—
Pn109	ND(1929)	—	Dollar. Silver. Memento. K#620	—
Pn110	ND(1929)	—	Dollar. Copper. K#620x	—
Pn111	ND(1929)	—	Dollar. White Metal. K#620y	—
Pn112	ND(1929)	—	Dollar. Silver. Wreath. K#620k	—
Pn113	ND(1929)	—	Dollar. White Metal. K#620m	—
Pn114	ND21(1932)	—	Cent. Bronze.	—
Pn115	ND21(1932)	—	Cent. Bronze. Without center hole	—
Pn118	ND21(1932)	—	2 Cents. Nickel. Milled edge. K#830	1,200
Pn119	ND21(1932)	—	2 Cents. Nickel. Plain edge. K#830a	1,200
Pn120	ND21(1932)	—	2 Cents. Nickel. Without center hole; K#830b	2,000
Pn121	ND21(1932)	—	5 Cents. Nickel. Milled edge. K#829	550
Pn122	ND21(1932)	—	5 Cents. Nickel. Plain edge. K#829a	550
Pn123	ND21(1932)	—	5 Cents. Nickel. Without center; K#329b	550
Pn136	ND21(1932)	—	Dollar. Copper. K#628x	—
Pn137	ND21(1932)	—	Dollar. Copper. Y#344, K#622x.	275
Pn138	ND22(1933)	—	Dollar. Copper. Y#345	—
Pn139	ND23(1934)	—	Dollar. Copper. Y#345	—
Pn140	ND24(1935)	—	5 Cents. Nickel. K#833	400
Pn141	ND24(1935)	—	5 Cents. Copper. K#833x	—
Pn142	ND24(1935)	—	10 Cents. Nickel. K#832	400
Pn143	ND24(1935)	—	10 Cents. Copper. K#832x	—
Pn144	ND24(1935)	—	20 Cents. Nickel. K#831	400
Pn145	ND24(1935)	—	20 Cents. Copper. K#831x	—
PnA146	ND24(1935)	—	1/2 Dollar. Silver. K#625k	—
PnB146	ND24(1935)	—	1/2 Dollar. Copper. K#625x	—
Pn146	ND24(1935)	—	Dollar. Silver. K#625	—
Pn146a	ND24(1935)	—	Dollar. Copper Or Brass. Reduced size Pn146	1,550
Pn147	ND24(1935)	—	Dollar. Copper. Y#345	—
Pn148	ND25//1936	—	Mei. Copper. Character "Chin".	—
Pn149	ND25//1936	—	Mei. Copper.	—
Pn150	ND25//1936	—	2 Mei. Copper.	—
Pn151	ND25//1936	—	5 Mei. Copper.	—
Pn152	ND25//1936	—	10 Mei. Copper.	—
Pn153	ND25//1936	—	50 Mei. Copper.	—
Pn154	ND25//1936	—	20 Wen. Copper.	—
PnA155	ND25//1936	—	1/2 Fen. Copper. Character "P'ing" lower.	—

Note: This may also exist with character under spade on reverse

KM#	Date	Mintage	Identification	Mkt Val
Pn155	ND25(1936)	—	Fen. Copper.	—
PnA156	ND25//1936	—	Fen. Copper. Character "P'ing" lower.	—
PnB156	ND25//1936	—	Fen. Copper. Character "P'ing" under spade.	—
PnC156	ND25//1936	—	Fen. Copper. Character "Ch'ing" lower.	—
PnD156	ND25//1936	—	Fen. Copper. Character "Ch'ing" under spade.	—
Pn156	ND25(1936)	—	5 Cents. Copper. Y#348	—
Pn157	ND25(1936)	—	10 Cents. Nickel. Character "Ch'ing" in field or on portrait.	450
Pn158	ND25(1936)	—	10 Cents. Nickel. Character "P'ing" in field or on portrait.	450
Pn159	ND25(1936)	—	10 Cents. Nickel. Character "Ch'ing" on side of portrait.	450
Pn160	ND25(1936)	—	10 Cents. Nickel. Character "P'ing" on side of portrait.	450
Pn161	ND25(1936)	—	10 Cents. Copper. Y#349	—
Pn162	ND25(1936)	—	10 Cents. Aluminum. Y#349	—
Pn163	ND25(1936)	—	10 Cents. Aluminum-Bronze. Y#349	—
Pn164	ND25(1936)	—	10 Cents. Lead. Y#349	—
Pn165	ND25(1936)	—	20 Cents. Copper. Y#350	—
Pn166	ND25(1936)	—	20 Cents. Aluminum. Y#350	—
Pn167	ND25(1936)	—	20 Cents. Aluminum-Bronze. Y#350	—
Pn168	ND25(1936)	—	20 Cents. Pewter. Y#350	75.00
Pn169	ND25(1936)	—	50 Cents. Silver. K#635	—
Pn170	ND25(1936)	—	50 Cents. Silver. K#633	—
Pn171	ND25(1936)	—	50 Cents. Silver. Similar to K#633 without Greek border.	—
Pn172	ND25(1936)	—	Dollar. Silver. K#634	—
Pn173	ND25(1936)	—	Dollar. Silver. Similar to K#632 without Greek border.	—
Pn174	ND25(1936)	—	Dollar. Silver. .K#632	9,000
Pn175	ND25(1936)	—	Dollar. Copper. K#632x	—
Pn176	ND25(1936)	—	Dollar. Nickel. K#632y	—
Pn177	ND25(1936)	—	Dollar. Brass. K#632z	—
Pn178	ND25(1936)	—	Dollar. Silver. Chiang Kai-shek	25,000
Pn179	ND25(1936)	—	Dollar. Copper. Chiang Kai-shek	7,500
Pn180	ND26(1937)	—	5 Cents. Nickel. Y#348.2	—
Pn181	ND26(1937)	—	10 Cents. Nickel. "P'ing" on side of portrait; Y#349.7	—
Pn183	ND26(1937)	—	20 Cents. Nickel. Y#350.1	—
Pn184	ND26(1937)S	—	50 Cents. Silver. K#637	—
Pn185	ND26(1937)S	—	Dollar. Silver. K#636	—
Pn186	ND27(1938)	—	5 Cents. Copper. Y#348	—
Pn187	ND27(1938)	—	10 Cents. Copper. Y#349	—
Pn188	ND27(1938)	—	20 Cents. Copper. Y#350	—
Pn189	ND27(1938)	—	20 Cents. Pewter. Y#350	150
Pn190	ND28(1939)	—	5 Cents. Copper. Y#348	—
Pn191	ND28(1939)	—	5 Cents. Brass. Y#348	—
PnA192	ND28(1939)	—	20 Cents. Copper. K#857x	175
PnB192	ND29(1940)	—	1/2 Dollar. Copper.	250
Pn192	ND30(1941)	—	10 Cents. Copper. Y#360	250
Pn193	ND30(1941)	—	10 Cents. Brass. Y#360	—
PnA194	ND30(1941)	—	20 Cents. Nickel. K#863 IV	250
PnB194	ND30(1941)	—	1/2 Dollar. Silver. . K#696x	—
PnC194	ND30(1941)	—	1/2 Dollar. Nickel. K#863 III	500
Pn194	ND31(1942)	—	10 Cents. Copper-Nickel. Character "Kuei" below the spade.	—
Pn195	ND31(1942)	—	10 Cents. Copper. Y#360	—
Pn196	ND31(1942)	—	10 Cents. Brass. Y#360	—
Pn197	ND31(1942)	—	20 Cents. Copper-Nickel. Character "Kuei" below spade.	—
Pn198	ND31(1942)	—	20 Cents. Copper. Y#361	—
Pn199	ND31(1942)	—	50 Cents. Copper-Nickel. Character "Kuei" between legs of space. K#866m	—
Pn200	ND31(1942)	—	50 Cents. Copper. Y#362	200
Pn201	ND31(1942)	—	50 Cents. Bronze. Y#362	200
Pn202	ND31(1942)	—	50 Cents. Silver. Y#362	500
PnA203	ND32(1943)	—	50 Cents. Copper-Nickel. Character "Kuei" between legs of spade.	—
Pn203	ND32(1943)	—	50 Cents. Copper. Y#362	200
Pn204	ND32(1943)	—	50 Cents. Bronze. Y#362	200
PnA205	ND37(1948)	—	50 Cents. Silver. Ch'ing right; K#698	—
Pn205	ND37(1948)	—	Dollar. Silver. K#637yII	—
Pn206	ND37(1948)	—	2 Dollars. Silver. K#637yI; denomination	200

PATTERNS

Gold Standard

KM#Pn124-135 were intended to be a gold standard coinage, but was not adopted. Though inscribed One Yuan Dollar, the proposed unit was called a Sun.

KM#	Date	Mintage	Identification	Mkt Val
Pn124	ND21(1932)	—	10 Cents. Silver. K#631	—
Pn125	ND21(1932)	—	10 Cents. Silver. Plain edge. K#631a	—
Pn126	ND21(1932)	—	10 Cents. Copper. K#631	—
Pn127	ND21(1932)	—	20 Cents. Silver. Milled edge. K#630	—
Pn128	ND21(1932)	—	20 Cents. Silver. Plain edge. K#630a	—
Pn129	ND21(1932)	—	20 Cents. Copper. K#630x	—
Pn130	ND21(1932)	—	1/2 Dollar. Silver. Milled edge. K#629	4,500
Pn131	ND21(1932)	—	1/2 Dollar. Silver. Plain edge. K#629a	4,500
Pn132	ND21(1932)	—	1/2 Dollar. Copper. K#629x	—
Pn133	ND21(1932)	—	Dollar. Silver. Milled edge. K#628	—
Pn134	ND21(1932)	—	Dollar. Silver. Plain edge. K#628a	10,000
Pn135	ND21(1932)	—	Dollar. Silver. Cherry blossom edge	10,000

TRIAL STRIKES

KM#	Date	Mintage	Identification	Mkt Val
TS1	ND(1912)	—	Dollar. Silver. Uniface. Chin Te-chuan; K#672b	8,000
TS2	ND37(1948)	—	50 Cents. Silver. 4.9800 g.. K#698w	750

TAIWAN

REPUBLIC

STANDARD COINAGE

Y# 531 CHIAO

Bronze **Obverse:** Bust of Sun Yat-sen left **Reverse:** Map, symbols on sides

Date	Mintage	F	VF	XF	Unc
38(1949)	157,600,000	0.15	0.30	1.00	4.00

Y# 533 CHIAO

Aluminum, 19 mm. **Obverse:** Bust of Sun Yat-sen left **Reverse:** Map, symbols on sides

Date	Mintage	F	VF	XF	Unc
44(1955)	583,980,000	—	0.10	0.15	1.00

Y# 545 CHIAO

Aluminum **Obverse:** Single-heart orchid **Reverse:** Two Chinese symbols

Date	Mintage	F	VF	XF	Unc
56(1967)	89,999,000	—	0.10	0.15	0.75
59(1970)	30,000,000	—	0.10	0.25	1.00
60(1971)	19,925,000	—	0.20	0.40	1.50
61(1972)	11,141,000	0.10	0.40	0.60	2.00
62(1973)	111,400,000	—	—	0.10	0.75
63(1974)	71,930,000	—	0.10	0.25	1.00

Y# 534 2 CHIAO

Aluminum, 22.9 mm. **Obverse:** Bust of Sun Yat-sen left **Reverse:** Map, symbols at sides

Date	Mintage	F	VF	XF	Unc
39(1950)	327,495,000	—	0.10	0.50	3.00

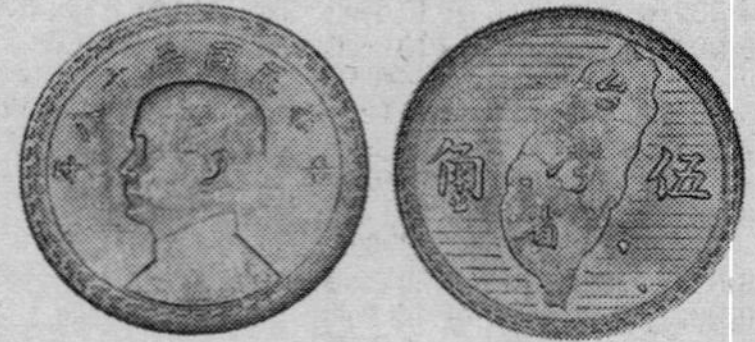

Y# 532 5 CHIAO

5.0000 g., 0.7200 Silver .1157 oz. ASW **Obverse:** Bust of Sun Yat-sen left **Reverse:** Map, symbols at sides

Date	Mintage	F	VF	XF	Unc
38(1949)	—	1.85	2.25	3.75	5.50

Y# 535 5 CHIAO

Brass, 27 mm. **Obverse:** Bust of Sun Yat-sen left **Reverse:** Map, symbols at sides

Date	Mintage	F	VF	XF	Unc
43(1954)	279,624,000	—	0.10	0.25	1.00

Y# 546 5 CHIAO

Brass, 22.5 mm. **Obverse:** Mayling orchid

Date	Mintage	F	VF	XF	Unc
56(1967)	109,999,000	—	0.10	0.15	0.50
59(1970)	6,010,000	0.15	0.30	0.60	1.25
60(1971)	4,434,000	0.20	0.40	0.80	1.50
61(1972)	21,171,000	—	0.10	0.20	1.00
62(1973)	88,840,000	—	0.10	0.20	1.00
69(1980)	3,972,000	—	0.10	0.20	1.00
70(1981)	100,000,000	—	0.10	0.20	1.00

Y# 550 5 CHIAO

Bronze, 18 mm. **Obverse:** Orchid **Reverse:** Value and Chinese symbols

Date	Mintage	F	VF	XF	Unc
70(1981)	103,800,000	—	0.10	0.20	1.00
70(1981) Proof	—	Value: 10.00			
75(1986)	22,000,000	—	0.10	0.20	1.00
77(1988)	10,000,000	—	0.15	0.30	1.25

Y# 536 YUAN

Copper-Nickel-Zinc, 25 mm. **Reverse:** Orchid

Date	Mintage	F	VF	XF	Unc
49(1960)	321,717,000	—	0.10	0.20	0.50
59(1970)	48,800,000	0.10	0.20	0.50	1.00
60(1971)	41,532,000	0.10	0.20	0.50	1.00
61(1972)	105,309,000	—	0.10	0.20	0.50
62(1973)	353,924,000	—	0.10	0.20	0.50
63(1974)	535,605,000	—	0.10	0.20	0.50
64(1975)	456,874,000	—	0.10	0.20	0.50
65(1976)	634,497,000	—	0.10	0.20	0.50
66(1977)	116,900,000	—	0.10	0.20	0.50
67(1978)	104,245,000	—	0.10	0.20	0.50
68(1979)	—	0.10	0.20	0.50	0.80
69(1980)	113,900,000	—	0.10	0.20	0.50

Y# A537 YUAN

Silver **Subject:** 50th Anniversary of the Republic **Obverse:** Chiang Kai-shek left **Reverse:** Value at center within flower wreath

Date	Mintage	F	VF	XF	Unc
50(1961)	—	—	—	—	285

Note: This coin was released accidentally or was released and quickly withdrawn and is very scarce today

Y# 543 YUAN

Copper-Nickel **Subject:** 80th Birthday of Chiang Kai-shek **Obverse:** Bust of Chiang Kai-shek **Reverse:** Chinese value in center

Date	Mintage	F	VF	XF	Unc
55(1966)	—	0.25	0.35	0.50	1.00

Y# 547 YUAN

Copper-Nickel-Zinc, 25 mm. **Series:** F.A.O. **Obverse:** Orchid **Reverse:** Farmer in field, value below

Date	Mintage	F	VF	XF	Unc
58(1969)	10,000,000	0.25	0.35	0.50	1.00

Y# 551 YUAN

Bronze, 20 mm. **Obverse:** Bust of Chiang Kai-shek left **Reverse:** Chinese value in center, 1 below

Date	Mintage	F	VF	XF	Unc
70(1981)	1,080,000,000	—	—	0.10	0.15
70(1981) Proof	—	Value: 12.50			
71(1982)	780,000,000	—	—	0.10	0.15
72(1983)	420,000,000	—	—	0.10	0.15
73(1984)	110,000,000	—	—	0.10	0.15
74(1985)	200,000,000	—	—	0.10	0.15
75(1986)	200,000,000	—	—	0.10	0.15
76(1987)	110,000,000	—	—	0.10	0.15
77(1988)	40,000,000	—	—	0.20	0.50
81(1992)	—	—	—	0.15	0.25
82(1993)	—	—	—	0.15	0.25
83(1994)	—	—	—	0.15	0.25
84(1995)	—	—	—	0.15	0.25
85(1996)	—	—	—	0.15	0.25
86(1997)	—	—	—	0.15	0.25

Y# 537 5 YUAN

Copper-Nickel **Obverse:** Bust of Sun Yat-sen left **Reverse:** Mausoleum in Nanking

Date	Mintage	F	VF	XF	Unc
54(1965)	—	0.35	0.75	1.50	5.00

Y# 548 5 YUAN

Copper-Nickel, 28.9 mm. **Obverse:** Bust of Chiang Kai-shek left **Reverse:** Chinese symbols in center

Date	Mintage	F	VF	XF	Unc
59(1970)	12,360,000	0.20	0.40	0.80	1.50
60(1971)	20,575,000	0.20	0.35	0.50	1.00
61(1972)	27,998,000	0.20	0.35	0.50	1.00
62(1973)	50,122,000	0.20	0.35	0.50	0.80
63(1974)	418,068,000	0.20	0.35	0.50	0.80
64(1975)	39,520,000	0.20	0.35	0.50	0.80
65(1976)	140,000,000	0.20	0.35	0.50	0.80
66(1977)	50,260,000	0.20	0.35	0.50	0.80
67(1978)	78,082,000	0.20	0.35	0.50	0.80
68(1979)	—	0.20	0.35	0.50	0.80
69(1980)	273,000,000	0.20	0.35	0.50	0.80
70(1981)	162,000,000	0.20	0.35	0.50	0.80

Y# 552 5 YUAN

Copper-Nickel **Obverse:** Bust of Chiang Kai-shek left **Reverse:** Chinese symbols in center, 5 below

Date	Mintage	F	VF	XF	Unc
70(1981)	522,432,000	—	0.15	0.20	0.50
70(1981) Proof	—	Value: 12.50			
71(1982)	6,600,000	—	0.15	0.20	0.50
72(1983)	34,000,000	—	0.15	0.20	0.50
73(1984)	280,000,000	—	0.15	0.20	0.50
77(1988)	200,000,000	—	0.15	0.20	0.50
78(1989)	—	—	0.15	0.20	0.50

Y# 538 10 YUAN

Copper-Nickel, 26 mm. **Obverse:** Bust of Sun Yat-sen left **Reverse:** Mausoleum in Nanking

Date	Mintage	F	VF	XF	Unc
54(1965)	—	0.50	1.00	2.00	6.00

Y# 553 10 YUAN

Copper-Nickel, 26 mm. **Obverse:** Bust of Chiang Kai-shek left **Reverse:** Chinese symbols in center, 10 below

Date	Mintage	F	VF	XF	Unc
70(1981)	123,000,000	—	0.30	0.45	0.75
70(1981) Proof	—	Value: 15.00			
71(1982)	361,000,000	—	0.30	0.45	0.75
72(1983)	196,000,000	—	0.30	0.45	0.75
73(1984)	220,000,000	—	0.30	0.45	0.75
74(1985)	200,000,000	—	0.30	0.45	0.75
75(1986)	100,000,000	—	0.30	0.45	0.75
76(1987)	90,000,000	—	0.30	0.45	0.75
77(1988)	100,000,000	—	0.30	0.45	0.75
78(1989)	—	—	0.30	0.45	0.75
79(1990)	—	—	0.30	0.45	0.75
80(1991)	—	—	0.30	0.45	0.75
81(1992)	—	—	0.30	0.45	0.75
82(1993)	—	—	0.30	0.45	0.75
83(1994)	—	—	0.30	0.45	0.75

Y# 555 10 YUAN

Copper-Nickel, 26 mm. **Subject:** 50th Anniversary - Taiwan's Liberation from Japan **Obverse:** Map with dates flanking **Reverse:** Chinese symbols in center, 10 below

Date	Mintage	F	VF	XF	Unc
84(1995)	—	—	—	—	2.50

Y# 558 10 YUAN

Copper-Nickel, 26 mm. **Subject:** 50th Anniversary - Taiwan Yuan (Dollar) **Obverse:** Coins **Reverse:** Anniversary dates above denomination

Date	Mintage	F	VF	XF	Unc
88(1999)	30,000,000	—	—	—	2.75

Y# 560 10 YUAN

7.5000 g., Copper-Nickel, 26 mm. **Subject:** Year of the Dragon **Obverse:** Stylized dragon above denomination **Reverse:** Dragon

Date	Mintage	F	VF	XF	Unc
89(2000)	—	—	—	—	3.00

Y# 539 50 YUAN

17.1000 g., 0.7500 Silver .4123 oz. ASW **Obverse:** Bust of Sun Yat-sen left **Reverse:** Chinese symbols in center, bird above, deer below

Date	Mintage	F	VF	XF	Unc
54(1965)	—	—	—	12.50	25.00

Y# 554 50 YUAN

Brass **Obverse:** Orchid burst **Reverse:** Chinese symbols center, 50 below, flower wreath circle

Date	Mintage	F	VF	XF	Unc
81(1992)	—	—	0.50	1.00	3.50
82(1993)	—	—	0.50	1.00	3.50

Y# 556 50 YUAN

Bi-Metallic Brass center in Copper-Nickel ring **Obverse:** Parliament building **Reverse:** Value left, Chinese symbols at bottom

Date	Mintage	F	VF	XF	Unc
85(1996)	—	—	—	—	5.75
86(1997)	—	—	—	—	5.75

Y# 562 50 YUAN

15.5680 g., 0.9990 Silver .5004 oz. ASW, 33 mm. **Mint:** Central Mint of China **Subject:** Late President - Chiang Ching-Kuo **Obverse:** Bust of Ching-kuo facing **Reverse:** Mausoleum above denomination **Edge:** Reeded

Date	Mintage	F	VF	XF	Unc
87 (1998)	70,000	—	—	—	25.00

Y# 559 50 YUAN

15.5500 g., 0.9250 Silver .4624 oz. ASW **Subject:** 50 Years - Taiwan Yuan (Dollar) **Obverse:** Coins **Reverse:** Denomination including coin design and date

Date	Mintage	F	VF	XF	Unc
88(1999)	390,000	—	—	—	20.00

Y# 564 50 YUAN

15.5680 g., 0.9990 Silver .5004 oz. ASW, 33 mm. **Mint:** Central Mint of China **Subject:** Year 2000 **Obverse:** Celestial globe **Reverse:** Dragon **Edge:** Reeded

Date	Mintage	F	VF	XF	Unc
89 (2000)	120,000	—	—	—	25.00

Y# 540 100 YUAN

22.2100 g., 0.7500 Silver .5335 oz. ASW .**Obverse:** Bust of Sun Yat-sen left

Date	Mintage	F	VF	XF	Unc
54(1965)	—	—	—	13.50	27.50

Y# 561 100 YUAN

15.5680 g., 0.9990 Silver .5000 oz. ASW, 33 mm. **Mint:** Central Mint of China **Subject:** 50th Anniversary - 2-28 Incident **Obverse:** Monument **Reverse:** Geometrical design **Edge:** Reeded

Date	Mintage	F	VF	XF	Unc
86(1997)	55,000	—	—	—	25.00

Y# 557 200 YUAN

31.1350 g., 0.9990 Silver 1.0000 oz. ASW **Subject:** First Popular Election Vote **Obverse:** Bust of President Lee Teng-hui and Vice President Lien Chan **Reverse:** National emblem above text

Date	Mintage	F	VF	XF	Unc
85(1996) Proof	—	Value: 65.00			

Y# 566 200 YUAN

31.3500 g., 0.9990 Silver 1.0069 oz. ASW, 38 mm. **Subject:** Second Popular Vote Presidential Election **Obverse:** Bust of the President and Vice-president **Reverse:** National emblem above inscription **Edge:** Reeded

Date	Mintage	F	VF	XF	Unc
89 (2000)	—	—	—	—	75.00

Y# 541 1000 YUAN

15.0000 g., 0.9000 Gold .4340 oz. AGW **Obverse:** Bust of Sun Yat-sen left

Date	Mintage	F	VF	XF	Unc
54(1965)	—	—	—	—	325

Y# 563 1000 YUAN

15.5540 g., 0.9990 Gold .5000 oz. AGW, 25 mm. **Mint:** Central Mint of China **Subject:** Late President - Chiang Ching-kuo **Obverse:** Bust of Ching-kuo facing **Reverse:** Mausoleum **Edge:** Reeded

Date	Mintage	F	VF	XF	Unc
87(1998)	30,000	—	—	—	325

Y# 542 2000 YUAN
30.0000 g., 0.9000 Gold .8681 oz. AGW **Obverse:** Bust of Sun Yat-sen left **Reverse:** Chinese symbols at center, budding branch wrappd around

Date	Mintage	F	VF	XF	Unc
54(1965)	—	—	—	—	675

Y# 544 2000 YUAN
31.0600 g., 0.9000 Gold .8988 oz. AGW **Subject:** 80th Birthday of Chiang Kai-shek **Reverse:** Two cranes standing on rock

Date	Mintage	F	VF	XF	Unc
55(1966)	—	—	—	—	700

PATTERNS

Yuan System; Including off metal strikes

KG numbers in reference to Coinage of the Chinese Emigre Government 1949-1957 by E. Kann and D. Graham.

KM#	Date	Mintage	Identification	Mkt Val
Pn1	38(1949)	—	Chiao. Bronze. KG#12a	150
Pn2	38(1949)	—	Chiao. Aluminum. KG#12b	150
Pn3	38(1949)	—	Chiao. Copper. KG#12c	150
Pn4	38(1949)	—	Chiao. Copper. KG#12d	150
Pn5	38(1949)	—	Chiao. Aluminum. K#12e; without reeded edge	150
Pn6	38(1949)	—	Chiao. Copper. k#13	150
Pn7	38(1949)	—	Chiao. Copper. KG#14	150
Pn8	38(1949)	—	5 Chiao. Aluminum-Bronze. KG#15a	350
Pn9	38(1949)	—	5 Chiao. Aluminum. KG#15b	250
Pn10	38(1949)	—	5 Chiao. Silver. KG#16	400
Pn11	38(1949)	—	5 Chiao. Copper. KG#16a	300
Pn12	38(1949)	—	5 Chiao. Silver. KG#17	375
Pn13	38(1949)	—	5 Chiao. Silver. KG#18	600
Pn14	38(1949)	—	5 Chiao. Silver. KG#19	725
Pn15	38(1949)	—	5 Chiao. Silver. KG#20	400
Pn16	38(1949)	—	Yuan. Silver. KG#21i	400
PnA17	38(1949)	—	Yuan. Nickel. Plain edge.	—
PnB17	38(1949)	—	20 Yuan. Bronze.	1,200
Pn17	39(1950)	—	2 Chiao. Aluminum. Reeded edge. KG#21a	150
Pn18	39(1950)	—	2 Chiao. Aluminum-Bronze. KG#21b	150
Pn19	39(1950)	—	2 Chiao. Aluminum-Bronze. KG#21c; without reeded edge	150
Pn20	39(1950)	—	2 Chiao. Copper. KG#21d	150
Pn21	39(1950)	—	Yuan. Silver.	700
Pn22	39(1950)	—	Yuan. Copper-Nickel.	300
Pn23	39(1950)	—	Yuan. Copper-Nickel.	300
Pn24	39(1950)	—	Yuan. Aluminum-Bronze. KG#22a	200
Pn25	39(1950)	—	Yuan. Aluminum. KG#22b	350
Pn26	43(1954)	—	5 Chiao. Aluminum-Bronze. KG#23	300
Pn27	43(1954)	—	5 Chiao. Aluminum-Bronze. Reeded edge. KG#23a	300
Pn28	43(1954)	—	5 Chiao. Copper. KG#23b	300
Pn29	43(1954)	—	5 Chiao. Aluminum-Bronze. KG#23c	300
Pn30	43(1954)	—	5 Chiao. Aluminum-Bronze. KG#24	300
Pn31	43(1954)	—	5 Chiao. Aluminum-Bronze. KG#25	300
Pn32	43(1954)	—	5 Chiao. Aluminum-Bronze. KG#25a	300
Pn33	43(1954)	—	5 Chiao. Bronze. KG#26a	300
Pn34	44(1955)	—	Chiao. Aluminum. Simplified "TAI", KG#27a	175
Pn35	44(1955)	—	Chiao. Bronze. KG#27b	175
Pn36	45(1956)	—	2 Chiao. Copper-Nickel. Y#534	175
PnA37	45(1956)	—	Yuan. Copper-Nickel. Ocean unlined.	—
PnB37	45(1956)	—	Yuan. Aluminum-Bronze. Pn37 with simplified "TAI" character.	—
Pn37	45(1956)	—	Yuan. Copper-Nickel.	300
Pn38	48(1959)	—	Yuan. Nickel.	350
Pn39	48(1959)	—	Yuan. Nickel-Silver.	250
Pn40	49(1960)	—	Yuan. Nickel-Silver. Y#536	250
Pn41	49(1960)	—	Yuan. Nickel-Silver. Large flan	275
Pn42	49(1960)	—	Yuan. Nickel-Silver. With Taiwan-sheng	275
Pn43	49(1960)	—	Yuan. Nickel-Silver. With 1 Yuan	275
Pn44	49(1960)	—	Yuan. Nickel-Silver. With 1 Kinmen	275
Pn45	49(1960)	—	5 Yuan. Nickel.	—
Pn46	49(1960)	—	5 Yuan. Nickel. Ancient Chinese symbols	—
PnA47	50(1961)	—	Yuan. Copper-Nickel. Y#536	—
Pn47	50(1961)	—	Yuan. Nickel-Silver. Sun Yat-sen.	225
Pn48	50(1961)	—	Yuan. Nickel-Aluminum. Chiang Kai-shek.	225
PnA49	50(1961)	—	Yuan. Nickel. Chiang Kai-shek	225
PnB49	50(1961)	—	Yuan. Nickel-Aluminum. Chiang Kai-shek	225
Pn49	50(1961)	—	Yuan. Nickel-Silver. Similar to Pn48 but eleven characters above bust.	225
Pn50	51(1962)	—	5 Yuan. Nickel.	300
Pn51	53(1964)	—	5 Yuan. Copper-Nickel.	300
Pn52	54(1965)	—	10 Yuan. Copper-Nickel. Clouds replace mountains. Y#538	400
Pn53	54(1965)	—	10 Yuan. Copper-Nickel. Without clouds. Y#538	400
Pn54	55(1966)	—	2000 Yuan. Gilt Silver. Madam and President Chiang. Y#544	650
Pn65	62(1973)	—	5 Yuan. Gold. Y#548	1,350
Pn66	64(1975)	—	Yuan. Gold. Y#536	950
Pn67	64(1975)	—	Yuan. Aluminum. Y#536	200

PATTERNS

Tael System; Including off metal strikes

KG numbers in reference to Coinage of the Chinese Emigre Government 1949-1957 by E. Kann and D. Graham.

KM#	Date	Mintage	Identification	Mkt Val
PnA36	45(1956)	—	2 Chiao. Aluminum-Bronze.	—
Pn55	38(1949)	—	Chien. Aluminum-Bronze. KG#7b	350
Pn56	38(1949)	—	Chien. Silver. KG#6a	500
Pn57	38(1949)	—	Chien. Aluminum-Bronze. KG#6b	350
Pn58	38(1949)	—	2 Chien. Aluminum-Bronze. KG#4b	350
Pn59	38(1949)	—	2 Chien. Aluminum-Bronze. KG#3b	350
Pn60	38(1949)	—	5 Chien. Aluminum-Bronze. KG#2b	350
Pn62	45(1956)	—	2 Chien. Copper-Nickel.	250
Pn63	45(1956)	—	2 Chien. Aluminum-Bronze.	250
Pn64	45(1956)	—	2 Chien. Aluminum.	250

MINT SETS

KM#	Date	Mintage	Identification	Issue Price	Mkt Val
MS1	54(1965) (4)	—	Y#537-540	—	75.00
MS2	70(1981) (4)	—	Y#550-553	—	—
MS3	88(1999) (2)	260,000	Y#558-559	—	25.00

PROOF SETS

KM#	Date	Mintage	Identification	Issue Price	Mkt Val
PS1	70(1981) (4)	—	Y#550-553	—	50.00
PS2	82(1993) (5)	50,000	Y#550-554	14.75	300
PS3	83(1994) (5)	70,000	Y#550-554	14.75	80.00
PS4	84(1995) (5)	70,000	Y#550-554	17.65	57.50
PS5	85(1996) (5)	70,000	Y#550-554	17.65	62.50
PS6	86(1997) (5)	70,000	Y#550-554	17.65	62.50
PS7	87(1998) (5)	100,000	Y#550-554	20.60	35.00
PS8	88(1999) (5)	100,000	Y#550-554	20.60	35.00
PS9	89(2000) (5)	100,000	Y#550-554	22.05	62.50

Shortly after World War I the greatest external threat to the territorial integrity of China was posed by Japan, which urgently needed room for an expanding population and raw materials for its industrial and military machines, and which recognized the necessity of controlling all of China if it was to realize its plan of dominating the rest of the Asiatic and South Sea countries. The Japanese had large investments in Manchuria (a name given by non-Chinese to the three northeastern provinces of China), which allowed them privileges that compromised Chinese sovereignty. The educated of China were not reconciled to Japan's growing power in Manchuria, and the resultant friction occasioned a series of vexing incidents, which Japan decided to circumvent by direct action. On the night of Sept. 18-19, 1931, with a contrived incident for an excuse, Japanese forces seized the city of Mukden (Shenyang), and within a few weeks completely demolished Chinese power north of the Great Wall.

In Feb. 1932, after the Japanese occupation of Manchuria, they set up Manchoukuo as an independent republic. Jehol (Rehe) was occupied by the Japanese in 1933 and added to Manchoukuo. Manchoukuo was established as an empire in 1934 with the deposed Manchu emperor Hsuan T'ung (the late Henry Pu Yi) as the puppet emperor K'ang Te. Lacking the means to face the Japanese armies in the field, the Chinese could only trade space for time.

Not content with confining its control of China to the areas north of the Great Wall, the Japanese launched a major campaign in 1937, and by the fall of 1938 had occupied in addition to Manchuria the provinces of Hopei (Hebei) and Chahar, most of the port cities, and the major cities as far west as Hankow (Hankou), now part of Wuhan. In addition, they dominated or threatened the provinces of Suiyuan, Shansi (Shanxi) and Shantung (Shandong).

Still the Chinese did not yield. The struggle was prolonged until the advent of World War II, which brought about the defeat of Japan and the return of the puppet states to Chinese control.

As the victorious Japanese armies swept deeper into China, Japan established central banks under control of the Bank of Japan in the conquered provinces for the purpose of establishing control over banking and finance in the puppet states, and eventually in all of China. These included the Chi Tung Bank, which had its main office in Tientsin (Tianjin) with branches in Peking (Beijing), Chinan (Jinan) and Tangshan, the Federal Reserve Bank of China with its main office in Peking (Beijing) and branches in 37 other cities; and the Hua Hsing Bank with its main office in Shanghai and two branches. The puppet states of Manchoukuo, previously detailed in this introduction, and Mengchiang, which comprised a greater part of Inner Mongolia, were also major coin-issuing entities.

EAST HOPEI

AUTONOMOUS

The Chi Tung Bank was the banking institution of the "East Hopei Anti-Comintern Autonomous Government" established by the Japanese in 1936 to undermine the political position of China in the northwest provinces. It issued both coins and notes between 1937 and 1939 with a restraint uncharacteristic of the puppet banks of the China-Japanese puppet states.

ANTI-COMINTERN AUTONOMOUS GOVERNMENT

STANDARD COINAGE

Y# 516 5 LI
Copper **Issuer:** Chi Tung Bank **Obv:** Japanese character 'first" **Rev:** Value in grain stalks

Date	Mintage	VG	F	VF	XF	Unc
26(1937)	—	4.00	10.00	20.00	35.00	100

Y# 517 FEN

Copper **Issuer:** Chi Tung Bank **Obv:** Japanese character 'first" **Rev:** Value in grain stalks

Date	Mintage	VG	F	VF	XF	Unc
26(1937)	—	1.25	3.00	6.00	9.00	30.00

Y# 518 5 FEN

Copper-Nickel **Issuer:** Chi Tung Bank **Obv:** Japanese character 'first" **Rev:** Value in grain stalks

Date	Mintage	VG	F	VF	XF	Unc
26(1937)	—	1.00	2.50	4.50	6.50	25.00

Y# 519 CHIAO

Copper-Nickel **Issuer:** Chi Tung Bank **Obv:** T'ien-ning Pagoda in Peking **Rev:** Value in grain stalks

Date	Mintage	VG	F	VF	XF	Unc
26(1937)	—	1.00	2.50	4.50	6.50	22.50

Y# 520 2 CHIAO

Copper-Nickel **Issuer:** Chi Tung Bank **Obv:** T'ien-ning Pagoda in Peking **Rev:** Value in grain stalks

Date	Mintage	VG	F	VF	XF	Unc
26(1937)	—	1.25	3.00	6.00	10.00	35.00

MANCHOUKUO

(Manchukuo)

The former Japanese puppet state of Manchoukuo (largely Manchuria), comprising the northeastern Chinese provinces of Fengtien (Liaoning), Kirin (Jilin), Heilungkiang (Heilongjiang) and Jehol (Rehe), had an area of 503,143 sq. mi. (1,303,134 sq. km.) and a population of 43.3 million. Capital: Changchun, renamed Hsinking. The area is rich in fertile soil, timber and mineral resources, including coal, iron and gold.

Until the closing years of the 19th century when Chinese influence became predominant, Manchuria was chiefly a domain of the tribal Manchus and their Mongol allies. Coincident with the rise of Chinese influence, foreign imperialistic powers began to appreciate the value of the area to their expansionist philosophy. Japan, overpopulated and poor in resources, desired it as a source of raw materials and for increased living area. Russia wanted it as the eastern terminus of the Trans-Siberian railway that was to unite its Asian empire. The inevitable conflict of Japanese, Chinese and Russian interests required that one or more of the powers be eliminated. After eliminating Russia in their war of 1904-05, Japan eliminated China on the night of Sept. 18, 1931, when, on the pretext of a contrived incident, it moved militarily to seize control of the Three Eastern Provinces. Early in 1932 Japan declared Manchuria independent by virtue of a voluntary separatist movement and established the state of Manchoukuo. To give the puppet state an aura of legitimacy, the deposed emperor of the former Manchu dynasty was recalled from retirement and designated "chief executive". The area was restored to China at the end of World War II.

RULERS

Ta T'ung, 1932-1934
K'ang Te, 1934-1945

The puppet emperor under the assumed name of K'ang Te was previously the last emperor of China (P'u-yi, or Hsuan T'ung, 1909-11).

MONETARY SYSTEM

10 Li = 1 Fen
10 Fen = 1 Chiao

IDENTIFICATION OF REIGN CHARACTERS

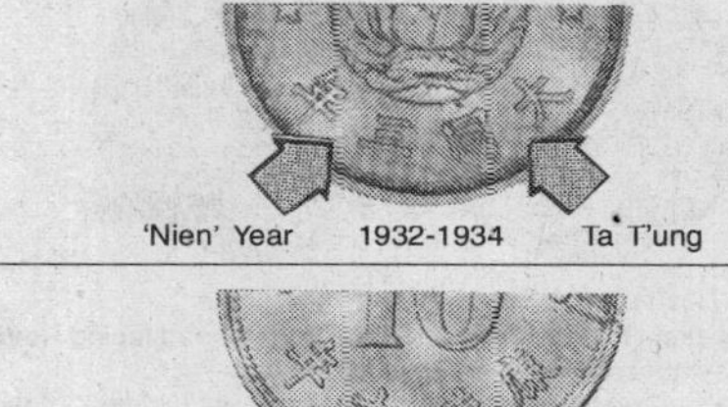

'Nien' Year 1932-1934 Ta T'ung

'Nien' Year 1934-1945 K'ang Te

DATE ABBREVIATIONS

TT - Ta T'ung
KT - K'ang Te

GREEK RIM BORDER VARIETIES

Narrow Design Wide Design

MARKET VALUATIONS

Uncirculated aluminum coins without any planchet defects are worth up to twice the market valuations given.

JAPANESE OCCUPATION

STANDARD COINAGE

Y# 1 5 LI

Bronze **Ruler:** Ta-t'ung **Obv:** Flag **Rev:** Value in floral sprays

Date	Mintage	VG	F	VF	XF	Unc
TT 2(1933)	—	8.00	20.00	35.00	50.00	100
TT 3(1934)	—	1.50	4.00	9.00	15.00	30.00

Y# 5 5 LI

Bronze **Ruler:** K'ang-te **Obv:** Character Yuan for "first", flag **Rev:** Value in floral sprays

Date	Mintage	VG	F	VF	XF	Unc
KT 1(1934)	—	1.25	3.00	7.50	10.00	25.00
KT 2(1935)	—	1.25	3.00	7.50	10.00	25.00
KT 3(1936)	—	7.00	17.50	27.50	40.00	70.00
KT 4(1937)	—	1.50	4.00	10.00	12.50	27.50
KT 6(1939)	—	75.00	150	200	275	375

Y# 2 FEN

Bronze **Ruler:** Ta-t'ung **Obv:** Flag **Rev: Value in floral sprays**

Date	Mintage	VG	F	VF	XF	Unc
TT 2(1933)	—	0.80	2.00	4.00	8.00	25.00
TT 3(1934)	—	0.60	1.50	3.00	5.00	20.00

Y# 6 FEN

Bronze **Ruler:** K'ang-te **Obv:** Character Yuan for "first", flag **Rev:** Value in floral sprays

Date	Mintage	VG	F	VF	XF	Unc
KT 1(1934)	—	0.40	1.00	3.00	6.00	15.00
KT 2(1935)	—	0.40	1.00	3.00	5.00	10.00
KT 3(1936)	—	0.40	1.00	3.00	5.00	10.00
KT 4(1937)	—	0.40	1.00	3.00	5.00	10.00
KT 5(1938)	—	0.40	1.00	3.00	5.00	10.00
KT 6(1939)	—	0.40	1.00	3.00	6.00	15.00

Y# 9 FEN

Aluminum, 19 mm. **Ruler:** K'ang-te **Obv:** National symbol **Rev:** Value in floral wreath

Date	Mintage	VG	F	VF	XF	Unc
KT 6(1939)	—	0.15	0.40	0.75	2.00	5.00
KT 7(1940)	—	0.15	0.40	0.75	2.00	5.00
KT 8(1941)	—	0.15	0.40	0.75	2.00	5.00
KT 9(1942)	—	0.15	0.40	0.75	2.00	5.00
KT 10(1943)	—	0.15	0.40	0.75	2.00	5.00

Y# 13 FEN

Aluminum **Ruler:** K'ang-te **Obv:** Legend around large "1" **Rev:** Floral wreath

Date	Mintage	VG	F	VF	XF	Unc
KT 10(1943)	—	0.35	0.75	2.00	5.00	10.00
KT 11(1944)	—	0.35	0.75	2.00	5.00	10.00

Y# 13a FEN

Red Fiber **Ruler:** K'ang-te **Obv:** Legend around large "1" **Rev:** Floral wreath

Date	Mintage	Good	VG	F	VF	XF
KT 12(1945)	—	1.75	2.75	4.50	9.00	15.00

Y# 13a.1 FEN

Brown Fiber **Ruler:** K'ang-te **Obv:** Legend around large "1" **Rev:** Floral wreath

Date	Mintage	Good	VG	F	VF	XF
KT 12(1945)	—	1.75	2.75	7.00	15.00	20.00

Y# 3 5 FEN

Copper-Nickel **Ruler:** Ta-t'ung **Obv:** Lotus flower **Rev:** Pearl above value between facing dragons

Date	Mintage	VG	F	VF	XF	Unc
TT 2(1933)	—	0.35	0.75	2.00	5.00	15.00
TT 3(1934)	—	0.15	0.40	1.00	2.00	10.00

Y# 7 5 FEN

Copper-Nickel **Ruler:** K'ang-te **Rev:** Pearl above value between facing dragons

Date	Mintage	VG	F	VF	XF	Unc
KT 1(1934)	—	0.25	0.60	1.50	3.00	6.00
Note: Character Yuan for "first".						
KT 2(1935)	—	0.25	0.60	1.50	3.00	6.00
KT 3(1936)	—	0.25	0.60	1.50	3.00	6.00

Date	Mintage	VG	F	VF	XF	Unc
Note: Narrow border design						
KT 3(1936)	—	0.50	1.25	3.00	6.00	12.00
Note: Wide border design						
KT 4(1937)	—	0.40	1.00	2.00	4.00	7.50
KT 6(1939)	—	0.40	1.00	2.00	4.00	7.50

Y# 11 5 FEN

Aluminum **Ruler:** K'ang-te **Obv:** Legend around large "5" **Rev:** National symbol above value in floral sprays

Date	Mintage	VG	F	VF	XF	Unc
KT 7 (1940)	—	0.25	0.60	1.50	3.00	6.00
KT 8 (1941)	—	0.15	0.40	0.75	2.00	4.00
KT 9 (1942)	—	0.15	0.40	0.75	2.00	4.00
KT 10 (1943)	—	0.15	0.40	0.75	2.00	4.00

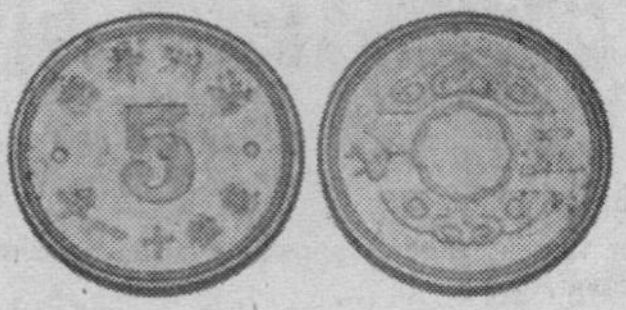

Y# A13 5 FEN

Aluminum **Ruler:** K'ang-te **Obv:** Legend around small "5" **Rev:** Wreath

Date	Mintage	VG	F	VF	XF	Unc
KT 10 (1943)	—	0.40	1.00	2.50	5.00	12.50
KT 11 (1944)	—	0.40	1.00	2.50	5.00	12.50

Y# A13a 5 FEN

Red Fiber **Ruler:** K'ang-te **Obv:** Legend around small "5" **Rev:** Wreath

Date	Mintage	VG	F	VF	XF	Unc
KT 11 (1944)	—	2.50	4.50	9.00	15.00	—
KT 12 (1945)	—	60.00	75.00	100	—	—

Y# A13a.1 5 FEN

Brown Fiber **Ruler:** K'ang-te **Obv:** Legend around small "5" **Rev:** Floral wreath

Date	Mintage	VG	F	VF	XF	Unc
KT 11 (1944)	—	5.00	10.00	15.00	25.00	—

Y# 4 CHIAO (10 Fen)

Copper-Nickel **Ruler:** Ta-t'ung **Obv:** Lotus flower **Rev:** Pearl above value between facing dragons

Date	Mintage	VG	F	VF	XF	Unc
TT 2 (1933)	—	0.60	1.50	3.00	7.00	15.00
TT 3 (1934)	—	0.30	0.80	2.00	3.75	12.50

Y# 8 CHIAO (10 Fen)

Copper-Nickel **Ruler:** K'ang-te **Rev:** Pearl above value between facing dragons

Date	Mintage	VG	F	VF	XF	Unc
KT 1 (1934)	—	0.30	0.80	2.00	3.00	8.00
Note: Character Yuan for "first".						
KT 2 (1935)	—	0.30	0.80	2.00	3.00	8.00
KT 5 (1938)	—	0.30	0.80	2.00	3.00	8.00
KT 6 (1939)	—	0.30	0.80	2.00	3.00	8.00
KT 6 (1939) Proof	—	—	—	—	—	—

Y# 10 CHIAO (10 Fen)

Copper-Nickel **Ruler:** K'ang-te **Obv:** Dragon head facing **Rev:** National symbol above value in floral sprays

Date	Mintage	VG	F	VF	XF	Unc
KT 7 (1940)	—	2.00	3.00	5.00	10.00	25.00

Y# 12 CHIAO (10 Fen)

Aluminum **Ruler:** K'ang-te **Obv:** Legend around "10" on "Fundo" weight outline **Rev:** National symbol above value in floral sprays

Date	Mintage	VG	F	VF	XF	Unc
KT 7 (1940)	—	0.35	0.80	2.00	3.00	8.00
KT 8 (1941)	—	0.35	0.80	2.00	3.00	8.00
KT 9 (1942)	—	0.35	0.80	2.00	3.00	8.00
KT 10 (1943)	—	115	275	400	500	600

Y# 14 CHIAO (10 Fen)

Aluminum **Ruler:** K'ang-te **Rev:** Legend around large "10"

Date	Mintage	VG	F	VF	XF	Unc
KT 10 (1943)	—	0.60	1.50	3.00	5.00	12.50

PATTERNS

Including off metal strikes

KM#	Date	Mintage	Identification	Mkt Val
Pn1	KT5(1938)	—	5 Chiao. Copper-Nickel. Medieval emperor's bust. Portrait.	—
Pn2	KT5(1938)	—	5 Chiao. Copper-Nickel. Two facing phoenix. Chinese characters.	—
Pn3	KT9(1942)	—	Chiao. Silver. Specimen	400
Pn4	KT9(1942)	—	Chiao. Copper-Nickel. Specimen	250
Pn5	KT9(1942)	—	Chiao. Brass. Specimen	200
Pn6	KT9(1942)	—	Chiao. Nickel-Bronze. Specimen	200
Pn7	KT12(1945)	—	Fen. Copper Plated Steel. Y#13a	—

MENG CHIANG

As Japanese troops moved into North China in 1937, the political situation became fluid in several provinces bordering on Manchoukuo, which were sometimes referred to as Inner Mongolia. On September 27, 1937, the Chanan Bank was established. As the situation became more settled the Japanese effected the merger of two local banks with the Bank of Chanan under a new title, Meng Chiang (Mongolian Borderlands or Mongol Territory) Bank. The Meng Chiang Bank was organized on November 27 and opened on December 1, 1937, with headquarters in Kalgan (Zhangjiakou) and branch offices in about a dozen locations throughout the region. Its notes were declared the exclusive currency for the area. The bank closed at the end of the war.

JAPANESE OCCUPATION

STANDARD COINAGE

Y# 521 5 CHIAO

Copper-Nickel **Obv:** Legend in floral design **Rev:** Value in facing dragons

Date	Mintage	VG	F	VF	XF	Unc
27(1938)	—	1.75	3.50	6.50	12.00	28.00

PATTERNS

Including off metal strikes

Note: KK indicates Kublai Khan dating system

KM#	Date	Mintage	Identification	Mkt Val
Pn1	738(1943)	—	Fen. Aluminum. Ram's head. Value above phoenix. This coin uses the Kublai Khan (KK) dating system.	—
Pn2	738(1943)	—	5 Fen. Aluminum. Ram's head. Value above phoenix. This coin uses the Kublai Khan (KK) dating system.	1,650
Pn3	738(1943)	—	Chiao. Aluminum. Ram's head. Value above phoenix. This coin uses the Kublai Khan (KK) dating system.	2,250

PROVISIONAL GOVT. OF CHINA

In late 1937 the Japanese North China Expeditionary Army established the "Provisional Government of China" at Peking (Beijing).

FEDERAL RESERVE BANK

The Federal Reserve Bank of China was opened in 1938 by Japanese military authorities in Peking (Beijing). It was the puppet financial agency of the Japanese in northeast China. The puppet bank issued both coins and currency, but in modest amounts.

JAPANESE OCCUPATION

STANDARD COINAGE

Y# 523 FEN

Aluminum **Issuer:** Federal Reserve Bank **Obv:** Legend around FR Bank symbol **Rev:** Temple of Heaven

Date	Mintage	VG	F	VF	XF	Unc
30 (1941)	—	0.20	0.50	1.00	2.50	7.00
31 (1942)	—	0.20	0.50	1.00	2.00	6.00
32 (1943)	—	1.25	3.00	6.00	10.00	30.00

Y# 524 5 FEN

Aluminum **Issuer:** Federal Reserve Bank **Obv:** Legend around FR Bank symbol **Rev:** Temple of Heaven **Note:** The 5 Fen pieces were struck on thick (1 gram) and thin (.8 gram) planchets.

Date	Mintage	VG	F	VF	XF	Unc
30 (1941)	—	0.35	0.75	2.00	4.00	10.00
31 (1942)	—	0.40	1.00	2.50	5.00	15.00
32 (1943)	—	1.50	3.50	7.50	15.00	45.00

Y# 525 CHIAO

Aluminum, 22 mm. **Issuer:** Federal Reserve Bank **Obv:** Legend around FR Bank symbol **Rev:** Temple of Heaven **Note:** The 1 Chiao pieces were struck on thick (1.5 gram), thin (1.2 gram), and very thin (1.0 gram) planchets.

Date	Mintage	VG	F	VF	XF	Unc
30 (1941)	—	0.15	0.40	1.00	2.00	6.00
31 (1942)	—	0.15	0.40	1.00	2.00	6.00
32 (1943)	—	0.60	1.50	3.00	6.50	20.00

PATTERNS

Including off metal strikes

KM#	Date	Mintage	Identification	Mkt Val
Pn1	30(1941)	—	Fen. Silver. KM#523, R.Y.30.	700
Pn2	30(1941)	—	5 Fen. Silver. KM#524, R.Y.30.	700

REFORMED GOVT. OF CHINA

On March 28, 1938 the Japanese Central China Expeditionary Army established the Reformed Government of the Republic of China at Nanking (Nanjing).

HUA HSING COMMERCIAL BANK

The Hua Hsing Commerce Bank was a financial agency created and established by the government of Japan and its puppet authorities in Shanghai in May 1939. Notes and coins were issued until sometime in 1941, with the quantities restricted by Chinese aversion to accepting them.

JAPANESE OCCUPATION

STANDARD COINAGE

Y# A522 FEN

Bronze **Obv:** Legend around character "Hua" above pair of wings **Rev:** Stylized character divides value

Date	Mintage	VG	F	VF	XF	Unc
29(1940)	—	50.00	100	200	300	400

Y# 522 10 FEN

Copper-Nickel **Obv:** Legend around character "Hua" above pair of wings **Rev:** Floral bouquet divides value

Date	Mintage	VG	F	VF	XF	Unc
29(1940)	—	0.40	1.00	2.00	3.50	7.00

Note: Metal alloys vary

PATTERNS

Including off metal strikes

KM#	Date	Mintage	Identification	Mkt Val
Pn1	29(1940)	—	Fen. Copper-Nickel.	650
Pn2	29(1940)	—	Fen. Silver.	750
Pn3	29(1940)	—	5 Fen. Copper-Nickel. Liu-ho Pagoda.	650
Pn4	29(1940)	—	20 Fen. Copper-Nickel. Junk.	2,250

CHINA, PEOPLE'S REPUBLIC

The Peoples Republic of China, located in eastern Asia, has an area of 3,696,100 sq. mi. (9,596,960 sq. km.) (including Manchuria and Tibet) and a population of *1.20 billion. Capital: Peking (Beijing). The economy is based on agriculture, mining, and manufacturing. Textiles, clothing, metal ores, tea and rice are exported.

China's ancient civilization began in east-central Henan's Huayang county, 2800-2300 B.C. The warring feudal states comprising early China were first united under Emperor Ch'in Shih (246-210 B.C.) who gave China its name and first central government. Subsequent dynasties alternated brilliant cultural achievements with internal disorder until the Empire was brought down by the revolution of 1911, and the Republic of China installed in its place. Chinese culture attained a pre-eminence in art, literature and philosophy, but a traditional backwardness in industry and administration ill prepared China for the demands of 19th century Western expansionism which exposed it to military and political humiliations, and mandated a drastic revision of political practice in order to secure an accommodation with the modern world.

The Republic of 1911 barely survived the stress of World War I, and was subsequently all but shattered by the rise of nationalism and the emergence of the Chinese Communist movement. Moscow, which practiced a policy of cooperation between Communists and other parties in movements for national liberation, sought to establish an entente between the Chinese Communist Party and the Kuomintang ('National Peoples Party') of Sun Yat-sen. The ensuing cooperation was based on little more than the hope each had of using the other.

An increasingly uneasy association between the Kuomintang and the Chinese Communist Party developed and continued until April 12, 1927, when Chiang Kai-shek, Sun Yat-sen's political heir, instituted a bloody purge to stamp out the Communists within the Kuomintang and the government and virtually paralyzed their ranks throughout China. Some time after the mid-1927 purges, the Chinese Communist Party turned to armed force to resist Chiang Kai-shek and during the period of 1930-34 acquired control over large parts of Kiangsi (Jiangxi), Fukien (Fujian), Hunan and Hupeh (Hubei). The Nationalist Nanking government responded with a series of campaigns against the soviet power bases and, by October of 1934, succeeded in driving the remnants of the Communist army to a refuge in Shensi (Shaanxi) Province. There the Communists reorganized under the leadership of Mao Tse-tung, defeated the Nationalist forces, and on Sept. 21, 1949, established the Peoples Republic of China. Thereafter relations between Russia and Communist China steadily deteriorated until 1958, when China emerged as an independent center of Communist power.

MONETARY SYSTEM

After 1949

10 Fen (Cents) = 1 Jiao

10 Jiao = 1 Renminbi Yuan

MINT MARKS

(b) - Beijing (Peking)

(s) - Shanghai

(y) - Shenyang (Mukden)

PEOPLES REPUBLIC

STANDARD COINAGE

Y# 1 FEN

0.6500 g., Aluminum, 18 mm. **Obv:** National emblem **Rev:** Denomination above wreath, date below

Date	Mintage	F	VF	XF	Unc	BU
1955	—	0.20	0.50	1.50	5.00	—
1956	—	0.40	1.00	2.50	7.50	—
1957	—	0.60	1.50	3.50	10.00	—
1958	—	0.10	0.25	0.75	2.50	—
1959	—	0.10	0.25	0.75	2.50	—
1961	—	0.10	0.25	0.75	2.50	—
1963	—	0.10	0.25	0.50	1.50	—
1964	—	0.10	0.25	0.50	1.00	—
1971	—	0.10	0.25	0.50	1.00	—
1972	—	0.10	0.25	0.50	1.00	—
1973	—	0.10	0.25	0.50	1.50	—
1974	—	0.10	0.25	0.50	1.00	—
1975	500,000	0.10	0.25	0.50	1.00	—
1976	—	—	0.10	0.25	0.50	—
1977	—	—	0.10	0.25	0.50	—
1978	—	—	0.10	0.25	0.50	—
1979	—	—	0.10	0.25	0.50	—
1980	—	—	0.10	0.25	0.50	—
1980 Proof	—	Value: 1.00				
1981	—	—	0.10	0.25	0.50	—
1981 Proof	—	Value: 1.00				
1982	—	—	—	0.25	0.50	—
1982 Proof	—	Value: 1.00				
1983	2,412,000	—	—	0.10	0.25	—
1984	3,283,000	—	—	0.10	0.25	—
1985	—	—	—	0.10	0.25	—
1985 Proof	—	Value: 1.00				
1986	—	—	—	0.10	0.25	—
1986 Proof	—	Value: 1.00				
1987	—	—	—	0.10	0.25	—
1991	—	—	—	0.10	0.25	—
1991 Proof	—	Value: 1.00				
1992	—	—	—	0.10	0.25	—
1992 Proof	—	Value: 1.00				
1993	—	—	—	—	0.75	—
Note: In sets only						
1993 Proof	—	Value: 1.00				
1994	—	—	—	—	0.75	—
Note: In sets only						
1994 Proof	—	Value: 1.00				
1995	—	—	—	—	0.75	—
Note: In sets only						
1995 Proof	—	Value: 1.00				
1996	—	—	—	—	0.75	—
Note: In sets only						
1996 Proof	—	Value: 1.00				
1997	—	—	—	0.10	0.25	—

Y# 2 2 FEN

1.0500 g., Aluminum, 21 mm. **Obv:** National emblem **Rev:** Denomination above wreath, date below

Date	Mintage	F	VF	XF	Unc	BU
1956	—	0.10	0.25	0.75	1.50	—
1959	—	0.20	0.50	1.00	4.00	—
1960	—	0.20	0.50	1.00	4.00	—
1961	—	0.10	0.25	0.75	1.50	—
1962	—	0.10	0.25	0.75	1.50	—
1963	—	0.10	0.25	0.75	1.50	—
1964	—	0.10	0.25	0.50	1.25	—
1974	—	0.10	0.25	0.50	1.50	—
1975	—	0.10	0.25	0.50	1.00	—
1976	—	0.10	0.25	0.50	1.00	—
1977	360,000	0.10	0.25	0.50	0.75	—
1978	—	0.10	0.20	0.40	0.60	—
1979	—	0.10	0.20	0.40	0.60	—
1980	—	0.10	0.20	0.40	0.60	—
1980 Proof	—	Value: 1.00				
1981	—	0.10	0.20	0.40	0.60	—
1981 Proof	—	Value: 1.00				
1982	—	0.10	0.20	0.40	0.60	—
1982 Proof	—	Value: 1.00				
1983	1,790,000	—	0.10	0.20	0.35	—
1984	1,963,000	—	0.10	0.20	0.35	—
1985	—	—	0.10	0.20	0.35	—
1985 Proof	—	Value: 1.00				
1986	—	—	0.15	0.35	0.75	—
1986 Proof	—	Value: 1.00				
1987	—	—	0.10	0.20	0.35	—
1988	—	—	0.10	0.20	0.35	—
1989	—	—	0.10	0.20	0.35	—
1990	—	—	0.10	0.20	0.35	—
1991	—	—	0.10	0.20	0.35	—
1991 Proof	—	Value: 1.00				
1992	—	—	0.10	0.20	0.35	—
1992 Proof	—	Value: 1.00				
1993	—	—	—	—	0.75	—
Note: In sets only						
1993 Proof	—	Value: 1.00				
1994	—	—	—	—	0.75	—
Note: In sets only						
1994 Proof	—	Value: 1.00				
1995	—	—	—	—	0.75	—
Note: In sets only						
1995 Proof	—	Value: 1.00				
1996	—	—	—	—	0.75	—
Note: In sets only						
1996 Proof	—	Value: 1.00				

Y# 3 5 FEN

1.6000 g., Aluminum, 24 mm. **Obv:** National emblem **Rev:** Denomination above wreath, date below

Date	Mintage	F	VF	XF	Unc	BU
1955	—	0.30	0.75	2.00	10.00	—
1956	—	0.15	0.35	0.75	2.00	—
1957	—	0.15	0.35	0.75	2.50	—
1974	—	0.15	0.25	0.50	1.50	—
1975	—	0.15	0.25	0.50	1.50	—
1976	350,000	0.15	0.25	0.50	0.75	—
1979	—	0.15	0.35	0.75	2.00	—
1980	—	0.15	0.25	0.50	0.75	—
1980 Proof	—	Value: 1.00				
1981	—	0.15	0.25	0.50	0.75	—
1981 Proof	—	Value: 1.00				
1982	—	0.15	0.25	0.50	0.75	—
1982 Proof	—	Value: 1.00				
1983	484,000	—	0.15	0.25	0.45	—
1984	600,000	—	0.15	0.25	0.45	—
1985	—	—	0.15	0.25	0.45	—
1985 Proof	—	Value: 1.00				
1986	—	—	0.15	0.25	0.45	—
1986 Proof	—	Value: 1.00				
1987	—	—	0.15	0.25	0.45	—
1988	—	—	0.15	0.25	0.45	—
1989	—	—	0.15	0.25	0.45	—
1990	—	—	0.15	0.25	0.45	—
1991	—	—	0.15	0.25	0.45	—
1991 Proof	—	Value: 1.00				
1992	—	—	0.15	0.25	0.45	—
1992 Proof	—	Value: 1.00				
1993	—	—	—	—	0.75	—
Note: In sets only						
1993 Proof	—	Value: 1.00				
1994	—	—	—	—	0.75	—
Note: In sets only						
1994 Proof	—	Value: 1.00				
1995	—	—	—	—	0.75	—
Note: In sets only						
1995 Proof	—	Value: 1.00				
1996	—	—	—	—	0.75	—
Note: In sets only						
1996 Proof	—	Value: 1.00				

Y# 24 JIAO

2.6000 g., Copper-Zinc, 20 mm. **Obv:** National emblem **Rev:** Denomination above wreath, date below

Date	Mintage	F	VF	XF	Unc	BU
1980	—	—	—	—	0.50	—
1980 Proof	—	Value: 1.00				
1981	—	—	—	—	0.50	—
1981 Proof	—	Value: 1.00				
1982 Proof	—	Value: 1.00				
1983	3,100,000	—	—	—	0.50	—
1984	3,500,000	—	—	—	0.50	—
1985 Proof	—	Value: 1.00				
1985	—	—	—	—	0.50	—
1986 Proof	—	Value: 1.00				

Y# 148 JIAO
Brass **Series:** 6th National Games **Subject:** Gymnast **Obv:** Stylized torch divides date below **Rev:** Gymnast above date, denomination at left

Date	Mintage	F	VF	XF	Unc	BU
1987	10,570,000	—	—	1.00	2.00	—

Y# 149 JIAO
Brass **Series:** 6th National Games **Subject:** Soccer **Obv:** Stylized torch divides date below **Rev:** Soccer player divides date and denomination

Date	Mintage	F	VF	XF	Unc	BU
1987	Inc. above	—	—	1.00	2.00	—

Y# 150 JIAO
Brass **Series:** 6th National Games **Subject:** Volleyball **Obv:** Stylized torch divides date below **Rev:** Volleyball player, date below, denomination at right

Date	Mintage	F	VF	XF	Unc	BU
1987	Inc. above	—	—	1.00	2.00	—

Y# 328 JIAO
Aluminum, 22.5 mm. **Obv:** National emblem, date below **Rev:** Peony blossom, denomination at right

Date	Mintage	F	VF	XF	Unc	BU
1991	—	—	—	—	0.50	—
1991 Proof	—	Value: 1.00				
1992	—	—	—	—	0.50	—
1992 Proof	—	Value: 1.00				
1993	—	—	—	—	0.50	—
1993 Proof	—	Value: 1.00				
1994	—	—	—	—	0.50	—
1994 Proof	—	Value: 1.00				
1995	—	—	—	—	0.50	—
1995 Proof	—	Value: 1.00				
1996	—	—	—	—	0.50	—
1996 Proof	—	Value: 1.00				
1997	—	—	—	—	0.50	—
1998	—	—	—	—	0.50	—
1999	—	—	—	—	0.50	—
1999 Proof	—	Value: 1.00				

Y# 1068 JIAO
Aluminum, 18.9 mm. **Obv:** Denomination, date below **Rev:** Orchid **Edge:** Plain

Date	Mintage	F	VF	XF	Unc	BU
1999	—	—	—	—	0.50	—
2000	—	—	—	—	0.50	—

Y# 25 2 JIAO
4.1500 g., Copper-Zinc, 23 mm. **Obv:** National emblem **Rev:** Denomination above wreath, date below

Date	Mintage	F	VF	XF	Unc	BU
1980	—	—	—	—	0.60	—
1980 Proof	—	Value: 1.25				
1981	—	—	—	—	0.60	—
1981 Proof	—	Value: 1.25				
1982 Proof	—	Value: 1.25				
1983	4,200,000	—	—	—	0.60	—
1984	2,500,000	—	—	—	0.60	—
1985 Proof	—	Value: 1.25				
1986 Proof	—	Value: 1.25				

Y# 26 5 JIAO
6.0000 g., Copper-Zinc, 26 mm. **Obv:** National emblem **Rev:** Denomination above wreath, date below

Date	Mintage	F	VF	XF	Unc	BU
1980	—	—	—	—	0.75	—
1980 Proof	—	Value: 1.50				
1981	—	—	—	—	0.75	—
1981 Proof	—	Value: 1.50				
1982 Proof	—	Value: 1.50				
1983	3,000,000	—	—	—	0.75	—
1984	3,500,000	—	—	—	0.75	—
1985	—	—	—	—	0.75	—
1985 Proof	—	Value: 1.50				
1986 Proof	—	Value: 1.50				

Y# 53 5 JIAO
2.2000 g., 0.9000 Silver .0637 oz. ASW **Obv:** Building divides date and denomination **Rev:** Marco Polo looking left, two dates below

Date	Mintage	F	VF	XF	Unc	BU
1983 Proof	7,050	Value: 90.00				

Y# 205 5 JIAO
2.0000 g., 0.9990 Silver .0643 oz. ASW **Obv:** Great wall, date below **Rev:** Denomination divides phoenix and dragon representing good luck

Date	Mintage	F	VF	XF	Unc	BU
1990 Proof	55,000	Value: 10.00				
1990 Proof	55,000	Value: 10.00				

Y# 329 5 JIAO
3.8300 g., Brass, 20.5 mm. **Obv:** National emblem, date below **Rev:** Denomination above flowers **Edge:** Segmented reeding

Date	Mintage	F	VF	XF	Unc	BU
1991	—	—	—	—	1.00	—
1991 Proof	—	Value: 1.50				
1992	—	—	—	—	1.00	—
1992 Proof	—	Value: 1.50				
1993	—	—	—	—	1.00	—
1993 Proof	—	Value: 1.50				
1994	—	—	—	—	1.00	—
1994 Proof	—	Value: 1.50				
1995	—	—	—	—	1.00	—
1995 Proof	—	Value: 1.50				
1996	—	—	—	—	1.00	—
1996 Proof	—	Value: 1.50				
1997	—	—	—	—	1.00	—
1998	—	—	—	—	1.00	—
1999	—	—	—	—	1.00	—
2000	—	—	—	—	1.00	—

Y# 10 YUAN
Brass **Series:** 1980 Olympics **Subject:** Archery **Obv:** National emblem above denomination **Rev:** Archers, date below, Olympic logo upper left

Date	Mintage	F	VF	XF	Unc	BU
1980 Proof	40,000	Value: 10.00				

Y# 11 YUAN
Brass **Series:** 1980 Olympics **Subject:** Wrestling **Obv:** National emblem, denomination below **Rev:** Wrestlers, date below, Olympic logo upper left

Date	Mintage	F	VF	XF	Unc	BU
1980 Proof	40,000	Value: 10.00				

Y# 12 YUAN
Brass **Series:** 1980 Olympics **Subject:** Equestrian **Obv:** National emblem, denomination below **Rev:** Equestrians, date below, Olympic logo, upper left

Date	Mintage	F	VF	XF	Unc	BU
1980 Proof	40,000	Value: 10.00				

Y# 13 YUAN
Brass **Series:** 1980 Olympics **Subject:** Soccer **Obv:** National emblem, denomination below **Rev:** 2 soccer players in ancient garb

Date	Mintage	F	VF	XF	Unc	BU
1980 Proof	40,000	Value: 10.00				

Y# 14 YUAN
Brass **Series:** Lake Placid - 13th Winter Olympic Games **Subject:** Alpine Skiing **Obv:** National emblem , Olympic logo at left, denomination below **Rev:** Skier within snowflake design

Date	Mintage	F	VF	XF	Unc	BU
1980 Proof	29,000	Value: 14.50				

Y# 15 YUAN
Brass **Series:** Lake Placid - 13th Winter Olympic Games **Subject:** Women's Speed Skating **Obv:** National emblem, Olympic logo at left, denomination below **Rev:** Speed skater within snowflake design

Date	Mintage	F	VF	XF	Unc	BU
1980 Proof	29,000	Value: 14.50				

Y# 16 YUAN

Brass **Series:** Lake Placid - 13th Winter Olympic Games **Subject:** Figure skating **Obv:** National emblem, Olympic logo at left, denomination below **Rev:** Woman figure skater within snowflake design

Date	Mintage	F	VF	XF	Unc	BU
1980 Proof	29,000	Value: 14.50				

Y# 17 YUAN

Brass **Series:** Lake Placid - 13th Winter Olympic Games **Subject:** Biathlon **Obv:** National emblem, Olympic logo at left, denomination below **Rev:** Biathlete within snowflake

Date	Mintage	F	VF	XF	Unc	BU
1980 Proof	29,000	Value: 14.50				

Y# 27 YUAN

9.3000 g., Copper-Nickel, 30 mm. **Obv:** National emblem, date below **Rev:** Great wall

Date	Mintage	F	VF	XF	Unc	BU
1980	—	—	—	—	2.00	—
1980 Proof	—	Value: 3.00				
1981	—	—	—	—	2.00	—
1981 Proof	—	Value: 3.00				
1982 Proof	—	Value: 3.00				
1983	3,100,000	—	—	—	2.00	—
1984	4,100,000	—	—	—	2.00	—
1985	—	—	—	—	2.00	—
1985 Proof	—	Value: 3.00				
1986 Proof	—	Value: 3.00				

Y# 34 YUAN

Brass **Subject:** World Cup Soccer **Obv:** National emblem, date below **Rev:** Soccer player, within ring, kicking the ball, denomination bottom right

Date	Mintage	F	VF	XF	Unc	BU
1982 Proof	20,000	Value: 10.00				

Y# 53 YUAN

Brass **Obv:** National emblem, date below **Rev:** Panda within octagon

Date	Mintage	F	VF	XF	Unc	BU
1983 Proof	30,000	Value: 25.00				
1984 Proof	30,000	Value: 25.00				

Y# 87 YUAN

Copper-Nickel **Subject:** 35th Anniversary - Peoples Republic **Obv:** National emblem above buildings, dates below **Rev:** Monument amid cranes in flight

Date	Mintage	F	VF	XF	Unc	BU
ND(1984)	Inc. above	—	—	—	6.00	—
ND(1984) Proof	—	Value: 7.50				

Y# 85 YUAN

Copper-Nickel **Subject:** 35th Anniversary - Peoples Republic **Obv:** National emblem above buildings, dates below **Rev:** Republic figures

Date	Mintage	F	VF	XF	Unc	BU
ND(1984)	20,410,000	—	—	—	6.00	—
ND(1984) Proof	—	Value: 7.50				

Y# 86 YUAN

Copper-Nickel **Subject:** 35th Anniversary - Peoples Republic **Obv:** National emblem **Rev:** Dancers

Date	Mintage	F	VF	XF	Unc	BU
ND(1984)	Inc. above	—	—	—	6.00	—
ND(1984) Proof	—	Value: 7.50				

Y# 96 YUAN

Copper-Nickel **Subject:** 20th Anniversary - Tibet Autonomous Region **Obv:** National emblem, date below **Rev:** Potala Palace

Date	Mintage	F	VF	XF	Unc	BU
1985	2,612,000	—	—	3.00	8.50	—
1985 Proof	10,000	Value: 12.00				

Y# 109 YUAN

Copper-Nickel **Subject:** 30th Anniversary - Xinjiang Autonomous Region

Date	Mintage	F	VF	XF	Unc	BU
1985	4,500,000	—	—	2.00	6.00	—
1985 Proof	10,000	Value: 7.50				

Y# 151 YUAN

Copper-Nickel **Subject:** Year of Peace **Obv:** National emblem, date below **Rev:** Seated woman with doves

Date	Mintage	F	VF	XF	Unc	BU
1986	27,048,000	—	—	—	5.00	—

Y# 140 YUAN

Copper-Nickel **Subject:** 40th Anniversary - Mongolian Autonomous Region **Obv:** Building, date below **Rev:** Riders, sheep below, denomination at left

Date	Mintage	F	VF	XF	Unc	BU
1987	9,054,000	—	—	2.00	6.00	—

Y# 198 YUAN

Copper-Nickel **Subject:** 30th Anniversary - Kwangsi Autonomous Region **Obv:** Mountains and water, inscription and date below **Rev:** Native dancers, denomination at right, two dates upper left

Date	Mintage	F	VF	XF	Unc	BU
1988	4,072,000	—	—	—	7.00	—

Y# 211 YUAN

Copper-Nickel **Subject:** 30th Anniversary - Ningxia Autonomous Region **Rev:** Women with plants, denomination at right, within circle, dates below

Date	Mintage	F	VF	XF	Unc	BU
1988	1,560,000	—	—	—	7.50	—

Y# 212 YUAN

Copper-Nickel **Subject:** 40th Anniversary - Peoples Bank **Obv:** National emblem, date below **Rev:** Building divides dates

Date	Mintage	F	VF	XF	Unc	BU
1988	2,068,000	—	—	5.00	20.00	—

Y# 204 YUAN

Copper-Nickel **Subject:** 40th Anniversary - Peoples Republic **Obv:** National emblem above buildings, date below **Rev:** Music score divides artistic year and dates

Date	Mintage	F	VF	XF	Unc	BU
1989	2,000,000	—	—	—	4.00	—

Y# 264 YUAN

Nickel Clad Steel **Series:** XI Asian Games **Obv:** Building, Roman numerals above, inscription and date below **Rev:** Sword Dancer, panda dancer at left, denomination at right

Date	Mintage	F	VF	XF	Unc	BU
1990	25,608,000	—	—	—	4.00	—

Y# 265 YUAN

Nickel Clad Steel **Series:** 11th Asian Games - Beijing 1990 **Obv:** Building, Roman numeral above, inscription and date below **Rev:** Female archer, denomination above, panda archer below

Date	Mintage	F	VF	XF	Unc	BU
1990	Inc. above	—	—	—	4.00	—

Y# 279 YUAN

Nickel Clad Steel, 25 mm. **Subject:** Planting Trees Festival **Rev:** Head of young woman

Date	Mintage	F	VF	XF	Unc	BU
1991	10,000,000	—	—	—	2.25	—

Y# 280 YUAN

Nickel Clad Steel, 25 mm. **Subject:** Planting Trees Festival **Obv:** Trees, inscription, and numbers within circle **Rev:** Monument on globe divides birds in flight, date below

Date	Mintage	F	VF	XF	Unc	BU
1991	10,000,000	—	—	—	2.25	—

Y# 281 YUAN

Nickel Clad Steel, 25 mm. **Subject:** Planting Trees Festival **Obv:** Trees, inscription, and numbers within circle **Rev:** Seedling, date below

Date	Mintage	F	VF	XF	Unc	BU
1991	10,000,000	—	—	—	2.25	—

Y# 284 YUAN

Nickel Plated Steel, 25 mm. **Subject:** 70th Anniversary of the Founding of the Chinese Communist Party **Obv:** National emblem, date below **Rev:** House of Shanghai

Date	Mintage	F	VF	XF	Unc	BU
1991	30,000,000	—	—	—	2.25	—

Y# 285 YUAN

Nickel Plated Steel, 25 mm. **Subject:** 70th Anniversary of the Founding of the Chinese Communist Party **Rev:** House in Tsun-i (Zunyi), Kweichow Province

Date	Mintage	F	VF	XF	Unc	BU
1991	30,000,000	—	—	—	2.25	—

Y# 286 YUAN

Nickel Plated Steel, 25 mm. **Subject:** 70th Anniversary of the Founding of the Chinese Communist Party - Meeting in Tiananmen Square, 1978 **Obv:** National emblem, date below **Rev:** Flags, monument, and building

Date	Mintage	F	VF	XF	Unc	BU
1991	30,000,000	—	—	—	2.25	—

Y# 316 YUAN

Nickel Plated Steel, 25 mm. **Subject:** 1st Women's World Football Cup **Obv:** Conjoined soccer balls, artistic woman design on top **Rev:** Goalie, date at right

Date	Mintage	F	VF	XF	Unc	BU
1991	10,000,000	—	—	—	2.50	—

Y# 317 YUAN

Nickel Plated Steel, 25 mm. **Subject:** 1st Women's World Football Cup **Obv:** Conjoined soccer balls, artistic woman design on top **Rev:** Player, soccer ball background, date at lower right

Date	Mintage	F	VF	XF	Unc	BU
1991	10,000,000	—	—	—	2.50	—

Y# 330 YUAN

Nickel Clad Steel, 25 mm. **Obv:** National emblem, date below **Rev:** Denomination above flowers

Date	Mintage	F	VF	XF	Unc	BU
1991	—	—	—	—	1.50	—
1991 Proof	—	Value: 2.50				
1992	—	—	—	—	1.50	—
1992 Proof	—	Value: 2.50				
1993	—	—	—	—	1.50	—
1993 Proof	—	Value: 2.50				
1994	—	—	—	—	1.50	—
1994 Proof	—	Value: 2.50				
1995	—	—	—	—	1.50	—
1995 Proof	—	Value: 2.50				
1996	—	—	—	—	1.50	—
1996 Proof	—	Value: 2.50				
1997	—	—	—	—	1.50	—
1997 Proof	—	Value: 2.50				
1998	—	—	—	—	1.50	—
1998 Proof	—	Value: 2.50				
1999	—	—	—	—	1.50	—
1999 Proof	—	Value: 2.50				

Y# 364 YUAN

Nickel Clad Steel, 25 mm. **Subject:** 10th Anniversary - Constitution **Obv:** National emblem, date below **Rev:** Constitution, denomination at right, dates and flower below

Date	Mintage	F	VF	XF	Unc	BU
1992	10,000,000	—	—	—	2.50	—

Y# 365 YUAN

Nickel Clad Steel, 25 mm. **Subject:** 100th Birthday of Soong Ching Ling - Second Wife of Sun Yat-sen **Obv:** Building, date below **Rev:** Bust of Ching-ling, 1892-1981, half left, revolutionary stateswoman

Date	Mintage	F	VF	XF	Unc	BU
1993	10,448,000	—	—	—	3.50	—
1993 Proof	—	Value: 5.00				

Y# 399 YUAN

Nickel Clad Steel, 25 mm. **Subject:** 100th Anniversary - Birth of Chairman Mao **Obv:** Buildings and mountains, date below **Rev:** Mao's head, left

Date	Mintage	F	VF	XF	Unc	BU
1993	20,000,000	—	—	—	3.50	—
1993 Prooflike	—	—	—	—	5.00	—

Y# 455 YUAN
Nickel Clad Steel, 25 mm. **Series:** Children's Year **Subject:** Project Hope **Obv:** National emblem, date below **Rev:** Two children, denomination lower left

Date	Mintage	F	VF	XF	Unc	BU
1994	—	—	—	—	2.50	—

Y# 487 YUAN
Nickel Plated Steel, 25 mm. **Subject:** Table Tennis **Obv:** Building divides design and date **Rev:** Table tennis player, denomination lower left

Date	Mintage	F	VF	XF	Unc	BU
1995	10,000,000	—	—	—	3.50	—
1995 Proof	20,000	Value: 6.50				

Y# 528 YUAN
Nickel Plated Steel, 25 mm. **Subject:** 50th Anniversary - Defeat of Fascism and Japan **Obv:** Great Wall and mountains, date below **Rev:** Statue of rock and soldiers, dates and denomination below

Date	Mintage	F	VF	XF	Unc	BU
1995	10,000,000	—	—	—	3.50	—

Y# 529 YUAN
Nickel Plated Steel, 25 mm. **Subject:** 50th Anniversary - United Nations **Obv:** National emblem above wall, denomination below **Rev:** United Nations logo and anniversary numbers, date lower right

Date	Mintage	F	VF	XF	Unc	BU
1995	10,000,000	—	—	—	3.00	—

Y# 530 YUAN
Nickel Plated Steel, 25 mm. **Subject:** 4th UN Women's Conference **Obv:** Small building within design **Rev:** Half moon and dove above inscription, denomination and dates below

Date	Mintage	F	VF	XF	Unc	BU
1995	10,000,000	—	—	—	3.00	—

Y# 1124 YUAN
6.0500 g., Nickel Plated Steel, 25 mm. **Obv:** Zhu De's home in Sichuan, date below **Rev:** Marshal Zhu De, 3/4 left **Edge:** Lettered **Edge Lettering:** "ZHONGGUO" twice

Date	Mintage	F	VF	XF	Unc	BU
1996	580,000	—	—	—	3.50	—

Y# 1057 YUAN
6.1000 g., Nickel Clad Steel, 24.9 mm. **Subject:** Liu Shao-chi **Obv:** Building, denomination and date **Rev:** Bust of Liu left **Edge Lettering:** ZHONGGUO twice

Date	Mintage	F	VF	XF	Unc	BU
1998	—	—	—	—	3.75	—

Y# 721 YUAN
Nickel Clad Steel, 25 mm. **Subject:** 100th Birthday - Chou (Zhou) Enlai **Obv:** Chou (Zhou) birth place, date below **Rev:** Chou (Zhou) bust left

Date	Mintage	F	VF	XF	Unc	BU
1998	—	—	—	—	3.50	—

Y# 1058 YUAN
6.1000 g., Nickel Clad Steel, 24.9 mm. **Subject:** 50th Anniversary - People's Political Consultative Conference **Obv:** Emblem, date within, above inscription and dates **Rev:** Building, date below

Date	Mintage	F	VF	XF	Unc	BU
1999	—	—	—	—	3.75	—

Y# 1069 YUAN
Nickel Plated Steel, 24.9 mm. **Obv:** Denomination, date below **Rev:** Chrysanthemum **Edge:** "RMB" three times

Date	Mintage	F	VF	XF	Unc	BU
1999	—	—	—	—	1.50	—
2000	—	—	—	—	1.50	—

Y# 1037 YUAN
6.1000 g., Nickel Clad Steel, 25 mm. **Subject:** Dunhuang Cave **Obv:** Pagoda, date below **Rev:** Standing and floating figures **Edge:** "RMB" 3 times

Date	Mintage	F	VF	XF	Unc	BU
2000	—	—	—	—	4.00	—

Y# 362 3 YUAN
15.0000 g., 0.9000 Silver .4340 oz. ASW **Subject:** Ancient Chinese Coins

Date	Mintage	F	VF	XF	Unc	BU
1992 Proof	23,000	Value: 16.50				

Y# 363 3 YUAN
15.0000 g., 0.9000 Silver .4340 oz. ASW **Subject:** Ancient Chinese Paper

Date	Mintage	F	VF	XF	Unc	BU
1992 Proof	Est. 20,000	Value: 16.50				

Y# 403 3 YUAN
15.0000 g., 0.9000 Silver .4340 oz. ASW **Rev:** Chinese gods Fu, Lu and Shu **Note:** Similar to 500 Yuan, Y#407.

Date	Mintage	F	VF	XF	Unc	BU
1993 Proof	20,000	Value: 18.50				

Y# 733 3 YUAN
15.0000 g., 0.9000 Silver .4340 oz. ASW **Subject:** Yin and Yang Concept **Obv:** Great Wall tower, date below **Rev:** Chinese gods Fu, Lu and Shu with Yin Yang symbol, denomination below

Date	Mintage	F	VF	XF	Unc	BU
1995 Proof	—	Value: 16.50				

Y# 734 3 YUAN
15.0000 g., 0.9000 Silver .4340 oz. ASW **Subject:** Great Wall of China **Obv:** Great Wall view, date below **Rev:** Great Wall construction scene, denomination above

Date	Mintage	F	VF	XF	Unc	BU
1995 Proof	—	Value: 16.50				

Y# 1081 3 YUAN
15.0000 g., 0.9000 Silver 0.434 oz. ASW, 30 mm. **Subject:** World Wildlife Federation **Obv:** State emblem, date below **Rev:** Panda seated right eating leaves, denomination at right **Edge:** Reeded

Date	Mintage	F	VF	XF	Unc	BU
1997 Proof	50,000	Value: 17.00				

Y# 54 5 YUAN
22.2200 g., 0.9000 Silver .6430 oz. ASW **Obv:** Building **Rev:** Marco Polo bust, right, facing left, above ships, denomination below, dates at left of bust

Date	Mintage	F	VF	XF	Unc	BU
1983 Proof	15,000	Value: 55.00				

Y# 61 5 YUAN
8.4500 g., 0.8000 Silver .2173 oz. ASW **Series:** 1984 Summer and Winter Olympics **Obv:** Mural of athletes divides emblem and date **Rev:** High jumper, Olympic torch below, denomination at left

Date	Mintage	F	VF	XF	Unc	BU
1984 Proof	10,000	Value: 25.00				

Y# 68 5 YUAN
22.2200 g., 0.9000 Silver .6430 oz. ASW **Rev:** Soldier statue, 3/4 left, from archaeological discovery, denomination lower left

Date	Mintage	F	VF	XF	Unc	BU
1984 Proof	14,000	Value: 20.00				

Y# 69 5 YUAN
22.2200 g., 0.9000 Silver .6430 oz. ASW **Rev:** Soldier statue, right, from archaeological discovery, denomination lower right

Date	Mintage	F	VF	XF	Unc	BU
1984 Proof	14,000	Value: 20.00				

Y# 70 5 YUAN
22.2200 g., 0.9000 Silver .6430 oz. ASW **Rev:** Soldier statue from archaeological discovery, kneeling, right, denomination lower right

Date	Mintage	F	VF	XF	Unc	BU
1984 Proof	14,000	Value: 20.00				

Y# 71 5 YUAN
22.2200 g., 0.9000 Silver .6430 oz. ASW **Rev:** Soldier statue with horse, right, from archaeological discovery, denomination below

Date	Mintage	F	VF	XF	Unc	BU
1984 Proof	14,000	Value: 20.00				

Y# 90 5 YUAN
22.2200 g., 0.9000 Silver .6430 oz. ASW **Subject:** Founders of Chinese Culture **Obv:** State seal **Rev:** Lao-Tse riding water buffalo

Date	Mintage	F	VF	XF	Unc	BU
1985 Proof	8,175	Value: 30.00				

Y# 91 5 YUAN
22.2200 g., 0.9000 Silver .6430 oz. ASW **Subject:** Founders of Chinese Culture **Rev:** Qu Yuan, left, facing , denomination at right

Date	Mintage	F	VF	XF	Unc	BU
1985 Proof	8,175	Value: 30.00				

Y# 92 5 YUAN
22.2200 g., 0.9000 Silver .6430 oz. ASW **Subject:** Founders of Chinese Culture **Rev:** Sun Wu, right, denomination at left

Date	Mintage	F	VF	XF	Unc	BU
1985 Proof	8,175	Value: 30.00				

Y# 93 5 YUAN
22.2200 g., 0.9000 Silver .6430 oz. ASW **Subject:** Founders of Chinese Culture **Rev:** Chen Sheng and Wu Guang, denomination at left

Date	Mintage	F	VF	XF	Unc	BU
1985 Proof	8,175	Value: 30.00				

Y# 106 5 YUAN
22.2200 g., 0.9000 Silver .6430 oz. ASW **Subject:** Wildlife **Obv:** National emblem, date below **Rev:** Giant panda divides mountains and denomination

Date	Mintage	F	VF	XF	Unc	BU
1986	20,000	—	—	—	—	35.00
1986 Proof	20,000	Value: 50.00				

Y# 112 5 YUAN
18.6100 g., 0.9250 Silver .5535 oz. ASW **Subject:** Soccer **Obv:** National emblem, inscription and date below **Rev:** Soccer player, denomination lower right

Date	Mintage	F	VF	XF	Unc	BU
1986 Proof	8,500	Value: 35.00				

Y# 112a 5 YUAN
17.0600 g., 0.8000 Silver .4388 oz. ASW

Date	Mintage	F	VF	XF	Unc	BU
1986	1,000	—	—	—	—	125

Note: Satin finish

Y# 113 5 YUAN
22.2200 g., 0.9000 Silver .6367 oz. ASW **Subject:** Chinese Culture **Rev:** Cai Lun - papermaking, denomination upper right

Date	Mintage	F	VF	XF	Unc	BU
1986 Proof	9,675	Value: 25.00				

Y# 114 5 YUAN
22.2200 g., 0.9000 Silver .6367 oz. ASW **Subject:** Chinese Culture **Rev:** Zhang Heng, Astronomer, left, denomination lower right

Date	Mintage	F	VF	XF	Unc	BU
1986 Proof	9,675	Value: 25.00				

Y# 115 5 YUAN
22.2200 g., 0.9000 Silver .6367 oz. ASW **Subject:** Chinese Culture **Rev:** Zu Chong Zhi, Mathematician, denomination at right

Date	Mintage	F	VF	XF	Unc	BU
1986 Proof	9,675	Value: 25.00				

Y# 116 5 YUAN

22.2200 g., 0.9000 Silver .6367 oz. ASW **Subject:** Chinese Culture **Rev:** Sima Qian, Historian, denomination below

Date	Mintage	F	VF	XF	Unc	BU
1986 Proof	9,675	Value: 25.00				

Y# 119 5 YUAN

18.6100 g., 0.9250 Silver .5535 oz. ASW **Subject:** Year of Peace **Obv:** National emblem, date below **Rev:** Seated woman, doves in flight, denomination at left

Date	Mintage	F	VF	XF	Unc	BU
1986 Proof	1,350	Value: 175				

Y# 197 5 YUAN

18.6100 g., 0.9250 Silver .5535 oz. ASW **Subject:** Soccer **Obv:** National emblem above inscription and date **Rev:** Two players, denomination above right

Date	Mintage	F	VF	XF	Unc	BU
1986 Proof	10,000	Value: 35.00				

Y# 197a 5 YUAN

16.8300 g., 0.8000 Silver .4328 oz. ASW

Date	Mintage	F	VF	XF	Unc	BU
1986 Satin finish	1,000	—	—	—	—	150

Y# 132 5 YUAN

22.2200 g., 0.9000 Silver .6367 oz. ASW **Obv:** Great Wall, date below **Rev:** The Ship Empress of China, denomination below

Date	Mintage	F	VF	XF	Unc	BU
1986	75,000	—	—	—	—	35.00

Y# 135 5 YUAN

31.4700 g., 0.9000 Silver .9107 oz. ASW **Rev:** Poet Li Bai, left, denomination at right

Date	Mintage	F	VF	XF	Unc	BU
1987 Proof	4,000	Value: 27.50				

Y# 136 5 YUAN

31.4700 g., 0.9000 Silver .9107 oz. ASW **Rev:** Poet Du Fu walking right, denomination at left

Date	Mintage	F	VF	XF	Unc	BU
1987 Proof	4,000	Value: 27.50				

Y# 137 5 YUAN

31.4700 g., 0.9000 Silver .9107 oz. ASW **Subject:** Bridge Builder - Li Chun **Rev:** Li Chun, left, denomination lower left

Date	Mintage	F	VF	XF	Unc	BU
1987 Proof	4,000	Value: 27.50				

Y# 138 5 YUAN

31.4700 g., 0.9000 Silver .9107 oz. ASW **Rev:** Princess Chen Wen and Song Zan Gan Bu strolling to left, denomination at left

Date	Mintage	F	VF	XF	Unc	BU
1987 Proof	4,000	Value: 27.50				

Y# 129 5 YUAN

31.4700 g., 0 9000 Silver .9107 oz. ASW **Series:** Winter Olympics **Obv:** National emblem, date below **Rev:** Downhill skier with snowflakes, denomination at left

Date	Mintage	F	VF	XF	Unc	BU
1988 Proof	10,000	Value: 50.00				

Y# 130 5 YUAN

31.4700 g., 0.9000 Silver .9107 oz. ASW **Series:** Seoul 1988 - 24th Summer Olympic Games **Obv:** National emblem, date below **Rev:** Woman hurdler, denomination below

Date	Mintage	F	VF	XF	Unc	BU
1988 Proof	20,000	Value: 32.50				

Y# 160 5 YUAN

22.2200 g., 0.9000 Silver .6430 oz. ASW **Subject:** Military Hero of Song Dynasty - Yue Fei **Rev:** Yue Fei, left, denomination at lower left

Date	Mintage	F	VF	XF	Unc	BU
1988 Proof	13,000	Value: 25.00				

Y# 161 5 YUAN

22.2200 g., 0.9000 Silver .6430 oz. ASW **Subject:** Inventor of Movable-type Printing **Rev:** Bi Sheng, 3/4 facing, denomination at right

Date	Mintage	F	VF	XF	Unc	BU
1988 Proof	14,000	Value: 25.00				

Y# 162 5 YUAN

22.2200 g., 0.9000 Silver .6430 oz. ASW **Subject:** Song Dynasty Poet **Rev:** Su Shi, waving, 3/4 facing, denomination at right

Date	Mintage	F	VF	XF	Unc	BU
1988 Proof	9,500	Value: 25.00				

Y# 163 5 YUAN

22.2200 g., 0.9000 Silver .6430 oz. ASW **Subject:** Poetess of Song Dynasty **Rev:** Li Qingzhao, facing, looking left, denomination at left

Date	Mintage	F	VF	XF	Unc	BU
1988 Proof	13,000	Value: 25.00				

Y# 171 5 YUAN

27.0000 g., 0.9000 Silver .7812 oz. ASW **Series:** Olympics **Obv:** National emblem, date below **Rev:** Sailboat racing, denomination at left

Date	Mintage	F	VF	XF	Unc	BU
1988 Proof	20,000	Value: 30.00				

Y# 172 5 YUAN

27.0000 g., 0.9000 Silver .7812 oz. ASW **Series:** Seoul 1988 - 24th Summer Olympic Games **Subject:** Woman fencer, date at left, denomination below **Obv:** National emblem, date below

Date	Mintage	F	VF	XF	Unc	BU
1988 Proof	20,000	Value: 30.00				

Y# 213 5 YUAN

22.2200 g., 0.9000 Silver .6431 oz. ASW **Obv:** National emblem, date below **Rev:** Kublai Khan, Emperor

Date	Mintage	F	VF	XF	Unc	BU
1989 Proof	10,000	Value: 35.00				

Y# 214 5 YUAN

22.2200 g., 0.9000 Silver .6431 oz. ASW **Rev:** Guan Hanqing, Playwright, denomination at left

Date	Mintage	F	VF	XF	Unc	BU
1989 Proof	8,000	Value: 30.00				

Y# 215 5 YUAN

22.2200 g., 0.9000 Silver .6431 oz. ASW **Rev:** Guo Shoujing, Scientist, right, denomination at left

Date	Mintage	F	VF	XF	Unc	BU
1989 Proof	8,500	Value: 30.00				

Y# 216 5 YUAN

22.2200 g., 0.9000 Silver .6431 oz. ASW **Obv:** National emblem, date below **Rev:** Huang Dao-po, facing, loooking left, 13th century inventor of hydraulic spinning, denomination at right

Date	Mintage	F	VF	XF	Unc	BU
1989 Proof	8,000	Value: 30.00				

Y# 230 5 YUAN

22.2200 g., 0.9000 Silver .6431 oz. ASW **Series:** Save The Children Fund **Obv:** National emblem, date below **Rev:** Children and panda, denomination at right

Date	Mintage	F	VF	XF	Unc	BU
1989	20,000	—	—	—	—	30.00

Y# 243 5 YUAN

27.0000 g., 0.9250 Silver .8030 oz. ASW **Subject:** Soccer **Rev:** 2 soccer players, date upper left, denomination below

Date	Mintage	F	VF	XF	Unc	BU
1989 Proof	30,000	Value: 35.00				

Y# 187 5 YUAN

1.5552 g., 0.9990 Gold .0500 oz. AGW **Series:** Olympics **Note:** Similar to 100 Yuan, Y#191.

Date	Mintage	F	VF	XF	Unc	BU
1989	Est. 334,000	—	—	—	—	45.00
1989 Proof	8,000	Value: 55.00				

Y# 257 5 YUAN

15.0000 g., 0.9000 Silver .4341 oz. ASW **Subject:** Bronze Archaeological Finds **Rev:** Elephant pitcher, left, denomination below

Date	Mintage	F	VF	XF	Unc	BU
1990 Proof	5,000	Value: 30.00				

Y# 258 5 YUAN

15.0000 g., 0.9000 Silver .4341 oz. ASW **Subject:** Bronze Archaeological Finds **Rev:** Mythical creature

Date	Mintage	F	VF	XF	Unc	BU
1990 Proof	5,000	Value: 30.00				

Y# 259 5 YUAN

15.0000 g., 0.9000 Silver .4341 oz. ASW **Subject:** Bronze Archaeological Finds **Rev:** Rhinoceros, left, denomination below

Date	Mintage	F	VF	XF	Unc	BU
1990 Proof	5,000	Value: 30.00				

Y# 260 5 YUAN

15.0000 g., 0.9000 Silver .4341 oz. ASW **Subject:** Bronze Archaeological Finds **Rev:** Leopard, left, denomination below

Date	Mintage	F	VF	XF	Unc	BU
1990 Proof	5,000	Value: 30.00				

Y# 297 5 YUAN

27.0000 g., 0.9250 Silver .8030 oz. ASW **Subject:** Soccer **Obv:** National emblem, date below **Rev:** 2 soccer players, denomination below

Date	Mintage	F	VF	XF	Unc	BU
1990 Proof	30,000	Value: 30.00				

Y# 298 5 YUAN
27.0000 g., 0.9250 Silver .8030 oz. ASW **Subject:** Soccer **Rev:** Goalie, denomination at left

Date	Mintage	F	VF	XF	Unc	BU
1990 Proof	30,000	Value: 30.00				

Y# 302 5 YUAN
22.2200 g., 0.9000 Silver .6431 oz. ASW **Rev:** Luo Guanzhong, Historian, seated left, denomination at right

Date	Mintage	F	VF	XF	Unc	BU
1990 Proof	Est. 30,000	Value: 27.50				

Y# 303 5 YUAN
22.2200 g., 0.9000 Silver .6431 oz. ASW **Rev:** Li Zicheng, Revolutionary, right, denomination upper right

Date	Mintage	F	VF	XF	Unc	BU
1990 Proof	Est. 30,500	Value: 27.50				

Y# 304 5 YUAN
22.2200 g., 0.9000 Silver .6431 oz. ASW **Rev:** Li Shi Zhen, Herbalist, seated left, denomination upper left

Date	Mintage	F	VF	XF	Unc	BU
1990 Proof	Est. 30,500	Value: 27.50				

Y# 305 5 YUAN
22.2200 g., 0.9000 Silver .6431 oz. ASW **Rev:** Zheng He, Seafarer, looking left, denomination at left

Date	Mintage	F	VF	XF	Unc	BU
1990 Proof	Est. 30,500	Value: 27.50				

Y# 322 5 YUAN
22.2200 g., 0.9000 Silver .6431 oz. ASW **Rev:** Song Yingxing, Scientist

Date	Mintage	F	VF	XF	Unc	BU
1991 Proof	Est. 25,000	Value: 27.50				

Y# 323 5 YUAN
22.2200 g., 0.9000 Silver .6431 oz. ASW **Rev:** Cao Xueqin, Writer

Date	Mintage	F	VF	XF	Unc	BU
1991 Proof	Est. 25,000	Value: 27.50				

Y# 324 5 YUAN
22.2200 g., 0.9000 Silver .6431 oz. ASW **Rev:** Lin Zexu, high ranking official

Date	Mintage	F	VF	XF	Unc	BU
1991 Proof	Est. 25,000	Value: 27.50				

Y# 325 5 YUAN
22.2200 g., 0.9000 Silver .6431 oz. ASW **Rev:** Hong Xuquan, Revolutionary

Date	Mintage	F	VF	XF	Unc	BU
1991 Proof	Est. 25,000	Value: 27.50				

Y# 331 5 YUAN
22.2200 g., 0.9000 Silver .6431 oz. ASW **Subject:** Archaeological Finds **Obv:** Great Wall, date below **Rev:** Ancient ships and shipbuilding, denomination at left

Date	Mintage	F	VF	XF	Unc	BU
1992 Proof	15,000	Value: 27.50				

Y# 332 5 YUAN
22.2200 g., 0.9000 Silver .6431 oz. ASW **Subject:** First Compass **Obv:** Great Wall, date below **Rev:** Ancient compass, men on horseback, empty biga, denomination below

Date	Mintage	F	VF	XF	Unc	BU
1992 Proof	15,000	Value: 25.00				

Y# 333 5 YUAN
22.2200 g., 0.9000 Silver .6431 oz. ASW **Subject:** First Seismograph **Obv:** Great wall, date below **Rev:** First seismograph

Date	Mintage	F	VF	XF	Unc	BU
1992 Proof	15,000	Value: 25.00				

Y# 334 5 YUAN
22.2200 g., 0.9000 Silver .6431 oz. ASW **Subject:** Ancient Kite Flying **Obv:** Great Wall, date below **Rev:** Butterfly, kites in background, denomination below

Date	Mintage	F	VF	XF	Unc	BU
1992 Proof	15,000	Value: 25.00				

Y# 335 5 YUAN
22.2200 g., 0.9000 Silver .6431 oz. ASW **Obv:** Great Wall, date below **Rev:** Bronze Age metal working scene, denomination below **Edge:** Fine or coarse reeding

Date	Mintage	F	VF	XF	Unc	BU
1992 Proof	15,000	Value: 25.00				

Y# 548 5 YUAN
22.2200 g., 0.9000 Silver .6430 oz. ASW **Subject:** United Nations Environmental Protection **Obv:** National emblem, date below **Rev:** Woman drawing water from stream, denomination below

Date	Mintage	F	VF	XF	Unc	BU
1992 Proof	20,000	Value: 20.00				

Y# 549 5 YUAN
22.2200 g., 0.9000 Silver .6430 oz. ASW **Obv:** National emblem, date below **Rev:** Zheng Chenggong portrait, pointing right, denomination upper left

Date	Mintage	F	VF	XF	Unc	BU
1992 Proof	—	Value: 30.00				

Y# 550 5 YUAN
22.2200 g., 0.9000 Silver .6430 oz. ASW **Obv:** National emblem **Rev:** Cai Wenji, 177-254AD, Poet, kneeling left, denomination at right

Date	Mintage	F	VF	XF	Unc	BU
1992 Proof	Est. 7,000	Value: 30.00				

Y# 551 5 YUAN

22.2200 g., 0.9000 Silver .6430 oz. ASW **Obv:** National emblem **Rev:** Hua Mulan, soldier, 2nd Century Heroine on horseback, denomination upper right

Date	Mintage	F	VF	XF	Unc	BU
1992 Proof	Est. 7,000	Value: 30.00				

Y# 552 5 YUAN

22.2200 g., 0.9000 Silver .6430 oz. ASW **Obv:** National emblem **Rev:** Wang Zhaojun, Princess, Peacemaker, Sponsor of the Arts, denomination at right

Date	Mintage	F	VF	XF	Unc	BU
1992 Proof	Est. 7,000	Value: 30.00				

Y# 676 5 YUAN

15.0000 g., 0.9000 Silver .4350 oz. ASW **Subject:** Taiwan Scenery Series **Obv:** Great Wall **Rev:** Tall, narrow building, denomination below

Date	Mintage	F	VF	XF	Unc	BU
1992 Proof	2,000	Value: 37.50				

Y# 677 5 YUAN

15.0000 g., 0.9000 Silver .4350 oz. ASW **Rev:** Pondside building, denomination below

Date	Mintage	F	VF	XF	Unc	BU
1992 Proof	2,000	Value: 37.50				

Y# 678 5 YUAN

15.0000 g., 0.9000 Silver .4350 oz. ASW **Rev:** Hillside building, denomination below

Date	Mintage	F	VF	XF	Unc	BU
1992 Proof	2,000	Value: 37.50				

Y# 679 5 YUAN

15.0000 g., 0.9000 Silver .4350 oz. ASW **Rev:** 3 buildings joined by bridges, denomination below

Date	Mintage	F	VF	XF	Unc	BU
1992 Proof	2,000	Value: 37.50				

Y# 750 5 YUAN

15.0000 g., 0.9000 Silver .4340 oz. ASW **Subject:** Archaeological Finds **Obv:** National emblem **Rev:** Resting deer with long antlers

Date	Mintage	F	VF	XF	Unc	BU
1992 Proof	3,000	Value: 35.00				

Y# 393 5 YUAN

15.0000 g., 0.9000 Silver .4341 oz. ASW **Obv:** National emblem, date below **Rev:** Marco Polo bust, looking right, buildings and dates at right, denomination below

Date	Mintage	F	VF	XF	Unc	BU
1992 Proof	12,000	Value: 25.00				

Y# 751 5 YUAN

15.0000 g., 0.9000 Silver .4340 oz. ASW **Subject:** Archeological Finds **Obv:** National emblem **Rev:** Panther sculpture

Date	Mintage	F	VF	XF	Unc	BU
1992 Proof	3,000	Value: 35.00				

Y# 752 5 YUAN

15.0000 g., 0.9000 Silver .4340 oz. ASW **Subject:** Archaeological Finds **Obv:** National emblem **Rev:** Bighorn sheep

Date	Mintage	F	VF	XF	Unc	BU
1992 Proof	3,000	Value: 35.00				

Y# 753 5 YUAN

15.0000 g., 0.9000 Silver .4340 oz. ASW **Subject:** Archaeological Finds **Obv:** National emblem **Rev:** Changzin court lantern

Date	Mintage	F	VF	XF	Unc	BU
1992 Proof	3,000	Value: 35.00				

Y# 553 5 YUAN

22.2200 g., 0.9000 Silver .6430 oz. ASW **Obv:** National emblem **Rev:** Xiao Zhuo, 953-1009AD, Strategist, left, denomination below

Date	Mintage	F	VF	XF	Unc	BU
1993 Proof	Est. 7,000	Value: 28.00				

Y# 558 5 YUAN

22.2200 g., 0.9000 Silver .6430 oz. ASW **Subject:** Mathematical Definition of Zero **Obv:** Great Wall, date below **Rev:** Mathematicians, abacus, denomination lower right

Date	Mintage	F	VF	XF	Unc	BU
1993 Proof	15,000	Value: 22.00				

Y# 559 5 YUAN

22.2200 g., 0.9000 Silver .6430 oz. ASW **Subject:** Invention of the Stirrup **Obv:** Great Wall **Rev:** Early polo game, denomination below

Date	Mintage	F	VF	XF	Unc	BU
1993 Proof	15,000	Value: 22.00				

Y# 560 5 YUAN

22.2200 g., 0.9000 Silver .6430 oz. ASW **Subject:** The Terracotta Army **Obv:** Great Wall, date below **Rev:** The unearthing of the terracotta figurines, denomination at right

Date	Mintage	F	VF	XF	Unc	BU
1993 Proof	15,000	Value: 22.00				

Y# 359 5 YUAN

Copper **Obv:** National emblem, date below **Obv. Legend:** ZHONGCHUA RENMIN GONGHEFUO **Rev:** 2 Pandas eating bamboo, denomination below

Date	Mintage	F	VF	XF	Unc	BU
1993	2,000,000	—	—	—	15.00	20.00

Y# 377 5 YUAN

22.2200 g., 0.9000 Silver .6431 oz. ASW **Subject:** Chin-Yin Yang **Rev:** Two figures, one standing and one kneeling, denomination below

Date	Mintage	F	VF	XF	Unc	BU
1993 Proof	15,000	Value: 35.00				

Y# 400 5 YUAN

22.2200 g., 0.9000 Silver .6431 oz. ASW **Subject:** Invention of the Umbrella **Obv:** Great Wall, date below **Rev:** Figures with umbrellas above umbrella makers, denomination at right

Date	Mintage	F	VF	XF	Unc	BU
1993 Proof	15,000	Value: 20.00				

Y# 441 5 YUAN

15.0000 g., 0.9000 Silver .4341 oz. ASW **Obv:** Great Wall **Rev:** Taiwan Temple Buddha Statue

Date	Mintage	F	VF	XF	Unc	BU
1993 Proof	2,000	Value: 27.50				

Y# 442 5 YUAN

15.0000 g., 0.9000 Silver .4341 oz. ASW **Subject:** Taiwan Temple **Obv:** Great Wall **Rev:** Large temple

Date	Mintage	F	VF	XF	Unc	BU
1993 Proof	2,000	Value: 27.50				

Y# 443 5 YUAN

15.0000 g., 0.9000 Silver .4341 oz. ASW **Subject:** Taiwan Temple **Obv:** Great Wall **Rev:** Small temple

Date	Mintage	F	VF	XF	Unc	BU
1993 Proof	2,000	Value: 27.50				

Y# 444 5 YUAN

15.0000 g., 0.9000 Silver .4341 oz. ASW **Subject:** Taiwan Temple **Obv:** Great Wall **Rev:** Tower temple

Date	Mintage	F	VF	XF	Unc	BU
1993 Proof	2,000	Value: 27.50				

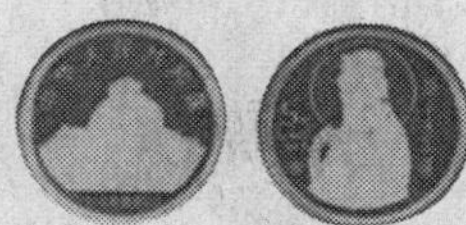

Y# 498 5 YUAN

1.5552 g., 0.9990 Gold .0500 oz. AGW **Subject:** Goddess of Mercy **Obv:** Great Wall, date below **Rev:** Goddess left, denomination at right

Date	Mintage	F	VF	XF	Unc	BU
1993 Prooflike	40,000	—	—	—	—	45.00

Y# 500 5 YUAN

1.5552 g., 0.9990 Gold .0500 oz. AGW **Rev:** Goddess Kuan Yin - Seated in Flowers

Date	Mintage	F	VF	XF	Unc	BU
1993 Proof	1,000	Value: 65.00				

Y# 534 5 YUAN

22.2200 g., 0.9000 Silver .6431 oz. ASW **Obv:** National emblem **Rev:** Chou En-Lai, facing, denomination upper left

Date	Mintage	F	VF	XF	Unc	BU
1993 Proof	Est. 25,000	Value: 30.00				

Y# 535 5 YUAN

22.2200 g., 0.9000 Silver .6431 oz. ASW **Obv:** National emblem **Rev:** Liu Shaoqi, 3/4 left, denomination at left

Date	Mintage	F	VF	XF	Unc	BU
1993 Proof	Est. 25,000	Value: 30.00				

Y# 536 5 YUAN

22.2200 g., 0.9000 Silver .6431 oz. ASW **Obv:** National emblem **Rev:** Chu Teh, 3/4 facing, arm raised, denomination upper right

Date	Mintage	F	VF	XF	Unc	BU
1993 Proof	Est. 25,000	Value: 30.00				

Y# 537 5 YUAN

22.2200 g., 0.9000 Silver .6431 oz. ASW **Obv:** National emblem **Rev:** Li Da-Chao, facing, denomination at right

Date	Mintage	F	VF	XF	Unc	BU
1993 Proof	Est. 25,000	Value: 30.00				

Y# 768 5 YUAN

15.0000 g., 0.9000 Silver .4340 oz. ASW **Subject:** Archeological Finds **Obv:** National emblem **Rev:** Ox lantern

Date	Mintage	F	VF	XF	Unc	BU
1993 Proof	2,000	Value: 37.50				

Y# 769 5 YUAN

15.0000 g., 0.9000 Silver .4340 oz. ASW **Subject:** Archeological Finds **Obv:** National emblem **Rev:** Human figure lantern

Date	Mintage	F	VF	XF	Unc	BU
1993 Proof	2,000	Value: 37.50				

Y# 770 5 YUAN

15.0000 g., 0.9000 Silver .4340 oz. ASW **Subject:** Archeological Finds **Obv:** National emblem **Rev:** Horse statue

Date	Mintage	F	VF	XF	Unc	BU
1993 Proof	2,000	Value: 37.50				

Y# 771 5 YUAN

15.0000 g., 0.9000 Silver .4340 oz. ASW **Subject:** Archeological Finds **Obv:** National emblem **Rev:** Pig statue

Date	Mintage	F	VF	XF	Unc	BU
1993 Proof	2,000	Value: 37.50				

Y# 773 5 YUAN

1.5552 g., 0.9990 Gold .0500 oz. AGW **Subject:** Homeland Scenery **Obv:** Great Wall **Rev:** Temple at Mount Song

Date	Mintage	F	VF	XF	Unc	BU
1993 Proof	8,888	Value: 45.00				

Y# 419 5 YUAN

1.5552 g., 0.9990 Gold .0500 oz. AGW **Obv:** Crowned figure on horseback, date lower right **Rev:** Unicorn, denomination at left

Date	Mintage	F	VF	XF	Unc	BU
1994 Proof	31,000	Value: 65.00				

Y# 506 5 YUAN

15.5517 g., 0.9990 Silver .5000 oz. ASW **Rev:** Goddess Kuan Yin - with child, denomination at left

Date	Mintage	F	VF	XF	Unc	BU
1994 Proof	3,000	Value: 28.50				

Y# 507 5 YUAN

15.5517 g., 0.9990 Silver .5000 oz. ASW **Rev:** Goddess Kuan Yin - with bottle

Date	Mintage	F	VF	XF	Unc	BU
1994 Proof	3,000	Value: 28.50				

Y# 508 5 YUAN

15.5517 g., 0.9990 Silver .5000 oz. ASW **Rev:** Goddess Kuan Yin - standing, denomination at right

Date	Mintage	F	VF	XF	Unc	BU
1994 Proof	3,000	Value: 28.50				

Y# 509 5 YUAN

15.5517 g., 0.9990 Silver .5000 oz. ASW **Rev:** Goddess Kuan Yin - seated

Date	Mintage	F	VF	XF	Unc	BU
1994 Proof	3,000	Value: 28.50				

Y# 616 5 YUAN

22.2200 g., 0.9000 Silver .6430 oz. ASW **Subject:** Oriental Inventions **Obv:** Great Wall, date below **Rev:** First tuned bells, denomination at left

Date	Mintage	F	VF	XF	Unc	BU
1994 Proof	15,000	Value: 18.00				

Y# 617 5 YUAN

22.2200 g., 0.9000 Silver .6430 oz. ASW **Subject:** Oriental Inventions **Obv:** Great Wall, date below **Rev:** First silken fabric, denomination lower right

Date	Mintage	F	VF	XF	Unc	BU
1994 Proof	15,000	Value: 20.00				

Y# 618 5 YUAN
22.2200 g., 0.9000 Silver .6430 oz. ASW **Subject:** Oriental Invention **Obv:** Great Wall, date below **Rev:** First records of comets, denomination at right

Date	Mintage	F	VF	XF	Unc	BU
1994 Proof	15,000	Value: 20.00				

Y# 619 5 YUAN
22.2200 g., 0.9000 Silver .6430 oz. ASW **Subject:** Oriental Inventions **Obv:** Great Wall, date below **Rev:** First masts for sailing, denomination lower right

Date	Mintage	F	VF	XF	Unc	BU
1994 Proof	15,000	Value: 20.00				

Y# 620 5 YUAN
22.2200 g., 0.9000 Silver .6430 oz. ASW **Subject:** Oriental Inventions **Obv:** Great Wall, date below **Rev:** First chain pumps used to draw water, denomination below

Date	Mintage	F	VF	XF	Unc	BU
1994 Proof	15,000	Value: 18.00				

Y# 481 5 YUAN
22.2200 g., 0.9000 Silver .6430 oz. ASW **Obv:** Temple, date below **Rev:** Sea goddess bust, 3/4 left, denomination at right

Date	Mintage	F	VF	XF	Unc	BU
1995 Proof	8,000,000	Value: 27.50				

Y# 516 5 YUAN
22.2200 g., 0.9000 Silver .6430 oz. ASW **Obv:** Temple, date below **Rev:** Goddess Kuan Yin, facing, - with Lotus flower, denomination at left

Date	Mintage	F	VF	XF	Unc	BU
1995 Proof	3,000	Value: 28.50				

Y# 517 5 YUAN
22.2200 g., 0.9000 Silver .6430 oz. ASW **Obv:** Temple, date below **Rev:** Goddess Kuan Yin - with wheel, 3/4 left, denomination at right

Date	Mintage	F	VF	XF	Unc	BU
1995 Proof	3,000	Value: 28.50				

Y# 518 5 YUAN
22.2200 g., 0.9000 Silver .6430 oz. ASW **Obv:** Temple, date below **Rev:** Goddess Kuan Yin, 3/4 left, - with scepter, denomination at left

Date	Mintage	F	VF	XF	Unc	BU
1995 Proof	3,000	Value: 28.50				

Y# 519 5 YUAN
22.2200 g., 0.9000 Silver .6430 oz. ASW **Obv:** Temple, date below **Rev:** Goddess Kuan Yin - with bowl, 3/4 left, denomination at right

Date	Mintage	F	VF	XF	Unc	BU
1995 Proof	3,000	Value: 28.50				

Y# 547 5 YUAN
Bronze **Obv:** National emblem, date below **Obv. Legend:** ZHONGHUA RENMIN GONGHEGUO **Rev:** Golden monkey, denomination at right

Date	Mintage	F	VF	XF	Unc	BU
1995	—	—	—	—	12.00	15.00

Y# 600 5 YUAN
22.2200 g., 0.9000 Silver .6430 oz. ASW **Rev:** 2 men leading camel, denomination below

Date	Mintage	F	VF	XF	Unc	BU
1995 Proof	15,000	Value: 35.00				

Y# 601 5 YUAN
22.2200 g., 0.9000 Silver .6430 oz. ASW **Rev:** Dancer, denomination lower right

Date	Mintage	F	VF	XF	Unc	BU
1995 Proof	15,000	Value: 27.50				

Y# 602 5 YUAN
22.2200 g., 0.9000 Silver .6430 oz. ASW **Rev:** Silk merchant and customer, denomination at right

Date	Mintage	F	VF	XF	Unc	BU
1995 Proof	15,000	Value: 25.00				

Y# 603 5 YUAN
22.2200 g., 0.9000 Silver .6430 oz. ASW **Rev:** Silk spinner, denomination at right

Date	Mintage	F	VF	XF	Unc	BU
1995 Proof	Est. 15,000	Value: 25.00				

Y# 627 5 YUAN
22.2200 g., 0.9000 Silver .6430 oz. ASW **Subject:** Oriental Inventions **Obv:** Great Wall, date below **Rev:** Soldiers with cannon and gunpowder, denomination lower left

Date	Mintage	F	VF	XF	Unc	BU
1995 Proof	15,000	Value: 25.00				

Y# 628 5 YUAN
22.2200 g., 0.9000 Silver .6430 oz. ASW **Subject:** Oriental Inventions **Obv:** Great Wall, date below **Rev:** Individual block printing, denomination at right

Date	Mintage	F	VF	XF	Unc	BU
1995 Proof	15,000	Value: 25.00				

Y# 629 5 YUAN
20.0000 g., 0.9000 Silver, 36 mm. **Subject:** Oriental Inventions - Chess **Obv:** The Great Wall, date below **Rev:** Chess players, denomination upper right

Date	Mintage	F	VF	XF	Unc	BU
1995 Proof	—	Value: 25.00				

Y# 630 5 YUAN
22.2200 g., 0.9000 Silver .6430 oz. ASW **Subject:** Oriental Inventions **Obv:** Great Wall, date below **Rev:** Potter, denomination lower left

Date	Mintage	F	VF	XF	Unc	BU
1995 Proof	15,000	Value: 25.00				

Y# 631 5 YUAN
22.2200 g., 0.9000 Silver .6430 oz. ASW **Subject:** Oriental Inventions **Obv:** Great Wall **Rev:** Teacher with chart of human body

Date	Mintage	F	VF	XF	Unc	BU
1995 Proof	15,000	Value: 25.00				

Y# 736 5 YUAN
1.5552 g., 0.9990 Gold .0500 oz. AGW **Obv:** Eastern unicorn rearing, left, date below **Rev:** Western unicorn with offspring, denomination at left

Date	Mintage	F	VF	XF	Unc	BU
1995 Proof	20,000	Value: 95.00				

Y# 794 5 YUAN
22.2223 g., 0.9000 Silver .6430 oz. ASW **Subject:** Chinese Culture Series **Obv:** Great Wall seen through arch, date below **Rev:** Pagoda of Six Harmonies, denomination at left

Date	Mintage	F	VF	XF	Unc	BU
1995 Proof	20,000	Value: 25.00				

Y# 795 5 YUAN
22.2223 g., 0.9000 Silver .6430 oz. ASW **Subject:** Chinese Culture Series **Obv:** Great Wall seen through arch, date below **Rev:** Mencius seated at table, denomination below

Date	Mintage	F	VF	XF	Unc	BU
1995 Proof	20,000	Value: 25.00				

Y# 796 5 YUAN
22.2223 g., 0.9000 Silver .6430 oz. ASW **Subject:** Chinese Culture Series **Obv:** Great Wall seen through arch, date below **Rev:** Tang Taizong seated, denomination at left

Date	Mintage	F	VF	XF	Unc	BU
1995 Proof	20,000	Value: 25.00				

Y# 797 5 YUAN
22.2223 g., 0.9000 Silver .6430 oz. ASW **Subject:** Chinese Culture Series **Obv:** Great Wall seen through arch **Rev:** Lion dance

Date	Mintage	F	VF	XF	Unc	BU
1995 Proof	20,000	Value: 25.00				

Y# 798 5 YUAN
22.2223 g., 0.9000 Silver .6430 oz. ASW **Subject:** Chinese Culture Series **Obv:** Great Wall seen through arch, date below **Rev:** Female opera role, denomination upper right

Date	Mintage	F	VF	XF	Unc	BU
1995 Proof	20,000	Value: 25.00				

Y# 604 5 YUAN
22.2200 g., 0.9000 Silver .6430 oz. ASW **Rev:** Caravan route market scene, denomination below

Date	Mintage	F	VF	XF	Unc	BU
1996 Proof	15,000	Value: 25.00				

Y# 605 5 YUAN
22.2200 g., 0.9000 Silver .6430 oz. ASW **Rev:** Fairy above Magao Sanctuary, denomination upper right

Date	Mintage	F	VF	XF	Unc	BU
1996 Proof	15,000	Value: 25.00				

Y# 606 5 YUAN
22.2200 g., 0.9000 Silver .6430 oz. ASW **Rev:** Various historic sculptures, denomination lower left

Date	Mintage	F	VF	XF	Unc	BU
1996 Proof	15,000	Value: 25.00				

Y# 607 5 YUAN
22.2200 g., 0.9000 Silver .6430 oz. ASW **Rev:** Musicians on camel, denomination at left

Date	Mintage	F	VF	XF	Unc	BU
1996 Proof	15,000	Value: 25.00				

Y# 729 5 YUAN
Bronze **Obv:** National emblem, date below **Obv. Legend:** ZONGHUA RENMIN GONGHEGUO **Rev:** Tiger, denomination at left

Date	Mintage	F	VF	XF	Unc	BU
1996	—	—	—	—	12.00	15.00

Y# 730 5 YUAN
Bronze **Obv:** National emblem, date below **Rev:** Pair of baiji dolphins, denomination above

Date	Mintage	F	VF	XF	Unc	BU
1996	—	—	—	—	12.00	15.00

Y# 740 5 YUAN
1.5552 g., 0.9990 Gold .0500 oz. AGW **Obv:** Eastern unicorn, date below **Rev:** Head of western unicorn, right, denomination at right

Date	Mintage	F	VF	XF	Unc	BU
1996	—	—	—	—	—	50.00
1996 Proof	5,000	Value: 130				

Y# 871 5 YUAN
22.2223 g., 0.9000 Silver .6430 oz. ASW **Subject:** Chinese Inventions and Discoveries Series **Obv:** Great Wall, date below **Rev:** Three musicians, denomination at left

Date	Mintage	F	VF	XF	Unc	BU
1996 Proof	15,000	Value: 30.00				

Y# 872 5 YUAN
22.2223 g., 0.9000 Silver .6430 oz. ASW **Subject:** Chinese Inventions and Discoveries Series **Obv:** Great Wall, date below **Rev:** Suspension bridge, denomination at right

Date	Mintage	F	VF	XF	Unc	BU
1996 Proof	15,000	Value: 30.00				

Y# 873 5 YUAN
22.2223 g., 0.9000 Silver .6430 oz. ASW **Subject:** Chinese Inventions and Discoveries Series **Obv:** Great Wall **Rev:** Astronomical clock, denomination at right

Date	Mintage	F	VF	XF	Unc	BU
1996 Proof	15,000	Value: 30.00				

Y# 874 5 YUAN
22.2223 g., 0.9000 Silver .6430 oz. ASW **Subject:** Chinese Inventions and Discoveries Series **Obv:** Great Wall **Rev:** Sailing ship, denomination at right

Date	Mintage	F	VF	XF	Unc	BU
1996 Proof	15,000	Value: 30.00				

Y# 875 5 YUAN
22.2223 g., 0.9000 Silver .6430 oz. ASW **Subject:** Chinese Inventions and Discoveries Series **Obv:** Great Wall **Rev:** Horse cart, denomination below

Date	Mintage	F	VF	XF	Unc	BU
1996 Proof	15,000	Value: 30.00				

Y# 883 5 YUAN
15.5517 g., 0.9990 Silver .5000 oz. ASW **Obv:** Eastern unicorn, date below **Rev:** Western unicorn rearing, left, denomination lower left

Date	Mintage	F	VF	XF	Unc	BU
1996	—	—	—	—	—	25.00

Y# 885 5 YUAN
1.5552 g., 0.9990 Gold .0500 oz. AGW **Subject:** Goddess Guanyin **Obv:** Temple, date below **Rev:** Goddess holding flower, denomination at left

Date	Mintage	F	VF	XF	Unc	BU
1996 Proof	5,000	Value: 45.00				

Y# 1196 5 YUAN
15.5500 g., 0.9990 Silver 0.4994 oz. ASW, 33 mm. **Obv:** Temple, date below **Rev:** Goddess holding vase and twig, denomination at right **Edge:** Reeded

Date	Mintage	F	VF	XF	Unc	BU
1996 Proof	5,000	Value: 35.00				

Y# 1197 5 YUAN
1.5550 g., 0.9990 Gold 0.0499 oz. AGW, 14 mm. **Subject:** Goddess Guanyin **Obv:** Temple **Rev:** Goddess holding vase and twig **Edge:** Reeded

Date	Mintage	F	VF	XF	Unc	BU
1996 Proof	35,000	Value: 42.50				

Y# 1198 5 YUAN
1.5550 g., 0.9990 Gold 0.0499 oz. AGW, 14 mm. **Obv:** Ornamental column **Rev:** Child holding a carp **Edge:** Reeded

Date	Mintage	F	VF	XF	Unc	BU
1997	100,000	—	—	—	—	42.50

Y# 1186 5 YUAN
22.0000 g., 0.9000 Silver 0.6366 oz. ASW, 36 mm. **Obv:** Great Wall view, date below **Rev:** Man with flag, denomination lower left **Edge:** Reeded

Date	Mintage	F	VF	XF	Unc	BU
1997(y)	35,000	—	—	—	22.50	—

Y# 1187 5 YUAN
22.0000 g., 0.9000 Silver 0.6366 oz. ASW, 36 mm. **Obv:** Great Wall **Rev:** Man with extended open hand, denomination at right **Edge:** Reeded

Date	Mintage	F	VF	XF	Unc	BU
1997(y)	35,000	—	—	—	22.50	—

Y# 1188 5 YUAN
22.0000 g., 0.9000 Silver 0.6366 oz. ASW, 36 mm. **Obv:** Great Wall **Rev:** Astronomer, denomination at left **Edge:** Reeded

Date	Mintage	F	VF	XF	Unc	BU
1997(y)	35,000	—	—	—	22.50	—

Y# 1189 5 YUAN
22.0000 g., 0.9000 Silver 0.6366 oz. ASW, 36 mm. **Obv:** Great Wall **Rev:** Gymnast, denomination at right **Edge:** Reeded

Date	Mintage	F	VF	XF	Unc	BU
1997(y)	35,000	—	—	—	22.50	—

Y# 1190 5 YUAN

22.0000 g., 0.9000 Silver 0.6366 oz. ASW, 36 mm. **Obv:** Great Wall **Rev:** Building, denomination below **Edge:** Reeded

Date	Mintage	F	VF	XF	Unc	BU
1997(y)	35,000	—	—	—	22.50	—

Y# 916.1 5 YUAN

15.5517 g., 0.9990 Silver .5000 oz. ASW **Subject:** Traditional Chinese Mascot **Obv:** Ornamental column **Rev:** Child holding carp

Date	Mintage	F	VF	XF	Unc	BU
1997	80,000	—	—	—	22.00	—

Y# 916.2 5 YUAN

15.5500 g., 0.9990 Silver 0.4994 oz. ASW, 36 mm. **Obv:** Ornamental column **Rev:** Multicolor child holding carp **Edge:** Reeded

Date	Mintage	F	VF	XF	Unc	BU
1997 Proof	100,000	Value: 35.00				

Y# 982 5 YUAN

1.5552 g., 0.9990 Gold .0500 oz. AGW **Subject:** Pu Tuo Mountain

Date	Mintage	F	VF	XF	Unc	BU
1997	35,000	—	—	—	—	42.50

Y# 731 5 YUAN

Bronze **Obv:** National emblem, date below **Obv. Legend:** ZHONGHUA RENMIN GONGHEGUO **Rev:** Crested Ibis, left, denomination at left

Date	Mintage	F	VF	XF	Unc	BU
1997	—	—	—	—	14.50	17.50

Y# 732 5 YUAN

Bronze **Obv:** National emblem, date below **Obv. Legend:** ZHONGHUA RENMIN GONGHEGUO **Rev:** Red-crowned Crane, right, denomination at right

Date	Mintage	F	VF	XF	Unc	BU
1997	—	—	—	—	14.50	17.50

Y# 911 5 YUAN

15.5517 g., 0.9990 Silver .5000 oz. ASW **Obv:** 2 Eastern unicorns, date below **Rev:** 1 Western unicorn, denomination below

Date	Mintage	F	VF	XF	Unc	BU
1997 Proof	—	Value: 20.00				

Y# 940 5 YUAN

Bronze **Subject:** Brown-eared Pheasant **Obv:** National emblem, date below **Rev:** Pheasant, left, denomination above

Date	Mintage	F	VF	XF	Unc	BU
1998	—	—	—	—	12.50	17.50

Y# 941 5 YUAN

Bronze **Subject:** Chinese Alligator **Obv:** National emblem, date below **Obv. Legend:** ZHONGHUA RENMIN GONGHEGUO **Rev:** Alligator, right, denomination above

Date	Mintage	F	VF	XF	Unc	BU
1998	—	—	—	—	15.00	20.00

Y# 1129 5 YUAN

15.6000 g., 0.9990 Silver 0.501 oz. ASW, 33 mm. **Obv:** Radiant winged pillar monument above flowers **Rev:** Child holding vase, elephant at left **Edge:** Reeded

Date	Mintage	F	VF	XF	Unc	BU
1998	80,000	—	—	—	22.00	—

Y# 1130 5 YUAN

15.6000 g., 0.9990 Silver 0.501 oz. ASW, 36 mm. **Obv:** Radiant winged pillar monument above flowers **Rev:** Multicolor child holding vase, elephant at left **Edge:** Reeded

Date	Mintage	F	VF	XF	Unc	BU
1998 Proof	100,000	Value: 35.00				

Y# 1053 5 YUAN

13.3000 g., Bronze, 31.9 mm. **Obv:** State emblem **Rev:** Butterfly **Edge:** Reeded and plain sections

Date	Mintage	F	VF	XF	Unc	BU
1999	—	—	—	—	12.00	15.00

Y# 1054 5 YUAN

13.3000 g., Bronze, 31.9 mm. **Obv:** State emblem **Rev:** Sturgeon **Edge:** Plain and reeded sections

Date	Mintage	F	VF	XF	Unc	BU
1999	—	—	—	—	12.00	14.50

Y# 55 10 YUAN

1.2000 g., 0.9000 Gold .0347 oz. AGW **Obv:** Building, denomination at right **Rev:** Marco Polo bust, left, dates below

Date	Mintage	F	VF	XF	Unc	BU
1983 Proof	50,000	Value: 55.00				

Y# 62 10 YUAN

16.8100 g., 0.9250 Silver .5000 oz. ASW **Subject:** Women's Decade **Obv:** National emblem, denomination below **Rev:** Heads of three women, dates upper right

Date	Mintage	F	VF	XF	Unc	BU
ND(1984) Proof	4,000	Value: 50.00				

Y# 63 10 YUAN

16.8100 g., 0.9250 Silver .5000 oz. ASW **Series:** Los Angeles 1984 - 23rd Summer Olympic Games **Obv:** National emblem, date below **Rev:** Volleyball player serving, denomination at left

Date	Mintage	F	VF	XF	Unc	BU
1984	1,000	—	—	—	70.00	—

Y# 63a 10 YUAN

17.0600 g., 0.8000 Silver .4388 oz. ASW

Date	Mintage	F	VF	XF	Unc	BU
1984 Proof	4,500	Value: 30.00				

Y# 64 10 YUAN

17.0600 g., 0.8000 Silver .4388 oz. ASW **Series:** Olympics **Obv:** National emblem, date below **Rev:** Speed skater, denomination lower right

Date	Mintage	F	VF	XF	Unc	BU
1984 Proof	6,000	Value: 40.00				

Y# 88 10 YUAN

27.0000 g., 0.9000 Silver .7813 oz. ASW **Subject:** 110th Anniversary - Birth of Dr. Cheng Jiageng **Obv:** Jie Mei School **Rev:** Bust, facing, divides dates

Date	Mintage	F	VF	XF	Unc	BU
1984 Proof	6,000	Value: 75.00				

Y# 97 10 YUAN

34.5600 g., 0.9000 Silver 1.0000 oz. ASW **Subject:** 20th Anniversary - Tibet Autonomous Region **Obv:** National emblem, date below **Rev:** Potala Palace, denomination upper right

Date	Mintage	F	VF	XF	Unc	BU
1985 Proof	3,000	Value: 50.00				

Y# 110 10 YUAN

34.5600 g., 0.9000 Silver 1.0000 oz. ASW **Subject:** 30th Anniversary - Xinjiang Autonomous Region **Obv:** Building, date below **Rev:** Woman carrying tray, animals below, denomination at right, circle surrounds

Date	Mintage	F	VF	XF	Unc	BU
1985 Proof	1,400	Value: 60.00				

Y# 111 10 YUAN

29.1900 g., 0.9250 Silver .8682 oz. ASW **Subject:** 120th Anniversary - Birth of Sun Yat-sen **Obv:** Bust, facing, divides dates, date below **Rev:** Sun Yat-sen's residence, denomination below

Date	Mintage	F	VF	XF	Unc	BU
1986 Proof	8,450	Value: 50.00				

Y# 165 10 YUAN

27.0000 g., 0.9250 Silver .5056 oz. ASW **Subject:** Rare Animal Protection **Rev:** Crested Ibis, right, denomination at right

Date	Mintage	F	VF	XF	Unc	BU
1988 Proof	35,000	Value: 35.00				

Y# 166 10 YUAN

27.0000 g., 0.9250 Silver .5056 oz. ASW **Subject:** Rare Animal Protection **Rev:** Baiji dolphins, denomination above

Date	Mintage	F	VF	XF	Unc	BU
1988 Proof	35,000	Value: 35.00				

Y# 177 10 YUAN

15.0000 g., 0.8500 Silver .4100 oz. ASW **Subject:** Year of the Snake **Obv:** Shanhaiguan City Gate, date below **Rev:** Snake left, denomination below

Date	Mintage	F	VF	XF	Unc	BU
1989 Proof	15,000	Value: 40.00				

Y# 199 10 YUAN

27.0000 g., 0.9250 Silver .8031 oz. ASW **Subject:** 1990 Asian Games **Obv:** Monument, stadium, Great Wall segment and sun **Rev:** Weight lifter, left, denomination at left

Date	Mintage	F	VF	XF	Unc	BU
1989 Proof	20,000	Value: 30.00				

Y# 200 10 YUAN

27.0000 g., 0.9250 Silver .8031 oz. ASW **Subject:** 11th Asian Games - Beijing 1990 **Obv:** Monument, stadium, Great Wall segment and sun **Rev:** Platform diver, denomination at left

Date	Mintage	F	VF	XF	Unc	BU
1989 Proof	20,000	Value: 30.00				

Y# 201 10 YUAN

27.0000 g., 0.9250 Silver .8031 oz. ASW **Subject:** 1990 Asian Games **Obv:** Monument, stadium, Great Wall segment and sun **Rev:** Tennis player, denomination above

Date	Mintage	F	VF	XF	Unc	BU
1989 Proof	20,000	Value: 30.00				

Y# 202 10 YUAN

27.0000 g., 0.9250 Silver .8031 oz. ASW **Subject:** 1990 Asian Games **Obv:** Monument, stadium, Great Wall segment and sun **Rev:** Bicyclist, denomination lower right

Date	Mintage	F	VF	XF	Unc	BU
1989 Proof	20,000	Value: 30.00				

Y# 235 10 YUAN

27.0000 g., 0.9250 Silver .8031 oz. ASW **Subject:** 40th Anniversary of Peoples Republic **Rev:** Tiananmen Square, birds flying above, denomination at right

Date	Mintage	F	VF	XF	Unc	BU
ND(1989) Proof	5,000	Value: 40.00				

Y# 236 10 YUAN

27.0000 g., 0.9250 Silver .8031 oz. ASW **Subject:** 40th Anniversary of Peoples Republic **Obv:** National emblem divides dates **Rev:** Great Wall with eagles in flight above, denomination at left

Date	Mintage	F	VF	XF	Unc	BU
ND(1989) Proof	5,000	Value: 40.00				

Y# 248 10 YUAN

27.0000 g., 0.9250 Silver .8031 oz. ASW **Subject:** Endangered Animals **Obv:** National emblem, date below **Rev:** Skia deer, denomination at left

Date	Mintage	F	VF	XF	Unc	BU
1989 Proof	10,000	Value: 35.00				

Y# 249 10 YUAN

27.0000 g., 0.9250 Silver .8031 oz. ASW **Subject:** Endangered Animals **Obv:** National emblem, date below **Rev:** Red-crowned crane, right, wings spread, denomination at left

Date	Mintage	F	VF	XF	Unc	BU
1989 Proof	10,000	Value: 37.50				

Y# 206 10 YUAN

1.0000 g., 0.9990 Gold .0322 oz. AGW **Obv:** Great Wall, date below **Rev:** Phoenix and dragon, denomination at left

Date	Mintage	F	VF	XF	Unc	BU
1990 Proof	34,000	Value: 40.00				

Y# 244 10 YUAN

27.0000 g., 0.9250 Silver .8031 oz. ASW **Obv:** National emblem, date below **Rev:** Half figure of Homer, Poet, denomination at right

Date	Mintage	F	VF	XF	Unc	BU
1990 Proof	30,000	Value: 25.00				

Y# 245 10 YUAN

27.0000 g., 0.9250 Silver .8031 oz. ASW **Obv:** National emblem, date below **Rev:** William Shakespeare, seated, denomination upper left

Date	Mintage	F	VF	XF	Unc	BU
1990 Proof	30,000	Value: 25.00				

Y# 246 10 YUAN

27.0000 g., 0.9250 Silver .8031 oz. ASW **Obv:** National emblem, date below **Rev:** Ludwig van Beethoven, seated at piano, denomination above

Date	Mintage	F	VF	XF	Unc	BU
1990 Proof	30,000	Value: 25.00				

Y# 247 10 YUAN

27.0000 g., 0.9250 Silver .8031 oz. ASW **Obv:** National emblem, date below **Rev:** Thomas Alva Edison holding lightbulb, facing, denomination at right

Date	Mintage	F	VF	XF	Unc	BU
1990 Proof	30,000	Value: 25.00				

Y# 251 10 YUAN

27.0000 g., 0.9250 Silver .8031 oz. ASW **Subject:** XI Asian Games **Rev:** Javelin thrower, denomination below

Date	Mintage	F	VF	XF	Unc	BU
1990 Proof	20,000	Value: 30.00				

Y# 252 10 YUAN

27.0000 g., 0.9250 Silver .8031 oz. ASW **Subject:** XI Asian Games **Rev:** Baseball player, denomination at left

Date	Mintage	F	VF	XF	Unc	BU
1990 Proof	20,000	Value: 30.00				

Y# 253 10 YUAN

27.0000 g., 0.9250 Silver .8031 oz. ASW **Subject:** XI Asian Games **Obv:** Roman numerals above building, date below **Rev:** Gymnast on rings, denomination lower right

Date	Mintage	F	VF	XF	Unc	BU
1990 Proof	20,000	Value: 30.00				

Y# 254 10 YUAN

27.0000 g., 0.9250 Silver .8031 oz. ASW **Subject:** XI Asian Games **Obv:** Roman numeral above building, date below **Rev:** Soccer player, denomination lower right

Date	Mintage	F	VF	XF	Unc	BU
1990 Proof	20,000	Value: 30.00				

Y# 261 10 YUAN

31.1000 g., 0.9990 Silver 1.0000 oz. ASW **Obv:** Great Wall, date below **Rev:** Phoenix and dragon, denomination at right

Date	Mintage	F	VF	XF	Unc	BU
1990 Proof	12,000	Value: 35.00				

Y# 283 10 YUAN

27.0000 g., 0.9000 Silver .7814 oz. ASW **Series:** Summer Olympics **Obv:** National emblem, date below **Rev:** Bicycle racers, denomination below

Date	Mintage	F	VF	XF	Unc	BU
1990 Proof	30,000	Value: 22.50				

Y# 300 10 YUAN

27.0000 g., 0.9000 Silver .7814 oz. ASW **Series:** Barcelona 1992 - 25th Summer Olympic Games **Obv:** National emblem, date below **Rev:** Woman high jumper, denomination at right

Date	Mintage	F	VF	XF	Unc	BU
1990 Proof	30,000	Value: 27.50				

Y# 366 10 YUAN
30.0000 g., 0.9000 Silver .8682 oz. ASW **Series:** Barcelona 1992 - 25th Summer Olympic Games **Obv:** National emblem, date below **Rev:** Platform diver, denomination lower left

Date	Mintage	F	VF	XF	Unc	BU
1990 Proof	30,000	Value: 27.50				

Y# 308.3 10 YUAN
31.1000 g., 0.9990 Silver 1.0000 oz. ASW **Obv:** Building, date below without bottom serifs

Date	Mintage	F	VF	XF	Unc	BU
1991	Inc. above	—	—	—	40.00	—

Y# 318 10 YUAN
27.0800 g., 0.9250 Silver .8030 oz. ASW **Subject:** 1st Women's World Football Championship **Obv:** 5 story building, date below **Rev:** Women's soccer, 2 players, denomination at right

Date	Mintage	F	VF	XF	Unc	BU
1991 Proof	2,800	Value: 45.00				

Y# 319 10 YUAN
27.0800 g., 0.9250 Silver .8030 oz. ASW **Subject:** Women's 1st World Football Championships **Obv:** 5 story building, date below **Rev:** Women's soccer, 3 players, denomination below

Date	Mintage	F	VF	XF	Unc	BU
1991 Proof	2,800	Value: 45.00				

Y# 347 10 YUAN
27.0800 g., 0.9250 Silver .8030 oz. ASW **Rev:** Mozart seated at piano, two dates upper right, denomination at left

Date	Mintage	F	VF	XF	Unc	BU
1991 Proof	—	Value: 25.00				

Y# 348 10 YUAN
27.0800 g., 0.9250 Silver .8030 oz. ASW **Rev:** Columbus

Date	Mintage	F	VF	XF	Unc	BU
1991 Proof	—	Value: 25.00				

Y# 349 10 YUAN
27.0800 g., 0.9250 Silver .8030 oz. ASW **Rev:** Einstein

Date	Mintage	F	VF	XF	Unc	BU
1991 Proof	—	Value: 25.00				

Y# 350 10 YUAN
27.0800 g., 0.9250 Silver .8030 oz. ASW **Obv:** National emblem, date below **Rev:** Mark Twain seated, with book, denomination at left

Date	Mintage	F	VF	XF	Unc	BU
1991 Proof	—	Value: 25.00				

Y# 367 10 YUAN
30.0000 g., 0.9000 Silver .8682 oz. ASW **Series:** Olympics **Obv:** National emblem, date below **Rev:** Downhill skier, denomination lower left

Date	Mintage	F	VF	XF	Unc	BU
1991 Proof	30,000	Value: 25.00				

Y# 456 10 YUAN
30.0000 g., 0.9000 Silver .8682 oz. ASW **Series:** Barcelona 1992 - 25th Summer Olympic Games **Obv:** National emblem, date below **Rev:** Woman playing table tennis, denomination at right

Date	Mintage	F	VF	XF	Unc	BU
1991 Proof	30,000	Value: 35.00				

Y# 476 10 YUAN
31.1035 g., 0.9990 Silver 1.0000 oz. ASW **Subject:** 80th Anniversary - 1911 Revolution **Obv:** Building, two dates below **Rev:** Sun Yat Sen in civilian clothes, denomination at right

Date	Mintage	F	VF	XF	Unc	BU
ND(1991) Proof	2,500	Value: 50.00				

Y# 351 10 YUAN
26.8300 g., 0.9000 Silver .7764 oz. ASW **Series:** 1994 Winter Olympics **Obv:** National emblem **Rev:** Slalom

Date	Mintage	F	VF	XF	Unc	BU
1992 Proof	7,500	Value: 50.00				

Y# 368 10 YUAN
26.8300 g., 0.9000 Silver .7764 oz. ASW **Series:** 1994 Winter Olympics **Obv:** National emblem, date below **Rev:** Cross country skier, denomination at right

Date	Mintage	F	VF	XF	Unc	BU
1992 Proof	7,500	Value: 50.00				

Y# 486 10 YUAN
27.0000 g., 0.9250 Silver .8031 oz. ASW **Subject:** Wildlife **Obv:** National emblem **Rev:** White storks, denomination at right

Date	Mintage	F	VF	XF	Unc	BU
1992 Proof	7,260	Value: 47.50				

Y# 490 10 YUAN
26.9500 g., 0.9000 Silver .7798 oz. ASW **Series:** Lillehammer 1994 - 17th Winter Olympic Games **Obv:** National emblem, date below **Rev:** Ski jumper, denomination at right

Date	Mintage	F	VF	XF	Unc	BU
1992 Proof	30,000	Value: 30.00				

Y# 584 10 YUAN
26.9500 g., 0.9000 Silver .7798 oz. ASW **Obv:** National emblem, date below **Rev:** Snow leopard, denomination above

Date	Mintage	F	VF	XF	Unc	BU
1992 Proof	7,260	Value: 47.50				

Y# 709 10 YUAN
27.1100 g., 0.9000 Silver .7844 oz. ASW **Obv:** National emblem, date below **Rev:** Tschaikovsky leaning against piano, denomination lower left

Date	Mintage	F	VF	XF	Unc	BU
1992 Proof	30,000	Value: 30.00				

Y# 755 10 YUAN
27.0000 g., 0.9250 Silver .8030 oz. ASW **Subject:** International Celebrities **Obv:** National emblem, date below **Rev:** Leonardo Da Vinci with painting of Mona Lisa, denomination below

Date	Mintage	F	VF	XF	Unc	BU
1992 Proof	30,000	Value: 30.00				

Y# 756 10 YUAN
27.0000 g., 0.9250 Silver .8030 oz. ASW **Subject:** International Celebrities **Obv:** National emblem, date below **Rev:** Wolfgang Von Goethe, denomination at right

Date	Mintage	F	VF	XF	Unc	BU
1992 Proof	30,000	Value: 30.00				

Y# 757 10 YUAN
27.0000 g., 0.9250 Silver .8030 oz. ASW **Subject:** International Celebrities **Obv:** National emblem, date below **Rev:** Alfred Nobel, denomination at left

Date	Mintage	F	VF	XF	Unc	BU
1992 Proof	30,000	Value: 30.00				

Y# 942 10 YUAN
31.1035 g., 0.9990 Silver 1.0000 oz. ASW **Subject:** Environmental Protection **Obv:** National emblem, date below **Rev:** Kneeling woman fetching water at stream, denomination below

Date	Mintage	F	VF	XF	Unc	BU
1992	60,000	—	—	—	30.00	—

Y# 352 10 YUAN
31.1000 g., 0.9990 Silver 1.0000 oz. ASW **Obv:** Temple of Harmony, date below **Rev:** Peacocks, denomination above **Rev. Designer:** Lang Shih Ning

Date	Mintage	F	VF	XF	Unc	BU
1993 Proof	7,000	Value: 55.00				
1997 Matte	50,000	—	—	—	40.00	—

Y# 412.1 10 YUAN
27.0000 g., 0.9250 Silver .8031 oz. ASW **Subject:** Mao Tse Tung **Obv:** Building on cliff **Rev:** Bust facing, denomination at right

Date	Mintage	F	VF	XF	Unc	BU
1993	30,000	—	—	—	45.00	—

Y# 412.2 10 YUAN
27.0000 g., 0.9250 Silver .8031 oz. ASW **Obv:** Building on cliff, date at right **Rev:** Revised bust facing, denomination at right

Date	Mintage	F	VF	XF	Unc	BU
1993	—	—	—	—	45.00	—

Y# 418 10 YUAN
24.2550 g., 0.9000 Silver .7799 oz. ASW **Subject:** World Cup Soccer - 1994 **Obv:** National emblem, date below **Rev:** Soccer players, denomination lower left

Date	Mintage	F	VF	XF	Unc	BU
1993 Proof	30,000	Value: 35.00				

Y# 474 10 YUAN
3.1103 g., 0.9990 Gold .1000 oz. AGW **Obv:** Temple of Harmony **Rev:** 2 peacocks, denomination above **Rev. Designer:** Lanf Shih Ning

Date	Mintage	F	VF	XF	Unc	BU
1993 Prooflike	—	—	—	—	—	100

Y# 492 10 YUAN
30.0000 g., 0.9000 Silver .8682 oz. ASW **Series:** Olympics **Obv:** National emblem, date below **Rev:** Runners, denomination below

Date	Mintage	F	VF	XF	Unc	BU
1993 Proof	30,000	Value: 30.00				

Y# 493 10 YUAN
30.0000 g., 0.9000 Silver .8682 oz. ASW **Subject:** Olympics Centennial **Obv:** National emblem, date below **Rev:** Fencing, denomination below

Date	Mintage	F	VF	XF	Unc	BU
1993 Proof	30,000	Value: 30.00				

Y# 499 10 YUAN
3.1103 g., 0.9990 Gold .1000 oz. AGW **Obv:** Building above date **Rev:** Goddess of Mercy holding flower, denomination at left

Date	Mintage	F	VF	XF	Unc	BU
1993 Prooflike	20,000	—	—	—	—	75.00

Y# 501 10 YUAN
3.1103 g., 0.9990 Gold .1000 oz. AGW **Rev:** Goddess Guanyin seated in flowers, denomination at left

Date	Mintage	F	VF	XF	Unc	BU
1993 Proof	1,000	Value: 90.00				

Y# 758 10 YUAN
30.0000 g., 0.9000 Silver .8681 oz. ASW **Obv:** National emblem **Rev:** Song Qingling, seated, denomination st right

Date	Mintage	F	VF	XF	Unc	BU
1993 Proof	20,000	Value: 35.00				

Y# 759 10 YUAN
30.0000 g., 0.9000 Silver .8681 oz. ASW **Obv:** National emblem **Rev:** 3/4-length figure of Soong Ching-ling, 1892-1981, half left, birds in background, denomination at right

Date	Mintage	F	VF	XF	Unc	BU
1993 Proof	20,000	Value: 35.00				

Y# 774 10 YUAN
3.1030 g., 0.9990 Gold .1000 oz. AGW, 18 mm. **Subject:** Homeland Scenery **Obv:** Great Wall **Rev:** Cliffside building

Date	Mintage	F	VF	XF	Unc	BU
1993 Proof	8,888	Value: 75.00				

Y# 779 10 YUAN
27.0000 g., 0.9250 Silver .8030 oz. ASW **Subject:** World Cup Soccer **Obv:** National emblem, date below **Rev:** 3 soccer players, denomination below

Date	Mintage	F	VF	XF	Unc	BU
1993 Proof	30,000	Value: 32.50				

Y# 932 10 YUAN
31.2000 g., 0.9990 Silver 1.0021 oz. ASW **Subject:** Homeland scenery **Obv:** Great Wall, date below **Rev:** Large building, islands in background, denomination upper right

Date	Mintage	F	VF	XF	Unc	BU
1993 Proof	60,000	Value: 35.00				

Y# 933 10 YUAN
31.2000 g., 0.9990 Silver 1.0021 oz. ASW **Subject:** Mt. Tai **Obv:** Great Wall, date below **Rev:** Small building with long staircase, denomination upper left

Date	Mintage	F	VF	XF	Unc	BU
1993 Proof	60,000	Value: 35.00				

Y# 934 10 YUAN
31.2000 g., 0.9990 Silver 1.0021 oz. ASW **Subject:** Mt. Hua **Obv:** Great Wall, date below **Rev:** Bird's eye view of mountain tops, shelter, denomination at left

Date	Mintage	F	VF	XF	Unc	BU
1993 Proof	60,000	Value: 35.00				

Y# 935 10 YUAN
31.2000 g., 0.9990 Silver 1.0021 oz. ASW **Subject:** Mt. Song **Obv:** Great Wall, date below **Rev:** Tall domed building, denomination at right

Date	Mintage	F	VF	XF	Unc	BU
1993 Proof	60,000	Value: 35.00				

Y# 1229 10 YUAN
31.2000 g., 0.9990 Silver 1.0021 oz. ASW, 39.9 mm. **Subject:** Mt. Heng **Obv:** Great Wall, date below **Rev:** Cliffside building, denomination below **Edge:** Reeded

Date	Mintage	F	VF	XF	Unc	BU
1993 Proof	60,000	Value: 35.00				

Y# 1077 10 YUAN
30.0000 g., 0.9000 Silver .8681 oz. ASW, 40 mm. **Subject:** Yin and Yang Concept **Obv:** Great Wall blockhouse, date below **Rev:** Four men studying the symbol,denomination below **Edge:** Reeded

Date	Mintage	F	VF	XF	Unc	BU
1993	—	—	—	—	27.50	—

Note: Probably minted at a much later date.

Y# 494 10 YUAN
31.1035 g., 0.9990 Silver 1.0000 oz. ASW **Series:** Olympics **Obv:** National emblem, date below **Rev:** Basketball player, denomination at left

Date	Mintage	F	VF	XF	Unc	BU
1994 Proof	30,000	Value: 35.00				

Y# 420 10 YUAN
31.1000 g., 0.9990 Silver 1.0000 oz. ASW **Obv:** Figure on Eastern unicorn, date below **Rev:** Unicorn, sprays of roses below, denomination at left

Date	Mintage	F	VF	XF	Unc	BU
1994	50,000	—	—	—	27.50	—
1994 Proof	4,000	Value: 40.00				

Y# 421 10 YUAN
3.1103 g., 0.9990 Gold .1000 oz. AGW **Rev:** Unicorn looking back towards right

Date	Mintage	F	VF	XF	Unc	BU
1994 Proof	5,100	Value: 110				

Y# 438 10 YUAN
27.0000 g., 0.9250 Silver .8031 oz. ASW **Subject:** Hiroshima 1994 - 12th Asian Games **Obv:** National emblem, athletic figures above date **Rev:** Swimming, denomination at left

Date	Mintage	F	VF	XF	Unc	BU
1994 Proof	5,000	Value: 30.00				

Y# 439 10 YUAN
27.0000 g., 0.9250 Silver .8031 oz. ASW **Subject:** Hiroshima 1994 - 12th Asian Games **Rev:** Runners, denomination lower right

Date	Mintage	F	VF	XF	Unc	BU
1994 Proof	5,000	Value: 30.00				

Y# 457 10 YUAN
31.1035 g., 0.9990 Silver 1.0000 oz. ASW **Subject:** Children at Play **Rev:** 2 children and cat, denomination below

Date	Mintage	F	VF	XF	Unc	BU
1994 Proof	8,500	Value: 30.00				

Y# 458 10 YUAN
31.1035 g., 0.9990 Silver 1.0000 oz. ASW **Subject:** Children at Play **Obv:** Building, date below **Rev:** 3 children and toy boat, denomination below

Date	Mintage	F	VF	XF	Unc	BU
1994 Proof	8,500	Value: 30.00				

Y# 482 10 YUAN
31.1035 g., 0.9990 Silver 1.0000 oz. ASW **Obv:** Great Wall, date below **Rev:** Guanyin - Goddess of Mercy, holding child, facing, denomination at left

Date	Mintage	F	VF	XF	Unc	BU
1994 Proof	30,000	Value: 30.00				

Y# 495 10 YUAN
31.1035 g., 0.9990 Silver 1.0000 oz. ASW **Series:** Olympics Centennial **Obv:** National emblem, date below **Rev:** Female archer shooting, denomination lower left

Date	Mintage	F	VF	XF	Unc	BU
1994 Proof	30,000	Value: 35.00				

Y# 496 10 YUAN
31.1035 g., 0.9990 Silver 1.0000 oz. ASW **Series:** Olympics **Obv:** National emblem, date below **Rev:** Boxing match, denomination at right

Date	Mintage	F	VF	XF	Unc	BU
1994 Proof	30,000	Value: 35.00				

Y# 510 10 YUAN
3.1103 g., 0.9990 Gold .1000 oz. AGW **Obv:** Great Wall above date **Rev:** Guanyin-Goddess of Mercy, holding child, facing, denomination at left

Date	Mintage	F	VF	XF	Unc	BU
1994 Prooflike	8,000	—	—	—	—	75.00

Y# 539 10 YUAN
27.0000 g., 0.9250 Silver .8031 oz. ASW **Obv:** National emblem **Rev:** Confucius, denomination at right

Date	Mintage	F	VF	XF	Unc	BU
1994 Proof	—	Value: 30.00				

Y# 540 10 YUAN
27.0000 g., 0.9250 Silver .8031 oz. ASW **Rev:** Socrates, denomination lower left

Date	Mintage	F	VF	XF	Unc	BU
1994 Proof	—	Value: 30.00				

Y# 541 10 YUAN
27.0000 g., 0.9250 Silver .8031 oz. ASW **Rev:** Rembrandt, denomination at left

Date	Mintage	F	VF	XF	Unc	BU
1994 Proof	—	Value: 30.00				

Y# 542 10 YUAN
27.0000 g., 0.9250 Silver .8031 oz. ASW **Rev:** Verdi, denomination at right

Date	Mintage	F	VF	XF	Unc	BU
1994 Proof	—	Value: 30.00				

Y# 579 10 YUAN
27.0000 g., 0.9250 Silver .8031 oz. ASW **Rev:** 2 Bactrian camels, denomination below

Date	Mintage	F	VF	XF	Unc	BU
1994 Proof	4,825	Value: 35.00				

Y# 580 10 YUAN
27.0000 g., 0.9250 Silver .8031 oz. ASW **Rev:** Pere David deer, denomination above

Date	Mintage	F	VF	XF	Unc	BU
1994 Proof	4,825	Value: 35.00				

Y# 615 10 YUAN
27.2000 g., 0.9250 Silver .8089 oz. ASW **Obv:** National emblem, date below **Rev:** Soccer player, denomination at left

Date	Mintage	F	VF	XF	Unc	BU
1994 Proof	—	Value: 30.00				

Y# 681 10 YUAN
20.7360 g., 0.9000 Silver .6013 oz. ASW **Obv:** Building, date below **Rev:** Black-billed Magpies on branch, denomination below **Shape:** 12-sided

Date	Mintage	F	VF	XF	Unc	BU
1994 Proof	3,900	Value: 45.00				

Y# 710 10 YUAN
31.1035 g., 0.9990 Silver 1.0000 oz. ASW **Subject:** Sino - Singapore Friendship **Obv:** Great Wall, date below **Rev:** City view of Singapore, denomination below

Date	Mintage	F	VF	XF	Unc	BU
1994 Proof	30,000	Value: 30.00				

Y# 783 10 YUAN
31.1035 g., 0.9990 Silver 1.0000 oz. ASW **Subject:** Children at Play **Obv:** Imperial Palace, corner building **Rev:** Three children carrying tray, denomination below

Date	Mintage	F	VF	XF	Unc	BU
1994 Proof	2,500	Value: 50.00				

Y# 784 10 YUAN
31.1035 g., 0.9990 Silver 1.0000 oz. ASW **Subject:** Children at Play **Obv:** Imperial Palace, corner building **Rev:** Three children playing on ground, denomination above

Date	Mintage	F	VF	XF	Unc	BU
1994 Proof	2,500	Value: 50.00				

Y# 469 10 YUAN
27.0000 g., 0.9250 Silver .8022 oz. ASW **Subject:** Dinosaurs **Rev:** Pterodactylus, denomination at right

Date	Mintage	F	VF	XF	Unc	BU
1995 Proof	Est. 5,000	Value: 50.00				

Y# 470 10 YUAN
27.0000 g., 0.9250 Silver .8022 oz. ASW **Subject:** Dinosaurs **Rev:** Stegosaurus, denomination below

Date	Mintage	F	VF	XF	Unc	BU
1995 Proof	Est. 5,000	Value: 47.50				

Y# 489 10 YUAN
31.1035 g., 0.9990 Silver 1.0000 oz. ASW **Obv:** Building, date below **Rev:** Guanyin, Goddess of Mercy with scepter, denomination at left

Date	Mintage	F	VF	XF	Unc	BU
1995 Prooflike	30,000	—	—	—	30.00	—

Y# 520 10 YUAN
3.1103 g., 0.9990 Gold .1000 oz. AGW **Obv:** Building, date below **Rev:** Guanyin - Goddess of Mercy with lotus flower, facing, denomination at left

Date	Mintage	F	VF	XF	Unc	BU
1995 Proof	3,000	Value: 115				

Y# 521 10 YUAN
3.1103 g., 0.9990 Gold .1000 oz. AGW **Obv:** Building, date below **Rev:** Guanyin, Goddess of Mercy with wheel, denomination at left

Date	Mintage	F	VF	XF	Unc	BU
1995 Proof	3,000	Value: 115				

Y# 522 10 YUAN
3.1103 g., 0.9990 Gold .1000 oz. AGW **Obv:** Building, date below **Rev:** Guanyin - Goddess of Mercy with scepter, denomination at left

Date	Mintage	F	VF	XF	Unc	BU
1995 Proof	3,000	Value: 115				

Y# 523 10 YUAN

3.1103 g., 0.9990 Gold .1000 oz. AGW **Obv:** Building, date below **Rev:** Guanyin, Goddess of Mercy with bowl, denomination at left

Date	Mintage	F	VF	XF	Unc	BU
1995 Proof	3,000	Value: 115				

Y# 531 10 YUAN

31.1035 g., 0.9990 Silver 1.0000 oz. ASW **Subject:** Return of Hong Kong to China **Obv:** Tiananmen Square, date below **Rev:** Deng Xiao Ping bust, left, buildings below, denomination at bottom

Date	Mintage	F	VF	XF	Unc	BU
1995 Proof	88,000	Value: 42.50				

Y# 588 10 YUAN

27.0000 g., 0.9250 Silver .8031 oz. ASW **Obv:** Dragon in inner circle, date below **Rev:** Huang Di in chariot, denomination at lower right

Date	Mintage	F	VF	XF	Unc	BU
1995 Proof	5,000	Value: 40.00				

Y# 589 10 YUAN

27.0000 g., 0.9250 Silver .8031 oz. ASW **Obv:** Dragon in inner circle **Rev:** Half figure of Yan Di, wearing skins, facing, denomination lower right

Date	Mintage	F	VF	XF	Unc	BU
1995 Proof	5,000	Value: 40.00				

Y# 590 10 YUAN

27.0000 g., 0.9250 Silver .8031 oz. ASW **Obv:** Dragon in inner circle **Rev:** Half figure of Yao holding feathers, facing, denomination lower right

Date	Mintage	F	VF	XF	Unc	BU
1995 Proof	5,000	Value: 40.00				

Y# 591 10 YUAN

27.0000 g., 0.9250 Silver .8031 oz. ASW **Obv:** Dragon in inner circle **Rev:** Half figure of Shun with urn, facing, denomination lower left

Date	Mintage	F	VF	XF	Unc	BU
1995 Proof	5,000	Value: 40.00				

Y# 647 10 YUAN

27.0000 g., 0.9250 Silver .8031 oz. ASW **Rev:** Sailing ship, denomination above

Date	Mintage	F	VF	XF	Unc	BU
1995 Proof	10,000	Value: 75.00				

Y# 650 10 YUAN

27.0000 g., 0.9250 Silver .8031 oz. ASW **Rev:** Junk, denomination below

Date	Mintage	F	VF	XF	Unc	BU
1995 Proof	10,000	Value: 75.00				

Y# 682 10 YUAN

27.0000 g., 0.9250 Silver .8031 oz. ASW **Series:** 50th Anniversary - United Nations **Obv:** UN logo **Rev:** UN building

Date	Mintage	F	VF	XF	Unc	BU
1995 Proof	115,000	Value: 30.00				

Y# 683 10 YUAN

31.1003 g., 0.9990 Silver 1.0001 oz. ASW **Obv:** Eastern Unicorn, date below **Rev:** Unicorn with offspring, denomination at left

Date	Mintage	F	VF	XF	Unc	BU
1995 Proof	—	Value: 30.00				

Y# 684 10 YUAN

31.1003 g., 0.9990 Silver 1.0001 oz. ASW **Subject:** 50th Anniversary of Anti-Japanese War **Obv:** National emblem, date below **Rev:** Chou and Mao above soldiers, denomination below

Date	Mintage	F	VF	XF	Unc	BU
1995 Proof	3,750	Value: 50.00				

Y# 685 10 YUAN

31.1003 g., 0.9990 Silver 1.0001 oz. ASW **Obv:** National emblem, date below **Rev:** Attacking soldiers above bridge guarded by lion, denomination at right

Date	Mintage	F	VF	XF	Unc	BU
1995 Proof	3,750	Value: 50.00				

Y# 686 10 YUAN

31.1003 g., 0.9990 Silver 1.0001 oz. ASW **Subject:** 4th UN World Women's Congress **Obv:** Logo above building **Rev:** Three women with flowers and birds

Date	Mintage	F	VF	XF	Unc	BU
1995 Proof	30,500	Value: 35.00				

Y# 713 10 YUAN

27.0000 g., 0.9250 Silver .8022 oz. ASW **Series:** 1996 Olympics **Obv:** National emblem, date below **Rev:** Handball player, denomination lower right

Date	Mintage	F	VF	XF	Unc	BU
1995 Proof	—	Value: 27.50				

Y# 714 10 YUAN

27.0000 g., 0.9250 Silver .8022 oz. ASW **Series:** 1996 Olympics **Obv:** National emblem, date below **Rev:** Kick boxer, denomination at right

Date	Mintage	F	VF	XF	Unc	BU
1995 Proof	—	Value: 27.50				

Y# 737 10 YUAN
3,1100 g., 0.9990 Gold .0999 oz. AGW **Obv:** Eastern unicorn, date below **Rev:** Western unicorn with offspring, denomination at left

Date	Mintage	F	VF	XF	Unc	BU
1995 Proof	5,000	Value: 110				

Y# 799 10 YUAN
3.1103 g., 0.9990 Gold .1000 oz. AGW **Subject:** Chinese Culture Series **Obv:** Great Wall seen through arch, date below **Rev:** Pagoda of six harmonies, denomination at left

Date	Mintage	F	VF	XF	Unc	BU
1995 Proof	25,000	Value: 75.00				

Y# 800 10 YUAN
3.1103 g., 0.9990 Gold .1000 oz. AGW **Subject:** Chinese Culture Series **Obv:** Great Wall seen through arch **Rev:** Mencius seated at table, denomination below

Date	Mintage	F	VF	XF	Unc	BU
1995 Proof	25,000	Value: 75.00				

Y# 801 10 YUAN
3.1103 g., 0.9990 Gold .1000 oz. AGW **Subject:** Chinese Culture Series **Obv:** Great Wall seen through arch **Rev:** Tang Taizong seated, denomination at left

Date	Mintage	F	VF	XF	Unc	BU
1995 Proof	25,000	Value: 75.00				

Y# 802 10 YUAN
3.1103 g., 0.9990 Gold .1000 oz. AGW **Subject:** Chinese Culture Series **Obv:** Great Wall seen through arch **Rev:** Lion dance, denomination lower left

Date	Mintage	F	VF	XF	Unc	BU
1995 Proof	25,000	Value: 75.00				

Y# 803 10 YUAN
3.1103 g., 0.9990 Gold .1000 oz. AGW **Subject:** Chinese Culture Series **Obv:** Great Wall seen through arch **Rev:** Female opera role

Date	Mintage	F	VF	XF	Unc	BU
1995 Proof	25,000	Value: 75.00				

Y# 809 10 YUAN
20.7333 g., 0.9000 Silver .5999 oz. ASW **Obv:** Great Wall, date below **Rev:** Eagle in flight, denomination at left **Shape:** 12-sided

Date	Mintage	F	VF	XF	Unc	BU
1995 Proof	3,900	Value: 65.00				

Y# 811 10 YUAN
31.1035 g., 0.9990 Silver 1.0000 oz. ASW **Subject:** 50th Anniversary - Return of Taiwan to China **Obv:** Great Wall **Rev:** Taiwan and China maps

Date	Mintage	F	VF	XF	Unc	BU
1995 Proof	5,000	Value: 75.00				

Y# 812 10 YUAN
31.1035 g., 0.9990 Silver 1.0000 oz. ASW **Subject:** 50th Anniversary - Return of Taiwan to China **Obv:** Great Wall **Rev:** Zhongshan Hall

Date	Mintage	F	VF	XF	Unc	BU
1995 Proof	5,000	Value: 75.00				

Y# 819 10 YUAN
27.0000 g., 0.9250 Silver .8030 oz. ASW **Subject:** Painter Zu Beihong **Obv:** Portrait, facing, divides dates **Rev:** Cat stalking, denomination at left

Date	Mintage	F	VF	XF	Unc	BU
1995 Proof	8,000	Value: 40.00				

Y# 820 10 YUAN
27.0000 g., 0.9250 Silver .8030 oz. ASW **Subject:** Painter Zu Beihong **Obv:** Portrait **Rev:** Horse running left, denomination at left

Date	Mintage	F	VF	XF	Unc	BU
1995 Proof	8,000	Value: 40.00				

Y# 825 10 YUAN
27.0000 g., 0.9250 Silver .8030 oz. ASW **Subject:** Romance of the Three Kingdoms Series **Obv:** Luo Guanzhong bust, facing, date below **Rev:** Liu Bei standing holding rod, denomination at right

Date	Mintage	F	VF	XF	Unc	BU
1995 Proof	7,000	Value: 60.00				

Y# 826 10 YUAN
27.0000 g., 0.9250 Silver .8030 oz. ASW **Subject:** Romance of the Three Kingdoms Series **Obv:** Luo Guanzhong bust **Rev:** Guan Yo reading, denomination above

Date	Mintage	F	VF	XF	Unc	BU
1995 Proof	7,000	Value: 60.00				

Y# 827 10 YUAN
27.0000 g., 0.9250 Silver .8030 oz. ASW **Subject:** Romance of the Three Kingdoms Series **Obv:** Luo Guanzhong bust **Rev:** Zhang Fei on horse, denomination at left

Date	Mintage	F	VF	XF	Unc	BU
1995 Proof	7,000	Value: 60.00				

Y# 828 10 YUAN
27.0000 g., 0.9250 Silver .8030 oz. ASW **Subject:** Romance of the Three Kingdoms Series **Obv:** Luo Guanzhong bust **Rev:** Zhuge Liang on throne, denomination at right

Date	Mintage	F	VF	XF	Unc	BU
1995 Proof	7,000	Value: 60.00				

Y# 836 10 YUAN
31.1035 g., 0.9990 Silver 1.0000 oz. ASW **Subject:** Table Tennis **Obv:** Tianjing Stadium **Rev:** Table tennis player, denomination at left

Date	Mintage	F	VF	XF	Unc	BU
1995 Proof	3,000	Value: 75.00				

Y# 837 10 YUAN

31.1035 g., 0.9990 Silver 1.0000 oz. ASW **Subject:** Table Tennis **Obv:** Tianjing Stadium **Rev:** Two table tennis players, denomination at left

Date	Mintage	F	VF	XF	Unc	BU
1995 Proof	3,000	Value: 75.00				

Y# 841 10 YUAN

31.1035 g., 0.9990 Silver 1.0000 oz. ASW **Series:** Olympics **Obv:** National emblem, date below **Rev:** Gymnast, denomination at right

Date	Mintage	F	VF	XF	Unc	BU
1995	30,000	—	—	—	27.50	—

Y# 842 10 YUAN

31.1035 g., 0.9990 Silver 1.0000 oz. ASW **Series:** 1996 Olympics **Obv:** National emblem, date below **Rev:** Female shooter, denomination below

Date	Mintage	F	VF	XF	Unc	BU
1995	30,000	—	—	—	27.50	—

Y# 741 10 YUAN

31.1700 g., 0.9990 Silver 1.0011 oz. ASW **Obv:** Eastern unicorn, date below **Rev:** Western unicorn in wreath, denomination lower left

Date	Mintage	F	VF	XF	Unc	BU
1996 Proof	8,000	Value: 50.00				

Y# 742 10 YUAN

3.1100 g., 0.9990 Gold .0999 oz. AGW **Obv:** Eastern unicorn, date below **Rev:** Western unicorn in wreath, denomination lower left

Date	Mintage	F	VF	XF	Unc	BU
1996 Proof	5,000	Value: 110				

Y# 845 10 YUAN

27.0000 g., 0.9250 Silver .8030 oz. ASW **Subject:** Ninth Asian Stamp Exhibition **Obv:** Temple of Heaven, date below, within circle, with additional legend **Rev:** Seated panda eating with cub

Date	Mintage	F	VF	XF	Unc	BU
1996 Proof	2,000	Value: 50.00				

Y# 846 10 YUAN

27.0000 g., 0.9250 Silver .8030 oz. ASW **Subject:** Beijing Coin Fair **Obv:** Temple of Heaven within inner circle with additional legend **Rev:** Seated panda eating with cub, gold insert

Date	Mintage	F	VF	XF	Unc	BU
1996 Proof	2,000	Value: 50.00				

Y# 858 10 YUAN

31.1035 g., 0.9990 Silver 1.0000 oz. ASW **Obv:** Building **Rev:** Sun Yat-Sen bust, facing, denomination below, 3/4 wreath of fans surrounds

Date	Mintage	F	VF	XF	Unc	BU
1996 Proof	20,000	Value: 30.00				

Y# 860 10 YUAN

31.1035 g., 0.9990 Silver 1.0000 oz. ASW **Subject:** Return of Hong Kong to China **Obv:** Tiananmen Square, date below **Rev:** Law book above Hong Kong harbor view, denomination below

Date	Mintage	F	VF	XF	Unc	BU
1996 Proof	88,000	Value: 30.00				

Y# 861 10 YUAN

31.1035 g., 0.9990 Silver 1.0000 oz. ASW **Subject:** 45th Anniversary - Chinese Aviation Industry **Obv:** National emblem, date below **Rev:** Propeller airplane, denomination below

Date	Mintage	F	VF	XF	Unc	BU
1996 Proof	20,000	Value: 30.00				

Y# 862 10 YUAN

31.1035 g., 0.9990 Silver 1.0000 oz. ASW **Subject:** 45th Anniversary - Chinese Aviation Industry **Obv:** National emblem **Rev:** Jet airplane, denomination at right

Date	Mintage	F	VF	XF	Unc	BU
1996 Proof	20,000	Value: 30.00				

Y# 863 10 YUAN

31.1035 g., 0.9990 Silver 1.0000 oz. ASW **Subject:** 40th Anniversary - Chinese Aviation Industry **Obv:** National emblem above Great Wall **Rev:** Satellites, denomination at left

Date	Mintage	F	VF	XF	Unc	BU
1996 Proof	20,000	Value: 30.00				

Y# 864 10 YUAN

31.1035 g., 0.9990 Silver 1.0000 oz. ASW **Subject:** 40th Anniversary - Chinese Aviation Industry **Obv:** National emblem above Great Wall **Rev:** Rocket and satellites, denomination at right

Date	Mintage	F	VF	XF	Unc	BU
1996 Proof	20,000	Value: 30.00				

Y# 865 10 YUAN
31.1035 g., 0.9990 Silver 1.0000 oz. ASW **Subject:** Centennial of Chinese Post Office **Obv:** Modern stamp **Rev:** Imperial stamp

Date	Mintage	F	VF	XF	Unc	BU
1996 Proof	20,000	Value: 25.00				

Y# 866 10 YUAN
31.1035 g., 0.9990 Silver 1.0000 oz. ASW **Subject:** 9th Asian Stamp Exhibition **Obv:** Stamp, date below **Rev:** Stamp, denomination at right, additional legend

Date	Mintage	F	VF	XF	Unc	BU
1996 Proof	20,000	Value: 55.00				

Y# 868 10 YUAN
31.1035 g., 0.9990 Silver 1.0000 oz. ASW **Subject:** 60th Anniversary - Long March **Obv:** Flag above building, date below **Rev:** Chairman Mao on horse, denomination above horse head

Date	Mintage	F	VF	XF	Unc	BU
1996 Proof	20,000	Value: 40.00				

Y# 869 10 YUAN
31.1035 g., 0.9990 Silver 1.0000 oz. ASW **Subject:** 60th Anniversary - Long March **Obv:** Flag above Baota Mountain, date below **Rev:** Two armies enjoined in battle, denomination below

Date	Mintage	F	VF	XF	Unc	BU
1996 Proof	20,000	Value: 40.00				

Y# 876 10 YUAN
27.0000 g., 0.9250 Silver .8030 oz. ASW **Subject:** Romance of the Three Kingdoms Series **Obv:** Luo Guanzhong portrait **Rev:** Cao Cao standing with spear, denomination at right

Date	Mintage	F	VF	XF	Unc	BU
1996 Proof	7,000	Value: 35.00				

Y# 877 10 YUAN
27.0000 g., 0.9250 Silver .8030 oz. ASW **Subject:** Romance of the Three Kingdoms Series **Obv:** Luo Guanzhong portrait **Rev:** Cao Pi seated at desk, denomination at right

Date	Mintage	F	VF	XF	Unc	BU
1996 Proof	7,000	Value: 35.00				

Y# 878 10 YUAN
27.0000 g., 0.9250 Silver .8030 oz. ASW **Subject:** Romance of the Three Kingdoms Series **Obv:** Luo Guanzhong portrait **Rev:** Cao Zhi standing with scroll and flags, denomination lower left

Date	Mintage	F	VF	XF	Unc	BU
1996 Proof	7,000	Value: 35.00				

Y# 879 10 YUAN
27.0000 g., 0.9250 Silver .8030 oz. ASW **Subject:** Romance of the Three Kingdoms Series **Obv:** Luo Guanzhong portrait **Rev:** Sima Yi on horse with spear, denomination at left

Date	Mintage	F	VF	XF	Unc	BU
1996 Proof	7,000	Value: 35.00				

Y# 886 10 YUAN
31.1035 g., 0.9990 Silver 1.0000 oz. ASW **Subject:** Goddess of Mercy - Guanyin **Obv:** Temple, date below **Rev:** Goddess holding flower, denomination at left

Date	Mintage	F	VF	XF	Unc	BU
1996 Proof	30,000	Value: 27.50				

Y# 887 10 YUAN
3.1101 g., 0.9990 Gold .1000 oz. AGW **Subject:** Goddess Guanyin **Obv:** Temple **Rev:** Goddess holding flower

Date	Mintage	F	VF	XF	Unc	BU
1996 Proof	10,000	Value: 75.00				

Y# 890 10 YUAN
27.0000 g., 0.9250 Silver .8030 oz. ASW **Series:** Olympics **Obv:** National emblem, date below **Rev:** Sailboarder, denomination at left

Date	Mintage	F	VF	XF	Unc	BU
1996 Proof	30,000	Value: 30.00				

Y# 711 10 YUAN
31.1035 g., 0.9990 Silver 1.0000 oz. ASW **Subject:** Sino - Thailand Friendship **Obv:** Forbidden City and Thai Royal Palace, date below **Rev:** Two Buddha statues, one in cameo, denomination lower left

Date	Mintage	F	VF	XF	Unc	BU
1997 Proof	45,000	Value: 22.50				

Y# 722 10 YUAN
Bi-Metallic Copper-Nickel center in Brass ring **Subject:** Return of Hong Kong **Obv:** Stylized flower within circle, date below **Rev:** City view, denomination above, circle surrounds

Date	Mintage	F	VF	XF	Unc	BU
1997	—	—	—	—	5.00	—

Note: 5,000 pieces were struck and issued in boxes with certificates and are valued at $350

Y# 723 10 YUAN

Bi-Metallic Brass center in Copper-Nickel ring **Subject:** Hong Kong - Constitution **Obv:** Stylized flower within circle, date below **Rev:** Document with state emblem within circle, denomination below

Date	Mintage	F	VF	XF	Unc	BU
1997	—	—	—	—	5.00	—

Y# 895 10 YUAN

31.1035 g., 0.9990 Silver 1.000 oz. ASW **Subject:** Shanghai International Stamp & Coin Expo **Obv:** Building within circle, legend outside **Rev:** Panda, left, denomination below, gold insert

Date	Mintage	F	VF	XF	Unc	BU
1997 Proof	30,000	Value: 40.00				

Y# 902 10 YUAN

31.1035 g., 0.9990 Silver 1.0000 oz. ASW **Subject:** Return of Hong Kong to China **Obv:** Tiananmen Square, date below **Rev:** Flag and fireworks over city, denomination below

Date	Mintage	F	VF	XF	Unc	BU
1997	800,000	—	—	—	35.00	—
1997 Proof	88,000	Value: 50.00				

Y# 905 10 YUAN

31.1035 g., 0.9990 Silver 1.0000 oz. ASW **Subject:** Return of Macao to China **Obv:** Tiananmen Square **Rev:** Deng Xiaoping viewing Macao, denomination at right

Date	Mintage	F	VF	XF	Unc	BU
1997 Proof	88,000	Value: 40.00				

Y# 903 10 YUAN

31.1035 g., 0.9990 Silver 1.0000 oz. ASW **Subject:** Peoples Liberation Army **Obv:** Radiant star above Great Wall, date below **Rev:** Founding of PLA scene, denomination below

Date	Mintage	F	VF	XF	Unc	BU
1997 Proof	30,000	Value: 25.00				

Y# 909 10 YUAN

31.1035 g., 0.9990 Silver 1.0000 oz. ASW **Obv:** Radiant star above Great Wall, date below **Rev:** Three members of the PRC Army, Air Force and Navy Airplanes, boats and missile in background, denomination at left

Date	Mintage	F	VF	XF	Unc	BU
1997 Proof	30,000	Value: 25.00				

Y# 985 10 YUAN

3.1103 g., 0.9990 Gold .1000 oz. AGW **Subject:** Goddess of Mercy - Guanyin

Date	Mintage	F	VF	XF	Unc	BU
1997	10,000	—	—	—	70.00	—

Y# 912a 10 YUAN

3.1100 g., 0.9990 Gold .1000 oz. AGW **Obv:** Eastern unicorn **Rev:** Western unicorn

Date	Mintage	F	VF	XF	Unc	BU
1997 Proof	5,000	Value: 120				

Y# 913 10 YUAN

3.1100 g., 0.9990 Gold .1000 oz. AGW **Subject:** Goddess Guanyin **Obv:** Putuo Hill Temple **Rev:** Goddess holding jug of dew

Date	Mintage	F	VF	XF	Unc	BU
1997 Proof	10,000	Value: 75.00				

Y# 914.1 10 YUAN

31.1035 g., 0.9990 Silver 1.0000 oz. ASW **Subject:** Celebrating Spring **Obv:** Radiant lantern, date below **Rev:** Children setting off firecrackers, denomination above

Date	Mintage	F	VF	XF	Unc	BU
1997	60,000	—	—	—	30.00	—
1997 Proof	60,000	Value: 30.00				

Y# 1079 10 YUAN

20.7333 g., 0.9000 Silver 0.5999 oz. ASW, 35 mm. **Subject:** Wildlife of China **Obv:** The Great Wall, date below **Rev:** Two penguins, denomination upper left **Edge:** Plain **Shape:** 12-sided

Date	Mintage	F	VF	XF	Unc	BU
1997 Proof	8,800	Value: 60.00				

Y# 1092 10 YUAN

31.4400 g., 0.9990 Silver 1.0098 oz. ASW, 39.8 mm. **Subject:** Forbidden City **Obv:** Exterior view of the Forbidden City **Rev:** Main interior approach and gatehouse to the palaces **Edge:** Reeded

Date	Mintage	F	VF	XF	Unc	BU
1997 Proof	—	Value: 40.00				

Y# 1093 10 YUAN

31.4400 g., 0.9990 Silver 1.0098 oz. ASW, 39.8 mm. **Subject:** Forbidden City **Obv:** Exterior view of the Forbidden City **Rev:** Causeway to palace **Edge:** Reeded

Date	Mintage	F	VF	XF	Unc	BU
1997 Proof	—	Value: 40.00				

Y# 1094 10 YUAN

31.4400 g., 0.9990 Silver 1.0098 oz. ASW, 39.8 mm. **Subject:** Forbidden City **Obv:** Exterior view of the Forbidden City **Rev:** Bronze lion statue **Edge:** Reeded

Date	Mintage	F	VF	XF	Unc	BU
1997 Proof	—	Value: 40.00				

Y# 1095 10 YUAN

31.4400 g., 0.9990 Silver 1.0098 oz. ASW, 39.8 mm. **Subject:** Forbidden City **Obv:** Exterior view of the Forbidden City **Rev:** Interior view **Edge:** Reeded

Date	Mintage	F	VF	XF	Unc	BU
1997 Proof	—	Value: 40.00				

Y# 1099 10 YUAN

27.0000 g., 0.9250 Silver 0.803 oz. ASW, 38 mm. **Subject:** Ancient Chinese Culture Series **Obv:** Dragon seal **Rev:** Bronze wares **Edge:** Reeded

Date	Mintage	F	VF	XF	Unc	BU
1997 Proof	10,000	Value: 45.00				

Y# 1100 10 YUAN

27.0000 g., 0.9250 Silver 0.803 oz. ASW, 38 mm. **Subject:** Ancient Chinese Culture Series **Obv:** Dragon seal **Rev:** Pottery **Edge:** Reeded

Date	Mintage	F	VF	XF	Unc	BU
1997 Proof	10,000	Value: 45.00				

Y# 1101 10 YUAN

27.0000 g., 0.9250 Silver 0.803 oz. ASW, 38 mm. **Subject:** Ancient Chinese Culture Series **Obv:** Dragon seal **Rev:** Calligraphy **Edge:** Reeded

Date	Mintage	F	VF	XF	Unc	BU
1997 Proof	10,000	Value: 45.00				

Y# 1102 10 YUAN

27.0000 g., 0.9250 Silver 0.803 oz. ASW, 38 mm. **Subject:** Ancient Chinese Culture Series **Obv:** Dragon seal **Rev:** Coinage **Edge:** Reeded

Date	Mintage	F	VF	XF	Unc	BU
1997 Proof	10,000	Value: 45.00				

Y# 1191 10 YUAN

3.1100 g., 0.9990 Gold 0.0999 oz. AGW, 18 mm. **Obv:** Great Wall, date below **Rev:** Man with flag, denomination at left **Edge:** Reeded

Date	Mintage	F	VF	XF	Unc	BU
1997(y)	16,000	—	—	—	90.00	—

Y# 1192 10 YUAN

3.1100 g., 0.9990 Gold 0.0999 oz. AGW, 18 mm. **Obv:** Great Wall, date below **Rev:** Man with extended open hand, denomination at right **Edge:** Reeded

Date	Mintage	F	VF	XF	Unc	BU
1997(y)	16,000	—	—	—	90.00	—

Y# 1193 10 YUAN
3.1100 g., 0.9990 Gold 0.0999 oz. AGW, 18 mm. **Obv:** Great Wall, date below **Rev:** Astronomer, denomination upper left **Edge:** Reeded

Date	Mintage	F	VF	XF	Unc	BU
1997(y)	16,000	—	—	—	90.00	—

Y# 1194 10 YUAN
3.1100 g., 0.9990 Gold 0.0999 oz. AGW, 18 mm. **Obv:** Great Wall, date below **Rev:** Gymnast, denomination at right **Edge:** Reeded

Date	Mintage	F	VF	XF	Unc	BU
1997(y)	16,000	—	—	—	90.00	—

Y# 1195 10 YUAN
3.1100 g., 0.9990 Gold 0.0999 oz. AGW, 18 mm. **Obv:** Great Wall, date below **Rev:** Building, denomination below **Edge:** Reeded

Date	Mintage	F	VF	XF	Unc	BU
1997(y)	16,000	—	—	—	90.00	—

Y# 1199.1 10 YUAN
3.1100 g., 0.9990 Gold 0.0999 oz. AGW, 18 mm. **Obv:** Ornamental column **Rev:** Child holding a carp **Edge:** Reeded

Date	Mintage	F	VF	XF	Unc	BU
1997	100,000	—	—	—	75.00	—

Y# 1199.2 10 YUAN
3.1100 g., 0.9990 Gold 0.0999 oz. AGW, 18 mm. **Obv:** Ornamental column **Rev:** Multicolor child holding a carp **Edge:** Reeded

Date	Mintage	F	VF	XF	Unc	BU
1997 Proof	20,000	Value: 90.00				

Y# 983 10 YUAN
3.1103 g., 0.9990 Gold .1000 oz. AGW **Subject:** Celebrating Spring **Obv:** Lantern **Rev:** Children setting off firecrackers

Date	Mintage	F	VF	XF	Unc	BU
1997	100,000	—	—	—	—	70.00

Y# 917.1 10 YUAN
31.1035 g., 0.9990 Silver 1.0000 oz. ASW **Subject:** Traditional Chinese Mascot **Obv:** Monument in Tiananmen Square, sprays below **Rev:** Child holding carp, denomination below

Date	Mintage	F	VF	XF	Unc	BU
1997 Proof	80,000	Value: 30.00				

Y# 917.2 10 YUAN
31.1035 g., 0.9990 Silver 1.0000 oz. ASW **Subject:** Traditional Chinese Mascot **Obv:** Monument in Tiananmen Square, sprays below, circle surrounds, date below **Rev:** Multicolor version of child holding carp, denomination below

Date	Mintage	F	VF	XF	Unc	BU
1997 Proof	100,000	Value: 35.00				

Y# 919 10 YUAN
31.1035 g., 0.9990 Silver 1.0000 oz. ASW **Subject:** Wildlife of China **Obv:** National emblem, date below **Rev:** Chinese white dolphins, denomination lower right

Date	Mintage	F	VF	XF	Unc	BU
1997 Proof	68,000	Value: 35.00				

Y# 920 10 YUAN
31.1035 g., 0.9990 Silver 1.0000 oz. ASW **Subject:** Wildlife of China **Obv:** National emblem, date below **Rev:** Swan with young, denomination lowe left

Date	Mintage	F	VF	XF	Unc	BU
1997 Proof	68,000	Value: 35.00				

Y# 936 10 YUAN
31.2000 g., 0.9990 Silver 1.0021 oz. ASW **Subject:** Gesal, King of Tibet **Obv:** Towered building, date below **Rev:** King on horseback, denomination at right, figures in a row below

Date	Mintage	F	VF	XF	Unc	BU
1997 Proof	28,000	Value: 25.00				

Y# 937 10 YUAN
31.2000 g., 0.9990 Silver 1.0021 oz. ASW **Subject:** Gadamellin of Mongolia **Obv:** Towered building, date below **Rev:** Cavalry attack with swords, denomination at right

Date	Mintage	F	VF	XF	Unc	BU
1997 Proof	28,000	Value: 25.00				

Y# 938 10 YUAN
31.2000 g., 0.9990 Silver 1.0021 oz. ASW **Subject:** Yi Nationality **Obv:** Towered building, date below **Rev:** Madame She Ziang with sword, soldiers at right above denomination

Date	Mintage	F	VF	XF	Unc	BU
1997 Proof	28,000	Value: 25.00				

Y# 939 10 YUAN
31.2000 g., 0.9990 Silver 1.0021 oz. ASW **Subject:** Li Nationality **Obv:** Towered building, date below **Rev:** Madame Zian reading scroll, denomination at right

Date	Mintage	F	VF	XF	Unc	BU
1997 Proof	28,000	Value: 25.00				

Y# 984 10 YUAN
3.1103 g., 0.9990 Gold .1000 oz. AGW **Obv:** Forbidden city, date below **Rev:** Bronze chinze, denomination upper right

Date	Mintage	F	VF	XF	Unc	BU
1997 Proof	11,000	Value: 75.00				

Y# 912 10 YUAN
31.1035 g., 0.9990 Silver 1.0000 oz. ASW **Obv:** Eastern unicorn, date below **Rev:** Western unicorn, denomination below

Date	Mintage	F	VF	XF	Unc	BU
1997 Prooflike	—	—	—	—	27.50	—
1997 Proof	8,000	Value: 60.00				

Y# 724 10 YUAN

31.0220 g., 0.9990 Silver .9963 oz. ASW **Subject:** 100th Birthday - Zhou Enlai **Obv:** Zhou Enlai Memorial Hall, date below **Rev:** Zhou on horseback, denomination at right, two dates at left

Date	Mintage	F	VF	XF	Unc	BU
1998 Proof	38,000	Value: 30.00				

Y# 725 10 YUAN

31.0220 g., 0.9990 Silver .9963 oz. ASW **Subject:** 100th Birthday - Zhou Enlai **Obv:** Zhou Enlai Memorial Hall, date below **Rev:** Zhou standing facing 3/4 right, denomination at right

Date	Mintage	F	VF	XF	Unc	BU
1998 Proof	38,000	Value: 30.00				

Y# 727 10 YUAN

31.3900 g., 0.9990 Silver 1.0082 oz. ASW **Obv:** National emblem, date below **Rev:** Portrait of Dr. Norman Bethune with surgery scene, denomination at left

Date	Mintage	F	VF	XF	Unc	BU
1998	61,000	Value: 20.00				

Note: In Proof sets only

Y# 744 10 YUAN

31.4700 g., 0.9990 Silver 1.0110 oz. ASW **Subject:** Celebrating Spring **Obv:** Radiant lantern, date below **Rev:** Three children about to fly kites, denomination below

Date	Mintage	F	VF	XF	Unc	BU
1998 Proof	60,000	Value: 27.50				
1998	80,000	—	—	—	25.00	—

Y# 987 10 YUAN

3.1103 g., 0.9990 Gold .1000 oz. AGW **Subject:** Culture of Dragons

Date	Mintage	F	VF	XF	Unc	BU
1998 Proof	6,000	Value: 75.00				

Y# 1063 10 YUAN

31.1035 g., 0.9990 Silver 1.0000 oz. ASW, 38 mm. **Subject:** World Wildlife Fund **Obv:** National emblem, date below **Rev:** Clouded leopard on branch, denomination below **Edge:** Reeded

Date	Mintage	F	VF	XF	Unc	BU
1998 Proof	40,000	Value: 35.00				

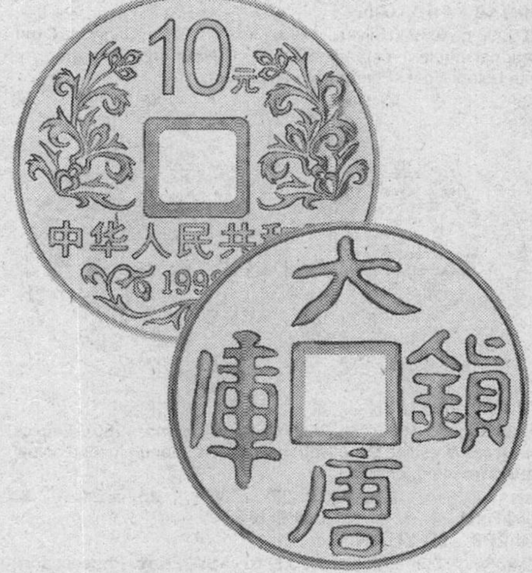

Y# 1064 10 YUAN

31.1035 g., 0.9990 Silver 1.0000 oz. ASW, 40 mm. **Subject:** Vault Protector **Obv:** Denomination, inscription and ornamental design,square cutout at center **Rev:** Old cash coin characters, square cutout at center **Edge:** Reeded **Note:** Square holed cash coin design.

Date	Mintage	F	VF	XF	Unc	BU
1998 Proof	100,000	Value: 22.50				

Y# 1065 10 YUAN

3.1100 g., 0.9990 Gold .0999 oz. AGW, 18 mm. **Subject:** Vault Protector **Obv:** Denomination, inscription and ornamental design **Rev:** Old cash coin characters **Edge:** Reeded **Note:** Square holed cash coin design.

Date	Mintage	F	VF	XF	Unc	BU
1998 Proof	6,000	Value: 120				

Y# 1131.1 10 YUAN

31.1000 g., 0.9990 Silver 0.9989 oz. ASW, 40 mm. **Obv:** Radiant winged pillar monument above flowers **Rev:** Child holding vase, elephant at left **Edge:** Reeded

Date	Mintage	F	VF	XF	Unc	BU
1998	80,000	—	—	—	27.50	—

Y# 1131.2 10 YUAN

31.1000 g., 0.9990 Silver 0.9989 oz. ASW, 40 mm. **Obv:** Radiant winged pillar monument above flowers **Rev:** Multicolor child holding vase, elephant at left **Edge:** Reeded

Date	Mintage	F	VF	XF	Unc	BU
1998 Proof	100,000	Value: 40.00				

Y# 914.2 10 YUAN

31.2600 g., 0.9990 Silver 1.0040 oz. ASW **Subject:** Celebrating Spring **Obv:** Radiant lantern, date below **Rev:** Multicolor, children lighting firecrackers, denomination above

Date	Mintage	F	VF	XF	Unc	BU
1999 Proof	—	Value: 42.50				

Y# 943 10 YUAN

31.1035 g., 0.9990 Silver 1.0000 oz. ASW **Obv:** Wan Chun Pavilion, date below **Rev:** Gold-plated Chinese roses, denomination at lower left

Date	Mintage	F	VF	XF	Unc	BU
1999	100,000	—	—	—	50.00	—

Y# 944 10 YUAN

31.1035 g., 0.9990 Silver 1.0000 oz. ASW **Obv:** Da Guan Tower in Kunming, date below **Rev:** Multicolor camellias, denomination upper right

Date	Mintage	F	VF	XF	Unc	BU
1999 Proof	100,000	Value: 50.00				

Y# 1055 10 YUAN

Bi-Metallic Copper-Nickel center in Brass ring, 25.5 mm. **Subject:** Return of Macau **Obv:** Stylized water lily **Rev:** Junk and building **Edge:** Reeded and plain sections

Date	Mintage	F	VF	XF	Unc	BU
1999	—	—	—	—	6.00	—

Y# 1056 10 YUAN

Bi-Metallic Copper-Nickel center in Brass ring, 25.5 mm. **Subject:** Return of Macau **Obv:** Stylized water lily **Rev:** Modern harbor and city view with document **Edge:** Reeded and plain sections

Date	Mintage	F	VF	XF	Unc	BU
1999	—	—	—	—	6.00	—

Y# 1059 10 YUAN

7.8000 g., Bi-Metallic Brass center in Copper-Nickel ring, 25.5 mm. **Subject:** 50th Anniversary - People's Republic **Obv:** Fireworks above building **Rev:** Birds above "50" **Edge:** Reeded and plain sections

Date	Mintage	F	VF	XF	Unc	BU
1999	—	—	—	—	8.00	—

Y# 1078 10 YUAN

30.9200 g., 0.9990 Silver .9931 oz. ASW, 40 mm. **Subject:** Yin and Yang Concept **Obv:** Gate, date below **Rev:** Gold-plated standing goddess, denomination at right **Edge:** Reeded

Date	Mintage	F	VF	XF	Unc	BU
1999	—	Value: 50.00				

Y# 1207 10 YUAN

31.1035 g., 0.9990 Silver 0.999 oz. ASW, 40 mm. **Obv:** Building on top of E Mei Mountain, date below **Rev:** The Kuan Yin Buddha, denomination at left **Edge:** Reeded

Date	Mintage	F	VF	XF	Unc	BU
1999	60,000	—	—	—	—	40.00

Y# 1228 10 YUAN

31.1035 g., 0.9990 Silver .999 oz. ASW, 40 mm. **Obv:** Radiant winged pillar above flowers **Rev:** Multicolor child holding a red carp above his head **Edge:** Reeded

Date	Mintage	F	VF	XF	Unc	BU
1999 Proof	—	Value: 40.00				

Y# 1235 10 YUAN

31.3300 g., 0.9990 Silver 1.0063 oz. ASW, 40 mm. **Subject:** Y2K **Obv:** Monument **Rev:** World Golbe as an eye above value **Edge:** Reeded

Date	Mintage	F	VF	XF	Unc	BU
2000 Proof	88,000	Value: 40.00				

Y# 993 10 YUAN

23.0375 g., 0.9000 Silver .6666 oz. ASW, 40 mm. **Obv:** Building within circle, date below **Rev:** Multicolor dragon, denomination at right

Date	Mintage	F	VF	XF	Unc	BU
2000	100,000	—	—	—	50.00	—

Y# 994 10 YUAN

3.1103 g., 0.9990 Gold .1000 oz. AGW **Subject:** Y2K

Date	Mintage	F	VF	XF	Unc	BU
2000	50,000	—	—	—	—	75.00

Y# 995 10 YUAN

3.1103 g., 0.9990 Gold .1000 oz. AGW **Subject:** Chinese Grotto Art

Date	Mintage	F	VF	XF	Unc	BU
2000	50,000	—	—	—	70.00	—

Y# 996 10 YUAN

3.1103 g., 0.9990 Gold .1000 oz. AGW, 18 mm. **Subject:** Goddess Kuan Yin **Obv:** Putuo Mountain Gate **Rev:** Standing Kuan Yin with holographic background **Edge:** Reeded

Date	Mintage	F	VF	XF	Unc	BU
2000	33,000	—	—	—	—	135

Y# 1048 10 YUAN

31.1035 g., 0.9990 Silver 1. oz. ASW, 40 mm. **Subject:** Dragons **Shape:** Round

Date	Mintage	F	VF	XF	Unc	BU
2000	50,000	—	—	—	—	40.00

Y# 1123 10 YUAN

7.8000 g., Bi-Metallic Copper-Nickel center in Brass ring, 25.5 mm. **Obv:** Rocket and city view above wheel **Rev:** Number two and eye above map of China **Edge:** Segmented reeding

Date	Mintage	F	VF	XF	Unc	BU
2000	—	—	—	—	8.00	—

Y# 745 15 YUAN

10.0000 g., 0.8000 Silver .2572 oz. ASW **Series:** Olympics **Obv:** National emblem, denomination below **Rev:** Ancient archers, date below **Note:** Piedfort-type planchet.

Date	Mintage	F	VF	XF	Unc	BU
1980	15,000	—	—	—	16.50	—

Y# 18 20 YUAN

10.3500 g., 0.8500 Silver .2829 oz. ASW **Series:** 1980 Olympics **Subject:** Wrestling **Obv:** National emblem, denomination below **Rev:** Wrestlers, date below

Date	Mintage	F	VF	XF	Unc	BU
1980 Proof	29,000	Value: 16.50				

Y# 207 20 YUAN

62.2060 g., 0.9990 Silver 2.0000 oz. ASW **Rev:** Phoenix and dragon

Date	Mintage	F	VF	XF	Unc	BU
1990 Proof	5,000	Value: 90.00				

Y# 888 20 YUAN

62.2060 g., 0.9990 Silver 2.0000 oz. ASW **Obv:** Great Wall, date below **Rev:** Horse and dragon, denomination at right

Date	Mintage	F	VF	XF	Unc	BU
1992 Proof	6,000	Value: 100				

Note: Issued in 1996

Y# 595 20 YUAN

62.2060 g., 0.9990 Silver 2.0000 oz. ASW **Obv:** Bai Di city gate, date at bottom **Rev:** Yangtze River scene, denomination at bottom **Shape:** Rectangular

Date	Mintage	F	VF	XF	Unc	BU
1996 Proof	8,000	Value: 65.00				

Y# 596 20 YUAN

62.2060 g., 0.9990 Silver 2.0000 oz. ASW **Obv:** Qu Yuan Temple, date at bottom **Rev:** River scene, denomination below **Shape:** Rectangular

Date	Mintage	F	VF	XF	Unc	BU
1996 Proof	8,000	Value: 65.00				

Y# 597 20 YUAN

62.2060 g., 0.9990 Silver 2.0000 oz. ASW **Obv:** Zhang Fei Temple, date at bottom **Rev:** River scene, denomination below **Shape:** Rectangular

Date	Mintage	F	VF	XF	Unc	BU
1996 Proof	8,000	Value: 65.00				

Y# 598 20 YUAN

62.2060 g., 0.9990 Silver 2.0000 oz. ASW **Obv:** Zhao Jun Temple, date at bottom **Rev:** River scene, denomination below **Shape:** Rectangular

Date	Mintage	F	VF	XF	Unc	BU
1996 Proof	8,000	Value: 65.00				

Y# 35 25 YUAN

19.4400 g., 0.8000 Silver .5000 oz. ASW **Subject:** World Soccer Cup **Obv:** National emblem, date below **Rev:** Soccer players, denomination upper right

Date	Mintage	F	VF	XF	Unc	BU
1982 Proof	40,000	Value: 27.50				

Y# 36 25 YUAN

19.4400 g., 0.8000 Silver .5000 oz. ASW **Subject:** World Soccer Cup **Obv:** National emblem, date below **Rev:** Soccer players, denomination below

Date	Mintage	F	VF	XF	Unc	BU
1982 Proof	40,000	Value: 27.50				

Y# 555 25 YUAN

8.4800 g., 0.9170 Gold .2500 oz. AGW **Subject:** Bronze Age Sculptures **Obv:** National emblem **Rev:** Ram

Date	Mintage	F	VF	XF	Unc	BU
1992 Proof	500	Value: 385				

Y# 556 25 YUAN

8.4800 g., 0.9170 Gold .2500 oz. AGW **Subject:** Bronze Age Sculptures **Rev:** Panther

Date	Mintage	F	VF	XF	Unc	BU
1992 Proof	500	Value: 385				

Y# 889 25 YUAN

7.7759 g., 0.9990 Gold .2500 oz. AGW **Obv:** Great Wall **Rev:** Horse and dragon

Date	Mintage	F	VF	XF	Unc	BU
1992 Proof	5,000	Value: 195				

Note: Issued in 1996

Y# 404 25 YUAN

7.7759 g., 0.9990 Gold .2500 oz. AGW **Rev:** Chinese Gods: Fu, Lu, and Shu

Date	Mintage	F	VF	XF	Unc	BU
1993	Est. 3,000	—	—	—	—	195

Y# 408 25 YUAN

8.4900 g., 0.9170 Gold .2500 oz. AGW **Subject:** Bronze Age Sculptures **Obv:** National emblem, date below **Rev:** Unicorn, right, denomination lower right

Date	Mintage	F	VF	XF	Unc	BU
1993 Proof	350	Value: 550				

Y# 475 25 YUAN

7.7758 g., 0.9990 Gold .2500 oz. AGW **Obv:** Temple of Heaven **Rev:** Two peacocks, denomination above

Date	Mintage	F	VF	XF	Unc	BU
1993 Prooflike	—	—	—	—	—	185

Y# 502 25 YUAN

7.7758 g., 0.9990 Gold .2500 oz. AGW **Rev:** Goddess Kuan Yin seated in flower, denomination at left

Date	Mintage	F	VF	XF	Unc	BU
1993 Proof	1,000	Value: 195				

Y# 775 25 YUAN

7.7758 g., 0.9990 Gold .2500 oz. AGW **Subject:** Homeland Scenery **Obv:** Great Wall **Rev:** Large temple at Mount Heng

Date	Mintage	F	VF	XF	Unc	BU
1993 Proof	8,888	Value: 220				

Y# 1072 25 YUAN

7.7758 g., 0.9995 Platinum .2500 oz. APW, 21.95 mm. **Series:** Chinese Inventions and Discoveries **Obv:** Great Wall **Rev:** Stirrup and equestrians **Edge:** Reeded

Date	Mintage	F	VF	XF	Unc	BU
1993 Proof	100	Value: 950				

Y# 1073 25 YUAN

7.7758 g., 0.9995 Platinum .2500 oz. APW **Series:** Chinese Inventions and Discoveries **Obv:** Great Wall **Rev:** Umbrella use and repair scene

Date	Mintage	F	VF	XF	Unc	BU
1993 Proof	100	Value: 950				

Y# 1074 25 YUAN

7.7758 g., 0.9995 Platinum .2500 oz. APW **Series:** Chinese Inventions and Discoveries **Obv:** Great Wall **Rev:** Mathematicians using an abacus

Date	Mintage	F	VF	XF	Unc	BU
1993 Proof	100	Value: 950				

Y# 1075 25 YUAN

7.7758 g., 0.9995 Platinum .2500 oz. APW **Series:** Chinese Inventions and Discoveries **Obv:** Great Wall **Rev:** Two men and Yin and Yang symbol

Date	Mintage	F	VF	XF	Unc	BU
1993 Proof	100	Value: 950				

Y# 1076 25 YUAN

7.7758 g., 0.9995 Platinum .2500 oz. APW **Series:** Chinese Inventions and Discoveries **Obv:** Great Wall **Rev:** Excavating the Terra-cotta army

Date	Mintage	F	VF	XF	Unc	BU
1993 Proof	100	Value: 950				

Y# 409 25 YUAN

8.4900 g., 0.9170 Gold .2500 oz. AGW **Subject:** Bronze Age Sculptures **Obv:** National emblem, date below **Rev:** Pig, left, denomination below

Date	Mintage	F	VF	XF	Unc	BU
1993 Proof	350	Value: 550				

Y# 1118 25 YUAN

7.7758 g., 0.9995 Platinum 0.2499 oz. APW, 21.95 mm. **Subject:** Oriental Inventions **Obv:** Great Wall **Rev:** First tuned bells

Date	Mintage	F	VF	XF	Unc	BU
1994 Proof	100	Value: 950				

Y# 1119 25 YUAN

7.7758 g., 0.9995 Platinum 0.2499 oz. APW, 21.95 mm. **Subject:** Oriental Inventions **Obv:** Great Wall **Rev:** First silken fabric

Date	Mintage	F	VF	XF	Unc	BU
1994 Proof	100	Value: 950				

Y# 1120 25 YUAN

7.7758 g., 0.9995 Platinum 0.2499 oz. APW, 21.95 mm. **Subject:** Oriental Inventions **Obv:** Great Wall **Rev:** First records of comets

Date	Mintage	F	VF	XF	Unc	BU
1994 Proof	100	Value: 950				

Y# 1121 25 YUAN

7.7758 g., 0.9995 Platinum 0.2499 oz. APW, 21.95 mm. **Subject:** Oriental Inventions **Obv:** Great Wall **Rev:** First masts for sailing

Date	Mintage	F	VF	XF	Unc	BU
1994 Proof	100	Value: 950				

Y# 1122 25 YUAN

7.7758 g., 0.9995 Platinum 0.2499 oz. APW, 21.95 mm. **Subject:** Oriental Inventions **Obv:** Great Wall **Rev:** First chain pumps used to draw water

Date	Mintage	F	VF	XF	Unc	BU
1994 Proof	100	Value: 950				

Y# 422 25 YUAN
7.7758 g., Bi-Metallic Gold center in Silver ring .2500 oz. **Obv:** Building within circle, date below **Rev:** Unicorn, denomination at left, within circle **Note:** Similar to 10 Yuan, Y#420.

Date	Mintage	F	VF	XF	Unc	BU
1994 Proof	1,100	Value: 220				

Y# 1181 25 YUAN
7.7759 g., 0.9999 Platinum 0.25 oz. APW **Subject:** Chinese Inventions **Rev:** First tuned bells

Date	Mintage	F	VF	XF	Unc	BU
1994	100	Value: 1,050				

Y# 1182 25 YUAN
7.7759 g., 0.9999 Platinum 0.25 oz. APW **Subject:** Chinese inventions **Rev:** First silk fabrics

Date	Mintage	F	VF	XF	Unc	BU
1994	100	Value: 1,050				

Y# 1183 25 YUAN
7.7759 g., 0.9999 Platinum 0.25 oz. APW **Subject:** Chinese inventions **Rev:** First recording of comets

Date	Mintage	F	VF	XF	Unc	BU
1994	100	Value: 1,150				

Y# 1184 25 YUAN
7.7759 g., 0.9999 Platinum 0.25 oz. APW **Subject:** Chinese inventions **Rev:** First masts for sailing

Date	Mintage	F	VF	XF	Unc	BU
1994	100	Value: 1,050				

Y# 1185 25 YUAN
7.7759 g., 0.9999 Platinum 0.25 oz. APW **Subject:** Chinese inventions **Rev:** First chain pumps used to draw water

Date	Mintage	F	VF	XF	Unc	BU
1994	100	Value: 1,050				

Y# 423 25 YUAN
7.7758 g., 0.9990 Gold .2500 oz. AGW **Obv:** Figure on Eastern unicorn, date below **Rev:** Unicorn, denomination at left, rose sprays below

Date	Mintage	F	VF	XF	Unc	BU
1994 Proof	5,100	Value: 220				

Y# 511 25 YUAN
3.1103 g., 0.9990 Gold .1000 oz. AGW **Obv:** Great Wall, date below **Rev:** Goddess Kuan Yin holding child, facing, denomination at left

Date	Mintage	F	VF	XF	Unc	BU
1994 Proof	1,000	Value: 220				

Y# 512 25 YUAN
3.1103 g., 0.9990 Gold .1000 oz. AGW **Obv:** Great Wall, date below **Rev:** Goddess Kuan Yin with bottle, 3/4 left, denomination at right

Date	Mintage	F	VF	XF	Unc	BU
1994 Proof	1,000	Value: 220				

Y# 513 25 YUAN
3.1103 g., 0.9990 Gold .1000 oz. AGW **Obv:** Great Wall, date below **Rev:** Goddess Kuan Yin standing, denomination at right

Date	Mintage	F	VF	XF	Unc	BU
1994 Proof	1,000	Value: 220				

Y# 514 25 YUAN
3.1103 g., 0.9990 Gold .1000 oz. AGW **Obv:** Great Wall, date below **Rev:** Goddess Kuan Yin seated, denomination at right

Date	Mintage	F	VF	XF	Unc	BU
1994 Proof	1,000	Value: 220				

Y# 524 25 YUAN
7.7758 g., 0.9990 Gold .2500 oz. AGW **Obv:** Pu-Tow temple **Rev:** Goddess of Mercy - with Lotus flower

Date	Mintage	F	VF	XF	Unc	BU
1995 Proof	1,000	Value: 220				

Y# 525 25 YUAN
7.7758 g., 0.9990 Gold .2500 oz. AGW **Rev:** Goddess of Mercy with wheel

Date	Mintage	F	VF	XF	Unc	BU
1995 Proof	1,000	Value: 220				

Y# 526 25 YUAN
7.7758 g., 0.9990 Gold .2500 oz. AGW **Rev:** Goddess of Mercy with scepter

Date	Mintage	F	VF	XF	Unc	BU
1995 Proof	1,000	Value: 220				

Y# 527 25 YUAN
7.7758 g., 0.9990 Gold .2500 oz. AGW **Rev:** Goddess of Mercy with bowl

Date	Mintage	F	VF	XF	Unc	BU
1995 Proof	1,000	Value: 220				

Y# 687 25 YUAN
7.7758 g., Bi-Metallic Gold center in Silver ring .2500 oz. **Obv:** Building within circle, date below **Rev:** Unicorn with offspring, denomination at left, circle surrounds

Date	Mintage	F	VF	XF	Unc	BU
1995 Proof	2,000	Value: 220				

Y# 738 25 YUAN
7.8300 g., 0.9990 Gold .2515 oz. AGW **Obv:** Eastern unicorn rearing, date below **Rev:** Western unicorn with offspring, denomination at left

Date	Mintage	F	VF	XF	Unc	BU
1995 Proof	5,000	Value: 220				

Y# 835 25 YUAN
7.8300 g., 0.9990 Gold .2515 oz. AGW **Subject:** Sea Goddess Mazhu **Obv:** Mazhu Temple **Rev:** Mazhu's portrayal

Date	Mintage	F	VF	XF	Unc	BU
1995 Proof	3,000	Value: 220				

Y# 1061 25 YUAN
Bi-Metallic 0.999 Gold center in 0.999 Silver ring, 30 mm. **Obv:** Eastern unicorn **Rev:** Western unicorn with offspring **Edge:** Reeded

Date	Mintage	F	VF	XF	Unc	BU
1995 Proof	—	Value: 220				

Y# 955 25 YUAN
7.7758 g., 0.9995 Platinum .2500 oz. APW, 21.9 mm. **Subject:** Unicorn **Obv:** Eastern unicorn, full body, date below **Rev:** Western unicorn head, right, denomination at right **Edge:** Reeded

Date	Mintage	F	VF	XF	Unc	BU
1996 Proof	500	Value: 375				

Y# 743 25 YUAN
7.7759 g., 0.9990 Gold .2500 oz. AGW **Obv:** Eastern unicorn, date below **Rev:** Western unicorn and maiden, denomination at left

Date	Mintage	F	VF	XF	Unc	BU
1996 Proof	3,000	Value: 300				

Y# 867 25 YUAN
7.7759 g., 0.9990 Gold .2500 oz. AGW **Subject:** Centennial of Chinese Post Office **Obv:** Modern postal stamp, date below **Rev:** Imperial postal stamp, denomination at right

Date	Mintage	F	VF	XF	Unc	BU
1996 Proof	3,000	Value: 195				

Y# 915 25 YUAN
7.7759 g., 0.9990 Gold .2500 oz. AGW **Subject:** Celebrating Spring **Obv:** Radiant lantern, date below **Rev:** Children setting off firecrackers, denomination above

Date	Mintage	F	VF	XF	Unc	BU
1997 Proof	10,000	Value: 185				

Y# 997 25 YUAN
7.7759 g., 0.9990 Gold .2500 oz. AGW **Subject:** China Palace Museum **Obv:** Forbidden City **Rev:** Imperial Gardens

Date	Mintage	F	VF	XF	Unc	BU
1997 Proof	4,000	Value: 195				

Y# 998 25 YUAN
7.7759 g., 0.9990 Gold .2500 oz. AGW **Subject:** China Palace Museum **Obv:** Forbidden City **Rev:** Jin Shui

Date	Mintage	F	VF	XF	Unc	BU
1997 Proof	4,000	Value: 195				

Y# 999 25 YUAN
7.7759 g., 0.9990 Gold .2500 oz. AGW **Subject:** China Palace Museum **Obv:** Forbidden City **Rev:** Quan Quin Palace

Date	Mintage	F	VF	XF	Unc	BU
1997 Proof	4,000	Value: 195				

Y# 1000 25 YUAN
7.7759 g., 0.9990 Gold .2500 oz. AGW **Subject:** China Palace Museum **Obv:** Forbidden City **Rev:** Inner view of palace

Date	Mintage	F	VF	XF	Unc	BU
1997 Proof	4,000	Value: 195				

Y# 743a 25 YUAN
7.7759 g., 0.9990 Platinum .2500 oz. APW

Date	Mintage	F	VF	XF	Unc	BU
1996 Proof	500	Value: 345				

Y# 1135 25 YUAN
7.7758 g., 0.9999 Gold 0.25 oz. AGW **Subject:** Greeting Spring

Date	Mintage	F	VF	XF	Unc	BU
1998	10,000	—	—	—	—	190

Y# 1136 25 YUAN
7.7758 g., 0.9999 Gold 0.25 oz. AGW **Subject:** Bird **Note:** Multicolored.

Date	Mintage	F	VF	XF	Unc	BU
2000	8,800	—	—	—	—	330

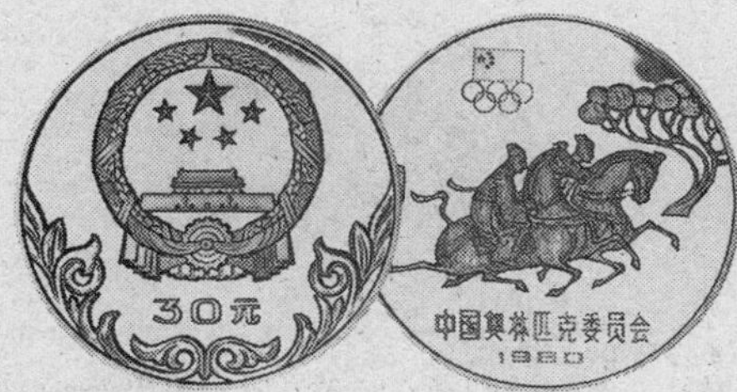

Y# 19 30 YUAN
15.0000 g., 0.8500 Silver .4099 oz. ASW **Series:** 1980 Olympics **Subject:** Equestrian **Obv:** National emblem, denomination below **Rev:** Horse racing, date below

Date	Mintage	F	VF	XF	Unc	BU
1980 Proof	29,000	Value: 17.50				

Y# 20 30 YUAN
15.0000 g., 0.8500 Silver .4099 oz. ASW **Series:** 1980 Olympics **Obv:** National emblem, denomination below **Rev:** Soccer, date below

Date	Mintage	F	VF	XF	Unc	BU
1980 Proof	29,000	Value: 17.50				

Y# 21 30 YUAN
15.0000 g., 0.8500 Silver .4099 oz. ASW **Series:** Lake Placid 1980 - 13th Winter Olympic Games **Obv:** National emblem, denomination below **Rev:** Woman speed skater, within snowflake

Date	Mintage	F	VF	XF	Unc	BU
1980 Proof	20,000	Value: 18.50				

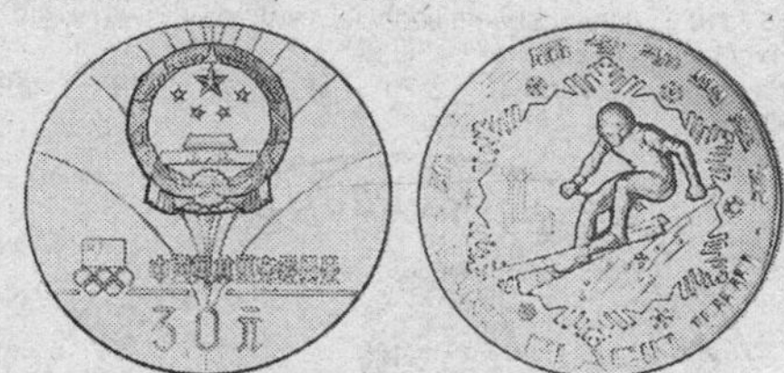

Y# 746 30 YUAN
16.0000 g., Silver .4373 oz. ASW **Series:** 1980 Olympics **Obv:** National emblem, denomination below **Rev:** Downhill skier, within snowflake

Date	Mintage	F	VF	XF	Unc	BU
1980 Proof	20,000	Value: 18.50				

Y# 747 30 YUAN
16.0000 g., Silver .4373 oz. ASW **Series:** Lake Placid 1980 - 13th Winter Olympic Games **Obv:** National emblem, denomination below **Rev:** Woman figure skater, within snowflake

Date	Mintage	F	VF	XF	Unc	BU
1980 Proof	20,000	Value: 18.50				

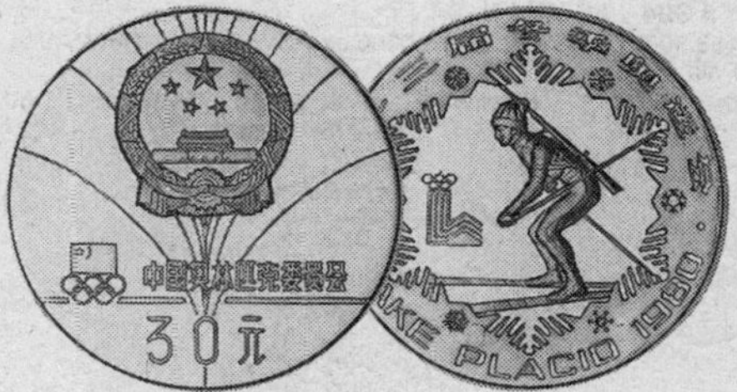

Y# 748 30 YUAN
16.0000 g., Silver .4373 oz. ASW **Series:** 1980 Olympics **Obv:** National emblem, denomination below **Rev:** Biathalon skier, within snowflake

Date	Mintage	F	VF	XF	Unc	BU
1980 Proof	20,000	Value: 18.50				

Y# 8 35 YUAN
19.4400 g., 0.8000 Silver .5000 oz. ASW **Subject:** UNICEF and IYC **Obv:** National emblem and date above sprays **Rev:** Children planting a flower, denomination below

Date	Mintage	F	VF	XF	Unc	BU
1979 Matte	1,000	—	—	—	150	—
1979 Proof	14,000	Value: 65.00				

Y# 46 35 YUAN
33.5800 g., 0.8000 Silver .8638 oz. ASW **Subject:** 70th Anniversary - 1911 Revolution **Obv:** Statue of Sun Yat-sen divides dates **Rev:** Mausoleum, denomination below

Date	Mintage	F	VF	XF	Unc	BU
1981 Proof	3,885	Value: 200				

Y# 108 50 YUAN
155.5000 g., 0.9990 Silver 5.0000 oz. ASW, 70 mm. **Subject:** 120th Anniversary - Birth of Sun Yat-sen **Rev:** Sun Yat-sen standing, facing, denomination at left, circle surrounds **Note:** Photo reduced.

Date	Mintage	F	VF	XF	Unc	BU
1986 Proof	3,000	Value: 175				

Y# 170 50 YUAN
155.5000 g., 0.9990 Silver 5.0000 oz. ASW, 70 mm. **Series:** Seoul 1988 - 24th Summer Olympic Games **Rev:** Volleyball game, denomination below **Note:** Photo reduced.

Date	Mintage	F	VF	XF	Unc	BU
1988 Proof	3,898	Value: 250				

Y# 220 50 YUAN
31.1030 g., 0.9990 Palladium 1.0000 oz. **Obv:** Building, date below **Rev:** Panda on grid background, denomination lower right

Date	Mintage	F	VF	XF	Unc	BU
1989	3,000	—	—	—	—	440

Y# 704 50 YUAN
15.5517 g., 0.9990 Gold .5000 oz. AGW **Subject:** Taiwan Scenery Series **Obv:** Great Wall **Rev:** Pagoda

Date	Mintage	F	VF	XF	Unc	BU
1990 Proof	4,000	Value: 360				

Y# 705 50 YUAN
15.5517 g., 0.9990 Gold .5000 oz. AGW **Subject:** Taiwan Scenery Series **Obv:** Great Wall **Rev:** Pondside building

Date	Mintage	F	VF	XF	Unc	BU
1990 Proof	4,000	Value: 360				

Y# 706 50 YUAN
15.5517 g., 0.9990 Gold .5000 oz. AGW **Subject:** Taiwan Scenery Series **Obv:** Great Wall **Rev:** Hillside building

Date	Mintage	F	VF	XF	Unc	BU
1990 Proof	4,000	Value: 360				

Y# 707 50 YUAN
15.5517 g., 0.9990 Gold .5000 oz. AGW **Subject:** Taiwan Scenery Series **Obv:** Great Wall **Rev:** Three buildings joined by docks and bridge

Date	Mintage	F	VF	XF	Unc	BU
1990 Proof	4,000	Value: 360				

Y# 321 50 YUAN
155.6800 g., 0.9990 Silver 5.0053 oz. ASW **Series:** Albertville 1992 - 16th Winter Olympic Games **Obv:** National emblem, date below **Rev:** 3 speed skaters, denomination above **Note:** Photo reduced.

Date	Mintage	F	VF	XF	Unc	BU
1990 Proof	10,000	Value: 165				

Y# 472 50 YUAN
155.5000 g., 0.9990 Silver 5.0000 oz. ASW **Series:** Barcelona 1992 - 25th Summer Olympic Games **Obv:** National emblem, date below **Rev:** Female runners, denomination above

Date	Mintage	F	VF	XF	Unc	BU
1991 Proof	10,000	Value: 175				

Y# 477 50 YUAN
155.5000 g., 0.9990 Silver 5.0000 oz. ASW **Subject:** 80th Anniversary - 1911 Revolution **Obv:** Similar to 10 Yuan, Y#476,(building with two dates below) **Rev:** Sun Yat-Sen in uniform, facing, denomination at left

Date	Mintage	F	VF	XF	Unc	BU
1991 Proof	1,000	Value: 350				

Y# 557 50 YUAN
16.9600 g., 0.9170 Gold .5000 oz. AGW **Subject:** Bronze Age Sculptures **Obv:** National emblem, date below **Rev:** Kneeling figure, denomination below

Date	Mintage	F	VF	XF	Unc	BU
1992 Proof	500	Value: 775				

Y# 353 50 YUAN
155.5000 g., 0.9990 Silver 5.0000 oz. ASW **Obv:** Temple of Harmony **Rev:** Two peacocks

Date	Mintage	F	VF	XF	Unc	BU
1993 Proof	888	Value: 275				

Y# 378 50 YUAN
15.5517 g., 0.9990 Gold .5000 oz. AGW **Subject:** Chinese Inventions and Discoveries **Obv:** Great Wall, denomination below **Rev:** Chin with Yin Yang, denomination below

Date	Mintage	F	VF	XF	Unc	BU
1993 Proof	1,200	Value: 380				

Y# 394 50 YUAN
155.5000 g., 0.9990 Silver 5.0000 oz. ASW, 70 mm. **Rev:** Marco Polo

Date	Mintage	F	VF	XF	Unc	BU
1993 Proof	500	Value: 275				

Y# 401 50 YUAN
15.5517 g., 0.9990 Gold .5000 oz. AGW **Subject:** Chinese Inventions and Discoveries **Obv:** Great Wall, date below **Rev:** Invention of the Umbrella, denomination at right

Date	Mintage	F	VF	XF	Unc	BU
1993 Proof	1,200	Value: 380				

Y# 405 50 YUAN
155.5175 g., 0.9990 Silver 5.0000 oz. ASW **Subject:** Chinese Gods: Fu, Lu and Shu **Obv:** Building and Great Wall, date below **Rev:** Three gods with symbol on panel and child

Date	Mintage	F	VF	XF	Unc	BU
1993 Proof	1,000	Value: 325				

Y# 410 50 YUAN
16.9800 g., 0.9170 Gold .5000 oz. AGW **Subject:** Bronze Age Sculptures **Obv:** National emblem, date below **Rev:** Kneeling man lantern, denomination at right

Date	Mintage	F	VF	XF	Unc	BU
1993 Proof	350	Value: 850				

Y# 414 50 YUAN
15.5517 g., 0.9990 Gold .5000 oz. AGW **Subject:** Chairman Mao **Rev:** Bust, 3/4 left, denomination at left

Date	Mintage	F	VF	XF	Unc	BU
1993 Proof	5,000	Value: 425				
1993(s) Proof	2,500	Value: 545				

Y# 445 50 YUAN
15.5517 g., 0.9990 Gold .5000 oz. AGW **Subject:** Taiwan Temples **Obv:** Great Wall, date below **Rev:** Buddha statue, denomination below

Date	Mintage	F	VF	XF	Unc	BU
1993 Proof	1,000	Value: 370				

Y# 446 50 YUAN
15.5517 g., 0.9990 Gold .5000 oz. AGW **Subject:** Taiwan Temples **Obv:** Great Wall, date below **Rev:** Large temple, denomination below

Date	Mintage	F	VF	XF	Unc	BU
1993 Proof	1,000	Value: 370				

Y# 447 50 YUAN
15.5517 g., 0.9990 Gold .5000 oz. AGW **Subject:** Taiwan Temples **Obv:** Great Wall, date below **Rev:** Small temple, denomination below

Date	Mintage	F	VF	XF	Unc	BU
1993 Proof	1,000	Value: 370				

Y# 448 50 YUAN
15.5517 g., 0.9990 Gold .5000 oz. AGW **Subject:** Taiwan Temples **Obv:** Great Wall, date below **Rev:** Tower temple, denomination below

Date	Mintage	F	VF	XF	Unc	BU
1993 Proof	—	Value: 370				

Y# 503 50 YUAN
15.5517 g., 0.9990 Gold .5000 oz. AGW **Obv:** Great Wall, date below **Rev:** Goddess Kuan Yin - seated in flower, denomination at left

Date	Mintage	F	VF	XF	Unc	BU
1993 Proof	1,000	Value: 380				

Y# 765 50 YUAN
15.5517 g., 0.9990 Gold .5000 oz. AGW **Subject:** Chinese Inventions and Discoveries **Obv:** Great Wall **Rev:** Stirrup

Date	Mintage	F	VF	XF	Unc	BU
1993 Proof	1,200	Value: 380				

Y# 766 50 YUAN
15.5517 g., 0.9990 Gold .5000 oz. AGW **Subject:** Chinese Inventions and Discoveries **Obv:** Great Wall **Rev:** Excavation of the Terra-cotta Army

Date	Mintage	F	VF	XF	Unc	BU
1993 Proof	1,200	Value: 380				

Y# 767 50 YUAN
15.5517 g., 0.9990 Gold .5000 oz. AGW **Subject:** Chinese Inventions and Discoveries **Obv:** Great Wall **Rev:** Discovery of mathematical zero

Date	Mintage	F	VF	XF	Unc	BU
1993 Proof	1,200	Value: 380				

Y# 776 50 YUAN
155.5518 g., 0.9990 Silver 5.0000 oz. ASW **Obv:** Great Wall **Rev:** Mount Hau and river

Date	Mintage	F	VF	XF	Unc	BU
1993 Proof	8,888	Value: 275				

Y# 413 50 YUAN
155.5175 g., 0.9990 Silver 5.0000 oz. ASW, 70 mm. **Rev:** Chairman Mao writing, denomination at right **Note:** Photo reduced.

Date	Mintage	F	VF	XF	Unc	BU
1993	1,500	—	—	—	300	—

Y# 772 50 YUAN
155.5518 g., 0.9990 Silver 5.0000 oz. ASW **Subject:** Chinese Wildlife **Obv:** National emblem, date below **Rev:** Brown bear and cub, denomination at right **Note:** Photo reduced.

Date	Mintage	F	VF	XF	Unc	BU
1993 Proof	4,500	Value: 350				

Y# 622 50 YUAN
15.5517 g., 0.9990 Gold 0.4995 oz. AGW **Subject:** Oriental Inventions **Obv:** Great Wall **Rev:** First silken fabric

Date	Mintage	F	VF	XF	Unc	BU
1994 Proof	1,200	Value: 380				

Y# 424 50 YUAN
155.5000 g., 0.9990 Silver 5.0000 oz. ASW **Obv:** Figure on Eastern unicorn, date below **Rev:** Unicorn looking right, denomination at left, rose sprays below

Date	Mintage	F	VF	XF	Unc	BU
1994 Proof	1,100	Value: 150				

Y# 425 50 YUAN
15.5517 g., 0.9990 Gold .5000 oz. AGW **Obv:** Figure on Eastern unicorn, date below **Rev:** Unicorn looking right, rose sprays below, denomination at left

Date	Mintage	F	VF	XF	Unc	BU
1994 Proof	1,100	Value: 400				

Y# 459 50 YUAN
15.5517 g., 0.9990 Gold .5000 oz. AGW **Subject:** Children At Play **Rev:** Two children with cat, denomination below

Date	Mintage	F	VF	XF	Unc	BU
1994 Proof	1,888	Value: 365				

Y# 460 50 YUAN
15.5517 g., 0.9990 Gold .5000 oz. AGW **Subject:** Children At Play **Obv:** Temple of Heaven **Rev:** Three children with toy boat, denomination below

Date	Mintage	F	VF	XF	Unc	BU
1994 Proof	1,888	Value: 365				

Y# 461 50 YUAN
155.5000 g., 0.9990 Silver 5.0000 oz. ASW **Subject:** Children At Play **Obv:** Temple of Heaven **Rev:** Two children with cat

Date	Mintage	F	VF	XF	Unc	BU
1994 Proof	500	Value: 375				

Y# 621 50 YUAN
15.5517 g., 0.9990 Gold .5000 oz. AGW **Subject:** Oriental Inventions **Obv:** Great Wall **Rev:** First tuned bells

Date	Mintage	F	VF	XF	Unc	BU
1994 Proof	1,200	Value: 380				

Y# 623 50 YUAN
15.5517 g., 0.9990 Gold .5000 oz. AGW **Subject:** Oriental Inventions - Astronomy **Obv:** Great Wall **Rev:** First records of comets

Date	Mintage	F	VF	XF	Unc	BU
1994 Proof	1,200	Value: 380				

Y# 624 50 YUAN
15.5517 g., 0.9990 Gold .5000 oz. AGW **Subject:** Oriental Inventions **Obv:** Great Wall **Rev:** First masts for sailing

Date	Mintage	F	VF	XF	Unc	BU
1994 Proof	1,200	Value: 380				

Y# 625 50 YUAN
15.5517 g., 0.9990 Gold .5000 oz. AGW **Subject:** Oriental Inventions **Obv:** Great Wall **Rev:** First chain pumps used to draw water

Date	Mintage	F	VF	XF	Unc	BU
1994 Proof	1,200	Value: 380				

Y# 708 50 YUAN
155.5175 g., 0.9990 Silver 5.0000 oz. ASW **Rev:** Taiwan temple

Date	Mintage	F	VF	XF	Unc	BU
1994 Proof	500	Value: 250				

Y# 785 50 YUAN
155.5175 g., 0.9990 Silver 5.0000 oz. ASW **Subject:** Sino-Singapore Friendship **Obv:** Great Wall **Rev:** Singapore harbor view

Date	Mintage	F	VF	XF	Unc	BU
1994 Proof	300	Value: 800				

Y# 471 50 YUAN
15.5517 g., 0.9990 Gold .5000 oz. AGW **Subject:** Dinosaur **Obv:** Tall building, date below **Rev:** Brontosaurus, denomination at left

Date	Mintage	F	VF	XF	Unc	BU
1995 Proof	2,000	Value: 365				

Y# 488 50 YUAN
15.5517 g., 0.9990 Gold .5000 oz. AGW **Series:** 50th Anniversary - United Nations **Obv:** United Nations logo, date below **Rev:** United Nations building, denomination upper left, dates at right

Date	Mintage	F	VF	XF	Unc	BU
1995 Proof	17,500	Value: 350				

Y# 532 50 YUAN
15.5517 g., 0.9990 Gold .5000 oz. AGW **Subject:** Return of Hong Kong to China - Series I **Obv:** Tiananmen building and monument **Rev:** Deng Xiaoping's portrait above Hong Kong skyline

Date	Mintage	F	VF	XF	Unc	BU
1995 Proof	11,800	Value: 365				

Y# 593 50 YUAN
15.5517 g., 0.9990 Gold .5000 oz. AGW **Subject:** Yellow River culture **Rev:** Nu Wa Rising, denomination below

Date	Mintage	F	VF	XF	Unc	BU
1995 Proof	2,500	Value: 400				

Y# 632 50 YUAN
15.5517 g., 0.9990 Gold .5000 oz. AGW **Subject:** Oriental Inventions **Obv:** Great Wall, date below **Rev:** Soldiers with cannon and gunpowder, denomination lower left

Date	Mintage	F	VF	XF	Unc	BU
1995 Proof	1,200	Value: 380				

Y# 633 50 YUAN
15.5517 g., 0.9990 Gold .5000 oz. AGW **Subject:** Oriental Inventions **Obv:** Great Wall, date below **Rev:** Individual block printing, denomination at right

Date	Mintage	F	VF	XF	Unc	BU
1995 Proof	1,200	Value: 380				

Y# 636 50 YUAN
15.5517 g., 0.9990 Gold .5000 oz. AGW **Subject:** Oriental Inventions **Obv:** Great Wall, date below **Rev:** Teacher with anatomy chart of human body, denomination at left

Date	Mintage	F	VF	XF	Unc	BU
1995 Proof	1,200	Value: 380				

Y# 648 50 YUAN
15.5517 g., 0.9990 Gold .5000 oz. AGW **Rev:** Sailing ship

Date	Mintage	F	VF	XF	Unc	BU
1995 Proof	1,000	Value: 425				

Y# 651 50 YUAN
15.5517 g., 0.9990 Gold .5000 oz. AGW **Rev:** Junk

Date	Mintage	F	VF	XF	Unc	BU
1995 Proof	1,000	Value: 425				

Y# 690 50 YUAN
15.5517 g., 0.9990 Gold .5000 oz. AGW **Subject:** 50th Anniversary - Anti-Japanese War **Obv:** National emblem, date below **Rev:** Zhou and Mao above soldiers, denomination below

Date	Mintage	F	VF	XF	Unc	BU
1995 Proof	2,500	Value: 365				

Y# 691 50 YUAN
10.3600 g., Bi-Metallic Gold center in Silver ring .3335 oz. **Ring Weight:** 5.1800 g. **Ring Composition:** 0.9990 Silver .1667 oz. ASW **Subject:** World Women's Conference **Obv:** Logo above building **Rev:** Three women, denomination above within circle

Date	Mintage	F	VF	XF	Unc	BU
1995 Proof	3,000	Value: 275				

Y# 739 50 YUAN
15.5517 g., 0.9990 Gold .5000 oz. AGW **Obv:** Eastern unicorn, rearing, date below **Rev:** Western unicorn with offspring, denomination at left

Date	Mintage	F	VF	XF	Unc	BU
1995 Proof	2,000	Value: 380				

Y# 739a 50 YUAN
15.5517 g., 0.9995 Platinum .5000 oz. APW, 26.8 mm. **Subject:** Unicorn **Obv:** Eastern unicorn, rearing, date below **Rev:** Western unicorn with offspring, denomination at left **Edge:** Reeded

Date	Mintage	F	VF	XF	Unc	BU
1995 Proof	1,015	Value: 700				

Y# 813 50 YUAN
155.5175 g., 0.9990 Silver 5.000 oz. ASW **Subject:** 50th Anniversary - For the return of Taiwan to China **Obv:** Great Wall **Rev:** Taiwan and China maps

Date	Mintage	F	VF	XF	Unc	BU
1995 Proof	999	Value: 575				

Y# 814 50 YUAN
15.5517 g., 0.9990 Gold .5000 oz. AGW **Subject:** 50th Anniversary - For the return of Taiwan to China **Obv:** Great Wall **Rev:** Taiwan and China maps

Date	Mintage	F	VF	XF	Unc	BU
1995 Proof	3,000	Value: 365				

Y# 815 50 YUAN
15.5517 g., 0.9990 Gold .5000 oz. AGW **Subject:** 50th Anniversary - For the return of Taiwan to China **Obv:** Great Wall **Rev:** Zhongshan Hall

Date	Mintage	F	VF	XF	Unc	BU
1995 Proof	3,000	Value: 365				

Y# 821 50 YUAN
7.9020 g., 0.9160 Gold .2327 oz. AGW **Obv:** Bust of painter Xu Beihong, facing, date below **Rev:** Lion, denomination lower right

Date	Mintage	F	VF	XF	Unc	BU
1995 Proof	3,000	Value: 195				

Y# 822 50 YUAN
155.5175 g., 0.9990 Silver 5.0000 oz. ASW **Obv:** Chiqian building **Rev:** Zheng Chenggong standing with flag and ships

Date	Mintage	F	VF	XF	Unc	BU
1995 Proof	250	Value: 475				

Y# 829 50 YUAN
155.5175 g., 0.9990 Silver 5.0000 oz. ASW **Subject:** Romance of Three Kingdoms **Obv:** Luo Guanzhong **Rev:** Three figures

Date	Mintage	F	VF	XF	Unc	BU
1995 Proof	7,000	Value: 475				

Y# 829a 50 YUAN
155.5517 g., 0.9990 Gold .5000 oz. AGW **Subject:** Romance of Three Kingdoms **Obv:** Luo Guanzhong **Rev:** Three figures

Date	Mintage	F	VF	XF	Unc	BU
1995 Proof	2,000	Value: 365				

Y# 838 50 YUAN
10.3678 g., 0.9990 Gold .3333 oz. AGW **Subject:** Table Tennis **Obv:** Tianjing Stadium **Rev:** Table tennis player

Date	Mintage	F	VF	XF	Unc	BU
1995 Proof	2,000	Value: 245				

Y# 634 50 YUAN
15.5517 g., 0.9990 Gold 0.4995 oz. AGW **Subject:** Oriental Inventions **Obv:** Great Wall **Rev:** Potter

Date	Mintage	F	VF	XF	Unc	BU
1995 Proof	1,200	Value: 380				

Y# 635 50 YUAN
15.5517 g., 0.9990 Gold 0.4995 oz. AGW **Subject:** Oriental Inventions **Obv:** Great Wall **Rev:** Chess players

Date	Mintage	F	VF	XF	Unc	BU
1995 Proof	1,200	Value: 380				

Y# 891 50 YUAN
155.5175 g., 0.9990 Silver 5.0000 oz. ASW **Series:** 1996 Summer Olympics **Obv:** National emblem, date below **Rev:** Table tennis player, date at right, denomination at left **Note:** Photo reduced.

Date	Mintage	F	VF	XF	Unc	BU
1995 Proof	—	Value: 125				
1996 Proof	3,000	Value: 140				

Y# 592 50 YUAN
1555.5175 g., 0.9990 Silver 5.0000 oz. ASW, 70 mm. **Rev:** Da Yu walking through water, denomination at left **Note:** Photo reduced.

Date	Mintage	F	VF	XF	Unc	BU
1995 Proof	500	Value: 325				

Y# 688 50 YUAN
155.5000 g., 0.9990 Silver 5.0000 oz. ASW, 69 mm. **Rev:** Unicorn with offspring, denomination at left **Note:** Photo reduced.

Date	Mintage	F	VF	XF	Unc	BU
1995 Proof	—	Value: 150				

Y# 689 50 YUAN
155.5000 g., 0.9990 Silver 5.0000 oz. ASW, 70 mm. **Rev:** Junk, denomination below **Note:** Photo reduced.

Date	Mintage	F	VF	XF	Unc	BU
1995 Proof	1,000	Value: 300				

Y# 608 50 YUAN
11.3180 g., 0.9160 Gold .3333 oz. AGW **Subject:** Silk Road **Obv:** National emblem, date below **Rev:** Man riding camel, denomination at right

Date	Mintage	F	VF	XF	Unc	BU
1995 Proof	10,000	Value: 245				

Y# 609 50 YUAN
11.3180 g., 0.9160 Gold .3333 oz. AGW **Subject:** Silk Road **Obv:** National emblem, date below **Rev:** Water vendor, denomination lower right

Date	Mintage	F	VF	XF	Unc	BU
1996 Proof	10,000	Value: 245				

Y# 859 50 YUAN
155.5517 g., 0.9990 Gold .5000 oz. AGW **Obv:** Building, date below **Rev:** Sun Yat-sen bust facing, denomination below, fan sprays 3/4 around

Date	Mintage	F	VF	XF	Unc	BU
1996 Proof	3,000	Value: 365				

Y# 870 50 YUAN
155.5517 g., 0.9990 Gold .5000 oz. AGW **Subject:** 60th Anniversary - Long March **Obv:** Flag above building, date below **Rev:** Chairman Mao portrait, denomination at right

Date	Mintage	F	VF	XF	Unc	BU
1996 Proof	6,000	Value: 365				

Y# 881 50 YUAN
15.5517 g., 0.9990 Gold .5000 oz. AGW **Subject:** Romance of the Three Kingdoms Series **Obv:** Luo Guanzhong portrait **Rev:** Guand Du on horseback, leading his troops

Date	Mintage	F	VF	XF	Unc	BU
1996 Proof	2,000	Value: 365				

Y# 658 50 YUAN
15.5517 g., 0.9990 Gold .5000 oz. AGW **Subject:** Return of Hong Kong to China Series II **Obv:** Hong Kong Harbor

Date	Mintage	F	VF	XF	Unc	BU
1996 Proof	11,800	Value: 350				

Y# 1039 50 YUAN
15.5517 g., 0.9990 Gold .5000 oz. AGW, 27 mm. **Subject:** Unicorn **Obv:** Eastern unicorn, full body **Rev:** Western unicorn in wreath **Edge:** Reeded

Date	Mintage	F	VF	XF	Unc	BU
1996 Proof	1,000	Value: 425				

Y# 880 50 YUAN
155.5175 g., 0.9990 Silver 5.0000 oz. ASW, 80 mm. **Subject:** Romance of the Three Kingdoms Series **Obv:** Bust of Luo Guanzhong, 3/4 right, date below **Rev:** Battle scene, denomination below **Note:** Photo reduced.

Date	Mintage	F	VF	XF	Unc	BU
1996 Proof	500	Value: 325				

Y# 1038 50 YUAN

155.5175 g., 0.9990 Silver 5.0000 oz. ASW, 70.2 mm. **Subject:** Unicorn **Obv:** Eastern unicorn, full body, date below **Rev:** Western unicorn with maiden, denomination at left **Edge:** Reeded **Note:** Photo reduced.

Date	Mintage	F	VF	XF	Unc	BU
1996 Proof	—	Value: 325				

Y# 1091 50 YUAN

15.5518 g., 0.9990 Gold 0.4995 oz. AGW, 27 mm. **Subject:** Unicorns **Obv:** Eastern unicorn **Rev:** Western unicorn **Edge:** Reeded

Date	Mintage	F	VF	XF	Unc	BU
1996 Proof	1,000	Value: 400				

Y# 599 50 YUAN

15.5517 g., 0.9990 Gold .5000 oz. AGW **Obv:** Yangtze River scene, denomination lower left corner **Rev:** Large dam **Shape:** Rectangular

Date	Mintage	F	VF	XF	Unc	BU
1996 Proof	6,000	Value: 445				

Y# 1179 50 YUAN

15.5517 g., 0.9999 Gold 0.4999 oz. AGW **Subject:** Romance of the Three Kingdoms **Rev:** Soldiers on a boat

Date	Mintage	F	VF	XF	Unc	BU
1997 Proof	3,000	Value: 365				

Y# 906 50 YUAN

155.5175 g., 0.9990 Silver 5.0000 oz. ASW, 80 mm. **Subject:** Return of Macao to China **Obv:** Tiananmen Square - Forbidden City, date above leaf sprays below **Rev:** Deng Xiaoping viewing Macao, denomination at right **Note:** Photo reduced.

Date	Mintage	F	VF	XF	Unc	BU
1997 Proof	—	Value: 200				

Y# 906a 50 YUAN

155.5517 g., 0.9990 Gold .5000 oz. AGW **Subject:** Return of Macao to China **Obv:** Tiananmen Square - Forbidden City **Rev:** Deng Xiaoping viewing Macao

Date	Mintage	F	VF	XF	Unc	BU
1997 Proof	11,800	Value: 345				

Y# 903 50 YUAN

15.5517 g., 0.9990 Gold .5000 oz. AGW **Subject:** Return of Hong Kong to China - Series III **Obv:** Tiananmen Square - Forbidden City **Rev:** Flag and fireworks above Hong Kong, denomination below

Date	Mintage	F	VF	XF	Unc	BU
1997 Proof	11,800	Value: 345				

Y# 1004 50 YUAN

15.5517 g., 0.9990 Gold .5000 oz. AGW **Subject:** Huang (Yellow) River Culture **Obv:** Archer **Rev:** Dragon

Date	Mintage	F	VF	XF	Unc	BU
1997 Proof	3,000	Value: 365				

Y# 910 50 YUAN

155.5517 g., 0.9990 Gold .5000 oz. AGW **Subject:** People's Liberation Army **Obv:** Radiant star above Great Wall **Rev:** Youthful Chairman Mao standing

Date	Mintage	F	VF	XF	Unc	BU
1997 Proof	12,000	Value: 345				

Y# 918 50 YUAN

155.5175 g., 0.9990 Silver 5.0000 oz. ASW **Subject:** Traditional Chinese Mascot **Obv:** Ornamental column **Rev:** Child holding carp

Date	Mintage	F	VF	XF	Unc	BU
1997 Proof	3,800	Value: 125				

Y# 921 50 YUAN

15.5517 g., 0.9990 Gold .50000 oz. AGW **Subject:** Chinese Wildlife **Obv:** National emblem, date below **Rev:** Two white dolphins, denomination at right

Date	Mintage	F	VF	XF	Unc	BU
1997 Proof	30,000	Value: 345				

Y# 1005 50 YUAN

15.5517 g., 0.9990 Gold .50000 oz. AGW **Obv:** Portrait of Qi Bashi **Rev:** Squirrels eating grapes **Shape:** Rectangular

Date	Mintage	F	VF	XF	Unc	BU
1997 Proof	5,000	Value: 400				

Y# 1007 50 YUAN

15.5517 g., 0.9990 Gold .5000 oz. AGW **Subject:** Zhou Enlai

Date	Mintage	F	VF	XF	Unc	BU
1998 Proof	8,000	Value: 345				

Y# 1180 50 YUAN

15.5517 g., 0.9999 Gold 0.4999 oz. AGW **Subject:** Liu Shao Qi **Obv:** Portrait **Rev:** Temple

Date	Mintage	F	VF	XF	Unc	BU
1998 Proof	8,000	Value: 360				

Y# 1008 50 YUAN

15.5517 g., 0.9990 Gold .5000 oz. AGW **Subject:** 50th Anniversary of People's Republic

Date	Mintage	F	VF	XF	Unc	BU
1999 Proof	15,700	Value: 400				

Y# 1049 50 YUAN

155.5175 g., 0.9990 Silver 5.0000 oz. ASW **Rev:** Dragons **Shape:** Rectangle

Date	Mintage	F	VF	XF	Unc	BU
2000 Proof	1,888	Value: 360				

Y# 1236 50 YUAN

17.0000 g., 0.9990 Gold, 27 mm. **Subject:** Y2K **Obv:** Monument **Rev:** World Globe as an eye above value within silver plated outer ring **Edge:** Reeded

Date	Mintage	F	VF	XF	Unc	BU
2000 Proof	20,000	Value: 370				

Y# 1050 50 YUAN

15.5518 g., 0.9990 Gold .5000 oz. AGW **Rev:** Dragons **Shape:** Fan

Date	Mintage	F	VF	XF	Unc	BU
2000	6,600	—	—	—	375	—

Y# 1137 50 YUAN

Bi-Metallic Gold center in Silver ring **Subject:** Y-2-K

Date	Mintage	F	VF	XF	Unc	BU
2000	20,000	Value: 385				

Y# 56 100 YUAN

11.0000 g., 0.9000 Gold .3183 oz. AGW **Obv:** Building, date at right **Rev:** Marco Polo bust, top right, ship below, denomination at bottom

Date	Mintage	F	VF	XF	Unc	BU
1983 Proof	1,030	Value: 550				

Y# 72 100 YUAN

11.3180 g., 0.9170 Gold .3337 oz. AGW **Obv:** National emblem, date below **Rev:** Emperor Huang Di, denomination below

Date	Mintage	F	VF	XF	Unc	BU
1984 Proof	10,000	Value: 250				

Y# 94 100 YUAN

11.3180 g., 0.9170 Gold .3337 oz. AGW, 23 mm. **Subject:** Founders of Chinese Culture **Rev:** Confucius, denomination at right

Date	Mintage	F	VF	XF	Unc	BU
1985 Proof	7,000	Value: 250				

Y# 107 100 YUAN

11.3180 g., 0.9170 Gold .3337 oz. AGW **Subject:** Wildlife **Obv:** National emblem, date below **Rev:** Wild Yak, left, denomination at left

Date	Mintage	F	VF	XF	Unc	BU
1986 Proof	3,000	Value: 275				

Y# 117 100 YUAN

11.3180 g., 0.9170 Gold .3337 oz. AGW, 23 mm. **Subject:** Chinese Culture **Obv:** National emblem, date below **Rev:** Revolutionary Soldier, Liu Bang on horseback, denomination at left

Date	Mintage	F	VF	XF	Unc	BU
1986 Proof	7,000	Value: 250				

Y# 120 100 YUAN

11.3180 g., 0.9170 Gold .3337 oz. AGW **Subject:** Year of Peace **Rev:** Statue of seated female **Note:** Similar to 5 Yuan, Y#119.

Date	Mintage	F	VF	XF	Unc	BU
1986 Proof	1,000	Value: 660				

Y# 131 100 YUAN
373.2360 g., 0.9990 Silver 12.0000 oz. ASW, 80 mm. **Subject:** 125th Anniversary - Birth of Zhan Tianyou **Obv:** National emblem, date below **Rev:** Bust of Zhan Tianyou facing above steam locomotive on bridge, denomination below, dates above **Note:** Photo reduced.

Date	Mintage	F	VF	XF	Unc	BU
1987 Proof	2,911	Value: 250				

Y# 139 100 YUAN
11.3180 g., 0.9170 Gold .3337 oz. AGW **Obv:** National emblem, date below **Rev:** Emperor Li Shih on horseback, denomination at right

Date	Mintage	F	VF	XF	Unc	BU
1987 Proof	7,000	Value: 275				

Y# 164 100 YUAN
11.3180 g., 0.9170 Gold .3337 oz. AGW **Rev:** Emperor Zhao Kuangyin, denomination at right

Date	Mintage	F	VF	XF	Unc	BU
1988 Proof	Est. 7,000	Value: 275				

Y# 167 100 YUAN
8.0000 g., 0.9170 Gold .2359 oz. AGW **Subject:** Rare Animal Protection **Obv:** National emblem, date below **Rev:** Golden monkey, denomination at left

Date	Mintage	F	VF	XF	Unc	BU
1988 Proof	29,000	Value: 195				

Y# 173 100 YUAN
15.5500 g., 0.9990 Gold .5000 oz. AGW **Series:** Seoul 1988 - 24th Summer Olympic Games **Obv:** National emblem, date below **Rev:** Rhythmic gymnast, denomination at right

Date	Mintage	F	VF	XF	Unc	BU
1988 Proof	5,500	Value: 380				

Y# 203 100 YUAN
8.0000 g., 0.9170 Gold .2359 oz. AGW **Subject:** 11th Asian Games - Beijing 1990 **Obv:** Stadium **Rev:** Ribbon dancer, denomination below

Date	Mintage	F	VF	XF	Unc	BU
1989 Proof	Est. 7,000	Value: 185				

Y# 217 100 YUAN
11.3180 g., 0.9170 Gold .3337 oz. AGW **Obv:** National emblem, date below **Rev:** Genghis Khan on horseback, denomination at left

Date	Mintage	F	VF	XF	Unc	BU
1989 Proof	Est. 7,000	Value: 300				

Y# 231 100 YUAN
11.3180 g., 0.9170 Gold .3337 oz. AGW **Series:** Save the Children Fund **Obv:** National emblem, date below **Rev:** Child running flying kites, denomination lower right

Date	Mintage	F	VF	XF	Unc	BU
1989 Proof	5,000	Value: 245				

Y# 250 100 YUAN
8.0000 g., 0.9170 Gold .2359 oz. AGW **Series:** Endangered Animals **Obv:** National emblem, date below **Rev:** Chinese tiger, denomination at left

Date	Mintage	F	VF	XF	Unc	BU
1989 Proof	14,000	Value: 195				

Y# 299 100 YUAN
7.7750 g., 0.9990 Gold .2500 oz. AGW **Subject:** 40th Anniversary of People's Republic **Obv:** National emblem, date at right **Rev:** Pair of flying cranes, denomination at left

Date	Mintage	F	VF	XF	Unc	BU
1989 Proof	1,000	Value: 275				

Y# 256 100 YUAN
8.0000 g., 0.9170 Gold .2359 oz. AGW **Subject:** XI Asian Games - Beijing 1990 **Obv:** Roman numeral above stadium, date below **Rev:** Swimmer, denomination lower left

Date	Mintage	F	VF	XF	Unc	BU
1990 Proof	10,000	Value: 175				

Y# 287 100 YUAN
10.3700 g., 0.9170 Gold .3054 oz. AGW **Obv:** National emblem, date below **Rev:** First emperor, Huang Di standing, denomination at right

Date	Mintage	F	VF	XF	Unc	BU
1990 Proof	20,000	Value: 275				

Y# 306 100 YUAN
11.3180 g., 0.9170 Gold .3333 oz. AGW **Obv:** National emblem, date below **Rev:** Emperor Zhu Yuanzhang seated, denomination upper left

Date	Mintage	F	VF	XF	Unc	BU
1990	Est. 7,000	—	—	—	—	300

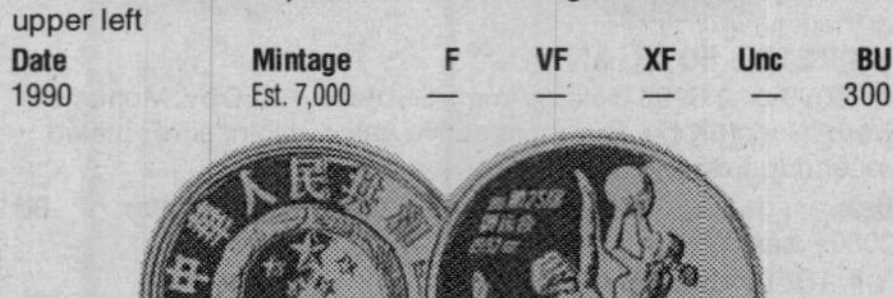

Y# 327 100 YUAN
11.3180 g., 0.9170 Gold .3333 oz. AGW **Series:** Barcelona 1992 - 25th Summer Olympic Games **Obv:** National emblem, date below **Rev:** 2 women playing basketball, denomination at right

Date	Mintage	F	VF	XF	Unc	BU
1990	10,000	—	—	—	—	245

Y# 320 100 YUAN
8.0000 g., 0.9160 Gold .2357 oz. AGW **Subject:** Women's 1st World Football Cup **Obv:** Stadium, date below **Rev:** Woman kicking ball, denomination at right

Date	Mintage	F	VF	XF	Unc	BU
1991 Proof	1,400	Value: 175				

Y# 326 100 YUAN
8.0000 g., 0.9160 Gold .2357 oz. AGW **Subject:** Emperor Kang Xi, denomination at left **Obv:** National emblem, date below

Date	Mintage	F	VF	XF	Unc	BU
1991 Proof	Est. 7,000	Value: 300				

Y# 473 100 YUAN
11.3180 g., 0.9170 Gold .3334 oz. AGW **Series:** Albertville 1992 - 16th Winter Olympic Games **Obv:** National emblem, date below **Rev:** Pairs figure skating, denomination lower right

Date	Mintage	F	VF	XF	Unc	BU
1991 Proof	10,000	Value: 245				

Y# 478 100 YUAN
8.6000 g., 0.9170 Gold .2533 oz. AGW **Subject:** 80th Anniversary - 1911 Revolution **Obv:** Building **Rev:** Sun Yat-sen writing, denomination at right

Date	Mintage	F	VF	XF	Unc	BU
1991 Proof	2,500	Value: 315				

Y# 545 100 YUAN
11.3180 g., 0.9170 Gold .3337 oz. AGW **Rev:** Emperor Yan Di, denomination upper right

Date	Mintage	F	VF	XF	Unc	BU
1991 Proof	10,000	Value: 275				

Y# 479 100 YUAN
31.1035 g., 0.9990 Gold 1.0000 oz. AGW **Obv:** Building, two dates below **Rev:** Sun Yat-sen in uniform, facing, denomination at left **Note:** Photo reduced.

Date	Mintage	F	VF	XF	Unc	BU
ND(1991) Proof	1,000	Value: 1,000				

Y# 754 100 YUAN
33.9600 g., 0.9160 Gold 1.000 oz. AGW **Subject:** Archeological Finds **Obv:** National emblem **Rev:** Resting deer with long antlers

Date	Mintage	F	VF	XF	Unc	BU
1992 Proof	500	Value: 1,325				

Y# 336 100 YUAN
31.1035 g., 0.9990 Gold 1.0000 oz. AGW **Subject:** Chinese Inventions **Obv:** Great Wall, date below **Rev:** Ancient ships and shipbuilding, denomination lower left

Date	Mintage	F	VF	XF	Unc	BU
1992 Proof	1,000	Value: 700				

Y# 337 100 YUAN
31.1035 g., 0.9990 Gold 1.0000 oz. AGW **Subject:** Chinese Inventions **Rev:** First compass, denomination below

Date	Mintage	F	VF	XF	Unc	BU
1992 Proof	1,000	Value: 700				

Y# 338 100 YUAN
31.1035 g., 0.9990 Gold 1.0000 oz. AGW **Subject:** Chinese Inventions **Rev:** First seismograph, denomination below

Date	Mintage	F	VF	XF	Unc	BU
1992 Proof	1,000	Value: 700				

Y# 339 100 YUAN
31.1035 g., 0.9990 Gold 1.0000 oz. AGW **Subject:** Chinese Inventions **Obv:** Great Wall **Rev:** First kite, denomination below

Date	Mintage	F	VF	XF	Unc	BU
1992 Proof	1,000	Value: 700				

Y# 340 100 YUAN
31.1035 g., 0.9990 Gold 1.0000 oz. AGW **Obv:** Great Wall, date below **Rev:** Bronze Age Metal Working, large urn, denomination below

Date	Mintage	F	VF	XF	Unc	BU
1992 Proof	1,000	Value: 700				

Y# 546 100 YUAN
10.3700 g., 0.9170 Gold .3054 oz. AGW **Obv:** National emblem, date below **Rev:** Emperor Da Yu, denomination at right

Date	Mintage	F	VF	XF	Unc	BU
1992 Proof	10,000	Value: 325				

Y# 554 100 YUAN
11.3180 g., 0.9170 Gold .3334 oz. AGW **Obv:** National emblem, date below **Rev:** Wu Zetian "The Iron Lady" 603-705AD, Stateswoman, denomination at right

Date	Mintage	F	VF	XF	Unc	BU
1992 Proof	25,000	Value: 245				

Y# 692 100 YUAN
11.3180 g., 0.9170 Gold .3334 oz. AGW **Series:** 1994 Olympics **Obv:** Temple of Heaven **Rev:** Male figure skater, denomination below

Date	Mintage	F	VF	XF	Unc	BU
1992 Proof	10,000	Value: 235				

Y# 693 100 YUAN
8.0000 g., 0.9170 Gold .2356 oz. AGW **Series:** Endangered Wildlife **Rev:** Mountain sheep, denomination below

Date	Mintage	F	VF	XF	Unc	BU
1992 Proof	5,000	Value: 250				

Y# 354 100 YUAN
31.1320 g., 0.9990 Gold 1.0000 oz. AGW **Obv:** Temple, date below **Rev:** Two peacocks, denomination above **Rev. Designer:** Lang Shih Ning

Date	Mintage	F	VF	XF	Unc	BU
1993 Proof	1,200	Value: 725				

Y# 406 100 YUAN
31.1035 g., 0.9990 Gold 1.0000 oz. AGW **Obv:** Building and Great Wall **Rev:** Chinese Gods: Fu, Lu, and Shu

Date	Mintage	F	VF	XF	Unc	BU
1993 Proof	888	Value: 875				

Y# 411 100 YUAN
33.9500 g., 0.9170 Gold 1.0000 oz. AGW **Subject:** Bronze Age Sculptures **Obv:** National emblem, date below **Rev:** Bull lantern, denomination at left

Date	Mintage	F	VF	XF	Unc	BU
1993 Proof	350	Value: 1,650				

Y# 491 100 YUAN
10.3600 g., 0.9170 Gold .3053 oz. AGW **Subject:** World Cup Soccer **Obv:** National emblem, date below **Rev:** Player kicking ball, denomination at left

Date	Mintage	F	VF	XF	Unc	BU
1993 Proof	5,000	Value: 220				

Y# 504 100 YUAN
31.1035 g., 0.9990 Gold 1.0000 oz. AGW **Obv:** Great Wall, date below **Rev:** Guanyin, Goddess of Mercy, seated in flower, denomination at left

Date	Mintage	F	VF	XF	Unc	BU
1993 Proof	1,000	Value: 725				

Y# 538 100 YUAN
11.3180 g., 0.9170 Gold .3337 oz. AGW **Obv:** National emblem, date below **Rev:** Bust of Chairman Mao Zedong, right, denomination at left

Date	Mintage	F	VF	XF	Unc	BU
1993 Proof	Est. 7,000	Value: 330				

Y# 760 100 YUAN
8.0000 g., 0.9160 Gold .2356 oz. AGW **Obv:** National emblem, date below **Rev:** Bust of Soong Ching-ling half left, 1892-1981, Revolutionary Stateswoman, denomination at right

Date	Mintage	F	VF	XF	Unc	BU
1993 Proof	2,000	Value: 225				

Y# 763 100 YUAN
31.1035 g., 0.9990 Gold 1.0000 oz. AGW **Obv:** Home of Sun Yat-sen **Rev:** Bust of Sun Yat-sen, facing, denomination at right

Date	Mintage	F	VF	XF	Unc	BU
1993 Proof	8,888	Value: 675				

Y# 777 100 YUAN
31.1035 g., 0.9990 Gold 1.0000 oz. AGW **Subject:** Mount Tai **Obv:** Great Wall **Rev:** Temple

Date	Mintage	F	VF	XF	Unc	BU
1993 Proof	8,888	Value: 675				

Y# 427 100 YUAN
31.1035 g., 0.9990 Gold 1.0000 oz. AGW **Obv:** Child riding Eastern Unicorn, date below **Rev:** Unicorn, denomination at left, rose sprays below

Date	Mintage	F	VF	XF	Unc	BU
1994 Proof	1,100	Value: 675				

Y# 440 100 YUAN
8.0000 g., 0.9170 Gold .2356 oz. AGW **Subject:** 12th Asian Games **Obv:** National emblem, row of athletic figures below, date at bottom **Rev:** Gymnast on bars, denomination at right

Date	Mintage	F	VF	XF	Unc	BU
1994 Proof	3,000	Value: 175				

Y# 497 100 YUAN
10.3600 g., 0.9170 Gold .3053 oz. AGW **Series:** Atlanta 1994 - 26th Summer Olympic Games **Rev:** Female torch runner, denomination lower left

Date	Mintage	F	VF	XF	Unc	BU
1994 Proof	5,000	Value: 220				

Y# 543 100 YUAN
10.3600 g., 0.9170 Gold .3053 oz. AGW **Obv:** National emblem **Rev:** Emperor Zhou Wenwang, denomination at left

Date	Mintage	F	VF	XF	Unc	BU
1994 Proof	10,000	Value: 375				

Y# 695 100 YUAN
15.5500 g., 0.9160 Gold .4579 oz. AGW **Obv:** Building, date below **Rev:** Black-billed magpie on branch, denomination below **Shape:** 12-sided

Date	Mintage	F	VF	XF	Unc	BU
1994 Proof	1,300	Value: 500				

Y# 426 100 YUAN
373.2360 g., 0.9990 Silver 12.0000 oz. ASW, 85 mm. **Rev:** Unicorn with offspring, denomination at left **Note:** Photo reduced.

Date	Mintage	F	VF	XF	Unc	BU
1994 Proof	2,000	Value: 300				

Y# 698 100 YUAN
373.2360 g., 0.9990 Silver 20.0000 oz. ASW, 98 mm. **Rev:** Unicorn with offspring, denomination at left **Note:** Photo reduced.

Date	Mintage	F	VF	XF	Unc	BU
1995 Proof	—	Value: 325				

Y# 843 100 YUAN
10.3678 g., 0.9990 Gold .3330 oz. AGW **Series:** 1996 Olympics **Obv:** National emblem, date below **Rev:** High diver, denomination below

Date	Mintage	F	VF	XF	Unc	BU
1995 Proof	10,000	Value: 240				

Y# 844 100 YUAN
10.3678 g., 0.9990 Gold .3330 oz. AGW **Series:** Olympics **Obv:** National emblem, date below **Rev:** Ribbon dancer, denomination at right

Date	Mintage	F	VF	XF	Unc	BU
1995 Proof	10,000	Value: 240				

Y# 1062 100 YUAN
31.1035 g., 0.9990 Gold 1.0000 oz. AGW, 32 mm. **Subject:** Unicorn **Obv:** Eastern unicorn **Rev:** Western unicorn with offspring **Edge:** Reeded

Date	Mintage	F	VF	XF	Unc	BU
1995 Proof	—	Value: 675				

Y# 1012 100 YUAN
31.1030 g., 0.9990 Gold 1.0000 oz. AGW **Rev:** Unicorn

Date	Mintage	F	VF	XF	Unc	BU
1995 Proof	1,500	Value: 675				

Y# 696 100 YUAN
31.1035 g., 0.9990 Gold 1.0000 oz. AGW **Subject:** 50th Anniversary - Anti-Japanese War **Rev:** People at wall, denomination below

Date	Mintage	F	VF	XF	Unc	BU
1995 Proof	1,400	Value: 680				

Y# 697 100 YUAN
31.1035 g., 0.9990 Gold 1.0000 oz. AGW **Rev:** Soldiers above bridge guarded by chinze, denomination at right

Date	Mintage	F	VF	XF	Unc	BU
1995 Proof	1,400	Value: 680				

Y# 804 100 YUAN
31.0103 g., 0.9990 Gold 1.0000 oz. AGW **Subject:** Chinese Culture Series **Obv:** Great Wall seen through arch **Rev:** Pagoda of Six Harmonies

Date	Mintage	F	VF	XF	Unc	BU
1995 Proof	1,000	Value: 665				

Y# 805 100 YUAN
31.0103 g., 0.9990 Gold 1.0000 oz. AGW **Subject:** Chinese Culture Series **Obv:** Great Wall seen through arch **Rev:** Mencius seated at table

Date	Mintage	F	VF	XF	Unc	BU
1995 Proof	1,000	Value: 665				

Y# 806 100 YUAN
31.0103 g., 0.9990 Gold 1.0000 oz. AGW **Subject:** Chinese Culture Series **Obv:** Great Wall seen through arch **Rev:** Tang Taizong seated

Date	Mintage	F	VF	XF	Unc	BU
1995 Proof	1,000	Value: 665				

Y# 807 100 YUAN
31.0103 g., 0.9990 Gold 1.0000 oz. AGW **Subject:** Chinese Culture Series **Obv:** Great Wall seen through arch **Rev:** Lion dance

Date	Mintage	F	VF	XF	Unc	BU
1995 Proof	1,000	Value: 665				

Y# 808 100 YUAN
31.0103 g., 0.9990 Gold 1.0000 oz. AGW **Subject:** Chinese Culture Series **Obv:** Great Wall seen through arch **Rev:** Female opera role

Date	Mintage	F	VF	XF	Unc	BU
1995 Proof	1,000	Value: 665				

Y# 810 100 YUAN
16.9779 g., 0.9160 Gold .5000 oz. AGW **Obv:** Great Wall, date below **Rev:** Perched eagle, denomination lower right **Shape:** 12-sided

Date	Mintage	F	VF	XF	Unc	BU
1995 Proof	1,300	Value: 350				

Y# 823 100 YUAN
373.2420 g., 0.9990 Silver 12.0000 oz. ASW **Subject:** Zheng Chenggong **Obv:** Chiqian building **Rev:** Standing figure with flag and ships

Date	Mintage	F	VF	XF	Unc	BU
1995 Proof	150	Value: 900				

Y# 830 100 YUAN
31.1035 g., 0.9990 Gold 1.0000 oz. AGW **Subject:** Romance of the Three Kingdoms **Obv:** Luo Guanzhong **Rev:** Standing Liu Bei with flags

Date	Mintage	F	VF	XF	Unc	BU
1995 Proof	1,500	Value: 665				

Y# 831 100 YUAN
31.1035 g., 0.9990 Gold 1.0000 oz. AGW **Subject:** Romance of the Three Kingdoms **Obv:** Luo Guanzhong **Rev:** Seated Guan Yu reading

Date	Mintage	F	VF	XF	Unc	BU
1995 Proof	1,500	Value: 665				

Y# 832 100 YUAN
31.1035 g., 0.9990 Gold 1.0000 oz. AGW **Subject:** Romance of the Three Kingdoms **Obv:** Luo Guanzhong **Rev:** Zhang Fei on horseback

Date	Mintage	F	VF	XF	Unc	BU
1995 Proof	1,500	Value: 665				

Y# 833 100 YUAN
31.1035 g., 0.9990 Gold 1.0000 oz. AGW **Subject:** Romance of the Three Kingdoms **Obv:** Luo Guanzhong **Rev:** Zhuge Liang seated on throne

Date	Mintage	F	VF	XF	Unc	BU
1995 Proof	1,500	Value: 665				

Y# 1014 100 YUAN
31.1035 g., 0.9990 Gold 1.0000 oz. AGW, 32.1 mm. **Subject:** Unicorn **Obv:** Eastern unicorn, full body **Rev:** Western unicorn **Edge:** Reeded

Date	Mintage	F	VF	XF	Unc	BU
1996 Proof	1,250	Value: 665				

Y# 956 100 YUAN
31.1035 g., 0.9990 Gold 1.0000 oz. AGW, 32 mm. **Obv:** Eastern unicorn **Rev:** Western unicorn in wreath **Edge:** Reeded

Date	Mintage	F	VF	XF	Unc	BU
1996 Proof	1,250	Value: 675				

Y# 956a 100 YUAN
31.1035 g., 0.9990 Platinum 1.0000 oz. APW, 32 mm. **Subject:** Unicorn **Obv:** Eastern unicorn, full body **Rev:** Western unicorn and maiden **Edge:** Reeded

Date	Mintage	F	VF	XF	Unc	BU
1996 Proof	500	Value: 1,350				

Y# 966 100 YUAN
31.1035 g., 0.9995 Platinum 1.0000 oz. APW **Obv:** Eastern unicorn **Rev:** Western unicorn

Date	Mintage	F	VF	XF	Unc	BU
1997 Proof	500	Value: 1,350				

Y# 1080 100 YUAN
16.9779 g., 0.9160 Gold 0.5 oz. AGW, 26.5 mm. **Subject:** Wildlife of China **Obv:** The Great Wall **Rev:** Penguin **Edge:** Plain

Date	Mintage	F	VF	XF	Unc	BU
1997 Proof	2,800	Value: 345				

Y# 1200 100 YUAN
373.2420 g., 0.9990 Silver 11.988 oz. ASW, 80 mm. **Obv:** Ornamental column **Rev:** Child holding a carp **Edge:** Reeded

Date	Mintage	F	VF	XF	Unc	BU
1997 Proof	2,000	Value: 265				

Y# 208 150 YUAN
622.0400 g., 0.9990 Silver 20.0000 oz. ASW **Rev:** Phoenix and dragon

Date	Mintage	F	VF	XF	Unc	BU
1990 Proof	1,500	Value: 650				

Y# 355 150 YUAN
373.2360 g., 0.9990 Silver 12.0000 oz. ASW **Obv:** Temple of Harmony **Rev:** Two peacocks, denomination below **Rev. Designer:** Lang Shih Ning

Date	Mintage	F	VF	XF	Unc	BU
1993 Proof	500	Value: 650				

Y# 428 150 YUAN
622.0400 g., 0.9990 Silver 20.0000 oz. ASW **Obv:** Figure on Eastern unicorn, date below **Rev:** Unicorn, denomination at left, rose sprays below

Date	Mintage	F	VF	XF	Unc	BU
1994 Proof	500	Value: 500				

Y# 699 150 YUAN
622.0400 g., 0.9990 Silver 20.0000 oz. ASW, 98 mm. **Obv:** Eastern unicorn, rearing, date below **Rev:** Unicorn with offspring **Note:** Photo reduced.

Date	Mintage	F	VF	XF	Unc	BU
1995	—	—	—	—	450	—

Y# 884 150 YUAN
622.0400 g., 0.9990 Silver 20.0000 oz. ASW **Obv:** Eastern unicorn, date below **Rev:** Western unicorn, rearing, denomination below

Date	Mintage	F	VF	XF	Unc	BU
1996 Proof	500	Value: 600				

Y# 28 200 YUAN
8.4700 g., 0.9170 Gold .2497 oz. AGW **Subject:** Chinese Bronze Age Finds **Obv:** National emblem **Rev:** Leopard, denomination below

Date	Mintage	F	VF	XF	Unc	BU
1981 Proof	1,000	Value: 400				

Y# 29 200 YUAN
8.4700 g., 0.9170 Gold .2497 oz. AGW **Subject:** Chinese Bronze Age Finds **Obv:** National emblem **Rev:** Winged creature, denomination below

Date	Mintage	F	VF	XF	Unc	BU
1981 Proof	1,000	Value: 625				

Y# 37 200 YUAN
8.4700 g., 0.9170 Gold .2497 oz. AGW **Subject:** World Cup Soccer **Obv:** National emblem, date below **Rev:** Player kicking, denomination below

Date	Mintage	F	VF	XF	Unc	BU
1982 Proof	1,261	Value: 425				

Y# 209 200 YUAN
62.2060 g., 0.9990 Gold 2.0000 oz. AGW **Obv:** Great Wall, date below **Rev:** Denomination between Phoenix and dragon

Date	Mintage	F	VF	XF	Unc	BU
1990 Proof	2,538	Value: 1,350				
1990 Proof	2,538	Value: 1,450				

Y# 816 200 YUAN
1000.0000 g., 0.9990 Silver 32.1895 oz. ASW, 100 mm. **Subject:** 50th Anniversary - Return of Taiwan to China **Obv:** Great Wall **Rev:** Taiwan and China maps

Date	Mintage	F	VF	XF	Unc	BU
1995 Proof	100	Value: 2,150				

Y# 712 200 YUAN
1000.0000 g., 0.9990 Silver 32.1895 oz. ASW **Subject:** Sino - Thailand Friendship **Obv:** Forbidden City and Thai Royal Palace **Rev:** 2 Buddha statues, one in cameo

Date	Mintage	F	VF	XF	Unc	BU
1997 Proof	880	Value: 1,000				

Y# 22 250 YUAN
8.0000 g., 0.9170 Gold .2358 oz. AGW **Subject:** 1980 Winter Olympics **Obv:** State seal **Rev:** Alpine skiing

Date	Mintage	F	VF	XF	Unc	BU
1980 Proof	10,000	Value: 170				

Y# 23 300 YUAN
10.0000 g., 0.9170 Gold .2948 oz. AGW **Series:** 1980 Olympics **Subject:** Archery **Obv:** National emblem, denomination below **Rev:** Two archers, date below

Date	Mintage	F	VF	XF	Unc	BU
1980 Proof	15,000	Value: 225				

Y# 515 300 YUAN
103.1250 g., 0.9990 Gold 3.3155 oz. AGW **Obv:** Great Wall, date below **Rev:** Guanyin, Goddess of Mercy, holding child, facing, denomination at left

Date	Mintage	F	VF	XF	Unc	BU
1994 Proof	128	Value: 3,150				

Y# 4 400 YUAN
16.9500 g., 0.9170 Gold .4997 oz. AGW **Obv:** National emblem, two dates below **Rev:** 30th Anniversary of People's Republic - Tiananmen, denomination below

Date	Mintage	F	VF	XF	Unc	BU
ND(1979) Proof	Est. 23,000	Value: 345				

Y# 5 400 YUAN
16.9500 g., 0.9170 Gold .4997 oz. AGW **Subject:** 30th Anniversary of People's Republic **Obv:** National emblem, two dates below **Rev:** People's Heroes Monument, denomination below

Date	Mintage	F	VF	XF	Unc	BU
ND(1979) Proof	Est. 23,000	Value: 345				

Y# 6 400 YUAN
16.9500 g., 0.9170 Gold .4997 oz. AGW **Subject:** 30th Anniversary of People's Republic **Obv:** National emblem, two dates below **Rev:** Chairman Mao Memorial Hall, denomination below

Date	Mintage	F	VF	XF	Unc	BU
ND(1979) Proof	Est. 23,000	Value: 345				

Y# 7 400 YUAN
16.9500 g., 0.9170 Gold .4997 oz. AGW **Subject:** 30th Anniversary of People's Republic **Obv:** National emblem **Rev:** Great Hall of the People

Date	Mintage	F	VF	XF	Unc	BU
ND(1979) Proof	Est. 23,000	Value: 345				

Y# 30 400 YUAN
16.9500 g., 0.9170 Gold .4997 oz. AGW **Subject:** Chinese Bronze Age Finds **Obv:** State seal **Rev:** Rhinoceros, left, denomination below

Date	Mintage	F	VF	XF	Unc	BU
1981 Proof	1,000	Value: 675				

Y# 47 400 YUAN
13.3600 g., 0.9170 Gold .3939 oz. AGW **Subject:** 70th Anniversary of 1911 Revolution **Obv:** Bust of Sun-Yat-sen, facing, two dates below **Rev:** Nationalist troops attacking, denomination and date below

Date	Mintage	F	VF	XF	Unc	BU
1981 Proof	1,338	Value: 1,100				

Y# 9 450 YUAN
17.1700 g., 0.9000 Gold .4968 oz. AGW **Series:** International Year of the Child **Obv:** State seal above floral sprays **Rev:** Two children planting flower

Date	Mintage	F	VF	XF	Unc	BU
1979 Proof	Est. 12,000	Value: 340				

Y# 1178 500 YUAN
15.5517 g., 0.9999 Gold 0.4999 oz. AGW **Subject:** Domestic Scene

Date	Mintage	F	VF	XF	Unc	BU
1993	8,888	Value: 340				

Y# 356 500 YUAN
155.5150 g., 0.9990 Gold 5.0000 oz. AGW **Obv:** Temple of Harmony **Rev:** Two peacocks **Rev. Designer:** Lang Shih Ning

Date	Mintage	F	VF	XF	Unc	BU
1993 Proof	99	Value: 4,250				

Y# 764 500 YUAN
155.5150 g., 0.9990 Gold 5.0000 oz. AGW **Subject:** Sun Yat-sen **Obv:** Home of Sun Yat-sen, date below **Rev:** Bust of Sun Yat-sen, facing, denomination at right

Date	Mintage	F	VF	XF	Unc	BU
1993 Proof	99	Value: 5,000				

Y# 778 500 YUAN
155.5150 g., 0.9990 Gold 5.0000 oz. AGW **Subject:** Tomb of Emperor Huang **Obv:** Great Wall, date below **Rev:** Tomb, denomination below

Date	Mintage	F	VF	XF	Unc	BU
1993 Proof	99	Value: 3,850				

Y# 395 500 YUAN
155.5150 g., 0.9990 Gold 5.0000 oz. AGW, 60 mm. **Subject:** Marco Polo bust on left, looking right, buildings at right, denomination below **Note:** Photo reduced.

Date	Mintage	F	VF	XF	Unc	BU
1993 Proof	100	Value: 3,450				

Y# 407 500 YUAN
155.5150 g., 0.9990 Gold 5.0000 oz. AGW, 60 mm. **Subject:** Chinese Gods: Fu, Lu and Shu, denomination below **Obv:** Building and Great Wall, date below **Rev:** Three gods with symbol on panel and child **Note:** Photo reduced.

Date	Mintage	F	VF	XF	Unc	BU
1993 Proof	99	Value: 3,450				

Y# 415 500 YUAN

155.5150 g., 0.9990 Gold 5.0000 oz. AGW, 60 mm. **Subject:** Chairman Mao **Obv:** Tall building, date at right **Rev:** 3/4 figure of Mao looking left, denomination at right **Note:** Photo reduced.

Date	Mintage	F	VF	XF	Unc	BU
1993 Proof	100	Value: 5,000				

Y# 417 500 YUAN

155.5150 g., 0.9990 Gold 5.0000 oz. AGW, 60 mm. **Subject:** Yandi, Semi-mythical First Emperor **Obv:** National emblem **Rev:** 3/4 figure looking left, denomination over right shoulder **Note:** Photo reduced.

Date	Mintage	F	VF	XF	Unc	BU
1993 Proof	99	Value: 3,450				

Y# 449 500 YUAN

155.5150 g., 0.9990 Gold 5.0000 oz. AGW, 60 mm. **Obv:** Taiwan Temple, date below **Rev:** Buddha statue, denomination below **Note:** Photo reduced.

Date	Mintage	F	VF	XF	Unc	BU
1994 Proof	76	Value: 4,000				

Y# 462 500 YUAN

155.5150 g., 0.9990 Gold 5.0000 oz. AGW, 60 mm. **Subject:** Children At Play **Rev:** Two children with cat, denomination below **Note:** Photo reduced.

Date	Mintage	F	VF	XF	Unc	BU
1994 Proof	99	Value: 3,550				

Y# 701 500 YUAN

155.5150 g., 0.9990 Gold 5.0000 oz. AGW **Subject:** Sino-Singapore Friendship **Obv:** Great Wall, date below **Rev:** Singapore Harbor, denomination below **Note:** Photo reduced.

Date	Mintage	F	VF	XF	Unc	BU
1994 Proof	91	Value: 3,550				

Y# 429 500 YUAN

155.5150 g., 0.9990 Gold 5.0000 oz. AGW **Obv:** Eastern unicorn with rider, date below **Rev:** Unicorn above sprays of roses, denomination at left

Date	Mintage	F	VF	XF	Unc	BU
1994 Proof	99	Value: 3,850				

Y# 533 500 YUAN

155.5150 g., 0.9990 Gold 5.0000 oz. AGW **Subject:** Return of Hong Kong to China - Series I **Obv:** Tiananmen Square, date below **Rev:** Bust of Deng Xiaoping over Hong Kong city view

Date	Mintage	F	VF	XF	Unc	BU
1995 Proof	228	Value: 3,750				

Y# 656 500 YUAN

155.5150 g., 0.9990 Gold 5.0000 oz. AGW, 60 mm. **Subject:** Unicorn **Obv:** Eastern unicorn **Rev:** Unicorn mother and baby **Edge:** Reeded

Date	Mintage	F	VF	XF	Unc	BU
1995 Proof	99	Value: 3,550				

Y# 824 500 YUAN

155.5175 g., 0.9999 Gold 5.0000 oz. AGW **Subject:** Zheng Chenggong **Obv:** Chiqian Building **Rev:** Standing figure with flag, war ships in background, two dates upper right, denomination lower right

Date	Mintage	F	VF	XF	Unc	BU
1995 Proof	99	Value: 3,450				

Y# 834 500 YUAN
155.5175 g., 0.9999 Gold 5.0000 oz. AGW **Subject:** Romance of the Three Kingdoms Series **Obv:** Bust of Luo Guanzhong, looking right **Rev:** Three heroes of Shu Han, denomination above

Date	Mintage	F	VF	XF	Unc	BU
1995 Proof	99	Value: 3,450				

Y# 594 500 YUAN
155.5150 g., 0.9990 Gold 5.0000 oz. AGW, 60 mm. **Subject:** Yellow River culture **Rev:** Nu Wa Rising, denomination below **Note:** Photo reduced.

Date	Mintage	F	VF	XF	Unc	BU
1995 Proof	99	Value: 3,550				

Y# 649 500 YUAN
155.5150 g., 0.9990 Gold 5.0000 oz. AGW, 60 mm. **Rev:** Dragon boat, denomination below **Note:** Photo reduced.

Date	Mintage	F	VF	XF	Unc	BU
1995 Proof	99	Value: 4,350				

Y# 817 500 YUAN
155.5175 g., 0.9999 Gold 5.0000 oz. AGW **Subject:** 50th Anniversary - Taiwan's Return to China **Obv:** Great Wall, date below **Rev:** Taiwan and China maps, date at right, denomination lower left **Note:** Photo reduced.

Date	Mintage	F	VF	XF	Unc	BU
1995 Proof	99	Value: 4,350				

Y# 882 500 YUAN
155.5175 g., 0.9990 Gold 5.0000 oz. AGW **Subject:** Romance of the Three Kingdoms Series **Obv:** Bust of Luo Guanzhong **Rev:** Guan Du on horseback leading troops, denomination at left **Note:** Photo reduced.

Date	Mintage	F	VF	XF	Unc	BU
1996 Proof	99	Value: 3,450				

Y# 657 500 YUAN
155.5175 g., 0.9999 Gold 5.0000 oz. AGW **Obv:** Western unicorn on hind legs, surrounded by roses **Rev:** Eastern unicorn standing

Date	Mintage	F	VF	XF	Unc	BU
1996 Proof	108	Value: 3,350				

Y# 659 500 YUAN
155.5175 g., 0.9999 Gold 5.0000 oz. AGW **Subject:** Return of Hong Kong to China - Series II

Date	Mintage	F	VF	XF	Unc	BU
1996 Proof	228	Value: 3,500				

Y# 904 500 YUAN
155.5175 g., 0.9990 Gold 5.0000 oz. AGW **Subject:** Return of Hong Kong to China - Series III **Obv:** Tiananmen Square **Rev:** Bust of Deng Xiaoping above city, denomination at left

Date	Mintage	F	VF	XF	Unc	BU
1997 Proof	228	Value: 3,500				

Y# 907 500 YUAN
155.5175 g., 0.9990 Gold 5.0000 oz. AGW **Subject:** Return of Macao to China **Obv:** Tiananmen Square **Rev:** Deng Xiaoping standing viewing Macao, denomination at right

Date	Mintage	F	VF	XF	Unc	BU
1997 Proof	228	Value: 3,500				

Y# 1022 500 YUAN
155.5175 g., 0.9990 Gold 5.0000 oz. AGW **Subject:** Greeting Spring **Obv:** Lantern **Rev:** Children lighting firecrackers

Date	Mintage	F	VF	XF	Unc	BU
1997 Proof	108	Value: 3,350				

Y# 1029 500 YUAN
155.5175 g., 0.9990 Gold 5.0000 oz. AGW **Obv:** Bust of Qi Bashi **Rev:** Squirrels eating grapes

Date	Mintage	F	VF	XF	Unc	BU
1997 Proof	99	Value: 3,850				

Y# 1023 500 YUAN
155.5175 g., 0.9990 Gold 5.0000 oz. AGW **Subject:** Greeting Spring **Obv:** Lantern **Rev:** Children making kites

Date	Mintage	F	VF	XF	Unc	BU
1998 Proof	128	Value: 3,250				

Y# 1026 500 YUAN
155.5175 g., 0.9990 Gold 5.0000 oz. AGW **Subject:** 50th Anniversary of People's Republic Founding Ceremony **Shape:** Rectangular

Date	Mintage	F	VF	XF	Unc	BU
1999 Proof	990	Value: 3,750				

Y# 1028 500 YUAN
155.5175 g., 0.9990 Gold 5.0000 oz. AGW **Subject:** Y2K

Date	Mintage	F	VF	XF	Unc	BU
2000 Proof	1,000	Value: 3,500				

Y# 31 800 YUAN
33.2000 g., 0.9170 Gold .9789 oz. AGW **Subject:** Chinese Bronze Age Finds **Obv:** National emblem, date below **Rev:** Elephant statue, left, denomination below

Date	Mintage	F	VF	XF	Unc	BU
1981 Proof	1,000	Value: 1,150				

Y# 210 1500 YUAN
622.6000 g., 0.9990 Gold 20.0000 oz. AGW **Obv:** Great Wall **Rev:** Denomination divides Phoenix and dragon

Date	Mintage	F	VF	XF	Unc	BU
1989 Proof	250	Value: 14,000				

Y# 232 1500 YUAN
622.6000 g., 0.9990 Gold 20.0000 oz. AGW, 90 mm. **Subject:** Anniversary of People's Republic **Obv:** National emblem above city view with fireworks in sky **Rev:** Man giving speech, people in background, denomination below **Note:** Photo reduced.

Date	Mintage	F	VF	XF	Unc	BU
1989 Proof	100	Value: 31,000				

Y# 505 1500 YUAN
562.5068 g., 0.9990 Gold 18.0850 oz. AGW, 85 mm. **Rev:** Guanyin, Goddess of Mercy, seated in flower, denomination at left **Note:** Photo reduced.

Date	Mintage	F	VF	XF	Unc	BU
1993 Proof	88	Value: 15,500				

Y# 357 1500 YUAN
622.6000 g., 0.9990 Gold 20.0000 oz. AGW **Obv:** Temple of Harmony **Rev:** Two peacocks **Rev. Designer:** Land Shih Ning

Date	Mintage	F	VF	XF	Unc	BU
1993 Proof	66	Value: 16,500				

Y# 749 2000 YUAN
1000.0000 g., 0.9990 Gold 32.1500 oz. AGW **Subject:** Chinese Inventions and Discoveries **Obv:** Great Wall **Rev:** Seismograph

Date	Mintage	F	VF	XF	Unc	BU
1992 Proof	Est. 4	Value: 31,500				

Y# 402 2000 YUAN
1000.0000 g., 0.9990 Gold 32.1500 oz. AGW, 100 mm. **Subject:** Chinese inventions **Rev:** First compass, denomination below **Note:** Photo reduced.

Date	Mintage	F	VF	XF	Unc	BU
1992 Proof	10	Value: 27,000				

Y# 703 2000 YUAN
1000.0000 g., 0.9990 Gold 32.1500 oz. AGW, 112 mm. **Subject:** Sino-Singapore Friendship **Obv:** Great Wall, date below **Rev:** Singapore Harbor, denomination below **Note:** Photo reduced.

Date	Mintage	F	VF	XF	Unc	BU
1994	15	—	—	—	—	22,500

Y# 430 2000 YUAN
1000.0000 g., 0.9990 Gold 32.1500 oz. AGW **Obv:** Figure on Eastern unicorn, date below **Rev:** Unicorn, denomination below, rose sprays below

Date	Mintage	F	VF	XF	Unc	BU
1994 Proof	20	Value: 22,000				

Y# 818 2000 YUAN
1000.0000 g., 0.9990 Gold 32.1500 oz. AGW **Subject:** 50th Anniversary - Taiwan's Return to China **Obv:** Great Wall **Rev:** Taiwan and China maps

Date	Mintage	F	VF	XF	Unc	BU
1995 Proof	25	Value: 23,500				

Y# 957 2000 YUAN
1000.0000 g., 0.9990 Gold 32.1500 oz. AGW **Obv:** Eastern unicorn **Rev:** Western unicorn with maiden

Date	Mintage	F	VF	XF	Unc	BU
1996 Proof	18	Value: 22,000				

Y# 1070 30000 YUAN
10000.0000 g., 0.9999 Gold 321.50 oz. AGW, 180 mm. **Subject:** Third Millennium **Obv:** China Centenary Altar **Rev:** Denominations **Edge:** Plain

Date	Mintage	F	VF	XF	Unc	BU
2000	20	—	—	—	—	210,000

SILVER BULLION COINAGE

Lunar Series

Y# 44 10 YUAN
15.0000 g., 0.8500 Silver .4099 oz. ASW **Subject:** Year of the Pig **Rev:** Pigs, denomination below

Date	Mintage	F	VF	XF	Unc	BU
1983 Proof	6,790	Value: 325				

Y# 59 10 YUAN
15.0000 g., 0.8500 Silver .4099 oz. ASW **Subject:** Year of the Rat **Obv:** Building, date below **Rev:** Rat eating squash, denomination below **Designer:** Qi Baishi

Date	Mintage	F	VF	XF	Unc	BU
1984 Proof	11,000	Value: 75.00				

Y# 78 10 YUAN
15.0000 g., 0.9000 Silver .4341 oz. ASW **Subject:** Year of the Ox **Rev:** Ox above denomination

Date	Mintage	F	VF	XF	Unc	BU
1985 Proof	22,000	Value: 45.00				

Y# 98 10 YUAN
15.0000 g., 0.9000 Silver .4341 oz. ASW **Subject:** Year of the Tiger **Obv:** Qing Dynasty Palace, date below **Rev:** Tiger, after a painting by He Ziang Ning, denomination upper left

Date	Mintage	F	VF	XF	Unc	BU
1986 Proof	15,000	Value: 45.00				

Y# 121 10 YUAN
15.0000 g., 0.9000 Silver .4341 oz. ASW **Subject:** Year of the Rabbit **Obv:** Yellow Crane Pavilion above legend **Rev:** 2 rabbits above denomination **Rev. Designer:** Lin Ji Yon

Date	Mintage	F	VF	XF	Unc	BU
1987 Proof	14,000	Value: 90.00				

Y# 141 10 YUAN
15.0000 g., 0.9000 Silver .4341 oz. ASW **Subject:** Year of the Dragon **Obv:** Great Wall, date below **Rev:** Dragon above denomination

Date	Mintage	F	VF	XF	Unc	BU
1988 Proof	15,000	Value: 65.00				

Y# 174 10 YUAN
31.1000 g., 0.9990 Silver 1.0000 oz. ASW **Subject:** Year of the Dragon **Obv:** Temple of Heaven, date below **Rev:** Dragons, denomination below center

Date	Mintage	F	VF	XF	Unc	BU
1988 Proof	20,000	Value: 65.00				

Y# 183 10 YUAN
31.1000 g., 0.9990 Silver 1.0000 oz. ASW **Subject:** Year of the Snake **Obv:** National emblem **Rev:** Snake above denomination

Date	Mintage	F	VF	XF	Unc	BU
1989 Proof	6,000	Value: 135				

Y# 221 10 YUAN
15.0000 g., 0.8500 Silver .4100 oz. ASW **Subject:** Year of the Horse **Obv:** Temple of Confucius, date below **Rev:** Horse galloping left, denomination below

Date	Mintage	F	VF	XF	Unc	BU
1990 Proof	15,000	Value: 45.00				

Y# 222 10 YUAN
31.1000 g., 0.9990 Silver 1.0000 oz. ASW **Subject:** Year of the Horse **Rev:** Saddled horse, left, denomination lower right

Date	Mintage	F	VF	XF	Unc	BU
1990 Proof	12,000	Value: 50.00				

Y# 270 10 YUAN
15.0000 g., 0.9000 Silver .4340 oz. ASW **Subject:** Year of the Goat **Obv:** Chinese building and legend **Rev:** Goat, denomination upper left

Date	Mintage	F	VF	XF	Unc	BU
1991 Proof	15,000	Value: 40.00				

Y# 271 10 YUAN
31.1000 g., 0.9990 Silver 1.0000 oz. ASW **Subject:** Year of the Goat **Obv:** National emblem, date below **Rev:** Three goats, denomination below

Date	Mintage	F	VF	XF	Unc	BU
1991 Proof	8,000	Value: 100				

Y# 288 10 YUAN
15.0000 g., 0.9000 Silver .4340 oz. ASW **Subject:** Year of the Monkey **Obv:** Building, date below **Rev:** Seated monkey, denomination at right

Date	Mintage	F	VF	XF	Unc	BU
1992 Proof	—	Value: 50.00				

Y# 294 10 YUAN
31.1000 g., 0.9990 Silver 1.0000 oz. ASW **Subject:** Year of the Monkey **Rev:** Monkey, denomination at left

Date	Mintage	F	VF	XF	Unc	BU
1992 Proof	8,000	Value: 60.00				

Y# 480 10 YUAN
20.7500 g., 0.9990 Silver .6640 oz. ASW **Subject:** Year of the Rooster **Obv:** Building, date below **Rev:** Rooster and sunflowers, denomination at left **Shape:** Scalloped

Date	Mintage	F	VF	XF	Unc	BU
1993 Proof	6,800	Value: 125				

Y# 567 10 YUAN
31.1000 g., 0.9990 Silver 1.0000 oz. ASW **Subject:** Year of the Rooster **Obv:** National emblem, date below **Rev:** Rooster and hen, denomination at left

Date	Mintage	F	VF	XF	Unc	BU
1993 Proof	Est. 9,000	Value: 75.00				

Y# 396 10 YUAN
31.1000 g., 0.9990 Silver 1.0000 oz. ASW **Subject:** Year of the Dog

Date	Mintage	F	VF	XF	Unc	BU
1994 Proof	8,000	Value: 65.00				

Y# 1246 10 YUAN
20.7500 g., 0.9990 Silver 0.6665 oz. ASW, 36 mm. **Subject:** Year of the Dog **Obv:** Traditional style building **Rev:** Value and dog **Edge:** Plain **Shape:** Scalloped

Date	Mintage	F	VF	XF	Unc	BU
1994 Proof	—	Value: 100				

Y# 450 10 YUAN
31.2400 g., 0.9990 Silver 1.0045 oz. ASW **Subject:** Year of the Pig **Obv:** National emblem, date below **Rev:** Pig, denomination at right

Date	Mintage	F	VF	XF	Unc	BU
1995 Proof	8,000	Value: 85.00				

Y# 452 10 YUAN
20.7500 g., 0.9990 Silver .6640 oz. ASW **Subject:** Year of the Pig **Obv:** Building, date below **Rev:** Two pigs, denomination lower left **Shape:** Scalloped

Date	Mintage	F	VF	XF	Unc	BU
1995 Proof	6,800	Value: 110				

Y# 585 10 YUAN
31.1035 g., 0.9990 Silver 1.0000 oz. ASW **Subject:** Year of the Rat **Rev:** Rat by oil lamp, denomination below

Date	Mintage	F	VF	XF	Unc	BU
1996 Proof	8,000	Value: 60.00				

Y# 854 10 YUAN
23.0375 g., 0.9000 Silver .6666 oz. ASW **Subject:** Year of the Rat **Obv:** Dengdu Pavilion **Rev:** Rat eating corn cob **Shape:** Scalloped

Date	Mintage	F	VF	XF	Unc	BU
1996 Proof	6,800	Value: 70.00				

Y# 896 10 YUAN
23.0375 g., 0.9000 Silver .6666 oz. ASW **Subject:** Year of the Ox **Obv:** Mingyuan Pavilion **Rev:** Bull, denomination below **Shape:** Scalloped

Date	Mintage	F	VF	XF	Unc	BU
1997 Proof	6,800	Value: 60.00				

Y# 899.1 10 YUAN
31.1035 g., 0.9990 Silver 1.0000 oz. ASW **Subject:** Year of the Ox **Obv:** State seal **Rev:** Water buffalo

Date	Mintage	F	VF	XF	Unc	BU
1997 Proof	8,000	Value: 70.00				

Y# 899.2 10 YUAN
31.1035 g., 0.9990 Silver 1.0000 oz. ASW, 40 mm. **Subject:** Year of the Ox **Obv:** National emblem, date below **Rev:** Bull, drinking, denomination below **Note:** Increased size.

Date	Mintage	F	VF	XF	Unc	BU
1997	50,000	—	—	—	35.00	—

Y# 922 10 YUAN
31.1035 g., 0.9990 Silver 1.0000 oz. ASW **Subject:** Year of the Tiger **Obv:** National emblem **Rev:** Tiger on rock, denomination at right

Date	Mintage	F	VF	XF	Unc	BU
1998	50,000	—	—	—	40.00	—

Y# 923 10 YUAN
31.1035 g., 0.9990 Silver 1.0000 oz. ASW **Subject:** Year of the Tiger **Obv:** Badaling building **Rev:** Multicolor tiger cub, denomination at right

Date	Mintage	F	VF	XF	Unc	BU
1998	100,000	—	—	—	50.00	—

Y# 926 10 YUAN
23.0375 g., 0.9000 Silver .6666 oz. ASW **Subject:** Year of the Tiger **Obv:** Badaling building, date below **Rev:** Tiger **Shape:** Scalloped

Date	Mintage	F	VF	XF	Unc	BU
1998 Proof	6,800	Value: 65.00				

Y# 978 10 YUAN
23.0375 g., 0.9000 Silver .6666 oz. ASW **Subject:** Year of the Dragon **Obv:** Building **Rev:** Dragon **Shape:** Scalloped

Date	Mintage	F	VF	XF	Unc	BU
2000 Proof	6,800	Value: 95.00				

Y# 1110 10 YUAN
31.1035 g., 0.9990 Silver 0.999 oz. ASW, 43.2 x 26.5 mm. **Subject:** Year of the Dragon **Obv:** Shanhaiguan gate tower of the Great, date above **Rev:** Dragon, denomination lower right **Edge:** Plain **Shape:** Fan

Date	Mintage	F	VF	XF	Unc	BU
2000 Proof	66,000	Value: 50.00				

Y# 38 20 YUAN
15.0000 g., 0.8500 Silver .4099 oz. ASW **Subject:** Year of the Dog **Obv:** Temple of Heaven, date lower right **Rev:** Dog above denomination

Date	Mintage	F	VF	XF	Unc	BU
1982 Proof	8,825	Value: 125				

Y# 32 30 YUAN
15.0000 g., 0.8500 Silver .4099 oz. ASW **Subject:** Year of the Rooster **Obv:** Shoreline temple, date lower left **Rev:** Rooster, denomination at left

Date	Mintage	F	VF	XF	Unc	BU
1981 Proof	10,000	Value: 225				

Y# 122 50 YUAN
155.5000 g., 0.9990 Silver 5.0000 oz. ASW **Subject:** Year of the Rabbit **Obv:** Pagoda, date below **Rev:** Two rabbits, denomination below

Date	Mintage	F	VF	XF	Unc	BU
1987 Proof	4,000	Value: 275				

Y# 142 50 YUAN
155.5000 g., 0.9990 Silver 5.0000 oz. ASW, 70 mm. **Subject:** Year of the Dragon **Obv:** Great Wall, date below **Rev:** Inner circle holds three dragons, four dragons surround, denomination below **Note:** Photo reduced.

Date	Mintage	F	VF	XF	Unc	BU
1988 Proof	5,000	Value: 265				

Y# 178 50 YUAN
155.5000 g., 0.9990 Silver 5.0000 oz. ASW, 70 mm. **Subject:** Year of the Snake **Obv:** Shanhaiguan Pass Gate **Rev:** Snake left, denomination below **Note:** Photo reduced.

Date	Mintage	F	VF	XF	Unc	BU
1989 Proof	1,000	Value: 365				

Y# 223 50 YUAN
155.5000 g., 0.9990 Silver 5.0000 oz. ASW, 70 mm. **Subject:** Year of the Horse **Obv:** Temple of Confucius **Rev:** Two horses drinking at stream, denomination below **Note:** Photo reduced.

Date	Mintage	F	VF	XF	Unc	BU
1990 Proof	2,000	Value: 225				

Y# 272 50 YUAN
155.5000 g., 0.9990 Silver 5.0000 oz. ASW, 60 mm. **Subject:** Year of the Goat **Obv:** Chinese building and legend **Rev:** Goats, denomination above **Note:** Photo reduced.

Date	Mintage	F	VF	XF	Unc	BU
1991 Proof	2,000	Value: 275				

Y# 289 50 YUAN
155.5000 g., 0.9990 Silver 5.0000 oz. ASW **Subject:** Year of the Monkey **Obv:** Building **Rev:** Monkey

Date	Mintage	F	VF	XF	Unc	BU
1992 Proof	1,000	Value: 325				

Y# 381 50 YUAN
155.5000 g., 0.9990 Silver 5.0000 oz. ASW **Subject:** Year of the Rooster

Date	Mintage	F	VF	XF	Unc	BU
1993 Proof	1,000	Value: 285				

Y# 386 50 YUAN
155.5000 g., 0.9990 Silver 5.0000 oz. ASW **Subject:** Year of the Dog

Date	Mintage	F	VF	XF	Unc	BU
1994 Proof	1,000	Value: 245				

Y# 464 50 YUAN
155.5175 g., 0.9990 Silver 5.0000 oz. ASW **Subject:** Year of the Pig **Obv:** Traditional building **Rev:** Sow and 4 piglets

Date	Mintage	F	VF	XF	Unc	BU
1995 Proof	1,000	Value: 245				

Y# 855 50 YUAN
155.5175 g., 0.9990 Silver 5.0000 oz. ASW **Subject:** Year of the Rat **Obv:** Dengdu Pavilion **Rev:** Rat and grapes, denomination above

Date	Mintage	F	VF	XF	Unc	BU
1996 Proof	1,000	Value: 255				

Y# 897 50 YUAN
155.5175 g., 0.9990 Silver 5.0000 oz. ASW, 80 mm. **Subject:** Year of the Ox **Obv:** Mingyuan Pavilion, date below **Rev:** Bull ox, left, denomination above **Note:** Photo reduced.

Date	Mintage	F	VF	XF	Unc	BU
1997 Proof	1,000	Value: 325				

Y# 927 50 YUAN
155.5175 g., 0.9990 Silver 5.0000 oz. ASW **Subject:** Year of the Tiger **Obv:** Badaling building **Rev:** Tiger on rock, denomination at right

Date	Mintage	F	VF	XF	Unc	BU
1998 Proof	1,000	Value: 325				

Y# 143 100 YUAN
373.2360 g., 0.9990 Silver 12.0000 oz. ASW, 80 mm. **Subject:** Year of the Dragon **Obv:** Great Wall, date below **Rev:** Two dragons facing, denomination below **Note:** Photo reduced.

Date	Mintage	F	VF	XF	Unc	BU
1988 Proof	3,000	Value: 450				

Y# 179 100 YUAN
373.2360 g., 0.9990 Silver 12.0000 oz. ASW **Subject:** Year of the Snake **Obv:** Shanhaiguan Pass Gate **Rev:** Snake left within beaded circle, denomination below **Note:** Photo reduced.

Date	Mintage	F	VF	XF	Unc	BU
1989 Proof	400	Value: 800				

Y# 224 100 YUAN
373.2360 g., 0.9990 Silver 12.0000 oz. ASW, 80 mm. **Subject:** Year of the Horse **Obv:** Temple of Confucius **Rev:** Two horses galloping left, denomination below **Note:** Photo reduced.

Date	Mintage	F	VF	XF	Unc	BU
1990 Proof	1,000	Value: 385				

Y# 273 100 YUAN
373.2360 g., 0.9990 Silver 12.0000 oz. ASW, 80 mm. **Subject:** Year of the Goat **Rev:** Two goats, denomination at left **Note:** Photo reduced.

Date	Mintage	F	VF	XF	Unc	BU
1991 Proof	1,000	Value: 385				

Y# 290 100 YUAN
373.2360 g., 0.9990 Silver 12.0000 oz. ASW **Subject:** Year of the Monkey **Obv:** Building **Rev:** Family of monkeys

Date	Mintage	F	VF	XF	Unc	BU
1992 Proof	500	Value: 475				

Y# 383 100 YUAN
373.2360 g., 0.9990 Silver 12.0000 oz. ASW **Subject:** Year of the Rooster

Date	Mintage	F	VF	XF	Unc	BU
1993 Proof	500	Value: 425				

Y# 569 100 YUAN
373.2420 g., 0.9990 Silver 12.0000 oz. ASW **Subject:** Year of the Rooster **Obv:** National emblem

Date	Mintage	F	VF	XF	Unc	BU
1993 Proof	Est. 500	Value: 500				

Y# 388 100 YUAN
373.2360 g., 0.9990 Silver 12.0000 oz. ASW **Subject:** Year of the Dog

Date	Mintage	F	VF	XF	Unc	BU
1994 Proof	500	Value: 425				

Y# 781 100 YUAN
373.2420 g., 0.9990 Silver 12.0000 oz. ASW **Subject:** Year of the Dog **Obv:** Phoenix Pavilion **Rev:** Large dog

Date	Mintage	F	VF	XF	Unc	BU
1994 Proof	500	Value: 575				

Y# 466 100 YUAN
373.2420 g., 0.9990 Silver 12.0000 oz. ASW, 80 mm. **Subject:** Year of the Pig **Rev:** Sow and five piglets

Date	Mintage	F	VF	XF	Unc	BU
1995 Proof	500	Value: 400				

Y# 669 100 YUAN
373.2360 g., 0.9990 Silver 12.0000 oz. ASW **Subject:** Year of the Ox

Date	Mintage	F	VF	XF	Unc	BU
1997	500	—	—	—	450	—

Y# 898 100 YUAN
373.2420 g., 0.9990 Silver 12.0000 oz. ASW **Subject:** Year of the Ox **Obv:** Minguan Pavilion **Rev:** Cow nursing calf, denomination below

Date	Mintage	F	VF	XF	Unc	BU
1997 Proof	500	Value: 475				

Y# 928 100 YUAN
373.2420 g., 0.9990 Silver 12.0000 oz. ASW **Subject:** Year of the Tiger **Obv:** Badaling building **Rev:** Tiger on rock, denomination at right

Date	Mintage	F	VF	XF	Unc	BU
1998 Proof	500	Value: 600				

Y# 700 200 YUAN
1000.0000 g., 0.9990 Silver 32.1895 oz. ASW, 120 mm. **Subject:** Completion of 150 Yuan Lunar - Animal Coin Series **Obv:** Monument divides date and denomination within circle **Rev:** Ying/Yang symbols within octagon surrounded by twelve animal coins **Note:** Photo reduced.

Date	Mintage	F	VF	XF	Unc	BU
1992 Proof	185	Value: 1,250				

Y# 976 200 YUAN
1000.2108 g., 0.9990 Silver 32.1253 oz. ASW **Subject:** Completion of 12-Year Lunar Cycle

Date	Mintage	F	VF	XF	Unc	BU
1999 Proof	1,000	Value: 1,200				

SILVER BULLION COINAGE

Panda Series

Y# 392 5 YUAN
15.5517 g., 0.9990 Silver .5000 oz. ASW **Obv:** Temple of Heaven within circle, date below **Rev:** Panda facing forward, denomination below

Date	Mintage	F	VF	XF	Unc	BU
1993	—	—	—	—	22.50	—

Y# 436 5 YUAN
15.5517 g., 0.9990 Silver .5000 oz. ASW **Rev:** Panda approaching water, denomination above

Date	Mintage	F	VF	XF	Unc	BU
1994	—	—	—	—	25.00	—

Y# 791 5 YUAN
15.7717 g., 0.9990 Silver .5000 oz. ASW **Obv:** Temple of Heaven **Rev:** Panda climbing tree branch

Date	Mintage	F	VF	XF	Unc	BU
1995 Proof	—	Value: 27.50				

Y# 847 5 YUAN
15.5517 g., 0.9990 Silver .5000 oz. ASW **Obv:** Temple of Heaven **Rev:** Panda seated on shore **Note:** Large and small date varieties exist.

Date	Mintage	F	VF	XF	Unc	BU
1996	—	—	—	—	13.50	20.00

Y# 728 5 YUAN
15.6300 g., 0.9990 Silver .5020 oz. ASW **Obv:** Temple of Heaven within circle, date below **Rev:** Panda crossing stream, denomination at lower left **Note:** Large and small date varieties exist.

Date	Mintage	F	VF	XF	Unc	BU
1997 Proof	—	Value: 22.00				

Y# 892 5 YUAN
15.5517 g., 0.9990 Silver .5000 oz. ASW **Obv:** Temple of Heaven **Rev:** Panda on branch **Note:** Large and small date varieties exist.

Date	Mintage	F	VF	XF	Unc	BU
1997	—	—	—	—	—	20.00

Y# 893 5 YUAN
15.5517 g., 0.9990 Silver .5000 oz. ASW **Obv:** Temple of Heaven with additional legend on Hong Kong's return **Rev:** Panda crossing stream, denomination lower left **Note:** Large and small date varieties exist.

Date	Mintage	F	VF	XF	Unc	BU
1997 Proof	30,000	Value: 50.00				

Y# 962 5 YUAN
15.6000 g., 0.9990 Silver .5000 oz. ASW, 36 mm. **Obv:** Temple of Heaven **Rev:** Multicolor panda and flora **Edge:** Reeded **Note:** Large and small date varieties exist.

Date	Mintage	F	VF	XF	Unc	BU
1997	100,000	—	—	—	22.00	—

Y# 964 5 YUAN
15.5517 g., 0.9990 Silver .5000 oz. ASW **Rev:** Multicolor panda **Note:** Large and small date varieties exist.

Date	Mintage	F	VF	XF	Unc	BU
1998	100,000	—	—	—	22.00	—

Y# 57 10 YUAN
27.0000 g., 0.9000 Silver .7813 oz. ASW **Obv:** Temple of Heaven, date below **Rev:** Two pandas, denomination below

Date	Mintage	F	VF	XF	Unc	BU
1983 Proof	10,000	Value: 225				
1983 Frosted Proof	Inc. above	Value: 235				

Y# 67 10 YUAN
27.0000 g., 0.9250 Silver .8031 oz. ASW **Obv:** Temple of Heaven, date below **Rev:** Panda and cub, denomination at right

Date	Mintage	F	VF	XF	Unc	BU
1984 Proof	10,000	Value: 95.00				

Y# 95 10 YUAN
27.0000 g., 0.9000 Silver .7813 oz. ASW **Obv:** Temple of Heaven, date below **Rev:** Panda with cub on back, denomination below

Date	Mintage	F	VF	XF	Unc	BU
1985 Proof	10,000	Value: 160				

Y# 133 10 YUAN
31.1000 g., 0.9990 Silver 1.0000 oz. ASW **Obv:** Temple of Heaven, date below **Rev:** Panda climbing tree, denomination at right

Date	Mintage	F	VF	XF	Unc	BU
1987 Proof	31,000	Value: 70.00				

Y# 186 10 YUAN

31.1000 g., 0.9990 Silver 1.0000 oz. ASW **Obv:** Temple of Heaven, date below **Rev:** Baby panda on grid background, date at bottom

Date	Mintage	F	VF	XF	Unc	BU
1989	250,000	—	—	—	27.50	—
1989 Proof	25,000	Value: 37.50				

Y# 237 10 YUAN

31.1000 g., 0.9990 Silver 1.0000 oz. ASW **Obv:** Temple of Heaven, date below **Rev:** Panda, denomination below

Date	Mintage	F	VF	XF	Unc	BU
1990	200,000	—	—	—	27.50	—
1990 Proof	20,000	Value: 37.50				

Y# 308.1 10 YUAN

31.1000 g., 0.9990 Silver 1.0000 oz. ASW **Obv:** Temple of Heaven, date below with bottom serifs **Rev:** Panda sitting with hind feet in water, denomination at left

Date	Mintage	F	VF	XF	Unc	BU
1991	100,000	—	—	—	65.00	—

Y# 308.2 10 YUAN

31.1000 g., 0.9990 Silver 1.0000 oz. ASW **Obv:** Temple of Heaven, date below **Rev:** P behind panda

Date	Mintage	F	VF	XF	Unc	BU
1991 Proof	20,000	Value: 75.00				

Y# 314 10 YUAN

62.2000 g., 0.9990 Silver 2.0000 oz. ASW **Obv:** Temple of Heaven, date below **Rev:** Panda climbing bamboo branch, denomination upper right

Date	Mintage	F	VF	XF	Unc	BU
1991 Proof	10,000	Value: 80.00				

Y# 346 10 YUAN

31.1000 g., 0.9990 Silver 1.0000 oz. ASW **Obv:** Temple of Heaven within circle, date below **Rev:** Panda climbing right on eucalyptus branch, denomination above

Date	Mintage	F	VF	XF	Unc	BU
1992	100,000	—	—	—	47.50	—
1992 Proof	5,202	Value: 65.00				

Y# 360 10 YUAN

31.1000 g., 0.9990 Silver 1.0000 oz. ASW **Obv:** Temple of Heaven, date below **Rev:** Mother panda nurturing cub

Date	Mintage	F	VF	XF	Unc	BU
1993 Proof	20,000	Value: 55.00				

Y# 361 10 YUAN

31.1000 g., 0.9990 Silver 1.0000 oz. ASW **Obv:** Temple of Heaven, date below **Rev:** Panda on flat rock

Date	Mintage	F	VF	XF	Unc	BU
1993	120,000	—	—	—	45.00	—

Y# 416 10 YUAN

31.1000 g., 0.9990 Silver 1.0000 oz. ASW **Obv:** Temple of Heaven within circle, date below **Rev:** Seated panda eating, denomination below

Date	Mintage	F	VF	XF	Unc	BU
1994	120,000	—	—	—	50.00	—

Y# 437 10 YUAN

31.1000 g., 0.9990 Silver 1.0000 oz. ASW **Obv:** Temple of Heaven, date below **Rev:** Panda sitting on branch of tree

Date	Mintage	F	VF	XF	Unc	BU
1994 Proof	20,000	Value: 55.00				

Y# 485.1 10 YUAN

31.1035 g., 0.9990 Silver 1.0000 oz. ASW **Subject:** Shanghai Mint **Obv:** Temple of Heaven **Rev:** Panda sitting on branch eating large twig

Date	Mintage	F	VF	XF	Unc	BU
1995	—	—	—	—	32.50	—

Y# 485.2 10 YUAN

31.1035 g., 0.9990 Silver 1.0000 oz. ASW **Subject:** Shenyang Mint **Obv:** Temple of Heaven, date below **Rev:** Panda eating small twig

Date	Mintage	F	VF	XF	Unc	BU
1995	—	—	—	—	32.50	—

Y# 787 10 YUAN

31.1035 g., 0.9990 Silver 1.0000 oz. ASW **Obv:** Temple of Heaven **Rev:** Panda approaching water from right

Date	Mintage	F	VF	XF	Unc	BU
1995 Proof	10,000	Value: 40.00				

Y# 792 10 YUAN

31.1035 g., 0.9990 Silver 1.0000 oz. ASW **Subject:** Beijing Stamp Fair **Obv:** Temple of Heaven with additional legend below **Rev:** Panda approaching water from right

Date	Mintage	F	VF	XF	Unc	BU
1995 Proof	18,000	Value: 40.00				

Y# 583 10 YUAN

31.1035 g., 0.9990 Silver 1.0000 oz. ASW **Obv:** Temple of Heaven within circle, date below **Rev:** Seated panda mother and cub, denomination upper left **Note:** Large and small date varieties exist.

Date	Mintage	F	VF	XF	Unc	BU
1996 Prooflike	—	—	—	—	32.50	—

Y# 1096 10 YUAN

31.2300 g., 0.9990 Silver 1.0031 oz. ASW, 39.8 mm. **Obv:** Temple of Heaven **Rev:** Seated panda facing left **Edge:** Reeded **Note:** Large and small date varieties exist.

Date	Mintage	F	VF	XF	Unc	BU
1996 Proof	8,000	Value: 75.00				

Y# 1060 10 YUAN

31.1035 g., 0.9990 Silver 1.0000 oz. ASW, 40 mm. **Obv:** Temple of Heaven within circle, date below **Rev:** Multicolor panda and flora, denomination at right **Edge:** Reeded **Note:** Large and small date varieties exist.

Date	Mintage	F	VF	XF	Unc	BU
1997	—	—	—	—	45.00	50.00

Y# 715 10 YUAN

31.1035 g., 0.9990 Silver 1.0000 oz. ASW **Obv:** Temple of Heaven within circle, date below **Rev:** Panda on thick branch, left, denomination below **Note:** Large and small date varieties exist.

Date	Mintage	F	VF	XF	Unc	BU
1997	50,000	—	—	—	28.50	—

Y# 726 10 YUAN
31.2200 g., 0.9990 Silver 1.0027 oz. ASW **Obv:** Temple of Heaven and date within circle, - "Visit China '97" around outside **Rev:** Panda on large tree branch, denomination below **Note:** Large and small date varieties exist.

Date	Mintage	F	VF	XF	Unc	BU
1997	50,000	—	—	—	—	30.00

Y# 894 10 YUAN
31.1035 g., 0.9990 Silver 1.0000 oz. ASW **Obv:** Temple of Heaven - "Founding of Chongqing Municipality" **Rev:** Panda on branch **Note:** Large and small date varieties exist.

Date	Mintage	F	VF	XF	Unc	BU
1997 Proof	50,000	Value: 35.00				

Y# 963 10 YUAN
31.1035 g., 0.9990 Silver 1.0000 oz. ASW **Obv:** Temple of Heaven, date below **Rev:** Multicolor panda **Note:** Large and small date varieties exist.

Date	Mintage	F	VF	XF	Unc	BU
1997	100,000	—	—	—	40.00	—

Y# 969 10 YUAN
31.1035 g., 0.9990 Silver 1.0000 oz. ASW **Obv:** Temple of Heaven, date below **Rev:** Panda **Note:** Large and small date varieties exist.

Date	Mintage	F	VF	XF	Unc	BU
1998	250,000	—	—	—	35.00	—

Y# 970 10 YUAN
31.1035 g., 0.9990 Silver 1.0000 oz. ASW **Obv:** Temple of Heaven, date below **Rev:** Multicolor panda **Note:** Large and small date varieties exist.

Date	Mintage	F	VF	XF	Unc	BU
1998	100,000	—	—	—	42.50	—

Y# 973 10 YUAN
31.1035 g., 0.9990 Silver 1.0000 oz. ASW **Obv:** Temple of Heaven, date below **Rev:** Panda **Note:** Large and small date varieties exist.

Date	Mintage	F	VF	XF	Unc	BU
1999	250,000	—	—	—	25.00	—

Y# 974 10 YUAN
31.1035 g., 0.9990 Silver 1.0000 oz. ASW **Obv:** Temple of Heaven, date below **Rev:** Multicolor panda **Note:** Large and small date varieties exist.

Date	Mintage	F	VF	XF	Unc	BU
1999	100,000	—	—	—	40.00	—

Y# 931 10 YUAN
31.1035 g., 0.9990 Silver 1.0000 oz. ASW **Obv:** Temple of Heaven within circle, date below **Rev:** Panda on rock, denomination at left **Note:** Large and small date varieties exist.

Date	Mintage	F	VF	XF	Unc	BU
1999	—	Value: 55.00				

Y# 979 10 YUAN
31.1035 g., 0.9990 Silver 1.0000 oz. ASW **Obv:** Temple of Heaven within circle, date below **Rev:** Panda seated, holding bamboo branch, denomination below **Note:** Large and small date varieties exist.

Date	Mintage	F	VF	XF	Unc	BU
2000	—	—	—	—	32.50	—

Note: Domestic Chinese examples struck with mirror fields, overseas examples struck with frosted fields

Y# 134 50 YUAN
155.5000 g., 0.9990 Silver 5.0000 oz. ASW, 70 mm. **Obv:** Temple of Heaven **Rev:** Panda clinging to tree trunk

Date	Mintage	F	VF	XF	Unc	BU
1987 Proof	8,540	Value: 110				

Y# 168 50 YUAN
155.5000 g., 0.9990 Silver 5.0000 oz. ASW **Obv:** Temple of Heaven **Rev:** Two pandas in tree

Date	Mintage	F	VF	XF	Unc	BU
1988 Proof	11,000	Value: 120				

Y# 218 50 YUAN
155.5000 g., 0.9990 Silver 5.0000 oz. ASW **Obv:** Temple of Heaven **Rev:** Mother panda with cub

Date	Mintage	F	VF	XF	Unc	BU
1989 Proof	9,599	Value: 130				

Y# 262 50 YUAN
155.5000 g., 0.9990 Silver 5.0000 oz. ASW **Obv:** Temple of Heaven **Rev:** Two pandas, one in tree

Date	Mintage	F	VF	XF	Unc	BU
1990 Proof	4,000	Value: 130				

Y# 373 50 YUAN
155.5000 g., 0.9990 Silver 5.0000 oz. ASW **Obv:** Temple of Heaven, date below **Rev:** Pandas at waters edge, denomination above

Date	Mintage	F	VF	XF	Unc	BU
1991 Proof	5,000	Value: 145				

Y# 374 50 YUAN
155.5000 g., 0.9990 Silver 5.0000 oz. ASW **Obv:** Temple of Heaven, date below **Rev:** Pandas

Date	Mintage	F	VF	XF	Unc	BU
1992 Proof	4,000	Value: 145				

Y# 379 50 YUAN
155.5000 g., 0.9990 Silver 5.0000 oz. ASW **Obv:** Temple of Heaven **Rev:** Pandas, denomination at left

Date	Mintage	F	VF	XF	Unc	BU
1993 Proof	Est. 3,000	Value: 165				

Y# 638 50 YUAN
155.5000 g., 0.9990 Silver 5.0000 oz. ASW **Obv:** Temple of Heaven **Rev:** Two pandas, one in tree

Date	Mintage	F	VF	XF	Unc	BU
1994 Proof	3,000	Value: 200				

Y# 645 50 YUAN
155.5000 g., 0.9990 Silver 5.0000 oz. ASW **Obv:** Temple of Heaven **Rev:** Two pandas on river bank, denomination above

Date	Mintage	F	VF	XF	Unc	BU
1995 Proof	3,000	Value: 200				

Y# 169 100 YUAN
373.2360 g., 0.9990 Silver 12.0000 oz. ASW, 70 mm. **Obv:** Temple of Heaven **Rev:** Two pandas in tree

Date	Mintage	F	VF	XF	Unc	BU
1988 Proof	5,000	Value: 300				

Y# 219 100 YUAN
373.2360 g., 0.9990 Silver 12.0000 oz. ASW **Obv:** Temple of Heaven **Rev:** Panda with two cubs

Date	Mintage	F	VF	XF	Unc	BU
1989 Proof	3,670	Value: 310				

Y# 263 100 YUAN
373.2360 g., 0.9990 Silver 12.0000 oz. ASW **Obv:** Temple of Heaven **Rev:** Three curious pandas

Date	Mintage	F	VF	XF	Unc	BU
1990 Proof	2,500	Value: 325				

Y# 375 100 YUAN
373.2360 g., 0.9990 Silver 12.0000 oz. ASW **Obv:** Temple of Heaven **Rev:** Pandas

Date	Mintage	F	VF	XF	Unc	BU
1991 Proof	Est. 2,500	Value: 350				

Y# 376 100 YUAN
373.2360 g., 0.9990 Silver 12.0000 oz. ASW, 80 mm. **Obv:** Temple of Heaven, date below **Rev:** Pandas

Date	Mintage	F	VF	XF	Unc	BU
1992 Proof	Est. 2,500	Value: 350				

Y# 380 100 YUAN
373.2360 g., 0.9990 Silver 12.0000 oz. ASW **Obv:** Temple of Heaven **Rev:** Pandas

Date	Mintage	F	VF	XF	Unc	BU
1993 Proof	Est. 2,500	Value: 375				

Y# 652 100 YUAN
373.2360 g., 0.9990 Silver 12.0000 oz. ASW **Obv:** Temple of Heaven **Rev:** Panda with two cubs at waters edge, denomination lower right, circle surrounds

Date	Mintage	F	VF	XF	Unc	BU
1994 Proof	2,500	Value: 350				

Y# 646 100 YUAN
373.2360 g., 0.9990 Silver 12.0000 oz. ASW **Obv:** Temple of Heaven **Rev:** Panda family

Date	Mintage	F	VF	XF	Unc	BU
1995 Proof	500	Value: 500				

Y# 968 200 YUAN
1000.0000 g., 0.9990 Silver 32.1895 oz. ASW **Obv:** Temple of Heaven **Rev:** Panda **Note:** Large and small date varieties exist.

Date	Mintage	F	VF	XF	Unc	BU
1998 Proof	1,998	Value: 775				

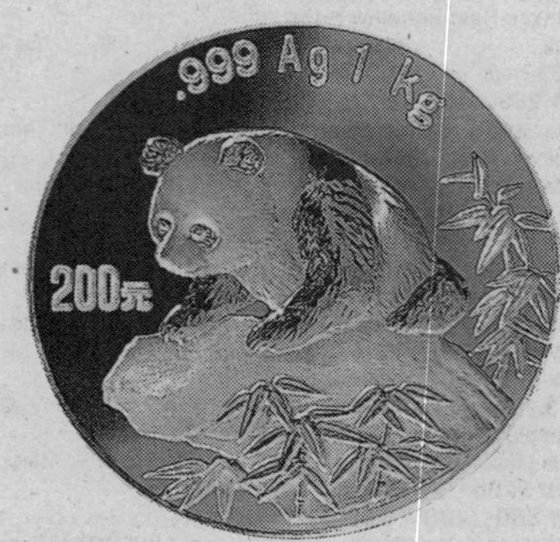

Y# 971 200 YUAN
1000.2108 g., 0.9990 Silver 32.1253 oz. ASW, 100 mm. **Obv:** Temple of Heaven within circle **Rev:** Panda on rock left, denomination at left **Note:** Photo reduced. Large and small date varieties exist.

Date	Mintage	F	VF	XF	Unc	BU
1999 Proof	—	Value: 850				

Y# 1071 300 YUAN
999.9775 g., 0.9990 Silver 32.1500 oz. ASW, 100 mm. **Obv:** Temple of Heaven **Rev:** Panda seated on leaves **Edge:** Plain **Note:** Large and small date varieties exist.

Date	Mintage	F	VF	XF	Unc	BU
2000 Proof	2,000	Value: 850				

GOLD BULLION COINAGE

Panda Series

Y# 307 3 YUAN
1.0000 g., 0.9990 Gold .0321 oz. AGW **Obv:** Temple of Heaven **Rev:** Seated panda left, denomination at left

Date	Mintage	F	VF	XF	Unc	BU
1991 Proof	110,000	Value: 37.50				

Y# 48 5 YUAN
1.5552 g., 0.9990 Gold .0500 oz. AGW **Obv:** Temple of Heaven, date below **Rev:** Panda on all fours right, within circle

Date	Mintage	F	VF	XF	Unc	BU
1983 Proof	Est. 58,000	Value: 70.00				

Y# 73 5 YUAN
1.5552 g., 0.9990 Gold .0500 oz. AGW **Obv:** Temple of Heaven, date below **Rev:** Panda holding bamboo branch, reclined, denomination at right

Date	Mintage	F	VF	XF	Unc	BU
1984 Proof	Est. 86,000	Value: 47.50				

Y# 80 5 YUAN
1.5552 g., 0.9990 Gold .0500 oz. AGW **Obv:** Temple of Heaven, date below **Rev:** Panda hanging from branch, denomination upper left

Date	Mintage	F	VF	XF	Unc	BU
1985 Proof	Est. 217,000	Value: 47.50				

Y# 101 5 YUAN
1.5552 g., 0.9990 Gold .0500 oz. AGW **Obv:** Temple of Heaven, date below **Rev:** Panda, denomination below

Date	Mintage	F	VF	XF	Unc	BU
1986	Est. 87,500	—	—	—	—	40.00
1986 P Proof	10,000	Value: 45.00				

Y# 124 5 YUAN
1.5552 g., 0.9990 Gold .0500 oz. AGW **Obv:** Temple of Heaven, date below **Rev:** Panda left, denomination below

Date	Mintage	F	VF	XF	Unc	BU
1987(s)	Est. 103,000	—	—	—	—	40.00
1987(y)	Est. 39,000	—	—	—	—	40.00
1987 P Proof	10,000	Value: 45.00				

Y# 152 5 YUAN
1.5552 g., 0.9990 Gold .0500 oz. AGW **Obv:** Temple of Heaven, date below **Rev:** Panda pawing bamboo

Date	Mintage	F	VF	XF	Unc	BU
1988	Est. 482,000	—	—	—	—	40.00
1988 Proof	10,000	Value: 45.00				

Y# 238 5 YUAN
1.5552 g., 0.9990 Gold .0500 oz. AGW **Obv:** Temple of Heaven, date below **Rev:** Panda climbing rock, denomination below

Date	Mintage	F	VF	XF	Unc	BU
1990	Est. 337,000	—	—	—	—	40.00
1990 Proof	5,000	Value: 47.50				

Y# 309 5 YUAN
1.5552 g., 0.9990 Gold .0500 oz. AGW **Obv:** Temple of Heaven **Rev:** Panda with hind feet in water eating bamboo

Date	Mintage	F	VF	XF	Unc	BU
1991	—	—	—	—	—	50.00
1991 Proof	3,500	Value: 60.00				

Y# 341 5 YUAN
1.5552 g., 0.9990 Gold .0500 oz. AGW **Obv:** Temple of Heaven **Rev:** Panda on branch

Date	Mintage	F	VF	XF	Unc	BU
1992	—	—	—	—	—	47.50
1992 Proof	2,000	Value: 65.00				

Y# 610 5 YUAN
1.5552 g., 0.9990 Gold .0500 oz. AGW **Obv:** Temple of Heaven, date below **Rev:** Panda pawing bamboo

Date	Mintage	F	VF	XF	Unc	BU
1993	—	—	—	—	—	45.00
1993 Proof	2,500	Value: 55.00				

Y# 1203 5 YUAN
1.5550 g., 0.9990 Gold 0.0499 oz. AGW, 14 mm. **Obv:** Temple of Heaven **Rev:** Panda seated on flat rock **Edge:** Reeded

Date	Mintage	F	VF	XF	Unc	BU
1993(y)	—	—	—	—	—	45.00
1993P(y) Proof	2,500	Value: 65.00				

Y# 431 5 YUAN
1.5552 g., 0.9990 Gold .0500 oz. AGW **Obv:** Temple of Heaven, date below **Rev:** Panda sitting, denomination below

Date	Mintage	F	VF	XF	Unc	BU
1994	—	—	—	—	—	45.00
1994 Proof	—	Value: 55.00				

Y# 640 5 YUAN
1.5552 g., 0.9990 Gold .0500 oz. AGW **Obv:** Temple of Heaven, date below **Rev:** Panda holding bamboo stick, denomination at left

Date	Mintage	F	VF	XF	Unc	BU
1995	—	—	—	—	—	45.00

Y# 716 5 YUAN
1.5552 g., 0.9990 Gold .0500 oz. AGW **Obv:** Temple of Heaven **Rev:** Panda on branch **Note:** Large and small date varieties exist.

Date	Mintage	F	VF	XF	Unc	BU
1997	—	—	—	—	—	45.00

Note: Exists in large and small date varieties

Y# 990 5 YUAN
1.5600 g., 0.9990 Gold .0500 oz. AGW **Obv:** Temple of Heaven **Rev:** Panda seated on rock

Date	Mintage	F	VF	XF	Unc	BU
1998	—	—	—	—	—	40.00

Y# 981 5 YUAN
1.5600 g., 0.9990 Gold .0500 oz. AGW **Obv:** Temple of Heaven **Rev:** Panda on ledge

Date	Mintage	F	VF	XF	Unc	BU
1999	—	—	—	—	—	40.00

Note: Exists in Large and Small date varieties.

Y# 945 5 YUAN
1.5600 g., 0.9990 Gold .0500 oz. AGW **Obv:** Temple of Heaven **Rev:** Panda seated on leaves **Note:** Large and small date varieties exist.

Date	Mintage	F	VF	XF	Unc	BU
2000	—	—	—	—	—	40.00

Note: Domestic Chinese examples struck with mirror fields, overseas examples struck with frosted fields

Y# 49 10 YUAN
3.1103 g., 0.9990 Gold .1000 oz. AGW **Obv:** Temple of Heaven, date below **Rev:** Panda right

Date	Mintage	F	VF	XF	Unc	BU
1983	Est. 74,000	—	—	—	—	85.00

Y# 74 10 YUAN
3.1103 g., 0.9990 Gold .1000 oz. AGW **Obv:** Temple of Heaven **Rev:** Panda holding bamboo branch, reclined, denomination at right

Date	Mintage	F	VF	XF	Unc	BU
1984	10,000	—	—	—	—	185

Y# 81 10 YUAN
3.1103 g., 0.9990 Gold .1000 oz. AGW **Obv:** Temple of Heaven, date below **Rev:** Panda hanging from branch, denomination upper left

Date	Mintage	F	VF	XF	Unc	BU
1985	Est. 150,000	—	—	—	—	85.00

Y# 102 10 YUAN
3.1103 g., 0.9990 Gold .1000 oz. AGW **Obv:** Temple of Heaven **Rev:** Panda, denomination below

Date	Mintage	F	VF	XF	Unc	BU
1986	Est. 45,000	—	—	—	—	75.00
1986 P Proof	10,000	Value: 80.00				

Y# 125 10 YUAN
3.1103 g., 0.9990 Gold .1000 oz. AGW **Obv:** Temple of Heaven, date below **Rev:** Panda, denomination below

Date	Mintage	F	VF	XF	Unc	BU
1987(s)	Est. 108,000	—	—	—	—	75.00
1987(y)	Est. 37,000	—	—	—	—	75.00
1987 P Proof	10,000	Value: 80.00				

Y# 153 10 YUAN
3.1103 g., 0.9990 Gold .1000 oz. AGW **Obv:** Temple of Heaven, date below **Rev:** Panda pawing bamboo, denomination below

Date	Mintage	F	VF	XF	Unc	BU
1988	Est. 290,000	—	—	—	—	70.00
1988 Proof	10,000	Value: 75.00				

Y# 188 10 YUAN
3.1103 g., 0.9990 Gold .1000 oz. AGW **Obv:** Temple of Heaven, date below **Rev:** Panda reclining, grid behind, denomination below

Date	Mintage	F	VF	XF	Unc	BU
1989	Est. 128,000	—	—	—	—	70.00
1989 Proof	8,000	Value: 75.00				

Y# 239 10 YUAN
3.1100 g., 0.9990 Gold .0322 oz. AGW **Obv:** Temple of Heaven, date below **Rev:** Panda, denomination below

Date	Mintage	F	VF	XF	Unc	BU
1990	Est. 214,000	—	—	—	—	75.00
1990 Proof	5,000	Value: 80.00				

Y# 310 10 YUAN
3.1100 g., 0.9990 Gold .10000 oz. AGW **Obv:** Temple of Heaven **Rev:** Panda with hind feet in water eating bamboo **Note:** Similar to 100 Yuan, KM#313.

Date	Mintage	F	VF	XF	Unc	BU
1991	—	—	—	—	—	75.00
1991 Proof	3,500	Value: 90.00				

Y# 342 10 YUAN
3.1103 g., 0.9990 Gold .1000 oz. AGW **Obv:** Temple of Heaven, date below **Rev:** Panda climbing right on eucalyptus branch

Date	Mintage	F	VF	XF	Unc	BU
1992	—	—	—	—	—	75.00
1992 Proof	2,000	Value: 95.00				

Y# 484 10 YUAN
3.1103 g., 0.9990 Gold .1000 oz. AGW **Obv:** Temple of Heaven **Rev:** Panda on flat rock

Date	Mintage	F	VF	XF	Unc	BU
1993	—	—	—	—	—	75.00
1993 Proof	2,500	Value: 95.00				

Y# 611 10 YUAN
Gold **Obv:** Temple of Heaven, date below **Rev:** Panda on flat rock

Date	Mintage	F	VF	XF	Unc	BU
1993 Proof	—	Value: 75.00				

Y# 432 10 YUAN
3.1103 g., 0.9990 Gold .1000 oz. AGW **Obv:** Temple of Heaven, date below **Rev:** Seated panda eating, denomination below

Date	Mintage	F	VF	XF	Unc	BU
1994	—	—	—	—	—	75.00
1994 Proof	2,500	Value: 95.00				

Y# 641 10 YUAN
3.1103 g., 0.9990 Gold .1000 oz. AGW **Obv:** Temple of Heaven **Rev:** Panda eating bamboo, denomination at left

Date	Mintage	F	VF	XF	Unc	BU
1995	—	—	—	—	—	75.00

Y# 581 10 YUAN
1.5552 g., 0.9990 Gold .0500 oz. AGW **Obv:** Temple of Heaven, date below **Rev:** Panda in tree looking down, denomination lower left **Note:** Large and small date varieties exist.

Date	Mintage	F	VF	XF	Unc	BU
1996	—	—	—	—	—	55.00

Y# 573 10 YUAN
3.1103 g., 0.9990 Gold .1000 oz. AGW **Obv:** Temple of Heaven, date below **Rev:** Panda in tree **Note:** Large and small date varieties exist.

Date	Mintage	F	VF	XF	Unc	BU
1996	—	—	—	—	—	75.00

Y# 848 10 YUAN
3.1103 g., 0.9990 Gold .1000 oz. AGW **Subject:** 15th Anniversary - Gold Panda Coins **Obv:** Temple of Heaven with additional legend **Rev:** Panda in tree **Note:** Large and small date varieties exist.

Date	Mintage	F	VF	XF	Unc	BU
1996 Proof	20,000	Value: 80.00				

Y# 717 10 YUAN
3.1103 g., 0.9990 Gold .1000 oz. AGW **Obv:** Temple of Heaven **Rev:** Panda on branch **Note:** Large and small date varieties exist.

Date	Mintage	F	VF	XF	Unc	BU
1997	—	—	—	—	—	70.00

Note: Exists in large and small date varieties

Y# 988 10 YUAN
3.1103 g. 0.9990 Gold .1000 oz. AGW **Obv:** Temple of Heaven **Rev:** Panda seated on rock **Note:** Large and small date varieties exist.

Date	Mintage	F	VF	XF	Unc	BU
1998	—	—	—	—	—	70.00

Y# 989 10 YUAN
3.1103 g., 0.9990 Gold .1000 oz. AGW **Obv:** Temple of Heaven **Rev:** Panda on ledge

Date	Mintage	F	VF	XF	Unc	BU
1999	—	—	—	—	—	70.00

Note: Exists in Large and Small date varieties.

Y# 946 10 YUAN
3.1103 g., 0.9990 Gold .1000 oz. AGW **Obv:** Temple of Heaven **Rev:** Panda seated on leaves **Note:** Large and small date varieties exist.

Date	Mintage	F	VF	XF	Unc	BU
2000 Proof	—	Value: 75.00				

Y# 50 25 YUAN
7.7758 g., 0.9990 Gold .2500 oz. AGW **Obv:** Temple of Heaven, date below **Rev:** Panda walking right, in inner circle, denomination below

Date	Mintage	F	VF	XF	Unc	BU
1983	Est. 39,000	—	—	—	—	180

Y# 75 25 YUAN
7.7758 g., 0.9990 Gold .2500 oz. AGW **Obv:** Temple of Heaven, date below **Rev:** Lounging Panda with bamboo

Date	Mintage	F	VF	XF	Unc	BU
1984	Est. 38,000	—	—	—	—	180

Y# 82 25 YUAN
7.7758 g., 0.9990 Gold .2500 oz. AGW **Obv:** Temple of Heaven, date below **Rev:** Panda hanging on bamboo branch, denomination upper left

Date	Mintage	F	VF	XF	Unc	BU
1985	Est. 95,000	—	—	—	—	200

Y# 103 25 YUAN
7.7758 g., 0.9990 Gold .2500 oz. AGW **Obv:** Temple of Heaven **Rev:** Facing panda standing, denomination below

Date	Mintage	F	VF	XF	Unc	BU
1986	Est. 33,000	—	—	—	—	170
1986 P Proof	10,000	Value: 175				

Y# 126 25 YUAN
7.7758 g., 0.9990 Gold .2500 oz. AGW **Obv:** Temple of Heaven, date below **Rev:** Panda drinking, denomination below

Date	Mintage	F	VF	XF	Unc	BU
1987(s)	Est. 81,000	—	—	—	—	170
1987(y)	Est. 31,000	—	—	—	—	170
1987 P Proof	10,000	Value: 175				

Y# 154 25 YUAN
7.7758 g., 0.9990 Gold .2500 oz. AGW **Obv:** Temple of Heaven **Rev:** Panda pawing bamboo

Date	Mintage	F	VF	XF	Unc	BU
1988	Est. 122,000	—	—	—	—	170
1988 Proof	10,000	Value: 175				

Y# 189 25 YUAN
7.7758 g., 0.9990 Gold .2500 oz. AGW **Obv:** Temple of Heaven, date below **Rev:** Panda reclining, grid behind, denomination below

Date	Mintage	F	VF	XF	Unc	BU
1989	Est. 71,000	—	—	—	—	170
1989 Proof	8,000	Value: 175				

Y# 240 25 YUAN
7.7758 g., 0.9990 Gold .2500 oz. AGW **Obv:** Temple of Heaven, date below **Rev:** Panda, denomination lower right

Date	Mintage	F	VF	XF	Unc	BU
1990	—	—	—	—	—	175
1990 Proof	5,000	Value: 180				

Y# 311 25 YUAN
7.7758 g., 0.9990 Gold .2500 oz. AGW, 22 mm. **Obv:** Temple of Heaven, date below **Edge:** Reeded

Date	Mintage	F	VF	XF	Unc	BU
1991	—	—	—	—	—	180
1991 Proof	—	Value: 200				

Y# 343 25 YUAN
7.7758 g., 0.9990 Gold .2500 oz. AGW **Obv:** Temple of Heaven, date below **Rev:** Panda on limb

Date	Mintage	F	VF	XF	Unc	BU
1992	—	—	—	—	—	175
1992 Proof	—	Value: 195				

Y# 612 25 YUAN
7.7758 g., 0.9990 Gold .2500 oz. AGW **Obv:** Temple of Heaven, date below **Rev:** Panda tugging on bamboo sprig, denomination below, within circle, date below

Date	Mintage	F	VF	XF	Unc	BU
1993	—	—	—	—	—	185
1993 Proof	—	Value: 200				

Y# 1204 25 YUAN
7.7758 g., 0.9990 Gold 0.2497 oz. AGW, 22 mm. **Obv:** Temple of Heaven **Rev:** Panda seated on flat rock **Edge:** Reeded

Date	Mintage	F	VF	XF	Unc	BU
1993P(y) Proof	2,500	Value: 175				
1993(y)	—	—	—	—	—	170

Y# 433 25 YUAN
7.7758 g., 0.9990 Gold .2500 oz. AGW **Obv:** Temple of Heaven, date below **Rev:** Panda tugging on bamboo sprig

Date	Mintage	F	VF	XF	Unc	BU
1994	35,000	—	—	—	—	195
1994 Proof	—	Value: 220				

Y# 642 25 YUAN
7.7600 g., 0.9990 Gold .2500 oz. AGW **Obv:** Temple of Heaven, date below **Rev:** Panda

Date	Mintage	F	VF	XF	Unc	BU
1995	—	—	—	—	—	195

Y# 576 25 YUAN

7.8300 g., 0.9990 Gold .2515 oz. AGW **Obv:** Temple of Heaven, date below **Rev:** Panda **Note:** Large and small date varieties exist.

Date	Mintage	F	VF	XF	Unc	BU
1996	—	—	—	—	—	195

Y# 849 25 YUAN

7.7759 g., 0.9990 Gold .2500 oz. AGW **Subject:** 15th Anniversary - Gold Panda Coinage **Obv:** Temple of Heaven with additional legend **Rev:** Panda in tree **Note:** Large and small date varieties exist.

Date	Mintage	F	VF	XF	Unc	BU
1996 Proof	8,000	Value: 220				

Y# 718 25 YUAN

7.7759 g., 0.9990 Gold .2500 oz. AGW **Obv:** Temple of Heaven **Rev:** Panda on branch

Date	Mintage	F	VF	XF	Unc	BU
1997	—	—	—	—	—	170

Note: Exists in Large and Small date varieties.

Y# 1002 25 YUAN

7.7758 g., 0.9990 Gold .2500 oz. AGW **Obv:** Temple of Heaven **Rev:** Panda seated on rock **Note:** Large and small date varieties exist.

Date	Mintage	F	VF	XF	Unc	BU
1998	—	—	—	—	—	170

Note: Exists in both large and small date varieties

Y# 1003 25 YUAN

7.7758 g., 0.9990 Gold .2500 oz. AGW **Obv:** Temple of Heaven **Rev:** Panda on ledge **Note:** Large and small date varieties exist.

Date	Mintage	F	VF	XF	Unc	BU
1999	—	—	—	—	—	170

Y# 947 25 YUAN

7.7758 g., 0.9990 Gold .2500 oz. AGW **Obv:** Temple of Heaven **Rev:** Panda seated on leaves **Note:** Large and small date varieties exist.

Date	Mintage	F	VF	XF	Unc	BU
2000	—	—	—	—	—	170

Note: Domestic Chinese examples struck with mirror fields, overseas examples struck with frosted fields

Y# 51 50 YUAN

15.5517 g., 0.9990 Gold .5000 oz. AGW **Obv:** Temple of Heaven, date below **Rev:** Panda walking right, in inner circle, date below

Date	Mintage	F	VF	XF	Unc	BU
1983 Proof	Est. 23,000	Value: 360				

Y# 76 50 YUAN

15.5517 g., 0.9990 Gold .5000 oz. AGW **Obv:** Temple of Heaven, date below **Rev:** Lounging panda with bamboo sprig, denomination at right

Date	Mintage	F	VF	XF	Unc	BU
1984 Proof	Est. 17,000	Value: 375				

Y# 83 50 YUAN

15.5517 g., 0.9990 Gold .5000 oz. AGW **Obv:** Temple of Heaven, date below **Rev:** Panda hanging from bamboo branch, denomination upper left

Date	Mintage	F	VF	XF	Unc	BU
1985	Est. 76,000	—	—	—	—	360

Y# 104 50 YUAN

15.5517 g., 0.9990 Gold .5000 oz. AGW **Obv:** Temple of Heaven, date below **Rev:** Facing panda standing, denomination below

Date	Mintage	F	VF	XF	Unc	BU
1986	Est. 60,000	—	—	—	—	360
1986 P Proof	10,000	Value: 375				

Y# 127 50 YUAN

15.5517 g., 0.9990 Gold .5000 oz. AGW **Obv:** Temple of Heaven, date below **Rev:** Panda drinking water, denomination below

Date	Mintage	F	VF	XF	Unc	BU
1987(s)	Est. 91,000	—	—	—	—	360
1987(y)	Est. 17,000	—	—	—	—	360
1987 P Proof	10,000	Value: 375				

Y# 155 50 YUAN

15.5517 g., 0.9990 Gold .5000 oz. AGW **Obv:** Temple of Heaven, date below **Rev:** Panda pawing bamboo within circle, denomination below

Date	Mintage	F	VF	XF	Unc	BU
1988	Est. 104,000	—	—	—	—	360
1988 Proof	10,000	Value: 375				

Y# 190 50 YUAN

15.5517 g., 0.9990 Gold .5000 oz. AGW **Obv:** Temple of Heaven **Rev:** Grid behind panda

Date	Mintage	F	VF	XF	Unc	BU
1989	Est. 46,000	—	—	—	—	360
1989 Proof	8,000	Value: 375				

Y# 241 50 YUAN

15.5517 g., 0.9990 Gold .5000 oz. AGW **Obv:** Temple of Heaven, date below **Rev:** Panda

Date	Mintage	F	VF	XF	Unc	BU
1990	Est. 35,000	—	—	—	—	375
1990 Proof	5,000	Value: 400				

Y# 312 50 YUAN

15.5517 g., 0.9990 Gold .5000 oz. AGW **Obv:** Temple of Heaven, date below **Rev:** Panda tugging on bamboo sprig, denomination below, within circle, date below

Date	Mintage	F	VF	XF	Unc	BU
1991	—	—	—	—	—	395
1991 Proof	3,500	Value: 425				

Y# 315 50 YUAN

31.1035 g., 0.9990 Gold 1.0000 oz. AGW **Subject:** 10th Anniversary of Panda Coinage **Obv:** Temple of Heaven, date below **Rev:** Panda climbing bamboo branch **Note:** Double thickness.

Date	Mintage	F	VF	XF	Unc	BU
1991 Proof	2,500	Value: 725				

Y# 344 50 YUAN

15.5660 g., 0.9990 Gold .5000 oz. AGW **Obv:** Temple of Heaven, date below **Rev:** Panda on tree branch

Date	Mintage	F	VF	XF	Unc	BU
1992	—	—	—	—	—	395
1992 Proof	2,000	Value: 450				

Y# 613 50 YUAN

15.5517 g., 0.9990 Gold .5000 oz. AGW **Obv:** Temple of Heaven **Rev:** Pandas

Date	Mintage	F	VF	XF	Unc	BU
1993	—	—	—	—	—	395
1993 Proof	2,500	Value: 450				

Y# 1205 50 YUAN

15.5500 g., 0.9990 Gold 0.4994 oz. AGW, 27 mm. **Obv:** Temple of Heaven **Rev:** Panda seated on flat rock **Edge:** Reeded

Date	Mintage	F	VF	XF	Unc	BU
1993(y)	—	—	—	—	395	—
1993P(y) Proof	2,500	Value: 450				

Y# 434 50 YUAN

15.5517 g., 0.9990 Gold .5000 oz. AGW **Obv:** Temple of Heaven **Rev:** Panda seated, eating bamboo shoots, denomination below

Date	Mintage	F	VF	XF	Unc	BU
1994	—	—	—	—	—	395
1994 Proof	2,500	Value: 450				

Y# 643 50 YUAN

15.5517 g., 0.9990 Gold .5000 oz. AGW **Obv:** Temple of Heaven **Rev:** Panda eating bamboo, denomination at left

Date	Mintage	F	VF	XF	Unc	BU
1995	—	—	—	—	—	395

Y# 577 50 YUAN

15.5517 g., 0.9990 Gold .5000 oz. AGW **Obv:** Temple of Heaven, date below **Rev:** Panda in tree **Note:** Large and small date varieties exist.

Date	Mintage	F	VF	XF	Unc	BU
1996	—	—	—	—	—	395

Y# 719 50 YUAN

15.5517 g., 0.9990 Gold .5000 oz. AGW **Obv:** Temple of Heaven within circle, date below **Rev:** Panda on large tree branch, denomination below

Date	Mintage	F	VF	XF	Unc	BU
1997	—	—	—	—	—	360

Note: Exists in Large and Small date varieties

Y# 1010 50 YUAN

15.5517 g., 0.9990 Gold .5000 oz. AGW **Obv:** Temple of Heaven **Rev:** Panda seated on rock

Date	Mintage	F	VF	XF	Unc	BU
1998	—	—	—	—	—	360

Note: Exists in Large and Small date varieties

Y# 1011 50 YUAN

15.5517 g., 0.9990 Gold .5000 oz. AGW **Obv:** Temple of Heaven **Rev:** Panda on ledge

Date	Mintage	F	VF	XF	Unc	BU
1999	—	—	—	—	—	360

Note: Exists in Large and Small date varieties

Y# 948 50 YUAN

15.5518 g., 0.9990 Gold .5000 oz. AGW **Obv:** Temple of Heaven **Rev:** Panda seated on leaves **Note:** Large and small date varieties exist.

Date	Mintage	F	VF	XF	Unc	BU
2000 Proof	—	Value: 365				

Note: Domestic Chinese examples struck with mirror fields, overseas examples struck with frosted fields.

Y# 52 100 YUAN

31.1320 g., 0.9990 Gold 1.0000 oz. AGW **Obv:** Temple of Heaven, date below **Rev:** Panda right within circle, date below

Date	Mintage	F	VF	XF	Unc	BU
1983	22,000	—	—	—	—	BV+10%

Y# 77 100 YUAN
31.1320 g., 0.9990 Gold 1.0000 oz. AGW **Obv:** Temple of Heaven, date below **Rev:** Lounging panda with bamboo sprigs, denomination at right

Date	Mintage	F	VF	XF	Unc	BU
1984	23,000	—	—	—	—	BV+10%

Y# 84 100 YUAN
31.1320 g., 0.9990 Gold 1.0000 oz. AGW **Obv:** Temple of Heaven, date below **Rev:** Panda hanging from branch, denomination upper left

Date	Mintage	F	VF	XF	Unc	BU
1985	164,000	—	—	—	—	BV+10%

Y# 105 100 YUAN
31.1320 g., 0.9990 Gold 1.0000 oz. AGW **Obv:** Temple of Heaven, date below **Rev:** Panda amongst bamboo plants

Date	Mintage	F	VF	XF	Unc	BU
1986	97,000	—	—	—	—	BV+10%
1986 P Proof	10,000	—	—	—	—	BV+15%

Y# 128 100 YUAN
31.1320 g., 0.9990 Gold 1.0000 oz. AGW **Obv:** Temple of Heaven, date below **Rev:** Panda drinking at stream, denomination below

Date	Mintage	F	VF	XF	Unc	BU
1987(s)	84,000	—	—	—	—	BV+10%
1987(y)	47,000	—	—	—	—	BV+10%
1987 P Proof	10,000	—	—	—	—	BV+15%

Y# 156 100 YUAN
31.1320 g., 0.9990 Gold 1.0000 oz. AGW **Obv:** Temple of Heaven, date below **Rev:** Panda pawing bamboo within circle, denomination below

Date	Mintage	F	VF	XF	Unc	BU
1988	167,000	—	—	—	—	BV+10%
1988 Proof	10,000	—	—	—	—	BV+15%

Y# 191 100 YUAN
31.1320 g., 0.9990 Gold 1.0000 oz. AGW **Obv:** Temple of Heaven, date below **Rev:** Panda reclining, grid behind, denomination below

Date	Mintage	F	VF	XF	Unc	BU
1989	—	—	—	—	—	BV+10%
1989 Proof	8,000	—	—	—	—	BV+15%

Y# 242 100 YUAN
31.1320 g., 0.9990 Gold 1.0000 oz. AGW **Obv:** Temple of Heaven, date below **Rev:** Panda climbing rock, denomination below

Date	Mintage	F	VF	XF	Unc	BU
1990	—	—	—	—	—	BV+10%
1990 Proof	5,000	BV+15%				

Y# 313 100 YUAN
31.1320 g., 0.9990 Gold 1.0000 oz. AGW **Obv:** Temple of Heaven, date below **Rev:** Seated panda with hind feet in water, eating bamboo, denomination at left

Date	Mintage	F	VF	XF	Unc	BU
1991	—	—	—	—	—	BV+10%
1991 Proof	3,500	BV+15%				

Y# 345 100 YUAN
31.1035 g., 0.9990 Gold 1.0000 oz. AGW **Obv:** Temple of Heaven within circle, date below **Rev:** Panda on branch, denomination above

Date	Mintage	F	VF	XF	Unc	BU
1992	—	—	—	—	—	BV+10%
1992 Proof	2,000	BV+15%				

Y# 614 100 YUAN
31.1035 g., 0.9990 Gold 1.0000 oz. AGW **Obv:** Temple of Heaven **Rev:** Panda seated on rock

Date	Mintage	F	VF	XF	Unc	BU
1993	—	—	—	—	—	BV+10%

Y# 435 100 YUAN
31.1035 g., 0.9990 Gold 1.0000 oz. AGW **Obv:** Temple of Heaven, date below **Rev:** Panda seated, eating bamboo shoots, denomination below

Date	Mintage	F	VF	XF	Unc	BU
1994	—	—	—	—	—	BV+10%

Y# 694 100 YUAN
8.0000 g., 0.9160 Gold .2361 oz. AGW **Obv:** National emblem, date below **Rev:** Panda climbing tree, denomination at right

Date	Mintage	F	VF	XF	Unc	BU
1994 Proof	5,000	Value: 225				

Y# 644 100 YUAN
31.1030 g., 0.9990 Gold 1.0000 oz. AGW **Obv:** Temple of Heaven **Rev:** Panda eating bamboo

Date	Mintage	F	VF	XF	Unc	BU
1995	—	—	—	—	—	BV+10%

Y# 790 100 YUAN
31.0103 g., 0.9990 Gold 1.0000 oz. AGW **Obv:** Temple of Heaven within circle, date below **Rev:** Panda approaching water from right, denomination below

Date	Mintage	F	VF	XF	Unc	BU
1995 Proof	2,000	BV+15%				

Y# 578 100 YUAN
31.1035 g., 0.9990 Gold 1.0000 oz. AGW **Obv:** Temple of Heaven within circle, date below **Rev:** Panda in tree, denomination at left **Note:** Large and small date varieties exist.

Date	Mintage	F	VF	XF	Unc	BU
1996	—	—	—	—	—	BV+10%

Y# 1013 100 YUAN
31.1035 g., 0.9990 Gold 1.0000 oz. AGW **Obv:** Temple of Heaven **Rev:** Panda sitting on rock **Note:** Large and small date varieties exist.

Date	Mintage	F	VF	XF	Unc	BU
1996 Proof	1,500	BV+15%				

Y# 850 100 YUAN
31.1035 g., 0.9990 Gold 1.0000 oz. AGW **Subject:** 15th Anniversary - Gold Panda Coins **Obv:** Temple of Heaven with additional legend **Rev:** Panda in tree **Note:** Large and small date varieties exist.

Date	Mintage	F	VF	XF	Unc	BU
1996 Proof	1,500	BV+15%				

Y# 720 100 YUAN
31.1035 g., 0.9990 Gold 1.0000 oz. AGW **Obv:** Temple of Heaven **Rev:** Panda on large branch, denomination below **Note:** Large and small date varieties exist.

Date	Mintage	F	VF	XF	Unc	BU
1997	—	—	—	—	—	BV+10%

Note: Exists in large and small date varieties

Y# 1016 100 YUAN
31.1320 g., 0.9990 Gold 1.0000 oz. AGW **Obv:** Temple of Heaven **Rev:** Panda seated on rock **Note:** Large and small date varieties exist.

Date	Mintage	F	VF	XF	Unc	BU
1998	—	—	—	—	—	BV+10%

Y# 1017 100 YUAN
31.1320 g., 0.9990 Gold 1.0000 oz. AGW **Obv:** Temple of Heaven **Rev:** Panda on ledge **Note:** Large and small date varieties exist.

Date	Mintage	F	VF	XF	Unc	BU
1999	—	—	—	—	—	BV+10%

Y# 949 100 YUAN
31.1036 g., 0.9990 Gold 1.0000 oz. AGW **Obv:** Temple of Heaven **Rev:** Panda seated on leaves **Note:** Large and small date varieties exist.

Date	Mintage	F	VF	XF	Unc	BU
2000	—	—	—	—	—	BV+10%

Note: Domestic Chinese examples struck with mirror fields, overseas examples struck with frosted fields

Y# 147 500 YUAN
155.5150 g., 0.9990 Gold 5.0000 oz. AGW, 60 mm. **Obv:** Temple of Heaven **Rev:** Panda with cub, denomination below **Note:** Photo reduced.

Date	Mintage	F	VF	XF	Unc	BU
1987 Proof	3,000	BV+15%				

Y# 233 500 YUAN
155.5150 g., 0.9990 Gold 5.0000 oz. AGW **Obv:** Temple of Heaven **Rev:** Two pandas in tree, denomination upper left

Date	Mintage	F	VF	XF	Unc	BU
1988 Proof	3,000	BV+15%				

Y# 369 500 YUAN
155.5150 g., 0.9990 Gold 5.0000 oz. AGW **Obv:** Temple of Heaven, date below **Rev:** Pandas

Date	Mintage	F	VF	XF	Unc	BU
1992 Proof	99	BV+25%				

Y# 761 500 YUAN
155.5150 g., 0.9990 Gold 5.0000 oz. AGW **Obv:** Temple of Heaven **Rev:** Two pandas climbing tree stumps

Date	Mintage	F	VF	XF	Unc	BU
1993 Proof	99	BV+25%				

Y# 639 500 YUAN
155.5150 g., 0.9990 Gold 5.0000 oz. AGW **Obv:** Temple of Heaven **Rev:** Two pandas, one in tree, denomination above

Date	Mintage	F	VF	XF	Unc	BU
1994 Proof	99	BV+25%				

Y# 66 1000 YUAN
373.2360 g., 0.9990 Gold 12.0000 oz. AGW, 70 mm. **Obv:** Temple of Heaven **Rev:** Panda seated left, denomination belo0w **Note:** Photo reduced.

Date	Mintage	F	VF	XF	Unc	BU
1984 Proof	250	BV+25%				

Note: A typical sealed proof exhibits some scuffing and is valued as above, while perfect examples can bring up to a 50% premium

Y# 118.1 1000 YUAN
373.2360 g., 0.9990 Gold 12.0000 oz. AGW, 70 mm. **Obv:** Temple of Heaven **Rev:** Panda eating bamboo shoot with cub, denomination at right **Note:** Photo reduced.

Date	Mintage	F	VF	XF	Unc	BU
1986 Proof	2,550	BV+15%				

Y# 118.2 1000 YUAN
373.2360 g., 0.9990 Gold 12.0000 oz. AGW **Obv:** Temple of Heaven **Rev:** Panda eating bamboo shoot with cub **Edge:** Plain

Date	Mintage	F	VF	XF	Unc	BU
1986 Proof	—	—	—	—	—	—

Note: 2 known; Last traded privately at $45,000

Y# 157 1000 YUAN
373.2360 g., 0.9990 Gold 12.0000 oz. AGW **Obv:** Temple of Heaven **Rev:** Panda with cub, denomination below **Shape:** 70 **Note:** Photo reduced.

Date	Mintage	F	VF	XF	Unc	BU
1987 Proof	2,445	BV+15%				

Y# 234 1000 YUAN
373.2360 g., 0.9990 Gold 12.0000 oz. AGW **Obv:** Temple of Heaven **Rev:** Pandas in tree **Note:** Similar to 500 Yuan, KM#233.

Date	Mintage	F	VF	XF	Unc	BU
1988 Proof	1,650	BV+15%				

Y# 282 1000 YUAN
373.2360 g., 0.9990 Gold 12.0000 oz. AGW, 70 mm. **Obv:** Temple of Heaven **Rev:** Three pandas, denomination upper right

Date	Mintage	F	VF	XF	Unc	BU
1990 Proof	500	BV+20%				

Y# 371 1000 YUAN
373.2360 g., 0.9990 Gold 12.0000 oz. AGW **Obv:** Temple of Heaven, date below **Rev:** Pandas

Date	Mintage	F	VF	XF	Unc	BU
1991 Proof	400	BV+20%				

Y# 372 1000 YUAN
373.2360 g., 0.9990 Gold 12.0000 oz. AGW **Obv:** Temple of Heaven **Rev:** Pandas

Date	Mintage	F	VF	XF	Unc	BU
1992 Proof	99	BV+30%				

Y# 762 1000 YUAN
373.2360 g., 0.9990 Gold 12.0000 oz. AGW **Obv:** Temple of Heaven **Rev:** Panda family of three

Date	Mintage	F	VF	XF	Unc	BU
1993 Proof	99	BV+30%				

Y# 1089 1000 YUAN
373.2420 g., 0.9990 Gold 11.988 oz. AGW, 70 mm. **Obv:** Temple of Heaven **Rev:** Panda and two cubs at water's edge **Edge:** Reeded

Date	Mintage	F	VF	XF	Unc	BU
1994 Proof	99	BV+30%				

Y# 1090 1000 YUAN
373.2420 g., 0.9990 Gold 11.988 oz. AGW, 70 mm. **Obv:** Temple of Heaven **Rev:** Two adult pandas with cub **Edge:** Reeded **Note:** Photo reduced.

Date	Mintage	F	VF	XF	Unc	BU
1995 Proof	99	BV+30%				

Y# 961 2000 YUAN
1000.0000 g., 0.9990 Gold 32.1500 oz. AGW **Obv:** Temple of Heaven **Rev:** Panda **Note:** Large and small date varieties exist.

Date	Mintage	F	VF	XF	Unc	BU
1997 Proof	58	BV+30%				

Y# 1036 2000 YUAN

1000.0000 g., 0.9990 Gold 32.1500 oz. AGW **Obv:** Temple of Heaven **Rev:** Panda **Note:** Large and small date varieties exist.

Date	Mintage	F	VF	XF	Unc	BU
1998 Proof	58	BV+20%				

Y# 972 2000 YUAN

1000.2108 g., 0.9990 Gold 32.1253 oz. AGW **Obv:** Temple of Heaven **Rev:** Panda on rock **Note:** Large and small date varieties exist.

Date	Mintage	F	VF	XF	Unc	BU
1999 Proof	68	BV+30%				

Y# 358 10000 YUAN

4851.6001 g., 0.9990 Gold 156.000 oz. AGW **Subject:** 10th Anniversary of Gold Panda Issue **Obv:** Temple of Heaven **Rev:** Panda on branch, denomination at right, in center of 10 panda coin designs

Date	Mintage	F	VF	XF	Unc	BU
1991 Proof, Rare	10	—	—	—	—	—

GOLD BULLION COINAGE

Lunar Series

Y# 901 10 YUAN

3.1103 g., 0.9990 Gold .1000 oz. AGW **Subject:** Year of the Ox **Obv:** Mingyuan Pavilion **Rev:** Calf

Date	Mintage	F	VF	XF	Unc	BU
1997 Proof	48,000	Value: 95.00				

Y# 924 10 YUAN

3.1103 g., 0.9990 Gold .1000 oz. AGW **Subject:** Year of the Tiger **Obv:** Badaling building, date below **Rev:** Tiger cub, denomination at right

Date	Mintage	F	VF	XF	Unc	BU
1998 Proof	48,000	Value: 100				

Y# 925 10 YUAN

3.1103 g., 0.9990 Gold .1000 oz. AGW **Subject:** Year of the Tiger **Obv:** Badaling building, date below **Rev:** Multicolor tiger head, facing, denomination at right

Date	Mintage	F	VF	XF	Unc	BU
1998 Proof	30,000	Value: 265				

Y# 991 10 YUAN

3.1103 g., 0.9990 Gold .1000 oz. AGW **Rev:** Multicolor rabbit

Date	Mintage	F	VF	XF	Unc	BU
1999 Proof	30,000	Value: 225				

Y# 980 10 YUAN

3.1103 g., 0.9990 Gold .1000 oz. AGW **Subject:** Year of the Rabbit

Date	Mintage	F	VF	XF	Unc	BU
1999 Proof	48,000	Value: 95.00				

Y# 992 10 YUAN

3.1103 g., 0.9990 Gold .1000 oz. AGW **Subject:** Year of the Dragon

Date	Mintage	F	VF	XF	Unc	BU
2000 Proof	48,000	Value: 165				

Y# 1006 50 YUAN

15.5518 g., 0.9990 Gold .5000 oz. AGW **Subject:** Year of the Dragon **Shape:** Fan

Date	Mintage	F	VF	XF	Unc	BU
2000	6,600	—	—	—	—	575

Y# 175 100 YUAN

31.1320 g., 0.9990 Gold 1.0000 oz. AGW **Subject:** Year of the Dragon **Obv:** Temple of Heaven **Rev:** 2 floating dragons

Date	Mintage	F	VF	XF	Unc	BU
1988 Proof	10,000	BV+10%				

Y# 184 100 YUAN

31.1320 g., 0.9990 Gold 1.0000 oz. AGW **Subject:** Year of the Snake **Obv:** National emblem **Rev:** Snake left, denomination below

Date	Mintage	F	VF	XF	Unc	BU
1989 Proof	3,000	BV+10%				

Y# 225 100 YUAN

31.1320 g., 0.9990 Gold 1.0000 oz. AGW **Subject:** Year of the Horse **Obv:** National emblem, date below **Rev:** Prancing horse left, denomination lower right

Date	Mintage	F	VF	XF	Unc	BU
1990 Proof	6,000	BV+10%				

Y# 274 100 YUAN

31.1320 g., 0.9990 Gold 1.0000 oz. AGW **Subject:** Year of the Goat **Obv:** National emblem **Rev:** Two goats butting heads, denomination below

Date	Mintage	F	VF	XF	Unc	BU
1991 Proof	1,300	BV+15%				

Y# 295 100 YUAN

31.1035 g., 0.9990 Gold 1.0000 oz. AGW **Subject:** Year of the Monkey **Rev:** Monkey seated on branch, denomination at left

Date	Mintage	F	VF	XF	Unc	BU
1992 Proof	1,800	BV+15%				

Y# 568 100 YUAN

15.5517 g., 0.9170 Gold .5000 oz. AGW **Subject:** Year of the Rooster **Obv:** City gate, date below **Rev:** Rooster with sunflowers, denomination at left **Shape:** Scalloped

Date	Mintage	F	VF	XF	Unc	BU
1993 Proof	2,300	BV+15%				

Y# 570 100 YUAN

31.1035 g., 0.9990 Gold 1.0000 oz. AGW **Subject:** Year of the Rooster **Obv:** National emblem **Rev:** Rooster and hen, denomination at left

Date	Mintage	F	VF	XF	Unc	BU
1993 Proof	1,900	BV+15%				

Y# 397 100 YUAN

31.1320 g., 0.9990 Gold 1.0000 oz. AGW **Subject:** Year of the Dog **Rev:** Two dogs, denomination lower left

Date	Mintage	F	VF	XF	Unc	BU
1994 Proof	1,800	BV+15%				

Y# 780 100 YUAN

16.3980 g., 0.9160 Gold .5000 oz. AGW **Subject:** Year of the Dog **Obv:** Phoenix Pavilion, date below **Rev:** Lap dog, denomination at left **Shape:** Scalloped

Date	Mintage	F	VF	XF	Unc	BU
1994 Proof	2,300	BV+20%				

Y# 451 100 YUAN

31.1030 g., 0.9990 Gold 1.0000 oz. AGW **Subject:** Year of the Pig **Obv:** National emblem, date below **Rev:** Pig, denomination at right

Date	Mintage	F	VF	XF	Unc	BU
1995 Proof	1,800	BV+15%				

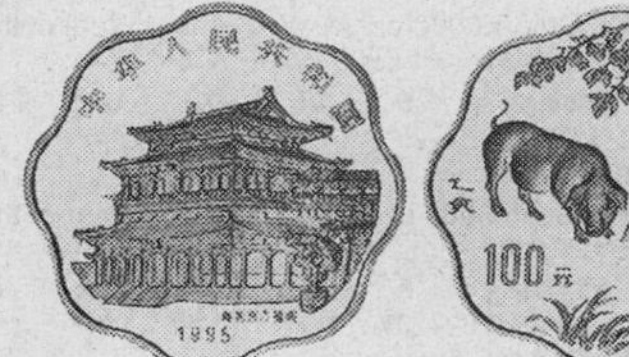

Y# 453 100 YUAN

15.5557 g., 0.9990 Gold .5000 oz. AGW **Subject:** Year of the Pig **Obv:** Building, date below **Rev:** Two pigs, denomination at lower left **Shape:** Scalloped

Date	Mintage	F	VF	XF	Unc	BU
1995 Proof	2,300	BV+20%				

Y# 586 100 YUAN
31.1035 g., 0.9990 Gold 1.0000 oz. AGW **Subject:** Year of the Rat **Rev:** Rat by oil lamp, denomination below

Date	Mintage	F	VF	XF	Unc	BU
1996 Proof	1,800	BV+20%				

Y# 856 100 YUAN
16.9779 g., 0.9160 Gold .5000 oz. AGW **Subject:** Year of the Rat **Obv:** Dengdu Pavilion, date below **Rev:** Rat on corn cob, denomination upper left **Shape:** Scalloped

Date	Mintage	F	VF	XF	Unc	BU
1996 Proof	2,300	BV+25%				

Y# 670 100 YUAN
15.5557 g., 0.9990 Gold .5000 oz. AGW **Subject:** Year of the Ox **Shape:** Scalloped

Date	Mintage	F	VF	XF	Unc	BU
1997 Proof	2,300	BV+20%				

Y# 900 100 YUAN
31.1035 g., 0.9990 Gold 1.0000 oz. AGW **Subject:** Year of the Ox **Obv:** National emblem, date below **Rev:** Ox, denomination below

Date	Mintage	F	VF	XF	Unc	BU
1997 Proof	1,600	BV+15%				

Y# 929 100 YUAN
31.1035 g., 0.9990 Gold 1.0000 oz. AGW **Subject:** Year of the Tiger **Obv:** State seal **Rev:** Tiger

Date	Mintage	F	VF	XF	Unc	BU
1998 Proof	1,600	BV+15%				

Y# 1015 100 YUAN
15.5557 g., 0.9990 Gold .5000 oz. AGW **Subject:** Year of the Tiger **Shape:** Scalloped

Date	Mintage	F	VF	XF	Unc	BU
1998 Proof	2,300	BV+20%				

Y# 1018 100 YUAN
31.1035 g., 0.9990 Gold 1.0000 oz. AGW **Subject:** Year of the Rabbit

Date	Mintage	F	VF	XF	Unc	BU
1999 Proof	—	BV+25%				

Y# 1019 100 YUAN
15.5551 g., 0.9990 Gold .5000 oz. AGW **Subject:** Year of the Rabbit **Shape:** Scalloped

Date	Mintage	F	VF	XF	Unc	BU
1999 Prof	—	BV+20%				

Y# 1051 100 YUAN
15.5518 g., 0.9160 Gold .4580 oz. AGW **Rev:** Dragons **Shape:** Scalloped

Date	Mintage	F	VF	XF	Unc	BU
2000 Proof	2,300	Value: 750				

Y# 45 150 YUAN
8.0000 g., 0.9170 Gold .2359 oz. AGW **Subject:** Year of the Pig **Obv:** Hillside pagoda, waterfront, date lower right **Rev:** Two pigs, denomination below

Date	Mintage	F	VF	XF	Unc	BU
1983 Proof	2,035	Value: 900				

Y# 60 150 YUAN
8.0000 g., 0.9170 Gold .2359 oz. AGW **Subject:** Year of the Rat **Obv:** Fortress, date lower right **Rev:** Rat with squash, denomination below **Rev. Designer:** Qi Baishi

Date	Mintage	F	VF	XF	Unc	BU
1984 Proof	2,248	Value: 2,400				

Y# 79 150 YUAN
8.0000 g., 0.9170 Gold .2359 oz. AGW **Subject:** Year of the Ox **Obv:** Houseboat in harbor **Rev:** Ox left, denomination below

Date	Mintage	F	VF	XF	Unc	BU
1985 Proof	Est. 16,000	Value: 190				

Note: 5,000 pieces were struck and issued in boxes with certificates and are valued at $275

Y# 99 150 YUAN
8.0000 g., 0.9170 Gold .2359 oz. AGW **Subject:** Year of the Tiger **Obv:** Qing Dynasty Palace, date below **Rev:** Tiger advancing left, after a painting by He Ziang Ning, denomination above

Date	Mintage	F	VF	XF	Unc	BU
1986 Proof	5,480	Value: 400				

Y# 123 150 YUAN
8.0000 g., 0.9170 Gold .2359 oz. AGW **Subject:** Year of the Rabbit **Obv:** Pagoda, date below **Rev:** Two rabbits, denomination below **Rev. Designer:** Lin Ji Yon

Date	Mintage	F	VF	XF	Unc	BU
1987 Proof	4,780	Value: 285				

Y# 144 150 YUAN
8.0000 g., 0.9170 Gold .2359 oz. AGW **Subject:** Year of the Dragon **Obv:** Great Wall of China, date below **Rev:** Dragon attacking, denomination below

Date	Mintage	F	VF	XF	Unc	BU
1988 Proof	7,600	Value: 285				

Y# 180 150 YUAN
8.0000 g., 0.9170 Gold .2359 oz. AGW **Subject:** Year of the Snake **Obv:** Shanhaiguan Pass Gate, date below **Rev:** Snake left, denomination below

Date	Mintage	F	VF	XF	Unc	BU
1989 Proof	7,500	Value: 210				

Y# 227 150 YUAN
8.0000 g., 0.9170 Gold .2359 oz. AGW **Subject:** Year of the Horse **Obv:** Temple of Confucius, date below **Rev:** Horse galloping, denomination at left

Date	Mintage	F	VF	XF	Unc	BU
1990 Proof	7,500	Value: 260				

Y# 276 150 YUAN
8.0000 g., 0.9170 Gold .2359 oz. AGW **Subject:** Year of the Goat **Obv:** Chinese building and legend **Rev:** Goat reclining, denomination below

Date	Mintage	F	VF	XF	Unc	BU
1991 Proof	7,500	Value: 210				

Y# 291 150 YUAN
8.0000 g., 0.9170 Gold .2359 oz. AGW **Subject:** Year of the Monkey **Obv:** Pavilion of Emperor Teng **Rev:** Monkey sitting, denomination at right

Date	Mintage	F	VF	XF	Unc	BU
1992 Proof	5,000	Value: 285				

Y# 39 200 YUAN
8.4700 g., 0.9170 Gold .2497 oz. AGW **Subject:** Year of the Dog **Obv:** Temple of Heaven, date below **Rev:** Dog, denomination below

Date	Mintage	F	VF	XF	Unc	BU
1982 Proof	2,500	Value: 525				

Y# 33 250 YUAN
8.0000 g., 0.9170 Gold .2358 oz. AGW **Subject:** Year of the Rooster **Obv:** Monument, date lower left **Rev:** Rooster left, denomination at left

Date	Mintage	F	VF	XF	Unc	BU
1981 Proof	5,015	Value: 475				

Y# 145 500 YUAN
155.5150 g., 0.9990 Gold 5.0000 oz. AGW, 60 mm. **Subject:** Year of the Dragon **Obv:** Great Wall **Rev:** Inner circle holds three dragons, four dragons surround, denomination below **Note:** Photo reduced.

Date	Mintage	F	VF	XF	Unc	BU
1988 Proof	3,000	Value: 3,750				

Y# 181 500 YUAN
155.5150 g., 0.9990 Gold 5.0000 oz. AGW, 60 mm. **Subject:** Year of the Snake **Obv:** National emblem **Rev:** Snake left, denomination below, within beaded circle **Note:** Photo reduced.

Date	Mintage	F	VF	XF	Unc	BU
1989 Proof	500	Value: 3,500				

Y# 228 500 YUAN
155.5150 g., 0.9990 Gold 5.0000 oz. AGW, 60 mm. **Obv:** Temple of Confucius **Rev:** Two horses drinking water, denomination below **Note:** Photo reduced.

Date	Mintage	F	VF	XF	Unc	BU
1990 Proof	500	Value: 3,750				

Y# 277 500 YUAN
155.5150 g., 0.9990 Gold 5.0000 oz. AGW, 60 mm. **Subject:** Year of the Goat **Obv:** Two goats, one nursing offspring, denomination above **Note:** Photo reduced.

Date	Mintage	F	VF	XF	Unc	BU
1991 Proof	250	Value: 4,000				

Y# 292 500 YUAN
155.5150 g., 0.9990 Gold 5.0000 oz. AGW, 60 mm. **Subject:** Year of the Monkey **Obv:** Chinese building **Rev:** Monkey seated, denomination at right **Note:** Photo reduced.

Date	Mintage	F	VF	XF	Unc	BU
1992 Proof	99	Value: 6,000				

Y# 384 500 YUAN
155.5150 g., 0.9990 Gold 5.0000 oz. AGW **Subject:** Year of the Rooster

Date	Mintage	F	VF	XF	Unc	BU
1993 Proof	99	Value: 5,000				

Y# 389 500 YUAN
155.5150 g., 0.9990 Gold 5.0000 oz. AGW **Subject:** Year of the Dog

Date	Mintage	F	VF	XF	Unc	BU
1994 Proof	99	Value: 5,000				

Y# 467 500 YUAN
155.5150 g., 0.9990 Gold 5.0000 oz. AGW **Subject:** Year of the Pig

Date	Mintage	F	VF	XF	Unc	BU
1995 Proof	99	Value: 5,000				

Y# 663 500 YUAN
155.5175 g., 0.9999 Gold 5.0000 oz. AGW **Subject:** Year of the Rat **Rev:** Rat eating grapes, denomination above

Date	Mintage	F	VF	XF	Unc	BU
1996 Proof	99	Value: 5,000				

Y# 672 500 YUAN
155.5175 g., 0.9990 Gold 5.0000 oz. AGW **Subject:** Year of the Ox

Date	Mintage	F	VF	XF	Unc	BU
1997 Proof	99	Value: 4,500				

Y# 1024 500 YUAN
155.5175 g., 0.9990 Gold 5.0000 oz. AGW **Subject:** Year of the Tiger

Date	Mintage	F	VF	XF	Unc	BU
1998 Proof	99	Value: 5,000				

Y# 1025 500 YUAN
155.5175 g., 0.9990 Gold 5.0000 oz. AGW **Subject:** Year of the Rabbit

Date	Mintage	F	VF	XF	Unc	BU
1999 Proof	99	Value: 4,500				

Y# 1027 500 YUAN
155.5175 g., 0.9990 Gold 5.0000 oz. AGW **Subject:** Year of the Dragon **Shape:** Rectangular

Date	Mintage	F	VF	XF	Unc	BU
2000 Proof	108	Value: 5,000				

Y# 146 1000 YUAN
373.2360 g., 0.9990 Gold 12.0000 oz. AGW, 70 mm. **Subject:** Year of the Dragon **Obv:** Great Wall **Rev:** Two facing dragons, denomination below **Note:** Photo reduced.

Date	Mintage	F	VF	XF	Unc	BU
1988 Proof	518	Value: 8,750				

Y# 182 1000 YUAN
373.2360 g., 0.9990 Gold 12.0000 oz. AGW, 70 mm. **Subject:** Year of the Snake **Obv:** National emblem **Rev:** Snake left within beaded circle, denomination below **Note:** Photo reduced.

Date	Mintage	F	VF	XF	Unc	BU
1989 Proof	200	Value: 8,500				

Y# 229 1000 YUAN
373.2360 g., 0.9990 Gold 12.0000 oz. AGW, 70 mm. **Subject:** Year of the Horse **Obv:** Temple of Confucius **Rev:** Two horses running, denomination below **Note:** Photo reduced.

Date	Mintage	F	VF	XF	Unc	BU
1990 Proof	500	Value: 8,250				

Y# 278 1000 YUAN
373.2360 g., 0.9990 Gold 12.0000 oz. AGW **Subject:** Year of the Goat **Obv:** Chinese building and legend **Rev:** Three goats, denomination at left **Note:** Photo reduced.

Date	Mintage	F	VF	XF	Unc	BU
1991 Proof	200	Value: 8,250				

Y# 293 1000 YUAN
373.2360 g., 0.9990 Gold 12.0000 oz. AGW **Subject:** Year of the Monkey **Obv:** Chinese building **Rev:** Five monkeys, denomination at left **Note:** Photo reduced.

Date	Mintage	F	VF	XF	Unc	BU
1992 Proof	99	Value: 9,000				

Y# 385 1000 YUAN
373.2360 g., 0.9990 Gold 12.0000 oz. AGW **Subject:** Year of the Rooster

Date	Mintage	F	VF	XF	Unc	BU
1993 Proof	99	Value: 8,750				

Y# 390 1000 YUAN
373.2360 g., 0.9990 Gold 12.0000 oz. AGW **Subject:** Year of the Dog

Date	Mintage	F	VF	XF	Unc	BU
1994 Proof	99	Value: 8,750				

Y# 468 1000 YUAN
373.2360 g., 0.9990 Gold 12.0000 oz. AGW **Subject:** Year of the Pig

Date	Mintage	F	VF	XF	Unc	BU
1995 Proof	99	Value: 9,000				

Y# 664 1000 YUAN
373.2360 g., 0.9990 Gold 12.0000 oz. AGW **Subject:** Year of the Rat

Date	Mintage	F	VF	XF	Unc	BU
1996 Proof	99	Value: 8,750				

Y# 673 1000 YUAN
373.2360 g., 0.9990 Gold 12.0000 oz. AGW **Subject:** Year of the Ox

Date	Mintage	F	VF	XF	Unc	BU
1997 Proof	99	Value: 8,750				

Y# 1030 1000 YUAN
373.2360 g., 0.9990 Gold 12.0000 oz. AGW **Subject:** Year of the Tiger

Date	Mintage	F	VF	XF	Unc	BU
1998 Proof	99	Value: 8,750				

Y# 1031 1000 YUAN
373.2360 g., 0.9990 Gold 12.0000 oz. AGW **Subject:** Year of the Rabbit

Date	Mintage	F	VF	XF	Unc	BU
1999 Proof	99	Value: 8,750				

Y# 702 2000 YUAN
1000.0000 g., 0.9990 Gold 32.1500 oz. AGW, 100 mm. **Subject:** Completion of 150 Yuan Lunar Animal Coin Series **Obv:** Monument divides date and denomination within circle **Rev:** Ying/Yang symbol within octagon, twelve animal coins surround **Note:** Photo reduced.Photo reduced.

Date	Mintage	F	VF	XF	Unc	BU
1992 Proof	21	Value: 35,000				

Y# 660 2000 YUAN
1000.0000 g., 0.9990 Gold 32.1500 oz. AGW **Subject:** Year of the Pig **Edge:** Scalloped

Date	Mintage	F	VF	XF	Unc	BU
1995 Proof	15	Value: 28,500				

Y# 665 2000 YUAN
1000.0000 g., 0.9990 Gold 32.1500 oz. AGW **Subject:** Year of the Rat **Shape:** Scalloped

Date	Mintage	F	VF	XF	Unc	BU
1996 Proof	15	Value: 28,500				

Y# 674 2000 YUAN
1000.0000 g., 0.9990 Gold 32.1500 oz. AGW **Subject:** Year of the Ox

Date	Mintage	F	VF	XF	Unc	BU
1997 Proof	15	Value: 28,500				

Y# 967 2000 YUAN
1000.0000 g., 0.9990 Gold 32.1500 oz. AGW **Subject:** Year of the Tiger **Shape:** Scalloped

Date	Mintage	F	VF	XF	Unc	BU
1998 Proof	15	Value: 28,500				

Y# 975 2000 YUAN
1000.0000 g., 0.9990 Gold 32.1500 oz. AGW **Subject:** Year of the Rabbit **Shape:** Scalloped

Date	Mintage	F	VF	XF	Unc	BU
1999 Proof	15	Value: 28,500				

Y# 977 2000 YUAN
1000.2108 g., 0.9990 Gold 32.1253 oz. AGW, Scalloped mm. **Subject:** Year of the Dragon

Date	Mintage	F	VF	XF	Unc	BU
2000 Proof	15	Value: 32,000				

Y# 1052 10000 YUAN
1000.2108 g., 0.9990 Gold 32.1575 oz. AGW **Subject:** Year of the Snake **Rev:** Dragons **Shape:** Scalloped

Date	Mintage	F	VF	XF	Unc	BU
2000 Proof	15	Value: 30,000				

PLATINUM BULLION COINAGE

Lunar Series

Y# 176 100 YUAN
31.1030 g., 0.9995 Platinum 1.0000 oz. APW **Subject:** Year of the Dragon **Obv:** Temple of Heaven **Rev:** 2 floating dragons

Date	Mintage	F	VF	XF	Unc	BU
1988 Proof	2,000	BV+20%				

Y# 185 100 YUAN
31.1030 g., 0.9995 Platinum 1.0000 oz. APW **Subject:** Year of the Snake **Obv:** National emblem **Rev:** Snake, left, denomination below

Date	Mintage	F	VF	XF	Unc	BU
1989 Proof	1,000	BV+20%				

Y# 274a 100 YUAN
31.1030 g., 0.9995 Platinum 1.0000 oz. APW **Subject:** Year of the Goat **Obv:** National emblem **Rev:** Two goats butting heads, denomination below

Date	Mintage	F	VF	XF	Unc	BU
1991 Proof	500	BV+30%				

Y# 295a 100 YUAN
31.1030 g., 0.9995 Platinum 1.0000 oz. APW **Subject:** Year of the Monkey **Rev:** Monkey seated on branch, denomination at left

Date	Mintage	F	VF	XF	Unc	BU
1992 Proof	300	BV+35%				

Y# 382 100 YUAN
31.1030 g., 0.9995 Platinum 1.0000 oz. APW **Subject:** Year of the Rooster

Date	Mintage	F	VF	XF	Unc	BU
1993 Proof	300	BV+35%				

Y# 397a 100 YUAN
31.1030 g., 0.9995 Platinum 1.0000 oz. APW **Subject:** Year of the Dog

Date	Mintage	F	VF	XF	Unc	BU
1994 Proof	300	BV+35%				

Y# 465 100 YUAN
31.1030 g., 0.9995 Platinum 1.0000 oz. APW **Subject:** Year of the Pig

Date	Mintage	F	VF	XF	Unc	BU
1995 Proof	300	BV+35%				

Y# 586a 100 YUAN
31.1035 g., 0.9995 Platinum 1.0000 oz. APW **Subject:** Year of the Rat **Rev:** Rat by oil lamp, denoination below

Date	Mintage	F	VF	XF	Unc	BU
1996 Proof	300	BV+35%				

Y# 900a 100 YUAN
31.1035 g., 0.9995 Platinum 1.0000 oz. APW **Subject:** Year of the Ox **Obv:** National emblem **Rev:** Ox, denomination below

Date	Mintage	F	VF	XF	Unc	BU
1997 Proof	300	BV+35%				

Y# 929a 100 YUAN
31.1035 g., 0.9990 Platinum 1.0000 oz. APW **Subject:** Year of the Tiger **Obv:** National emblem **Rev:** Tiger

Date	Mintage	F	VF	XF	Unc	BU
1998 Proof	300	BV+35%				

Y# 1018a 100 YUAN
31.1035 g., 0.9990 Platinum 1.0000 oz. APW **Subject:** Year of the Rabbit

Date	Mintage	F	VF	XF	Unc	BU
1999 Proof	—	BV+35%				

PLATINUM BULLION COINAGE

Panda Series

Y# 483 5 YUAN

1.5552 g., 0.9995 Platinum .0500 oz. APW **Obv:** Temple of Heaven within circle, date below **Rev:** Panda seated on rock, denomination upper left

Date	Mintage	F	VF	XF	Unc	BU
1993 Proof	2,500	Value: 75.00				

Y# 581a 5 YUAN

1.5552 g., 0.9990 Platinum .0500 oz. APW **Obv:** Temple of Heaven, date below **Rev:** Panda in tree looking down, denomination lower left

Date	Mintage	F	VF	XF	Unc	BU
1996	5,000	—	—	—	—	120

Y# 740a 5 YUAN

1.5552 g., 0.9990 Platinum .0500 oz. APW **Obv:** Eastern unicorn, date below **Rev:** Head of western unicorn, right, denomination at right

Date	Mintage	F	VF	XF	Unc	BU
1996	8,000	—	—	—	—	115

Y# 716a 5 YUAN

1.5552 g., 0.9990 Platinum 0.05 oz. APW **Obv:** Temple of Heaven **Rev:** Panda on branch

Date	Mintage	F	VF	XF	Unc	BU
1997 Prooflike	5,000	—	—	—	—	115

Y# 267 10 YUAN

3.1100 g., 0.9995 Platinum .1000 oz. APW **Obv:** Temple of Heaven, date below **Rev:** Panda with branch, denomination below

Date	Mintage	F	VF	XF	Unc	BU
1990 Proof	4,500	Value: 165				

Y# 484a 10 YUAN

3.1100 g., 0.9995 Platinum .1000 oz. APW **Obv:** Temple of Heaven within circle, date below **Rev:** Panda seated on rock, denomination upper left

Date	Mintage	F	VF	XF	Unc	BU
1993 Proof	2,500	—	—	—	—	165

Y# 432a 10 YUAN

3.1103 g., 0.9990 Platinum .1000 oz. APW **Obv:** Temple of Heaven, date below **Rev:** Seated panda eating, denomination below

Date	Mintage	F	VF	XF	Unc	BU
1994 Prooflike	2,500	—	—	—	—	235

Y# 641a 10 YUAN

3.1103 g., 0.9990 Platinum .1000 oz. APW **Obv:** Temple of Heaven, date below **Rev:** Panda eating bamboo, denomination at left

Date	Mintage	F	VF	XF	Unc	BU
1995 Prooflike	5,000	—	—	—	—	185

Y# 575a 10 YUAN

3.1103 g., 0.9990 Platinum .1000 oz. APW **Obv:** Temple of Heaven, date below **Rev:** Panda in tree

Date	Mintage	F	VF	XF	Unc	BU
1996 Prooflike	2,500	—	—	—	—	235

Y# 717a 10 YUAN

3.1100 g., 0.9990 Platinum .1000 oz. APW **Obv:** Temple of Heaven **Rev:** Panda on branch

Date	Mintage	F	VF	XF	Unc	BU
1997 Prooflike	2,500	—	—	—	—	165

Y# 894a 10 YUAN

3.1100 g., 0.9995 Platinum .1000 oz. APW **Obv:** Temple of Heaven, date below **Rev:** Panda on branch

Date	Mintage	F	VF	XF	Unc	BU
1997 Proof	2,500	Value: 140				

Y# 268 25 YUAN

7.7758 g., 0.9995 Platinum .2500 oz. APW **Obv:** Temple of Heaven, date below **Rev:** Panda climbing tree, denomination at right

Date	Mintage	F	VF	XF	Unc	BU
1990 Proof	3,500	Value: 345				

Y# 269 50 YUAN

15.5517 g., 0.9995 Platinum .5000 oz. APW **Obv:** Temple of Heaven, date below **Rev:** Panda eating bamboo on rock, denomination below

Date	Mintage	F	VF	XF	Unc	BU
1990 Proof	2,500	Value: 685				

Y# 158 100 YUAN

31.1030 g., 0.9995 Platinum 1.0000 oz. APW **Obv:** Temple of Heaven, date below **Rev:** Panda drinking at stream, denomination below

Date	Mintage	F	VF	XF	Unc	BU
1987 Proof	2,000	BV+20%				

Y# 159 100 YUAN

31.1030 g., 0.9995 Platinum 1.0000 oz. APW **Obv:** Temple of Heaven, date below **Rev:** Panda grasping bamboo shoot, within circle, denomination below

Date	Mintage	F	VF	XF	Unc	BU
1988 Proof	2,000	BV+20%				

Y# 191a 100 YUAN

31.1030 g., 0.9995 Platinum 1.0000 oz. APW **Obv:** Temple of Heaven, date below **Rev:** Panda reclining, grid behind, denomination lower right

Date	Mintage	F	VF	XF	Unc	BU
1989 Proof	3,000	—	—	—	—	BV+ 20%

Y# 735 100 YUAN

31.1400 g., 0.9995 Platinum 1.0077 oz. APW **Obv:** Temple of Heaven, date below **Rev:** Panda on rock, denomination below

Date	Mintage	F	VF	XF	Unc	BU
1990 Proof	1,300	—	—	—	—	BV+ 30%

BI-METALLIC MEDALLIC BULLION COINAGE

Silver / Gold

Y# 391 10 YUAN

3.1103 g., Bi-Metallic Gold center in Silver ring .1000 oz. **Obv:** Temple of Heaven within circle, date below **Rev:** Panda on branch, denomination above, within circle

Date	Mintage	F	VF	XF	Unc	BU
1992 Proof	2,000	Value: 150				

Y# 463 10 YUAN

3.1103 g., Bi-Metallic Gold center in Silver ring .1000 oz. **Rev:** Phoenix and dragon

Date	Mintage	F	VF	XF	Unc	BU
1994	2,500	—	—	—	—	150

Y# 680 10 YUAN

3.1103 g., Bi-Metallic Gold center in Silver ring .1000 oz. **Obv:** Temple of Heaven within circle, date below **Rev:** Panda tugging bamboo sprig, denomination below, within circle

Date	Mintage	F	VF	XF	Unc	BU
1994 Proof	3,000	Value: 150				

Y# 571 10 YUAN

3.1103 g., Bi-Metallic Gold center in Silver ring .1000 oz. **Obv:** Temple of Heaven, date below **Rev:** Panda at stream, denomination below

Date	Mintage	F	VF	XF	Unc	BU
1995 Proof set	2,000	Value: 150				

Y# 851 10 YUAN

3.1103 g., Bi-Metallic Gold center in Silver ring .1000 oz. **Obv:** Temple of Heaven **Rev:** Panda seated in rock

Date	Mintage	F	VF	XF	Unc	BU
1996 Proof	2,500	Value: 150				

Y# 986 10 YUAN

3.1103 g., Bi-Metallic Gold center in Silver ring .1000 oz. **Obv:** Temple of Heaven, date below **Rev:** Panda climbing tree

Date	Mintage	F	VF	XF	Unc	BU
1997 Proof	2,800	Value: 135				

Y# 301 25 YUAN

7.7758 g., Bi-Metallic Gold center in Silver ring .2500 oz. **Obv:** Temple of Heaven, date below **Rev:** Seated panda, denomination at left, date below

Date	Mintage	F	VF	XF	Unc	BU
1991 Proof	2,000	Value: 285				

Y# 930 25 YUAN

7.7758 g., Bi-Metallic Gold center in Silver ring .2500 oz. **Obv:** Temple of Heaven, date below **Rev:** Panda on rock

Date	Mintage	F	VF	XF	Unc	BU
1993 Proof	2,500	Value: 285				

Y# 544 25 YUAN
7.7758 g., Bi-Metallic Gold center in Silver ring .2500 oz. **Obv:** Temple of Heaven within circle, date below **Rev:** Panda tugging on bamboo sprig, denomination below, within circle, date below

Date	Mintage	F	VF	XF	Unc	BU
1994 Proof	2,500	Value: 255				

Y# 572 25 YUAN
7.7758 g., Bi-Metallic Gold center in Silver ring .2500 oz. **Obv:** Temple of Heaven, date below **Rev:** Panda at stream, denomination below, within circle

Date	Mintage	F	VF	XF	Unc	BU
1995 Proof	2,000	Value: 260				

Y# 852 25 YUAN
7.7759 g., Bi-Metallic Gold center in Silver ring .2500 oz. **Obv:** Temple of Heaven **Rev:** Panda seated on rock

Date	Mintage	F	VF	XF	Unc	BU
1996 Proof	2,500	Value: 255				

Y# 1001 25 YUAN
7.7758 g., 0.9990 Bi-Metallic Gold center in Silver ring .2500 oz. **Obv:** Temple of Heaven, date below **Rev:** Panda climbing tree

Date	Mintage	F	VF	XF	Unc	BU
1997 Proof	2,800	Value: 260				

Y# 266 50 YUAN
15.5517 g., 0.9990 Bi-Metallic Gold center in Silver ring .5000 oz. **Obv:** Temple of Heaven, date below, within circle **Rev:** Panda walking, denomination below, within circle, date below

Date	Mintage	F	VF	XF	Unc	BU
1990 Proof	2,000	Value: 385				

Y# 573 50 YUAN
21.7724 g., 0.9990 Bi-Metallic Gold center in Silver ring .5000 oz. **Obv:** Temple of Heaven within circle, date below **Rev:** Panda at stream, denomination below, within circle

Date	Mintage	F	VF	XF	Unc	BU
1995 Proof	2,000	Value: 395				

Y# 789 50 YUAN
15.5517 g., 9990.0000 Bi-Metallic Gold center in Silver ring .5000 oz. **Obv:** Temple of Heaven **Rev:** Panda approaching water from right

Date	Mintage	F	VF	XF	Unc	BU
1995 Proof	—	—	—	—	320	—

Y# 853 50 YUAN
15.5517 g., 0.9990 Bi-Metallic Gold center in Silver ring .5000 oz. **Obv:** Temple of Heaven **Rev:** Panda seated on rock

Date	Mintage	F	VF	XF	Unc	BU
1996 Proof	2,500	Value: 385				

Y# 1009 50 YUAN
15.5517 g., 0.9990 Bi-Metallic Gold center in Silver ring .5000 oz. **Obv:** Temple of Heaven, date below **Rev:** Panda climbing tree

Date	Mintage	F	VF	XF	Unc	BU
1997 Proof	2,800	Value: 385				

Y# 793 500 YUAN
155.5175 g., 0.9999 Bi-Metallic Gold center in Silver ring 5.0000 oz. **Obv:** Temple of Heaven **Rev:** Two pandas sitting on rock, denomination above, within circle

Date	Mintage	F	VF	XF	Unc	BU
1995 Proof	199	Value: 3,200				

Y# 1020 500 YUAN
155.5175 g., 0.9990 Bi-Metallic Gold center in Silver ring 5.0000 oz. **Obv:** Temple of Heaven, date below **Rev:** Panda

Date	Mintage	F	VF	XF	Unc	BU
1996 Proof	199	Value: 3,250				

Y# 1021 500 YUAN
155.5175 g., 0.9990 Bi-Metallic Gold center in Silver ring 5.0000 oz. **Obv:** Temple of Heaven **Rev:** Two pandas resting near stream

Date	Mintage	F	VF	XF	Unc	BU
1997 Proof	199	Value: 3,250				

PATTERNS

Including off metal strikes

KM#	Date	Mintage	Identification	Issue Price	Mkt Val
Pn1	1983	—	5 Yuan. Denomination between sprays. Marco Polo bust at upper right, ships below, dates at left, denomination below. Silvered base metal. Marco Polo.	—	600
Pn2	1983	—	100 Yuan. Gilt Bronze.	—	600
Pn3	1985	—	200 Yuan. Gold. Decade for Women, KM#89.	—	—
Pn4	1991	—	Yuan. Nickel Plated Steel. Raised character "pattern". Y#284.	—	100
Pn5	1991	—	Yuan. Nickel Plated Steel. Raised character "pattern". Y#285.	—	100
Pn6	1991	—	Yuan. Nickel Plated Steel. Raised character "pattern". Y#287.	—	100
Pn7	1991	—	Yuan. Nickel Plated Steel. Raised character "pattern". Y#315.	—	150
Pn8	1991	—	Yuan. Nickel Plated Steel. Raised character "pattern". Y#317.	—	150
Pn9	1991	—	10000 Yuan. Gold. Y#358.	—	—

PIEFORTS

KM#	Date	Mintage	Identification	Issue Price	Mkt Val
P1	1979	3,500	35 Yuan. 0.8000 Silver. Y#8.	—	200
P2	1979	500	450 Yuan. 0.9000 Gold. Y#9.	—	2,350
P3	1980	2,500	Yuan. Copper. Y#10.	—	15.00
P4	1980	2,500	Yuan. Copper. Y#11.	—	15.00
P5	1980	2,500	Yuan. Copper. Y#12.	—	15.00
P6	1980	2,500	Yuan. Copper. Y#13.	—	15.00
P7	1980	1,000	Yuan. Copper. Y#14.	—	25.00
P8	1980	1,000	Yuan. Copper. Y#15.	—	25.00
P9	1980	1,000	Yuan. Copper. Y#16.	—	25.00
P10	1980	1,000	Yuan. Copper. Y#17.	—	25.00
P11	1980	2,000	15 Yuan. 0.8000 Silver. Archery.	—	85.00
P12	1980	2,000	20 Yuan. 0.8000 Silver. Y#18, Wrestling.	—	85.00
P13	1980	1,000	30 Yuan. 0.8000 Silver. Equestrian, Y#19.	249	100
P14	1980	1,000	30 Yuan. 0.8000 Silver. Soccer.	249	100
P15	1980	2,000	30 Yuan. 0.8000 Silver. Speed skating, Y#21.	249	80.00
P16	1980	2,000	30 Yuan. 0.8000 Silver. Alpine skiing.	—	80.00
P17	1980	2,000	30 Yuan. 0.8000 Silver. Biathalon.	—	80.00
P18	1980	2,000	30 Yuan. 0.8000 Silver. Figure skating.	—	80.00
P19	1980	360	250 Yuan. 0.9170 Gold. Alpine skiing, Y#22.	1,750	900
P20	1980	500	300 Yuan. 0.9170 Gold. Archery, Y#23.	—	1,300
PA21	1991	—	10 Yuan. 0.9990 Silver. 62.2000g. Panda, hind feet in water.	—	200
P21	1992	—	5 Yuan. 0.9000 Silver. Ancient ship building, Y#331.	—	60.00
P22	1992	—	5 Yuan. 0.9000 Silver. First compass, Y#332.	—	60.00
P23	1992	—	5 Yuan. 0.9000 Silver. First seismograph, Y#333.	—	60.00
P24	1992	—	5 Yuan. 0.9000 Silver. Ancient kite flying, Y#334.	—	60.00
P25	1992	—	5 Yuan. 0.9000 Silver. Bronze metal working, Y#335.	—	60.00
P26	1996	5,000	5 Yuan. 0.9990 Silver. Goddess holding flower, Y-885.	—	—
P27	1996	5,000	5 Yuan. 0.9990 Silver. Goddess holding vase and twig, Y#1196.	—	—
P27	1996	5,000	5 Yuan. 0.9990 Silver. Goddess holding vase and twig, Y#1196.	—	—
P28	1997	80,000	5 Yuan. 0.9990 Silver. Prev. KM#P26. Y#916.	—	75.00
P29	1997	80,000	5 Yuan. 0.9990 Silver. Child w/carp, Y#916.1.	—	—
P30	1997	80,000	10 Yuan. 0.9990 Silver. Child w/carp, Y#917.1.	—	—
P31	1998	—	10 Yuan. 0.9990 Silver. Prev. KM#P27. Y#922.	—	60.00
P32	1998	100,000	10 Yuan. 0.9990 Silver. Prev. KM#P28. Y#917.	—	40.00

MINT SETS

KM#	Date	Mintage	Identification	Issue Price	Mkt Val
MS1	1979 (s) (3)	—	Y#1-3, Medal	—	7.50
MS2	1980(b) (7)	—	Y#1-3, 24-27	—	8.50
MS3	1982 (4)	—	Y#40-43	750	3,400
MS4	1986 (2)	—	KM#151 (2)	—	12.50
MS5	1990 (2)	—	Y#264-265	—	8.00
MS6	1991 (6)	—	Y#1-3, 328-330	—	5.50
MS7	1991 (2)	—	Y#316-317	—	5.00
MS8	1992 (6)	—	Y#1-3, 328-330	—	5.50
MS9	1993 (6)	—	Y#1-3, 328-330	—	5.50
MS10	1994 (6)	—	Y#1-3, 328-330	—	5.50
MS11	1995 (6)	—	Y#1-3, 328-330	—	5.50
MS12	1996 (6)	—	Y#1-3, 328-330	—	5.50

PROOF SETS

KM#	Date	Mintage	Identification	Issue Price	Mkt Val
PS1	1979 (4)	70,000	Y#4-7	1,695	800
PS2	1980 (14)	1,000	Y#10-23	1,750	425
PS3	1980 (7)	—	Y#1-3, 24-27	—	10.00
PS4	1980 (4)	—	Y#10-13	—	40.00
PS5	1980 (4)	—	Y#14-17	—	45.00
PS6	1980 (3)	1,000	Y#18-20	—	50.00
PS7	1981(s) (7)	10,000	Y#1-3, 24-27 Medal	—	12.00
PS8	1981 (4)	1,000	Y#28-31	2,950	2,550
PS9	1982(s) (7)	—	Y#1-3, 24-27 Medal	—	10.00
PS10	1983(s) (7)	—	Y#1-3, 24-27 Book	—	12.50
PS11	1983(s) (7)	—	Y#1-3, 24-27 Medal (paper cover)	—	140
PS12	1984(y) (7)	—	Y#1-3, 24-27 Medal	—	12.50
PS13	1984 (4)	—	Y#68-71	—	90.00
PS14	1984 (3)	—	Y#85-87	—	22.50
PS15	1985 (2)	—	Y#96-97	45.00	60.00
PS16	1985(y) (7)	—	Y#1-3, 24-27 Medal	—	12.00
PS17	1985 (2)	—	Y#109-110	45.00	65.00
PS18	1985 (4)	—	Y#90-93	—	115
PS19	1986(y) (7)	—	Y#1-3, 24-27 Medal	10.00	15.00
PS20	1986 (5)	10,000	Y#101-105	—	800
PS21	1986 (4)	—	Y#113-116	—	110
PS22	1987 (5)	10,000	Y#124-128	—	800
PS23	1987 (2)	—	Y#133-134	278	115
PS24	1987 (4)	—	Y#135-138	—	120
PS25	1988 (4)	—	Y#160-163	200	110
PS26	1988 (5)	10,000	Y#152-156	—	900
PS27	1989 (5)	8,000	Y#187-191	—	850
PS28	1989 (4)	—	Y#213-216	—	130
PS29	1990 (5)	5,000	Y#238-242	—	1,000
PS30	1990 (3)	2,500	Y#267-269	1,095	750
PS31	1990 (2)	2,000	Y#266 and medal	995	500
PSA32	1990 (5)	10,000	Y251-254, 256	—	265
PS32	1991 (6)	—	Y#1-3, 328-330	—	6.50
PS33	1991 (2)	2,000	Y#301 and medal	575	350
PS34	1991 (5)	350	Y#309-313	—	1,000
PS35	1992 (6)	—	Y#1-3, 328-330	—	6.50
PS36	1992 (5)	2,500	P#21-25 Piefort	—	350
PS37	1992 (5)	1,000	Y#336-340	—	4,500
PS38	1992 (5)	—	Y#341-345	—	1,000
PS39	1993 (4)	2,000	Y#441-444	200	140
PS40	1993 (4)	1,000	Y#445-448	1,600	1,350
PS41	1993 (3)	—	Y#352-354	—	925
PS42	1993 (5)	—	Y#610-614	—	600
PS43	1993 (6)	—	Y#1-3, 328-330	—	8.00
PSA44	1993 (5)	2,500	Y484, 930, 1203-1205	—	850
PS44	1993 (5)	100	Y#1072-1076	1,875	2,000
PS45	1994 (12)	50	Y#419, 420 Unc/Proof, 421-429	—	6,000
PS46	1994 (11)	50	Y#419, 420 Unc/Proof, 421-428	—	4,500
PS47	1994 (5)	1,000	Y#419, 421-423, 425	—	1,385
PS48	1994 (4)	2,500	Y#419-421, 423	645	655
PS49	1994 (3)	1,000	Y#420-424, 426	—	845
PS50	1994 (2)	400	Y#420, 428	—	1,270
PS51	1994 (5)	—	Y#431-434, 544	—	600
PS52	1994 (6)	—	Y#1-3, 328-330	—	8.00
PS53	1995 (3)	2,000	Y#469-471	485	500
PS54	1995 (3)	2,000	Y#571-573	—	710

KM#	Date	Mintage	Identification	Issue Price	Mkt Val
PS55	1995 (2)	3,000	Y#469-470	89.00	90.00
PS56	1995 (4)	15,000	Y#600-603	—	150
PS57	1995 (4)	9,000	Y#588-591	—	160
PS58	1995 (6)	—	Y#1-3, 328-330	—	8.00
PS59	1995 (5)	1,000	Y#687, 736-739	—	1,385
PS60	1996 (4)	15,000	Y#604-607	—	180
PS61	1996 (4)	8,000	Y#595-598	—	240
PS62	1996 (6)	—	Y#1-3, 328-330	—	8.00
PS63	1996 (4)	750	Y#740-743 Plus bottle	—	625
PS64	1997 (4)	28,000	Y#936-939	—	200
PS65	1997 (4)	10,000	Y#1099-1102	—	180
PS66	1998 (2)	61,000	China Y#727 and Canadian KM#316	72.50	70.00

CHINESE SOVIET REPUBLIC

In November, 1931, the first congress of the Chinese Soviet proclaimed and established the "Chinese Soviet Republic" under the Chairmanship of Mao Tse-Tung.

Prior to 1949, the People's Republic of China did not exist as such, but the Communists did control areas known as Soviets. Most of the Soviets were established on the borders of two or more provinces and were named according to the provinces involved. Thus there were such soviets as the Kiangsi-Hunan Soviet, the Hunan-Hupeh-Kiangsi Soviet, the Hupeh-Honan-Anhwei Soviet and others. In 1931 some of the soviets in the southern Kiangsi area were consolidated into the Chinese Soviet Republic, which lasted until the Long March of 1934.

MONETARY SYSTEM

10 Cash (Wen) = 1 Cent (Fen)

100 Cents (Fen) = 1 Dollar (Yuan)

CONSOLIDATED SOVIET REPUBLIC (Kiangsi)

STANDARD COINAGE

Y# 506 CENT

Copper **Ruler:** Mao Tse-tung **Obv:** Large "1" on hammer and sickle **Rev:** Star above value in wheat stalks

Date	Mintage	VG	F	VF	XF	Unc
ND(ca.1932)	—	10.00	20.00	35.00	65.00	—

Y# 506a CENT

Copper **Ruler:** Mao Tse-tung **Obv:** Large "1" on hammer and sickle **Rev:** Star above value in wheat stalks

Date	Mintage	F	VF	XF	Unc	BU
ND(ca.1960) Restrike	—	—	—	8.00	20.00	30.00

Y# 507 5 CENTS

Copper **Ruler:** Mao Tse-tung **Obv:** Hammer and sickle on map outline **Rev:** Star over value in wheat stalks **Edge:** Plain **Note:** Varieties exist.

Date	Mintage	VG	F	VF	XF	Unc
ND(ca.1932)	—	20.00	30.00	50.00	90.00	—

Y# 507.1 5 CENTS

Copper **Ruler:** Mao Tse-tung **Obv:** Hammer and sickle on map outline **Rev:** Star over value in wheat stalks **Edge:** Reeded **Note:** Varieties exist.

Date	Mintage	VG	F	VF	XF	Unc
ND(ca.1932)	—	20.00	30.00	50.00	90.00	—

Y# 507a 5 CENTS

Copper **Ruler:** Mao Tse-tung **Obv:** Hammer and sickle on map outline **Rev:** Star over value in wheat stalks

Date	Mintage	F	VF	XF	Unc	BU
ND(ca.1960) Restrike	—	—	—	10.00	25.00	35.00

Y# 508 20 CENTS

5.5000 g., Silver **Ruler:** Mao Tse-tung **Obv:** Star over hammer and sickle on globe in wheat stalks **Rev:** Denomination **Note:** Many minor varieties exist.

Date	Mintage	VG	F	VF	XF	Unc
1932	—	15.00	25.00	45.00	85.00	—
1933	—	10.00	20.00	35.00	75.00	—

KM# 5 DOLLAR

Silver **Ruler:** Mao Tse-tung **Obv:** Crude facing portrait of Lenin **Rev:** Hammer, sickle, and value within ornamental wreath

Date	Mintage	VG	F	VF	XF	Unc
1931 Rare	—	—	—	—	—	—

PATTERNS

Including off metal strikes

KM#	Date	Mintage	Identification	Mkt Val
Pn1	1932	—	20 Cents. Copper. Y#508.	265

HSIANG-O-HSI SOVIET

(Kiangsi-West Hupeh)

SOVIET CONTROLLED PROVINCE

STANDARD COINAGE

KM# 1 FEN

Copper **Obv:** Legend around large star **Rev:** Denomination within wreath, legend around

Date	Mintage	VG	F	VF	XF	Unc
ND(1931) Rare	—	—	—	—	—	—

HUNAN SOVIET

SOVIET CONTROLLED PROVINCE

STANDARD COINAGE

KM# 1.1 DOLLAR

Silver **Obv:** Large star **Obv. Legend:** "Hu-nan Sheng Su-wei-ai Cheng-fu" **Rev:** Denomination within sprays

Date	Mintage	VG	F	VF	XF	Unc
1931	—	200	350	—	—	—

KM# 1.2 DOLLAR

Silver **Obv:** Hammer and sickle within small star **Rev:** Denomination within sprays

Date	Mintage	VG	F	VF	XF	Unc
1931	—	100	200	350	—	—

HUPEH-HONAN-ANWHEI SOVIET

The Hupeh-Honan-Anhwei Soviet District was a large revolutionary base. It was formerly made up of three separate special districts: East Hupeh, South Honan and West Anhwei which united until after 1930. Between 1931 and 1932 this Bank has issued a quantity of copper and silver coins as well as banknotes.

SOVIET CONTROLLED PROVINCE

STANDARD COINAGE

Y# 503 DOLLAR

26.8000 g., Silver **Obv:** Hammer and sickle on globe at center **Rev:** Lower legend appears in crude Russian, denomination within circle at center **Rev. Legend:** "SOVETS...."

Date	Mintage	VG	F	VF	XF	Unc
1932	—	250	575	750	1,000	—

Note: Attribution of Y#503 to the Hupeh-Honan-Anhwei Soviet is not definite.

Y# 504 DOLLAR

27.2000 g., Silver **Obv:** Hammer and sickle on globe at center **Rev:** Denomination within center circle

Date	Mintage	VG	F	VF	XF	Unc
1932	—	175	275	400	700	—

P'ING CHIANG COUNTY SOVIET

SOVIET CONTROLLED PROVINCE

STANDARD COINAGE

KM# 1 DOLLAR
Silver **Obv:** Star in center circle holds sickle and hammer, legend in 8 Chinese characters **Obv. Legend:** "P'ing Chiang..." **Rev:** Denomination within wreath

Date	Mintage	VG	F	VF	XF	Unc
1931 Rare	—	—	—	—	—	—

SHENSI-NORTH SOVIET

SOVIET CONTROLLED PROVINCE

STANDARD COINAGE

Date is given in the 5th year of the Chinese Soviet Republic. They were issued after the Long March.

KM# 1.1 DOLLAR
Silver **Obv:** Large hammer and sickle **Rev:** Value in plain field, yr.5 at bottom

Date	Mintage	VG	F	VF	XF	Unc
5 (1936)	—	1,750	2,250	2,850	—	—

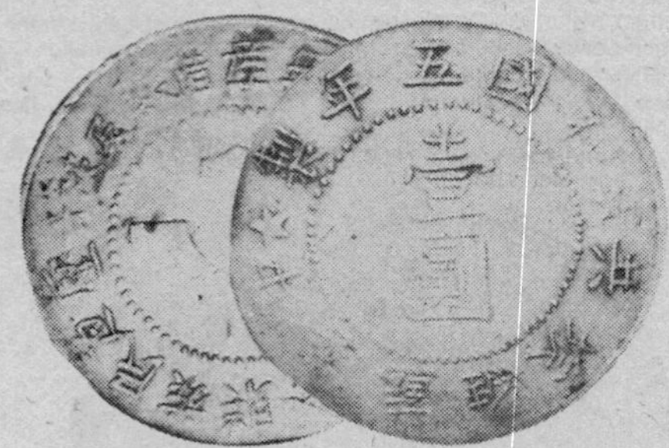

KM# 1.2 DOLLAR
Silver **Obv:** Star at left, slightly lower **Rev:** Denomination within center circle, legend rotated with yr.5 at top

Date	Mintage	VG	F	VF	XF	Unc
5 (1936)	—	1,750	2,250	2,850	—	—

KM# 2 DOLLAR
Silver **Obv:** Large hammer and sickle **Rev:** Value within wheat stalks

Date	Mintage	VG	F	VF	XF	Unc
5 (1936)	—	2,500	3,200	4,000	—	—

SZECHUAN-SHENSI SOVIET

SOVIET CONTROLLED PROVINCES

STANDARD COINAGE

Y# 510 200 CASH
Copper **Obv:** Three stars around hammer and sickle **Rev:** Denomination at center

Date	Mintage	Good	VG	F	VF	XF
1933	—	25.00	50.00	85.00	150	—

Y# 510.1 200 CASH
Copper **Obv:** Three stars around hammer and sickle **Rev:** Small "200" at center

Date	Mintage	Good	VG	F	VF	XF
1933	—	25.00	50.00	85.00	150	—

Y# 510.2 200 CASH
Copper **Obv:** Three stars around hammer and sickle **Rev:** Large "200" at center

Date	Mintage	Good	VG	F	VF	XF
1933	—	25.00	50.00	85.00	150	—

Y# 510.3 200 CASH
Copper **Obv:** Three stars around hammer and sickle **Rev:** Square 0's in "200" at center

Date	Mintage	Good	VG	F	VF	XF
1933	—	30.00	60.00	100	185	—

Y# 510.4 200 CASH
Copper **Obv:** Solid hammer and sickle reversed **Rev:** 200 retrograde at center

Date	Mintage	Good	VG	F	VF	XF
1933	—	35.00	75.00	125	250	—

Y# 510.5 200 CASH
Copper **Obv:** Shaded hammer and sickle reversed, three stars above **Rev:** Denomination within wreath at center **Note:** Varieties exist.

Date	Mintage	Good	VG	F	VF	XF
1933	—	30.00	60.00	100	185	—

Y# 511.1 200 CASH
Copper **Obv:** Hammer and sickle within large star, date with open 3 and backwards 4 **Rev:** Denomination within circle

Date	Mintage	VG	F	VF	XF	Unc
1934	—	22.50	45.00	75.00	150	—

Y# 511.2 200 CASH
Copper **Obv:** Hammer and sickle within large star, date with 4 corrected **Rev:** Denomination within circle

Date	Mintage	VG	F	VF	XF	Unc
1934	—	22.50	45.00	75.00	150	—

Y# 511 200 CASH
Copper **Obv:** Hammer and sickle at center of large star, date with closed 3 and backwards 4 **Rev:** Denomination within circle **Note:** Modern forgeries of this variety exist.

Date	Mintage	VG	F	VF	XF	Unc
1934	—	22.50	45.00	75.00	150	—

Y# 511a 200 CASH

Copper **Obv:** Hammer and sickle within large star, date with 4 corrected **Rev:** Denomination within circle

Date	Mintage	F	VF	XF	Unc	BU
1934 Restrike	—	—	—	12.50	25.00	35.00

Note: Many varieties of 200 Cash pieces exist; well struck, usually found in choice condition; unlisted varieties do not carry a premium

Y# 512 500 CASH

Copper **Obv:** Hammer and sickle within small star, small stars flanking date **Rev:** Denomination within circle

Date	Mintage	VG	F	VF	XF	Unc
1934	—	75.00	100	175	285	—

Y# 512.1 500 CASH

Copper **Obv:** Large stars flanking date; hammer handle across lower leg of star **Rev:** Denomination within circle

Date	Mintage	VG	F	VF	XF	Unc
1934	—	50.00	100	175	275	—

Y# 512.2 500 CASH

Copper, 33-34 mm. **Obv:** Hammer handle extends between right leg of star **Rev:** Denomination within circle

Date	Mintage	VG	F	VF	XF	Unc
1934	—	50.00	100	150	250	—

Note: Many varieties of 500 Cash pieces exist; unlisted varieties do not carry a premium

Y# 513.6 DOLLAR

26.3000 g., Silver **Obv:** Globe with outlined hammer and sickle, sickle blade over hammer handle **Rev:** Denomination within circle, small solid stars

Date	Mintage	VG	F	VF	XF	Unc
1934	—	100	200	275	400	—

Y# 513 DOLLAR

26.3000 g., Silver **Obv:** Globe with hammer and sickle **Rev:** Denomination within circle, large, decorative, solid stars

Date	Mintage	VG	F	VF	XF	Unc
1934	—	125	225	325	500	—

Y# 513.1 DOLLAR

26.3000 g., Silver **Obv:** Globe with outlined hammer and sickle, hammer handle over sickle blade **Rev:** Denomination within circle, medium solid stars

Date	Mintage	VG	F	VF	XF	Unc
1934	—	100	175	250	400	—

Y# 513.2 DOLLAR

26.3000 g., Silver **Obv:** Globe with outlined hammer and sickle **Rev:** Denomination within circle, small solid stars

Date	Mintage	VG	F	VF	XF	Unc
1933 Rare	—	—	—	—	—	—
1934	—	100	175	250	400	—

Y# 513.3 DOLLAR

26.3000 g., Silver **Obv:** Globe with hammer and sickle **Rev:** Denomination within circle, outlined stars

Date	Mintage	VG	F	VF	XF	Unc
1934	—	100	200	275	450	—

Y# 513.5 DOLLAR

26.3000 g., Silver **Obv:** Globe with outlined hammer and sickle **Rev:** Denomination within circle, large solid stars

Date	Mintage	VG	F	VF	XF	Unc
1934	—	100	200	275	450	—

Y# 513.4 DOLLAR

26.3000 g., Silver **Obv:** Globe with hammer and sickle **Rev:** Denomination within circle, pentagram stars **Note:** Many minor varieties exist.

Date	Mintage	VG	F	VF	XF	Unc
1934	—	75.00	150	225	375	—

COUNTERMARKED COINAGE

K# 650k DOLLAR

26.4000 g., Silver **Countermark:** Three Chinese characters in rectangular box **Obv:** Bust, left, countermark of uncertain origin meaning "SOVIET" **Rev:** Denomination within wreath **Note:** Countermark on Y#329.

CM Date	Host Date	Good	VG	F	VF	XF
ND(1934)	ND	62.50	125	200	325	600

WAN-HSI-PEI-SOVIET

(Northwest Anhwei)

SOVIET CONTROLLED PROVINCE

STANDARD COINAGE

KM# 1 50 CASH

Brass **Obv:** Legend around globe with hammer and sickle **Rev:** Value in star within wreath, all within legend

Date	Mintage	Good	VG	F	VF	XF
1931	—	150	250	—	—	—

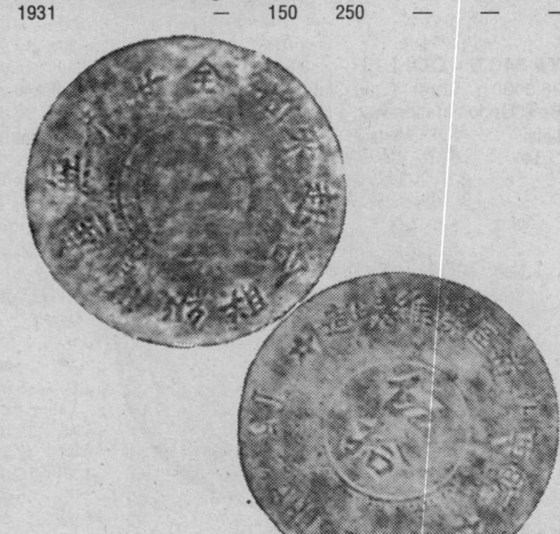

KM# 2 50 CASH

Copper **Obv:** Legend around globe with hammer and sickle **Rev:** Value in circle, Chinese legend above, Western legend below

Date	Mintage	VG	F	VF	XF	Unc
ND(1931-32) Rare	—	—	—	—	—	—

COLOMBIA

The Republic of Colombia, in the northwestern corner of South America, has an area of 440,831 sq. mi. (1,138,910 sq. km.) and a population of*42.3 million. Capital: Bogota. The economy is primarily agricultural with a mild, rich coffee being the chief crop. Colombia has the world's largest platinum deposits and important reserves of coal, iron ore, petroleum and limestone; other precious metals and emeralds are also mined. Coffee, crude oil, bananas, sugar and emeralds are exported.

The northern coast of present Colombia was one of the first parts of the American continent to be visited by Spanish navigators. At Darien in Panama is the site of the first permanent European settlement on the American mainland in 1510. New Granada, as Colombia was known until 1861, stemmed from the settlement of Santa Marta in 1525. New Granada was established as a Spanish colony in 1549. Independence was declared in 1810, and secured in 1819 when Simon Bolivar united Colombia, Venezuela, Panama and Ecuador as the Republic of Gran Colombia. Venezuela withdrew from the Republic in 1829; Ecuador in 1830; and Panama in 1903.

MINT MARKS

A, M – Medellin (capital), Antioquia (state)
B - BOGOTA
(D) Denver, USA
H – Birmingham (Heaton & Sons)
(m) - Medellin, w/o mint mark
(Mo) - Mexico City
NI - Numismatica Italiana, Arezzo, Italy
mint marks stylized in wreath
(P) - Philadelphia
(S) - San Francisco, USA.
(W) - Waterbury, CT (USA, Scoville mint)

REPUBLIC

DECIMAL COINAGE

100 Centavos = 1 Peso

KM# 275 CENTAVO

2.0000 g., Copper-Nickel **Obverse:** Liberty head right **Reverse:** Denomination within wreath **Note:** Erratically punched final two digits of date are common on these issues, especially 1935-1948. A very faint "17" is often observable beneath the final two digits on many dates of this type.

Date	Mintage	F	VF	XF	Unc
1918	430,000	6.00	15.00	35.00	125
1919	Inc. above	8.00	25.00	60.00	140
1920(D)	7,540,000	6.50	13.50	32.00	120
1921(D)	12,460,000	6.50	12.50	30.00	60.00
1933(P)	3,000,000	0.50	3.00	5.00	10.00
1935(P)	5,000,000	0.50	3.00	7.00	15.00
1936	1,540,000	2.00	5.00	15.00	45.00
1938(P)	7,920,000	0.25	0.50	2.00	6.00
1941B	1,000,000	0.50	1.00	3.00	10.00
1946B	2,096,000	0.35	0.75	2.50	6.50
1947/17B	1,835,000	1.00	3.50	6.00	12.00
1947/37B	Inc. above	1.00	3.50	6.00	12.00
1947/6B	Inc. above	1.00	3.50	6.00	12.00
1947B	Inc. above	0.50	1.00	2.00	5.00
1948/38B	1,139,000	1.00	3.50	6.00	12.00
1948B	Inc. above	0.50	1.00	2.00	5.00

KM# 205 CENTAVO

Bronze, 17 mm. **Obverse:** Liberty cap within wreath **Reverse:** Coffee bean sprigs flank denomination, cornucopia above **Note:** Several date varieties exist.

Date	Mintage	F	VF	XF	Unc
1942	1,000,000	1.00	2.00	4.50	12.50
1942B	Inc. above	1.00	3.50	9.00	28.00
1943	—	0.50	1.00	2.50	7.00
1943B	4,515,000	0.50	1.00	2.50	7.00
1944B	4,515,000	0.35	0.65	1.50	5.00
1945B	3,769,000	0.50	1.00	2.50	7.00
1945B over reversed B	—	0.35	0.65	1.50	5.00
1948B	585,000	0.50	1.00	3.00	10.00
1949B	4,255,000	0.35	0.65	1.50	5.00
1950B	5,827,000	0.45	0.75	2.50	8.00
1951B	Inc. above	0.35	0.65	1.75	5.50
1957	2,500,000	0.25	0.45	0.75	2.00
1958	590,000	0.25	0.45	1.00	2.25
1959	2,677,000	0.15	0.25	0.50	1.25
1960	2,500,000	0.15	0.25	0.50	1.25
1961 Widely spaced date	3,673,000	0.15	0.25	0.50	1.25
1961 Narrowly spaced date	Inc. above	0.15	0.25	0.45	1.00
1962	4,065,000	0.15	0.25	0.50	1.25
1963	1,845,000	0.15	0.25	0.75	2.00
1964/44	3,165,000	0.50	1.50	2.50	5.00
1964	Inc. above	0.15	0.25	0.50	1.25
1965 Large date	5,510,000	0.15	0.25	0.45	1.00
1965 Small date	Inc. above	0.15	0.25	0.45	1.00
1966	3,910,000	0.15	0.25	0.50	1.25

KM# 275a CENTAVO

Nickel Clad Steel, 17 mm. **Obverse:** Liberty head right **Reverse:** Denomination within wreath **Note:** Erratically punched final two digits of date are common on these issues.

Date	Mintage	F	VF	XF	Unc
1952/12B	—	0.20	0.50	1.50	4.00
1952B	Inc. above	0.10	0.15	0.75	3.00
1954B	5,080,000	0.10	0.15	0.50	2.00
1956	1,315,000	0.10	0.20	1.00	5.00
1957	900,000	0.35	0.75	2.50	7.50
1958/48	—	0.35	0.75	2.00	6.00
1958	1,596,000	0.20	0.45	1.00	3.00

KM# 218 CENTAVO

Bronze **Subject:** Uprising Sesquicentennial **Obverse:** Liberty cap within wreath **Reverse:** Coffee bean sprigs flank denomination, cornucopia above **Note:** This and the other issues in the uprising commemorative series offer the usual design of the period with the dates 1810-1960 added at the bottom of the obverse.

Date	Mintage	F	VF	XF	Unc
ND(1960)	500,000	0.60	1.50	3.00	8.00

KM# 205a CENTAVO

Copper Clad Steel, 17 mm. **Obverse:** Liberty cap within wreath **Reverse:** Coffee bean sprigs flank denomination, cornucopia above **Note:** Several date varieties exist.

Date	Mintage	F	VF	XF	Unc
1967	5,730,000	—	0.10	0.15	0.45
1968	7,390,000	—	0.10	0.15	0.45
1969	6,870,000	—	0.10	0.15	0.45
1970	3,839,000	—	0.10	0.20	0.60
1971	3,020,000	—	0.10	0.20	0.60
1972	3,100,000	—	0.10	0.20	0.60
1973	—	—	—	0.10	0.35
1974	2,000,000	—	—	0.10	0.35
1975	1,000,000	—	—	0.10	0.35
1976	1,000,000	—	—	0.10	0.35
1977	900,000	—	0.10	0.15	0.45
1978	224,000	—	0.10	0.20	0.65

KM# 198 2 CENTAVOS

3.0000 g., Copper-Nickel **Obverse:** Liberty head right, date below **Reverse:** Denomination within wreath **Note:** Erratically punched final two digits exist for 1946-1947. A very faint "17" is often observable beneath the final two digits on many dates of this type.

Date	Mintage	F	VF	XF	Unc
1918	930,000	7.00	15.00	30.00	80.00
1919	Inc. above	16.50	30.00	60.00	135
1920	3,855,000	3.00	6.50	18.50	50.00
1921(D)	11,145,000	2.50	5.00	15.00	40.00
1922 10 pieces known	—	1,350	2,800	—	—
1933(P)	3,500,000	0.50	1.50	4.00	10.00
1935(P)	2,500,000	0.35	1.00	3.50	8.00
1938(P)	3,872,000	0.35	1.00	3.25	7.00
1941B	500,000	1.00	2.00	7.00	20.00
1942B	500,000	1.50	2.50	8.00	16.50
1946/36B	2,593,000	1.00	2.50	6.00	12.50
1946B	Inc. above	0.75	1.50	4.75	11.00
1947/3B	1,337,000	0.75	1.50	4.00	10.00
1947/36B	Inc. above	0.75	1.50	4.00	10.00
1947B	Inc. above	0.35	1.00	3.00	8.00

KM# 210 2 CENTAVOS

Bronze **Mint:** Bogota **Obverse:** Liberty cap within wreath, date below **Reverse:** Coffee bean sprigs flank denomination, cornucopia above

Date	Mintage	F	VF	XF	Unc
1948B	2,648,000	0.35	1.00	4.00	10.00
1949B	1,278,000	0.75	2.00	7.00	15.00
1950B	2,285,000	0.75	1.50	7.00	18.00

KM# 211 2 CENTAVOS

Aluminum-Bronze **Obverse:** Head left, date below, divided legend **Reverse:** Denomination within wreath

Date	Mintage	F	VF	XF	Unc
1952B Small date	5,038,000	0.15	0.25	0.50	2.00
1965/3	1,830,000	0.10	0.20	0.40	1.00
1965 Large date	Inc. above	0.15	0.25	0.50	2.00

KM# 214 2 CENTAVOS

Aluminum-Bronze **Mint:** Bogota **Obverse:** Head left, date below, continuous legend **Reverse:** Denomination within wreath

Date	Mintage	F	VF	XF	Unc
1955 Large date	2,513,000	0.15	0.30	1.00	3.00
1955B Large date	Inc. above	0.15	0.30	0.75	2.00
1959 Small date	4,609,000	0.10	0.20	0.50	1.50

KM# 219 2 CENTAVOS

Aluminum-Bronze **Mint:** Bogota **Subject:** Uprising Sesquicentennial **Obverse:** Head left, date below **Reverse:** Denomination within wreath

Date	Mintage	F	VF	XF	Unc
ND(1960)	250,000	1.00	2.00	3.00	8.00

KM# 190 2-1/2 CENTAVOS

Copper-Nickel **Mint:** Waterbury **Obverse:** Liberty cap within circle **Reverse:** Denomination within circle

Date	Mintage	F	VF	XF	Unc
1902(W)	Est. 400,000	—	—	500	900

KM# 184 5 CENTAVOS

Copper-Nickel **Mint:** Waterbury **Obverse:** Head left, date below **Reverse:** Large denomination, sprays flank

Date	Mintage	F	VF	XF	Unc
1902(W)	Est. 400,000	—	—	650	1,000

KM# 191 5 CENTAVOS

1.2500 g., 0.6660 Silver .0268 oz. ASW **Mint:** Philadelphia **Obverse:** Head left, date below **Reverse:** Small denomination within two cornucopias **Edge:** Plain

Date	Mintage	F	VF	XF	Unc
1902(P)	400,000	0.75	1.50	3.50	8.00

KM# 199 5 CENTAVOS

4.0000 g., Copper-Nickel **Obverse:** Head right, date below **Reverse:** Denomination within wreath **Note:** Varieties exist. Erratically punched final two digits of date are common on these issues, especially 1935-1950. A very faint "17" is often observable beneath the final two digits on many dates of this type.

Date	Mintage	F	VF	XF	Unc
1918	767,000	11.00	25.00	50.00	100
1919	1,926,000	16.50	30.00	65.00	125
1920	2,062,000	11.00	25.00	50.00	100
1920H	—	10.00	27.50	45.00	100
1921	1,574,000	16.50	30.00	65.00	125
1921H	—	16.50	30.00	65.00	125
1922	2,623,000	16.50	30.00	65.00	125
1922H	—	16.50	30.00	65.00	125
1924	120,000	18.50	35.00	70.00	125
1933(P)	2,000,000	1.00	2.00	6.00	15.00
1935/24	1,616,000	5.00	12.00	30.00	60.00
1935(P)	10,000,000	0.75	1.75	3.50	10.00
1936	—	45.00	75.00	150	350
1938B	2,000,000	1.00	2.50	5.50	13.00
1938	3,867,000	2.00	3.75	8.00	15.00
1938 Large 38 in date	Inc. above	2.00	4.50	10.00	20.00
1939/5	2,000,000	1.75	3.00	6.00	13.00
1939	Inc. above	0.75	1.50	3.50	8.00
1941	—	2.50	5.50	9.00	23.00
1941B	500,000	3.00	6.00	10.00	25.00
1946(P) (S) Small date	40,000,000	0.20	0.50	1.00	3.00
1946(m) Large date	3,330,000	2.00	4.00	8.50	23.00
1949B	2,750,000	0.45	1.00	2.50	6.00
1950B Large 50 in date	3,611,000	6.00	12.00	25.00	45.00
1950B Small 50 in date	Inc. above	0.45	1.00	3.00	6.00

KM# 206 5 CENTAVOS

Bronze, 21 mm. **Obverse:** Liberty cap within wreath, date below **Reverse:** Coffee bean sprigs flank denomination, cornucopia above **Note:** Some coins of 1942-1956 have weak "B" mint mark.

Date	Mintage	F	VF	XF	Unc
1942	—	2.00	4.00	12.00	30.00
1942B	800,000	1.00	2.50	4.50	12.00
1943	—	5.00	9.00	18.00	35.00
1943B	6,053,000	0.75	1.50	3.00	10.00
1944	—	0.75	1.50	3.00	10.00
1944B	9,013,000	0.75	1.50	3.00	10.00
1945/4	—	0.75	1.50	3.00	10.00
1945	—	0.75	1.50	3.00	10.00
1945B	11,101,000	0.25	0.75	1.25	4.00
1946/5	—	1.25	3.50	4.50	12.50
1946	—	0.50	1.25	2.00	7.00
1952	—	1.25	2.50	3.50	10.00
1952B	3,985,000	0.15	0.40	1.00	2.50
1953B	5,180,000	0.10	0.25	0.75	2.00
1954B	1,159,000	0.10	0.25	0.75	2.00
1955B	6,819,000	0.10	0.25	0.75	2.00
1956	8,772,000	0.10	0.25	0.50	1.00
1956B	—	0.75	1.50	4.50	12.50
1957	8,912,000	0.10	0.25	0.75	2.00
1958	15,016,000	0.10	0.25	0.50	1.50
1959	14,271,000	0.10	0.25	0.50	1.50
1960/660	11,716,000	0.25	0.75	1.00	2.25
1960/70	Inc. above	0.25	0.75	1.00	2.25
1960	Inc. above	0.10	0.25	0.50	1.25
1961	11,200,000	0.10	0.25	0.50	1.25
CD1962	10,928,000	—	0.10	0.35	1.00
1963/53	15,113,000	—	—	—	—
1963	Inc. above	—	0.10	0.35	1.00
1964	9,336,000	—	0.10	0.35	1.00
1965	6,460,000	—	0.10	0.35	1.00
1966	7,170,000	—	0.10	0.35	1.00

KM# 206a 5 CENTAVOS

Copper Clad Steel **Obverse:** Liberty cap within wreath, date below **Reverse:** Coffee bean sprigs flank denomination, cornucopia above **Note:** Varieties exist for 1967, 1970, and 1973.

Date	Mintage	F	VF	XF	Unc
1967	10,280,000	—	—	0.10	1.00
1968	8,900,000	—	—	0.10	1.00
1969	17,800,000	—	—	0.10	1.00
1970	14,842,000	—	—	0.10	0.50
1971	10,730,000	—	—	0.10	0.50
1972	10,170,000	—	—	0.10	0.50
1973	10,525,000	—	—	0.10	0.50
1974	5,310,000	—	—	0.10	0.50
1975	5,631,000	—	—	0.10	0.50
1976	3,009,000	—	—	0.10	0.50
1977	2,000,000	—	—	0.10	0.50
1978	468,000	—	—	0.10	0.50
1979	8,087,000	—	—	—	—

KM# 220 5 CENTAVOS

Bronze **Subject:** Uprising Sesquicentennial **Obverse:** Liberty cap within wreath **Reverse:** Coffee bean sprigs flank denomination, cornucopia above

Date	Mintage	F	VF	XF	Unc
ND(1960)	400,000	1.75	3.50	7.50	25.00

KM# 196.1 10 CENTAVOS

2.5000 g., 0.9000 Silver .0723 oz. ASW **Obverse:** Simon Bolivar head right, date below **Reverse:** Arms and value **Note:** Varieties exist.

Date	Mintage	F	VF	XF	Unc
1911	5,065,000	1.00	1.75	10.00	25.00
1913	8,305,000	1.00	1.75	9.00	20.00
1914	3,840,000	1.00	1.75	10.00	25.00
1920	2,149,000	1.00	1.75	10.00	25.00
1934B B on obverse	140,000	3.00	7.00	18.00	40.00
1934/24	Inc. above	6.25	13.50	28.00	60.00
1934	Inc. above	6.00	12.50	28.00	60.00
1937B	—	5.00	11.50	22.50	45.00
1938/7B	2,055,000	1.75	3.75	6.50	20.00
1938B Wide date	Inc. above	1.00	2.00	4.00	10.00
1938 Narrow date	Inc. above	1.00	2.00	4.00	10.00
1940	450,000	1.50	2.50	4.50	15.00
1941	4,415,000	1.00	1.50	3.00	8.00
1942	3,140,000	5.00	10.00	16.50	38.00
1942B B on reverse	Inc. above	1.00	1.50	3.00	7.50

KM# 196.2 10 CENTAVOS

2.5000 g., 0.9000 Silver .0723 oz. ASW **Obverse:** Simon Bolivar head right **Reverse:** National arms recut

Date	Mintage	F	VF	XF	Unc
1920	Inc. above	2.00	6.00	12.00	30.00

KM# 207.1 10 CENTAVOS

2.5000 g., 0.5000 Silver .0401 oz. ASW **Obverse:** Francisco de Paula Santander head right **Reverse:** Denomination within wreath, mint mark at bottom **Designer:** Gilroy Roberts

Date	Mintage	F	VF	XF	Unc
1945B	4,830,000	0.75	1.50	3.50	9.00
1945 B-B	—	—	—	—	—
1945 Backwards B	—	1.00	2.00	4.00	10.00
1946/5B	—	0.65	1.50	4.50	13.00
1946B	—	0.65	1.50	4.50	13.00
1947/5B	7,366,000	1.50	3.00	5.00	15.00
1947/6B	Inc. above	1.50	3.00	5.00	15.00
1947B	Inc. above	1.50	3.00	5.00	15.00

KM# 207.2 10 CENTAVOS

2.5000 g., 0.5000 Silver .0401 oz. ASW **Obverse:** Head of Santander right, date below **Reverse:** Denomination within wreath, mint mark at top **Designer:** Gilroy Roberts **Note:** Varieties exist. Almost all dies for 1946-1951 show at least faint traces of overdating from 1945. Coins with absolutely no underdate, and those with very bold underdate, are generally worth more to advanced specialists.

Date	Mintage	F	VF	XF	Unc
1947/5B	Inc. above	2.00	4.00	7.50	20.00
1947B	Inc. above	2.00	4.00	7.50	20.00
1948/5B	3,629,000	0.75	1.50	5.00	15.00
1948B	Inc. above	0.65	1.25	3.00	10.00
1949/5B	5,923,000	3.00	6.50	12.50	28.00
1949B	Inc. above	0.65	1.25	2.25	8.00
1950B	6,783,000	0.65	1.50	2.75	9.00
1951/5B	5,185,000	0.65	1.50	2.75	9.00
1951B	Inc. above	0.65	1.25	2.25	8.00
1952B	1,060,000	1.25	2.25	4.50	13.00

KM# 212.1 10 CENTAVOS

Copper-Nickel, 18 mm. **Mint:** Bogota **Obverse:** Arms above date **Reverse:** Head of Chief Calarca right divides denomination

Date	Mintage	F	VF	XF	Unc
1952B	6,035,000	0.35	1.00	3.50	15.00
1953B	6,985,000	0.25	0.50	1.50	6.00

KM# 212.2 10 CENTAVOS

Copper-Nickel, 18.5 mm. **Mint:** Bogota **Obverse:** Arms above date **Reverse:** Head of Chief Calarca right divides denomination **Note:** Varieties exist.

Date	Mintage	F	VF	XF	Unc
1954B	13,006,000	0.20	0.50	1.25	3.00
1955B	9,968,000	0.20	0.50	1.25	3.00
1956	36,010,000	0.10	0.20	0.50	1.50
1956B	—	0.10	0.20	0.50	1.50
1958	41,695,000	—	—	—	—
1959	36,653,000	0.10	0.20	0.50	1.50
1960	32,290,000	0.10	0.20	0.50	2.00
1961	17,780,000	0.10	0.20	0.50	2.00
1962	8,930,000	0.10	0.20	0.50	2.00
1963	37,540,000	0.10	0.20	0.50	1.50
1964	61,672,000	0.10	0.20	0.50	1.50
1965	12,804,000	0.10	0.25	0.75	3.00
1966 Large date	23,544,000	0.10	0.20	0.50	1.50

KM# 221 10 CENTAVOS

Copper-Nickel **Subject:** Uprising Sesquicentennial **Obverse:** Arms above two dates **Reverse:** Head of Chief Calarca right divides denomination

Date	Mintage	F	VF	XF	Unc
ND(1960)	1,000,000	1.00	2.00	3.50	8.00

KM# 226 10 CENTAVOS

Nickel Clad Steel, 18.3 mm. **Obverse:** Head of Santander right, date below **Reverse:** Denomination within circular wreath

Date	Mintage	F	VF	XF	Unc
1967	26,980,000	—	0.10	0.20	1.00
1968	23,670,000	—	0.10	0.20	1.00
1969	29,450,000	—	0.10	0.20	1.00

KM# 236 10 CENTAVOS

Nickel Clad Steel, 18.3 mm. **Obverse:** Head of Santander right, date below **Reverse:** Denomination within wreath

Date	Mintage	F	VF	XF	Unc
1969	Inc. above	—	0.10	0.20	1.00
1970	38,935,000	—	0.10	0.20	1.00
1971	53,314,000	—	0.10	0.20	1.00

KM# 243 10 CENTAVOS

Nickel Clad Steel, 18.3 mm. **Obverse:** Legend divided after REPUBLICA

Date	Mintage	F	VF	XF	Unc
1970	—	—	—	—	—
1971	—	—	—	—	—

KM# 253 10 CENTAVOS

Nickel Clad Steel **Obverse:** Head right, date below, continuous legend **Reverse:** Denomination within wreath **Note:** Varieties exist.

Date	Mintage	F	VF	XF	Unc
1972	58,000,000	—	0.10	0.15	0.35
1973	46,549,000	—	0.10	0.15	0.35
1974	49,740,000	—	0.10	0.15	0.35
1975	46,037,000	—	0.10	0.15	0.35
1976	46,084,000	—	0.10	0.15	0.35
1977	8,127,000	—	0.10	0.15	0.35
1978	97,081,000	—	0.10	0.15	0.35
1980	18,929,000	—	0.10	0.15	0.35

KM# 197 20 CENTAVOS

5.0000 g., 0.9000 Silver .1446 oz. ASW **Obverse:** Head of Simon Bolivar right, date below **Reverse:** Arms, denomination above

Date	Mintage	F	VF	XF	Unc
1911	1,206,000	2.00	3.50	7.50	17.50
1913	1,630,000	2.00	3.50	7.50	22.50
1914	2,560,000	2.00	3.50	9.00	25.00
1920 Wide date	1,242,000	2.50	6.00	12.50	32.50
1920 Narrow date	Inc. above	2.50	6.00	12.50	32.50
1921	372,000	7.00	15.00	35.00	85.00
1922	45,000	30.00	55.00	85.00	225
1933B	330,000	3.50	7.50	15.00	35.00
Note: Mint mark on obverse					
1933B	Inc. above	12.50	25.00	45.00	125
Note: Mint mark on reverse					
1933B	Inc. above	5.00	10.00	20.00	50.00
Note: Mint mark on both sides					
1938/1	1,410,000	4.00	8.00	17.00	35.00
1938	Inc. above	2.25	5.00	10.00	22.00
1941	—	2.50	6.00	12.00	28.00
1942	155,000	9.00	20.00	32.50	65.00
1942B	Inc. above	2.00	3.50	7.50	20.00
Note: Mint mark on reverse					

KM# 208.1 20 CENTAVOS

5.0000 g., 0.5000 Silver .0803 oz. ASW **Obverse:** Francisco de Paula Santander **Reverse:** Mint mark in field below CENTAVOS **Designer:** Gilroy Roberts

Date	Mintage	F	VF	XF	Unc
1945B	1,675,000	1.25	3.00	7.00	15.00
1945BB	Inc. above	6.00	12.00	25.00	50.00
Note: 1945BB has extra B on wreath at bottom					
1946/5B	6,599,000	1.25	2.50	6.50	15.00
1946B	Inc. above	1.50	3.00	9.00	20.00
1947/5B	9,708,000	3.00	6.00	12.00	28.00
1947B	—	3.00	6.00	12.00	28.00

KM# 208.3 20 CENTAVOS

5.0000 g., 0.5000 Silver .0803 oz. ASW **Obverse:** Francisco de Paula Santander **Reverse:** Without mint mark **Designer:** Gilroy Roberts

Date	Mintage	F	VF	XF	Unc
1946(m)	—	3.00	7.50	15.00	32.50
1946/5(m)	—	3.75	9.50	16.50	37.50
1947(m)	1,748,000	5.00	8.50	15.00	35.00

KM# 208.2 20 CENTAVOS

5.0000 g., 0.5000 Silver .0803 oz. ASW **Obverse:** Francisco de Paula Santander **Reverse:** Mint mark on wreath at top **Designer:** Gilroy Roberts **Note:** Almost all dies for 1946-1951 show at least faint traces of overdating from 1945. Coins with absolutely no underdate, and those with very bold underdate, are generally worth more to advanced specialists. Varieties exist.

Date	Mintage	F	VF	XF	Unc
1947/5B	Inc. above	5.00	10.00	20.00	50.00
1948/5B	Inc. above	1.25	3.00	5.00	12.00
1948B	Inc. above	1.50	3.00	5.00	14.00
1949/5B	403,000	3.75	8.50	17.50	45.00
1949B	Inc. above	2.50	5.00	10.00	32.50
1950/45B	1,899,000	2.75	6.75	15.00	50.00
1950B	Inc. above	2.75	6.00	13.50	37.50
1951/45B	7,498,000	1.25	3.00	6.50	13.50
1951B	Inc. above	1.25	3.00	6.00	12.50

KM# 213 20 CENTAVOS

5.0000 g., 0.3000 Silver .0482 oz. ASW **Obverse:** Arms, date below **Reverse:** Bust of Simon Bolivar left, divides denomination

Date	Mintage	F	VF	XF	Unc
1952B Rare	3,887	—	—	—	—
1953B	17,819,000	1.00	1.50	3.50	7.50

KM# 215.1 20 CENTAVOS

Copper-Nickel, 23.4 mm. **Obverse:** Head of Simon Bolivar right, small date below **Reverse:** Denomination above arms, half circle of stars below

Date	Mintage	F	VF	XF	Unc
1956	39,778,000	0.10	0.15	0.50	1.50
1959	44,779,000	0.10	0.15	0.50	1.50
1961	10,740,000	0.15	0.25	0.75	2.50

KM# 215.2 20 CENTAVOS

Copper-Nickel, 23.4 mm. **Obverse:** Head of Simon Bolivar right, large date below **Reverse:** Denomination above arms, half circle of stars below

Date	Mintage	F	VF	XF	Unc
1963	12,035,000	—	0.10	0.50	1.50
1964	29,075,000	—	0.10	0.50	1.50
1965	19,180,000	0.10	0.25	0.75	2.50

KM# 215.3 20 CENTAVOS

Copper-Nickel, 23.4 mm. **Obverse:** Head of Simon Bolivar right, medium date **Reverse:** Denomination above arms, half circle of stars below

Date	Mintage	F	VF	XF	Unc
1966	23,060,000	0.10	0.15	0.50	1.50

KM# 222 20 CENTAVOS

Copper-Nickel **Subject:** Uprising Sesquicentennial **Obverse:** Head right divides dates below **Reverse:** Denomination above arms, half circle of stars below

Date	Mintage	F	VF	XF	Unc
ND(1960)	500,000	0.75	1.50	3.00	8.00

KM# 224 20 CENTAVOS

Copper-Nickel **Obverse:** Arms above denomination **Reverse:** Bust of Jorge Eliecer Gaitan left, date below

Date	Mintage	F	VF	XF	Unc
1965	1,000,000	—	0.10	0.50	1.50

KM# 227 20 CENTAVOS

Nickel Clad Steel **Obverse:** Head of Santander right, large date and legend **Reverse:** Denomination within wreath

Date	Mintage	F	VF	XF	Unc
1967	15,720,000	—	0.10	0.20	1.00
1968	26,680,000	—	0.10	0.20	1.00
1969	22,470,000	—	0.10	0.20	1.00

KM# 237 20 CENTAVOS

Nickel Clad Steel **Obverse:** Refined detailed portrait of Santander right, with smaller date and legend **Reverse:** Denomination within wreath

Date	Mintage	F	VF	XF	Unc
1969	Inc. above	—	—	—	—
1970	44,358,000	—	0.10	0.20	1.00

KM# 245 20 CENTAVOS

Nickel Clad Steel **Obverse:** Head right, legend divided after REPUBLICA DE **Reverse:** Denomination within wreath

Date	Mintage	F	VF	XF	Unc
1971	77,526,000	—	—	0.10	0.35

KM# 246.1 20 CENTAVOS

Nickel Clad Steel **Obverse:** Head right, date below, legend continuous **Reverse:** Denomination within wreath **Note:** Varieties exist with and without dots.

Date	Mintage	F	VF	XF	Unc
1971	Inc. above	—	—	0.10	0.35
1972	41,891,000	—	—	0.10	0.35
1973/1	41,440,000	—	—	0.10	0.35
1973	Inc. above	—	—	0.15	0.50
1974/1	45,941,000	—	—	0.35	1.00
1974	Inc. above	—	—	0.10	0.35
1975	28,635,000	—	—	0.10	0.35
1976	29,590,000	—	—	0.10	0.35
1977	2,054,000	—	—	0.15	0.50
1978	10,630,000	—	—	0.10	0.35

KM# 246.2 20 CENTAVOS

Nickel Clad Steel **Obverse:** Head right, date below, smaller letters in legend **Reverse:** Wreath with larger 20 and smaller CENTAVOS

Date	Mintage	F	VF	XF	Unc
1979	16,655,000	—	—	0.10	0.20

KM# 267 25 CENTAVOS

Aluminum-Bronze **Obverse:** Head of Simon Bolivar right, date below **Reverse:** Denomination within lines

Date	Mintage	F	VF	XF	Unc
1979	88,874,000	—	0.10	0.15	0.25
1980	46,168,000	—	0.10	0.15	0.25

KM# 186.2 50 CENTAVOS

12.5000 g., 0.8350 Silver .3356 oz. ASW **Mint:** Bogota **Obverse:** Liberty head left, incuse lettering on headband, date below **Reverse:** Denomination above arms **Edge Lettering:** DIOS LEI LIBERTAD **Note:** Similar to KM#186.1a.

Date	Mintage	VG	F	VF	XF	Unc
1906	446,000	6.50	13.50	25.00	40.00	75.00
1907	1,126,000	5.50	8.50	15.00	30.00	60.00
1908/7	871,000	20.00	30.00	45.00	65.00	135
1908	Inc. above	6.00	10.00	18.00	35.00	70.00

KM# 192 50 CENTAVOS

12.5000 g., 0.8350 Silver .3356 oz. ASW **Mint:** Philadelphia **Obverse:** Liberty head left, date below **Reverse:** Denomination above arms

Date	Mintage	F	VF	XF	Unc
1902(P)	960,000	13.50	27.50	50.00	125

KM# 193.1 50 CENTAVOS

12.5000 g., 0.9000 Silver .3617 oz. ASW **Obverse:** Simon Bolivar, sharper featured head right, date below **Reverse:** Denomination above arms, left wing and flags far from legend **Note:** Struck at Birmingham and Bogota mints. Date varieties exist.

Date	Mintage	F	VF	XF	Unc
1912	1,207,000	6.00	12.50	35.00	75.00
1912 Proof; rare	—	—	—	—	—
1913	417,000	6.00	12.50	35.00	75.00
1914 Closed 4	769,000	7.00	15.00	40.00	85.00
1915 Small date	946,000	6.00	12.50	30.00	70.00
1915 Small date; Proof; rare	—	—	—	—	—
1915 Large date	Inc. above	—	—	—	—
1915 Proof; rare	—	—	—	—	—
1916 Small date	1,060,000	5.00	10.00	22.50	50.00
1917 Normal 7	99,000	10.00	20.00	45.00	90.00
1917 Foot on 7	Inc. above	10.00	20.00	45.00	90.00
1917 Curved top	Inc. above	10.00	20.00	50.00	100
1918	400,000	5.00	10.00	25.00	75.00
1919	nc. above	15.00	25.00	40.00	85.00
1922	150,000	10.00	15.00	30.00	75.00
1923	150,000	10.00	15.00	30.00	75.00
1931/21B	—	5.00	10.00	22.50	50.00
1931B	700,000	5.00	10.00	22.50	50.00
1931	Inc. above	65.00	120	185	350
1932/12B	300,000	8.00	14.00	30.00	75.00
1932/22B	Inc. above	7.00	15.00	35.00	80.00
1932B	Inc. above	5.00	10.00	22.50	50.00
1932 Flat top 3, no B	Inc. above	20.00	30.00	45.00	90.00
1933/13B	1,000,000	5.00	10.00	20.00	45.00
1933/23B	Inc. above	5.00	10.00	25.00	50.00
1933B	Inc. above	BV	5.00	10.00	28.00

KM# 193.2 50 CENTAVOS

12.5000 g., 0.9000 Silver .3617 oz. ASW **Mint:** Medellin **Obverse:** Simon Bolivar, sharper featured head right, date below **Reverse:** Denomination above arms, larger letters, left wing and flags close to legend **Note:** Date varieties exist.

Date	Mintage	F	VF	XF	Unc
1914 Open 4	—	5.00	10.00	30.00	80.00
1915/4 Large date	—	45.00	75.00	125	200
1915 Large date	—	55.00	100	150	250
1918/4	—	10.00	20.00	35.00	75.00
1918	—	5.00	10.00	25.00	65.00
1919/8	—	7.50	15.00	30.00	70.00
1919	—	7.50	15.00	30.00	70.00
1921	300,000	7.50	15.00	30.00	70.00
1922	—	5.00	10.00	25.00	65.00
1932/22M	1,200,000	20.00	40.00	70.00	145
1932M	Inc. above	BV	5.00	15.00	30.00
1932 Round top 3, no M	Inc. above	18.00	35.00	60.00	125
1933M	800,000	BV	7.50	25.00	50.00
1933/23 Round top 3s, no M	Inc. above	15.00	25.00	35.00	75.00

KM# 274 50 CENTAVOS

12.5000 g., 0.9000 Silver .3617 oz. ASW **Obverse:** Simon Bolivar, rounded featured head right, date below **Reverse:** Denomination above arms **Note:** Struck at the Philadelphia and San Francisco mints.

Date	Mintage	F	VF	XF	Unc
1916(P)	1,300,000	BV	7.50	25.00	50.00
1917(P)	142,000	6.00	18.00	37.50	75.00
1921(P)	1,000,000	BV	6.00	20.00	45.00
1922(P)	3,000,000	BV	5.00	15.00	40.00
1934(S)	10,000,000	BV	5.00	15.00	40.00

KM# 209 50 CENTAVOS

12.5000 g., 0.5000 Silver .2009 oz. ASW **Mint:** Bogota **Obverse:** Simon Bolivar armored bust left, date below **Reverse:** Denomination within circular wreath

Date	Mintage	F	VF	XF	Unc
1947/6B	1,240,000	4.50	7.00	20.00	50.00
1947B	Inc. above	10.00	15.00	30.00	75.00
1948/6B	707,000	4.50	7.00	20.00	50.00
1948B/B inverted B	Inc. above	25.00	40.00	60.00	120
1948B	Inc. above	7.50	12.50	25.00	65.00

KM# 217 50 CENTAVOS

Copper-Nickel **Obverse:** Denomination below arms **Reverse:** Simon Bolivar head right, date below **Note:** Various sizes of date exist.

Date	Mintage	F	VF	XF	Unc
1958	3,596,000	0.15	0.50	1.25	3.50
1958 Medal Rotation	Inc. above	6.00	12.00	22.00	40.00
1959	13,466,000	0.15	0.30	1.00	3.00
1959 Medal Rotation	Inc. above	2.00	3.50	6.00	10.00
1960	4,360,000	0.15	0.30	1.50	4.00
1961	3,260,000	0.15	0.30	1.50	4.00
1962	2,336,000	0.15	0.30	1.50	4.00
1963	4,098,000	0.15	0.30	1.00	3.00
1964	9,274,000	0.15	0.30	1.00	3.00
1965	5,800,000	0.15	0.30	1.00	3.00
1966	2,820,000	0.15	0.30	1.00	3.00

KM# 223 50 CENTAVOS

Copper-Nickel **Subject:** Uprising Sesquicentennial **Obverse:** Denomination below arms **Reverse:** Head right, two dates below

Date	Mintage	F	VF	XF	Unc
ND(1960)	200,000	1.50	3.00	7.50	15.00

KM# 225 50 CENTAVOS

Copper-Nickel, 30.5 mm. **Obverse:** Arms and denomination **Reverse:** Jorge Eliecer Gaitan bust left, date below

Date	Mintage	F	VF	XF	Unc
1965	600,000	0.10	0.20	0.50	1.50

KM# 228 50 CENTAVOS

Nickel Clad Steel, 30 mm. **Obverse:** Head of Francisco de Paula Santander right, date below **Reverse:** Denomination within circular wreath

Date	Mintage	F	VF	XF	Unc
1967	3,460,000	0.10	0.15	0.25	1.00
1968	5,460,000	0.10	0.15	0.25	1.00
1969	1,590,000	0.10	0.15	0.25	1.00

KM# 244.1 50 CENTAVOS

Nickel Clad Steel **Obverse:** Head right, flat truncation, date below **Reverse:** Denomination within wreath, 5 far from wreath **Shape:** 12-sided **Note:** Date varieties exist.

Date	Mintage	F	VF	XF	Unc
1970	30,906,000	—	0.10	0.15	0.50
1971	32,650,000	—	0.10	0.15	0.50
1972	25,290,000	—	0.10	0.15	0.50
1973	8,060,000	—	0.10	0.15	0.50
1974	19,541,000	—	0.10	0.15	0.50
1975	4,325,000	—	0.10	0.15	0.60
1976	13,181,000	—	0.10	0.15	0.45
1977	10,413,000	—	0.10	0.15	0.45
1978	10,736,000	—	0.10	0.15	0.45

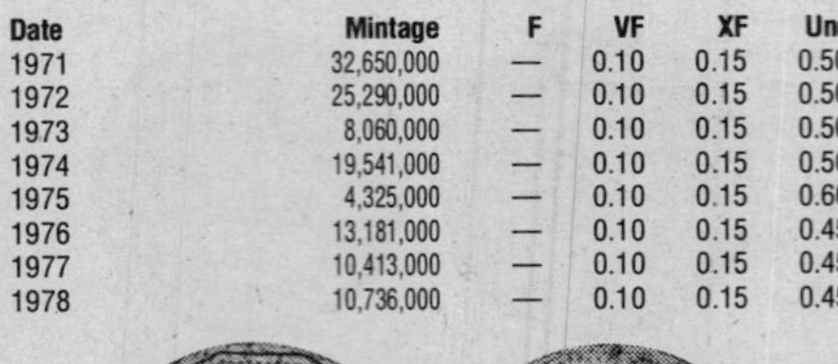

KM# 244.3 50 CENTAVOS

Nickel Clad Steel **Obverse:** Head right, angled truncation, date below **Reverse:** Denomination within wreath, 5 far from wreath **Shape:** Twelve sided **Note:** Mule.

Date	Mintage	F	VF	XF	Unc
1979	—	10.00	20.00	30.00	50.00

KM# 244.2 50 CENTAVOS

Nickel Clad Steel **Obverse:** Head right, angled truncation, date below **Reverse:** Denomination within wreath, 5 close to wreath **Shape:** 12-sided **Note:** Various sizes of dates exist.

Date	Mintage	F	VF	XF	Unc
1979	22,584,000	—	0.10	0.15	0.45
1980	16,433,000	—	0.10	0.15	0.45
1982	10,107,000	—	0.10	0.15	0.45

KM# 216 PESO

25.0000 g., 0.9000 Silver .7234 oz. ASW, 37 mm. **Mint:** Mexico City **Subject:** 200th Anniversary of Popayan Mint **Obverse:** Arms above denomination **Reverse:** Monument, sprays flank, date above

Date	Mintage	F	VF	XF	Unc
ND(1956)(Mo)	12,000	BV	10.00	15.00	25.00

KM# 229 PESO

Copper-Nickel, 30 mm. **Obverse:** Head of Simon Bolivar right, date below **Reverse:** Denomination within circular wreath **Shape:** 10-sided

Date	Mintage	F	VF	XF	Unc
1967	4,000,000	0.15	0.30	0.50	1.00

KM# 258.1 PESO

Copper-Nickel, 25.3 mm. **Obverse:** Bust of Simon Bolivar 3/4 facing, small date below **Reverse:** Denomination, ears of corn flank

Date	Mintage	F	VF	XF	Unc
1974	56,020,000	—	0.10	0.15	0.50
1975 medium date	117,714,000	—	0.10	0.15	0.40
1976	98,728,000	—	0.10	0.15	0.40

KM# 258.2 PESO

Copper-Nickel **Obverse:** Bust of Simon Bolivar 3/4 facing, large date below **Reverse:** Denomination, ears of corn flank

Date	Mintage	F	VF	XF	Unc
1976	Inc. above	—	0.10	0.15	0.40
1977	62,083,000	—	0.10	0.15	0.40
1978	48,624,000	—	0.10	0.15	0.40
1979	83,908,000	—	0.10	0.15	0.40
1980	93,406,000	—	0.10	0.15	0.40
1981	65,219,000	—	0.10	0.15	0.40

KM# 263 2 PESOS

Bronze, 23.8 mm. **Obverse:** Bust of Simon Bolivar 3/4 facing, date below **Reverse:** Denomination within wreath **Note:** Varieties exist.

Date	Mintage	F	VF	XF	Unc
1977	76,661,000	0.10	0.15	0.25	0.50
1978	69,575,000	0.10	0.15	0.25	0.50
1979	56,537,000	0.10	0.15	0.25	0.50
1980	108,521,000	0.10	0.15	0.25	0.50
1981	40,368,000	0.10	0.15	0.25	0.50
1983	8,358,000	0.10	0.15	0.25	0.50
1987	—	0.10	0.15	0.25	0.50
1988	16,200,000	0.10	0.15	0.25	0.50

KM# 194 2-1/2 PESOS

3.9940 g., 0.9170 Gold .1177 oz. AGW **Obverse:** Native, date below **Reverse:** Arms and denomination

Date	Mintage	F	VF	XF	Unc
1913	18,000	—	BV	85.00	125

KM# 200 2-1/2 PESOS

3.9940 g., 0.9170 Gold .1177 oz. AGW **Obverse:** Simon Bolivar large head right, date below **Reverse:** Arms and denomination

Date	Mintage	F	VF	XF	Unc
1919A	—	—	BV	80.00	110

Note: Two varieties, with large or small first 1 in date

Date	Mintage	F	VF	XF	Unc
1919B	—	—	—	—	—
1919	34,000	—	BV	80.00	110
1920/19A	—	—	BV	80.00	110
1920A	—	—	BV	80.00	110
1920	34,000	—	BV	90.00	150

KM# 203 2-1/2 PESOS
3.9940 g., 0.9170 Gold .1177 oz. AGW **Obverse:** Simon Bolivar small head, MEDELLIN below, date at bottom **Reverse:** Arms and denomination

Date	Mintage	F	VF	XF	Unc
1924	—	—	BV	80.00	110
1925 Rare	—	—	—	—	—
1927	—	—	BV	85.00	125
1928	14,000	—	BV	100	175
1929 Rare	—	—	—	—	—

KM# 195.2 5 PESOS
7.9881 g., 0.9170 Gold .2355 oz. AGW **Obverse:** Native, date below **Reverse:** Arms and denomination **Note:** Medallic die rotation.

Date	Mintage	F	VF	XF	Unc
1913	Inc. above	—	—	BV	165
1917	43,000	—	—	BV	165
1918	Inc. above	—	—	BV	165
1919	Inc. above	—	—	BV	165

KM# 195.1 5 PESOS
7.9881 g., 0.9170 Gold .2355 oz. AGW **Obverse:** Native, date below **Reverse:** Arms and denomination **Note:** Various rotations of dies exist.

Date	Mintage	F	VF	XF	Unc
1913	17,000	—	—	150	220
1918/3	423,000	—	—	BV	180
1918	Inc. above	—	—	BV	180
1919	2,181,000	—	—	BV	150
1919 Long-tail 9	Inc. above	—	—	BV	150
1919 Dot over 9	Inc. above	—	—	—	180

KM# 201.1 5 PESOS
7.9881 g., 0.9170 Gold .2355 oz. AGW **Obverse:** Simon Bolivar, large head right **Reverse:** Arms and denomination **Note:** 1920A dated coins come with mint mark centered or on right side of coat of arms; 1923B dated coins come with B on the left or right of coat of arms. The 1923B mint mark to right carries a 25% premium in value. Various rotations of dies exist.

Date	Mintage	F	VF	XF	Unc
1919	Inc. above	—	—	BV	150
Note: Narrow or wide dates, with multiple varieties of numeral alignment					
1919A	Inc. above	—	—	BV	150
Note: Narrow or wide date					
1919B	—	—	—	BV	155
1920	870,000	—	—	BV	150
1920A	Inc. above	—	—	BV	150
Note: Placement of A below coat of arms varies					
1920B	108,000	—	—	BV	155
Note: Placement of B varies					
1921A	—	—	—	—	—
1922B	29,000	—	—	BV	150
Note: Two varieties known, with B touching or separated from coat of arms					
1923B	74,000	—	—	BV	150
1924B	705,000	—	—	BV	150
Note: Placement of B varies					

KM# 201.2 5 PESOS
7.9881 g., 0.9170 Gold .2355 oz. AGW **Obverse:** Simon Bolivar, large head **Reverse:** Arms and denomination **Note:** Medallic die rotation.

Date	Mintage	F	VF	XF	Unc
1920	Inc. above	—	—	BV	150

KM# 204 5 PESOS
7.9881 g., 0.9170 Gold .2355 oz. AGW **Obverse:** Simon Bolivar, small head, MEDELLIN below, date at bottom **Reverse:** Arms and denomination **Note:** 1924 dated coins have several varieties in size of 2 and 4. 1925 dated coins exist with an Arabic and a Spanish style 5. 1930 dated coins have three varieties in size and placement of 3.

Date	Mintage	F	VF	XF	Unc
1924 Large 2	120,000	—	—	BV	155
1924 Large 4	Inc. above	—	—	BV	150
1924 Small 4	Inc. above	—	—	BV	155
1924 MFDELLIN	Inc. above	—	—	BV	165
1925/4	668,000	—	—	BV	150
1925 MFDELLIN	Inc. above	—	—	BV	150
Note: Wide or narrow date					
1925 MFDFLLIN	Inc. above	—	—	BV	150
Note: Wide or narrow date					
1926	383,000	—	—	BV	150
1926 MFDFLLIN	Inc. above	—	—	BV	150
1926 MFDFLLIN	Inc. above	—	—	BV	150
Note: With large 6 in date					
1927 MFDFLLIN	365,000	—	—	BV	150
Note: Wide or narrow date					
1928 MFDFLLIN	314,000	—	—	BV	150
Note: Narrow or wide date with large or normal 2					
1929 MFDFLLIN	321,000	—	—	BV	155
Note: Narrow or wide date					
1930 MFDFLLIN	502,000	—	—	BV	150
Note: Varieties known with aligned date or dropped 3 in date					

KM# 230 5 PESOS
Copper-Nickel, 35.5 mm. **Subject:** International Eucharistic Congress **Obverse:** Denomination within wheat stalks, date below **Reverse:** Design within circle, within square, at center

Date	Mintage	F	VF	XF	Unc
1968B	660,000	0.25	0.50	0.75	1.75

KM# 247 5 PESOS
Nickel Clad Steel, 30 mm. **Subject:** 6th Pan-American Games in Cali **Obverse:** Torches flank denomination at center, date below **Reverse:** Games logo

Date	Mintage	F	VF	XF	Unc
1971	2,000,000	0.15	0.35	0.60	1.50

KM# 268 5 PESOS
Bronze, 26.3 mm. **Obverse:** Seated figure right **Reverse:** Denomination and buildings

Date	Mintage	F	VF	XF	Unc
1980	146,268,000	0.15	0.35	0.60	1.25
1.981	9,148,000	0.15	0.35	0.60	1.25
1.982	—	0.15	0.35	0.75	1.50
1983	84,107,000	0.15	0.35	0.60	1.25
1985	—	0.15	0.35	0.60	1.25
1986	14,700,000	0.15	0.35	0.60	1.25
1987	—	0.15	0.35	0.60	1.25
1988 Small date	45,000,000	0.15	0.35	0.60	1.25
1988 Large inverted date	Inc. above	0.15	0.35	0.60	1.25
1989	—	0.15	0.35	0.60	1.25

KM# 280 5 PESOS
2.6000 g., Copper-Aluminum-Nickel, 17.3 mm. **Obverse:** Arms above date **Reverse:** Denomination within wreath **Note:** Varieties exist, such as 1989 where some have 72 beads on the obverse and reverse and some have 66 beads.

Date	Mintage	F	VF	XF	Unc
1989	—	—	—	—	0.50
1990	—	—	—	—	0.50
1991	—	—	—	—	0.50
1992	—	—	—	—	0.35
1993	—	—	—	—	0.35

KM# 202 10 PESOS
15.9761 g., 0.9170 Gold .4710 oz. AGW **Obverse:** Head of Simon Bolivar right, date below **Reverse:** Arms and denomination

Date	Mintage	F	VF	XF	Unc
1919	101,000	—	BV	315	365
1924B	55,000	—	BV	315	365
Note: Varieties with aligned date and dropped 4 in date					

KM# 270 10 PESOS
Copper-Nickel-Zinc, 28 mm. **Obverse:** Figure on horseback and standing, date at left **Reverse:** Map showing San Andreas Island and Providencia, denomination below **Note:** Date varieties exist.

Date	Mintage	F	VF	XF	Unc
1.981	104,554,000	—	0.15	0.25	1.25
1.982	83,605,000	—	0.15	0.25	1.25
1983	104,051,000	—	0.15	0.25	1.25
1985	80,000,000	—	0.15	0.25	1.25
1988	50,700,000	—	0.15	0.25	1.25
1989	—	—	0.15	0.25	1.25

KM# 281.1 10 PESOS
3.3000 g., Copper-Nickel-Zinc, 18.75 mm. **Obverse:** Flagged arms, date below **Reverse:** Denomination within wreath, wide 10 (5mm) - wreath nearly touches beads in rim **Note:** Varieties exist.

Date	Mintage	F	VF	XF	Unc
1989	—	—	—	—	0.75
1990	—	—	—	—	0.75
1991	—	—	—	—	0.75
1992	—	—	—	—	0.50
1993	—	—	—	—	0.50
1994	—	—	—	—	0.50

KM# 281.2 10 PESOS
3.3000 g., Copper-Nickel-Zinc, 18.75 mm. **Obverse:** Flagged arms, date below **Reverse:** Narrow 10 (4.5mm) - wreath is 1 mm away from beads in rim

Date	Mintage	F	VF	XF	Unc
1993	—	—	—	3.00	7.00
1994	—	—	—	3.00	7.00

KM# 271 20 PESOS
Aluminum-Bronze, 25 mm. **Obverse:** Vase, date below **Reverse:** Denomination within wreath **Note:** 1985 and 1988 coins exist with large and small dates.

Date	Mintage	F	VF	XF	Unc
1982	—	—	0.15	0.20	0.30
1984	64,066,000	—	0.15	0.20	0.30
1985	100,690,000	—	0.15	0.20	0.30
1986	18,300,000	—	0.15	0.20	0.30
1987	—	—	0.15	0.20	0.30
1988	72,000,000	—	0.15	0.20	0.30
1989	—	—	0.15	0.20	0.30

KM# 282.1 20 PESOS
3.6000 g., Copper-Aluminum-Nickel, 20.25 mm. **Obverse:** Flagged arms above date, 72 beads circle around the rim **Reverse:** Denomination within wreath **Note:** Varieties exist.

Date	Mintage	F	VF	XF	Unc
1989	—	—	—	—	0.75
1990	—	—	—	—	0.75
1991	—	—	—	—	0.75
1992	—	—	—	—	0.75
1993	—	—	—	—	0.75
1994	—	—	—	—	0.75

KM# 282.2 20 PESOS
3.6000 g., Copper-Aluminum-Nickel, 3.6 mm. **Obverse:** Flagged arms, 68 beads circle around the rim **Reverse:** Denomination within wreath

Date	Mintage	F	VF	XF	Unc
1994	—	—	—	—	0.50

KM# 272 50 PESOS
Copper-Nickel, 26.8 mm. **Subject:** National Constitution **Obverse:** Arms above denomination, sprigs flank date below **Reverse:** Building, stars below, within circle

Date	Mintage	F	VF	XF	Unc
1986	14,900,000	—	—	—	1.25
1987 Large date	—	—	—	—	1.25
1988 Small date	100,000,000	—	—	—	1.25
1989	—	—	—	—	1.25

KM# 283.1 50 PESOS
4.5000 g., Copper-Nickel-Zinc, 21.8 mm. **Obverse:** Flagged arms above date **Reverse:** Denomination within wreath, 66 beads circle around rim **Note:** Varieties exist.

Date	Mintage	F	VF	XF	Unc
1989	—	—	—	—	1.00
1990	—	—	—	—	1.00
1991	—	—	—	—	1.00
1992	—	—	—	—	1.00
1993	—	—	—	—	1.00
1994	—	—	—	—	1.00

KM# 283.2 50 PESOS
Copper-Nickel-Zinc **Obverse:** Flagged arms, date below **Reverse:** Denomination within wreath, 72 beads circle around rim

Date	Mintage	F	VF	XF	Unc
1990	—	—	—	—	1.00
1994	—	—	—	—	1.00

KM# 231 100 PESOS
4.3000 g., 0.9000 Gold .1244 oz. AGW **Subject:** International Eucharistic Congress **Obverse:** Arms divide denomination **Reverse:** Bust of Pope Paul VI left and Bogota's Cathedral at left, date below

Date	Mintage	F	VF	XF	Unc
1968 Proof	8,000	Value: 95.00			
1968	108,000	—	—	—	85.00

KM# 238 100 PESOS
4.3000 g., 0.9000 Gold .1244 oz. AGW **Subject:** Battle of Boyaca - Joachim Paris **Obverse:** Bust of Bolivar 3/4 facing **Reverse:** Bust of Paris 3/4 facing, dates above, denomination below

Date	Mintage	F	VF	XF	Unc
1969B Proof	6,000	Value: 100			
1969NI Proof	Inc. above	Value: 100			

KM# 248 100 PESOS
4.3000 g., 0.9000 Gold .1244 oz. AGW **Subject:** 6th Pan-American Games **Obverse:** Games logo, date below **Reverse:** Javelin thrower within circle, denomination below, 3/4 circle of athletes surround

Date	Mintage	F	VF	XF	Unc
1971 Proof	6,000	Value: 110			

KM# 285.1 100 PESOS
Brass **Obverse:** Flagged arms above date **Reverse:** Denomination within wreath, numerals 4.5mm tall

Date	Mintage	F	VF	XF	Unc
1992	—	—	—	—	1.75
1993	—	—	—	—	1.75
1994	—	—	—	—	1.75
1995	—	—	—	—	1.75

KM# 285.2 100 PESOS
Brass **Obverse:** Flagged arms above date **Reverse:** Denomination within wreath, numerals 6mm tall **Note:** Edge varieties exist.

Date	Mintage	F	VF	XF	Unc
1994	—	—	—	—	1.75
1995	—	—	—	—	1.75

KM# 232 200 PESOS
8.6000 g., 0.9000 Gold .2488 oz. AGW **Subject:** International Eucharistic Congress **Obverse:** Bust of Pope Paul VI left and Bogota's Cathedral at left, date below **Reverse:** Arms divide denomination

Date	Mintage	F	VF	XF	Unc
1968	108,000	—	—	—	165
1968 Proof	8,000	Value: 175			

KM# 239 200 PESOS
8.6000 g., 0.9000 Gold .2488 oz. AGW **Subject:** Battle of Boyaca - Carlos Soublette **Obverse:** Bust of Bolivar 3/4 facing **Reverse:** Bust of Soublette 3/4 facing, dates above, denomination below

Date	Mintage	F	VF	XF	Unc
1969B Proof	6,000	Value: 180			
1969NI Proof	Inc. above	Value: 180			

KM# 249 200 PESOS
8.6000 g., 0.9000 Gold .2488 oz. AGW **Subject:** 6th Pan-American Games in Cali **Obverse:** Games logo, date below **Reverse:** Runner within circle, denomination below, 3/4 circle of athletes surround

Date	Mintage	F	VF	XF	Unc
1971 Proof	6,000	Value: 190			

KM# 287 200 PESOS
Copper-Zinc-Nickel, 24.8 mm. **Obverse:** Denomination within lined circle, date below **Reverse:** Quimbaya artwork

Date	Mintage	F	VF	XF	Unc
1994	—	—	—	—	1.50
1995	—	—	—	—	1.50
1996	—	—	—	—	1.50

KM# 233 300 PESOS
12.9000 g., 0.9000 Gold .3733 oz. AGW **Subject:** International Eucharistic Congress **Obverse:** Bust of Pope Paul VI 3/4 left and Bogota's Cathedral at left, date below **Reverse:** Arms above denomination

Date	Mintage	F	VF	XF	Unc
1968	62,000	—	—	—	245
1968 Proof	8,000	Value: 260			

KM# 240 300 PESOS
12.9000 g., 0.9000 Gold .3733 oz. AGW **Subject:** Battle of Boyaca - Jose Anzoategui **Obverse:** Bust of Bolivar 3/4 facing **Reverse:** Bust of Anzoategui 3/4 facing, dates above, denomination below

Date	Mintage	F	VF	XF	Unc
1969NI Proof	Inc. above	Value: 265			
1969B Proof	6,000	Value: 265			

KM# 250 300 PESOS
12.9000 g., 0.9000 Gold .3733 oz. AGW **Subject:** 6th Pan-American Games **Obverse:** Games logo, date below **Reverse:** Two figures within circle, denomination below, 3/4 circle of athletes surround

Date	Mintage	F	VF	XF	Unc
1971 Proof	6,000	Value: 275			

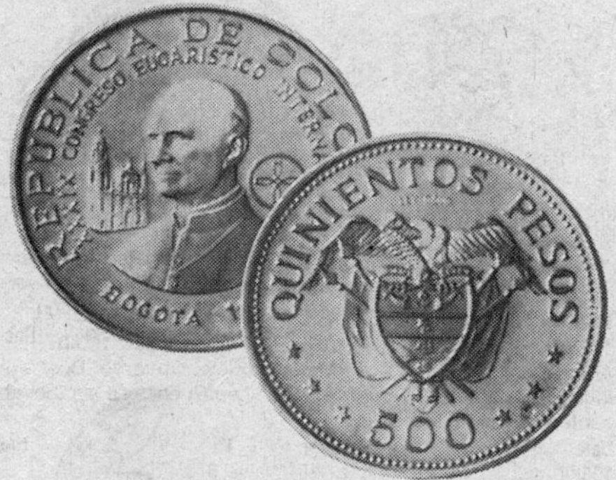

KM# 234 500 PESOS
21.5000 g., 0.9000 Gold .6221 oz. AGW **Subject:** International Eucharistic Congress **Obverse:** Bust of Pope Paul VI 3/4 left and Bogota's Cathedral left, date below **Reverse:** Arms above denomination

Date	Mintage	F	VF	XF	Unc
1968	14,000	—	—	—	415
1968 Proof	8,000	Value: 435			

KM# 241 500 PESOS
21.5000 g., 0.9000 Gold .6221 oz. AGW **Subject:** Battle of Boyaca **Obverse:** Bust of Simon Bolivar 3/4 facing **Reverse:** Bust of Juan Jose Rondon 3/4 facing, dates above, denomination below

Date	Mintage	F	VF	XF	Unc
ND(1969)B Proof	6,000	Value: 435			
ND(1969)NI Proof	Inc. above	Value: 435			

KM# 251 500 PESOS
21.5000 g., 0.9000 Gold .6221 oz. AGW **Subject:** 6th Pan-American Games in Cali **Obverse:** Games logo, date below **Reverse:** Two figures within circle, denomination below, 3/4 circle of athletes surround

Date	Mintage	F	VF	XF	Unc
1971 Proof	6,000	Value: 475			

KM# 264 500 PESOS
28.2800 g., 0.9250 Silver .8411 oz. ASW **Subject:** Conservation **Obverse:** Bust left, dates below **Reverse:** Orinoco Crocodile, denomination below

Date	Mintage	F	VF	XF	Unc
1978	2,678	—	—	—	28.00
1978 Proof	3,233	Value: 35.00			
1979 Proof	—	Value: 35.00			

KM# 286 500 PESOS
Bi-Metallic Aluminum-Bronze center in Copper-Nickel ring **Obverse:** Guacari tree within circle **Reverse:** Denomination within circle, date below

Date	Mintage	F	VF	XF	Unc
1993	—	—	—	—	4.00
1994	—	—	—	—	4.00
1995	—	—	—	—	4.00
1996	—	—	—	—	4.00
1997	—	—	—	—	4.00

KM# 265 750 PESOS
35.0000 g., 0.9250 Silver 1.0409 oz. ASW **Subject:** Conservation **Obverse:** Bust left **Reverse:** Chestnut-bellied hummingbird, denomination below

Date	Mintage	F	VF	XF	Unc
1978	2,656	—	—	—	28.00
1978 Proof	3,100	Value: 38.00			
1979 Proof	—	Value: 38.00			

KM# 254 1000 PESOS
4.3000 g., 0.9000 Gold .1244 oz. AGW **Subject:** 100th Anniversary - Birth of Guillermo Valencia **Obverse:** Shield above denomination **Reverse:** Head right

Date	Mintage	F	VF	XF	Unc
1973 Proof	10,003	Value: 85.00			

KM# 259 1000 PESOS
4.3000 g., 0.9000 Gold .1244 oz. AGW **Subject:** 450th Anniversary - City of Santa Marta **Obverse:** Bust 3/4 right, denomination below **Reverse:** Symbol at center, dates below

Date	Mintage	F	VF	XF	Unc
ND(1975) Proof	2,500	Value: 95.00			

KM# 260 1000 PESOS
4.3000 g., 0.9000 Gold .1244 oz. AGW **Subject:** Tricentennial - City of Medellin **Obverse:** City gate on shield, sprays flank, dates below **Reverse:** Symbol at center, denomination below **Shape:** Square

Date	Mintage	F	VF	XF	Unc
ND(1975) Proof	4,000	Value: 90.00			

KM# 288 1000 PESOS
Copper-Aluminum-Nickel **Obverse:** Armored bust 3/4 facing **Reverse:** Head right, arms divide dates above, denomination below **Edge:** Reeded and lettered **Edge Lettering:** CULTURA SINU MIL PESOS

Date	Mintage	F	VF	XF	Unc
1996	—	—	—	—	3.75
1997	—	—	—	—	3.75
1998	—	—	—	—	3.75

KM# 235 1500 PESOS
64.5000 g., 0.9000 Gold 1.8664 oz. AGW **Subject:** International Eucharistic Congress **Obverse:** Pope's bust 3/4 left, cathedral at left **Reverse:** Arms above denomination

Date	Mintage	F	VF	XF	Unc
1968	5,722	—	—	—	1,250
1968 Proof	8,000	Value: 1,300			

KM# 242 1500 PESOS
64.5000 g., 0.9000 Gold 1.8664 oz. AGW **Subject:** Battle of Boyaca **Obverse:** Armored bust of Bolivar 3/4 facing **Reverse:** Head of Santander right, arms divide dates above, denomination below

Date	Mintage	F	VF	XF	Unc
ND(1969)B Proof	6,000	Value: 1,350			
ND(1969)NI Proof	Inc. above	Value: 1,350			

KM# 252 1500 PESOS
64.5000 g., 0.9000 Gold 1.8664 oz. AGW **Subject:** 6th Pan-American Games **Obverse:** Games logo, date below **Reverse:** Symbols on raft within circle, denomination below, 3/4 circle of athletes surrounds

Date	Mintage	F	VF	XF	Unc
1971 Proof	6,000	Value: 1,450			

KM# 255 1500 PESOS
19.1000 g., 0.9000 Gold .5527 oz. AGW **Subject:** 50th Anniversary - Gold Museum of Central Bank of Bogota **Reverse:** Pre-Columbian urn made by Chibcha Indians

Date	Mintage	F	VF	XF	Unc
ND(1973) Proof	4,911	Value: 375			

KM# 257 2000 PESOS
12.9000 g., 0.9000 Gold .3733 oz. AGW **Subject:** 100th Anniversary - Birth of Guillermo Valencia **Obverse:** Shield above denomination, date below **Reverse:** Bust right, two dates below

Date	Mintage	F	VF	XF	Unc
1973 Proof	5,003	Value: 265			

KM# 261 2000 PESOS
8.6000 g., 0.9000 Gold .2488 oz. AGW **Subject:** 450th Anniversary - City of Santa Marta **Obverse:** Bust 3/4 right, denomination below **Reverse:** Symbol, dates below

Date	Mintage	F	VF	XF	Unc
ND(1975) Proof	2,500	Value: 175			

KM# 262 2000 PESOS
8.6000 g., 0.9000 Gold .2488 oz. AGW **Subject:** Tricentennial - City of Medellin **Obverse:** City gate on shield, sprays flank, two dates below **Reverse:** Symbol at center, denomination below **Shape:** Square

Date	Mintage	F	VF	XF	Unc
ND(1975) Proof	4,000	Value: 170			

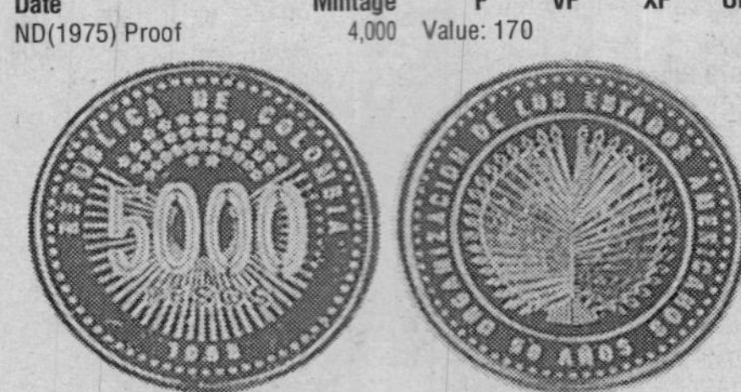

KM# 293 5000 PESOS
15.3000 g., Nickel **Subject:** 50th Anniversary - Organization of American States **Obverse:** Denomination, date below **Reverse:** Circle of flags

Date	Mintage	F	VF	XF	Unc
1998	—	—	—	—	5.50

KM# 284 10000 PESOS
27.0000 g., 0.9250 Silver .8029 oz. ASW **Series:** Ibero - American **Subject:** Bogota Mint **Obverse:** Arms at center, denomination below, shields surround **Reverse:** Ancient coin, two dates below

Date	Mintage	F	VF	XF	Unc
1991 Proof	70,000	Value: 55.00			

KM# 266 15000 PESOS
33.4370 g., 0.9000 Gold .9676 oz. AGW **Subject:** Conservation **Obverse:** Armored bust left **Reverse:** Ocelot left, denomination below

Date	Mintage	F	VF	XF	Unc
1978	490	—	—	—	700
1978 Proof	148	Value: 2,000			

KM# 276 15000 PESOS
17.2900 g., 0.9000 Gold .5000 oz. AGW **Subject:** 150th Anniversary - Death of Antonio Jose De Sucre **Obverse:** Armored bust 3/4 left divides dates **Reverse:** Cornucopias enclose symbol at center, denomination below

Date	Mintage	F	VF	XF	Unc
1980 Proof	250	Value: 375			

KM# 278 15000 PESOS
17.2900 g., 0.9000 Gold .5000 oz. AGW **Subject:** 150th Anniversary - Death of Jose Maria Cordova **Obverse:** Bust 3/4 facing, divides dates **Reverse:** Cornucopias enclose symbol at center, denomination below

Date	Mintage	F	VF	XF	Unc
1980 Proof	250	Value: 375			

KM# 289 20000 PESOS
8.6400 g., 0.9000 Gold .2500 oz. AGW **Subject:** Birth Centennial **Obverse:** Bust of Alfonso Lopez-Pumarejo facing divides dates **Reverse:** Building, denomination below

Date	Mintage	F	VF	XF	Unc
ND(1986) Proof	1,351	Value: 210			

KM# 269 30000 PESOS
34.5800 g., 0.9000 Gold 1.0007 oz. AGW **Subject:** Death of Bolivar **Obverse:** Funeral scene, dates below **Reverse:** Cornucopias flank symbol at center, denomination below

Date	Mintage	F	VF	XF	Unc
1980 Proof	500	Value: 725			

KM# 273 35000 PESOS
8.6400 g., 0.9000 Gold .2500 oz. AGW **Subject:** 100th Anniversary - Birth of President Santos **Obverse:** Bust facing divides dates **Reverse:** Inscription within wreath

Date	Mintage	F	VF	XF	Unc
ND(1988) Proof	900	Value: 210			

KM# 292 40000 PESOS
17.2800 g., 0.9000 Gold .5000 oz. AGW **Subject:** Centennial - Birthday of Alfonso Lopez-Pumarejo **Obverse:** Bust facing divides dates **Reverse:** Building, denomination below

Date	Mintage	F	VF	XF	Unc
ND(1986) Proof	1,351	Value: 410			

KM# 290 50000 PESOS
8.6400 g., 0.9000 Gold .2500 oz. AGW **Subject:** Centennial - Birthday of Mariano Ospina P **Obverse:** Portrait facing divides dates **Reverse:** Inscription within wreath

Date	Mintage	F	VF	XF	Unc
ND(1991) Proof	900	Value: 210			

KM# 277 70000 PESOS
17.2800 g., 0.9000 Gold .5000 oz. AGW **Subject:** 100th Anniversary - Birth of President Santos **Obverse:** Bust 3/4 facing divides dates **Reverse:** Inscription within wreath

Date	Mintage	F	VF	XF	Unc
ND(1988) Proof	600	Value: 380			

KM# 291 100000 PESOS
17.2800 g., 0.9000 Gold .5000 oz. AGW **Subject:** Centennial - Birthday of Mariano Ospina P **Obverse:** Head facing divides dates **Reverse:** Inscription within wreath

Date	Mintage	F	VF	XF	Unc
ND(1991) Proof	600	Value: 410			

INFLATIONARY COINAGE

P/M - Papel Moneda

Beginning about 1886, Colombia fell victim to rampant printing press inflation and a debased, vanishing coinage. Left without solid backing, the peso gradually fell until it was worth 1 centavo of the old silver-based currency. The copper-nickel 1, 2, and 5 peso p/m coins reflected this inflation, and later circulated at par with the newer 1, 2, and 5 centavo coins.

KM# A279 PESO (Papel Moneda)
2.0000 g., Copper-Nickel **Obverse:** Liberty head right **Reverse:** Denomination, p/m below, within wreath

Date	Mintage	F	VF	XF	Unc
1907 AM	2,860,000	1.25	3.50	13.50	37.50
1907 AM Proof	—	Value: 85.00			
1910 AM	1,205,000	3.50	9.00	17.50	45.00
1911 AM	2,816,000	2.75	7.50	17.50	45.00
1912 AM	6,094,000	2.00	7.00	16.50	40.00
1912 H Without crossbar	2,000,000	1.50	3.75	12.50	37.50
1912 H With crossbar	Inc. above	1.50	3.75	12.50	37.50
1913 AM	306,000	6.50	12.50	22.50	55.00
1914 AM	552,000	6.00	10.00	18.50	42.50
1916/4 AM	234,000	11.00	20.00	37.50	70.00
1916 AM	Inc. above	11.00	20.00	37.50	70.00

KM# B279 2 PESOS (Papel Moneda)
3.0000 g., Copper-Nickel **Obverse:** Liberty head right, date below **Reverse:** Denomination, p/m below, within wreath **Note:** Date varieties exist.

Date	Mintage	F	VF	XF	Unc
1907 AM	4,161,000	1.75	3.75	15.00	37.50
1907 AM Proof	—	Value: 100			
1910/07 AM	1,189,000	7.50	13.50	25.00	47.50

Date	Mintage	F	VF	XF	Unc
1910 AM	Inc. above	6.75	12.50	22.00	42.50
1914 AM	1,000,000	4.50	11.00	23.50	47.50

KM# 279 5 PESOS (Papel Moneda)
4.0000 g., Copper-Nickel **Obverse:** Liberty head right, date below **Reverse:** Denomination, p/m below, within wreath

Date	Mintage	F	VF	XF	Unc
1907 AM	6,143,000	2.50	9.00	20.00	40.00
1907 AM Proof	—	Value: 115			
1909 AM	4,000,000	2.75	8.50	18.50	40.00
1912 H	2,000,000	3.00	6.50	13.50	30.00
1912 AM	1,897,000	3.75	9.50	22.50	47.50
1913 AM	Inc. above	3.00	8.50	22.50	47.50
1914 AM	Inc. above	10.00	20.00	38.50	67.50

LEPROSARIUM COINAGE

Bogota Mint

Special coinage for use in the three government leper colonies of Agua de Dios, Cano de Lord, and Contratacion. The hospitals were closed in the late 1950s and patients were allowed to exchange these special coins for regular currency at any bank.

KM# L9 CENTAVO
2.0000 g., Copper-Nickel **Obverse:** LAZARETO on cross with circles at quarters, date below **Reverse:** Denomination within wreath

Date	Mintage	Good	VG	F	VF	XF
1921 RH	300,000	0.75	1.50	3.50	7.00	—

KM# L10 2 CENTAVOS
3.0000 g., Copper-Nickel **Obverse:** LAZARETO on cross with circles at quarters, date below **Reverse:** Denomination within wreath

Date	Mintage	Good	VG	F	VF	XF
1921 RH	350,000	0.50	0.65	1.75	6.75	—

KM# L1 2-1/2 CENTAVOS
1.3000 g., Brass **Obverse:** Denomination within circle, date below **Reverse:** LAZARETO on cross with circles at quarters

Date	Mintage	Good	VG	F	VF	XF
1901 Rare	20,000	—	—	—	—	3,500

Note: Only a few examples of this type are currently known to have survived.

KM# L2 5 CENTAVOS
Brass **Obverse:** Denomination within circle **Reverse:** LAZARETO on cross with circles at quarters, date below **Note:** Weight varies: 2.3-2.55 g.

Date	Mintage	Good	VG	F	VF	XF
1901 B	15,000	6.00	12.50	22.00	45.00	—

KM# L11 5 CENTAVOS
4.0000 g., Copper-Nickel **Obverse:** LAZARETO on cross with circles at quarters, date below **Reverse:** Denomination within wreath, large 5

Date	Mintage	Good	VG	F	VF	XF
1921 H	200,000	1.00	2.00	4.50	9.00	—

KM# L3 10 CENTAVOS
Brass **Obverse:** Denomination above date **Reverse:** LAZARETO on cross with circles at quarters **Note:** Weight varies: 3.3-3.69 g.

Date	Mintage	Good	VG	F	VF	XF
1901 B	10,000	10.00	15.00	28.00	50.00	—

KM# L12 10 CENTAVOS
5.1000 g., Copper-Nickel **Obverse:** LAZARETO on cross with circles at quarters, date below **Reverse:** Denomination within wreath

Date	Mintage	Good	VG	F	VF	XF
1921 RH	200,000	1.00	2.00	4.50	9.00	—

KM# L4 20 CENTAVOS
Brass **Obverse:** LAZARETO on cross with circles at quarters, date below **Reverse:** Denomination above arms **Note:** Weight varies: 4.85-5.1 g.

Date	Mintage	Good	VG	F	VF	XF
1901 B	30,000	10.00	15.00	28.00	50.00	—

KM# L5 50 CENTAVOS
Brass **Obverse:** LAZARETO on cross with circles at quarters, date below **Reverse:** Denomination above arms **Note:** Weight varies: 12-12.4 g.

Date	Mintage	Good	VG	F	VF	XF
1901 B	26,000	13.50	20.00	35.00	75.00	—

KM# L5a 50 CENTAVOS
Copper **Obverse:** LAZARETO on cross with circles at quarters, date below **Reverse:** Denomination above arms **Note:** Weight varies: 12-12.4 g.

Date	Mintage	Good	VG	F	VF	XF
1901 2 known	—	—	—	—	—	—

KM# L13 50 CENTAVOS
9.8000 g., Copper-Nickel

Date	Mintage	Good	VG	F	VF	XF
1921 RH	120,000	2.00	4.00	7.50	16.00	—

KM# L14 50 CENTAVOS
9.8000 g., Brass

Date	Mintage	Good	VG	F	VF	XF
1928 RH	50,000	2.00	4.50	9.00	18.00	—

KM# L14a 50 CENTAVOS
9.8000 g., Copper

Date	Mintage	Good	VG	F	VF	XF
1928 Proof; Rare	Inc. above	—	—	—	—	—

INFLATIONARY LEPROSARIUM COINAGE

P/M - Papel Moneda

1 Peso was equal in value to 1 Centavo of the old silver currency. It later circulated at par with the newer 1 Centavo coins.

KM# L6 PESO (Papel Moneda)

Copper-Nickel **Obverse:** Denomination, P.M., below, within wreath **Reverse:** LAZARETO within circle **Note:** Weight varies: 2.45-2.65 g.

Date	Mintage	Good	VG	F	VF	XF
1907/0	792,000	—	—	—	—	—
1907	Inc. above	5.00	10.00	20.00	45.00	—

KM# L7 5 PESOS (Papel Moneda)

4.7500 g., Copper-Nickel

Date	Mintage	Good	VG	F	VF	XF
1907	159,000	30.00	60.00	100	200	—

KM# L8 10 PESOS (Papal Moneda)

9.5000 g., Copper-Nickel

Date	Mintage	Good	VG	F	VF	XF
1907	129,000	40.00	75.00	125	250	—

PROVINCE OF SANTANDER

CIVIL WAR COINAGE

KM# A1 10 CENTAVOS

0.5000 g., Brass **Obverse:** Numeric denomination above 'C' **Note:** Uniface.

Date	Mintage	VG	F	VF	XF	Unc
ND(1902)	—	10.00	18.50	28.50	60.00	—

KM# A2 20 CENTAVOS

0.7000 g., Brass **Obverse:** Numeric denomination within "C" **Note:** Uniface.

Date	Mintage	VG	F	VF	XF	Unc
1902	—	18.00	35.00	55.00	80.00	—

KM# A3 50 CENTAVOS

1.4500 g., Brass **Obverse:** Numeric denomination within "C" **Note:** Uniface. Varieties exist in shape of "0" in denomination: a fully rounded zero commands double the listed values. Later 20th Century counterfeits are known.

Date	Mintage	VG	F	VF	XF	Unc
1902	—	1.75	3.75	7.00	15.00	—

Note: Varieties exist with round or elliptical "0" in denomination

PATTERNS

Including off metal strikes

KM#	Date	Mintage	Identification	Mkt Val
Pn84	1909	—	5 Centavos. Copper-Nickel.	—
Pn85	1913	—	5 Decimos. Thin Bolivar head.	—
Pn86	1913	—	5 Decimos. Thin Bolivar head, canceled obverse die.	—
Pn87	1913	—	2-1/2 Pesos. Gold. ENSAYO; KM#194.	—
Pn88	1913	—	5 Pesos. Gold. ENSAYO; KM#195.	—
Pn89	1915	—	2-1/2 Pesos. Gold. ENSAYO; KM#194.	—
Pn90	1917	—	5 Centavos. Copper-Nickel. PAZ on cap band; otherwise as KM#199.	—
Pn91	1917	—	5 Centavos. Copper-Nickel. KM#199.	—
Pn92	1923	—	2-1/2 Pesos. Gold. ENSAYO; KM#203.	2,450
Pn93	1923	—	2-1/2 Pesos. Silver. ESSAI; KM#203.	—
Pn94	1923	—	5 Pesos. Gold. ENSAYO, KM#204.	—
Pn95	1923	—	5 Pesos. Silver. ESSAI; KM#204.	—
Pn96	1941	—	5 Centavos. Copper-Nickel.	—
Pn97	1946	—	50 Centavos. Copper-Nickel. 10-sided planchet.	—
Pn98	1946	—	50 Centavos. 0.5000 Silver. Reeded edge.	—
Pn99	1950	—	20 Centavos. 0.5000 Silver.	100
Pn100	1950	—	50 Centavos. 0.9000 Silver. Bolivar military bust, condor over large shield.	100
Pn101	1950	—	50 Centavos. 0.9000 Silver. Condor over small shield.	100
Pn102	1950	—	50 Centavos. 0.9000 Silver.	—
Pn103	1951	—	50 Centavos. Silver.	100
Pn104	1952	—	50 Centavos. Silver.	100
PnA105	1956	—	20 Centavos. Copper-Nickel. 4.9400 g. 23.73 mm. Reeded edge.	—
Pn105	1956	—	50 Centavos. Copper-Nickel.	125
Pn106	1956	—	Peso. Gold.	—
Pn107	1957	—	50 Centavos. Copper-Nickel.	125
Pn108	1963	—	Peso. Copper-Nickel. Prev. KM#Pn57.	125
Pn109	1968	—	Peso. Copper-Nickel. Prev. KM#Pn58.	125
Pn110	1969	—	50 Centavos. Copper-Nickel. Prev. KM#Pn59.	75.00
Pn111	1969	—	50 Centavos. Copper-Nickel. Prev. KM#Pn60.	75.00
Pn112	1969	—	Peso. Copper-Nickel. . Prev. KM#Pn61.	125
Pn114	1969	—	Peso. Copper-Nickel. Prev. KM#Pn63.	125
Pn113	1969	—	Peso. Copper-Nickel. Prev. KM#Pn62.	125
Pn115	1970	—	Centavo. Aluminum. Prev. KM#Pn64.	25.00
Pn116	1970	—	5 Centavos. Aluminum. Prev. KM#Pn65.	25.00
Pn117	1971	—	10 Centavos. Aluminum. Prev. KMPn66.	30.00
Pn118	1971	—	50 Centavos. Copper-Nickel. Prev. KM#Pn67.	65.00
Pn119	1974	—	Peso. Silver. 6.7000 g. Prev. KM#Pn68.	150
Pn120	1979	—	5 Pesos. Copper-Nickel. Inverted date. Prev. KM#Pn69.	—

PIEFORTS

KM#	Date	Mintage	Identification	Mkt Val
P3	1913	—	50 Centavos. 0.9000 Silver. Ensayo	2,500
P4	1915	—	10 Centavos. 0.9000 Silver. Ensayo	—
P5	1915	—	20 Centavos. 0.9000 Silver. Ensayo	—

TRIAL STRIKES

KM#	Date	Mintage	Identification	Mkt Val
TS14	ND	—	50 Centavos. Lead.	—
TS15	1911	—	10 Centavos. Lead. Uniface.	—
TS16	1911	—	20 Centavos. Lead. Uniface.	—
TS17	1946	—	20 Centavos. Nickel.	—
TS18	1946	—	20 Centavos. Nickel.	—

PROOF SETS

KM#	Date	Mintage	Identification	Issue Price	Mkt Val
PS1	1968 (5)	8,000	KM#231-235	340	2,150
PS2	1969 (5)	6,000	KM#238-242	—	2,150
PS3	1971 (5)	6,000	KM#248-252	—	2,450
PS4	1973 (3)	—	KM#254, 256, 257	—	475
PS5	1975 (2)	2,500	KM#260, 262	195	245
PS6	1975 (2)	4,000	KM#259, 261	195	265
PS7	1979 (2)	—	KM#264-265	—	75.00

COMOROS

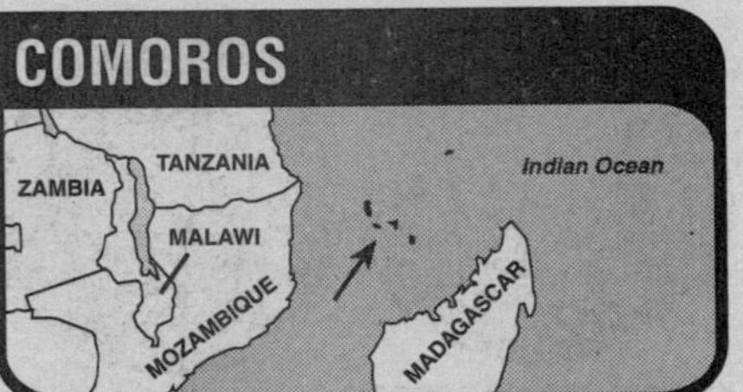

The Federal Islamic Republic of the Comoros, a volcanic archipelago located in the Mozambique Channel of the Indian Ocean 300 miles (483 km.) northwest of Madagascar, has an area of 719 sq. mi. (2,171 sq. km.) and a population of *714,000. Capital: Moroni. The economy of the islands is based on agriculture. There are practically no mineral resources. Vanilla, essence for perfumes, copra, and sisal are exported.

Ancient Phoenician traders were probably the first visitors to the Comoro Islands, but the first detailed knowledge of the area was gathered by Arab sailors. Arab dominion and culture were firmly established when the Portuguese, Dutch, and French arrived in the 16th century. In 1843 a Malagasy ruler ceded the island of Mayotte to France; the other three principal islands of the archipelago-Anjouan, Moheli, and Grand Comore came under French protection in 1886. The islands were joined administratively with Madagascar in 1912. The Comoros became partially autonomous, with the status of a French overseas territory, in 1946, and achieved complete internal autonomy in 1961. On Dec. 31, 1975, after 133 years of French association, the Comoro Islands became the independent Republic of the Comoros.

Mayotte retained the option of determining its future ties and in 1976 voted to remain French. Its present status is that of a French Territorial Collectivity. French currency now circulates there.

TITLES

Daulat Anjazanchiyah

RULERS

French, 1886-1975

MINT MARKS

(a) - Paris, privy marks only

A - Paris

MONETARY SYSTEM

100 Centimes = 1 Franc

FRENCH COLONIAL

DECIMAL COINAGE

KM# 4 FRANC

0.9000 Aluminum **Obv:** Winged Liberty bust left, headstones in background, date below **Obv. Designer:** G.B.L. Bazor **Rev:** Trees surrounding denomination

Date	Mintage	F	VF	XF	Unc	BU
1964(a)	500,000	0.15	0.25	0.40	1.25	4.00

KM# 5 2 FRANCS

Aluminum **Obv:** Winged Liberty bust left, date below, headstones in background **Obv. Designer:** G.B.L. Bazor **Rev:** Trees surround denomination

Date	Mintage	F	VF	XF	Unc	BU
1964(a)	600,000	0.15	0.25	0.50	1.50	5.00

KM# 6 5 FRANCS
Aluminum **Obv:** Winged Liberty bust left, date below, headstones in background **Obv. Designer:** G.B.L. Bazor **Rev:** Trees surround denomination

Date	Mintage	F	VF	XF	Unc	BU
1964(a)	1,000,000	0.20	0.40	0.65	2.00	6.00

KM# 7 10 FRANCS
Aluminum-Bronze **Obv:** Winged Liberty bust left, date below, headstones in background **Obv. Designer:** G.B.L. Bazor **Rev:** Plants on mantle, shells flank, denomination at center, fish below

Date	Mintage	F	VF	XF	Unc	BU
1964(a)	600,000	0.20	0.50	1.00	2.50	4.00

KM# 8 20 FRANCS
Aluminum-Bronze **Obv:** Winged Liberty bust left, date below, headstones in background **Obv. Designer:** G.B.L. Bazor **Rev:** Plants on mantle, shells flank, denomination at center, fish below

Date	Mintage	F	VF	XF	Unc	BU
1964(a)	500,000	0.30	0.65	1.25	3.00	6.00

TOKEN COINAGE

KM# Tn1 25 CENTIMES
1.2000 g., Aluminum **Issuer:** Societe Anonyme **Obv:** Legend at center and surrounding **Rev:** Denomination

Date	Mintage	F	VF	XF	Unc	BU
ND(1915)	—	30.00	60.00	125	250	—

KM# Tn1a 25 CENTIMES
4.6000 g., Brass **Issuer:** Societe Anonyme **Obv:** Legend at center and surrounding **Rev:** Denomination

Date	Mintage	F	VF	XF	Unc	BU
ND(1922)	—	—	—	175	300	—

KM# Tn2 50 CENTIMES
Aluminum **Obv:** Legend at center and surrounding **Rev:** Denomination

Date	Mintage	F	VF	XF	Unc	BU
ND(1915)	—	35.00	70.00	125	250	—

KM# Tn2a 50 CENTIMES
Brass **Obv:** Legend at center and surrounding **Rev:** Denomination

Date	Mintage	F	VF	XF	Unc	BU
ND(1915)	—	—	—	350	500	—

KM# Tn3 FRANC
1.3000 g., Aluminum **Obv:** Legend at center and surrounding **Rev:** Denomination

Date	Mintage	F	VF	XF	Unc	BU
ND(1915)	—	40.00	80.00	135	260	—

KM# Tn3a FRANC
Brass **Obv:** Legend at center and surrounding **Rev:** Denomination

Date	Mintage	F	VF	XF	Unc	BU
ND(1922)	—	—	—	225	400	—

KM# Tn4 2 FRANCS
Aluminum 1.7 oz. **Obv:** Legend at center and surrounding **Rev:** Denomination

Date	Mintage	F	VF	XF	Unc	BU
ND(1915)	—	50.00	100	175	325	—

KM# Tn5 2 FRANCS
Aluminum 1.7 oz. **Note:** Uniface.

Date	Mintage	F	VF	XF	Unc	BU
1915	—	50.00	100	175	325	—

FEDERAL ISLAMIC REPUBLIC

BANQUE CENTRAL COINAGE

KM# 15 5 FRANCS
Aluminum, 31 mm. **Subject:** World Fisheries Conference **Obv:** Trees surround denomination, date upper right **Rev:** Coelacanth fish left

Date	Mintage	F	VF	XF	Unc	BU
1984(a)	1,010,000	0.25	0.50	1.50	6.00	9.00
1992(a)	—	0.25	0.50	1.50	6.00	9.00

KM# 17 10 FRANCS
Aluminum-Bronze **Obv:** Half moon with four stars vertical from point to point **Rev:** Denomination above date

Date	Mintage	F	VF	XF	Unc	BU
1992(a)	—	—	—	—	1.65	2.00

KM# 14 25 FRANCS
Nickel, 20 mm. **Series:** F.A.O. **Obv:** Chickens **Rev:** Denomination above date

Date	Mintage	F	VF	XF	Unc	BU
1981(a)	1,000,000	1.50	3.00	6.00	16.00	—
1982(a)	2,007,000	0.20	0.40	0.80	2.00	4.00

KM# 16 50 FRANCS
Nickel **Obv:** Building with tall tower **Rev:** Moon and stars above denomination, date below

Date	Mintage	F	VF	XF	Unc	BU
1990(a)	—	0.50	0.80	1.50	2.50	3.50
1994(a)	—	0.50	0.80	1.50	2.50	3.50

KM# 18 100 FRANCS
10.0000 g., Nickel, 28 mm. **Subject:** Circulation Type **Obv:** Denomination, moon and stars above, date below **Rev:** Boat and fish **Edge:** Plain

Date	Mintage	F	VF	XF	Unc	BU
1999(a)	—	—	—	—	3.50	5.00

INSTITUT D'EMISSION COINAGE

KM# 9 50 FRANCS
Nickel **Subject:** Independence of Republic **Obv:** Building with tall tower **Rev:** Half moon on cross above denomination, date below

Date	Mintage	F	VF	XF	Unc	BU
1975(a)	1,200,000	0.40	0.75	1.25	2.25	3.00

KM# 13 100 FRANCS
Nickel **Series:** F.A.O. **Obv:** Half moon and stars above denomination, date below **Rev:** Boat and fish

Date	Mintage	F	VF	XF	Unc	BU
1977(a)	1,500,000	0.60	1.00	2.00	3.75	5.00

STANDARD COINAGE

KM# 10 5000 FRANCS
44.8300 g., 0.9250 Silver 1.3332 oz. ASW **Issuer:** Etat Comorien **Obv:** Flowers, date at left, denomination below **Rev:** Bust of Said Mohamed Cheikh facing divides dates

Date	Mintage	F	VF	XF	Unc	BU
1976	700	—	—	—	100	125
1976 Proof	1,000	Value: 160				

KM# 11 10000 FRANCS
3.0700 g., 0.9000 Gold .0888 oz. AGW **Issuer:** Etat Comorien **Obv:** Anjouan sunbird, denomination below **Rev:** Bust of Said Mohamed Cheikh facing divides dates

Date	Mintage	F	VF	XF	Unc	BU
1976	500	—	—	—	100	120
1976 Proof	500	Value: 140				

KM# 12 20000 FRANCS
6.1400 g., 0.9000 Gold .1776 oz. AGW **Issuer:** Etat Comorien **Obv:** Coelacanth fish right, denomination below **Rev:** Bust of Said Mohamed Cheikh facing divides dates

Date	Mintage	F	VF	XF	Unc	BU
1976	500	—	—	—	250	275
1976 Proof	500	Value: 300				

ESSAIS

Standard metals unless otherwise noted

KM#	Date	Mintage	Identification	Issue Price	Mkt Val
E1	1964(a)	1,700	Franc. KM4.	—	15.00
E2	1964(a)	1,700	2 Francs. KM5.	—	15.00
E3	1964(a)	1,700	5 Francs. KM6.	—	15.00
E4	1964(a)	1,700	10 Francs. KM7.	—	15.00
E5	1964(a)	1,700	20 Francs. KM8.	—	17.50
E6	1975(a)	1,800	50 Francs. KM9.	—	25.00
E7	1977(a)	1,900	100 Francs. KM13.	—	30.00
E8	1982(a)	1,900	25 Francs.	—	20.00
E9	1984(a)	1,700	5 Francs. KM15.	—	17.50

"FDC" SETS

KM#	Date	Mintage	Identification	Issue Price	Mkt Val
SS1	1964 (5)	—	KM4-8. Issued with Reunion set.	—	15.00

MINT SETS

KM#	Date	Mintage	Identification	Issue Price	Mkt Val
MS1	1976 (3)	500	KM10-12	—	450

PROOF SETS

KM#	Date	Mintage	Identification	Issue Price	Mkt Val
PS1	1976 (3)	500	KM10-12	229	600

CONGO FREE STATE

In ancient times the territory comprising former Zaire was occupied by Negrito peoples (Pygmies) pushed into the mountains by Bantu and Nilotic invaders. The interior was first explored by the American correspondent Henry Stanley, who was subsequently commissioned by King Leopold II of Belgium to conclude development treaties with the local chiefs. The Berlin conference of 1885 awarded the area to Leopold, who administered and exploited it as his private property until it was annexed to Belgium in 1908.

For later issues, see Belgian Congo.

RULER
Leopold II

ROYAL DOMAIN
1865-1908

STANDARD COINAGE

KM# 9 5 CENTIMES
Copper-Nickel **Ruler:** Leopold II **Obv:** Crowned monograms surround center hole, within circle **Rev:** Hole at center of radiant star, denomination above, date below

Date	Mintage	F	VF	XF	Unc	BU
1906	100,000	5.00	10.00	25.00	60.00	—
1908	180,000	4.00	8.00	20.00	50.00	—
1908/6	—	—	—	—	—	—

KM# 10 10 CENTIMES
Copper-Nickel **Ruler:** Leopold II **Obv:** Hole at center of crowned monograms within circle **Rev:** Hole at center of radiant star, denomination above, date below

Date	Mintage	F	VF	XF	Unc	BU
1906	100,000	5.00	12.00	35.00	90.00	—
1908	800,000	3.00	8.00	30.00	80.00	—

KM# 11 20 CENTIMES
Copper-Nickel **Ruler:** Leopold II **Obv:** Hole at center of crowned monograms within circle **Rev:** Hole at center of radiant star, denomination above, date below

Date	Mintage	F	VF	XF	Unc	BU
1906	100,000	5.00	12.00	40.00	110	—
1908	400,000	4.00	8.00	35.00	95.00	—

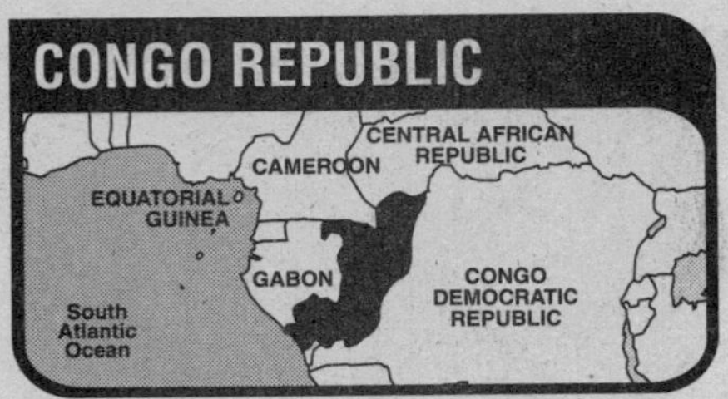

The Republic of the Congo (formerly the Peoples Republic of the Congo), located on the equator in west-central Africa, has an area of 132,047 sq. mi. (342,000 sq. km.) and a population of *2.98 million. Capital: Brazzaville. Agriculture forestry, mining, and food processing are the principal industries. Timber, industrial diamonds, potash, peanuts, and cocoa beans are exported.

The Portuguese were the first Europeans to explore the Congo (Brazzaville) area, 14th century. They conducted a slave trade with the tribal kingdoms of Teke, Loango, and Kongo without attempting developmental colonization. French influence was established in 1883 when the king of Teke signed a treaty with Savorgnan de Brazza, thereby placing his kingdom under the protection of France. While a French protectorate, the area was known as Middle Congo. In 1910 Middle Congo became a part of French Equatorial Africa, which also included Gabon, Ubangi-Shari (now the Central African Republic), and Chad. Following World War II, during which it was an important center of Free French activities, the Middle Congo was given a large measure of internal autonomy, and its inhabitants were made French citizens. Upon approval of the constitution of the Fifth French Republic, 1958, it became a member of the new French Community. On Aug. 15, 1960, Middle Congo became the independent Republic of the Congo-Brazzaville. In Jan. 1970 the country's name was changed to Peoples Republic of the Congo. A new constitution which asserts the government's advocacy of socialism was adopted in 1973.

In June and July of 1992, a new 125-member National Assembly was elected. Later that year a new president, Pascal Lissouba was elected. In November, President Lissouba dismissed the previous government and dissolved the National Assembly. A new 23-member government, including members of the opposition, was formed in December, 1992, and the name was changed to Republique du Congo.

NOTE: For earlier and related coinage see French Equatorial Africa and the Equatorial African States. For later coinage see Central African States.

RULERS
French until 1960

MINT MARKS
(a) - Paris, privy marks only

MONETARY SYSTEM
100 Centimes = 1 Franc

PEOPLE'S REPUBLIC
Republique Populaire du Congo

DECIMAL COINAGE

KM# 1 100 FRANCS
Nickel **Obv:** Three Giant Eland left **Obv. Designer:** G.B.L. Bazor **Rev:** Denomination within circle, date below

Date	Mintage	F	VF	XF	Unc	BU
1971(a)	2,700,000	8.00	15.00	25.00	40.00	—
1972(a)	2,500,000	8.00	15.00	25.00	40.00	—

KM# 2 100 FRANCS
Nickel **Obv:** Three Giant Eland left **Obv. Designer:** G.B.L. Bazor **Rev:** Denomination within circle, date below

Date	Mintage	F	VF	XF	Unc	BU
1975(a)	—	4.00	8.00	16.50	30.00	—
1982(a)	—	2.50	4.50	8.00	12.50	—
1983(a)	—	2.50	5.00	8.00	12.50	—
1985(a)	—	2.00	3.00	6.00	10.00	—
1990(a)	—	2.00	3.00	4.00	6.00	—

KM# 3 100 FRANCS

Copper-Nickel **Subject:** International Games **Obv:** Statue, date below **Rev:** Handball players, denomination below

Date	Mintage	F	VF	XF	Unc	BU
1984 Proof	—	Value: 16.50				

KM# 7 100 FRANCS

Nickel Plated Steel **Subject:** Olympics **Obv:** National arms, denomination below **Rev:** Boxers, date below

Date	Mintage	F	VF	XF	Unc	BU
1991	5,000	—	—	—	15.00	—

KM# 8 100 FRANCS

Nickel Plated Steel **Subject:** Olympics **Obv:** National arms, denomination below **Rev:** Hurdler, date lower right

Date	Mintage	F	VF	XF	Unc	BU
1991	5,000	—	—	—	15.00	—

KM# 10 100 FRANCS

Nickel Plated Steel **Series:** Old Ships **Obv:** National arms, denomination below **Rev:** Spanish galleon, date below

Date	Mintage	F	VF	XF	Unc	BU
1991	—	—	—	—	14.00	—

KM# 30 100 FRANCS

Copper **Series:** Old ships **Obv:** National arms, denomination below **Obv. Legend:** Republique Populaire du Congo **Rev:** Spanish galleon, date below

Date	Mintage	F	VF	XF	Unc	BU
1991 Proof	100	Value: 55.00				

KM# 22 100 FRANCS

Copper **Series:** Protection of Nature **Obv:** National arms, denomination below **Rev:** Congolese peacock

Date	Mintage	F	VF	XF	Unc	BU
1992	—	—	—	—	17.00	—

KM# 31 100 FRANCS

Copper-Nickel **Series:** Protection of Nature **Obv:** National arms, denomination below **Obv. Legend:** Republique Populaire du Congo **Rev:** Congolese peacock

Date	Mintage	F	VF	XF	Unc	BU
1992	333	—	—	—	50.00	—

KM# 4 500 FRANCS

Copper-Nickel **Obv:** Plants divide date and denomination, within octagon **Rev:** Inscription lower right of woman's head 3/4 left, within octagon

Date	Mintage	F	VF	XF	Unc	BU
1985(a)	—	3.50	6.50	10.00	18.50	—
1986(a)	—	3.50	6.50	10.00	18.50	—

KM# 5 500 FRANCS

16.0000 g., 0.9990 Silver .5144 oz. ASW **Series:** Old Ships **Obv:** National arms, denomination below **Rev:** Spanish galleon, date below

Date	Mintage	F	VF	XF	Unc	BU
1991 Proof	—	Value: 30.00				

KM# 6 500 FRANCS

12.0000 g., 0.9990 Silver .3858 oz. ASW **Subject:** World Cup Soccer **Obv:** National arms, denomination below **Rev:** Soccer players, date at left

Date	Mintage	F	VF	XF	Unc	BU
1991	—	—	—	—	27.50	—

KM# 9 500 FRANCS

16.0700 g., 0.9990 Silver .5170 oz. ASW **Subject:** Olympics **Obv:** National arms, denomination below **Rev:** Hurdler

Date	Mintage	F	VF	XF	Unc	BU
1991 Proof	—	Value: 25.00				

KM# 9a 500 FRANCS

20.0000 g., 0.9990 Silver .6425 oz. ASW **Subject:** Olympics **Obv:** National arms, denomination below **Rev:** Hurdler

Date	Mintage	F	VF	XF	Unc	BU
1991	5,000	—	—	—	27.50	—

KM# 11 500 FRANCS

20.0000 g., 0.9990 Silver .6430 oz. ASW **Subject:** World Cup Soccer **Obv:** National arms, denomination below **Rev:** Player and date left of Statue of Liberty

Date	Mintage	F	VF	XF	Unc	BU
1992 Proof	—	Value: 25.00				

KM# 12 500 FRANCS

19.9500 g., 0.9990 Silver .6415 oz. ASW **Subject:** Protection of Nature **Obv:** National arms, denomination below **Rev:** Congolese peacock

Date	Mintage	F	VF	XF	Unc	BU
1992 Proof	—	Value: 35.00				

REPUBLIC

Republique du Congo

DECIMAL COINAGE

KM# 18 100 FRANCS
Copper Nickel **Obv:** Woman seated with tablet, denomination below **Rev:** Four-masted sailing ship - "Herzogin Cecilie", date below

Date	Mintage	F	VF	XF	Unc	BU
1993	—	—	—	—	10.00	—

KM# 20 100 FRANCS
Copper **Subject:** Preservation of Nature **Obv:** Woman seated with tablet, denomination below **Rev:** Four elephants, tusks below, date at lower left

Date	Mintage	F	VF	XF	Unc	BU
1993	—	—	—	—	15.00	—

KM# 32 100 FRANCS
Copper **Obv:** Woman seated with tablet, denomination below **Rev:** Four-masted sailing ship - "Herzogin Cecilie", date below

Date	Mintage	F	VF	XF	Unc	BU
1993 Proof	100	Value: 50.00				

KM# 33 100 FRANCS
Copper **Subject:** Prehistoric Animals **Obv:** Woman seated with tablet, denomination below **Rev:** Brachiosaurus in water, date below

Date	Mintage	F	VF	XF	Unc	BU
1993 Proof	100	Value: 50.00				

KM# 16 100 FRANCS
Copper-Nickel **Subject:** Prehistoric Animals **Obv:** Woman seated with tablet, denomination below **Rev:** Polacanthus left, date below

Date	Mintage	F	VF	XF	Unc	BU
1994	—	—	—	—	30.00	—

KM# 19 100 FRANCS
Copper-Nickel **Subject:** Prehistoric Animals **Obv:** Woman seated with tablet, denomination below **Rev:** Spinosaurus left, date lower left

Date	Mintage	F	VF	XF	Unc	BU
1994	—	—	—	—	30.00	—

KM# 34 100 FRANCS
Copper-Nickel **Subject:** Prehistoric Animals **Obv:** Woman seated with tablet, denomination below **Rev:** Mammuthus 3/4 facing

Date	Mintage	F	VF	XF	Unc	BU
1994 Proof	100	Value: 50.00				

KM# 21 100 FRANCS
Copper-Nickel **Obv:** Woman seated with tablet, denomination below **Rev:** Junkers JU52 trimotor airplane left, date at right **Note:** Multicolored.

Date	Mintage	F	VF	XF	Unc	BU
1995	25,000	—	—	—	25.00	—

KM# 35 100 FRANCS
Copper-Nickel **Subject:** XXVII Olympiade **Obv:** Woman seated with tablet, denomination below **Rev:** Shot putter, date at left **Note:** Prev. KM#45.

Date	Mintage	F	VF	XF	Unc	BU
1999	10,000	—	—	—	7.00	9.00

KM# 42 500 FRANCS
13.8100 g., 0.9990 Silver, 30 mm. **Obv:** Woman seated with tablet, denomination below **Rev:** Multicolor lion head, date at right **Edge:** Plain

Date	Mintage	F	VF	XF	Unc	BU
1996 Proof	—	Value: 40.00				

KM# 38 500 FRANCS
9.9600 g., Silver, 29.9 mm. **Series:** 2000 Olympics **Subject:** Basketball **Obv:** Seated woman with tablet **Rev:** Basketball player and map of Australia

Date	Mintage	F	VF	XF	Unc	BU
1998 Proof	—	Value: 22.00				

KM# 13 1000 FRANCS
20.0000 g., 0.9990 Silver .6430 oz. ASW **Subject:** Preservation of Nature **Obv:** Woman seated with tablet, denomination below **Rev:** Elephants, tusks below, date lower left

Date	Mintage	F	VF	XF	Unc	BU
1993 Proof	—	Value: 40.00				

KM# 14 1000 FRANCS
15.9000 g., 0.9990 Silver .5107 oz. ASW **Subject:** Prehistoric Animals **Obv:** Woman seated with tablet, denomination below **Rev:** Brachiosaurus, date below

Date	Mintage	F	VF	XF	Unc	BU
1993 Proof	—	Value: 37.50				

KM# 15 1000 FRANCS
20.1000 g., 0.9990 Silver .6456 oz. ASW **Obv:** Woman seated with tablet, denomination below **Rev:** 4-masted sailing ship - "Herzogin Cecilie", date below

Date	Mintage	F	VF	XF	Unc	BU
1993	100	—	—	—	100	—
1993 Proof	—	Value: 40.00				

KM# 17 1000 FRANCS

15.8800 g., 0.9990 Silver .5106 oz. ASW **Subject:** Prehistoric Animals **Obv:** Woman seated with tablet, denomination below **Rev:** Mammoth, date lower left

Date	Mintage	F	VF	XF	Unc	BU
1994 Proof	—	Value: 35.00				

KM# 23 1000 FRANCS

20.0000 g., 0.9990 Silver .6430 oz. ASW **Subject:** 1996 Olympics **Obv:** Woman seated with tablet **Rev:** Discus throwing, date at left

Date	Mintage	F	VF	XF	Unc	BU
1995 Proof	15,000	Value: 30.00				

KM# 24 1000 FRANCS

20.0000 g., 0.9990 Silver .6430 oz. ASW **Obv:** Woman seated with tablet **Rev:** Multicolor Swiss airliner - Junkers JU 52, left, date at right

Date	Mintage	F	VF	XF	Unc	BU
1995 Proof	15,000	Value: 60.00				

KM# 25 1000 FRANCS

20.0000 g., 0.9990 Silver .6430 oz. ASW **Obv:** Woman seated with tablet, denomination below **Rev:** Multicolor Panther head facing, date upper right

Date	Mintage	F	VF	XF	Unc	BU
1996 Proof	—	Value: 60.00				

KM# 40 1000 FRANCS

20.0000 g., 0.9990 Silver 0.6424 oz. ASW, 38.1 mm. **Obv:** Woman seated with tablet, denomination below **Rev:** Multicolor elephant **Edge:** Reeded

Date	Mintage	F	VF	XF	Unc	BU
1996 Proof	—	Value: 60.00				

KM# 26 1000 FRANCS

20.0000 g., 0.9990 Silver .6430 oz. ASW **Subject:** World Cup Soccer **Obv:** Woman seated with tablet, denomination below **Rev:** Two soccer players, date at right

Date	Mintage	F	VF	XF	Unc	BU
1996	100	—	—	—	75.00	—
1996 Proof	—	Value: 45.00				

KM# 27 1000 FRANCS

20.0000 g., 0.9990 Silver .6430 oz. ASW **Subject:** World Cup Soccer **Obv:** Woman seated with tablet, denomination below **Rev:** Multicolor Eiffel Tower, soccer ball and French flag,

Date	Mintage	F	VF	XF	Unc	BU
1996 Proof	—	Value: 45.00				

KM# 28.1 1000 FRANCS

20.0000 g., 0.9990 Silver .6430 oz. ASW **Subject:** XXVII Olympiade **Obv:** Woman seated with tablet, denomination below **Rev:** Multicolored boxers

Date	Mintage	F	VF	XF	Unc	BU
1997	100	—	—	—	100	—
1997 Proof	500	Value: 55.00				

KM# 28.2 1000 FRANCS

15.8800 g., 0.9990 Silver .5106 oz. ASW **Subject:** XXVII Olympiade **Obv:** Woman seated with tablet, denomination below **Rev:** Multicolored boxers

Date	Mintage	F	VF	XF	Unc	BU
1998	100	—	—	—	100	—
1998 Proof	5,000	Value: 45.00				

KM# 41 1000 FRANCS

31.1000 g., 0.9990 Silver 0.9989 oz. ASW, 45 mm. **Obv:** Woman seated with tablet, denomination below **Rev:** Map of East Central African countries with two elephants and a crocodile **Edge:** Plain

Date	Mintage	F	VF	XF	Unc	BU
1997 Proof	—	Value: 150				

KM# 39 1000 FRANCS

15.0000 g., 0.9990 Silver 0.4818 oz. ASW, 35 mm. **Obv:** Woman seated with tablet, denomination below **Rev:** Soccer player, date lower right **Edge:** Plain

Date	Mintage	F	VF	XF	Unc	BU
1997 Proof	—	Value: 40.00				

KM# 37 1000 FRANCS

15.0000 g., 0.9990 Silver 0.4818 oz. ASW, 34.9 mm. **Subject:** Graf Zeppelin **Obv:** Woman with tablet **Rev:** Multicolor New York City view with Zeppelin in flight and a cameo insert at lower right of Count Zeppelin **Edge:** Plain **Note:** Prev. KM#107.

Date	Mintage	F	VF	XF	Unc	BU
ND(1997) Proof	—	Value: 45.00				

KM# 29 1000 FRANCS

15.0000 g., 0.9990 Silver .4818 oz. ASW **Obv:** Woman seated with tablet, denomination below **Rev:** Ancient Roman ship, date below

Date	Mintage	F	VF	XF	Unc	BU
1997 Proof	5,000	Value: 40.00				

KM# 36 1000 FRANCS

20.1000 g., 0.9990 Silver .6456 oz. ASW **Subject:** XXVII Olympiade **Obv:** Woman seated with tablet, denomination below **Rev:** Shot putter, date at left

Date	Mintage	F	VF	XF	Unc	BU
1999 Proof	5,000	Value: 32.50				

KM# 43 1000 FRANCS

15.0000 g., 0.9990 Silver 0.4818 oz. ASW, 35 mm. **Obv:** Woman seated with tablet, denomination below **Rev:** Charles Darwin **Edge:** Plain

Date	Mintage	F	VF	XF	Unc	BU
1999 Proof	—	Value: 40.00				

KM# 44 1000 FRANCS

15.0000 g., 0.9990 Silver 0.4818 oz. ASW, 35 mm. **Obv:** Woman seated with tablet, denomination below **Rev:** Graf Ferdinand von Zeppelin **Edge:** Plain

Date	Mintage	F	VF	XF	Unc	BU
ND(2000) Proof	—	Value: 40.00				

KM# 45 1000 FRANCS
15.0000 g., 0.9990 Silver 0.4818 oz. ASW, 35 mm. **Obv:** Woman seated with tablet, denomination below **Rev:** Ciconia bird, date at right **Edge:** Plain

Date	Mintage	F	VF	XF	Unc	BU
2000	—	—	—	—	35.00	—

ESSAIS

Standard metals unless otherwise noted

KM#	Date	Mintage	Identification	Mkt Val
E1	1971(a)	1,450	100 Francs.	25.00
E2	1971(a)	4	100 Francs. Gold.	1,350
E3	1975(a)	1,700	100 Francs.	20.00

KM#	Date	Mintage	Identification	Mkt Val
E5	1985(a)	1,700	500 Francs. Plants between denomination and date within octagon. Inscription at lower right of womans head.	35.00

PIEFORTS

KM#	Date	Mintage	Identification	Mkt Val

KM#	Date	Mintage	Identification	Mkt Val
P1	1991	110	500 Francs. 0.9990 Silver. National arms, denomination below. Spanish galleon, date below. KM5.	115

TRIAL STRIKES

KM#	Date	Mintage	Identification	Mkt Val
TS1	1984	3	10 Francs. Silver. Fencing. Uniface.	600
TS2	1984	3	50 Francs. Silver. Shot put. Uniface.	600

CONGO DEMOCRATIC REPUBLIC

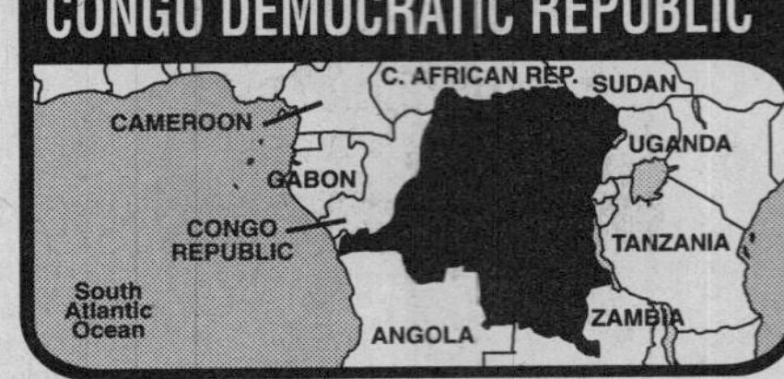

The Democratic Republic of the Congo (formerly the Republic of Zaire, and earlier the Belgian Congo), located in the south-central part of Africa, has an area of 905,568 sq. mi. (2,345,410 sq. km.) and a population of *47.4 million. Capital: Kinshasa. The mineral-rich country produces copper, tin, diamonds, gold, zinc, cobalt and uranium.

In ancient times the territory comprising former Zaire was occupied by Negrito peoples (Pygmies) pushed into the mountains by Bantu and Nilotic invaders. The interior was first explored by the American correspondent Henry Stanley, who was subsequently commissioned by King Leopold II of Belgium to conclude development treaties with the local chiefs. The Berlin conference of 1885 awarded the area to Leopold, who administered and exploited it as his private property until it was annexed to Belgium in 1908. Belgium received the mandate for the German territory of Ruanda-Urundi as a result of the international treaties after WWI. During World War II, Belgian Congolese troops fought on the side of the Allies, notably in Ethiopia. Following the eruption of bloody independence riots in 1959, Belgium granted the Belgian Congo independence as the Republic of the Congo on June 30, 1960. The nation officially changed its name to Zaire on Oct. 27, 1971, and following a Civil War in 1997 changed its name to the "Democratic Republic of the Congo."

REPUBLIC
1960 - 1971

DECIMAL COINAGE

KM# 1 10 FRANCS
Aluminum, 29.8 mm. **Obv:** Denomination above date **Rev:** Lion face **Note:** Most recalled and melted.

Date	Mintage	F	VF	XF	Unc	BU
1965(b)	Est. 100,000,000	0.60	1.50	3.00	7.00	10.00

KM# 2 10 FRANCS
3.2260 g., 0.9000 Gold .0934 oz. AGW **Subject:** 5th Anniversary of Independence **Obv:** President Joseph Kasa-Vubu **Rev:** Crossed palm trees, denomination below **Note:** Approximately 70 percent melted.

Date	Mintage	F	VF	XF	Unc	BU
1965 Proof	Est. 3,000	Value: 75.00				

KM# 3 20 FRANCS
6.4520 g., 0.9000 Gold .1867 oz. AGW **Subject:** 5th Anniversary of Independence **Obv:** Uniformed bust of President Joseph Kasa-Vubu 3/4 right **Rev:** Crossed palm trees, denomination below **Note:** Approximately 70 percent melted.

Date	Mintage	F	VF	XF	Unc	BU
1965 Proof	Est. 3,000	Value: 145				

KM# 4 25 FRANCS
8.0640 g., 0.9000 Gold .2334 oz. AGW **Subject:** 5th Anniversary of Independence **Rev:** Elephant left **Note:** Approximately 70 percent melted.

Date	Mintage	F	VF	XF	Unc	BU
1965 Proof	Est. 3,000	Value: 180				

KM# 4a 25 FRANCS
Silver **Subject:** 5th Anniversary of Independence **Rev:** Elephant left

Date	Mintage	F	VF	XF	Unc	BU
1965 Proof	—	Value: 60.00				

KM# 5 50 FRANCS
16.1290 g., 0.9000 Gold .4668 oz. AGW **Subject:** 5th Anniversary of Independence **Obv:** Uniformed President's bust 3/4 right **Rev:** Elephant left, denomination and date below **Note:** Approximately 70 percent melted.

Date	Mintage	F	VF	XF	Unc	BU
1965 Proof	Est. 3,000	Value: 360				

KM# 6 100 FRANCS
32.2580 g., 0.9000 Gold .9335 oz. AGW **Subject:** 5th Anniversary of Independence **Obv:** Uniformed bust of President Joseph Kasa-Vubu 3/4 right **Rev:** Elephant left **Note:** Approximately 70 percent melted.

Date	Mintage	F	VF	XF	Unc	BU
1965 Proof	Est. 3,000	Value: 675				

KM# 6a 100 FRANCS
Silver **Subject:** 5th Anniversary of Independence **Obv:** President Joseph Kasa-Vubu **Rev:** Elephant left

Date	Mintage	F	VF	XF	Unc	BU
1965 Proof	—	Value: 100				

REFORM COINAGE

100 Sengis = 1 Likuta; 100 Makuta (plural of Likuta) = 1 Zaire

KM# 7 10 SENGIS
Aluminum, 17 mm. **Obv:** Denomination within circle **Rev:** Leopard crouching on branch, date below

Date	Mintage	F	VF	XF	Unc	BU
1967	90,996,000	—	0.15	0.45	1.00	2.00

KM# 10 10 SENGIS
3.2000 g., 0.9000 Gold .0926 oz. AGW **Subject:** 5th Year of Mobutu Presidency **Obv:** Arms above denomination **Rev:** Military bust of President Joseph Desire Mobutu 3/4 facing, date below

Date	Mintage	F	VF	XF	Unc	BU
1970	1,000	—	—	—	70.00	—
1970 Proof	1,000	Value: 95.00				

KM# 10a 10 SENGIS
Gilt Brass **Subject:** 5th Year of Mobutu Presidency **Obv:** Arms **Rev:** Bust of President Joseph Desire Mobutu

Date	Mintage	F	VF	XF	Unc	BU
1970 Proof	—	Value: 70.00				

KM# 8 LIKUTA
Aluminum **Obv:** Denomination within circle **Rev:** Arms above date

Date	Mintage	F	VF	XF	Unc	BU
1967	49,180,000	—	0.15	0.50	1.25	—

KM# 9 5 MAKUTA
Copper-Nickel, 25 mm. **Obv:** Denomination within circle **Rev:** Bust of President Mobutu 3/4 left, date below

Date	Mintage	F	VF	XF	Unc	BU
1967	2,470,000	0.25	0.50	1.00	3.00	—

KM# 11 25 MAKUTAS
Gilt Brass **Subject:** 5th Year of Mobutu Presidency **Obv:** Arms above denomination **Rev:** President's bust 3/4 facing, date below

Date	Mintage	F	VF	XF	Unc	BU
1970 Proof	—	Value: 100				

KM# 11a 25 MAKUTAS
8.0000 g., 0.9000 Gold .2315 oz. AGW **Subject:** 5th Year of Mobutu Presidency **Obv:** Arms above denomination **Rev:** President's bust facing

Date	Mintage	F	VF	XF	Unc	BU
1970	1,000	—	—	—	165	—
1970 Proof	1,000	Value: 185				

KM# 12 50 MAKUTAS
Gilt Brass **Subject:** 5th Year of Mobutu Presidency **Obv:** Arms above denomination **Rev:** President's bust 3/4 facing

Date	Mintage	F	VF	XF	Unc	BU
1970 Proof	—	Value: 125				

KM# 12a 50 MAKUTAS
16.0000 g., 0.9000 Gold .4630 oz. AGW **Subject:** 5th Year of Mobutu Presidency **Obv:** Arms above denomination **Rev:** President's bust 3/4 facing, date below

Date	Mintage	F	VF	XF	Unc	BU
1970	1,000	—	—	—	325	—
1970 Proof	1,000	Value: 345				

KM# 13 ZAIRE
Gilt Brass **Subject:** 5th Year of Mobutu Presidency **Obv:** Arms above denomination **Rev:** President's bust 3/4 facing

Date	Mintage	F	VF	XF	Unc	BU
1970 Proof	—	Value: 150				

KM# 13a ZAIRE
32.0000 g., 0.9000 Gold .9261 oz. AGW **Subject:** 5th Year of Mobutu Presidency **Obv:** Arms above denomination **Rev:** President's bust, 3/4 facing, date below

Date	Mintage	F	VF	XF	Unc	BU
1970	1,000	—	—	—	665	—
1970 Proof	1,000	Value: 700				

DEMOCRATIC REPUBLIC
1998 -

REFORM COINAGE

Congo Francs replace Zaire; July 1998

KM# 73 5 FRANCS
24.3000 g., Copper Nickel, 38.5 mm. **Subject:** Royals of Europe **Obv:** Lion **Rev:** Multicolor portrait of Queen Juliana (1948-80) and crowned arms **Edge:** Reeded

Date	Mintage	F	VF	XF	Unc	BU
1999 Proof	—	—	—	—	12.00	—

KM# 84 5 FRANCS
24.3000 g., Copper Nickel, 38.5 mm. **Subject:** Anna Paulowna **Obv:** Lion within inner circle, denomination below in outer circle **Rev:** Multicolor portrait applique within inner circle **Edge:** Reeded

Date	Mintage	F	VF	XF	Unc	BU
1999 Proof	—	Value: 10.00				

KM# 85 5 FRANCS
24.3000 g., Copper Nickel, 38.5 mm. **Subject:** Willem I **Obv:** Lion within inner circle, denomination below in outer circle **Rev:** Multicolor portrait applique within inner circle **Edge:** Reeded

Date	Mintage	F	VF	XF	Unc	BU
1999 Proof	—	Value: 10.00				

KM# 86 5 FRANCS
24.3000 g., Copper Nickel, 38.5 mm. **Subject:** Willem III **Obv:** Lion within inner circle, denomination below in outer circle **Rev:** Multicolor portrait applique within inner circle **Edge:** Reeded

Date	Mintage	F	VF	XF	Unc	BU
1999 Proof	—	Value: 10.00				

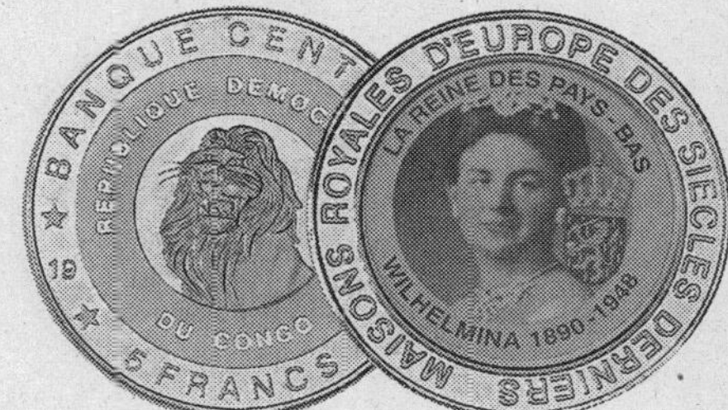

KM# 87 5 FRANCS
24.3000 g., Copper Nickel, 38.5 mm. **Subject:** Wilhelmina **Obv:** Lion within inner circle, denomination below in outer circle **Rev:** Multicolor portrait applique within inner circle **Edge:** Reeded

Date	Mintage	F	VF	XF	Unc	BU
1999 Proof	—	Value: 10.00				

KM# 88 5 FRANCS
24.3000 g., Copper Nickel, 38.5 mm. **Subject:** Bernhard **Obv:** Lion within inner circle, denomination in outer circle **Rev:** Multicolor portrait applique within inner circle **Edge:** Reeded

Date	Mintage	F	VF	XF	Unc	BU
1999 Proof	—	Value: 10.00				

KM# 89 5 FRANCS
24.3000 g., Copper-Nickel, 38.5 mm. **Subject:** Claus **Obv:** Lion within inner circle, denomination below in outer circle **Rev:** Multicolor portrait applique within inner circle **Edge:** Reeded

Date	Mintage	F	VF	XF	Unc	BU
1999 Proof	—	Value: 10.00				

KM# 90 5 FRANCS
24.3000 g., Copper-Nickel, 38.5 mm. **Subject:** Willem-Alexander **Obv:** Lion within inner circle, denomination below in outer circle **Rev:** Multicolor portrait applique within inner circle **Edge:** Reeded

Date	Mintage	F	VF	XF	Unc	BU
1999 Proof	—	Value: 10.00				

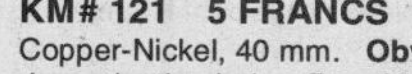

KM# 121 5 FRANCS
Copper-Nickel, 40 mm. **Obv:** Lion standing looking forward, denomination below **Rev:** Multicolor applique King Baudouin I (1930-1993) facing, dates at right **Edge:** Reeded

Date	Mintage	F	VF	XF	Unc	BU
2000	—	—	—	—	10.00	—

KM# 160 5 FRANCS
26.5300 g., Copper-Nickel, 37.3 mm. **Subject:** Marine-Life Protection **Obv:** Standing lion facing, denomination below **Rev:** Multicolor fish scene, date below **Edge:** Reeded

Date	Mintage	F	VF	XF	Unc	BU
2000 Proof	—	Value: 25.00				

KM# 63 5 FRANCS
28.7500 g., Copper-Nickel, 38 mm. **Subject:** Lady Diana - Visit to India **Obv:** Standing lion facing, denomination below **Rev:** Lady Diana at left, Taj Mahal at right, cameo of Queen Mother top center **Edge:** Reeded **Note:** Prev. KM#86.

Date	Mintage	F	VF	XF	Unc	BU
ND(2000) Proof	—	Value: 45.00				

KM# 64 5 FRANCS
28.7500 g., Copper-Nickel, 38 mm. **Subject:** Lady Diana - Meeting with Pope John Paul II **Obv:** Standing lion facing, denomination below **Rev:** Lady Diana front left, Pope John Paul II facing left, cameo of Queen Mother top center **Edge:** Reeded **Note:** Prev. KM#87.

Date	Mintage	F	VF	XF	Unc	BU
ND(2000) Proof	—	Value: 45.00				

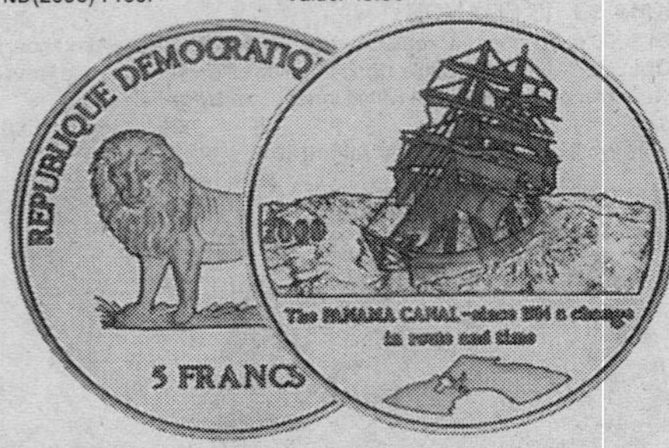

KM# 24 5 FRANCS
Copper-Nickel **Subject:** Panama Canal **Obv:** Standing lion facing, denomination below **Rev:** Sailing ship above inscription and map **Note:** Prev. KM#47.

Date	Mintage	F	VF	XF	Unc	BU
2000	—	—	—	—	9.00	—

KM# 39 5 FRANCS
27.1600 g., Copper Nickel, 37.3 mm. **Series:** Wild Life Protection **Obv:** Standing lion facing, denomination below **Rev:** Multicolor holographic parrot with folded wings right **Edge:** Reeded **Note:** Prev. KM#62.

Date	Mintage	F	VF	XF	Unc	BU
2000 Proof	—	Value: 27.50				

KM# 40 5 FRANCS
Copper Nickel 27.16, 37.3 mm. **Series:** Wild Life Protection **Obv:** Standing lion facing, denomination below **Rev:** Multicolor holographic parrot with open wings left **Edge:** Reeded **Note:** Prev. KM#63.

Date	Mintage	F	VF	XF	Unc	BU
2000 Proof	—	Value: 27.50				

KM# 41 5 FRANCS
27.1600 g., Copper Nickel, 37.3 mm. **Series:** Wild Life Protection **Obv:** Standing lion facing, denomination below **Rev:** Multicolor holographic toucan left **Note:** Prev. KM#64.

Date	Mintage	F	VF	XF	Unc	BU
2000 Proof	—	Value: 27.50				

KM# 17 10 FRANCS
20.0000 g., 0.9250 Silver .5948 oz. ASW **Series:** Endangered Wildlife **Obv:** Lion within inner circle, date below in outer circle **Rev:** Water chevrotain left, denomination below **Note:** Prev. KM#38.

Date	Mintage	F	VF	XF	Unc	BU
1999 Proof	10,000	Value: 40.00				

KM# 14 10 FRANCS
20.0000 g., 0.9250 Silver .5948 oz. ASW **Series:** Endangered Wildlife **Obv:** Lion within inner circle, date below in outer circle **Rev:** Bonobos female chimpanzee with young, denomination below **Note:** Prev. KM#35.

Date	Mintage	F	VF	XF	Unc	BU
1999 Proof	10,000	Value: 35.00				

KM# 15 10 FRANCS
20.0000 g., 0.9250 Silver .5948 oz. ASW **Series:** Endangered Wildlife **Obv:** Lion within inner circle, date below in outer circle **Rev:** Pygmy hippopotamus right, denomination below **Note:** Prev. KM#36.

Date	Mintage	F	VF	XF	Unc	BU
1999 Proof	10,000	Value: 35.00				

KM# 16 10 FRANCS
20.0000 g., 0.9250 Silver .5948 oz. ASW **Series:** Endangered Wildlife **Obv:** Lion within inner circle, date below in outer circle **Rev:** Crocodile left, denomination below **Note:** Prev. KM#37.

Date	Mintage	F	VF	XF	Unc	BU
1999 Proof	10,000	Value: 35.00				

KM# 18 10 FRANCS
20.0000 g., 0.9250 Silver .5948 oz. ASW **Series:** Endangered Wildlife **Obv:** Lion within inner circle, date below in outer circle **Rev:** Ground pangolin on branch right, denomination below **Note:** Prev. KM#39.

Date	Mintage	F	VF	XF	Unc	BU
1999 Proof	10,000	Value: 40.00				

KM# 19 10 FRANCS
20.0000 g., 0.9250 Silver .5948 oz. ASW **Series:** Endangered Wildlife **Obv:** Lion within inner circle, date below in outer circle **Rev:** Poto hanging on branches, denomination below **Note:** Prev. KM#40.

Date	Mintage	F	VF	XF	Unc	BU
1999 Proof	10,000	Value: 40.00				

KM# 20 10 FRANCS
25.3100 g., 0.9250 Silver .7524 oz. ASW **Subject:** Explorers of Africa-Dr. David Livingstone **Obv:** Lion within inner circle, date below in outer circle **Rev:** Head facing, land and ship in background, denomination at left **Note:** Prev. KM#41.

Date	Mintage	F	VF	XF	Unc	BU
1999 Proof	10,000	Value: 37.50				

KM# 21 10 FRANCS

25.3100 g., 0.9250 Silver .7524 oz. ASW **Subject:** Explorers of Africa-Sir Henry Morton Stanley **Obv:** Lion within inner circle, date below in outer circle **Rev:** Bust facing, denomination at right **Note:** Prev. KM#42.

Date	Mintage	F	VF	XF	Unc	BU
1999 Proof	10,000	Value: 37.50				

KM# 22 10 FRANCS

25.3100 g., 0.9250 Silver .7524 oz. ASW **Subject:** 30th Anniversary of the Lunar Landing **Obv:** Lion within inner circle, date below in outer circle **Rev:** First lunar landing scene, denomination at left, two dates above **Note:** Prev. KM#43.

Date	Mintage	F	VF	XF	Unc	BU
1999 Proof	10,000	Value: 37.50				

KM# 23 10 FRANCS

25.3100 g., 0.9250 Silver .7524 oz. ASW **Subject:** Sydney 2000 **Obv:** Roaring lion bust left within inner circle, date below in outer circle **Rev:** Diver and opera house, denomination at left **Note:** Prev. KM#44.

Date	Mintage	F	VF	XF	Unc	BU
1999 Proof	10,000	Value: 37.50				

KM# 25 10 FRANCS

25.1300 g., 0.9250 Silver .7474 oz. ASW **Subject:** Panama Canal **Obv:** Standing lion facing, denomination below **Rev:** Sailing ship above inscription and map **Note:** Prev. KM#48.

Date	Mintage	F	VF	XF	Unc	BU
2000 Proof	—	Value: 35.00				

KM# 26 10 FRANCS

25.1300 g., 0.9250 Silver .7474 oz. ASW **Subject:** Panama Canal **Obv:** Standing lion facing, denomination below **Rev:** Cargo ship over map of Panama, date at left **Note:** Prev. KM#49.

Date	Mintage	F	VF	XF	Unc	BU
2000 Proof	—	Value: 35.00				

KM# 27 10 FRANCS

25.1300 g., 0.9250 Silver .7474 oz. ASW **Subject:** 25th Anniversary - Visit of Pope John Paul II **Obv:** Standing lion facing, denomination below **Rev:** Bust 3/4 right of Pope John Paul II, date below **Note:** Prev. KM#50.

Date	Mintage	F	VF	XF	Unc	BU
2000 Proof	—	Value: 35.00				

KM# 28 10 FRANCS

25.1300 g., 0.9250 Silver .7474 oz. ASW **Subject:** 25th Anniversary - Visit of Pope John Paul II **Obv:** Standing lion facing, denomination below **Rev:** Half-length bust of Pope John Paul II facing, date below **Note:** Prev. KM#51.

Date	Mintage	F	VF	XF	Unc	BU
2000 Proof	—	Value: 35.00				

KM# 30 10 FRANCS

25.4500 g., 0.9250 Silver .7569 oz. ASW, 37.3 mm. **Subject:** Wild Life Protection **Obv:** Standing lion facing, denomination below **Rev:** Multicolor parrot with open wings left **Edge:** Reeded **Note:** Prev. KM#53.

Date	Mintage	F	VF	XF	Unc	BU
2000 Proof	—	Value: 50.00				

KM# 31 10 FRANCS

25.4500 g., 0.9250 Silver .7569 oz. ASW, 37.3 mm. **Subject:** Wild Life Protection **Obv:** Standing lion facing, denomination below **Rev:** Toucan with folded wings right **Edge:** Reeded **Note:** Prev. KM#54.

Date	Mintage	F	VF	XF	Unc	BU
2000 Proof	—	Value: 50.00				

KM# 32 10 FRANCS

31.2600 g., 0.9990 Silver 1.004 oz. ASW, 47.7 x 27.1 mm. **Subject:** Millennium - space travel **Obv:** Standing lion facing, denomination below **Rev:** Footprint on the moon **Edge:** Plain **Shape:** Rectangle **Note:** Prev. KM#55.

Date	Mintage	F	VF	XF	Unc	BU
2000 Proof	—	Value: 32.50				

KM# 33 10 FRANCS

31.2600 g., 0.9990 Silver 1.004 oz. ASW, 45.1 x 23.4 mm. **Subject:** Animal Protection **Obv:** Standing lion facing within triangle, denomination below **Rev:** Chimpanzee hanging from branches **Edge:** Plain **Shape:** Triangle **Note:** Prev. KM#56.

Date	Mintage	F	VF	XF	Unc	BU
2000 Proof	—	Value: 35.00				

KM# 34 10 FRANCS
31.2600 g., 0.9990 Silver 1.004 oz. ASW, 45.1 x 23.4 mm. **Subject:** Animal Protection **Obv:** Standing lion facing within triangle, denomination below **Rev:** 2 chimpanzees in trees **Edge:** Plain **Shape:** Triangle **Note:** Prev. KM#57.

Date	Mintage	F	VF	XF	Unc	BU
2000 Proof	—	Value: 35.00				

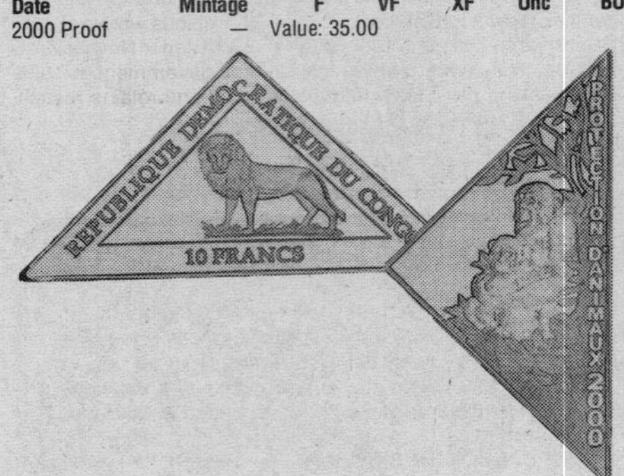

KM# 35 10 FRANCS
31.2600 g., 0.9990 Silver 1.004 oz. ASW, 45.1 x 23.4 mm. **Subject:** Animal Protection **Obv:** Standing lion facing within triangle, denomination below **Rev:** Female chimpanzee with young one **Edge:** Plain **Shape:** Triangle **Note:** Prev. KM#58.

Date	Mintage	F	VF	XF	Unc	BU
2000 Proof	—	Value: 35.00				

KM# 36 10 FRANCS
31.2600 g., 0.9990 Silver 1.004 oz. ASW, 45.1 x 23.4 mm. **Subject:** Animal Protection **Obv:** Standing lion facing within triangle, denomination below **Rev:** 2 chimpanzees on the ground **Edge:** Plain **Shape:** Triangle **Note:** Prev. KM#59.

Date	Mintage	F	VF	XF	Unc	BU
2000 Proof	—	Value: 35.00				

KM# 37 10 FRANCS
20.0000 g., 0.9250 Silver .5948 oz. ASW, 38 mm. **Subject:** Millennium - Jesus **Obv:** Standing lion facing, denomination below **Rev:** Portrait of Jesus facing within beaded circles, date below **Edge:** Plain **Note:** Prev. KM#60.

Date	Mintage	F	VF	XF	Unc	BU
2000 Proof	—	Value: 40.00				

KM# 44 10 FRANCS
19.9200 g., 0.9250 Silver .5924 oz. ASW, 41.1 mm. **Series:** Olympics **Obv:** Standing lion facing, date below **Rev:** Long jumper, denomination at right **Edge:** Reeded **Note:** Prev. KM#67.

Date	Mintage	F	VF	XF	Unc	BU
2000 Proof	—	Value: 40.00				

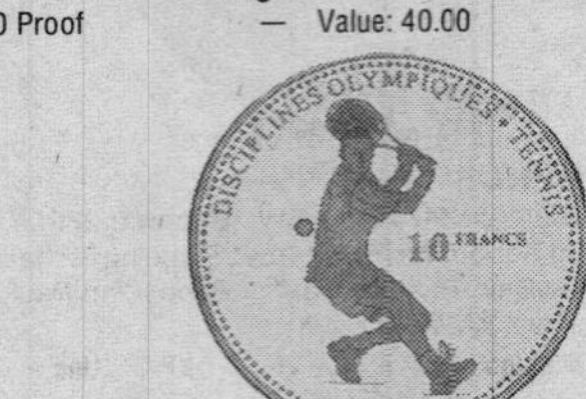

KM# 45 10 FRANCS
19.9200 g., 0.9250 Silver .5924 oz. ASW, 41.1 mm. **Series:** Olympics **Obv:** Standing lion facing, date below **Rev:** Two divers, denomination at left **Edge:** Reeded **Note:** Prev. KM#68.

Date	Mintage	F	VF	XF	Unc	BU
2000 Proof	—	Value: 40.00				

KM# 46 10 FRANCS
19.9200 g., 0.9250 Silver .5924 oz. ASW, 41.1 mm. **Series:** Olympics **Obv:** Standing lion facing, date below **Rev:** Tennis player, denomination at right **Edge:** Reeded **Note:** Prev. KM#69.

Date	Mintage	F	VF	XF	Unc	BU
2000 Proof	—	Value: 40.00				

KM# 47 10 FRANCS
19.9200 g., 0.9250 Silver .5924 oz. ASW, 41.1 mm. **Series:** Olympics **Obv:** Standing lion facing, date below **Rev:** Weight lifter, denomination at left **Edge:** Reeded **Note:** Prev. KM#70.

Date	Mintage	F	VF	XF	Unc	BU
2000 Proof	—	Value: 40.00				

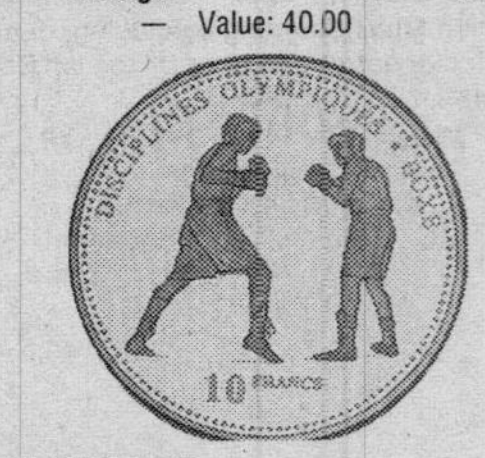

KM# 48 10 FRANCS
19.9200 g., 0.9250 Silver .5924 oz. ASW, 41.1 mm. **Series:** Olympics **Obv:** Standing lion facing, date below **Rev:** Two fencers, denomination below **Edge:** Plain **Note:** Prev. KM#71.

Date	Mintage	F	VF	XF	Unc	BU
2000 Proof	—	Value: 40.00				

KM# 49 10 FRANCS
19.9200 g., 0.9250 Silver .5924 oz. ASW, 41.1 mm. **Series:** Olympics **Obv:** Standing lion facing, date below **Rev:** Two boxers, denomination below **Edge:** Reeded **Note:** Prev. KM#72.

Date	Mintage	F	VF	XF	Unc	BU
2000 Proof	—	Value: 40.00				

KM# 50 10 FRANCS
19.9200 g., 0.9250 Silver .5924 oz. ASW, 41.1 mm. **Series:** Olympics **Obv:** Standing lion facing, date below **Rev:** Rowing, denomination below **Edge:** Reeded **Note:** Prev. KM#73.

Date	Mintage	F	VF	XF	Unc	BU
2000 Proof	—	Value: 40.00				

KM# 51 10 FRANCS
19.9200 g., 0.9250 Silver .5924 oz. ASW, 41.1 mm. **Series:** Olympics **Obv:** Standing lion facing, date below **Rev:** Archer, denomination at lower left **Edge:** Reeded **Note:** Prev. KM#74.

Date	Mintage	F	VF	XF	Unc	BU
2000 Proof	—	Value: 40.00				

KM# 52 10 FRANCS
19.9200 g., 0.9250 Silver .5924 oz. ASW, 41.1 mm. **Series:** Olympics **Obv:** Standing lion facing, date below **Rev:** Judo match, denomination below **Edge:** Reeded **Note:** Prev. KM#75.

Date	Mintage	F	VF	XF	Unc	BU
2000 Proof	—	Value: 40.00				

KM# 53 10 FRANCS
19.9200 g., 0.9250 Silver .5924 oz. ASW, 41.1 mm. **Series:** Olympics **Obv:** Standing lion facing, date below **Rev:** Ribbon dancer, denomination at right **Edge:** Reeded **Note:** Prev. KM#76.

Date	Mintage	F	VF	XF	Unc	BU
2000 Proof	—	Value: 40.00				

KM# 54 10 FRANCS
19.9200 g., 0.9250 Silver .5924 oz. ASW, 41.1 mm. **Series:** Olympics **Obv:** Standing lion facing, date below **Rev:** Badminton player, denomination below **Edge:** Reeded **Note:** Prev. KM#77.

Date	Mintage	F	VF	XF	Unc	BU
2000 Proof	—	Value: 40.00				

KM# 55 10 FRANCS
25.4500 g., 0.9250 Silver .7569 oz. ASW, 37.2 mm. **Series:** Wild Life Protection **Obv:** Standing lion facing, denomination below **Rev:** Multicolored toucan hologram left **Edge:** Reeded **Note:** Prev. KM#78.

Date	Mintage	F	VF	XF	Unc	BU
2000 Proof	—	Value: 50.00				

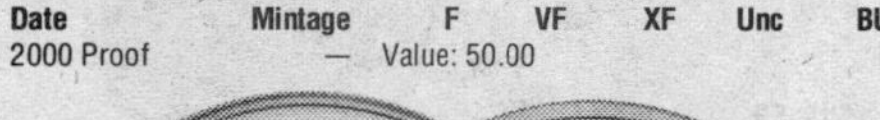

KM# 92 10 FRANCS
30.8700 g., 0.9990 Silver 0.9915 oz. ASW, 38.7 mm. **Obv:** Standing lion facing, date below **Rev:** African crocodile left, denomination below **Edge:** Reeded

Date	Mintage	F	VF	XF	Unc	BU
2000 Proof	—	Value: 45.00				

KM# 98 10 FRANCS
31.5500 g., 0.9250 Silver 0.9383 oz. ASW, 38.7 mm. **Subject:** Diogo Cao 1482 **Obv:** Standing lion facing, denomination below **Rev:** Portuguese sailing ship, date at right **Edge:** Reeded

Date	Mintage	F	VF	XF	Unc	BU
2000 Proof	—	Value: 40.00				

KM# 161 10 FRANCS
19.7600 g., 0.9250 Silver 0.5877 oz. ASW, 38.6 mm. **Obv:** Standing lion facing, denomination below **Rev:** Gorilla on all fours facing, date below **Edge:** Reeded

Date	Mintage	F	VF	XF	Unc	BU
2000 Proof	—	Value: 50.00				

KM# 29 20 FRANCS
1.5300 g., 0.9990 Gold .0492 oz. AGW **Subject:** 25th Anniversary - Visit of Pope John Paul II **Obv:** Standing lion facing, denomination below **Rev:** Bust right of Pope John Paul II **Note:** Prev. KM#52.

Date	Mintage	F	VF	XF	Unc	BU
2000 Proof	—	Value: 45.00				

KM# 62 20 FRANCS
62.2000 g., 0.9999 Silver 1.9996 oz. ASW, 40 mm. **Subject:** Japanese New 500 Yen Coin **Obv:** Standing lion facing, denomination below **Rev:** Japanese 500 yen coin Y-125, embedded over the obverse and reverse design of the Y-99 500 yen coin **Edge:** Reeded **Note:** Prev. KM#85.

Date	Mintage	F	VF	XF	Unc	BU
2000	1,500	—	—	—	65.00	—

KM# 177 100 FRANCS
39.2000 g., Gold **Obv:** Roaring lion **Rev:** Dr. Livingstone and river boat **Edge:** Reeded

Date	Mintage	F	VF	XF	Unc	BU
1999 Proof	—	—	—	—	—	—

KM# 42 100 FRANCS
31.5400 g., 0.9999 Gold 1.0139 oz. AGW, 37.3 mm. **Subject:** Wild Life Protection **Obv:** Standing lion facing, denomination below **Rev:** Multicolor holographic parrot with folded wings right **Edge:** Reeded **Note:** Prev. KM#65.

Date	Mintage	F	VF	XF	Unc	BU
2000 Proof	25	Value: 1,200				

KM# 43 100 FRANCS
31.5400 g., 0.9999 Gold 1.0139 oz. AGW, 37.3 mm. **Subject:** Wild Life Protection **Obv:** Standing lion facing, denomination below **Rev:** Multicolor holographic parrot with open wings left **Edge:** Reeded **Note:** Prev. KM#66.

Date	Mintage	F	VF	XF	Unc	BU
2000 Proof	25	Value: 1,200				

ESSAIS

KM#	Date	Mintage	Identification	Mkt Val
E1	1965	—	10 Francs. Silver.	—
E2	1965(b)	—	10 Francs. Gold.	—

Note: Aluminum and copper-nickel essais of the 10 Francs are valued at $175 and $250 respectively. These are considered off-metal pieces created as die trials or set-up strikes in the process of producing the official silver and gold coins.

KM#	Date	Mintage	Identification	Mkt Val
E3	1970	—	50 Makutas. Pewter. KM12.	250
E4	1970	—	Zaire. Pewter. KM13.	325
E5	1970	—	Zaire. Silver. KM13.	165
E6	1970	10	Zaire. Gold. ESSAI.	1,000

PIEFORTS WITH ESSAI

KM#	Date	Mintage	Identification	Mkt Val
PE1	1970	10	Zaire. Silver. 2.4 mm thick.	250
PE2	1970	10	Zaire. Silver. 4.7 mm thick.	365

MINT SETS

KM#	Date	Mintage	Identification	Issue Price	Mkt Val
MS1	1970 (4)	1,000	KM10-13	1,300	1,000

PROOF SETS

KM#	Date	Mintage	Identification	Issue Price	Mkt Val
PS1	1965 (5)	3,000	KM2-6. Approximately 70 percent melted.	490	1,300
PS2	1970 (4)	1,000	KM10-13	—	1,100

COOK ISLANDS

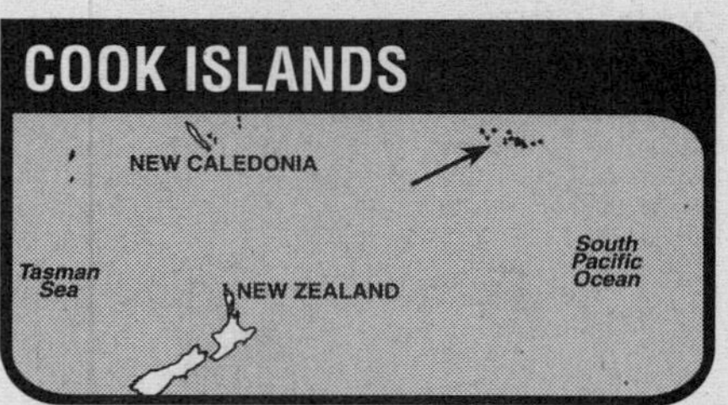

Cook Islands, a self-governing dependency of New Zealand consisting of 15 islands, is located in the South Pacific Ocean about 2,000 miles (3,218 km.) northeast of New Zealand. It has an area of 93 sq. mi. (234 sq. km.) and a population of 17,185. Capital: Avarua. The United States claims the islands of Danger, Manahiki, Penrhyn, and Rakahanga atolls. Citrus and canned fruits and juices, copra, clothing, jewelry, and mother-of-pearl shell are exported.

Spanish navigator Alvaro de Mendada first sighted the islands in 1595. Portuguese navigator Pedro Fernandes de Quieros landed on Rakahanga in 1606. English navigator Capt. James Cook sailed to the islands on three occasions: 1773, 1774 and 1777. He named them Hervey Islands, in honor of Augustus John Hervey, a lord of the Admiralty. The islands were declared a British protectorate in 1888, and were annexed to New Zealand in 1901. They were granted internal self-government in 1965. New Zealand provides an annual subsidy and retains responsibility for defense and foreign affairs.

RULERS
British

MINT MARKS
(b) - British Royal Mint
FM - Franklin Mint, U.S.A. *
PM - Pobjoy Mint

***NOTE:** From 1975-1985 the Franklin Mint produced coinage in up to three different qualities. Qualities of issue are designated in () after each date and are defined as follows:

(M) MATTE - Normal circulation strike or a dull finish produced by sandblasting special uncirculated (polish finish) or proof quality dies.

(U) SPECIAL UNCIRCULATED - Polished or proof-like in appearance without any frosted features.

(P) PROOF - The highest quality obtainable having mirror-like fields and frosted features.

MONETARY SYSTEM

(Until 1967)
12 Pence = 1 Shilling
20 Shillings = 1 Pound
(Commencing 1967)
100 Cents = 1 Dollar

DEPENDENCY OF NEW ZEALAND

DECIMAL COINAGE

KM# 1 CENT
Bronze **Ruler:** Elizabeth II **Obv:** Young bust right, date below **Rev:** Taro leaf, denomination at right **Rev. Designer:** James Berry

Date	Mintage	F	VF	XF	Unc	BU
1972	117,000	—	—	0.10	0.20	0.35
1972 Proof	17,000	Value: 0.50				
1973	8,500	—	—	0.10	0.20	0.35
1973 Proof	13,000	Value: 0.50				
1974	300,000	—	—	0.10	0.20	0.35
1974 Proof	7,300	Value: 0.50				
1975	429,000	—	—	0.10	0.20	0.35
1975FM (M)	1,000	—	—	—	0.50	0.65
1975FM (U)	2,251	—	—	—	0.20	0.35
1975FM (P)	21,000	Value: 0.50				
1976FM (M)	1,001	—	—	—	0.50	0.65
1976FM (U)	1,066	—	—	—	0.20	0.35
1976FM (P)	18,000	Value: 0.50				
1977FM (M)	1,171	—	—	—	0.50	0.65
1977FM (U)	1,002	—	—	—	0.20	0.35
1977FM (P)	5,986	Value: 0.50				
1979FM (M)	1,000	—	—	—	0.50	0.65
1979FM (U)	500	—	—	—	1.00	1.25
1979FM (P)	4,058	Value: 0.50				
1983	—	—	—	0.10	0.20	0.35
1983 Proof	10,000	Value: 0.50				

KM# 1a CENT
Bronze **Ruler:** Elizabeth II **Obv:** Young bust right, date below **Rev:** Taro leaf, denomination **Edge Lettering:** 1728 • CAPT. JAMES COOK • 1978

Date	Mintage	F	VF	XF	Unc	BU
1978FM (M)	1,000	—	—	—	0.85	1.15
1978FM (P)	6,287	Value: 0.50				
1978FM (U)	767	—	—	—	0.75	1.00

KM# 1b CENT

Bronze **Ruler:** Elizabeth II **Subject:** Wedding of Prince Charles and Lady Diana **Obv:** Young bust right **Edge Lettering:** THE ROYAL WEDDING 29 JULY 1981

Date	Mintage	F	VF	XF	Unc	BU
1981FM (M)	1,000	—	—	—	0.50	0.65
1981FM (U)	1,100	—	—	—	0.50	0.65
1981FM (P)	9,205	Value: 0.40				

KM# 2 2 CENTS

Bronze **Ruler:** Elizabeth II **Obv:** Young bust right, date below **Rev:** Pineapple, denomination at right **Rev. Designer:** James Berry

Date	Mintage	F	VF	XF	Unc	BU
1972	63,000	—	0.10	0.15	0.30	0.50
1972 Proof	17,000	Value: 0.75				
1973	8,500	—	0.15	0.20	0.40	0.60
1973 Proof	13,000	Value: 0.75				
1974	120,000	—	0.10	0.15	0.30	0.50
1974 Proof	7,300	Value: 0.75				
1975	129,000	—	0.10	0.15	0.25	0.45
1975FM (M)	1,000	—	—	—	0.50	0.75
1975FM (P)	21,000	Value: 0.75				
1975FM (U)	2,251	—	—	—	0.30	0.50
1976FM (M)	1,001	—	—	—	0.75	1.00
1976FM (P)	18,000	Value: 0.75				
1976FM (U)	1,066	—	—	—	0.30	0.50
1977FM (M)	1,171	—	—	—	0.75	1.00
1977FM (P)	5,986	Value: 0.75				
1977FM (U)	1,002	—	—	—	0.30	0.50
1979FM (M)	1,000	—	—	—	0.75	1.00
1979FM (U)	500	—	—	—	0.30	0.50
1979FM (P)	4,058	Value: 0.75				
1983	—	—	0.10	0.15	0.25	0.45
1983 Proof	10,000	Value: 0.75				

KM# 2a 2 CENTS

Bronze **Ruler:** Elizabeth II **Obv:** Young bust right **Rev:** Pineapple, denomination at right **Edge Lettering:** 1728 • CAPT. JAMES COOK • 1978

Date	Mintage	F	VF	XF	Unc	BU
1978FM (M)	1,000	—	—	—	0.75	1.00
1978FM (U)	767	—	—	—	0.85	1.15
1978FM (P)	6,287	Value: 0.50				

KM# 2b 2 CENTS

Bronze **Ruler:** Elizabeth II **Subject:** Wedding of Prince Charles and Lady Diana **Obv:** Young bust right, date below **Edge Lettering:** THE ROYAL WEDDING 29 JULY 1981

Date	Mintage	F	VF	XF	Unc	BU
1981FM (M)	1,000	—	—	—	0.75	1.00
1981FM (P)	9,205	Value: 0.50				
1981FM (U)	1,100	—	—	—	0.75	1.00

KM# 3 5 CENTS

Copper-Nickel, 19.41 mm. **Ruler:** Elizabeth II **Obv:** Young bust right, date below **Rev:** Hibiscus, denomination below **Rev. Designer:** James Berry

Date	Mintage	F	VF	XF	Unc	BU
1972	32,000	—	0.10	0.20	0.40	0.60
1972 Proof	17,000	Value: 1.00				
1973 Proof	13,000	Value: 1.00				
1973	8,500	—	0.15	0.25	0.50	0.75
1974	80,000	—	0.10	0.20	0.40	0.60
1974 Proof	7,300	Value: 1.00				
1975FM (M)	1,000	—	—	—	1.00	1.25
1975FM (U)	2,251	—	—	—	0.40	0.60
1975FM (P)	21,000	Value: 0.85				
1975	89,000	—	0.10	0.20	0.40	0.60
1976FM (M)	1,001	—	—	—	1.00	1.25
1976FM (U)	1,066	—	—	—	0.40	0.60
1976FM (P)	18,000	Value: 0.85				
1977FM (M)	1,171	—	—	—	1.00	1.25
1977FM (P)	5,986	Value: 1.00				
1977FM (U)	1,002	—	—	—	0.40	0.60
1979FM (P)	4,058	Value: 1.00				
1979FM (M)	1,000	—	—	—	1.00	1.25
1979FM (U)	500	—	—	—	0.40	0.60
1983	—	—	0.10	0.20	0.40	0.60
1983 Proof	10,000	Value: 1.00				

KM# 3a 5 CENTS

Copper-Nickel **Ruler:** Elizabeth II **Obv:** Young bust right, date below **Rev:** Hibiscus, denomination below **Edge Lettering:** 1728 • CAPT. JAMES COOK • 1978

Date	Mintage	F	VF	XF	Unc	BU
1978FM (M)	1,000	—	—	—	1.00	1.25
1978FM (U)	767	—	—	—	0.75	1.00
1978FM (P)	6,287	Value: 0.50				

KM# 3b 5 CENTS

Copper-Nickel, 19.41 mm. **Ruler:** Elizabeth II **Subject:** Wedding of Prince Charles and Lady Diana **Obv:** Young bust right, date below **Edge Lettering:** THE ROYAL WEDDING 29 JULY 1981

Date	Mintage	F	VF	XF	Unc	BU
1981FM (M)	1,000	—	—	—	1.00	1.25
1981FM (U)	1,100	—	—	—	1.00	1.25
1981FM (P)	9,205	Value: 0.50				

KM# 33 5 CENTS

Copper-Nickel, 19.41 mm. **Ruler:** Elizabeth II **Obv:** Crowned head right, date below **Rev:** Hibiscus **Rev. Designer:** James Berry

Date	Mintage	F	VF	XF	Unc	BU
1987	—	—	—	0.15	0.35	0.50
1987 Proof	—	Value: 1.00				
1988	—	—	—	0.15	0.35	0.50
1988 Proof	—	Value: 1.00				
1992	—	—	—	0.15	0.35	0.50
1992 Proof	—	Value: 1.00				
1994	20,000	—	—	0.15	0.35	0.50
1994 Proof	200	Value: 1.50				

KM# 369 5 CENTS

4.4300 g., Nickel Clad Steel, 24 mm. **Ruler:** Elizabeth II **Subject:** F.A.O. **Obv:** Head with tiara right, date below **Rev:** Statue of Tangaroa divides denomination **Rev. Designer:** James Berry **Edge:** Plain

Date	Mintage	F	VF	XF	Unc	BU
2000	—	—	—	—	1.00	1.50
2000 Proof	—	Value: 3.50				

KM# 4 10 CENTS

Copper-Nickel, 23.6 mm. **Ruler:** Elizabeth II **Obv:** Young bust right, date below **Rev:** Orange, denomination above **Rev. Designer:** James Berry

Date	Mintage	F	VF	XF	Unc	BU
1972	35,000	—	0.10	0.20	0.65	0.85
1972 Proof	17,000	Value: 1.25				
1973	59,000	—	0.10	0.20	0.65	0.85
1973 Proof	13,000	Value: 1.25				
1974 Proof	7,300	Value: 1.25				
1974	50,000	—	0.10	0.20	0.50	0.85
1975FM (M)	1,000	—	—	—	1.25	1.50
1975FM (P)	21,000	Value: 1.25				
1975	59,000	—	0.10	0.20	0.50	0.85
1975FM (U)	2,251	—	—	—	0.50	0.85
1976FM (M)	1,001	—	—	—	1.25	1.50
1976FM (U)	1,066	—	—	—	0.50	0.65
1976FM (P)	18,000	Value: 1.25				
1977FM (P)	5,986	Value: 1.25				
1977FM (M)	1,171	—	—	—	1.25	1.50
1977FM (U)	1,002	—	—	—	0.50	0.65
1983	—	—	0.10	0.20	0.50	0.65
1983 Proof	10,000	Value: 1.25				

KM# 4a 10 CENTS

Copper-Nickel, 23.6 mm. **Ruler:** Elizabeth II **Obv:** Young bust right, date below **Rev:** Orange, denomination above **Edge Lettering:** 1728 • CAPT. JAMES COOK • 1978

Date	Mintage	F	VF	XF	Unc	BU
1978FM (M)	1,000	—	—	—	1.25	1.50
1978FM (U)	767	—	—	—	1.25	1.50
1978FM (P)	6,287	Value: 1.00				

KM# 4b 10 CENTS

Copper-Nickel, 23.6 mm. **Ruler:** Elizabeth II **Series:** F.A.O. **Obv:** Young bust right, date below **Rev:** Orange, denomination above

Date	Mintage	F	VF	XF	Unc	BU
1979FM (M)	9,000	—	—	—	1.00	1.25
1979FM (P)	4,058	Value: 1.25				
1979FM (U)	500	—	—	—	1.50	1.75

KM# 4c 10 CENTS

Copper-Nickel, 23.6 mm. **Ruler:** Elizabeth II **Subject:** Wedding of Prince Charles and Lady Diana **Obv:** Young bust right, date below **Edge Lettering:** THE ROYAL WEDDING 29 JULY 1981

Date	Mintage	F	VF	XF	Unc	BU
1981FM (M)	1,000	—	—	—	1.25	1.50
1981FM (U)	1,100	—	—	—	1.25	1.50
1981FM (P)	9,205	Value: 0.75				

KM# 34 10 CENTS

Copper-Nickel, 23.6 mm. **Ruler:** Elizabeth II **Obv:** Crowned head right, date below **Rev:** Orange, denomination above **Rev. Designer:** James Berry

Date	Mintage	F	VF	XF	Unc	BU
1987	—	—	—	0.20	0.50	0.75
1987 Proof	—	Value: 1.25				
1988	—	—	—	0.20	0.50	0.75
1988 Proof	—	Value: 1.25				
1992	—	—	—	0.20	0.50	0.75
1992 Proof	—	Value: 1.25				
1994	20,000	—	—	0.20	0.50	0.75
1994 Proof	200	Value: 1.75				

KM# 5 20 CENTS

Copper-Nickel, 28.52 mm. **Ruler:** Elizabeth II **Obv:** Young bust right, date below **Rev:** Fairy Tern right, denomination below **Rev. Designer:** James Berry

Date	Mintage	F	VF	XF	Unc	BU
1972	31,000	—	0.20	0.40	0.75	1.00
1972 Proof	17,000	Value: 1.50				
1973	49,000	—	0.20	0.40	0.75	1.00
1973 Proof	13,000	Value: 1.50				
1974	5,500	—	0.20	0.45	0.85	1.25
1974 Proof	7,300	Value: 1.50				
1975	60,000	—	0.20	0.40	0.75	1.00
1975FM (M)	1,000	—	—	—	1.50	1.75
1975FM (U)	2,251	—	—	—	0.85	1.25
1975FM (P)	21,000	Value: 1.50				
1983	—	—	0.20	0.40	0.85	1.25
1983 Proof	10,000	Value: 1.50				

KM# 14 20 CENTS

Copper-Nickel, 28.52 mm. **Ruler:** Elizabeth II **Obv:** Young bust right, date below **Rev:** Two Pacific Triton shells, denomination lower right **Rev. Designer:** James Berry

Date	Mintage	F	VF	XF	Unc	BU
1976FM (M)	1,001	—	—	—	1.50	1.75
1976FM (U)	1,066	—	—	—	1.00	1.25
1976FM (P)	18,000	Value: 1.50				
1977FM (P)	5,986	Value: 1.50				
1977FM (M)	1,171	—	—	—	1.50	1.75
1977FM (U)	1,002	—	—	—	1.00	1.25

Date	Mintage	F	VF	XF	Unc	BU
1979FM (M)	1,000	—	—	—	1.50	1.75
1979FM (U)	500	—	—	—	2.00	1.50
1979FM (P)	4,058	Value: 1.50				

KM# 14a 20 CENTS

Copper-Nickel, 28.52 mm. **Ruler:** Elizabeth II **Obv:** Young bust right, date below **Rev:** Shells, denomination at right **Edge Lettering:** 1728 • CAPT. JAMES COOK • 1978

Date	Mintage	F	VF	XF	Unc	BU
1978FM (M)	1,000	—	—	—	1.50	1.75
1978FM (U)	767	—	—	—	2.00	2.50
1978FM (P)	6,287	Value: 1.50				

KM# 14b 20 CENTS

Copper-Nickel, 28.52 mm. **Ruler:** Elizabeth II **Subject:** Wedding of Prince Charles and Lady Diana **Obv:** Young bust right, date below **Rev:** Shells, denomination at right **Edge Lettering:** THE ROYAL WEDDING 29 JULY 1981

Date	Mintage	F	VF	XF	Unc	BU
1981FM (M)	1,000	—	—	—	1.50	1.75
1981FM (U)	1,100	—	—	—	1.50	1.75
1981FM (P)	9,205	Value: 1.00				

KM# 35 20 CENTS

Copper-Nickel, 28.52 mm. **Ruler:** Elizabeth II **Obv:** Crowned head right, date below **Rev:** Fairy Tern, denomination below **Rev. Designer:** James Berry

Date	Mintage	F	VF	XF	Unc	BU
1987	—	—	—	0.25	0.75	1.00
1987 Proof	—	Value: 1.50				
1988	—	—	—	0.25	0.75	1.00
1988 Proof	—	Value: 1.50				
1992	—	—	—	0.25	0.75	1.00
1992 Proof	—	Value: 1.50				
1994	20,000	—	—	0.25	0.75	1.00
1994 Proof	200	Value: 2.00				

KM# 6.1 50 CENTS

Copper-Nickel, 31.75 mm. **Ruler:** Elizabeth II **Obv:** Young bust right, date below **Obv. Designer:** Machin **Rev:** Bonito fish, denomination upper left **Rev. Designer:** James Berry

Date	Mintage	F	VF	XF	Unc	BU
1972	31,000	—	—	0.65	1.25	2.00
1972 Proof	17,000	Value: 3.00				
1973	19,000	—	—	0.65	1.25	2.00
1973 Proof	13,000	Value: 3.00				
1974	10,000	—	—	0.65	1.25	2.00
1974 Proof	7,300	Value: 3.00				
1975	19,000	—	—	0.65	1.25	2.00
1975FM (M)	1,000	—	—	—	2.00	3.00
1975FM (U)	2,251	—	—	—	1.50	2.00
1975FM (P)	21,000	Value: 2.50				
1976FM (M)	1,001	—	—	—	2.00	3.00
1976FM (U)	1,066	—	—	—	1.50	2.00
1976FM (P)	18,000	Value: 2.50				
1977FM (M)	1,171	—	—	—	2.00	3.00
1977FM (U)	1,002	—	—	—	1.50	2.00
1977FM (P)	5,986	Value: 3.00				
1983	—	—	—	0.65	1.25	2.00
1983 Proof	10,000	Value: 3.50				

KM# 6.2 50 CENTS

Copper-Nickel, 31.75 mm. **Ruler:** Elizabeth II **Obv:** Young bust right, date below **Edge Lettering:** 1728 • CAPT. JAMES COOK • 1978

Date	Mintage	F	VF	XF	Unc	BU
1978FM (M)	1,000	—	—	—	2.00	3.00
1978FM (P)	6,287	Value: 2.00				
1978FM (U)	767	—	—	—	2.00	3.00

KM# 6.3 50 CENTS

Copper-Nickel, 31.75 mm. **Ruler:** Elizabeth II **Series:** F.A.O. **Obv:** Young bust right, date below **Rev:** F.A.O. logo, Bonito fish, denomination upper left

Date	Mintage	F	VF	XF	Unc	BU
1979FM (M)	9,000	—	—	0.75	1.25	2.00
1979FM (U)	500	—	—	—	2.50	3.50
1979FM (P)	4,058	Value: 2.25				

KM# 6.4 50 CENTS

Copper-Nickel, 31.75 mm. **Ruler:** Elizabeth II **Subject:** Wedding of Prince Charles and Lady Diana **Obv:** Young bust right, date below **Edge Lettering:** THE ROYAL WEDDING 29 JULY 1981

Date	Mintage	F	VF	XF	Unc	BU
1981FM (M)	1,000	—	—	—	2.00	3.00
1981FM (U)	1,100	—	—	—	2.00	3.00
1981FM (P)	9,205	Value: 1.50				

KM# 36 50 CENTS

Copper-Nickel, 31.75 mm. **Ruler:** Elizabeth II **Obv:** Crowned head right, date below **Rev:** Bonito fish, denomination upper left **Rev. Designer:** James Berry

Date	Mintage	F	VF	XF	Unc	BU
1987	—	—	—	0.65	1.50	2.00
1987 Proof	—	Value: 2.00				
1992	—	—	—	0.65	1.50	2.00

KM# 307 50 CENTS

Copper-Nickel **Ruler:** Elizabeth II **Obv:** Crowned head right, date below **Rev:** Head 3/4 facing, dates and denomination below

Date	Mintage	F	VF	XF	Unc	BU
1997	—	—	—	—	6.00	—
1997 Proof	—	Value: 8.50				

KM# 338 50 CENTS

26.9000 g., Copper-Nickel **Ruler:** Elizabeth II **Obv:** Crowned head right, date below **Rev:** Multicolor cartoon cat "Garfield", denomination below **Edge:** Reeded

Date	Mintage	F	VF	XF	Unc	BU
1999 Proof	—	Value: 5.00				

KM# 41 50 TENE

13.6000 g., Copper-Nickel, 31.75 mm. **Ruler:** Elizabeth II **Obv:** Crowned head right, date below **Rev:** Hawksbill turtle right, denomination above **Rev. Designer:** Horst Hahne

Date	Mintage	F	VF	XF	Unc	BU
1988	60,000	—	—	0.50	1.50	3.00
1988 Proof	1,000	Value: 3.50				
1992	—	—	—	—	1.50	3.00
1992 Proof	—	Value: 3.50				
1994	20,000	—	—	—	1.50	3.00
1994 Proof	200	Value: 4.00				

KM# 7 DOLLAR

27.2000 g., Copper-Nickel, 38.5 mm. **Ruler:** Elizabeth II **Obv:** Young bust right, date below **Rev:** Tangaroa, Polynesian God of Creation, divides denominations **Rev. Designer:** James Berry

Date	Mintage	F	VF	XF	Unc	BU
1972	31,000	—	1.00	1.50	2.50	4.00
1972 Proof	27,000	Value: 4.00				
1973	49,000	—	1.00	1.50	2.50	4.00
1973 Proof	13,000	Value: 6.00				
1974	20,000	—	1.00	1.50	2.50	4.00
1974 Proof	7,300	Value: 6.00				
1975	29,000	—	1.00	1.50	2.50	4.00
1975FM (M)	1,000	—	—	—	4.50	6.00
1975FM (U)	2,251	—	—	—	3.50	5.00
1975FM (P)	21,000	Value: 6.00				
1976FM (M)	1,001	—	—	—	4.50	6.00
1976FM (U)	1,066	—	—	—	4.50	6.00
1976FM (P)	18,000	Value: 5.00				
1977FM (M)	1,171	—	—	—	4.50	6.00
1977FM (U)	1,002	—	—	—	4.50	6.00
1977FM (P)	5,986	Value: 6.50				
1979FM (M)	1,000	—	—	—	4.50	6.00
1979FM (U)	500	—	—	—	5.50	7.00
1979FM (P)	4,058	Value: 6.50				
1983	—	—	1.00	1.50	3.50	5.00
1983 Proof	10,000	Value: 5.00				

KM# 7a DOLLAR

27.2000 g., Copper-Nickel, 38.5 mm. **Ruler:** Elizabeth II **Obv:** Young bust right, date below **Rev:** Tangaroa, Polynesian God of Creation, divides denominations **Edge Lettering:** 1728 • CAPT. JAMES COOK • 1978

Date	Mintage	F	VF	XF	Unc	BU
1978FM (U)	767	—	—	—	6.00	7.50
1978FM (P)	6,287	Value: 5.50				
1978FM (M)	1,000	—	—	—	6.00	7.50

KM# 7b DOLLAR

27.2000 g., Copper-Nickel, 38.5 mm. **Ruler:** Elizabeth II **Subject:** Wedding of Prince Charles and Lady Diana **Obv:** Young bust right, date below **Rev:** Tangaroa, Polynesian God of Creation, divides denominations **Edge Lettering:** THE ROYAL WEDDING 29 JULY 1981

Date	Mintage	F	VF	XF	Unc	BU
1981FM (U)	1,100	—	—	—	5.00	6.50
1981FM (P)	9,205	Value: 5.00				
1981FM (M)	1,000	—	—	—	5.00	6.50

KM# 30 DOLLAR

27.2000 g., Copper-Nickel, 38.5 mm. **Ruler:** Elizabeth II **Subject:** 16th Forum, 2nd P.I.C. and Mini Games **Obv:** Young bust right, date below **Rev:** Tangaroa, Polynesian God of Creation **Rev. Designer:** James Berry

Date	Mintage	F	VF	XF	Unc	BU
1985	—	—	—	—	3.50	5.00

KM# 30a DOLLAR

27.2200 g., 0.9250 Silver .8096 oz. ASW, 38.5 mm. **Ruler:** Elizabeth II **Subject:** 16th Forum, 2nd P.I.C. and Mini Games **Obv:** Young bust right, date below **Rev:** Tangaroa, Polynesian God of Creation

Date	Mintage	F	VF	XF	Unc	BU
1985 Proof	Est. 2,500	Value: 12.50				

KM# 30b DOLLAR

39.8000 g., 0.9170 Gold 1.1735 oz. AGW, 38.5 mm. **Ruler:** Elizabeth II **Subject:** 16th Forum, 2nd P.I.C. and Mini Games **Obv:** Young bust right, date below **Rev:** Tangaroa, Polynesian God of Creation

Date	Mintage	F	VF	XF	Unc	BU
1985 Proof	Est. 25	Value: 1,750				

KM# 31 DOLLAR

27.2000 g., Copper-Nickel, 38.5 mm. **Ruler:** Elizabeth II **Subject:** 60th Birthday of Queen Elizabeth II **Obv:** Crowned bust right, date below **Rev:** Cameos of family members in circle

Date	Mintage	F	VF	XF	Unc	BU
1986	20,000	—	—	—	2.75	—

KM# 31a DOLLAR

27.2200 g., 0.9250 Silver .8096 oz. ASW, 38.5 mm. **Ruler:** Elizabeth II **Subject:** 60th Birthday of Queen Elizabeth II **Obv:** Crowned bust right, date below **Rev:** Busts of Andrew and Sarah facing each other within wreath

Date	Mintage	F	VF	XF	Unc	BU
1986 Proof	Est. 2,500	Value: 12.50				

KM# 31b DOLLAR

44.0000 g., 0.9170 Gold 1.2969 oz. AGW, 38.5 mm. **Ruler:** Elizabeth II **Subject:** 60th Birthday of Queen Elizabeth II **Obv:** Crowned bust right, date below **Rev:** Busts of Andrew and Sarah facing each other within wreath

Date	Mintage	F	VF	XF	Unc	BU
1986 Proof	Est. 60	Value: 950				

KM# 32 DOLLAR

27.2000 g., Copper-Nickel, 38.5 mm. **Ruler:** Elizabeth II **Subject:** Prince Andrew's Wedding **Obv:** Crowned head right, date below **Rev:** Busts of Andrew and Sarah facing each other within wreath **Rev. Designer:** John Savage

Date	Mintage	F	VF	XF	Unc	BU
1986	Est. 20,000	—	—	—	2.75	—

KM# 32a DOLLAR

27.2200 g., 0.9250 Silver .8096 oz. ASW, 38.5 mm. **Ruler:** Elizabeth II **Subject:** Prince Andrews Wedding **Obv:** Crowned bust right, date below **Rev:** Busts of Andrew and Sarah facing each other within wreath

Date	Mintage	F	VF	XF	Unc	BU
1986 Proof	Est. 2,500	Value: 12.50				

KM# 32b DOLLAR

44.0000 g., 0.9170 Gold 1.2969 oz. AGW, 38.5 mm. **Ruler:** Elizabeth II **Subject:** Prince Andrews Wedding **Obv:** Crowned bust right, date below **Rev:** Busts of Andrew and Sarah facing each other within wreath

Date	Mintage	F	VF	XF	Unc	BU
1986 Proof	Est. 75	Value: 950				

KM# 37 DOLLAR

Copper-Nickel, 28.52 mm. **Ruler:** Elizabeth II **Obv:** Crowned head right, date below **Rev:** Tangaroa statue divides denominations **Rev. Designer:** James Berry **Shape:** Scalloped

Date	Mintage	F	VF	XF	Unc	BU
1987	—	—	—	1.00	2.50	3.50
1987 Proof	—	Value: 4.50				
1988	—	—	—	1.00	2.50	3.50
1988 Proof	—	Value: 4.50				
1992	—	—	—	1.00	2.50	3.50
1992 Proof	—	Value: 4.50				
1994	20,000	—	—	1.00	2.50	3.50
1994 Proof	200	Value: 5.50				

KM# 147 DOLLAR

27.2000 g., Copper-Nickel, 38.5 mm. **Ruler:** Elizabeth II **Obv:** Crowned head right, date below **Rev:** Tangaroa, Polynesian God of Fertility **Rev. Designer:** James Berry

Date	Mintage	F	VF	XF	Unc	BU
1992	—	—	—	—	2.75	—

KM# 266 DOLLAR

27.2000 g., Copper-Nickel, 38.5 mm. **Ruler:** Elizabeth II **Obv:** Crowned head right, date below **Rev:** Queen Mother and daughters within circle, denomination below

Date	Mintage	F	VF	XF	Unc	BU
1995 Proof	Est. 30,000	Value: 3.00				

KM# 267 DOLLAR

10.0000 g., 0.5000 Silver .1607 oz. ASW **Ruler:** Elizabeth II **Subject:** 1996 Summer Olympics **Obv:** Crowned head right, date below **Rev:** Horse jumping left within circle, denomination below

Date	Mintage	F	VF	XF	Unc	BU
1996 Proof	Est. 10,000	Value: 4.50				

KM# 326 DOLLAR

31.1035 g., 0.9990 Silver 1.0000 oz. ASW **Ruler:** Elizabeth II **Subject:** Lunar Year of the Mouse **Obv:** Crowned head right, date below **Rev:** Mouse in basket

Date	Mintage	F	VF	XF	Unc	BU
1996 Proof	—	Value: 12.50				

KM# 327 DOLLAR

31.1035 g., 0.9990 Silver 1.0000 oz. ASW **Ruler:** Elizabeth II **Obv:** Crowned head right, date below **Rev:** Multicolor carnation

Date	Mintage	F	VF	XF	Unc	BU
1996 Proof	—	Value: 12.50				

KM# 268 DOLLAR

Copper-Nickel **Ruler:** Elizabeth II **Obv:** Crowned head right, date below **Rev:** Sir Francis Drake left and sailing ship right, denomination below

Date	Mintage	F	VF	XF	Unc	BU
1996 Proof	Est. 25,000	Value: 3.00				

KM# 277 DOLLAR

Copper-Nickel **Ruler:** Elizabeth II **Subject:** Yellowstone National Park **Obv:** Crowned head right, date below **Rev:** Multicolored Grizzly Bear and cub

Date	Mintage	F	VF	XF	Unc	BU
1996	—	—	—	—	5.50	—

KM# 278 DOLLAR

Copper-Nickel **Ruler:** Elizabeth II **Subject:** Olympic National Park **Obv:** Crowned head right, date below **Rev:** Multicolor Bald Eagle in flight

Date	Mintage	F	VF	XF	Unc	BU
1996	—	—	—	—	5.50	—

KM# 341 DOLLAR

Copper-Nickel **Ruler:** Elizabeth II **Subject:** Endangered Wildlife **Obv:** Crowned head right, date below **Rev:** Senegalese lion, denomination below

Date	Mintage	F	VF	XF	Unc	BU
1996	—	—	—	—	5.50	—

KM# 311 DOLLAR
9.9700 g., 0.5000 Silver .1603 oz. ASW **Ruler:** Elizabeth II **Subject:** Endangered Wildlife **Obv:** Crowned head right, date below **Rev:** Mother elephant with calf, denomination below

Date	Mintage	F	VF	XF	Unc	BU
1996 Proof	—	Value: 10.00				

KM# 342 DOLLAR
Copper-Nickel **Ruler:** Elizabeth II **Subject:** Endangered Wildlife **Obv:** Crowned head right, date below **Rev:** European otters, denomination below

Date	Mintage	F	VF	XF	Unc	BU
1996	—	—	—	—	6.50	—

KM# 343 DOLLAR
Copper-Nickel **Ruler:** Elizabeth II **Subject:** Endangered Wildlife **Obv:** Crowned head right, date below **Rev:** Jackass penguins

Date	Mintage	F	VF	XF	Unc	BU
1996	—	—	—	—	6.50	—

KM# 344 DOLLAR
Copper-Nickel **Ruler:** Elizabeth II **Subject:** Endangered Wildlife **Obv:** Crowned head right, date below **Rev:** Fallow deer, denomination

Date	Mintage	F	VF	XF	Unc	BU
1996	—	—	—	—	6.50	—

KM# 345 DOLLAR
Copper-Nickel **Ruler:** Elizabeth II **Subject:** Endangered Wildlife **Obv:** Crowned head right, date below **Rev:** Heaviside's dolphins, denomination below

Date	Mintage	F	VF	XF	Unc	BU
1996	—	—	—	—	6.50	—

KM# 346 DOLLAR
Copper-Nickel **Ruler:** Elizabeth II **Subject:** Endangered Wildlife **Obv:** Crowned head right, date below **Rev:** Cougar and cub, denomination below

Date	Mintage	F	VF	XF	Unc	BU
1996	—	—	—	—	6.50	—

KM# 347 DOLLAR
Copper-Nickel **Ruler:** Elizabeth II **Subject:** Endangered Wildlife **Obv:** Crowned head right, date below **Rev:** Lowland gorilla, denomination below

Date	Mintage	F	VF	XF	Unc	BU
1996	—	—	—	—	6.50	—

KM# 348 DOLLAR
Copper-Nickel **Ruler:** Elizabeth II **Subject:** Endangered Wildlife **Obv:** Crowned head right, date below **Rev:** Peregrine falcon, denomination

Date	Mintage	F	VF	XF	Unc	BU
1996	—	—	—	—	6.50	—

KM# 349 DOLLAR
Copper-Nickel **Ruler:** Elizabeth II **Subject:** Endangered Wildlife **Obv:** Crowned head right, date below **Rev:** Kangaroo, denomination

Date	Mintage	F	VF	XF	Unc	BU
1996	—	—	—	—	6.50	—

KM# 350 DOLLAR
Copper-Nickel **Ruler:** Elizabeth II **Subject:** Endangered Wildlife **Obv:** Crowned head right, date below **Rev:** Bee hummingbird, denomination

Date	Mintage	F	VF	XF	Unc	BU
1996	—	—	—	—	6.50	—

KM# 351 DOLLAR
Copper-Nickel **Ruler:** Elizabeth II **Subject:** Endangered Wildlife **Obv:** Crowned head right, date below **Rev:** Butterfly and thistle, denomination below

Date	Mintage	F	VF	XF	Unc	BU
1996	—	—	—	—	6.50	—

KM# 352 DOLLAR
Copper-Nickel **Ruler:** Elizabeth II **Subject:** Endangered Wildlife **Obv:** Crowned head right, date below **Rev:** Ring-tailed lemurs, denomination below

Date	Mintage	F	VF	XF	Unc	BU
1996	—	—	—	—	6.50	—

KM# 353 DOLLAR
Copper-Nickel **Ruler:** Elizabeth II **Subject:** Endangered Wildlife **Obv:** Crowned head right, date below **Rev:** Szechuan takins, denomination below

Date	Mintage	F	VF	XF	Unc	BU
1996	—	—	—	—	6.50	—

KM# 354 DOLLAR
Copper-Nickel **Ruler:** Elizabeth II **Subject:** Endangered Wildlife **Obv:** Crowned head right, date below **Rev:** Eagle owl, denomination

Date	Mintage	F	VF	XF	Unc	BU
1996	—	—	—	—	6.50	—

KM# 355 DOLLAR
Copper-Nickel **Ruler:** Elizabeth II **Subject:** Endangered Wildlife **Obv:** Crowned head right, date below **Rev:** White-tailed deer, denomination below

Date	Mintage	F	VF	XF	Unc	BU
1996	—	—	—	—	6.50	—

KM# 356 DOLLAR
Copper-Nickel **Ruler:** Elizabeth II **Subject:** Endangered Wildlife **Obv:** Crowned head right, date below **Rev:** Drill

Date	Mintage	F	VF	XF	Unc	BU
1996	—	—	—	—	6.50	—

KM# 387 DOLLAR
28.4000 g., Copper-Nickel, 38.6 mm. **Ruler:** Elizabeth II **Subject:** Endangered Wildlife **Obv:** Crowned head right, date below **Rev:** Alpine Ibex on mountain, denomination below **Edge:** Reeded

Date	Mintage	F	VF	XF	Unc	BU
1996	—	—	—	—	6.50	—

KM# 308.1 DOLLAR
31.4600 g., 0.9990 Silver 1.0104 oz. ASW **Ruler:** Elizabeth II **Obv:** Crowned head right, date below **Rev:** Princess Diana's portrait, dates **Note:** Polished fields with matte portraits.

Date	Mintage	F	VF	XF	Unc	BU
1997 Proof	—	Value: 12.50				

KM# 308.2 DOLLAR
34.4600 g., 0.9990 Silver 1.0104 oz. ASW **Ruler:** Elizabeth II **Obv:** Crowned head right, date below **Rev:** Princess Diana's bust facing, dates **Note:** Matte fields with polished portraits.

Date	Mintage	F	VF	XF	Unc	BU
1997 Matte Proof	—	—	—	BV	12.50	—

KM# 314 DOLLAR
31.6350 g., 0.9990 Silver 1.0160 oz. ASW **Ruler:** Elizabeth II **Subject:** Australian Fauna **Obv:** Crowned head right, date below **Rev:** Multicolor ring-tailed gecko, in beaded circle, denomination lower right

Date	Mintage	F	VF	XF	Unc	BU
1998 Proof	Est. 4,000	Value: 35.00				

KM# 315 DOLLAR
31.6350 g., 0.9990 Silver 1.0160 oz. ASW **Ruler:** Elizabeth II **Subject:** Australian Fauna **Obv:** Crowned head right, date below **Rev:** Multicolor bilby (mouse)

Date	Mintage	F	VF	XF	Unc	BU
1998 Proof	Est. 4,000	Value: 25.00				

KM# 316 DOLLAR
31.6350 g., 0.9990 Silver 1.0160 oz. ASW **Ruler:** Elizabeth II **Subject:** Australian Fauna **Obv:** Crowned head right, date below **Rev:** Multicolor platypus

Date	Mintage	F	VF	XF	Unc	BU
1998 Proof	Est. 4,000	Value: 25.00				

KM# 317 DOLLAR
31.6350 g., 0.9990 Silver 1.0160 oz. ASW **Ruler:** Elizabeth II **Subject:** Australian Fauna **Obv:** Crowned head right, date below **Rev:** Multicolor ghost bat

Date	Mintage	F	VF	XF	Unc	BU
1998 Proof	Est. 4,000	Value: 35.00				

KM# 318 DOLLAR
31.6350 g., 0.9990 Silver 1.0160 oz. ASW **Ruler:** Elizabeth II **Subject:** Australian Fauna **Obv:** Crowned head right, date below **Rev:** Multicolor hatback turtle

Date	Mintage	F	VF	XF	Unc	BU
1998 Proof	Est. 4,000	Value: 35.00				

KM# 361 DOLLAR
31.6800 g., 0.9990 Silver 1.0000 oz. ASW **Ruler:** Elizabeth II **Subject:** Tropical Fish **Obv:** Crowned head right, date below **Rev:** Multicolored lemonpeel angelfish **Edge:** Reeded

Date	Mintage	F	VF	XF	Unc	BU
1999 Proof	—	Value: 25.00				

KM# 365 DOLLAR
31.6800 g., 0.9990 Silver 1.0000 oz. ASW **Ruler:** Elizabeth II **Subject:** Tropical Fish **Obv:** Crowned head right, date below **Rev:** Multicolor clown fish on anemone **Edge:** Reeded

Date	Mintage	F	VF	XF	Unc	BU
1999 Proof	—	Value: 25.00				

KM# 362 DOLLAR
31.6800 g., 0.9990 Silver 1.0000 oz. ASW **Ruler:** Elizabeth II **Subject:** Tropical Fish **Obv:** Crowned head right, date below **Rev:** Multicolor clown triggerfish **Edge:** Reeded

Date	Mintage	F	VF	XF	Unc	BU
1999 Proof	—	Value: 25.00				

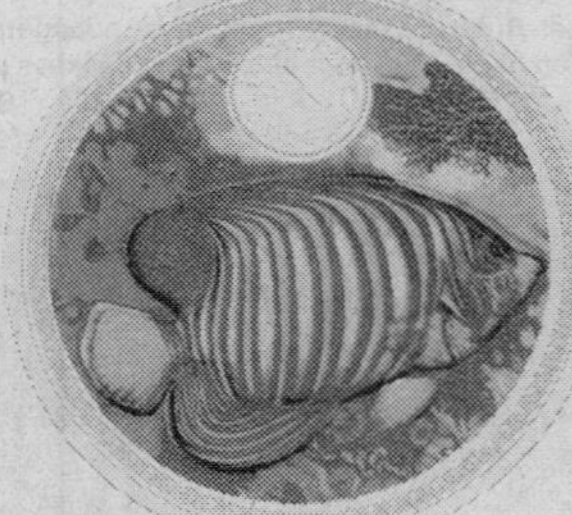

KM# 363 DOLLAR
31.6800 g., 0.9990 Silver 1.0000 oz. ASW **Ruler:** Elizabeth II **Subject:** Tropical Fish **Obv:** Crowned head right, date below **Rev:** Multicolor regal angelfish **Edge:** Reeded

Date	Mintage	F	VF	XF	Unc	BU
1999 Proof	—	Value: 25.00				

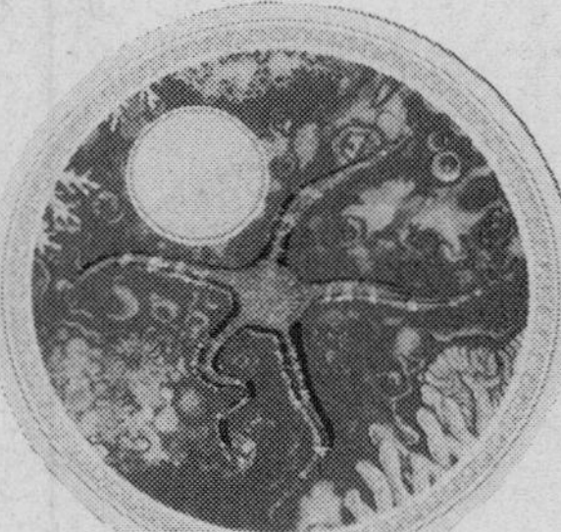

KM# 364 DOLLAR
Center Weight: 31.6800 g. **Center Composition:** 0.9990 Silver 1.0000 oz. ASW **Ruler:** Elizabeth II **Subject:** Tropical Fish **Obv:** Crowned head right, date below **Rev:** Multicolor serpent starfish **Edge:** Reeded

Date	Mintage	F	VF	XF	Unc	BU
1999 Proof	—	Value: 30.00				

KM# 437 DOLLAR
31.8000 g., 0.9990 Silver 1.0214 oz. ASW, 40.5 mm. **Ruler:** Elizabeth II **Obv:** Crowned head right, date below **Rev:** Queen Mother multicolor portrait **Edge:** Reeded

Date	Mintage	F	VF	XF	Unc	BU
2000 Proof	19,500	Value: 20.00				

KM# 380 DOLLAR
28.2800 g., 0.9250 Silver 0.841 oz. ASW, 38.6 mm. **Ruler:** Elizabeth II **Subject:** Queen's Golden Jubilee **Obv:** Crowned head right, date below **Rev:** Flags over roof tops, denomination below **Edge:** Reeded

Date	Mintage	F	VF	XF	Unc	BU
2000 Proof	15,000	Value: 12.00				

KM# 8 2 DOLLARS
25.7000 g., 0.9250 Silver .7646 oz. ASW **Ruler:** Elizabeth II **Subject:** 20th Anniversary of Coronation **Obv:** Young bust right, date below

Date	Mintage	F	VF	XF	Unc	BU
1973 Proof	46,000	Value: 11.50				
1973	16,000	—	—	BV	11.00	—

KM# 38 2 DOLLARS
Copper-Nickel, 28.52 mm. **Ruler:** Elizabeth II **Obv:** Crowned head right, date below **Rev:** Kumete table, morter and pestle from Atiu Island, denomination above **Rev. Designer:** Horst Hahne **Shape:** 3-sided

Date	Mintage	F	VF	XF	Unc	BU
1987	—	—	—	2.25	3.50	5.00
1987 Proof	—	Value: 6.00				
1988 Proof	—	Value: 6.00				
1988	—	—	—	2.25	3.50	5.00
1992	—	—	—	2.25	3.25	4.50
1992 Proof	—	Value: 6.00				
1994 Proof	200	Value: 6.50				
1994	20,000	—	—	2.25	3.25	4.50

KM# 279 2 DOLLARS
10.0000 g., 0.5000 Silver .1607 oz. ASW **Ruler:** Elizabeth II **Subject:** Yellowstone National Park **Obv:** Crowned head right, date below **Rev:** Grizzly bears, denomination below **Rev. Designer:** Alex Shagin

Date	Mintage	F	VF	XF	Unc	BU
1996 Proof	—	Value: 6.50				

KM# 280 2 DOLLARS
10.0000 g., 0.5000 Silver .1607 oz. ASW **Ruler:** Elizabeth II **Subject:** Olympic National Park **Obv:** Crowned head right, date below **Rev:** Eagle flying in the mountain tops **Rev. Designer:** Alex Shagin

Date	Mintage	F	VF	XF	Unc	BU
1996 Proof	—	Value: 6.50				

KM# 328 2 DOLLARS
10.0000 g., 0.5000 Silver .160736 oz. ASW **Ruler:** Elizabeth II **Subject:** Petrified Forest National Park **Obv:** Crowned head right, date below **Rev:** Pronghorn antelope **Rev. Designer:** Alex Shagin

Date	Mintage	F	VF	XF	Unc	BU
1997 Proof	—	—	—	—	—	—
1998 Proof	—	Value: 7.50				

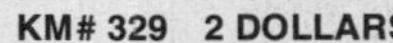

KM# 329 2 DOLLARS
10.0000 g., 0.5000 Silver .160736 oz. ASW **Ruler:** Elizabeth II **Subject:** Crater Lake National Park **Obv:** Crowned head right, date below **Rev:** White-tailed deer **Rev. Designer:** Alex Shagin

Date	Mintage	F	VF	XF	Unc	BU
1997 Proof	—	—	—	—	—	—
1998 Proof	—	Value: 5.50				

KM# 376 2 DOLLARS
15.8400 g., 0.9990 Silver .5088 oz. ASW, 28.3 mm. **Ruler:** Elizabeth II **Subject:** British Queen Mother **Obv:** Crowned head right, date below **Rev:** Queen Mother and daughters, circa 1936 within circle, denomination below **Edge:** Reeded

Date	Mintage	F	VF	XF	Unc	BU
1997 Proof	—	Value: 10.00				

KM# 371 2 DOLLARS
10.0000 g., 0.5000 Silver .1608 oz. ASW, 30 mm. **Ruler:** Elizabeth II **Subject:** Great Smoky Mountains National Park **Obv:** Crowned head right, date below **Rev:** Red wolf and two cubs **Rev. Designer:** Alex Shagin **Edge:** Reeded

Date	Mintage	F	VF	XF	Unc	BU
1997 Proof	—	Value: 6.00				

KM# 372 2 DOLLARS
10.0000 g., 0.5000 Silver .1608 oz. ASW, 30 mm. **Ruler:** Elizabeth II **Subject:** Theodore Roosevelt National Park **Obv:** Crowned head right, date below **Rev:** Bison, denomination below **Rev. Designer:** Alex Shagin **Edge:** Reeded

Date	Mintage	F	VF	XF	Unc	BU
1997 Proof	—	Value: 6.00				

KM# 373 2 DOLLARS
10,0000 g., 0.5000 Silver .1608 oz. ASW, 30 mm. **Ruler:** Elizabeth II **Subject:** Yosemite National Park **Obv:** Crowned head right, date below **Rev:** Peregrine falcon **Rev. Designer:** Alex Shagin **Edge:** Reeded

Date	Mintage	F	VF	XF	Unc	BU
1997 Proof	—	Value: 6.00				

KM# 436 2 DOLLARS
20.4000 g., 0.5000 Silver 0.3279 oz. ASW, 33.9 mm. **Ruler:** Elizabeth II **Obv:** Crowned head right, date below **Rev:** Queen Mother and daughters circa 1980 **Edge:** Reeded

Date	Mintage	F	VF	XF	Unc	BU
1997 Proof	—	Value: 7.50				

KM# 374 2 DOLLARS
10.0000 g., 0.5000 Silver .1608 oz. ASW, 30 mm. **Ruler:** Elizabeth II **Subject:** North Cascades National Park **Obv:** Crowned head right, date below **Rev:** Spotted owl, denomination below **Rev. Designer:** Alex Shagin **Edge:** Reeded

Date	Mintage	F	VF	XF	Unc	BU
1998 Proof	—	Value: 6.00				

KM# 321 2 DOLLARS
42.4139 g., 0.9250 Silver 1.2614 oz. ASW **Ruler:** Elizabeth II **Obv:** Crowned head right, date below **Rev:** Cook Islands attractions and features, denomination at right **Shape:** 1/3 circular segment

Date	Mintage	F	VF	XF	Unc	BU
1998 Proof	Est. 20,000	Value: 25.00				

Note: This coin is part of a tri-national, three coin matching set with Fiji and Western Samoa

KM# 339 2 DOLLARS
31.1035 g., 0.9990 Silver 1.0000 oz. ASW **Ruler:** Elizabeth II **Obv:** Crowned head right, date below **Rev:** Multicolor cartoon cat, Garfield, flipping coin **Edge:** Reeded

Date	Mintage	F	VF	XF	Unc	BU
1999 Proof	—	Value: 16.50				

KM# 340 2 DOLLARS
31.1035 g., 0.9990 Silver 1.0000 oz. ASW **Ruler:** Elizabeth II **Obv:** Crowned head right, date below **Rev:** Multicolor cartoon cat, Garfield, tricking Odie **Edge:** Reeded

Date	Mintage	F	VF	XF	Unc	BU
1999 Proof	—	Value: 16.50				

KM# 9 2-1/2 DOLLARS
27.3500 g., 0.9250 Silver .8133 oz. ASW **Ruler:** Elizabeth II **Subject:** Captain James Cook's 2nd Pacific Voyage **Obv:** Young bust right, date below **Rev:** H.M.S. Resolution and H.M.S. Adventure above world globe **Rev. Designer:** James Berry

Date	Mintage	F	VF	XF	Unc	BU
1973 Proof	12,000	Value: 8.00				
1973	6,000	—	—	BV	10.00	—
1974	2,000	—	—	BV	13.50	—
1974 Proof	12,000	Value: 8.00				

KM# 15 5 DOLLARS
27.3000 g., 0.5000 Silver .4388 oz. ASW **Ruler:** Elizabeth II **Subject:** Wildlife Conservation **Obv:** Young bust right, date below **Rev:** Mangara kingfisher, denomination below **Rev. Designer:** James Berry

Date	Mintage	F	VF	XF	Unc	BU
1976FM (M)	251	—	—	—	22.50	—
1976FM (P)	28,000	Value: 9.00				
1976FM (U)	2,192	—	—	—	13.50	—

KM# 17 5 DOLLARS
27.3000 g., 0.5000 Silver .4388 oz. ASW **Ruler:** Elizabeth II **Obv:** Young bust right, date below **Rev:** Atiu swiftlet, denomination below **Rev. Designer:** James Berry **Edge Lettering:** Wildlife Conservation

Date	Mintage	F	VF	XF	Unc	BU
1977FM (M)	252	—	—	—	30.00	—
1977FM (U)	4,032	—	—	—	12.50	—
1977FM (P)	11,000	Value: 7.00				

KM# 20 5 DOLLARS
27.3000 g., 0.5000 Silver .4388 oz. ASW **Ruler:** Elizabeth II **Subject:** Wildlife Conservation **Obv:** Young bust right, date below **Rev:** Polynesian warblers by nest in branches, denomination below **Edge Lettering:** 1728 • CAPT. JAMES COOK • 1978

Date	Mintage	F	VF	XF	Unc	BU
1978FM (U)	3,659	—	—	—	12.50	—
1978FM (P)	11,000	Value: 7.00				
1978FM (M)	250	—	—	—	20.00	—

KM# 24 5 DOLLARS
27.3000 g., 0.5000 Silver .4388 oz. ASW **Ruler:** Elizabeth II **Subject:** Wildlife Conservation **Obv:** Young bust right, date below **Rev:** Rarotongan fruit doves on branch, denomination below

Date	Mintage	F	VF	XF	Unc	BU
1979FM (U)	2,500	—	—	—	12.50	—
1979FM (P)	8,612	Value: 10.00				

KM# 39 5 DOLLARS
Aluminum-Bronze, 31.51 mm. **Ruler:** Elizabeth II **Obv:** Crowned head right, date below **Rev:** Conch shell, denomination above **Rev. Designer:** Horst Hahne **Shape:** 12-sided

Date	Mintage	F	VF	XF	Unc	BU
1987	—	—	—	3.50	5.50	7.50
1987 Proof	—	Value: 9.00				
1988	—	—	—	3.50	5.50	7.50
1988 Proof	—	Value: 9.00				

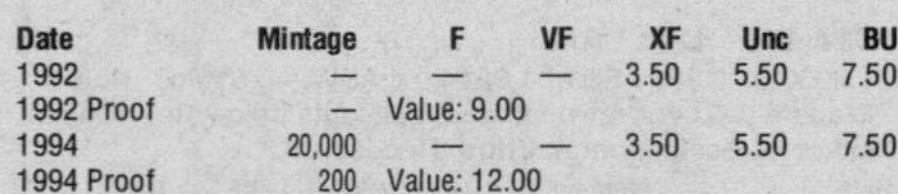

Date	Mintage	F	VF	XF	Unc	BU
1992	—	—	—	3.50	5.50	7.50
1992 Proof	—	Value: 9.00				
1994	20,000	—	—	3.50	5.50	7.50
1994 Proof	200	Value: 12.00				

KM# 39a 5 DOLLARS
Copper-Nickel, 31.51 mm. **Ruler:** Elizabeth II **Obv:** Crowned head right, date below **Rev:** Conch shell **Rev. Designer:** Horst Hahne **Shape:** 12-sided **Note:** Mint error, struck on Australian 50 cents planchet.

Date	Mintage	F	VF	XF	Unc	BU
1988	—	—	—	—	—	—

KM# 181 5 DOLLARS
Copper-Nickel **Ruler:** Elizabeth II **Subject:** Endangered World Wildlife **Obv:** Crowned head right, date below **Rev:** Tiger

Date	Mintage	F	VF	XF	Unc	BU
1990	—	—	—	—	7.00	9.00

KM# 149 5 DOLLARS
9.9500 g., 0.5000 Silver .1600 oz. ASW **Ruler:** Elizabeth II **Subject:** World Cup Soccer **Obv:** Crowned head right, date below **Rev:** Three soccer players

Date	Mintage	F	VF	XF	Unc	BU
1991 Proof	150,000	Value: 4.50				

KM# 217 5 DOLLARS
9.8500 g., 0.5000 Silver .1600 oz. ASW **Ruler:** Elizabeth II **Obv:** Crowned head right, date below **Rev:** Christopher Columbus 3/4 facing, ship at left, denomination below

Date	Mintage	F	VF	XF	Unc	BU
1991	Est. 50,000	—	—	—	6.00	—

KM# 218 5 DOLLARS
9.9500 g., 0.5000 Silver .1600 oz. ASW **Ruler:** Elizabeth II
Subject: Endangered Wildlife **Obv:** Crowned head right, date below **Rev:** European otters

Date	Mintage	F	VF	XF	Unc	BU
1991	Est. 100,000	—	—	—	7.50	9.50

KM# 219 5 DOLLARS
9.9500 g., 0.5000 Silver .1600 oz. ASW **Ruler:** Elizabeth II
Subject: Endangered Wildlife **Obv:** Crowned head right, date below **Rev:** Penguins

Date	Mintage	F	VF	XF	Unc	BU
1991	Est. 100,000	—	—	—	7.50	9.50

KM# 220 5 DOLLARS
9.9500 g., 0.5000 Silver .1600 oz. ASW **Ruler:** Elizabeth II
Subject: Endangered Wildlife **Obv:** Crowned head right, date below **Rev:** Deer

Date	Mintage	F	VF	XF	Unc	BU
1991	Est. 100,000	—	—	—	7.50	9.50

KM# 221 5 DOLLARS
9.9500 g., 0.5000 Silver .1600 oz. ASW **Ruler:** Elizabeth II
Subject: Endangered Wildlife **Obv:** Crowned head right, date below **Rev:** Cape dolphins

Date	Mintage	F	VF	XF	Unc	BU
1991	Est. 100,000	—	—	—	7.50	9.50

KM# 222 5 DOLLARS
9.9500 g., 0.5000 Silver .1600 oz. ASW **Ruler:** Elizabeth II
Subject: Endangered Wildlife **Obv:** Crowned head right, date below **Rev:** Cougar

Date	Mintage	F	VF	XF	Unc	BU
1991	Est. 100,000	—	—	—	7.50	9.50

KM# 223 5 DOLLARS
9.9500 g., 0.5000 Silver .1600 oz. ASW **Ruler:** Elizabeth II
Subject: Endangered Wildlife **Obv:** Crowned head right, date below **Rev:** Ibex

Date	Mintage	F	VF	XF	Unc	BU
1991	Est. 100,000	—	—	—	7.50	9.50

KM# 224 5 DOLLARS
9.9500 g., 0.5000 Silver .1600 oz. ASW **Ruler:** Elizabeth II
Subject: Endangered Wildlife **Obv:** Crowned head right, date below **Rev:** Eagle owl

Date	Mintage	F	VF	XF	Unc	BU
1991	Est. 100,000	—	—	—	7.50	9.50

KM# 225 5 DOLLARS
9.9500 g., 0.5000 Silver .1600 oz. ASW **Ruler:** Elizabeth II
Subject: Endangered Wildlife **Obv:** Crowned head right, date below **Rev:** Peregrine falcon

Date	Mintage	F	VF	XF	Unc	BU
1991	Est. 100,000	—	—	—	7.50	9.50

KM# 226 5 DOLLARS
9.9500 g., 0.5000 Silver .1600 oz. ASW **Ruler:** Elizabeth II
Subject: Endangered Wildlife **Obv:** Crowned head right, date below **Rev:** African lion

Date	Mintage	F	VF	XF	Unc	BU
1991	Est. 100,000	—	—	—	7.50	9.50

KM# 227 5 DOLLARS
9.9500 g., 0.5000 Silver .1600 oz. ASW **Ruler:** Elizabeth II
Subject: Endangered Wildlife **Obv:** Crowned head right, date below **Rev:** Bee hummingbird

Date	Mintage	F	VF	XF	Unc	BU
1991	Est. 100,000	—	—	—	7.50	9.50

KM# 228 5 DOLLARS
9.9500 g., 0.5000 Silver .1600 oz. ASW **Ruler:** Elizabeth II
Subject: Endangered Wildlife **Obv:** Crowned head right, date below **Rev:** Kangaroo

Date	Mintage	F	VF	XF	Unc	BU
1991	Est. 100,000	—	—	—	7.50	9.50

KM# 229 5 DOLLARS
9.9500 g., 0.5000 Silver .1600 oz. ASW **Ruler:** Elizabeth II
Subject: Endangered Wildlife **Obv:** Crowned head right, date below **Rev:** Persian fallow deer

Date	Mintage	F	VF	XF	Unc	BU
1991	Est. 100,000	—	—	—	7.50	9.50

KM# 230 5 DOLLARS
9.9500 g., 0.5000 Silver .1600 oz. ASW **Ruler:** Elizabeth II
Subject: Endangered Wildlife **Obv:** Crowned head right, date below **Rev:** Lowland gorilla

Date	Mintage	F	VF	XF	Unc	BU
1991	Est. 100,000	—	—	—	7.50	9.50

KM# 253 5 DOLLARS
10.1300 g., 0.5000 Silver .1628 oz. ASW **Ruler:** Elizabeth II
Obv: Crowned head right, date below **Rev:** First man on the moon, denomination below

Date	Mintage	F	VF	XF	Unc	BU
1991 Proof	—	Value: 6.00				

KM# 137 5 DOLLARS
10.0000 g., 0.5000 Silver .1607 oz. ASW **Ruler:** Elizabeth II
Subject: Environmental Protection **Obv:** Crowned head right, date below **Rev:** Child watching butterfly

Date	Mintage	F	VF	XF	Unc	BU
1992 Proof	Est. 25,000	Value: 5.50				

KM# 150 5 DOLLARS
10.0000 g., 0.5000 Silver .1607 oz. ASW **Ruler:** Elizabeth II **Obv:** Crowned head right, date below **Rev:** Johann Sebastian Bach

Date	Mintage	F	VF	XF	Unc	BU
1992 Proof	—	Value: 5.50				

KM# 160 5 DOLLARS
10.0000 g., 0.5000 Silver .1607 oz. ASW **Ruler:** Elizabeth II
Obv: Crowned head right, date below **Rev:** Sailing ship Astrolabe

Date	Mintage	F	VF	XF	Unc	BU
1992 Proof	—	Value: 5.50				

KM# 231 5 DOLLARS
10.0000 g., 0.5000 Silver .1607 oz. ASW **Ruler:** Elizabeth II
Subject: Endangered Wildlife **Obv:** Crowned head right, date below **Rev:** Mandrill right, denomination below

Date	Mintage	F	VF	XF	Unc	BU
1992	Est. 100,000	—	—	—	5.00	7.00

KM# 232 5 DOLLARS
10.0000 g., 0.5000 Silver .1607 oz. ASW **Ruler:** Elizabeth II
Subject: Endangered Wildlife **Obv:** Crowned head right, date below **Rev:** Butterfly

Date	Mintage	F	VF	XF	Unc	BU
1992	Est. 100,000	—	—	—	5.00	7.00

KM# 233 5 DOLLARS
10.0000 g., 0.5000 Silver .1607 oz. ASW **Ruler:** Elizabeth II
Subject: Endangered Wildlife **Obv:** Crowned head right, date below **Rev:** Takin

Date	Mintage	F	VF	XF	Unc	BU
1992	Est. 100,000	—	—	—	5.00	7.00

KM# 252 5 DOLLARS
9.9500 g., 0.5000 Silver .1600 oz. ASW **Ruler:** Elizabeth II
Subject: 1992 Olympics **Obv:** Crowned head right, date below **Rev:** High jump, denomination below

Date	Mintage	F	VF	XF	Unc	BU
1992 Proof	150,000	Value: 5.50				

KM# 255 5 DOLLARS
31.4700 g., 0.9250 Silver .9359 oz. ASW **Ruler:** Elizabeth II
Subject: Queen Elizabeth II's 25th Wedding Anniversary **Obv:** Crowned head right, date below **Rev:** St. Paul's Cathedral

Date	Mintage	F	VF	XF	Unc	BU
1995 Proof	Est. 30,000	Value: 14.00				

KM# 234 5 DOLLARS
10.0000 g., 0.5000 Silver .1607 oz. ASW **Ruler:** Elizabeth II
Subject: Endangered Wildlife **Obv:** Crowned head right, date below **Rev:** African elephant

Date	Mintage	F	VF	XF	Unc	BU
1995 Proof	Est. 25,000	Value: 7.50				

KM# 269 5 DOLLARS
31.4700 g., 0.9250 Silver .9359 oz. ASW **Ruler:** Elizabeth II
Subject: Endangered Wildlife **Obv:** Crowned head right, date below **Rev:** Cheetah

Date	Mintage	F	VF	XF	Unc	BU
1996 Proof	Est. 15,000	Value: 14.00				

KM# 281 5 DOLLARS
28.0000 g., 0.9250 Silver .8327 oz. ASW **Ruler:** Elizabeth II **Subject:** Yellowstone National Park **Obv:** Crowned head right, date below **Rev:** Multicolor grizzly bear and cub **Rev. Designer:** Alex Shagin

Date	Mintage	F	VF	XF	Unc	BU
1996 Proof	25,000	Value: 18.50				

KM# 282 5 DOLLARS
28.0000 g., 0.9250 Silver .8327 oz. ASW **Ruler:** Elizabeth II **Subject:** Olympic National Park **Obv:** Crowned head right, date below **Rev:** Multicolor bald eagle in flight **Rev. Designer:** Alex Shagin

Date	Mintage	F	VF	XF	Unc	BU
1996 Proof	25,000	Value: 18.50				

KM# 301 5 DOLLARS
28.0000 g., 0.9250 Silver .8327 oz. ASW **Ruler:** Elizabeth II **Subject:** Endangered Wildlife **Obv:** Crowned head right, date below **Rev:** Crocodile on river bank

Date	Mintage	F	VF	XF	Unc	BU
1996 Proof	—	Value: 27.50				

KM# 302 5 DOLLARS
28.0000 g., 0.9250 Silver .8327 oz. ASW **Ruler:** Elizabeth II **Subject:** Endangered Wildlife **Obv:** Crowned head right, date below **Rev:** Lion, lioness and cubs

Date	Mintage	F	VF	XF	Unc	BU
1996 Proof	—	Value: 18.50				

KM# 303 5 DOLLARS
28.0000 g., 0.9250 Silver .8327 oz. ASW **Ruler:** Elizabeth II **Subject:** Endangered Wildlife **Obv:** Crowned head right, date below **Rev:** Female gorilla and offspring

Date	Mintage	F	VF	XF	Unc	BU
1996 Proof	—	Value: 18.50				

KM# 304 5 DOLLARS
28.0000 g., 0.9250 Silver .8327 oz. ASW **Ruler:** Elizabeth II **Subject:** Endangered Wildlife **Obv:** Crowned head right, date below **Rev:** Penguin family

Date	Mintage	F	VF	XF	Unc	BU
1996 Proof	—	Value: 22.50				

KM# 368 5 DOLLARS
28.0000 g., 0.9250 Silver .8327 oz. ASW **Ruler:** Elizabeth II **Subject:** Great Smoky Mountains National Park **Obv:** Crowned head right, date below **Rev:** Red wolf and two cubs **Rev. Designer:** Alex Shagin **Edge:** Reeded

Date	Mintage	F	VF	XF	Unc	BU
1996 Proof	—	Value: 27.50				

KM# 379 5 DOLLARS
31.4700 g., 0.9250 Silver 0.9359 oz. ASW, 38.6 mm. **Ruler:** Elizabeth II **Subject:** Queen Mother **Obv:** Crowned head right, date below **Rev:** Queen Mother and daughters, circa 1936, within circle, denomination below **Edge:** Reeded

Date	Mintage	F	VF	XF	Unc	BU
1996 Proof	—	Value: 16.00				

KM# 366 5 DOLLARS
31.4700 g., 0.9250 Silver .9353 oz. ASW **Ruler:** Elizabeth II **Subject:** Protect Our World **Obv:** Crowned head right, date below **Rev:** Charles Darwin bust at right, map and tortoise, denomination below **Edge:** Reeded

Date	Mintage	F	VF	XF	Unc	BU
1996 Proof	—	Value: 25.00				

KM# 377 5 DOLLARS
31.5000 g., 0.9250 Silver 0.9368 oz. ASW, 38.6 mm. **Ruler:** Elizabeth II **Subject:** Endangered Wildlife **Obv:** Crowned head right, date below **Rev:** Two adult polar bears with cub **Edge:** Reeded

Date	Mintage	F	VF	XF	Unc	BU
1996 Proof	—	Value: 22.50				

KM# 370 5 DOLLARS
31.5000 g., 0.9250 Silver .9368 oz. ASW, 38.6 mm. **Ruler:** Elizabeth II **Subject:** Olympics **Obv:** Crowned head right, date below **Rev:** Pole vaulter and runner **Edge:** Reeded

Date	Mintage	F	VF	XF	Unc	BU
1996 Proof	—	Value: 17.50				

KM# 457 5 DOLLARS
1.2000 g., 0.9995 Platinum 0.0386 oz. APW **Ruler:** Elizabeth II **Subject:** Love Angels

Date	Mintage	F	VF	XF	Unc	BU
1997 Proof	250	Value: 45.00				

KM# 335 5 DOLLARS
15.5200 g., 0.9990 Silver .4985 oz. ASW **Ruler:** Elizabeth II **Subject:** Japanese Samurai **Obv:** Crowned head right, date below **Rev:** 3/4 bust Yoshinobu Tokugawa facing, denomination at right, 3/4 braided circle surrounds **Edge:** Reeded

Date	Mintage	F	VF	XF	Unc	BU
1997FM Proof	—	Value: 12.00				

KM# 312 5 DOLLARS
1.2441 g., 0.9999 Gold .04 oz. AGW **Ruler:** Elizabeth II **Obv:** Crowned head right, date below **Rev:** Portrait of Princess Diana, dates, denomination below

Date	Mintage	F	VF	XF	Unc	BU
1997 Proof	—	Value: 30.00				

KM# 367 5 DOLLARS
31.4500 g., 0.9250 Silver .9353 oz. ASW **Ruler:** Elizabeth II

Subject: Millennium - 2000 A.D. **Obv:** Crowned head right, date below **Rev:** Christian symbol above Tangaroa, Pagan God of Creation, denomination below **Edge:** Plain **Shape:** 7-sided

Date	Mintage	F	VF	XF	Unc	BU
1999 Proof	—	Value: 22.00				

KM# 444 5 DOLLARS

62.2070 g., 0.9990 Silver 1.998 oz. ASW, 50 mm. **Ruler:** Elizabeth II **Obv:** Crowned head right, date below **Rev:** SS Sofia Jane, steam and sail ship **Edge:** Reeded

Date	Mintage	F	VF	XF	Unc	BU
1999 Antiqued finish	5,000	—	—	—	65.00	—

KM# 445 5 DOLLARS

62.2070 g., 0.9990 Silver 1.998 oz. ASW, 50 mm. **Ruler:** Elizabeth II **Obv:** Crowned head right, date below **Rev:** Scottish Bard, barque type ship **Edge:** Reeded

Date	Mintage	F	VF	XF	Unc	BU
1999 Antiqued finish	5,000	—	—	—	65.00	—

KM# 446 5 DOLLARS

62.2070 g., 0.9990 Silver 1.998 oz. ASW, 50 mm. **Ruler:** Elizabeth II **Obv:** Crowned head right, date below **Rev:** Cutty Sark, clipper ship **Edge:** Reeded

Date	Mintage	F	VF	XF	Unc	BU
1999 Antiqued finish	5,000	—	—	—	65.00	—

KM# 447 5 DOLLARS

62.2070 g., 0.9990 Silver 1.998 oz. ASW, 50 mm. **Ruler:** Elizabeth II **Obv:** Crowned head right, date below **Rev:** HMS Sirius, 20 gun naval ship circa 1788 **Edge:** Reeded

Date	Mintage	F	VF	XF	Unc	BU
1999 Antiqued finish	5,000	—	—	—	65.00	—

KM# 448 5 DOLLARS

62.2070 g., 0.9990 Silver 1.998 oz. ASW, 50 mm. **Ruler:** Elizabeth II **Obv:** Crowned head right, date below **Rev:** 18 ft. Skiff **Edge:** Reeded

Date	Mintage	F	VF	XF	Unc	BU
1999 Antiqued finish	5,000	—	—	—	65.00	—

KM# 456 5 DOLLARS

31.5000 g., 0.9250 Silver 0.9368 oz. ASW, 38.6 mm. **Ruler:** Elizabeth II **Obv:** Crowned head right, date below **Rev:** Sail Ship Archimedes **Edge:** Reeded

Date	Mintage	F	VF	XF	Unc	BU
1999 Proof	—	Value: 32.50				

KM# 378 5 DOLLARS

31.5000 g., 0.9250 Silver 0.9368 oz. ASW, 38.6 mm. **Ruler:** Elizabeth II **Subject:** Takitumu Conservation Area **Obv:** Crowned head right, date below **Rev:** Rarotongan Monarch Flycatcher, denomination at left **Edge:** Reeded

Date	Mintage	F	VF	XF	Unc	BU
1999 Proof	—	Value: 27.50				

KM# 375 5 DOLLARS

28.1000 g., 0.9250 Silver with gold plated outer circle, 38.6 mm. **Ruler:** Elizabeth II **Subject:** Queen Mother's 100th Birthday **Obv:** Crowned head right, date below **Rev:** Queen Mother and daughters, circa 1980 **Edge:** Reeded

Date	Mintage	F	VF	XF	Unc	BU
2000 Proof	1,000	Value: 27.50				

KM# 10 7-1/2 DOLLARS

33.8000 g., 0.9250 Silver 1.0052 oz. ASW **Ruler:** Elizabeth II **Subject:** Capt. James Cook's 2nd Pacific Voyage **Obv:** Young bust right, date below **Rev:** H.M.S. Resolution and Cook's profile above map of Hervey Islands **Rev. Designer:** James Berry

Date	Mintage	F	VF	XF	Unc	BU
1973	6,000	—	—	BV	15.00	—
1973 Proof	12,000	Value: 13.50				
1974	2,000	—	—	BV	18.00	—
1974 Proof	13,000	Value: 13.50				

KM# 21 10 DOLLARS

27.9000 g., 0.9250 Silver .8297 oz. ASW **Ruler:** Elizabeth II **Subject:** 25th Anniversary of Coronation **Obv:** Young bust right, date below **Rev:** Crown with supporters, dates below, denomination at bottom

Date	Mintage	F	VF	XF	Unc	BU
1978FM (U)	5,350	—	—	—	13.50	—
1978FM Proof	11,000	Value: 12.50				

KM# 72 10 DOLLARS

10.0000 g., 0.9250 Silver .2974 oz. ASW **Ruler:** Elizabeth II **Subject:** Endangered World Wildlife **Obv:** Crowned head right, date below **Rev:** Elephants head left

Date	Mintage	F	VF	XF	Unc	BU
1990 Proof	25,000	Value: 7.50				

KM# 73 10 DOLLARS

10.0000 g., 0.9250 Silver .2974 oz. ASW **Ruler:** Elizabeth II **Subject:** Endangered World Wildlife **Obv:** Crowned head right, date below **Rev:** Tiger

Date	Mintage	F	VF	XF	Unc	BU
1990 Proof	Est. 25,000	Value: 7.50				

KM# 79 10 DOLLARS

10.0000 g., 0.9250 Silver .2974 oz. ASW **Ruler:** Elizabeth II **Subject:** Olympics **Obv:** Crowned head right, date below **Rev:** Runner

Date	Mintage	F	VF	XF	Unc	BU
1990 Proof	150,000	Value: 5.50				

KM# 80 10 DOLLARS

10.0000 g., 0.9250 Silver .2974 oz. ASW **Ruler:** Elizabeth II **Subject:** Endangered World Wildlife **Obv:** Crowned head right, date below **Rev:** African elephants

Date	Mintage	F	VF	XF	Unc	BU
1990 Proof	Est. 25,000	Value: 7.50				

KM# 81 10 DOLLARS

28.0000 g., 0.9250 Silver .8327 oz. ASW **Ruler:** Elizabeth II **Subject:** Save the Children **Obv:** Crowned head right, date below **Rev:** Grass-skirted dancers

Date	Mintage	F	VF	XF	Unc	BU
1990 Proof	20,000	Value: 12.50				

KM# 90 10 DOLLARS

10.0000 g., 0.9250 Silver .2974 oz. ASW **Ruler:** Elizabeth II **Subject:** 500 Years of America **Obv:** Crowned head right, date below **Rev:** Bust at left looking right, ship at right, denomination below

Date	Mintage	F	VF	XF	Unc	BU
1990 Proof	Est. 150,000	Value: 5.50				

KM# 91 10 DOLLARS

10.0000 g., 0.9250 Silver .2974 oz. ASW **Ruler:** Elizabeth II **Subject:** 1991 Winter Olympics **Obv:** Crowned head right, date below **Rev:** Cross-country skier, denomination below

Date	Mintage	F	VF	XF	Unc	BU
1990 Proof	150,000	Value: 6.00				

KM# 121 10 DOLLARS
10.0000 g., 0.9250 Silver .2974 oz. ASW **Ruler:** Elizabeth II
Subject: 500 Years of America **Obv:** Crowned head right, date below **Rev:** Columbus and ship

Date	Mintage	F	VF	XF	Unc	BU
1990 Proof	Est. 150,000	Value: 5.50				

KM# 136 10 DOLLARS
31.4700 g., 0.9250 Silver .9359 oz. ASW **Ruler:** Elizabeth II
Obv: Crowned head right, date below **Rev:** Bust with planet earth revolving around radiant sun in background

Date	Mintage	F	VF	XF	Unc	BU
1992 Proof	—	Value: 13.50				

KM# 254 10 DOLLARS
31.4700 g., 0.9250 Silver .9359 oz. ASW **Ruler:** Elizabeth II
Subject: World Cup '94 **Obv:** Crowned head right, date below **Rev:** Goalie catching ball

Date	Mintage	F	VF	XF	Unc	BU
1992 Proof	Est. 20,000	Value: 14.50				

KM# 358 10 DOLLARS
14.8000 g., 0.9250 Silver .4401 oz. ASW **Ruler:** Elizabeth II
Subject: Captain Cook **Obv:** Crowned head right, date below **Rev:** Captain Cook wading ashore, denomination at right **Edge:** Reeded

Date	Mintage	F	VF	XF	Unc	BU
1994FM Proof	—	Value: 7.50				

KM# 283 10 DOLLARS
28.0000 g., 0.9250 Silver .8327 oz. ASW **Ruler:** Elizabeth II
Subject: Olympic National Park **Obv:** Crowned head right, date below **Rev:** Multicolor Bald eagle in flight over mountain tops, denomination below **Rev. Designer:** Alex Shagin

Date	Mintage	F	VF	XF	Unc	BU
1996 Proof	10,000	Value: 18.00				

KM# 284 10 DOLLARS
28.0000 g., 0.9250 Silver .8327 oz. ASW **Ruler:** Elizabeth II
Subject: Yellowstone National Park **Obv:** Crowned head right, date below **Rev:** Multicolor Grizzly bear and cub **Rev. Designer:** Alex Shagin

Date	Mintage	F	VF	XF	Unc	BU
1996 Proof	10,000	Value: 22.00				

KM# 359 10 DOLLARS
28.0000 g., 0.9250 Silver .8327 oz. ASW **Ruler:** Elizabeth II
Subject: Theodore Roosevelt National Park **Obv:** Crowned head right, date below **Rev:** Multicolor bison **Rev. Designer:** Alex Shagin **Edge:** Reeded

Date	Mintage	F	VF	XF	Unc	BU
1996 Proof	—	Value: 22.50				
1997 Proof	—	Value: 22.50				

KM# 285 10 DOLLARS
1.2441 g., 0.9990 Gold .0399 oz. AGW **Ruler:** Elizabeth II
Subject: Olympic National Park **Obv:** Crowned head right, date below **Rev:** Eagle's head right, denomination below **Rev. Designer:** Alex Shagin

Date	Mintage	F	VF	XF	Unc	BU
1996 Proof	—	Value: 30.00				

KM# 286 10 DOLLARS
1.2441 g., 0.9990 Gold .0399 oz. AGW **Ruler:** Elizabeth II
Subject: Yellowstone National Park **Obv:** Crowned head right, date below **Rev. Designer:** Alex Shagin

Date	Mintage	F	VF	XF	Unc	BU
1996 Proof	—	Value: 30.00				

KM# 330 10 DOLLARS
28.0000 g., 0.9250 Silver .8327 oz. ASW **Ruler:** Elizabeth II
Subject: Great Smoky Mountains National Park **Obv:** Crowned head right, date below **Rev:** Multicolor red wolf with two cubs **Rev. Designer:** Alex Shagin

Date	Mintage	F	VF	XF	Unc	BU
1997 Proof	—	Value: 32.50				

KM# 331 10 DOLLARS
28.0000 g., 0.9250 Silver .8327 oz. ASW **Ruler:** Elizabeth II
Subject: Yosemite National Park **Obv:** Crowned head right, date below **Rev:** Multicolor Peregrine falcon **Rev. Designer:** Alex Shagin

Date	Mintage	F	VF	XF	Unc	BU
1997 Proof	—	Value: 22.50				

KM# 360 10 DOLLARS
28.0000 g., 0.9250 Silver .8327 oz. ASW **Ruler:** Elizabeth II
Subject: Glacier Bay National Park **Obv:** Crowned head right, date below **Rev:** Multicolor Humpback whale breaking the water **Rev. Designer:** Alex Shagin

Date	Mintage	F	VF	XF	Unc	BU
1997 Proof	—	Value: 22.50				

KM# 458 10 DOLLARS
2.5000 g., 0.9995 Platinum 0.0803 oz. APW **Ruler:** Elizabeth II
Subject: Love Angels

Date	Mintage	F	VF	XF	Unc	BU
1997 Proof	250	Value: 90.00				

KM# 332 10 DOLLARS
28.0000 g., 0.9250 Silver .8327 oz. ASW **Ruler:** Elizabeth II
Subject: Grand Teton National park **Obv:** Crowned head right, date below **Rev:** Multicolor Whooping crane **Rev. Designer:** Alex Shagin

Date	Mintage	F	VF	XF	Unc	BU
1998 Proof	—	Value: 27.50				

KM# 333 10 DOLLARS
28.0000 g., 0.9250 Silver .8327 oz. ASW **Ruler:** Elizabeth II
Subject: Grand Canyon National Park **Obv:** Crowned head right, date below **Rev:** Multicolor California condor in flight over canyon **Rev. Designer:** Alex Shagin

Date	Mintage	F	VF	XF	Unc	BU
1998 Proof	—	Value: 22.50				

KM# 28 20 DOLLARS
28.2800 g., 0.9250 Silver .8411 oz. ASW **Ruler:** Elizabeth II
Subject: International Year of the Scout **Obv:** Young bust right, date below **Rev:** Boy Scouts, dates at left, denomination at right

Date	Mintage	F	VF	XF	Unc	BU
1983	10,000	—	—	—	22.50	—
1983 Proof	10,000	Value: 25.00				

KM# 151 20 DOLLARS
31.4700 g., 0.9250 Silver .9359 oz. ASW **Ruler:** Elizabeth II
Obv: Crowned head right, date below **Rev:** Friedrich von Schiller

Date	Mintage	F	VF	XF	Unc	BU
1993 Proof	—	Value: 16.50				

KM# 152 20 DOLLARS
31.4700 g., 0.9250 Silver .9359 oz. ASW **Ruler:** Elizabeth II
Obv: Crowned head right, date below **Rev:** Bust of Charles Darwin facing left, tortoise and map, denomination below

Date	Mintage	F	VF	XF	Unc	BU
1993 Proof	10,000	Value: 16.50				

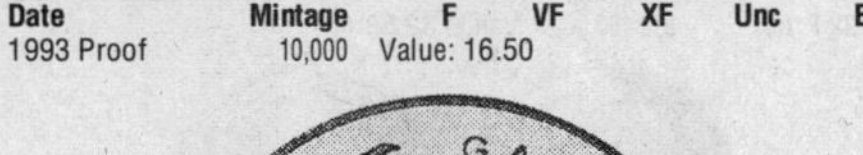

KM# 161 20 DOLLARS
31.4700 g., 0.9250 Silver .9359 oz. ASW **Ruler:** Elizabeth II
Subject: 1996 Olympics **Obv:** Crowned head right, date below **Rev:** Pole vaulter and sprinter

Date	Mintage	F	VF	XF	Unc	BU
1993 Proof	50,000	Value: 14.00				

KM# 235 20 DOLLARS
31.4700 g., 0.9250 Silver .9359 oz. ASW **Ruler:** Elizabeth II
Obv: Crowned head right, date below **Rev:** Tainui Catamaran

Date	Mintage	F	VF	XF	Unc	BU
1995 Proof	Est. 15,000	Value: 15.00				

KM# 236 20 DOLLARS
1.2441 g., 0.9990 Gold .04 oz. AGW **Ruler:** Elizabeth II **Subject:** 500 Years of America **Obv:** Crowned head right, date below **Rev:** Columbus claims the New World, denomination below

Date	Mintage	F	VF	XF	Unc	BU
1995	Est. 25,000	—	—	—	30.00	—

KM# 237 20 DOLLARS
1.2441 g., 0.9990 Gilt Silver .04 oz. **Ruler:** Elizabeth II **Subject:** 500 Years of America **Obv:** Crowned head right, date below **Rev:** Washington crossing the Delaware, denomination below

Date	Mintage	F	VF	XF	Unc	BU
1995	Est. 25,000	—	—	—	30.00	—

KM# 256 20 DOLLARS
31.4700 g., 0.9250 Silver .9359 oz. ASW **Ruler:** Elizabeth II
Obv: Crowned head right, date below **Rev:** Queen Mother and daughters within circle, denomination below

Date	Mintage	F	VF	XF	Unc	BU
1995 Proof	Est. 30,000	Value: 16.00				

KM# 257 20 DOLLARS
1.2441 g., 0.9999 Gold .0400 oz. AGW **Ruler:** Elizabeth II
Subject: 500 Years of America **Obv:** Crowned head right, date below **Rev:** Statue of Liberty, denomination below

Date	Mintage	F	VF	XF	Unc	BU
1995	Est. 25,000	—	—	—	30.00	—

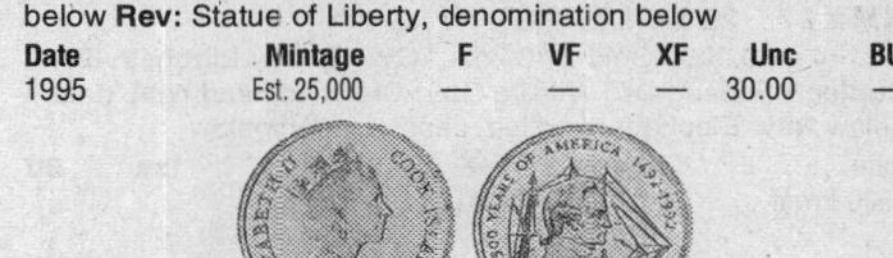

KM# 258 20 DOLLARS
1.2441 g., 0.9999 Gold .0400 oz. AGW **Ruler:** Elizabeth II
Subject: 500 Years of America **Obv:** Crowned head right, date below **Rev:** Capt. James Cook bust right, denomination below

Date	Mintage	F	VF	XF	Unc	BU
1995 Proof	Est. 25,000	Value: 30.00				

KM# 270 20 DOLLARS
1.2441 g., 0.9999 Gold .0400 oz. AGW **Ruler:** Elizabeth II
Subject: 500 Years of America **Obv:** Crowned head right, date below **Rev:** Astronaut on moon, denomination below

Date	Mintage	F	VF	XF	Unc	BU
1995 Proof	Est. 25,000	Value: 30.00				

KM# 287 20 DOLLARS
155.5175 g., 0.9990 Silver 4.9950 oz. ASW **Ruler:** Elizabeth II
Subject: Olympic National Park **Obv:** Crowned head right, date below **Rev:** Bald eagle

Date	Mintage	F	VF	XF	Unc	BU
1996 Proof	1,000	Value: 75.00				

KM# 288 20 DOLLARS
155.5175 g., 0.9990 Silver 4.9950 oz. ASW **Ruler:** Elizabeth II
Subject: Yellowstone National Park **Obv:** Crowned head right, date below **Rev:** Grizzly bear

Date	Mintage	F	VF	XF	Unc	BU
1996 Proof	1,000	Value: 75.00				

KM# 298 20 DOLLARS
3.0000 g., 0.9999 Gold .0964 oz. AGW **Ruler:** Elizabeth II **Subject:** Year of the Mouse **Obv:** Crowned head right, date below **Rev:** Multicolor Mickey Mouse portrait facing, denomination below

Date	Mintage	F	VF	XF	Unc	BU
1996 Proof	—	Value: 65.00				

KM# 334 20 DOLLARS
32.0200 g., 0.9250 Silver .9517 oz. ASW **Ruler:** Elizabeth II
Subject: 12th Century **Obv:** Crowned head right, date below **Rev:** Genghis Khan on horse left, soldier on camel at right, denominaition at left

Date	Mintage	F	VF	XF	Unc	BU
1997 Proof	—	Value: 14.50				

KM# 336 20 DOLLARS
31.8800 g., 0.9250 Silver .9481 oz. ASW **Ruler:** Elizabeth II
Subject: 18th Century **Obv:** Crowned head right, date below **Rev:** Signing of the Declaration of Independence, denomination lower right **Edge:** Reeded

Date	Mintage	F	VF	XF	Unc	BU
1997FM Proof	—	Value: 14.50				

KM# 337 20 DOLLARS
31.8800 g., 0.9250 Silver .9481 oz. ASW **Ruler:** Elizabeth II
Subject: 19th Century **Obv:** Crowned head right, date below **Rev:** Waving driver with two passengers in horseless carriage, bicycle at right in back, denomination at left **Edge:** Reeded

Date	Mintage	F	VF	XF	Unc	BU
1997FM Proof	—	Value: 14.50				

KM# 459 20 DOLLARS
5.0000 g., 0.9995 Platinum 0.1607 oz. APW **Ruler:** Elizabeth II
Subject: Love Angels

Date	Mintage	F	VF	XF	Unc	BU
1997 Proof	250	Value: 175				

KM# 18 25 DOLLARS
48.8500 g., 0.9250 Silver 1.4527 oz. ASW **Ruler:** Elizabeth II
Subject: Queen's Silver Jubilee **Obv:** Crowned head right, date below **Rev:** Crowned EIIR monogram between flowers **Rev. Designer:** James Berry

Date	Mintage	F	VF	XF	Unc	BU
1977FM (M)	100	—	—	—	47.50	—
1977FM (U)	4,068	—	—	—	22.50	—
1977FM Proof	17,000	Value: 20.00				

KM# 42 25 DOLLARS
37.0000 g., 0.9250 Silver 1.1005 oz. ASW **Ruler:** Elizabeth II
Subject: 100th Anniversary of British Rule **Obv:** Crowned head right, date below **Rev:** Sailing ship bottom right, bust of Makea Takau Ariki, island chief at left, mountains behind, denomination below

Date	Mintage	F	VF	XF	Unc	BU
1988 Proof	3,000	Value: 20.00				

KM# 83 25 DOLLARS
1.2144 g., 0.9990 Gold .0400 oz. AGW **Ruler:** Elizabeth II
Subject: Endangered Wildlife **Obv:** Crowned head right, date below **Rev:** Bison head left, denomination below

Date	Mintage	F	VF	XF	Unc	BU
1990 Proof	100,000	Value: 32.50				

KM# 84 25 DOLLARS
1.2144 g., 0.9990 Gold .0400 oz. AGW **Ruler:** Elizabeth II
Subject: Endangered Wildlife **Obv:** Crowned head right, date below **Rev:** Longhorn sheep head facing, denomination below

Date	Mintage	F	VF	XF	Unc	BU
1990 Proof	Est. 100,000	Value: 32.50				

KM# 85 25 DOLLARS
1.2144 g., 0.9990 Gold .0400 oz. AGW **Ruler:** Elizabeth II
Subject: Endangered Wildlife **Obv:** Crowned head right, date below **Rev:** Tiger head, denomination below

Date	Mintage	F	VF	XF	Unc	BU
1990 Proof	—	Value: 32.50				

KM# 86 25 DOLLARS
1.2144 g., 0.9990 Gold .0400 oz. AGW **Ruler:** Elizabeth II
Subject: Endangered Wildlife **Obv:** Crowned head right, date below **Rev:** Eagle

Date	Mintage	F	VF	XF	Unc	BU
1990 Proof	Est. 100,000	Value: 32.50				

KM# 87 25 DOLLARS
1.2144 g., 0.9990 Gold .0400 oz. AGW **Ruler:** Elizabeth II
Subject: Endangered Wildlife **Obv:** Crowned head right, date below **Rev:** Elephant head left, denomination below

Date	Mintage	F	VF	XF	Unc	BU
1990 Proof	Est. 100,000	Value: 32.50				

KM# 88 25 DOLLARS
1.2144 g., 0.9990 Gold .0400 oz. AGW **Ruler:** Elizabeth II
Subject: Endangered Wildlife **Obv:** Crowned head right, date below **Rev:** Lynx head left, denomination below

Date	Mintage	F	VF	XF	Unc	BU
1990 Proof	Est. 100,000	Value: 32.50				

KM# 239 25 DOLLARS
1.2144 g., 0.9990 Gold .0400 oz. AGW **Ruler:** Elizabeth II
Subject: Endangered Wildlife **Obv:** Crowned head right, date below **Rev:** Bee hummingbird right, denomination below

Date	Mintage	F	VF	XF	Unc	BU
1990 Proof	Est. 100,000	Value: 32.50				

KM# 240 25 DOLLARS
1.2144 g., 0.9990 Gold .0400 oz. AGW **Ruler:** Elizabeth II
Subject: Endangered Wildlife **Obv:** Crowned head right, date below **Rev:** Koala bear, denomination below

Date	Mintage	F	VF	XF	Unc	BU
1991 Proof	Est. 100,000	Value: 32.50				

KM# 241 25 DOLLARS
1.2144 g., 0.9990 Gold .0400 oz. AGW **Ruler:** Elizabeth II
Subject: Endangered Wildlife **Obv:** Crowned head right, date below **Rev:** Panda bear, denomination below

Date	Mintage	F	VF	XF	Unc	BU
1991 Proof	Est. 100,000	Value: 32.50				
1997PM Proof	—	Value: 37.50				

KM# 138 25 DOLLARS
1.2144 g., 0.9990 Gold .0400 oz. AGW **Ruler:** Elizabeth II **Subject:** Endangered Wildlife **Obv:** Crowned head right, date below **Rev:** Przewalski's horse galloping right, denomination below

Date	Mintage	F	VF	XF	Unc	BU
1992 Prooflike	—	—	—	—	32.50	—

KM# 242 25 DOLLARS
1.2144 g., 0.9990 Gold .0400 oz. AGW **Ruler:** Elizabeth II
Subject: Endangered Wildlife **Obv:** Crowned head right, date below **Rev:** African lion, denomination below

Date	Mintage	F	VF	XF	Unc	BU
1992 Proof	Est. 100,000	Value: 32.50				

KM# 243 25 DOLLARS
1.2144 g., 0.9990 Gold .0400 oz. AGW **Ruler:** Elizabeth II
Subject: Endangered Wildlife **Obv:** Crowned head right, date below **Rev:** Butterfly, denomination below

Date	Mintage	F	VF	XF	Unc	BU
1992 Proof	Est. 100,000	Value: 32.50				

KM# 238 25 DOLLARS
6.2200 g., 0.5830 Gold .1166 oz. AGW **Ruler:** Elizabeth II
Subject: 1996 Olympics **Obv:** Crowned head right, date below
Rev: Ancient archer within circle, denomination below

Date	Mintage	F	VF	XF	Unc	BU
1995 Proof	Est. 5,000	Value: 80.00				

KM# 271 25 DOLLARS
155.5175 g., 0.9990 Silver 5.000 oz. ASW **Ruler:** Elizabeth II **Subject:** Endangered Wildlife **Obv:** Crowned head right, date below **Rev:** Koala bear and baby, denomination below

Date	Mintage	F	VF	XF	Unc	BU
1996 Proof	Est. 10,000	Value: 70.00				

KM# 272 25 DOLLARS
155.5175 g., 0.9990 Silver 5.000 oz. ASW **Ruler:** Elizabeth II **Subject:** Endangered Wildlife **Obv:** Crowned head right, date below **Rev:** Family of chimpanzees

Date	Mintage	F	VF	XF	Unc	BU
1996 Proof	Est. 10,000	Value: 70.00				

KM# 273 25 DOLLARS
155.5175 g., 0.9990 Silver 5.000 oz. ASW **Ruler:** Elizabeth II **Subject:** Endangered Wildlife **Obv:** Crowned head right, date below **Rev:** Family of elephants

Date	Mintage	F	VF	XF	Unc	BU
1996 Proof	Est. 10,000	Value: 70.00				

KM# 274 25 DOLLARS
155.5175 g., 0.9990 Silver 5.000 oz. ASW **Ruler:** Elizabeth II **Subject:** Endangered Wildlife **Obv:** Crowned head right, date below **Rev:** Family of whooping cranes

Date	Mintage	F	VF	XF	Unc	BU
1996 Proof	Est. 10,000	Value: 70.00				

KM# 289 25 DOLLARS
155.5175 g., 0.9990 Silver 5.000 oz. ASW **Ruler:** Elizabeth II **Subject:** Olympic National Park **Obv:** Crowned head right, date below **Rev:** Multicolor Bald eagle in flight

Date	Mintage	F	VF	XF	Unc	BU
1996 Proof	1,000	Value: 75.00				

KM# 290 25 DOLLARS
155.5175 g., 0.9990 Silver 5.000 oz. ASW **Ruler:** Elizabeth II **Subject:** Yellowstone Natonal Park **Obv:** Crowned head right, date below **Rev:** Multicolor Grizzly bear and cub

Date	Mintage	F	VF	XF	Unc	BU
1996 Proof	1,000	Value: 75.00				

KM# 291 25 DOLLARS
3.1103 g., 0.9990 Gold .1000 oz. AGW **Ruler:** Elizabeth II **Subject:** Olympic National Park **Obv:** Crowned head right, date below **Rev:** Bald eagle head right, denomination below

Date	Mintage	F	VF	XF	Unc	BU
1996 Proof	—	Value: 70.00				

KM# 292 25 DOLLARS
3.1103 g., 0.9990 Gold .1000 oz. AGW **Ruler:** Elizabeth II **Subject:** Yellowstone National Park **Obv:** Crowned head right, date below **Rev:** Grizzly bear

Date	Mintage	F	VF	XF	Unc	BU
1996 Proof	—	Value: 70.00				

KM# 309 30 DOLLARS
10000.0996 g., 0.9990 Silver 32.1218 oz. ASW **Ruler:** Elizabeth II **Obv:** Crowned head right, date below **Rev:** Princess Diana's portrait, dates

Date	Mintage	F	VF	XF	Unc	BU
1997 Matte Proof	—	Value: 435				

KM# 11 50 DOLLARS
97.2000 g., 0.9250 Silver 2.8907 oz. ASW **Ruler:** Elizabeth II **Subject:** Winston Churchill Centenary **Obv:** Young bust right, date below **Rev:** Churchill head at right looking left, castle, Big Ben clock, flag, denomination below **Rev. Designer:** James Berry

Date	Mintage	F	VF	XF	Unc	BU
1974	1,202	—	—	BV	40.00	45.00
1974 Proof	2,502	Value: 42.50				

KM# 11a 50 DOLLARS
97.2000 g., 0.9250 Silver Gilt 2.8907 oz. ASW **Ruler:** Elizabeth II **Subject:** Winston Churchill Centenary **Obv:** Young bust right, date below **Rev:** Churchill head at right looking left, flag above castle and clock tower

Date	Mintage	F	VF	XF	Unc	BU
1974 Proof	2,002	Value: 40.00				

KM# 203 50 DOLLARS
3.9450 g., 0.5000 Gold 0.0634 oz. AGW **Ruler:** Elizabeth II **Obv:** Young bust right, date below **Rev:** Denomination above plant

Date	Mintage	F	VF	XF	Unc	BU
1980 Proof	—	Value: 47.50				

KM# 27 50 DOLLARS
3.9450 g., 0.5000 Gold 0.0634 oz. AGW **Ruler:** Elizabeth II **Subject:** Wedding of Prince Charles and Lady Diana **Obv:** Young bust right, date below **Rev:** Denomination below symbol

Date	Mintage	F	VF	XF	Unc	BU
1981	220	—	—	—	47.50	—
1981 Proof	1,309	Value: 52.50				

KM# 40 50 DOLLARS
28.2800 g., 0.9250 Silver .8411 oz. ASW **Ruler:** Elizabeth II **Subject:** 1988 Olympics **Obv:** Crowned bust right, date below **Rev:** Torch bearer, globe in background

Date	Mintage	F	VF	XF	Unc	BU
1987PM Proof	20,000	Value: 15.00				

KM# 61 50 DOLLARS
20.9400 g., 0.9250 Silver .6228 oz. ASW **Ruler:** Elizabeth II
Subject: Great Explorers **Obv:** Crowned head right, date below
Rev: Stanley and Livingstone, denomination lower right

Date	Mintage	F	VF	XF	Unc	BU
1988FM (P)	—	Value: 10.00				

KM# 62 50 DOLLARS
20.9400 g., 0.9250 Silver .6228 oz. ASW **Ruler:** Elizabeth II
Subject: Great Explorers **Obv:** Crowned head right, date below
Rev: Capt. James Cook

Date	Mintage	F	VF	XF	Unc	BU
1988FM (P)	—	Value: 10.00				

KM# 63 50 DOLLARS
20.9400 g., 0.9250 Silver .6228 oz. ASW **Ruler:** Elizabeth II
Subject: Great Explorers **Obv:** Crowned head right, date below
Rev: Vasco Nuñez de Balboa

Date	Mintage	F	VF	XF	Unc	BU
1988FM (P)	—	Value: 10.00				

KM# 64 50 DOLLARS
20.9400 g., 0.9250 Silver .6228 oz. ASW **Ruler:** Elizabeth II
Subject: Great Explorers **Obv:** Crowned head right, date below
Rev: Ferdinand Magellan's ships: Vittoria and Trinidad

Date	Mintage	F	VF	XF	Unc	BU
1988FM (P)	—	Value: 10.00				

KM# 65 50 DOLLARS
20.9400 g., 0.9250 Silver .6228 oz. ASW **Ruler:** Elizabeth II
Subject: Great Explorers **Obv:** Crowned head right, date below
Rev: Marco Polo on camel, denomination at right

Date	Mintage	F	VF	XF	Unc	BU
1988FM (P)	—	Value: 10.00				

KM# 66 50 DOLLARS
20.9400 g., 0.9250 Silver .6228 oz. ASW **Ruler:** Elizabeth II
Subject: Great Explorers **Obv:** Crowned head right, date below
Rev: Vasco da Gama

Date	Mintage	F	VF	XF	Unc	BU
1988FM (P)	—	Value: 10.00				

KM# 67 50 DOLLARS
20.9400 g., 0.9250 Silver .6228 oz. ASW **Ruler:** Elizabeth II
Subject: Great Explorers **Obv:** Crowned head right, date below
Rev: Christopher Columbus

Date	Mintage	F	VF	XF	Unc	BU
1988FM (P)	—	Value: 10.00				

KM# 68 50 DOLLARS
20.9400 g., 0.9250 Silver .6228 oz. ASW **Ruler:** Elizabeth II
Subject: Great Explorers **Obv:** Crowned head right, date below
Rev: Sir Francis Drake

Date	Mintage	F	VF	XF	Unc	BU
1988FM (P)	—	Value: 10.00				

KM# 69 50 DOLLARS
20.9400 g., 0.9250 Silver .6228 oz. ASW **Ruler:** Elizabeth II
Subject: Great Explorers **Obv:** Crowned head right, date below
Rev: Sieur de la Salle

Date	Mintage	F	VF	XF	Unc	BU
1988FM (P)	—	Value: 10.00				

KM# 96 50 DOLLARS
20.9400 g., 0.9250 Silver .6228 oz. ASW **Ruler:** Elizabeth II
Subject: Great Explorers **Obv:** Crowned head right, date below
Rev: Alexander the Great

Date	Mintage	F	VF	XF	Unc	BU
1988FM (P)	—	Value: 10.00				

KM# 97 50 DOLLARS
20.9400 g., 0.9250 Silver .6228 oz. ASW **Ruler:** Elizabeth II
Subject: Great Explorers **Obv:** Crowned head right, date below
Rev: Leif Ericson, denomination at right

Date	Mintage	F	VF	XF	Unc	BU
1988FM (P)	—	Value: 10.00				

KM# 98 50 DOLLARS
20.9400 g., 0.9250 Silver .6228 oz. ASW **Ruler:** Elizabeth II
Subject: Great Explorers **Obv:** Crowned head right, date below
Rev: Amerigo Vespucci

Date	Mintage	F	VF	XF	Unc	BU
1988FM (P)	—	Value: 10.00				

KM# 99 50 DOLLARS
20.9400 g., 0.9250 Silver .6228 oz. ASW **Ruler:** Elizabeth II
Subject: Great Explorers **Obv:** Crowned head right, date below
Rev: Bartolomeu Diaz

Date	Mintage	F	VF	XF	Unc	BU
1988FM (P)	—	Value: 10.00				

KM# 100 50 DOLLARS
20.9400 g., 0.9250 Silver .6228 oz. ASW **Ruler:** Elizabeth II
Subject: Great Explorers **Obv:** Crowned head right, date below
Rev: Juan Ponce de Léon

Date	Mintage	F	VF	XF	Unc	BU
1988FM (P)	—	Value: 10.00				

KM# 101 50 DOLLARS
20.9400 g., 0.9250 Silver .6228 oz. ASW **Ruler:** Elizabeth II
Subject: Great Explorers **Obv:** Crowned head right, date below
Rev: Hernando Cortés

Date	Mintage	F	VF	XF	Unc	BU
1988FM (P)	—	Value: 10.00				

KM# 102 50 DOLLARS
20.9400 g., 0.9250 Silver .6228 oz. ASW **Ruler:** Elizabeth II
Subject: Great Explorers **Obv:** Crowned head right, date below
Rev: Francisco Coronado

Date	Mintage	F	VF	XF	Unc	BU
1988FM (P)	—	Value: 10.00				

KM# 103 50 DOLLARS
20.9400 g., 0.9250 Silver .6228 oz. ASW **Ruler:** Elizabeth II
Subject: Great Explorers **Obv:** Crowned head right, date below
Rev: Francisco Pizarro and map, denomination at left

Date	Mintage	F	VF	XF	Unc	BU
1988FM (P)	—	Value: 10.00				

KM# 104 50 DOLLARS
20.9400 g., 0.9250 Silver .6228 oz. ASW **Ruler:** Elizabeth II
Subject: Great Explorers **Obv:** Crowned head right, date below
Rev: Samuel de Champlain

Date	Mintage	F	VF	XF	Unc	BU
1988FM (P)	—	Value: 10.00				

KM# 105 50 DOLLARS
20.9400 g., 0.9250 Silver .6228 oz. ASW **Ruler:** Elizabeth II
Subject: Great Explorers **Obv:** Crowned head right, date below
Rev: John Cabot

Date	Mintage	F	VF	XF	Unc	BU
1988FM (P)	—	Value: 10.00				

KM# 106 50 DOLLARS
20.9400 g., 0.9250 Silver .6228 oz. ASW **Ruler:** Elizabeth II
Subject: Great Explorers **Obv:** Crowned head right, date below
Rev: Abel Janszoon Tasman

Date	Mintage	F	VF	XF	Unc	BU
1988FM (P)	—	Value: 10.00				

KM# 107 50 DOLLARS
20.9400 g., 0.9250 Silver .6228 oz. ASW **Ruler:** Elizabeth II
Subject: Great Explorers **Obv:** Crowned head right, date below
Rev: Lewis and Clark, denomination at left

Date	Mintage	F	VF	XF	Unc	BU
1988FM (P)	—	Value: 10.00				

KM# 108 50 DOLLARS
20.9400 g., 0.9250 Silver .6228 oz. ASW **Ruler:** Elizabeth II
Subject: Great Explorers **Obv:** Crowned head right, date below
Rev: Fridtjof Nansen

Date	Mintage	F	VF	XF	Unc	BU
1988FM (P)	—	Value: 10.00				

KM# 109 50 DOLLARS
20.9400 g., 0.9250 Silver .6228 oz. ASW **Ruler:** Elizabeth II
Subject: Great Explorers **Obv:** Crowned head right, date below
Rev: Robert Peary

Date	Mintage	F	VF	XF	Unc	BU
1988FM (P)	—	Value: 10.00				

KM# 110 50 DOLLARS
20.9400 g., 0.9250 Silver .6228 oz. ASW **Ruler:** Elizabeth II
Subject: Great Explorers **Obv:** Crowned head right, date below
Rev: Roald Amundsen

Date	Mintage	F	VF	XF	Unc	BU
1988FM (P); Proof	—	Value: 10.00				

KM# 111 50 DOLLARS
20.9400 g., 0.9250 Silver .6228 oz. ASW **Ruler:** Elizabeth II
Subject: Great Explorers **Obv:** Crowned head right, date below
Rev: Richard Byrd, map at left, denomination above

Date	Mintage	F	VF	XF	Unc	BU
1988FM (P)	—	Value: 10.00				

KM# 45 50 DOLLARS
19.4000 g., 0.9250 Silver .5770 oz. ASW **Ruler:** Elizabeth II
Subject: 500 Years of America **Obv:** Crowned head right, date below **Rev:** Sir Francis Drake

Date	Mintage	F	VF	XF	Unc	BU
1989 Proof	15,000	Value: 10.00				
1990 Proof	—	Value: 9.00				

KM# 49 50 DOLLARS
31.1000 g., 0.9250 Silver .9250 oz. ASW **Ruler:** Elizabeth II
Subject: 500 Years of America **Obv:** Crowned head right, date below **Rev:** Ferdinand Magellan at right, map at left, denomination below

Date	Mintage	F	VF	XF	Unc	BU
1989 Proof	15,000	Value: 13.50				
1991 Proof	Est. 60,000	Value: 12.50				

KM# 46 50 DOLLARS
31.1000 g., 0.9990 Silver 1.0000 oz. ASW **Ruler:** Elizabeth II
Subject: 500 Years of America **Obv:** Crowned head right, date below **Rev:** Capt. James Cook

Date	Mintage	F	VF	XF	Unc	BU
1989 Proof	15,000	Value: 14.50				

KM# 47 50 DOLLARS
29.9000 g., 0.9250 Silver .8892 oz. ASW **Ruler:** Elizabeth II
Subject: 500 Years of America **Obv:** Crowned head right, date below **Rev:** Christopher Columbus **Edge Lettering:** CHRISTOPHER COLUMBUS WITH THE SANTA MARIA

Date	Mintage	F	VF	XF	Unc	BU
1989 Proof	Est. 15,000	Value: 16.00				

Note: Prior to the 27th edition, the illustration for KM#47 was incorrect. Please see KM#182 for correct listing.

KM# 60 50 DOLLARS
28.2800 g., 0.9250 Silver .8411 oz. ASW **Ruler:** Elizabeth II
Subject: 1990 Olympics **Obv:** Crowned bust right, date below **Rev:** Runners and biathalon

Date	Mintage	F	VF	XF	Unc	BU
1989 Proof	40,000	—	—	—	13.50	—

KM# 70 50 DOLLARS
28.2800 g., 0.9250 Silver .8411 oz. ASW **Ruler:** Elizabeth II
Subject: Soccer World Championship **Obv:** Crowned bust right, date below **Rev:** Two soccer players and ball

Date	Mintage	F	VF	XF	Unc	BU
1989 Proof	—	Value: 13.50				

KM# 43 50 DOLLARS
31.1000 g., 0.9250 Silver .9249 oz. ASW **Ruler:** Elizabeth II
Subject: 500 Years of America **Obv:** Crowned head right, date below **Rev:** Jacques Cartier

Date	Mintage	F	VF	XF	Unc	BU
1990 Proof	60,000	Value: 13.50				
1991 Proof	—	Value: 14.50				

KM# 44 50 DOLLARS
31.1000 g., 0.9990 Silver 1.0000 oz. ASW **Ruler:** Elizabeth II
Subject: 500 Years of America **Obv:** Crowned head right, date below **Rev:** Vasco Nunez de Balboa, left, denomination below

Date	Mintage	F	VF	XF	Unc	BU
1990 Proof	15,000	Value: 14.50				
1991 Proof	—	Value: 14.50				

KM# 265 50 DOLLARS
28.3000 g., 0.9250 Silver .8416 oz. ASW **Ruler:** Elizabeth II
Subject: World Cup Soccer **Obv:** Crowned head right, date below **Rev:** Soccer players, denomination below

Date	Mintage	F	VF	XF	Unc	BU
1990 Proof	—	Value: 12.50				

KM# 52 50 DOLLARS
19.4000 g., 0.9250 Silver .5770 oz. ASW **Ruler:** Elizabeth II
Subject: Endangered World Wildlife **Obv:** Crowned head right, date below **Rev:** Grizzly bear

Date	Mintage	F	VF	XF	Unc	BU
1990PM Proof	2,500	Value: 15.00				
1990PM Matte	550	Value: 45.00				

KM# 48 50 DOLLARS
31.1000 g., 0.9990 Silver 1.0000 oz. ASW **Ruler:** Elizabeth II
Subject: 500 Years of America **Obv:** Crowned head right, date below **Rev:** President Abraham Lincoln in foreground of capitol

Date	Mintage	F	VF	XF	Unc	BU
1990 Proof	15,000	Value: 15.00				
1991 Proof	—	Value: 15.00				

KM# 53 50 DOLLARS
19.4000 g., 0.9250 Silver .5770 oz. ASW **Ruler:** Elizabeth II
Subject: Endangered World Wildlife **Obv:** Crowned head right, date below **Rev:** African elephant

Date	Mintage	F	VF	XF	Unc	BU
1990 Matte	1,000	Value: 35.00				
1990 Proof	25,000	Value: 15.00				

KM# 54 50 DOLLARS
19.4000 g., 0.9250 Silver .5770 oz. ASW **Ruler:** Elizabeth II
Subject: Endangered World Wildlife **Obv:** Crowned head right, date below **Rev:** Lynx

Date	Mintage	F	VF	XF	Unc	BU
1990 Proof	25,000	Value: 17.50				

KM# 55 50 DOLLARS
19.4000 g., 0.9250 Silver .5770 oz. ASW **Ruler:** Elizabeth II
Subject: Endangered World Wildlife **Obv:** Crowned head right, date below **Rev:** Black rhinoceros

Date	Mintage	F	VF	XF	Unc	BU
1990 Proof	Est. 25,000	Value: 17.50				

KM# 56 50 DOLLARS
19.4000 g., 0.9250 Silver .5770 oz. ASW **Ruler:** Elizabeth II
Subject: Endangered World Wildlife **Obv:** Crowned head right, date below **Rev:** Bighorn sheep, denomination below

Date	Mintage	F	VF	XF	Unc	BU
1990 Proof	Est. 25,000	Value: 17.50				

KM# 57 50 DOLLARS
19.4000 g., 0.9250 Silver .5770 oz. ASW **Ruler:** Elizabeth II
Subject: Endangered World Wildlife **Obv:** Crowned head right, date below **Rev:** Koala bear

Date	Mintage	F	VF	XF	Unc	BU
1990 Proof	Est. 25,000	Value: 17.50				

KM# 58 50 DOLLARS
19.4000 g., 0.9250 Silver .5770 oz. ASW **Ruler:** Elizabeth II
Subject: Endangered World Wildlife **Obv:** Crowned head right, date below **Rev:** Buffalo, denomination below

Date	Mintage	F	VF	XF	Unc	BU
1990 Proof	25,000	Value: 17.50				
1990	600	—	—	—	40.00	—

KM# 59 50 DOLLARS
19.4000 g., 0.9250 Silver .5770 oz. ASW **Ruler:** Elizabeth II
Subject: Endangered World Wildlife **Obv:** Crowned head right, date below **Rev:** Chimpanzee, denomination below

Date	Mintage	F	VF	XF	Unc	BU
1990 Proof	Est. 25,000	Value: 17.50				

KM# 89 50 DOLLARS
31.1000 g., 0.9250 Silver .9250 oz. ASW **Ruler:** Elizabeth II
Subject: 500 Years of Amer ca **Obv:** Crowned head right, date below **Rev:** 3/4 figure of Henry Hudson at right looking left, ship at left, denomination below

Date	Mintage	F	VF	XF	Unc	BU
1990 Proof	60,000	Value: 13.50				

KM# 134 50 DOLLARS
31.1000 g., 0.9250 Silver .9250 oz. ASW **Ruler:** Elizabeth II
Subject: 500 Years of America **Obv:** Crowned head right, date below **Rev:** Cabral bust at right, two figures with cross at left, denomination below

Date	Mintage	F	VF	XF	Unc	BU
1990 Proof	Est. 60,000	Value: 13.50				

KM# 135 50 DOLLARS
31.1000 g., 0.9250 Silver .9250 oz. ASW **Ruler:** Elizabeth II
Subject: 500 Years of America **Obv:** Crowned head right, date below **Rev:** Half figure of Bo ivar at left facing right, denomination below

Date	Mintage	F	VF	XF	Unc	BU
1990 Proof	Est. 60,000	Value: 13.50				

KM# 139 50 DOLLARS
31.2600 g., 0.9250 Silver .9296 oz. ASW **Ruler:** Elizabeth II
Subject: 500 Years of America **Obv:** Crowned head right, date below **Rev:** Samuel Clemens at left looking right, steamboat in background, denomination below

Date	Mintage	F	VF	XF	Unc	BU
1990 Proof	Est. 60,000	Value: 13.50				

KM# 182 50 DOLLARS
31.3500 g., 0.9250 Silver .9324 oz. ASW **Ruler:** Elizabeth II
Subject: 500 Years of America **Obv:** Crowned head right, date below **Rev:** Columbus' portrait with Santa Maria in background

Date	Mintage	F	VF	XF	Unc	BU
1990 Proof	—	Value: 13.50				

KM# 184 50 DOLLARS
31.3500 g., 0.9250 Silver .9324 oz. ASW **Ruler:** Elizabeth II
Subject: 500 Years of America **Obv:** Crowned head right, date below **Rev:** Inca Prince

Date	Mintage	F	VF	XF	Unc	BU
1990 Proof	Est. 60,000	Value: 13.50				

KM# 185 50 DOLLARS
31.3500 g., 0.9250 Silver .9324 oz. ASW **Ruler:** Elizabeth II
Subject: 500 Years of America **Obv:** Crowned head right, date below **Rev:** Cortez and Montezuma, denomination below

Date	Mintage	F	VF	XF	Unc	BU
1990 Proof	Est. 60,000	Value: 13.50				

KM# 186 50 DOLLARS
31.3500 g., 0.9250 Silver .9324 oz. ASW **Ruler:** Elizabeth II
Subject: 500 Years of America **Obv:** Crowned head right, date below **Rev:** Samuel de Champlain bust looking right, denomination below

Date	Mintage	F	VF	XF	Unc	BU
1990 Proof	Est. 60,000	Value: 13.50				

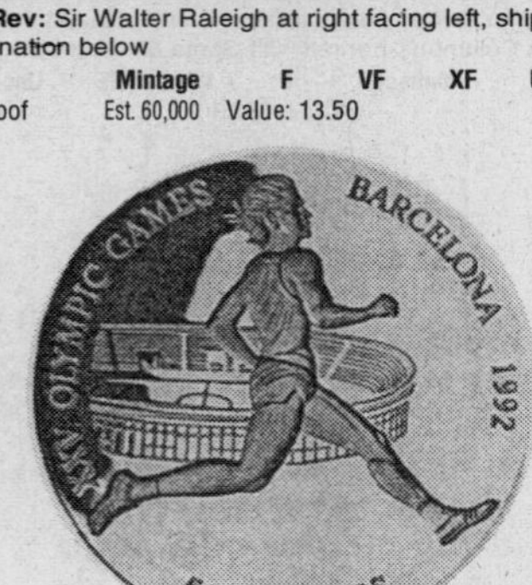

KM# 188 50 DOLLARS
31.3500 g., 0.9250 Silver .9324 oz. ASW **Ruler:** Elizabeth II
Subject: 500 Years of America **Obv:** Crowned head right, date below **Rev:** Sir Walter Raleigh at right facing left, ship at left, denomination below

Date	Mintage	F	VF	XF	Unc	BU
1990 Proof	Est. 60,000	Value: 13.50				

KM# 112 50 DOLLARS
19.2000 g., 0.9250 Silver .5710 oz. ASW **Ruler:** Elizabeth II
Subject: 1992 Olympics **Obv:** Crowned head right, date below **Rev:** Runner

Date	Mintage	F	VF	XF	Unc	BU
1990 Proof	40,000	Value: 10.00				

KM# 115 50 DOLLARS
19.8000 g., 0.9250 Silver .5888 oz. ASW **Ruler:** Elizabeth II
Subject: Endangered World Wildlife **Obv:** Crowned head right, date below **Rev:** Blackbuck left, denomination below

Date	Mintage	F	VF	XF	Unc	BU
1990 Proof	—	Value: 17.50				

KM# 117 50 DOLLARS
19.8000 g., 0.9250 Silver .5888 oz. ASW **Ruler:** Elizabeth II
Subject: Endangered World Wildlife **Obv:** Crowned head right, date below **Rev:** Whooping crane, denomination below

Date	Mintage	F	VF	XF	Unc	BU
1990 Proof	—	Value: 17.50				

KM# 144 50 DOLLARS
19.4000 g., 0.9250 Silver .5768 oz. ASW **Ruler:** Elizabeth II
Subject: Endangered World Wildlife **Obv:** Crowned head right, date below **Rev:** European hedgehog left, denomination below

Date	Mintage	F	VF	XF	Unc	BU
1990 Proof	Est. 25,000	Value: 17.50				

KM# 205 50 DOLLARS
19.2000 g., 0.9250 Silver .5768 oz. ASW **Ruler:** Elizabeth II
Subject: Endangered World Wildlife **Obv:** PM mint mark below truncation **Rev:** European bison and calf

Date	Mintage	F	VF	XF	Unc	BU
1990PM Proof	Est. 25,000	Value: 17.50				

KM# 206 50 DOLLARS
19.2000 g., 0.9250 Silver .5768 oz. ASW **Ruler:** Elizabeth II
Subject: Endangered World Wildlife **Obv:** Crowned head right, date below **Rev:** Tiger

Date	Mintage	F	VF	XF	Unc	BU
1990 Proof	Est. 25,000	Value: 17.50				

KM# 207 50 DOLLARS
19.2000 g., 0.9250 Silver .5768 oz. ASW **Ruler:** Elizabeth II
Subject: Endangered World Wildlife **Obv:** Crowned head right, date below **Rev:** Dama gazelles, denomination below

Date	Mintage	F	VF	XF	Unc	BU
1990 Proof	Est. 25,000	Value: 17.50				

KM# 208 50 DOLLARS
19.2000 g., 0.9250 Silver .5768 oz. ASW **Ruler:** Elizabeth II
Subject: Endangered World Wildlife **Obv:** Crowned head right, date below **Rev:** Cougars

Date	Mintage	F	VF	XF	Unc	BU
1990PM Proof	—	Value: 22.50				

KM# 209 50 DOLLARS
19.2000 g., 0.9250 Silver .5768 oz. ASW **Ruler:** Elizabeth II
Subject: Endangered World Wildlife **Obv:** Crowned head right, date below **Rev:** Eagle Owl, denomination below

Date	Mintage	F	VF	XF	Unc	BU
1990(b) Proof	—	Value: 22.50				

KM# 210 50 DOLLARS
19.2000 g., 0.9250 Silver .5768 oz. ASW **Ruler:** Elizabeth II
Subject: Endangered World Wildlife **Obv:** Crowned head right, date below **Rev:** Heaviside's dolphins

Date	Mintage	F	VF	XF	Unc	BU
1990(b) Proof	—	Value: 22.50				

KM# 211 50 DOLLARS
19.2000 g., 0.9250 Silver .5768 oz. ASW **Ruler:** Elizabeth II **Subject:** Endangered World Wildlife **Obv:** Crowned head right, date below **Rev:** European otters

Date	Mintage	F	VF	XF	Unc	BU
1990 Proof	—	Value: 25.00				

KM# 357 50 DOLLARS
19.2000 g., 0.9250 Silver .5768 oz. ASW **Ruler:** Elizabeth II **Subject:** Endangered World Wildlife **Obv:** Crowned head right, date below **Rev:** Peregrine falcon

Date	Mintage	F	VF	XF	Unc	BU
1990(b) Proof	—	Value: 22.50				

KM# 212 50 DOLLARS
19.2000 g., 0.9250 Silver .5768 oz. ASW **Ruler:** Elizabeth II **Subject:** Endangered World Wildlife **Obv:** Crowned head right, date below **Rev:** Alpine ibex

Date	Mintage	F	VF	XF	Unc	BU
1990 Proof	—	Value: 22.50				

KM# 213 50 DOLLARS
19.2000 g., 0.9250 Silver .5768 oz. ASW **Ruler:** Elizabeth II **Subject:** Endangered World Wildlife **Obv:** Crowned head right, date below **Rev:** Senegalese lion, denomination below

Date	Mintage	F	VF	XF	Unc	BU
1990 Proof	—	Value: 25.00				

KM# 214 50 DOLLARS
19.2000 g., 0.9250 Silver .5768 oz. ASW **Ruler:** Elizabeth II **Subject:** Endangered World Wildlife **Obv:** Crowned head right, date below **Rev:** Fallow deer, denomination below

Date	Mintage	F	VF	XF	Unc	BU
1990 Proof	—	Value: 22.50				

KM# 215 50 DOLLARS
19.2000 g., 0.9250 Silver .5768 oz. ASW **Ruler:** Elizabeth II **Subject:** Endangered World Wildlife **Obv:** Crowned head right, date below **Rev:** Bee hummingbird

Date	Mintage	F	VF	XF	Unc	BU
1990 Proof	—	Value: 25.00				

KM# 216 50 DOLLARS
19.2000 g., 0.9250 Silver .5768 oz. ASW **Ruler:** Elizabeth II **Subject:** Endangered World Wildlife **Obv:** Crowned head right, date below **Rev:** Jackass penguins

Date	Mintage	F	VF	XF	Unc	BU
1990 Proof	—	Value: 22.50				

KM# 93 50 DOLLARS
19.8000 g., 0.9250 Silver .5888 oz. ASW **Ruler:** Elizabeth II **Subject:** Endangered Wildlife **Obv:** Crowned head right, date below **Rev:** Eagle owl

Date	Mintage	F	VF	XF	Unc	BU
1991 Proof	Est. 25,000	Value: 22.50				

KM# 95 50 DOLLARS
19.2000 g., 0.9250 Silver .5768 oz. ASW **Ruler:** Elizabeth II **Subject:** Endangered Wildlife **Obv:** Crowned head right, date below **Rev:** Heaviside's dolphins

Date	Mintage	F	VF	XF	Unc	BU
1991 Proof	Est. 25,000	Value: 22.50				

KM# 118 50 DOLLARS
19.2000 g., 0.9250 Silver .5768 oz. ASW **Ruler:** Elizabeth II **Subject:** Endangered Wildlife **Obv:** Crowned head right, date below **Rev:** European otters

Date	Mintage	F	VF	XF	Unc	BU
1991 Proof	—	Value: 22.50				

KM# 119 50 DOLLARS
19.2000 g., 0.9250 Silver .5768 oz. ASW **Ruler:** Elizabeth II **Subject:** Endangered Wildlife **Obv:** Crowned head right, date below **Rev:** Peregrine falcon

Date	Mintage	F	VF	XF	Unc	BU
1991 Proof	Est. 25,000	Value: 22.50				

KM# 120 50 DOLLARS
19.2000 g., 0.9250 Silver .5768 oz. ASW **Ruler:** Elizabeth II **Subject:** Endangered Wildlife **Obv:** Crowned head right, date below **Rev:** Alpine ibex

Date	Mintage	F	VF	XF	Unc	BU
1991 Proof	Est. 25,000	Value: 17.50				

KM# 122 50 DOLLARS
19.2000 g., 0.9250 Silver .5768 oz. ASW **Ruler:** Elizabeth II
Subject: Endangered Wildlife **Obv:** Crowned head right, date below **Rev:** Senegalese lion

Date	Mintage	F	VF	XF	Unc	BU
1991 Proof	Est. 25,000	Value: 22.50				

KM# 123 50 DOLLARS
19.2000 g., 0.9250 Silver .5768 oz. ASW **Ruler:** Elizabeth II
Subject: Endangered Wildlife **Obv:** Crowned head right, date below **Rev:** Deer

Date	Mintage	F	VF	XF	Unc	BU
1991 Proof	Est. 25,000	Value: 22.50				

KM# 124 50 DOLLARS
19.2000 g., 0.9250 Silver .5768 oz. ASW **Ruler:** Elizabeth II
Subject: Endangered Wildlife **Qbv:** Crowned head right, date below **Rev:** Kangaroo

Date	Mintage	F	VF	XF	Unc	BU
1991 Proof	Est. 25,000	Value: 22.50				

KM# 125 50 DOLLARS
19.2000 g., 0.9250 Silver .5768 oz. ASW **Ruler:** Elizabeth II
Subject: Endangered Wildlife **Obv:** Crowned head right, date below **Rev:** Cougar and cub

Date	Mintage	F	VF	XF	Unc	BU
1991 Proof	Est. 25,000	Value: 22.50				

KM# 126 50 DOLLARS
19.2000 g., 0.9250 Silver .5768 oz. ASW **Ruler:** Elizabeth II
Subject: Endangered Wildlife **Obv:** Crowned head right, date below **Rev:** Fallow deer

Date	Mintage	F	VF	XF	Unc	BU
1991 Proof	Est. 25,000	Value: 22.50				

KM# 127 50 DOLLARS
19.2000 g., 0.9250 Silver .5768 oz. ASW **Ruler:** Elizabeth II
Subject: Endangered Wildlife **Obv:** Crowned head right, date below **Rev:** Bee hummingbird

Date	Mintage	F	VF	XF	Unc	BU
1991 Proof	Est. 25,000	Value: 22.50				

KM# 128 50 DOLLARS
19.2000 g., 0.9250 Silver .5768 oz. ASW **Ruler:** Elizabeth II
Subject: Endangered Wildlife **Obv:** Crowned head right, date below **Rev:** Jackass penguins

Date	Mintage	F	VF	XF	Unc	BU
1991 Proof	Est. 25,000	Value: 22.50				

KM# 94 50 DOLLARS
31.1000 g., 0.9250 Silver .9250 oz. ASW **Ruler:** Elizabeth II
Subject: 500 Years of America **Obv:** Crowned head right, date below **Rev:** Sitting Bull, denomination below

Date	Mintage	F	VF	XF	Unc	BU
1991 Proof	Est. 15,000	Value: 15.00				

KM# 140 50 DOLLARS
31.2600 g., 0.9250 Silver .9296 oz. ASW **Ruler:** Elizabeth II
Subject: 500 Years of America **Obv:** Crowned head right, date below **Rev:** Mayflower and pilgrims, denomination below

Date	Mintage	F	VF	XF	Unc	BU
1991 Proof	—	Value: 13.50				
1992 Proof	60,000	Value: 13.50				

KM# 141 50 DOLLARS
31.2600 g., 0.9250 Silver .9296 oz. ASW **Ruler:** Elizabeth II
Subject: 500 Years of America **Obv:** Crowned head right, date below **Rev:** Alexander Mackenzie bust looking right, figure in canoe at right, denomination below

Date	Mintage	F	VF	XF	Unc	BU
1991 Proof	60,000	Value: 13.50				

KM# 145 50 DOLLARS
7.7750 g., 0.5833 Gold .1458 oz. AGW **Ruler:** Elizabeth II
Subject: 500 Years of America **Obv:** Crowned head right, date below **Rev:** Columbus kneeling with flag, denomination below

Date	Mintage	F	VF	XF	Unc	BU
1991 Proof	Est. 60,000	Value: 95.00				

KM# 148 50 DOLLARS
31.1000 g., 0.9250 Silver .9249 oz. ASW **Ruler:** Elizabeth II
Subject: 500 Years of America **Obv:** Crowned head right, date below **Rev:** Aztec Priest, denomination below

Date	Mintage	F	VF	XF	Unc	BU
1991 Proof	Est. 15,000	Value: 13.50				

KM# 189 50 DOLLARS
31.1000 g., 0.9250 Silver .9249 oz. ASW **Ruler:** Elizabeth II **Subject:** 500 Years of America **Obv:** Crowned head right, date below **Rev:** Francisco Pizarro bust at left looking right, arms at right, denomination below

Date	Mintage	F	VF	XF	Unc	BU
1991 Proof	Est. 60,000	Value: 13.50				

KM# 190 50 DOLLARS
31.1000 g., 0.9250 Silver .9249 oz. ASW **Ruler:** Elizabeth II **Subject:** 500 Years of America **Obv:** Crowned head right, date below **Rev:** Jesuit Church in Cuzco, denomination below

Date	Mintage	F	VF	XF	Unc	BU
1991 Proof	Est. 60,000	Value: 13.50				

KM# 191 50 DOLLARS
31.1000 g., 0.9250 Silver .9249 oz. ASW **Ruler:** Elizabeth II **Subject:** 500 Years of America **Obv:** Crowned head right, date below **Rev:** Peter Minuit's purchase of Manhattan Island, denomination below

Date	Mintage	F	VF	XF	Unc	BU
1991 Proof	Est. 60,000	Value: 13.50				

KM# 192 50 DOLLARS
31.1000 g., 0.9250 Silver .9249 oz. ASW **Ruler:** Elizabeth II **Subject:** 500 Years of America **Obv:** Crowned head right, date below **Rev:** Boston Tea Party, denomination below

Date	Mintage	F	VF	XF	Unc	BU
1991 Proof	Est. 60,000	Value: 13.50				

KM# 193 50 DOLLARS
31.1000 g., 0.9250 Silver .9249 oz. ASW **Ruler:** Elizabeth II **Subject:** 500 Years of America **Obv:** Crowned head right, date below **Rev:** Marquis de Lafayette bust at right looking left, figures at left, denomination below

Date	Mintage	F	VF	XF	Unc	BU
1991 Proof	Est. 60,000	Value: 13.50				

KM# 194 50 DOLLARS
31.1000 g., 0.9250 Silver .9249 oz. ASW **Ruler:** Elizabeth II **Subject:** 500 Years of America **Obv:** Crowned head right, date below **Rev:** Robert Fulton, denomination below

Date	Mintage	F	VF	XF	Unc	BU
1991 Proof	Est. 60,000	Value: 13.50				

KM# 195 50 DOLLARS
31.1000 g., 0.9250 Silver .9249 oz. ASW **Ruler:** Elizabeth II **Subject:** 500 Years of America **Obv:** Crowned head right, date below **Rev:** First U.S. transcontinental railroad, two busts above at left, denomination below

Date	Mintage	F	VF	XF	Unc	BU
1991 Proof	Est. 60,000	Value: 13.50				

KM# 196 50 DOLLARS
31.1000 g., 0.9250 Silver .9249 oz. ASW **Ruler:** Elizabeth II **Subject:** 500 Years of America **Obv:** Crowned head right, date below **Rev:** Emperor Maximilian of Mexico on horseback, denomination below

Date	Mintage	F	VF	XF	Unc	BU
1991 Proof	Est. 60,000	Value: 13.50				

KM# 305 50 DOLLARS
31.1000 g., 0.9250 Silver .9249 oz. ASW **Ruler:** Elizabeth II **Subject:** 500 Years of America **Obv:** Crowned head right, date below **Rev:** Capt. James Cook

Date	Mintage	F	VF	XF	Unc	BU
1991 Proof	Est. 60,000	Value: 13.50				

KM# 44a 50 DOLLARS
31.1000 g., 0.9250 Silver .9250 oz. ASW **Ruler:** Elizabeth II **Subject:** 500 Years of America **Obv:** Crowned head right, date below **Rev:** Vasco Nuñez de Balboa

Date	Mintage	F	VF	XF	Unc	BU
1991 Proof	60,000	Value: 15.00				

KM# 46a 50 DOLLARS
31.1000 g., 0.9250 Silver .9249 oz. ASW **Ruler:** Elizabeth II **Subject:** 500 Years of America **Obv:** Crowned head right, date below **Rev:** Capt. James Cook

Date	Mintage	F	VF	XF	Unc	BU
1991 Proof	Est. 60,000	Value: 14.50				

KM# 244 50 DOLLARS
19.2000 g., 0.9250 Silver .5768 oz. ASW **Ruler:** Elizabeth II **Obv:** Crowned head right, date below **Rev:** Poplar Admiral Butterfly and thistle, denomination below

Date	Mintage	F	VF	XF	Unc	BU
1992 Proof	Est. 25,000	Value: 22.50				

KM# 114 50 DOLLARS
31.1000 g., 0.9250 Silver .9250 oz. ASW **Ruler:** Elizabeth II **Subject:** 500 Years of America **Obv:** Crowned head right, date below **Rev:** Coronado's discovery of the Grand Canyon, denomination below

Date	Mintage	F	VF	XF	Unc	BU
1992 Proof	Est. 15,000	Value: 14.50				

KM# 129 50 DOLLARS
7.7760 g., 0.5830 Gold .1458 oz. AGW **Ruler:** Elizabeth II **Subject:** Endangered Wildlife **Obv:** Crowned head right, date below **Rev:** Eagles head

Date	Mintage	F	VF	XF	Unc	BU
1992 Proof	—	Value: 95.00				

KM# 131 50 DOLLARS
7.7760 g., 0.5830 Gold .1458 oz. AGW **Ruler:** Elizabeth II **Subject:** Endangered Wildlife **Obv:** Crowned head right, date below **Rev:** Elephant head

Date	Mintage	F	VF	XF	Unc	BU
1992 Proof	—	Value: 95.00				

KM# 132 50 DOLLARS

7.7760 g., 0.5830 Gold .1458 oz. AGW **Ruler:** Elizabeth II
Subject: Endangered Wildlife **Obv:** Crowned head right, date below **Rev:** Tiger head

Date	Mintage	F	VF	XF	Unc	BU
1992 Proof	—	Value: 95.00				

KM# 142 50 DOLLARS

31.2600 g., 0.9250 Silver .9296 oz. ASW **Ruler:** Elizabeth II
Subject: 500 Years of America **Obv:** Crowned head right, date below **Rev:** John Davis' strait marked on map, ship at right, denomination below

Date	Mintage	F	VF	XF	Unc	BU
1992 Proof	Est. 60,000	Value: 13.50				

KM# 143 50 DOLLARS

31.2600 g., 0.9250 Silver .9296 oz. ASW **Ruler:** Elizabeth II
Subject: 500 Years of America **Obv:** Crowned head right, date below **Rev:** Vitus Bering, denomination below

Date	Mintage	F	VF	XF	Unc	BU
1992 Proof	Est. 60,000	Value: 13.50				

KM# 156 50 DOLLARS

31.1035 g., 0.9250 Silver .9250 oz. ASW **Ruler:** Elizabeth II
Subject: 500 Years of America **Obv:** Crowned head right, date below **Rev:** Pedro de Valdivia bust at left looking right, denomination below

Date	Mintage	F	VF	XF	Unc	BU
1992 Proof	—	Value: 13.50				

KM# 157 50 DOLLARS

31.1035 g., 0.9250 Silver .9250 oz. ASW **Ruler:** Elizabeth II
Subject: 500 Years of America **Obv:** Crowned head right, date below **Rev:** Diego de Almagro, denomination below

Date	Mintage	F	VF	XF	Unc	BU
1992 Proof	—	Value: 13.50				

KM# 162 50 DOLLARS

31.1035 g., 0.9250 Silver .9250 oz. ASW **Ruler:** Elizabeth II
Subject: 500 Years of America **Obv:** Crowned head right, date below **Rev:** Francisco de Coronado

Date	Mintage	F	VF	XF	Unc	BU
1992 Proof	—	Value: 13.50				

KM# 176 50 DOLLARS

7.7760 g., 0.5833 Gold .1458 oz. AGW **Ruler:** Elizabeth II
Subject: 500 Years of America **Obv:** Crowned head right, date below **Rev:** Robert de La Salle

Date	Mintage	F	VF	XF	Unc	BU
1992 Proof	—	Value: 95.00				

KM# 183 50 DOLLARS

31.1035 g., 0.9250 Silver .9250 oz. ASW **Ruler:** Elizabeth II
Subject: 500 Years of America **Obv:** Crowned head right, date below **Rev:** Giovanni da Verrazano, denomination below

Date	Mintage	F	VF	XF	Unc	BU
1992 Proof	Est. 60,000	Value: 13.50				

KM# 197 50 DOLLARS

31.1035 g., 0.9250 Silver .9250 oz. ASW **Ruler:** Elizabeth II
Subject: 500 Years of America **Obv:** Crowned head right, date below **Rev:** Juan Ponce de Leon, denomination below

Date	Mintage	F	VF	XF	Unc	BU
1992 Proof	Est. 60,000	Value: 13.50				

KM# 198 50 DOLLARS

31.1035 g., 0.9250 Silver .9250 oz. ASW **Ruler:** Elizabeth II
Subject: 500 Years of America **Obv:** Crowned head right, date below **Rev:** 3/4 bust of Pedro de Mendoza at left, historic monuments at right, denomination below

Date	Mintage	F	VF	XF	Unc	BU
1992 Proof	Est. 60,000	Value: 13.50				

KM# 199 50 DOLLARS

31.1035 g., 0.9250 Silver .9250 oz. ASW **Ruler:** Elizabeth II
Subject: 500 Years of America **Obv:** Crowned head right, date below **Rev:** Pedro Menendez de Aviles on horseback at lower right, monument at left, denomination below

Date	Mintage	F	VF	XF	Unc	BU
1992 Proof	—	Value: 13.50				

KM# 200 50 DOLLARS

31.1035 g., 0.9250 Silver .9250 oz. ASW **Ruler:** Elizabeth II
Subject: 500 Years of America **Obv:** Crowned head right, date below **Rev:** Independence Hall, figures above denomination

Date	Mintage	F	VF	XF	Unc	BU
1992 Proof	—	Value: 13.50				

KM# 201 50 DOLLARS

31.1035 g., 0.9250 Silver .9250 oz. ASW **Ruler:** Elizabeth II
Subject: 500 Years of America **Obv:** Crowned head right, date below **Rev:** Sacagawea guiding Lewis and Clark, denomination below

Date	Mintage	F	VF	XF	Unc	BU
1992 Proof	Est. 60,000	Value: 13.50				

KM# 202 50 DOLLARS

31.1035 g., 0.9250 Silver .9250 oz. ASW **Ruler:** Elizabeth II
Subject: 500 Years of America **Obv:** Crowned head right, date below **Rev:** Oregon Trail, conestoga wagon in front of U.S. map outline, denomination below

Date	Mintage	F	VF	XF	Unc	BU
1992 Proof	Est. 60,000	Value: 13.50				

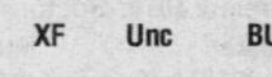

KM# 204 50 DOLLARS
7.7760 g., 0.5833 Gold .1458 oz. AGW **Ruler:** Elizabeth II **Subject:** 500 Years of America **Obv:** Crowned head right, date below **Rev:** Bust of John Cabot at left, ship at right, denomination below

Date	Mintage	F	VF	XF	Unc	BU
1992 Proof	5,000	Value: 95.00				

KM# 249 50 DOLLARS
7.7760 g., 0.5830 Gold .1458 oz. AGW **Ruler:** Elizabeth II **Subject:** 500 Years of America **Obv:** Crowned head right, date below **Rev:** Busts of Ferdinand and Isabella half right, denomination below

Date	Mintage	F	VF	XF	Unc	BU
1992 Proof	Est. 5,000	Value: 95.00				

KM# 259 50 DOLLARS
7.7760 g., 0.5830 Gold .1458 oz. AGW **Ruler:** Elizabeth II **Subject:** 500 Years of America **Obv:** Crowned head right, date below **Rev:** Paul de Maisonneuve, map and city view, denomination below

Date	Mintage	F	VF	XF	Unc	BU
1992 Proof	Est. 5,000	Value: 95.00				

KM# 260 50 DOLLARS
7.7760 g., 0.5830 Gold .1458 oz. AGW **Ruler:** Elizabeth II **Subject:** 500 Years of America **Obv:** Crowned head right, date below **Rev:** Jakob le Maire, ship and map, denomination below

Date	Mintage	F	VF	XF	Unc	BU
1992 Proof	Est. 5,000	Value: 95.00				

KM# 261 50 DOLLARS
19.2000 g., 0.9250 Silver .5710 oz. ASW **Ruler:** Elizabeth II **Subject:** Endangered Wildlife **Obv:** Crowned head right, date below **Rev:** Szechuan Takins, denomination below

Date	Mintage	F	VF	XF	Unc	BU
1992 Proof	25,000	Value: 20.00				

KM# 262 50 DOLLARS
19.2000 g., 0.9250 Silver .5710 oz. ASW **Ruler:** Elizabeth II **Subject:** Endangered Wildlife **Obv:** Crowned head right, date below **Rev:** Ring-tailed lemurs

Date	Mintage	F	VF	XF	Unc	BU
1992 Proof	25,000	Value: 20.00				

KM# 263 50 DOLLARS
19.2000 g., 0.9250 Silver .5710 oz. ASW **Ruler:** Elizabeth II **Subject:** Endangered Wildlife **Obv:** Crowned head right, date below **Rev:** Mandrill, denomination below

Date	Mintage	F	VF	XF	Unc	BU
1992 Proof	25,000	Value: 20.00				

KM# 264 50 DOLLARS
19.2000 g., 0.9250 Silver .5710 oz. ASW **Ruler:** Elizabeth II **Subject:** Endangered Wildlife **Obv:** Crowned head right, date below **Rev:** Lowland gorilla

Date	Mintage	F	VF	XF	Unc	BU
1992 Proof	25,000	Value: 20.00				

KM# 310 50 DOLLARS
31.0000 g., 0.9250 Silver .9219 oz. ASW **Ruler:** Elizabeth II **Obv:** Crowned head right, date below **Rev:** Aztec kneels before Alvarado, denomination below **Edge Lettering:** PEDRO DE ALVARADO CONQUEROR of the AZTEC EMPIRE

Date	Mintage	F	VF	XF	Unc	BU
1992 Proof	—	Value: 13.50				

KM# 153 50 DOLLARS
7.7760 g., 0.5833 Gold .1453 oz. AGW **Ruler:** Elizabeth II **Subject:** Endangered Wildlife **Obv:** Crowned head right, date below **Rev:** Ibex

Date	Mintage	F	VF	XF	Unc	BU
1993 Proof	—	Value: 97.50				

KM# 154 50 DOLLARS
7.7760 g., 0.5833 Gold .1453 oz. AGW **Ruler:** Elizabeth II **Subject:** Endangered Wildlife **Obv:** Crowned head right, date below **Rev:** Owl and parrot

Date	Mintage	F	VF	XF	Unc	BU
1993 Proof	—	Value: 97.50				

KM# 164 50 DOLLARS
31.1035 g., 0.9250 Silver .9250 oz. ASW **Ruler:** Elizabeth II **Subject:** 500 Years of America **Obv:** Crowned head right, date below **Rev:** Pinzon brothers, denomination below

Date	Mintage	F	VF	XF	Unc	BU
1993 Proof	—	Value: 13.50				

KM# 165 50 DOLLARS
31.1035 g., 0.9250 Silver .9250 oz. ASW **Ruler:** Elizabeth II **Subject:** 500 Years of America **Obv:** Crowned head right, date below **Rev:** Juan de la Cosa

Date	Mintage	F	VF	XF	Unc	BU
1993 Proof	—	Value: 13.50				

KM# 166 50 DOLLARS
31.1035 g., 0.9250 Silver .9250 oz. ASW **Ruler:** Elizabeth II **Subject:** 500 Years of America **Obv:** Crowned head right, date below **Rev:** William Penn

Date	Mintage	F	VF	XF	Unc	BU
1993 Proof	—	Value: 13.50				

KM# 167 50 DOLLARS
31.1035 g., 0.9250 Silver .9250 oz. ASW **Ruler:** Elizabeth II **Subject:** 500 Years of America **Obv:** Crowned head right, date below **Rev:** Diego de Velasquez

Date	Mintage	F	VF	XF	Unc	BU
1993 Proof	—	Value: 13.50				

KM# 168 50 DOLLARS
31.1035 g., 0.9250 Silver .9250 oz. ASW **Ruler:** Elizabeth II **Subject:** 500 Years of America **Obv:** Crowned head right, date below **Rev:** Miner panning for gold

Date	Mintage	F	VF	XF	Unc	BU
1993 Proof	—	Value: 13.50				

KM# 169 50 DOLLARS
31.1035 g., 0.9250 Silver .9250 oz. ASW **Ruler:** Elizabeth II **Subject:** 500 Years of America **Obv:** Crowned head right, date below **Rev:** Sir Martin Frobisher bust at left facing right, rocks at right, denomination below

Date	Mintage	F	VF	XF	Unc	BU
1993 Proof	—	Value: 13.50				

KM# 170 50 DOLLARS
31.1035 g., 0.9250 Silver .9250 oz. ASW **Ruler:** Elizabeth II **Subject:** 500 Years of America **Obv:** Crowned head right, date below **Rev:** George Vancouver

Date	Mintage	F	VF	XF	Unc	BU
1993 Proof	—	Value: 13.50				

KM# 171 50 DOLLARS
31.1035 g., 0.9250 Silver .9250 oz. ASW **Ruler:** Elizabeth II **Subject:** 500 Years of America **Obv:** Crowned head right, date below **Rev:** John Hawkins at right, ship at left, denomination below

Date	Mintage	F	VF	XF	Unc	BU
1993 Proof	—	Value: 13.50				

KM# 172 50 DOLLARS
31.1035 g., 0.9250 Silver .9250 oz. ASW **Ruler:** Elizabeth II **Subject:** 500 Years of America **Obv:** Crowned head right, date below **Rev:** Amerigo Vespucci head within map outline, ship at right, denomination below

Date	Mintage	F	VF	XF	Unc	BU
1993 Proof	—	Value: 13.50				

KM# 173 50 DOLLARS
7.7760 g., 0.5833 Gold .1458 oz. AGW **Ruler:** Elizabeth II **Subject:** 500 Years of America **Obv:** Crowned head right, date below **Rev:** George Washington

Date	Mintage	F	VF	XF	Unc	BU
1993 Proof	—	Value: 95.00				

KM# 174 50 DOLLARS
7.7760 g., 0.5833 Gold .1458 oz. AGW **Ruler:** Elizabeth II **Subject:** 500 Years of America **Obv:** Crowned head right, date below **Rev:** Alonso de Hojeda

Date	Mintage	F	VF	XF	Unc	BU
1993 Proof	—	Value: 95.00				

KM# 175 50 DOLLARS
7.7760 g., 0.5833 Gold .1458 oz. AGW **Ruler:** Elizabeth II **Subject:** 500 Years of America **Obv:** Crowned head right, date below **Rev:** Thomas Jefferson

Date	Mintage	F	VF	XF	Unc	BU
1993 Proof	—	Value: 95.00				

KM# 177 50 DOLLARS
7.7760 g., 0.5833 Gold .1458 oz. AGW **Ruler:** Elizabeth II **Subject:** 500 Years of America **Obv:** Crowned head right, date below **Rev:** Captain James Cook

Date	Mintage	F	VF	XF	Unc	BU
1993 Proof	—	Value: 95.00				

KM# 178 50 DOLLARS
7.7760 g., 0.5833 Gold .1458 oz. AGW **Ruler:** Elizabeth II **Subject:** 500 Years of America **Obv:** Crowned head right, date below **Rev:** Christopher Columbus

Date	Mintage	F	VF	XF	Unc	BU
1993 Proof	—	Value: 95.00				

KM# 179 50 DOLLARS
7.7760 g., 0.5833 Gold .1458 oz. AGW **Ruler:** Elizabeth II **Subject:** 500 Years of America **Obv:** Crowned head right, date below **Rev:** Statue of Liberty

Date	Mintage	F	VF	XF	Unc	BU
1993 Proof	—	Value: 95.00				

KM# 180 50 DOLLARS
7.7760 g., 0.5833 Gold .1458 oz. AGW **Ruler:** Elizabeth II **Subject:** 1996 Olympics **Obv:** Crowned head right, date below **Rev:** Ribbon dancer, denomination below **Rev. Designer:** Doris Waschk-Balz

Date	Mintage	F	VF	XF	Unc	BU
1993 Proof	Est. 5,000	Value: 95.00				

KM# 245 50 DOLLARS
7.7760 g., 0.5833 Gold .1458 oz. AGW **Ruler:** Elizabeth II **Subject:** Endangered Wildlife **Obv:** Crowned head right, date below **Rev:** African lion, denomination below

Date	Mintage	F	VF	XF	Unc	BU
1993 Proof	Est. 10,000	Value: 97.50				

KM# 248 50 DOLLARS
31.1035 g., 0.9250 Silver .9250 oz. ASW **Ruler:** Elizabeth II **Subject:** 500 Years of America **Obv:** Crowned head right, date below **Rev:** Jose de San Martin at right, figures on horseback at left, denomination below

Date	Mintage	F	VF	XF	Unc	BU
1993 Proof	Est. 60,000	Value: 13.50				

KM# 155 50 DOLLARS
31.1035 g., 0.9250 Silver .9250 oz. ASW **Ruler:** Elizabeth II **Subject:** 500 Years of America **Obv:** Crowned head right, date below **Rev:** Father Jacques Marquette, denomination below

Date	Mintage	F	VF	XF	Unc	BU
1993 Proof	—	Value: 13.50				

KM# 163 50 DOLLARS
31.1035 g., 0.9250 Silver .9250 oz. ASW **Ruler:** Elizabeth II **Subject:** 500 Years of America **Obv:** Crowned head right, date below **Rev:** Francisco de Orellana bust at right looking left, ship at left, denomination below

Date	Mintage	F	VF	XF	Unc	BU
1993 Proof	—	Value: 13.50				

KM# 246 50 DOLLARS
7.7760 g., 0.5830 Gold .1458 oz. AGW **Ruler:** Elizabeth II **Subject:** Endangered Wildlife **Obv:** Crowned head right, date below **Rev:** Sea otter head, denomination below

Date	Mintage	F	VF	XF	Unc	BU
1994 Proof	Est. 10,000	Value: 97.50				

KM# 247 50 DOLLARS
7.7760 g., 0.5830 Gold .1458 oz. AGW **Ruler:** Elizabeth II **Subject:** Endangered Wildlife **Obv:** Crowned head right, date below **Rev:** Przewalski's horse

Date	Mintage	F	VF	XF	Unc	BU
1994 Proof	Est. 10,000	Value: 97.50				

KM# 275 50 DOLLARS
7.7760 g., 0.5830 Gold .1458 oz. AGW **Ruler:** Elizabeth II **Subject:** Endangered Wildlife **Obv:** Crowned head right, date below **Rev:** Poplar Admiral butterflies

Date	Mintage	F	VF	XF	Unc	BU
1994 Proof	Est. 10,000	Value: 97.50				

KM# 276 50 DOLLARS
7.7760 g., 0.5830 Gold .1458 oz. AGW **Ruler:** Elizabeth II **Obv:** Crowned head right, date below **Rev:** Queen Mother and daughters

Date	Mintage	F	VF	XF	Unc	BU
1995 Proof	Est. 5,000	Value: 97.50				

KM# 299 50 DOLLARS
8.0000 g., 0.9999 Gold .2572 oz. AGW **Ruler:** Elizabeth II

Subject: Year of the Mouse **Obv:** Crowned head right, date below **Rev:** Mickey and Minnie Mouse portrait, denomination below

Date	Mintage	F	VF	XF	Unc	BU
1996 Proof	—	Value: 165				

KM# 322 50 DOLLARS
32.2225 g., 0.9250 Silver .9583 oz. ASW **Ruler:** Elizabeth II **Subject:** 2nd Century **Obv:** Crowned head right, date below **Rev:** Chinese papermaker, denomination at left

Date	Mintage	F	VF	XF	Unc	BU
1997 Proof	—	Value: 22.50				

KM# 323 50 DOLLARS
32.2225 g., 0.9250 Silver .9583 oz. ASW **Ruler:** Elizabeth II **Subject:** 8th Century **Obv:** Crowned head right, date below **Rev:** Coronation of Charlemagne

Date	Mintage	F	VF	XF	Unc	BU
1997 Proof	—	Value: 22.50				

KM# 324 50 DOLLARS
32.2225 g., 0.9250 Silver .9583 oz. ASW **Ruler:** Elizabeth II **Subject:** 12th Century **Obv:** Crowned head right, date below **Rev:** Genghis Khan **Rev. Inscription:** GENGHIS KHAN BEGINS ASIAN CONQUEST

Date	Mintage	F	VF	XF	Unc	BU
1997 Proof	—	Value: 22.50				

KM# 306 50 DOLLARS
Bi-Metallic Platinum center in Gold ring **Ruler:** Elizabeth II **Obv:** Crowned head right within circle, date below **Rev:** Mother seal with pup within circle, date below

Date	Mintage	F	VF	XF	Unc	BU
1997 Proof	—	Value: 185				

KM# 381 50 DOLLARS
4.6000 g., 0.5833 Gold 0.0863 oz. AGW, 20.9 mm. **Ruler:** Elizabeth II **Subject:** Explorers **Obv:** Crowned head right, date below **Rev:** Leif Ericson with battle axe facing, denomination at right **Edge:** Reeded

Date	Mintage	F	VF	XF	Unc	BU
1997 Proof	—	Value: 50.00				
1997FM Proof	—	Value: 65.00				

KM# 382 50 DOLLARS
4.6000 g., 0.5833 Gold 0.0863 oz. AGW, 20.9 mm. **Ruler:** Elizabeth II **Subject:** Explorers **Obv:** Crowned head right, date below **Rev:** Marco Polo on camel **Edge:** Reeded

Date	Mintage	F	VF	XF	Unc	BU
1997FM Proof	—	Value: 60.00				

KM# 383 50 DOLLARS
4.6000 g., 0.5833 Gold 0.0863 oz. AGW, 20.9 mm. **Ruler:** Elizabeth II **Subject:** Explorers **Obv:** Crowned head right, date below **Rev:** Vasco da Gama **Edge:** Reeded

Date	Mintage	F	VF	XF	Unc	BU
1997FM Proof	—	Value: 60.00				

KM# 384 50 DOLLARS
4.6000 g., 0.5833 Gold 0.0863 oz. AGW **Ruler:** Elizabeth II **Subject:** Explorers **Obv:** Crowned head right, date below **Rev:** Vasco de Nuñez Balboa **Edge:** Reeded

Date	Mintage	F	VF	XF	Unc	BU
1997FM Proof	—	Va ue: 60.00				

KM# 385 50 DOLLARS
4.6000 g., 0.5833 Gold 0.0863 oz. AGW, 20.9 mm. **Ruler:** Elizabeth II **Subject:** Explorers **Obv:** Crowned head right, date below **Rev:** Hernando Cortes **Edge:** Reeded

Date	Mintage	F	VF	XF	Unc	BU
1997FM Proof	—	Value: 60.00				

KM# 386 50 DOLLARS
4.6000 g., 0.5833 Gold 0.0863 oz. AGW, 20.9 mm. **Ruler:** Elizabeth II **Subject:** Explorers **Obv:** Crowned head right, date below **Rev:** Magellan's ships: Vittoria and Trinidad **Edge:** Reeded

Date	Mintage	F	VF	XF	Unc	BU
1997FM Proof	—	Value: 60.00				

KM# 390 50 DOLLARS
4.6000 g., 0.5833 Gold 0.0863 oz. AGW, 20.9 mm. **Ruler:** Elizabeth II **Subject:** Explorers **Obv:** Crowned head right, date below **Rev:** Alexander the Great with sword on horseback, denomination above **Edge:** Reeded

Date	Mintage	F	VF	XF	Unc	BU
1997FM Proof	—	Value: 60.00				

KM# 391 50 DOLLARS
4.6000 g., 0.5833 Gold 0.0863 oz. AGW, 20.9 mm. **Ruler:** Elizabeth II **Subject:** Explorers **Obv:** Crowned head right, date below **Rev:** Christopher Columbus **Edge:** Reeded

Date	Mintage	F	VF	XF	Unc	BU
1997FM Proof	—	Value: 60.00				

KM# 392 50 DOLLARS
4.6000 g., 0.5833 Gold 0.0863 oz. AGW, 20.9 mm. **Ruler:** Elizabeth II **Subject:** Explorers **Obv:** Crowned head right, date below **Rev:** Sir Francis Drake **Edge:** Reeded

Date	Mintage	F	VF	XF	Unc	BU
1997FM Proof	—	Value: 60.00				

KM# 393 50 DOLLARS
4.6000 g., 0.5833 Gold 0.0863 oz. AGW, 20.9 mm. **Ruler:** Elizabeth II **Subject:** Explorers **Obv:** Crowned head right, date below **Rev:** Abel Janszoon Tasman **Edge:** Reeded

Date	Mintage	F	VF	XF	Unc	BU
1997FM Proof	—	Value: 60.00				

KM# 394 50 DOLLARS
4.6000 g., 0.5833 Gold 0.0863 oz. AGW, 20.9 mm. **Ruler:** Elizabeth II **Subject:** Explorers **Obv:** Crowned head right, date below **Rev:** Capt. James Cook **Edge:** Reeded

Date	Mintage	F	VF	XF	Unc	BU
1997FM Proof	—	Value: 60.00				

KM# 395 50 DOLLARS
4.6000 g., 0.5833 Gold 0.0863 oz. AGW, 20.9 mm. **Ruler:** Elizabeth II **Subject:** Explorers **Obv:** Crowned head right, date below **Rev:** Richard E. Byrd **Edge:** Reeded

Date	Mintage	F	VF	XF	Unc	BU
1997FM Proof	—	Value: 60.00				

KM# 399 50 DOLLARS

31.9000 g., 0.9250 Silver 0.9487 oz. ASW, 38.7 mm. **Ruler:** Elizabeth II **Subject:** 1st Century **Obv:** Crowned head right, date below **Rev:** Nativity scene **Edge:** Reeded

Date	Mintage	F	VF	XF	Unc	BU
1997FM Proof	—	Value: 22.50				

KM# 400 50 DOLLARS

32.1000 g., 0.9250 Silver 0.9546 oz. ASW, 38.7 mm. **Ruler:** Elizabeth II **Subject:** 3rd Century **Obv:** Crowned head right, date below **Rev:** Roman citizens **Edge:** Reeded

Date	Mintage	F	VF	XF	Unc	BU
1997FM Proof	—	Value: 22.50				

KM# 401 50 DOLLARS

30.9100 g., 0.9250 Silver 0.9192 oz. ASW, 38.7 mm. **Ruler:** Elizabeth II **Subject:** 4th Century **Obv:** Crowned head right, date below **Rev:** Constantine the Great **Edge:** Reeded

Date	Mintage	F	VF	XF	Unc	BU
1997FM Proof	—	Value: 22.50				

KM# 402 50 DOLLARS

32.3200 g., 0.9250 Silver 0.9612 oz. ASW, 38.7 mm. **Ruler:** Elizabeth II **Subject:** 5th Century **Obv:** Crowned head right, date below **Rev:** The sacking of Rome **Edge:** Reeded

Date	Mintage	F	VF	XF	Unc	BU
1997FM Proof	—	Value: 22.50				

KM# 403 50 DOLLARS

30.8200 g., 0.9250 Silver 0.9166 oz. ASW, 38.7 mm. **Ruler:** Elizabeth II **Subject:** 6th Century **Obv:** Crowned head right, date below **Rev:** Emperor Justinian **Edge:** Reeded

Date	Mintage	F	VF	XF	Unc	BU
1997FM Proof	—	Value: 22.50				

KM# 404 50 DOLLARS

31.1000 g., 0.9250 Silver 0.9249 oz. ASW, 38.7 mm. **Ruler:** Elizabeth II **Subject:** 7th Century **Obv:** Crowned head right, date below **Rev:** Establishment of Islam, domed building, denomination at left **Edge:** Reeded

Date	Mintage	F	VF	XF	Unc	BU
1997FM Proof	—	Value: 22.50				

KM# 405 50 DOLLARS

29.5300 g., 0.9250 Silver 0.8782 oz. ASW, 38.7 mm. **Ruler:** Elizabeth II **Subject:** 9th Century **Obv:** Crowned head right, date below **Rev:** Caliph of Baghdad **Edge:** Reeded

Date	Mintage	F	VF	XF	Unc	BU
1997FM Proof	—	Value: 22.50				

KM# 406 50 DOLLARS

32.1300 g., 0.9250 Silver 0.9555 oz. ASW, 38.7 mm. **Ruler:** Elizabeth II **Subject:** 10th Century **Obv:** Crowned head right, date below **Rev:** Monk writing **Rev. Inscription:** THE DARK AGES OF EUROPE **Edge:** Reeded

Date	Mintage	F	VF	XF	Unc	BU
1997FM Proof	—	Value: 22.50				

KM# 407 50 DOLLARS

31.7600 g., 0.9250 Silver 0.9445 oz. ASW, 38.7 mm. **Ruler:** Elizabeth II **Subject:** 11th Century **Obv:** Crowned head right, date below **Rev:** Norman landing scene **Rev. Inscription:** THE NORMAN CONQUEST **Edge:** Reeded

Date	Mintage	F	VF	XF	Unc	BU
1997FM Proof	—	Value: 22.50				

KM# 325.2 50 DOLLARS

32.3400 g., 0.9250 Silver 0.9618 oz. ASW, 38.7 mm. **Ruler:** Elizabeth II **Subject:** 13th Century **Obv:** Crowned head right, date below **Rev:** Inscription in polished rectangle **Rev. Inscription:** MARCO POLO AT KUBLAI KHAN'S COURT **Edge:** Reeded

Date	Mintage	F	VF	XF	Unc	BU
1997FM Proof	—	Value: 15.00				

KM# 408 50 DOLLARS

31.7500 g., 0.9250 Silver 0.9442 oz. ASW, 38.7 mm. **Ruler:** Elizabeth II **Subject:** 14th Century **Obv:** Crowned head right, date below **Rev:** Renaissance buildings **Rev. Inscription:** BIRTH OF THE RENAISSANCE **Edge:** Reeded

Date	Mintage	F	VF	XF	Unc	BU
1997FM Proof	—	Value: 22.50				

KM# 409 50 DOLLARS

31.4400 g., 0.9250 Silver 0.935 oz. ASW, 38.7 mm. **Ruler:** Elizabeth II **Subject:** 15th Century **Obv:** Crowned head right, date below **Rev:** Columbus and ship **Rev. Inscription:** AGE OF EXPLORATION: CHRISTOPHER COLUMBUS **Edge:** Reeded

Date	Mintage	F	VF	XF	Unc	BU
1997FM Proof	—	Value: 22.50				

KM# 410 50 DOLLARS

32.6100 g., 0.9250 Silver 0.9698 oz. ASW, 38.7 mm. **Ruler:** Elizabeth II **Subject:** 16th Century **Obv:** Crowned head right, date below **Rev:** William Shakespeare **Edge:** Reeded

Date	Mintage	F	VF	XF	Unc	BU
1997FM Proof	—	Value: 22.50				

KM# 411 50 DOLLARS

32.0500 g., 0.9250 Silver 0.9531 oz. ASW, 38.7 mm. **Ruler:** Elizabeth II **Subject:** 17th Century **Obv:** Crowned head right, date below **Rev:** Isaac Newton **Edge:** Reeded

Date	Mintage	F	VF	XF	Unc	BU
1997FM Proof	—	Value: 22.50				

KM# 412 50 DOLLARS

32.3400 g., 0.9250 Silver 0.9618 oz. ASW, 38.7 mm. **Ruler:** Elizabeth II **Subject:** 18th Century **Obv:** Crowned head right, date below **Rev:** Declaration of Independence signing scene **Edge:** Reeded

Date	Mintage	F	VF	XF	Unc	BU
1997FM Proof	—	Value: 22.50				

KM# 413 50 DOLLARS

31.6300 g., 0.9250 Silver 0.9407 oz. ASW, 38.7 mm. **Ruler:** Elizabeth II **Subject:** 19th Century **Obv:** Crowned head right, date below **Rev:** Early automobile **Edge:** Reeded

Date	Mintage	F	VF	XF	Unc	BU
1997FM Proof	—	Value: 22.50				

KM# 414 50 DOLLARS

31.2400 g., 0.9250 Silver 0.9291 oz. ASW, 38.7 mm. **Ruler:** Elizabeth II **Subject:** 20th Century **Obv:** Crowned head right, date below **Rev:** Moon landing scene, denomination at left **Edge:** Reeded

Date	Mintage	F	VF	XF	Unc	BU
1997FM Proof	—	Value: 22.50				

KM# 395.1 50 DOLLARS

6.3700 g., 0.5833 Gold 0.1195 oz. AGW, 21 mm. **Ruler:** Elizabeth II **Obv:** Crowned head right, date below **Rev:** Admiral Richard C. Byrd **Edge:** Reeded

Date	Mintage	F	VF	XF	Unc	BU
1997FM Proof	8	Value: 400				

Note: Struck on thicker than normal planchet resulting in a 38.5% heavier weight. 8 Pieces known.

KM# 460 50 DOLLARS

10.0000 g., 0.9995 Platinum 0.3213 oz. APW **Ruler:** Elizabeth II **Subject:** Love Angels

Date	Mintage	F	VF	XF	Unc	BU
1997 Proof	250	Value: 350				

KM# 325.1 50 DOLLARS

32.2225 g., 0.9250 Silver .9583 oz. ASW **Ruler:** Elizabeth II **Subject:** 13th Century **Obv:** Crowned head right, date below **Rev:** Marco Polo and Kublai Khan **Note:** Prev. KM#325.

Date	Mintage	F	VF	XF	Unc	BU
1997 Proof	—	Value: 18.00				

KM# 461 75 DOLLARS
15.0000 g., 0.9995 Platinum 0.482 oz. APW **Ruler:** Elizabeth II **Subject:** Love Angels

Date	Mintage	F	VF	XF	Unc	BU
1997 Proof	250	Value: 525				

KM# 12 100 DOLLARS
16.7185 g., 0.9170 Gold .4929 oz. AGW, 27 mm. **Ruler:** Elizabeth II **Subject:** Winston Churchill Centenary **Obv:** Young bust right, date below **Rev:** Churchill head at right looking left, Big Ben and flag at left, denomination below **Rev. Designer:** James Berry

Date	Mintage	F	VF	XF	Unc	BU
1974	368	—	—	—	325	—
1974 Proof	1,453	Value: 325				

KM# 13 100 DOLLARS
9.6000 g., 0.9000 Gold .2778 oz. AGW, 26 mm. **Ruler:** Elizabeth II **Subject:** Bicentennial - Return of Captain James Cook from Second Pacific Voyage **Obv:** Young bust right, date below **Rev:** Ship divides portraits in cameos, denomination below **Rev. Designer:** James Berry

Date	Mintage	F	VF	XF	Unc	BU
1975FM (M)	100	—	—	—	210	—
1975FM (U)	7,447	—	—	—	180	—
1975FM Proof	17,000	Value: 185				

KM# 16 100 DOLLARS
9.6000 g., 0.9000 Gold .2778 oz. AGW, 26 mm. **Ruler:** Elizabeth II **Subject:** U.S. Bicentennial **Obv:** Young bust right, date below **Rev:** Conjoined heads of Benjamin Franklin and James Cook left, denomination below

Date	Mintage	F	VF	XF	Unc	BU
1976FM (M)	50	—	—	—	285	—
1976FM (U)	852	—	—	—	180	—
1976FM Proof	9,373	Value: 185				

KM# 19 100 DOLLARS
9.6000 g., 0.9000 Gold .2778 oz. AGW, 26 mm. **Ruler:** Elizabeth II **Subject:** Queen's Silver Jubilee **Obv:** Young bust right, date below **Rev:** Crowned EIIR monogram **Rev. Designer:** James Berry

Date	Mintage	F	VF	XF	Unc	BU
1977FM (M)	50	—	—	—	285	—
1977FM (P)	562	—	—	—	185	—
1977FM Proof	9,364	Value: 180				

KM# 25 100 DOLLARS
9.6000 g., 0.9000 Gold .2778 oz. AGW, 26 mm. **Ruler:** Elizabeth II **Subject:** Membership in Commonwealth of Nations **Obv:** Young bust right, date below **Rev:** Tangaroa head left, divides denomination, circle surrounds

Date	Mintage	F	VF	XF	Unc	BU
1979FM Proof	3,367	Value: 180				
1979FM (U)	400	—	—	—	185	—

KM# 74 100 DOLLARS
1.2441 g., 0.9990 Gold .0400 oz. AGW **Ruler:** Elizabeth II **Subject:** Endangered World Wildlife **Obv:** Crowned head right, date below **Rev:** American bald eagle head left, beak open, denomination below

Date	Mintage	F	VF	XF	Unc	BU
1990 Prooflike	1,320	—	—	—	30.00	—

KM# 75 100 DOLLARS
1.2441 g., 0.9990 Gold .0400 oz. AGW, 14 mm. **Ruler:** Elizabeth II **Subject:** Endangered World Wildlife **Obv:** Crowned head right, date below **Rev:** Bison

Date	Mintage	F	VF	XF	Unc	BU
1990 Prooflike	320	—	—	—	32.50	—

KM# 76 100 DOLLARS
1.2441 g., 0.9990 Gold .0400 oz. AGW, 14 mm. **Ruler:** Elizabeth II **Subject:** Endangered World Wildlife **Obv:** Crowned head right, date below **Rev:** Elephant

Date	Mintage	F	VF	XF	Unc	BU
1990 Prooflike	720	—	—	—	32.00	—

KM# 77 100 DOLLARS
1.2441 g., 0.9990 Gold .0400 oz. AGW, 14 mm. **Ruler:** Elizabeth II **Subject:** Endangered World Wildlife **Obv:** Crowned head right, date below **Rev:** Tiger

Date	Mintage	F	VF	XF	Unc	BU
1990 Prooflike	420	—	—	—	65.00	—

KM# 78 100 DOLLARS
1.2441 g., 0.9990 Gold .0400 oz. AGW, 14 mm. **Ruler:** Elizabeth II **Subject:** Encangered World Wildlife **Obv:** Crowned head right, date below **Rev:** European Mouflon

Date	Mintage	F	VF	XF	Unc	BU
1990 Prooflike	320	—	—	—	32.50	—

KM# 92 100 DOLLARS
3.4550 g., 0.9000 Gold .09999 oz. AGW, 18 mm. **Ruler:** Elizabeth II **Subject:** 1992 Summer Olympics **Obv:** Crowned head right, date below **Rev:** Bicyclists, denomination below

Date	Mintage	F	VF	XF	Unc	BU
1990 Proof	Est. 5,000	Value: 125				

KM# 113 100 DOLLARS
172.1100 g., 0.9250 Silver, 65 mm. **Ruler:** Elizabeth II **Subject:** 500 Years of America **Obv:** Crowned head right, date below **Rev:** Ferdinand Magellan **Note:** Photo reduced.

Date	Mintage	F	VF	XF	Unc	BU
1990 Proof	Est. 3,000	Value: 70.00				

KM# 319 100 DOLLARS
170.6000 g., 0.9250 Silver 5.0735 oz. ASW, 65 mm. **Ruler:** Elizabeth II **Subject:** 500 Years of America **Obv:** Crowned head right, date below **Rev:** Mt. Rushmore, eagle with wings spread below, denomination at bottom **Note:** Photo reduced.

Date	Mintage	F	VF	XF	Unc	BU
1991 Proof	—	Value: 70.00				

KM# 297 100 DOLLARS
155.6500 g., 0.9990 Silver 4.992 oz. ASW **Ruler:** Elizabeth II **Subject:** Endangered Wildlife **Obv:** Crowned head right, date below **Rev:** Three elephants **Note:** Photo reduced.

Date	Mintage	F	VF	XF	Unc	BU
1991 Proof	—	Value: 70.00				

KM# 320 100 DOLLARS
170.6000 g., 0.9250 Silver 5.0735 oz. ASW **Ruler:** Elizabeth II **Subject:** 500 Years of America **Obv:** Crowned head right, date below **Rev:** Bust of Columbus at left facing right, three ships at right, denomination below **Note:** Photo reduced.

Date	Mintage	F	VF	XF	Unc	BU
1992 Proof	—	Value: 70.00				

KM# 159 100 DOLLARS
155.5175 g., 0.9990 Silver 5.0000 oz. ASW **Ruler:** Elizabeth II **Subject:** 500 Years of America **Obv:** Crowned head right, date below **Rev:** Hudson's "Half Moon" and New York City skyline, denomination below **Note:** Photo reduced.

Date	Mintage	F	VF	XF	Unc	BU
1993 Proof	—	Value: 70.00				

KM# 158 100 DOLLARS
155.5176 g., 0.9990 Silver 5.0000 oz. ASW **Ruler:** Elizabeth II **Subject:** Endangered Wildlife **Obv:** Crowned head right, date below **Rev:** Manchurian cranes **Note:** Photo reduced.

Date	Mintage	F	VF	XF	Unc	BU
1993 Proof	—	Value: 70.00				

KM# 250 100 DOLLARS
7.7761 g., 0.9990 Platinum .1458 oz. APW **Ruler:** Elizabeth II **Obv:** Crowned head right, date below **Rev:** Javelin throwing

Date	Mintage	F	VF	XF	Unc	BU
1995 Proof	Est. 1,000	Value: 185				

KM# 293 100 DOLLARS
7.7800 g., 0.9990 Gold .2501 oz. AGW **Ruler:** Elizabeth II **Subject:** Olympic National Park **Obv:** Crowned head right, date below **Rev:** Eagles head right, denomination below **Rev. Designer:** Alex Shagin

Date	Mintage	F	VF	XF	Unc	BU
1996 Proof	—	Value: 165				

KM# 294 100 DOLLARS
7.7800 g., 0.9990 Gold .2501 oz. AGW **Ruler:** Elizabeth II **Subject:** Yellowstone National Park **Obv:** Crowned head right, date below **Rev:** Grizzly Bear, denomination below **Rev. Designer:** Alex Shagin

Date	Mintage	F	VF	XF	Unc	BU
1996 Proof	—	Value: 165				

KM# 300 100 DOLLARS
15.0000 g., 0.9999 Gold .4822 oz. AGW **Ruler:** Elizabeth II **Subject:** Year of the Mouse **Obv:** Crowned head right, date below **Rev:** Mickey Mouse sailboarding, denomination below

Date	Mintage	F	VF	XF	Unc	BU
1996 Proof	—	Value: 320				

KM# 388 100 DOLLARS
7.7800 g., 0.9990 Gold 0.2499 oz. AGW, 22 mm. **Ruler:** Elizabeth II **Subject:** Yellowstone National Park **Obv:** Crowned head right, date below **Rev:** Bear on tree branch **Rev. Designer:** Alex Shagin **Edge:** Reeded

Date	Mintage	F	VF	XF	Unc	BU
1996 Proof	—	Value: 165				

KM# 22 200 DOLLARS
16.6000 g., 0.9000 Gold .4803 oz. AGW **Ruler:** Elizabeth II **Subject:** Bicentennial - Discovery of Hawaii by Capt. James Cook **Obv:** Young bust right, date below **Rev:** Capt. James Cook with crew, denomination below

Date	Mintage	F	VF	XF	Unc	BU
1978FM (M)	26	—	—	—	425	—
1978FM (U)	621	—	—	—	325	—
1978FM Proof	3,216	Value: 320				

KM# 26 200 DOLLARS
16.6000 g., 0.9000 Gold .4803 oz. AGW **Ruler:** Elizabeth II **Subject:** Legacy of Capt. James Cook **Obv:** Young bust right, date below **Rev:** Bird flying right above banner, denomination below

Date	Mintage	F	VF	XF	Unc	BU
1979FM Proof	1,939	Value: 320				
1979FM (U)	271	—	—	—	325	—

KM# 29 200 DOLLARS
15.9800 g., 0.9170 Gold .4712 oz. AGW **Ruler:** Elizabeth II **Subject:** International Year of the Scout **Obv:** Young bust right, date below **Rev:** Circle of stars around symbol at center, dates at lower left, denomination at lower right

Date	Mintage	F	VF	XF	Unc	BU
1983 Proof	—	Value: 310				

KM# 251 200 DOLLARS
15.5520 g., 0.9990 Platinum .2916 oz. APW **Ruler:** Elizabeth II **Obv:** Crowned head right, date below **Rev:** Wrestling

Date	Mintage	F	VF	XF	Unc	BU
1995 Proof	1,000	Value: 365				

KM# 23 250 DOLLARS
17.9000 g., 0.9000 Gold .5180 oz. AGW **Ruler:** Elizabeth II **Subject:** 250th Anniversary - Birth of James Cook **Obv:** Young bust right, date below **Rev:** Head left, denomination below

Date	Mintage	F	VF	XF	Unc	BU
1978FM (U)	200	—	—	—	335	—
1978FM (M)	25	—	—	—	425	—
1978FM Proof	1,757	Value: 350				

KM# 50 250 DOLLARS
7.7750 g., 0.9990 Gold .2500 oz. AGW **Ruler:** Elizabeth II **Subject:** 500 Years of America **Obv:** Crowned head right, date below **Rev:** Cameos of Cook and Franklin flank sailing ship, denomination below

Date	Mintage	F	VF	XF	Unc	BU
1989 Proof	3,000	Value: 185				
1990 Proof	3,000	Value: 185				

KM# 51 250 DOLLARS
7.7750 g., 0.9990 Gold .2500 oz. AGW **Ruler:** Elizabeth II **Subject:** 500 Years of America **Obv:** Crowned head right, date below **Rev:** Amerigo Vespucci bust at right looking left, ship at left

Date	Mintage	F	VF	XF	Unc	BU
1990 Proof	Est. 3,000	Value: 185				

KM# 82 250 DOLLARS
9.6000 g., 0.9000 Gold .2778 oz. AGW **Ruler:** Elizabeth II **Subject:** Save the Children **Obv:** Crowned head right, date below **Rev:** Child behind large shell, denomination below

Date	Mintage	F	VF	XF	Unc	BU
1990 Proof	3,000	Value: 200				

KM# 71 250 DOLLARS
7.7750 g., 0.9990 Gold .2500 oz. AGW **Ruler:** Elizabeth II **Subject:** 1992 Olympics **Obv:** Crowned head right, date below **Rev:** Torch, denomination below

Date	Mintage	F	VF	XF	Unc	BU
1991 Proof	Est. 5,000	Value: 185				

KM# 295 250 DOLLARS
31.1035 g., 0.9990 Gold 1.0000 oz. AGW **Ruler:** Elizabeth II **Subject:** Olympic National Park **Obv:** Crowned head right, date below **Rev:** Multicolor bald eagle in flight

Date	Mintage	F	VF	XF	Unc	BU
1996 Proof	1,000	Value: 675				

KM# 296 250 DOLLARS
31.1035 g., 0.9990 Gold 1.0000 oz. AGW **Ruler:** Elizabeth II **Subject:** Yellowstone National Park **Obv:** Crowned head right, date below **Rev:** Multicolored grizzly bear and cub

Date	Mintage	F	VF	XF	Unc	BU
1996 Proof	1,000	Value: 675				

KM# 415 500 DOLLARS
14.7400 g., 0.9990 Platinum 0.4734 oz. APW, 25.8 mm. **Ruler:** Elizabeth II **Obv:** Crowned head right, date below **Rev:** Two of Ferdinand Magellan's ships **Edge:** Reeded

Date	Mintage	F	VF	XF	Unc	BU
1995FM Proof	1,000	Value: 625				

KM# 313 500 DOLLARS
14.7400 g., 0.9990 Platinum .4734 oz. APW **Ruler:** Elizabeth II **Obv:** Crowned head right, date below **Rev:** Marco Polo, oriental building in background, denomination below

Date	Mintage	F	VF	XF	Unc	BU
1995 Proof	Est. 1,000	Value: 625				

PIEFORTS

KM#	Date	Mintage	Identification	Mkt Val
P1	1985	250	Dollar. 0.9250 Silver.	200
P2	1986	500	Dollar. 0.9250 Silver.	45.00
P3	1986	500	Dollar. 0.9250 Silver.	45.00

MINT SETS

KM#	Date	Mintage	Identification	Issue Price	Mkt Val
MS1	1972 (7)	11,045	KM1-5, 6.1, 7	7.50	5.00
MS2	1973 (9)	3,652	KM1-5, 6.1, 7, 9, 10	52.50	40.00
MS3	1973 (7)	3,023	KM1-5, 6.1, 7	10.00	8.00
MS4	1973 (2)	2,348	KM9, 10	45.00	35.00
MS5	1974 (9)	913	KM1-5, 6.1, 7. 9. 10	5,250	50.00
MS6	1974 (7)	2,087	KM1-5, 6.1, 7	10.00	6.00
MS7	1974 (2)	587	KM9, 10	45.00	45.00
MS8	1975 (7)	2,251	KM1-5, 6.1, 7	10.00	6.00
MS9	1976 (8)	1,066	KM1-4, 6.1,7, 14, 15	20.00	25.00
MS10	1977 (8)	1,171	KM1-4, 6.1, 7, 14, 17	20.00	25.00
MS11	1978 (8)	767	KM1a-4a, 6.2, 7a, 14a, 20	20.00	30.00
MS12	1979 (8)	500	KM1-3, 4b, 6.3 7, 14, 24	—	30.00
MS13	1981 (7)	1,100	KM1b-3b, 4c, 6.4, 7b, 14b	—	1,500
MS14	1983	—	KM1-5, 6.1, 7	—	6.00
MS15	1987 (7)	—	KM33-39	—	15.00
MS16	1988 (7)	—	KM33-35, 37-39, 41	—	16.00
MS17	1992 (7)	—	KM33-35, 37-39, 41	—	16.00
MS18	1999 (5)	5,000	KM#444-448	418	418

PROOF SETS

KM#	Date	Mintage	Identification	Issue Price	Mkt Val
PS1	1972 (7)	17,101	KM1-5, 6.1, 7	20.00	9.00
PS2	1973 (9)	7,395	KM1-5, 6.1, 7, 9-10	89.50	45.00
PS3	1973 (7)	5,136	KM1-5, 6.1, 7	29.50	10.00
PS4	1973 (2)	4,754	KM9-10	60.00	35.00
PS5	1974 (9)	4,444	KM1-5, 6.1, 7, 9-10	95.00	50.00
PS6	1974 (7)	5,300	KM1-5, 6.1, 7	32.50	10.00
PS7	1974 (2)	2,856	KM9-10	65.00	35.00
PS8	1975 (7)	21,290	KM-15, 6.1, 7	31.50	10.00
PS9	1976 (8)	17,658	KM1-4, 6.1, 7, 14-15	40.00	22.50
PS10	1977 (8)	5,986	KM1-4, 6.1, 7, 14, 17	42.00	25.00
PS11	1978 (8)	6,287	KM1a-4a, 6.2, 7a, 14a, 20	42.00	25.00
PS12	1979 (8)	4,058	KM1-3,4b, 6.3, 7, 14, 24	44.00	25.00
PS13	1981 (7)	9,205	KM1b-3b, 4c, 6.4, 7b, 14b	39.50	12.50
PS14	1983 (7)	10,000	KM1-5, 6.1, 7	29.95	10.00
PS15	1987 (7)	—	KM33-39	—	32.50
PS16	1988 (7)	—	KM33-35, 37-39, 41	—	32.50
PSA16	1988 (25)	—	KM#61-69, 96-111	—	550
PS17	1991 (12)	1,000	KM93, 95, 118-120, 122-128	—	300
PS18	1992 (7)	—	KM33-35, 37-39, 41	—	32.50
PS19	1994 (7)	200	KM33-35, 37-39, 41	—	37.50
PS20	1996 (3)	—	KM298-300	—	500
PS21	1996 (6)	—	KM284, 286, 288, 292, 294, 296	—	935
PS22	1998 (5)	4,000	KM314-318	185	225
PS23	1999 (3)	—	KM338-340	98.00	110
PS24	1999 (5)	4,000	KM361-365	122	225

PROOF-LIKE SETS (PL)

KM#	Date	Mintage	Identification	Issue Price	Mkt Val
PLS1	1990 (5)	—	KM74-78	325	250
PLS2	1997 (5)	250	KM#457-461	—	1,200

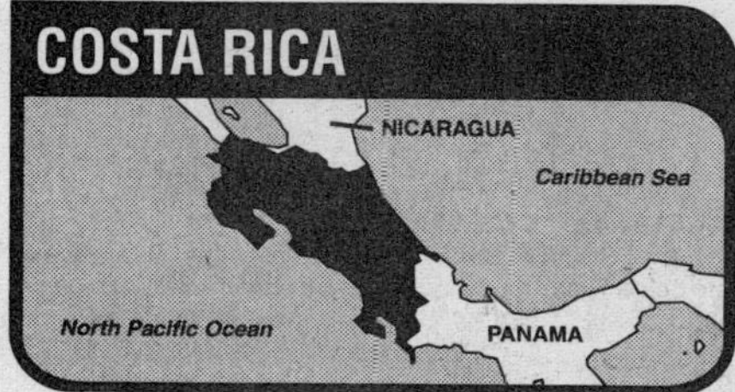

The Republic of Costa Rica, located in southern Central America between Nicaragua and Panama, has an area of 19,730 sq. mi. (51,100 sq. km.) and a population of 3.4 million. Capital: San Jose. Agriculture predominates; tourism and coffee, bananas, beef and sugar contribute heavily to the country's export earnings.

Costa Rica was discovered by Christopher Columbus in 1502, during his last voyage to the New World, and was a colony of Spain from 1522 until independence in 1821. Columbus named the territory Nueva Cartago; the name Costa Rica wasn't generally applied until 1540. Bartholomew Columbus attempted the first settlement but was driven off by Indian attacks and the country wasn't subdued until 1530. After centuries, as part of the Spanish Captaincy-General of Guatemala, Costa Rica was absorbed into the Mexican Empire of Augustin de Iturbide from 1821-1823. From 1823 to 1848, it was a constituent state of the Central American Republic (q.v.). Established as a republic in 1848, Costa Rica adopted democratic reforms in the 1870's and 80's. Today, Costa Rica remains a model of orderly democracy in Latin America, although, like most of the hemisphere - its economy is in stress.

MINT MARKS
CR - San Jose 1825-1947
(P) – Philadelphia, 1905-1961
(L) – London, 1937, 1948

ISSUING BANK INITIALS - MINTS
BCCR - Philadelphia 1951-1958,1961
BICR - Philadelphia 1935
BNCR - London 1937,1948
BNCR - San Jose 1942-1947
GCR - Philadelphia 1905-1908,1929
GCR - San Jose 1917-1941

ASSAYERS' INITIALS
CY – Carlos Yglesias, 1902
JCV – Jesus Cubrero Vargas, 1903
GCR – Gobierno de Costa Rica

MONETARY SYSTEM
8 Reales = 1 Peso
16 Pesos = 8 Escudos = 1 Onza

REPUBLIC

REFORM COINAGE

1897, 100 Centimos = 1 Colon

KM# 144 2 CENTIMOS
1.0000 g., Copper-Nickel **Obv:** Large numeral above date **Rev:** Denomination above sprays **Edge:** Plain

Date	Mintage	F	VF	XF	Unc	BU
1903(P)	630,000	0.50	1.00	2.25	5.00	8.50

Note: 274,342 of this type were used as blanks for KM178 in 1942.

KM# 145 5 CENTIMOS
1.0000 g., 0.9000 Silver .0289 oz. ASW **Obv:** National arms, date below **Rev:** Denomination within wreath **Edge:** Reeded

Date	Mintage	F	VF	XF	Unc	BU
1905(P)	500,000	BV	0.75	2.00	6.00	—
1910(P)	400,000	BV	0.75	2.00	7.50	—
1912(P)	540,000	BV	0.75	1.50	5.00	—
1914(P)	510,000	BV	0.75	1.50	5.50	—

KM# 146 10 CENTIMOS
2.0000 g., 0.9000 Silver .0578 oz. ASW **Obv:** National arms, date below **Rev:** Denomination within wreath

Date	Mintage	F	VF	XF	Unc	BU
1905(P)	400,000	0.80	1.25	3.00	10.00	—
1910(P)	400,000	0.80	1.25	3.00	12.00	—
1912(P)	270,000	0.80	1.25	3.00	12.00	—
1914(P)	150,000	0.85	1.50	4.00	15.00	—

KM# 143 50 CENTIMOS
10.0000 g., 0.9000 Silver .2893 oz. ASW **Obv:** National arms, date below **Rev:** Denomination within wreath

Date	Mintage	F	VF	XF	Unc	BU
1902 CY	120,000	15.00	30.00	60.00	135	—
1903 JCV	380,000	10.00	20.00	40.00	90.00	—

Note: Of the total mintage for this date, San Jose Mint struck 132,140 in 1903 and Philadelphia Mint struck an additional 250,000 in 1904 with the 1903 date; the two strikings are indistinguishable.

Date	Mintage	F	VF	XF	Unc	BU
1914(P) GCR	200,000	—	—	1,250	2,000	—

Note: Most coins dated 1914 were later counterstamped UN COLON/ 1923; See KM#164.

KM# 139 2 COLONES
1.5560 g., 0.9000 Gold .0456 oz. AGW **Obv:** National arms, date below **Rev:** Bust of Colombus right, denomination below

Date	Mintage	F	VF	XF	Unc	BU
1915(P)	5,000	35.00	50.00	75.00	125	—
1916(P)	5,000	37.50	55.00	75.00	150	—
1921(P)	3,000	40.00	65.00	100	200	—
1922(P)	13,000	35.00	45.00	60.00	100	—
1926(P)	15,000	35.00	45.00	60.00	85.00	—
1928(P)	25,000	35.00	45.00	55.00	80.00	—

REFORM COINAGE

1917, 100 Centavos = 1 Colon

KM# 147 5 CENTAVOS
1.0000 g., Brass **Obv:** National arms, date below **Rev:** Denomination within wreath **Edge:** Plain

Date	Mintage	F	VF	XF	Unc	BU
1917	400,000	3.00	10.00	22.00	75.00	—
1918	1,000,000	1.25	4.00	10.00	40.00	—
1919	500,000	1.25	4.50	12.00	35.00	—

KM# 148 10 CENTAVOS
2.0000 g., 0.5000 Silver .0321 oz. ASW **Obv:** National arms, date below **Rev:** Denomination within wreath **Edge:** Reeded

Date	Mintage	F	VF	XF	Unc	BU
1917	100,000	1.00	2.00	3.25	6.50	9.50

KM# 149.1 10 CENTAVOS
2.0000 g., Brass **Obv:** National arms, date below **Rev:** Denomination within wreath, GCR at lower right

Date	Mintage	F	VF	XF	Unc	BU
1917 GCR	500,000	1.50	5.00	13.50	60.00	—

KM# 149.2 10 CENTAVOS
2.0000 g., Brass **Obv:** National arms, date below **Rev:** Denomination within wreath, GCR at bottom center

Date	Mintage	F	VF	XF	Unc	BU
1917 GCR	Inc. above	3.50	8.00	20.00	70.00	—
1918 GCR	900,000	1.25	3.00	10.00	40.00	—
1919 GCR	250,000	1.75	4.50	13.50	50.00	—

KM# 150 50 CENTAVOS

10.0000 g., 0.5000 Silver .1607 oz. ASW **Obv:** National arms **Note:** All but 10 examples of the 1917 issue and the complete 1918 mintage were counterstamped UN COLON/1923. See KM#165.

Date	Mintage	F	VF	XF	Unc	BU
1917 GCR	9,400	—	—	1,250	2,500	—
1918 GCR	30,000	—	—	—	—	—

REFORM COINAGE

1920, 100 Centimos = 1 Colon

KM# 151 5 CENTIMOS

1.0000 g., Brass **Obv:** National arms, date below **Rev:** Denomination within wreath, G.C.R. lower right **Edge:** Plain

Date	Mintage	F	VF	XF	Unc	BU
1920	500,000	1.25	4.00	12.50	27.50	—
1921	500,000	2.00	5.00	15.00	37.50	—
1922	500,000	1.25	4.00	10.00	25.00	—
1936	1,500,000	0.40	0.75	2.00	7.50	—
1938	1,000,000	0.50	1.25	4.00	13.50	—
1940	1,300,000	0.40	0.75	1.50	7.50	—
1941	1,000,000	0.50	1.25	3.50	15.00	—

KM# 169 5 CENTIMOS

1.0000 g., Bronze **Obv:** National arms, date below **Rev:** Denomination within wreath, G.C.R. lower right

Date	Mintage	F	VF	XF	Unc	BU
1929(P)	1,500,000	0.60	1.25	3.00	6.25	11.00

KM# 178 5 CENTIMOS

1.0000 g., Copper-Nickel **Obv:** National arms, date below **Rev:** Denomination within wreath, star below divides B.N. at left from C.R. at right

Date	Mintage	F	VF	XF	Unc	BU
1942	274,000	0.65	1.00	3.00	8.50	—

Note: Struck over 2 Centimos, KM#144. Overstrikes with clear evidence of the undertype command a 10-15% premium.

KM# 179 5 CENTIMOS

1.0000 g., Brass **Obv:** National arms, date below **Rev:** Denomination within wreath, star below divides B.N. at left from C.R. at right

Date	Mintage	F	VF	XF	Unc	BU
1942	1,730,000	0.20	0.60	1.25	8.50	—
1942 Prooflike	—	Value: 35.00				
Note: Struck from specially polished dies.						
1943	1,000,000	0.20	1.00	3.00	8.50	—
1946	1,000,000	0.20	1.15	3.50	9.00	—
1946 Proof	—	Value: 100				
1947	3,000,000	0.10	0.45	1.00	3.50	—

KM# A184 5 CENTIMOS

1.0000 g., Copper-Nickel **Obv:** National arms, date below **Rev:** Denomination within wreath, star below divides B.C. at left from C.R. at right

Date	Mintage	F	VF	XF	Unc	BU
1951(P)	3,000,000	0.35	0.75	1.50	2.75	5.00

KM# 184.1 5 CENTIMOS

1.0000 g., Copper-Nickel **Obv:** National arms, ribbon above, date below **Rev:** Denomination within wreath, B.C.C.R. below

Date	Mintage	F	VF	XF	Unc	BU
1951(P)	7,000,000	0.10	0.15	0.40	1.00	—

KM# 184.1a 5 CENTIMOS

0.8750 g., Stainless Steel **Obv:** National arms, ribbon above, date below **Rev:** Denomination within wreath, B.C.C.R. below

Date	Mintage	F	VF	XF	Unc	BU
1953(P)	9,040,000	—	—	0.10	0.25	—
1958(P)	19,940,000	—	—	0.10	0.15	—
Note: Struck in 1959						
1967	6,020,000	—	—	0.10	0.20	—

KM# 184.2 5 CENTIMOS

Copper-Nickel **Obv:** Small ships, 7 stars on arms, no flag on near ship, date below **Rev:** Denomination within wreath, B.C.C.R. below **Note:** Varieties exist for shields of each date.

Date	Mintage	F	VF	XF	Unc	BU
1969	20,000,000	—	—	0.10	0.15	—
1976	—	—	—	0.10	0.15	—
1976 Proof	5,000	Value: 2.50				
1978	7,520,000	—	—	0.10	0.15	—

KM# 184.3 5 CENTIMOS

Copper-Nickel **Obv:** Large ships, 7 stars on arms, flag on near ship, date below arms **Rev:** Denomination within wreath, B.C.C.R. below **Note:** Dies vary for each date.

Date	Mintage	F	VF	XF	Unc	BU
1972	12,550,000	—	—	0.10	0.15	—
1973	20,000,000	—	—	0.10	0.15	—
1976	33,270,000	—	—	0.10	0.15	—

KM# 184.3a 5 CENTIMOS

Brass **Obv:** National arms, ribbon above, large date below **Rev:** Denomination within wreath, B.C.C.R. below

Date	Mintage	F	VF	XF	Unc	BU
1979	3,060,000	—	—	0.10	0.15	—

KM# 152 10 CENTIMOS

2.0000 g., Brass **Obv:** National arms, date below **Rev:** Denomination within wreath, G.C.R. at lower right

Date	Mintage	F	VF	XF	Unc	BU
1920 GCR	850,000	0.75	2.00	6.50	35.00	—
1921 GCR	750,000	1.00	2.50	10.00	47.50	—
1922 GCR	750,000	0.75	2.00	6.50	35.00	—

KM# 170 10 CENTIMOS

2.0000 g., Bronze **Obv:** National arms, date below **Rev:** Denomination within wreath, G.C.R. at bottom

Date	Mintage	F	VF	XF	Unc	BU
1929(P) GCR	500,000	1.00	2.00	5.00	22.50	—

KM# 174 10 CENTIMOS

Brass **Obv:** National arms, date below **Rev:** Denomination within wreath, G.C.R. below

Date	Mintage	F	VF	XF	Unc	BU
1936	750,000	0.35	0.65	3.00	10.00	—
1941	500,000	0.50	1.50	5.00	15.00	—

KM# 180 10 CENTIMOS

2.0000 g., Brass **Obv:** National arms, date below **Rev:** Denomination within wreath, B.N. - C.R. divided below

Date	Mintage	F	VF	XF	Unc	BU
1942	1,000,000	0.30	0.60	2.00	8.00	—
1943	500,000	0.35	0.75	3.50	12.00	—
1946	500,000	0.65	1.25	4.00	13.50	—
1947	1,500,000	0.25	0.50	1.50	5.50	—

Note: Edge varieties exist on 1947 strikes

KM# 185.1 10 CENTIMOS

2.0000 g., Copper-Nickel **Obv:** Small ships, 5 stars in shield, date below arms **Rev:** Denomination within wreath, B.C.C.R. below

Date	Mintage	F	VF	XF	Unc	BU
1951(P)	2,500,000	0.10	0.20	0.70	1.25	—

Note: Struck in 1952

KM# 185.1a 10 CENTIMOS

1.7500 g., Stainless Steel, 18 mm. **Obv:** National arms, date below **Rev:** Denomination within wreath, B.C.C.R. below

Date	Mintage	F	VF	XF	Unc	BU
1953(P)	5,290,000	—	—	0.10	0.75	—
1958(P)	10,470,000	—	—	0.10	0.25	—
Note: Struck in 1959						
1967	5,500,000	—	—	0.10	0.25	—

KM# 185.2 10 CENTIMOS

Copper-Nickel **Obv:** Small ships, 7 stars in field, date below arms **Rev:** Denomination within wreath, B.C.C.R. below **Note:** Dies vary for each date

Date	Mintage	F	VF	XF	Unc	BU
1969	10,000,000	—	—	0.10	0.15	—
1976	40,000,000	—	—	0.10	0.15	—
1976 Proof	5,000	Value: 2.50				

KM# 185.2a 10 CENTIMOS

Aluminum, 18 mm. **Obv:** National arms, small ships, 7 stars in field **Rev:** Denomination within wreath, B.C.C.R. below

Date	Mintage	F	VF	XF	Unc	BU
1982	40,000,000	—	—	0.10	0.15	—

KM# 185.2b 10 CENTIMOS

Nickel Clad Steel **Obv:** National arms **Rev:** Denomination within wreath, B.C.C.R. below

Date	Mintage	F	VF	XF	Unc	BU
1979	10,000,000	—	—	0.10	0.15	—

KM# 185.3 10 CENTIMOS

Copper-Nickel **Obv:** Large ships, 7 stars in field, date below arms **Rev:** Denomination within wreath B.C.C.R. below

Date	Mintage	F	VF	XF	Unc	BU
1972	20,000,000	—	—	0.10	0.15	—
1975	5,000,000	—	—	0.10	0.15	—

KM# 168 25 CENTIMOS

3.4500 g., 0.6500 Silver .0721 oz. ASW **Obv:** National arms, date below **Rev:** Denomination within wreath, G.C.R. below at left **Edge:** Reeded

Date	Mintage	F	VF	XF	Unc	BU
1924	1,340,000	1.25	2.25	5.00	12.50	18.50

Note: Typical examples of KM#168 are weak at centers, fully struck up XF and Unc pieces command a 50% premium.

KM# 171 25 CENTIMOS

3.4500 g., Copper-Nickel **Obv:** National arms, date below **Rev:** Denomination within wreath, B.I.C.R. below **Edge:** Incuse lettered

Date	Mintage	F	VF	XF	Unc	BU
1935(P)	1,200,000	0.25	0.75	2.50	15.00	—

KM# 175 25 CENTIMOS

Copper-Nickel **Obv:** National arms, date below **Rev:** Denomination within wreath, B.N.C.R. below

Date	Mintage	F	VF	XF	Unc	BU
1937(L)	1,600,000	0.25	0.75	1.75	8.00	—
1937(L) Proof	—	Value: 100				
1948(L)	9,200,000	0.10	0.20	0.40	1.25	—
1948(L) Proof	—	—	—	—	—	—

KM# 181 25 CENTIMOS

3.5000 g., Yellow Brass **Obv:** National arms, date below **Rev:** Denomination within wreath, star divides B.N. from C.R. below **Edge:** Reeded

Date	Mintage	F	VF	XF	Unc	BU
1944	800,000	0.50	1.00	3.25	11.00	16.50
1945	1,200,000	0.50	1.00	2.50	8.50	15.00
1946	1,200,000	0.50	1.00	2.75	9.00	12.50

KM# 181a 25 CENTIMOS

3.5000 g., Red Brass **Obv:** National arms, date below **Rev:** Denomination within wreath, star below divides B.N. and C.R. **Edge:** Reeded

Date	Mintage	F	VF	XF	Unc	BU
1945	Inc. above	2.00	4.00	10.00	20.00	35.00

KM# 188.1 25 CENTIMOS

Copper-Nickel **Obv:** Small ships, 7 stars on arms, date below **Rev:** Denomination within wreath, B.C.C.R. below **Note:** Dies vary for each date.

Date	Mintage	F	VF	XF	Unc	BU
1967	4,000,000	—	—	0.10	0.50	—
1969	4,000,000	—	—	0.10	0.50	—
1974	—	—	—	0.10	0.30	—
1976	12,000,000	—	—	0.10	0.30	—
1976 Proof	5,000	Value: 2.50				
1978	—	—	—	0.10	0.30	—

KM# 188.1a 25 CENTIMOS

Nickel Clad Steel **Obv:** National arms, date below **Rev:** Denomination within wreath, B.C.C.R. below **Note:** Beaded rims.

Date	Mintage	F	VF	XF	Unc	BU
1980	30,000,000	—	—	0.10	0.25	—

KM# 188.1b 25 CENTIMOS

Aluminum **Obv:** National arms, date below **Rev:** Denomination within wreath, B.C.C.R. below **Edge:** Plain

Date	Mintage	F	VF	XF	Unc	BU
1982	30,000,000	—	—	0.10	0.25	—

KM# 188.2 25 CENTIMOS

Aluminum **Obv:** Large ships, 7 stars on arms, flag, date below arms **Rev:** Denomination with n wreath, B.C.C.R. below

Date	Mintage	F	VF	XF	Unc	BU
1972	8,000,000	—	—	0.10	0.25	—

KM# 188.3 25 CENTIMOS

1.0500 g., Aluminum, 17 mm. **Obv:** National arms, date below **Rev:** Denomination within wreath, B.C.C.R. below **Edge:** Reeded **Note:** Reduced size. Dies vary for each date.

Date	Mintage	F	VF	XF	Unc	BU
1983	—	—	—	0.10	0.20	—
1986	—	—	—	0.10	0.20	—
1989	—	—	—	0.10	0.20	—

KM# 172 50 CENTIMOS

6.2500 g., Copper-Nickel **Obv:** National arms, date below **Rev:** Denomination within wreath, B.I.C.R. below

Date	Mintage	F	VF	XF	Unc	BU
1935(P)	700,000	0.50	2.00	8.00	30.00	—

KM# 176 50 CENTIMOS

Copper-Nickel **Obv:** National arms, date below **Rev:** Denomination within wreath, B.N.C.R. below

Date	Mintage	F	VF	XF	Unc	BU
1937(L)	600,000	0.30	1.00	3.00	15.00	—
1937(L) Proof	—	Value: 150				

KM# 182 50 CENTIMOS

Copper-Nickel, 26 mm. **Obv:** National arms, date below **Rev:** Denomination within wreath, B.N.C.R. below **Edge Lettering:** -BNCR- (repeated)

Date	Mintage	F	VF	XF	Unc	BU
1948(L)	4,000,000	0.15	0.25	0.50	2.00	—
1948(L) Proof	—	—	—	—	—	—

KM# 189.1 50 CENTIMOS

Copper-Nickel, 26 mm. **Obv:** Small ships, 7 stars on shield, date below arms **Rev:** Denomination within wreath, B.C.C.R. below **Note:** Medal rotation.

Date	Mintage	F	VF	XF	Unc	BU
1965	1,000,000	—	0.10	0.25	1.00	—

KM# 189.3 50 CENTIMOS

Copper-Nickel, 26 mm. **Obv:** National arms, date below **Rev:** Denomination within wreath, B.C.C.R. below, large 50 **Edge Lettering:** -BCCR- (repeated) **Note:** Dies vary for each date - the main variety is an open or closed "5" in "50".

Date	Mintage	F	VF	XF	Unc	BU
1968	2,000,000	—	0.10	0.15	0.50	—
1970	4,000,000	—	0.10	0.15	0.35	—
1976	6,000,000	—	0.10	0.15	0.35	—
1976 Proof	5,000	Value: 2.50				
1978	—	—	0.10	0.15	0.35	—

KM# 189.2 50 CENTIMOS

Copper-Nickel, 26 mm. **Obv:** Large ships, 7 stars in shield, date below arms **Rev:** Denomination within wreath, B.C.C.R. below, large 50

Date	Mintage	F	VF	XF	Unc	BU
1972 Large date	4,000,000	—	0.10	0.15	0.35	—
1972 Small date	Inc. above	—	0.10	0.15	0.35	—
1975 Large date	524,000	—	0.10	0.15	0.35	—
1975 Small date	Inc. above	—	0.10	0.15	0.35	—

KM# 209.1 50 CENTIMOS

2.2000 g., Stainless Steel, 18.95 mm. **Obv:** Large ships, letters incuse on ribbon, date below arms **Rev:** Denomination within wreath, B.C.C.R. below, thick 50

Date	Mintage	F	VF	XF	Unc	BU
1982	12,000,000	—	—	0.10	0.25	—
1983	—	—	—	0.10	0.25	—
1990	—	—	—	0.10	0.25	—

KM# 209.2 50 CENTIMOS

2.2000 g., Stainless Steel, 18.95 mm. **Obv:** Small ships, letters in relief on ribbon **Rev:** Denomination within wreath

Date	Mintage	F	VF	XF	Unc	BU
1984	—	—	—	0.10	0.25	—

KM# 173 COLON

10.0000 g., Copper-Nickel, 29 mm. **Obv:** National arms, date below **Rev:** Denomination within wreath, B.I.C.R below **Edge:** Incuse BICR; plain **Note:** Beaded rims.

Date	Mintage	F	VF	XF	Unc	BU
1935(P)	350,000	0.75	2.00	8.00	50.00	—

Note: Struck in 1936.

KM# 177 COLON

Copper-Nickel, 29 mm. **Obv:** National arms, date below **Rev:** Denomination within wreath, B.N.C.R. below **Edge Lettering:** -BNCR- (repeated)

Date	Mintage	F	VF	XF	Unc	BU
1937(L)	300,000	0.50	1.25	5.00	25.00	—
1937(L) Proof	—	Value: 200				
1948(L)	1,350,000	0.20	0.40	0.75	2.00	—
1948(L) Proof	—	—	—	—	—	—

KM# 186.1 COLON

8.6670 g., Stainless Steel, 29 mm. **Obv:** Small ships, 5 stars in shield, date below **Rev:** Denomination within wreath, B.C.C.R. below **Edge Lettering:** -BCCR- (repeated)

Date	Mintage	F	VF	XF	Unc	BU
1954(P)	987,000	0.20	0.35	1.00	10.00	—

KM# 186.1a COLON

10.0000 g., Copper-Nickel, 29 mm. **Obv:** National arms, date below **Rev:** Denomination within wreath, B.C.C.R. below

Date	Mintage	F	VF	XF	Unc	BU
1961(P)	1,000,000	0.10	0.20	0.50	2.00	—

KM# 186.2 COLON

Copper-Nickel, 29 mm. **Obv:** Small ships, 7 stars in shield, date below **Rev:** Denomination within wreath, B.C.C.R. below **Edge Lettering:** -BCCR- (repeated)

Date	Mintage	F	VF	XF	Unc	BU
1965	1,000,000	0.10	0.20	0.40	1.00	—
1968	2,000,000	0.10	0.20	0.30	0.65	—
1970	2,000,000	0.10	0.20	0.30	0.65	—
1974	—	0.10	0.20	0.30	0.65	—
1978	—	0.10	0.20	0.30	0.65	—

KM# 186.3 COLON

Copper-Nickel, 29 mm. **Obv:** Large ships, 7 stars in shield, date below **Rev:** Denomination within wreath, B.C.C.R. below

Date	Mintage	F	VF	XF	Unc	BU
1972	2,000,000	0.10	0.20	0.30	0.65	—
1975	1,028,000	0.10	0.20	0.30	0.65	—

KM# 186.4 COLON

Copper-Nickel, 29 mm. **Obv:** Small ships, 7 stars in shield **Rev:** Denomination within wreath, large "1" **Edge Lettering:** -BCCR- (repeated) **Note:** Dies vary for each date.

Date	Mintage	F	VF	XF	Unc	BU
1976	12,000,000	0.10	0.20	0.30	0.65	—
1976 Proof	5,000	Value: 2.50				
1977	22,000,000	0.10	0.20	0.30	0.65	—

KM# 210.1 COLON

3.2000 g., Stainless Steel, 21 mm. **Obv:** Large ships, letters incuse on ribbon, date below arms **Rev:** Denomination within wreath, B.C.C.R. below

Date	Mintage	F	VF	XF	Unc	BU
1982	12,000,000	—	—	0.15	0.35	—
1983	—	—	—	0.15	0.35	—
1984	—	—	—	0.15	0.35	—
1991	—	—	—	0.15	0.35	—

KM# 210.2 COLON

3.2000 g., Stainless Steel, 21 mm. **Obv:** Small ships, letters in relief on ribbon, date below arms **Rev:** Denomination within wreath, B.C.C.R. below **Note:** Varieties exist with a "slim 1" in the value for 1984 & 1989, and a "fat 1" in the value for 1993 & 1994.

Date	Mintage	F	VF	XF	Unc	BU
1984	—	—	—	0.15	0.35	—
1989	—	—	—	0.15	0.35	—
1993	—	—	—	0.15	0.35	—
1994	—	—	—	0.15	0.35	—

KM# 233 COLON

Brass **Obv:** National arms, date below **Rev:** Denomination above spray, B.C.C.R. below

Date	Mintage	F	VF	XF	Unc	BU
1998	—	—	—	0.10	0.35	—

KM# 183 2 COLONES

Copper-Nickel, 32 mm. **Obv:** National arms, date below **Rev:** Denomination within wreath, B.N.C.R. below **Edge Lettering:** -BNCR- (repeated)

Date	Mintage	F	VF	XF	Unc	BU
1948(L)	1,380,000	0.50	0.75	1.25	3.00	—
1948(L) Proof	—	Value: 250				

KM# 187.1 2 COLONES

12.0000 g., Stainless Steel, 32 mm. **Obv:** National arms with small ships, 5 stars in shield, date below arms **Rev:** Denomination within wreath, B.C.C.R. below **Edge Lettering:** -BCCR- (repeated)

Date	Mintage	F	VF	XF	Unc	BU
1954(P)	1,028,000	0.25	0.50	2.00	15.00	—

KM# 187.1a 2 COLONES

Copper-Nickel, 32 mm. **Obv:** National arms, date below **Rev:** Denomination within wreath, B.C.C.R. below **Edge Lettering:** -BCCR- (repeated)

Date	Mintage	F	VF	XF	Unc	BU
1961(P)	1,000,000	0.15	0.30	0.50	1.25	—

KM# 187.2 2 COLONES

Copper-Nickel, 32 mm. **Obv:** Small ships, 7 stars in shield, date below arms **Rev:** Denomination within wreath, B.C.C.R. below **Edge Lettering:** -BCCR- (repeated) **Note:** Dies vary for each date.

Date	Mintage	F	VF	XF	Unc	BU
1968	2,000,000	0.15	0.30	0.45	1.00	—
1970	1,000,000	0.15	0.30	0.45	1.25	—
1972	2,000,000	0.15	0.30	0.45	1.00	—
1976	—	0.15	0.30	0.45	1.00	—
1978	—	0.15	0.30	0.45	1.00	—

KM# 190 2 COLONES

4.3000 g., 0.9990 Silver .1381 oz. ASW **Subject:** 20th Anniversary of the Central Bank **Rev:** Bank above denomination

Date	Mintage	F	VF	XF	Unc	BU
1970 Proof	5,157	Value: 16.50				

Note: Also exists with a small oval with 1000 inside above the S in COLONES.

KM# 211.1 2 COLONES

4.2500 g., Stainless Steel, 23.1 mm. **Obv:** Large ships, letters incuse on ribbon, date below arms **Rev:** Denomination within wreath, B.C.C.R. below

Date	Mintage	F	VF	XF	Unc	BU
1982	12,000,000	—	—	0.20	0.60	—
1983	—	—	—	0.20	0.60	—

KM# 211.2 2 COLONES

4.2500 g., Stainless Steel, 23.1 mm. **Obv:** Small ship, letters in relief on ribbon, date below arms **Rev:** Denomination within wreath, B.C.C.R. below

Date	Mintage	F	VF	XF	Unc	BU
1984	—	—	—	0.20	0.60	—

KM# 191 5 COLONES
10.7800 g., 0.9990 Silver .3463 oz. ASW **Subject:** 400th Year - The Founding of New Carthage Juan Vazquez de Coronado **Obv:** National arms, date below **Rev:** Bust with ruffled collar facing, raised 1000 hallmark in oval below "o" of "Cartago" **Edge:** Reeded

Date	Mintage	F	VF	XF	Unc	BU
1970 Proof	5,157	Value: 22.50				

KM# 203 5 COLONES
Nickel **Subject:** 25th Anniversary of the Central Bank **Obv:** National arms, denomination below **Rev:** Plants with two dates at right

Date	Mintage	F	VF	XF	Unc	BU
ND(1975)	2,000,000	—	0.15	0.35	1.25	—
ND(1975) Proof	5,000	Value: 2.00				

KM# 214.1 5 COLONES
7.2500 g., Stainless Steel, 25.9 mm. **Obv:** Small ship, letters in relief on ribbon, date below arms **Rev:** Denomination above spray, B.C.C.R. below, thick '5' on lined background

Date	Mintage	F	VF	XF	Unc	BU
1983	—	—	0.10	0.25	0.75	—
1989	—	—	0.10	0.25	0.75	—
1993	—	—	0.10	0.25	0.75	—

KM# 214.2 5 COLONES
7.2500 g., Stainless Steel, 25.9 mm. **Obv:** Large ship, letters incuse on ribbon **Rev:** Numeral on lined background, B.C.C.R. below sprays

Date	Mintage	F	VF	XF	Unc	BU
1985	—	—	0.10	0.25	0.75	—

KM# 227 5 COLONES
Brass Plated Steel **Obv:** National arms, date below **Rev:** Denomination above sprays, B.C.C.R. below, thick '5'

Date	Mintage	F	VF	XF	Unc	BU
1995	—	—	—	0.25	0.75	—
1997	—	—	—	0.25	0.75	—
1999	—	—	—	0.25	0.75	—

KM# 227a 5 COLONES
4.0000 g., Brass, 21.6 mm. **Obv:** National arms, date below **Rev:** Denomination above spray, B.C.C.R. below, thick '5' **Edge:** Segmented reeding

Date	Mintage	F	VF	XF	Unc	BU
1997	—	—	—	—	0.50	—

KM# 227a.1 5 COLONES
4.0000 g., Brass, 21.6 mm. **Obv:** National arms, date below, smaller letters in legend **Rev:** Denomination above spray, B.C.C.R. below, smaller letters in legend, thick '5' **Edge:** Segmented reeding

Date	Mintage	F	VF	XF	Unc	BU
1999	—	—	—	—	0.65	—

KM# 192 10 COLONES
21.7000 g., 0.9990 Silver .6976 oz. ASW **Subject:** Attempt of Unification of Middle America **Obv:** National arms, date below **Rev:** Kapok tree (ceiba petandra), five mountains in background, denomination below

Date	Mintage	F	VF	XF	Unc	BU
1970 Proof	5,157	Value: 32.00				

KM# 204 10 COLONES
Nickel, 32 mm. **Subject:** 25th Anniversary of the Central Bank **Obv:** National arms, denomination below **Rev:** Two dates above tree at center

Date	Mintage	F	VF	XF	Unc	BU
ND(1975)	500,000	0.25	0.50	1.00	2.00	—
ND(1975) Proof	5,000	Value: 4.00				

KM# 215.1 10 COLONES
8.4500 g., Stainless Steel, 28.3 mm. **Obv:** Small ship, letters in relief on ribbon, date below arms **Rev:** Denomination above spray, B.C.C.R. below, thick number on lined background

Date	Mintage	F	VF	XF	Unc	BU
1983	—	—	0.20	0.35	1.25	—
1992	—	—	0.20	0.35	1.25	—

KM# 215.2 10 COLONES
8.4500 g., Stainless Steel, 28.3 mm. **Obv:** Large ship, letters incuse on ribbon, date below arms **Rev:** Denomination above spray, B.C.C.R. below, thick number on lined background

Date	Mintage	F	VF	XF	Unc	BU
1985	—	—	0.20	0.35	1.25	—

KM# 228 10 COLONES
Brass Plated Steel, 23.5 mm. **Obv:** National arms, date below **Rev:** Denomination above spray, B.C.C.R. below, thick numerals

Date	Mintage	F	VF	XF	Unc	BU
1995	—	—	—	0.35	1.25	—
1996	—	—	—	0.35	1.25	—
1997	—	—	—	0.35	1.25	—
1999	—	—	—	0.35	1.25	—

KM# 228a 10 COLONES
5.0500 g., Brass, 23.5 mm. **Obv:** National arms, date below **Rev:** Denomination above spray, B.C.C.R. below, thick numerals **Edge:** Segmented reeding

Date	Mintage	F	VF	XF	Unc	BU
1997	—	—	—	—	1.00	—

KM# 228a.1 10 COLONES
5.0000 g., Brass, 23.5 mm. **Obv:** Smaller letters in legend **Rev:** Smaller letters in legend **Edge:** Segmented reeding

Date	Mintage	F	VF	XF	Unc	BU
1999	—	—	—	—	1.15	—

KM# 193 20 COLONES
43.7000 g., 0.9990 Silver 1.4050 oz. ASW, 50.8 mm. **Rev:** Venus de Milo statue, raised 1000 hallmark in oval below "O" in "MILO"

Date	Mintage	F	VF	XF	Unc	BU
1970 Proof	7,500	Value: 42.50				

KM# 205 20 COLONES
Nickel, 36 mm. **Subject:** 25th Anniversary of the Central Bank **Obv:** National arms above denomination **Rev:** Flowers divide dates

Date	Mintage	F	VF	XF	Unc	BU
ND(1975)	250,000	0.50	1.00	2.00	4.00	—
ND(1975) Proof	5,000	Value: 9.00				

KM# 216.1 20 COLONES
9.7000 g., Stainless Steel, 31.25 mm. **Obv:** Letters in relief on ribbon, date below arms **Rev:** Denomination above spray, B.C.C.R. below, thick numerals on patterned background

Date	Mintage	F	VF	XF	Unc	BU
1983	—	—	0.35	0.65	1.75	—
1989	—	—	0.35	0.65	1.75	—
1994	—	—	0.35	0.65	1.75	—

KM# 216.2 20 COLONES
9.7000 g., Stainless Steel, 31.25 mm. **Obv:** Letters incuse on ribbon, date below arms **Rev:** Denomination above spray, B.C.C.R. below, thick numerals on patterned background

Date	Mintage	F	VF	XF	Unc	BU
1985	—	—	0.35	0.65	1.75	—
1994	—	—	0.35	0.65	1.75	—
1996	—	—	0.35	0.65	1.75	—

KM# 194 25 COLONES
53.9000 g., 0.9990 Silver 1.7312 oz. ASW **Subject:** 25 Years of Social Legislation **Obv:** National arms, date below **Rev:** "Materidad" sculpture by F. Zuniga, denomination below

Date	Mintage	F	VF	XF	Unc	BU
1970 Proof	6,800	Value: 55.00				

KM# 229 25 COLONES
Brass Plated Steel **Obv:** National arms, date below **Rev:** Denomination above spray, B.C.C.R. below, thick numerals

Date	Mintage	F	VF	XF	Unc	BU
1995	—	—	—	—	2.50	—

KM# 195.1 50 COLONES
7.4500 g., 0.9000 Gold .2155 oz. AGW **Subject:** Inter-American Human Rights Convention **Obv:** National arms, date below **Rev:** Nude on globe background, denomination below

Date	Mintage	F	VF	XF	Unc	BU
1970 Proof	3,507	Value: 150				

KM# 195.2 50 COLONES
7.4500 g., 0.9000 Gold .2155 oz. AGW **Obv:** National arms, date below **Rev:** "1 AR" countermark above fineness statement

Date	Mintage	F	VF	XF	Unc	BU
1970 Proof	Inc. above	Value: 165				

KM# 200 50 COLONES
25.5500 g., 0.5000 Silver .4107 oz. ASW **Subject:** Conservation **Obv:** National arms, date below **Rev:** Green turtles, denomination below **Rev. Designer:** Norman Sillman

Date	Mintage	F	VF	XF	Unc	BU
1974	7,599	—	—	—	20.00	—

KM# 200a 50 COLONES
28.2800 g., 0.9250 Silver .8411 oz. ASW **Subject:** Conservation **Obv:** National arms, date below **Rev:** Green Turtle, denomination below

Date	Mintage	F	VF	XF	Unc	BU
1974 Proof	11,000	Value: 25.00				

KM# 231 50 COLONES
Brass **Obv:** National arms, date below **Rev:** Denomination above spray, B.C.C.R. below, thick numerals

Date	Mintage	F	VF	XF	Unc	BU
1997	—	—	—	—	3.00	—

KM# 231.1 50 COLONES
7.8000 g., Brass, 27.5 mm. **Obv:** National arms, date below, smaller letters in legend **Rev:** Denomination above spray, B.C.C.R. below, thick numerals, smaller letters in legend **Edge:** Segmented reeding

Date	Mintage	F	VF	XF	Unc	BU
1999	—	—	—	—	3.00	—

KM# 196 100 COLONES
14.9000 g., 0.9000 Gold .4311 oz. AGW **Obv:** National arms **Rev:** Gold Vulture pendant in the style of the Chibcha Indians, denomination below

Date	Mintage	F	VF	XF	Unc	BU
1970 Proof	3,507	Value: 295				

KM# 201 100 COLONES
32.1000 g., 0.5000 Silver .5160 oz. ASW **Subject:** Conservation **Obv:** National arms, date below divides BC from CR **Rev:** Manatee, denomination below **Rev. Designer:** Norman Sillman

Date	Mintage	F	VF	XF	Unc	BU
1974	7,599	—	—	—	25.00	—

KM# 201a 100 COLONES
35.0000 g., 0.9250 Silver 1.0409 oz. ASW **Subject:** Conservation **Obv:** National arms **Rev:** Manatee

Date	Mintage	F	VF	XF	Unc	BU
1974 Proof	11,000	Value: 30.00				

KM# 206 100 COLONES
35.0000 g., 0.9250 Silver 1.0409 oz. ASW **Subject:** International Year of the Child **Rev:** Three birds in nest, date below

Date	Mintage	F	VF	XF	Unc	BU
1979	9,500	—	—	—	15.00	—
1979 Proof	5,000	Value: 28.00				

KM# 224 100 COLONES
Nickel **Obv:** National arms, denomination below **Rev:** Bust of President Dr. Oscar Arias S. divides dates

Date	Mintage	F	VF	XF	Unc	BU
1987	25,000	—	—	—	7.50	—

KM# 230 100 COLONES
Brass Plated Steel **Obv:** National arms **Rev:** Denomination above spray, B.C.C.R. below, thick numerals

Date	Mintage	F	VF	XF	Unc	BU
1995	—	—	—	—	4.50	—

KM# 230a 100 COLONES
Brass **Obv:** National arms, date below **Rev:** Denomination above spray, B.C.C.R. below, thick numerals

Date	Mintage	F	VF	XF	Unc	BU
1997	—	—	—	—	4.50	—
1998	—	—	—	—	4.50	—

KM# 230a.1 100 COLONES
9.0000 g., Brass, 29.5 mm. **Obv:** National arms, date below, smaller letters in legend **Rev:** Denomination above spray, B.C.C.R. below, thick numerals, smaller letters in legend **Edge:** Segmented reeding

Date	Mintage	F	VF	XF	Unc	BU
1999	—	—	—	—	4.50	—

KM# 240 100 COLONES
9.1000 g., Brass, 29.5 mm. **Obv:** New design with much smaller legend and date **Rev:** Value **Edge:** Segmented reeding

Date	Mintage	F	VF	XF	Unc	BU
2000	—	—	—	—	4.50	—

KM# 197 200 COLONES
29.8000 g., 0.9000 Gold .8623 oz. AGW **Obv:** National arms **Rev:** Juan Santamaria and cannon

Date	Mintage	F	VF	XF	Unc	BU
1970 Proof	3,507	Value: 585				

KM# 212 250 COLONES
30.3300 g., 0.9250 Silver .9020 oz. ASW **Subject:** Conservation **Obv:** National arms **Rev:** Jaguar head facing

Date	Mintage	F	VF	XF	Unc	BU
1982(P) FM Proof	1,109	Value: 125				

KM# 217 250 COLONES
30.3300 g., 0.9250 Silver .9020 oz. ASW **Obv:** National arms **Rev:** National flower, denomination below

Date	Mintage	F	VF	XF	Unc	BU
1983(P) FM Proof	393	Value: 75.00				

KM# 207 300 COLONES
10.9700 g., 0.9250 Silver .3262 oz. ASW **Subject:** 125th Anniversary - Death of Juan Santamaria **Obv:** National arms, denomination below **Rev:** Juan Santamaria standing with torch and rifle divides dates

Date	Mintage	F	VF	XF	Unc	BU
1981 Proof	10,000	Value: 12.50				

KM# 223 300 COLONES
10.9700 g., 0.9250 Silver .3262 oz. ASW **Subject:** 200th Anniversary - Founding of Alajuela **Obv:** National arms, denomination below **Rev:** Head facing, divides dates

Date	Mintage	F	VF	XF	Unc	BU
1981 Proof	—	Value: 12.50				

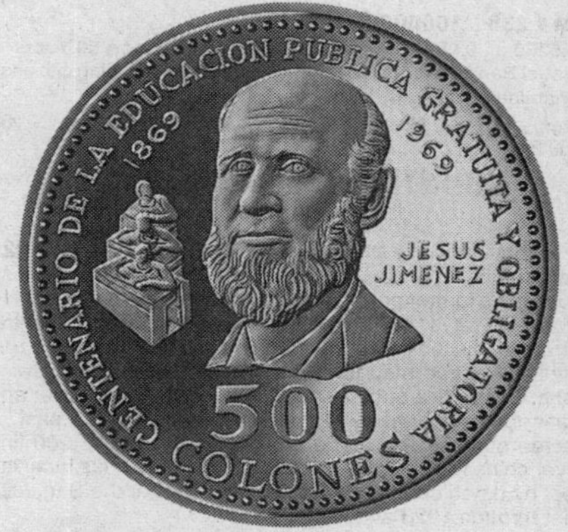

KM# 198 500 COLONES
74.5200 g., 0.9000 Gold 2.1565 oz. AGW **Subject:** 100th Anniversary of Public Education **Obv:** National arms **Rev:** Jesus Jimenez and students at desks

Date	Mintage	F	VF	XF	Unc	BU
1970 Proof	- 3,507	Value: 1,450				

KM# 236 500 COLONES
Brass **Subject:** 50 Years - Central Bank **Obv:** National arms, date below **Rev:** Bank building, denomination below

Date	Mintage	F	VF	XF	Unc	BU
2000	5,000	—	—	—	2.50	3.50

KM# 199 1000 COLONES
149.0400 g., 0.9000 Gold 4.3126 oz. AGW **Subject:** 150th Anniversary of Central American Independence **Obv:** National arms **Rev:** Face on radiant sun above mountains, water and map, denomination below **Note:** Photo reduced.

Date	Mintage	F	VF	XF	Unc	BU
1970 Proof	3,507	Value: 3,150				

KM# 225 1000 COLONES
10.9700 g., 0.9250 Silver .3272 oz. ASW **Obv:** National arms, denomination below **Rev:** Head of President Dr. Oscar Arias S. divides dates

Date	Mintage	F	VF	XF	Unc	BU
1987	10,000	—	—	—	30.00	—

KM# 202 1500 COLONES
33.4370 g., 0.9000 Gold .9676 oz. AGW **Subject:** Conservation **Obv:** National arms, date below divides B.C. from C.R. **Rev:** Giant anteater, denomination below

Date	Mintage	F	VF	XF	Unc	BU
1974	2,418	—	—	—	650	—
1974 Proof	726	Value: 725				

KM# 213 1500 COLONES
6.9800 g., 0.5000 Gold .1122 oz. AGW **Rev:** Busts of Francisco Coronado and Christopher Columbus, denomination above **Note:** Although considered legal tender, these coins were never officially authorized for circulation.

Date	Mintage	F	VF	XF	Unc	BU
1982FM (P)	724	Value: 125				

KM# 218 1500 COLONES
6.9800 g., 0.5000 Gold .1122 oz. AGW **Obv:** National arms, date below **Rev:** Native figurine, denomination above, spray below

Date	Mintage	F	VF	XF	Unc	BU
1983FM (P)	272	Value: 275				

KM# 234 3000 COLONES
25.3600 g., 0.9250 Silver .7542 oz. ASW **Subject:** 150th Anniversary San Juan de Dios Hospital **Obv:** National arms, denomination below **Rev:** Hospital building divides dates

Date	Mintage	F	VF	XF	Unc	BU
1994 Proof	—	Value: 50.00				

KM# 208 5000 COLONES
15.0000 g., 0.9000 Gold .4341 oz. AGW **Subject:** 125th Anniversary - Death of Juan Santamaria **Obv:** National arms, denomination below **Rev:** Figure standing with torch and rifle divides dates

Date	Mintage	F	VF	XF	Unc	BU
1981	—	—	—	—	295	—
1981 Proof	2,000	Value: 320				

KM# 232 5000 COLONES
15.0000 g., 0.9000 Gold .4341 oz. AGW **Subject:** Founding of Alajuela **Obv:** National arms **Rev:** Portrait of Ramirez

Date	Mintage	F	VF	XF	Unc	BU
1981 Proof	2,000	Value: 325				

KM# 235 5000 COLONES
25.0600 g., 0.9250 Silver .7453 oz. ASW **Subject:** Centennial of the Colon **Obv:** National arms, denomination below **Rev:** Bust of Columbus right, two dates below denomination

Date	Mintage	F	VF	XF	Unc	BU
1997 Proof	—	Value: 50.00				

KM# 237 5000 COLONES
31.1000 g., 0.9250 Silver .9429 oz. ASW **Subject:** 50 Years - Central Bank **Obv:** National arms, date below **Rev:** Man working screw press, denomination at right

Date	Mintage	F	VF	XF	Unc	BU
2000 Proof	7,500	Value: 30.00				

KM# 226 25000 COLONES
15.0000 g., 0.9000 Gold .4341 oz. AGW **Obv:** National arms, denomination below **Rev:** Bust of President Dr. Oscar Arias S., divides dates

Date	Mintage	F	VF	XF	Unc	BU
1987 Proof	5,000	Value: 320				

KM# 238 100000 COLONES
15.5500 g., 0.9000 Gold .4499 oz. AGW **Subject:** 50 Years - Central Bank **Obv:** National arms **Rev:** Three standing citizens, denomination at right

Date	Mintage	F	VF	XF	Unc	BU
2000 Proof	2,500	Value: 350				

COUNTERSTAMPED COINAGE

Type VIII • 1923

In the financially stressful years between 1914 and 1925 many Latin American countries saw their currencies lose much of its former purchasing power. Governments reacted in several ways: In Peru, Chile, Brazil and most of Central America, this took the form of devaluing their monetary unit relative to such standards as the U.S. dollar and Swiss franc. Costa Rica began issuing coins of .500 fine silver and brass to replace the .900 fine silver issues of the past. A decree of 1923 also made provisions for the old .900 fine silver coins to be revalued, doubling their previous face values, by dated counterstamping conducted at the San Jose Mint through 1923 and into 1924.

Obverse counterstamp: 1923 in 11mm circle.

Reverse counterstamp: 50/CENTIMOS in 11mm circle.

NOTE: The total mintage for KM#154-159 was 1,866,000 pieces.

KM# 156 50 CENTIMOS
6.2500 g., 0.7500 Silver .1507 oz. ASW **Counterstamp:** Type VIII **Note:** Counterstamped on 25 Centavos, KM#106.

CS Date	Host Date	Good	VG	F	VF	XF
1923	1865 GW	25.00	40.00	60.00	100	—
1923	1875 GW	20.00	30.00	40.00	80.00	—
1923	1864 GW	75.00	150	300	500	—

KM# 157 50 CENTIMOS
6.2500 g., 0.7500 Silver .1507 oz. ASW **Counterstamp:** Type VIII **Obv:** Liberty cap and flags above shield turned 3/4 right, date within circle on shield **Rev:** Denomination within circle, wreath surrounds, G.W. 9 DS. **Note:** Counterstamped on 25 Centavos, KM#127.1.

CS Date	Host Date	Good	VG	F	VF	XF
1923	1887 GW	—	3.50	6.00	9.50	15.00
1923	1886 GW	—	3.50	6.00	9.50	15.00

KM# 158 50 CENTIMOS
6.2500 g., 0.7500 Silver .1507 oz. ASW **Counterstamp:** Type VIII **Obv:** Date within circle, spray below **Rev:** Denomination within circle, wreath surrounds, 9Ds G.W. **Note:** Counterstamped on 25 Centavos, KM#127.2.

CS Date	Host Date	Good	VG	F	VF	XF
1923	1887 GW	—	3.50	6.00	9.50	15.00
1923	1886 GW	—	4.00	8.00	15.00	25.00

KM# 159 50 CENTIMOS
6.3000 g., 0.7500 Silver .1519 oz. ASW, 25 mm. **Counterstamp:** Type VIII **Obv:** Liberty cap and flags above shield turned 1/4 right, date within circle on shield, spray and date below **Rev:** Denomination within circle, wreath surrounds **Note:** Counterstamped on 25 Centavos, KM#130.

CS Date	Host Date	Good	VG	F	VF	XF
1923	1890/80HEATON	—	2.50	3.75	7.00	10.00
1923	1890HEATON	—	2.25	3.00	5.00	8.50
1923	1892HEATON	—	2.25	3.00	5.00	8.50
1923	1893HEATON	—	2.00	2.75	4.50	7.50
1923	1889HEATON	—	2.25	3.00	5.00	8.50

KM# 154 50 CENTIMOS
6.4000 g., 0.9030 Silver .1858 oz. ASW **Counterstamp:** Type VIII **Note:** Counterstamped on 1/4 Peso, KM#103.

CS Date	Host Date	Good	VG	F	VF	XF
1923	1850 JB	200	400	700	—	—

KM# 155 50 CENTIMOS
6.2500 g., 0.0750 Silver .1507 oz. ASW **Counterstamp:** Type VIII **Note:** Counterstamped on 25 Centavos, KM#105.

CS Date	Host Date	Good	VG	F	VF	XF
1923	1864 GW	150	325	550	—	—

COUNTERSTAMPED COINAGE

Type IX • 1923

Obverse counterstamp: 1923 in 14mm circle.

Reverse counterstamp: UN/COLON in 14mm circle.

NOTE: The total mintage for KM#162-164 was 421,810 pieces. Host dates of 1867 GW, 1870 GW and 1872 GW are listed, but no examples are currently known to exist.

KM# 162 COLON
12.5000 g., 0.7500 Silver **Counterstamp:** Type IX **Note:** Counterstamped on 50 Centavos, KM#112.

CS Date	Host Date	Good	VG	F	VF	XF
1923	1865 GW	25.00	40.00	75.00	—	—
1923	1866/5 GW	25.00	40.00	75.00	—	—
1923	1867 GW	100	200	—	—	—
1923	1870 GW	150	—	—	—	—
1923	1872 GW	200	—	—	—	—
1923	1875 GW	25.00	40.00	75.00	—	—

KM# 165 COLON
10.0000 g., 0.5000 Silver **Counterstamp:** Type IX **Obv:** Denomination on shield, date below **Rev:** Date within circle, wreath surrounds **Note:** Counterstamped on 50 Centimos, KM#150. For KM#165 the mintage were: 1917 host 9,390 pieces; 1918 host 28,800 pieces.

CS Date	Host Date	Good	VG	F	VF	XF
1923	1918 GCR	—	—	10.00	20.00	30.00
1923	1917 GCR	—	—	10.00	17.50	25.00

KM# 163 COLON (Un)
12.5000 g., 0.7500 Silver **Counterstamp:** Type IX **Obv:** Date within circle, wreath surrounds **Rev:** Liberty cap and flags above shield, turned 3/4 right, denomination within circle on shield **Note:** Counterstamped on 50 Centavos, KM#124.

CS Date	Host Date	Good	VG	F	VF	XF
1923	1885 GW	—	6.50	10.00	25.00	50.00
1923	1880 GW	—	6.50	10.00	25.00	50.00
1923	1886 GW	—	9.00	17.50	30.00	60.00
1923	1887 GW	—	6.50	10.00	27.50	55.00
1923	1890 GW	—	6.50	10.00	27.50	55.00

KM# 164 COLON (Un)
10.0000 g., 0.9000 Silver **Counterstamp:** Type IX **Obv:** Date within circle, wreath surrounds **Rev:** Denomination within circle on shield **Note:** Counterstamped on 50 Centimos, KM#143.

CS Date	Host Date	Good	VG	F	VF	XF
1923	1903 JCV	—	4.00	6.50	10.00	17.50
1923	1914 GCR	—	5.00	9.00	13.50	20.00
1923	1902 CY	—	5.00	9.00	13.50	22.50

LEPROSARIUM COINAGE

KM# L1 5 CENTIMOS
Copper Nickel **Note:** 4mm hole punched through 5 Centimos, KM#178. Prospective buyers should proceed with caution, as modern fabrications are prevalent.

Date	Mintage	VG	F	VF	XF	Unc
1942 (1944) Rare	2,000	—	—	—	—	—

KM# L2 25 CENTIMOS
Copper Nickel **Note:** 6mm hole punched through 25 Centimos, KM#171. Prospective buyers should proceed with caution, as modern fabrications are prevalent.

Date	Mintage	VG	F	VF	XF	Unc
1935 (1944) Rare	2,000	—	—	—	—	—

KM# L3 25 CENTIMOS
Copper-Nickel **Note:** 6mm hole punched through 25 Centimos, KM#175. Prospective buyers should proceed with caution, as modern fabrications are prevalent.

Date	Mintage	VG	F	VF	XF	Unc
1937 (1944) Rare	Inc. above	—	—	—	—	—

KM# L4 50 CENTIMOS
Copper Nickel **Note:** 8mm hole punched through 50 Centimos, KM#172. Prospective buyers should proceed with caution, as modern fabrications are prevalent.

Date	Mintage	VG	F	VF	XF	Unc
1935 (1944) Rare	800	—	—	—	—	—

KM# L5 50 CENTIMOS
Copper Nickel **Note:** 8mm hole punched through 50 Centimos, KM#176. Prospective buyers should proceed with caution, as modern fabrications are prevalent.

Date	Mintage	VG	F	VF	XF	Unc
1937 (1944) Rare	Inc. above	—	—	—	—	—

KM# L6 COLON
Copper Nickel **Note:** 9mm hole punched through 1 Colon, KM#173. Prospective buyers should proceed with caution, as modern fabrications are prevalent.

Date	Mintage	VG	F	VF	XF	Unc
1935 (1944) Rare	1,000	—	—	—	—	—

KM# L7 COLON
Copper Nickel **Note:** 9mm hole punched through 1 Colon, KM#177. Prospective buyers should proceed with caution, as modern fabrications are prevalent.

Date	Mintage	VG	F	VF	XF	Unc
1937 (1944) Rare	Inc. above	—	—	—	—	—

PATTERNS

Including off metal strikes

KM#	Date	Mintage	Identification	Mkt Val
Pn11	1917	—	10 Centavos. Silver. Similar to KM#129. As KM#148. Prev.# KMPn7. Existance of this type has been questioned.	—
PnA12	1923	—	25 Centimos. Brass. obverse of gold 5 pesos type. as KM#168. Obverse of gold 5 pesos type, reverse as KM#168	—
Pn12	1924	—	25 Centimos. Brass. KM#168. Considered false.	—

KM#	Date	Mintage	Identification	Mkt Val
Pn13	19xx	—	5 Centimos. Copper Nickel. Similar to 1929 issue	50.00
Pn14	19xx	—	5 Centimos. Brass. Similar to 1929 issues.	—

KM#	Date	Mintage	Identification	Mkt Val
Pn15	19xx	—	10 Centimos. Copper-Nickel. Similar to 1929 issue. Prev.# KMPn10.	60.00
Pn16	1944	—	25 Centimos. Silver.	—
Pn17	1944	—	25 Centimos. Brass. Polished dies.	100

PIEFORTS

KM#	Date	Mintage	Identification	Mkt Val
P6	1946	—	25 Centimos. Brass.	100
P7	1946	—	25 Centimos. Copper Nickel.	125

MINT SETS

KM#	Date	Mintage	Identification	Issue Price	Mkt Val
MS1	1972 (6)	—	KM#184.4, 185.3-186.3, 187.2, 188.2-189.2	—	10.00
MS2	1975 (3)	—	KM#203-205	—	7.50

PROOF SETS

KM#	Date	Mintage	Identification	Issue Price	Mkt Val
PS1	1889 (4)	—	KM#128-131	—	—
PS2	1937 (3)	—	KM#175-177	—	450
PS3	1970 (10)	570	KM#190-199	—	5,500
PS4	1970 (5)	4,650	KM#190-194	52.00	160
PS5	1970 (5)	3,000	KM#195-199	832	5,225
PS6	1974 (2)	30,000	KM#200a-201a	50.00	50.00
PS7	1975 (3)	—	KM#203-205	—	15.00
PS8	1976 (5)	5,000	KM#184.3, 185.2, 186.4, 188.1, 189.1	10.00	7.50

The island of Crete (Kriti), located 60 miles southeast of the Peloponnesus, was the center of a brilliant civilization that flourished before the advent of Greek culture. After being conquered by the Romans, Byzantines, Moslems and Venetians, Crete became part of the Turkish Empire in 1669. As a consequence of the Greek Revolution of the 1820s, it was ceded to Egypt. Egypt returned the island to the Turks in 1840, and they ceded it to Greece in 1913, after the Second Balkan War.

RULERS
Prince George, 1898-1906

MINT MARKS
A - Paris
(a) - Paris (privy marks only)

GREEK ADMINISTRATION

STANDARD COINAGE

KM# 1.2 LEPTON
Bronze, 16 mm. **Ruler:** Prince George **Obv:** Crown, date below **Rev:** Denomination within wreath

Date	Mintage	F	VF	XF	Unc	BU
1901A	1,710,717	6.00	12.00	27.50	100	200

KM# 2 2 LEPTA
Bronze **Ruler:** Prince George **Obv:** Crown, date below **Rev:** Denomination within wreath

Date	Mintage	F	VF	XF	Unc	BU
1901A	707,000	6.00	12.50	40.00	150	250

KM# 6 50 LEPTA
2.5000 g., 0.8350 Silver .0671 oz. ASW **Ruler:** Prince George **Obv:** Head right **Rev:** Crowned arms, denomination below

Date	Mintage	F	VF	XF	Unc	BU
1901(a)	600,000	25.00	55.00	135	500	1,000

KM# 7 DRACHMA
5.0000 g., 0.8350 Silver .1342 oz. ASW **Ruler:** Prince George **Obv:** Head right **Rev:** Crowned, mantled and supported arms, denomination below

Date	Mintage	F	VF	XF	Unc	BU
1901(a)	500,000	35.00	60.00	200	1,500	2,000

KM# 8 2 DRACHMAI
10.0000 g., 0.8350 Silver .2685 oz. ASW **Ruler:** Prince George **Obv:** Head right **Rev:** Crowned, mantled and supported arms, denomination below

Date	Mintage	F	VF	XF	Unc	BU
1901(a)	175,000	75.00	150	800	4,500	8,000

KM# 9 5 DRACHMAI
25.0000 g., 0.9000 Silver .7234 oz. ASW **Ruler:** Prince George **Obv:** Head right **Rev:** Crowned, mantled and supported arms, denomination below

Date	Mintage	F	VF	XF	Unc	BU
1901(a)	150,000	100	200	1,200	10,000	20,000

CROATIA

The Republic of Croatia, (Hrvatska) bordered on the west by the Adriatic Sea and the northeast by Hungary, has an area of 21,829 sq. mi. (56,538 sq. km.) and a population of 4.7 million. Capital: Zagreb.

The country was attached to the Kingdom of Hungary until Dec. 1, 1918, when it joined with the Serbs and Slovenes to form the Kingdom of the Serbs, Croats and Slovenes, which changed its name to the Kingdom of Yugoslavia on Oct. 3, 1929. On April 6, 1941, Hitler, angered by the coup d'etat that overthrew the pro-Nazi regime of regent Prince Paul, sent the Nazi armies crashing across the Yugoslav borders from Germany, Hungary, Romania and Bulgaria. Within a week the army of the Balkan Kingdom was prostrate and broken. Yugoslavia was dismembered to reward Hitler's Balkan allies. Croatia, reconstituted as a nominal kingdom, was given to the administration of an Italian princeling, who wisely decided to remain in Italy. By 1947 it was again totally part of the 6 Yugoslav Socialist Republics.

Croatia proclaimed their independence from Yugoslavia on Oct. 8, 1991.

Local Serbian forces, supported by the Yugoslav Federal Army, had developed a military stronghold and proclaimed an independent "SRPSKEKRAJINA" State in the area around Knin, located in southern Croatia having an estimated population of 350,000 Croat Serbs. In September 1995, Croat forces overwhelmed Croat Serb forces ending the short life of their proclaimed Serbian Republic.

NOTE: Coin dates starting with 1994 are followed with a period. Example: 1994.

MONETARY SYSTEM
100 Banica = 1 Kuna

The word kunas', related to the Russian Kunitsa, which means marten, reflects the use of furs for money in medieval Eastern Europe.

KINGDOM

DECIMAL COINAGE

KM# 1 KUNA
Zinc **Note:** Similar to 2 Kune, KM#2.

Date	Mintage	F	VF	XF	Unc	BU
1941 Rare	—	—	—	—	—	—

Note: Possibly unique

KM# 2 2 KUNE
Zinc **Designer:** Ivan Kerdic

Date	Mintage	F	VF	XF	Unc	BU
1941	—	3.00	7.00	15.00	40.00	—
1941 Proof	—	Value: 80.00				

KM# A3 500 KUNA
9.9500 g., 0.9000 Gold .2821 oz. AGW **Obv:** Ante Pavelió, date below **Rev:** Denomination above arms within braided circle **Designer:** Ivan Kerdic

Date	Mintage	F	VF	XF	Unc	BU
1941	170	—	1,750	2,250	3,000	—

KM# B3 500 KUNA
9.9500 g., 0.9000 Gold .2821 oz. AGW **Obv:** Kneeling figure with sheaf of grain, date below **Rev:** Denomination above arms within braided circle

Date	Mintage	F	VF	XF	Unc	BU
1941	—	—	—	—	3,400	—

REPUBLIC

REFORM COINAGE

May 30, 1994 - 1000 Dinara = 1 Kuna; 100 Lipa = 1 Kuna

For the circulating minor coins, the reverse legend (name of item) is in Croatian for odd dated years and Latin for even dated years.

KM# 3 LIPA
0.7000 g., Aluminum, 17 mm. **Obv:** Denomination above crowned arms **Rev:** Ears of corn, date below **Designer:** Kuzma Kovacic

Date	Mintage	F	VF	XF	Unc	BU
1993	57,834,100	—	—	0.20	0.50	—
1993 Proof	17,000	Value: 1.00				
1995. With dot	—	—	—	0.20	0.50	—
1995.	7,101,000	—	—	0.20	0.50	—
1995. With dot, Proof	4,000	Value: 2.00				
1997.	5,019,000	—	—	0.20	0.50	—
1997. Proof	—	Value: 1.00				
1999.	8,000,000	—	—	0.20	0.50	—
1999. Proof	2,000	Value: 1.50				

KM# 3a LIPA
Silver, 17 mm. **Obv:** Denomination above arms **Rev:** Ears of corn

Date	Mintage	F	VF	XF	Unc	BU
1993 Proof, Rare	5	—	—	—	—	—

KM# 3b LIPA
Gold, 17 mm. **Obv:** Denomination above arms **Rev:** Ears of corn

Date	Mintage	F	VF	XF	Unc	BU
1993 Proof, Rare	5	—	—	—	—	—

KM# 12 LIPA
0.7000 g., Aluminum, 17 mm. **Obv:** Denomination above crowned arms **Rev:** Ears of corn, date below **Rev. Legend:** ZEA MAYS

Date	Mintage	F	VF	XF	Unc	BU
1994.	2,003,097	—	—	0.40	1.00	—
1994. Proof	4,000	Value: 2.00				
1996.	2,000,000	—	—	0.40	1.00	—
1996. Proof	5,000	Value: 1.00				
1998.	2,000,000	—	—	0.40	1.00	—
1998. Proof	2,000	Value: 2.50				
2000.	2,000,000	—	—	0.40	1.00	—
2000. Proof	1,000	Value: 2.50				

KM# 13 LIPA
Aluminum, 17 mm. **Obv:** Denomination above crowned arms **Rev:** Ears of corn, date below **Rev. Legend:** FAO

Date	Mintage	F	VF	XF	Unc	BU
ND(1995)	1,000,000	—	—	0.30	1.00	—
ND(1995) Proof	5,000	Value: 1.50				

KM# 4 2 LIPE
0.9200 g., Aluminum, 19 mm. **Obv:** Denomination above crowned arms on half braid **Rev:** Grapevine, date below

Date	Mintage	F	VF	XF	Unc	BU
1993	17,958,962	—	—	0.40	1.00	—
1993 Proof	17,000	Value: 2.00				
1995. With dot	7,498,000	—	—	0.40	1.00	—
1995. With dot, Proof	4,000	Value: 2.00				
1997.	4,996,000	—	—	0.40	1.00	—
1997. Proof	2,000	Value: 2.50				
1999.	8,000,000	—	—	0.40	1.00	—
1999. Proof	2,000	Value: 2.50				

KM# 4a 2 LIPE
Silver, 19 mm. **Obv:** Denomination above crowned arms on half braid **Rev:** Grapevine above date

Date	Mintage	F	VF	XF	Unc	BU
1993 Proof, Rare	5	—	—	—	—	—

KM# 4b 2 LIPE
Gold, 19 mm. **Obv:** Denomination above crowned arms on half braid **Rev:** Grapevine

Date	Mintage	F	VF	XF	Unc	BU
1993 Proof, Rare	5	—	—	—	—	—

KM# 14 2 LIPE
0.9200 g., Aluminum, 19 mm. **Obv:** Denomination above crowned arms on half braid **Rev:** Grapevine, date below **Rev. Legend:** VITIS VINIFERA **Designer:** Kuzma Kovacic

Date	Mintage	F	VF	XF	Unc	BU
1994.	2,000,163	—	—	0.80	2.00	—
1994. Proof	4,000	Value: 2.25				
1996.	2,006,000	—	—	0.80	2.00	—
1996. Proof	5,000	Value: 2.25				
1998. Proof	2,000	Value: 2.50				
1998.	2,000,000	—	—	0.80	2.00	—
2000.	2,000,000	—	—	0.80	2.00	—
2000, Proof	1,000	Value: 3.00				

KM# 36 2 LIPE
0.9200 g., Aluminum, 19 mm. **Subject:** Olympics **Obv:** Denomination above crowned arms on half braid **Rev:** Olympic logo, torch above date below

Date	Mintage	F	VF	XF	Unc	BU
1996.	1,000,000	—	—	0.30	0.60	—
1996. Proof	5,000	Value: 1.00				

KM# 5 5 LIPA
2.5000 g., Brass Plated Steel, 18 mm. **Obv:** Denomination above crowned arms **Rev:** Oak leaves, date below **Designer:** Kuzma Kovacic

Date	Mintage	F	VF	XF	Unc	BU
1993	42,686,969	—	—	0.40	1.50	—
1993 Proof	17,000	Value: 2.00				
1995. With dot	17,308,000	—	—	0.40	1.00	—
1995. Proof	4,000	Value: 3.00				
1997.	29,964,000	—	—	0.40	1.00	—
1997. Proof	2,000	Value: 3.50				
1999.	25,402,000	—	—	0.40	1.00	—
1999. Proof	2,000	Value: 3.50				

KM# 5a 5 LIPA
Silver, 18 mm. **Obv:** Denomination above crowned arms **Rev:** Oak leaves, date below **Designer:** Kuzma Kovacic

Date	Mintage	F	VF	XF	Unc	BU
1993 Proof, Rare	5	—	—	—	—	—

KM# 5b 5 LIPA
Gold, 18 mm. **Obv:** Denomination above crowned arms **Rev:** Oak leaves, date below **Designer:** Kuzma Kovacic

Date	Mintage	F	VF	XF	Unc	BU
1993 Proof, Rare	5	—	—	—	—	—

KM# 15 5 LIPA
Brass Plated Steel, 18 mm. **Obv:** Denomination above crowned arms **Rev:** Oak leaves, date below **Rev. Legend:** QUERCUS ROBUR **Designer:** Kuzma Kovacic

Date	Mintage	F	VF	XF	Unc	BU
1994.	2,005,346	—	—	0.80	2.00	—
1994. Proof	4,000	Value: 2.25				
1996.	2,004,000	—	—	0.80	2.00	—
1996. Proof	5,000	Value: 2.50				
1998.	2,000,000	—	—	0.80	2.00	—
1998. Proof	2,000	Value: 3.00				
2000.	4,500,000	—	—	0.80	2.00	—
2000. Proof	1,000	Value: 4.00				

KM# 37 5 LIPA
Brass Plated Steel, 18 mm. **Subject:** Olympics **Obv:** Denomination above crowned arms **Rev:** Olympic logo, torch above, date below **Designer:** Kuzma Kovacic

Date	Mintage	F	VF	XF	Unc	BU
1996.	900,000	—	—	0.60	1.25	—
1996. Proof	5,000	Value: 2.00				

KM# 6 10 LIPA
Brass Plated Steel, 20 mm. **Obv:** Denomination above crowned arms **Rev:** Tobacco plant, date below **Designer:** Kuzma Kovacic

Date	Mintage	F	VF	XF	Unc	BU
1993	63,689,778	—	—	0.40	1.50	—
1993 Proof	17,000	Value: 3.00				
1995. With dot	26,335,500	—	—	0.40	1.50	—
1995. With dot, Proof	4,000	Value: 4.00				
1997.	39,995,500	—	—	0.40	1.50	—
1997. Proof	1,000	Value: 4.50				
1999.	49,500,000	—	—	0.40	1.50	—
1999. Proof	2,000	Value: 4.50				

KM# 6a 10 LIPA
Silver, 20 mm. **Obv:** Denomination above crowned arms on half braid **Rev:** Tobacco plant, date below **Designer:** Kuzma Kovacic

Date	Mintage	F	VF	XF	Unc	BU
1993 Proof, Rare	5	—	—	—	—	—

KM# 6b 10 LIPA
Gold, 20 mm. **Obv:** Denomination above crowned arms on half braid **Rev:** Oak leaves, date below **Designer:** Kuzma Kovacic

Date	Mintage	F	VF	XF	Unc	BU
1993 Proof, Rare	5	—	—	—	—	—

KM# 16 10 LIPA
Brass Plated Steel, 20 mm. **Obv:** Denomination above crowned arms on half braid **Rev:** Tobacco plant, date below **Rev. Legend:** NICOTIANA TABACUM **Designer:** Kuzma Kovacic

Date	Mintage	F	VF	XF	Unc	BU
1994.	2,000,127	—	—	0.80	2.50	—
1994. Proof	4,000	Value: 4.00				
1996.	2,000,000	—	—	0.80	2.50	—
1996. Proof	5,000	Value: 3.50				
1998.	2,000,000	—	—	0.80	2.50	—
1998. Proof	2,000	Value: 4.50				
2000.	3,000,000	—	—	0.80	2.50	—
2000. Proof	1,000	Value: 5.00				

KM# 38 10 LIPA
Brass, 20 mm. **Subject:** 50th Anniversary - UN **Obv:** Denomination above crowned arms above half braid **Rev:** UN logo, dates below **Designer:** Kuzma Kovacic

Date	Mintage	F	VF	XF	Unc	BU
ND(1995)	900,000	—	—	0.50	1.20	—
ND(1995)	5,000	Value: 4.00				

KM# 7 20 LIPA
2.9000 g., Nickel Plated Steel, 18.5 mm. **Obv:** Denomination above crowned arms on half braid **Rev:** Olive branch, date below **Designer:** Kuzma Kovacic

Date	Mintage	F	VF	XF	Unc	BU
1993	25,206,442	—	—	0.50	1.50	—
1993 Proof	17,000	Value: 3.00				
1995. With dot	—	—	—	0.50	1.50	—
1995.	39,718,500	—	—	0.50	1.50	—
1995. Proof	4,000	Value: 4.00				
1997.	9,999,000	—	—	0.45	1.50	—
1997. Proof	2,000	Value: 4.50				
1999.	33,500,000	—	—	0.45	1.50	—
1999. Proof	2,000	Value: 4.50				

KM# 7a 20 LIPA
Silver, 18.5 mm. **Obv:** Denomination above crowned arms on half braid **Rev:** Olive branch, date below **Designer:** Kuzma Kovacic

Date	Mintage	F	VF	XF	Unc	BU
1993 Proof, Rare	5	—	—	—	—	—

KM# 7b 20 LIPA
Gold, 18.5 mm. **Obv:** Denomination above crowned arms on half braid **Rev:** Olive branch, date below **Designer:** Kuzma Kovacic

Date	Mintage	F	VF	XF	Unc	BU
1993 Proof, Rare	5	—	—	—	—	—

KM# 17 20 LIPA
Nickel Plated Steel, 18.5 mm. **Obv:** Denomination above crowned arms on half braid **Rev:** Olive branch, date below **Rev. Legend:** OLEA EUROPAEA

Date	Mintage	F	VF	XF	Unc	BU
1994.	2,072,862	—	—	0.80	2.50	—
1994. Proof	4,000	Value: 3.00				
1996.	2,000,000	—	—	0.80	2.50	—
1996. Proof	5,000	Value: 4.00				
1998.	2,000,000	—	—	0.80	2.50	—
1998. Proof	2,000	Value: 4.50				
2000.	2,000,000	—	—	0.80	2.50	—
2000. Proof	1,000	Value: 5.00				

KM# 18 20 LIPA
2.9000 g., Nickel Plated Steel, 18.5 mm. **Subject:** F.A.O. **Obv:** Denomination above crowned arms on half braid **Rev:** Olive branch, date below **Designer:** Kuzma Kovacic

Date	Mintage	F	VF	XF	Unc	BU
ND(1995)	1,000,000	—	—	0.50	1.50	—
ND(1995) Proof	5,000	Value: 4.50				

KM# 8 50 LIPA
3.6500 g., Nickel Plated Steel, 20.5 mm. **Obv:** Denomination above crowned arms on half braid **Rev:** Flowers, date below **Designer:** Kuzma Kovacic

Date	Mintage	F	VF	XF	Unc	BU
1993	51,456,267	—	—	0.60	1.50	—
1993 Proof	17,000	Value: 4.00				
1995. With dot	23,077,000	—	—	0.60	1.50	—
1995. With dot, Proof	4,000	Value: 4.50				
1997.	1,473,000	—	—	0.60	1.50	—
1997. Proof	2,000	Value: 5.00				
1999.	1,000,000	—	—	0.60	1.50	—
1999. Proof	2,000	Value: 5.00				

KM# 8a 50 LIPA
Silver, 20.5 mm. **Obv:** Denomination above crowned arms on half braid **Rev:** Flowers, date below **Designer:** Kuzma Kovacic

Date	Mintage	F	VF	XF	Unc	BU
1993 Proof, Rare	5	—	—	—	—	—

KM# 8b 50 LIPA
Gold, 20.5 mm. **Obv:** Denomination above crowned arms on half braid **Rev:** Flowers, date below **Designer:** Kuzma Kovacic

Date	Mintage	F	VF	XF	Unc	BU
1993 Proof, Rare	5	—	—	—	—	—

KM# 19 50 LIPA
3.6500 g., Nickel Plated Steel, 20.5 mm. **Obv:** Denomination above crowned arms on half braid **Rev:** Flowers, date below **Rev. Legend:** DEGENIA VELEBITICA **Designer:** Kuzma Kovacic

Date	Mintage	F	VF	XF	Unc	BU
1994.	2,001,131	—	—	0.80	2.50	—

Date	Mintage	F	VF	XF	Unc	BU
1994. Proof	4,000	Value: 4.00				
1996.	2,000,000	—	—	0.80	2.50	—
1996. Proof	5,000	Value: 4.00				
1998.	2,000,000	—	—	0.80	2.50	—
1998. Proof	2,000	Value: 4.50				
2000.	3,500,000	—	—	0.80	2.50	—
2000. Proof	1,000	Value: 5.00				

KM# 39 50 LIPA

3.6500 g., Nickel Plated Steel, 20.5 mm. **Subject:** European soccer **Obv:** Denomination above crowned arms on half braid **Rev:** Checkered shield, soccer ball at bottom, date above **Designer:** Kuzma Kovacic

Date	Mintage	F	VF	XF	Unc	BU
1996.	900,000	—	—	0.40	1.50	—
1996. Proof	5,000	Value: 4.00				

KM# 9b KUNA

Gold **Obv:** Marten back of numeral, arms divide branches below **Rev:** Nightingale left

Date	Mintage	F	VF	XF	Unc	BU
1993 Proof, rare	5	—	—	—	—	—

KM# 9.1 KUNA

5.0000 g., Copper-Nickel, 22.5 mm. **Obv:** Marten back of numeral, arms divide branches below **Rev:** Nightingale left, two dates **Designer:** Kusma Kovacic

Date	Mintage	F	VF	XF	Unc	BU
1993	49,913,770	—	—	0.75	1.65	—
1993 Proof	17,000	Value: 3.00				
1995. With dot	32,707,000	—	—	0.75	1.65	—
1995. With dot, Proof	4,000	Value: 3.50				
1997.	6,205,000	—	—	0.75	1.65	—
1997. Proof	2,000	Value: 4.00				

KM# 9.2 KUNA

4.9300 g., Copper-Nickel, 22.5 mm. **Obv:** Crowned arms flanked by sprays, denomination above on marten **Rev:** Nightingale, left, '1994' above, date below **Edge:** Reeded

Date	Mintage	F	VF	XF	Unc	BU
1999.	18,000,000	—	—	0.75	1.65	—
1999. Proof	2,000	Value: 4.00				

KM# 9.1a KUNA

Silver, 22.5 mm. **Obv:** Marten back of numeral, arms divide branches below **Rev:** Nightingale left **Designer:** Kuzma Kovacic

Date	Mintage	F	VF	XF	Unc	BU
1993 Proof, Rare	5	—	—	—	—	—

KM# 9.1b KUNA

Gold, 22.5 mm. **Obv:** Marten back of numeral, arms divide branches below **Rev:** Nightingale left **Designer:** Kuzma Kovacic

Date	Mintage	F	VF	XF	Unc	BU
1993 Proof, Rare	5	—	—	—	—	—

KM# 20.1 KUNA

5.0000 g., Copper-Nickel, 22.5 mm. **Obv:** Marten back of numeral, arms divide branches below **Rev:** Nightingale left, date below **Rev. Legend:** Error spelling "LUSCINNIA" MEGARHYNCHOS **Designer:** Kuzma Kovacic **Note:** Formerly KM-20

Date	Mintage	F	VF	XF	Unc	BU
1994.	2,000,133	—	—	0.50	2.00	—
1994. Proof	4,000	Value: 4.00				

KM# 20.2 KUNA

5.0000 g., Copper-Nickel, 22.5 mm. **Obv:** Marten back of numeral, arms divide branches below **Rev:** Nightingale left, date below **Rev. Legend:** Correct spelling "LUSCINIA" MEGARHYNCHOS **Edge:** Reeded **Designer:** Kuzma Kovacic

Date	Mintage	F	VF	XF	Unc	BU
1996.	2,000,000	—	—	1.00	3.00	—
1996. Proof	5,000	Value: 5.00				
1998.	2,000,000	—	—	1.00	3.00	—
1998. Proof	1,000	Value: 5.00				
2000.	2,000,000	—	—	1.00	3.00	—
2000. Proof	1,000	Value: 5.00				

KM# 40 KUNA

Copper-Nickel, 22.5 mm. **Subject:** Olympics **Obv:** Marten back of numeral, arms divide branches below **Rev:** Olympic logo, torch above, date below

Date	Mintage	F	VF	XF	Unc	BU
1996.	1,000,000	—	—	0.40	1.50	—
1996. Proof	5,000	Value: 3.00				

KM# 10 2 KUNE

6.2000 g., Copper-Nickel, 24.5 mm. **Obv:** Marten back of numeral, arms divide branches below **Rev:** Bluefin tuna right, date below **Designer:** Kuzma Kovacic

Date	Mintage	F	VF	XF	Unc	BU
1993	19,774,119	—	—	1.00	2.00	—
1993 Proof	17,000	Value: 4.50				
1995. With dot	9,304,000	—	—	1.00	2.00	—
1995. With dot, Proof	4,000	Value: 5.50				
1997.	1,305,000	—	—	1.00	2.00	—
1997. Proof	1,000	Value: 6.00				
1999.	2,500,000	—	—	1.00	2.00	—
1999. Proof	2,000	Value: 6.00				

KM# 10a 2 KUNE

Silver, 24.5 mm. **Obv:** Marten back of numeral, arms divide branches below **Rev:** Tuna right, date below **Designer:** Kuzma Kovacic

Date	Mintage	F	VF	XF	Unc	BU
1993 Proof, Rare	5	—	—	—	—	—

KM# 10b 2 KUNE

Gold, 24.5 mm. **Obv:** Marten back of numeral, arms divide branches below **Rev:** Tuna right, date below **Designer:** Kuzma Kovacic

Date	Mintage	F	VF	XF	Unc	BU
1993 Proof, Rare	5	—	—	—	—	—

KM# 21 2 KUNE

6.2000 g., Copper-Nickel, 24.5 mm. **Obv:** Marten back of numeral, arms divide branches below **Rev:** Bluefin tuna right, date below **Rev. Legend:** THUNNUS - THYNNUS **Designer:** Kuzma Kovacic

Date	Mintage	F	VF	XF	Unc	BU
1994.	2,000,758	—	—	1.50	3.00	—
1994. Proof	4,000	Value: 5.00				
1996.	2,000,000	—	—	1.50	3.00	—
1996. Proof	5,000	Value: 4.50				
1998.	2,000,000	—	—	1.50	3.00	—
1998. Proof	1,000	Value: 5.50				
2000.	2,000,000	—	—	1.50	3.00	—
2000. Proof	1,000	Value: 6.00				

KM# 22 2 KUNE

6.2000 g., Copper-Nickel, 24.5 mm. **Obv:** Marten back of numeral, arms divide branches below **Rev:** Bluefin tuna right, date below **Rev. Legend:** FAO **Designer:** Kuzma Kovacic

Date	Mintage	F	VF	XF	Unc	BU
ND(1995)	500,000	—	—	0.60	2.00	—
ND(1995) Proof	5,000	Value: 5.50				

KM# 11 5 KUNA

7.5000 g., Copper-Nickel, 26.7 mm. **Obv:** Marten back of numeral, arms divide branches below **Rev:** Brown bear left, date below

Date	Mintage	F	VF	XF	Unc	BU
1993	4,989,300	—	—	1.50	4.00	6.00
1993 Proof	17,000	Value: 6.50				
1995. With dot	3,724,000	—	—	1.50	4.00	6.00
1995. With dot, Proof	4,000	Value: 7.00				
1997.	1,165,000	—	—	1.50	4.00	6.00
1997. Proof	2,000	Value: 7.50				
1999.	4,000,000	—	—	1.50	4.00	6.00
1999. Proof	2,000	Value: 7.50				

KM# 11a 5 KUNA

Silver, 26.7 mm. **Obv:** Marten back of numeral, arms divide branches below **Rev:** Brown bear left, date below

Date	Mintage	F	VF	XF	Unc	BU
1993 Proof, Rare	5	—	—	—	—	—

KM# 11b 5 KUNA

Gold, 26.7 mm. **Obv:** Marten back of numeral, arms divide branches below **Rev:** Brown bear left, date below

Date	Mintage	F	VF	XF	Unc	BU
1993 Proof, Rare	5	—	—	—	—	—

KM# 23 5 KUNA

Copper-Nickel, 26.7 mm. **Obv:** Marten back of numeral, arms divide branches below **Rev:** Brown bear left, date below **Rev. Legend:** URSUS ARCTOS

Date	Mintage	F	VF	XF	Unc	BU
1994.	2,001,442	—	—	2.00	4.00	6.00
1994. Proof	4,000	Value: 7.50				
1996.	2,000,000	—	—	2.00	4.00	6.00
1996. Proof	5,000	Value: 7.50				
1998. Proof	—	Value: 7.50				
2000.	7,700,000	—	—	2.00	4.00	6.00
2000. Proof	1,000	Value: 9.00				

KM# 24 5 KUNA

Copper-Nickel, 26.7 mm. **Subject:** 500th Anniversary - Senj **Obv:** Denomination on square divides arms above from shield below, circle surrounds **Rev:** Anniversary dates on symbol within circle

Date	Mintage	F	VF	XF	Unc	BU
1994.	1,000,000	—	—	—	3.50	—
1994. Proof	5,000	Value: 8.00				

KM# 24a 5 KUNA

Silver, 26.7 mm. **Subject:** 500th Anniversary - Senj **Obv:** Denomination on square divides arms above from shield below, circle surrounds **Rev:** Anniversary dates on symbols within circle

Date	Mintage	F	VF	XF	Unc	BU
1994. Proof	500	Value: 270				

Note: Reported not confirmed

KM# 24b 5 KUNA

12.0000 g., 0.9000 Gold, 26.7 mm. **Subject:** 500th Anniversary - Senj **Obv:** Denomination on square divides arms above from shield below, circle surrounds **Rev:** Anniversary dates on symbols within circle

Date	Mintage	F	VF	XF	Unc	BU
1994	200	—	—	—	450	—

KM# 47 25 KUNA
Bi-Metallic Brass center in Copper-Nickel ring, 31 mm. **Subject:** Danube Border Region **Obv:** 3D denomination on marten within circle, crowned arms below divide branches **Rev:** Regional map, date below **Shape:** 12-sided

Date	Mintage	F	VF	XF	Unc	BU
1997.	300,000	—	—	—	11.50	—
1997. Proof	2,000	Value: 22.50				

KM# 48 25 KUNA
Bi-Metallic Brass center in Copper-Nickel ring, 31 mm. **Subject:** 5th Anniversary - UN Membership **Obv:** 3D denomination on marten within circle, crowned arms divide branches below **Rev:** UN emblem within wreath, date below

Date	Mintage	F	VF	XF	Unc	BU
1997. Proof	2,000	Value: 22.50				
1997.	300,000	—	—	—	11.50	—

KM# 49 25 KUNA
Bi-Metallic Brass center in Copper-Nickel ring, 31 mm. **Subject:** First Croatian Esperanto Congress **Obv:** 3D denomination on marten within circle, crowned arms below divide branches **Rev:** Logo, date below

Date	Mintage	F	VF	XF	Unc	BU
1997. Proof	2,000	Value: 22.50				
1997.	300,000	—	—	—	11.50	—

KM# 63 25 KUNA
Bi-Metallic Brass center in Copper-Nickel ring, 31 mm. **Subject:** Lisbon Expo **Obv:** 3D denomination on marten within circle, crowned arms below divide branches **Rev:** Sailboat, date upper right

Date	Mintage	F	VF	XF	Unc	BU
1998.	300,000	—	—	—	11.50	—
1998. Proof	1,000	Value: 25.00				

KM# 64 25 KUNA
Bi-Metallic Brass center in Copper-Nickel ring, 31 mm. **Subject:** European Union **Obv:** 3D denomination on marten within circle, crowned arms below divide branches **Rev:** 12 stars on a large "E", date below **Edge:** Plain **Shape:** 12-sided

Date	Mintage	F	VF	XF	Unc	BU
1999.	300,000	—	—	—	11.50	—
1999. Proof	1,000	Value: 25.00				

KM# 65 25 KUNA
Bi-Metallic Brass center in Copper-Nickel ring, 31 mm. **Obv:** 3D denomination on marten within circle, crowned arms below divide branches **Rev:** Human fetus within radiant circle, date below **Edge:** Plain **Shape:** 12-sided

Date	Mintage	F	VF	XF	Unc	BU
2000.	300,000	—	—	—	11.50	—
2000. Proof	1,000	Value: 25.00				

KM# 25.1 100 KUNA
15.0000 g., Silver **Subject:** 900th Anniversary - St. Blaza Church **Obv:** Buildings divide arms and denomination **Rev:** Altar at St. Blaza divides dates

Date	Mintage	F	VF	XF	Unc	BU
ND(1994) Proof	3,000	Value: 47.50				

KM# 25.2 100 KUNA
15.0000 g., Silver **Subject:** 900th Anniversary - St. Blaza Church **Obv:** Buildings divide denomination and arms, series II mark added **Rev:** Altar at St. Blaza divides dates

Date	Mintage	F	VF	XF	Unc	BU
ND(1994) Proof	1,000	Value: 75.00				

KM# 26 100 KUNA
33.6300 g., Silver **Rev:** Half-length bust of Pope John Paul II

Date	Mintage	F	VF	XF	Unc	BU
1994. Proof	10,000	Value: 65.00				

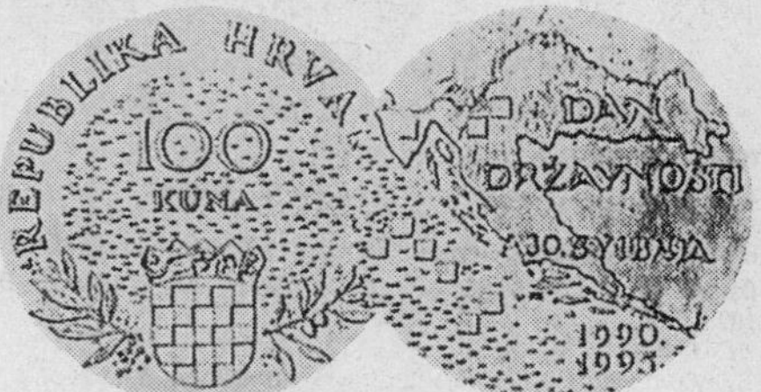

KM# 27 100 KUNA
20.0000 g., 0.9250 Silver .5947 oz. ASW **Subject:** 5th Anniversary of Independence

Date	Mintage	F	VF	XF	Unc	BU
ND(1995) Proof	6,000	Value: 35.00				

KM# 50 100 KUNA
20.0000 g., 0.9250 Silver .5947 oz. ASW **Subject:** City of Split **Obv:** Towered building, denomination at left **Rev:** Ancient depiction of king on throne, dates at left

Date	Mintage	F	VF	XF	Unc	BU
ND(1995) Proof	2,950	Value: 32.00				

KM# 41 100 KUNA
20.0000 g., 0.9250 Silver .5947 oz. ASW **Subject:** Olympics **Obv:** Sailboat racing, denomination above **Rev:** Wheelchair-bound javelin thrower, crowned arms above

Date	Mintage	F	VF	XF	Unc	BU
1996. Proof	2,000	Value: 40.00				

KM# 42 100 KUNA
20.0000 g., 0.9250 Silver .5947 oz. ASW **Subject:** Olympics **Obv:** Rowing, denomination above **Rev:** Water polo player, crowned arms above

Date	Mintage	F	VF	XF	Unc	BU
1996. Proof	2,000	Value: 40.00				

KM# 28 150 KUNA
24.0000 g., 0.9250 Silver .7136 oz. ASW **Subject:** 5th Anniversary of Independence **Obv:** Denomination below crowned arms **Rev:** Assorted symbols on portioned background

Date	Mintage	F	VF	XF	Unc	BU
1995. Proof	5,000	Value: 42.50				

KM# 43 150 KUNA
24.0000 g., 0.9250 Silver .7136 oz. ASW **Subject:** Olympics **Obv:** Gymnast, denomination at right **Rev:** Basketball players, crowned arms above

Date	Mintage	F	VF	XF	Unc	BU
1996. Proof	2,000	Value: 42.50				

KM# 44 150 KUNA
24.0000 g., 0.9250 Silver .7136 oz. ASW **Subject:** Olympics **Obv:** Table tennis and paddle, denomination at top **Rev:** Marksmanship eye design, crowned arms divide date above, circle surrounds

Date	Mintage	F	VF	XF	Unc	BU
1996.	2,000	Value: 42.50				

KM# 56 150 KUNA
24.0000 g., 0.9250 Silver .7136 oz. ASW **Subject:** 800th Anniversary - City of Osijek **Obv:** Crowned arms above denomination **Rev:** City view

Date	Mintage	F	VF	XF	Unc	BU
ND(1996) Proof	1,000	Value: 40.00				

KM# 59 150 KUNA
24.0000 g., 0.9250 Silver .7136 oz. ASW **Obv:** Denomination above arms, date divided below **Rev:** Bust left

Date	Mintage	F	VF	XF	Unc	BU
1997. Proof	10,000	Value: 40.00				

KM# 67 150 KUNA
24.0000 g., 0.9250 Silver 0.7137 oz. ASW, 37 mm. **Subject:** Vukovar **Obv:** Ceramic container, arms below **Rev:** Courtyard, date at right **Edge:** Plain

Date	Mintage	F	VF	XF	Unc	BU
1997. Proof	1,000	Value: 35.00				

KM# 69 150 KUNA
24.0000 g., 0.9250 Silver 0.7137 oz. ASW, 37 mm. **Obv:** Wild flowers, denomination at right, arms at top **Rev:** Eagle on branch **Edge:** Plain

Date	Mintage	F	VF	XF	Unc	BU
1997. Proof	1,000	Value: 40.00				

KM# 75 150 KUNA
24.0000 g., 0.9250 Silver 0.7137 oz. ASW, 37 mm. **Subject:** 150 Years of Croatian as an Official Language **Obv:** Two hands writing **Rev:** Old document **Edge:** Plain

Date	Mintage	F	VF	XF	Unc	BU
1997. Proof	1,000	Value: 40.00				

KM# 73 150 KUNA
24.0000 g., 0.9250 Silver 0.7137 oz. ASW, 37 mm. **Obv:** Small national arms above religious arms and value **Rev:** Cardinal Stepinac (1898-1960) right **Edge:** Plain

Date	Mintage	F	VF	XF	Unc	BU
1998. Proof	2,000	Value: 32.50				

KM# 29.1 200 KUNA
33.6300 g., 0.9250 Silver .9999 oz. ASW **Obv:** St. Marka Church **Rev:** Portal of St. Marka Church

Date	Mintage	F	VF	XF	Unc	BU
ND(1994) Proof	3,000	Value: 75.00				

KM# 29.2 200 KUNA
33.6300 g., 0.9250 Silver .9999 oz. ASW **Obv:** St. Marka Church, Series II mark added **Rev:** Portal of St. Marka Church

Date	Mintage	F	VF	XF	Unc	BU
ND(1994) Proof	1,000	Value: 90.00				

KM# 30 200 KUNA
33.6300 g., 0.9250 Silver .9999 oz. ASW **Subject:** 5th Anniversary of Independence

Date	Mintage	F	VF	XF	Unc	BU
ND(1995) Proof	4,000	Value: 75.00				

KM# 51 200 KUNA
33.6300 g., 0.9250 Silver .9999 oz. ASW **Subject:** Spalatum **Obv:** Diocletian's palace, denomination and arms above **Rev:** Sarcophagus, two dates above

Date	Mintage	F	VF	XF	Unc	BU
ND(1995) Proof	2,950	Value: 45.00				

KM# 45 200 KUNA
33.6300 g., 0.9250 Silver .9999 oz. ASW **Subject:** Olympics **Obv:** High jumper **Rev:** Tennis player

Date	Mintage	F	VF	XF	Unc	BU
ND Proof	2,000	Value: 45.00				

KM# 46 200 KUNA
33.6300 g., 0.9250 Silver .9999 oz. ASW **Subject:** Olympics **Obv:** Diving swimmers, denomination above **Rev:** Basketball game, crowned arms above

Date	Mintage	F	VF	XF	Unc	BU
1996. Proof	2,000	Value: 45.00				

KM# 54 200 KUNA
33.6300 g., 0.9250 Silver .9999 oz. ASW **Subject:** University in Zadar **Obv:** Circle of arches, denomination at top, arms below **Rev:** Saint reading within circle, dates below

Date	Mintage	F	VF	XF	Unc	BU
ND(1996) Proof	1,000	Value: 55.00				

KM# 57 200 KUNA
33.6300 g., 0.9250 Silver .9999 oz. ASW **Subject:** 500th Anniversary - City of Osijek **Obv:** National arms above denomination **Rev:** City view

Date	Mintage	F	VF	XF	Unc	BU
ND(1996) Proof	1,000	Value: 52.00				

KM# 60 200 KUNA
33.6300 g., 0.9250 Silver .9999 oz. ASW **Obv:** Denomination above national arms **Rev:** Bust left

Date	Mintage	F	VF	XF	Unc	BU
1997. Proof	5,000	Value: 45.00				

KM# 71 200 KUNA
33.6300 g., 0.9250 Silver 1.0001 oz. ASW, 40 mm. **Obv:** Wild flowers **Rev:** Three black storks **Edge:** Plain

Date	Mintage	F	VF	XF	Unc	BU
1997. Proof	1,000	Value: 45.00				

KM# 76 200 KUNA
33.6300 g., 0.9250 Silver 1.0001 oz. ASW, 40 mm. **Obv:** National arms above a page of illuminated text, denomination below **Rev:** Juraj Julija Klovic, 1498-1578, looking right **Edge:** Plain

Date	Mintage	F	VF	XF	Unc	BU
1998. Proof	2,000	Value: 45.00				

KM# 77 200 KUNA
33.6300 g., 0.9250 Silver 1.0001 oz. ASW, 40 mm. **Obv:** National arms and value above book, quill and oil lamp **Rev:** Ivana Brlic Mazuranic, seated looking right **Edge:** Plain

Date	Mintage	F	VF	XF	Unc	BU
1998. Proof	2,000	Value: 45.00				

KM# 80 200 KUNA
33.6300 g., 0.9250 Silver 1.0001 oz. ASW **Obv:** Cakovec old town view **Rev:** Katarina Zrinska **Edge:** Plain

Date	Mintage	F	VF	XF	Unc	BU
1999 Proof	2,000	Value: 45.00				

KM# 81 200 KUNA
33.6300 g., 0.9250 Silver 1.0001 oz. ASW **Obv:** Aquarelle painting **Rev:** Zlava Raskaj

Date	Mintage	F	VF	XF	Unc	BU
2000 Proof	2,000	Value: 45.00				

KM# 31.1 500 KUNA
3.5000 g., 0.9860 Gold .1109 oz. AGW **Obv:** Izborna Cathedral, denomination below **Rev:** Arms at top and bottom, cherubs flank

Date	Mintage	F	VF	XF	Unc	BU
1994. Proof	1,000	Value: 200				

KM# 31.2 500 KUNA
3.5000 g., 0.9860 Gold .1109 oz. AGW **Obv:** Izborna Cathedral, Series II added **Rev:** Arms at top and bottom, cherubs flank

Date	Mintage	F	VF	XF	Unc	BU
1994. Proof	1,000	Value: 185				

KM# 32 500 KUNA
3.5000 g., 0.9860 Gold .1109 oz. AGW **Subject:** 5th Anniversary of Independence

Date	Mintage	F	VF	XF	Unc	BU
1995. Proof	4,000	Value: 175				

KM# 52 500 KUNA
3.5000 g., 0.9860 Gold .1109 oz. AGW **Subject:** City of Split **Obv:** Towered building, denomination at left **Rev:** Ancient depiction of king on throne, dates at left

Date	Mintage	F	VF	XF	Unc	BU
ND(1995) Proof	3,950	Value: 150				

KM# 55 500 KUNA
3.5000 g., 0.9860 Gold .1109 oz. AGW **Subject:** University of Zadar **Obv:** Circle of arches, denomination at top, arms below **Rev:** Saint reading within circle, dates below

Date	Mintage	F	VF	XF	Unc	BU
ND(1996) Proof	1,000	Value: 185				

KM# 58 500 KUNA
3.5000 g., 0.9860 Gold .1109 oz. AGW **Subject:** 800th Anniversary - City of Osijek **Obv:** Crowned arms, denomination below **Rev:** City view

Date	Mintage	F	VF	XF	Unc	BU
ND(1996) Proof	1,000	Value: 185				

KM# 68 500 KUNA
3.5000 g., 0.9860 Gold 0.111 oz. AGW, 18 mm. **Subject:** Vukovar **Obv:** Ceramic container, denomination at upper right **Rev:** Courtyard, date at right **Edge:** Plain

Date	Mintage	F	VF	XF	Unc	BU
1997. Proof	2,000	Value: 115				

KM# 70 500 KUNA
3.5000 g., 0.9860 Gold 0.111 oz. AGW, 18 mm. **Obv:** Wild flowers, denomination at right, arms above **Rev:** Eagle on branch **Edge:** Plain

Date	Mintage	F	VF	XF	Unc	BU
1997. Proof	1,000	Value: 125				

KM# 74 500 KUNA
3.5000 g., 0.9860 Gold 0.111 oz. AGW, 18 mm. **Obv:** Small national arms above religious arms and value, date divided **Rev:** Bust of Cardinal Stepinac (1898-1960) right **Edge:** Plain

Date	Mintage	F	VF	XF	Unc	BU
1998. Proof	2,000	Value: 115				

KM# 82 500 KUNA
3.5000 g., 0.9860 Gold 0.111 oz. AGW **Subject:** 10th Anniversary of Parliament **Obv:** View of session **Rev:** Parliament building

Date	Mintage	F	VF	XF	Unc	BU
ND (2000) Proof	500	Value: 125				

KM# 33 1000 KUNA
7.0000 g., 0.9860 Gold .2218 oz. AGW **Obv:** Crowned arms divides date above denomination **Rev:** Half-length portrait of Pope John Paul II, looking left

Date	Mintage	F	VF	XF	Unc	BU
1994. Proof	4,000	Value: 285				

KM# 34 1000 KUNA
7.0000 g., 0.9860 Gold .2218 oz. AGW **Subject:** 5th Anniversary of Independence **Obv:** Arms divide sprays below denomination, dotted background **Rev:** Map, inscription, and dates, dotted background

Date	Mintage	F	VF	XF	Unc	BU
ND(1995) Proof	4,000	Value: 285				

KM# 53 1000 KUNA
7.0000 g., 0.9860 Gold .2218 oz. AGW **Subject:** Spalatum **Obv:** Diocletian's palace, denomination and arms above **Rev:** Sarcophagus, dates above

Date	Mintage	F	VF	XF	Unc	BU
ND(1995) Proof	1,950	Value: 285				

KM# 72 1000 KUNA
7.0000 g., 0.9860 Gold 0.2219 oz. AGW, 22 mm. **Obv:** Wild flowers, arms above, denomination at right **Rev:** Three Black Storks **Edge:** Plain

Date	Mintage	F	VF	XF	Unc	BU
1997. Proof	1,000	Value: 275				

KM# 61 1000 KUNA
7.0000 g., 0.9860 Gold 0.2219 oz. AGW, 22 mm. **Obv:** National arms **Rev:** Dr. Tudman **Edge:** Plain **Note:** Death of Dr. Tudman

Date	Mintage	F	VF	XF	Unc	BU
1997. Proof	3,000	Value: 245				

TRADE COINAGE

KM# 35 DUCAT
3.5000 g., 0.9860 Gold .1109 oz. AGW, 20 mm. **Obv:** Crowned arms with supporters, denomination below **Rev:** Ruder Boskovic bust at left facing, dates at left **Designer:** Kuzma Kovacic

Date	Mintage	F	VF	XF	Unc	BU
1994 Proof	5,000	Value: 160				

KM# 62 DUCAT
3.5000 g., 0.9860 Gold .1109 oz. AGW **Subject:** Liberation of Knin **Obv:** Crowned arms, denomination below **Rev:** Regional view within circle

Date	Mintage	F	VF	XF	Unc	BU
ND(1995)	3,000	—	—	—	160	—

PATTERNS

Including off metal strikes

KM#	Date	Mintage	Identification	Mkt Val
Pn5	1934	—	5 Kuna. Bronze.	350
Pn6	1934	—	5 Kuna. Copper Nickel.	400
Pn7	1934	—	5 Kuna. 0.9000 Silver.	450
Pn8	1934	—	5 Kuna. Zinc.	—
Pn9	1941	—	25 Banica. Zinc. With initials. 16 or 17 mm.	—
Pn10	1941	—	25 Banica. Zinc. Without initials. 16 or 17 mm.	—
Pn11	1941	—	25 Banica. Nickel. 16 or 17 mm.	—
Pn12	1941	—	25 Banica. Gold. 16 or 17 mm.	3,500
Pn13	1941	—	50 Banica. Nickel.	—
Pn14	1941	—	50 Banica. Zinc.	—
Pn15	1941	—	50 Banica. Silver.	—
Pn16	1941	—	50 Banica. Gold.	4,500
Pn17	1941	—	Kuna. Zinc.	—
Pn18	1941	—	Kuna. Copper.	—
Pn19	1941	—	Kuna. Aluminum.	175
Pn20	1941	—	Kuna. Nickel.	—
Pn21	1941	—	Kuna. Silver.	450
Pn22	1941	—	Kuna. Gold.	3,500
Pn23	1941	—	Kuna. Silver. 4.3800 g. 20 mm. Without undulating background.	—
Pn24	1941	—	2 Kune. Aluminum.	—
Pn25	1941	—	2 Kune. Nickel.	—
Pn26	1941	—	2 Kune. Silver. 4.8900 g. 22 mm.	—
Pn27	1941	—	2 Kune. Gold.	4,500
Pn28	1941	—	10 Kuna. Similar to Pn 19. 10 Kuna above shield within wheat border. Reported, not confirmed.	—
Pn29	1941	—	500 Kuna. Aluminum. Pn26. Similar to B3.	—
Pn30	1941	—	500 Kuna. Copper Nickel. Pn 26. Similar to B3.	—
Pn31	1941	—	500 Kuna. Aluminum. Chain.	—
Pn32	1941	—	500 Kuna. Aluminum-Bronze.	—
Pn33	1941	—	500 Kuna. Copper.	—
Pn34	1941	—	500 Kuna. Copper Nickel.	—
Pn35	1941	—	500 Kuna. Silver.	—

KM#	Date	Mintage	Identification	Mkt Val
Pn36	1941	—	500 Kuna. Aluminum. 1.6700 g. 22 mm. Head left, date below. Denomination above arms, wheat chain surrounds.	600
Pn37	1941	—	500 Kuna. Gold. 27 mm. Chain. KMA3.	—
Pn38	1941	—	500 Kuna. Nickel. 22 mm. KMA3.	—
Pn39	1941	—	500 Kuna. Aluminum. KMA3.	—
Pn40	1941	—	500 Kuna. Brass. 7.1100 g. 23 mm. KMA3.	400
Pn41	1943	—	5 Kuna.	—
Pn42	1943	—	10 Kuna.	—

MINT SETS

KM#	Date	Mintage	Identification	Issue Price	Mkt Val
MS1	1993 (9)	50,000	KM3-11	8.00	14.00

PROOF SETS

KM#	Date	Mintage	Identification	Issue Price	Mkt Val
PS1	1993 (9)	17,000	KM3-11	15.20	28.50
PS2	1993 (9)	10	KM3a-11a, rare	—	—
PS3	1993 (9)	5	KM3b-11b, rare	—	—
PS4	1994 (9)	4,000	KM12, 14-17, 19-21, 23	15.20	32.50
PS5	1994 (3)	500	KM21, 23, 24a	—	280
PS6	1994 (3)	250	KM21, 23, 24b	—	475
PS7	1994 (2)	1,000	KM26, 33	240	360
PS8	ND (1994) (3)	250	KM25.1, 29.1, 31.1	154	325
PS9	ND (1994) (3)	500	KM25.2, 29.2, 31.2	154	350
PS10	1994-95 (2)	1,000	KM22, 25.2	—	85.00
PS11	1994-95 (4)	—	KM13, 18, 22, 24	—	40.00
PS12	1994-96 (9)	5,000	KM13, 18, 22, 24, 36-40	8.00	33.50
PS13	1995 (9)	4,000	KM3-11	15.20	34.50
PS14	1995 (5)	—	KM27, 28, 30, 32, 34	—	625
PS15	ND (1995) (4)	1,000	KM50-53	375	525
PS16	ND (1995) (2)	1,000	KM50, 51	62.50	75.00
PS17	ND (1995) (2)	1,000	KM50, 52	125	190
PS18	ND (1995) (2)	1,000	KM51, 53	250	345
PS19	ND (1995) (2)	1,000	KM52, 53	312	445
PS20	ND (1995) (5)	1,000	KM 27, 28, 30, 32, 34	406	620
PS21	ND (1995) (3)	2,000	KM 27, 30, 34	270	400
PS22	1995 (2)	2,000	KM28, 32	135	225
PS23	1996 (6)	1,000	KM41-46	187	265
PS24	1996 (9)	5,000	KM12, 14-17, 19-21, 23	8.00	32.00
PS25	ND (1996) (2)	500	KM54-55	146	250
PS26	ND (1996) (3)	300	KM56-58	177	285
PS27	1997 (3)	300	KM59-61	281	370
PS28	1997 (2)	300	KM#69, 70	141	170
PS29	1997 (2)	300	KM#71, 72	260	325
PS30	1997 (4)	300	KM#69, 70, 71, 72	401	500
PS31	1998 (2)	500	KM#73, 74	141	150

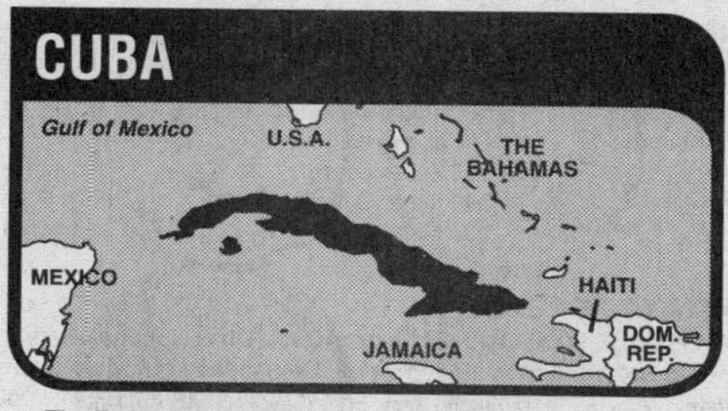

The Republic of Cuba, situated at the northern edge of the Caribbean Sea about 90 miles (145 km.) south of Florida, has an area of 42,804 sq. mi. (110,860 sq. km.) and a population of *11.2 million. Capital: Havana. The Cuban economy is based on the cultivation and refining of sugar, which provides 80 percent of export earnings.

Discovered by Columbus in 1492 and settled by Diego Velasquez in the early 1500s, Cuba remained a Spanish possession until 1898, except for a brief British occupancy of Havana in 1762-63. Cuban attempts to gain freedom were crushed, even while Spain was granting independence to its other American possessions. Ten years of warfare, 1868-78, between Spanish troops and Cuban rebels exacted guarantees of rights which were never implemented. The final revolt, begun in 1895, evoked American sympathy, and with the aid of U.S. troops independence was proclaimed on May 20, 1902. Fulgencio Batista seized the government in 1952 and established a dictatorship. Opposition to Batista, led by Fidel Castro, drove him into exile on Jan. 1, 1959. A communist-type, 25-member collective leadership headed by Castro was inaugurated in March, 1962.

RULERS

Spanish, until 1898

MINT MARKS

Key - Havana, 1977-

MONETARY SYSTEM

100 Centavos = 1 Peso

FIRST REPUBLIC

1902 - 1962

DECIMAL COINAGE

KM# 9.1 CENTAVO

Copper-Nickel **Obv:** National arms within wreath, denomination below **Rev:** Roman denomination within circle of star, date below, 2.5 G. 250M

Date	Mintage	F	VF	XF	Unc	BU
1915	9,396,000	—	1.00	2.00	40.00	200
1915 Proof	200	Value: 450				
1916	9,318,000	—	1.00	2.00	50.00	175
1916 Proof	104	Value: 950				
1920	19,378,000	—	1.50	3.00	50.00	175
1938	2,000,000	—	2.50	6.00	75.00	210

KM# 9.2 CENTAVO

Copper-Nickel **Obv:** National arms within wreath, denomination below **Rev:** Roman denomination within circle of star, 2.5 GR. 250M

Date	Mintage	F	VF	XF	Unc	BU
1946	50,000,000	—	0.20	1.00	4.00	60.00
1961	100,000,000	—	0.25	0.60	1.50	5.00

KM# 9.2a CENTAVO

Brass **Obv:** National arms within wreath, denomination below **Rev:** Roman denomination within circle of star, 2.3 GR. 300M

Date	Mintage	F	VF	XF	Unc	BU
1943	20,000,000	—	0.40	1.25	7.00	75.00

KM# 26 CENTAVO

Brass, 17 mm. **Subject:** Birth of Jose Marti Centennial **Obv:** Star on triangular shield divides denomination **Rev:** Bust, left **Designer:** Esteban Valderrama

Date	Mintage	F	VF	XF	Unc	BU
1953	50,000,000	—	0.15	0.75	12.00	60.00
1953 Proof; Rare	100	—	—	—	—	—

KM# 30 CENTAVO

Copper-Nickel, 17 mm. **Obv:** Star on triangular shield divides denomination **Rev:** Bust of Jose Marti left, date at left **Designer:** Esteban Valderrama

Date	Mintage	F	VF	XF	Unc	BU
1958	50,000,000	—	0.15	0.75	45.00	140

KM# A10 2 CENTAVOS

Copper-Nickel **Obv:** National arms within wreath, denomination below **Rev:** Roman denomination within circle of star, date below

Date	Mintage	F	VF	XF	Unc	BU
1915	6,090,000	—	1.25	3.00	40.00	175
1915 Proof	150	Value: 500				
1916	5,322,000	—	1.25	3.50	45.00	180
1916 Proof	100	Value: 1,000				

KM# 11.1 5 CENTAVOS

Copper-Nickel, 21 mm. **Obv:** National arms within wreath above denomination **Rev:** Roman denomination within circle of star, date below, 5.0 G. 250M

Date	Mintage	F	VF	XF	Unc	BU
1915	5,096,000	—	1.50	4.00	50.00	200
1915 Proof	150	Value: 600				
1916	1,714,000	—	1.50	5.00	50.00	210
1916 Proof	100	Value: 1,000				
1920	10,000,000	—	1.50	4.50	60.00	225

KM# 11.2 5 CENTAVOS

Copper-Nickel, 21 mm. **Obv:** National arms within wreath, denomination below **Rev:** Roman denomination within circle of star, 5.0 G 250M **Note:** No period after G

Date	Mintage	F	VF	XF	Unc	BU
1920	—	—	1.75	5.00	100	400

KM# 11.3 5 CENTAVOS

Copper-Nickel, 21 mm. **Obv:** National arms within wreath, denomination below **Rev:** Roman denomination within circle of star, date below, 5 GR. 250M **Note:** Prev. KM #11.2.

Date	Mintage	F	VF	XF	Unc	BU
1943	Inc. above	7.50	15.00	20.00	35.00	70.00
1946	40,000,000	—	0.50	0.75	5.00	45.00
1960	20,000,000	—	0.75	1.25	15.00	70.00
1961	70,000,000	—	0.15	0.40	1.00	2.00

KM# 11.3a 5 CENTAVOS

Brass **Rev:** 4.6 GR. 300M **Note:** Prev. KM#11.2a.

Date	Mintage	F	VF	XF	Unc	BU
1943	6,000,000	—	1.00	3.50	20.00	60.00

KM# A12 10 CENTAVOS

2.5000 g., 0.9000 Silver .0723 oz. ASW, 17.8 mm. **Obv:** National arms within wreath, denomination below **Rev:** Star

Date	Mintage	F	VF	XF	Unc	BU
1915	5,690,000	1.50	4.00	12.00	100	450
1915 Proof	125	Value: 1,500				
1916	560,000	7.00	20.00	75.00	500	2,000
1916 Proof	50	Value: 1,750				
1920	3,090,000	2.50	6.00	20.00	200	650
1948	5,120,000	—	1.25	2.00	9.00	20.00
1949	9,880,000	—	1.25	1.75	9.00	20.00

KM# 23 10 CENTAVOS

2.5000 g., 0.9000 Silver .0723 oz. ASW, 18 mm. **Subject:** 50th Year of Republic **Obv:** Two dates left of flag, tower at right, denomination below **Rev:** Star above tree, spoked wheel below **Designer:** Juan J. Sicre

Date	Mintage	F	VF	XF	Unc	BU
1952	10,000,000	—	1.25	2.50	4.50	20.00

KM# 13.1 20 CENTAVOS

5.0000 g., 0.9000 Silver .1446 oz. ASW, 23 mm. **Obv:** National arms within wreath **Rev:** High relief star

Date	Mintage	F	VF	XF	Unc	BU
1915 Fine reeding	—	3.00	8.00	35.00	245	800
1915 Coarse reeding	—	75.00	225	450	1,000	2,000
1915 Proof	125	Value: 2,000				

KM# 13.2 20 CENTAVOS

5.0000 g., 0.9000 Silver .1446 oz. ASW, 23 mm. **Obv:** National arms within wreath, denomination below **Rev:** Low relief star, date below **Note:** Coins with high relief stars normally exhibit a weak key and palm tree on the reverse. Coins with low relief stars tend to exhibit much more distinct lines in the valleys running towards the center of the star.

Date	Mintage	F	VF	XF	Unc	BU
1915 Coarse reeding	Inc. above	2.25	5.00	15.00	60.00	300
1915 Fine reeding	Inc. above	15.00	50.00	175	1,400	4,000
1916	2,535,000	2.50	6.50	18.00	300	875
1916 Proof	50	Value: 3,200				
1920	6,130,000	—	3.00	8.00	50.00	325
1932	184,000	22.00	75.00	300	1,000	1,750
1948	6,830,000	—	2.00	3.00	10.00	30.00
1949	13,170,000	—	2.00	3.00	10.00	30.00

KM# 24 20 CENTAVOS

5.0000 g., 0.9000 Silver .1446 oz. ASW, 23 mm. **Subject:** 50th Year of Republic **Obv:** Two dates left of flag, tower at right, denomination below **Rev:** Star above tree, spoked wheel below **Designer:** Juan J. Sicre

Date	Mintage	F	VF	XF	Unc	BU
1952	8,700,000	—	2.25	3.00	6.50	35.00

KM# 27 25 CENTAVOS

6.25 g., 0.90 Silver .1808 oz. ASW, 24 mm. **Subject:** Centennial - Birth of Jose Marti **Obv:** Liberty cap on post, denomination at right **Rev:** Bust, left **Designer:** Esteban Valderrama

Date	Mintage	F	VF	XF	Unc	BU
1953	19,000,000	—	2.50	3.50	7.00	20.00
1953 Proof; Rare	—	—	—	—	—	—

KM# 14.1 40 CENTAVOS

10.00 g., 0.9000 Silver .2893 oz. ASW **Obv:** National arms within wreath, denomination below **Rev:** High relief star, date below

Date	Mintage	F	VF	XF	Unc	BU
1915	2,633,000	4.50	12.00	25.00	300	750
1915 Proof	100	Value: 1,300				
1920	540,000	15.00	50.00	120	500	1,300
1920 Proof; Rare	—	—	—	—	—	—

KM# 14.2 40 CENTAVOS

10.0000 g., 0.9000 Silver .2893 oz. ASW **Obv:** National arms within wreath, denomination below **Rev:** Medium relief star, date below

Date	Mintage	F	VF	XF	Unc	BU
1915	Inc. above	30.00	100	275	1,250	1,750

KM# 14.3 40 CENTAVOS

10.0000 g., 0.9000 Silver .2893 oz. ASW **Obv:** National arms within wreath, denomination below **Rev:** Low relief star, date below **Note:** Coins with high relief stars normally exhibit a weak key and palm tree on the reverse. Coins with low relief stars tend to exhibit much more distinct lines in the valleys running towards the center of the star.

Date	Mintage	F	VF	XF	Unc	BU
1915	Inc. above	5.50	15.00	35.00	200	750

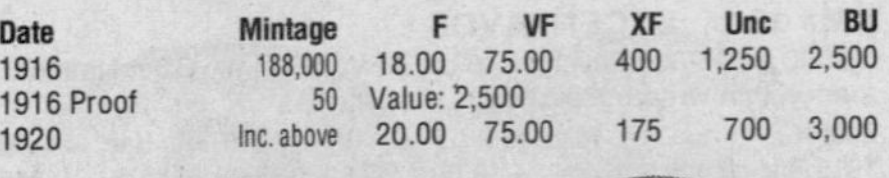

Date	Mintage	F	VF	XF	Unc	BU
1916	188,000	18.00	75.00	400	1,250	2,500
1916 Proof	50	Value: 2,500				
1920	Inc. above	20.00	75.00	175	700	3,000

KM# 25 40 CENTAVOS
10.0000 g., 0.9000 Silver .2893 oz. ASW, 28 mm. **Subject:** 50th Year of Republic **Obv:** Two dates left of flag, tower at right, denomination below **Rev:** Star abovetree, spoked wheel below **Designer:** Juan J. Sicre

Date	Mintage	F	VF	XF	Unc	BU
1952	1,250,000	—	4.00	6.00	25.00	75.00

KM# 28 50 CENTAVOS
12.5000 g., 0.9000 Silver .3617 oz. ASW, 31 mm. **Subject:** Centennial - Birth of Jose Marti **Obv:** Inscription on scroll, denomination at right **Rev:** Bust, left **Designer:** Esteban Valderrama

Date	Mintage	F	VF	XF	Unc	BU
ND(1953)	2,000,000	—	5.00	8.00	20.00	60.00
ND(1953) Proof; Rare	—	—	—	—	—	—

KM# 15.1 PESO
26.7295 g., 0.9000 Silver .7735 oz. ASW **Obv:** National arms within wreath, denomination below **Rev:** High relief star, date below

Date	Mintage	F	VF	XF	Unc	BU
1915	1,976,000	9.00	20.00	60.00	300	2,000
1915 Proof	100	Value: 2,000				

KM# 15.2 PESO
26.7295 g., 0.9000 Silver .7735 oz. ASW **Obv:** National arms within wreath, denomination below **Rev:** Low relief star, date below **Note:** Coins with high relief stars normally exhibit a weak key and palm tree on the reverse. Coins with low relief stars tend to exhibit much more distinct lines in the valleys running towards the center of the star.

Date	Mintage	F	VF	XF	Unc	BU
1915	Inc. above	75.00	225	600	2,500	8,500
1916	843,000	10.00	20.00	70.00	1,000	3,800
1916 Proof	50	Value: 3,500				
1932	3,550,000	—	11.00	28.00	175	750
1933	6,000,000	—	10.00	20.00	125	235
1934	3,000,000	—	11.00	30.00	150	275

KM# 16 PESO
1.6718 g., 0.9000 Gold .0483 oz. AGW **Obv:** National arms within wreath, denomination below **Rev:** Head of Jose Marti right, date below

Date	Mintage	F	VF	XF	Unc	BU
1915	6,850	50.00	100	150	275	600
1915 Proof	140	Value: 1,750				

Date	Mintage	F	VF	XF	Unc	BU
1916	11,000	50.00	100	150	300	700
1916 Proof	100	Value: 2,500				

KM# 22 PESO
26.7295 g., 0.9000 Silver .7735 oz. ASW **Obv:** National arms within wreath at right, denomination at left **Rev:** Laureate bust right, date lower right **Note:** Known as the "ABC" Peso.

Date	Mintage	F	VF	XF	Unc	BU
1934	7,000,000	11.00	25.00	60.00	225	600
1934 Matte proof	—	Value: 5,250				
1935	12,500,000	11.00	25.00	55.00	200	575
1936	16,000,000	11.00	25.00	65.00	250	750
1937	11,500,000	85.00	250	550	1,100	3,500
1938	10,800,000	10.00	22.50	45.00	150	525
1939	9,200,000	10.00	22.50	45.00	150	425

KM# 29 PESO
26.7295 g., 0.9000 Silver .7735 oz. ASW, 38 mm. **Subject:** Centennial of Jose Marti **Obv:** Radiant sun rising above water, denomination below **Rev:** Bust left, two dates **Designer:** Esteban Valderrama

Date	Mintage	F	VF	XF	Unc	BU
ND(1953)	1,000,000	—	BV	12.50	40.00	200
ND(1953) Proof; Rare	—	—	—	—	—	—

KM# 17 2 PESOS
3.3436 g., 0.9000 Gold .0967 oz. AGW **Obv:** National arms within wreath, denomination below **Rev:** Head right, date below

Date	Mintage	F	VF	XF	Unc	BU
1915	10,000	70.00	90.00	175	500	1,000
1915 Proof	100	Value: 3,000				
1916	150,000	65.00	75.00	90.00	200	450
1916 Proof; Rare	8	—	—	—	—	—

KM# 18 4 PESOS
6.6872 g., 0.9000 Gold .1935 oz. AGW **Obv:** National arms within wreath, denomination below **Rev:** Head right, date below

Date	Mintage	F	VF	XF	Unc	BU
1915	6,300	135	175	375	1,100	1,600
1915 Proof	100	Value: 3,000				
1916	129,000	125	135	160	500	750
1916 Proof	90	Value: 4,500				

KM# 19 5 PESOS
8.3592 g., 0.9000 Gold .2419 oz. AGW **Obv:** National arms within wreath, denomination below **Rev:** Head right, date below

Date	Mintage	F	VF	XF	Unc	BU
1915	696,000	—	BV	165	210	475
1915 Proof	—	Value: 3,200				
1916	1,132,000	—	BV	160	200	450
1916 Proof	—	Value: 6,500				

Note: American Numismatic Rarities Eliasberg sale 4-05, Proof 65 realized $13,800.

KM# 20 10 PESOS
16.7185 g., 0.9000 Gold .4838 oz. AGW **Obv:** National arms within wreath, denomination below **Rev:** Head right, date below

Date	Mintage	F	VF	XF	Unc	BU
1915	95,000	—	BV	330	550	800
1915 Proof	—	Value: 7,500				
1916	1,169,000	—	BV	320	400	750
1916 Proof, Rare	—	—	—	—	—	—

Note: David Akers John Jay Pittman sale 8-99 very choice Proof realized $19,550, choice Proof realized $14,950. American Numismatic Rarities Eliasberg sale 4-05, Proof 62 realized $29,900.

KM# 21 20 PESOS
33.4370 g., 0.9000 Gold .9676 oz. AGW **Subject:** Jose Marti **Obv:** National arms within wreath, denomination below **Rev:** Head right, date below

Date	Mintage	F	VF	XF	Unc	BU
1915	57,000	BV	675	800	1,500	3,000
1915 Proof; Rare	—	—	—	—	—	—

Note: David Akers John Jay Pittman sale 8-99 very choice proof 1915 realized $11,500.

Date	Mintage	F	VF	XF	Unc	BU
1916 Proof; Rare	10	—	—	—	—	—

Note: David Akers John Jay Pittman sale 8-99 nearly choice Proof 1916 realized $43,125.

SECOND REPUBLIC
1962 - Present
DECIMAL COINAGE

KM# 33.1 CENTAVO
Aluminum **Obv:** National arms within wreath, denomination below **Rev:** Roman denomination within circle of star, date below **Rev. Legend:** PATRIA Y LIBERTAD

Date	Mintage	F	VF	XF	Unc	BU
1963	200,020,000	—	0.10	0.30	0.60	1.25
1966	50,000,000	—	0.10	0.40	0.80	1.75
1967	—	—	—	—	—	—
1969	50,000,000	—	0.10	0.40	0.80	1.75
1970	50,000,000	—	0.10	0.40	0.80	1.75
1971	49,960,000	—	0.40	0.80	1.50	3.00
1972	100,000,000	—	0.10	0.40	0.80	1.75
1978	50,000,000	—	0.10	0.40	0.80	1.75
1979	100,000,000	—	0.10	0.40	0.80	1.75
1981	—	—	0.10	0.40	0.80	1.75
1982	—	—	0.10	0.40	0.80	1.75

KM# 33.2 CENTAVO
Aluminum **Obv:** National arms within wreath, denomination below **Rev:** Roman denomination within circle of star, date below **Rev. Legend:** PATRIA O MUERTE

Date	Mintage	F	VF	XF	Unc	BU
1983	—	—	0.10	0.40	0.80	1.75
1984	—	—	0.10	0.40	0.80	1.75
1985	—	—	0.10	0.40	0.80	1.75
1986	—	—	0.10	0.40	0.80	1.75
1987	—	—	0.10	0.40	0.80	1.75
1988	—	—	0.10	0.40	0.80	1.75

KM# 33.3 CENTAVO
0.7500 g., Aluminum, 16.76 mm. **Obv:** Cuban arms within wreath, denomination below **Rev:** Roman denomination within circle of star, date below

Date	Mintage	F	VF	XF	Unc	BU
1998	—	—	0.10	0.40	0.80	1.75

KM# 104.2 2 CENTAVOS
Aluminum **Obv:** National arms within wreath, denomination below **Rev:** Roman denomination within circle of star, date below **Note:** Large lettered legends, short edge denticles on both sides of coin

Date	Mintage	F	VF	XF	Unc	BU
1983	Inc. above	—	0.10	0.20	0.50	1.00
1984	—	—	0.10	0.25	1.00	2.00
1985	—	—	0.10	0.20	0.50	1.00
1986	—	—	0.10	0.20	0.50	1.00

KM# 104.1 2 CENTAVOS
Aluminum **Obv:** National arms within wreath, denomination below **Rev:** Roman denomination within circle of star, date below **Note:** Small lettered legends, long edge denticles on both sides of coin

Date	Mintage	F	VF	XF	Unc	BU
1983	3,996,000	—	0.10	0.25	1.00	2.00

KM# 34 5 CENTAVOS
Aluminum, 21 mm. **Obv:** National arms within wreath, denomination below **Rev:** Roman denomination within circle of star, date below

Date	Mintage	F	VF	XF	Unc	BU
1963	80,000,000	—	0.10	0.25	0.75	1.50
1966	50,000,000	—	0.15	0.35	1.50	3.00
1968	—	—	0.15	0.35	1.50	3.00
1969	—	—	0.25	0.50	2.50	5.00
1971	100,020,000	—	0.10	0.25	0.75	1.50
1972	100,000,000	—	0.10	0.25	0.75	1.50

KM# 31 20 CENTAVOS
Copper-Nickel, 24 mm. **Subject:** Jose Marti **Obv:** National arms within wreath, denomination below **Rev:** Bust left, date lower left

Date	Mintage	F	VF	XF	Unc	BU
1962	83,860,000	—	1.00	1.50	3.00	6.00
1968	25,750,000	—	1.25	2.00	4.00	8.00

KM# 35.1 20 CENTAVOS
2.0000 g., Aluminum, 24 mm. **Obv:** Cuban arms within wreath, denomination below **Rev:** Roman denomination within circle of star, date below

Date	Mintage	F	VF	XF	Unc	BU
1969	25,000,000	—	1.00	1.50	2.50	5.00
1970	29,560,000	0.35	1.25	1.75	4.00	—
1971	25,000,000	—	1.00	1.50	2.50	5.00
1972	—	—	1.00	1.50	2.50	5.00

KM# 35.2 20 CENTAVOS
Aluminum, 24 mm. **Obv:** National arms, revised shield **Rev:** Roman denomination within circle of star, date below

Date	Mintage	F	VF	XF	Unc	BU
ND	—	4.00	7.00	10.00	—	—

KM# 360 25 CENTAVOS
Copper-Nickel **Obv:** National arms within wreath, denomination below **Rev:** Bust at right looking left, dates below

Date	Mintage	F	VF	XF	Unc	BU
ND	—	—	—	3.00	6.00	9.00

KM# 361 25 CENTAVOS
Copper-Nickel **Subject:** Alexander von Humboldt **Obv:** National arms within wreath, denomination below **Rev:** Bust in cameo at left and bird at right divide dates

Date	Mintage	F	VF	XF	Unc	BU
1989	—	—	—	3.00	6.00	9.00

KM# 32 40 CENTAVOS
Copper-Nickel **Subject:** Camilo Cienfuegos Gornaran **Obv:** National arms within wreath, denomination below **Rev:** Uniformed bust right, date at left

Date	Mintage	F	VF	XF	Unc	BU
1962	15,250,000	—	3.00	5.00	7.00	12.00

KM# 186 PESO
Copper-Nickel **Subject:** Carlos Manuel de Cespedes

Date	Mintage	F	VF	XF	Unc	BU
ND(1977)	3,000	—	—	—	8.00	—

KM# 187 PESO
Copper-Nickel, 30 mm. **Subject:** Ignacio Agramonte **Obv:** National arms within wreath, denomination below **Rev:** Bust facing, date at left

Date	Mintage	F	VF	XF	Unc	BU
1977	3,000	—	—	—	8.00	—

KM# 188 PESO
Copper-Nickel, 30 mm. **Subject:** Maximo Gomez

Date	Mintage	F	VF	XF	Unc	BU
1977	3,000	—	—	—	8.00	—

KM# 189 PESO
Copper-Nickel, 30 mm. **Subject:** Antonio Maceo

Date	Mintage	F	VF	XF	Unc	BU
1977	3,000	—	—	—	8.00	—

KM# 190 PESO
Copper-Nickel, 30 mm. **Subject:** 60th Anniversary of Socialist Revolution - Lenin **Obv:** National arms within wreath, denomination below **Rev:** Bust left divides dates

Date	Mintage	F	VF	XF	Unc	BU
ND(1977)	6,000	—	—	—	15.00	—

KM# 191 PESO
Copper-Nickel, 30 mm. **Subject:** Nonaligned Nations Conference **Obv:** National arms within wreath, denomination below **Rev:** Design left of date

Date	Mintage	F	VF	XF	Unc	BU
1979	3,000	—	—	—	7.00	—

KM# 46 PESO

Copper-Nickel, 30 mm. **Subject:** Cuban Flower - Mariposa

Date	Mintage	F	VF	XF	Unc	BU
1980	3,000	—	—	—	8.00	—

KM# 192 PESO

Copper-Nickel, 30 mm. **Series:** Olympics **Obv:** National arms within wreath, denomination below **Rev:** Athletes in frames

Date	Mintage	F	VF	XF	Unc	BU
1980	3,000	—	—	—	6.50	—

KM# 193 PESO

Copper-Nickel, 30 mm. **Series:** Olympics **Rev:** Three athletic figures

Date	Mintage	F	VF	XF	Unc	BU
1980	3,000	—	—	—	6.50	—

KM# 194 PESO

Copper-Nickel, 30 mm. **Subject:** Soviet - Cuban Space Flight **Obv:** National arms within wreath, denomination below **Rev:** Shuttle orbiting planet, date below

Date	Mintage	F	VF	XF	Unc	BU
1980	3,000	—	—	—	7.50	—

KM# 53 PESO

Copper-Nickel, 30 mm. **Subject:** Cuban Flowers **Rev:** Azahar flower

Date	Mintage	F	VF	XF	Unc	BU
1981	3,000	—	—	—	8.00	—

KM# 54 PESO

Copper-Nickel, 30 mm. **Subject:** Cuban Flowers **Rev:** Orquidea flower

Date	Mintage	F	VF	XF	Unc	BU
1981	3,000	—	—	—	8.00	—

KM# 55 PESO

Copper-Nickel, 30 mm. **Subject:** Cuban Fauna **Obv:** National arms within wreath, denomination below **Rev:** Cuban Crocodiles, date above

Date	Mintage	F	VF	XF	Unc	BU
1981	5,000	—	—	—	9.00	—

KM# 56 PESO

Copper-Nickel, 30 mm. **Subject:** Cuban Fauna **Rev:** Emerald Hummingbird

Date	Mintage	F	VF	XF	Unc	BU
1981	5,000	—	—	—	9.00	—

KM# 57 PESO

Copper-Nickel, 30 mm. **Subject:** Cuban Fauna **Rev:** Bee Hummingbird

Date	Mintage	F	VF	XF	Unc	BU
1981	5,000	—	—	—	9.00	—

KM# 58 PESO

Copper-Nickel, 30 mm. **Subject:** Soccer World Championship - Spain 1982 **Obv:** National arms within wreath, denomination below **Rev:** Soccer player kicking ball, soccer ball background, date at right

Date	Mintage	F	VF	XF	Unc	BU
1981	10,000	—	—	—	7.00	—

KM# 59 PESO

Copper-Nickel, 30 mm. **Subject:** World Food Day - Sugar Production **Obv:** National arms within wreath, denomination below **Rev:** Sugarcane plants, date lower right

Date	Mintage	F	VF	XF	Unc	BU
1981	10,000	—	—	—	7.00	—

KM# 60 PESO

Copper-Nickel, 30 mm. **Subject:** XIV Central American and Caribbean Games **Obv:** National arms within wreath, denomination below **Rev:** Cartoon crocodile, date at left

Date	Mintage	F	VF	XF	Unc	BU
1981	5,000	—	—	—	9.00	—

KM# 61 PESO

Copper-Nickel, 30 mm. **Subject:** XIV Central American and Caribbean Games **Obv:** National arms within wreath, denomination below **Rev:** Three athletes

Date	Mintage	F	VF	XF	Unc	BU
1981	5,000	—	—	—	8.00	—

KM# 62 PESO

Copper-Nickel, 30 mm. **Subject:** XIV Central American and Caribbean Games **Obv:** National arms within wreath, denomination below **Rev:** Boxers

Date	Mintage	F	VF	XF	Unc	BU
1981	5,000	—	—	—	8.00	—

KM# 63 PESO

Copper-Nickel, 30 mm. **Subject:** Cuban Fauna **Obv:** National arms within wreath, denomination below **Rev:** Cuban Trogon

Date	Mintage	F	VF	XF	Unc	BU
1981	5,000	—	—	—	8.00	—

KM# 64 PESO
Copper-Nickel, 30 mm. **Subject:** Cuban Fauna **Obv:** National arms within wreath, denomination below **Rev:** Cuban Solendodon

Date	Mintage	F	VF	XF	Unc	BU
1981	5,000	—	—	—	8.00	—

KM# 65 PESO
Copper-Nickel, 30 mm. **Subject:** Cuban Fauna **Obv:** National arms within wreath, denomination below **Rev:** Giant Gar Fish

Date	Mintage	F	VF	XF	Unc	BU
1981	5,000	—	—	—	8.00	—

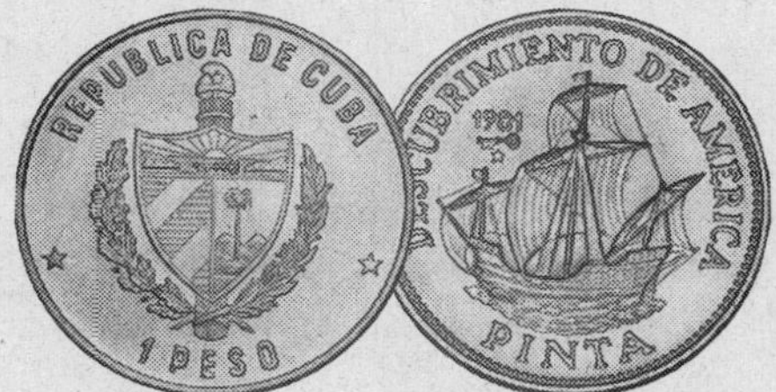

KM# 66 PESO
Copper-Nickel, 30 mm. **Obv:** National arms within wreath, denomination below **Rev:** Columbus' ship - Nina, date at right

Date	Mintage	F	VF	XF	Unc	BU
1981	10,000	—	—	—	12.00	—

KM# 67 PESO
Copper-Nickel, 30 mm. **Obv:** National arms within wreath, denomination below **Rev:** Columbus' ship - Pinta

Date	Mintage	F	VF	XF	Unc	BU
1981	10,000	—	—	—	12.00	—

KM# 68 PESO
Copper-Nickel, 30 mm. **Obv:** National arms within wreath, denomination below **Rev:** Columbus' ship - Santa Maria

Date	Mintage	F	VF	XF	Unc	BU
1981	10,000	—	—	—	12.00	—

KM# 88 PESO
Copper-Nickel, 30 mm. **Obv:** National arms within wreath, denomination below **Rev:** Bust facing, three dates

Date	Mintage	F	VF	XF	Unc	BU
1982	7,000	—	—	—	15.00	—

KM# 89 PESO
Copper-Nickel, 30 mm. **Subject:** Ernest Hemingway **Obv:** National arms within wreath, denomination below **Rev:** Fishing yacht

Date	Mintage	F	VF	XF	Unc	BU
1982	7,000	—	—	—	15.00	—

KM# 90 PESO
Copper-Nickel, 30 mm. **Subject:** Ernest Hemingway **Obv:** National arms within wreath, denomination below **Rev:** Small boat

Date	Mintage	F	VF	XF	Unc	BU
ND(1982)	7,000	—	—	—	15.00	—

KM# 91 PESO
Copper-Nickel, 30 mm. **Subject:** Miquel De Cervantes **Obv:** National arms within wreath, denomination below **Rev:** Bust with ruffled collar 3/4 right, three dates

Date	Mintage	F	VF	XF	Unc	BU
1982	7,000	—	—	—	8.00	—

KM# 92 PESO
Copper-Nickel, 30 mm. **Subject:** Hidalgo Don Quijote **Obv:** National arms within wreath, denomination below **Rev:** Figure on horseback with lance divides dates

Date	Mintage	F	VF	XF	Unc	BU
1982	7,000	—	—	—	8.00	—

KM# 93 PESO
Copper-Nickel, 30 mm. **Subject:** Hidalgo Don Quijote and Sancho Panza **Obv:** National arms within wreath **Rev:** Small figure on mule, larger figure with lance on horse

Date	Mintage	F	VF	XF	Unc	BU
1982	7,000	—	—	—	8.00	—

KM# 94 PESO
Copper-Nickel, 30 mm. **Series:** F.A.O. **Rev:** Citrus fruit

Date	Mintage	F	VF	XF	Unc	BU
1982	6,609	—	—	—	6.50	—

KM# 95 PESO
Copper-Nickel, 30 mm. **Series:** F.A.O. **Obv:** National arms within wreath **Rev:** Cow on grass left

Date	Mintage	F	VF	XF	Unc	BU
1982	5,684	—	—	—	8.00	—

KM# 105 PESO
Brass **Obv:** National arms within wreath, denomination below **Rev:** Star, date below

Date	Mintage	F	VF	XF	Unc	BU
1983	10,000,000	0.25	0.50	1.00	2.50	—
1984	—	0.25	0.50	1.00	2.50	—
1985	—	0.25	0.50	1.00	2.50	—
1986	—	0.25	0.50	1.00	2.50	—
1987	—	0.25	0.50	1.00	2.50	—
1988	—	0.25	0.50	1.00	2.50	—
1989	—	0.25	0.50	1.00	2.50	—

KM# 106 PESO
Copper-Nickel, 30 mm. **Subject:** Railroad **Obv:** National arms within wreath, denomination below **Rev:** Train engine, date below

Date	Mintage	F	VF	XF	Unc	BU
1983	7,000	—	—	—	7.50	—

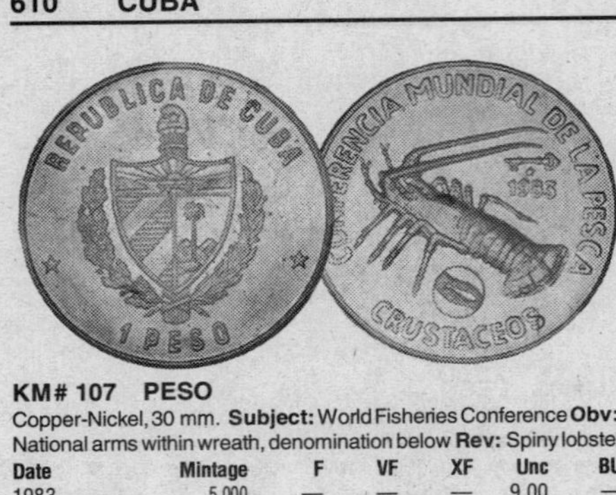

KM# 107 PESO
Copper-Nickel, 30 mm. **Subject:** World Fisheries Conference **Obv:** National arms within wreath, denomination below **Rev:** Spiny lobster

Date	Mintage	F	VF	XF	Unc	BU
1983	5,000	—	—	—	9.00	—

KM# 173 PESO
Copper-Nickel, 30 mm. **Series:** 1984 Olympics **Obv:** National arms within wreath, denomination **Rev:** Runner

Date	Mintage	F	VF	XF	Unc	BU
1983	3,000	—	—	—	8.00	—

KM# 174 PESO
Copper-Nickel, 30 mm. **Series:** 1984 Olympics **Obv:** National arms within wreath, denomination **Rev:** Discus thrower

Date	Mintage	F	VF	XF	Unc	BU
1983	3,000	—	—	—	8.00	—

KM# 175 PESO
Copper-Nickel, 30 mm. **Series:** 1984 Olympics **Obv:** National arms within wreath, denomination below **Rev:** Judo, date upper right

Date	Mintage	F	VF	XF	Unc	BU
1983	3,000	—	—	—	8.00	—

KM# 195 PESO
Copper-Nickel, 30 mm. **Series:** Olympics **Obv:** National arms within wreath, denomination **Rev:** Woman holding torch

Date	Mintage	F	VF	XF	Unc	BU
1983	3,000	—	—	—	8.00	—

KM# 196 PESO
Copper-Nickel, 30 mm. **Series:** Olympics **Rev:** Two hockey players

Date	Mintage	F	VF	XF	Unc	BU
1983	3,000	—	—	—	8.00	—

KM# 197 PESO
Copper-Nickel, 30 mm. **Series:** Olympics **Obv:** National arms within wreath, denomination **Rev:** Downhill skier

Date	Mintage	F	VF	XF	Unc	BU
1983	3,000	—	—	—	7.00	—

KM# 116 PESO
Copper-Nickel, 30 mm. **Subject:** Transportation **Obv:** National arms within wreath, denomination **Rev:** Freighter

Date	Mintage	F	VF	XF	Unc	BU
1984	5,000	—	—	—	8.00	—

KM# 118 PESO
Copper-Nickel, 30 mm. **Subject:** Santisima Trinidad **Obv:** National arms within wreath, denomination below **Rev:** Ship with full sails, date at left

Date	Mintage	F	VF	XF	Unc	BU
1984	3,000	—	—	—	12.00	—

KM# 130 PESO
Copper-Nickel, 30 mm. **Subject:** Transportation **Obv:** National arms within wreath, denomination **Rev:** Volanta coach

Date	Mintage	F	VF	XF	Unc	BU
1984	5,000	—	—	—	8.00	—

KM# 140 PESO
Copper-Nickel, 30 mm. **Subject:** Castillos **Obv:** National arms within wreath, denomination below **Rev:** El Morro La Habana

Date	Mintage	F	VF	XF	Unc	BU
1984	5,000	—	—	—	8.00	—

KM# 142 PESO
Copper-Nickel, 30 mm. **Subject:** Castillos **Obv:** National arms within wreath, denomination below **Rev:** La Fuerza La Habana

Date	Mintage	F	VF	XF	Unc	BU
1984	5,000	—	—	—	10.00	—

KM# 144 PESO
Copper-Nickel, 30 mm. **Subject:** Castillos **Obv:** National arms within wreath, denomination below **Rev:** El Morro Santiago De Cuba

Date	Mintage	F	VF	XF	Unc	BU
1984	5,000	—	—	—	8.00	—

KM# 172 PESO
Copper-Nickel, 30 mm. **Subject:** Transportation **Obv:** National arms within wreath, denomination below **Rev:** Hot air balloon, date at left

Date	Mintage	F	VF	XF	Unc	BU
1984	23	—	—	—	1,800	—

KM# 120 PESO
Copper-Nickel, 30 mm. **Subject:** International Year of Music **Obv:** National arms within wreath, denomination **Rev:** Bust of Bach at left, musical score at right

Date	Mintage	F	VF	XF	Unc	BU
1985	2,000	—	—	—	10.00	—

KM# 124 PESO
Copper-Nickel, 30 mm. **Subject:** Wildlife Preservation **Obv:** National arms within wreath, denomination below **Rev:** Cuban crocodile (head only)

Date	Mintage	F	VF	XF	Unc	BU
1985	5,000	—	—	—	17.50	—

KM# 126 PESO
Copper-Nickel, 30 mm. **Subject:** Wildlife Preservation **Obv:** National arms within wreath, denomination below **Rev:** Cuban rock iguana (half body)

Date	Mintage	F	VF	XF	Unc	BU
1985	5,000	—	—	—	17.50	—

KM# 128 PESO
Copper-Nickel, 30 mm. **Subject:** Wildlife Preservation **Obv:** National arms within wreath, denomination below **Rev:** Cuban amazon parrot (head)

Date	Mintage	F	VF	XF	Unc	BU
1985	5,000	—	—	—	17.50	—

KM# 132 PESO
Copper-Nickel, 30 mm. **Subject:** 40th Anniversary of F.A.O. **Obv:** National arms within wreath, denomination below **Rev:** Sugar cane, lobster, palm tree, and F.A.O. logo

Date	Mintage	F	VF	XF	Unc	BU
ND(1985)	5,000	—	—	—	7.00	—

KM# 133 PESO
Copper-Nickel, 30 mm. **Series:** F.A.O. **Obv:** National arms within wreath, denomination below **Rev:** Two people amid forest

Date	Mintage	F	VF	XF	Unc	BU
1985	5,000	—	—	—	6.50	—

KM# 181 PESO
Copper-Nickel, 30 mm. **Subject:** Wildlife Preservation **Obv:** National arms within wreath, denomination below **Rev:** Crocodile (full body)

Date	Mintage	F	VF	XF	Unc	BU
1985	Est. 3,000	—	—	—	25.00	35.00

KM# 182 PESO
Copper-Nickel, 30 mm. **Subject:** Wildlife Preservation **Obv:** National arms within wreath, denomination below **Rev:** Cuban rock iguana (full body)

Date	Mintage	F	VF	XF	Unc	BU
1985	Est. 3,000	—	—	—	25.00	35.00

KM# 183 PESO
Copper-Nickel, 30 mm. **Subject:** Wildlife Preservation **Obv:** National arms within wreath, denomination below **Rev:** Parrot, (full body), right, date at right

Date	Mintage	F	VF	XF	Unc	BU
1985	Est. 3,000	—	—	—	25.00	35.00

KM# 134 PESO
Copper-Nickel, 30 mm. **Subject:** 100th Anniversary of Automobile **Obv:** National arms within wreath, denomination below **Rev:** Daimler-Benz, two dates below

Date	Mintage	F	VF	XF	Unc	BU
ND(1986)	3,000	—	—	—	10.00	—

KM# 136 PESO
Copper-Nickel, 30 mm. **Subject:** 30th Anniversary - Voyage of the Granma **Obv:** National arms within wreath, denomination **Rev:** Large ship at sea, dates above

Date	Mintage	F	VF	XF	Unc	BU
ND(1986)	3,000	—	—	—	8.00	—

KM# 138 PESO
Copper-Nickel, 30 mm. **Series:** Olympics **Obv:** National arms within wreath, denomination below **Rev:** Speed skater

Date	Mintage	F	VF	XF	Unc	BU
1986	1,000	—	—	—	18.00	—

KM# 198 PESO
Copper-Nickel, 30 mm. **Obv:** National arms within wreath, denomination below **Rev:** Speed skater, without rings above skater, date lower left

Date	Mintage	F	VF	XF	Unc	BU
1986	3,000	—	—	—	8.00	—

KM# 122 PESO
Copper-Nickel, 30 mm. **Subject:** Soccer World Championship - Mexico '85 **Obv:** National arms within wreath, denomination **Rev:** Two soccer players

Date	Mintage	F	VF	XF	Unc	BU
ND(1986)	5,000	—	—	—	7.00	—

KM# 156 PESO
Copper-Nickel, 30 mm. **Subject:** International Year of Peace **Obv:** National arms within wreath, denomination below **Rev:** Dove with olive branch in flight, date at right

Date	Mintage	F	VF	XF	Unc	BU
1986	5,000	—	—	—	8.00	—
1986 Proof	5,000	Value: 15.00				

KM# 148 PESO
Copper-Nickel, 30 mm. **Obv:** National arms within wreath, denomination below **Rev:** Cathedral in Santiago

Date	Mintage	F	VF	XF	Unc	BU
1987	3,000	—	—	—	10.00	—

KM# 150 PESO

Copper-Nickel, 30 mm. **Obv:** National arms within wreath, denomination below **Rev:** Cathedral in Caridad del Cobre

Date	Mintage	F	VF	XF	Unc	BU
1987	3,000	—	—	—	10.00	—

KM# 152 PESO

Copper-Nickel, 30 mm. **Obv:** National arms within wreath, denomination below **Rev:** Cathedral in Trinidad, date below

Date	Mintage	F	VF	XF	Unc	BU
1987	3,000	—	—	—	10.00	—

KM# 154 PESO

Copper Nickel, 30 mm. **Subject:** 40th Anniversary - Expedition of Kon-Tiki **Obv:** National arms within wreath, denomination **Rev:** Full masted ships, dates

Date	Mintage	F	VF	XF	Unc	BU
ND(1987)	3,000	—	—	—	12.00	—

KM# 158 PESO

Copper-Nickel, 30 mm. **Subject:** 20th Anniversary - Demise of Ernesto Che Guevara **Obv:** National arms within wreath, denomination **Rev:** Facing bust divides dates

Date	Mintage	F	VF	XF	Unc	BU
ND(1987)	6,000	—	—	—	20.00	—
ND(1987) Proof	200	Value: 80.00				

KM# 160 PESO

Copper-Nickel, 30 mm. **Subject:** 70th Anniversary of Bolshevik Revolution **Obv:** National arms within wreath, denomination below **Rev:** Ship at sea, date at right

Date	Mintage	F	VF	XF	Unc	BU
1987	5,000	—	—	—	8.00	—

KM# 165 PESO

Copper-Nickel, 30 mm. **Subject:** 100th Anniversary of the Souvenir Peso **Obv:** National arms within wreath, denomination below **Rev:** Womans head right

Date	Mintage	F	VF	XF	Unc	BU
1987	3,000	—	—	—	10.00	—
1987 Proof	3,000	Value: 25.00				

KM# 167 PESO

Copper-Nickel, 30 mm. **Subject:** 100th Anniversary - Abolition of Slavery **Obv:** National arms within wreath, denomination below **Rev:** Half figure of slave breaking chains, three dates

Date	Mintage	F	VF	XF	Unc	BU
1987	2,000	—	—	—	12.50	—

KM# 179 PESO

Copper-Nickel, 30 mm. **Subject:** Chess Centennial **Obv:** National arms within wreath, denomination **Rev:** Jose Capablanca at match

Date	Mintage	F	VF	XF	Unc	BU
ND(1988)	1,000	—	—	—	15.00	—

KM# 184 PESO

Copper-Nickel, 30 mm. **Subject:** Soccer - 1986 Mexico **Obv:** National arms within wreath, denomination below **Rev:** Soccer players, date at left

Date	Mintage	F	VF	XF	Unc	BU
1988	1,000	—	—	—	15.00	—

KM# 200 PESO

Copper-Nickel, 30 mm. **Subject:** Chess Centennial **Rev:** Chess pieces

Date	Mintage	F	VF	XF	Unc	BU
ND(1988)	6,000	—	—	—	10.00	—

KM# 244 PESO

Copper-Nickel, 30 mm. **Subject:** Soccer World Championship - Italy 1990 **Obv:** Three towers above key on crowned shield within wreath **Rev:** Soccer players, date above

Date	Mintage	F	VF	XF	Unc	BU
1988	2,000	—	—	—	12.00	—

KM# 245 PESO

Copper-Nickel, 30 mm. **Subject:** European World Soccer Championship - Federal Republic of Germany **Obv:** National arms within wreath, denomination below **Rev:** Three players

Date	Mintage	F	VF	XF	Unc	BU
1988	2,000	—	—	—	12.00	—

KM# 246 PESO

Copper-Nickel, 30 mm. **Subject:** European World Soccer Championship - Federal Republic of Germany **Obv:** National arms within wreath, denomination below **Rev:** Four players

Date	Mintage	F	VF	XF	Unc	BU
1988	2,000	—	—	—	14.50	—

KM# 276 PESO

Copper-Nickel, 30 mm. **Subject:** 40th Anniversary of Cuban National Ballet **Obv:** National arms within wreath, denomination below **Rev:** Womans head right, looking up

Date	Mintage	F	VF	XF	Unc	BU
ND(1988)	2,000	—	—	—	10.00	—

KM# 277 PESO

Copper-Nickel, 30 mm. **Subject:** 150th Anniversary of Havana Grand Theater **Obv:** National arms within wreath, denomination below **Rev:** Theater building, dates at left

Date	Mintage	F	VF	XF	Unc	BU
ND(1977)	2,000	—	—	—	12.00	—

KM# 282 PESO

Copper-Nickel, 30 mm. **Obv:** National arms within wreath, denomination **Rev:** Carlos J. Finlay

Date	Mintage	F	VF	XF	Unc	BU
ND(1988)	2,000	—	—	—	11.50	—

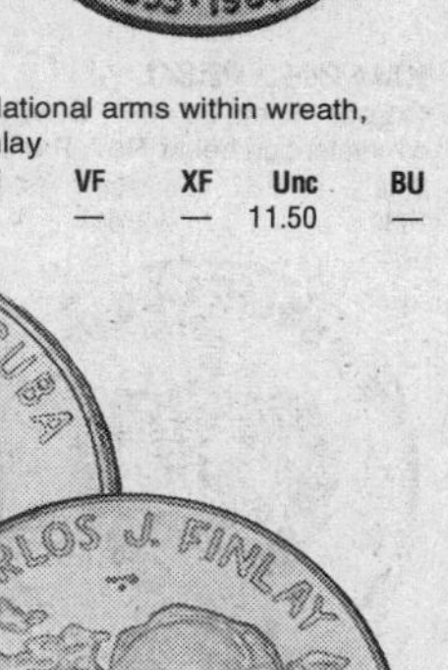

KM# 512 PESO

Copper **Obv:** National arms within wreath, denomination **Rev:** Bust at lower right looking left, dates below

Date	Mintage	F	VF	XF	Unc	BU
ND(1988)	2,500	—	—	—	10.00	—

KM# 258 PESO

Copper-Nickel, 30 mm. **Subject:** World Health Organization **Obv:** National arms within wreath, denomination below **Rev:** Nurse with baby, building in background

Date	Mintage	F	VF	XF	Unc	BU
1988	2,000	—	—	—	10.00	—

KM# 269 PESO

Copper-Nickel, 30 mm. **Subject:** Transportation **Obv:** National arms within wreath, denomination **Rev:** Zeppelin

Date	Mintage	F	VF	XF	Unc	BU
1988	1,000	—	—	—	45.00	—

KM# 324 PESO

Copper-Nickel, 30 mm. **Subject:** Assault of the Moncada Garrison **Obv:** National arms within wreath, denomination **Rev:** Battle scene

Date	Mintage	F	VF	XF	Unc	BU
1988	2,000	—	—	—	10.00	—

KM# 363 PESO

Brass, 30 mm. **Obv:** National arms within wreath, denomination below **Rev:** Head of Jose Marti right, date below

Date	Mintage	F	VF	XF	Unc	BU
1988	—	—	—	—	12.00	—

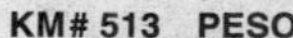

KM# 513 PESO

Copper **Subject:** Transportation **Obv:** National arms within wreath, denomination **Rev:** Zeppelin, date lower left

Date	Mintage	F	VF	XF	Unc	BU
1988	2,500	—	—	—	27.50	—

KM# 247 PESO

Copper-Nickel, 30 mm. **Subject:** World Soccer Championship - Italy 1990 **Obv:** National arms within wreath, denomination below **Rev:** Three players

Date	Mintage	F	VF	XF	Unc	BU
1989	4,000	—	—	—	10.00	—

KM# 248 PESO

Copper-Nickel, 30 mm. **Subject:** World Soccer Championship - Italy 1990 **Obv:** National arms within wreath, denomination below **Rev:** Colosseum

Date	Mintage	F	VF	XF	Unc	BU
1989	2,000	—	—	—	12.00	—

KM# 253 PESO

Copper-Nickel, 30 mm. **Subject:** 30th Anniversary of Revolution **Obv:** National arms within wreath, denomination below **Rev:** Castro with gun standing before radiant sun, dates at left

Date	Mintage	F	VF	XF	Unc	BU
ND(1989)	5,000	—	—	—	10.00	—

KM# 254 PESO

Copper-Nickel, 30 mm. **Subject:** 30th Anniversary of Revolution **Obv:** National arms within wreath, denomination below **Rev:** Facing busts of Jose Marti and Castro

Date	Mintage	F	VF	XF	Unc	BU
1989	5,000	—	—	—	10.00	—

KM# 255 PESO

Copper-Nickel, 30 mm. **Subject:** 30th Anniversary of Revolution **Obv:** National arms within wreath, denomination below **Rev:** Cienfuegos and Castro, dates at right

Date	Mintage	F	VF	XF	Unc	BU
ND(1989)	5,000	—	—	—	10.00	—

KM# 257 PESO

Copper-Nickel, 30 mm. **Subject:** Triumph of the Revolution **Obv:** National arms within wreath, denomination below **Rev:** Castro with revolutionaries, dates below

Date	Mintage	F	VF	XF	Unc	BU
1989	2,000	—	—	—	12.00	—

KM# 259 PESO

Copper-Nickel, 30 mm. **Subject:** Cuban Tobacco **Obv:** National arms within wreath, denomination below **Rev:** Native smoking above tobacco plant, parrot at right, date below

Date	Mintage	F	VF	XF	Unc	BU
1989	1,000	—	—	—	14.50	—

KM# 260 PESO

Copper-Nickel, 30 mm. **Subject:** 160th Anniversary of First Railroad in England **Obv:** National arms within wreath, denomination below **Rev:** Railroad carts, dates below and above

Date	Mintage	F	VF	XF	Unc	BU
1989	2,000	—	—	—	12.00	—

KM# 261 PESO
Copper-Nickel, 30 mm. **Subject:** 500th Anniversary - Discovery of America **Obv:** National arms within wreath, denomination below **Rev:** Three ships, date at left

Date	Mintage	F	VF	XF	Unc	BU
1989	3,145	—	—	—	12.00	—

KM# 270 PESO
Copper-Nickel, 30 mm. **Subject:** 30th Anniversary - The March to Victory **Obv:** National arms within wreath, denomination **Rev:** Uniformed figures marching, dates

Date	Mintage	F	VF	XF	Unc	BU
1989	2,000	—	—	—	10.00	—

KM# 271 PESO
Copper-Nickel, 30 mm. **Subject:** 200th Anniversary of French Revolution **Obv:** National arms within wreath, denomination below **Rev:** Female Allegory of Revolution

Date	Mintage	F	VF	XF	Unc	BU
ND(1989)	2,000	—	—	—	10.00	—

KM# 272 PESO
Copper-Nickel, 30 mm. **Subject:** 200th Anniversary of French Revolution - Bastille **Obv:** National arms within wreath, denomination below **Rev:** Castle scene, dates below

Date	Mintage	F	VF	XF	Unc	BU
ND(1989)	2,000	—	—	—	10.00	—

KM# 274 PESO
Copper-Nickel, 30 mm. **Subject:** First Spanish Railroad **Obv:** National arms within wreath, denomination below **Rev:** Train on track, three dates

Date	Mintage	F	VF	XF	Unc	BU
1989	2,000	—	—	—	10.00	—

KM# 275 PESO
Copper-Nickel, 30 mm. **Subject:** First Cuban Railroad **Obv:** National arms within wreath, denomination below **Rev:** Train engine divides dates

Date	Mintage	F	VF	XF	Unc	BU
1989	2,000	—	—	—	15.00	—

KM# 278 PESO
Copper-Nickel, 30 mm. **Subject:** 5th Centennial - Discovery of America **Obv:** National arms within wreath, denomination below **Rev:** Three ships at sea, date at left

Date	Mintage	F	VF	XF	Unc	BU
1989	2,000	—	—	—	10.00	—

KM# 283 PESO
Copper-Nickel, 30 mm. **Subject:** Alexander von Humboldt **Obv:** National arms within wreath, denomination below **Rev:** Cameo of Alexander von Humboldt, birds on branch

Date	Mintage	F	VF	XF	Unc	BU
1989	2,000	—	—	—	12.50	—

KM# 284 PESO
Copper-Nickel, 30 mm. **Series:** 1992 Olympics **Obv:** National arms within wreath, denomination below **Rev:** Two boxers

Date	Mintage	F	VF	XF	Unc	BU
1989	1,000	—	—	—	15.00	—

KM# 285 PESO
Copper-Nickel, 30 mm. **Obv:** National arms within wreath, denomination below **Rev:** Facing bust, date at left

Date	Mintage	F	VF	XF	Unc	BU
1989	2,000	—	—	—	10.00	—

KM# 286 PESO
Copper-Nickel, 30 mm. **Obv:** National arms within wreath, denomination below **Rev:** Profile of Ernesto Che Guevara

Date	Mintage	F	VF	XF	Unc	BU
1989	2,000	—	—	—	18.00	—

KM# 287 PESO
Copper-Nickel, 30 mm. **Obv:** National arms within wreath, denomination below **Rev:** Bust of Tania La Guerrillera, Argentinian revolutionary

Date	Mintage	F	VF	XF	Unc	BU
1989	2,000	—	—	—	10.00	—

KM# 436 PESO
Copper **Obv:** National arms within wreath, denomination below **Rev:** Cameo of Alexander von Humboldt, Condors

Date	Mintage	F	VF	XF	Unc	BU
1989	—	—	—	—	12.00	—

KM# 250 PESO
Copper, 30 mm. **Obv:** National arms within wreath, denomination below **Rev:** Esperanto at right, world globe at left

Date	Mintage	F	VF	XF	Unc	BU
1990	6,000	—	—	—	10.00	—

KM# 273 PESO
Copper, 30 mm. **Subject:** Discovery of America **Obv:** National arms within wreath, denomination below **Rev:** Scene depicting Columbus departing from Spain

Date	Mintage	F	VF	XF	Unc	BU
1990	12,000	—	—	—	12.00	—

KM# 279 PESO
Copper-Nickel, 30 mm. **Subject:** 5th Centennial of Columbus' Arrival in Cuba **Obv:** National arms within wreath, denomination below **Rev:** Ship at sea, map in background, date at right

Date	Mintage	F	VF	XF	Unc	BU
1990	2,000	—	—	—	12.00	—

KM# 288 PESO
Copper-Nickel, 30 mm. **Obv:** National arms within wreath, denomination below **Rev:** Columbus meeting natives

Date	Mintage	F	VF	XF	Unc	BU
1990	2,000	—	—	—	12.00	—

KM# 289 PESO
Copper-Nickel, 30 mm. **Obv:** National arms within wreath, denomination below **Rev:** Three soccer balls at left, map of Italy at right

Date	Mintage	F	VF	XF	Unc	BU
1990	—	—	—	—	10.00	—

KM# 306 PESO
Copper-Nickel, 30 mm. **Subject:** 500th Anniversary - Discovery of America **Obv:** National arms within wreath, denomination below **Rev:** King Ferdinand of Spain

Date	Mintage	F	VF	XF	Unc	BU
1990	3,000	—	—	—	9.00	—

KM# 307 PESO
Copper-Nickel, 30 mm. **Subject:** 500th Anniversary - Discovery of America **Obv:** National arms within wreath, denomination below **Rev:** Queen Isabella of Spain

Date	Mintage	F	VF	XF	Unc	BU
1990	3,000	—	—	—	9.00	—

KM# 308 PESO
Copper-Nickel, 30 mm. **Subject:** 500th Anniversary - Discovery of America **Obv:** National arms within wreath, denomination below **Rev:** Christopher Columbus 3/4 left

Date	Mintage	F	VF	XF	Unc	BU
1990	3,000	—	—	—	8.00	—

KM# 309 PESO
Copper Nickel, 30 mm. **Subject:** 500th Anniversary - Discovery of America **Obv:** National arms within wreath, denomination below **Rev:** Juan de la Cosa

Date	Mintage	F	VF	XF	Unc	BU
1990	3,000	—	—	—	6.50	—

KM# 310 PESO
Copper-Nickel, 30 mm. **Subject:** Pan American Games **Obv:** National arms within wreath, denomination below **Rev:** High jumper

Date	Mintage	F	VF	XF	Unc	BU
1990	5,000	—	—	—	8.00	—

KM# 311 PESO
Copper-Nickel, 30 mm. **Subject:** Pan American Games **Obv:** National arms within wreath, denomination below **Rev:** Volleyball

Date	Mintage	F	VF	XF	Unc	BU
1990	5,000	—	—	—	8.00	—

KM# 312 PESO
Copper-Nickel, 30 mm. **Subject:** Pan American Games **Obv:** National arms within wreath, denomination below **Rev:** Baseball game on baseball background

Date	Mintage	F	VF	XF	Unc	BU
1990	5,000	—	—	—	10.00	—

KM# 325 PESO
Copper-Nickel, 30 mm. **Obv:** National arms within wreath, denomination below **Rev:** Columbus' ships sailing west

Date	Mintage	F	VF	XF	Unc	BU
1990	12,000	—	—	—	7.50	—

KM# 340 PESO
Copper-Nickel, 30 mm. **Subject:** Celia Sanchez Manduley 1920-80, revolutionary **Obv:** National arms within wreath, denomination below **Rev:** Head looking left, dates below

Date	Mintage	F	VF	XF	Unc	BU
1990	—	—	—	—	8.00	—

KM# 387 PESO
Copper-Nickel, 30 mm. **Obv:** National arms within wreath, denomination below **Rev:** Route of first voyage by Columbus

Date	Mintage	F	VF	XF	Unc	BU
1990	2,000	—	—	—	12.00	—

KM# 471 PESO
Copper, 30 mm. **Obv:** National arms within wreath, denomination below **Rev:** Columbus meeting natives

Date	Mintage	F	VF	XF	Unc	BU
1990	—	—	—	—	12.00	—

KM# 514 PESO
Copper-Nickel, 30 mm. **Subject:** Simon Bolivar - Libertador **Obv:** National arms within wreath, denomination **Rev:** Uniformed bust facing, dates

Date	Mintage	F	VF	XF	Unc	BU
1990	2,000	—	—	—	8.00	—

KM# 364 PESO
Nickel Bonded Steel, 30 mm. **Obv:** National arms within wreath, denomination below **Rev:** Hatuey tribesman head left, date at right

Date	Mintage	F	VF	XF	Unc	BU
1991	3,000	—	—	—	9.00	—

KM# 365 PESO
Nickel Bonded Steel, 30 mm. **Obv:** National arms within wreath, denomination below **Rev:** Pinzon brothers

Date	Mintage	F	VF	XF	Unc	BU
1991	3,000	—	—	—	9.00	—

KM# 366 PESO
Nickel Bonded Steel, 30 mm. **Subject:** 500th Anniversary of New World **Obv:** National arms within wreath, denomination below **Rev:** Bust of Queen Joanna, 1479-1555, daughter of Isabella I

Date	Mintage	F	VF	XF	Unc	BU
1991	3,000	—	—	—	9.00	—

KM# 367 PESO
Nickel Bonded Steel, 30 mm. **Obv:** National arms within wreath, denomination below **Rev:** Diego Velazquez

Date	Mintage	F	VF	XF	Unc	BU
1991	3,000	—	—	—	9.00	—

KM# 388 PESO
Nickel Bonded Steel, 30 mm. **Subject:** Madrid **Obv:** National arms within wreath, denomination below **Rev:** Alcala Gate

Date	Mintage	F	VF	XF	Unc	BU
1991	10,000	—	—	—	9.00	—

KM# 389 PESO
Nickel Bonded Steel, 30 mm. **Subject:** Barcelona **Obv:** National arms within wreath, denomination below **Rev:** Olympic stadium

Date	Mintage	F	VF	XF	Unc	BU
1991	—	—	—	—	9.00	—

KM# 390 PESO
Nickel Bonded Steel, 30 mm. **Subject:** Seville **Obv:** National arms within wreath, denomination below **Rev:** La Giralda Tower

Date	Mintage	F	VF	XF	Unc	BU
1991	—	—	—	—	9.00	—

KM# 347 PESO
Brass Plated Steel **Subject:** Jose Marti **Obv:** National arms within wreath, denomination below **Rev:** Bust facing, denomination at left **Rev. Legend:** PATRIA O MUERTE

Date	Mintage	F	VF	XF	Unc	BU
1991	—	—	—	1.00	2.50	5.00
1992	—	—	—	1.00	2.00	4.00
1992 Proof	—	—	—	—	—	—
1994	—	—	—	1.00	2.00	4.00

KM# 368 PESO
Copper-Nickel, 30 mm. **Subject:** Postal Ship **Obv:** National arms within wreath, denomination below **Rev:** Ship at sea, date at left

Date	Mintage	F	VF	XF	Unc	BU
1992	—	—	—	—	12.00	—

KM# 391 PESO
Nickel Bonded Steel, 30 mm. **Subject:** 25th Anniversary - Death of Ernesto Che Guevara **Obv:** National arms within wreath, denomination below **Rev:** Ernesto Che Guevara

Date	Mintage	F	VF	XF	Unc	BU
1992	—	—	—	—	12.00	—

KM# 392 PESO
Nickel Bonded Steel, 30 mm. **Obv:** National arms within wreath, denomination below **Rev:** Bartolome de Las Casas

Date	Mintage	F	VF	XF	Unc	BU
1992	3,000	—	—	—	9.00	—

KM# 393 PESO
Nickel Bonded Steel, 30 mm. **Obv:** National arms within wreath, denomination below **Rev:** Half figure of Chief Guama blowing shell, date at left

Date	Mintage	F	VF	XF	Unc	BU
1992	3,000	—	—	—	9.00	—

KM# 394 PESO
Nickel Bonded Steel, 30 mm. **Obv:** National arms within wreath, denomination below **Rev:** King Philipp of Spain

Date	Mintage	F	VF	XF	Unc	BU
1992	3,000	—	—	—	9.00	—

KM# 395 PESO
Nickel Bonded Steel, 30 mm. **Subject:** Spanish Royalty **Obv:** National arms within wreath, denomination below **Rev:** Banners below royal busts at top and bottom, dates flanking

Date	Mintage	F	VF	XF	Unc	BU
ND(1992)	3,000	—	—	—	9.00	—

KM# 401 PESO
Copper-Nickel, 30 mm. **Obv:** National arms within wreath, denomination below **Rev:** Seville Tower of Gold

Date	Mintage	F	VF	XF	Unc	BU
1992	—	—	—	—	7.00	—

KM# 402 PESO
Copper-Nickel, 30 mm. **Subject:** El Escorial **Obv:** National arms within wreath, denomination below **Rev:** City view, date below

Date	Mintage	F	VF	XF	Unc	BU
1992	—	—	—	—	7.00	—

KM# 403 PESO
Copper-Nickel, 30 mm. **Obv:** National arms within wreath, denomination below **Rev:** St. Jorge Palace, date below

Date	Mintage	F	VF	XF	Unc	BU
1992	10,000	—	—	—	7.00	—

KM# 437 PESO
Copper **Subject:** 25th Anniversary - Death of Ernesto Che Guevara **Obv:** National arms within wreath, denomination **Rev:** Uniformed bust facing, dates

Date	Mintage	F	VF	XF	Unc	BU
ND(1992)	—	—	—	—	15.00	—

KM# 462 PESO
Nickel Bonded Steel, 30 mm. **Subject:** Introduction of Africans to America **Obv:** National arms within wreath, denomination below **Rev:** Figure with back facing at left, ship at sea at right, inscription below

Date	Mintage	F	VF	XF	Unc	BU
1992	—	—	—	—	11.50	—

KM# 396 PESO
Copper **Subject:** Millennium of St. Jacobi **Obv:** National arms within wreath, denomination **Rev:** Armored figure on rearing horse right

Date	Mintage	F	VF	XF	Unc	BU
1993	—	—	—	—	10.00	—

KM# 397 PESO
Copper **Subject:** 40th Anniversary of Moncada **Obv:** National arms within wreath, denomination **Rev:** Uniformed bust left

Date	Mintage	F	VF	XF	Unc	BU
1993	—	—	—	—	10.00	—

KM# 404 PESO
Copper-Nickel, 30 mm. **Series:** Prehistoric Animals **Obv:** National arms within wreath, denomination below **Rev:** Chalicotherium standing with tree, date below

Date	Mintage	F	VF	XF	Unc	BU
1993	—	—	—	—	22.00	—

KM# 429 PESO
Copper-Nickel, 30 mm. **Subject:** Federico Garcia Lorca **Obv:** National arms within wreath, denomination **Rev:** Bust facing, dates at left

Date	Mintage	F	VF	XF	Unc	BU
1993	—	—	—	—	10.00	—

KM# 509 PESO
Copper **Obv:** National arms within wreath, denomination below **Rev:** President Abraham Lincoln, map of United States behind

Date	Mintage	F	VF	XF	Unc	BU
1993	—	—	—	—	10.00	—

KM# 515 PESO
Copper **Obv:** National arms within wreath, denomination below **Rev:** Bolivar and Marti

Date	Mintage	F	VF	XF	Unc	BU
1993 Antiqued finish	—	—	—	—	12.00	—
1993 Plain finish	—	—	—	—	10.00	—

KM# 438 PESO
Copper-Nickel Plated Steel, 30 mm. **Series:** Prehistoric Animals **Obv:** National arms within wreath, denomination below **Rev:** Stegosaurus

Date	Mintage	F	VF	XF	Unc	BU
1994	—	—	—	—	25.00	—

KM# 439 PESO
Copper-Nickel, 30 mm. **Series:** Caribbean Fauna **Obv:** National arms within wreath, denomination below **Rev:** Multicolored Bottle-nosed Dolphins

Date	Mintage	F	VF	XF	Unc	BU
1994	25,000	—	—	—	15.00	—

KM# 460 PESO
Copper-Nickel, 30 mm. **Series:** Caribbean Fauna **Obv:** National

arms within wreath, denomination below **Rev:** Multicolored Spotted Eagle Ray left, date below

Date	Mintage	F	VF	XF	Unc	BU
1994	25,000	—	—	—	15.00	—

KM# 463 PESO
Nickel Bonded Steel, 30 mm. **Subject:** Isla del Evangelista **Obv:** National arms within wreath, denomination below **Rev:** Parrot, ship, and sea chest

Date	Mintage	F	VF	XF	Unc	BU
1994	—	—	—	—	8.00	—

KM# 464 PESO
Nickel Bonded Steel, 30 mm. **Subject:** Sailing Ships **Obv:** National arms within wreath, denomination below **Rev:** NAO VICTORIA

Date	Mintage	F	VF	XF	Unc	BU
1994	—	—	—	—	9.00	—

KM# 465 PESO
Nickel Bonded Steel, 30 mm. **Subject:** Sailing Ships **Obv:** National arms within wreath, denomination below **Rev:** LA INDIA

Date	Mintage	F	VF	XF	Unc	BU
1994	—	—	—	—	9.00	—

KM# 466.1 PESO
Copper-Nickel, 30 mm. **Series:** Caribbean Fauna **Obv:** National arms within wreath, denomination below **Rev:** Multicolored Yellow Sea Bass (Coney), 7 lines in the tail, slimmer fish

Date	Mintage	F	VF	XF	Unc	BU
1994	25,000	—	—	—	25.00	—

KM# 466.2 PESO
Copper-Nickel, 30 mm. **Subject:** Caribbean Fauna **Obv:** National arms within wreath, denomination below **Rev:** Multicolored Yellow Sea Bass (Coney), 5 lines in the tail

Date	Mintage	F	VF	XF	Unc	BU
1994	Inc. above	—	—	—	17.50	—

KM# 467.1 PESO
Copper-Nickel, 30 mm. **Series:** Caribbean Fauna **Obv:** National arms within wreath, denomination below **Rev:** Multicolored Swordfish, small water splashes, thin nose

Date	Mintage	F	VF	XF	Unc	BU
1994	25,000	—	—	—	25.00	—

KM# 467.2 PESO
Copper Nickel, 30 mm. **Subject:** Caribbean Fauna **Obv:** National arms within wreath, denomination below **Rev:** Multicolored Swordfish, large water splashes, wider nose

Date	Mintage	F	VF	XF	Unc	BU
1994	Inc. above	—	—	—	17.50	—

KM# 497 PESO
Copper-Nickel, 30 mm. **Series:** Caribbean Fauna **Obv:** National arms within wreath, denomination below **Rev:** Multicolor pelican

Date	Mintage	F	VF	XF	Unc	BU
1994	25,000	—	—	—	17.50	—

KM# 498.1 PESO
Copper-Nickel, 30 mm. **Series:** Caribbean Fauna **Obv:** National arms within wreath, denomination below **Rev:** Multicolored flamingos, thin water splashes

Date	Mintage	F	VF	XF	Unc	BU
1994	25,000	—	—	—	25.00	—

KM# 498.2 PESO
Copper-Nickel, 30 mm. **Subject:** Caribbean Fauna **Obv:** National arms within wreath, denomination below **Rev:** Multicolored flamingos, wide water splashes

Date	Mintage	F	VF	XF	Unc	BU
1994	Inc. above	—	—	—	17.50	—

KM# 516 PESO
Copper **Subject:** Montecristi Manifesto **Obv:** National arms within wreath, denomination below **Rev:** Two seated figures facing each other, date lower left

Date	Mintage	F	VF	XF	Unc	BU
1994 Antiqued finish	—	—	—	—	12.00	—
1994 Plain finish	—	—	—	—	12.00	—

KM# 517 PESO
Copper **Obv:** National arms within wreath, denomination below **Rev:** Nao Victoria

Date	Mintage	F	VF	XF	Unc	BU
1994	2,500	—	—	—	12.00	—

KM# 518 PESO
Nickel Bonded Steel, 30 mm. **Subject:** Fokker Dr. I **Obv:** National arms within wreath, denomination **Rev:** Multicolored fighter plane

Date	Mintage	F	VF	XF	Unc	BU
1994	—	—	—	—	18.50	—

KM# 547 PESO
Nickel Bonded Steel, 30 mm. **Subject:** Albatross DII **Obv:** National arms within wreath, denomination **Rev:** Multicolored fighter plane

Date	Mintage	F	VF	XF	Unc	BU
1994	25,000	—	—	—	18.50	—

KM# 606 PESO
Copper **Subject:** 500th Anniversary - Discovery of Evangelista Island **Obv:** National arms within wreath, denomination below **Rev:** Parrot, chest, and ship

Date	Mintage	F	VF	XF	Unc	BU
1994	—	—	—	—	12.50	—

KM# 472.1 PESO
Copper-Nickel, 30 mm. **Subject:** Pirates of the Caribbean **Obv:** Roman I in denomination, lower relief, more refined shield **Rev:** Blackbeard

Date	Mintage	F	VF	XF	Unc	BU
1995	Est. 25,000	—	—	—	12.00	—

KM# 472.2 PESO
Copper Nickel, 30 mm. **Subject:** Pirates of the Caribbean **Obv:** Arabic 1 in denomination, higher relief shield **Rev:** Blackbeard

Date	Mintage	F	VF	XF	Unc	BU
1995	Inc. above	—	—	—	12.00	—

KM# 472.3 PESO
Copper Nickel, 30 mm. **Subject:** Pirates of the Caribbean **Obv:** National arms within wreath, denomination below **Rev:** Blackbeard **Rev. Legend:** Mariposas del Caribe **Note:** Struck on trial planchet

Date	Mintage	F	VF	XF	Unc	BU
1995 Rare	—	—	—	—	—	—

KM# 473.1 PESO

Copper-Nickel, 30 mm. **Subject:** Pirates of the Caribbean **Obv:** Roman I in denomination, lower relief, more refined shield **Rev:** Sir Henry Morgan

Date	Mintage	F	VF	XF	Unc	BU
1995	25,000	—	—	—	12.00	—

KM# 473.2 PESO

Copper Nickel, 30 mm. **Subject:** Pirates of the Caribbean **Obv:** Arabic 1 in denomination, higher relief shield **Rev:** Sir Henry Morgan

Date	Mintage	F	VF	XF	Unc	BU
1995	Inc. above	—	—	—	12.00	—

KM# 473.3 PESO

Copper Nickel, 30 mm. **Subject:** Pirates of the Caribbean **Obv:** National arms within wreath, denomination below **Rev:** Sir Henry Morgan **Rev. Legend:** Mariposas del Caribe **Note:** Struck on trial planchet.

Date	Mintage	F	VF	XF	Unc	BU
1995 Rare	—	—	—	—	—	—

KM# 474.1 PESO

Copper-Nickel, 30 mm. **Subject:** Pirates of the Caribbean **Obv:** Roman I in denomination, lower relief, more refined shield **Rev:** Anne Bonny

Date	Mintage	F	VF	XF	Unc	BU
1995	Est. 25,000	—	—	—	12.00	—

KM# 474.2 PESO

Copper Nickel, 30 mm. **Subject:** Pirates of the Caribbean **Obv:** Arabic 1 in denomination, higher relief shield **Rev:** Anne Bonny

Date	Mintage	F	VF	XF	Unc	BU
1995	Inc. above	—	—	—	12.00	—

KM# 474.3 PESO

Copper Nickel, 30 mm. **Subject:** Pirates of the Caribbean **Obv:** National arms within wreath, denomination **Rev:** Anne Bonny **Rev. Legend:** Mariposas del Caribe **Note:** Struck on trial planchet.

Date	Mintage	F	VF	XF	Unc	BU
1995 Rare	—	—	—	—	—	—

KM# 475.1 PESO

Copper-Nickel, 30 mm. **Subject:** Pirates of the Caribbean **Obv:** Roman I in denomination, lower relief, more refined shield **Rev:** Mary Read

Date	Mintage	F	VF	XF	Unc	BU
1995	Est. 25,000	—	—	—	12.00	—

KM# 475.2 PESO

Copper Nickel, 30 mm. **Subject:** Pirates of the Caribbean **Obv:** Arabic 1 in denomination, higher relief shield **Rev:** Mary Read

Date	Mintage	F	VF	XF	Unc	BU
1995	Inc. above	—	—	—	12.00	—

KM# 475.3 PESO

Copper Nickel, 30 mm. **Subject:** Pirates of the Caribbean **Obv:** National arms within wreath, denomination below **Rev:** Mary Read **Rev. Legend:** Mariposas del caribe **Note:** Struck on trial planchet.

Date	Mintage	F	VF	XF	Unc	BU
1995 Rare	—	—	—	—	—	—

KM# 476.1 PESO

Copper-Nickel, 30 mm. **Subject:** Pirates of the Caribbean **Obv:** Roman I in denomination, lower relief, more refined shield **Rev:** Captain Kidd

Date	Mintage	F	VF	XF	Unc	BU
1995	Est. 25,000	—	—	—	12.00	—

KM# 476.2 PESO

Copper Nickel, 30 mm. **Subject:** Pirates of the Caribbean **Obv:** Arabic 1 in denomination, higher relief shield **Rev:** Captain Kidd

Date	Mintage	F	VF	XF	Unc	BU
1995	Inc. above	—	—	—	12.00	—

KM# 476.3 PESO

Copper Nickel, 30 mm. **Subject:** Pirates of the Caribbean **Obv:** National arms within wreath, denomination below **Rev:** Captain Kidd **Rev. Legend:** Mariposas del Caribe **Note:** Struck on trial planchet.

Date	Mintage	F	VF	XF	Unc	BU
1995 Rare	—	—	—	—	—	—

KM# 477.1 PESO

Copper-Nickel, 30 mm. **Subject:** Pirates of the Caribbean **Obv:** Roman I in denomination, lower relief, more refined shield **Rev:** Piet Heyn

Date	Mintage	F	VF	XF	Unc	BU
1995	Est. 25,000	—	—	—	12.00	—

KM# 477.2 PESO

Copper Nickel, 30 mm. **Subject:** Pirates of the Caribbean **Obv:** Arabic 1 in denomination, higher relief shield **Rev:** Piet Heyn

Date	Mintage	F	VF	XF	Unc	BU
1995	Inc. above	—	—	—	12.00	—

KM# 477.3 PESO

Copper Nickel, 30 mm. **Subject:** Pirates of the Caribbean **Obv:** National arms within wreath, denomination below **Rev:** Piet Heyn **Rev. Legend:** Mariposas del Caribe **Note:** Struck on trial planchet

Date	Mintage	F	VF	XF	Unc	BU
1995 Rare	—	—	—	—	—	—

KM# 519 PESO

Copper **Subject:** Centennial - Death of Jose Marti in combat **Obv:** National arms within wreath, denomination below **Rev:** Bust of Marti facing, date at right

Date	Mintage	F	VF	XF	Unc	BU
1995 Antiqued finish	3,000	—	—	—	12.00	—
1995 Plain finish	—	—	—	—	12.00	—

KM# 520 PESO

Copper **Subject:** Centennial 1895-1995 **Obv:** National arms within wreath, denomination below **Rev:** Three conjoined busts, right of sword, facing right, dates below

Date	Mintage	F	VF	XF	Unc	BU
ND(1995) Antiqued finish	2,000	—	—	—	12.00	—
ND(1995) Plain finish	Inc. above	—	—	—	12.00	—

KM# 521 PESO

Nickel Bonded Steel, 30 mm. **Subject:** Centennial - Jose Marti in combat **Obv:** National arms within wreath, denomination below **Rev:** Bust of Marti looking left, date at right

Date	Mintage	F	VF	XF	Unc	BU
1995	—	—	—	—	7.50	—

KM# 522 PESO

Nickel-Bonded Steel, 30 mm. **Obv:** National arms within wreath, denomination below **Rev:** Multicolored SIAI Marchetti Seaplane, date at left

Date	Mintage	F	VF	XF	Unc	BU
1995	—	—	—	—	18.50	—

KM# 523 PESO

Copper-Nickel **Subject:** 50th Anniversary - United Nations **Obv:** National arms within wreath, denomination below **Rev:** Five people, assorted ages and race, UN logo in front, dove outline behind, dates below

Date	Mintage	F	VF	XF	Unc	BU
ND(1995)	—	—	—	—	15.00	—

KM# 607 PESO

Nickel Bonded Steel, 30 mm. **Subject:** 50th Anniversary - F.A.O. **Obv:** National arms within wreath, denomination below **Rev:** Farmer plowing behind two oxen

Date	Mintage	F	VF	XF	Unc	BU
ND(1995)	—	—	—	—	8.50	—

KM# 549 PESO

Nickel-Bonded Steel, 30 mm. **Series:** Caribbean Fauna **Obv:** National arms within wreath, denomination below **Rev:** Multicolored Purple-throated Carib Hummingbird

Date	Mintage	F	VF	XF	Unc	BU
1996	10,000	—	—	—	12.00	—

KM# 550 PESO

Nickel Bonded Steel, 30 mm. **Series:** Caribbean Fauna **Obv:** National arms within wreath, denomination below **Rev:** Multicolored Yellow Perch

Date	Mintage	F	VF	XF	Unc	BU
1996	10,000	—	—	—	12.00	—

KM# 551 PESO

Nickel Bonded Steel, 30 mm. **Series:** Caribbean Fauna **Obv:** National arms within wreath, denomination below **Rev:** Multicolored Cuban Tody Bird

Date	Mintage	F	VF	XF	Unc	BU
1996	10,000	—	—	—	12.00	—

KM# 552 PESO

Nickel Bonded Steel, 30 mm. **Series:** Caribbean Fauna **Obv:** National arms within wreath, denomination below **Rev:** Multicolored Wood Duck

Date	Mintage	F	VF	XF	Unc	BU
1996	10,000	—	—	—	12.00	—

KM# 562 PESO

Nickel Bonded Steel, 30 mm. **Series:** Caribbean Fauna **Obv:** National arms within wreath, denomination below **Rev:** Multicolored Vaca Anil Fish

Date	Mintage	F	VF	XF	Unc	BU
1996	10,000	—	—	—	12.00	—

KM# 565 PESO

Nickel Bonded Steel, 30 mm. **Series:** Caribbean Fauna **Obv:** National arms within wreath, denomination below **Rev:** Multicolored Papilio butterfly

Date	Mintage	F	VF	XF	Unc	BU
1996	10,000	—	—	—	15.00	—

KM# 614 PESO

25.9100 Copper-Nickel, 37.9 mm. **Subject:** 40th Anniversary of the "Granma" Landing **Obv:** National arms within wreath, denomination below **Rev:** Portrait above ship **Edge:** Plain

Date	Mintage	F	VF	XF	Unc	BU
ND(1996)	—	Value: 15.00				

KM# 731 PESO

25.8300 g., Copper-Nickel, 37.9 mm. **Series:** F.A.O. **Obv:** National arms within wreath, denomination below **Rev:** Woman picking fruit **Edge:** Plain

Date	Mintage	F	VF	XF	Unc	BU
1996	—	—	—	—	18.50	—

KM# 617 PESO

Copper-Nickel, 37 mm. **Subject:** 30th Anniversary - Death of Ernesto Che Guevara **Obv:** National arms within wreath, denomination below **Rev:** Full figure of Guevara with rifle walking down road between anniversary dates, mountains behind

Date	Mintage	F	VF	XF	Unc	BU
1997	—	—	—	—	15.00	—

KM# 618 PESO

25.8600 g., Copper-Nickel, 37.9 mm. **Subject:** Che Guevara's Death **Obv:** National arms and inscription **Rev:** Bearded portrait **Edge:** Plain

Date	Mintage	F	VF	XF	Unc	BU
ND(1997)	—	—	—	—	15.00	—

KM# 619 PESO

12.9000 g., Copper-Nickel, 32.5 mm. **Subject:** Ruellia Tuberosa **Obv:** National arms within wreath, denomination **Rev:** Multicolor flower **Edge:** Plain

Date	Mintage	F	VF	XF	Unc	BU
1997	5,000	—	—	—	7.00	—

KM# 620 PESO

12.9000 g., Copper-Nickel, 32.5 mm. **Subject:** Turnera Ulmifola **Obv:** National arms within wreath, denomination **Rev:** Multicolor flower **Edge:** Plain

Date	Mintage	F	VF	XF	Unc	BU
1997	5,000	—	—	—	7.00	—

KM# 621 PESO

12.9000 g., Copper-Nickel, 32.5 mm. **Subject:** Cordia Sebestena **Obv:** National arms within wreath, denomination **Rev:** Multicolor flower **Edge:** Plain

Date	Mintage	F	VF	XF	Unc	BU
1997	5,000	—	—	—	7.00	—

KM# 737 PESO

12.9000 g., Copper-Nickel, 32.5 mm. **Subject:** Lochnera Rosea **Obv:** National arms within wreath, denomination **Rev:** Multicolor flower **Edge:** Plain

Date	Mintage	F	VF	XF	Unc	BU
1997	5,000	—	—	—	7.00	—

KM# 738 PESO

12.9000 g., Copper-Nickel, 32.5 mm. **Subject:** Bidens Pilosa **Obv:** National arms within wreath, denomination **Rev:** Multicolor flower **Edge:** Plain

Date	Mintage	F	VF	XF	Unc	BU
1997	5,000	—	—	—	7.00	—

KM# 722 PESO

Copper-Nickel 12.9 oz., 32.5 mm. **Subject:** Hibiscus Elatus **Obv:** National arms within wreath, denomination below **Rev:** Multicolored flower

Date	Mintage	F	VF	XF	Unc	BU
1997	5,000	Value: 12.00				

KM# 612 PESO

Copper-Nickel **Subject:** Fidel Castro's visit to the Vatican **Obv:** National arms within wreath, denomination below **Rev:** Pope and Castro meeting

Date	Mintage	F	VF	XF	Unc	BU
1997	—	—	—	—	15.00	—

KM# 622 PESO

11.3000 g., Copper-Nickel, 30 mm. **Subject:** AIDS **Obv:** National arms within wreath, denomination below **Rev:** AIDS ribbon on silhouette before world map

Date	Mintage	F	VF	XF	Unc	BU
1998	50,000	—	—	—	15.00	—

KM# 732 PESO

25.8300 g., Copper-Nickel, 37.9 mm. **Subject:** Papal Visit **Obv:** National arms within wreath, denomination below **Rev:** Half figure ofPope John Paul II facing left, cathedral at left **Edge:** Plain

Date	Mintage	F	VF	XF	Unc	BU
1998	—	—	—	—	16.50	—

KM# 662 PESO

Copper-Nickel **Subject:** 40th Anniversary - The Triumph of the Revolution

Date	Mintage	F	VF	XF	Unc	BU
1999	—	—	—	—	15.00	—

KM# 663 PESO

Copper Nickel **Subject:** Hacia un Nuevo Milenio - Towards a New Millennium

Date	Mintage	F	VF	XF	Unc	BU
2000	—	—	—	—	12.00	—

KM# 664 PESO

Copper Nickel **Subject:** Welcome the Third Millennium

Date	Mintage	F	VF	XF	Unc	BU
2000	—	—	—	—	12.00	—

KM# 665 PESO
Copper Nickel **Subject:** Welcome to the New Millennium

Date	Mintage	F	VF	XF	Unc	BU
2000	—	—	—	—	12.00	—

KM# 346 3 PESOS
Copper-Nickel, 26.3 mm. **Subject:** Ernesto Che Guevara **Obv:** National arms within wreath, denomination below **Rev:** Head facing, date below

Date	Mintage	F	VF	XF	Unc	BU
1990	4,050,000	—	—	3.00	6.00	8.00

KM# 346a 3 PESOS
8.2000 g., Nickel Clad Steel, 26.3 mm. **Obv:** National arms within wreath, denomination below **Rev:** Head facing, date below

Date	Mintage	F	VF	XF	Unc	BU
1992	—	—	—	3.00	6.00	8.00
1992 Proof	500	Value: 12.50				
1995	—	—	—	3.00	6.00	8.00

KM# 36 5 PESOS
13.3300 g., 0.9000 Silver .3857 oz. ASW **Subject:** 25th Anniversary - National Bank of Cuba **Obv:** Star behind arms above 1/2 wreath, denomination below **Rev:** Multi-storied building

Date	Mintage	F	VF	XF	Unc	BU
ND(1975) Proof	50,000	Value: 12.00				

KM# 47 5 PESOS
12.0000 g., 0.9990 Silver .3855 oz. ASW **Subject:** First Soviet-Cuban Space Flight **Obv:** National arms within wreath, denomination below **Rev:** Shuttle orbiting planet, date below

Date	Mintage	F	VF	XF	Unc	BU
1980	10,000	—	—	—	11.50	—
1980 Proof	5,000	Value: 50.00				

KM# 48 5 PESOS
12.0000 g., 0.9990 Silver .3855 oz. ASW **Subject:** Moscow Olympics **Obv:** National arms within wreath, denomination **Rev:** Three small squares depict athletes

Date	Mintage	F	VF	XF	Unc	BU
1980	10,000	—	—	—	10.00	—

KM# 49 5 PESOS
12.0000 g., 0.9990 Silver .3855 oz. ASW **Obv:** National arms within wreath, denomination below **Rev:** Cuban flower - Mariposa

Date	Mintage	F	VF	XF	Unc	BU
1980	10,000	—	—	—	12.50	—
1980 Proof	2,000	Value: 25.00				

KM# 69 5 PESOS
12.0000 g., 0.9990 Silver .3855 oz. ASW **Obv:** National arms within wreath, denomination below **Rev:** Cuban flower - Azahar

Date	Mintage	F	VF	XF	Unc	BU
1981	10,000	—	—	—	12.50	—
1981 Proof	2,000	Value: 25.00				

KM# 70 5 PESOS
12.0000 g., 0.9990 Silver .3855 oz. ASW **Obv:** National arms within wreath, denomination below **Rev:** Cuban flower - Orquidea

Date	Mintage	F	VF	XF	Unc	BU
1981	10,000	—	—	—	12.50	—
1981 Proof	2,000	Value: 25.00				

KM# 71 5 PESOS
12.0000 g., 0.9990 Silver .3855 oz. ASW **Obv:** National arms within wreath, denomination below **Rev:** Columbus' ship - Nina

Date	Mintage	F	VF	XF	Unc	BU
1981	10,000	—	—	—	22.50	—
1981 Proof	1,000	Value: 50.00				

KM# 72 5 PESOS
12.0000 g., 0.9990 Silver .3855 oz. ASW **Obv:** National arms within wreath, denomination below **Rev:** Columbus' ship - Pinta

Date	Mintage	F	VF	XF	Unc	BU
1981	10,000	—	—	—	22.50	—
1981 Proof	1,000	Value: 50.00				

KM# 73 5 PESOS
12.0000 g., 0.9990 Silver .3855 oz. ASW **Obv:** National arms within wreath, denomination below **Rev:** Columbus' ship - Santa Maria

Date	Mintage	F	VF	XF	Unc	BU
1981	10,000	—	—	—	22.50	—
1981 Proof	1,000	Value: 50.00				

KM# 74 5 PESOS
12.0000 g., 0.9990 Silver .3855 oz. ASW **Series:** Cuban Fauna **Obv:** National arms within wreath, denomination below **Rev:** Crocodiles, date above

Date	Mintage	F	VF	XF	Unc	BU
1981	5,000	—	—	—	20.00	—
1981 Proof	1,000	Value: 35.00				

KM# 75 5 PESOS
12.0000 g., 0.9990 Silver .3855 oz. ASW **Series:** Cuban Fauna **Obv:** National arms within wreath, denomination below **Rev:** Emerald Hummingbird

Date	Mintage	F	VF	XF	Unc	BU
1981	5,000	—	—	—	20.00	—
1981 Proof	1,000	Value: 35.00				

KM# 76 5 PESOS
12.0000 g., 0.9990 Silver .3855 oz. ASW **Series:** Cuban Fauna **Obv:** National arms within wreath, denomination below **Rev:** Bee Hummingbird

Date	Mintage	F	VF	XF	Unc	BU
1981	5,000	—	—	—	20.00	—
1981 Proof	1,000	Value: 35.00				

KM# 77 5 PESOS
12.0000 g., 0.9990 Silver .3855 oz. ASW **Subject:** Soccer Games - Spain 1982 **Obv:** National arms within wreath, denomination below **Rev:** Soccer player

Date	Mintage	F	VF	XF	Unc	BU
1981 Proof	4,000	Value: 22.50				

KM# 78 5 PESOS

12.0000 g., 0.9990 Silver .3855 oz. ASW **Subject:** World Food Day - Sugar Production **Obv:** National arms within wreath, denomination below **Rev:** Sugarcane plant, date at right

Date	Mintage	F	VF	XF	Unc	BU
1981	7,000	—	—	—	18.00	—
1981 Proof	1,560	Value: 25.00				

KM# 79 5 PESOS

12.0000 g., 0.9990 Silver .3855 oz. ASW **Subject:** XIV Central American and Caribbean Games **Obv:** National arms within wreath, denomination below **Rev:** Animated Mascot

Date	Mintage	F	VF	XF	Unc	BU
1981	5,000	—	—	—	15.00	—
1981 Proof	2,000	Value: 32.50				

KM# 80 5 PESOS

12.0000 g., 0.9990 Silver .3855 oz. ASW **Subject:** XIV Central American and Caribbean Games **Obv:** National arms within wreath, denomination below **Rev:** Three athletes

Date	Mintage	F	VF	XF	Unc	BU
1981	5,000	—	—	—	11.50	—
1981 Proof	2,000	Value: 30.00				

KM# 81 5 PESOS

12.0000 g., 0.9990 Silver .3855 oz. ASW **Subject:** XIV Central American and Caribbean Games **Obv:** National arms within wreath, denomination below **Rev:** Boxers

Date	Mintage	F	VF	XF	Unc	BU
1981	5,000	—	—	—	11.50	—
1981 Proof	2,000	Value: 30.00				

KM# 82 5 PESOS

12.0000 g., 0.9990 Silver .3855 oz. ASW **Series:** Cuban Fauna **Obv:** National arms within wreath, denomination below **Rev:** Cuban Tocororo

Date	Mintage	F	VF	XF	Unc	BU
1981	5,000	—	—	—	15.00	—
1981 Proof	1,000	Value: 30.00				

KM# 83 5 PESOS

12.0000 g., 0.9990 Silver .3855 oz. ASW **Series:** Cuban Fauna **Obv:** National arms within wreath, denomination below **Rev:** Cuban Solenodon left, date below

Date	Mintage	F	VF	XF	Unc	BU
1981	5,000	—	—	—	15.00	—
1981 Proof	1,000	Value: 30.00				

KM# 84 5 PESOS

12.0000 g., 0.9990 Silver .3855 oz. ASW **Series:** Cuban Fauna **Obv:** National arms within wreath, denomination below **Rev:** Giant Garfish left, date above

Date	Mintage	F	VF	XF	Unc	BU
1981	5,000	—	—	—	15.00	—
1981 Proof	1,000	Value: 30.00				

KM# 96 5 PESOS

12.0000 g., 0.9990 Silver .3855 oz. ASW **Obv:** National arms within wreath, denomination below **Rev:** Bust facing, three dates

Date	Mintage	F	VF	XF	Unc	BU
1982	5,000	—	—	—	20.00	—
1982 Proof	1,000	Value: 40.00				

KM# 97 5 PESOS

12.0000 g., 0.9990 Silver .3855 oz. ASW **Obv:** National arms within wreath, denomination below **Rev:** Ernest Hemingway's fishing yacht

Date	Mintage	F	VF	XF	Unc	BU
1982	5,000	—	—	—	20.00	—
1982 Proof	1,000	Value: 40.00				

KM# 98 5 PESOS

12.0000 g., 0.9990 Silver .3855 oz. ASW **Obv:** National arms within wreath, denomination below **Rev:** Ernest Hemingway - small boat

Date	Mintage	F	VF	XF	Unc	BU
1982	5,000	—	—	—	20.00	—
1982 Proof	1,000	Value: 40.00				

KM# 99 5 PESOS

12.0000 g., 0.9990 Silver .3855 oz. ASW **Obv:** National arms within wreath, denomination below **Rev:** Miguel De Cervantes

Date	Mintage	F	VF	XF	Unc	BU
1982	7,000	—	—	—	14.00	—
1982 Proof	2,000	Value: 40.00				

KM# 100 5 PESOS

12.0000 g., 0.9990 Silver .3855 oz. ASW **Obv:** National arms within wreath, denomination below **Rev:** Hidalgo Don Quijote on horse

Date	Mintage	F	VF	XF	Unc	BU
1982	7,000	—	—	—	14.00	—
1982 Proof	2,000	Value: 40.00				

KM# 101 5 PESOS

12.0000 g., 0.9990 Silver .3855 oz. ASW **Subject:** Hidalgo Don Quijote and Sancho Panza **Obv:** National arms within wreath, denomination below **Rev:** Small figure on mule, larger figure with lance on horse

Date	Mintage	F	VF	XF	Unc	BU
1982	7,000	—	—	—	14.00	—
1982 Proof	2,000	Value: 40.00				

KM# 102 5 PESOS

12.0000 g., 0.9990 Silver .3855 oz. ASW **Series:** F.A.O. **Obv:** National arms within wreath, denomination below **Rev:** Citrus fruit

Date	Mintage	F	VF	XF	Unc	BU
1982	3,125	—	—	—	20.00	—
1982 Proof	1,040	Value: 32.50				

KM# 103 5 PESOS

12.0000 g., 0.9990 Silver .3855 oz. ASW **Series:** F.A.O. **Obv:** National arms within wreath, denomination below **Rev:** Cow on grass left

Date	Mintage	F	VF	XF	Unc	BU
1982	4,177	—	—	—	20.00	—
1982 Proof	1,000	Value: 32.50				

KM# 108 5 PESOS

12.0000 g., 0.9990 Silver .3855 oz. ASW **Series:** 1984 Winter Olympics - Hockey **Obv:** National arms within wreath, denomination below **Rev:** Miguel De Cervantes

Date	Mintage	F	VF	XF	Unc	BU
1983 Proof	5,000	Value: 15.00				

KM# 109 5 PESOS

12.0000 g., 0.9990 Silver .3855 oz. ASW **Series:** 1984 Summer Olympics **Obv:** National arms within wreath, denomination below **Rev:** Runner

Date	Mintage	F	VF	XF	Unc	BU
1983 Proof	5,000	Value: 15.00				

KM# 110 5 PESOS

12.0000 g., 0.9990 Silver .3855 oz. ASW **Obv:** National arms within wreath, denomination below **Rev:** Train on track, date below

Date	Mintage	F	VF	XF	Unc	BU
1983	5,000	—	—	—	15.00	—
1983 Proof	2,000	Value: 30.00				

KM# 111 5 PESOS
12.0000 g., 0.9990 Silver .3855 oz. ASW **Subject:** World Fisheries **Obv:** National arms within wreath, denomination below **Rev:** Spiny lobster

Date	Mintage	F	VF	XF	Unc	BU
1983	5,000	—	—	—	20.00	—
1983 Proof	1,000	Value: 40.00				

KM# 112 5 PESOS
12.0000 g., 0.9990 Silver .3855 oz. ASW **Subject:** Winter Olympics **Obv:** National arms within wreath, denomination below **Rev:** Woman holding torch

Date	Mintage	F	VF	XF	Unc	BU
1983 Proof	5,000	Value: 15.00				

KM# 113 5 PESOS
12.0000 g., 0.9990 Silver .3855 oz. ASW **Series:** Winter Olympics **Obv:** National arms within wreath, denomination below **Rev:** Downhill skier

Date	Mintage	F	VF	XF	Unc	BU
1983 Proof	5,000	Value: 15.00				

KM# 114 5 PESOS
12.0000 g., 0.9990 Silver .3855 oz. ASW **Series:** Summer Olympics **Obv:** National arms within wreath, denomination below **Rev:** Discus thrower

Date	Mintage	F	VF	XF	Unc	BU
1983 Proof	5,000	Value: 15.00				

KM# 115 5 PESOS
12.0000 g., 0.9990 Silver .3855 oz. ASW **Series:** Summer Olympics **Obv:** National arms within wreath, denomination below **Rev:** Judo match, date at right

Date	Mintage	F	VF	XF	Unc	BU
1983 Proof	5,000	Value: 15.00				

KM# 117 5 PESOS
12.0000 g., 0.9990 Silver .3855 oz. ASW **Subject:** Transportation **Obv:** National arms within wreath, denomination below **Rev:** Freighter, date below

Date	Mintage	F	VF	XF	Unc	BU
1984	5,000	—	—	—	18.00	—
1984 Proof	1,000	Value: 40.00				

KM# 119 5 PESOS
12.0000 g., 0.9990 Silver .3855 oz. ASW **Obv:** National arms within wreath, denomination below **Rev:** Santisimo Trinidad, date at left

Date	Mintage	F	VF	XF	Unc	BU
1984	5,000	—	—	—	16.50	—

KM# 131 5 PESOS
12.0000 g., 0.9990 Silver .3855 oz. ASW **Subject:** Transportation **Obv:** National arms within wreath, denomination below **Rev:** Volanta coach

Date	Mintage	F	VF	XF	Unc	BU
1984	5,000	—	—	—	11.50	—
1984 Proof	1,000	Value: 40.00				

KM# 666 5 PESOS
12.0000 g., 0.9990 Silver .3855 oz. ASW **Subject:** Transportation **Obv:** National arms within wreath, denomination below **Rev:** Hot air balloon

Date	Mintage	F	VF	XF	Unc	BU
1984	2	—	—	—	4,000	—

KM# 141 5 PESOS
12.0000 g., 0.9990 Silver .3855 oz. ASW **Subject:** Fortress - El Morro La Habana **Obv:** National arms within wreath, denomination below **Rev:** Fortress, date at left

Date	Mintage	F	VF	XF	Unc	BU
1984	5,000	—	—	—	14.00	—
1984 Proof	1,000	Value: 45.00				

KM# 143 5 PESOS
12.0000 g., 0.9990 Silver .3855 oz. ASW **Subject:** La Fuerza La Habana **Obv:** National arms within wreath, denomination below **Rev:** Fortress

Date	Mintage	F	VF	XF	Unc	BU
1984	5,000	—	—	—	14.00	—
1984 Proof	1,000	Value: 45.00				

KM# 145 5 PESOS
12.0000 g., 0.9990 Silver .3855 oz. ASW **Subject:** El Morro Santiago De Cuba **Obv:** National arms within wreath, denomination below **Rev:** Fortress

Date	Mintage	F	VF	XF	Unc	BU
1984	5,000	—	—	—	14.00	—
1984 Proof	1,000	Value: 45.00				

KM# 121 5 PESOS
12.0000 g., 0.9990 Silver .3855 oz. ASW **Subject:** International Year of Music - Bach

Date	Mintage	F	VF	XF	Unc	BU
1985	2,000	—	—	—	32.50	—
1985 Proof	—	Value: 45.00				

KM# 123 5 PESOS
12.0000 g., 0.9990 Silver .3855 oz. ASW **Subject:** Soccer **Obv:** National arms within wreath, denomination below **Rev:** Two soccer players

Date	Mintage	F	VF	XF	Unc	BU
1985	5,000	—	—	—	18.00	—
1985 Proof	—	Value: 35.00				

KM# 125 5 PESOS
12.0000 g., 0.9990 Silver .3855 oz. ASW **Subject:** Wildlife Preservation **Obv:** National arms within wreath, denomination below **Rev:** Cuban crocodile

Date	Mintage	F	VF	XF	Unc	BU
1985	5,000	—	—	—	35.00	—

KM# 127 5 PESOS
12.0000 g., 0.9990 Silver .3855 oz. ASW **Subject:** Wildlife Preservation **Obv:** National arms within wreath, denomination below **Rev:** Cuban Rock Iquana

Date	Mintage	F	VF	XF	Unc	BU
1985	5,000	—	—	—	40.00	—

KM# 129 5 PESOS
12.0000 g., 0.9990 Silver .3855 oz. ASW **Subject:** Wildlife Preservation **Obv:** National arms within wreath, denomination below **Rev:** Cuban Amazon Parrot

Date	Mintage	F	VF	XF	Unc	BU
1985	5,000	—	—	—	30.00	—

KM# 146 5 PESOS

12.0000 g., 0.9990 Silver .3855 oz. ASW **Subject:** 40th Anniversary of F.A.O. **Obv:** National arms within wreath, denomination below **Rev:** Lobster, palm tree, and sugar cane

Date	Mintage	F	VF	XF	Unc	BU
ND(1985)	4,500	—	—	—	11.50	—
ND(1985) Proof	500	Value: 45.00				

KM# 147 5 PESOS

12.0000 g., 0.9990 Silver .3855 oz. ASW **Series:** F.A.O. **Subject:** Forestry **Obv:** National arms within wreath, denomination below **Rev:** Stylized forest

Date	Mintage	F	VF	XF	Unc	BU
ND(1985)	4,500	—	—	—	22.50	—
ND(1985) Proof	500	Value: 40.00				

KM# 135 5 PESOS

12.0000 g., 0.9990 Silver .3855 oz. ASW **Subject:** 100th Anniversary of the Automobile **Obv:** National arms within wreath, denomination below **Rev:** Daimler-Benz

Date	Mintage	F	VF	XF	Unc	BU
ND(1986)	2,500	—	—	—	22.50	—

KM# 137 5 PESOS

12.0000 g., 0.9990 Silver .3855 oz. ASW **Subject:** 30th Anniversary - Voyage of the Granma **Obv:** National arms within wreath, denomination below **Rev:** Large ship at sea, dates

Date	Mintage	F	VF	XF	Unc	BU
ND(1986)	2,500	—	—	—	20.00	—

KM# 139 5 PESOS

12.0000 g., 0.9990 Silver .3855 oz. ASW **Series:** Olympics **Obv:** National arms within wreath, denomination below **Rev:** Skater

Date	Mintage	F	VF	XF	Unc	BU
1986	2,500	—	—	—	30.00	—

KM# 157 5 PESOS

12.0000 g., 0.9990 Silver .3855 oz. ASW **Series:** F.A.O. **Subject:** International Year of Peace **Obv:** National arms within wreath, denomination below

Date	Mintage	F	VF	XF	Unc	BU
1986	10,000	—	—	—	22.50	—
1986 Proof	2,000	Value: 32.50				

KM# 199 5 PESOS

12.0000 g., 0.9990 Silver .3855 oz. ASW **Series:** Olympics **Obv:** National arms within wreath, denomination below **Rev:** Without rings above skater

Date	Mintage	F	VF	XF	Unc	BU
1986	10,000	—	—	—	10.00	—

KM# 149 5 PESOS

12.0000 g., 0.9990 Silver .3855 oz. ASW **Subject:** Cathedral in Santiago **Obv:** National arms within wreath, denomination below **Rev:** Cathedral, date above

Date	Mintage	F	VF	XF	Unc	BU
1987	2,500	—	—	—	25.00	—

KM# 151 5 PESOS

12.0000 g., 0.9990 Silver .3855 oz. ASW **Subject:** Cathedral in Caridad del Cobre **Obv:** National arms within wreath, denomination below **Rev:** Cathedral

Date	Mintage	F	VF	XF	Unc	BU
1987	2,500	—	—	—	25.00	—

KM# 153 5 PESOS

12.0000 g., 0.9990 Silver .3855 oz. ASW **Subject:** Cathedral in Trinidad **Obv:** National arms within wreath, denomination below **Rev:** Cathedral

Date	Mintage	F	VF	XF	Unc	BU
1987	2,500	—	—	—	25.00	—

KM# 155 5 PESOS

12.0000 g., 0.9990 Silver .3855 oz. ASW **Subject:** 40th Anniversary - Expedition of Kon-Tiki **Obv:** National arms within wreath, denomination below **Rev:** Full masted ships, dates

Date	Mintage	F	VF	XF	Unc	BU
ND(1987)	5,000	—	—	—	20.00	—

KM# 159 5 PESOS

12.0000 g., 0.9990 Silver .3855 oz. ASW **Subject:** 20th Anniversary - Demise of Ernesto Che Guevara **Obv:** National arms within wreath, denomination below **Rev:** Bust facing divides dates

Date	Mintage	F	VF	XF	Unc	BU
ND(1987)	5,000	—	—	—	35.00	—
ND(1987) Proof	200	Value: 150				

KM# 161 5 PESOS

12.0000 g., 0.9990 Silver .3855 oz. ASW **Subject:** 70th Anniversary - Bolshevik Revolution **Obv:** National arms within wreath, denomination below **Rev:** Ship at sea, date at right

Date	Mintage	F	VF	XF	Unc	BU
1987	3,000	—	—	—	22.50	—
1987 Proof	1,000	Value: 45.00				

KM# 166 5 PESOS

12.0000 g., 0.9990 Silver .3855 oz. ASW **Subject:** 100th Anniversary - Souvenir Peso **Obv:** National arms within wreath, denomination **Rev:** Head right

Date	Mintage	F	VF	XF	Unc	BU
1987	3,000	—	—	—	25.00	—

KM# 326 5 PESOS

12.0000 g., 0.9990 Silver .3855 oz. ASW **Subject:** Abolition of Slavery **Obv:** National arms within wreath, denomination **Rev:** Slave breaking chains, dates

Date	Mintage	F	VF	XF	Unc	BU
1987	2,000	—	—	—	32.50	—

KM# 180 5 PESOS

12.0000 g., 0.9990 Silver .3855 oz. ASW **Subject:** Jose Capablanca Chess Championship - Player **Obv:** National arms within wreath, denomination below **Rev:** Man with chessboard, dates at right

Date	Mintage	F	VF	XF	Unc	BU
ND	5,000	—	—	—	22.50	—

KM# 185 5 PESOS
12.0000 g., 0.9990 Silver .3855 oz. ASW **Subject:** Soccer - Mexico 1986 **Obv:** National arms within wreath, denomination below **Rev:** Soccer players, date at left

Date	Mintage	F	VF	XF	Unc	BU
1988	5,000	—	—	—	16.50	—
1988 Proof	—	Value: 30.00				

KM# 216 5 PESOS
6.0000 g., 0.9990 Silver .1927 oz. ASW **Subject:** Soccer - Italy 1990 **Obv:** Three towers above key on crowned shield within wreath **Rev:** Soccer players, date above

Date	Mintage	F	VF	XF	Unc	BU
1988	—	—	—	—	12.00	—

KM# 216a 5 PESOS
12.0000 g., 0.9990 Silver .3855 oz. ASW **Subject:** Soccer - Italy 1990 **Obv:** Three towers above key on crowned shield within wreath **Rev:** Soccer players, two dates

Date	Mintage	F	VF	XF	Unc	BU
1988	5,000	—	—	—	—	—

Note: Existence in doubt.

KM# 217 5 PESOS
12.0000 g., 0.9990 Silver .3855 oz. ASW **Subject:** Soccer - West Germany **Obv:** Three towers above key on crowned shield within wreath, denomination below **Rev:** Three players

Date	Mintage	F	VF	XF	Unc	BU
1988	5,000	—	—	—	18.50	—

KM# 218 5 PESOS
12.0000 g., 0.9990 Silver .3855 oz. ASW **Subject:** Soccer - West Germany **Obv:** Three towers above key on crowned shield within wreath, denomination below **Rev:** Four players

Date	Mintage	F	VF	XF	Unc	BU
1988	5,000	—	—	—	18.50	—

KM# 219 5 PESOS
16.0000 g., 0.9990 Silver .5145 oz. ASW **Subject:** 40th Anniversary - Cuban National Ballet **Obv:** National arms within wreath, denomination **Rev:** Head of Alicia Alonso right, ballet dancer, dates below

Date	Mintage	F	VF	XF	Unc	BU
ND(1988) Proof	2,000	Value: 47.50				

KM# 220.1 5 PESOS
16.0000 g., 0.9990 Silver .5145 oz. ASW **Obv:** National arms within wreath, denomination **Rev:** Graf Zeppelin

Date	Mintage	F	VF	XF	Unc	BU
1988 Proof	3,000	Value: 200				

KM# 220.2 5 PESOS
15.9400 g., 0.9990 Silver .5119 oz. ASW **Obv:** National arms within wreath, thicker wreath **Rev:** Graf Zeppelin

Date	Mintage	F	VF	XF	Unc	BU
1988 Proof	—	Value: 120				

KM# 221 5 PESOS
16.0000 g., 0.9990 Silver .5119 oz. ASW **Obv:** National arms within wreath, denomination below **Rev:** Carlos J. Finlay

Date	Mintage	F	VF	XF	Unc	BU
ND(1988) Proof	2,000	Value: 47.50				

KM# 222 5 PESOS
16.0000 g., 0.9990 Silver .5119 oz. ASW **Subject:** World Health Organization **Obv:** National arms within wreath, denomination **Rev:** Nurse with baby, building in background

Date	Mintage	F	VF	XF	Unc	BU
ND(1988) Proof	2,000	Value: 47.50				

KM# 223 5 PESOS
16.0000 g., 0.9990 Silver .5119 oz. ASW **Subject:** 150th Anniversary - Grand National Theater in Havana **Obv:** National arms within wreath, denomination below **Rev:** Theater building, dates and inscription at left

Date	Mintage	F	VF	XF	Unc	BU
ND(1988) Proof	2,000	Value: 55.00				

KM# 224.1 5 PESOS
16.0000 g., 0.9990 Silver .5119 oz. ASW **Series:** Olympics - Barcelona **Obv:** National arms within wreath, plain bars **Rev:** Boxing

Date	Mintage	F	VF	XF	Unc	BU
1989 Proof	10,000	Value: 30.00				

KM# 224.2 5 PESOS
16.0000 g., 0.9990 Silver 0.5139 oz. ASW **Subject:** Olympics - Barcelona **Obv:** National arms within wreath, striped bars **Rev:** Boxing

Date	Mintage	F	VF	XF	Unc	BU
1989 Proof	Inc. above	Value: 30.00				

KM# 225.1 5 PESOS
16.0000 g., 0.9990 Silver .5119 oz. ASW **Series:** Olympics - Italy **Obv:** Small thin towers, lower relief, larger rectangular indentations in the tower and the crown **Rev:** Three soccer players

Date	Mintage	F	VF	XF	Unc	BU
1989 Proof	10,000	Value: 30.00				

KM# 225.2 5 PESOS
16.0000 g., 0.9990 Silver .5139 oz. ASW **Subject:** Olympics - Italy **Obv:** Large, thick towers, higher relief, smaller oval indentations in the tower and the crown **Rev:** Three players

Date	Mintage	F	VF	XF	Unc	BU
1989 Proof	Inc. above	Value: 30.00				

KM# 226.1 5 PESOS
16.0000 g., 0.9990 Silver .5119 oz. ASW **Series:** Olympics - Italy **Obv:** Small, thin towers, lower relief, larger rectangular indentations in the towers and crown **Rev:** Colosseum

Date	Mintage	F	VF	XF	Unc	BU
1989 Proof	10,000	Value: 30.00				

KM# 226.2 5 PESOS
16.0000 g., 0.9990 Silver 0.5139 oz. ASW **Subject:** Olympics - Italy **Obv:** Large, thick towers, lower relief, smaller oval indentations in the towers and crown **Rev:** Colosseum

Date	Mintage	F	VF	XF	Unc	BU
1989 Proof	Inc. above	Value: 30.00				

KM# 226.3 5 PESOS
16.0000 g., 0.9990 Silver 0.5139 oz. ASW **Subject:** Olympics - Italy **Obv:** High relief **Rev:** Colosseum

Date	Mintage	F	VF	XF	Unc	BU
1989 Proof	Inc. above	Value: 30.00				

KM# 227.1 5 PESOS
16.0000 g., 0.9990 Silver .5119 oz. ASW **Subject:** Cuban tobacco **Obv:** Arms with plain field at lower right, thin wreath surrounds, denomination below **Rev:** Native smoking above tobacco plant, parrot at right, date below

Date	Mintage	F	VF	XF	Unc	BU
1989 Proof	2,000	Value: 55.00				

KM# 227.2 5 PESOS
16.0000 g., 0.9990 Silver 0.5139 oz. ASW **Subject:** Cuban tobacco **Obv:** Arms with striped field at lower right, thick wreath **Rev:** Native smoking above tobacco plant, parrot at right, date below

Date	Mintage	F	VF	XF	Unc	BU
1989 Proof	Inc. above	Value: 55.00				

KM# 231 5 PESOS
16.0000 g., 0.9990 Silver .5119 oz. ASW **Subject:** Alexander von Humboldt **Obv:** National arms within wreath, denomination **Rev:** Bust in cameo left of birds, dates

Date	Mintage	F	VF	XF	Unc	BU
1989 Proof	3,000	Value: 50.00				

KM# 251.1 5 PESOS
16.0000 g., 0.9990 Silver .5119 oz. ASW **Subject:** Universal Congress of Esperanto **Obv:** Arms with plain field at lower right, thin wreath surrounds, denomination below **Rev:** Bust to right of globe looking left, date below

Date	Mintage	F	VF	XF	Unc	BU
1990 Proof	6,000	Value: 45.00				

KM# 251.2 5 PESOS
16.0000 g., 0.9990 Silver 0.5139 oz. ASW **Subject:** Universal Congress of Esperanto **Obv:** Arms with striped field at lower right, thick wreath **Rev:** Bust to right of globe looking left

Date	Mintage	F	VF	XF	Unc	BU
1990 Proof	Inc. above	Value: 45.00				

KM# 290.1 5 PESOS
16.0000 g., 0.9990 Silver .5119 oz. ASW **Subject:** Soccer **Obv:** Small, thin towers, lower relief, larger rectangular indentations in the towers and crown **Rev:** Map of Italy and soccer balls

Date	Mintage	F	VF	XF	Unc	BU
1990 Proof	10,000	Value: 30.00				

KM# 290.2 5 PESOS
16.0000 g., 0.9990 Silver 0.5139 oz. ASW **Subject:** Soccer **Obv:** Large, thick towers, higher relief, smaller oval indentations in the towers and the crown **Rev:** Map of Italy and soccer balls

Date	Mintage	F	VF	XF	Unc	BU
1990 Proof	Inc. above	Value: 30.00				

KM# 290.3 5 PESOS
16.0000 g., 0.9990 Silver 0.5139 oz. ASW **Subject:** Soccer **Obv:** National arms within wreath, denomination **Rev:** Map of Italy and soccer balls **Note:** Mule

Date	Mintage	F	VF	XF	Unc	BU
1990 Proof	—	Value: 80.00				

KM# 338 5 PESOS
12.0000 g., 0.9990 Silver .3855 oz. ASW **Subject:** Soccer Championship **Obv:** National arms within wreath, denomination **Rev:** Two players

Date	Mintage	F	VF	XF	Unc	BU
1991 Proof	10,000	—	—	—	52.50	—

KM# 405 5 PESOS
6.0000 g., 0.9990 Silver .1927 oz. ASW **Series:** Prehistoric Animals **Obv:** National arms within wreath, denomination below **Rev:** Apatosaurus

Date	Mintage	F	VF	XF	Unc	BU
1993 Proof	30,000	Value: 27.50				

KM# 524.1 5 PESOS
15.0000 g., 0.9990 Silver .4818 oz. ASW **Subject:** Historia Postal de Cuba Steamship **Obv:** National arms within wreath, denomination below, thin letters **Rev:** Side-wheel steamship, date below

Date	Mintage	F	VF	XF	Unc	BU
1993 Proof	25,000	Value: 18.00				

KM# 524.2 5 PESOS
15.0000 g., 0.9990 Silver 0.4818 oz. ASW **Subject:** Historia Postal de Cuba Steamship **Obv:** National arms, thin letters and wreath **Rev:** Side-wheel steamship, curved end 9's in date

Date	Mintage	F	VF	XF	Unc	BU
1993 Proof	Inc. above	Value: 18.00				

KM# 524.3 5 PESOS
15.0000 g., 0.9990 Silver 0.4818 oz. ASW, 33 mm. **Subject:** Historia Postal de Cuba Steamship **Obv:** National arms, thick letters and wreath **Rev:** Side-wheel steamship, curved end 9's in date **Edge:** Reeded

Date	Mintage	F	VF	XF	Unc	BU
1993 Proof	—	Value: 35.00				

KM# 440 5 PESOS
16.0000 g., 0.9990 Silver .5145 oz. ASW **Series:** Prehistoric Animals **Obv:** National arms within wreath, denomination below **Rev:** Triceratops

Date	Mintage	F	VF	XF	Unc	BU
1994 Proof	10,000	Value: 50.00				

KM# 573 5 PESOS
16.0000 g., 0.9990 Silver .5145 oz. ASW **Series:** Prehistoric Animals **Obv:** National arms within wreath, denomination below **Rev:** Maiasaura

Date	Mintage	F	VF	XF	Unc	BU
1994 Proof	—	Value: 50.00				

KM# 581 5 PESOS
7.0000 g., 0.9990 Silver .2248 oz. ASW **Obv:** National arms within wreath, denomination below **Rev:** Multicolored hibiscus

Date	Mintage	F	VF	XF	Unc	BU
1997 Proof	—	Value: 20.00				

KM# 623 5 PESOS
7.0000 g., 0.9990 Silver .2248 oz. ASW, 30 mm. **Subject:** AIDS **Obv:** National arms within wreath, denomination below **Rev:** AIDS ribbon on silhouette before world map

Date	Mintage	F	VF	XF	Unc	BU
1998 Proof	50,000	Value: 18.50				

KM# 673 5 PESOS
0.9990 Gold .0500 oz. AGW **Subject:** Zunzuncita **Obv:** National arms within wreath, denomination **Rev:** Hummingbird

Date	Mintage	F	VF	XF	Unc	BU
1999 Proof	—	Value: 75.00				

KM# 655 5 PESOS
11.3000 g., 0.9990 Silver .3633 oz. ASW **Subject:** Expo 2000 - Philadelphia **Obv:** National arms within wreath, denomination below **Rev:** Cartoon above building

Date	Mintage	F	VF	XF	Unc	BU
1999 Proof	31,000	Value: 16.50				

KM# 656 5 PESOS
11.3000 g., 0.9990 Silver .3633 oz. ASW **Subject:** Expo 2000 - Hannover **Obv:** National arms within wreath, denomination below **Rev:** Cartoon above city hall

Date	Mintage	F	VF	XF	Unc	BU
1999 Proof	31,000	Value: 16.50				

KM# 657 5 PESOS
11.3000 g., 0.9990 Silver .3633 oz. ASW **Subject:** Expo 2000 - Osaka **Obv:** National arms within wreath, denomination below **Rev:** Cartoon above city view

Date	Mintage	F	VF	XF	Unc	BU
1999 Proof	31,000	Value: 16.50				

KM# 658 5 PESOS
11.3000 g., 0.9990 Silver .3633 oz. ASW **Subject:** Expo 2000 - Montreal **Obv:** National arms within wreath, denomination below **Rev:** Cartoon above sports buildings

Date	Mintage	F	VF	XF	Unc	BU
1999 Proof	31,000	Value: 16.50				

KM# 659 5 PESOS
11.3000 g., 0.9990 Silver .3633 oz. ASW **Subject:** Expo 2000 - Twipsy **Obv:** National arms within wreath, denomination below **Rev:** "Twipsy" in square

Date	Mintage	F	VF	XF	Unc	BU
1999 Proof	31,000	Value: 16.50				

KM# 660 5 PESOS
11.3000 g., 0.9990 Silver .3633 oz. ASW **Subject:** Expo 2000 **Obv:** National arms within wreath, denomination below **Rev:** World map with logo center square

Date	Mintage	F	VF	XF	Unc	BU
1999 Proof	31,000	Value: 16.50				

KM# 37 10 PESOS
26.6600 g., 0.9000 Silver .7715 oz. ASW **Subject:** 25th Anniversary - National Bank of Cuba **Obv:** Star behind national arms above half wreat, denomination below **Rev:** Multi-storied building

Date	Mintage	F	VF	XF	Unc	BU
1975 Proof	55,000	Value: 30.00				

KM# 50 10 PESOS
18.0000 g., 0.9990 Silver .5782 oz. ASW **Subject:** First Soviet-Cuban Space Flight **Obv:** National arms within wreath, denomination below **Rev:** Shuttle orbiting planet, date below

Date	Mintage	F	VF	XF	Unc	BU
1980	10,000	—	—	—	20.00	—
1980 Proof	5,000	Value: 35.00				
1980 Matte proof	—	—	—	—	45.00	—

KM# 51 10 PESOS
18.0000 g., 0.9990 Silver .5782 oz. ASW **Subject:** Moscow Olympics **Obv:** National arms within wreath, denomination **Rev:** Three athletic symbols in relief, date below

Date	Mintage	F	VF	XF	Unc	BU
1980	10,000	—	—	—	15.00	—
1980 Matte proof	—	Value: 65.00				

KM# 162 10 PESOS
31.1000 g., 0.9990 Silver 1.0000 oz. ASW **Subject:** Triumph of the Revolution **Obv:** National arms on star background above half wreath, denomination below **Rev:** Castro with revolutionaries divide dates

Date	Mintage	F	VF	XF	Unc	BU
1987 Proof	2,000	Value: 47.50				
1988 Proof	4,000	Value: 37.50				
1989 Proof	2,000	Value: 47.50				

KM# 163 10 PESOS
31.1000 g., 0.9990 Silver 1.0000 oz. ASW **Subject:** 60th Anniversary - Birth of Ernesto Che Guevara **Obv:** National arms on star background above half wreath, denomination below **Rev:** Bust right, date at left

Date	Mintage	F	VF	XF	Unc	BU
1987 Proof	2,000	Value: 47.50				
1988 Proof	4,000	Value: 37.50				
1989 Proof	2,000	Value: 47.50				

KM# 164 10 PESOS
31.1000 g., 0.9990 Silver 1.0000 oz. ASW **Subject:** 30th Anniversary - The March to Victory **Obv:** National arms on star background above half wreath, denomination below **Rev:** Uniformed figures on march

Date	Mintage	F	VF	XF	Unc	BU
1987 Proof	2,000	Value: 47.50				
1988 Proof	4,000	Value: 37.50				
1989 Proof	2,000	Value: 47.50				

KM# 205 10 PESOS
31.1000 g., 0.9990 Silver 1.0000 oz. ASW **Subject:** 150th Anniversary - First Railroad in Spanish America **Obv:** National arms on star background above half wreath, denomination below **Rev:** Train engine on track divides dates

Date	Mintage	F	VF	XF	Unc	BU
1988 Proof	5,000	Value: 40.00				

KM# 206 10 PESOS
31.1000 g., 0.9990 Silver 1.0000 oz. ASW **Subject:** 140th Anniversary - First Railroad in Spain **Obv:** National arms on star background above half wreath, denomination below **Rev:** Train on track, dates below

Date	Mintage	F	VF	XF	Unc	BU
1988 Proof	5,000	Value: 40.00				

KM# 207 10 PESOS
31.1000 g., 0.9990 Silver 1.0000 oz. ASW **Subject:** 160th Anniversary - World's First Railroad **Obv:** National arms on star background above half wreath, denomination below **Rev:** Railroad carts divide dates

Date	Mintage	F	VF	XF	Unc	BU
1988 Proof	5,000	Value: 40.00				

KM# 211 10 PESOS
3.1100 g., 0.9990 Gold .1000 oz. AGW **Obv:** National arms within wreath, denomination below **Rev:** Jose Marti

Date	Mintage	F	VF	XF	Unc	BU
1988	50	—	—	—	125	250
1988 Proof	10	Value: 250				
1989	50	—	—	—	125	250
1989 Proof	15	Value: 250				
1990	15	—	—	—	125	250
1990 Proof	12	Value: 250				

KM# 228 10 PESOS
31.1000 g., 0.9990 Silver 1.0000 oz. ASW **Subject:** Tania La Guerrillera, Argentinian revolutionary **Obv:** National arms on star background above half wreath, denomination below **Rev:** Bust facing

Date	Mintage	F	VF	XF	Unc	BU
1988 Proof	5,000	Value: 42.50				

KM# 229 10 PESOS
31.1000 g., 0.9990 Silver 1.0000 oz. ASW **Subject:** Camilo Cienfuegos **Obv:** National arms on star background above half wreath, denomination below **Rev:** Bust facing

Date	Mintage	F	VF	XF	Unc	BU
1988 Proof	5,000	Value: 42.50				

KM# 230 10 PESOS
31.1000 g., 0.9990 Silver 1.0000 oz. ASW **Subject:** 35th Anniversary - Assault of the Moncada Garrison **Obv:** National arms on star background above half wreat, denomination below **Rev:** Armed figures, dates below

Date	Mintage	F	VF	XF	Unc	BU
ND(1988) Proof	5,000	Value: 42.50				

KM# 238 10 PESOS
20.0000 g., 0.9990 Silver .6431 oz. ASW **Subject:** 5th Centennial - Discovery of America **Obv:** National arms within wreath, denomination below **Rev:** Three ships at sea, date below and at left

Date	Mintage	F	VF	XF	Unc	BU
1989	3,145	—	—	—	47.50	—

KM# 239 10 PESOS
26.7200 g., 0.9990 Silver .8592 oz. ASW **Subject:** 200th Anniversary of French Revolution - Lady Justice **Obv:** National arms within wreath, denomination below **Rev:** 3/4 Figure of Lady Justice, dates above

Date	Mintage	F	VF	XF	Unc	BU
ND(1989)	500	—	—	—	65.00	—
ND(1989) Proof	2,000	Value: 50.00				

KM# 240 10 PESOS
26.7200 g., 0.9990 Silver .8592 oz. ASW **Subject:** 200th Anniversary of French Revolution **Obv:** Small national arms within wreath, denomination below **Rev:** Bastille

Date	Mintage	F	VF	XF	Unc	BU
ND(1989)	500	—	—	—	65.00	—
ND(1989) Proof	2,000	Value: 50.00				

KM# 241.1 10 PESOS
31.1000 g., 0.9990 Silver 1.0000 oz. ASW **Subject:** 30th Anniversary of Revolution **Obv:** Arms with plain field at lower right, thin wreath **Rev:** Castro

Date	Mintage	F	VF	XF	Unc	BU
ND(1989)	5,000	—	—	—	40.00	—
ND(1989) Proof	5,000	Value: 50.00				

KM# 242.1 10 PESOS
31.1000 g., 0.9990 Silver 1.0000 oz. ASW **Subject:** 30th Anniversary of Revolution **Obv:** Arms with plain field at lower right, thin wreath **Rev:** Jose Marti and Castro

Date	Mintage	F	VF	XF	Unc	BU
1989	5,000	—	—	—	40.00	—
1989 Proof	5,000	Value: 50.00				

KM# 243.1 10 PESOS
31.1000 g., 0.9990 Silver 1.0000 oz. ASW **Subject:** 30th Anniversary of Revolution **Obv:** Arms with plain field at lower right, thin wreath **Rev:** Camilo Cienfuegos and Fidel Castro, inscription above, dates at right

Date	Mintage	F	VF	XF	Unc	BU
ND(1989)	5,000	—	—	—	40.00	—
ND(1989) Proof	5,000	Value: 70.00				

KM# 249.1 10 PESOS
20.0000 g., 0.9990 Silver .6431 oz. ASW **Subject:** Discovery of America **Obv:** Arms with plain field at lower right, thin wreath, denomination below **Rev:** Three sailing ships, date below and at left

Date	Mintage	F	VF	XF	Unc	BU
1989 Proof	8,855	Value: 40.00				

KM# 383 10 PESOS

3.1100 g., 0.9990 Gold .1000 oz. AGW **Obv:** National arms within wreath, denomination below **Rev:** Alexander von Humboldt

Date	Mintage	F	VF	XF	Unc	BU
1989	500	—	—	—	—	125
1989 Proof	—	Value: 100				

KM# 241.2 10 PESOS

31.1000 g., 0.9990 Silver 0.9989 oz. ASW **Subject:** 30th Anniversary of Revolution **Obv:** Arms with striped field at lower right, thick wreath **Rev:** Castro

Date	Mintage	F	VF	XF	Unc	BU
ND(1989)	Inc. above	—	—	—	40.00	—
ND(1989) Proof	Inc. above	Value: 50.00				

KM# 242.2 10 PESOS

31.1000 g., 0.9990 Silver 0.9989 oz. ASW **Subject:** 30th Anniversary of Revolution **Obv:** Arms with striped field at lower right, thick wreath **Rev:** Jose Marti and Castro

Date	Mintage	F	VF	XF	Unc	BU
1989	Inc. above	—	—	—	40.00	—
1989 Proof	Inc. above	Value: 70.00				

KM# 243.2 10 PESOS

31.1000 g., 0.9990 Silver 0.9989 oz. ASW **Subject:** 30th Anniversary of Revolution **Obv:** Arms with striped field at lower right, thick wreath **Rev:** Camilo Cienfuegos and Fidel Castro

Date	Mintage	F	VF	XF	Unc	BU
ND(1989)	Inc. above	—	—	—	40.00	—
ND(1989) Proof	Inc. above	Value: 50.00				

KM# 249.2 10 PESOS

20.0000 g., 0.9990 Silver 0.6424 oz. ASW **Subject:** Discovery of America **Obv:** Arms with striped field at lower right, thick wreath **Rev:** Three sailing ships

Date	Mintage	F	VF	XF	Unc	BU
1989 Proof	Inc. above	Value: 40.00				

KM# 252.2 10 PESOS

20.0000 g., 0.9990 Silver 0.6424 oz. ASW **Subject:** Discovery of America **Obv:** Arms with striped field at lower right, thick wreath **Rev:** Ship and map of Cuba

Date	Mintage	F	VF	XF	Unc	BU
1990 Proof	Inc. above	Value: 40.00				

KM# 256.2 10 PESOS

20.0000 g., 0.9990 Silver 0.6424 oz. ASW **Subject:** 500th Anniversary of Columbus Meeting Native Americans **Obv:** Arms with striped field at lower right, thick wreath

Date	Mintage	F	VF	XF	Unc	BU
1990 Proof	Inc. above	Value: 40.00				

KM# 262.2 10 PESOS

31.1030 g., 0.9990 Silver 0.999 oz. ASW **Obv:** Arms with striped bars at lower right, thick wreath **Rev:** Celia Sanchez Manduley

Date	Mintage	F	VF	XF	Unc	BU
1990 Proof	Inc. above	Value: 55.00				

KM# 267.2 10 PESOS

20.0000 g., 0.9990 Silver 0.6424 oz. ASW **Subject:** Discovery of America **Obv:** Arms with striped field at lower right, thick wreath **Rev:** Map of Columbus' route

Date	Mintage	F	VF	XF	Unc	BU
1990 Proof	Inc. above	Value: 35.00				

KM# 336.2 10 PESOS

28.0000 g., 0.9250 Silver 0.8327 oz. ASW **Subject:** Summer Olympics **Obv:** Large characters **Rev:** Hurdler

Date	Mintage	F	VF	XF	Unc	BU
1990 Proof	Inc. above	Value: 50.00				

KM# 344.2 10 PESOS

28.0000 g., 0.9250 Silver 0.8327 oz. ASW **Subject:** Summer Olympics **Obv:** Large characters **Rev:** Volleyball

Date	Mintage	F	VF	XF	Unc	BU
1990 Proof	Inc. above	Value: 50.00				

KM# 362.2 10 PESOS

28.0000 g., 0.9250 Silver 0.8327 oz. ASW **Subject:** Olympics **Obv:** Large characters **Rev:** Basketball

Date	Mintage	F	VF	XF	Unc	BU
1990 Proof	Inc. above	Value: 50.00				

KM# 252.1 10 PESOS

20.0000 g., 0.9990 Silver .6431 oz. ASW **Subject:** Discovery of America **Obv:** Arms with plain field at lower right, thin wreath **Rev:** Ship and map of Cuba, date at right

Date	Mintage	F	VF	XF	Unc	BU
1990 Proof	10,000	Value: 40.00				

KM# 256.1 10 PESOS

20.0000 g., 0.9990 Silver .6431 oz. ASW **Subject:** 500th Anniversary of Columbus Meeting Native Americans **Obv:** Arms with plain field at lower right, thin wreath **Rev:** Columbus meeting natives, date below

Date	Mintage	F	VF	XF	Unc	BU
1990 Proof	10,000	Value: 40.00				

KM# 262.1 10 PESOS

31.1030 g., 0.9990 Silver 1.0000 oz. ASW **Obv:** Arms with plain field at lower right, thin wreath **Rev:** Celia Sanchez Manduley

Date	Mintage	F	VF	XF	Unc	BU
1990 Proof	2,000	Value: 55.00				

KM# 263 10 PESOS

31.1030 g., 0.9990 Silver 1.0000 oz. ASW **Subject:** Discovery of America **Obv:** National arms within wreath, denomination **Rev:** King Ferdinand bust 3/4 right within wreath, two dates

Date	Mintage	F	VF	XF	Unc	BU
1990 Proof	5,000	Value: 50.00				

KM# 264 10 PESOS

31.1030 g., 0.9990 Silver 1.0000 oz. ASW **Subject:** Discovery of America **Obv:** National arms within wreath, denomination **Rev:** Queen Isabella

Date	Mintage	F	VF	XF	Unc	BU
1990 Proof	5,000	Value: 50.00				

KM# 265 10 PESOS

31.1030 g., 0.9990 Silver 1.0000 oz. ASW **Subject:** Discovery of America **Obv:** National arms within wreath, denomination below **Rev:** Christopher Columbus

Date	Mintage	F	VF	XF	Unc	BU
1990 Proof	5,000	Value: 50.00				

KM# 266 10 PESOS

31.1030 g., 0.9990 Silver 1.0000 oz. ASW **Subject:** Discovery of America **Obv:** National arms within wreath, denomination below **Rev:** Juan de la Casa

Date	Mintage	F	VF	XF	Unc	BU
1990 Proof	5,000	Value: 50.00				

KM# 267.1 10 PESOS

20.0000 g., 0.9990 Silver .6438 oz. ASW **Subject:** Discovery of America **Obv:** Arms with plain field at lower right, thin wreath **Rev:** Map of Columbus' route

Date	Mintage	F	VF	XF	Unc	BU
1990 Proof	10,000	Value: 35.00				

KM# 280 10 PESOS

25.0000 g., 0.9990 Silver .9037 oz. ASW **Subject:** Simon Bolivar **Obv:** National arms within wreath, denomination **Rev:** Uniformed bust right

Date	Mintage	F	VF	XF	Unc	BU
1990 Proof	3,300	Value: 47.50				

KM# 291 10 PESOS
31.1000 g., 0.9990 Silver 1.0000 oz. ASW **Subject:** Pan American Games **Obv:** National arms within wreath, denomination **Rev:** High jumper

Date	Mintage	F	VF	XF	Unc	BU
1990 Proof	3,000	Value: 55.00				

KM# 292 10 PESOS
31.1000 g., 0.9990 Silver 1.0000 oz. ASW **Subject:** Pan American Games **Obv:** National arms within wreath, denomination **Rev:** Volleyball

Date	Mintage	F	VF	XF	Unc	BU
1990 Proof	3,000	Value: 55.00				

KM# 293 10 PESOS
31.1000 g., 0.9990 Silver 1.0000 oz. ASW **Subject:** Pan American Games **Obv:** National arms within wreath, denomination **Rev:** Baseball game scene

Date	Mintage	F	VF	XF	Unc	BU
1990 Proof	3,000	Value: 57.50				

KM# 336.1 10 PESOS
28.0000 g., 0.9250 Silver .8327 oz. ASW **Series:** Summer Olympics **Obv:** Small characters **Rev:** Hurdler, tiny date at left

Date	Mintage	F	VF	XF	Unc	BU
1990 Proof	25,000	Value: 25.00				

KM# 342 10 PESOS
3.1100 g., 0.9990 Gold .1000 oz. AGW **Series:** Olympics **Obv:** National arms within wreath, denomination below **Rev:** Basketball hoop, ball and hands, small date between arms below

Date	Mintage	F	VF	XF	Unc	BU
1990 Proof	Est. 5,000	Value: 100				

KM# 344.1 10 PESOS
28.0000 g., 0.9250 Silver .8327 oz. ASW **Series:** Summer Olympics **Obv:** Small characters **Rev:** Volleyball

Date	Mintage	F	VF	XF	Unc	BU
1990 Proof	25,000	Value: 25.00				

KM# 345 10 PESOS
28.0000 g., 0.9250 Silver .8327 oz. ASW **Series:** Summer Olympics **Obv:** Small characters **Rev:** High jumper

Date	Mintage	F	VF	XF	Unc	BU
1990 Proof	25,000	Value: 25.00				

KM# 362.1 10 PESOS
28.0000 g., 0.9250 Silver .8327 oz. ASW **Series:** Olympics **Obv:** Small characters **Rev:** Basketball players

Date	Mintage	F	VF	XF	Unc	BU
1990 Proof	25,000	Value: 25.00				

KM# 369 10 PESOS
28.0000 g., 0.9990 Silver .8994 oz. ASW **Series:** Olympics **Obv. Designer:** Small characters **Rev:** Figure on pommel horse, date below

Date	Mintage	F	VF	XF	Unc	BU
1990 Proof	Est. 25,000	Value: 25.00				

KM# 327 10 PESOS
31.1000 g., 0.9990 Silver 1.0000 oz. ASW **Obv:** National arms within wreath, denomination **Rev:** Vicente and Martin Pinzon in cameos

Date	Mintage	F	VF	XF	Unc	BU
1991 Proof	3,000	Value: 55.00				

KM# 328 10 PESOS
31.1000 g., 0.9990 Silver 1.0000 oz. ASW **Obv:** National arms within wreath, denomination **Rev:** Hatuey tribesman

Date	Mintage	F	VF	XF	Unc	BU
1991 Proof	3,000	Value: 55.00				

KM# 329 10 PESOS
25.0000 g., 0.9990 Silver .8031 oz. ASW **Subject:** American International Monetary Conference **Obv:** National arms within wreath, denomination divided above **Rev:** Bust facing, dates below

Date	Mintage	F	VF	XF	Unc	BU
ND(1991) Proof	3,300	Value: 55.00				

KM# 337 10 PESOS
27.0000 g., 0.9990 Silver .8673 oz. ASW **Subject:** Ibero - American **Obv:** National arms within wreath, denomination below within inner circle, circle of arms surround **Rev:** Statue of Columbus at Gardenas, dates at right

Date	Mintage	F	VF	XF	Unc	BU
1991 Proof	51,000	Value: 40.00				

KM# 348 10 PESOS
31.1000 g., 0.9990 Silver 1.0000 oz. ASW **Subject:** Madrid **Obv:** National arms within wreath, denomination **Rev:** Alcala Gate

Date	Mintage	F	VF	XF	Unc	BU
1991 Proof	Est. 3,250	Value: 55.00				

KM# 349 10 PESOS
31.1000 g., 0.9990 Silver 1.0000 oz. ASW **Subject:** Seville **Obv:** National arms within wreath, denomination **Rev:** La Giralda Tower

Date	Mintage	F	VF	XF	Unc	BU
1991 Proof	Est. 3,250	Value: 55.00				

KM# 350 10 PESOS
31.1000 g., 0.9990 Silver 1.0000 oz. ASW **Subject:** Barcelona **Obv:** National arms within wreath, denomination **Rev:** Olympic Stadium

Date	Mintage	F	VF	XF	Unc	BU
1991 Proof	3,250	Value: 42.50				

KM# 525 10 PESOS
31.1000 g., 0.9990 Silver 1.0000 oz. ASW **Obv:** National arms within wreath, denomination **Rev:** Diego Velazquez

Date	Mintage	F	VF	XF	Unc	BU
1991 Proof	3,000	Value: 55.00				

KM# 526 10 PESOS
31.1000 g., 0.9990 Silver 1.0000 oz. ASW **Subject:** 500th Anniversary of New World **Obv:** National arms within wreath, denomination **Rev:** Head of Queen Joanna, right, 1479-1555, daughter of Isabella I

Date	Mintage	F	VF	XF	Unc	BU
1991 Proof	3,000	Value: 55.00				

KM# 341.1 10 PESOS
20.0000 g., 0.9990 Silver .6430 oz. ASW **Subject:** Postal History of Cuba **Obv:** 1992 style national arms **Rev:** Spanish galleon sailship, 1765 date

Date	Mintage	F	VF	XF	Unc	BU
1992 Proof	10,000	Value: 35.00				

KM# 341.2 10 PESOS
20.0000 g., 0.9990 Silver .6430 oz. ASW **Subject:** Postal History **Obv:** Pre-1990 detailed, styled arms **Rev:** Sailing ship

Date	Mintage	F	VF	XF	Unc	BU
1992 Proof	—	Value: 32.50				

KM# 351 10 PESOS
31.1000 g., 0.9990 Silver 1.0000 oz. ASW **Subject:** Seville **Obv:** National arms within wreath, denomination **Rev:** Tower of Gold

Date	Mintage	F	VF	XF	Unc	BU
1992 Proof	2,050	Value: 55.00				

KM# 352 10 PESOS
31.1000 g., 0.9990 Silver 1.0000 oz. ASW **Obv:** National arms within wreath, denomination **Rev:** El Escorial

Date	Mintage	F	VF	XF	Unc	BU
1992 Proof	2,050	Value: 55.00				

KM# 353 10 PESOS
31.1000 g., 0.9990 Silver 1.0000 oz. ASW **Subject:** 500th Anniversary of Philipp's rule **Obv:** National arms within wreath, denomination **Rev:** Bust of Philip I 3/4 right, date at right, within wreath

Date	Mintage	F	VF	XF	Unc	BU
1992 Proof	3,000	Value: 55.00				

KM# 354.1 10 PESOS
20.0000 g., 0.9990 Silver .6430 oz. ASW **Subject:** Ptolomeo and Toscanelli **Obv:** National arms within wreath, denomination **Rev:** Medieval symbolic table, figure at top with globe, bust lower right

Date	Mintage	F	VF	XF	Unc	BU
1992 Proof	—	Value: 37.50				

KM# 354.2 10 PESOS
20.0000 g., 0.9990 Silver .6430 oz. ASW **Obv:** Arms with thick wreath of the pre-1990 style **Rev:** Medieval symbolic table, figure at top with globe, bust lower right

Date	Mintage	F	VF	XF	Unc	BU
1992 Proof	—	Value: 35.00				

KM# 355 10 PESOS

31.1000 g., 0.9990 Silver 1.0000 oz. ASW **Obv:** National arms within wreath, denomination **Rev:** Guama tribesman

Date	Mintage	F	VF	XF	Unc	BU
1992 Proof	2,050	Value: 55.00				

KM# 370 10 PESOS

20.0000 g., 0.9990 Silver .6430 oz. ASW **Subject:** Postal History **Obv:** National arms within wreath, denomination **Rev:** Steam powered sailing ship, date below

Date	Mintage	F	VF	XF	Unc	BU
1992 Proof	10,000	Value: 32.50				

KM# 372 10 PESOS

31.0000 g., 0.9990 Silver 1.0000 oz. ASW **Obv:** National arms within wreath, denomination below **Rev:** Seated figure left, writing, date at left

Date	Mintage	F	VF	XF	Unc	BU
1992 Proof	2,050	Value: 50.00				

KM# 373 10 PESOS

31.0000 g., 0.9990 Silver 1.0000 oz. ASW **Subject:** Spanish Kings and Queens **Obv:** National arms within wreath **Rev:** Two heads left above and below banners

Date	Mintage	F	VF	XF	Unc	BU
ND(1992) Proof	2,050	Value: 55.00				

KM# 374 10 PESOS

31.0000 g., 0.9990 Silver 1.0000 oz. ASW **Subject:** San Jorge Palace **Obv:** National arms within wreath, denomination **Rev:** Palace view

Date	Mintage	F	VF	XF	Unc	BU
1992 Proof	2,050	Value: 40.00				

KM# 458.1 10 PESOS

20.0000 g., 0.9990 Silver .6430 oz. ASW **Subject:** World Cup Soccer **Obv:** Arms with plain field at lower right, thin wreath, thick characters **Rev:** Native in headdress on left, soccer player and date at right

Date	Mintage	F	VF	XF	Unc	BU
1992 Proof	—	Value: 35.00				

KM# 458.2 10 PESOS

20.0000 g., 0.9990 Silver .6430 oz. ASW **Subject:** World Cup Soccer **Obv:** Arms with plain field at lower right, thin wreath, thin characters **Rev:** Native in headdress on left, soccer player and date at right

Date	Mintage	F	VF	XF	Unc	BU
1992 Proof	—	Value: 35.00				

KM# 458.3 10 PESOS

20.0000 g., 0.9990 Silver 0.6424 oz. ASW **Subject:** World Cup Soccer **Obv:** Arms with striped field at lower right, thick wreath **Rev:** Native in headdress at left, soccer player and date at right

Date	Mintage	F	VF	XF	Unc	BU
1992 Proof	—	Value: 35.00				

KM# 527.1 10 PESOS

20.0000 g., 0.9990 Silver 0.6424 oz. ASW **Subject:** 25th Anniversary - Death of Ernesto Che Guevara **Obv:** Arms with plain field at lower right, thin wreath **Rev:** Bust facing, dates

Date	Mintage	F	VF	XF	Unc	BU
ND(1992) Proof	10,000	Value: 60.00				

KM# 527.2 10 PESOS

20.0000 g., 0.9990 Silver .6430 oz. ASW **Subject:** 25th Anniversary - Death of Ernesto Che Guevara **Obv:** Arms with striped field at lower right, thick wreath **Rev:** Bust facing, dates

Date	Mintage	F	VF	XF	Unc	BU
ND(1992) Proof	Inc. above	Value: 40.00				

KM# 561 10 PESOS

20.0000 g., 0.9990 Silver .6430 oz. ASW **Subject:** Postal History **Obv:** National arms within wreath, denomination **Rev:** Old steam and sailship, date at right

Date	Mintage	F	VF	XF	Unc	BU
1992 Proof	—	Value: 32.50				

KM# 371.1 10 PESOS

20.0000 g., 0.9990 Silver .6430 oz. ASW **Subject:** Introduction of Africans into America **Obv:** National arms within thin wreath **Rev:** Native at left, ship at sea on right

Date	Mintage	F	VF	XF	Unc	BU
1992 Proof	10,000	Value: 42.50				

KM# 371.2 10 PESOS

20.0000 g., 0.9990 Silver .6430 oz. ASW **Obv:** National arms within thick wreath **Rev:** Native at left, ship at sea at right

Date	Mintage	F	VF	XF	Unc	BU
1992 Proof	—	Value: 42.50				

KM# 375.1 10 PESOS

20.0000 g., 0.9990 Silver .6430 oz. ASW **Obv:** Arms with plain field at lower right, thin wreath **Rev:** President Abraham Lincoln

Date	Mintage	F	VF	XF	Unc	BU
1993 Proof	—	Value: 60.00				

KM# 375.2 10 PESOS

20.0000 g., 0.9990 Silver 0.6424 oz. ASW **Obv:** Arms with striped field at lower right, thick wreath **Rev:** President Abraham Lincoln

Date	Mintage	F	VF	XF	Unc	BU
1993 Proof	—	Value: 40.00				

KM# 398 10 PESOS

31.1000 g., 0.9990 Silver 1.0000 oz. ASW **Obv:** National arms within wreath, denomination **Rev:** Frosted bust of Fidel Castro left

Date	Mintage	F	VF	XF	Unc	BU
1993 Proof	5,000	Value: 47.50				

KM# 399 10 PESOS

31.1000 g., 0.9990 Silver 1.0000 oz. ASW **Subject:** St. Jacobi **Obv:** Two sets of shielded arms, denomination **Rev:** Armored figure on rearing horse right

Date	Mintage	F	VF	XF	Unc	BU
1993 Proof	5,000	Value: 50.00				

KM# 407.1 10 PESOS

31.1000 g., 0.9990 Silver 1.0000 oz. ASW **Subject:** Federico Garcia Lorca **Obv:** Arms with plain field at lower right, thin wreath **Rev:** Bust facing, dates at left

Date	Mintage	F	VF	XF	Unc	BU
1993 Proof	3,300	Value: 60.00				

KM# 407.2 10 PESOS

31.1000 g., 0.9990 Silver 0.9989 oz. ASW **Obv:** Arms with striped field at lower right, thick wreath **Rev:** Frederico Garcia Lorca

Date	Mintage	F	VF	XF	Unc	BU
1993 Proof	Inc. above	Value: 45.00				

KM# 496 10 PESOS

19.9600 g., 0.9990 Silver .6411 oz. ASW **Subject:** Postal History **Rev:** Steamship Almen Dares

Date	Mintage	F	VF	XF	Unc	BU
1993 Proof	—	Value: 45.00				

KM# 406.1 10 PESOS

31.1035 g., 0.9990 Silver 1.0000 oz. ASW **Obv:** Arms with plain field at lower right, thin wreath **Rev:** Bolivar and Marti

Date	Mintage	F	VF	XF	Unc	BU
1993 Proof	3,000	Value: 60.00				

KM# 406.2 10 PESOS

31.1035 g., 0.9990 Silver 1.0000 oz. ASW **Obv:** Arms with striped field at lower right, thick wreath **Rev:** Bolivar and Marti

Date	Mintage	F	VF	XF	Unc	BU
1993 Proof	Inc. above	Value: 45.00				

KM# 541 10 PESOS

27.0000 g., 0.9250 Silver .8030 oz. ASW **Subject:** Environmental Protection **Obv:** National arms within wreath, denomination **Rev:** Ivory-billed Woodpecker

Date	Mintage	F	VF	XF	Unc	BU
1994 Proof	20,000	Value: 45.00				

KM# 502.1 10 PESOS

20.0000 g., 0.9990 Silver .6424 oz. ASW **Series:** Caribbean Fauna **Obv:** Thin characters **Rev:** Multicolored Spotted Eagle Ray

Date	Mintage	F	VF	XF	Unc	BU
1994 Proof	10,000	Value: 45.00				

KM# 502.2 10 PESOS

20.0000 g., 0.9990 Silver 0.6424 oz. ASW **Subject:** Caribbean Fauna **Obv:** Thick characters **Rev:** Multicolored Spotter Eagle Ray

Date	Mintage	F	VF	XF	Unc	BU
1994 Proof	Inc. above	Value: 40.00				

KM# 408 10 PESOS

19.9600 g., 0.9990 Silver .6411 oz. ASW **Subject:** Montecristi Manifesto **Obv:** National arms within wreath, denomination below **Rev:** Two seated figures facing each other, date lower left

Date	Mintage	F	VF	XF	Unc	BU
1994 Proof	3,300	Value: 45.00				

KM# 427 10 PESOS

20.0000 g., 0.9990 Silver .6430 oz. ASW **Obv:** National arms within wreath, denomination below **Rev:** Sailing ship - LA INDIA

Date	Mintage	F	VF	XF	Unc	BU
1994 Proof	10,000	Value: 32.50				

KM# 428 10 PESOS

20.0000 g., 0.9990 Silver .6430 oz. ASW **Obv:** National arms within wreath, denomination below **Rev:** Sailing ship - NAO VICTORIA

Date	Mintage	F	VF	XF	Unc	BU
1994 Proof	10,000	Value: 32.50				

KM# 441 10 PESOS

20.0000 g., 0.9990 Silver .6430 oz. ASW **Subject:** Evangelista Island **Obv:** Map of island, small arms lower right **Rev:** Ship at sea, treasure chest, parrot

Date	Mintage	F	VF	XF	Unc	BU
1994 Proof	—	Value: 32.50				

KM# 442.1 10 PESOS

20.0000 g., 0.9990 Silver .6430 oz. ASW **Series:** Caribbean Fauna **Obv:** Thin characters **Rev:** Multicolored flamingos, thin water splashes

Date	Mintage	F	VF	XF	Unc	BU
1994 Proof	10,000	Value: 50.00				

KM# 442.2 10 PESOS

20.0000 g., 0.9990 Silver 0.6424 oz. ASW **Subject:** Caribbean Fauna **Obv:** Thick characters **Rev:** Multicolored flamingos, wide water splashes

Date	Mintage	F	VF	XF	Unc	BU
1994 Proof	Inc. above	Value: 40.00				

KM# 443.1 10 PESOS
20.0000 g., 0.9990 Silver .6430 oz. ASW **Series:** Caribbean Fauna **Obv:** Thin characters **Rev:** Multicolored Yellow Sea Bass (Coney), 7 lines in tail, slimmer fish

Date	Mintage	F	VF	XF	Unc	BU
1994 Proof	10,000	Value: 50.00				

KM# 443.2 10 PESOS
20.0000 g., 0.9990 Silver 0.6424 oz. ASW **Subject:** Caribbean Fauna **Obv:** Thin characters **Rev:** Multicolored Yellow Sea Bass (Coney), 5 lines in tail

Date	Mintage	F	VF	XF	Unc	BU
1994 Proof	Inc. above	Value: 40.00				

KM# 468 10 PESOS
20.0000 g., 0.9990 Silver .6430 oz. ASW **Subject:** Environmental Protection **Obv:** National arms within wreath, denomination **Rev:** Scale on left joined with tree on right, date lower right

Date	Mintage	F	VF	XF	Unc	BU
1994 Proof	Est. 5,000	Value: 45.00				

KM# 469 10 PESOS
20.0000 g., 0.9990 Silver .6430 oz. ASW **Series:** 1996 Olympics **Obv:** National arms within wreath, denomination **Rev:** Boxers

Date	Mintage	F	VF	XF	Unc	BU
1994 Proof	Est. 30,000	Value: 27.50				

KM# 470 10 PESOS
20.0000 g., 0.9990 Silver .6430 oz. ASW **Rev:** Red Baron Plane - multicolored Fokker Dr. I

Date	Mintage	F	VF	XF	Unc	BU
1994 Proof	—	Value: 55.00				

KM# 499.1 10 PESOS
20.0000 g., 0.9990 Silver .6424 oz. ASW **Series:** Caribbean Fauna **Obv:** Thin characters **Rev:** Multicolored bottle-nosed dolphins

Date	Mintage	F	VF	XF	Unc	BU
1994 Proof	Est. 10,000	Value: 45.00				

KM# 499.2 10 PESOS
20.0000 g., 0.9990 Silver 0.6424 oz. ASW **Subject:** Caribbean Fauna **Obv:** Thick characters **Rev:** Multicolored bottle-nosed dolphins

Date	Mintage	F	VF	XF	Unc	BU
1994 Proof	Inc. above	Value: 40.00				

KM# 500.1 10 PESOS
20.0000 g., 0.9990 Silver .6424 oz. ASW **Series:** Caribbean Fauna **Obv:** Thin characters **Rev:** Multicolored swordfish, smaller water splashes

Date	Mintage	F	VF	XF	Unc	BU
1994 Proof	10,000	Value: 50.00				

KM# 500.2 10 PESOS
20.0000 g., 0.9990 Silver 0.6424 oz. ASW **Subject:** Caribbean Fauna **Obv:** Thick characters **Rev:** Multicolored swordfish, larger water splashes

Date	Mintage	F	VF	XF	Unc	BU
1994 Proof	Inc. above	Value: 40.00				

KM# 501.1 10 PESOS
20.0000 g., 0.9990 Silver .6424 oz. ASW **Series:** Caribbean Fauna **Obv:** Thin characters **Rev:** Multicolored Brown Pelican

Date	Mintage	F	VF	XF	Unc	BU
1994 Proof	10,000	Value: 45.00				

KM# 501.2 10 PESOS
20.0000 g., 0.9990 Silver 0.6424 oz. ASW **Subject:** Caribbean Fauna **Obv:** Thick characters **Rev:** Multicolored Brown Pelican

Date	Mintage	F	VF	XF	Unc	BU
1994 Proof	Inc. above	Value: 40.00				

KM# 510.1 10 PESOS
20.0000 g., 0.9990 Silver .6424 oz. ASW **Subject:** World Cup Soccer **Obv:** Thin characters **Rev:** Two players with bridge in background, date above

Date	Mintage	F	VF	XF	Unc	BU
1994 Proof	Est. 10,000	Value: 45.00				

KM# 510.2 10 PESOS
20.0000 g., 0.9990 Silver .6424 oz. ASW **Subject:** World Cup Soccer **Obv:** Thick characters **Rev:** Two players with bridge in background, date above

Date	Mintage	F	VF	XF	Unc	BU
1994 Proof	Inc. above	Value: 45.00				

KM# 528 10 PESOS
20.0000 g., 0.9990 Silver .6424 oz. ASW **Obv:** National arms within wreath, denomination **Rev:** Multicolored Albatross DII fighter plane

Date	Mintage	F	VF	XF	Unc	BU
1994 Proof	—	Value: 42.50				

KM# 548 10 PESOS
Silver **Subject:** Seaplane **Obv:** National arms within wreath, denomination **Rev:** Multicolored SIAI Marchetti S55

Date	Mintage	F	VF	XF	Unc	BU
1995 Proof	15,000	Value: 45.00				

KM# 478 10 PESOS
20.0000 g., 0.9990 Silver .6430 oz. ASW **Subject:** Pirates of the Caribbean **Obv:** National arms within wreath, denomination below **Rev:** Blackbeard within circle, date below

Date	Mintage	F	VF	XF	Unc	BU
1995 Proof	Est. 10,000	Value: 60.00				

KM# 479 10 PESOS
20.0000 g., 0.9990 Silver .6430 oz. ASW **Subject:** Pirates of the Caribbean **Obv:** National arms within wreath, denomination below **Rev:** Sir Henry Morgan

Date	Mintage	F	VF	XF	Unc	BU
1995 Proof	Est. 10,000	Value: 60.00				

KM# 480 10 PESOS
20.0000 g., 0.9990 Silver .6430 oz. ASW **Subject:** Pirates of the Caribbean **Obv:** National arms within wreath, denomination below **Rev:** Anne Bonny

Date	Mintage	F	VF	XF	Unc	BU
1995 Proof	Est. 10,000	Value: 60.00				

KM# 481 10 PESOS
20.0000 g., 0.9990 Silver .6430 oz. ASW **Subject:** Pirates of the Caribbean **Obv:** National arms within wreath, denomination below **Rev:** Mary Read

Date	Mintage	F	VF	XF	Unc	BU
1995 Proof	Est. 10,000	Value: 60.00				

KM# 482 10 PESOS
20.0000 g., 0.9990 Silver .6430 oz. ASW **Subject:** Pirates of the Caribbean **Obv:** National arms within wreath, denomination below **Rev:** Captain Kidd

Date	Mintage	F	VF	XF	Unc	BU
1995 Proof	Est. 10,000	Value: 60.00				

KM# 483 10 PESOS
20.0000 g., 0.9990 Silver .6430 oz. ASW **Subject:** Pirates of the Caribbean **Obv:** National arms within wreath, denomination below **Rev:** Piet Heyn

Date	Mintage	F	VF	XF	Unc	BU
1995 Proof	Est. 10,000	Value: 60.00				

KM# 511 10 PESOS
20.0000 g., 0.9990 Silver .6430 oz. ASW **Obv:** National arms within wreath, denomination **Rev:** Arnaldo Tamayo Mendez

Date	Mintage	F	VF	XF	Unc	BU
1995 Proof	Est. 5,000	Value: 45.00				

KM# 529 10 PESOS
20.0000 g., 0.9990 Silver .6430 oz. ASW **Subject:** F.A.O. 50th Anniversary **Obv:** National arms within wreath, denomination below **Rev:** Farmer plowing with two oxen, logo and dates above

Date	Mintage	F	VF	XF	Unc	BU
ND(1995) Proof	3,000	Value: 35.00				

KM# 530 10 PESOS
31.1000 g., 0.9990 Silver 1.0000 oz. ASW **Subject:** Centennial 1895-1995 **Obv:** National arms within wreath, denomination **Rev:** Sword to right of three conjoined busts right, dates below

Date	Mintage	F	VF	XF	Unc	BU
ND(1995) Proof	500	Value: 60.00				

KM# 540 10 PESOS
28.2800 g., 0.9250 Silver .8411 oz. ASW **Subject:** 50th Anniversary - United Nations **Obv:** National arms within wreath, denomination below **Rev:** Five persons of assorted ages and race, UN logo in front, outline of dove in back

Date	Mintage	F	VF	XF	Unc	BU
ND(1995) Proof	Est. 105,000	Value: 40.00				

KM# 600 10 PESOS
15.0000 g., 0.9990 Silver .6423 oz. ASW **Subject:** Caribbean Flora **Obv:** National arms within wreath, denomination below **Rev:** Multicolor flower, Ruelia tuberosa

Date	Mintage	F	VF	XF	Unc	BU
ND(1995) Proof	3,000	Value: 40.00				

KM# 574 10 PESOS
20.0000 g., 0.9990 Silver .6430 oz. ASW **Subject:** Death of Jose Marti **Obv:** National arms within wreath, denomination below

Date	Mintage	F	VF	XF	Unc	BU
1995	—	—	—	—	45.00	—

KM# 584 10 PESOS
15.0000 g., 0.9990 Silver .6423 oz. ASW **Subject:** First Railroads - Switzerland **Obv:** National arms within wreath, denomination below **Rev:** First Swiss locomotive, date 1847-1997

Date	Mintage	F	VF	XF	Unc	BU
1996 Proof	—	Value: 32.50				

KM# 585 10 PESOS
15.0000 g., 0.9990 Silver .6423 oz. ASW **Subject:** El Mundo de la Aventura **Obv:** National arms within wreath, denomination below **Rev:** Multicolor submarine and cameo portrait of Capt. Nemo

Date	Mintage	F	VF	XF	Unc	BU
1996 Proof	—	Value: 40.00				

KM# 586 10 PESOS
20.0000 g., 0.9990 Silver .6430 oz. ASW **Subject:** Campeonato Mundial de Futbol - Francia **Obv:** National arms within wreath, denomination below **Rev:** Joan of Arc with France's flag before soccer ball

Date	Mintage	F	VF	XF	Unc	BU
1996 Proof	—	Value: 45.00				

KM# 587 10 PESOS
20.0000 g., 0.9990 Silver .6430 oz. ASW **Subject:** America - El Nuevo Mundo **Obv:** National arms within wreath, denomination below **Rev:** Ship and cameo portrait of Amerigo Vespucci

Date	Mintage	F	VF	XF	Unc	BU
1996 Proof	—	Value: 35.00				

KM# 588 10 PESOS
20.0000 g., 0.9990 Silver .6430 oz. ASW **Subject:** World Food Summit **Obv:** National arms within wreath, denomination below **Rev:** Woman picking fruit, F.A.O. logo, dates

Date	Mintage	F	VF	XF	Unc	BU
1996 Proof	—	Value: 45.00				

KM# 589 10 PESOS
31.1035 g., 0.9990 Silver 1.0000 oz. ASW **Subject:** 40th Anniversary of the Granma's Landing **Obv:** National arms within wreath, denomination below **Rev:** Castro's portrait above the Granma

Date	Mintage	F	VF	XF	Unc	BU
1996 Proof	—	Value: 50.00				

KM# 582 10 PESOS
15.0000 g., 0.9990 Silver .6423 oz. ASW **Subject:** First Railroads - Germany **Obv:** National arms within wreath, denomination below **Rev:** First German locomotive, date 1835-1996

Date	Mintage	F	VF	XF	Unc	BU
1996 Proof	—	Value: 32.50				

KM# 583 10 PESOS
15.0000 g., 0.9990 Silver .6423 oz. ASW **Subject:** First Railroads - Austria **Obv:** National arms within wreath, denomination below **Rev:** First Austrian locomotive, date 1848-1996

Date	Mintage	F	VF	XF	Unc	BU
1996 Proof	—	Value: 32.50				

KM# 553 10 PESOS
20.0000 g., 0.9990 Silver .6430 oz. ASW **Series:** Caribbean Fauna **Obv:** National arms within wreath, denomination below **Rev:** Multicolored Purple Throated Carib Hummingbird, right, date at right

Date	Mintage	F	VF	XF	Unc	BU
1996 Proof	5,000	Value: 45.00				

KM# 554 10 PESOS
Silver **Series:** Caribbean Fauna **Obv:** National arms within wreath, denomination below **Rev:** Multicolored Yellow Perch

Date	Mintage	F	VF	XF	Unc	BU
1996 Proof	5,000	Value: 40.00				

KM# 555 10 PESOS
20.0000 g., 0.9990 Silver .6430 oz. ASW **Series:** Caribbean Fauna **Obv:** National arms within wreath, denomination below **Rev:** Multicolored Cuban Tody Bird

Date	Mintage	F	VF	XF	Unc	BU
1996 Proof	5,000	Value: 40.00				

KM# 556 10 PESOS
20.0000 g., 0.9990 Silver .6430 oz. ASW **Series:** Caribbean Fauna **Obv:** National arms within wreath, denomination below **Rev:** Multicolored Wood Duck

Date	Mintage	F	VF	XF	Unc	BU
1996 Proof	5,000	—	—	—	40.00	—

KM# 566 10 PESOS
20.0000 g., 0.9990 Silver .6430 oz. ASW **Series:** Caribbean Fauna **Obv:** National arms within wreath, denomination below **Rev:** Multicolored Papilio Butterfly

Date	Mintage	F	VF	XF	Unc	BU
1996	5,000	Value: 50.00				

KM# 563 10 PESOS
20.0000 g., 0.9990 Silver .6430 oz. ASW **Series:** Caribbean Fauna **Obv:** National arms within wreath, denomination below **Rev:** Multicolored Vaca Anil (Blue Cow) Fish

Date	Mintage	F	VF	XF	Unc	BU
1996 Proof	5,000	Value: 40.00				

KM# 723 10 PESOS
31.1035 g., 0.9990 Silver 1.0000 oz. ASW, 42 mm. **Subject:** 25th Anniversary - Ernesto Che Guevara's Death **Obv:** National arms and inscription **Rev:** Ernesto Che Guevara walking

Date	Mintage	F	VF	XF	Unc	BU
ND(1997) Proof	10,000	Value: 50.00				

KM# 724 10 PESOS
31.1035 g., 0.9990 Silver 1.0000 oz. ASW, 42 mm. **Subject:** 30th Anniversary - Ernesto Che Guevara's Death **Obv:** National arms within wreath, denomination **Rev:** Bust left **Edge:** Reeded

Date	Mintage	F	VF	XF	Unc	BU
ND(1997) Proof	10,000	Value: 50.00				

KM# 747 10 PESOS
3.1100 g., Gold, 16 mm. **Obv:** National arms and inscription **Rev:** Che Guevara standing

Date	Mintage	F	VF	XF	Unc	BU
1997 Proof	500	Value: 195				

KM# 748 10 PESOS
3.1100 g., Gold, 16 mm. **Obv:** National arms within wreath, denomination **Rev:** Bust of Che Guevara

Date	Mintage	F	VF	XF	Unc	BU
1997 Proof	500	Value: 195				

KM# 593 10 PESOS
15.0000 g., 0.9990 Silver .6423 oz. ASW **Subject:** Wonders of the Ancient World **Obv:** National arms within wreath, denomination below **Rev:** Hanging Gardens of Babylon

Date	Mintage	F	VF	XF	Unc	BU
1997 Proof	—	Value: 32.50				

KM# 594 10 PESOS
15.0000 g., 0.9990 Silver .6423 oz. ASW **Subject:** Wonders of the Ancient World **Obv:** National arms within wreath, denomination below **Rev:** Temple of Artemis

Date	Mintage	F	VF	XF	Unc	BU
1997 Proof	—	Value: 32.50				

KM# 595 10 PESOS
15.0000 g., 0.9990 Silver .6423 oz. ASW **Subject:** Wonders of the Ancient World **Obv:** National arms within wreath, denomination below **Rev:** Lighthouse of Alexandria

Date	Mintage	F	VF	XF	Unc	BU
1997 Proof	—	Value: 32.50				

KM# 596 10 PESOS
15.0000 g., 0.9990 Silver .6423 oz. ASW **Subject:** Wonders of the Ancient World **Obv:** National arms within wreath, denomination below **Rev:** Statue of Colossus of Rhodes over breakwater

Date	Mintage	F	VF	XF	Unc	BU
1997 Proof	—	Value: 32.50				

KM# 597 10 PESOS
15.0000 g., 0.9990 Silver .6423 oz. ASW **Subject:** Wonders of the Ancient World **Obv:** National arms within wreath, denomination below **Rev:** Painting above Egyptian pyramids and excavation

Date	Mintage	F	VF	XF	Unc	BU
1997 Proof	—	Value: 32.50				

KM# 598 10 PESOS
15.0000 g., 0.9990 Silver .6423 oz. ASW **Subject:** Wonders of the Ancient World - Temple of Jupiter **Obv:** National arms within wreath, denomination below **Rev:** Statue of Jupiter inside temple

Date	Mintage	F	VF	XF	Unc	BU
1997 Proof	—	Value: 32.50				

KM# 601 10 PESOS
15.0000 g., 0.9990 Silver .6423 oz. ASW **Subject:** Caribbean Flora **Obv:** National arms within wreath, denomination below **Rev:** Multicolored flower, "Cordia sebestena"

Date	Mintage	F	VF	XF	Unc	BU
1997 Proof	—	Value: 32.50				

KM# 602 10 PESOS
15.0000 g., 0.9990 Silver .6423 oz. ASW **Subject:** Caribbean Flora **Obv:** National arms within wreath, denomination below **Rev:** Multicolor flower, "Lochnera rosea"

Date	Mintage	F	VF	XF	Unc	BU
1997 Proof	—	Value: 32.50				

KM# 603 10 PESOS
15.0000 g., 0.9990 Silver .6423 oz. ASW **Subject:** Caribbena Flora **Obv:** National arms within wreath, denomination below **Rev:** Multicolored flower, "Turnera ulmifolia"

Date	Mintage	F	VF	XF	Unc	BU
1997 Proof	—	Value: 32.50				

KM# 604 10 PESOS
15.0000 g., 0.9990 Silver .6423 oz. ASW **Subject:** Caribbean Flora **Obv:** National arms within wreath, denomination below **Rev:** Multicolored flower, "Bidens pilosa"

Date	Mintage	F	VF	XF	Unc	BU
1997 Proof	—	Value: 32.50				

KM# 609 10 PESOS
15.0000 g., 0.9990 Silver .4818 oz. ASW **Subject:** Sesquicentennial of First Stearn/Sail Powered Ship **Obv:** National arms within wreath, denomination below **Rev:** Ship, date

Date	Mintage	F	VF	XF	Unc	BU
1997 Proof	5,000	Value: 42.50				

KM# 613 10 PESOS
31.1035 g., 0.9990 Silver 1.0000 oz. ASW **Subject:** Castro Visit to Vatican **Obv:** National arms within wreath, denomination below **Rev:** Pope and Castro meeting

Date	Mintage	F	VF	XF	Unc	BU
1997	—	—	—	—	55.00	—

KM# 667 10 PESOS
15.0000 g., 0.9990 Silver .4818 oz. ASW **Subject:** 450th Anniversary - Birth of Cervantes

Date	Mintage	F	VF	XF	Unc	BU
1997 Proof	—	Value: 50.00				

KM# 625 10 PESOS
27.0000 g., 0.9250 Silver .8030 oz. ASW **Subject:** Ibero - American **Obv:** National arms and denomination within circle of arms **Rev:** Two rumba dancers, bongo drummer at left

Date	Mintage	F	VF	XF	Unc	BU
1997	—	—	—	—	50.00	—

KM# 590 10 PESOS
20.0000 g., 0.9990 Silver .6430 oz. ASW **Subject:** Circumnavigation of Cuba - Pinzon **Obv:** National arms within wreath, denomination below **Rev:** Sailship and cameo portrait of Vincente Pinzon

Date	Mintage	F	VF	XF	Unc	BU
1997 Proof	—	Value: 35.00				

KM# 591 10 PESOS
15.0000 g., 0.9990 Silver .6423 oz. ASW **Subject:** XXVII Olympics **Obv:** National arms within wreath, denomination below **Rev:** Two fencers

Date	Mintage	F	VF	XF	Unc	BU
1997 Proof	—	Value: 35.00				

KM# 592 10 PESOS
15.0000 g., 0.9990 Silver .6423 oz. ASW **Subject:** XXVII Olympics **Obv:** National arms within wreath, denomination below **Rev:** Multicolored baseball player at bat, baseball background, small date below

Date	Mintage	F	VF	XF	Unc	BU
1997 Proof	—	Value: 40.00				

KM# 635 10 PESOS
31.1000 g., 0.9990 Silver 0.9989 oz. ASW, 38 mm. **Obv:** National arms within wreath, denomination **Rev:** Pope John Paul II, cathedral

Date	Mintage	F	VF	XF	Unc	BU
1997 Proof	10,000	Value: 45.00				

KM# 624 10 PESOS
31.1000 g., 0.9990 Silver 0.9989 oz. ASW, 38 mm. **Obv:** National arms within wreath, denomination **Rev:** Deng Xiaoping bust facing

Date	Mintage	F	VF	XF	Unc	BU
1997 Proof	10,000	Value: 45.00				

KM# 750 10 PESOS
31.1000 g., 0.9990 Silver 0.9989 oz. ASW, 38 mm. **Obv:** National arms within wreath, denomination **Rev:** Deng Xiaoping viewing Hong Kong

Date	Mintage	F	VF	XF	Unc	BU
1997 Proof	10,000	Value: 45.00				

KM# 599 10 PESOS
15.0000 g., 0.9990 Silver .6423 oz. ASW **Subject:** Wonders of the Ancient World **Obv:** National arms within wreath, denomination below **Rev:** Mausoleum of Halicarnas

Date	Mintage	F	VF	XF	Unc	BU
1997 Proof	—	Value: 32.50				

KM# 610 10 PESOS
15.0000 g., 0.9990 Silver .4818 oz. ASW **Subject:** Mississippi **Obv:** National arms within wreath, denomination below **Rev:** Riverboat

Date	Mintage	F	VF	XF	Unc	BU
1998 Proof	5,000	Value: 37.50				

KM# 751 10 PESOS
20.0000 g., 0.9990 Silver 0.6424 oz. ASW **Obv:** National arms within wreath, denomination **Rev:** Cruise ship Hanseatic **Note:** 24 x 42mm

Date	Mintage	F	VF	XF	Unc	BU
1998 Proof	2,500	Value: 40.00				

KM# 644 10 PESOS
31.1035 g., 0.9990 Silver 1.0000 oz. ASW **Subject:** Centenary - Explosion del Maine **Obv:** National arms within wreath, denomination below **Rev:** Explosion scene

Date	Mintage	F	VF	XF	Unc	BU
1998 Proof	5,000	Value: 65.00				

KM# 611 10 PESOS
15.0000 g., 0.9990 Silver .4818 oz. ASW **Obv:** National arms within wreath, denomination below **Rev:** The ship Rio Bravo

Date	Mintage	F	VF	XF	Unc	BU
1998 Proof	—	Value: 35.00				

KM# 645 10 PESOS
31.1035 g., 0.9990 Silver 1.0000 oz. ASW **Subject:** Centenary - Naval battle of Santiago **Obv:** National arms within wreath,

denomination below **Rev:** Cameo of Admiral Cervera and burning ship

Date	Mintage	F	VF	XF	Unc	BU
1998 Proof	5,000	Value: 65.00				

KM# 646 10 PESOS

31.1035 g., 0.9990 Silver 1.0000 oz. ASW **Subject:** Centenary - Calixto Garcia - Combate en Oriente **Obv:** National arms within wreath, denomination below **Rev:** Portrait above three Cuban cavalry troopers

Date	Mintage	F	VF	XF	Unc	BU
1998 Proof	5,000	Value: 65.00				

KM# 647 10 PESOS

31.1035 g., 0.9990 Silver 1.0000 oz. ASW **Obv:** National arms within wreath, denomination **Rev:** Souvenir peso design, bust of Leonor Molina right

Date	Mintage	F	VF	XF	Unc	BU
1998 Proof	5,000	Value: 55.00				

KM# 648 10 PESOS

31.1035 g., 0.9990 Silver 1.0000 oz. ASW **Subject:** Expo 2000 - Twipsy **Obv:** National arms within wreath, denomination below **Rev:** "Twipsy" cartoon logo

Date	Mintage	F	VF	XF	Unc	BU
1998 Proof	19,000	Value: 35.00				

KM# 649 10 PESOS

31.1035 g., 0.9990 Silver 1.0000 oz. ASW **Subject:** Expo 2000 - Germany **Obv:** National arms within wreath, denomination below **Rev:** German map

Date	Mintage	F	VF	XF	Unc	BU
1998 Proof	19,000	Value: 35.00				

KM# 650 10 PESOS

31.1035 g., 0.9990 Silver 1.0000 oz. ASW **Subject:** Expo 2000 - London **Obv:** National arms within wreath, denomination below **Rev:** Cartoon over exhibit hall

Date	Mintage	F	VF	XF	Unc	BU
1998 Proof	19,000	Value: 35.00				

KM# 651 10 PESOS

31.1035 g., 0.9990 Silver 1.0000 oz. ASW **Subject:** Expo 2000 - Paris **Obv:** National arms within wreath, denomination below **Rev:** Cartoon and Eiffel Tower

Date	Mintage	F	VF	XF	Unc	BU
1998 Proof	19,000	Value: 35.00				

KM# 652 10 PESOS

31.1035 g., 0.9990 Silver 1.0000 oz. ASW **Subject:** Expo 2000 - Brussels **Obv:** National arms within wreath, denomination below **Rev:** Cartoon and Atomium structure

Date	Mintage	F	VF	XF	Unc	BU
1998 Proof	19,000	Value: 35.00				

KM# 653 10 PESOS

31.1035 g., 0.9990 Silver 1.0000 oz. ASW **Subject:** Expo 2000 - Postrimerias **Obv:** National arms within wreath, denomination below **Rev:** Cartoon on tree bearing world globe

Date	Mintage	F	VF	XF	Unc	BU
1998 Proof	19,000	Value: 35.00				

KM# 668 10 PESOS

31.1035 g., 0.9990 Silver 1.0015 oz. ASW, 45.2 x 35.1 mm. **Subject:** Havana Puzzle - Frigate Oquendo **Obv:** National arms within wreath, denomination below **Rev:** Two sailing ships **Edge:** Plain **Shape:** Rectangular

Date	Mintage	F	VF	XF	Unc	BU
1998 Proof	—	Value: 50.00				

KM# 669 10 PESOS

31.1035 g., 0.9990 Silver 1.0015 oz. ASW, 45.2 x 35.1 mm. **Subject:** Havana Puzzle - City of Havana **Obv:** National arms within wreath, denomination below **Rev:** Havana city view **Edge:** Plain **Shape:** Rectangular

Date	Mintage	F	VF	XF	Unc	BU
1998 Proof	3,000	Value: 50.00				

KM# 670 10 PESOS

31.1800 g., 0.9990 Silver 1.0015 oz. ASW, 45.2 x 35.1 mm. **Subject:** Havana Puzzle - Sailing Ship San Genaro **Obv:** National arms within wreath, denomination below **Rev:** Three sailing ships **Edge:** Plain **Shape:** Rectangular

Date	Mintage	F	VF	XF	Unc	BU
1998 Proof	3,000	Value: 50.00				

KM# 671 10 PESOS

31.1800 g., 0.9990 Silver 1.0015 oz. ASW, 45.2 x 35.1 mm. **Subject:** Havana Puzzle - El Morro **Obv:** National arms within wreath, denomination below **Rev:** Light house and sailing ships **Edge:** Plain **Shape:** Rectangular

Date	Mintage	F	VF	XF	Unc	BU
1998 Proof	3,000	Value: 50.00				

KM# 672 10 PESOS

31.1035 g., 0.9990 Silver 1.0000 oz. ASW **Subject:** 40th Anniversary - Triumph of the Revolution

Date	Mintage	F	VF	XF	Unc	BU
1999 Proof	—	Value: 45.00				

KM# 674 10 PESOS

31.1035 g., 0.9990 Silver 1.0000 oz. ASW **Subject:** Spanish Royal Visit - Fidel Castro receives King Juan Carlos I

Date	Mintage	F	VF	XF	Unc	BU
1999 Proof	—	Value: 75.00				

KM# 675 10 PESOS

31.1035 g., 0.9990 Silver 1.0000 oz. ASW **Subject:** Spanish Royal Visit - King Juan Carlos and Queen Sofia

Date	Mintage	F	VF	XF	Unc	BU
1999 Proof	—	Value: 75.00				

KM# 676 10 PESOS

31.1035 g., 0.9990 Silver 1.0000 oz. ASW **Subject:** Spanish Royal Visit - 2 Peoples United

Date	Mintage	F	VF	XF	Unc	BU
1999 Proof	—	Value: 75.00				

KM# 677 10 PESOS

31.1035 g., 0.9990 Silver 1.0000 oz. ASW **Subject:** Spanish Royal Visit - Homage to the Spanish Soldier

Date	Mintage	F	VF	XF	Unc	BU
1999 Proof	—	Value: 75.00				

KM# 661 10 PESOS

31.1035 g., 0.9990 Silver 1.0000 oz. ASW **Subject:** Zùnzuncito **Obv:** National arms **Rev:** Hummingbird **Edge:** Plain

Date	Mintage	F	VF	XF	Unc	BU
1999 Proof	—	Value: 60.00				

KM# 736 10 PESOS

14.9300 g., 0.9990 Silver 0.4795 oz. ASW, 35.1 mm. **Subject:** Johann Wolfgang von Goethe **Obv:** National arms **Rev:** Seated figure outdoors **Edge:** Plain

Date	Mintage	F	VF	XF	Unc	BU
1999 Proof	—	Value: 50.00				

KM# 749 10 PESOS

3.1100 g., Gold, 18 mm. **Obv:** National arms within wreath, denomination **Rev:** Hummingbird in flight

Date	Mintage	F	VF	XF	Unc	BU
1999 Proof	1,000	Value: 100				

KM# 725 10 PESOS

3.1100 g., 0.9990 Gold .1000 oz. AGW, 18 mm. **Subject:** Zunzuncito **Obv:** National arms **Rev:** Hummingbird **Edge:** Reeded

Date	Mintage	F	VF	XF	Unc	BU
1999 Proof	1,000	Value: 100				

KM# 752 10 PESOS

20.0000 g., 0.9990 Silver 0.6424 oz. ASW, 38 mm. **Subject:** First International Globalization Conference **Obv:** National arms within wreath, denomination **Rev:** World map

Date	Mintage	F	VF	XF	Unc	BU
1999 Proof	200	Value: 100				

KM# 753 10 PESOS
15.0000 g., 0.9990 Silver 0.4818 oz. ASW, 35 mm. **Subject:** Goethe's birthplace **Obv:** National arms within wreath, denomination **Rev:** Building at left, bust at right looking left

Date	Mintage	F	VF	XF	Unc	BU
1999 Proof	1,749	Value: 75.00				

KM# 754 10 PESOS
15.0000 g., 0.9990 Silver 0.4818 oz. ASW, 35 mm. **Subject:** Goeth's Weimar home **Obv:** National arms within wreath, denomination **Rev:** Building at right, bust at left looking right

Date	Mintage	F	VF	XF	Unc	BU
1999 Proof	1,749	Value: 75.00				

KM# 755 10 PESOS
15.0000 g., 0.9990 Silver 0.4818 oz. ASW, 35 mm. **Obv:** National arms within wreath, denomination **Rev:** Christopher Columbus, ship, and arms

Date	Mintage	F	VF	XF	Unc	BU
1999 Proof	1,950	Value: 65.00				

KM# 756 10 PESOS
31.1035 g., 0.9990 Silver 0.999 oz. ASW, 38 mm. **Obv:** National arms within wreath, denomination **Rev:** Hummingbird feeding nestlings

Date	Mintage	F	VF	XF	Unc	BU
2000 Proof	20,000	Value: 37.50				

KM# 757 10 PESOS
20.0000 g., 0.9990 Silver 0.6424 oz. ASW, 38 mm. **Subject:** Second International Globalization Conference **Obv:** National arms within wreath, denomination **Rev:** World map

Date	Mintage	F	VF	XF	Unc	BU
2000 Proof	100	Value: 125				

KM# 758 10 PESOS
15.0000 g., 0.9990 Silver 0.4818 oz. ASW, 35 mm. **Obv:** National arms within wreath, denomination **Rev:** Sailing ship Santisima Trinidad

Date	Mintage	F	VF	XF	Unc	BU
2000 Proof	2,500	Value: 60.00				

KM# 759 10 PESOS
15.0000 g., 0.9990 Silver 0.4818 oz. ASW, 35 mm. **Obv:** National arms within wreath, denomination **Rev:** Ship Vecero Rayo

Date	Mintage	F	VF	XF	Unc	BU
2000 Proof	2,500	Value: 60.00				

KM# 760 10 PESOS
15.0000 g., 0.9990 Silver 0.4818 oz. ASW, 35 mm. **Obv:** National arms within wreath, denomination **Rev:** Sailing ship, San Pedro De Alcantara

Date	Mintage	F	VF	XF	Unc	BU
2000 Proof	2,500	Value: 60.00				

KM# 761 10 PESOS
20.0000 g., 0.9990 Silver 0.6424 oz. ASW, 38 mm. **Obv:** National arms within wreath, denomination **Rev:** "50" in design

Date	Mintage	F	VF	XF	Unc	BU
2000 Proof	1,250	Value: 70.00				

KM# 679 10 PESOS
31.1035 g., 0.9990 Silver 1.0000 oz. ASW **Subject:** Maritime Relics - School Ship Galatea **Obv:** National arms within wreath, denomination **Rev:** Ship with full sails at sea

Date	Mintage	F	VF	XF	Unc	BU
2000 Proof	1,500	Value: 35.00				

KM# 678 10 PESOS
31.1035 g., 0.9990 Silver 1.0000 oz. ASW **Subject:** Maritime Relics - Peral Submarine **Obv:** National arms within wreath, denomination **Rev:** Submarine under water, small ship above

Date	Mintage	F	VF	XF	Unc	BU
2000 Proof	1,500	Value: 35.00				

KM# 680 10 PESOS
31.1035 g., 0.9990 Silver 1.0000 oz. ASW **Subject:** Maritime Relics - School Ship JS Elcano **Obv:** National arms within wreath, denomination **Rev:** Ship with many full sails at sea

Date	Mintage	F	VF	XF	Unc	BU
2000 Proof	1,500	Value: 35.00				

KM# 681 10 PESOS

31.1035 g., 0.9990 Silver 1.0000 oz. ASW **Subject:** Maritime Relics - Maritime Ambulance Buena Ventura **Obv:** National arms within wreath, denomination **Rev:** Two ships at sea

Date	Mintage	F	VF	XF	Unc	BU
2000 Proof	1,500	Value: 35.00				

KM# 683 10 PESOS

20.0000 g., 0.9990 Silver .6423 oz. ASW **Subject:** Hacia un Nuevo Milenio (Towards a New Millennium) **Obv:** National arms within wreath, denomination below **Rev:** Dove of Peace covering world map

Date	Mintage	F	VF	XF	Unc	BU
2000 Proof	3,000	Value: 45.00				

KM# 682 10 PESOS

20.0000 g., 0.9990 Silver .6423 oz. ASW **Subject:** Maritime Relics - Nautical Rose of Juan de la Cosa **Obv:** National arms within wreath, denomination **Rev:** Madonna and child with angels at center of radiant sun design

Date	Mintage	F	VF	XF	Unc	BU
2000 Proof	1,500	Value: 35.00				

KM# 684 10 PESOS

20.0000 g., 0.9990 Silver .6423 oz. ASW **Subject:** Welcome the Third Millennium **Obv:** National arms within wreath, denomination below **Rev:** Hot air balloons above earth

Date	Mintage	F	VF	XF	Unc	BU
2000 Proof	3,000	Value: 45.00				

KM# 685 10 PESOS

20.0000 g., 0.9990 Silver .6423 oz. ASW **Subject:** Welcome to the New Millennium **Obv:** National arms within wreath, denomination below **Rev:** Stars and Solar System

Date	Mintage	F	VF	XF	Unc	BU
2000 Proof	3,000	Value: 45.00				

KM# 687 10 PESOS

15.0000 g., 0.9990 Silver .4817 oz. ASW **Subject:** Palaces of the World **Obv:** National arms within wreath, denomination **Rev:** Windsor Palace

Date	Mintage	F	VF	XF	Unc	BU
2000 Proof	10	Value: 200				

KM# 688 10 PESOS

15.0000 g., 0.9990 Silver .4817 oz. ASW **Subject:** Palaces of the World **Obv:** National arms within wreath, denomination **Rev:** San Soucci Palace

Date	Mintage	F	VF	XF	Unc	BU
2000 Proof	10	Value: 200				

KM# 689 10 PESOS

15.0000 g., 0.9990 Silver .4817 oz. ASW **Subject:** Palaces of the World **Obv:** National arms within wreath, denomination **Rev:** Schonbrunn Palace

Date	Mintage	F	VF	XF	Unc	BU
2000 Proof	10	Value: 200				

KM# 690 10 PESOS

15.0000 g., 0.9990 Silver .4817 oz. ASW **Subject:** Palaces of the World - Neuschwanstein Castles

Date	Mintage	F	VF	XF	Unc	BU
2000 Proof	10	Value: 200				

KM# 691 10 PESOS

15.0000 g., 0.9990 Silver .4817 oz. ASW **Subject:** Palaces of the World - Hradschinn Castle

Date	Mintage	F	VF	XF	Unc	BU
2000 Proof	10	Value: 200				

KM# 735 10 PESOS

27.0000 g., 0.9250 Silver 0.803 oz. ASW, 40.1 mm. **Subject:** Ibero-America - Man and Horse **Obv:** National arms and denomination within circle of arms **Rev:** Horse in center within pictures of horses being ridden **Edge:** Reeded

Date	Mintage	F	VF	XF	Unc	BU
2000 Proof	—	Value: 75.00				

KM# 686 10 PESOS

15.0000 g., 0.9990 Silver .4817 oz. ASW **Subject:** Palaces of the World **Obv:** National arms within wreath, denomination **Rev:** Versailles Palace

Date	Mintage	F	VF	XF	Unc	BU
2000 Proof	10	Value: 200				

KM# 212 15 PESOS

3.8800 g., 0.9990 Gold .1250 oz. AGW **Obv:** National arms within wreath, denomination below **Rev:** Jose Marti head right, date below

Date	Mintage	F	VF	XF	Unc	BU
1988	50	—	—	—	200	—
1988 Proof	15	Value: 250				
1989	50	—	—	—	200	—
1989 Proof	15	Value: 250				
1990	15	—	—	—	250	—
1990 Proof	12	Value: 250				

KM# 38 20 PESOS

26.0000 g., 0.9250 Silver .7732 oz. ASW **Subject:** Ignacio Agramonte **Obv:** Flagged arms, liberty cap above **Rev:** Bust 3/4 facing, date at left

Date	Mintage	F	VF	XF	Unc	BU
1977 Proof	25,000	Value: 32.50				

KM# 39 20 PESOS

26.0000 g., 0.9250 Silver .7732 oz. ASW **Subject:** Maximo Gomez **Obv:** Liberty cap above flagged arms **Rev:** Bust facing

Date	Mintage	F	VF	XF	Unc	BU
1977 Proof	75,000	Value: 28.00				

KM# 40 20 PESOS

26.0000 g., 0.9250 Silver .7732 oz. ASW **Subject:** Antonio Maceo **Obv:** Liberty cap above flagged arms **Rev:** Bust facing looking right

Date	Mintage	F	VF	XF	Unc	BU
1977 Proof	75,000	Value: 28.00				

KM# 41 20 PESOS

26.0000 g., 0.9250 Silver .7732 oz. ASW **Subject:** 60th Anniversary Socialist Revolution - Lenin **Obv:** National arms within wreath, denomination **Rev:** Bust left

Date	Mintage	F	VF	XF	Unc	BU
1977 Proof	100	Value: 1,400				

KM# 44 20 PESOS

26.0000 g., 0.9250 Silver .7732 oz. ASW **Subject:** Nonaligned Nations Conference **Obv:** National arms within wreath, denomination below **Rev:** Design left of date

Date	Mintage	F	VF	XF	Unc	BU
1979	20,000	—	—	—	13.50	—
1979 Proof	—	Value: 60.00				
1979 Matte Proof	—	Value: 100				

KM# 169 20 PESOS

62.2000 g., 0.9990 Silver 2.0000 oz. ASW **Subject:** Triumph of the Revolution **Obv:** Arms on star background above half wreath **Rev:** Rejoicing scene

Date	Mintage	F	VF	XF	Unc	BU
1987 Proof	500	Value: 85.00				
1988 Proof	1,000	Value: 75.00				
1989 Proof	500	Value: 85.00				

KM# 170 20 PESOS

62.2000 g., 0.9990 Silver 2.0000 oz. ASW **Subject:** 60th Anniversary - Birth of Ernesto Che Guevara **Obv:** Arms on star background above half wreath **Rev:** Bust right

Date	Mintage	F	VF	XF	Unc	BU
1987 Proof	500	Value: 85.00				

Date	Mintage	F	VF	XF	Unc	BU
1988 Proof	1,000	Value: 75.00				
1989 Proof	500	Value: 85.00				

KM# 171 20 PESOS

62.2000 g., 0.9990 Silver 2.0000 oz. ASW **Subject:** 30th Anniversary - The March to Victory **Obv:** Arms on star background above half wreath **Rev:** Soldiers on the march

Date	Mintage	F	VF	XF	Unc	BU
1987 Proof	333	Value: 85.00				
1988 Proof	1,000	Value: 75.00				
1989 Proof	500	Value: 85.00				

KM# 232 20 PESOS

62.2000 g., 0.9990 Silver 2.0000 oz. ASW **Subject:** 150th Anniversary - First Railroad in Cuba **Obv:** Arms on star background above wreath **Rev:** Train engine right

Date	Mintage	F	VF	XF	Unc	BU
1988 Proof	Est. 1,000	Value: 80.00				

KM# 233 20 PESOS

62.2000 g., 0.9990 Silver 2.0000 oz. ASW **Subject:** 140th Anniversary - First Railroad in Spain **Obv:** Arms on star background above half wreath **Rev:** Train left, dates

Date	Mintage	F	VF	XF	Unc	BU
ND(1988) Proof	Est. 1,000	Value: 80.00				

KM# 234 20 PESOS

62.2000 g., 0.9990 Silver 2.0000 oz. ASW **Subject:** 160th Anniversary - First Railroad in England **Obv:** Arms on star background above half wreath **Rev:** Ancient train with boxcar, dates

Date	Mintage	F	VF	XF	Unc	BU
1988 Proof	Est. 1,000	Value: 80.00				

KM# 235 20 PESOS

62.2000 g., 0.9990 Silver 2.0000 oz. ASW **Subject:** Tania La Guerrillera, Argentinian revolutionary **Obv:** Arms on star background above half wreath **Rev:** Bust facing

Date	Mintage	F	VF	XF	Unc	BU
1988 Proof	1,000	Value: 75.00				

KM# 236 20 PESOS

62.2000 g., 0.9990 Silver 2.0000 oz. ASW **Subject:** Camilo Cienfuegos **Obv:** Arms on star background above half wreath **Rev:** Bust facing, dates

Date	Mintage	F	VF	XF	Unc	BU
1988 Proof	1,000	Value: 75.00				

KM# 237 20 PESOS

62.2000 g., 0.9990 Silver 2.0000 oz. ASW **Subject:** 35th Anniversary - Assault of the Moncada Garrison **Obv:** Arms on star background above half wreath **Rev:** Armed figures, dates below

Date	Mintage	F	VF	XF	Unc	BU
ND(1988) Proof	1,000	Value: 75.00				

KM# 531 20 PESOS

62.2000 g., 0.9990 Silver 2.0000 oz. ASW **Obv:** National arms within wreath, denomination **Rev:** Jose Raul playing chess

Date	Mintage	F	VF	XF	Unc	BU
ND(1988) Proof	1,000	Value: 90.00				

KM# 532 20 PESOS

62.2000 g., 0.9990 Silver 2.0000 oz. ASW **Subject:** 25th Anniversary - Death of Ernesto Che Guevara **Obv:** National arms **Rev:** Head facing, dates

Date	Mintage	F	VF	XF	Unc	BU
ND(1992) Proof	1,000	Value: 90.00				

KM# 471.1 20 PESOS

62.2000 g., 0.9990 Silver 2.0000 oz. ASW **Subject:** Fidel Castro - 40th Anniversary of Moncada **Obv:** National arms within wreath, denomination **Rev:** Uniformed bust left

Date	Mintage	F	VF	XF	Unc	BU
1993 Proof	—	Value: 90.00				

KM# 459 20 PESOS

62.2000 g., 0.9990 Silver 2.0000 oz. ASW **Subject:** Cuban Railroad **Obv:** National arms **Rev:** Train engine, date below

Date	Mintage	F	VF	XF	Unc	BU
1994 Proof	—	Value: 90.00				

KM# 533 20 PESOS

62.2000 g., 0.9990 Silver 2.0000 oz. ASW **Subject:** Transportation **Obv:** National arms **Rev:** Zeppelin, date below

Date	Mintage	F	VF	XF	Unc	BU
1995 Proof	1,000	Value: 110				

KM# 213 25 PESOS

7.7700 g., 0.9990 Gold .2500 oz. AGW **Subject:** Jose Marti **Obv:** National arms within wreath, denomination below **Rev:** Head right

Date	Mintage	F	VF	XF	Unc	BU
1988	50	—	—	—	300	—
1988 Proof	15	Value: 400				
1989	50	—	—	—	300	—
1989 Proof	15	Value: 400				
1990	12	—	—	—	350	—
1990 Proof	12	Value: 400				

KM# 692 25 PESOS

7.7700 g., 0.9990 Gold .2500 oz. AGW **Subject:** Zunzuncito **Obv:** National arms within wreath, denomination **Rev:** Hummingbird

Date	Mintage	F	VF	XF	Unc	BU
1999 Proof	—	Value: 200				

Y# 726 25 PESOS

7.7759 g., 0.9990 Gold .2500 oz. AGW, 20 mm. **Subject:** Zunzuncito **Obv:** National arms **Rev:** Hummingbird **Edge:** Reeded

Date	Mintage	F	VF	XF	Unc	BU
1999 Proof	1,000	Value: 185				

KM# 422 30 PESOS

93.2500 g., 0.9990 Silver 2.9951 oz. ASW **Rev:** Vincente and Martin Pinzon

Date	Mintage	F	VF	XF	Unc	BU
1991 Proof	1,000	Value: 150				

KM# 423 30 PESOS

93.2500 g., 0.9990 Silver 2.9951 oz. ASW **Rev:** Hatuey People

Date	Mintage	F	VF	XF	Unc	BU
1991 Proof	1,000	Value: 125				

KM# 430 30 PESOS

93.3000 g., 0.9990 Silver 2.9970 oz. ASW **Series:** 500th Anniversary of the New World **Subject:** Queen Joanna 1479-1555, dughter of Isabella I **Obv:** National arms within wreath **Rev:** Bust 3/4 right above half wreath

Date	Mintage	F	VF	XF	Unc	BU
1991 Proof	1,000	Value: 165				

KM# 431 30 PESOS
93.3000 g., 0.9990 Silver 2.9970 oz. ASW **Series:** 500th Anniversary of the New World **Subject:** Diego Velazquez **Obv:** National arms within wreath **Rev:** Bust 3/4 left above wreath

Date	Mintage	F	VF	XF	Unc	BU
1991 Proof	1,000	Value: 165				

KM# 376 30 PESOS
93.2500 g., 0.9990 Silver 2.9951 oz. ASW **Series:** 500th Anniversary of the New World **Subject:** Guama native **Obv:** National arms within wreath **Rev:** Native figure drinking from large shell

Date	Mintage	F	VF	XF	Unc	BU
1992 Proof	550	Value: 125				

KM# 377 30 PESOS
93.2500 g., 0.9990 Silver 2.9951 oz. ASW **Series:** 500th Anniversary of the New World **Subject:** Bartolome de Las Casas **Obv:** National arms within wreath **Rev:** Figure at desk writing a letter with a quill pen

Date	Mintage	F	VF	XF	Unc	BU
1992 Proof	550	Value: 125				

KM# 378 30 PESOS
93.2500 g., 0.9990 Silver 2.9951 oz. ASW **Series:** 500th Anniversary of the New World **Subject:** King Philipp **Obv:** National arms within wreath **Rev:** Bust 3/4 right above half wreath

Date	Mintage	F	VF	XF	Unc	BU
1992 Proof	550	Value: 125				

KM# 379 30 PESOS
93.2500 g., 0.9990 Silver 2.9951 oz. ASW **Series:** 500th Anniversary of the New World **Subject:** Fernando and Elisabeth, Philipp and Johanna **Obv:** National arms within wreath **Rev:** Spanish kings and queens

Date	Mintage	F	VF	XF	Unc	BU
ND(1992) Proof	550	Value: 125				

KM# 208 50 PESOS
15.5500 g., 0.9990 Gold .5000 oz. AGW **Subject:** 30th Anniversary - The March to Victory **Obv:** Arms on star background above half wreath **Rev:** Soldiers on the march, date above

Date	Mintage	F	VF	XF	Unc	BU
1988 Proof	150	Value: 360				

KM# 209 50 PESOS
15.5500 g., 0.9990 Gold .5000 oz. AGW **Subject:** 60th Anniversary - Birth of Ernesto Che Guevara **Obv:** Arms on star background above half wreath **Rev:** Bust right, date at left

Date	Mintage	F	VF	XF	Unc	BU
1988 Proof	150	Value: 360				

KM# 210 50 PESOS
15.5500 g., 0.9990 Gold .5000 oz. AGW **Subject:** Triumph of the Revolutionary **Obv:** Arms on star background above half wreath **Rev:** Castro with revolutionaries, divide dates

Date	Mintage	F	VF	XF	Unc	BU
1988 Proof	150	Value: 360				

KM# 214 50 PESOS
15.5500 g., 0.9990 Gold .5000 oz. AGW **Subject:** Jose Marti **Obv:** National arms within wreath, denomination **Rev:** Head right

Date	Mintage	F	VF	XF	Unc	BU
1988	12	—	—	—	450	—
1988 Proof	15	Value: 600				
1989	150	—	—	—	375	—
1989 Proof	15	Value: 600				
1990	15	—	—	—	450	—
1990 Proof	12	Value: 600				

KM# 313 50 PESOS
15.5500 g., 0.9990 Gold .5000 oz. AGW **Subject:** 160th Anniversary - First Train in England **Rev:** Train, Liverpool - Manchester

Date	Mintage	F	VF	XF	Unc	BU
1989 Proof	150	Value: 375				

KM# 314 50 PESOS
15.5500 g., 0.9990 Gold .5000 oz. AGW **Subject:** 150th Anniversary - First Train in Spanish America **Rev:** Train **Rev. Legend:** HABANA-BEJUCAL

Date	Mintage	F	VF	XF	Unc	BU
1989 Proof	150	Value: 375				

KM# 315 50 PESOS
15.5500 g., 0.9990 Gold .5000 oz. AGW **Subject:** 140th Anniversary - First Train in Spain **Rev:** Train **Rev. Legend:** BARCELONA-MATARD

Date	Mintage	F	VF	XF	Unc	BU
1989 Proof	150	Value: 375				

KM# 330 50 PESOS
15.5500 g., 0.9990 Gold .5000 oz. AGW **Subject:** Tania La Guerrillera **Rev:** Portrait of female guerilla fighter

Date	Mintage	F	VF	XF	Unc	BU
1989 Proof	150	Value: 375				

KM# 331 50 PESOS
15.5500 g., 0.9990 Gold .5000 oz. AGW **Subject:** Camilo Cienfuegos Gornaran **Rev:** Portrait of Camilo Cienfuegos

Date	Mintage	F	VF	XF	Unc	BU
1989 Proof	150	Value: 375				

KM# 332 50 PESOS
15.5500 g., 0.9990 Gold .5000 oz. AGW **Subject:** Assault of the Moncada Garrison **Rev:** Battle scene

Date	Mintage	F	VF	XF	Unc	BU
1989 Proof	150	Value: 375				

KM# 281 50 PESOS
15.5500 g., 0.9990 Gold .5000 oz. AGW **Subject:** Simon Bolivar **Rev:** Portrait of Simon Bolivar

Date	Mintage	F	VF	XF	Unc	BU
1990 Proof	50	Value: 375				

KM# 294 50 PESOS

155.5150 g., 0.9990 Silver 5.0000 oz. ASW **Subject:** 500th Anniversary - Discovery of America **Obv:** National arms within wreath **Rev:** Christopher Columbus

Date	Mintage	F	VF	XF	Unc	BU
1990 Proof	2,000	Value: 115				

KM# 295 50 PESOS

155.5150 g., 0.9990 Silver 5.0000 oz. ASW **Subject:** 500th Anniversary - Discovery of America **Obv:** National arms within wreath **Rev:** King Ferdinand of Spain

Date	Mintage	F	VF	XF	Unc	BU
1990 Proof	2,000	Value: 115				

KM# 296 50 PESOS

155.5150 g., 0.9990 Silver 5.0000 oz. ASW **Subject:** 500th Anniversary - Discovery of America **Obv:** National arms within wreath **Rev:** Queen Isabella of Spain

Date	Mintage	F	VF	XF	Unc	BU
1990 Proof	2,000	Value: 115				

KM# 297 50 PESOS

155.5150 g., 0.9990 Silver 5.0000 oz. ASW **Subject:** 500th Anniversary - Discovery of America **Obv:** National arms within wreath **Rev:** Juan de la Cosa

Date	Mintage	F	VF	XF	Unc	BU
1990 Proof	2,000	Value: 115				

KM# 298 50 PESOS

15.5500 g., 0.9990 Gold .5000 oz. AGW **Subject:** 500th Anniversary - Discovery of America **Obv:** National arms within wreath **Rev:** Portrait of Christopher Columbus

Date	Mintage	F	VF	XF	Unc	BU
1990 Proof	250	Value: 375				

KM# 299 50 PESOS

15.5500 g., 0.9990 Gold .5000 oz. AGW **Subject:** 500th Anniversary - Discovery of America **Obv:** National arms within wreath **Rev:** Portrait of King Ferdinand V

Date	Mintage	F	VF	XF	Unc	BU
1990 Proof	250	Value: 375				

KM# 300 50 PESOS

15.5500 g., 0.9990 Gold .5000 oz. AGW **Subject:** 500th Anniversary - Discovery of America **Obv:** National arms within wreath **Rev:** Portrait of Queen Isabella of Spain

Date	Mintage	F	VF	XF	Unc	BU
1990 Proof	250	Value: 375				

KM# 301 50 PESOS

15.5500 g., 0.9990 Gold .5000 oz. AGW **Subject:** 500th Anniversary - Discovery of America **Obv:** National arms within wreath **Rev:** Portrait of Juan de la Cosa

Date	Mintage	F	VF	XF	Unc	BU
1990 Proof	250	Value: 375				

KM# 321 50 PESOS

15.5500 g., 0.9990 Gold .5000 oz. AGW **Subject:** Pan American Games - Baseball **Obv:** National arms within wreath, denomination **Rev:** Baseball players

Date	Mintage	F	VF	XF	Unc	BU
1990 Proof	15	Value: 400				

KM# 322 50 PESOS

15.5500 g., 0.9990 Gold .5000 oz. AGW **Subject:** Pan American Games - High Jump **Obv:** National arms within wreath, denomination **Rev:** High jumper clearing pole

Date	Mintage	F	VF	XF	Unc	BU
1990 Proof	15	Value: 400				

KM# 323 50 PESOS

15.5500 g., 0.9990 Gold .5000 oz. AGW **Subject:** Pan American Games - Volleyball **Obv:** National arms within wreath, denomination **Rev:** Volleyball players

Date	Mintage	F	VF	XF	Unc	BU
1990 Proof	15	Value: 400				

KM# 339 50 PESOS

15.5500 g., 0.9990 Gold .5000 oz. AGW **Rev:** Hatuey tribesman

Date	Mintage	F	VF	XF	Unc	BU
1991 Proof	200	Value: 375				

KM# 343 50 PESOS

155.5000 g., 0.9990 Silver 5.0000 oz. ASW **Series:** Olympics **Obv:** National arms within wreath **Rev:** Stadium

Date	Mintage	F	VF	XF	Unc	BU
1991 Proof	1,050	Value: 240				

KM# 356 50 PESOS

155.5000 g., 0.9990 Silver 5.0000 oz. ASW **Subject:** Madrid - Alcala Gate **Obv:** National arms within wreath **Rev:** Building with arches

Date	Mintage	F	VF	XF	Unc	BU
1991 Proof	550	Value: 285				

KM# 357 50 PESOS

155.5000 g., 0.9990 Silver 5.0000 oz. ASW **Subject:** Seville - La Giralda Tower **Obv:** National arms within wreath **Rev:** Tower, date at right

Date	Mintage	F	VF	XF	Unc	BU
1991 Proof	550	Value: 285				

KM# 432 50 PESOS

155.5000 g., 0.9990 Silver 5.0000 oz. ASW **Series:** 500th Anniversary of the New World **Subject:** Queen Joanna 1479-1555, daughter of Isabella I **Obv:** National arms within wreath **Rev:** Head 3/4 right above half wreath

Date	Mintage	F	VF	XF	Unc	BU
1991 Proof	1,000	Value: 165				

KM# 433 50 PESOS

155.5000 g., 0.9990 Silver 5.0000 oz. ASW **Series:** 500th Anniversary of the New World **Subject:** Diego Valezquez **Obv:** National arms within wreath **Rev:** Bust 3/4 left above half wreath

Date	Mintage	F	VF	XF	Unc	BU
1991 Proof	1,000	Value: 165				

KM# 434 50 PESOS

155.5000 g., 0.9990 Silver 5.0000 oz. ASW **Series:** 500th Anneversary of the New World **Subject:** Pinzon Brothers **Obv:** National arms within wreath, denomination below **Rev:** Portraits in cameos, small ship above

Date	Mintage	F	VF	XF	Unc	BU
1991 Proof	1,000	Value: 165				

KM# 435 50 PESOS
155.5000 g., 0.9990 Silver 5.0000 oz. ASW **Series:** 500th Anniversary of the New World **Subject:** Hatuey Tribesman **Obv:** National arms within wreath, denomination **Rev:** Head stretching left

Date	Mintage	F	VF	XF	Unc	BU
1991 Proof	1,000	Value: 165				

KM# 444 50 PESOS
15.5500 g., 0.9990 Gold .5000 oz. AGW **Subject:** Queen Joanna

Date	Mintage	F	VF	XF	Unc	BU
1991 Proof	200	Value: 375				

KM# 445 50 PESOS
15.5500 g., 0.9990 Gold .5000 oz. AGW **Subject:** Diego Valezquez

Date	Mintage	F	VF	XF	Unc	BU
1991 Proof	200	Value: 375				

KM# 446 50 PESOS
15.5500 g., 0.9990 Gold .5000 oz. AGW **Subject:** Pinzon Brothers

Date	Mintage	F	VF	XF	Unc	BU
1991 Proof	200	Value: 375				

KM# 358 50 PESOS
155.5000 g., 0.9990 Silver 5.0000 oz. ASW **Series:** 500th Anniversary of the New World **Subject:** Philipp I **Obv:** National arms within wreath **Rev:** Bust right above half wreath

Date	Mintage	F	VF	XF	Unc	BU
1992 Proof	550	Value: 185				

KM# 359 50 PESOS
155.5000 g., 0.9990 Silver 5.0000 oz. ASW **Series:** 500th Anniversary of the New World **Subject:** Chief Guama **Obv:** National arms within wreath **Rev:** Native drinking from large shell

Date	Mintage	F	VF	XF	Unc	BU
1992 Proof	550	Value: 185				

KM# 380 50 PESOS
155.7300 g., 0.9990 Silver 5.0019 oz. ASW **Series:** 500th Anniversary of the New World **Subject:** Bartolome de Las Casas **Obv:** National arms within wreath, denomination below **Rev:** Seated figure writing with quill

Date	Mintage	F	VF	XF	Unc	BU
1992 Proof	550	Value: 185				

KM# 381 50 PESOS
155.7300 g., 0.9990 Silver 5.0019 oz. ASW **Series:** 500th Anniversary of the New World **Subject:** Ferdinand and Elisabeth, Philipp and Joanna **Obv:** National arms within wreath, denomination below **Rev:** Busts of Spanish Kings and Queens left

Date	Mintage	F	VF	XF	Unc	BU
ND(1992) Proof	550	Value: 185				

KM# 382 50 PESOS
155.7300 g., 0.9990 Silver 5.0019 oz. ASW **Obv:** National arms within wreath, denomination below **Rev:** San Jorge Palace

Date	Mintage	F	VF	XF	Unc	BU
1992 Proof	550	Value: 185				

KM# 568 50 PESOS
155.7300 g., 0.9990 Silver 5.0019 oz. ASW **Subject:** Cuban Fauna **Obv:** National arms within wreath, denomination below **Rev:** Multicolored Papilio butterfly

Date	Mintage	F	VF	XF	Unc	BU
1992 Proof	—	Value: 200				

KM# 641 50 PESOS
155.7300 g., 0.9990 Silver 5.0019 oz. ASW **Subject:** 1982 - Ano de Espana **Obv:** National arms within wreath, denomination below **Rev:** Seville's Tower of Gold

Date	Mintage	F	VF	XF	Unc	BU
1992 Proof	—	Value: 200				

KM# 400 50 PESOS
155.5150 g., 0.9990 Silver 5.0000 oz. ASW **Obv:** National arms, denomination below on left, crowned arms on right **Rev:** St. Jacobi on rearing horse

Date	Mintage	F	VF	XF	Unc	BU
1993 Proof	1,000	Value: 175				

KM# 693 50 PESOS
15.5518 g., 0.9990 Gold .4990 oz. AGW **Subject:** 40th Anniversary - Assault on Moncada Garrison

Date	Mintage	F	VF	XF	Unc	BU
1993 Proof	—	Value: 360				

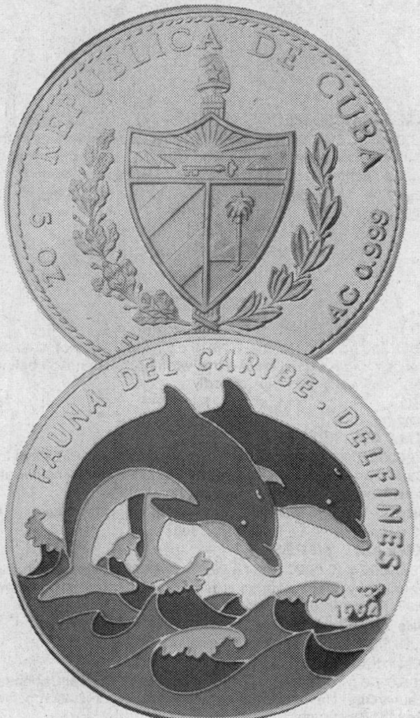

KM# 503 50 PESOS
155.5150 g., 0.9990 Silver 5.0000 oz. ASW **Subject:** Caribbean Fauna **Obv:** National arms within wreath, denomination below **Rev:** Multicolor bottle-nosed dophins **Edge:** Reeded

Date	Mintage	F	VF	XF	Unc	BU
1994 Proof	2,500	Value: 200				

KM# 504 50 PESOS
155.5150 g., 0.9990 Silver 5.0000 oz. ASW **Subject:** Caribbean Fauna **Obv:** National arms within wreath, denomination below **Rev:** Multicolor swordfish

Date	Mintage	F	VF	XF	Unc	BU
1994 Proof	2,500	Value: 200				

KM# 505 50 PESOS
155.5150 g., 0.9990 Silver 5.0000 oz. ASW **Subject:** Caribbean Fauna **Obv:** National arms within wreath, denomination below **Rev:** Multicolored brown pelican

Date	Mintage	F	VF	XF	Unc	BU
1994 Proof	2,500	Value: 200				

KM# 506 50 PESOS
155.5150 g., 0.9990 Silver 5.0000 oz. ASW **Subject:** Caribbean Fauna **Obv:** National arms within wreath, denomination below **Rev:** Multicolored flamingos

Date	Mintage	F	VF	XF	Unc	BU
1994 Proof	2,500	Value: 200				

KM# 507 50 PESOS
155.5150 g., 0.9990 Silver 5.0000 oz. ASW **Subject:** Caribbean Fauna **Obv:** National arms within wreath, denomination below **Rev:** Multicolored yellow sea bass (Coney)

Date	Mintage	F	VF	XF	Unc	BU
1994 Proof	2,500	Value: 200				

KM# 508 50 PESOS
155.5150 g., 0.9990 Silver 5.0000 oz. ASW **Subject:** Caribbean Fauna **Obv:** National arms within wreath, denomination below **Rev:** Multicolored spotted eagle ray

Date	Mintage	F	VF	XF	Unc	BU
1994 Proof	2,500	Value: 250				

KM# 484 50 PESOS
155.5150 g., 0.9990 Silver 5.0000 oz. ASW **Subject:** Pirates of the Caribbean **Obv:** National arms within wreath, denomination below **Rev:** Blackbeard within circle, date below

Date	Mintage	F	VF	XF	Unc	BU
1995 Proof	Est. 3,000	Value: 265				

KM# 485 50 PESOS
155.5150 g., 0.9990 Silver 5.0000 oz. ASW **Series:** Pirates of the Caribbean **Subject:** Sir Henry Morgan **Obv:** National arms within wreath, denomination below **Rev:** Pirate with rifle over right shoulder left

Date	Mintage	F	VF	XF	Unc	BU
1995 Proof	Est. 3,000	Value: 265				

KM# 486 50 PESOS
155.5150 g., 0.9990 Silver 5.0000 oz. ASW **Series:** Pirates of the Caribbean **Subject:** Anne Bonny **Obv:** National arms within wreath, denomination below **Rev:** Bare-breasted woman and pirates drinking within circle, date below

Date	Mintage	F	VF	XF	Unc	BU
1995 Proof	Est. 3,000	Value: 265				

KM# 487 50 PESOS
155.5150 g., 0.9990 Silver 5.0000 oz. ASW **Series:** Pirates of the Caribbean **Subject:** Mary Read **Obv:** National arms within wreath, denomination below **Rev:** Pirates fighting on the beach

Date	Mintage	F	VF	XF	Unc	BU
1995 Proof	Est. 3,000	Value: 265				

KM# 488 50 PESOS
155.5150 g., 0.9990 Silver 5.0000 oz. ASW **Series:** Pirates of the Caribbean **Subject:** Captain Kidd **Obv:** National arms within wreath, denomination below **Rev:** Pirates aboard ship

Date	Mintage	F	VF	XF	Unc	BU
1995 Proof	Est. 3,000	Value: 265				

KM# 489 50 PESOS
155.5150 g., 0.9990 Silver 5.0000 oz. ASW **Subject:** Piet Heyn **Obv:** National arms within wreath, denomination below **Rev:** Pirates having sword fight

Date	Mintage	F	VF	XF	Unc	BU
1995 Proof	Est. 3,000	Value: 265				

KM# 490 50 PESOS
13.0000 g., 0.9170 Gold .3829 oz. AGW **Series:** Pirates of the Caribbean **Subject:** Blackbeard **Obv:** National arms within wreath, denomination below **Rev:** Bust 3/4 facing within circle, date below

Date	Mintage	F	VF	XF	Unc	BU
1995 Proof	Est. 1,000	Value: 300				

KM# 491 50 PESOS
13.0000 g., 0.9170 Gold .3829 oz. AGW **Series:** Pirates of the Caribbean **Subject:** Sir Henry Morgan **Obv:** National arms within wreath, denomination below **Rev:** Bust 3/4 right

Date	Mintage	F	VF	XF	Unc	BU
1995 Proof	Est. 1,000	Value: 300				

KM# 492 50 PESOS
13.0000 g., 0.9170 Gold .3829 oz. AGW **Series:** Pirates of the Caribbean **Subject:** Anne Bonny **Obv:** National arms within wreath, denomination below **Rev:** Bust with bare breast looking left

Date	Mintage	F	VF	XF	Unc	BU
1995 Proof	Est. 1,000	Value: 300				

KM# 493 50 PESOS
13.0000 g., 0.9170 Gold .3829 oz. AGW **Series:** Pirates of the Caribbean **Subject:** Mary Read **Obv:** National arms within wreath, denomination below **Rev:** Bust with bare breasts 3/4 right

Date	Mintage	F	VF	XF	Unc	BU
1995 Proof	Est. 1,000	Value: 300				

KM# 494 50 PESOS
13.0000 g., 0.9170 Gold .3829 oz. AGW **Series:** Pirates of the Caribbean **Subject:** Captain Kidd **Obv:** National arms within wreath, denomination below **Rev:** Bust left looking right

Date	Mintage	F	VF	XF	Unc	BU
1995 Proof	Est. 1,000	Value: 300				

KM# 495 50 PESOS
13.0000 g., 0.9170 Gold .3829 oz. AGW **Series:** Pirates of the Caribbean **Subject:** Piet Heyn **Obv:** National arms within wreath, denomination below **Rev:** Bust facing

Date	Mintage	F	VF	XF	Unc	BU
1995 Proof	Est. 1,000	Value: 300				

KM# 557 50 PESOS
155.0000 g., 0.9990 Silver 4.9944 oz. ASW **Series:** Caribbean Fauna **Obv:** National arms within wreath, denomination below **Rev:** Purple-throated Carib Hummingbird

Date	Mintage	F	VF	XF	Unc	BU
1996 Proof	950	Value: 300				

KM# 558 50 PESOS
155.0000 g., 0.9990 Silver 4.9944 oz. ASW **Series:** Caribbean Fauna **Obv:** National arms within wreath, denomination below **Rev:** Yellow perch

Date	Mintage	F	VF	XF	Unc	BU
1996 Proof	950	Value: 300				

KM# 559 50 PESOS
155.0000 g., 0.9990 Silver 4.9944 oz. ASW **Series:** Caribbean Fauna **Obv:** National arms within wreath, denomination below **Rev:** Cuban Tody bird

Date	Mintage	F	VF	XF	Unc	BU
1996 Proof	950	Value: 300				

KM# 560 50 PESOS
155.0000 g., 0.9990 Silver 4.9944 oz. ASW **Series:** Caribbean Fauna **Obv:** National arms within wreath, denomination below **Rev:** Wood duck

Date	Mintage	F	VF	XF	Unc	BU
1996 Proof	950	Value: 300				

KM# 564 50 PESOS
155.0000 g., 0.9990 Silver 4.9944 oz. ASW **Series:** Caribbean Fauna **Obv:** National arms within wreath, denomination below **Rev:** Vaca anil fish

Date	Mintage	F	VF	XF	Unc	BU
1996 Proof	950	Value: 300				

KM# 567 50 PESOS
155.0000 g., 0.9990 Silver 4.9944 oz. ASW **Series:** Caribbean Fauna **Obv:** National arms within wreath, denomination below **Rev:** Papilio butterfly

Date	Mintage	F	VF	XF	Unc	BU
1996 Proof	950	Value: 300				

KM# 694 50 PESOS
155.0000 g., 0.9990 Silver 4.9944 oz. ASW **Subject:** Caribbean Flora **Obv:** National arms within wreath, denomination below **Rev:** Multicolor flower, "Bidens Romerillo"

Date	Mintage	F	VF	XF	Unc	BU
1997 Proof	—	Value: 300				

KM# 695 50 PESOS
155.0000 g., 0.9990 Silver 4.9944 oz. ASW **Subject:** Caribbean Flora **Obv:** National arms within wreath, denomination below **Rev:** Multicolor flower, "Cordia Vomitel"

Date	Mintage	F	VF	XF	Unc	BU
1997 Proof	—	Value: 300				

KM# 697 50 PESOS
155.0000 g., 0.9990 Silver 4.9944 oz. ASW **Subject:** Wonders of the Ancient World **Rev:** Temple of Artemis

Date	Mintage	F	VF	XF	Unc	BU
1997 Proof	—	Value: 250				

KM# 698 50 PESOS
155.0000 g., 0.9990 Silver 4.9944 oz. ASW **Subject:** Wonders of the Ancient World **Rev:** Pyramids

Date	Mintage	F	VF	XF	Unc	BU
1997 Proof	—	Value: 250				

KM# 699 50 PESOS
155.0000 g., 0.9990 Silver 4.9944 oz. ASW **Subject:** Wonders of the Ancient World **Rev:** Hanging Gardens of Babylon

Date	Mintage	F	VF	XF	Unc	BU
1997 Proof	—	Value: 250				

KM# 700 50 PESOS
155.0000 g., 0.9990 Silver 4.9944 oz. ASW **Subject:** Wonders of the Ancient World **Rev:** Statue of Jupiter at Olympus

Date	Mintage	F	VF	XF	Unc	BU
1997 Proof	—	Value: 250				

KM# 701 50 PESOS
155.0000 g., 0.9990 Silver 4.9944 oz. ASW **Subject:** Wonders of the Ancient World **Rev:** Colossus of Rhodes

Date	Mintage	F	VF	XF	Unc	BU
1997 Proof	—	Value: 250				

KM# 702 50 PESOS
155.0000 g., 0.9990 Silver 4.9944 oz. ASW **Subject:** Wonders of the Ancient World **Rev:** Mausoleum at Halicarnasos

Date	Mintage	F	VF	XF	Unc	BU
1997 Proof	—	Value: 250				

KM# 654 50 PESOS
15.5500 g., 0.9990 Gold .4999 oz. AGW **Subject:** Expo 2000 **Obv:** National arms within wreath **Rev:** Twipsy cartoon logo

Date	Mintage	F	VF	XF	Unc	BU
1998 Proof	3,125	Value: 360				

KM# 638 50 PESOS
15.5500 g., 0.9990 Gold .4999 oz. AGW, 30 mm. **Subject:** AIDS **Obv:** National arms within wreath **Rev:** AIDS ribbon on silhouette before world map

Date	Mintage	F	VF	XF	Unc	BU
1998 Proof	2,000	Value: 360				

KM# 727 50 PESOS
15.5518 g., 0.9990 Gold .5000 oz. AGW, 32.5 mm. **Obv:** National arms **Rev:** Hummingbird **Edge:** Reeded

Date	Mintage	F	VF	XF	Unc	BU
1999 Proof	1,000	Value: 375				

KM# 703 50 PESOS
15.5500 g., 0.9990 Gold .4999 oz. AGW **Subject:** 40th Anniversary - Triumph of the Revolution

Date	Mintage	F	VF	XF	Unc	BU
1999 Proof	—	Value: 450				

KM# 704 50 PESOS
15.5500 g., 0.9990 Gold .4999 oz. AGW **Obv:** National arms within wreath, denomination below **Rev:** Hummingbird

Date	Mintage	F	VF	XF	Unc	BU
1999 Proof	—	Value: 400				

KM# 705 50 PESOS
15.5500 g., 0.9990 Gold .4999 oz. AGW **Subject:** Welcome the New Millennium

Date	Mintage	F	VF	XF	Unc	BU
2000 Proof	—	Value: 350				

KM# 706 50 PESOS
15.5500 g., 0.9990 Gold .4999 oz. AGW **Subject:** Welcome the Third Millennium

Date	Mintage	F	VF	XF	Unc	BU
2000 Proof	—	Value: 350				

KM# 707 50 PESOS
15.5500 g., 0.9990 Gold .4999 oz. AGW **Subject:** Hacia un Nuevo Milenio (Towards a new Millennium)

Date	Mintage	F	VF	XF	Unc	BU
2000 Proof	—	Value: 350				

KM# 42 100 PESOS
12.0000 g., 0.9170 Gold .3538 oz. AGW **Subject:** 60th Anniversary of Socialist Revolution - Lenin **Obv:** National arms within wreath, denomination below **Rev:** Bust left divides dates

Date	Mintage	F	VF	XF	Unc	BU
ND(1977) Proof	10	Value: 10,000				

KM# 43 100 PESOS
12.0000 g., 0.9170 Gold .3538 oz. AGW **Obv:** Liberty cap above flagged arms, denomination **Rev:** Carlos Manuel de Cespedes

Date	Mintage	F	VF	XF	Unc	BU
ND(1977) Proof	25,000	Value: 260				

KM# 45 100 PESOS
12.0000 g., 0.9170 Gold .3538 oz. AGW **Subject:** Nonaligned Nations Conference **Obv:** National arms within wreath **Rev:** Number six within design

Date	Mintage	F	VF	XF	Unc	BU
1979	2,000	—	—	—	350	—
1979 Proof	20,000	Value: 275				

KM# 52 100 PESOS
12.0000 g., 0.9170 Gold .3538 oz. AGW **Subject:** First Soviet-Cuban space flight **Obv:** Arms **Rev:** Shuttle orbiting planet, date below

Date	Mintage	F	VF	XF	Unc	BU
1980	1,000	—	—	—	350	—

KM# 85 100 PESOS
12.0000 g., 0.9170 Gold .3538 oz. AGW **Obv:** National arms within wreath, denomination below **Rev:** Columbus' ship - Niña

Date	Mintage	F	VF	XF	Unc	BU
1981	2,000	—	—	—	325	—

KM# 86 100 PESOS
12.0000 g., 0.9170 Gold .3538 oz. AGW **Obv:** National arms within wreath, denomination below **Rev:** Columbus' ship - Pinta

Date	Mintage	F	VF	XF	Unc	BU
1981	2,000	—	—	—	325	—

KM# 87 100 PESOS
12.0000 g., 0.9170 Gold .3538 oz. AGW **Obv:** National arms within wreath, denomination below **Rev:** Columbus' ship - Santa Maria

Date	Mintage	F	VF	XF	Unc	BU
1981	2,000	—	—	—	325	—

KM# 202 100 PESOS
31.1030 g., 0.9990 Gold 1.0000 oz. AGW **Subject:** 30th Anniversary of March to Victory **Obv:** Arms on star background above half wreath **Rev:** Soldiers on the march

Date	Mintage	F	VF	XF	Unc	BU
1988 Proof	100	Value: 720				

KM# 203 100 PESOS
31.1030 g., 0.9990 Gold 1.0000 oz. AGW **Subject:** 60th Anniversary - Birth of Ernesto Che Guevara **Obv:** Arms on star background above half wreath **Rev:** Bust right, dates at left

Date	Mintage	F	VF	XF	Unc	BU
1988 Proof	100	Value: 720				

KM# 204 100 PESOS
31.1030 g., 0.9990 Gold 1.0000 oz. AGW **Subject:** 30th Anniversary - Triumph of the Revolution **Obv:** Arms on star background above half wreath **Rev:** Scene of triumph, dates

Date	Mintage	F	VF	XF	Unc	BU
1988 Proof	100	Value: 720				

KM# 215 100 PESOS
31.1030 g., 0.9990 Gold 1.0000 oz. AGW **Subject:** Jose Marti **Obv:** National arms within wreath, denomination below **Rev:** Head right, date below

Date	Mintage	F	VF	XF	Unc	BU
1988	50	—	—	—	800	—
1988 Proof	15	Value: 1,200				
1989	150	—	—	—	700	—
1989 Proof	15	Value: 1,200				
1990	15	—	—	—	1,000	—
1990 Proof	12	Value: 1,250				

KM# 316 100 PESOS
31.1030 g., 0.9990 Gold 1.0000 oz. AGW **Subject:** 160th Anniversary - First train in England **Rev:** Train **Rev. Legend:** LIVERPOOL-MANCHESTER

Date	Mintage	F	VF	XF	Unc	BU
1989 Proof	150	Value: 720				

KM# 317 100 PESOS
31.1030 g., 0.9990 Gold 1.0000 oz. AGW **Subject:** 150th Anniversary - First train in Spanish America **Rev:** Train **Rev. Legend:** HABANA-BEJUCAL

Date	Mintage	F	VF	XF	Unc	BU
1989 Proof	150	Value: 720				

KM# 318 100 PESOS
31.1030 g., 0.9990 Gold 1.0000 oz. AGW **Subject:** 140th Anniversary - First train in Spain **Rev:** Train **Rev. Legend:** BARCELONA-MATARO

Date	Mintage	F	VF	XF	Unc	BU
1989 Proof	150	Value: 720				

KM# 319 100 PESOS
31.1030 g., 0.9990 Gold 1.0000 oz. AGW **Subject:** 200th Anniversary of French Revolution - Lady Justice **Rev:** Female revolutionary raising flag

Date	Mintage	F	VF	XF	Unc	BU
1989 Proof	150	Value: 800				

KM# 320 100 PESOS
31.1030 g., 0.9990 Gold 1.0000 oz. AGW **Subject:** 200th Anniversary of French Revolution - Bastille **Rev:** Bastille, soldiers in foreground

Date	Mintage	F	VF	XF	Unc	BU
1989	150	—	—	—	800	—

KM# 333 100 PESOS
31.1030 g., 0.9990 Gold 1.0000 oz. AGW **Subject:** Tania La Guerrillera **Rev:** Portrait of female guerilla fighter

Date	Mintage	F	VF	XF	Unc	BU
1989 Proof	150	Value: 800				

KM# 334 100 PESOS
31.1030 g., 0.9990 Gold 1.0000 oz. AGW **Subject:** Camilo Cienfuegos Gornaran **Rev:** Portrait of Camilo Cienfuegos

Date	Mintage	F	VF	XF	Unc	BU
1989 Proof	150	Value: 800				

KM# 335 100 PESOS
31.1030 g., 0.9990 Gold 1.0000 oz. AGW **Subject:** 35th Anniversary - Assault of the Moncada Garrison **Rev:** Battle scene

Date	Mintage	F	VF	XF	Unc	BU
1989 Proof	150	Value: 800				

KM# 447 100 PESOS
31.1030 g., 0.9990 Gold 1.0000 oz. AGW **Subject:** 30th Anniversary of Revolution **Obv:** National arms within wreath, denomination **Rev:** Armed, uniformed figure standing right

Date	Mintage	F	VF	XF	Unc	BU
1989 Proof	250	Value: 715				

KM# 448 100 PESOS
31.1030 g., 0.9990 Gold 1.0000 oz. AGW **Subject:** 30th Anniversary of Revolution **Obv:** National arms within wreath, denomination **Rev:** Armed, uniformed figure standing right

Date	Mintage	F	VF	XF	Unc	BU
1989 Proof	250	Value: 715				

KM# 449 100 PESOS
31.1030 g., 0.9990 Gold 1.0000 oz. AGW **Subject:** 30th Anniversary of Revolution **Obv:** National arms within wreath, denomination **Rev:** Armed, uniformed figure standing right

Date	Mintage	F	VF	XF	Unc	BU
1989 Proof	250	Value: 715				

KM# 302 100 PESOS
31.1030 g., 0.9990 Gold 1.0000 oz. AGW **Subject:** 500th Anniversary - Discovery of America **Rev:** Portrait of Columbus

Date	Mintage	F	VF	XF	Unc	BU
1990 Proof	250	Value: 825				

KM# 303 100 PESOS
31.1030 g., 0.9990 Gold 1.0000 oz. AGW **Subject:** 500th Anniversary - Discovery of America **Rev:** Portrait of King Ferdinand V

Date	Mintage	F	VF	XF	Unc	BU
1990 Proof	250	Value: 825				

KM# 304 100 PESOS
31.1030 g., 0.9990 Gold 1.0000 oz. AGW **Subject:** 500th Anniversary - Discovery of America **Rev:** Portrait of Queen Isabella

Date	Mintage	F	VF	XF	Unc	BU
1990 Proof	250	Value: 825				

KM# 305 100 PESOS
31.1030 g., 0.9990 Gold 1.0000 oz. AGW **Subject:** 500th Anniversary - Discovery of America **Rev:** Portrait of Juan de la Cosa

Date	Mintage	F	VF	XF	Unc	BU
1990 Proof	250	Value: 825				

KM# 450 100 PESOS
31.1030 g., 0.9990 Gold 1.0000 oz. AGW **Subject:** Pinzon brothers **Obv:** National arms within wreath

Date	Mintage	F	VF	XF	Unc	BU
1991 Proof	200	Value: 750				

KM# 451 100 PESOS
31.1030 g., 0.9990 Gold 1.0000 oz. AGW **Subject:** 500th Anniversary of the New World **Rev:** Head of Queen Joanna half right, 1479-1555, daughter of Queen Isabella I

Date	Mintage	F	VF	XF	Unc	BU
1991 Proof	200	Value: 750				

KM# 452 100 PESOS
31.1030 g., 0.9990 Gold 1.0000 oz. AGW **Subject:** 500th Anniversary **Obv:** National arms within wreath **Rev:** Diego Velazquez

Date	Mintage	F	VF	XF	Unc	BU
1991 Proof	200	Value: 750				

KM# 534 100 PESOS
31.1030 g., 0.9990 Gold 1.0000 oz. AGW **Series:** Olympics **Rev:** Stadium

Date	Mintage	F	VF	XF	Unc	BU
1991 Proof	225	Value: 800				

KM# 535 100 PESOS
31.1030 g., 0.9990 Gold 1.0000 oz. AGW **Subject:** Madrid - Alcala Gate **Rev:** Building with arches

Date	Mintage	F	VF	XF	Unc	BU
1991 Proof	225	Value: 800				

KM# 569 100 PESOS
31.1030 g., 0.9990 Gold 1.0000 oz. AGW **Subject:** Hatuey People

Date	Mintage	F	VF	XF	Unc	BU
1991 Proof	—	Value: 800				

KM# 384 100 PESOS
31.1030 g., 0.9990 Gold 1.0000 oz. AGW **Subject:** Seville - Tower of Gold **Rev:** Tower of Gold in Seville

Date	Mintage	F	VF	XF	Unc	BU
1992 Proof	225	Value: 825				

KM# 385 100 PESOS
31.1030 g., 0.9990 Gold 1.0000 oz. AGW **Subject:** El Escorial **Rev:** El Escorial palace

Date	Mintage	F	VF	XF	Unc	BU
1992 Proof	225	Value: 825				

KM# 453 100 PESOS
31.1030 g., 0.9990 Gold 1.0000 oz. AGW **Subject:** 500th Anniversary **Obv:** National arms within wreath **Rev:** Bartolome de las Casas

Date	Mintage	F	VF	XF	Unc	BU
1992 Proof	100	Value: 750				

KM# 454 100 PESOS
31.1030 g., 0.9990 Gold 1.0000 oz. AGW **Subject:** 500th Anniversary **Obv:** National arms within wreath **Rev:** Guama Tribesman

Date	Mintage	F	VF	XF	Unc	BU
1992 Proof	100	Value: 750				

KM# 455 100 PESOS
31.1030 g., 0.9990 Gold 1.0000 oz. AGW **Subject:** 500th Anniversary **Obv:** National arms within wreath **Rev:** King Philipp

Date	Mintage	F	VF	XF	Unc	BU
1992 Proof	100	Value: 750				

KM# 456 100 PESOS
31.1030 g., 0.9990 Gold 1.0000 oz. AGW **Subject:** 500th Anniversary **Obv:** National arms within wreath **Rev:** Spanish kings and queens

Date	Mintage	F	VF	XF	Unc	BU
1992 Proof	100	Value: 750				

KM# 536 100 PESOS
31.1030 g., 0.9990 Gold 1.0000 oz. AGW **Subject:** San Jorge Palace

Date	Mintage	F	VF	XF	Unc	BU
1992 Proof	225	Value: 800				

KM# 570 100 PESOS
31.1030 g., 0.9990 Gold 1.0000 oz. AGW **Subject:** Ernesto Che Guevara **Obv:** National arms within wreath

Date	Mintage	F	VF	XF	Unc	BU
1992 Proof	—	Value: 715				

KM# 537 100 PESOS
31.1030 g., 0.9990 Gold 1.0000 oz. AGW **Subject:** 40th Anniversary of Moncada **Rev:** Fidel Castro

Date	Mintage	F	VF	XF	Unc	BU
1993 Proof	100	Value: 775				

KM# 538 100 PESOS
31.1030 g., 0.9990 Gold 1.0000 oz. AGW **Obv:** Two sets of arms and denomination **Rev:** St. Jacobi

Date	Mintage	F	VF	XF	Unc	BU
1993 Proof	100	Value: 775				

KM# 539 100 PESOS
31.1030 g., 0.9990 Gold 1.0000 oz. AGW **Rev:** Federico Garcia Lorca

Date	Mintage	F	VF	XF	Unc	BU
1993 Proof	100	Value: 775				

KM# 571 100 PESOS
31.1030 g., 0.9990 Gold 1.0000 oz. AGW **Obv:** National arms within wreath **Rev:** Jose Marti

Date	Mintage	F	VF	XF	Unc	BU
1994 Proof	—	Value: 715				

KM# 572 100 PESOS
31.1030 g., 0.9990 Gold 1.0000 oz. AGW **Subject:** Centennial of the Necessary War

Date	Mintage	F	VF	XF	Unc	BU
1995 Proof	—	Value: 715				

KM# 708 100 PESOS
31.1030 g., 0.9990 Gold 1.0000 oz. AGW **Subject:** Meeting of Fidel Castro and Pope John Paul II in the Vatican

Date	Mintage	F	VF	XF	Unc	BU
1997 Proof	—	Value: 800				

KM# 709 100 PESOS
31.1030 g., 0.9990 Gold 1.0000 oz. AGW **Subject:** Papal visit to Cuba

Date	Mintage	F	VF	XF	Unc	BU
1997 Proof	—	Value: 800				

KM# 710 100 PESOS
31.1030 g., 0.9990 Gold 1.0000 oz. AGW **Subject:** 90th Anniversary - Triumph of the Revolution

Date	Mintage	F	VF	XF	Unc	BU
1999 Proof	—	Value: 715				

KM# 719 100 PESOS
31.1030 g., 0.9990 Gold 1.0000 oz. AGW **Obv:** National arms within wreath **Rev:** Hummingbird

Date	Mintage	F	VF	XF	Unc	BU
1999 Proof	—	Value: 800				

KM# 728 100 PESOS
31.1035 g., 0.9990 Gold 1.0000 oz. AGW, 38 mm. **Obv:** National arms **Rev:** Hummingbird **Edge:** Reeded

Date	Mintage	F	VF	XF	Unc	BU
1999 Proof	1,000	Value: 715				

KM# 711 100 PESOS
31.1030 g., 0.9990 Gold 1.0000 oz. AGW **Subject:** Macia un Nuevo Milenio (Towards a new millennium)

Date	Mintage	F	VF	XF	Unc	BU
2000 Proof	—	Value: 850				

KM# 712 100 PESOS
31.1030 g., 0.9990 Gold 1.0000 oz. AGW **Subject:** Welcome to the third millennium

Date	Mintage	F	VF	XF	Unc	BU
2000 Proof	—	Value: 850				

KM# 713 100 PESOS
31.1030 g., 0.9990 Gold 1.0000 oz. AGW **Subject:** Welcome to the new millennium

Date	Mintage	F	VF	XF	Unc	BU
2000 Proof	—	Value: 850				

KM# 714 100 PESOS
31.1030 g., 0.9990 Gold 1.0000 oz. AGW **Subject:** Maritime relics - school ship Galatea

Date	Mintage	F	VF	XF	Unc	BU
2000 Proof	—	Value: 850				

KM# 715 100 PESOS
31.1030 g., 0.9990 Gold 1.0000 oz. AGW **Subject:** Maritime relics - maritime ambulance Buena Ventura

Date	Mintage	F	VF	XF	Unc	BU
2000 Proof	—	Value: 850				

KM# 716 100 PESOS
31.1030 g., 0.9990 Gold 1.0000 oz. AGW **Subject:** Maritime relics - nautical rise of Juan de la Cosa

Date	Mintage	F	VF	XF	Unc	BU
2000 Proof	—	Value: 850				

KM# 717 100 PESOS
31.1030 g., 0.9990 Gold 1.0000 oz. AGW **Subject:** Maritime relics - school ship JS Elcana

Date	Mintage	F	VF	XF	Unc	BU
2000 Proof	—	Value: 850				

KM# 718 100 PESOS
31.1030 g., 0.9990 Gold 1.0000 oz. AGW **Subject:** Maritime relics - Peral submarine

Date	Mintage	F	VF	XF	Unc	BU
2000 Proof	—	Value: 850				

KM# 642 150 PESOS
411.4225 g., 0.9990 Silver 13.2275 oz. ASW **Series:** Cuban Fauna **Obv:** National arms within wreath **Rev:** Multicolored Cuban Trogon **Note:** The Cuban Trogon is the Cuban National Bird.

Date	Mintage	F	VF	XF	Unc	BU
1996 Proof	Est. 420	Value: 600				

KM# 542 200 PESOS
31.1000 g., Gold **Obv:** National arms within wreath **Rev:** Bolivar and Marti

Date	Mintage	F	VF	XF	Unc	BU
1993	100	—	—	—	750	—
1993 Proof	100	Value: 800				

KM# 543 200 PESOS
31.1000 g., Gold **Series:** Prehistoric Animals **Obv:** National arms within wreath **Rev:** Apatosaurus

Date	Mintage	F	VF	XF	Unc	BU
1993 Proof	100	Value: 800				

KM# 544 200 PESOS
31.1000 g., Gold **Series:** Prehistoric Animals **Rev:** Chalicotherium

Date	Mintage	F	VF	XF	Unc	BU
1993 Proof	100	Value: 900				

KM# 545 200 PESOS
31.1000 g., Gold **Subject:** Montecristi Manifesto **Rev:** Two seated figures facing each other, date lower left

Date	Mintage	F	VF	XF	Unc	BU
1994 Proof	100	Value: 800				

KM# 643 300 PESOS
822.8449 g., 0.9990 Silver 27.5661 oz. ASW **Series:** Cuban Fauna **Obv:** National arms within wreath **Rev:** Multicolor Mariposa butterfly

Date	Mintage	F	VF	XF	Unc	BU
1996 Proof	Est. 420	Value: 975				

KM# 457 500 PESOS
155.5500 g., 0.9990 Gold 5.000 oz. AGW **Rev:** Christopher Columbus

Date	Mintage	F	VF	XF	Unc	BU
1990 Proof	15	Value: 5,500				

KM# 386 500 PESOS
155.5500 g., 0.9990 Gold 5.000 oz. AGW **Subject:** 500th Anniversary **Obv:** National arms within wreath **Rev:** Spanish Kings and Queens

Date	Mintage	F	VF	XF	Unc	BU
ND(1992) Proof	15	Value: 5,500				

KM# 605 500 PESOS
155.5500 g., 0.9990 Platinum 5.000 oz. APW **Subject:** Castro **Rev:** Fidel Castro

Date	Mintage	F	VF	XF	Unc	BU
1993 Proof	—	Value: 7,500				

KM# 720 500 PESOS
49.0000 g., 0.9990 Gold-Silver 25.0000 oz. **Subject:** Che Guevara

Date	Mintage	F	VF	XF	Unc	BU
2000 Proof	101	Value: 1,900				

PESO CONVERTIBLE SERIES

KM# 729 CENTAVO
1.7000 g., Copper Plated Steel, 15 mm. **Obv:** National arms within wreath, denomination below **Rev:** Tower and denomination **Edge:** Reeded

Date	Mintage	F	VF	XF	Unc	BU
2000	—	—	—	—	3.00	—

KM# 575.1 5 CENTAVOS
Stainless Steel **Obv:** National arms within wreath, denomination and date below **Rev:** Casa Colonial, denomination above **Note:** Medal alignment

Date	Mintage	F	VF	XF	Unc	BU
1994	—	—	—	—	1.00	—

KM# 575.2 5 CENTAVOS
2.6500 g., Nickel-Plated Steel, 18 mm. **Obv:** National arms **Rev:** Casa Colonial **Note:** Coin alignment, recut designs.

Date	Mintage	F	VF	XF	Unc	BU
1996	—	—	—	—	1.00	—
1998	—	—	—	—	1.00	—
1999	—	—	—	—	1.00	—
2000	—	—	—	—	1.00	—

KM# 576.1 10 CENTAVOS
Nickel-Bonded Steel, 20 mm. **Obv:** National arms within wreath, denomination and date below **Rev:** Castillo de la Fuerza, denomination above **Note:** Medal alignment.

Date	Mintage	F	VF	XF	Unc	BU
1994	—	—	—	—	2.00	—

KM# 576.2 10 CENTAVOS
Nickel Plated Steel **Obv:** National arms **Rev:** Castillo de la Fuerza **Note:** Coin alignment, recut designs.

Date	Mintage	F	VF	XF	Unc	BU
1996	—	—	—	—	2.00	—
1999	—	—	—	—	2.00	—
2000	—	—	—	—	2.00	—

KM# 577.1 25 CENTAVOS
Nickel Bonded Steel, 23 mm. **Obv:** National arms within wreath, denomination and date below **Rev:** Trinidad, denomination upper right **Note:** Medal alignment. Prev. KM#577.

Date	Mintage	F	VF	XF	Unc	BU
1994	—	—	—	—	3.00	—

KM# 577.2 25 CENTAVOS
5.6500 g., Nickel Plated Steel, 23 mm. **Obv:** National arms **Rev:** Trinidad **Note:** Coin alignment.

Date	Mintage	F	VF	XF	Unc	BU
1998	—	—	—	—	3.00	—
2000	—	—	—	—	3.00	—

KM# 578 50 CENTAVOS
7.5000 g., Nickel Plated Steel, 25 mm. **Obv:** National arms within wreath, denomination and date below **Rev:** Cathedral of Havana, denomination above

Date	Mintage	F	VF	XF	Unc	BU
1994	—	—	—	—	5.00	—

KM# 579.1 PESO
8.5000 g., Nickel Plated Steel, 27 mm. **Obv:** National arms within wreath, denomination and date below **Rev:** Guama, denomination upper left **Note:** Medal alignment.

Date	Mintage	F	VF	XF	Unc	BU
1994	—	—	—	—	5.00	—

KM# 579.2 PESO
8.5000 g., Nickel Plated Steel, 27 mm. **Obv:** National arms **Rev:** Guama **Note:** Coin alignment.

Date	Mintage	F	VF	XF	Unc	BU
1998	—	—	—	—	5.00	—
2000	—	—	—	—	5.00	—

KM# 730 5 PESOS
4.4600 g., Bi-Metallic Nickel Plated Steel center in Brass Plated Steel ring, 23 mm. **Obv:** National arms within wreath, denomination below **Rev:** Bust right, denomination at right, within circle **Edge:** Reeded **Note:** Medal alignment.

Date	Mintage	F	VF	XF	Unc	BU
1999	—	—	—	—	25.00	—

VISITOR'S COINAGE

KM# 409 CENTAVO
Copper-Nickel **Obv:** Stag, date below **Rev:** Palm tree within logo and denomination

Date	Mintage	F	VF	XF	Unc	BU
1988	—	—	0.50	1.50	3.00	—

KM# 410 CENTAVO
Aluminum **Obv:** Palm tree within logo **Rev:** Denomination

Date	Mintage	F	VF	XF	Unc	BU
1988	—	—	0.50	1.50	5.00	—

KM# 411 5 CENTAVOS
Copper-Nickel **Obv:** Mollusk and date **Rev:** Palm tree within logo, denomination

Date	Mintage	F	VF	XF	Unc	BU
1981	—	0.45	0.75	2.00	4.00	—

KM# 412.1 5 CENTAVOS
Copper-Nickel **Obv:** Mollusk and date **Rev:** Palm tree within logo, denomination

Date	Mintage	F	VF	XF	Unc	BU
1981	—	0.45	0.75	2.00	4.00	—

KM# 412.2 5 CENTAVOS
Copper-Nickel **Obv:** Mollusk and date **Rev:** Palm tree within logo, denomination

Date	Mintage	F	VF	XF	Unc	BU
1981	—	0.45	0.75	2.00	4.00	—

KM# 412.3 5 CENTAVOS
Copper-Nickel **Obv:** Mollusk and date **Rev:** Palm tree within logo, small 5

Date	Mintage	F	VF	XF	Unc	BU
1989	—	0.35	0.50	1.50	3.00	—

KM# 412.3a 5 CENTAVOS
Stainless Steel **Obv:** Palm tree within logo, denomination **Rev:** Mollusk and date

Date	Mintage	F	VF	XF	Unc	BU
1989	—	—	1.00	3.00	6.00	—

KM# 413 5 CENTAVOS
Aluminum **Obv:** Palm tree within logo, date below **Rev:** Denomination

Date	Mintage	F	VF	XF	Unc	BU
1988	—	0.50	1.00	3.00	5.00	—

KM# 414 10 CENTAVOS
Copper-Nickel **Obv:** Hummingbird in flight right, date below **Rev:** Palm tree within logo, denomination

Date	Mintage	F	VF	XF	Unc	BU
1981	—	—	0.65	2.00	4.00	—

KM# 415.1 10 CENTAVOS
Copper-Nickel **Obv:** Hummingbird in flight right, date below **Rev:** Palm tree within logo, large "10"

Date	Mintage	F	VF	XF	Unc	BU
1981	—	0.50	1.00	3.00	5.00	—

KM# 415.2 10 CENTAVOS
Copper-Nickel **Obv:** Hummingbird in flight right, date below **Rev:** Palm tree within logo, small "10"

Date	Mintage	F	VF	XF	Unc	BU
1981	—	—	0.65	2.00	4.00	—

KM# 415.2a 10 CENTAVOS
Stainless Steel **Obv:** Hummingbird in flight right **Rev:** Palm tree within logo, small 10

Date	Mintage	F	VF	XF	Unc	BU
1989	—	—	1.25	4.00	9.00	—

KM# 415.3 10 CENTAVOS
Copper-Nickel **Obv:** Hummingbird in flight right **Rev:** Palm tree within logo, denomination **Note:** Reduced size.

Date	Mintage	F	VF	XF	Unc	BU
1989	—	—	1.25	4.50	10.00	—

KM# 416 10 CENTAVOS
Aluminum **Obv:** Palm tree within logo, date below **Rev:** Denomination

Date	Mintage	F	VF	XF	Unc	BU
1988	—	—	0.65	2.00	4.00	—

KM# 417 25 CENTAVOS
Copper-Nickel **Obv:** Flower, date below **Rev:** Palm tree within logo, denomination

Date	Mintage	F	VF	XF	Unc	BU
1981	—	0.50	1.00	2.50	6.00	—

KM# 418.1 25 CENTAVOS
Copper-Nickel **Obv:** Flower, date below **Rev:** Palm tree within logo, large 25

Date	Mintage	F	VF	XF	Unc	BU
1981	—	—	1.00	3.00	7.00	—

KM# 418.2 25 CENTAVOS
Copper-Nickel **Obv:** Flower, date below **Rev:** Palm tree within logo, small 25

Date	Mintage	F	VF	XF	Unc	BU
1989	—	—	1.00	3.00	7.00	—

KM# 418.2a 25 CENTAVOS
Stainless Steel **Obv:** Flower and date **Rev:** Palm tree within logo, denomination

Date	Mintage	F	VF	XF	Unc	BU
1989	—	—	2.00	5.50	12.00	—

KM# 419 25 CENTAVOS
Aluminum **Obv:** Palm tree within logo, date below **Rev:** Denomination

Date	Mintage	F	VF	XF	Unc	BU
1988	—	—	0.75	2.50	5.00	—

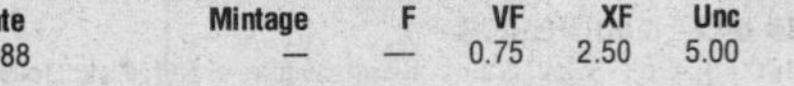

KM# 420 50 CENTAVOS

Copper-Nickel **Obv:** Palm tree within logo, date below **Rev:** Denomination and logo

Date	Mintage	F	VF	XF	Unc	BU
1981	—	—	2.50	7.50	15.00	—

Note: Varieties exist in the number of lines below the palm tree.

KM# 461 50 CENTAVOS

Copper-Nickel **Obv:** Palm tree within logo, denomination **Rev:** Denomination and logo

Date	Mintage	F	VF	XF	Unc	BU
1989	—	—	5.00	15.00	30.00	—

KM# 421 PESO

Copper-Nickel **Obv:** Lighthouse **Rev:** Palm tree within logo, denomination

Date	Mintage	F	VF	XF	Unc	BU
1981	—	—	4.00	12.00	24.00	—

KM# 580 PESO

Copper-Nickel **Obv:** Lighthouse **Rev:** Palm tree within logo, denomination

Date	Mintage	F	VF	XF	Unc	BU
1989	—	—	4.00	12.00	24.00	—

TRIAL STRIKES

KM#	Date	Mintage	Identification	Mkt Val
TS1	1977	—	20 Pesos. Brass. Antonio Maceo, KM40. Prev. KM#TS5.	300
TS2	1977	—	20 Pesos. Brass. Maximo Gomez, KM39. Prev. KM#TS6.	300
TS3	1977	—	20 Pesos. Brass. Ignacio Aramonte, KM38. Prev. KM#TS7.	300
TS4	1977	—	20 Pesos. Copper-Nickel. Antonio Maceo, KM40. Prev. KM#TS8.	500
TS5	1977	—	100 Pesos. Brass. de Cespedes, KM43. Prev. KM#TS9.	300
TS6	1994	10	100 Pesos. Gold. Reverse of KM467, uniface. Prev. KM#TS2.	2,000
TS7	1994	1	50 Pesos. Silver. KM503; dolphins green and red. Prev. KM#TS3.	—
TS8	1994	1	50 Pesos. Silver. KM503, dolphins green and red.	—

PATTERNS

Including off metal strikes

KM#	Date	Mintage	Identification	Mkt Val
PnA10	1915	—	Centavo. Bronze.	—
PnC10	1915	—	2 Centavos. Bronze.	2,000
PnA11	1970	—	Peso. 0.9990 Silver. KM158.	500
PnB11	1970	—	Peso. 0.9990 Silver. KM158.	500
PnC11	1986	—	5 Pesos. 0.9000 Copper. KM326.	—
PnD11	1986	—	5 Pesos. 0.0500 Silver. KM326.	—
PnE11	1986	—	5 Pesos. 0.0500 Gold. KM326.	—
PnF11	1987	—	5 Pesos. Copper. KM166.	—
PnG11	1987	—	5 Pesos. Copper. .900 Copper, 050 Silver, .050 Gold, KM#26.	—
Pn11	1987	3	5 Pesos. 0.9990 Gold. KM159.	6,500
PnA12	1988	6	5 Pesos. 0.9990 Silver.	1,150
Pn12	1988	6	5 Pesos. Silver.	1,150
PnA13	1988	6	100 Pesos. 0.9990 Gold.	5,500
PnB13	1988	—	100 Pesos. 0.9990 Gold.	5,500
Pn13	1988	6	100 Pesos. Gold.	—
Pn14	1993	34	10 Pesos. Silver. Mirror bust with frosted field. KM398.	500
Pn15	1994	25	10 Pesos. Silver. KM510, player's #9 on the back is matte.	385
Pn16	1995	22	10 Pesos. Silver. Key mint mark in proof.	385
Pn17	1995	100	Peso. Copper Nickel. Pirates del Carib, Sir Francis Drake, proof.	120
Pn106	1999	—	Peso. Copper-Nickel. KM662.	100
Pn107	1999	—	10 Pesos. Silver. KM672.	200
Pn108	1999	—	100 Pesos. Gold. KM710.	1,500
Pn109	2000	—	Peso. Copper-Nickel. KM665.	—
Pn110	2000	—	Peso. Copper-Nickel. KM664.	100
Pn111	2000	—	Peso. Copper-Nickel. KM663.	100
Pn112	2000	—	10 Pesos. Silver. KM685.	200
Pn113	2000	—	10 Pesos. Silver. KM681.	200
Pn114	2000	—	10 Pesos. Silver. KM678	200
Pn115	2000	—	10 Pesos. Silver. KM678.	200
Pn116	2000	—	10 Pesos. Silver. KM680.	200
Pn118	2000	—	10 Pesos. Silver. KM691.	200
Pn119	2000	—	10 Pesos. Silver. KM689.	200
Pn120	2000	—	10 Pesos. Silver. KM688.	200
Pn121	2000	—	10 Pesos. Silver. KM687.	200
Pn122	2000	—	10 Pesos. Silver. KM686.	200
Pn123	2000	—	10 Pesos. Silver. KM690.	200
Pn124	2000	—	10 Pesos. Silver. Ship Rays 1749-1805.	200
Pn125	2000	—	10 Pesos. Silver. Ship: Sand Pedro de Alcantara	200
Pn126	2000	—	10 Pesos. Silver. Ship: Santisma Trinidad.	200
Pn127	2000	—	10 Pesos. Silver. KM684.	200
Pn128	2000	—	10 Pesos. Silver. KM683.	200
Pn129	2000	—	100 Pesos. Gold. KM712.	1,500
Pn130	2000	—	100 Pesos. Gold. KM711.	1,500
Pn131	2000	—	100 Pesos. Gold. KM713	1,500
Pn132	2000	—	100 Pesos. Gold. KM718.	1,500
Pn133	2000	—	100 Pesos. Gold. KM717.	1,250
Pn134	2000	—	100 Pesos. Gold. KM714.	1,500
Pn135	2000	—	100 Pesos. Gold. KM715.	1,500
Pn136	2000	—	100 Pesos. Gold. KM716.	1,500

PIEFORTS

KM#	Date	Mintage	Identification	Mkt Val
P3	1983	100	5 Pesos. Silver. KM10.	200
P4	1988	30	10 Pesos. Gold. KM211.	1,200
P5	1988	30	10 Pesos. Gold. KM211.	1,200
P6	1988	15	15 Pesos. Gold. KM212.	1,200
P7	1988	15	15 Pesos. Gold. KM212.	1,200
P8	1988	10	25 Pesos. Gold. KM213.	1,600
P9	1988	10	25 Pesos. Gold. KM213.	1,600
P10	1988	10	50 Pesos. Gold. KM214.	1,600
P11	1988	10	50 Pesos. Gold. KM214.	1,600
P12	1988	10	100 Pesos. Gold. KM215.	2,200
P13	1988	10	100 Pesos. Gold. KM215.	2,200
P14	1989	30	10 Pesos. Gold. KM211.	1,200
P15	1989	30	10 Pesos. Gold. KM211.	1,200
P16	1989	150	10 Pesos. Silver. KM239.	200
P17	1989	150	10 Pesos. Silver. KM240.	200
P18	1989	15	15 Pesos. Gold. KM212.	1,200
P19	1989	15	15 Pesos. Gold. KM212.	1,200
P20	1989	10	25 Pesos. Gold. KM213.	1,600
P21	1989	15	25 Pesos. Gold. KM213.	1,600
P22	1989	10	50 Pesos. Gold. KM214.	2,200
P23	1989	15	50 Pesos. Gold. KM214.	2,200
P24	1989	12	50 Pesos. Gold. KM313.	1,800
P25	1989	12	50 Pesos. Gold. KM314.	1,800
P26	1989	12	50 Pesos. Gold. KM315.	1,800
P27	1989	15	100 Pesos. Silver. KM215.	—
P28	1989	10	100 Pesos. Gold. KM215.	2,200
P29	1989	15	100 Pesos. Gold. KM215.	2,200
P30	1989	12	100 Pesos. Gold. KM316.	1,800
P31	1989	12	100 Pesos. Gold. KM317.	1,800
P32	1989	12	100 Pesos. Gold. KM318.	1,800
P33	1989	12	100 Pesos. Gold. KM319.	2,200
P34	1989	12	100 Pesos. Gold. KM320.	2,200
P35	1990	50	10 Pesos. Silver. Ship and Cub; KM252.	400
P36	1990	15	10 Pesos. Silver. KM280.	900
P37	1990	100	10 Pesos. Silver. KM291.	250
P38	1990	100	10 Pesos. Silver. KM292.	160
P39	1990	100	10 Pesos. Silver. KM293.	160
P40	1990	12	10 Pesos. Gold. KM211.	1,200
P41	1990	12	10 Pesos. Gold. KM211.	1,200
P42	1990	12	15 Pesos. Gold. KM212.	1,200
P43	1990	12	15 Pesos. Gold. KM212.	1,200
P44	1990	12	25 Pesos. Gold. 15.5400 g. KM213.	—
P45	1990	12	25 Pesos. Gold. 15.5400 g. KM213.	—
P46	1990	12	50 Pesos. Gold. KM214.	2,200
P47	1990	12	50 Pesos. Gold. KM214.	2,200
P48	1990	12	50 Pesos. Gold. KM321.	2,200
P49	1990	12	50 Pesos. Gold. KM322.	2,200
P50	1990	12	50 Pesos. Gold. KM323.	2,200
P51	1990	12	100 Pesos. Gold. KM215.	2,200
P52	1990	15	100 Pesos. Gold. KM215.	2,200
P53	1992	50	10 Pesos. Silver. KM341.	150
P54	1993	150	5 Pesos. Silver. KM405.	200
P55	1993	—	10 Pesos. Silver. KM406.	250
P56	1993	15	200 Pesos. Gold. KM542.	2,200
P57	1994	10	100 Pesos. Gold. KM545.	1,750
P58	1993	—	100 Pesos. Gold. Similar to 200 Pesos; KM542.	—
P65	1999	—	10 Pesos. Silver. KM672.	200
P68	2000	—	10 Pesos. Silver. KM683.	200
P66	2000	—	10 Pesos. Silver. KM684.	200
P67	2000	—	10 Pesos. Silver. KM685.	200

MINT SETS

KM#	Date	Mintage	Identification	Issue Price	Mkt Val
MS1	1953 (4)	—	KM#26-29	—	125
MS2	1994 (5)	—	KM#575.1-576.1, 577-579	—	35.00

PROOF SETS

KM#	Date	Mintage	Identification	Issue Price	Mkt Val
PS1	1915 (7)	20	KM#9-15	—	3,600
PS2	1915 (6)	24	KM#16-21; Rare	—	—
PS3	1916 (7)	20	KM#9-15	—	6,250
PS4	1916 (6)	—	KM#16-21; Rare	—	—
PS5	1953 (4)	—	KM#26-29; Rare	—	—
PS6	1975 (2)	—	KM#36, 37	—	30.00
PS7	1977 (4)	—	KM#38-40, 43	290	335
PSA7	1977 (3)	—	KM#38-40	—	110
PS8	1979 (2)	—	KM#44, 45	240	260
PS9	1988 (5)	15	KM#211-215	—	1,650
PS10	1998 (4)	—	KM#668-671	—	200
PS11	1999 (5)	—	KM#671, 673, 692, 704, 719	—	1,250

The island of Curacao, the largest of the six islands that comprise the Netherlands Antilles, which is an autonomous part of the Kingdom of the Netherlands located in the Caribbean Sea 40 miles off the coast of Venezuela, has an area of 173 sq. mi. (472 sq. km.) and a population of 127,900. Capital: Willemstad. The chief industries are banking and tourism. Salt, phosphates and cattle are exported.

Curacao was discovered by Spanish navigator Alonsode Ojeda in 1499 and was settled by Spain in 1527. The Dutch West India Company took the island from Spain in 1634 and administered it until 1787, when it was surrendered to the United Netherlands. The Dutch held it thereafter except for two periods during the Napoleonic Wars, 1800-1803 and 1807-16, when it was occupied by the British. During World War II, Curacao refined 60 percent of the oil used by the Allies; the refineries were protected by U.S. troops after Germany invaded the Netherlands in1940.

During the second occupation of the Napoleonic period, the British created an emergency coinage for Curacao by cutting the Spanish dollar into 5 equal segments and countermarking each piece with a rosette indent.

MINT MARKS

D - Denver
P - Philadelphia
(u) - Utrecht

KINGDOM OF NETHERLANDS

1816

MONETARY REFORM

15 Realen = 1 Peso, 1818-22
7 Stuivers = 1 Reaal, 1822-27
10 Stuivers = 1 Franc, 1822-27
5 Francs = 1 Dollar
20 Stuivers = 1 Gulden, 1827-99
2/5 Peso = 1 Gulden, 1827-96
5/7 Peso = 1 Gulden, 1896-97
1 Peso = 1 Gulden, 1897-99

MODERN COINAGE

100 Cents = 1 Gulden

KM# 39 CENT

2.5000 g., Bronze, 19 mm. **Obv:** Rampant lion left within circle, date below **Rev:** Denomination within wreath **Edge:** Reeded

Date	Mintage	F	VF	XF	Unc	BU
1942P	2,500,000	1.25	2.50	5.00	10.00	25.00

Note: This coin was also circulated in Suriname. For similar coins dated 1943P & 1957-1960, see Suriname.

KM# 41 CENT

Bronze **Obv:** Rampant lion left within circle, date below **Rev:** Denomination within wreath

Date	Mintage	F	VF	XF	Unc	BU
1944D	3,000,000	1.25	2.50	5.00	10.00	20.00
1947 (u)	1,500,000	1.25	2.50	6.00	12.00	20.00
1947 (u) Proof	80	Value: 50.00				

KM# 42 2-1/2 CENTS

4.0000 g., Bronze, 23 mm. **Obv:** Rampant lion left within circle, date below **Rev:** Denomination within wreath **Edge:** Reeded

Date	Mintage	F	VF	XF	Unc	BU
1944D	1,000,000	1.25	2.50	6.00	12.00	20.00
1947 (u)	500,000	1.75	3.50	7.50	15.00	25.00
1947 (u) Proof	80	Value: 50.00				

Date	Mintage	F	VF	XF	Unc	BU
1948 (u)	1,000,000	1.25	2.50	6.00	12.00	20.00
1948 (u) Proof	75	Value: 50.00				

KM# 40 5 CENTS

4.5000 g., Copper-Nickel, 18 mm. **Obv:** Flower within inner circle **Rev:** Denomination within circle divides date at sides, shells at corners of coin **Edge:** Plain

Date	Mintage	F	VF	XF	Unc	BU
1943	8,595,000	1.25	2.50	4.00	8.50	19.00

Note: The above piece does not bear either a palm tree privy mark or a mint mark, but it was struck expressly for use in Curacao and Surinam. This homeland type of KM#153 was last issued in the Netherlands in 1940

KM# 47 5 CENTS

Copper-Nickel, 18 mm. **Obv:** Flower within inner circle **Rev:** Denomination within circle divides date at sides, shells at corners **Shape:** 4-sided

Date	Mintage	F	VF	XF	Unc	BU
1948	1,000,000	1.25	2.50	6.00	12.00	20.00
1948 Proof	75	Value: 50.00				

KM# 37 10 CENTS

1.4000 g., 0.6400 Silver .0288 oz. ASW, 15 mm. **Obv:** Head left **Rev:** Denomination and date within wreath **Edge:** Reeded

Date	Mintage	F	VF	XF	Unc	BU
1941P	800,000	3.75	8.00	17.50	35.00	45.00
1943P	4,500,000	2.50	6.00	15.00	30.00	40.00

Note: Both these coins were also circulated in Surinam. For coins dated 1942P, see Surinam.

KM# 38 25 CENTS

3.5800 g., 0.6400 Silver .0736 oz. ASW, 19 mm. **Obv:** Head left **Rev:** Denomination above date within wreath **Edge:** Reeded

Date	Mintage	F	VF	XF	Unc	BU
1941P	1,100,000	2.50	5.50	12.00	25.00	35.00
1943/1P	2,500,000	45.00	90.00	17.50	200	300
1943P	Inc. above	1.50	4.00	8.50	17.50	25.00

Note: Both coins were also circulated in Surinam. For similar coins dated 1943, 1944 & 1945-P with acorn mint mark, see Netherlands.

KM# 36 1/10 GULDEN

1.4000 g., 0.6400 Silver .0288 oz. ASW **Obv:** Head left **Rev:** Crowned arms divide denomination, date below

Date	Mintage	F	VF	XF	Unc	BU
1901 Proof	40	Value: 250				
1901	300,000	10.00	20.00	40.00	90.00	140

KM# 43 1/10 GULDEN

1.4000 g., 0.6400 Silver .0288 oz. ASW, 15 mm. **Obv:** Head left **Rev:** Denomination, date below **Edge:** Reeded

Date	Mintage	F	VF	XF	Unc	BU
1944D	1,500,000	1.50	4.00	8.50	17.50	35.00
1947	1,000,000	1.75	3.50	7.50	15.00	25.00
1947 Proof	80	Value: 60.00				

KM# 48 1/10 GULDEN

1.4000 g., 0.6400 Silver .0288 oz. ASW, 15 mm. **Obv:** Head left **Rev:** Denomination, date below **Edge:** Reeded

Date	Mintage	F	VF	XF	Unc	BU
1948	1,000,000	1.75	3.50	7.50	15.00	25.00
1948 Proof	75	Value: 60.00				

KM# 44 1/4 GULDEN

3.5800 g., 0.6400 Silver .0736 oz. ASW, 18.8 mm. **Obv:** Head left **Rev:** Denomination, date below **Edge:** Reeded

Date	Mintage	F	VF	XF	Unc	BU
1944D	1,500,000	1.50	4.00	8.50	17.50	35.00
1947 (u)	1,000,000	1.75	3.50	7.50	15.00	25.00
1947 (u) Proof	80	Value: 80.00				

KM# 45 GULDEN

10.0000 g., 0.7200 Silver .2315 oz. ASW, 20 mm. **Obv:** Head left **Edge Lettering:** GOD * ZU * MET * ONS *

Date	Mintage	F	VF	XF	Unc	BU
1944D	500,000	4.50	15.00	25.00	50.00	75.00

KM# 46 2-1/2 GULDEN

25.0000 g., 0.7200 Silver .5787 oz. ASW, 38 mm. **Obv:** Head left **Rev:** Crowned arms divide denomination, date belw **Edge Lettering:** GOD * ZU * MET * ONS *

Date	Mintage	F	VF	XF	Unc	BU
1944D	200,000	—	BV	8.50	12.50	20.00

Note: 60,000 coins melted down after minting.

PROOF SETS

KM#	Date	Mintage	Identification	Issue Price	Mkt Val
PS1	1901 (2)	40	KM36(1901), KM35(1900)	—	500
PS2	1947 (4)	80	KM41-44	—	200
PS3	1948 (3)	75	KM42, 47-48	—	150

The island of Cyprus lies in the eastern Mediterranean Sea 44 miles (71 km.) south of Turkey and 60 miles (97 km.) off the Syrian coast. It is the third largest island in the Mediterranean Sea, having an area of 3,572 sq. mi. (9,251 sq. km.) and a population of 736,636. Capital: Nicosia. Agriculture, light manufacturing and tourism are the chief industries. Citrus fruit, potatoes, footwear and clothing are exported

The importance of Cyprus dates from the Bronze Age when it was desired as a principal source of copper (from which the island derived its name) and as a strategic trading center. It was during this period that large numbers of Greeks settled on the island and gave it the predominantly Greek character. Its role as an international marketplace made it a prime disseminator of the then prevalent cultures, a role that still influences the civilization of Western man. Because of its fortuitous position and influential role, Cyprus was conquered by a succession of empires: the Assyrian, Egyptian, Persian, Macedonian, Ptolemaic, Roman and Byzantine. It was taken from Isaac Comnenus by Richard the Lion-Heart in 1191, sold to the Templar Knights and for the following 7 centuries was ruled by the Franks, the Venetians and the Ottomans. During the Ottoman period Cyprus acquired its Turkish community (18 percent of its population). In 1878 the island fell into British hands and was made a crown colony of Britain in 1925. Finally, on Aug. 16, 1960, it became an independent republic.

In 1964, the ethnic Turks withdrew from active participation in the government. Turkish forces invaded Cyprus in 1974, gained control of 40 percent of the island and forcibly separated the Greek and Turkish communities. In 1983, Turkish Cypriots proclaimed their own state in northern Cyprus, which remains without international recognition.

Cyprus is a member of the Commonwealth of Nations. The president is Chief of State and Head of Government.

RULERS

British, until 1960

MINT MARKS

no mint mark - Royal Mint, London, England
H - Birmingham, England

MONETARY SYSTEM

9 Piastres = 1 Shilling
20 Shillings = 1 Pound

BRITISH COLONY

PIASTRE COINAGE

KM# 1.2 1/4 PIASTRE

Bronze, 21 mm. **Obv:** Crowned bust right **Rev:** Denomination

Date	Mintage	F	VF	XF	Unc	BU
1901	72,000	20.00	50.00	100	200	—

KM# 8 1/4 PIASTRE

Bronze **Obv:** Crowned bust right **Rev:** Denomination within circle, date below **Shape:** 12-sided

Date	Mintage	F	VF	XF	Unc	BU
1902	72,000	20.00	30.00	50.00	150	—
1905	422,000	10.00	30.00	40.00	100	—
1908	36,000	50.00	100	200	350	—

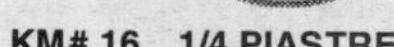

KM# 16 1/4 PIASTRE

Bronze **Obv:** Crowned bust left **Rev:** Denomination within circle, date below

Date	Mintage	F	VF	XF	Unc	BU
1922	72,000	10.00	25.00	40.00	100	—
1926 Proof	—	Value: 365				
1926	360,000	5.00	10.00	20.00	65.00	—

KM# 11 1/2 PIASTRE

Bronze **Obv:** Crowned bust right **Rev:** Denomination within circle, date at right

Date	Mintage	F	VF	XF	Unc	BU
1908	36,000	80.00	200	400	600	—

KM# 17 1/2 PIASTRE

Bronze **Obv:** Crowned bust left **Rev:** Denomination within circle, date at right

Date	Mintage	F	VF	XF	Unc	BU
1922	36,000	40.00	80.00	150	300	—
1927	108,000	10.00	20.00	50.00	120	—
1927 Proof	—	Value: 375				
1930 Proof	—	Value: 365				
1930	180,000	10.00	20.00	50.00	100	—
1931	90,000	15.00	30.00	80.00	140	—
1931 Proof	—	Value: 425				

KM# 20 1/2 PIASTRE

Copper-Nickel, 19.4 mm. **Obv:** Crowned bust left **Rev:** Denomination, date at right **Shape:** Scalloped

Date	Mintage	F	VF	XF	Unc	BU
1934	1,440,000	0.75	2.50	6.50	20.00	—
1934 Proof	—	Value: 325				

KM# 22 1/2 PIASTRE

Copper-Nickel, 19.4 mm. **Obv:** Crowned head left **Rev:** Denomination, date at right **Shape:** Scalloped

Date	Mintage	F	VF	XF	Unc	BU
1938	1,080,000	0.35	2.00	5.00	12.50	—
1938 Proof	—	Value: 325				

KM# 22a 1/2 PIASTRE

Bronze, 19.4 mm. **Obv:** Crowned head left **Rev:** Denomination, date at right **Shape:** Scalloped

Date	Mintage	F	VF	XF	Unc	BU
1942	1,080,000	2.00	4.00	10.00	25.00	—
Note: A large portion of the mintage was destroyed during WWII						
1942 Proof	—	Value: 400				
1943	1,620,000	0.25	1.00	2.50	15.00	—
1944	2,160,000	0.25	1.00	2.50	12.50	—
1945	1,080,000	0.25	1.00	2.50	15.00	—
1945 Proof	—	Value: 200				

KM# 29 1/2 PIASTRE

Bronze, 19.4 mm. **Obv:** Crowned head left **Rev:** Denomination, date at right **Shape:** Scalloped

Date	Mintage	F	VF	XF	Unc	BU
1949	1,080,000	0.15	0.35	1.00	3.50	—
1949 Proof	—	Value: 150				

KM# 12 PIASTRE

Bronze **Obv:** Crowned bust right **Rev:** Denomination within circle, date at right

Date	Mintage	F	VF	XF	Unc	BU
1908	27,000	100	200	350	700	—

KM# 18 PIASTRE

Bronze **Obv:** Crowned bust left **Rev:** Denomination within circle, date at right

Date	Mintage	F	VF	XF	Unc	BU
1922	54,000	15.00	50.00	150	300	—
1927 Proof	—	Value: 400				
1927	127,000	10.00	20.00	60.00	150	—
1930	96,000	10.00	25.00	100	200	—
1930 Proof	—	Value: 400				
1931	45,000	20.00	50.00	100	200	—
1931 Proof	—	Value: 725				

KM# 21 PIASTRE

Copper-Nickel **Obv:** Crowned bust left **Rev:** Denomination, date at right **Shape:** Scalloped

Date	Mintage	F	VF	XF	Unc	BU
1934	1,440,000	1.00	2.50	6.50	16.50	—
1934 Proof	—	Value: 325				

KM# 23 PIASTRE

Copper-Nickel **Obv:** Crowned head left **Rev:** Denomination, date at right **Shape:** Scalloped

Date	Mintage	F	VF	XF	Unc	BU
1938	2,700,000	0.60	1.50	3.00	12.50	—
1938 Proof	—	Value: 325				

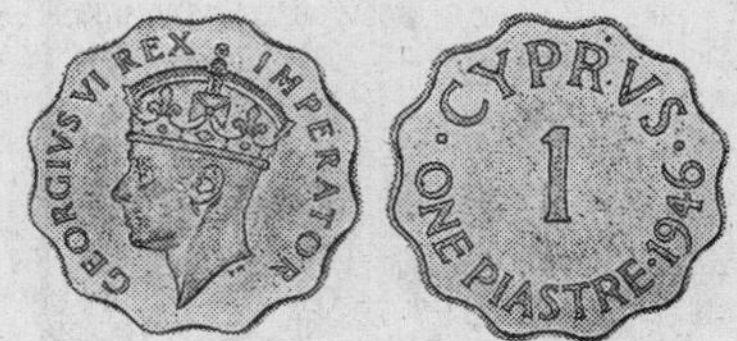

KM# 23a PIASTRE

Bronze **Obv:** Crowned head left **Rev:** Denomination, date at right

Date	Mintage	F	VF	XF	Unc	BU
1942 Proof	—	Value: 225				
1942	1,260,000	1.00	2.00	5.00	20.00	—
1943	2,520,000	0.50	1.00	2.50	15.00	—
1944	3,240,000	0.50	1.00	2.50	10.00	—
1945 Proof	—	Value: 200				
1945	1,080,000	0.60	1.50	3.00	20.00	—

Date	Mintage	F	VF	XF	Unc	BU
1946	1,080,000	0.60	1.50	3.00	20.00	—
1946 Proof	—	Value: 200				

KM# 30 PIASTRE
Bronze **Obv:** Crowned head left **Obv. Legend:** Legend ends ...DEI GRATIA REX **Rev:** Denomination, date at right **Shape:** Scalloped

Date	Mintage	F	VF	XF	Unc	BU
1949	1,080,000	0.25	0.75	2.00	4.00	—
1949 Proof	—	Value: 150				

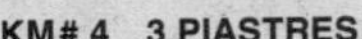

KM# 4 3 PIASTRES
1.8851 g., 0.9250 Silver .0561 oz. ASW **Obv:** Crowned and veiled bust left **Rev:** Crown over denomination divides date, circle surrounds

Date	Mintage	F	VF	XF	Unc	BU
1901 Proof	—	Value: 800				
1901	300,000	8.00	25.00	50.00	100	—

KM# 5 4-1/2 PIASTRES
2.8276 g., 0.9250 Silver .0841 oz. ASW, 19 mm. **Obv:** Crowned and veiled bust left **Rev:** Crowned arms divide date, denomination below

Date	Mintage	F	VF	XF	Unc	BU
1901 Proof	—	Value: 950				
1901	400,000	10.00	20.00	40.00	100	—

KM# 15 4-1/2 PIASTRES
2.8276 g., 0.9250 Silver .0841 oz. ASW, 19 mm. **Obv:** Crowned bust left **Rev:** Crowned arms divide date, denomination below

Date	Mintage	F	VF	XF	Unc	BU
1921	600,000	5.00	10.00	30.00	80.00	—

KM# 24 4-1/2 PIASTRES
2.8276 g., 0.9250 Silver .0841 oz. ASW, 19 mm. **Obv:** Crowned head left **Obv. Designer:** Percy Metcalfe **Rev:** Two stylized rampant lions left, denomination and date 3/4 surround **Rev. Designer:** George E. Kruger-Gray

Date	Mintage	F	VF	XF	Unc	BU
1938 Proof	—	Value: 400				
1938	192,000	2.00	6.00	15.00	30.00	—

KM# 6 9 PIASTRES
5.6552 g., 0.9250 Silver .1682 oz. ASW **Obv:** Crowned and veiled bust left **Rev:** Crowned arms divide date, denomination below

Date	Mintage	F	VF	XF	Unc	BU
1901	600,000	15.00	40.00	100	200	—
1901 Proof	—	Value: 1,250				

KM# 9 9 PIASTRES
5.6552 g., 0.9250 Silver .1682 oz. ASW **Obv:** Crowned bust right **Rev:** Crowned arms divide date, denomination below

Date	Mintage	F	VF	XF	Unc	BU
1907	60,000	35.00	100	275	500	—

KM# 13 9 PIASTRES
5.6552 g., 0.9250 Silver .1682 oz. ASW **Obv:** Crowned bust left **Rev:** Crowned arms divide date, denomination below

Date	Mintage	F	VF	XF	Unc	BU
1913	50,000	40.00	125	300	600	—
1919	400,000	5.00	10.00	30.00	100	—
1921	490,000	5.00	10.00	30.00	100	—

KM# 25 9 PIASTRES
5.6552 g., 0.9250 Silver .1682 oz. ASW **Obv:** Crowned head left **Obv. Designer:** Percy Metcalfe **Rev:** Two stylized rampant lions left, date at right, denomination below **Rev. Designer:** George E. Kruger-Gray

Date	Mintage	F	VF	XF	Unc	BU
1938	504,000	5.00	8.00	12.00	30.00	—
1938 Proof	—	Value: 400				
1940	800,000	2.75	5.00	10.00	27.50	—
1940 Proof	—	Value: 400				

KM# 27 SHILLING
Copper-Nickel **Obv:** Crowned head left **Obv. Designer:** Percy Metcalfe **Rev:** Two stylized rampant lions left, date below, denomination above **Rev. Designer:** George E. Kruger-Gray

Date	Mintage	F	VF	XF	Unc	BU
1947 Proof	—	Value: 300				
1947	1,440,000	2.00	4.00	10.00	30.00	—

KM# 31 SHILLING
Copper-Nickel **Obv:** Crowned head left **Obv. Legend:** Legend ends; DEI GRATIA REX **Obv. Designer:** Percy Metcalfe **Rev:** Two stylized rampant lions left, date below, denomination above **Rev. Designer:** George E. Kruger-Gray

Date	Mintage	F	VF	XF	Unc	BU
1949	1,440,000	2.00	4.00	10.00	30.00	—
1949 Proof	—	Value: 300				

KM# 7 18 PIASTRES
11.3104 g., 0.9250 Silver .3364 oz. ASW **Obv:** Crowned and veiled bust left **Rev:** Crowned arms divide date and denomination below

Date	Mintage	F	VF	XF	Unc	BU
1901	200,000	40.00	150	300	500	—
1901 Proof	—	Value: 2,500				

KM# 10 18 PIASTRES
11.3104 g., 0.9250 Silver .3364 oz. ASW **Obv:** Crowned bust right **Rev:** Crowned arms divide date and denomination below

Date	Mintage	F	VF	XF	Unc	BU
1907	20,000	80.00	225	485	1,250	—

KM# 14 18 PIASTRES
11.3104 g., 0.9250 Silver .3364 oz. ASW **Obv:** Crowned bust left **Rev:** Crowned arms divide date and denomination below

Date	Mintage	F	VF	XF	Unc	BU
1913	25,000	70.00	140	350	650	—
1921	155,000	25.00	60.00	150	350	—

KM# 26 18 PIASTRES
11.3104 g., 0.9250 Silver .3364 oz. ASW **Obv:** Crowned head left **Obv. Designer:** Percy Metcalfe **Rev:** Two stylized rampant lions left, date and denomination 3/4 surround **Rev. Designer:** George E. Kruger-Gray

Date	Mintage	F	VF	XF	Unc	BU
1938	200,000	5.50	20.00	30.00	50.00	—
1938 Proof	—	Value: 450				
1940	100,000	15.00	30.00	50.00	80.00	—
1940 Proof	—	Value: 450				

KM# 28 2 SHILLING
4.0000 g., Copper-Nickel, 28.3 mm. **Obv:** Crowned head left **Obv. Designer:** Percy Metcalfe **Rev:** Two stylized rampant lions left, date below, denomination above **Rev. Designer:** George E. Kruger-Gray

Date	Mintage	F	VF	XF	Unc	BU
1947 Proof	—	Value: 400				
1947	720,000	2.00	4.00	10.00	35.00	—

KM# 32 2 SHILLING

Copper-Nickel, 28.3 mm. **Obv:** Crowned head left **Obv. Designer:** Percy Metcalfe **Rev:** Two stylized rampant lions left, date below, denomination above **Rev. Designer:** George E. Kruger-Gray

Date	Mintage	F	VF	XF	Unc	BU
1949	720,000	4.00	8.00	15.00	40.00	—
1949 Proof	—	Value: 400				

KM# 19 45 PIASTRES

28.2759 g., 0.9250 Silver .8409 oz. ASW, 38 mm. **Subject:** 50th Anniversary of British Rule **Obv:** Crowned bust left **Obv. Designer:** E.B. MacKennal **Rev:** Two stylized rampant lions left, date at right, denomination below **Rev. Designer:** George E. Kruger-Gray

Date	Mintage	F	VF	XF	Unc	BU
ND(1928) Proof	517	Value: 550				
ND(1928)	80,000	25.00	35.00	60.00	150	—

DECIMAL COINAGE

50 Mils = 1 Shilling; 20 Shillings = 1 Pound; 1000 Mils = 1 Pound

KM# 33 3 MILS

Bronze, 20 mm. **Obv:** Crowned bust right **Rev:** Flying fish divides date and denomination

Date	Mintage	F	VF	XF	Unc	BU
1955	6,250,000	—	—	0.10	0.25	—
1955 Proof	2,000	Value: 2.50				

KM# 34 5 MILS

Bronze **Obv:** Crowned bust right **Rev:** Standing figure with open arms, date and denomination below

Date	Mintage	F	VF	XF	Unc	BU
1955	10,000,000	—	0.15	0.25	0.40	—
1955 Proof	2,000	Value: 3.00				
1956 Proof	—	Value: 300				
1956	2,950,000	—	0.15	0.30	0.50	—

KM# 35 25 MILS

Copper-Nickel **Obv:** Crowned bust right **Rev:** Bulls head above denomination, date below

Date	Mintage	F	VF	XF	Unc	BU
1955 Proof	2,000	Value: 3.00				
1955	2,500,000	—	0.25	0.35	1.00	—

KM# 36 50 MILS

Copper-Nickel **Obv:** Crowned bust right **Rev:** Fern leaves divide denomination, date below

Date	Mintage	F	VF	XF	Unc	BU
1955 Proof	2,000	Value: 3.00				
1955	4,000,000	—	0.35	0.50	1.00	—

KM# 37 100 MILS

Copper-Nickel, 28 mm. **Obv:** Crowned bust right **Rev:** Stylized ancient merchant ship, denomination upper left, date below

Date	Mintage	F	VF	XF	Unc	BU
1955 Proof	2,000	Value: 4.50				
1955	2,500,000	—	0.50	0.75	1.50	—
1957 Proof	—	Value: 440				
Note: All but 10,000 of 1957 issue were melted down.						
1957	Est. 500,000	—	10.00	15.00	50.00	—

REPUBLIC

DECIMAL COINAGE

50 Mils = 1 Shilling; 20 Shillings = 1 Pound; 1000 Mils = 1 Pound

KM# 38 MIL

Aluminum, 18.5 mm. **Obv:** Shielded arms within wreath, date above **Rev:** Denomination within wreath **Shape:** 12-sided

Date	Mintage	F	VF	XF	Unc	BU
1963 Proof	25,000	Value: 1.00				
1963	5,000,000	—	—	—	0.15	—
1971	500,000	—	—	0.10	0.25	—
1972	500,000	—	—	0.10	0.25	—
1972 Proof	—	Value: 2.00				

KM# 39 5 MILS

Bronze **Obv:** Shielded arms within wreath, date above **Rev:** Stylized ancient merchant ship, denomination upper left

Date	Mintage	F	VF	XF	Unc	BU
1963 Proof	25,000	Value: 1.25				
1963	12,000,000	—	—	0.10	0.35	—
1970	2,500,000	—	—	0.10	1.00	—
1971	2,500,000	—	—	0.10	0.35	—
1972	2,500,000	—	—	0.10	0.35	—
1973	5,000,000	—	—	0.10	0.35	—
1974	2,500,000	—	—	0.10	0.35	—
1976	2,000,000	—	—	0.10	0.35	—
1977	2,000,000	—	—	0.10	0.35	—
1978	2,000,000	—	—	0.10	0.35	—
1979	2,000,000	—	—	0.10	0.35	—
1980 Proof	—	Value: 2.50				
1980	4,000,000	—	—	0.10	0.35	—

KM# 50.1 5 MILS

1.2000 g., Aluminum, 20 mm. **Obv:** Shielded arms within wreath, date above **Rev:** Stylized ancient merchant ship, denomination upper left **Shape:** 12-sided

Date	Mintage	F	VF	XF	Unc	BU
1981	12,500,000	—	—	—	0.25	—

KM# 50.2 5 MILS

1.2000 g., Aluminum, 20 mm. **Obv:** Shielded arms within wreath, date above **Rev:** Stylized ancient merchant ship, denomination upper left **Shape:** 12-sided

Date	Mintage	F	VF	XF	Unc	BU
1982	15,000,000	—	—	—	0.25	—
1982 Proof	—	Value: 2.00				

KM# 40 25 MILS

2.8000 g., Copper-Nickel, 19.4 mm. **Obv:** Shielded arms within wreath, date above **Rev:** Cedar of Lebanon, denomination at left

Date	Mintage	F	VF	XF	Unc	BU
1963 Proof	25,000	Value: 1.50				
1963	2,500,000	—	0.10	0.15	0.45	—
1968	1,500,000	—	0.10	0.15	2.00	—
1971	1,000,000	—	0.10	0.15	0.45	—
1972	500,000	—	0.10	0.15	0.50	—
1973	1,000,000	—	0.10	0.15	0.45	—
1974	1,000,000	—	0.10	0.15	0.45	—
1976	2,000,000	—	0.10	0.15	0.45	—
1977	500,000	—	0.10	0.15	0.45	—
1978	500,000	—	0.10	0.15	0.45	—
1979	1,000,000	—	0.10	0.15	0.45	—
1980	2,000,000	—	0.10	0.15	0.45	—
1981	3,000,000	—	0.10	0.15	0.45	—
1982	1,000,000	—	0.10	0.15	0.45	—
1982 Proof	—	Value: 3.00				

KM# 41 50 MILS

5.6000 g., Copper-Nickel, 23.5 mm. **Obv:** Shielded arms within wreath, date above **Rev:** Bunch of grapes above denomination

Date	Mintage	F	VF	XF	Unc	BU
1963 Proof	25,000	Value: 1.75				
1963	2,800,000	—	0.20	0.30	1.00	—
1970	500,000	—	0.20	0.35	2.00	—
1971	500,000	—	0.20	0.35	1.25	—
1972	750,000	—	0.20	0.30	1.00	—
1973	750,000	—	0.20	0.30	1.00	—
1974	1,500,000	—	0.20	0.30	1.00	—
1976	1,500,000	—	0.20	0.30	1.00	—
1977	500,000	—	0.20	0.30	1.00	—
1978	500,000	—	0.20	0.30	3.00	—
1979	1,000,000	—	0.20	0.30	1.00	—
1980	3,000,000	—	0.20	0.30	1.00	—
1981	4,000,000	—	0.20	0.30	1.00	—
1982	2,000,000	—	0.20	0.30	1.00	—
1982 Proof	—	Value: 3.50				

KM# 42 100 MILS

11.3000 g., Copper-Nickel, 28.45 mm. **Obv:** Shielded arms within wreath, date above **Rev:** Cyprus Mouflon left, denomination below

Date	Mintage	F	VF	XF	Unc	BU
1963 Proof	25,000	Value: 2.50				
1963	1,750,000	—	0.40	0.70	2.00	3.00
1971	500,000	—	0.50	0.75	2.00	3.00
1973	750,000	—	0.40	0.70	2.00	3.00
1974	1,000,000	—	0.50	0.75	2.00	3.00
1976	1,500,000	—	0.40	0.70	2.00	3.00
1977	500,000	—	0.50	0.75	2.00	3.00
1978	1,000,000	—	0.50	0.75	2.00	3.00

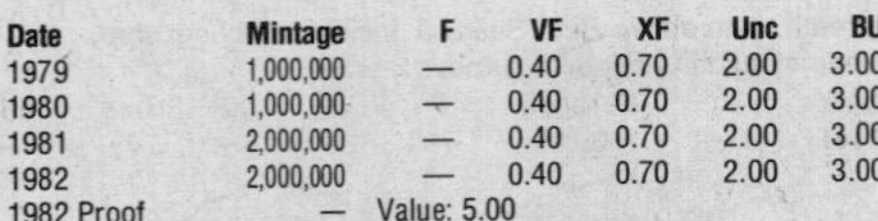

Date	Mintage	F	VF	XF	Unc	BU
1979	1,000,000	—	0.40	0.70	2.00	3.00
1980	1,000,000	—	0.40	0.70	2.00	3.00
1981	2,000,000	—	0.40	0.70	2.00	3.00
1982	2,000,000	—	0.40	0.70	2.00	3.00
1982 Proof	—	Value: 5.00				

KM# 43 500 MILS

Copper-Nickel **Series:** F.A.O. **Obv:** Double cornucopia, as on the ancient coins of Ptolemy II **Rev:** Figure holding tray of fruit, denomination at right **Designer:** Antis Ioannides

Date	Mintage	F	VF	XF	Unc	BU
1970	80,000	—	1.50	4.50	10.00	—

KM# 43a 500 MILS

22.6200 g., 0.8000 Silver .5818 oz. ASW **Series:** F.A.O **Obv:** Double cornucopia, as on the ancient coins of Ptolemy **Rev:** Figure holding tray of fruit, denomination

Date	Mintage	F	VF	XF	Unc	BU
1970 Proof	5,000	Value: 50.00				

KM# 44 500 MILS

Copper-Nickel **Obv:** Shielded arms within wreath, date above **Rev:** Hercules, denomination at right

Date	Mintage	F	VF	XF	Unc	BU
1975	500,000	—	1.25	1.75	4.00	—
1977	300,000	—	1.25	1.75	5.00	—
1977 Proof	—	Value: 15.00				

KM# 44a 500 MILS

14.1400 g., 0.8000 Silver .3637 oz. ASW **Obv:** Shielded arms within wreath **Rev:** Hercules and denomination

Date	Mintage	F	VF	XF	Unc	BU
1975 Proof	10,000	Value: 25.00				

KM# 45 500 MILS

Copper-Nickel **Subject:** Refugees, denomination and date at right **Obv:** Shielded arms within wreath, date above

Date	Mintage	F	VF	XF	Unc	BU
1976	25,000	—	1.25	2.00	4.00	—

KM# 45a 500 MILS

14.1400 g., 0.9250 Silver .4205 oz. ASW **Obv:** Shielded arms within wreath **Rev:** Refugees, denomination at right

Date	Mintage	F	VF	XF	Unc	BU
1976 Proof	25,000	Value: 25.00				

KM# 48 500 MILS

Copper-Nickel **Subject:** Human Rights **Obv:** Flame within wreath divides dates **Rev:** Stylized crying dove above denomination

Date	Mintage	F	VF	XF	Unc	BU
ND(1978)	50,000	—	1.25	2.00	4.00	—

KM# 48a 500 MILS

14.1400 g., 0.9250 Silver .4205 oz. ASW **Subject:** Human Rights **Obv:** Flame within wreath divides denomination **Rev:** Crying dove above denomination

Date	Mintage	F	VF	XF	Unc	BU
ND Proof	5,000	Value: 65.00				

KM# 49 500 MILS

Copper-Nickel **Series:** Summer Olympic Games **Obv:** Shielded arms within wreath, date above **Rev:** Olympic logo divides date and denomination, sprays surround

Date	Mintage	F	VF	XF	Unc	BU
1980	50,000	—	1.25	2.50	6.50	—

KM# 49a 500 MILS

14.1400 g., 0.9250 Silver .4205 oz. ASW **Obv:** Shielded arms within wreath **Rev:** Olympic logo divides date and denomination, sprays surround

Date	Mintage	F	VF	XF	Unc	BU
1980 Proof	7,500	Value: 50.00				

KM# 51 500 MILS

Copper-Nickel **Subject:** World Food Day **Obv:** Shielded arms within wreath, date above **Rev:** Denomination divides swordfish and grain sprig, date above

Date	Mintage	F	VF	XF	Unc	BU
ND(1978)	50,000	—	1.25	2.00	6.00	8.00

KM# 51a 500 MILS

14.1400 g., 0.9250 Silver .4205 oz. ASW **Obv:** Shielded arms within wreath **Rev:** Denomination divides swordfish and grain sprig

Date	Mintage	F	VF	XF	Unc	BU
ND(1978) Proof	7,500	Value: 50.00				

KM# 46 POUND

Copper-Nickel, 38.5 mm. **Obv:** Shielded arms within wreath, date above **Rev:** Refugees, date and denomination at right **Note:** Refugee Commemorative.

Date	Mintage	F	VF	XF	Unc	BU
1976	25,000	—	2.00	2.50	5.50	—

KM# 46a POUND

28.2800 g., 0.9250 Silver .8411 oz. ASW **Obv:** Shielded arms within wreath **Rev:** Refugees, denomination at right **Note:** Refugee Commemorative.

Date	Mintage	F	VF	XF	Unc	BU
1976 Proof	25,000	Value: 40.00				

KM# 47 50 POUNDS

15.9800 g., 0.9170 Gold .4711 oz. AGW **Obv:** Archbishop Makarios right, two dates **Rev:** Ship above map, dolphins, date and denomination below

Date	Mintage	F	VF	XF	Unc	BU
1977 Proof	51,000	Value: 350				
1977	39,000	—	—	—	345	—

REFORM COINAGE

100 Cents = 1 Pound

KM# 52 HALF CENT

Aluminum **Obv:** Shielded arms within wreath, date below **Rev:** Cyclamen, denomination at right **Shape:** 12-sided

Date	Mintage	F	VF	XF	Unc	BU
1983	10,000,000	—	—	0.10	0.15	0.25
1983 Proof	6,250	Value: 1.50				

KM# 53.1 CENT

Nickel-Brass **Obv:** Shielded arms within wreath, date below **Rev:** Stylized bird on a branch, value number surrounded by single line

Date	Mintage	F	VF	XF	Unc	BU
1983	15,000,000	—	—	0.10	0.20	0.30
1983 Proof	6,250	Value: 1.50				

KM# 53.2 CENT

Nickel-Brass **Obv:** Shielded arms within wreath, date below **Rev:** Stylized bird on a branch, value number surrounded by double line

Date	Mintage	F	VF	XF	Unc	BU
1985	5,000,000	—	—	0.10	0.20	0.30
1987	5,000,000	—	—	0.10	0.20	0.30
1988	5,000,000	—	—	0.10	0.20	0.30
1989	—	—	—	0.10	0.20	0.30
1990	4,000,000	—	—	0.10	0.20	0.30

KM# 53.3 CENT

Nickel-Brass **Obv:** Shielded arms within altered wreath, date below **Rev:** Stylized bird on a branch, denomination at left

Date	Mintage	F	VF	XF	Unc	BU
1991	4,000,000	—	—	0.10	0.20	0.30
1992	4,000,000	—	—	0.10	0.20	0.30
1993	7,000,000	—	—	0.10	0.20	0.30
1994	10,000,000	—	—	0.10	0.20	0.30
1996	12,000,000	—	—	0.10	0.20	0.30
1998	15,000,000	—	—	0.10	0.20	0.30

KM# 54.1 2 CENTS

Nickel-Brass, 19 mm. **Obv:** Shielded arms within wreath, date below **Rev:** Stylized goats, value number surrounded by single line

Date	Mintage	F	VF	XF	Unc	BU
1983	12,000,000	—	—	0.15	0.25	0.35
1983 Proof	6,250	Value: 1.50				

KM# 54.2 2 CENTS

Nickel-Brass, 19 mm. **Obv:** Shielded arms within wreath, date below **Rev:** Stylized goats; value number surrounded by double line

Date	Mintage	F	VF	XF	Unc	BU
1985	8,000,000	—	—	0.15	0.25	0.35
1987	—	—	—	0.15	0.25	0.35
1988	5,150,000	—	—	0.15	0.25	0.35
1989	—	—	—	0.15	0.25	0.35
1990	4,000,000	—	—	0.15	0.25	0.35

KM# 54.3 2 CENTS

Nickel-Brass, 19 mm. **Obv:** Shielded arms within altered wreath, date below **Rev:** Stylized goats, denomination upper right

Date	Mintage	F	VF	XF	Unc	BU
1991	4,000,000	—	—	0.15	0.25	0.35
1992	4,000,000	—	—	0.15	0.25	0.35
1993	4,000,000	—	—	0.15	0.25	0.35
1994	10,000,000	—	—	0.15	0.25	0.35
1996	12,000,000	—	—	0.15	0.25	0.35
1998	10,000,000	—	—	0.15	0.25	0.35

KM# 55.1 5 CENTS

Nickel-Brass, 22 mm. **Obv:** Shielded arms within wreath, date below **Rev:** Stylized bulls head, value number surrounded by single line **Note:** REV: Value number surrounded by single line

Date	Mintage	F	VF	XF	Unc	BU
1983	15,000,000	—	—	0.20	0.50	0.75
1983 Proof	6,250	Value: 2.00				

KM# 55.2 5 CENTS

Nickel-Brass, 22 mm. **Obv:** Shielded arms within wreath, date below **Rev:** Value number surrounded by double line

Date	Mintage	F	VF	XF	Unc	BU
1985	5,000,000	—	—	0.20	0.50	0.75
1987	5,000,000	—	—	0.20	0.50	0.75
1988	5,060,000	—	—	0.20	0.50	0.75
1989	—	—	—	0.20	0.50	0.75
1990	—	—	—	0.20	0.50	0.75

KM# 55.3 5 CENTS

Nickel-Brass, 22 mm. **Obv:** Altered wreath around arms **Rev:** Stylized bulls head above denomination

Date	Mintage	F	VF	XF	Unc	BU
1991	4,000,000	—	—	0.20	0.50	0.75
1992	4,000,000	—	—	0.20	0.50	0.75
1993	5,000,000	—	—	0.20	0.50	0.75
1994	8,000,000	—	—	0.20	0.50	0.75
1998	1,000,000	—	—	0.20	0.50	0.75

KM# 56.1 10 CENTS

Nickel-Brass **Obv:** Shielded arms within wreath, date below **Rev:** Decorative vase, value number surrounded by single line

Date	Mintage	F	VF	XF	Unc	BU
1983 Proof	6,250	Value: 3.00				
1983	10,000,000	—	—	0.35	0.75	1.00

KM# 56.2 10 CENTS

Nickel-Brass **Obv:** Shielded arms within wreath, date below **Rev:** Value number framed by double line

Date	Mintage	F	VF	XF	Unc	BU
1985	5,000,000	—	—	0.35	0.75	1.00
1987	—	—	—	0.35	0.75	1.00
1988	5,035,000	—	—	0.35	0.75	1.00
1989	—	—	—	0.35	0.75	1.00
1990	4,000,000	—	—	0.35	0.75	1.00

KM# 56.3 10 CENTS

Nickel-Brass **Obv:** Altered wreath around arms **Rev:** Decorative vase, denomination above

Date	Mintage	F	VF	XF	Unc	BU
1991	4,000,000	—	—	0.35	0.75	1.00
1992	3,000,000	—	—	0.35	0.75	1.00
1993	3,000,000	—	—	0.35	0.75	1.00
1994	8,000,000	—	—	0.35	0.75	1.00
1998	5,000,000	—	—	0.35	0.75	1.00

KM# 57.1 20 CENTS

Nickel-Brass, 27 mm. **Obv:** Shielded arms within wreath, date below **Rev:** Value number framed by single line

Date	Mintage	F	VF	XF	Unc	BU
1983	10,000,000	—	—	0.50	2.00	3.50
1983 Proof	6,200	Value: 5.00				

KM# 57.2 20 CENTS

Nickel-Brass, 27 mm. **Obv:** Shielded arms within wreath, date below **Rev:** Value number framed by double line

Date	Mintage	F	VF	XF	Unc	BU
1985	5,040,000	—	—	0.50	2.50	3.00
1987	—	—	—	0.50	2.50	3.00
1988	1,000,000	—	—	0.50	2.50	3.00

KM# 62.1 20 CENTS

Bronze, 27 mm. **Obv:** Shielded arms within wreath, date below **Rev:** Head left, denomination at right

Date	Mintage	F	VF	XF	Unc	BU
1989	2,000,000	—	—	—	1.00	1.50
1989 Proof	—	Value: 30.00				
1990	3,000,000	—	—	—	1.00	1.50

KM# 62.2 20 CENTS

Nickel-Brass, 27 mm. **Obv:** Altered wreath around arms **Rev:** Head left, denomination at right

Date	Mintage	F	VF	XF	Unc	BU
1991	4,000,000	—	—	—	1.00	1.50
1992	3,000,000	—	—	—	1.00	1.50
1993	4,000,000	—	—	—	1.00	1.50
1994	8,000,000	—	—	—	1.00	1.50
1998	5,000,000	—	—	—	1.00	1.50

KM# 58 50 CENTS

Copper-Nickel, 32 mm. **Series:** F.A.O. **Subject:** Forestry **Obv:** Shielded arms within wreath, date above **Rev:** Goddess Diana in the shape of a stylized tree, denomination at right

Date	Mintage	F	VF	XF	Unc	BU
1985	33,000	—	2.00	4.00	15.00	20.00

KM# 58a 50 CENTS

14.1400 g., 0.9250 Silver .4205 oz. ASW, 32 mm. **Series:** F.A.O. **Obv:** Shielded arms within wreath, date below **Rev:** Goddess Diana in the shape of a stylized tree

Date	Mintage	F	VF	XF	Unc	BU
1985 Proof	4,000	Value: 50.00				

KM# 60 50 CENTS

Copper-Nickel **Subject:** Olympics **Obv:** Shielded arms within wreath, date below **Rev:** Symbols divide denomination, Olympic logo at right **Rev. Designer:** Antis Ionnides

Date	Mintage	F	VF	XF	Unc	BU
1988	14,000	—	—	—	3.50	5.00

KM# 60a 50 CENTS

14.1400 g., 0.9250 Silver .4205 oz. ASW **Obv:** Shielded arms within wreath, date below **Rev:** Symbols divide denomination, logo at right

Date	Mintage	F	VF	XF	Unc	BU
1988 Proof	4,000	Value: 45.00				

KM# 66 50 CENTS

Copper-Nickel, 26 mm. **Subject:** Abduction of Europa **Obv:** Shielded arms within wreath, date below **Rev:** Figure riding bull within square, denomination below **Shape:** 7-sided

Date	Mintage	F	VF	XF	Unc	BU
1991 narrow date	3,005,000	—	—	—	2.50	3.25
1993 wide date	300,000	—	—	—	2.50	3.25
1994 wide date	500,000	—	—	—	2.50	3.25
1996	5,000,000	—	—	—	2.50	3.25
1998	5,000,000	—	—	—	2.50	3.25

KM# 66a 50 CENTS

7.0000 g., 0.9250 Silver .2082 oz. ASW, 26 mm. **Obv:** Shielded arms within wreath, date below **Rev:** Figure riding bull within square, denomination below

Date	Mintage	F	VF	XF	Unc	BU
1991 Proof	5,000	Value: 35.00				

KM# 59 POUND

Copper-Nickel **Subject:** World Wildlife Fund **Obv:** Shielded arms within wreath, date below **Rev:** Cyprian wild sheep (Moufflon), denomination below

Date	Mintage	F	VF	XF	Unc	BU
1986	39,000	—	—	—	10.00	12.50

KM# 59a POUND

0.9250 Silver **Obv:** Shielded arms within wreath, date below **Rev:** Wild sheep, denomination below

Date	Mintage	F	VF	XF	Unc	BU
1986 Proof	13,000	Value: 40.00				

KM# 61 POUND
Copper-Nickel **Series:** Olympics **Obv:** Shielded arms within wreath, date below **Rev:** Symbols, denomination below **Rev. Designer:** Antis Ionnides

Date	Mintage	F	VF	XF	Unc	BU
1988	14,000	—	—	—	6.50	8.00

KM# 61a POUND
28.2800 g., 0.9250 Silver .8411 oz. ASW **Obv:** Shielded arms within wreath, date below **Rev:** Symbols and denomination

Date	Mintage	F	VF	XF	Unc	BU
1988 Proof	4,000	Value: 55.00				

KM# 63 POUND
Copper-Nickel **Subject:** Small European States Games **Rev:** Winged figure divides Olympic logos, denomination below

Date	Mintage	F	VF	XF	Unc	BU
1989	19,000	—	—	—	5.50	7.50

Note: 4,000 issued in plastic case, 15,000 issued uncased

KM# 63a POUND
28.2800 g., 0.9250 Silver .8411 oz. ASW **Subject:** Small European States Games **Rev:** Winged figure divides logos, denomination below

Date	Mintage	F	VF	XF	Unc	BU
1989 Proof	4,000	Value: 50.00				

KM# 64 POUND
Copper-Nickel **Series:** Save the Children Fund **Obv:** Shielded arms within wreath **Rev:** Two boys at play **Rev. Designer:** Carl Gate

Date	Mintage	F	VF	XF	Unc	BU
1989	19,000	—	—	—	5.50	7.50

Note: 4,000 issued in plastic case, 15,000 issued uncased

KM# 64a POUND
28.2800 g., 0.9250 Silver .8411 oz. ASW **Series:** Save the Children Fund **Obv:** Shielded arms within wreath **Rev:** Two boys at play

Date	Mintage	F	VF	XF	Unc	BU
1989 Proof	4,000	Value: 42.50				

KM# 67 POUND
Copper-Nickel **Series:** Olympics **Obv:** Small arms **Rev:** Relay Racing, denomination above Olympic logo

Date	Mintage	F	VF	XF	Unc	BU
1992	8,000	—	—	—	8.50	10.00

KM# 67a POUND
28.2800 g., 0.9250 Silver .8411 oz. ASW **Series:** Olympics **Obv:** Small arms **Rev:** Relay racing, denomination above logo

Date	Mintage	F	VF	XF	Unc	BU
1992 Proof	4,000	Value: 50.00				

KM# 69 POUND
Copper-Nickel **Subject:** 50th Anniversary - United Nations **Obv:** Shielded arms within wreath, date below **Rev:** Tree of flag shields divides denomination and logo

Date	Mintage	F	VF	XF	Unc	BU
1995	—	—	—	—	8.50	10.00

KM# 69a POUND
28.2800 g., 0.9250 Silver .8411 oz. ASW **Series:** 50th Anniversary - United Nations **Obv:** Shielded arms within wreath, date below **Rev:** Tree of flag shields, denomination and logo

Date	Mintage	F	VF	XF	Unc	BU
1995	—	Value: 42.00				

KM# 70 POUND
Copper-Nickel **Series:** F.A.O. **Subject:** 50th Anniversary - United Nations **Obv:** Shielded arms within wreath, date below **Rev:** Bovine portrait, wheat and denominaton

Date	Mintage	F	VF	XF	Unc	BU
1995	—	—	—	—	12.50	14.50

KM# 70a POUND
28.2800 g., 0.9250 Silver .8411 oz. ASW **Series:** 50th Anniversary - F.A.O. **Obv:** Shielded arms within wreath, date below **Rev:** Bovine Portrait, wheat and denomination

Date	Mintage	F	VF	XF	Unc	BU
1995	4,000	Value: 55.00				

KM# 71 POUND
Copper-Nickel **Series:** 1996 Olympics **Obv:** Shielded arms within wreath, date below **Rev:** Olympic rings, stylized flames, olive branch, denomination above

Date	Mintage	F	VF	XF	Unc	BU
1996	3,000	—	—	—	20.00	22.50

KM# 71a POUND
28.2800 g., 0.9250 Silver .8410 oz. ASW **Series:** 1996 Olympics **Obv:** Shielded arms within wreath, date below **Rev:** Olympic rings, stylized flames, olive branch

Date	Mintage	F	VF	XF	Unc	BU
1996	4,000	Value: 45.00				

KM# 72 POUND
Copper-Nickel **Subject:** World Wildlife Fund - Conserving Nature **Obv:** Shielded arms within wreath, date below **Rev:** Green turtle, denomination above

Date	Mintage	F	VF	XF	Unc	BU
1997	3,000	—	—	—	25.00	32.00

KM# 72a POUND
28.2800 g., 0.9250 Silver .8411 oz. ASW **Obv:** Shielded arms within wreath, date below **Rev:** Green turtle

Date	Mintage	F	VF	XF	Unc	BU
1997 Proof	Est. 15,000	Value: 50.00				

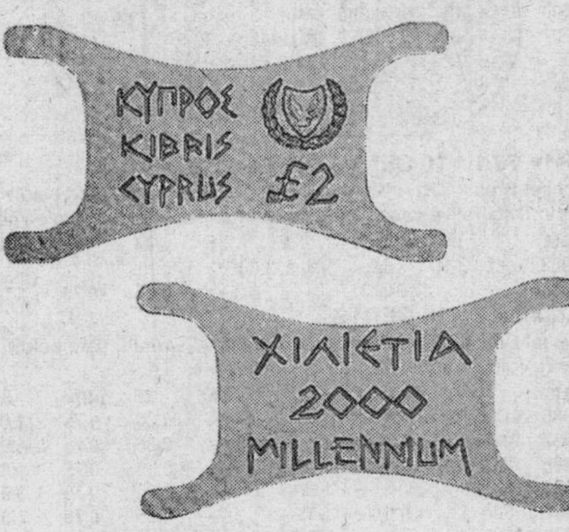

KM# 73 2 POUNDS
Bronze, 44.5 x 25 mm. **Subject:** Millennium **Obv:** National arms and denomination at right **Rev:** Three line inscription **Shape:** Ox-hide shape of ancient ingot

Date	Mintage	F	VF	XF	Unc	BU
2000	1,000	—	—	—	50.00	52.50

KM# 73a 2 POUNDS
15.0000 g., 0.9250 Silver .4461 oz. ASW, 44.5 x 25 mm. **Subject:** Millennium **Obv:** National arms and denomination **Rev:** Three line inscription **Edge:** Plain **Shape:** Ox-hide shape of ancient ingot

Date	Mintage	F	VF	XF	Unc	BU
2000	32,000	—	—	—	50.00	52.50

KM# 65 20 POUNDS

7.9881 g., 0.9170 Gold .2354 oz. AGW, 22 mm. **Subject:** 30th Anniversary of the Republic **Obv:** Shielded arms within wreath, date below **Rev:** Denomination within circle on stylized bird **Rev. Designer:** Antis Ionnides

Date	Mintage	F	VF	XF	Unc	BU
1990 Proof	5,000	Value: 250				

KM# 68 20 POUNDS

7.9881 g., 0.9170 Gold .2354 oz. AGW **Subject:** Museum Building Fund **Obv:** Shielded arms within wreath, date below **Rev:** Winged statue, left, denomination below

Date	Mintage	F	VF	XF	Unc	BU
1992 Proof	5,000	Value: 225				

KM# 74 100 POUNDS

Gold **Subject:** Millennium **Obv:** National arms and denomination at right **Rev:** Three line inscription **Shape:** Ox-hide shape of ancient ingot

Date	Mintage	F	VF	XF	Unc	BU
2000	750	—	—	—	1,000	—

TRIAL STRIKES

KM#	Date	Mintage	Identification	Mkt Val
TS2	ND	—	45 Piastres. 0.9170 Gold. 40.0000 g. Uniface.	3,000

Note: 1 known

MINT SETS

KM#	Date	Mintage	Identification	Issue Price	Mkt Val
MS1	1955 (5)	2,550	KM33-37	2.20	6.50
MS2	1963 (5)	8,050	KM38-42	1.95	5.00
MS3	1971 (5)	3,000	KM38-42	1.65	5.00
MS4	1972 (4)	30,000	KM38-41	2.35	5.00
MS5	1973 (4)	5,000	KM39-42	2.75	5.00
MS6	1974 (4)	5,000	KM39-42	3.25	5.00
MS7	1976 (3)	5,000	KM40-42	1.25	4.50
MS8	1976 (2)	25,000	KM45-46	6.50	6.00
MS9	1977 (5)	10,000	KM39-42, 44	—	6.50
MS10	1978 (5)	—	KM39-42, 48	5.50	6.50
MS11	1979 (4)	—	KM39-42	—	6.50
MS12	1980 (4)	—	KM39-42	—	6.50
MS13	1981 (5)	—	KM40-42, 50.1, 51	5.00	6.50
MS14	1981 (4)	—	KM40-42, 50.1	5.00	6.50
MS15	1982 (4)	5,000	KM40-42, 50.2	5.00	6.50
MS16	1983 (6)	11,400	KM52,53.1-57.1	15.00	10.00
MS17	1988 (5)	—	KM53.2-57.2	—	10.00
MS18	1989 (5)	—	KM53.2-56.2, 62.1	—	10.00
MS19	1990 (5)	—	KM53.2-56.2, 62.1	10.00	10.00

PROOF SETS

KM#	Date	Mintage	Identification	Issue Price	Mkt Val
PS1	1879 (3)	—	KM1.1, 2, 3.1	—	3,000
PS2	1881 (3)	—	KM1.1, 2, 3.1	—	1,800
PS3	1900 (3)	—	KM1.1, 2, 3.2	—	3,500
PS4	1901 (4)	—	KM4-7	—	5,500
PS5	1931 (2)	—	KM17-18	—	1,175
PS6	1934 (2)	—	KM20-21	—	650
PS7	1938 (5)	—	KM-22-26	—	2,000
PS8	1947 (2)	—	KM27-28	—	700
PS9	1949 (2)	—	KM31-32	—	700
PS10	1949 (4)	—	KM29-32	—	950
PS11	1955 (5)	2,000	KM33-37	5.50	16.00
PS12	1963 (5)	24,501	KM38-42	9.00	8.50
PS13	1963 (5)	500	KM38-42	8.70	8.00
PS14	1972, 1980, 1982 (6)	—	KM38(72), 39(80), 40-42(82), 50.2(82)	30.00	30.00
PS15	1976 (2)	25,000	KM45a-46a	50.00	35.00
PS16	1983 (6)	6,250	KM52, 53.1-57.1	20.00	40.00

CZECH REPUBLIC

The Czech Republic was formerly united with Slovakia as Czechoslovakia. It is bordered in the west by Germany, to the north by Poland, to the east by Slovakia and to the south by Austria. It consists of 3 major regions: Bohemia, Moravia and Silesia and has an area of 30,450 sq. mi. (78,864 sq. km.) and a population of 10.4 million. Capital: Prague (Praha). Agriculture and livestock are chief occupations while coal deposits are the main mineral resources.

The Czech lands were united with the Slovaks to form the Czechoslovak State, which came into existence on Oct. 28, 1918 upon the dissolution of the Austrian-Hungarian Empire. In 1938, this territory was broken up for the benefit of Germany, Poland, and Hungary by the Munich (Munchen) Agreement. In March 1939 the German influenced Slovak government proclaimed Slovakia independent. Germany incorporated the Czech lands into the Third Reich as the "Protectorate of Bohemia and Moravia." A Czech government-in-exile was set up in London in July 1940. The Soviets and USA forces liberated the area by May 1945. Communist influence increased steadily while pressure for liberalization culminated in the overthrow of the Stalinist leader Antonin Novotny and his associates in 1968. The Communist Party then introduced far reaching reforms which resulted in warnings from Moscow (Moskva), followed by occupation and stationing of Soviet forces. Mass demonstrations for reform began again in Nov. 1989 and the Federal Assembly abolished the Communist Party's sole right to govern. The new government formed was the Czech and Slovak Federal Republic. A movement for Democratic Slovakia was apparent in the June 1992 elections and on December 31, 1992, the CSFR was dissolved and the two new republics came into being on Jan. 1, 1993.

NOTE: For earlier issues see Czechoslovakia, Bohemia and Moravia or Slovakia listings.

MINT MARKS

(c) - castle = Hamburg
(cr) - cross = British Royal Mint
(l) - leaf = Royal Canadian
(m) - crowned *b* or *CM* = Jablonec nad Nisou
(mk) - *MK* in circle = Kremnica
(o) - broken circle = Vienna (Wien)

MONETARY SYSTEM

1 Czechoslovak Koruna (Kcs) = 1 Czech Koruna (Kc)
1 Koruna = 100 Haleru

REPUBLIC

STANDARD COINAGE

KM# 6 10 HALERU

0.9900 Aluminum 0.6 oz., 15.5 mm. **Obv:** Crowned Czech lion left, date below **Rev:** Denomination and stylized river **Edge:** Plain **Designer:** Jiri Pradler **Note:** Two varieties of mint marks exist for 1994.

Date	Mintage	F	VF	XF	Unc	BU
1993(c)	100,000,000	—	—	—	0.20	—
Note: 200 pieces destroyed						
1993(m)	94,902,000	—	—	—	0.20	—
1994(c) In sets only	2,500	—	—	—	2.50	—
1994(m)	53,127,024	—	—	—	0.20	—
1994(m) Proof, dull	2,000	—	—	—	—	—
1994(m) Proof, bright	27,500	—	—	—	—	—
1995(m)	106,118,596	—	—	—	0.20	—
1996(m)	61,498,678	—	—	—	0.20	—
1997(m)	40,968,395	—	—	—	0.20	—
Note: 85,778 pieces destroyed						
1997(m) Proof	1,500	Value: 3.50				
1998(m)	41,027,073	—	—	—	0.20	—
1998(m) Proof	2,600	Value: 2.00				
1999(m)	54,428,800	—	—	—	0.20	—
1999(m) Proof	2,000	Value: 2.00				
2000(m)	52,497,440	—	—	—	0.20	—
2000(m) Proof	2,500	Value: 2.00				

KM# 2.1 20 HALERU

0.7400 g., Aluminum, 17 mm. **Obv:** Crowned Czech lion left, date above **Rev:** Linden leaf within denomination; closed 2, "h" above flat line **Edge:** Milled **Designer:** Jaroslav Bejvl **Note:** Medallic coin alignment.

Date	Mintage	F	VF	XF	Unc	BU
1993(c)	80,000,000	—	—	—	0.30	—
1993(m)	30,558,000	—	—	—	0.30	—
1994(c)	9,310,000	—	—	—	0.30	—
1994(m) Proof, dull	2,500	—	—	—	3.00	—
1994(m) Proof, bright	17,500	—	—	—	1.00	—
1994(m)	81,289,000	—	—	—	0.30	—
1995(m)	80,960,374	—	—	—	0.30	—
1995(c)	450,000	—	—	—	1.75	—
1996(m)	61,086,142	—	—	—	0.30	—
1997(m)	51,013,450	—	—	—	0.30	—
Note: 78,835 pieces destroyed						
1997(m) Proof	1,500	Value: 5.00				

KM# 2.2 20 HALERU

Aluminum, 17 mm. **Obv:** Crowned Czech lion **Rev:** Linden leaf and value, "h" above flat line, closed 2 in denomination **Designer:** Jaroslav Bejvl **Note:** Coin alignment.

Date	Mintage	F	VF	XF	Unc	BU
1993(m)	Inc. above	—	—	—	4.00	—

KM# 2.3 20 HALERU

Aluminum **Obv:** Crowned Czech lion left, date above **Rev:** Open 2 in denomination, "h" above angle line **Note:** Medallic coin alignment.

Date	Mintage	F	VF	XF	Unc	BU
1998(m)	51,135,904	—	—	—	0.30	—
1998(m) Proof	2,600	Value: 3.00				
1999(m)	20,820,612	—	—	—	0.30	—
1999(m) Proof	2,000	Value: 3.00				
2000(m)	31,466,085	—	—	—	0.30	—
2000(m) Proof	2,500	Value: 3.00				

KM# 3.1 50 HALERU

Aluminum 0.9 oz., 19 mm. **Obv:** Crowned Czech lion left, date below **Rev:** Large denomination **Edge:** Part plain, part milled repeated **Designer:** Vladimir Oppl **Note:** Two styles of "9" exist for 1994; prev. KM#3.

Date	Mintage	F	VF	XF	Unc	BU
1993(c)	70,003,000	—	—	—	0.50	—
Note: 201 pieces destroyed						
1993(m)	30,940,000	—	—	—	0.50	—
1994(m)	21,109,425	—	—	—	0.50	—
1994(m) Proof, dull	2,500	—	—	—	3.00	—
1994(m) Proof, bright	Est. 27,500	—	—	—	1.00	—
1995(m)	30,940,000	—	—	—	0.50	—
1996(m)	35,904,000	—	—	—	0.50	—
1997(m)	25,713,443	—	—	—	0.50	—
Note: 35,610 pieces destroyed						
1997(m) Proof	1,500	Value: 5.00				
1998(m)	25,000	—	—	—	0.50	—
1998(m) Proof	2,600	Value: 3.00				
1999(m)	21,024,800	—	—	—	0.50	—
Note: 8,687 pieces destroyed						
1999(m) Proof	2,000	Value: 3.00				
2000(m)	15,753,440	—	—	—	0.50	—
2000(m) Proof	2,500	Value: 3.00				

KM# 7 KORUNA

Nickel Clad Steel, 20 mm. **Obv:** Crowned Czech lion left, date below **Rev:** Denomination above crown **Edge:** Milled **Designer:** Jarmila Truhlikova-Spevakova **Note:** Two varieties of mint marks exist for 1996. 2000-03 have two varieties in the artisit monogram.

Date	Mintage	F	VF	XF	Unc	BU
1993(l)	102,431,000	—	—	—	0.60	—
1994(m)	52,162,620	—	—	—	0.60	—
1995(m)	40,668,280	—	—	—	0.60	—
1996(m)	35,344,913	—	—	—	0.60	—
1997(m)	15,055,501	—	—	—	0.60	—
1997(m) Proof	1,500	Value: 6.50				
1998(m)	25,000	—	—	—	0.60	—
1998(m) Proof	2,600	Value: 4.00				
Note: 90 pieces destroyed.						
1999(m)	24,904	—	—	—	0.60	—
1999(m) Proof	2,000	Value: 4.00				
2000(m)	15,568,697	—	—	—	0.60	—
2000(m) Proof	2,500	Value: 4.00				

KM# 9 2 KORUN

3.7000 g., Nickel Clad Steel, 21.5 mm. **Obv:** Crowned Czech lion left, date below **Rev:** Large denomination, pendant design at left **Edge:** Plain **Shape:** 11-sided **Designer:** Jarmila Truhlikova-Spevakova **Note:** Two varieties of designer monograms exist for 2001-04.

Date	Mintage	F	VF	XF	Unc	BU
1993(l)	80,001,000	—	—	—	0.65	—
1994(m)	30,310,000	—	—	—	0.65	—
1994(l)	18,360,000	—	—	—	0.65	—
1995(m)	30,520,405	—	—	—	0.65	—
1996(m)	15,201,750	—	—	—	0.65	—
1997(m)	15,040,245	—	—	—	0.65	—
1997(m) Proof	1,500	Value: 8.50				
1998(m)	10,455,480	—	—	—	0.65	—
1998(m) Proof	2,510	Value: 5.00				
1999(m)	28,768	—	—	—	0.65	—
Note: 1098 pieces destroyed.						
1999(m) Proof	2,000	Value: 5.00				
2000(m)	25,000	—	—	—	0.65	—
2000(m) Proof	2,500	Value: 5.00				

KM# 8 5 KORUN

4.8000 g., Nickel Plated Steel, 23 mm. **Obv:** Crowned Czech lion left, date below **Rev:** Large denomination, Charles bridge and linden leaf **Edge:** Plain **Designer:** Jiri Harcuba

Date	Mintage	F	VF	XF	Unc	BU
1993(l)	70,001,000	—	—	—	1.00	—
1994(m)	30,475,491	—	—	—	1.00	—
1994(l)	14,400,000	—	—	—	1.00	—
1995(m)	20,155,218	—	—	—	1.00	—
1996(m)	5,053,730	—	—	—	1.00	—
1997(m)	40,000	—	—	—	1.00	—
1997(m) Proof	1,500	Value: 10.00				
1998(m)	25,000	—	—	—	1.00	—
Note: 10,207 pieces destroyed						
1998(m) Proof	2,600	Value: 6.00				
Note: 90 Pieces destroyed.						
1999(m)	29,490	—	—	—	1.00	—
1999(m) Proof	2,000	Value: 6.00				
2000(m)	26,431	—	—	—	1.00	—
2000(m) Proof	2,500	Value: 6.00				

KM# 4 10 KORUN

7.6200 g., Copper Plated Steel, 24.5 mm. **Obv:** Crowned Czech lion left, date below **Rev:** Brno Cathedral, denomination below **Edge:** Milled **Designer:** Ladislav Kozak **Note:** Position of designer's initials on reverse change during the 1995 strike.

Date	Mintage	F	VF	XF	Unc	BU
1993(c) Small 10	1,000	25.00	75.00	150	250	—
1993(c)	70,001,000	—	—	—	2.00	—
1994(m)	20,677,220	—	—	—	1.50	—
1994(m) bright	30,000	—	—	—	2.00	—
1995(m)	152,388	—	—	—	1.50	—
1995(m) LK below	20,530,459	—	—	—	1.50	—
1996(m)	20,644,143	—	—	—	1.50	—
1997(m)	48,215	—	—	—	1.50	—
1997(m) Proof	1,500	Value: 12.00				
1998(m)	25,000	—	—	—	1.50	—
1998(m) Proof	2,600	Value: 7.00				
Note: 90 pieces destroyed						
1999(m)	29,490	—	—	—	1.50	—
1999(m) Proof	2,000	Value: 7.00				
2000(m) Proof	2,500	Value: 7.00				
2000(m)	25,000	—	—	—	1.50	—

KM# 42 10 KORUN

7.5200 g., Copper Plated Steel, 24.5 mm. **Subject:** Year 2000 **Obv:** Crowned Czech lion left, date below **Rev:** Clock works above denomination, within circle **Edge:** Reeded

Date	Mintage	F	VF	XF	Unc	BU
2000	10,032,799	—	—	—	1.50	—
2000 Proof	2,500	Value: 7.50				

KM# 5 20 KORUN

8.4300 g., Brass Plated Steel, 26 mm. **Obv:** Crowned Czech lion left, date below **Rev:** St. Wenceslas (Duke Vaclav) on horse **Edge:** Plain **Shape:** 13-sided **Designer:** Vladimir Oppl **Note:** Two varieties of mint marks and style of 9's exist for 1997.

Date	Mintage	F	VF	XF	Unc	BU
1993(c)	55,001,000	—	—	1.00	3.00	—
1994(c)	100,000	—	—	—	3.50	—
1995(m)	101,837	—	—	—	2.50	—
1996(m)	101,152	—	—	—	2.50	—
1997(m)	8,091,219	—	—	—	2.50	—
1997(m) Proof	1,500	Value: 16.50				
1998(m)	15,725,000	—	—	—	2.50	—
Note: 41,786 pieces destroyed.						
1998(m) Proof	2,600	Value: 10.00				
Note: 90 pieces destroyed						
1999(m)	26,274,900	—	—	—	2.50	—
Note: 1,422 pieces destroyed.						
1999(m) Proof	2,000	Value: 10.00				
2000(m)	5,694,581	—	—	—	—	—
2000(m) Proof	2,500	—	—	—	—	—

KM# 43 20 KORUN

8.6000 g., Brass Plated Steel, 26 mm. **Subject:** Year 2000 **Obv:** Crowned Czech lion left, date below **Rev:** Astrolab and denomination within circle **Edge:** Plain **Shape:** 13-sided **Designer:** Vladimir Oppl

Date	Mintage	F	VF	XF	Unc	BU
2000	10,015,000	—	—	—	2.50	—
2000 Proof	2,500	Value: 10.00				

KM# 1 50 KORUN

9.7000 g., Bi-Metallic Brass plated Steel center in Copper plated Steel ring, 27.5 mm. **Obv:** Crowned Czech lion left **Rev:** Prague city view **Edge:** Plain **Designer:** Ladislav Kozak

Date	Mintage	F	VF	XF	Unc	BU
1993(c)	35,001,000	—	—	2.50	7.50	—
1994(c)	100,000	—	—	—	9.00	—
1995(m)	102,977	—	—	—	9.00	—
1996(m)	103,073	—	—	—	9.00	—
1997(m)	40,002	—	—	—	9.00	—
1997(m) Proof	1,500	Value: 35.00				
1998(m)	25,000	—	—	—	9.00	—
Note: 2,600 pieces destroyed.						
1998(m) Proof	2,600	Value: 20.00				
Note: 90 pieces destroyed						
1999(m)	29,490	—	—	—	9.00	—
1999(m) Proof	2,000	Value: 20.00				
2000(m) Proof	2,500	Value: 20.00				
2000(m)	26,436	—	—	—	9.00	—

KM# 10 200 KORUN

13.0000 g., 0.9000 Silver .3440 oz. ASW, 31 mm. **Subject:** 1st Anniversary of Constitution **Obv:** Quartered stylized arms above denomination and date **Rev:** Inscription above vertical dates **Designer:** Jitka Jelinkova **Note:** 22 pieces, Unc and Proof, were melted by the Czech National Bank in 1997.

Date	Mintage	F	VF	XF	Unc	BU
1993(o) Proof	3,968	Value: 30.00				
Note: Edge: CESKA NARODNI BANKA						
1993(o)	23,475	—	—	—	12.50	14.50
Note: Milled edge						

KM# 11.1 200 KORUN

13.0000 g., 0.9000 Silver .3440 oz. ASW, 31 mm. **Subject:** 650th Anniversary **Obv:** Quartered arms above denomination **Rev:** St. Vitus Cathedral and Archbishop's arms **Edge:** Reeded **Designer:** J. Truhlikova-Spevakova **Note:** See note with KM#11.2.

Date	Mintage	F	VF	XF	Unc	BU
ND(1994)(o)	23,888	—	—	—	12.50	14.50

KM# 11.2 200 KORUN

13.0000 g., 0.9000 Silver .3440 oz. ASW, 31 mm. **Subject:** 650th Anniversary **Rev:** St. Vitus Cathedral and Prague Archbishop's Arms **Edge:** Plain **Designer:** J. Truhlikova-Spevakova **Note:** 22 pieces, Unc and Proof of KM#11.1 and 11.2, were melted by the Czech National Bank in 1997.

Date	Mintage	F	VF	XF	Unc	BU
ND(1994)(o) Proof	2,500	Value: 400				

KM# 12 200 KORUN

13.0000 g., 0.9000 Silver .3440 oz. ASW, 31 mm. **Subject:** 50th Anniversary - Normandy Invasion **Obv:** Quartered arms, denomination at left, date below **Rev:** Spitfires in formation **Designer:** Jarmila Truhlikova-Spevakova **Note:** 6,445 pieces, Unc and Proof, were melted by the Czech National Bank in 1997.

Date	Mintage	F	VF	XF	Unc	BU
1994(cr)	29,980	—	—	—	16.50	18.50
Note: Milled edge						
1994(cr) Proof	5,000	Value: 150				
Note: Plain edge with CESKA NARODNI BANKA "0.900"						

KM# 13.1 200 KORUN

13.0000 g., 0.9000 Silver .3440 oz. ASW, 31 mm. **Subject:** 125th Anniversary of Brno Tramway **Obv:** Elongated, stylized, unbordered, quartered arms above date and denomination **Rev:** Tramway **Edge:** Reeded **Designer:** J. Harcuba **Note:** See note with KM#13.2.

Date	Mintage	F	VF	XF	Unc	BU
1994(mk)	20,138	—	—	—	14.00	16.00

KM# 13.2 200 KORUN

13.0000 g., 0.9000 Silver .3440 oz. ASW, 31 mm. **Subject:** 125th Anniversary Brno Tramway **Obv:** Quartered arms **Rev:** Tramway **Edge:** Plain **Designer:** J. Harcuba **Note:** 22 pieces, Unc and Proof, were melted by the Czech National Bank in 1997. Beginning with KM#14, all 200 Korun strikes come either reeded, or plain edges with the inscription, "CESKA NARODNI BANKA".

Date	Mintage	F	VF	XF	Unc	BU
1994 Proof	1,960	Value: 50.00				

KM# 14 200 KORUN

13.0000 g., 0.9000 Silver .3440 oz. ASW, 31 mm. **Subject:** Environmental Protection **Obv:** Stylized quartered arms divide date, denomination below **Rev:** Nude on globe, animals and plants in background **Designer:** Ladislav Kozak **Note:** 22 pieces, Unc and Proof, were melted by the Czech National Bank in 1997.

Date	Mintage	F	VF	XF	Unc	BU
1994(m)	21,236	—	—	—	14.00	16.00
Note: Milled edge						
1994(m) Proof	2,000	Value: 200				
Note: Edge: Plain with CESKA NARODNI BANKA *0.900*						

KM# 15 200 KORUN

13.0000 g., 0.9000 Silver .3440 oz. ASW, 31 mm. **Subject:** 50th Anniversary - Victory Over Fascism **Designer:** J. Jelinkova **Note:** 22 pieces, Unc and Proof, were melted by the Czech National Bank in 1997.

Date	Mintage	F	VF	XF	Unc	BU
ND(1995)	19,852	—	—	—	14.00	16.00
Note: Plain edge						
ND(1995) Proof	2,000	Value: 250				
Note: Plain edge with CESKA NARODNI BANKA *0.900*						

KM# 16 200 KORUN

13.0000 g., 0.9000 Silver .3440 oz. ASW, 31 mm. **Subject:** 200th Anniversary - Birth of Pavel Josef Safarik **Designer:** P. Horak **Note:** 22 pieces, Unc and Proof, were melted by the Czech National Bank in 1997.

Date	Mintage	F	VF	XF	Unc	BU
1995	19,192	—	—	—	14.00	16.00
Note: Plain edge						
1995 Proof	1,998	Value: 42.00				
Note: Plain edge with CESKA NARODNI BANKA *0.900*						

KM# 17 200 KORUN

13.0000 g., 0.9000 Silver .3440 oz. ASW, 31 mm. **Subject:** 50th Anniversary - United Nations **Obv:** Quartered arms above denomination **Rev:** UN logo, dates within wreath at left **Designer:** Frantisek Skrbek **Note:** 25 pieces, Unc and Proof, were melted by the Czech National Bank in 1997.

Date	Mintage	F	VF	XF	Unc	BU
ND(1995)	19,968	—	—	—	14.00	16.00
Note: Milled edge						

Date	Mintage	F	VF	XF	Unc	BU
ND(1995) Proof	2,500	Value: 40.00				
Note: Plain edge with CESKA NARODNI BANKA *0.900*						

KM# 23 200 KORUN

13.0000 g., 0.9000 Silver .3440 oz. ASW, 31 mm. **Subject:** Karel Svolinsky **Obv:** Stylized quartered arms above denomination **Rev:** Bird on vase holding bouquet **Designer:** Vladimir Oppl **Note:** 25 pieces, Unc and Proof, were melted by the Czech National Bank in 1997.

Date	Mintage	F	VF	XF	Unc	BU
ND(1996)	18,994	—	—	—	14.00	16.00
Note: Milled edge						
ND(1996) Proof	2,000	Value: 75.00				
Note: Plain edge with CESKA NARODNI BANKA *0.900*						

KM# 22 200 KORUN

13.0000 g., 0.9000 Silver .3440 oz. ASW, 31 mm. **Subject:** Czech Philharmonic **Obv:** Quartered arms above denomination **Rev:** Building and musical instruments, dates above **Designer:** Vladimir Oppl **Note:** Three varieties in the artist's monogram exist. 25 pieces, Unc and Proof, were melted by the Czech National Bank in 1997.

Date	Mintage	F	VF	XF	Unc	BU
1996 Proof	2,500	Value: 75.00				
Note: Plain edge with CESKA NARODNI BANKA *0.900*						
1996	19,231	—	—	—	14.00	16.00
Note: Milled edge						

KM# 24 200 KORUN

13.0000 g., 0.9000 Silver .3440 oz. ASW, 31 mm. **Subject:** Jean-Baptiste Gaspard Deburau **Obv:** Elongated, stylized, unbordered, quartered arms, denomination and date below **Rev:** Seated artistic portrait of Deburau **Designer:** Jiri Harcuba

Date	Mintage	F	VF	XF	Unc	BU
1996 Proof	2,000	Value: 35.00				
Note: Plain edge with CESKA NARODNI BANKA *0.900*						
1996	17,659	—	—	—	14.00	16.00
Note: Milled edge						

KM# 25 200 KORUN

13.0000 g., 0.9000 Silver .3761 oz. ASW, 31 mm. **Subject:** 200th Anniversary - Czech Christmas Mass by Jakub J. Ryba **Obv:** Quartered arms within circle, denomination below **Rev:** Angel with horn, stars above, church lower left, circle surrounds, dates at right **Designer:** Ladislav Kozak

Date	Mintage	F	VF	XF	Unc	BU
ND(1996) Proof	2,500	Value: 40.00				
Note: Plain edge with CESKA NARODNI BANKA *0.900*						
ND(1996)	19,311	—	—	—	14.00	16.00
Note: Milled edge						

KM# 26 200 KORUN

13.0000 g., 0.9000 Silver .3761 oz. ASW, 31 mm. **Subject:** Centennial - First Automobile in Bohemia **Obv:** National arms **Rev:** Side view of antique automobile - President **Designer:** Ladislav Kozak

Date	Mintage	F	VF	XF	Unc	BU
ND(1997)	18,778	—	—	—	14.00	16.00
Note: Milled edge						
ND(1997) Proof	3,000	Value: 32.00				
Note: Plain edge with CESKA NARODNI BANKA *0.900*						

KM# 27 200 KORUN

13.0000 g., 0.9000 Silver .3761 oz. ASW, 31 mm. **Subject:** Millennium - St. Adalbert's Death **Obv:** Unbordered quartered arms, denomination below **Rev:** Bishop's portrait right, dates at right **Designer:** Ladislav Kozak

Date	Mintage	F	VF	XF	Unc	BU
ND(1997) Proof	3,000	Value: 32.00				
Note: Plain edge with CESKA NARODNI BANKA *0.900*						
ND(1997)	20,567	—	—	—	14.00	16.00
Note: Milled edge						

KM# 28 200 KORUN

13.0000 g., 0.9000 Silver .3761 oz. ASW, 31 mm. **Subject:** Czech Amateur Athletic Union **Obv:** Unbordered arms **Rev:** Runners **Designer:** Jiri Harcuba

Date	Mintage	F	VF	XF	Unc	BU
ND(1997) Proof	3,000	Value: 35.00				
ND(1997)	17,215	—	—	—	14.00	16.00

KM# 29 200 KORUN

13.0000 g., 0.9000 Silver .3761 oz. ASW, 31 mm. **Subject:** 650th Anniversary - Na Slovanech-Emauzy Monastery **Obv:** Unbordered, quartered arms above denomination **Rev:** Seated saintly figure, date above **Designer:** Jiri Harcuba

Date	Mintage	F	VF	XF	Unc	BU
ND(1997)	18,100	—	—	—	14.00	16.00
Note: Milled edge						
ND(1997) Proof	2,966	Value: 32.00				
Note: Plain edge with CESKA NARODNI BANKA *0.900*						

KM# 30 200 KORUN

13.0000 g., 0.9000 Silver .3761 oz. ASW, 31 mm. **Subject:** 650th Anniversary - Charles University in Prague **Obv:** Quartered arms within circle, patterned circle surrounds **Rev:** Charles IV portrait and document seal **Designer:** M. Wichnerova

Date	Mintage	F	VF	XF	Unc	BU
ND(1998)	26,553	—	—	—	14.00	16.00
Note: Milled edge						
ND(1998) Proof	3,000	Value: 95.00				
Note: Plain edge with CESKA NARODNI BANKA *0.900*						

KM# 31 200 KORUN
13.0000 g., 0.9000 Silver .3761 oz. ASW, 31 mm. **Subject:** 200th Aniversary - Birth of Frantisek Palacky **Obv:** National arms **Rev:** Head of Palacky left **Designer:** Vladimir Oppl

Date	Mintage	F	VF	XF	Unc	BU
ND(1998)	16,881	—	—	—	14.00	16.00
Note: Milled edge						
ND(1998) Proof	2,941	Value: 30.00				
Note: Plain edge with CESKA NARODNI BANKA *0.900*						

KM# 32 200 KORUN
13.0000 g., 0.9000 Silver .3761 oz. ASW, 31 mm. **Subject:** 800th Anniversary - Coronation of King Premysl I. Otakar **Obv:** Quartered arms above denomination **Rev:** Half facing head at right, coin design at left **Designer:** J. Venecek

Date	Mintage	F	VF	XF	Unc	BU
ND(1998)(m)	17,392	—	—	—	14.00	16.00
Note: Milled edge						
ND(1998) Proof	3,000	Value: 30.00				
Note: Plain edge with CESKA NARODNI BANKA *0.900*						

KM# 33 200 KORUN
13.0000 g., 0.9000 Silver .3761 oz. ASW, 31 mm. **Subject:** 150th Anniversary - Birth of Frantisek Kmoch **Obv:** National arms **Rev:** Head of Kmoch facing left, dates **Designer:** Ladislav Kozak

Date	Mintage	F	VF	XF	Unc	BU
ND(1998)(m)	2,875	Value: 28.00				
Note: Plain edge with CESKA NARODNI BANKA *0.900*						
ND(1998)(m)	16,522	—	—	—	11.50	13.50
Note: Milled edge						

KM# 34 200 KORUN
13.0000 g., 0.9000 Silver .3761 oz. ASW, 31 mm. **Subject:** 50th Anniversary - NATO **Obv:** Unbordered, quartered arms, denomination below **Rev:** NATO style cross with dates on horizontals **Edge Lettering:** CESKA REPUBLIKA CLENSKA ZEME NATO 1996 **Designer:** Jiri Harcuba

Date	Mintage	F	VF	XF	Unc	BU
ND(1999) Proof	3,000	Value: 30.00				
Note: Plain edge with CESKA NARODNI BANKA *0.900*						
ND(1999)	18,133	—	—	—	14.00	16.00
Note: Edge: CESKA REPUBLIKA...						

KM# 35 200 KORUN
13.0000 g., 0.9000 Silver .3761 oz. ASW, 31 mm. **Subject:** 200 Years - Prague Fine Arts Academy **Obv:** Stylized and quartered national arms within 1/2 circle, denomination at left **Rev:** Stylized design, dates at left **Edge:** Reeded **Designer:** L. Rudolf

Date	Mintage	F	VF	XF	Unc	BU
ND(1999)	15,012	—	—	—	14.00	16.00
Note: Milled edge						
ND(1999) Proof	2,881	Value: 28.00				
Note: Plain edge with CESKA NARODNI BANKA *0.900*						

KM# 36 200 KORUN
13.0000 g., 0.9000 Silver .3761 oz. ASW, 31 mm. **Subject:** 100 Years - Brno University of Technology **Obv:** Unbordered, quartered arms, denomination below **Rev:** Stylized design, dates below **Designer:** Jiri Harcuba

Date	Mintage	F	VF	XF	Unc	BU
ND(1999) Proof	3,181	Value: 28.00				
Note: Plain edge with CESKA NARODNI BANKA *0.900*						
ND(1999)	17,304	—	—	—	14.00	16.00
Note: Milled edge						

KM# 37 200 KORUN
13.0000 g., 0.9000 Silver .3761 oz. ASW, 31 mm. **Subject:** 100th Birthday - Ondrej Sekora **Obv:** National arms **Rev:** Ant holding flowers **Designer:** J. Bejul

Date	Mintage	F	VF	XF	Unc	BU
ND(1999)	15,548	—	—	—	14.00	16.00
Note: Milled edge						
ND(1999) Proof	2,697	Value: 28.00				
Note: Plain edge with CESKA NARODNI BANKA *0.900*						

KM# 46 200 KORUN
13.0000 g., 0.9000 Silver .3761 oz. ASW **Subject:** 700th Anniversary - Currency Reform **Obv:** Quartered arms above coin design which divides denomination **Rev:** Seated figure divides coin designs **Designer:** Jiri Nemecek

Date	Mintage	F	VF	XF	Unc	BU
2000	14,855	—	—	—	15.00	—
Note: Milled edge						
2000 Proof	3,400	—	—	—	25.00	—
Note: Plain edge with CESKA NARODNI BANKA *0.900*						

KM# 47 200 KORUN
13.0000 g., 0.9000 Silver .3761 oz. ASW **Subject:** 100th Anniversary - Birth of Poet Vitezslav Nezval **Obv:** Quartered arms above denomination **Rev:** Stylized head left, dates at right **Designer:** Ladislav Kozak

Date	Mintage	F	VF	XF	Unc	BU
2000	13,486	—	—	—	15.00	—
Note: Milled edge						
2000 Proof	2,900	Value: 25.00				
Note: Plain edge with CESKA NARODNI BANKA *0.900*						

KM# 48 200 KORUN
13.0000 g., 0.9000 Silver .3762 oz. ASW, 31 mm. **Subject:** 150th Anniversary - Birth of Zdenek Fibich, Musical Composer **Obv:** National arms **Rev:** Portrait **Designer:** Vladimir Oppl

Date	Mintage	F	VF	XF	Unc	BU
2000	13,694	—	—	—	14.00	16.00
Note: Milled edge						
2000 Proof	2,900	Value: 28.00				
Note: Plain edge with CESKA NARODNI BANKA *0.900*						

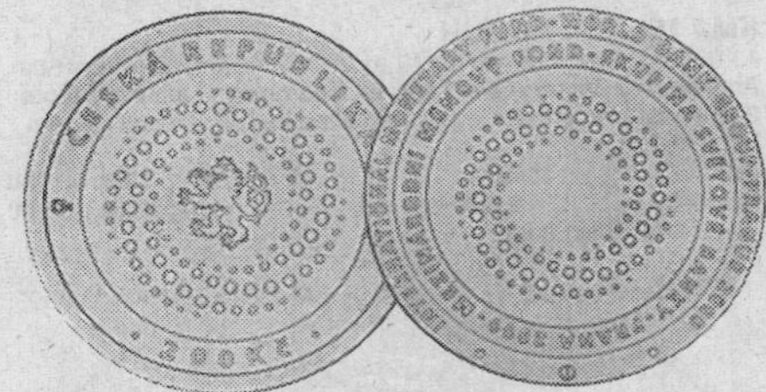

KM# 49 200 KORUN
13.0000 g., 0.9000 Silver .3762 oz. ASW, 31 mm. **Subject:** International Monetary Fund and Prague World Bank Group **Obv:** Crowned lion in swirling dots **Rev:** Circle of swirling dots **Designer:** Otakar Dusek

Date	Mintage	F	VF	XF	Unc	BU
2000	15,249	—	—	—	14.00	16.00
Note: Milled edge						
2000 Proof	4,299	Value: 28.00				
Note: Plain edge with CESKA NARODNI BANKA *0.900*						

KM# 50 200 KORUN
13.0000 g., 0.9000 Silver .3762 oz. ASW, 31 mm. **Subject:** New Millennium **Obv:** Elongated, stylized, unbordered arms, denomination below **Rev:** Stylized phoenix design, date below **Designer:** Jiri Harcuba

Date	Mintage	F	VF	XF	Unc	BU
2000	16,775	—	—	—	14.00	16.00
Note: Milled edge						
2000 Proof	3,500	Value: 28.00				
Note: Plain edge with CESKA NARODNI BANKA *0.900*						

KM# 44 2000 KORUN
34.2140 g., 0.9990 Bi-Metallic Gold And Silver .9990 oz., 40 mm. **Subject:** Millennium **Obv:** National arms hologram on gold inlay **Rev:** Stylized 2000 **Edge Lettering:** *CNB* Ag 0.999* 31.103 g *CNB* AU 999.9 *3. 111 g* **Designer:** O. Dusek **Note:** With a 3.1110 gram, .999 gold, .0999 ounce actual gold weight gold inlay.

Date	Mintage	F	VF	XF	Unc	BU
ND(1999)(m) Proof	2,999	Value: 165				
ND(1999)(m)	11,358	—	—	—	85.00	100

GOLD BULLION COINAGE

KM# 18 1000 KORUN
3.1103 g., 0.9999 Gold .1000 oz. AGW, 16 mm. **Subject:** Historic Coins - Tolar of Silesian Estates 12-1/2 tolar 1620. **Obv:** Imperial eagle, denomination below **Rev:** Tablet with four line inscription within circle **Designer:** Vladimir Oppl

Date	Mintage	F	VF	XF	Unc	BU
1995	1,997	—	—	—	—	100
1996	3,252	—	—	—	—	100
1996 Proof	741	Value: 145				
1997 Proof	2,247	Value: 120				

KM# 38 1000 KORUN
3.1103 g., 0.9999 Gold .1000 oz. AGW, 16 mm. **Obv:** Three shielded arms, dates below **Rev:** Old coin design at right, Quartered design in center **Designer:** J. Harcuba **Note:** Karlstejn Castle.

Date	Mintage	F	VF	XF	Unc	BU
1998	2,097	—	—	—	—	85.00

Note: Milled edge

Date	Mintage	F	VF	XF	Unc	BU
1998 Proof	2,206	Value: 100				

Note: Plain edge

Date	Mintage	F	VF	XF	Unc	BU
1999 Proof	1,997	Value: 100				

KM# 19 2500 KORUN
7.7759 g., 0.9999 Gold .2500 oz. AGW, 22 mm. **Subject:** Historic Coins - 1620 Tolar of Moravian Estates **Obv:** Imperial eagle within circle, denomination below **Rev:** Vine climbing tower within circle **Designer:** Vladimir Oppl

Date	Mintage	F	VF	XF	Unc	BU
1995	1,997	—	—	—	—	250
1996	1,253	—	—	—	—	250
1996 Proof	741	Value: 300				
1997 Proof	1,697	Value: 265				

KM# 39 2500 KORUN
7.7759 g., 0.9999 Gold .2500 oz. AGW, 22 mm. **Rev:** Seal of Karel IV with legal document **Designer:** Jarmila Truhlikova-Spevakova

Date	Mintage	F	VF	XF	Unc	BU
1998	1,122	—	—	—	—	175

Note: Milled edge

Date	Mintage	F	VF	XF	Unc	BU
1998 Proof	1,855	Value: 200				

Note: Plain edge

Date	Mintage	F	VF	XF	Unc	BU
1999 Proof	1,497	Value: 185				

KM# 20 5000 KORUN
15.5517 g., 0.9999 Gold .5000 oz. AGW, 28 mm. **Subject:** Historic Coins **Obv:** Czech lion left within circle, denomination below **Rev:** Bohemian Maley Gros of 1587 **Designer:** Vladimir Oppl

Date	Mintage	F	VF	XF	Unc	BU
1995	997	—	—	—	—	560
1996	1,253	—	—	—	—	560
1996 Proof	741	Value: 625				
1997 Proof	1,496	Value: 575				

KM# 40 5000 KORUN
15.5530 g., 0.9999 Gold .5000 oz. AGW, 28 mm. **Obv:** Three shielded arms, date above, denomination below **Rev:** Karel IV, Charles University founder **Designer:** M. Vitanovsky

Date	Mintage	F	VF	XF	Unc	BU
1998 Proof	1,854	Value: 375				

Note: Edge: CESKA NARODNI BANKA 18.553 g.

Date	Mintage	F	VF	XF	Unc	BU
1998	1,045	—	—	—	—	350

Note: Milled edge

Date	Mintage	F	VF	XF	Unc	BU
1999 Proof	1,497	Value: 350				

Note: Edge: CESKA NARODNI BANKA 18.553 g.

KM# 21 10000 KORUN
31.1035 g., 0.9999 Gold 1.0000 oz. AGW, 34 mm. **Subject:** Historic Coins **Obv:** Elongated, stylized, unbordered arms, date and denomination below **Rev:** Lion holding Prague Groschen **Designer:** Jiri Harcuba

Date	Mintage	F	VF	XF	Unc	BU
1995	997	—	—	—	—	975
1996	1,251	—	—	—	—	975
1996 Proof	740	Value: 1,100				
1997 Proof	1,497	Value: 1,000				

KM# 41 10000 KORUN
31.1070 g., 0.9999 Gold 1.0000 oz. AGW, 34 mm. **Rev:** Karel IV and seals of Nove Mesto **Designer:** Vladimir Oppl

Date	Mintage	F	VF	XF	Unc	BU
1998	1,111	—	—	—	—	700

Note: Milled edge

Date	Mintage	F	VF	XF	Unc	BU
1998 Proof	1,996	Value: 725				

Note: Edge: CESKA NARODNI BANKA 31.107 g.

Date	Mintage	F	VF	XF	Unc	BU
1999 Proof	1,297	Value: 700				

Note: Edge: CESKA NARODNI BANKA 31.107 g.

KM# 45 10000 KORUN
31.1070 g., 0.9990 Gold 1.0000 oz. AGW **Subject:** Karl IV **Obv:** 3 coats of arms **Rev:** Karl IV with 3 coin designs **Edge Lettering:** *CESKA NARODNI BANKA8 31.107 g*

Date	Mintage	F	VF	XF	Unc	BU
1999(m) Proof	6,000	Value: 675				

MINT SETS

KM#	Date	Mintage	Identification	Issue Price	Mkt Val
MS1	1993 (9)	20,000	KM1, 2.1, 3-9	—	14.00
MS2	1994 (9)	13,400	KM1, 2.1, 3-9	—	14.00
MS3	1995 (9)	19,400	KM1, 2.1, 3-9	—	14.00
MS4	1996 (9)	14,188	KM1, 2.1, 3-9	—	14.00
MS5	1996 (9)	11,052	KM1, 2.1, 3-9 w/EURO 96 medal	—	15.50
MS6	1997 (9)	15,000	KM1, 2.1, 3-9	—	14.00
MS7	1998 (9)	5,000	KM1, 2.3, 3-9, Olympic Hockey Folder	—	14.00
MS8	1998 (9)	—	KM1, 2.3, 3-9, Summer Winter Scene Folder	—	—
MS9	1999 (9)	5,000	KM1, 2.3, 3-9, Parler Folder	—	14.00
MS10	1999 (9)	2,500	KM1, 2.3, 3-9, Nato Folder	—	14.00
MS11	1999 (9)	2,500	KM1, 2.3, 3-9, Childrens Motif Folder	—	14.00
MS12	2001 (9)	6,000	KM#1, 2.3, 3-9 International Monetary Fund	—	14.00

PROOF SETS

KM#	Date	Mintage	Identification	Issue Price	Mkt Val
PS1	1994 (3)	2,000	KM2.1, 3, 6	—	—
PS2	1997 (9)	1,500	KM1, 2.1, 3-9, plus silver medal	35.00	300
PS3	1998 (9)	2,500	KM1, 2.3, 3-9, plus silver medal	35.00	60.00
PS4	1999 (9)	2,000	KM1, 2.3, 3-9, plus silver medal	35.00	60.00
PS5	2000 (9)	2,500	KM#1, 2.3, 3.1, 4, 5, 6, 7, 8, 9	35.00	60.00
PS6	2001 (9)	2,500	KM#1, 2.3, 3-9	35.00	60.00
PS7	2002 (9)	3,490	KM#1, 2.3, 3.2, 4, 5, 6, 7, 8, 9	35.00	60.00
PS8	2003 (9)	3,000	KM#1, 2.3, 3.2, 4, 5, 6, 7, 8, 9	35.00	60.00
PS9	2004 (9)	4,000	KM#1, 2.3, 3.2, 4, 5, 6, 7, 8, 9	35.00	60.00

CZECHOSLOVAKIA

The Republic of Czechoslovakia, founded at the end of World War I, was part of the old Austrian-Hungarian Empire. It had an area of 49,371 sq. mi. (127,870 sq. km.) and a population of 15.6 million. Capital: Prague (Praha).

Czechoslovakia proclaimed itself a republic on Oct. 28, 1918, with Tomas G. Masaryk as President. Hitler's rise to power in Germany provoked Czechoslovakia's German minority in the Sudetenland to agitate for autonomy. At Munich (Munchen) in Sept. of 1938, France and Britain, seeking to avoid World War II, forced the cession of the Sudetenland to Germany. In March, 1939, Germany invaded Czechoslovakia and established the "protectorate of Bohemia and Moravia". Bohemia is a historic province in northwest Czechoslovakia that includes the city of Prague, one of the oldest continually occupied sites in Europe. Moravia is an area of considerable mineral wealth in central Czechoslovakia. Slovakia, a province in southeastern Czechoslovakia under Nazi influence was constituted as a republic. The end of World War II saw the re-established independence of Czechoslovakia, while bringing it within the Russian sphere of influence. On Feb. 23-25, 1948, the Communists seized control of the government in a coup d'etat, and adopted a constitution making the country a 'people's republic'. A new constitution adopted June 11, 1960, converted the country into a 'socialist republic', which lasted until 1989. On Nov. 11, 1989, demonstrations against the communist government began and in Dec. of that same year, communism was overthrown, and the Czech and Slovak Federal Republic was formed. In 1993 the CSFR split into the Czech Republic and The Republic of Slovakia.

NOTE: For additional listings see Bohemia and Moravia, Czech Republic and Slovakia.

MINT MARKS
(k) - Kremnica
(l) - Leningrad

MONETARY SYSTEM
100 Haleru = 1 Koruna

REPUBLIC

DECIMAL COINAGE

KM# 5 2 HALERE
2.0000 g., Zinc, 17 mm. **Obv:** Czech lion with Slovak shield **Rev:** Charles Bridge in Praha, denomination below **Edge:** Plain **Designer:** O. Spaniel

Date	Mintage	F	VF	XF	Unc	BU
1923	2,700,000	3.00	5.00	10.00	16.00	—
1924	17,300,000	2.25	3.50	5.00	9.00	—
1925	2,000,000	3.00	5.00	7.50	17.00	—

KM# 6 5 HALERU
1.6600 g., Bronze, 16 mm. **Obv:** Czech lion with Slovak shield, date below **Rev:** Charles Bridge in Praha, denomination below **Edge:** Plain **Designer:** O. Spaniel

Date	Mintage	F	VF	XF	Unc	BU
1923	37,800,000	0.20	0.30	0.50	2.00	—
1924	10	—	—	2,500	5,000	—

Note: There are two varieties of the number 4 in 1924 dated coins: with and without seraphs

Date	Mintage	F	VF	XF	Unc	BU
1925	12,000,000	0.20	0.30	0.50	2.50	—
1926	1,084,000	1.50	4.00	20.00	60.00	—
1927	8,916,000	0.25	0.35	0.75	2.50	—
1928	5,320,000	0.30	0.45	0.75	2.50	—
1929	12,680,000	0.25	0.35	0.75	2.50	—
1930	5,000,000	0.35	3.50	15.00	50.00	—
1931	7,448,000	0.25	0.35	0.75	2.50	—
1932	3,556,000	0.65	3.50	12.00	35.00	—
1938	14,244,000	0.25	0.35	0.75	2.00	—

KM# 3 10 HALERU
Bronze, 18 mm. **Obv:** Czech lion with Slovak shield, date below **Rev:** Charles Bridge of Praha, denomination below **Edge:** Plain

Date	Mintage	F	VF	XF	Unc	BU
1922	6,000,000	0.30	0.45	1.00	2.75	—
1923	24,000,000	0.25	0.35	0.75	2.00	—

Date	Mintage	F	VF	XF	Unc	BU
1924	5,320,000	0.30	0.45	1.00	3.00	—
1925	24,680,000	0.25	0.35	0.60	2.25	—
1926	10,000,000	0.25	0.35	0.75	2.25	—
1927	10,000,000	0.25	0.35	0.75	2.25	—
1928	14,290,000	0.25	0.35	0.75	2.25	—
1929	5,710,000	1.25	2.50	10.00	25.00	—
1930	6,980,000	0.30	0.45	1.00	2.50	—
1931	6,740,000	0.30	0.45	1.00	2.50	—
1932	11,280,000	0.25	0.35	0.75	2.00	—
1933	4,190,000	1.50	3.50	12.00	25.00	—
1934	13,200,000	0.25	0.35	0.75	2.00	—
1935	3,420,000	1.50	3.50	12.00	25.00	—
1936	8,560,000	0.25	0.35	0.75	2.00	—
1937	20,200,000	0.25	0.35	0.75	2.00	—
1938	21,400,000	0.25	0.35	0.75	2.00	—

KM# 1 20 HALERU

3.3300 g., Copper-Nickel, 20 mm. **Obv:** Czech lion with Slovak shield, date below **Rev:** Sheaf with sickle, linden branch, denomination at left **Edge:** Plain **Designer:** O. Spaniel

Date	Mintage	F	VF	XF	Unc	BU
1921	40,000,000	0.25	0.35	0.60	2.50	—
1922	9,100,000	0.25	0.35	0.60	2.50	—
1924	20,931,000	0.25	0.35	0.60	2.50	—
1925	4,244,000	1.50	3.40	12.00	25.00	—
1926	14,825,000	0.25	0.35	0.60	2.50	—
1927	11,757,000	0.25	0.35	0.60	2.50	—
1928	14,018,000	0.25	0.35	0.60	2.50	—
1929	4,225,000	0.30	0.50	1.25	3.50	—
1930	—	1.00	2.00	5.00	14.00	—
1931	5,000,000	0.30	0.40	0.75	3.00	—
1933	Inc. above	9.00	25.00	80.00	160	—
1937	8,208,000	0.25	0.35	0.60	2.50	—
1938	18,787,000	0.25	0.35	0.60	2.50	—

KM# 16 25 HALERU

4.0000 g., Copper-Nickel, 21 mm. **Obv:** Czech lion with Slovak shield, date below **Rev:** Large denomination **Edge:** Milled **Designer:** O. Spaniel

Date	Mintage	F	VF	XF	Unc	BU
1932	—	—	1,250	2,250	3,000	—
1933	22,711,000	0.50	1.00	2.00	4.00	—

KM# 2 50 HALERU

5.0000 g., Copper-Nickel, 22 mm. **Obv:** Czech lion with Slovak shield, date below **Rev:** Linden branches and wheat sprigs bound with ribbon **Edge:** Milled **Designer:** O. Spaniel

Date	Mintage	F	VF	XF	Unc	BU
1921	3,000,000	0.25	0.50	1.00	3.00	—
1922	37,000,000	0.20	0.40	0.60	2.50	—
1924	10,000,000	0.20	0.40	0.60	3.00	—
1925	1,415,000	0.50	1.00	2.50	10.00	—
1926	1,585,000	3.50	9.00	20.00	45.00	—
1927	2,000,000	0.50	1.00	2.00	9.00	—
1931	6,000,000	0.25	0.50	1.00	2.50	—

KM# 4 KORUNA

6.6600 g., Copper-Nickel, 25 mm. **Obv:** Czech lion with Slovak shield, date below **Rev:** Woman with sheaf and sickle, denomination at left **Edge:** Milled **Designer:** O. Spaniel

Date	Mintage	F	VF	XF	Unc	BU
1922	50,000,000	0.30	0.50	0.75	2.00	—
1923	15,385,000	0.30	0.50	0.75	2.00	—
1924	21,041,000	0.30	0.50	0.75	2.00	—

Date	Mintage	F	VF	XF	Unc	BU
1925	8,574,000	0.40	0.60	1.25	4.00	—
1929	5,000,000	0.50	0.75	1.25	3.50	—
1930	5,000,000	0.40	0.60	1.25	5.00	—
1937	3,806,000	0.40	0.60	1.00	3.00	—
1938	8,582,000	0.40	0.60	1.00	3.00	—

KM# 10 5 KORUN

10.0000 g., Copper-Nickel, 30 mm. **Obv:** Czech lion with Slovak shield, date below **Rev:** Industrial factory and large value

Date	Mintage	F	VF	XF	Unc	BU
1925	16,474,500	1.50	2.50	3.50	9.00	—
1926	8,912,000	1.75	2.75	4.00	10.00	—
1927	4,613,500	8.00	20.00	80.00	160	—

KM# 11 5 KORUN

7.0000 g., 0.5000 Silver .125 oz. ASW, 27 mm. **Obv:** Czech lion with Slovak shield, date below **Rev:** Industrial factory and large value **Edge:** Plain with crosses and waves **Designer:** Ota Gutfreud

Date	Mintage	F	VF	XF	Unc	BU
1928	1,710,000	2.00	3.00	5.00	10.00	—
Note: Edge varieties exist for 1928						
1929	12,861,000	1.65	2.50	4.00	8.50	—
1930	10,429,000	1.65	2.50	4.00	8.50	—
1931	2,000,000	3.00	5.00	15.00	45.00	—
1932	1,000,000	5.00	7.50	20.00	60.00	—

KM# 11a 5 KORUN

8.0000 g., Nickel, 27 mm. **Obv:** Czech lion with Slovak shield, date below **Rev:** Industrial factory and large value **Designer:** O. Guttfreund

Date	Mintage	F	VF	XF	Unc	BU
1937	36,000	400	900	1,850	3,500	—
1938	17,200,000	1.25	2.50	4.00	6.50	—

KM# 12 10 KORUN

10.0000 g., 0.7000 Silver .2250 oz. ASW, 30 mm. **Subject:** 10th Anniversary of Independence **Obv:** Denomination above state shield within circle, dates below **Rev:** Bust right **Edge:** Milled **Designer:** O. Spaniel

Date	Mintage	F	VF	XF	Unc	BU
ND(1928)	1,000,000	3.00	4.50	7.00	11.50	—

KM# 15 10 KORUN

10.0000 g., 0.7000 Silver .2250 oz. ASW, 30 mm. **Obv:** State emblem, date below **Rev:** Republic holding linden tree, denomination above **Edge:** Milled **Designer:** J. Horejc

Date	Mintage	F	VF	XF	Unc	BU
1930	4,949,000	3.00	4.00	7.00	11.50	—
1931	6,689,000	2.85	3.75	6.00	10.00	—
1932	11,447,500	BV	3.50	5.00	9.00	—
1933	915,000	350	850	1,750	3,000	—

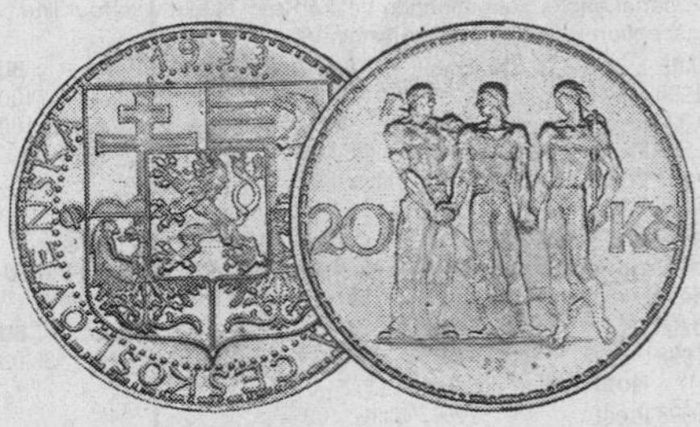

KM# 17 20 KORUN

12.0000 g., 0.7000 Silver .2700 oz. ASW, 34 mm. **Obv:** State emblem, date above **Rev:** Three figures: Industry, Agriculture, and Business, divide denomination **Edge:** Plain with crosses and waves **Designer:** J. Horejc

Date	Mintage	F	VF	XF	Unc	BU
1933	2,280,000	—	4.50	7.50	14.00	—
1934	3,280,000	—	4.50	7.50	14.00	—

KM# 18 20 KORUN

12.0000 g., 0.7000 Silver .2700 oz. ASW, 34 mm. **Subject:** Death of President Masaryk **Obv:** Denomination above state emblem **Obv. Designer:** J. Horejc **Rev:** Bust right, dates at left **Rev. Designer:** O. Spaniel **Edge:** Plain with crosses and waves

Date	Mintage	F	VF	XF	Unc	BU
ND(1937)	1,000,000	—	4.00	7.00	11.50	—

TRADE COINAGE

KM# 7 DUKAT

3.4900 g., 0.9860 Gold .1106 oz. AGW **Subject:** 5th Anniversary of the Republic **Obv:** Shield with Czech lion and Slovak shield **Obv. Designer:** J. Benda **Rev:** Duke Wenceslas (Vaclav) half-length figure facing **Rev. Designer:** O. Spaniel **Edge:** Milled **Note:** Serially numbered below the duke. The number is in the die.

Date	Mintage	F	VF	XF	Unc	BU
1923	1,000	—	1,000	2,500	5,000	—

KM# 8 DUKAT

3.4900 g., 0.9860 Gold .1106 oz. AGW **Obv:** Czech lion with Slovak shield, date below **Obv. Designer:** J. Benda **Rev:** Duke Wenceslas (Vaclav) half-length figure facing **Rev. Designer:** O. Spaniel **Edge:** Milled **Note:** Similar to KM#7 but without serial numbers.

Date	Mintage	F	VF	XF	Unc	BU
1923	61,861	—	BV	80.00	125	—
1924	32,814	—	BV	80.00	125	—

Date	Mintage	F	VF	XF	Unc	BU
1925	66,279	—	BV	80.00	125	—
1926	58,669	—	BV	80.00	125	—
1927	25,774	—	BV	80.00	125	—
1928	18,983	—	BV	80.00	135	—
1929	10,253	—	BV	85.00	165	—
1930	11,338	—	BV	85.00	165	—
1931	43,482	—	BV	80.00	125	—
1932	26,617	—	BV	80.00	125	—
1933	57,597	—	BV	80.00	125	—
1934	9,729	—	80.00	100	175	—
1935	13,178	—	BV	80.00	135	—
1936	14,566	—	BV	80.00	135	—
1937	324	—	275	650	1,000	—
1938	56	—	800	1,750	3,500	—
1939	276	—	—	—	—	—
Note: Czech reports show mintage of 20 for Czechoslovakia and 256 for state of Slovakia						
1951	500	—	325	725	1,500	—

KM# 9 2 DUKATY

6.9800 g., 0.9860 Gold .2212 oz. AGW, 25 mm. **Obv:** Czech lion with Slovak shield, denomination divides date below **Obv. Designer:** J. Benda **Rev:** Duke Wenceslas (Vaclav) half-length figure facing **Rev. Designer:** O. Spaniel **Edge:** Milled

Date	Mintage	F	VF	XF	Unc	BU
1923	4,000	—	160	300	400	—
1929	3,262	—	160	300	400	—
1930	Inc. above	—	165	375	500	—
1931	2,994	—	160	300	400	—
1932	5,496	—	160	300	400	—
1933	4,671	—	160	300	400	—
1934	2,403	—	165	325	450	—
1935	2,577	—	160	300	450	—
1936	819	—	300	600	900	—
1937	8	—	3,000	7,500	10,000	—
1938	186	—	700	2,500	3,500	—
Note: Czech reports show mintage of 14 for Czechoslovakia and 172 for state of Slovakia						
1951	200	—	600	2,500	3,500	—

KM# 13 5 DUKATU

17.4500 g., 0.9860 Gold .5532 oz. AGW, 34 mm. **Obv:** Czech lion with Slovak shield, denomination and date below **Obv. Designer:** J. Benda **Rev:** Duke Wenceslas (Vaclav) on horseback right **Rev. Designer:** O. Spaniel **Edge:** Milled

Date	Mintage	F	VF	XF	Unc	BU
1929	1,827	—	375	650	975	—
1930	543	—	500	1,000	1,500	—
1931	1,528	—	375	650	975	—
1932	1,827	—	375	650	975	—
1933	1,752	—	375	650	975	—
1934	1,101	—	375	650	975	—
1935	1,037	—	375	650	975	—
1936	728	—	600	1,200	1,950	—
1937 Rare	4	—	—	—	—	—
1938	56	—	2,500	4,500	6,500	—
Note: Czech reports show mintage of 12 for Czechoslovakia and 44 for state of Slovakia						
1951	100	—	2,000	4,000	5,500	—

KM# 14 10 DUKATU

34.9000 g., 0.9860 Gold 1.1064 oz. AGW, 42 mm. **Obv:** Czech lion with Slovak shield, denomination and date below **Obv. Designer:** J. Benda **Rev:** Duke Wenceslas (Vaclav) on horseback right **Rev. Designer:** O. Spaniel

Date	Mintage	F	VF	XF	Unc	BU
1929	1,564	—	750	1,700	2,250	—
1930	394	—	1,000	3,000	4,000	—
1931	1,239	—	750	1,700	2,250	—
1932	1,035	—	750	1,700	2,250	—
1933	1,780	—	750	1,700	2,250	—
1934	1,298	—	750	1,900	2,500	—
1935	600	—	800	2,000	3,000	—
1936	633	—	850	2,500	3,500	—
1937 Rare	34	—	—	—	—	—
1938	192	—	2,500	7,500	10,000	—
1951	100	—	3,000	7,500	10,000	—
Note: Czech reports show mintage of 20 for Czechoslovakia and 172 for state of Slovakia.						

POST WAR COINAGE

KM# 20 20 HALERU

Bronze, 18 mm. **Obv:** Czech lion with Slovak shield, date below **Rev:** Sheaf with sickle, linden branch, denomination at left **Edge:** Plain **Designer:** O. Spaniel

Date	Mintage	F	VF	XF	Unc	BU
1947	—	65.00	125	200	300	—
1948	24,340,000	0.10	0.15	0.40	1.50	—
1949	25,660,000	0.10	0.15	0.40	1.50	—
1950	11,132,000	0.10	0.15	0.40	2.00	—

KM# 31 20 HALERU

Aluminum, 16 mm. **Obv:** Czech lion with Slovak shield, date below **Rev:** Wheat sheaf, sickle, linden branch, denomination at left **Edge:** Plain **Designer:** O. Spaniel

Date	Mintage	F	VF	XF	Unc	BU
1951	46,800,000	0.10	0.15	0.25	1.00	—
1952	80,340,000	0.10	0.15	0.25	1.00	—

KM# 21 50 HALERU

Bronze, 20 mm. **Obv:** Czech lion with Slovak shield, date below **Rev:** Linden branches and wheat sprigs bound with ribbon **Edge:** Plain **Designer:** O. Spaniel

Date	Mintage	F	VF	XF	Unc	BU
1947	50,000,000	0.15	0.25	0.40	1.00	—
1948	20,000,000	0.15	0.25	0.40	1.50	—
1949	12,715,000	0.15	0.25	0.40	2.00	—
1950	17,415,000	0.15	0.25	0.40	1.80	—

KM# 32 50 HALERU

Aluminum, 18 mm. **Obv:** Czech lion with Slovak shield, date below **Rev:** Linden branches and wheat sprigs bound with ribbon **Edge:** Plain **Designer:** O. Spaniel

Date	Mintage	F	VF	XF	Unc	BU
1951	60,000,000	0.15	0.35	0.50	0.75	—
1952	60,000,000	0.25	0.45	0.60	1.00	—
1953	34,920,000	1.00	2.50	6.00	10.00	—

KM# 19 KORUNA

Copper-Nickel, 21 mm. **Obv:** Czech lion with Slovak shield, date below **Rev:** Woman with sheaf and sickle, denomination at left **Edge:** Milled **Designer:** Otakar Spaniel

Date	Mintage	F	VF	XF	Unc	BU
1946	88,000,000	0.15	0.25	0.50	1.00	—
1947	12,550,000	1.50	2.50	3.75	6.50	—
Note: Varieties exist for "4" in 1946 strikes						

KM# 22 KORUNA

Aluminum, 21 mm. **Obv:** Czech lion with Slovak shield, date below **Rev:** Woman with sheaf and sickle, denomination at left **Edge:** Milled **Designer:** O. Spaniel

Date	Mintage	F	VF	XF	Unc	BU
1947	—	150	450	1,000	2,000	—
Note: Counterfeits, with prooflike fields, are known.						
1950	62,190,000	0.20	0.35	0.45	1.00	—
1951	61,395,000	0.20	0.35	0.45	1.25	—
1952	101,105,000	0.20	0.30	0.40	0.80	—
1953	73,905,000	0.40	0.75	1.75	4.50	—

KM# 23 2 KORUNY

Copper-Nickel, 23.5 mm. **Obv:** Czech lion with Slovak shield, date below **Rev:** Juraj Janosik bust right, wearing hat, denomination at right **Edge:** Milled **Designer:** J. Wagner

Date	Mintage	F	VF	XF	Unc	BU
1947	20,000,000	0.20	0.40	0.60	1.25	—
1948	20,476,000	0.20	0.40	0.60	1.50	—

KM# 34 5 KORUN

Aluminum, 23 mm. **Obv:** Czech lion with Slovak shield, date below **Rev:** Industrial factory and large value **Designer:** O. Guttfreund

Date	Mintage	F	VF	XF	Unc	BU
1951	—	—	300	700	1,500	—
Note: Not released for circulation. Almost the entire mintage was melted						
1952	40,715,000	25.00	50.00	90.00	140	—
Note: Weakly struck counterfeits are known						

KM# 24 50 KORUN

10.0000 g., 0.5000 Silver .1607 oz. ASW, 28 mm. **Subject:** 1944 Slovak Uprising **Obv:** Czech lion with Slovak shield **Obv. Designer:** O. Spaniel **Rev:** Veiled female standing, holding linden branch, denomination at left **Rev. Designer:** R. Pribis **Edge:** Plain with stars and waves

Date	Mintage	F	VF	XF	Unc	BU
ND(1947)	1,000,000	—	2.75	4.50	6.50	—

KM# 25 50 KORUN
10.0000 g., 0.5000 Silver .1607 oz. ASW, 28 mm. **Subject:** 3rd Anniversary - Prague Uprising **Obv:** Czech lion with Slovak shield **Rev:** Liberator divides denomination, date at right **Edge:** Plain with stars and waves **Designer:** O. Spaniel

Date	Mintage	F	VF	XF	Unc	BU
ND(1948)	1,000,000	—	2.75	4.50	6.50	—

KM# 28 50 KORUN
10.0000 g., 0.5000 Silver .1607 oz. ASW, 28 mm. **Subject:** 70th Birthday - Josef Stalin **Obv:** Czech lion with Slovak shield within lined frame, denomination above **Rev:** Uniformed bust left **Edge:** Plain with stars and waves **Designer:** O. Spaniel

Date	Mintage	F	VF	XF	Unc	BU
ND(1949)	1,000,000	—	2.75	4.50	7.00	—

KM# 26 100 KORUN
14.0000 g., 0.5000 Silver .2250 oz. ASW, 31 mm. **Subject:** 600th Anniversary - Charles University **Obv:** Czech lion with Slovak shield, date below **Rev:** King Charles kneeling before Duke Wenceslas, two shields at left, denomination below **Designer:** O. Spaniel

Date	Mintage	F	VF	XF	Unc	BU
1948	1,000,000	—	3.25	4.75	7.50	—

KM# 27 100 KORUN
14.0000 g., 0.5000 Silver .2250 oz. ASW, 31 mm. **Subject:** 30th Anniversary of Independence **Obv:** Czech lion with Slovak shield within lined frame **Rev:** Man with flag and laurel branch divides dates, denomination below **Edge:** Plain with stars and waves **Designer:** O. Spaniel

Date	Mintage	F	VF	XF	Unc	BU
ND(1948)	1,000,000	—	3.25	4.75	7.50	—

KM# 29 100 KORUN
14.0000 g., 0.5000 Silver .2250 oz. ASW, 31 mm. **Subject:** 700th Anniversary - Jihlava Mining Privileges **Obv:** Czech lion with Slovak shield above inscription and date **Rev:** Seated figure, denomination below **Edge:** Plain with stars and waves **Designer:** O. Spaniel

Date	Mintage	F	VF	XF	Unc	BU
1949	1,000,000	—	3.25	4.75	7.50	—

KM# 30 100 KORUN
14.0000 g., 0.5000 Silver .2250 oz. ASW, 31 mm. **Subject:** 70th Birthday - Josef V. Stalin **Obv:** Czech lion with Slovak shield, denomination above **Rev:** Uniformed bust left, date at right **Edge:** Plain with stars and waves **Designer:** O. Spaniel

Date	Mintage	F	VF	XF	Unc	BU
ND(1949)	1,000,000	—	3.25	4.75	7.50	—

KM# 33 100 KORUN
14.0000 g., 0.5000 Silver .2250 oz. ASW, 31 mm. **Subject:** 30th Anniversary - Communist party **Obv:** Czech lion with Slovak shield, denomination above **Rev:** Party Chairman bust right divides dates **Edge:** Plain with stars and waves **Designer:** O. Spaniel

Date	Mintage	F	VF	XF	Unc	BU
ND(1951)	1,000,000	—	3.25	4.75	7.50	—

PEOPLES REPUBLIC

DECIMAL COINAGE

KM# 35 HALER
Aluminum, 16 mm. **Obv:** Czech lion with Slovak shield, date below **Rev:** Large denomination within linden wreath, star above **Edge:** Plain

Date	Mintage	F	VF	XF	Unc	BU
1953	188,885,000	—	—	0.10	0.25	—
1954	—	—	—	0.10	0.25	—
1955	—	—	—	0.15	0.50	—
1956	—	—	—	0.10	0.25	—
1957	—	—	—	0.10	0.25	—
1958	—	0.10	0.25	0.35	0.75	—
1959	—	—	—	0.15	0.50	—
1960	—	—	—	0.10	0.25	—

KM# 36 3 HALERE
Aluminum, 18 mm. **Obv:** Czech lion with Slovak shield, date below **Rev:** Large denomination within linden wreath, star above **Edge:** Plain

Date	Mintage	F	VF	XF	Unc	BU
1953	90,001,000	—	0.10	0.15	0.30	—
1954	Inc. above	—	0.10	0.15	0.30	—

KM# 37 5 HALERU
Aluminum, 20 mm. **Obv:** Czech lion with Slovak shield, date below **Rev:** Large denomination within linden wreath, star above **Edge:** Plain

Date	Mintage	F	VF	XF	Unc	BU
1953	160,233,000	0.10	0.15	0.25	0.50	—
1954	Inc. above	0.10	0.15	0.25	0.50	—
1955	Inc. above	1.50	3.50	30.00	120	—

KM# 38 10 HALERU
Aluminum, 22 mm. **Obv:** Czech lion with Slovak shield, date below **Rev:** Large denomination within linden wreath, star above

Date	Mintage	F	VF	XF	Unc	BU
1953	160,000	0.10	0.15	1.00	5.00	—
Note: Leningrad Mint-133 notches in milled edge						
1953	—	0.10	0.15	1.00	5.00	—
Note: Unknown Mint-125 notches in milled edge						
1954	—	0.25	0.50	2.00	7.00	—
1955	—	0.50	2.50	12.00	50.00	—
1956	—	0.10	0.15	1.00	5.00	—
1958	—	2.00	5.00	25.00	70.00	—

KM# 39 25 HALERU
Aluminum, 24 mm. **Obv:** Czech lion with Slovak shield, date below **Rev:** Large denomination within linden wreath, star above

Date	Mintage	F	VF	XF	Unc	BU
1953	Inc. above	0.30	0.50	0.60	6.00	—
Note: Leningrad Mint - 145 notches in milled edge						
1953	215,002,000	0.10	0.20	0.30	4.00	—
Note: Kremnica Mint - 134 notches in milled edge						
1954	Inc. above	9.00	18.00	35.00	140	—

KM# 46 KORUNA
Aluminum-Bronze, 23 mm. **Obv:** Czech lion with Slovak shield, date below **Rev:** Woman kneeling planting linden tree, denomination at left **Rev. Designer:** M. Uchitilova-Kucova **Edge:** Milled

Date	Mintage	F	VF	XF	Unc	BU
1957	137,000,000	0.20	0.30	0.45	5.00	—
1958	Inc. above	0.20	0.30	0.45	7.00	—
1959	Inc. above	0.15	0.25	0.35	4.50	—
1960	Inc. above	0.15	0.25	0.35	4.50	—

KM# 40 10 KORUN
12.0000 g., 0.5000 Silver .1929 oz. ASW, 30 mm. **Subject:** 10th Anniversary - Slovak Uprising **Obv:** Czech lion with Slovak shield **Obv. Designer:** O. Spaniel **Rev:** Soldier standing right, train and construction site in background, denomination at left, dates below **Rev. Designer:** R. Pribis **Edge:** Milled **Note:** 65,810 pieces, Unc and Proof, were melted by the Czech National Bank in 1999.

Date	Mintage	F	VF	XF	Unc	BU
ND(1954)	250,000	—	2.75	3.75	6.50	—
ND(1954) Proof	5,000	Value: 12.00				

KM# 42 10 KORUN

12.0000 g., 0.5000 Silver .1929 oz. ASW, 30 mm. **Subject:** 10th Anniversary - Liberation from Germany **Obv:** Czech lion with Slovak shield **Rev:** Soldier kneeling left holding child, denomination at left, dates at right **Edge:** Milled **Designer:** F. David **Note:** 95,552 pieces Unc and Proof, were melted by the Czech National Bank in 1999.

Date	Mintage	F	VF	XF	Unc	BU
ND(1955)	300,000	—	2.75	3.75	6.50	—
ND(1955) Proof	5,000	Value: 14.50				

KM# 48 10 KORUN

12.0000 g., 0.5000 Silver .1929 oz. ASW, 30 mm. **Obv:** Czech lion with Slovak shield, date above **Rev:** Bust right of the Bishop of the Moravian Brotherhood, denomination below **Edge:** Milled **Designer:** F. David **Note:** 7,854 pieces Unc and Proof, were melted by the Czech National Bank in 1999.

Date	Mintage	F	VF	XF	Unc	BU
1957	150,000	—	2.75	3.75	7.00	—
1957 Proof	5,000	Value: 14.50				

KM# 47.1 10 KORUN

12.0000 g., 0.5000 Silver .1929 oz. ASW, 30 mm. **Subject:** 250th Anniversary - Technical College **Obv:** Czech lion with Slovak shield, denomination below **Rev:** Bust left, hand on chin **Edge:** Plain with stars and waves **Designer:** F. David **Note:** Raised designer initials.

Date	Mintage	F	VF	XF	Unc	BU
1957	75,000	—	2.75	3.75	7.50	—

Note: See note below KM#47.2

KM# 47.2 10 KORUN

12.0000 g., 0.5000 Silver .1929 oz. ASW, 30 mm. **Obv:** Czech lion with Slovak shield **Rev:** Bust left, hand on chin **Designer:** F. David **Note:** Incuse designer initials.

Date	Mintage	F	VF	XF	Unc	BU
1957 Proof	Est. 5,000	Value: 14.50				

Note: 238 pieces, Unc and Proof, were melted by the Czech National Bank in 1999

KM# 41 25 KORUN

16.0000 g., 0.5000 Silver .2572 oz. ASW, 34 mm. **Subject:** 10th Anniversary - Slovak Unprising **Obv:** State emblem: Czech lion with Slovak shield **Obv. Designer:** O. Spaniel **Rev:** Soldier standing right, train and construction site in background, denomination at left, dates below **Rev. Designer:** R. Pribis **Edge:** Milled **Note:** 110,933 Pieces, Unc and Proof, were melted by the Czech National Bank in 1999.

Date	Mintage	F	VF	XF	Unc	BU
ND(1954)	250,000	—	—	5.00	8.00	—
ND(1954) Proof	Est. 5,000	Value: 25.00				

KM# 43 25 KORUN

16.0000 g., 0.5000 Silver .2572 oz. ASW, 34 mm. **Subject:** 10th Anniversary - Liberation from Germany **Obv:** Czech lion with Slovak shield **Rev:** Mother and child greeting soldier divides dates and denomination **Edge:** Milled **Designer:** F. David **Note:** 78,643 pieces, Unc and Proof, were melted by the Czech National Bank in 1999.

Date	Mintage	F	VF	XF	Unc	BU
ND(1955)	200,000	—	—	5.00	8.00	—
ND(1955) Proof	5,000	Value: 25.00				

KM# 44 50 KORUN

20.0000 g., 0.9000 Silver .5787 oz. ASW, 37 mm. **Subject:** 10th Anniversary - Liberation from Germany **Obv:** Czech lion with Slovak shield **Rev:** Soldier with rifle raised divides dates, denomination lower right **Edge:** Milled **Designer:** A. Sopr **Note:** 36,650 pieces were melted by the Czech National Bank in 1999.

Date	Mintage	F	VF	XF	Unc	BU
1955	120,000	—	8.00	10.00	17.50	—

KM# 45 100 KORUN

24.0000 g., 0.9000 Silver .6945 oz. ASW, 40 mm. **Subject:** 10th Anniversary - Liberation from Germany **Obv:** Czech lion with Slovak shield within circle **Rev:** Father and young boy greeting two returning soldiers, dates divided at top, denomination below **Designer:** Jaroslav Bruha **Note:** 22,244 pieces were melted by the Czech National Bank in 1999.

Date	Mintage	F	VF	XF	Unc	BU
ND(1955)	Est. 75,000	—	11.50	16.50	32.50	40.00

SOCIALIST REPUBLIC

DECIMAL COINAGE

KM# 51 HALER

Aluminum, 16 mm. **Obv:** Czech lion with socialist shield within shield, date below **Rev:** Denomination within linden wreath, star above **Edge:** Plain

Date	Mintage	F	VF	XF	Unc	BU
1962	20,056,000	—	—	0.10	0.15	—
1963	Inc. above	—	—	0.10	0.15	—
1986	3,360,000	—	—	—	1.00	—

KM# 52 3 HALERE

Aluminum, 18 mm. **Obv:** Czech lion with socialist shield within shield, date below **Rev:** Denomination within linden wreath, star above **Edge:** Plain

Date	Mintage	F	VF	XF	Unc	BU
1962	Inc. below	100	150	200	280	—
	Note: Counterfeits, with prooflike fields, are known.					
1963	5,130,000	—	—	0.10	0.15	—

KM# 53 5 HALERU

Aluminum, 20 mm. **Obv:** Czech lion with socialist shield within shield, date below **Rev:** Denomination within linden wreath, star above **Edge:** Plain

Date	Mintage	F	VF	XF	Unc	BU
1962	55,150,000	—	0.10	0.15	0.25	—
1963	Inc. above	—	0.10	0.15	0.25	—
1966	Inc. above	—	0.10	0.15	0.25	—
1967	20,770,000	—	0.10	0.15	0.25	—
1970	5,090,000	—	0.10	0.15	0.20	—
1972	10,090,000	—	0.10	0.15	0.20	—
1973	10,140,000	—	0.10	0.15	0.20	—
1974	15,510,000	—	0.10	0.15	0.20	—
1975	15,510,000	—	0.10	0.15	0.20	—
1976	15,550,000	—	0.10	0.15	0.20	—

KM# 53a 5 HALERU

2.0000 g., Brass **Obv:** Czech lion with socialist shield within shield **Rev:** Value within linden wreath, star above

Date	Mintage	F	VF	XF	Unc	BU
1967	Est. 20	—	—	300	500	—

KM# 86 5 HALERU

Aluminum, 16.2 mm. **Obv:** Czech lion with socialist shield within shield, date below **Rev:** Large denomination, star above **Edge:** Plain **Designer:** F. David

Date	Mintage	F	VF	XF	Unc	BU
1977	26,710,000	—	—	0.10	0.25	—
1978	51,110,000	—	—	0.10	0.25	—
1979	72,380,000	—	—	0.10	0.25	—
1980	50,600	—	—	—	0.25	—
	Note: In sets only					
1981	66,160	—	—	—	0.50	—
	Note: In sets only					
1982	53,847	—	—	—	1.00	—
	Note: In sets only					
1983	60,000	—	—	—	0.50	—
	Note: In sets only					
1984	39,957	—	—	—	0.75	—
	Note: In sets only					
1985	39,791	—	—	—	0.75	—
	Note: In sets only					
1986	20,020,000	—	—	0.10	0.25	—
1987	520,000	—	—	0.10	0.35	—
1988	8,029,999	—	—	0.10	0.25	—
1989	110,000	—	—	0.10	0.50	—
1990	13,950,000	—	—	0.10	0.25	—

KM# 49.1 10 HALERU

Aluminum **Obv:** Star above Czech lion with socialist shield within shield **Rev:** Large denomination within linden wreath, star above

Date	Mintage	F	VF	XF	Unc	BU
1961	314,480,000	—	0.10	0.20	0.35	—
1962	Inc. above	—	0.10	0.20	0.35	—
1963	Inc. above	—	0.10	0.20	0.35	—
1964	Inc. above	—	0.10	0.20	0.35	—
1965	Inc. above	—	0.10	0.20	0.35	—
1966	Inc. above	—	0.10	0.20	0.35	—
1967	46,990,000	—	0.10	0.20	0.35	—
1968	37,275,000	—	0.10	0.20	0.35	—
1969	80,000,000	—	0.10	0.15	0.35	—
1970	50,005,000	—	0.10	0.20	0.35	—
1971	30,450,000	—	0.10	0.20	0.35	—

KM# 49.2 10 HALERU

Aluminum, 22 mm. **Obv:** Star above Czech lion with socialist shield within shield, flat-top 3 in date below **Rev:** Denomination within linden wreath, star above **Note:** Obverse muled from 50 Haleru, KM 55.1.

Date	Mintage	F	VF	XF	Unc	BU
1963	Est. 3,600	12.50	25.00	60.00	150	—

Note: Weakly struck counterfeits are known.

KM# 49.1a 10 HALERU

2.4000 g., Brass **Obv:** Star above Czech lion with socialist shield within shield **Rev:** Large denomination within linden wreath, star above

Date	Mintage	F	VF	XF	Unc	BU
1968	Est. 20	—	—	300	500	—

KM# 80 10 HALERU

Aluminum, 18.2 mm. **Obv:** Czech lion with socialist shield within shield, fat date below **Rev:** Large thick denomination, star above **Designer:** F. David **Note:** Varieties exist.

Date	Mintage	F	VF	XF	Unc	BU
1974	11,470,000	—	—	0.10	0.25	—
1975	41,002,000	—	—	0.10	0.25	—
1976	182,000,000	—	—	0.10	0.25	—
1977	151,760,000	—	—	0.10	0.25	—
1978	62,620,000	—	—	0.10	0.25	—
1979	30,240,000	—	—	0.10	0.25	—
1980	31,280,000	—	—	0.10	0.25	—
1981	43,616,160	—	—	0.10	0.25	—
1982	74,568,847	—	—	0.10	0.25	—
1983	50,560,000	—	—	0.10	0.25	—
1984	40,369,957	—	—	0.10	0.25	—
1985	92,929,791	—	—	0.10	0.25	—
1986	87,260,000	—	—	0.10	0.25	—
1987	30,030,000	—	—	0.10	0.25	—
1988	47,479,999	—	—	0.10	0.25	—
1989	50,300,000	—	—	0.10	0.25	—
1990	25,220,000	—	—	0.10	0.25	—

KM# 74 20 HALERU

Brass, 19.5 mm. **Obv:** Czech lion with socialist shield within shield, thick date below **Rev:** Large thick denomination, star above **Designer:** F. David **Note:** Varieties exist.

Date	Mintage	F	VF	XF	Unc	BU
1972	25,820,000	—	0.10	0.20	0.40	—
1973	39,095,000	—	0.10	0.20	0.40	—
1974	24,795,000	—	0.10	0.20	0.40	—
1975	30,025,000	—	0.10	0.20	0.40	—
1976	30,540,000	—	0.10	0.20	0.40	—
1977	30,655,000	—	0.10	0.20	0.40	—
1978	30,095,000	—	0.10	0.20	0.40	—
1979	12,120,000	—	0.10	0.20	0.40	—
1980	52,301,000	—	0.10	0.15	0.30	—
1981	35,126,160	—	0.10	0.15	0.30	—
1982	41,238,847	—	0.10	0.15	0.30	—
1983	50,160,000	—	0.10	0.15	0.30	—
1984	33,684,957	—	0.10	0.15	0.30	—
1985	40,454,791	—	0.10	0.15	0.30	—
1986	37,055,000	—	0.10	0.15	0.30	—
1987	26,975,000	—	0.10	0.15	0.30	—
1988	18,259,999	—	0.10	0.15	0.30	—
1989	29,980,000	—	0.10	0.15	0.30	—
1990	15,030,000	—	0.10	0.15	0.30	—

KM# 54 25 HALERU

Aluminum, 24 mm. **Obv:** Czech lion with socialist shield within shield, date below **Rev:** Large denomination within linden wreath, star above **Edge:** Milled **Note:** This denomination ceased to be legal tender in 1972.

Date	Mintage	F	VF	XF	Unc	BU
1962	69,880,000	0.10	0.15	0.20	0.35	—
1963	Inc. above	0.10	0.15	0.20	0.35	—
1964	Inc. above	0.10	0.15	0.20	0.35	—

KM# 55.1 50 HALERU

Bronze, 21.5 mm. **Obv:** Czech lion with socialist shield within shield, date below **Rev:** Large denomination within linden wreath, star above

Date	Mintage	F	VF	XF	Unc	BU
1963	80,560,000	0.10	0.20	0.30	0.45	—
1964	Inc. above	0.10	0.20	0.30	0.45	—
1965	Inc. above	0.10	0.20	0.30	0.45	—
1969	9,876,000	0.10	0.20	0.30	0.45	—
1970	31,536,000	0.10	0.20	0.30	0.40	—
1971	20,800,000	0.10	0.20	0.30	0.40	—

KM# 55.2 50 HALERU

Bronze, 21.5 mm. **Obv:** Czech lion with socialist shield within shield, small date, without dots **Rev:** Value within linden wreath, star above **Note:** Obverse muled with 10 Haleru, KM 49.1.

Date	Mintage	F	VF	XF	Unc	BU
1969	—	12.50	22.50	40.00	75.00	—

KM# 89 50 HALERU

Copper-Nickel, 20.8 mm. **Obv:** Czech lion with socialist shield within shield, thick date below **Rev:** Thick denomination, star above **Edge:** Milled **Designer:** F. David **Note:** Date varieties exist.

Date	Mintage	F	VF	XF	Unc	BU
1977	Est. 5	—	—	500	1,000	—
1978	40,480,000	—	—	0.10	0.50	—
1979	76,116,000	—	—	0.10	0.50	—
1980	51,000	—	—	—	1.50	—
Note: In sets only						
1981	66,000	—	—	—	1.50	—
Note: In sets only						
1982	14,261,847	—	—	0.10	0.50	—
1983	16,168,000	—	—	0.10	0.50	—
1984	16,207,957	—	—	0.10	0.50	—
1985	10,467,791	—	—	0.10	0.50	—
1986	10,020,000	—	—	0.10	0.50	—
1987	5,138,000	—	—	0.10	0.50	—
1988	5,089,999	—	—	0.10	0.50	—
1989	13,030,000	—	—	0.10	0.50	—
1990	7,742,000	—	—	0.10	0.50	—

KM# 50 KORUNA

Aluminum-Bronze, 23 mm. **Obv:** Czech lion with socialist shield within shield, date below **Rev:** Woman planting linden tree, denomination at left **Rev. Designer:** Marie Uchytilova-Kucova **Edge:** Milled **Note:** Date varieties exist.

Date	Mintage	F	VF	XF	Unc	BU
1961	146,964,000	—	0.15	0.30	0.60	—
1962	Inc. above	—	0.15	0.30	0.60	—
1963	Inc. above	—	0.15	0.30	0.60	—
1964	Inc. above	—	0.15	0.30	0.60	—
1965	Inc. above	—	0.15	0.30	0.60	—
1966	Inc. above	0.40	0.65	0.90	1.25	—
1967	7,924,000	—	0.15	0.30	0.60	—
1968	10,696,000	—	0.15	0.30	0.60	—
1969	21,820,000	—	0.15	0.30	0.60	—
1970	31,036,000	—	0.15	0.30	0.60	—
1971	10,152,000	—	0.15	0.30	0.60	—
1975	6,657,000	—	0.15	0.30	0.60	—
1976	14,211,000	—	0.15	0.30	0.60	—
1977	10,434,000	—	0.15	0.30	0.75	—
1979	Inc. below	—	0.15	0.30	0.75	—
1980	24,513,000	—	0.15	0.30	0.75	—
1981	7,179,000	—	0.15	0.30	0.75	—
1982	17,162,847	—	0.15	0.30	0.75	—
1983	4,758,000	—	0.15	0.30	0.75	—
1984	9,732,957	—	0.15	0.30	0.75	—
1985	10,545,751	—	0.15	0.30	0.75	—
1986	2,789,000	—	0.15	0.30	0.75	—
1987	30,000	—	—	—	2.50	—
Note: In sets only						
1988	29,999	—	—	—	2.50	—
Note: In sets only						

Date	Mintage	F	VF	XF	Unc	BU
1989	1,038,000	—	0.15	0.30	0.75	—
1990	19,368,000	—	0.15	0.30	0.75	—

KM# 75 2 KORUNY

Copper-Nickel, 24 mm. **Obv:** Czech lion with socialist shield within shield, date below **Rev:** Star above hammer and sickle, large value at right **Edge:** Plain with crosses and waves **Designer:** J. Nalepa

Date	Mintage	F	VF	XF	Unc	BU
1972	20,344,000	—	0.25	0.45	1.00	—
1973	21,087,000	—	0.25	0.45	1.00	—
Note: 1973 date exists with edge of 5 Korun KM#60, value: $15.00						
1974	27,957,000	—	0.25	0.45	1.00	—
1975	35,094,000	—	0.25	0.45	1.00	—
1976	1,100,000	—	0.25	0.45	1.00	—
1977	4,201,000	—	0.25	0.65	1.50	—
1980	14,943,000	—	0.25	0.35	0.75	—
1981	17,264,000	—	0.25	0.35	0.75	—
1982	8,108,000	—	0.25	0.35	0.75	—
1983	10,190,000	—	0.25	0.35	0.75	—
1984	8,634,000	—	0.25	0.35	0.75	—
1985	6,772,000	—	0.25	0.35	0.75	—
1986	10,262,000	—	0.25	0.35	0.75	—
1987 In mint sets only	30,000	—	—	—	2.50	—
1988 In mint sets only	30,000	—	—	—	2.50	—
1989	9,092,000	—	0.25	0.35	0.75	—
1990	10,672,000	—	0.25	0.35	0.75	—

KM# 57 3 KORUNY

Copper-Nickel, 23.5 mm. **Obv:** Czech lion with socialist shield within shield, date below **Obv. Designer:** Zdenek Kolarsky **Rev:** Branch of five linden leaves within banner, large value at right **Rev. Designer:** E. Hajek **Edge:** Plain with lime leaves and waves

Date	Mintage	F	VF	XF	Unc	BU
1965	15,000,000	—	0.50	1.00	2.50	—
1966	Inc. above	—	0.50	1.00	2.50	—
1968	7,000,000	—	0.45	0.85	2.00	—
1969	10,080,000	—	0.40	0.75	1.50	—

KM# 60 5 KORUN

Copper-Nickel, 26 mm. **Obv:** Czech lion with socialist shield within shield, date below **Rev:** Geometric design and large denomination **Edge:** Plain with rhombs and waves **Designer:** J. Harcuba

Date	Mintage	F	VF	XF	Unc	BU
1966	6,383,000	—	0.75	1.00	2.00	—
Note: 1966 varieties on obverse of coin: large date: no space between letter B in REPUBLIC and coat of arms; small date: space between letter B in REPUBLIC and coat of arms; plain edge: no ornamental inscription on edge (error coin). So far there has been no indication of any of the varieties as being scarce						
1967	4,544,000	—	—	0.75	1.50	—
1968	14,120,000	—	—	0.75	1.50	—
1969	5,486,000	—	—	0.75	1.50	—
Note: Straight date						
1969	Inc. above	0.75	1.50	5.00	9.00	—
Note: Date in semi-circle						
1970	10,073,000	—	—	0.75	1.50	—
1973	15,620,000	—	—	0.75	1.25	—
Note: Two variations in 3 of date						
1974	20,053,000	—	—	0.75	1.25	—
Note: Three variations in 4 of date						
1975	17,158,000	—	—	0.75	1.25	—
1978	5,317,000	—	—	0.75	1.25	—
1979	9,219,000	—	—	0.75	1.25	—
1980	12,559,000	—	—	0.75	1.25	—
1981	8,620,160	—	—	0.75	1.25	—
1982	6,903,847	—	—	0.75	1.25	—
1983	6,704,000	—	—	0.75	1.25	—
1984	6,856,957	—	—	0.75	1.25	—
1985	6,763,791	—	—	0.75	1.25	—

Date	Mintage	F	VF	XF	Unc	BU
1986	20,000	—	—	—	35.00	—
Note: In sets only						
1987	30,000	—	—	—	7.00	—
Note: In sets only						
1988	29,999	—	—	—	5.00	—
1989	5,039,000	—	—	0.75	1.25	—
1990	2,783,000	—	—	0.75	1.25	—

KM# 56 10 KORUN

12.0000 g., 0.5000 Silver .1929 oz. ASW, 30 mm. **Subject:** 20th Anniversary - 1944 Slovak Uprising **Obv:** Star above Czech lion with socialist shield within shield **Obv. Designer:** A. Havelka **Rev:** Three hands and linden sprig divide dates and denomination **Rev. Designer:** Z. Kolarsky **Edge Lettering:** SLOVENSKE NARODNE POVSTANIE **Note:** 11,476 pieces were melted by the Czech National Bank in 1999.

Date	Mintage	F	VF	XF	Unc	BU
ND(1964)	120,000	—	—	3.50	5.50	—

KM# 58 10 KORUN

12.0000 g., 0.5000 Silver .1929 oz. ASW, 30 mm. **Subject:** 550th Anniversary - Death of Jan Hus **Obv:** Star above Czech lion with socialist shield within shield **Obv. Designer:** Z. Kolarsky **Rev:** Bust right, denomination below **Rev. Designer:** K. Lidicky **Edge Lettering:** 550 LET UPALENI M, JANA HUSA **Note:** 380 pieces, Unc and Proof, were melted by the Czech National Bank in 1999.

Date	Mintage	F	VF	XF	Unc	BU
ND(1965) Proof	5,000	Value: 20.00				
ND(1965)	55,000	—	—	7.00	15.00	—

KM# 61 10 KORUN

12.0000 g., 0.5000 Silver .1929 oz. ASW, 30 mm. **Subject:** 1100th Anniversary of Great Moravia **Obv:** Star above Czech lion with socialist shield within shield **Obv. Designer:** L. Ruzicka **Rev:** Medal with horseman with falcon and plot of church, denomination upper right **Rev. Designer:** Lubos Ruzicka and Jan Solpera **Edge:** Plain with ellipse and rings **Note:** 9,446 pieces, Unc and Proof, were melted by the Czech National Bank in 1999.

Date	Mintage	F	VF	XF	Unc	BU
1966 Proof	5,000	Value: 12.50				
1966	115,000	—	—	4.00	6.50	—

KM# 62 10 KORUN

12.0000 g., 0.5000 Silver .1929 oz. ASW, 30 mm. **Subject:** 500th Anniversary - Bratislava University **Obv:** Czech lion with socialist shield above stylized three mountains and river, denomination below **Rev:** University seal and building, date lower right **Edge:** Plain with Rhombs and waves **Designer:** Z. Kolarsky **Note:** 103 pieces, Unc and Proof, were melted by the Czech National Bank in 1999.

Date	Mintage	F	VF	XF	Unc	BU
ND(1967)	45,000	—	—	10.00	20.00	—
ND(1967) Proof	500	Value: 22.50				

KM# 63 10 KORUN

12.0000 g., 0.5000 Silver .1929 oz. ASW, 30 mm. **Subject:** Centennial - Prague (Praha) National Theater **Obv:** Czech lion with socialist shield within shield, denomination below **Rev:** Female goddess in three-horse chariot, dates below **Edge:** Plain with crosses and waves **Designer:** J. Harcuba **Note:** 50 pieces, Unc and Proof, were melted by the Czech National Bank in 1999.

Date	Mintage	F	VF	XF	Unc	BU
ND(1968)	55,000	—	—	15.00	20.00	—
ND(1968) Proof	5,000	Value: 40.00				

KM# 76 20 KORUN

9.0000 g., 0.5000 Silver .1446 oz. ASW, 29 mm. **Subject:** Centennial - Death of Andrej Sladkovic **Obv:** Czech lion with socialist shield within shield, denomination below **Rev:** Head left, dates below **Designer:** J. Kulich **Note:** 3,842 pieces, Unc and Proof, were melted by the Czech National Bank in 1999.

Date	Mintage	F	VF	XF	Unc	BU
ND(1972)	55,000	—	—	3.50	5.50	—
ND(1972) Proof	5,000	Value: 12.50				

KM# 59 25 KORUN

16.0000 g., 0.5000 Silver .2572 oz. ASW, 34 mm. **Subject:** 20th Anniversary - Czechoslovakian Liberation **Obv:** Czech lion with socialist shield within shield **Rev:** Female head left, dove with linden branch, denomination below, dates above and left **Edge Lettering:** 20 LET OSVOBOZENI CSSR **Designer:** Zdenek Kolarsky **Note:** 18,114 pieces, Unc and Proof, were melted by the Czech National Bank in 1999.

Date	Mintage	F	VF	XF	Unc	BU
ND(1965)	150,000	—	—	4.00	6.50	—
ND(1965) Proof	5,000	Value: 12.50				

KM# 64 25 KORUN

16.0000 g., 0.5000 Silver .2572 oz. ASW, 34 mm. **Subject:** 150th Anniversary - Prague (Praha) National Museum **Obv:** Czech lion with socialist shield within shield, three line inscription below **Rev:** National Museum building, denomination below **Edge:** Plain with crosses and waves **Designer:** M. Knobloch **Note:** 151 pieces, Unc and Proof, were melted by the Czech National Bank in 1999.

Date	Mintage	F	VF	XF	Unc	BU
ND(1968)	51,000	—	—	4.50	9.00	—
ND(1968) Proof	5,000	Value: 40.00				

KM# 66 25 KORUN

16.0000 g., 0.5000 Silver .2572 oz. ASW, 34 mm. **Subject:** 100th Anniversary - Death of J. E. Purkyne **Obv:** Czech lion with socialist shield within shield, denomination below **Obv. Designer:** J. Dostal **Rev:** Head right, dates at right **Rev. Designer:** J. Harcuba **Edge Lettering:** FYSIOLOG, FILOSOF, BUDITEL, BASNIK **Note:** Edge varieties exist; 140 pieces, Unc and Proof, were melted by the Czech National Bank in 1999.

Date	Mintage	F	VF	XF	Unc	BU
ND(1969) Proof	5,000	Value: 28.00				
ND(1969)	45,000	—	—	4.00	8.00	—

KM# 67 25 KORUN

16.0000 g., 0.5000 Silver .2572 oz. ASW, 34 mm. **Subject:** 25th Anniversary - 1944 Slovak Uprising **Obv:** Czech lion with socialist shield within shield, three line inscription and denomination below **Rev:** Three mountains and plant, date at top **Edge Lettering:** 25. VYROCIE SLOVENSKEHO NARODNEHO POVSTANIA **Designer:** J. Harcuba **Note:** Edge varieties exist; 40 pieces, Unc and Proof, were melted by the Czech National Bank in 1999.

Date	Mintage	F	VF	XF	Unc	BU
ND(1969)	25,000	—	—	45.00	75.00	—
ND(1969) Proof	5,000	Value: 95.00				

KM# 68 25 KORUN

10.0000 g., 0.5000 Silver .1607 oz. ASW, 30 mm. **Subject:** 50th Anniversary - Slovak National Theater **Obv:** Czech lion with socialist shield within square, denomination below **Obv. Designer:** Z. Kolarsky **Rev:** Stylized head of muse within square divides dates **Rev. Designer:** I. Strnad **Note:** 4,923 pieces, Unc and Proof, were melted by the Czech National Bank in 1999.

Date	Mintage	F	VF	XF	Unc	BU
ND(1970) Proof	5,000	Value: 60.00				
ND(1970)	45,000	—	—	5.00	10.00	—

KM# 69 25 KORUN

10.0000 g., 0.5000 Silver .1607 oz. ASW, 30 mm. **Subject:** 25th Anniversary of Liberation **Obv:** Czech lion with socialist shield within shield, three line inscription below **Obv. Designer:** I. Strnad **Rev:** Sun of Liberation, landscape, denomination below **Rev. Designer:** Z. Kovarsky **Edge:** - x - **Note:** 23,777 pieces, Unc and Proof, were melted by the Czech National Bank in 1999.

Date	Mintage	F	VF	XF	Unc	BU
ND(1970)	95,000	—	—	4.00	6.00	—
ND(1970) Proof	5,000	Value: 15.00				

KM# 65 50 KORUN

20.0000 g., 0.9000 Silver .5787 oz. ASW, 37 mm. **Subject:** 50th Anniversary of Czechoslovakia 20th Anniversary - People's Republic **Obv:** Czech lion with socialist shield divides dates, inscription and denomination below **Obv. Designer:** Imra Svitana and Jan Zoricak **Rev:** Woman's head left, wearing linden and floral wreath, date at left **Rev. Designer:** J. Harcuba **Note:** 650 pieces, Unc and Proof, were melted by the Czech National Bank in 1999.

Date	Mintage	F	VF	XF	Unc	BU
ND(1968)	58,000	—	—	18.00	32.00	40.00
ND(1968) Proof	2,000	Value: 75.00				

KM# 70 50 KORUN

13.0000 g., 0.7000 Silver .2926 oz. ASW, 31 mm. **Subject:** Centennial - Birth of Lenin **Obv:** Czech lion with socialist shield within shield, denomination below **Rev:** Head right, date at left **Designer:** F. David **Note:** 451 pieces, Unc and Proof, were melted by the Czech National Bank in 1999.

Date	Mintage	F	VF	XF	Unc	BU
ND(1970) Proof	6,200	Value: 30.00				
ND(1970)	44,000	—	—	4.50	8.50	—

KM# 71 50 KORUN

13.0000 g., 0.7000 Silver .2926 oz. ASW, 31 mm. **Subject:** 50th Anniversary - Czechoslovak Communist Party **Obv:** Czech lion with socialist shield within shield, denomination below **Rev:** Five figures standing within hammer and sickle, star above, dates below **Edge:** Wave, star, wave **Designer:** Jan Kulich **Note:** 4,850 pieces, Unc and Proof, were melted by the Czech National Bank in 1999.

Date	Mintage	F	VF	XF	Unc	BU
ND(1971)	45,000	—	—	4.50	8.50	—
ND(1971) Proof	5,000	Value: 22.00				

KM# 72 50 KORUN

13.0000 g., 0.7000 Silver .2926 oz. ASW, 31 mm. **Subject:** 50th Anniversary - Death of Pavol Orsagh-Hviezdoslav **Obv:** Czech lion with socialist shield within shield, denomination below **Rev:** Head left, dates at right **Designer:** F. David **Note:** 4,300 pieces, Unc and Proof, were melted by the Czech National Bank in 1999.

Date	Mintage	F	VF	XF	Unc	BU
ND(1971)	45,000	—	—	4.25	7.50	—
ND(1971) Proof	5,000	Value: 20.00				

KM# 77 50 KORUN

13.0000 g., 0.7000 Silver .2926 oz. ASW, 31 mm. **Subject:** 50th Anniversary - Death of J. V. Myslbek **Obv:** Czech lion with socialist shield within shield, denomination below **Obv. Designer:** A. Peter **Rev:** Head left, dates at right **Rev. Designer:** L. Picha **Edge Lettering:** J. V. MYSLBEK *1922-1972* **Note:** 6,439 pieces, Unc and Proof, were melted by the Czech National Bank in 1999.

Date	Mintage	F	VF	XF	Unc	BU
ND(1972) Proof	5,000	Value: 20.00				
ND(1972)	45,000	—	—	4.25	7.50	—

KM# 78 50 KORUN

13.0000 g., 0.7000 Silver .2926 oz. ASW, 31 mm. **Subject:** 25th Anniversary - Victory of Communist Party **Obv:** Czech lion with socialist shield within shield **Obv. Designer:** F. David **Rev:** Soldier standing before large star, hammer and sickle at right **Rev. Designer:** I. Liptak **Edge Lettering:** 25. VYROCI VITEZNEHO UNORA* **Note:** 5,340 pieces, Unc and Proof, were melted by the Czech National Bank in 1999.

Date	Mintage	F	VF	XF	Unc	BU
ND(1973)	55,000	—	—	4.25	7.50	—
ND(1973) Proof	5,000	Value: 20.00				

KM# 79 50 KORUN

13.0000 g., 0.7000 Silver .2926 oz. ASW, 31 mm. **Subject:** 200th Anniversary - Birth of Josef Jungmann **Obv:** Czech lion with socialist shield within shield, denomination below **Rev:** Head right, dates below **Designer:** P. Formanek **Note:** 2,084 pieces, Unc and Proof, were melted by the Czech National Bank in 1999.

Date	Mintage	F	VF	XF	Unc	BU
ND(1973)	45,000	—	—	4.25	7.50	—
ND(1973) Proof	5,000	Value: 11.50				

KM# 81 50 KORUN

13.0000 g., 0.7000 Silver .2926 oz. ASW, 31 mm. **Subject:** Centennial - Birth of Janko Jesensky **Obv:** Czech lion with socialist shield within shield, denomination below **Rev:** Head 3/4 right, date at right **Edge:** Plain with wave star wave **Designer:** J. Sturza **Note:** 112,038 pieces, Unc and Proof, were melted by the Czech National Bank in 1999.

Date	Mintage	F	VF	XF	Unc	BU
ND(1974)	55,000	—	—	4.25	6.75	—
ND(1974) Proof	5,000	Value: 11.50				

KM# 83 50 KORUN

13.0000 g., 0.7000 Silver .2926 oz. ASW, 31 mm. **Subject:** Centennial - Birth of S. K. Neumann **Obv:** Czech lion with socialist shield within shield, denomination below **Rev:** Head right, dates at right **Edge:** Milled **Designer:** F. David **Note:** 11,537 pieces, Unc and Proof, were melted by the Czech National Bank in 1999.

Date	Mintage	F	VF	XF	Unc	BU
ND(1975)	55,000	—	—	4.25	6.75	—
ND(1975) Proof	5,000	Value: 11.50				

KM# 87 50 KORUN

13.0000 g., 0.7000 Silver .2926 oz. ASW, 31 mm. **Subject:** 125th Anniversary - Death of Jan Kollar **Obv:** Czech lion with socialist shield within shield, denomination below **Rev:** Head facing, dates below **Edge:** Milled **Designer:** A. Peter **Note:** 19,743 pieces, Unc and Proof, were melted by the Czech National Bank in 1999.

Date	Mintage	F	VF	XF	Unc	BU
ND(1977) Proof	5,000	Value: 11.50				
ND(1977)	75,000	—	—	4.25	6.75	—

KM# 90 50 KORUN

13.0000 g., 0.7000 Silver .2926 oz. ASW, 31 mm. **Subject:** Centennial - Birth of Zdenek Nejedly **Obv:** Czech lion with socialist shield within shield, denomination below **Rev:** Bust right, dates at left **Edge:** Milled **Note:** 20,538 pieces, Unc and Proof, were melted by the Czech National Bank in 1999.

Date	Mintage	F	VF	XF	Unc	BU
ND(1978) Proof	5,000	Value: 11.50				
ND(1978)	75,000	—	—	4.25	6.75	—

KM# 91 50 KORUN

13.0000 g., 0.7000 Silver .2926 oz. ASW, 31 mm. **Subject:** 650th Anniversary of Kremnica Mint **Obv:** Czech lion with socialist shield within shield, denomination below **Rev:** Montage of five coin designs, dates below **Designer:** A. Peter **Note:** 22,037 pieces, Unc and Proof, were melted by the Czech National Bank in 1999.

Date	Mintage	F	VF	XF	Unc	BU
ND(1978)	93,000	—	—	4.25	6.75	—
ND(1978) Proof	7,000	Value: 11.50				

KM# 98 50 KORUN

13.0000 g., 0.7000 Silver .2926 oz. ASW, 31 mm. **Subject:** 30th Anniversary of 9th Congress **Obv:** Czech lion with socialist shield within shield, linden leaves flanking, three line inscription above denomination below **Rev:** Hammer and sickle in gear at center, linden leaves at left, dates below **Edge:** Milled **Designer:** A. Pavlica **Note:** 30,089 pieces, Unc and Proof, were melted by the Czech National Bank in 1999.

Date	Mintage	F	VF	XF	Unc	BU
ND(1979) Proof	6,000	Value: 11.50				
ND(1979)	94,000	—	—	4.25	6.75	—

KM# 121 50 KORUN

7.0000 g., 0.5000 Silver .1125 oz. ASW, 27 mm. **Obv:** Czech lion with socialist shield within shield, denomination and dates below **Rev:** Prague (Praha) city view **Designer:** L. Kozak **Note:** 6,838 pieces, Unc and Proof, were melted by the Czech National Bank in 1999.

Date	Mintage	F	VF	XF	Unc	BU
1986	90,000	—	—	—	6.00	—
1986 Proof	10,000	Value: 12.50				

KM# 122 50 KORUN

7.0000 g., 0.5000 Silver .1125 oz. ASW, 27 mm. **Obv:** Czech lion with socialist shield divides denomination, three line inscription and date below **Rev:** Levoca city view above three statues **Designer:** D. Zobek **Note:** 9,438 pieces Unc and Proof, were melted by the Czech National Bank in 1999.

Date	Mintage	F	VF	XF	Unc	BU
1986	69,000	—	—	—	6.00	—
1986 Proof	10,000	Value: 11.50				

KM# 124 50 KORUN

7.0000 g., 0.5000 Silver .1125 oz. ASW, 27 mm. **Obv:** Czech lion with socialist shield divides denomination, three line inscription and date below **Rev:** Three building facades in Telc **Designer:** J. Truhlikova **Note:** 13,438 pieces Unc and Proof, were melted by the Czech National Bank in 1999.

Date	Mintage	F	VF	XF	Unc	BU
1986	69,000	—	—	—	6.00	—
1986 Proof	10,000	Value: 11.50				

KM# 125 50 KORUN

7.0000 g., 0.5000 Silver .1125 oz. ASW, 27 mm. **Obv:** Czech lion with socialist shield divides denomination, three line inscription and date below **Rev:** Bratislava city view **Note:** 12,188 pieces, Unc and Proof, were melted by the Czech National Bank in 1999.

Date	Mintage	F	VF	XF	Unc	BU
1986	69,000	—	—	—	6.00	—
1986 Proof	10,000	Value: 11.50				

KM# 126 50 KORUN

7.0000 g., 0.5000 Silver .1125 oz. ASW, 27 mm. **Obv:** Czech lion with socialist shield within shield, date and denomination below **Rev:** Cesky Krumlov city view **Designer:** L. Kozak **Note:** 11,338 pieces Unc and Proof, were melted by the Czech National Bank in 1999.

Date	Mintage	F	VF	XF	Unc	BU
1986	69,000	—	—	—	6.00	—
1986 Proof	10,000	Value: 11.50				

KM# 127 50 KORUN

7.0000 g., 0.5000 Silver .1125 oz. ASW, 27 mm. **Subject:** Environmental Protection **Obv:** Czech lion with socialist shield within shield, date and denomination below **Rev:** Two Przewalski's horses **Designer:** A. Gabrik **Note:** 338 pieces Unc and Proof, were melted by the Czech National Bank in 1999.

Date	Mintage	F	VF	XF	Unc	BU
1987 Proof	5,000	Value: 30.00				
1987	55,000	—	—	—	25.00	—

KM# 129 50 KORUN

7.0000 g., 0.5000 Silver .1125 oz. ASW, 27 mm. **Subject:** 300th Anniversary - Birth of Juraj Janosik **Obv:** Czech lion with socialist shield divides denomination, three line inscription below **Rev:** Standing, caped man divides dates, bird at left **Note:** 735 pieces Unc and Proof, were melted by the Czech National Bank in 1999.

Date	Mintage	F	VF	XF	Unc	BU
ND(1988) Proof	5,000	Value: 15.00				
ND(1988)	53,000	—	—	—	7.00	—

KM# 133 50 KORUN

7.0000 g., 0.5000 Silver .1125 oz. ASW, 27 mm. **Subject:** 150th Anniversary - Breclav to Brno Railroad **Obv:** Czech lion with socialist shield within shield, denomination below **Rev:** Early steam locomotive, dates below **Designer:** V. Oppl **Note:** 1,835 pieces Unc and Proof, were melted by the Czech National Bank in 1999.

Date	Mintage	F	VF	XF	Unc	BU
ND(1989)	67,000	—	—	—	7.00	—
ND(1989) Proof	3,000	Value: 16.00				

KM# 73 100 KORUN

15.0000 g., 0.7000 Silver .3376 oz. ASW, 33 mm. **Subject:** Centennial - Death of Josef Manes **Obv:** Czech lion with socialist shield within shield, three line inscription and denomination below **Obv. Designer:** J. Kulich **Rev:** Bust right divides dates **Rev. Designer:** P. Formanek **Note:** 6,803 pieces, Unc and Proof, were melted by the Czech National Bank in 1999.

Date	Mintage	F	VF	XF	Unc	BU
ND(1971)	45,000	—	—	10.00	13.50	—
ND(1971) Proof	5,000	Value: 17.50				

KM# 82 100 KORUN

15.0000 g., 0.7000 Silver .3376 oz. ASW, 33 mm. **Subject:** Sesquicentennial - Birth of Bedrich Smetana **Obv:** Czech lion with socialist shield within shield, denomination below **Rev:** Head right, dates at left **Edge:** Plain with 150 LET OD NAROZENI **Designer:** M. Knobloch **Note:** 6,201 pieces, Unc and Proof, were melted by the Czech National Bank in 1999.

Date	Mintage	F	VF	XF	Unc	BU
ND(1974)	75,000	—	—	10.00	12.00	—
ND(1974) Proof	5,000	Value: 17.50				

KM# 84 100 KORUN

15.0000 g., 0.7000 Silver .3376 oz. ASW, 33 mm. **Subject:** Centennial - Death of Janko Kral **Obv:** Czech lion with socialist shield within shield, denomination below **Rev:** Head right, dates lower right **Edge Lettering:** BASNIK * REVOLUCIONAR **Designer:** A. Peter **Note:** 19,839 pieces, Unc and Proof, were melted by the Czech National Bank in 1999.

Date	Mintage	F	VF	XF	Unc	BU
ND(1976)	75,000	—	—	10.00	12.00	—
ND(1976) Proof	5,000	Value: 17.50				

KM# 85 100 KORUN

15.0000 g., 0.7000 Silver .3376 oz. ASW, 33 mm. **Subject:** Centennial - Birth of Viktor Kaplan **Obv:** Czech lion with socialist shield within shield, denomination below **Rev:** Bust right, dates at left **Edge:** - * - **Designer:** L. Havelka **Note:** 22,339 pieces, Unc and Proof, were melted by the Czech National Bank in 1999.

Date	Mintage	F	VF	XF	Unc	BU
ND(1976) Proof	5,000	Value: 17.50				
ND(1976)	75,000	—	—	10.00	12.00	—

KM# 88 100 KORUN

15.0000 g., 0.7000 Silver .3376 oz. ASW, 33 mm. **Subject:** 300th Anniversary - Death of Vaclav Hollar **Obv:** Czech lion with socialist shield within shield, denomination below **Rev:** Head left, dates lower left **Edge:** Plain with waves and dots **Designer:** F. David **Note:** 32,789 pieces, Unc and Proof, were melted by the Czech National Bank in 1999.

Date	Mintage	F	VF	XF	Unc	BU
ND(1977)	95,000	—	—	10.00	12.00	—
ND(1977) Proof	5,000	Value: 17.50				

KM# 93 100 KORUN

15.0000 g., 0.7000 Silver .3376 oz. ASW, 33 mm. **Subject:** 600th Anniversary - Death of Charles IV **Obv:** Czech lion with socialist shield within shield, three line inscription, denomination and date below **Rev:** Crowned bust right, dates below **Designer:** J. Stursa **Note:** 32,638 pieces, Unc and Proof, were melted by the Czech National Bank in 1999.

Date	Mintage	F	VF	XF	Unc	BU
1978 Proof	10,000	Value: 17.50				
1978	90,000	—	—	10.00	12.00	—

KM# 92 100 KORUN

15.0000 g., 0.7000 Silver .3376 oz. ASW, 33 mm. **Subject:** 75th Anniversary - Birth of Julius Fucik **Obv:** Czech lion with socialist shield within shield, denomination below **Rev:** Head left, dates at right **Edge Lettering:** LIDE, MEL JSEM VAS RAD, BDETE! **Designer:** V. Oppl **Note:** 24,840 pieces, Unc and Proof, were melted by the Czech National Bank in 1999.

Date	Mintage	F	VF	XF	Unc	BU
ND(1978)	75,000	—	—	10.00	12.00	—
ND(1978) Proof	5,000	Value: 17.50				

KM# 99 100 KORUN

15.0000 g., 0.7000 Silver .3376 oz. ASW, 33 mm. **Subject:** 150th Anniversary - Birth of Jan Botto **Obv:** Czech lion with socialist shield within shield, three line inscription above denomination below **Rev:** Head 3/4 left, date below **Edge:** ooo star ooo **Designer:** J. Harcuba **Note:** 26,740 pieces, Unc and Proof, were melted by the Czech National Bank in 1999.

Date	Mintage	F	VF	XF	Unc	BU
ND(1979) Proof	5,000	Value: 17.50				
ND(1979)	75,000	—	—	10.00	12.00	—

KM# 100 100 KORUN

15.0000 g., 0.7000 Silver .3376 oz. ASW, 33 mm. **Subject:** 150th Anniversary - Birth of Peter Parler **Obv:** Czech lion with socialist shield within shield, medieval arches in background, three line inscription above denomination below **Rev:** Bust facing, medieval arches in background, date at left and below **Edge:** Plain with waves and dots **Designer:** J. Harcuba **Note:** 54,738 pieces, Unc and Proof, were melted by the Czech National Bank in 1999.

Date	Mintage	F	VF	XF	Unc	BU
ND(1980) Proof	9,000	Value: 17.50				
ND(1980)	91,000	—	—	10.00	12.00	—

KM# 101 100 KORUN

9.0000 g., 0.5000 Silver .1446 oz. ASW, 29 mm. **Subject:** Fifth Spartakiade Games **Obv:** Czech lion with socialist shield within shield divides denomination, inscription below **Rev:** Seven female gymnastic figures, shadowing, date at left **Designer:** L. Kozak **Note:** 50,391 pieces, Unc and Proof, were melted by the Czech National Bank in 1999.

Date	Mintage	F	VF	XF	Unc	BU
1980	110,000	—	—	—	12.00	—
1980 Proof	10,000	Value: 18.50				

KM# 102 100 KORUN

9.0000 g., 0.5000 Silver .1446 oz. ASW, 29 mm. **Subject:** Centennial - Birth of Bohumir Smeral **Obv:** Czech lion with socialist shield within shield, denomination below **Rev:** Bust 3/4 facing, dates lower right **Edge:** Milled **Designer:** J. Harcuba **Note:** 29,943 pieces, Unc and Proof, were melted by the Czech National Bank in 1999.

Date	Mintage	F	VF	XF	Unc	BU
ND(1980)	74,000	—	—	—	12.00	—
ND(1980) Proof	6,000	Value: 17.50				

KM# 103 100 KORUN

9.0000 g., 0.5000 Silver .1446 oz. ASW, 29 mm. **Subject:** 20th Anniversary - Manned Space Flight **Obv:** Czech lion with socialist shield within shield, denomination below **Rev:** Cosmonaut Gagarin left, dates at right **Edge:** Milled **Designer:** J. Venecek **Note:** 31,639 pieces, Unc and Proof, were melted by the Czech National Bank in 1999.

Date	Mintage	F	VF	XF	Unc	BU
ND(1981) Proof	5,000	Value: 17.50				
ND(1981)	95,000	—	—	—	9.00	—

KM# 104 100 KORUN

9.0000 g., 0.5000 Silver .1446 oz. ASW, 29 mm. **Subject:** Centennial - Birth of Prof. Otakar Spaniel **Obv:** Czech lion with socialist shield within shield, denomination below **Rev:** Head left, dates below **Edge:** Milled **Designer:** M. Knobloch **Note:** 56,189 pieces, Unc and Proof, were melted by the Czech National Bank in 1999.

Date	Mintage	F	VF	XF	Unc	BU
ND(1981)	115,000	—	—	—	9.00	—
ND(1981) Proof	5,000	Value: 17.50				

KM# 106 100 KORUN

9.0000 g., 0.5000 Silver .1446 oz. ASW, 29 mm. **Subject:** Centennial - Birth of Ivan Olbracht **Obv:** Czech lion with socialist shield within shield divides denomination **Rev:** Head with hat left, dates at right **Edge:** Milled **Designer:** J. Malejovsky **Note:** 24,140 pieces, Unc and Proof, were melted by the Czech National Bank in 1999.

Date	Mintage	F	VF	XF	Unc	BU
ND(1982)	76,000	—	—	—	12.00	—
ND(1982) Proof	4,000	Value: 20.00				

KM# 107 100 KORUN

9.0000 g., 0.5000 Silver .1446 oz. ASW, 29 mm. **Subject:** 150th Anniversary - Ceske Budejovice Horse Drawn Railway **Obv:** Czech lion with socialist shield within shield, denomination and inscription below **Rev:** Horse-drawn train carriage, dates below **Designer:** L. Kozak **Note:** 14,939 pieces, Unc and Proof, were melted by the Czech National Bank in 1999.

Date	Mintage	F	VF	XF	Unc	BU
ND(1982) Proof	7,000	Value: 17.50				
ND(1982)	76,000	—	—	—	12.00	—

KM# 108 100 KORUN

9.0000 g., 0.5000 Silver .1446 oz. ASW, 29 mm. **Subject:** 100th Anniversary - Death of Karl Marx **Obv:** Czech lion with socialist shield within shield divides denomination, inscription below **Rev:** Head facing, dates at left **Edge:** Milled **Designer:** L. Kozak **Note:** 23,793 pieces, Unc and Proof, were melted by the Czech National Bank in 1999.

Date	Mintage	F	VF	XF	Unc	BU
ND(1983)	76,000	—	—	—	12.00	—
ND(1983) Proof	4,000	Value: 20.00				

KM# 109 100 KORUN

9.0000 g., 0.5000 Silver .1446 oz. ASW, 29 mm. **Subject:** Centennial - Birth of Jaroslav Hasek **Obv:** Czech lion with socialist shield within shield, denomination below **Rev:** Bust facing, date below **Edge:** Milled **Designer:** Stefen Novotny **Note:** 21,538 pieces, Unc and Proof, were melted by the Czech National Bank in 1999.

Date	Mintage	F	VF	XF	Unc	BU
ND(1983)	76,000	—	—	—	12.00	—
ND(1983) Proof	4,000	Value: 20.00				

KM# 110 100 KORUN

9.0000 g., 0.5000 Silver .1446 oz. ASW, 29 mm. **Subject:** Centennial - Death of Samo Chalupka **Obv:** Czech lion with socialist shield within shield, inscription and denomination below **Rev:** Bust 3/4 facing, dates at left **Edge:** Milled **Designer:** Stefen Novotny **Note:** 27,938 pieces, Unc and Proof, were melted by the Czech National Bank in 1999.

Date	Mintage	F	VF	XF	Unc	BU
ND(1983)	76,000	—	—	—	12.00	—
ND(1983) Proof	4,000	Value: 20.00				

KM# 111 100 KORUN

9.0000 g., 0.5000 Silver .1446 oz. ASW, 29 mm. **Subject:** 100th Anniversary of National Theater of Prague **Obv:** Czech lion with socialist shield within shield, denomination below **Rev:** View of the National Theater in Prague, dates below **Edge:** Milled **Designer:** V. Oppl **Note:** 23,538 pieces, Unc and Proof, were melted by the Czech National Bank in 1999.

Date	Mintage	F	VF	XF	Unc	BU
ND(1983)	140,000	—	—	—	9.00	—
ND(1983) Proof	10,000	Value: 17.50				

KM# 113 100 KORUN

9.0000 g., 0.5000 Silver .1446 oz. ASW, 29 mm. **Subject:** 300th Anniversary - Birth of Matej Bel **Obv:** Czech lion with socialist shield within shield, denomination below **Rev:** Seated figure, dates at right **Edge:** Milled **Designer:** Jan Kulich **Note:** 5288 pieces, Unc and Proof, were melted by the Czech National Bank in 1999.

Date	Mintage	F	VF	XF	Unc	BU
ND(1984) Proof	3,000	Value: 20.00				
ND(1984)	57,000	—	—	—	12.00	—

KM# 114 100 KORUN

9.0000 g., 0.5000 Silver .1446 oz. ASW, 29 mm. **Subject:** 150th Anniversary - Birth of Jan Neruda **Obv:** Czech lion with socialist shield within shield, denomination below **Rev:** Head 3/4 left, house and dates at left **Edge:** Milled **Designer:** Z. Kolarsky **Note:** 12,539 pieces, Unc and Proof, were melted by the Czech National Bank in 1999.

Date	Mintage	F	VF	XF	Unc	BU
ND(1984)	76,000	—	—	—	12.00	—
ND(1984) Proof	4,000	Value: 20.00				

KM# 115 100 KORUN

9.0000 g., 0.5000 Silver .1446 oz. ASW, 29 mm. **Subject:** Centennial - Birth of Antonin Zapotocky **Obv:** Czech lion with socialist shield within shield divides denomination, inscription below **Rev:** Head 3/4 right, dates at left **Edge:** Milled **Designer:** Jan Simota **Note:** 19,938 pieces, Unc and Proof, were melted by the Czech National Bank in 1999.

Date	Mintage	F	VF	XF	Unc	BU
ND(1984)	76,000	—	—	—	12.00	—
ND(1984) Proof	4,000	Value: 20.00				

KM# 117 100 KORUN

9.0000 g., 0.5000 Silver .1446 oz. ASW, 29 mm. **Subject:** 1985 Ice Hockey Championships **Obv:** Czech lion with socialist shield within shield, denomination below **Rev:** Hockey player skating left, dates at left **Edge:** Milled **Designer:** J. Kulich **Note:** 2,788 pieces, Unc and Proof, were melted by the Czech National Bank in 1999.

Date	Mintage	F	VF	XF	Unc	BU
1985 Proof	4,000	Value: 20.00				
1985	66,000	—	—	—	12.00	—

KM# 120 100 KORUN

9.0000 g., 0.5000 Silver .1446 oz. ASW, 29 mm. **Subject:** 250th Anniversary - Death of Petr Brandl **Obv:** Czech lion with socialist shield within shield, denomination below **Rev:** Bust facing, large rock in background, dates at right **Edge:** Milled **Designer:** V. Oppl **Note:** 16,038 pieces, Unc and Proof, were melted by the Czech National Bank in 1999.

Date	Mintage	F	VF	XF	Unc	BU
ND(1985) Proof	4,000	Value: 20.00				
ND(1985)	71,000	—	—	—	10.00	—

KM# 119 100 KORUN

9.0000 g., 0.5000 Silver .1446 oz. ASW, 29 mm. **Subject:** 10th Anniversary of Helsinki Conference **Obv:** Czech lion with socialist shield within shield divides denomination, inscription below **Rev:** Stylized dove embracing European map, dates at lower left **Edge:** Milled **Designer:** V. Oppl **Note:** 18,838 pieces, Unc and Proof, were melted by the Czech National Bank in 1999.

Date	Mintage	F	VF	XF	Unc	BU
ND(1985) Proof	5,000	Value: 20.00				
ND(1985)	75,000	—	—	—	10.00	—

KM# 118 100 KORUN

9.0000 g., 0.5000 Silver .1446 oz. ASW, 29 mm. **Subject:** 125th Anniversary - Birth of Martin Kukucin **Obv:** Czech lion with socialist shield within shield, denomination below **Rev:** Bust facing, dates at left **Edge:** Milled **Designer:** J. Kulich **Note:** 11,838 pieces, Unc and Proof, were melted by the Czech National Bank in 1999.

Date	Mintage	F	VF	XF	Unc	BU
ND(1985) Proof	3,000	Value: 20.00				
ND(1985)	62,000	—	—	—	12.00	—

KM# 116 100 KORUN

9.0000 g., 0.5000 Silver .1446 oz. ASW, 29 mm. **Subject:** 200th Anniversary - Birth of Jan Holly **Obv:** Czech lion with socialist shield within shield divides denomination, inscription below **Rev:** Head 3/4 facing, dates at left **Edge:** Milled **Designer:** Milan Kozuch **Note:** 9,338 pieces, Unc and Proof, were melted by the Czech National Bank in 1999.

Date	Mintage	F	VF	XF	Unc	BU
ND(1985) Proof	3,000	Value: 20.00				
ND(1985)	62,000	—	—	—	12.00	—

KM# 123 100 KORUN

13.0000 g., 0.5000 Silver .2090 oz. ASW, 31 mm. **Subject:** 150th Anniversary - Death of Karel Hynek Macha **Obv:** Czech lion with socialist shield within shield divides denomination, inscription below **Rev:** Head 3/4 left, dates at right **Edge:** Milled **Designer:** M. Vavro **Note:** 10,288 pieces, Unc and Proof, were melted by the Czech National Bank in 1999.

Date	Mintage	F	VF	XF	Unc	BU
ND(1986)	63,000	—	—	—	10.00	—
ND(1986) Proof	5,000	Value: 20.00				

KM# 128 100 KORUN

13.0000 g., 0.5000 Silver .2090 oz. ASW, 31 mm. **Subject:** 225th Anniversary of Mining Academy **Obv:** Czech lion with socialist shield within shield, denomination below **Rev:** Mining equipment, dates above small shield at right **Edge:** Milled **Designer:** O. Zobek **Note:** 6,438 pieces, Unc and Proof, were melted by the Czech National Bank in 1999.

Date	Mintage	F	VF	XF	Unc	BU
ND(1987) Proof	5,000	Value: 22.50				
ND(1987)	55,000	—	—	—	12.00	—

KM# 130 100 KORUN

13.0000 g., 0.5000 Silver .2090 oz. ASW, 31 mm. **Subject:** Prague Philatelic Exposition **Obv:** Czech lion with socialist shield within shield, denomination and date below **Rev:** City views of Prague presented as four stamps **Edge:** Milled **Designer:** V. Oppl **Note:** 4,235 pieces, Unc and Proof, were melted by the Czech National Bank in 1999.

Date	Mintage	F	VF	XF	Unc	BU
1988	66,000	—	—	—	12.00	—
1988 Proof	5,000	Value: 25.00				

KM# 132 100 KORUN

13.0000 g., 0.5000 Silver .2090 oz. ASW, 31 mm. **Subject:** Centennial - Birth of Martin Benka **Obv:** Czech lion with socialist shield within shield, denomination below **Rev:** Young Slovak woman in national costume with dove, dates at right, based on painting by Martin Benko **Edge:** Milled **Designer:** J. Kulich **Note:** 8,635 pieces, Unc and Proof, were melted by the Czech National Bank in 1999.

Date	Mintage	F	VF	XF	Unc	BU
ND(1988)	55,000	—	—	—	12.00	—
ND(1988) Proof	5,000	Value: 28.00				

KM# 135 100 KORUN

13.0000 g., 0.5000 Silver .2090 oz. ASW, 31 mm. **Subject:** 50th Anniversary of Student Organization Against Occupation and Fascism **Obv:** Czech lion with socialist shield within shield, denomination below **Rev:** Barbed wire and medieval document seal, dates above **Edge:** Milled **Designer:** J. Bradna **Note:** 4,335 pieces, Unc and Proof, were melted by the Czech National Bank in 1999.

Date	Mintage	F	VF	XF	Unc	BU
ND(1989) Proof	Est. 3,000	Value: 25.00				
ND(1989)	67,000	—	—	—	14.00	—

KM# 137 100 KORUN

13.0000 g., 0.5000 Silver .2090 oz. ASW, 31 mm. **Subject:** 100th Anniversary - Birth of Karel Capek **Obv:** Czech lion with socialist shield within shield, inscription and denomination below **Rev:** Head left, dates at right **Edge:** Milled **Designer:** A. Gabri **Note:** 7,920 pieces, Unc and Proof, were melted by the Czech National Bank in 1999.

Date	Mintage	F	VF	XF	Unc	BU
ND(1990)	67,000	—	—	—	14.00	—
ND(1990) Proof	3,500	Value: 25.00				

KM# 138 100 KORUN

13.0000 g., 0.5000 Silver .2090 oz. ASW, 31 mm. **Subject:** 250th Anniversary - Death of Jan Kupecky **Obv:** Czech lion with socialist shield within shield, denomination below **Rev:** Half-length figure holding paintbrush and palette right, dates at left **Edge:** Milled **Designer:** J. Truhilikova-Spevakova **Note:** 7,570 pieces, Unc and Proof, were melted by the Czech National Bank in 1999.

Date	Mintage	F	VF	XF	Unc	BU
ND(1990)	58,000	—	—	—	14.00	—
ND(1990) Proof	2,500	Value: 28.00				

KM# 105 500 KORUN

24.0000 g., 0.9000 Silver .6944 oz. ASW, 40 mm. **Subject:** 125th Anniversary - Death of Ludovit Stur **Obv:** Czech lion with socialist shield within shield, inscription and denomination below **Rev:** Head facing, dates below **Edge Lettering:** 125 ROKOV OD SMRTI L' STURA **Designer:** J. Kulich **Note:** 7,057 pieces, Unc and Proof, were melted by the Czech National Bank in 1999.

Date	Mintage	F	VF	XF	Unc	BU
ND(1981)	51,000	—	—	—	35.00	—
ND(1981) Proof	4,000	Value: 65.00				

KM# 112 500 KORUN

24.0000 g., 0.9000 Silver .6944 oz. ASW, 40 mm. **Subject:** 100th Anniversary of National Theater in Prague **Obv:** Czech lion with socialist shield within shield, denomination below **Rev:** Woman with book, theater facade at right, dates below **Edge Lettering:** NAROD SOBE **Designer:** Z. Kolarsky **Note:** 4,740 pieces, Unc and Proof, were melted by the Czech National Bank in 1999.

Date	Mintage	F	VF	XF	Unc	BU
ND(1983) Proof	5,000	Value: 75.00				
ND(1983)	55,000	—	—	—	40.00	—

KM# 136 500 KORUN

24.0000 g., 0.9000 Silver .6944 oz. ASW, 40 mm. **Subject:** 100th Anniversary - Birth of Josef Lada **Obv:** Czech lion with socialist shield within shield divides denomination, inscription below **Rev:** Town view, children building snowmen divide dates **Edge Lettering:** CESKY MALIR NARODNI UMELEC **Designer:** J. Bejvl **Note:** 2,238 pieces, Unc and Proof, were melted by the Czech National Bank in 1999.

Date	Mintage	F	VF	XF	Unc	BU
ND(1987)	48,000	—	—	—	45.00	—
ND(1987) Proof	5,000	Value: 70.00				

KM# 131 500 KORUN

24.0000 g., 0.9000 Silver .6944 oz. ASW, 40 mm. **Subject:** 20th Anniversary of National Federation **Obv:** Czech lion with socialist shield within shield, inscription and denomination below **Rev:** Stylized linden tree encircled by ribbon in shape of country, dates below **Edge Lettering:** 20. VYROCIE CESKOSLOVENSKEJ FEDERACIE oj **Designer:** J. Truhilkova **Note:** 6,435 pieces, Unc and Proof, were melted by the Czech National Bank in 1999.

Date	Mintage	F	VF	XF	Unc	BU
ND(1988) Proof	3,000	Value: 75.00				
ND(1988)	46,000	—	—	—	40.00	—

KM# 134 500 KORUN

24.0000 g., 0.9000 Silver .6944 oz. ASW, 40 mm. **Subject:** 125th Anniversary of Matica Slovenska Institute **Obv:** Czech lion with socialist shield within shield, denomination below **Rev:** Woman standing in national costume holding book and linden sprigs, dates at right **Edge Lettering:** HOJ VLAST MOJA TY ZEM DRAHA **Designer:** J. Kulich **Note:** 6,338 pieces, Unc and Proof, were melted by the Czech National Bank in 1999.

Date	Mintage	F	VF	XF	Unc	BU
ND(1988)	44,000	—	—	—	40.00	—
ND(1988) Proof	5,000	Value: 70.00				

CZECH SLOVAK FEDERAL REPUBLIC

DECIMAL COINAGE

KM# 149 HALER

Aluminum, 16 mm. **Obv:** CSFR above quartered shield, linden leaves flanking, date below **Rev:** Denomination within linden wreath **Edge:** Plain

Date	Mintage	F	VF	XF	Unc	BU
1991	55,000	—	—	—	2.50	—
1992	50,000	—	—	—	2.50	—

KM# 150 5 HALERU

0.7500 g., Aluminum, 16.2 mm. **Obv:** CSFR above quartered shield, linden leaves flanking, date below **Obv. Designer:** Miroslav Ronai **Rev:** Large, thick, denomination **Rev. Designer:** Frantisek David **Edge:** Plain

Date	Mintage	F	VF	XF	Unc	BU
1991	10,055,000	—	—	0.10	0.25	—
1992 In mint set only	50,000	—	—	—	2.00	—

KM# 146 10 HALERU

Aluminum, 18.2 mm. **Obv:** CSFR above quartered shield, linden leaves flanking, date below **Obv. Designer:** Miroslav Ronai **Rev:** Large, thick denomination **Rev. Designer:** Frantisek David

Date	Mintage	F	VF	XF	Unc	BU
1991	40,055,000	—	—	—	0.50	—
1992	45,050,000	—	—	—	0.50	—

KM# 143 20 HALERU

Aluminum-Bronze, 19.5 mm. **Obv:** CSFR above quartered shield, linden leaves flanking, date below **Obv. Designer:** Miroslav Ronai **Rev:** Large, thick denomination **Rev. Designer:** Frantisek David **Edge:** Milled

Date	Mintage	F	VF	XF	Unc	BU
1991	41,105,000	—	—	0.20	0.50	—
1992	35,050,000	—	—	0.20	0.50	—

KM# 144 50 HALERU

Copper-Nickel, 20.8 mm. **Obv:** CSFR above quartered shield, linden leaves flanking, date below **Obv. Designer:** Miroslav Ronai **Rev:** Large, thick denomination **Rev. Designer:** Frantisek David **Edge:** Milled

Date	Mintage	F	VF	XF	Unc	BU
1991	24,463,000	—	—	0.35	0.75	—
1992	15,062,000	—	—	0.35	0.75	—

KM# 151 KORUNA

Copper-Aluminum, 23 mm. **Obv:** CSFR above quartered shield, linden leaves flanking, date below **Obv. Designer:** Miroslav Ronai **Rev:** Female planting linden tree, denomination at left **Rev. Designer:** Marie Uchytilova-Kucova **Edge:** Milled

Date	Mintage	F	VF	XF	Unc	BU
1991	20,056,000	—	—	0.50	1.00	—
1992	20,387,000	—	—	0.50	1.00	—

KM# 148 2 KORUNY

Copper-Nickel, 24 mm. **Obv:** CSFR above quartered shield, linden leaves flanking, date below **Obv. Designer:** Miroslav Ronai **Rev:** Linden leaf, large value at right **Rev. Designer:** Josef Nalepa **Edge:** Plain with wave x wave

Date	Mintage	F	VF	XF	Unc	BU
1991(k)	25,201,000	—	—	0.60	1.25	—
1991(l)	20,000,000	—	—	0.60	1.25	—
1992	1,051,000	—	—	—	1.25	—

KM# 152 5 KORUN

Copper-Nickel, 26 mm. **Obv:** CSFR above quartered shield, linden leaves flanking, date below **Obv. Designer:** Jarmila Truhlikova-Spevakova **Rev:** Geometric design, large value **Rev. Designer:** Drahomir Zobek **Edge:** Eight plain and eight milled areas

Date	Mintage	F	VF	XF	Unc	BU
1991(l)	10,000,750	—	—	—	—	—
1991(k)	18,564,000	—	—	0.75	2.00	—
1992	50,000	—	—	2.50	6.00	—

Note: In sets only

KM# 139.1 10 KORUN

Nickel-Bronze, 24.5 mm. **Obv:** CSFR above quartered shield, date below, denomination at left **Obv. Designer:** J. Truhlikova-Spevakova **Rev:** Bust right, dates at left **Rev. Designer:** M. Ronai **Edge:** Eight plain and eight milled areas **Note:** Designer initials (MR) below bust, four varieties exist.

Date	Mintage	F	VF	XF	Unc	BU
1990	9,990,000	—	—	2.00	7.00	—
1993	2,500,000	—	—	2.00	6.00	—

KM# 139.2 10 KORUN

Nickel-Bronze, 24.5 mm. **Obv:** CSFR above shield, date below, denomination at left **Obv. Designer:** J. Truhlikova-Spevakova **Rev:** Tomas G. Masaryk bust, right, dates at left **Rev. Designer:** M. Ronai **Note:** Designer name below bust: RONAI.

Date	Mintage	F	VF	XF	Unc	BU
1990	Inc. above	—	2.00	5.00	10.00	—

KM# 153 10 KORUN

Nickel-Bronze, 24.5 mm. **Obv:** CSFR above quartered shield, date below, denomination at left **Obv. Designer:** J. Truhlikova-Spevakova **Rev:** Uniformed bust left, dates at right **Rev. Designer:** D. Zobek

Date	Mintage	F	VF	XF	Unc	BU
1991	10,036,000	—	—	2.00	5.00	—
1993	2,500,000	—	—	2.50	6.00	—

KM# 159 10 KORUN

Nickel-Bronze, 24.5 mm. **Obv:** CSFR above quartered shield, date below, denomination at left **Obv. Designer:** J. Truhlikova-Spevakova **Rev:** Bust right, dates at left **Rev. Designer:** J. Uprka **Edge:** Eight plain and eight milled areas

Date	Mintage	F	VF	XF	Unc	BU
1992	5,050,000	—	—	2.00	5.00	—

KM# 140.1 50 KORUN

7.0000 g., 0.5000 Silver .1125 oz. ASW, 27 mm. **Obv:** CSFR quartered shield with designer's initials (LK) below denomination **Obv. Designer:** Ladislav Kolar **Rev:** Veiled head left, date upper left **Rev. Designer:** Michal Vitanovsky **Edge:** Milled **Note:** See note with KM#140.2. Designer emblem exists with and without initials.

Date	Mintage	F	VF	XF	Unc	BU
1990 Proof	3,000	Value: 18.00				
1990	147,000	—	—	—	7.00	—

KM# 140.2 50 KORUN

7.0000 g., 0.5000 Silver .1125 oz. ASW, 27 mm. **Obv:** CSFR quartered shield, without designer's initials (LK) **Rev:** Veiled head left **Designer:** M. Vitanovsky **Note:** 12,070 pieces, Unc and Proof of either KM#140.1 or 140.2, were melted by the Czech National Bank in 1999.

Date	Mintage	F	VF	XF	Unc	BU
1990	Inc. above	—	—	10.00	25.00	—

KM# 155 50 KORUN

7.0000 g., 0.7000 Silver .1575 oz. ASW, 27 mm. **Obv:** CSFR quartered shield, denomination below **Rev:** Piestany Spa building, shield below **Rev. Designer:** V. Oppl **Edge:** Milled **Note:** 17,920 pieces, Unc and Proof, were melted by the Czech National Bank in 1999.

Date	Mintage	F	VF	XF	Unc	BU
1991	Est. 5,000	Value: 16.50				
1991	75,000	—	—	—	7.50	—

KM# 145 50 KORUN

7.0000 g., 0.5000 Silver .1125 oz. ASW, 27 mm. **Obv:** CSFR quartered shield, denomination below **Rev:** Steamship Bohemia, dates below **Edge:** Milled **Designer:** L. Kozak **Note:** 4,470 pieces, Unc and Proof, were melted by the Czech National Bank in 1999.

Date	Mintage	F	VF	XF	Unc	BU
ND(1991)	77,000	—	—	—	8.00	—
ND(1991) Proof	3,000	Value: 18.00				

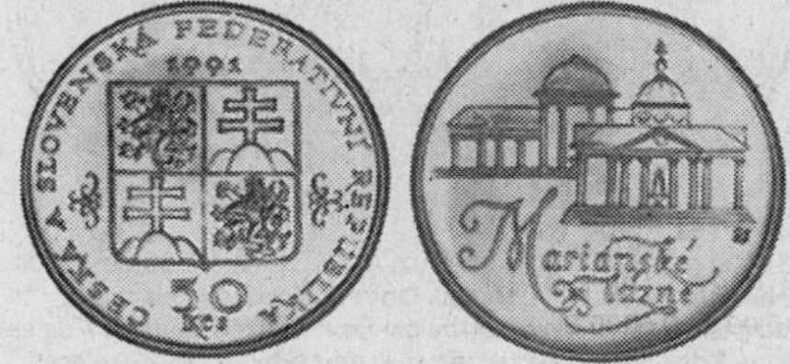

KM# 156 50 KORUN

7.0000 g., 0.7000 Silver .1575 oz. ASW, 27 mm. **Obv:** CSFR quartered shield, denomination below, date above **Rev:** Marianske Lazne Spa buildings **Rev. Designer:** J. Truhlikova-Spevakova **Edge:** Milled **Note:** 16,520 pieces, Unc and Proof, were melted by the Czech National Bank in 1999.

Date	Mintage	F	VF	XF	Unc	BU
1991	75,000	—	—	—	7.50	—
1991 Proof	5,000	Value: 16.50				

KM# 157 50 KORUN

7.0000 g., 0.7000 Silver .1575 oz. ASW, 27 mm. **Obv:** CSFR quartered shield, denomination above, date below **Rev:** Chamois on rock, Karlovy Vary Spa buildings **Rev. Designer:** J. Truhlikova-Spevakova **Edge:** Milled **Note:** 15,920, pieces, Unc and Proof, were melted by the Czech National Bank in 1999.

Date	Mintage	F	VF	XF	Unc	BU
1991	75,000	—	—	—	10.00	—
1991 Proof	5,000	Value: 20.00				

KM# 141 100 KORUN
13.0000 g., 0.5000 Silver .2090 oz. ASW, 31 mm. **Obv:** CSFR quartered shield, denomination at right **Rev:** Two horsemen right, date below **Edge:** Milled **Designer:** J. Truhlikova-Spevakova **Note:** 3,170 pieces, Unc and Proof, were melted by the Czech National Bank in 1999.

Date	Mintage	F	VF	XF	Unc	BU
1990	67,000	—	—	—	15.00	—
1990 Proof	3,000	Value: 25.00				

KM# 142 100 KORUN
13.0000 g., 0.5000 Silver .2090 oz. ASW, 31 mm. **Subject:** 100th Anniversary - Birth of Bohuslav Martinu **Obv:** CSFR quartered shield, denomination below **Rev:** Head facing, dates at right **Edge:** Milled **Designer:** L. Kolar **Note:** 8,170 pieces, Unc and Proof, were melted by the Czech National Bank in 1999.

Date	Mintage	F	VF	XF	Unc	BU
ND(1990)	53,000	—	—	—	15.00	—
ND(1990)	53,000	—	—	—	15.00	—
ND(1990) Proof	2,000	Value: 22.00				

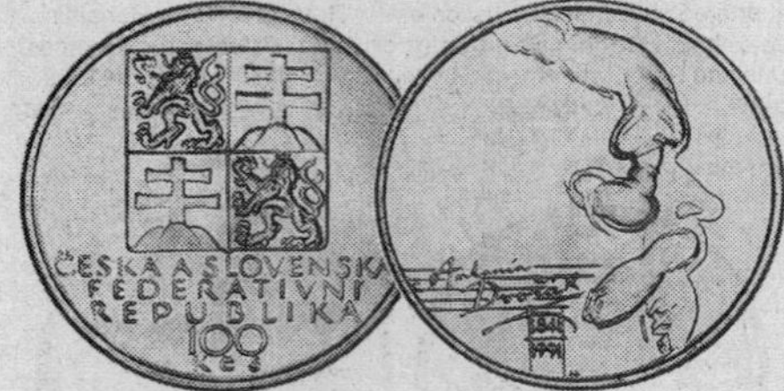

KM# 147 100 KORUN
13.0000 g., 0.5000 Silver .2926 oz. ASW, 31 mm. **Subject:** 150th Anniversary - Birth of A. Dvorák **Obv:** CSFR quartered shield, inscription and denomination below **Rev:** Stylized head right, dates below **Edge:** Milled **Designer:** J. Harcuba **Note:** 16,220 pieces, Unc and Proof, were melted by the Czech National Bank in 1999.

Date	Mintage	F	VF	XF	Unc	BU
1991	75,000	—	—	—	12.00	—
1991 Proof	5,000	Value: 20.00				

KM# 154 100 KORUN
13.0000 g., 0.7000 Silver .2926 oz. ASW, 31 mm. **Subject:** 200th Anniversary - Death of Wolfgang A. Mozart **Obv:** CSFR quartered shield, denomination below **Rev:** Bust right, dates below **Edge:** Milled **Designer:** J. Harcuba **Note:** 2,620 pieces, Unc and Proof, were melted by the Czech National Bank in 1999.

Date	Mintage	F	VF	XF	Unc	BU
ND(1991)	75,000	—	—	—	12.00	—
ND(1991) Proof	5,000	Value: 45.00				

KM# 160 100 KORUN
13.0000 g., 0.5000 Silver .2926 oz. ASW, 31 mm. **Subject:** 175th Anniversary - Moravian Museum **Obv:** CSFR quartered shield, denomination above, date below **Rev:** Moravian Museum, Moravian eagle **Edge:** Milled **Designer:** K. Zeman **Note:** 226,977 pieces, Unc and Proof, were melted by the Czech National Bank in 1999.

Date	Mintage	F	VF	XF	Unc	BU
1992	73,000	—	—	—	10.00	—
1992 Proof	5,000	Value: 22.00				

KM# 161 100 KORUN
13.0000 g., 0.5000 Silver .2926 oz. ASW, 31 mm. **Subject:** Nazi Massacres at Lidice and Lezaky **Obv:** CSFR quartered shield, denomination below, date above **Rev:** Cross with barbed wire loop **Edge:** Milled **Designer:** J. Truhlikova-Spevakova **Note:** 24,620 pieces, Unc and Proof, were melted by the Czech National Bank in 1999.

Date	Mintage	F	VF	XF	Unc	BU
1992	70,000	—	—	—	10.00	—
1992 Proof	3,000	Value: 22.00				

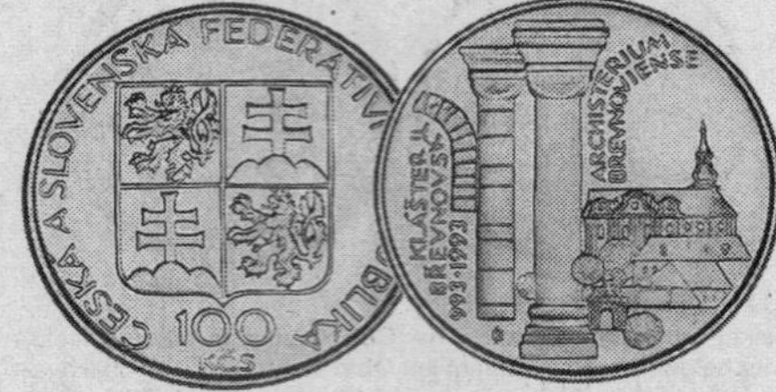

KM# 162 100 KORUN
13.0000 g., 0.5000 Silver .2926 oz. ASW, 31 mm. **Subject:** 1000 Years of Brevnov Monastery **Obv:** CSFR quartered shield, denomination below **Rev:** Church and cloister columns, dates at left **Edge:** Milled **Designer:** J. Bejvl **Note:** 25,932 pieces, Unc and Proof, were melted by the Czech National Bank in 1999.

Date	Mintage	F	VF	XF	Unc	BU
ND(1993) Proof	3,000	Value: 22.00				
ND(1993)	70,000	—	—	—	8.00	—

KM# 163 100 KORUN
13.0000 g., 0.5000 Silver .2926 oz. ASW, 31 mm. **Subject:** Slovak Museum Centennial **Obv:** CSFR quartered shield, inscription and denomination below **Rev:** Historic folk art designs, dates lower left **Edge:** Milled **Designer:** J. Truhlikova-Spevakova **Note:** 31,932 pieces, Unc and Proof, were melted by the Czech National Bank in 1999.

Date	Mintage	F	VF	XF	Unc	BU
ND(1993)	70,000	—	—	—	8.00	—
ND(1993) Proof	3,000	Value: 22.00				

KM# 158 500 KORUN
24.0000 g., 0.9000 Silver .6944 oz. ASW, 40 mm. **Subject:** 400th Anniversary - Birth of J. A. Komensky **Obv:** CSFR quartered shield, date above, denomination below **Rev:** J. A. Komensky standing, dates at left **Edge:** Milled **Designer:** M. Vitanovsky **Note:** 14,820 pieces, Unc and Proof, were melted by the Czech National Bank in 1999.

Date	Mintage	F	VF	XF	Unc	BU
1992	60,000	—	—	—	32.50	—
1992 Proof	5,000	Value: 55.00				

KM# 164 500 KORUN
24.0000 g., 0.9000 Silver .6944 oz. ASW, 40 mm. **Subject:** 100th Year of Czech Tennis **Obv:** CSFR quartered shield, inscription and denomination below **Rev:** Male tennis player, stadium at left, dates above **Edge:** Milled **Designer:** L. Kozak **Note:** 27,074 pieces, Unc and Proof, were melted by the Czech National Bank in 1999.

Date	Mintage	F	VF	XF	Unc	BU
ND(1993) Proof	3,000	Value: 65.00				
ND(1993)	62,000	—	—	—	35.00	—

PROBA

KM#	Date	Mintage	Identification	Mkt Val
Pr1	1922	—	Koruna. Aluminum.	—
Pr2	1922	—	Koruna. Copper-Nickel.	—
Pr3	1951	—	5 Koruna. Aluminum-Copper Magnesium.	—
Pr4	1932	2	25 Haleru. Copper-Nickel. W/dense notches.	—
Pr5	1932	2	25 Haleru. Copper-Nickel. Thin notches.	—
Pr6	1932	10	25 Haleru. Copper-Nickel.	—
Pr7	1976	—	3 Koruny.	—
Pr8	ND(1990)	2,500	100 Korun.	200

MINT SETS

KM#	Date	Mintage	Identification	Issue Price	Mkt Val
MS1	1980 (7)	50,000	KM50, 60, 74-75, 80, 86, 89	5.00	3.50
MS2	1981 (7)	66,000	KM50, 60, 74-75, 80, 86, 89	—	3.50
MS3	1982 (7)	53,000	KM50, 60, 74-75, 80, 86, 89	—	5.50
MS4	1983 (7)	50,000	KM50, 60, 74-75, 80, 86, 89	—	4.50
MS5	1984 (7)	39,000	KM50, 60, 74-75, 80, 86, 89	—	6.50
MS6	1985 (7)	39,000	KM50, 60, 74-75, 80, 86, 89	—	6.50
MS7	1986 (7)	20,000	KM50, 60, 74-75, 80, 86, 89	—	50.00
MS8	1987 (7)	30,000	km50, 60, 74-75, 80, 86, 89	—	15.00
MS9	1988 (7)	29,000	KM50, 60, 74-75, 80, 86, 89	—	10.00
MS10	1989 (7)	30,000	KM50, 60, 74-75, 80, 86, 89	—	10.00
MS11	1990 (7)	30,000	KM50, 60, 74-75, 80, 86, 89	—	10.00
MS12	1991 (9)	25,000	KM143-144, 146, 148-153	—	12.50
MS13	1991 (8)	30,000	KM143-144, 146, 148-152	—	12.50
MS14	1992 (9)	49,000	KM143-144, 146, 148-152, 159	—	15.00
MS15	1992 (8)	49,000	KM143-144,146, 148-152	—	10.00

PROOF SETS

KM#	Date	Mintage	Identification	Issue Price	Mkt Val
PS1	1966 (4)	—	KM49.1, 53, 57, 60	—	—
PS2	1981 (7)	—	KM50, 60, 74-75, 80, 86, 89	—	—

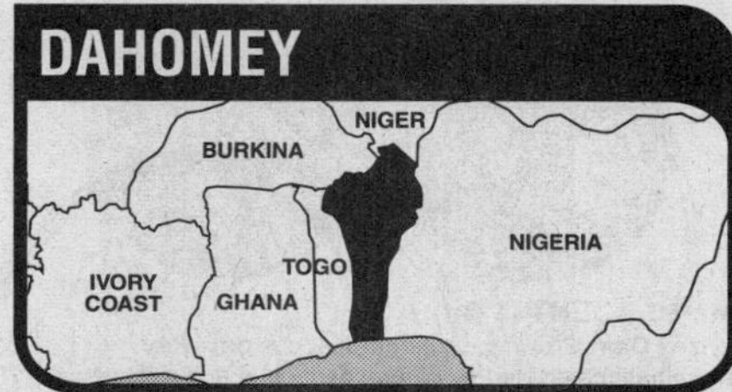

Porto-Novo, on the Bight of Benin, was founded as a trading post by the Portuguese in the 17th century. At that time, Dahomey (Benin) was composed of an aggregation of mutually suspicious tribes, the majority of which were tributary to the powerful northern Kingdom of Abomey. In 1863, the King of Porto-Novo petitioned France for protection from Abomey. The French subjugated other militant tribes as well, and in 1892 organized the area as a protectorate of France; in 1904 it was incorporated into French West Africa as the Territory of Dahomey. After the establishment of the Fifth French Republic, the Territory at Dahomey became an autonomous state within the French community. On Aug. 1, 1960, it became the fully independent Republic of Dahomey. In 1974, the republic began a transition to a socialist society with Marxism-Leninism as its revolutionary philosophy under Col. Ahmed Kerekow. On Nov. 30, 1975, the name of the Republic of Dahomey was changed to the Peoples Republic of Benin. As a result of Benin's first free presidential election in 30 years, Nicephore Soglo defeated Colonel Kerekou.

MINT MARKS

1 AR - Uno-A-Erre, Arezzo, Italy

REPUBLIC

STANDARD COINAGE

KM# 1.1 100 FRANCS

5.1000 g., 0.9990 Silver .1638 oz. ASW **Subject:** 10th Anniversary of Independence **Obv:** Facing cornucopias top supported arms, date above, denomination below **Rev:** Buildings on Lake Ganvié **Note:** Hallmark "999.9" above denomination.

Date	Mintage	F	VF	XF	Unc	BU
1971 Proof	4,650	Value: 45.00				

KM# 1.2 100 FRANCS

5.1000 g., 0.9990 Silver .1638 oz. ASW **Obv:** Facing cornucopias top supported arms, date above, denomination below **Rev:** Buildings on Lake Ganvié **Note:** Hallmark "999.9" right of denomination.

Date	Mintage	F	VF	XF	Unc	BU
1971 Proof	Inc. above	Value: 45.00				

KM# 1.3 100 FRANCS

5.1000 g., 0.9990 Silver .1638 oz. ASW **Obv:** Facing cornucopias top supported arms, date above, denomination below **Rev:** Buildings on Lake Ganvié **Note:** Hallmark "1000" lower right "S" in "FRANCS".

Date	Mintage	F	VF	XF	Unc	BU
1971 Proof	Inc. above	Value: 45.00				

KM# 2.1 200 FRANCS

10.2500 g., 0.9990 Silver .3292 oz. ASW **Subject:** 10th Anniversary of Independence **Obv:** Facing cornucopias top supported arms, date above, denomination below **Rev:** Abomey woman 3/4 left **Note:** Hallmark "999.9" between "200" and "FRANCS".

Date	Mintage	F	VF	XF	Unc	BU
1971 Proof	5,150	Value: 55.00				

KM# 2.2 200 FRANCS

10.2500 g., 0.9990 Silver .3292 oz. ASW **Obv:** Facing cornucopias top supported arms, date above, denomination below **Rev:** Abomey woman 3/4 left **Note:** Hallmark "1000" lower right of "S" in "FRANCS".

Date	Mintage	F	VF	XF	Unc	BU
1971 Proof	Inc. above	Value: 55.00				

KM# 2.3 200 FRANCS

10.2500 g., 0.9990 Silver .3292 oz. ASW **Obv:** Facing cornucopias top supported arms, date above, denomination below **Rev:** Abomey woman 3/4 left **Note:** Hallmark "999.9" lower right of "S" in "FRANCS".

Date	Mintage	F	VF	XF	Unc	BU
1971 Proof	Inc. above	Value: 55.00				

KM# 2.4 200 FRANCS

10.2500 g., 0.9990 Silver .3292 oz. ASW **Obv:** Facing cornucopias top supported arms, date above, denomination below **Rev:** Abomey woman 3/4 left **Note:** Hallmark "999.9" in oval below "F" in "CFA".

Date	Mintage	F	VF	XF	Unc	BU
1971 Proof	Inc. above	Value: 65.00				

KM# 3.1 500 FRANCS

25.2000 g., 0.9990 Silver .8094 oz. ASW **Subject:** 10th Anniversary of Independence **Obv:** Facing cornucopias top supported arms, date above, denomination below **Rev:** Ouémé woman right **Note:** "1000" in oval below "S" in "FRANCS".

Date	Mintage	F	VF	XF	Unc	BU
1971 Proof	5,550	Value: 95.00				

KM# 3.2 500 FRANCS

25.2000 g., 0.9990 Silver .8094 oz. ASW **Obv:** Facing cornucopias top supported arms, date above, denomination below **Rev:** Ouémé woman right **Note:** "1 AR" and "1000" to right of "CFA".

Date	Mintage	F	VF	XF	Unc	BU
1971 Proof	Inc. above	Value: 95.00				

KM# 4.1 1000 FRANCS

51.5000 g., 0.9990 Silver 1.6542 oz. ASW **Subject:** 10th Anniversary of Independence **Obv:** Facing cornucopias top supported arms, date above, denomination below **Rev:** Somba woman facing **Note:** "1000" in oval below "S" in "FRANCS".

Date	Mintage	F	VF	XF	Unc	BU
1971 Proof	6,500	Value: 150				

KM# 4.2 1000 FRANCS

51.5000 g., 0.9990 Silver 1.6542 oz. ASW **Obv:** Facing cornucopias top supported arms, date above, denomination below **Rev:** Somba woman facing **Note:** "1 AR" and "1000" to right of "CFA".

Date	Mintage	F	VF	XF	Unc	BU
1971 Proof	Inc. above	Value: 150				

KM# 6 2500 FRANCS
8.8800 g., 0.9000 Gold .2569 oz. AGW **Subject:** 10th Anniversary of Independence **Rev:** Dancers

Date	Mintage	F	VF	XF	Unc	BU
1971 Proof	960	Value: 275				

KM# 7 5000 FRANCS
17.7700 g., 0.9000 Gold .5142 oz. AGW **Subject:** 10th Anniversary of Independence **Obv:** Similar to 2500 Francs, KM#6 **Rev:** Water buffalos (suncerus caffer-bovidae)

Date	Mintage	F	VF	XF	Unc	BU
1971 Proof	610	Value: 550				

KM# 8 10000 FRANCS
35.5500 g., 0.9000 Gold 1.0287 oz. AGW **Subject:** 10th Anniversary of Independence **Obv:** Facing cornucopias top supported arms, date above, denomination below **Rev:** Acanthopholis

Date	Mintage	F	VF	XF	Unc	BU
1971 Proof	470	Value: 1,000				

KM# 9 25000 FRANCS
88.8800 g., 0.9000 Gold 2.5720 oz. AGW **Subject:** 10th Anniversary of Independence **Obv:** Facing cornucopias top supported arms, date above, denomination below **Rev:** Aligned Presidents busts, left

Date	Mintage	F	VF	XF	Unc	BU
1971 Proof	380	Value: 2,000				

PROOF SETS

KM#	Date	Mintage	Identification	Issue Price	Mkt Val
PS1	1971 (8)	380	KM#1.1-4.1, 6-9	—	4,175
PS2	1971 (4)	4,270	KM#1.1-4.1	36.00	345

DANISH WEST INDIES

The Danish West Indies (now the U.S. organized unincorporated territory of the Virgin Islands of the United States) consisted of the islands of St. Thomas, St. John, St. Croix, and 62 islets in the Caribbean Sea roughly 40 miles (64 km.) east of Puerto Rico. The islands have a combined area of 133 sq. mi. (352 sq. km.) and a population of *106,000. Capital: Charlotte Amalie. Tourism is the principal industry. Watch movements, costume jewelry, pharmaceuticals, and rum are exported.

The Virgin Islands were discovered by Columbus, in 1493, during his second voyage to America. During the 17th century, individual islands, actually the peaks of a submerged mountain range, were held by Spain, Holland, England, France and Denmark. These islands were also the favorite resorts of the buccaneers operating in the Caribbean and the coastal waters of eastern North America. Control of most of the 100-island group finally passed to Denmark, with England securing the easterly remainder. The Danish islands had their own coinage from the early 18th century, based on but unequal to, Denmark's homeland system. In the late 18th and early 19th centuries, Danish minor copper and silver coinage augmented the islands currency. The Danish islands were purchased by the United States in 1917 for $25 million, mainly to forestall their acquisition by Germany and because they command the Anegada Passage into the Caribbean Sea, a strategic point on the defense perimeter of the Panama Canal.

RULERS
Danish, until 1917

MINTMASTERS' INITIALS

Letter	Date	Name
P, VBP	1893-1918	Vilhelm Burchard Poulsen

MONEYERS' INITIALS

Letter	Date	Name
GJ	1901-1933	(Knud) Gunnar Jensen
AH	1908-1924	Andreas Frederik Vilhelm Hansen

MONETARY SYSTEM
(1904-1934)
5 Bit = 1 Cent
100 Bit = 1 Franc
5 Francs = 1 Daler

DANISH COLONY

The following listings are all believed to be spurious countermarks on a variety of host coins. The few genuine countermarked pieces are currently listed in the *Standard Catalog of World Coins, 1801-1900*.

DECIMAL COINAGE

20 Cents = 1 Franc

KM# 74 1/2 CENT (2-1/2 Bit)
Bronze **Ruler:** Christian IX **Obv:** Crowned monogram above date **Rev:** Denominations divided by trident, caduceus and sickle **Note:** Mintmaster's initial: P. Moneyer's initials: GJ.

Date	Mintage	F	VF	XF	Unc	BU
1905(h)	190,000	2.75	5.50	12.50	32.50	—
1905(h) Prooflike	—	—	—	—	—	—

Note: Specimen strike

KM# 75 CENT (5 Bit)
Bronze, 23 mm. **Ruler:** Christian IX **Rev:** Denominations divided by trident, caduceus and sickle **Note:** Mintmaster's initial: P. Moneyer's initials: GJ.

Date	Mintage	F	VF	XF	Unc	BU
1905(h)	500,000	3.50	7.50	20.00	55.00	—

KM# 83 CENT (5 Bit)
Bronze **Obv:** Crowned monogram above date **Rev:** Denominations divided by trident, caduceus and sickle **Note:** Mintmaster's initials: VBP. Moneyer's initials: AH-GJ.

Date	Mintage	F	VF	XF	Unc	BU
1913(h)	200,000	9.00	17.50	40.00	86.50	—

KM# 76 2 CENTS (10 Bit)
Bronze **Ruler:** Christian IX **Obv:** Crowned monogram above date **Rev:** Denominations divided by trident, caduceus and sickle **Note:** Mintmaster's initial: P. Moneyer's initials: GJ.

Date	Mintage	F	VF	XF	Unc	BU
1905(h)	150,000	5.00	13.50	30.00	70.00	—
1905(h) Prooflike	20	—	—	—	—	—

Note: Specimen strike

KM# 77 5 CENTS (25 Bit)
Nickel **Ruler:** Christian IX **Obv:** Crowned monogram above date **Rev:** Denominations divided by trident, caduceus and sickle **Note:** Mintmaster's initial: P. Moneyer's initials: GJ.

Date	Mintage	F	VF	XF	Unc	BU
1905(h)	199,000	3.00	7.50	18.50	62.50	—
1905(h) Prooflike	20	—	—	—	—	—

Note: Specimen strike

KM# 78 10 CENTS (50 Bit)
2.5000 g., 0.8000 Silver .0643 oz. ASW **Ruler:** Christian IX **Obv:** Head left **Rev:** Plant divides denominations **Note:** Mintmaster's initial: P. Moneyer's initials: GJ.

Date	Mintage	F	VF	XF	Unc	BU
1905(h)	175,000	4.00	8.50	18.50	63.50	—
1905(h) Prooflike	20	—	—	—	—	—

Note: Specimen strike

KM# 79 20 CENTS (1 Franc)
5.0000 g., 0.8000 Silver .1286 oz. ASW **Ruler:** Christian IX **Obv:** Uniformed bust left **Rev:** Three liberty figures divide denominations, date below **Note:** Mintmaster's initial: P. Moneyer's initials: GJ.

Date	Mintage	F	VF	XF	Unc	BU
1905(h)	150,000	12.50	27.50	67.50	135	—
1905(h) Prooflike	20	—	—	—	—	—

Note: Specimen strike

KM# 81 20 CENTS (1 Franc)
5.0000 g., 0.8000 Silver .1286 oz. ASW **Obv:** Head left **Rev:** Three liberty figures divide denominations, date below **Note:** Mintmaster's initial: P. Moneyer's initials: GJ.

Date	Mintage	F	VF	XF	Unc	BU
1907(h)	101,000	15.00	35.00	85.00	175	—
1907(h) Prooflike	10	—	—	—	—	—

Note: Specimen strike

KM# 80 40 CENTS (2 Francs)
10.0000 g., 0.8000 Silver .2572 oz. ASW **Ruler:** Christian IX **Note:** Mintmaster's initial: P. Moneyer's initials: GJ.

Date	Mintage	F	VF	XF	Unc	BU
1905(h)	38,000	30.00	60.00	160	325	—
1905(h) Prooflike	20	—	—	—	—	—

Note: Specimen strike

KM# 82 40 CENTS (2 Francs)
10.0000 g., 0.8000 Silver .2572 oz. ASW **Obv:** Head left **Rev:** Three liberty figures divide denominations, date below **Note:** Mintmaster's initial: P. Moneyer's initials: GJ.

Date	Mintage	F	VF	XF	Unc	BU
1907(h)	25,000	55.00	115	225	420	—
1907(h) Prooflike	10	—	—	—	—	1,100

Note: Specimen strike

KM# 72 4 DALER (20 Francs)
6.4516 g., 0.9000 Gold .1867 oz. AGW **Ruler:** Christian IX **Obv:** Head left **Rev:** Seated liberty figure divides denominations **Note:** Mintmaster's initial: P. Moneyer's initials: GJ.

Date	Mintage	F	VF	XF	Unc	BU
1904(h)	121,000	150	250	400	650	—
1905(h)	Inc. above	150	275	425	775	—

KM# 73 10 DALER (50 Francs)
16.1290 g., 0.9000 Gold .4667 oz. AGW **Ruler:** Christian IX **Obv:** Head left **Rev:** Seated liberty figure divides denominations, date below **Note:** Mintmaster's initial: P. Moneyer's initials: GJ.

Date	Mintage	F	VF	XF	Unc	BU
1904(h)	2,005	1,250	2,000	4,275	6,900	—

TRIAL STRIKES

KM#	Date	Mintage	Identification	Mkt Val
TS1	1904	—	20 Francs. Copper. 10.8000 g. KM#72.	—
TS2	1904	—	20 Francs. Copper. 10.8000 g. KM#72.	—

PROOF-LIKE SETS (PL)

KM#	Date	Mintage	Identification	Issue Price	Mkt Val
PL1	1859 (5)	10	KM#63-67	—	—
PL2	1862 (2)	—	KM#66-67	—	—
PL3	1878 (3)	—	KM#69-71	—	—
PL4	1905 (5)	20	KM#76-80	—	—
PL5	1907 (2)	10	KM#81-82	—	—

DANZIG

Danzig is an important seaport on the northern coast of Poland with access to the Baltic Sea. It has at different times belonged to the Teutonic Knights, Pomerania, Russia, and Prussia. It was part of the Polish Kingdom from 1587-1772.

Danzig (Gdansk) was a free city from 1919 to 1939 during which most of its modern coinage was made.

MONETARY SYSTEM

Until 1923
100 Pfennig = 1 Mark

Commencing 1923
100 Pfennig = 1 Gulden

FREE CITY

STANDARD COINAGE

KM# 140 PFENNIG
Bronze **Obv:** Denomination **Rev:** Arms divide date

Date	Mintage	F	VF	XF	Unc	BU
1923	4,000,000	1.00	3.00	5.00	10.00	18.00
1923 Proof	—	Value: 60.00				
1926	1,500,000	1.50	4.00	8.00	16.00	35.00
1929	1,000,000	2.50	7.50	12.00	20.00	40.00
1930	2,000,000	1.25	3.50	6.50	12.00	22.00
1937	3,000,000	1.25	3.50	6.50	12.00	22.00

KM# 141 2 PFENNIG
Bronze **Obv:** Denomination **Rev:** Arms divide date

Date	Mintage	F	VF	XF	Unc	BU
1923	1,000,000	1.75	4.50	7.50	15.00	35.00
1923 Proof	—	Value: 75.00				
1926	1,750,000	1.75	4.50	7.50	15.00	35.00
1937	500,000	2.75	6.50	12.50	20.00	40.00

KM# 142 5 PFENNIG
Copper-Nickel **Obv:** Denomination **Rev:** Arms divide date within snowflake design

Date	Mintage	F	VF	XF	Unc	BU
1923	3,000,000	1.25	2.75	6.00	12.50	22.50
1923 Proof	—	Value: 100				
1928	1,000,000	3.50	8.50	16.00	30.00	60.00
1928 Proof	—	Value: 175				

KM# 151 5 PFENNIG
Aluminum-Bronze **Obv:** Denomination **Rev:** Turbot left, date below

Date	Mintage	F	VF	XF	Unc	BU
1932	4,000,000	1.50	2.50	7.00	16.00	35.00

KM# 143 10 PFENNIG
Copper-Nickel **Obv:** Denomination **Rev:** Arms divide date within snowflake design

Date	Mintage	F	VF	XF	Unc	BU
1923	5,000,000	2.50	3.50	9.00	18.00	37.50
1923 Proof	—	Value: 125				

KM# 152 10 PFENNIG
Aluminum-Bronze **Obv:** Denomination **Rev:** Codfish (godus morrhua) left, date below

Date	Mintage	F	VF	XF	Unc	BU
1932	5,000,000	1.75	2.75	8.00	17.00	36.00

KM# 144 1/2 GULDEN
2.5000 g., 0.7500 Silver .0603 oz. ASW **Obv:** Date divided by shielded arms, denomination above **Rev:** Ship at sea

Date	Mintage	F	VF	XF	Unc	BU
1923	1,000,000	7.50	20.00	35.00	75.00	—
1923 Proof	—	Value: 150				
1927	400,000	17.50	35.00	75.00	140	—
1927 Proof	—	Value: 250				

KM# 153 1/2 GULDEN
Nickel **Obv:** Crowned vertical crosses **Rev:** Denomination above date

Date	Mintage	F	VF	XF	Unc	BU
1932	1,400,000	8.00	25.00	37.50	70.00	—

KM# 145 GULDEN
5.0000 g., 0.7500 Silver .1206 oz. ASW **Obv:** Ship and star divide denomination **Rev:** Shielded arms with supporters, star above, date below

Date	Mintage	F	VF	XF	Unc	BU
1923	2,500,000	12.50	27.50	40.00	95.00	—
1923 Proof	—	Value: 200				

KM# 154 GULDEN
Nickel **Obv:** Large numeric denomination within circle **Rev:** Arms divide date

Date	Mintage	F	VF	XF	Unc	BU
1932	2,500,000	8.00	25.00	35.00	60.00	90.00

KM# 146 2 GULDEN
10.0000 g., 0.7500 Silver .2411 oz. ASW **Obv:** Ship and star divide denomination **Rev:** Shielded arms with supporters, star above, date below

Date	Mintage	F	VF	XF	Unc	BU
1923	1,250,000	30.00	70.00	125	245	—
1923 Proof	—	Value: 325				

KM# 155 2 GULDEN
10.0000 g., 0.5000 Silver .1608 oz. ASW **Obv:** Ship afloat within circle, denomination below **Rev:** Shielded arms with supporters, date above

Date	Mintage	F	VF	XF	Unc	BU
1932	1,250,000	100	150	200	375	—

KM# 147 5 GULDEN
25.0000 g., 0.7500 Silver .6028 oz. ASW **Obv:** Marienkirche within circle **Rev:** Shielded arms with supporters, denomination below, star above

Date	Mintage	F	VF	XF	Unc	BU
1923	700,000	65.00	135	225	475	—
1923 Proof	—	Value: 550				
1927	160,000	150	250	385	675	—
1927 Proof	—	Value: 1,000				

KM# 156 5 GULDEN
14.8200 g., 0.5000 Silver .2382 oz. ASW **Obv:** Marienkirche within circle, denomination below **Rev:** Shielded arms with supporters, date above

Date	Mintage	F	VF	XF	Unc	BU
1932	430,000	125	225	350	950	—

KM# 157 5 GULDEN
14.8200 g., 0.5000 Silver .2382 oz. ASW **Obv:** Grain elevator by harbor within circle, denomination below **Rev:** Shielded arms with supporters, date above

Date	Mintage	F	VF	XF	Unc	BU
1932	430,000	150	350	850	1,500	—

KM# 158 5 GULDEN
Nickel **Obv:** Ship with three crowns asea, numeric denomination at left, circle surrounds, denomination below circle, date at right **Rev:** Arms with supporters on oval shield

Date	Mintage	F	VF	XF	Unc	BU
1935	800,000	120	180	265	500	—

KM# 159 10 GULDEN
Nickel **Obv:** Town hall tower, numeric denomination at right, circle surrounds, denomination below, date at right **Rev:** Arms with supporters on oval shield

Date	Mintage	F	VF	XF	Unc	BU
1935	380,000	.300	500	750	1,400	—

KM# 148 25 GULDEN
7.9881 g., 0.9170 Gold .2354 oz. AGW **Obv:** Arms between columns with supporters, date below **Rev:** Statue from the Nepture fountain, denomination at left and divided below **Note:** Presented to senate members.

Date	Mintage	F	VF	XF	Unc	BU
1923	800	—	1,650	2,000	3,000	—
1923 Proof	200	Value: 4,000				

KM# 150 25 GULDEN
7.9881 g., 0.9170 Gold .2354 oz. AGW **Obv:** Shielded arms with supporters, date below **Rev:** Statue from the Nepture fountain, denomination at left and divided below **Note:** Not released for circulation. A few were distributed on Sept. 1, 1939, in VIP presentation cases.

Date	Mintage	F	VF	XF	Unc	BU
1930	Est. 4,000	—	—	7,000	10,000	—

TOKEN COINAGE

KM# Tn1 10 PFENNIG
Zinc **Obv:** Angel head above oval arms within circle, date below **Rev:** Denomination within cartouche **Note:** Small "10" in cartouche.

Date	Mintage	F	VF	XF	Unc	BU
1920	876,000	12.00	18.00	35.00	75.00	—

KM# Tn2 10 PFENNIG
Zinc **Note:** Large "10".

Date	Mintage	F	VF	XF	Unc	BU
1920	124,000	100	150	225	350	—

PATTERNS

Including off metal strikes

KM#	Date	Mintage	Identification	Mkt Val
Pn43	1920	30	10 Pfennig. Silver.	3,250
Pn44	1920	30	10 Pfennig. Silver. Large 10.	3,250
Pn45	1923	—	5 Pfennig. Brass.	165
Pn46	1923	—	10 Pfennig. Brass.	170
Pn47	1923	10	Gulden. Gold. KM145.	7,500
Pn49	1935	—	5 Gulden. Nickel. PROBE.	—
Pn48	1927	—	2 Pfennig. Brass.	—
Pn50	1935	—	10 Gulden. Nickel. PROBE.	—
Pn51	1935	—	10 Gulden. Tin.	110

PROOF SETS

KM#	Date	Mintage	Identification	Issue Price	Mkt Val
PS1	1923 (8)	—	KM140-147	—	1,600

DENMARK

The Kingdom of Denmark (Danmark), a constitutional monarchy located at the mouth of the Baltic Sea, has an area of 16,639 sq. mi. (43,070 sq. km.) and a population of 5.2 million. Capital: Copenhagen. Most of the country is arable. Agriculture is conducted by large farms served by cooperatives. The largest industries are food processing, iron and metal, and shipping. Machinery, meats (chiefly bacon), dairy products and chemicals are exported.

Denmark, a great power during the Viking period of the 9th-11th centuries, conducted raids on western Europe and England, and in the 11th century united England, Denmark and Norway under the rule of King Canute. Despite a struggle between the crown and the nobility (13th-14th centuries) which forced the King to grant a written constitution, Queen Margaret (Margrethe) (1387-1412) succeeded in uniting Denmark, Norway, Sweden, Finland and Greenland under the Danish crown, placing all of the Nordic countries under the rule of Denmark. An unwise alliance with Napoleon caused the loss of Norway to Sweden in 1814. In the following years a liberal movement was fostered, which succeeded in making Denmark a constitutional monarchy in 1849.

In 1864, Denmark lost Schleswig and Holstein to Prussia. In 1920, Denmark regained North-Schleswig by plebiscite.

The present decimal system of currency was introduced in 1874. As a result of a referendum held September 28, 2000, the currency of the European Monetary Union, the Euro, will not be introduced in Denmark in the foreseeable future.

RULERS
Christian IX, 1863-1906
Frederik VIII, 1906-1912
Christian X, 1912-1947
Frederik IX, 1947-1972
Margrethe II, 1972—

MINT MARKS
(h) - Copenhagen, heart

MINT OFFICIALS' INITIALS

Copenhagen

Letter	Date	Name
*P, VBP	1893-1918	Vilhelm Buchard Poulsen
HCN	1919-1927	Hans Christian Nielsen
N	1927-1955	Niels Peter Nielsen
C	1956-1971	Alfred Frederik Christiansen
S	1971-1978	Vagn Sorensen
B	1978-1981	Peter M Bjarno
R, NR	1982-1989	N. Norregaard Rasmussen
LG	1989-2001	Laust Grove

NOTE: The letter P was only used on Danish West Indies coins and on Denmark, KM#802.

MONEYERS' INITIALS

Copenhagen

Letter	Date	Name
GI, GJ	1901-1933	Knud Gunnar Jensen
AH	1908-1924	Andreas Frederik Vilhelm Hansen
HS, S	1933-1968	Harald Salomon
B	1968-1983	Frode Bahnsen
A	1986-	Johan Alkjaer (designer)
HV	1986-	Hanne Varming (sculptor)
JP	1989-	Jan Petersen

MONETARY SYSTEM
100 Øre = 1 Krone

KINGDOM

DECIMAL COINAGE

100 Øre = 1 Krone; 1874-present

KM# 792.2 ORE
2.0000 g., Bronze **Ruler:** Christian IX **Obv:** Crowned CIX monogram, date at lower left, initials VBP at lower right **Rev:** Value above porpoise and barley ear

Date	Mintage	F	VF	XF	Unc	BU
1902/802(h) VBP	2,977,000	2.75	4.50	10.00	30.00	—
1902(h) VBP	Inc. above	1.75	2.75	6.50	25.00	—
1904/804(h) VBP	4,962,000	1.75	3.50	6.25	18.00	—
1904(h) VBP	Inc. above	1.25	2.25	4.75	16.00	—

KM# 804 ORE
2.0000 g., Bronze **Ruler:** Frederik VIII **Obv:** Denomination within circle, date and initials VBP below **Rev:** Crowned F8F monogram, initials GJ at lower right **Rev. Legend:** "THE KINGDOM OF DENMARK"

Date	Mintage	F	VF	XF	Unc	BU
1907(h) VBP, GJ	5,975,000	1.25	2.75	5.50	16.00	—

Date	Mintage	F	VF	XF	Unc	BU
1909(h) VBP; GJ	2,985,000	1.25	2.75	5.50	18.50	—
1910(h) VBP; GJ	2,994,000	1.75	4.50	12.00	30.00	—
1912(h) VBP; GJ	3,006,000	1.25	3.75	8.00	25.00	—

KM# 812.1 ORE

2.0000 g., Bronze **Ruler:** Christian X **Obv:** Crowned CX monogram, initials VBP and mint mark at lower left, date and initials GJ at lower right **Rev:** Thick denomination, ornaments flanking

Date	Mintage	F	VF	XF	Unc	BU
1913(h) VBP; GJ	5,011,000	1.00	1.50	2.00	6.00	—
1915(h) VBP; GJ	4,940,000	1.35	2.25	3.75	10.00	—
1916(h) VBP; GJ	2,439,000	1.35	2.75	5.00	14.00	—
1917(h) VBP; GJ	4,564,000	16.00	25.00	45.00	90.00	—

KM# 812.1a ORE

1.7400 g., Iron **Ruler:** Christian X **Obv:** Crowned CX monogram, initials VBP and mint mark at lower left, date and initials GJ at lower right **Rev:** Thick denomination, ornaments flanking

Date	Mintage	F	VF	XF	Unc	BU
1918(h) VBP; GJ	6,776,000	2.00	5.50	20.00	65.00	—

KM# 812.2 ORE

2.0000 g., Bronze **Ruler:** Christian X **Obv:** Crowned CX monogram, initials HCN and mint mark at lower left, date and initials GJ at lower right **Rev:** Value, ornaments flanking

Date	Mintage	F	VF	XF	Unc	BU
1919(h) HCN; GJ	4,586,000	1.00	1.50	4.00	8.50	—
1920(h) HCN; GJ	2,367,000	6.00	12.50	30.00	60.00	—
1921(h) HCN; GJ	3,121,000	1.35	2.25	3.25	8.50	—
1922(h) HCN; GJ	3,267,000	1.75	2.50	4.00	9.50	—
1923(h) HCN; GJ	2,938,000	1.75	2.50	3.75	8.50	—

KM# 812.2a ORE

1.7400 g., Iron **Ruler:** Christian X **Obv:** Crowned CX monogram, initials HCN and mint mark at lower left, date and initials GJ at lower right **Rev:** Value, ornaments flanking

Date	Mintage	F	VF	XF	Unc	BU
1919(h) HCN; GJ	931,000	5.00	15.00	42.50	110	—

KM# 826.1 ORE

1.9000 g., Bronze **Ruler:** Christian X **Obv:** Crowned CXC monogram within title "KING OF DENMARK", initials GJ below **Rev:** Country name and date above center hole, denomination, mint mark, and initials HCN below

Date	Mintage	F	VF	XF	Unc	BU
1926(h) HCN; GJ	1,572,000	3.00	6.50	20.00	65.00	—
1927(h) HCN; GJ	Inc. above	0.10	0.30	4.50	25.00	—

KM# 826.2 ORE

1.9000 g., Bronze **Ruler:** Christian X **Obv:** Crowned CXC monogram within title "KING OF DENMARK", initials GJ below **Rev:** Country name and date above center hole, denomination, mint mark, and initial N below **Note:** For coins dated 1941 refer to Faeroe Islands listings.

Date	Mintage	F	VF	XF	Unc	BU
1927(h) N; GJ	Inc. above	4.00	11.00	30.00	90.00	—
1928(h) N; GJ	29,691,000	0.10	0.25	2.75	12.50	—
1929(h) N; GJ	5,172,000	0.10	0.25	2.75	17.50	—
1930(h) N; GJ	5,306,000	0.10	0.20	2.75	20.00	—
1932(h) N; GJ	5,089,000	0.10	0.20	2.75	18.00	—
1933(h) N; GJ	2,095,000	0.25	1.50	5.50	35.00	—
1934(h) N; GJ	3,665,000	—	0.15	1.00	9.50	—
1935(h) N; GJ	5,668,000	—	0.15	1.00	7.00	—
1936(h) N; GJ	5,584,000	—	0.15	0.40	4.00	—
1937(h) N; GJ	6,877,000	—	0.15	0.40	3.25	—
1938(h) N; GJ	3,850,000	—	0.15	0.40	2.50	—
1939(h) N; GJ	5,662,000	—	0.15	0.30	2.50	—
1940(h) N; GJ	1,965,000	—	0.15	0.30	2.00	—

KM# 832 ORE

1.6000 g., Zinc **Ruler:** Christian X **Obv:** Crowned monogram divides date, mint mark and initials N-S below **Rev:** Oak and beech leaves divide denomination

Date	Mintage	F	VF	XF	Unc	BU
1941(h) N; S	21,570,000	0.10	0.30	9.00	40.00	—
1942(h) N; S	6,997,000	0.10	0.30	9.00	40.00	—
1943(h) N; S	15,082,000	0.10	0.30	9.00	40.00	—
1944(h) N; S	11,981,000	0.10	0.30	9.00	40.00	—
1945(h) N; S	916,000	1.00	2.00	20.00	60.00	—
1946(h) N; S	712,000	3.00	7.50	25.00	75.00	—

KM# 839.1 ORE

1.6000 g., Zinc, 16 mm. **Ruler:** Frederik IX **Obv:** Crowned F IX R monogram and date **Rev:** Mint mark, initials N-S below value

Date	Mintage	F	VF	XF	Unc	BU
1948(h) N; S	460,000	1.00	2.25	9.50	55.00	—
1949(h) N; S	2,513,000	0.35	0.80	3.50	45.00	—
1950(h) N; S	9,453,000	0.25	0.40	3.25	40.00	—
1951(h) N; S	2,931,000	0.35	1.00	3.50	55.00	—
1952(h) N; S	7,626,000	0.15	0.30	2.25	30.00	—
1953(h) N; S	11,994,000	0.10	0.20	2.25	30.00	—
1954(h) N; S	12,642,000	0.10	0.20	2.25	25.00	—
1955(h) N; S	14,177,000	0.10	0.20	1.75	25.00	—

KM# 839.2 ORE

1.6000 g., Zinc, 16 mm. **Ruler:** Frederik IX **Obv:** Crowned F R monogram, IX below, crown divides date **Rev:** Mint mark, initials C-S below denomination

Date	Mintage	F	VF	XF	Unc	BU
1956(h) C; S	20,211,000	0.10	0.20	0.80	7.00	—
1957(h) C; S	20,900,000	0.10	0.20	0.80	7.00	—
1958(h) C; S	16,021,000	—	0.10	0.60	6.00	—
1959(h) C; S	15,929,000	—	0.10	0.60	6.00	—
1960(h) C; S	23,982,000	—	0.10	0.60	4.00	—
1961(h) C; S	18,986,000	—	0.10	0.50	3.00	—
1962(h) C; S	16,992,000	—	0.10	0.50	1.75	—
1963(h) C; S	28,986,000	—	0.10	0.40	1.75	—
1964(h) C; S	21,971,000	—	0.10	0.40	1.75	—
1965(h) C; S	29,943,000	—	0.10	0.30	1.75	—
1966(h) C; S	35,907,000	—	0.10	0.20	1.75	—
1967(h) C; S	32,959,000	—	0.10	0.20	1.75	—
1968(h) C; S	21,889,000	—	—	0.20	0.80	—
1969(h) C; S	29,243,000	—	—	0.10	0.80	—
1970(h) C; S	22,970,000	—	—	0.10	0.50	—
1971(h) C; S	21,983,000	—	—	0.10	0.50	—

KM# 839.3 ORE

1.6000 g., Zinc, 16 mm. **Ruler:** Frederik IX **Obv:** Crowned F IX R monogram and date **Rev:** Mint mark, initials C-S below value

Date	Mintage	F	VF	XF	Unc	BU
1972(h) S; S	13,000,000	—	—	0.10	0.60	—

KM# 846 ORE

1.8000 g., Bronze **Ruler:** Frederik IX **Obv:** Crowned F IX R monogram, date **Rev:** Two barley stalks around value, initials below **Note:** Never released for circulation, see note at 2 Ore, KM#847.

Date	Mintage	F	VF	XF	Unc	BU
1960(h) C; S	8,990,000	—	—	1.00	1.50	—
1962(h) C; S	Inc. above	—	—	1.00	1.50	—
1963(h) C; S	9,980,000	—	—	1.00	1.50	—
1964(h) C; S	2,990,000	—	—	1.00	1.50	—

KM# 793.2 2 ORE

4.0000 g., Bronze **Ruler:** Christian IX **Obv:** Crowned CIX monogram, date at lower left, initials VBP at lower right **Rev:** Denomination above porpoise and barley sprig

Date	Mintage	F	VF	XF	Unc	BU
1902/802(h) VBP	3,502,000	3.00	6.00	12.00	45.00	—
1902(h) VBP	Inc. above	1.50	3.00	6.00	37.50	—
1906(h) VBP	2,498,000	3.50	10.00	22.50	45.00	—

KM# 805 2 ORE

4.0000 g., Bronze **Ruler:** Frederik VIII **Obv:** Denomination within circle, date and initials VBP below **Rev:** Crowned F8F monogram, initials GJ at lower right

Date	Mintage	F	VF	XF	Unc	BU
1907(h) VBP; GJ	2,502,000	1.50	3.00	12.00	32.50	—
1909(h) VBP; GJ	2,485,000	2.25	5.00	20.00	70.00	—
1912(h) VBP; GJ	2,480,000	2.25	5.00	14.00	45.00	—

KM# 813.1 2 ORE

4.0000 g., Bronze **Ruler:** Christian X **Obv:** Crowned CX monogram, initials VBP and mint mark at lower left, date and initials GJ at lower right **Rev:** Value, ornament flanking

Date	Mintage	F	VF	XF	Unc	BU
1913(h) VBP; GJ	373,000	27.50	50.00	85.00	220	—
1914(h) VBP; GJ	2,126,000	2.25	4.00	6.50	22.50	—
1915(h) VBP; GJ	2,485,000	1.75	4.00	6.50	25.00	—
1916(h) VBP; GJ	1,383,000	2.75	4.00	7.50	27.50	—
1917(h) VBP; GJ	1,837,000	14.00	27.50	45.00	90.00	125

KM# 813.1a 2 ORE

3.4700 g., Iron **Ruler:** Christian X **Obv:** Crowned CX monogram, initials VBP and mint mark at lower left, date and initials GJ at lower right **Rev:** Value, ornament flanking

Date	Mintage	F	VF	XF	Unc	BU
1918(h) VBP; GJ	4,160,999	2.25	7.50	30.00	90.00	—

KM# 813.2 2 ORE

4.0000 g., Bronze **Ruler:** Christian X **Obv:** Crowned CX monogram, initials HCN and mint mark at lower left, date and initials GJ at lower right **Rev:** Thick denomination, ornaments flanking

Date	Mintage	F	VF	XF	Unc	BU
1919(h) HCN; GJ	5,503,000	6.00	12.00	27.50	60.00	—
1920(h) HCN; GJ	2,528,000	1.00	1.50	3.50	22.50	—
1921(h) HCN; GJ	2,158,000	3.25	5.00	8.50	20.00	—
1923(h) HCN; GJ	2,625,000	2.25	4.00	7.00	20.00	—

KM# 813.2a 2 ORE

3.4700 g., Iron **Ruler:** Christian X **Obv:** Crowned CX monogram, initials HCN and mint mark at lower left, date and initials GJ at lower right **Rev:** Value, ornament flanking

Date	Mintage	F	VF	XF	Unc	BU
1919(h) HCN; GJ	1,944,000	20.00	45.00	100	250	—

KM# 827.1 2 ORE

3.8000 g., Bronze **Ruler:** Christian X **Obv:** Crowned CXC monogram within title "KING OF DENMARK", initials GJ below **Rev:** Country name and date above center hole, denomination, mint mark, and initials HCN below

Date	Mintage	F	VF	XF	Unc	BU
1926(h) HCN; GJ	301,000	42.50	80.00	250	1,050	—
1927(h) HCN; GJ	15,359,000	0.10	0.20	3.25	25.00	—

KM# 827.2 2 ORE

3.8000 g., Bronze **Ruler:** Christian X **Obv:** Crowned CXC monogram within title "KING OF DENMARK", initials GJ below **Rev:** Country name and date above center hole, denomination, mint mark, and initial N below **Note:** For coins dated 1941 refer to Faeroe Islands listings.

Date	Mintage	F	VF	XF	Unc	BU
1927(h) N; GJ	Inc. above	1.00	2.25	55.00	190	290
1928(h) N; GJ	5,758,000	0.10	0.20	2.50	22.50	—
1929(h) N; GJ	6,817,000	0.10	0.20	2.50	42.50	—
1930(h) N; GJ	2,327,000	0.75	1.50	8.50	80.00	—
1931(h) N; GJ	5,135,000	0.10	0.20	2.25	30.00	—
1932(h) N; GJ	Inc. above	1.25	2.25	35.00	150	—
1934(h) N; GJ	756,000	0.50	1.00	8.00	42.50	—
1935(h) N; GJ	1,391,000	0.10	0.20	1.50	22.50	—
1936(h) N; GJ	2,973,000	0.10	0.20	1.00	22.50	—
1937(h) N; GJ	3,437,000	0.10	0.20	1.00	12.50	—
1938(h) N; GJ	2,177,000	—	0.10	0.50	5.50	—
1939(h) N; GJ	3,165,000	—	0.10	0.50	3.25	—
1940(h) N; GJ	1,582,000	—	0.10	0.50	2.25	—

KM# 833 2 ORE

1.2000 g., Aluminum **Ruler:** Christian X **Obv:** Crowned CX monogram and date within title: "KING OF DENMARK"; mint mark and initials N-S below **Rev:** Oak and beach leaves divide denomination

Date	Mintage	F	VF	XF	Unc	BU
1941(h) N; S	26,205,000	0.10	0.60	2.25	14.00	—
1941(h) N; S Proof	—	Value: 150				

KM# 833a 2 ORE

3.2000 g., Zinc **Ruler:** Christian X **Obv:** Crowned CX monogram divides date, mint mark and initials N-S below **Rev:** Oak and beach leaves divide denomination

Date	Mintage	F	VF	XF	Unc	BU
1942(h) N; S	12,934,000	0.10	0.40	10.00	55.00	—
1943(h) N; S	9,603,000	0.10	0.40	10.00	55.00	—
1944(h) N; S	6,069,000	0.10	0.40	10.00	55.00	—
1945(h) N; S	329,000	4.25	8.50	45.00	120	—
1947(h) N; S	589,000	1.50	3.00	22.50	90.00	—

KM# 840.1 2 ORE

3.2000 g., Zinc, 20.8 mm. **Ruler:** Frederik IX **Obv:** Crowned F IX R monogram and date **Rev:** Mint mark, initials N-S below value

Date	Mintage	F	VF	XF	Unc	BU
1948(h) N; S	1,927,000	0.40	1.00	5.50	50.00	—
1949(h) N; S	1,603,000	3.75	14.50	55.00	225	—
1950(h) N; S	4,544,000	0.75	1.35	5.50	55.00	—
1951(h) N; S	3,766,000	1.50	2.50	11.00	85.00	—
1952(h) N; S	4,874,000	0.10	0.20	2.50	45.00	—
1953(h) N; S	8,112,000	0.10	0.20	2.50	35.00	—
1954(h) N; S	6,497,000	0.10	0.20	2.50	25.00	—
1955(h) N; S	6,968,000	—	0.10	1.50	15.00	—

KM# 840.2 2 ORE

3.2000 g., Zinc, 20.8 mm. **Ruler:** Frederik IX **Obv:** Crowned FR monogram divides date, IX below **Rev:** Mint mark, initials C-S below denomination

Date	Mintage	F	VF	XF	Unc	BU
1956(h) C; S	10,004,000	—	0.10	1.00	7.50	—
1957(h) C; S	15,329,000	—	0.10	1.00	6.00	—
1958(h) C; S	8,119,999	—	0.10	1.00	5.00	—
1959(h) C; S	10,462,000	—	0.10	1.00	4.00	—
1960(h) C; S	16,504,000	—	0.10	0.80	3.00	—
1961(h) C; S	15,504,000	—	0.10	0.80	2.50	—
1962(h) C; S	10,980,000	—	0.10	0.80	2.50	—
1963(h) C; S	19,470,000	—	0.10	0.30	1.50	—
1964(h) C; S	15,411,000	—	0.10	0.30	1.00	—
1965(h) C; S	20,173,000	—	0.10	0.20	1.00	—
1966(h) C; S	21,949,000	—	0.10	0.20	1.00	—
1967(h) C; S	22,439,000	—	0.10	0.20	1.00	—
1968(h) C; S	17,632,000	—	—	0.10	0.80	—
1969(h) C; S	29,276,000	—	—	0.10	0.80	—
1970(h) C; S	23,864,000	—	—	0.10	0.50	—
1971(h) C; S	35,811,000	—	—	0.10	0.50	—

KM# 840.3 2 ORE

3.2000 g., Zinc **Ruler:** Frederik IX **Obv:** Crowned F IX R monogram and date **Rev:** Mint mark, initials S-S below value

Date	Mintage	F	VF	XF	Unc	BU
1972(h) S; S	6,496,000	—	0.15	0.30	0.85	—

KM# 847 2 ORE

3.6000 g., Bronze **Ruler:** Frederik IX **Obv:** Crowned F IX R monogram, date **Rev:** Two barley stalks around value, mint mark and initials C-S below **Note:** KM#847 was never released for circulation. Together with the 4 dates of 1 Øre, KM#846, they were sold as a 10 coin set to collectors by the mint. Approximately 100,000 sets were sold, remaining coins were melted.

Date	Mintage	F	VF	XF	Unc	BU
1960(h) C; S	Inc. above	—	—	1.00	1.50	—
1962(h) C; S	Inc. above	—	—	1.00	1.50	—
1963(h) C; S	100,000	—	—	1.00	1.50	—
1964(h) C; S	3,990,000	—	—	1.00	1.50	—
1965(h) C; S	11,980,000	—	—	1.00	1.50	—
1966(h) C; S	12,000,000	—	—	1.00	1.50	—

KM# 794.2 5 ORE

8.0000 g., Bronze **Ruler:** Christian IX **Obv:** Crowned CIX monogram, date at lower left, initials VBP at lower right **Rev:** Denomination above porpoise and barley sprig

Date	Mintage	F	VF	XF	Unc	BU
1902(h) VBP	601,000	12.50	25.00	47.50	140	—
1904(h) VBP	397,000	25.00	50.00	125	275	—
1906(h) VBP	1,000,000	17.50	40.00	85.00	200	—

KM# 806 5 ORE

8.0000 g., Bronze **Ruler:** Frederik VIII **Obv:** Crowned F VIII F monogram, initials VBP at lower right **Rev:** Denomination within circle, date and initials VP below

Date	Mintage	F	VF	XF	Unc	BU
1907(h) VBP; GJ	1,000,000	8.00	15.00	40.00	95.00	—
1908(h) VBP; GJ	1,198,000	9.00	17.00	45.00	105	—
1912(h) VBP; GJ	999,000	10.00	19.00	50.00	120	160

KM# 814.1 5 ORE

8.0000 g., Bronze **Ruler:** Christian X **Obv:** Crowned CX monogram, initials VBP and mint mark lower at left, date and initials GJ at lower right **Rev:** Thick denomination, ornaments flanking

Date	Mintage	F	VF	XF	Unc	BU
1913(h) VBP; GJ	216,000	60.00	110	150	275	425
1914(h) VBP; GJ	785,000	8.00	16.00	20.00	45.00	—
1916(h) VBP; GJ	887,000	10.00	20.00	30.00	60.00	—
1917(h) VBP; GJ	494,000	10.00	20.00	40.00	80.00	225

KM# 814.1a 5 ORE

6.9400 g., Iron **Ruler:** Christian X **Obv:** Crowned CX monogram, initials VBP and mint mark at lower left, date and initials GJ at lower right **Rev:** Value, ornament flanking

Date	Mintage	F	VF	XF	Unc	BU
1918(h) VBP; GJ	1,918,000	7.00	14.00	40.00	130	—

KM# 814.2 5 ORE

8.0000 g., Bronze **Ruler:** Christian X **Obv:** Crowned CX monogram, initials HCN and mint mark at lower left, date and initials GJ at lower right **Rev:** Thick denomination, ornaments flanking

Date	Mintage	F	VF	XF	Unc	BU
1919(h) HCN; GJ	994,000	3.25	5.50	8.50	22.50	—
1920(h) HCN; GJ	2,618,000	7.00	13.50	22.50	45.00	—
1921(h) HCN; GJ	3,248,000	4.50	8.00	11.50	25.00	—
1923(h) HCN; GJ	369,000	85.00	175	240	425	—

KM# 814.2a 5 ORE

6.9400 g., Iron **Ruler:** Christian X **Obv:** Crowned CX monogram, initials HCN and mint mark at lower left, date and initials GJ at lower right **Rev:** Value, ornament flanking

Date	Mintage	F	VF	XF	Unc	BU
1919(h) HCN; GJ	1,034,999	17.50	50.00	110	265	—

KM# 828.1 5 ORE

7.6000 g., Bronze **Ruler:** Christian X **Obv:** Crowned CXC monogram within title "KING OF DENMARK", initials GJ below **Rev:** Country name and date above center hole, denomination, mint mark, and initials HCN below

Date	Mintage	F	VF	XF	Unc	BU
1927(h) HCN; GJ	7,129,000	0.10	0.25	3.50	30.00	—

KM# 828.2 5 ORE

7.6000 g., Bronze **Ruler:** Christian X **Obv:** Crowned CXC monogram within title "KING OF DENMARK", initials GJ below **Rev:** Country name and date above center hole, denomination, mint mark, and initial N below **Note:** For coins dated 1941 refer to Faeroe Islands.

Date	Mintage	F	VF	XF	Unc	BU
1927(h) N; GJ	Inc. above	4.00	8.00	90.00	700	1,000
1928(h) N; GJ	4,685,000	0.10	0.40	3.50	32.50	—
1929(h) N; GJ	1,387,000	0.30	0.60	5.00	75.00	—
1930(h) N; GJ	1,339,000	0.40	0.80	15.00	80.00	—
1932(h) N; GJ	1,010,999	0.30	0.60	9.50	75.00	100
1932(h) N; GJ Proof	—	Value: 150				
1934(h) N; GJ	524,000	0.30	0.60	8.00	55.00	—
1935(h) N; GJ	1,124,000	2.25	4.50	27.50	125	—
1936(h) N; GJ	1,091,000	0.20	0.40	3.25	37.50	—
1937(h) N; GJ	1,209,000	0.20	0.40	1.50	25.00	—
1938(h) N; GJ	1,093,000	0.40	1.00	2.25	15.00	—
1939(h) N; GJ	1,402,000	0.15	0.20	0.50	4.25	—
1940(h) N; GJ	2,735,000	0.15	0.20	0.50	4.25	—

KM# 834 5 ORE

2.4000 g., Aluminum **Ruler:** Christian X **Obv:** Crowned CX monogram divides date, mint mark and initials N-S below **Rev:** Oak and beech leaves divide denomination

Date	Mintage	F	VF	XF	Unc	BU
1941(h) N; S Proof	—	Value: 150				
1941(h) N; S	16,984,000	0.10	1.00	3.75	20.00	—

KM# 834a 5 ORE

6.4000 g., Zinc **Ruler:** Christian X **Obv:** Crowned CX monogram and date within title: "KING OF DENMARK"; mint mark and initials N-S below **Rev:** Value between oak and beech leaves

Date	Mintage	F	VF	XF	Unc	BU
1942(h) N; S	2,963,000	1.50	3.00	30.00	90.00	—
1943(h) N; S	4,522,000	0.50	1.75	22.50	75.00	—
1944(h) N; S	3,744,000	0.60	2.00	22.50	75.00	—
1945(h) N; S	864,000	4.00	10.00	45.00	125	—

KM# 843.1 5 ORE

6.4000 g., Zinc **Ruler:** Frederik IX **Obv:** Crowned FR monogram, IX below, divides date **Rev:** Mint mark, initials N-S below denomination

Date	Mintage	F	VF	XF	Unc	BU
1950(h) N; S	657,000	6.00	12.50	50.00	120	—
1951(h) N; S Straight 5	1,858,000	1.25	3.00	14.00	60.00	—
1951(h) N; S Slant 5	Inc. above	1.00	2.50	12.00	55.00	—
1952(h) N; S	3,562,000	0.60	1.00	6.50	35.00	—

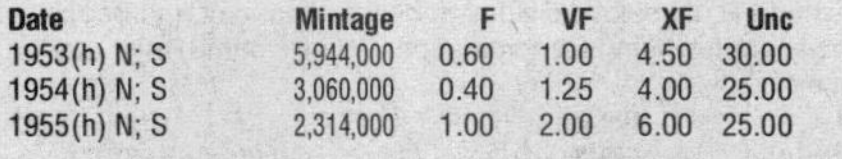

Date	Mintage	F	VF	XF	Unc	BU
1953(h) N; S	5,944,000	0.60	1.00	4.50	30.00	—
1954(h) N; S	3,060,000	0.40	1.25	4.00	25.00	—
1955(h) N; S	2,314,000	1.00	2.00	6.00	25.00	—

KM# 843.2 5 ORE

6.4000 g., Zinc **Ruler:** Frederik IX **Obv:** Crowned FR monogram, IX below, divides date **Rev:** Mint mark, initials C-S below denomination

Date	Mintage	F	VF	XF	Unc	BU
1956(h) C; S	5,888,000	0.40	1.25	2.75	11.00	—
1957(h) C; S	8,606,000	0.20	0.50	1.50	6.50	—
1958(h) C; S	9,598,000	0.20	0.50	1.50	5.50	—
1959(h) C; S	6,110,000	0.10	0.20	1.00	5.50	—
1960(h) C; S	11,800,000	0.10	0.20	1.00	3.50	—
1961(h) C; S	8,995,000	0.20	0.40	1.00	2.75	—
1962(h) C; S	9,729,000	0.10	0.20	0.80	2.75	—
1963(h) C; S	8,980,000	0.10	0.20	0.80	2.50	—
1964(h) C; S	6,738,000	0.75	1.25	3.50	7.00	—

KM# 848.1 5 ORE

6.0000 g., Bronze, 24 mm. **Ruler:** Frederik IX **Obv:** Crowned FR monogram, IX below, divides date **Rev:** Two barley stalks around denomination, initials C-S below

Date	Mintage	F	VF	XF	Unc	BU
1960(h) C; S	3,760,000	0.10	0.25	1.25	6.00	—
1962(h) C; S	5,873,000	0.25	0.75	2.25	20.00	—
1963(h) C; S	23,287,000	—	0.10	0.50	2.75	—
1964(h) C; S	41,521,000	—	0.10	0.50	2.75	—
1965(h) C; S	14,229,000	—	0.10	0.50	2.75	—
1966(h) C; S	23,410,000	—	0.10	0.50	2.75	—
1967(h) C; S	15,094,000	—	0.10	0.50	2.75	—
1968(h) C; S	16,105,000	—	0.10	0.40	1.75	—
1969(h) C; S	23,594,000	—	0.10	0.30	1.00	—
1970(h) C; S	26,176,000	—	—	0.10	1.00	—
1971(h) C; S	10,076,000	—	—	0.10	1.00	—

KM# 848.2 5 ORE

6.0000 g., Bronze, 24 mm. **Ruler:** Frederik IX **Obv:** Crowned F IX R monogram, date **Rev:** Two barley stalks around value, initials S-S below

Date	Mintage	F	VF	XF	Unc	BU
1972(h) S; S	27,938,000	—	—	0.10	1.00	—

KM# 859.1 5 ORE

1.6000 g., Copper Clad Iron, 15.5 mm. **Ruler:** Margrethe II **Obv:** Crowned MIIR monogram divides date; mint mark, initials S-B **Rev:** "DANMARK" above denomination

Date	Mintage	F	VF	XF	Unc	BU
1973(h) S; B	75,138,000	—	—	0.10	0.70	—
1974(h) S; B	71,796,000	—	—	0.10	0.70	—
1975(h) S; B	45,004,000	—	—	0.10	0.70	—
1976(h) S; B	73,296,000	—	—	0.10	0.70	—
1977(h) S; B	74,066,000	—	—	0.10	0.70	—
1978(h) S; B	52,425,000	—	—	0.10	0.70	—

KM# 859.2 5 ORE

1.6000 g., Copper Clad Iron, 15.5 mm. **Ruler:** Margrethe II **Obv:** Crowned MIIR monogram divides date; mint mark, initials B-B **Rev:** "DANMARK" above denomination

Date	Mintage	F	VF	XF	Unc	BU
1979(h) B; B	58,953,000	—	—	0.10	0.70	—
1980(h) B; B	54,362,000	—	—	0.10	0.70	—
1981(h) B; B	52,201,000	—	—	0.10	0.35	—

KM# 859.3 5 ORE

1.6000 g., Copper Clad Iron, 15.5 mm. **Ruler:** Margrethe II **Obv:** Crowned MIIR monogram divides date; mint mark, initials R-B **Rev:** "DANMARK" above value

Date	Mintage	F	VF	XF	Unc	BU
1982(h) R; B	74,296,000	—	—	0.10	0.30	—
1983(h) R; B	70,655,000	—	—	0.10	0.30	—
1984(h) R; B	27,599,000	—	—	0.10	0.30	—
1985(h) R; B	56,676,000	—	—	0.10	0.30	—
1986(h) R; B	62,496,000	—	—	0.10	0.30	—
1987(h) R; B	71,798,000	—	—	0.10	0.30	—
1988(h) R; B	48,925,000	—	—	0.10	0.30	—

KM# 795.2 10 ORE

1.4500 g., 0.4000 Silver .0186 oz. ASW **Ruler:** Christian IX **Obv:** Head of Christian IX, date, mint mark and initials VBP **Rev:** Value above porpoise and barley ear, star at top

Date	Mintage	F	VF	XF	Unc	BU
1903/803(h) VBP	3,007,000	4.00	6.50	12.50	32.00	—
1903(h) VBP	Inc. above	2.50	5.00	10.00	25.00	—
1904(h) VBP	2,449,000	20.00	30.00	47.50	95.00	—
1905(h) VBP	1,571,000	2.25	4.50	9.50	22.50	—

KM# 807 10 ORE

1.4500 g., 0.4000 Silver .0186 oz. ASW **Ruler:** Frederik VIII **Obv:** Head left, initials GJ below **Rev:** Denomination, date, mint mark, initials VBP within circle, lily ornamentation surrounds

Date	Mintage	F	VF	XF	Unc	BU
1907(h) VBP; GJ	3,068,000	3.25	5.50	11.50	27.50	—
1910(h) VBP; GJ	2,530,000	3.25	5.50	10.00	25.00	—
1911(h) VBP; GJ	579,000	27.50	45.00	70.00	140	—
1912(h) VBP; GJ	1,951,000	3.75	7.00	12.00	27.50	—

KM# 818.1 10 ORE

1.4500 g., 0.4000 Silver .0186 oz. ASW **Ruler:** Christian X **Obv:** Crowned CX monogram, initials VBP and mint mark at lower left, date and initials GJ at lower right **Rev:** Denomination, ornaments flanking

Date	Mintage	F	VF	XF	Unc	BU
1914(h) VBP; GJ	2,128,000	4.00	7.00	11.00	20.00	—
1915(h) VBP; GJ	915,000	5.50	10.00	14.00	22.50	—
1916(h) VBP; GJ	2,699,000	4.00	7.00	11.50	17.50	—
1917(h) VBP; GJ	6,003,000	2.25	4.00	6.00	10.00	—
1918(h) VBP; GJ	5,042,000	1.35	2.50	4.25	7.00	—

KM# 818.2 10 ORE

1.4500 g., 0.4000 Silver .0186 oz. ASW **Ruler:** Christian X **Obv:** Crowned CX monogram, initials HCN and mint mark at lower left, date and initials GJ at lower right **Rev:** Value, ornament flanking

Date	Mintage	F	VF	XF	Unc	BU
1919(h) HCN; GJ	10,184,000	1.00	1.50	2.75	4.25	—

KM# 818.2a 10 ORE

1.5000 g., Copper-Nickel **Ruler:** Christian X **Obv:** Crowned CX monogram, initials HCN and mint mark at lower left, date and initials GJ at lower right **Rev:** Denomination, ornaments flanking

Date	Mintage	F	VF	XF	Unc	BU
1920(h) HCN; GJ	10,234,000	2.75	4.00	9.50	40.00	—
1921(h) HCN; GJ	8,064,000	2.75	3.75	8.00	32.50	—
1922(h) HCN; GJ	3,065,000	20.00	30.00	50.00	95.00	—
1923(h) HCN; GJ	1,790,000	300	450	600	850	—

KM# 822.1 10 ORE

3.0000 g., Copper-Nickel **Ruler:** Christian X **Obv:** Crowned CXR monogram around center hole, date, mint mark and initials HCN-GJ below hole **Rev:** Center hole flanked by design divides denomination

Date	Mintage	F	VF	XF	Unc	BU
1924(h) HCN; GJ	14,661,000	0.25	1.50	3.00	20.00	—
1925(h) HCN; G	8,678,000	0.30	1.50	8.00	40.00	—
1925(h) HCN; GJ	—	—	—	—	—	—
1926(h) HCN; GJ	4,107,000	0.30	1.50	8.00	45.00	—

KM# 822.2 10 ORE

3.0000 g., Copper-Nickel **Ruler:** Christian X **Obv:** Crowned CXR monogram around center hole, date, mint mark and initial N-GJ below hole **Rev:** Value above, ornaments flanking center hole **Note:** For coins dated 1941 without mint mark or initials refer to Faeroe Islands listings.

Date	Mintage	F	VF	XF	Unc	BU
1929(h) N; GJ	5,037,000	0.75	1.25	8.00	45.00	—
1931(h) N; GJ Large N	—	1.35	2.50	11.00	55.00	—
1931(h) N; GJ Small N	3,054,000	1.35	2.50	11.00	55.00	—
1933(h) N; GJ	1,274,000	7.50	15.00	35.00	90.00	—
1934(h) N; GJ	2,013,000	1.00	2.50	8.00	30.00	—
1935(h) N; GJ	2,848,000	1.35	2.50	7.00	27.50	—
1936(h) N; GJ	3,320,000	1.35	2.50	6.00	45.00	—
1937(h) N; GJ	2,234,000	1.00	1.75	6.00	20.00	—
1938(h) N; GJ	2,991,000	1.75	3.00	5.50	17.50	—
1939(h) N; GJ	2,973,000	1.00	2.00	5.50	17.50	—
1940(h) N; GJ	2,998,000	0.50	1.00	2.00	12.50	—
1941(h) N; GJ	748,000	2.75	4.50	8.00	20.00	—
1946(h) N; GJ	460,000	2.50	4.25	6.00	10.00	—
1947(h) N; GJ	1,292,000	85.00	110	170	230	—

KM# 822.2a 10 ORE

2.4000 g., Zinc **Ruler:** Christian X **Obv:** Crowned CXR monogram around center hole, date, mint mark and initials N-GJ below hole **Rev:** Center hole flanked by design divides denomination

Date	Mintage	F	VF	XF	Unc	BU
1941(h) N; GJ	7,706,000	1.00	2.00	14.00	40.00	—
1942(h) N; GJ	8,676,000	1.00	2.00	14.00	40.00	—
1943(h) N; GJ	2,181,000	1.75	3.25	15.00	42.50	—
1944(h) N; GJ	7,994,000	1.35	2.50	10.00	32.50	—
1945(h) N; GJ	1,280,000	45.00	70.00	110	225	325

KM# 841.1 10 ORE

3.0000 g., Copper-Nickel, 18 mm. **Ruler:** Frederik IX **Obv:** Crowned FR, IX below, divides date, oak and beech branches below **Rev:** Denomination, country name, mint mark, initials N-S

Date	Mintage	F	VF	XF	Unc	BU
1948(h) N; S	5,317,000	0.20	0.60	4.00	25.00	—
1949(h) N; S	7,595,000	0.10	0.20	3.00	22.50	—
1950(h) N; S	6,886,000	0.10	0.20	3.00	20.00	—
1951(h) N; S	8,763,000	0.10	0.20	4.00	30.00	—
1952(h) N; S	6,810,000	0.10	0.20	3.00	22.50	—
1953(h) N; S	11,946,000	0.10	0.20	3.00	20.00	—
1954(h) N; S	19,739,000	—	0.10	1.50	10.00	—
1955(h) N; S	17,623,000	—	0.10	1.50	10.00	—

KM# 841.2 10 ORE

3.0000 g., Copper-Nickel, 18 mm. **Ruler:** Frederik IX **Obv:** Crowned FR, IX below divides date, oak and beech branches below **Rev:** Denomination, country name, mint mark, initials C-S

Date	Mintage	F	VF	XF	Unc	BU
1956(h) C; S	12,323,000	—	0.10	2.25	12.50	—
1957(h) C; S	13,227,000	—	0.10	1.00	6.50	—
1958(h) C; S	10,870,000	—	0.10	1.00	6.50	—
1959(h) C; S	1,255,000	30.00	45.00	65.00	140	—
1960(h) C; S	5,107,000	0.10	0.30	1.00	4.25	—

KM# 849.1 10 ORE

3.0000 g., Copper-Nickel, 18 mm. **Ruler:** Frederik IX **Obv:** Crowned FR, IX below, divides date, mint mark and initials C-S below **Rev:** Denomination, country name above oak branches

Date	Mintage	F	VF	XF	Unc	BU
1960(h) C; S	Inc. above	0.10	0.30	0.75	4.00	—
1961(h) C; S	20,258,000	—	0.15	0.40	5.00	—
1962(h) C; S	12,785,000	—	0.15	0.40	5.00	—
1963(h) C; S	17,171,000	—	0.15	0.40	4.00	—
1964(h) C; S	14,282,000	—	0.15	0.40	3.25	—
1965(h) C; S	21,857,000	—	0.15	0.40	3.25	—
1966(h) C; S	24,160,000	—	0.15	0.20	2.75	—
1967(h) C; S	21,544,000	—	0.15	0.20	1.75	—

Date	Mintage	F	VF	XF	Unc	BU
1968(h) C; S	7,586,000	—	0.15	0.20	1.50	—
1969(h) C; S	31,534,000	—	—	0.10	1.00	—
1970(h) C; S	37,813,000	—	—	0.10	0.30	—
1971(h) C; S	17,719,000	—	—	0.10	0.30	—

KM# 849.2 10 ORE

3.0000 g., Copper-Nickel, 18 mm. **Ruler:** Frederik IX **Obv:** Crowned FIXR above mint mark and initials S-S **Rev:** Value, country name above oak branches

Date	Mintage	F	VF	XF	Unc	BU
1972(h) S; S	46,959,000	—	—	0.10	0.30	—

KM# 860.1 10 ORE

3.0000 g., Copper-Nickel, 18 mm. **Ruler:** Margrethe II **Obv:** Crowned MIIR monogram divides date, mint mark and initials S-B below **Rev:** Denomination flanked by oak leaves

Date	Mintage	F	VF	XF	Unc	BU
1973(h) S; B	37,538,000	—	—	0.10	0.30	—
1974(h) S; B	38,570,000	—	—	0.10	0.30	—
1975(h) S; B	62,633,000	—	—	0.10	0.50	—
1976(h) S; B	64,358,999	—	—	0.10	0.50	—
1977(h) S; B	61,994,000	—	—	0.10	0.50	—
1978(h) S; B	30,302,000	—	—	0.10	0.50	—

KM# 860.2 10 ORE

3.0000 g., Copper-Nickel, 18 mm. **Ruler:** Margrethe II **Obv:** Crowned MIIR monogram divides date, mint mark and initials B-B below **Rev:** Denomination flanked by oak leaves

Date	Mintage	F	VF	XF	Unc	BU
1979(h) B; B	10,224,000	—	—	0.10	0.30	—
1980(h) B; B	37,233,000	—	—	0.10	0.30	—
1981(h) B; B	51,565,000	—	—	0.10	0.20	—

KM# 860.3 10 ORE

3.0000 g., Copper-Nickel, 18 mm. **Ruler:** Margrethe II **Obv:** Crowned MIIR monogram divides date, mint mark and initials R-B below **Rev:** Value flanked by oak leaves

Date	Mintage	F	VF	XF	Unc	BU
1982(h) R; B	40,195,000	—	—	0.10	0.20	—
1983(h) R; B	35,634,000	—	—	0.10	0.20	—
1984(h) R; B	17,828,000	—	—	0.10	0.20	—
1985(h) R; B	29,317,000	—	—	0.10	0.20	—
1986(h) R; B	46,254,000	—	—	0.10	0.20	—
1987(h) R; B	27,898,000	—	—	0.10	0.20	—
1988(h) R; B	29,400,000	—	—	0.10	0.20	—

KM# 796.2 25 ORE

2.4200 g., 0.6000 Silver .0467 oz. ASW **Ruler:** Christian IX **Obv:** Head right, date, mint mark and initials VBP **Rev:** Denomination above porpoise and barley sprig, star at top

Date	Mintage	F	VF	XF	Unc	BU
1904(h) VBP	1,922,000	15.00	30.00	45.00	100	—
1905/805(h) VBP	1,722,000	9.00	15.00	35.00	65.00	—
1905(h) VBP	Inc. above	7.00	12.50	30.00	55.00	—

KM# 808 25 ORE

2.4200 g., 0.6000 Silver .0467 oz. ASW **Ruler:** Frederik VIII **Obv:** Head left, initials GJ below **Rev:** Denomination, date, mint mark, initials VBP within circle, lily ornamentation surrounds

Date	Mintage	F	VF	XF	Unc	BU
1907(h) VBP; GJ	2,009,000	6.00	11.00	20.00	45.00	—
1911(h) VBP; GJ	2,015,000	6.00	11.00	20.00	45.00	—

KM# 815.1 25 ORE

2.4200 g., 0.6000 Silver .0467 oz. ASW **Ruler:** Christian X **Obv:** Crowned CX monogram, initials VBP and mint mark lower left, date and initials GJ lower right **Rev:** Denomination, ornaments flanking

Date	Mintage	F	VF	XF	Unc	BU
1913(h) VBP; GJ	2,016,000	4.00	7.50	12.50	25.00	—
1914(h) VBP; GJ	347,000	95.00	150	210	325	—
1915(h) VBP; GJ	2,862,000	3.25	6.00	10.00	20.00	—
1916(h) VBP; GJ	938,000	10.00	16.00	27.50	40.00	—
1917(h) VBP; GJ	1,354,000	42.50	70.00	105	170	—
1918(h) VBP; GJ	2,089,999	6.00	9.50	15.00	23.00	—

KM# 815.2 25 ORE

2.4200 g., 0.6000 Silver .0467 oz. ASW **Ruler:** Christian X **Obv:** Crowned CX monogram, initials HCN and mint mark lower left, date and initials GJ lower right **Rev:** Value, ornament flanking

Date	Mintage	F	VF	XF	Unc	BU
1919(h) HCN; GJ	9,295,000	1.25	2.00	3.00	6.00	—

KM# 815.2a 25 ORE

2.4000 g., Copper-Nickel **Ruler:** Christian X **Obv:** Crowned CX monogram, initials HCN and mint mark lower left, date and initials GJ lower right **Rev:** Value, ornament flanking

Date	Mintage	F	VF	XF	Unc	BU
1920(h) HCN; GJ	12,288,000	3.00	5.00	16.00	50.00	—
1921(h) HCN; GJ	9,444,000	2.50	4.00	16.00	50.00	—
1922(h) HCN; GJ	5,701,000	30.00	40.00	55.00	100	—

KM# 823.1 25 ORE

4.5000 g., Copper-Nickel **Ruler:** Christian X **Obv:** Crowned CXR monogram around center hole, date, mint mark and initials HCN-GJ below hole **Rev:** Center hole flanked by designs divide denomination

Date	Mintage	F	VF	XF	Unc	BU
1924(h) HCN; GJ	8,035,000	0.30	1.75	4.50	17.50	—
1925(h) HCN; GJ	1,906,000	5.00	9.00	20.00	70.00	240
1926(h) HCN; GJ	2,659,000	1.50	2.75	8.00	50.00	—

KM# 823.2 25 ORE

4.5000 g., Copper-Nickel **Ruler:** Christian X **Obv:** Crowned CXR monogram around center hole, date, mint mark and initials N-GJ below hole **Rev:** Center hole flanked by designs divides denomination **Note:** For coins dated 1941 refer to Faeroe Islands listings.

Date	Mintage	F	VF	XF	Unc	BU
1929(h) N; GJ	886,000	1.75	3.75	10.00	50.00	—
1930(h) N; GJ	3,423,000	2.25	4.50	15.00	60.00	—
1932(h) N; GJ	846,000	8.50	12.50	22.50	75.00	—
1933(h) N; GJ	479,000	30.00	42.50	60.00	140	—
1934(h) N; GJ	1,660,000	2.25	3.75	9.50	42.50	—
1935(h) N; GJ	1,032,000	12.50	25.00	42.50	95.00	—
1936(h) N; GJ	1,453,000	1.75	2.75	7.50	37.50	—
1937(h) N; GJ	1,612,000	3.25	5.50	9.50	25.00	—
1938(h) N; GJ	1,794,000	2.75	4.00	8.00	25.00	—
1939(h) N; GJ	1,972,000	12.50	22.50	37.50	75.00	—
1940(h) N; GJ	1,356,000	1.35	2.25	4.00	15.00	—
1946(h) N; GJ	2,323,000	1.25	2.75	4.00	10.00	—
1947(h) N; GJ	1,751,000	5.00	10.00	16.00	25.00	—

KM# 823.2a 25 ORE

3.6000 g., Zinc **Ruler:** Christian X **Obv:** Crowned CXR monogram around center hole, date, mint mark and initials N-GJ below hole **Rev:** Value above, ornaments flanking center hole

Date	Mintage	F	VF	XF	Unc	BU
1941(h) N; GJ	15,332,000	4.00	7.50	20.00	50.00	—
1942(h) N; GJ	997,000	1.50	3.50	12.50	40.00	—
1943(h) N; GJ	5,784,000	4.00	9.00	20.00	45.00	—
1944(h) N; GJ	10,665,000	1.50	4.00	12.50	40.00	60.00
1945(h) N; GJ	4,543,000	2.50	5.00	12.50	40.00	60.00

KM# 842.1 25 ORE

4.5000 g., Copper-Nickel, 23 mm. **Ruler:** Frederik IX **Obv:** Crowned FR, IX below, divides denomination, oak and beech branches below **Rev:** Denomination, country name, mint mark, initials N-S

Date	Mintage	F	VF	XF	Unc	BU
1948(h) N; S	1,853,000	2.25	5.00	10.00	55.00	—
1949(h) N; S	15,000,000	0.20	0.50	2.25	17.50	—
1950(h) N; S	13,771,000	0.20	0.50	3.75	30.00	—
1951(h) N; S	5,045,000	0.20	0.50	4.50	35.00	—
1952(h) N; S	2,017,999	0.75	3.00	14.00	45.00	—
1953(h) N; S	9,553,000	0.20	0.50	2.25	11.00	—
1954(h) N; S	11,337,000	0.20	0.50	1.50	6.50	—
1955(h) N; S	6,385,000	0.20	0.50	1.50	6.50	—

KM# 842.2 25 ORE

4.5000 g., Copper-Nickel, 23 mm. **Ruler:** Frederik IX **Obv:** Crowned FR, IX below divides date, oak and beech branches below **Rev:** Denomination, country name, mint mark, initials C-S

Date	Mintage	F	VF	XF	Unc	BU
1956(h) C; S	10,228,000	0.20	0.50	1.00	5.50	—
1957(h) C; S	7,421,000	0.20	0.50	0.75	4.50	—
1958(h) C; S	3,600,000	0.30	0.60	1.00	5.00	—
1959(h) C; S	2,211,000	2.25	4.25	7.00	11.00	—
1960(h) C; S	3,453,000	0.30	0.60	1.25	6.00	—

KM# 850 25 ORE

4.5000 g., Copper-Nickel, 23 mm. **Ruler:** Frederik IX **Obv:** Crowned FR, IX below, divides date, oak and beech branches below **Rev:** Denomination, country name, mint mark, initials C-S

Date	Mintage	F	VF	XF	Unc	BU
1960(h) C; S	Inc. above	6.50	11.00	15.00	27.50	—
1961(h) C; S	20,860,000	0.20	0.35	1.00	6.00	—
1962(h) C; S	12,563,000	0.20	0.35	1.00	5.00	—
1964(h) C; S	6,175,000	0.20	0.35	1.00	5.00	—
1965(h) C; S	13,492,000	0.20	0.35	1.00	5.00	—
1966(h) C; S	50,220,000	0.20	0.35	1.00	5.00	—
1967(h) C; S	87,468,000	6.00	12.50	16.00	27.50	—

KM# 855.1 25 ORE

4.3000 g., Copper-Nickel, 23 mm. **Ruler:** Frederik IX **Obv:** Crowned F IX R monogram, date below, to left of center hole, beech branch to right, initials C-S and mint mark at bottom **Rev:** Center flanked by grain sprigs divides denomination

Date	Mintage	F	VF	XF	Unc	BU
1966(h) C; S	Inc. above	—	0.20	0.40	3.00	—
1967(h) C; S	Inc. above	—	0.20	0.40	2.50	—
1968(h) C; S	39,142,000	—	0.20	0.40	1.50	—
1969(h) C; S	16,974,000	—	0.20	0.40	1.25	—
1970(h) C; S	5,393,000	—	—	0.20	0.80	—
1971(h) C; S	12,725,000	—	—	0.20	0.70	—

KM# 855.2 25 ORE

4.3000 g., Copper-Nickel, 23 mm. **Ruler:** Frederik IX **Obv:** Crowned F IX R monogram and date to left of center hole, beech branch to right, initial S-S and mint mark at bottom **Rev:** Value, country name and 2 stalks of barley around center hole

Date	Mintage	F	VF	XF	Unc	BU
1972(h) S; S	31,422,000	—	—	0.20	0.50	—

KM# 861.1 25 ORE

4.3000 g., Copper-Nickel, 23 mm. **Ruler:** Margrethe II **Obv:** Crowned MIIR monogram to left, oak branch to right of center hole, date above, mint mark and initials S-B below **Rev:** Denomination divided by center hole, stylized stalks flank

Date	Mintage	F	VF	XF	Unc	BU
1973(h) S; B	30,834,000	—	—	0.20	0.50	—
1974(h) S; B	22,178,000	—	—	0.20	0.50	—

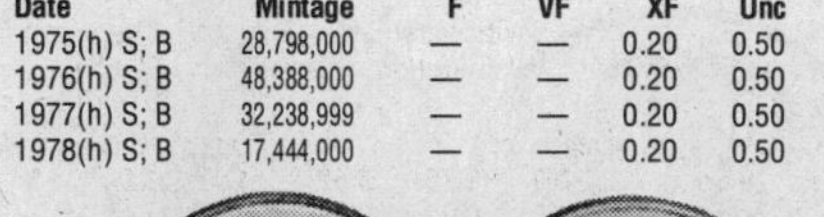

Date	Mintage	F	VF	XF	Unc	BU
1975(h) S; B	28,798,000	—	—	0.20	0.50	—
1976(h) S; B	48,388,000	—	—	0.20	0.50	—
1977(h) S; B	32,238,999	—	—	0.20	0.50	—
1978(h) S; B	17,444,000	—	—	0.20	0.50	—

KM# 861.2 25 ORE

4.3000 g., Copper-Nickel, 23 mm. **Ruler:** Margrethe II **Obv:** Denomination divided by center hole, stylized stalks flank **Rev:** Date above center hole, crowned monogram at left, oak branch at right, mint mark and B-B below

Date	Mintage	F	VF	XF	Unc	BU
1979(h) B; B	24,261,000	—	—	0.20	0.50	—
1980(h) B; B	30,448,000	—	—	0.20	0.50	—
1981(h) B; B	1,427,000	—	—	0.20	0.50	—

KM# 861.3 25 ORE

4.3000 g., Copper-Nickel, 23 mm. **Ruler:** Margrethe II **Obv:** Denomination divided by center hole, stylized stalks flank **Rev:** Crowned MIIR monogram to left, oak branch to right of center hole, date above, mint mark and initials R-B below

Date	Mintage	F	VF	XF	Unc	BU
1982(h) R; B	24,671,000	—	—	0.20	0.50	—
1983(h) R; B	32,706,000	—	—	0.20	0.50	—
1984(h) R; B	22,882,000	—	—	0.20	0.50	—
1985(h) R; B	29,048,000	—	—	0.20	0.50	—
1986(h) R; B	53,496,000	—	—	0.20	0.50	—
1987(h) R; B	30,575,000	—	—	0.20	0.50	—
1988(h) R; B	23,370,000	—	—	0.20	0.50	—

KM# 868.1 25 ORE

2.8000 g., Bronze **Ruler:** Margrethe II **Obv:** Large crown divides date above, initial to right of country **Rev:** Denomination, small heart above, mint mark and initials LG-JP below **Note:** Beginning in 1996 and ending with 1998, the words "DANMARK" and "ØRE" have raised edges. Heart mint mark under "ØRE"; Prev. KM#868.

Date	Mintage	F	VF	XF	Unc	BU
1990 LG; JP; A	109,084,000	—	—	—	0.40	—
1991 LG; JP; A	102,162,000	—	—	—	0.40	—
1992 LG; JP; A	6,293,000	—	—	—	1.25	—
1993 LG; JP; A	14,756,000	—	—	—	0.40	—
1994 LG; JP; A	35,750,000	—	—	—	0.40	—
1995 LG; JP; A	40,000,000	—	—	—	0.40	—
1996 LG; JP; A	46,760,000	—	—	—	0.15	—
1997 LG; JP; A	30,306,000	—	—	—	0.15	—
1998 LG; JP; A	17,200,000	—	—	—	0.15	—
1999 LG; JP; A	18,748,000	—	—	—	0.15	—
2000 LG; JP; A	14,500,000	—	—	—	0.15	—

KM# 866.1 50 ORE

4.3000 g., Bronze **Ruler:** Margrethe II **Obv:** Date above large crown, country name below, initial A to right **Rev:** Large heart above value, mint mark and initials NR-JP below **Note:** Heart mint mark under the word "Øre".

Date	Mintage	F	VF	XF	Unc	BU
1989 NR; JP; A	92,236,000	—	—	—	0.50	—
1989 NR; JP and A	92,236,000	—	—	—	0.15	—

KM# 866.2 50 ORE

4.3000 g., Bronze **Ruler:** Margrethe II **Obv:** Large crown divides date above, initial to right of country name **Rev:** Large heart above value, mint mark and initials LG-JP below **Note:** Beginning in 1996 and ending with 1998, the words "DANMARK" and "ØRE" have raised edges. Heart mint mark under the word "ØRE".

Date	Mintage	F	VF	XF	Unc	BU
1990 LG; JP; A	63,518,000	—	—	—	0.50	—
1991 LG; JP; A	11,115,000	—	—	—	0.50	—
1992 LG; JP; A	14,397,000	—	—	—	0.50	—
1993 LG; JP; A	14,328,000	—	—	—	0.50	—
1994 LG; JP; A	25,055,000	—	—	—	0.35	—
1995 LG; JP; A	15,988,000	—	—	—	0.35	—
1996 LG; JP; A	11,536,000	—	—	—	0.35	—
1997 LG; JP; A	15,574,000	—	—	—	0.25	—
1998 LG; JP; A	13,120,000	—	—	—	0.25	—
1999 LG; JP; A	14,186,000	—	—	—	0.25	—
2000 LG; JP; A	15,500,000	—	—	—	0.25	—

KM# 831.1 1/2 KRONE

3.0000 g., Aluminum-Bronze **Ruler:** Christian X **Obv:** Crowned CXC monogram, date, mint mark, and initials HCN-GJ **Rev:** Value above, country name below large crown

Date	Mintage	F	VF	XF	Unc	BU
1924(h) HCN; GJ	2,150,000	4.00	9.00	17.50	72.50	—
1925(h) HCN; GJ	3,432,000	4.00	9.00	20.00	80.00	—
1926(h) HCN; GJ	716,000	11.50	25.00	40.00	95.00	—

KM# 831.2 1/2 KRONE

3.0000 g., Aluminum-Bronze **Ruler:** Christian X **Obv:** Crowned CXC monogram, date, mint mark, and initial N-GJ **Rev:** Value above, country name below large crown

Date	Mintage	F	VF	XF	Unc	BU
1939(h) N; GJ	226,000	70.00	100	130	200	—
1940(h) N; GJ	1,871,000	4.50	8.50	12.50	22.50	—

KM# 819 KRONE

7.5000 g., 0.8000 Silver .1929 oz. ASW **Ruler:** Christian X **Obv:** Head of Christian X, right, with titles, date, mint mark and initials AH at neck, and VBP at date **Rev:** Crowned royal arms with porpoise to left, barley stalk to right, value below

Date	Mintage	F	VF	XF	Unc	BU
1915(h) VBP; AH	1,410,000	2.75	5.00	8.00	22.50	—
1916(h) VBP; AH	992,000	3.75	8.00	15.00	27.50	—

KM# 824.1 KRONE

6.5000 g., Aluminum-Bronze, 25.5 mm. **Ruler:** Christian X **Obv:** Crowned CXC monogram, date, mint mark, and initials HCN-GJ **Rev:** Denomination above large crown, country name below

Date	Mintage	F	VF	XF	Unc	BU
1924(h) HCN; GJ	999,000	160	450	1,000	2,400	—
1925(h) HCN; GJ	6,314,000	2.00	8.50	40.00	105	—
1926(h) HCN; GJ	2,706,000	2.00	8.50	42.50	110	—

KM# 824.2 KRONE

6.5000 g., Aluminum-Bronze, 25.5 mm. **Ruler:** Christian X **Obv:** Crowned CXC monogram, date, mint mark, and initials N-GJ **Rev:** Denomination above large crown, country name below

Date	Mintage	F	VF	XF	Unc	BU
1929(h) N; GJ	501,000	8.00	15.00	85.00	210	—
1930(h) N; GJ	540,000	22.50	42.50	115	340	—
1931(h) N; GJ	540,000	9.00	20.00	60.00	190	—
1934(h) N; GJ	529,000	6.50	11.50	40.00	150	265
1935(h) N; GJ	505,000	35.00	50.00	100	230	—
1936(h) N; GJ	558,000	10.00	20.00	60.00	185	—
1938(h) N; GJ	407,000	17.50	27.50	55.00	170	—
1939(h) N; GJ	1,517,000	2.75	4.50	10.00	50.00	—
1940(h) N; GJ	1,496,000	2.75	5.00	90.00	55.00	—
1941(h) N; GJ	661,000	10.00	20.00	60.00	250	—

KM# 835 KRONE

6.5000 g., Aluminum-Bronze, 25.5 mm. **Ruler:** Christian X **Obv:** Head right, with titles, mint mark, initials N-S **Rev:** Value divided by stalk of wheat and oats crossed, date

Date	Mintage	F	VF	XF	Unc	BU
1942(h) N; S	3,952,000	2.00	3.25	10.00	55.00	—
1943(h) N; S	798,000	10.00	22.50	100	350	—
1944(h) N; S	1,760,000	2.00	4.00	17.50	72.50	—
1945(h) N; S	2,581,000	2.00	3.00	8.00	55.00	—
1946(h) N; S	4,321,000	2.00	3.00	5.00	32.50	—
1947(h) N; S	5,060,000	2.00	2.50	3.00	12.50	—

KM# 837.1 KRONE

6.5000 g., Aluminum-Bronze, 25.5 mm. **Ruler:** Frederik IX **Obv:** Head right, titles, mint mark, initials N-S **Rev:** Crowned royal arms divide date, value above

Date	Mintage	F	VF	XF	Unc	BU
1947(h) N; S	Inc. above	3.00	6.00	11.50	30.00	—
1948(h) N; S	4,248,000	2.00	3.00	6.50	14.00	—
1949(h) N; S	1,300,000	4.25	8.50	18.00	45.00	—
1952(h) N; S	2,124,000	3.00	5.00	10.00	24.00	—
1953(h) N; S	573,000	4.25	7.00	13.00	26.00	—
1954(h) N; S	584,000	14.00	22.50	45.00	75.00	140
1955(h) N; S	1,359,000	5.50	8.75	13.00	25.00	—

KM# 837.2 KRONE

6.5000 g., Aluminum-Bronze, 25.5 mm. **Ruler:** Frederik IX **Obv:** Head right, titles, mint mark, initials C-S **Rev:** Crowned royal arms divide date, value above

Date	Mintage	F	VF	XF	Unc	BU
1956(h) C; S	2,858,000	1.75	2.75	4.00	8.00	—
1957(h) C; S	10,896,000	0.60	1.00	1.50	4.00	—
1958(h) C; S	1,507,000	1.00	1.75	2.25	4.25	—
1959(h) C; S	243,000	15.00	25.00	30.00	42.50	—
1960(h) C; S	100	—	—	3,000	3,750	—

Note: 1960 dated coins were not released into circulation, however, approximately 50 pieces did eventually make their way into the collector's market in 1969.

KM# 851.1 KRONE

6.8000 g., Copper-Nickel, 25.5 mm. **Ruler:** Frederik IX **Obv:** Older head right, titles, mint mark, initials C-S **Rev:** Crowned and quartered royal arms divide date, value above

Date	Mintage	F	VF	XF	Unc	BU
1960(h) C; S	1,000,000	1.00	1.50	2.75	9.00	—
1961(h) C; S	10,348,000	—	0.50	1.75	14.00	—
1962(h) C; S	27,068,000	—	0.50	1.75	12.00	—
1963(h) C; S	32,083,000	—	0.50	1.50	6.50	—
1964(h) C; S	5,984,000	—	0.50	1.50	6.50	—
1965(h) C; S	13,799,000	—	0.50	1.25	7.00	—
1966(h) C; S	10,890,000	—	0.50	1.25	5.00	—
1967(h) C; S	18,304,000	—	0.50	1.25	5.00	—
1968(h) C; S	8,212,999	—	0.50	1.00	3.75	—
1969(h) C; S	9,597,000	—	0.50	1.00	2.00	—
1970(h) C; S	9,460,000	—	—	0.50	2.00	—
1971(h) C; S	13,985,000	—	—	0.50	2.00	—

KM# 851.2 KRONE

6.8000 g., Copper-Nickel, 25.5 mm. **Ruler:** Frederik IX **Obv:** Older head right, titles, mint mark, initials S-S **Rev:** Crowned royal arms divide date, value above

Date	Mintage	F	VF	XF	Unc	BU
1972(h) S; S	21,019,000	—	—	0.40	1.25	—

KM# 862.1 KRONE

6.8000 g., Copper-Nickel, 25.5 mm. **Ruler:** Margrethe II **Obv:** Head right, with titles, mint mark, initials S-B **Rev:** Crowned and quartered royal arms divide date, value below

Date	Mintage	F	VF	XF	Unc	BU
1973(h) S; B	18,268,000	—	—	0.40	1.00	—
Note: Narrow rim (0.7mm)						
1973(h) S; B	Inc. above	—	—	0.40	1.00	—
Note: Wide rim (1.1mm)						
1974(h) S; B	17,742,000	—	—	0.40	0.80	—
1975(h) S; B	20,136,000	—	—	0.40	0.80	—
1976(h) S; B	28,049,000	—	—	0.40	0.80	—

Date	Mintage	F	VF	XF	Unc	BU
1977(h) S; B	25,685,000	—	—	0.40	0.80	—
1978(h) S; B	11,286,000	—	—	0.40	0.80	—

KM# 862.2 KRONE

6.8000 g., Copper-Nickel, 25.5 mm. **Ruler:** Margrethe II **Obv:** Head right, with titles, mint mark, initials S-B **Rev:** Crowned and quartered royal arms divide date, value below

Date	Mintage	F	VF	XF	Unc	BU
1979(h) B; B	25,216,000	—	—	0.35	0.80	—
1980(h) B; B	25,825,000	—	—	0.35	0.80	—
1981(h) B; B	8,889,000	—	—	0.35	0.80	—

KM# 862.3 KRONE

6.8000 g., Copper-Nickel, 25.5 mm. **Ruler:** Margrethe II **Obv:** Head right with titles, mint mark, initials **Rev:** Crowned and quartered royal arms divide date, value below

Date	Mintage	F	VF	XF	Unc	BU
1982(h) R; B	5,011,000	—	—	0.35	0.80	—
1983(h) R; B	13,946,000	—	—	0.35	0.80	—
1984(h) R; B	36,439,000	—	—	0.35	0.70	—
1985(h) R; B	10,843,000	—	—	0.35	0.70	—
1986(h) R; B	12,556,000	—	—	0.35	0.70	—
1987(h) R; B	20,120,000	—	—	0.35	0.70	—
1988(h) R; B	32,073,999	—	—	0.35	0.70	—
1989(h) R; B	15,704,000	—	—	0.35	0.70	—

KM# 873.1 KRONE

3.6000 g., Copper-Nickel **Ruler:** Margrethe II **Obv:** Designs surround center hole, denomination above, hearts flank **Rev:** 3 crowned MII monograms around center hole, date and initials LG-JP-A below **Note:** Prev. KM#873.

Date	Mintage	F	VF	XF	Unc	BU
1992 LG; JP; A	81,621,000	—	—	—	0.50	—
1993 LG; JP; A	15,844,000	—	—	—	0.50	—
1994 LG; JP; A	23,658,000	—	—	—	0.50	—
1995 LG; JP; A	34,966,000	—	—	—	0.50	—
1996 LG; JP; A	10,081,000	—	—	—	0.50	—
1997 LG; JP; A	10,121,807	—	—	—	0.40	—
1998 LG; JP; A	13,100,000	—	—	—	0.40	—
1999 LG; JP; A	6,479,000	—	—	—	0.40	—
2000 LG; JP; A	21,500,000	—	—	—	0.40	—

KM# 802 2 KRONER

15.0000 g., 0.8000 Silver .3858 oz. ASW, 31 mm. **Ruler:** Christian IX **Subject:** 40th Anniversary of Reign **Obv:** Armored bust right, with titles and anniversary dates, date below bust **Rev:** Seated woman holding royal shield; flying dove to the left; Motto: "With God for honor and justice"; denomination in exergue **Designer:** Gunnar Jensen

Date	Mintage	F	VF	XF	Unc	BU
1903(h) P; GJ	103,000	7.00	15.00	35.00	60.00	120

KM# 803 2 KRONER

15.0000 g., 0.8000 Silver .3858 oz. ASW, 31 mm. **Ruler:** Frederik VIII **Subject:** Death of Christian IX and Accession of Frederik VIII **Obv:** Armored bust left with titles, motto, date, initials VBP **Rev:** Bust left with titles, date of death, value, initials GJ **Designer:** Gunnar Jensen

Date	Mintage	F	VF	XF	Unc	BU
1906(h) VBP GJ	151,000	6.00	9.00	30.00	55.00	110

KM# 811 2 KRONER

15.0000 g., 0.8000 Silver .3858 oz. ASW, 31 mm. **Ruler:** Christian X **Subject:** Death of Frederik VIII and Accession of Christian X **Obv:** Head right with initials AH at neck, date, mint mark and initials VBP below **Rev:** Head right with initials AH, value below, date of death **Designer:** Gunnar Jensen **Note:** Coin rotation.

Date	Mintage	F	VF	XF	Unc	BU
1912(h) VBP; AH	102,000	8.00	17.50	37.50	70.00	125

KM# 820 2 KRONER

15.0000 g., 0.8000 Silver .3858 oz. ASW, 31 mm. **Ruler:** Christian X **Obv:** Head right with initials AH at neck, date, mint mark and initial VBP below **Rev:** Crowned royal arms, porpoise and barley stalk flanking, value below

Date	Mintage	F	VF	XF	Unc	BU
1915(h) AH	657,000	15.00	27.50	45.00	80.00	—
1916(h) AH	402,000	10.00	13.50	20.00	40.00	—

KM# 821 2 KRONER

15.0000 g., 0.8000 Silver .3858 oz. ASW, 31 mm. **Ruler:** Christian X **Subject:** Silver Wedding Anniversary **Obv:** Heads of Christian X and Queen Alexandrine right, initials GJ **Rev:** Crowned arms within anniversary dates, initials HCN, denomination below **Designer:** Gunnar Jensen

Date	Mintage	F	VF	XF	Unc	BU
1923(h) HCN; GJ	203,000	—	—	15.00	30.00	60.00

KM# 825.1 2 KRONER

13.0000 g., Aluminum-Bronze, 31 mm. **Ruler:** Christian X **Obv:** Crowned CXC monogram, date, mint mark, and initials HCN-GJ **Rev:** Denomination above large crown, country name below

Date	Mintage	F	VF	XF	Unc	BU
1924(h) HCN; GJ	1,138,000	25.00	160	550	1,800	—
1925(h) HCN; GJ	3,248,000	2.50	15.00	50.00	125	—
1926(h) HCN; GJ	1,126,000	2.50	15.00	50.00	175	—

KM# 825.2 2 KRONER

13.0000 g., Aluminum-Bronze, 31 mm. **Ruler:** Christian X **Obv:** Crowned CXC monogram, date, mint mark, and initials N-GJ **Rev:** Denomination above large crown, country name below

Date	Mintage	F	VF	XF	Unc	BU
1936(h) N; GJ	400,000	7.00	17.00	75.00	330	—
1938(h) N; GJ	191,000	17.50	27.50	105	275	—
1939(h) N; GJ	723,000	2.00	3.75	10.00	45.00	—
1940(h) N; GJ	743,000	7.00	12.00	25.00	70.00	—
1941(h) N; GJ	129,000	40.00	65.00	225	475	—

KM# 829 2 KRONER

15.0000 g., 0.8000 Silver .3858 oz. ASW, 31 mm. **Ruler:** Christian X **Subject:** King's 60th Birthday **Obv:** Head right, date, mint mark, initials AH at neck, N below **Rev:** Draped and supported national arms, value below, initials HS, two dates at top **Designer:** Andreas Hansen

Date	Mintage	F	VF	XF	Unc	BU
1930(h) N; AH/HS	303,000	—	—	8.00	14.00	30.00

KM# 830 2 KRONER

15.0000 g., 0.8000 Silver .3858 oz. ASW, 31 mm. **Ruler:** Christian X **Subject:** 25th Anniversary of Reign **Obv:** Head right, mint mark and initials N-S below **Rev:** Crowned royal arms, value below **Designer:** Andreas Hansen

Date	Mintage	F	VF	XF	Unc	BU
ND(1937)(h) N; S	209,000	—	—	9.00	18.00	32.50

KM# 836 2 KRONER

15.0000 g., 0.8000 Silver .3858 oz. ASW, 31 mm. **Ruler:** Christian X **Subject:** King's 75th Birthday **Obv:** Head right, mint mark and initials N-S below **Rev:** Dates of birth and 75th birthday year within wreath, legend around, denomination below **Rev. Legend:** "IN ONE WITH HIS PEOPLE IN SORROW AND VICTORY" **Designer:** Harald Salomon

Date	Mintage	F	VF	XF	Unc	BU
ND(1945)(h) N; S	157,000	—	—	12.00	24.00	60.00

KM# 838.1 2 KRONER

13.0000 g., Aluminum-Bronze, 31.4 mm. **Ruler:** Frederik IX **Obv:** Head right, mint mark and initials N-S below **Rev:** Crowned royal arms divide date, value above

Date	Mintage	F	VF	XF	Unc	BU
1947(h) N; S	1,151,000	2.25	4.50	12.50	40.00	—
1948(h) N; S	857,000	1.75	3.00	8.00	32,50	—
1949(h) N; S	272,000	4.50	9.50	30.00	85.00	—
1951(h) N; S	1,576,000	1.35	2.25	4.50	22.50	—
1952(h) N; S	1,958,000	1.00	2.00	5.00	20.00	—
1953(h) N; S	432,000	2.25	4.50	12.50	45.00	—
1954(h) N; S	716,000	2.25	4.00	9.50	37.50	—
1955(h) N; S	457,000	3.75	6.50	11.00	37.50	—

KM# 838.2 2 KRONER

13.0000 g., Aluminum-Bronze, 31.4 mm. **Ruler:** Frederik IX **Obv:** Head right, mint mark and initials C-S below **Rev:** Crowned royal arms divide date, value above

Date	Mintage	F	VF	XF	Unc	BU
1956(h) C; S	1,444,000	2.00	3.25	5.50	11.50	—
1957(h) C; S	2,610,000	1.50	2.25	3.50	7.00	—
1958(h) C; S	2,605,000	1.50	2.25	3.25	8.00	—
1959(h) C; S	192,000	17.50	25.00	35.00	55.00	—

KM# 844 2 KRONER

15.0000 g., 0.8000 Silver .3858 oz. ASW, 31 mm. **Ruler:** Frederik IX **Subject:** Foundation for the Campaign against Tuberculosis in Greenland **Obv:** Conjoined heads right, date, mint mark and initials N-S below **Rev:** Map of Greenland, country name in Greenlandic language, denomination below **Designer:** Harald Salomon **Note:** Greenland Commemorative.

Date	Mintage	F	VF	XF	Unc	BU
1953(h) N; S	152,000	—	6.50	17.50	40.00	200

KM# 845 2 KRONER

15.0000 g., 0.8000 Silver .3858 oz. ASW, 31 mm. **Ruler:** Frederik IX **Subject:** Princess Margrethe's 18th Birthday **Obv:** Head right with titles, mint mark and initials C-S below **Rev:** Head left, date of 18th birthday, value below **Designer:** Harold Salomon

Date	Mintage	F	VF	XF	Unc	BU
ND(1958)(h) C; S	301,000	—	—	8.50	17.50	30.00

KM# 874.1 2 KRONER

Copper-Nickel **Ruler:** Margrethe II **Obv:** 3 crowned MII monograms around center hole, date and initials LG-JP-A below **Rev:** Design surrounds center hole, denomination above, hearts flank **Note:** Prev. KM#874.

Date	Mintage	F	VF	XF	Unc	BU
1992 LG; JP; A	41,648,000	—	—	—	0.65	—
1993 LG; JP; A	43,864,000	—	—	—	0.65	—
1994 LG; JP; A	27,629,000	—	—	—	0.65	—
1995 LG; JP; A	19,850,000	—	—	—	0.65	—
1996 LG; JP; A	2,884,000	—	—	—	0.65	—
1997 LG; JP; A	25,874,000	—	—	—	0.50	—
1998 LG; JP; A	4,360,000	—	—	—	0.50	—
1999 LG; JP; A	20,608,000	—	—	—	0.50	—
2000 LG; JP; A	10,400,000	—	—	—	0.50	—

KM# 852 5 KRONER

17.0000 g., 0.8000 Silver .4372 oz. ASW, 33 mm. **Ruler:** Frederik IX **Subject:** Silver Wedding Anniversary **Obv:** Conjoined heads right, within titles **Rev:** Crowned double FI monogram, silver anniversary dates above, 2 barley ears, denomination, mint mark and initials C-S below

Date	Mintage	F	VF	XF	Unc	BU
ND(1960)(h) C; S	410,000	—	6.50	8.00	15.00	32.50

KM# 853.1 5 KRONER

15.0000 g., Copper-Nickel, 33 mm. **Ruler:** Frederik IX **Obv:** Head right, titles, mint mark and initials C-S **Rev:** Crownedand quartered arms divide date within two oak branches, value above

Date	Mintage	F	VF	XF	Unc	BU
1960(h) C; S	6,418,000	—	2.00	4.00	17.50	—
1961(h) C; S	9,744,000	—	2.00	4.00	22.50	—
1962(h) C; S	2,073,999	—	2.50	4.50	22.50	—
1963(h) C; S	709,000	—	2.25	4.50	30.00	—
1964(h) C; S	1,443,000	—	2.00	4.00	25.00	—
1965(h) C; S	2,574,000	—	2.00	2.50	20.00	—
1966(h) C; S	4,370,000	—	1.75	2.25	12.50	—
1967(h) C; S	1,864,000	—	1.75	2.25	9.00	—
1968(h) C; S	4,131,999	—	1.75	2.00	9.00	—
1969(h) C; S	72,000	2.00	4.50	7.50	15.00	—
1970(h) C; S	2,246,000	—	—	1.75	4.00	—
1971(h) C; S	4,767,000	—	—	1.75	3.25	—

KM# 853.2 5 KRONER

15.0000 g., Copper-Nickel, 33 mm. **Ruler:** Frederik IX **Obv:** Head right, mint mark and initials S-S **Rev:** Crowned and quartered arms divide date within two oak branches, value above

Date	Mintage	F	VF	XF	Unc	BU
1972(h) S; S	2,599,000	—	—	1.75	2.75	—

KM# 854 5 KRONER

17.0000 g., 0.8000 Silver .4372 oz. ASW, 33 mm. **Ruler:** Frederik IX **Subject:** Wedding of Princess Anne Marie **Obv:** Head right, mint mark and initials C-S **Rev:** Head left within title and wedding date

Date	Mintage	F	VF	XF	Unc	BU
1964(h) C; S	359,000	—	—	7.50	15.00	—

KM# 863.1 5 KRONER

15.0000 g., Copper-Nickel, 33 mm. **Ruler:** Margrethe II **Obv:** Head right, mint mark and initial S-B below **Rev:** Crowned and quartered royal arms divide date and oak leaves, value below

Date	Mintage	F	VF	XF	Unc	BU
1973(h) S; B	3,774,000	—	—	1.75	3.75	—
Note: Narrow rim (1.0mm)						
1973(h) S; B	Inc. above	—	—	1.75	3.75	—
Note: Wide rim (1.5mm)						
1974(h) S; B	5,239,000	—	—	1.75	3.75	—
1975(h) S; B	5,810,000	—	—	3.25	8.00	—
1976(h) S; B	7,651,000	—	—	1.60	5.00	—
1977(h) S; B	6,885,000	—	—	1.60	5.00	—
1978(h) S; B	2,984,000	—	—	1.60	5.00	—

KM# 863.2 5 KRONER

15.0000 g., Copper-Nickel, 33 mm. **Ruler:** Margrethe II **Obv:** Head right, mint mark and initials B-B below **Rev:** Crowned and quartered royal arms divide date and oak leaves, value below

Date	Mintage	F	VF	XF	Unc	BU
1979(h) B; B	2,861,000	—	—	1.50	4.00	—
1980(h) B; B	3,622,000	—	—	2.50	6.50	—
1981(h) B; B	1,057,000	—	—	1.50	4.00	—

KM# 863.3 5 KRONER

15.0000 g., Copper-Nickel, 33 mm. **Ruler:** Margrethe II **Obv:** Head right, mint mark and initials R-B below **Rev:** Crowned and quartered royal arms divide date and oak leaves, value below

Date	Mintage	F	VF	XF	Unc	BU
1982(h) R; B	1,002,000	—	—	2.50	6.50	—
1983(h) R; B	1,044,000	—	—	1.50	3.00	—
1984(h) R; B	713,000	—	—	1.50	3.00	—
1985(h) R; B	621,000	—	—	1.50	3.00	—
1986(h) R; B	1,042,000	—	—	1.50	3.00	—
1987(h) R; B	611,000	—	—	1.50	3.00	—
1988(h) R; B	648,000	—	—	1.50	3.00	—

KM# 869.1 5 KRONER

9.2000 g., Copper-Nickel, 28 mm. **Ruler:** Margrethe II **Obv:** Design surrounds center hole, denomination above, hearts flank **Rev:** 3 crowned MII monograms around center hole, date and initials LG-JP-A below **Note:** Large and small date varieties exist.

Date	Mintage	F	VF	XF	Unc	BU
1990 LG; JP; A	46,745,000	—	—	—	2.00	—
1991 LG; JP; A	3,752,000	—	—	—	2.00	—
1992 LG; JP; A	2,426,000	—	—	—	1.75	—
1993 LG; JP; A	1,538,000	—	—	—	1.75	—
1994 LG; JP; A	7,920,000	—	—	—	1.75	—
1995 LG; JP; A	5,850,000	—	—	—	1.75	—
1997 LG; JP; A	5,258,000	—	—	—	1.60	—
1998 LG; JP; A	6,450,000	—	—	—	1.60	—
1999 LG; JP; A	4,786,000	—	—	—	1.60	—
2000 LG; JP; A	2,800,000	—	—	—	1.60	—

KM# 809 10 KRONER

4.4803 g., 0.9000 Gold .1296 oz. AGW **Ruler:** Frederik VIII **Obv:** Head left with titles **Rev:** Draped crowned national arms above date, value, mint mark and initials VBP

Date	Mintage	F	VF	XF	Unc	BU
1908(h) VBP; GJ	308,000	—	100	120	140	—
1909(h) VBP; GJ	153,000	—	100	120	140	—

KM# 816 10 KRONER

4.4803 g., 0.9000 Gold .1296 oz. AGW **Ruler:** Christian X **Obv:** Head right with title, date, mint mark, initials VBP. Initials AH at neck **Rev:** Draped crowned national arms above date, value, mint mark and initials VBP

Date	Mintage	F	VF	XF	Unc	BU
1913(h) AH/ GJ	312,000	—	100	120	135	—
1917(h) AH/ GJ	132,000	—	100	130	145	—

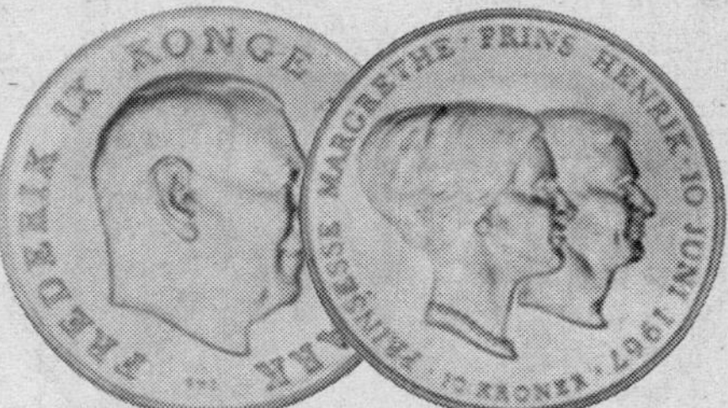

KM# 856 10 KRONER

20.4000 g., 0.8000 Silver .5247 oz. ASW **Ruler:** Frederik IX **Subject:** Wedding of Princess Margrethe **Obv:** Head right with titles, mint mark, initials C-S **Rev:** Heads of Prince and Princess right, value below

Date	Mintage	F	VF	XF	Unc	BU
ND(1967)(h) C; S	419,000	—	—	8.00	14.00	45.00
Note: 78,383 pieces were melted.						

KM# 857 10 KRONER
20.4000 g., 0.8000 Silver .5247 oz. ASW **Ruler:** Frederik IX **Subject:** Wedding of Princess Benedikte **Obv:** Head right, mint mark and initials C-S below **Rev:** Head left, value below

Date	Mintage	F	VF	XF	Unc	BU
ND(1968)(h) C; S	254,000	—	—	8.50	17.50	50.00

Note: 42,923 were melted.

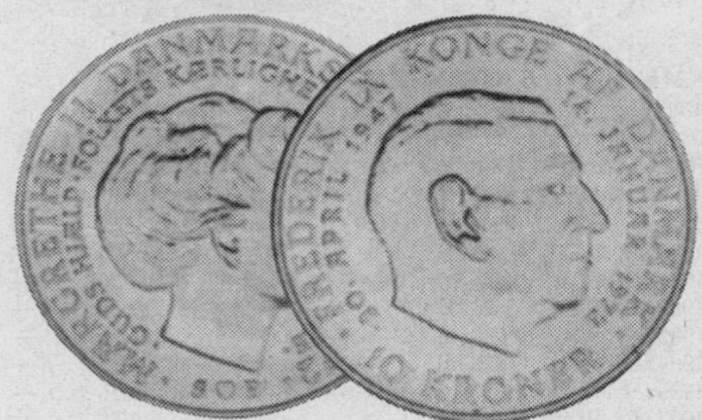

KM# 858 10 KRONER
20.4000 g., 0.8000 Silver .5247 oz. ASW **Ruler:** Margrethe II **Subject:** Death of Frederik IX and Accession of Margrethe II **Obv:** Head right, motto, titles, mint mark and initials S-B **Rev:** Head right with titles, date of death, value below

Date	Mintage	F	VF	XF	Unc	BU
1972(h) S; S	402,000	—	—	7.50	9.50	17.50

KM# 864.1 10 KRONER
12.5000 g., Copper-Nickel, 28 mm. **Ruler:** Margrethe II **Obv:** Head right with tiara, mint mark and initials B-B below **Rev:** Large 10 on horizontal grid, two rye stalks flanking, date above

Date	Mintage	F	VF	XF	Unc	BU
1979(h) B; B	76,801,000	—	—	2.00	5.00	—
1981(h) B; B	10,520,000	—	2.50	5.00	13.00	—

KM# 864.2 10 KRONER
12.5000 g., Copper-Nickel, 28 mm. **Ruler:** Margrethe II **Obv:** Head right with tiara, mint mark and initials R-B below **Rev:** Large 10 on horizontal grid, two rye stalks flanking, date above

Date	Mintage	F	VF	XF	Unc	BU
1982(h) R; B	1,065,000	—	2.50	5.00	13.50	—
1983(h) R; B	1,123,000	—	2.50	5.00	13.50	—
1984(h) R; B	748,000	—	3.00	6.00	16.00	—
1985(h) R; B	720,000	—	3.00	6.00	16.00	—
1987(h) R; B	719,000	—	2.50	4.75	13.50	—
1988(h) R; B	718,000	—	2.25	4.50	12.50	—

KM# 865 10 KRONER
12.5000 g., Copper-Nickel, 28 mm. **Ruler:** Margrethe II **Subject:** Crown Prince's 18th Birthday **Obv:** Head with tiara right, mint mark and initials R-A below **Rev:** Head left, date of 18th birthday, value below **Edge:** Plain

Date	Mintage	F	VF	XF	Unc	BU
ND(1986)(h) R; A	1,090,351	—	—	5.00	15.00	—
ND(1986)(h) R; A Proof	2,000	Value: 240				

KM# 865a 10 KRONER
14.3000 g., 0.8000 Silver .3678 oz. ASW, 28 mm. **Ruler:** Margrethe II **Obv:** Head with tiara right, mint mark and initials R-A below **Rev:** Head of Crown Prince Frederik left, date of 18th birthday, value below

Date	Mintage	F	VF	XF	Unc	BU
1986(h) R; A Proof	24,000	Value: 120				

KM# 867.1 10 KRONER
7.0000 g., Aluminum-Bronze, 23.4 mm. **Ruler:** Margrethe II **Obv:** Head with tiara right, titles, date, initials NR-JP-A **Rev:** Crowned arms within ornaments, value below **Edge:** Plain

Date	Mintage	F	VF	XF	Unc	BU
1989 NR; JP; A	38,346,000	—	—	—	4.00	—

KM# 867.2 10 KRONER
7.0000 g., Aluminum-Bronze, 23.4 mm. **Ruler:** Margrethe II **Obv:** Head with tiara right, titles, date, initials LG-JP-A **Rev:** Crowned arms within ornaments, value below **Edge:** Plain

Date	Mintage	F	VF	XF	Unc	BU
1990 LG; JP; A	12,193,000	—	—	—	4.00	—
1991 LG; JP; A	1,065,000	—	—	—	5.50	—
1992 LG; JP; A	484,000	—	—	3.00	6.50	—
1993 LG; JP; A	1,069,000	—	—	2.50	4.50	—

KM# 877 10 KRONER
7.0000 g., Aluminum-Bronze, 23.4 mm. **Ruler:** Margrethe II **Obv:** New portrait right, date below **Rev:** Crowned arms within ornaments, value below **Edge:** Plain **Note:** Beginning with strikes in 1995 and ending in 1998, letters and numbers on reverse have raised edges.

Date	Mintage	F	VF	XF	Unc	BU
1994 LG; JP; A	4,058,000	—	—	—	4.00	—
1995 LG; JP; A	9,461,000	—	—	—	4.00	—
1997 LG; JP; A	3,725,000	—	—	—	4.00	—
1998 LG; JP; A	6,000,000	—	—	—	3.50	—
1999 LG; JP; A	4,034,749	—	—	—	3.50	—

KM# 810 20 KRONER
8.9606 g., 0.9000 Gold .2592 oz. AGW **Ruler:** Frederik VIII **Obv:** Head left, with titles **Rev:** Crowned and mantled arms above date, value, mint mark and initials VBP

Date	Mintage	F	VF	XF	Unc	BU
1908(h) VBP; GJ	243,000	—	175	210	250	—
1909(h) VBP; GJ	365,000	—	180	220	260	—
1910(h) VBP; GJ	200,000	—	200	225	275	—
1911(h) VBP; GJ	183,000	—	180	220	260	—
1912(h) VBP; GJ	184,000	—	180	220	260	—

KM# 817.1 20 KRONER
8.9606 g., 0.9000 Gold .2592 oz. AGW **Ruler:** Christian X **Obv:** Head right with title, date, mint mark, initials VBP, initials AH at neck **Rev:** Crowned and mantled arms above date, value, mint mark and initials VBP

Date	Mintage	F	VF	XF	Unc	BU
1913(h) AH/GJ	815,000	—	175	210	250	—
1914(h) AH/GJ	920,000	—	175	210	250	—
1915(h) AH/GJ	532,000	—	180	215	255	—
1916(h) AH/GJ	1,401,000	—	180	220	265	—
1917(h) AH/GJ	Inc. above	—	180	220	260	—

KM# 817.2 20 KRONER
8.9606 g., 0.9000 Gold .2592 oz. AGW **Ruler:** Christian X **Obv:** Head right with title, date, mint mark, and initials HCN, initials AH at neck **Rev:** Crowned and mantled arms above date, value, mint mark, and initials HCN **Note:** 1926-1927 dated 20 Kroners were not released for circulation.

Date	Mintage	F	VF	XF	Unc	BU
1926(h) HCN	358,000	—	—	3,000	6,000	—
1927(h) HCN	Inc. above	—	—	3,000	6,000	—

KM# 817.3 20 KRONER
8.9606 g., 0.9000 Gold .2592 oz. AGW **Ruler:** Christian X **Obv:** Head right with title, date, mint mark, and initials HCN. Initials AH at neck **Rev:** Crowned and mantled arms above date, value, mint mark and initials HCN **Note:** The 1930-1931 dated 20 Kroners were not released for circulation.

Date	Mintage	F	VF	XF	Unc	BU
1930(h) N	1,285,000	—	—	3,000	6,000	—
1931(h) N	Inc. above	—	—	3,000	6,000	—

KM# 870 20 KRONER
9.3000 g., Aluminum-Bronze **Ruler:** Margrethe II **Subject:** 50th Birthday of Queen Margrethe **Obv:** Head with hat right, mint mark after 2 in legend, initials LG left of shoulder **Rev:** Large crown above daisy flower divides dates, value below **Edge:** Alternate reeded and plain sections **Designer:** Jan Petersen

Date	Mintage	F	VF	XF	Unc	BU
ND(1990)(h) LG	1,101,000	—	—	—	5.50	—

KM# 871 20 KRONER
9.3000 g., Aluminum-Bronze **Ruler:** Margrethe II **Obv:** Head with tiara right, titles, date, initials LG-JP-A, mint mark after II in legend **Rev:** Crowned arms within ornaments and value **Edge:** Alternate reeded and plain sections **Note:** Large and small date varieties exist.

Date	Mintage	F	VF	XF	Unc	BU
1990(h) LG; JP ; A	34,368,000	—	—	—	6.50	—
1991(h) LG; JP; A	11,563,000	—	—	—	7.00	—
1993(h) LG; JP; A	674,000	—	—	—	8.00	—

KM# 875 20 KRONER
9.3000 g., Aluminum-Bronze **Ruler:** Margrethe II **Subject:** Silver Wedding Anniversary **Obv:** Heads of Prince Henrik and Margrethe II facing each other, anniversary dates below **Rev:** Fairy tale house, mint mark and initials LG at lower left, denomination at left **Edge:** Alternate reeded and plain sections **Designer:** Jan Petersen

Date	Mintage	F	VF	XF	Unc	BU
ND(1992)(h) LG	994,000	—	—	—	5.50	—

KM# 878 20 KRONER
9.3000 g., Aluminum-Bronze **Ruler:** Margrethe II **Obv:** New portrait right, date, mint mark and initials LG-JP-A below **Rev:** Crowned arms within ornament and value **Edge:** Alternating reeded and plain sections **Note:** Strikes dated 1996 and 1998 have letters and numbers on reverse with raised edges.

Date	Mintage	F	VF	XF	Unc	BU
1994(h) LG, JP; A	2,565,000	—	—	—	6.50	—
1996(h) LG, JP; A	8,651,000	—	—	—	6.00	—
1998(h) LG, JP; A	4,000,000	—	—	—	5.50	—
1999(h) LG, JP; A	4,133,363	—	—	—	5.50	—

KM# 879 20 KRONER

9.3000 g., Aluminum-Bronze **Ruler:** Margrethe II **Subject:** 1000 Years of Danish Coinage **Obv:** Head with cloche left, inner legend in runic letters **Rev:** Large crown on cross, mint mark and initials LG **Edge:** Alternate reeded and plain sections **Designer:** Jan Petersen

Date	Mintage	F	VF	XF	Unc	BU
ND(1995)(h) LG; JP; A	1,000,000	—	—	—	5.50	—

KM# 881 20 KRONER

9.3000 g., Aluminum-Bronze **Ruler:** Margrethe II **Subject:** Wedding of Prince Joachim **Obv:** New portrait right, mint mark after II in legend, initials LG below at date **Rev:** Schackenborg castle at center, value below **Edge:** Alternate reeded and plain sections **Designer:** Jan Petersen

Date	Mintage	F	VF	XF	Unc	BU
1995(h) LG, JP	1,000,000	—	—	—	5.00	—

Note: Although dated 1995, this coin was minted at the end of the year and included in a 1996 mint set.

KM# 883 20 KRONER

9.3000 g., Aluminum-Bronze **Ruler:** Margrethe II **Subject:** 25th Anniversary - Queen's Reign **Obv:** Full-length portrait, mint mark and initials LG **Rev:** Crowned arms within anniversary date and value **Edge:** Alternate reeded and plain sections **Designer:** Jan Petersen

Date	Mintage	F	VF	XF	Unc	BU
ND(1997)(h) LG; JP	1,000,000	—	—	—	5.50	—

KM# 885 20 KRONER

9.3600 g., Aluminum-Bronze **Ruler:** Margrethe II **Subject:** 60th Birthday of Queen Margrethe II **Obv:** Bust right **Rev:** Crown divides dates above daisy flowers, denomination below **Edge:** Alternating reeded and plain sections **Designer:** Mogens Moeller

Date	Mintage	F	VF	XF	Unc	BU
ND(2000)(h) LG	1,000,000	—	—	—	5.50	—

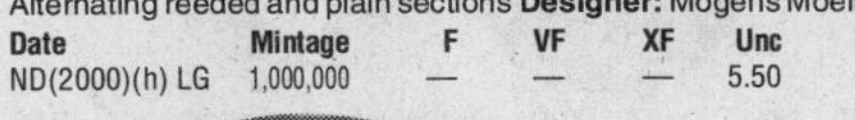

KM# 872 200 KRONER

31.1000 g., 0.8000 Silver .8000 oz. ASW, 38 mm. **Ruler:** Margrethe II **Subject:** 50th Birthday of Queen Margrethe **Obv:** Bust with hat right, mint mark after 2 in legend, initials LG and Fox mark above shoulder **Rev:** Large crown above daisy flower divides dates, value below **Edge:** Plain **Designer:** Jan Petersen

Date	Mintage	F	VF	XF	Unc	BU
ND(1990)(h) LG	132,655	—	—	—	40.00	—

KM# 876 200 KRONER

31.1000 g., 0.9990 Silver 1.0000 oz. ASW, 38 mm. **Ruler:** Margrethe II **Subject:** Silver Wedding Anniversary **Obv:** Heads of Prince Henrik and Queen Margrethe II facing each other, anniversary dates below **Rev:** Fairy tale house, mint mark and initials LG at lower left, denomination **Edge:** Plain **Designer:** Jan Petersen

Date	Mintage	F	VF	XF	Unc	BU
ND(1992)(h) LG	100,300	—	—	—	42.50	—

KM# 880 200 KRONER

31.1000 g., 0.9990 Silver 1.0000 oz. ASW, 38 mm. **Ruler:** Margrethe II **Subject:** 1000 Year of Danish Coinage **Obv:** Head with cloche left, runic lettering within legend **Rev:** Large crown on cross, mint mark at left, initials LG at bottom, denomination at left **Edge:** Plain **Designer:** Jan Petersen

Date	Mintage	F	VF	XF	Unc	BU
ND(1995)(h) LG	33,727	—	—	—	65.00	—

KM# 882 200 KRONER

31.1000 g., 0.9990 Silver 1.0000 oz. ASW, 38 mm. **Ruler:** Margrethe II **Subject:** Wedding of Prince Joachim **Obv:** New portrait right, date below **Rev:** Schackenburg Castle, denomination below **Edge:** Plain **Designer:** Jan Petersen

Date	Mintage	F	VF	XF	Unc	BU
1995(h) LG	56,100	—	—	—	50.00	—

KM# 884 200 KRONER

31.1000 g., 0.9990 Silver 1.0000 oz. ASW, 38 mm. **Ruler:** Margrethe II **Subject:** 25th Anniversary - Queen's Reign **Obv:** Full-length portrait **Rev:** Quartered arms, denomination below, anniversary date at right **Edge:** Plain **Designer:** Jan Petersen

Date	Mintage	F	VF	XF	Unc	BU
ND(1997)(h) LG	62,022	—	—	—	50.00	—

KM# 886 200 KRONER

31.1000 g., 0.9990 Silver 1.0000 oz. ASW, 38 mm. **Ruler:** Margrethe II **Subject:** 60th Birthday of Queen Margrethe II **Obv:** Bust with tiara right **Rev:** Crown above flowers divides dates, denomination below **Edge:** Plain **Designer:** Mogens Møller

Date	Mintage	F	VF	XF	Unc	BU
ND(2000)(h) LG	60,000	—	—	—	50.00	—

PATTERNS

Including off metal strikes

KM#	Date	Mintage	Identification	Mkt Val
PnB63	1940	—	25 Ore. Zinc. KM#823.	—
Pn63	1941	—	Ore. Aluminum. KM#832.	3,300
PnA64	1941	—	2 Ore. Zinc. KM#833.	—
PnB64	1941	—	5 Ore. Zinc. KM#834.	—
Pn64	19xxC	—	Krone. Copper-Nickel. KM#837.2.	700

KM#	Date	Mintage	Identification	Mkt Val
Pn65	1947	—	5 Kroner. Nickel. Without denomination.	3,650
Pn66	1948N	—	5 Ore. Zinc. KM#843. Unique.	—
Pn67	1926(h) HCN; GJ	—	5 Ore. Bronze. KM#828.1. Thomas Holland Sale 11-00 $8600. Beware of counterfeits. Another example of the 1926 5 Øre was auctioned at Thomas Holland Auction 20, lot 1574. The coin was defaced on the obv. which the catalogers see as a proof that the coin is a pattern.	—

PROVAS

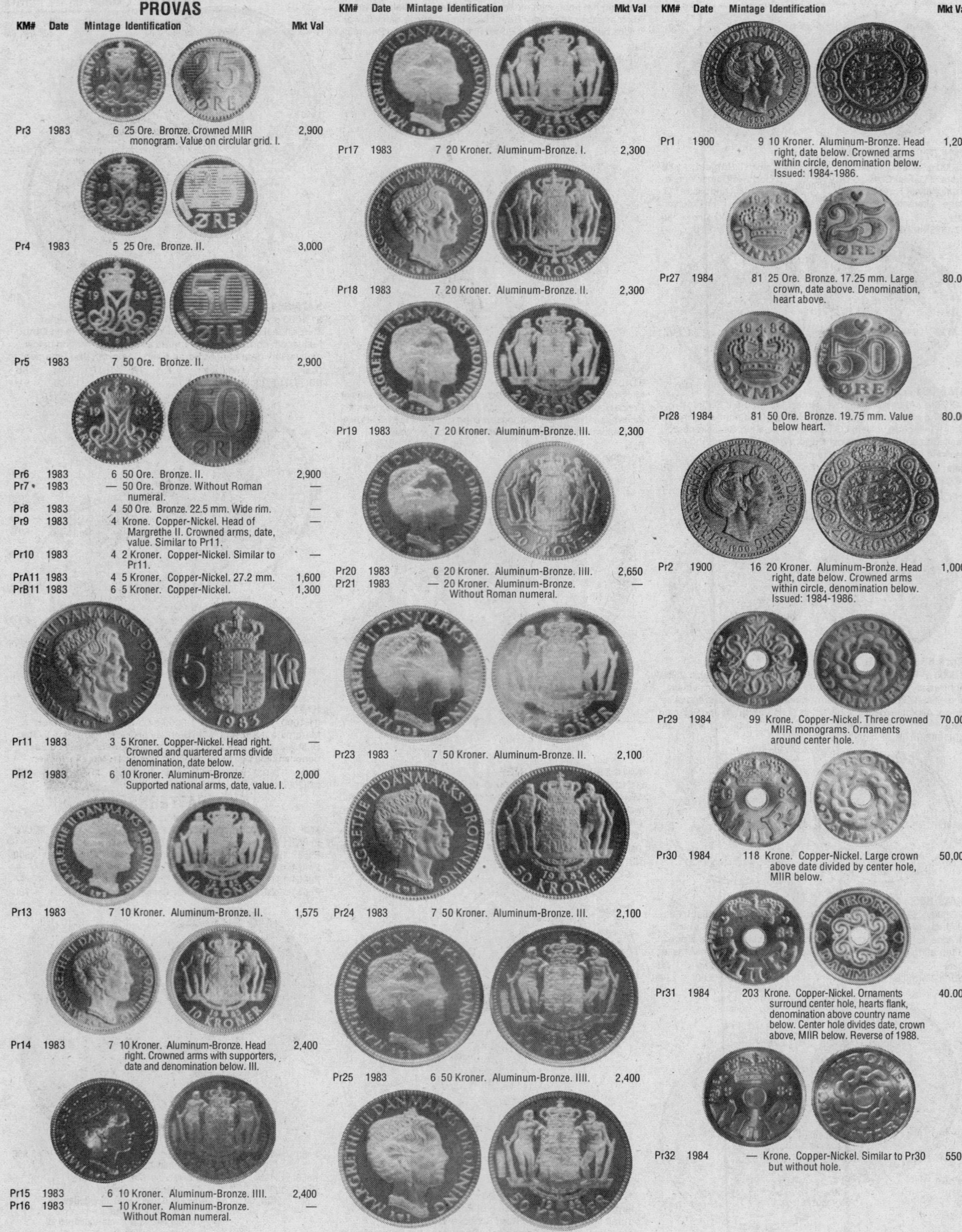

KM#	Date	Mintage	Identification	Mkt Val
Pr3	1983	6	25 Ore. Bronze. Crowned MIIR monogram. Value on circular grid. I.	2,900
Pr4	1983	5	25 Ore. Bronze. II.	3,000
Pr5	1983	7	50 Ore. Bronze. II.	2,900
Pr6	1983	6	50 Ore. Bronze. II.	2,900
Pr7	1983	—	50 Ore. Bronze. Without Roman numeral.	—
Pr8	1983	4	50 Ore. Bronze. 22.5 mm. Wide rim.	—
Pr9	1983	4	Krone. Copper-Nickel. Head of Margrethe II. Crowned arms, date, value. Similar to Pr11.	—
Pr10	1983	4	2 Kroner. Copper-Nickel. Similar to Pr11.	—
PrA11	1983	4	5 Kroner. Copper-Nickel. 27.2 mm.	1,600
PrB11	1983	6	5 Kroner. Copper-Nickel.	1,300
Pr11	1983	3	5 Kroner. Copper-Nickel. Head right. Crowned and quartered arms divide denomination, date below.	—
Pr12	1983	6	10 Kroner. Aluminum-Bronze. Supported national arms, date, value. I.	2,000
Pr13	1983	7	10 Kroner. Aluminum-Bronze. II.	1,575
Pr14	1983	7	10 Kroner. Aluminum-Bronze. Head right. Crowned arms with supporters, date and denomination below. III.	2,400
Pr15	1983	6	10 Kroner. Aluminum-Bronze. IIII.	2,400
Pr16	1983	—	10 Kroner. Aluminum-Bronze. Without Roman numeral.	—
Pr17	1983	7	20 Kroner. Aluminum-Bronze. I.	2,300
Pr18	1983	7	20 Kroner. Aluminum-Bronze. II.	2,300
Pr19	1983	7	20 Kroner. Aluminum-Bronze. III.	2,300
Pr20	1983	6	20 Kroner. Aluminum-Bronze. IIII.	2,650
Pr21	1983	—	20 Kroner. Aluminum-Bronze. Without Roman numeral.	—
Pr23	1983	7	50 Kroner. Aluminum-Bronze. II.	2,100
Pr24	1983	7	50 Kroner. Aluminum-Bronze. III.	2,100
Pr25	1983	6	50 Kroner. Aluminum-Bronze. IIII.	2,400
Pr26	1983	22	50 Kroner. Aluminum-Bronze. Without Roman numeral.	1,475
Pr1	1900	9	10 Kroner. Aluminum-Bronze. Head right, date below. Crowned arms within circle, denomination below. Issued: 1984-1986.	1,200
Pr27	1984	81	25 Ore. Bronze. 17.25 mm. Large crown, date above. Denomination, heart above.	80.00
Pr28	1984	81	50 Ore. Bronze. 19.75 mm. Value below heart.	80.00
Pr2	1900	16	20 Kroner. Aluminum-Bronze. Head right, date below. Crowned arms within circle, denomination below. Issued: 1984-1986.	1,000
Pr29	1984	99	Krone. Copper-Nickel. Three crowned MIIR monograms. Ornaments around center hole.	70.00
Pr30	1984	118	Krone. Copper-Nickel. Large crown above date divided by center hole, MIIR below.	50,00
Pr31	1984	203	Krone. Copper-Nickel. Ornaments surround center hole, hearts flank, denomination above country name below. Center hole divides date, crown above, MIIR below. Reverse of 1988.	40.00
Pr32	1984	—	Krone. Copper-Nickel. Similar to Pr30 but without hole.	550

KM#	Date	Mintage	Identification	Mkt Val
Pr33	1984	191	2 Kroner. Copper-Nickel. Triple monogram. Ornaments around center hole, value above.	40.00
Pr34	1984	103	2 Kroner. Copper-Nickel. Milled edge.	75.00
Pr35	1984	201	2 Kroner. Copper-Nickel. Interrupted milling 6 or 7 notches.	40.00
Pr36	1984	85	5 Kroner. Copper-Nickel. Triple monogram. Ornament around center hole, value.	70.00
Pr37	1984	108	5 Kroner. Copper-Nickel. Milled edge.	75.00
Pr38	1984	202	5 Kroner. Copper-Nickel. Milled edge.	40.00
Pr39	1984	6	5 Kroner. Copper-Nickel. As Pr36 except for added date at top and country name at bottom. Large 5 above ornament and denomination.	2,000
Pr40	1984	85	10 Kroner. Aluminum-Bronze. Crowned arms, ornament, value.	100
PrA41	1984	4	10 Kroner. Aluminum-Bronze. Without "Prove".	—
PrB41	1984	3	10 Kroner. Aluminum-Bronze. Different ornaments and value style. Without "Prove".	—

KM#	Date	Mintage	Identification	Mkt Val
Pr41	1984	112	20 Kroner. Aluminum-Bronze. Head right, date below. Crowned arms within circle, denomination below.	80.00
Pr42	1984	4	20 Kroner. Aluminum-Bronze. Without "PROVE".	—
PrA43	1984	51	20 Kroner. Aluminum-Bronze. Without "Prove".	150
Pr43	1986	183	25 Ore. Bronze. 17.5 mm.	60.00
Pr44	1986	210	25 Ore. Bronze. 18 mm.	50.00
Pr45	19(86)	23	50 Ore. Bronze. 19.75 mm.	250
Pr46	1986	181	50 Ore. Bronze.	50.00
Pr47	19(86)	1	Krone. Copper-Nickel. Crowned MIIR monogram, date. Ornaments around center hole, value, country name. Crown lacks lower rim.	500
Pr48	19(86)	1	Krone. Copper-Nickel. Center hole within crowned monogram. Full crown (miscolored).	600
Pr49	198(6)	6	Krone. Copper-Nickel. Three digits in date.	1,400
Pr50	198(6)	9	Krone. Copper-Nickel. Without hole.	850

KM#	Date	Mintage	Identification	Mkt Val
Pr51	1986	185	Krone. Copper-Nickel. Full date.	40.00
PrA52	1986	2	Krone. Copper-Nickel. Without hole.	—
Pr52a	1986	91	2 Kroner. Copper-Nickel. Two crowned MIIR monograms, date. Ornaments around center hole, value, country name. With hole interrupted milling 7x5 grooves.	100
Pr52b	1986	196	2 Kroner. Copper-Nickel. Without hole, interrupted milling, 6x6 grooves.	20.00
Pr52c	1986	196	2 Kroner. Copper-Nickel. Without hole, interrupted milling, 8x7 grooves, widely spaced notches.	20.00
Pr52d	1986	196	2 Kroner. Copper-Nickel. Without hole, interrupted milling, 8x9 grooves.	20.00
Pr52e	1986	196	2 Kroner. Copper-Nickel. Without hole, interrupted milling, 8x8 grooves, no notches.	20.00
Pr52f	1986	196	2 Kroner. Copper-Nickel. Without hole, interrupted milling, 8x8 grooves, with notches.	20.00
Pr52g	1986	196	2 Kroner. Copper-Nickel. Without hole, interrupted milling, 6x7 grooves.	20.00
Pr52h	1986	196	2 Kroner. Copper-Nickel. Interrupted milling, 8x7 grooves, narrowly spaced notches.	20.00
Pr53	1986	2	2 Kroner. Copper-Nickel. Three crowned MIIR monograms, date. Ornaments around center hole, denomination. Without hole.	—
Pr54	1986	190	2 Kroner. Copper-Nickel. With hole.	20.00
Pr55	1986	102	5 Kroner. Copper-Nickel. Three crowned MIIr monograms, mint mark, date. Ornaments with value and country name.	120
Pr56	1986	212	5 Kroner. Copper-Nickel. Turned 120 degrees.	25.00
Pr57	1986	5	5 Kroner. Copper-Nickel. Without hole.	2,100

KM#	Date	Mintage	Identification	Mkt Val
Pr58	1986	302	10 Kroner. Aluminum-Bronze. 23 mm. Head of Margrethe II. Crowned arms, ornaments, value.	55.00
Pr59a	1986	198	20 Kroner. Aluminum-Bronze. Interrupted milling, 12x4 grooves.	25.00
Pr59b	1986	198	20 Kroner. Aluminum-Bronze. Interrupted milling, 8x8 grooves, notches widely spaced.	25.00
Pr59c	1986	198	20 Kroner. Aluminum-Bronze. Interrupted milling, 8x6 grooves.	25.00
Pr59d	1986	198	20 Kroner. Aluminum-Bronze. Interrupted milling, 16x3 grooves, no notches.	25.00
Pr59e	1986	198	20 Kroner. Aluminum-Bronze. Interrupted milling, 8x8 grooves, notches narrowly spaced.	25.00
Pr59f	1986	198	20 Kroner. Aluminum-Bronze. Interrupted milling, 8x8 grooves.	25.00
Pr60	1987	190	50 Ore. Bronze.	25.00
Pr61	1988	171	25 Ore. Bronze.	60.00
Pr62	1988	178	50 Ore. Bronze.	60.00
Pr63	1988	56	50 Ore. Bronze. A above cross on crown.	65.00
Pr64	1988	187	Krone. Copper-Nickel. Three crowned MIIR monograms, date, mint mark. Ornaments around center hole, value, country name.	60.00
Pr65	1988	175	2 Kroner. Copper-Nickel.	60.00
Pr66	1988	174	5 Kroner. Copper-Nickel. Ornaments surround center hole, hearts flank, denomination above country name below. Three crowns and monograms surround center hole, date below, hearts at top sides.	60.00
Pr67	1988	171	10 Kroner. Aluminum-Bronze.	50.00
Pr68	1988	171	20 Kroner. Aluminum-Bronze.	28.00
Pr69	1990 LG-JP	—	Krone. Copper-Nickel.	8.00
Pr70	1990 LG-JP	—	2 Kroner. Copper-Nickel.	8.00

TRIAL STRIKES

KM#	Date	Mintage	Identification	Mkt Val
TS3	1907	—	10 Kroner. Bronze. KM#809.	—
TS4	1907	—	10 Kroner. Bronze. KM#809.	—
TS5	1907	—	20 Kroner. Bronze. KM#810.	—
TS6	1907	—	20 Kroner. Bronze. KM#810.	—

MINT SETS

KM#	Date	Mintage	Identification	Issue Price	Mkt Val
MS1	1956 (7)	—	KM#837.2-843.2	—	120
MS2	1957 (7)	—	KM#837.2-843.2	—	90.00
MS3	1958 (7)	—	KM#837.2-843.2	—	90.00
MS4	1959 (7)	—	KM#837.2-843.2	—	245
MS5	1960 (8)	—	KM#837.2, 839.2-843.2, 849.1, 850	—	135
MS6	1961 (7)	—	KM#839.2-840.2, 843.2, 849.1, 850, 851.1, 853.1	—	80.00
MS7	1962 (8)	—	KM#839.2-840.2, 843.2, 848.1-849.1, 850, 851.1, 853.1	—	65.00
MS8	1963 (7)	—	KM#839.2-840.2, 843.2, 848.1-849.1, 851.1, 853.1	—	40.00
MS9	1964 (8)	—	KM#839.2-840.2, 843.2, 848.1-849.1, 850, 851.1, 853.1	—	40.00
MS10	1965 (7)	—	KM#839.2-840.2, 848.1-849.1, 850, 851.1, 853.1	—	40.00
MS11	1966 (8)	—	KM#839.2-840.2, 848.1-849.1, 850, 851.1, 853.1, 855.1	—	35.00
MSA12	1960-66 (10)	10,000	KM#846 (1960, 1962, 1963, 1964), KM#847 (1960, 1962, 1963, 1964, 1965, 1966)	—	9.00
MS12	1967 (8)	—	KM#839.2-840.2, 848.1-849.1, 850, 851.1, 853.1, 855.1	—	45.00
MS13	1968 (7)	—	KM#839.2-840.2, 848.1-849.1, 851.1, 853.1, 855.1	—	28.00
MS14	1969 (7)	—	KM#839.2-840.2, 848.1-849.1, 851.1, 853.1, 855.1	—	28.00
MS15	1970 (7)	—	KM#839.2-840.2, 848.1-849.1, 851.1, 853.1, 855.1	—	13.50
MS16	1971 (7)	—	KM#839.2-840.2, 848.1-849.1, 851.1, 853.1, 855.1	—	13.50
MS17	1972 (7)	—	KM#839.3-840.3, 848.2-849.2, 851.2, 853.2, 855.2	—	9.00
MS18	1973 (5)	—	KM#859.1-863.1	—	10.00
MS19	1974 (5)	—	KM#859.1-863.1	6.00	9.00
MS20	1975 (5)	4,300	KM#859.1-863.1	6.00	100
MS21	1976 (5)	6,000	KM#859.1-863.1	3.55	45.00
MS22	1977 (5)	6,000	KM#859.1-863.1	—	45.00
MS23	1978 (5)	6,000	KM#859.1-863.1	—	20.00
MS24	1979 (6)	6,000	KM#859.2-863.2, 864.1	—	18.00
MS25	1980 (5)	4,000	KM#859.2-863.2	—	150
MS26	1981 (6)	15,767	KM#859.2-863.2, 864.1	—	16.50
MS27	1982 (6)	17,031	KM#859.3-863.3, 864.2	—	14.00
MS28	1983 (6)	14,595	KM#859.3-863.3, 864.2	—	14.00
MS29	1984 (6)	14,041	KM#859.3-863.3, 864.2	—	14.00
MS30	1985 (6)	14,000	KM#859.3-863.3, 864.2	—	14.00
MS31	1986 (6)	20,000	KM#859.3-863.3, 865	—	25.00
MS32	1987 (6)	15,000	KM#859.3-863.3, 864.2	—	25.00
MS33	1988 (6)	19,692	KM#859.3-863.3, 864.2	—	14.00
MS34	1989 (3)	27,123	KM#862.3, 866.1, 867.1	12.00	10.00
MS35	1990 (6)	39,258	KM#866.2, 867.2, 868-871	15.00	16.50
MS36	1991 (5)	33,258	KM#866.2, 867.2, 868-869, 871	15.00	22.50
MS37	1992 (7)	40,000	KM#866.2, 867.2, 868-869, 873-875	15.00	25.00
MS38	1993 (7)	35,000	KM#866.2, 867.2, 868-869, 871, 873-874	15.00	20.00
MS39	1994 (7)	30,000	K#866.2, 868-869, 873-874, 877-878	15.00	16.50
MS40	1995 (7)	25,000	KM#866.2, 868-869, 873-874, 877, 879	15.00	16.50
MS41	1996 (6)	25,000	KM#866.2, 868, 873-874, 878, 881 (1995 date)	15.00	16.50
MS42	1997 (7)	25,000	KM#866.2, 868-869, 873-874, 877, 883	15.00	25.00
MS43	1998 (7)	28,000	KM#866.2, 868, 869, 873-874, 877, 878	15.00	22.50
MS44	1999 (7)	30,100	KM#866.2, 868-869, 873-874, 877, 878	15.00	22.50
MS45	2000 (6)	28,000	KM#866.2, 868, 869, 873, 874, 885	15.00	50.00

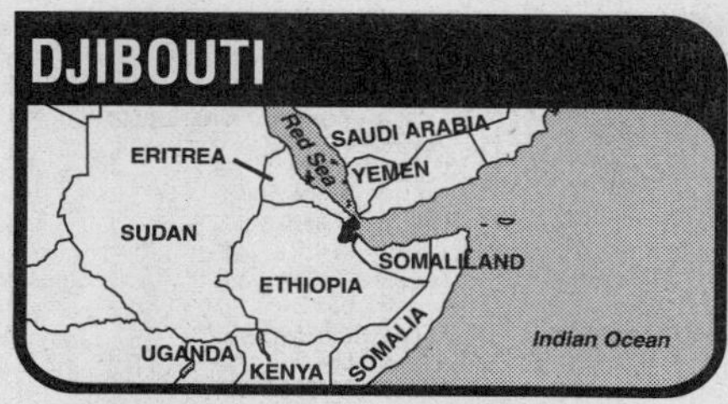

The Republic of Djibouti (formerly French Somaliland and the French Overseas Territory of Afars and Issas), located in northeast Africa at the Bab el Mandeb Strait connecting the Suez Canal and the Red Sea with the Gulf of Aden and the Indian Ocean, has an area of 8,950 sq. mi. (22,000 sq. km.) and a population of 421,320. Capital: Djibouti. The tiny nation has less than one sq. mi. of arable land, and no natural resources except salt, sand, and camels. The commercial activities of the transshipment port of Djibouti and the Addis Abada-Djibouti railroad are the basis of the economy. Salt, fish and hides are exported.

French interest in former French Somaliland began in 1839 with concessions obtained by a French naval lieutenant from the provincial sultans. French Somaliland was made a protectorate in 1884 and its boundaries were delimited by the Franco-British and Ethiopian accords of 1887 and 1897. It became a colony in 1896 and a territory within the French Union in 1946. In 1958 it voted to join the new French Community as an overseas territory, and reaffirmed that choice by a referendum in March, 1967. Its name was changed from French Somaliland to the French Territory of Afars and Issas on July 5, 1967.

The French Tricolor, which had flown over the strategically important territory for 115 years, was lowered for the last time on June 27, 1977, when French Afars and Issas became Africa's 49th independent state, under the name of the Republic of Djibouti.

Djibouti, a seaport and capital city of the Republic of Djibouti (and formerly of French Somaliland and French Afars and Issas) is located on the east coast of Africa at the southernmost entrance to the Red Sea. The capital was moved from Obok to Djibouti in 1892 and established as the transshipment point for Ethiopia's foreign trade via the Franco-Ethiopian railway linking Djibouti and Addis Ababa.

RULERS

French, until 1977

COLONY

TOKEN COINAGE

KM# Tn1 5 CENTIMES

Zinc **Issuer:** Chamber of Commerce

Date	Mintage	VG	F	VF	XF	Unc
1920	—	12.00	25.00	70.00	150	300

KM# Tn5 5 CENTIMES

Aluminum **Issuer:** Chamber of Commerce **Obv:** Horned deer left of tree, date below **Rev:** Denomination within wreath

Date	Mintage	VG	F	VF	XF	Unc
1921	—	10.00	20.00	50.00	100	225

KM# Tn2 10 CENTIMES

Zinc **Issuer:** Chamber of Commerce

Date	Mintage	VG	F	VF	XF	Unc
1920	—	15.00	30.00	80.00	165	325

KM# Tn6 10 CENTIMES

Aluminum **Issuer:** Chamber of Commerce

Date	Mintage	VG	F	VF	XF	Unc
1921	—	12.00	25.00	65.00	125	250

KM# Tn7 25 CENTIMES

Aluminum **Issuer:** Chamber of Commerce **Obv:** Horned deer left of tree, date below **Rev:** Denomination within wreath

Date	Mintage	VG	F	VF	XF	Unc
1921	—	15.00	30.00	80.00	165	325

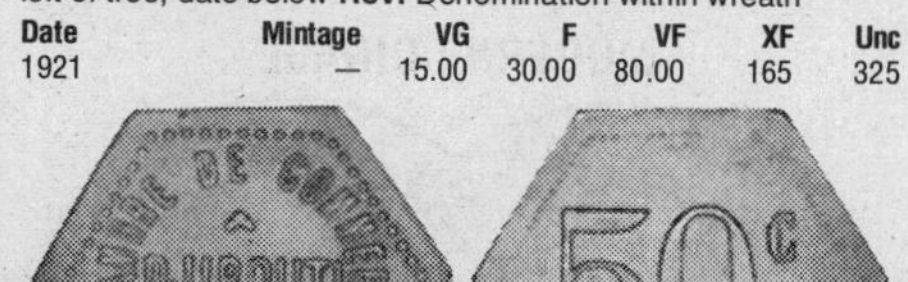

KM# Tn3 50 CENTIMES

Zinc **Issuer:** Chamber of Commerce

Date	Mintage	VG	F	VF	XF	Unc
1920	—	20.00	40.00	100	200	400

KM# Tn8 50 CENTIMES

Bronze-Aluminum **Issuer:** Chamber of Commerce **Obv:** Country name between hearts at center, date below, beaded outline surrounds **Rev:** Large denomination **Shape:** Six sided coin

Date	Mintage	VG	F	VF	XF	Unc
1921	—	15.00	30.00	80.00	160	320

KM# Tn9 50 CENTIMES

Bronze **Issuer:** Chamber of Commerce

Date	Mintage	VG	F	VF	XF	Unc
1921	—	20.00	40.00	100	200	400

KM# Tn10 50 CENTIMES

Aluminum **Issuer:** Chamber of Commerce

Date	Mintage	VG	F	VF	XF	Unc
1922	—	22.50	45.00	120	250	500

KM# Tn4 FRANC

Aluminum **Issuer:** Chamber of Commerce

Date	Mintage	VG	F	VF	XF	Unc
1920	—	25.00	50.00	135	275	550

REPUBLIC

STANDARD COINAGE

KM# 20 FRANC

1.3000 g., Aluminum, 23 mm. **Obv:** National arms within wreath, date below **Rev:** Giant eland head with headdress facing, divides denomination, shell on fish flank below

Date	Mintage	F	VF	XF	Unc	BU
1977(a)	300,000	0.50	0.75	1.50	3.00	5.00
1996(a)	—	0.50	0.75	1.50	3.00	5.00
1997(a)	350	—	—	—	12.00	14.00
Note: In sets only						
1999(a)	—	0.50	0.75	1.50	3.00	5.00

KM# 21 2 FRANCS

2.2000 g., Aluminum, 27.1 mm. **Obv:** National arms within wreath, date below **Rev:** Giant eland head with headdress facing, divides denomination, shell on fish flank below

Date	Mintage	F	VF	XF	Unc	BU
1977(a)	200,000	0.75	1.00	1.75	3.50	5.50
1991(a)	—	0.75	1.00	1.75	3.50	5.50
1996(a)	—	0.75	1.00	1.75	3.50	5.50
1997(a)	350	—	—	—	12.00	14.00
Note: In sets only						

KM# 22 5 FRANCS

3.7500 g., Aluminum, 31.1 mm. **Obv:** National arms within wreath, date below **Rev:** Giant eland head with headdress facing, divides denomination, shell on fish flank below

Date	Mintage	F	VF	XF	Unc	BU
1977(a)	400,000	0.75	1.25	2.00	4.00	6.00
1986(a)	—	0.75	1.00	1.75	3.50	5.50
1989(a)	—	0.75	1.00	1.75	3.50	5.50
1991(a)	—	0.75	1.00	1.75	3.50	5.50
1996(a)	—	0.75	1.00	1.75	3.50	5.50
1997(a)	350	—	—	—	12.00	14.00
Note: In sets only						

KM# 23 10 FRANCS

3.0000 g., Aluminum-Bronze, 20 mm. **Obv:** National arms within wreath, date below **Rev:** Boats on water, denomination above **Note:** Varieties exist.

Date	Mintage	F	VF	XF	Unc	BU
1977(a)	600,000	0.45	0.85	1.50	3.00	5.00
1983(a)	—	0.50	1.00	1.75	3.50	5.50
1989(a)	—	0.45	0.75	1.25	2.50	4.50
1991(a)	—	0.45	0.75	1.25	2.50	4.50
1996(a)	—	0.45	0.75	1.25	2.50	4.50
1997(a)	350	—	—	—	12.00	14.00
Note: In sets only						
1999(a)	—	0.50	0.75	1.25	2.50	4.50

KM# 24 20 FRANCS

4.0000 g., Aluminum-Bronze, 23.5 mm. **Obv:** National arms within wreath, date below **Rev:** Boats on water, denomination above **Note:** Varieties exist.

Date	Mintage	F	VF	XF	Unc	BU
1977(a)	700,000	0.50	1.00	1.50	3.00	5.00
1982(a)	—	0.50	1.00	1.75	3.50	5.50
1983(a)	—	0.50	1.00	1.50	3.00	5.00
1986(a)	—	0.45	0.75	1.25	2.50	4.50
1991(a)	—	0.45	0.75	1.25	2.50	4.50
1996(a)	—	0.45	0.75	1.25	2.50	4.50
1997(a)	350	—	—	—	12.00	14.00
Note: In sets only						
1999(a)	—	0.50	0.75	1.25	2.50	4.50

KM# 25 50 FRANCS

6.9000 g., Copper-Nickel, 25.5 mm. **Obv:** National arms within wreath, date below **Rev:** Pair of dromedary camels right, denomination above

Date	Mintage	F	VF	XF	Unc	BU
1977(a)	1,500,000	0.75	1.50	3.00	6.00	8.00
1982(a)	—	0.75	1.50	3.00	6.00	8.00
1983(a)	—	0.50	1.00	2.25	6.00	8.00
1986(a)	—	0.50	1.00	2.25	6.00	8.00
1989(a)	—	0.50	1.00	2.25	6.00	8.00
1991(a)	—	0.50	1.00	2.25	6.00	8.00
1997(a)	350	—	—	—	12.00	14.00
Note: In sets only						
1999(a)	—	0.50	1.00	2.25	6.00	8.00

KM# 26 100 FRANCS

12.0000 g., Copper-Nickel, 30 mm. **Obv:** National arms within wreath, date below **Rev:** Pair of dromedary camels right, denomination above

Date	Mintage	F	VF	XF	Unc	BU
1977(a)	1,500,000	1.00	2.00	3.00	7.50	9.50
1983(a)	—	1.00	2.50	3.50	8.00	10.00
1991(a)	—	1.00	1.75	2.75	7.50	9.50
1996(a)	—	1.00	1.75	2.25	7.00	9.00
1997(a)	350	—	—	—	15.00	17.00
Note: In sets only						
1999(a)	—	1.00	1.75	2.25	7.00	9.00

KM# 29 100 FRANCS
31.4700 g., 0.9250 Silver **Subject:** World Cup Soccer **Obv:** National arms within wreath, date below **Rev:** Soccer player divides maps, denomination below

Date	Mintage	F	VF	XF	Unc	BU
1994 Proof	Est. 15,000	Value: 40.00				

KM# 30 100 FRANCS
31.4700 g., 0.9250 Silver **Series:** 1996 Olympic Games **Obv:** National arms within wreath, date below **Rev:** Runner, denomination at right

Date	Mintage	F	VF	XF	Unc	BU
1994 Proof	Est. 30,000	Value: 37.50				

KM# 31 100 FRANCS
31.4700 g., 0.9250 Silver **Obv:** National arms within wreath, date below **Rev:** Frigate "Bateau" flag and denomination below

Date	Mintage	F	VF	XF	Unc	BU
1994 Proof	Est. 15,000	Value: 45.00				

KM# 32 100 FRANCS
31.4700 g., 0.9250 Silver **Subject:** Endangered Wildlife **Obv:** National arms within wreath, date below **Rev:** Grevy zebras running right, denomination below

Date	Mintage	F	VF	XF	Unc	BU
1994 Proof	Est. 15,000	Value: 45.00				

KM# 33 100 FRANCS
31.4700 g., 0.9250 Silver **Obv:** National arms within wreath, date below **Rev:** Portuguese "Nao" ship within circle, denomination below

Date	Mintage	F	VF	XF	Unc	BU
1996 Proof	Est. 15,000	Value: 45.00				

KM# 36 250 FRANCS
1.2440 g., 0.9990 Gold, 13.95 mm. **Obv:** National arms within wreath, date below **Rev:** Old Portuguese Ship

Date	Mintage	F	VF	XF	Unc	BU
1996 Proof	—	Value: 75.00				

KM# 27 500 FRANCS
Aluminum-Bronze **Obv:** National arms within wreath, date below **Rev:** Denomination within sprays

Date	Mintage	F	VF	XF	Unc	BU
1989(a)	—	3.00	4.00	6.00	10.00	12.00
1991(a)	—	3.00	4.00	6.00	10.00	12.00
1997(a)	350	—	—	—	15.00	17.00

Note: In sets only

KM# 35 500 FRANCS
0.9250 Silver **Subject:** Wildlife of Africa **Rev:** One lion in a tree, two lions under a tree

Date	Mintage	F	VF	XF	Unc	BU
1997 Proof	—	Value: 65.00				

KM# 28 15000 FRANCS
24.3000 g., 0.9990 Silver .7710 oz. ASW **Obv:** National arms within wreath, date below **Rev:** Map at center, denomination below

Date	Mintage	F	VF	XF	Unc	BU
1991	Est. 10,000	—	—	—	95.00	—

ESSAIS

Standard metals unless otherwise noted

KM#	Date	Mintage	Identification	Issue Price	Mkt Val
E1	1977(a)	1,700	Franc. KM20.	—	12.50
E2	1977(a)	1,700	2 Francs. KM21.	—	12.50
E3	1977(a)	1,700	5 Francs. KM22.	—	12.50
E4	1977(a)	1,700	10 Francs. KM23.	—	14.50
E5	1977(a)	1,700	20 Francs. KM24.	—	14.50
E6	1977(a)	1,700	50 Francs. KM25.	—	17.50
E7	1977(a)	1,700	100 Francs. KM26.	—	20.00

MINT SETS

KM#	Date	Mintage	Identification	Issue Price	Mkt Val
MS1	1997 (8)	350	KM#20-27	—	100

PROOF SETS

KM#	Date	Mintage	Identification	Issue Price	Mkt Val
PS1	1997 (8)	—	KM#20-27	—	150

DOMINICA

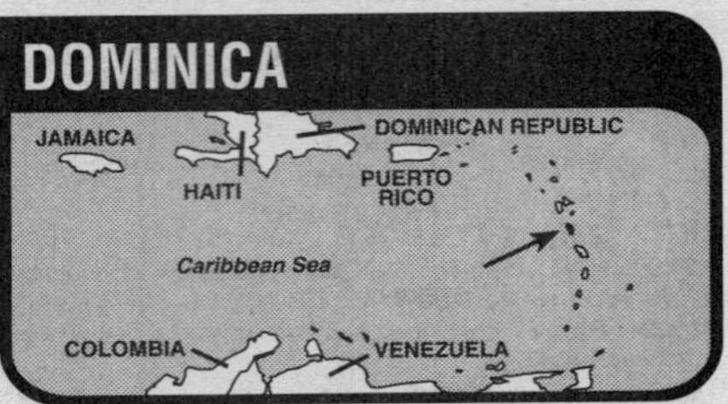

The Commonwealth of Dominica, situated in the Lesser Antilles midway between Guadeloupe to the north and Martinique to the south, has an area of 290 sq. mi. (750 sq. km.) and a population of 82,608. Capital: Roseau. Agriculture is the chief economic activity of the mountainous island. Bananas are the chief export.

Columbus discovered and named the island on Nov. 3, 1493. Spain neglected it and it was finally colonized by the French in 1632. The British drove the French from the island in 1756. Thereafter it changed hands between the French and British a dozen or more times before becoming permanently British in 1805. Around 1761, pierced or mutilated silver from Martinique was used on the island. A council in 1798 acknowledged and established value for these mutilated coins and ordered other cut and countermarked to be made in Dominica. These remained in use until 1862, when they were demonetized and sterling became the standard. Throughout the greater part of its British history, Dominica was a presidency of the Leeward Islands. In 1940 its administration was transferred to the Windward Islands and it was established as a separate colony with considerable local autonomy. From 1955, Dominica was a member of the currency board of the British Caribbean Territories (Eastern Group), which issued its own coins until 1965. Dominica became a West Indies associated state with a built in option for independence in 1967. Full independence was attained on Nov. 3, 1978. Dominica, which has a republican form of government, is a member of the Commonwealth of Nations.

RULERS

British, until 1978

MINT MARKS

CHI in circle - Valcambi, Chiasso, Italy
(ml) - maple leaf - Canadian Royal Mint

MONETARY SYSTEM

(Commencing 1813)
16 Bits = 12 Shillings = 1 Dollar (Spanish)
100 Cents = 1 Dollar (Dominican)

BRITISH COLONY

MODERN COINAGE

KM# 11 4 DOLLARS
Copper-Nickel, 38.5 mm. **Series:** F.A.O. **Rev:** Sugar cane and banana tree branch, denomination below **Note:** This 4-dollar F.A.O. commemorative coin is part of a group. The others are listed individually under their respective country names: Antigua, Barbados, Dominica, Grenada, Montserrat, St. Kitts, St. Lucia, and St. Vincent.

Date	Mintage	F	VF	XF	Unc	BU
1970	13,000	—	6.00	10.00	20.00	30.00
1970 Proof	2,000	Value: 35.00				

COMMONWEALTH

MODERN COINAGE

KM# 12.1 10 DOLLARS
20.5000 g., 0.9250 Silver .6097 oz. ASW **Subject:**

Independence - History of Carnival **Obv:** Young bust right **Obv. Designer:** Arnold Machin **Rev:** Six dancing women, denomination below, with mint mark

Date	Mintage	F	VF	XF	Unc	BU
ND(1978)CHI	1,500	—	—	9.00	18.50	22.00
ND(1978)CHI Proof	2,000	Value: 25.00				

KM# 12.2 10 DOLLARS

20.5000 g., 0.9250 Silver .6097 oz. ASW **Subject:** Independence - History of Carnival **Obv:** Young bust right **Obv. Designer:** Arnold Machin **Rev:** Six dancing women, denomination below, without mint mark

Date	Mintage	F	VF	XF	Unc	BU
ND(1978)	—	—	—	9.00	18.50	22.00

KM# 12.3 10 DOLLARS

20.5000 g., 0.9250 Silver .6097 oz. ASW **Subject:** Independence - History of Carnival **Obv:** Young bust right **Obv. Designer:** Arnold Machin **Rev:** Six dancing women, denomination below, Canadian mint mark and fineness

Date	Mintage	F	VF	XF	Unc	BU
ND(1978)(ml)	18	—	—	—	—	—
ND(1978)(ml) Proof	233	Value: 80.00				

KM# 16 10 DOLLARS

20.5000 g., 0.9250 Silver .6097 oz. ASW **Subject:** Visit of Pope John Paul II **Obv:** Young bust right **Obv. Designer:** Arnold Machin **Rev:** Head with beanie left, denomination below

Date	Mintage	F	VF	XF	Unc	BU
ND(1979)CHI	1,150	—	—	9.50	20.00	25.00
ND(1979)CHI Proof	3,450	Value: 28.00				

KM# 20 10 DOLLARS

Copper Nickel **Subject:** Royal Visit **Obv:** Crowned bust right **Obv. Designer:** Raphael Maklouf **Rev:** Lion tops arms with parrots, circle surrounds

Date	Mintage	F	VF	XF	Unc	BU
1985	Est. 100,000	—	—	6.00	10.00	16.50

KM# 20a 10 DOLLARS

28.2800 g., 0.9250 Silver .8409 oz. ASW **Subject:** Royal Visit **Obv:** Crowned bust right **Rev:** Lion tops arms with parrots, circle surrounds

Date	Mintage	F	VF	XF	Unc	BU
1985 Proof	Est. 5,000	Value: 30.00				

KM# 20b 10 DOLLARS

47.5400 g., 0.9170 Gold 1.4013 oz. AGW **Subject:** Royal Visit **Obv:** Crowned bust right **Rev:** Lion tops arms with parrots, circle surrounds

Date	Mintage	F	VF	XF	Unc	BU
1985 Proof	Est. 250	Value: 975				

KM# 13.1 20 DOLLARS

40.9100 g., 0.9250 Silver 1.2167 oz. ASW **Subject:** Independence and 50th Anniversary of Graf Zeppelin **Obv:** Young bust right divides dates **Rev:** Blimp above denomination

Date	Mintage	F	VF	XF	Unc	BU
ND(1978)CHI	500	—	—	30.00	65.00	75.00
ND(1978)CHI Proof	1,000	Value: 85.00				

KM# 13.2 20 DOLLARS

40.9100 g., 0.9250 Silver 1.2167 oz. ASW **Subject:** Independence and 50th Anniversary of Graf Zeppelin **Obv:** Young bust right divides dates **Rev:** Blimp above denomination, Canadian mint mark and .925 fineness stamp added

Date	Mintage	F	VF	XF	Unc	BU
ND(1978)(ml)	—	—	—	—	—	—
ND(1978)(ml) Proof	233	Value: 120				

KM# 13.3 20 DOLLARS

Silver, 45.2 mm. **Obv:** Young bust right **Obv. Designer:** Arnold Machin **Rev:** Blimp above denomination **Edge:** Reeded **Note:** No mint marks or fineness.

Date	Mintage	F	VF	XF	Unc	BU
ND(1978) Proof	—	Value: 150				

KM# 17 20 DOLLARS

40.9100 g., 0.9250 Silver 1.2167 oz. ASW **Subject:** Israel and Egypt Peace Treaty **Obv:** Young bust right **Obv. Designer:** Arnold Machin **Rev:** Portrait of Sadat, Begin, and Carter, with small flags, denomination below

Date	Mintage	F	VF	XF	Unc	BU
ND(1979)CHI	200	—	—	35.00	75.00	85.00
ND(1979)CHI Proof	200	Value: 95.00				

KM# 21 100 DOLLARS

129.5900 g., 0.9250 Silver 3.8543 oz. ASW, 63 mm. **Subject:** Tropical Birds - Imperial Parrots **Obv:** Lion tops arms with parrots, circle surrounds, date below **Rev:** Parrots in trees, denomination above **Note:** Photo reduced.

Date	Mintage	F	VF	XF	Unc	BU
1988 Proof	Est. 10,000	Value: 150				

KM# 14.1 150 DOLLARS

9.6000 g., 0.9000 Gold .2778 oz. AGW **Subject:** Independence - Imperial Parrot **Obv:** Young bust right **Obv. Designer:** Arnold Machin **Rev:** Map of Dominica and parrot, without fineness, denomination at left

Date	Mintage	F	VF	XF	Unc	BU
ND(1978)	300	—	—	—	225	—
ND(1978) Proof	400	Value: 250				

KM# 14.2 150 DOLLARS

9.6000 g., 0.9000 Gold .2778 oz. AGW **Subject:** Independence - Imperial Parrot **Obv:** Young bust right **Obv. Designer:** Arnold

Machin **Rev:** Parrot and map, denomination at left, Canadian mint mark and .900 fineness added

Date	Mintage	F	VF	XF	Unc	BU
ND(1978)(ml)	18	—	—	—	—	—
ND(1978)(ml) Proof	116	Value: 300				

KM# 18 150 DOLLARS

9.6000 g., 0.9000 Gold .2778 oz. AGW **Subject:** Israel and Egypt Peace Treaty **Obv:** Young bust right **Obv. Designer:** Arnold Machin **Rev:** Heads of Carter, Sadat, and Begin with flags, denomination below

Date	Mintage	F	VF	XF	Unc	BU
ND(1979)CHI	100	—	—	—	500	—
ND(1979)CHI Proof	100	Value: 550				

KM# 15.1 300 DOLLARS

19.2000 g., 0.9000 Gold .5556 oz. AGW **Subject:** Independence - Arms **Obv:** Young bust right **Obv. Designer:** Arnold Machin **Rev:** Lion tops arms with parrots, denomination below, without fineness

Date	Mintage	F	VF	XF	Unc	BU
ND(1978)	500	—	—	—	400	—
ND(1978) Proof	800	Value: 450				

KM# 15.2 300 DOLLARS

19.2000 g., 0.9000 Gold .5556 oz. AGW **Subject:** Independence - Arms **Obv:** Young bust right **Obv. Designer:** Arnold Machin **Rev:** National arms, Canadian mint mark and .900 fineness added

Date	Mintage	F	VF	XF	Unc	BU
ND(1978)(ml)	18	—	—	—	—	—
ND(1978)(ml) Proof	82	Value: 500				

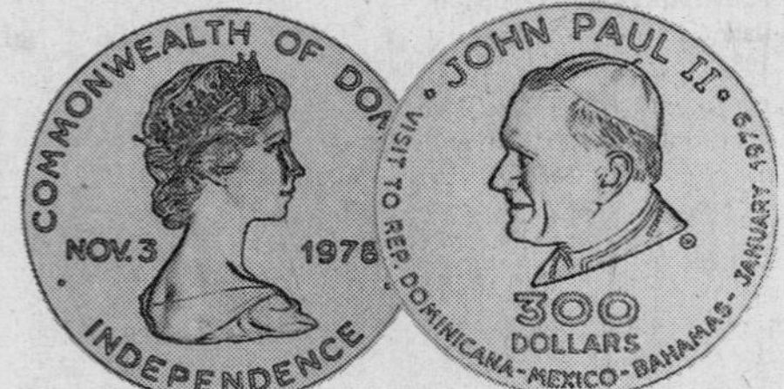

KM# 19 300 DOLLARS

19.2000 g., 0.9000 Gold .5556 oz. AGW **Subject:** Visit of Pope John Paul II **Obv:** Young bust right **Obv. Designer:** Arnold Machin **Rev:** Head with beanie left, denomination below

Date	Mintage	F	VF	XF	Unc	BU
ND(1979)CHI	5,000	—	—	—	375	—
ND(1979)CHI	300	—	—	—	550	—

PROOF SETS

KM#	Date	Mintage	Identification	Issue Price	Mkt Val
PS1	1978 (2)	—	KM#12.3, 13.2	—	200
PS2	1978 (4)	—	KM#12.3, 13.2, 14.2, 15.2	—	1,000

DOMINICAN REPUBLIC

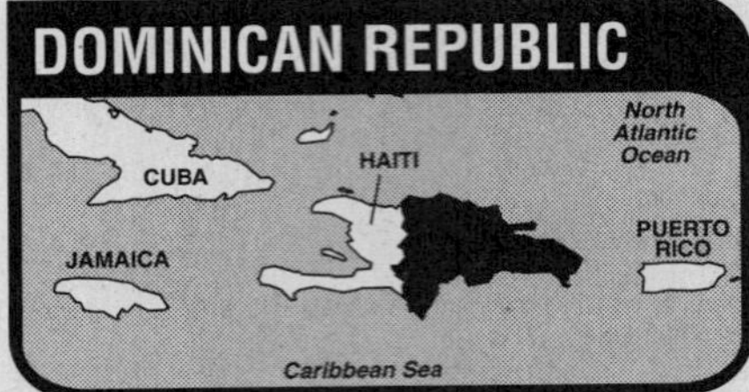

The Dominican Republic, which occupies the eastern two-thirds of the island of Hispaniola, has an area of 18,704 sq. mi. (48,734 sq. km.) and a population of 7.9 million. Capital: Santo Domingo. The largely agricultural economy produces sugar, coffee, tobacco and cocoa. Tourism and casino gaming are also a rising source of revenue.

Columbus discovered Hispaniola in 1492, and named it La Isla Espanola - 'the Spanish Island'. Santo Domingo, the oldest white settlement in the Western Hemisphere, was the base from which Spain conducted its exploration of the New World. Later, French buccaneers settled the western third of Hispaniola, naming the colony St. Dominique, which in 1697, was ceded to France by Spain. In 1804, following a bloody revolt by former slaves, the French colony became the Republic of Haiti - mountainous country'. The Spanish called their part of Hispaniola Santo Domingo. In 1822, the Haitians conquered the entire island and held it until 1844, when Juan Pablo Duarte, the national hero of the Dominican Republic, drove them out of Santo Domingo and established an independent Dominican Republic. The republic returned voluntarily to Spanish dominion from 1861 to 1865, after being rejected by France, Britain and the United States. Independence was reclaimed in 1866.

MINT MARKS

(c) - Stylized maple leaf, Royal Canadian Mint
Mo – Mexico City
(o) - CHI in oval - Valcambi, Chiasso, Italy
(t) - Tower, Tower Mint, London

MONETARY SYSTEM

100 Centavos = 1 Peso Oro

REPUBLIC

REFORM COINAGE

1937

100 Centavos = 1 Peso Oro

KM# 17 CENTAVO

Bronze **Obv:** National arms **Rev:** Palm tree divides denomination and weight, date below

Date	Mintage	F	VF	XF	Unc	BU
1937	1,000,000	0.50	1.50	7.50	75.00	100
1937 Proof	—	Value: 350				
1939	2,000,000	0.50	1.25	5.00	40.00	60.00
1941	2,000,000	0.25	0.50	3.00	12.00	25.00
1942	2,000,000	0.25	0.50	3.00	15.00	30.00
1944	5,000,000	0.20	0.50	1.50	10.00	20.00
1947	3,000,000	0.20	0.50	1.00	8.00	15.00
1949	3,000,000	0.20	0.40	1.00	8.00	15.00
1951	3,000,000	0.20	0.35	0.75	8.00	15.00
1952	3,000,000	0.20	0.35	0.75	8.00	15.00
1955	3,000,000	0.15	0.35	0.75	6.00	12.00
1956	3,000,000	0.15	0.35	0.75	6.00	12.00
1957	5,000,000	0.10	0.25	0.75	5.00	10.00
1959	5,000,000	0.10	0.25	0.75	5.00	10.00
1961	5,000,000	0.10	0.20	0.50	2.00	5.00

KM# 25 CENTAVO

Bronze **Subject:** 100th Anniversary - Restoration of the Republic **Obv:** National arms, date below **Rev:** Taino Indian divides denomination and weight, date below **Rev. Designer:** T. H. Paget

Date	Mintage	F	VF	XF	Unc	BU
1963	13,000,000	—	—	0.10	0.40	0.80

KM# 31 CENTAVO

Bronze **Obv:** National arms **Rev:** Profile of native princess left divides denomination and weight, date below

Date	Mintage	F	VF	XF	Unc	BU
1968	5,000,000	—	—	0.10	0.20	0.50
1971	6,000,000	—	—	0.10	0.20	0.50
1972	3,000,000	—	—	0.10	0.20	0.50
1972 Proof	500	Value: 15.00				
1975	500,000	—	—	0.10	0.20	0.50

KM# 32 CENTAVO

Bronze **Series:** F.A.O. **Obv:** National arms, date below **Rev:** Profile of native princess left divides denomination and weight, date below **Rev. Designer:** T. H. Paget

Date	Mintage	F	VF	XF	Unc	BU
1969	5,000,000	—	—	0.10	0.30	0.60

KM# 40 CENTAVO

Bronze **Subject:** Centennial - Death of Juan Pablo Duarte **Obv:** National arms, two dates below **Rev:** Bust facing divides denomination and weight, date below

Date	Mintage	F	VF	XF	Unc	BU
1976	3,995,000	—	—	0.10	0.20	0.50
1976 Proof	5,000	Value: 1.00				

KM# 48 CENTAVO

Bronze **Subject:** Death of Juan Pablo Duarte **Obv:** National arms without memorial legend **Rev:** Bust facing divides denomination and weight, date below

Date	Mintage	F	VF	XF	Unc	BU
1978	2,995,000	—	—	0.10	0.15	0.30
1978 Proof	5,000	Value: 2.00				
1979	2,985,000	—	—	0.10	0.15	0.30
1979 Proof	500	Value: 15.00				
1980	200,000	—	—	0.10	0.15	0.30
1980 Proof	3,000	Value: 1.00				
1981 Proof	3,000	Value: 1.00				

Note: KM#48a previously listed here has been moved to the Pattern section

KM# 64 CENTAVO

2.0000 g., Copper Plated Zinc, 19.1 mm. **Subject:** Human Rights **Obv:** National arms, denomination at left, date below **Rev:** Bust of Caonabo right

Date	Mintage	F	VF	XF	Unc	BU
1984Mo	10,000,000	—	—	—	0.25	0.50
1984Mo Proof	1,600	Value: 1.50				
1986	18,067,000	—	—	—	0.25	0.50
1986 Proof	1,600	Value: 1.50				
1987	15,000,000	—	—	—	0.25	0.50
1987(t) Proof	1,600	Value: 1.50				

KM# 64a CENTAVO

2.0000 g., 0.9000 Silver .0578 oz. ASW, 19.1 mm. **Subject:** Human Rights **Obv:** National arms, date below **Rev:** Bust of Caonabo right

Date	Mintage	F	VF	XF	Unc	BU
1984Mo Proof	100	Value: 20.00				
1986 Proof	100	Value: 20.00				

KM# 72a CENTAVO

3.7000 g., 0.9250 Silver .1100 oz. ASW, 19.1 mm. **Obv:** National arms, date below **Rev:** Triangular artifact

Date	Mintage	F	VF	XF	Unc	BU
1989 Proof	2,600	—	—	—	—	—

KM# 72 CENTAVO

Copper Plated Zinc, 19.1 mm. **Obv:** National arms, date below **Rev:** Triangular artifact, denomination below

Date	Mintage	F	VF	XF	Unc	BU
1989	1,115	—	—	—	1.25	1.75

KM# 18 5 CENTAVOS

Copper-Nickel, 21 mm. **Obv:** National arms **Rev:** Profile of native princess left divides denomination and weight, date below **Rev. Designer:** T. H. Paget

Date	Mintage	F	VF	XF	Unc	BU
1937	2,000,000	1.00	1.75	5.00	50.00	65.00
1937 Proof	—	Value: 600				
1939	200,000	5.00	15.00	60.00	350	400
1951	2,000,000	0.75	1.25	2.00	20.00	35.00
1956	1,000,000	0.20	0.50	0.80	3.50	5.00
1959	1,000,000	0.20	0.50	0.80	3.50	5.00
1961	4,000,000	0.10	0.20	0.35	0.75	1.25
1971	440,000	0.10	0.15	0.20	0.50	1.00
1972	2,000,000	0.10	0.15	0.20	0.40	0.90
1972 Proof	500	Value: 15.00				
1974	5,000,000	—	—	0.10	0.40	0.90
1974 Proof	500	Value: 15.00				

KM# 18a 5 CENTAVOS

5.0000 g., 0.3500 Silver .0563 oz. ASW, 21 mm. **Obv:** National arms **Rev:** Profile of native princess left divides denomination and weight, date below

Date	Mintage	F	VF	XF	Unc	BU
1944	2,000,000	1.50	3.50	7.50	50.00	75.00

KM# 26 5 CENTAVOS

Copper-Nickel, 21 mm. **Subject:** 100th Anniversary - Restoration of the Republic **Obv:** National arms, two dates below **Rev:** Profile of native princess left divides denomination and weight, date below **Rev. Designer:** T. H. Paget

Date	Mintage	F	VF	XF	Unc	BU
1963	4,000,000	—	0.10	0.15	0.60	1.25

KM# 41 5 CENTAVOS

Copper-Nickel, 41 mm. **Subject:** Centennial - Death of Juan Pablo Duarte **Obv:** National arms, two dates below **Rev:** Bust facing divides denomination and weight, date below

Date	Mintage	F	VF	XF	Unc	BU
1976	5,595,000	—	—	0.10	0.50	1.00
1976 Proof	5,000	Value: 2.00				

KM# 49 5 CENTAVOS

Copper-Nickel, 21 mm. **Obv:** National arms without memorial legend **Rev:** Bust facing divides denomination and weight, date below

Date	Mintage	F	VF	XF	Unc	BU
1978	1,996,000	—	—	0.10	0.35	0.90
1978 Proof	5,000	Value: 1.50				
1979	2,988,000	—	—	0.10	0.35	0.90
1979 Proof	500	Value: 15.00				
1980	5,300,000	—	—	0.10	0.35	0.90
1980 Proof	3,000	Value: 2.00				
1981	4,500,000	—	—	0.10	0.35	0.90
1981 Proof	3,000	Value: 2.00				

Note: KM#49a previously listed here has been moved to the Pattern section

KM# 59 5 CENTAVOS

5.0000 g., Copper Nickel, 21 mm. **Subject:** Human Rights **Obv:** National arms, date below **Rev:** Conjoined busts right, denomination above

Date	Mintage	F	VF	XF	Unc	BU
1983	3,998,000	—	—	0.10	0.30	0.90
1983(t) Proof	1,600	Value: 2.00				
1984Mo	10,000,000	—	—	0.10	0.30	0.90
1984Mo Proof	1,600	Value: 2.00				
1986	12,898,000	—	—	0.10	0.30	0.90
1986 Proof	1,600	Value: 2.00				
1987	10,000,000	—	—	0.10	0.30	0.90
1987(t) Proof	1,700	Value: 2.00				

KM# 59a 5 CENTAVOS

5.0000 g., 0.9000 Silver .1447 oz. ASW, 21 mm. **Subject:** Human Rights **Obv:** National arms, date below **Rev:** Conjoined busts right, denomination above

Date	Mintage	F	VF	XF	Unc	BU
1983(t) Proof	100	Value: 30.00				
1984Mo Proof	100	Value: 30.00				
1986 Proof	100	Value: 30.00				

KM# 69 5 CENTAVOS

Nickel Clad Steel, 21 mm. **Subject:** Native Culture **Obv:** National arms, date below **Rev:** Native drummer, denomination at left

Date	Mintage	F	VF	XF	Unc	BU
1989	50,000,000	—	—	—	0.35	0.90

KM# 69a 5 CENTAVOS

5.8300 g., 0.9250 Silver .1734 oz. ASW, 21 mm. **Subject:** Native Culture **Obv:** National arms, date below **Rev:** Native drummer, denomination at left

Date	Mintage	F	VF	XF	Unc	BU
1989 Proof	2,600	—	—	—	—	—

KM# 19 10 CENTAVOS

2.5000 g., 0.9000 Silver .0723 oz. ASW, 17.9 mm. **Obv:** National arms **Rev:** Profile of native princess left divides denomination and weight

Date	Mintage	F	VF	XF	Unc	BU
1937	1,000,000	BV	2.00	5.00	40.00	60.00
1937 Proof	—	Value: 700				
1939	150,000	5.00	15.00	40.00	300	350
1942	2,000,000	1.25	2.00	3.00	30.00	40.00
1944	1,000,000	1.25	2.00	4.00	75.00	95.00
1951	500,000	1.25	2.00	3.00	10.00	17.50
1952	500,000	1.25	2.00	3.00	10.00	17.50
1953	750,000	1.25	2.00	3.00	8.00	15.00
1956	1,000,000	1.00	1.75	2.50	8.00	15.00
1959	2,000,000	BV	1.25	2.25	7.00	12.50
1961	2,000,000	BV	1.25	2.00	6.00	12.00

KM# 19a 10 CENTAVOS

Copper-Nickel, 17.9 mm. **Obv:** National arms **Rev:** Profile of native princess left divides denomination and weight, date below **Edge:** Plain

Date	Mintage	F	VF	XF	Unc	BU
1967	10,000,000	—	—	0.15	0.50	1.00
1973	8,000,000	—	—	0.15	0.50	1.00
1973 Proof	500	Value: 20.00				
1975	8,000,000	—	—	0.15	0.50	1.00

KM# 27 10 CENTAVOS

2.5000 g., 0.6500 Silver .0522 oz. ASW, 17.9 mm. **Subject:** 100th Anniversary - Restoration of the Republic **Obv:** National arms **Rev:** Profile of native princess left divides denomination and weight **Rev. Designer:** T. H. Paget

Date	Mintage	F	VF	XF	Unc	BU
1963	4,000,000	—	BV	1.00	2.00	3.00

KM# 42 10 CENTAVOS

Copper-Nickel, 17.9 mm. **Subject:** Centennial - Death of Juan Pablo Duarte **Obv:** National arms **Rev:** Bust facing, date below

Date	Mintage	F	VF	XF	Unc	BU
1976	5,595,000	—	—	0.10	0.75	1.50
1976 Proof	5,000	Value: 2.00				

KM# 50 10 CENTAVOS

Copper-Nickel, 17.9 mm. **Obv:** National arms **Rev:** Bust facing divides denomination and weight, date below

Date	Mintage	F	VF	XF	Unc	BU
1978	3,000,000	—	—	0.10	0.50	1.00
1978 Proof	5,000	Value: 2.00				
1979	4,020,000	—	—	0.10	0.50	1.00
1979 Proof	500	Value: 20.00				
1980	4,400,000	—	—	0.10	0.35	1.00
1980 Proof	3,000	Value: 3.00				
1981	6,000,000	—	—	0.10	0.35	1.00
1981 Proof	3,000	Value: 3.00				

Note: KM#50a previously listed here has been moved to the Pattern section

KM# 60 10 CENTAVOS

2.5000 g., Copper-Nickel, 17.9 mm. **Subject:** Human Rights **Obv:** National arms, date below **Rev:** Head left, denomination above

Date	Mintage	F	VF	XF	Unc	BU
1983	4,998,000	—	—	0.10	0.35	0.90
1983(t)	4,000,000	—	—	0.10	0.35	0.90
1983(t) Proof	1,600	Value: 2.50				
1984Mo	15,000,000	—	—	0.10	0.25	0.75
Note: Coarse reeding						
1984Mo Proof	1,600	Value: 2.50				
Note: Coarse reeding						
1986	15,515,000	—	—	0.10	0.25	0.75
1986 Proof	1,600	Value: 2.50				
1987	20,000,000	—	—	0.10	0.25	0.75
1987(t) Proof	1,700	Value: 2.50				

KM# 60a 10 CENTAVOS

2.5000 g., 0.9000 Silver .0723 oz. ASW, 17.9 mm. **Subject:** Human Rights **Obv:** National arms **Rev:** Head left, denomination above

Date	Mintage	F	VF	XF	Unc	BU
1983(t) Proof	100	Value: 30.00				
1984Mo Proof	100	Value: 30.00				
1986 Proof	100	Value: 30.00				

KM# 70 10 CENTAVOS

Nickel Clad Steel, 17.9 mm. **Obv:** National arms, date below **Rev:** Indigenous fruits and vegetables divide denomination

Date	Mintage	F	VF	XF	Unc	BU
1989	40,000,000	—	—	—	0.40	0.90
1991	3,500,000	—	—	—	0.40	0.90

KM# 70a 10 CENTAVOS

2.9000 g., 925.0000 Silver .0863 oz. ASW, 17.9 mm. **Obv:** National arms **Rev:** Indigenous fruits and vegetables divide denomination

Date	Mintage	F	VF	XF	Unc	BU
1989 Proof	2,600	—	—	—	—	—

KM# 20 25 CENTAVOS

6.2500 g., 0.9000 Silver .1808 oz. ASW, 24 mm. **Obv:** National arms **Rev:** Profile of native princess left divides denomination and weight, date below **Rev. Designer:** T. H. Paget

Date	Mintage	F	VF	XF	Unc	BU
1937 Proof	—	Value: 1,000				
1937	560,000	BV	5.00	15.00	65.00	75.00
1939	160,000	5.00	15.00	50.00	500	650
1942	560,000	2.50	4.00	10.00	100	125
1944	400,000	2.50	4.00	8.00	100	125
1947	400,000	2.50	4.00	8.00	80.00	100
1951	400,000	2.50	4.00	8.00	80.00	100
1952	400,000	BV	3.00	5.00	12.50	15.00
1956	400,000	BV	2.50	4.00	10.00	12.50
1960	600,000	BV	2.50	4.00	10.00	12.50
1961	800,000	BV	2.50	4.00	10.00	12.50

KM# 20a.1 25 CENTAVOS

Copper Nickel, 24 mm. **Obv:** National arms **Rev:** Profile of native princess left divides denomination and weight, date below **Rev. Designer:** T. H. Paget **Edge:** Plain

Date	Mintage	F	VF	XF	Unc	BU
1967	5,000,000	—	0.10	0.20	0.75	1.00
1972	800,000	—	0.10	0.40	1.00	1.50
1972 Proof	500	Value: 20.00				

KM# 20a.2 25 CENTAVOS

Copper-Nickel, 24 mm. **Obv:** National arms **Rev:** Profile of native princess left divides denomination and weight, date below **Rev. Designer:** T. H. Paget **Edge:** Reeded

Date	Mintage	F	VF	XF	Unc	BU
1974	2,000,000	—	0.10	0.40	1.00	1.50
1974 Proof	500	Value: 20.00				

KM# 28 25 CENTAVOS

6.2500 g., 0.6500 Silver .1306 oz. ASW, 24 mm. **Subject:** 100th Anniversary - Restoration of the Republic **Obv:** National arms, two dates below **Rev:** Profile of native princess left divides denomination and weight, date below **Rev. Designer:** T. H. Paget

Date	Mintage	F	VF	XF	Unc	BU
1963	2,400,000	—	BV	2.00	3.00	5.00

KM# 43 25 CENTAVOS

Copper-Nickel, 24 mm. **Subject:** Centennial - Death of Juan Pablo Duarte **Obv:** National arms, two dates below **Rev:** Bust facing divides denomination and weight, date below

Date	Mintage	F	VF	XF	Unc	BU
1976	3,195,000	—	0.10	0.40	1.00	1.50
1976 Proof	5,000	Value: 2.50				

KM# 51 25 CENTAVOS

Copper-Nickel, 24 mm. **Obv:** National arms without memorial legend **Rev:** Bust facing divides denomination and weight, date below

Date	Mintage	F	VF	XF	Unc	BU
1978	996,000	—	—	0.35	0.75	1.00
1978 Proof	5,000	Value: 3.00				
1979	2,089,000	—	—	0.15	0.50	0.75
1979 Proof	500	Value: 25.00				
1980	2,600,000	—	—	0.15	0.50	0.75
1980 Proof	3,000	Value: 3.00				
1981	3,200,000	—	—	0.15	0.50	0.75
1981 Proof	3,000	Value: 3.00				

Note: KM#51a previously listed here has been moved to the Pattern section

KM# 61a 25 CENTAVOS

6.2500 g., 0.9000 Silver .1808 oz. ASW, 24 mm. **Subject:** Human Rights **Obv:** National arms **Rev:** Profile of the Mirabel sisters left

Date	Mintage	F	VF	XF	Unc	BU
1983(t) Proof	100	Value: 40.00				
1984Mo Proof	100	Value: 40.00				
1986 Proof	100	Value: 40.00				

KM# 61 25 CENTAVOS

6.2500 g., Copper-Nickel, 24 mm. **Subject:** Human Rights **Obv:** National arms, date below, denomination at left **Rev:** Profiles of the Mirabel sisters, left, Patria, Minerva & Maria Teresa, human rights martyrs murdered 25.11.1960 by Trujillo **Note:** Coin and medal rotations and edge reeding varieties exist.

Date	Mintage	F	VF	XF	Unc	BU
1983	793,000	—	0.10	0.20	0.50	1.00
Note: Medal rotation						
1983(t)	5,000	—	—	—	2.50	4.00
1983(t) Proof	1,600	Value: 8.00				
1984Mo	6,400,000	—	—	0.15	0.40	1.00
Note: Medal rotation						
1984Mo Proof	1,600	Value: 8.00				
1986	10,132,000	—	—	0.15	0.40	1.00
1986 Proof	1,600	Value: 8.00				
1987	6,000,000	—	—	0.15	0.40	1.00
1987(t) Proof	1,700	Value: 8.00				

KM# 71.2 25 CENTAVOS

Nickel Clad Steel, 24 mm. **Subject:** Native Culture **Obv:** National arms, date below **Rev:** Two oxen pulling cart, denomination above **Note:** Obverse and reverse legends and designs in beaded circle. Varieties exist.

Date	Mintage	F	VF	XF	Unc	BU
1989	Inc. above	—	—	—	0.60	1.25
1990	20,000,000	—	—	—	0.60	1.25

KM# 71.1 25 CENTAVOS

Nickel Clad Steel, 24 mm. **Subject:** Native Culture **Obv:** National arms, date below **Rev:** Two oxen pulling cart, denomination above

Date	Mintage	F	VF	XF	Unc	BU
1989	16,000,000	—	—	—	0.60	1.25
1991	38,000,000	—	—	—	0.60	1.25

KM# 71.1a 25 CENTAVOS

6.7400 g., 0.9250 Silver .2005 oz. ASW, 24 mm. **Subject:** Native Culture **Obv:** National arms **Rev:** Two oxen pulling cart

Date	Mintage	F	VF	XF	Unc	BU
1989 Proof	2,600	—	—	—	—	—

KM# 21 1/2 PESO

12.5000 g., 0.9000 Silver .3617 oz. ASW, 30.5 mm. **Obv:** National arms **Rev:** Profile of native princess left divides denomination and weight **Rev. Designer:** T. H. Paget

Date	Mintage	F	VF	XF	Unc	BU
1937	500,000	BV	7.50	12.50	70.00	100
1937 Proof	—	Value: 1,500				
1944	100,000	BV	15.00	40.00	400	450
1947	200,000	BV	10.00	30.00	350	500
1951	200,000	BV	7.50	15.00	150	200
1952	140,000	BV	7.50	12.50	70.00	100
1959	100,000	BV	6.00	10.00	40.00	75.00
1960	100,000	BV	6.00	9.00	30.00	55.00
1961	400,000	BV	5.00	7.00	25.00	50.00

KM# 21a.1 1/2 PESO

Copper-Nickel, 30.5 mm. **Obv:** National arms **Rev:** Profile of native princess left divides denomination and weight **Rev. Designer:** T.H. Pajet **Edge:** Plain

Date	Mintage	F	VF	XF	Unc	BU
1967	1,500,000	—	0.20	0.40	1.50	3.00
1968	600,000	—	0.30	0.50	2.50	5.00

KM# 29 1/2 PESO

12.5000 g., 0.6500 Silver .2612 oz. ASW, 30.5 mm. **Subject:** 100th Anniversary - Restoration of the Republic **Obv:** National arms **Rev:** Profile of native princess left divides denomination and weight **Rev. Designer:** T. H. Paget

Date	Mintage	F	VF	XF	Unc	BU
1963	300,000	—	BV	4.50	7.50	9.00

KM# 21a.2 1/2 PESO

Copper-Nickel, 30.5 mm. **Obv:** National arms **Rev:** Profile of native princess left divides denomination and weight **Edge:** Reeded

Date	Mintage	F	VF	XF	Unc	BU
1973	600,000	—	0.20	0.40	1.50	2.00
1973 Proof	500	Value: 30.00				
1975	600,000	—	0.20	0.40	1.50	2.00

KM# 44 1/2 PESO

Copper-Nickel, 30.5 mm. **Subject:** Centennial - Death of Juan Pablo Duarte **Obv:** National arms, two dates below **Rev:** Bust facing divides denomination and weight, date below

Date	Mintage	F	VF	XF	Unc	BU
1976	195,000	—	0.20	0.40	1.50	2.00
1976 Proof	5,000	Value: 3.00				

KM# 52 1/2 PESO

Copper-Nickel, 30.5 mm. **Obv:** National arms without memorial legend **Rev:** Bust facing divides denomination and weight, date below

Date	Mintage	F	VF	XF	Unc	BU
1978	296,000	—	0.20	0.40	1.50	2.00
1978 Proof	5,000	Value: 4.00				
1979	967,000	—	0.20	0.40	1.50	2.00
1979 Proof	500	Value: 30.00				
1980	1,000,000	—	0.20	0.40	1.50	2.00
1980 Proof	3,000	Value: 5.00				
1981	1,300,000	—	0.20	0.40	1.50	2.00
1981 Proof	3,000	Value: 5.00				

Note: KM#52a previously listed here has been moved to the Pattern section

KM# 62 1/2 PESO

12.5000 g., Copper-Nickel, 30.5 mm. **Subject:** Human Rights **Obv:** National arms, date below, denomination at left **Rev:** Three profiles right **Note:** Coin and medal rotations exist.

Date	Mintage	F	VF	XF	Unc	BU
1983	393,000	—	0.20	0.40	1.50	2.00
1983(t)	5,000	—	—	—	4.00	5.00
1983(t) Proof	1,600	Value: 15.00				
1984Mo	3,200,000	—	0.20	0.40	1.50	2.00
1984Mo Proof	1,600	Value: 15.00				
1986	5,225,000	—	0.20	0.40	1.50	2.00
1986 Proof	1,600	Value: 15.00				
1987	3,000,000	—	0.20	0.40	1.50	2.00
1987(t) Proof	1,700	Value: 15.00				

KM# 62a 1/2 PESO

12.5000 g., 0.9000 Silver .3617 oz. ASW, 30.5 mm. **Subject:** Human Rights **Obv:** National arms, date below **Rev:** Three profiles right

Date	Mintage	F	VF	XF	Unc	BU
1983(t) Proof	100	Value: 50.00				
1984Mo Proof	100	Value: 50.00				
1986 Proof	100	Value: 50.00				

KM# 73.1 1/2 PESO

Nickel Clad Steel, 30.5 mm. **Subject:** National Culture **Obv:** National arms **Rev:** Beacon at Colon

Date	Mintage	F	VF	XF	Unc	BU
1989	8,000,000	—	—	—	2.00	3.00

KM# 73.1a 1/2 PESO

14.6500 g., 0.9250 Silver .4357 oz. ASW, 30.5 mm. **Subject:** National Culture **Obv:** National arms **Rev:** Beacon at Colon

Date	Mintage	F	VF	XF	Unc	BU
1989 Proof	2,600	—	—	—	—	—

KM# 73.2 1/2 PESO

Nickel-Clad Steel, 30.5 mm. **Subject:** National Culture **Obv:** National arms, date below **Rev:** Beacon at Colon, denomination at left

Date	Mintage	F	VF	XF	Unc	BU
1990	1,500,000	—	—	—	2.00	3.00

KM# 22 PESO

26.7000 g., 0.9000 Silver .7725 oz. ASW **Obv:** National arms **Rev:** HP below head of native princess left **Rev. Designer:** T. H. Paget

Date	Mintage	F	VF	XF	Unc	BU
1939	15,000	15.00	45.00	200	1,500	—
1939 Proof	—	Value: 2,250				
1952	20,000	BV	10.00	12.00	16.00	30.00

KM# 23 PESO

26.7000 g., 0.9000 Silver .7725 oz. ASW, 38 mm. **Subject:** 25th Anniversary of Trujillo Regime **Obv:** National arms **Rev:** Bust right divides date and denomination **Note:** 30,550 officially melted following Trujillo's assassination in 1961.

Date	Mintage	F	VF	XF	Unc	BU
1955	50,000	10.00	12.00	15.00	25.00	35.00

KM# 30 PESO

26.7000 g., 0.6500 Silver .5579 oz. ASW **Subject:** 100th Anniversary - Restoration of the Republic **Obv:** Memorial legend around national arms, two dates below **Rev:** Profile of native princess left divides denomination and weight, date below **Rev. Designer:** T. H. Paget

Date	Mintage	F	VF	XF	Unc	BU
1963	20,000	—	—	7.50	10.00	16.00
1963 Proof	—	—	—	—	—	—

KM# 33 PESO

Copper-Nickel, 38 mm. **Subject:** 125th Anniversary of the Republic **Obv:** Memorial legend around national arms, two dates below **Rev:** Pueblo entrance within circle holding legend divides denomination and weight, date below

Date	Mintage	F	VF	XF	Unc	BU
1969	30,000	—	—	2.00	4.50	6.00

KM# 34 PESO

26.7000 g., 0.9000 Silver .7725 oz. ASW **Subject:** 25th Anniversary - Central Bank **Obv:** Memorial legend around national arms **Rev:** Bank door in inner circle divides denomination and weight, date below

Date	Mintage	F	VF	XF	Unc	BU
1972	27,000	—	—	—	11.00	13.00
1972 Proof	3,000	Value: 16.00				

KM# 35 PESO

26.7000 g., 0.9000 Silver .7725 oz. ASW **Subject:** 12th Central American and Caribbean Games **Obv:** National arms without memorial legend **Rev:** Coat of arms within circle, on map, denomination and date below

Date	Mintage	F	VF	XF	Unc	BU
1974	50,000	—	—	—	11.00	13.00
1974 Proof	5,000	Value: 16.00				

KM# 45 PESO

Copper-Nickel **Subject:** Centennial - Death of Juan Pablo Duarte **Obv:** National arms, two dates below **Rev:** Bust facing divides denomination and weight, date below

Date	Mintage	F	VF	XF	Unc	BU
1976	25,000	—	—	1.00	2.00	4.00
1976 Proof	5,000	Value: 7.50				

KM# 53 PESO

Copper-Nickel **Obv:** National arms without memorial legend **Rev:** Bust facing divides denomination and weight, date below

Date	Mintage	F	VF	XF	Unc	BU
1978	35,000	—	—	1.00	2.00	4.00
1978 Proof	5,000	Value: 7.50				
1979	45,000	—	—	1.00	2.00	4.00
1979 Proof	500	Value: 35.00				
1980	20,000	—	—	1.00	2.00	4.00
1980 Proof	3,000	Value: 6.50				
1981 Proof	3,000	Value: 6.50				

Note: KM#53a previously listed here has been moved to the Pattern section

KM# 63 PESO

16.9000 g., Copper Nickel, 33.2 mm. **Subject:** Human Rights **Obv:** National arms, date below, denomination at left **Rev:** Three profiles right **Shape:** 10-sided **Note:** Coin and medal rotations exist.

Date	Mintage	F	VF	XF	Unc	BU
1983	5,000	—	—	—	6.00	12.00
1983(t)	93,000	—	—	1.00	2.50	4.00
1983(t) Proof	1,600	Value: 15.00				
1984Mo	120,000	—	—	1.00	2.50	4.00
1984Mo Proof	1,600	Value: 15.00				
1986	—	—	—	1.00	2.50	4.00

KM# 63a PESO

17.0000 g., 0.9000 Silver .4919 oz. ASW **Subject:** Human Rights **Obv:** National arms, denomination **Rev:** Three profiles right **Shape:** 10-sided

Date	Mintage	F	VF	XF	Unc	BU
1983(T) Proof	100	Value: 100				
1984 Proof	100	Value: 100				

KM# 65 PESO

Nickel Bonded Steel **Subject:** 15th Central American and Caribbean Games **Obv:** National arms, date below, denomination at left **Rev:** St. George and coat of arms **Shape:** Round

Date	Mintage	F	VF	XF	Unc	BU
1986	100,000	—	—	1.00	3.00	5.00
1986 Proof	1,700	Value: 15.00				

KM# 65a PESO

6.5000 g., Copper-Nickel **Subject:** 15th Central American and Caribbean Games **Obv:** National arms, denomination **Rev:** St. George and coat of arms **Shape:** Round

Date	Mintage	F	VF	XF	Unc	BU
1986 Proof	48	—	—	—	—	—
1986	548	—	—	—	40.00	60.00

KM# 65b PESO

10.0000 g., Copper-Nickel **Subject:** 15th Central American and Caribbean Games **Obv:** National arms and denomination **Rev:** St. George and coat of arms **Shape:** Round

Date	Mintage	F	VF	XF	Unc	BU
1986	550	—	—	—	40.00	60.00
1986 Proof	50	—	—	—	—	—

KM# 66 PESO

19.8400 g., Copper-Nickel **Subject:** 500th Anniversary - Discovery and Evangelization **Obv:** National arms, date below, denomination at left **Rev:** 3 ships at sea, date below

Date	Mintage	F	VF	XF	Unc	BU
1988(c)	150,000	—	—	—	2.50	3.50
1988(c) Proof	1,500	Value: 12.50				

KM# 66a PESO

21.1035 g., 0.9990 Silver 1 oz. ASW **Subject:** 500th Anniversary - Discovery and Evangelization **Obv:** Denomination, national arms **Rev:** 3 ships at sea

Date	Mintage	F	VF	XF	Unc	BU
1988 Proof	10,000	Value: 18.50				

KM# 66b PESO

31.1035 g., 0.9990 Gold 1 oz. AGW **Subject:** 500th Anniversary - Discovery and Evangelization **Obv:** Denomination, national arms **Rev:** 3 ships at sea

Date	Mintage	F	VF	XF	Unc	BU
1988 Proof	—	Value: 1,250				

KM# 74 PESO

Copper-Nickel **Subject:** 500th Anniversary - Discovery and Evangelization **Obv:** Denomination, national arms **Rev:** Sailship landing

Date	Mintage	F	VF	XF	Unc	BU
1989(c)	—	—	—	—	2.50	3.50

KM# 74a PESO

31.1035 g., 0.9990 Silver 1 oz. ASW **Subject:** 500th Anniversary - Discovery and Evangelization **Obv:** Denomination, national arms **Rev:** Sailship landing

Date	Mintage	F	VF	XF	Unc	BU
1989 Proof	10,000	Value: 18.50				

KM# 74b PESO

31.1035 g., 0.9990 Gold 1 oz. AGW **Subject:** 500th Anniversary - Discovery and Evangelization **Obv:** Denomination, national arms **Rev:** Sailship landing

Date	Mintage	F	VF	XF	Unc	BU
1989(c) Proof	30	Value: 1,250				

KM# 77 PESO

Copper-Nickel **Subject:** 500th Anniversary - Discovery and Evangelization **Obv:** National arms, date below, denomination at left **Rev:** Two standing figures, date below

Date	Mintage	F	VF	XF	Unc	BU
1990(c)	30,000	—	—	—	2.50	3.50

KM# 77a PESO

31.1035 g., 0.9990 Silver 1 oz. ASW **Subject:** 500th Anniversary - Discovery and Evangelization **Obv:** National arms and denomination **Rev:** Two standing figures

Date	Mintage	F	VF	XF	Unc	BU
1990 Proof	10,000	Value: 18.00				

KM# 77b PESO

31.1035 g., 0.9990 Gold 1 oz. AGW **Subject:** 500th Anniversary - Discovery and Evangelization **Obv:** National arms **Rev:** Two standing figures

Date	Mintage	F	VF	XF	Unc	BU
1990 Proof	50	—	—	—	1,000	—

KM# 80.1 PESO

Copper-Zinc, 25 mm. **Subject:** Juan Pablo Duarte **Countermark:** 11-sided **Obv:** National arms and denomination **Rev:** DUARTE on bust 3/4 left, date below **Note:** Coin die alignment.

Date	Mintage	F	VF	XF	Unc	BU
1991	40,000,000	—	—	—	2.00	2.50
1992	35,000,000	—	—	—	2.00	2.50
1993	—	—	—	—	2.00	2.50
2000	—	—	—	—	2.00	2.50

KM# 80.2 PESO

Copper-Zinc, 25 mm. **Subject:** Juan Pablo Duarte **Obv:** National arms and denomination **Rev:** DUARTE below bust, date below

Date	Mintage	F	VF	XF	Unc	BU
1992	35,000,000	—	—	—	2.00	2.50
1993	40,000,000	—	—	—	2.00	2.50
1997	—	—	—	—	2.00	2.50
Note: Medal alignment						
2000	—	—	—	—	2.00	2.50

KM# 81 PESO

Copper-Nickel **Subject:** Pinzon brothers on ship at sea **Obv:** National arms, date below, denomination at left **Rev:** Conjoined busts 3/4 left, on ship at sea, date below

Date	Mintage	F	VF	XF	Unc	BU
1991(c)	50,000	—	—	—	2.50	3.50

KM# 81a PESO

31.1035 g., 0.9990 Silver 1 oz. ASW **Subject:** Pinzon brothers on ship at sea **Obv:** Denomination, national arms **Rev:** Conjoined busts left on ship at sea

Date	Mintage	F	VF	XF	Unc	BU
1991 Proof	10,000	Value: 20.00				

KM# 81b PESO

31.1035 g., 0.9990 Gold 1 oz. AGW **Subject:** Pinzon brothers on ship at sea **Obv:** Denomination, national arms **Rev:** Conjoined busts left on ship at sea

Date	Mintage	F	VF	XF	Unc	BU
1991 Proof	35	Value: 1,150				

KM# 82 PESO

Copper-Nickel **Subject:** Christopher Columbus **Obv:** National arms, date below, denomination at left **Rev:** Bust 3/4 left, date below

Date	Mintage	F	VF	XF	Unc	BU
1992(c)	50,000	—	—	—	2.50	3.50

KM# 82a PESO

31.1035 g., 0.9990 Silver 1 oz. ASW **Subject:** Christopher Columbus **Obv:** Denomination, national arms **Rev:** Bust 3/4 left

Date	Mintage	F	VF	XF	Unc	BU
1992 Proof	10,000	Value: 20.00				

KM# 82b PESO

31.1035 g., 0.9990 Gold 1 oz. AGW **Subject:** Christopher Columbus **Obv:** Denomination, national arms **Rev:** Bust 3/4 left

Date	Mintage	F	VF	XF	Unc	BU
1992(c) Proof	35	Value: 1,150				

KM# 87 PESO

Copper-Nickel **Subject:** UN - Peace **Obv:** National arms, stars flank date below, denomination at left, **Rev:** UN logo, two doves, two dates above

Date	Mintage	F	VF	XF	Unc	BU
1995	—	—	—	—	8.00	9.00

KM# 87a PESO

28.4400 g., 0.9250 Silver .8458 oz. ASW **Subject:** UN - Peace **Obv:** Denomination, arms, stars **Rev:** UN logo, two doves

Date	Mintage	F	VF	XF	Unc	BU
1995 Proof	—	Value: 35.00				

KM# 88 5 PESOS

Bi-Metallic Stainless Steel center in Brass ring, 23 mm. **Subject:** 50th Anniversary - Central Bank **Obv:** Denomination and national arms within circle, date below **Rev:** Head facing within circle, two dates below

Date	Mintage	F	VF	XF	Unc	BU
1997	—	—	—	—	2.50	3.00

KM# 37 10 PESOS

28.0000 g., 0.9000 Silver .8102 oz. ASW **Subject:** International Bankers' Conference - First Hispaniola Coinage of Carlos and Johanna **Obv:** National arms, denomination and date below **Rev:** Arms of Castille in inner ring

Date	Mintage	F	VF	XF	Unc	BU
1975	26,000	—	—	—	12.00	15.00
1975 Proof	4,000	Value: 17.50				

KM# 38 10 PESOS

30.0000 g., 0.9000 Silver .8681 oz. ASW **Subject:** Taino Art **Obv:** National arms **Rev:** Ancient figurine "Pueblo Viejo Mine" divides dates, date below

Date	Mintage	F	VF	XF	Unc	BU
1975	Est. 45,000	—	—	—	—	—
Note: Reported, not confirmed						
1975 Proof	5,000	Value: 14.50				

KM# 57 10 PESOS

23.3300 g., 0.9250 Silver .6938 oz. ASW **Subject:** International Year of the Child **Obv:** National arms **Rev. Designer:** Michael Rizzello

Date	Mintage	F	VF	XF	Unc	BU
1982(o) Proof	8,712	Value: 12.50				

KM# 91 10 PESOS

2.4500 g., 0.9990 Silver 0.0787 oz. ASW, 18 mm. **Obv:** National arms **Rev:** St. Andrews Chapel

Date	Mintage	F	VF	XF	Unc	BU
2000	3,000	—	—	—	10.00	12.50

KM# 92 10 PESOS

2.4500 g., 0.9990 Silver 0.0787 oz. ASW, 18 mm. **Obv:** National arms **Rev:** Our Lady of Carmen Church

Date	Mintage	F	VF	XF	Unc	BU
2000	3,000	—	—	—	10.00	12.50

KM# 93 10 PESOS

2.4500 g., 0.9990 Silver 0.0787 oz. ASW, 18 mm. **Obv:** National arms **Rev:** Regina Angelorum Church

Date	Mintage	F	VF	XF	Unc	BU
2000	3,000	—	—	—	10.00	12.50

KM# 94 10 PESOS

2.4500 g., 0.9990 Silver 0.0787 oz. ASW, 18 mm. **Obv:** National arms **Rev:** Chapel of the Remedies

Date	Mintage	F	VF	XF	Unc	BU
2000	3,000	—	—	—	10.00	12.50

KM# 95 10 PESOS

2.4500 g., 0.9990 Silver 0.0787 oz. ASW, 18 mm. **Obv:** National arms **Rev:** St. Lazarus Church

Date	Mintage	F	VF	XF	Unc	BU
2000	3,000	—	—	—	10.00	12.50

KM# 96 10 PESOS

2.4500 g., 0.9990 Silver 0.0787 oz. ASW, 18 mm. **Obv:** National arms **Rev:** St. Michael's Church

Date	Mintage	F	VF	XF	Unc	BU
2000	3,000	—	—	—	10.00	12.50

KM# 97 10 PESOS

2.4500 g., 0.9990 Silver 0.0787 oz. ASW, 18 mm. **Obv:** National arms **Rev:** Church of Santa Barbara

Date	Mintage	F	VF	XF	Unc	BU
2000	3,000	—	—	—	10.00	12.50

KM# 98 10 PESOS

2.4500 g., 0.9990 Silver 0.0787 oz. ASW, 18 mm. **Obv:** National arms **Rev:** Our Lady of the Rosary Church

Date	Mintage	F	VF	XF	Unc	BU
2000	3,000	—	—	—	10.00	12.50

KM# 99 10 PESOS

2.4500 g., 0.9990 Silver 0.0787 oz. ASW, 18 mm. **Obv:** National arms **Rev:** Church of Banica

Date	Mintage	F	VF	XF	Unc	BU
2000	3,000	—	—	—	10.00	12.50

KM# 100 10 PESOS

2.4500 g., 0.9990 Silver 0.0787 oz. ASW, 18 mm. **Obv:** National arms **Rev:** Church of Boya

Date	Mintage	F	VF	XF	Unc	BU
2000	3,000	—	—	—	10.00	12.50

KM# 101 10 PESOS

2.4500 g., 0.9990 Silver 0.0787 oz. ASW, 18 mm. **Obv:** National arms **Rev:** Santo Domingo Cathedral

Date	Mintage	F	VF	XF	Unc	BU
2000	3,000	—	—	—	10.00	12.50

KM# 102 10 PESOS

2.4500 g., 0.9990 Silver 0.0787 oz. ASW, 18 mm. **Obv:** National arms **Rev:** Holy Cross Cathedral of El Seibo

Date	Mintage	F	VF	XF	Unc	BU
2000	3,000	—	—	—	10.00	12.50

KM# 103 10 PESOS

2.4500 g., 0.9990 Silver 0.0787 oz. ASW, 18 mm. **Obv:** National arms **Rev:** Higney Sanctuary

Date	Mintage	F	VF	XF	Unc	BU
2000	3,000	—	—	—	10.00	12.50

KM# 54 25 PESOS

65.0000 g., 0.9250 Silver .9332 oz. ASW **Subject:** Pope John Paul II's Visit **Obv:** National arms, denomination below **Rev:** Bust left, Vatican City and date at left

Date	Mintage	F	VF	XF	Unc	BU
ND(1979)	3,000	—	—	—	37.50	45.00
ND(1979) Proof	6,000	Value: 50.00				

KM# 24 30 PESOS

29.6220 g., 0.9000 Gold .8572 oz. AGW, 32 mm. **Subject:** 25th Anniversary of Trujillo regime **Obv:** National arms, denomination below **Rev:** Head left, date below

Date	Mintage	F	VF	XF	Unc	BU
1955	33,000	—	—	BV	575	600

KM# 36 30 PESOS

11.7000 g., 0.9000 Gold .3385 oz. AGW **Subject:** 12th Central American and Caribbean Games **Obv:** National arms **Rev:** Games symbol, denomination and date below

Date	Mintage	F	VF	XF	Unc	BU
1974	25,000	—	—	—	225	245
1974 Proof	5,000	Value: 265				

KM# 46 30 PESOS

78.0000 g., 0.9250 Silver 2.3199 oz. ASW **Subject:** 30th Anniversary of Central Bank **Obv:** National arms, denomination at left, date below **Rev:** Bank building, two dates below

Date	Mintage	F	VF	XF	Unc	BU
1977	5,000	—	—	—	32.50	37.50
1977 Proof	2,000	Value: 45.00				

KM# 104 50 PESOS

28.3500 g., 0.9250 Silver 0.8431 oz. ASW, 38 mm. **Subject:** 50th Anniversary - Central Bank **Obv:** National arms **Rev:** Seated woman holding up coin **Edge:** Reeded

Date	Mintage	F	VF	XF	Unc	BU
ND (1997)	3,000	—	—	—	—	35.00
ND (1997) Proof	2,000	Value: 50.00				

KM# 39 100 PESOS

10.0000 g., 0.9000 Gold .2893 oz. AGW **Subject:** Taino Art **Obv:** National arms, date below **Rev:** Native art divides denomination, date below

Date	Mintage	F	VF	XF	Unc	BU
1975	18,000	—	—	—	200	210
1975 Proof	2,000	Value: 225				

KM# 55 100 PESOS

12.0000 g., 0.9000 Gold .3472 oz. AGW **Subject:** Pope John Paul II's Visit **Obv:** National arms, denomination below **Rev:** Bust left, Vatican City and date at left

Date	Mintage	F	VF	XF	Unc	BU
ND(1979)	1,000	—	—	—	235	245
ND(1979) Proof	3,000	Value: 260				

KM# 67 100 PESOS

155.5000 g., 0.9990 Silver 5 oz. ASW, 65 mm. **Subject:** Discovery of America - Native Americans

Date	Mintage	F	VF	XF	Unc	BU
1988 Proof	5,300	Value: 90.00				

KM# 75 100 PESOS

155.5000 g., 0.9990 Silver 5 oz. ASW **Subject:** 500th Anniversary of Discovery and Evangelization of America **Obv:** Arms **Rev:** Columbus and crew, date below

Date	Mintage	F	VF	XF	Unc	BU
1989(c) Proof	1,500	Value: 125				

KM# 75a 100 PESOS
155.5000 g., 0.9990 Gold 5 oz. AGW **Subject:** 500th Anniversary of Discovery and Evangelization of America **Obv:** Arms **Rev:** Columbus and crew

Date	Mintage	F	VF	XF	Unc	BU
1989 Proof	30	Value: 3,600				

KM# 78 100 PESOS
155.5000 g., 0.9990 Silver 5 oz. ASW, 65 mm. **Subject:** 500th Anniversary of Discovery and Evangelization of America **Obv:** National arms **Rev:** Building a stockade, date below **Note:** Photo reduced.

Date	Mintage	F	VF	XF	Unc	BU
1990 Proof	1,000	Value: 145				

KM# 78a 100 PESOS
155.5300 g., 0.9990 Gold 5 oz. AGW, 65 mm. **Subject:** 500th Anniversary of Discovery and Evangelization of America **Obv:** National arms **Rev:** Building a stockade **Note:** Photo reduced.

Date	Mintage	F	VF	XF	Unc	BU
1990 Proof	50	Value: 3,350				

KM# 83 100 PESOS
155.5300 g., 0.9990 Silver 5 oz. ASW, 65 mm. **Subject:** 500th Anniversary of Discovery and Evangelization of America **Obv:** National arms **Rev:** Columbus Presenting Native American to Court **Note:** Photo reduced.

Date	Mintage	F	VF	XF	Unc	BU
1991 Proof	1,500	Value: 125				

KM# 83a 100 PESOS
155.5300 g., 0.9990 Gold 5 oz. AGW, 65 mm. **Subject:** 500th Anniversary of Discovery and Evangelization of America **Obv:** National arms **Rev:** Columbus Presenting Native American to Court **Note:** Photo reduced.

Date	Mintage	F	VF	XF	Unc	BU
1991 Proof	35	Value: 3,500				

KM# 84 100 PESOS
155.5300 g., 0.9990 Silver 5 oz. ASW, 65 mm. **Subject:** 500th Anniversary - Discovery and Evangelization of America **Obv:** National arms **Rev:** Columbus bust left, and anchored ship, date below **Note:** Photo reduced.

Date	Mintage	F	VF	XF	Unc	BU
1992 Proof	1,500	Value: 135				

KM# 84a 100 PESOS
155.5300 g., 0.9990 Gold 5 oz. AGW, 65 mm. **Subject:** 500th Anniversary - Discovery and Evangelization of America **Obv:** National arms **Rev:** Bust left and anchored ship

Date	Mintage	F	VF	XF	Unc	BU
1992 Proof	35	Value: 3,500				

KM# 47 200 PESOS
31.0000 g., 0.8000 Gold .7974 oz. AGW **Subject:** Centennial - Death of Juan Pablo Duarte **Obv:** National arms, date below **Rev:** Head facing divides denomination, two dates below **Note:** Large quantities of both varieties were melted for bullion.

Date	Mintage	F	VF	XF	Unc	BU
1977	1,000	—	—	—	525	545
1977 Proof	2,000	Value: 575				

KM# 58 200 PESOS
17.1700 g., 0.9000 Gold .4969 oz. AGW **Subject:** International Year of the Child **Obv:** National arms, date below **Rev:** Children dancing, denomination below

Date	Mintage	F	VF	XF	Unc	BU
1982 Proof	4,303	Value: 345				

KM# 105 200 PESOS
12.0000 g., 0.9000 Gold 0.3472 oz. AGW, 25 mm. **Subject:** 50th Anniversary - Central Bank **Obv:** National arms **Rev:** Seated woman holding up coin **Edge:** Reeded

Date	Mintage	F	VF	XF	Unc	BU
ND (1997) Proof	2,000	Value: 450				
ND (1997)	500	—	—	—	—	375

KM# 56 250 PESOS
31.1000 g., 0.9000 Gold .9000 oz. AGW **Subject:** Visit of Pope John Paul II

Date	Mintage	F	VF	XF	Unc	BU
1979	1,000	—	—	—	600	625
1979 Proof	3,000	Value: 650				

KM# 68 500 PESOS
31.1000 g., 0.9990 Gold .9989 oz. AGW **Subject:** Discovery of America - Columbus

Date	Mintage	F	VF	XF	Unc	BU
1988 Proof	2,600	Value: 720				

KM# 76 500 PESOS
31.1000 g., 0.9990 Gold .9989 oz. AGW **Subject:** 500th Anniversary - Discovery and Evangelization of America **Obv:** National arms, denomination below **Rev:** Portraits of Ferdinand and Isabella, date below

Date	Mintage	F	VF	XF	Unc	BU
1989 Proof	600	Value: 845				

KM# 76a 500 PESOS
31.1000 g., 0.9990 Platinum .9989 oz. APW **Subject:** 500th Anniversary - Discovery and Evangelization of America **Obv:** National arms **Rev:** Portraits of Ferdinand and Isabella

Date	Mintage	F	VF	XF	Unc	BU
1989 Proof	—	Value: 1,350				

KM# 79 500 PESOS
16.9600 g., 0.9170 Gold .5 oz. AGW **Subject:** 500th Anniversary - Discovery and Evangelization of America **Obv:** National arms, denomination below **Rev:** Santa Maria and landing crew, date below

Date	Mintage	F	VF	XF	Unc	BU
1990 Proof	1,500	Value: 375				

KM# 79a 500 PESOS
15.5500 g., 0.9990 Platinum .5 oz. APW **Subject:** 500th Anniversary - Discovery and Evangelization of America **Obv:** National arms **Rev:** Santa Maria and landing crew

Date	Mintage	F	VF	XF	Unc	BU
1990 Proof	50	Value: 700				

KM# 85 500 PESOS
16.9600 g., 0.9170 Gold .5 oz. AGW **Subject:** 500th Anniversary - Discovery and Evangelization of America **Obv:** National arms, denomination below **Rev:** American fruits, date below

Date	Mintage	F	VF	XF	Unc	BU
1991 Proof	1,500	Value: 375				

KM# 85a 500 PESOS
15.5500 g., 0.9990 Platinum .5 oz. APW **Subject:** 500th Anniversary - Discovery and Evangelization of America **Obv:** National arms **Rev:** American fruits

Date	Mintage	F	VF	XF	Unc	BU
1991 Proof	35	Value: 745				

KM# 86 500 PESOS
16.9600 g., 0.9170 Gold .5 oz. AGW **Subject:** 500th Anniversary - Discovery and Evangelization of America **Obv:** National arms, denomination below **Rev:** Enshrined tomb of Christopher Columbus, date below

Date	Mintage	F	VF	XF	Unc	BU
1992 Proof	2,000	Value: 360				

KM# 86a 500 PESOS
15.5000 g., 0.9990 Platinum .5 oz. APW **Subject:** 500th Anniversary - Discovery and Evangelization of America **Obv:** National arms **Rev:** Enshrined tomb of Christopher Columbus

Date	Mintage	F	VF	XF	Unc	BU
1992 Proof	35	Value: 745				

PATTERNS

Including off metal strikes

KM#	Date	Mintage	Identification	Mkt Val
Pn6	1937	—	50 Centavos. Silver. Obverse only.	—
Pn7	1937	—	50 Centavos. Copper. Obverse only.	—
Pn8	1937	—	50 Centavos. Silver. Reverse only.	—
Pn9	1961	—	5 Centavos. Copper-Bonded Steel.	—
Pn10	1961	—	5 Centavos. Copper-Bonded Steel.	—
Pn11	1961	—	5 Centavos. Copper-Bonded Steel. Same design both sides.	—
Pn12	1961	—	10 Centavos. Copper-Bonded Steel.	—
Pn13	1961	—	25 Centavos. Chrome Plated Steel.	—
Pn14	1968	3	50 Centavos. Reeded edge.	—
Pn15	1972	1	25 Centavos. Reeded edge.	—
Pn16	1975	1	10 Pesos. Silver.	—
Pn17	1975	11	10 Pesos. 0.5000 Gold.	—
Pn18	1975	1	10 Pesos. 0.2940 Gold.	—
Pn19	1975	1	10 Pesos. 0.4000 Gold.	—
Pn20	1975	1	10 Pesos. 0.8000 Gold.	—
Pn21	1975	1	100 Pesos. 0.9000 Gold. without matte details.	—

KM#	Date	Mintage	Identification	Mkt Val
Pn22	1975	1	100 Pesos. 0.8000 Gold. alloyed with .050 Silver and .150 Copper.	—
Pn23	1975	5	100 Pesos. 0.8000 Gold. alloyed with .150 Silver.	—
Pn24	1975	5	100 Pesos. 0.8000 Gold. alloyed with .150 Silver and .050 Copper, Proof.	—
Pn25	1976	3	10 Centavos. Plain rim.	—
Pn26	1977	5	30 Pesos. Gold. Proof.	—
Pn27	1978	3	Centavo. Aluminum.	—
Pn28	1978	3	Centavo. Copper And Zinc.	100
Pn29	1978	—	Centavo. 0.9000 Silver. 3.5800 g.	125
Pn30	1978	—	5 Centavos. 0.9000 Silver. 5.8600 g. Without memorial legend.	125
Pn31	1978	—	10 Centavos. 0.9000 Silver. 2.9500 g. Without memorial legend.	125
Pn32	1978	3	25 Centavos. 6-1/2 Gramos.	—
Pn33	1978	—	25 Centavos. 0.9000 Silver. 7.3200 g. Without memorial legend.	150
Pn34	1978	—	1/2 Peso. 0.9000 Silver. 14.5500 g. Without memorial legend.	150
Pn35	1978	—	Peso. 0.9000 Silver. 30.9200 g. Without memorial legend. Portrait of Duarte.	300
Pn36	1979	—	Centavo. 0.9000 Silver. 3.5800 g.	125
Pn37	1979	—	5 Centavos. 0.9000 Silver. 5.8600 g. Without memorial legend.	125
Pn38	1979	—	10 Centavos. 0.9000 Silver. 2.9500 g. Without memorial legend.	125
Pn39	1979	3	25 Centavos. 6-1/2 Gramos.	—
Pn40	1979	—	25 Centavos. 0.9000 Silver. 7.3200 g. Without memorial legend.	150
Pn41	1979	—	1/2 Peso. 0.9000 Silver. 14.5500 g. Without memorial legend.	150
Pn42	1979	—	Peso. 0.9000 Silver. 30.9200 g. Without memorial legend. Portrait of Duarte.	300
Pn43	1980	—	Centavo. 0.9000 Silver. 3.5800 g.	125
Pn44	1980	—	5 Centavos. 0.9000 Silver. 5.8600 g. Without memorial legend.	125
Pn45	1980	—	10 Centavos. 0.9000 Silver. 2.9500 g. Without memorial legend.	125
Pn46	1980	—	25 Centavos. 0.9000 Silver. 7.3200 g. Without memorial legend.	150
Pn47	1980	—	1/2 Peso. 0.9000 Silver. 14.5500 g. Without memorial legend.	150
Pn48	1980	—	Peso. 0.9000 Silver. 30.9200 g. Without memorial legend. Portrait of Duarte.	300
Pn49	1981	—	Centavo. 0.9000 Silver. 3.5800 g.	125
Pn50	1981	—	5 Centavos. 0.9000 Silver. 5.8600 g. Without memorial legend.	125
Pn51	1981	—	10 Centavos. 0.9000 Silver. 2.9500 g. Without memorial legend.	125
Pn52	1981	—	25 Centavos. 0.9000 Silver. 7.3200 g. Without memorial legend.	150
Pn53	1981	—	1/2 Peso. 0.9000 Silver. 14.5500 g. Without memorial legend.	150
Pn54	1981	—	Peso. 0.9000 Silver. 30.9200 g. Without memorial legend. Portrait of Duarte.	300
Pn55	1982	80	10 Pesos. Silver. KM#57.	—
Pn56	1983	15	25 Centavos. Nickel Bonded Steel.	200
Pn57	1984	3	25 Centavos. Nickel Bonded Steel.	200
Pn58	1984	5	Peso. Nickel Bonded Steel.	—
Pn59	1986	500	Peso. Copper-Nickel.	—

Note: Several issues previously listed under Patterns have now been correctly identified as commercially inspired, privately contracted Medallic Issues and have been moved to that section. The remaining patterns have been renumbered

PIEFORTS

KM#	Date	Mintage	Identification	Mkt Val
P1	1977	5	30 Pesos. Gold. Piefort.	—
P2	1982	262	10 Pesos.	150
P3	1982	42	200 Pesos.	2,250
P4	1983 H	300	5 Centavos.	20.00
P5	1983 H	300	10 Centavos. Nickel Bonded Steel.	30.00
P6	1983	300	25 Centavos. Copper-Nickel. KM#61.	35.00
P7	1983 H	300	25 Centavos. Copper-Nickel.	35.00
P8	1983	300	1/2 Peso. Copper-Nickel center. KM#62.	40.00
P9	1983	300	Peso. Copper-Nickel. KM#63.	50.00
P10	1984	300	Centavo.	5.00
P11	1984	300	5 Centavos.	5.00
P12	1984	300	10 Centavos.	5.00
P13	1984	300	25 Centavos.	8.00
P14	1984	300	1/2 Peso.	10.00
P15	1984	300	Peso.	12.00
P16	1986	300	Peso. Nickel Bonded Steel.	15.00
P17	1986	50	Peso. Copper Nickel. 20.0000 g.	—
P18	1986	300	Centavo. Copper Plated Zinc.	5.00
P19	1986	300	5 Centavos. Copper-Nickel.	5.00
P20	1986	300	10 Centavos. Copper-Nickel.	8.00
P21	1986	300	25 Centavos. Copper-Nickel.	10.00
P22	1986	300	1/2 Peso. Copper-Nickel.	12.00
P23	1987	300	Centavo. 0.9250 Silver.	—
P24	1987	300	5 Centavos. 0.9250 Silver.	—
P25	1987	300	10 Centavos. 0.9250 Silver.	—
P26	1987	300	25 Centavos. 0.9250 Silver.	—
P27	1987	300	1/2 Peso. 0.9250 Silver.	—
P28	1988	100	Peso. 0.9990 Silver. KM#67.	50.00
P29	1988	100	100 Pesos. 0.9990 Silver. KM#67.	325
P30	1989	300	Centavo. 0.9250 Silver. KM#72a.	—
P31	1989	300	5 Centavos. 0.9250 Silver. KM#69a.	—
P32	1989	300	10 Centavos. 0.9250 Silver. KM#70a.	—
P33	1989	300	25 Centavos. 0.9250 Silver. KM#71a.	—
P34	1989	300	1/2 Peso. 0.9250 Silver. KM#73a.	—
P35	1989	10,000	Peso. 0.9990 Silver. KM#74.	40.00
P36	1989	200	100 Pesos. 0.9990 Silver. KM#75.	375
P37	1990	10,000	Peso. 0.9990 Silver. KM#77.	40.00
P38	1990	200	100 Pesos. 0.9990 Silver. KM#78.	300
P39	1991	10,000	Peso. 0.9990 Silver. KM#81.	40.00
P40	1992	10,000	Peso. 0.9990 Silver. KM#82.	40.00

MINT SETS

KM#	Date	Mintage	Identification	Issue Price	Mkt Val
MS1	1983 (5)	2,000	KM#59-63	10.00	15.00
MS2	1984 (6)	2,000	KM#59-64	—	15.00
MS3	1986 (5)	2,000	KM#59-62, 64	10.00	14.00
MS4	1987 (5)	1,000	KM#59-62, 64	10.00	14.00
MS5	1989 (5)	1,000	KM#69,70,71.1,72,73.1	—	14.00

PROOF SETS

KM#	Date	Mintage	Identification	Issue Price	Mkt Val
PS1	1937 (5)	—	KM#17-21	—	5,000
PS2	1972 (4)	500	KM#18, 20a.1, 31, 34	20.00	65.00
PS3	1973 (2)	500	KM#19a, 21a.2	5.00	50.00
PS4	1974 (2)	500	KM#18, 20a.2	5.00	35.00
PS5	1974 (2)	500	KM#35-36	120	190
PS6	1975 (2)	500	KM#38-39	200	165
PS7	1976 (6)	5,000	KM#40-45	10.00	20.00
PS8	1978 (6)	5,000	KM#48-53	10.00	20.00
PS9	1978 (6)	15	KM#Pn29-31, Pn33-35	175	900
PS10	1979 (6)	500	KM#48-53	15.00	135
PS11	1979 (6)	15	KM#Pn36-38, Pn40-42	255	900
PS12	1980 (6)	3,000	KM#48-53	15.00	20.00
PS13	1980 (6)	15	KM#Pn43-48	255	900
PS14	1981 (6)	3,000	KM#48-53	15.00	20.00
PS15	1981 (6)	15	KM#Pn49-54	300	900
PS16	1983 (2)	1,600	KM#59-60	10.00	10.00
PS17	1983 (2)	300	KM-P4, P5	25.00	50.00
PS18	1983 (2)	100	KM#59a, 60a	45.00	45.00
PS19	1983 (3)	1,570	KM#61-63	20.00	20.00
PS20	1983 (3)	270	KM-P7, 8, 9	45.00	115
PS21	1983 (3)	70	KM#61a-63a	125	125
PS22	1984 (6)	1,570	KM#59-64	20.00	45.00
PS23	1984 (6)	270	KM-P10, 11, 12, 13, 14, 15	30.00	30.00
PS24	1984 (6)	70	KM#59a-64a	250	250
PS25	1986 (5)	1,570	KM#59-62, 64	30.00	20.00
PS26	1986 (5)	270	KM-P17, 19, 20, 21, 22	40.00	40.00
PS27	1986 (5)	70	KM#59a-62a, 64a	150	150
PS28	1987 (5)	1,600	KM#59-62, 64	—	30.00
PS29	1987 (5)	300	KM-P23, 24, 25, 26, 27	—	75.00
PS30	1989 (5)	2,500	KM#69a-70a, 71.1a, 72a, 73.1a	—	—
PS31	1989 (5)	300	KM-P30, 31, 32, 33, 34	—	—

SPECIAL SETS

KM#	Date	Mintage	Identification	Issue Price	Mkt Val
SS1	1983 (15)	30	KM#61-63, 61a-63a, all mint marks, including Piefort	200	200
SS2	1984 (24)	30	KM#59-64, including Piefort	400	400
SS3	1986 (20)	30	KM#59-64	300	300
SS4	1986 (2)	1,700	KM65	35.00	25.00
SS5	1986 (3)	300	KM#65, KM-P16	75.00	75.00
SS6	1986 (2)	23	KM#65a	—	—
SS7	1986 (3)	25	KM#65a, KM-P17	—	—
SS8	1986 (2)	25	KM#65b	—	—
SS9	1986 (3)	25	KM#65b, KM-P17	—	—
SS10	1987 (15)	100	KM#59-62, 64, KM-P23, 24, 25, 26, 27	—	125
SS11	1989 (15)	100	KM#69-73, KM-P31, 32, 33, 34, 35	—	—

EAST AFRICA

East Africa was an administrative grouping of five separate British territories: Kenya, Uganda, the Sultanate of Zanzibar and British Somaliland.

The common interest of Kenya, Tanganyika and Uganda invited cooperation in economic matters and consideration of political union. The territorial governors, organized as the East Africa High Commission, met periodically to administer such common activities as taxation, industrial development and education. The authority of the Commission did not infringe upon the constitution and internal autonomy of the individual colonies. A common coinage and banknotes, which were also legal tender in Aden, were provided for use of the member colonies by the East Africa Currency Board. The coinage through 1919 had the legend "East Africa and Uganda Protectorate".

NOTE: For later coinage see Kenya, Tanzania and Uganda.

RULERS

British

MINT MARKS

A - Ackroyd & Best, Morley
I - Bombay Mint
H - Heaton Mint, Birmingham, England
K, KN - King's Norton Mint, Birmingham, England
SA - Pretoria Mint, South Africa
No mint mark – British Royal Mint, London

EAST AFRICA AND UGANDA PROTECTORATES

DECIMAL COINAGE

50 Cents = 1 Shilling; 100 Cents = 1 Florin

KM# 6 1/2 CENT

Aluminum **Ruler:** Edward VII **Edge:** Plain

Date	Mintage	F	VF	XF	Unc	BU
1908	900,000	15.00	25.00	60.00	90.00	—

KM# 6a 1/2 CENT

Copper-Nickel **Ruler:** Edward VII **Obv:** Center hole divides crown and denomination, fleurs flank **Rev:** Tusks flank center hole, denomination above, circle surrounds **Edge:** Plain

Date	Mintage	F	VF	XF	Unc	BU
1909	900,000	6.00	12.00	35.00	60.00	95.00

KM# 5 CENT

Aluminum **Ruler:** Edward VII **Obv:** Center hole divides crown and denomination, fleurs flank **Rev:** Tusks flank center hole, denomination above, circle surrounds **Edge:** Plain

Date	Mintage	F	VF	XF	Unc	BU
1907	6,948,000	5.00	10.00	30.00	50.00	—
1908	2,871,000	8.00	16.00	35.00	60.00	—

KM# 5a CENT

Copper-Nickel **Ruler:** Edward VII **Obv:** Center hole divides crown and denomination, fleurs flank **Rev:** Tusks flank center hole, denomination above, circle surrounds **Edge:** Plain

Date	Mintage	F	VF	XF	Unc	BU
1909	25,000,000	0.50	1.25	3.00	7.00	—
1910	6,000,000	0.50	1.25	4.00	12.00	—

KM# 7 CENT

Copper-Nickel **Ruler:** George V **Obv:** Center hole divides crown and denomination, fleurs flank **Rev:** Tusks flank center hole, denomination above, circle surrounds **Edge:** Plain

Date	Mintage	F	VF	XF	Unc	BU
1911H	25,000,000	0.25	1.00	5.00	15.00	—
1912H	20,000,000	0.25	1.00	3.00	8.00	—
1913	4,529,000	0.75	1.50	8.00	20.00	—
1914 S	6,000,000	0.75	1.75	5.00	15.00	—
1914H	2,500,000	1.00	3.00	8.00	20.00	—
1916H	1,824,000	1.25	4.00	10.00	25.00	—
1917H	3,176,000	0.75	2.00	5.00	15.00	—
1918H	10,000,000	0.50	1.00	3.25	12.00	—

KM# A11 5 CENTS

Copper-Nickel **Ruler:** Edward VII

Date	Mintage	F	VF	XF	Unc	BU
1907 Rare	—	—	—	—	—	—

KM# 11 5 CENTS

Copper-Nickel **Ruler:** George V **Obv:** Center hole divides crown and denomination, fleurs flank **Rev:** Tusks flank center hole, denomination above, circle surrounds **Edge:** Plain

Date	Mintage	F	VF	XF	Unc	BU
1913H	300,000	1.50	4.00	20.00	35.00	—
1914K	1,240,000	0.75	3.25	12.00	22.50	—
1914K Proof	—	Value: 200				

Note: The 1914K was issued with British West Africa KM#8 in a double (4 pieces) Specimen Set

Date	Mintage	F	VF	XF	Unc	BU
1919H	200,000	10.00	15.00	40.00	120	—

KM# 2 10 CENTS

Copper-Nickel **Ruler:** Edward VII **Obv:** Center hole divides crown and denomination, fleurs flank **Rev:** Tusks flank center hole, denomination above, circle surrounds **Edge:** Plain

Date	Mintage	F	VF	XF	Unc	BU
1906	—	1,000	1,500	2,000	3,000	—
1907	1,000,000	1.50	4.00	16.00	30.00	50.00
1910	500,000	4.00	8.00	35.00	60.00	—

KM# 8 10 CENTS

Copper-Nickel **Ruler:** George V **Obv:** Center hole divides crown and denomination, fleurs flank **Rev:** Tusks flank center hole, denomination above, circle surrounds **Edge:** Plain

Date	Mintage	F	VF	XF	Unc	BU
1911H	1,250,000	2.00	5.00	25.00	40.00	—
1912H	1,050,000	2.00	5.00	30.00	55.00	—
1913	50,000	75.00	150	300	500	—
1918H	400,000	10.00	20.00	80.00	150	—

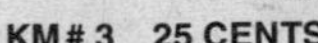

KM# 3 25 CENTS

2.9160 g., 0.8000 Silver .0750 oz. ASW **Ruler:** Edward VII **Obv:** Bust of King Edward VII right **Obv. Designer:** G.W. DeSaulles **Rev:** Lion and mountains within 3/4 circle with fleur ends, denomination and date below **Edge:** Reeded

Date	Mintage	F	VF	XF	Unc	BU
1906	400,000	3.00	7.00	35.00	60.00	—
1910H	200,000	4.00	8.00	50.00	90.00	—

KM# 10 25 CENTS

2.9160 g., 0.8000 Silver .0750 oz. ASW **Ruler:** George V **Obv:** Bust of King George V left **Obv. Designer:** E.B. MacKennal **Rev:** Lion and mountains within 3/4 circle with fleur ends, date and denomination below **Edge:** Reeded

Date	Mintage	F	VF	XF	Unc	BU
1912	180,000	4.00	15.00	45.00	80.00	—
1913	300,000	3.50	10.00	35.00	60.00	—
1914H	80,000	20.00	35.00	60.00	100	—
1914H Proof	—	Value: 400				
1918H	40,000	150	300	500	900	—

KM# 4 50 CENTS

5.8319 g., 0.8000 Silver .1500 oz. ASW **Ruler:** Edward VII **Obv:** Bust of King Edward VII right **Obv. Designer:** G.W. DeSaulles **Rev:** Lion and mountains within circle with fleur ends, denomination and date below **Edge:** Reeded

Date	Mintage	F	VF	XF	Unc	BU
1906	200,000	4.50	30.00	80.00	140	—
1906 Proof	—	Value: 400				
1909	100,000	15.00	50.00	155	300	—
1910	100,000	10.00	45.00	110	225	—

KM# 9 50 CENTS

5.8319 g., 0.8000 Silver .1500 oz. ASW **Ruler:** George V **Obv:** Bust of King George V left **Obv. Designer:** E.B. MacKennal **Rev:** Lion and mountains within circle with fleur ends, denomination and date below **Edge:** Reeded

Date	Mintage	F	VF	XF	Unc	BU
1911	150,000	7.50	35.00	85.00	140	—
1911 Proof	—	Value: 250				
1912	100,000	8.00	45.00	125	200	—
1913	200,000	5.00	30.00	65.00	135	—
1914H	180,000	5.00	30.00	65.00	135	—
1918H	60,000	60.00	200	350	500	—
1919	100,000	250	350	900	1,500	—

BRITISH COLONY

DECIMAL COINAGE

50 Cents = 1 Shilling; 100 Cents = 1 Florin

KM# 12 CENT

Copper-Nickel **Ruler:** George V **Obv:** Center hole divides crown and denomination, fleurs flank **Rev:** Tusks flank center hole, denomination above, circle surrounds **Edge:** Plain

Date	Mintage	F	VF	XF	Unc	BU
1920H	Est. 2,908,000	30.00	60.00	110	225	—

Note: Only about 30% of the total mintage was released into circulation

Date	Mintage	F	VF	XF	Unc	BU
1920	—	—	—	—	750	—
1921	920,000	—	—	—	3,000	—

Note: Not released for circulation

KM# 13 5 CENTS

Copper-Nickel **Ruler:** George V **Obv:** Center hole divides crown and denomination, fleurs flank **Rev:** Tusks flank center hole, denomination above, circle surrounds **Edge:** Plain

Date	Mintage	F	VF	XF	Unc	BU
1920H	Est. 550,000	75.00	250	300	425	—

Note: Only about 30% of the total mintage was released into circulation

KM# 14 10 CENTS

Copper-Nickel **Ruler:** George V **Obv:** Center hole divides crown and denomination, fleurs flank **Rev:** Tusks flank center hole, denomination above, circle surrounds **Edge:** Plain

Date	Mintage	F	VF	XF	Unc	BU
1920H	Est. 700,000	120	150	225	375	—
1920H Proof	—	Value: 600				

Note: 20-30 pcs

KM# 15 25 CENTS

2.9160 g., 0.5000 Silver .0469 oz. ASW **Ruler:** George V **Obv:** Bust of King George V left **Obv. Designer:** E.B. MacKennal **Rev:** Lion and mountains within circle with fleur ends, date and denomination below **Edge:** Reeded

Date	Mintage	F	VF	XF	Unc	BU
1920H	748,000	25.00	35.00	75.00	150	—
1920H Proof	—	Value: 250				

Note: 20-30 pieces

KM# 16 50 CENTS

5.8319 g., 0.5000 Silver .0937 oz. ASW **Ruler:** George V **Obv:** Bust of King George V left **Obv. Designer:** E.B. MacKennal **Rev:** Lion and mountains within circle with fleur ends, date and denomination below **Edge:** Reeded **Note:** Not released for circulation.

Date	Mintage	F	VF	XF	Unc	BU
1920A	12,000	1,500	2,000	3,000	4,000	—

Date	Mintage	F	VF	XF	Unc	BU
1920H	62,000	500	1,000	1,500	2,500	—
1920H Proof	—	Value: 600				

Note: 20-30 pieces

KM# 17 FLORIN

11.6638 g., 0.5000 Silver .1875 oz. ASW **Ruler:** George V **Obv:** Bust of King George V left **Obv. Designer:** E.B. MacKennal **Rev:** Lion and mountains within circle with fleur ends, denomination and date below **Edge:** Reeded

Date	Mintage	F	VF	XF	Unc	BU
1920	1,479,000	15.00	75.00	200	325	—
1920A	542,000	200	500	1,100	2,000	—
1920H	9,689,000	12.50	60.00	125	275	—
1920H Proof	—	Value: 800				
Note: 20-30 pieces						
1921*	2	—	—	—	4,500	—

REFORM COINAGE

Commencing May 1921

100 Cents = 1 Shilling

KM# 22 CENT

Bronze **Ruler:** George V **Obv:** Center hole divides crown and denomination, fleurs flank **Rev:** Tusks flank center hole, denomination above, circle surrounds **Edge:** Plain

Date	Mintage	F	VF	XF	Unc	BU
1922	8,250,000	0.25	1.00	8.00	15.00	22.00
1922H	43,750,000	0.25	0.50	3.50	6.50	9.00
1923	50,000,000	0.25	0.50	3.50	6.50	9.00
1924	Inc. above	0.25	0.75	5.00	10.00	15.00
1924H	17,500,000	0.25	0.75	4.00	8.00	11.00
1924KN	10,720,000	0.25	0.75	4.00	8.00	11.00
1924KN Proof	—	Value: 125				
1925	6,000,000	50.00	100	225	350	—
1925KN	6,780,000	2.00	4.00	18.00	35.00	52.00
1927	10,000,000	0.25	0.75	5.00	10.00	15.00
1927 Proof	—	Value: 125				
1928H	12,000,000	0.25	0.75	4.00	8.00	11.00
1928KN	11,764,000	0.50	2.00	8.00	18.00	27.00
1928KN Proof	—	Value: 125				
1930	15,000,000	0.25	0.75	2.50	5.00	8.00
1930 Proof	—	Value: 125				
1935	10,000,000	0.25	0.50	1.75	3.50	6.00

KM# 29 CENT

Bronze **Ruler:** George VI **Obv:** Center hole divides crown and denomination, fleurs flank **Rev:** Tusks flank center hole, denomination above, circle surrounds **Edge:** Plain

Date	Mintage	F	VF	XF	Unc	BU
1942	25,000,000	0.10	0.25	1.25	2.50	4.00
1942I	15,000,000	0.15	0.30	1.50	3.00	5.00

KM# 32 CENT

Bronze **Ruler:** George VI **Obv:** Center hole divides crown and denomination, fleurs flank **Obv. Legend:** ET IND. IMP. dropped from legend **Rev:** Tusks flank center hole, denomination above, circle surrounds **Edge:** Plain

Date	Mintage	F	VF	XF	Unc	BU
1949	4,000,000	0.35	0.75	2.00	4.00	7.00
1949 Proof	—	Value: 125				
1950	16,000,000	0.10	0.25	1.25	2.50	5.00
1950 Proof	—	Value: 150				
1951H	9,000,000	0.10	0.25	1.25	2.50	5.00
1951H Proof	—	Value: 125				

Date	Mintage	F	VF	XF	Unc	BU
1951KN	11,140,000	0.10	0.25	1.25	2.50	5.00
1951KN Proof	—	Value: 125				
1952	7,000,000	0.10	0.25	1.25	2.50	5.00
1952 Proof	—	Value: 150				
1952H	13,000,000	0.10	0.25	1.25	2.50	5.00
1952H Proof	—	Value: 125				
1952KN	5,230,000	0.10	0.35	1.50	5.00	8.00

KM# 35 CENT

Bronze, 20 mm. **Ruler:** Elizabeth II **Obv:** Center hole divides crown and denomination, fleurs flank **Rev:** Tusks flank center hole, denomination above, circle surrounds **Edge:** Plain

Date	Mintage	F	VF	XF	Unc	BU
1954	8,000,000	0.10	0.25	0.85	2.50	5.00
1954 Proof	—	Value: 150				
1955	5,000,000	0.10	0.25	0.50	1.75	3.00
1955H	6,384,000	0.10	0.20	0.65	1.75	3.00
1955KN	4,000,000	0.10	0.20	0.65	1.75	3.00
1956H	15,616,000	0.10	0.15	0.30	1.25	3.00
1956KN	9,680,000	0.10	0.20	0.40	1.25	3.00
1957	15,000,000	0.10	0.20	0.65	1.75	3.00
1957H	5,000,000	1.50	3.00	6.00	15.00	21.00
1957KN	Inc. above	0.10	0.20	0.65	1.75	3.00
1959H	10,000,000	0.10	0.20	0.40	1.25	2.00
1959KN	10,000,000	0.10	0.20	0.40	1.25	2.00
1961	1,800,000	0.15	0.40	2.00	3.50	5.00
1961 Proof	—	Value: 100				
1961H	1,800,000	0.15	0.40	2.00	3.50	5.00
1962H	10,320,000	0.10	0.20	0.40	1.25	2.00

KM# 18 5 CENTS

Bronze **Ruler:** George V **Edge:** Plain

Date	Mintage	F	VF	XF	Unc	BU
1921	1,000,000	2.00	4.00	15.00	32.00	50.00
1922	2,500,000	0.50	1.25	4.50	12.50	15.00
1923	2,400,000	0.50	1.25	6.00	15.00	18.00
1923 Proof	—	Value: 150				
1924	4,800,000	0.50	1.00	5.00	15.00	21.00
1925	6,600,000	0.50	1.00	4.00	10.00	15.00
1925 Proof	—	Value: 125				
1928	1,200,000	1.50	3.00	10.00	25.00	35.00
1928 Proof	—	Value: 150				
1933	5,000,000	0.50	1.00	5.00	10.00	15.00
1934	3,910,000	0.50	1.00	7.50	15.00	21.00
1934 Proof	—	Value: 150				
1935	5,800,000	0.50	1.00	5.00	10.00	15.00
1935 Proof	—	Value: 150				
1936	1,000,000	2.00	15.00	30.00	50.00	—

KM# 23 5 CENTS

Bronze, 26 mm. **Ruler:** Edward VIII **Obv:** Center hole divides crown and denomination, fleurs flank **Rev:** Tusks flank center hole, denomination above, circle surrounds **Edge:** Plain

Date	Mintage	F	VF	XF	Unc	BU
1936H	3,500,000	0.25	0.50	2.00	5.50	9.00
1936H Proof	—	Value: 150				
1936KN	2,150,000	0.25	0.50	2.00	5.50	9.00
1936KN Proof	—	Value: 150				

KM# 25.1 5 CENTS

Bronze **Ruler:** George VI **Obv:** Center hole divides crown and denomination, fleurs flank **Rev:** Tusks flank center hole, denomination above, circle surrounds **Edge:** Plain **Note:** Thick flan.

Date	Mintage	F	VF	XF	Unc	BU
1937H	3,000,000	0.50	1.00	2.00	4.00	7.00
1937KN	3,000,000	0.50	1.00	2.00	6.00	10.00
1939H	2,000,000	0.50	1.00	5.00	13.50	20.00
1939KN	2,000,000	0.50	1.00	5.00	13.50	20.00
1941	—	3.00	10.00	25.00	40.00	65.00
1941I	20,000,000	0.50	1.00	2.00	5.00	8.00

KM# 25.2 5 CENTS

Bronze **Ruler:** George VI **Obv:** Center hole divides crown and denomination, fleurs flank **Rev:** Tusks flank center hole, denomination above, circle surrounds **Edge:** Plain **Note:** Thin flan, reduced weight.

Date	Mintage	F	VF	XF	Unc	BU
1941I	Inc. above	0.50	1.00	2.00	5.00	8.00
1942	16,000,000	0.50	1.00	2.00	4.00	7.00
1942SA	4,120,000	1.00	6.00	15.00	30.00	42.00
1943SA	17,880,000	Value: 3.00				

KM# 25.3 5 CENTS

Bronze **Ruler:** George VI **Edge:** Plain **Note:** Similar to KM#25.2, but hole not punched.

Date	Mintage	F	VF	XF	Unc	BU
1942	—	—	—	—	100	—

KM# 33 5 CENTS

Bronze **Ruler:** George VI **Obv:** Center hole divides crown and denomination, fleurs flank **Obv. Legend:** ET IND. IMP. dropped from legend **Rev:** Tusks flank center hole, denomination above, circle surrounds **Edge:** Plain

Date	Mintage	F	VF	XF	Unc	BU
1949	4,000,000	0.25	0.50	3.00	6.00	10.00
1949 Proof	—	Value: 175				
1951H	6,000,000	0.25	0.50	2.00	5.00	8.00
1951H Proof	—	Value: 175				
1952	11,200,000	0.20	0.40	1.00	3.00	6.00
1952 Proof	—	Value: 200				

KM# 37 5 CENTS

Bronze **Ruler:** Elizabeth II **Obv:** Center hole divides crown and denomination, fleurs flank **Rev:** Tusks flank center hole, denomination above, circle surrounds **Edge:** Plain

Date	Mintage	F	VF	XF	Unc	BU
1955	2,000,000	0.10	0.25	0.75	2.00	3.50
1955 Proof	—	Value: 150				
1955H	4,000,000	0.20	0.50	1.25	3.50	5.00
1955H Proof	—	Value: 150				
1955KN	2,000,000	0.35	0.80	2.50	5.00	8.00
1956H	3,000,000	0.15	0.35	1.00	3.00	5.00
1956KN	3,000,000	3.00	5.00	8.00	10.00	15.00
1956KN Proof	—	Value: 125				
1957H	5,000,000	0.10	0.25	0.75	2.00	3.50
1957KN	5,000,000	0.10	0.25	0.75	2.00	3.50
1961H	4,000,000	0.15	0.35	1.00	3.00	5.50
1963	12,600,000	—	0.10	0.30	0.75	1.50
1963 Proof	—	Value: 150				

KM# 39 5 CENTS

Bronze **Ruler:** Elizabeth II **Obv:** Fleurs flank center hole, country name below, denomination above and right **Rev:** Tusks flank center hole, denomination above, circle surrounds **Edge:** Plain **Note:** Post-independence issue.

Date	Mintage	F	VF	XF	Unc	BU
1964	7,600,000	—	0.10	0.20	0.50	0.85

KM# 19 10 CENTS

Bronze **Ruler:** George V **Obv:** Center hole divides crown and denomination, fleurs flank **Rev:** Tusks flank center hole, denomination above, circle surrounds **Edge:** Plain

Date	Mintage	F	VF	XF	Unc	BU
1921	130,000	5.00	20.00	45.00	80.00	—
1922	7,120,000	1.00	3.00	8.00	20.00	—
1923	1,200,000	1.25	4.00	20.00	40.00	—
1924	4,900,000	0.65	2.25	14.00	25.00	—
1925	4,800,000	0.65	2.25	14.00	25.00	—
1927	2,000,000	0.75	2.50	12.50	20.00	—
1928	3,800,000	0.75	2.50	15.00	30.00	—
1928 Proof	—	Value: 175				
1933	6,260,000	0.75	2.50	6.50	17.50	—
1934	3,649,000	0.75	2.50	15.00	30.00	—
1935	7,300,000	0.65	2.00	8.00	18.00	—
1936	500,000	1.50	15.00	30.00	50.00	—

KM# 24 10 CENTS

Bronze, 30.5 mm. **Ruler:** Edward VIII **Obv:** Center hole divides crown and denomination, fleurs flank **Rev:** Tusks flank center hole, denomination above, circle surrounds **Edge:** Plain **Note:** For listing of mule dated 1936H with obverse of KM#24 and reverse of British West Africa KM#16 refer to British West Africa listings.

Date	Mintage	F	VF	XF	Unc	BU
1936	2,000,000	1.00	3.50	8.00	25.00	40.00
1936 Proof	—	Value: 200				
1936H	4,330,000	0.25	0.50	1.50	6.50	10.00
1936H Proof	—	Value: 325				
1936KN	4,142,000	0.25	0.50	1.50	6.50	10.00
1936KN Proof	—	Value: 145				

KM# 24a 10 CENTS

Copper-Nickel **Ruler:** Edward VIII **Obv:** Center hole divides crown and denomination, fleurs flank **Rev:** Tusks flank center hole, denomination above, circle surrounds **Edge:** Plain

Date	Mintage	F	VF	XF	Unc	BU
1936KN	—	—	—	—	—	—

KM# 26.1 10 CENTS

Bronze **Ruler:** George VI **Obv:** Center hole divides crown and denomination, fleurs flank **Rev:** Tusks flank center hole, denomination above, circle surrounds **Edge:** Plain **Note:** Thick flan.

Date	Mintage	F	VF	XF	Unc	BU
1937	2,000,000	0.25	0.75	2.50	6.00	9.00
1937 Proof	—	Value: 175				
1937H	2,500,000	0.25	0.75	2.50	8.00	13.00
1937H Proof	—	Value: 175				
1937KN	2,500,000	0.25	0.75	2.50	8.00	13.00
1937KN Proof	—	Value: 175				
1939H	2,000,000	0.25	0.70	5.50	15.00	21.00
1939KN	2,029,999	0.25	0.70	5.50	12.50	16.00
1939KN Proof	—	Value: 175				
1941I	15,682,000	0.35	1.00	6.00	15.00	23.00
1941I Proof	—	Value: 175				
1941	—	0.50	1.50	7.50	16.00	21.00
1941 Proof	—	Value: 175				

KM# 26.2 10 CENTS

Bronze **Ruler:** George VI **Obv:** Center hole divides crown and denomination, fleurs flank **Rev:** Tusks flank center hole, denomination above, circle surrounds **Edge:** Plain **Note:** Thin flan, reduced weight.

Date	Mintage	F	VF	XF	Unc	BU
1942	12,000,000	0.20	0.50	1.75	4.00	7.00
1942 Proof	—	Value: 175				
1942I	4,317,000	3.00	5.00	12.00	20.00	28.00

Date	Mintage	F	VF	XF	Unc	BU
1943SA	14,093,000	0.25	0.50	4.50	10.00	15.00
1945SA	5,000,000	0.25	0.50	5.00	12.50	16.00

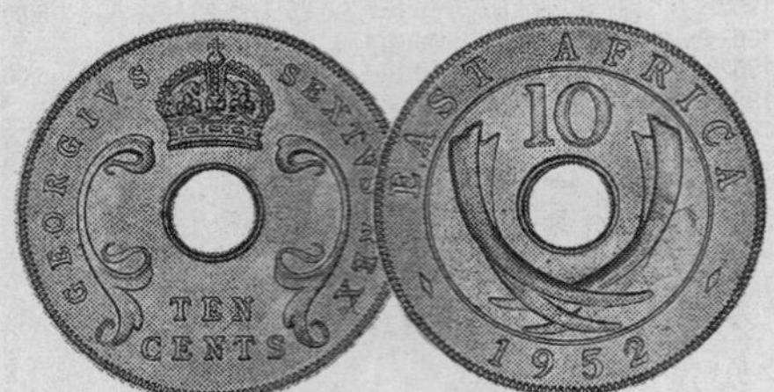

KM# 34 10 CENTS

Bronze **Ruler:** George VI **Obv:** Center hole divides crown and denomination, fleurs flank **Obv. Legend:** ET IND. IMP. dropped from legend **Rev:** Tusks flank center hole, denomination above, circle surrounds **Edge:** Plain

Date	Mintage	F	VF	XF	Unc	BU
1949	4,000,000	0.25	2.50	5.00	15.00	21.00
1949 Proof	—	Value: 175				
1950	8,000,000	0.20	0.40	1.75	4.00	7.00
1950 Proof	—	Value: 200				
1951	14,500,000	0.20	0.40	1.25	3.00	6.00
1951 Proof	—	Value: 175				
1952	15,800,000	0.20	0.40	1.25	3.00	6.00
1952 Proof	—	Value: 250				
1952H	2,000,000	3.00	5.00	10.00	20.00	30.00

KM# 38 10 CENTS

Bronze **Ruler:** Elizabeth II **Obv:** Center hole divides crown and denomination, fleurs flank **Rev:** Tusks flank center hole, denomination above, circle surrounds **Edge:** Plain

Date	Mintage	F	VF	XF	Unc	BU
1956	6,001,000	0.35	1.00	2.50	10.00	15.00
1956 Proof	—	Value: 175				
1964H Rare	—	—	—	—	—	—

KM# 40 10 CENTS

Bronze **Ruler:** Elizabeth II **Obv:** Fleurs flank center hole, country name below, denomination above and right **Rev:** Tusks flank center hole, denomination above, circle surrounds **Edge:** Plain **Note:** Post-independence issue.

Date	Mintage	F	VF	XF	Unc	BU
1964H	10,002,000	0.10	0.15	0.30	1.00	1.50

KM# 20 50 CENTS

3.8879 g., 0.2500 Silver .0312 oz. ASW **Ruler:** George V **Obv:** Crowned bust of King George V left **Obv. Designer:** E.B. MacKennal **Rev:** Lion and mountains within 3/4 circle with fleur ends, date below divides denominations **Edge:** Reeded

Date	Mintage	F	VF	XF	Unc	BU
1921	6,200,000	1.00	5.00	17.50	30.00	—
1922	Inc. above	1.00	4.00	16.00	27.50	—
1923	396,000	5.00	18.00	55.00	80.00	—
1924	1,000,000	2.00	14.00	25.00	40.00	—

KM# 27 50 CENTS

3.8879 g., 0.2500 Silver .0312 oz. ASW **Ruler:** George VI **Obv:** Crowned head of King George VI left **Obv. Designer:** Percy Metcalfe **Rev:** Lion and mountains within 3/4 circle with fleur ends, date and denomination below and right **Edge:** Reeded

Date	Mintage	F	VF	XF	Unc	BU
1937H	4,000,000	0.75	1.25	5.50	12.50	—
1937H Proof	—	Value: 275				
1942H	5,000,000	0.75	1.25	9.00	20.00	—
1943I	2,000,000	1.50	5.00	17.50	30.00	—
1944SA	1,000,000	2.00	6.00	18.00	32.50	—

KM# 30 50 CENTS

Copper-Nickel **Ruler:** George VI **Obv:** Crowned head of King George VI left **Obv. Legend:** ET INDIA IMPERATOR dropped from legend **Obv. Designer:** Percy Metcalfe **Rev:** Lion and mountains within 3/4 circle with fleur ends, date divides denominations below **Edge:** Reeded

Date	Mintage	F	VF	XF	Unc	BU
1948	7,290,000	0.20	0.40	2.00	6.00	8.50
1948 Proof	—	Value: 250				
1949	12,960,000	0.15	0.30	1.50	5.00	7.50
1949 Proof	—	Value: 325				
1952KN	2,000,000	0.20	0.40	2.00	7.50	9.00

KM# 36 50 CENTS

Copper-Nickel **Ruler:** Elizabeth II **Obv:** Crowned bust right **Obv. Designer:** Cecil Thomas **Rev:** Lion and mountains within 3/4 circle with fleur ends, date divides denominations below **Edge:** Reeded **Note:** The KHN mint marks above exist because the master dies were produced with both the KN and H mint marks for use at either mint. Each mint was required to remove the other's mint mark before striking, but this was not always meticulously done. When one or the other mint mark was not fully removed a weak trace would remain creating the appearance of a wide space K N with a weak H in the middle or an H flanked by a weak K and N, in the field below the lion.

Date	Mintage	F	VF	XF	Unc	BU
1954	3,720,000	0.15	0.35	1.00	4.00	7.50
1954 Proof	—	Value: 225				
1955H	1,600,000	1.00	3.00	6.00	15.00	—
1955H Proof	—	Value: 225				
1955KHN	—	10.00	20.00	55.00	85.00	—
1955KN	—	0.15	0.35	1.75	5.00	7.00
1956H	2,000,000	0.15	0.25	1.25	4.00	6.00
1956H Proof	—	Value: 225				
1956KHN	—	10.00	20.00	35.00	65.00	—
1956KN	2,000,000	0.15	0.35	1.75	5.00	7.00
1958H	2,600,000	0.15	0.40	2.00	5.00	7.00
1960	4,000,000	0.10	0.25	1.25	4.00	6.00
1962KN	4,000,000	0.15	0.35	1.75	5.00	7.00
1963	6,000,000	0.10	0.25	1.25	4.00	6.00

KM# 21 SHILLING

7.7759 g., 0.2500 Silver .0625 oz. ASW, 27.8 mm. **Ruler:** George V **Obv:** Bust of King George V left **Obv. Designer:** E.B. MacKennal **Edge:** Reeded

Date	Mintage	F	VF	XF	Unc	BU
1921	6,141,000	1.50	5.75	18.00	30.00	—
1921H	4,240,000	1.75	3.00	25.00	40.00	—
1922	18,858,000	1.25	2.25	13.00	28.00	—
1922H	20,052,000	1.25	2.25	13.00	28.00	—
1923	4,000,000	5.00	10.00	30.00	45.00	—
1924	44,604,000	1.00	2.00	7.00	18.00	—
1925	28,405,000	1.00	2.00	7.00	20.00	—
1925 Proof	—	Value: 250				

KM# 28.1 SHILLING

7.7759 g., 0.2500 Silver .0625 oz. ASW **Ruler:** George VI **Obv:** Crowned head of King George VI left **Obv. Designer:** Percy Metcalfe **Rev:** Lion and mountains within 3/4 circle with fleur ends, date divides denominations below **Edge:** Reeded **Note:** REV; Type I, thin rim and short milling, EAST AFRICA further from edge than Type II, larger loop on right side of coin below diamond in legend. Edge reeding spaced out

Date	Mintage	F	VF	XF	Unc	BU
1937H	7,672,000	1.00	2.00	12.50	22.00	—

Date	Mintage	F	VF	XF	Unc	BU
1937H Proof	—	Value: 300				
1941I	7,000,000	1.25	2.25	14.00	28.00	—
1942H	4,430,000	1.25	2.25	14.00	28.00	—
1942H Proof	—	Value: 300				
1944H	10,000,000	1.25	2.25	17.00	32.00	—

KM# 28.2 SHILLING

7.7759 g., 0.2500 Silver .0625 oz. ASW **Ruler:** George VI **Obv:** Crowned head left **Rev:** Type II, thicker rim and larger milling, EAST AFRICA and leaves very near the edge, small leaf (loop) under diamond on right side **Edge:** Reeded

Date	Mintage	F	VF	XF	Unc	BU
1941I Rare	—	—	—	—	—	—

KM# 28.3 SHILLING

7.7759 g., 0.2500 Silver .0625 oz. ASW **Ruler:** George VI **Obv:** Crowned head left **Rev:** Type III, retouched central image, especially tuft of grass in front of lion **Edge:** Reeded

Date	Mintage	F	VF	XF	Unc	BU
1942I	3,900,000	1.00	2.00	13.00	25.00	—
1943I	—	500	750	1,200	1,500	—

Note: 25-50 pieces

KM# 28.4 SHILLING

7.7759 g., 0.2500 Silver .0625 oz. ASW **Ruler:** George VI **Obv:** Crowned head left **Rev:** Lion and mountains within 3/4 circle with fleur ends, date divides denominations below **Edge:** Reeded **Note:** Obverse and reverse as KM#28.1, edge reeding close. For more in-depth comparison of these reverse variety types, see The Guidebook and Catalogue of British Commonwealth Coins, 1649-1971, 3rd Edition, Remick, J. Winnipeg, Regency Coin and Stamp, 1971.

Date	Mintage	F	VF	XF	Unc	BU
1944SA	5,820,000	1.25	2.25	17.00	30.00	—
1945SA	10,080,000	1.25	2.25	13.00	27.50	—
1946SA	18,260,000	1.00	2.00	12.00	20.00	—

KM# 31 SHILLING

Copper-Nickel, 27.8 mm. **Ruler:** George VI **Obv:** Crowned head of King George VI left **Obv. Legend:** ET INDIA IMPERATOR dropped from legend **Obv. Designer:** Percy Metcalfe **Rev:** Lion and mountains within 3/4 circle with fleur ends, date and denomination below **Edge:** Reeded

Date	Mintage	F	VF	XF	Unc	BU
1948	19,704,000	0.50	0.90	2.00	6.50	12.00
1949	38,318,000	0.50	0.90	2.00	6.50	12.00
1949 Proof	—	Value: 250				
1949H	12,584,000	0.50	0.90	2.25	7.50	12.50
1949KN	15,060,000	0.50	0.90	3.25	7.50	12.50
1950	56,362,000	0.35	0.60	1.50	5.00	12.00
1950 Proof	—	Value: 250				
1950H	12,416,000	0.50	0.90	3.25	6.00	12.00
1950KN	10,040,000	0.40	0.70	2.00	5.00	12.00
1952	55,605,000	0.35	0.60	1.50	5.00	12.00
1952 Proof	—	Value: 175				
1952H	8,023,999	0.35	0.60	1.75	5.00	12.00
1952KN	9,360,000	0.35	0.60	1.75	5.00	12.00

PATTERNS

Including off metal strikes

KM#	Date	Mintage	Identification	Mkt Val
Pn6	1906	—	Cent. Aluminum. KM#5.	1,500
Pn7	1907	5	1/2 Cent. Aluminum. KM#6.	2,000
Pn8	1907	—	5 Cents. Copper-Nickel. KM#11.	2,500
Pn9	1908	—	Cent. Copper-Nickel. KM#5a.	—
Pn10	1920 (a)	—	50 Cents. Aluminum. KM#16.	3,000
Pn11	1920 (a)	—	Florin. Aluminum. KM#17.	2,000
Pn12	1925KN	—	Cent. Bronze. Uniface.	250
Pn13	1929KN	—	Cent. Bronze. Uniface.	250

MINT SETS

KM#	Date	Mintage	Identification	Issue Price	Mkt Val
MS1	1921-1922 (5)	—	KM#18-22. The 5 cent coin is dated 1921, all others are 1922.	—	2,000

PROOF SETS

KM#	Date	Mintage	Identification	Issue Price	Mkt Val
PS1	1906-1907 (4)	—	KM#2-5, Pn7-8; Rare	—	—
PSA1	1920H (6)	—	KM#12-17; 20-30 pieces	—	3,000
PS2	1949 (5)	—	KM#30-34	—	1,000
PS3	1950 (3)	—	KM#31, 32, 34	—	600
PS4	1952 (3)	—	KM#32, 33, 34	—	600

EAST CARIBBEAN STATES

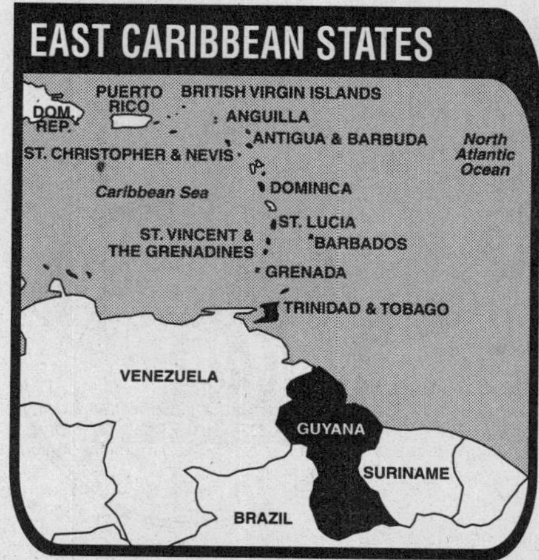

The East Caribbean States, formerly the British Caribbean Territories (Eastern group), formed a currency board in 1950 to provide the constituent territories of Trinidad & Tobago, Barbados, British Guiana (now Guyana), British Virgin Islands, Anguilla, St. Kitts, Nevis, Antigua, Dominica, St. Lucia, St. Vincent and Grenada with a common currency, thereby permitting withdrawal of the regular British Pound currency. This was dissolved in 1965 and after the breakup, the East Caribbean Territories, a grouping including Barbados, the Leeward and Windward Islands, came into being. Coinage of the dissolved 'Eastern Group' continues to circulate. Paper currency of the East Caribbean Authority was first issued in 1965 and although Barbados withdrew from the group they continued using them prior to 1973 when Barbados issued a decimal coinage.

A series of 4-dollar coins tied to the FAO coinage program were released in 1970 under the name of the Caribbean Development Bank by eight loosely federated island groupings in the eastern Caribbean. These issues are listed individually in this volume under Antigua, Barbados, Dominica, Grenada, Montserrat, St. Kitts, St. Lucia and St. Vincent.

RULERS
British

BRITISH CARIBBEAN TERRITORIES

STANDARD COINAGE

100 Cents = 1 British West Indies Dollar

KM# 1 1/2 CENT

Bronze, 20.4 mm. **Ruler:** Elizabeth II **Obv:** Crowned bust right **Rev:** Denomination above date

Date	Mintage	F	VF	XF	Unc	BU
1955	500,000	0.30	0.50	1.00	2.50	—
1955 Proof	2,000	Value: 3.00				
1958	200	0.50	0.75	1.50	3.00	—
1958 Proof	20	Value: 145				

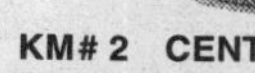

KM# 2 CENT

Bronze **Ruler:** Elizabeth II **Obv:** Crowned bust right **Rev:** Denomination within wreath, date below

Date	Mintage	F	VF	XF	Unc	BU
1955	8,000,000	0.15	0.25	0.60	1.00	—
1955 Proof	2,000	Value: 3.00				
1957	3,000,000	0.15	0.25	1.75	3.00	—
1957 Proof	—	Value: 100				
1958	1,500,000	0.35	0.50	4.50	7.50	—
1958 Proof	20	Value: 165				
1959	500,000	0.40	0.60	6.00	20.00	—
1959 Proof	—	Value: 100				
1960	2,500,000	0.15	0.25	0.60	1.25	—
1960 Proof	—	Value: 100				
1961	2,280,000	0.25	0.35	0.75	1.25	—
1961 Proof	—	Value: 100				
1962	2,000,000	0.15	0.25	0.50	1.25	—
1962 Proof	—	Value: 100				
1963	750,000	0.45	0.70	1.20	2.50	—

Date	Mintage	F	VF	XF	Unc	BU
1963 Proof	—	Value: 100				
1964	2,500,000	—	—	0.20	0.35	—
1964 Proof	—	Value: 100				
1965	4,800,000	—	—	0.20	0.35	—
1965 Prooflike	—	—	—	—	0.75	—
1965 Proof	—	Value: 5.00				

KM# 3 2 CENTS

Bronze, 30.5 mm. **Ruler:** Elizabeth II **Obv:** Crowned bust right **Rev:** Denomination within wreath, date below

Date	Mintage	F	VF	XF	Unc	BU
1955	5,500,000	0.15	0.25	0.50	1.00	—
1955 Proof	2,000	Value: 3.00				
1957	1,250,000	0.15	0.25	1.25	2.50	—
1957 Proof	—	Value: 110				
1958	1,250,000	0.15	0.25	2.50	5.00	—
1958 Proof	20	Value: 185				
1960	750,000	0.15	0.25	1.75	3.50	—
1960 Proof	—	Value: 110				
1961	788,000	0.15	0.25	1.75	3.50	—
1961 Proof	—	Value: 110				
1962	1,060,000	0.10	0.20	0.30	0.85	—
1962 Proof	—	Value: 110				
1963	250,000	0.50	0.75	1.50	5.00	—
1963 Proof	—	Value: 110				
1964	1,188,000	0.10	0.20	0.30	0.75	—
1964 Proof	—	Value: 110				
1965	2,001,000	—	0.10	0.20	0.45	—
1965 Prooflike	—	—	—	—	0.75	—
1965 Proof	—	Value: 5.00				

KM# 4 5 CENTS

Nickel-Brass, 21 mm. **Ruler:** Elizabeth II **Obv:** Crowned head right **Rev:** Sir Francis Drake's Golden Hind divides denomination, date below

Date	Mintage	F	VF	XF	Unc	BU
1955	8,600,000	0.15	0.25	0.60	1.25	—
1955 Proof	2,000	Value: 4.50				
1956	2,000,000	0.15	0.25	0.60	1.00	—
1956 Proof	—	Value: 300				
1960	1,000,000	0.20	0.30	0.90	1.50	—
1960 Proof	—	Value: 150				
1962	1,300,000	0.15	0.25	0.50	1.00	—
1962 Proof	—	Value: 150				
1963	200,000	0.25	0.35	1.20	2.00	—
1963 Proof	—	Value: 150				
1964	1,350,000	—	0.10	0.30	0.75	—
1964 Proof	—	Value: 150				
1965	2,400,000	—	0.10	0.20	0.50	—
1965 Prooflike	—	—	—	—	0.75	—
1965 Proof	—	Value: 5.00				

KM# 5 10 CENTS

Copper-Nickel, 18 mm. **Ruler:** Elizabeth II **Obv:** Crowned head right **Rev:** Sir Francis Drake's Golden Hind divides denomination, date below

Date	Mintage	F	VF	XF	Unc	BU
1955	5,000,000	0.15	0.25	0.45	0.75	—
1955 Proof	2,000	Value: 4.50				
1956	4,000,000	0.15	0.25	0.45	0.75	—
1956 Proof	—	Value: 175				
1959	2,000,000	0.15	0.25	0.60	1.00	—
1959 Proof	—	Value: 175				
1961	1,260,000	0.20	0.30	0.50	1.00	—
1961 Proof	—	Value: 175				
1962	1,200,000	0.15	0.25	0.50	1.00	—
1962 Proof	—	Value: 175				
1964	1,400,000	0.10	0.20	0.35	0.65	—
1965	3,200,000	0.10	0.20	0.30	0.50	—
1965 Prooflike	—	—	—	—	0.75	—
1965 Proof	—	Value: 5.00				

KM# 6 25 CENTS
Copper-Nickel **Ruler:** Elizabeth II **Obv:** Crowned bust right **Rev:** Sir Francis Drake's Golden Hind divides denomination, date below

Date	Mintage	F	VF	XF	Unc	BU
1955	7,000,000	0.35	0.50	0.70	1.00	—
1955 Proof	2,000	Value: 6.50				
1957	800,000	0.75	1.00	2.25	4.50	—
1957 Proof	—	Value: 225				
1959	1,000,000	0.35	0.50	1.25	2.25	—
1959 Proof	—	Value: 225				
1961	744,000	0.50	0.75	2.50	5.00	—
1961 Proof	—	Value: 225				
1962	480,000	0.25	0.50	1.25	2.50	—
1962 Proof	—	Value: 225				
1963	480,000	0.25	0.50	1.25	2.50	—
1963 Proof	—	Value: 225				
1964	480,000	0.25	0.50	1.00	1.75	—
1964 Proof	—	Value: 225				
1965	1,280,000	0.25	0.50	0.75	1.00	—
1965 Prooflike	—	—	—	—	1.50	
1965 Proof	—	Value: 7.50				

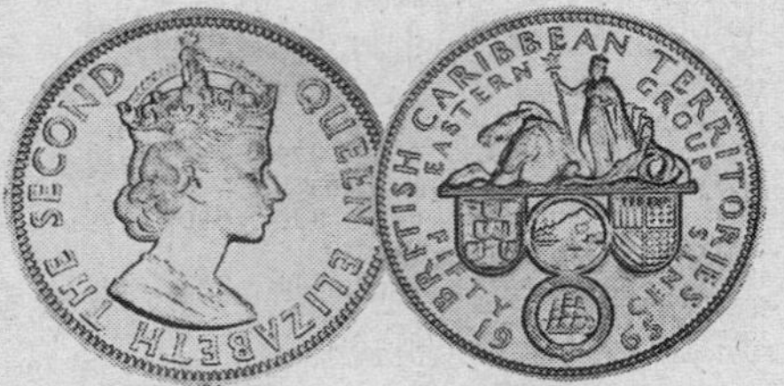

KM# 7 50 CENTS
13.0000 g., Copper-Nickel, 30 mm. **Ruler:** Elizabeth II **Obv:** Crowned bust right **Rev:** Figure and horseheads above shielded arms and circular pictures, denomination and date divided below

Date	Mintage	F	VF	XF	Unc	BU
1955	1,500,000	1.00	1.50	2.00	3.50	5.00
1955 Proof	2,000	Value: 12.50				
1965	100,000	2.00	5.00	7.50	15.00	—
1965 Prooflike	—	—	—	—	7.50	—
1965 Proof	—	Value: 10.00				

EAST CARIBBEAN TERRITORIES

STANDARD COINAGE

100 Cents = 1 Dollar

KM# 8 10 DOLLARS
Copper-Nickel, 38.8 mm. **Ruler:** Elizabeth II **Subject:** 10th Anniversary of Caribbean Development Bank **Obv:** Sir Francis Drake's Golden Hind divides denomination, date below **Rev:** Map on grid within circle, dates below **Note:** Prev. KM#1.

Date	Mintage	F	VF	XF	Unc	BU
1980	—	—	—	—	7.00	9.00

KM# 8a 10 DOLLARS
28.2800 g., 0.9250 Silver .8411 oz. ASW, 38.8 mm. **Ruler:** Elizabeth II **Obv:** Sir Francis Drake's Golden Hind divides denomination, date below **Rev:** Map on grid within circle, two dates below **Note:** Prev. KM#1a.

Date	Mintage	F	VF	XF	Unc	BU
1980 Proof	10,000	Value: 45.00				

KM# 9 10 DOLLARS
Copper-Nickel, 38.8 mm. **Ruler:** Elizabeth II **Subject:** Wedding of Prince Charles and Lady Diana **Obv:** Young bust right **Rev:** Sir Francis Drake's Golden Hind and map of island chain, denomination below **Note:** Prev. KM#2.

Date	Mintage	F	VF	XF	Unc	BU
1981	50,000	—	—	—	7.00	9.00

KM# 9a 10 DOLLARS
28.2800 g., 0.9250 Silver .8411 oz. ASW, 38.8 mm. **Ruler:** Elizabeth II **Obv:** Young bust right **Rev:** Sir Francis Drake's Golden Hind and map of island chain, denomination below **Note:** Prev. KM#2a.

Date	Mintage	F	VF	XF	Unc	BU
1981 Proof	30,000	Value: 30.00				

EAST CARIBBEAN STATES

British Administration

STANDARD COINAGE

100 Cents = 1 Dollar

KM# 10 CENT
0.9000 g., Aluminum, 18.4 mm. **Ruler:** Elizabeth II **Obv:** Young bust right **Rev:** Wreath divides denomination, date upper right **Shape:** Scalloped **Note:** Prev. KM#1.

Date	Mintage	F	VF	XF	Unc	BU
1981	—	—	—	—	0.20	0.30
1981 Proof	5,000	Value: 1.25				
1983	—	—	—	—	0.20	0.30
1984	—	—	—	—	0.20	0.30
1986	—	—	—	—	0.20	0.30
1986 Proof	2,500	Value: 1.25				
1987	—	—	—	—	0.20	0.30
1989	—	—	—	—	0.20	0.30
1991	—	—	—	—	0.20	0.30
1992	—	—	—	—	0.20	0.30
1993	—	—	—	—	0.20	0.30
1994	—	—	—	—	0.20	0.30
1995	—	—	—	—	0.20	0.30
1996	—	—	—	—	0.20	0.30
1997	—	—	—	—	0.20	0.30
1998	—	—	—	—	0.20	0.30
1999	—	—	—	—	0.20	0.30
2000	—	—	—	—	0.20	0.30

KM# 11 2 CENTS
1.1000 g., Aluminum, 18.25 mm. **Ruler:** Elizabeth II **Obv:** Young bust right **Rev:** Wreath divides denomination, date upper right **Shape:** Square **Note:** Prev. KM#2.

Date	Mintage	F	VF	XF	Unc	BU
1981	—	—	—	0.10	0.25	0.35
1981 Proof	5,000	Value: 1.50				
1984	—	—	—	0.10	0.25	0.35
1986	—	—	—	0.10	0.25	0.35
1986 Proof	2,500	Value: 1.50				
1987	—	—	—	0.10	0.25	0.35
1989	—	—	—	0.10	0.25	0.35
1991	—	—	—	0.10	0.25	0.35
1992	—	—	—	0.10	0.25	0.35
1993	—	—	—	0.10	0.25	0.35
1994	—	—	—	0.10	0.25	0.35
1995	—	—	—	0.10	0.25	0.35
1996	—	—	—	0.10	0.25	0.35
1997	—	—	—	0.10	0.25	0.35
1998	—	—	—	0.10	0.25	0.35
1999	—	—	—	0.10	0.25	0.35
2000	—	—	—	0.10	0.25	0.35

KM# 12 5 CENTS
1.4000 g., Aluminum, 23.1 mm. **Ruler:** Elizabeth II **Obv:** Young bust right **Rev:** Wreath divides denomination, date upper right **Shape:** Scalloped **Note:** Prev. KM#3.

Date	Mintage	F	VF	XF	Unc	BU
1981	—	—	—	0.10	0.30	0.45
1981 Proof	5,000	Value: 2.25				
1984	—	—	—	0.10	0.30	0.45
1986	—	—	—	0.10	0.30	0.45
1986 Proof	2,500	Value: 2.25				
1987	—	—	—	0.10	0.30	0.45
1989	—	—	—	0.10	0.30	0.45
1991	—	—	—	0.10	0.30	0.45
1992	—	—	—	0.10	0.30	0.45
1993	—	—	—	0.10	0.30	0.45
1994	—	—	—	0.10	0.30	0.45
1995	—	—	—	0.10	0.30	0.45
1996	—	—	—	0.10	0.30	0.45
1997	—	—	—	0.10	0.30	0.45
1998	—	—	—	0.10	0.30	0.45
1999	—	—	—	0.10	0.30	0.45
2000	—	—	—	0.10	0.30	0.45

KM# 13 10 CENTS
2.6000 g., Copper-Nickel, 18.1 mm. **Ruler:** Elizabeth II **Obv:** Young bust right **Rev:** Sir Francis Drake's Golden Hind, denomination below and left, date at right **Note:** Prev. KM#4.

Date	Mintage	F	VF	XF	Unc	BU
1981	—	—	0.10	0.15	0.40	0.60
1981 Proof	5,000	Value: 3.00				
1986	—	—	0.10	0.15	0.40	0.60
1986 Proof	2,500	Value: 3.00				
1987	—	—	0.10	0.15	0.40	0.60
1989	—	—	0.10	0.15	0.40	0.60
1991	—	—	0.10	0.15	0.40	0.60
1992	—	—	0.10	0.15	0.40	0.60
1993	—	—	0.10	0.15	0.40	0.60
1994	—	—	0.10	0.15	0.40	0.60
1995	—	—	0.10	0.15	0.40	0.60
1996	—	—	0.10	0.15	0.40	0.60
1997	—	—	0.10	0.15	0.40	0.60
1998	—	—	0.10	0.15	0.40	0.60
1999	—	—	0.10	0.15	0.40	0.60
2000	—	—	0.10	0.15	0.40	0.60

KM# 14 25 CENTS
6.5000 g., Copper-Nickel, 24 mm. **Ruler:** Elizabeth II **Obv:** Young bust right **Rev:** Sir Francis Drake's Golden Hind, divides denomination, date at right **Note:** Prev. KM#5.

Date	Mintage	F	VF	XF	Unc	BU
1981	—	—	0.15	0.20	0.50	0.75
1981 Proof	5,000	Value: 4.00				
1986	—	—	0.15	0.20	0.50	0.75
1986 Proof	2,500	Value: 4.00				
1987	—	—	0.15	0.20	0.50	0.75
1989	—	—	0.15	0.20	0.50	0.75
1991	—	—	0.15	0.20	0.50	0.75
1992	—	—	0.15	0.20	0.50	0.75
1993	—	—	0.15	0.20	0.50	0.75
1994	—	—	0.15	0.20	0.50	0.75
1995	—	—	0.15	0.20	0.50	0.75
1996	—	—	0.15	0.20	0.50	0.75
1997	—	—	0.15	0.20	0.50	0.75
1998	—	—	0.15	0.20	0.50	0.75
1999	—	—	0.15	0.20	0.50	0.75
2000	—	—	0.15	0.20	0.50	0.75

KM# 15 DOLLAR

8.2000 g., Aluminum-Bronze, 26.9 mm. **Ruler:** Elizabeth II **Obv:** Young bust right **Rev:** Sir Francis Drake's Golden Hind divides denomination, date at right **Note:** Prev. KM#6.

Date	Mintage	F	VF	XF	Unc	BU
1981	—	—	0.50	0.75	1.50	2.50
1981 Proof	5,000	Value: 8.00				
1986	—	—	0.50	0.75	1.50	2.50
1986 Proof	2,500	Value: 8.00				

KM# 20 DOLLAR

Copper-Nickel, 27.5 mm. **Ruler:** Elizabeth II **Obv:** Young bust right **Rev:** Sir Francis Drake's Golden Hind divides denomination, date at right **Shape:** 10-sided **Note:** Prev. KM#11.

Date	Mintage	F	VF	XF	Unc	BU
1989	—	—	—	—	2.25	3.25
1991	—	—	—	—	2.25	3.25
1992	—	—	—	—	2.25	3.25
1993	—	—	—	—	2.25	3.25
1994	—	—	—	—	2.25	3.25
1995	—	—	—	—	2.25	3.25
1996	—	—	—	—	2.25	3.25
1997	—	—	—	—	2.00	3.00
1998	—	—	—	—	2.00	3.00
1999	—	—	—	—	2.00	3.00
2000	—	—	—	—	2.00	3.00

KM# 24 2 DOLLARS

Copper-Nickel **Ruler:** Elizabeth II **Subject:** 10th Anniversary of Central Bank **Obv:** Bank building, dates below **Rev:** Bust facing, denomination below **Note:** Prev. KM#15.

Date	Mintage	F	VF	XF	Unc	BU
ND(1993)	—	—	—	—	8.50	10.00

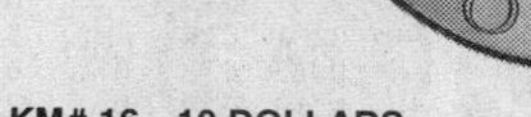

KM# 16 10 DOLLARS

Copper-Nickel **Ruler:** Elizabeth II **Series:** F.A.O. **Subject:** World Food Day **Obv:** Denomination within wreath, date below **Rev:** Grain sprig within circle divides date and FAO logo **Note:** Prev. KM#7.

Date	Mintage	F	VF	XF	Unc	BU
1981	—	—	—	—	14.50	16.50

KM# 16a 10 DOLLARS

28.2800 g., 0.5000 Silver .4546 oz. ASW **Ruler:** Elizabeth II **Obv:** Denomination within wreath, date below **Rev:** Grain sprig within circle divides date and FAO logo **Note:** Prev. KM#7a.

Date	Mintage	F	VF	XF	Unc	BU
1981	10,000	—	—	—	17.50	20.00
1981 Proof	5,000	Value: 47.50				

KM# 22 10 DOLLARS

28.2800 g., 0.9250 Silver .8411 oz. ASW **Ruler:** Elizabeth II **Subject:** Queen Mother's 90th Birthday **Obv:** Crowned bust right, denomination below **Rev:** Crowned monogram with flowers flanking, dates below **Rev. Designer:** Robert Elderton **Note:** Prev. KM#13.

Date	Mintage	F	VF	XF	Unc	BU
ND(1990) Proof	—	Value: 50.00				

KM# 23 10 DOLLARS

28.2800 g., 0.9250 Silver .8411 oz. ASW **Ruler:** Elizabeth II **Subject:** 40th Anniversary - Coronation of Queen Elizabeth **Obv:** Crowned bust right, denomination below **Rev:** Crowned and seated 1/2 figure holding scepter and royal orb, dates below **Note:** Prev. KM#14.

Date	Mintage	F	VF	XF	Unc	BU
ND(1993) Proof	10,000	Value: 47.50				

KM# 25 10 DOLLARS

28.2800 g., 0.9250 Silver .8411 oz. ASW **Ruler:** Elizabeth II **Subject:** 10th Anniversary of Central Bank **Obv:** Bank building, dates below **Rev:** Bust facing, denomination below **Note:** Prev. KM#16.

Date	Mintage	F	VF	XF	Unc	BU
ND(1993) Proof	2,500	Value: 55.00				

KM# 27 10 DOLLARS

31.4700 g., 0.9250 Silver .9359 oz. ASW **Ruler:** Elizabeth II **Subject:** World Cup Soccer **Rev:** Buildings, soccer ball at right, denomination below **Note:** Prev. KM#18.

Date	Mintage	F	VF	XF	Unc	BU
1994 Proof	10,000	Value: 45.00				

KM# 33 10 DOLLARS

28.5000 g., 0.9250 Silver 0.8476 oz. ASW, 38.5 mm. **Ruler:** Elizabeth II **Subject:** Reeded **Obv:** Queens portrait **Rev:** The Royal Launch, denomination divides dates below **Edge:** Reeded

Date	Mintage	F	VF	XF	Unc	BU
1996 Proof	—	Value: 50.00				

KM# 32 10 DOLLARS

28.5000 g., 0.9250 Silver 0.8476 oz. ASW, 38.5 mm. **Ruler:** Elizabeth II **Subject:** Queen Elizabeth and Philip's Golden Wedding Anniversary **Obv:** Crowned bust right, date below **Rev:** The royal couple waving behind gold inset shield, within circle, denomination below **Edge:** Reeded

Date	Mintage	F	VF	XF	Unc	BU
1997 Proof	—	Value: 45.00				

KM# 30 10 DOLLARS

28.2800 g., 0.9250 Silver .8410 oz. ASW **Ruler:** Elizabeth II **Subject:** Montserrat Volcano Appeal Fund **Obv:** Queens portrait **Rev:** Multicolor rainbow and volcano, date below **Note:** Prev. KM#30.

Date	Mintage	F	VF	XF	Unc	BU
1998 Proof	10,000	Value: 60.00				

KM# 28 10 DOLLARS
28.2800 g., 0.9250 Silver .8410 oz. ASW **Ruler:** Elizabeth II **Subject:** 50th Anniversary - University of the West Indies **Obv:** Bust facing, denomination below **Rev:** University arms, dates below, Pelican above **Note:** Prev. KM#19.

Date	Mintage	F	VF	XF	Unc	BU
ND(1999) Proof	1,000	Value: 60.00				

KM# 31 2000 CENTS (20 Dollars)
7.9800 g., 0.9170 Gold .2353 oz. AGW **Ruler:** Elizabeth II **Series:** Millennium **Subject:** British Royal Mint **Obv:** Young bust right **Rev:** Ship, palm trees and radiant sun within circle divided by words "millennium", denomination below **Edge:** Reeded **Note:** Prev. KM#22.

Date	Mintage	F	VF	XF	Unc	BU
2000	—	—	—	—	165	185

KM# 19 50 DOLLARS
28.2800 g., 0.9250 Silver .8411 oz. ASW **Ruler:** Elizabeth II **Series:** International Year of Disabled Persons **Obv:** Young bust right **Rev:** Two winged figures divide date and denomination **Note:** Prev. KM#10.

Date	Mintage	F	VF	XF	Unc	BU
1981	10,000	—	—	—	30.00	—
1981 Proof	10,000	Value: 45.00				

KM# 17 50 DOLLARS
28.2800 g., 0.9250 Silver .8411 oz. ASW **Ruler:** Elizabeth II **Series:** International Year of the Scout **Rev:** Boy scouts, denomination below, date at left **Note:** Prev. KM#8.

Date	Mintage	F	VF	XF	Unc	BU
ND(1983)	10,000	—	—	—	30.00	—
ND(1983) Proof	10,000	Value: 47.50				

KM# 26 100 DOLLARS
15.9760 g., 0.9170 Gold .4708 oz. AGW **Ruler:** Elizabeth II **Subject:** 10th Anniversary of Central Bank **Obv:** Bank building, dates below **Rev:** Bust facing, denomination below **Note:** Prev. KM#17.

Date	Mintage	F	VF	XF	Unc	BU
1993 Proof	150	Value: 525				

KM# 29 100 DOLLARS
15.9760 g., 0.9170 Gold .4708 oz. AGW **Ruler:** Elizabeth II **Subject:** 50th Anniversary - University of West Indies **Obv:** Bust facing, denomination below **Rev:** University arms, pelican above, dates below **Note:** Prev. KM#20.

Date	Mintage	F	VF	XF	Unc	BU
ND(1999) Proof	300	Value: 535				

KM# 21 500 DOLLARS
15.9800 g., 0.9170 Gold .4712 oz. AGW **Ruler:** Elizabeth II **Series:** International Year of Disabled Persons **Obv:** Young bust right **Rev:** Two figures raising center figure, denomination above, date at right **Note:** Prev. KM#12.

Date	Mintage	F	VF	XF	Unc	BU
1981	—	—	—	—	500	525
1981 Proof	—	Value: 750				

KM# 18 500 DOLLARS
15.9800 g., 0.9170 Gold .4712 oz. AGW **Ruler:** Elizabeth II **Series:** International Year of the Scout **Obv:** Queens portrait **Rev:** One scout standing, pointing; one scout kneeling with map, denomination below, date at right **Note:** Prev. KM#9.

Date	Mintage	F	VF	XF	Unc	BU
ND(1983)	2,000	—	—	—	375	425
ND(1983) Proof	2,000	Value: 550				

PIEFORTS

KM#	Date	Mintage	Identification	Mkt Val
P1	1981	1,000	50 Dollars. Silver. KM#19.	65.00
P2	1981	—	500 Dollars. Gold. KM#21.	1,600

MINT SETS

KM#	Date	Mintage	Identification	Issue Price	Mkt Val
MS1	1986 (6)	—	KM#10-15	—	7.50
MS2	1991 (6)	—	KM#10-14, 20	19.95	20.00
MS3	1992 (6)	—	KM#10-14, 20	—	15.00
MS4	1993 (6)	—	KM#10-14, 20	30.00	15.00
MS5	1994 (6)	—	KM#10-14,20	30.00	15.00
MS6	1995 (6)	—	KM#10-14, 20	30.00	15.00
MS7	1995-97 (6)	—	KM#10-11 (1995), 12-14, 20 (1997)	25.00	25.00
MS8	1996 (6)	—	KM#10-14, 20	30.00	15.00
MS9	1997 (6)	—	KM#10-14, 20	30.00	15.00
MS10	1998 (6)	—	KM#10-14, 20	30.00	15.00
MS11	1999 (6)	—	KM#10-14, 20	25.00	25.00
MS12	2000 (7)	—	KM#10-14, 20, 31	139	145

PROOF SETS

KM#	Date	Mintage	Identification	Issue Price	Mkt Val
PS1	1955 (7)	2,000	KM#1-7	—	30.00
PS2	1958 (3)	20	KM#1-3	—	500
PS3	1965 (6)	—	KM#2-7	—	35.00
PS5	1981 (6)	5,000	KM#10-15	29.00	20.00
PS6	1986 (6)	2,500	KM#10-15	30.75	20.00

ECUADOR

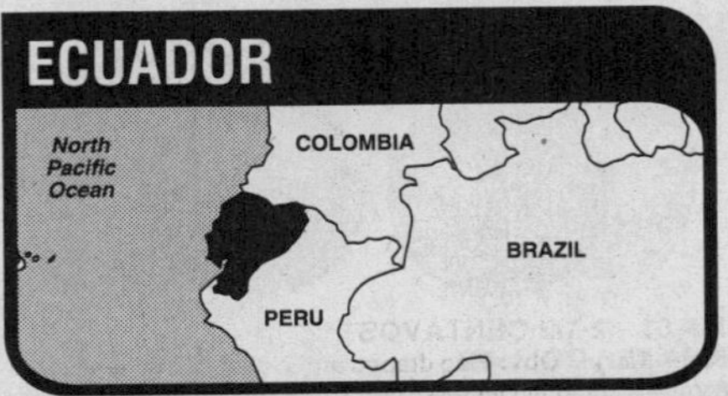

The Republic of Ecuador, located astride the equator on the Pacific Coast of South America, has an area of 105,037 sq. mi. (283,560 sq. km.) and a population of 10.9 million. Capital: Quito. Agriculture is the mainstay of the economy but there are appreciable deposits of minerals and petroleum. It is one of the world's largest exporters of bananas and balsa wood. Coffee, cacao, sugar and petroleum are also valuable exports.

Ecuador was first sighted in 1526 by Francisco Pizarro. Conquest was undertaken by Sebastian de Benalcazar, who founded Quito in 1534. Ecuador was part of the Viceroyalty of New Granada through the 16th and 17th centuries. After previous attempts to attain independence were crushed, Antonio Sucre, the able lieutenant of Bolivar, secured Ecuador's freedom in the Battle of Pinchincha, May 24, 1822. It then joined Venezuela and Colombia in a confederation known as Gran Colombia, and became an independent republic when it left the confederacy in 1830.

MINT MARKS

BIRMm - Birmingham, Heaton
Birmingham - Birmingham
D - Denver
H - Heaton, Birmingham
HF - LeLocle (Swiss)
LIMA - Lima
Mo - Mexico
PHILA.U.S.A. - Philadelphia
PHILADELPHIA - Philadelphia
PHILA - Philadelphia

MONETARY SYSTEM

10 Centavos = 1 Decimo
10 Decimos = 1 Sucre
25 Sucres = 1 Condor

REPUBLIC

DECIMAL COINAGE

10 Centavos = 1 Decimo; 10 Decimos = 1 Sucre; 25 Sucres = 1 Condor

KM# 57 1/2 CENTAVO (Medio)
Copper-Nickel **Obv:** Flag draped arms, date below **Rev:** Denomination within laurels

Date	Mintage	F	VF	XF	Unc	BU
1909H	4,000,000	4.00	9.00	20.00	40.00	—

KM# 58 CENTAVO (Un)
Copper-Nickel **Obv:** Flag draped arms, date below **Rev:** Denomination within laurels

Date	Mintage	F	VF	XF	Unc	BU
1909H	3,000,000	4.50	10.00	22.00	45.00	—

KM# 67 CENTAVO (Un)
Bronze **Obv:** Flag draped arms, date below **Rev:** Denomination within laurels

Date	Mintage	F	VF	XF	Unc	BU
1928	2,016,000	1.00	2.00	7.50	25.00	—

KM# 59 2 CENTAVOS (Dos)
Copper-Nickel **Obv:** Flag draped arms, date below **Rev:** Denomination within laurels

Date	Mintage	F	VF	XF	Unc	BU
1909H	2,500,000	5.00	12.00	25.00	60.00	—
1909H Proof	—	Value: 200				

KM# 61 2-1/2 CENTAVOS

Copper-Nickel **Obv:** Flag draped arms, date below **Rev:** Denomination within laurels

Date	Mintage	F	VF	XF	Unc	BU
1917	1,600,000	6.00	15.00	55.00	175	—

KM# 68 2-1/2 CENTAVOS

Nickel **Obv:** Flag draped arms, date below **Rev:** Denomination within laurels

Date	Mintage	F	VF	XF	Unc	BU
1928	4,000,000	2.00	4.00	20.00	50.00	—

KM# 55.1 1/2 DECIMO (Medio)

1.2500 g., 0.9000 Silver .0361 oz. ASW **Obv:** Head of Sucre left, date below **Rev:** Flag-draped arms, denomination upper left

Date	Mintage	F	VF	XF	Unc	BU
1902/892LIMA JF	1,000,000	1.00	2.00	8.50	20.00	—
1902/802LIMA JF	Inc. above	1.00	2.00	8.50	20.00	—
1902LIMA JF	Inc. above	0.75	1.50	6.00	20.00	—
1905/805LIMA JF	500,000	3.00	5.00	15.00	40.00	—
1905/2LIMA JF	Inc. above	3.50	6.00	18.00	50.00	—
1905LIMA JF	Inc. above	0.75	1.50	7.00	15.00	—
1912/05LIMA FG	20,000	3.00	6.00	18.00	50.00	—
1912LIMA FG	Inc. above	0.75	1.50	6.00	15.00	—
1912LIMA FG	Inc. above	2.00	3.00	8.50	20.00	—

Note: FCUADOR (obverse error)

KM# 55.2 1/2 DECIMO (Medio)

1.2500 g., 0.9000 Silver .0361 oz. ASW **Obv:** Head of Sucre left, date below **Rev:** Modified flag draped arms, denomination upper left

Date	Mintage	F	VF	XF	Unc	BU
1915BIRMm	2,000,000	0.75	1.25	5.00	10.00	—
1915BIRMm Proof	—	Value: 200				

KM# 60.1 5 CENTAVOS (Cinco)

Copper-Nickel **Obv:** Flag draped arms with tails on flagpoles pointing outward, date below **Rev:** Denomination within laurels

Date	Mintage	F	VF	XF	Unc	BU
1909H	2,000,000	4.50	10.00	30.00	80.00	—

KM# 60.2 5 CENTAVOS (Cinco)

Copper-Nickel **Obv:** Flag draped arms with tails on flagpoles pointing downward, date below **Rev:** Denomination within laurels **Note:** Thin planchet.

Date	Mintage	F	VF	XF	Unc	BU
1917	1,200,000	8.50	25.00	80.00	200	—
1918	7,980,000	4.00	8.50	17.50	75.00	—

KM# 63 5 CENTAVOS (Cinco)

Copper-Nickel **Obv:** Flag draped arms, date below **Rev:** Denomination within laurels

Date	Mintage	F	VF	XF	Unc	BU
1919	12,000,000	1.00	2.00	8.00	15.00	—
Note: 3 berries to left of "C" on reverse						
1919	Inc. above	1.25	2.50	20.00	40.00	—
Note: 4 berries loose to left of "C" on reverse						
1919	Inc. above	1.25	2.50	20.00	40.00	—
Note: 4 berries tight to left of "C" on reverse						

KM# 65 5 CENTAVOS (Cinco)

Copper-Nickel **Obv:** Flag draped arms, date below **Rev:** Head right within wreath, denomination below

Date	Mintage	F	VF	XF	Unc	BU
1924H	10,000,000	2.00	5.00	15.00	35.00	—

KM# 69 5 CENTAVOS (Cinco)

Nickel **Obv:** Flag draped arms, date below **Rev:** Head right within wreath, denomination below

Date	Mintage	F	VF	XF	Unc	BU
1928	16,000,000	1.00	2.00	3.00	6.50	—

KM# 75 5 CENTAVOS (Cinco)

Nickel **Obv:** Flag draped arms, date below **Rev:** Denomination within wreath

Date	Mintage	F	VF	XF	Unc	BU
1937HF	15,000,000	0.10	0.20	0.75	2.00	—

KM# 75a 5 CENTAVOS (Cinco)

Brass **Obv:** Flag draped arms, date below **Rev:** Denomination within wreath

Date	Mintage	F	VF	XF	Unc	BU
1942	2,000,000	1.00	2.00	6.00	15.00	—
1944D	3,000,000	1.00	2.00	5.00	10.00	—

KM# 75b 5 CENTAVOS (Cinco)

Copper-Nickel, 18 mm. **Obv:** Flag draped arms **Rev:** Denomination within wreath

Date	Mintage	F	VF	XF	Unc	BU
1946	40,000,000	—	—	0.40	1.00	—

KM# 75c 5 CENTAVOS (Cinco)

Nickel Clad Steel **Obv:** Flag draped arms, date below **Rev:** Denomination within wreath

Date	Mintage	F	VF	XF	Unc	BU
1970	—	—	—	0.15	0.50	—
1970	—	—	—	—	—	—
Note: ECADOR (obverse legend error)						

KM# 50.3 DECIMO (Un)

2.5000 g., 0.9000 Silver .0723 oz. ASW **Obv:** Head of Sucre left, date below, legend without "LEY" **Rev. Legend:** Flag draped arms, denomination upper left

Date	Mintage	VG	F	VF	XF	Unc
1902LIMA JF	519,000	—	1.75	4.50	10.00	22.00
Note: With JR below fasces on reverse						
1902LIMA JF	Inc. above	—	1.75	4.50	10.00	22.00
Note: Without JR below fasces on reverse						
1902LIMA JF/TF	—	—	1.50	3.00	10.00	20.00
1905LIMA JF	250,000	—	1.50	3.00	10.00	20.00
1912LIMA FG	30,000	—	3.00	6.00	15.00	35.00

KM# 50.4 DECIMO (Un)

2.5000 g., 0.9000 Silver .0723 oz. ASW **Obv:** Head of Sucre left, date below **Rev:** Flag draped arms, denomination upper left

Date	Mintage	VG	F	VF	XF	Unc
1915BIRMm	1,000,000	—	BV	1.25	2.00	7.00
1915BIRMm Proof	—	Value: 300				

KM# 50.5 DECIMO (Un)

2.5000 g., 0.9000 Silver .0723 oz. ASW **Obv:** Head of Sucre left **Rev:** Flag draped arms

Date	Mintage	VG	F	VF	XF	Unc
1916PHILA	2,000,000	—	BV	1.25	2.00	7.00

KM# 62 10 CENTAVOS (Diez)

Copper-Nickel **Obv:** Flag draped arms, date below **Rev:** Denomination within wreath

Date	Mintage	F	VF	XF	Unc	BU
1918	1,000,000	10.00	20.00	40.00	90.00	—

KM# 64 10 CENTAVOS (Diez)

Copper-Nickel **Obv:** Flag draped arms, date below **Rev:** Denomination within wreath

Date	Mintage	F	VF	XF	Unc	BU
1919	2,000,000	2.00	4.00	10.00	25.00	—
1919 Proof	—	Value: 300				

KM# 66 10 CENTAVOS (Diez)

Copper-Nickel **Obv:** Flag draped arms, date below **Rev:** Head of Bolivar left within wreath, denomination below **Note:** The H mint mark is very small and is located above the date.

Date	Mintage	F	VF	XF	Unc	BU
1924H	5,000,000	1.25	2.50	7.50	20.00	—
1924H Proof	—	Value: 100				

KM# 70 10 CENTAVOS (Diez)

Nickel **Obv:** Flag draped arms, date below **Rev:** Head of Bolivar right within wreath, denomination below

Date	Mintage	F	VF	XF	Unc	BU
1928	16,000,000	1.00	2.00	6.50	20.00	—

KM# 76 10 CENTAVOS (Diez)

Nickel **Obv:** Flag draped arms **Rev:** Denomination in wreath

Date	Mintage	F	VF	XF	Unc	BU
1937HF	7,500,000	0.25	0.50	1.00	3.50	—

KM# 76a 10 CENTAVOS (Diez)
Brass **Obv:** Flag draped arms, date below **Rev:** Denomination within wreath

Date	Mintage	F	VF	XF	Unc	BU
1942	5,000,000	0.60	1.00	5.00	15.00	—

KM# 76b 10 CENTAVOS (Diez)
Copper-Nickel **Obv:** Flag draped arms, date below **Rev:** Denomination within wreath

Date	Mintage	F	VF	XF	Unc	BU
1946	40,000,000	0.10	0.15	0.25	1.00	—

KM# 76c 10 CENTAVOS (Diez)
Nickel Clad Steel **Obv:** Flag draped arms, date below **Rev:** Denomination within wreath **Note:** Varieties exist.

Date	Mintage	F	VF	XF	Unc	BU
1964	20,000,000	—	—	0.20	0.75	—
1968	15,000,000	—	—	0.20	0.75	—
1972	20,000,000	—	—	0.15	0.65	—

KM# 76d 10 CENTAVOS (Diez)
Copper-Nickel Clad Steel **Obv:** Flag draped arms, date below **Rev:** Denomination within wreath

Date	Mintage	F	VF	XF	Unc	BU
1976	10,000,000	—	—	0.15	0.65	—

KM# 51.3 2 DECIMOS (Dos)
5.0000 g., 0.9000 Silver .1446 oz. ASW **Obv:** Head of Sucre left, date below **Rev:** Flag-draped arms, denomination upper left, legend without "LEY"

Date	Mintage	F	VF	XF	Unc	BU
1912/18 FG	50,000	5.00	12.50	30.00	75.00	—
1912 FG	Inc. above	2.75	6.00	20.00	50.00	—
1914 FG LIMA.	110,000	3.00	7.00	14.50	40.00	—
1914 FG LIMA	Inc. above	2.50	5.50	11.50	30.00	—
1915 FG	157,000	5.00	15.00	50.00	100	—

Note: Small "R" below fasces on reverse

KM# 51.4 2 DECIMOS (Dos)
5.0000 g., 0.9000 Silver .1446 oz. ASW **Obv:** Head of Sucre left, date below **Rev:** Flag-draped arms, denomination upper left

Date	Mintage	F	VF	XF	Unc	BU
1914PHILADELPHIA TF	2,500,000	2.25	3.50	7.50	15.00	—
1916PHILADELPHIA TF	1,000,000	2.25	3.50	7.50	15.00	—

KM# 77.1 20 CENTAVOS
Nickel, 21 mm. **Obv:** Flag draped arms, date below **Rev:** Denomination within wreath

Date	Mintage	F	VF	XF	Unc	BU
1937HF	7,500,000	0.25	0.50	1.00	5.00	—

KM# 77.1a 20 CENTAVOS
Brass, 21 mm. **Obv:** Flag draped arms, date below **Rev:** Denomination within wreath

Date	Mintage	F	VF	XF	Unc	BU
1942	5,000,000	0.60	1.00	6.00	15.00	—
1944 D	15,000,000	0.40	0.75	4.00	10.00	—

KM# 77.1b 20 CENTAVOS
Copper Nickel, 21 mm. **Obv:** Flag draped arms **Rev:** Denomination within wreath

Date	Mintage	F	VF	XF	Unc	BU
1946	30,000,000	0.25	0.75	2.00	5.00	—

KM# 77.1c 20 CENTAVOS
Nickel Clad Steel, 21 mm. **Obv:** Flag draped arms, date below **Rev:** Denomination within wreath

Date	Mintage	F	VF	XF	Unc	BU
1959	14,400,000	—	—	0.20	1.00	—
1962	14,400,000	—	—	0.20	1.00	—
1966	24,000,000	—	—	0.20	1.00	—
1969	24,000,000	—	—	0.20	1.00	—
1971	12,000,000	—	—	0.20	1.00	—
1972	48,432,000	—	—	0.20	1.00	—

KM# 77.2 20 CENTAVOS
Copper-Nickel, 21 mm. **Obv:** Modified flag draped arms, date below **Rev:** Denomination within wreath

Date	Mintage	F	VF	XF	Unc	BU
1974	19,562,000	—	—	0.15	0.50	—

KM# 77.2a 20 CENTAVOS
Nickel Coated Steel, 21 mm. **Obv:** Flag draped arms, date below **Rev:** Denomination within wreath

Date	Mintage	F	VF	XF	Unc	BU
1975	52,437,000	—	—	0.15	0.35	—
1978	37,500,000	—	—	0.15	0.35	—
1980	18,000,000	—	—	0.15	0.35	—
1981	21,000,000	—	—	0.15	0.35	—

KM# 71 50 CENTAVOS (Cincuenta)
2.5000 g., 0.7200 Silver .0579 oz. ASW **Obv:** Head of Sucre left, date below **Rev:** Flag draped arms, denomination above

Date	Mintage	F	VF	XF	Unc	BU
1928PHILA•U•S•A•	1,000,000	1.50	3.00	15.00	40.00	—
1930PHILA•U•S•A•	155,000	2.00	5.00	25.00	60.00	—

KM# 81 50 CENTAVOS (Cincuenta)
Nickel Clad Steel **Obv:** Flag draped arms, date below **Rev:** Denomination within wreath

Date	Mintage	F	VF	XF	Unc	BU
1963	20,000,000	—	0.15	0.25	0.85	—
1971	5,000,000	—	0.15	0.25	0.85	—
1974	—	—	0.15	0.25	0.85	—
1975	—	—	0.15	0.25	0.85	—
1977	40,000,000	—	0.10	0.20	0.75	—
1979	25,000,000	—	0.10	0.20	0.75	—
1982	20,000,000	—	0.10	0.20	0.75	—

KM# 87 50 CENTAVOS (Cincuenta)
Nickel Clad Steel **Obv:** Modified flag draped arms, date below **Rev:** Denomination within wreath

Date	Mintage	F	VF	XF	Unc	BU
1985	30,000,000	—	0.10	0.20	0.40	—

KM# 90 50 CENTAVOS (Cincuenta)
Nickel Clad Steel **Obv:** Flag draped arms, date below **Rev:** Denomination within square **Note:** The circulation strikes were withdrawn from circulation and remelted. Approximately 100,000 pieces were released.

Date	Mintage	F	VF	XF	Unc	BU
1988	—	—	—	—	0.30	—
1988 Proof	25	—	—	—	—	—

KM# 72 SUCRE (Un)
5.0000 g., 0.7200 Silver .1157 oz. ASW **Obv:** Head of Sucre left, date below **Rev:** Flag draped arms, denomination above

Date	Mintage	F	VF	XF	Unc	BU
1928PHILA•U•S•A•	3,000,000	2.00	4.00	12.50	35.00	—
1930PHILA•U•S•A•	400,000	3.00	10.00	30.00	70.00	—
1934PHILA•U•S•A•	2,000,000	BV	2.00	10.00	30.00	—

KM# 78.1 SUCRE (Un)
Nickel, 26.5 mm. **Obv:** Flag draped arms, date below **Rev:** Head of Sucre left within wreath, denomination below

Date	Mintage	F	VF	XF	Unc	BU
1937 HF	9,000,000	0.50	1.00	2.00	7.00	—

KM# 78.2 SUCRE (Un)
Nickel, 25.9 mm. **Obv:** Flag draped arms **Rev:** Head of Sucre left

Date	Mintage	F	VF	XF	Unc	BU
1946	18,000,000	0.40	0.60	0.80	2.00	—

KM# 78a SUCRE (Un)
Copper-Nickel, 26 mm. **Obv:** Different ship in flag draped arms, date below **Rev:** Head of Sucre left within wreath, denomination below

Date	Mintage	F	VF	XF	Unc	BU
1959	8,400,000	0.25	0.50	0.65	1.00	—
1959 Proof	—	Value: 250				

KM# 78b SUCRE (Un)

Nickel Clad Steel, 26 mm. **Obv:** Flag draped arms, date below **Rev:** Head left within wreath, denomination below **Note:** Ship in arms similar to KM#78

Date	Mintage	F	VF	XF	Unc	BU
1964	20,000,000	—	0.10	0.25	0.75	—
1970	24,000,000	—	0.10	0.25	0.75	—
1971	8,092,000	—	0.10	0.25	0.75	—
1974	40,308,000	—	0.10	0.25	0.50	—
1978	32,000,000	—	0.10	0.25	0.50	—
1979	32,000,000	—	0.10	0.25	0.50	—
1980	110,000,000	—	0.10	0.25	0.50	—
1981	70,000,000	—	0.10	0.25	0.50	—

KM# 83 SUCRE (Un)

Nickel Clad Steel, 26 mm. **Obv:** Modified flag draped arms, date below **Rev:** Head left within wreath, denomination below **Note:** Ship in arms similar to KM #78

Date	Mintage	F	VF	XF	Unc	BU
1974	32,000,000	—	0.10	0.20	0.40	—
1975	32,000,000	—	0.10	0.20	0.40	—
1975 Proof	—	Value: 150				
1977	32,000,000	—	0.10	0.20	0.35	—

KM# 85.1 SUCRE (Un)

Nickel Clad Steel, 26 mm. **Obv:** Modified coat of arms **Rev:** Large head right within wreath

Date	Mintage	F	VF	XF	Unc	BU
1985	—	—	—	—	0.50	—

KM# 85.2 SUCRE (Un)

Nickel Clad Steel, 26 mm. **Obv:** Flag draped arms, date below **Rev:** Small head left within wreath, denomination below

Date	Mintage	F	VF	XF	Unc	BU
1986	—	—	—	—	0.50	—

KM# 89 SUCRE (Un)

Nickel Clad Steel **Obv:** Flag draped arms, date below **Rev:** Head left within wreath, denomination below **Note:** The 1988 circulation strikes were reportedly withdrawn from circulation and remelted. Approximately 100,000 pieces were released.

Date	Mintage	F	VF	XF	Unc	BU
1988	—	—	—	—	0.40	—
1988 Proof	25	—	—	—	—	—
1990	—	—	—	—	0.40	—
1992	—	—	—	—	0.40	—

KM# 111 SUCRE (Un)

31.1000 g., 0.9000 Gold 0.8999 oz. AGW, 40 mm. **Subject:** Central Bank's 70th Anniversary **Obv:** Partial view of bank building **Rev:** Coin designs of 1 escudo KM-15 **Edge:** Reeded

Date	Mintage	F	VF	XF	Unc	BU
ND (1997) Proof	2,000	Value: 665				

KM# 73 2 SUCRES (Dos)

10.0000 g., 0.7200 Silver .2315 oz. ASW **Obv:** Head of Sucre left, date below **Rev:** Flag draped arms, denomination above

Date	Mintage	F	VF	XF	Unc	BU
1928PHILA•U•S•A•	500,000	3.50	10.00	30.00	70.00	—
1930PHILA•U•S•A•	100,000	7.00	25.00	50.00	90.00	—

KM# 80 2 SUCRES (Dos)

10.0000 g., 0.7200 Silver .2315 oz. ASW **Obv:** Head of Sucre left, date below **Rev:** Flag draped arms, denomination above

Date	Mintage	F	VF	XF	Unc	BU
1944Mo	1,000,000	3.50	5.00	8.00	16.00	—

KM# 82 2 SUCRES (Dos)

Copper-Nickel **Obv:** Flag draped arms, date below **Rev:** Head 3/4 facing, divides denomination **Note:** Not released to circulation. All but approximatley 35 pieces remelted.

Date	Mintage	F	VF	XF	Unc	BU
1973	2,000,000	—	—	200	300	—

KM# 79 5 SUCRES (Cinco)

25.0000 g., 0.7200 Silver .5787 oz. ASW **Obv:** Head of Sucre left, date below **Rev:** Flag draped arms, denomination above

Date	Mintage	F	VF	XF	Unc	BU
1943Mo	1,000,000	—	BV	8.50	16.50	27.50
1944Mo	2,600,000	—	BV	8.00	14.00	22.50

KM# 84 5 SUCRES (Cinco)

Copper-Nickel **Obv:** Flag draped arms, date below **Rev:** Head of Sucre left within wreath, denomination below

Date	Mintage	F	VF	XF	Unc	BU
1973	500	—	—	—	1,200	—

Note: Only 7 pieces were distributed to Ecuadorian government officials, while 8 pieces (5 of these cancelled) reside in the Central Bank Collection; the remaining 485 pieces have been remelted

KM# 91 5 SUCRES (Cinco)

Nickel Clad Steel, 22 mm. **Obv:** Flag draped arms, date below **Rev:** Denomination within lines, design in background **Note:** The 1988 circulation strikes were reportedly withdrawn from circulation and remelted. Approximately 100,000 pieces released.

Date	Mintage	F	VF	XF	Unc	BU
1988	—	—	—	—	0.50	—
1988 Proof	25	—	—	—	—	—
1991	—	—	—	—	0.50	—

KM# 92.1 10 SUCRES (Diez)

Nickel Clad Steel, 24 mm. **Obv:** Flag draped arms, date below **Rev:** Denomination to right of statuette **Note:** Similar to KM#92.2 but small arms and letters. The circulation strikes were withdrawn from circulation and remelted. Approximately 100,000 pieces were released.

Date	Mintage	F	VF	XF	Unc	BU
1988	—	—	—	—	1.00	—
1988 Proof	25	—	—	—	—	—

KM# 92.2 10 SUCRES (Diez)

Nickel Clad Steel, 24 mm. **Obv:** Flag draped arms, date below, large arms and letters **Rev:** Denomination to right of statuette

Date	Mintage	F	VF	XF	Unc	BU
1991	—	—	—	—	1.00	—

KM# 94.1 20 SUCRES

Nickel Clad Steel, 26 mm. **Obv:** Flag draped arms, date below **Rev:** Denomination to right of small monument **Note:** The circulation strikes were withdrawn from circulation and remelted. Approximately 100,000 pieces released.

Date	Mintage	F	VF	XF	Unc	BU
1988	—	—	—	—	1.75	—
1988 Proof	25	—	—	—	—	—

KM# 94.2 20 SUCRES

Nickel Clad Steel, 26 mm. **Obv:** Modified coat of arms **Rev:** Denomination to right of small monument

Date	Mintage	F	VF	XF	Unc	BU
1991	—	—	—	—	1.75	—

KM# 93 50 SUCRES

Nickel Clad Steel, 29 mm. **Obv:** Flag draped arms, date below **Rev:** Denomination to left of native mask **Note:** The 1988 circulation strikes were withdrawn from circulation and remelted. Approximately 100,000 pieces released.

Date	Mintage	F	VF	XF	Unc	BU
1988 Narrow date	—	—	—	—	3.00	—
Note: 141 denticles in obverse border						
1988 Proof	25	—	—	—	—	—
1991 Wide date	—	—	—	—	3.00	—
Note: 141 denticles in obverse border						

Date	Mintage	F	VF	XF	Unc	BU
1991 Narrow date	—	—	—	—	3.00	—

Note: 161 denticles in obverse border

KM# 96 100 SUCRES
Bi-Metallic Bronze plated Steel center in Nickel plated Steel ring, 19 mm. **Subject:** National Bicentennial **Obv:** Flag draped arms within circle, date below **Rev:** Bust left within circle, denomination below

Date	Mintage	F	VF	XF	Unc	BU
1995	—	—	0.35	0.55	2.00	3.00

KM# 101 100 SUCRES
Bi-Metallic Brass clad steel center in Stainless Steel ring, 19 mm. **Subject:** 70th Anniversary - Central Bank **Obv:** Bust of Antonio Jose de Sucre left within circle, dates below **Rev:** Denomination within circle, grain sprigs flank

Date	Mintage	F	VF	XF	Unc	BU
ND(1997)	—	—	0.25	0.50	2.00	3.00

KM# 97 500 SUCRES
Bi-Metallic Bronze plated Steel center in Nickel plated Steel ring, 21.5 mm. **Subject:** State Reform **Obv:** Flag draped arms within circle, date below **Rev:** Isidro Ayora facing within circle, denomination below

Date	Mintage	F	VF	XF	Unc	BU
1995	—	—	—	—	3.00	4.00

KM# 102 500 SUCRES
Bi-Metallic Aluminumn-Bronze center in Copper-Nickel ring, 21.5 mm. **Subject:** 70th Anniversary - Central Bank **Obv:** Isidro Ayora head facing within circle, dates below **Rev:** Denomination within circle, grain sprigs flank

Date	Mintage	F	VF	XF	Unc	BU
ND(1997)	—	—	—	—	3.00	4.00

KM# 86 1000 SUCRES
23.3300 g., 0.9250 Silver .6938 oz. ASW **Subject:** Championship Soccer **Obv:** Flag draped arms, date below **Rev:** Soccer player, globe in background, denomination below

Date	Mintage	F	VF	XF	Unc	BU
1986 Proof	8,125	Value: 50.00				

KM# 88 1000 SUCRES
23.3300 g., 0.9250 Silver .6938 oz. ASW **Subject:** Championship Soccer **Obv:** Flag draped arms, date below **Rev:** Soccer players, globe in background, denomination below

Date	Mintage	F	VF	XF	Unc	BU
1986 Proof	Est. 10,000	Value: 50.00				

KM# 99 1000 SUCRES
Bi-Metallic Brass center in Stainless Steel ring, 23.5 mm. **Obv:** Flag draped arms within circle, date below **Rev:** Eugenio Espejo head right within circle, denomination below

Date	Mintage	F	VF	XF	Unc	BU
1996	—	—	—	—	5.00	6.00

KM# 103 1000 SUCRES
Bi-Metallic Aluminumn-Bronze center in Copper-Nickel ring, 23.5 mm. **Subject:** 70th Anniversary - Central Bank **Obv:** Eugenio Espejo head right within circle, dates below **Rev:** Denomination within circle, grain sprigs flank

Date	Mintage	F	VF	XF	Unc	BU
ND(1997)	—	—	—	—	5.00	6.00

KM# 95 5000 SUCRES
27.0000 g., 0.9250 Silver .8029 oz. ASW **Subject:** Ibero - American Series **Obv:** Flag draped arms and date within inner circle, circle of shields surround **Rev:** Native mask and dates above three ships, denomination below

Date	Mintage	F	VF	XF	Unc	BU
1991 Proof	50,000	Value: 75.00				

KM# 98 5000 SUCRES
27.0000 g., 0.9250 Silver .8029 oz. ASW **Subject:** Environmental Protection - Galapagos Penguins **Rev:** Two penguins, date at right, denomination below

Date	Mintage	F	VF	XF	Unc	BU
1994 Proof	20,000	Value: 75.00				

KM# 100 5000 SUCRES
27.0000 g., 0.9250 Silver .8029 oz. ASW **Subject:** Ibero-American Series - Native Costumes

Date	Mintage	F	VF	XF	Unc	BU
1997 Proof	20,000	Value: 60.00				

KM# 109 5000 SUCRES
27.1000 g., 0.9250 Silver 0.8059 oz. ASW, 40 mm. **Subject:** Ibero-America Series **Obv:** Flag draped arms within a circle of arms **Rev:** Man on horse with condor in background, date at left, denomination below **Edge:** Reeded

Date	Mintage	F	VF	XF	Unc	BU
1999 Proof	—	Value: 60.00				

KM# 74 CONDOR (Un)
8.3592 g., 0.9000 Gold .2419 oz. AGW **Obv:** Head of Bolivar left, date below **Rev:** Flag draped arms, denomination above
Note: 5,000 were released into circulation; the remainder are held as the Central Bank gold reserve.

Date	Mintage	F	VF	XF	Unc	BU
1928Birmingham	20,000	BV	170	200	350	425

REFORM COINAGE

100 Centavos = 1 Dollar

KM# 104 CENTAVO (Un)
2.5200 g., Brass, 19 mm. **Obv:** Map of the Americas within circle **Rev:** Denomination **Edge:** Plain

Date	Mintage	F	VF	XF	Unc	BU
2000	—	—	—	—	0.20	0.40

KM# 105 5 CENTAVOS (Cinco)
5.0000 g., Steel, 21.2 mm. **Subject:** Juan Montalvo **Obv:** Bust 3/4 facing and arms **Rev:** Denomination **Edge:** Plain

Date	Mintage	F	VF	XF	Unc	BU
2000	—	—	—	—	0.50	0.75

KM# 106 10 CENTAVOS (Diez)
2.2400 g., Steel, 17.9 mm. **Subject:** Eugenio Espejo **Obv:** Bust 3/4 left and arms **Rev:** Denomination **Edge:** Plain

Date	Mintage	F	VF	XF	Unc	BU
2000	—	—	—	—	0.75	1.00

KM# 107 25 CENTAVOS
5.6500 g., Steel, 24.2 mm. **Subject:** Jose Joaquin De Olmedo **Obv:** Bust facing and arms **Rev:** Denomination **Edge:** Reeded

Date	Mintage	F	VF	XF	Unc	BU
2000	—	—	—	—	1.00	1.50

KM# 108 50 CENTAVOS (Cincuenta)
11.3200 g., Steel, 30.6 mm. **Subject:** Eloy Alfaro **Obv:** Head at left 3/4 facing and arms **Rev:** Denomination **Edge:** Reeded

Date	Mintage	F	VF	XF	Unc	BU
2000	—	—	—	2.00	5.00	6.50

KM# 110 SUCRE (Un)
11.2500 g., Nickel Clad Steel, 30.5 mm. **Obv:** Denomination **Rev:** Antonio Jose De Sucre and small national arms **Edge:** Reeded

Date	Mintage	F	VF	XF	Unc	BU
2000	—	—	—	—	—	—

PATTERNS

Including off metal strikes

KM#	Date	Mintage	Identification	Mkt Val
Pn11	1928	—	Condor. Copper-Nickel. KM#74.	—
Pn12	1928	—	Condor. Copper. KM#74.	—
Pn13	1974	—	20 Centavos. Brass. 3.6000 g. KM#77.2	150
Pn14	1975	—	50 Centavos. Brass. 5.2100 g. KM#81.	150
Pn15	1975	—	Sucre. Brass. 6.7900 g. KM#83.	150
Pn16	1976	—	10 Centavos. Brass. 2.9100 g. KM#76d.	150

PIEFORTS

KM#	Date	Mintage	Identification	Mkt Val
P1	1915H	—	1/2 Decimo. Copper Nickel.	—
P2	1915H	—	Decimo. Copper Nickel.	—

MINT SETS

KM#	Date	Mintage	Identification	Issue Price	Mkt Val
MS35	1975	10,000	8 circulating coins and 1 commemorative dollar Polo	30.00	42.00
MS36	2000 (5)	—	KM#104-108	30.00	30.00

PROOF SETS

KM#	Date	Mintage	Identification	Issue Price	Mkt Val
PS2	1988 (6)	25	KM#89-94	—	—

EGYPT

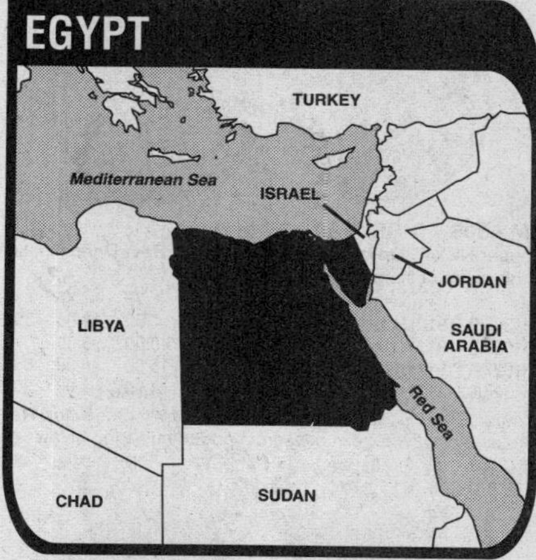

The Arab Republic of Egypt, located on the northeastern corner of Africa, has an area of 385,229 sq. mi. (1,1001,450 sq. km.) and a population of 62.4 million. Capital: Cairo. Although Egypt is an almost rainless expanse of desert, its economy is predominantly agricultural. Cotton, rice and petroleum are exported. Other main sources of income are revenues from the Suez Canal, remittances of Egyptian workers abroad and tourism.

Egyptian history dates back to about 3000 B.C. when the empire was established by uniting the upper and lower kingdoms. Following its 'Golden Age' (16th to 13th centuries B.C.), Egypt was conquered by Persia (525 B.C.) and Alexander the Great (332 B.C.). The Ptolemies, descended from one of Alexander's generals, ruled until the suicide of Cleopatra (30 B.C.) when Egypt became the private domain of the Roman emperor, and subsequently part of the Byzantine world. Various Muslim dynasties ruled Egypt from 641 on, including Ayyubid Sultans to 1250 and Mamluks to 1517, when it was conquered by the Ottoman Turks, interrupted by the occupation of Napoleon (1798-1801). A semi-independent dynasty was founded by Muhammad Ali in 1805 which lasted until 1952. Turkish rule became increasingly casual, permitting Great Britain to inject its influence by purchasing shares in the Suez Canal. British troops occupied Egypt in 1882, becoming the de facto rulers. On Dec. 14, 1914, Egypt was made a protectorate of Britain. British occupation ended on Feb. 28, 1922, when Egypt became a sovereign, independent kingdom. The monarchy was abolished and a republic proclaimed on June 18, 1953.

On Feb. 1, 1958, Egypt and Syria formed the United Arab Republic. Yemen joined on March 8 in an association known as the United Arab States. Syria withdrew from the United Arab Republic on Sept. 29, 1961, and on Dec. 26 Egypt dissolved its ties with Yemen in the United Arab States. On Sept. 2, 1971, Egypt finally shed the name United Arab Republic in favor of the Arab Republic of Egypt.

RULERS
British, 1882-1922
Kingdom, 1922-1953
Ahmed Fuad I, 1922-1936
Farouk, 1936-1952
Fuad II, 1952-1953
Republic, 1953-

MONETARY SYSTEM

(1885-1916)
10 Ushr-al-Qirsh = 1 Piastre

(Commencing 1916)
10 Milliemes = 1 Piastre (Qirsh)
100 Piastres = 1 Pound (Gunayh)

MINT MARKS

Egyptian coins issued prior to the advent of the British Protectorate series of Sultan Hussein Kamil introduced in 1916 were very similar to Turkish coins of the same period. They can best be distinguished by the presence of the Arabic word *Misr* Egypt) on the reverse, which generally appears immediately above the Muslim accession date of the ruler, which is presented in Arabic numerals. Each coin is individually dated according to the regnal years.

BP - Budapest, Hungary
H - Birmingham, England
KN - King's Norton, England

ENGRAVER

W - Emil Weigand, Berlin

INITIAL LETTERS

Letters, symbols and numerals were placed on coins during the reigns of Mustafa II (1695) until Selim III (1789). They have been observed in various positions but the most common position being over *bin* in the third row of the obverse. In Egypt these letters and others used on the Paras (Medins) above the word *duribe* on the reverse during this period.

REGNAL YEAR IDENTIFICATION

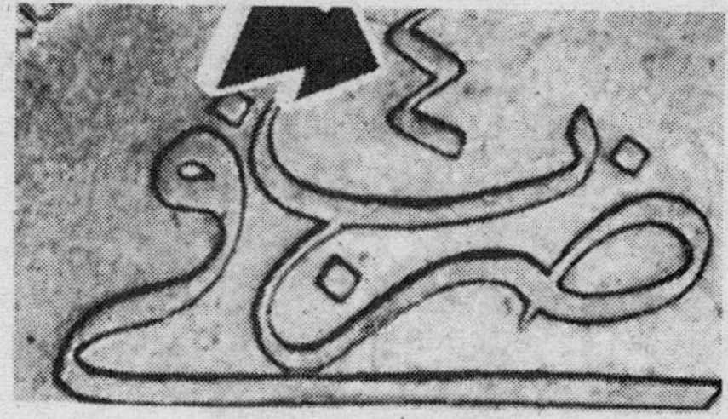

4
Duriba fi

Misr **Accession Date**

DENOMINATIONS

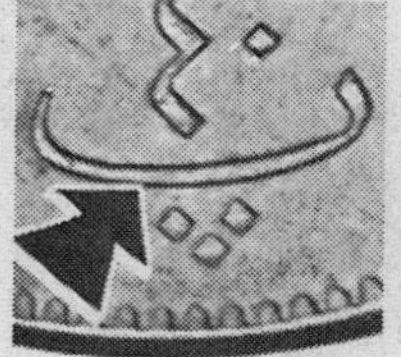

Para

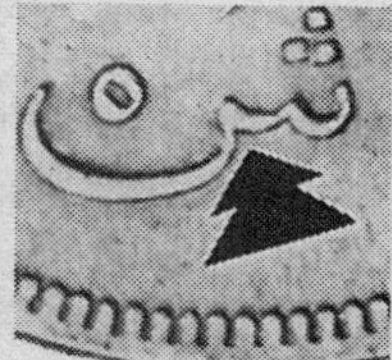

Qirsh

NOTE: The unit of value on coins of this period is generally presented on the obverse immediately below the toughra, as shown in the illustrations above.

Piastres **1916-1933**

Milliemes

Piastres **1934 –**

TITLES

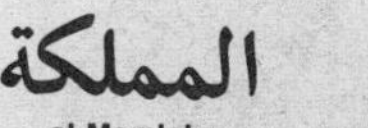

al-Mamlaka

al-Misriya

(The Kingdom of Egypt)

U.A.R. EGYPT

The legend illustrated is *Jumhuriyat Misr* al-*Arabiyya* which translates to 'The Arab Republic of Egypt'. Similar legends are found on the modern issues of Syria.

OTTOMAN EMPIRE
1595 - 1914AD
Muhammad V
AH1327-1332/1909-1914AD
MILLED COINAGE

KM# 300 1/40 QIRSH
Bronze **Obv:** Tughra **Rev:** Denomination

Date	Mintage	F	VF	XF	Unc
AH1327/2 (1910) H	2,000,000	1.50	3.00	7.50	25.00
AH1327/4 (1911) H	1,200,000	1.50	3.00	7.50	25.00
AH1327/3 (1911) H	2,000,000	1.50	3.00	7.50	25.00
AH1327/6 (1913) H	1,200,000	1.00	2.00	5.00	20.00

KM# 301 1/20 QIRSH
Bronze **Obv:** Tughra **Rev:** Denomination

Date	Mintage	F	VF	XF	Unc
AH1327/2 (1910) H	2,000,000	1.00	5.00	11.00	18.00
AH1327/3 (1911) H	2,000,000	1.50	5.00	15.00	25.00
AH1327/4 (1911) H	2,400,000	1.00	5.00	11.00	18.00
AH1327/6 (1913) H	1,400,000	0.75	4.00	11.00	18.00

KM# 302 1/10 QIRSH
Copper-Nickel **Obv:** Tughra **Rev:** Denomination

Date	Mintage	F	VF	XF	Unc
AH1327/2-6 (1910) H Proof	—	Value: 110			
Note: Above value for common date of proof					
AH1327/2 (1910) H	3,000,000	3.00	6.00	15.00	25.00
AH1327/3 (1911)	1,000,000	5.00	12.00	30.00	50.00
AH1327/4 (1911) H	3,000,000	1.00	2.00	5.00	12.50
AH1327/6 (1913) H	3,000,000	0.75	1.50	3.00	12.50

KM# 303 2/10 QIRSH
Copper-Nickel **Obv:** Tughra within wreath **Rev:** Denomination

Date	Mintage	F	VF	XF	Unc
AH1327/2 (1910) H	1,000,000	2.00	6.00	15.00	25.00
AH1327/3 (1911)	500,000	3.00	10.00	15.00	35.00
AH1327/4 (1911) H	1,000,000	2.00	6.00	15.00	25.00
AH1327/6 (1913) H	1,000,000	1.25	6.00	15.00	25.00
AH1327/2-6 (1914) H Proof	—	Value: 120			

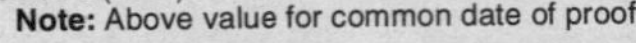
Note: Above value for common date of proof

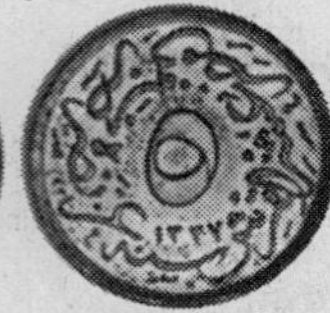

KM# 304 5/10 QIRSH
Copper-Nickel **Obv:** Tughra within wreath **Rev:** Denomination

Date	Mintage	F	VF	XF	Unc
AH1327/2 (1910) H	2,131,000	2.50	12.00	20.00	50.00
AH1327/3 (1911)	1,000,000	5.00	22.00	45.00	75.00
AH1327/4 (1911) H	3,327,000	1.00	5.00	11.00	25.00
AH1327/6 (1913) H	3,000,000	1.00	5.00	11.00	25.00

KM# 305 QIRSH
1.4000 g., 0.8330 Silver .0375 oz. ASW **Obv:** Tughra **Rev:** Denomination

Date	Mintage	F	VF	XF	Unc
AH1327/2 (1910) H	251,000	2.00	6.00	18.00	28.00
AH1327/3 (1911) H	171,000	2.25	6.00	18.00	35.00

KM# 306 QIRSH
Copper-Nickel **Obv:** Tughra within wreath **Rev:** Denomination within circle of stars

Date	Mintage	F	VF	XF	Unc
AH1327/2 (1910) H	1,000,000	2.00	7.00	18.00	35.00
AH1327/3 (1911)	300,000	20.00	40.00	95.00	150
AH1327/4 (1911) H	500,000	4.00	15.00	40.00	65.00
AH1327/6 (1913) H	2,500,000	2.00	4.00	8.00	20.00

KM# 307 2 QIRSH
2.8000 g., 0.8330 Silver .0750 oz. ASW **Obv:** Tughra, spray below **Rev:** Denomination within wreath

Date	Mintage	F	VF	XF	Unc
AH1327/2 (1910) H	250,000	5.00	10.00	45.00	90.00
AH1327/3 (1911) H	300,000	5.00	10.00	45.00	90.00

KM# 308 5 QIRSH
7.0000 g., 0.8330 Silver .1875 oz. ASW **Obv:** Tughra above spray **Rev:** Denomination within wreath

Date	Mintage	F	VF	XF	Unc
AH1327/2-6 (1910) H Proof	—	Value: 350			
Note: Above value for common date of proof					
AH1327/2 (1910) H	574,000	10.00	40.00	90.00	150
AH1327/3 (1911) H	2,400,000	5.00	10.00	40.00	70.00
AH1327/4 (1911) H	1,351,000	6.00	22.00	40.00	85.00
AH1327/6 (1913) H	7,400,000	4.00	15.00	27.00	55.00

KM# 309 10 QIRSH
14.0000 g., 0.8330 Silver .3749 oz. ASW **Obv:** Tughra, spray below **Rev:** Denomination within wreath

Date	Mintage	F	VF	XF	Unc
AH1327/2-6 (1910) H Proof	—	Value: 475			
Note: Above value for common date of proof					
AH1327/2 (1910) H	300,000	20.00	50.00	110	200
AH1327/3 (1911) H	1,300,000	8.00	25.00	75.00	115
AH1327/4 (1911) H	300,000	10.00	50.00	110	200
AH1327/6 (1913) H	4,212,000	6.00	15.00	35.00	80.00

KM# 310 20 QIRSH
28.0000 g., 0.8330 Silver .7499 oz. ASW **Obv:** Tughra, spray below **Rev:** Denomination within wreath

Date	Mintage	F	VF	XF	Unc
AH1327/2-6 (1910) H Proof	—	Value: 950			
Note: Above value for common date of proof					
AH1327/2 (1910) H	75,000	35.00	65.00	210	500
AH1327/3 (1911) H	600,000	22.50	65.00	100	325
AH1327/4 (1911) H	100,000	30.00	55.00	135	425
AH1327/6 (1913) H	875,000	21.50	32.50	70.00	200

OTTOMAN EMPIRE
Resumed
Abdul Hamid II
AH1293-1327/1876-1909AD
REFORM COINAGE

KM# 287 1/40 QIRSH
Bronze **Obv:** Tughra

Date	Mintage	F	VF	XF	Unc
AH1293/27 (1901)	1,200,000	1.50	4.00	11.00	18.00
AH1293/29 (1903)	2,000,000	1.00	3.00	6.00	15.00
AH1293/31 (1905) H	2,400,000	1.00	3.00	6.00	15.00
AH1293/32 (1906) H	Inc. below	1.00	4.00	11.00	18.00
AH1293/33 (1907) H	1,200,000	1.00	4.00	11.00	18.00
AH1293/35 (1909) H	1,200,000	2.00	5.00	7.00	15.00

KM# 288 1/20 QIRSH
Bronze **Obv:** Tughra

Date	Mintage	F	VF	XF	Unc
AH1293/27 (1901)	1,402,000	1.00	3.00	5.00	12.00
AH1293/29 (1903)	3,200,000	1.00	3.00	5.00	12.00
AH1293/31 (1905) H	3,000,000	1.00	3.00	5.00	12.00
AH1293/32 (1906) H	Inc. below	1.00	3.00	5.00	12.00
AH1293/33 (1907) H	1,400,000	2.00	3.00	7.00	15.00
AH1293/35 (1909) H	1,400,000	3.00	6.00	12.00	20.00

KM# 289 1/10 QIRSH
Copper-Nickel **Obv:** Tughra **Rev:** Denomination

Date	Mintage	F	VF	XF	Unc
AH1293/27-35 (1901) Proof	—	Value: 100			
Note: Above value for common date proof					
AH1293/27 (1901)	3,010,000	1.00	2.00	5.00	10.00
AH1293/28 (1902)	6,000,000	1.00	2.00	5.00	10.00
AH1293/29 (1903)	1,500,000	1.00	3.00	6.00	15.00
AH1293/30 (1904)	1,000,000	1.00	3.00	6.00	15.00
AH1293/31 (1905) H	3,000,000	1.00	3.00	6.00	15.00
AH1293/32 (1906) H	Inc. below	1.00	3.00	6.00	15.00
AH1293/33 (1907) H	2,000,000	1.00	3.00	5.00	10.00
AH1293/35 (1909) H	2,000,000	1.25	5.00	12.00	20.00

KM# 290 2/10 QIRSH
Copper-Nickel **Obv:** Tughra **Rev:** Denomination

Date	Mintage	F	VF	XF	Unc
AH1293/27 (1901)	1,002,000	1.00	5.00	12.00	20.00
AH1293/28 (1902)	2,000,000	1.00	5.00	12.00	20.00
AH1293/29 (1903)	1,500,000	1.00	5.00	12.00	20.00
AH1293/30 (1904)	—	3.00	12.00	22.00	40.00
AH1293/31 (1905) H	1,000,000	1.00	5.00	12.00	20.00
AH1293/33 (1907) H	1,500,000	1.00	5.00	12.00	20.00
AH1293/35 (1909) H	750,000	2.00	10.00	20.00	35.00

KM# 291 5/10 QIRSH
Copper-Nickel

Date	Mintage	F	VF	XF	Unc
AH1293/27 (1901)	4,999,000	0.30	5.00	11.00	20.00
AH1293/27 (1901)	4,999,000	0.30	5.00	11.00	20.00
AH1293/27-33 (1901) Proof	—	Value: 145			
Note: Above value for common date proof					
AH1293/27-33 (1901) Proof	—	Value: 145			
Note: Above value for common date proof					
AH1293/29 (1903)	12,000,000	0.30	2.00	6.00	12.00
AH1293/30 (1904)	2,000,000	0.50	4.00	12.00	25.00
AH1293/33 (1907) H	1,000,000	2.00	9.00	22.50	40.00

KM# 299 QIRSH

Copper-Nickel **Obv:** Tughra

Date	Mintage	F	VF	XF	Unc
AH1293/27 (1901)	999,000	2.00	12.00	32.00	50.00
AH1293/27 (1901)	999,000	2.00	12.00	32.00	50.00
AH1293/29 (1903)	3,500,000	2.00	5.00	15.00	30.00
AH1293/29 (1903)	3,500,000	2.00	5.00	15.00	30.00
AH1293/30 (1904)	500,000	2.50	14.00	35.00	55.00
AH1293/30 (1904)	500,000	2.50	14.00	35.00	55.00
AH1293/33 (1907) H	1,000,000	2.00	8.00	21.00	40.00
AH1293/33 (1907) H	1,000,000	2.00	8.00	21.00	40.00

KM# 292 QIRSH

1.4000 g., 0.8330 Silver .0375 oz. ASW **Obv:** Tughra

Date	Mintage	F	VF	XF	Unc
AH1293/27-33 (1901) Proof	—	Value: 135			
Note: Above value for common date proof					
AH1293/27 (1901) W	200,000	1.25	7.00	15.00	27.50
AH1293/29 (1903) W	100,000	1.50	7.00	16.00	30.00
AH1293/29 (1903) H	100,000	1.25	5.00	12.00	25.00
AH1293/29 (1903) H	100,000	1.25	5.00	12.00	25.00
AH1293/33 (1907) H	100,000	1.25	5.00	12.00	25.00
AH1293/33 (1907) H	100,000	1.25	5.00	12.00	25.00

KM# 299 QIRSH

Copper-Nickel **Obv:** Tughra

Date	Mintage	F	VF	XF	Unc
AH1293/27 (1901)	999,000	2.00	12.00	32.00	50.00
AH1293/27 (1901)	999,000	2.00	12.00	32.00	50.00
AH1293/29 (1903)	3,500,000	2.00	5.00	15.00	30.00
AH1293/29 (1903)	3,500,000	2.00	5.00	15.00	30.00
AH1293/30 (1904)	500,000	2.50	14.00	35.00	55.00
AH1293/30 (1904)	500,000	2.50	14.00	35.00	55.00
AH1293/33 (1907) H	1,000,000	2.00	8.00	21.00	40.00
AH1293/33 (1907) H	1,000,000	2.00	8.00	21.00	40.00

KM# 292 QIRSH

1.4000 g., 0.8330 Silver .0375 oz. ASW **Obv:** Tughra

Date	Mintage	F	VF	XF	Unc
AH1293/27-33 (1901) Proof	—	Value: 135			
Note: Above value for common date proof					
AH1293/27 (1901) W	200,000	1.25	7.00	15.00	27.50
AH1293/29 (1903) W	100,000	1.50	7.00	16.00	30.00
AH1293/29 (1903) H	100,000	1.25	5.00	12.00	25.00
AH1293/29 (1903) H	100,000	1.25	5.00	12.00	25.00
AH1293/33 (1907) H	100,000	1.25	5.00	12.00	25.00
AH1293/33 (1907) H	100,000	1.25	5.00	12.00	25.00

KM# 293 2 QIRSH

2.8000 g., 0.8330 Silver, 19 mm. **Obv:** Flower to right of tughra **Rev:** Denomination

Date	Mintage	F	VF	XF	Unc
AH1293/17-33 (1901) Proof	—	Value: 145			
Note: Above value for common date of proof					
AH1293/27 (1901) W	1,000,000	2.00	8.00	21.00	35.00
AH1293/29 (1903) W	450,000	2.00	10.00	25.00	45.00
AH1293/29 (1903) H	1,250,000	2.00	6.00	15.00	30.00
AH1293/30 (1904) H	500,000	3.00	10.00	22.00	40.00
AH1293/31 (1905) H	Inc. above	3.00	10.00	22.00	40.00
AH1293/33 (1907) H	450,000	2.00	10.00	22.00	35.00

KM# 294 5 QIRSH

7.0000 g., 0.8330 Silver 0.1875 oz. ASW **Obv:** Flower at right of toughra

Date	Mintage	F	VF	XF	Unc
AH1293/27 (1902) W	448,000	5.00	12.50	30.00	50.00
AH1293/29 (1904) W	600,000	5.00	10.00	30.00	50.00
AH1293/29 (1904) H	3,465,000	5.00	10.00	30.00	50.00
AH1293/30 (1905) H	1,213,000	5.00	10.00	32.50	60.00
AH1293/31 (1906) H	1,959,000	5.00	10.00	32.50	60.00
AH1293/32 (1907) H	Inc. above	5.00	10.00	30.00	50.00
AH1293/33 (1908) H	2,800,000	3.00	7.50	30.00	50.00

KM# 298 5 QIRSH

0.4200 g., 0.8750 Gold .0118 oz. AGW **Obv:** "Al-Ghazi" at right of tughra **Rev:** Denomination

Date	Mintage	F	VF	XF	Unc
AH1293//34 (1908)	8,000	35.00	60.00	90.00	120

KM# 295 10 QIRSH

14.0000 g., 0.8330 Silver .3749 oz. ASW **Obv:** Flower at right of tughra **Rev:** Denomination

Date	Mintage	F	VF	XF	Unc
AH1293/27-33 (1901) Proof	—	Value: 435			
Note: Above value for common date of proof					
AH1293/27 (1901) W	250,000	15.00	50.00	95.00	150
AH1293/29 (1903) W	Est. 2,450,000	8.00	25.00	60.00	100
AH1293/29 (1903) H	2,950,000	8.00	25.00	65.00	100
AH1293/30 (1904) H	1,000,000	8.00	25.00	65.00	100
AH1293/31 (1905) H	1,250,000	10.00	28.00	65.00	150
AH1293/32 (1906) H	Inc. below	8.00	16.00	65.00	100
AH1293/33 (1907) H	2,400,000	8.00	16.50	65.00	100

KM# 282 10 QIRSH

0.8544 g., 0.8750 Gold .0240 oz. AGW **Obv:** Al-Ghazi at right of tughra **Rev:** Denomination

Date	Mintage	F	VF	XF	Unc
AH1293/34 (1908)	5,000	45.00	90.00	150	—

KM# 296 20 QIRSH

28.0000 g., 0.8330 Silver .7499 oz. ASW **Obv:** Tughra

Date	Mintage	F	VF	XF	Unc
AH1293/27-33 (1901) Proof	—	Value: 825			
Note: Above value for common date of proof					
AH1293/27 (1901) W	25,000	17.50	70.00	250	500
AH1293/29 (1903) W	50,000	15.00	60.00	200	425
AH1293/29 (1903) H	425,000	12.00	50.00	180	400
AH1293/30 (1904) H	200,000	12.00	55.00	200	400
AH1293/31 (1905) H	250,000	12.00	55.00	200	400
AH1293/32 (1906) H	Inc. below	12.00	55.00	200	400
AH1293/33 (1907) H	300,000	12.00	45.00	175	350

BRITISH OCCUPATION

AH1333-1341 / 1914-1922AD

Hussein Kamil

As Sultan, AH1333-1336/1914-1917AD

OCCUPATION COINAGE

KM# 312 1/2 MILLIEME

Bronze **Obv:** Tughra, date below **Rev:** Dates below denominations

Date	Mintage	F	VF	XF	Unc
AH1335-1917	4,000,000	1.35	5.00	12.50	25.00

KM# 313 MILLIEME

Copper-Nickel **Obv:** Center hole divides date and legend **Rev:** Center hole divides denomination, date below

Date	Mintage	F	VF	XF	Unc
AH1335-1917	4,002,000	1.25	4.00	11.00	20.00
AH1335-1917H	12,000,000	0.40	2.00	7.00	12.00

KM# 314 2 MILLIEMES

Copper-Nickel **Obv:** Center hole divides date **Rev:** Center hole divides denomination, date below

Date	Mintage	F	VF	XF	Unc
AH1335-1916H	300,000	1.25	5.00	7.50	30.00
AH1335-1917	3,006,000	1.00	4.00	12.00	22.00
AH1335-1917H	9,000,000	0.40	2.00	5.00	14.00

KM# 315 5 MILLIEMES

Copper-Nickel **Obv:** Center hole divides dates **Rev:** Center hole divides denomination

Date	Mintage	F	VF	XF	Unc
AH1335-1916	3,000,000	2.00	5.00	10.00	20.00
AH1335-1916H	3,000,000	1.35	5.50	10.00	20.00
AH1335-1917	6,776,000	1.00	2.50	6.00	15.00
AH1335-1917H	37,000,000	0.60	1.50	2.50	8.00

KM# 316 10 MILLIEMES

Copper-Nickel **Obv:** Center hole divides dates **Rev:** Center hole divides denomination

Date	Mintage	F	VF	XF	Unc
AH1335-1916H	1,000,000	1.50	6.00	18.00	35.00
AH1335-1916	1,006,999	2.00	6.00	18.00	35.00
AH1335-1917	1,010,999	2.00	6.00	18.00	35.00
AH1335-1917KN	4,000,000	1.25	3.00	8.00	20.00
AH1335-1917H	6,000,000	0.75	2.00	7.00	15.00

KM# 317.1 2 PIASTRES

2.8000 g., 0.8330 Silver .0749 oz. ASW **Obv:** Text above date and sprays **Rev:** Denomination, legend within wreath

Date	Mintage	F	VF	XF	Unc
AH1335-1916	2,505,000	2.00	6.00	15.00	30.00
AH1335-1917	4,461,000	1.50	4.50	10.00	20.00

KM# 317.2 2 PIASTRES

2.8000 g., 0.8330 Silver .0749 oz. ASW **Obv:** Without inner circle **Rev:** Without inner circle

Date	Mintage	F	VF	XF	Unc
AH1335-1917H	2,180,000	1.50	4.00	8.00	15.00

KM# 318.1 5 PIASTRES

7.0000 g., 0.8330 Silver .1874 oz. ASW **Obv:** Text within wreath **Rev:** Denomination within wreath

Date	Mintage	F	VF	XF	Unc
AH1335-1916	6,000,000	3.50	9.00	20.00	35.00
AH1335-1917	9,218,000	2.75	5.00	17.50	32.00

KM# 318.2 5 PIASTRES

7.0000 g., 0.8330 Silver .1874 oz. ASW **Obv:** Without inner circle **Rev:** Without inner circle

Date	Mintage	F	VF	XF	Unc
AH1335-1917H	5,036,000	3.50	9.00	22.00	45.00
AH1335-1917H Proof	—	Value: 325			

KM# 319 10 PIASTRES

14.0000 g., 0.8330 Silver .3749 oz. ASW **Obv:** Text above date within wreath **Rev:** Denomination within wreath, dates below

Date	Mintage	F	VF	XF	Unc
AH1335-1916	2,900,000	6.00	15.00	40.00	95.00
AH1335-1917	4,859,000	6.00	12.00	22.00	85.00

KM# 320 10 PIASTRES

14.0000 g., 0.8330 Silver .3749 oz. ASW **Obv:** Text above date within wreath, without inner circle **Rev:** Denomination within wreath, without inner circle

Date	Mintage	F	VF	XF	Unc
AH1335-1917H	2,000,000	6.00	15.00	45.00	100

KM# 321 20 PIASTRES

28.0000 g., 0.8330 Silver .7499 oz. ASW **Obv:** Text above date within wreath **Rev:** Denomination within wreath, dates below

Date	Mintage	F	VF	XF	Unc
AH1335-1916	1,500,000	12.00	25.00	85.00	160

Date	Mintage	F	VF	XF	Unc
AH1335-1917	840,000	12.00	20.00	95.00	180
AH1335-1917 Proof	—	Value: 750			

KM# 322 20 PIASTRES

28.0000 g., 0.8330 Silver .7499 oz. ASW **Obv:** Without inner circle **Rev:** Without inner circle

Date	Mintage	F	VF	XF	Unc
AH1335-1917H	250,000	22.00	65.00	155	300

KM# 324 100 PIASTRES

8.5000 g., 0.8750 Gold .2391 oz. AGW **Obv:** Text above date within wreath **Rev:** Denomination within wreath, dates below

Date	Mintage	F	VF	XF	Unc
AH1335-1916 Proof	—	Value: 1,500			
Note: Restrikes may exist					
AH1335-1916	10,000	—	BV	180	275

Fuad I

As Sultan, AH1335-1341/1917-1922AD

OCCUPATION COINAGE

KM# 325 2 PIASTRES

2.8000 g., 0.8330 Silver .0749 oz. ASW **Obv:** Text above date **Rev:** Denomination and dates

Date	Mintage	F	VF	XF	Unc
AH1338-1920H	2,820,000	37.50	110	200	365

KM# 326 5 PIASTRES

7.0000 g., 0.8330 Silver .1874 oz. ASW **Obv:** Text above date **Rev:** Denomination and dates

Date	Mintage	F	VF	XF	Unc
AH1338-1920H	1,000,000	17.50	55.00	165	340

KM# 327 10 PIASTRES

14.0000 g., 0.8330 Silver .3749 oz. ASW **Obv:** Text above date **Rev:** Denomination and dates

Date	Mintage	F	VF	XF	Unc
AH1338-1920H	500,000	17.50	65.00	200	350

KM# 328 20 PIASTRES

28.0000 g., 0.8330 Silver .7499 oz. ASW **Obv:** Text above date **Rev:** Denomination and dates

Date	Mintage	F	VF	XF	Unc
AH1338-1920H Rare	2	—	—	—	—

KINGDOM

AH1341-1372 / 1922-1952AD

Fuad I

As King, AH1341-1355/1922-1936AD

DECIMAL COINAGE

KM# 330 1/2 MILLIEME

Bronze **Obv:** Bust right **Rev:** Denomination, dates above

Date	Mintage	F	VF	XF	Unc
AH1342-1924H Proof	—	Value: 120			
AH1342-1924H	3,000,000	2.00	5.00	14.00	25.00

KM# 343 1/2 MILLIEME

Bronze **Obv:** Uniformed bust left **Rev:** Dates above denomination

Date	Mintage	F	VF	XF	Unc
AH1348-1929BP	1,000,000	6.00	20.00	30.00	50.00
AH1351-1932H	1,000,000	3.00	20.00	30.00	50.00
AH1351-1932H Proof	—	Value: 160			

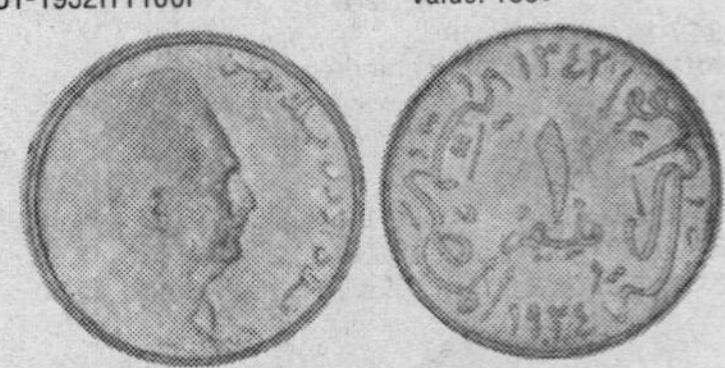

KM# 331 MILLIEME

Bronze **Obv:** Bust right **Rev:** Denomination divides dates

Date	Mintage	F	VF	XF	Unc
AH1342-1924H	6,500,000	1.25	3.00	6.00	15.00

KM# 344 MILLIEME

Bronze **Obv:** Uniformed bust left **Rev:** Denomination divides dates

Date	Mintage	F	VF	XF	Unc
AH1348-1929BP	4,500,000	1.50	4.00	10.00	20.00
AH1351-1932H	2,500,000	0.50	1.25	6.00	15.00
AH1351-1932H Proof	—	Value: 120			

Date	Mintage	F	VF	XF	Unc
AH1352-1933H	5,110,000	1.25	3.00	6.00	15.00
AH1354-1935H	18,000,000	0.20	0.50	2.00	8.00

KM# 332 2 MILLIEMES

Copper-Nickel **Obv:** Bust right **Rev:** Denomination divides dates

Date	Mintage	F	VF	XF	Unc
AH1342-1924H Proof	—	Value: 120			
AH1342-1924H	4,500,000	1.25	3.00	10.00	20.00

KM# 345 2 MILLIEMES

Copper-Nickel **Obv:** Uniformed bust left **Rev:** Denomination divides dates

Date	Mintage	F	VF	XF	Unc
AH1348-1929BP	Est. 3,500,000	0.40	1.00	3.00	10.00

KM# 356 2-1/2 MILLIEMES

Copper-Nickel **Obv:** Uniformed bust left **Rev:** Denomination divides dates **Shape:** 8-sided

Date	Mintage	F	VF	XF	Unc
AH1352-1933	4,000,000	1.25	7.00	10.00	30.00

KM# 333 5 MILLIEMES

Copper-Nickel **Obv:** Bust right **Rev:** Denomination divides dates

Date	Mintage	F	VF	XF	Unc
AH1342-1924	6,000,000	1.25	6.00	17.50	28.00

KM# 346 5 MILLIEMES

Copper-Nickel **Obv:** Uniformed bust left **Rev:** Denomination divides dates

Date	Mintage	F	VF	XF	Unc
AH1348-1929BP	4,000,000	0.75	5.00	14.00	25.00
AH1352-1933H	3,000,000	1.50	4.00	18.00	35.00
AH1354-1935H	8,000,000	0.80	1.00	6.00	12.50
AH1354-1935H Proof	—	Value: 120			

KM# 334 10 MILLIEMES

Copper-Nickel **Obv:** Bust right **Rev:** Denomination divides dates

Date	Mintage	F	VF	XF	Unc
AH1342-1924	2,000,000	2.00	15.00	30.00	50.00

KM# 347 10 MILLIEMES

Copper-Nickel **Obv:** Uniformed bust left **Rev:** Denomination divides dates

Date	Mintage	F	VF	XF	Unc
AH1348-1929BP	1,500,000	1.35	8.50	20.00	38.00
AH1352-1933H	1,500,000	1.35	8.50	25.00	45.00
AH1354-1935H	4,000,000	0.75	3.00	11.50	20.00

KM# 335 2 PIASTRES

2.8000 g., 0.8330 Silver .0749 oz. ASW **Obv:** Bust right **Rev:** Denomination above center circle, dates flank below

Date	Mintage	F	VF	XF	Unc
AH1342-1923H	2,500,000	2.00	6.00	11.00	35.00

KM# 348 2 PIASTRES

2.8000 g., 0.8330 Silver .0749 oz. ASW **Obv:** Uniformed bust left **Rev:** Denomination above center circle, dates flank below

Date	Mintage	F	VF	XF	Unc
AH1348-1929BP	500,000	2.00	5.00	11.00	20.00

Note: Edge varieties exist

KM# 336 5 PIASTRES

7.0000 g., 0.8330 Silver .1874 oz. ASW **Obv:** Bust right **Rev:** Denomination above center circle, dates flank below

Date	Mintage	F	VF	XF	Unc
AH1341-1923	800,000	4.50	15.00	35.00	60.00
AH1341-1923H	1,800,000	3.50	10.00	30.00	60.00
AH1341-1923H Proof	—	Value: 250			

KM# 349 5 PIASTRES

7.0000 g., 0.8330 Silver .1874 oz. ASW **Obv:** Uniformed bust left **Rev:** Denomination above center circle, dates flank below

Date	Mintage	F	VF	XF	Unc
AH1348-1929BP	800,000	4.50	15.00	35.00	65.00
AH1352-1933	1,300,000	3.50	7.50	25.00	55.00
AH1352-1933 Proof	—	Value: 250			

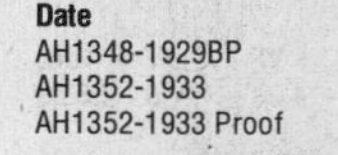
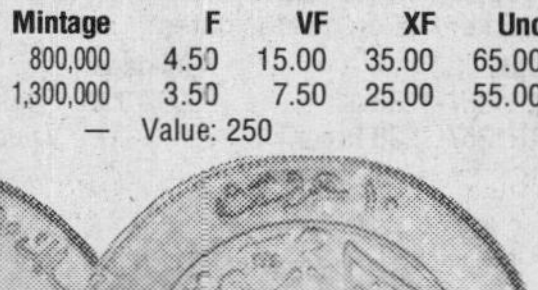

KM# 337 10 PIASTRES

14.0000 g., 0.8330 Silver .3749 oz. ASW, 32.5 mm. **Obv:** Bust right **Rev:** Denomination above center circle, dates flank below

Date	Mintage	F	VF	XF	Unc
AH1341-1923H Proof	—	Value: 450			

Date	Mintage	F	VF	XF	Unc
AH1341-1923	400,000	7.00	22.50	70.00	120
AH1341-1923H	1,000,000	7.00	22.50	60.00	100

KM# 350 10 PIASTRES

14.0000 g., 0.8330 Silver .3749 oz. ASW **Obv:** Uniformed bust left **Rev:** Denomination above center circle, dates flank below

Date	Mintage	F	VF	XF	Unc
AH1348-1929BP	400,000	6.50	20.00	55.00	100
AH1352-1933	Est. 350,000	6.50	20.00	55.00	100
AH1352-1933 Proof	—	Value: 475			

KM# 338 20 PIASTRES

28.0000 g., 0.8330 Silver .7499 oz. ASW **Obv:** Bust right **Rev:** Denomination above center circle, dates flank below

Date	Mintage	F	VF	XF	Unc
AH1341-1923	100,000	20.00	60.00	210	425
AH1341-1923H	50,000	20.00	70.00	240	425
AH1341-1923H Proof	—	Value: 875			

KM# 339 20 PIASTRES

1.7000 g., 0.8750 Gold .0478 oz. AGW **Obv:** Bust right **Rev:** Denomination above center inscription, dates flank below

Date	Mintage	F	VF	XF	Unc
AH1341-1923	65,000	40.00	75.00	125	325

KM# 351 20 PIASTRES

1.7000 g., 0.8750 Gold .0478 oz. AGW **Obv:** Bust left

Date	Mintage	F	VF	XF	Unc
AH1348 Proof	—	—	—	—	—
AH1348-1929	—	37.50	55.00	70.00	120
AH1349-1930	—	37.50	55.00	70.00	120
AH1349-1930 Proof	—	—	—	—	—

KM# 352 20 PIASTRES

28.0000 g., 0.8330 Silver .7499 oz. ASW **Obv:** Uniformed bust left **Rev:** Denomination above center circle, dates flank below

Date	Mintage	F	VF	XF	Unc
AH1348-1929BP	50,000	15.00	70.00	165	350
AH1352-1933 Proof	—	—	—	—	—
AH1352-1933	25,000	12.50	70.00	150	300

KM# 340 50 PIASTRES
4.2500 g., 0.8750 Gold .1195 oz. AGW **Obv:** Bust right **Rev:** Denomination above inscription, dates flank

Date	Mintage	F	VF	XF	Unc
AH1341-1923	18,000	BV	85.00	100	160

KM# 353 50 PIASTRES
4.2500 g., 0.8750 Gold .1195 oz. AGW **Obv:** Bust left **Rev:** Denomination above inscription, dates flank below

Date	Mintage	F	VF	XF	Unc
AH1348-1929	—	BV	90.00	110	175
AH1348-1929 Proof	—	—	—	—	—
AH1349-1930	—	BV	80.00	95.00	150
AH1349-1930 Proof	—	—	—	—	—

KM# 341 100 PIASTRES
8.5000 g., 0.8750 Gold .2391 oz. AGW **Obv:** Bust right **Rev:** Denomination above center circle, dates flank below

Date	Mintage	F	VF	XF	Unc
AH1340-1922	25,000	BV	160	175	250

KM# 354 100 PIASTRES
8.5000 g., 0.8750 Gold .2391 oz. AGW **Obv:** Bust left

Date	Mintage	F	VF	XF	Unc
AH1348-1929	—	BV	165	185	265
AH1349-1930	—	BV	160	175	250
AH1349-1930 Proof	—	—	—	—	—

KM# 342 500 PIASTRES
42.5000 g., 0.8750 Gold 1.1957 oz. AGW **Obv:** Bust right **Rev:** Denomination above center circle, dates flank below

Date	Mintage	F	VF	XF	Unc
AH1340-1922 Proof	—	Value: 1,500			
Note: Circulation coins were struck in both red and yellow gold					
AH1340-1922	1,800	—	—	875	1,350

KM# 355 500 PIASTRES
42.5000 g., 0.8750 Gold 1.1957 oz. AGW **Obv:** Uniformed bust left **Rev:** Denomination above center circle, dates flank below

Date	Mintage	F	VF	XF	Unc
AH1348-1929	—	—	—	850	1,250
AH1349-1930	—	—	—	850	1,250
AH1351-1932 Proof	—	Value: 1,500			
AH1351-1932	—	—	—	850	1,250

Farouk
AH1355-1372/1936-1952AD

DECIMAL COINAGE

KM# 357 1/2 MILLIEME
Bronze **Obv:** Uniformed bust looking left **Rev:** Denomination, dates below

Date	Mintage	F	VF	XF	Unc
AH1357-1938 Proof	—	Value: 100			
AH1357-1938	4,000,000	1.50	5.00	9.00	18.00

KM# 358 MILLIEME
Bronze **Obv:** Uniformed bust looking left **Rev:** Denomination, dates below

Date	Mintage	F	VF	XF	Unc
AH1357-1938 Proof	—	Value: 120			
AH1357-1938	26,240,000	0.20	0.50	2.00	7.00
AH1364-1945	10,000,000	1.25	7.00	26.00	50.00
AH1366-1947	—	1.25	7.00	26.00	50.00
AH1369-1950 Proof	—	Value: 85.00			
AH1369-1950	5,000,000	0.40	1.00	3.00	10.00

KM# 362 MILLIEME
3.9600 g., Copper-Nickel, 18.1 mm.

Date	Mintage	F	VF	XF	Unc
AH1357-1938	3,500,000	1.00	3.50	8.00	15.00

KM# 359 2 MILLIEMES
Copper-Nickel **Obv:** Uniformed bust looking left **Rev:** Denomination divides dates

Date	Mintage	F	VF	XF	Unc
AH1357-1938	2,500,000	1.50	4.00	14.00	25.00
AH1357-1938 Proof	—	Value: 140			

KM# 360 5 MILLIEMES
Bronze **Obv:** Uniformed bust looking left **Rev:** Denomination divides dates **Shape:** Scalloped

Date	Mintage	F	VF	XF	Unc
AH1357-1938	—	0.40	1.00	3.00	10.00
AH1357-1938 Proof	—	Value: 65.00			
AH1362-1943	—	0.40	1.00	3.00	10.00

KM# 363 5 MILLIEMES
Copper-Nickel **Obv:** Uniformed bust looking left **Rev:** Denomination divides dates

Date	Mintage	F	VF	XF	Unc
AH1357-1938 Proof	—	Value: 75.00			
AH1357-1938	7,000,000	0.40	1.00	4.00	10.00
AH1360-1941	11,500,000	0.20	1.00	4.00	8.00

KM# 361 10 MILLIEMES
Bronze **Obv:** Uniformed bust looking left **Rev:** Denomination divides dates **Shape:** Scalloped

Date	Mintage	F	VF	XF	Unc
AH1357-1938	—	0.40	1.00	4.00	10.00
AH1357-1938 Proof	—	Value: 140			
AH1362-1943	—	—	0.75	4.00	10.00

KM# 364 10 MILLIEMES
Copper-Nickel, 23 mm. **Obv:** Uniformed bust looking left **Rev:** Denomination divides dates

Date	Mintage	F	VF	XF	Unc
AH1357-1938	3,500,000	0.40	1.00	5.00	12.50
AH1357-1938 Proof	—	Value: 85.00			
AH1360-1941	5,322,000	0.40	1.00	5.00	12.50

KM# 365 2 PIASTRES
2.8000 g., 0.8330 Silver .0749 oz. ASW

Date	Mintage	F	VF	XF	Unc
AH1356-1937	500,000	1.25	1.75	3.00	8.00
Note: Fine and coarse edge reeding exist					
AH1356-1937 Proof	—	Value: 300			
AH1358-1939	500,000	1.50	4.00	10.00	75.00
AH1358-1939 Proof	—	Value: 200			
AH1361-1942	10,000,000	1.25	1.75	4.00	10.00
Note: Normal and flat rim varieties exist for AH1361 coins					

KM# 369 2 PIASTRES
2.8000 g., 0.5000 Silver .0450 oz. ASW **Obv:** Uniformed bust looking left **Rev:** Denomination and dates within tasseled wreath **Shape:** 6-sided

Date	Mintage	F	VF	XF	Unc
AH1363-1944	32,000	0.85	1.45	2.75	5.50

KM# 366 5 PIASTRES
7.0000 g., 0.8330 Silver .1874 oz. ASW

Date	Mintage	F	VF	XF	Unc
AH1356-1937	—	2.75	3.75	6.50	15.00
AH1356-1937 Proof	—	Value: 275			
AH1358-1939	8,000,000	2.75	3.75	6.50	15.00
AH1358-1939 Proof	—	Value: 275			

KM# 367 10 PIASTRES
14.0000 g., 0.8330 Silver .3749 oz. ASW

Date	Mintage	F	VF	XF	Unc
AH1356-1937	2,800,000	5.50	9.00	17.50	35.00
AH1356-1937 Proof	—	Value: 375			
AH1358-1939	2,850,000	5.50	9.00	17.50	35.00
AH1358-1939 Proof	—	Value: 300			

KM# 368 20 PIASTRES
28.0000 g., 0.8330 Silver .7499 oz. ASW **Obv:** Uniformed bust looking left **Rev:** Denomination and dates within tasseled wreath

Date	Mintage	F	VF	XF	Unc
AH1356-1937	—	12.00	26.00	50.00	90.00
AH1356-1937 Proof	—	Value: 1,000			
AH1358-1939	—	12.00	26.00	50.00	90.00
AH1358-1939 Proof	—	Value: 1,200			

KM# 370 20 PIASTRES
1.7000 g., 0.8750 Gold .0478 oz. AGW **Subject:** Royal Wedding **Obv:** Uniformed bust looking left **Rev:** Dates within circle, denomination above, decorative vine surrounds

Date	Mintage	F	VF	XF	Unc
AH1357-1938	20,000	BV	65.00	90.00	125

KM# 371 50 PIASTRES
4.2500 g., 0.8750 Gold .1195 oz. AGW **Subject:** Royal Wedding **Obv:** Uniformed bust looking left **Rev:** Dates within circle, denomination above, decorative vine surrounds

Date	Mintage	F	VF	XF	Unc
AH1357-1938	10,000	BV	95.00	140	240

KM# 372 100 PIASTRES
8.5000 g., 0.8750 Gold .2391 oz. AGW **Subject:** Royal Wedding **Obv:** Uniformed bust looking left **Rev:** Dates within circle, denomination above, decorative vine surrounds

Date	Mintage	F	VF	XF	Unc
AH1357-1938	5,000	BV	165	195	300

Note: Circulation coins were struck in both red and yellow gold

KM# 373 500 PIASTRES
42.5000 g., 0.8750 Gold 1.1957 oz. AGW **Subject:** Royal Wedding **Obv:** Uniformed bust looking left **Rev:** Dates within circle, denomination above, decorative vine surrounds

Date	Mintage	F	VF	XF	Unc
AH1357-1938	—	—	—	1,250	1,850
AH1357-1938 Proof	—	Value: 2,200			

FIRST REPUBLIC
AH1373-1378 / 1953-1958AD
DECIMAL COINAGE

KM# 375 MILLIEME
Aluminum-Bronze **Obv:** Denomination divides dates **Rev:** Small sphinx without outlined base

Date	Mintage	F	VF	XF	Unc
AH1373-1954	—	—	50.00	100	200
AH1374-1954	—	—	3.00	12.00	25.00
AH1374-1955	—	—	2.00	7.00	15.00
AH1375-1955	—	—	2.00	7.00	15.00
AH1375-1956	—	—	2.00	7.00	15.00

KM# 376 MILLIEME
Aluminum-Bronze **Obv:** Denomination divides dates **Rev:** Small sphinx with base outlined

Date	Mintage	F	VF	XF	Unc
AH1373-1954	—	—	—	—	—
AH1374-1954	—	—	2.00	7.00	15.00
AH1375-1955	—	—	1.00	2.00	5.00
AH1374-1955	—	—	1.00	2.00	5.00
AH1375-1956	—	—	1.50	4.00	10.00
AH1376-1957	—	—	—	—	—

KM# 377.1 MILLIEME
Aluminum-Bronze **Rev:** Large sphinx; without outlined base **Note:** Prev. KM#377.

Date	Mintage	F	VF	XF	Unc
AH1375-1956	—	—	0.50	2.00	4.00
AH1376-1957	—	—	0.75	2.50	5.00
AH1377-1958	—	—	0.75	2.50	5.00

KM# 377.2 MILLIEME
Aluminum **Obv:** Denomination divides dates **Rev:** Small sphinx with outlined base

Date	Mintage	F	VF	XF	Unc
AH1376-1957BP	—	—	0.75	1.50	5.00
AH1377-1958BP	—	—	0.75	1.50	5.00

KM# 378 5 MILLIEMES
Aluminum-Bronze **Obv:** Denomination divides dates **Rev:** Small sphinx with outlined base

Date	Mintage	F	VF	XF	Unc
AH1373-1954	—	—	5.00	10.00	35.00
AH1374-1954	—	—	4.00	8.00	25.00
AH1374-1955	—	—	10.00	20.00	50.00
AH1375-1956	—	—	3.00	6.00	15.00

KM# 379 5 MILLIEMES
Aluminum-Bronze **Obv:** Denomination divides dates **Rev:** Large sphinx

Date	Mintage	F	VF	XF	Unc
AH1376-1957	—	—	2.00	4.00	10.00
AH1377-1957	—	—	2.00	4.00	10.00
AH1377-1958	—	—	2.00	4.00	10.00

Thin "milliemes"

Thick "milliemes"

KM# 380 10 MILLIEMES
Aluminum-Bronze **Obv:** Denomination divides dates **Rev:** Small sphinx without base outlined

Date	Mintage	F	VF	XF	Unc
AH1373-1954	—	—	5.00	12.00	25.00
Note: Thin milliemes					
AH1374-1954	—	—	4.00	10.00	20.00
AH1374-1955	—	—	3.00	7.00	15.00
Note: Thick milliemes					

KM# 381 10 MILLIEMES
Aluminum-Bronze **Rev:** Large sphinx

Date	Mintage	F	VF	XF	Unc
AH1374-1955	—	—	50.00	85.00	150
AH1375-1956	—	—	3.00	7.00	15.00
AH1376-1957	—	—	2.00	6.00	12.00
AH1377-1958	—	—	2.00	6.00	12.00

KM# 382.1 5 PIASTRES
3.5000 g., 0.7200 Silver .0810 oz. ASW **Obv:** Denomination within wings **Rev:** Small sphinx without outlined base **Note:** Prev. KM#382.

Date	Mintage	F	VF	XF	Unc
AH1375-1956	—	BV	1.50	3.00	8.00
AH1376-1956	—	1.50	3.00	5.00	10.00
AH1376-1957	—	BV	1.50	3.00	8.00

KM# 382.2 5 PIASTRES
3.5000 g., 0.7200 Silver 0.081 oz. ASW **Obv:** Denomination within wings **Rev:** With outlined base

Date	Mintage	F	VF	XF	Unc
AH1375-1956	—	BV	1.50	3.00	8.00
AH1376-1957	—	1.50	3.00	5.00	10.00
AH1377-1958	—	BV	1.50	3.00	8.00

KM# 383 10 PIASTRES
7.0000 g., 0.6250 Silver .1406 oz. ASW **Obv:** Denomination within wings **Rev:** Large sphinx

Date	Mintage	F	VF	XF	Unc
AH1374-1955	1,408,000	2.00	4.00	9.00	18.00

Note: Varieties in date sizes exist

KM# 383a 10 PIASTRES
7.0000 g., 0.7200 Silver .1620 oz. ASW **Obv:** Denomination within wings **Rev:** Sphinx, dates

Date	Mintage	F	VF	XF	Unc
AH1375-1956	—	BV	3.50	7.00	15.00
AH1376-1957	—	BV	3.50	6.00	12.00

KM# 384 20 PIASTRES
14.0000 g., 0.7200 Silver .3241 oz. ASW **Obv:** Denomination within wings

Date	Mintage	F	VF	XF	Unc
AH1375-1956	—	BV	5.50	9.00	18.00

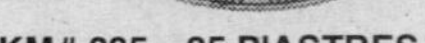

KM# 385 25 PIASTRES
17.5000 g., 0.7200 Silver .4051 oz. ASW, 35 mm. **Subject:** Suez Canal Nationalization **Obv:** Denomination and dates above wings **Rev:** Headquarter building in Port Said Rev. Designer: A. Wahba

Date	Mintage	F	VF	XF	Unc
AH1375-1956	258,000	BV	6.50	10.00	20.00

KM# 389 25 PIASTRES
17.5000 g., 0.7200 Silver .4051 oz. ASW, 35 mm. **Subject:** National Assembly Inauguration **Obv:** Denomination and dates above wings **Rev:** Radiant sun behind building Rev. Designer: A. Wahba

Date	Mintage	F	VF	XF	Unc
AH1376-1957	246,000	BV	6.00	9.00	17.00

KM# 386 50 PIASTRES
28.0000 g., 0.9000 Silver .8102 oz. ASW, 40 mm. **Subject:** Evacuation of the British **Obv:** Denomination and dates above wings **Rev:** Figure with torch and broken chains Rev. Designer: A. Wahba

Date	Mintage	F	VF	XF	Unc
AH1375-1956	250,000	BV	12.00	16.00	22.50

KM# 387 POUND
8.5000 g., 0.8750 Gold .2391 oz. AGW **Subject:** 3rd and 5th Anniversaries of Revolution **Obv:** Denomination and dates above wings **Rev:** Pharoah Ramses II in a war chariot

Date	Mintage	F	VF	XF	Unc
AH1374-1955	16,000	—	—	160	220
AH1377-1957	10,000	—	—	165	230

Note: Struck in red and yellow gold

KM# 388 5 POUNDS
42.5000 g., 0.8750 Gold 1.1957 oz. AGW **Subject:** 3rd and 5th Anniversaries of Revolution **Obv:** Denomination and dates above wings **Rev:** Horse, chariot, and archer

Date	Mintage	F	VF	XF	Unc
AH1374-1955	—	—	—	825	1,250
AH1377-1957	—	—	—	850	1,300

Note: Struck in red and yellow gold

UNITED ARAB REPUBLIC
AH1378-1391 / 1958-1971AD
DECIMAL COINAGE

KM# 393 MILLIEME
Aluminum-Bronze **Obv:** Denomination divides dates, legend above **Rev:** Eagle with shield on breast

Date	Mintage	F	VF	XF	Unc
AH1380-1960	—	—	0.10	0.15	0.30
AH1386-1966 Proof	—	Value: 3.00			

KM# 403 2 MILLIEMES
Aluminum-Bronze **Obv:** Denomination divides dates, legend above **Rev:** Eagle with shield on breast

Date	Mintage	F	VF	XF	Unc
AH1381-1962	—	—	0.15	0.35	0.65
AH1386-1966 Proof	—	Value: 3.00			

KM# 394 5 MILLIEMES
Aluminum-Bronze **Obv:** Denomination divides dates, legend above **Rev:** Eagle with shield on breast

Date	Mintage	F	VF	XF	Unc
AH1380-1960	—	—	0.15	0.45	0.85
AH1386-1966 Proof	—	Value: 3.00			

KM# 410 5 MILLIEMES
Aluminum

Date	Mintage	F	VF	XF	Unc
AH1386-1967	—	—	0.15	0.40	0.75

KM# 395 10 MILLIEMES
Aluminum-Bronze **Obv:** Denomination divides dates, legend above **Obv. Legend:** Misr **Rev:** Eagle with shield on breast

Date	Mintage	F	VF	XF	Unc
AH1377-1958	—	—	15.00	20.00	40.00
AH1380-1960	16,079,999	—	0.80	1.20	2.25
AH1386-1966 Proof	—	Value: 4.00			

KM# 396 10 MILLIEMES
Aluminum-Bronze **Obv:** Denomination divides dates, legend above, without Misr above denomination **Rev:** Eagle with shield on breast

Date	Mintage	F	VF	XF	Unc
AH1377-1958	—	—	15.00	25.00	40.00
AH1377-1958 Proof	—	Value: 300			

KM# 411 10 MILLIEMES
Aluminum **Obv:** Denomination divides dates **Rev:** Eagle with shield on breast

Date	Mintage	F	VF	XF	Unc
AH1386-1967	—	—	0.15	0.35	0.75

KM# 390 20 MILLIEMES
Aluminum-Bronze, 24 mm. **Subject:** Agriculture and Industrial Fair in Cairo **Obv:** Denomination divides dates, legend above **Rev:** Symbols of agriculture and industry

Date	Mintage	F	VF	XF	Unc
AH1378-1958	—	—	0.75	1.50	5.00

KM# 397 5 PIASTRES
3.5000 g., 0.7200 Silver .0810 oz. ASW **Obv:** Denomination divides dates, legend above **Rev:** Eagle with shield on breast

Date	Mintage	F	VF	XF	Unc
AH1380-1960	—	—	1.75	3.00	5.00
AH1386-1966	—	Value: 8.00			

KM# 404 5 PIASTRES
2.5000 g., 0.7200 Silver .0578 oz. ASW **Subject:** Diversion of the Nile **Obv:** Denomination divides dates, legend above **Rev:** Sadd el-Ali Dam, Nile River basin scene

Date	Mintage	F	VF	XF	Unc
AH1384-1964	500,000	—	1.25	2.50	4.00
AH1384-1964 Proof	2,000	Value: 8.00			

KM# 412 5 PIASTRES
Copper-Nickel, 25 mm. **Obv:** Denomination divides dates, legend above **Rev:** Eagle with shield on breast

Date	Mintage	F	VF	XF	Unc
AH1387-1967	10,800,000	—	0.50	0.75	1.50

Note: Edge varieties, narrow and gapped milling, exist

KM# 414 5 PIASTRES
Copper-Nickel **Subject:** International Industrial Fair **Obv:** Denomination, legend above **Rev:** Globe with cogwheel section around, dates below

Date	Mintage	F	VF	XF	Unc
AH1388-1968	500,000	—	0.75	1.00	2.50

KM# 417 5 PIASTRES
Copper-Nickel, 25 mm. **Subject:** 50th Anniversary - International Labor Organization **Obv:** Denomination, legend **Rev:** Hands holding open-ended wrenches within wreath, dates divided below

Date	Mintage	F	VF	XF	Unc
AH1389-1969	500,000	—	0.75	1.00	2.50

KM# 392 10 PIASTRES
7.0000 g., 0.7200 Silver .1620 oz. ASW, 24 mm. **Subject:** First Anniversary of U.A.R. Founding **Obv:** Denomination divides dates, legend above **Rev:** Eagle with shield on breast

Date	Mintage	F	VF	XF	Unc
AH1378-1959	—	—	3.25	6.00	17.50

KM# 398 10 PIASTRES
7.0000 g., 0.7200 Silver .1620 oz. ASW **Obv:** Denomination divides dates, legend above **Rev:** Eagle with shield on breast

Date	Mintage	F	VF	XF	Unc
AH1380-1960	500,000	—	3.00	4.50	7.50
AH1386-1966 Proof	—	Value: 12.50			

KM# 405 10 PIASTRES
5.0000 g., 0.7200 Silver .1157 oz. ASW **Subject:** Diversion of the Nile **Obv:** Denomination divides dates, legend above **Rev:** Sadd el-Ali Dam, Nile River basin scene

Date	Mintage	F	VF	XF	Unc
AH1384-1964 Proof	2,000	Value: 12.50			
AH1384-1964	500,000	—	2.50	3.50	6.00

KM# 413 10 PIASTRES
Copper-Nickel, 27 mm. **Obv:** Denomination divides dates, legend above **Rev:** Eagle with shield on breast

Date	Mintage	F	VF	XF	Unc
AH1387-1967	13,200,000	—	0.60	0.90	2.00

KM# 419 10 PIASTRES
Copper-Nickel **Subject:** Cairo International Agricultural Fair **Obv:** Denomination divides dates, legend above **Rev:** Grain sprig above globe and name

Date	Mintage	F	VF	XF	Unc
AH1389-1969	1,000,000	—	0.75	1.25	3.00

KM# 418 10 PIASTRES
Copper-Nickel **Series:** F.A.O. **Obv:** Denomination divides dates, legend above **Rev:** People with oxen, eagle above, logo below

Date	Mintage	F	VF	XF	Unc
ND(1970)	500,000	—	0.75	1.25	3.50

KM# 420 10 PIASTRES
Copper-Nickel **Subject:** 50 Years - Banque Misr **Obv:** Crowned head within wreath left of denomination and date **Rev:** Sun above building

Date	Mintage	F	VF	XF	Unc
AH1390-1970	500,000	—	0.60	1.00	2.00

KM# 421.1 10 PIASTRES
Copper-Nickel **Subject:** Cairo International Industrial Fair **Obv:** Denomination **Rev:** Ship within cogwheel, dates in box below

Date	Mintage	F	VF	XF	Unc
AH1390-1970	500,000	—	0.60	1.00	3.25

KM# 421.2 10 PIASTRES
Copper-Nickel, 27 mm. **Subject:** Cairo International Industrial Fair **Obv:** New shorter Arabic inscriptions, denomination at center **Rev:** Ship within cogwheel, dates in box below

Date	Mintage	F	VF	XF	Unc
AH1391-1971	500,000	—	0.60	1.00	2.75

KM# 399 20 PIASTRES
14.0000 g., 0.7200 Silver .3241 oz. ASW **Obv:** Denomination divides dates, legend above **Rev:** Eagle with shield on breast

Date	Mintage	F	VF	XF	Unc
AH1380-1960	400,000	—	7.00	15.00	25.00
AH1386-1966 Proof	—	Value: 32.50			

KM# 400 25 PIASTRES
17.5000 g., 0.7200 Silver .4051 oz. ASW **Subject:** 3rd Year of National Assembly **Obv:** Denomination and dates above wings **Rev:** Radiant sun back of building, hand on book in front

Date	Mintage	F	VF	XF	Unc
AH1380-1960	250,000	—	6.50	9.00	18.00

KM# 406 25 PIASTRES
10.0000 g., 0.7200 Silver .2315 oz. ASW **Subject:** Diversion of the Nile **Obv:** Denomination divides dates, legend above **Rev:** Sadd el-Ali Dam, Nile River basin scene

Date	Mintage	F	VF	XF	Unc
AH1384-1964	250,000	—	3.75	5.50	9.50
AH1384-1964 Proof	2,000	Value: 35.00			

KM# 422 25 PIASTRES
6.0000 g., 0.7200 Silver .1388 oz. ASW **Subject:** President Nasser **Obv:** Head of President Nasser right

Date	Mintage	F	VF	XF	Unc
AH1390-1970	700 000	—	2.50	4.00	6.50

KM# 407 50 PIASTRES
20.0000 g., 0.7200 Silver .4630 oz. ASW **Subject:** Diversion of the Nile **Rev:** Nile River basin scene

Date	Mintage	F	VF	XF	Unc
AH1384-1964	250,000	—	6.50	8.00	10.00
AH1384-1964 Proof	2,000	Value: 40.00			

KM# 423 50 PIASTRES
12.5000 g., 0.7200 Silver .2893 oz. ASW **Subject:** President Nasser **Obv:** Head of President Nasser right **Rev:** Denomination and dates

Date	Mintage	F	VF	XF	Unc
AH1390-1970	400,000	—	4.50	6.00	9.00

KM# 391 1/2 POUND
4.2500 g., 0.8750 Gold .1195 oz. AGW, 20 mm. **Subject:** U.A.R. Founding **Obv:** Denomination and dates above wings **Rev:** Pharoah Ramses II in a war chariot

Date	Mintage	F	VF	XF	Unc
AH1377-1958	30,000	—	—	—	185

KM# 401 POUND
8.5000 g., 0.8750 Gold .2391 oz. AGW **Rev:** Aswan Dam

Date	Mintage	F	VF	XF	Unc
AH1379-1960	252,000	—	—	—	170

KM# 415 POUND
25.0000 g., 0.7200 Silver .5787 oz. ASW **Obv:** Denomination and dates **Rev:** Power station for Aswan Dam, grain sprigs flank

Date	Mintage	F	VF	XF	Unc
AH1387-1968	100,000	—	8.00	9.00	12.00

KM# 424 POUND
25.0000 g., 0.7200 Silver .5787 oz. ASW **Subject:** 1000th Anniversary - Al Azhar Mosque **Obv:** Center circle divides dates **Rev:** Al Azhar Mosque

Date	Mintage	F	VF	XF	Unc
AH1359-1361 - 1970-1972	100,000	—	8.00	9.50	13.00

KM# 425 POUND
25.0000 g., 0.7200 Silver .5787 oz. ASW **Subject:** President Nasser **Obv:** Head of President Nasser right **Rev:** Denomination divides dates, legend above

Date	Mintage	F	VF	XF	Unc
AH1390-1970	400,000	—	8.00	9.00	12.00

KM# 426 POUND
8.0000 g., 0.8750 Gold .2251 oz. AGW **Subject:** President Nasser **Obv:** Head of President Nasser right **Rev:** Denomination divides dates, legend above

Date	Mintage	F	VF	XF	Unc
AH1390-1970	10,000	—	—	—	160

KM# 402 5 POUNDS
42.5000 g., 0.8750 Gold 1.1957 oz. AGW **Obv:** Denomination and dates above wings **Rev:** Aswan Dam

Date	Mintage	F	VF	XF	Unc
AH1379-1960	5,000	—	—	—	800

KM# 408 5 POUNDS
26.0000 g., 0.8750 Gold .7315 oz. AGW **Subject:** Diversion of the Nile **Obv:** Denomination divides dates, legend above **Rev:** Nile River basin scene

Date	Mintage	F	VF	XF	Unc
AH1384-1964	—	—	—	—	520

KM# 416 5 POUNDS
26.0000 g., 0.8750 Gold .7315 oz. AGW **Subject:** 1400th Anniversary of the Koran **Obv:** Denomination and dates within center circle **Rev:** Open Koran book above globe with radiant sun in back

Date	Mintage	F	VF	XF	Unc
AH1388-1968	10,000	—	—	—	500

KM# 427 5 POUNDS
26.0000 g., 0.8750 Gold .7315 oz. AGW **Subject:** 1000th Anniversary - Al Azhar Mosque **Rev:** Al Azhar Mosque

Date	Mintage	F	VF	XF	Unc
AH1390-1970	—	—	—	—	510

KM# 428 5 POUNDS
26.0000 g., 0.8750 Gold .7315 oz. AGW **Subject:** President Nasser **Obv:** Head of President Nasser right

Date	Mintage	F	VF	XF	Unc
AH1390-1970	3,000	—	—	—	510

KM# 409 10 POUNDS
52.0000 g., 0.8750 Gold 1.4630 oz. AGW **Subject:** Diversion of the Nile **Obv:** Denomination divides dates **Rev:** Nile River basin scene

Date	Mintage	F	VF	XF	Unc
AH1384-1964	2,000	—	—	—	1,000

ARAB REPUBLIC
AH1391- / 1971- AD

DECIMAL COINAGE

KM# A423 MILLIEME
Aluminum **Obv:** Denomination divides dates, legend above **Rev:** Eagle with shield on breast

Date	Mintage	F	VF	XF	Unc
AH1392-1972	—	—	0.10	0.30	0.50

KM# A424 5 MILLIEMES
Aluminum **Obv:** Denomination divides dates, legend above **Rev:** Corn ears and grain sprigs encircle figure below sun **Note:** Mule.

Date	Mintage	F	VF	XF	Unc
AH1392-1972	—	—	10.00	20.00	45.00

KM# A425 5 MILLIEMES

Aluminum **Obv:** Denomination divides dates, legend above **Rev:** Eagle with shield on breast

Date	Mintage	F	VF	XF	Unc
AH1392-1972	16,000,000	—	0.20	0.50	2.50

KM# 432 5 MILLIEMES

2.0000 g., Brass, 18 mm. **Obv:** Denomination divides dates, legend above **Rev:** Eagle with shield on breast

Date	Mintage	F	VF	XF	Unc
AH1393-1973	—	—	0.10	0.15	0.30

KM# A433 5 MILLIEMES

Aluminum, 18 mm. **Obv:** Denomination divides dates, legend above **Rev:** Eagle with shield on breast **Note:** Mule.

Date	Mintage	F	VF	XF	Unc
AH1393-1973	—	—	10.00	20.00	45.00

KM# 433 5 MILLIEMES

Aluminum **Series:** F.A.O. **Obv:** Denomination divides dates, legend above **Rev:** Corn ears and grain sprigs encircle figure below sun

Date	Mintage	F	VF	XF	Unc
AH1393-1973	10,000,000	—	0.10	0.20	0.35

KM# 434 5 MILLIEMES

2.0000 g., Brass, 18 mm. **Obv:** Denomination divides dates, legend above **Rev:** Nefertiti head right and grain sprig **Note:** Mule.

Date	Mintage	F	VF	XF	Unc
AH1393-1973	—	—	5.00	10.00	20.00

KM# 445 5 MILLIEMES

Brass, 18 mm. **Series:** International Women's Year **Obv:** Denomination divides dates, legend above **Rev:** Nefertiti head right and grain sprig

Date	Mintage	F	VF	XF	Unc
AH1395-1975	10,000,000	—	0.10	0.15	0.30

KM# 462 5 MILLIEMES

Brass, 18 mm. **Series:** F.A.O. **Obv:** Denomination divides dates, legend above **Rev:** People, animals, and building

Date	Mintage	F	VF	XF	Unc
AH1397-1977	5,000,000	—	0.10	0.20	0.50

KM# 463 5 MILLIEMES

Brass **Subject:** 1971 Corrective Revolution **Obv:** Denomination divides dates, legend above **Rev:** City scene

Date	Mintage	F	VF	XF	Unc
AH1397-1977	2,500,000	—	0.10	0.20	0.50
AH1399-1979	2,500,000	—	0.10	0.20	0.50

KM# A426 10 MILLIEMES

Aluminum, 21 mm.

Date	Mintage	F	VF	XF	Unc
AH1392-1972	20,000,000	—	0.50	2.00	6.00

Note: Two varieties of edge letterings exist

KM# 435 10 MILLIEMES

3.2000 g., Brass, 21 mm.

Date	Mintage	F	VF	XF	Unc
AH1393-1973	—	—	0.10	0.25	0.50
AH1396-1976	—	—	0.75	1.50	3.00

KM# 446 10 MILLIEMES

Brass, 21 mm. **Series:** F.A.O. **Obv:** Denomination divides dates, legend above **Rev:** Family scene

Date	Mintage	F	VF	XF	Unc
AH1395-1975	10,000,000	—	0.10	0.20	0.35

KM# 449 10 MILLIEMES

Brass, 21 mm. **Series:** F.A.O. **Obv:** Denomination divides dates, legend above **Rev:** Osiris seated, wheat ear at right

Date	Mintage	F	VF	XF	Unc
AH1396-1976	10,000,000	—	0.10	0.20	0.30

KM# 464 10 MILLIEMES

Brass, 21 mm. **Series:** F.A.O. **Obv:** Denomination divides dates, legend above **Rev:** Various laborers surround center design

Date	Mintage	F	VF	XF	Unc
AH1397-1977	10,000,000	—	0.10	0.20	0.85

KM# 465 10 MILLIEMES

Brass, 21 mm. **Subject:** 1971 Corrective Revolution **Obv:** Denomination divides dates, legend above **Rev:** Date and denomination left of head

Date	Mintage	F	VF	XF	Unc
AH1397-1977	2,500,000	—	0.10	0.20	0.65
AH1399-1979	2,500,000	—	0.20	0.40	1.00

KM# 476 10 MILLIEMES

Brass, 21 mm. **Series:** F.A.O. **Obv:** Denomination divides dates, legend above **Rev:** Woman looking into microscope

Date	Mintage	F	VF	XF	Unc
AH1398-1978	2,000,000	—	0.10	0.20	0.80

KM# 483 10 MILLIEMES

Brass, 21 mm. **Series:** International Year of the Child **Obv:** Denomination divides dates, legend above **Rev:** Seated woman and child

Date	Mintage	F	VF	XF	Unc
AH1399-1979	2,000,000	—	0.10	0.20	0.65

KM# 498 10 MILLIEMES

Aluminum-Bronze, 21 mm. **Subject:** Sadat's Corrective Revolution **Obv:** Fist raised holding grain stalk **Rev:** Denomination divides dates, legend above

Date	Mintage	F	VF	XF	Unc
AH1400-1980	2,500,000	—	0.10	0.25	1.00

KM# 499 10 MILLIEMES

Aluminum-Bronze, 21 mm. **Series:** F.A.O.

Date	Mintage	F	VF	XF	Unc
AH1400-1980	2,000,000	—	0.10	0.20	0.60

KM# 553.1 PIASTRE

Aluminum-Bronze, 18 mm. **Obv:** Christian date left of denomination, tughra above **Rev:** Pyramids

Date	Mintage	F	VF	XF	Unc
AH1404-1984	—	—	—	0.15	0.35

KM# 553.2 PIASTRE

Aluminum-Bronze, 18 mm. **Obv:** Islamic date left of denomination, tughra above **Rev:** Pyramids

Date	Mintage	F	VF	XF	Unc
AH1404-1984	—	—	—	0.15	0.35

KM# 500 2 PIASTRES

4.9000 g., Aluminum-Bronze, 21 mm.

Date	Mintage	F	VF	XF	Unc
AH1400-1980	—	—	0.20	0.30	0.60

KM# 554.1 2 PIASTRES

4.9000 g., Aluminum-Bronze, 21 mm. **Obv:** Christian date left of denomination

Date	Mintage	F	VF	XF	Unc
AH1404-1984	—	—	—	0.20	0.50

KM# 554.2 2 PIASTRES

4.9000 g., Aluminum-Bronze, 21 mm. **Obv:** Islamic date left of denomination

Date	Mintage	F	VF	XF	Unc
AH1404-1984	—	—	—	0.20	0.50

KM# A427 5 PIASTRES

Copper-Nickel, 24.5 mm. **Subject:** 25th Anniversary of UNICEF

Date	Mintage	F	VF	XF	Unc
AH1392-1972	500,000	—	0.75	1.00	3.00

Note: Error in spelling "UNICFE".

KM# A428 5 PIASTRES

4.5000 g., Copper-Nickel, 25 mm. **Obv:** Denomination divides dates, legend above **Rev:** Islamic falcon

Date	Mintage	F	VF	XF	Unc
AH1392-1972	—	—	0.50	0.75	2.00

KM# 436 5 PIASTRES
Copper-Nickel, 25 mm. **Subject:** Cairo State Fair **Obv:** Denomination divides dates, legend above **Rev:** Stylized design

Date	Mintage	F	VF	XF	Unc
AH1393-1973	500,000	—	0.60	0.75	2.25

KM# 437 5 PIASTRES
Copper-Nickel, 25 mm. **Subject:** 75th Anniversary - National Bank of Egypt **Obv:** Denomination divides dates, legend above **Rev:** Bank building in front of globe at left

Date	Mintage	F	VF	XF	Unc
AH1393-1973	1,000,000	—	0.60	0.75	2.00

KM# A441 5 PIASTRES
Copper-Nickel, 25 mm. **Subject:** First Anniversary - October War **Obv:** Denomination divides dates, legend above **Rev:** Soldier with gun facing right

Date	Mintage	F	VF	XF	Unc
AH1394-1974	2,000,000	—	0.60	0.75	2.00

KM# 447 5 PIASTRES
Copper-Nickel, 25 mm. **Series:** International Women's Year **Obv:** Denomination divides dates, legend above **Rev:** Bust of Nefertiti right, grain sprig at left

Date	Mintage	F	VF	XF	Unc
AH1395-1975	2,000,000	—	0.50	0.65	1.25

KM# 451 5 PIASTRES
Copper-Nickel, 25 mm. **Subject:** 1976 Cairo Trade Fair **Obv:** Denomination divides dates, legend above **Rev:** Legend forms square around design, florals flank

Date	Mintage	F	VF	XF	Unc
AH1396-1976	500,000	—	0.60	0.75	2.00

KM# 450 5 PIASTRES
Copper-Nickel, 25 mm. **Obv:** Denomination divides dates, legend above **Rev:** Islamic falcon **Note:** Mule.

Date	Mintage	F	VF	XF	Unc
AH1396-1976	—	—	5.00	10.00	20.00

KM# 466 5 PIASTRES
Copper-Nickel, 25 mm. **Subject:** 1971 Corrective Revolution

Date	Mintage	F	VF	XF	Unc
AH1397-1977	1,000,000	—	0.50	0.60	1.50
AH1399-1979	—	—	0.50	0.60	1.25

KM# 467 5 PIASTRES
Copper-Nickel, 25 mm. **Subject:** 50th Anniversary - Textile Industry **Obv:** Crowned head within wreath at right of denomination and dates **Rev:** Figure between dates

Date	Mintage	F	VF	XF	Unc
AH1397-1977	1,000,000	—	0.50	0.75	1.65

KM# 468 5 PIASTRES
Copper-Nickel, 25 mm. **Series:** F.A.O. **Obv:** Denomination divides dates, legend above **Rev:** People, animals, and building

Date	Mintage	F	VF	XF	Unc
AH1397-1977	—	—	0.50	0.75	1.65

Note: Edge varieties exist

KM# 477 5 PIASTRES
Copper-Nickel, 25 mm. **Subject:** Portland Cement **Obv:** Denomination divides dates, legend above **Rev:** Cement factory, dates at top

Date	Mintage	F	VF	XF	Unc
AH1398-1978	500,000	—	0.50	0.75	1.65

KM# 478 5 PIASTRES
Copper-Nickel, 25 mm. **Series:** F.A.O. **Obv:** Denomination divides dates, legend above **Rev:** Woman looking into microscope

Date	Mintage	F	VF	XF	Unc
AH1398-1978	1,000,000	—	0.50	0.75	1.65

KM# 484 5 PIASTRES
Copper-Nickel, 25 mm. **Series:** International Year of the Child **Obv:** Denomination divides dates, legend above **Rev:** Woman seated with child

Date	Mintage	F	VF	XF	Unc
AH1399-1979	1,000,000	—	0.50	0.75	1.65

KM# 501 5 PIASTRES
Copper-Nickel, 25 mm. **Subject:** Applied Professions **Obv:** Denomination divides dates, legend above **Rev:** Various professions depicted, date and shield below

Date	Mintage	F	VF	XF	Unc
AH1400-1980	500,000	—	0.50	0.75	1.35

KM# 502 5 PIASTRES
Copper-Nickel, 25 mm. **Subject:** Sadat's Corrective Revolution of May 15, 1971 **Obv:** Denomination divides dates, legend above **Rev:** Raised fist holding stalk of grain

Date	Mintage	F	VF	XF	Unc
AH1400-1980	1,000,000	—	0.50	0.75	1.75

KM# 555.1 5 PIASTRES
Aluminum-Bronze **Obv:** Christian date left of denomination, tughra above **Rev:** Pyramids

Date	Mintage	F	VF	XF	Unc
AH1404-1984	—	—	—	0.25	0.75

Note: Varieties exist with wide and narrow rims

KM# 555.2 5 PIASTRES
Aluminum-Bronze **Obv:** Islamic date left of denomination, tughra above **Rev:** Pyramids

Date	Mintage	F	VF	XF	Unc
AH1404-1984	—	—	—	0.25	0.75

KM# 622.1 5 PIASTRES
Aluminum-Bronze **Obv:** Tughra below dates and denomination, denomination not shaded **Rev:** Pyramids

Date	Mintage	F	VF	XF	Unc
AH1404-1984	—	—	—	0.25	0.85

KM# 622.2 5 PIASTRES
Aluminum-Bronze, 23 mm. **Obv:** Denomination shaded, tughra below **Rev:** Pyramids

Date	Mintage	F	VF	XF	Unc
AH1404-1984	—	—	—	0.25	0.85

KM# 731 5 PIASTRES
Brass, 21 mm. **Obv:** Denomination divides dates, legend above **Rev:** Decorated vase

Date	Mintage	F	VF	XF	Unc
AH1413-1992	—	—	—	—	0.85

KM# 429 10 PIASTRES
Copper-Nickel, 27 mm. **Subject:** Cairo International Fair **Obv:** Denomination, legend **Rev:** Dates in box below ship with mast

Date	Mintage	F	VF	XF	Unc
AH1392-1972	500,000	—	0.60	1.00	2.50

KM# 430 10 PIASTRES
Copper-Nickel, 27 mm. **Rev:** Islamic falcon

Date	Mintage	F	VF	XF	Unc
AH1392-1972	—	—	0.60	1.00	4.00

KM# 431 10 PIASTRES
Copper-Nickel, 27 mm. **Obv:** Denomination divides dates, legend above **Rev:** Islamic falcon **Note:** Mule.

Date	Mintage	F	VF	XF	Unc
AH1392-1972	—	—	5.50	17.50	27.50

Note: Wide and narrow inscriptions exist for obverse

KM# 442 10 PIASTRES
Copper-Nickel, 27 mm. **Subject:** First Anniversary - October War **Obv:** Denomination divides dates, legend above **Rev:** Wreath above 3/4 figure of soldier, dates below

Date	Mintage	F	VF	XF	Unc
AH1394-1974	2,000,000	—	0.60	1.00	4.00

KM# 448 10 PIASTRES
Copper-Nickel, 27 mm. **Series:** F.A.O. **Obv:** Denomination divides dates, legend above **Rev:** Family scene

Date	Mintage	F	VF	XF	Unc
AH1395-1975	2,000,000	—	0.60	1.00	4.00

KM# 452 10 PIASTRES
Copper-Nickel, 27 mm. **Subject:** Reopening of the Suez Canal **Obv:** Denomination divides dates, legend above **Rev:** Canal scene

Date	Mintage	F	VF	XF	Unc
AH1396-1976	5,000,000	—	0.60	1.00	4.00

Note: Wide and narrow inscriptions exist for the obverse

KM# 469 10 PIASTRES
Copper-Nickel, 27 mm. **Series:** F.A.O. **Obv:** Denomination divides dates, legend above **Rev:** Various laborers surround center design

Date	Mintage	F	VF	XF	Unc
AH1397-1977	1,000,000	—	0.60	1.00	3.00

KM# 470 10 PIASTRES
Copper-Nickel, 27 mm. **Subject:** 1971 Corrective Revolution **Obv:** Denomination divides dates, legend above **Rev:** Date and denomination left of head

Date	Mintage	F	VF	XF	Unc
AH1397-1977	1,000,000	—	0.50	0.85	3.00
AH1399-1979	1,000,000	—	0.50	0.85	3.00

KM# 471 10 PIASTRES
Copper-Nickel, 27 mm. **Subject:** 20th Anniversary - Economic Union

Date	Mintage	F	VF	XF	Unc
AH1397-1977	1,000,000	—	0.50	0.85	3.00

KM# 479 10 PIASTRES
Copper-Nickel, 27 mm. **Subject:** Cairo International Fair **Obv:** Denomination divides dates, legend above **Rev:** Legend forms square around design at top

Date	Mintage	F	VF	XF	Unc
AH1398-1978	—	—	0.50	0.85	3.50

KM# 485 10 PIASTRES
Copper-Nickel, 27 mm. **Subject:** 25th Anniversary of Abbasia Mint **Obv:** Denomination divides dates, legend above **Rev:** Dates at top corners of building, cogwheel design above

Date	Mintage	F	VF	XF	Unc
AH1399-1979	1,000,000	—	0.50	0.85	3.00

KM# 486 10 PIASTRES
Copper-Nickel, 27 mm. **Subject:** National Education Day **Obv:** Denomination divides dates, legend above **Rev:** Teachers, back to back and students, wreath in background

Date	Mintage	F	VF	XF	Unc
AH1399-1979	1,000,000	—	0.50	0.85	3.00

KM# 503 10 PIASTRES
Copper-Nickel, 27 mm. **Subject:** Doctor's Day **Obv:** Denomination divides dates, legend above **Rev:** Seated Egyptian healer with staff left

Date	Mintage	F	VF	XF	Unc
AH1400-1980	1,000,000	—	0.50	0.85	3.00

KM# 504 10 PIASTRES
Copper-Nickel, 27 mm. **Subject:** Egyptian-Israeli Peace Treaty **Obv:** Denomination divides dates, legend above **Rev:** Anwar Sadat at right facing left, dove of peace, hand with quill signing treaty

Date	Mintage	F	VF	XF	Unc
AH1400-1980	1,000,000	—	1.00	2.00	4.50

KM# 505 10 PIASTRES
Copper-Nickel, 27 mm. **Series:** F.A.O.

Date	Mintage	F	VF	XF	Unc
AH1400-1980	1,000,000	—	0.50	0.85	3.00

KM# 506 10 PIASTRES
Copper-Nickel, 27 mm. **Series:** F.A.O. **Subject:** Sadat's Corrective Revolution of May 15, 1971 **Obv:** Denomination divides dates, legend above **Rev:** Raised fist with grain stalk

Date	Mintage	F	VF	XF	Unc
AH1400-1980	1,000,000	—	0.50	0.85	3.00
AH1401-1981	—	—	0.60	1.20	3.50

KM# 520 10 PIASTRES
Copper-Nickel, 27 mm. **Subject:** Scientist's Day **Obv:** Denomination, seated figure at left **Rev:** Cogwheel center of spray below sun and satellite dish

Date	Mintage	F	VF	XF	Unc
AH1401-1981	—	—	0.50	0.85	3.00

KM# 521 10 PIASTRES
Copper-Nickel, 27 mm. **Subject:** 25th Anniversary - Trade Unions **Obv:** Denomination divides dates, legend above **Rev:** Half cogwheel above shield

Date	Mintage	F	VF	XF	Unc
AH1402-1981	—	—	1.00	2.00	4.50

KM# 599 10 PIASTRES
Copper-Nickel, 27 mm. **Subject:** 50th Anniversary of Egyptian Products Co. **Obv:** Denomination divides dates, legend above **Rev:** Head within crowned wreath at top, triangle in background

Date	Mintage	F	VF	XF	Unc
AH1402-1982	—	—	0.50	0.85	3.00

KM# 556 10 PIASTRES
Copper-Nickel, 25 mm. **Obv:** Denomination divides dates, legend above **Rev:** Mohamad Ali Mosque

Date	Mintage	F	VF	XF	Unc
AH1404-1984	—	—	—	0.50	1.00

KM# 570 10 PIASTRES
Copper-Nickel, 25 mm. **Subject:** 25th Anniversary - National Planning Institute **Obv:** Arabic legends, dates below **Rev:** Shield divides dates

Date	Mintage	F	VF	XF	Unc
AH1405-1985	100,000	—	—	—	2.00

KM# 573 10 PIASTRES
Copper-Nickel, 25 mm. **Subject:** 60th Anniversary - Egyptian Parliament **Obv:** Arabic legends, dates below **Rev:** Dates above building

Date	Mintage	F	VF	XF	Unc
AH1405-1985	250,000	—	—	—	2.00

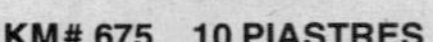

KM# 675 10 PIASTRES
Copper-Nickel, 25 mm. **Subject:** 1973 October War **Obv:** Tughra below dates, denomination at right **Rev:** Figure with flag left, building at right, dates below

Date	Mintage	F	VF	XF	Unc
AH1410-1989	250,000	—	—	—	2.00

KM# 732 10 PIASTRES
Brass, 23 mm. **Obv:** Denomination divides dates, legend above **Rev:** Mohamad Ali Mosque

Date	Mintage	F	VF	XF	Unc
AH1413-1992	—	—	—	—	2.00

KM# 507 20 PIASTRES
10.0000 g., Copper-Nickel, 30 mm. **Obv:** Denomination divides dates, legend above **Rev:** Eagle with shield on breast

Date	Mintage	F	VF	XF	Unc
AH1400-1980	—	—	0.75	1.00	3.00

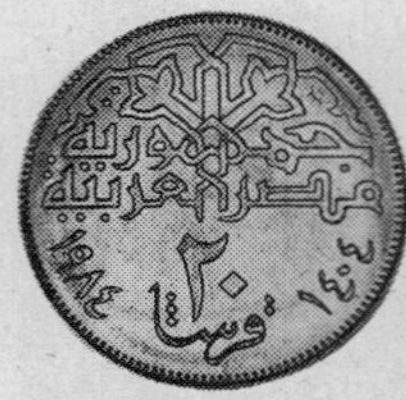

KM# 557 20 PIASTRES
6.0000 g., Copper-Nickel, 27 mm. **Obv:** Denomination divides dates, legend above **Obv. Legend:** Mohammad Ali Mosque **Rev:** Mohammad Ali Mosque

Date	Mintage	F	VF	XF	Unc
AH1404-1984	—	—	—	0.70	2.00

KM# 596 20 PIASTRES
6.0000 g., Copper-Nickel, 27 mm. **Subject:** 25th Anniversary - Cairo International Airport **Obv:** Arabic legends, dates below **Rev:** Birds in flight, wings and tails form diamond at center

Date	Mintage	F	VF	XF	Unc
AH1405-1985	50,000	—	—	—	5.00

KM# 597 20 PIASTRES
Copper-Nickel, 27 mm. **Subject:** Professions **Obv:** Arabic legends, dates below **Rev:** People doing various jobs

Date	Mintage	F	VF	XF	Unc
AH1406-1985	100,000	—	—	—	3.00

KM# 606 20 PIASTRES
Copper-Nickel, 27 mm. **Subject:** Soldiers **Obv:** Arabic legends, dates below **Rev:** Torch on crossed swords within wreath

Date	Mintage	F	VF	XF	Unc
AH1406-1986	50,000	—	—	—	5.00

KM# 607 20 PIASTRES
Copper-Nickel, 27 mm. **Subject:** Census **Obv:** Arabic legends, dates below **Rev:** City scene

Date	Mintage	F	VF	XF	Unc
AH1407-1986	500,000	—	—	—	3.00

KM# 652 20 PIASTRES
Copper-Nickel, 27 mm. **Subject:** Investment Bank **Obv:** Tughra divides dates **Rev:** Design in center of toothed circle, within circle

Date	Mintage	F	VF	XF	Unc
AH1407-1987	250,000	—	—	—	3.00

KM# 646 20 PIASTRES
Copper-Nickel, 27 mm. **Subject:** Police Day **Obv:** Arabic legends, dates below **Rev:** Eagle with wings spread on pedestal within wreath

Date	Mintage	F	VF	XF	Unc
AH1408-1988	250,000	—	—	—	3.00

KM# 650 20 PIASTRES
Copper-Nickel, 27 mm. **Subject:** Dedication of Cairo Opera House **Obv:** Arabic legends, dates below **Rev:** Building

Date	Mintage	F	VF	XF	Unc
AH1409-1988	250,000	—	—	—	3.00

KM# 676 20 PIASTRES
Copper-Nickel, 27 mm. **Subject:** 1973 October War **Obv:** Tughra below denomination and dates **Rev:** Figure with flag at left, building at right, dates below

Date	Mintage	F	VF	XF	Unc
AH1410-1989	250,000	—	—	—	3.00

KM# 685 20 PIASTRES
Copper-Nickel, 27 mm. **Subject:** National Health Insurance **Obv:** Denomination and dates within circle at top **Rev:** People within half moon design at left, rock in background, dates below

Date	Mintage	F	VF	XF	Unc
AH1409-1989	250,000	—	—	—	3.00

KM# 690 20 PIASTRES
Copper-Nickel, 25 mm. **Subject:** Cairo Subway **Obv:** Four patterned tiles divide dates **Rev:** Designs within circles flank 3/4 wreath surrounding train

Date	Mintage	F	VF	XF	Unc
AH1409-1989	250,000	—	—	—	3.00

KM# 733 20 PIASTRES
Copper-Nickel, 25 mm. **Subject:** Mosque **Obv:** Denomination divides dates Rev. Designer: Buildings with towers

Date	Mintage	F	VF	XF	Unc
AH1413-1992	—	—	—	—	2.50

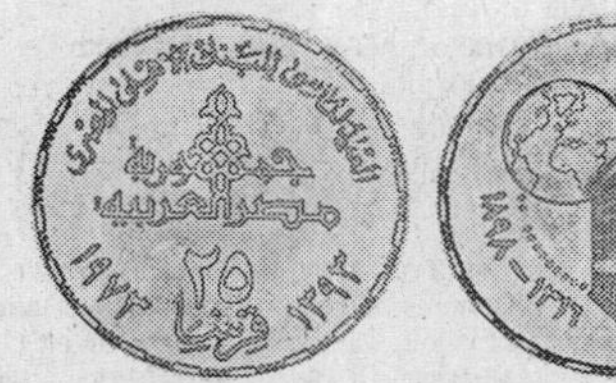

KM# 438 25 PIASTRES
6.0000 g., 0.7200 Silver .1388 oz. ASW **Subject:** 75th Anniversary - National Bank of Egypt **Obv:** Denomination divides dates **Rev:** National Bank building, globe at back, divides dates

Date	Mintage	F	VF	XF	Unc
AH1393-1973	100,000	—	4.00	6.00	9.00

KM# 734 25 PIASTRES
Copper-Nickel, 734 mm. **Obv:** Chain surrounds center hole, dates below **Rev:** Chain surrounds center hole, denomination below

Date	Mintage	F	VF	XF	Unc
AH1413-1993	—	—	—	—	2.75

KM# 834 1/2 POUND
4.0000 g., 0.8750 Gold .1125 oz. AGW **Subject:** El Akkad **Obv:** Legend and vase **Rev:** Portrait

Date	Mintage	F	VF	XF	Unc
AH1413-1992	600	—	—	—	250

KM# 809 1/2 POUND
4.0000 g., 0.8750 Gold .1125 oz. AGW **Subject:** 20th Anniversary - October War **Obv:** Smoking chimney text **Rev:** Soldier with flag

Date	Mintage	F	VF	XF	Unc
AH1414-1993	Est. 5,000	—	—	—	250

KM# 760 1/2 POUND
4.0000 g., 0.8750 Gold .1125 oz. AGW **Subject:** Salah El Din El-Ayubi **Obv:** Denomination **Rev:** Portrait

Date	Mintage	F	VF	XF	Unc
AH1414-1994	500	—	—	—	250

KM# 439 POUND
25.0000 g., 0.7200 Silver .5787 oz. ASW **Series:** F.A.O. **Obv:** Denomination divides dates, legend above **Rev:** Corn ears and grain sprigs flank Aswan Dam

Date	Mintage	F	VF	XF	Unc
AH1393-1973	50,000	—	8.00	9.00	15.00

KM# 440 POUND
8.0000 g., 0.8750 Gold .2250 oz. AGW **Subject:** 75th Anniversary - National Bank of Egypt **Obv:** Denomination divides dates **Rev:** National Bank of Egypt building, globe at back, divides dates

Date	Mintage	F	VF	XF	Unc
AH1393-1973	7,000	—	—	—	160

KM# 443 POUND
15.0000 g., 0.7200 Silver .3472 oz. ASW **Subject:** First Anniversary - October War **Obv:** Denomination divides dates **Rev:** Half-figure of soldier within 3/4 wreath above

Date	Mintage	F	VF	XF	Unc
AH1394-1974	50,000	—	—	—	20.00

KM# 453 POUND
15.0000 g., 0.7200 Silver .3472 oz. ASW **Series:** F.A.O. **Obv:** Denomination divides dates **Rev:** Osiris seated, wheat sprig at right

Date	Mintage	F	VF	XF	Unc
AH1396-1976	50,000	—	—	—	20.00

KM# 454 POUND
15.0000 g., 0.7200 Silver .3472 oz. ASW **Subject:** Reopening of Suez Canal **Obv:** Denomination divides dates **Rev:** Sun above canal scene

Date	Mintage	F	VF	XF	Unc
AH1396-1976	250,000	—	—	—	10.00

KM# 455 POUND
15.0000 g., 0.7200 Silver .3472 oz. ASW **Rev:** Om Kalsoum right, singer, music symbol in hair

Date	Mintage	F	VF	XF	Unc
AH1396-1976	250,000	—	—	—	10.00

KM# 456 POUND
8.0000 g., 0.8750 Gold .2250 oz. AGW **Rev:** Om Kalsoum right

Date	Mintage	F	VF	XF	Unc
AH1396-1976	5,000	—	—	—	170

KM# 457 POUND
15.0000 g., 0.7200 Silver .3472 oz. ASW **Obv:** Denomination divides dates **Rev:** Bust of King Faisal half right

Date	Mintage	F	VF	XF	Unc
AH1396-1976	100,000	—	—	—	10.00

KM# 458 POUND
8.0000 g., 0.8750 Gold .2250 oz. AGW **Obv:** Denomination divides dates **Rev:** Bust of King Faisal half right

Date	Mintage	F	VF	XF	Unc
AH1396-1976	8,000	—	—	—	165

KM# 472 POUND
15.0000 g., 0.7200 Silver .3472 oz. ASW **Series:** F.A.O. **Obv:** Denomination divides dates **Rev:** Various laborers surround center design

Date	Mintage	F	VF	XF	Unc
AH1397-1977	50,000	—	—	—	10.00

KM# 473 POUND
15.0000 g., 0.7200 Silver .3472 oz. ASW **Subject:** 1971 Corrective Revolution **Obv:** Denomination divides dates **Rev:** Sun above head at right, date and denomination at left

Date	Mintage	F	VF	XF	Unc
AH1397-1977	50,000	—	—	—	10.00
AH1399-1979	49,000	—	—	—	11.00
AH1399-1979 Proof	1,500	Value: 11.50			

KM# 474 POUND
15.0000 g., 0.7200 Silver .3472 oz. ASW **Subject:** 20th Anniversary - Economic Union **Obv:** Denomination divides dates **Rev:** Design above grasped hands divides dates, grain stalks divided by cogwheel below flank

Date	Mintage	F	VF	XF	Unc
AH1397-1977	50,000	—	—	—	10.00

KM# 475 POUND

8.0000 g., 0.8750 Gold .2250 oz. AGW **Subject:** 20th Anniversary - Economic Union

Date	Mintage	F	VF	XF	Unc
AH1397-1977	5,000	—	—	—	170

KM# 480 POUND

15.0000 g., 0.7200 Silver .3472 oz. ASW **Subject:** Portland Cement **Obv:** Denomination divides dates **Rev:** Cement factory

Date	Mintage	F	VF	XF	Unc
AH1398-1978	50,000	—	—	—	10.00

KM# 481 POUND

15.0000 g., 0.7200 Silver .3472 oz. ASW **Subject:** 25th Anniversary - Ain Shams University **Obv:** Denomination divides dates **Rev:** Birds flank center design, dates below

Date	Mintage	F	VF	XF	Unc
AH1398-1978	50,000	—	—	—	10.00

KM# 482 POUND

15.0000 g., 0.7200 Silver .3472 oz. ASW **Series:** F.A.O. **Rev:** Female looking into microscope

Date	Mintage	F	VF	XF	Unc
AH1398-1978	50,000	—	—	—	10.00

KM# 488 POUND

15.0000 g., 0.7200 Silver .3472 oz. ASW **Subject:** 25th Anniversary - Abbasia Mint **Obv:** Denomination divides dates **Rev:** Dates above building at corners, cogwheel at top

Date	Mintage	F	VF	XF	Unc
AH1399-1979	23,000	—	—	—	20.00
AH1399-1979 Proof	2,000	Value: 25.00			

KM# 489 POUND

15.0000 g., 0.7200 Silver .3472 oz. ASW **Series:** F.A.O. and I.Y.C. **Obv:** Denomination divides dates **Rev:** Seated woman with child, logo and designs at right, FAO below chair

Date	Mintage	F	VF	XF	Unc
AH1399-1979	48,000	—	—	—	10.00
AH1399-1979 Proof	2,500	Value: 20.00			

KM# 490 POUND

15.0000 g., 0.7200 Silver .3472 oz. ASW **Subject:** National Education Day **Obv:** Denomination divides dates **Rev:** Back to back teachers and students, wreath in background

Date	Mintage	F	VF	XF	Unc
AH1399-1979	98,000	—	—	—	10.50
AH1399-1979 Proof	2,000	Value: 20.00			

KM# 491 POUND

15.0000 g., 0.7200 Silver .3472 oz. ASW **Subject:** 100th Anniversary - Bank of Land Reform **Rev:** Seated figure, workers harvesting grain at back, farmers and oxen above

Date	Mintage	F	VF	XF	Unc
AH1399-1979	98,000	—	—	—	10.50
AH1399-1979 Proof	2,000	Value: 20.00			

KM# 492 POUND

8.0000 g., 0.8750 Gold .2250 oz. AGW **Subject:** 100th Anniversary - Bank of Land Reform

Date	Mintage	F	VF	XF	Unc
AH1399-1979	4,200	—	—	—	165
AH1399-1979 Proof	800	Value: 225			

KM# 493 POUND

15.0000 g., 0.7200 Silver .3472 oz. ASW **Subject:** 1400th Anniversary - Mohammed's Flight **Obv:** Denomination divides dates **Rev:** Birds and eggs in front of web design

Date	Mintage	F	VF	XF	Unc
AH1400-1979	97,000	—	—	—	10.50
AH1400-1979 Proof	3,000	Value: 15.00			

KM# 494 POUND

8.0000 g., 0.8750 Gold .2250 oz. AGW **Subject:** 1400th Anniversary - Mohammed's Flight

Date	Mintage	F	VF	XF	Unc
AH1400-1979	2,000	—	—	—	170
AH1400-1979 Proof	2,000	Value: 225			

KM# 508 POUND

15.0000 g., 0.7200 Silver .3472 oz. ASW **Subject:** Egyptian-Israeli Peace Treaty **Obv:** Denomination divides dates **Rev:** Head of Anwar Sadat at right facing left, with dove of peace at left

Date	Mintage	F	VF	XF	Unc
AH1400-1980	95,000	—	—	—	10.00
AH1400-1980 Proof	5,000	Value: 15.50			

KM# 509 POUND

8.0000 g., 0.8750 Gold .2250 oz. AGW **Subject:** Egyptian-Israeli Peace Treaty **Obv:** Denomination divides dates **Rev:** Head of Anwar Sadat left, with dove of peace at left

Date	Mintage	F	VF	XF	Unc
AH1400-1980	9,500	—	—	—	160
AH1400-1980 Proof	500	Value: 200			

KM# 510 POUND

15.0000 g., 0.7200 Silver .3472 oz. ASW **Subject:** Applied Professions in Egypt **Obv:** Denomination divides dates **Rev:** Various professions depicted, date and shield below

Date	Mintage	F	VF	XF	Unc
AH1400-1980	22,000	—	—	—	20.00
AH1400-1980 Proof	3,000	Value: 15.00			

KM# 511 POUND

15.0000 g., 0.7200 Silver .3472 oz. ASW **Subject:** Doctor's Day **Obv:** Denomination divides dates **Rev:** Seated healer with staff facing left

Date	Mintage	F	VF	XF	Unc
AH1400-1980	97,000	—	—	—	10.00
AH1400-1980 Proof	3,000	Value: 15.00			

KM# 512 POUND

8.0000 g., 0.8750 Gold .2250 oz. AGW **Subject:** Doctor's Day **Rev:** Seated healer with staff facing left

Date	Mintage	F	VF	XF	Unc
AH1400-1980 Proof	5,000	Value: 185			

KM# 513 POUND

15.0000 g., 0.7200 Silver .3472 oz. ASW **Series:** F.A.O. **Obv:** Denomination divides dates **Rev:** Kneeling figure with book and birds, city scene at right, pyramids and tractor at left

Date	Mintage	F	VF	XF	Unc
AH1400-1980	97,000	—	—	—	10.00
AH1400-1980 Proof	3,000	Value: 15.00			

KM# 514 POUND
15.0000 g., 0.7200 Silver .3472 oz. ASW **Subject:** Sadat's Corrective Revolution of May 15, 1971 **Obv:** Denomination divides dates **Rev:** Raised clenched fist holding grain sprig

Date	Mintage	F	VF	XF	Unc
AH1400-1980	47,000	—	—	—	15.00
AH1400-1980 Proof	3,000	Value: 15.00			

KM# 515 POUND
15.0000 g., 0.7200 Silver .3472 oz. ASW **Obv:** Denomination divides dates **Rev:** Cairo University Law facility

Date	Mintage	F	VF	XF	Unc
AH1400-1980	47,000	—	—	—	15.00
AH1400-1980 Proof	3,000	Value: 15.00			

KM# 516 POUND
8.0000 g., 0.8750 Gold .2250 oz. AGW **Obv:** Denomination divides dates **Rev:** Cairo University Law facility

Date	Mintage	F	VF	XF	Unc
AH1400-1980	2,000	—	—	—	170
AH1400-1980 Proof	—	Value: 225			

KM# 528 POUND
15.0000 g., 0.7200 Silver .3472 oz. ASW **Subject:** 25th Anniversary - Nationalization of Suez Canal **Obv:** Denomination divides dates **Rev:** Central design divides dates, grain spray below

Date	Mintage	F	VF	XF	Unc
AH1401-1981	25,000	—	—	—	20.00
AH1401-1981 Proof	1,500	Value: 30.00			

KM# 522 POUND
15.0000 g., 0.7200 Silver .3472 oz. ASW **Subject:** Scientists' Day **Obv:** Denomination within circle, seated figure at left **Rev:** Sun above satellite dish, cogwheel divides spray below

Date	Mintage	F	VF	XF	Unc
AH1401-1981	25,000	—	—	—	20.00

KM# 530 POUND
15.0000 g., 0.7200 Silver .3472 oz. ASW **Subject:** 100th Anniversary - Revolt by Arabi Pasha **Rev:** Pasha mounted on horse in front of his followers

Date	Mintage	F	VF	XF	Unc
AH1402-1981	50,000	—	—	—	10.00
AH1402-1981 Proof	1,500	Value: 30.00			

KM# 523 POUND
15.0000 g., 0.7200 Silver .3472 oz. ASW **Series:** World Food Day **Obv:** Denomination divides dates **Rev:** Standing figure with food tray, animals at right, figure harvesting grain at left

Date	Mintage	F	VF	XF	Unc
AH1401-1981	50,000	—	—	—	10.50
AH1401-1981 Proof	1,500	Value: 30.00			

KM# 524 POUND
15.0000 g., 0.7200 Silver .3472 oz. ASW **Subject:** 3rd Anniversary - Suez Canal Reopening **Obv:** Denomination divides dates **Rev:** Grain stalk right of canal scene

Date	Mintage	F	VF	XF	Unc
AH1401-1981	50,000	—	—	—	10.00
AH1401-1981 Proof	2,000	Value: 25.00			

KM# 525 POUND
8.0000 g., 0.8750 Gold .2250 oz. AGW **Subject:** 3rd Anniversary - Suez Canal Reopening

Date	Mintage	F	VF	XF	Unc
AH1401-1981 Proof	150	Value: 250			

KM# 526 POUND
15.0000 g., 0.7200 Silver .3472 oz. ASW **Subject:** 25th Anniversary - Egyptian Industry

Date	Mintage	F	VF	XF	Unc
AH1402-1981	25,000	—	—	—	15.00

KM# 527 POUND
15.0000 g., 0.7200 Silver .3472 oz. ASW **Subject:** 25th Anniversary - Trade Unions **Obv:** Denomination divides dates **Rev:** Hands holding up factories, flower below, all within oval on shield with 1/2 cogwheel above, dates at left

Date	Mintage	F	VF	XF	Unc
AH1402-1981	25,000	—	—	—	15.00

KM# 529 POUND
8.0000 g., 0.8750 Gold .2250 oz. AGW **Subject:** 25th Anniversary - Nationalization of Suez Canal **Obv:** Denomination divides dates **Rev:** Central design divides dates, grain spray below

Date	Mintage	F	VF	XF	Unc
AH1401-1981	3,000	—	—	—	180

KM# 531 POUND
8.0000 g., 0.8750 Gold .2250 oz. AGW **Subject:** 100th Anniversary - Revolt by Arabi Pasha **Rev:** Pasha mounted on horse in front of his followers

Date	Mintage	F	VF	XF	Unc
AH1402-1981	3,000	—	—	—	180

KM# 532 POUND
15.0000 g., 0.7200 Silver .3472 oz. ASW **Series:** F.A.O. **Obv:** Denomination divides dates **Rev:** Figures flank design at center

Date	Mintage	F	VF	XF	Unc
AH1401-1981	50,000	—	—	—	10.00

KM# 539 POUND
15.0000 g., 0.7200 Silver .3472 oz. ASW **Subject:** Golden Jubilee - Egypt Air **Obv:** Denomination divides dates **Rev:** Stylized bird on globe, dates above

Date	Mintage	F	VF	XF	Unc
AH1402-1982	20,000	—	—	—	15.00

KM# 540 POUND

15.0000 g., 0.7200 Silver .3472 oz. ASW **Subject:** 1000th Anniversary - Al Azhar Mosque **Obv:** Denomination within circle, divides dates **Rev:** Mosque

Date	Mintage	F	VF	XF	Unc
AH1402-1982	23,000	—	—	—	12.00
AH1402-1982 Proof	4,000	Value: 15.00			

KM# 541 POUND

8.0000 g., 0.8750 Gold .2250 oz. AGW **Subject:** 1000th Anniversary - Al Azhar Mosque **Rev:** Mosque

Date	Mintage	F	VF	XF	Unc
AH1402-1982 Proof	2,000	Value: 190			

KM# 544 POUND

15.0000 g., 0.7200 Silver .3472 oz. ASW **Subject:** 50th Anniversary - Egyptian Products Co. **Obv:** Denomination divides dates **Rev:** Head within crowned wreath at top, triangle in background

Date	Mintage	F	VF	XF	Unc
AH1402-1982	5,000	—	—	—	20.00
AH1402-1982 Proof	2,000	Value: 25.00			

KM# 545 POUND

15.0000 g., 0.7200 Silver .3472 oz. ASW **Subject:** Return of Sinai to Egypt **Obv:** Denomination divides dates **Rev:** Grain sprigs form 'V', bird above

Date	Mintage	F	VF	XF	Unc
AH1402-1982(1983)	50,000	—	—	—	10.00
AH1402-1982(1983) Proof	2,000	Value: 25.00			

KM# 542 POUND

15.0000 g., 0.7200 Silver .3472 oz. ASW **Subject:** 50th Anniversary of Air Force **Rev:** Air Force insignia within wreath

Date	Mintage	F	VF	XF	Unc
AH1403-1982	10,000	—	—	—	20.00
AH1403-1982 Proof	2,260	Value: 25.00			

KM# 543 POUND

8.0000 g., 0.8750 Gold .2250 oz. AGW **Subject:** 50th Anniversary of Air Force **Rev:** Air Force insignia within wreath

Date	Mintage	F	VF	XF	Unc
AH1403-1982 Proof	2,000	Value: 190			

KM# 549 POUND

15.0000 g., 0.7200 Silver .3472 oz. ASW **Subject:** 50th Anniversary - Deaths of Shawky and Hafez **Obv:** Denomination divides dates **Rev:** Two busts, flowers flank

Date	Mintage	F	VF	XF	Unc
AH1403-1983	25,000	—	—	—	15.00

KM# 551 POUND

15.0000 g., 0.7200 Silver .3472 oz. ASW **Subject:** Misr Insurance Company **Obv:** Denomination divides dates **Rev:** Design within center oval divides dates

Date	Mintage	F	VF	XF	Unc
AH1404-1984	20,000	—	—	—	15.00

KM# 559 POUND

15.0000 g., 0.7200 Silver .3472 oz. ASW **Subject:** Helwan University Faculty of Fine Arts **Obv:** Flower head at top, denomination and dates **Rev:** Artist's tools within design

Date	Mintage	F	VF	XF	Unc
AH1404-1984	25,000	—	—	—	15.00
AH1404-1984 Proof	25	Value: 200			

KM# 583 POUND

8.0000 g., 0.8750 Gold .2250 oz. AGW **Subject:** 50th Anniversary - Egyptian Radio Broadcasting

Date	Mintage	F	VF	XF	Unc
AH1404-1984	2,000	—	—	—	190

KM# 571 POUND

8.0000 g., 0.8750 Gold .2250 oz. AGW **Subject:** 25th Anniversary - National Planning Institute

Date	Mintage	F	VF	XF	Unc
AH1405-1985	200	—	—	—	275

KM# 574 POUND

8.0000 g., 0.8750 Gold .2250 oz. AGW **Subject:** 60th Anniversary - Egyptian Parliament **Rev:** Parliament building

Date	Mintage	F	VF	XF	Unc
AH1405-1985	1,000	—	—	—	210

KM# 577 POUND

8.0000 g., 0.8750 Gold .2250 oz. AGW **Subject:** 25th Anniversary - Cairo Stadium **Rev:** Stadium

Date	Mintage	F	VF	XF	Unc
AH1405-1985	300	—	—	—	250

KM# 580 POUND

8.0000 g., 0.8750 Gold .2250 oz. AGW **Subject:** 25th Anniversary - Egyptian Television

Date	Mintage	F	VF	XF	Unc
AH1405-1985	150	—	—	—	275

KM# 604 POUND

8.0000 g., 0.8750 Gold .2250 oz. AGW **Subject:** Commerce Day **Rev:** Stylized depictions of commercial activity

Date	Mintage	F	VF	XF	Unc
AH1405-1985 Proof	2,000	Value: 190			

KM# 605 POUND

8.0000 g., 0.8750 Gold .2250 oz. AGW **Subject:** Faculty of Economics and Political Science **Obv:** Arabic legends, seals, and date **Rev:** Graph within wreath, partial gear wheel

Date	Mintage	F	VF	XF	Unc
AH1405-1985 Proof	250	Value: 250			

KM# 635 POUND

8.0000 g., 0.8750 Gold .2250 oz. AGW **Subject:** 25th Anniversary - Cairo International Airport **Obv:** Stylized legend above dates, dividing two seals **Rev:** Two circling vultures within Arabic and English legends

Date	Mintage	F	VF	XF	Unc
AH1405-1985	200	—	—	—	250

KM# 632 POUND

8.0000 g., 0.8750 Gold .2250 oz. AGW **Subject:** Prophet's Mosque **Obv:** Minaret, globe, denomination, legends **Rev:** Crescent, mosque, minaret below legend arch

Date	Mintage	F	VF	XF	Unc
AH1406-1985	800	—	—	—	215

KM# 636 POUND

8.0000 g., 0.8750 Gold .2250 oz. AGW **Subject:** Cairo University Faculty of Commerce **Obv:** Stylized legend above dates, dividing two seals **Rev:** Ancient Egyptian commerce related scenes

Date	Mintage	F	VF	XF	Unc
AH1406-1986	200	—	—	—	250

KM# 637 POUND

8.0000 g., 0.8750 Gold .2250 oz. AGW **Subject:** 25th Anniversary - Egyptian Central Bank **Obv:** Stylized flowers, gear wheel and cotton within legend **Rev:** Ancient Egyptian sculptures, legends above and below within ornamental border

Date	Mintage	F	VF	XF	Unc
AH1406-1986	200	—	—	—	275

KM# 638 POUND

8.0000 g., 0.8750 Gold .2250 oz. AGW **Subject:** 100th Anniversary - Petroleum Industry **Obv:** Stylized legend above dates, dividing two seals **Rev:** Oil well and landscape within ornamental circle

Date	Mintage	F	VF	XF	Unc
AH1406-1986	800	—	—	—	215

KM# 640 POUND

8.0000 g., 0.8750 Gold .2250 oz. AGW **Subject:** 50th Anniversary - National Theater **Obv:** Stylized stage curtain, legend within **Rev:** Large building, two masks in foreground, legend above

Date	Mintage	F	VF	XF	Unc
AH1406-1986	250	—	—	—	235

KM# 644 POUND

8.0000 g., 0.8750 Gold .2250 oz. AGW **Subject:** Restoration of Parliament Building **Obv:** Arabic legends **Rev:** Dome and tower with scaffolding

Date	Mintage	F	VF	XF	Unc
AH1406-1986	400	—	—	—	220

KM# 639 POUND

8.0000 g., 0.8750 Gold .2250 oz. AGW **Subject:** Census **Obv:** Arabic legends, seals, date **Rev:** City view with paper doll cutout human figures

Date	Mintage	F	VF	XF	Unc
AH1407-1986	200	—	—	—	235

KM# 643 POUND

8.0000 g., 0.8750 Gold .2250 oz. AGW **Subject:** 40th Anniversary - Engineer's Syndicate **Obv:** Arabic legends, seals, dates **Rev:** Three triangles, legend, ornamentation

Date	Mintage	F	VF	XF	Unc
AH1407-1986	400	—	—	—	220

KM# 645 POUND

8.0000 g., 0.8750 Gold .2250 oz. AGW **Subject:** Parliament Museum **Obv:** Arabic legends, seals, dates **Rev:** Documents, quill, carriage, building with national emblem

Date	Mintage	F	VF	XF	Unc
AH1407-1987	400	—	—	—	220

KM# 653 POUND

8.0000 g., 0.8750 Gold .2250 oz. AGW **Subject:** Investment Bank **Obv:** Toughra, legends above and below, dates **Rev:** Symbol within stylized circle, legend around

Date	Mintage	F	VF	XF	Unc
AH1407-1987	600	—	—	—	215

KM# 673 POUND

8.0000 g., 0.8750 Gold .2250 oz. AGW **Subject:** First African Subway **Obv:** Stylized legends and denomination **Rev:** Subway emerging from tunnel with legend around rim

Date	Mintage	F	VF	XF	Unc
AH1408-1987 Proof	500	Value: 230			

KM# 647 POUND

8.0000 g., 0.8750 Gold .2250 oz. AGW **Subject:** Police Day **Obv:** Arabic and English legends, seals, dates **Rev:** Police emblem - eagle in wreath, legends

Date	Mintage	F	VF	XF	Unc
AH1408-1988	500	—	—	—	215

KM# 654 POUND

8.0000 g., 0.8750 Gold .2250 oz. AGW **Subject:** Dedication of Cairo Opera House **Obv:** Arabic legends, seals, dates **Rev:** Opera house, legends above and below

Date	Mintage	F	VF	XF	Unc
AH1409-1988	1,500	—	—	—	225

KM# 661 POUND

8.0000 g., 0.8750 Gold .2250 oz. AGW **Subject:** Naquib Mahfouz, Nobel Laureate **Obv:** Stylized quill ink and paper design with legend above **Rev:** Head of Mahfouz left

Date	Mintage	F	VF	XF	Unc
AH1409-1988 Proof	1,000	Value: 190			

KM# 664 POUND

8.0000 g., 0.8750 Gold .2250 oz. AGW **Subject:** United Parliamentary Union **Obv:** Kufic legend above denomination and dates **Rev:** Anniversary dates, map in wreath above domed building, and legend

Date	Mintage	F	VF	XF	Unc
AH1409-1989 Proof	200	Value: 275			

KM# 666 POUND

8.0000 g., 0.8750 Gold .2250 oz. AGW **Subject:** First Arab Olympics **Obv:** Kufic legend above denomination and dates **Rev:** 5 Olympic rings and map as part of torch held by hand within wreath and legend

Date	Mintage	F	VF	XF	Unc
AH1409-1989 Proof	300	Value: 250			

KM# 668 POUND

8.0000 g., 0.8750 Gold .2250 oz. AGW **Subject:** National Research Center **Obv:** Kufic legend above denomination and dates **Rev:** Stylized ancient and modern research elements

Date	Mintage	F	VF	XF	Unc
AH1409-1989 Proof	250	Value: 250			

KM# 677 POUND

8.0000 g., 0.8750 Gold .2250 oz. AGW **Subject:** University of Cairo, School of Agriculture **Obv:** Denomination between wheat ears above legend **Rev:** Ancient farming scene and coat of arms, building in background

Date	Mintage	F	VF	XF	Unc
AH1410-1989 Proof	200	Value: 275			

KM# 695 POUND

8.0000 g., 0.8750 Gold .2250 oz. AGW **Subject:** Export Trade Show **Obv:** Toughra, inscription above **Rev:** Display of symbols

Date	Mintage	F	VF	XF	Unc
AH1410-1989 Proof	200	Value: 275			

KM# 696 POUND

8.0000 g., 0.8750 Gold .2250 oz. AGW **Subject:** Union of African Parliament **Obv:** Toughra, denomination, date within circle and legend **Rev:** Map of Africa, laurel branch and Parliament building

Date	Mintage	F	VF	XF	Unc
AH1410-1990 Proof	200	Value: 275			

KM# 699 POUND

8.0000 g., 0.8750 Gold .2250 oz. AGW **Subject:** 5th African Games - Cairo **Obv:** Torch with legend and inscription **Rev:** Logo above rings within legend

Date	Mintage	F	VF	XF	Unc
AH1411-1991 Proof	200	Value: 275			

KM# 832 POUND

8.0000 g., 0.8750 Gold .2250 oz. AGW **Subject:** Library of Alexandria **Obv:** Legend and inscription **Rev:** Waterfront building with tower

Date	Mintage	F	VF	XF	Unc
AH1411-1991	300	—	—	—	400

KM# 726 POUND

8.0000 g., 0.8750 Gold .2250 oz. AGW **Subject:** Mohamed Abdel Wahab **Rev:** Bust of Mohamed Abdel Wahab left with music sheet in background

Date	Mintage	F	VF	XF	Unc
AH1412-1991	1,000	—	—	—	200

KM# 835 POUND

15.0000 g., 0.7200 Silver .3472 oz. ASW **Subject:** Gorgui Zidane **Obv:** Legend and vase **Rev:** Portrait **Edge:** Reeded

Date	Mintage	F	VF	XF	Unc
AH1413-1992	3,000	—	—	—	20.00

KM# 836 POUND

8.0000 g., 0.8750 Gold .2250 oz. AGW **Subject:** Rifa'a El Tahtaoui **Obv:** Legend and vase **Rev:** Portrait

Date	Mintage	F	VF	XF	Unc
AH1413-1992	800	—	—	—	400

KM# 810 POUND

15.0000 g., 0.7200 Silver .3472 oz. ASW **Subject:** 20th Anniversary - October War **Obv:** Smoking chimneys divide dates, text **Rev:** Soldier with flag

Date	Mintage	F	VF	XF	Unc
AH1414-1993	Est. 25,000	—	—	—	30.00

KM# 811 POUND

8.0000 g., 0.8750 Gold .2250 oz. AGW **Subject:** 20th Anniversary - October War **Obv:** Smoking chimney, text **Rev:** Soldier with flag

Date	Mintage	F	VF	XF	Unc
AH1414-1993	Est. 3,000	—	—	—	400

KM# 761 POUND

15.0000 g., 0.7200 Silver .3472 oz. ASW **Subject:** Salah El Din El-Ayubi **Obv:** Denomination **Rev:** Portrait

Date	Mintage	F	VF	XF	Unc
AH1414-1994	5,000	—	—	—	25.00

KM# 762 POUND

8.0000 g., 0.8750 Gold .2250 oz. AGW **Subject:** Salah El Din El-Ayubi **Obv:** Denomination **Rev:** Portrait

Date	Mintage	F	VF	XF	Unc
AH1414-1994	300	—	—	—	400

KM# 764 POUND

15.0000 g., 0.7200 Silver .3472 oz. ASW **Subject:** 125 Years - Suez Canal **Obv:** Toughra **Rev:** Building and canal scenes

Date	Mintage	F	VF	XF	Unc
AH1415-1994	3,000	—	—	—	20.00

KM# 766 POUND

15.0000 g., 0.7200 Silver .3472 oz. ASW **Subject:** 75 Years - Bank of Misr **Obv:** Inscription **Rev:** Bank building and emblem, dates upper left

Date	Mintage	F	VF	XF	Unc
AH1415-1994	2,500	—	—	—	30.00

KM# 839 POUND

15.0000 g., 0.7200 Silver .3472 oz. ASW **Subject:** Abd Al Halem Hafez **Obv:** Tughra, date and denomination **Rev:** Head left

Date	Mintage	F	VF	XF	Unc
AH1416-1995	3,000	—	—	—	20.00

KM# 767 POUND

8.0000 g., 0.8750 Gold .2250 oz. AGW **Subject:** 75 Years - Bank of Misr

Date	Mintage	F	VF	XF	Unc
AH1415-1995	1,000	—	—	—	275

KM# 769 POUND

15.0000 g., 0.7200 Silver .3472 oz. ASW **Series:** F.A.O. **Rev:** Workers

Date	Mintage	F	VF	XF	Unc
AH1415-1995	3,000	—	—	—	40.00

KM# 771 POUND

8.0000 g., 0.8750 Gold .2250 oz. AGW **Subject:** Pediatrics International Conference **Obv:** Tughra divides dates and denomination **Rev:** Children and pyramids on globe, dates divided below

Date	Mintage	F	VF	XF	Unc
AH1416-1995	300	—	—	—	400

KM# 840 POUND

8.0000 g., 0.8750 Gold .2250 oz. AGW **Obv:** Denomination **Rev:** Abd Al Halem Hafez

Date	Mintage	F	VF	XF	Unc
AH1416-1995	500	—	—	—	400

KM# 844 POUND

15.0000 g., 0.7200 Silver .3472 oz. ASW **Subject:** Centennial - Electrification **Obv:** Legend and inscription **Rev:** Electric bolt on Pyramid

Date	Mintage	F	VF	XF	Unc
AH1417-1996	3,000	—	—	—	15.00

KM# 845 POUND

15.0000 g., 0.7200 Silver .3472 oz. ASW **Subject:** 65 Years - Egyptian Air Force **Obv:** Denomination **Rev:** Flying eagle in wreath

Date	Mintage	F	VF	XF	Unc
AH1418-1997	226	—	—	—	85.00

KM# 847 POUND

15.0000 g., 0.7200 Silver .3472 oz. ASW **Subject:** 50 Years Arab Land Bank **Obv:** Denomination **Rev:** Arab Real Estate domed Bank building

Date	Mintage	F	VF	XF	Unc
AH1418-1997	3,000	—	—	—	35.00

KM# 849 POUND
15.0000 g., 0.7200 Silver .3472 oz. ASW **Subject:** 95th Interparliamentary Union Conference **Obv:** Circular design above inscription **Rev:** Pyramids in wreath

Date	Mintage	F	VF	XF	Unc
AH1418-1997	375	—	—	—	85.00

KM# 926 POUND
15.0000 g., 0.7200 Silver 0.3472 oz. ASW, 35 mm. **Subject:** Soccer FIFA-JVC Cup **Obv:** Value, ornamental design and inscription **Rev:** Games logo **Edge:** Reeded

Date	Mintage	F	VF	XF	Unc
AH1418-1997	—	—	—	—	90.00

KM# 851 POUND
15.0000 g., 0.7200 Silver .3472 oz. ASW **Subject:** Centennial - Chemical Department **Obv:** Denomination **Rev:** Symbolic design

Date	Mintage	F	VF	XF	Unc
AH1419-1998	1,000	—	—	—	35.00

KM# 855 POUND
15.0000 g., 0.7200 Silver .3472 oz. ASW **Series:** Centennial - National Bank **Obv:** Denomination **Rev:** Large "100"

Date	Mintage	F	VF	XF	Unc
AH1419-1998	2,000	—	—	—	85.00

KM# 857 POUND
15.0000 g., 0.7200 Silver .3472 oz. ASW **Subject:** 25th Anniversary - October War **Obv:** Denomination **Rev:** Symbolic design

Date	Mintage	F	VF	XF	Unc
AH1419-1998	2,000	—	—	—	40.00

KM# 859 POUND
15.0000 g., 0.7200 Silver .3472 oz. ASW **Subject:** Death of Imam Metwaly El Sharawi **Obv:** Open book **Rev:** Bust of El Sharawi facing

Date	Mintage	F	VF	XF	Unc
AH1419-1998	2,000	—	—	—	40.00

KM# 861 POUND
15.0000 g., 0.7200 Silver .3472 oz. ASW **Subject:** Centennial - Land Surveying **Obv:** Denomination **Rev:** "100" above ancient surveyors

Date	Mintage	F	VF	XF	Unc
AH1419-1998	1,000	—	—	—	35.00

KM# 863 POUND
15.0000 g., 0.7200 Silver .3472 oz. ASW **Series:** Centennial - Solidarity **Obv:** Denomination **Rev:** Symbolic design

Date	Mintage	F	VF	XF	Unc
AH1419-1998	2,000	—	—	—	35.00

KM# 865 POUND
15.0000 g., 0.7200 Silver .3472 oz. ASW **Subject:** Golden Jubilee of Ash Shanns University **Obv:** Denomination **Rev:** Monument

Date	Mintage	F	VF	XF	Unc
AH1420-1999	1,000	—	—	—	35.00

KM# 928 POUND
15.0000 g., 0.7200 Silver 0.3472 oz. ASW, 35 mm. **Subject:** National Insurance Company Centennial **Obv:** Value **Rev:** Ancient seated figure with "100" **Edge:** Reeded

Date	Mintage	F	VF	XF	Unc
AH1421-2000	2,500	—	—	—	35.00

KM# 441 5 POUNDS
26.0000 g., 0.8750 Gold .7315 oz. AGW **Subject:** 75th Anniveresary - National Bank of Egypt **Obv:** Denomination and dates **Rev:** World globe back of bank building divides dates

Date	Mintage	F	VF	XF	Unc
AH1393-1973	1,000	—	—	—	525
AH1393-1973 Proof	—	Value: 650			

KM# 444 5 POUNDS
26.0000 g., 0.8750 Gold .7315 oz. AGW **Subject:** 1973 October War **Obv:** Denomination, dates, and legend **Rev:** Half-figure of soldier, 3/4 wreath surrounds above

Date	Mintage	F	VF	XF	Unc
AH1394-1974	1,000	—	—	—	550

KM# 459 5 POUNDS
26.0000 g., 0.8750 Gold .7315 oz. AGW **Subject:** King Faisal of Saudi Arabia **Obv:** Denomination divides dates **Rev:** Head 3/4 right

Date	Mintage	F	VF	XF	Unc
AH1396-1976	2,500	—	—	—	575

KM# 460 5 POUNDS
26.0000 g., 0.8750 Gold .7315 oz. AGW **Subject:** Reopening of Suez Canal

Date	Mintage	F	VF	XF	Unc
AH1396-1976	2,000	—	—	—	525

KM# 461 5 POUNDS
26.0000 g., 0.8750 Gold .7315 oz. AGW **Subject:** Om Kalsoum **Obv:** Denomination divides dates **Rev:** Head right, music symbol in hair

Date	Mintage	F	VF	XF	Unc
AH1396-1976	1,000	—	—	—	800

KM# 495 5 POUNDS
26.0000 g., 0.8750 Gold .7315 oz. AGW **Subject:** 100th Anniversary - Bank of Land Reform **Rev:** Seated man, farmer tilling soil with three oxen behind, mural showing workers cutting grain sheaves

Date	Mintage	F	VF	XF	Unc
AH1399-1979	1,750	—	—	—	500
AH1399-1979 Proof	250	Value: 625			

KM# 496 5 POUNDS
26.0000 g., 0.8750 Gold .7315 oz. AGW **Subject:** 1400th Anniversary - Mohammed's Flight **Obv:** Denomination divides dates, legend above **Rev:** Two doves with eggs in front of spider web

Date	Mintage	F	VF	XF	Unc
AH1400-1979	2,000	—	—	—	500

KM# 517 5 POUNDS
26.0000 g., 0.8750 Gold .7315 oz. AGW **Subject:** Egyptian-Israeli Peace Treaty **Obv:** Denomination divides dates, legend above **Rev:** Head of Anwar Sadat at right facing left, dove of peace at left behind

Date	Mintage	F	VF	XF	Unc
AH1400-1980	2,375	—	—	—	500
AH1400-1980 Proof	125	Value: 650			

KM# 518 5 POUNDS
26.0000 g., 0.8750 Gold .7315 oz. AGW **Subject:** Doctors' Day

Date	Mintage	F	VF	XF	Unc
AH1400-1980	1,000	—	—	—	585

KM# 534 5 POUNDS
26.0000 g., 0.8750 Gold .7315 oz. AGW **Subject:** 3rd Anniversary - Suez Canal Reopening

Date	Mintage	F	VF	XF	Unc
AH1401-1981	925	—	—	—	525
AH1401-1981 Proof	75	Value: 675			

KM# 533 5 POUNDS
24.0000 g., 0.9250 Silver .7138 oz. ASW **Series:** International Year of the Child **Rev:** Children holding hands and dancing around stylistic globe

Date	Mintage	F	VF	XF	Unc
AH1401-1981 Proof	10,000	Value: 30.00			

KM# 535 5 POUNDS
26.0000 g., 0.8750 Gold .7315 oz. AGW **Subject:** 25th Anniversary - Ministry of Industry

Date	Mintage	F	VF	XF	Unc
AH1402-1981 Proof	1,500	Value: 500			

KM# 536 5 POUNDS
26.0000 g., 0.8750 Gold .7315 oz. AGW **Subject:** 100th Anniversary - Revolt by Arabi Pasha **Rev:** Pasha mounted on horse in front of his followers

Date	Mintage	F	VF	XF	Unc
AH1402-1981	1,000	—	—	—	520

KM# 537 5 POUNDS
26.0000 g., 0.8750 Gold .7315 oz. AGW **Subject:** 25th Anniversary - Nationalization of Suez Canal **Obv:** Denomination divides dates, legend above **Rev:** Design at center, grain spray below

Date	Mintage	F	VF	XF	Unc
AH1401-1981	1,000	—	—	—	520

KM# 546 5 POUNDS
26.0000 g., 0.8750 Gold .7315 oz. AGW **Subject:** 1000th Anniversary - Al Azhar Mosque **Rev:** Mosque

Date	Mintage	F	VF	XF	Unc
AH1402-1982	1,500	—	—	—	500

KM# 547 5 POUNDS
26.0000 g., 0.8750 Gold .7315 oz. AGW **Subject:** 50th Anniversary - Air Force **Rev:** Air Force insignia within wreath

Date	Mintage	F	VF	XF	Unc
AH1403-1982	1,000	—	—	—	520

KM# 552 5 POUNDS
17.5000 g., 0.7200 Silver .4051 oz. ASW **Subject:** 75th Anniversary - Cairo University **Obv:** Denomination within circle divides dates **Rev:** Buildings, shield within wreath at right

Date	Mintage	F	VF	XF	Unc
AH1404-1983	25,000	—	—	—	18.00

KM# 558 5 POUNDS
17.5000 g., 0.7200 Silver .4051 oz. ASW **Subject:** Los Angeles Olympics **Obv:** Torch above Olympic rings, dates below **Rev:** Athletes above symbols Rev. Designer: Ibrahim el-Helw

Date	Mintage	F	VF	XF	Unc
AH1404-1984	20,000	—	—	—	13.50

KM# 560 5 POUNDS
17.5000 g., 0.7200 Silver .4051 oz. ASW **Subject:** Academy of Arabic Languages **Obv:** Denomination within circle divides dates **Rev:** World globe above book

Date	Mintage	F	VF	XF	Unc
AH1404-1984	25,000	—	—	—	13.50

KM# 561 5 POUNDS
17.5000 g., 0.7200 Silver .4051 oz. ASW **Subject:** 50th Anniversary - Egyptian Radio Broadcasting **Obv:** Designs within small circles flank design at top, dates below **Rev:** Radio tower divides dates

Date	Mintage	F	VF	XF	Unc
AH1404-1984	25,000	—	—	—	13.50

KM# 565 5 POUNDS
17.5000 g., 0.7200 Silver .4051 oz. ASW **Subject:** Sculptor Mahmoud Mokhtar **Obv:** Denomination within circle divides dates **Rev:** Bust left

Date	Mintage	F	VF	XF	Unc
AH1404-1984	10,000	—	—	—	12.50

KM# 566 5 POUNDS
17.5000 g., 0.7200 Silver .4051 oz. ASW **Subject:** Golden Jubilee of Petroleum Industry **Obv:** Denomination within circle divides dates **Rev:** Radiant flame above three rings

Date	Mintage	F	VF	XF	Unc
AH1404-1984	10,000	—	—	—	13.50

KM# 567 5 POUNDS
17.5000 g., 0.7200 Silver .4051 oz. ASW **Subject:** Diamond Jubilee of Cooperation **Obv:** Arabic legends, dates below **Rev:** Seven joined hexagons with different scenes

Date	Mintage	F	VF	XF	Unc
AH1404-1984	10,000	—	—	—	12.50

KM# 671 5 POUNDS
26.0000 g., 0.8750 Gold .7315 oz. AGW **Subject:** 50th Anniversary - Egyptian Radio **Obv:** Arabic legends **Rev:** Tall buildings with transmitter

Date	Mintage	F	VF	XF	Unc
AH1404-1984 Proof	500	Value: 525			

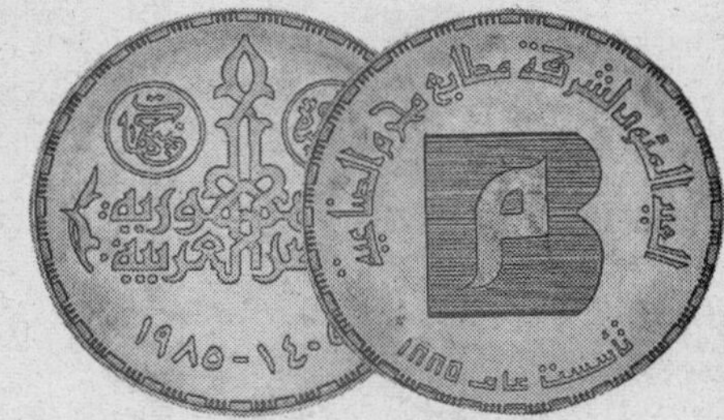

KM# 563 5 POUNDS
17.5000 g., 0.7205 Silver .4051 oz. ASW **Subject:** 100th Anniversary - Moharram Printing Press Co. **Obv:** Arabic legends, date below **Rev:** Printing design on shaded field that resembles the letter 'B'

Date	Mintage	F	VF	XF	Unc
AH1405-1985	20,000	—	—	—	14.50

KM# 564 5 POUNDS
40.0000 g., 0.8750 Gold 1.1253 oz. AGW **Subject:** 100th Anniversary - Moharram Printing Press Co.

Date	Mintage	F	VF	XF	Unc
AH1405-1985	200	—	—	—	1,850

KM# 572 5 POUNDS
17.5000 g., 0.7200 Silver .4051 oz. ASW **Subject:** 25th Anniversary - National Planning Institute **Obv:** Arabic legends, dates below **Rev:** Design on shield divides dates

Date	Mintage	F	VF	XF	Unc
AH1405-1985	15,000	—	—	—	15.50

KM# 575 5 POUNDS
17.5000 g., 0.7200 Silver .4051 oz. ASW **Subject:** 60th Anniversary - Egyptian Parliament **Obv:** Arabic legends, dates below **Rev:** Parliament building, dates above

Date	Mintage	F	VF	XF	Unc
AH1405-1985	25,000	—	—	—	12.50

KM# 576 5 POUNDS
26.0000 g., 0.8750 Gold .7315 oz. AGW **Subject:** 60th Anniversary - Egyptian Parliament **Rev:** Parliament building

Date	Mintage	F	VF	XF	Unc
AH1405-1985	500	—	—	—	1,750

KM# 578 5 POUNDS
17.5000 g., 0.7200 Silver .4051 oz. ASW **Subject:** 25th Anniversary - Cairo Stadium **Obv:** Arabic legends, dates below **Rev:** Stadium

Date	Mintage	F	VF	XF	Unc
AH1405-1985	25,000	—	—	—	12.50

KM# 581 5 POUNDS
17.5000 g., 0.7200 Silver .4051 oz. ASW **Subject:** 25th Anniversary - Egyptian Television **Obv:** Arabic legends, dates below **Rev:** Television tower emitting signal divides dates

Date	Mintage	F	VF	XF	Unc
AH1405-1985	5,000	—	—	—	12.50

KM# 585 5 POUNDS
17.5000 g., 0.7200 Silver .4051 oz. ASW **Subject:** 25th Anniversary - Cairo International Airport **Rev:** Buzzards in flight adapted from ancient Egyptian art

Date	Mintage	F	VF	XF	Unc
AH1405-1985	20,000	—	—	—	12.50

KM# 592 5 POUNDS
17.5000 g., 0.7200 Silver .4051 oz. ASW **Subject:** Tutankhamen **Obv:** Arabic legends, dates below **Rev:** Bust left

Date	Mintage	F	VF	XF	Unc
AH1405-1985	6,000	—	—	—	18.00
AH1405-1985 Proof	2,000	Value: 30.00			

KM# 593 5 POUNDS
17.5000 g., 0.7200 Silver .4051 oz. ASW **Subject:** XV UIA Congress **Obv:** Arabic legends, dates below **Rev:** Pyramid

Date	Mintage	F	VF	XF	Unc
AH1405-1985	10,000	—	—	—	15.50
AH1405-1985 Proof	Est. 500	Value: 25.00			

KM# 598 5 POUNDS
17.5000 g., 0.7200 Silver .4051 oz. ASW **Subject:** Faculty of Economics and Political Science **Obv:** Arabic legends, dates below **Rev:** Grid on globe, dentiled arch above, spray below, divides dates above

Date	Mintage	F	VF	XF	Unc
AH1405-1985	8,000	—	—	—	10.00

KM# 600 5 POUNDS
17.5000 g., 0.7200 Silver .4051 oz. ASW **Subject:** Commerce Day **Obv:** Arabic legends, dates below **Rev:** Ship above head on grid, vendors and shoppers flank

Date	Mintage	F	VF	XF	Unc
AH1405-1985	20,000	—	—	—	11.50
AH1405-1985 Proof	1,000	Value: 40.00			

KM# 584 5 POUNDS
17.5000 g., 0.7200 Silver .4051 oz. ASW **Subject:** The Prophet's Mosque **Obv:** Towers at left of stylized globe **Rev:** Mosque

Date	Mintage	F	VF	XF	Unc
AH1406-1985	25,000	—	—	—	11.50
AH1406-1985 Proof	1,000	Value: 40.00			

KM# 587 5 POUNDS
17.5000 g., 0.7200 Silver .4051 oz. ASW **Subject:** Professions **Obv:** Arabic legends, dates below **Rev:** Various professions illustrated on coin

Date	Mintage	F	VF	XF	Unc
AH1406-1985	8,000	—	—	—	18.00

KM# 633 5 POUNDS
26.0000 g., 0.8750 Gold .7315 oz. AGW **Subject:** Prophet's Mosque **Obv:** Minaret, globe, denomination, legends **Rev:** Crescent, mosque, minaret below legend arch

Date	Mintage	F	VF	XF	Unc
AH1406-1985	400	—	—	—	525

KM# 579 5 POUNDS
26.0000 g., 0.8750 Gold .7315 oz. AGW **Subject:** 25th Anniversary - Cairo Stadium **Rev:** Stadium

Date	Mintage	F	VF	XF	Unc
AH1405-1985	200	—	—	—	1,850

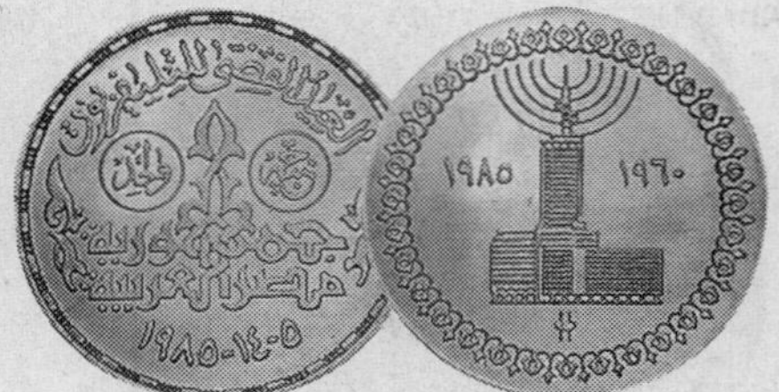

KM# 582 5 POUNDS
26.0000 g., 0.8750 Gold .7315 oz. AGW **Subject:** 25th Anniversary - Egyptian Television **Obv:** Arabic legends, dates below **Rev:** Television tower emitting signal divides dates

Date	Mintage	F	VF	XF	Unc
AH1405-1985	100	—	—	—	1,150

KM# 609a 5 POUNDS
26.0000 g., 0.8750 Gold .7315 oz. AGW **Subject:** Mecca **Obv:** Denomination and dates **Rev:** Building within circle

Date	Mintage	F	VF	XF	Unc
AH1406-1986 Proof	1,400	Value: 500			

KM# 586 5 POUNDS
17.5000 g., 0.7200 Silver .4051 oz. ASW **Subject:** Cairo University Faculty of Commerce **Obv:** Arabic legends, dates below **Rev:** Scribes and merchant vessel

Date	Mintage	F	VF	XF	Unc
AH1406-1986	20,000	—	—	—	13.50

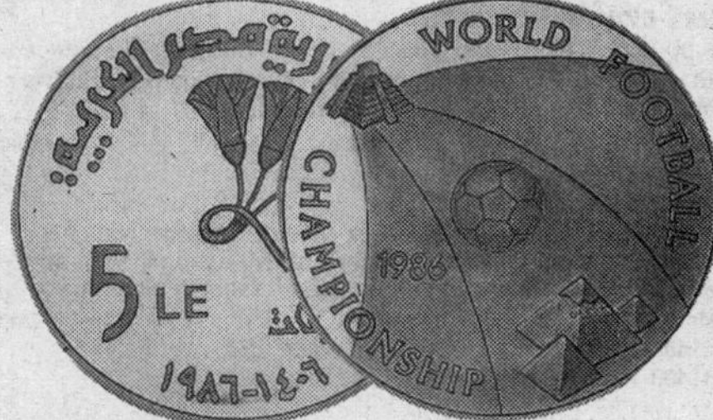

KM# 588 5 POUNDS
17.5000 g., 0.7200 Silver .4051 oz. ASW **Subject:** 25th Anniversary - Egyptian National Bank **Obv:** Denomination divides dates, buds above, cogwheel at left **Rev:** Monument divides dates

Date	Mintage	F	VF	XF	Unc
AH1406-1986	6,000	—	—	—	18.00

KM# 589 5 POUNDS
17.6800 g., 0.7200 Silver .4093 oz. ASW **Subject:** World Soccer Championships **Obv:** Grain heads above denomination and dates **Rev:** Soccer ball, three pyramids

Date	Mintage	F	VF	XF	Unc
AH1406-1986 Prooflike	5,000	—	—	—	20.00
AH1406-1986 Proof	2,150	Value: 30.00			

KM# 590 5 POUNDS
17.5000 g., 0.7200 Silver .4051 oz. ASW **Subject:** African Soccer Championship Games **Rev:** Two soccer players at right

Date	Mintage	F	VF	XF	Unc
AH1406-1986	15,000	—	—	—	14.00
AH1406-1986 Proof	2,000	Value: 30.00			

KM# 594 5 POUNDS
17.5000 g., 0.7200 Silver .4051 oz. ASW **Subject:** 50th Anniversary - Ministry of Health **Obv:** Denomination and dates within circle **Rev:** Figures on heart, within half moon design, below surgeon holding snake and glass

Date	Mintage	F	VF	XF	Unc
AH1406-1986	10,000	—	—	—	20.00
AH1406-1986 Proof	Est. 500	Value: 55.00			

KM# 601 5 POUNDS
17.5000 g., 0.7200 Silver .4051 oz. ASW **Rev:** Crossed swords within wreath

Date	Mintage	F	VF	XF	Unc
AH1406-1986	16,000	—	—	—	13.50

KM# 602 5 POUNDS
17.5000 g., 0.7200 Silver .4051 oz. ASW **Subject:** 100th Anniversary - Petroleum Industry **Obv:** Arabic legends, dates below **Rev:** Oil derrick with building behind

Date	Mintage	F	VF	XF	Unc
AH1406-1986	6,000	—	—	—	18.00

KM# 608 5 POUNDS
17.5000 g., 0.7200 Silver .4051 oz. ASW **Subject:** 50th Anniversary - National Theater **Obv:** Drapes enclose text **Rev:** Theater building, masks below

Date	Mintage	F	VF	XF	Unc
AH1406-1986	6,000	—	—	—	18.00

KM# 609 5 POUNDS
17.5000 g., 0.7200 Silver .4051 oz. ASW **Subject:** Mecca **Obv:** Denomination and dates **Rev:** Building within circle

Date	Mintage	F	VF	XF	Unc
AH1406-1986	30,000	—	—	—	12.50
AH1406-1986 Proof	—	Value: 22.50			

KM# 614 5 POUNDS
17.5000 g., 0.7200 Silver .4051 oz. ASW **Subject:** Restoration of Parliament Building **Obv:** Arabic legends, dates below **Rev:** Dome and tower with scaffolding

Date	Mintage	F	VF	XF	Unc
AH1406-1986	5,000	—	—	—	15.00

KM# 614a 5 POUNDS
26.0000 g., 0.8750 Gold .7315 oz. AGW **Subject:** Restoration of Parliament Building **Obv:** Arabic legends **Rev:** Dome and tower with scaffolding

Date	Mintage	F	VF	XF	Unc
AH1406-1986	300	—	—	—	525

KM# 615 5 POUNDS
17.5000 g., 0.7200 Silver .4051 oz. ASW **Subject:** 30th Anniversary - Atomic Energy Organization **Obv:** Arabic legends, dates below **Rev:** Atoms within circle above center design, figures flank

Date	Mintage	F	VF	XF	Unc
AH1406-1986	5,000	—	—	—	15.00

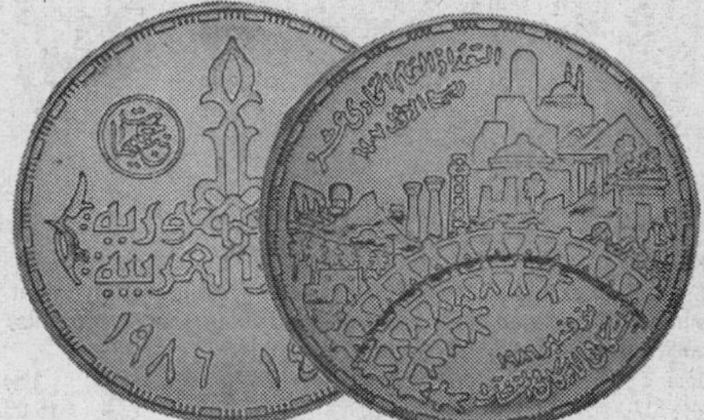

KM# 603 5 POUNDS
17.5000 g., 0.7200 Silver .4051 oz. ASW **Subject:** Census **Obv:** Arabic legends, dates below **Rev:** Joined figures below city scene

Date	Mintage	F	VF	XF	Unc
AH1407-1986	6,000	—	—	—	18.00

KM# 610 5 POUNDS
17.5000 g., 0.7200 Silver .4051 oz. ASW **Subject:** 40th Anniversary - Engineer's Syndicate **Obv:** Arabic legends, dates below **Rev:** Stylized train and pyramids within square formed by outer designs

Date	Mintage	F	VF	XF	Unc
AH1407-1986	6,000	—	—	—	15.00

KM# 616 5 POUNDS
17.5000 g., 0.7200 Silver .4051 oz. ASW **Subject:** 30th Anniversary - Egyptian Industry **Obv:** Arabic legends, dates below **Rev:** Split dentiled design at center

Date	Mintage	F	VF	XF	Unc
AH1407-1986	5,000	—	—	—	15.00

KM# 611 5 POUNDS
17.5000 g., 0.7200 Silver .4051 oz. ASW **Subject:** Aida Opera **Obv:** Towers, sun, date, names and inscriptions **Rev:** Scene from the opera, 'AIDA'

Date	Mintage	F	VF	XF	Unc
ND(1407-1987)	25,000	—	—	—	35.00

KM# 617 5 POUNDS
17.5000 g., 0.7200 Silver .4051 oz. ASW **Subject:** Parliament Museum **Obv:** Arabic legends, seals and dates **Rev:** Documents, quill, carriage, building with national emblem

Date	Mintage	F	VF	XF	Unc
AH1407-1987	5,000	—	—	—	15.00

KM# 617a 5 POUNDS
26.0000 g., 0.8750 Gold .7315 oz. AGW **Subject:** Parliament Museum **Obv:** Arabic legends, seals and dates **Rev:** Documents, quill, carriage, building with national emblem

Date	Mintage	F	VF	XF	Unc
AH1407-1987	300	—	—	—	525

KM# 618 5 POUNDS
17.5000 g., 0.7200 Silver .4051 oz. ASW **Subject:** Veterinarian Day **Obv:** Arabic legends, dates below **Rev:** Squatting figure with ox, caduceus within large 'V' above ox at left

Date	Mintage	F	VF	XF	Unc
AH1407-1987	5,000	—	—	—	15.50

KM# 619 5 POUNDS
17.5000 g., 0.7200 Silver .4051 oz. ASW **Subject:** 75th Anniversary - Misr Petroleum Company **Obv:** Arabic legends, dates below **Rev:** Pyramids within circle divides dates

Date	Mintage	F	VF	XF	Unc
AH1407-1987	10,000	—	—	—	10.00

KM# 630 5 POUNDS
17.5000 g., 0.7200 Silver .4051 oz. ASW **Subject:** Faculty of Fine Arts **Obv:** Denomination, dates and legend **Rev:** Design above dates

Date	Mintage	F	VF	XF	Unc
AH1407-1987	5,000	—	—	—	15.50

KM# 651 5 POUNDS
17.7800 g., 0.7200 Silver .4052 oz. ASW **Subject:** Investment Bank **Obv:** Tughra divides dates **Rev:** Design within inner dentiled circle

Date	Mintage	F	VF	XF	Unc
AH1407-1987	8,000	—	—	—	15.50

KM# 620 5 POUNDS
17.5000 g., 0.7200 Silver .4051 oz. ASW **Subject:** First African Subway **Obv:** Four square designs divide dates **Rev:** Train leaving tunnel

Date	Mintage	F	VF	XF	Unc
AH1408-1987	15,000	—	—	—	12.50

KM# 623 5 POUNDS
17.5000 g., 0.7200 Silver .4051 oz. ASW **Subject:** 25th Anniversary - Hellwan Company **Obv:** Circles flank smoking towers at top, dates below **Rev:** Design within inner circle, legends and dentiled circle surrounds

Date	Mintage	F	VF	XF	Unc
AH1408-1987	8,000	—	—	—	13.50

KM# 674 5 POUNDS
26.0000 g., 0.8750 Gold .7315 oz. AGW **Subject:** First African Subway **Obv:** Stylized legends and denomination **Rev:** Subway emerging from tunnel with legend around rim

Date	Mintage	F	VF	XF	Unc
AH1408-1987 Proof	200	Value: 575			

KM# 670 5 POUNDS
26.0000 g., 0.8750 Gold .7315 oz. AGW **Subject:** National Research Center **Obv:** Kufic legend above denomination and date **Rev:** Stylized ancient and modern research elements

Date	Mintage	F	VF	XF	Unc
AH1408-1988 Proof	—	Value: 575			
AH1409-1989 Proof	200	Value: 575			

KM# 626 5 POUNDS
17.5000 g., 0.7200 Silver .4051 oz. ASW **Series:** Summer Olympics **Obv:** Denomination and date above design and legend **Rev:** Athletes and mythological figures, dates below

Date	Mintage	F	VF	XF	Unc
AH1408-1988	24,000	—	—	—	13.50
AH1408-1988 Matte	—	—	—	—	55.00
AH1408-1988 Proof	5,000	Value: 30.00			

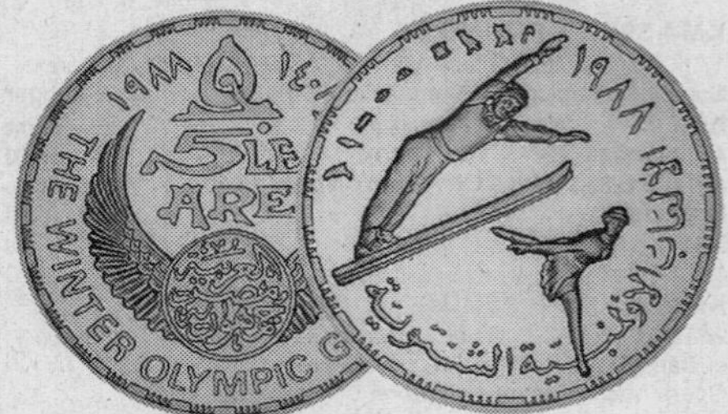

KM# 628 5 POUNDS
17.5000 g., 0.7200 Silver .4051 oz. ASW **Series:** Winter Olympics **Rev:** Ski jumper and figure skater

Date	Mintage	F	VF	XF	Unc
AH1408-1988	8,000	—	—	—	13.50

Date	Mintage	F	VF	XF	Unc
AH1408-1988 Matte	—	—	—	—	55.00
AH1408-1988 Proof	2,000	Value: 30.00			

KM# 621 5 POUNDS

17.5000 g., 0.7200 Silver .4051 oz. ASW **Subject:** Police Day **Obv:** Arabic legends **Rev:** Eagle with wings spread within oval wreath

Date	Mintage	F	VF	XF	Unc
AH1408-1988	35,000	—	—	—	13.50

KM# 624 5 POUNDS

17.5000 g., 0.7200 Silver .4051 oz. ASW **Series:** Summer Olympics **Obv:** Denomination and date above design and legend **Rev:** Pharoah and athletes

Date	Mintage	F	VF	XF	Unc
AH1408-1988 Matte	—	—	—	—	55.00
AH1408-1988 Proof	2,000	Value: 27.50			
AH1408-1988	30,000	—	—	—	13.50

KM# 631 5 POUNDS

17.5000 g., 0.7200 Silver .4051 oz. ASW **Subject:** 50th Anniversary of Air Travel **Obv:** Torch above shield within eagles wings **Rev:** Stylized airplane above text divides dates

Date	Mintage	F	VF	XF	Unc
AH1408-1988	5,000	—	—	—	13.50

KM# 649 5 POUNDS

17.5000 g., 0.7200 Silver .4051 oz. ASW **Subject:** Dedication of Cairo Opera House **Obv:** Arabic legends, seals and dates **Rev:** Opera house

Date	Mintage	F	VF	XF	Unc
AH1409-1988	30,000	—	—	—	12.50

KM# 655 5 POUNDS

26.0000 g., 0.8750 Gold .7315 oz. AGW **Subject:** Dedication of Cairo Opera House **Obv:** Arabic legends, seals, dates **Rev:** Opera house, legends above and below

Date	Mintage	F	VF	XF	Unc
AH1409-1988	200	—	—	—	560

KM# 660 5 POUNDS

17.5000 g., 0.7200 Silver .4051 oz. ASW **Subject:** Ministry of Agriculture **Obv:** Tughra divides dates and denomination **Rev:** Tractor above corn ears, within grain sprigs and flowers

Date	Mintage	F	VF	XF	Unc
AH1409-1988	5,000	—	—	—	15.50

KM# 662 5 POUNDS

17.5000 g., 0.7200 Silver .4051 oz. ASW **Subject:** Naguib Mahfouz, Nobel Laureate **Obv:** Quill in inkwell designed as globe, divides date and denomination **Rev:** Head left

Date	Mintage	F	VF	XF	Unc
AH1409-1988	15,000	—	—	—	12.00

KM# 663 5 POUNDS

17.5000 g., 0.7200 Silver .4051 oz. ASW **Subject:** Advista Arabia II **Obv:** Arabic legends, seals and dates **Rev:** Head with art tools left, date at right

Date	Mintage	F	VF	XF	Unc
AH1409-1989	5,000	—	—	—	12.50

KM# 665 5 POUNDS

17.5000 g., 0.7200 Silver .4051 oz. ASW **Subject:** United Parliamentary Union **Obv:** Denomination divides dates below text **Rev:** Globe within wreath divides buildings, date on top building

Date	Mintage	F	VF	XF	Unc
AH1409-1989	5,000	—	—	—	12.50

KM# 667 5 POUNDS

17.5000 g., 0.7200 Silver .4051 oz. ASW **Subject:** First Arab Olympics **Obv:** Kufic legend below denomination and date within circle **Rev:** Wreath surrounds hand holding pillar with map and rings on top

Date	Mintage	F	VF	XF	Unc
AH1409-1989	8,000	—	—	—	12.50

KM# 669 5 POUNDS

17.5000 g., 0.7200 Silver .4051 oz. ASW **Subject:** National Research Center **Rev:** Stylized ancient and modern research elements

Date	Mintage	F	VF	XF	Unc
AH1409-1989	5,000	—	—	—	12.50

KM# 686 5 POUNDS

17.5000 g., 0.7200 Silver .4051 oz. ASW **Subject:** National Health Insurance **Obv:** Dates and denomination within circle, text below **Rev:** Figures within half moon design on rock, dates below

Date	Mintage	F	VF	XF	Unc
AH1409-1989	3,000	—	—	—	16.00

KM# 678 5 POUNDS

17.5000 g., 0.7200 Silver .4051 oz. ASW **Subject:** University of Cairo - School of Agriculture **Obv:** Denomination and dates within wreath of grain sprigs, text below **Rev:** Shield to right of farmers and oxen, building in background

Date	Mintage	F	VF	XF	Unc
AH1410-1989	4,000	—	—	—	22.00

KM# 679 5 POUNDS
17.5000 g., 0.7200 Silver .4051 oz. ASW **Series:** Soccer World Championship - Italy **Obv:** Circle of text at center of wings, denomination and dates above **Rev:** Ancient gods in front of pyramid with soccer ball above

Date	Mintage	F	VF	XF	Unc
AH1410-1990	600	—	—	—	35.00
AH1410-1990 Proof	8,000	Value: 25.00			

KM# 682 5 POUNDS
17.5000 g., 0.7200 Silver .4051 oz. ASW **Series:** Soccer World Championship - Italy **Obv:** Text within circle at center of wings, denomination and dates above **Rev:** Player chasing ball

Date	Mintage	F	VF	XF	Unc
AH1410-1990 Matte	400	—	—	—	40.00
AH1410-1990 Proof	4,000	Value: 30.00			

KM# 687 5 POUNDS
17.5000 g., 0.7200 Silver .4051 oz. ASW **Subject:** Export Drive **Obv:** Tughra, date and text **Rev:** Stylized symbols

Date	Mintage	F	VF	XF	Unc
AH1410-1990	4,000	—	—	—	15.00

KM# 688 5 POUNDS
17.5000 g., 0.7200 Silver .4051 oz. ASW **Subject:** National Population Center **Obv:** Tughra below dates **Rev:** Repeated design of people forms square at center, which holds text

Date	Mintage	F	VF	XF	Unc
AH1410-1990	5,000	—	—	—	13.50

KM# 689 5 POUNDS
17.5000 g., 0.7200 Silver .4051 oz. ASW **Subject:** Union of African Parliaments **Obv:** Tughra below dates and denomination, within circle **Rev:** Map in background divides grain sprig and building

Date	Mintage	F	VF	XF	Unc
AH1410-1990	5,000	—	—	—	13.50

KM# 691 5 POUNDS
17.8200 g., 0.9000 Silver .5156 oz. ASW **Subject:** Dar-el-Eloun Faculty **Obv:** Denomination and dates within circle above text **Rev:** Bust and shield left of dates, text below

Date	Mintage	F	VF	XF	Unc
AH1410-1990	5,000	—	—	—	14.00

KM# 697 5 POUNDS
17.5000 g., 0.7200 Silver .4051 oz. ASW **Subject:** Newly Populated Areas Organization

Date	Mintage	F	VF	XF	Unc
AH1410-1990	2,000	—	—	—	45.00

KM# 698 5 POUNDS
17.5000 g., 0.7200 Silver .4051 oz. ASW **Subject:** Alexandria Sports Club **Obv:** Denomination and dates within circle above text **Rev:** Athletes surround center circles with text and designs

Date	Mintage	F	VF	XF	Unc
AH1411-1990	5,000	—	—	—	20.00

KM# 692 5 POUNDS
17.8200 g., 0.9000 Silver .5156 oz. ASW **Subject:** Islamic Development Bank **Obv:** Globe back of towered buildings above grasped hands, dentiled design below, grain stalks flank **Rev:** Tughra divided dates above inscription and denomination

Date	Mintage	F	VF	XF	Unc
AH1411-1991	5,000	—	—	—	20.00

KM# 700 5 POUNDS
17.8200 g., 0.9000 Silver .5156 oz. ASW **Subject:** 5th African Games - Cairo

Date	Mintage	F	VF	XF	Unc
AH1411-1991	3,000	—	—	—	30.00

KM# 727 5 POUNDS
17.5000 g., 0.7200 Silver .4051 oz. ASW **Subject:** Muhamed Abdel Wahab **Obv:** Arabic legends and inscriptions **Rev:** Bust left with music sheet in background

Date	Mintage	F	VF	XF	Unc
AH1412-1991	30,000	—	—	—	13.50

KM# 728 5 POUNDS
26.0000 g., 0.8750 Gold .7314 oz. AGW **Subject:** Muhamed Abdel Wahab **Obv:** Arabic legends and inscriptions **Rev:** Bust left with music sheet in background

Date	Mintage	F	VF	XF	Unc
AH1412-1991 Proof	400	—	—	—	540

KM# 791 5 POUNDS
17.4200 g., 0.7200 Silver .4032 oz. ASW **Subject:** National Zoo **Obv:** Zoo entrance, dates and denomination **Rev:** Five zoo animals

Date	Mintage	F	VF	XF	Unc
AH1411-1991	—	—	—	—	25.00

KM# 804 5 POUNDS
17.5000 g., 0.7200 Silver .4051 oz. ASW **Subject:** Atomic Energy **Obv:** Denomination **Rev:** Ancient statue and pyramid within rings

Date	Mintage	F	VF	XF	Unc
AH1411-1991	Est. 5,000	—	—	—	15.00

KM# 805 5 POUNDS
17.5000 g., 0.7200 Silver .4051 oz. ASW **Subject:** Library of Alexandria **Obv:** Arabic inscription, dates **Rev:** Library building complex

Date	Mintage	F	VF	XF	Unc
AH1411-1991	Est. 8,000	—	—	—	15.00

KM# 805a 5 POUNDS
26.0000 g., 0.8750 Gold .7314 oz. AGW **Subject:** Library of Alexandria **Obv:** Arabic inscription **Rev:** Library building complex **Edge:** Reeded **Note:** Struck at Cairo.

Date	Mintage	F	VF	XF	Unc
AH1411-1991 Proof	200	—	—	—	550

KM# 833 5 POUNDS
26.0000 g., 0.8750 Gold .7315 oz. AGW **Subject:** Library of Alexandria **Obv:** Legend and inscription **Rev:** Waterfront building with tower

Date	Mintage	F	VF	XF	Unc
AH1411-1991	200	—	—	—	550

KM# 701 5 POUNDS
17.5000 g., 0.7200 Silver .4051 oz. ASW **Series:** Summer Olympics **Obv:** Text within circle at center of wings, denomination and dates above **Rev:** Two men fencing

Date	Mintage	F	VF	XF	Unc
AH1412-1992	999	—	—	—	42.50
AH1412-1992 Proof	2,999	Value: 40.00			

KM# 702 5 POUNDS
17.5000 g., 0.7200 Silver .4051 oz. ASW **Series:** Summer Olympics **Obv:** Text within circle at center of wings, denomination and dates above **Rev:** Pairs wrestling, half globe below

Date	Mintage	F	VF	XF	Unc
AH1412-1992	999	—	—	—	42.50
AH1412-1992 Proof	2,999	Value: 40.00			

KM# 703 5 POUNDS
17.5000 g., 0.7200 Silver .4051 oz. ASW **Series:** Summer Olympics **Obv:** Text within circle at center of wings, denomination and dates above **Rev:** Archery demonstrated

Date	Mintage	F	VF	XF	Unc
AH1412-1992	999	—	—	—	42.50
AH1412-1992 Proof	2,999	Value: 40.00			

KM# 704 5 POUNDS
17.5000 g., 0.7200 Silver .4051 oz. ASW **Series:** Summer Olympics **Obv:** Text within circle at center of wings, denomination and dates above **Rev:** Many men wrestling an ox

Date	Mintage	F	VF	XF	Unc
AH1412-1992	999	—	—	—	42.50
AH1412-1992 Proof	2,999	Value: 40.00			

KM# 705 5 POUNDS
17.5000 g., 0.7200 Silver .4051 oz. ASW **Series:** Summer Olympics **Obv:** Text within circle at center of wings, denomination and dates above **Rev:** Swimmer stalking a duck

Date	Mintage	F	VF	XF	Unc
AH1412-1992	999	—	—	—	42.50
AH1412-1992 Proof	2,999	Value: 40.00			

KM# 706 5 POUNDS
17.5000 g., 0.7200 Silver .4051 oz. ASW **Series:** Summer Olympics **Rev:** Handball player

Date	Mintage	F	VF	XF	Unc
AH1412-1992	999	—	—	—	42.50
AH1412-1992 Proof	25,000	Value: 20.00			

KM# 707 5 POUNDS
17.5000 g., 0.7200 Silver .4051 oz. ASW **Series:** Summer Olympics **Rev:** Field hockey player

Date	Mintage	F	VF	XF	Unc
AH1412-1992	999	—	—	—	42.50
AH1412-1992 Proof	25,000	Value: 20.00			

KM# 708 5 POUNDS
17.5000 g., 0.7200 Silver .4051 oz. ASW **Series:** Summer Olympics **Obv:** Text within circle at center of wings, denomination and dates above **Rev:** Soccer player kicking ball

Date	Mintage	F	VF	XF	Unc
AH1412-1992	999	—	—	—	42.50
AH1412-1992 Proof	25,000	Value: 20.00			

KM# 806 5 POUNDS
17.5000 g., 0.7200 Silver .4051 oz. ASW **Subject:** Lighthouse of Alexandria **Obv:** Denomination and dates within circle above text **Rev:** Ancient tower and Egyptian

Date	Mintage	F	VF	XF	Unc
AH1412-1992	Est. 3,000	—	—	—	17.50

KM# 807 5 POUNDS
17.5000 g., 0.7200 Silver .4051 oz. ASW **Subject:** 50 Years - University of Alexandria **Obv:** Arabic inscription, dates **Rev:** University emblem divides dates

Date	Mintage	F	VF	XF	Unc
AH1413-1992	Est. 3,000	—	—	—	18.50

KM# 808 5 POUNDS
17.5000 g., 0.7200 Silver .4051 oz. ASW **Subject:** Naguib Mahfouz, Nobel Laureate **Obv:** Vase and inscriptions, dates below **Rev:** Bust right

Date	Mintage	F	VF	XF	Unc
AH1413-1992	Est. 6,000	—	—	—	15.00

KM# 746 5 POUNDS

22.5000 g., 0.9990 Silver .7227 oz. ASW **Subject:** Menkaure Triad **Obv:** Vulture, denomination above and dates below **Rev:** Three figures

Date	Mintage	F	VF	XF	Unc
AH1414-1993 Proof	50,000	Value: 30.00			

KM# 735 5 POUNDS

22.5000 g., 0.9990 Silver .7227 oz. ASW **Subject:** Cleopatra - queen and statesperson, 69-30BC **Obv:** Vulture, denomination above and dates below **Rev:** Bust in formal headdress left

Date	Mintage	F	VF	XF	Unc
AH1413-1993 Proof	50,000	Value: 36.50			

KM# 740 5 POUNDS

22.5000 g., 0.9990 Silver .7227 oz. ASW **Subject:** Pyramids **Obv:** Vulture, denomination above and dates below **Rev:** Three pyramids

Date	Mintage	F	VF	XF	Unc
AH1414-1993 Proof	50,000	Value: 36.50			

KM# 741 5 POUNDS

22.5000 g., 0.9990 Silver .7227 oz. ASW **Obv:** Vulture, denomination above and dates below **Rev:** Sphinx

Date	Mintage	F	VF	XF	Unc
AH1414-1993 Proof	50,000	Value: 36.50			

KM# 742 5 POUNDS

22.5000 g., 0.9990 Silver .7227 oz. ASW **Subject:** King Narmur Smiting a Foe **Obv:** Vulture, denomination above and dates below **Rev:** Decorative vase depicting punishment scene

Date	Mintage	F	VF	XF	Unc
AH1414-1993 Proof	50,000	Value: 30.00			

KM# 743 5 POUNDS

22.5000 g., 0.9990 Silver .7227 oz. ASW **Obv:** Vulture, denomination above and dates below **Rev:** Guardian Goddess Serket

Date	Mintage	F	VF	XF	Unc
AH1414-1993 Proof	50,000	Value: 30.00			

KM# 744 5 POUNDS

22.5000 g., 0.9990 Silver .7227 oz. ASW **Subject:** Amulet of Hathor **Obv:** Vulture, denomination above and dates below **Rev:** Sculpture of head

Date	Mintage	F	VF	XF	Unc
AH1414-1993 Proof	50,000	Value: 30.00			

KM# 745 5 POUNDS

22.5000 g., 0.9990 Silver .7227 oz. ASW **Obv:** Vulture, denomination above and dates below **Rev:** Standing Ramses II

Date	Mintage	F	VF	XF	Unc
AH1414-1993 Proof	50,000	Value: 30.00			

KM# 747 5 POUNDS

22.5000 g., 0.9990 Silver .7227 oz. ASW **Subject:** Symbol of Unification **Obv:** Vulture, denomination above and dates below **Rev:** Two females representing the upper and lower Nile

Date	Mintage	F	VF	XF	Unc
AH1414-1993 Proof	50,000	Value: 30.00			

KM# 748 5 POUNDS

22.5000 g., 0.9990 Silver .7227 oz. ASW **Series:** World Cup Soccer **Obv:** Vulture, denomination above and dates below **Rev:** Kneeling King Pepi I facing

Date	Mintage	F	VF	XF	Unc
AH1414-1993 Proof	—	Value: 32.50			
AH1415-1994 Proof	50,000	Value: 30.00			

KM# 759 5 POUNDS

17.5000 g., 0.7200 Silver .4051 oz. ASW **Subject:** Beram El Tunsi, Poet **Obv:** Inscription and seals, dates below **Rev:** Bust 3/4 left

Date	Mintage	F	VF	XF	Unc
AH1413-1993	3,000	—	—	—	25.00

KM# 793 5 POUNDS

22.5000 g., 0.9990 Silver .7227 oz. ASW **Obv:** Vulture, denomination above and dates below **Rev:** Tutankhamen's burial mask

Date	Mintage	F	VF	XF	Unc
AH1414-1993 Proof	—	Value: 37.50			

KM# 812 5 POUNDS
17.5000 g., 0.7200 Silver .4051 oz. ASW **Subject:** 20th Anniversary - October War **Obv:** Smoking towers divide dates **Rev:** Soldier with flag

Date	Mintage	F	VF	XF	Unc
AH1414-1993	Est. 5,000	—	—	—	15.00

KM# 837 5 POUNDS
17.5000 g., 0.7200 Silver .4051 oz. ASW **Subject:** 125th Anniversary of Taalat Harb Birth **Obv:** Denomination and date in circle above inscription **Rev:** Taalat Harb wearing fez **Edge:** Reeded

Date	Mintage	F	VF	XF	Unc
AH1413-1993	5,000	—	—	—	25.00

KM# 869 5 POUNDS
22.5500 g., 0.9990 Silver .7243 oz. ASW **Subject:** King Kha-Sekhem **Obv:** Vulture, denomination above and dates below **Rev:** Seated figure **Edge:** Reeded

Date	Mintage	F	VF	XF	Unc
AH1414-1993 Proof	15,000	—	—	—	45.00

KM# 879 5 POUNDS
26.0000 g., 0.8750 Gold .7315 oz. AGW **Subject:** Symbol of Unification **Obv:** Vulture, denomination above and dates below **Rev:** Two females representing the upper and lower Nile

Date	Mintage	F	VF	XF	Unc
AH1414-1993 Proof	3,000	—	—	—	500

KM# 736 5 POUNDS
17.5000 g., 0.9250 Silver .5205 oz. ASW **Series:** World Cup Soccer **Obv:** Text within circle at center of wings, dates above divided by oval shield **Rev:** Two players, pyramid with Statue of Liberty at left

Date	Mintage	F	VF	XF	Unc
AH1415-1994	499	—	—	—	45.00
AH1415-1994 Proof	15,000	Value: 40.00			

KM# 738 5 POUNDS
17.5000 g., 0.9250 Silver .5205 oz. ASW **Series:** World Cup Soccer **Rev:** Stylized player

Date	Mintage	F	VF	XF	Unc
AH1415-1994	499	—	—	—	45.00
AH1415-1994 Proof	15,000	Value: 40.00			

KM# 749 5 POUNDS
22.5000 g., 0.9990 Silver .7227 oz. ASW **Obv:** Vulture, denomination above and dates below **Rev:** Sphinx and pyramids

Date	Mintage	F	VF	XF	Unc
AH1414-1994 Proof	50,000	Value: 32.50			

KM# 750 5 POUNDS
22.5000 g., 0.9990 Silver .7227 oz. ASW **Obv:** Vulture, denomination above and dates below **Rev:** King Djoser wearing the Red Crown right

Date	Mintage	F	VF	XF	Unc
AH1415-1994 Proof	50,000	Value: 30.00			

KM# 751 5 POUNDS
22.5000 g., 0.9990 Silver .7227 oz. ASW **Obv:** Vulture, denomination above and dates below **Rev:** King Khonsu facing

Date	Mintage	F	VF	XF	Unc
AH1415-1994 Proof	50,000	Value: 30.00			

KM# 752 5 POUNDS
22.5000 g., 0.9990 Silver .7227 oz. ASW **Obv:** Vulture, denomination above and dates below **Rev:** RE (Sun God) presenting the Ankh (Symbol of Life) to Sesostris I wearing Double Crown

Date	Mintage	F	VF	XF	Unc
AH1415-1994 Proof	50,000	Value: 30.00			

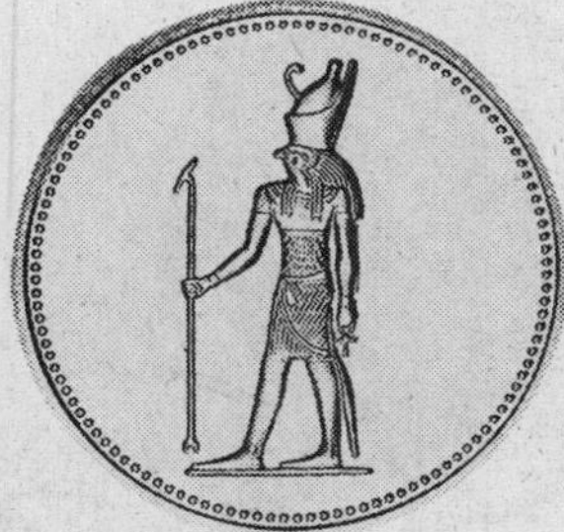

KM# 753 5 POUNDS
22.5000 g., 0.9990 Silver .7227 oz. ASW **Obv:** Vulture, denomination above and dates below **Rev:** God Horus wearing Double Crown

Date	Mintage	F	VF	XF	Unc
AH1415-1994 Proof	50,000	Value: 30.00			

KM# 754 5 POUNDS
22.5000 g., 0.9990 Silver .7227 oz. ASW **Obv:** Vulture, denomination above and dates below **Rev:** Standing god Seth left

Date	Mintage	F	VF	XF	Unc
AH1415-1994 Proof	50,000	Value: 30.00			

KM# 757 5 POUNDS
22.5000 g., 0.9990 Silver .7227 oz. ASW **Obv:** Vulture, denomination above and dates below **Rev:** Queen Nefretari, wife of Ramses II kneeling right

Date	Mintage	F	VF	XF	Unc
AH1415-1994 Proof	Est. 25,000	Value: 37.50			

KM# 763 5 POUNDS
17.5000 g., 0.7200 Silver .4051 oz. ASW **Subject:** Salah El Din El-Ayubi **Obv:** Dates and denomination within circle above text **Rev:** Bust at center, mosque behind at left, mounted rider with sword at right

Date	Mintage	F	VF	XF	Unc
AH1414-1994	5,000	—	—	—	25.00

KM# 783 5 POUNDS
22.5000 g., 0.9990 Silver .7227 oz. ASW **Obv:** Ancient style vulture **Rev:** Bust of Nefertiti right

Date	Mintage	F	VF	XF	Unc
AH1415-1994 Proof	50,000	Value: 36.50			

KM# 784 5 POUNDS
22.5000 g., 0.9990 Silver .7227 oz. ASW **Obv:** Vulture, denomination above and dates below **Rev:** Archer in chariot

Date	Mintage	F	VF	XF	Unc
AH1415-1994 Proof	50,000	Value: 37.50			

KM# 785 5 POUNDS
22.5000 g., 0.9990 Silver .7227 oz. ASW **Obv:** Vulture, denomination above and dates below **Rev:** Five birds

Date	Mintage	F	VF	XF	Unc
AH1415-1994 Proof	50,000	Value: 40.00			

KM# 786 5 POUNDS
22.5000 g., 0.9990 Silver .7227 oz. ASW **Obv:** Vulture, denomination above and dates below **Rev:** Hippopotamus right

Date	Mintage	F	VF	XF	Unc
AH1415-1994 Proof	50,000	Value: 40.00			

KM# 787 5 POUNDS
22.5000 g., 0.9990 Silver .7227 oz. ASW **Obv:** Vulture, denomination above and dates below **Rev:** Ruins of Karnak

Date	Mintage	F	VF	XF	Unc
AH1415-1994 Proof	50,000	Value: 30.00			

KM# 788 5 POUNDS
22.5000 g., 0.9990 Silver .7227 oz. ASW **Obv:** Vulture, denomination above and dates below **Rev:** Standing Goddess Neith wearing the Red Crown

Date	Mintage	F	VF	XF	Unc
AH1415-1994 Proof	50,000	Value: 30.00			

KM# 789 5 POUNDS
22.5000 g., 0.9990 Silver .7227 oz. ASW **Obv:** Vulture, denomination above and dates below **Rev:** Statue of King Amenemhat III

Date	Mintage	F	VF	XF	Unc
AH1415-1994 Proof	50,000	Value: 30.00			

KM# 790 5 POUNDS
22.5000 g., 0.9990 Silver .7227 oz. ASW **Obv:** Vulture, denomination above and dates below **Rev:** Ritual mask of Queen Hatshepsut, female Pharoah, peacemaker, died 1468BC

Date	Mintage	F	VF	XF	Unc
AH1415-1994 Proof	50,000	Value: 30.00			

KM# 792 5 POUNDS
15.0000 g., 0.7200 Silver .3472 oz. ASW **Subject:** ICPD Cairo **Obv:** Inscription and seals **Rev:** Stylized design

Date	Mintage	F	VF	XF	Unc
AH1415-1994	—	—	—	—	17.50

KM# 794 5 POUNDS
22.5950 g., 0.9990 Silver .7264 oz. ASW **Obv:** Vulture, denomination above and dates below **Rev:** Seated, jeweled cat

Date	Mintage	F	VF	XF	Unc
AH1415-1994 Proof	—	Value: 40.00			

KM# 795 5 POUNDS
22.5950 g., 0.9990 Silver .7264 oz. ASW **Obv:** Vulture, denomination above and dates below **Rev:** Sacred falcon at Edfu

Date	Mintage	F	VF	XF	Unc
AH1415-1994 Proof	—	Value: 40.00			

KM# 797 5 POUNDS
22.5950 g., 0.9990 Silver .7264 oz. ASW **Obv:** Vulture, denomination above and dates below **Rev:** Tutankhamen's throne

Date	Mintage	F	VF	XF	Unc
AH1415-1994 Proof	—	Value: 31.50			

KM# 798 5 POUNDS
22.5950 g., 0.9990 Silver .7264 oz. ASW **Obv:** Vulture, denomination above and dates below **Rev:** King Au as high priest

Date	Mintage	F	VF	XF	Unc
AH1415-1994 Proof	—	Value: 31.50			

KM# 799 5 POUNDS
22.5950 g., 0.9990 Silver .7264 oz. ASW **Obv:** Vulture, denomination above and dates below **Rev:** Akhnaton

Date	Mintage	F	VF	XF	Unc
AH1415-1994 Proof	—	Value: 40.00			

KM# 800 5 POUNDS
22.5950 g., 0.9990 Silver .7264 oz. ASW **Obv:** Vulture, denomination above and dates below **Rev:** Osiris, seated right

Date	Mintage	F	VF	XF	Unc
AH1415-1994 Proof	—	Value: 30.00			

KM# 801 5 POUNDS
22.5950 g., 0.9990 Silver .7264 oz. ASW **Obv:** Vulture, denomination above and dates below **Rev:** RE, the sun god, walking left

Date	Mintage	F	VF	XF	Unc
AH1415-1994 Proof	—	Value: 30.00			

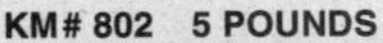

KM# 802 5 POUNDS
22.5950 g., 0.9990 Silver .7264 oz. ASW **Obv:** Vulture, denomination above and dates below **Rev:** The God Khnoum, walking right

Date	Mintage	F	VF	XF	Unc
AH1415-1994 Proof	—	Value: 37.50			

KM# 803 5 POUNDS
22.5950 g., 0.9990 Silver .7264 oz. ASW **Obv:** Vulture, denomination above and dates below **Rev:** Sobek, Crocodile God, walking left

Date	Mintage	F	VF	XF	Unc
AH1415-1994 Proof	—	Value: 37.50			

KM# 813 5 POUNDS
22.5500 g., 0.9990 Silver .7243 oz. ASW **Obv:** Vulture, denomination above and dates below **Rev:** Ancient seated scribe **Edge:** Reeded

Date	Mintage	F	VF	XF	Unc
AH1415-1994 Proof	—	Value: 37.50			

KM# 823 5 POUNDS
22.5000 g., 0.9990 Silver .7227 oz. ASW **Obv:** Vulture, denomination above and dates below **Rev:** Temple of Ramses II

Date	Mintage	F	VF	XF	Unc
AH1415-1994 Proof	—	Value: 36.50			

KM# 824 5 POUNDS
22.5000 g., 0.9990 Silver .7227 oz. ASW **Obv:** Vulture, denomination above and dates below **Rev:** Ancient ruins

Date	Mintage	F	VF	XF	Unc
AH1415-1994 Proof	—	Value: 30.00			

KM# 825 5 POUNDS
22.5000 g., 0.9990 Silver .7227 oz. ASW **Obv:** Vulture, denomination above and dates below **Rev:** Egyptian gazelle right

Date	Mintage	F	VF	XF	Unc
AH1415-1994 Proof	—	Value: 35.00			

KM# 826 5 POUNDS
22.5000 g., 0.9990 Silver .7227 oz. ASW **Obv:** Vulture, denomination above and dates below **Rev:** King Thoutmosis III, kneeling, left

Date	Mintage	F	VF	XF	Unc
AH1415-1994 Proof	—	Value: 30.00			

KM# 827 5 POUNDS
22.5000 g., 0.9990 Silver .7227 oz. ASW **Obv:** Vulture, denomination above and dates below **Rev:** Seated King Khufu

Date	Mintage	F	VF	XF	Unc
AH1415-1994 Proof	—	Value: 30.00			

KM# 828 5 POUNDS
22.5000 g., 0.9990 Silver .7227 oz. ASW **Obv:** Vulture, denomination above and dates below **Rev:** Standing Goddess Hathor left

Date	Mintage	F	VF	XF	Unc
AH1415-1994 Proof	—	Value: 30.00			

KM# 829 5 POUNDS
22.5000 g., 0.9990 Silver .7227 oz. ASW **Obv:** Vulture, denomination above and dates below **Rev:** Standing God Ptah of Memphis right

Date	Mintage	F	VF	XF	Unc
AH1415-1994 Proof	—	Value: 30.00			

KM# 830 5 POUNDS
22.5000 g., 0.9990 Silver .7227 oz. ASW **Obv:** Vulture, denomination above and dates below **Rev:** Seated Goddess Isis nursing child

Date	Mintage	F	VF	XF	Unc
AH1415-1994 Proof	—	Value: 30.00			

KM# 831 5 POUNDS
22.5000 g., 0.9990 Silver .7227 oz. ASW **Obv:** Vulture, denomination above and dates below **Rev:** Dwarf Seneb and family

Date	Mintage	F	VF	XF	Unc
AH1415-1994 Proof	—	Value: 30.00			

KM# 874 5 POUNDS
26.0000 g., 0.8750 Gold .7315 oz. AGW **Rev:** Sphinx and pyramids

Date	Mintage	F	VF	XF	Unc
AH1415-1994 Proof	5,000	—	—	—	500

KM# 875 5 POUNDS
22.5000 g., 0.9990 Silver .7227 oz. ASW **Rev:** 3/4-length standing Sheikh El Balad

Date	Mintage	F	VF	XF	Unc
AH1415-1994 Proof	15,000	Value: 40.00			

KM# 876 5 POUNDS
26.0000 g., 0.8750 Gold .7315 oz. AGW **Rev:** 3/4-length standing Sheikh El Balad

Date	Mintage	F	VF	XF	Unc
AH1415-1994 Proof	3,000	Value: 500			

KM# 878 5 POUNDS
26.0000 g., 0.8750 Gold .7315 oz. AGW **Obv:** Vulture, denomination above and dates below **Rev:** Dwarf Seneb and family

Date	Mintage	F	VF	XF	Unc
AH1415-1994 Proof	3,000	—	—	—	500

KM# 880 5 POUNDS
26.0000 g., 0.8750 Gold .7315 oz. AGW **Rev:** Kneeling King Pepi I facing

Date	Mintage	F	VF	XF	Unc
AH1415-1994 Proof	3,000	—	—	—	500

KM# 881 5 POUNDS
26.0000 g., 0.8750 Gold .7315 oz. AGW **Rev:** Statue of King Amenemhat III

Date	Mintage	F	VF	XF	Unc
AH1415-1994 Proof	3,000	—	—	—	500

KM# 883 5 POUNDS
22.5000 g., 0.9990 Silver .7227 oz. ASW **Rev:** Seated King Horemheb

Date	Mintage	F	VF	XF	Unc
AH1415-1994 Proof	15,000	Value: 40.00			

KM# 889 5 POUNDS
22.5000 g., 0.9990 Silver .7227 oz. ASW **Obv:** Vulture, denomination above and dates below **Rev:** Akhnaton and family

Date	Mintage	F	VF	XF	Unc
AH1415-1994 Proof	15,000	Value: 40.00			

KM# 894 5 POUNDS
22.5000 g., 0.9990 Silver .7227 oz. ASW **Obv:** Vulture, denomination above and dates below **Rev:** Bust amulet of Hathor

Date	Mintage	F	VF	XF	Unc
AH1415-1994 Proof	15,000	Value: 40.00			

KM# 896 5 POUNDS
22.5000 g., 0.9990 Silver .7227 oz. ASW **Rev:** Pair of geese

Date	Mintage	F	VF	XF	Unc
AH1415-1994 Proof	15,000	Value: 40.00			

KM# 765 5 POUNDS
17.5000 g., 0.7200 Silver .4051 oz. ASW **Subject:** 50 Years - Arab League **Obv:** Dates and denomination within circle above text **Rev:** Buildings and emblem

Date	Mintage	F	VF	XF	Unc
AH1415-1995	5,000	—	—	—	22.50

KM# 768 5 POUNDS
17.5000 g., 0.7200 Silver .4051 oz. ASW **Subject:** 75 Years - Bank of Misr

Date	Mintage	F	VF	XF	Unc
AH1415-1995	2,500	—	—	—	28.00

KM# 770 5 POUNDS
17.5000 g., 0.7200 Silver .4051 oz. ASW **Series:** F.A.O. **Obv:** Tughra above logo **Rev:** People working

Date	Mintage	F	VF	XF	Unc
AH1415-1995	5,000	—	—	—	50.00

KM# 772 5 POUNDS
17.5000 g., 0.7200 Silver .4051 oz. ASW **Subject:** Pediatrics International Conference

Date	Mintage	F	VF	XF	Unc
AH1416-1995	4,000	—	—	—	22.00

KM# 773 5 POUNDS
17.5000 g., 0.7200 Silver .4051 oz. ASW **Subject:** 75 Years - Architects Association **Obv:** Outline of building divides dates **Rev:** Seated statue

Date	Mintage	F	VF	XF	Unc
AH1416-1995	3,000	—	—	—	50.00

KM# 838 5 POUNDS
17.5000 g., 0.7200 Silver .4051 oz. ASW **Subject:** 75 Years - American University in Cairo **Rev:** Design in center surrounded by inscriptions and border

Date	Mintage	F	VF	XF	Unc
AH1415-1995	3,000	—	—	—	25.00

KM# 841 5 POUNDS
17.5000 g., 0.7200 Silver .4051 oz. ASW **Obv:** Tughra **Rev:** Abd Al Halem Hafez left

Date	Mintage	F	VF	XF	Unc
AH1416-1995	5,000	—	—	—	45.00

KM# 774 5 POUNDS
26.0000 g., 0.8750 Gold .7315 oz. AGW **Subject:** 75 Years - Architects Association **Obv:** Tughra **Rev:** Head left

Date	Mintage	F	VF	XF	Unc
AH1416-1995	300	—	—	—	550

KM# 842 5 POUNDS
26.0000 g., 0.8750 Gold .7315 oz. AGW **Rev:** Abd Al Halem Hafez

Date	Mintage	F	VF	XF	Unc
AH1416-1995	500	—	—	—	550

KM# 843 5 POUNDS
17.5000 g., 0.9000 Silver .5084 oz. ASW **Subject:** Centennial - Mining and Geology **Obv:** Denomination with toughra **Rev:** Building in circle

Date	Mintage	F	VF	XF	Unc
AH1416-1996	700	—	—	—	75.00

KM# 846 5 POUNDS
17.5000 g., 0.9000 Silver .5084 oz. ASW **Subject:** 65 Years - Egyptian Air Force **Rev:** Flying eagle in wreath

Date	Mintage	F	VF	XF	Unc
AH1418-1997	300	—	—	—	85.00

KM# 848 5 POUNDS
17.5000 g., 0.9000 Silver .5084 oz. ASW **Subject:** 50 Years Arab Land Bank **Rev:** Arab Real Estate domed Bank building

Date	Mintage	F	VF	XF	Unc
AH1418-1997	3,000	—	—	—	37.50

KM# 850 5 POUNDS
17.5000 g., 0.9000 Silver .5084 oz. ASW **Subject:** 95th Interparliamentary Union Conference **Obv:** Circular design above inscription **Rev:** Pyramids in wreath

Date	Mintage	F	VF	XF	Unc
AH1418-1997	375	—	—	—	85.00

KM# 852 5 POUNDS
17.5000 g., 0.9000 Silver .5084 oz. ASW **Subject:** Centennial - Chemical Department **Rev:** Symbolic design

Date	Mintage	F	VF	XF	Unc
AH1419-1998	1,000	—	—	—	40.00

KM# 853 5 POUNDS
17.5000 g., 0.9000 Silver .5084 oz. ASW **Subject:** Restoration of Al Azhar Mosque

Date	Mintage	F	VF	XF	Unc
AH1419-1998	4,000	—	—	—	37.50

KM# 856 5 POUNDS
17.5000 g., 0.9000 Silver .5084 oz. ASW **Subject:** Centennial of National Bank **Rev:** Large "100"

Date	Mintage	F	VF	XF	Unc
AH1419-1998	2,000	—	—	—	85.00

KM# 858 5 POUNDS
17.5000 g., 0.9000 Silver .5084 oz. ASW **Subject:** 25th Anniversary - October War **Rev:** Symbolic design

Date	Mintage	F	VF	XF	Unc
AH1419-1998	1,500	—	—	—	40.00

KM# 860 5 POUNDS
17.5000 g., 0.9000 Silver .5084 oz. ASW **Subject:** Death of El Sheikh M. Metwaly El Sharawy **Rev:** Bust of Imam Metwaly El Sharawi facing

Date	Mintage	F	VF	XF	Unc
AH1419-1998	3,000	—	—	—	40.00

KM# 862 5 POUNDS
17.5000 g., 0.9000 Silver .5084 oz. ASW **Subject:** Centennial - Land Surveying **Rev:** "100" above ancient surveyors

Date	Mintage	F	VF	XF	Unc
AH1419-1998	6,000	—	—	—	40.00

KM# 864 5 POUNDS
17.5000 g., 0.9000 Silver .5084 oz. ASW **Subject:** Centennial - Solidarity **Rev:** Symbolic design

Date	Mintage	F	VF	XF	Unc
AH1419-1998	9,500	—	—	—	37.50

KM# 854 5 POUNDS
17.5000 g., 0.9000 Silver .5084 oz. ASW **Subject:** 16th Men's World Handball Championship **Obv:** Denomination and dates **Rev:** Handball game

Date	Mintage	F	VF	XF	Unc
AH1420-1999	6,500	—	—	—	45.00

KM# 867 5 POUNDS
17.5000 g., 0.9000 Silver .5084 oz. ASW **Subject:** 50 Years Cairo Metropolitan Mass Transit System **Rev:** Water above subway train

Date	Mintage	F	VF	XF	Unc
AH1420-1999	2,000	—	—	—	40.00

KM# 897 5 POUNDS
17.5000 g., 0.9000 Silver .5084 oz. ASW **Subject:** 75 Years - Dar El-Eloum University

Date	Mintage	F	VF	XF	Unc
AH1420-1999	2,000	—	—	—	40.00

KM# 898 5 POUNDS
17.3300 g., 0.9750 Silver 0.5432 oz. ASW, 37 mm. **Subject:** Sacred falcon **Obv:** Denomination and inscription **Rev:** Ancient sacred falcon **Edge:** Reeded

Date	Mintage	F	VF	XF	Unc
AH1420-1999 Proof	—	Value: 50.00			

KM# 899 5 POUNDS
17.3300 g., 0.9750 Silver 0.5432 oz. ASW, 37 mm. **Obv:** Denomination and inscription **Rev:** Two statues of Ramses II **Edge:** Reeded

Date	Mintage	F	VF	XF	Unc
AH1420-1999 Proof	—	Value: 50.00			

KM# 900 5 POUNDS
17.3300 g., 0.9750 Silver 0.5432 oz. ASW, 37 mm. **Obv:** Denomination and inscription **Rev:** Tutankhamen's Death Mask **Edge:** Reeded

Date	Mintage	F	VF	XF	Unc
AH1420-1999 Proof	—	Value: 50.00			

KM# 901 5 POUNDS
17.3300 g., 0.9750 Silver 0.5432 oz. ASW, 37 mm. **Obv:** Denomination and inscription **Rev:** Bust of Nefertiti right **Rev. Designer:** Dominic Angelini **Edge:** Reeded

Date	Mintage	F	VF	XF	Unc
AH1420-1999 Proof	—	Value: 50.00			

KM# 902 5 POUNDS
17.3300 g., 0.9750 Silver 0.5432 oz. ASW, 37 mm. **Obv:** Denomination and inscription **Rev:** Imaginary bust of Cleopatra left **Edge:** Reeded

Date	Mintage	F	VF	XF	Unc
AH1420-1999 Proof	—	Value: 50.00			

KM# 927 5 POUNDS
17.5000 g., 0.7200 Silver 0.4051 oz. ASW, 37 mm. **Subject:** Ain Shams University **Obv:** Value **Rev:** Shams University logo above anniversary dates 2000-1950 **Edge:** Reeded

Date	Mintage	F	VF	XF	Unc
1999-1420AH	1,000	—	—	—	45.00

KM# 929 5 POUNDS
17.5000 g., 0.7250 Silver 0.4079 oz. ASW, 37 mm. **Subject:** National Insurance Company Centennial **Obv:** Value **Rev:** Ancient seated figure with "100" **Edge:** Reeded

Date	Mintage	F	VF	XF	Unc
2000-1421AH	2,500	—	—	—	45.00

KM# 519 10 POUNDS
40.0000 g., 0.8750 Gold 1.1254 oz. AGW **Subject:** Egyptian-Israeli Peace Treaty **Obv:** Denomination divides dates **Rev:** Head at right facing left, dove with olive branch at left

Date	Mintage	F	VF	XF	Unc
AH1400-1980	950	—	—	—	875
AH1400-1980 Proof	50	Value: 1,200			

KM# 538 10 POUNDS
40.0000 g., 0.8750 Gold 1.1254 oz. AGW **Subject:** 25th Anniversary - Ministry of Industry **Obv:** Text, denomination and dates **Rev:** Factory building, cogwheel at right

Date	Mintage	F	VF	XF	Unc
AH1402-1981	18	—	—	—	1,500
AH1402-1981 Proof	1,000	Value: 800			

KM# 548 10 POUNDS
40.0000 g., 0.8750 Gold 1.1254 oz. AGW **Subject:** 1000th Anniversary - Al Azhar Mosque **Obv:** Text within circle divides dates **Rev:** Mosque

Date	Mintage	F	VF	XF	Unc
AH1402-1982 Proof	1,322	Value: 800			

KM# 634 10 POUNDS
40.0000 g., 0.8750 Gold 1.1254 oz. AGW **Subject:** Prophet's Mosque **Obv:** Minaret, globe, denomination, legends **Rev:** Crescent, mosque, minaret below legend arch

Date	Mintage	F	VF	XF	Unc
AH1406-1985 Proof	300	Value: 800			

KM# 672 50 POUNDS
8.5000 g., 0.9000 Gold .2460 oz. AGW **Series:** World Soccer Championships **Obv:** Stylized flowers, denomination, date and legends **Rev:** Soccer ball on road between Mexican and Egyptian pyramids

Date	Mintage	F	VF	XF	Unc
AH1406-1986	250	—	—	—	275
AH1406-1986 Proof	250	Value: 325			

KM# 641 50 POUNDS
8.5000 g., 0.9000 Gold .2460 oz. AGW **Subject:** Mecca **Obv:** Arabic legend, ornamentation **Rev:** Interior view of the Kaaba

Date	Mintage	F	VF	XF	Unc
AH1406-1986	14,000	—	—	—	200

KM# 612 50 POUNDS
8.5000 g., 0.9000 Gold .2460 oz. AGW **Subject:** Aida Opera **Obv:** Radiant sun, pillars and inscriptions **Rev:** Ancient figures among ruins

Date	Mintage	F	VF	XF	Unc
AH1407-1987	40,000	—	—	—	225

KM# 625 50 POUNDS
8.5000 g., 0.9000 Gold .2460 oz. AGW **Series:** Summer Olympics **Obv:** Arabic legend and ornamentation within English legend **Rev:** Pharoah and athletes

Date	Mintage	F	VF	XF	Unc
AH1408-1988	150	—	—	—	325
AH1408-1988 Proof	50	Value: 375			

KM# 627 50 POUNDS
8.5000 g., 0.9000 Gold .2460 oz. AGW **Series:** Summer Olympics **Rev:** Athletes and mythological figures

Date	Mintage	F	VF	XF	Unc
AH1408-1988	750	—	—	—	275
AH1408-1988 Proof	250	Value: 325			

KM# 629 50 POUNDS
8.5000 g., 0.9000 Gold .2460 oz. AGW **Series:** Winter Olympics **Obv:** Winged design, English legend, Arabic inscription **Rev:** Ski jumper and figure skater within Arabic legend

Date	Mintage	F	VF	XF	Unc
AH1408-1988	150	—	—	—	325
AH1408-1988 Proof	50	Value: 375			

KM# 680 50 POUNDS
8.5000 g., 0.9000 Gold .2460 oz. AGW **Subject:** Soccer World Championship - Italy **Obv:** Text within circle at center of wings, denomination and dates above **Rev:** Ancient gods

Date	Mintage	F	VF	XF	Unc
AH1410-1990 Proof	225	Value: 450			

KM# 683 50 POUNDS
8.5000 g., 0.9000 Gold .2460 oz. AGW **Subject:** Soccer World Championship **Rev:** Player chasing ball

Date	Mintage	F	VF	XF	Unc
AH1410-1990 Proof	75	Value: 525			

KM# 709 50 POUNDS
8.5000 g., 0.9000 Gold .2460 oz. AGW **Series:** Summer Olympics **Obv:** Text within circle at center of wings, denomination and dates above **Rev:** Fencing

Date	Mintage	F	VF	XF	Unc
AH1412-1992	49	—	—	—	475
AH1412-1992 Proof	99	Value: 475			

KM# 710 50 POUNDS
8.5000 g., 0.9000 Gold .2460 oz. AGW **Series:** Summer Olympics **Obv:** Text within circle at center of wings, denomination and dates above **Rev:** Wrestling, half globe below

Date	Mintage	F	VF	XF	Unc
AH1412-1992	49	—	—	—	475
AH1412-1992 Proof	99	Value: 475			

KM# 711 50 POUNDS
8.5000 g., 0.9000 Gold .2460 oz. AGW **Series:** Summer Olympics **Obv:** Text within circle at center of wings, denomination and dates above **Rev:** Archery

Date	Mintage	F	VF	XF	Unc
AH1412-1992	49	—	—	—	475
AH1412-1992 Proof	99	Value: 475			

KM# 712 50 POUNDS
8.5000 g., 0.9000 Gold .2460 oz. AGW **Series:** Summer Olympics **Obv:** Text within circle at center of wings, denomination and dates above **Rev:** Many men wrestling an ox

Date	Mintage	F	VF	XF	Unc
AH1412-1992	49	—	—	—	475
AH1412-1992 Proof	99	Value: 475			

KM# 713 50 POUNDS
8.5000 g., 0.9000 Gold .2460 oz. AGW **Series:** Summer Olympics **Obv:** Text within circle at center of wings, denomination and dates above **Rev:** Swimmer stalking a duck

Date	Mintage	F	VF	XF	Unc
AH1412-1992	49	—	—	—	475
AH1412-1992 Proof	99	Value: 475			

KM# 714 50 POUNDS
8.5000 g., 0.9000 Gold .2460 oz. AGW **Series:** Summer Olympics **Obv:** Text within circle at center of wings, denomination and dates above **Rev:** Handball player

Date	Mintage	F	VF	XF	Unc
AH1412-1992	49	—	—	—	475
AH1412-1992 Proof	99	Value: 475			

KM# 715 50 POUNDS
8.5000 g., 0.9000 Gold .2460 oz. AGW **Series:** Summer Olympics **Obv:** Text within circle at center of wings, denomination and dates above **Rev:** Field hockey player

Date	Mintage	F	VF	XF	Unc
AH1412-1992	49	—	—	—	475
AH1412-1992 Proof	99	Value: 475			

KM# 716 50 POUNDS
8.5000 g., 0.9000 Gold .2460 oz. AGW **Series:** Summer Olympics **Obv:** Text within circle at center of wings, denomination and dates above **Rev:** Soccer player kicking ball

Date	Mintage	F	VF	XF	Unc
AH1412-1992	49	—	—	—	475
AH1412-1992 Proof	115	Value: 475			

KM# 755 50 POUNDS
8.5000 g., 0.9000 Gold .2460 oz. AGW **Obv:** Vulture, denomination above and dates below **Rev:** King Tutankhamen's burial mask

Date	Mintage	F	VF	XF	Unc
AH1414-1993 Proof	—	Value: 275			

KM# 756 50 POUNDS
8.5000 g., 0.9000 Gold .2460 oz. AGW **Subject:** Cleopatra **Obv:** Vulture, denomination above and dates below **Rev:** Bust left

Date	Mintage	F	VF	XF	Unc
AH1414-1993 Proof	—	Value: 250			

KM# 776 50 POUNDS
8.5000 g., 0.9000 Gold .2460 oz. AGW **Obv:** Vulture, denomination above and dates below **Rev:** Sphinx head

Date	Mintage	F	VF	XF	Unc
AH1414-1993 Proof	—	Value: 225			

KM# 777 50 POUNDS
8.5000 g., 0.9000 Gold .2460 oz. AGW **Obv:** Vulture, denomination above and dates below **Rev:** Standing Ramses II

Date	Mintage	F	VF	XF	Unc
AH1414-1993 Proof	—	Value: 225			

KM# 778 50 POUNDS
8.5000 g., 0.9000 Gold .2460 oz. AGW **Obv:** Vulture, denomination above and dates below **Rev:** Crowned falcon left

Date	Mintage	F	VF	XF	Unc
AH1414-1993 Proof	—	Value: 240			

KM# 868 50 POUNDS
8.5000 g., 0.9000 Gold .2460 oz. AGW **Subject:** King Narmer Palette **Obv:** Vulture, denomination above and dates below **Rev:** King killing a wounded foe

Date	Mintage	F	VF	XF	Unc
AH1414-1993 Proof	3,000	Value: 265			

KM# 870 50 POUNDS
8.5000 g., 0.9000 Gold .2460 oz. AGW **Subject:** King Kna-Sekhem **Obv:** Vulture, denomination above and dates below **Rev:** Seated king

Date	Mintage	F	VF	XF	Unc
AH1414-1993 Proof	3,000	Value: 265			

KM# 873 50 POUNDS
8.5000 g., 0.9000 Gold .2460 oz. AGW **Subject:** Menkaure Triad **Obv:** Vulture, denomination above and dates below **Rev:** Three carved figurines

Date	Mintage	F	VF	XF	Unc
AH1414-1993 Proof	3,000	Value: 265			

KM# 885 50 POUNDS
8.5000 g., 0.9000 Gold .2460 oz. AGW **Subject:** Thoutmosis III **Obv:** Vulture, denomination above and dates below **Rev:** Kneeling figure holding jar

Date	Mintage	F	VF	XF	Unc
AH1414-1993 Proof	3,000	Value: 265			

KM# 775 50 POUNDS
8.5000 g., 0.9000 Gold .2460 oz. AGW **Obv:** Vulture, denomination above and dates below **Rev:** Three pyramids

Date	Mintage	F	VF	XF	Unc
AH1414-1993 Proof	—	Value: 225			

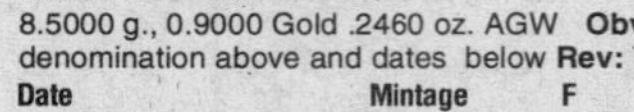

KM# 737 50 POUNDS
8.5000 g., 0.9000 Gold .2460 oz. AGW **Series:** World Cup Soccer **Obv:** Text within circle at center of wings, oval shield above divides dates **Rev:** Two players, pyramid and Statue of Liberty

Date	Mintage	F	VF	XF	Unc
AH1415-1994	99	—	—	—	325
AH1415-1994 Proof	99	Value: 325			

KM# 739 50 POUNDS
8.5000 g., 0.9000 Gold .2460 oz. AGW **Series:** World Cup Soccer **Obv:** Text within circle at center of wings, oval shield above divides dates **Rev:** Stylized player

Date	Mintage	F	VF	XF	Unc
AH1415-1994	99	—	—	—	325
AH1415-1994 Proof	99	Value: 325			

KM# 779 50 POUNDS
8.5000 g., 0.9000 Gold .2460 oz. AGW **Subject:** Queen Nefertiti **Obv:** Vulture, denomination above and dates below **Rev:** Bust right

Date	Mintage	F	VF	XF	Unc
AH1415-1994 Proof	—	Value: 230			

KM# 780 50 POUNDS
8.5000 g., 0.9000 Gold .2460 oz. AGW **Obv:** Vulture, denomination above and dates below **Rev:** Seated cat right

Date	Mintage	F	VF	XF	Unc
AH1415-1994 Proof	—	Value: 230			

KM# 781 50 POUNDS
8.5000 g., 0.9000 Gold .2460 oz. AGW **Obv:** Vulture, denomination above and dates below **Rev:** Archer in chariot

Date	Mintage	F	VF	XF	Unc
AH1415-1994 Proof	—	Value: 245			

KM# 782 50 POUNDS
8.5000 g., 0.9000 Gold .2460 oz. AGW **Obv:** Vulture, denomination above and dates below **Rev:** Standing God Seth left

Date	Mintage	F	VF	XF	Unc
AH1415-1994 Proof	—	Value: 215			

KM# 814 50 POUNDS
8.5000 g., 0.9000 Gold .2460 oz. AGW **Obv:** Vulture, denomination above and dates below **Rev:** Hippopotamus

Date	Mintage	F	VF	XF	Unc
AH1415-1994 Proof	—	Value: 215			

KM# 815 50 POUNDS
8.5000 g., 0.9000 Gold .2460 oz. AGW **Obv:** Vulture, denomination above and dates below **Rev:** Egyptian gazelle

Date	Mintage	F	VF	XF	Unc
AH1415-1994 Proof	—	Value: 215			

KM# 816 50 POUNDS
8.5000 g., 0.9000 Gold .2460 oz. AGW **Obv:** Vulture, denomination above and dates below **Rev:** Phoenix birds

Date	Mintage	F	VF	XF	Unc
AH1415-1994 Proof	—	Value: 215			

KM# 817 50 POUNDS
8.5000 g., 0.9000 Gold .2460 oz. AGW **Obv:** Vulture, denomination above and dates below **Rev:** Egyptian geese

Date	Mintage	F	VF	XF	Unc
AH1415-1994 Proof	—	Value: 215			

KM# 818 50 POUNDS
8.5000 g., 0.9000 Gold .2460 oz. AGW **Obv:** Vulture, denomination above and dates below **Rev:** King Taharqa

Date	Mintage	F	VF	XF	Unc
AH1415-1994 Proof	—	Value: 215			

KM# 819 50 POUNDS
8.5000 g., 0.9000 Gold .2460 oz. AGW **Obv:** Vulture, denomination above and dates below **Rev:** Amenhotep Temple

Date	Mintage	F	VF	XF	Unc
AH1415-1994 Proof	—	Value: 215			

KM# 820 50 POUNDS
8.5000 g., 0.9000 Gold .2460 oz. AGW **Obv:** Vulture, denomination above and dates below **Rev:** Karnak Temple

Date	Mintage	F	VF	XF	Unc
AH1415-1994 Proof	—	Value: 215			

KM# 821 50 POUNDS
8.5000 g., 0.9000 Gold .2460 oz. AGW **Obv:** Vulture, denomination above and dates below **Rev:** Philae Temple

Date	Mintage	F	VF	XF	Unc
AH1415-1994 Proof	—	Value: 215			

KM# 822 50 POUNDS
8.5000 g., 0.9000 Gold .2460 oz. AGW **Obv:** Vulture, denomination above and dates below **Rev:** Khonsu Temple

Date	Mintage	F	VF	XF	Unc
AH1415-1994 Proof	—	Value: 215			

KM# 871 50 POUNDS
8.5000 g., 0.9000 Gold .2460 oz. AGW **Obv:** Vulture, denomination above and dates below **Rev:** King Djoser wearing the Red Crown

Date	Mintage	F	VF	XF	Unc
AH1415-1994 Proof	3,000	Value: 260			

KM# 872 50 POUNDS
8.5000 g., 0.9000 Gold .2460 oz. AGW **Obv:** Vulture, denomination above and dates below **Rev:** Seated King Khufu with flat-top hat

Date	Mintage	F	VF	XF	Unc
AH1415-1994 Proof	3,000	Value: 260			

KM# 882 50 POUNDS
8.5000 g., 0.9000 Gold .2460 oz. AGW **Subject:** King Sesostris I **Obv:** Vulture, denomination above and dates below **Rev:** RE (sun god) presenting the ANKH (symbol of life) to the king wearing the Double Crown

Date	Mintage	F	VF	XF	Unc
AH1415-1994 Proof	3,000	Value: 275			

KM# 884 50 POUNDS
8.5000 g., 0.9000 Gold .2460 oz. AGW **Subject:** King Horemheb **Obv:** Vulture, denomination above and dates below **Rev:** Seated King Horemheb

Date	Mintage	F	VF	XF	Unc
AH1415-1994 Proof	3,000	Value: 275			

KM# 886 50 POUNDS
8.5000 g., 0.9000 Gold .2460 oz. AGW **Subject:** King Khonsu **Obv:** Vulture, denomination above and dates below **Rev:** 1/2-length King Khonsu

Date	Mintage	F	VF	XF	Unc
AH1415-1994 Proof	3,000	Value: 275			

KM# 887 50 POUNDS
8.5000 g., 0.9000 Gold .2460 oz. AGW **Subject:** Tutankhamen's Throne **Obv:** Vulture, denomination above and dates below **Rev:** King Tut seated on throne with servant

Date	Mintage	F	VF	XF	Unc
AH1415-1994 Proof	3,000	Value: 300			

KM# 888 50 POUNDS
8.5000 g., 0.9000 Gold .2460 oz. AGW **Subject:** Queen Hatshepsut **Obv:** Vulture, denomination above and dates below **Rev:** Queen's facial sculpture

Date	Mintage	F	VF	XF	Unc
AH1415-1994 Proof	3,000	Value: 275			

KM# 890 50 POUNDS
8.5000 g., 0.9000 Gold .2460 oz. AGW **Subject:** Akhnaton and Family **Obv:** Vulture, denomination above and dates below **Rev:** Family scene

Date	Mintage	F	VF	XF	Unc
AH1415-1994 Proof	3,000	Value: 275			

KM# 891 50 POUNDS
8.5000 g., 0.9000 Gold .2460 oz. AGW **Obv:** Vulture, denomination above and dates below **Rev:** Akhnaton

Date	Mintage	F	VF	XF	Unc
AH1415-1994 Proof	3,000	Value: 275			

KM# 892 50 POUNDS
8.5000 g., 0.9000 Gold .2460 oz. AGW **Subject:** Queen Nefertari **Obv:** Vulture, denomination above and dates below **Rev:** Kneeling Queen Nefertari

Date	Mintage	F	VF	XF	Unc
AH1415-1994 Proof	5,000	Value: 275			

KM# 893 50 POUNDS
8.5000 g., 0.9000 Gold .2460 oz. AGW **Subject:** Ramses III **Obv:** Vulture, denomination above and dates below **Rev:** 3/4-length Ramses III

Date	Mintage	F	VF	XF	Unc
AH1415-1994 Proof	3,000	Value: 300			

KM# 895 50 POUNDS
8.5000 g., 0.9000 Gold .2460 oz. AGW **Obv:** Vulture, denomination above and dates below **Rev:** Amulet of Hathor

Date	Mintage	F	VF	XF	Unc
AH1415-1994 Proof	3,000	Value: 275			

KM# 877 50 POUNDS
26.0000 g., 0.8750 Gold .7315 oz. AGW **Obv:** Vulture, denomination above and dates below **Rev:** Seated scribe

Date	Mintage	F	VF	XF	Unc
AH1415-1994 Proof	3,000	Value: 500			

KM# 921 50 POUNDS
8.5000 g., 0.9000 Gold 0.246 oz. AGW, 24 mm. **Obv:** Value and inscription **Rev:** Statue of Ramses II seated **Edge:** Reeded

Date	Mintage	F	VF	XF	Unc
AH1420-1999 Proof	—	Value: 275			

KM# 550 100 POUNDS
17.1500 g., 0.9000 Gold .4963 oz. AGW **Obv:** Denomination, dates and text **Rev:** Bust of Queen Nefertiti right **Rev. Designer:** Dominic Angelini

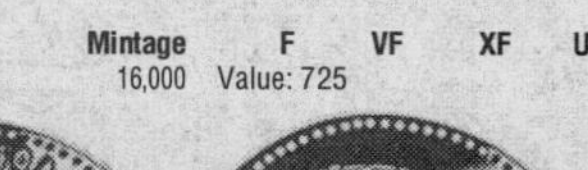

Date	Mintage	F	VF	XF	Unc
AH1404-1983 Proof	16,000	Value: 725			

KM# 562 100 POUNDS
17.1500 g., 0.9000 Gold .4963 oz. AGW **Obv:** Denomination, dates and text **Rev:** Bust of Cleopatra VII in formal headdress left 69-30BC, Queen and statesperson

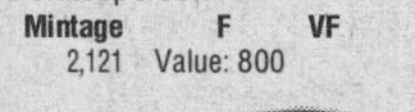

Date	Mintage	F	VF	XF	Unc
AH1404-1984 Proof	2,121	Value: 800			

KM# 569 100 POUNDS

17.1500 g., 0.9000 Gold .4963 oz. AGW **Obv:** Denomination, dates and text **Rev:** The golden falcon, from an ancient breastplate found in King Tutankhamen's tomb

Date	Mintage	F	VF	XF	Unc
AH1405-1985 Proof	1,800	Value: 500			

KM# 591 100 POUNDS
17.1500 g., 0.9000 Gold .4963 oz. AGW **Rev:** Tutankhamen

Date	Mintage	F	VF	XF	Unc
AH1406-1986 Proof	7,500	Value: 775			

KM# 642 100 POUNDS
17.0000 g., 0.9000 Gold .4918 oz. AGW **Subject:** Mecca **Obv:** Arabic legend, ornamentation **Rev:** Interior view of the Kaaba

Date	Mintage	F	VF	XF	Unc
AH1406-1986	700	—	—	—	425

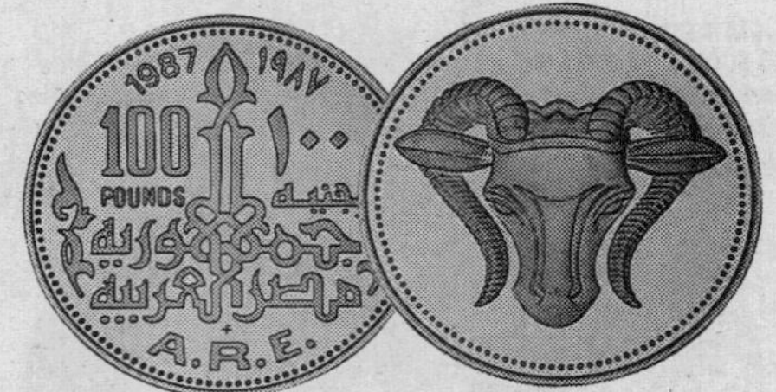

KM# 613 100 POUNDS
17.0000 g., 0.9000 Gold .4918 oz. AGW **Obv:** Denomination, dates and text **Rev:** The golden ram

Date	Mintage	F	VF	XF	Unc
AH1407-1987 Proof	7,500	Value: 475			

KM# 648 100 POUNDS
17.0000 g., 0.9000 Gold .4918 oz. AGW **Obv:** Denomination, dates and text **Rev:** The golden warrior

Date	Mintage	F	VF	XF	Unc
AH1408-1988 Proof	5,500	Value: 500			

KM# 656 100 POUNDS
17.1500 g., 0.9000 Gold .4963 oz. AGW **Obv:** Denomination, dates and text **Rev:** The golden cat

Date	Mintage	F	VF	XF	Unc
AH1409-1989 FM Proof	Est. 7,500	Value: 475			

KM# 681 100 POUNDS
17.0000 g., 0.9000 Gold .4918 oz. AGW **Series:** World Soccer Championship - Italy **Rev:** Ancient gods

Date	Mintage	F	VF	XF	Unc
AH1410-1990 Proof	125	Value: 800			

KM# 684 100 POUNDS
17.0000 g., 0.9000 Gold .4918 oz. AGW **Series:** World Soccer Championship - Italy **Rev:** Player chasing ball

Date	Mintage	F	VF	XF	Unc
AH1410-1990 Proof	75	Value: 825			

KM# 693 100 POUNDS
17.0000 g., 0.9000 Gold .4918 oz. AGW **Series:** Ancient Egyptian Culture **Obv:** Denomination, dates and text **Rev:** Sphinx

Date	Mintage	F	VF	XF	Unc
AH1410-1990 FM Proof	Est. 5,000	Value: 575			

KM# 729 100 POUNDS
17.0000 g., 0.9000 Gold .4918 oz. AGW **Series:** Ancient Egyptian Culture **Obv:** Denomination, dates and text **Rev:** Pyramids of Giza

Date	Mintage	F	VF	XF	Unc
AH1411-1991 Proof	Est. 5,000	Value: 575			

KM# 717 100 POUNDS
17.0000 g., 0.9000 Gold .4918 oz. AGW **Series:** Summer Olympics **Rev:** Fencing

Date	Mintage	F	VF	XF	Unc
AH1412-1992	49	—	—	—	845
AH1412-1992 Proof	99	Value: 845			

KM# 718 100 POUNDS
17.0000 g., 0.9000 Gold .4918 oz. AGW **Series:** Summer Olympics **Obv:** Text within circle at center of wings, denomination and dates above **Rev:** Wrestling matches

Date	Mintage	F	VF	XF	Unc
AH1412-1992	49	—	—	—	845
AH1412-1992 Proof	99	Value: 845			

KM# 720 100 POUNDS
17.0000 g., 0.9000 Gold .4918 oz. AGW **Series:** Summer Olympics **Obv:** Text within circle at center of wings, denomination and dates above **Rev:** Many men wrestling an ox

Date	Mintage	F	VF	XF	Unc
AH1412-1992	49	—	—	—	845
AH1412-1992 Proof	99	Value: 845			

KM# 721 100 POUNDS
17.0000 g., 0.9000 Gold .4918 oz. AGW **Series:** Summer Olympics **Rev:** Swimmer stalking a duck

Date	Mintage	F	VF	XF	Unc
AH1412-1992	49	—	—	—	845
AH1412-1992 Proof	99	Value: 845			

KM# 722 100 POUNDS
17.0000 g., 0.9000 Gold .4918 oz. AGW **Series:** Summer Olympics **Rev:** Handball player

Date	Mintage	F	VF	XF	Unc
AH1412-1992	49	—	—	—	845
AH1412-1992 Proof	99	Value: 845			

KM# 723 100 POUNDS
17.0000 g., 0.9000 Gold .4918 oz. AGW **Series:** Summer Olympics **Rev:** Field hockey player

Date	Mintage	F	VF	XF	Unc
AH1412-1992	49	—	—	—	845
AH1412-1992 Proof	99	Value: 845			

KM# 724 100 POUNDS
17.0000 g., 0.9000 Gold .4918 oz. AGW **Series:** Summer Olympics **Rev:** Soccer player

Date	Mintage	F	VF	XF	Unc
AH1412-1992	49	—	—	—	845
AH1412-1992 Proof	115	Value: 845			

KM# 730 100 POUNDS
17.1500 g., 0.9000 Gold .4963 oz. AGW **Subject:** The Golden Guardians **Obv:** Denomination, dates and text **Rev:** Two statues of Ramses II

Date	Mintage	F	VF	XF	Unc
1992 Proof	Est. 5,000	Value: 525			

KM# 719 100 POUNDS
17.0000 g., 0.9000 Gold .4918 oz. AGW **Series:** Summer Olympics **Obv:** Text within circle at center of wings, denomination and dates above **Rev:** Archery demonstration

Date	Mintage	F	VF	XF	Unc
AH1412-1992	49	—	—	—	845
AH1412-1992 Proof	99	Value: 845			

PATTERNS

Including off metal strikes

KM#	Date	Mintage	Identification	Mkt Val
Pn26	AH1917	—	1/2 Millieme. Copper-Nickel.	125
Pn27	AH1942	—	2 Piastres. Platinum. KM#365	—
Pn28	AH1960	—	25 Piastres. Silver. KM#400 but with hand pointing to right	—
Pn29	AH1962	—	5 Piastres. Bronze. ESSAi	—
Pn30	AH1962	—	5 Piastres. Brass Or Aluminum-Bronze. 7.3400 g.	1,600
Pn31	AH1964	—	10 Piastres. Copper-Nickel.	—

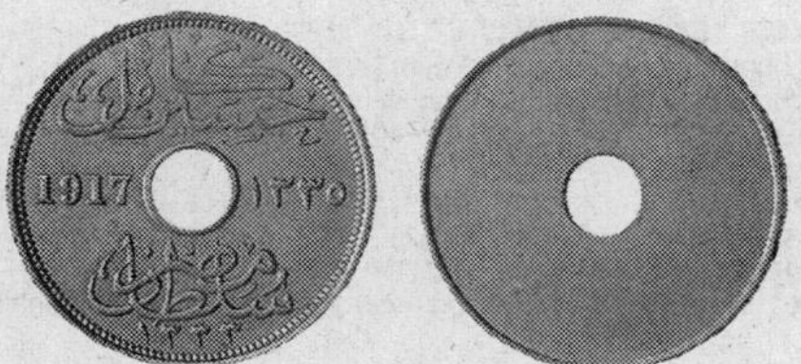

KM#	Date	Mintage	Identification	Mkt Val
Pn32	AH1917	—	10 Milliemes. Copper-Nickel. 5.7200 g. 25.9 mm. Design of KM-316 obverse. Blank. Plain edge. Obverse die trial of KM-316	—

KM#	Date	Mintage	Identification	Mkt Val
Pn33	AHND (1917)KN	—	10 Milliemes. Copper-Nickel. 5.7000 g. 25.9 mm. Blank. Design of KM-316 reverse. Plain edge. Reverse die trial of KM-316	—

PIEFORTS

KM#	Date	Mintage	Identification	Mkt Val
P1	AH1981	152	5 Pounds. 0.9000 Silver. KM533	200

PROOF SETS

KM#	Date	Mintage	Identification	Issue Price	Mkt Val
PS1	1938 (4)	—	KM#370, 371, 372, 373	4,200	4,500
PS2	1964 (4)	2,000	KM#404, 405, 406, 407	18.00	90.00
PS3	1966 (7)	2,500	KM#393, 394, 395, 397, 398, 399, 403	9.00	75.00
PS4	1980 (4)	—	KM#508, 509, 517, 519	—	2,000
PS5	1980 (3)	—	KM#509, 517, 519	—	1,975

SPECIMEN SETS (SS)

KM#	Date	Mintage	Identification	Issue Price	Mkt Val
SS1	1916/7 (10)	—	KM#312-316, 317.1, 318.1, 319, 321, 324	—	1,700

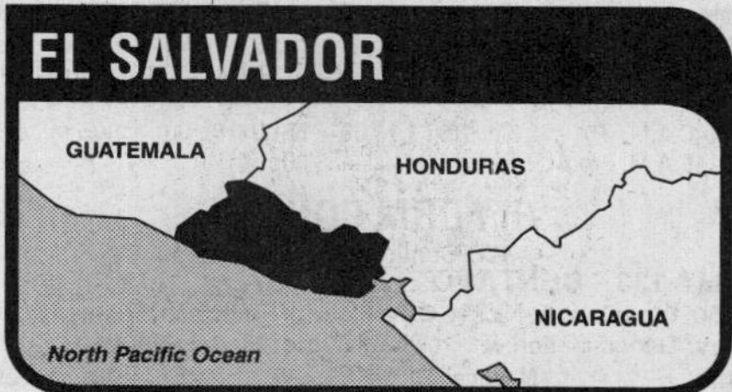

The Republic of El Salvador, a Central American country bordered by Guatemala, Honduras and the Pacific Ocean, has an area of 8,124 sq. mi. (21,040 sq. km.) and a population of 6.0 million. Capital: San Salvador. This most intensely cultivated of Latin America countries produces coffee (the major crop), sugar and balsam for export. Gold, silver and other metals are largely unexploited.

The first Spanish attempt to subjugate the area was undertaken in 1523 by Pedro de Alvarado, Cortes' lieutenant. He was forced to retreat by Indian forces, but returned in 1525 and succeeded in bringing the region under control of the Captaincy General of Guatemala. In 1821, El Salvador and the other Central American provinces jointly declared independence from Spain. In 1823, the Republic of Central America was formed by the five Central American states; this federation dissolved in 1839. El Salvador then became an independent republic in 1841.

Since 1960, El Salvador has been a part of the Central American Common Market. During the 1980's El Salvador went through a 12 year Civil War that ended in 1992 with the signing of a United Nations-sponsored Peace Accord. Free elections, with full participation of all political parties, were held in 1994, 1997 and 1999. Armando Calderon-Sol was elected president in 1994 for a 5-year term and Francisco Flores was elected in 1999 for a 5-year term as well.

MINT MARKS

C.A.M. - Central American Mint, San Salvador
H - Heaton Mint, Birmingham
S - San Francisco
Mo - Mexico
(a) - British Royal Mint, England
(b) - Denver Mint, USA
(c) - Deutsche Nickel A.G., Germany
(d) - Guatemala City Mint, Guatemala
(e) - Mexico City Mint, Mexico
(f) - San Francisco Mint, USA
(g) - Sherrit Mint, Canada
(h) - Vereingte Deutsche Metall, Germany
(i) - Royal Canadian Mint, Canada
(P) – Philadelphia Mint, USA

NOTE: The Monetary Integration Law of November 2000 resulted in the elimination of the Colon coinage and notes by early October 2002. No new coins are expected to be minted.

REPUBLIC OF EL SALVADOR

DECIMAL COINAGE

100 Centavos = 1 Peso

KM# 120 1/4 REAL
3.2000 g., Bronze **Obv:** Flag draped arms within wreath, liberty cap on top, swords above cap **Rev:** Denomination and date within wreath **Note:** The decimal value of this coin was about 3 Centavos. It was apparently struck in response to the continuing use of the Reales monetary system in rural areas.

Date	Mintage	F	VF	XF	Unc	BU
1909	—	20.00	40.00	75.00	150	—

KM# 106 CENTAVO
2.5000 g., Copper-Nickel **Obv:** Head of Francisco Morazan left, date below **Obv. Legend:** REPUBLICA DEL SALVADOR **Rev:** Denomination within wreath **Note:** Medal rotation.

Date	Mintage	F	VF	XF	Unc	BU
1913H	2,500,000	1.50	3.50	6.00	40.00	—

KM# 127 CENTAVO
2.5000 g., Copper-Nickel **Obv:** Head of Francisco Morazan left, date below **Rev:** Denomination within wreath **Note:** Medal rotation.

Date	Mintage	F	VF	XF	Unc	BU
1915(P)	5,000,000	1.25	4.50	12.50	35.00	—
1919(P)	1,000,000	2.25	7.00	20.00	60.00	—
1920(P)	1,490,000	1.50	6.00	15.00	40.00	—
1925(f)	200,000	4.00	12.00	25.00	70.00	—
1926(f)	400,000	3.00	10.00	20.00	55.00	—
1928S	5,000,000	1.25	7.00	16.00	40.00	—
Note: Varieties exist with large or small "S"						
1936(P)	2,500,000	1.25	4.50	12.50	35.00	—

KM# 107 3 CENTAVOS
3.3000 g., Copper-Nickel **Obv:** Head of Francisco Morazan left **Obv. Legend:** REPUBLICA DEL SALVADOR **Rev:** Denomination within wreath **Note:** Medal rotation.

Date	Mintage	F	VF	XF	Unc	BU
1913H	1,000,000	2.00	8.00	20.00	65.00	125

KM# 128 3 CENTAVOS
3.5000 g., Copper Nickel **Obv:** Head of Francisco Morazan left, date below **Rev:** Denomination within wreath **Note:** Medal rotation.

Date	Mintage	F	VF	XF	Unc	BU
1915(P)	2,700,000	2.00	8.00	20.00	65.00	200

KM# 121 5 CENTAVOS
1.2500 g., 0.8350 Silver .0336 oz. ASW **Obv:** Arms **Rev:** Denomination within wreath

Date	Mintage	F	VF	XF	Unc	BU
1911	1,000,000	3.00	10.00	20.00	45.00	—

KM# 124 5 CENTAVOS
1.2500 g., 0.8350 Silver .0336 oz. ASW **Obv:** Flag draped triangular arms within wreath **Rev:** Denomination within wreath

Date	Mintage	F	VF	XF	Unc	BU
1914(P)	2,000,000	3.00	7.00	15.00	35.00	—
1914(P) Proof	20	Value: 750				

KM# 129 5 CENTAVOS
5.0000 g., Copper-Nickel **Obv:** Head of Francisco Morazan left, date below **Rev:** Denomination, within wreath **Note:** Medal rotation.

Date	Mintage	F	VF	XF	Unc	BU
1915(P)	2,500,000	2.25	6.00	15.00	60.00	—
1916(P)	1,500,000	2.50	7.00	20.00	65.00	—
1917(P)	1,000,000	3.00	8.00	20.00	70.00	—
1918/7(P)	1,000,000	2.50	7.00	20.00	60.00	—
1918(P)	Inc. above	2.50	7.00	17.50	70.00	—
1919/8(P)	—	2.50	7.00	17.50	70.00	—
1919(P)	2,000,000	2.50	7.00	17.50	70.00	—
1920(P)	2,000,000	1.75	4.50	10.00	50.00	—
1921(f)	1,780,000	2.00	5.00	12.00	55.00	—
1925(f)	4,000,000	1.25	3.50	10.00	55.00	—

KM# 122 10 CENTAVOS
2.5000 g., 0.8350 Silver **Obv:** Flag draped arms, liberty cap on top, dates below **Rev:** Denomination within wreath

Date	Mintage	F	VF	XF	Unc	BU
1911	1,000,000	3.00	7.00	15.00	65.00	—

KM# 123 25 CENTAVOS
6.2500 g., 0.8350 Silver .1678 oz. ASW **Obv:** Flag draped arms, liberty cap above, dates below **Rev:** Denomination within wreath

Date	Mintage	F	VF	XF	Unc	BU
1911	600,000	5.00	9.00	18.00	50.00	—

KM# 125 10 CENTAVOS
2.5000 g., 0.8350 Silver **Obv:** Flag draped triangular arms within wreath, dates below **Rev:** Denomination within wreath

Date	Mintage	F	VF	XF	Unc	BU
1914(P)	1,500,000	2.50	6.50	12.50	45.00	—
1914(P) Proof	20	Value: 750				

KM# 126 25 CENTAVOS
6.2500 g., 0.8350 Silver .1678 oz. ASW **Obv:** Flag draped triangular arms within wreath, dates below **Rev:** Denomination within wreath

Date	Mintage	F	VF	XF	Unc	BU
1914(P) 15 DE SEPT DE 1821	1,400,000	5.50	6.50	10.00	30.00	—
1914(P) 15 SET DE 1821	Inc. above	5.50	6.50	10.00	30.00	—
1914(P) Proof	20	Value: 1,500				

KM# 115.1 PESO (Colon)
25.0000 g., 0.9000 Silver .7234 oz. ASW **Obv:** Arms **Obv. Legend:** REPUBLICA DEL SALVADOR **Rev:** Columbus bust left

Date	Mintage	F	VF	XF	Unc	BU
1904C.A.M.	600,000	10.00	15.00	30.00	160	—
1908C.A.M.	1,600,000	10.00	14.00	28.00	140	—
1911C.A.M.	500,000	10.00	15.00	30.00	150	—
1914C.A.M.	700,000	—	—	—	625	—

Note: 1914 struck at the Brussels mint, but then remelted

KM# 115.2 PESO (Colon)
25.0000 g., 0.9000 Silver .7234 oz. ASW **Obv:** Flag draped arms, liberty cap and swords above, dates below **Rev:** Columbus bust left, denomination below, heavier portrait (wider right shoulder) **Note:** Struck at United States mints.

Date	Mintage	F	VF	XF	Unc	BU
1904C.A.M. (f)	400,000	12.00	20.00	40.00	250	—
1909C.A.M. (f)	690,000	11.00	17.50	32.50	200	—

Date	Mintage	F	VF	XF	Unc	BU
1911C.A.M. (P) (S)	1,020,000	10.00	15.00	30.00	175	—

Note: Of the total mintage, 510, 993 struck at Philadelphia Mint (P), and 511,108 were struck at San Francisco Mint (f)

Date	Mintage	F	VF	XF	Unc	BU
1914C.A.M. (P)	2,100,000	10.00	15.00	30.00	175	425
1914C.A.M. Proof	Est. 20	Value: 3,000				

REFORM COINAGE

100 Centavos = 1 Colon

KM# 133 CENTAVO
2.5000 g., Copper-Nickel **Obv:** Head of Francisco Morazan right **Rev:** Denomination within wreath **Note:** Medal rotation.

Date	Mintage	F	VF	XF	Unc	BU
1940(P)	1,000,000	2.00	6.00	15.00	45.00	—

KM# 135.1 CENTAVO
2.5000 g., Bronze, 15 mm. **Obv:** Head of Francisco Morazan left, date below **Rev:** Denomination within wreath

Date	Mintage	F	VF	XF	Unc	BU
1942(f)	5,000,000	0.20	0.50	1.00	4.50	—

Note: Struck in 1943

Date	Mintage	F	VF	XF	Unc	BU
1943(f)	5,000,000	0.20	0.50	1.00	4.50	—

Note: Struck in 1944

Date	Mintage	F	VF	XF	Unc	BU
1945(P)	5,000,000	0.20	0.40	0.75	3.50	—
1947(f)	5,000,000	0.20	0.50	1.00	4.00	—
1951(f)	10,000,000	0.10	0.30	0.75	2.50	—
1952(f)	10,000,000	0.10	0.20	0.40	2.00	—

Note: Struck in 1953

Date	Mintage	F	VF	XF	Unc	BU
1956(P)	10,000,000	0.10	0.20	0.40	2.00	—

Note: Struck in 1957

Date	Mintage	F	VF	XF	Unc	BU
1966	5,000,000	—	—	0.10	0.75	—
1968 (f)	5,000,000	—	—	0.10	0.75	—
1969 (b)	5,000,000	—	—	0.10	0.75	—
1972 (f)	20,000,000	—	—	0.10	0.50	—

KM# 135.1a CENTAVO
2.5000 g., Bronze Clad Steel **Obv:** Head of Francisco Morazan left **Rev:** Denomination within wreath **Note:** Prev. KM#135d. Medal rotation.

Date	Mintage	F	VF	XF	Unc	BU
1989(h)	36,000,000	—	—	0.10	0.20	0.35
1992(h)	—	—	—	0.10	0.20	0.35

KM# 135.2 CENTAVO
2.5000 g., Brass **Obv:** Head of Francisco Morazan left **Rev:** Denomination within wreath **Note:** Prev. KM#135a. Medal rotation.

Date	Mintage	F	VF	XF	Unc	BU
1976(g)	20,000,000	—	—	0.10	0.20	0.35
1977(g)	40,000,000	—	—	0.10	0.20	0.35

KM# 135.2a CENTAVO
2.5000 g., Copper-Zinc **Obv:** DH monogram at truncation, smaller Morazan portrait **Rev:** Denomination in wreath, SM at right base of 1 **Note:** Previously KM#135c.

Date	Mintage	F	VF	XF	Unc	BU
1981(d)	50,000,000	—	—	0.10	0.20	0.35

KM# 135.2b CENTAVO
2.5000 g., Copper Clad Steel **Obv:** DH monogram at truncation, smaller Morazan portrait **Rev:** Denomination in wreath, SM at right base of 1 **Note:** Prev. KM#135b.

Date	Mintage	F	VF	XF	Unc	BU
1986 (a)	30,000,000	—	—	0.10	0.20	0.35

KM# 135.2c CENTAVO
2.5000 g., Brass Clad Steel **Obv:** DH monogram at truncation, smaller portrait **Rev:** Denomination in wreath, SM at right base of 1

Date	Mintage	F	VF	XF	Unc	BU
1995(a)	—	—	—	0.10	0.20	0.35

KM# 147 2 CENTAVOS
2.6000 g., Nickel-Brass **Obv:** Head of Francisco Morazan left **Rev:** Denomination within wreath **Note:** Medal rotation.

Date	Mintage	F	VF	XF	Unc	BU
1974(a)	10,002,000	—	0.10	0.20	1.00	—
1974(a)	2,000	Value: 30.00				

Note: In proof sets only

KM# 148 3 CENTAVOS
4.0000 g., Nickel-Brass, 19 mm. **Obv:** Head of Francisco Morazan left **Rev:** Denomination within wreath **Note:** Medal rotation.

Date	Mintage	F	VF	XF	Unc	BU
1974(a)	10,002,000	0.10	0.15	0.20	1.00	—
1974(a)	2,000	Value: 35.00				

Note: In proof sets only

KM# 134 5 CENTAVOS
5.0000 g., Copper-Nickel, 23 mm. **Obv:** Head of Francisco Morazan left **Rev:** Denomination within wreath **Note:** Medal rotation.

Date	Mintage	F	VF	XF	Unc	BU
1939	—	—	—	—	—	—
1940(P)	800,000	1.00	3.00	10.00	30.00	—
1951	2,000,000	0.75	2.00	6.00	15.00	—
1956	8,000,000	0.10	0.15	0.25	1.00	—
1959	6,000,000	0.10	0.15	0.25	1.00	—
1963	10,000,000	—	0.10	0.15	0.50	—
1966	6,000,000	0.10	0.15	0.25	0.75	—
1967 (f)	10,000,000	—	0.10	0.15	0.50	—
1972 (f)	10,000,000	—	0.10	0.15	0.50	—
1974 (g)	10,002,000	—	0.10	0.15	0.50	—
1974 (g)	2,000	Value: 35.00				

Note: In proof sets only

KM# 134a 5 CENTAVOS
5.0000 g., Nickel-Silver, 23 mm. **Obv:** Head of Francisco Morazan left, date below **Rev:** Denomination within wreath

Date	Mintage	F	VF	XF	Unc	BU
1944(f)	5,000,000	0.25	0.50	1.50	5.00	—
1948(f)	3,000,000	0.25	0.50	1.00	2.50	—
1950(f)	2,000,000	0.25	0.50	1.50	5.00	—
1952(f)	4,000,000	0.20	0.35	0.75	4.00	—

Note: Half the total mintage was struck in 1952, the remainder in 1953

KM# 149 5 CENTAVOS
5.0000 g., Copper-Nickel Clad Steel, 23 mm. **Obv:** Head of Francisco Morazan left, date below **Rev:** Denomination within wreath **Note:** Medal rotation.

Date	Mintage	F	VF	XF	Unc	BU
1975 (a)	15,000,000	—	0.10	0.15	0.30	0.50
1975	2,000	Value: 40.00				

Note: In proof sets only

Date	Mintage	F	VF	XF	Unc	BU
1986 (h)	30,000,000	—	0.10	0.15	0.30	0.50

KM# 149a 5 CENTAVOS
5.0000 g., Nickel Clad Steel, 23 mm. **Obv:** Head of Francisco Morazan left **Rev:** Denomination within wreath

Date	Mintage	F	VF	XF	Unc	BU
1976 (g)	15,000,000	—	0.10	0.15	0.30	0.50
1984 (a)	15,000,000	—	0.10	0.15	0.30	0.50

KM# 149b 5 CENTAVOS
5.0000 g., Copper-Nickel-Zinc, 23 mm. **Obv:** Head of Francisco Morazan left **Rev:** Denomination within wreath **Note:** Previously KM#149a.

Date	Mintage	F	VF	XF	Unc	BU
1977(h)	26,000,000	—	0.10	0.15	0.30	0.50

KM# 154 5 CENTAVOS

2.0000 g., Stainless Steel **Obv:** Head of Francisco Morazan left, date below **Rev:** Denomination within wreath

Date	Mintage	F	VF	XF	Unc	BU
1987(h)	30,000,000	—	0.10	0.15	0.30	0.50
1987(h) Proof	—	Value: 50.00				
1999(h)	—	—	0.10	0.15	0.30	0.50

KM# 154a 5 CENTAVOS

2.0000 g., Copper-Nickel Clad Steel **Obv:** Head of Francisco Morazan left **Rev:** Denomination within wreath **Note:** Medal rotation.

Date	Mintage	F	VF	XF	Unc	BU
1991 (h)	—	—	0.10	0.15	0.30	0.50
1998 (c)	—	—	0.10	0.15	0.30	0.50

KM# 154b 5 CENTAVOS

2.0000 g., Nickel Clad Steel, 17 mm. **Obv:** Head of Francisco Morazan left, date below **Rev:** Denomination within wreath **Note:** Medal rotation.

Date	Mintage	F	VF	XF	Unc	BU
1992 (g)	—	—	0.10	0.15	0.30	0.50
1993 (g)	—	—	0.10	0.15	0.30	0.50
1994 (h)	—	—	0.10	0.15	0.30	0.50
1994(h) Proof	—	Value: 40.00				
1995 (g)	—	—	0.10	0.15	0.30	0.50
1998	—	—	0.10	0.15	0.30	0.50
1999	—	—	0.10	0.15	0.30	0.50

KM# 130 10 CENTAVOS

7.0000 g., Copper-Nickel, 26 mm. **Obv:** Head of Francisco Morazan left, date below **Rev:** Denomination within wreath **Note:** Medal rotation.

Date	Mintage	F	VF	XF	Unc	BU
1921(f)	2,000,000	4.50	10.00	30.00	200	300
1925(f)	2,000,000	5.00	12.50	55.00	—	—
1940(f)	500,000	6.50	15.00	40.00	90.00	—
1951(f)	1,000,000	1.00	3.50	12.50	30.00	—
1967(f)	2,000,000	—	0.10	0.50	2.00	—
1968(b)	3,000,000	—	0.10	0.40	1.25	—
1969(b)	3,000,000	—	0.10	0.40	1.25	—
1972(f)	7,000,000	—	0.10	0.25	1.00	—

KM# 130a 10 CENTAVOS

7.0000 g., Copper-Nickel-Zinc, 26 mm. **Obv:** Head of Francisco Morazan left **Rev:** Denomination within wreath

Date	Mintage	F	VF	XF	Unc	BU
1952(f)	2,000,000	0.15	0.25	0.75	4.00	—

Note: Of the 2,000,000 struck, 336,000 were struck in 1952 and the remaining 1,664,000 struck in 1953

Date	Mintage	F	VF	XF	Unc	BU
1985 Mo	15,000,000	—	0.10	0.15	0.30	—

KM# 150 10 CENTAVOS

7.0000 g., Copper-Nickel Clad Steel, 26 mm. **Obv:** Head of Francisco Morazan left date below **Rev:** Denomination within wreath **Note:** Medal rotation.

Date	Mintage	F	VF	XF	Unc	BU
1975(a)	15,000,000	—	0.15	0.25	0.50	—
1975(a)	2,000	Value: 35.00				

Note: In proof sets only

KM# 150a 10 CENTAVOS

7.0000 g., Copper-Nickel-Zinc, 26 mm. **Obv:** Head of Francisco Morazan left **Rev:** Denomination within wreath **Note:** Medal rotation.

Date	Mintage	F	VF	XF	Unc	BU
1977(h)	24,000,000	—	0.10	0.20	0.45	—
1977(h) Proof	—	Value: 40.00				

KM# 155 10 CENTAVOS

7.0000 g., Stainless Steel **Obv:** Head of Francisco Morazan left date below **Rev:** Denomination within wreath **Note:** Medal rotation.

Date	Mintage	F	VF	XF	Unc	BU
1987 (h)	30,000,000	—	0.10	0.20	0.40	0.60
1987(h) Proof	—	Value: 40.00				
1999 (i)	—	—	0.10	0.20	0.40	0.60

KM# 155a 10 CENTAVOS

Nickel Clad Steel **Obv:** Head of Francisco Morazan left **Rev:** Denomination within wreath **Note:** Medal rotation.

Date	Mintage	F	VF	XF	Unc	BU
1992 (a)	—	—	0.10	0.20	0.40	0.60
1993 (g)	—	—	0.10	0.20	0.40	0.60
1994 (h)	—	—	0.10	0.20	0.40	0.60
1994 Proof	—	Value: 40.00				

KM# 155b 10 CENTAVOS

Copper-Nickel Clad Steel **Obv:** Head of Francisco Morazan left **Rev:** Denomination within wreath

Date	Mintage	F	VF	XF	Unc	BU
1995 (c)	—	—	0.10	0.20	0.40	0.60
1998 (c)	—	—	0.10	0.20	0.40	0.60
1999	—	—	0.10	0.20	0.40	0.60

KM# 136 25 CENTAVOS

7.5000 g., 0.9000 Silver .217 oz. ASW **Obv:** Head of Francisco Morazan left, date below **Rev:** Denomination within wreath

Date	Mintage	F	VF	XF	Unc	BU
1943	1,000,000	3.00	4.00	8.00	16.00	—
1944	1,000,000	3.00	4.00	8.00	16.00	—

KM# 137 25 CENTAVOS

2.5000 g., 0.9000 Silver .0723 oz. ASW **Obv:** Head of Jose Matias Delgado left, date below **Rev:** Denomination within wreath **Designer:** Gilroy Roberts

Date	Mintage	F	VF	XF	Unc	BU
1953	14,000,000	1.00	1.50	2.50	4.50	—

KM# 139 25 CENTAVOS

2.5000 g., Nickel, 17.8 mm. **Obv:** Head of Jose Matias Delgado left, date below **Rev:** Denomination within wreath

Date	Mintage	F	VF	XF	Unc	BU
1970 (a)	14,000,000	—	0.10	0.20	0.60	0.80
1973 (g)	28,000,000	—	0.10	0.20	0.50	0.75
1975 (g)	20,000,000	—	0.10	0.20	0.50	0.75
1977 (a)	22,400,000	—	0.10	0.20	0.50	0.75

KM# 139a 25 CENTAVOS

2.5000 g., Copper-Nickel **Obv:** Head of Jose Matias Delgado left **Rev:** Denomination within wreath

Date	Mintage	F	VF	XF	Unc	BU
1986Mo	21,000,000	—	0.10	0.20	0.50	0.75
1986Mo Proof	—	Value: 50.00				

KM# 157 25 CENTAVOS

4.0000 g., Stainless Steel **Obv:** Head of Jose Matias Delgado left, date below **Rev:** Denomination within wreath **Note:** Medal rotation.

Date	Mintage	F	VF	XF	Unc	BU
1988 (h)	20,000,000	—	0.10	0.20	0.50	0.75
1988(h) Proof	—	Value: 50.00				
1999 (i)	—	—	0.10	0.20	0.50	0.75

KM# 157a 25 CENTAVOS

4.0000 g., Copper-Nickel Clad Steel **Obv:** Bust of Jose Matias Delgado left **Rev:** Denomination

Date	Mintage	F	VF	XF	Unc	BU
1992(c)	—	—	0.10	0.20	0.50	0.75
1995(c)	—	—	0.10	0.20	0.50	0.75

KM# 157b 25 CENTAVOS

4.0000 g., Nickel Clad Steel **Obv:** Head of Jose Matias Delgado left, date below **Rev:** Denomination within wreath **Note:** Medal rotation.

Date	Mintage	F	VF	XF	Unc	BU
1993 (a)	—	—	0.10	0.20	0.50	0.75
1994 (g)	—	—	0.10	0.20	0.50	0.75
1998	—	—	0.10	0.20	0.50	0.75
1999	—	—	0.10	0.20	0.50	0.75

KM# 138 50 CENTAVOS

5.0000 g., 0.9000 Silver .1446 oz. ASW **Obv:** Head of Jose Matias Delgado left, date below **Rev:** Denomination within wreath **Designer:** Gilroy Roberts

Date	Mintage	F	VF	XF	Unc	BU
1953	3,000,000	2.00	3.00	4.00	8.00	—

KM# 140.1 50 CENTAVOS

5.0000 g., Nickel, 20 mm. **Obv:** Head of Jose Matias Delgado left, date below **Rev:** Denomination within wreath **Note:** 1.65 mm thick.

Date	Mintage	F	VF	XF	Unc	BU
1970(a)	3,000,000	—	0.20	0.30	0.60	0.80

KM# 140.2 50 CENTAVOS

5.1000 g., Nickel, 20 mm. **Obv:** Head of Jose Matias Delgado left **Rev:** Denomination **Note:** Two millimeters thick.

Date	Mintage	F	VF	XF	Unc	BU
1977(a)	1,500,000	—	0.20	0.30	0.60	0.80

KM# 131 COLON

25.0000 g., 0.9000 Silver .7234 oz. ASW, 37 mm. **Subject:** 400th Anniversary - San Salvador **Obv:** Flags flank triangular arms within wreath, denomination below **Obv. Designer:** Ignacio Cortes **Rev:** Alvarado and Quinonez busts left, dates above **Rev. Designer:** Jose C. Tovar

Date	Mintage	F	VF	XF	Unc	BU
ND(1925)Mo	2,000	50.00	90.00	135	225	—

KM# 141 COLON
2.3000 g., 0.9990 Silver .0738 oz. ASW **Subject:** 150th Anniversary of Independence **Obv:** Flags flank triangular arms within wreath, bust at right **Rev:** Salvador Dali image, "La Fecandida" within circle, denomination below

Date	Mintage	F	VF	XF	Unc	BU
1971 Proof	21,000	Value: 7.50				

KM# 153 COLON
9.2500 g., Copper-Nickel, 29 mm. **Obv:** Head of Christopher Columbus left, date below **Rev:** Denomination within wreath

Date	Mintage	F	VF	XF	Unc	BU
1984Mo	10,000,000	—	0.50	1.00	2.50	3.50
1984Mo Proof	—	Value: 125				
1985Mo	20,000,000	—	0.50	1.00	2.50	3.50
1985Mo Proof	—	Value: 200				

KM# 156 COLON
6.0000 g., Stainless Steel, 25 mm. **Obv:** Head of Christopher Columbus left, date below **Rev:** Denomination within wreath

Date	Mintage	F	VF	XF	Unc	BU
1988 (h)	30,000,000	—	0.40	0.80	2.25	3.00
1988 Proof	—	Value: 40.00				
1999 (i)	—	—	—	0.80	2.25	3.00

KM# 156a COLON
6.0000 g., Copper-Nickel Clad Steel, 25 mm. **Obv:** Head of Christopher Columbus left **Rev:** Denomination within wreath **Note:** Medal rotation.

Date	Mintage	F	VF	XF	Unc	BU
1991(h)	—	—	0.40	0.80	2.25	3.00

KM# 156b COLON
6.0000 g., Nickel Clad Steel, 25 mm. **Obv:** Head of Christopher Columbus left **Rev:** Denomination within wreath **Note:** Medal rotation.

Date	Mintage	F	VF	XF	Unc	BU
1993 (a)	—	—	0.40	0.80	2.25	3.00
1994 (g)	—	—	0.40	0.80	2.25	3.00
1995 (h)	—	—	0.40	0.80	2.25	3.00
1998	—	—	0.40	0.80	2.25	3.00
1999	—	—	0.40	0.80	2.25	3.00

KM# 142 5 COLONES
11.5000 g., 0.9990 Silver .3694 oz. ASW **Subject:** 150th Anniversary of Independence **Obv:** Flags flank triangular arms within wreath, date below **Rev:** Liberty statue, Cañas bust at right, dates at left, denomination below

Date	Mintage	F	VF	XF	Unc	BU
1971 Proof	18,000	Value: 12.50				

KM# 162 5 COLONES
7.5000 g., Bi-Metallic Bronze Plated Steel center in Nickel-plated Steel ring, 26 mm. **Obv:** Columbus' ships sailing west on world map within circle, date below **Rev:** Denomination within circle, wreath surrounds **Edge:** Segmented reeding **Note:** Viridian mint. Not released for circulation.

Date	Mintage	F	VF	XF	Unc	BU
1997	—	—	—	—	—	—

KM# 163 5 COLONES
7.5000 g., Bi-Metallic, 25.9 mm. **Obv:** Y2K motif **Rev:** Denomination **Note:** Not released for circulation.

Date	Mintage	F	VF	XF	Unc	BU
2000	—	—	—	—	—	—

KM# 132 20 COLONES
15.5600 g., 0.9000 Gold .4502 oz. AGW, 27 mm. **Subject:** 400th Anniversary - San Salvador **Obv:** Flags flank triangular arms within wreath, denomination below **Obv. Designer:** Ignacio Cortes **Rev:** Alvarado and Quinonez busts left, dates above **Rev. Designer:** Jose C. Tovar

Date	Mintage	F	VF	XF	Unc	BU
ND(1925)Mo	200	—	800	1,600	2,500	—

KM# 143 25 COLONES
2.9400 g., 0.9000 Gold .0850 oz. AGW **Subject:** 150th Anniversary of Independence **Obv:** Flags flank triangular arms within wreath **Rev:** Salvador Dali image, "La Fecundida" within circle, denomination below

Date	Mintage	F	VF	XF	Unc	BU
1971 Proof	7,650	Value: 85.00				

KM# 151 25 COLONES
25.0000 g., 0.9000 Silver .7234 oz. ASW **Subject:** 18th Annual Governors' Assembly **Obv:** Flags flank triangular arms within wreath, denomination below **Rev:** First coin of C.A. Federation 1874, date below **Note:** Medal rotation.

Date	Mintage	F	VF	XF	Unc	BU
1977	2,000	—	—	—	27.50	32.50
1977 Proof	20,000	Value: 37.50				

KM# 144 50 COLONES
5.9000 g., 0.9000 Gold .1707 oz. AGW **Subject:** 150th Anniversary of Independence **Obv:** Flags flank triangular arms within wreath **Rev:** Liberty statue, Cañas bust at right, dates at left, denomination below

Date	Mintage	F	VF	XF	Unc	BU
1971 Proof	3,530	Value: 145				

KM# 145 100 COLONES
11.8000 g., 0.9000 Gold .3414 oz. AGW **Subject:** 150th Anniversary of Independence **Obv:** Flags flank triangular arms within wreath **Rev:** Map of El Salvador, denomination below

Date	Mintage	F	VF	XF	Unc	BU
1971 Proof	2,750	Value: 250				

KM# 158 150 COLONES
25.0000 g., 0.9000 Silver .7235 oz. ASW, 37 mm. **Subject:** Union for Peace **Obv:** Four clasped hands, date below **Rev:** Denomination within wreath **Edge:** Lettered

Date	Mintage	F	VF	XF	Unc	BU
1992	—	—	—	—	42.50	—

KM# 160 150 COLONES
25.0000 g., 0.9000 Silver .7235 oz. ASW, 37 mm. **Subject:** Discovery of America **Obv:** Columbus' ships and world map, date below **Rev:** Denomination within wreath **Edge:** Lettered

Date	Mintage	F	VF	XF	Unc	BU
1992	—	—	—	—	47.50	—

KM# 146 200 COLONES
23.6000 g., 0.9000 Gold .6829 oz. AGW **Subject:** 150th Anniversary of Independence **Obv:** Flags flank triangular arms within wreath, bust at right, date below **Rev:** Panchimalco Church, denomination below

Date	Mintage	F	VF	XF	Unc	BU
1971 Proof	2,245	Value: 485				

KM# 152 250 COLONES
16.0000 g., 0.9170 Gold .4717 oz. AGW **Subject:** 18th Annual Governors' Assembly **Obv:** Flags flank triangular arms within wreath, denomination below **Rev:** First coin of C.A. Federation 1824, dates below

Date	Mintage	F	VF	XF	Unc	BU
1977	4,000	—	—	—	325	350
1977 Proof	400	Value: 385				

KM# 159 2500 COLONES
16.0000 g., 0.9170 Gold .4715 oz. AGW **Subject:** Union for Peace **Obv:** Four clasped hands, date below **Rev:** Denomination within wreath

Date	Mintage	F	VF	XF	Unc	BU
1992	—	—	—	—	375	—

KM# 161 2500 COLONES
16.0000 g., 0.9170 Gold .4715 oz. AGW **Subject:** Discovery of America **Obv:** Columbus' ships and world map, date below **Rev:** Denomination within wreath

Date	Mintage	F	VF	XF	Unc	BU
1992	—	—	—	—	375	—

PATTERNS

Including off metal strikes

KM#	Date	Mintage	Identification	Mkt Val
Pn51	1996	—	5 Colones. Nickel-Plated Steel ring. 7.4000 g. 25.9 mm. Columbus' ships and world map, date below. Denomination within wreath. Prev.KM#Pn15.	400

PROOF SETS

KM#	Date	Mintage	Identification	Issue Price	Mkt Val
PS3	1914 (4)	—	KM#115.2, 124-126	—	6,000
PS4	1971 (6)	—	KM#141-146	—	900
PS5	1971 (4)	—	KM#143-146	250	885
PS6	1971 (2)	—	KM#141-142	6.00	20.00
PS7	1974 (3)	2,000	KM#134, 147-148	—	100
PS8	1975 (2)	2,000	KM#149.1, 150	—	70.00

EQUATORIAL AFRICAN STATES

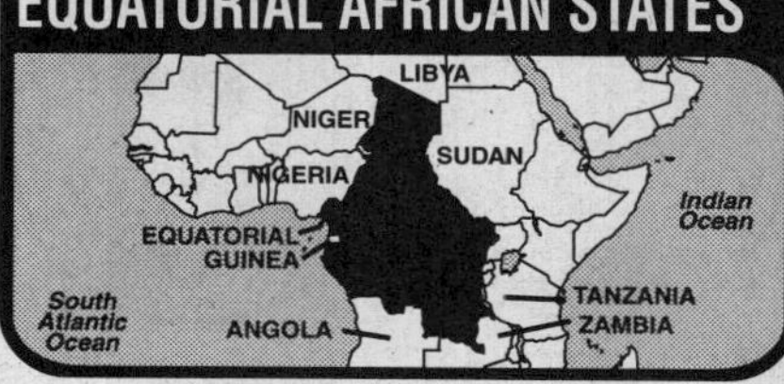

For historical background, see the introduction to Central African States.

CURRENCY UNION

DECIMAL COINAGE

100 Centimes = 1 Franc

KM# 6 FRANC
Aluminum **Obv:** Three giant eland left, date below **Obv. Designer:** G.B.L. Bazor **Rev:** Denomination within wreath **Designer:** G. B. L. Bazor

Date	Mintage	F	VF	XF	Unc	BU
1969(a)	2,500,000	0.25	0.65	1.00	2.25	—
1971(a)	3,000,000	0.25	0.65	1.00	2.25	—

KM# 1 5 FRANCS
Aluminum-Bronze **Obv:** Three giant eland left **Rev:** Denomination within wreath **Designer:** G. B. L. Bazor

Date	Mintage	F	VF	XF	Unc	BU
1961(a)	10,000,000	0.35	1.00	1.50	2.50	—
1962(a)	5,000,000	0.35	1.00	1.50	2.50	—

KM# 1a 5 FRANCS
Aluminum-Nickel-Bronze **Obv:** Three giant eland left, date below **Obv. Designer:** G.B.L. Bazor **Rev:** Denomination within wreath **Designer:** G. B. L. Bazor

Date	Mintage	F	VF	XF	Unc	BU
1965(a)	7,000,000	0.35	1.00	1.50	3.00	—
1967(a)	4,000,000	0.35	1.00	1.25	2.50	—
1968(a)	5,000,000	0.35	1.00	1.25	2.50	—
1970(a)	9,000,000	0.35	1.00	1.25	2.50	—
1972(a)	5,000,000	0.35	1.00	1.25	2.50	—
1973(a)	5,010,000	0.35	1.00	1.25	2.50	—

KM# 2 10 FRANCS
Aluminum-Bronze **Obv:** Three giant eland left **Rev:** Denomination within wreath **Designer:** G. B. L. Bazor

Date	Mintage	F	VF	XF	Unc	BU
1961(a)	10,000,000	0.40	1.00	1.75	3.00	—
1962(a)	5,000,000	0.40	1.00	1.75	3.00	—

KM# 2a 10 FRANCS
Aluminum-Nickel-Bronze **Obv:** Three giant eland left, date below **Obv. Designer:** G.B.L. Bazor **Rev:** Denomination within wreath **Designer:** G. B. L. Bazor

Date	Mintage	F	VF	XF	Unc	BU
1965(a)	7,000,000	1.00	1.75	2.75	5.00	—
1967(a)	10,000,000	0.40	1.00	1.75	3.00	—
1968(a)	2,000,000	1.50	2.25	3.50	6.00	—
1969(a)	10,000,000	0.40	1.00	1.75	3.00	—
1972(a)	5,000,000	0.40	1.00	1.75	3.00	—
1973(a)	5,000,000	0.75	1.50	2.50	4.50	—

KM# 4 25 FRANCS
Aluminum-Bronze **Obv:** Three giant eland left, date below **Obv. Designer:** G.B.L. Bazor **Rev:** Denomination within wreath

Date	Mintage	F	VF	XF	Unc	BU
1962(a)	6,000,000	0.50	1.25	2.25	4.00	—

KM# 4a 25 FRANCS
Aluminum-Nickel-Bronze **Obv:** Three giant eland left, date below **Obv. Designer:** G.B.L. Bazor **Rev:** Denomination, within wreath

Date	Mintage	F	VF	XF	Unc	BU
1970(a)	3,019,000	0.50	1.25	2.25	4.00	—
1972(a)	5,000,000	0.50	1.25	2.00	3.00	—

KM# 3 50 FRANCS
Copper-Nickel, 30.7 mm. **Obv:** Three giant eland left, date below **Obv. Designer:** G.B.L. Bazor **Rev:** Denomination within wreath

Date	Mintage	F	VF	XF	Unc	BU
1961(a)	5,000,000	2.00	4.00	6.00	10.00	—
1963(a)	5,000,000	2.00	4.00	6.00	10.00	—

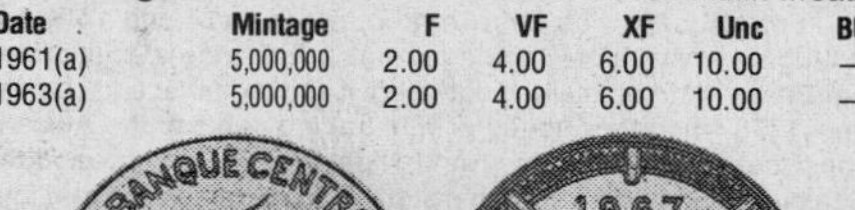

KM# 5 100 FRANCS
Nickel **Obv:** Three giant eland left **Obv. Designer:** G.B.L. Bazor **Rev:** Denomination, date above **Note:** KM#5 was issued double thick and should not be considered a piefort.

Date	Mintage	F	VF	XF	Unc	BU
1966(a)	6,000,000	2.00	4.00	7.00	12.00	—
1967(a)	5,800,000	2.00	4.00	7.00	12.00	—
1968(a)	6,200,000	2.00	4.00	7.00	12.00	—

ESSAIS

Standard metals unless otherwise noted

KM#	Date	Mintage	Identification	Issue Price	Mkt Val
E1	1961(a)	—	5 Francs. KM#1.	—	10.00
E2	1961(a)	—	10 Francs. KM#2.	—	15.00

KM#	Date	Mintage	Identification	Issue Price	Mkt Val
E3	1961(a)	—	50 Francs. Three Giant Eland, left, date below. Denomination within wreath. KM#3.	—	30.00
E4	1961(a)	—	50 Francs. Gold. KM#4.	—	1,250
E5	1962(a)	—	25 Francs. KM#4. This is a mule, having an old reverse die with a wing privy mark.	—	60.00
E6	1966(a)	—	100 Francs. KM#5.	—	20.00
E7	1969(a)	—	Franc. KM#6.	—	12.00

PIEFORTS

KM#	Date	Mintage	Identification	Issue Price	Mkt Val
P1	1965(a)	—	100 Francs. Gold. 23.4800 g. Three Giant Eland, left. Denomination, date above. KM#5. With ESSAI.	—	1,000

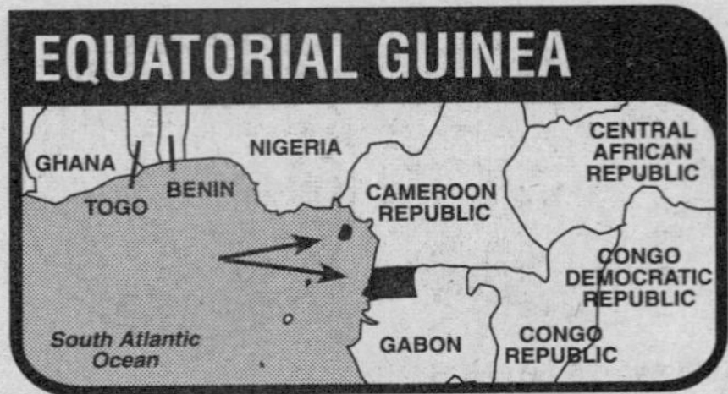

The Republic of Equatorial Guinea (formerly Spanish Guinea) consists of Rio Muni, located on the coast of West-Central Africa between Cameroon and Gabon, and the off-shore islands of Fernando Po, Annobon, Corisco, Elobey Grande and Elobey Chico. The equatorial country has an area of 10,831 sq. mi. (28,050 sq. km.) and a population of 420,293. Capital: Malabo. The economy is based on agriculture and forestry. Cacao, wood and coffee are exported.

Fernando Po was discovered between 1474 and 1496 by Portuguese navigators charting a route to the spice islands of the Far East. Portugal retained control of it and the adjacent islands until 1778 when they, together with trading rights to the African coast between the Ogooue and Niger Rivers, were ceded to Spain. Fernando Po was administered, with Spanish consent, by the British from 1827 to 1844 when it was reclaimed by Spain. Mainland Rio Muni was granted to Spain by the Berlin Conference of 1885. The name of the colony was changed from Spanish Guinea to Equatorial Guinea in Dec. of 1963. Independence was attained on Oct. 12, 1968.

Equatorial Guinea converted to the CFA currency system as issued for the Central African States issuing its first 100 Franc denomination in 1985.

NOTE: The 1969 coinage carries the actual minting date in the stars at the sides of the large date.

MINT MARKS

(a) - Paris, privy marks only

REPUBLIC

PESETA COINAGE

KM# 1 PESETA

Aluminum-Bronze, 19.5 mm.

Date	Mintage	F	VF	XF	Unc	BU
1969(69)	—	0.35	0.75	1.25	2.50	—

KM# 2 5 PESETAS

Copper-Nickel

Date	Mintage	F	VF	XF	Unc	BU
1969(69)	—	0.75	1.50	2.50	8.00	—

KM# 3 25 PESETAS

Copper-Nickel, 24 mm. **Obv:** Crossed tusks, date below **Rev:** Denomination at left, shielded arms at right, stars above arms

Date	Mintage	F	VF	XF	Unc	BU
1969(69)	—	1.50	2.50	6.50	12.00	—

KM# 5 25 PESETAS

5.0000 g., 0.9990 Silver .1606 oz. ASW **Subject:** World Bank **Obv:** Crossed tusks divide arms above and denomination below **Rev:** Banner crosses globe

Date	Mintage	F	VF	XF	Unc	BU
1970 Proof	2,475	Value: 10.00				

KM# 6 25 PESETAS

5.0000 g., 0.9990 Silver .1606 oz. ASW **Subject:** United Nations **Obv:** Crossed tusks divide arms above and denomination below **Rev:** UN logo

Date	Mintage	F	VF	XF	Unc	BU
1970 Proof	2,475	Value: 10.00				

KM# 4 50 PESETAS

Copper-Nickel **Obv:** Head right, date below **Rev:** Denomination at left, arms at right

Date	Mintage	F	VF	XF	Unc	BU
1969(69)	—	2.00	3.00	7.50	15.00	—

KM# 7 50 PESETAS

10.0000 g., 0.9990 Silver .3212 oz. ASW **Obv:** Crossed tusks divide arms above and denomination below **Rev:** Durer's Praying Hands

Date	Mintage	F	VF	XF	Unc	BU
1970 Proof	3,840	Value: 12.00				

KM# 8 75 PESETAS

15.0000 g., 0.9990 Silver .4818 oz. ASW **Obv:** Crossed tusks divide arms above and denomination below **Rev:** Pope John XXIII bust left

Date	Mintage	F	VF	XF	Unc	BU
1970 Proof	4,000	Value: 21.50				

KM# 9.1 75 PESETAS

15.0000 g., 0.9990 Silver .4818 oz. ASW **Subject:** Centennial - Birth of Vladimir Ilyich Lenin **Obv:** Crossed tusks divide arms above and denomination below, fineness stamp in field behind denomination **Rev:** Head left divides dates **Note:** Prev. KM#9.

Date	Mintage	F	VF	XF	Unc	BU
1970 Proof	4,000	Value: 21.50				

KM# 9.2 75 PESETAS

15.1400 g., 1.0000 Silver 0.4868 oz. ASW, 35.8 mm. **Subject:** Centennial of Lenin's birth **Obv:** Crossed tusks divide arms above and denomination below, fineness stamp at truncation of left tusk **Rev:** Head left divides dates

Date	Mintage	F	VF	XF	Unc	BU
1970 Proof	—	Value: 21.50				

KM# 10.1 75 PESETAS

15.0000 g., 0.9990 Silver .4818 oz. ASW **Subject:** Abraham Lincoln **Obv:** Crossed tusks divide arms above and denomination below, hallmark "1000" in oval at left tusk base **Rev:** Bust facing divides dates

Date	Mintage	F	VF	XF	Unc	BU
1970 Proof	4,390	Value: 16.50				

KM# 10.2 75 PESETAS

15.0000 g., 0.9990 Silver .4818 oz. ASW **Obv:** "1 AR" Hallmark above "E" in "Pesetas"

Date	Mintage	F	VF	XF	Unc	BU
1970 Proof	Inc. above	Value: 30.00				

KM# 11 75 PESETAS

15.0000 g., 0.9990 Silver .4818 oz. ASW **Subject:** Centennial - Birth of Mahatma Gandhi **Obv:** Crossed tusks divide arms above and denomination below **Rev:** Bust looking right divides dates

Date	Mintage	F	VF	XF	Unc	BU
1970 Proof	4,000	Value: 28.00				

KM# 12.1 100 PESETAS

20.0000 g., 0.9990 Silver .6430 oz. ASW **Obv:** Crossed tusk divide arms above and denomination below **Rev:** Durer's Praying Hands

Date	Mintage	F	VF	XF	Unc	BU
1970 Proof	4,000	Value: 16.50				

KM# 12.2 100 PESETAS

20.0000 g., 0.9990 Silver .6430 oz. ASW **Obv:** Crossed tusks divide arms above and denomination below, "1 AR" hallmark **Rev:** Durer's Praying Hands

Date	Mintage	F	VF	XF	Unc	BU
1970 Proof	Inc. above	Value: 27.50				

KM# 13.1 100 PESETAS

20.0000 g., 0.9990 Silver .6430 oz. ASW, 40 mm. **Obv:** Crossed tusks divide arms above and denomination below **Rev:** Goya's Naked Maja

Date	Mintage	F	VF	XF	Unc	BU
1970 Proof	30,000	Value: 30.00				

KM# 13.2 100 PESETAS

20.0000 g., 0.9990 Silver .6430 oz. ASW, 40 mm. **Obv:** Crossed tusks divide arms above and denomination below, fineness stamp at base of right tusk **Rev:** Goya's Naked Maja

Date	Mintage	F	VF	XF	Unc	BU
1970 Proof	Inc. above	Value: 30.00				

KM# 13.3 100 PESETAS

20.0000 g., 0.9990 Silver .6430 oz. ASW, 40 mm. **Obv:** Crossed tusks divide arms above and denomination below, fineness stamp below base of right tusk **Rev:** Goya's Naked Maja

Date	Mintage	F	VF	XF	Unc	BU
1970 Proof	Inc. above	Value: 30.00				

KM# 13.4 100 PESETAS

20.0000 g., 0.9990 Silver .6430 oz. ASW, 40 mm. **Obv:** Crossed tusks divide arms above and denomination below, fineness stamp above letters AN **Rev:** Goya's Naked Maja

Date	Mintage	F	VF	XF	Unc	BU
1970 Proof	Inc. above	Value: 30.00				

KM# 13.5 100 PESETAS

20.0000 g., 0.9990 Silver .6430 oz. ASW, 40 mm. **Obv:** Crossed tusks divide arms above and denomination below, 1000 in oval at base of right tusk **Rev:** Goya's Naked Maja

Date	Mintage	F	VF	XF	Unc	BU
1970 Proof	Inc. above	Value: 30.00				

KM# 14 150 PESETAS

30.0000 g., 0.9990 Silver .9636 oz. ASW, 30 mm. **Subject:** Centennial of the Capital Rome **Obv:** Crossed tusks divide arms above and denomination below **Rev:** Symbols of Rome, dates at left

Date	Mintage	F	VF	XF	Unc	BU
1970 Proof	3,520	Value: 32.50				

KM# 15 150 PESETAS

30.0000 g., 0.9990 Silver .9636 oz. ASW **Subject:** Centennial of the Capital Rome **Obv:** Crossed tusks divide arms above and denomination below **Rev:** Coliseum

Date	Mintage	F	VF	XF	Unc	BU
1970 Proof	3,520	Value: 32.50				

KM# 16 150 PESETAS

30.0000 g., 0.9990 Silver .9636 oz. ASW **Subject:** Centennial of the Capital Rome **Obv:** Crossed tusks divide arms above and denomination below **Rev:** Athena divides dates and buildings

Date	Mintage	F	VF	XF	Unc	BU
1970 Proof	3,520	Value: 32.50				

KM# 17 150 PESETAS

30.0000 g., 0.9990 Silver .9636 oz. ASW **Subject:** Centennial of the Capital Rome **Obv:** Crossed tusks divide arms above and denomination below **Rev:** Mercury left, dates lower left

Date	Mintage	F	VF	XF	Unc	BU
1970 Proof	3,520	Value: 40.00				

KM# 18.1 200 PESETAS

40.0000 g., 0.9990 Silver 1.2848 oz. ASW **Subject:** World Soccer Championship in Mexico **Obv:** Crossed tusks divide arms above and denomination below **Rev:** Statue flanked by countries with dates, four on each side

Date	Mintage	F	VF	XF	Unc	BU
1970 Proof	4,200	Value: 55.00				

KM# 18.2 200 PESETAS

40.0000 g., 0.9990 Silver 1.2848 oz. ASW **Subject:** World Soccer Championship in Mexico **Obv:** Fineness stamp in oval at base of right tusk; mint mark stamp "1 AR" at base of left tusk; incuse serial number below denomination **Rev:** Statue flanked by countries with dates, four on each side

Date	Mintage	F	VF	XF	Unc	BU
1970 Proof	Inc. above	Value: 75.00				

KM# 19 200 PESETAS

40.0000 g., 0.9990 Silver 1.2848 oz. ASW **Subject:** First President Francisco Macias **Obv:** Crossed tusks divide arms above and denomination below **Rev:** Head 3/4 right

Date	Mintage	F	VF	XF	Unc	BU
1970 Proof	4,000	Value: 45.00				

KM# 20.1 250 PESETAS

3.5200 g., 0.9000 Gold .1018 oz. AGW **Obv:** Crossed tusks divide arms above and denomination below, fineness countermark at 8 o'clock by tusk base **Rev:** Goya's Naked Maja **Note:** Prev. KM#20.

Date	Mintage	F	VF	XF	Unc	BU
1970 Proof	3,500	Value: 100				

KM# 20.2 250 PESETAS

3.5200 g., 0.9000 Gold 0.1019 oz. AGW **Obv:** Crossed tusks divide arms above and denomination below, fineness countermark at 4o'clock by tusk base **Rev:** Goya's Naked Maja

Date	Mintage	F	VF	XF	Unc	BU
1970 Proof	—	Value: 100				

KM# 21 250 PESETAS

3.5200 g., 0.9000 Gold .1018 oz. AGW **Obv:** Crossed tusks divide arms above and denomination below **Rev:** Durer's Praying Hands

Date	Mintage	F	VF	XF	Unc	BU
1970 Proof	2,000	Value: 85.00				

KM# 22 500 PESETAS

7.0500 g., 0.9000 Gold .2040 oz. AGW **Obv:** Crossed tusks divide arms above and denomination below **Rev:** Bust of Pope John XXIII

Date	Mintage	F	VF	XF	Unc	BU
1970 Proof	1,680	Value: 165				

KM# 23 500 PESETAS

7.0500 g., 0.9000 Gold .2040 oz. AGW **Subject:** Vladimer Illyich Lenin **Obv:** Crossed tusks divide arms above and denomination below **Rev:** Head left divides dates

Date	Mintage	F	VF	XF	Unc	BU
1970 Proof	1,680	Value: 170				

KM# 24 500 PESETAS

7.0500 g., 0.9000 Gold .2040 oz. AGW **Obv:** Crossed tusks divide arms above and denomination below **Rev:** President Abraham Lincoln

Date	Mintage	F	VF	XF	Unc	BU
1970 Proof	1,700	Value: 160				

KM# 25 500 PESETAS

7.0500 g., 0.9000 Gold .2040 oz. AGW **Subject:** Centennial - Birth of Mahatma Gandhi **Obv:** Crossed tusks divide arms above and denomination below **Rev:** Portrait of Gandhi

Date	Mintage	F	VF	XF	Unc	BU
1970 Proof	1,680	Value: 170				

KM# 26 750 PESETAS

10.5700 g., 0.9000 Gold .3058 oz. AGW **Subject:** Centennial of the Capital Rome **Obv:** Crossed tusks divide arms above and denomination below **Rev:** Symbols of Rome

Date	Mintage	F	VF	XF	Unc	BU
1970 Proof	1,650	Value: 240				

KM# 27 750 PESETAS
10.5700 g., 0.9000 Gold .3058 oz. AGW **Subject:** Centennial of the Capital Rome **Obv:** Crossed tusks divide arms above and denomination below **Rev:** Colisseum

Date	Mintage	F	VF	XF	Unc	BU
1970 Proof	1,550	Value: 250				

KM# 28 750 PESETAS
10.5700 g., 0.9000 Gold .3058 oz. AGW **Subject:** Centennial of the Capital Rome **Obv:** Crossed tusks divide arms above and denomination below **Rev:** Athena divides dates and buildings

Date	Mintage	F	VF	XF	Unc	BU
1970 Proof	1,550	Value: 245				

KM# 29 750 PESETAS
10.5700 g., 0.9000 Gold .3058 oz. AGW **Subject:** Centennial of the Capital Rome **Obv:** Crossed tusks divide arms above and denomination below **Rev:** Head of Mercury left

Date	Mintage	F	VF	XF	Unc	BU
1970 Proof	1,550	Value: 245				

KM# 30 1000 PESETAS
14.1000 g., 0.9000 Gold .4080 oz. AGW **Subject:** World Soccer Championship in Mexico **Obv:** Crossed tusks divide arms above and denomination below **Rev:** Statue flanked by countries with dates, four on each side

Date	Mintage	F	VF	XF	Unc	BU
1970 Proof	1,190	Value: 320				

KM# 31 5000 PESETAS
70.5200 g., 0.9000 Gold 2.0407 oz. AGW **Subject:** First President - Francisco Macias **Obv:** Crossed tusks divide arms above and denomination below **Rev:** Head 3/4 right

Date	Mintage	F	VF	XF	Unc	BU
1970 Proof	330	Value: 1,600				

REFORM COINAGE

1975-1980

KM# 32 EKUELE
Brass **Obv:** Head left, date below **Rev:** Assorted tools divide denomination **Note:** Withdrawn from circulation.

Date	Mintage	F	VF	XF	Unc	BU
1975	3,000,000	1.00	2.00	3.00	5.00	7.00

KM# 33 5 EKUELE
Copper-Nickel **Obv:** Head left, date below **Rev:** Figures on split shields divide denomination **Note:** Withdrawn from circulation.

Date	Mintage	F	VF	XF	Unc	BU
1975	2,800,000	1.00	2.00	3.50	6.00	8.00

KM# 34 10 EKUELE
Copper-Nickel **Obv:** Head left, date below **Rev:** Rooster within shield divides denomination **Note:** Withdrawn from circulation.

Date	Mintage	F	VF	XF	Unc	BU
1975	1,300,000	1.50	2.50	4.50	9.00	12.00

KM# 35 1000 EKUELE
21.4300 g., 0.9250 Silver .6373 oz. ASW **Obv:** Bank building, denomination below **Rev:** Head right, date below

Date	Mintage	F	VF	XF	Unc	BU
1978 Proof	31,000	Value: 18.50				

KM# 36 2000 EKUELE
42.8700 g., 0.9250 Silver 1.2749 oz. ASW **Obv:** Assorted tools, denomination below, rooster above **Rev:** President Masie Nguema Biyogo head, right, date below

Date	Mintage	F	VF	XF	Unc	BU
1978 Proof	31,000	Value: 32.50				

KM# 37 2000 EKUELE
31.1000 g., 0.9270 Silver .9270 oz. ASW **Subject:** XXII Olympics **Rev:** Discus thrower, building at left, Olympic logo at right

Date	Mintage	F	VF	XF	Unc	BU
ND(1979) Proof	11,000	Value: 18.00				

KM# 56 2000 EKUELE
31.0000 g., 0.9270 Silver .9270 oz. ASW **Rev:** Impalas

Date	Mintage	F	VF	XF	Unc	BU
1980 (1983) Proof	1,000	Value: 30.00				

KM# 55 2000 EKUELE
31.0000 g., 0.9270 Silver .9270 oz. ASW **Rev:** Burchell's zebra

Date	Mintage	F	VF	XF	Unc	BU
1980 (1983) Proof	1,000	Value: 30.00				

KM# 57 2000 EKUELE
31.0000 g., 0.9270 Silver .9270 oz. ASW **Obv:** Bank building, denomination below **Rev:** Tiger's head 3/4 left, date below

Date	Mintage	F	VF	XF	Unc	BU
1980 (1983) Proof	1,000	Value: 32.50				

KM# 58 2000 EKUELE
31.0000 g., 0.9270 Silver .9270 oz. ASW **Rev:** Cheetah running left, date below

Date	Mintage	F	VF	XF	Unc	BU
1980 (1983) Proof	1,000	Value: 32.50				

KM# 39 5000 EKUELE
6.9600 g., 0.9170 Gold .2052 oz. AGW **Obv:** Bank building, denomination below **Rev:** Head right, date below

Date	Mintage	F	VF	XF	Unc	BU
1978 Proof	31,000	Value: 165				

KM# 40 10000 EKUELE
13.9200 g., 0.9170 Gold .4104 oz. AGW **Obv:** Assorted tools, denomination below, rooster above **Rev:** Head right, date below

Date	Mintage	F	VF	XF	Unc	BU
1978 Proof	31,000	Value: 325				

KM# 41 10000 EKUELE
13.9200 g., 0.9170 Gold .4104 oz. AGW **Subject:** Soccer Games - Argentina 1978 **Obv:** Assorted tools, denomination below, rooster above **Rev:** Country name and map at center, soccer players flank, shields above and below

Date	Mintage	F	VF	XF	Unc	BU
ND(1979) Proof	121	Value: 550				

REFORM COINAGE

1980-1982

KM# 50 EKUELE

Aluminum-Bronze **Obv:** T. E. Nkogo head right, date below **Rev:** Denomination at left, shielded arms at right, stars above arms **Note:** Two digit incuse date within star to left of date on obverse

Date	Mintage	F	VF	XF	Unc	BU
1980(80)	Est. 200,000	—	—	—	60.00	65.00

KM# 54 EKUELE

62.2900 g., 0.9990 Gold 2.0009 oz. AGW **Obv:** Coat of arms **Rev:** Pope John Paul II

Date	Mintage	F	VF	XF	Unc	BU
1982	—	—	—	—	1,650	—

KM# 51 5 BIPKWELE

Copper-Nickel **Obv:** T. E. Nkogo right **Rev:** Value and arms **Note:** Two digit incuse date within star to left of date on obverse

Date	Mintage	F	VF	XF	Unc	BU
1980(80)	Est. 200,000	—	65.00	125	175	—

KM# 52 25 BIPKWELE

Copper-Nickel **Obv:** T. E. Nkogo head right, date below **Rev:** Denomination at left, arms at right **Note:** Two digit incuse date within star to left of date on obverse

Date	Mintage	F	VF	XF	Unc	BU
1980(80)	Est. 200,000	—	15.00	25.00	45.00	50.00
1981	Est. 800,000	—	—	—	—	—

KM# 53 50 BIPKWELE

Copper-Nickel **Obv:** T. E. Nkogo right **Rev:** Value and arms **Note:** Two digit incuse date within star to left of date on obverse

Date	Mintage	F	VF	XF	Unc	BU
1980(80)	Est. 200,000	—	—	—	50.00	55.00
1981	Est. 500,000	—	—	—	—	—

REFORM COINAGE

1985-

KM# 62 5 FRANCOS

Aluminum-Bronze **Obv:** Three Giant Eland left **Obv. Designer:** G.B.L. Bazor **Rev:** Denomination above date

Date	Mintage	F	VF	XF	Unc	BU
1985(a)	—	—	2.50	4.50	8.00	—

KM# 60 25 FRANCOS

Aluminum-Bronze **Obv:** Three Giant Eland left **Obv. Designer:** G.B.L. Bazor **Rev:** Denomination above date

Date	Mintage	F	VF	XF	Unc	BU
1985(a)	—	—	3.50	7.00	15.00	—

KM# 64 50 FRANCOS

Nickel **Obv:** Three Giant Eland left **Obv. Designer:** G.B.L. Bazor **Rev:** Denomination above date

Date	Mintage	F	VF	XF	Unc	BU
1985(a)	—	—	8.00	16.00	28.00	—
1986(a)	—	—	6.00	12.00	20.00	—

KM# 59 100 FRANCOS

Nickel **Obv:** Three Giant Eland left **Obv. Designer:** G.B.L. Bazor **Rev:** Denomination above date

Date	Mintage	F	VF	XF	Unc	BU
1985(a)	—	—	10.00	20.00	35.00	—
1986(a)	—	—	7.00	14.00	25.00	—

KM# 68 1000 FRANCOS

Copper-Nickel **Obv:** Arms above denomination **Rev:** Brandenburg Gate, dates below

Date	Mintage	F	VF	XF	Unc	BU
1991 Proof	5,150	Value: 10.00				

KM# 81 1000 FRANCOS

Copper-Nickel **Subject:** Jurassic Dinosaurs **Obv:** Arms divide date, denomination below **Rev:** Diplodocus **Note:** Multicolored.

Date	Mintage	F	VF	XF	Unc	BU
1993	—	—	—	—	27.50	—

KM# 115 1000 FRANCOS

25.5600 g., Copper-Nickel, 38 mm. **Subject:** Jurassic Dinosaurs **Obv:** Arms divide date, denomination below **Rev:** Multicolor stegosaurus **Edge:** Reeded

Date	Mintage	F	VF	XF	Unc	BU
1993	—	—	—	—	27.50	—

KM# 82 1000 FRANCOS

Copper-Nickel **Subject:** Jurassic Dinosaurs **Obv:** Arms divide date, denomination below **Rev:** Styracosaurus

Date	Mintage	F	VF	XF	Unc	BU
1993	—	—	—	—	27.50	—

KM# 83 1000 FRANCOS

Copper-Nickel **Subject:** Jurassic Dinosaurs **Obv:** Arms divide date, denomination below **Rev:** Tyrannosaurus

Date	Mintage	F	VF	XF	Unc	BU
1993	—	—	—	—	35.00	—

KM# 87 1000 FRANCOS

Copper-Nickel **Subject:** Jurassic Dinosaurs **Obv:** Arms divide date, denomination below **Rev:** Allosaurus

Date	Mintage	F	VF	XF	Unc	BU
1993	—	—	—	—	27.50	—

KM# 88 1000 FRANCOS

Copper-Nickel **Subject:** Jurassic Dinosaurs **Obv:** Arms divide date, denomination below **Rev:** Plateosaurus

Date	Mintage	F	VF	XF	Unc	BU
1993	—	—	—	—	27.50	—

KM# 89 1000 FRANCOS

Copper-Nickel **Subject:** African Bird Wildlife - Kingfisher **Obv:** Arms divide date, denomination below **Rev:** Pair of multicolored kingfishers

Date	Mintage	F	VF	XF	Unc	BU
1994	10,000	—	—	—	25.00	—

KM# 90 1000 FRANCOS

Copper-Nickel **Subject:** World Soccer Championship - 1994 **Obv:** Arms divide date, denomination below **Rev:** Soccer players with trophy

Date	Mintage	F	VF	XF	Unc	BU
1994	—	—	—	—	27.50	—

KM# 112 1000 FRANCOS

26.0000 g., Copper-Nickel, 38 mm. **Obv:** Arms divide date, denomination below **Rev:** Multicolor Spanish Salvador Dali stamp design **Edge:** Reeded

Date	Mintage	F	VF	XF	Unc	BU
1994 Proof	15,000	Value: 20.00				

KM# 91 1000 FRANCOS

Copper-Nickel **Subject:** World's Famous Dogs **Obv:** Arms divide date, denomination below **Rev:** St. Bernards **Note:** Multicolored.

Date	Mintage	F	VF	XF	Unc	BU
1994	10,000	—	—	—	25.00	—

KM# 92 1000 FRANCOS

Copper-Nickel **Subject:** 25th Anniversary - Moon Landing **Obv:** Arms divide date, denomination below **Rev:** Placing the flag

Date	Mintage	F	VF	XF	Unc	BU
1994	15,000	—	—	—	22.50	—

KM# 93 1000 FRANCOS

Copper-Nickel **Subject:** Famous Stamps of the World - Swiss **Obv:** Arms divide date, denomination below **Rev:** Imprint of stamp

Date	Mintage	F	VF	XF	Unc	BU
1994	15,000	—	—	—	20.00	—

KM# 84.1 1000 FRANCOS

Copper-Nickel **Subject:** 150th Anniversary - Basel "Taube" Stamp **Obv:** Arms divide date, denomination below **Rev:** Stamp within circle **Note:** Multicolored.

Date	Mintage	F	VF	XF	Unc	BU
1995	15,000	—	—	—	20.00	—

KM# 84.2 1000 FRANCOS

Copper-Nickel **Subject:** 150th Anniversary - Basel "Taube" Stamp **Obv:** Arms divide date, denomination below **Rev. Legend:** Stamp within circle, error, "TAUBER" **Note:** Multicolored.

Date	Mintage	F	VF	XF	Unc	BU
1995	Inc. above	—	—	—	30.00	—

KM# 95 1000 FRANCOS

Copper-Nickel **Subject:** Famous Places in the World - Altdorf **Obv:** Arms divide date, denomination below **Rev:** Multicolor applique of Wilhelm Tell

Date	Mintage	F	VF	XF	Unc	BU
1996 Proof	—	Value: 27.50				

KM# 96 1000 FRANCOS

Copper-Nickel **Subject:** Famous Stamps of the World - Pintores Famosos dei Mundo - Rolf Knie **Obv:** Arms divide date, denomination below **Rev:** Multicolor applique of Swiss circus stamp design

Date	Mintage	F	VF	XF	Unc	BU
1996 Proof	—	Value: 35.00				

KM# 97 1000 FRANCOS

Copper-Nickel **Subject:** Famous Stamps of the World - XXVI Juegos Olimpicos de Verano **Obv:** Arms divide date, denomination below **Rev:** Stamp with downhill skier

Date	Mintage	F	VF	XF	Unc	BU
1996 Proof	—	Value: 35.00				

KM# 118 1000 FRANCOS

29.5000 g., Copper-Nickel, 38 mm. **Subject:** Famous Places - les Diablerets **Obv:** Arms divide date, denomination below **Rev:** Multicolor stamp design **Edge:** Reeded

Date	Mintage	F	VF	XF	Unc	BU
1996	—	—	—	—	—	—

KM# 66 7000 FRANCOS

26.3000 g., 0.9990 Silver .8455 oz. ASW **Obv:** Arms above denomination **Rev:** President Mbasogo bust above three shields

Date	Mintage	F	VF	XF	Unc	BU
1991 Proof	—	Value: 42.50				

KM# 67 7000 FRANCOS

25.7000 g., 0.9990 Silver .8263 oz. ASW **Subject:** Soccer - Italy 1990 **Obv:** Arms above denomination **Rev:** Soccer players, small statue at left

Date	Mintage	F	VF	XF	Unc	BU
1991 Proof	6,000	Value: 45.00				

KM# 69 7000 FRANCOS

20.0000 g., 0.9990 Silver .6430 oz. ASW **Subject:** Discovery of America **Obv:** Arms above denomination **Rev:** Santa Maria, date below

Date	Mintage	F	VF	XF	Unc	BU
1991 Proof	15,000	Value: 40.00				

KM# 70 7000 FRANCOS

20.0000 g., 0.9990 Silver .6430 oz. ASW **Subject:** Seville Expo **Obv:** Arms above denomination **Rev:** Symbols from expo

Date	Mintage	F	VF	XF	Unc	BU
1991 Proof	15,000	Value: 40.00				

KM# 71 7000 FRANCOS
20.0000 g., 0.9990 Silver .6430 oz. ASW **Subject:** Barcelona Olympics **Obv:** Arms above denomination **Rev:** Athletes covering Olympic rings

Date	Mintage	F	VF	XF	Unc	BU
1991 Proof	15,000	Value: 42.50				

KM# 76 7000 FRANCOS
510.3000 g., 0.9990 Silver 16.4062 oz. ASW, 75.1 mm. **Subject:** Endangered Wildlife **Obv:** Arms at lower left, figures and wildlife scene **Rev:** Lions, denomination below **Note:** Photo reduced.

Date	Mintage	F	VF	XF	Unc	BU
1992 Proof	1,700	Value: 250				

KM# 80 7000 FRANCOS
10.4800 g., 0.9990 Silver .3366 oz. ASW **Subject:** Barcelona Olympics - 1992 **Obv:** Arms above denomination **Rev:** Katrin Krabbe, German sprinter

Date	Mintage	F	VF	XF	Unc	BU
1992 Proof	15,000	Value: 22.50				

KM# 105 7000 FRANCOS
7.7700 g., 0.9000 Gold .2248 oz. AGW **Subject:** Endangered Wildlife **Obv:** Arms above denomination **Rev:** Lions

Date	Mintage	F	VF	XF	Unc	BU
1992 Proof	450	Value: 200				

KM# 121 7000 FRANCOS
10.5100 g., 0.9990 Silver 0.3376 oz. ASW, 34.9 mm. **Obv:** Arms above denomination **Rev:** Elephant in profile, no trees or fineness statement in background **Edge:** Reeded

Date	Mintage	F	VF	XF	Unc	BU
1993 Proof	—	Value: 55.00				

KM# 122 7000 FRANCOS
10.2700 g., 0.9990 Silver 0.3299 oz. ASW, 34.8 mm. **Subject:** Protection of Endangered Wildlife **Obv:** Arms divide date, denomination below **Rev:** Two gorillas **Edge:** Reeded

Date	Mintage	F	VF	XF	Unc	BU
1993 Proof	—	Value: 55.00				

KM# 123 7000 FRANCOS
19.7300 g., 0.9990 Silver 0.6337 oz. ASW, 38.1 mm. **Obv:** Arms divide date, denomination below **Rev:** Lucerne city view **Edge:** Reeded

Date	Mintage	F	VF	XF	Unc	BU
1993 Proof	—	Value: 45.00				

KM# 126 7000 FRANCOS
0.9990 Silver, 34.8 mm. **Subject:** Endangered Wildlife **Obv:** Arms divide date, denomination below **Rev:** Rhino **Edge:** Reeded

Date	Mintage	F	VF	XF	Unc	BU
1993	—	Value: 60.00				

KM# 127 7000 FRANCOS
0.9990 Silver, 34.8 mm. **Subject:** Endangered Wildlife **Obv:** Arms divide date, denomination below **Rev:** Buffalo **Edge:** Reeded

Date	Mintage	F	VF	XF	Unc	BU
1993 Proof	—	Value: 50.00				

KM# 128 7000 FRANCOS
0.9990 Silver, 34.8 mm. **Subject:** Endangered Wildlife **Obv:** Arms divide date, denomination below **Rev:** Lion **Edge:** Reeded

Date	Mintage	F	VF	XF	Unc	BU
1993 Proof	—	Value: 60.00				

KM# 129 7000 FRANCOS
0.9990 Silver, 34.8 mm. **Subject:** Endangered Wildlife **Obv:** Arms divide date, denomination below **Rev:** Springbok **Edge:** Reeded

Date	Mintage	F	VF	XF	Unc	BU
1993 Proof	—	Value: 50.00				

KM# 77 7000 FRANCOS
10.5100 g., 0.9990 Silver .3379 oz. ASW **Subject:** African Elephant Protection **Obv:** Arms divide date, denomination below **Rev:** Elephant

Date	Mintage	F	VF	XF	Unc	BU
1993 Proof	Est. 25,000	Value: 30.00				

KM# 78 7000 FRANCOS
20.0000 g., 0.9990 Silver .6430 oz. ASW **Subject:** Barcelona Olympics **Obv:** Arms divide date, denomination below **Rev:** Athletes covering Olympic rings

Date	Mintage	F	VF	XF	Unc	BU
1993 Proof	—	Value: 65.00				

KM# 94 7000 FRANCOS
20.1700 g., 0.9990 Silver .6478 oz. ASW **Subject:** Jurassic Dinosaurs **Obv:** Arms divide date, denomination below **Rev:** Multicolor stegosaurus scene applique

Date	Mintage	F	VF	XF	Unc	BU
1993 Proof	—	Value: 65.00				

KM# 114 7000 FRANCOS
9.9300 g., 0.7400 Silver .2362 oz. ASW, 34.8 mm. **Subject:** Endangered Wildlife **Obv:** Arms divide date, denomination below **Rev:** Giraffe family **Edge:** Reeded

Date	Mintage	F	VF	XF	Unc	BU
1993 Proof	—	Value: 50.00				

KM# 119 7000 FRANCOS
20.0000 g., 0.9990 Silver 0.6424 oz. ASW **Obv:** Arms divide date, denomination below **Rev:** Zebras

Date	Mintage	F	VF	XF	Unc	BU
1993 Proof	—	Value: 50.00				

KM# 86 7000 FRANCOS
20.1700 g., 0.9990 Silver .6651 oz. ASW **Subject:** World Cup Soccer **Obv:** Arms divide date, denomination below **Rev:** Soccer net and players

Date	Mintage	F	VF	XF	Unc	BU
1994 Proof	—	Value: 40.00				

KM# 113 7000 FRANCOS
20.3500 g., 0.9990 Silver 0.6536 oz. ASW, 38 mm. **Obv:** Arms divide date, denomination below **Rev:** Multicolor Spanish Salvador Dali stamp design **Edge:** Reeded

Date	Mintage	F	VF	XF	Unc	BU
1994 Proof	—	Value: 50.00				

KM# 125 7000 FRANCOS
20.3500 g., 0.9990 Silver 0.6536 oz. ASW, 38.1 mm. **Obv:** Arms divide date, denomination below **Rev:** Multicolor Bulldog on cross **Edge:** Reeded

Date	Mintage	F	VF	XF	Unc	BU
1994 Proof	—	Value: 45.00				

KM# 98 7000 FRANCOS
20.3500 g., 0.9990 Silver .6536 oz. ASW **Subject:** African Bird

Wildlife - Kingfisher **Obv:** Arms divide date, denomination below **Rev:** Pair of multicolor kingfishers

Date	Mintage	F	VF	XF	Unc	BU
1994 Proof	—	Value: 42.50				

KM# 99 7000 FRANCOS
20.3500 g., 0.9990 Silver .6536 oz. ASW **Subject:** World Famous Dogs - St. Bernard **Obv:** Arms divide date, denomination below **Rev:** Pair of multicolor St. Bernards

Date	Mintage	F	VF	XF	Unc	BU
1994 Proof	—	Value: 50.00				

KM# 108 7000 FRANCOS
20.3500 g., 0.9990 Silver .6536 oz. ASW **Subject:** 25th Anniversary - Moon Landing **Obv:** Arms divide date, denomination below **Rev:** Multicolor moon landing scene

Date	Mintage	F	VF	XF	Unc	BU
1994 Proof	10,000	Value: 42.50				

KM# 85 7000 FRANCOS
21.0000 g., 0.9990 Silver .6752 oz. ASW **Subject:** 50th Anniversary - United Nations **Obv:** Arms divide date, denomination below **Rev:** Building and laurel sprigs, dates below

Date	Mintage	F	VF	XF	Unc	BU
1995 Proof	—	Value: 37.50				

KM# 100 7000 FRANCOS
157.5500 g., 0.9990 Silver 5.0603 oz. ASW, 64.9 mm. **Subject:** Endangered wildlife **Obv:** Topical map of Africa **Rev:** Elephant head facing, denomination below **Note:** Photo reduced.

Date	Mintage	F	VF	XF	Unc	BU
1995 Proof	555	Value: 120				

KM# 109 7000 FRANCOS
20.3500 g., 0.9990 Silver .6536 oz. ASW **Subject:** 150th Anniversary - Basel "Taube" Stamp **Obv:** Arms divide date, denomination below **Rev:** Multicolored stamp

Date	Mintage	F	VF	XF	Unc	BU
1995 Proof	7,500	Value: 30.00				

KM# 101 7000 FRANCOS
157.5500 g., 0.9990 Silver 5.0603 oz. ASW **Subject:** Endangered wildlife **Obv:** Topical map of Africa **Rev:** Mother elephant with calf, denomination below **Note:** Photo reduced.

Date	Mintage	F	VF	XF	Unc	BU
1995 Proof	555	Value: 120				

KM# 102 7000 FRANCOS
157.5500 g., 0.9990 Silver 5.0603 oz. ASW **Subject:** Endangered wildlife **Obv:** Topical map of Africa **Rev:** Elephants at watering hole, denomination below **Note:** Photo reduced.

Date	Mintage	F	VF	XF	Unc	BU
1995 Proof	555	Value: 120				

KM# 103 7000 FRANCOS
157.5500 g., 0.9990 Silver 5.0603 oz. ASW **Subject:** Endangered wildlife **Obv:** Topical map of Africa **Rev:** Elephant family, denomination below **Note:** Photo reduced.

Date	Mintage	F	VF	XF	Unc	BU
1995 Proof	555	Value: 120				

KM# 104 7000 FRANCOS
157.5500 g., 0.9990 Silver 5.0603 oz. ASW **Subject:** Endangered wildlife **Obv:** Topical map of Africa **Rev:** Adolescent elephant with adult **Note:** Photo reduced.

Date	Mintage	F	VF	XF	Unc	BU
1995 Proof	555	Value: 120				

KM# 120 7000 FRANCOS
19.6000 g., 0.9999 Silver 0.6301 oz. ASW, 37.9 mm. **Subject:** Charlemagne **Obv:** Arms divide date, denomination below **Rev:** King on horse **Edge:** Reeded

Date	Mintage	F	VF	XF	Unc	BU
1997 Proof	—	Value: 35.00				

KM# 116 8000 FRANCOS
7.7700 g., 0.9990 Gold 0.2496 oz. AGW, 26.9 mm. **Subject:** World's Famous Dogs **Obv:** Arms divide date, denomination below **Rev:** Pekingese dog and Chinese building **Edge:** Reeded

Date	Mintage	F	VF	XF	Unc	BU
1994 Proof	—	Value: 250				

KM# 72 15000 FRANCOS
7.0000 g., 0.9170 Gold .2063 oz. AGW **Subject:** Discovery of America - Columbus **Obv:** Arms above denomination

Date	Mintage	F	VF	XF	Unc	BU
1991 Proof	1,500	Value: 165				

KM# 73 15000 FRANCOS
7.0000 g., 0.9170 Gold .2063 oz. AGW **Subject:** Expo Seville

Obv: Arms above denomination **Rev:** Ship and Space Shuttle, dates below

Date	Mintage	F	VF	XF	Unc	BU
1991 Proof	1,500	Value: 165				

KM# 74 15000 FRANCOS

7.0000 g., 0.9170 Gold .2063 oz. AGW **Series:** Barcelona Olympics **Obv:** Arms above denomination **Rev:** Equestrian jumping

Date	Mintage	F	VF	XF	Unc	BU
1991 Proof	1,500	Value: 170				

KM# 74a 15000 FRANCOS

20.3300 g., 0.9990 Silver .6350 oz. ASW **Series:** Barcelona Olympics **Obv:** Arms above denomination **Rev:** Equestrian jumping

Date	Mintage	F	VF	XF	Unc	BU
1992 Proof	—	Value: 50.00				

KM# 79 15000 FRANCOS

855.3422 g., 0.9990 Silver 27.49 oz. ASW, 106 mm. **Subject:** Endangered Wildlife **Obv:** Topical map of Africa **Rev:** Elephant mother and calf, denomination below **Note:** Photo reduced.

Date	Mintage	F	VF	XF	Unc	BU
1992 Proof	2,200	Value: 400				

KM# 106 15000 FRANCOS

15.5500 g., 0.9000 Gold .4499 oz. AGW **Subject:** Endangered Wildlife **Obv:** Topical map of Africa **Rev:** Elephant

Date	Mintage	F	VF	XF	Unc	BU
1992 Proof	450	Value: 350				

KM# 107 30000 FRANCOS

33.9300 g., 0.9170 Gold 1.0003 oz. AGW, 32.8 mm. **Subject:** Elephant Protection **Obv:** Arms above denomination **Rev:** Elephant **Edge:** Reeded

Date	Mintage	F	VF	XF	Unc	BU
1993 Proof	700	Value: 750				

Note: 400 pieces remelted at mint

ESSAIS

KM#	Date	Mintage	Identification	Issue Price	Mkt Val
E1	1978	25	1000 Ekuele. Aluminum. KM#35.	—	45.00
E2	1978	20	1000 Ekuele. Copper. KM#35.	—	50.00
E3	1978	25	2000 Ekuele. Aluminum. KM#36.	—	55.00
E4	1978	—	2000 Ekuele. Copper. KM#36.	—	60.00
E5	1978	—	5000 Ekuele. Aluminum. KM#39.	—	35.00
E6	1978	—	5000 Ekuele. Copper. KM#39.	—	40.00
E7	1978	—	10000 Ekuele. Aluminum. KM#40.	—	45.00
E8	1978	—	10000 Ekuele. Copper. KM#40.	—	50.00
E9	ND(1979)	—	2000 Ekuele. Aluminum. KM#38.	—	25.00
E10	ND(1979)	—	2000 Ekuele. Copper. KM#38.	—	90.00
E11	ND(1979)	—	10000 Ekuele. Aluminum. KM#41.	—	25.00
E12	ND(1979)	—	10000 Ekuele. Copper. KM#41.	—	60.00
E13	1980	—	Bipkwele. Copper. KM#5.	—	20.00
E28	1985	—	5 Francos. Aluminum-Bronze. KM#62.	—	17.50
E29	1985	—	25 Francos. Aluminum-Bronze. Three Giant Eland, left. Denomination above date. KM#60.	—	22.50
E30	1985	—	50 Francos. Nickel. KM#64.	—	25.00
E31	1985	—	100 Francos. Nickel. Three Giant Eland, left. Denomination above date. KM#59.	—	27.50

PATTERNS

Including off metal strikes

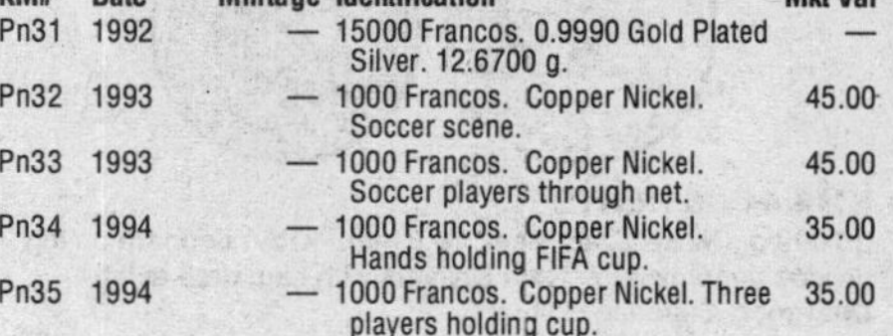

KM#	Date	Mintage	Identification	Mkt Val
Pn31	1992	—	15000 Francos. 0.9990 Gold Plated Silver. 12.6700 g.	—
Pn32	1993	—	1000 Francos. Copper Nickel. Soccer scene.	45.00
Pn33	1993	—	1000 Francos. Copper Nickel. Soccer players through net.	45.00
Pn34	1994	—	1000 Francos. Copper Nickel. Hands holding FIFA cup.	35.00
Pn35	1994	—	1000 Francos. Copper Nickel. Three players holding cup.	35.00
Pn36	1994	—	7000 Francos. 0.9990 Silver. 19.9100 g. Dalmations.	—
Pn37	1995	—	1000 Francos. Copper-Nickel. 26.4000 g. 38.2 mm. National arms. "UN" letters with German inscription and the UN logo in background. Reeded edge.	—
Pn38	1996	—	1000 Francos. Brass. 28.5000 g. 38 mm. National arms. French postage stamp design. Reeded edge.	300

PIEFORTS

KM#	Date	Mintage	Identification	Issue Price	Mkt Val
P1	1978	—	1000 Ekuele. Copper. KM#35.	—	200
P2	1978	—	1000 Ekuele. 0.9250 Silver. KM#35.	—	250
P3	1978	—	2000 Ekuele. Copper. 6.8 mm. Plain edge. KM#36.	—	300
P4	1978	—	5000 Ekuele. Copper. 2.6 mm. Milled edge. KM#39.	—	175
P5	1978	—	5000 Ekuele. Copper. 4.1 mm. Plain edge.	—	150
P6	1978	—	10000 Ekuele. Copper. 3.4 mm. Milled edge. KM#41.	—	110
P7	ND(1979)	—	2000 Ekuele. Copper. KM#38.	—	215
P8	ND(1979)	—	2000 Ekuele. 0.9250 Silver. KM#38.	—	300
P9	ND(1979)	—	2000 Ekuele. Gilt Copper.	—	215
P10	ND(1979)	—	10000 Ekuele. Copper. KM#41.	—	225
P11	ND(1979)	—	10000 Ekuele. Gold. KM#41.	—	1,200
P12	ND(1979)	—	10000 Ekuele. Gilt Copper. KM#41.	—	200

TRIAL STRIKES

KM#	Date	Mintage	Identification	Issue Price	Mkt Val
TS1	1978	—	2000 Ekuele. Copper. 3.9 mm. KM#36. PRUEBA.	—	150
TS2	1978	—	2000 Ekuele. Copper. 3.9 mm. PRUEBA. KM#36.	—	150
TS3	1978	—	5000 Ekuele. Copper. 2.8 mm. KM39. PRUEBA.	—	75.00
TS4	1978	—	5000 Ekuele. Copper. 2.8 mm. KM39. PRUEBA.	—	75.00

KM#	Date	Mintage	Identification	Issue Price	Mkt Val
TS5	1978	—	10000 Ekuele. Copper. 3.6 mm. KM40. PRUEBA.	—	75.00

KM#	Date	Mintage	Identification	Issue Price	Mkt Val
TS6	1978	—	10000 Ekuele. Copper. PRUEBA. KM#40.	—	75.00

KM#	Date	Mintage	Identification	Issue Price	Mkt Val
TS7	1978(80)	—	2000 Bipkwele. 0.9250 Silver. 25.2100 g. M3. PRUEBA.	—	150

MINT SETS

KM#	Date	Mintage	Identification	Issue Price	Mkt Val
MS1	1975 (3)	—	KM#32-34	—	22.00

PROOF SETS

KM#	Date	Mintage	Identification	Issue Price	Mkt Val
PS1	1970 (27)	330	KM#5-31	—	3,500
PS2	1970 (15)	2,475	KM#5-19	127	350
PS3	1970 (12)	330	KM#20-31	—	3,150

ERITREA

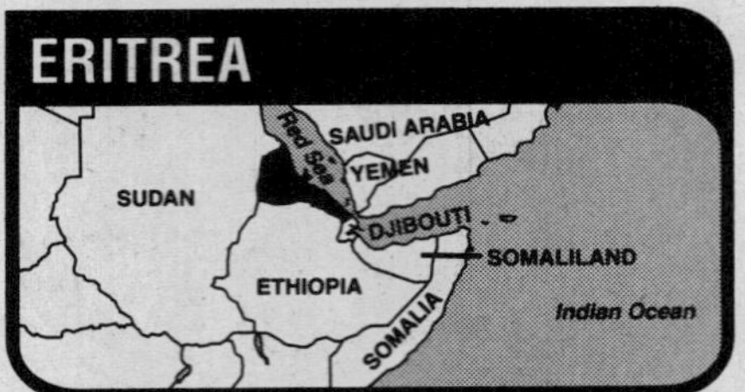

The State of Eritrea, a former Ethiopian province fronting on the Red Sea, has an area of 45,300 sq. mi. (117,600 sq. km.) and a population of 3.6 million. It was an Italian colony from 1889 until its incorporation into Italian East Africa in 1936. It was under the British Military Administration from 1941 to Sept. 15, 1952, when the United Nations designated it an autonomous unit within the federation of Ethiopia and Eritrea. On Nov. 14, 1962, it was annexed with Ethiopia. In 1991 the Eritrean Peoples Liberation Front extended its control over the entire territory of Eritrea. Following 2 years of provisional government, Eritrea held a referendum on independence in May 1993. Overwhelming popular approval led to the proclamation of an independent Republic of Eritrea on May 24.

RULERS
Umberto I, 1889-1900
Vittorio Emanuele III, 1900-1945

MINT MARKS
M - Milan
PM - Pobjoy
R – Rome

MONETARY SYSTEM
100 Centesimi = 1 Lira
5 Lire = 1 Tallero
100 Cents = 1 Nakfa (from 1997)

ITALIAN COLONY

COLONIAL COINAGE

KM# 5 TALLERO
28.0668 g., 0.8350 Silver .7535 oz. ASW, 40 mm. **Ruler:** Vittorio Emanuele III **Obv:** Bust with loose hair right, date at right **Rev:** Crowned imperial eagle with shield on breast

Date	Mintage	F	VF	XF	Unc	BU
1918R	510,000	40.00	100	300	650	1,000

REPUBLIC

DECIMAL COINAGE

100 Cents = 1 Dollar

KM# 43 CENT
2.2000 g., Nickel Clad Steel, 17 mm. **Obv:** Red-fronted gazelle right, divides denomination **Rev:** Soldiers with flag, date at left **Designer:** Clarence Holbert

Date	Mintage	F	VF	XF	Unc	BU
1997	—	—	—	—	0.50	1.00

KM# 44 5 CENTS
2.7000 g., Nickel Clad Steel, 18.9 mm. **Obv:** Leopard on log divides denomination **Rev:** Soldiers with flag, date at left **Designer:** Clarence Holbert

Date	Mintage	F	VF	XF	Unc	BU
1997	—	—	—	—	0.75	1.50

KM# 45 10 CENTS
3.3000 g., Nickel Clad Steel, 20.95 mm. **Obv:** Ostrich left divides denomination **Rev:** Soldiers with flag, date at left **Designer:** Clarence Holbert

Date	Mintage	F	VF	XF	Unc	BU
1997	—	—	—	—	1.00	1.75

KM# 46 25 CENTS
5.8000 g., Nickel Clad Steel, 23 mm. **Obv:** Grevy's zebra left divides denomination **Rev:** Soldiers with flag, date at left **Designer:** Clarence Holbert

Date	Mintage	F	VF	XF	Unc	BU
1997	—	—	—	—	1.25	2.00

KM# 47 50 CENTS
7.8000 g., Nickel Clad Steel, 24.95 mm. **Obv:** Greater Kudu left divides denomination **Rev:** Soldiers with flag, date at left **Designer:** Clarence Holbert

Date	Mintage	F	VF	XF	Unc	BU
1997	—	—	—	—	1.50	2.25

KM# 48 100 CENTS
10.3000 g., Nickel Clad Steel, 26.2 mm. **Obv:** African elephant and calf left, divide denomination **Rev:** Soldiers with flag, date at left **Designer:** Clarence Holbert

Date	Mintage	F	VF	XF	Unc	BU
1997	—	—	—	—	2.00	3.00

KM# 6 DOLLAR
Copper-Nickel **Subject:** Independence Day **Obv:** Dhow, camel and palm tree, date below, all within circle **Rev:** Tree within laurel wreath, dates below, circle surrounds, denomination below

Date	Mintage	F	VF	XF	Unc	BU
1993	—	—	—	—	8.50	—

KM# 10 DOLLAR
Copper-Nickel **Subject:** Preserve Planet Earth **Obv:** Dhow, camel and palm tree, date below, all within circle **Rev:** Triceratops, denomination below

Date	Mintage	F	VF	XF	Unc	BU
1993	—	—	—	—	12.00	—

KM# 13 DOLLAR
Copper-Nickel **Subject:** Preserve Planet Earth **Obv:** Dhow, camel and palm tree, date below, all within circle **Rev:** Ankylosaurus, denomination below

Date	Mintage	F	VF	XF	Unc	BU
1993	—	—	—	—	12.00	—

KM# 14 DOLLAR
Copper-Nickel **Subject:** Preserve Planet Earth **Obv:** Dhow, camel and palm tree, date below, all within circle **Rev:** Pteranodon, denomination below

Date	Mintage	F	VF	XF	Unc	BU
1993	—	—	—	—	14.00	—

KM# 15 DOLLAR
Copper-Nickel **Subject:** Preserve Planet Earth **Obv:** Dhow, camel and palm tree, date below, all within circle **Rev:** Cheetah, denomination below

Date	Mintage	F	VF	XF	Unc	BU
1994	—	—	—	—	12.00	—

KM# 16 DOLLAR
Copper-Nickel **Subject:** Preserve Planet Earth **Obv:** Dhow, camel and palm tree, date below, all within circle **Rev:** Black Rhinoceros, denomination below

Date	Mintage	F	VF	XF	Unc	BU
1994	—	—	—	—	12.00	—

KM# 17 DOLLAR
Copper-Nickel **Subject:** Preserve Planet Earth **Obv:** Dhow, camel and palm tree, date below, all within circle **Rev:** Black and White Colobus Monkey, denomination below

Date	Mintage	F	VF	XF	Unc	BU
1994	—	—	—	—	12.00	—

KM# 28 DOLLAR
Copper-Nickel **Subject:** Preserve Planet Earth **Obv:** Dhow, camel and palm tree, date below, all within circle **Rev:** Lions

Date	Mintage	F	VF	XF	Unc	BU
1995PM	—	—	—	—	12.00	—

KM# 31 DOLLAR
Copper-Nickel **Subject:** Preserve Planet Earth **Obv:** Dhow, camel and palm tree, date below, all within circle **Rev:** Cape Eagle owl

Date	Mintage	F	VF	XF	Unc	BU
1995PM	—	—	—	—	12.00	—

KM# 34 DOLLAR
Copper-Nickel **Subject:** Preserve Planet Earth **Obv:** Dhow, camel and palm tree, date below, all within circle **Rev:** Wattled Cranes

Date	Mintage	F	VF	XF	Unc	BU
1996	—	—	—	—	12.00	—

KM# 37 DOLLAR
Copper-Nickel **Subject:** Preserve Planet Earth **Obv:** Dhow, camel and palm tree, date below, all within circle **Rev:** Laner falcon

Date	Mintage	F	VF	XF	Unc	BU
1996	—	—	—	—	12.00	—

KM# 40 DOLLAR
Copper-Nickel **Subject:** Jurassic Park **Obv:** Dhow, camel and palm tree, date below, all within circle **Rev:** Triceratops, Jurassic Park logo

Date	Mintage	F	VF	XF	Unc	BU
1997	—	—	—	—	12.00	—

KM# 7 10 DOLLARS
31.1030 g., 0.9999 Silver 1.0000 oz. ASW **Subject:** Independence Day **Obv:** Dhow, camel and palm tree, date below, within circle **Rev:** Tree within laurel wreath, dates below, circle surrounds, denomination below

Date	Mintage	F	VF	XF	Unc	BU
1993 Proof	Est. 30,000	Value: 45.00				

KM# 11 10 DOLLARS
28.2800 g., 0.9250 Silver .8411 oz. ASW **Subject:** Preserve Planet Earth **Obv:** Dhow, camel and palm tree, date below, all within circle **Rev:** Triceratops, denomination below

Date	Mintage	F	VF	XF	Unc	BU
1993 Proof	Est. 30,000	Value: 45.00				

KM# 24 10 DOLLARS
28.2800 g., 0.9250 Silver .8411 oz. ASW **Subject:** Preserve Planet Earth **Obv:** Dhow, camel and palm tree, date below, all within circle **Rev:** Ankylosaurus

Date	Mintage	F	VF	XF	Unc	BU
1993 Proof	Est. 30,000	Value: 45.00				

KM# 25 10 DOLLARS
28.2800 g., 0.9250 Silver .8411 oz. ASW **Subject:** Preserve Planet Earth **Obv:** Dhow, camel and palm tree, date below, all within circle **Rev:** Pteranodon

Date	Mintage	F	VF	XF	Unc	BU
1993 Proof	Est. 30,000	Value: 45.00				

KM# 18 10 DOLLARS
28.2800 g., 0.9250 Silver .8411 oz. ASW **Subject:** Preserve Planet Earth **Obv:** Dhow, camel and palm tree, date below, all within circle **Rev:** Cheetah, denomination below

Date	Mintage	F	VF	XF	Unc	BU
1994 Proof	Est. 30,000	Value: 45.00				

KM# 19 10 DOLLARS
28.2800 g., 0.9250 Silver .8411 oz. ASW **Subject:** Preserve Planet Earth **Obv:** Dhow, camel and palm tree, date below, all within circle **Rev:** Black rhinoceros, denomination below

Date	Mintage	F	VF	XF	Unc	BU
1994 Proof	Est. 30,000	Value: 45.00				

KM# 20 10 DOLLARS
28.2800 g., 0.9250 Silver .8411 oz. ASW **Subject:** Preserve Planet Earth **Obv:** Dhow, camel and palm tree, date below, all within circle **Rev:** Colobus monkey, denomination below

Date	Mintage	F	VF	XF	Unc	BU
1994 Proof	Est. 30,000	Value: 45.00				

KM# 29 10 DOLLARS
28.2800 g., 0.9250 Silver .8411 oz. ASW **Subject:** Preserve Planet Earth **Obv:** Dhow, camel and palm tree, date below, all within circle **Rev:** Lions, denomination below

Date	Mintage	F	VF	XF	Unc	BU
1995PM Proof	5,000	Value: 45.00				

KM# 32 10 DOLLARS
28.2800 g., 0.9250 Silver .8411 oz. ASW **Subject:** Preserve Planet Earth **Obv:** Dhow, camel and palm tree, date below, all within circle **Rev:** Cape Eagle owl, denomination below

Date	Mintage	F	VF	XF	Unc	BU
1995PM Proof	Est. 30,000	Value: 50.00				

KM# 35 10 DOLLARS
28.2800 g., 0.9250 Silver .8411 oz. ASW **Subject:** Preserve Planet Earth **Obv:** Dhow, camel and palm tree, date below, all within circle **Rev:** Wattled cranes, denomination below

Date	Mintage	F	VF	XF	Unc	BU
1996 Proof	Est. 30,000	Value: 45.00				

KM# 38 10 DOLLARS
28.2800 g., 0.9250 Silver .8411 oz. ASW **Subject:** Preserve Planet Earth **Obv:** Dhow, camel and palm tree, date below, all within circle **Rev:** Laner falcon, denomination below

Date	Mintage	F	VF	XF	Unc	BU
1996 Proof	Est. 30,000	Value: 45.00				

KM# 41 10 DOLLARS
28.2800 g., 0.9250 Silver .8411 oz. ASW **Subject:** Jurassic Park **Obv:** Dhow, camel and palm tree, date below, all within circle **Rev:** Triceratops, Jurassic Park logo, denomination below

Date	Mintage	F	VF	XF	Unc	BU
1997 Proof	Est. 10,000	Value: 45.00				

KM# 8 50 DOLLARS
3.1100 g., 0.9990 Gold .1000 oz. AGW **Subject:** Independence Day **Obv:** Dhow, camel and tree within circle, denomination below **Rev:** Tree within laurel wreath, dates below, circle surrounds, denomination below

Date	Mintage	F	VF	XF	Unc	BU
1993 Proof	Est. 20,000	Value: 100				

KM# 9 100 DOLLARS
6.2200 g., 0.9990 Gold .2000 oz. AGW **Subject:** Independence Day **Obv:** Dhow, camel and palm tree, date below, all within circle **Rev:** Tree within laurel wreath, dates below, circle surrounds, denomination below

Date	Mintage	F	VF	XF	Unc	BU
1993 Proof	Est. 5,000	Value: 200				

KM# 12 100 DOLLARS
6.2200 g., 0.9990 Gold .2000 oz. AGW **Subject:** Preserve Planet Earth **Obv:** Dhow, camel and tree within circle, denomination below **Rev:** Triceratops, denomination below

Date	Mintage	F	VF	XF	Unc	BU
1993 Proof	Est. 5,000	Value: 175				

KM# 26 100 DOLLARS
6.2200 g., 0.9990 Gold .2000 oz. AGW **Subject:** Preserve Planet Earth **Obv:** Dhow, camel and palm tree, date below, all within circle **Rev:** Ankylosaurus

Date	Mintage	F	VF	XF	Unc	BU
1993 Proof	Est. 5,000	Value: 175				

KM# 27 100 DOLLARS
6.2200 g., 0.9990 Gold .2000 oz. AGW **Subject:** Preserve Planet Earth **Obv:** Dhow, camel and palm tree, date below, all within circle **Rev:** Pteranodon

Date	Mintage	F	VF	XF	Unc	BU
1993 Proof	Est. 5,000	Value: 175				

KM# 21 100 DOLLARS
6.2200 g., 0.9990 Gold .2000 oz. AGW **Subject:** Preserve Planet Earth **Obv:** Dhow, camel and palm tree, date below, all within circle **Rev:** Mother and baby cheetah

Date	Mintage	F	VF	XF	Unc	BU
1994 Proof	5,000	Value: 175				

KM# 22 100 DOLLARS
6.2200 g., 0.9990 Gold .2000 oz. AGW **Subject:** Preserve Planet Earth **Obv:** Dhow, camel and palm tree, date below, all within circle **Rev:** Rhinoceros head right

Date	Mintage	F	VF	XF	Unc	BU
1994 Proof	5,000	Value: 175				

KM# 23 100 DOLLARS
6.2200 g., 0.9990 Gold .2000 oz. AGW **Subject:** Preserve Planet Earth **Obv:** Dhow, camel and palm tree, date below, all within circle **Rev:** Colobus monkey

Date	Mintage	F	VF	XF	Unc	BU
1994 Proof	5,000	Value: 175				

KM# 30 100 DOLLARS
6.2200 g., 0.9990 Gold .2000 oz. AGW **Subject:** Preserve Planet Earth **Obv:** Dhow, camel and palm tree, date below, all within circle **Rev:** Female lion and cub

Date	Mintage	F	VF	XF	Unc	BU
1995 Proof	Est. 5,000	Value: 185				

KM# 33 100 DOLLARS
6.2200 g., 0.9990 Gold .2000 oz. AGW **Subject:** Preserve Planet Earth **Obv:** Dhow, camel and palm tree, date below, all within circle **Rev:** Cape eagle owl

Date	Mintage	F	VF	XF	Unc	BU
1995 Proof	Est. 5,000	Value: 175				

KM# 36 100 DOLLARS
6.2200 g., 0.9990 Gold .2000 oz. AGW **Subject:** Preserve Planet Earth **Obv:** Dhow, camel and palm tree, date below, all within circle **Rev:** Wattled cranes

Date	Mintage	F	VF	XF	Unc	BU
1996 Proof	Est. 5,000	Value: 175				

KM# 39 100 DOLLARS
6.2200 g., 0.9990 Gold .2000 oz. AGW **Subject:** Preserve Planet Earth **Obv:** Dhow, camel and palm tree, date below, all within circle **Rev:** Laner falcon

Date	Mintage	F	VF	XF	Unc	BU
1996 Proof	Est. 5,000	Value: 175				

KM# 42 100 DOLLARS
6.2200 g., 0.9990 Gold .2000 oz. AGW **Subject:** Jurassic Park **Obv:** Dhow, camel and tree within circle, denomination below **Rev:** Triceratops, Jurassic Park logo

Date	Mintage	F	VF	XF	Unc	BU
1997 Proof	Est. 2,500	Value: 185				

PROVAS

KM#	Date	Mintage	Identification	Mkt Val
PR1	1918R	—	Tallero. Bust with loose hair right. Crowned imperial eagle, shield on breast. KM5.	1,250

The Republic of Estonia (formerly the Estonian Soviet Socialist Republic of the U.S.S.R.) is the northernmost of the three Baltic States in Eastern Europe. It has an area of 17,462 sq. mi. (45,100 sq. km.) and a population of 1.6 million. Capital: Tallinn. Agriculture and dairy farming are the principal industries. Butter, eggs, bacon, timber and petroleum are exported.

This small and ancient Baltic state had enjoyed but two decades of independence since the 13th century until the present time. After having been conquered by the Danes, the Livonian Knights, the Teutonic Knights of Germany (who reduced the people to serfdom), the Swedes, the Poles and Russia, Estonia declared itself an independent republic on Feb. 24, 1918 but was not freed until Feb. 1919. The peace treaty was signed Feb. 2, 1920. Shortly after the start of World War II, it was again occupied by Russia and incorporated as the 16th state of the U.S.S.R Germany occupied the tiny state from 1941 to 1944, after which it was retaken by Russia. Most of the nations of the world, including the United States and Great Britain, did not recognize Estonia's incorporation into the Soviet Union.

The coinage, issued during the country's brief independence, is obsolete.

On August 20, 1991, the Parliament of the Estonian Soviet Socialist Republic voted to reassert the republic's independence.

REPUBLIC
1918 - 1941
REPUBLIC COINAGE

KM# 1 MARK
Copper-Nickel, 18 mm. **Obv:** Three Czech lions left divide date **Rev:** Denomination **Edge:** Milled

Date	Mintage	F	VF	XF	Unc	BU
1922	5,025,000	3.00	4.00	7.00	12.50	—

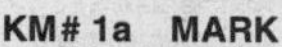

KM# 1a MARK
2.6000 g., Nickel-Bronze, 18 mm. **Obv:** Three Czech lions left divide date **Rev:** Denomination **Edge:** Milled

Date	Mintage	F	VF	XF	Unc	BU
1924	1,985,000	3.00	6.00	8.00	15.00	—

KM# 5 MARK
Nickel-Bronze **Obv:** Three Czech lions left divide date **Rev:** Denomination

Date	Mintage	F	VF	XF	Unc	BU
1926	3,979,000	5.00	8.00	15.00	30.00	—

KM# 2 3 MARKA
Copper-Nickel **Obv:** Three Czech lions left divide date **Rev:** Denomination

Date	Mintage	F	VF	XF	Unc	BU
1922	2,089,000	3.00	6.00	8.00	14.00	—

KM# 2a 3 MARKA
Nickel-Bronze **Obv:** Three Czech lions left divide date **Rev:** Denomination

Date	Mintage	F	VF	XF	Unc	BU
1925	1,134,000	5.00	8.00	15.00	30.00	—

KM# 6 3 MARKA
Nickel-Bronze **Obv:** Three Czech lions on shield within wreath **Rev:** Denomination, date below

Date	Mintage	F	VF	XF	Unc	BU
1926	903,000	25.00	50.00	80.00	150	—

KM# 3 5 MARKA
5.0000 g., Copper-Nickel, 23 mm. **Obv:** Three Czech lions left divide date **Rev:** Denomination **Edge:** Milled

Date	Mintage	F	VF	XF	Unc	BU
1922	3,983,000	5.00	8.00	10.00	20.00	—

KM# 3a 5 MARKA
5.0000 g., Nickel-Bronze, 23 mm. **Obv:** Three Czech lions left divide date **Rev:** Denomination **Edge:** Milled

Date	Mintage	F	VF	XF	Unc	BU
1924	1,335,000	5.00	8.00	11.00	25.00	—

KM# 7 5 MARKA
Nickel-Bronze **Obv:** Three Czech lions on shield within wreath **Rev:** Denomination above date

Date	Mintage	F	VF	XF	Unc	BU
1926	1,038,000	75.00	150	200	350	—

KM# 4 10 MARKA
6.0000 g., Nickel-Bronze, 26 mm. **Obv:** Three Czech lions left divide date **Rev:** Denomination **Edge:** Milled

Date	Mintage	F	VF	XF	Unc	BU
1925	2,200,000	7.00	12.00	20.00	40.00	—

KM# 8 10 MARKA
Nickel-Bronze **Obv:** Three Czech lions on shield within wreath **Rev:** Denomination above date

Date	Mintage	F	VF	XF	Unc	BU
1926	2,789,000	650	1,000	1,500	2,000	—

Note: Most of this issue was melted down; Not released to circulation

REFORM COINAGE
100 Senti = 1 Kroon

KM# 10 SENT
2.0000 g., Bronze, 17 mm. **Obv:** Three Czech lions left above date **Rev:** Denomination, oak leaves in background **Edge:** Plain

Date	Mintage	F	VF	XF	Unc	BU
1929	23,553,000	1.00	2.00	3.00	4.00	—

KM# 19.1 SENT
2.0000 g., Bronze, 16 mm. **Obv:** Three Czech lions left above date **Rev:** Denomination **Edge:** Plain **Note:** 1mm thick planchet.

Date	Mintage	F	VF	XF	Unc	BU
1939	5,000,000	4.00	8.00	15.00	35.00	—

KM# 19.2 SENT
Bronze **Obv:** Three Czech lions left divide date **Rev:** Denomination **Note:** 0.9mm thick planchet.

Date	Mintage	F	VF	XF	Unc	BU
1939	Inc. above	6.00	10.00	15.00	35.00	—

KM# 15 2 SENTI
3.5000 g., Bronze, 19 mm. **Obv:** Three Czech lions left above date **Rev:** Denomination **Edge:** Plain

Date	Mintage	F	VF	XF	Unc	BU
1934	5,838,000	2.00	3.00	6.00	10.00	—

KM# 11 5 SENTI
3.5000 g., Bronze, 23.3 mm. **Obv:** Three Czech lions left above date **Rev:** Denomination **Edge:** Plain

Date	Mintage	F	VF	XF	Unc	BU
1931	11,000,000	2.00	3.00	6.00	10.00	—

KM# 12 10 SENTI
Nickel-Bronze, 18 mm. **Obv:** Three Czech lions within shield divide date **Rev:** Denomination **Edge:** Plain

Date	Mintage	F	VF	XF	Unc	BU
1931	4,089,000	2.00	3.00	6.00	12.00	—

KM# 17 20 SENTI
Nickel-Bronze, 21 mm. **Obv:** Three Czech lions within shield divide date **Rev:** Denomination **Edge:** Plain

Date	Mintage	F	VF	XF	Unc	BU
1935	4,250,000	4.00	6.00	8.00	15.00	—

KM# 9 25 SENTI
Nickel-Bronze **Obv:** Three Czech lions within shield, wreath surrounds **Rev:** Denomination above date

Date	Mintage	F	VF	XF	Unc	BU
1928	2,025,000	6.00	9.00	20.00	35.00	—

KM# 18 50 SENTI
7.5000 g., Nickel-Bronze, 27.5 mm. **Obv:** Three Czech lions within shield divide date **Rev:** Denomination **Edge:** Plain

Date	Mintage	F	VF	XF	Unc	BU
1936	1,256,000	6.00	9.00	17.00	35.00	—

KM# 14 KROON
6.0000 g., 0.5000 Silver .0965 oz. ASW, 26 mm. **Subject:** 10th Singing Festival **Obv:** Three Czech lions within shield, wreath surrounds, date below **Obv. Designer:** Gunther Reidorf **Rev:** Harp divides dates, denomination below **Rev. Designer:** Georg Vestenberg

Date	Mintage	F	VF	XF	Unc	BU
1933	350,000	15.00	25.00	40.00	55.00	75.00

KM# 16 KROON
Aluminum-Bronze, 25 mm. **Obv:** Three Czech lions within shield, wreath surrounds, date below **Rev:** Ship of Vikings, denomination below **Edge:** Plain **Note:** 1990 restrikes which exist are private issues.

Date	Mintage	F	VF	XF	Unc	BU
1934	3,304,000	5.00	8.00	14.00	40.00	60.00

KM# 20 2 KROONI
12.0000 g., 0.5000 Silver .1929 oz. ASW, 30 mm. **Subject:** Toompea Fortress at Tallinn **Obv:** Three Czech lions within shield, wreath surrounds, date below **Rev:** Castle denomination below **Edge:** Milled

Date	Mintage	F	VF	XF	Unc	BU
1930	1,276,000	4.50	9.00	16.00	35.00	55.00

KM# 13 2 KROONI
12.0000 g., 0.5000 Silver .1929 oz. ASW, 30 mm. **Subject:** Tercentenary - University of Tartu **Obv:** Three Czech lions within shield, wreath surrounds, date below **Obv. Designer:** Gunther Reidorf **Rev:** University building, denomination below **Rev. Designer:** Georg Vestenberg **Edge:** Plain

Date	Mintage	F	VF	XF	Unc	BU
1932	100,000	15.00	25.00	35.00	50.00	70.00

MODERN REPUBLIC

1991 - present

STANDARD COINAGE

KM# 21 5 SENTI
1.2900 g., Brass, 15.9 mm. **Obv:** Three Czech lions left divide date **Rev:** Denomination **Edge:** Plain

Date	Mintage	F	VF	XF	Unc	BU
1991	—	—	—	—	0.25	—
1992	—	—	—	—	0.25	—
1995	—	—	—	—	0.25	—

KM# 22 10 SENTI
1.8500 g., Copper-Aluminum-Nickel, 17.1 mm. **Obv:** Three Czech lions left divide date **Rev:** Denomination **Edge:** Plain

Date	Mintage	F	VF	XF	Unc	BU
1991	—	—	—	—	0.35	—
1992	—	—	—	—	0.35	—
1994	—	—	—	—	0.35	—
1996	—	—	—	—	0.35	—
1997	—	—	—	—	0.35	—
1998	—	—	—	—	0.35	—

KM# 23 20 SENTI
2.2700 g., Brass, 18.9 mm. **Obv:** Three Czech lions left divide date **Rev:** Denomination **Edge:** Plain

Date	Mintage	F	VF	XF	Unc	BU
1992	—	—	—	—	0.65	—
1996	—	—	—	—	0.65	—

KM# 23a 20 SENTI
2.0000 g., Nickel Plated Steel, 18.9 mm. **Obv:** Three Czech lions left divide date **Rev:** Denomination **Edge:** Plain

Date	Mintage	F	VF	XF	Unc	BU
1997	—	—	—	—	0.65	—
1999	—	—	—	—	0.65	—

KM# 24 50 SENTI
2.9000 g., Brass, 19.5 mm. **Obv:** Three Czech lions left divide date **Rev:** Denomination **Edge:** Plain

Date	Mintage	F	VF	XF	Unc	BU
1992	—	—	—	—	1.00	—

KM# 28 KROON
5.4400 g., Copper-Nickel, 23.5 mm. **Obv:** Three Czech lions within shield divide date **Rev:** Large, thick denomination **Edge:** Plain

Date	Mintage	F	VF	XF	Unc	BU
1992	20,000	—	—	—	—	—
Note: In sets only						
1993	—	—	—	—	1.50	—
1995	—	—	—	—	1.50	—

KM# 35 KROON
5.0000 g., Brass, 23.5 mm. **Obv:** Three Czech lions within shield divide date **Rev:** Large, thick denomination **Edge:** Three reeded and plain sections

Date	Mintage	F	VF	XF	Unc	BU
1998	—	—	—	—	1.25	—
2000	—	—	—	—	1.25	—

KM# 36 KROON
Brass, 23.5 mm. **Obv:** Bird above date **Rev:** Festival building and denomination

Date	Mintage	F	VF	XF	Unc	BU
1999	100,000	—	—	—	5.00	—

KM# 29 5 KROONI
7.1000 g., Brass, 26.2 mm. **Subject:** 75th Anniversary - Declaration of Independence **Obv:** Three Czech lions within shield divide date **Rev:** Small deer right, denomination at right **Edge:** Plain

Date	Mintage	F	VF	XF	Unc	BU
1993	—	—	—	—	4.00	6.00
1993 Prooflike	—	Value: 4.50				

KM# 30 5 KROONI
7.1000 g., Brass, 26.1 mm. **Subject:** 75th Anniversary - Estonian National Bank **Obv:** Three Czech lions within shield divide date **Rev:** Denomination on design **Edge:** Plain

Date	Mintage	F	VF	XF	Unc	BU
1994	—	—	—	—	3.00	—

KM# 25 10 KROONI
28.2800 g., 0.9250 Silver .8411 oz. ASW **Series:** Olympics **Obv:** Three Czech lions within shield, wreath surrounds, date below **Rev:** Two sail boats, denomination below

Date	Mintage	F	VF	XF	Unc	BU
1992 Proof	Est. 20,000	Value: 50.00				

KM# 26 10 KROONI
28.2800 g., 0.9250 Silver .8411 oz. ASW **Obv:** Three Czech lions within shield, wreath surrounds, date below **Rev:** Barn Swallow, denomination below

Date	Mintage	F	VF	XF	Unc	BU
1992 Proof	Est. 10,000	Value: 50.00				

KM# 32 10 KROONI
16.0000 g., 0.9250 Silver .4758 oz. ASW **Subject:** 80th Anniversary of Nation **Obv:** Framed dates **Rev:** Farmer plowing field, denomination above

Date	Mintage	F	VF	XF	Unc	BU
ND(1998) Prooflike	Est. 15,000	—	—	—	22.50	—

KM# 37 15.65 KROONI
1.7300 g., 0.9000 Gold .0501 oz. AGW **Subject:** Estonia's Euro Equivalent **Obv:** Three Czech lions within shield, wreath surrounds, date below **Rev:** Cross and stars design, denomination below

Date	Mintage	F	VF	XF	Unc	BU
1999 Proof	Est. 5,000	Value: 40.00				

KM# 27 100 KROONI
24.0000 g., 0.9250 Silver .7135 oz. ASW **Obv:** Three Czech lions left **Rev:** Barn Swallows, date below, denomination above

Date	Mintage	F	VF	XF	Unc	BU
1992 Proof	Est. 50,000	Value: 40.00				

KM# 31 100 KROONI
28.2800 g., 0.9250 Silver .8411 oz. ASW **Obv:** Three Czech lions within shield, wreath surrounds, date below **Rev:** Olympics - Nike crowning Wrestler, denomination below

Date	Mintage	F	VF	XF	Unc	BU
1996	—	—	—	—	30.00	—
1996 Proof	10,000	Value: 40.00				

KM# 33 100 KROONI
27.0000 g., 0.9250 Silver .8030 oz. ASW **Subject:** 80th Anniversary of Nation **Obv:** Framed dates **Rev:** Male figure and stylized eagle head, denomination below

Date	Mintage	F	VF	XF	Unc	BU
ND(1998) Proof	Est. 12,000	Value: 50.00				
ND(1998)	—	—	—	—	35.00	—

KM# 34 500 KROONI
8.6400 g., 0.9000 Gold .2500 oz. AGW **Subject:** 80th Anniversary of Nation **Obv:** Framed dates **Rev:** Male figure on horse, denomination above

Date	Mintage	F	VF	XF	Unc	BU
ND(1998) Proof	Est. 3,000	Value: 195				

MINT SETS

KM#	Date	Mintage	Identification	Issue Price	Mkt Val
MS1	1992 (5)	20,000	KM#21-24, 28	—	40.00

ETHIOPIA

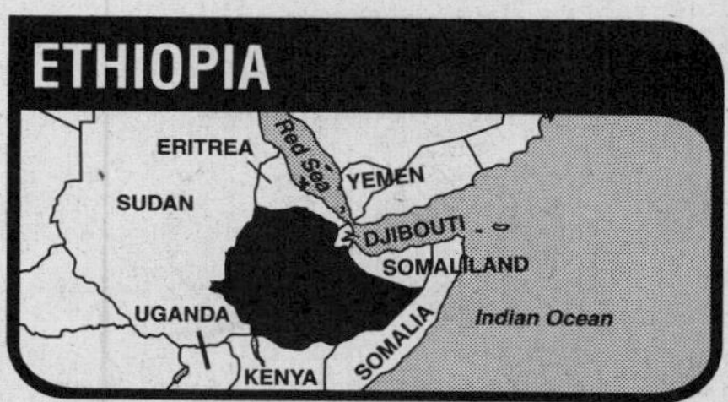

The People's Federal Republic of Ethiopia (formerly the Peoples Democratic Republic and the Empire of Ethiopia), Africa's oldest independent nation, faces the Red Sea in East-Central Africa. The country has an area of 424,214 sq. mi. (1,004,390 sq. km.) and a population of 56 million people who are divided among 40 tribes that speak some 270 languages and dialects. Capital: Addis Ababa. The economy is predominantly agricultural and pastoral. Gold and platinum are mined and petroleum fields are being developed. Coffee, oilseeds, hides and cereals are exported.

Legend claims that Menelik I, the son born to Solomon, King of Israel, by the Queen of Sheba, settled in Axum in North Ethiopia to establish the dynasty, which reigned with only brief interruptions until 1974. Modern Ethiopian history began with the reign of Emperor Menelik II (1889-1913) under whose guidance the country emerged from medieval isolation. Progress continued throughout the reigns of Menelik's daughter, Empress Zauditu, and her successor Emperor Haile Selassie I who was coronated in 1930. Ethiopia was invaded by Italy in 1935, and together with Italian Somaliland and Eritrea became part of Italian East Africa. Victor Emmanuel III, as declared by Mussolini, would be Ethiopia's emperor as well as a king of Italy. Liberated by British and Ethiopian troops in 1941, Ethiopia reinstated Haile Selassie I to the throne. The 225th consecutive Solomonic ruler was deposed by a military committee on Sept 12, 1974. In July 1976 Ethiopia's military provisional government referred to the country as Socialist Ethiopia. After establishing a new regime in 1991, Ethiopia became a federated state and is now the Federal Republic of Ethiopia. Following 2 years of provisional government, the province of Eritrea held a referendum on independence in May 1993 leading to the proclamation of its independence on May 24.

No coins, patterns or presentation pieces are known bearing Emperor Lij Yasu's likeness or titles. Coins of Menelik II were struck during this period with dates frozen.

RULERS

Menelik II, 1889-1913
Lij Yasu, 1913-1916
Zauditu, Empress, 1916-1930
Haile Selassie I
1930-36, 1941-1974
Victor Emmanuel III, of Italy
1936-1941

MINT MARKS

A - Paris
(a) - Paris, privy marks only
(b)

Coinage of Menelik II, 1889-1913

NOTE: The first national issue coinage, dated 1887 and 1888 E.E., carried a cornucopia, A, and fasces on the reverse. Subsequent dates have a torch substituted for the fasces, the A being dropped. All issues bearing these marks were struck at the Paris Mint. Coins without mint marks were struck in Addis Ababa.

MONETARY SYSTEM

(Until about 1903)
40 Besa = 20 Gersh = 1 Birr
(After 1903)
32 Besa = 16 Gersh = 1 Birr

DATING

Ethiopian coinage is dated by the Ethiopian Era calendar (E.E.), which commenced 7 years and 8 months after the advent of A.D. dating.

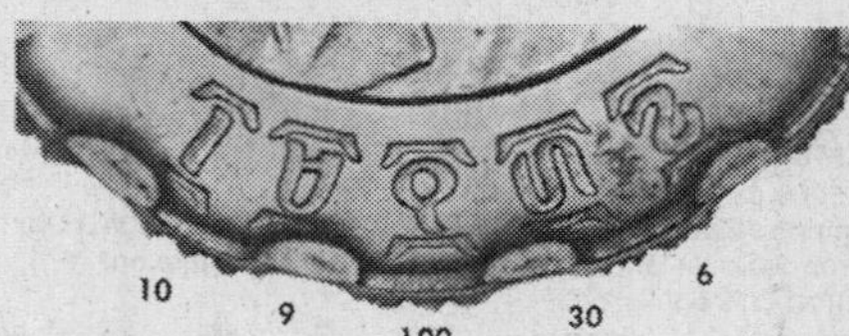

EXAMPLE

1900 (10 and 9 = 19 x 100)
36 (Add 30 and 6)
1936 E.E.
8 (Add)
1943/4 AD

EMPIRE OF ETHIOPIA

REFORM COINAGE

KM# 12 GERSH
1.4038 g., 0.8350 Silver .0377 oz. ASW, 16.5 mm. **Ruler:** Manelik II EE1882-1906 / 1889-1913AD **Obv:** Crowned bust right **Rev:** Crowned lion left, right foreleg raised holding ribboned cross

Date	Mintage	F	VF	XF	Unc	BU
EE1895A	44,789,000	2.00	3.50	6.00	20.00	—

Note: Struck between 1903-1928

KM# 3 1/4 BIRR
7.1088 g., 0.8350 Silver .1884 oz. ASW, 25 mm. **Ruler:** Manelik II EE1882-1906 / 1889-1913AD **Obv:** Crowned bust right **Rev:** Crowned lion left, right foreleg raised holding ribboned cross

Date	Mintage	F	VF	XF	Unc	BU
EE1895A	821,000	5.00	10.00	25.00	100	—

Note: Struck between 1903 and 1925

KM# 19 BIRR
28.0750 g., 0.8350 Silver .7537 oz. ASW, 40 mm. **Ruler:** Manelik II EE1882-1906 / 1889-1913AD **Obv:** Crowned bust right **Rev:** Crowned lion left, right foreleg raised holding ribboned cross

Date	Mintage	F	VF	XF	Unc	BU
EE1895	459,000	25.00	90.00	150	500	—

Note: Struck in 1901, 1903 and 1904

Date	Mintage	
EE1895 Proof	—	Value: 1,200

KM# 20 1/2 WERK
3.5000 g., 0.9000 Gold .1012 oz. AGW, 18 mm. **Ruler:** Empress Zauditu (Waizero) EE1909-1923 / 1916-1930AD **Obv:** Crowned bust left, laurels below **Rev:** Haloed figure on horseback, right

Date	Mintage	F	VF	XF	Unc	BU
EE1923	—	250	500	900	1,500	—

KM# 21 WERK
7.0000 g., 0.9000 Gold .2025 oz. AGW, 21 mm. **Ruler:** Empress Zauditu (Waizero) EE1909-1923 / 1916-1930AD **Obv:** Crowned bust left, laurels below **Rev:** Haloed figure on horseback, right

Date	Mintage	F	VF	XF	Unc	BU
EE1923	—	500	750	1,500	2,500	—

DECIMAL COINAGE

100 Santeems (Cents) = 1 Birr (Dollar)

100 Matonas = 100 Santeems

KM# 27 MATONA
Copper **Ruler:** Empress Zauditu (Waizero) EE1909-1923 / 1916-1930AD **Obv:** Crowned head right **Rev:** Crowned lion right, right foreleg raised holding ribboned cross

Date	Mintage	F	VF	XF	Unc	BU
EE1923	1,250,000	1.50	2.50	5.00	15.00	20.00

Note: Struck by ICI in Birmingham, England. Other denominations in the Matona series were struck in Addis Ababa

KM# 32 CENT (Ande Santeem)
Copper, 17 mm. **Ruler:** Haile Selassie I EE1923-1929 / 1930-1936AD **Obv:** Bust left, date below **Rev:** Crowned lion right, right foreleg raised holding ribboned cross **Designer:** Gilroy Roberts

Date	Mintage	F	VF	XF	Unc	BU
EE1936	20,000,000	—	0.10	0.20	0.50	1.00

Note: Struck at Philadelphia, Birmingham and the Royal Mint, London between 1944 and 1975 with the date EE1936 frozen

KM# 28.1 5 MATONAS
Copper **Ruler:** Empress Zauditu (Waizero) EE1909-1923 / 1916-1930AD **Obv:** Crowned head right **Rev:** Crowned lion right, right foreleg raised holding ribboned cross **Edge:** Plain

Date	Mintage	F	VF	XF	Unc	BU
EE1923	1,363,000	2.00	3.50	6.00	20.00	25.00

KM# 28.2 5 MATONAS
Copper **Ruler:** Empress Zauditu (Waizero) EE1909-1923 / 1916-1930AD **Obv:** Crowned head right **Rev:** Crowned lion right, right foreleg raised holding ribboned cross **Edge:** Reeded

Date	Mintage	F	VF	XF	Unc	BU
EE1923	Inc. above	3.00	4.50	8.00	25.00	40.00

KM# 33 5 CENTS (Amist Santeem)
Copper, 20 mm. **Ruler:** Haile Selassie I EE1923-1929 / 1930-1936AD **Obv:** Bust left, date below **Rev:** Crowned lion right, right foreleg raised holding ribboned cross **Designer:** Gilroy Roberts

Date	Mintage	F	VF	XF	Unc	BU
EE1936	219,000,000	—	0.10	0.20	0.50	1.25

Note: Struck between 1944-1962 in Philadelphia and 1964-1966 in Birmingham

KM# 29 10 MATONAS
Nickel **Ruler:** Empress Zauditu (Waizero) EE1909-1923 / 1916-1930AD **Obv:** Crowned bust right **Rev:** Crowned lion right, right foreleg raised holding ribboned cross

Date	Mintage	F	VF	XF	Unc	BU
EE1923	936,000	1.50	2.50	4.50	12.50	—

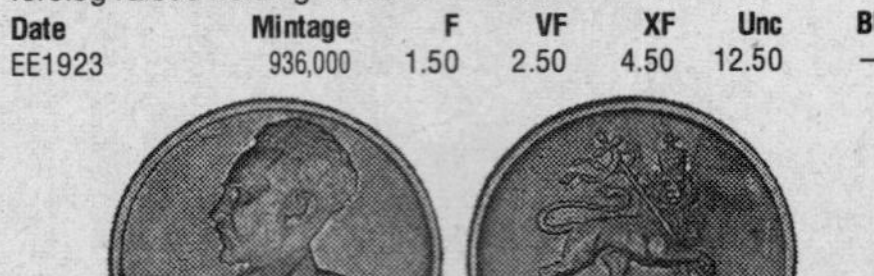
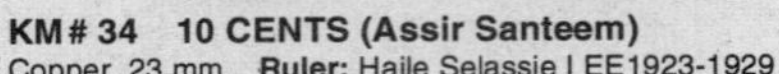

KM# 34 10 CENTS (Assir Santeem)
Copper, 23 mm. **Ruler:** Haile Selassie I EE1923-1929 / 1930-1936AD **Obv:** Bust left, date below **Rev:** Crowned lion right, right foreleg raised holding ribboned cross **Designer:** Gilroy Roberts

Date	Mintage	F	VF	XF	Unc	BU
EE1936	348,998,000	—	0.10	0.25	0.75	1.50

Note: Struck between 1945-1963 in Philadelphia, 1964-1966 in Birmingham and 1974-1975 in London

KM# 30 25 MATONAS
Nickel **Ruler:** Empress Zauditu (Waizero) EE1909-1923 / 1916-1930AD **Obv:** Crowned head right **Rev:** Crowned lion right, right foreleg raised holding ribboned cross

Date	Mintage	F	VF	XF	Unc	BU
EE1923	2,742,000	1.25	2.00	3.25	10.00	—

KM# 35 25 CENTS (Haya Amist Santeem)
Copper, 26 mm. **Ruler:** Haile Selassie I EE1923-1929 / 1930-1936AD **Obv:** Bust left, date below **Rev:** Crowned lion right, right foreleg raised holding ribboned cross **Designer:** Gilroy Roberts

Date	Mintage	F	VF	XF	Unc	BU
EE1936	10,000,000	5.00	10.00	20.00	45.00	—

Note: 421,500 issued and 1952 withdrawn and replaced by KM#36

KM# 36 25 CENTS (Haya Amist Santeem)
Copper, 25.5 mm. **Ruler:** Haile Selassie I EE1923-1929 / 1930-1936AD **Obv:** Bust left, date below **Rev:** Crowned lion right, right foreleg raised holding ribboned cross **Shape:** Scalloped **Designer:** Gilroy Roberts

Date	Mintage	F	VF	XF	Unc	BU
EE1936	30,000,000	0.25	0.50	1.00	3.50	6.00

Note: Issued in 1952 and 1953. Crude and refined edges

KM# 31 50 MATONAS
Nickel **Ruler:** Empress Zauditu (Waizero) EE1909-1923 / 1916-1930AD **Obv:** Crowned head right **Rev:** Crowned lion right, right foreleg raised holding ribboned cross

Date	Mintage	F	VF	XF	Unc	BU
EE1923	1,621,000	1.50	3.00	5.00	15.00	—

KM# 37 50 CENTS (Hamsa Santeem)
7.0307 g., 0.8000 Silver .1808 oz. ASW **Ruler:** Haile Selassie I EE1923-1929 / 1930-1936AD **Obv:** Bust left, date below **Rev:** Crowned lion right, right foreleg raised holding ribboned cross **Designer:** Gilroy Roberts

Date	Mintage	F	VF	XF	Unc	BU
EE1936	30,000,000	3.00	5.00	12.00	25.00	—

Note: Struck in 1944-1945

KM# 37a 50 CENTS (Hamsa Santeem)
7.0307 g., 0.7000 Silver .1582 oz. ASW **Ruler:** Haile Selassie I EE1923-1929 / 1930-1936AD **Obv:** Bust left, date below **Rev:** Crowned lion right, right foreleg raised holding ribboned cross

Date	Mintage	F	VF	XF	Unc	BU
EE1936	20,434,000	2.50	4.50	12.00	25.00	—

Note: Struck in 1947

KM# 48 5 DOLLARS
20.0000 g., 0.9250 Silver .5948 oz. ASW **Ruler:** Haile Selassie Second Reign **Rev:** Bust facing, dates below

Date	Mintage	F	VF	XF	Unc	BU
EE1964 F-NI	—	—	—	—	75.00	—
EE1964 NI Proof	55,000	Value: 40.00				

KM# 49 5 DOLLARS
20.0000 g., 0.9250 Silver .5948 oz. ASW **Ruler:** Haile Selassie Second Reign **Rev:** Crowned bust facing, dates below

Date	Mintage	F	VF	XF	Unc	BU
EE1964 F-NI	—	—	—	—	75.00	—
EE1964 NI Proof	55,000	Value: 40.00				

KM# 50 5 DOLLARS
20.0000 g., 0.9250 Silver .5948 oz. ASW **Ruler:** Haile Selassie Second Reign **Rev:** Crowned lion right, right foreleg raised holding ribboned cross

Date	Mintage	F	VF	XF	Unc	BU
EE1964 F-NI	—	—	—	—	85.00	—
EE1964 NI Proof	60,000	Value: 40.00				

KM# 51 5 DOLLARS
20.0000 g., 0.9250 Silver .5948 oz. ASW **Ruler:** Haile Selassie Second Reign **Rev:** Veiled bust left, dates at right

Date	Mintage	F	VF	XF	Unc	BU
EE1964 F-NI	—	—	—	—	90.00	—
EE1964 NI Proof	60,000	Value: 42.50				

KM# 52 5 DOLLARS
25.0000 g., 0.9999 Silver .8030 oz. ASW **Ruler:** Haile Selassie Second Reign **Obv:** Uniformed bust right, crown at left, shield at right **Rev:** Crowned lion right, right foreleg raised holding ribboned cross

Date	Mintage	F	VF	XF	Unc	BU
1972 (1972) HF Proof	100,000	Value: 22.50				

KM# 38 10 DOLLARS
4.0000 g., 0.9000 Gold .1157 oz. AGW **Ruler:** Haile Selassie Second Reign **Subject:** 75th Anniverary of Birth and 50th Jubilee of Reign of Emperor Haile Selassie I **Obv:** Bust 3/4 left divides crown and shield **Rev:** Crowned lion right, right foreleg raised holding ribboned cross

Date	Mintage	F	VF	XF	Unc	BU
EE1958 (1966) NI Proof	28,000	Value: 100				

KM# 53 10 DOLLARS
40.0000 g., 0.9250 Silver 1.1895 oz. ASW **Ruler:** Haile Selassie Second Reign **Obv:** Uniformed bust 3/4 facing **Rev:** Crowned lion right, right foreleg raised holding ribboned cross

Date	Mintage	F	VF	XF	Unc	BU
EE1964 (1972) F-NI	—	—	—	—	175	—
EE1964 (1972) NI Proof	50,000	Value: 85.00				

KM# 39 20 DOLLARS
8.0000 g., 0.9000 Gold .2315 oz. AGW **Ruler:** Haile Selassie Second Reign **Subject:** 75th Anniversary of Birth and 50th Jubilee of Reign of Emperor Haile Selassie I **Obv:** Bust 3/4 left divides crown and shield **Rev:** Crowned lion right, right foreleg raised holding ribboned cross

Date	Mintage	F	VF	XF	Unc	BU
EE1958 (1966) NI Proof	25,000	Value: 185				

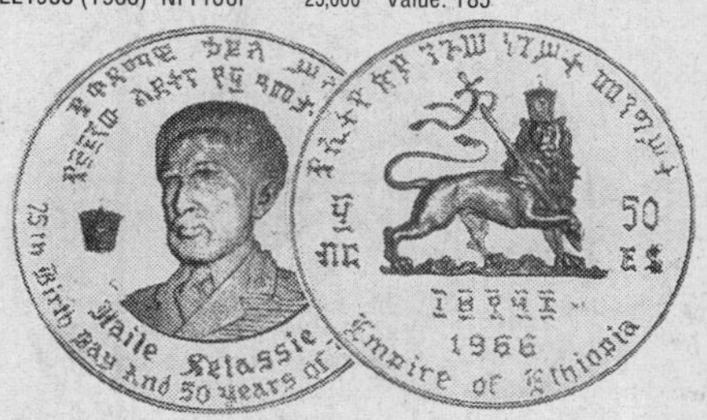

KM# 40 50 DOLLARS
20.0000 g., 0.9000 Gold .5787 oz. AGW **Ruler:** Haile Selassie Second Reign **Subject:** 75th Anniversary of Birth and 50th Jubilee of Reign of Emperor Haile Selassie I **Obv:** Bust 3/4 left divides crown and shield **Rev:** Crowned lion right, right foreleg raised holding ribboned cross

Date	Mintage	F	VF	XF	Unc	BU
EE1958 (1966) NI Proof	15,000	Value: 385				

KM# 55 50 DOLLARS
20.0000 g., 0.9000 Gold .5787 oz. AGW **Ruler:** Haile Selassie Second Reign **Obv:** Bust of Theodros II **Rev:** Lion

Date	Mintage	F	VF	XF	Unc	BU
EE1964 (1972) NI Proof	12,000	Value: 400				

KM# 56 50 DOLLARS
20.0000 g., 0.9000 Gold .5787 oz. AGW **Ruler:** Haile Selassie Second Reign **Obv:** Bust of Yohannes IV

Date	Mintage	F	VF	XF	Unc	BU
EE1964 (1972) NI Proof	12,000	Value: 400				

KM# 57 50 DOLLARS
20.0000 g., 0.9000 Gold .5787 oz. AGW **Ruler:** Haile Selassie Second Reign **Obv:** Bust of Menelik II

Date	Mintage	F	VF	XF	Unc	BU
EE1964 (1972) NI Proof	20,000	Value: 400				

KM# 58 50 DOLLARS
20.0000 g., 0.9000 Gold .5787 oz. AGW **Ruler:** Haile Selassie Second Reign **Obv:** Bust of Empress Zauditu

Date	Mintage	F	VF	XF	Unc	BU
EE1964 (1972) NI Proof	16,000	Value: 400				

KM# 41 100 DOLLARS
40.0000 g., 0.9000 Gold 1.1575 oz. AGW **Ruler:** Haile Selassie Second Reign **Subject:** 75th Anniversary of Birth and 50th Jubilee of Reign of Emperor Haile Selassie I **Rev:** Crowned lion right, right foreleg raised holding ribboned cross

Date	Mintage	F	VF	XF	Unc	BU
EE1958 (1966) NI Proof	11,000	Value: 800				

KM# 59 100 DOLLARS
40.0000 g., 0.9000 Gold 1.1575 oz. AGW **Ruler:** Haile Selassie Second Reign **Obv:** Uniformed bust 3/4 facing **Rev:** Crowned lion right, right foreleg raised holding ribboned cross

Date	Mintage	F	VF	XF	Unc	BU
EE1964 (1972) NI Proof	10,000	Value: 800				

KM# 42 200 DOLLARS
80.0000 g., 0.9000 Gold 2.3151 oz. AGW **Ruler:** Haile Selassie Second Reign **Subject:** 75th Anniversary of Birth and 50th Jubilee of Reign of Emperor Haile Selassie I **Rev:** Crowned lion right, right foreleg raised holding ribboned cross

Date	Mintage	F	VF	XF	Unc	BU
EE1958 (1966) NI Proof	8,823	Value: 1,600				

TOKEN COINAGE

KM# Tn1 PIASTRE (1/16 Thaler)
Aluminum **Ruler:** Empress Zauditu (Waizero) EE1909-1923 / 1916-1930AD **Obv:** Seven line inscription **Rev:** Denomination and date

Date	Mintage	VG	F	VF	XF	Unc
1922	—	12.00	25.00	40.00	60.00	—

Note: Issued by a commercial syndicate in Dire Dawa

KM# Tn2 PIASTRE (1/16 Thaler)
Aluminum **Obv:** Legend within circle and surrounding **Rev:** Denomination

Date	Mintage	VG	F	VF	XF	Unc
ND	—	10.00	20.00	35.00	55.00	—

Note: Issued by P. P. Trohalis in Addis Ababa

KM# Tn3 PIASTRE (1/16 Thaler)
Copper-Nickel-Zinc **Obv:** Legend surrounds center **Rev:** Denomination

Date	Mintage	VG	F	VF	XF	Unc
ND	—	25.00	40.00	65.00	90.00	—

Note: Issued by Magdalinos Freres in Addis Ababa

KM# Tn4 PIASTRE (1/16 Thaler)
Aluminum **Obv. Designer:** PRASSO within beaded circle, legend surrounds **Rev:** Denomination

Date	Mintage	VG	F	VF	XF	Unc
ND	—	20.00	35.00	60.00	85.00	—

Note: Issued by Prasso Concessions En Abyssinie

KM# Tn5 PIASTRE (1/16 Thaler)
Aluminum **Note:** Uniface

Date	Mintage	VG	F	VF	XF	Unc
ND	—	25.00	45.00	75.00	95.00	—

Note: Issued by F. L. in Addis Abada

PEOPLES DEMOCRATIC REPUBLIC

We have two varieties for KM#43.1 to KM#46.1. One was minted at the British Royal Mint, the other at the Berlin Mint. The main difference is where the lion's chin whiskers end above the date (easiest to see on the 2nd, 3rd and 4th characters).

British Royal Mint

Berlin Mint

DECIMAL COINAGE

100 Santeems (Cents) = 1 Birr (Dollar)

100 Matonas = 100 Santeems

KM# 43.1 CENT
0.6000 g., Aluminum, 17 mm. **Ruler:** Haile Selassie Second Reign **Series:** F.A.O. **Obv:** Small lion head right, uniform chin whiskers **Rev:** Farmer with two oxen, denomination above **Designer:** Stuart Devlin

Date	Mintage	F	VF	XF	Unc	BU
EE1969	35,034,000	0.20	0.30	0.50	1.00	—

KM# 43.2 CENT
0.6000 g., Aluminum, 17 mm. **Ruler:** Haile Selassie Second Reign **Obv:** Small lion head right, two long chin whiskers at left nearly touch date **Rev:** Farmer with two oxen, denomination above

Date	Mintage	F	VF	XF	Unc	BU
EE1969	Inc. above	0.25	0.35	0.65	1.25	—

KM# 43.3 CENT
0.6000 g., Aluminum, 17 mm. **Ruler:** Haile Selassie Second Reign **Obv:** Large lion head right **Rev:** Farmer with two oxen, denomination above **Designer:** Stuart Devlin

Date	Mintage	F	VF	XF	Unc	BU
EE1969 FM Proof	12,000	Value: 2.50				

KM# 44.1 5 CENTS
3.0000 g., Copper-Zinc, 20 mm. **Ruler:** Haile Selassie Second Reign **Obv:** Small lion head right, uniform chin whiskers **Rev:** Denomination left of figure **Designer:** Stuart Devlin

Date	Mintage	F	VF	XF	Unc	BU
EE1969	201,275,000	0.20	0.30	0.50	1.00	—

KM# 44.2 5 CENTS
3.0000 g., Copper-Zinc, 20 mm. **Ruler:** Haile Selassie Second Reign **Obv:** Lion head right, date below **Rev:** Denomination left of figure

Date	Mintage	F	VF	XF	Unc	BU
EE1969	Inc. above	0.25	0.35	0.65	1.25	—

KM# 44.3 5 CENTS
3.0000 g., Copper-Zinc, 20 mm. **Obv:** Large lion head, right **Rev:** Denomination left of figure **Designer:** Stuart Devlin

Date	Mintage	F	VF	XF	Unc	BU
EE1969 FM Proof	12,000	Value: 2.50				

KM# 45.1 10 CENTS
4.5000 g., Copper-Zinc, 23 mm. **Ruler:** Haile Selassie Second Reign **Obv:** Small lion head right, uniform chin whiskers **Rev:** Mountain Nyala, denomination at right **Designer:** Stuart Devlin

Date	Mintage	F	VF	XF	Unc	BU
EE1969	202,722,000	0.20	0.30	0.60	1.50	2.50

KM# 45.2 10 CENTS
4.5000 g., Copper-Zinc, 23 mm. **Ruler:** Haile Selassie Second Reign **Obv:** Small lion head, two long chin whiskers at left nearly touch date **Rev:** Mountain Nyala and denomination

Date	Mintage	F	VF	XF	Unc	BU
EE1969	Inc. above	0.25	0.40	0.75	1.75	2.75

KM# 45.3 10 CENTS
4.5000 g., Copper-Zinc, 23 mm. **Obv:** Large lion head right **Rev:** Mountain Nyala, denomination at right **Designer:** Stuart Devlin

Date	Mintage	F	VF	XF	Unc	BU
EE1969 FM	—	—	—	—	2.00	3.00
EE1969 FM Proof	12,000	Value: 4.00				

KM# 46.1 25 CENTS
3.7000 g., Copper-Nickel, 21.45 mm. **Ruler:** Haile Selassie Second Reign **Obv:** Small lion head right, uniform chin whiskers **Rev:** Man and woman with arms raised divide denomination **Designer:** Stuart Devlin

Date	Mintage	F	VF	XF	Unc	BU
EE1969	44,983,000	0.20	0.30	0.60	1.25	2.00

KM# 46.2 25 CENTS
3.7000 g., Copper-Nickel, 21.45 mm. **Ruler:** Haile Selassie Second Reign **Obv:** Small lion head, two long chin whiskers at left nearly touch date **Rev:** Man and woman with arms raised divide denomination

Date	Mintage	F	VF	XF	Unc	BU
EE1969	Inc. above	0.25	0.40	0.75	1.50	—

KM# 46.3 25 CENTS

3.7000 g., Copper-Nickel, 21.45 mm. **Obv:** Large lion head right **Rev:** Man and woman with arms raised divide denomination **Designer:** Stuart Devlin

Date	Mintage	F	VF	XF	Unc	BU
EE1969 FM Proof	12,000	Value: 4.50				

KM# 47.1 50 CENTS

6.0000 g., Copper-Nickel, 25 mm. **Ruler:** Haile Selassie Second Reign **Obv:** Small lion head right, uniform chin whiskers **Rev:** People of the Republic, denomination above **Designer:** Stuart Devlin

Date	Mintage	F	VF	XF	Unc	BU
EE1969	27,772,000	0.40	0.75	1.25	3.00	—

KM# 47.2 50 CENTS

6.0000 g., Copper-Nickel, 25 mm. **Ruler:** Haile Selassie Second Reign **Obv:** Small lion head, two long chin whiskers at left nearly touch date **Rev:** People of the republic, denomination above

Date	Mintage	F	VF	XF	Unc	BU
EE1969	Inc. above	0.50	0.85	1.50	3.00	—

KM# 47.3 50 CENTS

6.0000 g., Copper-Nickel, 25 mm. **Ruler:** Haile Selassie Second Reign **Obv:** Large lion head **Rev:** People of the republic, denomination above **Designer:** Stuart Devlin **Note:** Prev. KM#47.2.

Date	Mintage	F	VF	XF	Unc	BU
EE1969 FM Proof	12,000	Value: 7.50				

KM# 64 2 BIRR

Copper-Nickel **Ruler:** Haile Selassie Second Reign **Subject:** World Soccer Games 1982 **Obv:** Lion head right **Rev:** Soccer players in front of two joined globes, denomination above

Date	Mintage	F	VF	XF	Unc	BU
EE1964 (error)	7	—	—	—	145	—
EE1974	—	—	—	—	12.00	—

KM# 61 10 BIRR

25.3100 g., 0.9250 Silver .7527 oz. ASW **Ruler:** Haile Selassie Second Reign **Subject:** Conservation **Obv:** Lion within circle divides wreath surrounding symbols in center **Rev:** Bearded Vulture

Date	Mintage	F	VF	XF	Unc	BU
EE1970	4,002	—	—	—	25.00	—

KM# 61a 10 BIRR

28.2800 g., 0.9250 Silver .8411 oz. ASW **Ruler:** Haile Selassie Second Reign **Obv:** Lion within circle divides wreath surrounding symbols in center **Rev:** Bearded Vulture

Date	Mintage	F	VF	XF	Unc	BU
EE1970 Proof	3,460	Value: 35.00				

KM# 54 20 BIRR

23.3300 g., 0.9250 Silver .6938 oz. ASW **Ruler:** Haile Selassie Second Reign **Subject:** International Year of the Child **Obv:** Silhouette of child flanked by laurels, logo above **Rev:** Children, logo above, denomination below

Date	Mintage	F	VF	XF	Unc	BU
EE1972 Proof	16,000	Value: 20.00				

KM# 65 20 BIRR

23.3300 g., 0.9250 Silver .6938 oz. ASW **Ruler:** Haile Selassie Second Reign **Subject:** World Soccer Games 1982 **Obv:** Lion head right **Rev:** Soccer players in front of two joined globes, denomination above

Date	Mintage	F	VF	XF	Unc	BU
EE1974 Proof	10,000	Value: 35.00				

KM# 73 20 BIRR

23.3300 g., 0.9250 Silver .6938 oz. ASW **Subject:** Decade for Women **Rev:** Woman in field

Date	Mintage	F	VF	XF	Unc	BU
1984 Proof	372	Value: 150				

KM# 74 20 BIRR

23.3300 g., 0.9250 Silver .6938 oz. ASW **Subject:** 50th Anniversary UNICEF - Folk Dance **Obv:** Two dancing girls and huts, denomination below **Rev:** UNICEF logo divides date **Edge:** Reeded

Date	Mintage	F	VF	XF	Unc	BU
1998 Proof	—	Value: 50.00				

KM# 62 25 BIRR

31.6500 g., 0.9250 Silver .9413 oz. ASW **Ruler:** Haile Selassie Second Reign **Subject:** Conservation **Obv:** Lion within circle divides wreath surrounding symbols in center **Rev:** Mountain Nyala left, right foreleg raised

Date	Mintage	F	VF	XF	Unc	BU
EE1970	4,002	—	—	—	30.00	—

KM# 62a 25 BIRR

35.0000 g., 0.9250 Silver 1.0409 oz. ASW **Ruler:** Haile Selassie Second Reign **Obv:** Lion within circle divides wreath surrounding symbols in center **Rev:** Mountain Nyala left, right foreleg raised

Date	Mintage	F	VF	XF	Unc	BU
EE1970 Proof	3,295	Value: 40.00				

KM# 66 50 BIRR

28.2800 g., 0.9250 Silver .8411 oz. ASW **Ruler:** Haile Selassie Second Reign **Subject:** International Year of Disabled Persons **Obv:** Symbol within wreath **Rev:** Hand grasping wrist, denomination below, initials above

Date	Mintage	F	VF	XF	Unc	BU
EE1974	11,000	—	—	—	25.00	—
EE1974 Proof	10,000	Value: 35.00				

KM# 67 200 BIRR

7.1300 g., 0.9000 Gold .2063 oz. AGW **Subject:** World Soccer Games 1982 **Obv:** Lion head right **Rev:** Soccer players in front of two joined globes, denomination above

Date	Mintage	F	VF	XF	Unc	BU
1982 Proof	1,310	Value: 200				

KM# 72 200 BIRR

7.1300 g., 0.9000 Gold .2063 oz. AGW **Subject:** Decade for Women **Obv:** Small lion head right, denomination below **Rev:** Woman with child, writing

Date	Mintage	F	VF	XF	Unc	BU
1984 Proof	298	Value: 340				

KM# 60 400 BIRR
17.1700 g., 0.9000 Gold .4968 oz. AGW **Ruler:** Haile Selassie Second Reign **Subject:** International Year of the Child **Obv:** Silhouette of child, laurels flanking, logo above **Rev:** Children playing, denomination below, logo above

Date	Mintage	F	VF	XF	Unc	BU
EE1972 Proof	3,387	Value: 330				

KM# 68 500 BIRR
15.9800 g., 0.9170 Gold .5006 oz. AGW **Ruler:** Haile Selassie Second Reign **Subject:** International Year of the Disabled Persons **Obv:** Symbol within wreath **Rev:** Flanking figures on steps holding arms of central figure, denomination below

Date	Mintage	F	VF	XF	Unc	BU
EE1974	2,007	—	—	—	330	—
EE1974 Proof	2,042	Value: 345				

KM# 63 600 BIRR
33.4370 g., 0.9000 Gold .9676 oz. AGW **Ruler:** Haile Selassie Second Reign **Subject:** Conservation **Obv:** Lion within circle divides wreath surrounding symbols at center **Rev:** Walia Ibex right

Date	Mintage	F	VF	XF	Unc	BU
EE1970	547	—	—	—	800	—
EE1970 Proof	160	Value: 1,000				

PATTERNS

Including off metal strikes

KM#	Date	Mintage	Identification	Mkt Val
Pn7	EE1921	—	1/2 Werk. Gold. Similar to KM20. Proof	—
Pn8	EE1921	—	Werk. Gold. Similar to KM21. Proof	—

TRIAL STRIKES

KM#	Date	Mintage	Identification	Mkt Val
TS9	EE1917	—	1/2 Birr. Pewter. KM M3. (thin)	300
TS10	EE1917	—	Birr. Pewter. KM M4. (thin)	500
TS11	1966	—	10 Dollars. Gilt Bronze. KM38	50.00
TS12	1966	—	20 Dollars. Gilt Bronze. KM39	80.00
TS13	1966	—	50 Dollars. Gilt Bronze. KM40	130
TS14	1966	—	100 Dollars. Gilt Bronze. KM41	240
TS15	1966	—	200 Dollars. Gilt Bronze. KM42	450

Note: Issued in cased set of five pieces

PIEFORTS

KM#	Date	Mintage	Identification	Issue Price	Mkt Val
P1	1980	39	20 Birr. Silver. KM54	—	150
P2	1980	8	400 Birr. Gold. KM60	—	775
P3	1981	1,100	50 Birr. Silver. KM66	—	55.00
P4	1982	520	500 Birr. Gold. KM68	—	650

MINT SETS

KM#	Date	Mintage	Identification	Issue Price	Mkt Val
MS1	1972 (5)	—	KM48-51, 53	—	475

PROOF SETS

KM#	Date	Mintage	Identification	Issue Price	Mkt Val
PS2	1966 (5)	8,823	KM38-42	—	2,450
PS3	1972 (10)	—	KM48-51, 53, 55-59	—	2,600
PS5	1972 (5)	10,000	KM55-59	—	2,300
PS6	1972 (5)	50,000	KM48-51, 53	46.00	220
PS7	1977 (5)	11,724	KM43.2-47.2	25.00	25.00
PS8	1979 (2)	—	KM61a-62a	—	75.00

FAEROE ISLANDS

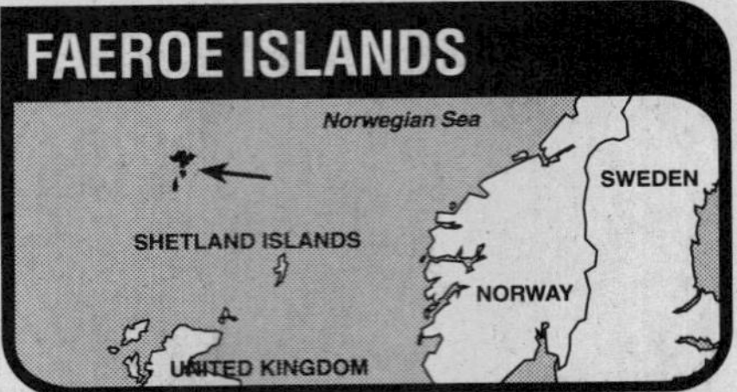

The Faeroe Islands, a self-governing community within the kingdom of Denmark, are situated in the North Atlantic between Iceland and the Shetland Islands. The 17 inhabited islands and numerous islets and reefs have an area of 540 sq. mi. (1,400 sq. km.)and a population of 46,000. Capital: Thorshavn. The principal industries are fishing and livestock. Fish and fish products are exported.

While it is thought that Irish hermits lived on the islands in the 7th and 8th centuries, the present inhabitants are descended from 6th century Norse settlers. The Faeroe Islands became a Norwegian fief in 1035 and became Danish in 1380 when Norway and Denmark were united. They have ever since remained in Danish possession and were granted self-government (except for an appointed governor-general) with their own legislature, executive and flag in 1948.

The islands were occupied by British troops during World War II, after the German occupation of Denmark. The Faeroe island coinage was struck in London during World War II.

RULER
Danish

MONETARY SYSTEM
100 Øre = 1 Krone

DANISH STATE

DECIMAL COINAGE

KM# 1 ORE
Bronze **Obv:** Center hole divides date and denomination **Rev:** Center hole within crowned monogram

Date	Mintage	F	VF	XF	Unc	BU
1941	Est. 200,000	20.00	40.00	60.00	92.50	—

Note: Also struck in 1942 with 1941 dies

1941 Proof	—	Value: 565

KM# 2 2 ORE
Bronze **Obv:** Center hole divides date and denomination **Rev:** Center hole within crowned monogram

Date	Mintage	F	VF	XF	Unc	BU
1941	Est. 200,000	5.00	10.00	22.50	55.00	—

Note: Also struck in 1942 with 1941 dies

1941 Proof	—	Value: 565

KM# 3 5 ORE
Bronze **Obv:** Center hole divides date and denomination **Rev:** Center hole within crowned monogram

Date	Mintage	F	VF	XF	Unc	BU
1941	Est. 200,000	4.00	8.00	18.50	55.00	—

Note: Also struck in 1942 with 1941 dies

1941 Proof	—	Value: 565

KM# 4 10 ORE
Copper-Nickel **Obv:** Center hole divides crowned monogram, date below **Rev:** Center hole with ornaments divides denomination

Date	Mintage	F	VF	XF	Unc	BU
1941	Est. 300,000	5.50	11.00	27.50	83.50	—

Note: Also struck in 1942 with 1941 dies

1941 Proof	—	Value: 585

KM# 5 25 ORE
Copper-Nickel **Obv:** Center hole divides crowned monogram, date below **Rev:** Center hole with ornaments divides denominatio

Date	Mintage	F	VF	XF	Unc	BU
1941	Est. 250,000	7.00	12.50	30.00	95.00	—

Note: Also struck in 1942 with 1941 dies

1941 Proof	—	Value: 585

PROOF SETS

KM#	Date	Mintage	Identification	Issue Price	Mkt Val
PS1	1941 (5)	—	KM1-5	—	2,850

FALKLAND ISLANDS

The Colony of the Falkland Islands and Dependencies, a British colony located in the South Atlantic about 500 miles northeast of Cape Horn, has an area of 4,700 sq. mi. (12,170 sq. km.) and a population of 2,121. East Falkland, West Falkland, South Georgia, and South Sandwich are the largest of the 200 islands. Capital: Stanley. Sheep grazing is the main industry. Wool, whale oil, and seal oil are exported.

The Falklands were discovered by British navigator John Davis (Davys) in 1592, and named by Capt. John Strong - for Viscount Falkland, treasurer of the British navy - in 1690. French navigator Louis De Bougainville established the first settlement, at Port Louis, in 1764. The following year Capt. John Byron claimed the islands for Britain and left a small party at Saunders Island. Spain later forced the French and British to abandon their settlements but did not implement its claim to the islands. In 1829 the Republic of Buenos Aires, which claimed to have inherited the Spanish rights, sent Louis Vernet to develop a colony on the islands. In 1831 he seized three American sealing vessels, whereupon the men of the corvette, the U.S.S. Lexington, destroyed his settlement and proclaimed the Falklands to be 'free of all governance'. Britain, which had never renounced its claim, then re-established its settlement in 1833.

RULERS
British

MONETARY SYSTEM
100 Pence = 1 Pound

BRITISH COLONY

DECIMAL COINAGE

KM# 1 1/2 PENNY
1.7820 g., Bronze, 17.14 mm. **Ruler:** Elizabeth II **Obv:** Young bust right **Rev:** Salmon behind denomination, date at right **Designer:** William Gardner

Date	Mintage	F	VF	XF	Unc	BU
1974	140,000	—	—	0.10	0.35	0.50
1974 Proof	23,000	Value: 1.50				
1980	—	—	—	0.10	0.25	0.35
1980 Proof	10,000	Value: 1.50				
1982	—	—	—	0.10	0.25	0.35
1982 Proof	—	Value: 1.50				
1983	—	—	—	0.10	0.25	0.35

KM# 2 PENNY
3.6000 g., Bronze, 20.3 mm. **Ruler:** Elizabeth II **Obv:** Young bust right **Rev:** Gentoo penguins flank denomination, date below **Designer:** William Gardner

Date	Mintage	F	VF	XF	Unc	BU
1974	96,000	—	0.10	0.20	0.60	0.75
1974 Proof	23,000	Value: 2.00				
1980	—	—	0.10	0.20	0.60	0.75
1980 Proof	10,000	Value: 2.00				
1982	—	—	0.10	0.20	0.60	0.75
1982 Proof	—	Value: 2.00				
1983	—	—	0.10	0.20	0.60	0.75
1985	—	—	0.10	0.20	0.60	0.75
1987	111,000	—	—	0.20	0.60	0.75
1987 Proof	—	Value: 2.50				
1992	—	—	0.10	0.20	0.60	0.75
1992 Proof	—	Value: 2.50				

KM# 2a PENNY
Copper Plated Steel, 20.3 mm. **Ruler:** Elizabeth II **Obv:** Young bust right **Rev:** Denomination divides penguins, date below

Date	Mintage	F	VF	XF	Unc	BU
1998	2,500	—	—	—	0.50	0.75
1999	—	—	—	—	0.50	0.75
1999 Proof	2,500	Value: 2.00				

KM# 3 2 PENCE
7.1000 g., Bronze, 25.9 mm. **Ruler:** Elizabeth II **Obv:** Young bust right **Rev:** Upland goose, wings open, denomination above, date at right **Designer:** William Gardner

Date	Mintage	F	VF	XF	Unc	BU
1974	72,000	—	0.10	0.15	0.50	1.50
1974 Proof	23,000	Value: 3.00				
1980	—	—	0.10	0.15	0.50	1.50
1980 Proof	10,000	Value: 3.00				
1982	—	—	0.10	0.15	0.50	1.50
1982 Proof	—	Value: 3.00				
1983	—	—	0.10	0.15	0.50	1.50
1985	—	—	0.10	0.15	0.50	1.50
1987	106,000	—	—	0.15	0.50	1.50
1987 Proof	—	Value: 3.50				
1992	—	—	0.10	0.15	0.50	1.50
1992 Proof	—	Value: 3.50				

KM# 3a 2 PENCE
Copper Plated Steel, 25.9 mm. **Ruler:** Elizabeth II **Obv:** Young bust right **Rev:** Upland goose, wings open, denomination above, date at right

Date	Mintage	F	VF	XF	Unc	BU
1998	—	—	—	—	0.35	1.00
1999	—	—	—	—	0.35	1.00
1999 Proof	2,500	Value: 3.00				

KM# 4.1 5 PENCE
5.6500 g., Copper-Nickel, 23.6 mm. **Ruler:** Elizabeth II **Obv:** Young bust right **Rev:** Blackbrowed albatross in flight, denomination and date below **Designer:** William Gardner

Date	Mintage	F	VF	XF	Unc	BU
1974	67,000	—	0.10	0.25	0.75	1.00
1974 Proof	23,000	Value: 3.50				
1980	—	—	0.10	0.25	0.75	1.00
1980 Proof	10,000	Value: 4.00				
1982	—	—	0.10	0.25	0.75	1.00
1982 Proof	—	Value: 4.00				
1983	—	—	0.10	0.25	0.75	1.00
1985	—	—	0.10	0.20	0.75	1.00
1987	5,000	—	—	0.25	0.75	1.00
1987 Proof	—	Value: 4.50				
1992	—	—	0.10	0.25	0.75	1.00
1992 Proof	—	Value: 4.50				

KM# 4.2 5 PENCE
Copper-Nickel, 18 mm. **Ruler:** Elizabeth II **Obv:** Young bust right **Rev:** Blackbrowed albatross in flight, denomination and date below **Designer:** William Gardner

Date	Mintage	F	VF	XF	Unc	BU
1998	—	—	—	—	0.75	1.00
1999	—	—	—	—	0.75	1.00
1999 Proof	2,500	Value: 4.00				

KM# 5.1 10 PENCE
11.3100 g., Copper-Nickel, 28.5 mm. **Ruler:** Elizabeth II **Obv:** Young bust right **Rev:** Ursine seal with cub, denomination below, date at left **Designer:** William Gardner

Date	Mintage	F	VF	XF	Unc	BU
1974	87,000	—	0.20	0.40	1.50	3.50
1974 Proof	23,000	Value: 5.00				
1980	—	—	0.20	0.40	1.50	3.50
1980 Proof	10,000	Value: 5.00				
1982	—	—	0.20	0.40	1.50	3.50
1982 Proof	—	Value: 5.00				
1983	—	—	0.20	0.40	1.50	3.50
1985	—	—	0.20	0.40	1.50	3.50
1987	4,000	—	—	0.40	1.50	3.50
1987 Proof	—	Value: 5.50				
1992	—	—	0.20	0.40	1.50	3.50
1992 Proof	—	Value: 5.50				

KM# 5.2 10 PENCE
Copper-Nickel, 24.5 mm. **Ruler:** Elizabeth II **Obv:** Young bust right **Rev:** Ursine seal with cub, denomination below, date at left **Designer:** William Gardner

Date	Mintage	F	VF	XF	Unc	BU
1998	—	—	—	—	1.50	3.00
1999	—	—	—	—	1.50	3.00
1999 Proof	2,500	Value: 5.00				

KM# 17 20 PENCE
5.0000 g., Copper-Nickel, 21.95 mm. **Ruler:** Elizabeth II **Obv:** Young bust right **Rev:** Romney marsh sheep left, denomination above **Shape:** 7-sided **Designer:** William Gardner

Date	Mintage	F	VF	XF	Unc	BU
1982	—	—	0.40	0.65	2.00	4.00
1982 Proof	—	Value: 5.00				
1983	—	—	0.40	0.65	2.00	4.00
1985	—	—	0.40	0.65	2.00	4.00
1987	4,250	—	0.40	0.65	2.00	4.00
1987 Proof	—	Value: 5.50				
1992	—	—	0.40	0.65	2.00	4.00
1992 Proof	—	Value: 5.50				
1998	—	—	0.40	0.65	2.00	4.00
1999	—	—	—	—	2.00	4.00
1999 Proof	2,500	Value: 5.00				

KM# 10 50 PENCE
Copper-Nickel, 38.5 mm. **Ruler:** Elizabeth II **Subject:** Queen's Silver Jubilee **Obv:** Young bust right, dates at left **Rev:** Sheep above ship on shield within wreath, denomination below

Date	Mintage	F	VF	XF	Unc	BU
ND(1977)	100,000	—	1.00	1.50	3.00	4.50

KM# 10a 50 PENCE
28.2800 g., 0.9250 Silver .8411 oz. ASW, 38.5 mm. **Ruler:** Elizabeth II **Obv:** Young bust right **Rev:** Sheep above ship on shield within wreath, denomination below

Date	Mintage	F	VF	XF	Unc	BU
ND(1977) Proof	22,000	Value: 14.50				

KM# 14.1 50 PENCE
13.6500 g., Copper-Nickel, 30 mm. **Ruler:** Elizabeth II **Obv:** Young bust right **Rev:** Falkland Island fox (extinct), date at right, denomination above **Shape:** 7-sided

Date	Mintage	F	VF	XF	Unc	BU
1980	—	—	1.00	2.00	5.00	7.50
1980 Proof	—	Value: 8.00				
1982	—	—	1.00	2.00	5.00	7.50
1982 Proof	—	Value: 8.00				
1983	—	—	1.00	2.00	5.00	7.50
1985	—	—	1.00	2.00	5.00	7.50

Date	Mintage	F	VF	XF	Unc	BU
1987	4,000	—	1.00	2.00	5.00	7.50
1987 Proof	—	Value: 9.00				
1992	—	—	1.00	2.00	5.00	7.50
1992 Proof	—	Value: 9.00				
1995	—	—	—	2.00	5.00	7.50

KM# 14.2 50 PENCE
Copper-Nickel, 27.5 mm. **Ruler:** Elizabeth II **Obv:** Young bust right **Rev:** Falkland Island fox (extinct) **Shape:** 7-sided **Note:** Reduced size.

Date	Mintage	F	VF	XF	Unc	BU
1998	—	—	—	2.00	5.00	7.50
1999	—	—	—	2.00	5.00	7.50
1999 Proof	2,500	Value: 8.00				

KM# 15 50 PENCE
Copper-Nickel, 38.5 mm. **Ruler:** Elizabeth II **Subject:** 80th Anniversary - Birth of Queen Mother **Obv:** Young bust right **Rev:** Queen Mother's bust left

Date	Mintage	F	VF	XF	Unc	BU
ND(1980)	—	—	1.00	1.50	3.50	6.00

KM# 15a 50 PENCE
28.2800 g., 0.9250 Silver .8411 oz. ASW, 38.5 mm. **Ruler:** Elizabeth II **Subject:** 80th Anniversary-Birth of Queen Mother **Obv:** Young bust right **Rev:** Queen Mothers bust left

Date	Mintage	F	VF	XF	Unc	BU
ND(1980) Proof	—	Value: 14.50				

KM# 16 50 PENCE
Copper-Nickel, 38.5 mm. **Ruler:** Elizabeth II **Subject:** Wedding of Prince Charles and Lady Diana **Obv:** Young bust right **Rev:** Conjoined busts of royal couple right

Date	Mintage	F	VF	XF	Unc	BU
1981	—	—	1.00	1.50	3.00	4.50

KM# 16a 50 PENCE
28.2800 g., 0.9250 Silver .8411 oz. ASW, 38.5 mm. **Ruler:** Elizabeth II **Subject:** Wedding of Prince Charles and Lady Diana **Obv:** Young bust right **Rev:** Conjoined busts of royal couple right

Date	Mintage	F	VF	XF	Unc	BU
1981 Proof	40,000	Value: 20.00				

KM# 18 50 PENCE
Copper-Nickel, 38.5 mm. **Subject:** Liberation from Argentina Forces **Obv:** Young bust right, denomination below **Rev:** Flag design in background, state shield at left, date below **Designer:** Philip Nathan

Date	Mintage	F	VF	XF	Unc	BU
ND(1982)	—	—	1.00	1.50	3.00	4.50

KM# 18a 50 PENCE
28.2800 g., 0.9250 Silver .8411 oz. ASW, 38.5 mm. **Ruler:** Elizabeth II **Obv:** Young bust right, denomination below **Rev:** Flag design in background, state shield at left, date below

Date	Mintage	F	VF	XF	Unc	BU
ND(1982) Proof	Est. 25,000	Value: 16.00				

KM# 18b 50 PENCE
47.5000 g., 0.9170 Gold 1.4005 oz. AGW, 38.5 mm. **Ruler:** Elizabeth II **Subject:** Liberation From Argentina Forces **Obv:** Young bust right, denomination below **Rev:** Flag design in background, state shield at left, date below

Date	Mintage	F	VF	XF	Unc	BU
ND(1982) Proof	25	Value: 5,500				

KM# 19 50 PENCE
Copper-Nickel, 38.5 mm. **Ruler:** Elizabeth II **Subject:** 150th Anniversary of British Rule **Obv:** Young bust right **Rev:** Ship divides dates **Designer:** Robert Elderton

Date	Mintage	F	VF	XF	Unc	BU
ND(1983)	Est. 50,000	—	1.00	2.00	5.00	7.00

KM# 19a 50 PENCE
28.2800 g., 0.9250 Silver .8411 oz. ASW, 38.5 mm. **Ruler:** Elizabeth II **Obv:** Young bust right **Rev:** Ship divides dates

Date	Mintage	F	VF	XF	Unc	BU
ND(1983) Proof	Est. 10,000	Value: 18.50				

KM# 19b 50 PENCE
47.5400 g., 0.9170 Gold 1.4017 oz. AGW, 38.5 mm. **Ruler:** Elizabeth II **Subject:** 150th Anniversary of British Rule **Obv:** Young bust right **Rev:** Ship divides dates

Date	Mintage	F	VF	XF	Unc	BU
ND(1983) Proof	150	Value: 1,250				

KM# 21 50 PENCE
Copper-Nickel, 38.5 mm. **Ruler:** Elizabeth II **Subject:** Opening of Mount Pleasant Airport **Obv:** Crowned bust right, denomination below **Rev:** Bust left, date at right

Date	Mintage	F	VF	XF	Unc	BU
ND(1985)	—	—	—	—	3.00	4.50

KM# 21a 50 PENCE
28.2750 g., 0.9250 Silver .8410 oz. ASW, 38.5 mm. **Obv:** Crowned bust right, denomination below **Rev:** Bust left

Date	Mintage	F	VF	XF	Unc	BU
ND (1985) Proof	Est. 5,000	Value: 16.00				

KM# 25 50 PENCE
Copper-Nickel, 38.5 mm. **Ruler:** Elizabeth II **Subject:** World Wildlife Fund **Obv:** Crowned bust right **Rev:** King penguins, denomination and date

Date	Mintage	F	VF	XF	Unc	BU
1987	—	—	—	—	7.00	12.00

KM# 25a 50 PENCE
28.2800 g., 0.9250 Silver .8411 oz. ASW, 38.5 mm. **Ruler:** Elizabeth II **Subject:** World Wildlife Fund **Obv:** Crowned bust right **Rev:** King Penguins, denomination and date

Date	Mintage	F	VF	XF	Unc	BU
1987 Proof	Est. 25,000	Value: 35.00				

KM# 26 50 PENCE
Copper-Nickel, 38.5 mm. **Ruler:** Elizabeth II **Subject:** Children's Fund **Obv:** Crowned bust right **Rev:** Woman on horseback, dog herding animals, denomination below

Date	Mintage	F	VF	XF	Unc	BU
1990	Est. 20,000	—	—	—	5.00	8.00

KM# 26a 50 PENCE
28.2800 g., 0.9250 Silver .8411 oz. ASW, 38.5 mm. **Ruler:** Elizabeth II **Subject:** Children's Fund **Obv:** Crowned bust right **Rev:** Woman on horseback, dog herding animals, denomination below

Date	Mintage	F	VF	XF	Unc	BU
1990 Proof	—	Value: 37.50				

KM# 34 50 PENCE
Copper-Nickel, 38.5 mm. **Ruler:** Elizabeth II **Subject:** 40th Anniversary - Reign of Queen Elizabeth II **Obv:** Crowned bust right **Rev:** Three figures, one at left is silhouette, dates below **Rev. Designer:** Willem Vis

Date	Mintage	F	VF	XF	Unc	BU
ND(1992)	—	—	—	—	4.50	6.50

KM# 34a 50 PENCE
28.2800 g., 0.9250 Silver .8411 oz. ASW, 38.5 mm. **Ruler:** Elizabeth II **Subject:** 40th Anniversary - Reign of Queen Elizabeth II **Obv:** Crowned bust right **Rev:** Three figures, one at left is silhouette, dates below

Date	Mintage	F	VF	XF	Unc	BU
ND(1992) Proof	5,000	Value: 50.00				

KM# 34b 50 PENCE
47.5400 g., 0.9170 Gold 1.4011 oz. AGW, 38.5 mm. **Ruler:** Elizabeth II **Subject:** 40th Anniversary - Reign of Queen Elizabeth **Obv:** Crowned bust right **Rev:** Three figures, one at left is silhouette, dates below

Date	Mintage	F	VF	XF	Unc	BU
ND(1992) Proof	150	Value: 985				

KM# 43 50 PENCE
Copper-Nickel, 38.5 mm. **Ruler:** Elizabeth II **Subject:** 40th Anniversary - Coronation of Queen Elizabeth II **Obv:** Crowned bust right **Rev:** Queen on horseback, dates and denomination below

Date	Mintage	F	VF	XF	Unc	BU
ND(1993)	—	—	—	—	6.50	8.50

KM# 43a 50 PENCE
28.2800 g., 0.9250 Silver .8411 oz. ASW, 38.5 mm. **Ruler:** Elizabeth II **Subject:** 40th Anniversary - Coronation of Queen Elizabeth II **Obv:** Crowned bust right **Rev:** Queen on horseback, dates and denomination below

Date	Mintage	F	VF	XF	Unc	BU
ND(1993) Proof	Est. 10,000	Value: 55.00				

KM# 45 50 PENCE
Copper-Nickel, 38.5 mm. **Ruler:** Elizabeth II **Subject:** V. E. Day - 50th Anniversary **Obv:** Crowned bust right **Rev:** Denomination and dove divide flags, date below

Date	Mintage	F	VF	XF	Unc	BU
1995	—	—	—	—	5.50	7.50

KM# 45a 50 PENCE
28.2800 g., 0.9250 Silver .8411 oz. ASW, 38.5 mm. **Ruler:** Elizabeth II **Subject:** V. E. Day - 50th Anniversary **Obv:** Crowned bust right **Rev:** Denomination and dove divide flags, date below

Date	Mintage	F	VF	XF	Unc	BU
1995 Proof	Est. 10,000	Value: 50.00				

KM# 45b 50 PENCE
47.5400 g., 0.9170 Gold 1.4011 oz. AGW, 38.5 mm. **Ruler:** Elizabeth II **Subject:** V.E. Day - 50th Anniversary **Obv:** Crowned bust right **Rev:** Denomination and dove divide flags, date below

Date	Mintage	F	VF	XF	Unc	BU
1995 Proof	Est. 100	Value: 985				

KM# 46 50 PENCE
Copper-Nickel, 38.5 mm. **Ruler:** Elizabeth II **Subject:** Queen Elizabeth II's 70th Birthday **Obv:** Crowned bust right **Rev:** Queen and Prince Philip as young adults, denomination and date below

Date	Mintage	F	VF	XF	Unc	BU
1996	—	—	—	—	7.00	9.00

KM# 46a 50 PENCE
28.2800 g., 0.9250 Silver .8411 oz. ASW, 38.5 mm. **Ruler:** Elizabeth II **Subject:** Queen Elizabeth II's 70th Birthday **Obv:** Crowned bust right **Rev:** Queen and Prince Philip as young adults, denomination and date below

Date	Mintage	F	VF	XF	Unc	BU
1996 Proof	—	Value: 50.00				

KM# 72 50 PENCE
28.2800 g., Copper-Nickel, 38.6 mm. **Ruler:** Elizabeth II **Obv:** Crowned bust right, date below **Rev:** Queen Mother holding infant on lap, date below, circle surrounds, denmination below **Edge:** Reeded

Date	Mintage	F	VF	XF	Unc	BU
1995	—	—	—	—	7.00	9.00

KM# 72a 50 PENCE
28.2800 g., 0.9250 Silver 0.841 oz. ASW, 38.6 mm. **Ruler:** Elizabeth II **Obv:** Crowned bust right, date below **Rev:** Queen Mother holding infant on lap, date below, circle surrounds, denmination below

Date	Mintage	F	VF	XF	Unc	BU
1995 Proof	—	Value: 35.00				

KM# 72a.1 50 PENCE
15.9200 g., 0.9250 Silver 0.4735 oz. ASW, 28.3 mm. **Ruler:** Elizabeth II **Obv:** Crowned bust right, date below **Rev:** Queen Mother holding the baby, date below, circle surrounds, denomination below **Edge:** Reeded

Date	Mintage	F	VF	XF	Unc	BU
1997 Proof	—	Value: 25.00				

KM# 59 50 PENCE
Copper-Nickel, 38.5 mm. **Ruler:** Elizabeth II **Subject:** WWF - Conserving Nature **Obv:** Crowned bust right **Rev:** Pair of Black-browed Albatross, date above

Date	Mintage	F	VF	XF	Unc	BU
1997	—	—	—	—	12.00	—

KM# 59a 50 PENCE
28.2800 g., 0.9250 Silver .8410 oz. ASW, 38.5 mm. **Ruler:** Elizabeth II **Subject:** WWF - Conserving Nature **Obv:** Crowned bust right **Rev:** Pair of Black-browed Albatross, date above

Date	Mintage	F	VF	XF	Unc	BU
1997 Proof	Est. 15,000	Value: 40.00				

KM# 60 50 PENCE
Copper-Nickel, 38.5 mm. **Ruler:** Elizabeth II **Subject:** WWF - Conserving Nature **Obv:** Crowned bust right **Rev:** Peale's dolphin, date above

Date	Mintage	F	VF	XF	Unc	BU
1998	—	—	—	—	12.00	—

KM# 60a 50 PENCE
28.2800 g., 0.9250 Silver 0.841 oz. ASW, 38.5 mm. **Ruler:** Elizabeth II **Subject:** WWF - Conserving Nature **Obv:** Crowned bust right **Rev:** Peale's dolphin

Date	Mintage	F	VF	XF	Unc	BU
1998 Proof	—	Value: 40.00				

KM# 71a 50 PENCE
28.2800 g., 0.9250 Silver 0.841 oz. ASW, 38.5 mm. **Ruler:** Elizabeth II **Obv:** Crowned bust right **Rev:** Uncrowned portrait left **Edge:** Reeded

Date	Mintage	F	VF	XF	Unc	BU
1999 Proof	10,000	Value: 50.00				

KM# 66 50 PENCE
28.2800 g., Copper-Nickel, 38.5 mm. **Ruler:** Elizabeth II **Subject:** Winston Churchill **Obv:** Crowned bust right **Rev:** Churchill in Admiral's uniform, date below ship at left

Date	Mintage	F	VF	XF	Unc	BU
1999	—	—	—	—	7.00	9.00

KM# 66a 50 PENCE
28.2800 g., 0.9250 Silver .8410 oz. ASW, 38.5 mm. **Ruler:** Elizabeth II **Subject:** Winston Churchill **Obv:** Crowned bust right **Rev:** Churchill in Admiral's uniform

Date	Mintage	F	VF	XF	Unc	BU
1999 Proof	2,500	Value: 40.00				

KM# 66b 50 PENCE
47.5400 g., 0.9160 Gold 1.4010 oz. AGW, 38.5 mm. **Ruler:** Elizabeth II **Obv:** Crowned bust right **Rev:** Churchill in Admiral's uniform

Date	Mintage	F	VF	XF	Unc	BU
1999 Proof	125	Value: 1,500				

KM# 6 1/2 POUND
3.9900 g., 0.9170 Gold .1176 oz. AGW **Ruler:** Elizabeth II **Obv:** Young bust right **Rev:** Romney marsh sheep left, date above **Rev. Designer:** William Gardner

Date	Mintage	F	VF	XF	Unc	BU
1974 Proof	2,673	Value: 165				

KM# 7 POUND
7.9900 g., 0.9170 Gold .2356 oz. AGW **Ruler:** Elizabeth II **Obv:** Young bust right **Rev:** Romney marsh sheep left, date above **Rev. Designer:** William Gardner

Date	Mintage	F	VF	XF	Unc	BU
1974 Proof	2,675	Value: 265				

KM# 24 POUND
9.5000 g., Nickel-Brass, 22.5 mm. **Ruler:** Elizabeth II **Obv:** Crowned bust right **Rev:** State shield, date and denomination **Edge Lettering:** DESIRE THE RIGHT

Date	Mintage	F	VF	XF	Unc	BU
1987	—	—	—	—	3.50	—
1987 Proof	2,500	Value: 12.50				

Date	Mintage	F	VF	XF	Unc	BU
1992	—	—	—	—	3.50	—
1992 Proof	—	Value: 12.50				
1999	—	—	—	—	3.50	—
1999 Proof	2,500	Value: 12.50				

KM# 24a POUND

9.5000 g., 0.9250 Silver .2825 oz. ASW, 22.5 mm. **Ruler:** Elizabeth II **Obv:** Crowned bust right **Rev:** State shield, date and denomination

Date	Mintage	F	VF	XF	Unc	BU
1987 Proof	Est. 5,000	Value: 22.50				

KM# 24b POUND

19.6500 g., 0.9170 Gold .5791 oz. AGW, 22.5 mm. **Ruler:** Elizabeth II **Obv:** Crowned bust right **Rev:** State shield, date and denomination

Date	Mintage	F	VF	XF	Unc	BU
1987 Proof	Est. 200	Value: 625				

KM# 8 2 POUNDS

15.9800 g., 0.9170 Gold .4712 oz. AGW **Ruler:** Elizabeth II **Obv:** Young bust right **Rev:** Romney marsh sheep left, date above **Rev. Designer:** William Gardner

Date	Mintage	F	VF	XF	Unc	BU
1974 Proof	2,158	Value: 520				

KM# 22 2 POUNDS

28.2800 g., 0.5000 Silver .4546 oz. ASW, 38.61 mm. **Ruler:** Elizabeth II **Subject:** Commonweatlth Games **Obv:** Crowned bust right, denomination below **Rev:** Marksman

Date	Mintage	F	VF	XF	Unc	BU
1986	Est. 50,000	—	—	—	30.00	—

KM# 22a 2 POUNDS

28.2800 g., 0.9250 Silver .8411 oz. ASW, 38.61 mm. **Ruler:** Elizabeth II **Obv:** Crowned bust right, denomination below **Rev:** Marksman

Date	Mintage	F	VF	XF	Unc	BU
1986	Est. 20,000	Value: 40.00				

KM# 32 2 POUNDS

28.2800 g., 0.9250 Silver .8411 oz. ASW, 38.61 mm. **Ruler:** Elizabeth II **Subject:** 10th Wedding Anniversary - Prince Charles and Lady Diana **Obv:** Crowned bust right **Rev:** Facing cameos divide cathedral and crown design, wreath surrounds

Date	Mintage	F	VF	XF	Unc	BU
1991 Proof	Est. 10,000	Value: 40.00				

KM# 35 2 POUNDS

Copper-Nickel, 38.61 mm. **Ruler:** Elizabeth II **Subject:** Heritage Year **Obv:** Crowned bust right **Rev:** State shield below flowers, ferns flank

Date	Mintage	F	VF	XF	Unc	BU
1992	—	—	—	—	11.50	—

KM# 35a 2 POUNDS

28.2800 g., 0.9250 Silver .8411 oz. ASW, 38.61 mm. **Ruler:** Elizabeth II **Subject:** Heritage year **Obv:** Crowned bust right **Rev:** State shield below flowers, ferns flank

Date	Mintage	F	VF	XF	Unc	BU
1992 Proof	Est. 7,500	Value: 37.50				

KM# 47 2 POUNDS

28.2800 g., 0.9250 Silver .8410 oz. ASW, 38.61 mm. **Ruler:** Elizabeth II **Subject:** Royal Heritage - Egbert of Wessex **Obv:** Crowned bust right **Rev:** Egbert in archway, dates divided

Date	Mintage	F	VF	XF	Unc	BU
1996 Proof	10,000	Value: 50.00				

KM# 47a 2 POUNDS

28.1500 g., 0.9250 Bi-Metallic Silver center in Gold-plated Silver ring .8411 oz., 38.61 mm. **Ruler:** Elizabeth II **Subject:** Royal Heritage - Egbert of Wessex **Obv:** Crowned bust right **Rev:** Egbert in archway, dates divided

Date	Mintage	F	VF	XF	Unc	BU
1996 Proof	Est. 10,000	Value: 45.00				

KM# 47b 2 POUNDS

28.2800 g., Copper-Nickel, 38.6 mm. **Ruler:** Elizabeth II **Subject:** Royal Heritage - Egbert of Wessex **Obv:** Crowned bust right **Rev:** Egbert in archway, dates divided **Edge:** Reeded

Date	Mintage	F	VF	XF	Unc	BU
1996	—	—	—	—	8.50	—

KM# 48 2 POUNDS

28.2800 g., 0.9250 Silver .8410 oz. ASW, 38.61 mm. **Ruler:** Elizabeth II **Subject:** Royal Heritage - Alfred the Great **Obv:** Crowned bust right **Rev:** Alfred with axe, scroll, ancient coin, dates divided

Date	Mintage	F	VF	XF	Unc	BU
1996 Proof	10,000	Value: 50.00				

KM# 48a 2 POUNDS

28.1500 g., 0.9250 Bi-Metallic Silver center in Gold-plated Silver ring .8411 oz., 38.61 mm. **Ruler:** Elizabeth II **Subject:** Royal Heritage - Alfred the Great **Obv:** Crowned bust right **Rev:** Alfred with axe, scroll, ancient coin, dates divided

Date	Mintage	F	VF	XF	Unc	BU
1996 Proof	Est. 10,000	Value: 35.00				

KM# 48b 2 POUNDS

28.2800 g., Copper-Nickel, 38.6 mm. **Ruler:** Elizabeth II **Subject:** Royal Heritage - Alfred the Great **Obv:** Crowned bust right **Rev:** Alfred with axe, scroll, ancient coin, dates divided **Edge:** Reeded

Date	Mintage	F	VF	XF	Unc	BU
1996	—	—	—	—	8.50	—

KM# 49 2 POUNDS

28.2800 g., 0.9250 Silver .8410 oz. ASW, 38.61 mm. **Ruler:** Elizabeth II **Subject:** Royal Heritage - Edward the Confessor **Obv:** Crowned bust right **Rev:** Edward with halo offering miniature church within wreath, dates divided

Date	Mintage	F	VF	XF	Unc	BU
1996 Proof	10,000	Value: 50.00				

KM# 49a 2 POUNDS

28.1500 g., 0.9250 Bi-Metallic Silver center in Gold-plated Silver ring .8411 oz., 38.61 mm. **Ruler:** Elizabeth II **Subject:** Royal Heritage - Edward the Confessor **Obv:** Crowned bust right **Rev:** Edward with halo offering miniature church; dates divided

Date	Mintage	F	VF	XF	Unc	BU
1996 Proof	Est. 10,000	Value: 35.00				

KM# 49b 2 POUNDS

28.2800 g., Copper-Nickel, 38.6 mm. **Ruler:** Elizabeth II **Subject:** Royal Heritage - Edward the Confessor 1042-66 **Obv:** Crowned bust right **Rev:** Edward with halo offering miniature church within wreath, dates divided **Edge:** Reeded

Date	Mintage	F	VF	XF	Unc	BU
1996	—	—	—	—	8.50	—

KM# 50 2 POUNDS

28.2800 g., 0.9250 Silver .8410 oz. ASW, 38.61 mm. **Ruler:** Elizabeth II **Subject:** Royal Heritage - William I **Obv:** Crowned bust right **Rev:** Seated William holding miniature church, Doomsday Book at left, shield at right, dates below

Date	Mintage	F	VF	XF	Unc	BU
1996 Proof	10,000	Value: 50.00				

KM# 50a 2 POUNDS

28.1500 g., 0.9250 Bi-Metallic Silver center in Gold-plated ring .8411 oz., 38.61 mm. **Ruler:** Elizabeth II **Subject:** Royal Heritage - William I **Obv:** Crowned bust right **Rev:** Seated William holding miniature church, Doomsday Book at left, shield at right, dates below

Date	Mintage	F	VF	XF	Unc	BU
1996 Proof	Est. 10,000	Value: 35.00				

KM# 50b 2 POUNDS

28.2800 g., Copper-Nickel, 38.6 mm. **Ruler:** Elizabeth II **Subject:** Royal Heritage - William I the Conqueror 1066-87 **Obv:** Crowned bust right **Rev:** Seated William holding miniature church, Doomsday Book at left, shield at right, dates below **Edge:** Reeded

Date	Mintage	F	VF	XF	Unc	BU
1996	—	—	—	—	8.50	—

KM# 51 2 POUNDS

28.2800 g., 0.9250 Silver .8410 oz. ASW, 38.61 mm. **Ruler:** Elizabeth II **Subject:** Royal Heritage - Henry II 1154-89 **Obv:** Crowned bust right **Rev:** Crowned bust of Henry II 3/4 facing, dates at right

Date	Mintage	F	VF	XF	Unc	BU
1996 Proof	10,000	Value: 50.00				

KM# 51a 2 POUNDS

28.1500 g., 0.9250 Bi-Metallic Silver center in Gold-plated Silver ring .8411 oz., 38.61 mm. **Ruler:** Elizabeth II **Subject:** Royal Heritage - Henry II 1154-89 **Obv:** Crowned bust right **Rev:** Crowned bust of Henry II 3/4 facing, dates at right

Date	Mintage	F	VF	XF	Unc	BU
1996 Proof	Est. 10,000	Value: 35.00				

KM# 51b 2 POUNDS

28.2800 g., Copper-Nickel, 38.6 mm. **Ruler:** Elizabeth II **Subject:** Royal Heritage - Henry II 1154-89 **Obv:** Crowned bust right **Rev:** Crowned bust of Henry II 3/4 facing, dates at right **Edge:** Reeded

Date	Mintage	F	VF	XF	Unc	BU
1996	—	—	—	—	8.50	—

KM# 52 2 POUNDS

28.2800 g., 0.9250 Silver .8410 oz. ASW, 38.61 mm. **Ruler:** Elizabeth II **Subject:** Royal Heritage - Richard I The Lionheart 1189-99 **Obv:** Crowned bust right **Rev:** Seated Richard flanked by sun and crescent moon, dates divided

Date	Mintage	F	VF	XF	Unc	BU
1996 Proof	10,000	Value: 50.00				

KM# 52a 2 POUNDS

28.1500 g., 0.9250 Bi-Metallic Silver center in Gold-plated Silver ring .8411 oz., 38.61 mm. **Ruler:** Elizabeth II **Subject:** Royal Heritage - Richard I The Lionheart 1189-99 **Obv:** Crowned bust right **Rev:** Seated Richard flanked by sun and crescent moon; dates divided

Date	Mintage	F	VF	XF	Unc	BU
1996 Proof	Est. 10,000	Value: 35.00				

KM# 52b 2 POUNDS

28.2800 g., Copper-Nickel, 38.6 mm. **Ruler:** Elizabeth II **Subject:** Royal Heritage - Richard the Lionheart 1189-99 **Obv:** Crowned bust right **Rev:** Seated Richard flanked by sun and crescent moon, dates divided **Edge:** Reeded

Date	Mintage	F	VF	XF	Unc	BU
1996	—	—	—	—	8.50	—

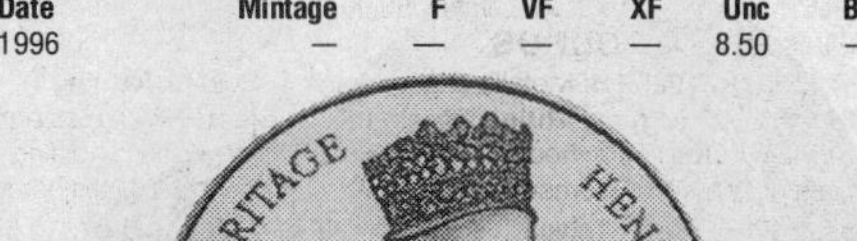

KM# 53 2 POUNDS

28.2800 g., 0.9250 Silver .8410 oz. ASW, 38.61 mm. **Ruler:** Elizabeth II **Subject:** Royal Heritage - Henry IV 1399-1413 **Obv:** Crowned bust right **Rev:** Portrait of Henry in crown and cape right, dates below

Date	Mintage	F	VF	XF	Unc	BU
1996 Proof	10,000	Value: 50.00				

KM# 53a 2 POUNDS

28.1500 g., 0.9250 Bi-Metallic Silver center in Gold-plated Silver ring .8411 oz., 38.61 mm. **Ruler:** Elizabeth II **Subject:** Royal Heritage - Henry IV 1399-1413 **Obv:** Crowned bust right **Rev:** Portrait of Henry in crown and cape right, dates below

Date	Mintage	F	VF	XF	Unc	BU
1996 Proof	Est. 10,000	Value: 35.00				

KM# 53b 2 POUNDS

28.2800 g., Copper-Nickel, 38.6 mm. **Ruler:** Elizabeth II **Subject:** Royal Heritage - Henry IV 1399-1413 **Obv:** Crowned bust right **Rev:** Portrait of Henry in crown and cape right, dates below **Edge:** Reeded

Date	Mintage	F	VF	XF	Unc	BU
1996	—	—	—	—	8.50	—

KM# 54 2 POUNDS

28.2800 g., 0.9250 Silver .8410 oz. ASW, 38.61 mm. **Ruler:** Elizabeth II **Subject:** Royal Heritage - Edward IV 1461-83 **Obv:** Crowned bust right **Rev:** Youthful Edward bust looking left, castle and ship at left, dates divided

Date	Mintage	F	VF	XF	Unc	BU
1996 Proof	10,000	Value: 50.00				

KM# 54a 2 POUNDS

28.1500 g., 0.9250 Bi-Metallic Silver center in Gold-plated Silver ring .8411 oz., 38.61 mm. **Ruler:** Elizabeth II **Subject:** Royal Heritage - Edward IV 1461-83 **Obv:** Crowned bust right **Rev:** Youthful Edward bust looking left, castle and ship at left, dates divided

Date	Mintage	F	VF	XF	Unc	BU
1996 Proof	Est. 10,000	Value: 35.00				

KM# 54b 2 POUNDS

28.2800 g., Copper-Nickel, 38.6 mm. **Ruler:** Elizabeth II **Subject:** Royal Heritage - Edward IV 1461-83 **Obv:** Crowned bust right **Rev:** Youthful Edward bust looking left, castle and ship at left, dates divided **Edge:** Reeded

Date	Mintage	F	VF	XF	Unc	BU
1996	—	—	—	—	8.50	—

KM# 55 2 POUNDS

28.2800 g., 0.9250 Silver .8410 oz. ASW, 38.61 mm. **Ruler:** Elizabeth II **Subject:** Royal Heritage - Henry VIII 1509-47 **Obv:** Crowned bust right **Rev:** Standing Henry with shield; dates below at left

Date	Mintage	F	VF	XF	Unc	BU
1996 Proof	10,000	Value: 50.00				

KM# 55a 2 POUNDS

28.1500 g., 0.9250 Bi-Metallic Silver center in Gold-plated Silver ring .8411 oz., 38.61 mm. **Ruler:** Elizabeth II **Subject:** Royal Heritage - Henry VIII 1509-47 **Obv:** Crowned bust right **Rev:** Standing Henry with shield; dates

Date	Mintage	F	VF	XF	Unc	BU
1996 Proof	Est. 10,000	Value: 35.00				

KM# 55b 2 POUNDS

28.2800 g., Copper-Nickel, 38.6 mm. **Ruler:** Elizabeth II **Subject:** Royal Heritage - Henry VIII 1509-47 **Obv:** Crowned bust right **Rev:** Standing Henry with shield; dates below at left **Edge:** Reeded

Date	Mintage	F	VF	XF	Unc	BU
1996	—	—	—	—	8.50	—

KM# 56 2 POUNDS

28.2800 g., 0.9250 Silver .8410 oz. ASW, 38.61 mm. **Ruler:** Elizabeth II **Subject:** Royal Heritage - Elizabeth I 1558-1603 **Obv:** Crowned bust right **Rev:** Bust with high ruffled collar 3/4 facing, dates below

Date	Mintage	F	VF	XF	Unc	BU
1996 Proof	10,000	Value: 50.00				

KM# 56a 2 POUNDS

28.1500 g., 0.9250 Bi-Metallic Silver center in Gold-plated Silver ring .8411 oz., 38.61 mm. **Ruler:** Elizabeth II **Subject:** Royal Heritage - Elizabeth I 1558-1603 **Obv:** Crowned bust right **Rev:** Bust with high ruffled collar 3/4 facing, dates below

Date	Mintage	F	VF	XF	Unc	BU
1996 Proof	Est. 10,000	Value: 35.00				

KM# 56b 2 POUNDS

28.2800 g., Copper-Nickel, 38.6 mm. **Ruler:** Elizabeth II **Subject:** Royal Heritage - Elizabeth I 1558-1603 **Obv:** Crowned bust right **Rev:** Bust with high ruffled collar 3/4 facing, dates below **Edge:** Reeded

Date	Mintage	F	VF	XF	Unc	BU
1996	—	—	—	—	8.50	—

KM# 57 2 POUNDS

28.2800 g., 0.9250 Silver .8410 oz. ASW, 38.61 mm. **Ruler:** Elizabeth II **Subject:** Royal Heritage - Charles I 1625-49 **Obv:** Crowned bust right **Rev:** Smiling portrait of Charles 3/4 right, small shield and dates at right

Date	Mintage	F	VF	XF	Unc	BU
1996 Proof	10,000	Value: 50.00				

KM# 57a 2 POUNDS

28.1500 g., 0.9250 Bi-Metallic Silver center in Gold-plated Silver ring .8411 oz., 38.61 mm. **Ruler:** Elizabeth II **Subject:** Royal Heritage - Charles I 1625-49 **Obv:** Crowned bust right **Rev:** Smiling portrait of Charles 3/4 right, small shield and dates at right

Date	Mintage	F	VF	XF	Unc	BU
1996 Proof	Est. 10,000	Value: 35.00				

KM# 57b 2 POUNDS

28.2800 g., Copper-Nickel, 38.6 mm. **Ruler:** Elizabeth II **Subject:** Royal Heritage - Charles I 1625-49 **Obv:** Crowned bust right **Rev:** Smiling portrait of Charles 3/4 right, small shield and dates at right **Edge:** Reeded

Date	Mintage	F	VF	XF	Unc	BU
1996	—	—	—	—	8.50	—

KM# 58 2 POUNDS

28.2800 g., 0.9250 Silver .8410 oz. ASW, 38.61 mm. **Ruler:** Elizabeth II **Subject:** Royal Heritage - Victoria 1837-1901 **Obv:**

Crowned bust right **Rev:** Seated Queen Victoria with scepter and shield, dates at right

Date	Mintage	F	VF	XF	Unc	BU
1996 Proof	10,000	Value: 50.00				

KM# 58a 2 POUNDS
28.1500 g., 0.9250 Bi-Metallic Silver center in Gold-plated Silver ring .8411 oz., 38.61 mm. **Ruler:** Elizabeth II **Subject:** Royal Heritage - Victoria 1837-1901 **Obv:** Crowned bust right **Rev:** Seated Queen Victoria with sceptre and shield, dates at right

Date	Mintage	F	VF	XF	Unc	BU
1996 Proof	Est. 10,000	Value: 35.00				

KM# 58b 2 POUNDS
28.2800 g., Copper-Nickel, 38.6 mm. **Ruler:** Elizabeth II **Subject:** Royal Heritage - Victoria 1837-1901 **Obv:** Crowned bust right **Rev:** Seated Queen Victoria with scepter and shield, dates at right **Edge:** Reeded

Date	Mintage	F	VF	XF	Unc	BU
1996	—	—	—	—	8.50	—

KM# 104 2 POUNDS
1.2428 g., 0.9990 Gold 0.0399 oz. AGW, 14 mm. **Ruler:** Elizabeth II **Obv:** Crowned bust right **Rev:** Egbert of Wessex 802-839 **Edge:** Reeded

Date	Mintage	F	VF	XF	Unc	BU
1997 Proof	—	Value: 45.00				

KM# 105 2 POUNDS
1.2428 g., 0.9990 Gold 0.0399 oz. AGW, 14 mm. **Ruler:** Elizabeth II **Obv:** Crowned bust right **Rev:** Alfred the Great 871-899 **Edge:** Reeded

Date	Mintage	F	VF	XF	Unc	BU
1997 Proof	—	Value: 45.00				

KM# 106 2 POUNDS
1.2428 g., 0.9990 Gold 0.0399 oz. AGW, 14 mm. **Ruler:** Elizabeth II **Obv:** Crowned bust right **Rev:** Edward the Confessor **Edge:** Reeded

Date	Mintage	F	VF	XF	Unc	BU
1997 Proof	—	Value: 45.00				

KM# 107 2 POUNDS
1.2428 g., 0.9990 Gold 0.0399 oz. AGW, 14 mm. **Ruler:** Elizabeth II **Obv:** Crowned bust right **Rev:** William I the Conqueror 1066-87 **Edge:** Reeded

Date	Mintage	F	VF	XF	Unc	BU
1997 Proof	—	Value: 45.00				

KM# 108 2 POUNDS
1.2428 g., 0.9990 Gold 0.0399 oz. AGW, 14 mm. **Ruler:** Elizabeth II **Obv:** Crowned bust right **Rev:** Henry II 1154-89 **Edge:** Reeded

Date	Mintage	F	VF	XF	Unc	BU
1997 Proof	—	Value: 45.00				

KM# 109 2 POUNDS
1.2428 g., 0.9990 Gold 0.0399 oz. AGW, 14 mm. **Ruler:** Elizabeth II **Obv:** Crowned bust right **Rev:** Richard I the Lion Hearted, 1189-99 **Edge:** Reeded

Date	Mintage	F	VF	XF	Unc	BU
1997 Proof	—	Value: 45.00				

KM# 110 2 POUNDS
1.2428 g., 0.9990 Gold 0.0399 oz. AGW, 14 mm. **Ruler:** Elizabeth II **Obv:** Crowned bust right **Rev:** Henry IV 1399-1413 **Edge:** Reeded

Date	Mintage	F	VF	XF	Unc	BU
1997 Proof	—	Value: 45.00				

KM# 111 2 POUNDS
1.2428 g., 0.9990 Gold 0.0399 oz. AGW, 14 mm. **Ruler:** Elizabeth II **Obv:** Crowned bust right **Rev:** Edward IV 1461-83 **Edge:** Reeded

Date	Mintage	F	VF	XF	Unc	BU
1997 Proof	—	Value: 45.00				

KM# 112 2 POUNDS
1.2428 g., 0.9990 Gold 0.0399 oz. AGW, 14 mm. **Ruler:** Elizabeth II **Obv:** Crowned bust right **Rev:** Henry VIII 1509-47 **Edge:** Reeded

Date	Mintage	F	VF	XF	Unc	BU
1997 Proof	—	Value: 45.00				

KM# 113 2 POUNDS
1.2428 g., 0.9990 Gold 0.0399 oz. AGW, 14 mm. **Ruler:** Elizabeth II **Obv:** Crowned bust right **Rev:** Elizabeth I 1558-1603 **Edge:** Reeded

Date	Mintage	F	VF	XF	Unc	BU
1997 Proof	—	Value: 45.00				

KM# 114 2 POUNDS
1.2428 g., 0.9990 Gold 0.0399 oz. AGW, 14 mm. **Ruler:** Elizabeth II **Obv:** Crowned bust right **Rev:** Charles I 1625-49 **Edge:** Reeded

Date	Mintage	F	VF	XF	Unc	BU
1997 Proof	—	Value: 45.00				

KM# 115 2 POUNDS
1.2428 g., 0.9990 Gold 0.0399 oz. AGW, 14 mm. **Ruler:** Elizabeth II **Obv:** Crowned bust right **Rev:** Victoria 1837-1901 **Edge:** Reeded

Date	Mintage	F	VF	XF	Unc	BU
1998 Proof	—	Value: 45.00				

KM# 116 2 POUNDS
7.8000 g., 0.5830 Gold 0.2505 oz. AGW, 24.9 mm. **Ruler:** Elizabeth II **Subject:** Royal Heritage - Egbert of Wessex 802-839 **Obv:** Crowned bust right **Rev:** Egbert in archway, dates divided **Edge:** Reeded

Date	Mintage	F	VF	XF	Unc	BU
1997 Proof	—	Value: 175				

KM# 117 2 POUNDS
7.8000 g., 0.5830 Gold 0.2505 oz. AGW, 24.9 mm. **Ruler:** Elizabeth II **Obv:** Crowned bust right **Rev:** Alfred the Great 871-899 **Edge:** Reeded

Date	Mintage	F	VF	XF	Unc	BU
1997 Proof	—	Value: 175				

KM# 118 2 POUNDS
7.8000 g., 0.5830 Gold 0.2505 oz. AGW, 24.9 mm. **Ruler:** Elizabeth II **Obv:** Crowned bust right **Rev:** Edward the Confessor 1042-66 **Edge:** Reeded

Date	Mintage	F	VF	XF	Unc	BU
1997 Proof	—	Value: 175				

KM# 119 2 POUNDS
7.8000 g., 0.5830 Gold 0.2505 oz. AGW, 24.9 mm. **Ruler:** Elizabeth II **Obv:** Crowned bust right **Rev:** William I the Conqueror 1066-87 **Edge:** Reeded

Date	Mintage	F	VF	XF	Unc	BU
1997 Proof	—	Value: 175				

KM# 120 2 POUNDS
7.8000 g., 0.5830 Gold 0.2505 oz. AGW, 24.9 mm. **Ruler:** Elizabeth II **Obv:** Crowned bust right **Rev:** Henry II 1154-89 **Edge:** Reeded

Date	Mintage	F	VF	XF	Unc	BU
1997 Proof	—	Value: 175				

KM# 121 2 POUNDS
7.8000 g., 0.5830 Gold 0.2505 oz. AGW, 24.9 mm. **Ruler:** Elizabeth II **Obv:** Crowned bust right **Rev:** Richard I the Lion Hearted 1189-99 **Edge:** Reeded

Date	Mintage	F	VF	XF	Unc	BU
1997 Proof	—	Value: 175				

KM# 122 2 POUNDS
7.8000 g., 0.5830 Gold 0.2505 oz. AGW, 24.9 mm. **Ruler:** Elizabeth II **Obv:** Crowned bust right **Rev:** Henry IV 1399-1413 **Edge:** Reeded

Date	Mintage	F	VF	XF	Unc	BU
1997 Proof	—	Value: 175				

KM# 123 2 POUNDS
7.8000 g., 0.5830 Gold 0.2505 oz. AGW, 24.9 mm. **Ruler:** Elizabeth II **Obv:** Crowned bust right **Rev:** Edward IV 1461-83 **Edge:** Reeded

Date	Mintage	F	VF	XF	Unc	BU
1997 Proof	—	Value: 175				

KM# 124 2 POUNDS
7.8700 g., 0.5830 Gold 0.2505 oz. AGW, 24.9 mm. **Ruler:** Elizabeth II **Obv:** Crowned bust right **Rev:** Henry VIII 1509-47, shield at right, dates at left **Edge:** Reeded

Date	Mintage	F	VF	XF	Unc	BU
1997 Proof	—	Value: 175				

KM# 125 2 POUNDS
7.8000 g., 0.5830 Gold 0.2505 oz. AGW, 24.9 mm. **Ruler:** Elizabeth II **Subject:** Royal Heritage - Elizabeth I 1558-1603 **Obv:** Crowned bust right **Rev:** Bust with high ruffled collar 3/4 facing, dates below **Edge:** Reeded

Date	Mintage	F	VF	XF	Unc	BU
1998 Proof	—	Value: 175				

KM# 126 2 POUNDS
7.8000 g., 0.5830 Gold 0.2505 oz. AGW, 24.9 mm. **Ruler:** Elizabeth II **Obv:** Crowned bust right **Rev:** Charles I 1625-49 **Edge:** Reeded

Date	Mintage	F	VF	XF	Unc	BU
1998 Proof	—	Value: 175				

KM# 127 2 POUNDS
7.8000 g., 0.5830 Gold 0.2505 oz. AGW, 24.9 mm. **Ruler:** Elizabeth II **Obv:** Crowned bust right **Rev:** Victoria 1837-1901 **Edge:** Reeded

Date	Mintage	F	VF	XF	Unc	BU
1998 Proof	—	Value: 175				

KM# 61 2 POUNDS
Copper-Nickel **Ruler:** Elizabeth II **Subject:** Flying Doctor Service **Obv:** Crowned bust right **Rev:** Two airplanes in flight, denomination below

Date	Mintage	F	VF	XF	Unc	BU
1998	—	—	—	—	8.50	—

KM# 61a 2 POUNDS
28.2800 g., 0.9250 Silver .8411 oz. ASW **Ruler:** Elizabeth II **Subject:** Flying Doctor Service **Obv:** Crowned bust right **Rev:** Two airplanes in flight

Date	Mintage	F	VF	XF	Unc	BU
1998 Proof	Est. 10,000	Value: 50.00				

KM# 128 2 POUNDS
7.6700 g., 0.5830 Gold 0.1438 oz. AGW, 24.9 mm. **Ruler:** Elizabeth II **Obv:** Crowned bust right, date below **Rev:** Queen Mother holding the baby within circle, denomination below **Edge:** Reeded

Date	Mintage	F	VF	XF	Unc	BU
1998 Proof	—	Value: 150				

KM# 64 2 POUNDS
Copper-Nickel **Ruler:** Elizabeth II **Subject:** Sir Ernest Henry Shackleton **Obv:** Crowned bust right **Rev:** Cameo portrait and icebound ship "Endurance", denomination below divides dates

Date	Mintage	F	VF	XF	Unc	BU
1999	—	—	—	—	8.50	—

KM# 64a 2 POUNDS
28.2800 g., 0.9250 Silver .8411 oz. ASW **Ruler:** Elizabeth II **Subject:** Sir Ernest Henry Shackleton **Obv:** Crowned bust right **Rev:** Cameo portrait and icebound ship "Endurance"

Date	Mintage	F	VF	XF	Unc	BU
1999 Proof	Est. 10,000	Value: 50.00				

KM# 69 2 POUNDS
28.2800 g., Bi-Metallic Copper-Nickel center in Nickel-Brass ring, 38.61 mm. **Ruler:** Elizabeth II **Obv:** Crowned bust right **Rev:** Island map, radiant sun and denomination within circle of wildlife **Rev. Designer:** Matthew Bonaccorsi **Edge:** Plain

Date	Mintage	F	VF	XF	Unc	BU
1999	—	—	—	—	10.00	—
1999 Proof	2,500	Value: 20.00				

KM# 69a 2 POUNDS
28.1500 g., 0.9250 Bi-Metallic Silver center in Gold-plated Silver ring 0.8372 oz., 38.61 mm. **Ruler:** Elizabeth II **Obv:** Crowned bust right within circle, dates below **Rev:** Islands map, radiant sun, and denomination within circle of local wildlife **Rev. Designer:** Matthew Bonaccorsi **Edge:** Reeded

Date	Mintage	F	VF	XF	Unc	BU
1999-2000 Proof	—	Value: 55.00				

KM# 85 2 POUNDS
28.4000 g., 0.9250 Silver with gold gilt outer ring 0.8446 oz. ASW, 38.4 mm. **Ruler:** Elizabeth II **Subject:** Queen Mother **Obv:** Crowned bust right within beaded circle, date below **Rev:** Queen Mother holding baby and date within beaded circle, denomination below **Edge:** Reeded

Date	Mintage	F	VF	XF	Unc	BU
2000 Proof	10,000	Value: 50.00				

KM# 67 2 POUNDS
28.2800 g., Copper-Nickel **Ruler:** Elizabeth II **Subject:** The Gold Rush - "Vicar of Bray" Ship **Obv:** Crowned bust right, date below **Rev:** Ship in harbor, denomination below **Edge:** Reeded

Date	Mintage	F	VF	XF	Unc	BU
2000	—	—	—	—	8.50	—

KM# 67a 2 POUNDS
28.2800 g., 0.9250 Silver .8411 oz. ASW **Ruler:** Elizabeth II **Subject:** The Gold Rush - "Vicar of Bray" Ship **Obv:** Crowned bust right **Rev:** Ship in harbor, denomination below **Edge:** Reeded

Date	Mintage	F	VF	XF	Unc	BU
2000 Proof	10,000	Value: 47.50				

KM# 9 5 POUNDS
39.9400 g., 0.9170 Gold 1.1773 oz. AGW **Ruler:** Elizabeth II **Obv:** Young bust right **Rev:** Romney marsh sheep left, date above **Rev. Designer:** William Gardner

Date	Mintage	F	VF	XF	Unc	BU
1974 Proof	2,158	Value: 1,150				

KM# 11 5 POUNDS
28.2800 g., 0.9250 Silver .8411 oz. ASW **Ruler:** Elizabeth II **Subject:** Conservation **Obv:** Young bust right **Rev:** Humpback whale

Date	Mintage	F	VF	XF	Unc	BU
1979	3,998	—	—	—	30.00	—
1979 Proof	3,432	Value: 45.00				

KM# 27 5 POUNDS
Copper-Nickel **Ruler:** Elizabeth II **Subject:** 90th Birthday of Queen Mother **Obv:** Crowned bust right, denomination below **Rev:** Crowned monogram, flowers flank, dates below

Date	Mintage	F	VF	XF	Unc	BU
1990	—	—	—	—	17.50	—

KM# 27a 5 POUNDS
28.2800 g., 0.9250 Silver .8411 oz. ASW **Ruler:** Elizabeth II **Subject:** 90th Birthday of Queen Mother **Obv:** Crowned bust right, denomination below **Rev:** Flowers flank crowned monogram, dates below

Date	Mintage	F	VF	XF	Unc	BU
1990 Proof	Est. 10,000	Value: 37.50				

KM# 33 5 POUNDS
39.9400 g., 0.9170 Gold 1.1773 oz. AGW **Ruler:** Elizabeth II **Subject:** 10th Wedding Anniversary - Prince Charles and Lady Diana **Obv:** Crowned bust right **Rev:** Facing cameo portraits of Prince Charles and Princess Diana

Date	Mintage	F	VF	XF	Unc	BU
1991 Proof	Est. 200	Value: 900				

KM# 36 5 POUNDS
Copper-Nickel **Ruler:** Elizabeth II **Subject:** 10th Anniversary of Liberation **Obv:** Crowned bust right **Rev:** Statue at center, inscription at right within 1/2 wreath

Date	Mintage	F	VF	XF	Unc	BU
1992	—	—	—	—	15.00	—

KM# 36a 5 POUNDS
28.2800 g., 0.9250 Silver .8411 oz. ASW **Ruler:** Elizabeth II **Subject:** 10th Anniversary of Liberation **Obv:** Crowned bust right **Rev:** Statue at center, inscription at right

Date	Mintage	F	VF	XF	Unc	BU
1992 Proof	Est. 5,000	Value: 42.50				

KM# 36b 5 POUNDS
39.9400 g., 0.9170 Gold 1.1773 oz. AGW **Ruler:** Elizabeth II **Subject:** 10th Anniversary of Liberation **Obv:** Crowned bust right **Rev:** Statue at center, inscription at right

Date	Mintage	F	VF	XF	Unc	BU
1992 Proof	100	Value: 1,100				

KM# 37 5 POUNDS
28.2800 g., 0.9250 Silver .8411 oz. ASW **Ruler:** Elizabeth II **Subject:** 400th Anniversary of Discovery - Ship "Desire" **Obv:** Crowned bust right **Rev:** Map above ship, "Desire" at sea, dates at right

Date	Mintage	F	VF	XF	Unc	BU
ND(1992) Proof	Est. 20,000	Value: 40.00				

KM# 63 5 POUNDS
Copper-Nickel **Ruler:** Elizabeth II **Subject:** Queen's Golden Wedding Anniversary **Obv:** Crowned bust right **Rev:** Royal couple with gold inlay shield, dates at right

Date	Mintage	F	VF	XF	Unc	BU
1997	—	—	—	—	20.00	—

KM# 63a 5 POUNDS
28.2800 g., 0.9250 Silver 0.841 oz. ASW, 38.6 mm. **Ruler:** Elizabeth II **Subject:** Queen's Golden Wedding Anniversary **Obv:** Crowned bust right **Rev:** Royal couple with gold inlay shield **Edge:** Reeded

Date	Mintage	F	VF	XF	Unc	BU
1997 Proof	—	Value: 45.00				

KM# 12 10 POUNDS
35.0000 g., 0.9250 Silver 1.0409 oz. ASW **Ruler:** Elizabeth II **Subject:** Conservation **Obv:** Young bust right **Rev:** Flightless steamer ducks, denomination below, date at right

Date	Mintage	F	VF	XF	Unc	BU
1979	3,996	—	—	—	35.00	—
1979 Proof	3,247	Value: 50.00				

KM# 28 10 POUNDS
3.1300 g., 0.9990 Gold .1000 oz. AGW **Ruler:** Elizabeth II **Subject:** 90th Birthday of Queen Mother **Obv:** Crowned bust right **Rev:** Crowned arms with supporters, dates below

Date	Mintage	F	VF	XF	Unc	BU
ND(1990) Proof	Est. 750	Value: 85.00				

KM# 38 10 POUNDS
3.1300 g., 0.9990 Gold .1000 oz. AGW **Ruler:** Elizabeth II **Subject:** 400th Anniversary of Discovery - Ship "Desire" **Obv:** Crowned bust right **Rev:** Map above ship "Desire" at sea, dates at right

Date	Mintage	F	VF	XF	Unc	BU
ND(1992) Proof	Est. 400	Value: 75.00				

KM# 62 20 POUNDS
6.2200 g., 0.9990 Gold .2000 oz. AGW **Ruler:** Elizabeth II **Subject:** Flying Doctor Service **Obv:** Crowned bust right **Rev:** Two airplanes in flight

Date	Mintage	F	VF	XF	Unc	BU
1998 Proof	Est. 1,000	Value: 180				

KM# 65 20 POUNDS
6.2200 g., 0.9990 Gold .2000 oz. AGW **Ruler:** Elizabeth II **Subject:** Sir Ernest H. Shackleton **Obv:** Crowned bust right **Rev:** Cameo portrait and icebound ship

Date	Mintage	F	VF	XF	Unc	BU
1999 Proof	Est. 1,000	Value: 180				

KM# 68 20 POUNDS
6.2200 g., 0.9990 Gold .2000 oz. AGW **Ruler:** Elizabeth II **Subject:** The Gold Rush **Obv:** Crowned bust right **Rev:** "Vicar of Bray" in harbor **Edge:** Reeded

Date	Mintage	F	VF	XF	Unc	BU
2000 Proof	1,000	Value: 180				

KM# 20 25 POUNDS
150.0000 g., 0.9250 Silver 4.4614 oz. ASW **Ruler:** Elizabeth II **Subject:** 100 Years of Self Sufficiency **Obv:** Crowned bust right **Rev:** S.S. Great Britain a steam and sailing ship which was scuttled in the Falkland Islands, dates below **Rev. Designer:** Michael Hibbit

Date	Mintage	F	VF	XF	Unc	BU
ND(1985) Proof	Est. 20,000	Value: 70.00				

KM# 23 25 POUNDS
150.0000 g., 0.9250 Silver 4.4614 oz. ASW **Ruler:** Elizabeth II **Subject:** Prince Andrew's Wedding **Obv:** Crowned bust right **Rev:** Profiles of Prince Andrew and Sarah Ferguson facing, date above **Rev. Designer:** Robert Elderton

Date	Mintage	F	VF	XF	Unc	BU
1986 Proof	Est. 20,000	Value: 60.00				

KM# 29 25 POUNDS
7.8100 g., 0.9990 Gold .2500 oz. AGW **Ruler:** Elizabeth II **Subject:** 90th Birthday of Queen Mother **Obv:** Crowned bust right **Rev:** Queen Mother head left, within wreath and flowers, dates below

Date	Mintage	F	VF	XF	Unc	BU
ND(1990) Proof	Est. 750	Value: 220				

KM# 40 25 POUNDS
7.8100 g., 0.9990 Gold .2500 oz. AGW **Ruler:** Elizabeth II **Subject:** 100th Anniversary of Christchurch Cathedral **Obv:** Crowned bust right, denomination below **Rev:** Cathedral, cross, scepter, and mitre, dates at left

Date	Mintage	F	VF	XF	Unc	BU
1992 Proof	Est. 400	Value: 185				

KM# 39 25 POUNDS
155.5800 g., 0.9990 Silver 4.9970 oz. ASW **Ruler:** Elizabeth II **Subject:** 400th Anniversary - First Sighting of Falkland Islands **Obv:** Crowned bust right **Rev:** Map above ship at sea, dates at right

Date	Mintage	F	VF	XF	Unc	BU
ND(1992) Proof	Est. 3,000	Value: 200				

KM# 30 50 POUNDS
15.6100 g., 0.9990 Gold .5000 oz. AGW **Ruler:** Elizabeth II **Subject:** 90th Birthday of Queen Mother **Obv:** Crowned bust right

Date	Mintage	F	VF	XF	Unc	BU
ND(1990) Proof	Est. 750	Value: 360				

KM# 41 50 POUNDS
15.6100 g., 0.9990 Gold .5000 oz. AGW **Ruler:** Elizabeth II **Subject:** 100th Anniversary of Defense **Obv:** Crowned bust right **Rev:** Soldier with shield, dates at right

Date	Mintage	F	VF	XF	Unc	BU
ND(1992) Proof	Est. 400	Value: 345				

KM# 44 50 POUNDS
47.5400 g., 0.9170 Gold 1.4013 oz. AGW **Ruler:** Elizabeth II **Subject:** 40th Anniversary - Coronation of Queen Elizabeth II

Date	Mintage	F	VF	XF	Unc	BU
ND(1993) Proof	Est. 100	Value: 1,150				

KM# 31 100 POUNDS
31.2100 g., 0.9990 Gold 1.0000 oz. AGW **Ruler:** Elizabeth II **Subject:** 90th Birthday of Queen Mother **Obv:** Crowned bust right **Rev:** Queen Mother's head left, within wreath and flowers, dates below

Date	Mintage	F	VF	XF	Unc	BU
ND(1990) Proof	Est. 750	Value: 725				

KM# 42 100 POUNDS
31.2100 g., 0.9990 Gold 1.0000 oz. AGW **Ruler:** Elizabeth II **Subject:** 400th Anniversary of Discovery - Ship "Desire' **Obv:** Crowned bust right **Rev:** Map above ship "Desire" at sea, dates at right

Date	Mintage	F	VF	XF	Unc	BU
ND(1992) Proof	Est. 400	Value: 710				

KM# 13 150 POUNDS
33.4370 g., 0.9000 Gold .9676 oz. AGW **Ruler:** Elizabeth II **Subject:** Conservation **Obv:** Young bust right **Rev:** Falkland Fur Seal, denomination below, date at right

Date	Mintage	F	VF	XF	Unc	BU
1979	488	—	—	—	765	—
1979 Proof	164	Value: 1,600				

PIEFORTS

KM#	Date	Mintage	Identification	Mkt Val
P1	1987	2,500	Pound. 0.9250 Silver. KM24a.	42.50
P2	1992	750	50 Pence. 0.9250 Silver. KM34a	60.00
P3	1995	—	50 Pence. 0.9250 Silver. KM48a	85.00

MINT SETS

KM#	Date	Mintage	Identification	Issue Price	Mkt Val
MS1	1987 (7)	—	KM2-3, 4.1-5.1, 14.1, 17, 24	10.00	12.00
MS2	1992 (8)	—	KM2-3, 4.1-5.1, 14.1, 17, 24, 35	24.50	25.00
MS3	1999 (8)	—	KM2a-3a, 4.2-5.2, 14.2, 17, 24, 69	20.00	22.50

PROOF SETS

KM#	Date	Mintage	Identification	Issue Price	Mkt Val
PS1	1974 (5)	20,000	KM1-3, 4.1-5.1	12.00	15.50
PS2	1974 (4)	2,000	KM6-9	1,100	2,000
PS3	1979 (2)	10,000	KM11-12	—	115
PS4	1980 (6)	10,000	KM1-3, 4.1-5.1, 14.1	35.00	20.00
PS5	1982 (8)	5,000	KM1-3, 4.1-5.1, 14.1, 17, 18a	—	45.00
PS6	1982 (7)	5,000	KM1-3, 4.1-5.1, 14.1, 17	—	27.50
PS7	1987 (7)	2,500	KM2-3, 4.1-5.1, 14.1, 17, 24	35.00	40.00
PS8	1990 (4)	750	KM28-31	1,595	1,150
PS9	1992 (8)	2,500	KM2-3, 4.1-5.1, 14.1, 17, 24, 35a	89.50	90.00
PS10	1992 (4)	400	KM38, 40-42	1,595	1,075
PS11	1999 (8)	2,500	KM2a-3a, 4.2-5.2, 14.2, 17, 24, 69	50.00	55.00

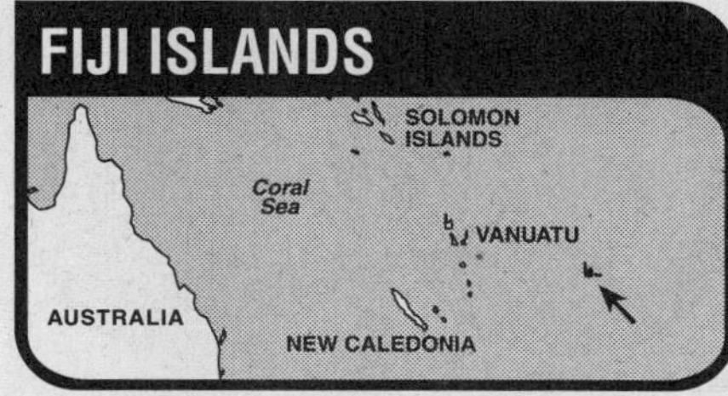

The Republic of Fiji, consists of about 320 islands located in the southwestern Pacific 1,100 miles (1,770 km.) north of New Zealand. The islands have a combined area of 7,056 sq. mi. (18,274 sq. km.) and a population of 772,891. Capital: Suva. Fiji's economy is based on agriculture and mining. Sugar, coconut products, manganese, and gold are exported.

The first European to sight Fiji was the Dutch navigator Abel Tasman in 1643 and the islands were visited by British naval captain James Cook in 1774. The first complete survey of the island was conducted by the United States in 1840. Settlement by mercenaries from Tonga, and traders attracted by the sandalwood trade, began in 1801. Following a lengthy period of intertribal warfare, the islands were unconditionally ceded to Great Britain in 1874 by King Cakobau. Fiji became a sovereign and independent nation on Oct. 10, 1970, the 96th anniversary of the cession of the islands to Queen Victoria.

Fiji was declared a Republic in 1987 following two military coups. It left the British Commonwealth and Queen Elizabeth ceased to be the Head of State. A new constitution was introduced in 1991. The country returned to the Commonwealth in 1997 with a revised constitution.

RULERS
British until 1970

MINT MARKS
(c) - Australian Mint, Canberra
(H) – The Mint, Birmingham
(l) – Royal Mint, Llatrisant
(o) - Royal Canadian Mint, Ottawa
S - San Francisco, U.S.A.

MONETARY SYSTEM
12 Pence = 1 Shilling
2 Shillings = 1 Florin
20 Shillings = 1 Pound

REPUBLIC

British Administration until 1970

POUND STERLING COINAGE

KM# 1 1/2 PENNY

Copper-Nickel **Ruler:** George V **Obv:** Crown above center hole **Rev:** Center hole divides date, denomination above

Date	Mintage	F	VF	XF	Unc	BU
1934	96,000	0.75	1.75	4.00	15.00	20.00
1934 Proof	—	—	—	—	—	—

KM# 14 1/2 PENNY

Copper-Nickel **Ruler:** George VI **Obv:** Crown above center hole **Rev:** Center hole divides date, denomination above

Date	Mintage	F	VF	XF	Unc	BU
1940	24,000	2.50	7.50	12.50	30.00	50.00
1940 Proof	—	Value: 350				
1941 Proof	—	Value: 200				
1941	96,000	0.75	1.50	4.00	10.00	20.00

KM# 14a 1/2 PENNY

Brass **Ruler:** George VI **Obv:** Crown above center hole **Rev:** Center hole divides date, denomination above

Date	Mintage	F	VF	XF	Unc	BU
1942S	250,000	—	0.35	2.50	10.00	20.00
1943S	250,000	—	0.35	2.50	12.50	20.00

KM# 16 1/2 PENNY

Copper-Nickel **Ruler:** George VI **Obv:** Crown above center hole, EMPEROR dropped from legend **Rev:** Center hole divides date, denomination above

Date	Mintage	F	VF	XF	Unc	BU
1949	—	Value: 210				
1949	96,000	—	0.50	2.00	7.50	12.50
1950	115,000	—	0.35	1.50	6.00	10.00
1950 Proof	—	Value: 230				
1951 Proof	—	Value: 190				
1951	115,000	—	0.35	1.50	5.00	7.50
1952	228,000	—	0.25	0.75	1.50	2.00
1952 Proof	—	—	—	—	—	—

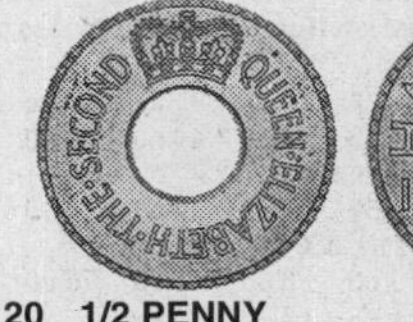

KM# 20 1/2 PENNY

Copper-Nickel **Obv:** Crown above center hole **Rev:** Center hole divides date, denomination above

Date	Mintage	F	VF	XF	Unc	BU
1954	228,000	—	0.25	0.50	1.00	1.50
1954 Proof	—	Value: 180				

KM# 2 PENNY

Copper-Nickel, 26 mm. **Ruler:** George V **Obv:** Crown above center hole **Rev:** Center hole divides date, denomination below

Date	Mintage	F	VF	XF	Unc	BU
1934	480,000	0.50	1.00	5.00	12.50	22.50
1934 Proof	—	—	—	—	—	—
1935 Proof	—	—	—	—	—	—
1935	240,000	0.65	1.25	5.00	15.00	25.00
1936	240,000	0.65	1.25	5.00	17.50	27.50
1936 Proof	—	—	—	—	—	—

KM# 6 PENNY

Copper-Nickel, 26 mm. **Ruler:** Edward VIII **Obv:** Crown above center hole **Rev:** Center hole divides date, denomination below

Date	Mintage	F	VF	XF	Unc	BU
1936	120,000	0.50	1.00	2.00	4.00	7.50
1936 Proof	—	Value: 225				

KM# 7 PENNY

Copper-Nickel, 26 mm. **Ruler:** George VI **Obv:** Crown above center hole **Rev:** Center hole divides cate, denomination below

Date	Mintage	F	VF	XF	Unc	BU
1937	360,000	0.50	1.00	3.00	7.50	12.50
1937 Proof	—	Value: 225				
1940	144,000	1.50	3.00	15.00	45.00	75.00
1940 Proof	—	Value: 225				
1941	228,000	0.50	1.00	2.00	10.00	15.00
1941 Proof	—	Value: 225				
1945	240,000	1.00	2.00	6.00	15.00	25.00
1945 Proof	—	Value: 225				

KM# 7a PENNY

Brass, 26 mm. **Ruler:** George VI **Obv:** Crown above center hole **Rev:** Center hole divides date, denomination below

Date	Mintage	F	VF	XF	Unc	BU
1942S	1,000,000	0.25	1.00	3.50	10.00	20.00
1943S	1,000,000	0.25	1.00	3.50	7.50	20.00

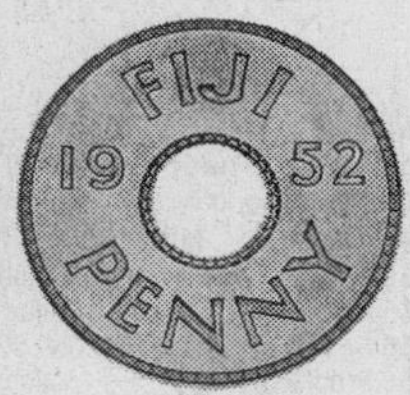

KM# 17 PENNY

Copper-Nickel, 26 mm. **Ruler:** George VI **Obv:** Crown above center hole, "EMPEROR" dropped from legend **Rev:** Center hole divides date, denomination below

Date	Mintage	F	VF	XF	Unc	BU
1949 Proof	—	Value: 325				
1949	120,000	0.25	0.50	1.00	4.50	7.50
1950	58,000	1.50	3.50	12.50	65.00	100
1950 Proof	—	Value: 200				
1952 Proof	—	Value: 175				
1952	230,000	0.25	0.50	1.00	3.75	7.00

KM# 21 PENNY

Copper-Nickel, 26 mm. **Ruler:** Elizabeth II **Obv:** Crown above center hole **Rev:** Center hole divides date, denomination below

Date	Mintage	F	VF	XF	Unc	BU
1954	511,000	0.20	0.50	1.00	3.00	4.50
1954 Proof	—	Value: 175				
1955	230,000	0.20	0.50	1.25	5.00	9.00
1955 Proof	—	Value: 175				
1956 Proof	—	Value: 175				
1956	230,000	0.20	0.50	1.25	3.50	7.50
1957	360,000	0.10	0.25	0.75	3.00	7.00
1957 Proof	—	Value: 175				
1959	864,000	—	0.20	0.35	2.00	3.50
1959 Proof	—	Value: 175				
1961	432,000	0.15	0.35	0.50	1.25	3.00
1961 Proof	—	Value: 175				
1963 Proof	—	Value: 175				
1963	432,000	0.15	0.35	0.50	1.25	3.00
1964 Proof	—	Value: 150				
1964	864,000	—	0.15	0.25	0.85	2.00
1965	1,440,000	—	—	0.20	0.75	2.00
1966	720,000	—	—	0.20	0.85	2.50
1967	720,000	—	—	0.20	0.75	1.50
1968	720,000	—	—	0.20	0.75	1.50

KM# 15 THREEPENCE

Nickel-Brass **Ruler:** George VI **Obv:** Crowned head left **Rev:** Native dwelling, date above, denomination below **Shape:** 12-sided

Date	Mintage	F	VF	XF	Unc	BU
1947	450,000	1.50	2.50	6.00	20.00	45.00
1947 Proof	—	Value: 190				

KM# 18 THREEPENCE

Nickel-Brass **Ruler:** George VI **Obv:** Crowned head left, EMPEROR dropped from legend **Rev:** Native dwelling, date above, denomination below **Shape:** 12-sided

Date	Mintage	F	VF	XF	Unc	BU
1950	450,000	0.50	1.00	4.00	15.00	25.00
1950 Proof	—	Value: 190				
1952 Proof	—	Value: 190				
1952	400,000	0.50	1.00	5.00	22.50	35.00

KM# 22 THREEPENCE
Nickel-Brass **Ruler:** Elizabeth II **Obv:** Crowned head right **Rev:** Native dwelling, date above, denomination below **Shape:** 12-sided

Date	Mintage	F	VF	XF	Unc	BU
1955	400,000	0.50	1.00	4.00	17.50	35.00
1955 Proof	—	Value: 130				
1956	200,000	0.50	1.00	4.00	20.00	40.00
1956 Proof	—	Value: 155				
1958	200,000	0.50	1.00	4.00	20.00	40.00
1958 Proof	—	Value: 140				
1960	240,000	0.25	0.50	3.00	8.50	15.00
1960 Proof	—	Value: 125				
1961 Proof	—	Value: 125				
1961	240,000	0.25	0.50	1.25	6.00	12.50
1963	240,000	0.15	0.30	0.75	5.00	10.00
1963 Proof	—	Value: 115				
1964	240,000	0.15	0.30	0.50	2.00	5.00
1965	800,000	—	0.15	0.25	1.50	3.50
1967	800,000	—	0.15	0.25	1.50	3.50

KM# 3 SIXPENCE
2.8276 g., 0.5000 Silver .0455 oz. ASW, 19.5 mm. **Ruler:** George V **Obv:** Crowned bust left **Rev:** Sea turtle divides date, denomination below

Date	Mintage	F	VF	XF	Unc	BU
1934	160,000	1.25	2.50	10.00	35.00	45.00
1934 Proof	—	Value: 450				
1935 Proof	—	Value: 350				
1935	120,000	1.50	3.50	12.50	45.00	55.00
1936	40,000	2.00	4.00	15.00	55.00	70.00
1936 Proof	—	Value: 350				

KM# 8 SIXPENCE
2.8276 g., 0.5000 Silver .0455 oz. ASW, 19.5 mm. **Ruler:** George VI **Obv:** Crowned head left **Rev:** Sea turtle divides date, denomination below

Date	Mintage	F	VF	XF	Unc	BU
1937 Proof	—	Value: 400				
1937	40,000	2.00	4.00	16.00	50.00	75.00

KM# 11 SIXPENCE
2.8276 g., 0.5000 Silver .0455 oz. ASW, 19.5 mm. **Ruler:** George VI **Obv:** Smaller head **Rev:** Sea turtle divides date, denomination below

Date	Mintage	F	VF	XF	Unc	BU
1938	40,000	2.00	4.00	13.50	45.00	60.00
1938 Proof	—	Value: 500				
1940	40,000	2.00	4.00	13.50	45.00	60.00
1940 Proof	—	Value: 350				
1941	40,000	3.00	8.00	20.00	60.00	85.00
1941 Proof	—	Value: 350				

KM# 11a SIXPENCE
2.8276 g., 0.9000 Silver .0818 oz. ASW, 19.5 mm. **Ruler:** George VI **Obv:** Crowned head left **Rev:** Sea turtle divides date, denomination below

Date	Mintage	F	VF	XF	Unc	BU
1942S	400,000	—	1.25	2.50	6.50	8.50
1943S	400,000	—	1.25	2.50	6.50	8.50

KM# 19 SIXPENCE
Copper-Nickel, 19.5 mm. **Ruler:** Elizabeth II **Obv:** Crowned head right **Rev:** Sea turtle divides date, denomination below

Date	Mintage	F	VF	XF	Unc	BU
1953 Proof	—	Value: 210				
1953	800,000	0.25	0.50	1.00	3.00	7.50
1958	400,000	0.25	0.50	1.50	4.50	8.00
1958 Proof	—	Value: 200				
1961 Proof	—	Value: 200				
1961	400,000	0.25	0.50	1.00	3.50	7.00
1962	400,000	0.25	0.50	1.00	3.00	7.00
1962 Proof	—	Value: 200				
1965	800,000	0.15	0.30	1.00	2.50	6.00
1967	800,000	0.15	0.30	1.00	2.50	6.00

KM# 4 SHILLING
5.6552 g., 0.5000 Silver .0909 oz. ASW, 23.5 mm. **Ruler:** George V **Obv:** Crowned bust left **Rev:** Outrigger divides dates, denomination above

Date	Mintage	F	VF	XF	Unc	BU
1934	360,000	1.50	4.00	14.50	60.00	75.00
1934 Proof	—	Value: 650				
1935	180,000	1.50	4.00	14.50	75.00	90.00
1935 Proof	—	Value: 550				
1936	140,000	1.50	6.00	15.50	75.00	90.00
1936 Proof	—	—	—	—	—	—

KM# 9 SHILLING
5.6552 g., 0.5000 Silver .0909 oz. ASW, 23.5 mm. **Ruler:** George VI **Obv:** Crowned head left **Rev:** Outrigger divides dates, denomination above

Date	Mintage	F	VF	XF	Unc	BU
1937 Proof	—	Value: 500				
1937	40,000	1.50	7.00	17.50	80.00	100

KM# 12 SHILLING
5.6552 g., 0.5000 Silver .0909 oz. ASW, 23.5 mm. **Ruler:** George VI **Obv:** Smaller head **Rev:** Outrigger divides date, denomination above

Date	Mintage	F	VF	XF	Unc	BU
1938	40,000	1.50	7.00	17.50	80.00	100
1938 Proof	—	Value: 450				
1941	40,000	1.50	7.00	17.50	80.00	100
1941 Proof	—	Value: 450				

KM# 12a SHILLING
5.6552 g., 0.9000 Silver .1636 oz. ASW, 23.5 mm. **Ruler:** George VI **Obv:** Crowned head left **Rev:** Outrigger divides date, denomination above

Date	Mintage	F	VF	XF	Unc	BU
1942S	500,000	—	2.50	3.50	7.50	10.00
1943S	500,000	—	2.50	3.50	7.50	10.00

KM# 23 SHILLING
Copper-Nickel, 23.5 mm. **Ruler:** Elizabeth II **Obv:** Crowned head right **Rev:** Outrigger divides date, denomination above

Date	Mintage	F	VF	XF	Unc	BU
1957	400,000	0.50	0.75	2.00	10.00	12.50
1957 Proof	—	Value: 350				
1958	400,000	0.50	0.75	2.25	10.00	12.50
1958 Proof	—	Value: 300				
1961	200,000	0.75	1.00	2.25	7.50	10.00
1961 Proof	—	Value: 275				
1962	400,000	0.35	0.75	1.25	4.00	6.50
1962 Proof	—	Value: 250				
1965	800,000	0.25	0.50	0.75	2.00	3.50

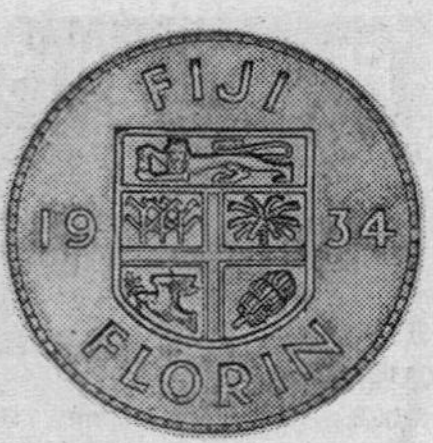

KM# 5 FLORIN
11.3104 g., 0.5000 Silver .1818 oz. ASW **Ruler:** George V **Obv:** Crowned bust left **Rev:** Shield of arms divides date, denomination below

Date	Mintage	F	VF	XF	Unc	BU
1934 Proof	—	Value: 750				
1934	200,000	2.50	4.50	17.50	125	145
1935	50,000	2.75	9.00	20.00	190	210
1935 Proof	—	Value: 700				
1936	65,000	2.75	9.00	20.00	170	190
1936 Proof	—	Value: 725				

KM# 10 FLORIN
11.3104 g., 0.5000 Silver .1818 oz. ASW **Ruler:** George VI **Obv:** Crowned head left **Rev:** Shield of arms divides date, denomination below

Date	Mintage	F	VF	XF	Unc	BU
1937	30,000	2.65	7.00	17.50	150	170
1937 Proof	—	Value: 850				

KM# 13 FLORIN
11.3104 g., 0.5000 Silver .1818 oz. ASW **Ruler:** George VI **Obv:** Smaller head **Rev:** Shield of arms divides dates, denomination below

Date	Mintage	F	VF	XF	Unc	BU
1938	20,000	4.00	12.00	25.00	185	215
1938 Proof	—	Value: 750				
1941	20,000	4.00	12.00	25.00	185	215
1941 Proof	—	Value: 775				
1945	100,000	9.00	20.00	35.00	230	275
1945 Proof	—	Value: 750				

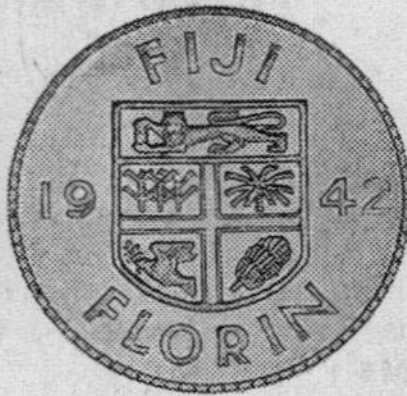

KM# 13a FLORIN
11.3104 g., 0.9000 Silver .3273 oz. ASW **Ruler:** George VI **Obv:** Crowned head left **Rev:** Shield of arms divides date, denomination below

Date	Mintage	F	VF	XF	Unc	BU
1942S	250,000	—	4.50	6.00	12.50	17.50
1943S	250,000	—	4.50	6.50	15.00	20.00

Note: BU coins must display full face of leopard at top of arms

KM# 24 FLORIN
Copper-Nickel **Ruler:** Elizabeth II **Obv:** Crowned head right **Rev:** Shield of arms divides date, denomination below

Date	Mintage	F	VF	XF	Unc	BU
1957	300,000	0.50	1.00	4.00	15.00	20.00
1957 Proof	—	Value: 375				
1958	220,000	0.50	1.00	4.00	15.00	20.00
1958 Proof	—	Value: 375				
1962	200,000	0.25	0.50	2.00	10.00	15.00
1962 Proof	—	Value: 375				
1964	200,000	0.25	0.50	1.50	5.00	10.00
1964 Proof	—	Value: 400				
1965	400,000	0.25	0.50	1.00	3.00	5.00

DECIMAL COINAGE

100 Cents = 1 Dollar

KM# 27 CENT

1.9000 g., Bronze, 17.5 mm. **Ruler:** Elizabeth II **Rev:** Tanoa kava bowl divides denomination **Rev. Designer:** Ken Payne

Date	Mintage	F	VF	XF	Unc	BU
1969(h)	11,000,000	—	—	0.10	0.20	1.00
1969 Proof	10,000	Value: 0.50				
1973(c)	3,000,000	—	—	0.10	0.50	2.00
1975(c)	2,064,000	—	—	0.10	0.50	1.00
1976(c)	—	—	—	0.10	0.50	1.00
1983(c)	3,000,000	—	—	0.10	0.50	1.00
1983 Proof	3,000	Value: 1.00				
1984(c)	2,295,000	—	—	0.10	0.35	1.00
1985(c)	—	—	—	0.10	0.35	1.00

KM# 27a CENT

2.2600 g., 0.9250 Silver .0672 oz. ASW, 17.5 mm. **Ruler:** Elizabeth II **Rev:** Tanoa kava bowl divides denomination

Date	Mintage	F	VF	XF	Unc	BU
1976 Proof	3,012	Value: 3.50				

KM# 39 CENT

1.9000 g., Bronze, 17.5 mm. **Ruler:** Elizabeth II **Series:** F.A.O. **Obv:** Young bust right **Rev:** Rice plant at left, denomination at right

Date	Mintage	F	VF	XF	Unc	BU
1977(c)	3,000,000	—	—	0.10	0.50	1.50
1978(c)	3,032,000	—	—	0.10	0.50	1.50
1978 Proof	2,000	Value: 2.50				
1979(c)	2,500,000	—	—	0.10	2.00	4.00
1980(c)	314,000	—	—	0.10	0.50	1.50
1980 Proof	2,500	Value: 1.50				
1981(c)	4,040,000	—	—	0.10	0.50	1.00
1982 Proof	3,000	Value: 1.00				
1982(c)	5,000,000	—	—	0.10	0.50	1.00

KM# 49 CENT

1.9000 g., Bronze, 17.5 mm. **Ruler:** Elizabeth II **Obv:** Crowned head right, date at right **Rev:** Tanoa kava bowl divides denomination **Rev. Designer:** Ken Payne

Date	Mintage	F	VF	XF	Unc	BU
1986(c)	3,400,000	—	—	0.10	0.50	1.00
1987(c)	3,400,000	—	—	0.15	0.50	1.00

KM# 49a CENT

Copper Plated Zinc, 17.5 mm. **Ruler:** Elizabeth II **Obv:** Crowned head right, date at right **Rev:** Tanoa kava bowl divides denomination

Date	Mintage	F	VF	XF	Unc	BU
1990(o)	8,500,000	—	—	0.10	0.25	0.75
1992(o)	16,200,000	—	—	0.10	0.25	0.75
1994(o)	7,800,000	—	—	—	0.25	0.75
1995(o)	6,000,000	—	—	—	0.25	2.00
1997(o)	12,000,000	—	—	—	0.25	1.00
1999(o)	14,000,000	—	—	—	0.25	0.75

KM# 28 2 CENTS

3.8500 g., Bronze, 21.1 mm. **Ruler:** Elizabeth II **Obv:** Young bust right, date at right **Rev:** Palm fan and denomination **Rev. Designer:** Ken Payne

Date	Mintage	F	VF	XF	Unc	BU
1969 Proof	10,000	Value: 0.75				
1969(h)	8,000,000	—	—	0.10	0.50	0.75
1973(c)	2,110,000	—	0.10	0.15	0.75	2.50
1975(c)	1,500,000	—	0.10	0.15	0.75	1.50
1976(c)	1,004,999	—	0.10	0.15	0.75	1.50
1977	1,250,000	—	—	0.10	0.75	1.50
1978 Proof	2,000	Value: 3.50				
1978(c)	1,502,000	—	—	0.10	0.75	1.50
1979(c)	500,000	—	—	0.10	2.50	5.00
1980(c)	4,019,999	—	—	0.10	1.00	1.75
1980 Proof	2,500	Value: 2.50				
1981(c)	3,250,000	—	—	0.10	1.00	2.00
1982(c)	4,000,000	—	—	0.10	1.00	1.75
1982 Proof	3,000	Value: 2.00				
1983(c)	3,000,000	—	—	0.10	0.75	1.75
1983 Proof	3,000	Value: 1.50				
1984(c)	1,845,000	—	—	0.10	0.75	1.75
1985(c)	1,700,000	—	—	0.10	0.75	2.00

KM# 28a 2 CENTS

4.5300 g., 0.9250 Silver .1347 oz. ASW, 21.1 mm. **Ruler:** Elizabeth II **Obv:** Young bust right **Rev:** Palm fan and denomination

Date	Mintage	F	VF	XF	Unc	BU
1976 Proof	3,012	Value: 4.50				

KM# 50 2 CENTS

3.8500 g., Bronze, 21.1 mm. **Ruler:** Elizabeth II **Obv:** Crowned head right, date at right **Rev:** Palm fan and denomination **Rev. Designer:** Ken Payne

Date	Mintage	F	VF	XF	Unc	BU
1986(c)	1,700,000	—	—	0.15	0.75	1.50
1987(c)	1,700,000	—	—	0.15	0.75	1.50

KM# 50a 2 CENTS

3.8500 g., Copper Plated Zinc, 21.1 mm. **Ruler:** Elizabeth II **Obv:** Crowned head right, date at right **Rev:** Palm fan and denomination

Date	Mintage	F	VF	XF	Unc	BU
1990(o)	5,500,000	—	—	—	0.75	1.00
1992(o)	10,000,000	—	—	—	0.50	1.00
1994(o)	6,000,000	—	—	—	0.35	2.00
1995(o)	5,000,000	—	—	—	0.35	1.00

KM# 29 5 CENTS

2.8000 g., Copper-Nickel, 19.35 mm. **Ruler:** Elizabeth II **Obv:** Young bust right, date at right **Rev:** Fijian drum - lali divides denomination **Rev. Designer:** Ken Payne

Date	Mintage	F	VF	XF	Unc	BU
1969 Proof	10,000	Value: 0.75				
1969(l)	9,200,000	—	0.10	0.20	0.75	1.00
1973(c)	600,000	—	0.10	0.30	1.50	2.00
1974(c)	608,000	—	0.10	0.30	1.25	2.00
1975(c)	1,008,000	—	0.10	0.20	1.00	2.00
1976(c)	1,205,000	—	0.10	0.20	1.00	2.00
1977	960,000	—	0.10	0.20	1.00	2.00
1978(c)	880,000	—	0.10	0.20	1.00	2.00
1978 Proof	2,000	Value: 5.00				
1979(c)	1,500,000	—	0.10	0.25	2.00	4.50
1980(c)	2,506,000	—	0.10	0.15	1.00	1.50
1980 Proof	2,500	Value: 3.50				
1981(c)	1,980,000	—	0.10	0.15	1.00	1.50
1982 Proof	3,000	Value: 3.00				
1982(c)	2,700,000	—	0.10	0.15	1.00	1.50
1983 Proof	3,000	Value: 2.00				
1983(c)	3,000,000	—	0.10	0.15	1.00	1.50
1984(c)	5,005,000	—	0.10	0.20	1.00	1.50

KM# 29a 5 CENTS

3.2800 g., 0.9250 Silver .0975 oz. ASW, 19.35 mm. **Ruler:** Elizabeth II **Series:** F.A.O. **Obv:** Young bust right **Rev:** Fijian drum - lali divides denomination

Date	Mintage	F	VF	XF	Unc	BU
1976 Proof	3,012	Value: 6.00				

KM# 51 5 CENTS

2.8000 g., Copper-Nickel, 19.35 mm. **Ruler:** Elizabeth II **Obv:** Crowned head right, date at right **Rev:** Fijian drum - lali divides denomination **Rev. Designer:** Ken Payne

Date	Mintage	F	VF	XF	Unc	BU
1986(c)	1,200,000	—	0.10	0.20	1.00	1.50
1987(c)	1,200,000	—	0.10	0.20	1.00	2.00

KM# 51a 5 CENTS

Nickel Bonded Steel, 19.35 mm. **Ruler:** Elizabeth II **Obv:** Crowned head right **Rev:** Fijian drum - lali divides denomination

Date	Mintage	F	VF	XF	Unc	BU
1990(o)	4,000,000	—	—	—	1.00	1.50
1992(o)	7,700,000	—	—	—	0.75	1.00
1994(o)	500,000	—	—	—	0.75	1.00
1995	—	—	—	—	0.75	2.50
1997(l)	4,000,000	—	—	—	0.75	1.00
1998(l)	3,000,000	—	—	—	0.75	1.00
1999(l)	3,000,000	—	—	—	0.75	1.00
2000(l)	3,000,000	—	—	—	0.75	1.00

KM# 77 5 CENTS

Nickel Bonded Steel, 19.35 mm. **Ruler:** Elizabeth II **Series:** F.A.O. **Subject:** Harvest From the Sea **Obv:** Crowned head right, date at right **Rev:** Fish, F.A.O. logo below denomination

Date	Mintage	F	VF	XF	Unc	BU
1995(o)	300,000	—	—	—	1.00	1.50

KM# 30 10 CENTS

5.6000 g., Copper-Nickel, 23.6 mm. **Ruler:** Elizabeth II **Rev:** Throwing club - ula tava tava **Rev. Designer:** Ken Payne

Date	Mintage	F	VF	XF	Unc	BU
1969 Proof	10,000	Value: 1.00				
1969	3,500,000	—	0.20	0.40	1.00	1.50
1973	750,000	—	0.20	0.50	2.50	4.00
1975	752,000	—	0.20	0.50	1.75	3.00
1976	805,000	—	0.20	0.50	1.50	2.50
1977	240,000	—	0.25	0.65	1.50	2.50
1978 Proof	2,000	Value: 6.00				
1978	664,000	—	0.20	0.50	1.50	2.50
1979	702,000	—	0.20	0.50	1.50	2.50
1980 Proof	2,500	Value: 4.50				
1980	1,000,000	—	0.15	0.30	1.50	2.50
1981	1,200,000	—	0.20	0.50	1.25	2.00
1982	1,500,000	—	0.20	0.50	1.25	2.00
1982 Proof	3,000	Value: 4.00				
1983	3,003,000	—	0.25	0.65	1.25	2.00
1983 Proof	3,000	Value: 3.00				
1984	5,000,000	—	0.25	0.65	1.25	2.00
1985	660,000	—	0.20	0.50	1.25	2.00

KM# 30a 10 CENTS

6.5500 g., 0.9250 Silver .1948 oz. ASW, 23.6 mm. **Ruler:** Elizabeth II **Rev:** Throwing club - ula tava tava

Date	Mintage	F	VF	XF	Unc	BU
1976 Proof	3,012	Value: 6.50				

KM# 52 10 CENTS

5.6000 g., Copper-Nickel, 23.6 mm. **Ruler:** Elizabeth II **Obv:** Crowned head right, date at right **Rev:** Throwing club - ula tava tava divides denomination **Rev. Designer:** Ken Payne

Date	Mintage	F	VF	XF	Unc	BU
1986(c)	740,000	—	0.20	0.40	1.50	2.25
1987(c)	740,000	—	0.20	0.40	1.50	2.25

KM# 52a 10 CENTS

Nickel Bonded Steel, 23.6 mm. **Ruler:** Elizabeth II **Obv:** Crowned head right **Rev:** Throwing club - ula tava tava

Date	Mintage	F	VF	XF	Unc	BU
1990	2,000,000	—	—	—	1.25	1.75
1992	31,640,000	—	—	—	1.25	1.75
1994	1,000,000	—	—	—	1.25	1.75
1995	736,000	—	—	—	1.25	2.00
1996	1,000,000	—	—	—	1.25	2.50
1997	2,000,000	—	—	—	1.00	1.50
1998(l)	2,000,000	—	—	—	1.00	1.25
1999(l)	2,000,000	—	—	—	1.00	1.25
2000(l)	1,340,000	—	—	—	1.00	1.25

KM# 31 20 CENTS

11.2500 g., Copper-Nickel, 28.5 mm. **Ruler:** Elizabeth II **Obv:** Young bust right, date at right **Rev:** Tabua on braided sennit cord divides denomination **Rev. Designer:** Ken Payne

Date	Mintage	F	VF	XF	Unc	BU
1969	2,000,000	—	0.30	0.80	1.50	2.00
1969 Proof	10,000	Value: 1.75				
1973	250,000	—	0.35	1.00	2.25	3.00
1974	252,000	—	0.35	0.75	2.00	2.75
1975	352,000	—	0.35	0.75	3.00	4.50
1976	405,000	—	0.25	0.65	1.75	2.25
1977	200,000	—	0.35	0.75	3.50	4.00
1978	406,000	—	0.25	0.50	1.75	2.25
1978 Proof	2,000	Value: 8.00				
1979	500,000	—	0.25	0.60	1.75	2.25
1980 Proof	2,500	Value: 6.50				
1980	1,014,000	—	0.25	0.60	1.75	2.25

Date	Mintage	F	VF	XF	Unc	BU
1981	1,200,000	—	0.25	0.60	1.75	2.25
1982	1,500,000	—	0.25	0.60	1.50	2.00
1982 Proof	3,000	Value: 6.00				
1983 Proof	3,000	Value: 5.00				
1983	3,003,000	—	0.35	0.75	1.50	2.00
1984	5,005,000	—	0.35	0.75	1.50	2.00
1985	240,000	—	0.20	0.35	1.75	2.25

KM# 31a 20 CENTS

13.0900 g., 0.9250 Silver .3893 oz. ASW, 28.5 mm. **Ruler:** Elizabeth II **Obv:** Young bust right **Rev:** Tabua on braided sennit cord divides denomination

Date	Mintage	F	VF	XF	Unc	BU
1976 Proof	3,012	Value: 8.50				

KM# 53 20 CENTS

11.2500 g., Copper-Nickel, 28.5 mm. **Ruler:** Elizabeth II **Obv:** Crowned head right, date at right **Rev:** Tabua on braided sennit cord divides denomination **Rev. Designer:** Ken Payne

Date	Mintage	F	VF	XF	Unc	BU
1986(c)	360,000	—	0.25	0.60	2.00	2.50
1987(c)	360,000	—	0.25	0.60	2.00	2.50

KM# 53a 20 CENTS

11.2500 g., Nickel Bonded Steel, 28.5 mm. **Ruler:** Elizabeth II **Obv:** Crowned head right **Rev:** Tabua on braided sennit cord divides denomination

Date	Mintage	F	VF	XF	Unc	BU
1990	1,500,000	—	0.20	0.35	1.50	2.00
1992	1,000,000	—	0.20	0.35	1.75	3.50
1994	500,000	—	0.20	0.35	1.50	3.00
1995	200,000	—	0.20	0.35	1.50	2.00
1996(l)	1,000,000	—	0.20	0.35	1.25	1.50
1997(l)	153,000	—	0.20	0.35	1.50	3.00
1998	1,000,000	—	0.20	0.35	1.25	1.50
1999(l)	1,000,000	—	0.20	0.35	1.25	1.50
2000(l)	1,000,000	—	0.20	0.35	1.25	1.50

KM# 36 50 CENTS

15.5500 g., Copper-Nickel, 31.5 mm. **Ruler:** Elizabeth II **Obv:** Young bust right, date at right **Rev:** Sailing canoe - Takia, denomination below **Shape:** 12-sided

Date	Mintage	F	VF	XF	Unc	BU
1975	1,000,000	—	0.75	1.50	4.00	6.50
1976	805,000	—	0.50	1.00	2.00	3.50
1978 Proof	2,000	Value: 13.00				
1978	4,006	—	1.25	2.00	5.00	6.50
1979(c)	258,000	—	0.75	1.00	5.00	6.50
1980 Proof	2,500	Value: 11.50				
1980	316,000	—	0.75	1.00	2.00	3.50
1981	511,000	—	0.75	1.00	4.00	7.00
1982	1,000,000	—	0.75	1.00	3.00	5.00
1982 Proof	3,000	Value: 10.00				
1983 Proof	3,000	Value: 9.00				
1983	3,000,000	—	0.65	1.00	2.50	4.00
1984	5,000,000	—	0.65	1.00	2.25	3.50

KM# 36a 50 CENTS

18.0000 g., 0.9250 Silver .5353 oz. ASW, 31.5 mm. **Ruler:** Elizabeth II **Obv:** Young bust right **Rev:** Sailing canoe - Takia, denomination below **Shape:** 12-sided

Date	Mintage	F	VF	XF	Unc	BU
1976 Proof	3,012	Value: 13.50				

KM# 44 50 CENTS

15.5500 g., Copper-Nickel, 31.5 mm. **Ruler:** Elizabeth II **Series:** F.A.O. **Subject:** First Indians in Fiji Centennial **Obv:** Young bust right, date at right **Rev:** Rice plants, denomination and date at right **Shape:** 12-sided

Date	Mintage	F	VF	XF	Unc	BU
1979	258,000	—	—	—	2.50	—
1979 Proof	6,004	Value: 7.50				

KM# 45 50 CENTS

15.5500 g., Copper-Nickel, 31.5 mm. **Ruler:** Elizabeth II **Subject:** 10th Anniversary of Independence **Obv:** Arms with supporters, date below **Rev:** Prince Charles 3/4 facing, denomination below **Rev. Designer:** Michael Rizzello **Shape:** 12-sided

Date	Mintage	F	VF	XF	Unc	BU
1980	10,000	—	—	—	2.50	—

KM# 54 50 CENTS

15.5500 g., Copper-Nickel, 31.5 mm. **Ruler:** Elizabeth II **Obv:** Crowned head right, date at right **Rev:** Sailing canoe - Takia, denomination below **Shape:** 12-sided

Date	Mintage	F	VF	XF	Unc	BU
1986(c)	160,000	—	0.75	1.00	2.00	4.00
1987(c)	160,000	—	0.50	0.75	2.00	4.00

KM# 54a 50 CENTS

Nickel Bonded Steel, 31.5 mm. **Ruler:** Elizabeth II **Obv:** Crowned head right **Rev:** Sailing canoe - Takia, denomination below **Shape:** 12-sided

Date	Mintage	F	VF	XF	Unc	BU
1990(o)	800,000	—	—	0.60	1.75	2.50
1992(o)	280,000	—	—	0.60	1.75	2.50
1994(o)	480,000	—	—	0.60	1.50	2.50
1995(l)	480,000	—	—	0.60	1.50	2.50
1996(l)	560,000	—	—	0.60	1.50	2.50
1997(l)	536,000	—	—	0.60	1.50	2.50
1998(l)	536,000	—	—	0.60	1.50	2.50
1999(l)	536,000	—	—	0.60	1.50	2.50
2000(l)	536,000	—	—	0.60	1.50	2.50

KM# 32 DOLLAR

Copper-Nickel, 38.5 mm. **Ruler:** Elizabeth II **Obv:** Young bust right **Rev:** Arms with supporters, date below

Date	Mintage	F	VF	XF	Unc	BU
1969	70,000	—	—	1.00	3.00	—
1969 Proof	10,000	Value: 3.50				
1976	5,007	—	1.00	2.00	5.00	—

KM# 32a DOLLAR

28.2800 g., 0.9250 Silver .8411 oz. ASW **Ruler:** Elizabeth II **Obv:** Young bust right **Rev:** Arms with supporters divide denomination

Date	Mintage	F	VF	XF	Unc	BU
1976 Proof	3,012	Value: 20.00				

KM# 33a DOLLAR

28.2800 g., 0.9250 Silver .8411 oz. ASW **Ruler:** Elizabeth II **Subject:** Independence Commemorative **Obv:** Young bust right **Rev:** Crown above dove on shield, palm trees flank

Date	Mintage	F	VF	XF	Unc	BU
1970 Proof	1,000	Value: 75.00				

KM# 33 DOLLAR

Copper-Nickel **Ruler:** Elizabeth II **Subject:** Independence Commemorative **Obv:** Young bust right, date at right **Rev:** Dove with olive branch on shield, crown above, palm trees flank

Date	Mintage	F	VF	XF	Unc	BU
1970	15,000	—	—	—	3.00	—
1970 Proof	15,000	Value: 4.00				

Note: Variety with medallic alignment exists; Value: $100

KM# 71 DOLLAR

Copper-Nickel **Ruler:** Elizabeth II **Subject:** Move to Buckingham Palace **Obv:** Crowned head right **Rev:** Buckingham Palace and soldier within circle, denomination below

Date	Mintage	F	VF	XF	Unc	BU
1995	Est. 300,000	—	—	—	3.00	—

KM# 73 DOLLAR

Brass **Ruler:** Elizabeth II **Obv:** Crowned head right, date at right **Rev:** "Saqamoli" drinking vessel, denomination above

Date	Mintage	F	VF	XF	Unc	BU
1995	5,000,000	—	—	1.00	2.00	3.50
1996(l)	1,000,000	—	—	1.00	2.00	3.50
1997(l)	1,000,000	—	—	1.00	2.00	3.50
1998(l)	1,000,000	—	—	1.00	2.00	3.50
1999(l)	1,000,000	—	—	1.00	2.00	3.50
2000(l)	1,000,000	—	—	1.00	2.00	3.50

KM# 78 2 DOLLARS

42.4139 g., 0.9250 Silver 1.3636 oz. ASW **Ruler:** Elizabeth II **Subject:** Soft Coral Capital of the World **Obv:** Crowned head at left facing right **Rev:** Denomination at right, coral industry scenes **Shape:** 1/3 circle segment

Date	Mintage	F	VF	XF	Unc	BU
1998 Proof	20,000	Value: 30.00				

Note: Part of a tri-nation, three coin matching set with Cook Islands and Western Samoa

KM# 81 5 DOLLARS
20.0000 g., 0.5000 Silver .3215 oz. ASW **Ruler:** Elizabeth II
Subject: Protect Our World **Obv:** Crowned head right **Rev:** Reef-heron, fish and tree, denomination below **Edge:** Reeded

Date	Mintage	F	VF	XF	Unc	BU
1993 Proof	25,000	Value: 6.50				

KM# 69 5 DOLLARS
20.0000 g., 0.5000 Silver .3215 oz. ASW **Ruler:** Elizabeth II
Subject: Queen Mother's London House **Obv:** Crowned head right **Rev:** Clarence House within circle, denomination below

Date	Mintage	F	VF	XF	Unc	BU
1994 Proof	50,000	Value: 5.00				

KM# 80 5 DOLLARS
31.4400 g., 0.9250 Silver .9350 oz. ASW **Ruler:** Elizabeth II
Subject: Millennium 2000 **Obv:** Crowned head right, date at right **Rev:** Woman, map of Tavenui with 180 meridian and branch, denomination above **Shape:** 5-sided

Date	Mintage	F	VF	XF	Unc	BU
1999 Proof	10,000	Value: 22.50				

KM# 40 10 DOLLARS
30.3000 g., 0.9250 Silver .9012 oz. ASW **Ruler:** Elizabeth II
Subject: Queen's Silver Jubilee **Obv:** Young bust right, date at right **Rev:** Arms with supporters, crown divides dates above, denomination below

Date	Mintage	F	VF	XF	Unc	BU
1977 Proof	3,010	Value: 15.00				

KM# 41 10 DOLLARS
28.2800 g., 0.5000 Silver .4547 oz. ASW **Ruler:** Elizabeth II
Subject: Conservation **Obv:** Young bust right **Rev:** Pink-billed parrot finch on branch right

Date	Mintage	F	VF	XF	Unc	BU
1978	3,582	—	—	—	17.00	—

KM# 41a 10 DOLLARS
28.2800 g., 0.9250 Silver .8411 oz. ASW **Ruler:** Elizabeth II
Subject: Conservation **Obv:** Young bust right **Rev:** Pink-billed parrot finch

Date	Mintage	F	VF	XF	Unc	BU
1978 Proof	4,026	Value: 20.00				

KM# 46 10 DOLLARS
28.4400 g., 0.5000 Silver .4572 oz. ASW **Ruler:** Elizabeth II
Subject: 10th Anniversary of Independence **Obv:** Arms with supporters, date below **Rev:** Bust 3/4 left, denomination below
Rev. Designer: Michael Rizzello

Date	Mintage	F	VF	XF	Unc	BU
1980	5,001	—	—	—	9.00	—

KM# 46a 10 DOLLARS
30.4800 g., 0.9250 Silver .9066 oz. ASW **Ruler:** Elizabeth II
Subject: 10th Anniversary of Independence **Obv:** Arms with supporters **Rev:** Bust of Prince Charles 3/4 left

Date	Mintage	F	VF	XF	Unc	BU
1980 Proof	3,001	Value: 15.00				

KM# 48 10 DOLLARS
30.0000 g., 0.9250 Silver .8922 oz. ASW **Ruler:** Elizabeth II
Subject: Wedding of Prince Charles and Lady Diana **Obv:** Young bust right **Rev:** Head 3/4 left **Rev. Designer:** Michael Rizzello

Date	Mintage	F	VF	XF	Unc	BU
1981 Proof	5,000	Value: 13.50				

KM# 55 10 DOLLARS
28.2800 g., 0.9250 Silver .8411 oz. ASW **Ruler:** Elizabeth II
Subject: 25th Anniversary - World Wildlife Fund **Obv:** Crowned head right **Rev:** Fijian ground frog, denomination at right

Date	Mintage	F	VF	XF	Unc	BU
1986 Proof	25,000	Value: 24.00				

KM# 60 10 DOLLARS
28.2800 g., 0.9250 Silver .8411 oz. ASW **Ruler:** Elizabeth II
Subject: Save the Children Fund **Obv:** Crowned head right **Rev:** Children reading by lantern light, denomination upper right

Date	Mintage	F	VF	XF	Unc	BU
1991 Proof	20,000	Value: 12.50				

KM# 62 10 DOLLARS
28.2800 g., 0.9250 Silver .8411 oz. ASW **Ruler:** Elizabeth II
Subject: 40th Anniversary - Coronation of Queen Elizabeth II
Obv: Crowned head right **Rev:** Queen seated on throne flanked by church figures

Date	Mintage	F	VF	XF	Unc	BU
1993 Proof	10,000	Value: 12.50				

KM# 63 10 DOLLARS
31.1035 g., 0.9250 Silver .9250 oz. ASW **Ruler:** Elizabeth II
Subject: Discovery of Fiji **Obv:** Crowned head right **Rev:** Cameo of Abel J. Tasman upper right, ships below

Date	Mintage	F	VF	XF	Unc	BU
1993 Proof	10,000	Value: 14.50				

KM# 64 10 DOLLARS
31.1035 g., 0.9250 Silver .9250 oz. ASW **Ruler:** Elizabeth II
Subject: Discovery of Fiji **Obv:** Crowned head right **Rev:** Cameo of William Bligh upper right, long boat with sailors, denomination below

Date	Mintage	F	VF	XF	Unc	BU
1993 Proof	10,000	Value: 14.50				

KM# 66 10 DOLLARS

31.4600 g., 0.9250 Silver .9357 oz. ASW **Ruler:** Elizabeth II **Subject:** Protect Our World **Obv:** Crowned head right **Rev:** Island scene within palm of hand, denomination below

Date	Mintage	F	VF	XF	Unc	BU
1993 Proof	—	Value: 15.00				

KM# 67 10 DOLLARS

31.4600 g., 0.9250 Silver .9357 oz. ASW **Ruler:** Elizabeth II **Series:** 1996 Olympics **Obv:** Crowned head right **Rev:** Judo match, denomination below

Date	Mintage	F	VF	XF	Unc	BU
1993 Proof	20,000	Value: 14.00				

KM# 68 10 DOLLARS

31.6400 g., 0.9250 Silver .9409 oz. ASW **Ruler:** Elizabeth II **Subject:** World Cup Soccer **Obv:** Crowned head right **Rev:** Soccer player

Date	Mintage	F	VF	XF	Unc	BU
1993 Proof	30,000	Value: 14.00				

KM# 70 10 DOLLARS

31.4700 g., 0.9250 Silver .9359 oz. ASW **Ruler:** Elizabeth II **Subject:** Lunar Module "Eagle" **Obv:** Crowned head right **Rev:** Lunar module on moon, eagle outline in background, denomination below

Date	Mintage	F	VF	XF	Unc	BU
1994 Proof	Est. 10,000	Value: 14.00				

KM# 74 10 DOLLARS

31.3700 g., 0.9250 Silver .9329 oz. ASW **Ruler:** Elizabeth II **Subject:** Endangered Wildlife **Obv:** Crowned head right **Rev:** Streaked Fantail on branch, denomination below

Date	Mintage	F	VF	XF	Unc	BU
1995 Proof	—	Value: 24.00				

KM# 75 10 DOLLARS

34.4600 g., 0.9250 Silver .9357 oz. ASW **Ruler:** Elizabeth II **Subject:** Silver Jubilee of Independence **Obv:** Crowned head right **Rev:** Arms with supporters, crown above divides dates, denomination below

Date	Mintage	F	VF	XF	Unc	BU
1995 Proof	—	Value: 14.00				

KM# 79 10 DOLLARS

31.5200 g., 0.9250 Silver .9368 oz. ASW **Ruler:** Elizabeth II **Series:** Olympic Games 1996 **Obv:** Crowned head right **Rev:** Two sailboarders, denomination at right

Date	Mintage	F	VF	XF	Unc	BU
1995 Proof	—	Value: 14.00				

KM# 86 10 DOLLARS

31.3500 g., 0.9250 Silver 0.9323 oz. ASW, 38.7 mm. **Ruler:** Elizabeth II **Subject:** Queen Elizabeth II and The Queen Mother - Move to Buckingham Palace **Obv:** Crowned head right **Rev:** 1/2 bust of soldier at right in front of Buckingham Palace within circle, denomination below **Edge:** Reeded

Date	Mintage	F	VF	XF	Unc	BU
1995 Proof	—	Value: 14.00				

KM# 100 10 DOLLARS

31.4700 g., 0.9250 Silver 0.9359 oz. ASW, 38.61 mm. **Ruler:** Elizabeth II **Subject:** Victorian Age - Queen Victoria's Coronation, 28 June 1838 **Obv:** Crowned head right **Rev:** Crowned Queen Victoria **Edge:** Reeded

Date	Mintage	F	VF	XF	Unc	BU
1996 Proof	10,000	Value: 14.50				

KM# 90 10 DOLLARS

28.5000 g., 0.9250 Silver 0.8476 oz. ASW, 38.5 mm. **Ruler:** Elizabeth II **Subject:** Queen's 70th Birthday **Obv:** Crowned head right **Rev:** Native dancer, denomination divides dates below **Edge:** Reeded

Date	Mintage	F	VF	XF	Unc	BU
1996 Proof	—	Value: 13.50				

KM# 92 10 DOLLARS

31.6000 g., 0.9250 Silver 0.9398 oz. ASW, 38.6 mm. **Ruler:** Elizabeth II **Subject:** Princess Diana **Obv:** Crowned head right **Rev:** Diana with sick child **Edge:** Reeded

Date	Mintage	F	VF	XF	Unc	BU
1997 Proof	—	Value: 14.00				

KM# 87 10 DOLLARS

19.7000 g., 0.9250 Silver 0.5859 oz. ASW, 33.9 mm. **Ruler:** Elizabeth II **Subject:** Queen Elizabeth II's Golden Jubilee **Obv:** Crowned head right **Rev:** The royal couple, shield and treehouse **Edge:** Reeded

Date	Mintage	F	VF	XF	Unc	BU
1997 Proof	—	Value: 16.00				

KM# 85 10 DOLLARS

28.2800 g., 0.9250 Silver 0.841 oz. ASW, 38.6 mm. **Ruler:** Elizabeth II **Subject:** UNICEF **Obv:** Crowned head right **Rev:** Two young folk dancers, denomination below **Edge:** Reeded

Date	Mintage	F	VF	XF	Unc	BU
1997 Proof	25,000	Value: 12.50				

KM# 76 10 DOLLARS

31.3300 g., 0.9250 Silver .9317 oz. ASW **Ruler:** Elizabeth II **Subject:** Endangered Wildlife **Obv:** Crowned head right **Rev:** Banded iguana left

Date	Mintage	F	VF	XF	Unc	BU
1997 Proof	—	Value: 25.00				

KM# 96 10 DOLLARS

34.4700 g., 0.9250 Silver 1.0251 oz. ASW, 38.6 mm. **Ruler:** Elizabeth II **Subject:** HM Barge [sic] "Endeavour" **Obv:** Crowned head right **Rev:** Endeavour **Edge:** Reeded

Date	Mintage	F	VF	XF	Unc	BU
1998(o) Proof	20,000	Value: 15.00				

KM# 97 10 DOLLARS

1.2500 g., 0.9990 Gold 0.0401 oz. AGW **Ruler:** Elizabeth II **Subject:** Discovery of Gold in Fiji - 1932 **Obv:** Crowned head right **Rev:** Gold panning

Date	Mintage	F	VF	XF	Unc	BU
1998 Proof	—	Value: 28.50				

KM# 91 10 DOLLARS

28.1000 g., 0.9250 Silver Gold plated outer ring 0.8357 oz. ASW, 38.6 mm. **Ruler:** Elizabeth II **Subject:** Queen Mother's Centennial **Obv:** Crowned head right within beaded circle, date at right **Rev:** Elizabeth and David as children within beaded circle, denomination below **Edge:** Reeded

Date	Mintage	F	VF	XF	Unc	BU
2000 Proof	10,000	Value: 13.50				

KM# 42 20 DOLLARS
35.0000 g., 0.5000 Silver .5627 oz. ASW **Ruler:** Elizabeth II **Subject:** Conservation **Obv:** Young bust right **Rev:** Golden cowrie, denomination below

Date	Mintage	F	VF	XF	Unc	BU
1978	3,584	—	—	—	17.00	—

KM# 42a 20 DOLLARS
35.0000 g., 0.9250 Silver 1.0409 oz. ASW **Ruler:** Elizabeth II **Subject:** Conservation **Obv:** Young bust right **Rev:** Golden cowrie

Date	Mintage	F	VF	XF	Unc	BU
1978 Proof	3,869	Value: 24.00				

KM# 34 25 DOLLARS
48.6000 g., 0.9250 Silver 1.4455 oz. ASW **Ruler:** Elizabeth II **Subject:** 100th Anniversary - Cession to Great Britian **Obv:** Young bust right **Rev:** Bust of King Cakobau, facing, denomination below, dates above

Date	Mintage	F	VF	XF	Unc	BU
1974	2,400	—	—	—	22.50	—
1974 Proof	8,299	Value: 20.00				

KM# 37 25 DOLLARS
48.6000 g., 0.9250 Silver 1.4455 oz. ASW **Ruler:** Elizabeth II **Obv:** Young bust right **Rev:** King Cakobau bust facing, denomination below, dates above

Date	Mintage	F	VF	XF	Unc	BU
1975	836	—	—	—	30.00	—
1975 Proof	5,157	Value: 20.00				

KM# 57 25 DOLLARS
7.7750 g., 0.7500 Gold .1875 oz. AGW **Ruler:** Elizabeth II **Obv:** Denomination at center of designs **Rev:** Balikula mint mark of Pacific Sovereign Mint, Fijian thatched temple **Designer:** David Holland

Date	Mintage	F	VF	XF	Unc	BU
ND(1990)	443	—	—	—	130	—
Note: Boar tusks						
ND(1991)	512	—	—	—	130	—
Note: War fan						
ND(1992)	50	—	—	—	150	—

KM# 58 50 DOLLARS
15.5500 g., 0.7500 Gold .3750 oz. AGW **Ruler:** Elizabeth II **Obv:** Denomination at center of patterns **Rev:** Balikula mint mark of Pacific Sovereign Mint, Fijian warrior **Designer:** David Holland

Date	Mintage	F	VF	XF	Unc	BU
ND(1990)	168	—	—	—	265	—
Note: Boar tusks						
ND(1991)	141	—	—	—	265	—
Note: War fan						
ND(1992)	43	—	—	—	300	—

KM# 72 50 DOLLARS
7.7760 g., 0.5833 Gold .1458 oz. AGW **Ruler:** Elizabeth II **Subject:** Olympics **Obv:** Crowned head right, date at right **Rev:** Two field hockey players, denomination below

Date	Mintage	F	VF	XF	Unc	BU
1996	Est. 3,000	—	—	—	100	—

KM# 88 50 DOLLARS
1000.0000 g., 0.9990 Silver 32.1186 oz. ASW, 100 mm. **Ruler:** Elizabeth II **Subject:** 70th Birthday of Queen Elizabeth II **Obv:** Crowned head right **Rev:** Queen and Queen mother side by side facing **Edge:** Reeded **Note:** Photo reduced.

Date	Mintage	F	VF	XF	Unc	BU
1996 Proof	99	Value: 460				

KM# 35 100 DOLLARS
31.3600 g., 0.5000 Gold .5042 oz. AGW **Ruler:** Elizabeth II **Subject:** 100th Anniversary - Cession to Great Britain **Obv:** Young bust right **Rev:** Bust of King Cakobau facing, denomination below

Date	Mintage	F	VF	XF	Unc	BU
1974 Proof	2,321	Value: 365				
1974	1,109	—	—	—	345	—

KM# 38 100 DOLLARS
31.3000 g., 0.5000 Gold .5032 oz. AGW **Ruler:** Elizabeth II **Obv:** Young bust right **Rev:** King Cakobau, facing denomination below

Date	Mintage	F	VF	XF	Unc	BU
1975 Proof	3,197	Value: 350				
1975	593	—	—	—	365	—

KM# 59 100 DOLLARS
31.1000 g., 0.7500 Gold .7500 oz. AGW **Ruler:** Elizabeth II **Obv:** Denomination within center, diamonds on pattern at top, bottom, right and left **Rev:** Balikula mint mark of Pacific Sovereign Mint **Designer:** David Holland **Note:** Dates are privy marks; 1990 - Boar Tusks; 1991 - War Fan; 1992 - ?.

Date	Mintage	F	VF	XF	Unc	BU
ND(1990)	161	—	—	—	530	—
ND(1991)	131	—	—	—	530	—
ND(1992)	41	—	—	—	575	—

KM# 65 100 DOLLARS
7.5000 g., 0.9170 Gold .2209 oz. AGW **Ruler:** Elizabeth II **Subject:** Discovery of Fiji **Obv:** Crowned head right, date at right **Rev:** James Cook in cameo right of sailing ship, denomination below

Date	Mintage	F	VF	XF	Unc	BU
1993 Proof	3,000	Value: 155				

KM# 98 100 DOLLARS
0.9990 Gold **Ruler:** Elizabeth II **Subject:** Silver Jubilee of Independence **Obv:** Crowned head right **Rev:** Arms

Date	Mintage	F	VF	XF	Unc	BU
1995 Proof	—	Value: 160				

KM# 47 200 DOLLARS
15.9800 g., 0.9170 Gold .4712 oz. AGW **Ruler:** Elizabeth II **Subject:** 10th Anniversary of Independence **Obv:** Arms with supporters, date below **Rev:** Bust 3/4 facing, denomination below **Rev. Designer:** Michael Rizzello

Date	Mintage	F	VF	XF	Unc	BU
1980	500	—	—	—	325	—
1980 Proof	1,166	Value: 315				

KM# 56 200 DOLLARS
15.9800 g., 0.9170 Gold .4712 oz. AGW **Ruler:** Elizabeth II **Subject:** 25th Anniversary - World Wildlife Fund **Obv:** Young bust right **Rev:** Ogmodon

Date	Mintage	F	VF	XF	Unc	BU
1986 Proof	5,000	Value: 310				

KM# 61 200 DOLLARS
10.0000 g., 0.9170 Gold .2948 oz. AGW **Ruler:** Elizabeth II **Subject:** Save the Children Fund **Obv:** King Cakobau facing divides date **Rev:** Child with toy boat, figure in background with spear, denomination below

Date	Mintage	F	VF	XF	Unc	BU
1991 Proof	32,000	Value: 195				

KM# 43 250 DOLLARS
33.4370 g., 0.9000 Gold .9676 oz. AGW **Ruler:** Elizabeth II **Subject:** Conservation **Obv:** Young bust right **Rev:** Banded iguana, denomination at right

Date	Mintage	F	VF	XF	Unc	BU
1978 Proof	252	Value: 825				
1978	810	—	—	—	675	—

TRIAL STRIKES

KM#	Date	Mintage	Identification	Mkt Val
TS1	1974	—	100 Dollars. Bronze. KM35.	950
TS2	1974	—	Cent. Bronze. Fijian planting taro.	275
TS3	1974	—	Cent. Copper-Nickel. Fijian planting taro.	310

MINT SETS

KM#	Date	Mintage	Identification	Issue Price	Mkt Val
MSA1	1934 (3)	—	KM3-5	—	750
MSB1	1969 (6)	—	KM27-32	—	5.00
MS1	1976 (7)	5,001	KM27-32, 36	9.00	11.50
MS2	1976 (6)	—	KM27-31, 36	—	6.50
MS3	1978 (6)	4,006	KM28-31, 36, 39	4.50	7.00
MS4	1978 (3)	—	KM41-43	444	750
MS5	1978 (2)	—	KM41-42	44.00	45.00
MS6	1983 (6)	3,000	KM27-31, 36	5.00	4.50
MS7	1984 (6)	5,000	KM27-31, 36	3.60	4.00
MS8	1990 (8)	—	KM49a-54a	—	5.00
MS9	1990 (3)	—	KM57-59	905	875

PROOF SETS

KM#	Date	Mintage	Identification	Issue Price	Mkt Val
PS1	1969 (6)	10,000	KM#27-32	7.20	6.50
PS2	1976 (7)	3,023	KM#27a-32a, 36a	87.50	35.00
PS3	1978 (6)	2,000	KM#28-31, 36, 39	31.00	20.00
PS4	1978 (2)	—	KM#41a, 42a	76.00	55.00
PS5	1978 (3)	—	KM#41a, 42a, 43	726	865
PS6	1980 (6)	2,500	KM#28-31, 36, 39	45.00	20.00
PS7	1982 (6)	3,000	KM#28-31, 36, 39	32.00	20.00
PS8	1983 (6)	3,000	KM#27-31, 36	27.00	20.00
PS9	1993 (3)	—	KM#63-65	370	225

FINLAND

The Republic of Finland, the third northernmost state of the European continent, has an area of 130,559 sq. mi. (338,127 sq. km.) and a population of 5.1 million. Capital: Helsinki. Lumbering, shipbuilding, metal and woodworking are the leading industries. Paper, timber, wood pulp, plywood and metal products are exported.

The Finns, who probably originated in the Volga region of Russia, took Finland from the Lapps late in the 7th century. They were conquered in the 12th century by Eric IX of Sweden, and brought into contact with Western Christendom. In 1809, Sweden was conquered by Alexander I of Russia, and the peace terms gave Finland to Russia which became a grand duchy, with autonomy, within the Russian Empire until Dec. 6, 1917, when, shortly after the Bolshevik revolution it declared its independence. After a brief but bitter civil war between the Russian communists and Finnish nationalists in which the Whites (nationalists) were victorious, a new constitution was adopted, and on Dec. 6, 1917 Finland was established as a republic. In 1939 Soviet troops attacked Finland over disputed territorial concessions which were later granted in the peace treaty of 1940. When the Germans invaded Russia, Finland became involved and in the Armistice of 1944 lost the Petsamo area to the Soviets.

RULERS

Nicholas II, 1894-1917

MONETARY SYSTEM

100 Pennia = 1 Markka

Commencing 1963

100 Old Markka = 1 New Markka

MINT MARKS

H - Birmingham 1921
Heart (h) - Copenhagen 1922
No mm – Helsinki

MINT OFFICIALS' INITIALS

Letter	Date	Name
H	1948-1958	Peippo Uolevi Helle
H-M	1990	Raimo Heino & Raimo Makkonen
K	1976-1983	Timo Koivuranta
K-H	1977, 1979	Timo Koivuranta & Heikki Haivaoja (Designer)
K-M	1983	Timo Koivuranta & Pertti Makinen
K-N	1978	Timo Koivuranta & Antti Neuvonen
K-T	1982	Timo Koivuranta & Erja Tielinen
L	1885-1912	Johan Conrad Lihr
L	1948	Vesa Uolevi Liuhto
L-M	1991	Arto Lappalainen & Raimo Makkonen
L-M	2000	Maija Lavonen & Raimo Makkonen
M	1987	Raimo Makkonen
M-G	1998	Raimo Makkonen & Henrik Gummerus
M-L	1997	Raimo Makkonen & Tero Lounas
M-L-L	1995	Raimo Makkonen & Arto Lappalainen & Marita Lappalainen
M-L-M	1989	Marjo Lahtinen & Raimo Makkonen
M-M	2004, 2006	:ertti Mäkinen & Raimo Makkonen
M-O	1998	Raimo Makkonen & Harri Ojala
M-S	1992, 1997	Raimo Makkonen & Erkki Salmela
N	1983-1987	Tapio Nevalainen
P-M	1989-1991, 1994-1995, 1997, 2000	Reijo Paavilainen & Raimo Makkonen
P-M	2003	Matti Peltokangas & Raimo Makkonen
P-N	1985	Reijo Paavilainen & Tapio Nevalainen
P-V-M	1999	Juhani Pallasmaa, Jukka Veistola & Raimo Makkonen
R-M	1999	Jarkko Roth & Raimo Makkonen
S	1912-1947	Isak Gustaf Sundell
S	1958-1975	Allan Alarik Soiniemi
S-H	1967-1971	Allan Alarik Soiniemi & Heikki Haivaoja (Designer)
S-J	1960	Allan Alarik Soiniemi & Toivo Jaatinen
S-M	1995	Terho Sakki & Raimo Makkonen
S-M	2003	Anneli Sijriläinen & Raimo Makkonen
T-M	1996, 2000	Erja Tielinen & Raimo Makkonen
W-M	2002	Erkki Vainio & Hannu Veijalainen & Raimo Makkonen

GRAND DUCHY

DECIMAL COINAGE

KM# 13 PENNI
1.2800 g., Copper, 15 mm. **Ruler:** Nicholas II **Obv:** Crowned monogram **Rev:** Denomination and date **Designer:** Aleksander Fadejev

Date	Mintage	F	VF	XF	Unc	BU
1901	1,520,000	0.75	1.25	2.50	8.00	—
1902	1,000,000	0.75	1.25	5.00	12.00	—
1903	1,145,000	0.75	1.25	5.00	12.00	—
Note: Small 3						
1903	Inc. above	1.50	2.50	10.00	20.00	—
Note: Large 3						
1904	500,000	2.50	5.00	10.00	20.00	—
1905	1,390,000	0.50	1.00	2.00	6.00	—
1906	1,020,000	0.50	1.00	2.00	5.00	—
1907	Inc. above	0.30	0.75	1.75	4.00	—
Note: Without serif on 7 arm						
1907	2,490,000	0.75	1.25	2.50	4.00	—
Note: Normal 7						
1908	950,000	0.50	1.00	3.00	7.00	—
1909	3,060,000	0.25	0.65	1.25	2.50	—
1911	2,550,000	0.25	0.65	1.25	2.50	—
1912	2,450,000	0.25	0.65	1.25	2.50	—
1913	1,650,000	0.25	0.65	1.25	3.00	—
1914	1,900,000	0.25	0.65	1.25	3.50	—
1915	2,250,000	0.25	0.65	1.25	2.50	—
1916	3,040,000	0.25	0.50	1.00	2.00	—

KM# 15 5 PENNIA
6.4000 g., Copper, 25 mm. **Ruler:** Nicholas II **Obv:** Crowned monogram **Rev:** Denomination and date **Designer:** Aleksander Fadejev

Date	Mintage	F	VF	XF	Unc	BU
1901	990,000	1.00	5.00	15.00	80.00	—
1905	620,000	2.00	10.00	40.00	125	—
1906	960,000	1.00	5.00	20.00	100	—
1907	770,000	2.00	10.00	75.00	150	—
1908	1,660,000	0.75	2.50	15.00	50.00	—
1910	60,000	25.00	50.00	120	250	—
1911	1,050,000	0.75	2.50	6.00	30.00	—
1912	460,000	1.50	5.00	25.00	75.00	—
1913	1,060,000	0.65	1.25	4.00	15.00	—
1914	820,000	0.65	1.25	3.00	15.00	—
1915	2,080,000	0.30	0.75	3.00	10.00	—
1916	4,470,000	0.30	0.75	3.00	10.00	—
1917	4,070,000	0.30	0.75	3.00	10.00	—

KM# 14 10 PENNIA
12.8000 g., Copper, 30 mm. **Ruler:** Nicholas II **Obv:** Crowned monogram **Rev:** Denomination and date within wreath **Designer:** Aleksander Fadejev

Date	Mintage	F	VF	XF	Unc	BU
1905	500,000	2.00	10.00	70.00	175	—
1907	503,000	2.00	10.00	70.00	175	—
1908	320,000	1.50	10.00	35.00	100	—
1909	180,000	3.00	20.00	100	225	—
1910	241,000	1.50	7.50	35.00	100	—
1911	370,000	1.00	5.00	20.00	60.00	—
1912	191,000	1.50	7.50	25.00	100	—
1913	150,000	2.50	10.00	50.00	150	—
1914	605,000	0.75	1.50	10.00	30.00	—
1915	420,000	0.50	1.00	5.00	15.00	—
1916	1,952,000	0.50	1.00	3.00	10.00	—
1917	1,600,000	0.75	1.50	4.00	12.00	—

KM# 6.2 25 PENNIA
1.2747 g., 0.7500 Silver .0307 oz. ASW, 16 mm. **Ruler:** Nicholas II **Obv:** Crowned imperial double eagle with sceptre and orb **Rev:** Denomination and date within wreath **Designer:** Aleksander Fadejev **Note:** Dentilated border.

Date	Mintage	F	VF	XF	Unc	BU
1901 L	993,000	1.00	2.00	8.00	35.00	—
1902 L	210,000	3.00	10.00	30.00	100	—
1906 L	281,000	2.00	5.00	15.00	60.00	—
1907 L	590,000	1.00	2.00	5.00	25.00	—
1908 L	340,000	1.00	2.50	20.00	50.00	—
1909 L	1,099,000	0.75	1.50	5.00	15.00	—
1910 L	392,000	2.50	5.00	15.00	50.00	—
1913 S	832,000	0.50	1.00	1.50	3.00	—
1915 S	2,400,000	0.50	0.75	1.00	1.50	—
1916 S	6,392,000	0.50	0.75	1.00	1.50	—
1917 S	5,820,000	0.50	0.75	1.00	1.50	—

KM# 2.2 50 PENNIA
2.5494 g., 0.7500 Silver .0615 oz. ASW, 18.6 mm. **Ruler:** Nicholas II **Obv:** Crowned imperial double eagle with sceptre and orb **Rev:** Denomination and date within wreath **Designer:** Aleksander Fadejev **Note:** Dentilated border.

Date	Mintage	F	VF	XF	Unc	BU
1907 L	260,000	1.00	5.00	30.00	90.00	—
1908 L	353,000	0.90	2.00	10.00	30.00	—
1911 L	616,000	0.85	1.25	2.50	5.00	—
1914 S	600,000	0.85	1.00	1.50	4.00	—
1915 S	1,000,000	0.85	1.00	1.50	2.50	—
1916 S	4,752,000	0.85	1.00	1.50	2.50	—
1917 S	3,972,000	0.85	1.00	1.50	2.50	—

KM# 3.2 MARKKA
5.1828 g., 0.8680 Silver .1446 oz. ASW, 24 mm. **Ruler:** Nicholas II **Obv:** Crowned imperial double eagle holding orb and scepter, fineness around (text in Finnish) **Rev:** Denomination and date within wreath **Designer:** Aleksander Fadejev **Note:** Obverse text translates to: "94.48 pieces from one pound of fine silver." Dentilated border.

Date	Mintage	F	VF	XF	Unc	BU
1907 L	350,000	6.00	8.00	10.00	25.00	—
1908 L	153,000	8.00	12.00	25.00	50.00	—
1915 S	1,212,000	5.00	7.00	10.00	12.00	—

KM# 7.2 2 MARKKAA
10.3657 g., 0.8680 Silver .2893 oz. ASW, 27.5 mm. **Ruler:** Nicholas II **Obv:** Crowned imperial double eagle holding orb and scepter, fineness around (Finnish text) **Rev:** Denomination and date within wreath **Designer:** Aleksander Fadejev **Note:** Obverse text translates to: "47.24 pieces from one pound of fine silver." Dentilated border.

Date	Mintage	F	VF	XF	Unc	BU
1905 L	24,000	100	170	500	1,200	—
1906 L	225,000	12.00	17.00	50.00	80.00	—
1907 L	125,000	15.00	25.00	75.00	250	—
1908 L	124,000	15.00	25.00	50.00	75.00	—

KM# 8.2 10 MARKKAA
3.2258 g., 0.9000 Gold .0933 oz. AGW, 18.9 mm. **Ruler:** Nicholas II **Obv:** Crowned imperial double eagle holding orb and scepter **Rev:** Denomination and date within circle, fineness around **Note:** Regal issues

Date	Mintage	F	VF	XF	Unc	BU
1904 L	102,000	250	350	400	500	—
1905 L	43,000	1,500	2,000	2,800	3,000	—
1913 L	396,000	100	150	175	200	—

KM# 9.2 20 MARKKAA
6.4516 g., 0.9000 Gold .1867 oz. AGW, 21.3 mm. **Ruler:** Nicholas II **Obv:** Crowned imperial double eagle holding orb and scepter **Rev:** Denomination and date within circle, fineness around **Note:** Regal issues.

Date	Mintage	F	VF	XF	Unc	BU
1903 L	112,000	150	180	210	230	—
1904 L	188,000	150	180	200	220	—
1910 L	201,000	150	180	200	220	—
1911 L	161,000	150	180	200	220	—
1912 L	881,000	2,500	4,500	6,000	7,000	—
1912 S	Inc. above	150	180	200	220	—
1913 S	214,000	150	180	200	220	—

CIVIL WAR COINAGE

Kerenski Government Issue

KM# 16 PENNI
1.2800 g., Copper, 15 mm. **Ruler:** Nicholas II

Date	Mintage	F	VF	XF	Unc	BU
1917	1,650,000	0.25	0.75	1.00	1.50	—

KM# 17 5 PENNIA
6.4000 g., Copper, 25 mm. **Ruler:** Nicholas II **Obv:** Imperial double eagle holding royal orb and scepter, shield on breast within circle **Rev:** Denomination above date

Date	Mintage	F	VF	XF	Unc	BU
1917	Inc. above	0.30	0.75	3.00	7.00	—

KM# 18 10 PENNIA
12.8000 g., Copper, 30 mm. **Ruler:** Nicholas II

Date	Mintage	F	VF	XF	Unc	BU
1917	Inc. above	0.50	1.00	4.00	10.00	—

KM# 19 25 PENNIA
1.2747 g., 0.7500 Silver .0307 oz. ASW, 16 mm. **Ruler:** Nicholas II **Obv:** Crown above eagle removed

Date	Mintage	F	VF	XF	Unc	BU
1917 S	2,310,000	—	BV	1.00	1.50	—

KM# 20 50 PENNIA
2.5494 g., 0.7500 Silver .0615 oz. ASW, 18.6 mm. **Ruler:** Nicholas II **Obv:** Imperial double eagle holding royal orb and scepter, shield on breast **Rev:** Denomination and date within wreath **Note:** No crown above eagle

Date	Mintage	F	VF	XF	Unc	BU
1917 S	570,000	—	BV	1.25	2.00	—

CIVIL WAR COINAGE

Liberated Finnish Government Issue

KM# 21 5 PENNIA
2.5000 g., Copper, 17.9 mm. **Obv:** Flag and 3 trumpets within wreath, wreath knot centered between 9 and 1 of date below **Obv. Legend:** • KANSAN TYÖ, KANSAN VALTA • - SUOMI - FINLAND **Rev:** Large value flanked by flower heads **Note:** Prev. KM#21.1. For previously listed KM#21.2, refer to Unusual World Coins, X#B1.

Date	Mintage	F	VF	XF	Unc	BU
1918	35,000	20.00	30.00	45.00	60.00	—

REPUBLIC

DECIMAL COINAGE

KM# 23 PENNI
1.0000 g., Copper, 14 mm. **Rev:** Denomination flanked by rosettes **Designer:** Isak Sundell

Date	Mintage	F	VF	XF	Unc	BU
1919	1,200,000	0.25	0.65	1.75	3.00	—
1920	720,000	0.25	0.65	1.75	3.00	—
1921	510,000	0.35	1.00	2.00	4.00	—
1922	1,060,000	0.25	0.65	1.75	3.00	—
1923	990,000	0.25	0.65	1.75	3.00	—
1924	2,180,000	0.25	0.65	1.75	3.00	—

KM# 22 5 PENNIA
2.5000 g., Copper, 18 mm. **Obv:** Rampant lion left with sword divides date **Rev:** Rosettes flank denomination **Designer:** Isak Sundell

Date	Mintage	F	VF	XF	Unc	BU
1918	4,270,000	0.10	0.25	1.00	4.00	—
1919	4,640,000	0.10	0.25	1.00	4.00	—
1920	7,710,000	0.10	0.25	1.00	3.00	—
1921	5,910,000	0.10	0.25	1.00	3.00	—
1922	8,540,000	0.10	0.25	1.00	3.00	—
1927	1,520,000	0.75	1.50	3.50	15.00	—
1928	2,110,000	0.25	0.50	1.50	8.00	—
1929	1,500,000	0.25	0.50	1.50	8.00	—
1930	2,140,000	0.75	1.25	3.00	12.00	—
1932	2,130,000	0.15	0.50	1.00	4.00	—
1934	2,180,000	0.15	0.50	1.00	4.00	—
1935	1,610,000	0.15	0.35	1.00	3.00	—
1936	2,610,000	0.15	0.35	1.00	3.00	—
1937	3,830,000	0.10	0.25	1.00	3.00	—
1938	4,300,000	0.10	0.25	1.00	3.00	—
1939	2,270,000	0.10	0.25	1.00	3.00	—
1940	1,610,000	0.25	0.50	1.50	5.00	—

KM# 64.1 5 PENNIA
1.2700 g., Copper, 16 mm. **Obv:** Rosette above center hole flanked by leaves dividing date below **Rev:** Center hole divides denomination, rosettes flank **Designer:** Isak Sundell **Note:** Punched center hole.

Date	Mintage	F	VF	XF	Unc	BU
1941	5,950,000	0.10	0.20	0.50	1.25	—
1942	4,280,000	0.10	0.20	0.50	1.25	—
1943	1,530,000	0.10	0.50	1.25	2.50	—

KM# 64.2 5 PENNIA
Copper, 16 mm. **Designer:** Isak Sundell **Note:** Without punched center hole. These issues were not authorized by the government and any that exist were illegally removed from the mint.

Date	Mintage	F	VF	XF	Unc	BU
1941	Inc. above	25.00	30.00	70.00	100	—
1942	Inc. above	25.00	30.00	70.00	100	—
1943	Inc. above	50.00	70.00	100	125	—

KM# 24 10 PENNIA
5.0000 g., Copper, 22 mm. **Obv:** Rampant lion left, holding sword divides date **Designer:** Isak Sundell

Date	Mintage	F	VF	XF	Unc	BU
1919	3,670,000	0.10	0.25	1.00	5.00	—
1920	2,380,000	0.10	0.25	1.00	5.00	—
1921	3,970,000	0.10	0.25	1.00	5.00	—
1922	2,180,000	0.10	0.25	2.00	7.00	—
1923	910,000	1.00	2.00	10.00	30.00	—
1924	1,350,000	0.25	0.50	3.00	12.00	—
1926	1,690,000	0.25	0.50	2.00	10.00	—
1927	1,330,000	0.50	1.00	5.00	15.00	—
1928	1,006,000	0.50	1.00	2.50	10.00	—
1929	1,560,000	0.35	0.85	2.00	7.00	—
1930	650,000	0.75	1.50	7.00	15.00	—
1931	1,040,000	1.00	2.00	10.00	30.00	—
1934	1,680,000	0.35	0.85	2.00	7.00	—
1935	1,690,000	0.15	0.25	1.00	5.00	—
1936	2,009,999	0.15	0.25	1.00	5.00	—
1937	2,420,000	0.10	0.25	0.50	3.50	—
1938	2,940,000	0.10	0.25	0.50	3.50	—
1939	2,100,000	0.10	0.25	0.50	3.50	—
1940	2,009,999	0.25	0.50	1.00	5.00	—

KM# 33.1 10 PENNIA
2.5500 g., Copper, 18.5 mm. **Obv:** Rosette above center hole flanked by leaves dividing date below **Rev:** Center hole divides denomination, rosettes flank **Designer:** Isak Sundell

Date	Mintage	F	VF	XF	Unc	BU
1941	3,610,000	0.10	0.25	0.50	1.25	—

Date	Mintage	F	VF	XF	Unc	BU
1942	4,970,000	0.10	0.25	0.50	1.25	—
1943	1,860,000	0.25	0.75	1.50	2.50	—

KM# 33.2 10 PENNIA

2.6000 g., Copper, 18.5 mm. **Obv:** Rosette above center hole flanked by leaves dividing date below **Rev:** Center hole divides denomination, rosettes flank **Designer:** Isak Sundell **Note:** Without punched center hole. These issues were not authorized by the government and any that exist were illegally removed from the mint.

Date	Mintage	F	VF	XF	Unc	BU
1941	Inc. above	20.00	30.00	50.00	75.00	—
1942	Inc. above	20.00	30.00	50.00	75.00	—
1943	Inc. above	30.00	50.00	70.00	100	—

KM# 34.2 10 PENNIA

Iron **Obv:** Sprigs divide date, rosette above **Rev:** Rosettes and denomination **Designer:** Isak Sundell **Note:** Without punched center hole. These issues were not authorized by the government and any that exist were illegally removed from the mint.

Date	Mintage	F	VF	XF	Unc	BU
1943	Inc. above	30.00	50.00	70.00	100	—
1944	Inc. above	30.00	50.00	70.00	100	—
1945	Inc. above	50.00	70.00	100	150	—

KM# 34.1 10 PENNIA

1.1200 g., Iron, 16 mm. **Obv:** Rosette above center hole flanked by leaves dividing date below **Rev:** Center hole flanked by rosettes divides denomination **Designer:** Isak Sundell **Note:** Reduced planchet size.

Date	Mintage	F	VF	XF	Unc	BU
1943	1,430,000	0.10	0.25	1.00	5.00	—
1944	3,040,000	0.10	0.25	1.00	5.00	—
1945	1,810,000	0.25	0.50	2.00	10.00	—

KM# 25 25 PENNIA

1.2700 g., Copper-Nickel, 16 mm. **Obv:** Rampant lion left holding sword divides date **Rev:** Denomination flanked by grain sprigs **Designer:** Isak Sundell

Date	Mintage	F	VF	XF	Unc	BU
1921 H	20,096,000	0.10	0.25	1.00	3.00	—
1925 S	1,250,000	0.50	1.50	15.00	25.00	—
1926 S	2,820,000	0.40	1.25	5.00	12.00	—
1927 S	1,120,000	0.50	1.50	10.00	20.00	—
1928 S	2,920,000	0.40	1.00	5.00	12.00	—
1929 S	200,000	2.00	4.00	25.00	50.00	—
1930 S	1,090,000	0.50	1.50	5.00	15.00	—
1934 S	1,260,000	0.40	0.75	3.00	10.00	—
1935 S	2,190,000	0.30	0.50	2.00	8.00	—
1936 S	2,300,000	0.20	0.40	2.00	5.00	—
1937 S	4,019,999	0.20	0.40	1.00	3.00	—
1938 S	4,500,000	0.20	0.40	1.00	3.00	—
1939 S	2,712,000	0.20	0.40	1.00	3.00	—
1940 S	4,840,000	0.15	0.30	0.75	2.00	—

KM# 25a 25 PENNIA

1.2700 g., Copper, 16 mm. **Obv:** Rampant lion left divides date **Rev:** Grain sprigs flank denomination **Designer:** Isak Sundell

Date	Mintage	F	VF	XF	Unc	BU
1940 S	72,000	0.50	1.00	5.00	20.00	—
1941 S	5,980,000	0.10	0.35	2.00	5.00	—
1942 S	6,464,000	0.10	0.35	2.00	5.00	—
1943 S	4,912,000	0.25	0.50	2.00	7.00	—

KM# 25b 25 PENNIA

Iron, 16 mm. **Obv:** Rampant lion left divides dates **Rev:** Grain sprigs flank denomination **Designer:** Isak Sundell

Date	Mintage	F	VF	XF	Unc	BU
1943 S	2,700,000	0.15	0.50	3.00	12.00	—
1944 S	5,480,000	0.15	0.50	2.00	8.00	—
Note: Small closed 4's						
1944 S	Inc. above	0.15	0.50	2.00	8.00	—
Note: Large open 4's						
1945 S	6,810,000	0.25	0.75	3.00	12.00	—

KM# 26 50 PENNIA

2.5500 g., Copper-Nickel, 18.5 mm. **Obv:** Rampant lion left divides date **Designer:** Isak Sundell

Date	Mintage	F	VF	XF	Unc	BU
1921 H	10,072,000	0.15	0.30	1.00	3.00	—
1923 S	6,000,000	0.25	1.00	3.00	12.00	—
1929 S	984,000	1.00	2.00	15.00	40.00	—
1934 S	612,000	1.00	2.50	15.00	40.00	—
1935 S	610,000	1.00	2.50	10.00	35.00	—
1936 S	1,520,000	0.30	0.50	3.00	12.00	—
1937 S	2,350,000	0.15	0.25	1.00	5.00	—
1938 S	2,330,000	0.15	0.25	1.00	5.00	—
1939 S	1,280,000	0.15	0.25	1.00	5.00	—
1940 S	3,152,000	0.15	0.25	1.00	3.00	—

KM# 26a 50 PENNIA

2.5500 g., Copper, 18.5 mm. **Obv:** Rampant lion left divides date **Rev:** Grain sprigs flank denomination **Designer:** Isak Sundell

Date	Mintage	F	VF	XF	Unc	BU
1940 S	480,000	1.25	2.50	8.00	20.00	—
1941 S	3,860,000	0.15	0.40	3.00	8.00	—
1942 S	5,900,000	0.15	0.40	3.00	8.00	—
1943 S	3,140,000	0.25	0.50	3.00	8.00	—

KM# 26b 50 PENNIA

2.2500 g., Iron, 18.5 mm. **Obv:** Rampant lion left divides date **Rev:** Grain sprigs flank denomination **Designer:** Isak Sundell

Date	Mintage	F	VF	XF	Unc	BU
1943 S	1,580,000	0.25	0.50	5.00	20.00	—
1944 S	7,600,000	0.15	0.40	3.00	12.00	—
1945 S	4,700,000	0.15	0.40	3.00	15.00	—
1946 S	2,632,000	0.30	0.50	3.00	15.00	—
1947 S	1,748,000	0.50	2.00	10.00	25.00	—
1948 L	1,112,000	3.00	10.00	20.00	35.00	—

KM# 27 MARKKA

5.1000 g., Copper-Nickel, 24 mm. **Designer:** Isak Sundell

Date	Mintage	F	VF	XF	Unc	BU
1921 H	10,048,000	1.00	2.00	3.00	10.00	—
1922 Heart	10,000,000	1.00	2.00	5.00	15.00	—
1923 S	1,780,000	10.00	20.00	35.00	70.00	—
1924 S	3,270,000	5.00	10.00	20.00	40.00	—

KM# 30 MARKKA

4.0000 g., Copper-Nickel, 21 mm. **Obv:** Rampant lion left divides date **Rev:** Denomination flanked by branches **Designer:** Isak Sundell **Note:** Reduced size.

Date	Mintage	F	VF	XF	Unc	BU
1928 S	3,000,000	0.15	1.00	5.00	20.00	—
1929 S	3,862,000	0.15	1.00	5.00	20.00	—
1930 S	10,284,000	0.15	1.00	5.00	15.00	—
1931 S	2,830,000	0.15	1.00	5.00	15.00	—
1932 S	4,140,000	0.15	1.00	5.00	15.00	—
1933 S	4,032,000	0.15	1.00	5.00	15.00	—
1936 S	562,000	1.00	3.00	15.00	50.00	—
1937 S	4,930,000	0.15	1.00	3.00	6.00	—
1938 S	4,410,000	0.15	1.00	3.00	6.00	—
1939 S	3,070,000	0.15	1.00	3.00	6.00	—
1940 S	3,372,000	0.15	1.00	3.00	6.00	—

Note: Coins dated 1928S, 1929S and 1930S are known to be restruck on 1921-24, KM#27 coins; 1928S: 2 or 3 known

KM# 30a MARKKA

4.0000 g., Copper, 21 mm. **Obv:** Rampant lion left divides date **Rev:** Denomination flanked by branches **Designer:** Isak Sundell

Date	Mintage	F	VF	XF	Unc	BU
1940 S	84,000	1.50	3.50	8.00	20.00	—
1941 S	8,970,000	0.15	0.50	2.00	8.00	—
1942 S	11,200,000	0.15	0.50	2.00	8.00	—
1943 S	7,460,000	0.15	0.50	2.00	8.00	—
1949 H	250	3,000	4,000	6,000	8,000	—
Note: Counterfeits exist						
1950 H	320,000	0.50	1.00	3.00	10.00	—
1951 H	4,630,000	0.25	0.50	2.00	8.00	—

KM# 30b MARKKA

3.5000 g., Iron, 21 mm. **Obv:** Rampant lion left divides date **Rev:** Branches flank denomination **Designer:** Isak Sundell

Date	Mintage	F	VF	XF	Unc	BU
1943 S	7,460,000	0.15	0.25	5.00	20.00	—
1944 S	12,830,000	0.15	0.25	5.00	20.00	—
1945 S	21,950,000	0.15	0.25	5.00	20.00	—
1946 S	2,630,000	0.15	0.30	5.00	20.00	—
1947 S	1,750,000	0.25	0.50	5.00	25.00	—
1948 L	20,500,000	0.15	0.25	3.00	10.00	—
1949 H	17,358,000	0.15	0.25	2.00	8.00	—
1950 H	14,654,000	0.15	0.25	2.00	7.00	—
1951 H	21,414,000	0.15	0.25	2.00	7.00	—
1952 H	5,410,000	0.25	0.50	5.00	20.00	—

KM# 36 MARKKA

1.1500 g., Iron, 16 mm. **Obv:** Four joined loops form design, date below **Rev:** Grasped hands flank denomination **Designer:** Peippo Uolevi Helle

Date	Mintage	F	VF	XF	Unc	BU
1952	22,050,000	0.15	0.35	1.00	7.00	—
1953	28,618,000	0.15	0.35	1.00	7.00	—

KM# 36a MARKKA

1.1500 g., Nickel Plated Iron, 16 mm. **Obv:** Four joined loops form design, date below **Rev:** Grasped hands flank denomination **Designer:** Peippo Uolevi Helle

Date	Mintage	F	VF	XF	Unc	BU
1953	6,000,000	5.00	8.00	15.00	25.00	—
1954	36,400,000	—	0.10	0.25	0.50	—
1955	38,100,000	—	0.10	0.25	0.50	—
1956	35,600,000	—	0.10	0.25	1.00	—
1957	29,100,000	—	0.10	0.25	0.50	—
1958	19,940,000	0.10	0.20	0.35	0.70	—
1959	Inc. above	—	0.10	0.25	1.00	—
Note: Thin letters						
1959	23,920,000	—	0.10	0.25	0.50	—
Note: Thick letters						
1960	22,020,000	—	0.10	0.25	0.50	—
1961	32,220,000	—	0.10	0.25	0.50	—
1962	29,040,000	—	0.10	0.25	0.50	—

KM# 31 5 MARKKAA

4.5000 g., Aluminum-Bronze, 23 mm. **Obv:** Wreath divides denomination **Rev:** Shielded arms within wreath divide date **Designer:** Isak Sundell

Date	Mintage	F	VF	XF	Unc	BU
1928 S	580,000	50.00	80.00	150	350	—
1929 S	Inc. above	50.00	80.00	150	350	—
1930 S	592,000	1.00	3.00	40.00	100	—
1931 S	3,090,000	1.00	2.00	20.00	40.00	—
1932 S	964,000	10.00	25.00	200	400	—
1933 S	1,050,000	1.00	3.00	30.00	100	—
1935 S	440,000	2.00	5.00	30.00	100	—
1936 S	470,000	2.00	5.00	30.00	100	—
1937 S	1,032,000	1.00	3.00	20.00	40.00	—
1938 S	912,000	1.00	3.00	20.00	40.00	—
1939 S	752,000	1.00	3.00	20.00	40.00	—
1940 S	820,000	2.00	5.00	25.00	50.00	—
1941 S	1,452,000	1.00	3.00	12.00	25.00	—
1942 S	1,390,000	1.00	2.00	10.00	20.00	—
1946 S	618,000	5.00	10.00	30.00	100	—

KM# 31a 5 MARKKAA

4.5500 g., Brass, 23 mm. **Obv:** Denomination divided by wreath **Rev:** Shielded arms within wreath divides date below **Designer:** Isak Sundell

Date	Mintage	F	VF	XF	Unc	BU
1946 S	5,538,000	0.50	1.00	2.00	7.00	—
1947 S	6,550,000	1.00	2.00	3.00	12.00	—
1948 L	8,210,000	0.50	1.00	2.00	10.00	—
1949 H	Inc. above	1.00	2.00	3.00	7.00	—
Note: Wide H						
1949 H	11,014,000	2.00	5.00	10.00	20.00	—
Note: Thin H						
1950 H	4,760,000	0.50	1.00	3.00	7.00	—
1951 H	7,800,000	0.50	1.00	2.00	5.00	—
1952 H	1,210,000	3.00	8.00	15.00	30.00	—

KM# 37 5 MARKKAA

2.5500 g., Iron, 18 mm. **Obv:** Four joined loops form design, date below **Rev:** Grasped hands flank denomination **Designer:** Peippo Uolevi Helle

Date	Mintage	F	VF	XF	Unc	BU
1952	10,820,000	0.20	0.35	2.00	8.00	—
1953	9,772,000	0.20	0.35	3.00	10.00	—

KM# 37a 5 MARKKAA

2.5500 g., Nickel Plated Iron, 18 mm. **Obv:** Four joined loops form design, date below **Rev:** Grasped hands flank denomination **Designer:** Peippo Uolevi Helle

Date	Mintage	F	VF	XF	Unc	BU
1953	Inc. above	60.00	100	130	200	—
1954	6,696,000	—	0.20	1.00	5.00	—
1955	9,894,000	—	0.20	1.00	5.00	—
1956	8,220,000	—	0.20	1.00	5.00	—

Date	Mintage	F	VF	XF	Unc	BU
1957	4,276,000	—	0.20	1.00	5.00	—
1958	3,300,000	—	0.20	1.00	7.00	—
1959	5,874,000	—	0.20	1.00	5.00	—
1960	3,066,000	0.10	0.25	1.00	5.00	—
1961	7,254,000	0.10	0.25	0.50	3.00	—
1962	4,542,000	0.50	2.00	5.00	8.00	—

KM# 63 10 MARKKAA

8.0000 g., Aluminum-Bronze, 27 mm. **Obv:** Wreath divides denomination **Rev:** Shielded arms within wreath divide date below **Designer:** Isak Sundell

Date	Mintage	F	VF	XF	Unc	BU
1928 S	730,000	3.00	15.00	70.00	200	—
1929 S	Inc. above	2.00	8.00	50.00	150	—
1930 S	260,000	1.00	5.00	35.00	100	—
1931 S	1,530,000	1.00	3.00	20.00	90.00	—
1932 S	1,010,000	1.00	2.50	10.00	70.00	—
1934 S	154,000	2.00	8.00	50.00	120	—
1935 S	81,000	3.00	12.00	70.00	180	—
1936 S	304,000	2.00	8.00	50.00	100	—
1937 S	181,000	1.50	5.00	20.00	90.00	—
1938 S	631,000	1.00	3.00	15.00	60.00	—
1939 S	133,000	5.00	10.00	30.00	75.00	—

KM# 38 10 MARKKAA

3.0000 g., Aluminum-Bronze, 20 mm. **Obv:** Rampant lion left within circle, date below **Rev:** Tree right of denomination **Designer:** Peippo Uolevi Helle

Date	Mintage	F	VF	XF	Unc	BU
1952 H	6,390,000	0.20	1.00	5.00	12.00	—
1953 H	22,650,000	0.15	0.35	1.00	5.00	—
1954 H	2,452,000	0.50	1.00	5.00	15.00	—
1955 H	2,342,000	0.20	0.50	5.00	12.00	—
1956 H	4,240,000	0.20	0.40	3.00	10.00	—
1958 H	3,292,000	3.00	10.00	20.00	35.00	—
Note: Thin 1						
1958 H	Inc. above	0.20	0.40	3.00	8.00	—
Note: Wide 1						
1960 S	740,000	2.00	5.00	10.00	20.00	—
1961 S	3,580,000	2.00	5.00	10.00	20.00	—
Note: Wide 1						
1961 S	Inc. above	0.20	0.50	2.00	5.00	—
1962 S	1,852,000	0.30	1.00	3.00	7.00	—

Note: The "1" in the denomination on all 1952 to 1956 issues is the thin variety; 1960 issues are the wide variety, and 1961's and 1962's are thin; Varieties exist in root length of tree

KM# 32 20 MARKKAA

13.0000 g., Aluminum-Bronze, 31 mm. **Obv:** Wreath divides denomination **Rev:** Shielded arms within wreath divide date below **Designer:** Isak Sundell

Date	Mintage	F	VF	XF	Unc	BU
1931 S	16,000	20.00	30.00	50.00	75.00	—
1932 S	14,000	30.00	40.00	60.00	90.00	—
1934 S	390,000	2.00	10.00	50.00	100	—
1935 S	250,000	2.00	10.00	50.00	100	—
1936 S	110,000	3.00	15.00	50.00	150	—
1937 S	510,000	1.50	5.00	15.00	50.00	—
1938 S	360,000	1.50	5.00	15.00	50.00	—
1939 S	960,000	1.00	2.00	6.00	20.00	—

KM# 39 20 MARKKAA

4.5000 g., Aluminum-Bronze, 25.5 mm. **Obv:** Rampant lion left within circle, date below **Rev:** Tree right of denomination **Designer:** Peippo Uolevi Helle

Date	Mintage	F	VF	XF	Unc	BU
1952 H	83,000	7.00	10.00	20.00	40.00	—
1953 H	2,880,000	0.25	0.50	3.00	15.00	—
1954 H	17,034,000	0.15	0.50	2.00	10.00	—
1955 H	2,800,000	0.25	0.50	5.00	15.00	—
1956 H	2,540,000	0.25	0.50	5.00	15.00	—
1957 H	1,050,000	0.50	1.00	8.00	20.00	—
1958 H	515,000	2.50	5.00	20.00	40.00	—
1959 S	1,580,000	0.25	0.50	5.00	15.00	—
1960 S	3,850,000	0.15	0.50	3.00	10.00	—
1961 S	4,430,000	0.15	0.50	3.00	10.00	—
1962 S	2,280,000	0.15	0.50	3.00	8.00	—

KM# 40 50 MARKKAA

5.5000 g., Aluminum-Bronze, 25 mm. **Obv:** Rampant lion left within circle, date below **Rev:** Tree right of denomination **Designer:** Peippo Uolevi Helle

Date	Mintage	F	VF	XF	Unc	BU
1952 H	991,000	2.00	5.00	20.00	40.00	—
1953 H	10,300,000	0.25	0.50	3.00	10.00	—
1954 H	1,170,000	2.00	5.00	20.00	40.00	—
1955 H	583,000	2.50	5.00	25.00	50.00	—
1956 H	792,000	2.00	5.00	20.00	40.00	—
1958 H	242,000	25.00	40.00	60.00	75.00	—
1960 S	110,000	25.00	50.00	75.00	100	—
1961 S	1,811,000	1.00	2.00	5.00	15.00	—
1962 S	405,000	2.00	4.00	15.00	25.00	—

KM# 28 100 MARKKAA

4.2105 g., 0.9000 Gold .1218 oz. AGW, 18.5 mm. **Obv:** Rampant lion left divides date **Rev:** Denomination flanked by sprigs **Designer:** Isak Sundell

Date	Mintage	F	VF	XF	Unc	BU
1926 S	50,000	—	950	1,150	1,300	—

KM# 41 100 MARKKAA

5.2000 g., 0.5000 Silver .0836 oz. ASW, 24 mm. **Obv:** Shielded arms above date **Rev:** Denomination surrounded by trees and tree tops **Designer:** Peippo Uolevi Helle

Date	Mintage	F	VF	XF	Unc	BU
1956 H	3,012,000	—	BV	1.50	3.00	—
1957 H	3,012,000	—	BV	1.50	3.00	—
1958 H	1,704,000	BV	2.00	5.00	8.00	—
1959 H	1,270,000	5.00	7.50	18.00	25.00	—
1960 S	290,000	3.50	7.00	12.00	18.00	—

KM# 29 200 MARKKAA

8.4210 g., 0.9000 Gold .2436 oz. AGW, 22.5 mm. **Obv:** Rampant lion left divides date **Rev:** Denomination flanked by sprigs **Designer:** Isak Sundell

Date	Mintage	F	VF	XF	Unc	BU
1926 S	50,000	—	1,300	1,800	2,000	—

KM# 42 200 MARKKAA

8.3000 g., 0.5000 Silver .1334 oz. ASW, 27.5 mm. **Obv:** Shielded arms above date **Rev:** Denomination surrounded by trees and tree tops **Designer:** Peippo Uolevi Helle

Date	Mintage	F	VF	XF	Unc	BU
1956 H	1,552,000	—	BV	3.00	7.00	—
1957 H	2,157,000	—	BV	3.00	7.00	—
1958 H	1,477,000	BV	2.50	5.00	10.00	—
1958 S	34,000	400	600	750	850	—
1959 S	70,000	25.00	40.00	55.00	70.00	—

KM# 35 500 MARKKAA

12.0000 g., 0.5000 Silver .1929 oz. ASW, 32 mm. **Obv:** Wreath divides denomination **Rev:** Olympic logo above date **Designer:** Aarre Aaltonen and Matti Visanti

Date	Mintage	F	VF	XF	Unc	BU
1951 H	19,000	200	300	375	425	—
1952 H	586,000	20.00	28.00	40.00	50.00	—

KM# 43 1000 MARKKAA

14.0000 g., 0.8750 Silver .3938 oz. ASW, 32 mm. **Subject:** Markka Currency System Centennial - Snellman **Obv:** Head left, date below **Rev:** Denomination within wreath **Designer:** Toivo Jaatinen

Date	Mintage	F	VF	XF	Unc	BU
1960 S-J	201,000	7.00	10.00	20.00	30.00	—

REFORM COINAGE

100 Old Markka = 1 New Markka 1963

KM# 44 PENNI

1.6000 g., Copper, 15.8 mm. **Obv:** Four joined loops form design, date below **Rev:** Grasped hands flank denomination **Designer:** Peippo Uolevi Helle

Date	Mintage	F	VF	XF	Unc	BU
1963	171,333,000	—	0.15	0.25	1.50	—
Note: Struck at Leningrad Mint						
1964	49,300,000	—	0.15	0.50	2.00	—
1965	43,112,000	—	0.15	0.50	2.00	—
1966	36,880,000	—	0.15	0.50	2.00	—
1967	62,792,000	—	0.15	0.50	2.00	—
1968	73,416,000	—	—	0.50	2.00	—
1969	51,748,000	—	—	0.50	2.00	—

KM# 44a PENNI

0.4500 g., Aluminum, 15.8 mm. **Obv:** Four joined loops form design, date below **Rev:** Grasped hands flank denomination **Designer:** Peippo Uolevi Helle

Date	Mintage	F	VF	XF	Unc	BU
1969	28,524,000	—	—	0.50	2.00	—
1970	85,140,000	—	—	0.20	1.00	—
1971	70,240,000	—	—	0.20	1.00	—
1972	95,096,000	—	—	0.20	1.00	—
1973	115,532,000	—	—	0.20	0.50	—
1974	100,132,000	—	—	0.20	0.50	—

Date	Mintage	F	VF	XF	Unc	BU
1975	111,906,000	—	—	0.20	0.50	—
1976	34,965,000	—	—	0.20	0.50	—
1977	61,393,000	—	—	0.20	0.50	—
1978	90,132,000	—	—	0.20	0.50	—
1979	33,388,000	—	—	0.20	0.50	—

KM# 45 5 PENNIA
2.6000 g., Copper, 18.5 mm. **Obv:** Four joined loops form design, date below **Rev:** Grasped hands flank denomination **Designer:** Peippo Uolevi Helle

Date	Mintage	F	VF	XF	Unc	BU
1963	60,320,000	—	0.15	0.50	1.50	—
1964	4,634,000	0.50	1.00	5.00	15.00	—
1965	10,264,000	—	0.15	0.50	2.00	—
1966	8,064,000	—	0.15	0.50	3.00	—
1967	9,968,000	—	0.15	0.50	2.00	—
1968	6,144,000	—	0.15	0.50	2.00	—
1969	3,598,000	—	0.15	0.50	2.00	—
1970	13,772,000	—	0.15	0.25	1.00	—
1971	20,010,000	—	—	0.25	1.00	—
1972	24,122,000	—	—	0.25	1.00	—
1973	25,644,000	—	—	0.25	1.00	—
1974	21,530,000	—	—	0.25	1.00	—
1975	25,010,000	—	—	0.25	1.00	—
1976	25,551,000	—	—	0.25	1.00	—
1977	1,489,000	—	0.10	0.50	1.50	—

KM# 45a 5 PENNIA
0.8000 g., Aluminum, 18 mm. **Obv:** Four joined loops form design, date below **Rev:** Grasped hands flank denomination **Designer:** Peippo Uolevi Helle

Date	Mintage	F	VF	XF	Unc	BU
1977	30,552,000	—	—	0.15	0.50	—
1978	26,112,000	—	—	0.15	0.50	—
1979	40,042,000	—	—	0.15	0.50	—
1980	60,026,000	—	—	0.15	0.50	—
1981	2,044,000	—	0.20	0.40	1.00	—
1982	10,012,000	—	—	0.25	0.75	—
1983	33,885,000	—	—	—	0.25	—
1984	25,001,000	—	—	—	0.25	—
1985	25,000,000	—	—	—	0.25	—
1986	20,000,000	—	—	—	0.25	—
1987	2,020,000	—	—	—	0.25	—
1988	33,005,000	—	—	—	0.15	—
1989	2,200,000	—	—	—	0.50	—
1990	2,506,000	—	—	—	0.50	—

KM# 46 10 PENNIA
3.0000 g., Aluminum-Bronze, 20 mm. **Obv:** Rampant lion left, date below **Rev:** Tree right of denomination **Designer:** Peippo Uolevi Helle

Date	Mintage	F	VF	XF	Unc	BU
1963 S	38,420,000	—	0.15	0.50	1.50	—
1964 S	6,926,000	—	0.15	1.00	3.00	—
1965 S	4,524,000	—	0.15	0.50	3.00	—
1966 S	3,094,000	—	0.15	0.50	2.00	—
1967 S	1,050,000	0.15	0.30	3.00	10.00	—
1968 S	3,004,000	—	0.15	0.25	1.50	—
1969 S	5,046,000	—	—	0.20	1.50	—
1970 S	3,996,000	—	—	0.20	1.50	—
1971 S	15,026,000	—	—	0.10	1.00	—
1972 S	19,900,000	—	—	0.10	1.00	—
1973 S	9,196,000	—	—	0.10	1.00	—
1974 S	8,930,000	—	—	0.10	1.00	—
1975 S	15,064,000	—	—	0.10	0.50	—
1976 K	10,063,000	—	—	0.10	0.50	—
1977 K	10,043,000	—	—	0.10	0.50	—
1978 K	10,062,000	—	—	0.10	0.50	—
1979 K	13,072,000	—	—	0.10	0.50	—
1980 K	23,654,000	—	—	0.10	0.50	—
1981 K	30,036,000	—	—	0.10	0.50	—
1982 K	35,548,000	—	—	0.10	0.50	—

KM# 46a 10 PENNIA
1.0000 g., Aluminum, 20 mm. **Obv:** Rampant lion left, date below **Rev:** Tree right of denomination **Designer:** Peippo Uolevi Helle

Date	Mintage	F	VF	XF	Unc	BU
1983 K	6,320,000	—	—	0.25	1.00	—
1983 N	4,191,000	—	—	0.25	1.00	—
1984 N	20,061,000	—	—	0.10	0.50	—
1985 N	20,000,000	—	—	0.10	0.50	—

Date	Mintage	F	VF	XF	Unc	BU
1986 N	15,000,000	—	—	0.10	0.50	—
1987 N	1,400,000	—	—	0.25	1.00	—
1987 M	8,654,000	—	—	0.25	1.00	—
1988 M	23,197,000	—	—	0.10	0.50	—
1989 M	2,400,000	—	—	0.25	0.50	—
1990 M	2,254,000	—	—	0.25	0.50	—

KM# 65 10 PENNIA
1.8000 g., Copper-Nickel, 16.3 mm. **Obv:** Flower pods and stems, date at right **Rev:** Denomination to right of honeycombs **Designer:** Antti Neuvonen

Date	Mintage	F	VF	XF	Unc	BU
1990 M	338,100,000	—	—	0.10	0.15	—
1991 M	263,899,000	—	—	0.10	0.15	—
1992 M	136,131,000	—	—	0.10	0.15	—
1993 M	56,206,000	—	—	0.10	0.15	—
1994 M	59,946,000	—	—	0.10	0.15	—
1994 M Proof	5,000	Value: 7.00				
1995 M Proof	3,000	Value: 7.00				
1995 M	85,000,000	—	—	0.10	0.15	—
1996 M	123,000,000	—	—	0.10	0.15	—
1996 M Proof	1,200	Value: 7.00				
1997 M	43,406,000	—	—	0.10	0.15	—
1997 M Proof	2,000	Value: 7.00				
1998 M	95,322,000	—	—	0.10	0.15	—
1998 M Proof	2,000	Value: 7.00				
1999 M	46,375,000	—	—	0.10	0.15	—
1999 M Proof	—	Value: 7.00				
2000 M	114,903,000	—	—	—	0.15	—
2000 M Proof	—	Value: 7.00				

KM# 47 20 PENNIA
4.5000 g., Aluminum-Bronze, 22.5 mm. **Obv:** Rampant lion left, date below **Rev:** Tree right of denomination **Designer:** Peippo Uolevi Helle

Date	Mintage	F	VF	XF	Unc	BU
1963 S	39,970,000	—	0.15	0.20	1.50	—
1964 S	4,248,000	0.50	1.00	2.50	5.00	—
1965 S	5,704,000	0.10	0.50	1.00	3.00	—
1966 S	4,085,000	0.10	0.50	1.00	3.00	—
1967 S	1,716,000	0.10	0.50	1.00	3.00	—
1968 S	1,330,000	0.10	0.50	1.00	3.00	—
1969 S	201,000	0.50	1.00	2.00	4.00	—
1970 S	230,000	0.50	1.00	2.00	3.50	—
1971 S	5,150,000	—	0.25	0.50	1.00	—
Note: Some coins dated 1971 are magnetic and command a higher premium						
1972 S	10,001,000	—	0.25	0.50	1.00	—
1973 S	9,462,000	—	0.25	0.50	1.00	—
1974 S	12,705,000	—	0.25	0.50	1.00	—
1975 S	12,068,000	—	0.25	0.50	1.00	—
1976 K	20,058,000	—	0.25	0.50	1.00	—
1977 K	10,063,000	—	0.25	0.50	1.00	—
1978 K	10,014,000	—	0.25	0.50	1.00	—
1979 K	7,513,000	—	0.25	0.50	1.00	—
1980 K	20,047,000	—	—	0.25	0.50	—
1981 K	30,002,000	—	—	0.25	0.50	—
1982 K	35,050,000	—	—	0.25	0.50	—
1983 K	7,113,000	—	—	0.25	0.50	—
1983 N	12,889,000	—	—	0.25	0.50	—
1984 N	20,029,000	—	—	0.25	0.50	—
1985 N	15,004,000	—	—	0.25	0.50	—
1986 N	20,001,000	—	—	0.25	0.50	—
1987 N	1,200,000	—	0.25	0.50	1.00	—
1987 M	25,670,000	—	—	0.25	0.50	—
1988 M	13,853,000	—	—	0.25	0.50	—
1989 M	40,695,000	—	—	0.25	0.50	—
1990 M	9,168,000	—	—	0.25	0.50	—

KM# 48 50 PENNIA
5.5000 g., Aluminum-Bronze, 25.0 mm. **Obv:** Rampant lion left, date below **Rev:** Tree right of denomination **Designer:** Peippo Uolevi Helle

Date	Mintage	F	VF	XF	Unc	BU
1963 S	17,316,000	—	0.20	0.50	3.00	—
1964 S	3,101,000	—	0.25	3.00	10.00	—
1965 S	1,667,000	—	0.20	2.00	5.00	—

Date	Mintage	F	VF	XF	Unc	BU
1966 S	1,051,000	—	0.20	2.00	5.00	—
1967 S	400,000	0.25	0.50	2.00	5.00	—
1968 S	816,000	—	0.25	1.00	4.00	—
1969 S	1,341,000	—	0.20	0.50	3.00	—
1970 S	2,250,000	—	0.20	0.50	2.00	—
1971 S	10,003,000	—	0.20	0.50	1.50	—
Note: Some coins dated 1971 are magnetic and command a higher premium						
1972 S	7,892,000	—	0.20	0.50	1.50	—
1973 S	5,428,000	—	0.20	0.50	1.50	—
1974 S	5,049,000	—	0.20	0.50	1.50	—
1975 S	4,305,000	—	0.20	0.50	1.50	—
1976 K	7,022,000	—	0.20	0.50	1.50	—
1977 K	8,077,000	—	0.20	0.50	1.50	—
1978 K	8,048,000	—	0.20	0.50	1.50	—
1979 K	8,004,000	—	0.20	0.50	1.50	—
1980 K	5,349,000	—	0.20	0.50	1.50	—
1981 K	20,031,000	—	0.20	0.50	1.00	—
1982 K	5,042,000	—	0.20	0.50	1.00	—
1983 K	4,043,999	—	—	0.25	1.00	—
1983 N	1,016,000	—	0.20	0.50	1.50	—
1984 N	3,006,000	—	—	0.25	1.00	—
1985 N	10,000,000	—	—	0.25	1.00	—
1986 N	9,002,000	—	—	0.25	1.00	—
1987 N	700,000	—	0.30	0.75	1.50	—
1987 M	4,305,000	—	—	0.25	1.00	—
1988 M	14,735,000	—	—	0.25	1.00	—
1989 M	10,651,000	—	—	0.25	1.00	—
1990 M	5,391,000	—	—	0.50	2.00	—

KM# 66 50 PENNIA
3.3000 g., Copper-Nickel, 19.7 mm. **Obv:** Polar bear, date below **Rev:** Denomination above flower heads **Designer:** Antti Neuvonen

Date	Mintage	F	VF	XF	Unc	BU
1990 M	70,459,000	—	—	0.20	0.75	—
1991 M	90,480,000	—	—	0.20	0.75	—
1992 M	58,996,000	—	—	0.20	0.75	—
1993 M	10,066,000	—	—	0.20	0.75	—
1994 M	3,005,000	—	—	0.20	0.75	—
1994 M Proof	5,000	Value: 8.00				
1995 M	1,048,000	—	—	0.20	0.75	—
1995 M Proof	3,000	Value: 8.00				
1996 M	17,000,000	—	—	0.20	0.75	—
1996 M Proof	1,200	Value: 8.00				
1997 M	524,000	—	—	0.20	0.75	—
1997 M Proof	2,000	Value: 8.00				
1998 M Proof	2,000	Value: 8.00				
1998 M	3,345,500	—	—	0.20	0.75	—
1999 M	100,000	—	—	0.20	0.75	—
1999 M Proof	—	Value: 8.00				
2000 M	100,000	—	—	0.20	0.75	—
2000 M Proof	—	Value: 8.00				

KM# 49 MARKKA
6.4000 g., 0.3500 Silver .0720 oz. ASW, 24 mm. **Obv:** Rampant lion left, date below **Obv. Designer:** Olof Eriksson **Rev:** Stylized fir trees with denomination in center **Rev. Designer:** Heikki Haivaoja **Edge Lettering:** SUOMI FINLAND

Date	Mintage	F	VF	XF	Unc	BU
1964 S	9,999,000	BV	1.20	2.00	5.00	—
1965 S	15,107,000	—	BV	1.50	4.00	—
1966 S	15,183,000	—	BV	1.50	3.00	—
1967 S	6,249,000	—	BV	1.50	3.00	—
1968 S	3,063,000	—	BV	1.50	3.00	—

KM# 49a MARKKA
6.1000 g., Copper-Nickel, 24 mm. **Obv:** Rampant lion left, date below **Obv. Designer:** Olof Eriksson **Rev:** Denomination flanked by stylized fir trees **Rev. Designer:** Heikki Haivaoja **Edge Lettering:** SUOMI FINLAND

Date	Mintage	F	VF	XF	Unc	BU
1969 S	1,308,000	0.25	0.50	1.00	2.00	—
1970 S	12,255,000	—	0.35	0.50	1.00	—
1971 S	19,676,000	—	0.35	0.50	1.00	—
1972 S	19,885,000	—	0.35	0.50	1.00	—
1973 S	17,060,000	—	0.35	0.50	1.00	—
1974 S	18,065,000	—	0.35	0.50	1.00	—
1975 S	11,523,000	—	0.35	0.50	1.00	—
1976 K	12,048,000	—	0.35	0.50	1.00	—
1977 K	10,077,000	—	0.35	0.50	1.00	—
1978 K	10,022,000	—	0.35	0.50	1.00	—
1979 K	11,311,000	—	0.35	0.50	1.00	—
1980 K	19,306,000	—	—	0.35	0.75	—

Date	Mintage	F	VF	XF	Unc	BU
1981 K	32,003,000	—	—	0.35	0.75	—
1982 K	30,001,000	—	—	0.35	0.75	—
1983 K	8,074,999	—	—	0.35	0.75	—
1983 N	11,927,000	—	—	0.35	0.75	—
1984 N	15,000,000	—	—	0.35	0.75	—
1985 N	19,001,000	—	—	0.35	0.75	—
1986 N	10,000,000	—	—	0.35	0.75	—
1987 M	9,303,000	—	—	0.35	0.75	—
1987 N	700,000	—	0.50	1.00	2.00	—
1988 M	27,535,000	—	—	0.35	0.75	—
1989 M	37,520,000	—	—	0.35	0.75	—
1990 M	50,305,000	—	—	0.35	0.75	—
1991 M	15,026,000	—	—	0.35	0.75	—
1992 M	3,628,000	—	—	0.35	0.75	—
1993 M	1,036,000	—	—	0.50	1.00	—

KM# 76a MARKKA

Copper-Nickel **Obv:** Rampant lion left within circle, date below **Rev:** Ornaments flank denomination

Date	Mintage	F	VF	XF	Unc	BU
1993 M	100,000	—	—	—	—	—

Note: In sets only

KM# 76 MARKKA

4.9000 g., Aluminum-Bronze, 22 mm. **Obv:** Rampant lion left within circle, date below **Rev:** Ornaments flank denomination within circle

Date	Mintage	F	VF	XF	Unc	BU
1993 M	91,588,000	—	—	0.35	0.75	—
1994 M	152,011,000	—	—	0.35	0.75	—
1994 M Proof	5,000	Value: 10.00				
1995 M	40,008,000	—	—	0.35	0.75	—
1995 M Proof	3,000	Value: 10.00				
1996 M Proof	1,200	Value: 10.00				
1996 M	21,000,000	—	—	0.35	0.75	—
1997 M	23,775,200	—	—	0.35	0.75	—
1997 M Proof	2,000	Value: 10.00				
1998 M	33,955,200	—	—	0.35	0.75	—
1998 M Proof	2,000	Value: 10.00				
1999 M	100,000	—	—	0.35	0.75	—
1999 M Proof	—	Value: 10.00				
2000 M Proof	—	Value: 10.00				
2000 M	100,000	—	—	0.35	0.75	—

KM# 53 5 MARKKAA

8.0000 g., Aluminum-Bronze, 26.3 mm. **Obv:** Icebreaker "Varma", date below **Rev:** Stylized flock of birds **Edge Lettering:** REPUBLIKEN FINLAND SUOMEN TASAVALTA **Designer:** Heikki Haivaoja

Date	Mintage	F	VF	XF	Unc	BU
1972 S	400,000	1.50	2.00	2.50	4.00	—
1973 S	2,188,000	—	1.25	2.00	3.00	—
1974 S	300,000	—	1.25	2.00	3.00	—
1975 S	300,000	—	1.25	2.00	3.00	—
1976 K	400,000	—	1.25	2.00	3.00	—
1977 K	300,000	—	1.25	2.00	3.00	—
1978 K	300,000	—	1.25	2.00	3.00	—

KM# 57 5 MARKKAA

8.0000 g., Aluminum-Bronze, 26.3 mm. **Obv:** Icebreaker "Urho", date below **Rev:** Stylized flock of birds with denomination at top **Designer:** Heikki Haivaoja

Date	Mintage	F	VF	XF	Unc	BU
1979 K	2,005,000	—	—	1.50	2.25	—
1980 K	501,000	—	1.50	2.00	3.00	—
1981 K	1,009,000	—	—	1.50	2.25	—
1982 K	3,004,000	—	—	1.50	2.25	—
1983 K	8,776,000	—	—	1.50	2.25	—
1983 N	11,230,000	—	—	1.50	2.25	—
1984 N	15,001,000	—	—	1.50	2.25	—
1985 N	8,005,000	—	—	1.50	2.25	—
1986 N	5,006,000	—	—	1.50	2.25	—
1987 N	660,000	—	1.50	2.00	3.00	—

Date	Mintage	F	VF	XF	Unc	BU
1987 M	2,348,000	—	—	1.50	2.25	—
1988 M	3,042,000	—	—	1.50	2.25	—
1989 M	10,175,000	—	—	1.50	2.25	—
1990 M	9,925,000	—	—	1.50	2.25	—
1991 M	9,910,000	—	—	2.00	3.00	—
1992 M	547,000	—	—	2.00	3.00	—
1993 M	911,000	—	—	2.00	3.00	—

KM# 73 5 MARKKAA

5.5000 g., Copper-Aluminum-Nickel, 24.5 mm. **Obv:** Lake Saimaa ringed seal, date below **Rev:** Denomination, dragonfly and lilypad leaves

Date	Mintage	F	VF	XF	Unc	BU
1992 M	800,000	—	—	—	3.50	5.00
1993 M	46,034,000	—	—	—	2.00	4.00
1994 M	19,003,000	—	—	—	2.00	4.00
1994 M Proof	5,000	Value: 12.00				
1995 M	9,016,000	—	—	—	2.50	4.50
1995 M Proof	3,000	Value: 12.00				
1996 M	7,000,000	—	—	—	2.50	4.50
1996 M Proof	1,200	Value: 12.00				
1997 M	537,700	—	—	2.00	3.00	5.00
1997 M Proof	2,000	Value: 12.00				
1998 M	813,650	—	—	—	2.50	4.50
1998 M Proof	2,000	Value: 12.00				
1999 M	100,000	—	—	—	2.50	4.50
1999 M Proof	—	Value: 12.00				
2000 M	100,000	—	—	—	2.50	4.50
2000 M Proof	—	Value: 12.00				

KM# 50 10 MARKKAA

23.7500 g., 0.9000 Silver .6872 oz. ASW, 35 mm. **Subject:** 50th Anniversary of Independence **Obv:** Five Whooper swans in flight, date above **Rev:** Design above denomination **Edge Lettering:** ITSENAINEN SUOMI 50 FINLAND SJALVSTANDIGT 50 **Designer:** Heikki Haivaoja

Date	Mintage	F	VF	XF	Unc	BU
1967 S-H	1,000,000	—	—	BV	10.00	12.00

KM# 51 10 MARKKAA

22.7500 g., 0.5000 Silver .3657 oz. ASW, 35 mm. **Subject:** Centennial - Birth of President Paasikivi **Obv:** Denomination below date, brick wall background **Rev:** Head facing **Designer:** Heikki Haivaoja

Date	Mintage	F	VF	XF	Unc	BU
1970 S-H	600,000	—	—	BV	5.50	6.50

KM# 52 10 MARKKAA

24.2000 g., 0.5000 Silver .3890 oz. ASW, 35 mm. **Subject:** 10th European Athletic Championships **Obv:** Denomination above city scene **Rev:** Runners on track, date lower right **Designer:** Heikki Haivaoja

Date	Mintage	F	VF	XF	Unc	BU
1971 S-H	1,000,000	—	—	BV	5.50	6.50

KM# 54 10 MARKKAA

23.5000 g., 0.5000 Silver .3778 oz. ASW, 35 mm. **Subject:** 75th Birthday of President Kekkonen **Obv:** Denomination below trees, hills in background **Rev:** Head facing **Designer:** Heikki Haivaoja

Date	Mintage	F	VF	XF	Unc	BU
1975 S-H	1,000,000	—	—	BV	5.50	6.50

KM# 55 10 MARKKAA

21.7800 g., 0.5000 Silver .3501 oz. ASW, 35 mm. **Subject:** 60th Anniversary of Independence **Obv:** Four line inscription superimposed over five line inscription, date at left **Rev:** Crowds of people, denomination upper right **Designer:** Heikki Haivaoja

Date	Mintage	F	VF	XF	Unc	BU
1977 K-H	400,000	—	—	BV	5.50	6.50

KM# 77 10 MARKKAA

8.8000 g., Bi-Metallic Brass center in Copper-Nickel ring, 27.25 mm. **Obv:** Capercaillie bird within circle, date above **Rev:** Denomination and branches

Date	Mintage	F	VF	XF	Unc	BU
1993 M	30,002,000	—	—	2.00	3.50	4.50
1994 M	19,979,000	—	—	2.00	3.50	4.50
1994 M Proof	5,000	Value: 18.00				
1995 M	4,008,000	—	—	2.00	3.50	4.50
1995 M Proof	3,000	Value: 18.00				
1996 M Proof	1,200	Value: 18.00				
1996 M	3,300,000	—	—	2.00	3.50	4.50
1997 M Proof	2,000	Value: 18.00				
1997 M	917,607	—	—	2.00	3.50	4.50
1998 M	797,713	—	—	2.00	3.50	4.50
1998 M Proof	2,000	Value: 18.00				
1999 M	100,000	—	—	3.00	5.00	6.00
1999 M Proof	—	Value: 18.00				
2000 M	100,000	—	—	3.00	5.00	6.00
2000 M Proof	—	Value: 18.00				

KM# 82 10 MARKKAA
8.0000 g., Bi-Metallic Brass center in Copper-Nickel ring, 27.25 mm. **Subject:** European Unity **Obv:** Swan in flight within circle, date upper right **Rev:** Denomination and branches **Designer:** Pertti Makinen and Antti Neuvonen

Date	Mintage	F	VF	XF	Unc	BU
1995 M	500,000	—	—	2.50	4.50	6.00

KM# 82a 10 MARKKAA
Bi-Metallic Gold center in Silver ring, 27.25 mm. **Subject:** European Unity **Obv:** Swan in flight left within circle **Rev:** Denomination and branches **Designer:** Pertti Makinen and Antti Neuvonen **Note:** Total weight 12.200 grams.

Date	Mintage	F	VF	XF	Unc	BU
1995 M Proof	2,000	Value: 2,500				

KM# 91a 10 MARKKAA
13.2000 g., Bi-Metallic Gold And Silver **Ring Composition:** 0.7500 Gold **Center Composition:** 0.9250 Silver, 27.25 mm. **Obv:** Fire breathing profile left **Rev:** Denomination and branches **Edge:** Lettered **Designer:** Jarkko Roth and Antti Neuvonen **Note:** Total weight 13.200 grams.

Date	Mintage	F	VF	XF	Unc	BU
1999	3,000	—	—	—	1,000	1,150

KM# 91 10 MARKKAA
8.8200 g., Bi-Metallic Copper-Nickel center in Brass ring, 27.25 mm. **Obv:** Fire breathing profile left, date at right **Rev:** Denomination and branches **Note:** Finnish Presidency of the EU.

Date	Mintage	F	VF	XF	Unc	BU
1999	100,000	—	—	7.50	10.00	—

KM# 56 25 MARKKAA
26.3000 g., 0.5000 Silver .4228 oz. ASW, 37 mm. **Subject:** Winter Games in Lahti **Obv:** Ski trail, denomination at left **Rev. Designer:** Cross country skier, date at left **Designer:** Antti Neuvonen

Date	Mintage	F	VF	XF	Unc	BU
1978 K-N	500,000	—	—	6.00	7.00	—

KM# 58 25 MARKKAA
26.3000 g., 0.5000 Silver .4228 oz. ASW, 37 mm. **Subject:** 750th Anniversary of Turku **Obv:** School of fish, denomination above **Rev:** City scene with dates **Designer:** Heikki Haivaoja

Date	Mintage	F	VF	XF	Unc	BU
1979 K-H	300,000	—	—	6.00	7.00	12.00

KM# 85 25 MARKKAA
20.2000 g., Bi-Metallic Brass center in Copper-Nickel ring, 35 mm. **Subject:** 80th Anniversary of Independence **Obv:** Stylized landscape, dates below **Rev:** Stylized city view, denomination below **Designer:** Tero Lounas

Date	Mintage	F	VF	XF	Unc	BU
ND(1997) M-L	100,000	—	—	10.00	12.00	—
ND(1997) M-L Proof	2,000	Value: 16.50				

Note: In sets only

KM# 59 50 MARKKAA
20.0000 g., 0.5000 Silver .3216 oz. ASW, 30 mm. **Subject:** 80th Birthday of President Kekkonen **Obv:** Head 3/4 facing **Rev:** Horses, denomination above **Designer:** Nina Terno

Date	Mintage	F	VF	XF	Unc	BU
1981 K	500,000	—	—	8.50	10.00	15.00

KM# 60 50 MARKKAA
23.1000 g., 0.5000 Silver .3698 oz. ASW, 35 mm. **Subject:** World Ice Hockey Championship Games **Obv:** Denomination **Rev:** Hockey player, date at right **Designer:** Erja Tielinen

Date	Mintage	F	VF	XF	Unc	BU
1982 K-T	400,000	—	—	10.00	12.00	15.00

KM# 61 50 MARKKAA
21.8000 g., 0.5000 Silver .3537 oz. ASW, 35 mm. **Subject:** 1st World Athletics Championships **Obv:** Trees divide denomination **Rev:** Hurdler, date at right **Designer:** Pertti Makinen and Toivo Pelkonen

Date	Mintage	F	VF	XF	Unc	BU
1983 K-M	450,000	—	—	10.00	12.00	15.00

KM# 62 50 MARKKAA
19.9000 g., 0.5000 Silver .3216 oz. ASW, 35 mm. **Subject:** National Epic - The Kalevala **Obv:** Trees with reflections, denomination at right **Rev:** Stylized waves with figure, dates below **Designer:** Tapio Nevalainen

Date	Mintage	F	VF	XF	Unc	BU
1985 P-N	300,000	—	—	13.00	15.00	18.00

KM# 75 100 MARKKAA
24.0000 g., 0.8300 Silver .6405 oz. ASW **Subject:** Pictorial Arts of Finland **Obv:** Artistic design, denomination above **Rev:** Two figures holding artists palette, date at right **Designer:** Reijo Paavilainen

Date	Mintage	F	VF	XF	Unc	BU
1989 P-M	100,000	—	—	25.00	35.00	42.50

KM# 67 100 MARKKAA
24.0000 g., 0.8300 Silver .6405 oz. ASW **Subject:** 50th Anniversary of Disabled War Veterans Association **Obv:** Home and landscape scene, denomination above **Rev:** Cross superimposed on people, date below **Designer:** Reijo Paavilainen

Date	Mintage	F	VF	XF	Unc	BU
1990 P-M	100,000	—	—	25.00	35.00	40.00

KM# 68 100 MARKKAA
24.0000 g., 0.8300 Silver .6405 oz. ASW **Subject:** 350th Anniversary - University of Helsinki **Obv:** Owl, denomination below **Rev:** Harp within square, dates below **Designer:** Raimo Heino

Date	Mintage	F	VF	XF	Unc	BU
1990 H-M	150,000	—	—	25.00	45.00	60.00

KM# 69 100 MARKKAA
24.0000 g., 0.8300 Silver .6405 oz. ASW **Subject:** Ice Hockey

World Championship Games **Obv:** Stylized design, date lower right **Rev:** Stylized hockey player, denomination below **Designer:** Arto Lappalainen

Date	Mintage	F	VF	XF	Unc	BU
1991 L-M	200	Value: 350				
Note: Struck with polished dies to prooflike quality and encapsulated in hard plastic 60 mm x 83 mm square; these pieces were given out as business gifts to selected mint visitors						
1991 L-M	150,000	—	—	25.00	35.00	40.00

KM# 70 100 MARKKAA

24.0000 g., 0.9250 Silver .7137 oz. ASW **Subject:** 70th Anniversary - Autonomy of Aland **Obv:** Masted ship at sea, denomination above **Rev:** Stag on crowned shield, dates below **Designer:** Reijo Paavilainen

Date	Mintage	F	VF	XF	Unc	BU
1991 P-M	100,000	—	—	25.00	35.00	40.00
1991 P-M	Est. 700	Value: 400				
Note: Encapsulated as KM#69 above, but struck to higher prooflike quality						

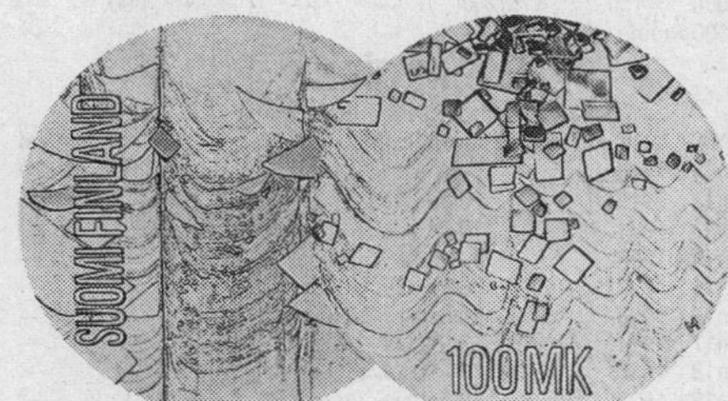

KM# 71 100 MARKKAA

24.0000 g., 0.9250 Silver .7137 oz. ASW **Subject:** 75th Anniversary of Independence **Obv:** Pine trees **Rev:** Artistic design, denomination below **Designer:** Erkki Salmela

Date	Mintage	F	VF	XF	Unc	BU
1992 M-S	300,000	—	—	20.00	22.50	25.00

KM# 78 100 MARKKAA

24.0000 g., 0.9250 Silver .7137 oz. ASW **Subject:** Stadium of Friendship **Obv:** Laurel sprig, stylized stadium, denomination above **Rev:** Sprinters, date above **Designer:** Reijo Paavilainen

Date	Mintage	F	VF	XF	Unc	BU
1994 P-M	80,000	—	—	—	22.50	25.00
Note: Encapsulated as KM#69 above, but struck to higher proof quality						
1994 P-M Proof	15,000	Value: 30.00				

KM# 80 100 MARKKAA

24.0000 g., 0.9250 Silver .7137 oz. ASW **Subject:** 100th Birthday - Artturi Ilmari Virtanen **Obv:** Budding branch, denomination below **Rev:** Head right **Designer:** Terho Sakki

Date	Mintage	F	VF	XF	Unc	BU
1995 S-M	40,000	—	—	30.00	35.00	40.00
1995 S-M Proof	3,000	Value: 65.00				

KM# 81 100 MARKKAA

24.0000 g., 0.9250 Silver .7137 oz. ASW **Subject:** 50th Anniversary - United Nations **Obv:** Design, denomination at left, date below **Rev:** Face foreward, dates at right **Designer:** Reijo Paavilainen

Date	Mintage	F	VF	XF	Unc	BU
1995 P-M	40,000	—	—	—	35.00	40.00
1995 P-M Proof	3,000	Value: 65.00				

KM# 83 100 MARKKAA

24.0000 g., 0.9250 Silver .7137 oz. ASW **Subject:** Helene Schjerfbeck - Painter - 50th Anniversary of Her Death **Designer:** Erja Tielinen

Date	Mintage	F	VF	XF	Unc	BU
1996 T-M	300,000	—	—	—	60.00	75.00
1996 T-M Proof	3,000	Value: 150				

KM# 84 100 MARKKAA

22.0000 g., 0.9250 Silver .6543 oz. ASW **Subject:** 100th Birthday - Paavo Nurmi **Obv:** Two gymnasts **Rev:** Facial portrait and running Paavo Nurmi, denomination below **Designer:** Erkki Salmela

Date	Mintage	F	VF	XF	Unc	BU
1997 M-S	45,000	—	—	30.00	35.00	40.00
1997 M-S Proof	6,500	Value: 65.00				

KM# 87 100 MARKKAA

22.0000 g., 0.9250 Silver .6543 oz. ASW **Subject:** 100th Birthday - Alvar Aalto **Obv:** Walls above cliffs and denominations **Rev:** Mature rye plants, dates in vertical at right **Designer:** Henrik Gummerus

Date	Mintage	F	VF	XF	Unc	BU
1998 M-G	Est. 44,000	—	—	—	25.00	30.00
1998 M-G Proof	4,000	Value: 65.00				

KM# 88 100 MARKKAA

22.0000 g., 0.9250 Silver .6543 oz. ASW **Subject:** Suomenlinna Fortress **Obv:** Stylized island view, denomination below **Rev:** Sailship and fortress gate, dates at right **Designer:** Harri Ojala

Date	Mintage	F	VF	XF	Unc	BU
1998 M-O Proof	3,300	Value: 65.00				
1998 M-O	30,000	—	—	25.00	30.00	35.00

KM# 89 100 MARKKAA

22.0000 g., 0.9250 Silver .6543 oz. ASW **Subject:** Jean Sibelius - Composer **Obv:** Head left **Rev:** Finlandia musical score divides date and denomination **Designer:** Juhani Pallasmaa and Jukka Veistola

Date	Mintage	F	VF	XF	Unc	BU
1999 P-V-M	30,000	—	—	30.00	35.00	40.00
1999 P-V-M Proof	6,000	Value: 65.00				

KM# 92 100 MARKKAA

22.0000 g., 0.9250 Silver .6543 oz. ASW **Subject:** Jubilee Year 2000 **Obv:** Turku Cathedral vault ceiling design, denomination below **Rev:** Leaf within circle, date below **Edge:** Plain **Designer:** Maija Lavonen

Date	Mintage	F	VF	XF	Unc	BU
2000 L-M	15,000	—	—	35.00	50.00	60.00
2000 L-M Proof	3,000	Value: 80.00				

KM# 93 100 MARKKAA

22.0000 g., 0.9250 Silver .6543 oz. ASW **Subject:** 450th Anniversary - Helsinki Cultural Capital **Obv:** Symbolic column design **Rev:** Carved city view, denomination upper left **Edge:** Plain **Designer:** Reijo Paavilainen

Date	Mintage	F	VF	XF	Unc	BU
2000 P-M	10,000	—	—	35.00	50.00	60.00

KM# 94 100 MARKKAA
22.0000 g., 0.9250 Silver .6543 oz. ASW, 35 mm. **Subject:** Aleksis Kivi **Obv:** Books on shelves, denomination below **Rev:** Portrait on partial disc, facing left, date at left **Edge:** Plain

Date	Mintage	F	VF	XF	Unc	BU
2000	10,000	—	—	—	35.00	50.00
2000 Proof	6,000	Value: 65.00				

KM# 72 1000 MARKKAA
9.0000 g., 0.9000 Gold .2604 oz. AGW, 22.1 mm. **Subject:** 75th Anniversary of Independence **Obv:** Dates above design **Rev:** Denomination below design **Designer:** Erkki Salmela

Date	Mintage	F	VF	XF	Unc	BU
1992 M-S	35,000	—	—	—	200	250

KM# 86 1000 MARKKAA
8.6400 g., 0.9000 Gold .2500 oz. AGW **Subject:** 80th Anniversary of Independence **Obv:** New shoot growing from tree stump, denomination above **Rev:** Symbolic design separating dates **Designer:** Reijo Paavilainen

Date	Mintage	F	VF	XF	Unc	BU
ND (1997) M-P Proof	20,000	Value: 330				

KM# 90 1000 MARKKAA
8.6400 g., 0.9000 Gold .2500 oz. AGW **Subject:** Jean Sibelius - Composer **Obv:** Head left **Rev:** Finlandia musical score, denomination above, date below **Designer:** Juhani Pallasmaa and Jukka Veistola

Date	Mintage	F	VF	XF	Unc	BU
1999 P-V-M Proof	25,000	Value: 350				

KM# 79 2000 MARKKAA
16.9700 g., 0.9000 Gold .4910 oz. AGW, 28 mm. **Subject:** 50 Years of Peace **Obv:** Design at center, date below **Rev:** Design above denomination **Designer:** Arto Lappalainen and Marita Lappalainen

Date	Mintage	F	VF	XF	Unc	BU
1995 M-L-L Proof	6,900	Value: 700				

EURO COINAGE

European Economic Community Issues

KM# 98 EURO CENT
2.2700 g., Copper Plated Steel, 16.3 mm. **Obv:** Rampant lion left surrounded by stars, date at left **Obv. Designer:** Heikki Haivaoja **Rev:** Denomination and globe **Rev. Designer:** Luc Luycx **Edge:** Plain

Date	Mintage	F	VF	XF	Unc	BU
1999	8,170,000	—	—	—	1.25	—
1999 Proof	—	—	—	—	—	—
2000	7,670,000	—	—	—	3.50	—
2000 Proof	—	—	—	—	—	—

KM# 99 2 EURO CENTS
3.0000 g., Copper Plated Steel, 18.7 mm. **Obv:** Rampant lion surrounded by stars, date at left **Obv. Designer:** Heikki Haivaoja **Rev:** Denomination and globe **Rev. Designer:** Luc Luycx **Edge:** Grooved

Date	Mintage	F	VF	XF	Unc	BU
1999	1,855,000	—	—	—	1.25	—
1999 Proof	—	—	—	—	—	—
2000	14,007,000	—	—	—	3.50	—
2000 Proof	—	—	—	—	—	—

KM# 100 5 EURO CENTS
3.8600 g., Copper Plated Steel, 21.2 mm. **Obv:** Rampant lion left surrounded by stars, date at left **Obv. Designer:** Heikki Haivaoja **Rev:** Denomination and globe **Rev. Designer:** Luc Luycx **Edge:** Plain

Date	Mintage	F	VF	XF	Unc	BU
1999	63,450,000	—	—	—	1.00	—
1999 Proof	—	—	—	—	—	—
2000	56,730,000	—	—	—	1.00	—
2000 Proof	—	—	—	—	—	—

KM# 101 10 EURO CENTS
4.0000 g., Brass, 19.7 mm. **Obv:** Rampant lion left surrounded by stars, date at left **Obv. Designer:** Heikki Haivaoja **Rev:** Denomination and map **Rev. Designer:** Luc Luycx **Edge:** Reeded

Date	Mintage	F	VF	XF	Unc	BU
1999	133,590,000	—	—	—	1.25	—
1999 Proof	—	—	—	—	—	—
2000	167,519,000	—	—	—	1.75	—
2000 Proof	—	—	—	—	—	—

KM# 102 20 EURO CENTS
5.7300 g., Brass, 22.2 mm. **Obv:** Rampant lion left surrounded by stars, date at left **Obv. Designer:** Heikki Haivaoja **Rev:** Denomination and map **Rev. Designer:** Luc Luycx **Edge:** Notched

Date	Mintage	F	VF	XF	Unc	BU
1999	42,420,000	—	—	—	1.25	—
1999 Proof	—	—	—	—	—	—
2000	570,000	—	—	—	12.00	—
2000 Proof	—	—	—	—	—	—

KM# 103 50 EURO CENTS
7.8100 g., Brass, 24.2 mm. **Obv:** Rampant lion left surrounded by stars, date at left **Obv. Designer:** Heikki Haivaoja **Rev:** Denomination and map **Rev. Designer:** Luc Luycx **Edge:** Reeded

Date	Mintage	F	VF	XF	Unc	BU
1999	20,766,000	—	—	—	1.75	—
1999 Proof	—	—	—	—	—	—
2000	67,167,000	—	—	—	1.50	—
2000 Proof	—	—	—	—	—	—

KM# 104 EURO
7.5000 g., Bi-Metallic Copper-nickel center in Brass ring, 23.2 mm. **Obv:** 2 flying swans, date below, surrounded by stars on outer ring **Obv. Designer:** Pertti Makinen **Rev:** Denomination and map **Rev. Designer:** Luc Luycx **Edge:** Reeded and plain sections

Date	Mintage	F	VF	XF	Unc	BU
1999	16,280,000	—	—	—	4.50	—
1999 Proof	—	—	—	—	—	—
2000	36,709,000	—	—	—	4.50	—
2000 Proof	—	—	—	—	—	—

KM# 105 2 EURO
8.5200 g., Bi-Metallic Brass center in Copper-nickel ring, 25.6 mm. **Obv:** 2 cloudberry flowers surrounded by stars on outer ring **Obv. Designer:** Raimo Heino **Rev:** Denomination and map **Rev. Designer:** Luc Luycx **Edge:** Reeded and lettered **Edge Lettering:** SUOMI FINLAND

Date	Mintage	F	VF	XF	Unc	BU
1999	16,160,000	—	—	—	4.00	—
1999 Proof	—	—	—	—	—	—
2000	8,750,000	—	—	—	4.00	—
2000 Proof	—	—	—	—	—	—

PATTERNS

Including off metal strikes

KM#	Date	Mintage	Identification	Mkt Val
Pn11	1918	—	5 Pennia. Silver.	3,500
Pn12	1919	—	Penni. Nickel.	—
Pn13	1921	—	10 Pennia. Iron.	—
Pn14	1922	—	5 Pennia. Silver.	—
Pn15	1923	—	50 Pennia. Copper.	—
Pn16	1923	—	Markkaa. Copper.	—
Pn17	1924	—	10 Pennia. Nickel.	—
Pn18	1926	—	200 Markkaa. Copper.	—
Pn19	1927	—	10 Pennia. Copper.	—
Pn20	1936	—	25 Pennia. Copper.	—
Pn21	1936	—	Markkaa. Iron.	—
Pn22	1941	—	10 Pennia. Iron.	250
Pn23	1942	—	25 Pennia. Aluminum.	—
Pn24	1942	—	50 Pennia. Aluminum.	—
Pn25	1942	—	Markkaa. Aluminum.	—
Pn26	1942	—	Markka. Iron - Blued.	—
Pn27	1942	—	5 Markkaa. Brass.	—
Pn28	1945	—	Markkaa. Brass.	3,000
Pn29	1946	—	5 Markkaa. Nickel.	—
Pn30	1947	—	5 Markkaa. Iron.	—
Pn31	1948	—	Markkaa. Aluminum.	—
Pn32	1948	—	Markkaa. Bronze.	—
Pn33	1948	—	5 Markkaa. Nickel.	—
Pn34	1949	—	Markkaa. Copper.	5,000
Pn35	1949	—	5 Markkaa. Iron.	—
Pn36	1950 H	—	Markkaa. Brass.	2,500
Pn37	1951	—	500 Markkaa. Aluminum - Blued.	—
Pn38	1952	—	Markkaa. Iron - Blued.	—
Pn39	1952	—	5 Markkaa. Iron - Blued.	—
Pn40	1952	—	10 Markkaa. Iron.	500
Pn41	1952	—	10 Markkaa. Copper.	—
Pn42	1953	—	Markka. Aluminum. With pearls.	—
Pn43	1953	—	Markka. Iron. Lion head.	—
Pn44	1953	—	Markka. Iron. With pearls.	—
Pn45	1953	—	5 Markkaa. Iron - Blued.	—
Pn46	1953	—	50 Markkaa. Nickel.	—
Pn47	1954	—	Markkaa. Nickel Plated Iron.	1,000
Pn48	1954	—	Markkaa. Iron. With pearls.	—
Pn49	1954	—	5 Markkaa. Iron. With pearls.	—
Pn50	1954	—	20 Markkaa. Nickel.	—
Pn51	1956	—	20 Markkaa. Nickel.	—
Pn52	1956	—	20 Markkaa. Silver.	—
Pn53	1956	—	500 Markkaa. Silver. With waves.	—
Pn54	1956	—	500 Markkaa. Silver. With plain field.	—
Pn55	1969	—	5 Markkaa. Copper-Nickel.	—

TRIAL STRIKES

KM#	Date	Mintage	Identification	Mkt Val
TS6	1918	—	5 Pennia. Iron.	2,000
TS7	1960	—	(1000 Markkaa). Brass.	—
TS8	1960	—	(1000 Markkaa). Brass.	—

MINT SETS

KM#	Date	Mintage	Identification	Issue Price	Mkt Val
MS1	1973 (7)	9,978	KM#44a, 45-48, 49a, 53 Soft plastic holder	10.00	60.00
MS2	1973 (7)	10,029	KM#44a, 45-48, 49a, 53 Hard plastic holder	5.00	25.00
MS3	1974	79,258	KM#44a, 45-48, 49a, 53	3.75	8.00
MS4	1975 (7)	58,820	KM#44a, 45-48, 49a, 53	3.75	8.00
MS5	1976 (7)	45,263	KM#44a, 45-48, 49a, 53	3.75	8.00
MS6	1977 (7)	40,392	KM#44a, 45-48, 49a, 53	4.00	10.00
MS7	1978 (7)	39,745	KM#44a-45a, 46-48, 49a, 53	4.45	8.00

KM#	Date	Mintage	Identification	Issue Price	Mkt Val
MS8	1979 (7)	36,000	KM#44a-45a, 46-48, 49a, 57	4.85	10.00
MS9	1980 (6)	33,805	KM#45a, 46-48, 49a, 57	5.00	8.00
MS10	1981 (6)	63,100	KM#45a, 46-48, 49a, 57	5.25	8.00
MS11	1982 (6)	35,500	KM#45a, 46-48, 49a, 57	5.50	8.00
MS12	1983 (6)	30,100	KM#45a-46a, 47-48, 49a, 57	3.25	8.00
MS13	1983 (6)	9,250	KM#45a-46a, 47-48, 49a, 57	3.25	20.00
MS14	1984 (6)	30,500	KM#45a-46a, 47-48, 49a, 57	3.25	6.00
MS15	1984 (6)	600	KM#45a-46a, 47-48, 49a, 57 Russian text	3.75	50.00
MS16	1985 (6)	38,385	KM#45a-46a, 47-48, 49a, 57 Finnish text	3.25	6.00
MS17	1985 (6)	1,500	KM#45a-46a, 47-48, 49a, 57 Russian text	4.65	20.00
MS18	1985 (6)	1,560	KM#45a-46a, 47-48, 49a, 57 English text	3.75	20.00
MS19	1986 (6)	37,100	KM#45a-46a, 47-48, 49a, 57 Finnish text	3.25	6.00
MS20	1986 (6)	1,300	KM#45a-46a, 47-48, 49a, 57 Russian text	5.00	20.00
MS21	1986 (6)	1,780	KM#45a-46a, 47-48, 49a, 57 English text	4.25	20.00
MS22	1987 (6)	34,300	KM#45a-46a, 47-48, 49a, 57 Finnish text	—	6.00
MS23	1987 (6)	1,120	KM#45a-46a, 47-48, 49a, 57 Russian text	—	20.00
MS24	1987 (6)	1,400	KM#45a-46a, 47-48, 49a, 57 English text	—	20.00
MS25	1987 (6)	15,900	KM#45a-46a, 47-48, 49a, 57 Finnish text	—	10.00
MS26	1987 (6)	300	KM#45a-46a, 47-48, 57 Russian text	—	50.00
MS27	1987 (6)	180	KM#45a-46a, 47-48, 49a, 57 English text	—	50.00
MS28	1988 (6)	35,750	KM#45a-46a, 47-48, 49a, 57 Finnish text	—	6.00
MS29	1988 (6)	1,450	KM#45a-46a, 47-48, 49a, 57 English text	—	15.00
MS30	1988 (6)	1,220	KM#45a-46a, 47-48, 49a, 57 Russian text	—	15.00
MS31	1989 (6)	33,000	KM#45a-46a, 47-48, 49a, 57 Finnish text, bronze medal	—	6.00
MS32	1989 (6)	1,450	KM#45a-46a, 47-48, 49a, 57 English text, bronze medal	—	10.00
MS33	1989 (6)	1,700	KM#45a-46a, 47-48, 49a, 57 Russian text, bronze medal	—	10.00
MS34	1989 (6)	15,982	KM#45a-46a, 47-48, 49a, 57 Finnish text, silver medal	—	22.00
MS35	1989 (6)	1,000	KM#45a-46a, 47-48, 49a, 57 English text, silver medal	—	35.00
MS36	1989 (6)	1,150	KM#45a-46a, 47-48, 49a, 57 Russian text, silver-medal	—	35.00
MS37	1990 (6)	29,400	KM#45a-46a, 47-48, 49a, 57 Finnish text	—	6.00
MS38	1990 (6)	1,000	KM#45a-46a, 47-48, 49a, 57 English text	—	10.00
MS39	1990 (6)	1,500	KM#45a-46a, 47-48, 49a, 57 Russian text	—	10.00
MS40	1990 (4)	41,750	KM#49a, 57, 65-66 Finnish text	—	9.00
MS41	1990 (4)	3,500	KM#49a, 57, 65-66 English text	—	10.00
MS42	1991 (4)	30,000	KM#49a, 57, 65-66 Finnish-Swedish text	—	10.00
MS43	1991 (4)	5,000	KM#49a, 57, 65-66 English text	—	10.00
MS44	1992 (5)	28,000	KM#49a, 57, 65-55, 73	—	12.50
MS45	1993 (6)	100,000	KM#49a, 65-66, 73, 76a, 77	—	21.50
MS46	1993 (5)	—	KM#65-66, 73, 76-77	13.30	13.50
MS47	1993 (4)	20,000	KM#49a, 65-66, 73 Silver medal	—	15.00
MS48	1994 (5)	25,000	KM#65-66, 73, 76-77 Medal (August Frederick Soldan)	—	18.00
MS49	1995 (5)	23,190	KM#65-66, 73, 76-77 Ecu medal	—	20.00
MS50	1995 (5)	15,000	KM#65-66, 73, 76-77 Medal (John Conrad Lihr)	—	20.00
MS51	1996 (5)	16,300	KM#65-66, 73, 76-77 Medal (Isak Gustaf Sundell)	—	20.00
MS52	1997 (5)	18,000	KM#65-66, 73, 76-77 Medal (Peippo Uolevi Helle)	—	20.00
MS53	1998 (5)	18,000	KM#65-66, 73, 76-77 Medal, (Allan Alarik Soiniemi)	—	20.00
MS54	1999 (5)	—	KM#65-66, 73, 76-77 Medal (Euro Summit)	—	20.00
MS55	1999 (5)	—	KM#65-66, 73, 76-77 Medal, Finnish presidency of the EU	12.50	20.00
MS56	2000 (5)	—	KM#65-66, 73, 76-77 Medal (Byzantine imitation coin found in Finland)	12.50	20.00
MS57	2000 (5)	—	KM#65-66, 73, 76-77 Medal (Time)	12.50	20.00

PROOF SETS

KM#	Date	Mintage	Identification	Issue Price	Mkt Val
PS1	1994 (5)	1,000	KM#65-66, 73, 76-77 Medal (August Frederik Soldan)	—	150
PS2	1995 (2)	500	KM#80, 82a	802	1,350
PS3	1995 (5)	1,810	KM#65-66, 73, 76-77 Medal (Ecu)	—	55.00
PS4	1996 (5)	1,200	KM#65-66, 73, 76-77 Medal (Johan Conrad Lihr)	—	55.00
PS5	1997 (6)	2,000	KM#65-66, 73, 76-77, 85	67.50	70.00
PS6	1998 (5)	1,600	KM#65-66, 73, 76-77 Medal (10 Euro Suomenlinna Fortress)	—	55.00
PS7	1999 (5)	—	KM#65-66, 73, 76-77 Medal (Euro Summit)	—	55.00
PS8	2000 (5)	—	KM#65-66, 73, 76-77, medal (Nykyaika)	—	55.00

FRANCE

The French Republic, largest of the West European nations, has an area of 210,026 sq. mi. (547,030 sq. km.) and a population of 58.1 million. Capital: Paris. Agriculture, manufacturing, tourist industry and financial services are the most important elements of France's diversified economy. Textiles and clothing, steel products, machinery and transportation equipment, chemicals, pharmaceuticals, nuclear electricity, agricultural products and wine are exported.

France, the Gaul of ancient times, emerged from the Renaissance as a modern centralized national state which reached its zenith during the reign of Louis XIV (1643-1715) when it became an absolute monarchy and the foremost power in Europe. Although his reign marks the golden age of French culture, the domestic abuses and extravagance of Louis XIV plunged France into a series of costly wars. This, along with a system of special privileges granted the nobility and other favored groups, weakened the monarchy and brought France to bankruptcy. This laid the way for the French Revolution of 1789-99 that shook Europe and affected the whole world.

The monarchy was abolished and the First Republic formed in 1793. The new government fell in 1799 to a coup led by Napoleon Bonaparte who, after declaring himself First Consul for life, in 1804 had himself proclaimed Emperor of France and King of Italy.

Napoleon's military victories made him master of much of Europe, but his disastrous Russian campaign of 1812 initiated a series of defeats that led to his abdication in 1814 and exile to the island of Elba. The monarchy was briefly restored under Louis XVIII. Napoleon returned to France in March 1815, but his efforts to uphold his power were totally crushed at the battle of Waterloo. He was exiled to the island of St. Helena where he died in 1821.

The monarchy under Louis XVIII was again restored in 1815, but the ultra reactionary regime of Charles X (1824-30) was overthrown by a liberal revolution and Louis Philippe of Orleans replaced him as monarch. The monarchy was ousted by the Revolution of 1848 and the Second Republic proclaimed. Louis Napoleon Bonaparte (nephew of Napoleon I) was elected president of the Second Republic. He was proclaimed emperor in 1852. As Napoleon III, he gave France two decades of prosperity under a stable, autocratic regime, but led it to defeat in the Franco-Prussian War of 1870, after which the Third Republic was established.

The Third Republic endured until 1940 and the capitulation of France to the swiftly maneuvering German forces. Marshal Philippe Petain formed a puppet government that sued for peace and ruled unoccupied France until 1942 from Vichy. Meanwhile, General Charles de Gaulle escaped to London where he formed a wartime government in exile and the Free French army. De Gaulle's provisional exile government was officially recognized by the Allies after the liberation of Paris in 1944, and De Gaulle, who had been serving as head of the provisional government, tacitly maintained that position. In October 1945, the people overwhelmingly rejected a return to the prewar government, thus paving the way for the formation of the Fourth Republic in 1947 just after the dismissal of De Gaulle, at grips with a coalition of rival parties, the Communists especially.

In actual operation, the Fourth Republic was remarkably like the Third, with the National Assembly the focus of power causing a constant governmental instability. The later years of the Fourth Republic were marked by a burst of industrial expansion unmatched in modern French history. The growth rate, however, was marred by a two colonial wars, nagging inflationary trend that weakened the franc and undermined the betterment of the people's buying power. This and the Algerian conflict led to the recall of De Gaulle to power, the adoption of a new constitution vesting strong powers in the executive, and the establishment in 1959 of the current Fifth Republic.

RULERS

Third Republic, 1871-1940
Vichy State, 1940-1944
De Gaulle's Provisional Govt., 1944-1946
Fourth Republic, 1947-1958
Fifth Republic, 1959—

MINT MARKS AND PRIVY MARKS

In addition to the date and mint mark which are customary on western civilization coinage, most coins manufactured by the French Mints contain two or three small 'Marks or Differents' as the French call them. These privy marks represent the men responsible for the dies which struck the coins. One privy mark is sometimes for the Engraver General (since 1880 the title is Chief Engraver). The other privy mark is the signature of the Mint Director of each mint; another one is the different' of the local engraver. Three other marks appeared at the end of Louis XIV's reign: one for the Director General of Mints, one for the General Engineer of Mechanical edge-marking, one identifying over struck coins in 1690-1705 and in 1715-1723. Equally amazing and unique is that sometimes the local assayer's or Judge-custody's 'different' or 'secret pellet' appears. Since 1880 this privy mark has represented the office rather than the personage of both the Administration of Coins & Medals and the Mint Director, and a standard privy mark has been used (cornucopia).

For most dates these privy marks are important though minor features for advanced collectors or local researchers. During some issue dates, however, the marks changed. To be even more accurate sometimes the marks changed when the date didn't, even though it should have. These coins can be attributed to the proper mintage report only by considering the privy marks. Previous references (before G. Sobin and F. Droulers) have by and large ignored these privy marks. It is entirely possible that unattributed varieties may exist for any privy mark transition. All transition years which may have two or three varieties or combinations of privy marks have the known attribution indicated after the date (if it has been confirmed).

ENGRAVER GENERAL'S PRIVY MARKS

Mark	Desc.	Date	Name
	Torch	1896-1930	Henry Patey
	Wing	1931-Oct. 1958	Lucien Bazor
	Owl	1958-74	Raymond Joly
	Dolphin	1974-94	Rousseau
	Bee	1994-	Pierre Rodier

MINT DIRECTOR'S PRIVY MARKS

Some modern coins struck from dies produced at the Paris Mint have the 'A' mint mark. In the absence of a mint mark, the cornucopia privy mark serves to attribute a coin to Paris design.

A – Paris, Central Mint

B – Beaumont – Le Roger

Cornucopia 1943-58

(b) – Brussels

Legend ending BD, see PAU

C - Castelsarrasin

C 1914, 1943-46

Thunderbolt (tb) - Poissy

Cornucopia 1922-24

Star (s) - Madrid

★ 1916

MONETARY SYSTEM

(Commencing 1960)

1 Old Franc = 1 New Centime

100 New Centimes = 1 New Franc

MODERN REPUBLICS

1870-

DECIMAL COINAGE

KM# 840 CENTIME

Bronze **Obv:** Liberty head right **Rev:** Denomination above date within wreath **Note:** Without mint mark or privy mark.

Date	Mintage	F	VF	XF	Unc	BU
1901	1,000,000	1.00	2.00	15.00	35.00	50.00
1902	1,000,000	0.75	1.50	4.00	15.00	—
1903	2,000,000	0.50	1.50	3.00	15.00	—
1904	1,000,000	0.75	1.50	4.00	15.00	—
1908	4,500,000	2.00	4.00	10.00	20.00	—
1909	1,500,000	3.00	5.00	12.00	30.00	50.00
1910	1,500,000	10.00	20.00	40.00	100	185
1911	5,000,000	0.25	0.75	1.50	5.00	—
1912	2,000,000	0.50	1.00	2.00	7.00	—
1913	1,500,000	0.50	1.00	2.00	7.00	—
1914	1,000,000	0.75	1.50	3.00	9.50	—
1916	1,996,000	0.50	1.00	2.00	6.50	—
1919	2,407,000	0.25	0.75	1.50	4.00	—
1920	2,594,000	0.25	0.75	1.50	4.00	—

KM# 841 2 CENTIMES

Bronze **Obv:** Liberty head right **Rev:** Denomination and date within wreath **Note:** Without mint mark or privy mark.

Date	Mintage	F	VF	XF	Unc	BU
1901	1,000,000	1.00	2.50	4.00	11.50	55.00
1902	750,000	1.50	3.50	5.50	15.00	—
1903	750,000	1.50	3.50	5.50	16.50	—
1904	500,000	2.00	4.50	7.50	18.50	60.00
1907	250,000	10.00	25.00	55.00	130	200
1908	3,500,000	0.35	0.75	2.00	6.00	—
1909	1,750,000	6.00	12.00	30.00	50.00	90.00
1910	1,750,000	0.50	1.00	5.00	12.50	—
1911	5,000,000	0.15	0.50	1.25	5.00	—
1912	1,500,000	0.25	1.00	2.00	7.00	—
1913	1,750,000	0.25	1.00	2.00	7.00	—
1914	2,000,000	0.15	0.50	1.25	5.00	—
1916	500,000	0.75	1.50	3.00	9.00	—
1919	902,000	0.50	1.00	2.00	6.00	—
1920	598,000	0.75	1.50	3.00	8.00	—

KM# 842 5 CENTIMES

Bronze, 25.1 mm. **Obv:** Liberty head right **Rev:** Republic protecting her child, denomination at right, date below **Note:** Without mint mark.

Date	Mintage	F	VF	XF	Unc	BU
1901 (c)	6,000,000	1.75	3.50	15.00	55.00	75.00
1902	7,900,000	1.75	3.50	10.00	50.00	70.00
1903	2,879,000	5.00	10.00	25.00	75.00	100
1904	8,000,000	1.00	3.00	6.50	25.00	50.00
1905	2,100,000	6.00	16.00	45.00	115	225
1906	8,394,000	0.75	2.50	6.00	24.00	—
1907	7,900,000	0.75	2.50	6.00	24.00	—
1908	6,090,000	2.00	4.00	12.00	32.00	—
1909	8,000,000	0.75	2.50	6.00	25.00	—
1910	4,000,000	1.50	2.50	9.00	50.00	85.00
1911	15,386,000	0.25	0.75	1.75	9.00	—
1912	20,000,000	0.25	0.75	1.75	9.00	—
1913	12,603,000	0.25	0.75	1.75	9.00	—
1914	7,000,000	0.25	0.75	1.75	9.00	—
1915	6,032,000	0.25	0.75	1.75	9.00	—
1916	41,531,000	0.25	0.75	1.75	7.50	—
1916 (s)	Inc. above	0.25	0.75	1.75	7.50	—
1917	16,963,000	0.25	0.75	1.75	7.50	—
1920	8,151,999	2.00	4.00	9.00	28.00	—
1921	142,000	250	450	850	1,350	—

KM# 865 5 CENTIMES

Copper-Nickel, 17 mm. **Obv:** Monogram within wreath divided by center hole, liberty cap above **Rev:** Denomination divided by plant and center hole

Date	Mintage	F	VF	XF	Unc	BU
1914 Rare	—	—	—	—	—	—
1917	10,458,000	1.00	1.75	4.00	18.00	40.00
1918	35,592,000	0.25	0.75	1.75	4.50	—
1919	43,848,000	0.25	0.75	1.75	4.00	—
1920	51,321,000	0.25	0.50	1.75	3.50	—

KM# 875 5 CENTIMES

2.0000 g., Copper-Nickel, 17 mm. **Obv:** Monogram divided by center hole, liberty cap above, wreath surrounds **Rev:** Denomination divided by plant and center hole, date below

Date	Mintage	F	VF	XF	Unc	BU
1920	Inc. above	5.00	15.00	28.00	75.00	150
1921	32,908,000	0.25	0.50	1.75	4.00	—
1922	31,700,000	0.25	0.50	1.75	4.00	—
1922 (tb)	17,717,000	1.50	2.50	5.00	13.50	—
1923	23,322,000	0.50	1.50	2.00	6.50	—
1923 (tb)	45,097,000	0.25	0.50	1.00	3.50	—
1924	47,018,000	0.25	0.50	1.00	3.50	—
1924 (tb)	21,210,000	0.50	1.50	2.00	5.50	—
1925	66,837,999	0.25	0.50	1.00	2.50	—
1926	19,820,000	0.25	1.50	2.00	5.50	—
1927	6,066,000	2.50	8.50	25.00	70.00	—
1930	31,902,000	0.20	0.50	1.00	2.25	—
1931	34,711,000	0.20	0.50	1.00	2.25	—
1932	31,112,000	0.20	0.50	1.00	2.25	—
1933	12,970,000	1.00	1.75	4.00	10.00	—
1934	27,144,000	0.30	0.65	2.00	5.00	—
1935	57,221,000	0.25	0.50	1.00	2.25	—
1936	64,340,999	0.15	0.25	0.75	2.25	—
1937	26,329,000	0.15	0.25	0.75	2.25	—
1938	21,614,000	0.15	0.25	0.75	2.25	—

KM# 875a 5 CENTIMES

1.5000 g., Nickel-Bronze, 17 mm. **Obv:** Center hole divides monogram, liberty cap above, wreath surrounds **Rev:** Center hole and plant divide denomination, date below

Date	Mintage	F	VF	XF	Unc	BU
.1938.	26,330,000	0.15	0.50	1.00	3.00	—
.1938. star	Inc. above	100	200	300	425	—
.1939.	52,673,000	0.10	0.25	0.75	2.00	—

KM# 843 10 CENTIMES

Bronze, 30 mm. **Obv:** Liberty head right **Rev:** Republic protecting her child **Note:** Without mint mark.

Date	Mintage	F	VF	XF	Unc	BU
1901 (c)	2,700,000	1.50	3.00	20.00	50.00	75.00
1902	3,800,000	0.75	1.75	6.50	25.00	—
1903	3,650,000	0.75	1.75	6.50	25.00	—
1904	3,800,000	0.75	1.75	6.50	25.00	—
1905	950,000	25.00	50.00	125	275	—
1906	3,000,000	2.00	5.00	12.00	40.00	65.00
1907	4,000,000	0.75	1.75	4.50	20.00	—
1908	3,500,000	0.75	1.75	4.50	20.00	—
1909	2,933,000	0.75	1.75	4.50	25.00	—
1910	3,567,000	0.75	1.75	4.50	20.00	—
1911	7,903,000	0.50	1.25	2.75	12.00	—
1912	9,500,000	0.50	1.25	2.75	12.00	—
1913	9,000,000	0.50	1.25	2.75	12.00	—
1914	6,000,000	0.75	1.75	3.50	14.00	—
1915	4,362,000	0.50	1.25	2.75	12.00	—
1916	22,477,000	0.25	0.75	1.50	7.00	—
1916 (s)	Inc. above	0.25	0.75	1.50	7.00	—
1917	11,914,000	0.25	0.75	1.50	7.00	—
1920	4,119,000	1.50	3.00	10.00	40.00	65.00
1921	1,896,000	8.00	16.00	40.00	85.00	140

KM# 866 10 CENTIMES

Nickel, 21.3 mm. **Obv:** Monogram divided by center hole, liberty cap above, wreath surrounds **Rev:** Denomination divided by plant and center hole, date below

Date	Mintage	F	VF	XF	Unc	BU
1914 dash	3,972	400	700	1,000	1,600	—

KM# 866a 10 CENTIMES

Copper-Nickel, 21.3 mm. **Obv:** Center hole divides monogram, liberty cap above, wreath surrounds **Rev:** Center hole and plant divides denomination, date below

Date	Mintage	F	VF	XF	Unc	BU
1917	8,170,999	0.75	1.50	3.50	20.00	—
1918	30,605,000	0.25	0.50	1.00	3.50	—
1919	33,488,999	0.25	0.50	1.00	3.50	—
1920	38,845,000	0.25	0.50	1.00	3.50	—
1921	42,768,000	0.10	0.35	0.75	2.50	—
1922	23,033,000	0.35	0.75	1.25	4.00	—
1922 (tb)	12,412,000	0.75	1.50	2.50	6.50	—
1923	18,701,000	0.50	1.00	2.00	4.50	—
1923 (tb)	30,016,000	0.25	0.50	1.00	3.00	—
1924	43,949,000	0.10	0.35	0.75	2.00	—
1924 (tb)	13,591,000	1.50	4.50	12.50	40.00	65.00
1925	46,266,000	0.10	0.35	0.75	2.00	—
1926	25,660,000	0.25	0.50	1.00	3.00	—
1927	16,203,000	0.40	0.75	1.25	4.00	—
1928	6,967,000	1.00	2.50	8.00	28.00	—
1929	24,531,000	0.10	0.35	1.00	2.00	—
1930	22,146,000	0.10	0.35	1.00	2.00	—
1931	49,107,000	0.10	0.35	1.00	2.00	—
1932	30,317,000	0.10	0.35	1.00	2.00	—
1933	13,042,000	0.35	0.75	1.50	4.00	—
1934	24,067,000	0.10	0.50	1.00	2.00	—
1935	47,487,000	0.10	0.50	1.00	2.00	—
1936	57,738,000	0.10	0.50	1.00	2.00	—
1937	25,308,000	0.10	0.50	1.00	2.00	—
1938	17,063,000	0.25	0.75	1.75	4.50	—

KM# 889.1 10 CENTIMES

Nickel-Bronze, 21.3 mm. **Obv:** Monogram divided by center hole, liberty cap above, wreath surrounds **Rev:** Denomination divided by plant and center hole, date below

Date	Mintage	F	VF	XF	Unc	BU
.1938.	24,151,000	0.25	0.50	1.00	2.00	—
1.938.	Inc. above	—	—	—	—	—
.1939.	62,269,000	0.15	0.30	0.65	1.75	—

KM# 889.2 10 CENTIMES

Nickel-Bronze, 21.3 mm. **Obv:** Center hole divides monogram, liberty cap above **Rev:** Center hole and plant divide denomination **Note:** Thin flan: 1.35-1.45mm thickness

Date	Mintage	F	VF	XF	Unc	BU
.1939.	Inc. above	0.10	0.20	0.50	1.25	—

KM# 898.1 10 CENTIMES

Zinc, 21 mm. **Obv:** Grain sprigs flank center hole **Rev:** Center hole divides denomination, oak leaves flank, date below **Note:** Issued for Vichy French State, thickness 1.5 mm.

Date	Mintage	F	VF	XF	Unc	BU
1941	70,860,000	0.35	0.65	1.50	6.00	—
1942	139,598,000	0.30	0.60	1.25	4.00	—
1943	21,520,000	1.00	2.00	4.00	15.00	—

KM# 898.2 10 CENTIMES

Zinc, 21.3 mm. **Obv:** Grain sprigs flank center hole **Rev:** Center hole divides denomination, oak leaves flank, date below **Note:** Thin flan, 1.3mm.

Date	Mintage	F	VF	XF	Unc	BU
1941	Inc. above	0.25	0.50	1.25	3.00	—
1942	Inc. above	0.20	0.40	1.00	2.25	—
1943	Inc. above	0.75	1.50	2.75	6.00	—

KM# 895 10 CENTIMES

Zinc **Rev:** Without dash below MES in C MES

Date	Mintage	F	VF	XF	Unc	BU
1941	235,875,000	1.00	2.00	6.00	15.00	—

KM# 896 10 CENTIMES

Zinc **Obv:** Monogram within wreath divided by center hole, liberty cap above **Rev:** Center hole within wreath divides denomination, date below, dash below MES in C MES

Date	Mintage	F	VF	XF	Unc	BU
1941	Inc. above	0.75	1.25	4.00	10.00	—

KM# 897 10 CENTIMES

Zinc, 21 mm. **Obv:** Monogram within wreath divided by center hole, liberty cap above **Rev:** Center hole within wreath divides denomination, dot before and after date below

Date	Mintage	F	VF	XF	Unc	BU
.1941.	Inc. above	0.25	0.50	1.00	4.00	—
1941.	Inc. above	0.25	0.50	1.00	4.00	—

KM# 903 10 CENTIMES

Zinc, 17 mm. **Obv:** Grain sprigs flank center hole **Rev:** Center hole divides denomination, oak leaves flank, date below **Note:** Reduced size.

Date	Mintage	F	VF	XF	Unc	BU
1943	22,008,000	0.25	0.75	2.50	7.00	—
1944	58,463,000	0.25	0.50	2.00	5.00	—

KM# 906.1 10 CENTIMES

Zinc, 17 mm. **Obv:** Monogram divided by center hole, liberty cap above, wreath surrounds **Rev:** Center hole and plant divide denomination, date below **Note:** Reduced size.

Date	Mintage	F	VF	XF	Unc	BU
1945	38,174,000	1.00	1.75	3.25	12.00	—
1946 Rare	—	—	—	—	—	—

KM# 906.2 10 CENTIMES

Zinc **Obv:** Monogram divided by center hole, liberty cap above, wreath surrounds **Rev:** Center hole and plant divide denomination

Date	Mintage	F	VF	XF	Unc	BU
1945B	7,246,000	1.50	3.00	6.00	16.00	—
1946B	10,566,000	2.50	5.00	10.00	25.00	—

KM# 906.3 10 CENTIMES

Zinc **Obv:** Monogram divided by center hole, liberty cap above, wreath surrounds **Rev:** Center hole and plant divide denomination

Date	Mintage	F	VF	XF	Unc	BU
1945C	8,379,000	2.00	4.00	8.00	20.00	45.00

KM# 899 20 CENTIMES

Zinc **Obv:** Grain sprigs flank center hole **Rev:** Center hole divides denomination, oak leaves flank, date below **Note:** Issued for Vichy French State.

Date	Mintage	F	VF	XF	Unc	BU
1941	54,044,000	1.00	2.00	4.00	17.00	—

KM# 900.1 20 CENTIMES

3.5000 g., Zinc **Obv:** Grain sprigs flank center hole **Rev:** Center hole divides denomination, oak leaves flank, date below **Note:** Thick flan.

Date	Mintage	F	VF	XF	Unc	BU
1941	31,397,000	1.00	2.00	4.00	15.00	—
1942	112,868,000	0.50	1.00	2.00	7.00	—
1943	64,138,000	0.75	1.50	2.50	8.50	—

KM# 900.2 20 CENTIMES

3.0000 g., Zinc **Obv:** Grain sprigs flank center hole **Rev:** Center hole divides denomination, leaves flank **Note:** Thin flan. Struck at Paris Mint.

Date	Mintage	F	VF	XF	Unc	BU
1941	Inc. above	0.50	0.75	2.00	8.50	—
1942	Inc. above	0.50	0.75	2.00	7.50	—
1943	Inc. above	0.50	0.75	2.00	6.50	—
1944	5,250,000	15.00	30.00	80.00	165	—

KM# 900.2a 20 CENTIMES

Iron **Obv:** Grain sprigs flank center hole **Rev:** Center hole divides denomination, leaves flank

Date	Mintage	F	VF	XF	Unc	BU
1944	695,000	25.00	50.00	150	185	250

KM# 907.1 20 CENTIMES

Zinc **Obv:** Monogram divided by center hole, liberty cap above, wreath surrounds **Rev:** Center hole and plant divide denomination, date below **Note:** Fourth Republic.

Date	Mintage	F	VF	XF	Unc	BU
1945	6,003,000	2.00	4.00	9.00	22.00	—
1946	2,662,000	8.00	18.00	35.00	70.00	140

KM# 907.2 20 CENTIMES

Zinc **Obv:** Monogram divided by center hole, liberty cap above, wreath surrounds **Rev:** Center hole and plant divide denomination, date below

Date	Mintage	F	VF	XF	Unc	BU
1945B	100,000	85.00	165	285	470	—
1946B	5,525,000	75.00	150	260	450	—

KM# 907.3 20 CENTIMES

Zinc **Obv:** Monogram divided by center hole, liberty cap above, wreath surrounds **Rev:** Center hole and plant divide denomination, date below

Date	Mintage	F	VF	XF	Unc	BU
1945C	299,000	20.00	40.00	85.00	150	220

KM# 855 25 CENTIMES

Nickel, 24 mm. **Obv:** Laureate liberty head left **Rev:** Denomination and date flanked by cornucopias **Note:** Without mint mark.

Date	Mintage	F	VF	XF	Unc	BU
1903	16,000,000	0.25	1.00	2.00	11.50	—

KM# 856 25 CENTIMES

Nickel, 24 mm. **Obv:** Laureate bust left **Rev:** Oak leaves divide date and denomination, column with axe head on top at left **Shape:** 22-sided

Date	Mintage	F	VF	XF	Unc	BU
1904	16,000,000	0.25	0.75	2.00	13.50	—
1905	8,000,000	0.50	1.50	3.50	20.00	—

KM# 867 25 CENTIMES

Nickel, 24 mm. **Obv:** Monogram divided by center hole, liberty cap above, wreath surrounds **Rev:** Center hole and plant divide denomination, dash under "MES" in denomination

Date	Mintage	F	VF	XF	Unc	BU
1914	941,000	1.50	3.00	7.00	22.50	—
1915	535,000	2.50	4.00	8.00	32.00	—
1916	100,000	15.00	30.00	60.00	120	—
1917	65,000	30.00	50.00	85.00	185	—

KM# 867a 25 CENTIMES

Copper-Nickel, 24 mm. **Obv:** Monogram divided by center hole, liberty cap above, wreath surrounds **Rev:** Without dash under "MES" in denomination

Date	Mintage	F	VF	XF	Unc	BU
1917	3,085,000	2.00	4.00	12.00	22.00	—
1918	18,330,000	0.25	0.50	1.50	3.50	—
1919	5,106,000	1.00	2.00	3.00	7.00	—
1920	18,108,000	0.15	0.50	1.00	3.00	—
1921	18,531,000	0.15	0.50	1.00	3.00	—
1922	17,766,000	0.15	0.50	1.00	3.00	—
1923	19,718,000	0.15	0.50	1.00	3.00	—
1924	24,535,000	0.15	0.50	1.00	3.00	—
1925	17,807,000	0.15	0.50	1.00	3.00	—
1926	13,226,000	0.15	0.50	1.00	3.00	—
1927	13,465,000	0.15	0.50	1.00	3.00	—
1928	9,960,000	0.25	0.50	1.50	3.50	—
1929	12,887,000	0.15	0.50	1.00	2.50	—
1930	28,363,000	0.15	0.50	1.00	2.50	—
1931	22,121,000	0.15	0.50	1.00	2.50	—
1932	30,364,000	0.15	0.50	1.00	2.50	—
1933	28,562,000	0.15	0.50	1.00	2.50	—
1936	4,657,000	1.50	3.00	8.00	18.00	—
1937	7,780,000	0.25	0.50	1.50	3.50	—

KM# 867b 25 CENTIMES

Nickel-Bronze, 24 mm. **Obv. Designer:** Monogram divided by center hole, liberty cap above, wreath surrounds **Rev:** Center hole and plant divide denomination, date below **Note:** Listings below appear with a period before and after the date.

Date	Mintage	F	VF	XF	Unc	BU
1938	5,170,000	0.25	0.50	1.00	2.50	—
1939	42,964,000	0.15	0.35	0.75	1.50	—
Note: Thick flan (1.55mm)						
1939	Inc. above	0.15	0.35	0.75	1.50	—
Note: Thin flan (1.35mm)						
1940	3,446,000	6.00	12.00	18.00	35.00	—

KM# 854 50 CENTIMES

2.5000 g., 0.8350 Silver .0671 oz. ASW, 18 mm. **Obv:** Figure sowing seed **Rev:** Leafy branch divides date and denomination **Designer:** Louis Oscar Roty **Note:** Without mint mark.

Date	Mintage	F	VF	XF	Unc	BU
1901	4,960,000	2.00	4.00	12.00	45.00	90.00
1902	3,778,000	2.50	5.00	15.00	55.00	80.00
1903	2,222,000	12.00	25.00	50.00	150	200
1904	4,000,000	1.50	3.50	10.00	45.00	90.00

Date	Mintage	F	VF	XF	Unc	BU
1905	2,381,000	5.00	9.00	20.00	100	200
1906	2,679,000	2.50	5.00	15.00	55.00	85.00
1907	7,332,000	1.50	3.50	10.00	30.00	—
1908	14,304,000	1.00	1.50	4.00	15.00	—
1909	9,900,000	1.00	1.50	4.00	15.00	—
1910	15,923,000	BV	1.25	3.00	10.00	—
1911	1,330,000	20.00	50.00	110	200	—
1912	16,000,000	BV	1.00	1.50	5.00	—
1913	14,000,000	BV	1.00	1.50	5.00	—
1914	9,657,000	BV	1.00	1.50	6.00	—
1915	20,893,000	BV	1.00	1.25	3.00	—
1916	52,963,000	BV	1.00	1.25	2.50	—
1917	48,629,000	BV	1.00	1.25	2.50	—
1918	36,492,000	BV	1.00	1.25	2.50	—
1919	24,299,000	BV	1.00	1.25	2.50	—
1920	8,509,000	1.00	1.50	3.00	6.00	—

KM# 884 50 CENTIMES

Aluminum-Bronze, 18 mm. **Obv:** Denomination within circle **Rev:** Mercury seated left, caduceus at left, shield on right, date below

Date	Mintage	F	VF	XF	Unc	BU
1921	8,692,000	0.75	2.00	6.00	18.00	—
1922	86,226,000	0.15	0.25	1.00	4.00	—
1923	119,584,000	0.15	0.25	0.75	2.50	—
1924	97,036,000	0.15	0.25	1.00	3.00	—
1925	48,017,000	0.25	0.50	1.25	5.00	—
1926	46,447,000	0.25	0.50	1.25	5.00	—
1927	23,703,000	0.75	1.50	3.00	8.50	—
1928	10,329,000	0.75	2.00	5.00	16.00	—
1929	6,669,000	2.50	6.00	12.50	25.00	60.00

KM# 894.1 50 CENTIMES

Aluminum-Bronze, 18 mm. **Obv:** Laureate head left **Rev:** Denomination above date, cornucopias flank **Designer:** Pierre Alexandre Marlon

Date	Mintage	F	VF	XF	Unc	BU
1931	62,775,000	0.15	0.25	1.00	3.00	—
1932 Closed 9	Inc. above	0.15	0.25	0.50	2.00	—
1932 Open 9	108,839,000	0.15	0.25	0.50	2.00	—
1933 Open 9	41,937,000	0.15	0.25	0.75	3.00	—
1933 Closed 9	Inc. above	0.15	0.25	0.75	3.00	—
1936	16,602,000	0.50	1.00	2.00	5.00	—
1937	43,950,000	0.15	0.25	0.75	3.00	—
1938	55,707,000	0.15	0.25	0.75	3.00	—
1939	96,594,000	0.15	0.25	0.50	2.00	—
1940	10,854,000	0.50	1.00	2.00	5.00	—
1941	82,958,000	0.15	0.25	1.00	3.00	—
1947	Est. 2,170,000	60.00	125	225	350	—

Note: 1947 date was struck for colonial use in Africa

KM# 894.2a 50 CENTIMES

Aluminum, 18 mm. **Obv:** Laureate liberty head left **Rev:** Cornucopias flank denomination and date

Date	Mintage	F	VF	XF	Unc	BU
1944B	20,000	—	—	—	—	—

Note: Reported, not confirmed

Date	Mintage	F	VF	XF	Unc	BU
1945B	6,357,000	0.50	1.00	3.00	8.00	—
1946B	29,344,000	0.15	0.25	1.00	4.00	—
1947B	18,504,000	2.00	5.00	10.00	20.00	—

KM# 894.3a 50 CENTIMES

Aluminum, 18 mm. **Obv:** Laureate liberty head left **Rev:** Cornucopias flank denomination and date

Date	Mintage	F	VF	XF	Unc	BU
1944C	17,220,000	—	—	—	—	—

Note: Reported, not confirmed

Date	Mintage	F	VF	XF	Unc	BU
1945C	2,968,000	1.00	3.00	6.00	12.00	—

KM# 894.1a 50 CENTIMES

Aluminum, 18 mm. **Obv:** Laureate liberty head left **Rev:** Cornucopias flank denomination and date **Note:** Without mint mark. Thick and thin planchets exist.

Date	Mintage	F	VF	XF	Unc	BU
1941	129,758,000	0.15	0.25	0.50	2.00	—
1944	9,898,000	0.50	1.00	2.50	6.00	—
1945	26,224,000	0.15	0.25	1.00	3.00	—
1946	24,605,000	0.15	0.25	1.00	3.00	—
1947	51,744,000	0.15	0.25	0.60	2.00	—

KM# 894.2 50 CENTIMES

Aluminum-Bronze, 18 mm. **Obv:** Laureate liberty head left **Rev:** Cornucopias flank denomination and date

Date	Mintage	F	VF	XF	Unc	BU
1939B	6,200,000	0.50	1.00	2.50	10.00	—

KM# 914.2 50 CENTIMES

Aluminum, 18 mm. **Obv:** Grain sprigs flank double bit axe **Rev:** Denomination above date, oak leaves flank

Date	Mintage	F	VF	XF	Unc	BU
1943B	21,916,000	5.00	10.00	28.00	50.00	70.00
1944B	27,334,000	1.50	3.00	7.00	15.00	25.00

KM# 914.3 50 CENTIMES

Aluminum, 18 mm. **Obv:** Grain sprigs flank double bit axe **Rev:** Denomination above date, oak leaves flank

Date	Mintage	F	VF	XF	Unc	BU
1944C Small C	27,213,000	2.00	4.00	8.00	26.00	40.00
1944C Large C	Inc. above	—	—	—	—	—

KM# 914.4 50 CENTIMES

Aluminum, 18 mm. **Obv:** Grain sprigs flank double bit axe **Rev:** Denomination above date, oak leaves flank **Note:** Without mint mark. Thin flan. Struck at Paris Mint.

Date	Mintage	F	VF	XF	Unc	BU
1942	—	0.15	0.25	1.00	2.50	—
1943	—	0.15	0.25	0.50	1.25	—

KM# 914.1 50 CENTIMES

Aluminum, 18 mm. **Obv:** Double bit axe, grain sprigs flank **Rev:** Denomination above date, oak leaves flank **Designer:** Lucien Bazor **Note:** Without mint mark. Vichy French State. Thick and thin planchets exist.

Date	Mintage	F	VF	XF	Unc	BU
1942	50,134,000	0.15	0.25	0.75	2.00	—
1943	84,462,000	0.15	0.25	0.75	1.50	—
1944	57,410,000	1.50	3.00	6.00	18.00	—

KM# 844.1 FRANC

5.0000 g., 0.8350 Silver .1342 oz. ASW, 23 mm. **Obv:** Figure sowing seed **Rev:** Leafy branch divides date and denomination **Designer:** Louis Oscar Roty **Note:** Without mint mark.

Date	Mintage	F	VF	XF	Unc	BU
1901	6,200,000	2.00	4.00	20.00	75.00	130
1902	6,000,000	2.00	4.00	20.00	75.00	130
1903	472,000	40.00	80.00	325	650	1,000
1904	7,000,000	2.00	4.00	17.50	75.00	130
1905	6,004,000	2.00	4.00	15.00	65.00	110
1906	1,908,000	6.00	20.00	40.00	100	175
1907	2,563,000	4.00	9.00	30.00	90.00	150
1908	3,961,000	2.50	5.00	20.00	65.00	110
1909	10,924,000	2.00	2.50	5.00	22.00	75.00
1910	7,725,000	2.00	2.50	5.00	22.00	75.00
1911	5,542,000	2.25	3.00	12.00	45.00	90.00
1912	10,001,000	2.00	2.50	5.00	22.00	75.00
1913	13,654,000	2.00	2.50	4.00	18.00	—
1914	14,361,000	2.00	2.50	3.50	15.00	—
1915	47,955,000	BV	1.85	2.25	5.50	—
1916	92,029,000	—	BV	2.00	3.50	—
1917	57,153,000	—	BV	2.00	3.50	—
1918	50,112,000	—	BV	2.00	3.50	—
1919	46,112,000	—	BV	2.00	3.50	—
1920	19,322,000	BV	1.85	2.50	5.50	—

KM# 844.2 FRANC

5.0000 g., 0.8350 Silver .1342 oz. ASW, 23 mm. **Obv:** Figure sowing seed **Rev:** Leafy branch divides date and denomination **Designer:** Louis Oscar Roty

Date	Mintage	F	VF	XF	Unc	BU
1914C	43,000	135	250	350	500	700

KM# 876 FRANC

Aluminum-Bronze, 23 mm. **Rev:** Mercury seated left **Note:** Without mint mark. Chamber of Commerce.

Date	Mintage	F	VF	XF	Unc	BU
1920	590,000	3.00	5.00	12.50	32.00	—
1921	54,572,000	0.25	0.50	1.50	5.50	—
1922	111,343,000	0.15	0.25	1.00	4.50	—
1923	140,138,000	0.15	0.25	1.00	3.50	—
1924 Open 4	87,715,000	0.15	0.25	1.00	4.50	—
1924 Closed 4	Inc. above	0.35	0.60	2.00	6.50	—
1925	36,523,000	0.25	0.50	1.50	5.50	—
1926	1,580,000	3.00	8.00	20.00	45.00	75.00
1927	11,330,000	0.50	1.50	3.50	8.50	—

KM# 885 FRANC

Aluminum-Bronze, 23 mm. **Obv:** Laureate head left **Rev:** Cornucopias flank denomination and date **Designer:** Pierre Alexandre Marlon

Date	Mintage	F	VF	XF	Unc	BU
1931	15,504,000	0.25	0.50	2.00	6.50	—
1932	29,768,000	0.15	0.25	1.00	4.00	—
1933	15,356,000	0.25	0.50	2.00	6.50	—
1934	17,286,000	0.25	0.50	2.00	5.00	—
1935	1,166,000	6.00	15.00	25.00	60.00	100
1936	23,817,000	0.15	0.25	1.00	4.00	—
1937	30,940,000	0.15	0.25	1.00	3.00	—
1938	66,165,000	0.15	0.25	1.00	2.50	—
1939	48,434,000	0.15	0.25	1.00	3.00	—
1940	25,525,000	0.15	0.25	1.00	3.50	—
1941	34,705,000	0.15	0.25	1.00	3.00	—

KM# 885a.1 FRANC

Aluminum, 23 mm. **Obv:** Laureate head left **Rev:** Cornucopias flank denomination and date **Note:** Thick and thin planchets exist.

Date	Mintage	F	VF	XF	Unc	BU
1941	60,877,000	0.10	0.20	1.00	4.00	—
1943	4,400	1,200	1,500	2,250	4,000	6,000
1944	22,608,000	0.10	0.20	1.50	5.00	—
1945	61,780,000	0.10	0.15	0.50	2.00	—
1946	52,516,000	0.10	0.15	0.25	2.00	—
1947	110,448,000	0.10	0.15	0.25	2.00	—
1948	96,092,000	0.10	0.15	0.25	2.00	—
1949	41,090,000	0.10	0.15	0.25	2.00	—
1950	27,882,000	0.10	0.15	0.50	2.50	—
1957	16,497,000	0.10	0.15	0.75	3.00	—
1958	21,197,000	0.10	0.15	0.75	3.00	—
1959	41,985,000	0.10	0.15	0.25	1.25	—

KM# 902.1 FRANC

Aluminum, 23 mm. **Obv:** Double bit axe, grain sprigs flank **Rev:** Denomination above date, oak leaves flank **Designer:** Lucien Bazor **Note:** Without mint mark. Vichy French State Issues. Thick and thin planchets exist.

Date	Mintage	F	VF	XF	Unc	BU
1942	152,144,000	0.25	0.50	1.50	4.00	—
1942 Without LB	Inc. above	—	—	—	—	—
1943	205,564,000	0.10	0.25	1.00	2.50	—
1943 Thin flan	Inc. above	0.10	0.25	1.00	2.50	—
1944	50,605,000	0.50	1.25	2.00	10.00	—

KM# 902.2 FRANC

Aluminum, 23 mm. **Obv:** Grain sprigs flank double bit axe **Rev:** Leaves flank denomination, date below

Date	Mintage	F	VF	XF	Unc	BU
1943B	68,082,000	5.00	9.00	28.00	80.00	120
1944B	13,622,000	1.50	3.00	12.00	25.00	—
1944 large C	74,859,000	0.50	1.50	3.50	12.50	—
1944 small C	—	50.00	100	200	400	600

KM# 885b FRANC

Zinc, 23 mm. **Obv:** Laureate head left **Rev:** Cornucopias flank denomination and date **Note:** Struck for colonial use in Africa.

Date	Mintage	F	VF	XF	Unc	BU
1943A	Est. 17,000	750	1,100	1,700	3,200	—

KM# 885a.3 FRANC

Aluminum, 23 mm. **Obv:** Laureate head left **Rev:** Cornucopias flank denomination and date

Date	Mintage	F	VF	XF	Unc	BU
1944C	33,600,000	0.50	1.50	3.50	12.00	—
1945C	5,220,000	1.50	3.50	9.00	25.00	60.00

KM# 885a.2 FRANC

Aluminum, 23 mm. **Obv:** Laureate head left **Rev:** Cornucopias flank denomination and date

Date	Mintage	F	VF	XF	Unc	BU
1945B	4,251,000	1.00	3.50	9.00	28.00	75.00
1946B	26,493,000	0.10	0.20	1.50	5.00	—
1947B	51,562,000	0.10	0.20	1.00	4.00	—
1948B	45,481,000	0.10	0.20	1.00	3.50	—
1949B	35,840,000	0.10	0.20	1.00	4.00	—
1950B	18,800,000	1.00	2.00	3.50	15.00	—
1957B	63,976,000	0.10	0.20	1.00	4.00	—
1958B	13,412,000	0.25	0.75	2.00	5.50	—

KM# 902.3 FRANC

Aluminum, 23 mm. **Obv:** Grain sprigs flank double bit axe **Rev:** Leaves flank denomination, date below

Date	Mintage	F	VF	XF	Unc	BU
1944 Large C	74,859,000	0.25	0.75	1.50	5.50	—
1944 Small C	Inc. above	15.00	30.00	70.00	325	—

KM# 845.1 2 FRANCS

10.0000 g., 0.8350 Silver .2684 oz. ASW, 27 mm. **Obv:** Figure sowing seed **Rev:** Leafy branch divides denomination and date **Designer:** Louis Oscar Roty **Note:** Without mint mark.

Date	Mintage	F	VF	XF	Unc	BU
1901	1,860,000	6.50	18.00	50.00	150	250
1902	2,000,000	6.50	18.00	50.00	125	210
1904	1,500,000	7.50	18.00	40.00	175	250
1905	2,000,000	6.50	18.00	50.00	150	225
1908	2,502,000	3.75	6.00	20.00	75.00	100
1909	1,000,000	8.00	18.00	35.00	175	250
1910	2,190,000	3.75	6.00	20.00	75.00	100
1912	1,000,000	7.00	18.00	40.00	125	200
1913	500,000	15.00	25.00	45.00	150	225
1914	5,719,000	BV	3.75	7.00	25.00	50.00
1915	13,963,000	—	BV	4.00	18.00	—
1916	17,887,000	—	BV	4.00	18.00	—
1917	16,555,000	—	BV	4.00	18.00	—
1918	12,026,000	—	BV	4.00	18.00	—
1919	9,261,000	—	BV	4.00	15.00	—
1920	3,014,000	BV	4.00	7.00	25.00	—

KM# 845.2 2 FRANCS

10.0000 g., 0.8352 Silver .2684 oz. ASW, 27 mm. **Obv:** Figure sowing seed **Rev:** Leafy branch divides date and denomination

Date	Mintage	F	VF	XF	Unc	BU
1914C	462,000	9.00	16.00	35.00	60.00	150
1914C Matte Proof	—	Value: 650				

KM# 877 2 FRANCS

Aluminum-Bronze, 27 mm. **Subject:** French Chamber of Commerce **Obv:** Denomination within circle **Rev:** Mercury seated left, caduceus at left, shield on right, date below **Note:** Without mint mark.

Date	Mintage	F	VF	XF	Unc	BU
1920	14,363,000	6.00	15.00	40.00	90.00	—
1921	Inc. above	0.75	1.50	3.00	12.50	—
1922	29,463,000	0.50	1.00	2.00	7.50	—
1923	43,960,000	0.50	1.00	2.00	7.50	—
1924 Open 4	29,631,000	0.50	1.00	2.00	7.50	—
1924 Closed 4	Inc. above	0.65	1.50	3.00	10.00	—
1925/3	31,607,000	0.75	1.75	4.00	12.50	—
1925	Inc. above	0.50	1.00	2.00	8.00	—
1926	2,962,000	7.00	18.00	50.00	100	—
1927	1,678,000	100	150	300	700	—

KM# 886 2 FRANCS

Aluminum-Bronze, 27 mm. **Obv:** Laureate head left **Rev:** Denomination and date flanked by cornucopias **Designer:** Pierre Alexandre Marlon

Date	Mintage	F	VF	XF	Unc	BU
1931	1,717,000	3.00	6.00	12.00	35.00	—
1932	8,943,000	0.75	1.50	3.00	10.00	—
1933	8,413,000	0.75	1.50	3.00	10.00	—
1934	6,896,000	1.25	2.50	6.00	12.00	—
1935	298,000	12.00	20.00	40.00	90.00	—
1936	12,394,000	0.25	1.00	2.00	6.00	—
1937	11,055,000	0.25	1.00	2.00	6.00	—
1938	28,072,000	0.20	0.50	1.00	5.00	—
1939	25,403,000	0.20	0.50	1.00	5.00	—
1940	9,716,000	1.00	2.00	3.50	10.00	—
1941	16,684,000	0.25	1.00	2.00	6.00	—

KM# 886a.1 2 FRANCS

Aluminum, 27 mm. **Obv:** Laureate head left **Rev:** Denomination and date flanked by cornucopias

Date	Mintage	F	VF	XF	Unc	BU
1941	Inc. above	0.25	0.50	1.00	3.00	—
1944	7,224,000	0.75	1.50	4.00	12.00	—
1945	16,636,000	0.50	1.00	2.50	7.00	—
1946	34,930,000	0.20	0.50	1.00	3.50	—
1947	78,984,000	0.20	0.30	1.00	2.50	—
1948	32,354,000	0.20	0.50	1.00	3.50	—
1949	13,683,000	0.25	0.50	1.00	2.50	—
1950	12,191,000	0.25	0.50	1.00	2.50	—
1958	9,906,000	0.20	0.50	1.00	3.50	—
1959	17,774,000	0.20	0.50	1.00	3.50	—

KM# 904.2 2 FRANCS

Aluminum, 27 mm. **Obv:** Grain sprigs flank double bit axe **Rev:** Oak leaves flank denomination, date below

Date	Mintage	F	VF	XF	Unc	BU
1943B	34,131,000	3.50	7.00	15.00	25.00	—
1944B	10,298,000	1.50	3.00	6.00	18.00	—

KM# 904.1 2 FRANCS

Aluminum, 27 mm. **Obv:** Double bit axe, grain sprigs flank **Rev:** Oak leaves flank denomination, date below **Designer:** Lucien Bazor **Note:** Without mint mark. Issued for Vichy French State.

Date	Mintage	F	VF	XF	Unc	BU
1943	106,997,000	0.20	0.50	1.00	6.00	—
1944	25,546,000	0.75	1.50	3.50	8.00	—

KM# 905 2 FRANCS

Brass, 27 mm. **Obv:** FRANCE within wreath **Rev:** Large denomination above date **Note:** Without mint mark. Issued during Allied Occupation.

Date	Mintage	F	VF	XF	Unc	BU
1944	50,000,000	1.00	2.00	5.00	25.00	60.00

KM# 886a.2 2 FRANCS

Aluminum, 27 mm. **Obv:** Laureate head left **Rev:** Denomination and date flanked by cornucopias

Date	Mintage	F	VF	XF	Unc	BU
1944B	170,000	—	—	—	—	—
1945B	1,726,000	3.00	7.00	15.00	35.00	—
1946B	6,018,000	2.00	4.00	8.00	20.00	—
1947B	26,220,000	0.20	0.50	1.00	3.50	—
1948B	39,090,000	0.20	0.50	1.00	3.00	—
1949B	23,955,000	0.20	0.50	1.00	3.50	—
1950B	18,185,000	0.50	1.00	3.00	5.00	—

KM# 904.3 2 FRANCS

Aluminum, 27 mm. **Obv:** Grain sprigs flank double bit axe **Rev:** Oak leaves flank denomination, date below

Date	Mintage	F	VF	XF	Unc	BU
1944C	19,470,000	1.25	2.50	5.00	18.00	—

KM# 886a.3 2 FRANCS

Aluminum, 27 mm. **Obv:** Laureate head left **Rev:** Denomination and date flanked by cornucopias

Date	Mintage	F	VF	XF	Unc	BU
1945C	1,165,000	5.00	10.00	25.00	65.00	110

KM# 887 5 FRANCS

Nickel **Obv:** Head right, date below **Rev:** Denomination flanked by grain sprigs **Note:** Without mint mark.

Date	Mintage	F	VF	XF	Unc	BU
1933 (a)	160,078,000	0.75	1.50	3.50	9.00	—

KM# 888 5 FRANCS

Nickel, 31 mm. **Obv:** Laureate head left **Rev:** Denomination above date within sectioned wreath **Note:** Without mint mark.

Date	Mintage	F	VF	XF	Unc	BU
1933 (a)	56,686,000	0.25	0.75	2.50	8.00	—
1935 (a)	54,164,000	0.25	0.75	2.50	8.00	—
1936 (a)	117,000	400	700	1,200	1,850	—
1937 (a)	157,000	35.00	60.00	120	225	—
1938 (a)	4,977,000	12.00	25.00	50.00	120	—
1939 (a)	—	700	1,200	2,000	4,000	—

KM# 888a.1 5 FRANCS

Aluminum-Bronze, 31 mm. **Obv:** Laureate head left **Rev:** Denomination above date within sectioned wreath **Note:** Struck for Colonial use in Algeria.

Date	Mintage	F	VF	XF	Unc	BU
1938 (a)	10,144,000	6.00	10.00	18.00	85.00	120
1939 (a)	Inc. above	2.50	5.00	12.00	30.00	60.00
1940 (a)	38,758,000	1.00	2.00	3.50	10.00	40.00

KM# 901 5 FRANCS

Copper-Nickel **Obv:** Double bit axe divides denomination, date below **Rev:** Head with collar left **Note:** Without mint mark.

Date	Mintage	F	VF	XF	Unc	BU
1941 (a)	13,782,000	65.00	100	150	250	400

Note: Never released into circulation.

KM# 888b.1 5 FRANCS

Aluminum, 31 mm. **Obv:** Laureate head left **Rev:** Denomination above date within sectioned wreath **Note:** Without mint mark.

Date	Mintage	F	VF	XF	Unc	BU
1945 (a) Open 9	95,399,000	0.20	0.35	1.50	6.00	—
1946 (a) Open 9	61,332,000	0.20	0.35	1.50	6.00	—
1947 (a) Open 9	46,576,000	0.20	0.35	1.50	6.00	—
1947 (a) Closed 9	Inc. above	0.20	0.35	1.50	6.00	—
1948 (a) Open 9	104,473,000	1.00	3.00	6.00	12.50	—
1948 (a) Closed 9	Inc. above	5.00	10.00	30.00	50.00	—
1949 (a) Closed 9	203,252,000	0.20	0.35	0.75	3.00	—
1950 (a) Closed 9	128,372,000	0.20	0.35	0.75	3.00	—
1952 (a) Closed 9	4,000,000	20.00	40.00	100	225	—

KM# 888a.3 5 FRANCS

Aluminum-Bronze, 31 mm. **Obv:** Laureate head left **Rev:** Denomination above date within sectioned wreath

Date	Mintage	F	VF	XF	Unc	BU
1945C Open 9	Inc. above	3.00	7.00	15.00	30.00	—
1946C Open 9	Inc. above	5.00	15.00	30.00	60.00	—

KM# 888b.2 5 FRANCS

Aluminum, 31 mm. **Obv:** Laureate head left **Rev:** Denomination above date within sectioned wreath

Date	Mintage	F	VF	XF	Unc	BU
1945B Open 9	6,043,000	1.50	3.00	5.00	15.00	—
1946B Open 9	13,360,000	0.75	1.50	3.00	12.00	—
1947B Open 9	30,839,000	0.50	1.00	2.50	8.00	—
1947B Closed 9	Inc. above	0.50	1.00	2.50	8.00	—
1948B Open 9	28,047,000	20.00	40.00	100	175	—
1949B Closed 9	48,414,000	0.50	1.00	2.50	8.00	—
1950B Closed 9	28,952,000	0.75	1.50	3.50	9.00	—

KM# 888b.3 5 FRANCS

Aluminum, 31 mm. **Obv:** Laureate head left **Rev:** Denomination above date within sectioned wreath

Date	Mintage	F	VF	XF	Unc	BU
1945C Open 9	2,208,000	7.00	15.00	28.00	60.00	85.00
1946C Open 9	1,269,000	8.00	18.00	38.00	75.00	95.00

KM# 888a.2 5 FRANCS

Aluminum-Bronze, 31 mm. **Obv:** Laureate head left **Rev:** Denomination above date within sectioned wreath **Note:** Struck for Colonial use in Africa.

Date	Mintage	F	VF	XF	Unc	BU
1945 (a) Open 9	13,044,000	1.00	2.00	4.00	11.00	—
1946 (a) Open 9	21,790,000	1.00	2.00	4.00	11.00	—
1947 (a)	2,662,000	165	400	600	1,200	—

Note: Date exists with both open and closed 9's.

KM# 846 10 FRANCS

3.2258 g., 0.9000 Gold .0933 oz. AGW

Date	Mintage	F	VF	XF	Unc	BU
1901	2,100,000	—	BV	65.00	85.00	125
1901	2,100,000	—	BV	65.00	85.00	125
1905	1,426,000	—	BV	65.00	85.00	125
1905	1,426,000	—	BV	65.00	85.00	125
1906	3,665,000	—	BV	65.00	85.00	125
1907	3,364,000	—	BV	65.00	85.00	125
1908	1,650,000	—	BV	65.00	85.00	125
1909	599,000	—	BV	70.00	120	255
1910	2,110,000	—	BV	65.00	85.00	125
1911	1,881,000	—	BV	65.00	85.00	125
1912	1,756,000	—	BV	65.00	85.00	125
1914	3,041,000	—	BV	65.00	85.00	125

KM# 878 10 FRANCS

10.0000 g., 0.6800 Silver .2186 oz. ASW, 28 mm. **Note:** Without mint mark.

Date	Mintage	F	VF	XF	Unc	BU
1929	16,292,000	BV	3.50	5.50	12.00	—
1930	36,986,000	BV	3.00	4.50	9.00	—
1931	35,468,000	BV	3.00	4.50	9.00	—
1932	40,288,000	BV	3.00	3.50	7.00	—
1933	31,146,000	BV	3.00	3.50	7.00	—
1934	52,001,000	BV	3.00	3.50	7.00	—
1936	—	—	—	—	—	—
1937	52,000	65.00	125	250	360	500
1938	14,090,000	BV	3.00	6.00	12.50	—
1939	8,298,999	3.00	4.00	8.00	17.50	—

KM# 908.1 10 FRANCS
Copper-Nickel, 26 mm. **Obv:** Laureate head right, long leaves and short leaves **Rev:** Denomination above date, inscription below, grain columns flank **Note:** Large head.

Date	Mintage	F	VF	XF	Unc	BU
1945 (ll)	6,557,000	0.25	0.75	2.00	6.00	—
1945 (sl)	Inc. above	15.00	30.00	50.00	90.00	140
1946 (ll)	24,409,000	185	300	400	—	—
1946 (sl)	Inc. above	0.25	0.50	2.00	5.00	—
1947	41,627,000	0.25	0.50	1.00	3.00	—

KM# 908.2 10 FRANCS
Copper-Nickel, 26 mm. **Obv:** Laureate head right **Rev:** Denomination above date, inscription below, grain columns flank **Note:** Large head

Date	Mintage	F	VF	XF	Unc	BU
1946B (ll)	8,452,000	20.00	35.00	50.00	85.00	—
1946B (sl)	Inc. above	0.25	0.75	2.00	6.00	—
1947B	17,188,000	0.25	0.50	2.00	5.00	—

KM# 909.1 10 FRANCS
Copper-Nickel, 26 mm. **Obv:** Laureate head right, small head **Rev:** Denomination above date, inscription below, grain columns flank **Note:** Without mint mark.

Date	Mintage	F	VF	XF	Unc	BU
1947	Inc. above	0.30	0.75	1.50	3.50	—
1948	155,945,000	0.20	0.35	0.75	2.00	—
1949	118,149,000	0.20	0.35	0.75	2.00	—

KM# 909.2 10 FRANCS
Copper-Nickel, 26 mm. **Obv:** Large head **Rev:** Denomination above date, inscription below, grain columns flank

Date	Mintage	F	VF	XF	Unc	BU
1947B	Inc. above	1.00	2.50	6.00	17.00	—
1948B	40,500,000	0.35	0.75	2.00	4.00	—
1949B	29,518,000	0.35	0.75	2.00	4.00	—

KM# 915.1 10 FRANCS
Aluminum-Bronze, 20 mm. **Obv:** Head left **Rev:** Denomination above date at right, rooster above laurel leaves at left **Designer:** Georges Guiraud **Note:** Without mint mark.

Date	Mintage	F	VF	XF	Unc	BU
1950	13,534,000	0.35	0.65	1.50	5.00	—
1951	153,689,000	0.20	0.35	0.75	2.00	—
1952	76,810,000	0.20	0.35	0.75	2.00	—
1953	46,272,000	0.25	0.50	0.75	2.50	—
1954	2,207,000	4.00	12.00	30.00	50.00	—
1955	47,466,000	0.20	0.35	0.75	2.50	—
1956	2,570,000	—	—	—	—	—
Note: Reported, not confirmed.						
1957	26,351,000	0.50	1.00	2.00	4.50	—
1958 (w)	27,213,000	0.50	1.00	2.00	4.50	—
1959	125,000	—	—	—	—	—
Note: Reported, not confirmed.						

KM# 915.2 10 FRANCS
Aluminum-Bronze, 20 mm. **Obv:** Head left **Rev:** Rooster above laurel sprig, denominaton at right **Designer:** Georges Guiraud

Date	Mintage	F	VF	XF	Unc	BU
1950B	4,808,000	1.00	3.00	6.00	17.50	—
1951B	106,866,000	0.20	0.35	0.75	2.00	—
1952B	72,346,000	0.20	0.35	0.75	2.00	—
1953B	36,466,000	0.25	0.50	1.00	3.00	—
1954B	21,634,000	0.75	1.50	3.50	7.00	—
1958B	1,500,000	—	—	—	—	—
Note: Reported, not confirmed.						

KM# 1400 10 FRANCS
22.2000 g., 0.9000 Silver 0.6424 oz. ASW, 36.9 mm. **Obv:** Liberty bust by Dupre **Rev:** Value **Edge:** Plain

Date	Mintage	F	VF	XF	Unc	BU
2000 Proof	—	Value: 40.00				

KM# 1401 10 FRANCS
22.2000 g., 0.9000 Silver 0.6424 oz. ASW, 36.9 mm. **Obv:** Liberty bust by Lagriffoul **Rev:** Value **Edge:** Plain

Date	Mintage	F	VF	XF	Unc	BU
2000 Proof	—	Value: 40.00				

KM# 847 20 FRANCS
6.4516 g., 0.9000 Gold .1867 oz. AGW **Edge Lettering:** DIEU PROTEGE LA FRANCE

Date	Mintage	F	VF	XF	Unc	BU
1901A	2,643,000	—	—	BV	140	185
1901A	2,643,000	—	—	BV	140	185
1902A	2,394,000	—	—	BV	140	185
1902A	2,394,000	—	—	BV	140	185
1903A	4,405,000	—	—	BV	140	185
1904A	7,706,000	—	—	BV	140	185
1905A	9,158,000	—	—	BV	140	185
1906A	14,613,000	—	—	BV	140	185

KM# 857 20 FRANCS
6.4516 g., 0.9000 Gold .1867 oz. AGW **Obv:** Oak leaf wreath encircles liberty head right **Rev:** Rooster divides denomination, date below **Edge Lettering:** LIBERTE EGALITE FRATERNITE **Note:** All dates from 1907-1914 have been officially restruck.

Date	Mintage	F	VF	XF	Unc	BU
1906	—	—	—	BV	130	165
1907	17,716,000	—	—	BV	130	165
1908	6,721,000	—	—	BV	130	165
1909	9,637,000	—	—	BV	130	165
1910	5,779,000	—	—	BV	130	165
1911	5,346,000	—	—	BV	130	165
1912	10,332,000	—	—	BV	130	165
1913	12,163,000	—	—	BV	130	165
1914	6,518,000	—	—	BV	130	165

KM# 879 20 FRANCS
20.0000 g., 0.6800 Silver .4372 oz. ASW **Obv:** Laureate head right, long and short leaves **Rev:** Denomination above date, inscription below, grain columns flank **Note:** Without mint mark.

Date	Mintage	F	VF	XF	Unc	BU
1929 (ll)	3,234,000	BV	6.50	9.00	35.00	60.00
1933 (sl)	—	BV	6.00	7.00	18.00	40.00
Note: Counterfeits exist in bronze-aluminum with thin silver sheath.						
1933 (ll)	Inc. above	BV	6.00	7.00	18.00	40.00
1934 (sl)	11,785,000	BV	6.00	10.00	30.00	45.00
1936 (sl)	48,000	200	300	450	700	—
1937 (sl)	1,189,000	10.00	15.00	25.00	50.00	70.00
1938 (sl)	10,910,000	BV	6.00	7.50	20.00	35.00
1939 (sl)	3,918	1,000	2,000	2,750	4,500	—

KM# 916.1 20 FRANCS
Aluminum-Bronze, 23 mm. **Obv:** Head left, "GEORGES GUIRAUD" behind head **Rev:** Denomination above date at right, rooster above laurel branch at left

Date	Mintage	F	VF	XF	Unc	BU
1950	5,779,000	0.50	1.00	2.50	7.00	—
Note: 3 plumes						
1950	—	125	200	350	700	—
Note: 4 plumes						

KM# 916.2 20 FRANCS
Aluminum-Bronze, 23 mm. **Obv:** Head left **Rev:** Rooster above laurel sprig, denomination at right

Date	Mintage	F	VF	XF	Unc	BU
1950B	—	1.50	3.00	7.00	20.00	—
Note: 3 plumes						
1950B	—	40.00	85.00	150	225	—
Note: 4 plumes						

KM# 917.2 20 FRANCS
Aluminum-Bronze, 23 mm. **Obv:** "G. GUIRAUD" behind head **Rev:** Rooster above laurel sprig, denomination at right

Date	Mintage	F	VF	XF	Unc	BU
1950B	43,355,000	25.00	35.00	50.00	135	—
Note: 3 plumes						
1950B	Inc. above	0.50	1.00	3.00	6.50	—
Note: 4 plumes						
1951B	46,815,000	0.30	0.50	1.75	3.50	—
Note: 4 plumes						
1952B	54,381,000	0.30	0.50	1.75	3.50	—
Note: 4 plumes						
1953B	42,410,000	0.30	0.50	1.75	3.50	—
Note: 4 plumes						
1954B	1,573,000	125	200	350	800	—
Note: 4 plumes						

KM# 917.1 20 FRANCS
Aluminum-Bronze, 23 mm. **Obv:** Head left, "G. GUIRAUD" behind head **Rev:** Denomination above date at right, rooster above laurel branch at left **Note:** Without mint mark.

Date	Mintage	F	VF	XF	Unc	BU
1950	120,656,000	2.00	6.00	12.00	40.00	—
Note: 3 plumes						
1950	Inc. above	0.25	0.40	1.00	2.50	—
Note: 4 plumes						
1951	97,922,000	0.25	0.40	1.00	2,50	—
Note: 4 plumes						
1952	130,281,000	0.25	0.40	1.00	2.50	—
Note: 4 plumes						
1953	60,158,000	0.30	0.50	1.00	2.50	—
Note: 4 plumes						

KM# 831 50 FRANCS
16.1290 g., 0.9000 Gold .4467 oz. AGW **Obv:** Standing Genius writing the Constitution, rooster at right, fasces at left **Rev:** Denomination above date within circular wreath

Date	Mintage	F	VF	XF	Unc	BU
1904A	20,000	325	550	900	1,650	—

KM# 918.1 50 FRANCS
Aluminum-Bronze, 27 mm. **Obv:** Head left **Rev:** Denomination above date at right, rooster above laurel branch at left **Designer:** Georges Guiraud **Note:** Without mint mark.

Date	Mintage	F	VF	XF	Unc	BU
1950	600,000	75.00	150	350	625	—
1951	68,630,000	0.50	1.00	2.25	5.50	—
1952	74,212,000	0.50	1.00	2.25	5.50	—
1953	63,172,000	0.50	1.00	2.25	5.50	—
1954	997,000	15.00	35.00	65.00	110	—
1958 (w)	501,000	25.00	50.00	85.00	240	—

KM# 918.2 50 FRANCS
Aluminum-Bronze, 27 mm. **Obv:** Head left **Rev:** Rooster above laurel, denomination at right

Date	Mintage	F	VF	XF	Unc	BU
1951B	11,829,000	0.75	1.50	3.00	9.00	—
1952B	13,432,000	1.00	2.00	5.00	15.00	—
1953B	23,376,000	0.65	1.25	2.50	8.00	—
1954B	6,531,000	3.00	5.50	11.50	30.00	—

KM# 832 100 FRANCS
32.2581 g., 0.9000 Gold .9335 oz. AGW **Obv:** Standing Genius writing the Constitution, rooster on right, fasces on left **Rev:** Denomination above date within circular wreath **Edge Lettering:** DIEU PROTEGE LA FRANCE

Date	Mintage	F	VF	XF	Unc	BU
1901A	10,000	—	BV	625	800	1,200
1901A	10,000	—	BV	625	800	1,200
1902A	10,000	—	BV	625	800	1,200
1902A	10,000	—	BV	625	800	1,200
1903A	10,000	—	BV	625	800	1,200
1904A	20,000	—	BV	625	800	1,200
1905A	10,000	—	BV	625	800	1,200
1906A	30,000	—	BV	626	800	1,200

KM# 858 100 FRANCS
32.2581 g., 0.9000 Gold .9335 oz. AGW **Obv:** Standing Genius writing the constitution, rooster on right, column on the left **Rev:** Denomination and date within wreath **Edge Lettering:** LIBERTE EGALITE FRATERNITE

Date	Mintage	F	VF	XF	Unc	BU
1907A	20,000	—	—	BV	645	900
1908A	23,000	—	—	BV	645	900
1909A	20,000	—	—	BV	645	900
1910A	20,000	—	—	BV	645	900
1911A	30,000	—	—	BV	645	900
1912A	20,000	—	—	BV	645	900
1913A	30,000	—	—	BV	645	900
1914A Rare	1,281	—	—	—	—	—

KM# 880 100 FRANCS
6.5500 g., 0.9000 Gold .1895 oz. AGW **Obv:** Winged head left **Rev:** Denomination above grain sprig, date below, laurel and oak branches flank **Note:** Without mint mark.

Date	Mintage	F	VF	XF	Unc	BU
1929	50	—	—	2,500	4,000	—
1932	Est. 50	—	—	3,250	4,750	—
1933	Est. 300	—	—	1,650	2,500	—
1934 Rare	—	—	—	—	—	—
1935	6,102,000	—	—	500	800	—
1936	7,689,000	—	—	500	800	—

KM# 919.1 100 FRANCS
Copper-Nickel, 24 mm. **Obv:** Liberty bust with torch right **Rev:** Denomination above date at left, grain sprigs at right

Date	Mintage	F	VF	XF	Unc	BU
1954	97,285,000	0.50	1.00	2.50	7.00	—
1955	152,517,000	0.25	0.75	1.50	4.50	—
1956	7,578,000	3.50	7.50	15.00	40.00	—
1957	11,312,000	1.50	3.00	6.00	18.00	—
1958 (w)	3,256,000	2.50	5.50	12.50	35.00	—
1958 (o)	Inc. above	20.00	40.00	90.00	175	—

KM# 919.2 100 FRANCS
Copper-Nickel, 24 mm. **Obv:** Liberty bust with torch right **Rev:** Denomination and date left of grain sprigs

Date	Mintage	F	VF	XF	Unc	BU
1954B	86,261,000	0.50	1.25	2.50	5.00	—
1955B	136,585,000	0.25	0.75	1.50	3.50	—
1956B	19,154,000	1.00	2.00	4.50	10.00	—
1957B	25,702,000	1.00	2.00	4.50	12.50	—
1958B	54,072,000	1.00	2.00	4.50	11.50	—

REFORM COINAGE

(Commencing 1960)

1 Old Franc = 1 New Centime; 100 New Centimes = 1 New Franc

KM# 928 CENTIME
Chrome-Steel **Obv:** Cursive legend surrounds grain sprig **Rev:** Cursive denomination, date at top **Note:** 1991-1993 dated coins, non-Proof, exist in both coin and medal alignment. Values given here are for medal alignment examples. Pieces struck in coin alignment have been traded for as much as $50.00.

Date	Mintage	F	VF	XF	Unc	BU
1962	34,200,000	—	—	0.10	0.25	0.35
1963	16,811,000	—	0.10	0.15	0.35	0.50
1964	22,654,000	—	—	0.10	0.25	0.35
1965	47,799,000	—	—	0.10	0.25	0.35
1966	19,688,000	—	—	0.10	0.25	0.35
1967	52,308,000	—	—	0.10	0.25	0.35
1968	40,890,000	—	—	0.10	0.25	0.35
1969	35,430,000	—	—	0.10	0.25	0.35
1970	29,600,000	—	—	0.10	0.25	0.35
1971	3,082,000	—	—	0.10	0.25	0.35
1972	1,014,999	—	0.10	0.15	0.35	0.50
1973	1,806,000	—	0.10	0.15	0.35	0.50
1974	7,949,000	—	—	0.10	0.25	0.35
1975	771,000	—	0.10	0.25	1.00	1.50
1976	4,482,000	—	—	0.10	0.25	0.35
1977	6,425,000	—	—	0.10	0.25	0.35
1978	1,236,000	—	0.10	0.15	0.35	0.50
1979	2,213,000	—	—	0.10	0.25	0.35
1980	60,000	—	—	—	1.00	1.50
1981	50,000	—	—	—	1.00	1.50
1982	69,000	—	—	—	1.00	1.50
1983	101,000	—	—	—	1.00	1.50
1984	50,000	—	—	—	1.00	1.50
1985	20,000	—	—	—	1.00	1.50
1986	48,000	—	—	—	1.00	1.50
Note: In sets only						
1987	100,000	—	—	—	1.00	1.50
1988	100,000	—	—	—	1.00	1.50
1989	83,000	—	—	—	1.00	1.50
1990	15,000	—	—	—	1.00	1.50
1991	5,000	—	—	—	1.00	1.50
1991 Proof	10,000	Value: 2.00				
1992	85,000	—	—	—	1.00	1.50
1992 Proof	15,000	Value: 2.00				
1993	40,000	—	—	—	1.00	1.50
1993 Proof	10,000	Value: 2.00				
1994 bee	20,000	—	—	—	1.00	1.50
1994 fish	10,000	—	—	—	1.00	1.50
1995	25,000	—	—	—	1.00	1.50
1995 Proof	10,000	Value: 2.00				
1996	17,000	—	—	—	1.00	1.50
1996 Proof	8,000	Value: 2.00				
1997	15,000	—	—	—	1.00	1.50
Note: In sets only						
1997 Proof	10,000	Value: 2.00				
1998	—	—	—	—	1.00	1.50
Note: In sets only						
1998 Proof	—	Value: 2.00				
1999	—	—	—	—	1.00	1.50
Note: In sets only						
1999 Proof	—	Value: 2.00				
2000	—	—	—	—	1.00	1.50
Note: In sets only						
2000 Proof	—	Value: 2.00				

KM# 928a CENTIME
2.5000 g., 0.7500 Gold .0603 oz. AGW **Obv:** Cursive legend surrounds grain sprig, medallic alignment **Rev:** Cursive denomination, date above, medallic alignment **Edge:** Plain **Note:** Last Centime.

Date	Mintage	F	VF	XF	Unc	BU
2000	25,000	—	—	—	—	55.00

KM# 927 5 CENTIMES
Chrome-Steel **Obv:** Cursive legend surrounds grain sprig **Rev:** Cursive denomination, date above

Date	Mintage	F	VF	XF	Unc	BU
1961	39,000,000	0.10	0.20	0.50	2.00	3.00
1962	166,360,000	0.10	0.15	0.20	0.75	1.00
1963	71,900,000	0.10	0.20	0.40	1.00	1.50
1964	126,480,000	0.10	0.15	0.30	0.75	1.00

KM# 933 5 CENTIMES
2.0000 g., Aluminum-Bronze, 17 mm. **Obv:** Liberty bust left **Obv. Designer:** Henri Lagriffoul **Rev:** Denomination above date, grain sprig below, laurel branch at left **Rev. Designer:** Adrien Dieudonne **Note:** 1991-1993 dated coins, non-Proof exist in both coin and medal alignment.

Date	Mintage	F	VF	XF	Unc	BU
1966	502,512,000	—	—	—	0.10	0.15
1967	11,747,000	—	—	0.10	0.25	0.35
1968	110,395,000	—	—	—	0.10	0.15
1969	94,955,000	—	—	—	0.10	0.15
1970	58,900,000	—	—	—	0.10	0.15
1971	93,190,000	—	—	—	0.10	0.15
1972	100,515,000	—	—	—	0.10	0.15
1973	100,344,000	—	—	—	0.10	0.15
1974	103,890,000	—	—	—	0.10	0.15
1975	95,835,000	—	—	—	0.10	0.15
1976	148,395,000	—	—	—	0.10	0.15
1977	115,285,000	—	—	—	0.10	0.15
1978	189,804,000	—	—	—	0.10	0.15
1979	180,000,000	—	—	—	0.10	0.15
1980	180,010,000	—	—	—	0.10	0.15
1981	134,974,000	—	—	—	0.10	0.15
1982	138,000,000	—	—	—	0.10	0.15
1983	132,000,000	—	—	—	0.10	0.15
1984	150,000,000	—	—	—	0.10	0.15
1985	170,000,000	—	—	—	0.10	0.15
1986	280,000,000	—	—	—	0.10	0.15
1987	310,000,000	—	—	—	0.10	0.15
1988	200,000,000	—	—	—	0.10	0.15
1989	84,000	—	—	—	1.00	1.50
1990	79,992,000	—	—	—	0.20	0.30
1991	49,994,000	—	—	—	0.20	0.30
1991 Proof	10,000	Value: 1.00				
1992	179,996,000	—	—	—	0.20	0.30
1992 Proof	15,000	Value: 1.00				
1993	154,988,000	—	—	—	0.20	0.30
1993 Proof	10,000	Value: 1.00				
1994	—	—	—	—	0.20	0.30
1994 fish	60,000,000	—	—	—	0.20	0.30
1994 fish Proof	10,000	—	—	—	—	—
1994 bee	59,996,000	—	—	—	0.20	0.30
1995	129,991,999	—	—	—	0.20	0.30

Date	Mintage	F	VF	XF	Unc	BU
1995 Proof	10,000	Value: 1.00				
1996	139,990,000	—	—	—	0.20	0.30
1996 Proof	8,000	Value: 1.00				
1997	199,995,000	—	—	—	0.20	0.30
1997 Proof	10,000	Value: 1.00				
1998	300,084,000	—	—	—	0.20	0.30
1998 Proof	—	Value: 1.00				
1999	—	—	—	—	1.50	2.50
Note: In sets only						
1999 Proof	—	Value: 1.00				
2000	—	—	—	—	1.50	2.50
Note: In sets only						
2000 Proof	—	Value: 1.00				

KM# 929 10 CENTIMES

3.0000 g., Aluminum-Bronze, 20 mm. **Obv:** Liberty bust left **Obv. Designer:** Henri Lagriffoul **Rev:** Denomination above date, grain sprig below, laurel branch at left **Rev. Designer:** Adrien Dieudonne **Note:** Without mint mark. 1991-1993 dated coins, non-Proof, exist in both coin and medal alignment.

Date	Mintage	F	VF	XF	Unc	BU
1962	29,100,000	—	—	0.10	0.40	0.60
1963	217,601,000	—	—	—	0.10	0.15
1964	93,409,000	—	—	0.10	0.20	0.30
1965	41,220,000	—	—	0.10	0.30	0.50
1966	16,428,999	—	0.10	0.15	0.40	0.60
1967	196,728,000	—	—	—	0.10	0.15
1968	111,700,000	—	—	—	0.10	0.15
1969	129,530,000	—	—	—	0.10	0.15
1970	77,020,000	—	—	—	0.10	0.15
1971	26,280,000	—	—	—	0.10	0.15
1972	45,700,000	—	—	—	0.10	0.15
1973	58,000,000	—	—	—	0.10	0.15
1974	91,990,000	—	—	—	0.10	0.15
1975	74,450,000	—	—	—	0.10	0.15
1976	137,320,000	—	—	—	0.10	0.15
1977	140,110,000	—	—	—	0.10	0.15
1978	154,360,000	—	—	—	0.10	0.15
1979	140,000,000	—	—	—	0.10	0.15
1980	140,010,000	—	—	—	0.10	0.15
1981	135,000,000	—	—	—	0.10	0.15
1982	110,000,000	—	—	—	0.10	0.15
1983	150,000,000	—	—	—	0.10	0.15
1984	200,000,000	—	—	—	0.10	0.15
1985	170,000,000	—	—	—	0.10	0.15
1986	150,000,000	—	—	—	0.10	0.15
1987	150,000,000	—	—	—	0.10	0.15
1988	145,000,000	—	—	—	0.10	0.15
1989	179,984,000	—	—	—	0.10	0.15
1990	179,992,000	—	—	—	0.10	0.15
1991	179,986,000	—	—	—	0.10	0.15
1991 Proof	10,000	Value: 1.00				
1992	179,996,000	—	—	—	0.10	0.15
1992 Proof	15,000	Value: 1.00				
1993	154,988,000	—	—	—	0.10	0.15
1993 Proof	10,000	Value: 1.00				
1994 Fish	103,000,000	—	—	—	0.10	0.15
1994	—	—	—	—	0.10	0.15
1994 Fish Proof	10,000	Value: 1.00				
1994 Bee	76,988,000	—	—	—	0.10	0.15
1995	169,996,000	—	—	—	0.10	0.15
1995 Proof	10,000	Value: 1.00				
1996	179,981,000	—	—	—	0.10	0.15
1996 Proof	8,000	Value: 1.00				
1997	551,991,000	—	—	—	0.10	0.15
1997 Proof	10,000	Value: 1.00				
1998	350,000,000	—	—	—	0.10	0.15
1998 Proof	—	Value: 1.00				
1999	—	—	—	—	2.00	3.00
Note: In sets only						
1999 Proof	—	Value: 1.00				
2000	60,000,000	—	—	—	0.10	0.15
2000 Proof	—	Value: 1.00				

KM# 930 20 CENTIMES

4.0000 g., Aluminum-Bronze, 23.5 mm. **Obv:** Liberty bust left **Obv. Designer:** Henri Lagriffoul **Rev:** Denomination above date, grain sprig below, laurel branch at left **Rev. Designer:** Adrien Dieudonne **Note:** Without mint mark. 1991-1993 dated coins, non-Proof, exist in both coin and medal alignment.

Date	Mintage	F	VF	XF	Unc	BU
1962	48,200,000	—	—	0.10	0.40	0.60
1963	190,330,000	—	—	0.10	0.30	0.50
1964	127,521,000	—	—	0.10	0.30	0.50
1965	27,024,000	—	0.10	0.20	0.40	0.60
1966	21,762,000	—	0.10	0.20	0.40	0.60
1967	138,780,000	—	—	0.10	0.15	0.25
1968	77,408,000	—	—	0.10	0.20	0.30
1969	50,570,000	—	—	0.10	0.20	0.30
1970	70,040,000	—	—	0.10	0.15	0.25
1971	31,080,000	—	—	0.10	0.15	0.25
1972	39,740,000	—	—	0.10	0.15	0.25
1973	45,240,000	—	—	0.10	0.15	0.25
1974	54,250,000	—	—	0.10	0.15	0.25
1975	40,570,000	—	—	0.10	0.15	0.25
1976	117,610,000	—	—	—	0.10	0.15
1977	100,340,000	—	—	—	0.10	0.15
1978	125,015,000	—	—	—	0.10	0.15
1979	70,000,000	—	—	—	0.10	0.15
1980	20,010,000	—	—	0.10	0.15	0.25
1981	125,000,000	—	—	—	0.10	0.15
1982	150,000,000	—	—	—	0.10	0.15
1983	110,000,000	—	—	—	0.10	0.15
1984	200,000,000	—	—	—	0.10	0.15
1985	150,000,000	—	—	—	0.10	0.15
1986	40,000,000	—	—	—	0.10	0.15
1987	60,000,000	—	—	—	0.10	0.15
1988	220,000,000	—	—	—	0.10	0.15
1989	139,985,000	—	—	—	0.10	0.15
1990	49,990,000	—	—	—	0.10	0.15
1991	39,992,000	—	—	—	0.10	0.15
1991 1 Proof	10,000	Value: 1.00				
1992	89,985,000	—	—	—	0.10	0.15
1992 1 Proof	15,000	Value: 1.00				
1993	10,990,000	—	—	—	0.10	0.15
1993 1 Proof	10,000	Value: 1.00				
1994	—	—	—	—	0.10	0.15
1994 Fish	60,000,000	—	—	—	0.10	0.15
1994 Fish Proof	10,000	Value: 1.00				
1994 Bee	79,900,000	—	—	—	0.10	0.15
1995	109,995,000	—	—	—	0.10	0.15
1995 Proof	10,000	Value: 1.00				
1996	139,987,000	—	—	—	0.10	0.15
1996 Proof	8,000	Value: 1.00				
1997	436,216,500	—	—	—	0.10	0.15
1997 Proof	10,000	Value: 1.00				
1998	—	—	—	—	2.00	3.00
Note: In sets only						
1998 Proof	—	Value: 1.00				
1999	—	—	—	—	2.00	3.00
Note: In sets only						
1999 Proof	—	Value: 1.00				
2000	85,385,000	—	—	—	0.10	0.15
2000 Proof	—	Value: 1.00				

KM# 939.1 50 CENTIMES

Aluminum-Bronze, 25 mm. **Obv:** Liberty bust left, 3 folds in collar **Obv. Designer:** Henri Lagriffoul **Rev:** Denomination above date, grain sprig below, laurel branch at left **Rev. Designer:** Adrien Dieudonne

Date	Mintage	F	VF	XF	Unc	BU
1962	37,560,000	0.30	0.60	1.50	3.00	5.00
1963	62,482,000	0.20	0.40	1.00	2.00	3.00

KM# 939.2 50 CENTIMES

Aluminum-Bronze, 25 mm. **Obv:** 4 folds in collar **Rev:** Denomination above grain sprig, laurel at left

Date	Mintage	F	VF	XF	Unc	BU
1962	Inc. above	30.00	70.00	120	170	275
1963	Inc. above	0.20	0.40	1.00	2.00	3.00
1964	41,471,000	0.45	0.90	2.00	6.00	9.00

KM# 931.1 1/2 FRANC

4.5000 g., Nickel, 19.5 mm. **Obv:** The seed sower **Rev:** Laurel divides denomination and date **Edge:** Reeded **Designer:** Louis Oscar Roty **Note:** Without mint mark.

Date	Mintage	F	VF	XF	Unc	BU
1965	184,834,000	—	—	0.15	0.30	0.50
Note: Small legends						
1965	Inc. above	—	—	0.15	0.30	0.50
Note: Large legends						
1966	88,890,000	—	—	0.15	0.30	0.50
1967	28,394,000	—	—	0.15	0.40	0.60
1968	57,548,000	—	—	0.15	0.30	0.50
1969	47,144,000	—	—	0.15	0.30	0.50
1970	42,298,000	—	—	0.15	0.30	0.50
1971	36,068,000	—	—	0.15	0.30	0.50
1972	42,302,000	—	—	0.15	0.30	0.50
1972	Inc. above	25.00	50.00	100	150	—
Note: Without "O. ROTY"						
1973	48,372,000	—	—	0.15	0.30	0.60
1974	37,072,000	—	—	0.15	0.30	0.50
1975	22,803,000	—	—	0.15	0.40	0.60
1976	115,314,000	—	—	0.15	0.30	0.50
1977	131,644,000	—	—	0.15	0.30	0.50
1978	63,360,000	—	—	0.15	0.30	0.50
1979	51,000	—	—	—	0.50	0.75
1980	60,000	—	—	—	0.50	0.75
Note: In sets only						
1981	50,000	—	—	—	0.50	0.75
1982	78,000	—	—	—	0.50	0.75
1983	50,000,000	—	—	0.15	0.30	0.50
1984	80,000,000	—	—	0.15	0.30	0.50
1985	50,000,000	—	—	—	1.50	2.50
1986	110,000,000	—	—	—	1.50	2.50
1987	50,000,000	—	—	—	0.30	0.50
1988	100,000	—	—	—	0.40	0.60
1989	83,000	—	—	—	0.40	0.60
1990	15,000	—	—	—	0.40	0.60
1991	49,988,000	—	—	—	0.40	0.60
Note: Exists in both coin and medal alignment						
1992	29,968,000	—	—	—	0.40	0.60
Note: Exists in both coin and medal alignment						
1993	24,972,000	—	—	—	0.40	0.60
1994 Fish	10,000,000	—	—	—	0.40	0.60
1994 Bee	29,972,000	—	—	—	0.40	0.60
1995	29,976,000	—	—	—	0.40	0.60
1996	55,978,000	—	—	—	0.40	0.60
1997	99,976,000	—	—	—	0.40	0.60
1998	—	—	—	—	2.00	3.00
Note: In sets only						
1999	—	—	—	—	2.00	3.00
Note: In sets only						
2000	75,000,000	—	—	—	0.40	0.60

KM# 931.2 1/2 FRANC

4.5000 g., Nickel, 19.5 mm. **Obv:** Modified sower, engraver's signature: "O. ROTY" preceded by "D'AP" **Rev:** Laurel divides date and denomination **Edge:** Plain

Date	Mintage	F	VF	XF	Unc	BU
1991	—	—	—	—	0.40	0.60
1991 Proof	10,000	Value: 1.50				
1992	—	—	—	—	0.40	0.60
1992 Proof	15,000	Value: 1.50				
1993	—	—	—	—	0.40	0.60
1993 Proof	10,000	Value: 1.50				
1994 Fish	—	—	—	—	0.40	0.60
1994 Fish Proof	10,000	Value: 1.50				
1994 Bee	—	—	—	—	0.40	0.60
1995 Proof	10,000	Value: 1.50				
1995	—	—	—	—	0.40	0.60
1996	—	—	—	—	0.40	0.60
1996 Proof	8,000	Value: 1.50				
1997 Proof	10,000	Value: 1.50				
1997	—	—	—	—	0.40	0.60
1998 Proof	—	Value: 1.50				
1999 Proof	—	Value: 1.50				
2000	—	—	—	—	0.40	0.60
2000 Proof	—	Value: 1.50				

KM# 925.1 FRANC

6.0000 g., Nickel, 24 mm. **Obv:** The seed sower **Obv. Designer:** Louis Oscar Roty **Rev:** Laurel branch divides denomination and date **Edge:** Reeded **Note:** Without mint mark.

Date	Mintage	F	VF	XF	Unc	BU
1960	406,375,000	—	—	0.20	0.40	0.60
1961	119,611,000	—	—	0.20	0.40	0.60
1962	14,014,000	—	—	0.25	0.50	0.75
1964	77,425,000	—	—	0.20	0.40	0.60
1965	44,252,000	—	—	0.20	0.40	0.60
1966	38,038,000	—	—	0.20	0.40	0.60
1967	11,322,000	—	—	0.25	0.50	0.75
1968	51,550,000	—	—	0.20	0.40	0.60
1969	70,595,000	—	—	0.20	0.40	0.60
1970	42,560,000	—	—	0.20	0.40	0.60
1971	42,475,000	—	—	0.20	0.40	0.60
1972	48,250,000	—	—	0.20	0.40	0.60
1973	70,000,000	—	—	0.20	0.40	0.60
1974	82,235,000	—	—	0.20	0.40	0.60
1975	101,685,000	—	—	0.20	0.40	0.60
1976	192,520,000	—	—	0.20	0.40	0.60
1977	230,085,000	—	—	0.20	0.40	0.60
1978	136,580,000	—	—	0.20	0.40	0.60
1979	51,000	—	—	—	3.00	5.00
1980	60,000	—	—	—	3.00	5.00
Note: In sets only						
1981	50,000	—	—	—	3.00	5.00
1982	92,000	—	—	—	3.00	5.00
1983	101,000	—	—	—	3.00	5.00

Date	Mintage	F	VF	XF	Unc	BU
1984	50,000	—	—	—	3.00	5.00
1985	7,002,000	—	—	—	2.00	3.00
1986	48,000	—	—	—	3.00	5.00
1987	100,000	—	—	—	2.50	4.00
1988	100,000	—	—	—	2.50	4.00
1989	83,000	—	—	—	3.00	5.00
1990	15,000	—	—	—	4.00	6.00
1991	54,988,000	—	—	—	0.40	0.60
Note: Exists in both coin and medal alignment						
1992	30,000,000	—	—	—	0.40	0.60
Note: Exists in both coin and medal alignment						
1993	20,000	—	—	—	4.00	6.00
1994 Bee	4,792,000	—	—	—	0.40	0.60
1995	15,000	—	—	—	0.40	0.60
1996	—	—	—	—	3.00	5.00
Note: In sets only						
1997	—	—	—	—	3.00	5.00
Note: In sets only						
1998	—	—	—	—	3.00	5.00
Note: In sets only						
1999	80,432,000	—	—	—	0.40	0.60
2000	—	—	—	—	3.00	5.00
Note: In sets only						

KM# 963 FRANC

6.0000 g., Nickel, 24 mm. **Subject:** 30th Anniversary of Fifth Republic **Obv:** Head right **Rev:** Denomination within six sided wreath, dates below

Date	Mintage	F	VF	XF	Unc	BU
1988	49,921,000	—	—	—	1.00	2.00

KM# 978 FRANC

22.2000 g., 0.9000 Silver .6424 oz. ASW, 24 mm. **Subject:** 30th Anniversary of Fifth Republic

Date	Mintage	F	VF	XF	Unc	BU
1988 Proof	60,000	Value: 30.00				

KM# 979 FRANC

9.0000 g., 0.9200 Gold .2662 oz. AGW, 24 mm. **Subject:** 30th Anniversary of Fifth Republic

Date	Mintage	F	VF	XF	Unc	BU
1988 Proof	20,000	Value: 200				

KM# 967 FRANC

6.0000 g., Nickel, 24 mm. **Subject:** 200th Anniversary of Estates General **Obv:** Denomination within wreath, date below **Rev:** Three figure monument

Date	Mintage	F	VF	XF	Unc	BU
1989	5,010,000	—	—	—	2.50	4.50

KM# 925.2 FRANC

6.0000 g., Nickel, 24 mm. **Obv:** Modified sower, engraver's signature: O. ROTY, preceded by D'AP **Rev:** Laurel divides date and denomination **Edge:** Plain

Date	Mintage	F	VF	XF	Unc	BU
1991	—	—	—	—	0.40	0.60
1991 Proof	10,000	Value: 2.50				
1992	—	—	—	—	0.40	0.60
1992 Proof	15,000	Value: 2.50				
1993	—	—	—	—	0.40	0.60
1993 Proof	10,000	Value: 2.50				
1994 Bee	—	—	—	—	0.40	0.60
1994 Fish Proof	10,000	Value: 2.50				
1995	35,000	—	—	—	0.40	0.60
1995 Proof	10,000	Value: 2.50				
1996	5,000	—	—	—	0.40	0.60
1996 Proof	8,000	Value: 2.50				
1997	15,000	—	—	—	0.40	0.60
1997 Proof	—	Value: 2.50				
1998 Proof	—	Value: 2.50				
1999 Proof	—	Value: 2.50				
2000	—	—	—	—	0.40	0.60
2000 Proof	—	Value: 2.50				

KM# 1004.1 FRANC

6.0000 g., Nickel, 24 mm. **Subject:** 200th Anniversary of French Republic **Obv:** Liberty bust left **Rev:** Denomination within wreath, date below

Date	Mintage	F	VF	XF	Unc	BU
1992	30,000,000	—	—	—	1.25	2.00

KM# 1004.1a FRANC

9.0000 g., 0.9200 Gold .2662 oz. AGW, 24 mm. **Subject:** 200th Anniversary of the French Republic **Obv:** Liberty bust left **Rev:** Denomination within wreath

Date	Mintage	F	VF	XF	Unc	BU
1992 Proof	5,000	Value: 200				

KM# 1004.1b FRANC

11.0000 g., 0.9990 Platinum .3537 oz. APW, 24 mm. **Obv:** Liberty bust left **Rev:** Denomination within wreath

Date	Mintage	F	VF	XF	Unc	BU
1992 Proof	2,000	Value: 400				

KM# 1005 FRANC

15.5500 g., 0.9000 Silver .4500 oz. ASW **Obv:** Liberty bust left **Rev:** Denomination within wreath, date below

Date	Mintage	F	VF	XF	Unc	BU
1992	—	—	—	—	17.50	25.00
1992 Proof	30,000	Value: 35.00				

KM# 1014 FRANC

22.2000 g., 0.9000 Silver .6424 oz. ASW **Obv:** American soldiers storming Omaha Beach **Rev:** Head of Liberty Statue, flags, denomination and date

Date	Mintage	F	VF	XF	Unc	BU
1993	1,000,000	—	—	—	14.00	20.00
1993 Proof	150,000	Value: 30.00				

KM# 1015 FRANC

17.0000 g., 0.9250 Gold .5028 oz. AGW **Subject:** Normandy Invasion **Obv:** American soldiers storming Omaha beach **Rev:** Head of Liberty Statue, flags, denomination and date

Date	Mintage	F	VF	XF	Unc	BU
1993 Proof	Est. 20,000	Value: 360				

KM# 1133 FRANC

6.0000 g., Nickel, 24 mm. **Subject:** 200th Anniversary of Institute of France **Obv:** Institut de France building divides denomination, date below **Rev:** Framed arms, date below, branches flank three sides

Date	Mintage	F	VF	XF	Unc	BU
1995	4,976,000	—	—	—	1.50	2.00

KM# 1160 FRANC

6.0000 g., Nickel, 24 mm. **Subject:** 100th Anniversary - Birth of Jacques Rueff **Obv:** Head at right facing **Rev:** Figure at center, flanked by branches, divides denomination

Date	Mintage	F	VF	XF	Unc	BU
1996	2,976,000	—	—	—	1.50	2.50

KM# 1211 FRANC

12.0000 g., 0.9000 Silver .3472 oz. ASW **Subject:** 1998 World Cup Soccer Games **Obv:** Games logo above denomination **Rev:** Soccer ball on world globe

Date	Mintage	F	VF	XF	Unc	BU
1997	250,000	—	—	—	25.00	30.00

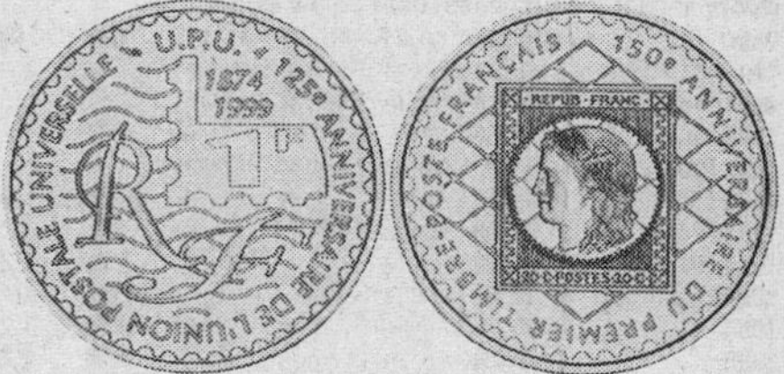

KM# 1214 FRANC

11.9400 g., 0.9000 Silver .3455 oz. ASW **Subject:** 125th Anniversary - Universal Postal Union **Obv:** Partial stamp design, monograms, dates above denomination **Rev:** Head left on stamp design, patterned coin background **Edge:** Reeded

Date	Mintage	F	VF	XF	Unc	BU
ND(1999)	—	—	—	—	20.00	25.00

KM# 1291 FRANC

13.0000 g., 0.9000 Silver 0.3762 oz. ASW, 30 mm. **Subject:** Rugby **Obv:** Players in a scrum, date above **Rev:** Players jumping for a ball, denomination below **Edge:** Plain

Date	Mintage	F	VF	XF	Unc	BU
1999	50,000	—	—	—	25.00	30.00

KM# 1262 FRANC

13.0000 g., 0.9000 Silver .3762 oz. ASW **Subject:** World Soccer Championship **Obv:** Soccer ball design, denomination on ball divides "R" and "F", date below **Rev:** Soccer player **Edge:** Reeded

Date	Mintage	F	VF	XF	Unc	BU
2000	10,000	—	—	—	25.00	30.00

KM# 925.1a FRANC

8.0000 g., 0.7500 Gold .1929 oz. AGW, 24 mm. **Obv:** The seed sower **Rev:** Laurel divides date and denomination **Edge:** Reeded **Designer:** Louis Oscar Roty **Note:** Medallic alignment. Struck at Paris Mint.

Date	Mintage	F	VF	XF	Unc	BU
2000	5,000	—	—	—	140	160

KM# 942.1 2 FRANCS

7.5000 g., Nickel, 26.5 mm. **Obv:** The seed sower **Rev:** Denomination on branches, date below **Edge:** Reeded **Designer:** Louis Oscar Roty

Date	Mintage	F	VF	XF	Unc	BU
1979	130,000,000	—	—	0.40	0.65	1.00
1980	100,010,000	—	—	0.40	0.65	1.00
1981	120,000,000	—	—	0.40	0.65	1.00
1982	90,000,000	—	—	0.40	0.65	1.00
1983	90,000,000	—	—	0.40	0.65	1.00
1984	50,000	—	—	—	0.75	1.25
1985	20,000	—	—	—	2.00	3.00
1986	48,000	—	—	—	2.00	3.00
1987	100,000	—	—	—	0.75	1.25
1988	100,000	—	—	—	0.75	1.25
1989	83,000	—	—	—	0.75	1.25
1990	15,000	—	—	—	0.75	1.25
1994 Fish	—	—	—	—	0.75	1.25
1994 Bee	—	—	—	—	14.00	20.00
1995	—	—	—	—	0.75	1.25
1996	—	—	—	—	0.75	1.25
1997	—	—	—	—	0.75	1.25
1998	—	—	—	—	0.75	1.25
1999	—	—	—	—	0.75	1.25
2000	—	—	—	—	0.75	1.25

KM# 942.2 2 FRANCS

7.5000 g., Nickel, 26.5 mm. **Obv:** The seed sower **Rev:** Denomination on branches, date below **Edge:** Plain

Date	Mintage	F	VF	XF	Unc	BU
1991	5,000	—	—	—	—	—
1991 Proof	10,000	Value: 3.50				
1992	15,000	—	—	—	0.75	1.25
1992 Proof	85,000	Value: 3.50				
1993	40,000	—	—	—	0.75	1.25
1993 Proof	10,000	Value: 3.50				
1994 Fish	9,870,000	—	—	—	0.75	1.25
1994 Fish Proof	10,000	Value: 3.50				
1994 Bee	20,000	—	—	—	0.75	1.25
1995	20,000	—	—	—	0.75	1.25
1995 Proof	10,000	Value: 3.50				
1996	11,980,000	—	—	—	0.75	1.25
1996 Proof	8,000	Value: 3.50				
1997	9,990,000	—	—	—	0.75	1.25
1997 Proof	10,000	Value: 3.50				
1998	45,000,000	—	—	—	0.75	1.25
1998 Proof	—	Value: 3.50				
1999 Proof	—	Value: 3.50				
2000	25,000,000	—	—	—	0.75	1.25
2000 Proof	—	Value: 3.50				

KM# 1062 2 FRANCS

7.5000 g., Nickel, 26.5 mm. **Obv:** Bust with hat facing, double cross in background **Rev:** Denomination on branches, date below

Date	Mintage	F	VF	XF	Unc	BU
1993	30,000,000	—	—	—	1.00	1.50

KM# 1119 2 FRANCS

7.5000 g., Nickel, 26.5 mm. **Obv:** Head of Louis Pasteur facing, building at left **Rev:** Denomination to right of bottles, date below

Date	Mintage	F	VF	XF	Unc	BU
1995	9,975,000	—	—	—	2.00	2.75

KM# 1187 2 FRANCS

7.5000 g., Nickel, 26.5 mm. **Obv:** Georges Guynemer, WWI fighter pilot ace, looking left, date below **Rev:** Guynemer's stork emblem below denomination

Date	Mintage	F	VF	XF	Unc	BU
1997	—	—	—	—	2.25	3.00

KM# 1213 2 FRANCS

7.5000 g., Nickel, 26.5 mm. **Subject:** 50th Anniversary-Declaration of Human Rights **Obv:** Head right, initials above inscription, dates and building below **Rev:** Denomination on world globe, laurel spray and date below

Date	Mintage	F	VF	XF	Unc	BU
1998	—	—	—	—	2.25	3.00

KM# 926 5 FRANCS

12.0000 g., 0.8350 Silver .3221 oz. ASW, 29 mm. **Obv:** Figure sowing seed **Rev:** Branches divide denomination and date **Edge Lettering:** LIBERTE EGALITE FRATERNITE **Designer:** Louis Oscar Roty

Date	Mintage	F	VF	XF	Unc	BU
1960	55,182,000	—	—	BV	5.00	6.50
1961	15,630,000	—	—	BV	5.00	6.50
1962	42,500,000	—	—	BV	5.00	6.50
1963	37,936,000	—	—	BV	5.00	6.50
1964	32,378,000	—	—	BV	5.00	6.50
1965	5,156,000	—	—	BV	6.00	7.50
1966	5,017,000	—	—	BV	6.00	7.50
1967	502,000	—	BV	6.00	12.00	15.00
1968	557,000	—	BV	5.00	10.00	12.50
1969	504,000	—	BV	5.00	10.00	12.50

KM# 926a.1 5 FRANCS

Nickel Clad Copper-Nickel, 29 mm. **Obv:** The seed sower **Rev:** Branches divide denomination and date **Edge:** Reeded **Designer:** Louis Oscar Roty

Date	Mintage	F	VF	XF	Unc	BU
1970	57,890,000	—	—	1.00	1.25	1.75
1971	142,204,000	—	—	1.00	1.25	1.75
1972	45,492,000	—	—	1.00	1.50	2.25
1973	45,079,000	—	—	1.00	1.25	1.75
1974	26,888,000	—	—	1.00	1.25	1.75
1975	16,712,000	—	—	1.00	1.25	1.75
1976	1,662,000	—	1.00	1.25	2.00	3.00
1977	485,000	—	1.00	1.50	2.25	3.50
1978	30,022,000	—	—	1.00	1.25	1.75
1979	51,000	—	—	2.00	3.50	5.50
1980	60,000	—	—	—	5.00	7.50
Note: In sets only						
1981	50,000	—	—	2.00	3.00	5.50
1982	60,000	—	—	2.00	3.50	5.50
1983	101,000	—	—	2.00	3.50	5.50
1984	49,000	—	—	2.00	3.50	5.50
1985	20,000	—	—	2.00	6.00	9.00
1986	48,000	—	—	—	5.00	7.50
Note: In sets only						
1987	20,000,000	—	—	—	1.65	2.50
1988	100,000	—	—	—	1.65	2.85
1989	83,000	—	—	—	1.65	3.00
1990	14,990,000	—	—	—	1.65	2.50
1991	7,488,000	—	—	—	1.65	2.50
1992	9,966,000	—	—	—	1.65	2.50
1993	14,970,000	—	—	—	1.65	2.50
1994 Bee	6,000,000	—	—	—	1.65	2.50
1994 Fish	3,990,000	—	—	—	1.65	2.50
1995	19,986,000	—	—	—	1.65	2.50
1996	12,000	—	—	3.00	5.00	7.50
1997	—	—	—	—	5.00	7.50
Note: In sets only						
1998	—	—	—	—	5.00	7.50
Note: In sets only						
1999	—	—	—	—	5.00	7.50
Note: In sets only						
2000	—	—	—	—	5.00	7.50
Note: In sets only						

KM# 968 5 FRANCS

Copper-Nickel, 29 mm. **Subject:** Centennial - Erection of Eiffel Tower **Obv:** Base of tower, denomination above **Obv. Designer:** Joaquin Jimenez **Rev:** Eiffel Tower, dates at right **Rev. Designer:** Frederic Soubert

Date	Mintage	F	VF	XF	Unc	BU
1989	9,910,000	—	—	—	6.50	9.00

KM# 968a 5 FRANCS

12.0000 g., 0.9000 Silver .3473 oz. ASW, 29 mm. **Subject:** Centennial - Erection of Eiffel Tower **Obv:** Denomination above tower base **Rev:** Tower view from bottom

Date	Mintage	F	VF	XF	Unc	BU
1989 Proof	80,000	Value: 28.00				

KM# 968b 5 FRANCS

14.0000 g., 0.9250 Gold .4141 oz. AGW, 29 mm. **Subject:** Centennial - Erection of Eiffel Tower **Obv:** Denomination above tower base **Rev:** Tower view from bottom

Date	Mintage	F	VF	XF	Unc	BU
1989 Proof	30,000	Value: 300				

KM# 968c 5 FRANCS

16.0000 g., 0.9990 Platinum .5145 oz. APW, 29 mm. **Subject:** Centennial - Erection of Eiffel Tower **Obv:** Denomination above base **Rev:** Tower view from base

Date	Mintage	F	VF	XF	Unc	BU
1989 Proof	Est. 3,000	Value: 500				

Note: 1,800 pieces were melted by MTB Banking

KM# 926a.2 5 FRANCS

Nickel Clad Copper-Nickel, 29 mm. **Obv:** Modified sower, engraver's signature: "O. ROTY" preceded by "D'AP" **Rev:** Branches divide date and denomination **Edge:** Plain

Date	Mintage	F	VF	XF	Unc	BU
1991	7,490,000	—	—	—	1.65	2.50
1991 Proof	10,000	Value: 6.50				
1992	9,986,000	—	—	—	1.65	2.50
1992 Proof	15,000	Value: 6.50				
1993	14,990,000	—	—	—	1.65	2.50
1993 Proof	10,000	Value: 6.50				
1994 Fish	6,000,000	—	—	—	1.65	2.50
1994 Fish Proof	10,000	Value: 6.50				
1994 Bee	3,990,000	—	—	—	1.65	2.50
1995	20,006,000	—	—	—	1.65	2.50
1995 Proof	—	Value: 6.50				
1996	17,000	—	—	—	1.65	2.50
1996 Proof	8,000	Value: 6.50				
1997	15,000	—	—	—	1.65	2.50
1997 Proof	—	Value: 6.50				
1998 Proof	—	Value: 6.50				
1999 Proof	—	Value: 6.50				
2000	—	—	—	—	1.65	2.50
2000 Proof	—	Value: 6.50				

KM# 1006 5 FRANCS

Copper-Nickel, 29 mm. **Obv:** Denomination within design **Rev:** Bust of Pierre Mendes France facing

Date	Mintage	F	VF	XF	Unc	BU
1992	10,000,000	—	—	—	4.50	6.00

KM# 1006a 5 FRANCS

12.0000 g., 0.9000 Silver .3473 oz. ASW, 29 mm. **Obv:** Denomination within design **Rev:** Bust of Pierre Mendes France facing

Date	Mintage	F	VF	XF	Unc	BU
1992 Proof	10,000	Value: 30.00				

KM# 1006b 5 FRANCS

14.0000 g., 0.9200 Gold .4141 oz. AGW, 29 mm. **Obv:** Denomination within design **Rev:** Bust of Pierre Mendes France facing

Date	Mintage	F	VF	XF	Unc	BU
1992 Proof	1,000	Value: 300				

KM# 1007 5 FRANCS
12.0000 g., 0.9000 Silver .3473 oz. ASW, 29 mm. **Subject:** French Antarctic Territories **Rev:** 3 albatross in flight

Date	Mintage	F	VF	XF	Unc	BU
1992 Proof	15,000	Value: 50.00				

KM# 1063 5 FRANCS
Nickel Clad Copper-Nickel, 29 mm. **Obv:** Head of Voltaire the poet 3/4 facing **Rev:** Quill divides building and date from denomination

Date	Mintage	F	VF	XF	Unc	BU
1994	15,000,000	—	—	—	4.00	5.00

KM# 1118 5 FRANCS
12.0000 g., 0.9000 Silver .3473 oz. ASW, 29 mm. **Subject:** 50th Anniversary - United Nations **Obv:** Dove and branch at left, denomination at right **Rev:** UN logo, dates below

Date	Mintage	F	VF	XF	Unc	BU
1995 Proof	250,000	Value: 27.50				

KM# 1118a 5 FRANCS
14.0000 g., 0.9200 Gold .4141 oz. AGW, 29 mm. **Obv:** Dove and branch left of denomination **Rev:** UN logo and dates

Date	Mintage	F	VF	XF	Unc	BU
1995 Proof	125,000	Value: 300				

KM# 1155 5 FRANCS
Nickel Clad Steel, 29 mm. **Obv:** Denomination and date within wreath **Rev:** Hercules group design **Designer:** Augustine Dupré

Date	Mintage	F	VF	XF	Unc	BU
1996	4,976,000	—	—	—	4.50	6.00

KM# 1212 5 FRANCS
12.0000 g., 0.9000 Silver .3472 oz. ASW, 29 mm. **Subject:** 1998 World Cup Soccer Games: French Victory **Obv:** Game logo above denomination **Rev:** Handheld trophy with stadium in background

Date	Mintage	F	VF	XF	Unc	BU
1998 Proof	Est. 100,000	Value: 45.00				

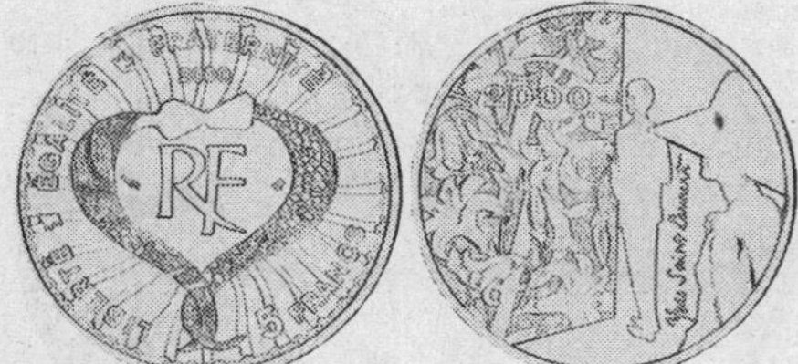

KM# 1215 5 FRANCS
12.0000 g., 0.9000 Silver .3472 oz. ASW, 29 mm. **Subject:** Yves St. Laurent **Obv:** RF monogram within entwined snake design, denomination below **Rev:** Fashion show scene

Date	Mintage	F	VF	XF	Unc	BU
2000	—	—	—	—	30.00	—

KM# 1222 5 FRANCS
10.0000 g., Copper-Nickel Plated Nickel, 29 mm. **Subject:** 2000 Years of French Coinage **Obv:** Denomination and date within wreath **Rev:** 1st century B.C. Celtic Parisii Stater coin design **Edge:** Reeded

Date	Mintage	F	VF	XF	Unc	BU
2000	50,000	—	—	—	10.00	12.00

KM# 1223 5 FRANCS
10.0000 g., Copper-Nickel Plated Nickel, 29 mm. **Subject:** 2000 Years of French Coinage **Obv:** Denomination and date within wreath **Rev:** Charlemagne Denar coin design **Edge:** Reeded

Date	Mintage	F	VF	XF	Unc	BU
2000	50,000	—	—	—	10.00	12.00

KM# 1224 5 FRANCS
10.0000 g., Copper-Nickel Plated Nickel, 29 mm. **Subject:** 2000 Years of French Coinage **Obv:** Denomination and date within wreath **Rev:** Louis IX Gold Ecu design **Edge:** Reeded

Date	Mintage	F	VF	XF	Unc	BU
2000	50,000	—	—	—	9.50	11.50

KM# 1255 6.55957 FRANCS
22.2000 g., 0.9000 Silver .6424 oz. ASW **Obv:** Europa allegorical portrait **Rev:** Country names and euro-currency equivalents around RF and denomination in center plus French coin designs **Edge:** Plain

Date	Mintage	F	VF	XF	Unc	BU
1999 Proof	25,000	Value: 40.00				

KM# 1254 6.55957 FRANCS
13.0000 g., 0.9000 Silver .3762 oz. ASW **Subject:** Euro Conversion Series **Obv:** Europa allegorical portrait, denomination and date at left **Rev:** Country names and euro-currency equivalents around "RF" and denomination in center **Edge:** Plain **Note:** Struck at Paris Mint.

Date	Mintage	F	VF	XF	Unc	BU
1999	200,000	—	—	—	30.00	35.00

KM# 1225 6.55957 FRANCS
22.2000 g., 0.9000 Silver .6424 oz. ASW **Subject:** European Art Styles Renaissance **Obv:** Europa allegorical portrait, denomination and date at left **Rev:** Renaissance style buildings **Edge Lettering:** "Europa" repeated four times

Date	Mintage	F	VF	XF	Unc	BU
2000 Proof	15,000	Value: 35.00				

KM# 1226 6.55957 FRANCS
22.2000 g., 0.9000 Silver .6424 oz. ASW **Series:** European Art Styles - Renaissance Classic and Baroque **Obv:** Europa allegorical portrait, denomination and date at left **Rev:** Buildings, top and left of artistic design

Date	Mintage	F	VF	XF	Unc	BU
2000 Proof	15,000	Value: 35.00				

KM# 1227 6.55957 FRANCS
22.2000 g., 0.9000 Silver .6424 oz. ASW **Series:** European Art Styles Renaissance - Art Nouveau **Rev:** Artistic designs

Date	Mintage	F	VF	XF	Unc	BU
2000 Proof	15,000	Value: 35.00				

KM# 1228 6.55957 FRANCS
22.2000 g., 0.9000 Silver .6424 oz. ASW **Series:** European Art Styles Renaissance - Modern **Obv:** Europa allegorical portrait, denomination and date at left **Rev:** Modern artistic designs

Date	Mintage	F	VF	XF	Unc	BU
2000 Proof	15,000	Value: 35.00				

KM# 1244 6.55957 FRANCS
22.2000 g., 0.9000 Silver .6424 oz. ASW **Series:** European Art Styles Renaissance - Greek and Roman **Rev:** Greek and Roman columns

Date	Mintage	F	VF	XF	Unc	BU
2000 Proof	15,000	Value: 35.00				

KM# 1245 6.55957 FRANCS
22.2000 g., 0.9000 Silver .6424 oz. ASW **Series:** European Art Styles Renaissance - Roman Art and Structures **Rev:** Figure on shield, columns in background

Date	Mintage	F	VF	XF	Unc	BU
2000 Proof	15,000	Value: 35.00				

KM# 1246 6.55957 FRANCS
22.2000 g., 0.9000 Silver .6424 oz. ASW **Series:** European Art Styles Renaissance - Gothic **Rev:** Religious figure in foreground, designs in background

Date	Mintage	F	VF	XF	Unc	BU
2000 Proof	15,000	Value: 35.00				

KM# 1258 6.55957 FRANCS
13.0000 g., 0.9000 Silver .3762 oz. ASW **Obv:** Country names and euro-currency equivalents around "RF" and denomination **Rev:** Europa allegorical portrait, date below **Edge:** Plain

Date	Mintage	F	VF	XF	Unc	BU
2000	200,000	—	—	—	30.00	35.00

KM# 1259 6.55957 FRANCS
22.2000 g., 0.9000 Silver .3762 oz. ASW **Obv:** Country names and euro-currency equivalents around "RF", denomination and French euro coin designs **Edge:** Plain

Date	Mintage	F	VF	XF	Unc	BU
2000 Proof	10,000	Value: 40.00				

KM# 932 10 FRANCS
25.0000 g., 0.9000 Silver .7234 oz. ASW **Obv:** Denomination and date within wreath **Rev:** Hercules group **Designer:** Augustine Dupré **Note:** Without mint mark.

Date	Mintage	F	VF	XF	Unc	BU
1965	8,051,000	—	BV	10.00	12.50	15.00
1966	9,800,000	—	BV	10.00	12.50	15.00
1967	10,100,000	—	BV	10.00	12.50	15.00
1968	3,887,000	—	BV	12.00	14.00	17.50
1969	761,000	—	BV	14.00	16.00	20.00
1970	5,013,000	—	BV	10.00	12.50	15.00
1971	513,000	—	BV	14.00	18.00	22.50
1972	915,000	—	BV	12.00	14.00	17.50
1973	207,000	—	BV	14.00	20.00	25.00

KM# 940 10 FRANCS
Nickel-Brass, 26 mm. **Obv. Designer:** Electric bursts, some forming outline map of France, date below **Rev:** High tension towers and electric transmission wires, denomination at center **Designer:** Georges Mathieu

Date	Mintage	F	VF	XF	Unc	BU
1974	22,447,000	—	—	1.50	2.00	2.50
1975	59,013,000	—	—	1.50	2.00	2.50
1976	104,093,000	—	—	1.50	2.00	2.50
1977	100,028,000	—	—	1.50	2.00	2.50
1978	97,590,000	—	—	1.50	2.00	2.50
1979	110,000,000	—	—	1.50	2.00	2.50
1980	80,010,000	—	—	1.50	2.00	2.50
1981	50,000	—	—	—	2.75	3.75
1982	74,000	—	—	—	2.75	3.75
1983	101,000	—	—	—	2.75	3.75
1984	39,988,000	—	—	1.50	2.00	2.50
1985	30,000,000	—	—	1.50	2.00	2.50
1987	Est. 50,000,000	—	—	—	2.50	2.50

KM# 950 10 FRANCS
Nickel-Bronze, 26 mm. **Subject:** 100th Anniversary - Death of Leon Gambetta **Obv:** Denomination and date, flags in background **Rev:** Head left

Date	Mintage	F	VF	XF	Unc	BU
1982	3,045,000	—	—	2.50	4.00	5.00

KM# 952 10 FRANCS
Nickel-Bronze, 26 mm. **Subject:** 200th Anniversary - Montgolfier Balloon **Obv:** Denomination and date below balloon basket **Rev:** Balloon, figures and date below **Designer:** D. Ponce

Date	Mintage	F	VF	XF	Unc	BU
1983	3,001,000	—	—	2.50	4.00	5.00

KM# 953 10 FRANCS
Nickel-Bronze, 26 mm. **Subject:** 200th Anniversary - Birth of Stendhal **Obv:** Head 3/4 facing **Rev:** Quill, branch, book, and buildings divide date and denomination

Date	Mintage	F	VF	XF	Unc	BU
1983	2,951,000	—	—	2.50	4.00	5.00

KM# 954 10 FRANCS
Nickel-Bronze, 26 mm. **Subject:** 200th Anniversary - Birth of Francois Rude **Obv:** Head 3/4 right, RF below **Rev:** Armed figure divides denomination and date

Date	Mintage	F	VF	XF	Unc	BU
1984	10,000,000	—	—	2.50	3.50	4.50

KM# 956 10 FRANCS
Nickel-Bronze, 26 mm. **Subject:** Centennial - Death of Victor Hugo **Obv:** Denomination above armed figures, quill and book at right, date below **Rev:** Head facing

Date	Mintage	F	VF	XF	Unc	BU
1985	10,000,000	—	—	2.50	3.50	4.50

KM# 956a 10 FRANCS
12.0000 g., 0.9000 Silver .3472 oz. ASW, 26 mm. **Subject:** Centennial - Death of Victor Hugo **Obv:** Figures left of quill and book, denomination above **Rev:** Head facing

Date	Mintage	F	VF	XF	Unc	BU
1985	20,000	—	—	—	20.00	25.00

KM# 956b 10 FRANCS
12.0000 g., 0.9990 Silver .3854 oz. ASW, 26 mm. **Subject:** Centennial - Death of Victor Hugo **Obv:** Figures left of quill and book, denomination above **Rev:** Head facing

Date	Mintage	F	VF	XF	Unc	BU
1985 Proof	8,000	Value: 40.00				

KM# 959 10 FRANCS
Nickel, 21 mm. **Obv:** Designs divide denomination and date **Rev:** Madam Republic head, map in background **Designer:** Joaquin Jimenez

Date	Mintage	F	VF	XF	Unc	BU
1986	110,015,000	—	—	3.00	10.00	12.00

Note: Recalled and melted, no longer legal tender

KM# 958 10 FRANCS
Nickel **Subject:** 100th Anniversary - Birth of Robert Schuman **Obv:** Rooster at left, denomination right **Rev:** Half head right

Date	Mintage	F	VF	XF	Unc	BU
1986	9,961,000	—	—	3.00	6.50	7.50

KM# 958a 10 FRANCS
7.0000 g., 0.9000 Silver .2025 oz. ASW **Obv:** Rooster at left, denomination right **Rev:** Half head right

Date	Mintage	F	VF	XF	Unc	BU
1986	20,000	—	—	—	18.50	22.50

KM# 958b 10 FRANCS
7.0000 g., 0.9500 Silver .2138 oz. ASW **Obv:** Rooster at left, denomination right **Rev:** Half head right

Date	Mintage	F	VF	XF	Unc	BU
1986 Proof	6,000	Value: 45.00				

KM# 958c 10 FRANCS
7.0000 g., 0.9200 Gold .2071 oz. AGW **Subject:** 100th Anniversary - Birth of Robert Schuman **Obv:** Rooster at left, denomination right **Rev:** Half head right

Date	Mintage	F	VF	XF	Unc	BU
1986 Proof	5,000	Value: 160				

KM# 961c 10 FRANCS
14.0000 g., 0.9990 Platinum .4497 oz. APW **Subject:** Millennium of King Capet and France **Obv:** Denomination and date within circle **Rev:** Crowned figure standing at center, rosettes in background

Date	Mintage	F	VF	XF	Unc	BU
1987 Proof	1,000	Value: 600				

KM# 961 10 FRANCS
12.0000 g., 0.9000 Silver .3473 oz. ASW **Subject:** Millennium of King Hugo Capet first King of France **Obv:** Denomination and date within circle **Rev:** Crowned figure standing at center divides dates below, rosettes in background

Date	Mintage	F	VF	XF	Unc	BU
1987	20,000	—	—	—	18.50	22.50

KM# 961a 10 FRANCS
12.0000 g., 0.9500 Silver .3665 oz. ASW **Subject:** Millennium of King Capet and France **Obv:** Denomination and date within circle **Rev:** Crowned figure standing at center, rosettes in background

Date	Mintage	F	VF	XF	Unc	BU
1987 Proof	10,000	Value: 40.00				

KM# 961b 10 FRANCS
12.0000 g., 0.9200 Gold .3549 oz. AGW **Subject:** Millennium of King Capet and France **Obv:** Denomination and date within circle **Rev:** Crowned figure standing at center, rosettes in background

Date	Mintage	F	VF	XF	Unc	BU
1987 Proof	6,000	Value: 275				

KM# 961d 10 FRANCS
Nickel-Bronze, 21 mm. **Subject:** Millennium of King Capet and France **Obv:** Denomination and date within circle **Rev:** Crowned figure standing at center, rosettes in background

Date	Mintage	F	VF	XF	Unc	BU
1987	70,000,000	—	—	3.00	6.50	9.00

KM# 964.1 10 FRANCS
6.5000 g., Bi-Metallic Steel center in Aluminum-Bronze ring, 23 mm. **Subject:** Spirit of Bastille **Obv:** Winged figure divides RF within circle **Rev:** Patterned denomination above date within circle

Date	Mintage	F	VF	XF	Unc	BU
1988	100,000,000	—	—	2.50	6.00	7.50
1989	249,980,000	—	—	2.50	6.00	7.50
1990	250,000,000	—	—	2.50	6.00	7.50
1991	249,987,000	—	—	2.50	6.00	7.50
Note: Exist in both medal and coin alignment						
1992	99,966,000	—	—	2.50	6.00	7.50
Note: Exist in both medal and coin alignment						
1995	15,000	—	—	6.00	10.00	12.50
1996	12,000	—	—	6.00	10.00	12.50
2000	28,065,000	—	—	2.50	6.00	7.50

KM# 964.1a 10 FRANCS
Bi-Metallic .920 Gold center in Gold with Palladium and Silver alloy ring, 23 mm. **Subject:** Spirit of Bastille **Obv:** Winged figure divides RF **Rev:** Patterned denomination above date

Date	Mintage	F	VF	XF	Unc	BU
1988 Proof	5,000	Value: 350				

KM# 965 10 FRANCS
Aluminum-Bronze, 26 mm. **Subject:** 100th Anniversary - Birth of Roland Garros **Obv:** Denomination below wings **Rev:** Dates and plane above head right **Designer:** H. Duetthe

Date	Mintage	F	VF	XF	Unc	BU
1988	30,000,000	—	—	2.50	4.00	5.00

KM# 965a 10 FRANCS
12.0000 g., 0.9000 Silver .3472 oz. ASW, 26 mm. **Obv:** Wings above denomination **Rev:** Airplane above head right

Date	Mintage	F	VF	XF	Unc	BU
1988	10,000	—	—	—	18.50	22.50

KM# 965b 10 FRANCS
12.0000 g., 0.9500 Silver .3665 oz. ASW, 26 mm. **Obv:** Wings above denomination **Rev:** Airplane above head right

Date	Mintage	F	VF	XF	Unc	BU
1988 Proof	10,000	Value: 35.00				

KM# 965c 10 FRANCS
12.0000 g., 0.9200 Gold .3550 oz. AGW, 26 mm. **Subject:** 100th Anniversary - Birth of Roland Garros **Obv:** Wings above denomination **Rev:** Airplane above head right

Date	Mintage	F	VF	XF	Unc	BU
1988 Proof	3,000	Value: 275				

KM# 969 10 FRANCS
Bi-Metallic Steel center in Aluminum-Bronze ring, 23 mm. **Subject:** 300th Anniversary - Birth of Montesquieu **Obv:** Bust right **Rev:** Patterned denomination above date

Date	Mintage	F	VF	XF	Unc	BU
1989	15,000	—	—	6.50	17.50	20.00

KM# 969a 10 FRANCS
Bi-Metallic Gold, Palladium and Silver alloy center in .920 Gold ring, 23 mm. **Subject:** 300th Anniversary - Birth of Montesquieu **Obv:** Bust right **Rev:** Patterned denomination above date

Date	Mintage	F	VF	XF	Unc	BU
1989 Proof	5,000	Value: 345				

KM# 964.2 10 FRANCS
Aluminum-Bronze, 23 mm. **Obv:** Winged figure divides RF **Rev:** Patterned denomination above date **Edge:** Plain

Date	Mintage	F	VF	XF	Unc	BU
1991	—	—	—	—	—	—
Note: Exist in both medal and coin alignment.						
1991 Proof	10,000	Value: 15.00				
1992	—	—	—	—	6.00	7.50
Note: Exist in both medal and coin alignment.						
1992 Proof	15,000	Value: 15.00				
1993	20,000	—	—	—	6.00	7.50
1993 Proof	10,000	Value: 15.00				
1994 Bee	20,000	—	—	—	6.00	7.50
1994 Fish Proof	10,000	Value: 15.00				
1995	25,000	—	—	—	6.00	7.50
1995 Proof	10,000	Value: 15.00				
1996	17,000	—	—	—	6.00	7.50
1996 Proof	8,000	Value: 15.00				
1997	15,000	—	—	—	6.00	7.50
1997 Proof	10,000	Value: 15.00				
1998	—	—	—	—	6.00	7.50
1998 Proof	—	Value: 15.00				
1999	—	—	—	—	6.00	7.50
1999 Proof	—	Value: 15.00				
2000	—	—	—	—	6.00	7.50
2000 Proof	—	Value: 15.00				

KM# 1144 10 FRANCS
21.1600 g., 0.9000 Silver .6412 oz. ASW **Subject:** World Cup

- Coupe du Monde 1998 **Obv:** World Cup 1998 logo above denomination **Rev:** Soccer ball breaking net, stylized dove, date upper right

Date	Mintage	F	VF	XF	Unc	BU
1996 Proof	Est. 40,000	Value: 40.00				

KM# 1166 10 FRANCS
21.1600 g., 0.9000 Silver .6412 oz. ASW **Subject:** World Cup - Uruguay 1930 1958 **Obv:** World Cup 1998 logo above denomination **Rev:** Stylized gaucho and soccer player, date below

Date	Mintage	F	VF	XF	Unc	BU
1996 Proof	100,000	Value: 35.00				

KM# 1161 10 FRANCS
21.1600 g., 0.9000 Silver .6412 oz. ASW **Subject:** World Cup - Argentina 1978 1986 **Obv:** World Cup 1998 logo above denomination **Rev:** Stylized bull and soccer player, date below

Date	Mintage	F	VF	XF	Unc	BU
1997 Proof	100,000	Value: 35.00				

KM# 1163 10 FRANCS
21.1600 g., 0.9000 Silver .6412 oz. ASW **Subject:** World Cup - England 1966 **Obv:** World Cup 1998 logo above denomination **Rev:** Big Ben and soccer player, date below

Date	Mintage	F	VF	XF	Unc	BU
1997 Proof	100,000	Value: 35.00				

KM# 1164 10 FRANCS
21.1600 g., 0.9000 Silver .6412 oz. ASW **Subject:** World Cup - Germany 1954 1974 1990 **Obv:** World Cup 1998 logo above denomination **Rev:** Brandenburg gate, soccer player, date below

Date	Mintage	F	VF	XF	Unc	BU
1997 Proof	100,000	Value: 35.00				

KM# 1165 10 FRANCS
21.1600 g., 0.9000 Silver .6412 oz. ASW **Subject:** World Cup - Italy 1934 1938 1982 **Obv:** World Cup 1998 logo above denomination and date **Rev:** Colosseum and soccer player, date below

Date	Mintage	F	VF	XF	Unc	BU
1997 Proof	100,000	Value: 35.00				

KM# 1162 10 FRANCS
21.1600 g., 0.9000 Silver .6412 oz. ASW **Subject:** World Cup - Brazil 1958 1968 1970 1994 **Obv:** World Cup 1998 logo above denomination **Rev:** Pavilion and soccer player, date below

Date	Mintage	F	VF	XF	Unc	BU
1998 Proof	100,000	Value: 35.00				

KM# 1167 10 FRANCS
21.1600 g., 0.9000 Silver .6412 oz. ASW **Subject:** World Cup - Coupe du Monte **Obv:** World Cup 1998 logo above denomination and date **Rev:** World Cup trophy and 11 French city arms

Date	Mintage	F	VF	XF	Unc	BU
1998 Proof	100,000	Value: 35.00				

KM# 1205 10 FRANCS
22.2000 g., 0.9000 Silver .6424 oz. ASW **Series:** Treasures of the Nile - J.F. Champollion **Obv:** Portrait and obelisk **Rev:** Sphinx and pyramids, date at left, denomination below

Date	Mintage	F	VF	XF	Unc	BU
1998 Proof	15,000	Value: 38.50				

KM# 1206 10 FRANCS
22.2000 g., 0.9000 Silver .6424 oz. ASW **Series:** Treasures of the Nile **Subject:** Nefertiti 1372-1350BC, Queen and monotheist **Obv:** Crowned bust 3/4 right **Rev:** Sphinx and pyramids, date at left, denomination below

Date	Mintage	F	VF	XF	Unc	BU
1998 Proof	15,000	Value: 38.50				

KM# 1207 10 FRANCS
22.2000 g., 0.9000 Silver .6424 oz. ASW **Series:** Treasures of the Nile **Subject:** Ramses II **Rev:** Kneeling figure right

Date	Mintage	F	VF	XF	Unc	BU
1998 Proof	15,000	Value: 38.50				

KM# 1398 10 FRANCS
22.2000 g., 0.9000 Silver 0.6424 oz. ASW, 37 mm. **Obv:** Partial postage stamp with denomination below, Initials, "RF" on wavy field **Rev:** First French postage stamp **Edge:** Plain

Date	Mintage	F	VF	XF	Unc	BU
ND (1999)A Proof	—	Value: 45.00				

KM# 1294 10 FRANCS
22.2300 g., 0.9000 Silver 0.6432 oz. ASW, 36.9 mm. **Subject:** Rugby **Obv:** Players in a "scrum" **Rev:** Players jumping for a ball **Edge:** Plain

Date	Mintage	F	VF	XF	Unc	BU
1999A Proof	10,000	Value: 35.00				

KM# 1216 10 FRANCS
22.2300 g., 0.9000 Silver .6432 oz. ASW **Series:** XXth Century - Biology and Medicine **Obv:** Double X design divides date and denomination **Rev:** Parents, fetus, hands **Edge:** Plain

Date	Mintage	F	VF	XF	Unc	BU
2000 Proof	10,000	Value: 40.00				

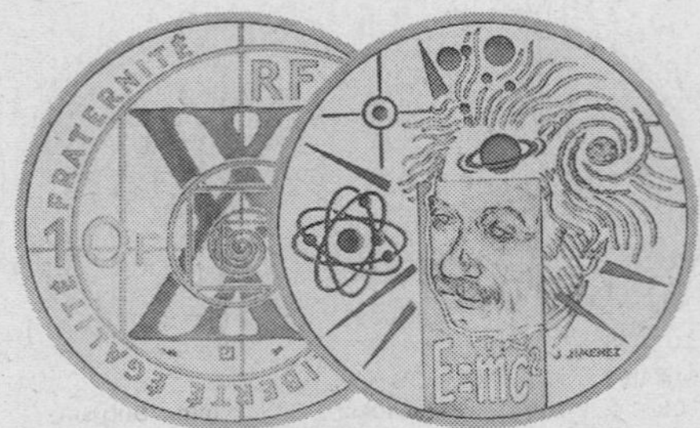

KM# 1217 10 FRANCS
22.2300 g., 0.9000 Silver .6432 oz. ASW **Series:** XXth Century - Physical Sciences **Rev:** Einstein's portrait, atom and planets

Date	Mintage	F	VF	XF	Unc	BU
2000 Proof	10,000	Value: 40.00				

KM# 1218 10 FRANCS
22.2300 g., 0.9000 Silver .6432 oz. ASW **Series:** XXth Century - Communications **Rev:** World, satellites and keyboard

Date	Mintage	F	VF	XF	Unc	BU
2000 Proof	10,000	Value: 40.00				

KM# 1219 10 FRANCS
22.2300 g., 0.9000 Silver .6432 oz. ASW **Series:** XXth Century - The Automobile **Rev:** Race cars above horse

Date	Mintage	F	VF	XF	Unc	BU
2000 Proof	10,000	Value: 40.00				

KM# 1220 10 FRANCS
22.2300 g., 0.9000 Silver .6432 oz. ASW **Series:** XXth Century - Flight **Rev:** Icarus in flight above Bleriot monoplane

Date	Mintage	F	VF	XF	Unc	BU
2000 Proof	10,000	Value: 40.00				

KM# 1221 10 FRANCS
22.2300 g., 0.9000 Silver .6432 oz. ASW **Series:** XXth Century - Space Travel **Rev:** Astronaut weightless in space amidst planets

Date	Mintage	F	VF	XF	Unc	BU
2000 Proof	10,000	Value: 40.00				

KM# 1229 10 FRANCS
22.2000 g., 0.9000 Silver .6424 oz. ASW **Subject:** 2000 Years - French Coinage **Obv:** Denomination and date within wreath **Rev:** 1st century B.C. Celtic Parisii Stater coin design **Edge:** Plain

Date	Mintage	F	VF	XF	Unc	BU
2000 Proof	10,000	Value: 40.00				

KM# 1230 10 FRANCS
22.2000 g., 0.9000 Silver .6424 oz. ASW **Rev:** Charlemagne Denar coin design, laureate head right

Date	Mintage	F	VF	XF	Unc	BU
2000 Proof	10,000	Value: 40.00				

KM# 1231 10 FRANCS
22.2000 g., 0.9000 Silver .6424 oz. ASW **Subject:** 2000 Years of French Coinage **Obv:** Denomination **Rev:** Louis IX gold ecu coin design, arms on shield within scalloped wreath **Edge:** Plain

Date	Mintage	F	VF	XF	Unc	BU
2000 Proof	10,000	Value: 37.50				

KM# 1235 10 FRANCS
22.2000 g., 0.9000 Silver .6424 oz. ASW **Subject:** Yves St. Laurent **Obv:** RF monogram within entwined snake design, date above, denomination lower right **Rev:** Fashion show scene

Date	Mintage	F	VF	XF	Unc	BU
2000 Proof	30,000	Value: 37.50				

KM# 1263 10 FRANCS
22.2000 g., 0.9000 Silver .6424 oz. ASW **Subject:** Antoine de St. Exupery **Obv:** RF Monogram, portrait and bi-plane **Rev:** Multicolor "Little Prince" character, denomination at left, date below

Date	Mintage	F	VF	XF	Unc	BU
2000 Proof	10,000	Value: 47.50				

KM# 1008.2 20 FRANCS
Tri-Metallic Copper-Aluminum-Nickel center plug, Nickel inner ring, Copper-Aluminum-Nickel outer ring, 27 mm. **Obv:** Mont St. Michel **Rev:** Patterned denomination above date **Edge:** 5 milled bands

Date	Mintage	F	VF	XF	Unc	BU
1992	59,986,000	—	—	—	6.50	8.50
Note: Closed V in outer ring, exist in both coin and medal alignment						
1992	Inc. above	—	—	—	6.50	8.50
Note: Open V in outer ring, exist in both coin and medal alignment						
1992 Proof	15,000	Value: 25.00				
1993	54,990,000	—	—	—	7.00	9.00
Note: Exist in both coin and medal alignment						
1993 Proof	10,000	Value: 25.00				
1994	—	—	—	—	8.00	10.00
1994 Proof	—	Value: 25.00				
1994 Fish	5,000,000	—	—	—	10.00	12.50
1994 Fish Proof	10,000	Value: 25.00				
1994 Bee	9,990,000	—	—	—	9.00	11.00
1995	9,996,000	—	—	—	9.00	11.00
1995 Proof	10,000	Value: 25.00				
1996	17,000	—	—	—	6.50	8.50
1996 Proof	8,000	Value: 25.00				
1997	15,000	—	—	—	8.00	10.00
1997 Proof	10,000	Value: 25.00				
1998	—	—	—	—	8.00	10.00
1998 Proof	—	Value: 25.00				
1999	—	—	—	—	8.00	10.00
1999 Proof	—	Value: 25.00				
2000	—	—	—	—	8.00	10.00
2000 Proof	—	Value: 25.00				

KM# 1008.1 20 FRANCS
Tri-Metallic Copper-Aluminum-Nickel center plug%2C Nickel inner ring%2C Copper-Aluminum-Nickel outer ring, 27 mm. **Obv:** Mont St. Michel **Rev:** Patterned denomination above date within circle **Edge:** 4 milled bands

Date	Mintage	F	VF	XF	Unc	BU
1992	Inc. above	—	—	—	15.00	18.00
Note: Open V in outer ring						
1992	60,000,000	—	—	—	15.00	18.00
Note: Closed V in outer ring						

KM# 1008.2a 20 FRANCS
12.6600 g., Tri-Metallic .720 Gold center plug, .950 Silver inner ring, .750 Gold outer ring., 27 mm. **Obv:** Mont St. Michel; 5 bands of stripes in outer ring **Rev:** Patterned denomination above date

Date	Mintage	F	VF	XF	Unc	BU
1992 Proof	15,000	Value: 210				

KM# 1008.2b 20 FRANCS
16.4600 g., Tri-Metallic .920 Gold center plug, .750 Gold inner ring, .920 Gold outer ring, 27 mm. **Obv:** Mont St. Michel **Rev:** Patterned denomination above date

Date	Mintage	F	VF	XF	Unc	BU
1992 Proof	5,000	Value: 375				

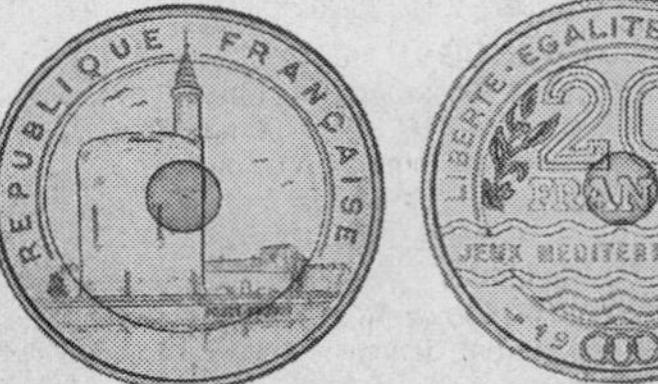

KM# 1016 20 FRANCS
Tri-Metallic Aluminum-Bronze center plug, Nickel inner ring, Copper-Aluminum-Nickel outer ring, 27 mm. **Subject:** Mediterranean Games **Obv:** Tower of Adge **Rev:** Denomination flanked by laurels, wavy design below, rings divide date at bottom

Date	Mintage	F	VF	XF	Unc	BU
1993	5,001,000	—	—	—	10.00	12.00

KM# 1036 20 FRANCS
Tri-Metallic Aluminum-Bronze center plug, Nickel inner ring, Copper-Aluminum-Nickel outer ring, 26.8 mm. **Subject:** Founder of Modern Day Olympics - Pierre de Coubertin **Obv:** Head left, 'RF' below, torch at right **Rev:** Building at left, denomination and date divided by Olympic logo at right

Date	Mintage	F	VF	XF	Unc	BU
1994	15,000,000	—	—	—	10.00	12.00

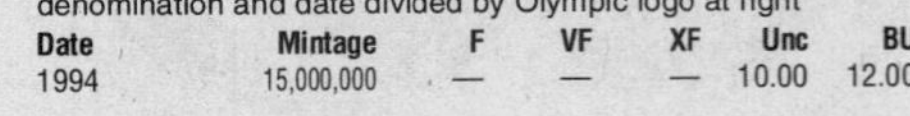

KM# 941.1 50 FRANCS
30.0000 g., 0.9000 Silver .8682 oz. ASW **Obv:** Denomination within wreath **Rev:** Hercules group **Designer:** Augustine Dupré
Note: Without mint mark.

Date	Mintage	F	VF	XF	Unc	BU
1974	4,299,000	—	—	BV	12.00	14.00
1975	4,551,000	—	—	BV	14.50	17.50
1976	7,739,000	—	—	BV	13.50	16.00
1977	7,884,000	—	—	BV	12.00	14.00
1978	12,028,000	—	—	BV	12.00	14.00

Date	Mintage	F	VF	XF	Unc	BU
1979	12,041,000	—	—	BV	12.00	14.00
1980	60,000	—	—	25.00	50.00	65.00

Note: In sets only

KM# 941.2 50 FRANCS

30.0000 g., 0.9000 Silver .8682 oz. ASW **Obv:** Denomination within wreath **Rev:** Legend begins at the level of the beltline of the goddess of Hercules' at left

Date	Mintage	F	VF	XF	Unc	BU
1974	—	15.00	25.00	40.00	65.00	80.00

KM# 1145 50 FRANCS

8.4521 g., 0.9200 Gold .2500 oz. AGW **Subject:** World Class Soccer **Obv:** Soccer ball, denomination and date below **Rev:** Stylized dove, soccer ball

Date	Mintage	F	VF	XF	Unc	BU
1996 Proof	Est. 10,000	Value: 200				

KM# 1208 50 FRANCS

8.4521 g., 0.9200 Gold .2500 oz. AGW **Subject:** Treasures of the Nile **Obv:** Portrait above 'RF', obelisk at right **Rev:** Sphinx and pyramids, date at left, denomination below

Date	Mintage	F	VF	XF	Unc	BU
1998 Proof	3,000	Value: 275				

KM# 1236 50 FRANCS

8.4521 g., 0.9200 Gold .2500 oz. AGW **Subject:** Yves St. Laurent **Obv:** RF monogram, denomination **Rev:** Fashion show scene **Edge:** Plain

Date	Mintage	F	VF	XF	Unc	BU
2000 Proof	2,000	Value: 275				

KM# 1256 65.5997 FRANCS

8.4500 g., 0.9250 Gold .2499 oz. AGW **Series:** Euro Conversion Series **Obv:** Country names with euro currency equivalents around "RF", denomination and French coin designs **Rev:** Europa allegorical portrait **Edge:** Plain

Date	Mintage	F	VF	XF	Unc	BU
1999 Proof	10,000	Value: 275				

KM# 1260 65.5997 FRANCS

8.4500 g., 0.9250 Gold .2499 oz. AGW **Obv:** Country names with euro-currency equivalents around "RF", denomination and French euro coin designs

Date	Mintage	F	VF	XF	Unc	BU
2000 Proof	3,000	Value: 275				

KM# 951.1 100 FRANCS

15.0000 g., 0.9000 Silver .4340 oz. ASW **Obv:** Pantheon, date below **Rev:** Leafy design above denomination **Note:** Without mint mark.

Date	Mintage	F	VF	XF	Unc	BU
1982	3,030,000	—	—	—	27.50	37.50
1982 Proof	25,000	Value: 45.00				
1983	5,001,000	—	—	—	27.50	37.50
1983 Proof	17,000	Value: 45.00				
1984	5,000,000	—	—	—	27.50	37.50
1985	999,000	—	—	—	30.00	40.00
1985 Proof	13,000	Value: 45.00				
1986	519,000	—	—	—	30.00	40.00
1987	100,000	—	—	—	30.00	40.00
1988	100,000	—	—	—	30.00	40.00
1989	83,000	—	—	—	30.00	40.00
1990	15,000	—	—	—	35.00	45.00
1991	5,000	—	—	—	35.00	45.00
1991 Proof	10,000	Value: 55.00				
1992 Proof	15,000	Value: 45.00				
1993 Proof	15,000	Value: 45.00				
1994 Proof	15,000	Value: 45.00				
1995	4,011	—	—	—	32.00	42.00
1995 Proof	10,000	Value: 48.00				
1996	2,013	—	—	—	40.00	50.00
1996 Proof	8,000	Value: 60.00				
1997	—	—	—	—	40.00	50.00

Date	Mintage	F	VF	XF	Unc	BU
1997 Proof	—	Value: 60.00				
1998	—	—	—	—	40.00	50.00
1998 Proof	—	Value: 60.00				
1999	—	—	—	—	40.00	50.00
1999 Proof	—	Value: 60.00				
2000	—	—	—	—	40.00	50.00
2000 Proof	—	Value: 60.00				

KM# 955 100 FRANCS

15.0000 g., 0.9000 Silver .4340 oz. ASW **Subject:** 50th Anniversary - Death of Marie Curie **Obv:** Leafy branches divide date and denomination **Rev:** Head right, dates below

Date	Mintage	F	VF	XF	Unc	BU
1984	3,964,000	—	—	—	25.00	30.00

KM# 955a 100 FRANCS

15.0000 g., 0.9500 Silver .4582 oz. ASW **Obv:** Leafy branches divide date and denomination **Rev:** Head right, two dates

Date	Mintage	F	VF	XF	Unc	BU
1984 Proof	1,000	Value: 200				

KM# 955b 100 FRANCS

17.0000 g., 0.9200 Gold .5028 oz. AGW **Subject:** 50th Anniversary - Death of Marie Curie **Obv:** Leafy branches divide date and denomination **Rev:** Head right, two dates

Date	Mintage	F	VF	XF	Unc	BU
1984 Proof	5,000	Value: 400				

KM# 957 100 FRANCS

15.0000 g., 0.9000 Silver .4340 oz. ASW **Subject:** Centennial of Emile Zola's Novel **Rev:** Head right

Date	Mintage	F	VF	XF	Unc	BU
1985	3,980,000	—	—	—	28.00	35.00
1985 Proof	13,000	Value: 55.00				

KM# 957a 100 FRANCS

15.0000 g., 0.9500 Silver .4582 oz. ASW **Subject:** Centennial of Emile Zola's Novel **Rev:** Head right

Date	Mintage	F	VF	XF	Unc	BU
1985 Proof	5,000	Value: 115				

KM# 957b 100 FRANCS

17.0000 g., 0.9200 Gold .5028 oz. AGW **Subject:** Centennial of Emile Zola's Novel **Rev:** Head right

Date	Mintage	F	VF	XF	Unc	BU
1985 Proof	5,000	Value: 375				

KM# 960 100 FRANCS

15.0000 g., 0.9000 Silver .4340 oz. ASW, 31 mm. **Subject:** Centennial - Statue of Liberty **Obv:** Top of statue facing, dates at right **Rev:** Liberty cap over inscription above denomination, date below **Designer:** Michel Durand Megret

Date	Mintage	F	VF	XF	Unc	BU
1986	4,427,000	—	—	—	11.50	16.50

KM# 960a 100 FRANCS

15.0000 g., 0.9500 Silver .4582 oz. ASW **Subject:** Centennial of Statue of Liberty **Obv:** Top of statue facing **Rev:** Liberty cap over inscription above denomination, date below

Date	Mintage	F	VF	XF	Unc	BU
1986 Proof	18,000	Value: 45.00				

KM# 960b 100 FRANCS

17.0000 g., 0.9200 Gold .5028 oz. AGW **Subject:** Centennial - Statue of Liberty **Obv:** Top of statue facing **Rev:** Liberty cap over inscription above denomination, date below

Date	Mintage	F	VF	XF	Unc	BU
1986	13,000	—	—	—	340	360
1986 Proof	17,000	Value: 375				

KM# 960c 100 FRANCS

20.0000 g., 0.9990 Platinum .6430 oz. APW **Subject:** Centennial - Statue of Liberty **Obv:** Top of statue facing **Rev:** Liberty cap over inscription above denomination, date below

Date	Mintage	F	VF	XF	Unc	BU
1986 Proof	9,500	Value: 875				

KM# 960d 100 FRANCS

17.0000 g., 0.9000 Palladium .4920 oz. **Subject:** Centennial - Statue of Liberty **Obv:** Top of statue facing **Rev:** Liberty cap over inscription above denomination, date below

Date	Mintage	F	VF	XF	Unc	BU
1986 Proof	1,250	Value: 425				

KM# 962 100 FRANCS

15.0000 g., 0.9000 Silver .4340 oz. ASW, 31 mm. **Subject:** 230th Anniversary - Birth of General Lafayette **Obv:** Bust left **Rev:** Liberty cap over inscription above denomination, date below

Date	Mintage	F	VF	XF	Unc	BU
1987	4,801,000	—	—	—	20.00	25.00

KM# 962a 100 FRANCS

15.0000 g., 0.9500 Silver .4582 oz. ASW **Subject:** 230th Anniversary - Birth of General Lafayette **Obv:** Bust left **Rev:** Liberty cap over inscription above denomination, date below

Date	Mintage	F	VF	XF	Unc	BU
1987 Proof	30,000	Value: 35.00				

KM# 962b 100 FRANCS

17.0000 g., 0.9200 Gold .5028 oz. AGW **Subject:** 230th Anniversary - Birth of General Lafayette **Obv:** Bust left **Rev:** Liberty cap over inscription above denomination, date below

Date	Mintage	F	VF	XF	Unc	BU
1987	10,000	—	—	—	340	360
1987 Proof	20,000	Value: 375				

KM# 962c 100 FRANCS

20.0000 g., 0.9990 Platinum .6430 oz. APW **Subject:** 230th Anniversary - Birth of General Lafayette **Obv:** Bust left **Rev:** Liberty cap over inscription above denomination, date below

Date	Mintage	F	VF	XF	Unc	BU
1987 Proof	8,500	Value: 875				

KM# 962d 100 FRANCS

17.0000 g., 0.9000 Palladium .4920 oz. **Subject:** 230th Anniversary - Birth of General Lafayette **Obv:** Bust left **Rev:** Liberty cap over inscription above denomination, date below

Date	Mintage	F	VF	XF	Unc	BU
1987 Proof	7,000	Value: 300				

KM# 966 100 FRANCS

15.0000 g., 0.9000 Silver .4340 oz. ASW **Subject:** Fraternity **Obv:** Radiant head left with crown of cherubs **Rev:** Liberty cap over inscription above denomination, date below

Date	Mintage	F	VF	XF	Unc	BU
1988	4,853,000	—	—	—	26.50	32.50

KM# 966a 100 FRANCS

15.0000 g., 0.9500 Silver .4582 oz. ASW **Subject:** Fraternity **Obv:** Radiant head left with crown of cherubs

Date	Mintage	F	VF	XF	Unc	BU
1988 Proof	20,000	Value: 40.00				

KM# 966b 100 FRANCS

17.0000 g., 0.9200 Gold .5028 oz. AGW **Subject:** Fraternity **Obv:** Radiant head left with crown of cherubs **Rev:** Liberty cap over inscription above denomination, date below

Date	Mintage	F	VF	XF	Unc	BU
1988	3,000	—	—	—	450	475
1988 Proof	12,000	Value: 375				

KM# 966c 100 FRANCS

20.0000 g., 0.9990 Platinum .6430 oz. APW **Subject:** Fraternity **Obv:** Radiant head left with crown of cherubs **Rev:** Liberty cap over inscription above denomination, date below

Date	Mintage	F	VF	XF	Unc	BU
1988 Proof	5,000	Value: 875				

KM# 966d 100 FRANCS

17.0000 g., 0.9000 Palladium .4920 oz. **Subject:** Fraternity **Obv:** Radiant head left with crown of cherubs **Rev:** Liberty cap over inscription above denomination, date below

Date	Mintage	F	VF	XF	Unc	BU
1988 Proof	7,000	Value: 300				

KM# 970 100 FRANCS
15.0000 g., 0.9000 Silver .4340 oz. ASW **Subject:** Human Rights **Obv:** Standing Genius writing the constitution **Rev:** Liberty cap over inscription above denomination, date below

Date	Mintage	F	VF	XF	Unc	BU
1989	4,823,000	—	—	—	32.50	37.50

KM# 970a 100 FRANCS
15.0000 g., 0.9500 Silver .4582 oz. ASW **Subject:** Human Rights **Obv:** Standing Genius writing the constitution **Rev:** Liberty cap over inscription above denomination, date below

Date	Mintage	F	VF	XF	Unc	BU
1989 Proof	40,000	Value: 47.50				

KM# 971 100 FRANCS
22.2000 g., 0.9000 Silver .6424 oz. ASW **Subject:** 1992 Olympics **Obv:** Alpine skiing **Rev:** Cross on flame, date and denomination, logo below

Date	Mintage	F	VF	XF	Unc	BU
1989 Proof	136,000	Value: 30.00				

KM# 972 100 FRANCS
22.2000 g., 0.9000 Silver .6424 oz. ASW **Subject:** 1992 Olympics **Obv:** Ice Skating Couple **Rev:** Cross on flame, date and denomination, logo below

Date	Mintage	F	VF	XF	Unc	BU
1989 Proof	179,000	Value: 27.50				

KM# 970b 100 FRANCS
17.0000 g., 0.9200 Gold .5028 oz. AGW **Subject:** Human Rights **Obv:** Standing Genius writing the constitution **Rev:** Liberty cap over inscription above denomination, date below

Date	Mintage	F	VF	XF	Unc	BU
1989	1,000	—	—	—	600	650
1989 Proof	20,000	Value: 365				

KM# 970c 100 FRANCS
20.0000 g., 0.9990 Platinum .6430 oz. APW **Subject:** Human Rights **Obv:** Standing Genius writing the constitution **Rev:** Liberty cap over inscription above denomination, date below

Date	Mintage	F	VF	XF	Unc	BU
1989 Proof	1,000	Value: 900				

KM# 970d 100 FRANCS
17.0000 g., 0.9000 Palladium .4920 oz. **Subject:** Human Rights **Obv:** Standing Genius writing the constitution **Rev:** Liberty cap over inscription above denomination, date below

Date	Mintage	F	VF	XF	Unc	BU
1989 Proof	1,250	Value: 400				

KM# 980 100 FRANCS
22.2000 g., 0.9000 Silver .6424 oz. ASW **Series:** 1992 Olympics **Obv:** Speed skaters and alpine marmot **Rev:** Crossed flame divides date and denomination, Olympic logo below

Date	Mintage	F	VF	XF	Unc	BU
1990 Proof	137,000	Value: 30.00				

KM# 981 100 FRANCS
22.2000 g., 0.9000 Silver .6424 oz. ASW **Series:** 1992 Olympics **Obv:** Bobsledding **Rev:** Games logo, value and legend

Date	Mintage	F	VF	XF	Unc	BU
1990 Proof	127,000	Value: 30.00				

KM# 982 100 FRANCS
15.0100 g., 0.9000 Silver .4340 oz. ASW **Subject:** Charlemagne **Obv:** Date and denomination divided by monogram, laurel spray below, circle surrounds **Rev:** Stylized head facing

Date	Mintage	F	VF	XF	Unc	BU
1990	4,950,000	—	—	—	37.50	40.00

KM# 983 100 FRANCS
22.2000 g., 0.9000 Silver .6423 oz. ASW **Series:** 1992 Olympics **Obv:** Free-style skier and chamois **Rev:** Crossed flame, date and denomination, logo below

Date	Mintage	F	VF	XF	Unc	BU
1990 Proof	110,000	Value: 32.50				

KM# 984 100 FRANCS
22.2000 g., 0.9000 Silver .6423 oz. ASW **Subject:** 1992 Olympics **Obv:** Slalom skiers **Rev:** Crossed flame, date and denomination, logo below

Date	Mintage	F	VF	XF	Unc	BU
1990 Proof	110,000	Value: 30.00				

KM# 991 100 FRANCS
22.2000 g., 0.9000 Silver .6423 oz. ASW **Subject:** 100th Anniversary of Basketball **Obv:** 2 players **Rev:** Star, ring, and globe above denomination and date

Date	Mintage	F	VF	XF	Unc	BU
1991 Proof	13,000	Value: 65.00				

KM# 992 100 FRANCS
22.2000 g., 0.9000 Silver .6423 oz. ASW **Subject:** 100th Anniversary of Basketball **Obv:** 1 player, hoops in background

Date	Mintage	F	VF	XF	Unc	BU
1991 Proof	13,000	Value: 65.00				

KM# 993 100 FRANCS
22.2000 g., 0.9000 Silver .6423 oz. ASW **Series:** 1992 Olympics **Obv:** Hockey players and Ibex **Rev:** Crossed flame divides date and denomination, Olympic logo below

Date	Mintage	F	VF	XF	Unc	BU
1991 Proof	93,000	Value: 37.50				

KM# 994 100 FRANCS
22.2000 g., 0.9000 Silver .6423 oz. ASW **Series:** 1992 Olympics **Obv:** Cross-country skier, building at left **Rev:** Crossed flame, date and denomination, logo below

Date	Mintage	F	VF	XF	Unc	BU
1991 Proof	93,000	Value: 35.00				

KM# 995 100 FRANCS
22.2000 g., 0.9000 Silver .6423 oz. ASW **Series:** 1992 Olympics **Obv:** Ski jumpers **Rev:** Crossed flame, date and denomination, logo below

Date	Mintage	F	VF	XF	Unc	BU
1991 Proof	90,000	Value: 37.50				

KM# 996 100 FRANCS
15.0100 g., 0.9000 Silver .4340 oz. ASW **Obv:** Finger pointing on starred paper, denomination below **Rev:** Head 3/4 facing, date below

Date	Mintage	F	VF	XF	Unc	BU
1991	3,985,000	—	—	—	32.50	35.00

KM# 1009 100 FRANCS
22.2000 g., 0.9000 Silver .6423 oz. ASW **Subject:** Paralympics **Obv:** Segmented flying birds, denomination and date below **Rev:** Designs

Date	Mintage	F	VF	XF	Unc	BU
1992 Proof	5,000	Value: 95.00				

KM# 1010 100 FRANCS
22.2000 g., 0.9000 Silver .6423 oz. ASW **Subject:** French Antarctic Territories **Obv:** Head at left facing, ship, mountains and "RF" in background, denomination below **Rev:** Fur seals above date

Date	Mintage	F	VF	XF	Unc	BU
1992 Proof	15,000	Value: 75.00				

KM# 1011 100 FRANCS
22.2000 g., 0.9000 Silver .6423 oz. ASW **Subject:** French Antarctic Territories **Rev:** Emperor Penguins, date below

Date	Mintage	F	VF	XF	Unc	BU
1992 Proof	15,000	Value: 75.00				

KM# 1120 100 FRANCS
15.0100 g., 0.9000 Silver .4340 oz. ASW **Subject:** Jean Monet **Rev:** Denomination above date within legend, rings surround, RF at bottom

Date	Mintage	F	VF	XF	Unc	BU
1992	3,925,000	—	—	—	35.00	37.50

KM# 1017 100 FRANCS
22.2000 g., 0.9000 Silver .6423 oz. ASW **Series:** Bicentennial of the Louvre **Obv:** Mona Lisa **Rev:** Patterned pyramids front museum, date and denomination below

Date	Mintage	F	VF	XF	Unc	BU
1993	—	—	—	—	—	—
1993 Proof	200,000	Value: 45.00				

KM# 1018.1 100 FRANCS
15.0000 g., 0.9000 Silver .4340 oz. ASW, 31 mm. **Series:** Bicentennial of the Louvre **Obv:** Liberty **Rev:** Patterned pyramids front museum, date and denomination below

Date	Mintage	F	VF	XF	Unc	BU
1993	—	—	—	—	35.00	40.00

KM# 1018.2 100 FRANCS
22.2000 g., 0.9000 Silver .6423 oz. ASW **Series:** Bicentennial of the Louvre **Obv:** Liberty **Rev:** Patterned pyramids front museum, date and denomination below

Date	Mintage	F	VF	XF	Unc	BU
1993	—	—	—	—	—	—
1993 Proof	20,000	Value: 37.50				

KM# 1018.2a 100 FRANCS
17.0000 g., 0.9200 Gold .5028 oz. AGW **Series:** Bicentennial of the Louvre **Obv:** Liberty **Rev:** Patterned pyramids front museum, date and denomination below

Date	Mintage	F	VF	XF	Unc	BU
1993	—	—	—	—	—	—
1993 Proof	5,000	Value: 400				

KM# 1019 100 FRANCS
22.2000 g., 0.9000 Silver .6420 oz. ASW **Series:** Bicentennial of the Louvre **Obv:** Victory **Rev:** Patterned pyramids front museum, date and denomination below

Date	Mintage	F	VF	XF	Unc	BU
1993	—	—	—	—	—	—
1993 Proof	20,000	Value: 37.50				

KM# 1019a 100 FRANCS
17.0000 g., 0.9200 Gold .5028 oz. AGW **Series:** Bicentennial of the Louvre **Obv:** Victory **Rev:** Patterned pyramids front museum, date and denomination below

Date	Mintage	F	VF	XF	Unc	BU
1993	—	—	—	—	—	—
1993 Proof	5,000	Value: 400				

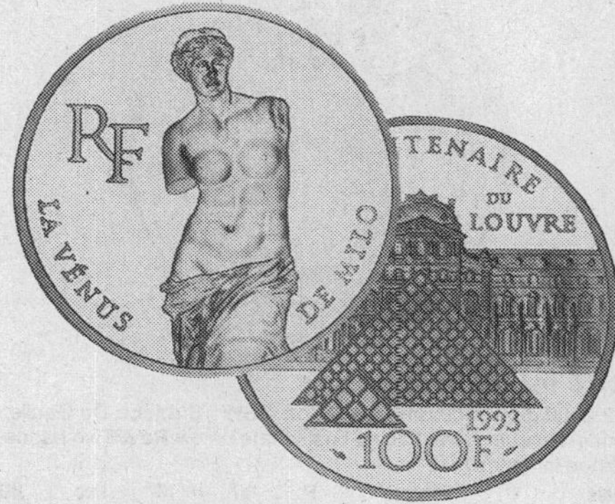

KM# 1020 100 FRANCS
22.2600 g., 0.9000 Silver .6420 oz. ASW **Series:** Bicentennial of the Louvre **Obv:** Venus de Milo **Rev:** Patterned pyramids front museum, date and denomination below

Date	Mintage	F	VF	XF	Unc	BU
1993	—	—	—	—	—	—
1993 Proof	20,000	Value: 40.00				

KM# 1021 100 FRANCS
22.2600 g., 0.9000 Silver .6420 oz. ASW **Series:** Bicentennial of the Louvre **Obv:** Marie-Marguerite **Rev:** Patterned pyramids front museum, date and denomination below

Date	Mintage	F	VF	XF	Unc	BU
1993 Proof	20,000	Value: 35.00				
1993	—	—	—	—	—	—

KM# 1021a 100 FRANCS
17.0000 g., 0.9200 Gold .5028 oz. AGW **Series:** Bicentennial of the Louvre **Obv:** Marie-Marguerite **Rev:** Patterned pyramids front museum, date and denomination below

Date	Mintage	F	VF	XF	Unc	BU
1993	—	—	—	—	—	—
1993 Proof	5,000	Value: 400				

KM# 1022 100 FRANCS
22.2600 g., 0.9000 Silver .6420 oz. ASW **Series:** Bicentennial of the Louvre **Obv:** Napoleon crowning Josephine as Empress, 1763-1814 **Rev:** Patterned pyramids front museum, date and denomination below

Date	Mintage	F	VF	XF	Unc	BU
1993	—	—	—	—	—	—
1993 Proof	20,000	Value: 42.50				

KM# 1022a 100 FRANCS
17.0000 g., 0.9200 Gold .5028 oz. AGW **Series:** Bicentennial of the Louvre **Obv:** Napoleon crowning Josephine **Rev:** Patterned pyramids front museum, date and denomination below

Date	Mintage	F	VF	XF	Unc	BU
1993	—	—	—	—	—	—
1993 Proof	5,000	Value: 400				

KM# 1023 100 FRANCS
22.2000 g., 0.9000 Silver .6424 oz. ASW **Obv:** Head with hat facing **Rev:** Flaming torch, denomination below

Date	Mintage	F	VF	XF	Unc	BU
1993	100,000	—	—	—	25.00	—
1993 Proof	50,000	Value: 40.00				

KM# 1037 100 FRANCS
22.2000 g., 0.9000 Silver .6424 oz. ASW **Subject:** Winston Churchill **Obv:** Uniformed bust right

Date	Mintage	F	VF	XF	Unc	BU
1994 Proof	Est. 30,000	Value: 42.50				

KM# 1038 100 FRANCS
22.2000 g., 0.9000 Silver .6424 oz. ASW **Subject:** General de Gaulle **Obv:** Bust right at microphone **Rev:** Map of France, inscription overlay

Date	Mintage	F	VF	XF	Unc	BU
1994 Proof	Est. 30,000	Value: 45.00				

KM# 1039 100 FRANCS
22.2000 g., 0.9000 Silver .6424 oz. ASW **Subject:** General Leclerc **Obv:** Bust facing **Rev:** Flag, inscription, fort, denomination

Date	Mintage	F	VF	XF	Unc	BU
1994 Proof	Est. 30,000	Value: 42.50				

KM# 1040 100 FRANCS
22.2000 g., 0.9000 Silver .6424 oz. ASW **Subject:** General Marie Pierre Koenig **Obv:** Bust facing looking left **Rev:** Battle scene

Date	Mintage	F	VF	XF	Unc	BU
1994 Proof	Est. 30,000	Value: 42.50				

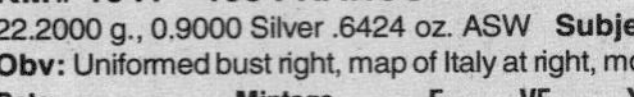

KM# 1041 100 FRANCS
22.2000 g., 0.9000 Silver .6424 oz. ASW **Subject:** General Juin **Obv:** Uniformed bust right, map of Italy at right, mountaintop building

Date	Mintage	F	VF	XF	Unc	BU
1994 Proof	Est. 30,000	Value: 42.50				

KM# 1042 100 FRANCS
22.2000 g., 0.9000 Silver .6424 oz. ASW **Subject:** General Dwight David Eisenhower **Obv:** Bust 3/4 left **Rev:** Flags representing allied countries under Supreme Commander Eisenhower

Date	Mintage	F	VF	XF	Unc	BU
1994 Proof	Est. 30,000	Value: 42.50				

KM# 1043 100 FRANCS
22.2000 g., 0.9000 Silver .6424 oz. ASW **Subject:** Sainte - Mere - Eglise **Rev:** Church, parachute behind

Date	Mintage	F	VF	XF	Unc	BU
1994 Proof	Est. 30,000	Value: 42.50				

KM# 1044 100 FRANCS
22.2000 g., 0.9000 Silver .6424 oz. ASW **Subject:** General de Lattre de Tassigny **Obv:** Face in profile right **Rev:** Waving flags below denomination

Date	Mintage	F	VF	XF	Unc	BU
1994 Proof	Est. 30,000	Value: 42.50				

KM# 1046 100 FRANCS
22.2000 g., 0.9000 Silver .6424 oz. ASW **Subject:** De Gaulle and Adenauer **Obv:** Facing busts, date below **Rev:** Two hands joined in handshake

Date	Mintage	F	VF	XF	Unc	BU
1994 Proof	Est. 30,000	Value: 42.50				

KM# 1047 100 FRANCS
33.6300 g., 0.9250 Silver 1.0000 oz. ASW **Series:** 1996 Olympics **Obv:** Head facing, denomination and date below **Rev:** Discus thrower **Edge Lettering:** CITIUS ALTIUS FORTIUS **Designer:** Joaquin Jimenez

Date	Mintage	F	VF	XF	Unc	BU
1994 Proof	250,000	Value: 32.50				

KM# 1048 100 FRANCS
33.6300 g., 0.9250 Silver 1.0000 oz. ASW **Subject:** 1996 Olympics **Obv:** Head facing, denomination and date below **Rev:** Javelin Thrower **Edge:** CITIUS ALTIUS FORTIUS **Designer:** Joaquin Jimenez

Date	Mintage	F	VF	XF	Unc	BU
1994 Proof	250,000	Value: 32.50				

KM# 1072 100 FRANCS
22.2000 g., 0.9000 Silver .6424 oz. ASW **Series:** Centennial of Cinema **Subject:** Lumiere Brothers **Obv:** Antique movie camera, denomination at right **Rev:** Conjoined busts right

Date	Mintage	F	VF	XF	Unc	BU
1994 Proof	15,000	Value: 32.50				

KM# 1073 100 FRANCS
17.0000 g., 0.9200 Gold .5028 oz. AGW **Series:** Centennial of Cinema **Subject:** Lumiere Brothers **Obv:** Antique movie camera **Rev:** Conjoined busts right

Date	Mintage	F	VF	XF	Unc	BU
1994 Proof	5,000	Value: 400				

KM# 1076 100 FRANCS
22.2000 g., 0.9000 Silver .6424 oz. ASW **Series:** Centennial of Cinema **Subject:** Charlie Chaplan **Obv:** Antique movie camera **Rev:** Head facing

Date	Mintage	F	VF	XF	Unc	BU
1994 Proof	15,000	Value: 42.00				

KM# 1077 100 FRANCS
17.0000 g., 0.9200 Gold .5028 oz. AGW **Series:** Centennial of Cinema **Subject:** Charlie Chaplan **Obv:** Antique movie camera **Rev:** Head facing

Date	Mintage	F	VF	XF	Unc	BU
1994 Proof	5,000	Value: 400				

KM# 1182 100 FRANCS
22.2000 g., 0.9000 Silver .6424 oz. ASW **Rev:** Voltaire

Date	Mintage	F	VF	XF	Unc	BU
1994 Proof	3,000	Value: 55.00				

KM# 1045.1 100 FRANCS
15.0000 g., 0.9000 Silver .4340 oz. ASW, 31 mm. **Subject:** Liberation of Paris **Obv:** Battle scene, denomination below **Rev:** Triumphant troops marching down Champs Elysees **Note:** Smaller size.

Date	Mintage	F	VF	XF	Unc	BU
1994	1,598,000	—	—	—	35.00	40.00

KM# 1045.2 100 FRANCS
22.2000 g., 0.9000 Silver .6424 oz. ASW **Subject:** Liberation of Paris **Obv:** Battle scene, denomination **Rev:** Triumphant troops marching down Champs Elysees

Date	Mintage	F	VF	XF	Unc	BU
1994	—	—	—	—	30.00	35.00
1994 Proof	Est. 30,000	Value: 42.50				

KM# 1080 100 FRANCS
22.2000 g., 0.9000 Silver .6424 oz. ASW **Series:** Centennial of Cinema **Subject:** Leon Gaumont **Obv:** Antique movie camera **Rev:** Head facing

Date	Mintage	F	VF	XF	Unc	BU
1995 Proof	15,000	Value: 40.00				

KM# 1081 100 FRANCS
17.0000 g., 0.9200 Gold .5028 oz. AGW **Series:** Centennial of Cinema **Subject:** Leon Gaumont **Obv:** Antique movie camera **Rev:** Head facing

Date	Mintage	F	VF	XF	Unc	BU
1995 Proof	5,000	Value: 400				

KM# 1084 100 FRANCS
22.2000 g., 0.9000 Silver .6424 oz. ASW **Series:** Centennial of Cinema **Subject:** Jean Renoir **Obv:** Antique movie camera **Rev:** Head right

Date	Mintage	F	VF	XF	Unc	BU
1995 Proof	15,000	Value: 30.00				

KM# 1085 100 FRANCS
17.0000 g., 0.9200 Gold .5028 oz. AGW **Series:** Centennial of Cinema **Subject:** Jean Renoir **Obv:** Antique movie camera **Rev:** Head right

Date	Mintage	F	VF	XF	Unc	BU
1995 Proof	5,000	Value: 400				

KM# 1088 100 FRANCS
22.2000 g., 0.9000 Silver .6424 oz. ASW **Series:** Centennial of Cinema **Subject:** Alfred Hitchcock **Obv:** Antique movie camera **Rev:** Head 1/4 left

Date	Mintage	F	VF	XF	Unc	BU
1995 Proof	15,000	Value: 40.00				

KM# 1089 100 FRANCS
17.0000 g., 0.9200 Gold .5028 oz. AGW **Series:** Centennial of Cinema **Subject:** Alfred Hitchcock **Obv:** Antique movie camera **Rev:** Head 1/4 left

Date	Mintage	F	VF	XF	Unc	BU
1995 Proof	5,000	Value: 425				

KM# 1092 100 FRANCS
22.2000 g., 0.9000 Silver .6424 oz. ASW **Series:** Centennial of Cinema **Subject:** Greta Garbo **Obv:** Antique movie camera **Rev:** Head right

Date	Mintage	F	VF	XF	Unc	BU
1995 Proof	15,000	Value: 37.50				

KM# 1093 100 FRANCS
17.0000 g., 0.9200 Gold .5028 oz. AGW **Series:** Centennial of Cinema **Subject:** Greta Garbo 1905-1990, actress in "Camille & Ninotchka" **Obv:** Antique movie camera **Rev:** Head right

Date	Mintage	F	VF	XF	Unc	BU
1995 Proof	5,000	Value: 450				

KM# 1096 100 FRANCS
22.2000 g., 0.9000 Silver .6424 oz. ASW **Series:** Centennial of Cinema **Subject:** Audrey Hepburn **Obv:** Antique movie camera **Rev:** Head 3/4 left

Date	Mintage	F	VF	XF	Unc	BU
1994 Proof	15,000	Value: 37.50				

KM# 1097 100 FRANCS
17.0000 g., 0.9200 Gold .5028 oz. AGW **Series:** Centennial of Cinema **Subject:** Audrey Hepburn **Obv:** Antique movie camera **Rev:** Head 3/4 left

Date	Mintage	F	VF	XF	Unc	BU
1994 Proof	5,000	Value: 425				

KM# 1100 100 FRANCS
22.2000 g., 0.9000 Silver .6424 oz. ASW **Series:** Centennial of Cinema **Subject:** Federico Fellini **Obv:** Antique movie camera **Rev:** Bust 3/4 right

Date	Mintage	F	VF	XF	Unc	BU
1995 Proof	15,000	Value: 30.00				

KM# 1101 100 FRANCS
17.0000 g., 0.9200 Gold .5028 oz. AGW **Series:** Centennial of Cinema **Subject:** Federico Fellini **Obv:** Antique movie camera **Rev:** Bust 3/4 right

Date	Mintage	F	VF	XF	Unc	BU
1995 Proof	5,000	Value: 425				

KM# 1104 100 FRANCS
22.2000 g., 0.9000 Silver .6424 oz. ASW **Series:** Centennial of Cinema **Subject:** Yves Montand **Obv:** Antique movie camera **Rev:** Bust 3/4 facing

Date	Mintage	F	VF	XF	Unc	BU
1994 Proof	15,000	Value: 30.00				

KM# 1105 100 FRANCS
17.0000 g., 0.9200 Gold .5028 oz. AGW **Series:** Centennial of Cinema **Subject:** Yves Montand **Obv:** Antique movie camera **Rev:** Bust 3/4 facing

Date	Mintage	F	VF	XF	Unc	BU
1994 Proof	5,000	Value: 400				

KM# 1108 100 FRANCS
22.2000 g., 0.9000 Silver .6424 oz. ASW **Series:** Centennial of Cinema **Subject:** Romy Schneider **Obv:** Antique movie camera **Rev:** Bust 3/4 left

Date	Mintage	F	VF	XF	Unc	BU
1995 Proof	15,000	Value: 30.00				

KM# 1109 100 FRANCS
17.0000 g., 0.9200 Gold .5028 oz. AGW **Series:** Centennial of Cinema **Subject:** Romy Schneider **Obv:** Antique movie camera **Rev:** Bust 3/4 left

Date	Mintage	F	VF	XF	Unc	BU
1995 Proof	5,000	Value: 400				

KM# 1116.2 100 FRANCS
22.2000 g., 0.9000 Silver .6424 oz. ASW **Obv:** Victory in Europe date, May 8,1945 **Rev:** Birds in flight above banners, PAX below

Date	Mintage	F	VF	XF	Unc	BU
1995 Proof	30,000	Value: 45.00				

KM# 1134 100 FRANCS
22.2000 g., 0.9000 Silver .6424 oz. ASW **Obv:** Bust facing **Rev:** Lab bottles, denomination and date

Date	Mintage	F	VF	XF	Unc	BU
1995 Proof	10,000	Value: 45.00				

KM# 1136 100 FRANCS
22.2000 g., 0.9000 Silver .6424 oz. ASW **Obv:** Bust 1/4 left **Rev:** Bird in tree, denomination at right, fox and date below

Date	Mintage	F	VF	XF	Unc	BU
1995 Proof	10,000	Value: 45.00				

KM# 1116.1 100 FRANCS
15.0000 g., 0.9000 Silver .4340 oz. ASW, 31 mm. **Subject:** V.E. Day **Obv:** Victory in Europe date, May 8, 1945 **Rev:** Birds in flight above banners, PAX below **Note:** Smaller size.

Date	Mintage	F	VF	XF	Unc	BU
1995	1,990,000	—	—	—	40.00	45.00

KM# 1138 100 FRANCS
22.2000 g., 0.9000 Silver .6424 oz. ASW **Subject:** 300th Anniversary of the Death of Marie de Sevigne; letter writer, 1626-1696 **Obv:** Bust 1/4 left **Rev:** Crowned double arms with supporters divide date and denomination

Date	Mintage	F	VF	XF	Unc	BU
1996 Proof	5,000	Value: 65.00				

KM# 1180 100 FRANCS
15.0500 g., 0.9000 Silver .4340 oz. ASW **Subject:** King Clovis I **Obv:** Bust facing **Rev:** Baptism scene, date and denomination below

Date	Mintage	F	VF	XF	Unc	BU
1996	2,000,000	—	—	—	32.50	37.50
1996 Proof	—	Value: 60.00				

KM# 1172 100 FRANCS
17.0000 g., 0.9200 Gold .5028 oz. AGW **Subject:** Coupe du Monde 1998 - France **Obv:** World Cup 1998 logo above denomination and date **Rev:** Segment of Eiffel tower, soccer player

Date	Mintage	F	VF	XF	Unc	BU
1996 Proof	25,000	Value: 385				

KM# 1168 100 FRANCS
17.0000 g., 0.9200 Gold .5028 oz. AGW **Subject:** Coupe du Monde 1998 - Africa **Obv:** World Cup 1998 logo above denomination and date **Rev:** Soccer player and map of Africa, date below **Designer:** Joaquin Jimenez

Date	Mintage	F	VF	XF	Unc	BU
1997 Proof	25,000	Value: 400				

KM# 1169 100 FRANCS
17.0000 g., 0.9200 Gold .5028 oz. AGW **Subject:** Coupe du Monde 1998 - America **Obv:** World Cup 1998 logo above denomination and date below **Rev:** Soccer player and map of North & South America **Designer:** Joaquin Jimenez

Date	Mintage	F	VF	XF	Unc	BU
1997 Proof	25,000	Value: 400				

KM# 1170 100 FRANCS
17.0000 g., 0.9200 Gold .5028 oz. AGW **Subject:** Coupe du Monde 1998 - Asia **Rev:** Soccer player and map of Asia, date below **Designer:** Joaquin Jimenez

Date	Mintage	F	VF	XF	Unc	BU
1997 Proof	25,000	Value: 400				

KM# 1173 100 FRANCS
17.0000 g., 0.9200 Gold .5028 oz. AGW **Subject:** Coupe du Monde 1998 - Oceania **Rev:** Soccer player and map of the Pacific, with Australia highlighted in a box, date below **Designer:** Joaquin Jimenez

Date	Mintage	F	VF	XF	Unc	BU
1997 Proof	25,000	Value: 400				

KM# 1188 100 FRANCS
15.1500 g., 0.9000 Silver .4384 oz. ASW **Obv:** Head facing **Rev:** Two cats flanking denomination

Date	Mintage	F	VF	XF	Unc	BU
1997 Proof	3,000	Value: 50.00				
1997	3,000	—	—	—	32.50	37.50

KM# 1195 100 FRANCS
8.4500 g., 0.9200 Gold .2499 oz. AGW **Obv:** Pantheon, date below **Rev:** Denomination and tree design

Date	Mintage	F	VF	XF	Unc	BU
1997 Proof	500	Value: 350				

KM# 1196 100 FRANCS
22.2000 g., 0.9000 Silver .6424 oz. ASW **Subject:** Georges Guynemer **Obv:** Bust 3/4 facing **Rev:** Guynemer's stork and denomination

Date	Mintage	F	VF	XF	Unc	BU
1997 Proof	3,000	Value: 50.00				

KM# 1198 100 FRANCS
22.2000 g., 0.9000 Silver .6424 oz. ASW **Subject:** Pierre and Marie Curie, 1867-1934, physicist - chemist **Obv:** Conjoined busts left **Rev:** Denomination

Date	Mintage	F	VF	XF	Unc	BU
1997 Proof	3,000	Value: 50.00				

KM# 1171 100 FRANCS
17.0000 g., 0.9200 Gold .5028 oz. AGW **Subject:** Coupe du Monte 1998 - Europe **Obv:** World Cup 1998 logo, denomination and date below **Rev:** Soccer player and map of Europe, date below **Designer:** Joaquin Jimenez

Date	Mintage	F	VF	XF	Unc	BU
1998 Proof	25,000	Value: 400				

KM# 1201 100 FRANCS
22.2000 g., 0.9000 Silver .6424 oz. ASW **Subject:** Marie Caritat Marquis de Condorcet **Obv:** Bust 3/4 right **Rev:** Denomination

Date	Mintage	F	VF	XF	Unc	BU
1998 Proof	3,000	Value: 50.00				

KM# 1203 100 FRANCS

22.2000 g., 0.9000 Silver .6424 oz. ASW **Subject:** Gaspard Monge **Obv:** Bust 3/4 right, building at right **Rev:** Denomination

Date	Mintage	F	VF	XF	Unc	BU
1998 Proof	3,000	Value: 50.00				

KM# 1209 100 FRANCS

17.0000 g., 0.9200 Gold .5028 oz. AGW **Subject:** Treasures of the Nile - King Tutankhamon **Obv:** Burial mask and dog **Rev:** Sphinx and pyramids

Date	Mintage	F	VF	XF	Unc	BU
1998 Proof	2,000	Value: 475				

KM# 1210 100 FRANCS

17.0000 g., 0.9200 Gold .5028 oz. AGW **Subject:** Treasures of the Nile - The Scribe Accroupi **Obv:** Seated scribe **Rev:** Pyramids, Sphinx, date at left, denomination below

Date	Mintage	F	VF	XF	Unc	BU
1998 Proof	2,000	Value: 475				

KM# 1397 100 FRANCS

22.1400 g., 0.9000 Silver 0.6406 oz. ASW, 37 mm. **Subject:** Human Rights Declaration **Obv:** Bust right, building and dates below **Rev:** Denomination on globe, laurel spray below **Edge:** Plain

Date	Mintage	F	VF	XF	Unc	BU
1998A Proof	—	Value: 50.00				

KM# 1295 100 FRANCS

22.3000 g., 0.9000 Silver 0.6453 oz. ASW, 36.7 mm. **Subject:** Louis Braille **Obv:** Portrait, dots and fingers **Rev:** Braille text, tools and fingers **Edge:** Plain

Date	Mintage	F	VF	XF	Unc	BU
1999 Proof	3,000	Value: 50.00				

KM# 1296 100 FRANCS

22.3000 g., 0.9000 Silver 0.6453 oz. ASW, 36.7 mm. **Subject:** Jean Jaures **Obv:** Bearded portrait **Rev:** Floor plan and dome **Edge:** Plain

Date	Mintage	F	VF	XF	Unc	BU
1999 Proof	3,000	Value: 50.00				

KM# 1232 100 FRANCS

17.0000 g., 0.9200 Gold .5028 oz. AGW **Subject:** 2000 Years - French Coinage **Obv:** Denomination **Rev:** 1st century B.C. Celtic Parisii Stater coin design **Edge:** Plain

Date	Mintage	F	VF	XF	Unc	BU
2000 Proof	1,000	Value: 450				

KM# 1233 100 FRANCS

17.0000 g., 0.9200 Gold .5028 oz. AGW **Subject:** 2000 Years - French Coinage **Rev:** Charlemagne Denar coin design

Date	Mintage	F	VF	XF	Unc	BU
2000 Proof	1,000	Value: 450				

KM# 1234 100 FRANCS

17.0000 g., 0.9200 Gold .5028 oz. AGW **Subject:** 2000 Years - French Coinage **Rev:** Louis IX gold Ecu coin design

Date	Mintage	F	VF	XF	Unc	BU
2000 Proof	1,000	Value: 450				

KM# 1238 100 FRANCS

17.0000 g., 0.9200 Gold .5028 oz. AGW **Series:** XXth Century **Subject:** Biology and Medicine **Obv:** Double X design **Rev:** Parents, fetus, hands

Date	Mintage	F	VF	XF	Unc	BU
2000 Proof	1,000	Value: 450				

KM# 1239 100 FRANCS

17.0000 g., 0.9200 Gold .5028 oz. AGW **Series:** XXth Century **Subject:** Physics **Rev:** Einstein's portrait, atom and formula

Date	Mintage	F	VF	XF	Unc	BU
2000 Proof	1,000	Value: 450				

KM# 1240 100 FRANCS

17.0000 g., 0.9200 Gold .5028 oz. AGW **Series:** XXth Century **Subject:** Communications **Rev:** World, satellites, keyboard

Date	Mintage	F	VF	XF	Unc	BU
2000 Proof	1,000	Value: 450				

KM# 1241 100 FRANCS

17.0000 g., 0.9200 Gold .5028 oz. AGW **Series:** XXth Century **Subject:** Automobile **Rev:** Race cars above horse

Date	Mintage	F	VF	XF	Unc	BU
2000 Proof	1,000	Value: 450				

KM# 1242 100 FRANCS

17.0000 g., 0.9200 Gold .5028 oz. AGW **Series:** XXth Century **Subject:** Flight **Rev:** Icarus in flight above Bleriot monoplane

Date	Mintage	F	VF	XF	Unc	BU
2000 Proof	1,000	Value: 450				

KM# 1243 100 FRANCS

17.0000 g., 0.9200 Gold .5028 oz. AGW **Series:** XXth Century **Subject:** Space Travel **Rev:** Astronaut, footprint on moon, planets

Date	Mintage	F	VF	XF	Unc	BU
2000 Proof	1,000	Value: 450				

KM# 1264 100 FRANCS

17.0000 g., 0.9200 Gold .5028 oz. AGW **Subject:** Antoine de St. Exupery **Obv:** Portrait, bi-plane **Rev:** The "Little Prince" standing on a small planet

Date	Mintage	F	VF	XF	Unc	BU
2000 Proof	1,000	Value: 450				

KM# 974 500 FRANCS

17.0000 g., 0.9200 Gold .5029 oz. AGW **Series:** 1992 Olympics **Obv:** Ice skating couple **Obv. Designer:** Georges Yoldjoglou **Rev:** Cross on flame divides date and denomination, Olympic logo below

Date	Mintage	F	VF	XF	Unc	BU
1989 Proof	Est. 17,000	Value: 360				

KM# 973 500 FRANCS

17.0000 g., 0.9200 Gold .5029 oz. AGW **Series:** 1992 Olympics **Obv:** Alpine skiing **Obv. Designer:** Guy Brun **Rev:** Cross on flame, date and denomination, Olympic logo below **Note:** Without mint mark.

Date	Mintage	F	VF	XF	Unc	BU
1989 Proof	19,000	Value: 350				

KM# 985 500 FRANCS

17.0000 g., 0.9200 Gold .5029 oz. AGW **Series:** 1992 Olympics **Obv:** Speed skating **Rev:** Crossed flame, date and denomination, logo below

Date	Mintage	F	VF	XF	Unc	BU
1990 Proof	13,000	Value: 355				

KM# 986 500 FRANCS

17.0000 g., 0.9200 Gold .5029 oz. AGW **Series:** 1992 Olympics **Obv:** Bobsledding **Rev:** Games logo, value and legend

Date	Mintage	F	VF	XF	Unc	BU
1990 Proof	13,000	Value: 355				

KM# 987 500 FRANCS

17.0000 g., 0.9200 Gold .5029 oz. AGW **Series:** 1992 Olympics **Subject:** Pierre de Coubertin **Obv:** Free-style skier watched by chamois **Rev:** Head facing

Date	Mintage	F	VF	XF	Unc	BU
1990 Proof	8,000	Value: 360				

KM# 988 500 FRANCS

17.0000 g., 0.9200 Gold .5029 oz. AGW **Series:** 1992 Olympics **Obv:** Modern and old style slalom skiers

Date	Mintage	F	VF	XF	Unc	BU
1990 Proof	8,000	Value: 360				

KM# 977 500 FRANCS

17.0000 g., 0.9200 Gold .5029 oz. AGW **Subject:** 100th Anniversary of Basketball **Obv:** Player jumping for lay-up shot, hoop behind **Rev:** Star, ring, and globe, denomination and date below

Date	Mintage	F	VF	XF	Unc	BU
1991 Proof	5,000	Value: 365				

KM# 997 500 FRANCS

17.0000 g., 0.9200 Gold .5029 oz. AGW **Series:** 1992 Olympics **Obv:** 2 hockey players and large ibex ram

Date	Mintage	F	VF	XF	Unc	BU
1991 Proof	8,000	Value: 350				

KM# 998 500 FRANCS

17.0000 g., 0.9200 Gold .5029 oz. AGW

Date	Mintage	F	VF	XF	Unc	BU
1991 Proof	8,000	Value: 350				

KM# 999 500 FRANCS

17.0000 g., 0.9200 Gold .5029 oz. AGW **Series:** 1992 Olympics **Obv:** Old style and modern ski jumpers

Date	Mintage	F	VF	XF	Unc	BU
1991 Proof	8,000	Value: 360				

KM# 1000 500 FRANCS

17.0000 g., 0.9200 Gold .5029 oz. AGW **Series:** 1992 Olympics **Subject:** Pierre de Coubertin **Obv:** Head facing **Rev:** Cross on flame divides date and denomination, Olympic logo below

Date	Mintage	F	VF	XF	Unc	BU
1991 Proof	28,000	Value: 350				

KM# 1001 500 FRANCS

17.0000 g., 0.9200 Gold .5029 oz. AGW **Obv:** Building, denomination and date below **Rev:** Mozart in Paris at piano

Date	Mintage	F	VF	XF	Unc	BU
1991 Proof	Est. 5,000	Value: 365				

KM# 1024 500 FRANCS

31.1040 g., 0.9990 Gold 1.0000 oz. AGW **Series:** Bicentennial of the Louvre **Obv:** Mona Lisa **Obv. Designer:** Emile Rousseau **Rev:** Pyramids front building, date and denomination below

Date	Mintage	F	VF	XF	Unc	BU
1993	—	—	—	—	—	—
1993 Proof	5,000	Value: 750				
1994 Proof	5,000	Value: 800				

KM# 1025.1 500 FRANCS

31.1040 g., 0.9990 Gold 1.0000 oz. AGW **Series:** Bicentennial of the Louvre **Obv:** Venus de Milo

Date	Mintage	F	VF	XF	Unc	BU
1993	—	—	—	—	—	—
1993 Proof	5,000	Value: 750				

KM# 1026 500 FRANCS

155.5175 g., 0.9990 Gold 5.0000 oz. AGW **Series:** Bicentennial of the Louvre **Obv:** Liberty **Rev:** Pyramids front building, date and denomination below

Date	Mintage	F	VF	XF	Unc	BU
1993 Proof	99	Value: 3,500				
1994 Proof	99	Value: 3,750				

KM# 1027 500 FRANCS

155.5175 g., 0.9990 Gold 5.0000 oz. AGW **Series:** Bicentennial of the Louvre **Obv:** Mona Lisa **Rev:** Patterned pyramids front building

Date	Mintage	F	VF	XF	Unc	BU
1993 Proof	99	Value: 3,750				
1994 Proof	99	Value: 3,800				

KM# 1028 500 FRANCS

17.0000 g., 0.9200 Gold .5028 oz. AGW **Subject:** Jean Moulin **Obv:** Head facing

Date	Mintage	F	VF	XF	Unc	BU
1993 Proof	5,000	Value: 375				

KM# 1183 500 FRANCS

155.5175 g., 0.9990 Gold 5.0000 oz. AGW **Series:** Bicentennial of the Louvre **Obv:** Victory

Date	Mintage	F	VF	XF	Unc	BU
1993 Proof	99	Value: 4,150				
1994 Proof	99	Value: 4,250				

KM# 1184 500 FRANCS

155.5175 g., 0.9990 Gold 5.0000 oz. AGW **Series:** Bicentennial of the Louvre **Obv:** Napoleon and Josephine

Date	Mintage	F	VF	XF	Unc	BU
1993 Proof	99	Value: 3,750				
1994 Proof	99	Value: 3,800				

KM# 1185 500 FRANCS

155.5175 g., 0.9990 Gold 5.0000 oz. AGW **Series:** Bicentennial of the Louvre **Obv:** Marie Marguerite

Date	Mintage	F	VF	XF	Unc	BU
1993 Proof	99	Value: 3,750				
1994 Proof	99	Value: 3,800				

KM# 1025.2 500 FRANCS

155.5000 g., 0.9990 Gold 4.9944 oz. AGW, 50 mm. **Obv:** Venus de Milo **Rev:** The Louvre Building entrance above value

Date	Mintage	F	VF	XF	Unc	BU
1993 Proof	99	Value: 3,500				

KM# 1399 500 FRANCS

155.5175 g., 0.9990 Gold 4.995 oz. AGW, 50 mm. **Subject:** Venus De Milo **Edge:** Plain

Date	Mintage	F	VF	XF	Unc	BU
1993A Proof	99	Value: 3,750				

KM# 1049 500 FRANCS

17.0000 g., 0.9200 Gold .5028 oz. AGW **Subject:** Winston Churchill **Obv:** Bust right, denomination and date **Rev:** Eleven line inscription on flag design, rampant lion at right

Date	Mintage	F	VF	XF	Unc	BU
1994 Proof	Est. 2,000	Value: 375				

KM# 1051 500 FRANCS

17.0000 g., 0.9200 Gold .5028 oz. AGW **Subject:** General Leclerc **Obv:** Bust facing

Date	Mintage	F	VF	XF	Unc	BU
1994 Proof	Est. 2,000	Value: 375				

KM# 1050 500 FRANCS

17.0000 g., 0.9200 Gold .5028 oz. AGW **Subject:** General de Gaulle **Obv:** 3/4 bust of General de Gaulle in front of microphone

Date	Mintage	F	VF	XF	Unc	BU
1994 Proof	Est. 5,000	Value: 375				

KM# 1052 500 FRANCS

17.0000 g., 0.9200 Gold .5028 oz. AGW **Subject:** General Marie Pierre Koenig **Obv:** Bust looking left

Date	Mintage	F	VF	XF	Unc	BU
1994 Proof	Est. 2,000	Value: 375				

KM# 1053 500 FRANCS

17.0000 g., 0.9200 Gold .5028 oz. AGW **Subject:** General Juin **Obv:** Bust right, map of Italy at right

Date	Mintage	F	VF	XF	Unc	BU
1994 Proof	Est. 2,000	Value: 375				

KM# 1054 500 FRANCS

17.0000 g., 0.9200 Gold .5028 oz. AGW **Subject:** Dwight David Eisenhower **Obv:** Uniformed bust left

Date	Mintage	F	VF	XF	Unc	BU
1994 Proof	Est. 2,000	Value: 375				

KM# 1055 500 FRANCS

17.0000 g., 0.9200 Gold .5028 oz. AGW **Rev:** Church of Sainte - Mere - Eglise, parachute behind

Date	Mintage	F	VF	XF	Unc	BU
1994 Proof	Est. 2,000	Value: 375				

KM# 1056 500 FRANCS

17.0000 g., 0.9200 Gold .5028 oz. AGW **Subject:** General de Lattre de Tassigny **Obv:** Head right

Date	Mintage	F	VF	XF	Unc	BU
1994 Proof	Est. 2,000	Value: 375				

KM# 1057 500 FRANCS

17.0000 g., 0.9200 Gold .5028 oz. AGW **Subject:** Liberation of Paris **Obv:** Triumphant troops marching down Champs Elysees

Date	Mintage	F	VF	XF	Unc	BU
1994 Proof	Est. 5,000	Value: 375				

KM# 1058 500 FRANCS

17.0000 g., 0.9200 Gold .5028 oz. AGW **Obv:** Heads of de Gaulle and Adenauer facing the center, date below

Date	Mintage	F	VF	XF	Unc	BU
1994 Proof	Est. 2,000	Value: 365				

KM# 1059 500 FRANCS

16.9700 g., 0.9170 Gold .5000 oz. AGW **Subject:** 1996 Olympics **Obv:** Head facing, date and denomination **Rev:** Archer in front of Eiffel Tower **Rev. Designer:** Joaquin Jimenez **Edge Lettering:** CITIUS ALTIUS FORTTUS

Date	Mintage	F	VF	XF	Unc	BU
1994 Proof	60,000	Value: 350				

KM# 1074 500 FRANCS
31.0350 g., 0.9990 Gold 1.0000 oz. AGW **Series:** Centennial of Cinema **Subject:** Lumiere Brothers **Obv:** Antique camera **Rev:** Conjoined busts right

Date	Mintage	F	VF	XF	Unc	BU
1994 Proof	3,000	Value: 900				

KM# 1078 500 FRANCS
31.0350 g., 0.9990 Gold 1.0000 oz. AGW **Series:** Centennial of Cinema **Subject:** Charlie Chaplan **Obv:** Antique movie camera **Rev:** Head facing

Date	Mintage	F	VF	XF	Unc	BU
1994 Proof	3,000	Value: 900				

KM# 1079 500 FRANCS
155.5175 g., 0.9990 Gold 5.0000 oz. AGW **Series:** Centennial of Cinema **Subject:** Charlie Chaplan **Obv:** Antique movie camera **Rev:** Head facing

Date	Mintage	F	VF	XF	Unc	BU
1994 Proof	99	Value: 3,750				

KM# 1186 500 FRANCS
17.0000 g., 0.9200 Gold .5028 oz. AGW **Series:** Centennial of Cinema **Rev:** Voltaire

Date	Mintage	F	VF	XF	Unc	BU
1994 Proof	350	Value: 385				

KM# 1082 500 FRANCS
31.0350 g., 0.9990 Gold 1.0000 oz. AGW **Series:** Centennial of Cinema **Subject:** Leon Gaumont **Obv:** Antique movie camera **Rev:** Head facing

Date	Mintage	F	VF	XF	Unc	BU
1995 Proof	3,000	Value: 900				

KM# 1083 500 FRANCS
155.5175 g., 0.9990 Gold 5.0000 oz. AGW **Series:** Centennial of Cinema **Subject:** Leon Gaumont **Obv:** Antique movie camera **Rev:** Head facing

Date	Mintage	F	VF	XF	Unc	BU
1995 Proof	99	Value: 3,500				

KM# 1086 500 FRANCS
31.0350 g., 0.9990 Gold 1.0000 oz. AGW **Series:** Centennial of Cinema **Subject:** Jean Renoir **Obv:** Antique movie camera **Rev:** Head 3/4 right

Date	Mintage	F	VF	XF	Unc	BU
1995 Proof	3,000	Value: 900				

KM# 1087 500 FRANCS
155.5175 g., 0.9990 Gold 5.0000 oz. AGW **Series:** Centennial of Cinema **Subject:** Jean Renoir **Obv:** Antique movie camera **Rev:** Head 3/4 right

Date	Mintage	F	VF	XF	Unc	BU
1995 Proof	99	Value: 3,750				

KM# 1090 500 FRANCS
31.0350 g., 0.9990 Gold 1.0000 oz. AGW **Series:** Centennial of Cinema **Subject:** Alfred Hitchcock **Obv:** Antique movie camera **Rev:** Bust 3/4 facing

Date	Mintage	F	VF	XF	Unc	BU
1995 Proof	3,000	Value: 900				

KM# 1091 500 FRANCS
155.5175 g., 0.9990 Gold 5.0000 oz. AGW **Series:** Centennial of Cinema **Subject:** Alfred Hitchcock **Obv:** Antique movie camera **Rev:** Bust 3/4 facing

Date	Mintage	F	VF	XF	Unc	BU
1995 Proof	99	Value: 3,500				

KM# 1094 500 FRANCS
31.0350 g., 0.9990 Gold 1.0000 oz. AGW **Series:** Centennial of Cinema **Subject:** Greta Garbo 1905-1990; actress in "Camille & Ninotchka" **Obv:** Antique movie camera **Rev:** Head with high collar right

Date	Mintage	F	VF	XF	Unc	BU
1995 Proof	3,000	Value: 900				

KM# 1095 500 FRANCS
155.5175 g., 0.9990 Gold 5.0000 oz. AGW **Series:** Centennial of Cinema **Subject:** Greta Garbo 1905-1990; actress in "Camille & Ninotchka" **Obv:** Antique movie camera **Rev:** Head with high collar right

Date	Mintage	F	VF	XF	Unc	BU
1995 Proof	99	Value: 3,750				

KM# 1098 500 FRANCS
31.0350 g., 0.9990 Gold 1.0000 oz. AGW **Series:** Centennial of Cinema **Subject:** Audrey Hepburn **Obv:** Antique movie camera **Rev:** Head 3/4 left

Date	Mintage	F	VF	XF	Unc	BU
1994 Proof	3,000	Value: 900				

KM# 1099 500 FRANCS
155.5175 g., 0.9990 Gold 5.0000 oz. AGW **Series:** Centennial of Cinema **Subject:** Audrey Hepburn **Obv:** Antique movie camera **Rev:** Head 3/4 left

Date	Mintage	F	VF	XF	Unc	BU
1994 Proof	99	Value: 3,500				

KM# 1102 500 FRANCS
31.0350 g., 0.9990 Gold 1.0000 oz. AGW **Series:** Centennial of Cinema **Subject:** Federico Fellini **Obv:** Antique movie camera **Rev:** Bust 3/4 right

Date	Mintage	F	VF	XF	Unc	BU
1995 Proof	3,000	Value: 900				

KM# 1103 500 FRANCS
155.5175 g., 0.9990 Gold 5.0000 oz. AGW **Series:** Centennial of Cinema **Subject:** Federico Fellini **Obv:** Antique movie camera **Rev:** Bust 3/4 right

Date	Mintage	F	VF	XF	Unc	BU
1995 Proof	99	Value: 3,500				

KM# 1106 500 FRANCS
31.0350 g., 0.9990 Gold 1.0000 oz. AGW **Series:** Centennial of Cinema **Subject:** Yves Montand **Obv:** Antique movie camera **Rev:** Bust 3/4 facing

Date	Mintage	F	VF	XF	Unc	BU
1994 Proof	3,000	Value: 900				

KM# 1107 500 FRANCS
155.5175 g., 0.9990 Gold 5.0000 oz. AGW **Series:** Centennial of Cinema **Subject:** Yves Montand **Obv:** Antique movie camera **Rev:** Bust 3/4 facing

Date	Mintage	F	VF	XF	Unc	BU
1994 Proof	99	Value: 3,500				

KM# 1110 500 FRANCS
31.0350 g., 0.9990 Gold 1.0000 oz. AGW **Series:** Centennial of Cinema **Subject:** Romy Schneider **Obv:** Antique movie camera **Rev:** Bust 3/4 left

Date	Mintage	F	VF	XF	Unc	BU
1995 Proof	3,000	Value: 900				

KM# 1111 500 FRANCS
155.5175 g., 0.9990 Gold 5.0000 oz. AGW **Series:** Centennial of Cinema **Subject:** Romy Schneider **Obv:** Antique movie camera **Rev:** Bust 3/4 left

Date	Mintage	F	VF	XF	Unc	BU
1995 Proof	99	Value: 3,450				

KM# 1117 500 FRANCS
17.0000 g., 0.9200 Gold .5028 oz. AGW **Subject:** V.E. Day **Obv:** Victory in Europe date May 8, 1945, denomination **Rev:** Birds in flight above banners, PAX below

Date	Mintage	F	VF	XF	Unc	BU
1995 Proof	5,000	Value: 375				

KM# 1135 500 FRANCS
17.0000 g., 0.9200 Gold .5028 oz. AGW **Obv:** Louis Pasteur

Date	Mintage	F	VF	XF	Unc	BU
1995 Proof	1,000	Value: 385				

KM# 1137 500 FRANCS
17.0000 g., 0.9200 Gold .5028 oz. AGW **Obv:** Jean de la Fountain

Date	Mintage	F	VF	XF	Unc	BU
1995 Proof	1,000	Value: 385				

KM# 1311 500 FRANCS
155.5000 g., 0.9990 Gold 4.9944 oz. AGW, 50 mm. **Series:** Centennial of Cinema **Subject:** Gerard Philipe **Obv:** Antique movie camera **Rev:** Bust 3/4 facing

Date	Mintage	F	VF	XF	Unc	BU
1995 Proof	99	Value: 3,500				

KM# 1312 500 FRANCS
155.5000 g., 0.9990 Gold 4.9944 oz. AGW, 50 mm. **Series:** Centennial of Cinema **Subject:** George Melies **Obv:** Antique movie camera **Rev:** Head facing

Date	Mintage	F	VF	XF	Unc	BU
1995 Proof	99	Value: 3,500				

KM# 1313 500 FRANCS
155.5000 g., 0.9990 Gold 4.9944 oz. AGW, 50 mm. **Series:** Centennial of Cinema **Subject:** Arletty **Obv:** Antique movie camera **Rev:** Head left

Date	Mintage	F	VF	XF	Unc	BU
1995 Proof	99	Value: 3,500				

KM# 1314 500 FRANCS
155.5000 g., 0.9990 Gold 4.9944 oz. AGW, 50 mm. **Series:** Centennial of Cinema **Subject:** Marcel Pagnol **Obv:** Antique movie camera **Rev:** Head 3/4 left

Date	Mintage	F	VF	XF	Unc	BU
1995 Proof	—	Value: 3,500				

KM# 1139 500 FRANCS
17.0000 g., 0.9200 Gold .5028 oz. AGW **Subject:** 300th Anniversary - Death of Marie de Sevigne; letter writer, 1626-1696 **Obv:** Bust 1/2 left

Date	Mintage	F	VF	XF	Unc	BU
1996 Proof	500	Value: 675				

KM# 1181 500 FRANCS
17.0000 g., 0.9200 Gold .5028 oz. AGW **Subject:** King Clovis I **Obv:** Bust facing

Date	Mintage	F	VF	XF	Unc	BU
1996 Proof	250	Value: 700				

KM# 1197 500 FRANCS
17.0000 g., 0.9200 Gold .5028 oz. AGW **Subject:** Georges Guynemer **Obv:** Bust 3/4 facing **Rev:** Stork emblem and denomination

Date	Mintage	F	VF	XF	Unc	BU
1997 Proof	300	Value: 600				

KM# 1199 500 FRANCS
17.0000 g., 0.9200 Gold .5028 oz. AGW **Subject:** Pierre and Marie Curie 1867-1934, physicist - chemist **Obv:** Conjoined busts left **Rev:** Denomination

Date	Mintage	F	VF	XF	Unc	BU
1997 Proof	300	Value: 600				

KM# 1200 500 FRANCS
17.0000 g., 0.9200 Gold .5028 oz. AGW **Subject:** Andre Malraux **Obv:** Head facing **Rev:** Cats flanking denomination

Date	Mintage	F	VF	XF	Unc	BU
1997 Proof	300	Value: 600				

KM# 1202 500 FRANCS
17.0000 g., 0.9200 Gold .5028 oz. AGW **Subject:** Marquis de Condorcet **Obv:** Head right **Rev:** Denomination

Date	Mintage	F	VF	XF	Unc	BU
1998 Proof	300	Value: 600				

KM# 1204 500 FRANCS
17.0000 g., 0.9200 Gold .5028 oz. AGW **Subject:** Gaspard Monge **Obv:** Head 1/2 right **Rev:** Denomination

Date	Mintage	F	VF	XF	Unc	BU
1998 Proof	300	Value: 600				

KM# 1237 500 FRANCS
31.1040 g., 0.9990 Gold .9990 oz. AGW **Subject:** Yves St. Laurent **Obv:** RF monogram within entwined snake design divides denomination and date **Rev:** Fashion show scene **Edge:** Plain

Date	Mintage	F	VF	XF	Unc	BU
2000 Proof	1,000	Value: 850				

KM# 1315 500 FRANCS - 75 EURO
155.5000 g., 0.9990 Gold 4.9944 oz. AGW, 50 mm. **Subject:** "The Thinker" by Auguste Rodin **Obv:** Seated statue left **Rev:** Denominations-(francs and euros)

Date	Mintage	F	VF	XF	Unc	BU
1996 Proof	99	Value: 3,500				

KM# 1316 500 FRANCS - 75 EURO
155.5000 g., 0.9990 Gold 4.9944 oz. AGW, 50 mm. **Subject:** Chinese Horseman **Obv:** Equestrian statue **Rev:** Denominations-(francs and euros)

Date	Mintage	F	VF	XF	Unc	BU
1996 Proof	99	Value: 3,500				

KM# 1317 500 FRANCS - 75 EURO
155.5000 g., 0.9990 Gold 4.9944 oz. AGW, 50 mm. **Subject:** Klimt's "The Kiss" **Obv:** Two figures embraced **Rev:** Denominations-(francs and euros)

Date	Mintage	F	VF	XF	Unc	BU
1997 Proof	—	Value: 3,500				

KM# 1318 500 FRANCS - 75 EURO
155.5000 g., 0.9990 Gold 4.9944 oz. AGW, 50 mm. **Subject:** Durer's Self Portrait **Obv:** Bust facing **Rev:** Denominations-(francs and euros)

Date	Mintage	F	VF	XF	Unc	BU
1997 Proof	99	Value: 3,500				

KM# 1319 500 FRANCS - 75 EURO
155.5000 g., 0.9990 Gold 4.9944 oz. AGW, 50 mm. **Obv:** Japanese woman carrying a case **Rev:** Denominations-(francs and euros)

Date	Mintage	F	VF	XF	Unc	BU
1997 Proof	99	Value: 3,500				

KM# 1320 500 FRANCS - 75 EURO
155.5000 g., 0.9990 Gold 4.9944 oz. AGW, 50 mm. **Subject:** "The Little Dancer" by Degas **Obv:** Figure in tutu left **Rev:** Denominations-(francs and euros)

Date	Mintage	F	VF	XF	Unc	BU
1997 Proof	99	Value: 3,500				

KM# 1257 655.957 FRANCS
31.1040 g., 0.9990 Gold .9990 oz. AGW **Series:** Euro conversion **Obv:** Country names with euro-currency equivalents around "RF", denomination and French coin designs **Rev:** Europa allegorical portrait **Edge:** Plain

Date	Mintage	F	VF	XF	Unc	BU
1999 Proof	2,000	Value: 775				

KM# 1261 655.957 FRANCS
31.1040 g., 0.9990 Gold .9990 oz. AGW **Obv:** Country names with euro-currency equivalents around "RF", denomination and French euro coin design

Date	Mintage	F	VF	XF	Unc	BU
2000 Proof	2,000	Value: 775				

KM# 1247 655.957 FRANCS
15.5520 g., 0.9990 Gold .4995 oz. AGW **Series:** European Art Styles - Renaissance **Obv:** Europe allegorical portrait **Rev:** Greek and Roman style buildings

Date	Mintage	F	VF	XF	Unc	BU
2000 Proof	2,000	Value: 485				

KM# 1248 655.957 FRANCS
15.5520 g., 0.9990 Gold .4995 oz. AGW **Series:** European Art Styles - Roman **Rev:** Roman sculpture and ancient buildings

Date	Mintage	F	VF	XF	Unc	BU
2000 Proof	2,000	Value: 485				

KM# 1249 655.957 FRANCS
15.5520 g., 0.9990 Gold .4995 oz. AGW **Series:** European Art Styles - Gothic **Rev:** Gothic sculpture and buildings

Date	Mintage	F	VF	XF	Unc	BU
2000 Proof	2,000	Value: 485				

KM# 1250 655.957 FRANCS
15.5520 g., 0.9990 Gold .4995 oz. AGW **Series:** European Art Styles - Renaissance **Rev:** Renaissance buildings

Date	Mintage	F	VF	XF	Unc	BU
2000 Proof	2,000	Value: 485				

KM# 1251 655.957 FRANCS
15.5520 g., 0.9990 Gold .4995 oz. AGW **Series:** European Art Styles - Classic and Baroque **Rev:** Classic and Baroque art

Date	Mintage	F	VF	XF	Unc	BU
2000 Proof	2,000	Value: 485				

KM# 1252 655.957 FRANCS
15.5520 g., 0.9990 Gold .4995 oz. AGW **Series:** European Art Styles - Art Nouveau **Rev:** Arches and scrollwork

Date	Mintage	F	VF	XF	Unc	BU
2000 Proof	2,000	Value: 485				

KM# 1253 655.957 FRANCS
15.5520 g., 0.9990 Gold .4995 oz. AGW **Series:** European Art Styles - Modern **Rev:** Modern artistic designs

Date	Mintage	F	VF	XF	Unc	BU
2000 Proof	2,000	Value: 485				

ECU / FRANCS COINAGE

European Currency Units

KM# 989 100 FRANCS - 15 ECUS
22.2000 g., 0.9000 Silver .6424 oz. ASW **Obv:** Center monogram divides date and denomination, laurel spray below **Rev:** Stylized head facing, denomination below

Date	Mintage	F	VF	XF	Unc	BU
1990 Proof	30,000	Value: 95.00				

KM# 1002 100 FRANCS - 15 ECUS
22.2000 g., 0.9000 Silver .6424 oz. ASW **Subject:** Descartes **Obv:** Finger pointing to starred paper, denomination below **Rev:** Head 3/4 facing, denomination and date below

Date	Mintage	F	VF	XF	Unc	BU
1991 Proof	20,000	Value: 65.00				

KM# 1012 100 FRANCS - 15 ECUS
22.2000 g., 0.9000 Silver .6424 oz. ASW **Subject:** Jean Monet **Obv:** Denomination in center within legend and chain above RF **Rev:** Head left, denomination at right

Date	Mintage	F	VF	XF	Unc	BU
1992 Proof	30,000	Value: 55.00				

KM# 1029 100 FRANCS - 15 ECUS
22.2000 g., 0.9000 Silver .6424 oz. ASW **Subject:** Mediterranean Games **Obv:** Head left, denomination below **Rev:** Swimming, denomination below, rings divide date below

Date	Mintage	F	VF	XF	Unc	BU
1993 Proof	15,000	Value: 47.50				

KM# 1030 100 FRANCS - 15 ECUS
22.2000 g., 0.9000 Silver .6424 oz. ASW **Subject:** Mediterranean Games **Obv:** Head left, denomination below **Rev:** Soccer, denomination below, rings divide date below

Date	Mintage	F	VF	XF	Unc	BU
1993 Proof	15,000	Value: 47.50				

KM# 1031 100 FRANCS - 15 ECUS
22.2000 g., 0.9000 Silver .6424 oz. ASW **Rev:** Arc de Triumph

Date	Mintage	F	VF	XF	Unc	BU
1993 Proof	20,000	Value: 42.50				

KM# 1032 100 FRANCS - 15 ECUS
22.2000 g., 0.9000 Silver .6424 oz. ASW **Rev:** Brandenburg Gate

Date	Mintage	F	VF	XF	Unc	BU
1993 Proof	20,000	Value: 42.50				

KM# 1060 100 FRANCS - 15 ECUS
22.2000 g., 0.9000 Silver .6424 oz. ASW **Rev:** Stylized Tunnel View - Map

Date	Mintage	F	VF	XF	Unc	BU
1994 Proof	20,000	Value: 32.50				

KM# 1068 100 FRANCS - 15 ECUS
22.2000 g., 0.9000 Silver .6424 oz. ASW **Obv:** Denominations-(francs/ecus) **Rev:** St. Mark's Cathedral, Venice

Date	Mintage	F	VF	XF	Unc	BU
1994 Proof	20,000	Value: 32.50				

KM# 1070 100 FRANCS - 15 ECUS
22.2000 g., 0.9000 Silver .6424 oz. ASW **Obv:** Stars surround denominations, (francs/euros) **Rev:** Big Ben, London, date below

Date	Mintage	F	VF	XF	Unc	BU
1994 Proof	20,000	Value: 32.50				

KM# 1112 100 FRANCS - 15 ECUS
22.2000 g., 0.9000 Silver .6424 oz. ASW **Rev:** The Alhambra, Granada, date below

Date	Mintage	F	VF	XF	Unc	BU
1995 Proof	20,000	Value: 35.00				

KM# 1114 100 FRANCS - 15 ECUS
22.2000 g., 0.9000 Silver .6424 oz. ASW **Rev:** The Parthenon, Greece, date below

Date	Mintage	F	VF	XF	Unc	BU
1995 Proof	20,000	Value: 35.00				

KM# 990 500 FRANCS - 70 ECUS
17.0000 g., 0.9200 Gold .5029 oz. AGW **Obv:** Center monogram divides date and denomination, laurel spray below **Rev:** Stylized head facing above denomination

Date	Mintage	F	VF	XF	Unc	BU
1990 Proof	5,000	Value: 385				

KM# 990a 500 FRANCS - 70 ECUS
20.0000 g., 0.9990 Platinum .6431 oz. APW **Obv:** Monogram divides denomination and date, spray below **Rev:** Stylized head facing, denomintion below

Date	Mintage	F	VF	XF	Unc	BU
1990 Proof	2,000	Value: 825				

KM# 1003a 500 FRANCS - 70 ECUS
20.0000 g., 0.9990 Platinum .6431 oz. APW **Subject:** Descartes **Obv:** Finger pointing to page with stars, denomination **Rev:** Head 3/4 facing

Date	Mintage	F	VF	XF	Unc	BU
1991 Proof	1,000	Value: 825				

KM# 1003 500 FRANCS - 70 ECUS
17.0000 g., 0.9200 Gold .5029 oz. AGW **Subject:** Descartes **Obv:** Finger pointing to page with stars **Rev:** Head 3/4 facing

Date	Mintage	F	VF	XF	Unc	BU
1991 Proof	3,000	Value: 425				

KM# 1013 500 FRANCS - 70 ECUS
17.0000 g., 0.9200 Gold .5029 oz. AGW **Subject:** Jean Monet **Obv:** Denomination and date within legend at center, chain surrounds, RF below **Rev:** Head left, denomination at right

Date	Mintage	F	VF	XF	Unc	BU
1992 Proof	5,000	Value: 400				

KM# 1013a 500 FRANCS - 70 ECUS
20.0000 g., 0.9990 Platinum .6431 oz. APW **Subject:** Jean Monet **Obv:** Denomination and date within legend at center, chain surrounds, RF below **Rev:** Head 3/4 left

Date	Mintage	F	VF	XF	Unc	BU
1992 Proof	2,000	Value: 825				

KM# 1033 500 FRANCS - 70 ECUS
17.0000 g., 0.9200 Gold .5029 oz. AGW **Subject:** Mediterranean Games **Obv:** Head left, denomination below **Rev:** Statue divides denomination above, rings divide date below

Date	Mintage	F	VF	XF	Unc	BU
1993 Proof	3,000	Value: 425				

KM# 1034 500 FRANCS - 70 ECUS
17.0000 g., 0.9200 Gold .5029 oz. AGW **Obv:** Denominations-(francs/ecus) **Rev:** Arc de Triumph, date below

Date	Mintage	F	VF	XF	Unc	BU
1993 Proof	5,000	Value: 385				

KM# 1034a 500 FRANCS - 70 ECUS
19.8000 g., 0.9900 Platinum .6303 oz. APW **Obv:** Denominations-(francs/ecus) **Rev:** Arc de Triumph

Date	Mintage	F	VF	XF	Unc	BU
1993 Proof	2,000	Value: 800				

KM# 1035 500 FRANCS - 70 ECUS
17.0000 g., 0.9200 Gold .5029 oz. AGW **Obv:** Denominations-(francs/ecus) **Rev:** Brandenburg Gate, date above

Date	Mintage	F	VF	XF	Unc	BU
1993 Proof	5,000	Value: 385				

KM# 1035a 500 FRANCS - 70 ECUS
19.8000 g., 0.9900 Platinum .6303 oz. APW **Obv:** Denominations-(francs/ecus) **Rev:** Brandenburg Gate

Date	Mintage	F	VF	XF	Unc	BU
1993 Proof	2,000	Value: 800				

KM# 1061 500 FRANCS - 70 ECUS
17.0000 g., 0.9200 Gold .5029 oz. AGW **Obv:** Stars surround denominations, (francs/euros) **Rev:** Channel Tunnel

Date	Mintage	F	VF	XF	Unc	BU
1994 Proof	5,000	Value: 375				

KM# 1069 500 FRANCS - 70 ECUS
17.0000 g., 0.9200 Gold .5028 oz. AGW **Obv:** Stars surround denominations, (francs/euros) **Rev:** St. Mark's Cathedral, Venice, date below

Date	Mintage	F	VF	XF	Unc	BU
1994 Proof	5,000	Value: 385				

KM# 1069a 500 FRANCS - 70 ECUS
20.0000 g., 0.9990 Platinum .6431 oz. APW **Obv:** Stars surround denominations, (francs/euros) **Rev:** St. Mark's Cathedral, Venice

Date	Mintage	F	VF	XF	Unc	BU
1994 Proof	2,000	Value: 825				

KM# 1071 500 FRANCS - 70 ECUS
17.0000 g., 0.9200 Gold .5028 oz. AGW **Obv:** Stars surround denominations, (francs/euros) **Rev:** Big Ben, London, date below

Date	Mintage	F	VF	XF	Unc	BU
1994 Proof	5,000	Value: 385				

KM# 1071a 500 FRANCS - 70 ECUS
20.0000 g., 0.9990 Platinum .6431 oz. APW **Obv:** Stars surround denominations, (francs/euros) **Rev:** Big Ben, London

Date	Mintage	F	VF	XF	Unc	BU
1994 Proof	2,000	Value: 825				

KM# 1113 500 FRANCS - 70 ECUS
17.0000 g., 0.9200 Gold .5028 oz. AGW **Obv:** Stars surround denominations, (francs/euros) **Rev:** The Alhambra, Granada

Date	Mintage	F	VF	XF	Unc	BU
1995 Proof	5,000	Value: 385				

KM# 1113a 500 FRANCS - 70 ECUS
20.0000 g., 0.9990 Platinum .6431 oz. APW **Obv:** Stars surround denominations, (francs/euros) **Rev:** The Alhambra, Granada

Date	Mintage	F	VF	XF	Unc	BU
1995 Proof	2,000	Value: 825				

KM# 1115 500 FRANCS - 70 ECUS
17.0000 g., 0.9200 Gold .5028 oz. AGW **Obv:** Stars surround denominations, (francs/euros) **Rev:** The Parthenon, Athens

Date	Mintage	F	VF	XF	Unc	BU
1995 Proof	5,000	Value: 385				

KM# 1115a 500 FRANCS - 70 ECUS
20.0000 g., 0.9990 Platinum .6431 oz. APW **Obv:** Stars surround denominations, (francs/euros) **Rev:** The Parthenon, Athens

Date	Mintage	F	VF	XF	Unc	BU
1995 Proof	2,000	Value: 825				

EURO / FRANCS COINAGE

KM# 1121 10 FRANCS - 1.5 EURO
22.2000 g., 0.9000 Silver .6424 oz. ASW **Series:** Museum Treasures **Subject:** La Source by Raphael Jean A.D. Ingres **Obv:** Standing nude facing, RF and date at left **Rev:** Denominations, (francs/euros), on lined field, stars surround

Date	Mintage	F	VF	XF	Unc	BU
1996 Proof	15,000	Value: 37.50				

KM# 1122 10 FRANCS - 1.5 EURO
22.2000 g., 0.9000 Silver .6424 oz. ASW **Series:** Museum Treasures **Subject:** Fife player by Edouard Manet **Obv:** Standing figure facing, RF and date at left **Rev:** Denominations, (francs/euros), on lined field, stars surround

Date	Mintage	F	VF	XF	Unc	BU
1996 Proof	15,000	Value: 35.00				

KM# 1123 10 FRANCS - 1.5 EURO
22.2000 g., 0.9000 Silver .6424 oz. ASW **Series:** Museum Treasures **Subject:** Shang Dynasty Elephant **Obv:** Elephant left, RF and date at left **Rev:** Denominations, (francs/euros), on lined field, stars surround

Date	Mintage	F	VF	XF	Unc	BU
1996 Proof	15,000	Value: 35.00				

KM# 1146 10 FRANCS - 1.5 EURO
22.2000 g., 0.9000 Silver .6424 oz. ASW **Series:** Museum Treasures **Subject:** David by Michaelangelo **Obv:** Standing nude facing, RF and date at right **Rev:** Denominations, (francs/euros), on lined field, stars surround

Date	Mintage	F	VF	XF	Unc	BU
1996 Proof	15,000	Value: 32.50				

KM# 1147 10 FRANCS - 1.5 EURO
22.2000 g., 0.9000 Silver .6424 oz. ASW **Series:** Museum Treasures **Subject:** Vincent Van Gogh, self portrait **Obv:** Bust 3/4 left, RF and date at left **Rev:** Denominations, (francs/euros), on lined field, stars surround

Date	Mintage	F	VF	XF	Unc	BU
1996 Proof	15,000	Value: 35.00				

KM# 1148 10 FRANCS - 1.5 EURO
22.2000 g., 0.9000 Silver .6424 oz. ASW **Series:** Museum Treasures **Subject:** Clothed Maya by Goya **Obv:** Reclining figure, RF and date at left **Rev:** Denominations, (francs/euros), on lined field, stars surround

Date	Mintage	F	VF	XF	Unc	BU
1996 Proof	15,000	Value: 32.50				

KM# 1158 10 FRANCS - 1.5 EURO
22.2000 g., 0.9000 Silver .6424 oz. ASW **Series:** Museum Treasures **Subject:** Chinese Horseman **Obv:** Equestrian statue right, RF and date at right **Rev:** Denominations, (francs/euros), on lined field, stars surround

Date	Mintage	F	VF	XF	Unc	BU
1996 Proof	15,000	Value: 32.50				

KM# 1124 10 FRANCS - 1.5 EURO
22.2000 g., 0.9000 Silver .6424 oz. ASW **Series:** Museum Treasures **Subject:** "The Thinker" by Auguste Rodin **Obv:** Seated statue left, RF and date at left **Rev:** Denominations, (francs/euros), on lined field, stars surround **Note:** Silver coins sold as a set only.

Date	Mintage	F	VF	XF	Unc	BU
1996 Proof	15,000	Value: 35.00				

KM# 1292 10 FRANCS - 1.5 EURO
22.2200 g., 0.9000 Silver 0.643 oz. ASW, 36.9 mm. **Subject:** Museum Treasures **Obv:** Figure wearing tutu left, RF and date at right **Rev:** Denominations, (francs/euros), on lined field, stars surround **Edge:** Plain

Date	Mintage	F	VF	XF	Unc	BU
1997 Proof	15,000	Value: 35.00				

KM# 1297 10 FRANCS - 1.5 EURO
22.2200 g., 0.9000 Silver 0.643 oz. ASW **Series:** Museum Treasures **Obv:** Japanese woman carrying a glass box **Rev:** Denominations, (francs/euros), on lined field, stars surround

Date	Mintage	F	VF	XF	Unc	BU
1997 Proof	15,000	Value: 30.00				

KM# 1298 10 FRANCS - 1.5 EURO
22.2200 g., 0.9000 Silver 0.643 oz. ASW **Series:** Museum Treasures **Subject:** Durer's "Self Portrait" **Obv:** Bust facing **Rev:** Denominations, (francs/euros), on lined field, stars surround

Date	Mintage	F	VF	XF	Unc	BU
1997 Proof	15,000	Value: 30.00				

KM# 1299 10 FRANCS - 1.5 EURO
22.2200 g., 0.9000 Silver 0.643 oz. ASW **Series:** Museum Treasures **Subject:** Klimt's "The Kiss" **Obv:** Two figures embraced **Rev:** Denominations, (francs/euros), on lined field, stars surround

Date	Mintage	F	VF	XF	Unc	BU
1997 Proof	15,000	Value: 32.50				

KM# 1140 100 FRANCS - 15 EURO
22.2000 g., 0.9000 Silver .6424 oz. ASW **Obv:** Stars surround denominations, (francs/euros) **Rev:** St. Stephen's Cathedral, Vienna, date at right

Date	Mintage	F	VF	XF	Unc	BU
1996 Proof	20,000	Value: 50.00				

KM# 1125 100 FRANCS - 15 EURO
17.0000 g., 0.9200 Gold .5028 oz. AGW **Series:** Museum Treasures **Subject:** La Source by Raphael Jean A.D. Ingres **Obv:** Standing nude facing **Rev:** Denominations, (francs/euros), on lined field, stars surround

Date	Mintage	F	VF	XF	Unc	BU
1996 Proof	5,000	Value: 395				

KM# 1126 100 FRANCS - 15 EURO
17.0000 g., 0.9200 Gold .5028 oz. AGW **Series:** Museum Treasures **Subject:** Fife Player by Edouard Manet **Obv:** Standing figure facing **Rev:** Denominations, (francs/euros), on lined field, stars surround

Date	Mintage	F	VF	XF	Unc	BU
1996 Proof	5,000	Value: 385				

KM# 1127 100 FRANCS - 15 EURO
17.0000 g., 0.9200 Gold .5028 oz. AGW **Series:** Museum Treasures **Subject:** Shang Dynasty Elephant **Obv:** Elephant left **Rev:** Denominations, (francs/euros), on lined field, stars surround

Date	Mintage	F	VF	XF	Unc	BU
1996 Proof	5,000	Value: 385				

KM# 1142 100 FRANCS - 15 EURO
22.2000 g., 0.9000 Silver .6424 oz. ASW **Obv:** Stars surround denominations, (francs/euros) **Rev:** Grand Place, Bruxelles, date below

Date	Mintage	F	VF	XF	Unc	BU
1996 Proof	20,000	Value: 37.50				

KM# 1149 100 FRANCS - 15 EURO
17.0000 g., 0.9200 Gold .5028 oz. AGW **Series:** Museum Treasures **Subject:** Van Gogh, Self Portrait **Obv:** Bust 3/4 left **Rev:** Denominations, (francs/euros), on lined field, stars surround

Date	Mintage	F	VF	XF	Unc	BU
1996 Proof	5,000	Value: 385				

KM# 1150 100 FRANCS - 15 EURO
17.0000 g., 0.9200 Gold .5028 oz. AGW **Series:** Museum Treasures **Subject:** Clothed Maya by Goya **Obv:** Reclined figure **Rev:** Stars surround denominations, (francs/euros), on lined field

Date	Mintage	F	VF	XF	Unc	BU
1996 Proof	5,000	Value: 385				

KM# 1156 100 FRANCS - 15 EURO
22.2000 g., 0.9000 Silver .6424 oz. ASW **Subject:** Amsterdam - Magere Brug **Obv:** Denominations, (francs/euros), on field of stars **Rev:** Bridge, date below

Date	Mintage	F	VF	XF	Unc	BU
1996 Proof	20,000	Value: 37.50				

KM# 1159 100 FRANCS - 15 EURO
17.0000 g., 0.9200 Gold .5028 oz. AGW **Series:** Museum Treasures **Subject:** Chinese Horseman **Obv:** Equestrian statue **Rev:** Stars surround denominations, (francs/euros), on lined field

Date	Mintage	F	VF	XF	Unc	BU
1996 Proof	5,000	Value: 385				

KM# 1174 100 FRANCS - 15 EURO
22.2000 g., 0.9000 Silver .6424 oz. ASW **Subject:** Lisbon **Obv:** Denominations-(francs/ecus), on field of stars **Rev:** Castle-like building Tour de Belem, date below

Date	Mintage	F	VF	XF	Unc	BU
1997 Proof	20,000	Value: 50.00				

KM# 1176 100 FRANCS - 15 EURO
22.2000 g., 0.9000 Silver .6424 oz. ASW **Subject:** Helsinki **Obv:** Denominations-(francs/ecus) **Rev:** Cathedral, Cathedrale Saint - Nicolas, date below

Date	Mintage	F	VF	XF	Unc	BU
1997 Proof	20,000	Value: 50.00				

KM# 1178 100 FRANCS - 15 EURO
22.2000 g., 0.9000 Silver .6424 oz. ASW **Subject:** Copenhagen **Obv:** Denominations-(francs/ecus) **Rev:** Statue of the Copenhagen mermaid, Petite Sirene, date at right

Date	Mintage	F	VF	XF	Unc	BU
1997 Proof	20,000	Value: 55.00				

KM# 1189 100 FRANCS - 15 EURO
22.2000 g., 0.9000 Silver .6424 oz. ASW **Subject:** Irlande - Rock of Cashel **Obv:** Denomination **Rev:** Celtic cross and castle, date below

Date	Mintage	F	VF	XF	Unc	BU
1997 Proof	20,000	Value: 50.00				

KM# 1191 100 FRANCS - 15 EURO
22.2000 g., 0.9000 Silver .6424 oz. ASW **Subject:** Luxembourg - Wenceslaus Wall **Obv:** Denomination **Rev:** Walled palace, date above

Date	Mintage	F	VF	XF	Unc	BU
1997 Proof	20,000	Value: 50.00				

KM# 1193 100 FRANCS - 15 EURO
22.2000 g., 0.9000 Silver .6424 oz. ASW **Subject:** Stockholm - Hotel de Ville **Obv:** Denomination **Rev:** Tower and building, date at right

Date	Mintage	F	VF	XF	Unc	BU
1997 Proof	20,000	Value: 50.00				

KM# 1141a 500 FRANCS - 75 EURO
20.0000 g., 0.9990 Platinum .6431 oz. APW **Subject:** St. Stephen's Cathedral, Vienna **Obv:** Denominations-(francs/ecus) **Rev:** Cathedral

Date	Mintage	F	VF	XF	Unc	BU
1996 Prof	2,000	Value: 825				

KM# 1143a 500 FRANCS - 75 EURO
20.0000 g., 0.9990 Platinum .6431 oz. APW **Subject:** Grand Place, Bruxelles **Obv:** Denominations-(francs/ecus) **Rev:** Buildings with tower

Date	Mintage	F	VF	XF	Unc	BU
1996 Proof	2,000	Value: 825				

KM# 1157a 500 FRANCS - 75 EURO
20.0000 g., 0.9990 Platinum .6431 oz. APW **Subject:** Amsterdam Magere Brug

Date	Mintage	F	VF	XF	Unc	BU
1996 Proof	2,000	Value: 825				

KM# 1128 500 FRANCS - 75 EURO
31.1035 g., 0.9990 Gold 1.0000 oz. AGW **Series:** Museum Treasures **Subject:** "The Thinker", by Auguste Rodin **Obv:** Seated statue left **Rev:** Stars surround denominations, (francs/euros), on lined field

Date	Mintage	F	VF	XF	Unc	BU
1996 Proof	5,000	Value: 725				

KM# 1129 500 FRANCS - 75 EURO
155.5175 g., 0.9990 Gold 5.0000 oz. AGW **Series:** Museum Treasures **Subject:** La Source by Raphael Jean A.D. Ingres **Obv:** Standing nude facing **Rev:** Stars surround denominations, (francs/euros), on lined field

Date	Mintage	F	VF	XF	Unc	BU
1996 Prof	99	Value: 3,500				

KM# 1130 500 FRANCS - 75 EURO
155.5175 g., 0.9990 Gold 5.0000 oz. AGW **Series:** Museum Treasures **Subject:** Fife Player by Edouard Manet **Obv:** Standing figure facing **Rev:** Stars surround denominations, (francs/euros), on lined field

Date	Mintage	F	VF	XF	Unc	BU
1996 Proof	99	Value: 3,500				

KM# 1131 500 FRANCS - 75 EURO
155.5175 g., 0.9990 Gold 5.0000 oz. AGW **Series:** Museum Treasures **Subject:** Shang Dynasty Elephant **Obv:** Elephant left **Rev:** Stars surround denominations, (francs/euros), on lined field

Date	Mintage	F	VF	XF	Unc	BU
1996 Proof	99	Value: 3,500				

KM# 1141 500 FRANCS - 75 EURO
17.0000 g., 0.9200 Gold .5028 oz. AGW **Subject:** St. Stephen's Cathedral, Vienna **Obv:** Denominations, (francs/euro), on field of stars **Rev:** Cathedral, date at right

Date	Mintage	F	VF	XF	Unc	BU
1996 Proof	5,000	Value: 385				

KM# 1143 500 FRANCS - 75 EURO
17.0000 g., 0.9200 Gold .5028 oz. AGW **Subject:** Grand Place, Bruxelles **Obv:** Denominations-(francs/ecus) **Rev:** Buildings with tower, date below

Date	Mintage	F	VF	XF	Unc	BU
1996 Proof	5,000	Value: 385				

KM# 1151 500 FRANCS - 75 EURO
31.1035 g., 0.9990 Gold 1.0000 oz. AGW **Series:** Museum Treasures **Subject:** David by Michaelangelo **Obv:** Standing nude **Rev:** Denominations, (francs/euros), on lined field, stars surround

Date	Mintage	F	VF	XF	Unc	BU
1996 Proof	5,000	Value: 725				

KM# 1152 500 FRANCS - 75 EURO
155.5175 g., 0.9990 Gold 5.0000 oz. AGW **Series:** Museum Treasures **Subject:** David by Michaelangelo **Obv:** Standing nude **Rev:** Denominations-(francs/ecus), on lined field, stars surround

Date	Mintage	F	VF	XF	Unc	BU
1996 Proof	99	Value: 3,500				

KM# 1153 500 FRANCS - 75 EURO
155.5175 g., 0.9990 Gold 5.0000 oz. AGW **Series:** Museum Treasures **Subject:** Vincent Van Gogh, Self Portrait **Obv:** Bust 3/4 left, RF and date at left **Rev:** Denominations-(francs/ecus), on lined field, stars surround

Date	Mintage	F	VF	XF	Unc	BU
1996 Proof	99	Value: 3,500				

KM# 1154 500 FRANCS - 75 EURO
155.5175 g., 0.9990 Gold 5.0000 oz. AGW **Series:** Museum Treasures **Subject:** Clothed Maya by Goya **Obv:** Reclined figure, RF and date at left **Rev:** Denominations-(francs/ecus), on lined field, stars surround

Date	Mintage	F	VF	XF	Unc	BU
1996 Proof	99	Value: 3,500				

KM# 1157 500 FRANCS - 75 EURO
17.0000 g., 0.9200 Gold .5028 oz. AGW **Subject:** Amsterdam Magere Brug

Date	Mintage	F	VF	XF	Unc	BU
1996 Proof	5,000	Value: 385				

KM# 1175 500 FRANCS - 75 EURO
17.0000 g., 0.9200 Gold .5028 oz. AGW **Subject:** Lisbon **Obv:** Denominations **Rev:** Castle-like building Tour de Belem, date below

Date	Mintage	F	VF	XF	Unc	BU
1997 Proof	5,000	Value: 395				

KM# 1175a 500 FRANCS - 75 EURO
20.0000 g., 0.9990 Platinum .6431 oz. APW **Subject:** Lisbon **Obv:** Denominations **Rev:** Castle-like building Tour de Belem

Date	Mintage	F	VF	XF	Unc	BU
1997 Proof	2,000	Value: 825				

KM# 1179a 500 FRANCS - 75 EURO
20.0000 g., 0.9990 Platinum .6431 oz. APW **Subject:** Copenhagen **Obv:** Denominations **Rev:** Statue of Copenhagen's Little Mermaid, Petite Siren

Date	Mintage	F	VF	XF	Unc	BU
1997 Proof	2,000	Value: 845				

KM# 1190a 500 FRANCS - 75 EURO
20.0000 g., 0.9990 Platinum .6431 oz. APW **Subject:** Ireland - Rock of Cashel **Obv:** Denomination **Rev:** Celtic cross and castle

Date	Mintage	F	VF	XF	Unc	BU
1997 Proof	2,000	Value: 825				

KM# 1192a 500 FRANCS - 75 EURO
20.0000 g., 0.9990 Platinum .6431 oz. APW **Subject:** Luxembourg - Wenceslas Wall **Obv:** Denomination **Rev:** Walled palace

Date	Mintage	F	VF	XF	Unc	BU
1997 Proof	2,000	Value: 825				

KM# 1179 500 FRANCS - 75 EURO
17.0000 g., 0.9200 Gold .5028 oz. AGW **Subject:** Copenhagen **Obv:** Denominations, (francs/euros), on field of stars **Rev:** Statue of Copenhagen's Little Mermaid, Petite Siren, date at right

Date	Mintage	F	VF	XF	Unc	BU
1997 Proof	5,000	Value: 500				

KM# 1190 500 FRANCS - 75 EURO
17.0000 g., 0.9200 Gold .5028 oz. AGW **Subject:** Ireland - Rock of Cashel **Obv:** Denomination **Rev:** Celtic cross and castle

Date	Mintage	F	VF	XF	Unc	BU
1997 Proof	5,000	Value: 450				

KM# 1192 500 FRANCS - 75 EURO
17.0000 g., 0.9200 Gold .5028 oz. AGW **Subject:** Luxembourg - Wenceslas Wall **Obv:** Denomination **Rev:** Walled palace

Date	Mintage	F	VF	XF	Unc	BU
1997 Proof	5,000	Value: 450				

KM# 1194 500 FRANCS - 75 EURO
17.0000 g., 0.9990 Gold .5028 oz. AGW **Subject:** Stockholm - Hotel de Ville **Obv:** Denomination **Rev:** Tower and building

Date	Mintage	F	VF	XF	Unc	BU
1997 Proof	5,000	Value: 450				

KM# 1177 500 FRANCS - 75 EURO
17.0000 g., 0.9200 Gold .5028 oz. AGW **Subject:** Helsinki **Obv:** Denominations **Rev:** Cathedrale Saint Nicholas, date below

Date	Mintage	F	VF	XF	Unc	BU
1997 Proof	5,000	Value: 400				

KM# 1194a 500 FRANCS - 75 EURO
20.0000 g., 0.9990 Platinum .5028 oz. APW **Subject:** Stockholm - Hotel de Ville **Obv:** Denomination **Rev:** Tower and building

Date	Mintage	F	VF	XF	Unc	BU
1997 Proof	2,000	Value: 700				

KM# 1177a 500 FRANCS - 75 EURO
20.0000 g., 0.9990 Platinum .6431 oz. APW **Subject:** Helsinki **Obv:** Denominations **Rev:** Cathedral, Cathedrale Saint Nicholas

Date	Mintage	F	VF	XF	Unc	BU
1997 Proof	2,000	Value: 825				

EURO COINAGE

European Union Issues

KM# 1282 EURO CENT
2.2700 g., Copper Plated Steel, 16.3 mm. **Obv:** Human face **Obv. Designer:** Fabienne Courtiade **Rev:** Denomination and globe **Rev. Designer:** Luc Luycx **Edge:** Plain

Date	Mintage	F	VF	XF	Unc	BU
1999	794,054,000	—	—	—	0.35	0.50
1999 Proof	15,000	Value: 10.00				
2000	605,267,000	—	—	—	0.35	0.50
2000 Proof	15,000	Value: 10.00				

KM# 1283 2 EURO CENTS
3.0300 g., Copper-Plated-Steel, 18.7 mm. **Obv:** Human face **Obv. Designer:** Fabienne Courtiade **Rev:** Denomination and globe **Rev. Designer:** Luc Luycx **Edge:** Grooved

Date	Mintage	F	VF	XF	Unc	BU
1999	702,104,000	—	—	—	0.50	0.75
1999 Proof	Est. 15,000	Value: 10.00				
2000	510,155,000	—	—	—	0.50	0.75
2000 Proof	15,000	Value: 10.00				

KM# 1284 5 EURO CENTS
3.8600 g., Copper-Plated-Steel, 21.2 mm. **Obv:** Human face **Obv. Designer:** Fabienne Courtiade **Rev:** Denomination and globe **Rev. Designer:** Luc Luycx

Date	Mintage	F	VF	XF	Unc	BU
1999	616,227,000	—	—	—	0.75	1.25
1999 Proof	Est. 15,000	Value: 12.00				
2000	280,099,000	—	—	—	0.75	1.25
2000 Proof	15,000	Value: 12.00				

KM# 1285 10 EURO CENTS
4.0700 g., Brass, 19.7 mm. **Obv:** The seed sower divides date and RF **Obv. Designer:** Laurent Jorb **Rev:** Denomination and map **Rev. Designer:** Luc Luycx **Edge:** Reeded

Date	Mintage	F	VF	XF	Unc	BU
1999	447,284,600	—	—	—	0.75	1.25
1999 Proof	15,000	Value: 12.00				
2000	297,467,000	—	—	—	0.75	1.25
2000 Proof	15,000	Value: 12.00				

KM# 1286 20 EURO CENTS
5.7300 g., Brass, 22.2 mm. **Obv:** The seed sower divides date and RF **Obv. Designer:** Laurent Jorb **Rev:** Denomination and map **Rev. Designer:** Luc Luycx **Edge:** Notched

Date	Mintage	F	VF	XF	Unc	BU
1999	454,326,200	—	—	—	1.00	1.50
1999 Proof	15,000	Value: 14.00				
2000	148,988,600	—	—	—	1.25	2.00
2000 Proof	15,000	Value: 14.00				

KM# 1287 50 EURO CENTS
7.8100 g., Brass, 24.2 mm. **Obv:** The seed sower divides date and RF **Obv. Designer:** Laurent Jorb **Rev:** Denomination and map **Rev. Designer:** Luc Luycx **Edge:** Reeded

Date	Mintage	F	VF	XF	Unc	BU
1999	150,788,600	—	—	—	1.50	2.25
1999 Proof	15,000	Value: 15.00				
2000	179,531,000	—	—	—	1.25	2.00
2000 Proof	15,000	Value: 15.00				

KM# 1288 EURO
7.5000 g., Bi-Metallic Copper-Nickel center in Brass ring, 23.3 mm. **Obv:** Stylized tree divides RF within circle, date below **Obv. Designer:** Joaquin Jimenez **Rev:** Denomination and map **Rev. Designer:** Luc Luycx **Edge:** Reeded and plain sections

Date	Mintage	F	VF	XF	Unc	BU
1999	301,085,000	—	—	—	2.50	3.75
1999 Proof	15,000	Value: 18.00				
2000	297,305,000	—	—	—	2.50	3.75
2000 Proof	15,000	Value: 18.00				

KM# 1289 2 EUROS
8.5200 g., Bi-Metallic Brass center in Copper-Nickel ring, 25.6 mm. **Obv:** Stylized tree divides RF within circle, date below **Obv. Designer:** Joaquin Jimenez **Rev:** Denomination and map **Rev. Designer:** Luc Luycx **Edge:** Reeding with 2's and stars

Date	Mintage	F	VF	XF	Unc	BU
1999	56,730,000	—	—	—	4.50	7.00
1999 Proof	15,000	Value: 20.00				
2000	171,155,000	—	—	—	3.75	6.00
2000 Proof	15,000	Value: 20.00				

ESSAIS

Standard metals unless otherwise noted

KM#	Date	Mintage	Identification	Mkt Val
E38	1903 (a)	—	25 Centimes. Nickel. Denomination within square, date below. KM#855.	160

KM#	Date	Mintage	Identification	Mkt Val
E-A39	1904 (a)	—	25 Centimes. Nickel. Laureate bust left. Denomination above date. Without square around denomination, 22 sided flan.	165

KM#	Date	Mintage	Identification	Mkt Val
E39	1904 (a)	—	25 Centimes. Nickel. Laureate bust left. Leafy branch divides denomination and date, axe on column at left. KM#856.	150

KM#	Date	Mintage	Identification	Mkt Val
E-A40	1904 (a)	—	25 Centimes. Nickel. 22 sided flan, KM#856.	150

KM#	Date	Mintage	Identification	Mkt Val
E-B40	1904 (a)	—	25 Centimes. Nickel. 18 sided flan, KM#856.	150

KM#	Date	Mintage	Identification	Mkt Val
E-C40	1908 (a)	—	5 Centimes. Bronze. Head right. Woman and child, denomination at right, date below. KM#842.	175
E40	1908 (a)	—	10 Centimes. Aluminum. KM#843.	150

KM#	Date	Mintage	Identification	Mkt Val
E41	1910 (a)	—	5 Centimes. Bronze. KM#842.	160
E42	1913 (a)	—	25 Centimes. Nickel. KM#867.	110
E43	1914 (a)	104	5 Centimes. Copper-Nickel. KM#865.	550
E44	1914 (a)	—	25 Centimes. Nickel. KM#867.	110

KM#	Date	Mintage	Identification	Mkt Val
E45	1929 (a)	—	10 Francs. Silver. Delannoy.	675

KM#	Date	Mintage	Identification	Mkt Val
E46	1929 (a)	—	10 Francs. Aluminum-Bronze. Republic above denomination and date. Laureate head right.	60.00
E47	1929 (a)	—	10 Francs. Aluminum-Bronze. Oak leaves on head right, date at right. Hand holding supported torch divides denomination.	75.00
E48	1929 (a)	—	10 Francs. Silver. KM#878.	75.00
E49	1929 (a)	—	20 Francs. Silver. KM#879.	950
E50	1929 (a)	—	20 Francs. Aluminum-Bronze. KM#879.	120

KM#	Date	Mintage	Identification	Mkt Val
E51	1929 (a)	15	100 Francs. Gold. Winged head left. Leafy branches flank grain sprig, denomination above, date below.	3,850

KM#	Date	Mintage	Identification	Mkt Val
E52	1929	15	100 Francs. Gold. Globe with sprays flanking, denomination below.	3,850

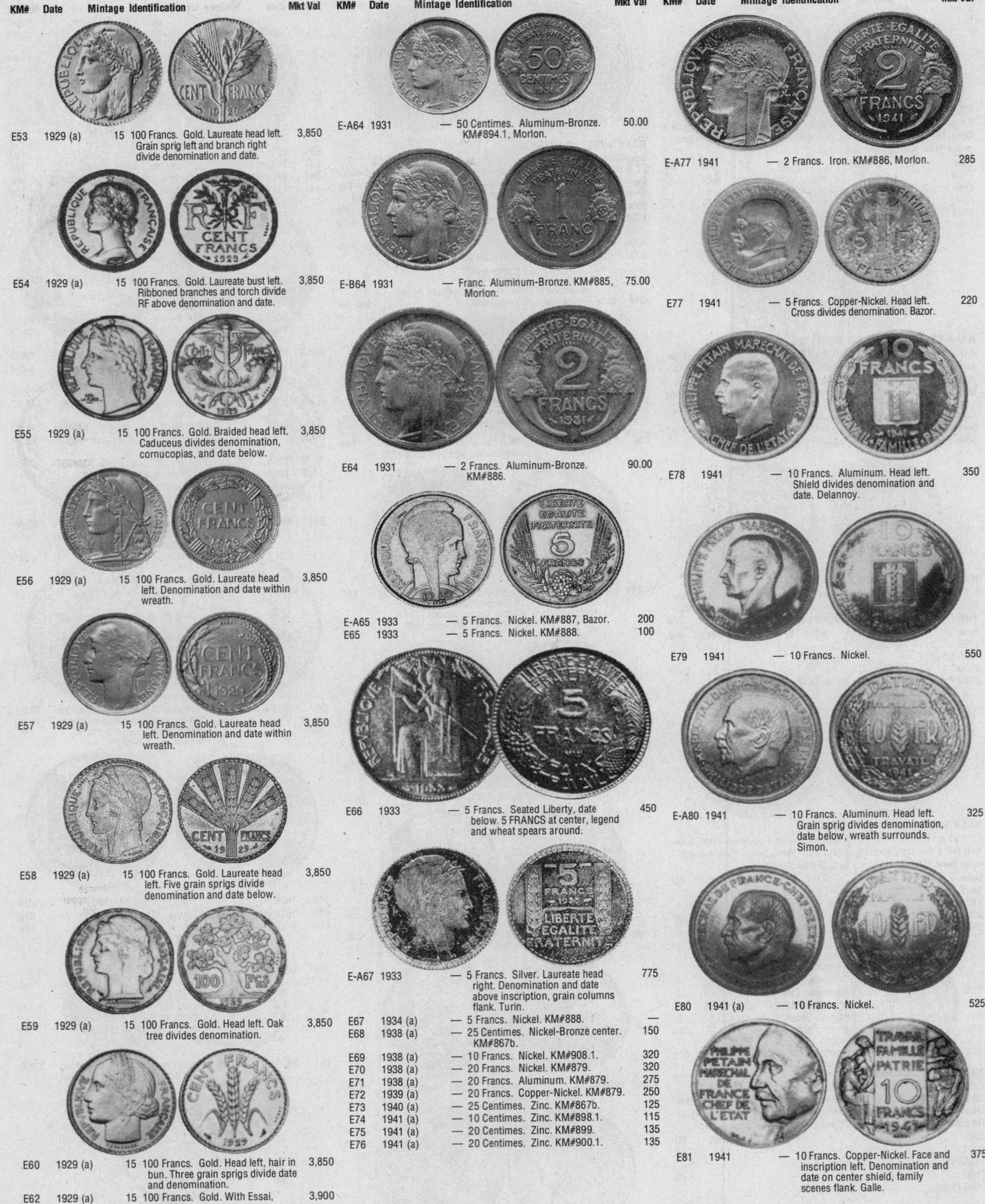

KM#	Date	Mintage	Identification	Mkt Val
E53	1929 (a)	15	100 Francs. Gold. Laureate head left. Grain sprig left and branch right divide denomination and date.	3,850
E54	1929 (a)	15	100 Francs. Gold. Laureate bust left. Ribboned branches and torch divide RF above denomination and date.	3,850
E55	1929 (a)	15	100 Francs. Gold. Braided head left. Caduceus divides denomination, cornucopias, and date below.	3,850
E56	1929 (a)	15	100 Francs. Gold. Laureate head left. Denomination and date within wreath.	3,850
E57	1929 (a)	15	100 Francs. Gold. Laureate head left. Denomination and date within wreath.	3,850
E58	1929 (a)	15	100 Francs. Gold. Laureate head left. Five grain sprigs divide denomination and date below.	3,850
E59	1929 (a)	15	100 Francs. Gold. Head left. Oak tree divides denomination.	3,850
E60	1929 (a)	15	100 Francs. Gold. Head left, hair in bun. Three grain sprigs divide date and denomination.	3,850
E62	1929 (a)	15	100 Francs. Gold. With Essai, KM#880.	3,900

KM#	Date	Mintage	Identification	Mkt Val
E-A64	1931	—	50 Centimes. Aluminum-Bronze. KM#894.1, Morlon.	50.00
E-B64	1931	—	Franc. Aluminum-Bronze. KM#885, Morlon.	75.00
E64	1931	—	2 Francs. Aluminum-Bronze. KM#886.	90.00
E-A65	1933	—	5 Francs. Nickel. KM#887, Bazor.	200
E65	1933	—	5 Francs. Nickel. KM#888.	100
E66	1933	—	5 Francs. Seated Liberty, date below. 5 FRANCS at center, legend and wheat spears around.	450
E-A67	1933	—	5 Francs. Silver. Laureate head right. Denomination and date above inscription, grain columns flank. Turin.	775
E67	1934 (a)	—	5 Francs. Nickel. KM#888.	—
E68	1938 (a)	—	25 Centimes. Nickel-Bronze center. KM#867b.	150
E69	1938 (a)	—	10 Francs. Nickel. KM#908.1.	320
E70	1938 (a)	—	20 Francs. Nickel. KM#879.	320
E71	1938 (a)	—	20 Francs. Aluminum. KM#879.	275
E72	1939 (a)	—	20 Francs. Copper-Nickel. KM#879.	250
E73	1940 (a)	—	25 Centimes. Zinc. KM#867b.	125
E74	1941 (a)	—	10 Centimes. Zinc. KM#898.1.	115
E75	1941 (a)	—	20 Centimes. Zinc. KM#899.	135
E76	1941 (a)	—	20 Centimes. Zinc. KM#900.1.	135

KM#	Date	Mintage	Identification	Mkt Val
E-A77	1941	—	2 Francs. Iron. KM#886, Morlon.	285
E77	1941	—	5 Francs. Copper-Nickel. Head left. Cross divides denomination. Bazor.	220
E78	1941	—	10 Francs. Aluminum. Head left. Shield divides denomination and date. Delannoy.	350
E79	1941	—	10 Francs. Nickel.	550
E-A80	1941	—	10 Francs. Aluminum. Head left. Grain sprig divides denomination, date below, wreath surrounds. Simon.	325
E80	1941 (a)	—	10 Francs. Nickel.	525
E81	1941	—	10 Francs. Copper-Nickel. Face and inscription left. Denomination and date on center shield, family scenes flank. Galle.	375

KM#	Date	Mintage	Identification	Mkt Val
E82	1941	—	20 Francs. Aluminum. Head left, date below. Leaves at center of grain sheaf divide denomination. Cochet.	285
E-A92	1941	—	20 Francs. Aluminum. Denomination and date below center inscription. Bouchard.	365
E83	1942	—	Franc. Aluminum. KM#902.1.	175
E84	1943 (a)	300	10 Centimes. Zinc. KM#903.	165
E85	1943 (a)	300	2 Francs. Aluminum. KM#904.	225
E86	1943	—	10 Francs. Copper-Nickel. Bazor.	265
E86a	1943	—	10 Francs. Aluminum. Head left. Statues below denomination, date at bottom. Bazor.	320
E87	1944 (a)	300	10 Centimes. Zinc. KM#906.	165
E88	1945 (a)	40	20 Centimes. Zinc. KM#907.	325
E89	1945 (a)	1,100	5 Francs. KM#888b.	110
E90	1945 (a)	1,100	10 Francs. Copper-Nickel. KM#909.	85.00
E91	1950 (g)	1,700	10 Francs. Aluminum-Bronze. KM#915.	40.00
E92	1950 (a)	25	20 Francs. Aluminum-Bronze. Georges Guiraud, KM#916.	550
E93	1950 (a)	1,700	20 Francs. Silver. G. Guiraud, KM#971.	40.00
E94	1950 (a)	1,700	50 Francs. Aluminum-Bronze. KM#918.	95.00
E95	1950 (a)	50	100 Francs.	250

KM#	Date	Mintage	Identification	Mkt Val
E-A96	1950	—	100 Francs. Copper-Nickel. KM#919.1.	4,000
E96	1951 (a)	28	20 Francs. Aluminum-Bronze. KM#917.	625
E97	1954 (a)	1,200	100 Francs. Copper-Nickel. KM#919.	85.00
E98	1959 (a)	4,000	Franc. Nickel. KM#925.	65.00
E99	1959 (a)	4,000	Franc. Nickel. KM#925.	50.00
E100	1959	—	2 Francs. Silver. KM#845.1.	950
E101	1959 (a)	4,000	5 Francs. Silver. KM#926.	60.00
E102	1959 (a)	I.A.	5 Francs. Silver. Small 5 in date, KM#926.	65.00
E103	1961 (a)	3,500	Centime. Chrome-Steel. KM#928.	30.00
E104	1961 (a)	3,500	5 Centimes. Chrome-Steel. KM#927.	30.00
E105	1961	—	20 Centimes. Aluminum-Bronze. KM#930.	40.00
E106	1961	—	20 Centimes. Laureate head with short hair left. Denomination and date within wreath.	40.00
E107	1961	—	20 Centimes. Head with long hair left. Denomination above date within wreath.	75.00
E108	1962 (a)	3,500	10 Centimes. Aluminum-Bronze. KM#929.	25.00
E109	1962 (a)	3,500	20 Centimes. Aluminum-Bronze. KM#930.	25.00
E110	1962 (a)	3,500	50 Centimes. Aluminum-Bronze. KM#939.	25.00
E111	1964 (a)	3,500	10 Francs. Silver. KM#932.	135

KM#	Date	Mintage	Identification	Mkt Val
E112	1965 (a)	4,700	1/2 Franc. Nickel. KM#931.	35.00
E113	1966 (a)	4,128	5 Centimes. Aluminum-Bronze. KM#933.	30.00
E114	1970 (a)	5,000	5 Francs. Silver. KM#926a.	40.00
E115	1974	7,300	10 Francs. Nickel-Brass. KM#940.	45.00
E116	1974	9	10 Francs. Gold. KM#940.	2,750
E117	1974	13,800	50 Francs. Silver. KM#941.	70.00
E118	1974	5	50 Francs. Gold. KM#941.	3,250
E119	1978	6,000	2 Francs. Nickel. KM#942.	45.00
E120	1978	22	2 Francs. Silver. KM#942.	450
E121	1978	12	2 Francs. Gold. KM#942.	1,350
E122	1982	—	10 Francs. Copper-Nickel. Gambetta, KM#950.	60.00
E123	1982	—	100 Francs. Silver. KM#951.	90.00
E124	1983	4,000	10 Francs. Nickel-Bronze. Baloon, KM#952.	45.00
E125	1983	9	10 Francs. Gold. Baloon, KM#952.	1,850
E126	1983	4,000	10 Francs. Nickel-Bronze. Standhal, KM#953.	45.00
E127	1983	9	10 Francs. Gold. Standhal, KM#953.	1,850
E128	1984	—	10 Francs. Nickel-Bronze. Rude, KM#954.	45.00
E129	1984	—	100 Francs. Silver. Curie, KM#955.	75.00
E130	1985	1,700	10 Francs. Nickel-Bronze. Hugo, KM#956.	45.00
E131	1985	1,700	100 Francs. Silver. Zola, KM#957.	60.00
E132	1986	1,750	10 Francs. Nickel. KM#959.	45.00
E133	1986	9	10 Francs. Gold. KM#959.	1,850
E134	1986	1,750	10 Francs. Nickel. Schuman, KM#958d.	45.00
E135	1986	1,750	100 Francs. Silver. Liberty, KM#960.	85.00
E136	1987	1,850	10 Francs. Nickel-Bronze. Capet, KM#916.1.	50.00
E137	1987	1,850	100 Francs. Silver. Lafayette, KM#962.	140
E138	1988	1,850	Franc. Nickel. KM#963.	75.00
E139	1988	1,850	10 Francs. Aluminum-Bronze. Garros, KM#965.	35.00
E140	1988	1,850	10 Francs. Steel center. Aluminum-Bronze ring. Bastille, KM#964.	50.00
E141	1988	1,850	100 Francs. Silver. Fraternity, KM#966.	60.00
E142	1989	—	Franc. Nickel. KM#967.	45.00
E143	1989	—	5 Francs. Nickel. Eiffel TOwer, KM#968.	60.00
E144	1989	—	10 Francs. Steel center. Aluminum-Bronze ring. Montesquien, KM#969.	50.00
E145	1989	—	100 Francs. Silver. Human Rights, KM#970.	65.00
E146	1994	—	20 Francs. Aluminum-Bronze center. Nickel inner ring, Copper-Aluminum-Nickel outer ring, KM#1036.	75.00

PATTERNS

Including off metal strikes

KM#	Date	Mintage	Identification	Mkt Val
Pn102	1929	—	100 Francs. Aluminum-Bronze. Bust left. Date. CENT FRANCS.	140
Pn103	1933	—	5 Francs. Liberty bust left. Legend above, date below. CENT FRANCS.	180
Pn104	1939	—	20 Francs. Copper-Nickel.	600
Pn105	1941	—	10 Francs. Copper-Nickel. Petain bust left, legend in front. People working at sides. TRAVAIL/ FAMILLE/PATRIE/10/FRANCS/1941	325
Pn106	1941	—	20 Francs. Copper-Nickel. Petain bust left. Sheaves of wheat bent outward divide denomination, legend above.	325

KM#	Date	Mintage	Identification	Mkt Val
Pn107	1941	—	20 Francs. Copper-Nickel. Petain bust left. Family group above FAMILLE divide 20-FR.	325
Pn108	1941	—	20 Francs. Nickel. Petain bust left. 3 figures, 2 standing, 1 sitting.	325
Pn109	1942	—	5 Francs. Copper-Nickel. Petain bust left. TRAVAIL/FAMILLE/ PATRIE/5/FRANCS/1942	325
Pn110	1943	—	10 Francs. Copper-Nickel. Petain bust left. 3 figures, 2 standing, 1 sitting.	325
Pn111	1950	—	20 Francs. Liberty left. 20-FR divided by symbol.	55.00
Pn112	1950	—	20 Francs. Liberty left. Inscription above 20 dividing flowers, FRANCS and date below.	55.00
Pn113	1950	—	20 Francs. Liberty bust left. 20 over branch at left, FRANCS in center at right, date below.	55.00
Pn114	1950	—	20 Francs. Liberty bust left. 20 in small circle of branches, 4 branches to edge of coin.	55.00
Pn115	1950	—	100 Francs. Copper-Nickel.	250
Pn116	1964	131	10 Francs. Silver. KM#756. KM#932.	250
Pn117	1964	3,500	10 Francs. Silver. KM#932.	100
Pn118	1977	253	2 Francs. Nickel. KM#942.	70.00

PIEFORTS

Standard metals unless otherwise noted

KM#	Date	Mintage	Identification	Mkt Val
P251	1903	—	25 Centimes. Copper-Nickel-Zinc.	150
P270	1914	—	10 Centimes. Nickel. KM#866.	120
P272	1914	—	25 Centimes. Nickel. KM#867.	165
P280	1920	—	5 Centimes. Copper-Nickel. KM#875.	135
P-A297	1920	—	2 Francs. Aluminum-Bronze. KM#877.	125
P297	1928	—	2 Francs. Silver. KM#845.	320
P300	1929	—	100 Francs. Gold. KM#880.	3,500
P305	1941	—	10 Centimes. Zinc. KM#895.	220
P341	1962	500	Centime. Chrome-Steel. KM#928.	25.00
P342	1962	50	Centime. Silver. KM#928.	65.00
P343	1962	20	Centime. Gold. KM#928.	325
P344	1962	500	10 Centimes. Aluminum-Bronze. KM#929.	25.00
P345	1962	50	10 Centimes. Silver. KM#929.	85.00
P346	1962	20	10 Centimes. Gold. KM#929.	375
P347	1962	500	20 Centimes. Aluminum-Bronze. KM#930.	25.00
P348	1962	50	20 Centimes. Silver. KM#930.	120
P349	1962	20	20 Centimes. Gold. KM#930.	400
P350	1962	500	50 Centimes. Aluminum-Bronze. KM#939.	25.00
P351	1962	50	50 Centimes. Silver. KM#939.	130
P352	1962	20	50 Centimes. Gold. KM#939.	500
P353	1965	500	1/2 Franc. Nickel. KM#931.	30.00
P354	1965	50	1/2 Franc. Silver. KM#931.	75.00
P355	1965	20	1/2 Franc. Gold. KM#931.	400
P356	1965	500	10 Francs. Silver center. KM#932.	75.00
P357	1965	50	10 Francs. Gold. KM#932.	1,950
P358	1966	500	5 Centimes. Aluminum-Bronze. KM#933.	20.00
P359	1966	50	5 Centimes. Silver. KM#933.	80.00
P360	1966	20	5 Centimes. Gold. KM#933.	350
P361	1967	500	Centime. Chrome-Steel center. KM#928.	20.00
P362	1967	50	Centime. Silver. KM#928.	35.00
P363	1967	20	Centime. Gold. KM#928.	375
P364	1967	500	5 Centimes. Aluminum-Bronze. KM#933.	20.00
P365	1967	50	5 Centimes. Silver. KM#933.	50.00
P366	1967	20	5 Centimes. Gold. KM#933.	350
P367	1967	500	10 Centimes. Aluminum-Bronze. KM#929.	20.00
P368	1967	50	10 Centimes. Silver. KM#929.	65.00
P369	1967	20	10 Centimes. Gold. KM#929.	350
P370	1967	500	20 Centimes. Aluminum-Bronze. KM#930.	20.00
P371	1967	50	20 Centimes. Silver. KM#930.	125
P372	1967	20	20 Centimes. Gold. KM#930.	400
P373	1967	500	25 Centimes. Aluminum-Bronze. KM#939.	20.00
P374	1967	50	50 Centimes. Silver. KM#939.	125
P375	1967	20	50 Centimes. Gold. KM#939.	675
P376	1967	500	1/2 Franc. Nickel. KM#931.	25.00
P377	1967	50	1/2 Franc. Silver. KM#931.	85.00
P378	1967	20	1/2 Franc. Gold. KM#931.	450
P379	1967	500	Franc. Nickel. KM#925.	25.00
P380	1967	50	Franc. Silver. KM#925.	85.00
P382	1967	500	5 Francs. Silver. KM#926.	35.00
P383	1967	50	5 Francs. Gold. KM#926.	850
P384	1967	500	10 Francs. Silver. KM#932.	50.00
P385	1967	50	10 Francs. Gold. KM#932.	1,950
P386	1968	500	Centime. Chrome-Steel. KM#928.	35.00
P387	1968	50	Centime. Silver. KM#928.	60.00
P388	1968	20	Centime. Gold. KM#928.	375
P389	1968	500	5 Centimes. Aluminum-Bronze. KM#933.	35.00
P390	1968	50	5 Centimes. Silver. KM#933.	60.00
P391	1968	20	5 Centimes. Gold. KM#933.	225
P392	1968	500	10 Centimes. Aluminum-Bronze. KM#929.	35.00
P393	1968	50	10 Centimes. Silver. KM#929.	60.00
P394	1968	20	10 Centimes. Gold. KM#929.	325
P395	1968	500	20 Centimes. Aluminum-Bronze. KM#930.	35.00
P396	1968	50	20 Centimes. Silver. KM#930.	60.00
P397	1968	20	20 Centimes. Gold. KM#930.	425
P398	1968	500	1/2 Franc. Nickel. KM#931.	35.00
P399	1968	50	1/2 Franc. Silver. KM#931.	65.00
P400	1968	20	1/2 Franc. Gold. KM#931.	425
P401	1968	500	Franc. Nickel. KM#925.	35.00
P402	1968	50	Franc. Silver. KM#925.	65.00
P404	1968	500	5 Francs. Silver. KM#926.	35.00
P405	1968	50	5 Francs. Gold. KM#926.	875
P406	1968	500	10 Francs. Silver. KM#932.	45.00
P407	1968	50	10 Francs. Gold. KM#932.	850
P408	1970	500	5 Francs. Nickel Clad Copper-Nickel. KM#926a.	40.00
P409	1970	200	5 Francs. Silver. KM#926a.	60.00
P410	1970	100	5 Francs. Gold. KM#926a.	875
P411	1970	100	5 Francs. Platinum. KM#926a.	1,950
P412	1971	500	Centime. Chrome-Steel. KM#928.	20.00
P413	1971	250	Centime. Silver. KM#928.	30.00
P414	1971	100	Centime. Gold. KM#928.	140
P415	1971	500	5 Centimes. Aluminum-Bronze. KM#933.	20.00
P416	1971	250	5 Centimes. Silver. KM#933.	30.00
P417	1971	100	5 Centimes. Gold. KM#933.	165
P418	1971	500	10 Centimes. Aluminum-Bronze. KM#929.	20.00
P419	1971	250	10 Centimes. Silver. KM#929.	35.00
P420	1971	100	10 Centimes. Gold. KM#929.	250
P421	1971	500	20 Centimes. Aluminum-Bronze. KM#930.	20.00
P422	1971	250	20 Centimes. Silver. KM#930.	35.00
P423	1971	100	20 Centimes. Gold. KM#930.	375
P424	1971	500	1/2 Franc. Nickel. KM#931.	20.00
P425	1971	250	1/2 Franc. Silver. KM#931.	35.00
P426	1971	100	1/2 Franc. Gold. KM#931.	365
P427	1971	500	Franc. Nickel. KM#925.	25.00
P428	1971	250	Franc. Silver. KM#925.	35.00
P429	1971	100	Franc. Gold. KM#925.	450
P430	1971	1,000	5 Francs. Nickel Clad Copper-Nickel. KM#926a.	20.00
P431	1971	500	5 Francs. Silver. KM#926a.	30.00
P432	1971	250	5 Francs. Gold. KM#926a.	875
P433	1971	100	5 Francs. Platinum. KM#926a.	1,950
P435	1971	500	10 Francs. Silver. KM#932.	50.00
P436	1971	250	10 Francs. Gold. KM#932.	1,875
P437	1972	250	Centime. Chrome-Steel. KM#928.	20.00
P438	1972	150	Centime. Silver. KM#928.	25.00
P439	1972	75	Centime. Gold. KM#928.	140
P440	1972	250	5 Centimes. Aluminum-Bronze. KM#933.	20.00
P441	1972	150	5 Centimes. Silver. KM#933.	25.00
P442	1972	75	5 Centimes. Gold. KM#933.	200
P443	1972	250	10 Centimes. Aluminum-Bronze. KM#929.	20.00
P444	1972	150	10 Centimes. Silver. KM#929.	25.00
P445	1972	75	10 Centimes. Gold. KM#929.	285
P446	1972	250	20 Centimes. Aluminum-Bronze. KM#930.	25.00
P447	1972	150	20 Centimes. Silver. KM#930.	35.00
P448	1972	75	20 Centimes. Gold. KM#930.	345
P449	1972	250	1/2 Franc. Nickel. KM#931.	25.00
P450	1972	150	1/2 Franc. Silver. KM#931.	35.00
P451	1972	75	1/2 Franc. Gold. KM#931.	380
P452	1972	250	Franc. Nickel. KM#925.	25.00
P453	1972	150	Franc. Silver. KM#925.	40.00
P454	1972	75	Franc. Gold. KM#925.	500
P455	1972	500	5 Francs. Nickel Clad Copper-Nickel. KM#926a.	25.00
P456	1972	250	5 Francs. Silver. KM#926a.	35.00
P457	1972	200	5 Francs. Gold. KM#926a.	875
P458	1972	500	10 Francs. Silver. KM#932.	70.00
P459	1972	200	10 Francs. Gold. KM#932.	1,875
P460	1972	20	10 Francs. Platinum. KM#932.	3,950
P461	1973	250	Centime. Chrome-Steel. KM#928.	20.00
P462	1973	150	Centime. Silver. KM#928.	25.00
P463	1973	75	Centime. Gold. KM#928.	175
P464	1973	250	5 Centimes. Aluminum-Bronze center. KM#933.	20.00
P465	1973	150	5 Centimes. Silver. KM#933.	25.00
P466	1973	75	5 Centimes. Gold. KM#933.	200
P467	1973	250	10 Centimes. Aluminum-Bronze. KM#929.	20.00
P468	1973	150	10 Centimes. Silver. KM#929.	25.00
P469	1973	75	10 Centimes. Gold. KM#929.	285
P470	1973	250	20 Centimes. Aluminum-Bronze. KM#930.	20.00
P471	1973	150	20 Centimes. Silver. KM#930.	25.00
P472	1973	75	20 Centimes. Gold. KM#930.	375
P473	1973	250	1/2 Franc. Nickel. KM#931.	20.00
P474	1973	150	1/2 Franc. Silver. KM#931.	25.00
P475	1973	75	1/2 Franc. Gold. KM#931.	385
P476	1973	250	Franc. Nickel. KM#925.	20.00
P477	1973	150	Franc. Silver. KM#925.	25.00
P478	1973	75	Franc. Gold. KM#925.	385
P479	1973	500	5 Francs. Nickel Clad Copper-Nickel. KM#926a.	20.00
P480	1973	250	5 Francs. Silver. KM#926a.	35.00
P481	1973	200	5 Francs. Gold. KM#926a.	875
P482	1973	500	10 Francs. Silver. KM#932.	25.00
P483	1973	200	10 Francs. Gold. KM#932.	1,950
P484	1973	20	10 Francs. Platinum. KM#932.	3,950
P485	1974	127	Centime. Chrome-Steel. KM#928.	30.00
P486	1974	242	Centime. Silver. KM#928.	35.00
P487	1974	96	Centime. Gold. KM#928.	160
P488	1974	98	5 Centimes. Aluminum-Bronze. KM#933.	30.00
P489	1974	247	5 Centimes. Silver. KM#933.	35.00
P490	1974	96	5 Centimes. Gold. KM#933.	200
P491	1974	97	10 Centimes. Aluminum-Bronze. KM#929.	30.00
P492	1974	246	10 Centimes. Silver. KM#929.	35.00
P493	1974	94	10 Centimes. Gold. KM#929.	275
P494	1974	101	20 Centimes. Aluminum-Bronze. KM#930.	30.00
P495	1974	247	20 Centimes. Silver. KM#930.	35.00
P496	1974	98	20 Centimes. Gold. KM#930.	365
P497	1974	102	1/2 Franc. Nickel. KM#931.	30.00
P498	1974	241	1/2 Franc. Silver. KM#931.	35.00
P499	1974	91	1/2 Franc. Gold. KM#931.	380
P500	1974	118	Franc. Nickel. KM#925.	35.00
P501	1974	246	Franc. Silver. KM#925.	40.00
P502	1974	95	Franc. Gold. KM#925.	485
P503	1974	162	5 Francs. Nickel Clad Copper-Nickel. KM#926a.	35.00
P504	1974	245	5 Francs. Silver. KM#926a.	40.00
P505	1974	107	5 Francs. Gold. KM#926a.	875
P506	1974	493	10 Francs. Nickel-Brass. KM#940.	35.00
P507	1974	491	10 Francs. Silver. KM#940.	40.00
P508	1974	172	10 Francs. Gold. KM#940.	875
P509	1974	982	50 Francs. Silver. KM#941.	85.00
P510	1974	241	50 Francs. Gold. KM#941.	2,150
P511	1974	18	50 Francs. Platinum. KM#941.	4,500
P512	1975	147	Centime. Chrome-Steel. KM#928.	20.00
P513	1975	228	Centime. Silver. KM#928.	25.00
P514	1975	67	Centime. Gold. KM#928.	160
P515	1975	129	5 Centimes. Aluminum-Bronze. KM#933.	20.00
P516	1975	203	5 Centimes. Silver. KM#933.	25.00
P517	1975	44	5 Centimes. Gold. KM#933.	200
P518	1975	127	10 Centimes. Aluminum-Bronze. KM#929.	20.00
P519	1975	198	10 Centimes. Silver. KM#929.	25.00
P520	1975	39	10 Centimes. Gold. KM#929.	270
P521	1975	133	20 Centimes. Aluminum-Bronze. KM#930.	20.00
P522	1975	212	20 Centimes. Silver. KM#930.	25.00
P523	1975	42	20 Centimes. Gold. KM#930.	365
P524	1975	131	1/2 Franc. Nickel. KM#931.	20.00
P525	1975	213	1/2 Franc. Silver. KM#931.	25.00
P526	1975	40	1/2 Franc. Gold. KM#931.	395
P527	1975	145	Franc. Nickel. KM#925.	20.00
P528	1975	250	Franc. Silver. KM#925.	25.00
P529	1975	51	Franc. Gold. KM#925.	500
P530	1975	202	5 Francs. Nickel Clad Copper-Nickel. KM#926a.	20.00
P531	1975	250	5 Francs. Silver. KM#926a.	30.00
P532	1975	60	5 Francs. Gold. KM#926a.	875
P533	1975	356	10 Francs. Nickel-Brass. KM#940.	25.00
P534	1975	500	10 Francs. Silver. KM#940.	35.00
P535	1975	62	10 Francs. Gold. KM#940.	875
P536	1975	955	50 Francs. Silver. KM#941.	85.00
P537	1975	74	50 Francs. Gold. KM#941.	2,150
P538	1975	10	50 Francs. Platinum. KM#941.	4,600
P539	1976	200	Centime. Chrome-Steel. KM#928.	20.00
P540	1976	300	Centime. Silver. KM#928.	25.00
P541	1976	100	Centime. Gold. KM#928.	160
P542	1976	200	5 Centimes. Aluminum-Bronze. KM#933.	20.00
P543	1976	300	5 Centimes. Silver. KM#933.	25.00
P544	1976	100	5 Centimes. Gold. KM#933.	160
P545	1976	200	10 Centimes. Aluminum-Bronze. KM#929.	20.00
P546	1976	300	10 Centimes. Silver. KM#929.	25.00
P547	1976	100	10 Centimes. Gold. KM#929.	270
P548	1976	200	20 Centimes. Aluminum-Bronze. KM#930.	20.00
P549	1976	300	20 Centimes. Silver. KM#930.	25.00
P550	1976	100	20 Centimes. Gold. KM#930.	365
P551	1976	200	1/2 Franc. Nickel. KM#931.	20.00
P552	1976	250	1/2 Franc. Silver. KM#931.	25.00
P553	1976	100	1/2 Franc. Gold. KM#931.	500
P554	1976	126	Franc. Nickel. KM#925.	30.00
P555	1976	88	Franc. Silver. KM#925.	35.00
P556	1976	38	Franc. Gold. KM#925.	500

KM#	Date	Mintage	Identification	Mkt Val
P557	1976	178	5 Francs. Nickel Clad Copper-Nickel center. KM#926a.	30.00
P558	1976	104	5 Francs. Silver. KM#926a.	37.50
P559	1976	26	5 Francs. Gold. KM#926a.	875
P560	1976	175	10 Francs. Nickel-Brass. KM#940.	30.00
P561	1976	121	10 Francs. Silver. KM#940.	40.00
P562	1976	36	10 Francs. Gold. KM#940.	875
P563	1976	213	50 Francs. Silver. KM#941.	150
P564	1976	54	50 Francs. Gold. KM#941.	2,200
P565	1976	6	50 Francs. Platinum. KM#941.	7,000
P566	1977	118	Centime. Chrome-Steel. KM#928.	25.00
P567	1977	247	Centime. Silver. KM#928.	30.00
P568	1977	53	Centime. Gold. KM#928.	160
P569	1977	89	5 Centimes. Aluminum-Bronze. KM#933.	25.00
P570	1977	232	5 Centimes. Silver. KM#933.	30.00
P571	1977	41	5 Centimes. Gold. KM#933.	195
P572	1977	85	10 Centimes. Aluminum-Bronze. KM#929.	25.00
P573	1977	231	10 Centimes. Silver. KM#929.	30.00
P574	1977	32	10 Centimes. Gold. KM#929.	270
P575	1977	88	20 Centimes. Aluminum-Bronze. KM#930.	30.00
P576	1977	243	20 Centimes. Silver. KM#930.	35.00
P577	1977	32	20 Centimes. Gold. KM#930.	365
P578	1977	89	1/2 Franc. Nickel. KM#931.	30.00
P579	1977	234	1/2 Franc. Silver. KM#931.	35.00
P580	1977	32	1/2 Franc. Gold. KM#931.	395
P581	1977	100	Franc. Nickel. KM#925.	30.00
P582	1977	259	Franc. Silver. KM#925.	35.00
P583	1977	42	Franc. Gold. KM#925.	500
P584	1977	139	5 Francs. Nickel Clad Copper-Nickel. KM#926a.	30.00
P585	1977	282	5 Francs. Silver. KM#926a.	35.00
P586	1977	35	5 Francs. Gold. KM#926a.	875
P587	1977	146	10 Francs. Nickel-Brass center. KM#940.	30.00
P588	1977	296	10 Francs. Silver. KM#940.	40.00
P589	1977	43	10 Francs. Gold. KM#940.	875
P590	1977	465	50 Francs. Silver. KM#941.	115
P591	1977	50	50 Francs. Gold. KM#941.	2,150
P592	1977	19	50 Francs. Platinum. KM#941.	4,500
P593	1978	150	Centime. Chrome-Steel. KM#928.	20.00
P594	1978	294	Centime. Silver. KM#928.	25.00
P595	1978	144	Centime. Gold. KM#928.	160
P596	1978	148	5 Centimes. Aluminum-Bronze center. KM#933.	20.00
P597	1978	295	5 Centimes. Silver. KM#933.	25.00
P598	1978	144	5 Centimes. Gold. KM#933.	195
P599	1978	147	10 Centimes. Aluminum-Bronze. KM#929.	20.00
P600	1978	290	10 Centimes. Silver. KM#929.	25.00
P601	1978	139	10 Centimes. Gold. KM#929.	270
P602	1978	148	20 Centimes. Aluminum-Bronze. KM#930.	20.00
P603	1978	296	20 Centimes. Silver. KM#930.	25.00
P604	1978	141	20 Centimes. Gold. KM#930.	365
P605	1978	149	1/2 Franc. Nickel. KM#931.	20.00
P606	1978	296	1/2 Franc. Silver. KM#931.	25.00
P607	1978	141	1/2 Franc. Gold. KM#931.	395
P608	1978	149	Franc. Nickel. KM#925.	20.00
P609	1978	297	Franc. Silver. KM#925.	25.00
P610	1978	142	Franc. Gold. KM#925.	500
P611	1978	350	2 Francs. Silver. KM#942.	30.00
P612	1978	—	2 Francs. Nickel. KM#942.	100
P613	1978	150	5 Francs. Nickel Clad Copper-Nickel. KM#926a.	20.00
P614	1978	306	5 Francs. Silver. KM#926a.	25.00
P615	1978	143	5 Francs. Gold. KM#926a.	875
P616	1978	174	10 Francs. Nickel-Brass. KM#940.	25.00
P617	1978	345	10 Francs. Silver. KM#940.	35.00
P618	1978	144	10 Francs. Gold. KM#940.	875
P619	1978	599	50 Francs. Silver. KM#941.	85.00
P620	1978	149	50 Francs. Gold. KM#941.	2,150
P621	1978	25	50 Francs. Platinum. KM#941.	4,500
P622	1979	300	Centime. Chrome-Steel. KM#928.	15.00
P623	1979	600	Centime. Silver. KM#928.	20.00
P624	1979	300	Centime. Gold. KM#928.	160
P625	1979	299	5 Centimes. KM#935.	15.00
P626	1979	600	5 Centimes. Silver. KM#933.	20.00
P627	1979	300	5 Centimes. Gold. KM#933.	160
P628	1979	300	10 Centimes. Aluminum-Bronze. KM#929.	15.00
P629	1979	600	10 Centimes. Silver. KM#929.	20.00
P630	1979	300	10 Centimes. Gold. KM#929.	270
P631	1979	300	20 Centimes. Aluminum-Bronze. KM#930.	15.00
P632	1979	600	20 Centimes. Silver. KM#930.	20.00
P633	1979	300	20 Centimes. Gold. KM#930.	365
P634	1979	300	1/2 Franc. Nickel. KM#931.	15.00
P635	1979	600	1/2 Franc. Silver. KM#931.	20.00
P636	1979	300	1/2 Franc. Gold. KM#931.	395
P637	1979	500	Franc. Nickel. KM#925.	20.00
P638	1979	1,250	Franc. Silver. KM#925.	85.00
P639	1979	600	Franc. Gold. KM#925.	500
P640	1979	500	2 Francs. Nickel. KM#942.	20.00
P641	1979	1,250	2 Francs. Silver. KM#942.	30.00
P642	1979	600	2 Francs. Gold. KM#942.	710
P643	1979	40	2 Francs. Platinum. KM#942.	1,325
P644	1979	300	5 Francs. Nickel Clad Copper-Nickel. KM#926a.	20.00
P645	1979	600	5 Francs. Silver. KM#926a.	30.00
P646	1979	300	5 Francs. Gold. KM#926a.	875
P647	1979	349	10 Francs. Nickel-Brass. KM#940.	25.00
P648	1979	700	10 Francs. Silver. KM#940.	35.00
P649	1979	300	10 Francs. Gold. KM#940.	895
P650	1979	2,250	50 Francs. Silver. KM#941.	85.00
P651	1979	400	50 Francs. Gold. KM#941.	2,100
P652	1979	30	50 Francs. Platinum. KM#941.	4,500
P653	1980	155	Centime. Chrome-Steel center. KM#928.	15.00
P654	1980	570	Centime. Silver. KM#928.	20.00
P655	1980	176	Centime. Gold. KM#928.	160
P656	1980	142	5 Centimes. Aluminum-Bronze center. KM#933.	15.00
P657	1980	547	5 Centimes. Silver. KM#933.	20.00
P658	1980	137	5 Centimes. Gold. KM#933.	195
P659	1980	148	10 Centimes. Aluminum-Bronze. KM#929.	15.00
P660	1980	528	10 Centimes. Silver. KM#929.	20.00
P661	1980	127	10 Centimes. Gold. KM#929.	270
P662	1980	140	20 Centimes. Aluminum-Bronze. KM#930.	15.00
P663	1980	569	20 Centimes. Silver. KM#930.	20.00
P664	1980	136	20 Centimes. Gold. KM#930.	365
P665	1980	156	1/2 Franc. Nickel. KM#931.	15.00
P666	1980	537	1/2 Franc. Silver. KM#931.	20.00
P667	1980	118	1/2 Franc. Gold. KM#931.	395
P668	1980	132	Franc. Nickel. KM#925.	15.00
P669	1980	563	Franc. Silver. KM#925.	20.00
P670	1980	193	Franc. Gold. KM#925.	500
P671	1980	194	2 Francs. Nickel. KM#942.	15.00
P672	1980	772	2 Francs. Silver. KM#942.	20.00
P673	1980	130	2 Francs. Gold. KM#942.	710
P674	1980	271	5 Francs. Nickel Clad Copper-Nickel. KM#926a.	15.00
P675	1980	580	5 Francs. Silver. KM#926a.	20.00
P676	1980	213	5 Francs. Gold. KM#926a.	895
P677	1980	148	10 Francs. Nickel-Brass. KM#940.	15.00
P678	1980	730	10 Francs. Silver KM#940.	20.00
P679	1980	157	10 Francs. Gold. KM#940.	890
P680	1980	2,500	50 Francs. Silver. KM#941.	100
P681	1980	500	50 Francs. Gold. KM#941.	2,250
P682	1980	34	50 Francs. Platinum. KM#941.	4,500
P683	1981	150	Centime. Chrome-Steel. KM#928.	15.00
P684	1981	362	Centime. Silver. KM#928.	20.00
P685	1981	69	Centime. Gold. KM#928.	160
P686	1981	105	5 Centimes. Aluminum-Bronze. KM#933.	15.00
P687	1981	358	5 Centimes. Silver. KM#933.	20.00
P688	1981	42	5 Centimes. Gold. KM#933.	195
P689	1981	104	10 Centimes. Aluminum-Bronze. KM#929.	15.00
P690	1981	357	10 Centimes. Silver. KM#929.	20.00
P691	1981	32	10 Centimes. Gold. KM#929.	250
P692	1981	106	20 Centimes. Aluminum-Bronze. KM#930.	15.00
P693	1981	359	20 Centimes. Silver. KM#930.	20.00
P694	1981	30	20 Centimes. Gold. KM#930.	365
P695	1981	110	1/2 Franc. Nickel. KM#931.	15.00
P696	1981	358	1/2 Franc. Silver. KM#931.	20.00
P697	1981	33	1/2 Franc. Gold. KM#931.	395
P698	1981	16	1/2 Franc. Platinum. KM#931.	1,000
P699	1981	122	Franc. Nickel. KM#925.	15.00
P700	1981	358	Franc. Silver. KM#925.	20.00
P701	1981	42	Franc. Gold. KM#925.	450
P702	1981	16	Franc. Platinum. KM#925.	1,350
P703	1981	131	2 Francs. Nickel. KM#942.	15.00
P704	1981	359	2 Francs. Silver. KM#942.	25.00
P705	1981	37	2 Francs. Gold. KM#942.	710
P706	1981	16	2 Francs. Platinum. KM#942.	1,500
P707	1981	150	5 Francs. Nickel Clad Copper-Nickel. KM#926a.	15.00
P708	1981	261	5 Francs. Silver. KM#926a.	20.00
P709	1981	52	5 Francs, Gold. KM#926a.	890
P710	1981	16	5 Francs. Platinum. KM#926a.	1,750
P711	1981	150	10 Francs. Nickel-Brass. KM#940.	15.00
P712	1981	365	10 Francs. Silver. KM#940.	30.00
P713	1981	52	10 Francs. Gold. KM#940.	890
P714	1981	17	10 Francs. Platinum. KM#940.	1,850
P715	1982	70	Centime. Steel. KM#928.	20.00
P716	1982	195	Centime. Silver. KM#928.	25.00
P717	1982	36	Centime. Gold. KM#928.	225
P718	1982	53	5 Centimes. Aluminum-Bronze. KM#933.	25.00
P719	1982	164	5 Centimes. Silver. KM#933.	25.00
P720	1982	26	5 Centimes. Gold. KM#933.	250
P721	1982	53	10 Centimes. Aluminum-Bronze. KM#929.	25.00
P722	1982	163	10 Centimes. Silver. KM#929.	25.00
P723	1982	29	10 Centimes. Gold. KM#929.	275
P724	1982	53	20 Centimes. Aluminum-Bronze. KM#930.	25.00
P725	1982	171	20 Centimes. Silver. KM#930.	25.00
P726	1982	26	20 Centimes. Gold. KM#930.	385
P727	1982	54	1/2 Franc. Nickel. KM#931.	25.00
P728	1982	165	1/2 Franc. Silver. KM#931.	25.00
P729	1982	26	1/2 Franc. Gold. KM#931.	385
P730	1982	4	1/2 Franc. Platinum. KM#931.	2,750
P731	1982	57	Franc. Nickel. KM#925.	25.00
P732	1982	252	Franc. Silver. KM#925.	25.00
P733	1982	29	Franc. Gold. KM#925.	450
P734	1982	6	Franc. Platinum. KM#925.	1,800
P735	1982	62	2 Francs. Nickel. KM#942.	25.00
P736	1982	203	2 Francs. Silver. KM#942.	25.00
P737	1982	27	2 Francs. Gold. KM#942.	925
P738	1982	4	2 Francs. Platinum. KM#942.	3,000
P739	1982	69	5 Francs. Nickel Clad Copper-Nickel. KM#926a.	25.00
P740	1982	188	5 Francs. Silver. KM#926a.	25.00
P741	1982	27	5 Francs. Gold. KM#926a.	950
P742	1982	4	5 Francs. Platinum. KM#926a.	3,500
P743	1982	80	10 Francs. Nickel-Brass. KM#940.	25.00
P744	1982	239	10 Francs. Silver. KM#940.	30.00
P745	1982	33	10 Francs. Gold. KM#940.	890
P746	1982	4	10 Francs. Platinum. KM#940.	3,700
P747	1982	326	10 Francs. Nickel-Bronze. KM#950.	20.00
P748	1982	812	10 Francs. Silver. KM#950.	30.00
P749	1982	87	10 Francs. Gold. KM#950.	890
P750	1982	14	10 Francs. Platinum. KM#950.	1,700
P751	1982	999	100 Francs. Silver. KM#951.	55.00
P752	1982	93	100 Francs. Gold. KM#951.	1,100
P753	1982	16	100 Francs. Platinum. KM#951.	2,250
P754	1983	50	Centime. Steel. KM#928.	20.00
P755	1983	98	Centime. Silver. KM#928.	25.00
P756	1983	17	Centime. Gold. KM#928.	225
P757	1983	42	Centime. Aluminum-Bronze. KM#933.	20.00
P758	1983	90	5 Centimes. Silver. KM#933.	25.00
P759	1983	7	5 Centimes. Gold. KM#933.	650
P760	1983	42	10 Centimes. Aluminum-Bronze. KM#929.	25.00
P761	1983	90	10 Centimes. Silver. KM#929.	30.00
P762	1983	6	10 Centimes. Gold. KM#929.	700
P763	1983	44	20 Centimes. Aluminum-Bronze. KM#930.	25.00
P764	1983	95	20 Centimes. Silver. KM#930.	30.00
P765	1983	5	20 Centimes. Gold. KM#930.	775
P766	1983	43	1/2 Franc. Nickel. KM#931.	25.00
P767	1983	89	1/2 Franc. Silver. KM#931.	35.00
P768	1983	5	1/2 Franc. Gold. KM#931.	825
P769	1983	3	1/2 Franc. Platinum. KM#931.	7,150
P770	1983	46	Franc. Nickel center. KM#925.	25.00
P771	1983	98	Franc. Silver. KM#925.	35.00
P772	1983	11	Franc. Gold. KM#925.	550
P773	1983	3	Franc. Platinum. KM#925.	7,150
P774	1983	51	2 Francs. Nickel. KM#942.	25.00
P775	1983	121	2 Francs. Silver. KM#942.	35.00
P776	1983	9	2 Francs. Gold. KM#942.	750
P777	1983	3	2 Francs. Platinum. KM#942.	6,950
P778	1983	58	5 Francs. Nickel Clad Copper-Nickel. KM#926a.	25.00
P779	1983	97	5 Francs. Silver. KM#926a.	35.00
P780	1983	8	5 Francs. Gold. KM#926a.	950
P781	1983	3	5 Francs. Platinum. KM#926a.	7,350
P782	1983	286	10 Francs. Nickel-Bronze. KM#952.	20.00
P783	1983	454	10 Francs. Silver. KM#952.	35.00
P784	1983	34	10 Francs. Gold. KM#952.	890
P785	1983	13	10 Francs. Platinum. KM#952.	2,350
P786	1983	74	10 Francs. Nickel-Brass. KM#940.	25.00
P787	1983	118	10 Francs. Silver. KM#940.	45.00
P788	1983	12	10 Francs. Gold. KM#940.	900
P789	1983	5	10 Francs. Platinum. KM#940.	2,800
P790	1983	206	10 Francs. Nickel-Bronze. KM#953.	20.00
P791	1983	314	10 Francs. Silver. KM#953.	45.00
P792	1983	29	10 Francs. Gold. KM#953.	890
P793	1983	5	10 Francs. Platinum. KM#953.	2,800
P794	1983	242	100 Francs. Silver. KM#951.	55.00
P795	1983	14	100 Francs. Gold. KM#951.	1,250
P796	1983	7	100 Francs. Platinum. KM#951.	2,350
P797	1984	56	Centime. Steel. KM#928.	25.00
P798	1984	64	Centime. Silver. KM#928.	25.00
P799	1984	10	Centime. Gold. KM#928.	225
P800	1984	36	5 Centimes. Copper-Nickel. KM#933.	30.00
P801	1984	49	5 Centimes. Silver. KM#933.	25.00
P802	1984	6	5 Centimes. Gold. KM#933.	650
P803	1984	34	10 Centimes. Copper-Nickel. KM#929.	30.00
P804	1984	54	10 Centimes. Silver. KM#929.	25.00
P805	1984	4	10 Centimes. Gold. KM#929.	1,000
P806	1984	34	20 Centimes. Copper-Nickel. KM#930.	30.00
P807	1984	60	20 Centimes. Silver. KM#930.	25.00
P808	1984	4	20 Centimes. Gold. KM#930.	1,325
P809	1984	34	1/2 Franc. Nickel. KM#931.	30.00
P900	1984	59	1/2 Franc. Silver. KM#931.	25.00
P901	1984	8	1/2 Franc. Gold. KM#931.	550
P902	1984	5	1/2 Franc. Platinum. KM#931.	1,450
P903	1984	40	Franc. Nickel. KM#925.	30.00
P904	1984	69	Franc. Silver. KM#925.	25.00
P905	1984	6	Franc. Gold. KM#925.	850
P906	1984	5	Franc. Platinum. KM#925.	2,500
P907	1984	42	2 Francs. Nickel. KM#942.	30.00
P908	1984	79	2 Francs. Silver. KM#942.	25.00
P909	1984	9	2 Francs. Gold. KM#942.	800
P910	1984	5	2 Francs. Platinum. KM#942.	1,750
P911	1984	55	5 Francs. Nickel Clad Copper-Nickel. KM#926a.	30.00
P912	1984	59	5 Francs. Silver. KM#926a.	30.00
P913	1984	4	5 Francs. Gold. KM#926a.	1,650
P914	1984	5	5 Francs. Platinum. KM#926a.	2,400
P915	1984	50	10 Francs. Copper-Nickel-Aluminum. KM#940.	30.00
P916	1984	79	10 Francs. Silver. KM#940.	30.00
P917	1984	6	10 Francs. Gold. KM#940.	1,000
P918	1984	5	10 Francs. Platinum. KM#940.	2,000
P919	1984	184	10 Francs. Copper-Nickel-Aluminum. KM#954.	25.00
P920	1984	244	10 Francs. Silver. KM#954.	30.00

KM#	Date	Mintage	Identification	Mkt Val
P921	1984	18	10 Francs. Gold. KM#954.	950
P922	1984	5	10 Francs. Platinum. KM#954.	2,000
P923	1984	500	100 Francs. Silver. KM#955.	50.00
P924	1984	34	100 Francs. Gold. KM#955.	1,300
P925	1984	9	100 Francs. Platinum. KM#955.	1,950
P926	1984	100	100 Francs. Silver. KM#951.	65.00
P927	1984	10	100 Francs. Gold. KM#951.	1,450
P928	1984	5	100 Francs. Platinum. KM#951.	3,200
P929	1985	100	Centime. 0.9250 Silver. KM#928.	20.00
P930	1985	18	Centime. 0.9200 Gold. KM#928.	225
P931	1985	60	5 Centimes. 0.9250 Silver. KM#933.	30.00
P932	1985	6	5 Centimes. 0.9200 Gold. KM#933.	500
P933	1985	65	10 Centimes. 0.9250 Silver. KM#929.	32.00
P934	1985	4	10 Centimes. 0.9200 Gold. KM#929.	775
P935	1985	85	20 Centimes. 0.9250 Silver. KM#930.	35.00
P936	1985	4	20 Centimes. 0.9200 Gold. KM#930.	1,100
P937	1985	80	1/2 Franc. 0.9250 Silver. KM#931.	35.00
P938	1985	16	1/2 Franc. 0.9200 Gold. KM#931.	475
P939	1985	5	1/2 Franc. Platinum. KM#931.	2,000
P940	1985	90	Franc. 0.9250 Silver. KM#925.	35.00
P941	1985	5	Franc. 0.9200 Gold. KM#925.	750
P942	1985	5	Franc. Platinum. KM#925.	1,600
P943	1985	90	2 Francs. 0.9250 Silver. KM#942.	35.00
P944	1985	17	2 Francs. 0.9200 Gold. KM#942.	750
P945	1985	5	2 Francs. Platinum. KM#942.	1,600
P946	1985	70	5 Francs. 0.9250 Silver. KM#926a.	50.00
P947	1985	4	5 Francs. 0.9200 Gold. KM#926a.	1,750
P948	1985	•5	5 Francs. Platinum. KM#926a.	2,350
P949	1985	120	10 Francs. 0.9250 Silver. KM#940.	45.00
P950	1985	12	10 Francs. 0.9200 Gold. KM#940.	1,150
P951	1985	5	10 Francs. Platinum. KM#940.	2,150
P952	1985	8	10 Francs. 0.9200 Gold. KM#952.	1,150
P953	1985	8	10 Francs. 0.9200 Gold. KM#953.	1,150
P954	1985	45	10 Francs. 0.9250 Silver. KM#954.	60.00
P955	1985	8	10 Francs. 0.9200 Gold. KM#954.	1,100
P956	1985	215	10 Francs. 0.9250 Silver. KM#956.	45.00
P957	1985	17	10 Francs. 0.9200 Gold. KM#956.	1,000
P958	1985	15	10 Francs. Platinum. KM#956.	2,400
P959	1985	100	100 Francs. 0.9250 Silver. KM#951.	65.00
P960	1985	18	100 Francs. 0.9200 Gold. KM#951.	1,325
P961	1985	10	100 Francs. Platinum. KM#951.	2,850
P962	1985	200	100 Francs. 0.9250 Silver. KM#955a.	55.00
P963	1985	8	100 Francs. 0.9200 Gold. KM#955b.	1,650
P964	1985	440	100 Francs. 0.9250 Silver. KM#957.	45.00
P965	1985	30	100 Francs. 0.9200 Gold. KM#957.	1,225
P966	1985	15	100 Francs. Platinum. KM#957.	2,400
P967	1986	10	10 Francs. Platinum. KM#958.	1,850
P968	1986	200	10 Francs. 0.9500 Silver. KM#959.	50.00
P969	1986	5	10 Francs. Platinum. KM#959.	2,150
P970	1986	5	100 Francs. Platinum. KM#951.	3,000
P971	1986	250	100 Francs. Silver. KM#951.	50.00
P972	1986	5,000	100 Francs. 0.9000 Silver. KM#960.	12.50
P973	1986	15	100 Francs. Platinum. KM#960.	2,150
P973b	1986	50	100 Francs. Gold. KM#960b.	1,375
P974	1987	50	Centime. 0.9500 Silver. KM#928.	40.00
P975	1987	50	5 Centimes. 0.9500 Silver. KM#933.	50.00
P976	1987	50	10 Centimes. 0.9500 Silver. KM#929.	50.00
P977	1987	50	20 Centimes. 0.9500 Silver. KM#930.	50.00
P978	1987	50	1/2 Franc. 0.9500 Silver. KM#931.	50.00
P979	1987	50	Franc. 0.9500 Silver. KM#925.	40.00
P980	1987	50	2 Francs. 0.9500 Silver. KM#942.	50.00
P981	1987	50	5 Francs. 0.9500 Silver. KM#926a.	65.00
P982	1987	50	10 Francs. 0.9500 Silver. KM#940.	65.00
P983	1987	15	10 Francs. 0.9200 Gold. KM#940.	950
P984	1987	5	10 Francs. 0.9990 Platinum. KM#940.	2,200
P985	1987	1,000	10 Francs. 0.9500 Silver. KM#961.	45.00
P986	1987	25	10 Francs. 0.9200 Gold. KM#961.	890
P987	1987	10	10 Francs. 0.9990 Platinum. KM#961.	1,650
P988	1987	30	100 Francs. 0.9000 Silver. KM#951.	65.00
P989	1987	15	100 Francs. 0.9200 Gold. KM#951.	1,200
P990	1987	5	100 Francs. 0.9990 Platinum. KM#951.	2,850
P991	1987	51,000	100 Francs. 0.9500 Silver. KM#962, Proof.	20.00
P991a	1987	100,000	100 Francs. 0.9000 Silver. KM#962, Unc.	12.50
P992	1987	50	100 Francs. 0.9200 Gold. KM#962.	1,300
P993	1987	15	100 Francs. 0.9990 Platinum. KM#962.	2,400
P994	1988	5	Centime. Platinum. KM#928.	500
P995	1988	—	10 Francs. 0.9000 Silver. KM#965a, Proof.	100
P996	1988	—	10 Francs. Gold. KM#965c, Proof.	1,300
P997	1988	10	10 Francs. Platinum. KM#965.	1,150
P998	1988	5	100 Francs. Platinum. KM#951.	2,100
PSA999	1988	—	100 Francs. 0.9000 Silver. KM#966, Proof.	2,200
P999	1988	20,000	100 Francs. 0.9000 Silver. KM#966, Unc.	14.00
P1000	1988	10	100 Francs. Platinum. KM#966.	2,350
P1001	1989	5	Centime. Platinum. KM#928.	450
P1002	1989	10	Franc. Platinum. KM#925.	1,250
P1003	1989	300	Franc. Silver. KM#967.	35.00
P1004	1989	25	Franc. Gold. KM#967.	800
P1005	1989	10	Franc. Platinum. KM#967.	1,250
P1006	1989	10	5 Francs. Platinum. KM#968.	1,850
P1007	1989	5	100 Francs. Platinum. KM#951.	2,150
PA1008	1989	—	100 Francs. 0.9000 Silver. KM#970, Proof.	25.00
P1008	1989	10,000	100 Francs. 0.9000 Silver. KM#970, Unc.	16.00
P1009	1989	10	100 Francs. Platinum. KM#970.	2,150
P1010	1990	50	Centime. Silver. KM#928.	—
P1011	1990	10	Centime. Gold. KM#928.	440
P1012	1990	5	Centime. Platinum. KM#928.	550
P1013	1990	50	5 Centimes. Silver. KM#933.	40.00
P1014	1990	50	10 Centimes. Silver. KM#929.	40.00
P1015	1990	50	20 Centimes. Silver. KM#930.	40.00
P1016	1990	5	20 Centimes. Gold. KM#930.	700
P1017	1990	50	1/2 Franc. Silver. KM#931.	40.00
P1018	1990	50	Franc. Silver. KM#925.	40.00
P1019	1990	50	2 Francs. Silver. KM#942.	40.00
P1020	1990	5	2 Francs. Gold. KM#942.	1,000
P1021	1990	50	5 Francs. Silver. KM#926a.	40.00
P1022	1990	10	10 Francs. Gold. Gold Alloy Spirit of Bastille.	650
P1023	1990	50	100 Francs. Silver. KM#951.	65.00
P1024	1990	10	100 Francs. Gold. KM#951.	1,250
P1025	1990	5	100 Francs. Platinum. KM#951.	2,100
P1026	1990	100	100 Francs. Silver. KM#982.	60.00
P1027	1990	10	100 Francs. Gold. KM#982.	1,250
P1028	1990	5	100 Francs. Platinum. KM#982.	1,900
P1029	1991	—	100 Francs. Silver. KM#951.	65.00
P1030	1991	—	100 Francs. Silver. KM#996.	65.00

PIEFORTS WITH ESSAI

Double thickness; standard metals unless otherwise noted

KM#	Date	Mintage	Identification	Mkt Val
PE271	1914	—	10 Centimes. Nickel. Center hole divides RF within wreath, liberty cap above. Denomination divided by plant and center hole, date below. KM#866.	600
PE272	1914	—	25 Centimes. Nickel. KM#867.	550
PE282	1920	—	Franc. Bronze-Aluminum. Denomination within circle, legend surrounds. Mercury seated left, caduceus on left, shield on right, date below.	120
PE-A281	1920	—	5 Centimes. Copper-Nickel. KM#875.	120
PE281	1920	—	50 Centimes. Aluminum-Bronze. Denomination within circle, legend surrounds. Mercury seated left, caduceus on left, shield on right, date below. KM#875.	120
PE299	1929	—	20 Francs. Silver. KM#879.	400
PE298	1929	—	10 Francs. Silver. KM#878.	350
PE301	1931	—	50 Centimes. Aluminum-Bronze. KM#894.1.	—
PE302	1931	—	Franc. Aluminum-Bronze. KM#885.	—
PE303	1931	—	2 Francs. Aluminum-Bronze. KM#886.	—
PE304	1941	—	20 Centimes. Zinc. KM#899.	140
PE307	1941	—	20 Centimes. Zinc. KM#900.	120
PE308	1941	—	5 Francs. Copper-Nickel. KM#901.	450
PE306	1941	—	10 Centimes. Zinc. KM#898.	120
PE309	1943	—	2 Francs. Aluminum. KM#904.	150
PE311	1945	104	5 Francs. Nickel. KM#888.	120
PE310	1945	104	20 Centimes. Zinc. KM#907.	165
PE312	1945	104	20 Francs. Copper-Nickel. KM#879.	185
PE315	1946	104	2 Francs. Aluminum. KM#886a.	120
PE313	1946	104	50 Centimes. Aluminum. KM#894.1a.	90.00
PE314	1946	104	Franc. Aluminum. KM#885a.	100
PE316	1946	104	10 Francs. Copper-Nickel. Laureate head right. Denomination above date, inscription below, grain columns flank. KM#909.	175
PE317	1950	—	10 Francs. Aluminum-Bronze. KM#915.	70.00
PE318	1950	—	20 Francs. Aluminum-Bronze. KM#916.	85.00
PE319	1950	—	50 Francs. Aluminum-Bronze. KM#918.	135
PE320	1952	104	10 Francs. Aluminum-Bronze. KM#915.	70.00
PE321	1952	104	20 Francs. Aluminum-Bronze. KM#917.	85.00
PE322	1952	104	50 Francs. Aluminum-Bronze. KM#918.	115
PE323	1954	104	100 Francs. Copper-Nickel. KM#919.	115
PE324	1958	65	100 Francs. Silver. KM#919.	550
PE327	1959	104	5 Francs. Silver. KM#926.	375
PE325	1959	104	Franc. Nickel. KM#925.	85.00
PE326	1959	104	5 Francs. Silver. KM#926.	135
PE329	1960	20	Franc. Gold. KM#925.	675
PE332	1960	50	5 Francs. Gold. KM#926.	900
PE328	1960	50	Franc. Silver. KM#925.	165
PE330	1960	500	Franc. Nickel. KM#925.	45.00
PE331	1960	500	5 Francs. Silver. KM#926.	115
PE333	1961	104	Centime. Chrome-Steel. KM#928.	65.00
PE334	1961	104	5 Centimes. Chrome-Steel. KM#927.	65.00
PE335	1961	500	5 Centimes. Chrome-Steel. KM#927.	30.00
PE337	1961	20	5 Centimes. Gold. KM#927.	590
PE336	1961	50	5 Centimes. Silver. KM#927.	120
PE340	1962	104	50 Centimes. Aluminum-Bronze. KM#939.	85.00
PE338	1962	104	10 Centimes. Aluminum-Bronze. KM#929.	50.00
PE339	1962	104	20 Centimes. Aluminum-Bronze. KM#930.	50.00
PE434	1971	100	5 Francs. Platinum. KM#926a.	1,500

MINT SETS

KM#	Date	Mintage	Identification	Issue Price	Mkt Val
MS1	1986 (10)	20,000	KM#925.1, 926a, 928-931, 933, 942, 951.1, 959 (sets with perfect case and no PVC damage on coins command a 25% premium)	—	90.00

KM#	Date	Mintage	Identification	Issue Price	Mkt Val
MS2	1987 (10)	4,000	KM#925.1, 926a, 928-931, 933, 940, 942, 961d	—	60.00
MS3	1988 (10)	2,000	KM#925.1, 926a, 928-931, 933, 942, 964-965	—	65.00
MS4	1989 (10)	2,000	KM#925.1, 926a, 928-931, 933, 942, 964, 969	—	65.00
MS6	1991 (9)	2,500	KM#925.1, 926a.1, 928-930, 931.1, 933, 942.1, 964.1, medal rotation	50.00	40.00
MS7	1992 (10)	20,000	KM#925.1, 926a.1, 928-930, 931.1, 933, 942.1, 964.1, 1008.2, medal rotation	—	45.00
MS8	1993 (10)	20,000	KM#925.1, 926a.1, 928-930, 931.1, 933, 942.1, 964.1, 1008.2, medal rotation	—	40.00
MS9	1994 (10)	20,000	KM#925.1, 926a.1, 928-930, 931.1, 933, 942.1, 964.2, 1008.2 bee privy mark	—	50.00
MS10	1995 (10)	20,000	KM#925.1, 926a.1, 928, 930, 931.1, 933, 942.1, 964.2, 1008.2	—	50.00
MS11	1996 (10)	5,000	KM#925.1, 926a.1, 928-930, 931.1, 933, 942.1, 964.2, 1008.2	—	60.00
MS12	1996 (3)	2,500	KM#1155, 1160, 1180	—	35.00
MS13	1997 (10)	15,000	KM#925.1, 926a.1, 928-930, 931.1, 933, 942.1, 964.2, 1008.2	—	50.00
MS14	1998 (10)	—	KM#925.1, 926a.1, 928-930, 931.1, 933, 942.1, 964.2, 1008.2	—	50.00
MS15	1999 (10)	—	KM#925.1, 926a.1, 928-930, 931.1, 933, 942.1, 964.2, 1008.2	—	50.00
MS18	1999 (8)	35,000	KM#1282-1289	20.25	50.00
MS16	2000 (3)	—	KM#1222-1224	—	30.00
MS17	2000 (10)	50,000	KM#925, 926a, 928-931, 933, 942, 964.2, 1008.2	—	50.00
MS19	2000 (8)	35,000	KM#1282-1289	20.25	50.00

PROOF SETS

KM#	Date	Mintage	Identification	Issue Price	Mkt Val
PS6	1990-91 (9)	—	KM#971-972, 980-981, 983-984, 993-995	—	500
PS7	1991 (10)	10,000	KM#925.2, 926a.2, 928-930, 931.2, 933, 942.2, 951.2, 964.2	160	145
PS8	1991 (3)	15,000	KM#977, 991-992	—	500
PS9	1992 (11)	15,000	KM#925.2, 926a.2, 928-930, 931-2, 933, 942.2, 951.2, 964.2, 1008.2	—	125
PS10	1992 (3)	2,000	KM#1007, 1010-1011	—	200
PS11	1993 (11)	10,000	KM#925.1, 926a.1, 928-930, 931.2, 933, 942.1, 964.1, 961.1, 1008.2	—	135
PS12	1994 (11)	10,000	KM#925.2, 926a.2, 928-930, 931.2, 933, 942.2, 951.1, 964.2, 1008.2, fish privy mark	—	135
PS13	1995 (11)	10,000	KM#925.2, 926a.2, 928-930, 931.2, 933, 942.2, 951.1, 964.2, 1008.2	—	135
PS14	1996 (11)	8,000	KM#925.2, 926a.2, 928-930, 931.2, 933, 942.2, 951.1, 964.2, 1008.2	—	140
PS15	1997 (11)	10,000	KM#925.2, 926a.2, 928, 930, 931.2, 933, 942.2, 951.1, 964.2, 1008.2	—	135
PS16	1998 (11)	—	KM#925.2, 926a.2, 928, 930, 931.2, 933, 942.2, 951.1, 964.2, 1008.2	—	135
PS17	1999 (11)	—	KM#925.2, 926a.2, 928, 930, 941.2, 933, 942.2, 951.1, 964.2, 1008.2	—	135
PS19	1999 (8)	15,000	KM#1282-1289	59.00	110
PS18	2000 (11)	—	KM#925.2, 926a.2, 928, 930, 931.2, 933, 942.2, 951.1, 964.2, 1008.2	—	135
PS20	2000 (8)	15,000	KM#1282-1289	59.00	110

SPECIMEN FDC SETS (FLEUR DE COIN)

KM#	Date	Mintage	Identification	Issue Price	Mkt Val
SS1	1964 (7)	25,600	KM#925-930, 939	4.00	25.00
SS2	1965 (7)	35,000	KM#925-926, 928-932	7.60	35.00
SS3	1966 (8)	7,171	KM#925-926, 928-933	9.00	70.00
SS4	1967 (8)	2,305	KM#925-926, 928-933	10.00	220
SS5	1968 (8)	3,000	With perfect box KM#925-926, 928-933	10.00	450
SS5A	1968 (8)	I.A.	KM#925-926, 928-933 without box	—	120
SS6	1969 (8)	6,050	KM#925-926, 928-933	10.00	120
SS7	1970 (8)	10,000	KM#925, 926a, 928-933	9.00	35.00
SS8	1971 (8)	12,000	KM#925, 926a, 928-933	9.00	35.00
SS9	1972 (8)	15,000	KM#925, 926a, 928-933	9.00	35.00
SS10	1973 (8)	79,000	KM#925, 926a, 928-933	12.00	32.00
SS11	1974 (9)	98,800	KM#925, 926a, 928-931, 933, 940-941	31.00	30.00
SS12	1975 (9)	52,000	KM#925, 926a, 928-931, 933, 940-941	35.00	35.00
SS13	1976 (9)	35,700	KM#925, 926a, 928-931, 933, 940-941	35.00	35.00
SS14	1977 (9)	25,000	KM#925, 926a, 928-931, 933, 940-941	36.00	40.00
SS15	1978 (9)	24,000	KM#925, 926a, 928-931, 933, 940-941	39.00	50.00
SS16	1979 (10)	40,500	KM#925, 926a, 928-931, 933, 940--942	55.00	70.00
SS17	1980 (10)	60,000	KM#925, 926a, 928-931, 933, 940-942	90.00	60.00
SS18	1981 (9)	26,000	KM#925, 926a, 928-931, 933, 940, 942	—	55.00
SS19	1982 (11)	27,500	KM#925, 926a, 928-931, 933, 940, 942, 950-951	—	85.00
SS20	1983 (12)	16,561	KM#925, 926a, 928-931, 933, 940, 942, 951-953	—	120
SS21	1984 (12)	13,388	KM#825, 926a, 928-931, 933, 940, 942, 951, 954, 955	—	175
SS22	1985 (12)	12,224	KM#925, 926a, 928-931, 933, 940, 942, 951, 956-957	—	150
SS23	1986 (12)	13,000	KM#925.1, 926a.1, 928-931.1, 933, 942.1, 951, 958, 959, 960	—	165
SS24	1987 (12)	15,000	KM#925.1, 926a.1, 928-931.1, 933, 940, 942.1, 951, 961, 962	68.00	165
SS25	1987 (2)	—	KMP991-991a, Proof and BU	120	60.00
SS26	1988 (13)	13,000	KM#925.1, 926a.1, 928-931.1, 933, 941.1, 951, 963-966	—	175
SS27	1989 (14)	10,000	KM#925.1, 926a.1, 928-931.1, 933, 942.1, 951, 964, 967-970	—	185
SS28	1990 (13)	10,000	KM#925.1, 926a.1, 928-931.1, 933, 942.1, 951, 964, 980-982	—	175
SS29	1990 (11)	10,000	KM#925.1, 926a.1, 928-931.1, 933, 942.1, 951, 964, 982	—	165

FRENCH AFARS & ISSAS

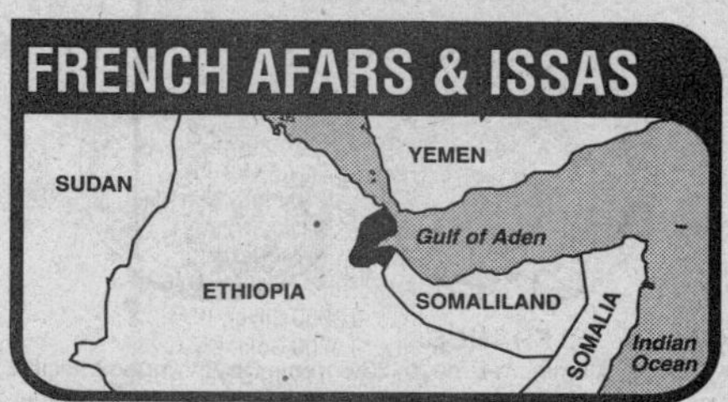

MINT MARKS

(a) - Paris (privy marks only)

MONETARY SYSTEM

100 Centimes = 1 Franc

Note

For later coinage, see Djibouti

For earlier coinage, see French Somaliland

FRENCH COLONY

DECIMAL COINAGE

KM# 16 FRANC

1.3000 g., Aluminum, 24 mm. **Obv:** Winged bust left, date below **Obv. Designer:** G.B.L. Bazor **Rev:** Lyre antelope divides denomination

Date	Mintage	F	VF	XF	Unc	BU
1969(a)	100,000	1.00	2.00	3.50	6.00	—
1971(a)	100,000	1.00	2.00	3.50	6.00	—
1975(a)	300,000	0.75	1.25	2.00	3.00	—

KM# 13 2 FRANCS

2.2000 g., Aluminum, 27 mm. **Obv:** Winged bust left, date below **Obv. Designer:** G.B.L. Bazor **Rev:** Lyre antelope divides denomination

Date	Mintage	F	VF	XF	Unc	BU
1968(a)	100,000	1.00	2.00	3.50	6.00	—
1975(a)	180,000	0.75	1.50	2.50	5.00	—

KM# 14 5 FRANCS

3.8000 g., Aluminum, 31.1 mm. **Obv:** Winged bust left, date below **Obv. Designer:** G.B.L. Bazor **Rev:** Lyre antelope divides denomination

Date	Mintage	F	VF	XF	Unc	BU
1968(a)	100,000	1.00	2.00	3.50	6.00	—
1975(a)	300,000	0.75	1.25	2.00	4.00	—

KM# 17 10 FRANCS

3.0000 g., Aluminum-Bronze, 20 mm. **Obv:** Winged bust left, date below **Obv. Designer:** G.B.L. Bazor **Rev:** Dhow, ocean liner, denomination above

Date	Mintage	F	VF	XF	Unc	BU
1969(a)	100,000	1.50	3.00	6.00	9.00	—
1970(a)	300,000	1.00	2.00	4.00	7.00	—
1975(a)	360,000	0.75	1.50	3.00	5.00	—

KM# 15 20 FRANCS
4.1000 g., Aluminum-Bronze, 23.6 mm. **Obv:** Winged bust left, date below **Obv. Designer:** G.B.L. Bazor **Rev:** Dhow, ocean liner, denomination above

Date	Mintage	F	VF	XF	Unc	BU
1968(a)	300,000	1.50	2.50	4.50	8.00	—
1975(a)	300,000	1.25	2.00	4.00	7.00	—

KM# 18 50 FRANCS
7.0000 g., Copper Nickel, 25.5 mm. **Obv:** Hooded head left, date below **Obv. Designer:** R. Joly **Rev:** Pair of dromedary camels, denomination above

Date	Mintage	F	VF	XF	Unc	BU
1970(a)	600,000	1.50	3.00	6.00	10.00	12.00
1975(a)	180,000	1.50	3.00	6.00	10.00	12.00

KM# 19 100 FRANCS
11.9000 g., Copper-Nickel, 30 mm. **Obv:** Hooded head left, date below **Obv. Designer:** R. Joly **Rev:** Pair of dromedary camels, denomination below

Date	Mintage	F	VF	XF	Unc	BU
1970(a)	600,000	2.50	4.00	7.00	11.50	15.00
1975(a)	400,000	2.50	4.50	7.50	12.50	16.00

ESSAIS

Standard metals unless otherwise noted

KM#	Date	Mintage	Identification	Issue Price	Mkt Val
E1	1968(a)	1,700	2 Francs. KM13.	—	12.00
E2	1968(a)	1,700	5 Francs. KM14.	—	15.00
E3	1968(a)	1,700	20 Francs. KM15.	—	20.00
E4	1969(a)	1,700	Franc. KM16.	—	15.00
E5	1969(a)	1,700	10 Francs. KM17.	—	20.00
E6	1970(a)	1,700	50 Francs. KM18.	—	30.00
E7	1970(a)	1,700	100 Francs. KM19.	—	35.00

FRENCH EQUATORIAL AFRICA

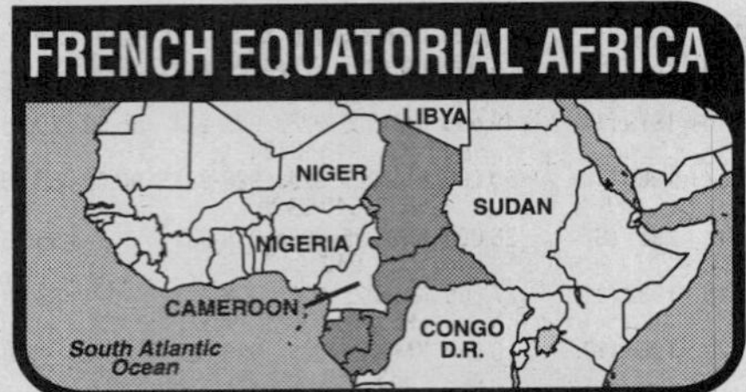

French Equatorial Africa, an area consisting of four self governing dependencies (Middle Congo, Ubangi-Shari, Chad and Gabon) in West-Central Africa, had an area of 969,111 sq. mi. (2,509,987 sq. km.). Capital: Brazzaville. The area, rich in natural resources, exported cotton, timber, coffee, cacao, diamonds and gold.

Little is known of the history of these parts of Africa prior to French occupation - which began with no thought of territorial acquisition. France's initial intent was simply to establish a few supply stations along the west coast of Africa to service the warships assigned to combat the slave trade in the early part of the 19th century. French settlement began in 1839. Gabon (then Gabun) and the Middle Congo were secured between 1885 and 1891; Chad and Ubangi-Shari between 1894 and 1897. The four colonies were joined to form French Equatorial Africa in 1910. The dependencies were changed from colonies to territories within the French Union in 1946, and all the inhabitants were made French citizens. In 1958 they voted to become autonomous republics within the new French Community, and attained full independence in 1960.

For later coinage see Central African States, Congo Peoples Republic, Gabon and Chad.

RULERS
French, until 1960

MINT MARKS
(a) - Paris, privy marks only
(t) - Poissy, privy marks only, thunderbolt
SA - Pretoria (1942-1943)

ENGRAVERS INITIALS
GLS – Steynberg

MONETARY SYSTEM
100 Centimes = 1 Franc

FRENCH COLONY

DECIMAL COINAGE

KM# 3 5 CENTIMES
Aluminum-Bronze **Note:** Similar to 10 Centimes, KM#4.

Date	Mintage	F	VF	XF	Unc	BU
1943	Est. 44,000,000	90.00	150	325	650	750

Note: Not released for circulation

KM# 4 10 CENTIMES
Aluminum-Bronze

Date	Mintage	F	VF	XF	Unc	BU
1943	Est. 13,000,000	75.00	100	160	375	450

Note: Not released for circulation

KM# 5 25 CENTIMES
Aluminum-Bronze **Note:** Similar to 10 Centimes, KM#4.

Date	Mintage	F	VF	XF	Unc	BU
1943	Est. 4,160,000	200	350	550	850	1,000

Note: Not released for circulation

KM# 1 50 CENTIMES
Brass **Rev:** Double cross divides denomination, date below

Date	Mintage	F	VF	XF	Unc	BU
1942SA	8,000,000	1.50	3.00	8.00	20.00	25.00

KM# 1a 50 CENTIMES
Bronze **Rev:** Double cross divides denomination

Date	Mintage	F	VF	XF	Unc	BU
1943SA	16,000,000	1.25	2.50	7.00	18.00	25.00

KM# 2 FRANC
Brass **Obv:** Rooster, small shield above **Rev:** Double cross divides denomination, date below

Date	Mintage	F	VF	XF	Unc	BU
1942SA	3,000,000	2.00	3.50	10.00	22.50	30.00

KM# 2a FRANC
Bronze **Obv:** Rooster left, small shield above **Rev:** Double cross divides denomination

Date	Mintage	F	VF	XF	Unc	BU
1943SA	6,000,000	1.75	2.75	9.00	20.00	30.00

KM# 6 FRANC
Aluminum, 23 mm. **Obv:** Winged bust left, date below **Obv. Designer:** G.B.L. Bazor **Rev:** Loder's gazelle divides denomination

Date	Mintage	F	VF	XF	Unc	BU
1948(a)	15,000,000	0.15	0.25	0.50	2.00	—

KM# 7 2 FRANCS
Aluminum **Obv:** Winged bust left, date below **Obv. Designer:** G.B.L. Bazor **Rev:** Loder's gazelle divides denomination

Date	Mintage	F	VF	XF	Unc	BU
1948(a)	5,040,000	0.25	0.50	1.50	4.00	—

TOKEN COINAGE

Middle Congo

KM# TnA1 NON-DENOMINATED
Aluminum **Obv:** Center hole, date below, MC above **Rev:** Center hole within Elephant walking left **Note:** Prev. KM#Tn1.

Date	Mintage	F	VF	XF	Unc	BU
1925(t)	—	35.00	65.00	115	300	425

KM# TnA2 NON-DENOMINATED
Aluminum **Rev:** Center hole within Leopard walking left **Note:** Previous KM#Tn2.

Date	Mintage	F	VF	XF	Unc	BU
1926	—	40.00	75.00	150	325	475

ESSAIS

Standard metals unless otherwise noted

KM#	Date	Mintage	Identification	Mkt Val
E1	1948(a)	2,000	Franc. Copper-Nickel. KM#7	30.00
E2	1948(a)	2,000	2 Francs. Copper-Nickel. KM#7	35.00

PIEFORTS WITH ESSAI

Standard metals unless otherwise noted

KM#	Date	Mintage	Identification	Mkt Val
PE1	1948(a)	104	Franc. Aluminum. KM#6	60.00
PE2	1948(a)	104	2 Francs. Aluminum. KM#7	70.00

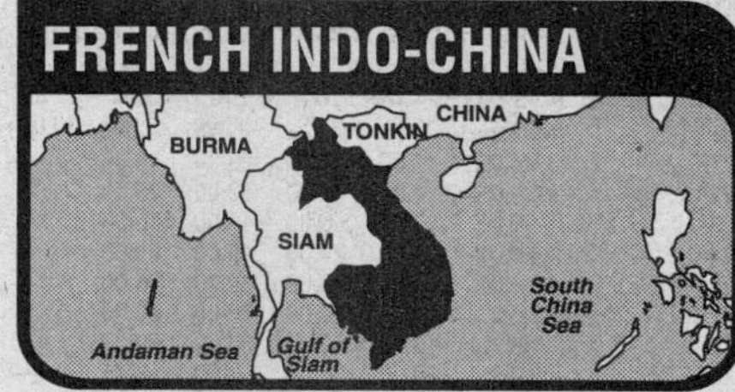

French Indo-China, made up of the protectorates of Annam, Tonkin, Cambodia and Laos and the colony of Cochin-China was located on the Indo-Chinese peninsula of Southeast Asia. The colony had an area of 286,194 sq. mi. (741,242 sq. km.). and a population of 30 million. Principal cities: Saigon, Haiphong, Vientiane, Pnom-Penh and Hanoi.

The forebears of the modern Indo-Chinese people originated in the Yellow River Valley of Northern China. From there, they were driven into the Indo-Chinese peninsula by the Han Chinese. The Chinese followed southward in the second century B.C., conquering the peninsula and ruling it until 938, leaving a lingering heritage of Chinese learning and culture. Indo-Chinese independence was basically maintained until the arrival of the French in the mid-19th century who established control over all of Vietnam, Laos and Cambodia. Activities directed toward obtaining self-determination accelerated during the Japanese occupation of World War II. The dependencies were changed from colonies to territories within the French Union in 1946, and all the inhabitants were made French citizens.

In Aug. of 1945, an uprising erupted involving the French and Vietnamese Nationalists, culminated in the French military disaster at Dien Bien Phu (May, 1954) and the subsequent Geneva Conference that brought an end to French colonial rule in Indo-China.

For later coinage see Kampuchea, Laos and Vietnam.

RULERS
French, until 1954

MINT MARKS
A - Paris
(a) - Paris, privy marks only
B - Beaumont-le-Roger
C - Castlesarrasin
H - Heaton, Birmingham
(p) - Thunderbolt - Poissy
S - San Francisco, U.S.A.
None - Osaka, Japan
None - Hanoi, Tonkin

MONETARY SYSTEM
5 Sapeques = 1 Cent
100 Cents = 1 Piastre

FRENCH COLONY

STANDARD COINAGE

KM# 6 2 SAPEQUE

Bronze

Date	Mintage	F	VF	XF	Unc	BU
1901A	4,843,000	2.50	7.50	15.00	45.00	90.00
1902A	2,500,000	7.50	20.00	40.00	125	200

KM# 25 1/4 CENT

Zinc **Obv:** Square surrounds center hole, grain sprigs flank, date below **Rev:** Square around center hole, corners section coin, denomination divided by hole **Note:** Lead counterfeits dated 1941 and 1942 are known.

Date	Mintage	F	VF	XF	Unc	BU
1941	—	12.00	25.00	45.00	—	—
1942	221,800,000	8.00	15.00	35.00	75.00	100
1943	279,450,000	15.00	35.00	55.00	125	150
1944	46,122,000	100	180	250	750	1,250

KM# 20 1/2 CENT

Bronze, 21 mm. **Obv:** Center hole divides RF, liberty cap above, wreath surrounds **Rev:** Denomination divided by grain sprigs around center hole, date below

Date	Mintage	F	VF	XF	Unc	BU
1935(a)	26,365,000	0.25	0.50	2.00	10.00	—
1936(a)	23,635,000	0.25	0.50	2.00	10.00	—
1937(a)	10,244,000	0.50	1.50	5.00	15.00	—
1938(a)	16,665,000	0.25	0.75	2.50	12.00	—
1939(a)	17,305,000	0.25	0.75	2.50	12.00	—
1940(a)	11,218,000	4.00	8.00	20.00	40.00	75.00

KM# 20a 1/2 CENT

Zinc, 21 mm. **Obv:** Center hole divides RF, liberty cap above, wreath surrounds **Rev:** Denomination divided by center hole and grain sprigs

Date	Mintage	F	VF	XF	Unc	BU
1939(a)	185,000	200	400	600	900	—
1940(a)	Inc. above	350	500	800	1,200	—

KM# 8 CENT

Bronze, 27.5 mm. **Obv:** Center hole within statue, denomination below **Rev:** Symbols at four sides of center hole within circle, date below

Date	Mintage	F	VF	XF	Unc	BU
1901	9,750,000	2.00	3.00	7.50	25.00	—
1902	6,050,000	4.00	7.00	15.00	50.00	—
1903	8,000,000	2.50	4.00	8.00	30.00	—
1906	2,000,000	8.00	15.00	35.00	100	—

KM# 12.1 CENT

Bronze, 26 mm. **Obv:** Center hole within statue, denomination below, mint mark "A" for Paris mint **Rev:** Symbols at four sides of center hole within circle, date below

Date	Mintage	F	VF	XF	Unc	BU
1908	3,000,000	10.00	20.00	55.00	235	350
1909	5,000,000	20.00	40.00	80.00	275	—
1910	7,703,000	2.00	5.00	15.00	35.00	—
1911	15,234,000	0.75	3.00	10.00	20.00	—
1912	17,027,000	0.75	2.00	7.50	20.00	—
1913	3,945,000	2.00	7.00	18.00	45.00	—
1914	11,027,000	0.75	3.00	15.00	30.00	—
1916	1,312,000	8.00	15.00	30.00	65.00	—
1917	9,762,000	1.00	4.00	10.00	20.00	—
1918	2,372,000	6.00	12.50	25.00	50.00	—
1919	9,148,000	1.00	4.00	7.50	20.00	—
1920	18,305,000	0.75	3.00	5.00	12.50	—
1921	14,272,000	0.75	2.00	3.00	10.00	—
1922	8,850,000	1.00	3.00	5.00	20.00	—
1923	1,079,000	40.00	90.00	180	350	—
1926	11,672,000	0.75	2.00	4.00	15.00	—
1927	3,328,000	5.00	15.00	35.00	70.00	—
1930	4,682,000	1.25	2.75	5.00	15.00	—
1931	5,318,000	30.00	85.00	200	550	—
Note: Torch privy mark						
1931	Inc. above	60.00	120	300	800	—
Note: Wing privy mark						
1937	8,902,000	1.50	3.00	6.00	25.00	—
1938	15,499,000	1.00	2.00	4.00	16.00	—
1939	17,589,000	1.00	2.00	4.00	16.00	—

KM# 12.2 CENT

Bronze, 26 mm. **Obv:** No mint mark at bottom, (San Francisco mint) **Rev:** Four symbols surround center hole **Note:** Without mint mark.

Date	Mintage	F	VF	XF	Unc	BU
1920	13,290,000	2.00	4.00	10.00	25.00	—
1921	1,710,000	35.00	70.00	180	350	—

KM# 12.3 CENT

Bronze, 26 mm. **Obv:** Center hole within statue, denomination below **Rev:** Four symbols surround center hole

Date	Mintage	F	VF	XF	Unc	BU
1922(p)	9,476,000	1.00	1.75	5.00	12.00	—
1923(p)	35,524,000	0.50	0.75	1.50	7.50	—

KM# 24.1 CENT

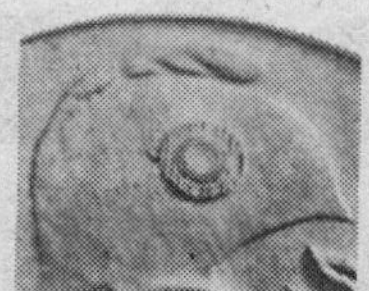

Circles

KM# 24.1 CENT

Zinc **Obv:** Wreath surrounds center hole, liberty cap above, denomination below **Rev:** Center hole divides denomination, wreath surrounds, date below **Note:** Vichy Government issue. Type 1: Circles on Phrygian cap.

Date	Mintage	F	VF	XF	Unc	BU
1940	1,990,000	10.00	16.00	40.00	75.00	—

Rosettes

KM# 24.2 CENT

Zinc **Obv:** Wreath surrounds center hole, liberty cap above, denomination below **Rev:** Center hole divides denomination, wreath surrounds, date below **Note:** Vichy Government issue. Type 2: Rosette on Phrygian cap, variety 2 with 12 petals.

Date	Mintage	F	VF	XF	Unc	BU
1940	150,000	18.00	35.00	70.00	140	—

KM# 24.3 CENT

Zinc **Obv:** Wreath surrounds, cap above, denomination below **Rev:** Wreath surrounds center hole, denomination divided **Note:** Vichy Government issue. Type 2: Rosette on Phrygian cap. Variety 2: 11 petals.

Date	Mintage	F	VF	XF	Unc	BU
1940	2,360,000	8.00	18.00	35.00	70.00	—
1941	2,500,000	7.00	16.00	32.50	70.00	—

KM# 26 CENT

Aluminum **Obv:** Center hole flanked by leafy sprays, date below **Rev:** Denomination left and top of center hole **Note:** Edge varieties exist - plain, grooved, and partially grooved.

Date	Mintage	F	VF	XF	Unc	BU
1943	15,000,000	0.75	2.00	4.00	8.00	—

KM# 18 5 CENTS

5.0000 g., Copper-Nickel, 24 mm. **Obv:** Cornucopias flank center hole, laureate head left above **Rev:** Center hole within wreath divides denomination, date below **Designer:** A. Patey **Note:** 1.6 mm thick; prev. KM#18.1.

Date	Mintage	F	VF	XF	Unc	BU
1923(a)	1,611,000	10.00	20.00	40.00	80.00	—
1924(a)	3,389,000	6.00	12.00	24.00	45.00	—
1925(a)	6,000,000	5.00	10.00	20.00	35.00	—
1930(a) Torch	4,000,000	5.00	10.00	20.00	35.00	—
1937(a) Wing	10,000,000	2.00	5.00	10.00	20.00	—
1938(a)	1,480,000	15.00	30.00	75.00	160	—
1938(a) Proof	—	Value: 275				

KM# 18.1a 5 CENTS
4.0000 g., Nickel-Brass, 24 mm. **Obv:** Cornucopias flank center hole, laureate head left above **Rev:** Center hole divides denomination, wreath surrounds, date below **Note:** 1.3 mm thick.

Date	Mintage	F	VF	XF	Unc	BU
1938(a)	50,569,000	0.75	2.00	5.00	12.00	—
1939(a)	38,501,000	0.75	2.00	5.00	12.00	—

KM# 27 5 CENTS
Aluminum **Note:** Vichy Government issue. Edge varieties exist: reeded - rare, plain, grooved, and partially grooved.

Date	Mintage	F	VF	XF	Unc	BU
1943A	10,000,000	1.00	2.00	5.00	10.00	—

KM# 30.1 5 CENTS
Aluminum **Obv:** Bust right holding laurel, date below **Rev:** Plant divides denomination

Date	Mintage	F	VF	XF	Unc	BU
1946(a)	28,000,000	0.25	0.60	1.00	5.00	—

KM# 30.2 5 CENTS
Aluminum **Obv:** Bust right holding laurel, date below **Rev:** Plant divide denomination

Date	Mintage	F	VF	XF	Unc	BU
1946B	22,000,000	0.25	0.60	1.00	5.00	—

KM# 9 10 CENTS
2.7000 g., 0.8350 Silver .0725 oz. ASW **Obv:** Liberty seated left with fasces **Rev:** Denomination within wreath **Rev. Legend:** TITRE 0.835. POIDS 2 GR. 7 **Designer:** Barre

Date	Mintage	F	VF	XF	Unc	BU
1901	2,950,000	7.00	25.00	60.00	200	350
1902	7,050,000	4.00	12.00	30.00	125	—
1903	1,300,000	12.00	30.00	80.00	325	—
1908	1,000,000	50.00	100	200	575	—
1909	1,000,000	30.00	75.00	130	425	—
1910	2,689,000	25.00	60.00	100	350	—
1911	2,311,000	25.00	40.00	80.00	325	—
1912	2,500,000	25.00	35.00	70.00	275	—
1913	4,847,000	7.50	12.50	30.00	125	—
1914	2,667,000	10.00	30.00	60.00	175	—
1916	2,000,000	10.00	30.00	60.00	185	—
1917	1,500,000	25.00	50.00	100	300	—
1919	1,500,000	30.00	60.00	125	350	—

KM# 14 10 CENTS
3.0000 g., 0.4000 Silver .0386 oz. ASW **Obv:** Liberty seated, date below **Rev:** Denomination within wreath, without fineness indicated **Designer:** Barre **Note:** Without mint mark.

Date	Mintage	F	VF	XF	Unc	BU
1920	10,000,000	10.00	20.00	50.00	120	150

KM# 16.1 10 CENTS
2.7000 g., 0.6800 Silver .0590 oz. ASW **Obv:** Liberty seated, date below **Rev:** Denomination within wreath **Rev. Legend:** TITRE 0.680 POIDS 2 GR. 7 **Designer:** Barre

Date	Mintage	F	VF	XF	Unc	BU
1921A	12,516,000	1.50	3.00	9.00	25.00	30.00
1922A	22,381,000	1.50	3.00	9.00	20.00	25.00
1923A	21,755,000	1.50	3.00	9.00	20.00	25.00
1924A	2,816,000	4.00	9.00	25.00	60.00	80.00
1925A	4,909,000	2.00	5.00	15.00	35.00	50.00
1927A	6,471,000	2.50	7.00	17.50	40.00	60.00
1928A	1,593,000	40.00	100	200	480	750
1929A	5,831,000	1.50	3.00	10.00	30.00	50.00
1930A	6,608,000	1.50	3.00	10.00	30.00	50.00
1931A Proof	100	Value: 400				

KM# 16.2 10 CENTS
2.7000 g., 0.6800 Silver .0590 oz. ASW **Obv:** Liberty seated left, date below **Rev:** Denomination within wreath **Rev. Legend:** TITRE 0.680 POIDS 2 GR. 7 **Designer:** Barre

Date	Mintage	F	VF	XF	Unc	BU
1937(a)	25,000,000	1.00	1.50	3.00	8.00	10.00

KM# 21.1 10 CENTS
Nickel, 18 mm. **Obv:** Bust right holding laurel, date without dots **Obv. Designer:** P. Turin **Rev:** Plant divides denomination **Note:** These coins are magnetic.

Date	Mintage	F	VF	XF	Unc	BU
1939(a)	16,841,000	0.50	1.00	2.00	8.00	10.00
1940(a)	25,505,000	0.50	1.00	2.00	8.00	10.00

KM# 21.1a 10 CENTS
Copper-Nickel, 18 mm. **Obv:** Date without dots **Rev:** Plant divides denomination **Designer:** P. Turin **Note:** These coins are not magnetic.

Date	Mintage	F	VF	XF	Unc	BU
1939(a)	—	45.00	100	200	375	—
Note: Mintage included in KM#21.2						
1941S	50,000,000	0.50	1.00	3.00	8.00	—

KM# 21.2 10 CENTS
Copper-Nickel, 18 mm. **Obv:** Date between two dots **Rev:** Plant divides denomination **Designer:** P. Turin **Note:** These coins are not magnetic.

Date	Mintage	F	VF	XF	Unc	BU
.1939.(a)	2,237,000	65.00	140	250	475	—

KM# 28.1 10 CENTS
Aluminum, 23 mm. **Obv:** Bust right holding laurel, date below **Obv. Designer:** P. Turin **Rev:** Plant divides denomination

Date	Mintage	F	VF	XF	Unc	BU
1945(a)	40,170,000	0.25	0.50	1.00	4.50	—

KM# 28.2 10 CENTS
Aluminum, 23 mm. **Obv:** Bust right holding laurel, date below **Obv. Designer:** P. Turin **Rev:** Plant divides denomination

Date	Mintage	F	VF	XF	Unc	BU
1945B	9,830,000	1.00	2.00	5.00	12.50	—

KM# 10 20 CENTS
5.4000 g., 0.8350 Silver .1450 oz. ASW **Designer:** Barre

Date	Mintage	F	VF	XF	Unc	BU
1901	1,375,000	20.00	50.00	100	300	—
1902	3,525,000	7.50	15.00	40.00	175	—
1903	675,000	50.00	100	150	600	—
1908	500,000	100	250	400	850	—
1909	500,000	100	200	350	850	—
1911	2,340,000	7.50	15.00	35.00	120	—
1912	160,000	100	200	400	900	1,100
1913	1,252,000	50.00	100	150	400	—
1914	2,500,000	7.50	15.00	25.00	120	—
1916	1,000,000	20.00	45.00	120	280	—

KM# 13 20 CENTS
0.8350 Silver **Obv:** KM#10 **Rev:** KM#3a **Note:** Mule.

Date	Mintage	F	VF	XF	Unc	BU
1909	—	100	250	650	1,000	1,400

KM# 15 20 CENTS
6.0000 g., 0.4000 Silver .0772 oz. ASW **Rev:** Without fineness indicated **Note:** Without mint mark.

Date	Mintage	F	VF	XF	Unc	BU
1920	4,000,000	12.50	25.00	50.00	125	—

KM# 17.1 20 CENTS
5.4000 g., 0.6800 Silver .1181 oz. ASW **Obv:** Seated liberty left, date below **Rev:** Denomination within wreath **Rev. Legend:** TITRE O.680 POIDS 5 GR. 4 **Designer:** Barre

Date	Mintage	F	VF	XF	Unc	BU
1921A	3,663,000	4.00	10.00	20.00	40.00	—
1922A	5,812,000	3.00	6.00	12.00	25.00	—
1923A	7,109,000	3.00	6.00	12.00	25.00	—
1924A	1,400,000	8.00	20.00	40.00	90.00	—
1925A	2,556,000	6.00	15.00	30.00	75.00	—
1927A	3,245,000	4.00	10.00	20.00	40.00	—
1928A	794,000	15.00	40.00	80.00	225	—
1929A	644,000	20.00	50.00	100	275	—
1930A	5,576,000	3.00	6.00	12.00	25.00	—

KM# 17.2 20 CENTS
5.4000 g., 0.6800 Silver .1181 oz. ASW **Obv:** Liberty seated, date below **Rev:** Denomination within wreath **Rev. Legend:** TITRE O.680 POIDS 5 GR. 4 **Designer:** Barre

Date	Mintage	F	VF	XF	Unc	BU
1937(a)	17,500,000	1.75	2.50	6.00	12.00	—

KM# 23 20 CENTS
Nickel, 24 mm. **Obv:** Bust right holding laurel, date below **Obv. Designer:** P. Turin **Rev:** Plant divides denomination **Note:** Magnetic coin with security edge.

Date	Mintage	F	VF	XF	Unc	BU
1939(a)	344,500	15.00	30.00	70.00	125	—

KM# 23a.1 20 CENTS
Copper-Nickel, 24 mm. **Obv:** Bust right holding laurel, date below **Obv. Designer:** P. Turin **Rev:** Plant divides denomination **Edge:** Reeded **Note:** Non-magnetic coin.

Date	Mintage	F	VF	XF	Unc	BU
1939(a)	14,676,000	0.50	1.00	2.00	10.00	—
Note: Date between dots						

KM# 23a.2 20 CENTS
Copper-Nickel, 24 mm. **Obv:** Bust right holding laurel, date below **Obv. Designer:** P. Turin **Rev:** Plant divides denomination **Edge:** Reeded **Note:** Non-magnetic coin.

Date	Mintage	F	VF	XF	Unc	BU
1941S	25,000,000	0.50	1.00	2.00	6.00	—
Note: Date between dots						

KM# 29.1 20 CENTS
Aluminum **Obv:** Bust right holding laurel, date below **Obv. Designer:** P. Turin **Rev:** Plant divides denomination

Date	Mintage	F	VF	XF	Unc	BU
1945(a)	15,412,000	0.50	1.00	2.50	10.00	—

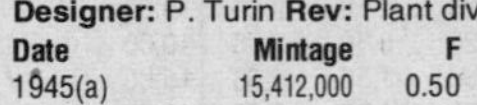

KM# 29.2 20 CENTS
Aluminum **Obv:** Bust right holding laurel, date below **Obv. Designer:** P. Turin **Rev:** Plant divides denomination

Date	Mintage	F	VF	XF	Unc	BU
1945B	6,665,000	2.00	4.00	8.00	25.00	—

KM# 29.3 20 CENTS
Aluminum **Obv:** Bust right holding laurel, date below **Obv. Designer:** P. Turin **Rev:** Plant divides denomination

Date	Mintage	F	VF	XF	Unc	BU
1945C	22,423,000	0.50	1.00	3.00	15.00	—

KM# 4a.2 50 CENTS
13.5000 g., 0.9000 Silver .3906 oz. ASW **Obv:** Liberty seated, date below **Rev:** Denomination within wreath **Rev. Legend:** TITRE 0.900. POIDS 13 GR. 5 **Designer:** Barre

Date	Mintage	F	VF	XF	Unc	BU
1936(a)	4,000,000	5.50	6.50	12.00	25.00	—

KM# 31 50 CENTS
Copper-Nickel **Obv:** Liberty seated, date below **Rev:** Denomination within wreath **Rev. Legend:** BRONZE DE NICKEL **Designer:** Barre

Date	Mintage	F	VF	XF	Unc	BU
1946(a)	32,292,000	2.00	4.00	9.00	25.00	—

KM# 5a.1 PIASTRE
27.0000 g., 0.9000 Silver .7812 oz. ASW **Obv:** Liberty seated left with fasces **Rev:** Denomination within wreath **Rev. Legend:** TITRE 0.900 POIDS 27 GR. **Designer:** Barre

Date	Mintage	F	VF	XF	Unc	BU
1901A	3,150,000	11.50	15.00	25.00	150	275
1902A	3,327,000	11.50	15.00	25.00	150	275
1903A	10,077,000	11.50	13.50	17.50	110	—
1904A	5,751,000	11.50	15.00	20.00	130	—
1905A	3,561,000	11.50	15.00	20.00	130	—
1906A	10,194,000	11.50	13.50	20.00	110	—
1907A	14,062,000	11.50	13.50	20.00	110	—
1908A	13,986,000	11.50	13.50	20.00	110	—
1909A	9,201,000	11.50	13.50	20.00	100	—
1910A	761,000	25.00	50.00	120	320	450
1913A	3,244,000	11.50	15.00	22.50	110	—
1924A	2,831,000	11.50	13.50	22.50	150	—
1925A	2,882,000	11.50	13.50	22.50	150	—
1926A	6,383,000	11.50	13.50	20.00	110	—
1927A	8,183,999	11.50	13.50	20.00	90.00	110
1928A	5,290,000	11.50	13.50	20.00	110	—

KM# 5a.2 PIASTRE
27.0000 g., 0.9000 Silver .7812 oz. ASW **Rev:** Denomination within wreath **Designer:** Barre **Note:** Without mint mark.

Date	Mintage	F	VF	XF	Unc	BU
1921	4,850,000	12.00	20.00	40.00	150	175
1922	1,150,000	13.50	30.00	60.00	225	275

KM# 5a.3 PIASTRE
27.0000 g., 0.9000 Silver .7812 oz. ASW **Rev:** Denomination within wreath **Designer:** Barre

Date	Mintage	F	VF	XF	Unc	BU
1921H	3,580,000	12.00	20.00	40.00	150	—
1922H	7,420,000	11.50	13.50	20.00	100	—

KM# 19 PIASTRE
20.0000 g., 0.9000 Silver .5787 oz. ASW **Obv:** Laureate head left **Rev:** Denomination and date within keyhole shape wreath

Date	Mintage	F	VF	XF	Unc	BU
1931(a)	16,000,000	10.00	20.00	50.00	110	—

FEDERATED STATES
French Union

STANDARD COINAGE

KM# 32.1 PIASTRE
Copper-Nickel, 34.5 mm. **Obv:** Bust right holding laurel, date below **Obv. Designer:** P. Turin **Rev:** Grain sprigs below denomination **Note:** Security edge.

Date	Mintage	F	VF	XF	Unc	BU
1946(a)	2,520,000	7.50	12.50	20.00	85.00	135
1947(a)	261,000	15.00	35.00	75.00	160	300

KM# 32.2 PIASTRE
Copper-Nickel, 34.5 mm. **Obv:** Bust right holding laurel, date below **Obv. Designer:** P. Turin **Rev:** Denomination above plants **Edge:** Reeded **Note:** Similar coins dated 1946 with reverse legend: INDOCHINE - FRANCAISE are Essais.

Date	Mintage	F	VF	XF	Unc	BU
1947(a)	54,480,000	2.00	4.00	7.50	15.00	30.00

ESSAIS

Standard metals unless otherwise noted

KM#	Date	Mintage	Identification	Mkt Val
E7	1910	—	Cent. Copper-Nickel. ESSAI. KM#12.1	450
E8	1919	—	10 Cents. Silver. Fineness 0.700/0.835 incuse plus 0.700 incuse on field on reverse; KM#9.	650
E9	ND	—	20 Cents. Silver center. Mule. Two reverses. KM#3.	500
E10	1923(p)	—	Cent. Bronze center. ESSAI in field; KM#12.1.	550
E11	1923(p)	—	Cent. Bronze. ESSAI at rim; KM#12.1.	550

KM#	Date	Mintage	Identification	Mkt Val
E12	1923(a)	—	5 Cents. Cornucopias flank center hole, laureate liberty, left, above. Center hole within wreath divides denomination. KM#18.1	180
E13	1928	—	20 Cents. Brass. Plain edge. KM#17.1	250
E14	1928(a)	—	20 Cents. Bronze. KM#17.1	250
E15	19(30a)	—	Cent. Silver. KM#12.1	750
E16	19(30a)	—	Cent. Aluminum-Bronze. KM#12.1	600
E17	1930(a)	—	Piastre. Silver. Uniface.	4,650
E18	19(31)	—	10 Cents. Silver.	500
E19	19(31a)	—	10 Cents. Silver-Bronze. KM#16.1, medallic alignment.	900
E20	19(31)	—	20 Cents. Silver.	650
E21	19(31a)	—	20 Cents. Silver-Bronze. KM#17.1, medallic alignment.	1,000
E22	1(931)	—	50 Cents. Medallic alignment.	—

KM#	Date	Mintage	Identification	Mkt Val
E23	1(931a)	—	50 Cents. Silver-Bronze. Liberty seated, date below. Denomination within wreath.	1,000
E24	19(31a)	—	Piastre. Silver. KM#19	9,000
E25	19(31a)	—	Piastre. Silver-Bronze. KM#19	350
EA26	1931(a)	—	Piastre. Aluminum. Unique.	—
E26	1931(a)	—	Piastre. Silver. KM#19	425
E27	1935(a)	—	1/2 Cent. Bronze. KM#20	90.00

KM#	Date	Mintage	Identification	Mkt Val
E28	1936(a)	—	50 Cents. Aluminum. Liberty seated, date below. Denomination within wreath.	250
E29	1937(a)	—	10 Cents. Nickel. KM#16.2	200
E30	1937(a)	—	20 Cents. Silver. KM#17.2	300
E31	1937(a)	—	20 Cents. Nickel. KM#17.2	250
E32	1939(a)	—	10 Cents. Nickel. KM#21	110
E33	1939(a)	—	20 Cents. Nickel. Plain edge. KM#23	225
E34	1939(a)	—	20 Cents. Nickel. Security edge; KM#23	200
E35	1939(a)	—	20 Cents. Copper-Nickel. Reeded edge. KM#23a.1	260
E36	1940(a)	—	Cent. Zinc. KM#24.1	150
E37	1940(a)	—	Cent. Aluminum-Bronze. KM#24.1	450
E45	ND(1943)	—	Tael. Silver. KM#2.	—
E46	ND(1943)	—	1/2 Tael. Silver. KM#1	—
E38	1945(a)	1,100	10 Cents. Aluminum. KM#28.1	55.00
E39	1945(a)	1,100	20 Cents. Aluminum. KM#29	65.00
E40	1946(a)	1,100	5 Cents. Aluminum. KM#30.1	40.00

KM#	Date	Mintage	Identification	Mkt Val
E42	1946(a)	1,100	Piastre. Federation.	120

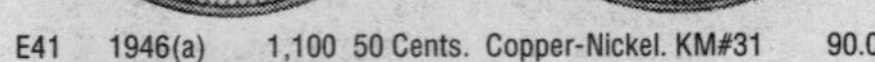

KM#	Date	Mintage	Identification	Mkt Val
E41	1946(a)	1,100	50 Cents. Copper-Nickel. KM#31	90.00

KM#	Date	Mintage	Identification	Mkt Val
E43	1946(a)	1,100	Piastre. Copper-Nickel. Indochina. KM#32.1.	215

KM#	Date	Mintage	Identification	Mkt Val
E44	1947(a)	104	Piastre. Bust right holding laurel, date below. Grain sprigs below denomination. Federation.	650

PIEFORTS

KM#	Date	Mintage	Identification	Mkt Val
P2	1908	—	Cent. Bronze. KM#12.1	480
P3	1920	—	20 Cents. Brass. Reeded edge. Medallic alignment. KM#15.	—
P4	1923	—	Cent. Bronze. Filled center hole. KM#12.1.	—
P5	19(30)	—	Cent. Bronze. France Y#81. Filled center hole; KM#12.1.	—
P6	19(30)	—	Cent. Aluminum-Bronze. France Y#81. Filled center hole; KM#12.1.	750
P7	19(31)	—	20 Cents. Medallic alignment.	500
P8	1939	—	1/2 Cent. Zinc. KM#20a.	325

PIEFORTS WITH ESSAI

Double thickness - Standard metals unless otherwise noted

KM#	Date	Mintage	Identification	Mkt Val
PE1	1908	—	Cent. Bronze. KM#12.1.	235
PE2	1923	—	5 Cents. Nickel-Brass. KM#18.1.	350

KM#	Date	Mintage	Identification	Mkt Val
PE3	1931(a)	—	Piastre. Silver. Laureate head left. Denomination and date within keyhole shape wreath. KM#19.	2,000
PE4	1945(a)	104	10 Cents. Aluminum. KM#28.1.	180
PE5	1945(a)	104	20 Cents. Aluminum. KM#29.1.	200
PE6	1946(a)	104	5 Cents. Aluminum. KM#30.1.	120
PE7	1946(a)	104	50 Cents. Copper-Nickel center. KM#31.	275
PE8	1947(a)	104	Piastre. Copper-Nickel. KM#32.	425

TRIAL STRIKES

KM#	Date	Mintage	Identification	Mkt Val
TS1	1921	—	Piastre. 0.9000 Silver. Without collar.	—
TS2	ND(1931)	—	Piastre. Uniface.	1,200

KM#	Date	Mintage	Identification	Mkt Val
TS3	1931	—	Piastre. Uniface, denomination and date within keyhole shape wreath.	650

The Colony of French Oceania (now the Territory of French Polynesia), comprising 130 basalt and coral islands scattered among five archipelagoes in the South Pacific, had an area of 1,544 sq. mi. (3,999 sq. km.). Capital: Papeete. The colony produced phosphates, copra and vanilla.

Tahiti of the Society Islands, the hub of French Oceania, was visited by Capt. Cook in 1769 and by Capt. Bligh on the Bounty 1788-89. The Society Islands were claimed by France in 1768, and in 1903 grouped with the Marquesas Islands, the Tuamotu Archipelago, the Gambier Islands and the Austral Islands under a single administrative head located at Papeete, Tahiti, to form the colony of French Oceania.

RULERS

French

MINT MARKS

(a) - Paris, privy marks only

(b)

MONETARY SYSTEM

100 Centimes = 1 Franc

FRENCH COLONY

DECIMAL COINAGE

KM# 1 50 CENTIMES

Aluminum **Obv:** Seated Liberty with torch and cornucopia right, date below **Obv. Designer:** G.B.L. Bazor **Rev:** Inscription and island scene divide denomination

Date	Mintage	F	VF	XF	Unc	BU
1949(a)	795,000	0.50	0.75	1.50	3.00	6.50

KM# 2 FRANC

Aluminum **Obv. Designer:** G.B.L. Bazor

Date	Mintage	F	VF	XF	Unc	BU
1949(a)	2,000,000	0.20	0.35	1.00	2.00	3.00

KM# 3 2 FRANCS

Aluminum, 31 mm. **Obv:** Seated Liberty with torch and cornucopia right, date below **Obv. Designer:** G.B.L. Bazor

Date	Mintage	F	VF	XF	Unc	BU
1949(a)	1,000,000	0.40	0.60	1.25	2.50	4.00

KM# 4 5 FRANCS

Aluminum **Obv:** Seated Liberty with torch and cornucopia right, date below **Obv. Designer:** G.B.L. Bazor **Rev:** Inscription and island scene divide denomination

Date	Mintage	F	VF	XF	Unc	BU
1952	2,000,000	0.50	0.75	1.50	3.50	5.50

ESSAIS

Standard metals unless otherwise noted

KM#	Date	Mintage	Identification	Issue Price	Mkt Val
E1	1948	1,100	50 Centimes. Incuse design.	—	25.00
E2	1948	1,100	50 Centimes. Raised design.	—	25.00
E3	1948	1,100	Franc. Incuse design.	—	30.00
E4	1948	1,100	Franc. Raised design.	—	30.00

KM#	Date	Mintage	Identification	Issue Price	Mkt Val

KM#	Date	Mintage	Identification	Issue Price	Mkt Val
E5	1948	1,100	2 Francs. Copper-Nickel. 9.9800 g. 26.9 mm. Republic seated with grain spray and shield. Dhow divides denomination and date. Plain edge. Incuse design.	—	35.00
E6	1948	1,100	2 Francs. Copper-Nickel. 9.9800 g. 26.9 mm. Raised design.	—	35.00
E7	1949(a)	2,000	50 Centimes. Copper-Nickel. KM1	—	20.00
E8	1949(a)	2,000	Franc. Copper-Nickel. KM2	—	25.00
E9	1949(a)	2,000	2 Francs. Copper-Nickel. KM3	—	30.00
E10	1952(a)	1,200	5 Francs. Copper-Nickel. KM4.	—	35.00

PIEFORTS WITH ESSAI

Double thickness - Standard metals unless otherwise noted

KM#	Date	Mintage	Identification	Issue Price	Mkt Val
PE1	1949(a)	104	50 Centimes.	—	60.00
PE2	1949(a)	104	Franc.	—	70.00
PE3	1949(a)	104	2 Francs.	—	80.00
PE4	1952(a)	104	5 Francs.	—	95.00

FRENCH POLYNESIA

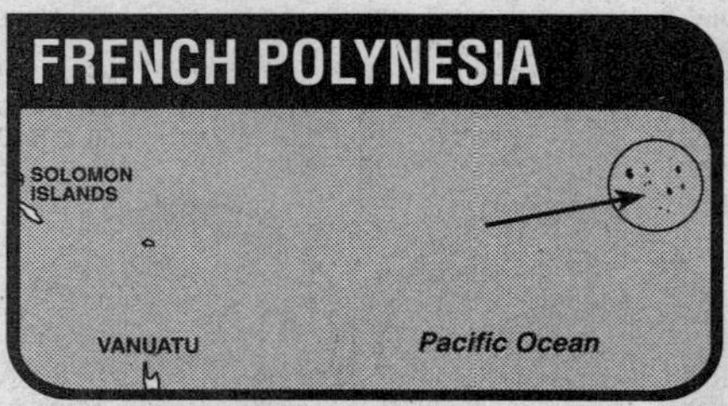

The Territory of French Polynesia (formerly French Oceania) has an area of 1,544 sq. mi. (3,941 sq. km.) and a population of 220,000. It is comprised of the same five archipelagoes that were grouped administratively to form French Oceania.

The colony of French Oceania became the Territory of French Polynesia by act of the French National Assembly in March, 1957. In Sept. of 1958 it voted in favor of the new constitution of the Fifth Republic, thereby electing to remain within the new French Community.

Picturesque, mountainous Tahiti, the setting of many tales of adventure and romance, is one of the most inspiringly beautiful islands in the world. Robert Louis Stevenson called it 'God's sweetest works'. It was there that Paul Gaugin, one of the pioneers of the Impressionist movement, painted the brilliant, exotic pictures that later made him famous. The arid coral atolls of Tuamotu comprise the most economically valuable area of French Polynesia. Pearl oysters thrive in the warm, limpid lagoons, and extensive portions of the atolls are valuable phosphate rock.

RULERS
French

MINT MARKS
(a) - Paris, privy marks only
(b)

MONETARY SYSTEM
100 Centimes = 1 Franc

FRENCH OVERSEAS TERRITORY

DECIMAL COINAGE

KM# 1 50 CENTIMES
Aluminum **Obv:** Seated Liberty with torch and cornucopia right, date below **Obv. Designer:** G.B.L. Bazor **Rev:** Legend and island scene divides denomination

Date	Mintage	F	VF	XF	Unc	BU
1965(a)	400,000	0.10	0.25	0.50	1.50	4.50

KM# 2 FRANC
Aluminum **Obv:** Seated Liberty with torch and cornucopia right, date below **Obv. Designer:** G.B.L. Bazor **Rev:** Legend and island scene divide denomination

Date	Mintage	F	VF	XF	Unc	BU
1965(a)	3,300,000	—	0.10	0.20	0.75	2.50

KM# 11 FRANC
1.3000 g., Aluminum, 23 mm. **Obv:** Seated Liberty with torch and cornucopia right, date below, legend added flanking figure's feet **Obv. Legend:** I. E. O. M. **Obv. Designer:** G.B.L. Bazor **Rev:** Legend and island scene divide denomination

Date	Mintage	F	VF	XF	Unc	BU
1975(a)	2,000,000	—	0.10	0.15	0.45	2.50
1977(a)	2,000,000	—	0.10	0.15	0.45	1.75
1979(a)	1,500,000	—	0.10	0.15	0.45	1.25
1981(a)	2,000,000	—	0.10	0.15	0.45	1.25
1982(a)	1,000,000	—	0.10	0.15	0.45	1.25
1983(a)	2,200,000	—	0.10	0.15	0.45	1.25
1984(a)	1,500,000	—	0.10	0.15	0.45	1.25
1985(a)	2,000,000	—	0.10	0.15	0.45	1.25
1986(a)	2,000,000	—	0.10	0.15	0.45	1.25
1987(a)	2,000,000	—	0.10	0.15	0.45	1.25
1989(a)	1,000,000	—	0.10	0.15	0.45	1.25
1990(a)	1,500,000	—	0.10	0.15	0.45	1.00
1991(a)	1,400,000	—	0.10	0.15	0.35	1.00
1992(a)	800,000	—	0.10	0.15	0.35	1.00
1993(a)	2,300,000	—	0.10	0.15	0.35	1.00
1994(a)	1,000,000	—	0.10	0.15	0.30	1.00
1995(a)	1,000,000	—	0.10	0.15	0.30	1.00
1996(a)	2,700,000	—	0.10	0.15	0.30	1.00
1997(a)	1,100,000	—	0.10	0.15	0.25	0.75
1998(a)	1,600,000	—	0.10	0.15	0.25	0.75
1999(a)	2,600,000	—	0.10	0.15	0.25	0.75
2000(a)	3,000,000	—	0.10	0.15	0.25	0.75

KM# 3 2 FRANCS
Aluminum **Obv:** Seated Liberty with torch and cornucopia right, date below **Obv. Designer:** G.B.L. Bazor **Rev:** Legend and island scene divide denomination

Date	Mintage	F	VF	XF	Unc	BU
1965(a)	1,750,000	—	0.10	0.25	1.00	2.50

KM# 10 2 FRANCS
2.7000 g., Aluminum, 27 mm. **Obv:** Seated Liberty with torch and cornucopia right, date below, legend added flanking figure's feet **Obv. Legend:** I. E. O. M. **Obv. Designer:** G.B.L. Bazor **Rev:** Legend and island scene divide denomination

Date	Mintage	F	VF	XF	Unc	BU
1973(a)	400,000	—	0.10	0.25	0.75	3.00
1975(a)	1,000,000	—	0.10	0.25	0.75	2.00
1977(a)	1,000,000	—	0.10	0.25	0.75	2.00
1979(a)	2,000,000	—	0.10	0.25	0.75	1.75
1982(a)	1,000,000	—	0.10	0.25	0.75	1.75
1983(a)	1,500,000	—	0.10	0.25	0.75	1.75
1984(a)	1,200,000	—	0.10	0.25	0.75	1.75
1985(a)	1,400,000	—	0.10	0.25	0.75	1.50
1986(a)	1,500,000	—	0.10	0.25	0.75	1.50
1987(a)	1,000,000	—	0.10	0.25	0.75	1.50
1988(a)	500,000	—	0.10	0.25	0.75	1.50
1989(a)	1,000,000	—	0.10	0.25	0.75	1.50
1990(a)	1,500,000	—	0.10	0.25	0.75	1.50
1991(a)	1,500,000	—	0.10	0.25	0.60	1.50
1992(a)	—	—	0.10	0.25	0.60	1.25
1993(a)	1,400,000	—	0.10	0.25	0.50	1.25
1995(a)	1,200,000	—	0.10	0.20	0.40	1.25
1996(a)	2,200,000	—	0.10	0.20	0.40	1.25
1997(a)	1,300,000	—	0.10	0.20	0.40	1.25
1998(a)	600,000	—	0.10	0.20	0.40	1.25
1999(a)	2,800,000	—	0.10	0.20	0.40	1.00
2000(a)	1,600,000	—	0.10	0.20	0.40	1.00

KM# 4 5 FRANCS
3.7500 g., Aluminum, 31 mm. **Obv:** Seated Liberty with torch and cornucopia right, date below **Obv. Designer:** G.B.L. Bazor **Rev:** Legend and island scene divide denomination

Date	Mintage	F	VF	XF	Unc	BU
1965(a)	1,520,000	0.10	0.25	0.50	1.75	3.50

KM# 12 5 FRANCS

3.7500 g., Aluminum, 31 mm. **Obv:** Seated Liberty with torch and cornucopia right, date below, legend added flanking figure's feet **Obv. Legend:** I. E. O. M. **Obv. Designer:** G.B.L. Bazor **Rev:** Legend and island divide denomination

Date	Mintage	F	VF	XF	Unc	BU
1975(a)	500,000	0.10	0.20	0.40	1.25	3.25
1977(a)	500,000	0.10	0.20	0.40	1.25	2.25
1982(a)	500,000	0.10	0.20	0.40	1.25	2.25
1983(a)	800,000	0.10	0.20	0.40	1.25	2.00
1984(a)	600,000	0.10	0.20	0.40	1.25	2.00
1985(a)	—	0.10	0.20	0.40	1.25	2.00
1986(a)	600,000	0.10	0.20	0.40	1.25	2.00
1987(a)	400,000	0.10	0.20	0.40	1.25	1.75
1988(a)	400,000	0.10	0.20	0.40	1.25	1.75
1989(a)	—	0.10	0.20	0.40	1.25	1.75
1990(a)	500,000	0.10	0.20	0.40	1.25	1.75
1991(a)	700,000	0.10	0.20	0.40	1.00	1.50
1992(a)	500,000	0.10	0.20	0.40	1.00	1.50
1993(a)	400,000	0.10	0.20	0.35	0.85	1.25
1994(a)	500,000	0.10	0.20	0.35	0.70	1.25
1996(a)	100,000	0.10	0.20	0.35	0.75	1.25
1997(a)	500,000	0.10	0.20	0.35	0.85	1.25
1998(a)	800,000	0.10	0.20	0.35	0.70	1.25
1999(a)	600,000	0.10	0.20	0.35	0.65	1.25
2000(a)	900,000	—	—	—	0.50	1.00

KM# 5 10 FRANCS

Nickel **Obv:** Capped head left, date below **Obv. Designer:** R. Joly **Rev:** Native art above denomination **Rev. Designer:** A. Guzman

Date	Mintage	F	VF	XF	Unc	BU
1967(a)	1,000,000	0.25	0.50	0.75	1.85	4.75

KM# 8 10 FRANCS

6.0000 g., Nickel, 24 mm. **Obv:** Capped head left, date and legend below **Obv. Legend:** I. E. O. M. **Obv. Designer:** R. Joly **Rev:** Native art, denomination below **Rev. Designer:** A. Guzman

Date	Mintage	F	VF	XF	Unc	BU
1972(a)	300,000	0.25	0.50	0.75	2.75	4.50
1973(a)	400,000	0.25	0.50	0.75	2.75	3.00
1975(a)	1,000,000	0.25	0.50	0.75	1.75	2.75
1979(a)	500,000	0.25	0.50	0.75	1.75	2.75
1982(a)	500,000	0.25	0.50	0.75	1.75	2.75
1983(a)	1,000,000	0.25	0.50	0.75	1.75	2.75
1984(a)	800,000	0.25	0.50	0.75	1.75	2.75
1985(a)	800,000	0.25	0.50	0.75	1.75	2.75
1986(a)	800,000	0.25	0.50	0.75	1.75	2.50
1991(a)	600,000	0.25	0.50	0.75	1.50	2.50
1992(a)	400,000	0.25	0.50	0.75	1.25	2.50
1993(a)	600,000	0.25	0.50	0.75	1.25	2.25
1995(a)	500,000	0.25	0.50	0.70	1.00	2.00
1996(a)	300,000	0.25	0.50	0.70	1.00	2.00
1997(a)	300,000	0.25	0.50	0.70	1.00	2.00
1998(a)	1,000,000	0.25	0.45	0.65	0.85	1.75
1999(a)	2,000,000	0.25	0.45	0.65	0.85	1.75
2000(a)	1,200,000	0.25	0.45	0.65	0.85	1.75

KM# 6 20 FRANCS

10.0000 g., Nickel, 28.3 mm. **Obv:** Capped head left, date below **Obv. Designer:** R. Joly **Rev:** Flowers, vanilla shoots, bread fruit **Rev. Designer:** A. Guzman

Date	Mintage	F	VF	XF	Unc	BU
1967(a)	750,000	0.35	0.75	1.25	3.00	4.50
1969(a)	250,000	0.35	1.00	2.00	7.00	9.00
1970(a)	500,000	0.35	0.75	1.25	3.25	3.75

KM# 9 20 FRANCS

10.0000 g., Nickel, 28.3 mm. **Obv:** Capped head left, date and legend below **Obv. Legend:** I. E. O. M. **Obv. Designer:** R. Joly **Rev:** Flowers, vanilla shoots, bread fruit **Rev. Designer:** A. Guzman

Date	Mintage	F	VF	XF	Unc	BU
1972(a)	300,000	0.30	0.50	1.00	3.00	5.50
1973(a)	300,000	0.30	0.50	1.00	3.00	4.50
1975(a)	700,000	0.30	0.50	1.00	2.25	3.50
1977(a)	350,000	0.35	0.75	1.50	4.50	7.50
1979(a)	500,000	0.30	0.50	1.00	2.25	3.50
1983(a)	800,000	0.30	0.50	1.00	2.25	3.50
1984(a)	600,000	0.30	0.50	1.00	2.25	3.50
1986(a)	400,000	0.30	0.50	1.00	2.25	3.00
1988(a)	250,000	0.30	0.50	1.00	2.25	3.00
1991(a)	—	0.30	0.50	1.00	2.00	3.00
1992(a)	—	0.30	0.50	1.00	2.00	3.00
1993(a)	—	0.30	0.50	1.00	1.75	2.50
1995(a)	—	0.30	0.50	1.00	1.75	2.50
1996(a)	—	0.30	0.50	0.85	1.50	2.25
1997(a)	—	0.30	0.50	0.85	1.50	2.25
1998(a)	—	0.30	0.50	0.85	1.35	2.00
1999(a)	—	0.30	0.50	0.85	1.35	2.00
2000(a)	—	—	—	—	1.25	1.75

KM# 7 50 FRANCS

15.0000 g., Nickel, 33 mm. **Obv:** Capped head left, date below **Obv. Designer:** R. Joly **Rev:** Denomination above Moorea Harbor **Rev. Designer:** A. Guzman

Date	Mintage	F	VF	XF	Unc	BU
1967(a)	600,000	0.60	1.00	2.00	5.00	8.00

KM# 13 50 FRANCS

15.0000 g., Nickel, 33 mm. **Obv:** Capped head left, date and legend below **Obv. Legend:** I. E. O. M. **Obv. Designer:** R. Joly **Rev:** Denomination above Moorea Harbor **Rev. Designer:** A. Guzman

Date	Mintage	F	VF	XF	Unc	BU
1975(a)	500,000	0.60	0.80	1.25	4.00	7.50
1982(a)	500,000	0.60	0.80	1.25	4.00	6.00
1985(a)	Inc. above	0.60	0.80	1.25	4.00	6.00
1988(a)	125,000	0.60	0.80	1.25	4.00	7.00
1991(a)	—	0.60	0.80	1.25	3.50	5.00
1995(a)	—	0.60	0.75	1.20	2.00	3.00
1996(a)	—	0.60	0.75	1.00	1.50	2.50
1998(a)	—	0.60	0.75	1.00	1.50	2.50
1999(a)	—	0.60	0.75	1.00	1.50	2.50
2000(a)	—	—	—	—	1.50	2.50

KM# 14 100 FRANCS

10.0000 g., Nickel-Bronze, 30 mm. **Obv:** Capped head left, date below **Obv. Designer:** R. Joly **Rev:** Denomination above Moorea Harbor **Rev. Designer:** A. Guzman

Date	Mintage	F	VF	XF	Unc	BU
1976(a)	2,000,000	1.20	1.50	2.00	4.00	9.00
1979(a)	150	—	—	—	—	—
1982(a)	1,000,000	1.20	1.50	2.25	5.00	8.50
1984(a)	500,000	1.20	1.50	2.25	5.00	8.00
1986(a)	400,000	1.20	1.50	2.25	5.00	8.00
1987(a)	500,000	1.20	1.50	2.25	5.00	8.00
1988(a)	500,000	1.20	1.50	2.25	5.00	7.50
1991(a)	—	1.20	1.50	2.25	4.25	7.00
1992(a)	—	1.20	1.50	2.25	4.00	7.00
1995(a)	—	1.20	1.50	2.25	3.50	6.50
1996(a)	—	1.20	1.50	2.00	3.00	6.50
1997(a)	—	1.20	1.50	2.00	3.00	6.00
1998(a)	—	1.00	1.25	1.75	2.50	5.00
1999(a)	—	—	—	—	2.50	5.00
2000(a)	—	—	—	—	2.00	3.50

ESSAIS

Standard metals unless otherwise noted

KM#	Date	Mintage	Identification	Issue Price	Mkt Val
E1	1967(a)	1,700	10 Francs. Nickel. KM5.	—	20.00
E2	1967(a)	1,700	20 Francs. Nickel. KM6.	—	25.00
E3	1967(a)	1,700	50 Francs. Nickel. KM7.	—	30.00
E4	1976(a)	1,900	100 Francs. Nickel-Bronze center. KM14.	—	35.00

PIEFORTS

KM#	Date	Mintage	Identification	Issue Price	Mkt Val
P1	1967(a)	500	10 Francs. Nickel. KM5.	—	25.00
P2	1967(a)	50	10 Francs. 0.9500 Silver. KM5.	—	120
P3	1967(a)	20	10 Francs. 0.9200 Gold. KM5.	—	950
P4	1967(a)	500	20 Francs. Nickel. KM6.	—	25.00
P5	1967(a)	50	20 Francs. 0.9500 Silver. KM6.	—	140
P6	1967(a)	20	20 Francs. 0.9200 Gold. KM6.	—	1,250
P7	1967(a)	500	50 Francs. Nickel. KM7.	—	30.00
P8	1967(a)	50	50 Francs. 0.9500 Silver. KM7.	—	180
P9	1967(a)	20	50 Francs. 0.9200 Gold. KM7.	—	1,450
P10	1979(a)	150	50 Centimes. Aluminum. KM11.	—	20.00
P11	1979(a)	250	50 Centimes. 0.9250 Silver. KM11.	—	75.00
P12	1979(a)	93	50 Centimes. 0.9200 Gold. KM11.	—	450
P13	1979(a)	150	2 Francs. Aluminum. KM10.	—	30.00
P14	1979(a)	250	2 Francs. 0.9250 Silver. KM10.	—	85.00
P15	1979(a)	94	2 Francs. 0.9200 Gold. KM10.	—	650
P16	1979(a)	150	5 Francs. Aluminum. KM12.	—	40.00
P17	1979(a)	250	5 Francs. 0.9250 Silver. KM12.	—	90.00
P18	1979(a)	95	5 Francs. 0.9200 Gold. KM12.	—	900
P19	1979(a)	150	10 Francs. Nickel. KM8.	—	50.00
P20	1979(a)	250	10 Francs. 0.9250 Silver. KM8.	—	90.00
P21	1979(a)	94	10 Francs. 0.9200 Gold. KM8.	—	700
P22	1979(a)	150	20 Francs. Nickel. KM9.	—	55.00
P23	1979(a)	250	20 Francs. 0.9250 Silver. KM9.	—	110
P24	1979(a)	93	20 Francs. 0.9200 Gold. KM9.	—	850
P25	1979(a)	150	50 Francs. Nickel. KM13.	—	60.00
P26	1979(a)	250	50 Francs. 0.9250 Silver. KM13.	—	130
P27	1979(a)	94	50 Francs. 0.9200 Gold. KM13.	—	1,200
P28	1979(a)	150	100 Francs. Nickel-Bronze. KM14.	—	75.00
P29	1979(a)	350	100 Francs. 0.9250 Silver. KM14.	—	150
P30	1979(a)	98	100 Francs. 0.9200 Gold. KM14.	—	1,250

"FDC" SETS

KM#	Date	Mintage	Identification	Issue Price	Mkt Val
SS1	1965 (4)	2,200	KM1-4	—	10.00
SS2	1967 (3)	2,200	K5-7	10.00	17.00

FRENCH SOMALILAND

French Somaliland is located in northeast Africa at the Bab el Mandeb Strait connecting the Suez Canal and the Red Sea with the Gulf of Aden and the Indian Ocean. French interest in French Somaliland began in 1839 with concessions obtained by a French naval lieutenant from the provincial sultans. French Somaliland was made a protectorate in 1884 and its boundaries were delimited by the Franco-British and Ethiopian accords of 1887 and 1897. It became a colony in 1896 and a territory within the French Union in 1946.

NOTE: For later coinage see French Afars & Issas.

MINT MARKS

(a) - Paris (privy marks only)

MONETARY SYSTEM

100 Centimes = 1 Franc

FRENCH COLONY

DECIMAL COINAGE

KM# 4 FRANC

Aluminum **Obv:** Winged head left, date below **Obv. Designer:** G.B.L. Bazor **Rev:** Lyre antelope divides denomination

Date	Mintage	F	VF	XF	Unc	BU
1948(a)	200,000	6.50	12.50	25.00	45.00	75.00
1949(a)	Inc. above	8.00	15.00	30.00	60.00	—

KM# 8 FRANC

Aluminum, 22.8 mm. **Obv:** Winged head left, date below **Obv. Designer:** G.B.L. Bazor **Rev. Designer:** Lyre antelope divides denomination

Date	Mintage	F	VF	XF	Unc	BU
1959(a)	500,000	0.25	0.50	1.50	3.00	5.00
1965(a)	200,000	0.35	0.60	2.00	4.00	6.00

KM# 5 2 FRANCS

Aluminum **Obv:** Winged head left, date below **Obv. Designer:** G.B.L. Bazor **Rev:** Lyre antelope divides denomination

Date	Mintage	F	VF	XF	Unc	BU
1948(a)	200,000	6.50	12.50	25.00	60.00	80.00
1949(a)	Inc. above	8.00	15.00	30.00	70.00	—

KM# 9 2 FRANCS

Aluminum **Obv:** Winged head left, date below **Obv. Designer:** G.B.L. Bazor **Rev:** Lyre antelope divides denomination

Date	Mintage	F	VF	XF	Unc	BU
1959(a)	200,000	0.25	0.75	2.50	5.00	7.00
1965(a)	240,000	0.25	0.75	2.50	5.00	7.00

KM# 6 5 FRANCS

Aluminum **Obv:** Winged head left, date below **Obv. Designer:** G.B.L. Bazor **Rev:** Lyre antelope divides denomination

Date	Mintage	F	VF	XF	Unc	BU
1948(a)	500,000	5.00	10.00	25.00	45.00	75.00

KM# 10 5 FRANCS

Aluminum **Obv:** Winged head left, date below **Obv. Designer:** G.B.L. Bazor **Rev:** Lyre antelope divides denomination

Date	Mintage	F	VF	XF	Unc	BU
1959(a)	500,000	0.25	0.75	2.50	5.50	7.50
1965(a)	200,000	0.25	0.75	3.00	6.50	8.50

KM# 11 10 FRANCS

Aluminum-Bronze **Obv:** Winged head left, date below **Obv. Designer:** G.B.L. Bazor **Rev:** Dhow, ocean liner, denomination above

Date	Mintage	F	VF	XF	Unc	BU
1965(a)	250,000	0.50	1.00	3.00	6.00	8.00

KM# 7 20 FRANCS

Aluminum-Bronze **Obv:** Winged head left, date below **Obv. Designer:** G.B.L. Bazor **Rev:** Dhow, ocean liner, denomination above

Date	Mintage	F	VF	XF	Unc	BU
1952(a)	500,000	1.25	2.50	4.50	10.00	12.00

KM# 12 20 FRANCS

Aluminum-Bronze **Obv:** Winged head left, date below **Obv. Designer:** G.B.L. Bazor **Rev:** Dhow, ocean liner, denomination above

Date	Mintage	F	VF	XF	Unc	BU
1965(a)	200,000	1.00	2.00	4.00	8.00	10.00

ESSAIS

Standard metals unless otherwise noted

KM#	Date	Mintage	Identification	Issue Price	Mkt Val
E1	1948(a)	2,000	Franc. Copper-Nickel. KM4.	—	12.00
E2	1948(a)	2,000	2 Francs. Copper-Nickel. KM5.	—	15.00
E3	1948(a)	2,000	5 Francs. Copper-Nickel. KM6	—	18.00
E4	1952(a)	1,200	20 Francs. Aluminum-Bronze. KM7	—	22.00
E5	1965(a)	2,000	10 Francs. Aluminum-Bronze center. KM11	—	20.00

PIEFORTS WITH ESSAI

Standard metals unless otherwise noted

KM#	Date	Mintage	Identification	Issue Price	Mkt Val
PE1	1948(a)	104	Franc.	—	80.00
PE2	1948(a)	104	2 Francs.	—	100
PE3	1948(a)	104	5 Francs.	—	110
PE4	1952(a)	104	20 Francs.	—	125

"FDC" SETS

KM#	Date	Mintage	Identification	Issue Price	Mkt Val
SS1	1965 (5)	1,898	KM#8-12; Issued with French Polynesia	—	40.00

FRENCH WEST AFRICA

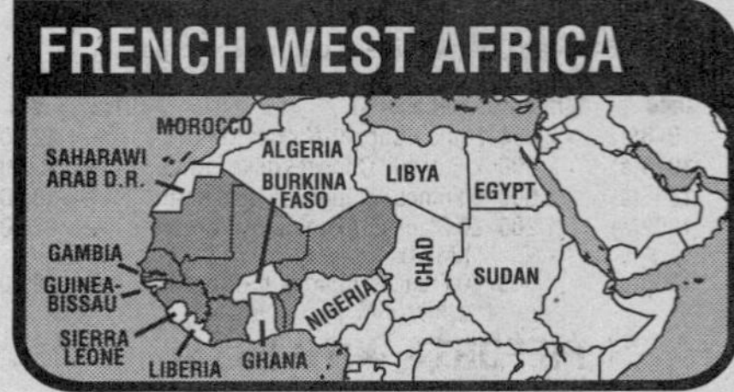

French West Africa (Afrique Occidentale Francaise), a former federation of French colonial territories on the northwest coast of Africa, had an area of 1,831,079 sq. mi. (4,742,495 sq. km.) and a population of about 17.4 million. Capital: Dakar. The constituent territories were Mauritania, Senegal, Dahomey, French Sudan, Ivory Coast, Upper Volta, Niger, French Guinea, and later on the mandated area of Togo. Peanuts, palm kernels, cacao, coffee and bananas were exported.

Prior to the mid-19th century, France, as the other European states, maintained establishments on the west coast of Africa for the purpose of trading in slaves and gum, but made no serious attempt at colonization. From 1854 onward, the coastal settlements were gradually extended into the interior until, by the opening of the 20th century, acquisition ended and organization and development began. French West Africa was formed in 1895 by grouping the several colonies under one administration (at Dakar) while retaining a large measure of autonomy to each of the constituent territories. The inhabitants of French West Africa were made French citizens in 1946. With the exception of French Guinea, all of the colonies voted in 1958 to become autonomous members of the new French Community. French Guinea voted to become the fully independent Republic of Guinea. The present-day independent states are members of the "Union Monetaire Ouest-Africaine". For later coinage see West African States.

RULERS
French

MINT MARKS
(a) - Paris, privy marks only
(L) – London

MONETARY SYSTEM
100 Centimes = 1 Franc
5 Francs = 1 Unit

FRENCH COLONY

COLONIAL COINAGE

KM# 1 50 CENTIMES
Aluminum-Bronze **Obv:** Laureate head left **Rev:** Cornucopias flank denomination and date

Date	Mintage	F	VF	XF	Unc	BU
1944(L)	10,000,000	2.00	4.00	15.00	28.00	32.00
1944(L) Proof	—	Value: 200				

KM# 2 FRANC
Aluminum-Bronze **Obv:** Laureate head left **Rev:** Cornucopias flank denomination and date

Date	Mintage	F	VF	XF	Unc	BU
1944(L)	15,000,000	1.00	2.00	10.00	20.00	24.00
1944(L) Proof	—	Value: 250				

KM# 3 FRANC
Aluminum **Obv:** Winged head left, date below **Rev:** Rhim gazelle facing divides denomination **Designer:** G. B. L. Bazor

Date	Mintage	F	VF	XF	Unc	BU
1948(a)	30,110,000	0.15	0.20	2.00	4.00	5.00
1955(a)	5,200,000	0.20	0.35	1.00	3.00	4.00

KM# 4 2 FRANCS
Aluminum, 27 mm. **Obv:** Winged head left, date below **Rev:** Rhim gazelle facing divides denomination **Designer:** G. B. L. Bazor

Date	Mintage	F	VF	XF	Unc	BU
1948(a)	12,665,000	0.20	0.30	0.50	1.75	2.75
1955(a)	1,400,000	0.25	0.40	5.00	12.00	14.00

KM# 5 5 FRANCS
Aluminum-Bronze **Obv:** Head left divides date above **Rev:** Rhim gazelle facing, divides denomination **Rev. Designer:** G.B.L. Bazor

Date	Mintage	F	VF	XF	Unc	BU
1956(a)	85,000,000	0.35	0.50	1.00	2.50	5.00

KM# 6 10 FRANCS
Aluminum-Bronze, 23.5 mm. **Obv:** Head left, divides date above **Rev:** Rhim gazelle facing divides denomination **Rev. Designer:** G.B.L. Bazor

Date	Mintage	F	VF	XF	Unc	BU
1956(a)	20,000,000	0.50	1.00	1.50	3.50	6.00

KM# 8 10 FRANCS
Aluminum-Bronze **Obv:** Fish divides denomination **Rev:** Rhim gazelle facing, date below **Rev. Designer:** G.B.L. Bazor **Note:** Issued for circulation in French West Africa, including Togo.

Date	Mintage	F	VF	XF	Unc	BU
1957(a)	30,000,000	0.50	1.00	1.50	3.00	5.00

KM# 7 25 FRANCS
Aluminum-Bronze **Obv:** Head left divides date above **Rev:** Rhim gazelle facing, divides denomination **Rev. Designer:** G.B.L. Bazor

Date	Mintage	F	VF	XF	Unc	BU
1956(a)	37,877,000	0.50	1.00	2.00	5.50	8.00

KM# 9 25 FRANCS
Aluminum-Bronze **Obv:** Fish divides denomination **Rev:** Rhim gazelle facing, date below **Rev. Designer:** G.B.L. Bazor **Note:** Also issued for circulation in Togo

Date	Mintage	F	VF	XF	Unc	BU
1957(a)	30,000,000	0.50	1.00	2.00	5.00	7.00

ESSAIS

Standard metals unless otherwise noted

KM#	Date	Mintage	Identification	Issue Price	Mkt Val
E1	1948(a)	2,000	Franc. Copper-Nickel. KM3.	—	25.00
E2	1948	2,000	2 Francs. Copper-Nickel. KM4.	—	30.00
E5	1956(a)	2,300	25 Francs. Aluminum-Bronze. KM7	—	22.00
E3	1956(a)	2,300	5 Francs. Aluminum-Bronze. KM5	—	16.00
E4	1956(a)	2,300	10 Francs. Aluminum-Bronze. KM6.	—	20.00
E6	1957(a)	—	10 Francs. Aluminum-Bronze. KM8	—	20.00
E7	1957(a)	—	25 Francs. Aluminum-Bronze. KM9	—	22.00

PIEFORTS WITH ESSAI

Double thickness - Standard metals unless otherwise noted

KM#	Date	Mintage	Identification	Issue Price	Mkt Val
PE1	1948(a)	104	Franc. Aluminum. KM3	—	60.00
PE2	1948(a)	104	2 Francs. Aluminum. KM4.	—	70.00

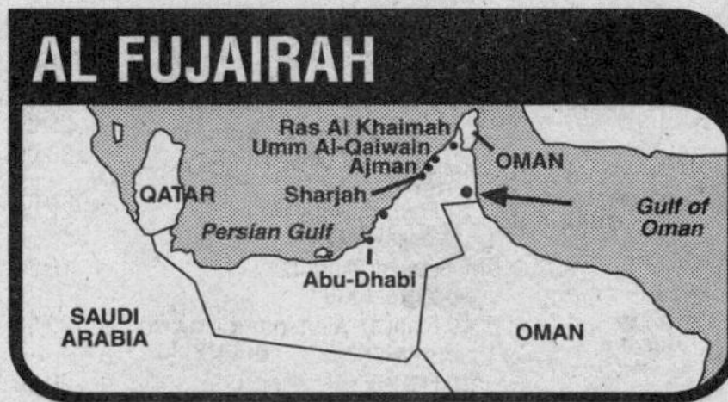

An original member of the United Arab Emirates, al-Fujairah is the only emirate that does not have territory on the Persian Gulf. It is on the eastern side of the "horn" of Oman. It has an estimated area of 450 sq. mi. (1200 sq. km.) and a population of 27,000. Al-Fujairah has been, historically a frequent rival of Sharjah. As recently as 1952 Great Britain recognized al-Fujairah as an autonomous state.

TITLES

al Fujaira(t)

RULERS

Muhammad bin Hamad al-Sharqi, 1952-74
Hamad bin Muhammad al-Sharqi, 1974--

EMIRATE

NON-CIRCULATING LEGAL TENDER COINAGE

KM# 1 RIYAL

3.0000 g., 1.0000 Silver .0964 oz. ASW **Ruler:** Muhammad bin Hamad al-Sharqi **Subject:** Desert Fort **Obv:** Arms-flags above rifles on pointed shield **Rev:** Arms below fort

Date	Mintage	F	VF	XF	Unc	BU
AH1388 - 1969 Proof	4,050	Value: 25.00				
AH1389 - 1970 Proof	Inc. above	Value: 25.00				

KM# 2 2 RIYALS

6.0000 g., 1.0000 Silver .1928 oz. ASW **Ruler:** Muhammad bin Hamad al-Sharqi **Subject:** President Richard Nixon **Obv:** Arms-flags above rifles on pointed shield **Rev:** Head 3/4 right

Date	Mintage	F	VF	XF	Unc	BU
AH1388 - 1969 Proof	6,250	Value: 30.00				
AH1389 - 1970 Proof	Inc. above	Value: 30.00				

KM# 3 5 RIYALS

15.0000 g., 1.0000 Silver .4823 oz. ASW **Ruler:** Muhammad bin Hamad al-Sharqi **Series:** 1972 Munich Olympics **Obv:** Arms-flags above rifles on pointed shield **Rev:** Olympic rings, logo and torch

Date	Mintage	F	VF	XF	Unc	BU
AH1388 - 1969 Proof	3,550	Value: 55.00				
AH1389 - 1970 Proof	1,300	Value: 60.00				

KM# 4.1 10 RIYALS

30.0000 g., 1.0000 Silver .9645 oz. ASW **Ruler:** Muhammad bin Hamad al-Sharqi **Subject:** Apollo XI **Obv:** Arms, fineness in oval at lower left, mintage figure at lower right **Rev:** Astronauts, moon and stars, dates at upper left

Date	Mintage	F	VF	XF	Unc	BU
AH1388 - 1969 Proof	14,000	Value: 60.00				

KM# 4.2 10 RIYALS

30.0000 g., 1.0000 Silver .9645 oz. ASW **Ruler:** Muhammad bin Hamad al-Sharqi **Obv:** Arms, mintage figure stamped at lower left, fineness in oval at lower right **Rev:** Astronauts, moon and stars, dates upper left

Date	Mintage	F	VF	XF	Unc	BU
AH1389 - 1969 Proof	—	Value: 60.00				

KM# 5 10 RIYALS

30.0000 g., 1.0000 Silver .9645 oz. ASW **Ruler:** Muhammad bin Hamad al-Sharqi **Subject:** Apollo XII **Obv:** Arms **Rev:** Four shields on moon background at left, astronauts aligned on large shield at right

Date	Mintage	F	VF	XF	Unc	BU
AH1388 - 1969 Proof	15,000	Value: 50.00				
AH1389 - 1969 Proof	15,000	Value: 50.00				

KM# 19 10 RIYALS

30.0000 g., 1.0000 Silver .9645 oz. ASW **Ruler:** Muhammad Hamad al-Sharqi **Subject:** Apollo XIII **Obv:** Arms **Rev:** Five shields at left, Arab riders and sun at right

Date	Mintage	F	VF	XF	Unc	BU
AH1389 - 1969 Proof	15,000	Value: 55.00				

KM# 20 10 RIYALS

30.0000 g., 1.0000 Silver .9645 oz. ASW **Ruler:** Muhammad Hamad al-Sharqi **Subject:** Visit of Pope Paul VI to Philippines **Obv:** Arms-flags above rifles on pointed shield **Rev:** Buildings, Pope's profile at right

Date	Mintage	F	VF	XF	Unc	BU
AH1389 - 1969 Proof	300	Value: 85.00				

KM# 21 10 RIYALS

30.0000 g., 1.0000 Silver .9645 oz. ASW **Ruler:** Muhammad bin Hamad al-Sharqi **Subject:** Visit of Pope Paul VI to Australia **Obv:** Arms-flags above rifles on pointed shield **Rev:** Pope's profile at left, crown with keys and kangaroo on map at right

Date	Mintage	F	VF	XF	Unc	BU
AH1389 - 1969 Proof	12,000	Value: 85.00				

KM# 22 10 RIYALS

30.0000 g., 1.0000 Silver .9645 oz. ASW **Ruler:** Muhammad bin Hamad al-Sharqi **Subject:** Apollo XIV **Obv:** Arms-flags above rifles on pointed shield **Rev:** Moon above shooting star within ring, planet lower left

Date	Mintage	F	VF	XF	Unc	BU
AH1389 - 1969 Proof	14,000	Value: 75.00				

KM# 7 25 RIYALS

5.1800 g., 0.9000 Gold .1499 oz. AGW **Ruler:** Muhammad Hamad al-Sharqi **Subject:** U.S. President Richard Nixon **Obv:** Arms-flags above rifles on pointed shield **Rev:** Head 3/4 right

Date	Mintage	F	VF	XF	Unc	BU
AH1388 - 1969 Proof	3,280	Value: 150				
Note: Fineness incuse						
AH1389 - 1970 Proof	Inc. above	Value: 150				
Note: Fineness both raised and incuse						

KM# 8 50 RIYALS

10.3600 g., 0.9000 Gold .2998 oz. AGW **Ruler:** Muhammad bin Hamad al-Sharqi **Series:** 1972 Munich Olympics **Obv:** Arms-flags above rifles on pointed shield **Rev:** Olympic logo and symbols with date

Date	Mintage	F	VF	XF	Unc	BU
AH1388 - 1969 Proof	1,230	Value: 260				
AH1389 - 1970 Proof	400	Value: 275				

KM# 9 100 RIYALS

20.7300 g., 0.9000 Gold .5999 oz. AGW **Ruler:** Muhammad bin Hamad al-Sharqi **Subject:** Apollo X **Obv:** Arms-flags above rifles on pointed shield **Rev:** Three astronauts and moon

Date	Mintage	F	VF	XF	Unc	BU
AH1388 - 1969 Proof	2,140	Value: 450				

KM# 10 100 RIYALS

20.7300 g., 0.9000 Gold .5999 oz. AGW **Ruler:** Muhammad bin Hamad al-Sharqi **Subject:** Apollo XII **Obv:** Arms-flags above rifles on pointed shield **Rev:** Four shields on moon surface at left, three astronauts on shield at right

Date	Mintage	F	VF	XF	Unc	BU
AH1388 - 1969 Proof	3,040	Value: 435				
AH1389 - 1970 Proof	—	Value: 435				

KM# 23 100 RIYALS

20.7300 g., 0.9000 Gold .5999 oz. AGW **Ruler:** Muhammad bin Hamad al-Sharqi **Subject:** Apollo XIII **Obv:** Arms-flags above rifles on pointed shield **Rev:** Five shields at left, Arab riders and sun at right

Date	Mintage	F	VF	XF	Unc	BU
AH1389 - 1970 Proof	600	Value: 475				

KM# 24 100 RIYALS

20.7300 g., 0.9000 Gold .5999 oz. AGW **Ruler:** Muhammad Hamad al-Sharqi **Subject:** Visit of Pope Paul VI to Philippines **Obv:** Arms-flags above rifles on pointed shield **Rev:** Buildings, Pope's profile at right

Date	Mintage	F	VF	XF	Unc	BU
AH1389 - 1970 Proof	290	Value: 550				

KM# 26 100 RIYALS

20.7300 g., 0.9000 Gold .5999 oz. AGW **Ruler:** Muhammad Hamad al-Sharqi **Subject:** Visit of Pope Paul VI to Australia **Obv:** Arms-flags above rifles on pointed shield **Rev:** Pope's profile at left, crown with keys and kangaroo on map at right

Date	Mintage	F	VF	XF	Unc	BU
AH1389 - 1970 Proof	250	Value: 550				

KM# 25 100 RIYALS

20.7300 g., 0.9000 Gold .5999 oz. AGW **Ruler:** Muhammad bin Hamad al-Sharqi **Subject:** Apollo XIV **Obv:** Arms-flags above rifles on pointed shield **Rev:** Moon above shooting star within ring, planet lower left

Date	Mintage	F	VF	XF	Unc	BU
AH1389 - 1971 Proof	550	Value: 435				

KM# 11 200 RIYALS

41.4600 g., 0.9000 Gold 1.1998 oz. AGW **Ruler:** Muhammad bin Hamad al-Sharqi **Subject:** Mohamad bin Hamad al-Sharqi **Obv:** Arms-flags above rifles on pointed shield **Rev:** Bust left

Date	Mintage	F	VF	XF	Unc	BU
AH1388 - 1969 Proof	680	Value: 850				
Note: Serially numbered on the obverse						

PROOF SETS

KM#	Date	Mintage	Identification	Issue Price	Mkt Val
PS1	1969-71 (18)	—		—	—
PS2	1969-71 (9)	—	KM#1-4.2, 5, 19-22	—	475
PS3	1969-71 (8)	—	KM#4.2, 5, 19, 22, 9, 10, 23, 25	—	2,000
PS4	1969 (8)	—	KM#1-4.2, 7-9, 11	—	1,875
PS5	1969 (5)	2,550	KM#1-4.2, 5	40.00	220
PS6	1969 (5)	5,000	KM#7-11	280	2,150
PS7	1969 (4)	—	KM#1-4.2	—	170
PS8	1970 (5)	200	KM#1-4.2, 5	40.00	220

GABON

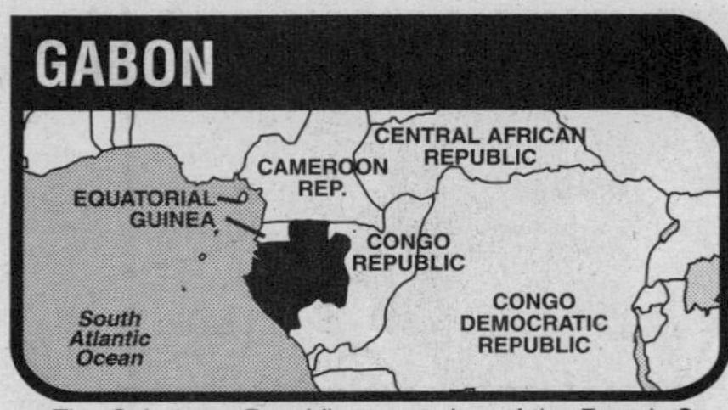

The Gabonese Republic, a member of the French Community, straddles the equator on the west coast of Africa. The hot and humid rain forest country has an area of 103,347 sq. mi. (267,670 sq. km.) and a population of 1.2 million, almost all of Bantu origin. Capital: Libreville. Extravagantly rich in resources, Gabon exports crude oil, manganese ore, gold and timbers.

Gabon was first visited by Portuguese navigator Diego Cam in the 15th century. Dutch, French and British traders, lured by the rich stands of hard woods and oil palms, quickly followed. The French founded their first settlement on the left bank of the Gabon River in 1839 and established their presence by signing treaties with the tribal chiefs. After gradually extending their influence into the interior during the last half of the 19th century, France occupied Gabon in 1885 and, in 1910, organized it as one of the four territories of French Equatorial Africa. It became an autonomous republic within the French Union in 1946, and on Aug. 17, 1960, became a completely independent republic within the new French Community.

For earlier coinage see French Equatorial Africa, Central African States and the Equatorial African States.

MINT MARKS

(a) - Paris, privy marks only
(t) - Poissy, privy marks only, thunderbolt

REPUBLIC

DECIMAL COINAGE

KM# 1 10 FRANCS

4.2000 g., 0.9000 Gold .1215 oz. AGW **Subject:** Independence **Obv:** Head of Mba right, date below **Rev:** Arms with supporters, denomination below

Date	Mintage	F	VF	XF	Unc	BU
1960 Proof	500	Value: 110				

KM# 2 25 FRANCS

8.0000 g., 0.9000 Gold .2315 oz. AGW **Subject:** Independence **Obv:** Head of Mba right, date below **Rev:** Arms with supporters, denomination below

Date	Mintage	F	VF	XF	Unc	BU
1960	10,000	—	—	—	165	—
1960 Proof	500	Value: 185				

KM# 3 50 FRANCS

16.0000 g., 0.9000 Gold .4630 oz. AGW **Subject:** Independence **Obv:** Head of Mba right, date below **Rev:** Arms with supporters, denomination below

Date	Mintage	F	VF	XF	Unc	BU
1960 Proof	500	Value: 325				

KM# 4 100 FRANCS
32.0000 g., 0.9000 Gold .9260 oz. AGW **Subject:** Independence **Obv:** Head of Mba right, date below **Rev:** Arms with supporters, denomination

Date	Mintage	F	VF	XF	Unc	BU
1960 Proof	500	Value: 650				

KM# 12 100 FRANCS
Nickel, 25 mm. **Obv:** Three great eland left **Obv. Designer:** G.B.L. Bazor **Rev:** Denomination within circle, date below

Date	Mintage	F	VF	XF	Unc	BU
1971(a)	1,300,000	4.50	9.00	17.50	25.00	—
1972(a)	2,000,000	4.50	9.00	17.50	25.00	—

KM# 13 100 FRANCS
Nickel, 25 mm. **Obv:** Three great eland left **Obv. Designer:** G.B.L. Bazor **Rev:** Denomination within circle, date below

Date	Mintage	F	VF	XF	Unc	BU
1975(a)	—	2.00	4.00	7.50	15.00	22.00
1977(a)	—	3.00	6.50	12.50	24.00	30.00
1978(a)	—	2.50	4.50	9.00	18.50	26.00
1982(a)	—	1.75	3.50	6.50	10.00	15.00
1983(a)	—	1.75	3.50	6.50	10.00	15.00
1984(a)	—	1.75	3.50	6.50	10.00	15.00
1985(a)	—	1.75	3.50	6.50	10.00	15.00

KM# 14 500 FRANCS
Copper-Nickel **Obv:** Leafy plants divide denomination and date **Rev:** Head left, inscription at right

Date	Mintage	F	VF	XF	Unc	BU
1985(a)	—	4.00	7.00	12.00	20.00	—

KM# 6 1000 FRANCS
3.5000 g., 0.9000 Gold .1012 oz. AGW **Obv:** Head of Bongo left **Rev:** Stump of okume tree, denomination below, arms above

Date	Mintage	F	VF	XF	Unc	BU
1969 Proof	4,000	Value: 100				

KM# 7 3000 FRANCS
10.5000 g., 0.9000 Gold .3038 oz. AGW **Obv:** Head of Bongo left **Rev:** Arms with supporters, denomination below

Date	Mintage	F	VF	XF	Unc	BU
1969 Proof	4,000	Value: 215				

KM# 8 5000 FRANCS
17.5000 g., 0.9000 Gold .5064 oz. AGW **Obv:** Head of Bongo left **Rev:** Reliquary figure of Bakota, denomination below, arms above

Date	Mintage	F	VF	XF	Unc	BU
1969 Proof	4,000	Value: 345				

KM# 11 5000 FRANCS
17.5000 g., 0.9000 Gold .5064 oz. AGW **Subject:** Visit of French President Georges Pompidou **Rev:** Head left

Date	Mintage	F	VF	XF	Unc	BU
1971 Proof	—	Value: 525				

KM# 9 10000 FRANCS
35.0000 g., 0.9000 Gold 1.0128 oz. AGW **Subject:** 1st Moon landing **Obv:** Head of Bongo left **Rev:** Lunar module, denomination below

Date	Mintage	F	VF	XF	Unc	BU
1969 Proof	4,000	Value: 700				

KM# 10 20000 FRANCS
70.0000 g., 0.9000 Gold 2.0257 oz. AGW **Subject:** 1st Moon landing - Cape Kennedy **Obv:** Head of Bongo left **Rev:** Apollo XI at launching pad, denomination below

Date	Mintage	F	VF	XF	Unc	BU
1969 Proof	4,000	Value: 1,375				

FRENCH EQUATORIAL AFRICAN TERRITORY

TOKEN COINAGE

Believed to be initially used for payment of taxes. These tokens do not show a denomination, but circulated until 1930 with varying values corresponding to the animals shown. All have center hole.

KM# Tn1 NON-DENOMINATED
Aluminum **Obv:** Date below center hole, "GABON" above **Rev:** Hole within elephant walking left

Date	Mintage	F	VF	XF	Unc	BU
1925(t)	—	55.00	100	180	350	600

KM# Tn2 NON-DENOMINATED
Aluminum **Obv:** Date below center hole, "GABON" above **Rev:** Center hole within leopard walking left

Date	Mintage	F	VF	XF	Unc	BU
1926	—	100	175	325	550	700

KM# Tn3 NON-DENOMINATED
Aluminum **Obv:** Date below center hole, "GABON" above **Rev:** Center hole within ox head facing

Date	Mintage	F	VF	XF	Unc	BU
1927(t)	—	75.00	150	250	450	650

KM# Tn4 NON-DENOMINATED
Aluminum **Obv:** Date below center hole, "GABON" above **Rev:** Center hole within pelican right

Date	Mintage	F	VF	XF	Unc	BU
1928	—	125	200	350	550	700

KM# Tn5 NON-DENOMINATED
Aluminum **Obv:** "Gabon" above center hole, date below **Rev:** Rhinoceros walking left

Date	Mintage	F	VF	XF	Unc	BU
1929	—	85.00	175	300	550	700

ESSAIS

Standard metals unless otherwise noted

KM#	Date	Mintage	Identification	Issue Price	Mkt Val
E1	1960	10	25 Francs. Gold. KM2.	—	750
E2	1960	—	25 Francs. Silver. KM2.	—	250
E3	1971(a)	1,450	100 Francs. KM12.	—	30.00
E4	1971(a)	4	100 Francs. Gold. KM12.	—	1,800
E5	1971(a)	—	5000 Francs. Copper-Aluminum-Nickel. KM11.	—	200

KM#	Date	Mintage	Identification	Issue Price	Mkt Val
E6	1975(a)	1,700	100 Francs. Three great eland left. Denomination within circle, date below. KM13.	—	20.00

KM#	Date	Mintage	Identification	Issue Price	Mkt Val
E7	1985(a)	1,700	500 Francs. Plants divide denomination and date. Head left, inscription at right. KM14.	—	30.00

PROOF SETS

KM#	Date	Mintage	Identification	Issue Price	Mkt Val
PS1	1960 (4)	500	KM1-4	—	1,275
PS2	1969 (5)	4,000	KM6-10	—	2,740

GAMBIA

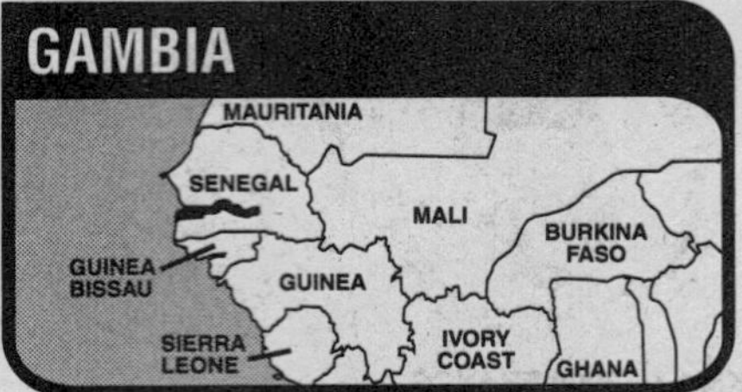

The Republic of The Gambia, occupies a strip of land 7 miles (11km.) to 20 miles (32 km.) wide and 200 miles (322 km.) long encompassing both sides of West Africa's Gambia River, and completely surrounded by Senegal. The republic, one of Africa's smallest countries, has an area of 4,127 sq. mi. (11,300 sq. km.) and a population of 989,273. Capital: Banjul. Agriculture and tourism are the principal industries. Peanuts constitute 95 per cent of export earnings.

The Gambia was once part of the great empires of Ghana and Songhay. When Portuguese gold seekers and slave traders visited The Gambia in the 15th century, it was part of the Kingdom of Mali. In 1588 the territory became, through purchase, the first British colony in Africa. English slavers established Fort James, the first settlement, on a small island a dozen miles up the Gambia River in 1664. After alternate periods of union with Sierra Leone and existence as a separate colony The Gambia became a British colony in 1888. On Feb. 18, 1965, The Gambia achieved independence as a constitutional monarchy within the Commonwealth of Nations, with Elizabeth II as Head of State as Queen of The Gambia. It became a republic on April 24, 1970, remaining a member of the Commonwealth, but with the president as Chief of State and Head of Government.

Together with Senegal, The Gambia formed a confederation on February 1, 1982. This confederation was officially dissolved on September 21, 1989. In July, 1994 a military junta took control of The Gambia and disbanded its elected government.

For earlier coinage see British West Africa.

RULERS
British until 1970

MONETARY SYSTEM
12 Pence = 1 Shilling
20 Shillings = 1 Pound

COLONIAL

STERLING COINAGE

KM# 1 PENNY
Bronze, 25.5 mm. **Obv:** Young bust right **Obv. Designer:** Arnold Machin **Rev:** Sailing vessel, denomination at right **Edge:** Smooth

Date	Mintage	F	VF	XF	Unc	BU
1966	3,600,000	—	0.20	0.40	1.00	1.25
1966 Proof	6,600	Value: 1.00				

KM# 2 3 PENCE
Nickel-Brass, 21.5 mm. **Obv:** Young bust right **Obv. Designer:** Arnold Machin **Rev:** Double-spurred francolin, denomination above **Edge:** Smooth

Date	Mintage	F	VF	XF	Unc	BU
1966	2,000,000	—	0.30	0.50	1.50	2.00
1966 Proof	6,600	Value: 1.50				

KM# 3 6 PENCE
Copper-Nickel, 19.5 mm. **Obv:** Young bust right **Obv. Designer:** Arnold Machin **Rev:** Peanuts divide denomination **Edge:** Reeded

Date	Mintage	F	VF	XF	Unc	BU
1966	1,500,000	—	0.30	0.50	1.75	2.00
1966 Proof	6,600	Value: 1.75				

KM# 4 SHILLING
Copper-Nickel, 23.5 mm. **Obv:** Young bust right **Obv. Designer:** Arnold Machin **Rev:** Oil palm, denomination above **Edge:** Reeded

Date	Mintage	F	VF	XF	Unc	BU
1966	2,500,000	—	0.50	0.80	2.00	2.50
1966 Proof	6,600	Value: 2.00				

KM# 5 2 SHILLINGS
Copper-Nickel, 28.3 mm. **Obv:** Young bust right **Rev:** African domestic ox divides denomination **Edge:** Reeded

Date	Mintage	F	VF	XF	Unc	BU
1966	1,600,000	—	0.75	1.50	2.50	3.00
1966 Proof	6,600	Value: 2.50				

KM# 6 4 SHILLINGS
Copper-Nickel, 34 mm. **Obv:** Young bust right **Obv. Designer:** Arnold Machin **Rev:** Slender-snouted crocodile, denomination at right **Edge:** Reeded

Date	Mintage	F	VF	XF	Unc	BU
1966	800,000	—	1.50	2.50	5.50	8.00
1966 Proof	6,600	Value: 8.00				

KM# 7 8 SHILLINGS
Copper-Nickel **Obv:** Young bust right **Obv. Designer:** Arnold Machin **Rev:** Hippopotamus, denomination above

Date	Mintage	F	VF	XF	Unc	BU
1970	25,000	—	2.00	4.00	12.00	15.00

KM# 7a 8 SHILLINGS
32.4000 g., 0.9250 Silver .9635 oz. ASW **Obv:** Young bust right **Rev:** Hippopotamus, denomination above

Date	Mintage	F	VF	XF	Unc	BU
1970 Proof	4,500	Value: 35.00				

Note: VIP issued proofs have a frosted relief, value: $175.00.

REPUBLIC

DECIMAL COINAGE

100 Bututs = 1 Dalasi

KM# 8 BUTUT

1.8000 g., Bronze, 17.15 mm. **Obv:** President's bust left **Obv. Designer:** Michael Rizzello **Rev:** Peanuts, denomination at right

Date	Mintage	F	VF	XF	Unc	BU
1971	12,449,000	—	—	0.10	0.20	0.30
1971 Proof	32,000	Value: 0.50				
1973	3,000,000	—	—	0.10	0.25	0.35
1974	19,060,000	—	0.25	0.50	1.50	2.00

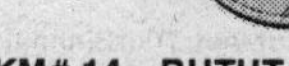

KM# 14 BUTUT

Bronze **Series:** F.A.O. **Obv:** President's bust left **Obv. Designer:** Michael Rizzello **Rev:** Peanuts, denomination at right

Date	Mintage	F	VF	XF	Unc	BU
1974	26,062,000	—	—	0.10	0.20	0.30
1985	4,500,000	—	—	0.15	0.25	0.35

KM# 54 BUTUT

Copper Plated Steel **Obv:** National arms, date below **Rev:** Peanuts, denomination at right

Date	Mintage	F	VF	XF	Unc	BU
1998	—	—	—	—	0.20	0.30

KM# 9 5 BUTUTS

3.5500 g., Bronze, 20.3 mm. **Obv:** President's bust left **Obv. Designer:** Michael Rizzello **Rev:** Sailing vessel, denomination at right

Date	Mintage	F	VF	XF	Unc	BU
1971	5,400,000	—	—	0.10	0.35	0.50
1971 Proof	32,000	Value: 0.60				

KM# 55 5 BUTUTS

Copper Plated Steel **Obv:** National arms, date below **Rev:** Sailboat, denomination at right

Date	Mintage	F	VF	XF	Unc	BU
1998	—	—	—	—	0.35	0.50

KM# 10 10 BUTUTS

6.2000 g., Nickel-Brass, 25.9 mm. **Obv:** President's bust left **Obv. Designer:** Michael Rizzello **Rev:** Double-spurred francolin, denomination at right

Date	Mintage	F	VF	XF	Unc	BU
1971	3,000,000	—	0.15	0.35	1.50	2.00
1971 Proof	32,000	Value: 2.00				

KM# 64 10 BUTUTS

24.7000 g., Copper-Nickel, 38.5 mm. **Subject:** Marine Life Protection **Obv:** National arms **Rev:** Multicolor fish scene **Edge:** Reeded

Date	Mintage	F	VF	XF	Unc	BU
1997	—	—	—	—	27.50	—

KM# 56 10 BUTUTS

Brass Plated Steel **Obv:** National arms, date below **Rev:** Double-spurred francolin, denomination at right

Date	Mintage	F	VF	XF	Unc	BU
1998	—	—	—	—	1.00	1.50

KM# 11 25 BUTUTS

5.6500 g., Copper-Nickel, 23.6 mm. **Obv:** President's bust left **Obv. Designer:** Michael Rizzello **Rev:** Oil palm, denomination above

Date	Mintage	F	VF	XF	Unc	BU
1971	3,040,000	—	0.15	0.30	0.75	1.00
1971 Proof	32,000	Value: 1.25				

KM# 57 25 BUTUTS

Copper-Nickel **Obv:** National arms, date below **Rev:** Oil palm, denomination above

Date	Mintage	F	VF	XF	Unc	BU
1998	—	—	—	—	1.00	1.25

KM# 12 50 BUTUTS

11.3000 g., Copper-Nickel, 28.5 mm. **Obv:** President's bust left **Obv. Designer:** Michael Rizzello **Rev:** African domestic ox divides denomination

Date	Mintage	F	VF	XF	Unc	BU
1971	1,700,000	—	0.35	0.65	1.75	2.50
1971 Proof	32,000	Value: 1.75				

KM# 60 50 BUTUTS

24.9700 g., 0.9800 Silver .7867 oz. ASW **Subject:** Marine Life Protection **Obv:** National arms, date and denomination below **Rev:** Pair of multicolor fish

Date	Mintage	F	VF	XF	Unc	BU
1997 Proof	—	Value: 40.00				

KM# 58 50 BUTUTS

Copper-Nickel **Obv:** National arms, date below **Rev:** African domestic ox divides denomination

Date	Mintage	F	VF	XF	Unc	BU
1998	—	—	—	—	1.50	2.00

KM# 62 2000 BUTUTS

0.9250 g., Silver, 37.5 mm. **Subject:** Millennium **Obv:** National arms, dates below **Rev:** Gambian map on radiant sun, denomination below **Edge:** Reeded **Shape:** 10-sided **Note:** Struck at British Royal Mint.

Date	Mintage	F	VF	XF	Unc	BU
ND(1999) Proof	30,000	Value: 55.00				

KM# 13 DALASI

Copper-Nickel **Obv:** President's bust left **Obv. Designer:** Michael Rizzello **Rev:** Slender-snouted crocodile, denomination at right

Date	Mintage	F	VF	XF	Unc	BU
1971	1,300,000	—	2.00	3.50	8.00	10.00
1971 Proof	32,000	Value: 5.00				

KM# 29 DALASI

12.2000 g., Copper-Nickel, 30.8 mm. **Obv:** President's bust left **Obv. Designer:** Michael Rizzello **Rev:** Slender-snouted crocodile, denomination at right **Edge:** Reeded, smooth alternating edge **Shape:** 7-sided

Date	Mintage	F	VF	XF	Unc	BU
1987	—	—	1.75	2.75	6.00	7.50

KM# 65 DALASI
28.1100 g., Copper Nickel, 38.6 mm. **Subject:** Queen Mother **Obv:** National arms, date below **Rev:** Oval portraits of George V, Edward VIII and George VI within circle, denomination below **Edge:** Reeded

Date	Mintage	F	VF	XF	Unc	BU
1996	30,000	—	—	—	16.50	—

KM# 59 DALASI
Copper Nickel, 28 mm. **Obv:** National arms, date below **Rev:** Slender-snouted crocodile, denomination at right **Shape:** 7-sided

Date	Mintage	F	VF	XF	Unc	BU
1998	—	—	1.75	2.75	6.00	7.50

KM# 46 2 DALASIS
9.9200 g., 0.5000 Silver .1595 oz. ASW **Subject:** Olympic Games 1996 **Obv:** National arms, date below **Rev:** Two runners crossing a finish line, denomination at right

Date	Mintage	F	VF	XF	Unc	BU
1996 Proof	Est. 10,000	Value: 15.00				

KM# 49 2 DALASIS
Copper-Nickel **Subject:** 70th Birthday of Queen Elizabeth II **Obv:** National arms

Date	Mintage	F	VF	XF	Unc	BU
1996	5,000	—	—	—	10.00	12.00

KM# 16 10 DALASIS
28.2800 g., 0.5000 Silver .4546 oz. ASW **Subject:** 10th Anniversary of Independence **Obv:** President's bust left **Obv. Designer:** Michael Rizzello **Rev:** National arms, denomination below

Date	Mintage	F	VF	XF	Unc	BU
1975	50,000	—	—	—	10.00	12.50

KM# 16a 10 DALASIS
28.2800 g., 0.9250 Silver .8411 oz. ASW **Subject:** 10th Anniversary of Independence **Obv:** President's bust left **Rev:** National arms, denomination

Date	Mintage	F	VF	XF	Unc	BU
1975 Proof	20,000	Value: 16.50				

KM# 23 10 DALASIS
28.2800 g., 0.5000 Silver .4546 oz. ASW, 38.61 mm. **Subject:** Commonwealth Games **Obv:** President's bust left **Rev:** Hurdlers, denomination below

Date	Mintage	F	VF	XF	Unc	BU
1986	Est. 50,000	—	—	—	12.50	14.00

KM# 23a 10 DALASIS
28.2800 g., 0.9250 Silver .8411 oz. ASW, 38.61 mm. **Subject:** Commonwealth Games **Obv:** President's bust left **Rev:** Hurdlers, denomination

Date	Mintage	F	VF	XF	Unc	BU
1986 Proof	Est. 20,000	Value: 22.50				

KM# 28 10 DALASIS
28.2800 g., 0.9250 Silver .8411 oz. ASW **Subject:** Silver Jubilee of Independence **Obv:** President's bust left **Obv. Designer:** Michael Rizzello **Rev:** National arms, denomination below

Date	Mintage	F	VF	XF	Unc	BU
1990 Proof	2,000	Value: 42.50				

KM# 30 10 DALASIS
Copper-Nickel **Subject:** Papal Visit **Obv:** National arms, denomination below **Rev:** Half-figure of Pope 3/4 facing, right arm raised

Date	Mintage	F	VF	XF	Unc	BU
1992	—	—	—	—	6.50	8.00

KM# 30a 10 DALASIS
28.2800 g., 0.9250 Silver .8411 oz. ASW **Subject:** Papal Visit **Obv:** National arms, denomination **Rev:** Half figure of Pope 3/4 facing with right arm raised

Date	Mintage	F	VF	XF	Unc	BU
1992 Proof	5,000	Value: 55.00				

KM# 50 10 DALASIS
Copper Nickel **Subject:** 70th Birthday of H.M. Queen Elizabeth II **Obv:** National arms, date **Rev:** Queen inspecting guard, denomination

Date	Mintage	F	VF	XF	Unc	BU
1996	—	—	—	—	8.00	10.00

KM# 50a 10 DALASIS
28.2800 g., 0.9250 Silver .8411 oz. ASW **Subject:** 70th Birthday of H.M. Queen Elizabeth II **Obv:** National arms, date below **Rev:** Queen inspecting guard, denomination divides dates

Date	Mintage	F	VF	XF	Unc	BU
1996 Proof	70,000	Value: 42.50				

KM# 17 20 DALASIS
28.6300 g., 0.9250 Silver .8514 oz. ASW **Subject:** Conservation **Obv:** President's bust left **Obv. Designer:** Michael Rizzello **Rev:** Spur-winged goose divides denomination

Date	Mintage	F	VF	XF	Unc	BU
1977	4,302	—	—	—	22.00	—

KM# 17a 20 DALASIS
28.2800 g., 0.9250 Silver .8411 oz. ASW **Subject:** Conservation **Obv:** President's bust left **Rev:** Spur-winged goose divides denomination

Date	Mintage	F	VF	XF	Unc	BU
1977 Proof	4,404	Value: 25.00				

KM# 20 20 DALASIS
28.2800 g., 0.9250 Silver .8411 oz. ASW **Subject:** World Food Day **Obv:** President's bust left **Rev:** Logo above field worker, denomination below

Date	Mintage	F	VF	XF	Unc	BU
1981	10,000	—	—	—	25.00	30.00
1981 Proof	5,000	Value: 45.00				

KM# 21 20 DALASIS

28.2800 g., 0.9250 Silver .8411 oz. ASW **Subject:** Year of the Scout **Obv:** President's bust in beret left **Rev:** Scout emblem above motto, denomination

Date	Mintage	F	VF	XF	Unc	BU
1983	Est. 10,000	—	—	—	25.00	30.00
1983 Proof	Inc. above	Value: 40.00				

KM# 24 20 DALASIS

28.2800 g., 0.9250 Silver .8411 oz. ASW **Subject:** World Wildlife Fund **Rev:** Temminck's colobus monkey divides denomination

Date	Mintage	F	VF	XF	Unc	BU
1987 Proof	Est. 25,000	Value: 27.50				

KM# 26 20 DALASIS

28.2800 g., 0.9250 Silver .8411 oz. ASW **Subject:** Save the Children Fund **Obv:** Bust of President Alhaji Sir Dawda Dairaba Jawara **Rev:** Girls playing "akara" (rythmic clapping and dancing game), denomination below

Date	Mintage	F	VF	XF	Unc	BU
1989	Est. 20,000	Value: 25.00				

KM# 32 20 DALASIS

31.4700 g., 0.9250 Silver .9359 oz. ASW **Subject:** 40th Anniversary - Coronation of Queen Elizabeth II **Obv:** President's bust left **Obv. Designer:** Michael Rizzello **Rev:** Royal crown above denomination

Date	Mintage	F	VF	XF	Unc	BU
1993 Proof	Est. 10,000	Value: 45.00				

KM# 33 20 DALASIS

31.2600 g., 0.9250 Silver .9296 oz. ASW **Series:** Olympics **Obv:** President's bust left **Rev:** Wrestlers, denomination below

Date	Mintage	F	VF	XF	Unc	BU
1993 Proof	Est. 40,000	Value: 22.50				

KM# 34 20 DALASIS

31.4700 g., 0.9250 Silver .9359 oz. ASW **Subject:** Prince Henry the Navigator **Obv:** President's bust left **Rev:** Ship at sea at left, 3/4 figure at right above denomination

Date	Mintage	F	VF	XF	Unc	BU
1993 Proof	Est. 15,000	Value: 22.50				

KM# 36 20 DALASIS

31.4700 g., 0.9250 Silver .9359 oz. ASW **Subject:** Rendezvous in Space **Obv:** President's bust left **Rev:** Space Shuttle at left, astronauts at right, denomination below

Date	Mintage	F	VF	XF	Unc	BU
1993 Proof	Est. 10,000	Value: 30.00				

KM# 35 20 DALASIS

31.4700 g., 0.9250 Silver .9359 oz. ASW **Subject:** Soccer - World Cup 1994 **Obv:** President's bust left **Rev:** Maps on globe, soccer ball and players, denomination below

Date	Mintage	F	VF	XF	Unc	BU
1994 Proof	Est. 15,000	Value: 30.00				

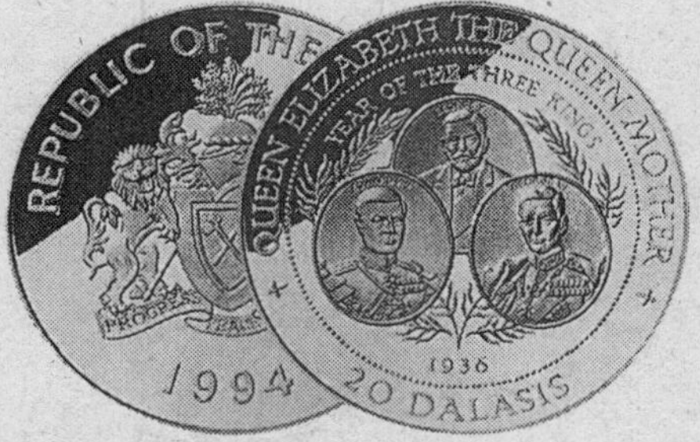

KM# 40 20 DALASIS

31.4700 g., 0.9250 Silver .9359 oz. ASW **Subject:** Elizabeth, the Queen Mother **Obv:** National arms, date below **Rev:** Busts of Edward VIII, George V and George VI facing within circles, inscription above **Rev. Inscription:** Year of the Three Kings

Date	Mintage	F	VF	XF	Unc	BU
1994 Proof	Est. 30,000	Value: 37.50				

KM# 38 20 DALASIS

31.4700 g., 0.9250 Silver .9359 oz. ASW **Subject:** Endangered Wildlife **Obv:** President's bust left **Obv. Designer:** Michael Rizzello **Rev:** Chimpanzee, denomination below

Date	Mintage	F	VF	XF	Unc	BU
1994 Proof	Est. 15,000	Value: 35.00				

KM# 39 20 DALASIS

31.4700 g., 0.9250 Silver .9359 oz. ASW **Subject:** Mungo Park **Obv:** President's bust left **Obv. Designer:** Michael Rizzello **Rev:** Bust left at right, figures piloting raft at left, denomination above

Date	Mintage	F	VF	XF	Unc	BU
1994 Proof	Est. 10,000	Value: 32.50				

KM# 47 20 DALASIS

31.4700 g., 0.9250 Silver .9359 oz. ASW **Subject:** Olympic Games 1996 **Obv:** National arms, date below **Rev:** Two runners crossing a finish line, denomination at right

Date	Mintage	F	VF	XF	Unc	BU
1994 Proof	—	Value: 22.50				

KM# 37 20 DALASIS
Copper-Nickel **Subject:** 50th Anniversary - United Nations **Obv:** National arms, date below **Rev:** Dove with olive branch above UN logo, map in background, denomination below

Date	Mintage	F	VF	XF	Unc	BU
1995	—	—	—	—	8.00	9.50

KM# 37a 20 DALASIS
28.2800 g., 0.9250 Silver .8411 oz. ASW **Subject:** 50th Anniversary - United Nations **Obv:** National arms, date **Rev:** Dove with olive branch above logo, map in background

Date	Mintage	F	VF	XF	Unc	BU
1995 Proof	—	Value: 32.50				

KM# 41 20 DALASIS
31.4700 g., 0.9250 Silver .9359 oz. ASW **Subject:** Protect Our World **Obv:** National arms, date below **Rev:** Nudes in forest, birds and snake in trees, denomination below

Date	Mintage	F	VF	XF	Unc	BU
1995 Proof	Est. 10,000	Value: 40.00				

KM# 42 20 DALASIS
7.7760 g., 0.5833 Gold .1458 oz. AGW **Subject:** Endangered Wildife **Obv:** National arms, date below **Rev:** Black rhinoceros, denomination below

Date	Mintage	F	VF	XF	Unc	BU
1995	Est. 2,000	—	—	—	120	135

KM# 43 20 DALASIS
7.7760 g., 0.5833 Gold .1458 oz. AGW **Subject:** Endangered Wildife **Obv:** National arms, date below **Rev:** African elephant, denomination below

Date	Mintage	F	VF	XF	Unc	BU
1995	Est. 2,000	—	—	—	120	135

KM# 44 20 DALASIS
31.4700 g., 0.9250 Silver .9359 oz. ASW **Subject:** Victorian Age **Obv:** National arms, date below **Rev:** Queen Victoria with first steam locomotive in background within circle, denomination below

Date	Mintage	F	VF	XF	Unc	BU
1996	Est. 10,000	—	—	—	42.50	—

KM# 51 20 DALASIS
31.4700 g., 0.9990 Silver 1.0108 oz. ASW **Subject:** World Cup 1998 **Obv:** National arms, date below **Rev:** Two soccer players, denomination below

Date	Mintage	F	VF	XF	Unc	BU
1996 Proof	10,000	Value: 40.00				

KM# 63 20 DALASIS
31.3600 g., 0.9250 Silver 0.9326 oz. ASW, 38.5 mm. **Subject:** British Queen Mother **Obv:** National arms, date below **Rev:** 1909 Portrait of the Queen Mother, denomination below **Edge:** Reeded

Date	Mintage	F	VF	XF	Unc	BU
1996 Proof	—	Value: 40.00				

KM# 18 40 DALASIS
35.2900 g., 0.9250 Silver 1.0495 oz. ASW **Subject:** Conservation **Obv:** President's bust left **Obv. Designer:** Michael Rizzello **Rev:** Aardvark divides denomination

Date	Mintage	F	VF	XF	Unc	BU
1977	4,304	—	—	—	25.00	—

KM# 18a 40 DALASIS
35.0000 g., 0.9250 Silver 1.0409 oz. ASW **Subject:** Conservation **Obv:** President's bust left **Rev:** Aardvark left divides denomination

Date	Mintage	F	VF	XF	Unc	BU
1977 Proof	4,183	Value: 35.00				

KM# 52 50 DALASIS
1.2441 g., 0.9990 Gold .0400 oz. AGW **Subject:** Kankan Manga Musa **Obv:** National arms, date below **Rev:** Seated king and supplicant, denomination below

Date	Mintage	F	VF	XF	Unc	BU
1997 Proof	—	Value: 45.00				

KM# 45 100 DALASIS
1000.0000 g., 0.9990 Silver 32.1186 oz. ASW, 100 mm. **Subject:** Endangered Wildlife **Obv:** National arms, date below **Rev:** Lion family within circle, denomination below **Note:** Illustration reduced.

Date	Mintage	F	VF	XF	Unc	BU
1996 Proof	1,000	Value: 520				

KM# 53 100 DALASIS
3.1100 g., 0.5833 Gold .0583 oz. AGW **Series:** Olympic Games 2000 **Obv:** National arms, date below **Rev:** Silhouette of three runners, denomination below

Date	Mintage	F	VF	XF	Unc	BU
1997 Proof	5,000	Value: 60.00				

KM# 61 150 DALASIS
7.7760 g., 0.5830 Gold .1458 oz. AGW **Subject:** British Year of 3 Kings and Queen Mother **Obv:** National arms, date below **Rev:** Busts of Edward VIII, George V and George VI facing within circles

Date	Mintage	F	VF	XF	Unc	BU
1996 Proof	—	Value: 175				

KM# 48 200 DALASIS
31.1035 g., 0.9990 Gold 1 oz. AGW **Subject:** Endangered Wildlife **Rev:** Lion right, denomination below

Date	Mintage	F	VF	XF	Unc	BU
1996 Proof	1,000	Value: 725				

KM# 22 250 DALASIS
15.9800 g., 0.9170 Gold .4712 oz. AGW **Subject:** Year of the Scout **Obv:** President's bust in beret left **Rev:** Scout emblem above motto, denomination below

Date	Mintage	F	VF	XF	Unc	BU
1983	2,000	—	—	—	335	—
1983 Proof	2,000	Value: 360				

KM# 31 250 DALASIS
47.5400 g., 0.9170 Gold 1.4011 oz. AGW **Subject:** Papal Visit **Obv:** National arms **Rev:** Pope John Paul II giving a blessing

Date	Mintage	F	VF	XF	Unc	BU
1992 Proof	100	Value: 1,250				

KM# 19 500 DALASIS
33.4370 g., 0.9000 Gold .9676 oz. AGW **Subject:** Conservation **Obv:** President's bust left **Obv. Designer:** Michael Rizzello **Rev:** Sitatunga divides denomination

Date	Mintage	F	VF	XF	Unc	BU
1977	699	—	—	—	675	—
1977 Proof	285	Value: 820				

KM# 25 1000 DALASIS
10.0000 g., 0.9170 Gold .2948 oz. AGW **Subject:** World Wildlife Fund **Obv:** President's bust left **Obv. Designer:** Michael Rizzello **Rev:** Gambian puffback bird divides denomination

Date	Mintage	F	VF	XF	Unc	BU
1987 Proof	Est. 5,000	Value: 215				

KM# 27 1000 DALASIS
10.0000 g., 0.9170 Gold .2948 oz. AGW **Subject:** Save the Children Fund **Obv:** President's bust left **Obv. Designer:** Michael Rizzello

Date	Mintage	F	VF	XF	Unc	BU
1989 Proof	Est. 3,000	Value: 235				

PROOF SETS

KM#	Date	Mintage	Identification	Issue Price	Mkt Val
PS1	1966 (6)	5,100	KM1-6	13.00	16.50
PS2	1966 and 1970 (7)	1,500	KM1-6, 7a	25.00	42.50
PS3	1971 (6)	26,249	KM8-13	—	9.00
PS4	1977 (2)	—	KM17a, 18a	60.00	55.00

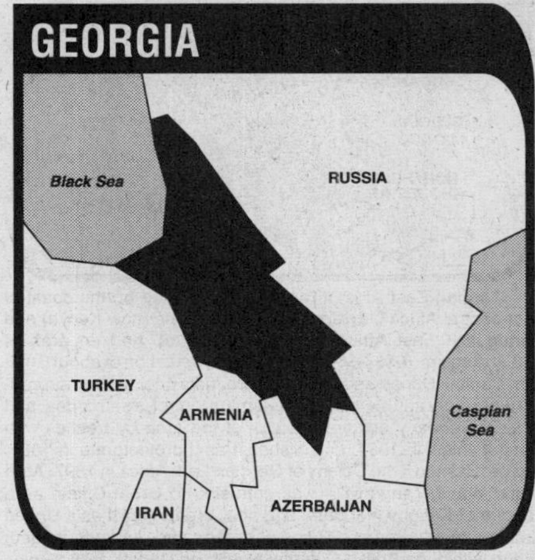

Georgia (formerly the Georgian Social Democratic Republic under the U.S.S.R.), is bounded by the Black Sea to the west and by Turkey, Armenia and Azerbaijan. It occupies the western part of Transcaucasia covering an area of 26,900 sq. mi. (69,700 sq. km.) and a population of 5.7 million. Capitol: Tbilisi. Hydro-electricity, minerals, forestry and agriculture are the chief industries.

After the Russian Revolution the Georgians, Armenians, and Azerbaijanis formed the short-lived Transcaucasian Federal Republic on Sept. 20, 1917, which broke up into three independent republics on May 26, 1918. A Germano-- Georgian treaty was signed on May 28, 1918, followed by a Turko-Georgian peace treaty on June 4. The end of WW I and the collapse of the central powers allowed free elections.

On May 20, 1920, Soviet Russia concluded a peace treaty, recognizing its independence, but later invaded on Feb. 11, 1921 and a soviet republic was proclaimed. On March 12, 1922 Stalin included Georgia in a newly formed Transcaucasian Soviet Federated Socialist Republic. On Dec. 5, 1936 the T.S.F.S.R. was dissolved and Georgia became a direct member of the U.S.S.R. The collapse of the U.S.S.R. allowed full transition to independence and on April 9, 1991 a unanimous vote declared the republic an independent state based on its original treaty of independence of May 1918.

INDEPENDENT STATE (C.I.S.)

STANDARD COINAGE

100 Thetri = 1 Lari

KM# 76 THETRI
1.3500 g., Stainless Steel, 14.9 mm. **Obv:** Stylized candelabra design divides date within circle **Rev:** Denomination above grapes **Edge:** Smooth

Date	Mintage	F	VF	XF	Unc	BU
1993	—	—	—	—	0.25	0.35

KM# 77 2 THETRI
1.8500 g., Stainless Steel, 17.4 mm. **Obv:** Stylized candelabra divides date within circle **Rev:** Stylized eagle above denomination **Edge:** Smooth

Date	Mintage	F	VF	XF	Unc	BU
1993	—	—	—	—	0.35	0.50

KM# 78 5 THETRI
2.4500 g., Stainless Steel, 19.9 mm. **Obv:** Stylized candelabra divides date within circle **Rev:** Stylized lion above denomination **Edge:** Smooth

Date	Mintage	F	VF	XF	Unc	BU
1993	—	—	—	—	0.75	1.00

KM# 79 10 THETRI
2.9500 g., Stainless Steel, 21.9 mm. **Obv:** Stylized candelabra divides date within circle **Rev:** St. Mamas riding lion right, denomination **Edge:** Smooth

Date	Mintage	F	VF	XF	Unc	BU
1993	—	—	—	—	1.25	1.50

KM# 80 20 THETRI
4.9500 g., Stainless Steel, 25 mm. **Obv:** Stylized candelabra divides date within circle **Rev:** Red Deer left, denomination **Edge:** Smooth

Date	Mintage	F	VF	XF	Unc	BU
1993	—	—	—	—	1.50	2.00

KM# 81 50 THETRI
2.4500 g., Brass, 19 mm. **Obv:** Stylized candelabra divides date within circle **Rev:** Stylized griffin left, above denomination **Edge:** Smooth

Date	Mintage	F	VF	XF	Unc	BU
1993	—	—	—	—	2.00	2.50

KM# 83 10 LARI
28.2800 g., 0.9250 Silver .8410 oz. ASW, 28.4 mm. **Subject:** State System 3,000 Years **Obv:** Denomination within circle **Rev:** Eagle and lion within circle **Edge:** Reeded

Date	Mintage	F	VF	XF	Unc	BU
2000 Proof	1,000	Value: 55.00				

KM# 84 10 LARI
28.2800 g., 0.9250 Silver .8410 oz. ASW **Subject:** Birth of Jesus 2,000th Anniversary **Obv:** Denomination within circle **Rev:** Christian arms within circle

Date	Mintage	F	VF	XF	Unc	BU
2000 Proof	1,000	Value: 55.00				

KM# 85 10 LARI
10.6000 g., Bi-Metallic Copper-Nickel center in Brass ring, 26 mm. **Subject:** State System: 3000 Years **Obv:** Denomination within circle **Rev:** Eagle above lion within circle **Edge:** Reeding over "GEORGIA . TEN LARI"

Date	Mintage	F	VF	XF	Unc	BU
2000	1,000	—	—	—	18.00	20.00

KM# 86 10 LARI
10.6000 g., Bi-Metallic Copper-Nickel center in Brass ring, 25.9 mm. **Subject:** Christianity: 2000 Years **Obv:** Denomination within circle **Rev:** Christian arms within circle **Edge:** Reeding over "GEORGIA . TEN LARI"

Date	Mintage	F	VF	XF	Unc	BU
2000	25,000	—	—	—	15.00	16.50

KM# 86a 10 LARI
16.0000 g., 0.9000 Silver 0.463 oz. ASW, 28.3 mm. **Obv:** Denomination **Rev:** Christian arms **Edge:** Reeded and lettered **Edge Lettering:** "GEORGIA TEN LARI"

Date	Mintage	F	VF	XF	Unc	BU
2000 Proof	—	Value: 75.00				

KM# 87 10 LARI
28.2800 g., Copper-Nickel, 38.61 mm. **Subject:** 300th Anniversary of Statehood **Obv:** Eagle above lion **Rev:** Denomination

Date	Mintage	F	VF	XF	Unc	BU
2000	2,000	—	—	—	25.00	28.00

KM# 88 10 LARI
28.2800 g., Copper-Nickel, 38.61 mm. **Subject:** 2000th Anniversary of the Birth of Christ

Date	Mintage	F	VF	XF	Unc	BU
2000	2,000	—	—	—	25.00	28.00

KM# 82 500 LARI
17.0000 g., 0.9170 Gold .5010 oz. AGW **Subject:** 50th Anniversary - Defeat of Fascism **Obv:** Stylized candelabra divides date above denomination **Rev:** Profiles of Stalin, Roosevelt, Churchill and de Gaulle left, date below

Date	Mintage	F	VF	XF	Unc	BU
1995 Proof	2,000	Value: 500				

MINT SETS

KM#	Date	Mintage	Identification	Issue Price	Mkt Val
MS1	1993 (6)	—	KM76-81	—	7.50

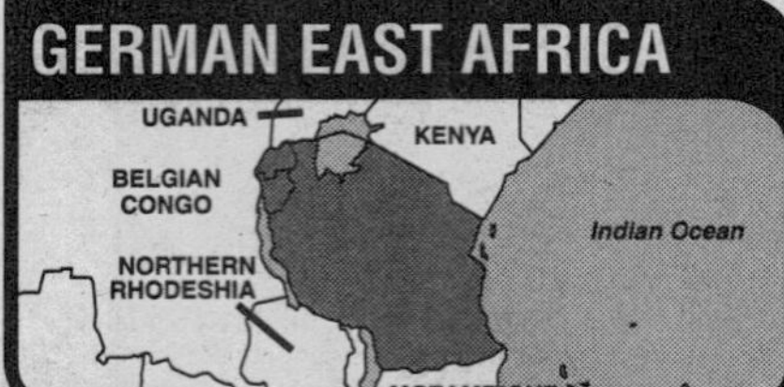

German East Africa (Tanganyika), located on the coast of east-central Africa between British East Africa (now Kenya) and Portuguese East Africa (now Mozambique), had an area of 362,284 sq. mi. (938,216 sq. km.) and a population of about 6 million. Capital: Dar es Salaam. Chief products prior to German control were ivory and slaves; after German control, sisal, coffee, and rubber. Germany acquired control of the area by treaties with coastal chiefs in 1884, established it as a protectorate in 1891, and proclaimed it the Colony of German East Africa in 1897. After World War I, Tanganyika was entrusted to Great Britain as a League of Nations mandate, and after World War II as a United Nations trust territory. Tanganyika became an independent nation within the British Commonwealth on Dec. 9, 1961. Coins dated up until 1902 were issued by the German East Africa Company. From 1904 onwards, the government issued coins.

NOTE: For later coinage see East Africa.

TITLE

شراكة المانيا

Sharaka(t) Almania

RULER
Wilhelm II, 1888-1918

MINT MARKS
A - Berlin
J - Hamburg
T - Tabora

MONETARY SYSTEM
Until 1904
64 Pesa = 1 Rupie
Commencing 1904
100 Heller = 1 Rupie

COLONIAL

STANDARD COINAGE

64 Pesa = 1 Rupee until 1904; 100 Heller = 1 Rupie commencing 1904

KM# 6 1/2 HELLER
Bronze **Ruler:** Wihelm II **Obv:** Crown with ribbon above date **Rev:** Denomination within wreath

Date	Mintage	F	VF	XF	Unc	BU
1904A	1,201,000	2.00	6.00	10.00	35.00	50.00
1905A	7,192,000	2.25	5.25	9.00	32.50	45.00
1905J	4,000,000	2.25	5.25	9.00	32.50	45.00
1906J	6,000,000	1.25	3.50	6.50	28.00	40.00
1906J Proof	—	Value: 250				

KM# 7 HELLER
Bronze **Ruler:** Wihelm II **Obv:** Crown with ribbon above date **Rev:** Denomination within wreath

Date	Mintage	F	VF	XF	Unc	BU
1904A	10,256,000	0.75	2.25	4.00	20.00	30.00
1904A Proof	—	Value: 125				
1904J	2,500,000	0.75	2.25	7.00	25.00	35.00
1905A	3,760,000	0.75	2.25	7.00	25.00	35.00
1905A Proof	—	Value: 125				
1905J	7,556,000	0.75	2.25	4.00	25.00	35.00
1906A	3,004,000	0.75	2.25	7.00	25.00	40.00
1906A Proof	—	Value: 200				
1906J	1,962,000	0.75	2.25	7.00	30.00	50.00
1907J	17,790,000	0.75	1.50	4.00	20.00	25.00
1908J	12,205,000	0.75	1.50	4.00	20.00	25.00
1908J Proof	—	Value: 135				
1909J	1,698,000	2.50	7.50	15.00	35.00	50.00
1909J Proof	—	Value: 135				
1910J	5,096,000	0.75	1.50	4.00	20.00	25.00
1910J Proof	—	Value: 135				
1911J	6,420,000	0.75	1.50	4.00	20.00	25.00

Date	Mintage	F	VF	XF	Unc	BU
1911J Proof	—	Value: 135				
1912J	7,012,000	0.75	1.50	4.00	25.00	40.00
1912J Proof	—	Value: 135				
1913A	—	0.75	1.50	4.00	20.00	30.00
1913A Proof	—	Value: 135				
1913J	5,186,000	0.75	1.50	4.00	20.00	30.00
1913J Proof	—	Value: 150				

KM# 11 5 HELLER
Bronze **Ruler:** Wihelm II **Obv:** Crown with ribbon above date **Rev:** Denomination within wreath

Date	Mintage	F	VF	XF	Unc	BU
1908J	600,000	20.00	45.00	85.00	550	650
1908J Proof	—	Value: 1,200				
1909J	756,000	22.00	50.00	90.00	550	650
1909J Proof	60	Value: 1,200				

KM# 13 5 HELLER
Copper-Nickel **Ruler:** Wihelm II **Obv:** Center hole divides date, crown with ribbon above, legend below **Rev:** Center hole divides denomination, sprigs flank

Date	Mintage	F	VF	XF	Unc	BU
1913A	1,000,000	6.00	15.00	25.00	55.00	100
1913A Proof	—	Value: 250				
1913J	1,000,000	6.00	15.00	25.00	60.00	100
1913J Proof	—	Value: 250				
1914J	1,000,000	5.00	12.00	22.00	50.00	100
1914J Proof	—	Value: 250				

KM# 14.1 5 HELLER
Brass **Ruler:** Wihelm II **Obv:** Crown with ribbon above date, oval base on crown **Rev:** Denomination within wreath **Note:** 1-1/2 -2mm thick. Tabora emergency issue.

Date	Mintage	F	VF	XF	Unc	BU
1916T	30,000	10.00	20.00	40.00	80.00	150

KM# 14.2 5 HELLER
Brass **Ruler:** Wihelm II **Obv:** Crown with ribbon above date, flat base on crown **Rev:** Denomination within wreath **Note:** 1mm or less thick.

Date	Mintage	F	VF	XF	Unc	BU
1916T	Inc. above	4.00	12.00	30.00	60.00	100

KM# 12 10 HELLER
Copper-Nickel **Ruler:** Wihelm II **Obv:** Center hole divides date, crown with ribbon above, legend below **Rev:** Center hole divides denomination, sprigs flank

Date	Mintage	F	VF	XF	Unc	BU
1908J	—	5.00	15.00	30.00	90.00	125

Date	Mintage	F	VF	XF	Unc	BU
1908J Proof	—	Value: 350				
1909J	1,990,000	3.00	10.00	20.00	80.00	125
1909J Proof	—	Value: 275				
1910J	500,000	3.00	10.00	20.00	80.00	150
1910J Proof	—	Value: 275				
1911A	500,000	5.00	15.00	35.00	100	150
1911A Proof	—	Value: 300				
1914J	200,000	10.00	30.00	60.00	125	200
1914 Proof	—	Value: 285				

Reverse A
Curled tip on second L

Reverse B
Pointed tips on L's

Reverse C
Curled tips on L's

KM# 15 20 HELLER

Copper **Ruler:** Wihelm II **Obv:** Crown with ribbon above date **Rev:** Denomination within wreath **Note:** Tabora Emergency Coinage.

Date	Mintage	F	VF	XF	Unc	BU
1916T	300,000	6.00	10.00	20.00	85.00	100
Note: Obverse A and reverse A						
1916T	Inc. above	125	200	350	—	—
Note: Obverse A and reverse B						
1916T	Inc. above	60.00	85.00	140	—	—
Note: Obverse B and reverse A						
1916T	Inc. above	6.00	10.00	20.00	60.00	80.00
Note: Obverse B and reverse B						
1916T Rare	Inc. above	—	—	—	—	—
Note: Obverse A and reverse C						
1916T Rare	Inc. above	—	—	—	—	—
Note: Obverse B and reverse C						

KM# 15a 20 HELLER

Brass **Ruler:** Wihelm II **Obv:** Crown with ribbon above date **Rev:** Denomination within wreath **Note:** Tabora Emergency Issue.

Date	Mintage	F	VF	XF	Unc	BU
1916T	1,600,000	6.00	10.00	20.00	75.00	90.00
Note: Obverse A and reverse A						
1916T	Inc. above	7.00	12.50	25.00	85.00	100
Note: Obverse A and reverse B						
1916T	Inc. above	7.00	12.50	25.00	85.00	100
Note: Obverse B and reverse A						
1916T	Inc. above	6.00	10.00	20.00	65.00	80.00
Note: Obverse B and reverse B						
1916T	Inc. above	10.00	30.00	45.00	125	150
Note: Obverse A and reverse C						
1916T	Inc. above	12.00	35.00	50.00	135	150
Note: Obverse B and reverse C						

KM# 3 1/4 RUPIE

2.9160 g., 0.9170 Silver .0859 oz. ASW **Ruler:** Wihelm II **Obv:** Armored bust left **Rev:** Shielded arms, denomination below

Date	Mintage	F	VF	XF	Unc	BU
1901	350,000	6.00	18.00	45.00	140	160

KM# 8 1/4 RUPIE

2.9160 g., 0.9170 Silver .0859 oz. ASW **Ruler:** Wihelm II **Obv:** Armored bust left **Rev:** Shielded arms, denomination below

Date	Mintage	F	VF	XF	Unc	BU
1904A	300,000	5.00	12.00	37.50	110	150
1904A Proof	—	Value: 300				
1906A	300,000	5.00	12.00	37.50	110	150
1906A Proof	—	Value: 300				
1906J	100,000	20.00	60.00	125	300	400
1907J	200,000	10.00	25.00	75.00	200	275
1907J Proof	—	Value: 375				
1909A	300,000	6.00	13.50	40.00	185	225
1910J	600,000	5.00	12.00	37.50	110	140
1910J Proof	—	Value: 350				
1912J	400,000	6.00	13.50	40.00	120	175
1912J Proof	—	Value: 350				
1913A	200,000	6.50	14.50	42.50	135	225
1913A Proof	—	Value: 350				
1913J	400,000	5.00	12.00	37.50	110	140
1913J Proof	—	Value: 300				
1914J	200,000	6.50	14.50	42.50	125	200
1914J Proof	—	Value: 300				

KM# 4 1/2 RUPIE

5.8319 g., 0.9170 Silver .1719 oz. ASW **Ruler:** Wihelm II **Obv:** Armored bust left **Rev:** Shielded arms, denomination below

Date	Mintage	F	VF	XF	Unc	BU
1901	215,000	15.00	40.00	100	240	300

KM# 9 1/2 RUPIE

5.8319 g., 0.9170 Silver .1719 oz. ASW **Ruler:** Wihelm II **Obv:** Armored bust left **Rev:** Shielded arms, denomination below

Date	Mintage	F	VF	XF	Unc	BU
1904A	400,000	15.00	40.00	95.00	275	300
1904A Proof	—	Value: 450				
1906A	50,000	125	225	350	750	1,000
1906A Proof	—	Value: 1,000				
1906J	50,000	125	225	350	750	1,000
1907J	140,000	20.00	50.00	125	300	350
1907J Proof	—	Value: 550				
1909A	100,000	30.00	65.00	150	350	500
1910J	300,000	20.00	40.00	100	250	275
1910J Proof	—	Value: 450				
1912J	200,000	15.00	40.00	95.00	250	300
1913A	100,000	20.00	45.00	110	300	400
1913J	200,000	15.00	40.00	95.00	200	250
1914J	100,000	20.00	45.00	100	285	350

KM# 2 RUPIE

11.6638 g., 0.9170 Silver .3437 oz. ASW **Ruler:** Wihelm II **Obv:** Armored bust left **Rev:** Shielded arms, denomination below

Date	Mintage	F	VF	XF	Unc	BU
1901	319,000	12.50	25.00	75.00	175	225
1902	151,000	20.00	40.00	125	450	550

KM# 10 RUPIE

11.6638 g., 0.9170 Silver .3437 oz. ASW **Ruler:** Wihelm II **Obv:** Armored bust left **Rev:** Shielded arms, denomination below

Date	Mintage	F	VF	XF	Unc	BU
1904A	1,000,000	11.50	22.50	45.00	130	150
1904A Proof	—	Value: 425				
1905A	300,000	15.00	27.50	60.00	185	250
1905A Proof	—	Value: 450				
1905J	1,000,000	11.50	22.50	45.00	130	160
1905J Proof	—	Value: 400				
1906A	950,000	11.50	22.50	45.00	130	160
1906J	700,000	15.00	27.50	65.00	175	200
1907J	880,000	9.00	15.00	45.00	180	200
1908J	500,000	12.50	25.00	55.00	190	225
1908J Proof	—	Value: 450				
1909A	200,000	15.00	27.50	65.00	275	350
1910J	270,000	9.00	15.00	45.00	200	275
1911A	300,000	12.50	25.00	55.00	175	250
1911A Proof	—	Value: 450				
1911J	1,400,000	9.00	15.00	45.00	150	175
1911J Proof	—	Value: 400				
1912J	300,000	12.50	25.00	55.00	165	250
1912J Proof	—	Value: 450				
1913A	400,000	12.50	25.00	55.00	160	225
1913J	1,400,000	9.00	15.00	45.00	150	175
1913J Proof	—	Value: 400				
1914J	500,000	11.50	22.50	50.00	175	250

KM# 16.1 15 RUPIEN

7.1680 g., 0.7500 Gold .1728 oz. AGW **Ruler:** Wihelm II **Obv:** Crowned imperial eagle, right arabesque ends below "T" of "OSTAFRIKA" **Rev:** Elephant roaring right above date **Note:** Tabora Emergency Issue.

Date	Mintage	F	VF	XF	Unc	BU
1916T	9,803	650	950	1,400	2,250	2,750

KM# 16.2 15 RUPIEN

7.1680 g., 0.7500 Gold .1728 oz. AGW **Ruler:** Wihelm II **Obv:** Crowned imperial eagle above denomination, right arabesque ends below first "A" of "OSTAFRIKA" **Rev:** Elephant roaring right above date **Note:** Tabora Emergency Issue.

Date	Mintage	F	VF	XF	Unc	BU
1916T	6,395	650	1,000	1,500	2,250	2,750

PATTERNS

Including off metal strikes

KM#	Date	Mintage	Identification	Mkt Val
Pn1	1908	—	5 Heller. Bronze.	1,000

KM#	Date	Mintage	Identification	Mkt Val
Pn2	1908	—	10 Heller. Copper-Nickel. Crown with ribbon above center hole dividing date. Center hole divides denomination.	350
Pn2a	1908/1908	—	10 Heller. Copper-Nickel. Two obverses.	375
Pn3	1908J	—	25 Pfennig. Nickel. With sprigs.	250
Pn4	1908J	—	25 Pfennig. Nickel. With sprigs.	—
Pn5	ND	—	5 Rupien. White Metal. Uniface.	450
pn6	1913A	—	Rupie. Aluminum.	—

Although the origin of the German Empire can be traced to the Treaty of Verdun that ceded Charlemagne's lands east of the Rhine to German Prince Louis, it was for centuries little more than a geographic expression, con- sisting of hundreds of effectively autonomous big and little states. Nominally the states owed their allegiance to the Holy Roman Emperor, who was also a German king, but as the Emperors exhibited less and less concern for Germany the actual power devolved on the lords of the individual states. The fragmentation of the empire climaxed with the tragic denouement of the Thirty Years War, 1618-48, which devastated much of Germany, destroyed its agriculture and medieval commercial eminence and ended the attempt of the Hapsburgs to unify Germany. Deprived of administrative capacity by a lack of resources, the imperial authority became utterly powerless. At this time Germany contained an estimated 1,800 individual states, some with a population of as little as 300. The German Empire of recent history (the creation of Bis- marck) was formed on April 14, 1871, when the king of Prussia became German Emperor William I. The new empire comprised 4 kingdoms, 6 grand duchies, 12 duchies and principalities, 3 free cities and the nonautonomous province of Alsace-Lorraine. The states had the right to issue gold and silver coins of higher value than 1 Mark; coins of 1 Mark and under were general issues of the empire.

MINT MARKS

A - Berlin, 1750-date
D - Munich (Germany), 1872-date
E - Muldenhutten (Germany), 1887-1953
F - Stuttgart (Germany) 1872-date
G - Karlsruhe (Germany) 1872-date
J - Hamburg (Germany) 1873-date

MONETARY SYSTEM

After the German unification in 1871 when the old Thaler system was abandoned in favor of the Mark system (100 Pfennig = 1 Mark) the Vereinsthaler continued to circulate as a legal tender 3 Mark coin, and the double Thaler as a 6 Mark coin until 1908. In 1908 the Vereinsthalers were officially demonetized and the Thaler coinage was replaced by the new 3 Mark coin which had the same specifications as the old Vereinsthaler. The double Thaler coinage was not replaced as there was no great demand for a 6 Mark coin. Until the 1930's the German public continued to refer to the 3 Mark piece as a "Thaler".

Commencing 1871
100 Pfennig = 1 Mark

VERRECHNUNGS & GUTSCHRIFTS TOKENS

These were metallic indebtedness receipts used for commercial and banking purposes due to the lack of available subsidiary coinage. These tokens could be redeemed in sufficient quantities.

ANHALT-DESSAU

Anhalt-Dessau was part of the 1252 division that included Zerbst and Köthen. In 1396, Anhalt-Zerbst was divided into Anhalt-Zerbst and Anhalt-Dessau. In 1508, Anhalt-Zerbst was absorbed into Anhalt-Dessau. The latter was given to the eldest son of Joachim Ernst in the division of 1603. As other lines became extinct, they fell to Anhalt-Dessau, which united all territories of the dynasty in 1863. The last ruler was forced to give up power at the end of World War I.

RULERS

Friedrich I, 1871-1904
Friedrich II, 1904-1918
Ernst, 1918

MINT MARK

A – Berlin Mint, 1839-1914

DUCHY

REFORM COINAGE

KM# 27 2 MARK
11.1110 g., 0.9000 Silver .3215 oz. ASW, 28 mm. **Ruler:** Friedrich II **Obv:** Head left **Rev:** Crowned imperial German eagle, shield on breast

Date	Mintage	F	VF	XF	Unc	BU
1904A	50,000	150	320	550	750	1,000
1904A Proof	150	Value: 1,500				

KM# 29 3 MARK
16.6670 g., 0.9000 Silver .4823 oz. ASW, 33 mm. **Ruler:** Friedrich II **Obv:** Head left **Rev:** Crowned imperial German eagle, shield on breast

Date	Mintage	F	VF	XF	Unc	BU
1909A	100,000	35.00	75.00	150	275	320
1911A	100,000	40.00	85.00	165	300	350
Common date Proof	—	Value: 400				
Common date Proof	—	Value: 400				

KM# 30 3 MARK
16.6670 g., 0.9000 Silver .4823 oz. ASW, 33 mm. **Ruler:** Friedrich II **Subject:** Silver Wedding Anniversary **Obv:** Jugate heads left **Rev:** Crowned imperial German eagle, shield on breast

Date	Mintage	F	VF	XF	Unc	BU
1914A	200,000	25.00	60.00	85.00	100	130
1914A Proof	1,000	Value: 300				

KM# 31 5 MARK
27.7770 g., 0.9000 Silver .8038 oz. ASW, 38 mm. **Ruler:** Friedrich II **Subject:** Silver Wedding Anniversary **Obv:** Jugate heads left **Rev:** Crowned imperial German eagle, shield on breast

Date	Mintage	F	VF	XF	Unc	BU
1914A	30,000	65.00	180	285	450	500
1914A Proof	1,000	Value: 700				

KM# 25 10 MARK
3.9820 g., 0.9000 Gold .1152 oz. AGW **Ruler:** Friedrich I **Obv:** Head right **Rev:** Crowned imperial German eagle

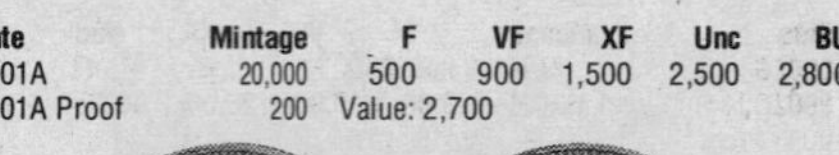

Date	Mintage	F	VF	XF	Unc	BU
1901A	20,000	500	900	1,500	2,500	2,800
1901A Proof	200	Value: 2,700				

KM# 26 20 MARK
7.9650 g., 0.9000 Gold .2304 oz. AGW **Ruler:** Friedrich I **Obv:** Small head right **Rev:** Crowned imperial German eagle

Date	Mintage	F	VF	XF	Unc	BU
1901A	15,000	700	1,000	1,600	2,200	3,200
1901A Proof	200	Value: 3,250				

KM# 28 20 MARK
7.9650 g., 0.9000 Gold .2304 oz. AGW **Ruler:** Friedrich II **Obv:** Head left **Rev:** Crowned imperial German eagle, shield on breast

Date	Mintage	F	VF	XF	Unc	BU
1904A	25,000	450	1,000	1,400	2,000	3,000
1904A Proof	200	Value: 3,250				

PATTERNS

Including off metal strikes

KM#	Date	Mintage	Identification	Mkt Val
Pn1	1901A	—	2 Mark. Silver. KM23.	—
Pn2	1901A	—	5 Mark. Silver. KM24.	—
Pn3	1914	—	3 Mark. Silver. Wreath around rim. KM30.	—
Pn4	1914	—	3 Mark. Brass.	—
Pn5	1914	—	5 Mark. Silver. Pn6. KM31.	—
Pn6	1914	—	5 Mark. Silver. Lettered edge.	—
Pn7	1914	—	5 Mark. Silver. Plain edge.	—

BADEN

The earliest rulers of Baden, in the southwestern part of Germany along the Rhine, descended from the dukes of Zähringen in the late 11th century. The first division of the territory occurred in 1190, when separate lines of margraves were established in Baden and in Hachberg. Immediately prior to its extinction in 1418, Hachberg was sold back to Baden, which underwent several minor divisions itself during the next century. Baden acquired most of the countship of Sponheim from Electoral Pfalz near the end of the 15th century. In 1515, the most significant division of the patrimony took place, in which the Baden-Baden and Baden-(Pforzheim) Durlach lines were established.

Although Baden-Durlach was founded upon the division of Baden in 1515, the youngest son of Christoph I did not begin ruling in his own right until the demise of his father. This part of Baden was called Pforzheim until 1565, when the margrave moved his seat from the former to Durlach, located to the west and nearer the Rhine. After the male line of Baden-Baden failed in 1771 and the two parts of Baden were reunited, the fortunes of the margraviate continued to grow. Karlsruhe, near Durlach, was developed into a well-planned capital city. The ruler was given the rank of elector in 1803, only to be raised to grand duke three years later. The grand duchy came to an end in 1918, but had by this time become one of the largest states in Germany.

RULERS

Friedrich I, Prince Regent 1852-1856,
Grand Duke 1856-1907
Friedrich II, 1907-1918

UNITED BADEN LINE

REFORM COINAGE

KM# 269 2 MARK
11.1110 g., 0.9000 Silver .3215 oz. ASW, 28 mm. **Ruler:** Friedrich I as Grand Duke **Obv:** Head left **Rev:** Crowned imperial German eagle, shield on breast

Date	Mintage	F	VF	XF	Unc	BU
1901G	451,000	35.00	95.00	300	950	1,100
1901G Proof	—	Value: 2,500				

Date	Mintage	F	VF	XF	Unc	BU
1902G	5,368	275	800	1,900	4,000	5,000
1902G Proof	—	Value: 3,500				

KM# 271 2 MARK

11.1110 g., 0.9000 Silver .3215 oz. ASW, 28 mm. **Ruler:** Friedrich I as Grand Duke **Subject:** 50th Year of Reign **Obv:** Head right **Rev:** Crowned imperial German eagle, shield on breast

Date	Mintage	F	VF	XF	Unc	BU
1902	375,000	12.00	28.00	40.00	50.00	60.00

KM# 272 2 MARK

11.1110 g., 0.9000 Silver .3215 oz. ASW, 28 mm. **Ruler:** Friedrich I as Grand Duke **Obv:** Head right **Rev:** Crowned imperial German eagle, shield on breast

Date	Mintage	F	VF	XF	Unc	BU
1902G	198,000	25.00	60.00	120	250	300
1903G	494,000	20.00	45.00	110	250	300
1904G	1,122,000	20.00	40.00	80.00	250	300
1905G	610,000	20.00	45.00	70.00	175	200
1906G	108,000	45.00	90.00	250	800	1,200
1907G	913,000	20.00	40.00	65.00	150	180

KM# 276 2 MARK

11.1110 g., 0.9000 Silver .3215 oz. ASW, 28 mm. **Ruler:** Friedrich I as Grand Duke **Subject:** Golden Wedding Anniversary **Obv:** Heads of royal couple right **Rev:** Crowned imperial German eagle, shield on breast

Date	Mintage	F	VF	XF	Unc	BU
1906	350,000	15.00	30.00	40.00	60.00	70.00
1906 Matte proof	—	—	—	—	—	—

KM# 278 2 MARK

11.1110 g., 0.9000 Silver .3215 oz. ASW, 28 mm. **Ruler:** Friedrich I as Grand Duke **Subject:** Death of Friedrich **Obv:** Head right **Rev:** Crowned imperial German eagle, shield on breast

Date	Mintage	F	VF	XF	Unc	BU
1907	350,000	20.00	50.00	70.00	90.00	100
1907 Proof	—	Value: 150				

KM# 283 2 MARK

11.1110 g., 0.9000 Silver .3215 oz. ASW, 28 mm. **Ruler:** Friedrich II **Obv:** Head left **Rev:** Crowned imperial German eagle, shield on breast

Date	Mintage	F	VF	XF	Unc	BU
1911G	80,000	125	250	375	750	900

Date	Mintage	F	VF	XF	Unc	BU
1913G	140,000	100	250	400	700	800
(1911-1913) Proof	—	Value: 1,200				

KM# 280 3 MARK

16.6670 g., 0.9000 Silver .4823 oz. ASW, 33 mm. **Ruler:** Friedrich II **Obv:** Head left **Rev:** Crowned imperial German eagle, shield on breast

Date	Mintage	F	VF	XF	Unc	BU
1908G	300,000	12.00	28.00	45.00	100	120
1909G	760,000	12.00	28.00	40.00	75.00	100
1910G	670,000	12.00	28.00	40.00	75.00	100
1911G	380,000	12.00	28.00	40.00	75.00	100
1912G	840,000	12.00	28.00	40.00	75.00	100
1914G	410,000	12.00	25.00	35.00	70.00	100
1915G	170,000	20.00	60.00	95.00	225	250
(1908-1915)G Proof	—	Value: 225				

KM# 268 5 MARK

27.7770 g., 0.9000 Silver .8038 oz. ASW, 38 mm. **Ruler:** Friedrich I as Grand Duke **Obv:** Head left **Rev:** Crowned imperial German eagle, shield on breast

Date	Mintage	F	VF	XF	Unc	BU
1901G	128,000	30.00	75.00	425	2,000	2,800
1902G	43,000	35.00	85.00	445	2,000	3,000
(1891-1902)G Proof	—	Value: 2,500				

KM# 273 5 MARK

27.7770 g., 0.9000 Silver .8038 oz. ASW, 38 mm. **Ruler:** Friedrich I as Grand Duke **Subject:** 50th Year of Reign **Obv:** Head right **Rev:** Crowned imperial German eagle, shield on breast

Date	Mintage	F	VF	XF	Unc	BU
1902	50,000	45.00	90.00	150	225	300
1902 Proof	—	Value: 625				

KM# 274 5 MARK

27.7770 g., 0.9000 Silver .8038 oz. ASW, 38 mm. **Ruler:** Friedrich I as Grand Duke **Obv:** Head right **Rev:** Crowned imperial German eagle, shield on breast

Date	Mintage	F	VF	XF	Unc	BU
1902G	128,000	35.00	70.00	225	600	800
1903G	439,000	20.00	50.00	165	585	650
1904G	238,000	20.00	50.00	165	585	650

Date	Mintage	F	VF	XF	Unc	BU
1907G	244,000	20.00	50.00	165	585	700
(1902-1907)G Proof	—	Value: 800				

KM# 277 5 MARK

27.7770 g., 0.9000 Silver .8038 oz. ASW, 38 mm. **Ruler:** Friedrich I as Grand Duke **Subject:** Golden Wedding Anniversary **Obv:** Jugate busts right **Rev:** Crowned imperial German eagle, shield on breast

Date	Mintage	F	VF	XF	Unc	BU
1906	60,000	40.00	80.00	145	220	275
1906 Proof	—	Value: 300				

KM# 279 5 MARK

27.7770 g., 0.9000 Silver .8038 oz. ASW, 38 mm. **Ruler:** Friedrich I as Grand Duke **Subject:** Death of Friedrich **Obv:** Head right **Rev:** Crowned imperial German eagle, shield on breast

Date	Mintage	F	VF	XF	Unc	BU
1907	60,000	60.00	125	175	250	300
1907 Proof	—	Value: 320				

KM# 281 5 MARK

27.7770 g., 0.9000 Silver .8038 oz. ASW, 38 mm. **Ruler:** Friedrich II **Obv:** Head left **Rev:** Crowned imperial German eagle, shield on breast

Date	Mintage	F	VF	XF	Unc	BU
1908G	180,000	40.00	60.00	175	600	700
1913G	240,000	30.00	50.00	165	400	500
(1908-1913)G Proof	—	Value: 1,000				

KM# 267 10 MARK

3.9820 g., 0.9000 Gold .1152 oz. AGW **Ruler:** Friedrich I as Grand Duke **Obv:** Head left **Rev:** Crowned imperial German eagle, shield on breast

Date	Mintage	F	VF	XF	Unc	BU
1901G	91,000	125	250	350	500	600
1901G Proof	—	Value: 1,700				

KM# 275 10 MARK

3.9820 g., 0.9000 Gold .1152 oz. AGW **Ruler:** Friedrich I as

Grand Duke **Obv:** Head right **Rev:** Crowned imperial German eagle, shield on breast

Date	Mintage	F	VF	XF	Unc	BU
1902G	30,000	175	300	450	750	1,000
1903G	110,000	125	200	265	450	550
1904G	150,000	110	170	245	400	550
1905G	96,000	125	200	265	500	700
1906G	120,000	125	170	245	400	550
1907G	120,000	110	170	245	400	550
(1902-1907)G Proof	—	Value: 1,600				

KM# 282 10 MARK
3.9820 g., 0.9000 Gold .1152 oz. AGW **Ruler:** Friedrich II **Obv:** Head right **Rev:** Crowned imperial German eagle, shield on breast

Date	Mintage	F	VF	XF	Unc	BU
1909G	86,000	225	500	650	950	1,200
1910G	61,000	225	500	650	950	1,200
1911G	29,000	2,000	4,000	5,000	6,750	7,500
1912G	26,000	700	1,200	1,500	1,750	2,000
1913G	42,000	500	800	1,000	1,250	1,600
(1909-1913)G Proof	—	Value: 2,000				

KM# 284 20 MARK
7.9650 g., 0.9000 Gold .2304 oz. AGW **Ruler:** Friedrich II **Obv:** Head left **Rev:** Crowned imperial German eagle, shield on breast

Date	Mintage	F	VF	XF	Unc	BU
1911G	190,000	BV	175	225	320	400
1912G	310,000	BV	165	220	300	400
1913G	85,000	BV	170	225	350	425
1914G	280,000	BV	165	220	320	400
(1911-1914)G Proof	—	Value: 1,200				

BAVARIA

(Bayern)

Located in south Germany. In 1180 the Duchy of Bavaria was given to the Count of Wittelsbach by the emperor. He is the ancestor of all who ruled in Bavaria until 1918. Primogeniture was proclaimed in 1506 and in 1623 the dukes of Bavaria were given the electoral right. Bavaria, which had been divided for the various heirs, was reunited in 1799. The title of king was granted to Bavaria in 1805.

RULERS
Otto, 1886-1913, Prince Regent Luitpold, 1886-1912
Ludwig III, 1913-1918

MINT MARKS
D - Munich

KINGDOM

REFORM COINAGE

KM# 511 2 MARK
11.1110 g., 0.9000 Silver .3215 oz. ASW, 28 mm. **Ruler:** Otto Prince Regent Luitpold **Obv:** Head left **Rev:** Crowned imperial eagle, shield on breast **Note:** Open and closed curl varieties exist.

Date	Mintage	F	VF	XF	Unc	BU
1901D	809,000	12.00	28.00	55.00	135	175
1902D	1,321,000	10.00	22.00	45.00	120	150
1903D	1,406,000	10.00	22.00	45.00	110	150
1904D	2,320,000	9.00	20.00	35.00	100	150
1905D	1,406,000	10.00	22.00	45.00	95.00	150
1906D	1,055,000	10.00	22.00	55.00	120	150
1907D	2,106,000	9.00	20.00	35.00	85.00	150
1908D	633,000	10.00	22.00	45.00	95.00	150
1912D	214,000	12.00	28.00	60.00	125	150
1913D	98,000	40.00	80.00	160	250	300

KM# 516 2 MARK
11.1110 g., 0.9000 Silver .3215 oz. ASW **Ruler:** Otto Prince Regent Luitpold **Subject:** 90th Birthday of Prince Regent Luitpold **Obv:** Head right **Rev:** Crowned imperial eagle, shield on breast

Date	Mintage	F	VF	XF	Unc	BU
1911D	640,000	12.00	22.00	35.00	45.00	55.00
1911D Proof	—	Value: 100				

KM# 519 2 MARK
11.1110 g., 0.9000 Silver .3215 oz. ASW, 28 mm. **Ruler:** Ludwig III **Obv:** Head left **Rev:** Crowned imperial eagle, shield on breast

Date	Mintage	F	VF	XF	Unc	BU
1914D	574,000	30.00	65.00	100	165	185

KM# 515 3 MARK
16.6670 g., 0.9000 Silver .4823 oz. ASW, 33 mm. **Ruler:** Otto Prince Regent Luitpold **Obv:** Head left **Rev:** Crowned imperial eagle, shield on breast

Date	Mintage	F	VF	XF	Unc	BU
1908D	681,000	12.00	20.00	35.00	60.00	70.00
1909D	1,827,000	10.00	18.00	30.00	50.00	65.00
1910D	1,496,000	10.00	18.00	30.00	50.00	65.00
1911D	843,000	12.00	20.00	35.00	60.00	70.00
1912D	1,014,000	12.00	20.00	35.00	60.00	70.00
1913D	731,000	12.00	20.00	35.00	60.00	70.00
1913D Proof	—	Value: 100				

KM# 517 3 MARK
16.6670 g., 0.9000 Silver .4823 oz. ASW, 33 mm. **Ruler:** Otto Prince Regent Luitpold **Subject:** 90th Birthday of Prince Regent Luitpold **Obv:** Head right **Rev:** Crowned imperial eagle, shield on breast

Date	Mintage	F	VF	XF	Unc	BU
1911D	640,000	12.00	22.00	35.00	50.00	65.00
1911D Proof	—	Value: 100				

KM# 520 3 MARK
16.6670 g., 0.9000 Silver .4823 oz. ASW, 33 mm. **Ruler:** Ludwig III **Obv:** Head left **Rev:** Crowned imperial eagle, shield on breast

Date	Mintage	F	VF	XF	Unc	BU
1914D	717,000	17.50	32.50	50.00	75.00	90.00
1914D Proof	—	Value: 150				

KM# 523 3 MARK
16.6670 g., 0.9000 Silver .4823 oz. ASW, 33 mm. **Ruler:** Ludwig III **Subject:** Golden Wedding Anniversary **Obv:** Jugate heads right **Rev:** Crowned imperial eagle, shield on breast

Date	Mintage	F	VF	XF	Unc	BU
1918D	130	—	16,000	26,000	32,000	40,000

KM# 512 5 MARK
27.7770 g., 0.9000 Silver .8038 oz. ASW, 38 mm. **Ruler:** Otto **Obv:** Head left **Rev:** Crowned imperial eagle, shield on breast **Note:** Varieties in the hair locks and curls exist.

Date	Mintage	F	VF	XF	Unc	BU
1901D	275,000	14.00	25.00	85.00	300	400
1902D	486,000	14.00	25.00	65.00	250	350
1903D	1,012,000	14.00	25.00	65.00	250	350
1904D	548,000	16.00	30.00	70.00	250	350
1906D	70,000	35.00	75.00	200	1,100	1,300
1907D	753,000	14.00	20.00	50.00	225	275
1908D	537,000	14.00	20.00	50.00	225	275
1913D	420,000	14.00	20.00	40.00	150	225
(1901-1913)D Proof	—	Value: 650				

KM# 518 5 MARK
27.7770 g., 0.9000 Silver .8038 oz. ASW, 38 mm. **Ruler:** Otto Prince Regent Luitpold **Subject:** 90th Birthday of Prince Regent Luitpold **Obv:** Head right **Rev:** Crowned imperial eagle, shield on breast

Date	Mintage	F	VF	XF	Unc	BU
1911D	160,000	25.00	65.00	95.00	170	200
1911D Proof	—	Value: 220				

KM# 521 5 MARK
27.7770 g., 0.9000 Silver .8038 oz. ASW, 38 mm. **Ruler:** Ludwig III **Obv:** Head left

Date	Mintage	F	VF	XF	Unc	BU
1914D	142,000	40.00	90.00	175	225	275

KM# 514 10 MARK
3.9820 g., 0.9000 Gold .1152 oz. AGW **Ruler:** Otto **Obv:** Head left **Obv. Legend:** V. BAYERN **Rev:** Crowned imperial eagle, shield on breast

Date	Mintage	F	VF	XF	Unc	BU
1901D	141,000	90.00	135	210	325	400
1902D	68,000	90.00	135	210	325	600
1903D	534,000	90.00	130	185	275	300
1904D	211,000	90.00	130	185	275	300
1905D	281,000	90.00	130	185	275	300
1906D	141,000	90.00	135	200	300	400
1907D	211,000	90.00	130	195	275	300
1909D	209,000	90.00	130	195	275	300
1910D	141,000	90.00	130	195	275	350
1911D	72,000	90.00	135	215	325	400
1912D	141,000	90.00	135	200	285	350
(1901-1912)D Proof	—	Value: 1,000				

KM# 513 20 MARK
7.9650 g., 0.9000 Gold .2304 oz. AGW **Ruler:** Otto **Obv:** Head left **Rev:** Crowned imperial eagle, shield on breast, type III

Date	Mintage	F	VF	XF	Unc	BU
1905D	501,000	BV	165	200	275	325
1905D Proof	—	Value: 1,250				
1913D	311,000	—	17,500	22,500	25,000	—
1913D Proof	—	Value: 35,000				

KM# 522 20 MARK
7.9650 g., 0.9000 Gold .2304 oz. AGW **Ruler:** Ludwig III **Obv:** Head left **Rev:** Crowned imperial eagle, shield on breast **Note:** Never officially released.

Date	Mintage	F	VF	XF	Unc	BU
1914D	533,000	—	2,000	2,500	3,000	3,500
1914D Proof	—	Value: 3,750				

PATTERNS

Including off metal strikes

KM#	Date	Mintage	Identification	Mkt Val
Pn14	1904	—	5 Mark. Silver. Eagle in ring. Reeded edge.	—
Pn15	1904D	—	5 Mark. Silver. Eagle in ring. Lettered edge.	—
Pn16	1904D	—	5 Mark. Silver. Without inner circle.	—
Pn17	1905D	—	5 Mark. Copper. Pn6. KM512.	—
Pn18	1911	—	3 Mark. Silver.	—
Pn19	1911D	—	3 Mark. Copper.	—
Pn25	1913D	—	3 Mark. Silver. Plain edge.	—
Pn35	1914D	—	3 Mark. Silver. Bust faces right.	—
Pn36	1914D	—	5 Mark. Silver. Larger lettering, KM521.	—
Pn37	1914D	—	5 Mark. Silver. Plain edge. KM521.	—
Pn38	1914D	—	20 Mark. Gold. Lettered edge.	—
Pn39	1914D	—	20 Mark. Silver Gilt. Hallmarked, plain edge.	150
Pn40	1914D	—	20 Mark. Silver Gilt. Hallmarked, plain edge. KM522.	—
Pn41	1914D	—	20 Mark. Gold. Denticled rim. KM522. Plain edge.	—
Pn42	1914D	—	20 Mark. Silver Gilt. Denticled rim. KM522. Hallmarked, plain edge.	—
Pn43	1914D	—	20 Mark. Gold. 18-millimeter bust. KM522. Lettered edge.	8,000
Pn44	1914D	—	20 Mark. Silver Gilt. 18-millimeter bust. KM522. Hallmarked, plain edge.	—
Pn45	1914D	—	20 Mark. Gold. Plain rim. KM522. Plain edge.	—
Pn46	1914D	—	20 Mark. Gold. Plain rim. KM522. Lettered edge.	—
Pn47	1914D	—	20 Mark. Gold. Round "O" in KOENIG. Lettered edge.	—
Pn48	1914D	—	20 Mark. Silver Gilt. Round "O" in KOENIG. KM522. Hallmarked, plain edge.	—
Pn49	ND J	—	Gulden. Gold. Bust of Ludwig III in uniform. Main bridge of Wurzburger.	—

BREMEN

Established at about the same time as the bishopric in 787, Bremen was under the control of the bishops and archbishops until joining the Hanseatic League in 1276. Archbishop Albrecht II granted the mint right to the city in 1369, but this was not formalized by imperial decree until 1541. In 1646, Bremen was raised to free imperial status and continued to strike its own coins into the early 20th century. The city lost its free imperial status in 1803 and was controlled by France from 1806 until 1813. Regaining it independence in 1815, Bremen joined the North German Confederation in 1867 and the German Empire in 1871. Since 1369, there was practically continuous coinage until 1907.

FREE CITY

REGULAR COINAGE

KM# 250 2 MARK
11.1110 g., 0.9000 Silver .3215 oz. ASW, 28 mm. **Obv:** Key on crowned shield with supporters **Rev:** Crowned imperial eagle, shield on breast, date at right, denomination below

Date	Mintage	F	VF	XF	Unc	BU
1904 J	100,000	30.00	60.00	90.00	150	175
1904 J Proof	200	Value: 400				

KM# 251 5 MARK
27.7770 g., 0.9000 Silver .8038 oz. ASW, 38 mm. **Obv:** Key on crowned shield with supporters **Rev:** Crowned imperial eagle, shield on breast, date at right, denomination below

Date	Mintage	F	VF	XF	Unc	BU
1906 J	41,000	85.00	200	300	450	500
1906 J Proof	600	Value: 750				

KM# 253 10 MARK
3.9820 g., 0.9000 Gold .1152 oz. AGW **Obv:** Key on crowned shield with supporters **Rev:** Crowned imperial eagle, shield on breast, date at right, denomination below

Date	Mintage	F	VF	XF	Unc	BU
1907 J	20,000	425	800	1,250	1,700	2,100
1907 J Proof	—	Value: 2,250				

KM# 252 20 MARK
7.9650 g., 0.9000 Gold .2304 oz. AGW

Date	Mintage	F	VF	XF	Unc	BU
1906 J	20,000	425	725	1,150	1,750	—
1906 J Proof	—	Value: 2,500				

TOKEN COINAGE

Reckoning Tokens

These vouchers, issued March 18, 1924, were based on the American dollar. Issued in conjunction with Bremens issue of treasury. Due to monies being held to purchase Bremens 5% Dollar Bond, they rarely circulated. The tokens were withdrawn September 30 of that same year.

KM# Tn1 2 VERRECHNUNGS-PFENNIG
Brass **Obv:** State arms-key within circle **Rev:** Denomination within circle

Date	Mintage	F	VF	XF	Unc	BU
ND(1924)	501,000	10.00	25.00	45.00	85.00	—

KM# Tn2 5 VERRECHNUNGS-PFENNIG
Aluminum **Obv:** State arms-key within circle **Rev:** Denomination within circle

Date	Mintage	F	VF	XF	Unc	BU
ND(1924)	669,000	9.00	18.00	30.00	70.00	—

KM# Tn3 10 VERRECHNUNGS-PFENNIG
Aluminum **Obv:** State arms-key within circle **Rev:** Denomination within circle

Date	Mintage	F	VF	XF	Unc	BU
ND(1924)	695,000	10.00	20.00	35.00	75.00	—

KM# Tn4 20 VERRECHNUNGS-PFENNIG
Aluminum **Obv:** State arms-key within circle **Rev:** Denomination within circle

Date	Mintage	F	VF	XF	Unc	BU
ND(1924)	382,000	17.00	35.00	60.00	120	—

KM# Tn5 50 VERRECHNUNGS-PFENNIG
Aluminum **Obv:** Key on crowned shield with supporters **Rev:** Denomination within circle

Date	Mintage	F	VF	XF	Unc	BU
ND(1924)	483,000	30.00	55.00	100	200	—

KM# Tn6 VERRECHNUNGSMARK
Aluminum **Obv:** Crowned shield with supporters on pedestal, key on shield **Rev:** Large, thick denomination **Note:** This coin is listed in Jaeger & Funck as struck in aluminum. Kunker has listed it as having an iron core but doesn't indicate what metal clads or plates the piece.

Date	Mintage	F	VF	XF	Unc	BU
ND(1924)	382,000	75.00	150	275	500	—

PATTERNS

Including off metal strikes

KM#	Date	Mintage	Identification	Mkt Val
Pn40	1904 J	—	5 Mark. KM251.	—
Pn41	1905 J	—	2 Mark. KM250.	—
Pn42	1905 J	—	5 Mark. Silver. Larger lettering without beaded rim. KM251.	15,000
Pn43	1905 J	—	5 Mark. Tin.	—
Pn44	1906	—	5 Mark. Bronze.	—
Pn45	1906	—	5 Mark. Silver.	—
Pn46	1906	—	5 Mark. Tin.	—
Pn47	ND	—	S.M.. Copper.	—

BRUNSWICK-WOLFENBUTTEL

(Braunschweig-Wolfenbüttel)

Located in north-central Germany. Wolfenbüttel was annexed to Brunswick in 1257. One of the five surviving sons of Albrecht II founded the first line in Wolfenbüttel in 1318. A further division in Wolfenbüttel and Lüneburg was undertaken in 1373. Another division occurred in 1495, but the Wolfenbüttel duchy survived in the younger line. Heinrich IX was forced out of his territory during the religious wars of the mid-sixteenth century by Duke Johann Friedrich I of Saxony and Landgrave Philipp of Hessen in 1542, but was restored to his possessions in 1547. Duke Friedrich Ulrich was forced to cede the Grubenhagen lands, which had been acquired by Wolfenbüttel in 1596, to Lüneburg in 1617. When the succession died out in 1634, the lands and titles fell to the cadet line in Dannenberg. The line became extinct once again and passed to Brunswick-Bevern in 1735 from which a new succession of Wolfenbüttel dukes descended. The ducal family was beset by continual personal and political tragedy during the nineteenth century. Two of the dukes were killed in battles with Napoleon, the territories were occupied by the French and became part of the Kingdom of Westphalia, another duke was forced out by a revolt in 1823. From 1884 until 1913, Brunswick-Wolfenbüttel was governed by Prussia and then turned over to the only surviving (of 3) prince of Brunswick who married the only daughter of Kaiser Wilhelm II. His reign was short, however, as he was forced to abdicate at the end of World War I.

RULERS

Prussian rule, 1884-1913
Ernst August, 1913-1918

DUCHY

REFORM COINAGE

KM# 1161 3 MARK
16.6670 g., 0.9000 Silver .4823 oz. ASW, 33 mm. **Ruler:** Ernst August **Subject:** Ernst August Wedding and Accession **Obv:** Jugate heads right **Rev:** Crowned imperial eagle, shield on breast

Date	Mintage	F	VF	XF	Unc	BU
1915A	1,700	600	1,150	1,850	2,500	3,000
1915A Proof	—	Value: 3,250				

KM# 1162 3 MARK
16.6670 g., 0.9000 Silver .4823 oz. ASW, 33 mm. **Ruler:** Ernst August **Subject:** Ernst August Wedding and Accession **Obv:** Jugate heads right **Obv. Legend:** U LUNEB added **Rev:** Crowned imperial eagle, shield on breast

Date	Mintage	F	VF	XF	Unc	BU
1915A	32,000	50.00	120	200	250	300
1915A Proof	—	Value: 400				

KM# 1163 5 MARK
27.7770 g., 0.9000 Silver .8038 oz. ASW, 38 mm. **Ruler:** Ernst August **Subject:** Ernst August Wedding and Accession **Obv:** Jugate heads right **Rev:** Crowned imperial eagle, shield on breast

Date	Mintage	F	VF	XF	Unc	BU
1915A	1,400	800	1,650	2,750	3,500	4,000
1915A Proof	—	Value: 4,250				

KM# 1164 5 MARK
27.7770 g., 0.9000 Silver .8038 oz. ASW, 38 mm. **Ruler:** Ernst August **Subject:** Ernst August Wedding and Accession **Obv:** Jugate heads right **Obv. Legend:** U. LUNEB added **Rev:** Crowned imperial eagle, shield on breast

Date	Mintage	F	VF	XF	Unc	BU
1915A	8,600	185	400	700	1,150	1,400
1915A Proof	—	Value: 1,500				

PATTERNS

Including off metal strikes

KM#	Date	Mintage	Identification	Mkt Val
Pn54	1913	—	3 Mark. Silver.	—
Pn55	1913	—	5 Mark. Silver.	—
Pn56	1915A	—	3 Mark. Silver. Plain edge. KM1161.	—
Pn57	1915A	—	3 Mark. Silver. Beaded rim. Weak 5 in date. Plain edge. KM1162.	—
Pn58	191x	—	5 Mark. Silver. Beaded rim, wedding portraits facing left. Partial date. Plain edge.	—

HAMBURG

The city of Hamburg is located on the Elbe River about 75 miles (125 kilometers) from the North Sea. Tradition states that it was founded by Charlemagne in the early 9th century. At first, the town was controlled by the archbishopric of Bremen and Hamburg (see Bremen). In 1110, Hamburg and the territory of Holstein came under the rule of Count Adolf I of Schauenburg (Schaumburg, ruled 1106-1128), which inaugurated a period stretching for four centuries in which the Holstein dynasty exercised authority over the city. Hamburg joined with Lübeck in 1241 to form the first partnership in what was to become the Hanseatic League. Count Adolf VI of Schauenburg (1290-1315) gave civic autonomy to Hamburg in 1292 and leased the mint right to the citizens the next year. Local *hohlpfennige* had already been struck fifty years previous. From this early time, the city struck an almost continuous series of coins throughout the centuries up to World War I. In 1510, Hamburg was granted the status of a Free City of the Empire, although it had actually been free for about 250 years. It was occupied by the French during the period of the Napoleonic Wars. In 1866, Hamburg joined the North German Confederation and became a part of the German Empire in 1871.

FREE CITY

REFORM COINAGE

KM# 294 2 MARK
11.1110 g., 0.9000 Silver .3215 oz. ASW, 28 mm. **Obv:** Three tower castle on helmeted shield with supporters **Rev:** Crowned imperial eagle, shield on breast

Date	Mintage	F	VF	XF	Unc	BU
1901J	482,000	15.00	25.00	60.00	200	300
1902J	779,000	12.50	25.00	60.00	200	240
1903J	817,000	12.50	25.00	50.00	200	240
1904J	1,248,000	12.50	25.00	50.00	180	225
1905J	204,000	35.00	65.00	125	450	550
1906J	1,225,000	12.50	25.00	50.00	180	200
1907J	1,226,000	12.50	25.00	50.00	180	200
1908J	368,000	12.50	30.00	55.00	180	200
1911J	204,000	12.50	30.00	55.00	180	200
1912J	79,000	20.00	50.00	110	300	400
1913J	105,000	12.50	30.00	65.00	180	200
1914J	328,000	10.00	25.00	50.00	140	160
(1901-1914)J Proof	—	Value: 350				

KM# 296 3 MARK
16.6670 g., 0.9000 Silver .4823 oz. ASW, 33 mm. **Obv:** Three tower castle on helmeted shield with supporters **Rev:** Crowned imperial eagle, shield on breast

Date	Mintage	F	VF	XF	Unc	BU
1908J	408,000	12.50	25.00	40.00	80.00	100
1909J	1,389,000	12.50	25.00	40.00	80.00	100
1910J	526,000	12.50	25.00	40.00	80.00	100
1911J	922,000	12.50	25.00	40.00	80.00	100
1912J	491,000	12.50	25.00	40.00	80.00	100
1913J	344,000	12.50	25.00	40.00	80.00	100
1914J	575,000	12.50	25.00	40.00	80.00	100
(1908-1914) Proof	—	Value: 250				

KM# 293 5 MARK
27.7770 g., 0.9000 Silver .8038 oz. ASW, 38 mm. **Obv:** Three tower castle on helmeted shield with supporters **Rev:** Crowned imperial eagle, shield on breast

Date	Mintage	F	VF	XF	Unc	BU
1901J	172,000	20.00	40.00	100	500	600
1902J	294,000	17.50	35.00	80.00	400	500
1903J	588,000	17.50	35.00	75.00	275	350
1904J	319,000	16.00	32.00	75.00	275	350
1907J	326,000	16.00	32.00	75.00	275	325
1908J	458,000	16.00	32.00	75.00	220	325
1913J	327,000	16.00	32.00	60.00	165	250
(1901-1913)J Proof	—	Value: 1,500				

KM# 292 10 MARK
3.9820 g., 0.9000 Gold .1152 oz. AGW **Obv:** Three tower castle on helmeted shield with supporters **Rev:** Crowned imperial eagle, shield on breast, type II

Date	Mintage	F	VF	XF	Unc	BU
1901J	82,000	90.00	150	225	385	485
1902J	41,000	120	225	350	650	750
1903J	310,000	90.00	150	225	350	400
1905J	164,000	90.00	150	225	350	400
1906J	164,000	90.00	150	225	350	400
1907J	111,000	90.00	150	225	350	400
1908J	32,000	150	300	500	800	950
1909J	122,000	90.00	150	225	350	400
1909J Proof	—	Value: 850				
1910J	41,000	120	225	350	600	700
1910J Proof	—	Value: 1,200				
1911J	75,000	95.00	175	250	300	375
1911J Proof	—	Value: 8,000				
1912J	48,000	145	245	350	500	600
1912J Proof	—	Value: 1,000				
1913J	41,000	145	245	300	400	500
1913J Proof	—	Value: 1,000				

KM# 295 20 MARK
7.9650 g., 0.9000 Gold .2304 oz. AGW **Obv:** Three tower castle on helmeted shield with supporters **Rev:** Crowned imperial eagle, shield on breast, type III

Date	Mintage	F	VF	XF	Unc	BU
1908J Rare	14	—	—	—	—	—
1913J	491,000	—	BV	160	200	275
1913J Proof	—	Value: 1,000				

TOKEN COINAGE

Reckoning Tokens

KM# Tn1 1/100 VERRECHNUNGSMARKE
Aluminum, 20.5 mm. **Issuer:** Hamburg Bank **Obv:** City arms-three tower castle on helmeted shield with supporters **Rev:** Denomination within circle

Date	Mintage	F	VF	XF	Unc	BU
1923	9,128,000	3.00	6.00	12.50	25.00	—

KM# Tn2 5/100 VERRECHNUNGSMARKE

Aluminum, 23 mm. **Issuer:** Hamburg Bank **Obv:** City arms-three tower castle on helmeted shield with supporters **Rev:** Denomination within circle

Date	Mintage	F	VF	XF	Unc	BU
1923	8,100,000	2.75	4.50	9.00	18.00	—

KM# Tn3 1/10 VERRECHNUNGSMARKE

Aluminum, 26.5 mm. **Issuer:** Hamburg Bank **Obv:** City arms-three tower castle on helmeted shield with supporters **Rev:** Denomination within circle

Date	Mintage	F	VF	XF	Unc	BU
1923	8,600,000	2.75	4.50	10.00	20.00	—

PATTERNS

Including off metal strikes

KM#	Date	Mintage	Identification	Mkt Val
Pn20	1906J	—	5 Mark. Copper. Plain edge. KM293.	—
Pn21	1913	—	5 Mark. Silver. Plain edge. KM293.	1,100
Pn22	1913J	—	5 Mark. Silver. Plain edge. KM293.	—
Pn23	1914J	—	3 Mark. Silver. Plain edge. KM296.	—
Pn24	1922J	—	1/2 Mark. Aluminum. Plain edge.	—
Pn25	1922J	—	1/2 Mark. Iron. Plain edge.	—
Pn26	1922J	—	1/2 Mark. Nickel. Plain edge.	—

KM#	Date	Mintage	Identification	Mkt Val
Pn27	1922J	—	1/2 Mark. Copper. Plain edge. 19 mm.	225
Pn28	1922J	—	Mark. Aluminum. Plain edge.	—
Pn29	1922J	—	Mark. Copper. Plain edge.	—
Pn30	1922J	—	Mark. Nickel. Plain edge.	—
Pn31	1922J	—	Mark. Iron. Plain edge.	—
Pn32	1922J	—	2 Mark. Nickel. Plain edge.	—
Pn33	1922J	—	2 Mark. Aluminum. Plain edge.	—
Pn34	1922J	—	2 Mark. Zinc. Plain edge.	—
Pn35	1922J	—	3 Mark. Iron. Plain edge. Copper-nickel plated.	—
Pn36	1922J	—	3 Mark. Aluminum. Plain edge.	—
Pn37	1922J	—	3 Mark. Nickel. Plain edge.	—
Pn38	1922J	—	5 Mark. Nickel Plated Iron. Plain edge.	—
Pn39	1922J	—	5 Mark. Aluminum. Plain edge.	—
Pn40	1922J	—	5 Mark. Nickel. Plain edge.	—
Pn41	1922J	—	5 Mark. Zinc. Plain edge.	—

HESSE-DARMSTADT

(Hessen-Darmstadt)

Founded by the youngest of Philipp I's four sons upon the death of their father in 1567, Hesse-Darmstadt was one of the two main branches of the family which survived past the beginning of the 17th century. The Countship of Hanau-Lichtenberg was through marriage when the male line failed in 1736. Ludwig X was forced to cede that territory to France in 1801. In 1803, Darmstadt acquired part of the Palatinate, the city of Friedberg, part of the city of Mainz, and the Duchy of Westphalia in a general settlement with France. The Landgrave was elevated to the status of Grand Duke in 1806 and reacquired Hesse-Homburg, which got its souveranity back in 1816. In 1815 the Congress of Vienna awarded Hesse-Darmstadt the city of Worms and all of Mainz. These were relinquished, along with Hesse-Homburg, to Prussia in 1866 and Hesse-Darmstadt was called just Hesse from 1867 onwards. Hesse became part of the German Empire in 1871, but ceased to exist as a semi-sovereign state at the end of World War I.

RULERS

Ernst Ludwig, 1892-1918

GRAND DUCHY

REFORM COINAGE

Grossherzogtum within the German Empire

KM# 372 2 MARK

11.1110 g., 0.9000 Silver .3215 oz. ASW, 28 mm. **Ruler:** Ernst Ludwig **Subject:** 400th Birthday of Philipp the Magnanimous **Obv:** Jugate heads left, dates below **Rev:** Crowned imperial eagle with shield on breast

Date	Mintage	F	VF	XF	Unc	BU
1904	100,000	30.00	60.00	90.00	140	200
1904 Proof	2,250	Value: 400				

Note: Obverse matte, reverse polished

KM# 375 3 MARK

16.6670 g., 0.9000 Silver .4823 oz. ASW, 33 mm. **Ruler:** Ernst Ludwig **Obv:** Head left **Rev:** Crowned imperial eagle, shield on breast

Date	Mintage	F	VF	XF	Unc	BU
1910A	200,000	50.00	100	150	400	550
1910A Proof	Est. 500	Value: 500				

KM# 376 3 MARK

16.6670 g., 0.9000 Silver .4823 oz. ASW, 33 mm. **Ruler:** Ernst Ludwig **Subject:** 25-Year Jubilee **Obv:** Head left **Rev:** Crowned imperial eagle, shield on breast **Note:** All minted pieces are proof. Values in circulated grades are for impaired proofs.

Date	Mintage	F	VF	XF	Unc	BU
1917A	1,333	—	3,000	4,600	6,000	8,000
1917A Proof	Inc. above	Value: 8,500				

KM# 373 5 MARK

27.7770 g., 0.9000 Silver .8038 oz. ASW, 38 mm. **Ruler:** Ernst Ludwig **Subject:** 400th birthday of Philipp the Magnanimous **Obv:** Jugate heads left, dates below **Rev:** Crowned imperial eagle, shield on breast

Date	Mintage	F	VF	XF	Unc	BU
1904	40,000	70.00	130	200	350	—
1904 Proof	700	Value: 660				

Note: Obverse matte, reverse polished

KM# 371 20 MARK

7.9650 g., 0.9000 Gold .2304 oz. AGW **Ruler:** Ernst Ludwig **Obv:** Head left **Rev:** Crowned imperial eagle, shield on breast

Date	Mintage	F	VF	XF	Unc	BU
1901A	80,000	220	400	700	1,400	2,000
1901A Proof	600	Value: 2,500				
1903A	40,000	220	400	700	1,400	2,000
1903A Proof	100	Value: 2,500				

KM# 374 20 MARK

7.9650 g., 0.9000 Gold .2304 oz. AGW **Ruler:** Ernst Ludwig **Obv:** Head left **Rev:** Crowned imperial eagle, shield on breast

Date	Mintage	F	VF	XF	Unc	BU
1905A	45,000	350	450	1,000	1,200	900
1905A Proof	200	Value: 1,950				
1906A	85,000	155	310	400	900	1,100
1906A Proof	199	Value: 1,750				
1908A	40,000	165	350	450	1,000	1,200
1908A Proof	—	Value: 1,750				
1911A	150,000	165	310	400	900	1,100
1911A Proof	—	Value: 1,500				

PATTERNS

Including off metal strikes

KM#	Date	Mintage	Identification	Mkt Val
Pn31	1910A	—	3 Mark. Silver.	—
Pn32	1917	—	3 Mark. Silver.	—
Pn33	1917A	—	3 Mark. Silver. Plain edge. Y82.	—

LIPPE-DETMOLD

After the division of 1613, the Counts of Lippe-Detmold, as the senior branch of the family, ruled over the largest portion of Lippe (see), a small patrimony in northwestern Germany. In 1620, Lippe-Sternberg became extinct and its lands and titles reverted to Lippe-Detmold. The younger brother of Hermann Adolf founded the line of Lippe-Sternberg-Schwalenberg (Biesterfeld) in 1652, which lasted into the 20th century. In 1720, the count was raised to the rank of prince, but did not use the title until 1789. Lippe joined the North German Confederation in 1866 and became part of the German Empire in 1871. Prince Alexander was declared insane and placed under a regency during his entire reign. There ensued a ten-year testamentary dispute between the Lippe-Biesterfeld and the Schaumburg-Lippe lines over the succession to the childless Alexander - a Wilhelmine cause célèbre. Leopold (V) of the Biesterfeld line gained the principality in 1905, but was forced to abdicate in 1918, at the end of World War I. In 1947, Lippe was absorbed by the German state of North Rhine-Westphalia.

RULERS

Alexander, 1895-1905
Leopold IV, 1905-1918

MINT MARKS

A - Berlin mint, 1843-1918

PRINCIPALITY

REFORM COINAGE

KM# 270 2 MARK

11.1110 g., 0.9000 Silver .3215 oz. ASW, 28 mm. **Ruler:** Leopold IV **Obv:** Head left **Rev:** Crowned imperial eagle, shield on breast

Date	Mintage	F	VF	XF	Unc	BU
1906A	20,000	125	250	350	500	575
1906A Proof	1,100	Value: 750				

KM# 275 3 MARK
16.6670 g., 0.9000 Silver .4823 oz. ASW, 33 mm. **Ruler:** Leopold IV **Obv:** Head left **Rev:** Crowned imperial eagle, shield on breast

Date	Mintage	F	VF	XF	Unc	BU
1913A	15,000	150	300	425	550	700
1913A Proof	100	Value: 750				

LUBECK

The original settlement was called Liubice, the capital of a Slavic principality. It was located at the confluence of the Schwartau with the Trave Rivers and contained a castle with a merchant town on a harbor. The town was burned down in 1138 and Count Adolf II of Holstein (1128-64) refounded the city four miles (6.5 kilometers) up the Trave in 1143. Duke Heinirich III the Lion of Saxony (1153-80) forced Adolf II to relinquish Lübeck to him as his feudal overlord. Heinrich III no sooner had the city in his possession when a fire destroyed it. Heinrich III began rebuilding it in 1159 and this is now considered the traditional date of it founding. As the city and its trade on the Baltic grew in importance, special rights and privileges were granted to it in 1188 by Emperor Friedrich I Barbarossa. In 1226, Friedrich II raised Lübeck to the status of a free imperial city and a long period of self-government began. From about 1190 and into the 13th century, an imperial mint operated in the town. Although Lübeck was granted the mint right in 1188, reiterated in 1226 and 1340, its earliest civic coinage only began about 1350. The commercial importance of the city became even greater when it joined with Hamburg in 1241 to form the nucleus of what was to become the Hanseatic League. In 1358, the member cities of the League, which had grown very powerful during the preceding century, elected Lübeck as the administrative capital. By the beginning of the 15th century, the city was second only to Cologne as the largest in northern Germany.

The Protestant Reformation swept through Lübeck in 1529-30 (see Bishopric) and changes came rapidly as the governing city council was removed from office, only to be replaced by a revolutionary *burgomeister*, Jürgen Wullenwever. An unsuccessful war ensued against Denmark, Sweden and the Netherlands and caused the city to lose its powerful position in northern Europe. This began the dismemberment of the Hanseatic League and even a victorious war against Sweden during 1563-1570 was not enough to prevent the decline of Lübeck's fortunes. The demise of the League in 1630, during the Thirty Years' War, may have actually been beneficial to the city as it was able to remain neutral during the long years of struggle throughout Germany. The city was able to regain much of its lost economic power during the 18th century, partly due to increased trade with Russia through its new Baltic port of St. Petersburg. Lübeck's economy was completely ruined, however, during the Napoleonic Wars (1792-1815). Occupied by the French from 1811 to 1813, it was restored as a free city in the latter year. After 1815, the city was a member of the German Confederation and joined the North German Confederation in 1866. It remained a free city as part of the German Empire from 1871 until the end of World War I in 1918, However, its status as a self-governing entity, which had begun in 1226, did not end until 1937, when it was made a part of the province of Schleswig-Holstein.

FREE CITY

REFORM COINAGE

KM# 210 2 MARK
11.1110 g., 0.9000 Silver .3215 oz. ASW, 28 mm. **Obv:** Double imperial eagle with divided shield on breast **Rev:** Crowned imperial eagle, shield on breast

Date	Mintage	F	VF	XF	Unc	BU
1901A	25,000	100	200	300	475	525
1901A Proof	—	Value: 550				

KM# 212 2 MARK
11.1110 g., 0.9000 Silver .3215 oz. ASW, 28 mm. **Obv:** Double imperial eagle with divided shield on breast **Designer:** Crowned imperial eagle, shield on breast

Date	Mintage	F	VF	XF	Unc	BU
1904A	25,000	45.00	85.00	135	220	275
1904A Proof	200	Value: 300				
1905A	25,000	45.00	85.00	135	225	275
1905A Proof	178	Value: 300				
1906A	25,000	45.00	85.00	135	225	275
1906A Proof	200	Value: 300				
1907A	25,000	45.00	85.00	135	225	275
1911A	25,000	45.00	85.00	135	225	275
1911A Proof	—	Value: 350				
1912A	25,000	45.00	85.00	135	225	275
1912A Proof	—	Value: 350				

KM# 215 3 MARK
16.6670 g., 0.9000 Silver .4823 oz. ASW, 33 mm. **Obv:** Double imperial eagle with divided shield on breast **Rev:** Crowned imperial eagle, shield on breast

Date	Mintage	F	VF	XF	Unc	BU
1908	33,000	25.00	70.00	125	200	225
1909A	33,000	25.00	70.00	125	200	225
1910A	33,000	25.00	70.00	125	200	225
1911A	33,000	25.00	70.00	125	200	225
1912A	34,000	25.00	70.00	125	200	225
1913A	30,000	25.00	70.00	125	200	225
1914A	10,000	35.00	85.00	150	250	275
(1908-1914)A Proof	—	Value: 285				

KM# 213 5 MARK
27.7770 g., 0.9000 Silver .8038 oz. ASW, 38 mm. **Obv:** Double imperial eagle with divided shield on breast **Rev:** Crowned imperial eagle, shield on breast

Date	Mintage	F	VF	XF	Unc	BU
1904A	10,000	120	275	400	550	650
1904A Proof	200	Value: 875				
1907A	10,000	120	275	400	575	675
1908A	10,000	120	300	425	600	700
1913A	6,000	120	300	450	650	750

KM# 211 10 MARK
3.9820 g., 0.9000 Gold .1152 oz. AGW **Obv:** Double imperial eagle with divided shield on breast **Rev:** Crowned imperial eagle, shield on breast

Date	Mintage	F	VF	XF	Unc	BU
1901A	10,000	375	800	1,200	1,650	2,000
1901A Proof	200	Value: 2,250				
1904A	10,000	375	800	1,200	1,650	2,000
1904A Proof	130	Value: 2,250				

KM# 214 10 MARK
3.9820 g., 0.9000 Gold .1152 oz. AGW **Obv:** Double imperial eagle with divided shield on breast **Rev:** Crowned imperial eagle, shield on breast

Date	Mintage	F	VF	XF	Unc	BU
1905A	10,000	300	550	1,100	1,350	1,800
1905A Proof	247	Value: 2,750				
1906A	10,000	300	550	1,100	1,350	1,800
1906A Proof	216	Value: 2,750				
1909A	10,000	300	550	1,100	1,350	1,800
1909A Proof	—	Value: 2,750				
1910A	10,000	300	550	1,100	1,350	1,800
1910A Proof	—	Value: 3,000				

PATTERNS

Including off metal strikes

KM#	Date	Mintage	Identification	Mkt Val
Pn38	1915A	—	3 Mark. Copper. Aluminum plated.	—
Pn39	1915A	—	3 Mark. Zinc. Aluminum-plated.	—
Pn40	1915A	—	3 Mark. Silver.	—

MECKLENBURG-SCHWERIN

The Duchy of Mecklenburg was divided in 1592 to form the branches of Mecklenburg-Schwerin and Mecklenburg-Güstrow. During the Thirty Years' War, the several dukes of the Mecklenburg states sided with the Protestant forces against the emperor. Albrecht von Wallenstein, Duke of Friedland and imperial general, ousted the Mecklenburg dukes from their territories in 1628. The rightful rulers were each restored to their lands in 1632. In 1658, Mecklenburg-Schwerin was divided by the four sons of Adolf Friedrich into the lines of Mecklenburg-Schwerin, Mecklenburg-Grabow, Mecklenburg-Mirow (extinct in 1675) and Mecklenburg-Strelitz (see). Mecklenburg-Schwerin and Mecklenburg-Güstrow fell extinct in the male line in 1692 and 1695 respectively, becoming a source of dispute between Mecklenburg-Grabow and Mecklenburg-Strelitz. Both parties finally agreed to a settlement in 1701 which awarded about eighty percent of all Mecklenburg territory to Grabow, which became the main Schwerin line, and the rest to Strelitz. No coinage was produced for Mecklenburg-Schwerin from 1708 until 1750. In 1815, the Congress of Vienna elevated the ruler to the rank of Grand Duke. Mecklenburg-Schwerin became a part of the German Empire in 1871. The last grand duke abdicated at the end of World War I in 1918.

RULERS
Friedrich Franz IV, 1897-1918

MINT MARKS
A - Berlin mint, 1852-1915

GRAND DUCHY

REFORM COINAGE

KM# 330 2 MARK
11.1110 g., 0.9000 Silver .3215 oz. ASW, 28 mm. **Ruler:** Friedrich Franz IV **Subject:** Grand Duke Coming of Age **Obv:** Head right **Rev:** Crowned imperial eagle, shield on breast

Date	Mintage	F	VF	XF	Unc	BU
1901A	50,000	125	300	465	1,100	1,250
1901A Proof	1,000	Value: 1,300				

KM# 333 2 MARK
11.1110 g., 0.9000 Silver .3215 oz. ASW, 28 mm. **Ruler:** Friedrich Franz IV **Subject:** Friedrich Franz IV Wedding **Obv:** Jugate heads left **Rev:** Crowned imperial eagle, shield on breast

Date	Mintage	F	VF	XF	Unc	BU
1904A	100,000	18.00	40.00	65.00	100	120
1904A Proof	6,000	Value: 175				

KM# 340 3 MARK
16.6670 g., 0.9000 Silver .4823 oz. ASW, 33 mm. **Ruler:** Friedrich Franz IV **Subject:** 100 Years as Grand Duchy **Obv:** Uniformed jugate busts left **Rev:** Crowned imperial eagle, shield on breast within circle

Date	Mintage	F	VF	XF	Unc	BU
1915A	33,000	50.00	100	175	250	300
1915A Proof	—	Value: 500				

KM# 334 5 MARK
27.7770 g., 0.9000 Silver .8038 oz. ASW, 38 mm. **Ruler:** Friedrich Franz IV **Subject:** Friedrich Franz IV Wedding **Obv:** Jugate heads left **Rev:** Crowned imperial eagle, shield on breast

Date	Mintage	F	VF	XF	Unc	BU
1904A	40,000	45.00	100	175	250	325
1904A Proof	2,500	Value: 600				

KM# 341 5 MARK
27.7770 g., 0.9000 Silver .8038 oz. ASW, 38 mm. **Ruler:** Friedrich Franz IV **Subject:** 100 Years as Grand Duchy **Obv:** Uniformed jugate busts left **Rev:** Crowned imperial eagle, shield on breast within circle

Date	Mintage	F	VF	XF	Unc	BU
1915A	10,000	135	375	500	900	1,200
1915A Proof	—	Value: 1,250				

KM# 331 10 MARK
3.9820 g., 0.9000 Gold .1152 oz. AGW **Ruler:** Friedrich Franz IV **Subject:** Grand Duke Coming of Age **Obv:** Head right **Rev:** Crowned imperial eagle, shield on breast, type III

Date	Mintage	F	VF	XF	Unc	BU
1901A	10,000	750	1,600	2,500	3,250	4,000
1901A Proof	200	Value: 4,500				

KM# 332 20 MARK
7.9650 g., 0.9000 Gold .2304 oz. AGW **Ruler:** Friedrich Franz IV **Subject:** Grand Duke Coming of Age **Obv:** Head right **Rev:** Crowned imperial eagle, shield on breast, type III

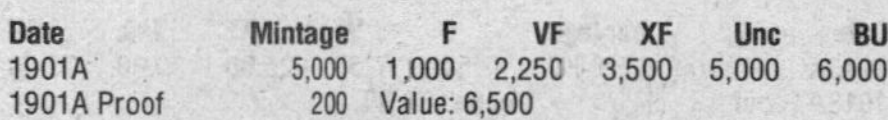

Date	Mintage	F	VF	XF	Unc	BU
1901A	5,000	1,000	2,250	3,500	5,000	6,000
1901A Proof	200	Value: 6,500				

PATTERNS

Including off metal strikes

KM#	Date	Mintage	Identification	Mkt Val
Pn26	1915A	—	3 Mark. Silver. Plain edge. KM340.	—
Pn27	1915A	—	3 Mark. Silver.	—
Pn28	1915A	—	5 Mark. Silver. KM341.	—

MECKLENBURG-STRELITZ

The Duchy of Mecklenburg-Strelitz was the youngest branch of the dynasty established when Mecklenburg-Schwerin was divided in 1658. Like its parent senior line, Mecklenburg-Strelitz became a grand duchy in 1815 as enacted by the Congress of Vienna. It became a constituent part of the German Empire in 1871, but all sovereignty ended with the conclusion of World War I in 1918.

RULERS
Friedrich Wilhelm, 1860-1904
Adolf Friedrich V, 1904-1914
Adolf Friedrich VI, 1914-1918

GRAND DUCHY

REFORM COINAGE

KM# 115 2 MARK
11.1110 g., 0.9000 Silver .3215 oz. ASW, 28 mm. **Ruler:** Adolph Friedrich V **Obv:** Head left **Rev:** Crowned imperial eagle, shield on breast

Date	Mintage	F	VF	XF	Unc	BU
1905A	10,000	150	350	575	800	1,200
1905A Proof	2,500	Value: 1,100				

KM# 120 3 MARK
16.6670 g., 0.9000 Silver .4823 oz. ASW, 33 mm. **Ruler:** Adolph Friedrich V **Obv:** Head left **Rev:** Crowned imperial eagle, shield on breast

Date	Mintage	F	VF	XF	Unc	BU
1913A	7,000	250	500	950	1,600	2,000
1913A Proof	—	Value: 2,100				

KM# 116 10 MARK
3.9820 g., 0.9000 Gold .1152 oz. AGW **Ruler:** Adolph Friedrich V **Obv:** Head left **Rev:** Crowned imperial eagle, shield on breast

Date	Mintage	F	VF	XF	Unc	BU
1905A	1,000	1,750	3,000	4,500	6,500	7,000
1905A Proof	150	Value: 7,500				

KM# 117 20 MARK
7.9650 g., 0.9000 Gold .2304 oz. AGW **Ruler:** Adolph Friedrich V **Obv:** Head left **Rev:** Crowned imperial eagle, shield on breast, type III

Date	Mintage	F	VF	XF	Unc	BU
1905A	1,000	2,000	4,000	5,500	8,000	10,000
1905A Proof	160	Value: 10,500				

PATTERNS

Including off metal strikes

KM#	Date	Mintage	Identification	Mkt Val
Pn41	1913	—	3 Mark. Silver. KM120.	—

OLDENBURG

The county of Oldenburg was situated on the North Seacoast, to the east of the principality of East Friesland. It was originally part of the old duchy of Saxony and the first recorded lord ruled from the beginning of the 11th century. The first count was named in 1091 and had already acquired the county of Delmenhorst prior to that time. The first identifiable Oldenburg coinage was struck in the first half of the 13th century. Oldenburg was divided into Oldenburg and Delmenhorst in 1270, but the two lines were reunited by marriage five generations later. Through another marriage to the heiress of the duchy of Schleswig and county of Holstein, the royal house of Denmark descended through the Oldenburg line beginning in 1448, while a junior branch continued as counts of Oldenburg. The lordship of Jever was added to the county's domains in 1575. In 1667, the last count died without a direct heir and Oldenburg reverted to Denmark until 1773. In the following year, Oldenburg was given to the bishop of Lübeck, of the Holstein-Gottorp line, and raised to the status of a duchy. Oldenburg was occupied several times during the Napoleonic Wars and became a grand duchy in 1829. In 1817, Oldenburg acquired the principality of Birkenfeld from Prussia and struck coins in denominations used there. World War I spelled the end of temporal power for the Grand Duke in 1918, but the title has continued up to the present time. Grand Duke Anton Günther was born in 1923.

RULERS
Friedrich August, 1900-1918

MINT MARKS
A - Berlin mint, 1891-1901

DUCHY

REFORM COINAGE

KM# 202 2 MARK
11.1110 g., 0.9000 Silver .3215 oz. ASW, 28 mm. **Ruler:** Friedrich August **Obv:** Head left **Rev:** Crowned imperial eagle, shield on breast

Date	Mintage	F	VF	XF	Unc	BU
1901A	75,000	BV	225	400	900	1,100
1901A Proof	260	Value: 1,200				

KM# 203 5 MARK
27.7770 g., 0.9000 Silver .8038 oz. ASW, 38 mm. **Ruler:** Friedrich August **Obv:** Head left **Rev:** Crowned imperial eagle, shield on breast

Date	Mintage	F	VF	XF	Unc	BU
1901A	10,000	350	800	1,650	3,750	4,250
1901A Proof	170	Value: 4,500				

PRUSSIA

(Preussen)

Elector Friedrich III of Brandenburg-Prussia (1688-1713) was accorded the title of "King in Prussia" in 1701 as a reward for his support of Austria during the War of the Spanish Succession. Under successive strong leaders, Prussia gained increasing importance and added to its territories to become one of the leading countries of Europe in the course of the 18th century. As part of the reforms instituted by Friedrich II, the system of single letter mintmarks representing specific mints replaced the traditional incorporation of mint officials' symbols and/or initials as part of coin designs. Some of these very same mintmarks are still in use on modern German coins up to the present day. During the Napoleonic Wars (1792-1815), Prussia was allied with Saxony and they were soundly defeated at Jena in 1806. Prussia was forced to cede large portions of its territory at the time, but played a large part in the final defeat of Napoleon. The Congress of Vienna awarded Prussia part of Pomerania, the northern half of Saxony, much of Westphalia and the Rhineland, thus making it the largest state in Germany and a major power in European affairs. After defeating Denmark in 1864 and Austria in 1866, Prussia acquired Schleswig-Holstein, Hannover, Hesse-Cassel, Nassau and Frankfurt am Main. By this time, Prussia encompassed a large part of German territory and its population included two-thirds of all the German people. By winning the Franco-Prussian War (1870-71), Prussia became the pivotal state in the unification of Germany in 1871. King Wilhelm I was proclaimed Kaiser (Emperor) of all Germany, but World War I brought an end to both the Empire and the Kingdom of Prussia in 1918.

NOTE:

For coins of Neuchatel previously listed here, see Switzerland.

RULERS

Wilhelm II, 1888-1918

MINT MARKS

A - Berlin = Prussia, East Friesland, East Prussia, Posen

KINGDOM

REFORM COINAGE

KM# 522 2 MARK

11.1110 g., 0.9000 Silver .2215 oz. ASW, 28 mm. **Ruler:** Wilhelm II **Obv:** Head right **Rev:** Crowned imperial eagle with shield on breast

Date	Mintage	F	VF	XF	Unc	BU
1901	398,000	70.00	160	320	450	700
1901 Proof	—	Value: 2,500				
1902	3,948,000	7.50	16.00	55.00	100	140
1903	4,079,000	7.50	16.00	55.00	100	125
1904A	9,981,000	7.50	16.00	55.00	100	125
1905A	6,493,000	7.00	15.00	50.00	100	125
1905A Proof	620	Value: 500				
1906A	4,019,000	7.00	15.00	50.00	100	125
1906A Proof	85	Value: 600				
1907A	8,110,000	7.00	15.00	50.00	100	125
1908A	2,389,000	7.00	15.00	45.00	100	125
1911A	1,181,000	10.00	22.00	55.00	110	140
1912A	733,000	12.00	28.00	58.00	125	180

KM# 525 2 MARK

11.1110 g., 0.9000 Silver .3215 oz. ASW, 28 mm. **Ruler:** Wilhelm II **Subject:** 200 Years - Kingdom of Prussia **Obv:** Friedrich I, Wilhelm II left **Rev:** Crowned imperial eagle with shield on breast

Date	Mintage	F	VF	XF	Unc	BU
1901A	2,600,000	7.50	17.50	24.00	30.00	40.00
1901A Proof	—	Value: 80.00				

KM# 532 2 MARK

11.1110 g., 0.9000 Silver .3215 oz. ASW, 28 mm. **Ruler:** Wilhelm II **Subject:** 100 Years - Defeat of Napoleon **Obv:** Eagle with snake in talons, denomination below **Rev:** Figure on horseback surrounded by people

Date	Mintage	F	VF	XF	Unc	BU
1913A	1,500,000	7.50	17.50	25.00	30.00	35.00
1913A Proof	—	Value: 80.00				

KM# 533 2 MARK

11.1110 g., 0.9000 Silver .3215 oz. ASW, 28 mm. **Ruler:** Wilhelm II **Subject:** 25th Year of Reign **Obv:** Uniformed bust right **Rev:** Crowned imperial eagle with shield on breast

Date	Mintage	F	VF	XF	Unc	BU
1913A	1,500,000	7.50	17.50	24.00	30.00	35.00
1913A Proof	5,000	Value: 75.00				

KM# 527 3 MARK

16.6670 g., 0.9000 Silver .4823 oz. ASW, 33 mm. **Ruler:** Wilhelm II **Obv:** Head right **Rev:** Crowned imperial eagle with shield on breast

Date	Mintage	F	VF	XF	Unc	BU
1908A	2,859,000	7.00	14.00	24.00	60.00	80.00
1909A	6,344,000	7.00	14.00	24.00	50.00	70.00
1910A	5,591,000	7.00	14.00	24.00	50.00	70.00
1911A	3,242,000	7.00	14.00	24.00	50.00	70.00
1912A	4,626,000	7.00	14.00	24.00	45.00	60.00
(1908-1912)A Proof	—	Value: 190				

KM# 530 3 MARK

16.6670 g., 0.9000 Silver .4823 oz. ASW, 33 mm. **Ruler:** Wilhelm II **Subject:** Berlin University **Obv:** Friedrich Wilhelm III and Wilhelm II left divide dates **Rev:** Crowned imperial eagle with shield on breast

Date	Mintage	F	VF	XF	Unc	BU
1910A	200,000	22.00	55.00	85.00	125	150
1910A Proof	2,000	Value: 325				

KM# 531 3 MARK

16.6670 g., 0.9000 Silver .4823 oz. ASW, 33 mm. **Ruler:** Wilhelm II **Subject:** Breslau University **Obv:** Friedrich Wilhelm III, Wilhelm II left within circle **Rev:** Crowned imperial eagle with shield on breast

Date	Mintage	F	VF	XF	Unc	BU
1911A	400,000	18.00	45.00	70.00	85.00	110
1911A Proof	—	Value: 300				

KM# 534 3 MARK

16.6670 g., 0.9000 Silver .4823 oz. ASW, 33 mm. **Ruler:** Wilhelm II **Subject:** 100 Years - Defeat of Napoleon **Obv:** Eagle with snake in talons, denomination below **Rev:** Figure on horseback surrounded by people

Date	Mintage	F	VF	XF	Unc	BU
1913A	2,000,000	8.00	20.00	25.00	30.00	35.00
1913A Proof	—	Value: 120				

KM# 535 3 MARK

16.6670 g., 0.9000 Silver .4823 oz. ASW, 33 mm. **Ruler:** Wilhelm II **Subject:** 25th Year of Reign **Obv:** Uniformed bust right **Rev:** Crowned imperial eagle with shield on breast

Date	Mintage	F	VF	XF	Unc	BU
1913A	2,000,000	8.00	20.00	25.00	30.00	35.00
1913A Proof	6,000	Value: 90.00				

KM# 538 3 MARK

16.6670 g., 0.9000 Silver .4823 oz. ASW, 33 mm. **Ruler:** Wilhelm II **Obv:** Uniformed bust right **Rev:** Crowned imperial eagle with shield on breast

Date	Mintage	F	VF	XF	Unc	BU
1914A	2,564,000	10.00	20.00	25.00	70.00	90.00
1914A Proof	—	Value: 120				

KM# 539 3 MARK

16.6670 g., 0.9000 Silver .4823 oz. ASW, 33 mm. **Ruler:** Wilhelm II **Subject:** Centenary - Absorption of Mansfeld **Obv:** St. George slaying the dragon **Rev:** Crowned imperial eagle with shield on breast

Date	Mintage	F	VF	XF	Unc	BU
1915A	30,000	220	400	600	1,000	1,200
1915A Proof	—	Value: 1,500				

KM# 523 5 MARK

27.7770 g., 0.9000 Silver .8038 oz. ASW, 38 mm. **Ruler:** Wilhelm II **Obv:** Head right **Rev:** Crowned imperial eagle with shield on breast, type III

Date	Mintage	F	VF	XF	Unc	BU
1901A	668,000	9.00	20.00	100	450	550
1902A	1,951,000	8.00	17.50	95.00	300	400
1903A	3,856,000	8.00	17.50	95.00	300	400
1904A	2,060,000	8.00	17.50	95.00	300	400
1906A	231,000	20.00	40.00	155	800	1,100
1907A	2,902,000	8.00	16.00	65.00	200	275
1908A	2,231,000	8.00	16.00	60.00	250	300
(1891-1908)A Common date proof	—	Value: 1,300				

KM# 526 5 MARK

27.7770 g., 0.9000 Silver .8038 oz. ASW, 38 mm. **Ruler:** Wilhelm II **Subject:** 200 Years - Kingdom of Prussia **Obv:** Friedrich I, Wilhelm II left **Rev:** Crowned imperial eagle with shield on breast

Date	Mintage	F	VF	XF	Unc	BU
1901A	460,000	30.00	50.00	80.00	110	140
1901A Proof	—	Value: 175				

KM# 536 5 MARK

27.7770 g., 0.9000 Silver .8038 oz. ASW, 38 mm. **Ruler:** Wilhelm II **Obv:** Uniformed bust right **Rev:** Crowned imperial eagle, shield on breast

Date	Mintage	F	VF	XF	Unc	BU
1913A	1,962,000	14.00	28.00	40.00	150	200
1914A	1,587,000	13.00	24.00	35.00	150	200
(1913-1914)A Proof	—	Value: 600				

KM# 520 10 MARK

3.9820 g., 0.9000 Gold .1152 oz. AGW **Ruler:** Wilhelm II **Obv:** Head, right **Rev:** Crowned imperial eagle with shield on breast, type III

Date	Mintage	F	VF	XF	Unc	BU
1901A	702,000	BV	95.00	120	250	275
1901A Proof	—	Value: 900				
1902A	271,000	BV	135	185	275	325
1902A Proof	—	Value: 900				
1903A	1,685,000	BV	95.00	125	250	275
1903A Proof	—	Value: 900				
1904A	1,178,000	BV	95.00	125	250	275
1905A	1,063,000	BV	95.00	125	250	275
1905A Proof	117	Value: 900				
1906A	542,000	BV	100	135	265	300
1906A Proof	150	Value: 900				
1907A	813,000	BV	95.00	125	250	275
1907A Proof	—	Value: 900				
1909A	532,000	BV	100	135	265	300
1909A Proof	—	Value: 900				
1910A	803,000	BV	95.00	125	250	275
1911A	271,000	BV	130	180	275	325
1911A Proof	—	Value: 1,000				
1912A	542,000	BV	95.00	125	250	275
1912A Proof	—	Value: 900				

KM# 521 20 MARK

7.9650 g., 0.9000 Gold .2304 oz. AGW **Ruler:** Wilhelm II **Obv:** Head right **Rev:** Crowned imperial eagle with shield on breast, type III

Date	Mintage	F	VF	XF	Unc	BU
1901A	5,188,000	—	BV	160+10%	225	275
1901A Proof	—	Value: 600				
1902A	4,138,000	—	BV	160+10%	225	275
1902A Proof	—	Value: 600				
1903A	2,870,000	—	BV	160+10%	225	275
1903A Proof	—	Value: 600				
1904A	3,453,000	—	BV	160+10%	225	275
1904A Proof	—	Value: 600				
1905A	4,176,000	—	BV	160+10%	225	275
1905A Proof	287	Value: 600				
1905J	921,000	BV+5%	BV+10%	190	300	350
1906A	7,788,000	—	BV	160+10%	250	300
1906A Proof	124	Value: 600				
1906J	82,000	BV+5%	290	380	600	700
1907A	2,576,000	—	BV	160+10%	225	275
1907A Proof	—	Value: 600				
1908A	3,274,000	—	BV	160+10%	225	275
1908A Proof	—	Value: 600				
1909A	5,213,000	—	BV	160+10%	225	275
1909J	350,000	BV+5%	BV+10%	190	300	350
1909A Proof	—	Value: 600				
1909J Proof	—	Value: 800				
1910A	8,646,000	—	BV	160+10%	225	275
1910J	753,000	—	BV	160+10%	225	275
1911A	4,746,000	—	BV	160+10%	225	275
1912A	5,569,000	—	BV	160+10%	225	275
1912J	503,000	BV+3%	BV+5%	190	300	350
1913A	6,102,000	—	BV	160+10%	225	275
1913A Proof	—	Value: 600				

KM# 537 20 MARK

7.9650 g., 0.9000 Gold .2304 oz. AGW **Ruler:** Wilhelm II **Obv:** Uniformed bust right **Rev:** Crowned imperial eagle with shield on breast

Date	Mintage	F	VF	XF	Unc	BU
1913A	—	BV	BV+5%	180	250	300
1913A Proof	—	Value: 1,200				
1914A	2,137,000	BV	BV+5%	180	250	300
1914A Proof	—	Value: 1,200				
1915A	1,271,000	—	1,100	1,600	2,000	2,500

PATTERNS

Including off metal strikes

KM#	Date	Mintage	Identification	Mkt Val
Pn28	1901	—	5 Mark. Silver. Larger design. KM526.	—
Pn29	1901A	—	5 Mark. Silver. Larger design. KM526.	—
PnA30	1901A	—	20 Mark. Silver. Plain edge.	—
Pn30	1904A	—	2 Mark. Silver. Plain edge. Broader rim. KM522.	—
Pn31	1904A	—	5 Mark. Silver.	—
Pn32	1904A	—	5 Mark. Copper. "N.A." countermarked.	—
Pn33	1904A	—	5 Mark. Silver. Reeded edge. Without beaded rims. KM523.	—
Pn34	1904A	—	5 Mark. Silver. Smaller lettering. KM523.	—
Pn35	1904A	—	5 Mark. Silver. Eagle in ornamental in inner border.	—
Pn36	1905A	—	3 Mark. Silver.	—
Pn37	1905A	—	3 Mark. Silver. Legend in different position.	—
Pn38	1905A	—	3 Mark. Copper.	—
Pn39	1905A	—	3 Mark. Silver. KM527.	—
PnA40	1907A	—	20 Mark. Copper. 4.1100 g.	—
Pn40	1908A	—	5 Mark. Silver.	—
Pn41	1908A	—	5 Mark. Brass.	—
Pn42	1908J	—	20 Mark. Gold. KM521.2	—
Pn43	1909A	—	2 Mark. Nickel. KM522.	—
Pn44	1910	—	3 Mark. Silver.	—
Pn45	1910	—	3 Mark. Copper.	—
Pn46	1911	—	3 Mark. Silver. KM531.	—
Pn47	1911	—	3 Mark. Silver.	—
Pn48	1911A	—	3 Mark. Silver. KM531.	400
Pn49	1912A	—	2 Mark. Silver. KM533.	—
Pn51	1912	—	3 Mark. Bronze.	—
Pn52	1912A	—	3 Mark. Silver.	—
Pn53	1912A	—	3 Mark. Bronze.	—
Pn54	1913A	—	2 Mark. Silver. Dots above "O" in KONIG. KM533.	—
Pn55	1913	—	3 Mark. Silver.	—
Pn56	1913	—	3 Mark. Bronze.	—
Pn57	1913A	—	3 Mark. Silver.	—
Pn58	1913A	—	3 Mark. Bronze.	—
Pn59	1913A	—	3 Mark. Silver. Dots above O in KONIG. KM535.	—
Pn60	1913A	—	3 Mark. Copper.	—
Pn61	1913A	—	5 Mark. Silver. Extra sharp design. KM536.	—
Pn62	1914A	—	3 Mark. Silver. Extra sharp design. KM538.	—
Pn63	1915	—	3 Mark. Silver. Gothic script. KM539.	—
Pn64	1915	—	3 Mark. White Metal.	—
Pn65	1915	—	3 Mark. Iron, Tinned. Tin-iron.	—

REUSS

The Reuss family, whose lands were located in Thuringia, was founded c. 1035. By the end of the 12th century, the custom of naming all males in the ruling house Heinrich had been established. The Elder Line modified this strange practice in the late 17th century to numbering all males from 1 to 100, then beginning over again. The Younger Line, meanwhile, decided to start the numbering of Heinrichs with the first male born in each century. Greiz was founded in1303. Upper and Lower Greiz lines were founded in 1535 and the territories were divided until 1768. In 1778 the ruler was made a prince of the Holy Roman Empire. The principality endured until 1918.

MINT MARKS

A - Berlin

B - Hannove

REUSS-OBERGREIZ

The other branch of the division of 1635, Obergreiz went through a number of consolidations and further divisions. Upon the extinction of the Ruess-Untergreiz linein 1768, the latter passed to Reuss-Obergreiz and this line continued on into the 20th century, obtaining the rank of count back in 1673 and that of prince in 1778.

RULERS

Heinrich XXII, 1859-1902

Heinrich XXIV, 1902-1918

PRINCIPALITY

REFORM COINAGE

KM# 128 2 MARK

11.1110 g., 0.9000 Silver .3215 oz. ASW, 28 mm. **Ruler:** Heinrich XXII **Obv:** Head right **Rev:** Crowned imperial eagle with shield on breast

Date	Mintage	F	VF	XF	Unc	BU
1901A	10,000	125	225	375	625	750
1901A Proof	—	Value: 900				

KM# 130 3 MARK

16.6670 g., 0.9000 Silver .4823 oz. ASW, 33 mm. **Ruler:** Heinrich XXIV **Obv:** Head right **Rev:** Crowned imperial eagle with shield on breast

Date	Mintage	F	VF	XF	Unc	BU
1909A	10,000	120	285	450	800	900
1909A Proof	400	Value: 1,250				

PATTERNS

Including off metal strikes

KM#	Date	Mintage	Identification	Mkt Val
Pn4	1909A	—	3 Mark. Silver. Head faces left. KM130	—

SAXE-ALTENBURG

(Sachsen-Neu-Altenburg)

A new line was established at Altenburg when the Duke of Saxe-Hildburghausen exchanged Hildburghausen for Altenburg in 1826. This line lasted until the end of World War I, when the last duke was forced to abdicate.

RULERS

Ernst I, 1853-1908
Ernst II, 1908-1918

MINT MARKS

A – Berlin Mint, 1886-1918

DUCHY

REFORM COINAGE

KM# 144 2 MARK

11.1110 g., 0.9000 Silver .3215 oz. ASW, 28 mm. **Ruler:** Ernst I **Subject:** Ernst 75th Birthday **Obv:** Head right **Rev:** Crowned imperial eagle with shield on breast

Date	Mintage	F	VF	XF	Unc	BU
1901A	50,000	120	250	450	675	800
1901A Proof	500	Value: 850				

KM# 145 5 MARK

27.7770 g., 0.9000 Silver .8038 oz. ASW, 38 mm. **Ruler:** Ernst I **Subject:** Ernst 75th Birthday **Obv:** Head right **Rev:** Crowned imperial eagle with shield on breast

Date	Mintage	F	VF	XF	Unc	BU
1901A	20,000	200	425	800	1,400	1,750
1901A Proof	500	Value: 1,850				

KM# 147 5 MARK

27.7770 g., 0.9000 Silver .8038 oz. ASW, 38 mm. **Ruler:** Ernst I **Subject:** Ernst's 50th Year of Reign **Obv:** Head right, date and sprays below **Rev:** Crowned imperial eagle with shield on breast

Date	Mintage	F	VF	XF	Unc	BU
1903	20,000	100	200	325	500	700
1903A Proof	300	Value: 750				

SAXE-COBURG-GOTHA

(Sachsen-Coburg-Gotha)

Upon the extinction of the ducal line in Saxe-Gotha-Altenburg in 1826, Gotha was assigned to Saxe-Coburg-Saalfeld and Saxe-Meiningen received Saalfeld. The resulting duchy became called Saxe-Coburg-Gotha. Albert, the son of Ernst I and younger brother of Ernst II, married Queen Victoria of Great Britain and the British royal dynastic name was that of Saxe-Coburg-Gotha. Their son, Alfred was made the Duke of Edinburgh and succeeded his uncle, Ernst II, as Duke of Saxe-Coburg-Gotha. Alfred's older brother, Eduard Albert, followed their mother as King Edward VII (1901-1910). The last duke of Saxe-Coburg-Gotha was Alfred's nephew, Karl Eduard, forced to abdicate in 1918 as a result of World War I, which was fought in part against his cousin, King George V.

RULERS

Karl Eduard, 1900-1918

MINT MARKS

A – Berlin Mint, 1886-1911

DUCHY

REFORM COINAGE

KM# 152 2 MARK

11.1110 g., 0.9000 Silver .3215 oz. ASW, 28 mm. **Ruler:** Karl Eduard **Obv:** Head right

Date	Mintage	F	VF	XF	Unc	BU
1905A	10,000	135	285	600	1,100	1,300
1905A Proof	2,000	Value: 1,350				
1911A Proof	100	Value: 12,500				

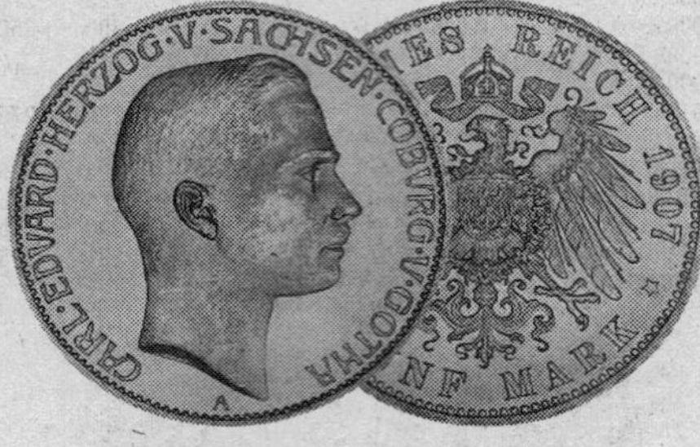

KM# 153 5 MARK

27.7770 g., 0.9000 Silver .8038 oz. ASW, 38 mm. **Ruler:** Karl Eduard **Obv:** Head right **Rev:** Crowned imperial eagle with shield on breast

Date	Mintage	F	VF	XF	Unc	BU
1907A	10,000	300	600	1,000	1,600	2,000
1907A Proof	—	Value: 2,250				

KM# 154 10 MARK

3.9820 g., 0.9000 Gold .1152 oz. AGW **Ruler:** Karl Eduard **Obv:** Head right **Rev:** Crowned imperial eagle with shield on breast

Date	Mintage	F	VF	XF	Unc	BU
1905A	9,511	650	1,100	1,800	2,250	2,750
1905A Proof	489	Value: 4,000				

KM# 155 20 MARK

7.9650 g., 0.9000 Gold .2304 oz. AGW **Ruler:** Karl Eduard **Obv:** Head, right **Rev:** Crowned imperial eagle with shield on breast, type I

Date	Mintage	F	VF	XF	Unc	BU
1905A	10,000	700	1,200	1,900	2,500	2,800
1905A Proof	484	Value: 4,250				

SAXE-MEININGEN

(Sachsen-Meiningen)

The duchy of Saxe-Meiningen was located in Thuringia (Thüringen), sandwiched between Saxe-Weimar-Eisenach on the west and north and the enclave of Schmalkalden belonging to Hesse-Cassel on the east. It was founded upon the division of the Ernestine line in Saxe-Gotha in 1680. In 1735, due to an exchange of some territory, the duchy became known as Saxe-Coburg-Meiningen. In 1826, Saxe-Coburg-Gotha assigned Saalfeld to Saxe-Meiningen. The duchy came under the strong influence of Prussia from 1866, when Bernhard II was forced to abdicate because of his support of Austria. The last duke was forced to give up his sovereign power at the end of World War I in 1918.

RULERS

Georg II, 1866-1914
Bernhard III, 1914-1918

DUCHY

REFORM COINAGE

KM# 196 2 MARK

11.1110 g., 0.9000 Silver .3215 oz. ASW, 28 mm. **Ruler:** Georg II **Subject:** Duke's 75th Birthday **Obv:** Head right **Rev:** Crowned imperial eagle with shield on breast

Date	Mintage	F	VF	XF	Unc	BU
1901D	20,000	100	250	400	750	900
1901D Proof	—	Value: 1,000				

KM# 198 2 MARK

11.1110 g., 0.9000 Silver .3215 oz. ASW, 28 mm. **Ruler:** Georg II **Obv:** Head left, long beard **Rev:** Crowned imperial eagle with shield on breast

Date	Mintage	F	VF	XF	Unc	BU
1902D	20,000	250	800	1,450	2,200	2,750

KM# 199 2 MARK

11.1110 g., 0.9000 Silver .3215 oz. ASW, 28 mm. **Ruler:** Georg II **Obv:** Head left, short beard **Rev:** Crowned imperial eagle with shield on breast

Date	Mintage	F	VF	XF	Unc	BU
1902D	Inc. above	100	200	350	750	850
1913D	5,000	150	275	500	1,250	1,400

KM# 206 2 MARK

11.1110 g., 0.9000 Silver .3215 oz. ASW, 28 mm. **Ruler:** Bernhard III **Subject:** Death of Georg II **Obv:** Head left, long beard **Rev:** Crowned imperial eagle with shield on breast

Date	Mintage	F	VF	XF	Unc	BU
1915	30,000	35.00	75.00	150	220	250

KM# 203 3 MARK

16.6670 g., 0.9000 Silver .4823 oz. ASW, 33 mm. **Ruler:**

Georg II **Obv:** Head left, long beard **Rev:** Crowned imperial eagle with shield on breast

Date	Mintage	F	VF	XF	Unc	BU
1908D	35,000	35.00	110	165	250	350
1908D Proof	—	Value: 450				
1913D	20,000	35.00	110	165	300	400

KM# 207 3 MARK
16.6670 g., 0.9000 Silver .4823 oz. ASW, 33 mm. **Ruler:** Bernhard III **Subject:** Death of Georg II **Obv:** Head left, long beard **Rev:** Crowned imperial eagle with shield on breast

Date	Mintage	F	VF	XF	Unc	BU
1915	30,000	30.00	70.00	150	220	260
1915 Proof	—	Value: 275				

KM# 197 5 MARK
27.7770 g., 0.9000 Silver .8038 oz. ASW, 38 mm. **Ruler:** Georg II **Subject:** Duke's 75th Birthday **Obv:** Head right, long beard **Rev:** Crowned imperial eagle with shield on breast

Date	Mintage	F	VF	XF	Unc	BU
1901D	20,000	85.00	250	450	1,000	1,400
1901D Proof	—	Value: 1,500				

KM# 200 5 MARK
27.7770 g., 0.9000 Silver .8038 oz. ASW, 38 mm. **Ruler:** Georg II **Obv:** Long beard **Rev:** Crowned imperial eagle with shield on breast

Date	Mintage	F	VF	XF	Unc	BU
1902D	20,000	60.00	185	350	1,000	1,250

KM# 201 5 MARK
27.7770 g., 0.9000 Silver .8038 oz. ASW, 38 mm. **Ruler:** Georg II **Obv:** Head left, long beard **Rev:** Crowned imperial eagle with shield on breast

Date	Mintage	F	VF	XF	Unc	BU
1902D	Inc. above	60.00	175	400	1,200	1,800
1908D	60,000	50.00	160	275	850	900

KM# 202 10 MARK
3.9820 g., 0.9000 Gold .1152 oz. AGW **Ruler:** Georg II **Obv:** Head left, long beard **Rev:** Crowned imperial eagle with shield on breast

Date	Mintage	F	VF	XF	Unc	BU
1902D	2,000	900	2,000	2,750	4,000	5,000
1902D Proof	—	Value: 5,500				
1909D	2,000	900	2,000	2,750	4,000	5,000
1909D Proof	—	Value: 5,500				
1914D	1,002	950	2,150	3,000	4,500	5,500
1914D Proof	—	Value: 5,750				

KM# 195 20 MARK
7.9650 g., 0.9000 Gold .2304 oz. AGW **Ruler:** Georg II **Obv:** Head left, short beard **Rev:** Crowned imperial eagle with shield on breast, type III

Date	Mintage	F	VF	XF	Unc	BU
1905D	1,000	3,000	5,000	7,500	12,500	15,000
1905D Proof	—	Value: 12,500				

KM# 205 20 MARK
7.9650 g., 0.9000 Gold .2304 oz. AGW **Ruler:** Georg II **Obv:** Head left, long beard **Rev:** Crowned imperial eagle with shield on breast

Date	Mintage	F	VF	XF	Unc	BU
1910D	1,004	1,500	3,000	4,500	6,000	7,500
1910D Proof	—	Value: 8,000				
1914D	1,000	1,500	3,000	4,500	6,000	7,500
1914D Proof	—	Value: 8,000				

PATTERNS

Including off metal strikes

KM#	Date	Mintage	Identification	Mkt Val
Pn16	1901D	—	10 Mark. Gold. With neck and beard variety. KM202.	—
Pn17	1901D	—	10 Mark. Gold. KM202.	—
Pn18	1915D	—	2 Mark. KM206.	—
Pn19	1915D	—	3 Mark. KM207.	—

SAXE-WEIMAR-EISENACH

(Sachsen-Weimar-Eisenach)

When the death of the duke of Saxe-Eisenach in 1741 heralded the extinction of that line, its possessions reverted to Saxe-Weimar, which henceforth was known as Saxe-Weimar-Eisenach. Because of the strong role played by the duke during the Napoleonic Wars, Saxe-Weimar-Eisenach was raised to the rank of a grand duchy in 1814 and granted the territory of Neustadt, taken from Saxony. The last grand duke abdicated at the end of World War I.

RULERS
Karl Alexander, 1853-1901
Wilhelm Ernst, 1901-1918

MINT MARKS
A – Berlin Mint, 1840-1915

GRAND DUCHY

REFORM COINAGE

Y# 170 2 MARK
11.1110 g., 0.9000 Silver .3215 oz. ASW, 28 mm. **Ruler:** Wilhelm Ernst **Obv:** Head left **Rev:** Crowned imperial eagle with shield on breast

Date	Mintage	F	VF	XF	Unc	BU
1901A	100,000	100	300	450	850	1,200
1901A Proof	—	Value: 1,250				

Y# 172 2 MARK
11.1110 g., 0.9000 Silver .3215 oz. ASW, 28 mm. **Ruler:** Wilhelm Ernst **Subject:** Grand Duke's First Marriage - Caroline **Obv:** Jugate heads left **Rev:** Crowned imperial eagle with shield on breast

Date	Mintage	F	VF	XF	Unc	BU
1903A	40,000	35.00	60.00	100	145	180
1903A Proof	Est. 1,000	Value: 185				

Y# 174 2 MARK
11.1110 g., 0.9000 Silver .3215 oz. ASW, 28 mm. **Ruler:** Wilhelm Ernst **Subject:** Jena University 350th Anniversary **Obv:** Johan Friedrich I the Magnanimous 3/4 right **Rev:** Crowned imperial eagle with shield on breast

Date	Mintage	F	VF	XF	Unc	BU
1908	50,000	25.00	55.00	110	135	180

Y# 176 3 MARK
16.6670 g., 0.9000 Silver .4823 oz. ASW, 33 mm. **Ruler:** Wilhelm Ernst **Subject:** Grand Duke's Second Marriage - Feodora **Obv:** Jugate heads left **Rev:** Crowned imperial eagle with shield on breast

Date	Mintage	F	VF	XF	Unc	BU
1910	133,000	20.00	40.00	85.00	100	140
1910A Proof	—	Value: 200				

Y# 177 3 MARK
16.6670 g., 0.9000 Silver .4823 oz. ASW, 33 mm. **Ruler:** Wilhelm Ernst **Subject:** Centenary of Grand Duchy **Obv:** Wilhelm Ernst and Carl August right **Rev:** Crowned imperial eagle with shield on breast

Date	Mintage	F	VF	XF	Unc	BU
1915A	50,000	25.00	50.00	100	150	225
1915A Proof	200	Value: 400				

Y# 173 5 MARK
27.7770 g., 0.9000 Silver .8038 oz. ASW, 38 mm. **Ruler:** Wilhelm Ernst **Subject:** Grand Duke's First Marriage - Caroline **Obv:** Jugate heads left **Rev:** Crowned imperial eagle with shield on breast

Date	Mintage	F	VF	XF	Unc	BU
1903A	24,000	60.00	125	225	315	350
1903A Proof	Est. 1,000	Value: 425				

Y# 175 5 MARK
27.7770 g., 0.9000 Silver .8038 oz. ASW, 38 mm. **Ruler:** Wilhelm Ernst **Subject:** Jena University 350th Anniversary **Obv:** Johan Friedrich I the Magnanimous 3/4 right **Rev:** Crowned imperial eagle with shield on breast

Date	Mintage	F	VF	XF	Unc	BU
1908A	40,000	60.00	110	200	300	350
1908A Proof	—	Value: 625				

Y# 171 20 MARK
7.9650 g., 0.9000 Gold .2304 oz. AGW **Ruler:** Wilhelm Ernst **Subject:** Golden Wedding of Carl Alexander **Obv:** Head left **Rev:** Crowned imperial eagle with shield on breast

Date	Mintage	F	VF	XF	Unc	BU
1901A	5,000	1,000	2,000	2,800	4,000	5,000
1901A Proof	—	Value: 5,500				

PATTERNS

Including off metal strikes

KM#	Date	Mintage	Identification	Mkt Val
Pn1	1908	—	5 Mark. Silver. Figure smaller. Y#175.	—
Pn2	1910	—	3 Mark. Silver.	—
Pn3	1910	—	3 Mark. Brass.	—

SAXONY

Saxony, located in southeast Germany was founded in 850. The first coinage was struck c. 990. It was divided into two lines in 1464. The electoral right was obtained by the elder line in 1547. During the time of the Reformation, Saxony was one of the more powerful states in central Europe. It became a kingdom in 1806. At the Congress of Vienna in 1815, they were forced to cede half its territories to Prussia.

RULERS
Albert, 1873-1902
Georg, 1902-1904
Friedrich August III, 1904-1918

MINT MARKS
L - Leipzig

KINGDOM

REFORM COINAGE

KM# 1245 2 MARK
11.1110 g., 0.9000 Silver .3215 oz. ASW **Ruler:** Albert **Note:** Similar to KM#185.

Date	Mintage	F	VF	XF	Unc	BU
1901E	440,000	12.50	55.00	110	300	400
1902E	543,000	10.00	55.00	110	275	350

KM# 1255 2 MARK
11.1110 g., 0.9000 Silver .3215 oz. ASW, 28 mm. **Ruler:** Georg **Subject:** Death of Albert **Obv:** Head right **Rev:** Crowned imperial eagle with shield on breast

Date	Mintage	F	VF	XF	Unc	BU
1902E	168,000	15.00	40.00	65.00	125	175
1902E Proof	250	Value: 225				

KM# 1257 2 MARK
11.1110 g., 0.9000 Silver .3215 oz. ASW, 28 mm. **Ruler:** Georg **Obv:** Head right **Rev:** Crowned imperial eagle with shield on breast

Date	Mintage	F	VF	XF	Unc	BU
1903E	746,000	30.00	60.00	140	250	400
1903E Proof	50	Value: 600				
1904E	1,266,000	17.50	50.00	100	200	350

KM# 1261 2 MARK
11.1110 g., 0.9000 Silver .3215 oz. ASW, 28 mm. **Ruler:** Friedrich August III **Subject:** Death of Georg **Obv:** Head right **Rev:** Crowned imperial eagle with shield on breast

Date	Mintage	F	VF	XF	Unc	BU
1904E	150,000	15.00	35.00	70.00	100	130
1904E Proof	55	Value: 250				

KM# 1263 2 MARK
11.1110 g., 0.9000 Silver .3215 oz. ASW, 28 mm. **Ruler:** Friedrich August III **Obv:** Head right **Rev:** Crowned imperial eagle with shield on breast

Date	Mintage	F	VF	XF	Unc	BU
1905E	559,000	20.00	45.00	75.00	160	225
1905E Proof	100	Value: 300				
1906E	559,000	20.00	45.00	75.00	160	225
1907E	1,118,000	20.00	45.00	70.00	155	175
1908E	336,000	20.00	45.00	70.00	155	175
1911E	186,000	20.00	45.00	75.00	200	300
1912E	168,000	20.00	45.00	75.00	200	300
1914E	298,000	20.00	45.00	70.00	125	160
(1905-1914)E Proof	—	Value: 300				

KM# 1268 2 MARK
11.1110 g., 0.9000 Silver .3215 oz. ASW, 28 mm. **Ruler:** Friedrich August III **Subject:** 500th Anniversary - Leipzig University **Obv:** Crown Prince Friedrich the Pugnacious and Friedrich August III left **Rev:** Crowned imperial eagle with shield on breast

Date	Mintage	F	VF	XF	Unc	BU
1909	125,000	15.00	35.00	65.00	100	120
1909 Proof	300	Value: 200				

KM# 1267 3 MARK
16.6670 g., 0.9000 Silver .4823 oz. ASW, 33 mm. **Ruler:** Friedrich August III **Obv:** Head right **Rev:** Crowned imperial eagle with shield on breast

Date	Mintage	F	VF	XF	Unc	BU
1908E	276,000	10.00	22.00	40.00	100	140
1909E	1,197,000	10.00	20.00	35.00	80.00	110
1910E	745,000	10.00	20.00	35.00	90.00	125
1911E	581,000	10.00	20.00	35.00	90.00	120
1912E	379,000	10.00	20.00	35.00	90.00	120
1913E	307,000	10.00	20.00	35.00	90.00	120
(1908-1913)E Proof	—	Value: 225				

KM# 1275 3 MARK
16.6670 g., 0.9000 Silver .4823 oz. ASW, 33 mm. **Ruler:** Friedrich August III **Subject:** Battle of Leipzig Centennial **Obv:** Monument divides date above **Rev:** Crowned imperial eagle with shield on breast

Date	Mintage	F	VF	XF	Unc	BU
1913E	1,000,000	12.00	18.00	28.00	45.00	60.00
1913E Proof	17,000	Value: 150				

KM# 1276 3 MARK
16.6670 g., 0.9000 Silver .4823 oz. ASW, 33 mm. **Ruler:** Friedrich August III **Subject:** Jubilee of Reformation **Obv:** Friederich the Wise right, Protector of Martin Luther **Rev:** Crowned imperial eagle with shield on breast

Date	Mintage	F	VF	XF	Unc	BU
1917E Proof	100	Value: 70,000				

KM# 1246 5 MARK
27.7770 g., 0.9000 Silver .8038 oz. ASW, 38 mm. **Ruler:** Albert **Obv:** Head right **Rev:** Crowned imperial eagle with shield on breast

Date	Mintage	F	VF	XF	Unc	BU
1901E	156,000	25.00	55.00	300	750	1,200
1902E	168,000	20.00	45.00	275	650	1,150
1902E Proof	—	Value: 2,400				

KM# 1256 5 MARK
27.7770 g., 0.9000 Silver .8038 oz. ASW, 38 mm. **Ruler:** Georg **Subject:** Death of Albert **Obv:** Head right **Rev:** Crowned imperial eagle with shield on breast

Date	Mintage	F	VF	XF	Unc	BU
1902E	100,000	30.00	65.00	125	300	275
1902E Proof	250	Value: 450				

KM# 1258 5 MARK
27.7770 g., 0.9000 Silver .8038 oz. ASW, 38 mm. **Ruler:** Georg **Obv:** Head right **Rev:** Crowned imperial eagle with shield on breast

Date	Mintage	F	VF	XF	Unc	BU
1903E	536,000	25.00	50.00	200	650	750
1903E Proof	50	Value: 1,000				
1904E	291,000	30.00	60.00	220	750	900
1904E Proof	—	Value: 1,100				

KM# 1262 5 MARK
27.7770 g., 0.9000 Silver .8038 oz. ASW, 38 mm. **Ruler:** Friedrich August III **Subject:** Death of Georg **Obv:** Head right **Rev:** Crowned imperial eagle with shield on breast

Date	Mintage	F	VF	XF	Unc	BU
1904E	37,000	45.00	150	200	350	400
1904E Proof	70	Value: 550				

KM# 1266 5 MARK
27.7770 g., 0.9000 Silver .8038 oz. ASW, 38 mm. **Ruler:** Friedrich August III **Obv:** Head right **Rev:** Crowned imperial eagle with shield on breast

Date	Mintage	F	VF	XF	Unc	BU
1907E	398,000	20.00	40.00	90.00	300	350
1908E	317,000	20.00	40.00	85.00	250	275
1914E	298,000	17.50	35.00	80.00	200	225
1914E Proof	—	Value: 1,100				

KM# 1269 5 MARK
27.7770 g., 0.9000 Silver .8038 oz. ASW, 38 mm. **Ruler:** Friedrich August III **Subject:** 500th Anniversary - Leipzig University **Obv:** Crown Prince Friedrich the Pugracious and Friederich August III left **Rev:** Crowned imperial eagle with shield on breast

Date	Mintage	F	VF	XF	Unc	BU
1909	50,000	40.00	95.00	175	245	300
1909 Proof	300	Value: 525				

KM# 1247 10 MARK
3.9820 g., 0.9000 Gold .1152 oz. AGW **Ruler:** Albert **Rev:** Crowned imperial eagle with shield on breast, type III

Date	Mintage	F	VF	XF	Unc	BU
1901E	75,000	100	175	250	500	650
1902E	37,000	100	175	250	500	650
1902E Proof	—	Value: 1,500				

KM# 1259 10 MARK
3.9820 g., 0.9000 Gold .1152 oz. AGW **Ruler:** Georg **Obv:** Head right **Rev:** Crowned imperial eagle with shield on breast

Date	Mintage	F	VF	XF	Unc	BU
1903E	284,000	100	210	350	600	700
1903E Proof	100	Value: 1,600				
1904E	149,000	100	210	350	600	700

KM# 1264 10 MARK
3.9820 g., 0.9000 Gold .1152 oz. AGW **Ruler:** Friedrich August III **Obv:** Head right **Rev:** Crowned imperial eagle with shield on breast

Date	Mintage	F	VF	XF	Unc	BU
1905E	112,000	120	250	325	500	650
1905E Proof	100	Value: 1,400				
1906E	75,000	120	250	325	500	650
1906E Proof	—	Value: 1,500				
1907E	112,000	120	250	325	500	650
1907E Proof	—	Value: 1,500				
1909E	112,000	120	250	325	500	650
1910E	75,000	120	250	325	500	650
1910E Proof	—	Value: 1,400				
1911E	38,000	120	250	325	500	650
1912E	75,000	120	250	325	500	650

KM# 1260 20 MARK
7.9650 g., 0.9000 Gold .2304 oz. AGW **Ruler:** Georg **Obv:** Head right **Rev:** Crowned imperial eagle with shield on breast, type III

Date	Mintage	F	VF	XF	Unc	BU
1903E	250,000	BV	200	300	450	550
1903E Proof	—	Value: 1,800				

KM# 1265 20 MARK
7.9650 g., 0.9000 Gold .2304 oz. AGW **Ruler:** Friedrich August III **Obv:** Head right **Rev:** Crowned imperial eagle with shield on breast

Date	Mintage	F	VF	XF	Unc	BU
1905E	500,000	BV	200	400	500	600
1905E Proof	86	Value: 1,500				
1913E	121,000	BV	200	500	600	750
1914E	325,000	BV	200	375	450	550
1914E Proof	—	Value: 1,750				

PATTERNS

Including off metal strikes

KM#	Date	Mintage	Identification	Mkt Val
Pn78	1902 E	—	5 Mark. Silver. KM1258.	—
PnA78	1905E	—	20 Mark. Copper. 4.0600 g.	—
PnB78	1905E	—	20 Mark. Copper. 4.8900 g. Bust in uniform.	—
Pn79	1913	—	3 Mark. Silver.	—
Pn80	1917 E	—	3 Mark. Aluminum. KM1267.	—

SCHAUMBURG-LIPPE

The tiny countship of Schaumburg-Lippe, with an area of only 131 square miles (218 square kilometers) in northwest Germany, was surrounded by the larger states of Brunswick-Lüneburg-Calenberg, an enclave of Hesse-Cassel, and the bishopric of Minden (part of Brandenburg-Prussia from 1648). It was founded in 1640 when Schaumburg-Gehmen was divided between Hesse-Cassel and Lippe-Alverdissen. The two became known as Schaumburg-Hessen and Schaumburg-Lippe. Philipp II, the youngest son of Count Simon VI of Lippe came into the possession of Alverdissen and Lipperode upon his father's death in 1613. In 1640, he also inherited half of Schaumburg-Bückeburg, becoming the first Count of Schaumburg-Lippe. A separate line of Schaumburg-Alverdissen was established in 1681 and, upon the extinction of the elder line in 1777, the lands and titles devolved onto Alverdissen, becoming the ruling line in the countship. In 1806, the count was raised to the rank of prince and Schaumburg-Lippe was incorporated into the Rhine Confederation. It became a part of the German Confederation in 1815 and joined the North German Confederation in 1866. The principality became a member state in the German Empire in 1871. The last sovereign prince resigned as a result of World War I.

RULERS
Albrecht Georg, 1893-1911
Adolf II Bernhard, 1911-1918

MINT MARKS
A - Berlin mint, 1858-1911

PRINCIPALITY

REFORM COINAGE

Y# 203 2 MARK
11.1110 g., 0.9000 Silver 0.3215 oz. ASW, 28 mm. **Ruler:** Albrecht Georg **Subject:** Death of Prince Georg **Obv:** Head left **Rev:** Crowned imperial eagle with shield on breast

Date	Mintage	F	VF	XF	Unc	BU
1904A	5,000	200	400	500	850	950
1904A Proof	200	Value: 1,300				

Y# 206 3 MARK
16.6670 g., 0.9000 Silver 0.4823 oz. ASW, 33 mm. **Ruler:** Albrecht Georg **Subject:** Death of Prince Georg **Obv:** Head left **Rev:** Crowned imperial eagle with shield on breast

Date	Mintage	F	VF	XF	Unc	BU
1911A	50,000	30.00	65.00	95.00	220	225
1911A Proof	—	Value: 300				

Y# 204 5 MARK
27.7770 g., 0.9000 Silver 0.8038 oz. ASW, 38 mm. **Ruler:** Albrecht Georg **Subject:** Death of Prince Georg **Obv:** Head left **Rev:** Crowned imperial eagle with shield on breast

Date	Mintage	F	VF	XF	Unc	BU
1904A	3,000	350	775	1,250	2,400	2,650
1904A Proof	200	Value: 3,500				

Y# 205 20 MARK
7.9650 g., 0.9000 Gold 0.2304 oz. AGW **Ruler:** Albrecht Georg **Subject:** Death of Prince Georg **Obv:** Head left **Rev:** Crowned imperial eagle with shield on breast

Date	Mintage	F	VF	XF	Unc	BU
1904A	5,500	750	1,400	2,000	3,000	3,750
1904A Proof	132	Value: 4,700				

SCHLESWIG-HOLSTEIN

Schleswig-Holstein is located along the border area between Denmark and Germany. The Duchy of Schleswig was predominantly Danish while the Duchy of Holstein was mostly German. Holstein-Gottorp was the ruling line in most of the territory from 1533 and lost Schleswig to Denmark permanently in 1721. Holstein-Gottorp was transferred by the 1773 Treaty of Zarskoje Selo to Denmark in exchange for Oldenburg. There was a great deal of trouble in the area during the 19th century and as a result of a war with Denmark, Prussia annexed the territory in 1864. After World War I, a plebiscite was held and the area was divided in 1920. North Slesvig went to Denmark while South Schleswig and Holstein became a permanent part of Germany.

STATE

GUTSCHRIFTSMARKE COINAGE

KM# Tn1 5/100 GUTSCHRIFTSMARKE
Aluminum, 23 mm. **Obv:** Provincial arms **Rev:** Denomination

Date	Mintage	F	VF	XF	Unc	BU
1923	3,330,000	3.00	7.00	14.00	22.50	—

KM# Tn2 10/100 GUTSCHRIFTSMARKE
Aluminum, 27 mm. **Obv:** Provincial arms **Rev:** Denomination

Date	Mintage	F	VF	XF	Unc	BU
1923	4,500,000	4.00	8.00	16.00	25.00	—

SCHWARZBURG-RUDOLSTADT

The Countship of Schwarzburg-Rudolstadt came into being as the younger line upon the division of Schwarzburg-Blankenburg in 1552. Its territory of about 360 square miles (600 square kilometers) is located in the center of Thuringia (Thüringen), surrounded by several of the Saxon duchies and Reuss-Obergreiz. The count attained the rank of prince in 1711 and the small state was able to weather the political perils of the Napoleonic Wars (1792-1815). Schwarzburg-Rudolstadt joined the German Confederation at the end of hostilities and subsequently became a member of the North German Confederation in 1867, then the German Empire in 1871. The last prince obtained Schwarzburg-Sondershausen upon the latter's extinction in 1909, then was forced to abdicate in 1918.

RULERS
Günther Viktor, 1890-1918

MINT MARKS
A - Berlin mint, 1841-1901

PATTERNS

Including off metal strikes

KM#	Date	Mintage	Identification	Mkt Val
Pn3	1901 A	—	2 Mark. Silver. Y207.	—

SCHWARZBURG-SONDERSHAUSEN

The Countship of Schwarzburg-Sondershausen contains territory of about 330 square miles (550 square kilometers) and is located just north of Thuringia (Thüringen), surrounded by the Prussian province of Saxony, between the ducal enclaves of Gotha and Weimar. The count was raised to the rank of prince in 1697 and underwent several minor divisions during the 18th century. Schwarzburg-Sondershausen joined the German Confederation in 1815 and became a member of the North German Confederation in 1867, as well as the German Empire in 1871. When Karl Günther died without an heir in 1909, his lands and titles went to Schwarzburg-Rudolstadt.

RULERS
Karl Günther, 1880-1909

MINT MARKS
A - Berlin mint, 1846-1909

PRINCIPALITY

REFORM COINAGE

Y# 211 2 MARK
11.1110 g., 0.9000 Silver .3215 oz. ASW, 28 mm. **Ruler:** Karl Gunther **Subject:** 25th Anniversary of Reign **Obv:** Head right, leafy spray below **Rev:** Crowned imperial eagle with shield on breast **Note:** Thick rim.

Date	Mintage	F	VF	XF	Unc	BU
1905	13,000	40.00	80.00	145	220	275
1905 Proof	5,000	Value: 300				

Y# 211a 2 MARK
11.1110 g., 0.9000 Silver .3215 oz. ASW, 28 mm. **Ruler:** Karl Gunther **Subject:** 25th Anniversary of Reign **Obv:** Head right, leafy spray below **Rev:** Crowned imperial eagle with shield on breast **Note:** Thin rim.

Date	Mintage	F	VF	XF	Unc	BU
1905	62,000	25.00	50.00	95.00	135	160
1905 Proof	5,000	Value: 175				

Y# 212 3 MARK
16.6670 g., 0.9000 Silver .4823 oz. ASW, 33 mm. **Ruler:** Karl Gunther **Subject:** Death of Karl Gunther **Obv:** Head right **Rev:** Crowned imperial eagle with shield on breast

Date	Mintage	F	VF	XF	Unc	BU
1909A	70,000	30.00	60.00	100	175	200
1909A Proof	100	Value: 350				

PATTERNS

Including off metal strikes

KM#	Date	Mintage	Identification	Mkt Val
Pn1	1901A	—	2 Mark. Silver. Y209.	—
Pn2	1901A	—	2 Mark. Silver. Y211.	—
Pn3	1909A	—	3 Mark. Silver.	—

WALDECK-PYRMONT

The Count of Waldeck-Eisenberg inherited the Countship of Pyrmont, located between Lippe and Hannover, in 1625, thus creating an entity which encompassed about 672 square miles (1120 square kilometers). Waldeck and Pyrmont were permanently united in 1668, thus continuing the Eisenberg line as Waldeck-Pyrmont from that date. The count was raised to the rank of prince in 1712 and the unification of the two territories was confirmed in 1812. Waldeck-Pyrmont joined the German Confederation in 1815 and the North German Confederation in 1867. The prince renounced his sovereignty on 1 October of that year and Waldeck-Pyrmont was incorporated into Prussia. However, coinage was struck into the early 20th century for Waldeck-Pyrmont as a member of the German Empire. The hereditary territorial titles were lost along with the war in 1918. Some coins were struck for issue in Pyrmont only in the 18th through 20th centuries and those are listed separately under that name.

RULERS
Friedrich, 1893-1918 (d.1946)

MINT OFFICIALS
AW - Albert Welle, mintmaster in Arolsen 1827-1840
FW, F*w, W, .W. – Friedrich Welle

MINT MARKS
A - Berlin mint, 1842-1903
B - Hannover mint, 1867

PRINCIPALITY

REFORM COINAGE

Y# 213 5 MARK
27.7770 g., 0.9000 Silver .8038 oz. ASW, 38 mm. **Ruler:** Friedrich **Obv:** Head left **Rev:** Crowned imperial eagle with shield on breast

Date	Mintage	F	VF	XF	Unc	BU
1903A	2,000	—	3,000	4,000	5,000	6,000
1903A Proof	300	Value: 8,000				

Y# 214 20 MARK
7.9650 g., 0.9000 Gold .2304 oz. AGW **Ruler:** Friedrich **Obv:** Head left **Rev:** Crowned imperial eagle with shield on breast

Date	Mintage	F	VF	XF	Unc	BU
1903A	2,000	2,400	4,000	5,800	8,000	10,000
1903A Proof	150	Value: 12,000				

WURTTEMBERG

Located in South Germany, between Baden and Bavaria, Württemberg takes its name from the ancestral castle of the ruling dynasty. The early countship was located in the old duchy of Swabia, most of which was given to Count Ulrich II (1265-79) in 1268 by Conradin von Hohenstaufen. Ulrich's son, Eberhard II (1279-1325) moved the seat of his rule to Stuttgart. Württemberg obtained the mint right in 1374 and joined the Swabian monetary union two years later. The countship was divided into the lines of Württemberg-Urach and Württemberg-Stuttgart in 1441 and the elder Urach branch was raised to the rank of duke in 1495. It became extinct in the following year and the younger line in Württemberg-Stuttgart inherited the lands and ducal title. A cadet line of the family had been established in Mömpelgard in 1473 and, when the Württemberg-Stuttgart line fell extinct in 1593, the primacy of the dynasty fell to Württemberg-Mömpelgard. The latter took the Stuttgart title and spun off several cadet branches in Neustadt, Neuenburg and Weiltingen-Brenz. Meanwhile, the duke in Stuttgart succumbed to the French advances under Napoleon. Land west of the Rhine was exchanged with France for territories in and around Reutlingen, Heilbronn and seven other towns in 1802. More territories were added in Swabia at the expense of Austria in 1805. Napoleon elevated the duke to the status of elector in 1803 and then to king in 1806. Even more land was given to Württemberg that year, doubling the kingdom's size, and it joined the Confederation of the Rhine. At the close of the Napoleonic Wars (1792-1815), Württemberg joined the German Confederation, but sided with Austria in its war with Prussia in 1866. It sided with Prussia against France in 1870 and became a member of the German Empire in 1871. King Wilhelm II was forced to abdicate at the end of World War I in 1918.

RULERS
Wilhelm II, 1891-1918

MINT MARKS
C, CT - Christophstal Mint
F - Freudenstadt Mint
S - Stuttgart Mint
T - Tübingen Mint

KINGDOM

REFORM COINAGE

KM# 631 2 MARK
11.1110 g., 0.9000 Silver .3215 oz. ASW, 28 mm. **Ruler:** Wilhelm II **Obv:** Head right **Rev:** Crowned imperial eagle with shield on breast

Date	Mintage	F	VF	XF	Unc	BU
1901F	592,000	9.00	19.00	45.00	125	175
1902F	816,000	8.00	17.00	45.00	125	175
1903F	811,000	9.00	19.00	45.00	125	175
1904F	1,988,000	8.00	15.00	35.00	100	140
1905F	250,000	9.00	20.00	40.00	100	180
1906F	1,505,000	9.00	20.00	40.00	100	150
1907F	1,504,000	8.00	15.00	35.00	100	140
1908F	451,000	8.00	22.00	45.00	125	185
1912F	251,000	8.00	15.00	35.00	100	160
1913F	226,000	8.00	17.00	45.00	125	185
1914F	318,000	8.00	17.00	40.00	100	140
(1901-1914) Proof	—	Value: 250				

KM# 635 3 MARK
16.6670 g., 0.9000 Silver .4823 oz. ASW, 33 mm. **Ruler:** Wilhelm II **Obv:** Head right **Rev:** Crowned imperial eagle with shield on breast

Date	Mintage	F	VF	XF	Unc	BU
1908F	300,000	10.00	20.00	30.00	70.00	110
1909F	1,907,000	10.00	20.00	30.00	65.00	100
1910F	837,000	10.00	20.00	30.00	65.00	100
1911F	425,000	10.00	20.00	30.00	65.00	100
1912F	849,000	10.00	17.50	25.00	60.00	100
1913F	267,000	10.00	20.00	30.00	75.00	115
1914F	733,000	10.00	17.50	25.00	60.00	90.00
(1908-1914)F Proof	—	Value: 250				

KM# 636 3 MARK
16.6670 g., 0.9000 Silver .4823 oz. ASW, 33 mm. **Ruler:** Wilhelm II **Subject:** Silver Wedding Anniversary **Obv:** Conjoined heads right, normal bar in "H" of "CHARLOTTE" **Rev:** Crowned imperial eagle with shield on breast

Date	Mintage	F	VF	XF	Unc	BU
1911F	493,000	12.00	18.00	35.00	60.00	80.00
1911F Proof	—	Value: 125				

KM# 637 3 MARK
16.6670 g., 0.9000 Silver .4823 oz. ASW, 33 mm. **Ruler:** Wilhelm II **Subject:** Silver Wedding Anniversary **Obv:** High bar in "H" of "CHARLOTTE" **Rev:** Crowned imperial eagle with shield on breast

Date	Mintage	F	VF	XF	Unc	BU
1911F	7,000	125	275	475	650	800
1911F Proof	—	Value: 1,100				

KM# 638 3 MARK
16.6670 g., 0.9000 Silver .4823 oz. ASW, 33 mm. **Ruler:** Wilhelm II **Subject:** 25th Year of Reign **Obv:** Head right **Rev:** Crowned imperial eagle with shield on breast **Note:** 5,650 were melted.

Date	Mintage	F	VF	XF	Unc	BU
1916F Proof	1,000	Value: 8,500				

KM# 632 5 MARK
27.7770 g., 0.9000 Silver .8038 oz. ASW, 38 mm. **Ruler:** Wilhelm II **Obv:** Head right **Rev:** Crowned imperial eagle with shield on breast

Date	Mintage	F	VF	XF	Unc	BU
1901F	211,000	15.00	35.00	90.00	600	1,100
1902F	361,000	15.00	35.00	90.00	400	600
1903F	722,000	15.00	30.00	75.00	375	550
1904F	391,000	15.00	30.00	75.00	375	550
1906F	64,000	25.00	65.00	200	1,200	1,750
1906F Proof	50	Value: 1,500				
1907F	417,000	15.00	30.00	65.00	300	450
1908F	532,000	15.00	30.00	55.00	250	350
1913F	401,000	15.00	30.00	50.00	200	225
(1901-1913)F Proof	—	Value: 700				

KM# 633 10 MARK
3.9820 g., 0.9000 Gold .1152 oz. AGW **Ruler:** Wilhelm II **Obv:** Head right **Rev:** Crowned imperial eagle with shield on breast

Date	Mintage	F	VF	XF	Unc	BU
1901F	110,000	80.00	135	175	300	350
1902F	50,000	125	150	200	400	500
1903F	180,000	80.00	120	175	300	350
1903F Proof	—	Value: 1,200				
1904F	350,000	80.00	125	175	300	350
1904F Proof	—	Value: 1,200				
1905F	200,000	80.00	125	175	300	350
1905F Proof	—	Value: 1,200				
1906F	100,000	80.00	125	175	300	350
1906F Proof	50	Value: 1,200				
1907F	150,000	80.00	125	175	300	350
1907F Proof	—	Value: 1,200				
1909F	100,000	80.00	125	175	300	350
1909F Proof	—	Value: 1,200				
1910F	150,000	80.00	125	175	300	350
1910F Proof	—	Value: 1,200				
1911F	50,000	140	275	425	650	700
1911F Proof	—	Value: 1,200				
1912F	49,000	140	275	375	600	700
1912F Proof	—	Value: 1,500				
1913F	50,000	140	275	375	600	700
1913F Proof	—	Value: 1,500				

KM# 634 20 MARK
7.9650 g., 0.9000 Gold .2304 oz. AGW **Ruler:** Wilhelm II **Obv:** Head right **Rev:** Crowned imperial eagle with shield on breast

Date	Mintage	F	VF	XF	Unc	BU
1905F	506,000	—	BV	200	250	300
1905F Proof	—	Value: 1,200				
1913F	43,000	5,000	12,500	25,000	35,000	—
1913F Proof	—	Value: 50,000				
1914F	558,000	1,750	3,250	4,750	8,000	10,000
1914F Proof	—	Value: 10,000				

PATTERNS

Including off metal strikes

KM#	Date	Mintage	Identification	Mkt Val
Pn42	19xxF	—	5 Mark. Copper. Lettered edge.	—
Pn43	1904	—	5 Mark. Silver.	—
Pn44	1904F	—	5 Mark. Copper. Y222. Eagle within irregular inner circle, countermarked "N.A.".	—
Pn45	1905	—	5 Mark. Silver.	—
Pn46	1905	—	5 Mark. Silver. Beaded rim.	—
Pn47	1905F	—	5 Mark. Silver. Lettered edge.	—
Pn48	1905F	—	5 Mark. Silver. Reeded edge.	—
Pn49	1910F	—	3 Mark. Silver. Irregular "LH" under neck. Y225a.	—
Pn50	1911	—	3 Mark. Silver.	—
Pn51	1911	—	3 Mark. Silver. Busts divide date.	—
Pn52	1911F	—	3 Mark. Aluminum.	—
PnA53	1911F	—	3 Mark. Iron. Aluminum-plated.	—
Pn53	1911F	—	3 Mark. Silver.	—
Pn54	1911F	—	3 Mark. Silver.	—
Pn55	1911F	—	3 Mark. Copper.	—
Pn56	1911F	—	3 Mark. Silver.	—
Pn57	1911F	—	3 Mark. Copper.	—
Pn58	1911F	—	3 Mark. Silver.	—
Pn59	1911F	—	3 Mark. Copper.	—
Pn60	1913F	—	2 Mark. Aluminum.	—
Pn61	1913	—	5 Mark. Nickel.	—
Pn62	1916F	—	3 Mark. Aluminum.	—
Pn63	1916F	—	3 Mark. Silver.	—

TRIAL STRIKES

KM#	Date	Mintage	Identification	Mkt Val
TS3	1905	—	3 Mark. Silver. Uniface.	—
TS4	19xx	—	5 Mark. Silver. Uniface.	200

1871-1918

Germany, a nation of north-central Europe which from1871 to 1945 was, successively, an empire, a republic and a totalitarian state, attained its territorial peak as an empire when it comprised a 208,780 sq. mi. (540,740 sq. km.) homeland and an overseas colonial empire.

As the power of the Roman Empire waned, several war-like tribes residing in northern Germany moved south and west, invading France, Belgium, England, Italy and Spain. In 800 A.D. the Frankish king Charlemagne, who ruled most of France and Germany, was crowned Emperor of the Holy Roman Empire, a loose federation of an estimated 1,800 German States that lasted until 1806. Modern Germany was formed from the eastern part of Charlemagne's empire.

After 1812, the German States were reduced to a federation of 32, of which Prussia was the strongest. In 1871, Prussian chancellor Otto von Bismarck united the German States into an empire ruled by William I, the Prussian king. The empire initiated a colonial endeavor and became one of the world's greatest powers. Germany disintegrated as a result of World War I.

It was reestablished as the Weimar Republic. The humiliation of defeat, economic depression, poverty and discontent gave rise to Adolf Hitler, 1933, who reconstituted Germany as the Third Reich and after initial diplomatic and military triumphs, expanded his goals beyond Europe into Africa and USSR which led it into final disaster in World War II, ending on VE Day, May 7, 1945.

RULERS

Wilhelm II, 1888-1918

MINT MARKS

A - Berlin
D - Munich
E - Muldenhutten (1887-1953)
F - Stuttgart
G - Karlsruhe
J - Hamburg

MONETARY SYSTEM

(Until 1923)
100 Pfennig = 1 Mark

(Commencing 1945)
100 Pfennig = 1 Mark

EMPIRE

STANDARD COINAGE

KM# 10 PFENNIG

Copper **Ruler:** Wilhelm II **Obv:** Denomination, date at right **Rev:** Crowned imperial eagle with shield on breast **Note:** Struck from 1890-1916.

Date	Mintage	F	VF	XF	Unc	BU
1901A	21,045,000	0.20	1.25	4.00	22.00	25.00
1901D	5,337,000	0.50	2.00	9.00	40.00	45.00
1901E	1,397,000	1.00	6.00	27.50	80.00	100
1901F	2,925,000	0.60	4.00	17.50	60.00	80.00
1901G	1,977,000	2.50	9.00	32.50	110	130
1901J	2,011,000	4.00	12.50	40.00	180	225
1902A	7,474,000	0.50	2.00	4.00	25.00	30.00
1902D	2,811,000	0.60	3.50	6.00	40.00	45.00
1902E	1,183,000	1.00	6.00	25.00	110	130
1902F	1,250,000	1.00	6.00	20.00	100	120
1902G	881,000	4.00	22.50	60.00	200	230
1902J	150	475	1,600	2,200	5,000	6,000
1903A	12,690,000	0.20	1.00	4.00	30.00	35.00
1903D	3,140,000	0.80	2.00	8.00	40.00	50.00
1903E	1,956,000	1.50	3.00	10.00	50.00	60.00
1903F	2,945,000	0.80	2.00	10.00	45.00	55.00
1903G	1,377,000	3.00	6.00	25.00	100	125
1903J	2,832,000	1.00	4.00	20.00	60.00	80.00
1904A	28,625,000	0.20	1.00	3.00	25.00	30.00
1904D	4,118,000	0.80	2.00	8.00	40.00	45.00
1904E	2,778,000	1.00	3.00	9.00	40.00	50.00
1904F	4,520,000	1.00	3.00	8.00	40.00	50.00
1904G	3,232,000	2.00	6.00	18.00	80.00	90.00
1904J	4,467,000	1.00	2.50	10.00	40.00	50.00
1905A	19,631,000	0.20	1.00	3.50	18.00	22.00
1905D	6,084,000	0.50	2.00	5.50	30.00	35.00
1905E	3,564,000	0.50	2.00	5.50	30.00	35.00
1905E	Inc. above	—	—	2,500	—	—
Note: Cross under denomination						
1905F	4,153,000	0.80	3.00	6.50	40.00	45.00
1905G	3,051,000	0.80	3.00	18.00	70.00	80.00
1905J	4,085,000	1.00	5.00	12.00	55.00	65.00
1906A	46,921,000	0.20	0.80	2.50	18.00	20.00
1906D	5,633,000	0.20	0.80	5.00	30.00	35.00
1906E	7,278,000	0.20	0.80	5.00	20.00	25.00
1906F	7,173,000	0.20	0.80	5.00	25.00	30.00
1906G	5,194,000	0.20	0.80	5.00	40.00	45.00
1906J	3,622,000	0.20	1.00	6.00	45.00	55.00
1907A	33,711,000	0.20	0.80	1.50	14.00	16.00
1907D	14,691,000	0.20	1.00	2.00	20.00	23.00
1907E	3,719,000	0.20	1.50	5.00	20.00	25.00
1907F	7,026,000	0.20	1.00	3.00	20.00	23.00
1907G	3,052,000	0.20	1.50	6.00	30.00	35.00
1907J	6,722,000	0.20	1.50	6.00	20.00	25.00
1908A	21,922,000	0.20	0.60	1.25	12.00	15.00
1908D	10,629,000	0.20	0.80	2.25	20.00	23.00
1908E	3,400,000	0.20	1.50	5.00	22.00	26.00
1908F	6,112,000	0.20	1.50	5.00	22.00	26.00
1908G	3,663,000	0.20	2.00	6.00	40.00	45.00
1908J	5,581,000	0.20	1.50	5.00	22.00	26.00
1909A	21,430,000	0.20	0.75	3.00	20.00	23.00
1909D	2,814,000	0.20	1.25	7.00	55.00	65.00
1909E	2,562,000	1.00	3.00	8.00	45.00	50.00
1909F	2,425,000	1.50	4.00	10.00	50.00	60.00
1909G	1,220,000	1.50	5.00	12.00	80.00	90.00
1909J	1,634,000	1.50	5.00	11.00	80.00	90.00
1910A	10,761,000	0.20	0.75	2.50	15.00	18.00
1910D	4,221,000	0.20	1.00	3.00	20.00	24.00
1910E	1,600,000	0.50	3.00	5.00	38.00	42.00
1910F	3,009,000	0.30	2.00	6.00	30.00	35.00
1910G	1,834,000	0.50	3.00	16.00	85.00	95.00
1910J	2,450,000	0.50	3.00	9.00	60.00	70.00
1911A	38,172,000	0.20	0.75	2.00	14.00	16.00
1911D	8,657,000	0.20	1.00	3.00	20.00	23.00
1911E	5,236,000	0.20	1.00	3.00	20.00	23.00
1911F	5,780,000	0.20	1.00	3.00	20.00	23.00
1911G	2,075,000	0.20	1.50	5.00	35.00	40.00
1911J	5,594,000	0.20	1.00	3.00	15.00	18.00
1912A	42,693,000	0.10	0.75	1.50	10.00	13.00
1912D	10,173,000	0.10	0.80	2.00	12.00	15.00
1912E	5,689,000	0.10	0.80	2.50	13.00	16.00
1912F	7,441,000	0.10	0.80	3.00	13.00	16.00
1912G	5,526,000	0.10	0.80	3.00	15.00	20.00
1912J	5,615,000	0.10	0.80	3.00	25.00	30.00
1913A	32,671,000	0.10	0.50	2.00	10.00	13.00
1913D	8,161,000	0.20	1.00	3.00	12.00	15.00
1913E	2,258,000	1.00	2.00	4.00	20.00	23.00
1913F	6,620,000	0.20	1.00	3.00	14.00	16.00
1913G	3,209,000	0.20	1.00	2.00	25.00	30.00
1913J	1,456,000	0.10	5.00	11.00	45.00	50.00
1914A	9,976,000	0.20	0.80	2.00	8.00	10.00
1914D	1,842,000	0.20	1.25	2.50	14.00	17.00
1914E	2,926,000	0.30	2.00	3.00	15.00	18.00
1914F	3,316,000	0.20	1.00	2.00	15.00	18.00
1914G	2,100,000	0.20	1.75	2.50	15.00	18.00
1914J	4,368,000	0.20	1.75	2.50	15.00	18.00
1915A	14,738,000	0.10	0.75	1.50	8.00	10.00
1915D	1,771,000	0.20	1.00	2.50	20.00	22.00
1915E	2,779,000	0.20	1.00	3.50	20.00	22.00
1915F	1,411,000	0.20	1.00	4.00	25.00	30.00
1915G	2,041,000	0.20	1.00	4.00	25.00	30.00
1915J	2,981,000	0.20	1.00	4.00	20.00	25.00
1916A	5,960,000	0.20	0.75	2.50	10.00	12.00
1916D	5,401,000	0.20	1.00	4.00	25.00	30.00
1916E	818,000	1.00	6.00	8.00	35.00	40.00
1916F	1,104,000	0.80	3.00	8.00	35.00	40.00
1916G	671,000	1.50	6.00	20.00	60.00	70.00
1916J	898,000	1.00	5.00	10.00	50.00	55.00
1901-16 Common date proof	—	Value: 100				

KM# 24 PFENNIG

Aluminum **Ruler:** Wilhelm II **Obv:** Denomination, date at right **Rev:** Crowned imperial eagle with shield on breast

Date	Mintage	F	VF	XF	Unc	BU
1916G	—	—	260	380	8,000	1,000
1917A	27,159,000	0.15	0.75	2.00	6.00	8.00
1917A Proof	—	Value: 90.00				
1917D	6,940,000	0.15	0.75	2.50	10.00	12.00
1917E	3,862,000	0.50	2.00	5.00	15.00	18.00
1917E Proof	—	Value: 90.00				
1917F	5,125,000	0.25	2.00	3.00	10.00	12.00
1917G	3,139,000	0.25	2.00	4.00	10.00	13.00
1917G Proof	—	Value: 90.00				
1917J	4,182,000	0.50	2.50	3.00	24.00	28.00
1917J Proof	—	Value: 90.00				
1918A	—	—	2,000	3,000	4,000	5,000
1918D	318,000	10.00	20.00	45.00	100	125
1918F	—	—	2,500	4,000	—	—
Note: The 1918F 1 Pfennigs are from the burned-out ruins of the Stuttgart Mint destroyed in World War II						
1916-18 Common date proof	—	Value: 90.00				

KM# 16 2 PFENNIG

Copper **Ruler:** Wilhelm II **Obv:** Denomination, date at right **Rev:** Crowned imperial eagle with shield on breast

Date	Mintage	F	VF	XF	Unc	BU
1904A	5,414,000	0.20	1.00	5.00	25.00	30.00
1904D	1,404,000	0.50	2.00	10.00	30.00	35.00
1904E	744,000	2.00	6.00	16.00	70.00	80.00
1904F	1,002,000	0.20	3.50	12.00	45.00	55.00
1904G	495,000	3.00	7.00	28.00	140	160
1904J	44,000	2.00	11.00	25.00	180	200
1905A	5,172,000	0.10	0.50	2.50	20.00	22.00
1905D	1,570,000	0.20	2.00	10.00	30.00	35.00
1905E	924,000	0.40	3.50	12.00	55.00	65.00
1905F	1,115,000	0.40	3.00	10.00	60.00	70.00
1905G	1,030,000	0.40	3.50	16.00	80.00	100
1905J	1,609,000	0.40	3.00	12.00	90.00	100
1906A	8,459,000	0.20	1.00	5.00	30.00	35.00
1906D	3,539,000	0.20	1.75	6.00	35.00	40.00
1906E	2,055,000	0.20	1.50	7.50	40.00	45.00
1906F	2,840,000	0.20	1.50	6.50	35.00	40.00
1906G	1,527,000	0.40	2.00	12.00	80.00	90.00
1906J	1,908,000	0.40	2.00	12.00	60.00	70.00
1907A	13,468,000	0.10	0.50	3.00	16.00	20.00
1907D	1,921,000	0.20	0.75	4.50	28.00	30.00
1907E	744,000	0.50	2.50	8.00	55.00	65.00
1907F	1,059,000	0.20	2.50	12.00	70.00	80.00
1907G	610,000	0.50	3.00	12.00	70.00	80.00
1907J	952,000	0.20	2.50	10.00	60.00	65.00
1908A	5,421,000	0.10	1.00	4.00	20.00	25.00
1908D	1,407,000	0.10	2.00	7.00	25.00	30.00
1908E	745,000	1.00	3.00	10.00	50.00	55.00
1908F	1,003,000	0.10	3.00	10.00	50.00	55.00
1908G	610,000	0.25	4.00	14.00	70.00	80.00
1908J	817,000	0.10	3.00	12.00	60.00	70.00
1910A	5,421,000	0.20	1.00	5.00	18.00	22.00
1910D	1,407,000	0.50	2.00	8.00	30.00	35.00
1910E	745,000	1.00	4.50	10.00	55.00	60.00
1910F	1,003,000	0.40	2.00	8.00	50.00	55.00
1910G	517,000	0.40	3.00	15.00	90.00	110
1910J	568,000	0.40	3.00	15.00	80.00	90.00
1911A	8,187,000	0.20	1.00	3.00	17.00	20.00
1911D	2,100,000	0.20	2.00	4.00	22.00	26.00
1911E	1,133,000	0.50	3.00	5.00	26.00	30.00
1911F	1,490,000	0.40	2.00	4.00	22.00	26.00
1911G	1,313,000	0.40	2.00	6.00	30.00	35.00
1911J	1,883,000	0.40	2.00	4.00	22.00	26.00
1912A	13,580,000	0.20	0.75	3.00	18.00	20.00
1912D	3,109,000	0.30	1.00	4.00	22.00	26.00
1912E	1,808,000	0.30	2.00	5.00	22.00	26.00
1912F	2,366,000	0.30	1.00	6.00	22.00	26.00
1912G	1,395,000	0.50	2.50	7.50	50.00	60.00
1912J	1,605,000	0.50	2.00	6.00	30.00	35.00
1913A	4,212,000	0.20	0.75	3.00	16.00	18.00
1913D	2,525,000	0.20	1.00	6.00	24.00	28.00
1913E	413,000	0.50	3.00	12.00	65.00	75.00
1913F	1,602,000	0.40	2.00	12.00	60.00	70.00
1913G	741,000	1.50	9.00	13.00	70.00	80.00
1913J	1,254,000	0.40	2.00	9.00	60.00	70.00
1914A	5,350,000	0.10	1.00	3.00	14.00	16.00
1914E	1,201,000	1.00	5.00	8.00	40.00	45.00
1914F	158,000	12.00	45.00	90.00	300	325
1914G	610,000	2.00	9.00	25.00	120	140
1914J	817,000	0.10	6.00	17.00	70.00	80.00
1915A	3,897,000	0.40	1.00	3.00	12.00	15.00
1915D	1,407,000	0.40	2.00	6.00	20.00	25.00
1915E	288,000	3.00	15.00	28.00	50.00	60.00
1915F	904,000	0.20	2.00	7.00	25.00	30.00
1916A	3,524,000	0.20	1.00	3.00	12.00	14.00
1916D	915,000	0.40	1.50	8.00	18.00	22.00
1916E	484,000	1.00	3.50	10.00	32.00	36.00
1916F	651,000	0.25	1.50	5.00	20.00	25.00
1916G	397,000	1.00	3.50	14.00	50.00	60.00
1916J	531,000	0.50	2.50	12.00	40.00	50.00
1904-16 Common date proof	—	Value: 150				

KM# 11 5 PFENNIG

Copper-Nickel **Ruler:** Wilhelm II **Obv:** Denomination, date at right **Rev:** Crowned imperial eagle with shield on breast **Note:** Struck from 1890-1915.

Date	Mintage	F	VF	XF	Unc	BU
1901A	8,155,000	0.20	0.60	5.00	40.00	50.00
1901D	2,779,000	0.20	1.50	12.00	75.00	85.00
1901E	1,492,000	0.40	2.50	12.00	100	120
1901F	1,810,000	0.40	2.50	10.00	90.00	110
1901G	915,000	0.50	3.50	35.00	300	350
1901J	1,226,000	0.50	3.50	25.00	150	170
1902A	8,949,000	0.20	0.75	5.00	40.00	50.00
1902D	2,812,000	0.40	2.50	12.00	90.00	110
1902E	1,120,000	1.00	3.50	12.00	70.00	80.00
1902F	1,800,000	1.00	3.00	11.00	60.00	70.00
1902G	1,220,000	1.50	6.00	25.00	150	170
1902J	1,636,000	1.50	6.00	20.00	130	150
1903A	5,932,000	0.20	4.00	6.00	70.00	80.00
1903D	1,406,000	0.60	2.00	15.00	100	120
1903E	1,114,000	0.80	3.50	18.00	80.00	100
1903F	1,209,000	1.00	4.00	20.00	175	225
1903G	610,000	2.00	9.00	55.00	275	300
1903J	817,000	1.00	6.00	45.00	225	250
1904A	6,791,000	0.20	6.00	10.00	65.00	75.00
1904D	1,408,000	1.00	2.50	15.00	80.00	100
1904E	746,000	1.50	6.00	20.00	130	150
1904F	1,006,000	1.00	3.50	20.00	100	120
1904G	610,000	2.00	8.00	25.00	300	350
1904J	818,000	1.00	5.00	28.00	200	225
1905A	8,129,000	0.20	0.75	2.50	35.00	45.00
1905D	2,109,000	0.20	1.00	6.00	80.00	90.00
1905E	1,117,000	0.40	1.75	7.00	60.00	70.00
1905F	1,505,000	0.20	1.00	6.00	70.00	80.00
1905G	915,000	1.00	3.00	16.00	130	145
1905J	1,226,000	0.60	2.50	12.00	120	135
1906A	18,970,000	0.20	0.75	2.00	25.00	35.00
1906D	4,922,000	0.20	1.00	5.00	40.00	50.00
1906E	2,605,000	0.20	1.25	5.00	45.00	55.00
1906F	3,512,000	0.20	1.00	5.00	50.00	60.00
1906G	2,136,000	0.50	2.00	15.00	130	150
1906J	2,859,000	0.20	1.75	13.00	130	150
1907A	11,930,000	0.20	0.75	2.25	20.00	25.00
1907D	2,113,000	0.20	1.00	5.00	40.00	50.00
1907E	1,517,000	0.30	1.75	5.00	40.00	50.00
1907F	1,845,000	0.30	1.75	5.00	40.00	45.00
1907G	915,000	1.00	2.50	6.00	60.00	80.00
1907J	1,636,000	0.50	2.00	5.00	45.00	50.00
1908A	22,114,000	0.20	0.50	2.50	18.00	20.00
1908D	4,991,000	0.20	1.00	3.00	20.00	25.00
1908E	2,919,000	0.30	1.50	5.00	35.00	40.00
1908/7F	5,124,000	30.00	60.00	80.00	125	150
1908F	Inc. above	0.50	1.50	5.00	40.00	50.00
1908G	3,357,000	0.50	2.00	8.00	70.00	80.00
1908J	3,264,000	0.50	2.00	10.00	110	130
1909A	5,797,000	0.40	1.50	9.00	60.00	70.00
1909D	2,753,000	0.60	2.50	14.00	110	130
1909E	984,000	1.50	4.50	18.00	120	140
1909F	252,000	2.00	18.00	50.00	250	300
1909/8J	1,632,000	1.00	5.00	5.00	45.00	50.00
1909J	Inc. above	1.00	9.00	28.00	170	190
1910A	7,344,000	0.20	0.50	3.00	25.00	30.00
1910D	2,814,000	0.20	0.80	6.00	40.00	50.00
1910E	1,290,000	0.20	1.00	9.00	60.00	70.00
1910F	1,721,000	0.20	1.50	11.00	65.00	75.00
1910G	1,222,000	0.30	1.75	20.00	120	130
1910J	152,000	30.00	42.50	70.00	150	175
1911A	15,660,000	0.20	0.50	1.50	10.00	12.00
1911D	2,221,000	0.20	1.00	2.50	15.00	18.00
1911E	1,770,000	0.40	2.00	3.00	15.00	18.00
1911F	2,714,000	0.40	2.00	3.00	15.00	18.00
1911G	1,833,000	0.40	1.00	2.50	15.00	18.00
1911J	3,116,000	0.20	1.00	2.00	18.00	22.00
1912A	19,320,000	0.20	0.80	2.00	12.00	15.00
1912D	4,015,000	0.20	0.80	2.50	16.00	18.00
1912E	2,568,000	0.20	1.00	2.50	20.00	25.00
1912F	3,679,000	0.20	1.00	2.50	22.00	25.00
1912G	2,440,000	0.20	1.00	3.00	30.00	35.00
1912J	3,020,000	0.20	1.00	2.50	20.00	25.00
1913A	15,506,000	0.20	0.50	1.50	12.00	15.00
1913D	5,519,000	0.20	0.50	2.00	15.00	18.00
1913E	2,373,000	0.50	2.00	3.00	17.00	20.00
1913F	2,054,000	0.50	2.00	3.00	17.00	20.00
1913G	1,221,000	1.00	5.00	9.00	70.00	80.00
1913J	253,000	10.00	16.00	35.00	160	180
1914A	23,605,000	0.20	0.50	1.00	9.00	10.00
1914D	3,014,000	0.20	0.80	1.50	12.00	15.00
1914E	1,710,000	0.20	1.00	3.50	12.00	15.00
1914F	2,206,000	0.20	1.00	2.50	18.00	22.00
1914G	1,218,000	0.20	1.00	3.00	20.00	25.00
1914J	3,235,000	0.20	1.00	2.50	20.00	25.00
1915D	3,516,000	0.10	1.00	2.00	18.00	22.00
1915E	834,000	1.00	8.00	13.00	60.00	70.00
1915F	1,894,000	0.10	2.00	5.00	35.00	40.00
1915G	894,000	0.50	7.00	18.00	70.00	80.00
1915J	1,669,000	0.10	6.00	14.00	60.00	70.00
1901-15 Common date proof	—	Value: 120				

KM# 19 5 PFENNIG

Iron **Obv:** Denomination, date below **Rev:** Crowned imperial eagle with shield on breast

Date	Mintage	F	VF	XF	Unc	BU
1915A	34,631,000	0.20	0.50	3.00	15.00	20.00
1915D	2,021,000	2.00	7.00	13.00	60.00	70.00
1915E	4,670,000	1.00	4.00	9.00	40.00	45.00
1915F	3,500,000	0.80	3.00	6.00	35.00	40.00
1915G	3,676,000	0.80	3.00	6.00	35.00	40.00
1915J	2,100,000	1.50	6.00	12.00	50.00	60.00
1916A	51,003,000	0.20	0.50	2.50	12.00	15.00
1916D	19,590,000	0.20	0.50	3.00	18.00	22.00
1916E	2,271,000	2.00	6.00	15.00	50.00	60.00
1916F	10,479,000	0.20	0.80	5.00	25.00	30.00
1916G	5,599,000	0.50	1.50	5.50	35.00	40.00
1916J	10,253,000	0.30	1.00	4.00	30.00	35.00
1917A	87,315,000	0.10	0.30	1.50	12.00	15.00
1917D	19,581,000	0.20	1.00	2.50	14.00	17.00
1917E	11,092,000	0.50	1.00	3.00	18.00	20.00
1917F	10,930,000	0.20	0.50	3.50	20.00	22.00
1917F	—	600	1,000	1,600	2,250	2,500
Note: Mule with Polish reverse of Y#5, see Poland						
1917G	6,720,000	0.20	1.00	4.00	18.00	22.00
1917J	11,686,000	0.20	1.00	4.50	20.00	25.00
1918A	223,516,000	0.10	0.50	1.00	6.00	8.00
1918D	29,130,000	0.10	0.50	1.00	8.00	10.00
1918E	23,600,000	0.20	1.00	2.00	10.00	14.00
1918F	24,598,000	0.10	0.30	1.25	10.00	12.00
1918G	12,697,000	0.20	1.00	2.00	10.00	14.00
1918J	20,240,000	0.10	0.50	1.00	8.00	10.00
1919A	112,102,000	0.10	0.50	0.75	6.00	8.00
1919D	41,163,000	0.10	0.50	1.00	8.00	10.00
1919E	20,608,000	0.10	0.50	1.00	8.00	10.00
1919F	32,700,000	0.10	0.50	1.00	8.00	10.00
1919G	13,925,000	0.20	1.00	2.00	15.00	20.00
1919J	16,249,000	0.50	1.50	6.00	15.00	20.00
1920A	80,300,000	0.10	0.40	1.00	5.00	8.00
1920D	25,502,000	0.10	0.50	1.00	6.00	9.00
1920E	11,646,000	0.50	1.00	3.00	25.00	30.00
1920F	24,300,000	0.10	0.40	1.00	10.00	12.00
1920G	10,244,000	0.10	0.50	1.25	16.00	18.00
1920J	16,857,000	0.20	0.30	1.00	14.00	16.00
1921A	143,418,000	0.10	0.20	0.75	7.00	9.00
1921D	38,133,000	0.10	0.20	1.00	7.00	9.00
1921E	21,104,000	0.50	1.00	3.50	25.00	30.00
1921F	24,800,000	0.10	0.20	1.00	8.00	10.00
1921G	21,289,000	0.10	0.20	1.00	8.00	10.00
1921J	28,928,000	0.15	1.00	2.50	8.00	10.00
1922A Rare	89,062,000	—	—	—	—	—
1922D	31,240,000	0.10	0.20	0.50	12.00	14.00
1922E	19,156,000	0.50	1.00	8.00	20.00	25.00
1922F	16,436,000	0.10	0.20	1.00	12.00	14.00
1922G	19,708,000	0.10	0.25	1.00	8.00	10.00
1922J	16,820,000	0.10	0.20	1.25	15.00	18.00
1915-22 Common date proof	—	Value: 110				

KM# 12 10 PFENNIG

Copper-Nickel **Ruler:** Wilhelm II **Obv:** Denomination, date at right **Rev:** Crowned imperial eagle with shield on breast **Note:** Struck from 1890-1916.

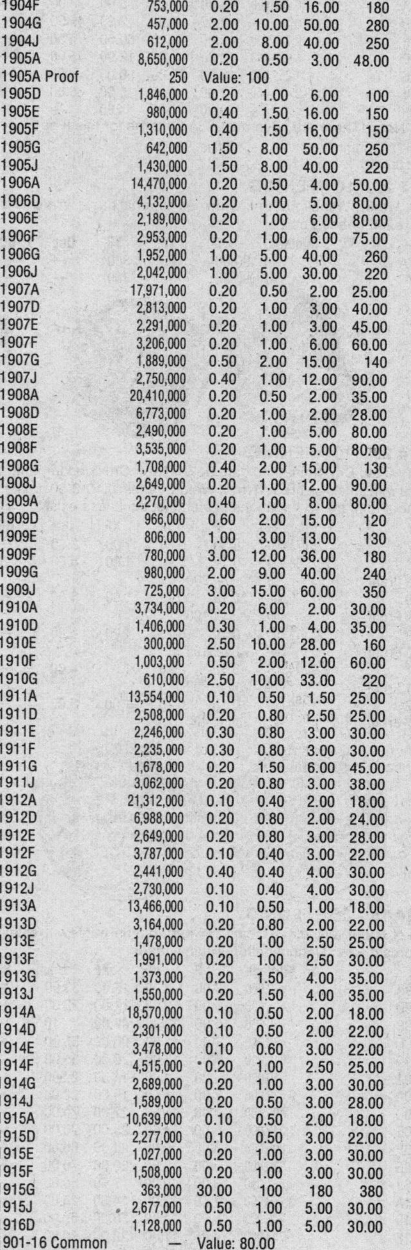

Date	Mintage	F	VF	XF	Unc	BU
1901A	10,200,000	0.20	1.00	8.00	70.00	—
1901D	3,259,000	1.00	4.00	22.00	150	—
1901E	1,863,000	1.00	5.00	20.00	170	—
1901F	2,594,000	1.00	5.00	16.00	130	—
1901G	1,527,000	2.00	17.00	60.00	280	—
1901J	1,225,000	2.00	14.00	60.00	280	—
1902A	5,878,000	0.20	1.00	4.00	60.00	—
1902D	1,406,000	0.20	1.00	15.00	120	—
1902E	502,000	1.00	5.00	45.00	280	—
1902F	1,003,000	0.20	1.00	15.00	110	—
1902G	610,000	0.20	10.00	50.00	280	—
1902J	815,000	1.50	8.00	30.00	220	—
1903A	5,131,000	0.20	0.50	5.00	90.00	—
1903D	1,406,000	0.40	1.00	15.00	150	—
1903E	988,000	0.40	1.00	15.00	120	—
1903F	1,003,000	0.50	2.00	22.00	175	—
1903G	610,000	2.00	8.00	50.00	250	—
1903J	816,000	1.50	6.00	45.00	250	—
1904A	5,189,000	0.20	0.50	4.00	70.00	—
1904D	1,056,000	0.20	1.50	14.00	140	—
1904E	559,000	0.20	1.50	14.00	130	—
1904F	753,000	0.20	1.50	16.00	180	—
1904G	457,000	2.00	10.00	50.00	280	—
1904J	612,000	2.00	8.00	40.00	250	—
1905A	8,650,000	0.20	0.50	3.00	48.00	—
1905A Proof	250	Value: 100				
1905D	1,846,000	0.20	1.00	6.00	100	—
1905E	980,000	0.40	1.50	16.00	150	—
1905F	1,310,000	0.40	1.50	16.00	150	—
1905G	642,000	1.50	8.00	50.00	250	—
1905J	1,430,000	1.50	8.00	40.00	220	—
1906A	14,470,000	0.20	0.50	4.00	50.00	—
1906D	4,132,000	0.20	1.00	5.00	80.00	—
1906E	2,189,000	0.20	1.00	6.00	80.00	—
1906F	2,953,000	0.20	1.00	6.00	75.00	—
1906G	1,952,000	1.00	5.00	40.00	260	—
1906J	2,042,000	1.00	5.00	30.00	220	—
1907A	17,971,000	0.20	0.50	2.00	25.00	—
1907D	2,813,000	0.20	1.00	3.00	40.00	—
1907E	2,291,000	0.20	1.00	3.00	45.00	—
1907F	3,206,000	0.20	1.00	6.00	60.00	—
1907G	1,889,000	0.50	2.00	15.00	140	—
1907J	2,750,000	0.40	1.00	12.00	90.00	—
1908A	20,410,000	0.20	0.50	2.00	35.00	—
1908D	6,773,000	0.20	1.00	2.00	28.00	—
1908E	2,490,000	0.20	1.00	5.00	80.00	—
1908F	3,535,000	0.20	1.00	5.00	80.00	—
1908G	1,708,000	0.40	2.00	15.00	130	—
1908J	2,649,000	0.20	1.00	12.00	90.00	—
1909A	2,270,000	0.40	1.00	8.00	80.00	—
1909D	966,000	0.60	2.00	15.00	120	—
1909E	806,000	1.00	3.00	13.00	130	—
1909F	780,000	3.00	12.00	36.00	180	—
1909G	980,000	2.00	9.00	40.00	240	—
1909J	725,000	3.00	15.00	60.00	350	—
1910A	3,734,000	0.20	6.00	2.00	30.00	—
1910D	1,406,000	0.30	1.00	4.00	35.00	—
1910E	300,000	2.50	10.00	28.00	160	—
1910F	1,003,000	0.50	2.00	12.00	60.00	—
1910G	610,000	2.50	10.00	33.00	220	—
1911A	13,554,000	0.10	0.50	1.50	25.00	—
1911D	2,508,000	0.20	0.80	2.50	25.00	—
1911E	2,246,000	0.30	0.80	3.00	30.00	—
1911F	2,235,000	0.30	0.80	3.00	30.00	—
1911G	1,678,000	0.20	1.50	6.00	45.00	—
1911J	3,062,000	0.20	0.80	3.00	38.00	—
1912A	21,312,000	0.10	0.40	2.00	18.00	—
1912D	6,988,000	0.20	0.80	2.00	24.00	—
1912E	2,649,000	0.20	0.80	3.00	28.00	—
1912F	3,787,000	0.10	0.40	3.00	22.00	—
1912G	2,441,000	0.40	0.40	4.00	30.00	—
1912J	2,730,000	0.10	0.40	4.00	30.00	—
1913A	13,466,000	0.10	0.50	1.00	18.00	—
1913D	3,164,000	0.20	0.80	2.00	22.00	—
1913E	1,478,000	0.20	1.00	2.50	25.00	—
1913F	1,991,000	0.20	1.00	2.50	30.00	—
1913G	1,373,000	0.20	1.50	4.00	35.00	—
1913J	1,550,000	0.20	1.50	4.00	35.00	—
1914A	18,570,000	0.10	0.50	2.00	18.00	—
1914D	2,301,000	0.10	0.50	2.00	22.00	—
1914E	3,478,000	0.10	0.60	3.00	22.00	—
1914F	4,515,000	0.20	1.00	2.50	25.00	—
1914G	2,689,000	0.20	1.00	3.00	30.00	—
1914J	1,589,000	0.20	0.50	3.00	28.00	—
1915A	10,639,000	0.10	0.50	2.00	18.00	—
1915D	2,277,000	0.10	0.50	3.00	22.00	—
1915E	1,027,000	0.20	1.00	3.00	30.00	—
1915F	1,508,000	0.20	1.00	3.00	30.00	—
1915G	363,000	30.00	100	180	380	—
1915J	2,677,000	0.50	1.00	5.00	30.00	—
1916D	1,128,000	0.50	1.00	5.00	30.00	—
1901-16 Common date proof	—	Value: 80.00				

KM# 20 10 PFENNIG

Iron **Obv:** Denomination, date below **Rev:** Crowned imperial eagle with shield on breast, beaded border

Date	Mintage	F	VF	XF	Unc	BU
1916A	69,143,000	0.20	0.60	1.50	8.00	—
1916D	11,609,000	0.20	0.60	1.50	12.00	—
1916E	8,280,000	0.30	1.00	2.50	12.00	—
1916F	7,473,000	0.30	2.00	4.50	15.00	—
1916G	5,878,000	0.30	2.00	4.50	18.00	—
1916J	11,683,000	0.30	1.00	2.50	15.00	—
1916 Rare	—	180	220	—	—	—
1917A	53,198,000	0.20	0.60	1.50	4.00	—
1917D	16,370,000	0.20	0.60	1.50	5.00	—
1917E	9,182,000	0.30	1.00	3.00	7.00	—
1917F	11,341,000	0.20	1.50	3.00	7.00	—
1917F	—	—	—	—	—	—
Note: Mule with Polish reverse of Y#6, see Poland						
1917G	7,088,000	0.30	1.50	8.00	25.00	—
1917J	9,205,000	0.30	1.00	8.00	25.00	—

Date	Mintage	F	VF	XF	Unc	BU
1918D	42,000	0.50	1,250	2,400	—	—
1921A	16,265,000	0.80	3.00	8.00	33.00	—
1922D	—	2.00	6.00	12.00	45.00	—
1922E	2,235,000	10.00	30.00	60.00	200	—
1922F	1,928,000	2.00	6.00	12.00	45.00	—
1922G	1,358,000	10.00	30.00	60.00	200	—
1922J	2,420,000	2.00	6.00	15.00	60.00	—
1922	—	40.00	130	200	—	—

Note: There are several 1915A patterns for this type

Date	Mintage	F	VF	XF	Unc	BU
1916-22 Common date proof	—	Value: 95.00				

KM# 25 10 PFENNIG

Zinc **Ruler:** Wilhelm II **Rev:** Crowned imperial eagle with shield on breast, beaded border

Date	Mintage	F	VF	XF	Unc	BU
1917A	—	90.00	180	380	—	—
1917	—	90.00	180	380	—	—

KM# 26 10 PFENNIG

Zinc **Obv:** Denomination, date below **Rev:** Crowned imperial eagle with shield on breast **Note:** Weight varies: 3.10-3.60 grams. Without mint mark. Variations in planchet thickness exist.

Date	Mintage	F	VF	XF	Unc	BU
1917	75,073,000	0.10	0.20	1.00	8.00	—
1918	202,008,000	0.10	0.20	1.00	8.00	—
1918 Proof	28	Value: 300				
1919	147,800,000	0.10	0.20	1.00	8.00	—
1919 Proof	50	Value: 100				
1920	223,019,000	0.10	0.20	1.00	6.00	—
1920 Proof	40	Value: 100				
1921	319,334,000	0.10	0.20	1.00	4.00	—
1921 Proof	24	Value: 300				
1922	274,499,000	0.10	0.20	1.00	8.00	—
1922 Proof	12	Value: 400				

KM# 18 25 PFENNIG

Nickel **Ruler:** Wilhelm II **Obv:** Crowned imperial eagle with shield on breast **Rev:** Denomination within wreath

Date	Mintage	F	VF	XF	Unc	BU
1909A	962,000	3.00	9.00	15.00	33.00	—
1909D	1,406,000	3.00	9.00	12.00	22.00	—
1909E	250,000	15.00	33.00	48.00	110	—
1909F	400,000	3.00	11.00	20.00	55.00	—
1909G	610,000	5.00	13.00	20.00	55.00	—
1909J	10,000	100	220	500	1,000	2,500
1910A	9,522,000	2.00	6.00	10.00	22.00	—
1910D	1,408,000	4.00	11.00	22.00	70.00	—
1910E	1,242,000	5.00	14.00	23.00	70.00	—
1910F	1,605,000	3.00	9.00	20.00	60.00	—
1910G	330,000	3.00	9.00	20.00	70.00	—
1910J	1,561,000	3.00	9.00	17.00	50.00	—
1911A	3,179,000	2.50	8.00	14.00	25.00	—
1911D	506,000	5.00	14.00	28.00	60.00	—
1911E	747,000	4.00	11.00	22.00	70.00	—
1911G	892,000	4.00	11.00	22.00	70.00	—
1911J	516,000	6.00	11.00	26.00	80.00	—
1912A	2,590,000	3.00	9.00	12.00	35.00	—
1912D	900,000	4.50	12.00	15.00	45.00	—
1912F	1,003,000	4.50	12.00	15.00	45.00	—
1912J	362,000	12.50	25.00	35.00	90.00	—
1909-12 Common date proof	—	Value: 175				

KM# 15 50 PFENNIG

2.7770 g., 0.9000 Silver .0803 oz. ASW **Ruler:** Wilhelm II **Obv:** Denomination within wreath **Rev:** Crowned imperial eagle with shield on breast within wreath

Date	Mintage	F	VF	XF	Unc	BU
1901A	194,000	160	300	400	650	750
1902F	95,000	250	300	500	850	1,000
1902F Proof	—	Value: 800				
1903A	384,000	130	220	280	500	600
1901-03 Common date proof	—	Value: 500				

KM# 17 1/2 MARK

2.7770 g., 0.9000 Silver .0803 oz. ASW **Obv:** Denomination within wreath **Rev:** Crowned imperial eagle with shield on breast within wreath **Note:** Some coins dated from 1918-19 were issued with a black finish to prevent hoarding.

Date	Mintage	F	VF	XF	Unc	BU
1905A	37,766,000	0.85	1.25	2.50	22.00	—
1905D	7,636,000	0.85	1.25	3.00	33.00	—
1905E	4,908,000	0.85	1.25	3.00	30.00	—
1905F	6,310,000	0.85	1.25	4.00	28.00	—
1905G	3,886,000	1.00	4.00	6.00	45.00	—
1905J	6,316,000	1.00	3.00	9.00	75.00	—
1906A	29,754,000	0.80	1.50	3.00	25.00	—
1906D	11,977,000	0.90	2.00	4.00	30.00	—
1906E	5,821,000	0.90	2.00	4.00	30.00	—
1906F	8,036,000	1.00	3.00	6.00	30.00	—
1906G	4,273,000	1.00	3.00	6.00	30.00	—
1906J	2,179,000	2.00	8.00	25.00	250	—
1907A	14,168,000	0.80	1.25	3.00	85.00	—
1907D	2,884,000	0.90	1.50	4.50	33.00	—
1907E	600,000	2.00	10.00	28.00	90.00	—
1907F	1,202,000	1.50	5.00	20.00	165	—
1907G	927,000	1.50	4.00	30.00	165	—
1907J	3,268,000	1.00	3.00	18.00	110	—
1908A	5,018,000	0.90	3.00	15.00	100	—
1908D	400,000	5.00	15.00	50.00	200	—
1908E	591,000	3.00	10.00	18.00	140	—
1908F	1,000	2,000	5,000	8,000	10,000	—
1908G	675,000	3.00	30.00	60.00	500	—
1808/7J	1,309,000	3.00	30.00	60.00	500	—
1908J	Inc. above	3.00	26.00	100	1,200	—
1909A	5,404,000	0.85	2.00	9.00	100	—
1909/5D	1,001,000	1.00	4.00	20.00	120	—
1909D	Inc. above	1.00	4.00	20.00	120	—
1909E	745,000	3.00	9.00	20.00	120	—
1909F	999,000	1.00	4.00	20.00	130	—
1909G	607,000	4.00	15.00	24.00	400	—
1909J	816,000	3.00	10.00	20.00	180	—
1911A	2,710,000	1.00	2.00	9.00	90.00	—
1911/05D	703,000	1.00	3.00	12.00	85.00	—
1911D	Inc. above	1.00	3.00	12.00	85.00	—
1911E	376,000	1.00	4.00	14.00	70.00	—
1911F	502,000	3.00	9.00	22.00	140	—
1911G	610,000	3.00	9.00	22.00	110	—
1911J	418,000	5.00	15.00	40.00	380	—
1912A	2,709,000	1.00	3.00	9.00	45.00	—
1912/5D	703,000	3.00	10.00	20.00	60.00	—
1912D	Inc. above	3.00	10.00	20.00	60.00	—
1912E	369,000	3.00	10.00	30.00	170	—
1912F	501,000	4.00	12.00	22.00	170	—
1912J	399,000	11.00	30.00	60.00	350	—
1913A	5,419,000	0.90	2.00	7.00	25.00	—
1913/05D	1,406,000	1.00	3.00	9.00	30.00	—
1913D	Inc. above	1.00	3.00	9.00	30.00	—
1913E	745,000	2.00	5.00	10.00	55.00	—
1913F	1,003,000	1.50	4.00	8.00	55.00	—
1913G	610,000	3.00	9.00	18.00	80.00	—
1913J	817,000	3.00	10.00	20.00	140	—
1914A	13,525,000	0.85	1.50	4.00	24.00	—
1914/05D	328,000	3.00	10.00	25.00	50.00	—
1914D	Inc. above	3.00	10.00	25.00	50.00	—
1914J	2,292,000	1.00	3.00	10.00	70.00	—
1915A	13,015,000	0.85	1.25	4.00	11.00	—
1915/05D	5,117,000	0.90	1.50	3.00	10.00	—
1915D	Inc. above	0.85	1.25	5.00	12.00	—
1915E	3,308,000	0.85	1.25	3.00	12.00	—
1915F	5,309,000	0.85	1.25	3.00	12.00	—
1915G	2,730,000	0.85	2.00	6.00	18.00	—
1915J	2,285,000	0.85	2.00	4.00	18.00	—
1916A	9,750,000	0.85	1.25	3.00	14.00	—
1916/616D	4,397,000	0.90	1.50	3.00	10.00	—
1916/05D	Inc. above	0.90	1.50	3.00	10.00	—
1916/5D	Inc. above	0.90	1.50	3.00	10.00	—
1916D	Inc. above	0.90	2.00	7.00	15.00	—
1916E	1,640,000	0.90	2.00	7.00	10.00	—
1916F	2,410,000	0.90	2.00	7.00	15.00	—
1916G	1,779,000	1.00	3.00	8.00	30.00	—
1916J	1,464,000	1.00	3.00	8.00	35.00	—
1917A	14,692,000	0.85	1.25	3.00	10.00	—
1917/05D	979,000	0.90	2.00	5.00	16.00	—
1917D	Inc. above	0.90	2.00	5.00	16.00	—
1917E	1,561,000	0.90	1.50	3.00	10.00	—
1917F	450,000	3.00	10.00	30.00	220	—
1917G	619,000	3.00	10.00	30.00	180	—
1917J	1,039,000	1.50	5.00	10.00	30.00	—
1918A	14,622,000	0.85	1.25	3.00	10.00	—
1918/05D	3,670,000	0.90	1.50	3.00	10.00	—
1918D	Inc. above	0.90	1.50	3.00	10.00	—
1918E	2,807,000	1.50	5.00	12.00	25.00	—
1918E Proof	19	—	—	—	—	—
1918F	4,010,000	3.00	9.00	20.00	80.00	—
1918G	1,032,000	2.00	6.00	14.00	60.00	—
1918J	3,452,000	1.50	5.00	12.00	30.00	—
1919A	9,124,000	0.85	1.25	4.00	12.00	—
1919/1619D	2,195,000	0.90	1.50	5.00	15.00	—
1919/05D	Inc. above	0.90	1.50	5.00	15.00	—
1919D	Inc. above	2.00	6.00	12.00	50.00	—
1919E	1,767,000	2.00	6.00	12.00	25.00	—
1919F	1,559,000	3.00	9.00	18.00	80.00	—
1919J	1,875,000	2.00	6.00	22.00	35.00	—
1905-19 Common date proof	—	Value: 150				

KM# 14 MARK

5.5500 g., 0.9000 Silver .1606 oz. ASW **Ruler:** Wilhelm II **Obv:** Denomination within wreath **Rev:** Crowned imperial eagle with shield on breast **Note:** Struck from 1890-1916.

Date	Mintage	F	VF	XF	Unc	BU
1901A	3,821,000	2.00	6.00	20.00	50.00	—
1901/800D	914,000	2.50	5.00	12.00	35.00	—
1901/801D	915,000	2.50	5.00	12.00	35.00	—
1901D	Inc. above	2.00	6.00	20.00	50.00	—
1901E	484,000	3.00	10.00	20.00	250	—
1901F	802,000	2.00	6.00	18.00	220	—
1901G	579,000	3.00	10.00	40.00	320	—
1901J	531,000	3.50	12.00	45.00	320	—
1902A	5,222,000	1.75	5.00	14.00	150	—
1902D	1,546,000	1.75	4.00	14.00	120	—
1902E	819,000	2.50	9.00	30.00	300	—
1902F	953,000	2.00	7.00	30.00	200	—
1902G	270,000	5.00	20.00	60.00	800	—
1902J	898,000	3.00	10.00	40.00	800	—
1903A	3,965,000	1.65	4.00	12.00	100	—
1903/803D	914,000	1.75	5.00	12.00	60.00	—
1903D	Inc. above	1.75	5.00	12.00	60.00	—
1903E	485,000	3.00	9.00	33.00	280	—
1903F	652,000	3.00	8.00	25.00	250	—
1903G	614,000	3.00	8.00	45.00	400	—
1903J	531,000	3.50	10.00	30.00	1,000	—
1904A	3,243,000	1.65	3.00	12.00	100	—
1904D	1,761,000	1.65	3.50	16.00	60.00	—
1904E	931,000	1.65	4.00	20.00	200	—
1904F	1,255,000	1.65	4.00	18.00	120	—
1904G	664,000	2.50	8.00	26.00	200	—
1904J	1,021,000	2.50	8.00	35.00	1,000	—
1905A	10,303,000	1.65	3.50	14.00	50.00	—
1905D	1,759,000	1.65	4.00	15.00	100	—
1905E	931,000	2.00	5.00	22.00	170	—
1905F	Inc. above	—	—	—	—	—
1905G	860,000	2.00	6.00	20.00	280	—
1905J	1,021,000	2.50	7.00	35.00	750	—
1906A	5,414,000	1.65	3.50	11.00	150	—
1906D	1,412,000	1.65	4.00	11.00	110	—
1906E	745,000	2.50	9.00	22.00	220	—
1906F	2,257,000	1.75	5.00	16.00	120	—
1906G	609,000	3.00	11.00	40.00	400	—
1906G Proof	—	—	—	—	—	—
1906J	372,000	5.00	15.00	50.00	2,000	—
1907A	9,201,000	1.65	2.50	5.00	55.00	—
1907D	2,387,000	1.65	2.75	9.00	50.00	—
1907E	1,265,000	1.65	3.00	11.00	80.00	—
1907F	1,704,000	1.65	3.00	8.00	65.00	—
1907G	1,035,000	1.25	4.00	12.00	130	—
1907J	1,833,000	1.75	5.00	25.00	350	—
1908A	4,338,000	1.65	3.00	9.00	85.00	—
1908D	1,126,000	1.65	3.00	9.00	60.00	—
1908E	596,000	2.50	7.00	18.00	100	—
1908F	802,000	1.65	5.00	15.00	85.00	—
1908G	488,000	2.50	9.00	24.00	210	—
1908J	653,000	2.50	8.00	30.00	420	—
1909A	4,151,000	1.65	5.00	13.00	200	—
1909D	1,968,000	1.65	5.00	12.00	75.00	—
1909E	Inc. below	40.00	120	180	420	—
1909G	854,000	3.00	10.00	24.00	170	—
1909J	53,000	85.00	175	285	650	—
1910A	5,870,000	1.65	3.50	12.00	55.00	—
1910D	1,406,000	1.75	4.00	6.00	50.00	—
1910E	1,050,000	1.75	5.00	12.00	80.00	—
1910F	1,631,000	1.75	5.00	10.00	70.00	—
1910G	610,000	2.00	7.00	22.00	170	—
1910J	1,094,000	2.50	8.00	30.00	330	—
1911A	5,693,000	1.65	3.00	9.00	60.00	—
1911D	126,000	8.00	30.00	48.00	170	—
1911E	738,000	1.75	5.00	8.00	60.00	—
1911F	773,000	2.50	9.00	50.00	900	—
1911G	305,000	3.50	11.00	40.00	100	—
1911J	812,000	2.50	9.00	35.00	100	—
1912A	2,439,000	1.65	2.50	6.00	70.00	—
1912D	632,000	1.75	4.00	10.00	100	—
1912E	708,000	2.00	5.00	10.00	70.00	—
1912F	502,000	2.00	6.00	16.00	145	—
1912J	409,000	5.00	25.00	50.00	750	—
1913F	450,000	5.00	15.00	30.00	130	—
1913G	275,000	15.00	40.00	60.00	180	—
1913J	368,000	7.00	20.00	40.00	270	—

Date	Mintage	F	VF	XF	Unc	BU
1914A	11,304,000	1.65	2.25	4.00	15.00	—
1914/9D	3,515,000	1.65	2.50	6.00	18.00	—
1914D	Inc. above	1.65	2.50	6.00	18.00	—
1914E	2,235,000	1.65	3.00	7.00	18.00	—
1914F	2,300,000	1.65	2.25	3.75	15.00	—
1914G	1,911,000	1.65	4.00	8.00	20.00	—
1914J	2,978,000	1.65	4.00	8.00	18.00	—
1915A	13,817,000	1.65	2.25	4.00	15.00	—
1915D	4,218,000	1.65	3.00	5.00	15.00	—
1915E	2,235,000	1.65	3.00	5.00	15.00	—
1915F	2,911,000	1.65	3.00	9.00	20.00	—
1915G	1,749,000	1.65	3.00	6.00	15.00	—
1915J	1,634,000	1.75	4.00	8.00	15.00	—
1916F	306,000	10.00	30.00	45.00	90.00	—
1901-16 Common date proof	—	Value: 150				

MILITARY COINAGE - WWI

Issued under the authority of the German Military Commander of the East for use in Estonia, Latvia, Lithuania, Poland, and Northwest Russia.

KM# 21 KOPEK

Iron **Ruler:** Wilhelm II **Obv:** Inscription **Rev:** Denomination and date within iron cross

Date	Mintage	F	VF	XF	Unc	BU
1916A	11,942,000	2.00	6.00	15.00	40.00	—
1916A Proof	—	Value: 150				
1916J	8,000,000	2.50	7.00	20.00	50.00	—
1916J Proof	—	Value: 150				

KM# 22 2 KOPEKS

Iron **Ruler:** Wilhelm II **Obv:** Inscription **Rev:** Denomination and date within iron cross

Date	Mintage	F	VF	XF	Unc	BU
1916A	6,973,000	2.00	6.00	15.00	40.00	—
1916A Proof	—	Value: 150				
1916J	8,000,000	2.50	6.00	15.00	40.00	—
1916J Proof	—	Value: 150				

KM# 23 3 KOPEKS

Iron **Ruler:** Wilhelm II **Obv:** Inscription **Rev:** Denomination and date within iron cross

Date	Mintage	F	VF	XF	Unc	BU
1916A	8,670,000	2.50	6.00	18.00	45.00	—
1916A Proof	—	Value: 150				
1916J	8,000,000	2.50	6.00	18.00	45.00	—
1916J Proof	—	Value: 150				

PATTERNS

Including off metal strikes

KM#	Date	Mintage	Identification	Mkt Val
Pn66	1901A	—	50 Pfennig. Silver. Plain 2mm edge. KM#15.	200
Pn67	1901A	—	50 Pfennig. Silver. Plain 3.5mm edge. KM#15.	200
Pn68	1901A	—	50 Pfennig. Silver. Coarse reeding. KM#15.	200
Pn69	1901A	—	50 Pfennig. Silver. Coarse wavy reeding. KM#15.	200
Pn70	1901A	—	1/2 Mark. Silver.	400
Pn71	1901D	—	1/2 Mark. Silver. Date.	400
Pn72	1901D	—	1/2 Mark. Silver. Incuse diamond.	400
Pn73	1901D	—	1/2 Mark. Brass. Incuse diamond.	200
Pn74	1901D	—	1/2 Mark. Brass. Incuse diamond, beaded circle.	200
Pn75	1901D	—	1/2 Mark. Silver. Diamond within beads.	375
Pn76	1901D	—	1/2 Mark. Brass. Beaded diamond.	200
Pn77	1901D	—	1/2 Mark. Silver. Beaded diamond.	375
Pn78	1901D	—	1/2 Mark. Silver. Beaded circle.	375
Pn79	1901D	—	1/2 Mark. Brass. Beaded circle.	200
Pn80	1901D	—	1/2 Mark. Silver. Diamond within beads.	375
Pn81	1901D	—	1/2 Mark. Silver. Incuse diamond.	375
Pn82	1901D	—	1/2 Mark. Brass. Incuse diamond.	200
Pn83	1901D	—	1/2 Mark. Silver. Date.	375
Pn84	1901D	—	1/2 Mark. Silver. Beaded circle.	375
Pn85	1901D	—	1/2 Mark. Brass. Beaded circle.	200
Pn86	1902A	—	50 Pfennig. Silver. Without beaded rims, coarse reeding; KM#15.	375
Pn87	1902A	—	50 Pfennig. Silver. Without beaded rims, reeded edge; KM#15.	375
Pn88	1902A	—	50 Pfennig. 0.7100 Silver. Incuse circle.	500
Pn89	1902A	—	1/2 Mark. Silver. Incuse circle.	400
Pn90	1903A	—	50 Pfennig. Silver. Without beaded rim, coarse reeding; KM#15.	375
Pn91	1903A	—	50 Pfennig. Silver. Coarse reeding; KM#15.	375
Pn92	1903D	—	50 Pfennig. Silver. Crown.	400
Pn93	1903D	—	50 Pfennig. Eagle.	400
Pn94	1903D	—	50 Pfennig. Brass. Otto of Bavaria.	375
Pn95	1903D	—	50 Pfennig. Copper. Otto of Bavaria.	375
Pn96	1903	—	50 Pfennig. Brass. Crown. Otto of Bavaria.	375
Pn97	1903D	—	50 Pfennig. Brass. Germania.	350
Pn98	1904A	—	1/2 Mark. Silver. KM#17.	400
Pn99	NDA	—	25 Pfennig. Nickel-Silver. Value within beaded circle.	200
Pn100	NDA	—	25 Pfennig. Copper-Nickel. Beaded circle.	200
Pn101	NDA	—	25 Pfennig. Tin Alloy. Beaded circle.	200
Pn102	1907	—	25 Pfennig. Nickel. Germania.	150
Pn103	1907A	—	25 Pfennig. Copper. Crown.	150
Pn104	1907A	—	25 Pfennig. Nickel. Crown.	150
Pn105	1907D	—	1/2 Mark. Silver. Coarse reeding; KM#17.	200
Pn106	1908A	—	25 Pfennig. Nickel.	300
Pn107	1908A	—	25 Pfennig. Nickel-Silver. Eagle plain.	200
Pn108	1908A	—	25 Pfennig. Silver. Eagle plain.	300
Pn109	1908A	—	25 Pfennig. Nickel-Silver. Eagle within beads.	200
Pn110	1908A	—	25 Pfennig. Nickel-Silver. Eagle within beads.	200
Pn111	1908A	—	25 Pfennig. Eagle plain.	200
Pn112	1908A	—	25 Pfennig. Copper-Nickel.	200
Pn113	1908A	—	25 Pfennig. Nickel-Silver.	200
Pn114	1908A	—	25 Pfennig. Nickel.	200
Pn115	1908A	—	25 Pfennig. Nickel-Silver.	200
Pn116	1908A	—	25 Pfennig. Aluminum.	200
Pn117	1908A	—	25 Pfennig. Copper-Nickel.	150
Pn118	1908A	—	25 Pfennig. Silver.	250
Pn119	1908A	—	25 Pfennig. Bronze.	150
Pn120	1908A	—	25 Pfennig. Copper.	150
Pn121	1908A	—	25 Pfennig. Silver. Eagle in crown.	400
Pn122	1908A	—	25 Pfennig. Silver. Cross in crown.	400
Pn123	1908A	—	25 Pfennig. Silver.	400
Pn124	1908A	—	25 Pfennig. Copper-Nickel.	200
Pn125	1908A	—	25 Pfennig. Silver.	400
Pn126	1908A	—	25 Pfennig. Nickel.	200
Pn127	1908A	—	25 Pfennig. Copper-Nickel.	250
Pn128	1908A	—	25 Pfennig. Nickel.	250
Pn129	1908A	—	25 Pfennig. Nickel. Germania.	250
Pn130	1908A	—	25 Pfennig. Nickel. Kaiser Wilhelm.	225
Pn131	1908A	—	25 Pfennig. Iron. Kaiser Wilhelm.	200
Pn132	1908A	—	25 Pfennig. Copper. Kaiser Wilhelm.	250
PnA133	1908D	—	25 Pfennig. Copper. Eagle head in order collar.	100
Pn133	1908D	—	25 Pfennig. Silvered Copper Alloy.	150
Pn134	1908D	—	25 Pfennig. Silvered Copper Alloy.	150
Pn135	1908A	—	25 Pfennig. Lead. Without circle around eagle, or crown above value.	150
PnA136	1908D	—	25 Pfennig. Nickel.	150
Pn136	1908J	—	25 Pfennig. Copper-Nickel. Gothic style.	250
Pn137	1908J	—	25 Pfennig. Copper-Nickel. Block style.	250
Pn138	1908A	—	25 Pfennig. Copper-Nickel. Crown.	250
Pn139	1908A	—	25 Pfennig. Tin. Crown.	200
Pn140	1908A	—	25 Pfennig. Aluminum. Crown.	200
Pn141	1908	—	25 Pfennig. Silver. Eagle within beads.	350
Pn142	1908/09	—	25 Pfennig. Nickel-Silver. Eagle within beads.	250
Pn143	1909A	—	25 Pfennig. Silver. Large eagle.	300
Pn144	1909A	—	10 Pfennig. Nickel. 2mm rims, KM#12.	250
Pn145	1909	—	25 Pfennig. Nickel.	200
Pn146	1909	—	25 Pfennig. Bronze.	200
Pn147	1909A	—	25 Pfennig. Antique Silvered Copper Alloy.	175
Pn148	1909A	—	25 Pfennig. Cast	200
Pn149	1909A	—	25 Pfennig. Copper-Nickel.	200
Pn150	1909A	—	25 Pfennig. Nickel.	200
Pn151	1909A	—	25 Pfennig. Nickel.	200
Pn152	1909A	—	25 Pfennig. Nickel-Silver.	200
Pn153	1909A	—	25 Pfennig. Nickel.	200
Pn154	1909A	—	25 Pfennig. Iron.	175
Pn155	1909A	—	25 Pfennig. Nickel.	200
Pn156	1909A	—	25 Pfennig. Nickel.	200
Pn157	1909A	—	25 Pfennig. Silver.	350
Pn158	1909A	—	25 Pfennig. Silver. Standing eagle right.	350
Pn159	1909A	—	25 Pfennig. Silver.	350
Pn160	1909A	—	25 Pfennig. Silver. Standing eagle right.	350
Pn161	1909A	—	25 Pfennig. Silver.	300
Pn162	1909A	—	25 Pfennig. Nickel.	200
Pn163	1909A	—	25 Pfennig. Copper-Nickel.	200
Pn168	1909A	—	25 Pfennig. Silver. Eagle within legend.	300
Pn169	1909A	—	25 Pfennig. Silver. Large eagle, legend above crowned value.	300
Pn170	1909A	—	25 Pfennig. Silver.	350
PnA171	1909A	—	25 Pfennig.	250
Pn171	1909A	—	25 Pfennig. Silver.	300
Pn172	1909A	—	25 Pfennig. Silver.	300
Pn173	1909A	—	25 Pfennig. Nickel. GOTT MITUNS above crowned eagle with spread wings. DEUTSCHES REICH above large numerals.	250
Pn174	1909A	—	25 Pfennig. Nickel. Stockier eagle, countermarked mm. Large munerals and countermarked date.	250
Pn175	1909A	—	25 Pfennig.	250
Pn176	1909E	—	25 Pfennig. Silver Or Copper-Nickel.	300
Pn177	1909A	—	25 Pfennig. Antique Silvered Copper Alloy.	250
Pn178	NDA	—	25 Pfennig. Silver. Large eagle.	350
Pn179	1910E	—	25 Pfennig. Silver. Eagle within legend.	250
Pn180	1910A	—	1/2 Mark. Silver. KM#17.	350
Pn181	1910	—	Mark. Silver. Without mint mark, KM#7.	—
PnD182	1910A	—	3 Mark. Ernst Ludwig	—
PnA182	1911D	—	Mark. Aluminum Clad Zinc.	—
PnB182	1911D	—	2 Mark. Aluminum Clad Zinc. Bavaria	—
PnC182	1912D	—	3 Mark. Aluminum Clad Zinc. Bavaria	—
PnE182	1913	—	3 Mark. Silver. Without mint mark, Kaiser on horseback.	—
PnF182	1913	—	3 Mark. Copper.	—
Pn182	1914A	—	5 Pfennig. Unknown Metal. Reeded edge. KM#11	—
PnA183	1915	—	Non-Denominated. Gilt Bronze.	—
Pn183	1915A	—	Pfennig. Zinc. Reeded edge. KM#10	—
Pn184	1915A	—	Pfennig. Iron. Date below value, KM#24.	—
Pn185	1915A	—	Pfennig. Aluminum.	—
Pn186	1915	—	5 Pfennig. Copper-Nickel center. Without mint mark, KM#11.	—
Pn187	1915A	—	10 Pfennig. Brass. KM#17. KM#12.	—
Pn188	1915A	—	10 Pfennig. Brass. Broad rims, KM#12.	—
Pn189	1915A	—	10 Pfennig. Nickel. Broad rims.	—
Pn190	1915A	—	10 Pfennig. Copper-Nickel. Broad rims.	—
Pn191	1915A	—	10 Pfennig. Rusted Iron. Broad rims.	100
Pn192	1915A	—	10 Pfennig. Brass. Date above value.	—
Pn193	1915A	—	10 Pfennig. Nickel. Date above value.	—
Pn194	1915A	—	10 Pfennig. Iron. Date above value.	—
Pn195	1915A	—	10 Pfennig. Small "10".	—
Pn196	1915A	—	10 Pfennig. Large "10".	—
Pn197	1915A	—	10 Pfennig. Brass. Small "10", KM#20.	—
Pn198	1915A	—	10 Pfennig. Nickel. Small "10", KM#20.	—
Pn199	1915A	—	10 Pfennig. Iron. 67 beads on rim.	—
Pn200	1915A	—	10 Pfennig. Nickel. 67 beads on rim.	—
Pn201	1915A	—	10 Pfennig. Copper-Nickel. KM#20.	—
Pn202	1915A	—	10 Pfennig. Iron. KM#20.	500
Pn203	1915A	—	1/2 Mark. Silver. Large eagle.	—
Pn204	1915A	—	Mark. Aluminum. GOTT MIT UNS on rim, KM#14.	—
PnA205	ND	—	Pfennig. Copper. KM#24.	—
Pn205	1916A	—	Pfennig. Aluminum. KM#24.	—
Pn206	1916F	—	Pfennig. Aluminum. KM#24.	—
Pn207	1917	—	Pfennig. Aluminum. Without mint mark, KM#24.	—
Pn208	1917	—	10 Pfennig. Iron. Without mint mark, KM#20.	—
Pn209	1917A	—	10 Pfennig. Zinc. Mint mark, KM#26.	—

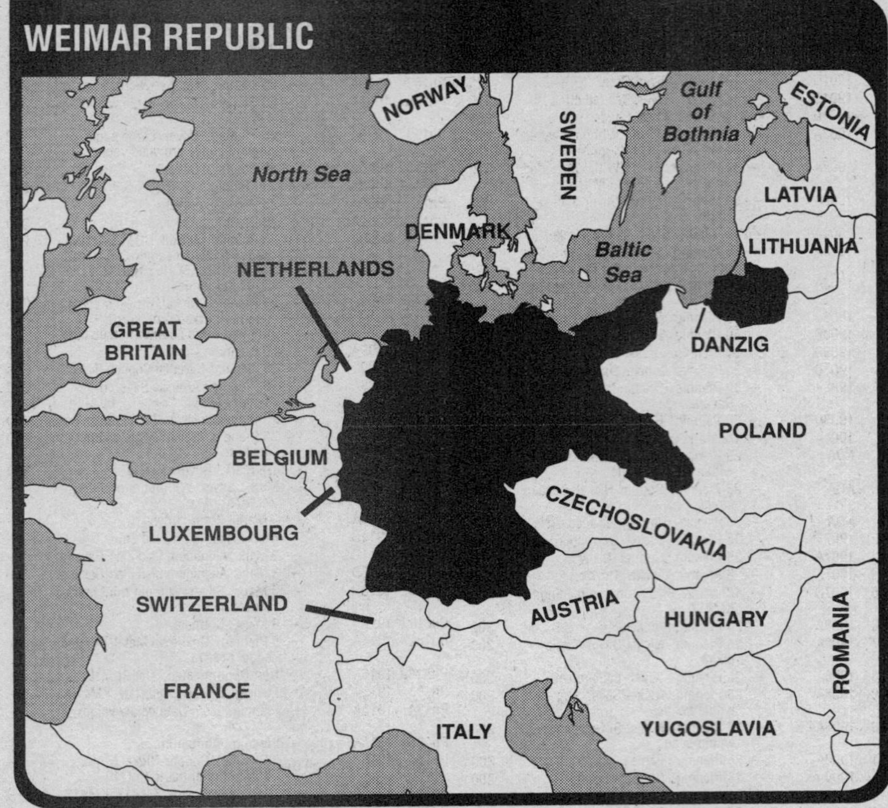

1919-1933

The Imperial German government disintegrated in a flurry of royal abdications as World War I ended. Desperate German parliamentarians, fearful of impending anarchy and civil war, hastily declared a German Republic. The new National Assembly, which was convened Feb. 6, 1919 in Weimar had to establish a legal government, draft a constitution, and then conclude a peace treaty with the Allies. Friedrich Ebert was elected as Reichs President. The harsh terms of the peace treaty imposed on Germany were economically and psychologically unacceptable to the German population regardless of political persuasion and the problem of German treaty compliance was to plague the Republic until the worldwide Great Depression of 1929. The new constitution paid less attention to fundamental individual rights and concentrated more power in the President and Central Government to insure a more stable social and economic order. The German bureaucracy survived the transition intact and had a stifling effect on the democratic process. The army started training large numbers of reservists in conjunction with the U.S.S.R. thereby circumventing treaty limitations on the size of the German military.

New anti-democratic ideologies were forming. Communism and Fascism were spreading. The National Socialist German Workers Party, under Hitler's leadership, incorporated the ever-present anti-Semitism into a new virulent Nazi Catechism.

In spite of the historic German inflation, the French occupation of the Rhineland, and the loss of vast territories and resources, the republic survived. By 1929 the German economy had been restored to its pre-war level. Much of the economic gains however were dependent on the extensive assistance provided by the U.S.A. and collapsed along with the world economy in 1929. Even during the good times, the Republic was never able to muster any loyal public support or patriotism. By 1930, Nationalists, Nazis, and Communists held nearly half of the Reichstag seats and the government was forced to rely more and more on presidential decrees as the only means to effectuate policy. In 1932, the Nazis won 230 Reichstag seats. As head of the largest party, Hitler claimed the right to form the next government. President Hindenburg's opposition forced a second election in which the Nazis lost 34 seats. Von Papen, however, convinced Hindenburg to name Hitler Chancellor by arguing that Hitler could be controlled! Hitler formed his cabinet and immediately began consolidating his power and laying the groundwork for the Third Reich.

MONETARY SYSTEM

(During 1923-1924)
100 Rentenpfennig = 1 Rentenmark

(Commencing 1924)
100 Reichspfennig = 1 Reichsmark

WEIMAR REPUBLIC

MARK COINAGE

1922-1923

KM# 27 50 PFENNIG

Aluminum, 23 mm. **Obv:** Denomination above date **Rev:** Sheaf behind inscription

Date	Mintage	F	VF	XF	Unc	BU
1919A	7,173,000	0.25	1.00	3.50	20.00	25.00
1919D	791,000	5.00	11.00	22.00	70.00	90.00
1919E	930,000	2.00	6.00	15.00	60.00	80.00
1919E Proof	35	Value: 350				
1919F	160,000	10.00	20.00	40.00	120	150
1919G	660,000	2.00	4.00	10.00	40.00	48.00
1919J	800,000	5.00	10.00	24.00	70.00	85.00
1920A	119,793,000	0.10	0.50	1.00	7.00	10.00
1920D	28,306,000	0.10	0.50	1.50	9.00	12.00
1920E	14,400,000	0.25	1.00	2.50	12.00	15.00
1920E Proof	226	Value:.150				
1920F	10,932,000	0.25	1.00	2.50	12.00	15.00
1920G	5,040,000	0.25	1.00	3.00	20.00	25.00
1920J	15,423,000	0.25	1.00	3.00	12.00	15.00
1921A	184,468,000	0.10	0.15	0.50	3.00	5.00
1921D	48,729,000	0.10	0.15	0.75	6.00	8.00
1921E	31,210,000	0.15	1.00	2.00	10.00	12.00
1921E Proof	332	Value: 115				
1921F	46,950,000	0.10	0.15	0.75	10.00	12.00
1921G	19,107,000	0.10	0.25	1.00	6.00	8.00
1921J	28,013,000	0.10	0.25	1.00	6.00	8.00
1922A	145,215,000	0.10	0.25	1.00	6.00.	8.00
1922D	58,019,000	0.10	0.25	1.00	6.00	8.00
1922E	33,930,000	0.15	1.00	2.00	10.00	14.00
1922E Proof	333	Value: 115				
1922F	33,000,000	0.10	0.25	1.00	6.00	8.00
1922G	36,745,000	0.10	0.25	1.00	6.00	8.00
1922J	36,202,000	0.10	0.25	1.00	6.00	8.00

KM# 28 3 MARK

Aluminum **Obv:** Denomination above date **Rev:** Imperial eagle **Edge:** Reeded

Date	Mintage	F	VF	XF	Unc	BU
1922A	15,497,000	0.25	2.50	7.00	14.00	20.00
1922A Proof	—	Value: 85.00				
1922E	2,000	60.00	100	200	600	700
1922E Proof	1,000	Value: 300				
1922F Rare	—	—	—	—	—	—

KM# 29 3 MARK

Aluminum **Subject:** 3rd Anniversary Weimar Constitution

Date	Mintage	F	VF	XF	Unc	BU
1922A	32,514,000	0.25	1.00	3.00	10.00	12.00
1922D	8,441,000	140	200	300	800	1,000
1922D Proof	—	Value: 1,100				
1922E	2,440,000	0.50	2.00	4.00	12.00	15.00
1922E Proof	22,000	Value: 50.00				
1922F	6,023,000	2.00	6.00	12.00	35.00	45.00
1922G	3,655,000	0.50	2.00	4.00	12.00	15.00
1922J	4,896,000	0.50	2.00	4.00	12.00	15.00
1923E	2,060,000	6.00	12.00	25.00	70.00	80.00
1923E Proof	2,291	Value: 75.00				
1923F	—	300	650	1,000	2,250	2,750

Note: The 1923F 3 Mark pieces are from the burned-out ruin of the Stuttgart Mint, destroyed in World War II

KM# 35 200 MARK

Aluminum, 23 mm. **Obv:** Denomination above date **Rev:** Imperial eagle

Date	Mintage	F	VF	XF	Unc	BU
1923A	174,900,000	0.15	0.50	0.75	2.00	3.00
1923A Proof	—	Value: 125				
1923D	35,189,000	0.20	0.50	1.00	2.20	3.00
1923D Proof, unique	—	—	—	—	—	—
1923E	11,250,000	0.20	1.00	3.00	7.00	9.00
1923E Proof	4,095	Value: 100				
1923F	20,090,000	0.25	0.75	2.00	3.00	4.00
1923F Proof	—	Value: 125				
1923G	24,923,000	0.25	0.75	2.00	3.00	4.00
1923G Proof	—	Value: 125				
1923J	16,258,000	0.20	1.00	3.00	7.00	9.00
1923J Proof	—	Value: 125				

KM# 36 500 MARK

Aluminum **Obv:** Denomination above date **Rev:** Imperial eagle

Date	Mintage	F	VF	XF	Unc	BU
1923A	59,278,000	0.20	1.00	1.50	5.00	6.00
1923A Proof	—	Value: 125				
1923D	13,683,000	0.25	1.00	3.00	5.00	7.00
1923D Proof	—	Value: 125				
1923E	2,128,000	2.00	5.00	12.00	30.00	35.00
1923E Proof	2,053	Value: 100				
1923F	7,963,000	0.25	1.00	3.00	8.00	9.00
1923F Proof	—	Value: 125				
1923G	4,404,000	0.25	1.75	6.00	14.00	16.00
1923G Proof	—	Value: 125				
1923J	1,008,000	10.00	20.00	40.00	90.00	100
1923J Proof	—	Value: 250				

RENTENMARK COINAGE

1923-1929

KM# 30 RENTENPFENNIG

Bronze **Obv:** Denomination within circle **Rev:** Wheat sheaf divides date

Date	Mintage	F	VF	XF	Unc	BU
1923A	12,629,000	0.25	1.00	3.00	15.00	16.00
1923D	Est. 2,314,000	0.25	2.00	7.00	30.00	33.00
1923E	2,200,000	1.00	3.00	8.00	30.00	33.00
1923F	160,000	2.00	8.00	24.00	80.00	90.00
1923G	1,004,000	1.00	4.00	8.00	30.00	33.00
1923J	1,470,000	2.00	8.00	20.00	85.00	100
1924A	55,273,000	25.00	0.50	3.00	12.00	14.00
1924D	17,540,000	25.00	1.50	4.00	15.00	17.00
1924E	6,838,000	1.00	1.50	6.00	24.00	27.00
1924F	10,347,000	1.00	2.50	6.00	24.00	27.00
1924G	7,366,000	1.00	3.00	9.00	30.00	33.00
1924J	11,024,000	1.00	2.50	6.00	24.00	26.00
1925A	—	750	1,250	2,500	—	—
1929F	—	150	250	500	1,000	1,200
1923-29 Common date proof	—	Value: 120				

KM# 31 2 RENTENPFENNIG

Bronze **Obv:** Denomination within circle **Rev:** Wheat sheaf divides date

Date	Mintage	F	VF	XF	Unc	BU
1923A	8,587,000	0.20	1.00	3.00	20.00	22.00
1923D	1,490,000	0.20	1.00	6.00	35.00	40.00
1923F	Inc. above	1.00	3.50	9.00	35.00	45.00
1923G	Inc. above	1.00	2.00	10.00	40.00	50.00
1923J	Inc. above	2.00	6.00	15.00	70.00	80.00
1924A	80,864,000	0.20	0.50	1.00	8.00	10.00
1924D	19,899,000	0.25	1.00	3.00	15.00	17.00
1924E	6,595,000	0.25	1.00	3.00	15.00	17.00
1924F	14,969,000	0.25	1.00	3.00	15.00	17.00
1924G	10,349,000	0.25	1.00	4.00	18.00	20.00
1924J	21,196,000	0.25	1.00	3.00	15.00	17.00
1923-24 Common date proof	—	Value: 140				

KM# 32 5 RENTENPFENNIG

Aluminum-Bronze

Date	Mintage	F	VF	XF	Unc	BU
1923A	3,083,000	1.00	3.00	10.00	50.00	55.00
1923D	Inc. below	1.00	3.00	12.00	60.00	65.00
1923F	Inc. below	35.00	70.00	120	300	320
1923G	Inc. below	10.00	25.00	50.00	200	220
1924A	171,966,000	0.25	1.00	3.00	20.00	24.00
1924D	31,163,000	0.25	1.00	5.00	28.00	30.00
1924E	12,206,000	0.25	1.00	6.00	30.00	33.00
1924F	29,032,000	0.25	1.00	5.00	30.00	33.00
1924G	19,217,000	0.25	1.00	6.00	30.00	33.00
1924J	32,332,000	0.25	1.00	5.00	25.00	27.00
1925F 1 known	—	—	5,000	—	—	—
1923-25 Common date proof	—	Value: 160				

KM# 33 10 RENTENPFENNIG

Aluminum-Bronze **Obv:** Denomination within square, oak leaf on each side **Rev:** Six grain sprigs form center triangle above date

Date	Mintage	F	VF	XF	Unc	BU
1923A	Inc. below	0.25	3.00	10.00	30.00	33.00
1923D	Inc. below	0.50	6.00	12.00	48.00	53.00
1923F	Inc. below	70.00	100	180	400	420
1923G	Inc. below	2.50	15.00	25.00	120	140
1924A	169,956,000	0.25	1.00	3.00	15.00	17.00
1924D	33,894,000	0.25	1.00	4.00	18.00	20.00
1924E	18,679,000	0.25	1.50	4.50	22.00	24.00
1924F	42,237,000	0.25	1.50	5.00	22.00	24.00
1924F Proof	—	Value: 160				
1924G	18,758,000	0.25	1.50	5.00	22.00	25.00
1924J	33,928,000	0.25	1.50	6.00	25.00	28.00
1925F	13,000	900	1,500	2,000	—	—
1923-1925 Common date proof	—	Value: 160				

KM# 34 50 RENTENPFENNIG

Aluminum-Bronze **Obv:** Denomination within square, oak leaf on each side **Rev:** Six grain sprigs form center triangle above date

Date	Mintage	F	VF	XF	Unc	BU
1923A	451,000	10.00	20.00	32.00	80.00	90.00
1923D	192,000	15.00	30.00	48.00	180	200
1923F	120,000	40.00	90.00	125	420	450
1923G	120,000	20.00	40.00	55.00	220	240
1923J	4,000	500	800	1,600	2,500	2,800
1924A	117,365,000	5.00	12.00	20.00	60.00	70.00
1924D	30,971,000	6.00	15.00	25.00	80.00	90.00
1924E	14,668,000	6.00	15.00	25.00	80.00	90.00
1924F	21,968,000	10.00	15.00	25.00	85.00	100
1924G	13,349,000	12.00	22.00	36.00	130	150
1924J	17,252,000	10.00	20.00	35.00	100	120
1923-24 Common date proof	—	Value: 225				

REICHSMARK COINAGE

1924-1938

KM# 37 REICHSPFENNIG

Bronze **Obv:** Denomination within circle **Rev:** Wheat sheaf divides date

Date	Mintage	F	VF	XF	Unc	BU
1924A	13,496,000	0.20	0.50	1.00	10.00	11.00
1924D	6,206,000	0.20	0.50	1.00	12.00	13.00
1924E	1,100,000	100	250	400	850	900
1924F	2,650,000	0.20	0.50	1.00	12.00	13.00
1924G	5,100,000	0.25	0.75	3.00	15.00	16.00
1924J	24,400,000	0.20	0.50	1.00	12.00	13.00
1925A	40,925,000	0.20	0.50	1.00	5.00	10.00
1925D	1,558,000	5.00	15.00	35.00	100	120
1925E	10,460,000	0.20	0.50	1.00	10.00	11.00
1925F	5,673,000	0.20	0.50	1.00	10.00	11.00
1925G	13,502,000	0.20	0.50	1.00	10.00	11.00
1925J	30,300,000	0.20	0.50	1.00	10.00	11.00
1927A	4,671,000	0.30	1.00	3.00	18.00	19.00
1927D	4,203,000	0.30	1.00	3.00	18.00	19.00
1927E	8,000,000	0.30	1.00	3.00	18.00	19.00
1927F	2,350,000	0.50	2.00	10.00	35.00	37.00
1927G	3,236,000	0.50	2.00	8.00	30.00	32.00
1928A	19,300,000	0.20	0.50	1.00	10.00	11.00
1928D	10,200,000	0.20	0.50	1.00	11.00	12.00
1928F	8,672,000	0.20	0.50	1.00	12.00	13.00
1928G	3,764,000	0.50	2.00	5.00	24.00	26.00
1929A	37,170,000	0.20	0.50	1.00	6.00	10.00
1929D	9,337,000	0.20	0.50	1.00	6.00	10.00
1929E	6,600,000	0.20	0.50	1.00	6.00	11.00
1929F	3,150,000	0.20	0.50	1.50	6.00	11.00
1929G	1,986,000	0.20	0.75	3.00	13.00	15.00
1930A	40,997,000	0.20	0.50	1.00	8.00	10.00
1930D	6,441,000	0.20	0.50	1.00	10.00	12.00
1930E	1,412,000	6.00	15.00	40.00	140	160
1930F	6,415,000	0.20	0.50	1.50	10.00	11.00
1930G	5,017,000	0.20	0.50	1.00	10.00	11.00
1931A	38,481,000	0.20	0.50	3.00	8.00	10.00
1931D	5,998,000	0.20	0.50	1.00	11.00	12.00
1931E	12,800,000	0.20	0.50	2.50	14.00	16.00
1931F	12,591,000	0.20	0.50	1.00	11.00	12.00
1931G	2,622,000	0.20	0.50	8.00	30.00	33.00
1932A	17,096,000	0.20	0.75	2.50	20.00	24.00
1933A	37,846,000	0.20	0.50	1.00	8.00	10.00
1933E	2,945,000	0.30	2.00	8.00	30.00	33.00
1933F	5,023,000	0.20	0.50	1.00	11.00	12.00
1934A	51,214,000	0.20	0.50	1.00	7.00	9.00
1934D	7,408,000	0.20	0.50	1.00	10.00	12.00
1934E	4,628,000	0.50	3.50	10.00	35.00	40.00
1934F	5,667,000	0.20	0.50	1.00	11.00	13.00
1934G	2,450,000	0.20	0.50	3.00	15.00	17.00
1934J	4,271,000	0.20	0.50	3.00	15.00	17.00
1935A	35,894,000	0.20	0.50	1.00	7.00	9.00
1935D	15,489,000	0.20	0.50	1.00	8.00	10.00
1935E	8,351,000	0.20	0.50	2.00	11.00	14.00
1935F	12,094,000	0.20	0.50	1.50	8.00	10.00
1935G	7,454,000	0.20	0.50	1.00	11.00	14.00
1935J	8,505,000	0.20	0.50	1.00	10.00	12.00
1936A	Est. 50,949,000	0.20	0.50	1.00	7.00	8.00
1936D	12,262,000	0.20	0.50	1.00	9.00	10.00
1936E	2,576,000	0.50	3.00	7.00	30.00	33.00
1936F	6,915,000	0.20	0.50	1.00	10.00	12.00
1936G	Est. 2,940,000	0.20	0.50	1.00	11.00	13.00
1936J	Est. 5,421,000	0.20	0.50	1.00	11.00	13.00
1924-36 Common date proof	—	Value: 85.00				

KM# 38 2 REICHSPFENNIG

Bronze **Obv:** Denomination within circle **Rev:** Wheat sheaf divides date

Date	Mintage	F	VF	XF	Unc	BU
1923F Proof	—	Value: 4,500				
1924A	19,620,000	0.20	0.50	1.00	10.00	12.00
1924D	3,482,000	0.30	1.00	2.00	20.00	22.00
1924E	4,253,000	0.30	2.00	5.00	25.00	28.00
1924F	4,567,000	0.30	0.60	1.50	15.00	17.00
1924G	7,560,000	0.30	0.60	1.50	15.00	17.00
1924J	7,489,000	0.30	0.50	1.00	15.00	17.00
1925A	22,433,000	0.20	0.50	1.00	7.00	8.00
1925D	2,412,000	0.20	1.00	4.00	30.00	32.00
1925E	5,414,000	0.30	0.60	2.00	18.00	20.00
1925F	4,851,000	0.30	0.60	2.00	18.00	20.00
1925G	2,456,000	2.00	7.00	15.00	75.00	80.00
1936A	3,220,000	0.50	2.00	5.00	24.00	26.00
1936D	6,525,000	0.20	0.50	1.50	8.00	10.00
1936E	573,000	5.00	12.00	22.00	80.00	90.00
1936F	3,100,000	0.20	0.60	4.00	23.00	25.00
1923-36 Common date proof	—	Value: 90.00				

KM# 75 4 REICHSPFENNIG

Bronze **Obv:** Large denomination within circle, date at right **Rev:** Imperial eagle

Date	Mintage	F	VF	XF	Unc	BU
1932A	27,101,000	—	9.00	15.00	35.00	40.00
1932A Proof	—	Value: 150				
1932D	7,055,000	—	12.00	18.00	40.00	50.00
1932D Proof	—	Value: 150				
1932E	3,729,000	—	15.00	23.00	45.00	55.00
1932E Proof	—	Value: 150				
1932F	5,022,000	—	12.00	18.00	48.00	60.00
1932F Proof	—	Value: 150				
1932G	3,050,000	—	15.00	25.00	80.00	100
1932G Proof	—	Value: 150				
1932J	4,094,000	—	12.00	18.00	65.00	75.00
1932J Proof	—	Value: 150				

KM# 39 5 REICHSPFENNIG

Aluminum-Bronze **Obv:** Denomination within square, oak leaf on each side **Rev:** Six grain sprigs form center triangle above date

Date	Mintage	F	VF	XF	Unc	BU
1924A	14,469,000	0.30	0.60	3.00	20.00	22.00
1924D	8,139,000	0.50	1.00	4.00	20.00	23.00
1924E	5,976,000	0.50	1.00	5.00	25.00	28.00
1924E Proof, Rare	166	—	—	—	—	—
1924F	3,134,000	0.50	1.00	4.00	25.00	28.00
1924G	4,790,000	0.50	1.00	7.00	30.00	33.00
1924J	2,200,000	0.50	2.00	10.00	40.00	44.00
1925A	85,239,000	0.20	0.50	2.50	13.00	15.00
1925D	39,750,000	0.20	0.50	2.50	15.00	17.00
1925E	17,554,000	0.20	1.00	4.00	18.00	20.00
1925E Proof, Rare	61	—	—	—	—	—
1925F Large 5	20,990,000	6.00	14.00	28.00	130	150
1925F Small 5	Inc. above	0.20	0.50	4.00	25.00	28.00
1925G	10,232,000	0.20	1.00	5.00	26.00	30.00
1925J	10,950,000	0.50	4.00	9.00	40.00	45.00
1926A	22,377,000	0.50	1.00	5.00	30.00	35.00
1926E	5,990,000	10.00	25.00	50.00	260	290
1926E Proof, Rare	33	—	—	—	—	—
1926F	2,871,000	5.00	16.00	38.00	190	220
1930A	7,418,000	0.30	3.00	6.00	25.00	30.00
1935A	19,178,000	0.20	0.50	1.00	10.00	12.00
1935D	5,480,000	0.20	0.50	2.00	12.00	14.00
1935E	2,384,000	0.30	0.60	3.00	20.00	22.00
1935F	4,585,000	0.20	0.50	2.00	16.00	18.00
1935G	2,652,000	0.30	3.00	6.00	20.00	22.00
1935J	2,614,000	0.30	3.00	6.00	24.00	26.00
1936A	36,992,000	0.20	0.30	1.00	10.00	12.00
1936D	8,108,000	0.20	0.50	2.00	12.00	14.00
1936E	2,981,000	0.20	0.60	3.00	18.00	20.00
1936F	6,643,000	0.20	0.60	3.00	15.00	17.00
1936G	2,274,000	0.20	0.60	3.00	18.00	20.00

Date	Mintage	F	VF	XF	Unc	BU
1936J	4,470,000	0.20	0.60	3.00	18.00	20.00
1924-36 Common date proof	—	Value: 100				

KM# 40 10 REICHSPFENNIG

Aluminum-Bronze **Obv:** Denomination within square, oak leaf on each side **Rev:** Six grain sprigs form center triangle above date

Date	Mintage	F	VF	XF	Unc	BU
1924A	20,883,000	0.20	1.00	6.00	32.00	35.00
1924D	9,639,000	0.20	1.00	9.00	52.00	60.00
1924E	5,185,000	0.20	1.00	6.00	35.00	40.00
1924E Proof, Rare	166	—	—	—	—	—
1924F	2,758,000	1.00	9.00	28.00	160	180
1924G	4,363,000	0.30	2.00	11.00	70.00	85.00
1924J	3,993,000	0.30	2.00	11.00	70.00	85.00
1925A	102,319,000	0.20	0.50	2.00	15.00	20.00
1925D	36,853,000	0.20	1.00	4.00	28.00	32.00
1925E	18,700,000	0.30	2.00	9.00	45.00	52.00
1925E Proof, Rare	61	—	—	—	—	—
1925F	12,516,000	0.20	3.00	15.00	55.00	62.00
1925G	10,360,000	0.30	4.00	15.00	60.00	70.00
1925J	8,755,000	1.00	5.00	17.00	80.00	90.00
1926A	14,390,000	0.30	2.00	10.00	50.00	55.00
1926G	1,481,000	2.00	10.00	28.00	130	150
1928A	2,308,000	2.00	6.00	12.00	45.00	60.00
1928G	Inc. below	50.00	120	200	600	700
1929A	25,712,000	0.20	1.00	2.00	22.00	25.00
1929D	7,049,000	0.20	1.00	2.00	35.00	40.00
1929E	3,138,000	0.30	2.00	12.00	75.00	90.00
1929F	3,740,000	0.30	2.00	12.00	65.00	75.00
1929G	2,729,000	0.30	4.00	18.00	90.00	100
1929J	4,086,000	0.30	2.00	12.00	75.00	85.00
1930A	7,540,000	0.20	1.00	3.00	20.00	24.00
1930D	2,148,000	0.30	2.00	5.00	35.00	40.00
1930E	2,090,000	1.00	4.00	13.00	90.00	110
1930F	2,006,000	1.00	4.00	13.00	60.00	75.00
1930G	1,542,000	2.00	5.00	20.00	100	130
1930J	1,637,000	2.00	4.00	12.00	100	120
1931A	9,661,000	0.30	2.00	4.00	25.00	35.00
1931D	664,000	15.00	35.00	70.00	180	200
1931F	1,482,000	7.50	20.00	45.00	150	180
1931G	38,000	170	260	430	1,600	2,000
1932A	4,528,000	0.30	2.00	4.00	24.00	28.00
1932D	2,812,000	0.50	4.00	10.00	50.00	60.00
1932E	1,491,000	2.50	5.00	12.00	75.00	90.00
1932F	1,806,000	3.00	8.00	15.00	90.00	115
1932G	137,000	350	850	1,250	2,000	2,500
1933A	1,349,000	15.00	25.00	45.00	170	200
1933G	1,046,000	5.00	15.00	30.00	80.00	100
1933J	1,634,000	3.00	9.00	20.00	60.00	75.00
1934A	3,200,000	0.30	1.00	6.00	30.00	35.00
1934D	1,252,000	2.00	7.00	18.00	110	125
1934E	Inc. below	18.00	35.00	65.00	180	215
1934F	100,000	12.00	30.00	55.00	170	205
1934G	150,000	15.00	40.00	75.00	290	335
1935A	35,890,000	0.20	0.50	2.00	15.00	17.00
1935D	8,960,000	0.20	0.50	2.00	18.00	20.00
1935E	5,966,000	0.20	0.50	2.00	20.00	22.00
1935F	7,944,000	0.20	0.30	1.50	18.00	20.00
1935G	4,847,000	0.20	0.50	3.00	20.00	22.00
1935J	8,995,000	0.20	0.50	3.00	16.00	18.00
1936A	24,527,000	0.20	0.80	2.00	18.00	20.00
1936D	8,092,000	0.20	1.00	3.00	23.00	25.00
1936E	2,441,000	0.20	1.00	6.00	28.00	31.00
1936F	4,889,000	0.20	1.00	3.00	24.00	27.00
1936G	1,715,000	0.20	3.00	12.00	50.00	56.00
1936J	1,632,000	0.50	4.00	18.00	70.00	80.00
1924-36 Common date proof	—	Value: 100				

KM# 41 50 REICHSPFENNIG

Aluminum-Bronze **Obv:** Denomination within square, oak leaf on each side **Rev:** Six grain sprigs form center triangle above date

Date	Mintage	F	VF	XF	Unc	BU
1924A	801,000	600	1,000	1,600	2,800	3,200
1924A	—	Value: 3,500				
1924E	Inc. below	1,650	3,000	4,000	5,000	5,500
1924F	55,000	3,200	7,000	10,000	17,000	20,000
1924F Proof	—	Value: 22,500				

Note: Peus Auction #324 4-89 proof realized $10,360

Date	Mintage	F	VF	XF	Unc	BU
1924G	11,000	6,000	12,000	18,000	25,000	30,000
1924G Proof	—	Value: 15,000				
1925E	1,805,000	800	1,200	2,000	3,500	4,000

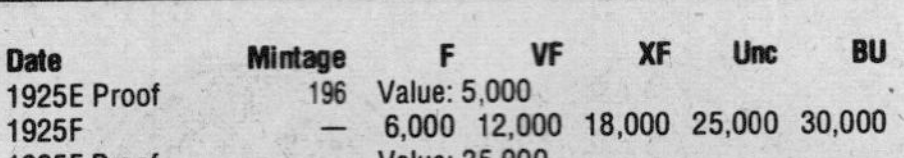

Date	Mintage	F	VF	XF	Unc	BU
1925E Proof	196	Value: 5,000				
1925F	—	6,000	12,000	18,000	25,000	30,000
1925F Proof	—	Value: 35,000				

Note: Peus Auction #324 4-89 proof realized $23,830. Kurdfälzische Munzhandlung Mannheim 6-91 proof realized $37,600

KM# 49 50 REICHSPFENNIG

Nickel **Obv:** Imperial eagle within circle, leaf spray below **Rev:** Denomination within lined circle, oak leaves and acorns above

Date	Mintage	F	VF	XF	Unc	BU
1927A	16,309,000	2.00	3.00	7.00	23.00	25.00
1927D	2,228,000	3.00	7.00	15.00	65.00	75.00
1927E	1,070,000	4.00	9.00	18.00	70.00	80.00
1927F	1,940,000	2.50	6.00	12.00	60.00	70.00
1927G	1,756,000	5.00	15.00	25.00	100	120
1927J	4,056,000	2.50	6.00	12.00	60.00	70.00
1928A	43,864,000	0.80	2.00	4.00	18.00	20.00
1928D	14,088,000	1.00	3.00	6.00	30.00	35.00
1928E	8,618,000	1.00	3.00	6.00	30.00	35.00
1928F	9,954,000	1.00	3.00	6.00	30.00	35.00
1928G	6,177,000	1.00	3.50	7.00	40.00	50.00
1928J	6,565,000	1.00	3.00	6.00	40.00	50.00
1929A	10,298,000	1.00	3.00	7.00	40.00	50.00
1929D	1,965,000	2.00	6.00	15.00	70.00	85.00
1929F	1,162,000	9.00	20.00	45.00	150	170
1930A	4,128,000	1.00	4.00	8.00	40.00	48.00
1930D	1,406,000	4.00	8.00	15.00	75.00	88.00
1930E	745,000	20.00	35.00	70.00	220	250
1930F	320,000	50.00	100	140	360	420
1930G	610,000	18.00	40.00	80.00	250	280
1930J	526,000	20.00	50.00	100	280	320
1931A	5,624,000	1.00	4.00	8.00	21.00	24.00
1931D	1,125,000	2.00	7.00	16.00	32.00	35.00
1931F	1,484,000	2.00	6.00	15.00	30.00	33.00
1931G	60,000	190	290	420	900	1,000
1931J	291,000	45.00	120	200	400	500
1932E	598,000	40.00	90.00	150	400	500
1932G	96,000	800	1,300	1,900	2,900	3,500
1933G	333,000	55.00	120	180	430	475
1933J	654,000	45.00	100	155	360	390
1935A	6,390,000	1.00	4.00	9.00	32.00	36.00
1935D	2,812,000	3.00	7.00	15.00	42.00	48.00
1935E	745,000	10.00	25.00	40.00	130	150
1935F	2,006,000	3.00	6.00	12.00	40.00	50.00
1935G	650,000	15.00	35.00	48.00	140	180
1935J	1,635,000	3.00	14.00	34.00	100	120
1936A	7,696,000	2.00	4.00	10.00	25.00	35.00
1936D	844,000	7.00	20.00	42.00	155	175
1936E	1,190,000	7.00	20.00	40.00	165	190
1936F	602,000	9.00	25.00	52.00	180	220
1936G	936,000	6.00	18.00	35.00	110	130
1936J	490,000	30.00	70.00	120	260	290
1937A	10,842,000	1.00	2.50	5.00	12.00	14.00
1937D	2,814,000	1.00	4.00	12.00	36.00	40.00
1937F	1,700,000	1.00	4.00	12.00	36.00	40.00
1937J	300,000	60.00	120	200	380	420
1938E	1,200,000	8.00	15.00	30.00	110	125
1938G	1,299,000	7.00	13.00	26.00	90.00	105
1938J	1,333,000	7.00	13.00	26.00	90.00	105
1927-38 Common date proof	—	Value: 200				

KM# 42 MARK

5.0000 g., 0.5000 Silver .0803 oz. ASW **Obv:** Denomination above date **Rev:** Imperial eagle

Date	Mintage	F	VF	XF	Unc	BU
1924A	75,536,000	5.00	12.00	24.00	65.00	75.00
1924D	17,099,000	6.00	13.00	26.00	75.00	90.00
1924E	12,293,000	7.00	16.00	32.00	170	190
1924E Proof	115	Value: 275				
1924F	16,550,000	6.00	13.00	26.00	120	140
1924G	10,065,000	7.00	15.00	30.00	160	190
1924J	13,481,000	6.00	12.00	25.00	110	130
1925A	13,878,000	14.00	28.00	56.00	270	290
1925D	6,100,000	9.00	20.00	40.00	130	150
1924-25 Common date proof	—	Value: 250				

KM# 43 3 MARK

15.0000 g., 0.5000 Silver .2411 oz. ASW, 30 mm. **Obv:** Denomination above date **Rev:** Imperial eagle

Date	Mintage	F	VF	XF	Unc	BU
1924A	24,386,000	16.00	40.00	80.00	110	130
1924D	3,769,000	20.00	45.00	90.00	280	320
1924E	3,353,000	20.00	42.00	80.00	280	320
1924E Proof	115	Value: 450				
1924F	4,518,000	20.00	40.00	80.00	200	230
1924G	2,745,000	25.00	50.00	100	300	340
1924J	3,677,000	20.00	40.00	80.00	220	250
1925D	2,558,000	40.00	100	200	700	790
1924-25 Common date proof	—	Value: 280				

KM# 44 REICHSMARK

5.0000 g., 0.5000 Silver .0803 oz. ASW **Obv:** Imperial eagle above date **Rev:** Denomination within wreath

Date	Mintage	F	VF	XF	Unc	BU
1925A	34,527,000	5.00	12.00	24.00	50.00	55.00
1925A Proof	600	Value: 380				
1925D	13,854,000	6.00	16.00	28.00	60.00	70.00
1925E	6,460,000	8.00	20.00	32.00	110	125
1925F	8,035,000	8.00	17.00	27.00	135	155
1925G	4,520,000	9.00	23.00	38.00	120	140
1925J	6,800,000	9.00	22.00	36.00	115	135
1926A	35,555,000	8.00	17.00	26.00	95.00	110
1926D	4,424,000	10.00	21.00	38.00	120	140
1926E	3,225,000	14.00	32.00	70.00	230	260
1926E Proof	31	Value: 450				
1926F	3,045,000	12.00	30.00	50.00	190	210
1926G	3,410,000	14.00	32.00	55.00	240	260
1926J	1,290,000	50.00	110	180	480	540
1927A	364,000	250	390	600	1,300	1,400
1927F	1,959,000	40.00	70.00	110	280	310
1927J	2,451,000	30.00	55.00	100	240	265

KM# 45 2 REICHSMARK

10.0000 g., 0.5000 Silver .1608 oz. ASW, 28 mm. **Obv:** Imperial eagle above date **Rev:** Denomination within wreath

Date	Mintage	F	VF	XF	Unc	BU
1925A	16,145,000	8.00	16.00	24.00	80.00	90.00
1925D	2,272,000	10.00	20.00	32.00	120	135
1925E	1,971,000	12.00	25.00	43.00	160	175
1925E Proof	101	Value: 350				
1925F	2,414,000	11.00	23.00	37.00	100	115
1925G	929,000	15.00	32.00	65.00	210	230
1925J	2,326,000	10.00	20.00	32.00	96.00	110
1926A	31,645,000	8.00	16.00	25.00	70.00	80.00
1926D	11,322,000	8.00	16.00	25.00	80.00	90.00
1926E	5,107,000	11.00	23.00	45.00	170	190
1926E Proof	30	—	750	—	—	—
1926F	7,115,000	8.00	16.00	32.00	105	120
1926G	5,171,000	10.00	20.00	42.00	150	170
1926J	5,305,000	10.00	18.00	38.00	115	130
1927A	6,399,000	12.00	25.00	40.00	135	150
1927D	466,000	800	1,200	2,000	5,000	6,000
1927E	373,000	200	325	700	1,400	1,600
1927E Proof	53	Value: 3,000				
1927F	502,000	60.00	200	300	950	1,100
1927J	540,000	45.00	100	185	500	580
1931D	2,109,000	20.00	36.00	53.00	160	180
1931E	1,118,000	26.00	50.00	85.00	240	270
1931F	1,505,000	22.00	40.00	65.00	190	230
1931G	915,000	30.00	55.00	100	250	300
1931J	1,226,000	30.00	55.00	100	520	600
1925-31 Common date proof	—	Value: 300				

KM# 46 3 REICHSMARK
15.0000 g., 0.5000 Silver .2411 oz. ASW, 30 mm. **Subject:** 1000th Year of the Rhineland **Obv:** Armored figure behind shield divides date, right arm raised **Rev:** Denomination within wreath **Designer:** Wackerle

Date	Mintage	F	VF	XF	Unc	BU
1925A	3,052,000	25.00	45.00	55.00	100	110
1925A Proof	—	Value: 200				
1925D	1,123,000	25.00	50.00	60.00	110	125
1925D Proof	—	Value: 240				
1925E	441,000	25.00	55.00	65.00	120	145
1925E Proof	229	Value: 250				
1925F	173,000	30.00	60.00	75.00	135	155
1925F Proof	—	Value: 280				
1925G	300,000	30.00	55.00	70.00	115	130
1925G Proof	—	Value: 240				
1925J	492,000	30.00	55.00	70.00	115	130
1925J Proof	—	Value: 240				

KM# 48 3 REICHSMARK
15.0000 g., 0.5000 Silver .2411 oz. ASW, 30 mm. **Subject:** 700 Years of Freedom for Lubeck **Obv:** Denomination within circle, leaf spray below **Rev:** Double imperial eagle on shield within circle, dates above

Date	Mintage	F	VF	XF	Unc	BU
1926A	200,000	60.00	110	180	240	260
1926A Proof	—	Value: 300				

KM# 50 3 REICHSMARK
15.0000 g., 0.5000 Silver .2411 oz. ASW, 30 mm. **Subject:** 100th Anniversary of Bremerhaven **Obv:** Imperial eagle on shield within scalloped design **Rev:** Shield divides date below ship

Date	Mintage	F	VF	XF	Unc	BU
1927A	150,000	70.00	130	190	270	290
1927A Proof	—	Value: 360				

KM# 52 3 REICHSMARK
15.0000 g., 0.5000 Silver .2411 oz. ASW, 30 mm. **Subject:** 1000th Anniversary - Founding of Nordhausen **Obv:** Large denomination within scalloped design **Rev:** Heinrich I and Mathilde **Designer:** Maxmillian Dasio

Date	Mintage	F	VF	XF	Unc	BU
1927A	100,000	60.00	120	190	260	290
1927A Proof	—	Value: 500				

KM# 53 3 REICHSMARK
15.0000 g., 0.5000 Silver .2411 oz. ASW, 30 mm. **Subject:** 400th Anniversary - Philipps University in Marburg **Obv:** Imperial eagle, denomination below **Rev:** Arms of Philip I the Magnanimous **Designer:** Maxmillian Dasio

Date	Mintage	F	VF	XF	Unc	BU
1927A	130,000	60.00	115	160	240	265
1927A Proof	—	Value: 290				

KM# 54 3 REICHSMARK
15.0000 g., 0.5000 Silver .2411 oz. ASW, 30 mm. **Subject:** 450th Anniversary - Tubingen University **Obv:** Imperial eagle, denomination below **Rev:** Count Eberhard the Bearded left

Date	Mintage	F	VF	XF	Unc	BU
1927F	50,000	190	380	520	720	760
1927F Proof	—	Value: 980				

KM# 57 3 REICHSMARK
15.0000 g., 0.5000 Silver .2411 oz. ASW, 30 mm. **Subject:** 900th Anniversary - Founding of Naumburg **Obv:** Imperial eagle above denomination **Rev:** Margrave Hermann, City Founder

Date	Mintage	F	VF	XF	Unc	BU
1928A	100,000	70.00	115	170	230	250
1928A Matte proof	—	Value: 480				

KM# 58 3 REICHSMARK
15.0000 g., 0.5000 Silver .2411 oz. ASW, 30 mm. **Subject:** 400th Anniversary - Death of Albrecht Durer **Obv:** Imperial eagle above denomination **Rev:** Head left within circle, date below **Designer:** Nida Rumelin

Date	Mintage	F	VF	XF	Unc	BU
1928D	50,000	150	330	530	710	750
1928D Matte proof	—	Value: 900				

KM# 59 3 REICHSMARK
15.0000 g., 0.5000 Silver .2411 oz. ASW, 30 mm. **Subject:** 1000th Anniversary - Founding of Dinkelsbuhl **Obv:** Imperial eagle above denomination **Rev:** Shield below figure holding sickle and sheaf, towers flank, date is divided in fourths by the above **Designer:** Karl Roth

Date	Mintage	F	VF	XF	Unc	BU
1928D	40,000	250	500	750	900	1,000
1928D Proof	—	Value: 1,400				
1928D Matte proof	—	Value: 2,250				

KM# 65 3 REICHSMARK
15.0000 g., 0.5000 Silver .2411 oz. ASW, 30 mm. **Subject:** 1000th Anniversary - Meissen **Obv:** Imperial eagle within circle, denomination below **Rev:** Central figure holding shields on poles divides date, five crosses above

Date	Mintage	F	VF	XF	Unc	BU
1929E	200,000	30.00	50.00	75.00	115	125
1929E Proof	—	Value: 330				

KM# 62 3 REICHSMARK
15.0000 g., 0.5000 Silver .2411 oz. ASW, 30 mm. **Subject:** Waldeck-Prussia Union **Obv:** Imperial eagle above denomination **Rev:** Eagle with wings lowered holds shield at left, date below **Designer:** Kruschker

Date	Mintage	F	VF	XF	Unc	BU
1929A	170,000	55.00	125	175	250	270
1929A Proof	—	Value: 450				

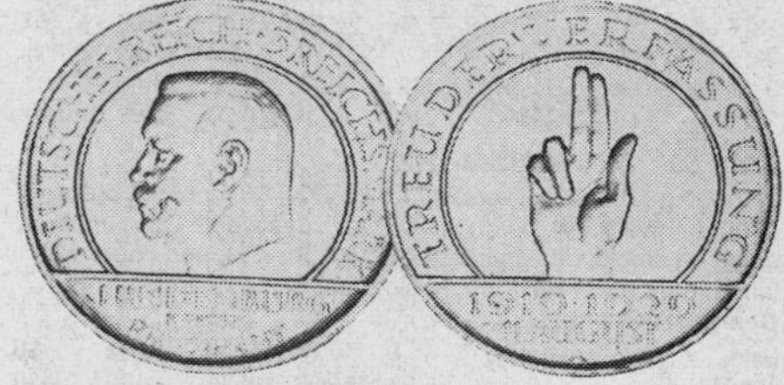

KM# 63 3 REICHSMARK
15.0000 g., 0.5000 Silver .2411 oz. ASW, 30 mm. **Subject:** 10th Anniversary - Weimar Constitution **Obv:** Paul Von Beneckendorff Und Von Hindenburg **Rev:** Hand with two fingers raised within circle, dates below **Designer:** Rudolf Bosselt

Date	Mintage	F	VF	XF	Unc	BU
1929A	1,421,000	20.00	35.00	65.00	80.00	70.00
1929A Proof	—	Value: 250				
1929A Matte proof	—	—	—	—	—	—
1929D	499,000	20.00	40.00	75.00	90.00	98.00
1929D Proof	—	Value: 250				
1929E	122,000	24.00	50.00	85.00	100	110
1929E Proof	—	Value: 280				
1929F	370,000	20.00	40.00	80.00	95.00	105
1929F Proof	—	Value: 280				
1929G	256,000	20.00	40.00	80.00	95.00	105
1929G Proof	—	Value: 280				
1929J	342,000	20.00	40.00	75.00	90.00	105
1929J Proof	—	Value: 280				

KM# 60 3 REICHSMARK
15.0000 g., 0.5000 Silver .2411 oz. ASW, 30 mm. **Subject:** 200th Anniversary - Birth of Gotthold Lessing **Obv:** Small imperial eagle, denomination below **Rev:** Head left divides dates **Designer:** Rudolf Bosselt

Date	Mintage	F	VF	XF	Unc	BU
1929A	217,000	25.00	50.00	80.00	130	140
1929A Proof	—	Value: 290				

Date	Mintage	F	VF	XF	Unc	BU
1929D	56,000	30.00	55.00	85.00	145	155
1929D Proof	—	Value: 330				
1929E	30,000	30.00	65.00	95.00	160	170
1929E Proof	—	Value: 330				
1929F	40,000	25.00	45.00	90.00	140	150
1929F Proof	—	Value: 330				
1929G	24,000	25.00	40.00	85.00	160	170
1929G Proof	—	Value: 330				
1929J	33,000	25.00	40.00	85.00	150	160
1929J Proof	—	Value: 330				

KM# 67 3 REICHSMARK

15.0000 g., 0.5000 Silver .2411 oz. ASW, 30 mm. **Subject:** Graf Zeppelin Flight **Obv:** Imperial eagle, denomination below **Rev:** Zeppelin across globe, date below

Date	Mintage	F	VF	XF	Unc	BU
1930A	542,000	35.00	65.00	90.00	140	150
1930A Proof	—	Value: 325				
1930D	141,000	35.00	70.00	95.00	150	160
1930D Proof	—	Value: 360				
1930E	75,000	45.00	90.00	125	170	185
1930E Proof	—	Value: 360				
1930F	100,000	35.00	70.00	95.00	145	155
1930F Proof	—	Value: 325				
1930G	61,000	45.00	90.00	125	170	185
1930G Proof	—	Value: 360				
1930J	82,000	50.00	100	115	155	170
1930J Proof	—	Value: 360				

KM# 69 3 REICHSMARK

15.0000 g., 0.5000 Silver .2411 oz. ASW, 30 mm. **Subject:** 700th Anniversary - Death of Von Der Vogelweide **Obv:** Imperial eagle on shield, design in background **Rev:** Robed figure with tablet, harp and shield at left, birds at right, date below **Rev. Designer:** Grienauer

Date	Mintage	F	VF	XF	Unc	BU
1930A	163,000	35.00	55.00	95.00	120	130
1930A Proof	—	Value: 290				
1930A Matte proof	—	Value: 500				
1930D	42,000	35.00	65.00	100	140	150
1930D Proof	—	Value: 290				
1930E	22,000	37.50	75.00	120	160	175
1930E Proof	—	Value: 290				
1930F	30,000	37.50	85.00	110	200	220
1930F Proof	—	Value: 290				
1930G	18,000	45.00	80.00	130	175	190
1930G Proof	—	Value: 290				
1930J	25,000	45.00	80.00	120	165	180
1930J Proof	—	Value: 290				

KM# 70 3 REICHSMARK

15.0000 g., 0.5000 Silver .2411 oz. ASW, 30 mm. **Subject:** Liberation of Rhineland **Obv:** Imperial eagle on shield, design in background **Rev:** Eagle left on bridge divides date

Date	Mintage	F	VF	XF	Unc	BU
1930A	1,734,000	25.00	48.00	65.00	100	110
1930A Proof	—	Value: 240				
1930A Matte proof	—	—	—	—	—	—
1930D	450,000	25.00	55.00	75.00	120	135
1930D Proof	—	Value: 240				
1930E	38,000	75.00	120	200	330	360
1930E Proof	—	Value: 450				
1930F	321,000	35.00	60.00	90.00	110	125
1930F Proof	—	Value: 240				
1930G	195,000	35.00	65.00	100	130	145

Date	Mintage	F	VF	XF	Unc	BU
1930G Proof	—	Value: 240				
1930J	261,000	35.00	60.00	90.00	120	135
1930J Proof	—	Value: 240				

KM# 72 3 REICHSMARK

15.0000 g., 0.5000 Silver .2411 oz. ASW, 30 mm. **Subject:** 300th Anniversary - Magdeburg Rebuilding **Obv:** Eagle on shield, scalloped design in background **Rev:** Shield divides dates above city scene

Date	Mintage	F	VF	XF	Unc	BU
1931A	100,000	90.00	170	255	340	370
1931A Proof	—	Value: 450				

KM# 73 3 REICHSMARK

15.0000 g., 0.5000 Silver .2411 oz. ASW, 30 mm. **Subject:** Centenary - Death of von Stein **Obv:** Imperial eagle divides dates, denomination below **Rev:** Head left, name below

Date	Mintage	F	VF	XF	Unc	BU
1931A	150,000	55.00	120	180	240	260
1931A Proof	—	Value: 380				

KM# 74 3 REICHSMARK

15.0000 g., 0.5000 Silver .2411 oz. ASW, 30 mm. **Obv:** Imperial eagle above date **Rev:** Denomination within wreath

Date	Mintage	F	VF	XF	Unc	BU
1931A	13,324,000	130	260	360	660	750
1931D	2,232,000	160	300	400	790	900
1931E	2,235,000	190	330	430	1,050	1,200
1931F	2,357,000	160	300	400	730	860
1931G	1,468,000	190	360	490	1,160	1,320
1931J	1,115,000	230	330	460	1,140	1,300
1932A	2,933,000	140	260	400	730	860
1932D	1,986,000	150	280	460	900	1,050
1932F	653,000	230	430	880	2,100	2,600
1932G	210,000	500	900	1,700	4,500	5,800
1932J	1,336,000	190	320	470	970	1,060
1933G	152,000	900	1,750	3,100	7,200	9,000

Note: Less than 10 percent of issue was released

Date	Mintage	F	VF	XF	Unc	BU
1931-33 Common date proof	—	Value: 1,400				

KM# 76 3 REICHSMARK

15.0000 g., 0.5000 Silver .2411 oz. ASW, 30 mm. **Subject:** Centenary - Death of Goethe **Obv:** Imperial eagle divides dates, denomination below **Rev:** Head left, name below

Date	Mintage	F	VF	XF	Unc	BU
1932A	217,000	35.00	80.00	110	160	175
1932A Proof	—	Value: 240				
1932D	56,000	40.00	80.00	115	180	195
1932D Proof	—	Value: 240				
1932E	30,000	45.00	85.00	125	200	220
1932E Proof	—	Value: 280				

Date	Mintage	F	VF	XF	Unc	BU
1932F	40,000	35.00	80.00	115	180	195
1932F Proof	—	Value: 240				
1932F Matte proof	—	Value: 600				
1932G	24,000	45.00	85.00	125	200	220
1932G Proof	—	Value: 320				
1932J	33,000	45.00	80.00	115	180	195
1932J Proof	—	Value: 280				

KM# 47 5 REICHSMARK

25.0000 g., 0.5000 Silver .4019 oz. ASW, 37 mm. **Subject:** 1000th Year of the Rhineland **Obv:** Armored figure behind shield divides date, right arm raised **Rev:** Denomination within wreath **Designer:** Wackerle

Date	Mintage	F	VF	XF	Unc	BU
1925A	684,000	50.00	95.00	125	210	225
1925A Proof	—	Value: 600				
1925D	452,000	50.00	95.00	140	240	265
1925D Proof	—	Value: 700				
1925E	204,000	55.00	110	160	255	285
1925E Proof	226	Value: 700				
1925F	212,000	55.00	105	150	245	275
1925F Proof	—	Value: 700				
1925G	89,000	60.00	120	170	300	350
1925G Proof	—	Value: 700				
1925J	43,000	95.00	190	290	520	580
1925J Proof	—	Value: 800				

KM# 51 5 REICHSMARK

25.0000 g., 0.5000 Silver .4019 oz. ASW, 37 mm. **Subject:** 100th Anniversary - Bremerhaven **Obv:** Imperial eagle on shield, scalloped design in background **Rev:** Crowned shield divides date below ship

Date	Mintage	F	VF	XF	Unc	BU
1927A	50,000	220	420	580	760	850
1927A Proof	—	Value: 980				

KM# 55 5 REICHSMARK

25.0000 g., 0.5000 Silver .4019 oz. ASW, 37 mm. **Subject:** 450th Anniversary - University of Tubingen **Rev:** Bust left within circle

Date	Mintage	F	VF	XF	Unc	BU
1927F	40,000	130	290	550	720	850
1927F Proof	—	Value: 1,100				

KM# 56 5 REICHSMARK
25.0000 g., 0.5000 Silver .4019 oz. ASW, 37 mm. **Obv:** Imperial eagle within circle, denomination below **Rev:** Oaktree divides date

Date	Mintage	F	VF	XF	Unc	BU
1927A	7,926,000	35.00	90.00	140	260	280
1927D	1,471,000	40.00	100	160	340	370
1927E	1,100,000	50.00	120	175	430	470
1927F	700,000	50.00	130	220	550	630
1927G	759,000	60.00	160	260	880	1,000
1927J	1,006,000	50.00	125	190	480	520
1928A	15,466,000	40.00	100	135	290	320
1928D	4,613,000	45.00	110	145	400	440
1928E	2,310,000	60.00	130	190	520	580
1928F	3,771,000	50.00	120	160	420	480
1928G	1,923,000	65.00	145	180	450	500
1928J	2,450,000	60.00	125	170	430	490
1929A	6,730,000	45.00	100	130	300	330
1929D	2,020,000	50.00	130	190	490	535
1929E	860,000	140	320	540	1,650	1,900
1929F	814,000	70.00	175	260	760	850
1929G	950,000	90.00	190	290	880	990
1929J	779,000	90.00	190	300	800	890
1930A	3,790,000	60.00	120	170	410	440
1930D	606,000	175	450	600	1,700	1,900
1930E	354,000	500	1,550	2,200	5,100	5,700
1930F	630,000	300	650	930	1,650	1,800
1930G	367,000	600	1,350	1,850	4,600	5,100
1930J	740,000	300	660	880	1,800	2,000
1931A	14,651,000	40.00	100	140	270	300
1931D	3,254,000	50.00	120	165	385	420
1931E	2,245,000	60.00	135	180	450	490
1931F	4,152,000	50.00	120	165	385	420
1931G	1,620,000	75.00	190	330	950	1,080
1931J	3,092,000	60.00	140	210	460	500
1932A	32,303,000	40.00	100	140	270	300
1932D	8,556,000	45.00	115	160	300	340
1932E	4,013,000	55.00	125	180	320	360
1932F	5,019,000	50.00	120	170	310	350
1932G	3,504,000	60.00	150	220	500	570
1932J	3,752,000	60.00	150	220	520	590
1933J	423,000	700	1,400	2,600	5,400	6,000
1933J Proof	—	Value: 6,500				
1927-33 Common date proof	—	Value: 900				

KM# 66 5 REICHSMARK
25.0000 g., 0.5000 Silver .4019 oz. ASW, 37 mm. **Subject:** 1000th Anniversary - Meissen **Obv:** Imperial eagle **Rev:** Central figure holding shields on poles divides date, five crosses above

Date	Mintage	F	VF	XF	Unc	BU
1929E	120,000	160	250	400	550	600
1929E Proof	—	Value: 1,000				

KM# 61 5 REICHSMARK
25.0000 g., 0.5000 Silver .4019 oz. ASW, 37 mm. **Subject:** 200th Anniversary - Birth of Gotthold Lessing **Obv:** Small imperial eagle, denomination below **Rev:** Head left divides date

Date	Mintage	F	VF	XF	Unc	BU
1929A	87,000	60.00	100	145	255	275
1929A Proof	—	Value: 600				
1929D	22,000	60.00	110	160	280	310
1929D Proof	—	Value: 670				
1929E	12,000	60.00	125	200	300	330
1929E Proof	—	Value: 670				
1929F	16,000	60.00	120	180	290	320
1929F Proof	—	Value: 670				
1929G	9,760	80.00	150	225	350	400
1929G Proof	—	Value: 800				
1929J	13,000	70.00	130	210	330	360
1929J Proof	—	Value: 670				

KM# 64 5 REICHSMARK
25.0000 g., 0.5000 Silver .4019 oz. ASW, 37 mm. **Subject:** 10th Anniversary - Weimar Constitution **Obv:** Hand with two fingers raised, dates below **Rev:** Head left, denomination above

Date	Mintage	F	VF	XF	Unc	BU
1929A	325,000	55.00	100	160	260	290
1929A Proof	—	Value: 500				
1929D	84,000	60.00	120	180	290	330
1929D Proof	—	Value: 500				
1929E	45,000	70.00	140	200	320	360
1929E Proof	—	Value: 500				
1929F	60,000	70.00	130	190	350	380
1929F Proof	—	Value: 500				
1929G	37,000	70.00	140	200	370	410
1929G Proof	—	Value: 500				
1929J	49,000	70.00	130	190	350	380
1929J Proof	—	Value: 500				

KM# 68 5 REICHSMARK
25.0000 g., 0.5000 Silver .4019 oz. ASW, 37 mm. **Subject:** Graf Zeppelin Flight **Obv:** Imperial eagle, denomination below **Rev:** Zeppelin across globe, date below

Date	Mintage	F	VF	XF	Unc	BU
1930A	217,000	70.00	120	190	300	330
1930A Proof	—	Value: 500				
1930A Matte proof	—	—	—	—	—	—
1930D	56,000	75.00	130	200	325	360
1930D Proof	—	Value: 700				
1930E	30,000	80.00	150	210	350	390
1930E Proof	—	Value: 550				
1930F	40,000	75.00	140	200	340	380
1930F Proof	—	Value: 500				
1930G	24,000	85.00	160	235	350	390
1930G Proof	—	Value: 660				
1930J	33,000	80.00	150	220	340	380
1930J Proof	—	Value: 660				

KM# 71 5 REICHSMARK
25.0000 g., 0.5000 Silver .4019 oz. ASW, 37 mm. **Subject:** Liberation of Rhineland **Obv:** Imperial eagle on shield, design in background **Rev:** Eagle left on bridge divides date

Date	Mintage	F	VF	XF	Unc	BU
1930A	325,000	70.00	125	190	310	340
1930A Proof	—	Value: 500				
1930D	84,000	70.00	135	220	375	400
1930D Proof	—	Value: 550				
1930E	45,000	80.00	150	275	420	450
1930E Proof	—	Value: 500				
1930F	60,000	70.00	135	235	400	440
1930F Proof	—	Value: 500				
1930G	37,000	90.00	170	280	440	490
1930G Proof	—	Value: 670				
1930J	49,000	80.00	150	250	420	460
1930J Proof	—	Value: 620				

KM# 77 5 REICHSMARK
25.0000 g., 0.5000 Silver .4019 oz. ASW, 37 mm. **Subject:** Centenary - Death of Goethe **Obv:** Imperial eagle divides dates, denomination below **Rev:** Head left, name below

Date	Mintage	F	VF	XF	Unc	BU
1932A	11,000	950	2,300	2,850	3,450	3,800
1932A Proof	—	Value: 4,500				
1932D	2,812	1,000	2,400	3,000	3,800	4,200
1932D Proof	—	Value: 5,000				
1932E	1,490	1,000	2,500	3,150	4,200	4,500
1932E Proof	—	Value: 5,000				
1932F	2,006	1,000	2,400	3,000	4,000	4,500
1932F Proof	—	Value: 5,000				
1932G	1,220	1,050	2,550	3,200	4,250	4,750
1932G Proof	—	Value: 5,000				
1932J	1,634	1,000	2,450	3,100	4,100	4,500
1932J Proof	—	Value: 5,000				

PATTERNS

Including off metal strikes

KM#	Date	Mintage	Identification	Mkt Val
Pn212	1919A	—	50 Pfennig. Brass.	250
Pn213	1919A	—	50 Pfennig. Silver.	350
Pn214	1919A	—	50 Pfennig. Nickel.	175
Pn215	1919A	—	50 Pfennig. Aluminum.	175
Pn216	1919A	—	50 Pfennig. Zinc.	175
Pn217	1919A	—	50 Pfennig. Zinc. Reeded edge.	—
Pn218	1919A	—	50 Pfennig. Aluminum. Reeded edge.	125
Pn219	1919A	—	50 Pfennig. Aluminum. Plain edge.	—
Pn220	1919A	—	50 Pfennig. Aluminum. Ornamental edge.	—
Pn221	1919A	—	50 Pfennig. Zinc. Ornamental edge.	—
Pn222	1919G	—	1/2 Mark. KM#17.	—
Pn223	1919G	—	Mark. Copper. KM#14.	—
Pn224	19xxA	—	Mark. Aluminum.	—
Pn225	1921A	—	Mark. Brass Plated Aluminum.	—
Pn226	1921A	—	Mark. Zinc.	—
Pn227	1921A	—	Mark.	—
Pn228	1921A	—	Mark. Aluminum Plated Steel.	—
Pn229	1921A	—	Mark. Nickel.	150
Pn230	1921A	—	Mark. Silver.	—
Pn231	1921A	—	Mark. Iron.	—
Pn232	1921A	—	Mark. Copper Strips Inlaid On Silver Or Copper-Nickel.	—
Pn233	1921A	—	Mark. Copper Strips Inlaid On Aluminum.	—
PnA234	1922A	—	10 Pfennig. Iron.	225
Pn234	1922A	—	50 Pfennig. Iron. Plain with 6 ridges edge. KM#27.	—
Pn235	1922F	—	3 Mark. Aluminum. KM#28; GOTT MIT UNS.	850

Note: Most 1922F lettered-edge 3 Marks were recovered from the burned out ruins of the Stuttgart Mint destroyed in World War II; the above value is for the one known perfect example, blackened VF examples are valued between $200 and $400

KM#	Date	Mintage	Identification	Mkt Val
Pn236	1922F	—	3 Mark. Aluminum. Reeded edge. KM#28.	—
Pn237	1922F	—	3 Mark. Aluminum. Plain edge. KM#28.	—
Pn238	1922G	—	3 Mark. Aluminum. Reeded edge. KM#28.	—
Pn239	1922A	—	5 Mark. Aluminum.	125
Pn239a	1922A	—	5 Mark. Aluminum Plated Copper.	750
Pn240	1922A	—	5 Mark. Roman lettering.	—
Pn248	1923F	—	1000 Mark. Silver. Reeded edge.	—
Pn249	1923F	—	1000 Mark. Aluminum. Plain edge.	—
Pn241	1923	—	2 Pfennig. Bronze. Without mintmark; KM#31.	—
Pn242	1923	—	50 Pfennig. Aluminum-Bronze. Without mintmark; KM#34.	—
Pn243	1923F	—	3 Mark. KM#29.4.	250

Note: All pattern 1923F 3 Marks were recovered from the burned out ruins of the Stuttgart Mint destroyed in World War II; blackened VF examples range in value from $250 to $450

KM#	Date	Mintage	Identification	Mkt Val
Pn244	1923A	—	20 Mark. Aluminum.	—
Pn245	1923A	—	100 Mark. Aluminum.	—
Pn246	1923F	—	200 Mark. Aluminum. Doubled reeding; KM#35.	—
Pn247	1923F	—	1000 Mark. Aluminum. Reeded edge.	325
Pn252	1924E	—	10 Pfennig. Aluminum.	—
Pn257	1924A	—	Mark. Silver. Reeded, lettered edge.	—
Pn258	1924A	—	3 Mark. 0.5000 Silver. Ornamental edge.	—
Pn259	1924E	—	5 Mark. Silver.	—
PnA250	1924	—	2 Pfennig. Brass. KM#31.	150
Pn254	1924E	—	10 Pfennig. Aluminum. Full eagle	—
Pn256	1924D	—	50 Pfennig. Lead. KM#41.	—
Pn250	1924E	—	2 Pfennig. Copper. Eagle head left.	—
Pn251	1924E	—	10 Pfennig. Copper.	—
Pn253	1924E	—	10 Pfennig. Copper. Full eagle	—
Pn255	1924E	—	10 Pfennig. Nickel. Full eagle.	—
Pn261	1925E	—	2 Pfennig. Copper.	—
Pn262	1925E	—	5 Pfennig. Copper-Nickel.	—
Pn263	1925E	—	5 Pfennig. Copper-Nickel. Larger eagle head.	—
Pn265	1925	6	50 Pfennig. Aluminum-Bronze. KM#41.	17,500

Note: An XF-AU example brought $15,957, Emporium Hamburg 1987 sale

KM#	Date	Mintage	Identification	Mkt Val
Pn266	1925F	—	50 Pfennig. Brass. Bundle.	125
Pn273	1925E	—	Mark. Silver. Thick wreath.	—
Pn274	1925E	—	Mark. Nickel. Thick wreath.	—
Pn278	1925E	—	3 Mark. Silver.	450
Pn260	1925E	—	Pfennig. Copper.	—
Pn264	1925E	—	10 Pfennig. Copper-Nickel.	—
Pn267	1925F	—	50 Pfennig. Bronze. Bundle.	125
Pn268	1925F	—	50 Pfennig. Copper-Nickel. Bundle.	125
Pn271	1925F	—	50 Pfennig. Nickel. Mercury	150
Pn272	1925F	—	50 Pfennig. Brass. Mercury	—
Pn275	1925E	—	Mark. 0.4500 Silver. Thin wreath.	—
Pn276	1925E	—	2 Mark. 0.5000 Silver. Thick wreath.	175
Pn277	1925J	—	3 Mark. Iron. KM#46.	—
Pn281a	1925F	—	5 Mark. Silvered-Bronze.	175
Pn282	1925E	—	5 Mark. Silver.	1,500

KM#	Date	Mintage	Identification	Mkt Val
Pn279	1925E	—	5 Reichsmark. Silver.	850
Pn281	1925F	—	5 Mark. Silver.	1,850
Pn283	1925E	—	20 Mark. Gold.	7,500
Pn284	1925E	—	20 Mark. Brass.	—
Pn269	1925F	—	50 Pfennig. Nickel. Bundle.	125
Pn270	1925F	—	50 Pfennig. Nickel-Silver. Mercury	150
PnA276	1925F	—	3 Mark. Brass.	—
PnA277	1925	—	3 Mark. Brass. Woman's head.	—
Pn280	1925E	—	5 Mark. Silver.	850
Pn285	1926E	—	50 Pfennig. Copper-Nickel.	—
Pn286	1926	—	50 Pfennig.	—
Pn287	1926E	—	50 Pfennig. Copper-Nickel. Leaves through value	150
Pn292	1926E	—	50 Pfennig. Copper-Nickel. Two leaves.	—
Pn300	1926E	—	50 Pfennig. Copper-Nickel. Eagle.	—
Pn307	1926A	—	Mark. Brass.	125
PnA308	1926	—	3 Mark.	—
Pn309	1926	—	5 Mark. Silver. Wreath aaround eagle.	—
Pn318	1926F	—	5 Mark. Silver. With motto.	700
Pn306	1926J	—	50 Pfennig. Nickel. Smaller eagle.	—
Pn307a	1926A	—	Mark. Silver.	—
Pn308	1926A	—	5 Mark. Silver.	—
Pn310	1926A	—	5 Mark. Silver.	850
Pn312	1926A	—	5 Mark. Silver.	1,000
Pn317	1926F	—	5 Mark. Silver. "PROBE"; with motto.	—
Pn289	1926E	—	50 Pfennig. Copper-Nickel. Leaves below value	—
Pn290	1926	—	50 Pfennig. Leaves below value.	—
Pn291	1926E	—	50 Pfennig. Copper-Nickel. Cornucopia.	150
Pn293	1926E	—	50 Pfennig. Copper-Nickel. Wreath.	—
Pn294	1926E	—	50 Pfennig. Copper-Nickel. Wheat.	—
Pn295	1926E	—	50 Pfennig. Copper-Nickel. Eagle.	—
Pn297	1926E	—	50 Pfennig. Copper-Nickel. Eagle.	—
Pn298	1926E	—	50 Pfennig. Copper-Nickel. Wheat.	—
Pn299	1926E	—	50 Pfennig. Copper-Nickel. Two leaves.	—
Pn303	1926A	—	50 Pfennig. Nickel.	—
Pn304	1926E	—	50 Pfennig. Copper-Nickel.	—
Pn305	1926J	—	50 Pfennig. Nickel.	125
Pn311	1926A	—	5 Mark. Silver.	850
Pn313	1926E	—	5 Mark. Silver. Large eagle, small mint mark.	600
Pn319	1926F	—	5 Mark. Silver. "PROBE" without motto.	—
Pn320	1926F	—	5 Mark. Silver. Without motto..	850
Pn288	1926A	—	50 Pfennig. Leaves below value	—
Pn296	1926E	—	50 Pfennig. Copper-Nickel. Two leaves.	—
Pn301	1926E	—	50 Pfennig. Copper-Nickel. "Reichspfennig"	—
Pn302	1926E	—	50 Pfennig. Copper-Nickel.	—
Pn312a	1926D	—	5 Mark. Silver. Ship sailing right.	600
Pn314	1926	—	5 Mark. Silver. Small eagle, large mint mark.	600
Pn315	1926E	—	5 Mark. Silver.	850
Pn316	1926E	—	5 Mark. Silver.	850
Pn327a	1927A	—	3 Mark. Copper-Nickel.	1,000
PnA331	1927F	—	3 Mark. Silver. Justus Von Liebig; never issued.	—
Pn321	1927A	—	50 Pfennig. Nickel center. Deeper relief, KM#49.	—
Pn326	1927F	—	Mark. 0.9930 Silver. Plain edge.	250
Pn327	1927A	—	3 Mark. 0.9930 Silver.	—
Pn331	1927A	—	5 Mark. Silver. Large eagle.	—
Pn322	1927E	—	50 Pfennig. Silver.	—
Pn323	1927F	—	50 Pfennig. Copper-Nickel.	175
Pn324	1927	—	Mark. Brass. Pn307.	—
Pn332	NDA	—	5 Mark. Silvered Tin. Small eagle.	—
Pn334	1927A	—	5 Mark. Silver. 50 stars; KM#56.	—
Pn325	1927F	—	Mark. 0.5000 Silver. Ornamental edge.	200
Pn328	1927F	—	3 Mark. Silver. Lettered edge. "PROBE"	—

KM#	Date	Mintage	Identification	Mkt Val
Pn329	1927F	—	3 Mark. Silver. Lettered edge.	—
Pn330	1927F	—	3 Mark. Plain edge.	875
Pn335	1927A	—	5 Mark. Silver. 47 stars; KM#56.	—
Pn336	1927A	—	5 Mark. Silver. 73 stars; KM#56.	—
Pn339	1929A	—	5 Mark. Silver. Plain rims; "PROBE".	—
Pn337	1929A	—	3 Mark. Silver. Script on edge; KM#60.	875
Pn338	1929A	—	3 Mark. Silver. "PROBE"; KM#62.	—
Pn340	1929A	—	5 Mark. Silver. Star rims; "PROBE".	—
Pn341	1929A	—	5 Mark. Silver. "PROBE".	1,850
Pn342	1929A	—	5 Mark. Silver. Pn346.	—
PnA343	1929E	—	3 Mark. PROBE	—
Pn343	1930	—	3 Mark. Silver. "PROBE"; KM#70.	—
Pn344	1930	—	3 Mark. Silver. "PROBE"	900
Pn345	1930A	—	3 Mark. Silver. "PROBE"; KM#69.	900
Pn347	1930	—	5 Mark. Silver.	—
Pn346	1930A	—	5 Mark. Silver. "PROBE"; KM#68.	—
Pn349	1931	—	5 Mark.	—
PnA347	1931G	—	Pfennig. Brass.	100
Pn348	1931A	—	3 Mark.	—
Pn350	1932A	—	4 Pfennig. Silvered Copper. "PROBE"	—
PnA351	1932	—	3 Mark. Silver.	—
Pn351	1932D	—	3 Mark. 0.7500 Silver. KM#74.	750
Pn352	1932F	—	3 Mark. Silver. Reeded edge. "PROBE"; KM#74.	—
Pn353	1932F	—	3 Mark. Silver. Reeded edge. Without "PROBE"; KM#74.	—
Pn353a	1932A	—	5 Mark. Nickel. "PROBE". KM#76.	400

Date	Mintage	F	VF	XF	Unc	BU
1940J	7,450,000	0.60	2.75	4.50	10.00	20.00
1936-1940 Common date proof	—	Value: 140				

1933-1945

A wide range of factors, such as humiliation of defeat, economic depression, poverty, and a pervasive feeling of discontent aided Hitler in his climb to power. After the unsuccessful Putsch (uprising against the Bavarian Government) in 1923, Hitler was imprisoned in Landsberg Fortress. While imprisoned Hitler dictated his book *"Mein Kampf"* which became the cornerstone of Nazism espousing Hitler's irrational ideology and the manipulation of power without moral constraint as the basis of strategy.

Master propagandist Josef Goebbels tried to attract the sympathetic attention of the German public. The usual tactic was to have Hitler promise all things to all people provided that they in turn would pledge to him their complete faith and obedience.

Once in power, coercion was used to elicit the appearance of unanimous endorsement. Public works and military rearmament helped overcome the depression. It took the Nazis only about two years to consolidate their system politically. The combined terrorism of the storm troops and the police forces, including the Gestapo, stifled potential opposition. By 1935, Nazi affiliated organizations controlled all German cultural, professional, and economic fields, assuring strict compliance with the party line.

With the passage of the Nurnberg Laws in 1935, the more ominous aspects of Nazi anti-Semitism came to light. Jews were deprived of their citizenship and forbidden to marry non-Jews. This was followed by confiscation of property and the required wearing of the Star of David for identification purposes, eventually culminating in the mass deportation to concentration and death camps.

By 1936, unemployment was virtually eliminated and economic production was up to 1929 levels. All sources of information were under the control of Josef Goebbels, while all police power was in the hands of Heinrich Himmler. Himmler's Gestapo would silence Germans who were not convinced by Goebbel's propaganda machine. Usually the implied threat was enough. The majority of Germans did not suffer any ill effects at first and national pride stirred once again.

Hitler's audacity in foreign affairs met with success due to the trend of appeasement by the western powers. First, Germany withdrew from the League of Nations and the World Disarmament Council. In 1935, the Saar voted to return to Germany and Hitler renounced the reviled 1921 peace treaty and related pacts. In 1936, German forces reoccupied the Rhineland. In 1938, Austria was annexed and at the Munich Conference, which excluded Czechoslovakia, Great Britain and France agreed that the Sudetenland was to become German territory. In 1939, Slovakia became an independent Nazi Puppet State and the "Protectorate" of Bohemia and Moravia was established. Next came the German-Soviet non-aggression pact, which secretly divided up Poland between the two totalitarian powers. Great Britain and France finally declared war when Poland was invaded. The years of 1939-1942 were a period of impressive victories for Germany's well-trained and equipped forces. However, when Hitler expanded his war beyond Western Europe by invading Africa and Russia and declaring war on the U.S.A., it started the chain of events, which would culminate in the total and final German defeat on May 8, 1945, VE Day, ending the European theater of the Second World War and The Third Reich.

MINT MARKS

A - Berlin
B - Vienna, 1938-1944
D - Munich
E - Muldenhutten
F - Stuttgart
G - Karlsruhe
J - Hamburg

MONETARY SYSTEMS

(During 1923-1924)
100 Rentenpfennig = 1 Rentenmark

(Commencing 1924)
100 Reichspfennig = 1 Reichsmark

THIRD REICH

STANDARD COINAGE

KM# 89 REICHSPFENNIG

Bronze **Obv:** Imperial eagle above swastika within wreath **Rev:** Denomination, oak leaves below

Date	Mintage	F	VF	XF	Unc	BU
1936A	—	2.00	5.50	15.00	50.00	75.00
Note: Mintage included with KM#37						
1936E	150,000	27.50	55.00	110	165	275
1936F	4,600,000	25.00	50.00	90.00	200	300
1936G	—	15.00	25.00	60.00	110	200
Note: Mintage included with KM#37						
1936J	—	10.00	22.50	50.00	100	125
Note: Mintage included with KM#37						
1937A	67,180,000	0.20	0.35	1.00	3.50	6.00
1937D	14,060,000	0.20	0.35	1.25	6.00	12.00
1937E	10,700,000	0.20	0.40	1.25	6.00	12.00
1937F	11,058,000	0.20	0.40	1.25	6.00	12.00
1937G	4,250,000	0.20	0.40	2.50	6.00	14.00
1937J	6,714,000	0.20	0.40	1.25	6.00	12.00
1938A	75,707,000	0.15	0.35	0.50	5.00	9.00
1938B	2,378,000	0.50	4.00	6.50	15.00	30.00
1938D	13,930,000	0.15	0.35	0.60	6.00	9.00
1938E	14,503,000	0.15	0.35	0.60	6.00	9.00
1938F	11,714,000	0.15	0.35	0.60	6.00	9.00
1938G	8,390,000	0.15	0.35	1.25	6.00	11.00
1938J	15,458,000	0.15	0.35	0.60	6.00	9.00
1939A	97,541,000	0.15	0.35	0.60	4.00	9.00
1939B	22,732,000	0.20	0.40	0.90	6.00	11.00
1939D	20,760,000	0.15	0.30	0.60	5.00	9.00
1939E	12,478,000	0.15	0.35	0.60	6.00	11.00
1939F	12,482,000	0.15	0.35	0.60	5.00	9.00
1939G	12,250,000	0.15	0.35	0.60	5.00	9.00
1939J	8,368,000	0.15	0.35	0.60	6.00	11.00
1940A	27,094,000	0.15	0.35	0.60	5.00	10.00
1940F	7,850,000	0.20	0.45	1.25	7.00	12.00
1940G	3,875,000	1.00	4.00	11.00	20.00	35.00

KM# 97 REICHSPFENNIG

Zinc **Obv:** Imperial eagle above swastika within wreath **Rev:** Denomination, oak leaves below

Date	Mintage	F	VF	XF	Unc	BU
1940A	223,948,000	0.15	0.25	1.00	5.00	8.00
1940B	62,198,000	0.15	0.25	1.00	5.00	8.00
1940D	43,951,000	0.15	0.25	1.00	5.00	8.00
1940E	20,749,000	0.25	1.00	4.50	11.00	17.50
1940F	33,854,000	0.15	0.25	1.00	6.00	10.00
1940G	20,165,000	0.15	0.25	1.00	6.00	12.00
1940J	24,459,000	0.15	0.25	1.00	6.00	10.00
1941A	281,618,000	0.15	0.20	0.50	4.00	7.00
1941B	62,285,000	0.20	1.00	1.50	5.00	7.00
1941D	73,745,000	0.15	0.20	0.60	5.00	7.00
1941E	49,041,000	0.15	0.50	1.50	8.50	15.00
1941F	51,017,000	0.15	0.20	0.60	5.00	8.00
1941G	44,810,000	0.15	0.50	1.00	7.50	10.00
1941J	57,625,000	0.15	0.20	0.60	6.00	10.00
1942A	558,877,000	0.15	0.20	0.50	5.00	6.00
1942B	124,740,000	0.15	0.25	1.00	6.00	7.00
1942D	134,145,000	0.15	0.20	0.60	6.00	7.00
1942E	84,674,000	0.20	1.25	2.00	8.00	10.00
1942F	90,788,000	0.15	0.20	0.60	6.00	7.00
1942G	59,858,000	0.15	0.20	0.60	6.00	9.00
1942J	122,934,000	0.15	0.50	1.00	6.00	7.00
1943A	372,401,000	0.15	0.20	0.50	6.00	7.00
1943B	79,315,000	0.15	0.50	0.90	6.00	7.00
1943D	91,629,000	0.15	0.20	0.50	6.00	7.00
1943E	34,191,000	0.50	2.25	6.50	12.00	18.00
1943F	70,269,000	0.15	0.50	0.90	6.00	7.00
1943G	24,688,000	0.20	1.25	2.00	8.00	11.00
1943J	37,695,000	0.20	1.25	2.00	6.00	7.00
1944A	124,421,000	0.15	0.50	1.50	5.00	7.00
1944B	87,850,000	0.25	1.00	1.75	6.00	9.00
1944D	56,755,000	0.25	1.00	2.00	7.00	10.00
1944E	41,729,000	0.25	1.75	4.00	12.00	18.00
1944F	15,580,000	0.50	3.50	6.50	17.50	25.00
1944G	34,967,000	0.15	0.60	1.50	6.00	11.00
1945A	17,145,000	0.50	2.50	7.00	20.00	30.00
1945E	6,800,000	45.00	60.00	100	175	275
1940-1945 Common date proof	—	Value: 140				

KM# 90 2 REICHSPFENNIG

Bronze **Obv:** Imperial eagle above swastika within wreath **Rev:** Denomination, oak leaves below

Date	Mintage	F	VF	XF	Unc	BU
1936A	Inc. below	0.60	3.50	10.00	40.00	50.00
1936D	Inc. below	0.60	3.50	8.00	30.00	35.00
1936F	3,100,000	5.00	15.00	40.00	100	160
1937A	34,404,000	0.20	0.60	1.25	7.00	11.00
1937D	9,016,000	0.20	0.60	1.25	7.00	11.00
1937E	Inc. below	12.50	17.50	35.00	70.00	110
1937F	7,487,000	0.20	0.60	1.75	8.00	12.00
1937G	490,000	2.00	7.50	14.00	40.00	50.00
1937J	450,000	2.00	7.50	14.00	30.00	35.00
1938A	27,264,000	0.20	0.30	0.60	6.00	9.00
1938B	2,714,000	1.50	3.50	8.00	30.00	40.00
1938D	8,770,000	0.20	0.35	1.00	6.00	9.00
1938E	5,450,000	0.35	1.00	2.00	7.00	10.00
1938F	10,090,000	0.20	0.35	1.00	6.00	9.00
1938G	3,685,000	0.20	0.35	5.50	15.00	22.00
1938J	7,243,000	0.20	0.35	1.25	7.00	13.00
1939A	37,348,000	0.20	0.35	1.00	6.00	9.00
1939B	9,361,000	0.20	0.35	1.00	6.00	9.00
1939D	7,555,000	0.20	0.35	1.00	6.00	9.00
1939E	6,650,000	0.35	1.00	2.00	7.00	11.00
1939F	7,019,000	0.20	0.35	1.00	6.00	10.00
1939G	4,885,000	0.20	0.35	1.25	9.00	15.00
1939J	6,996,000	0.20	0.35	1.25	7.00	10.00
1940A	22,681,000	0.20	0.35	1.00	8.00	12.00
1940D	3,855,000	0.60	2.50	5.50	20.00	25.00
1940E	3,412,000	2.00	8.00	12.50	20.00	30.00
1940G	1,161,000	40.00	80.00	120	225	375
1940J	2,357,000	1.50	7.00	13.50	35.00	50.00
1936-1940 Common date proof	—	Value: 175				

KM# 91 5 REICHSPFENNIG

Aluminum-Bronze **Obv:** Imperial eagle above swastika within wreath **Rev:** Denomination, oak leaves below

Date	Mintage	F	VF	XF	Unc	BU
1936A	Inc. below	30.00	65.00	90.00	130	180
1936D	Inc. below	30.00	65.00	90.00	160	225
1936G	Inc. below	50.00	90.00	150	300	375
1937A	29,700,000	0.50	1.00	2.00	7.00	10.00
1937D	4,992,000	0.50	1.00	2.00	12.50	20.00
1937E	4,474,000	0.50	1.50	3.50	20.00	30.00
1937F	2,092,000	0.50	1.00	6.00	20.00	40.00
1937G	2,749,000	2.50	6.50	12.50	35.00	50.00
1937J	6,991,000	0.50	2.50	5.00	20.00	30.00
1938A	54,012,000	0.50	2.50	4.00	9.00	12.50
1938B	3,447,000	0.50	2.00	4.00	15.00	20.00
1938D	17,708,000	0.50	1.00	2.00	8.00	10.00
1938E	8,602,000	0.50	1.00	4.00	12.00	20.00
1938F	8,147,000	0.50	1.00	2.00	10.00	20.00
1938G	7,323,000	0.50	1.00	2.00	10.00	20.00
1938J	7,646,000	0.50	1.00	2.00	10.00	20.00
1939A	35,337,000	0.50	1.00	2.00	7.00	10.00
1939B	8,313,000	0.50	1.00	1.50	7.00	10.00
1939D	8,304,000	0.50	1.50	2.00	7.50	12.00
1939E	5,138,000	0.50	1.50	2.00	7.50	12.00
1939F	10,339,000	0.50	1.00	1.50	7.00	10.00
1939G	4,266,000	0.50	2.50	6.50	15.00	22.00
1939J	4,177,000	0.50	2.00	6.50	12.50	22.00
1936-1939 Common date proof	—	Value: 150				

KM# 100 5 REICHSPFENNIG

Zinc **Obv:** Imperial eagle above swastika within wreath **Rev:** Denomination, oak leaves below

Date	Mintage	F	VF	XF	Unc	BU
1940A	174,684,000	0.20	0.25	0.75	6.00	8.00
1940B	63,469,000	0.25	1.00	1.50	6.00	8.00
1940D	44,364,000	0.25	1.00	1.50	6.00	8.00
1940E	25,800,000	0.30	1.00	3.50	7.00	10.00
1940F	31,381,000	0.25	1.00	2.00	7.00	10.00
1940G	24,148,000	0.25	1.00	2.75	8.00	15.00
1940J	30,518,000	0.25	1.00	2.00	7.00	10.00
1941A	246,216,000	0.20	0.25	0.75	5.00	7.00
1941B	60,297,000	0.20	0.40	1.75	7.50	10.00
1941D	51,100,000	0.20	0.40	1.75	7.50	10.00
1941E	26,354,000	0.20	0.40	1.75	7.50	10.00
1941F	36,725,000	0.20	0.40	1.75	7.50	10.00
1941G	21,276,000	0.20	0.40	2.00	8.50	12.00
1941J	52,872,000	0.20	0.40	2.00	7.50	10.00
1942A	161,042,000	0.20	0.25	0.75	6.00	9.00
1942B	12,405,000	0.25	1.50	4.50	10.00	15.00
1942D	15,486,000	0.20	0.45	2.25	8.00	12.00
1942E	8,800,000	6.00	15.00	20.00	40.00	50.00
1942F	24,662,000	0.20	0.35	1.50	8.00	12.00
1942G	12,749,000	0.20	0.40	2.25	10.00	15.00
1943A	46,830,000	0.20	0.50	1.75	7.00	10.00
1943B	833,000	30.00	50.00	75.00	160	200
1943D	13,650,000	0.20	0.50	3.50	9.00	13.00
1943E	16,581,000	2.00	6.00	10.00	20.00	25.00
1943F	9,891,000	0.25	1.00	2.50	8.00	12.00
1943G	7,237,000	0.20	0.75	2.25	9.00	15.00
1944A	23,699,000	3.50	12.50	25.00	40.00	50.00
1944D	26,340,000	0.25	1.25	2.50	7.00	10.00
1944E	19,720,000	0.50	2.50	5.00	10.00	14.00
1944F	6,853,000	0.25	1.50	2.75	8.00	12.00
1944G	3,540,000	100	200	275	400	500
1940-1944 Common date proof	—	Value: 225				

KM# 92 10 REICHSPFENNIG

Aluminum-Bronze **Obv:** Imperial eagle above swastika within wreath **Rev:** Denomination, oak leaves below

Date	Mintage	F	VF	XF	Unc	BU
1936A	Inc. below	20.00	40.00	60.00	100	120
1936E	245,000	90.00	150	200	300	375
1936G	129,000	175	225	300	450	700
1937A	36,830,000	0.50	1.00	2.25	12.00	20.00
1937D	6,882,000	0.50	2.00	3.50	12.00	22.00
1937E	3,786,000	2.00	9.00	18.00	45.00	60.00
1937F	5,934,000	1.00	2.50	6.00	25.00	40.00
1937G	2,131,000	1.00	5.50	9.00	30.00	60.00
1937J	4,439,000	1.00	2.00	5.00	20.00	30.00
1938A	70,068,000	0.50	1.00	2.00	7.00	12.00
1938B	7,852,000	1.00	2.00	4.50	15.00	20.00
1938D	16,990,000	0.50	1.00	2.00	9.00	16.00
1938E	10,739,000	0.50	2.00	2.50	10.00	18.00
1938F	12,307,000	0.50	2.00	2.75	11.00	18.00
1938G	8,584,000	0.50	2.00	3.00	12.00	22.00
1938J	10,389,000	0.50	2.00	2.75	12.00	20.00
1939A	40,171,000	0.50	2.00	2.25	9.00	15.00
1939B	7,814,000	0.50	2.00	2.25	10.00	16.00
1939D	11,307,000	0.50	2.00	2.25	12.00	20.00
1939E	5,079,000	1.00	2.00	6.50	15.00	20.00
1939F	6,993,000	0.50	2.00	3.00	12.00	20.00
1939G	5,532,000	1.00	4.50	9.00	16.00	22.00
1939J	5,557,000	0.50	2.00	2.50	12.00	20.00
1936-1939 Common date proof	—	Value: 175				

KM# 101 10 REICHSPFENNIG

Zinc **Obv:** Imperial eagle above swastika within wreath **Rev:** Denomination, oak leaves below

Date	Mintage	F	VF	XF	Unc	BU
1940A	212,948,000	0.20	0.40	1.75	8.00	15.00
1940B	76,274,000	0.20	0.75	3.00	12.00	20.00
1940D	45,434,000	0.20	0.75	2.50	12.00	20.00
1940E	34,350,000	0.20	0.75	2.50	12.00	25.00
1940F	27,603,000	0.20	1.50	6.00	17.50	40.00
1940G	27,308,000	0.20	1.50	8.00	25.00	50.00
1940J	41,678,000	0.20	1.25	2.50	12.00	25.00
1941A	240,284,000	0.20	0.40	1.50	7.00	14.00
1941B	70,747,000	0.20	0.75	3.00	9.00	15.00
1941D	77,560,000	0.20	0.75	3.50	12.00	20.00
1941E	36,548,000	0.20	0.75	3.50	12.00	20.00
1941F	42,834,000	0.20	0.75	3.50	12.00	20.00
1941G	28,765,000	0.20	2.25	9.00	25.00	40.00
1941J	30,525,000	0.20	0.75	2.50	12.00	25.00
1942A	184,545,000	0.20	0.30	0.75	9.00	15.00
1942B	16,329,000	1.00	3.00	12.00	30.00	50.00
1942D	40,852,000	0.20	1.25	3.50	12.00	25.00
1942E	18,334,000	1.00	2.00	12.00	30.00	50.00
1942F	32,690,000	0.20	0.50	3.50	12.00	25.00
1942G	20,295,000	1.00	2.00	12.00	35.00	60.00
1942J	29,957,000	0.50	1.75	3.50	12.00	25.00
1943A	157,357,000	0.20	1.50	2.50	9.00	15.00
1943B	11,940,000	2.50	7.50	14.00	30.00	60.00
1943D	17,304,000	0.25	1.75	4.50	16.00	25.00
1943E	10,445,000	2.50	7.50	14.00	35.00	60.00
1943F	24,804,000	0.25	2.50	5.00	20.00	25.00
1943G	3,618,000	4.00	14.00	35.00	80.00	150
1943J	1,821,000	25.00	45.00	85.00	200	300
1944A	84,164,000	0.20	1.00	2.50	10.00	15.00
1944B	40,781,000	0.50	1.50	2.50	12.00	20.00
1944D	30,369,000	0.50	1.50	2.50	12.00	20.00
1944E	29,963,000	0.50	2.00	4.50	12.00	20.00
1944F	19,639,000	0.50	2.50	5.00	14.00	25.00
1944G	13,023,000	0.75	3.50	10.00	30.00	50.00
1945A	7,112,000	5.00	12.50	30.00	90.00	150
1945E	4,897,000	15.00	35.00	80.00	140	200
1940-1945 Common date proof	—	Value: 250				

KM# 87 50 REICHSPFENNIG

Aluminum **Obv:** Imperial eagle above date **Rev:** Denomination, oak leaves below

Date	Mintage	F	VF	XF	Unc	BU
1935A	75,912,000	1.00	2.25	9.00	35.00	80.00
1935A Proof	—	Value: 250				
1935D	19,688,000	1.00	2.25	12.00	60.00	100
1935D Proof	—	Value: 250				
1935E	10,418,000	1.00	3.50	12.00	60.00	100
1935E Proof	—	Value: 250				
1935F	14,061,000	1.00	2.25	12.00	60.00	100
1935F Proof	—	Value: 250				
1935G	8,540,000	2.00	4.50	14.00	65.00	110
1935G Proof	—	Value: 250				
1935J	11,438,000	2.00	4.50	14.00	65.00	110
1935J Proof	—	Value: 250				

KM# 95 50 REICHSPFENNIG

Nickel **Obv:** Imperial eagle above swastika within wreath **Rev:** Denomination within circle, oak leaves and acorns below

Date	Mintage	F	VF	XF	Unc	BU
1938A	5,051,000	17.50	32.50	42.50	55.00	75.00
1938B	1,124,000	25.00	40.00	50.00	80.00	100
1938D	1,260,000	25.00	40.00	55.00	80.00	100
1938E	949,000	25.00	40.00	60.00	100	125
1938F	1,210,000	15.00	30.00	50.00	90.00	125
1938G	460,000	30.00	70.00	90.00	160	225
1938J	730,000	30.00	90.00	120	225	300
1939A	15,037,000	20.00	30.00	40.00	50.00	60.00
1939B	2,826,000	20.00	35.00	45.00	60.00	90.00
1939D	3,648,000	17.50	35.00	45.00	60.00	90.00
1939E	1,924,000	17.50	35.00	50.00	85.00	100
1939F	2,602,000	17.50	35.00	50.00	70.00	90.00
1939G	1,565,000	17.50	35.00	75.00	130	170
1939J	2,114,000	17.50	35.00	60.00	100	120
1938-1939 Common date proof	—	Value: 275				

KM# 96 50 REICHSPFENNIG

Aluminum **Obv:** Imperial eagle above swastika within wreath **Rev:** Denomination, oak leaves below

Date	Mintage	F	VF	XF	Unc	BU
1939A	5,000,000	2.50	6.00	20.00	65.00	100
1939B	5,482,000	2.50	6.00	20.00	65.00	100
1939D	600,000	6.00	16.00	35.00	120	170
1939E	2,000,000	2.50	6.00	25.00	70.00	110
1939F	3,600,000	2.50	11.00	30.00	70.00	120
1939G	560,000	12.50	22.50	60.00	150	200
1939J	1,000,000	12.50	22.50	50.00	150	200
1940A	56,128,000	2.50	4.50	11.00	35.00	50.00
1940B	10,016,000	5.00	9.00	25.00	70.00	100
1940D	13,800,000	8.00	15.00	30.00	100	150
1940E	5,618,000	8.00	15.00	30.00	100	150
1940F	6,663,000	5.00	10.00	25.00	65.00	100
1940G	5,616,000	15.00	27.00	55.00	130	200
1940J	7,335,000	8.00	15.00	30.00	100	150
1941A	31,263,000	5.00	9.00	20.00	65.00	100
1941B	4,291,000	3.00	10.00	25.00	80.00	110
1941D	7,200,000	2.00	10.00	25.00	80.00	110
1941E	3,806,000	5.00	15.00	27.50	85.00	125
1941F	5,128,000	2.50	10.00	25.00	65.00	100
1941G	3,091,000	10.00	20.00	40.00	110	150
1941J	4,165,000	10.00	20.00	35.00	110	150
1942A	11,580,000	2.00	5.00	10.00	30.00	50.00
1942B	2,876,000	5.00	12.00	25.00	70.00	100
1942D	2,247,000	2.00	20.00	35.00	80.00	120
1942E	3,810,000	5.00	20.00	40.00	110	150
1942F	5,133,000	2.00	15.00	30.00	80.00	120
1942G	1,400,000	10.00	25.00	70.00	125	200
1943A	29,325,000	2.00	5.00	10.00	30.00	40.00
1943B	8,229,000	2.00	5.00	10.00	25.00	40.00
1943D	5,315,000	2.00	7.00	16.00	50.00	75.00
1943G	2,892,000	10.00	20.00	50.00	110	180
1943J	4,166,000	5.00	9.00	14.00	30.00	45.00
1944B	5,622,000	2.50	8.00	12.00	50.00	70.00
1944D	4,886,000	7.50	16.00	40.00	100	130
1944F	3,739,000	5.00	10.00	20.00	75.00	100
1944G	1,190,000	60.00	100	180	400	600
1940-1944 Common date proof	—	Value: 275				

KM# 78 REICHSMARK

Nickel **Obv:** Denomination within wreath, date below **Rev:** Imperial eagle

Date	Mintage	F	VF	XF	Unc	BU
1933A	6,030,000	1.00	2.75	8.00	35.00	45.00
1933D	4,562,000	1.00	3.50	10.00	35.00	45.00
1933E	3,500,000	2.50	7.50	10.00	25.00	45.00
1933F	1,400,000	4.00	8.50	16.00	45.00	65.00
1933G	2,000,000	2.50	10.00	20.00	90.00	130

Date	Mintage	F	VF	XF	Unc	BU
1934A	52,345,000	1.00	1.75	3.00	10.00	15.00
1934D	30,597,000	1.00	1.75	5.00	16.00	22.00
1934E	15,135,000	1.00	3.00	7.00	16.00	22.00
1934F	23,672,000	1.00	2.75	5.00	15.00	20.00
1934G	13,252,000	1.50	5.00	10.00	20.00	25.00
1934J	16,820,000	1.00	3.50	7.50	16.00	20.00
1935A	57,896,000	1.00	2.50	5.00	12.50	15.00
1935J	3,621,000	10.00	15.00	30.00	110	150
1936A	20,287,000	1.25	4.50	8.00	20.00	25.00
1936D	4,940,000	2.50	7.50	15.00	40.00	50.00
1936E	3,200,000	10.00	15.00	35.00	110	150
1936F	2,075,000	20.00	30.00	50.00	110	150
1936G	620,000	30.00	75.00	150	225	275
1936J	2,975,000	7.50	15.00	30.00	110	150
1937A	49,976,000	1.00	1.75	3.00	9.00	13.00
1937D	10,529,000	2.00	5.00	10.00	20.00	30.00
1937E	2,926,000	4.00	12.50	22.50	50.00	70.00
1937F	6,221,000	4.00	12.50	22.50	65.00	90.00
1937G	2,143,000	3.00	9.00	16.00	45.00	70.00
1937J	4,721,000	3.00	9.00	16.00	60.00	90.00
1938A	9,829,000	2.00	5.00	12.00	30.00	45.00
1938E	2,073,000	5.00	18.00	35.00	90.00	130
1938F	2,739,000	6.00	20.00	25.00	75.00	100
1938G	4,381,000	15.00	35.00	70.00	140	225
1938J	1,269,000	30.00	65.00	100	160	250
1939A	52,150,000	6.00	12.50	16.00	40.00	50.00
1939B	9,836,000	60.00	110	160	275	375
1939D	12,522,000	10.00	22.50	37.50	80.00	100
1939E	6,570,000	25.00	40.00	70.00	130	160
1939F	10,033,000	15.00	25.00	45.00	110	150
1939G	5,475,000	70.00	140	200	350	450
1939J	8,478,000	20.00	40.00	60.00	120	175
1933-1939 Common date proof	—	Value: 250				

KM# 79 2 REICHSMARK

8.0000 g., 0.6250 Silver .1607 oz. ASW, 27 mm. **Subject:** 450th Anniversary - Birth of Martin Luther **Obv:** Imperial eagle above denomination **Rev:** Head left, dates below

Date	Mintage	F	VF	XF	Unc	BU
1933A	542,000	10.00	22.50	30.00	50.00	70.00
1933A Proof	—	Value: 250				
1933D	141,000	12.00	25.00	35.00	60.00	75.00
1933D Proof	—	Value: 250				
1933E	75,000	15.00	30.00	40.00	60.00	90.00
1933E Proof	—	Value: 275				
1933F	100,000	12.00	25.00	35.00	60.00	80.00
1933F Proof	—	Value: 275				
1933G	61,000	16.00	30.00	42.00	75.00	120
1933G Proof	—	Value: 275				
1933J	82,000	12.00	25.00	40.00	60.00	85.00
1933J Proof	—	Value: 265				

KM# 81 2 REICHSMARK

8.0000 g., 0.6250 Silver .1607 oz. ASW, 27 mm. **Subject:** 1st Anniversary - Nazi Rule March 21, 1933 **Obv:** Imperial eagle divides dates, denomination below **Rev:** Potsdam Garrison Church

Date	Mintage	F	VF	XF	Unc	BU
1934A	2,710,000	4.50	10.00	22.00	50.00	90.00
1934A Proof	—	Value: 250				
1934D	703,000	5.50	12.00	28.00	70.00	110
1934D Proof	—	Value: 250				
1934E	373,000	7.50	16.50	40.00	100	130
1934E Proof	—	Value: 250				
1934F	502,000	6.00	12.00	32.50	75.00	110
1934F Proof	—	Value: 250				
1934G	305,000	7.00	15.00	45.00	110	140
1934G Proof	—	Value: 250				
1934J	409,000	7.00	15.00	40.00	100	120
1934J Proof	—	Value: 250				

KM# 84 2 REICHSMARK

8.0000 g., 0.6250 Silver .1607 oz. ASW, 27 mm. **Subject:** 175th Anniversary - Birth of Schiller **Obv:** Imperial eagle, oak leaves flank, denomination below **Rev:** Head left, date below **Designer:** Hubert Zimmerman

Date	Mintage	F	VF	XF	Unc	BU
1934F	300,000	40.00	70.00	90.00	120	145
1934F Proof	—	Value: 250				

KM# 93 2 REICHSMARK

8.0000 g., 0.6250 Silver .1607 oz. ASW, 27 mm. **Subject:** Swastika-Hindenburg Issue **Obv:** Imperial eagle above swastika within wreath **Rev:** Large head, right

Date	Mintage	F	VF	XF	Unc	BU
1936D	840,000	4.00	7.00	20.00	60.00	90.00
1936E	Inc. below	9.00	28.00	45.00	110	170
1936G	Inc. below	8.00	18.00	30.00	80.00	140
1936J	Inc. below	30.00	70.00	160	400	550
1937A	23,425,000	2.50	3.00	4.50	11.00	16.00
1937D	6,190,000	2.50	3.00	4.50	16.00	20.00
1937E	3,725,000	2.50	3.50	6.00	22.00	30.00
1937F	5,015,000	2.50	3.00	6.00	16.00	22.00
1937G	1,913,000	2.50	4.50	10.00	30.00	45.00
1937J	2,756,000	2.50	3.50	5.50	20.00	35.00
1938A	13,201,000	2.50	3.00	5.00	11.00	20.00
1938B	13,163,000	2.50	3.00	5.00	15.00	22.00
1938D	3,711,000	2.50	3.00	5.00	16.00	30.00
1938E	4,731,000	2.50	3.00	5.00	16.00	30.00
1938F	1,882,000	3.00	4.00	6.50	20.00	40.00
1938G	2,313,000	2.50	3.00	5.50	17.00	30.00
1938J	2,306,000	2.50	3.50	5.50	17.00	30.00
1939A	26,855,000	2.25	3.00	4.50	11.00	15.00
1939B	3,522,000	2.50	3.25	5.50	14.00	30.00
1939D	5,357,000	2.50	3.25	5.00	14.00	25.00
1939E	251,000	15.00	30.00	45.00	100	160
1939F	3,180,000	2.50	3.25	5.50	14.00	30.00
1939G	2,305,000	2.50	3.50	7.50	20.00	40.00
1939J	3,414,000	2.50	3.25	7.00	17.50	30.00
1936-1939 Common date proof	—	Value: 225				

KM# 80 5 REICHSMARK

13.8800 g., 0.9000 Silver .4016 oz. ASW, 29 mm. **Subject:** 450th Anniversary - Birth of Martin Luther **Obv:** Imperial eagle, denomination below **Rev:** Head left, dates below

Date	Mintage	F	VF	XF	Unc	BU
1933A	108,000	60.00	100	150	200	275
1933A Proof	—	Value: 400				
1933D	28,000	60.00	125	175	200	300
1933D Proof	—	Value: 450				
1933E	12,000	80.00	145	190	225	300
1933E Proof	—	Value: 450				
1933F	20,000	60.00	125	160	200	300
1933F Proof	—	Value: 525				
1933G	12,000	100	175	250	300	400
1933G Proof	—	Value: 550				
1933J	16,000	85.00	145	180	250	350
1933J Proof	—	Value: 550				

KM# 82 5 REICHSMARK

13.8800 g., 0.9000 Silver .4016 oz. ASW, 29 mm. **Subject:** 1st Anniversary - Nazi Rule **Obv:** Imperial eagle divides date, denomination below **Rev:** Potsdam Garrison Church

Date	Mintage	F	VF	XF	Unc	BU
1934A	2,168,000	10.00	12.00	40.00	100	120
1934D	562,000	10.00	15.00	45.00	120	140
1934E	298,000	10.00	18.00	50.00	150	180
1934F	401,000	10.00	14.00	40.00	120	160
1934G	244,000	10.00	20.00	50.00	160	190
1934J	327,000	10.00	18.00	45.00	160	190
1934 Proof	—	Value: 300				

Note: Impaired proofs are common and valued around $200

KM# 83 5 REICHSMARK

13.8800 g., 0.9000 Silver .4016 oz. ASW, 29 mm. **Subject:** 1st Anniversary - Nazi Rule **Obv:** Imperial eagle divides date, denomination below **Rev:** Potsdam Garrison Church, date 21 MARZ 1933 dropped

Date	Mintage	F	VF	XF	Unc	BU
1934A	14,526,000	5.00	6.00	10.00	35.00	40.00
1934D	6,303,000	5.00	6.00	13.00	40.00	50.00
1934E	2,739,000	5.00	7.00	15.00	55.00	65.00
1934F	4,844,000	5.00	6.00	13.00	40.00	50.00
1934G	2,304,000	5.00	7.50	15.00	55.00	65.00
1934J	4,294,000	5.00	6.50	14.00	50.00	60.00
1935A	23,407,000	4.00	5.00	9.00	30.00	40.00
1935D	3,539,000	5.00	6.50	14.00	40.00	50.00
1935E	2,476,000	5.00	7.50	15.00	55.00	65.00
1935F	2,177,000	5.00	7.50	17.50	50.00	70.00
1935G	1,966,000	5.00	7.50	16.00	65.00	75.00
1935J	1,425,000	6.00	10.00	22.50	90.00	110
1934-1935 Common date proof	—	Value: 275				

KM# 85 5 REICHSMARK

13.8800 g., 0.9000 Silver .4016 oz. ASW, 29 mm. **Subject:** 175th Anniversary - Birth of Schiller **Obv:** Imperial eagle, oak leaves flank, denomination below **Rev:** Head left, dates below

Date	Mintage	F	VF	XF	Unc	BU
1934F	100,000	150	200	285	425	475
1934F Proof	—	Value: 750				

KM# 86 5 REICHSMARK

13.8800 g., 0.9000 Silver .4016 oz. ASW, 29 mm. **Subject:** Hindenburg issue **Obv:** Imperial eagle divides date, denomination below **Rev:** Large head, right

Date	Mintage	F	VF	XF	Unc	BU
1935A	19,325,000	4.00	5.00	9.00	16.00	20.00
1935D	6,596,000	4.00	6.00	9.00	20.00	25.00
1935E	3,260,000	4.00	6.00	11.00	25.00	30.00

Date	Mintage	F	VF	XF	Unc	BU
1935F	4,372,000	4.00	6.00	9.00	25.00	30.00
1935G	2,371,000	4.00	6.50	12.50	35.00	45.00
1935J	2,830,000	4.00	6.50	12.50	40.00	60.00
1936A	30,611,000	4.00	5.50	9.00	16.00	20.00
1936D	7,032,000	4.00	6.00	9.00	20.00	25.00
1936E	3,320,000	4.00	6.00	11.00	25.00	30.00
1936F	4,926,000	4.00	6.00	11.00	25.00	30.00
1936G	2,734,000	4.00	6.50	15.00	50.00	70.00
1936J	3,706,000	4.00	6.50	14.00	40.00	50.00
1935-1936 Common date proof	—	Value: 250				

KM# 94 5 REICHSMARK

13.8800 g., 0.9000 Silver .4016 oz. ASW, 29 mm. **Subject:** Swastika-Hindenburg Issue **Obv:** Imperial eagle above swastika within wreath **Rev:** Large head, right

Date	Mintage	F	VF	XF	Unc	BU
1936A	8,430,000	4.00	6.00	10.00	20.00	30.00
1936D	1,872,000	4.00	7.00	14.00	30.00	40.00
1936E	870,000	5.00	8.00	16.00	35.00	50.00
1936F	1,732,000	4.00	7.00	14.00	40.00	50.00
1936G	743,000	5.00	9.00	20.00	65.00	80.00
1936J	640,000	8.00	18.00	30.00	80.00	110
1937A	6,662,000	4.00	6.00	9.00	20.00	30.00
1937D	2,173,000	4.00	6.00	10.00	25.00	35.00
1937E	1,490,000	5.00	8.00	14.00	30.00	50.00
1937F	1,578,000	4.00	7.50	14.00	35.00	45.00
1937G	1,472,000	5.00	8.00	14.00	35.00	45.00
1937J	2,191,000	4.00	6.00	12.50	30.00	40.00
1938A	6,789,000	4.00	6.00	9.00	20.00	25.00
1938D	1,304,000	4.00	6.00	12.50	25.00	35.00
1938E	425,000	5.00	8.00	14.00	40.00	60.00
1938F	740,000	4.00	6.50	12.50	40.00	60.00
1938G	861,000	4.00	7.50	14.00	40.00	60.00
1938J	1,302,000	4.00	6.50	12.50	30.00	40.00
1939A	3,428,000	4.00	7.50	12.50	25.00	40.00
1939B	1,942,000	5.00	8.00	14.00	25.00	50.00
1939D	1,216,000	7.00	11.00	18.00	40.00	50.00
1939E	1,320,000	15.00	20.00	40.00	80.00	110
1939F	1,060,000	7.50	12.50	25.00	70.00	100
1939G	567,000	12.50	20.00	35.00	100	140
1939J	1,710,000	5.00	10.00	20.00	60.00	75.00
1936-1939 Common date proof	—	Value: 250				

MILITARY COINAGE

WWII

KM# 98 5 REICHSPFENNIG

Zinc **Note:** Circulated only in occupied territories.

Date	Mintage	F	VF	XF	Unc	BU
1940A	—	15.00	20.00	30.00	60.00	90.00
1940B	3,020,000	100	160	325	550	750
1940D	—	30.00	45.00	75.00	120	190
1940E	2,445,000	100	200	325	550	750
1940F	—	200	300	425	675	900
1940G	—	6,000	10,000	—	—	—
1940J	—	100	225	325	500	750
1941A	—	300	500	800	1,500	2,500
1941F	—	5,000	10,000	—	—	—
1940-1941 Common date proof	—	Value: 850				

KM# 99 10 REICHSPFENNIG

Zinc **Rev:** Eagle head above center hole, denomination below **Note:** Circulated only in occupied territories.

Date	Mintage	F	VF	XF	Unc	BU
1940A	—	15.00	20.00	30.00	50.00	80.00
1940B	840,000	200	325	650	950	1,250
1940D	—	5,000	6,000	10,000	15,000	20,000
1940E	5,100,000	3,000	4,500	6,000	10,000	12,000
1940F	—	300	450	1,250	1,750	2,250
1940G	150,000	100	125	225	400	550
1940J	—	400	900	1,400	2,500	2,750
1941A	—	600	1,000	1,800	2,500	2,750
1941F 2 known	—	—	12,000	—	15,000	—
1940-1941 Proof	—	Value: 1,150				

ALLIED OCCUPATION

POST WW II COINAGE

KM# A102 REICHSPFENNIG

Zinc **Obv:** Modified design, swastika and wreath removed **Rev:** Eagle missing tail feathers

Date	Mintage	F	VF	XF	Unc	BU
1944D	—	—	—	10,000	—	—

Note: Possibly a pattern, only one known

KM# A103 REICHSPFENNIG

Zinc **Obv:** Imperial eagle above date **Rev:** Denomination

Date	Mintage	F	VF	XF	Unc	BU
1945F	2,984,000	6.00	12.00	20.00	40.00	60.00
1946F	1,633,000	20.00	40.00	70.00	140	165
1946G	1,500,000	40.00	70.00	110	170	225
1945-1946 Common date proof	—	Value: 250				

KM# A105 5 REICHSPFENNIG

Zinc **Obv:** Imperial eagle, date below **Rev:** Denomination

Date	Mintage	F	VF	XF	Unc	BU
1947A	—	3.00	7.50	15.00	40.00	55.00
1947D	16,528,000	3.00	5.00	7.00	20.00	40.00
1948A	—	5.00	12.50	20.00	45.00	70.00
1948E	7,666,000	150	300	400	700	850
1947-1948 Proof	—	Value: 250				

KM# A104 10 REICHSPFENNIG

Zinc **Obv:** Imperial eagle **Rev:** Denomination

Date	Mintage	F	VF	XF	Unc	BU
1945F	5,942,000	4.50	7.50	15.00	35.00	60.00
1946F	3,738,000	15.00	25.00	35.00	90.00	120
1946G	1,600,000	40.00	70.00	120	200	300
1947A	—	4.50	10.00	20.00	35.00	65.00
1947E	2,612,000	250	350	575	775	950
1947F	1,269,000	2.00	4.00	9.00	20.00	28.00
1948A	—	5.00	18.00	22.50	35.00	55.00
1948F	19,579,000	2.00	4.00	9.00	30.00	40.00
1946-1948 Common date proof	—	Value: 225				

PATTERNS

Including off metal strikes

KM#	Date	Mintage	Identification	Mkt Val
Pn354	1933	—	Mark. Nickel. Legend above eagle. PROBE.	300
Pn355	1933A	—	Mark. Nickel. "PROBE."	300
Pn356	1933A	—	Mark. Nickel. Rays above eagle.	300
Pn357	1933A	—	Mark. Nickel. Plain above eagle.	300
Pn358	1933A	—	Mark. Nickel. Large 1 with rays. "PROBE."	300
Pn359	1933A	—	Mark. Nickel. "PROBE."	300
Pn360	1933J	—	Mark. Nickel. KM78.	300
PnA361	1933/6	—	5 Mark. Copper-Nickel. Martin Luther. Eagle. KM94.	—
Pn361	1934	—	2 Mark. KM79. KM81.	—
Pn362	1934A	—	2 Mark. Silver. KM84.	—
Pn364	1934A	—	5 Mark. Silver. KM85. "PROBE".	—
Pn363	NDD	—	5 Mark. Silver. Similar to Pn351 edge. KM80.	—
Pn365	1934A	—	5 Pfennig. Brass. KM91.	—
Pn366	1934A	—	5 Pfennig. Aluminum-Bronze. KM91.1. "PROBE."	—
Pn370	1935A	—	5 Mark. Silver. "PROBE."	—
Pn367	1935A	—	50 Pfennig. Aluminum.	—
Pn371	1935A	—	5 Mark. Silver. "PROBE."	—
Pn368	1935A	—	50 Pfennig. Oak leaves next to date. "PROBE". Wavy edge.	—
Pn372	1935A	—	5 Mark. Silver. Masses entering. "PROBE."	—
Pn369	1935E	—	Mark. Nickel. KM78.	—
Pn373	1935A	—	5 Mark. 0.9000 Silver. Family entering. "PROBE."	—
Pn374	1935A	—	5 Mark. Electrotype.	—

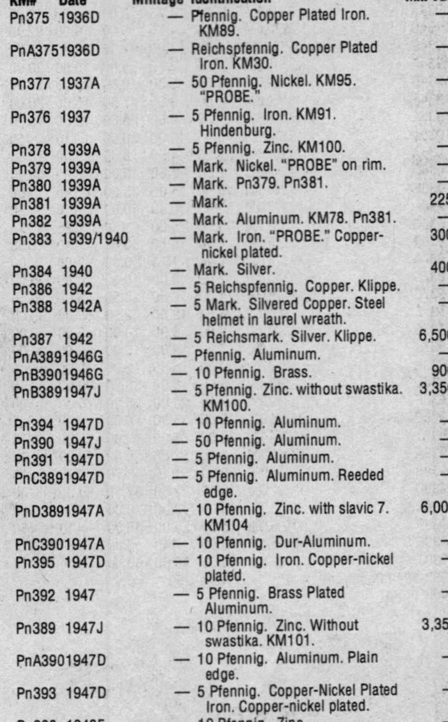

KM#	Date	Mintage	Identification	Mkt Val
Pn375	1936D	—	Pfennig. Copper Plated Iron. KM89.	—
PnA375	1936D	—	Reichspfennig. Copper Plated Iron. KM30.	—
Pn377	1937A	—	50 Pfennig. Nickel. KM95. "PROBE."	—
Pn376	1937	—	5 Pfennig. Iron. KM91. Hindenburg.	—
Pn378	1939A	—	5 Pfennig. Zinc. KM100.	—
Pn379	1939A	—	Mark. Nickel. "PROBE" on rim.	—
Pn380	1939A	—	Mark. Pn379. Pn381.	—
Pn381	1939A	—	Mark.	225
Pn382	1939A	—	Mark. Aluminum. KM78. Pn381.	—
Pn383	1939/1940	—	Mark. Iron. "PROBE." Copper-nickel plated.	300
Pn384	1940	—	Mark. Silver.	400
Pn386	1942	—	5 Reichspfennig. Copper. Klippe.	—
Pn388	1942A	—	5 Mark. Silvered Copper. Steel helmet in laurel wreath.	—
Pn387	1942	—	5 Reichsmark. Silver. Klippe.	6,500
PnA389	1946G	—	Pfennig. Aluminum.	—
PnB390	1946G	—	10 Pfennig. Brass.	900
PnB389	1947J	—	5 Pfennig. Zinc. without swastika. KM100.	3,350
Pn394	1947D	—	10 Pfennig. Aluminum.	—
Pn390	1947J	—	50 Pfennig. Aluminum.	—
Pn391	1947D	—	5 Pfennig. Aluminum.	—
PnC389	1947D	—	5 Pfennig. Aluminum. Reeded edge.	—
PnD389	1947A	—	10 Pfennig. Zinc. with slavic 7. KM104	6,000
PnC390	1947A	—	10 Pfennig. Dur-Aluminum.	—
Pn395	1947D	—	10 Pfennig. Iron. Copper-nickel plated.	—
Pn392	1947	—	5 Pfennig. Brass Plated Aluminum.	—
Pn389	1947J	—	10 Pfennig. Zinc. Without swastika. KM101.	3,350
PnA390	1947D	—	10 Pfennig. Aluminum. Plain edge.	—
Pn393	1947D	—	5 Pfennig. Copper-Nickel Plated Iron. Copper-nickel plated.	—
Pn396	1948F	—	10 Pfennig. Zinc.	—

The Federal Republic of Germany, located in north-central Europe, has an area of 137,744 sq. mi. (356,910sq. km.) and a population of 81.1 million. Capital: Berlin. The economy centers about one of the world's foremost industrial establishments. Machinery, motor vehicles, iron, steel, yarns and fabrics are exported.

During the post-Normandy phase of World War II, Allied troops occupied the western German provinces of Schleswig-Holstein, Hamburg, Lower Saxony, Bremen, North Rhine-Westphalia, Hesse, Rhineland-Palatinate, Baden-Wurttemberg, Bavaria and Saarland. The conquered provinces were divided into American, British and French occupation zones. Five eastern German provinces were occupied and administered by the forces of the Soviet Union.

The post-World War II division of Germany was ended Oct. 3, 1990, when the German Democratic Republic (East Germany) ceased to exist and its five constituent provinces were formally admitted to the Federal Republic of Germany. An election Dec. 2, 1990, chose representatives to the united federal parliament (Bundestag), which then conducted its opening session in Berlin in the old Reichstag building. Berlin is again the capital of a United Germany.

MINT MARKS

A - Berlin
D - Munich
F - Stuttgart
G - Karlsruhe
J - Hamburg

MONETARY SYSTEM

100 Pfennig = 1 Deutsche Mark (DM)

FEDERAL REPUBLIC

STANDARD COINAGE

KM# A101 PFENNIG

Bronze-Clad Steel, 16.5 mm. **Obv. Legend:** BANK DEUTSCHER LÄNDER

Date	Mintage	F	VF	XF	Unc	BU
1948D	46,325,000	—	0.50	15.00	40.00	—
1948F	68,203,000	—	0.50	8.00	32.50	—
1948F Proof	250	Value: 150				
1948G	45,604,000	—	0.50	15.00	60.00	—
1948J	79,304,000	—	0.50	15.00	50.00	—
1949D	99,863,000	—	0.50	6.00	27.50	—
1949D Proof	—	Value: 100				
1949F	70,900,000	—	0.50	6.00	22.50	—
1949F Proof	250	Value: 60.00				
1949G	70,950,000	—	0.50	10.00	40.00	—
1949J	101,932,000	—	0.50	6.00	27.50	—
1949J Proof	—	Value: 85.00				

KM# 105 PFENNIG

2.0000 g., Copper Plated Steel, 16.5 mm. **Obv:** Five oak leaves, date below **Obv. Legend:** BUNDES REPUBLIK DEUTSCHLAND **Rev:** Denomination

Date	Mintage	F	VF	XF	Unc	BU
1950D	772,592,000	—	—	0.10	2.00	—
1950F	898,277,000	—	—	0.10	2.00	—
1950F Proof	620	Value: 27.50				
1950G	515,673,000	—	—	0.10	3.00	—
1950G Proof	1,800	Value: 5.00				
1950J	784,424,000	—	—	0.10	2.00	—
1950J Proof	—	Value: 12.00				
1966D	65,063,000	—	—	0.10	3.00	—
1966F	75,031,000	—	—	0.10	3.00	—
1966F Proof	100	Value: 35.00				
1966G	48,261,000	—	—	0.10	5.00	—
1966G Proof	3,070	Value: 4.00				
1966J	66,842,000	—	—	0.10	3.00	—
1966J Proof	1,000	Value: 8.00				
1967D	39,082,000	—	0.10	2.00	8.00	—
1967F	45,003,000	—	0.10	1.50	8.00	—
1967F Proof	1,500	Value: 6.00				
1967G	20,787,000	—	0.20	4.50	17.00	—
1967G Proof	4,500	Value: 3.50				
1967J	42,583,000	—	0.10	1.50	8.00	—
1967J Proof	1,500	Value: 8.00				
1968D	32,796,999	—	0.10	1.50	7.00	—
1968F	26,338,000	—	0.10	1.50	7.00	—
1968F Proof	3,000	Value: 5.00				
1968G	20,382,000	—	0.10	1.50	8.00	—
1968G Proof	6,023	Value: 4.00				
1968J	23,414,000	—	0.10	1.50	8.00	—
1968J Proof	2,000	Value: 6.50				
1969D	78,177,000	—	—	0.10	1.00	—
1969F	90,172,000	—	—	0.10	1.00	—
1969F Proof	5,100	Value: 1.50				
1969G	61,836,000	—	—	0.10	2.00	—
1969G Proof	8,700	Value: 1.25				
1969J	80,221,000	—	—	0.10	1.00	—
1969J Proof	5,000	Value: 1.50				
1970D	91,151,000	—	—	0.10	1.00	—
1970F	105,236,000	—	—	0.10	1.00	—
1970F Proof	5,240	Value: 1.50				
1970G	82,421,000	—	—	0.10	1.00	—
1970G Proof	10,200	Value: 1.00				
1970 Small J	93,455,000	—	—	0.10	1.00	—
1970 Large J	Inc. above	—	—	0.10	1.00	—
1970J Proof	5,000	Value: 1.50				
1971D	116,612,000	—	—	0.10	0.50	—

Date	Mintage	F	VF	XF	Unc	BU
1971D Proof	8,000	Value: 1.00				
1971F	157,393,000	—	—	0.10	0.50	—
1971F Proof	8,000	Value: 1.00				
1971G	77,674,000	—	—	0.10	1.00	—
1971G Proof	10,200	Value: 1.00				
1971J	120,218,000	—	—	0.10	0.50	—
1971J Proof	8,000	Value: 1.00				
1972D	90,696,000	—	—	0.10	0.25	—
1972D Proof	8,000	Value: 1.00				
1972F	105,006,000	—	—	0.10	0.25	—
1972F Proof	8,000	Value: 1.00				
1972G	60,660,000	—	—	0.10	0.25	—
1972G Proof	10,000	Value: 1.00				
1972J	93,492,000	—	—	0.10	0.25	—
1972J Proof	8,000	Value: 1.00				
1973D	38,976,000	—	—	0.10	0.25	—
1973D Proof	9,000	Value: 1.00				
1973F	45,006,000	—	—	0.10	0.25	—
1973F Proof	9,000	Value: 1.00				
1973G	25,811,000	—	—	0.10	0.25	—
1973G Proof	9,000	Value: 1.00				
1973J	40,057,000	—	—	0.10	0.25	—
1973J Proof	9,000	Value: 1.00				
1974D	90,951,000	—	—	0.10	0.25	—
1974D Proof	35,000	Value: 0.40				
1974F	105,091,000	—	—	0.10	0.25	—
1974F Proof	35,000	Value: 0.40				
1974G	60,548,000	—	—	0.10	0.25	—
1974G Proof	35,000	Value: 0.40				
1974J	93,527,000	—	—	0.10	0.25	—
1974J Proof	35,000	Value: 0.40				
1975D	91,053,000	—	—	0.10	0.25	—
1975D Proof	43,000	Value: 0.40				
1975F	105,007,000	—	—	0.10	0.25	—
1975F Proof	43,000	Value: 0.40				
1975G	60,704,000	—	—	0.10	0.25	—
1975G Proof	43,000	Value: 0.40				
1975J	93,495,000	—	—	0.10	0.25	—
1975J Proof	43,000	Value: 0.40				
1976D	130,227,000	—	—	0.10	0.25	—
1976D Proof	43,000	Value: 0.40				
1976F	150,037,000	—	—	0.10	0.25	—
1976F Proof	43,000	Value: 0.40				
1976G	86,586,000	—	—	0.10	0.25	—
1976G Proof	43,000	Value: 0.40				
1976J	133,500,000	—	—	0.10	0.25	—
1976J Proof	43,000	Value: 0.40				
1977D	143,000,000	—	—	0.10	0.25	—
1977D Proof	52,000	Value: 0.40				
1977F	165,000,000	—	—	0.10	0.25	—
1977F Proof	51,000	Value: 0.40				
1977G	95,201,000	—	—	0.10	0.25	—
1977G Proof	51,000	Value: 0.40				
1977J	146,788,000	—	—	0.10	0.25	—
1977J Proof	51,000	Value: 0.40				
1978D	156,000,000	—	—	0.10	0.25	—
1978D Proof	54,000	Value: 0.40				
1978F	180,000,000	—	—	0.10	0.25	—
1978F Proof	54,000	Value: 0.40				
1978G	103,800,000	—	—	0.10	0.25	—
1978G Proof	54,000	Value: 0.40				
1978J	160,200,000	—	—	0.10	0.25	—
1978J Proof	54,000	Value: 0.40				
1979D	156,000,000	—	—	0.10	0.25	—
1979D Proof	89,000	Value: 0.40				
1979F	180,000,000	—	—	0.10	0.25	—
1979F Proof	89,000	Value: 0.40				
1979G	103,800,000	—	—	0.10	0.25	—
1979G Proof	89,000	Value: 0.40				
1979J	160,200,000	—	—	0.10	0.25	—
1979J Proof	89,000	Value: 0.40				
1980D	200,080,000	—	—	0.10	0.25	—
1980D Proof	110,000	Value: 0.40				
1980F	200,620,000	—	—	0.10	0.25	—
1980F Proof	110,000	Value: 0.40				
1980G	71,940,000	—	—	0.10	0.25	—
1980G Proof	110,000	Value: 0.40				
1980J	143,110,000	—	—	0.10	0.25	—
1980J Proof	110,000	Value: 0.40				
1981D	169,550,000	—	—	0.10	0.25	—
1981D Proof	91,000	Value: 0.40				
1981F	274,010,000	—	—	0.10	0.25	—
1981F Proof	91,000	Value: 0.40				
1981G	178,010,000	—	—	0.10	0.25	—
1981G Proof	91,000	Value: 0.40				
1981J	189,090,000	—	—	0.10	0.25	—
1981J Proof	91,000	Value: 0.40				
1982D	130,090,000	—	—	0.10	0.20	—
1982D Proof	78,000	Value: 0.40				
1982F	108,390,000	—	—	0.10	0.20	—
1982F Proof	78,000	Value: 0.40				
1982G	77,740,000	—	—	0.10	0.20	—
1982G Proof	78,000	Value: 0.40				
1982J	124,720,000	—	—	0.10	0.20	—
1982J Proof	78,000	Value: 0.40				
1983D	46,800,000	—	—	0.10	0.20	—
1983D Proof	75,000	Value: 0.40				
1983F	54,000,000	—	—	0.10	0.20	—
1983F Proof	75,000	Value: 0.40				
1983G	31,140,000	—	—	0.10	0.20	—
1983G Proof	75,000	Value: 0.40				
1983J	48,060,000	—	—	0.10	0.20	—

Date	Mintage	F	VF	XF	Unc	BU
1983J Proof	75,000	Value: 0.40				
1984D	58,500,000	—	—	0.10	0.20	—
1984D Proof	64,000	Value: 0.40				
1984F	67,500,000	—	—	0.10	0.20	—
1984F Proof	64,000	Value: 0.40				
1984G	38,900,000	—	—	0.10	0.20	—
1984G Proof	64,000	Value: 0.40				
1984J	60,100,000	—	—	0.10	0.20	—
1984J Proof	64,000	Value: 0.40				
1985D	19,500,000	—	—	0.10	0.20	—
1985D Proof	56,000	Value: 0.40				
1985F	22,500,000	—	—	0.10	0.20	—
1985F Proof	54,000	Value: 0.40				
1985G	13,000,000	—	—	—	0.10	—
1985G Proof	55,000	Value: 0.40				
1985J	20,000,000	—	—	—	0.10	—
1985J Proof	54,000	Value: 0.40				
1986D	39,000,000	—	—	—	0.10	—
1986D Proof	44,000	Value: 0.40				
1986F	45,000,000	—	—	—	0.10	—
1986F Proof	44,000	Value: 0.40				
1986G	25,900,000	—	—	—	0.10	—
1986G Proof	44,000	Value: 0.40				
1986J	40,100,000	—	—	—	0.10	—
1986J Proof	44,000	Value: 0.40				
1987D	6,500,000	—	—	—	0.10	—
1987D Proof	45,000	Value: 0.40				
1987F	7,500,000	—	—	—	0.10	—
1987F Proof	45,000	Value: 0.40				
1987G	4,330,000	—	—	—	0.10	—
1987G Proof	45,000	Value: 0.40				
1987J	6,680,000	—	—	—	0.10	—
1987J Proof	45,000	Value: 0.40				
1988D	52,000,000	—	—	—	0.10	—
1988D Proof	45,000	Value: 0.40				
1988F	60,000,000	—	—	—	0.10	—
1988F Proof	45,000	Value: 0.40				
1988G	34,600,000	—	—	—	0.10	—
1988G Proof	45,000	Value: 0.40				
1988J	53,400,000	—	—	—	0.10	—
1988J Proof	45,000	Value: 0.40				
1989D	104,000,000	—	—	—	0.10	—
1989D Proof	45,000	Value: 0.40				
1989F	120,000,000	—	—	—	0.10	—
1989F Proof	45,000	Value: 0.40				
1989G	69,200,000	—	—	—	0.10	—
1989G Proof	45,000	Value: 0.40				
1989J	106,800,000	—	—	—	0.10	—
1989J Proof	45,000	Value: 0.40				
1990D	169,000,000	—	—	—	0.10	—
1990D Proof	45,000	Value: 0.40				
1990F	195,000,000	—	—	—	0.10	—
1990F Proof	45,000	Value: 0.40				
1990G	112,450,000	—	—	—	0.10	—
1990G Proof	45,000	Value: 0.40				
1990J	173,550,000	—	—	—	0.10	—
1990J Proof	45,000	Value: 0.40				
1991A	260,000,000	—	—	—	0.10	—
1991A Proof	45,000	Value: 0.40				
1991D	273,000,000	—	—	—	0.10	—
1991D Proof	45,000	Value: 0.40				
1991F	312,000,000	—	—	—	0.10	—
1991F Proof	45,000	Value: 0.40				
1991G	182,000,000	—	—	—	0.10	—
1991G Proof	45,000	Value: 0.40				
1991J	273,000,000	—	—	—	0.10	—
1991J Proof	45,000	Value: 0.40				
1992A	40,000,000	—	—	—	0.10	—
1992A Proof	45,000	Value: 0.40				
1992D	42,000,000	—	—	—	0.10	—
1992D Proof	45,000	Value: 0.40				
1992F	48,000,000	—	—	—	0.10	—
1992F Proof	45,000	Value: 0.40				
1992G	28,000,000	—	—	—	0.10	—
1992G Proof	45,000	Value: 0.40				
1992J	42,000,000	—	—	—	0.10	—
1992J Proof	45,000	Value: 0.40				
1993A	40,000,000	—	—	—	0.10	—
1993A Proof	45,000	Value: 0.40				
1993D	42,000,000	—	—	—	0.10	—
1993D Proof	45,000	Value: 0.40				
1993F	48,000,000	—	—	—	0.10	—
1993F Proof	45,000	Value: 0.40				
1993G	28,000,000	—	—	—	0.10	—
1993G Proof	45,000	Value: 0.40				
1993J	42,000,000	—	—	—	0.10	—
1993J Proof	45,000	Value: 0.40				
1994A	100,000,000	—	—	—	0.10	—
1994A Proof	45,000	Value: 0.40				
1994D	105,000,000	—	—	—	0.10	—
1994D Proof	45,000	Value: 0.40				
1994F	120,000,000	—	—	—	0.10	—
1994F Proof	45,000	Value: 0.40				
1994G	70,000,000	—	—	—	0.10	—
1994G Proof	45,000	Value: 0.40				
1994J	105,000,000	—	—	—	0.10	—
1994J Proof	45,000	Value: 0.40				
1995A	100,000,000	—	—	—	0.15	—
1995A Proof	45,000	Value: 0.45				
1995D	105,000,000	—	—	—	0.15	—
1995D Proof	45,000	Value: 0.45				
1995F	120,000,000	—	—	—	0.15	—
1995F Proof	45,000	Value: 0.45				
1995G	70,000,000	—	—	—	0.15	—
1995G Proof	45,000	Value: 0.45				
1995J	105,000,000	—	—	—	0.15	—
1995J Proof	45,000	Value: 0.45				
1996A	80,000,000	—	—	—	0.20	—
1996A Proof	45,000	Value: 0.50				
1996D	84,000,000	—	—	—	0.20	—
1996D Proof	45,000	Value: 0.50				
1996F	96,000,000	—	—	—	0.20	—
1996F Proof	45,000	Value: 0.50				
1996G	56,000,000	—	—	—	0.20	—
1996G Proof	45,000	Value: 0.50				
1996J	84,000,000	—	—	—	0.20	—
1996J Proof	45,000	Value: 0.50				
1997A	70,000	—	—	—	1.75	—
Note: In sets only						
1997A Proof	45,000	Value: 2.00				
1997D	70,000	—	—	—	1.75	—
Note: In sets only						
1997D Proof	45,000	Value: 2.00				
1997F	70,000	—	—	—	1.75	—
Note: In sets only						
1997F Proof	45,000	Value: 2.00				
1997G	70,000	—	—	—	1.75	—
Note: In sets only						
1997G Proof	45,000	Value: 2.00				
1997J	70,000	—	—	—	1.75	—
Note: In sets only						
1997J Proof	45,000	Value: 2.00				
1998A	70,000	—	—	—	1.75	—
Note: In sets only						
1998A Proof	45,000	Value: 2.00				
1998D	70,000	—	—	—	1.75	—
Note: In sets only						
1998D Proof	45,000	Value: 2.00				
1998F	70,000	—	—	—	1.75	—
Note: In sets only						
1998F Proof	45,000	Value: 2.00				
1998G	70,000	—	—	—	1.75	—
Note: In sets only						
1998G Proof	45,000	Value: 2.00				
1998J	70,000	—	—	—	1.75	—
Note: In sets only						
1998J Proof	45,000	Value: 2.00				
1999A	70,000	—	—	—	1.75	—
Note: In sets only						
1999A Proof	45,000	Value: 2.00				
1999D	70,000	—	—	—	1.75	—
Note: In sets only						
1999D Proof	45,000	Value: 2.00				
1999F	70,000	—	—	—	1.75	—
Note: In sets only						
1999F Proof	45,000	Value: 2.00				
1999G	70,000	—	—	—	1.75	—
Note: In sets only						
1999G Proof	45,000	Value: 2.00				
1999J	70,000	—	—	—	1.75	—
Note: In sets only						
1999J Proof	45,000	Value: 2.00				
2000A	20,000	—	—	—	1.75	—
Note: In sets only						
2000A Proof	45,000	Value: 2.00				
2000D	20,000	—	—	—	1.75	—
Note: In sets only						
2000D Proof	45,000	Value: 2.00				
2000F	20,000	—	—	—	1.75	—
Note: In sets only						
2000F Proof	45,000	Value: 2.00				
2000G	20,000	—	—	—	1.75	—
Note: In sets only						
2000G Proof	45,000	Value: 2.00				
2000J	20,000	—	—	—	1.75	—
Note: In sets only						
2000J Proof	45,000	Value: 2.00				

KM# 106 2 PFENNIG

Bronze, 19.25 mm. **Obv:** Five oak leaves, date below **Rev:** Denomination

Date	Mintage	F	VF	XF	Unc	BU
1950D	26,263,000	—	0.10	2.50	12.00	—
1950D Proof	—	Value: 50.00				
1950F	30,278,000	—	0.10	2.00	10.00	—
1950F Proof	200	—	—	—	—	—
1950G	17,151,000	—	0.10	25.00	75.00	—
1950G Proof	—	Value: 90.00				
1950J	27,216,000	—	0.10	2.50	12.00	—
1950J Proof	—	Value: 40.00				
1958D	19,440,000	—	0.10	3.00	14.00	—
1958F	24,122,000	—	0.10	2.00	10.00	—
1958F Proof	100	—	—	—	—	—
1958G	15,255,000	—	0.10	4.00	18.00	—
1958J	21,250,000	—	0.10	2.00	10.00	—
1959D	19,690,000	—	0.10	2.00	10.00	—
1959F	25,017,000	—	0.10	1.50	10.00	—
1959F Proof	75	—	—	—	—	—
1959G	12,899,000	—	0.10	3.00	14.00	—
1959J	25,482,000	—	0.10	2.00	10.00	—
1960D	21,979,000	—	0.10	1.50	9.00	—
1960F	13,060,000	—	—	0.10	10.00	—
1960F Proof	75	—	—	—	—	—
1960G	5,657,000	—	0.10	2.00	18.00	—
1960J	17,799,000	—	0.10	2.00	10.00	—
1961D	26,662,000	—	0.10	1.50	9.00	—
1961F	24,990,000	—	0.10	1.50	8.00	—
1961G	18,060,000	—	0.10	1.50	9.00	—
1961J	22,147,000	—	0.10	1.50	8.00	—
1962D	21,297,000	—	0.10	1.50	9.00	—
1962F	42,189,000	—	0.10	1.00	6.00	—
1962G	17,297,000	—	0.10	2.00	12.00	—
1962J	30,706,000	—	0.10	1.00	8.00	—
1963D	7,648,000	—	0.10	2.00	10.00	—
1963F	18,299,000	—	0.10	1.50	9.00	—
1963G	35,838,000	—	0.10	1.50	8.00	—
1963G Proof		—	—	—	—	—
1963J	42,884,000	—	0.10	1.50	6.00	—
1964D	20,336,000	—	0.10	1.50	10.00	—
1964F	31,400,000	—	0.10	1.50	7.00	—
1964G	18,431,000	—	0.10	1.50	8.00	—
1964G Proof	Est. 600	Value: 12.00				
1964J	13,370,000	—	0.10	1.50	8.00	—
1965D	48,541,000	—	0.10	1.00	4.00	—
1965F	27,000,000	—	0.10	1.00	6.00	—
1965F Proof	Est. 80	Value: 70.00				
1965G	13,584,000	—	0.10	1.50	7.00	—
1965G Proof	1,200	Value: 5.00				
1965J	33,397,000	—	0.10	1.00	4.00	—
1966D	65,077,000	—	—	0.50	3.00	—
1966F	52,543,000	—	—	0.50	3.00	—
1966F Proof	100	Value: 80.00				
1966G	40,804,000	—	—	0.50	3.00	—
1966G Proof	3,070	Value: 5.50				
1966J	46,754,000	—	—	0.50	3.00	—
1966J Proof	1,000	Value: 40.00				
1967D	25,997,000	—	0.10	1.00	6.00	—
1967F	30,004,000	—	0.10	1.00	5.00	—
1967F Proof	1,500	Value: 7.00				
1967G	6,280,000	—	0.10	1.50	10.00	—
1967G Proof	4,500	Value: 4.50				
1967J	26,725,000	—	0.10	1.00	6.00	—
1967J Proof	1,500	Value: 10.00				
1968D	19,523,000	—	0.10	1.00	5.00	—
1968G	15,357,000	—	0.10	1.00	6.00	—
1968G Proof	3,651	Value: 4.00				
1968J	—	—	200	400	600	—
Note: A 1968J error of 1963J exists with coin alignment						
1969J	—	—	200	400	600	—

KM# 106a 2 PFENNIG

2.9000 g., Bronze Clad Steel, 19.25 mm. **Obv:** Five oak leaves, date below **Rev:** Denomination

Date	Mintage	F	VF	XF	Unc	BU
1967G Proof	520	Value: 950				
1968D	19,523,000	—	—	0.50	2.50	—
1968F	30,000,000	—	—	0.50	2.50	—
1968F Proof	3,000	Value: 6.00				
1968G	13,004,000	—	—	0.50	2.50	—
1968G Proof	2,372	Value: 4.00				
1968J	20,026,000	—	—	0.25	2.00	—
1968J Proof	2,000	Value: 7.50				
1969D	39,012,000	—	—	0.25	1.00	—
1969D Proof	—	Value: 1.25				
1969F	45,029,000	—	—	0.25	1.00	—
1969F Proof	5,100	Value: 1.25				
1969G	32,156,999	—	—	0.25	1.00	—
1969G Proof	8,700	Value: 1.25				
1969J	40,102,000	—	—	0.25	1.00	—
1969J Proof	5,000	Value: 2.50				
1970D	45,525,000	—	—	0.10	0.25	—
1970F	73,851,000	—	—	0.10	0.25	—
1970F Proof	5,140	Value: 1.25				
1970G	30,330,000	—	—	0.10	0.25	—
1970G Proof	10,200	Value: 1.25				
1970 Small J	46,730,000	—	—	0.10	0.25	—
1970 Large J	Inc. above	—	—	0.10	0.25	—
1970J Proof	5,000	Value: 1.75				
1971D	71,755,000	—	—	0.10	0.25	—
1971D Proof	8,000	Value: 1.25				
1971F	82,765,000	—	—	0.10	0.25	—
1971F Proof	8,000	Value: 1.25				
1971G	47,850,000	—	—	0.10	0.25	—
1971G Proof	10,000	Value: 1.25				
1971J	73,641,000	—	—	0.10	0.25	—
1971J Proof	8,000	Value: 1.25				
1972D	52,403,000	—	—	0.10	0.25	—
1972D Proof	8,000	Value: 1.00				

Date	Mintage	F	VF	XF	Unc	BU
1972F	60,272,000	—	—	0.10	0.25	—
1972F Proof	8,000	Value: 1.00				
1972G	34,864,000	—	—	0.10	0.25	—
1972G Proof	10,000	Value: 1.00				
1972J	53,673,000	—	—	0.10	0.25	—
1972J Proof	8,000	Value: 1.00				
1973D	26,190,000	—	—	0.10	0.25	—
1973D Proof	9,000	Value: 1.00				
1973F	30,160,000	—	—	0.10	0.25	—
1973F Proof	9,000	Value: 1.00				
1973G	17,379,000	—	—	0.10	0.25	—
1973G Proof	9,000	Value: 1.00				
1973J	26,830,000	—	—	0.10	0.25	—
1973J Proof	9,000	Value: 1.00				
1974D	58,667,000	—	—	0.10	0.25	—
1974D Proof	35,000	Value: 0.50				
1974F	67,596,000	—	—	0.10	0.25	—
1974F Proof	35,000	Value: 0.50				
1974G	39,007,000	—	—	0.10	0.25	—
1974G Proof	35,000	Value: 0.50				
1974J	60,195,000	—	—	0.10	0.25	—
1974J Proof	35,000	Value: 0.50				
1975D	58,634,000	—	—	0.10	0.25	—
1975D Proof	43,000	Value: 0.50				
1975F	67,685,000	—	—	0.10	0.25	—
1975F Proof	43,000	Value: 0.50				
1975G	39,391,000	—	—	0.10	0.25	—
1975G Proof	43,000	Value: 0.50				
1975J	60,207,000	—	—	0.10	0.25	—
1975J Proof	43,000	Value: 0.50				
1976D	78,074,000	—	—	0.10	0.25	—
1976D Proof	43,000	Value: 0.50				
1976F	90,130,000	—	—	0.10	0.25	—
1976F Proof	43,000	Value: 0.50				
1976G	51,988,000	—	—	0.10	0.25	—
1976G Proof	43,000	Value: 0.50				
1976J	80,145,000	—	—	0.10	0.25	—
1976J Proof	43,000	Value: 0.50				
1977D	84,516,000	—	—	0.10	0.20	—
1977D Proof	51,000	Value: 0.40				
1977F	97,504,000	—	—	0.10	0.20	—
1977F Proof	51,000	Value: 0.40				
1977G	56,276,000	—	—	0.10	0.20	—
1977G Proof	51,000	Value: 0.40				
1977J	86,888,000	—	—	0.10	0.20	—
1977J Proof	51,000	Value: 0.40				
1978D	84,500,000	—	—	0.10	0.20	—
1978D Proof	54,000	Value: 0.40				
1978F	97,500,000	—	—	0.10	0.20	—
1978F Proof	54,000	Value: 0.40				
1978G	56,225,000	—	—	0.10	0.20	—
1978G Proof	54,000	Value: 0.40				
1978J	86,775,000	—	—	0.10	0.20	—
1978J Proof	54,000	Value: 0.40				
1979D	91,000,000	—	—	0.10	0.20	—
1979D Proof	89,000	Value: 0.40				
1979F	105,000,000	—	—	0.10	0.20	—
1979F Proof	89,000	Value: 0.40				
1979G	60,550,000	—	—	0.10	0.20	—
1979G Proof	89,000	Value: 0.40				
1979J	93,480,000	—	—	0.10	0.20	—
1979J Proof	89,000	Value: 0.40				
1980D	93,360,000	—	—	0.10	0.20	—
1980D Proof	110,000	Value: 0.40				
1980F	120,360,000	—	—	0.10	0.20	—
1980F Proof	110,000	Value: 0.40				
1980G	50,830,000	—	—	0.10	0.20	—
1980G Proof	110,000	Value: 0.40				
1980J	102,260,000	—	—	0.10	0.20	—
1980J Proof	110,000	Value: 0.40				
1981D	93,910,000	—	—	0.10	0.20	—
1981D Proof	91,000	Value: 0.40				
1981F	83,710,000	—	—	0.10	0.20	—
1981F Proof	91,000	Value: 0.40				
1981G	89,850,000	—	—	0.10	0.20	—
1981G Proof	91,000	Value: 0.40				
1981J	87,250,000	—	—	0.10	0.20	—
1981J Proof	91,000	Value: 0.40				
1982D	64,390,000	—	—	0.10	0.20	—
1982D Proof	78,000	Value: 0.40				
1982F	36,870,000	—	—	0.10	0.20	—
1982F Proof	78,000	Value: 0.40				
1982G	58,590,000	—	—	0.10	0.20	—
1982G Proof	78,000	Value: 0.40				
1982J	57,690,000	—	—	0.10	0.20	—
1982J Proof	78,000	Value: 0.40				
1983D	71,500,000	—	—	0.10	0.20	—
1983D Proof	75,000	Value: 0.40				
1983F	82,500,000	—	—	0.10	0.20	—
1983F Proof	75,000	Value: 0.40				
1983G	47,575,000	—	—	0.10	0.20	—
1983G Proof	75,000	Value: 0.40				
1983J	73,425,000	—	—	0.10	0.20	—
1983J Proof	75,000	Value: 0.40				
1984D	58,500,000	—	—	0.10	0.20	—
1984D Proof	64,000	Value: 0.40				
1984F	67,500,000	—	—	0.10	0.20	—
1984F Proof	64,000	Value: 0.40				
1984G	38,900,000	—	—	0.10	0.20	—
1984G Proof	64,000	Value: 0.40				
1984J	60,100,000	—	—	0.10	0.20	—
1984J Proof	64,000	Value: 0.40				

Date	Mintage	F	VF	XF	Unc	BU
1985D	19,500,000	—	0.10	1.00	3.00	—
1985D Proof	56,000	Value: 0.40				
1985F	22,500,000	—	0.25	1.00	3.00	—
1985F Proof	54,000	Value: 0.40				
1985G	13,000,000	0.25	0.75	2.50	8.00	—
1985G Proof	55,000	Value: 0.40				
1985J	20,000,000	0.25	0.50	2.00	7.00	—
1985J Proof	54,000	Value: 0.40				
1986D	39,000,000	—	—	—	0.25	—
1986D Proof	44,000	Value: 0.40				
1986F	45,000,000	—	—	—	0.25	—
1986F Proof	44,000	Value: 0.40				
1986G	25,900,000	—	—	—	0.50	—
1986G Proof	44,000	Value: 0.40				
1986J	40,100,000	—	—	—	0.25	—
1986J Proof	44,000	Value: 0.40				
1987D	6,500,000	0.50	1.00	2.50	5.00	—
1987D Proof	45,000	Value: 0.40				
1987F	7,500,000	0.50	1.00	2.50	5.00	—
1987F Proof	45,000	Value: 0.40				
1987G	4,330,000	0.75	1.25	2.75	6.00	—
1987G Proof	45,000	Value: 0.40				
1987J	6,680,000	0.50	1.00	2.50	5.00	—
1987J Proof	45,000	Value: 0.40				
1988D	52,000,000	—	—	—	0.25	—
1988D Proof	45,000	Value: 0.40				
1988F	60,000,000	—	—	—	0.25	—
1988F Proof	45,000	Value: 0.40				
1988G	34,600,000	—	—	—	0.25	—
1988G Proof	45,000	Value: 0.40				
1988J	53,400,000	—	—	—	0.25	—
1988J Proof	45,000	Value: 0.40				
1989D	52,000,000	—	—	—	0.25	—
1989D Proof	45,000	Value: 0.40				
1989F	60,000,000	—	—	—	0.25	—
1989F Proof	45,000	Value: 0.40				
1989G	34,600,000	—	—	—	0.25	—
1989G Proof	45,000	Value: 0.40				
1989J	53,400,000	—	—	—	0.25	—
1989J Proof	45,000	Value: 0.40				
1990D	71,500,000	—	—	—	0.25	—
1990D Proof	45,000	Value: 0.40				
1990F	82,500,000	—	—	—	0.25	—
1990F Proof	45,000	Value: 0.40				
1990G	47,570,000	—	—	—	0.25	—
1990G Proof	45,000	Value: 0.40				
1990J	73,420,000	—	—	—	0.25	—
1990J Proof	45,000	Value: 0.40				
1991A	115,000,000	—	—	—	0.25	—
1991A Proof	45,000	Value: 0.40				
1991D	120,750,000	—	—	—	0.25	—
1991D Proof	45,000	Value: 0.40				
1991F	138,000,000	—	—	—	0.25	—
1991F Proof	45,000	Value: 0.40				
1991G	80,500,000	—	—	—	0.25	—
1991G Proof	45,000	Value: 0.40				
1991J	120,750,000	—	—	—	0.25	—
1991J Proof	45,000	Value: 0.40				
1992A	60,000,000	—	—	—	0.25	—
1992A Proof	45,000	Value: 0.40				
1992D	63,000,000	—	—	—	0.25	—
1992D Proof	45,000	Value: 0.40				
1992F	72,000,000	—	—	—	0.25	—
1992F Proof	45,000	Value: 0.40				
1992G	42,000,000	—	—	—	0.25	—
1992G Proof	45,000	Value: 0.40				
1992J	63,000,000	—	—	—	0.25	—
1992J Proof	45,000	Value: 0.40				
1993A	10,000,000	—	0.25	1.00	4.00	—
1993A Proof	45,000	Value: 0.40				
1993D	10,500,000	—	0.25	1.00	4.00	—
1993D Proof	45,000	Value: 0.40				
1993F	12,000,000	—	0.25	1.00	4.00	—
1993F Proof	45,000	Value: 0.40				
1993G	7,000,000	—	0.25	1.00	4.00	—
1993G Proof	45,000	Value: 0.40				
1993J	10,000,000	—	0.25	1.00	4.00	—
1993J Proof	45,000	Value: 0.40				
1994A	55,000,000	—	—	—	0.15	—
1994A Proof	45,000	Value: 0.40				
1994D	57,750,000	—	—	—	0.15	—
1994D Proof	45,000	Value: 0.40				
1994F	66,000,000	—	—	—	0.15	—
1994F Proof	45,000	Value: 0.40				
1994G	38,500,000	—	—	—	0.25	—
1994G Proof	45,000	Value: 0.40				
1994J	57,750,000	—	—	—	0.15	—
1994J Proof	45,000	Value: 0.40				
1995A	1,000,000,000	—	—	—	0.15	—
1995A Proof	45,000	Value: 0.45				
1995D	105,000,000	—	—	—	0.15	—
1995D Proof	45,000	Value: 0.45				
1995F	120,000,000	—	—	—	0.15	—
1995F Proof	45,000	Value: 0.45				
1995G	70,000,000	—	—	—	0.25	—
1995G Proof	45,000	Value: 0.45				
1995J	105,000,000	—	—	—	0.15	—
1995J Proof	45,000	Value: 0.45				
1996A	40,000,000	—	—	—	0.20	—
1996A Proof	45,000	Value: 0.50				
1996D	42,000,000	—	—	—	0.20	—
1996D Proof	45,000	Value: 0.50				

Date	Mintage	F	VF	XF	Unc	BU
1996F	48,000,000	—	—	—	0.20	—
1996F Proof	45,000	Value: 0.50				
1996G	28,000,000	—	—	—	0.25	—
1996G Proof	45,000	Value: 0.50				
1996J	42,000,000	—	—	—	0.20	—
1996J Proof	45,000	Value: 0.50				
1997A	70,000	—	—	—	1.75	—
Note: In sets only						
1997A Proof	45,000	Value: 2.00				
1997D	70,000	—	—	—	1.75	—
Note: In sets only						
1997D Proof	45,000	Value: 2.00				
1997F	70,000	—	—	—	1.75	—
Note: In sets only						
1997F Proof	45,000	Value: 2.00				
1997G	70,000	—	—	—	1.75	—
Note: In sets only						
1997G Proof	45,000	Value: 2.00				
1997J	70,000	—	—	—	1.75	—
Note: In sets only						
1997J Proof	45,000	Value: 2.00				
1998A	70,000	—	—	—	1.75	—
Note: In sets only						
1998A Proof	45,000	Value: 2.00				
1998D	70,000	—	—	—	1.75	—
Note: In sets only						
1998D Proof	45,000	Value: 2.00				
1998F	70,000	—	—	—	1.75	—
Note: In sets only						
1998F Proof	45,000	Value: 2.00				
1998G	70,000	—	—	—	1.75	—
Note: In sets only						
1998G Proof	45,000	Value: 2.00				
1998J	70,000	—	—	—	1.75	—
Note: In sets only						
1998J Proof	45,000	Value: 2.00				
1999A	70,000	—	—	—	1.75	—
Note: In sets only						
1999A Proof	45,000	Value: 2.00				
1999D	70,000	—	—	—	1.75	—
Note: In sets only						
1999D Proof	45,000	Value: 2.00				
1999F	70,000	—	—	—	1.75	—
Note: In sets only						
1999F Proof	45,000	Value: 2.00				
1999G	70,000	—	—	—	1.75	—
Note: In sets only						
1999G Proof	45,000	Value: 2.00				
1999J	70,000	—	—	—	1.75	—
Note: In sets only						
1999J Proof	45,000	Value: 2.00				
2000A	70,000	—	—	—	1.75	—
Note: In sets only						
2000A Proof	45,000	Value: 2.00				
2000D	70,000	—	—	—	1.75	—
Note: In sets only						
2000D Proof	45,000	Value: 2.00				
2000F	70,000	—	—	—	1.75	—
Note: In sets only						
2000F Proof	45,000	Value: 2.00				
2000G	70,000	—	—	—	1.75	—
Note: In sets only						
2000G Proof	45,000	Value: 2.00				
2000J	70,000	—	—	—	1.75	—
Note: In sets only						
2000J Proof	45,000	Value: 2.00				

KM# 102 5 PFENNIG

Bronze-Clad Steel, 18.5 mm. **Obv:** Five oak leaves, date below **Obv. Legend:** BANK DEUTSCHER LÄNDER **Rev:** Denomination

Date	Mintage	F	VF	XF	Unc	BU
1949D	60,026,000	0.25	1.00	10.00	45.00	—
1949D Proof	—	Value: 150				
1949F	66,081,999	0.25	1.00	7.50	35.00	—
1949F Proof	250	Value: 85.00				
1949G	57,356,000	0.25	1.50	12.50	50.00	—
1949J	68,977,000	0.25	1.00	10.00	40.00	—
1949J Proof	—	Value: 85.00				

KM# 107 5 PFENNIG

3.0000 g., Brass Plated Steel, 18.5 mm. **Obv:** Five oak leaves, date below **Obv. Legend:** BUNDES REPUBLIK DEUTSCHLAND **Rev:** Denomination

Date	Mintage	F	VF	XF	Unc	BU
1950D	271,962,000	—	—	.1.50	5.00	—

Date	Mintage	F	VF	XF	Unc	BU
1950F	362,880,000	—	—	1.50	5.00	—
1950F Proof	500	Value: 65.00				
1950G	180,492,000	—	—	1.50	5.00	—
1950G Proof	1,800	Value: 25.00				
1950J Large J	285,283,000	—	—	1.50	5.00	—
1950J Small J	Inc. above	—	—	1.50	5.00	—
1966D	26,036,000	—	—	1.50	8.50	—
1966F	30,047,000	—	—	1.50	8.50	—
1966F Proof	100	Value: 60.00				
1966G	17,333,000	—	—	1.50	8.50	—
1966G Proof	3,070	Value: 7.50				
1966J	26,741,000	—	—	1.50	8.50	—
1966J Proof	1,000	Value: 17.50				
1967D	10,418,000	—	—	1.50	8.50	—
1967F	12,012,000	—	—	1.50	8.50	—
1967F Proof	1,500	Value: 15.00				
1967G	1,736,000	0.50	2.50	7.00	25.00	—
1967G Proof	4,500	Value: 7.50				
1967J	10,706,000	—	—	1.50	8.50	—
1967J Proof	1,500	Value: 15.00				
1968D	13,047,000	—	—	1.00	6.00	—
1968F	15,026,000	—	—	1.00	5.00	—
1968F Proof	3,000	Value: 9.00				
1968G	13,855,000	—	—	1.00	7.00	—
1968G Proof	6,023	Value: 6.00				
1968J	13,362,000	—	—	1.00	7.00	—
1968J Proof	2,000	Value: 15.00				
1969D	23,488,000	—	—	0.50	2.50	—
1969F	27,046,000	—	—	0.50	2.50	—
1969F Proof	5,000	Value: 3.00				
1969G	15,631,000	—	—	0.50	3.00	—
1969G Proof	8,700	Value: 2.50				
1969J	24,120,000	—	—	0.50	2.50	—
1969J Proof	5,000	Value: 2.00				
1970D	39,940,000	—	—	0.10	1.00	—
1970F	45,517,000	—	—	0.10	1.00	—
1970F Proof	5,140	Value: 2.50				
1970G	27,638,000	—	—	0.10	1.00	—
1970G Proof	10,200	Value: 1.50				
1970J	40,873,000	—	—	0.10	1.00	—
1970J Proof	5,000	Value: 2.50				
1971D	57,345,000	—	—	0.10	1.00	—
1971D Proof	8,000	Value: 1.50				
1971F	66,426,000	—	—	0.10	1.00	—
1971F Proof	8,000	Value: 1.50				
1971G	38,284,000	—	—	0.10	1.00	—
1971G Proof	10,000	Value: 1.50				
1971J	58,566,000	—	—	0.10	1.00	—
1971J Proof	8,000	Value: 1.50				
1972D	52,325,000	—	—	0.10	1.00	—
1972D Proof	8,000	Value: 1.50				
1972F	60,292,000	—	—	0.10	1.00	—
1972F Proof	8,000	Value: 1.50				
1972G	34,719,000	—	—	0.10	1.00	—
1972G Proof	10,000	Value: 1.50				
1972J	54,218,000	—	—	0.10	1.00	—
1972J Proof	8,000	Value: 1.50				
1973D	15,596,000	—	—	0.10	1.00	—
1973D Proof	9,000	Value: 1.50				
1973F	18,039,000	—	—	0.10	1.00	—
1973F Proof	9,000	Value: 1.50				
1973G	10,391,000	—	—	0.10	1.00	—
1973G Proof	9,000	Value: 1.50				
1973J	16,035,000	—	—	0.10	1.00	—
1973J Proof	9,000	Value: 1.50				
1974D	15,769,000	—	—	0.10	1.00	—
1974D Proof	35,000	Value: 0.50				
1974F	18,143,000	—	—	0.10	1.00	—
1974F Proof	35,000	Value: 0.50				
1974G	10,508,000	—	—	0.10	1.00	—
1974G Proof	35,000	Value: 0.50				
1974J	16,055,000	—	—	0.10	1.00	—
1974J Proof	35,000	Value: 0.50				
1975D	15,715,000	—	—	0.10	1.00	—
1975D Proof	43,000	Value: 0.50				
1975F	18,013,000	—	—	0.10	0.35	—
1975F Proof	43,000	Value: 0.50				
1975G	10,466,000	—	—	0.10	0.35	—
1975G Proof	43,000	Value: 0.50				
1975J	16,201,000	—	—	0.10	0.35	—
1975J Proof	43,000	Value: 0.50				
1976D	47,091,000	—	—	0.10	0.35	—
1976D Proof	43,000	Value: 0.50				
1976F	54,370,000	—	—	0.10	0.35	—
1976F Proof	43,000	Value: 0.50				
1976G	31,367,000	—	—	0.10	0.35	—
1976G Proof	43,000	Value: 0.50				
1976J	48,321,000	—	—	0.10	0.35	—
1976J Proof	43,000	Value: 0.50				
1977D	52,159,000	—	—	0.10	0.35	—
1977D Proof	51,000	Value: 0.45				
1977F	60,124,000	—	—	0.10	0.35	—
1977F Proof	51,000	Value: 0.45				
1977G	34,600,000	—	—	0.10	0.35	—
1977G Proof	51,000	Value: 0.45				
1977J	53,481,000	—	—	0.10	0.35	—
1977J Proof	51,000	Value: 0.45				
1978D	41,600,000	—	—	0.10	0.35	—
1978D Proof	54,000	Value: 0.45				
1978F	48,000,000	—	—	0.10	0.35	—
1978F Proof	54,000	Value: 0.45				
1978G	27,680,000	—	—	0.10	0.35	—

Date	Mintage	F	VF	XF	Unc	BU
1978G Proof	54,000	Value: 0.45				
1978J	42,720,000	—	—	0.10	0.35	—
1978J Proof	54,000	Value: 0.45				
1979D	41,600,000	—	—	0.10	0.20	—
1979D Proof	89,000	Value: 0.40				
1979F	48,000,000	—	—	0.10	0.20	—
1979F Proof	89,000	Value: 0.40				
1979G	27,680,000	—	—	0.10	0.20	—
1979G Proof	89,000	Value: 0.40				
1979J	42,711,000	—	—	0.10	0.20	—
1979J Proof	89,000	Value: 0.40				
1980D	39,880,000	—	—	0.10	0.20	—
1980D Proof	110,000	Value: 0.40				
1980F	53,270,000	—	—	0.10	0.20	—
1980F Proof	110,000	Value: 0.40				
1980G	43,070,000	—	—	0.10	0.20	—
1980G Proof	110,000	Value: 0.40				
1980J	59,130,000	—	—	0.10	0.20	—
1980J Proof	110,000	Value: 0.40				
1981D	82,250,000	—	—	0.10	0.20	—
1981D Proof	91,000	Value: 0.40				
1981F	84,910,000	—	—	0.10	0.20	—
1981F Proof	91,000	Value: 0.40				
1981G	41,910,000	—	—	0.10	0.20	—
1981G Proof	91,000	Value: 0.40				
1981J	49,290,000	—	—	0.10	0.20	—
1981J Proof	91,000	Value: 0.40				
1982D	57,500,000	—	—	0.10	0.20	—
1982D Proof	78,000	Value: 0.40				
1982F	53,290,000	—	—	0.10	0.20	—
1982F Proof	78,000	Value: 0.40				
1982G	23,750,000	—	—	0.10	0.20	—
1982G Proof	78,000	Value: 0.40				
1982J	62,000,000	—	—	0.10	0.20	—
1982J Proof	78,000	Value: 0.40				
1983D	46,800,000	—	—	0.10	0.20	—
1983D Proof	75,000	Value: 0.40				
1983F	54,000,000	—	—	0.10	0.20	—
1983F Proof	75,000	Value: 0.40				
1983G	31,140,000	—	—	0.10	0.20	—
1983G Proof	75,000	Value: 0.40				
1983J	48,060,000	—	—	0.10	0.20	—
1983J Proof	75,000	Value: 0.40				
1984D	36,400,000	—	—	0.10	0.20	—
1984D Proof	64,000	Value: 0.40				
1984F	42,000,000	—	—	0.10	0.20	—
1984F Proof	64,000	Value: 0.40				
1984G	24,200,000	—	—	0.10	0.20	—
1984G Proof	64,000	Value: 0.40				
1984J	37,400,000	—	—	0.10	0.20	—
1984J Proof	64,000	Value: 0.40				
1985D	15,600,000	—	—	0.10	0.50	—
1985D Proof	56,000	Value: 0.50				
1985F	18,000,000	—	—	0.10	0.50	—
1985F Proof	54,000	Value: 0.50				
1985G	10,400,000	—	—	0.10	0.50	—
1985G Proof	55,000	Value: 0.50				
1985J	16,000,000	—	—	0.10	0.50	—
1985J Proof	54,000	Value: 0.50				
1986D	36,400,000	—	—	—	0.25	—
1986D Proof	44,000	Value: 0.40				
1986F	42,000,000	—	—	—	0.25	—
1986F Proof	44,000	Value: 0.40				
1986G	24,200,000	—	—	—	0.25	—
1986G Proof	44,000	Value: 0.40				
1986J	37,400,000	—	—	—	0.25	—
1986J Proof	44,000	Value: 0.40				
1987D	52,000,000	—	—	—	0.25	—
1987D Proof	45,000	Value: 0.40				
1987F	60,000,000	—	—	—	0.25	—
1987F Proof	45,000	Value: 0.40				
1987G	34,600,000	—	—	—	0.25	—
1987G Proof	45,000	Value: 0.40				
1987J	53,400,000	—	—	—	0.25	—
1987J Proof	45,000	Value: 0.40				
1988D	52,400,000	—	—	—	0.25	—
1988D Proof	45,000	Value: 0.40				
1988F	72,000,000	—	—	—	0.25	—
1988F Proof	45,000	Value: 0.40				
1988G	41,500,000	—	—	—	0.25	—
1988G Proof	45,000	Value: 0.40				
1988J	64,099,999	—	—	—	0.25	—
1988J Proof	45,000	Value: 0.40				
1989D	93,600,000	—	—	—	0.25	—
1989D Proof	45,000	Value: 0.40				
1989F	108,000,000	—	—	—	0.25	—
1989F Proof	45,000	Value: 0.40				
1989G	62,280,000	—	—	—	0.25	—
1989G Proof	45,000	Value: 0.40				
1989J	96,120,000	—	—	—	0.25	—
1989J Proof	45,000	Value: 0.40				
1990A	70,000,000	—	—	—	0.10	—
1990D	93,600,000	—	—	—	0.10	—
1990D Proof	45,000	Value: 0.40				
1990F	108,000,000	—	—	—	0.10	—
1990F Proof	45,000	Value: 0.40				
1990G	62,280,000	—	—	—	0.10	—
1990G Proof	45,000	Value: 0.40				
1990J	96,120,000	—	—	—	0.10	—
1990J Proof	45,000	Value: 0.40				
1991A	128,000,000	—	—	—	0.10	—
1991A Proof	45,000	Value: 0.40				

Date	Mintage	F	VF	XF	Unc	BU
1991D	134,400,000	—	—	—	0.10	—
1991D Proof	45,000	Value: 0.40				
1991F	153,600,000	—	—	—	0.10	—
1991F Proof	45,000	Value: 0.40				
1991G	89,600,000	—	—	—	0.10	—
1991G Proof	45,000	Value: 0.40				
1991J	134,400,000	—	—	—	0.10	—
1991J Proof	45,000	Value: 0.40				
1992A	28,000,000	—	—	—	0.10	—
1992A Proof	45,000	Value: 0.40				
1992D	29,400,000	—	—	—	0.10	—
1992D Proof	45,000	Value: 0.40				
1992F	33,600,000	—	—	—	0.10	—
1992F Proof	45,000	Value: 0.40				
1992G	19,600,000	—	—	—	0.10	—
1992G Proof	45,000	Value: 0.40				
1992J	29,400,000	—	—	—	0.10	—
1992J Proof	45,000	Value: 0.40				
1993A	36,000,000	—	—	—	0.10	—
1993A Proof	45,000	Value: 0.40				
1993D	37,800,000	—	—	—	0.10	—
1993D Proof	45,000	Value: 0.40				
1993F	43,200,000	—	—	—	0.10	—
1993F Proof	45,000	Value: 0.40				
1993G	25,200,000	—	—	—	0.10	—
1993G Proof	45,000	Value: 0.40				
1993J	37,800,000	—	—	—	0.10	—
1993J Proof	45,000	Value: 0.40				
1994A	38,000,000	—	—	—	0.10	—
1994A Proof	45,000	Value: 0.40				
1994D	39,900,000	—	—	—	0.10	—
1994D Proof	45,000	Value: 0.40				
1994F	45,600,000	—	—	—	0.10	—
1994F Proof	45,000	Value: 0.40				
1994G	26,600,000	—	—	—	0.10	—
1994G Proof	45,000	Value: 0.40				
1994J	39,900,000	—	—	—	0.10	—
1994J Proof	45,000	Value: 0.40				
1995A	48,000,000	—	—	—	0.15	—
1995A Proof	45,000	Value: 0.45				
1995D	50,400,000	—	—	—	0.15	—
1995D Proof	45,000	Value: 0.45				
1995F	57,600,000	—	—	—	0.15	—
1995F Proof	45,000	Value: 0.45				
1995G	33,600,000	—	—	—	0.15	—
1995G Proof	45,000	Value: 0.45				
1995J	50,400,000	—	—	—	0.15	—
1995J Proof	45,000	Value: 0.45				
1996A	48,000,000	—	—	—	0.20	—
1996A Proof	45,000	Value: 0.50				
1996D	50,400,000	—	—	—	0.20	—
1996D Proof	45,000	Value: 0.50				
1996F	57,600,000	—	—	—	0.20	—
1996F Proof	45,000	Value: 0.50				
1996G	33,600,000	—	—	—	0.20	—
1996G Proof	45,000	Value: 0.50				
1996J	50,400,000	—	—	—	0.20	—
1996J Proof	45,000	Value: 0.50				
1997A	70,000	—	—	—	1.75	—
Note: In sets only						
1997A Proof	45,000	Value: 2.00				
1997D	70,000	—	—	—	1.75	—
Note: In sets only						
1997D Proof	45,000	Value: 2.00				
1997F	70,000	—	—	—	1.75	—
Note: In sets only						
1997F Proof	45,000	Value: 2.00				
1997G	70,000	—	—	—	1.75	—
Note: In sets only						
1997G Proof	45,000	Value: 2.00				
1997J	70,000	—	—	—	1.75	—
Note: In sets only						
1997J Proof	45,000	Value: 2.00				
1998A	70,000	—	—	—	1.75	—
Note: In sets only						
1998A Proof	45,000	Value: 2.00				
1998D	70,000	—	—	—	1.75	—
Note: In sets only						
1998D Proof	45,000	Value: 2.00				
1998F	70,000	—	—	—	1.75	—
Note: In sets only						
1998F Proof	45,000	Value: 2.00				
1998G	70,000	—	—	—	1.75	—
Note: In sets only						
1998G Proof	45,000	Value: 2.00				
1998J	70,000	—	—	—	1.75	—
Note: In sets only						
1998J Proof	45,000	Value: 2.00				
1999A	70,000	—	—	—	1.75	—
Note: In sets only						
1999A Proof	45,000	Value: 2.00				
1999D	70,000	—	—	—	1.75	—
Note: In sets only						
1999D Proof	45,000	Value: 2.00				
1999F	70,000	—	—	—	1.75	—
Note: In sets only						
1999F Proof	45,000	Value: 2.00				
1999G	70,000	—	—	—	1.75	—
Note: In sets only						
1999G Proof	45,000	Value: 2.00				
1999J	70,000	—	—	—	1.75	—

Date	Mintage	F	VF	XF	Unc	BU
Note: In sets only						
1999J Proof	45,000	Value: 2.00				
2000A	45,000	—	—	—	1.75	—
Note: In sets only						
2000A Proof	70,000	Value: 2.00				
2000D	45,000	—	—	—	1.75	—
Note: In sets only						
2000D Proof	70,000	Value: 2.00				
2000F	45,000	—	—	—	1.75	—
Note: In sets only						
2000F Proof	70,000	Value: 2.00				
2000G	45,000	—	—	—	1.75	—
Note: In sets only						
2000G Proof	70,000	Value: 2.00				
2000J	45,000	—	—	—	1.75	—
Note: In sets only						
2000J Proof	70,000	Value: 2.00				

KM# 103 10 PFENNIG

Brass Clad Steel, 21.5 mm. **Obv:** Five oak leaves, date below **Obv. Legend:** BANK DEUTSCHER LÄNDER **Rev:** Denomination

Date	Mintage	F	VF	XF	Unc	BU
1949D	140,558,000	—	0.50	7.50	30.00	—
1949D Proof	—	Value: 150				
1949F	120,932,000	—	0.50	10.00	35.00	—
1949F Proof	250	Value: 140				
1949G	82,933,000	—	1.00	10.00	40.00	—
1949J Large J	154,095,000	—	0.50	7.50	30.00	—
1949J Proof	—	Value: 60.00				
1949J Small J	Inc. above	—	0.50	7.50	32.00	—
1949J Proof	—	Value: 60.00				

KM# 108 10 PFENNIG

4.0000 g., Brass Plated Steel, 21.5 mm. **Obv:** Five oak leaves, date below **Obv. Legend:** BUNDES REPUBLIK DEUTSCHLAND **Rev:** Denomination **Edge:** Plain

Date	Mintage	F	VF	XF	Unc	BU
1950D	393,209,000	—	—	0.50	4.00	—
1950F	584,340,000	—	—	0.50	4.00	—
1950F Proof	500	Value: 45.00				
1950G	309,045,000	—	0.20	1.00	8.00	—
1950G Proof	1,800	Value: 5.00				
1950J	402,452,000	—	—	0.50	4.00	—
1950J Proof	—	Value: 20.00				
1966D	31,220,000	—	0.20	1.50	8.00	—
1966F	36,097,000	—	0.20	1.50	8.00	—
1966F Proof	100	Value: 75.00				
1966G	25,338,000	—	0.20	1.50	9.00	—
1966G Proof	3,070	Value: 7.50				
1966J	32,116,000	—	0.20	1.50	8.00	—
1966J Proof	1,000	Value: 12.50				
1967D	15,632,000	—	0.20	3.00	10.00	—
1967F	18,049,000	—	0.20	2.00	9.00	—
1967F Proof	1,500	Value: 15.00				
1967G	1,518,000	0.20	2.00	7.00	30.00	—
1967G Proof	4,500	Value: 7.50				
1967J	16,050,999	—	0.20	3.00	10.00	—
1967J Proof	1,500	Value: 12.50				
1968D	5,207,000	—	0.20	2.00	10.00	—
1968F	6,010,000	—	0.20	2.00	8.00	—
1968F Proof	3,000	Value: 10.00				
1968G	12,384,000	—	0.15	1.50	7.00	—
1968G Proof	6,023	Value: 5.00				
1968J	5,422,000	—	0.20	2.00	10.00	—
1968J Proof	2,000	Value: 10.00				
1969D	41,693,000	—	—	0.15	2.00	—
1969F	48,084,000	—	—	0.15	2.00	—
1969F Proof	5,000	Value: 3.00				
1969G	48,760,000	—	—	0.15	2.00	—
1969G Proof	8,700	Value: 2.50				
1969J	42,756,000	—	—	0.15	2.00	—
1969J Proof	5,000	Value: 2.50				
1970D	54,085,000	—	—	0.15	2.00	—
1970F	60,086,000	—	—	0.15	2.00	—
1970F Proof	5,140	Value: 3.00				
1970G	35,900,000	—	—	0.15	1.00	—
1970G Proof	10,200	Value: 2.00				
1970J	40,115,000	—	—	0.15	1.00	—
1970J Proof	5,000	Value: 2.50				
1971D	54,022,000	—	—	0.15	0.25	—
1971D Proof	8,000	Value: 2.50				
1971F	92,534,000	—	—	0.15	0.25	—
1971F Proof	8,000	Value: 2.50				
1971G	88,614,000	—	—	0.15	0.25	—
1971G Proof	10,000	Value: 2.00				
1971 Small J	65,622,000	—	—	0.15	0.25	—
1971 Large J	Inc. above	—	—	0.15	0.25	—
1971J Proof	8,000	Value: 1.50				
1972D	104,345,000	—	—	0.15	0.25	—
1972D Proof	8,000	Value: 1.50				
1972F	110,177,000	—	—	0.15	0.25	—
1972F Proof	8,000	Value: 1.50				
1972G	71,766,000	—	—	0.15	0.25	—
1972G Proof	10,000	Value: 1.50				
1972J	96,991,000	—	—	0.15	0.25	—
1972J Proof	8,000	Value: 1.50				
1973D	26,052,000	—	—	0.15	0.25	—
1973D Proof	9,000	Value: 1.50				
1973F	30,070,000	—	—	0.15	0.25	—
1973F Proof	9,000	Value: 1.50				
1973G	17,294,000	—	—	0.15	0.25	—
1973G Proof	9,000	Value: 1.50				
1973J	26,774,000	—	—	0.15	0.25	—
1973J Proof	9,000	Value: 1.50				
1974D	15,707,000	—	—	0.15	0.25	—
1974D Proof	35,000	Value: 0.75				
1974F	18,135,000	—	—	0.15	0.25	—
1974F Proof	35,000	Value: 0.75				
1974G	10,450,000	—	—	0.15	0.25	—
1974G Proof	35,000	Value: 0.75				
1974J	16,056,000	—	—	0.15	0.25	—
1974J Proof	35,000	Value: 0.75				
1975D	15,654,000	—	—	0.15	0.25	—
1975D Proof	43,000	Value: 0.75				
1975F	18,043,000	—	—	0.15	0.25	—
1975F Proof	43,000	Value: 0.75				
1975G	10,403,000	—	—	0.15	0.25	—
1975G Proof	43,000	Value: 0.75				
1975J	16,111,000	—	—	0.15	0.25	—
1975J Proof	43,000	Value: 0.75				
1976D	65,200,000	—	—	0.15	0.25	—
1976D Proof	43,000	Value: 0.75				
1976F	75,282,000	—	—	0.15	0.25	—
1976F Proof	43,000	Value: 0.75				
1976G	43,372,000	—	—	0.15	0.25	—
1976G Proof	43,000	Value: 0.75				
1976J	66,930,000	—	—	0.15	0.25	—
1976J Proof	43,000	Value: 0.75				
1977D	64,989,000	—	—	0.10	0.20	—
1977D Proof	51,000	Value: 0.50				
1977F	75,052,000	—	—	0.10	0.20	—
1977F Proof	51,000	Value: 0.50				
1977G	43,300,000	—	—	0.10	0.20	—
1977G Proof	51,000	Value: 0.50				
1977J	66,800,000	—	—	0.10	0.20	—
1977J Proof	51,000	Value: 0.50				
1978D	91,000,000	—	—	0.10	0.20	—
1978D Proof	54,000	Value: 0.50				
1978F	105,000,000	—	—	0.10	0.20	—
1978F Proof	54,000	Value: 0.50				
1978G	60,590,000	—	—	0.10	0.20	—
1978G Proof	54,000	Value: 0.50				
1978J	93,490,000	—	—	0.10	0.20	—
1978J Proof	54,000	Value: 0.50				
1979D	104,000,000	—	—	0.10	0.20	—
1979D Proof	89,000	Value: 0.50				
1979F	120,000,000	—	—	0.10	0.20	—
1979F Proof	89,000	Value: 0.50				
1979G	69,200,000	—	—	0.10	0.20	—
1979G Proof	89,000	Value: 0.50				
1979J	106,800,000	—	—	0.10	0.20	—
1979J Proof	89,000	Value: 0.50				
1980D	65,450,000	—	—	0.10	0.20	—
1980D Proof	110,000	Value: 0.50				
1980F	122,780,000	—	—	0.10	0.20	—
1980F Proof	110,000	Value: 0.50				
1980G	75,410,000	—	—	0.10	0.20	—
1980G Proof	110,000	Value: 0.50				
1980J	70,960,000	—	—	0.10	0.20	—
1980J Proof	110,000	Value: 0.50				
1981D	135,200,000	—	—	0.10	0.20	—
1981D Proof	91,000	Value: 0.50				
1981F	117,410,000	—	—	0.10	0.20	—
1981F Proof	91,000	Value: 0.50				
1981G	69,440,000	—	—	0.10	0.20	—
1981G Proof	91,000	Value: 0.50				
1981J	138,360,000	—	—	0.10	0.20	—
1981J Proof	91,000	Value: 0.50				
1982D	74,690,000	—	—	0.10	0.20	—
1982D Proof	78,000	Value: 0.50				
1982F	85,140,000	—	—	0.10	0.20	—
1982F Proof	78,000	Value: 0.50				
1982G	50,840,000	—	—	0.10	0.20	—
1982G Proof	78,000	Value: 0.50				
1982J	80,620,000	—	—	0.10	0.20	—
1982J Proof	78,000	Value: 0.50				
1983D	33,800,000	—	—	0.10	0.20	—
1983D Proof	75,000	Value: 0.50				
1983F	39,000,000	—	—	0.10	0.20	—
1983F Proof	75,000	Value: 0.50				
1983G	22,490,000	—	—	0.10	0.20	—
1983G Proof	75,000	Value: 0.50				
1983J	34,710,000	—	—	0.10	0.20	—
1983J Proof	75,000	Value: 0.50				
1984D	52,000,000	—	—	0.10	0.20	—
1984D Proof	64,000	Value: 0.50				
1984F	60,000,000	—	—	0.10	0.20	—
1984G Proof	64,000	Value: 0.50				
1984G	34,600,000	—	—	0.10	0.20	—
1984G Proof	64,000	Value: 0.50				
1984J	53,400,000	—	—	0.10	0.20	—
1984J Proof	64,000	Value: 0.50				
1985D	78,000,000	—	—	—	0.15	—
1985D Proof	56,000	Value: 0.50				
1985F	90,000,000	—	—	—	0.15	—
1985F Proof	54,000	Value: 0.50				
1985G	51,900,000	—	—	—	0.15	—
1985G Proof	55,000	Value: 0.50				
1985J	80,100,000	—	—	—	0.15	—
1985J Proof	54,000	Value: 0.50				
1986D	41,600,000	—	—	—	0.15	—
1986D Proof	44,000	Value: 0.50				
1986F	48,000,000	—	—	—	0.15	—
1986F Proof	44,000	Value: 0.50				
1986G	27,700,000	—	—	—	0.15	—
1986G Proof	44,000	Value: 0.50				
1986J	42,700,000	—	—	—	0.15	—
1986J Proof	44,000	Value: 0.15				
1987D	58,500,000	—	—	—	0.10	—
1987D Proof	45,000	Value: 0.15				
1987F	67,500,000	—	—	—	0.10	—
1987F Proof	45,000	Value: 0.15				
1987G	38,900,000	—	—	—	0.10	—
1987G Proof	45,000	Value: 0.50				
1987J	60,100,000	—	—	—	0.15	—
1987J Proof	45,000	Value: 0.50				
1988D	109,200,000	—	—	—	0.15	—
1988D Proof	45,000	Value: 0.50				
1988F	126,000,000	—	—	—	0.15	—
1988F Proof	45,000	Value: 0.50				
1988G	72,700,000	—	—	—	0.15	—
1988G Proof	45,000	Value: 0.50				
1988J	112,100,000	—	—	—	0.15	—
1988J Proof	45,000	Value: 0.50				
1989D	119,600,000	—	—	—	0.15	—
1989D Proof	45,000	Value: 0.50				
1989F	138,000,000	—	—	—	0.15	—
1989F Proof	45,000	Value: 0.50				
1989G	79,580,000	—	—	—	0.15	—
1989G Proof	45,000	Value: 0.50				
1989J	122,820,000	—	—	—	0.15	—
1989J Proof	45,000	Value: 0.50				
1990A	100,000,000	—	—	—	0.15	—
1990D	156,000,000	—	—	—	0.15	—
1990D Proof	45,000	Value: 0.50				
1990F	180,000,000	—	—	—	0.15	—
1990F Proof	45,000	Value: 0.50				
1990G	103,800,000	—	—	—	0.15	—
1990G Proof	45,000	Value: 0.50				
1990J	160,200,000	—	—	—	0.15	—
1990J Proof	45,000	Value: 0.50				
1991A	170,000,000	—	—	—	0.15	—
1991A Proof	45,000	Value: 0.40				
1991D	178,550,000	—	—	—	0.15	—
1991D Proof	45,000	Value: 0.40				
1991F	204,000,000	—	—	—	0.15	—
1991F Proof	45,000	Value: 0.40				
1991G	119,000,000	—	—	—	0.15	—
1991G Proof	45,000	Value: 0.40				
1991J	178,500,000	—	—	—	0.15	—
1991J Proof	45,000	Value: 0.40				
1992A	80,000,000	—	—	—	0.10	—
1992A Proof	45,000	Value: 0.40				
1992D	84,000,000	—	—	—	0.10	—
1992D Proof	45,000	Value: 0.40				
1992F	96,000,000	—	—	—	0.10	—
1992F Proof	45,000	Value: 0.40				
1992G	56,000,000	—	—	—	0.10	—
1992G Proof	45,000	Value: 0.40				
1992J	84,000,000	—	—	—	0.10	—
1992J Proof	45,000	Value: 0.40				
1993A	80,000,000	—	—	—	0.10	—
1993A Proof	45,000	Value: 0.40				
1993D	84,000,000	—	—	—	0.10	—
1993D Proof	45,000	Value: 0.40				
1993F	96,000,000	—	—	—	0.10	—
1993F Proof	45,000	Value: 0.40				
1993G	56,000,000	—	—	—	0.10	—
1993G Proof	45,000	Value: 0.40				
1993J	84,000,000	—	—	—	0.10	—
1993J Proof	45,000	Value: 0.40				
1994A	100,000,000	—	—	—	0.10	—
1994A Proof	45,000	Value: 0.40				
1994D	105,000,000	—	—	—	0.10	—
1994D Proof	45,000	Value: 0.40				
1994F	120,000,000	—	—	—	0.10	—
1994F Proof	45,000	Value: 0.40				
1994G	70,000,000	—	—	—	0.10	—
1994G Proof	45,000	Value: 0.40				
1994J	105,000,000	—	—	—	0.10	—
1994J Proof	45,000	Value: 0.40				
1995A	110,000,000	—	—	—	0.15	—
1995A Proof	45,000	Value: 0.45				
1995D	115,000,000	—	—	—	0.15	—
1995D Proof	45,000	Value: 0.45				
1995F	132,000,000	—	—	—	0.15	—
1995F Proof	45,000	Value: 0.45				

Date	Mintage	F	VF	XF	Unc	BU
1995G	77,000,000	—	—	—	0.15	—
1995G Proof	45,000	Value: 0.45				
1995J	115,500,000	—	—	—	0.15	—
1995J Proof	45,000	Value: 0.45				
1996A	90,000,000	—	—	—	0.20	—
1996A Proof	45,000	Value: 0.50				
1996D	94,500,000	—	—	—	0.20	—
1996D Proof	45,000	Value: 0.50				
1996F	108,000,000	—	—	—	0.20	—
1996F Proof	45,000	Value: 0.50				
1996G	63,000,000	—	—	—	0.20	—
1996G Proof	45,000	Value: 0.50				
1996J	94,500,000	—	—	—	0.20	—
1996J Proof	45,000	Value: 0.50				
1997A	70,000	—	—	—	1.75	—
Note: In sets only						
1997A Proof	45,000	Value: 2.00				
1997D	70,000	—	—	—	1.75	—
Note: In sets only						
1997D Proof	45,000	Value: 2.00				
1997F	70,000	—	—	—	1.75	—
Note: In sets only						
1997F Proof	45,000	Value: 2.00				
1997G	70,000	—	—	—	1.75	—
Note: In sets only						
1997G Proof	45,000	Value: 2.00				
1997J	70,000	—	—	—	1.75	—
Note: In sets only						
1997J Proof	45,000	Value: 2.00				
1998A	—	—	—	—	1.75	—
1998A Proof	—	Value: 2.00				
1998D	—	—	—	—	1.75	—
1998D Proof	—	Value: 2.00				
1998F	70,000	—	—	—	1.75	—
Note: In sets only						
1998F Proof	45,000	Value: 2.00				
1998G	—	—	—	—	1.75	—
1998G Proof	—	Value: 2.00				
1998J	—	—	—	—	1.75	—
1998J Proof	—	Value: 2.00				
1999A	—	—	—	—	1.75	—
1999A Proof	—	Value: 2.00				
1999D	—	—	—	—	1.75	—
1999D Proof	—	Value: 2.00				
1999F	70,000	—	—	—	1.75	—
Note: In sets only						
1999F Proof	45,000	Value: 2.00				
1999G	—	—	—	—	1.75	—
1999G Proof	—	Value: 2.00				
1999J	—	—	—	—	1.75	—
1999J Proof	—	Value: 2.00				
2000A	70,000	—	—	—	1.75	—
Note: In sets only						
2000A Proof	45,000	Value: 2.00				
2000D	70,000	—	—	—	1.75	—
Note: In sets only						
2000D Proof	45,000	Value: 2.00				
2000F	70,000	—	—	—	1.75	—
Note: In sets only						
2000F Proof	45,000	Value: 2.00				
2000G	70,000	—	—	—	1.75	—
Note: In sets only						
2000G Proof	45,000	Value: 2.00				
2000J	70,000	—	—	—	1.75	—
Note: In sets only						
2000J Proof	45,000	Value: 2.00				

KM# 104 50 PFENNIG

3.5000 g., Copper-Nickel, 20 mm. **Obv:** Denomination **Obv. Legend:** BANK DEUTSCHER LÄNDER **Rev:** Woman planting an oak seedling, date below

Date	Mintage	F	VF	XF	Unc	BU
1949D	39,108,000	—	0.75	4.50	45.00	—
1949F	45,118,000	—	0.50	3.00	35.00	—
1949F Proof	200	Value: 125				
1949G	25,924,000	—	0.75	5.00	55.00	—
1949J	42,303,000	—	0.75	3.50	35.00	—
1949J Proof	—	Value: 135				
1950G	30,000	—	350	475	750	—

Note: The 1950G dated coin was restruck without authorization by a mint official using genuine dies - quantity unknown

KM# 109.1 50 PFENNIG

3.5000 g., Copper-Nickel, 20 mm. **Obv:** Denomination **Obv. Legend:** BUNDESREPUBLIK DEUTSCHLAND **Rev:** Woman planting an oak seedling **Edge:** Reeded

Date	Mintage	F	VF	XF	Unc	BU
1950D	100,735,000	—	0.50	0.75	7.00	—
1950F	143,510,000	—	0.50	0.75	7.00	—
1950F Proof	450	Value: 85.00				
1950G	66,421,000	—	0.50	1.50	12.00	—
1950G Proof	1,800	Value: 5.00				
1950J	102,736,000	—	0.50	0.75	9.00	—
1950J Proof	—	Value: 25.00				
1966D	8,327,999	—	0.50	1.00	15.00	—
1966F	9,605,000	—	0.50	1.00	15.00	—
1966F Proof	100	Value: 125				
1966G	5,543,000	—	0.50	1.50	15.00	—
1966G Proof	3,070	Value: 10.00				
1966J	8,569,000	—	1.00	7.00	35.00	—
1966J Proof	1,000	Value: 20.00				
1967D	5,207,000	—	0.50	1.00	15.00	—
1967F	6,005,000	—	0.50	1.00	15.00	—
1967F Proof	1,500	Value: 18.00				
1967G	1,843,000	—	1.00	5.00	22.00	—
1967G Proof	4,500	Value: 15.00				
1967J	10,684,000	—	0.50	1.50	20.00	—
1967J Proof	1,500	Value: 18.00				
1968D	7,809,000	—	0.50	1.50	12.00	—
1968F	3,000,000	—	0.50	1.50	12.00	—
1968F Proof	3,000	Value: 15.00				
1968G	6,818,000	—	0.50	1.50	12.00	—
1968G Proof	6,023	Value: 8.00				
1968J	2,672,000	—	1.00	5.00	30.00	—
1968J Proof	2,000	Value: 15.00				
1969D	14,561,000	—	0.45	0.55	2.50	—
1969F	16,804,000	—	0.45	0.55	2.50	—
1969F Proof	5,000	Value: 4.00				
1969G	9,704,000	—	0.45	0.55	2.50	—
1969G Proof	8,700	Value: 3.50				
1969J	14,969,000	—	0.45	0.55	2.50	—
1969J Proof	5,000	Value: 10.00				
1970D	25,294,000	—	0.45	0.55	1.50	—
1970F	26,455,000	—	0.45	0.55	1.50	—
1970F Proof	5,140	Value: 3.50				
1970G	11,955,000	—	0.45	0.55	1.50	—
1970G Proof	10,200	Value: 3.00				
1970J	10,683,000	—	0.45	0.55	1.50	—
1970J Proof	5,000	Value: 3.50				
1971D	23,393,000	—	0.45	0.55	1.25	—
1971D Proof	8,000	Value: 3.00				
1971F	29,746,000	—	0.45	0.55	1.25	—
1971F Proof	8,000	Value: 3.00				
1971G	15,556,000	—	0.45	0.55	1.25	—
1971G Proof	10,000	Value: 3.00				
1971 Large J	24,044,000	—	0.45	0.55	1.25	—
1971 Small J	Inc. above	—	0.45	0.55	1.25	—
1971J Proof	8,000	Value: 3.00				

KM# 109.2 50 PFENNIG

3.5000 g., Copper-Nickel, 20 mm. **Obv:** Denomination **Rev:** Woman planting an oak seedling **Edge:** Plain **Note:** Counterfeits of 1972 dated coins with reeded edges exist.

Date	Mintage	F	VF	XF	Unc	BU
1972D	26,008,000	—	—	0.45	0.60	—
1972D Proof	8,000	Value: 2.00				
1972F	30,043,000	—	—	0.45	0.60	—
1972F Proof	8,000	Value: 2.00				
1972G	17,337,000	—	—	0.45	0.60	—
1972G Proof	10,000	Value: 2.00				
1972J	26,707,000	—	—	0.45	0.60	—
1972J Proof	8,000	Value: 2.00				
1973D	7,810,000	—	—	0.45	1.00	—
1973D Proof	9,000	Value: 2.00				
1973F	8,994,000	—	—	0.45	0.60	—
1973F Proof	9,000	Value: 2.00				
1973G	5,201,000	—	—	0.45	0.60	—
1973G Proof	9,000	Value: 2.00				
1973J	8,010,999	—	—	0.45	0.60	—
1973J Proof	9,000	Value: 2.00				
1974D	18,264,000	—	—	0.45	1.00	—
1974D Proof	35,000	Value: 1.00				
1974 Large F	21,036,000	—	—	0.45	1.00	—
1974 Small F	Inc. above	—	—	0.45	1.00	—
1974F Proof	35,000	Value: 1.00				
1974G	12,159,000	—	—	0.45	1.50	—
1974G Proof	35,000	Value: 1.00				
1974J	18,752,000	—	—	0.45	1.00	—
1974J Proof	35,000	Value: 1.00				
1975D	13,055,000	—	—	0.45	1.00	—
1975D Proof	43,000	Value: 1.00				
1975F	15,003,000	—	—	0.45	1.00	—
1975F Proof	43,000	Value: 1.00				
1975G	8,675,000	—	—	0.45	1.50	—
1975G Proof	43,000	Value: 1.00				
1975J	13,379,000	—	—	0.45	1.00	—
1975J Proof	43,000	Value: 1.00				
1976D	10,411,000	—	—	0.45	0.60	—
1976D Proof	43,000	Value: 1.00				
1976F	12,048,000	—	—	0.45	0.60	—
1976F Proof	43,000	Value: 1.00				
1976G	6,653,000	—	—	0.45	1.25	—
1976G Proof	43,000	Value: 1.00				
1976J	10,716,000	—	—	0.45	0.60	—
1976J Proof	43,000	Value: 1.00				
1977D	10,400,000	—	—	0.45	0.60	—
1977D Proof	51,000	Value: 0.75				
1977F	12,000,000	—	—	0.45	0.60	—
1977F Proof	51,000	Value: 0.75				
1977G	6,921,000	—	—	0.45	1.00	—
1977G Proof	51,000	Value: 0.75				
1977J	10,708,000	—	—	0.45	0.60	—
1977J Proof	51,000	Value: 0.75				
1978D	10,400,000	—	—	0.45	1.00	—
1978D Proof	54,000	Value: 0.75				
1978F	12,000,000	—	—	0.45	0.60	—
1978F Proof	54,000	Value: 0.75				
1978G	6,640,000	—	—	0.45	1.00	—
1978G Proof	54,000	Value: 0.75				
1978J	10,680,000	—	—	0.45	0.60	—
1978J Proof	54,000	Value: 0.75				
1979D	10,400,000	—	—	0.45	1.00	—
1979D Proof	89,000	Value: 0.75				
1979F	12,000,000	—	—	0.45	0.60	—
1979F Proof	89,000	Value: 0.75				
1979G	6,920,000	—	—	0.45	1.00	—
1979G Proof	89,000	Value: 0.75				
1979J	10,680,000	—	—	0.45	0.60	—
1979J Proof	89,000	Value: 0.75				
1980D	23,250,000	—	—	0.45	0.60	—
1980D Proof	110,000	Value: 0.75				
1980F	17,440,000	—	—	0.45	0.60	—
1980F Proof	110,000	Value: 0.75				
1980G	22,460,000	—	—	0.45	1.00	—
1980G Proof	110,000	Value: 0.75				
1980J	24,030,000	—	—	0.45	0.60	—
1980J Proof	110,000	Value: 0.75				
1981D	17,900,000	—	—	0.45	1.25	—
1981D Proof	91,000	Value: 0.75				
1981F	29,810,000	—	—	0.45	1.25	—
1981F Proof	91,000	Value: 0.75				
1981G	10,880,000	—	—	0.45	1.50	—
1981G Proof	91,000	Value: 0.75				
1981J	24,140,000	—	—	0.45	1.25	—
1981J Proof	91,000	Value: 0.75				
1982D	21,540,000	—	—	0.45	1.25	—
1982D Proof	78,000	Value: 0.75				
1982F	28,900,000	—	—	0.45	1.25	—
1982F Proof	78,000	Value: 0.75				
1982G	19,710,000	—	—	0.45	1.50	—
1982G Proof	78,000	Value: 0.75				
1982J	17,210,000	—	—	0.45	1.25	—
1982J Proof	78,000	Value: 0.75				
1983D	20,800,000	—	—	0.45	1.25	—
1983D Proof	75,000	Value: 0.75				
1983F	24,000,000	—	—	0.45	1.25	—
1983F Proof	75,000	Value: 0.75				
1983G	13,840,000	—	—	0.45	1.50	—
1983G Proof	75,000	Value: 0.75				
1983J	21,360,000	—	—	0.45	1.25	—
1983J Proof	75,000	Value: 0.75				
1984D	11,700,000	—	—	0.45	1.50	—
1984D Proof	64,000	Value: 0.75				
1984F	13,500,000	—	—	0.45	1.50	—
1984F Proof	64,000	Value: 0.75				
1984G	7,800,000	—	—	0.45	1.50	—
1984G Proof	64,000	Value: 0.75				
1984J	12,000,000	—	—	0.45	1.50	—
1984J Proof	64,000	Value: 0.75				
1985D	15,700,000	—	—	0.45	1.50	—
1985D Proof	56,000	Value: 0.75				
1985F	18,000,000	—	—	0.45	1.50	—
1985F Proof	54,000	Value: 0.75				
1985G	10,400,000	—	—	0.45	1.50	—
1985G Proof	55,000	Value: 0.75				
1985J	16,100,000	—	—	0.45	1.50	—
1985J Proof	54,000	Value: 0.75				
1986D	2,100,000	—	1.00	2.00	8.00	—
1986D Proof	44,000	Value: 0.75				
1986F	2,400,000	—	1.00	2.00	7.00	—
1986F Proof	44,000	Value: 0.75				
1986G	1,400,000	1.00	2.00	4.00	10.00	—
1986G Proof	44,000	Value: 0.75				
1986J	2,100,000	—	1.50	3.50	12.50	—
1986J Proof	44,000	Value: 0.75				
1987D	520,000	2.00	5.00	10.00	30.00	—
1987D Proof	45,000	Value: 0.75				
1987F	600,000	1.00	3.00	6.00	15.00	—
1987F Proof	45,000	Value: 0.75				
1987G	350,000	2.50	5.00	8.00	28.00	—
1987G Proof	45,000	Value: 0.75				
1987J	530,000	1.00	3.00	6.00	15.00	—
1987J Proof	45,000	Value: 0.75				
1988D	4,160,000	—	—	0.50	2.00	—
1988D Proof	45,000	Value: 0.75				
1988F	4,800,000	—	—	0.50	2.00	—
1988F Proof	45,000	Value: 0.75				
1988G	2,770,000	—	—	1.00	3.00	—
1988G Proof	45,000	Value: 0.75				
1988J	4,300,000	—	—	0.50	2.00	—
1988J Proof	45,000	Value: 0.75				
1989D	36,400,000	—	—	—	0.50	—
1989D Proof	45,000	Value: 0.75				

Date	Mintage	F	VF	XF	Unc	BU
1989F	42,000,000	—	—	—	0.50	—
1989F Proof	45,000	Value: 0.75				
1989G	24,220,000	—	—	—	0.50	—
1989G Proof	45,000	Value: 0.75				
1989J	37,380,000	—	—	—	0.50	—
1989J Proof	45,000	Value: 0.75				
1990A	150,000,000	—	—	—	0.50	—
1990D	58,500,000	—	—	—	0.50	—
1990D Proof	45,000	Value: 0.75				
1990F	67,500,000	—	—	—	0.50	—
1990F Proof	45,000	Value: 0.75				
1990G	38,920,000	—	—	—	0.50	—
1990G Proof	45,000	Value: 0.75				
1990J	60,070,000	—	—	—	0.50	—
1990J Proof	45,000	Value: 0.75				
1991A	22,000,000	—	—	—	0.50	—
1991A Proof	45,000	Value: 0.75				
1991D	23,100,000	—	—	—	0.50	—
1991D Proof	45,000	Value: 0.75				
1991F	26,400,000	—	—	—	0.50	—
1991F Proof	45,000	Value: 0.75				
1991G	15,400,000	—	—	—	0.50	—
1991G Proof	45,000	Value: 0.75				
1991J	23,100,000	—	—	—	0.50	—
1991J Proof	45,000	Value: 0.75				
1992A	18,000,000	—	—	—	0.50	—
1992A Proof	45,000	Value: 0.75				
1992D	18,900,000	—	—	—	0.50	—
1992D Proof	45,000	Value: 0.75				
1992F	21,600,000	—	—	—	0.50	—
1992F Proof	45,000	Value: 0.75				
1992G	12,600,000	—	—	—	1.00	—
1992G Proof	45,000	Value: 0.75				
1992J	18,900,000	—	—	—	0.50	—
1992J Proof	45,000	Value: 0.75				
1993A	16,000,000	—	—	—	0.50	—
1993A Proof	45,000	Value: 0.75				
1993D	16,800,000	—	—	—	0.50	—
1993D Proof	45,000	Value: 0.75				
1993F	19,200,000	—	—	—	0.50	—
1993F Proof	45,000	Value: 0.75				
1993G	11,200,000	—	—	—	1.50	—
1993G Proof	45,000	Value: 0.75				
1993J	16,800,000	—	—	—	0.50	—
1993J Proof	45,000	Value: 0.75				
1994A	7,500,000	—	—	—	1.50	—
1994A Proof	45,000	Value: 0.75				
1994D	Est. 7,875,000	—	—	—	3.00	—
1994D Proof	45,000	Value: 0.75				
1994F	9,000,000	—	—	—	1.50	—
1994F Proof	45,000	Value: 0.75				
1994G	5,250,000	—	—	—	1.50	—
1994G Proof	45,000	Value: 0.75				
1994J	7,875,000	—	—	—	1.00	—
1994J Proof	45,000	Value: 0.75				
1995A	1,300,000	—	—	—	2.25	—
1995A Proof	45,000	Value: 6.00				
1995D	1,365,000	—	—	—	2.25	—
1995D Proof	45,000	Value: 6.00				
1995F	20,000	—	—	—	90.00	—
1995F Proof	45,000	Value: 12.00				
1995G	20,000	—	—	—	100	—
1995G Proof	45,000	Value: 12.00				
1995J	150,000	—	—	—	14.00	—
1995J Proof	45,000	Value: 12.00				
1996A	50,000	—	—	—	12.00	—
Note: In sets only						
1996A Proof	45,000	Value: 13.50				
1996D	50,000	—	—	—	12.00	—
Note: In sets only						
1996D Proof	45,000	Value: 13.50				
1996F	50,000	—	—	—	12.00	—
Note: In sets only						
1996F Proof	45,000	Value: 13.50				
1996G	50,000	—	—	—	12.00	—
Note: In sets only						
1996G Proof	45,000	Value: 13.50				
1996J	50,000	—	—	—	12.00	—
Note: In sets only						
1996J Proof	45,000	Value: 13.50				
1997A	70,000	—	—	—	4.75	—
Note: In sets only						
1997A Proof	45,000	Value: 5.00				
1997D	70,000	—	—	—	4.75	—
Note: In sets only						
1997D Proof	45,000	Value: 5.00				
1997F	70,000	—	—	—	4.75	—
Note: In sets only						
1997F Proof	45,000	Value: 5.00				
1997G	70,000	—	—	—	4.75	—
Note: In sets only						
1997G Proof	45,000	Value: 5.00				
1997J	70,000	—	—	—	4.75	—
Note: In sets only						
1997J Proof	45,000	Value: 5.00				
1998A	70,000	—	—	—	4.75	—
Note: In sets only						
1998A Proof	45,000	Value: 5.00				
1998D	70,000	—	—	—	4.75	—
Note: In sets only						
1998D Proof	45,000	Value: 5.00				

Date	Mintage	F	VF	XF	Unc	BU
1998F	70,000	—	—	—	4.75	—
Note: In sets only						
1998F Proof	45,000	Value: 5.00				
1998G	70,000	—	—	—	4.75	—
Note: In sets only						
1998G Proof	45,000	Value: 5.00				
1998J	70,000	—	—	—	4.75	—
Note: In sets only						
1998J Proof	45,000	Value: 5.00				
1999A	70,000	—	—	—	4.75	—
Note: In sets only						
1999A Proof	45,000	Value: 5.00				
1999D	70,000	—	—	—	4.75	—
Note: In sets only						
1999D Proof	45,000	Value: 5.00				
1999F	70,000	—	—	—	4.75	—
Note: In sets only						
1999F Proof	45,000	Value: 5.00				
1999G	70,000	—	—	—	4.75	—
Note: In sets only						
1999G Proof	45,000	Value: 5.00				
1999J	70,000	—	—	—	4.75	—
Note: In sets only						
1999J Proof	45,000	Value: 5.00				
2000A	70,000	—	—	—	5.00	—
Note: In sets only						
2000A Proof	45,000	Value: 5.00				
2000D	70,000	—	—	—	5.00	—
Note: In sets only						
2000D Proof	45,000	Value: 5.00				
2000F	70,000	—	—	—	5.00	—
Note: In sets only						
2000F Proof	45,000	Value: 5.00				
2000G	70,000	—	—	—	5.00	—
Note: In sets only						
2000G Proof	45,000	Value: 5.00				
2000J	70,000	—	—	—	5.00	—
Note: In sets only						
2000J Proof	45,000	Value: 5.00				

KM# 110 MARK

5.5000 g., Copper-Nickel, 23.5 mm. **Obv:** Imperial eagle **Rev:** Denomination flanked by oak leaves, date below

Date	Mintage	F	VF	XF	Unc	BU
1950D	60,467,000	—	1.50	12.00	75.00	—
1950D Proof	—	Value: 200				
1950F	69,183,000	—	1.50	12.00	70.00	—
1950F Proof	150	Value: 450				
1950G	39,826,000	—	2.00	15.00	110	—
1950G Proof	Est. 200	Value: 375				
1950J	61,483,000	—	1.00	10.00	65.00	—
1950J Proof	—	Value: 200				
1954D	5,202,000	2.00	8.00	100	425	—
1954D Proof	—	Value: 925				
1954F	6,000,000	2.50	10.00	200	650	—
1954F Proof	175	Value: 1,000				
1954G	3,459,000	4.00	25.00	450	1,900	—
1954G Proof	15	Value: 2,250				
1954J	5,341,000	1.50	7.00	55.00	400	—
1954J Proof	—	Value: 1,000				
1955D	3,093,000	2.00	9.00	125	550	—
1955D Proof	—	Value: 900				
1955F	4,909,000	1.00	6.00	50.00	500	—
1955F Proof	Est. 20	Value: 750				
1955G	2,500,000	4.00	40.00	400	1,650	—
1955G Proof	—	Value: 2,750				
1955J	5,294,000	1.00	6.00	50.00	220	—
1955J Proof	—	Value: 650				
1956D	13,231,000	1.00	4.00	35.00	325	—
1956D Proof	—	Value: 525				
1956F	14,700,000	1.00	4.00	35.00	375	—
1956F Proof	100	Value: 500				
1956G	8,362,000	1.00	4.00	35.00	275	—
1956G Proof	—	Value: 650				
1956J	11,478,000	1.00	5.00	40.00	220	—
1956J Proof	—	Value: 850				
1957D	6,820,000	1.00	5.00	75.00	325	—
1957D Proof	100	Value: 475				
1957F	6,390,000	1.00	5.00	75.00	325	—
1957F Proof	100	Value: 485				
1957G	3,841,000	2.50	10.00	145	800	—
1957G Proof	27	Value: 1,350				
1957J	6,632,000	1.00	6.00	100	500	—
1957J Proof	200	Value: 385				
1958D	4,150,000	1.00	4.00	40.00	275	—
1958D Proof	200	Value: 400				
1958F	4,109,000	1.00	5.00	45.00	375	—
1958F Proof	100	Value: 525				
1958G	3,460,000	2.50	8.00	135	1,100	—
1958G Proof	20	Value: 2,100				
1958J	4,656,000	1.00	5.00	50.00	500	—
1958J Proof	37	Value: 850				
1959D	10,409,000	—	2.00	20.00	225	—
1959D Proof	40	Value: 850				
1959F	11,972,000	—	2.00	20.00	225	—
1959F Proof	100	Value: 475				
1959G	6,921,000	1.00	5.00	40.00	375	—
1959G Proof	20	Value: 2,100				
1959J	10,691,000	1.00	4.00	35.00	650	—
1959J Proof	25	Value: 1,250				
1960D	5,453,000	—	2.00	25.00	750	—
1960D Proof	100	Value: 550				
1960F	5,709,000	—	2.00	25.00	250	—
1960F Proof	100	Value: 800				
1960G	3,632,000	1.00	6.00	50.00	600	—
1960G Proof	100	Value: 650				
1960J	5,612,000	2.50	8.00	200	750	—
1960J Proof	36	Value: 1,650				
1961D	7,536,000	—	2.00	20.00	275	—
1961D Proof	60	Value: 800				
1961F	6,029,000	—	2.00	20.00	175	—
1961F Proof	50	Value: 800				
1961G	4,843,000	1.00	6.00	50.00	475	—
1961G Proof	70	Value: 700				
1961J	7,483,000	1.50	7.00	75.00	850	—
1961J Proof	28	Value: 1,000				
1962D	10,327,000	—	1.50	15.00	400	—
1962D Proof	40	Value: 800				
1962F	11,122,000	—	1.50	10.00	125	—
1962F Proof	45	Value: 750				
1962G	6,054,000	—	2.00	25.00	800	—
1962G Proof	100	Value: 550				
1962J	10,822,000	—	2.00	17.50	220	—
1962J Proof	28	Value: 1,100				
1963D	12,624,000	—	1.00	10.00	110	—
1963D Proof	40	Value: 550				
1963F	18,292,000	—	1.50	15.00	135	—
1963F Proof	45	Value: 650				
1963G	11,253,000	—	1.50	12.50	165	—
1963G Proof	200	Value: 300				
1963J	15,906,000	—	1.50	15.00	200	—
1963J Proof	28	Value: 1,200				
1964D	8,048,000	—	0.85	4.00	100	—
1964D Proof	30	Value: 1,000				
1964F	12,796,000	—	0.85	4.00	90.00	—
1964F Proof	25	Value: 1,900				
1964G	3,465,000	—	2.00	20.00	250	—
1964G Proof	368	Value: 275				
1964J	6,958,000	—	0.85	4.00	85.00	—
1964J Proof	33	Value: 900				
1965D	9,388,000	—	0.75	3.00	37.50	—
1965F	9,013,000	—	0.75	3.00	40.00	—
1965F Proof	Est. 80	Value: 175				
1965G	6,232,000	—	0.75	3.00	47.50	—
1965G Proof	1,200	Value: 65.00				
1965J	8,023,999	—	0.75	3.00	55.00	—
1966D	11,717,000	—	0.75	3.00	42.50	—
1966F	11,368,000	—	0.75	3.00	42.50	—
1966F Proof	100	Value: 200				
1966G	7,799,000	—	0.75	3.00	55.00	—
1966G Proof	3,070	Value: 45.00				
1966J	12,030,000	—	0.75	3.00	42.50	—
1966J Proof	1,000	Value: 85.00				
1967D	13,017,000	—	0.75	3.00	32.50	—
1967F	7,500,000	—	0.75	5.00	100	—
1967F Proof	1,500	Value: 95.00				
1967G	4,324,000	—	0.75	3.00	55.00	—
1967G Proof	4,500	Value: 50.00				
1967J	13,357,000	—	0.75	3.00	40.00	—
1967J Proof	1,500	Value: 85.00				
1968D	1,303,000	—	1.00	10.00	65.00	—
1968F	1,500,000	—	0.75	4.00	40.00	—
1968F Proof	3,000	Value: 65.00				
1968G	5,198,000	—	1.50	7.00	60.00	—
1968G Proof	6,023	Value: 35.00				
1968J	1,338,000	1.00	12.50	145	375	—
1968J Proof	2,000	Value: 85.00				
1969D	13,025,000	—	0.75	1.50	22.00	—
1969F	15,021,000	—	0.75	1.50	20.00	—
1969F Proof	5,000	Value: 15.00				
1969G	8,665,000	—	0.75	1.50	32.50	—
1969G Proof	8,700	Value: 14.50				
1969J	13,370,000	—	0.75	1.50	25.00	—
1969J Proof	5,000	Value: 18.00				
1970D	17,928,000	—	0.75	1.00	20.00	—
1970F	19,408,000	—	0.75	1.00	25.00	—
1970F Proof	5,140	Value: 15.00				
1970G	20,386,000	—	0.75	1.00	32.50	—
1970G Proof	10,200	Value: 9.00				
1970J	10,707,000	—	0.75	1.00	20.00	—
1970J Proof	5,000	Value: 15.00				
1971D	24,513,000	—	0.75	1.00	10.00	—
1971D Proof	8,000	Value: 8.00				
1971F	28,275,000	—	0.75	1.00	10.00	—
1971F Proof	8,000	Value: 8.00				
1971G	16,375,000	—	0.75	1.00	12.50	—
1971G Proof	10,000	Value: 8.00				
1971J	25,214,000	—	0.75	1.00	10.00	—
1971J Proof	8,000	Value: 8.00				
1972D	20,904,000	—	0.75	1.00	10.00	—
1972D Proof	8,000	Value: 7.00				
1972F	24,086,000	—	0.75	1.00	10.00	—
1972F Proof	8,000	Value: 7.00				
1972G	13,868,000	—	0.75	1.00	10.00	—

Date	Mintage	F	VF	XF	Unc	BU
1972G Proof	10,000	Value: 7.00				
1972J	21,360,000	—	0.75	1.00	10.00	—
1972J Proof	8,000	Value: 7.00				
1973D	14,327,000	—	0.75	1.00	6.00	—
1973D Proof	9,000	Value: 5.00				
1973F	16,591,999	—	0.75	1.00	6.00	—
1973F Proof	9,000	Value: 5.00				
1973G	10,409,000	—	0.75	1.00	6.00	—
1973G Proof	9,000	Value: 5.00				
1973J	14,704,000	—	0.75	1.00	6.00	—
1973J Proof	9,000	Value: 5.00				
1974D	20,876,000	—	0.75	1.00	6.00	—
1974D Proof	35,000	Value: 4.00				
1974F	24,057,000	—	0.75	1.00	6.00	—
1974F Proof	35,000	Value: 4.00				
1974G	13,931,000	—	0.75	1.00	6.00	—
1974G Proof	35,000	Value: 4.00				
1974J	21,440,000	—	0.75	1.00	6.00	—
1974J Proof	35,000	Value: 4.00				
1975D	18,241,000	—	0.75	1.00	6.00	—
1975D Proof	43,000	Value: 4.00				
1975F	21,059,000	—	0.75	1.00	6.00	—
1975F Proof	43,000	Value: 4.00				
1975G	12,142,000	—	0.75	1.00	6.50	—
1975G Proof	43,000	Value: 4.00				
1975J	18,770,000	—	0.75	1.00	6.00	—
1975J Proof	43,000	Value: 4.00				
1976D	15,670,000	—	0.75	1.00	6.00	—
1976D Proof	43,000	Value: 4.00				
1976F	18,105,000	—	0.75	1.00	6.00	—
1976F Proof	43,000	Value: 4.00				
1976G	10,382,000	—	0.75	1.00	6.00	—
1976G Proof	43,000	Value: 4.00				
1976J	16,046,000	—	0.75	1.00	6.00	—
1976J Proof	43,000	Value: 4.00				
1977D	20,801,000	—	0.75	0.85	3.00	—
1977D Proof	51,000	Value: 2.00				
1977F	24,026,000	—	0.75	0.85	3.00	—
1977F Proof	51,000	Value: 2.00				
1977G	13,849,000	—	0.75	0.85	3.00	—
1977G Proof	51,000	Value: 2.00				
1977J	21,416,000	—	0.75	0.85	3.00	—
1977J Proof	51,000	Value: 2.00				
1978D	15,600,000	—	0.75	0.85	2.00	—
1978D Proof	54,000	Value: 1.25				
1978F	18,000,000	—	0.75	0.85	2.00	—
1978F Proof	54,000	Value: 1.25				
1978G	10,380,000	—	0.75	0.85	2.00	—
1978G Proof	54,000	Value: 1.25				
1978J	16,020,000	—	0.75	0.85	2.00	—
Note: Error with coin alignment exists						
1978J Proof	54,000	Value: 1.25				
1979D	18,200,000	—	0.75	0.85	2.00	—
1979D Proof	89,000	Value: 1.25				
1979F	21,000,000	—	0.75	0.85	2.00	—
1979F Proof	89,000	Value: 1.25				
1979G	12,110,000	—	0.75	0.85	2.00	—
1979G Proof	89,000	Value: 1.25				
1979J	18,690,000	—	0.75	0.85	2.00	—
1979J Proof	89,000	Value: 1.25				
1980D	24,330,000	—	—	0.75	0.90	—
1980D Proof	110,000	Value: 1.00				
1980F	9,670,000	—	—	0.75	0.90	—
1980F Proof	110,000	Value: 1.00				
1980G	8,540,000	—	—	0.75	0.90	—
1980G Proof	110,000	Value: 1.00				
1980J	16,010,000	—	—	0.75	0.90	—
1980J Proof	110,000	Value: 1.00				
1981D	21,150,000	—	—	1.50	4.00	—
1981D Proof	91,000	Value: 1.00				
1981F	25,910,000	—	—	1.50	4.00	—
1981F Proof	91,000	Value: 1.00				
1981G	14,090,000	—	—	1.50	4.00	—
1981G Proof	91,000	Value: 1.00				
1981J	18,800,000	—	—	1.50	4.00	—
1981J Proof	91,000	Value: 1.00				
1982D	20,590,000	—	—	1.50	4.00	—
1982D Proof	78,000	Value: 1.00				
1982F	22,990,000	—	—	1.50	4.00	—
1982F Proof	78,000	Value: 1.00				
1982G	14,900,000	—	—	1.50	4.00	—
1982G Proof	78,000	Value: 1.00				
1982J	11,520,000	—	—	1.50	4.00	—
1982J Proof	78,000	Value: 1.00				
1983D	18,200,000	—	—	1.50	4.00	—
1983D Proof	75,000	Value: 1.00				
1983F	21,000,000	—	—	1.50	4.00	—
1983F Proof	75,000	Value: 1.00				
1983G	12,100,000	—	—	1.50	4.00	—
1983G Proof	75,000	Value: 1.00				
1983J	18,690,000	—	—	1.50	4.00	—
1983J Proof	75,000	Value: 1.00				
1984D	8,400,000	—	—	1.50	4.00	—
1984D Proof	64,000	Value: 1.50				
1984F	9,700,000	—	—	1.50	4.00	—
1984F Proof	64,000	Value: 1.50				
1984G	5,600,000	—	—	1.50	4.00	—
1984G Proof	64,000	Value: 1.50				
1984J	8,700,000	—	—	1.50	4.00	—
1984J Proof	64,000	Value: 1.50				
1985D	11,700,000	—	—	1.50	4.00	—
1985D Proof	56,000	Value: 1.50				
1985F	13,500,000	—	—	1.50	4.00	—
1985F Proof	54,000	Value: 1.50				
1985G	7,800,000	—	—	1.50	4.00	—
1985G Proof	55,000	Value: 1.50				
1985J	12,000,000	—	—	1.50	4.00	—
1985J Proof	54,000	Value: 1.50				
1986D	10,400,000	—	—	1.50	5.00	—
1986D Proof	44,000	Value: 1.50				
1986F	12,000,000	—	—	1.50	5.00	—
1986F Proof	44,000	Value: 1.50				
1986G	6,900,000	—	—	1.50	5.00	—
1986G Proof	44,000	Value: 1.50				
1986J	10,700,000	—	—	1.50	5.00	—
1986J Proof	44,000	Value: 1.50				
1987D	3,120,000	—	3.50	7.50	15.00	—
1987D Proof	45,000	Value: 1.50				
1987F	3,600,000	—	3.50	7.50	15.00	—
1987F Proof	45,000	Value: 1.50				
1987G	2,080,000	—	3.50	7.50	15.00	—
1987G Proof	45,000	Value: 1.50				
1987J	3,200,000	—	3.50	7.50	15.00	—
1987J Proof	45,000	Value: 1.50				
1988D	20,800,000	—	—	0.75	2.00	—
1988D Proof	45,000	Value: 1.50				
1988F	24,000,000	—	—	0.75	2.00	—
1988F Proof	45,000	Value: 1.50				
1988G	13,800,000	—	—	0.75	2.00	—
1988G Proof	45,000	Value: 1.50				
1988J	21,400,000	—	—	0.75	2.00	—
1988J Proof	45,000	Value: 1.50				
1989D	39,000,000	—	—	—	1.00	—
1989D Proof	45,000	Value: 1.50				
1989F	45,000,000	—	—	—	1.00	—
1989F Proof	45,000	Value: 1.50				
1989G	25,950,000	—	—	—	1.00	—
1989G Proof	45,000	Value: 1.50				
1989J	40,050,000	—	—	—	1.00	—
1989J Proof	45,000	Value: 1.50				
1990A	55,000,000	—	—	—	1.00	—
1990D	77,740,000	—	—	—	1.00	—
1990D Proof	45,000	Value: 1.50				
1990F	89,700,000	—	—	—	1.00	—
1990F Proof	45,000	Value: 1.50				
1990G	51,720,000	—	—	—	1.00	—
1990G Proof	45,000	Value: 1.50				
1990J	79,830,000	—	—	—	1.00	—
1990J Proof	45,000	Value: 1.50				
1991A	30,000,000	—	—	—	1.00	—
1991A Proof	45,000	Value: 1.50				
1991D	31,500,000	—	—	—	1.00	—
1991D Proof	45,000	Value: 1.50				
1991F	36,000,000	—	—	—	1.00	—
1991F Proof	45,000	Value: 1.50				
1991G	21,000,000	—	—	—	1.00	—
1991G Proof	45,000	Value: 1.50				
1991J	31,500,000	—	—	—	1.00	—
1991J Proof	45,000	Value: 1.50				
1992A	30,000,000	—	—	—	1.00	—
1992A Proof	45,000	Value: 1.50				
1992D	31,500,000	—	—	—	1.00	—
1992D Proof	45,000	Value: 1.50				
1992F	36,000,000	—	—	—	1.00	—
1992F Proof	45,000	Value: 1.50				
1992G	21,000,000	—	—	—	1.00	—
1992G Proof	45,000	Value: 1.50				
1992J	31,500,000	—	—	—	1.00	—
1992J Proof	45,000	Value: 1.50				
1993A	8,000,000	—	—	—	1.00	—
1993A Proof	45,000	Value: 1.50				
1993D	8,400,000	—	—	—	1.00	—
1993D Proof	45,000	Value: 1.50				
1993F	9,600,000	—	—	—	1.00	—
1993F Proof	45,000	Value: 1.50				
1993G	5,600,000	—	—	—	1.00	—
1993G Proof	45,000	Value: 1.50				
1993J	8,400,000	—	—	—	1.00	—
1993J Proof	45,000	Value: 1.50				
1994A	18,000,000	—	—	—	1.00	—
1994A Proof	45,000	Value: 1.50				
1994D	18,900,000	—	—	—	1.00	—
1994D Proof	45,000	Value: 1.50				
1994F	21,800,000	—	—	—	1.00	—
1994F Proof	45,000	Value: 1.50				
1994G	12,800,000	—	—	—	1.00	—
1994G Proof	45,000	Value: 1.50				
1994J	18,900,000	—	—	—	1.00	—
1994J Proof	45,000	Value: 1.50				
1995A	20,000	—	—	—	70.00	—
Note: In sets only						
1995A Proof	45,000	Value: 20.00				
1995D	20,000	—	—	—	70.00	—
Note: In sets only						
1995D Proof	45,000	Value: 20.00				
1995F	20,000	—	—	—	70.00	—
Note: In sets only						
1995F Proof	45,000	Value: 20.00				
1995G	20,000	—	—	—	70.00	—
Note: In sets only						
1995G Proof	45,000	Value: 20.00				
1995J	100,000	—	—	—	18.00	—
1995J Proof	45,000	Value: 20.00				
1996A	50,000	—	—	—	12.50	—
Note: In sets only						
1996A Proof	45,000	Value: 14.00				
1996D	50,000	—	—	—	12.50	—
Note: In sets only						
1996D Proof	45,000	Value: 14.00				
1996F	50,000	—	—	—	12.50	—
Note: In sets only						
1996F Proof	45,000	Value: 14.00				
1996G	50,000	—	—	—	12.50	—
Note: In sets only						
1996G Proof	45,000	Value: 14.00				
1996J	50,000	—	—	—	12.50	—
Note: In sets only						
1996J Proof	45,000	Value: 14.00				
1997A	70,000	—	—	—	4.75	—
Note: In sets only						
1997A Proof	45,000	Value: 5.00				
1997D	70,000	—	—	—	4.75	—
Note: In sets only						
1997D Proof	45,000	Value: 5.00				
1997F	70,000	—	—	—	4.75	—
Note: In sets only						
1997F Proof	45,000	Value: 5.00				
1997G	70,000	—	—	—	4.75	—
Note: In sets only						
1997G Proof	45,000	Value: 5.00				
1997J	70,000	—	—	—	4.75	—
Note: In sets only						
1997J Proof	45,000	Value: 5.00				
1998A	70,000	—	—	—	4.75	—
Note: In sets only						
1998A Proof	45,000	Value: 5.00				
1998D	70,000	—	—	—	4.75	—
Note: In sets only						
1998D Proof	45,000	Value: 5.00				
1998F	70,000	—	—	—	4.75	—
Note: In sets only						
1998F Proof	45,000	Value: 5.00				
1998G	70,000	—	—	—	4.75	—
Note: In sets only						
1998G Proof	45,000	Value: 5.00				
1998J	70,000	—	—	—	4.75	—
Note: In sets only						
1998J Proof	45,000	Value: 5.00				
1999A	70,000	—	—	—	4.75	—
Note: In sets only						
1999A Proof	45,000	Value: 5.00				
1999D	70,000	—	—	—	4.75	—
Note: In sets only						
1999D Proof	45,000	Value: 5.00				
1999F	70,000	—	—	—	4.75	—
Note: In sets only						
1999F Proof	45,000	Value: 5.00				
1999G	70,000	—	—	—	4.75	—
Note: In sets only						
1999G Proof	45,000	Value: 5.00				
1999J	70,000	—	—	—	4.75	—
Note: In sets only						
1999J Proof	45,000	Value: 5.00				
2000A	70,000	—	—	—	5.00	—
Note: In sets only						
2000A Proof	45,000	Value: 5.00				
2000D	70,000	—	—	—	5.00	—
Note: In sets only						
2000D Proof	45,000	Value: 5.00				
2000F	70,000	—	—	—	5.00	—
Note: In sets only						
2000F Proof	45,000	Value: 5.00				
2000G	70,000	—	—	—	5.00	—
Note: In sets only						
2000G Proof	45,000	Value: 5.00				
2000J	70,000	—	—	—	5.00	—
Note: In sets only						
2000J Proof	45,000	Value: 5.00				

KM# 111 2 MARK

7.0000 g., Copper-Nickel, 26.75 mm. **Obv:** Imperial eagle **Rev:** Denomination flanked by leaves, grapes, and grain sprigs, date above

Date	Mintage	F	VF	XF	Unc	BU
1951D	19,564,000	—	25.00	30.00	100	—
1951D Proof	200	Value: 450				
1951F	22,609,000	—	25.00	30.00	100	—
1951F Proof	150	Value: 500				
1951G	Est. 13,012,000	—	50.00	75.00	200	—
Note: The 1951G dated coin was restruck without authorization by a mint official using genuine dies - quantity unknown						
1951G Proof	33	Value: 1,200				
1951J	20,104,000	—	25.00	30.00	100	—
1951J Proof	180	Value: 450				

KM# 116 2 MARK

7.0000 g., Copper-Nickel, 26.75 mm. **Subject:** Max Planck **Obv:** Imperial eagle above denomination **Rev:** Head left, dates below

Date	Mintage	F	VF	XF	Unc	BU
1957D	7,452,000	—	2.00	6.00	65.00	—
1957D Proof	350	Value: 235				
1957F	6,337,000	—	2.00	6.00	65.00	—
1957F Proof	100	Value: 325				
1957G	2,598,000	—	3.00	7.50	135	—
1957G Proof	56	Value: 600				
1957J	11,210,000	—	2.00	6.00	60.00	—
1957J Proof	370	Value: 175				
1958D	12,623,000	—	1.50	5.00	50.00	—
1958D Proof	1,240	Value: 85.00				
1958F	16,825,000	—	1.50	4.00	45.00	—
1958F Proof	300	Value: 200				
1958G	10,744,000	—	1.50	4.00	45.00	—
1958G Proof	45	Value: 700				
1958J	9,408,000	—	1.50	4.00	45.00	—
1958J Proof	100	Value: 400				
1959D	1,020,000	—	4.00	15.00	240	—
1959D Proof	38	Value: 1,150				
1959F	203,000	—	15.00	60.00	425	—
1959F Proof	24	Value: 1,850				
1960D	3,535,000	—	1.50	4.00	35.00	—
1960D Proof	100	Value: 325				
1960F	3,692,000	—	1.50	4.00	35.00	—
1960F Proof	50	Value: 600				
1960G	2,695,000	—	2.00	4.00	35.00	—
1960G Proof	130	Value: 300				
1960J	4,676,000	—	1.50	4.00	35.00	—
1960J Proof	36	Value: 800				
1961D	3,918,000	—	1.50	4.00	35.00	—
1961D Proof	50	Value: 600				
1961F	3,872,000	—	1.50	4.00	35.00	—
1961F Proof	46	Value: 650				
1961G	2,776,000	—	2.00	4.00	35.00	—
1961G Proof	100	Value: 325				
1961J	2,940,000	—	1.50	4.00	35.00	—
1961J Proof	28	Value: 800				
1962D	4,105,000	—	2.00	6.00	35.00	—
1962D Proof	50	Value: 600				
1962F	3,344,000	—	2.00	6.00	35.00	—
1962F Proof	42	Value: 625				
1962G	1,800,000	—	2.00	6.00	45.00	—
1962G Proof	130	Value: 300				
1962J	3,609,000	—	2.00	6.00	25.00	—
1962J Proof	28	Value: 750				
1963D	4,411,000	—	1.50	4.00	25.00	—
1963D Proof	40	Value: 650				
1963F	3,752,000	—	1.50	4.00	25.00	—
1963F Proof	47	Value: 600				
1963G	3,448,000	—	1.50	4.00	25.00	—
1963G Proof	200	Value: 350				
1963J	7,348,000	—	1.50	4.00	25.00	—
1963J Proof	32	Value: 700				
1964D	5,205,000	—	1.50	4.00	20.00	—
1964D Proof	40	Value: 650				
1964F	4,834,000	—	1.50	4.00	20.00	—
1964F Proof	36	Value: 800				
1964G	3,044,000	5.00	10.00	25.00	125	—
1964G Proof	368	Value: 150				
1964J	2,681,000	—	1.50	4.00	20.00	—
1964J Proof	43	Value: 600				
1965D	3,903,000	—	1.50	2.50	15.00	—
1965D Proof	35	Value: 800				
1965F	4,045,000	—	1.50	2.50	15.00	—
1965F Proof	300	Value: 250				
1965G	2,599,000	—	1.50	2.50	15.00	—
1965G Proof	8,233	Value: 5.00				
1965J	4,006,999	—	1.50	2.50	15.00	—
Note: Error exists without edge inscription						
1965J Proof	36	Value: 750				
1966D	5,855,000	—	1.50	2.50	12.00	—
1966D Proof	20	Value: 900				
1966F	3,750,000	—	1.50	2.50	12.00	—
1966F Proof	450	Value: 250				
1966G	3,895,000	—	1.50	2.50	12.00	—
1966G Proof	3,070	Value: 20.00				
1966J	6,014,000	—	1.50	2.50	12.00	—
1966J Proof	1,000	Value: 35.00				
1967D	3,254,000	—	1.50	2.50	12.00	—
1967D Proof	20	Value: 900				
1967F	3,758,000	—	1.50	2.50	12.00	—
1967F Proof	1,600	Value: 32.00				
1967G	1,878,000	—	1.50	4.00	16.50	—
1967G Proof	5,363	Value: 28.00				
1967J	6,684,000	—	1.25	2.50	12.00	—
1967J Proof	1,500	Value: 32.00				
1968D	4,166,000	—	1.50	2.50	15.00	—
1968D Proof	30	Value: 850				
1968F	1,050,000	—	2.00	5.00	20.00	—
1968F Proof	3,100	Value: 22.00				
1968G	3,060,000	—	2.00	2.50	12.00	—
1968G Proof	6,023	Value: 15.00				
1968J	939,000	—	2.00	4.00	20.00	—
1968J Proof	2,000	Value: 28.00				
1969D	2,602,000	—	2.00	2.50	15.00	—
1969F	3,005,000	—	2.00	2.50	15.00	—
1969F Proof	5,100	Value: 6.00				
1969G	1,754,000	—	2.00	2.50	16.50	—
1969G Proof	8,700	Value: 6.00				
1969J	2,680,000	—	2.00	2.50	10.00	—
1969J Proof	5,000	Value: 6.00				
1970D	5,203,000	—	1.50	2.00	4.00	—
1970F	6,018,000	—	1.50	2.00	4.00	—
1970F Proof	5,140	Value: 7.50				
1970G	3,461,000	—	1.50	2.00	4.00	—
1970G Proof	10,000	Value: 5.00				
1970J	5,691,000	—	1.50	2.00	4.00	—
1970J Proof	5,000	Value: 6.00				
1971D	8,451,000	—	1.00	1.25	3.00	—
1971D Proof	8,000	Value: 5.00				
1971F	10,017,000	—	1.00	1.25	3.00	—
1971F Proof	8,000	Value: 5.00				
1971G	5,631,000	—	1.00	1.25	3.00	—
1971G Proof	10,000	Value: 5.00				
1971J	8,786,000	—	1.00	1.25	3.00	—
1971J Proof	8,000	Value: 6.00				

KM# 124 2 MARK

7.0000 g., Copper-Nickel Clad Nickel, 26.75 mm. **Subject:** Konrad Adenauer **Obv:** Imperial eagle above denomination **Rev:** Head left, dates below

Date	Mintage	F	VF	XF	Unc	BU
1969D	7,001,000	—	—	1.50	3.00	—
1969F	7,006,000	—	—	1.50	3.00	—
1969G	7,010,000	—	—	1.50	3.00	—
1969J	7,000,000	—	—	1.50	3.00	—
1970D	7,318,000	—	—	1.50	3.00	—
1970F	8,422,000	—	—	1.50	3.00	—
1970G	4,844,000	—	—	1.50	3.00	—
1970J	7,476,000	—	—	1.50	3.00	—
1971D	7,287,000	—	—	1.50	3.00	—
1971F	8,400,000	—	—	1.50	3.00	—
1971G	4,848,000	—	—	1.50	3.00	—
1971J	7,476,000	—	—	1.50	3.00	—
1972D	7,286,000	—	—	1.50	3.00	—
1972D Proof	8,000	Value: 4.50				
1972F	8,392,000	—	—	1.50	3.00	—
1972F Proof	8,000	Value: 4.50				
1972G	4,848,000	—	—	1.50	3.00	—
1972G Proof	10,000	Value: 4.50				
1972J	7,476,000	—	—	1.50	3.00	—
1972J Proof	8,000	Value: 4.50				
1973D	10,393,000	—	—	1.50	3.00	—
1973D Proof	9,000	Value: 4.50				
1973F	11,015,000	—	—	1.50	3.00	—
Note: Errors exist without edge inscription						
1973F Proof	9,000	Value: 4.50				
1973G	9,022,000	—	—	1.50	3.00	—
1973G Proof	9,000	Value: 4.50				
1973J	12,272,000	—	—	1.50	3.00	—
Note: Errors with coin alignment exist						
1973J Proof	9,000	Value: 4.50				
1974D	5,151,000	—	—	1.50	3.00	—
1974D Proof	35,000	Value: 2.25				
1974F	5,894,000	—	—	1.50	3.00	—
1974F Proof	35,000	Value: 2.25				
1974G	3,790,000	—	—	1.50	3.00	—
1974G Proof	35,000	Value: 2.25				
1974J	5,282,000	—	—	1.50	3.00	—
1974J Proof	35,000	Value: 2.25				
1975D	4,553,000	—	—	1.50	2.50	—
1975D Proof	43,000	Value: 2.25				
1975F	5,270,000	—	—	1.50	2.50	—
1975F Proof	43,000	Value: 2.25				
1975G	3,035,000	—	—	1.50	2.50	—
1975G Proof	43,000	Value: 2.25				
1975J	4,673,000	—	—	1.50	2.50	—
1975J Proof	43,000	Value: 2.25				
1976D	4,576,000	—	—	1.50	2.50	—
1976D Proof	43,000	Value: 2.25				
1976F	5,257,000	—	—	1.50	2.50	—
1976F Proof	43,000	Value: 2.25				
1976G	3,028,000	—	—	1.50	2.50	—
1976G Proof	43,000	Value: 2.25				
1976J	4,673,000	—	—	1.50	2.50	—
1976J Proof	43,000	Value: 2.25				
1977D	5,906,000	—	—	1.50	2.50	—
1977D Proof	51,000	Value: 2.00				
1977F	6,765,000	—	—	1.50	2.50	—
1977F Proof	51,000	Value: 2.00				
1977G	3,892,000	—	—	1.50	2.50	—
1977G Proof	51,000	Value: 2.00				
1977J	6,007,000	—	—	1.50	2.50	—
1977J Proof	51,000	Value: 2.00				
1978D	3,304,000	—	—	1.50	2.50	—
1978D Proof	54,000	Value: 2.00				
1978F	3,804	—	—	1.50	2.50	—
1978F Proof	54,000	Value: 2.00				
1978G	2,217,000	—	—	1.50	2.50	—
1978G Proof	54,000	Value: 2.00				
1978J	3,392,000	—	—	1.50	2.50	—
1978J Proof	54,000	Value: 2.00				
1979D	3,209,000	—	—	1.50	2.50	—
1979D Proof	89,000	Value: 2.00				
1979F	3,689,000	—	—	1.50	2.50	—
1979F Proof	89,000	Value: 2.00				
1979G	2,165,000	—	—	1.50	2.50	—
1979G Proof	89,000	Value: 2.00				
1979J	3,293,000	—	—	1.50	2.50	—
1979J Proof	89,000	Value: 2.00				
1980D	10,810,000	—	—	1.50	2.00	—
1980D Proof	110,000	Value: 2.00				
1980F	8,910,000	—	—	1.50	2.00	—
1980F Proof	110,000	Value: 2.00				
1980G	1,170,000	—	—	1.50	2.00	—
1980G Proof	110,000	Value: 2.00				
1980J	4,670,000	—	—	1.50	2.00	—
1980J Proof	110,000	Value: 2.00				
1981D	8,180,000	—	—	1.50	2.00	—
1981D Proof	91,000	Value: 2.00				
1981F	7,690,000	—	—	1.50	2.00	—
1981F Proof	91,000	Value: 2.00				
1981G	7,070,000	—	—	1.50	2.00	—
1981G Proof	91,000	Value: 2.00				
1981J	8,289,999	—	—	1.50	2.00	—
1981J Proof	91,000	Value: 2.00				
1982D	9,220,000	—	—	1.50	2.00	—
1982D Proof	78,000	Value: 2.00				
1982F	11,260,000	—	—	1.50	2.00	—
1982F Proof	78,000	Value: 2.00				
1982G	6,640,000	—	—	1.50	2.00	—
1982G Proof	78,000	Value: 2.00				
1982J	9,790,000	—	—	1.50	2.00	—
1982J Proof	78,000	Value: 2.00				
1983D	1,560,000	—	—	1.50	2.00	—
1983D Proof	75,000	Value: 2.00				
1983F	1,800,000	—	—	1.50	2.00	—
1983F Proof	75,000	Value: 2.00				
1983G	1,030,000	—	—	1.50	2.00	—
1983G Proof	75,000	Value: 2.00				
1983J	1,600,000	—	—	1.50	2.00	—
1983J Proof	75,000	Value: 2.00				
1984D	52,000	—	2.00	4.50	8.50	—
1984D Proof	64,000	Value: 2.00				
1984F	60,000	—	2.00	4.50	8.50	—
1984F Proof	64,000	Value: 2.00				
1984G	35,000	—	3.00	6.00	11.50	—
1984G Proof	64,000	Value: 2.00				
1984J	53,000	—	2.00	4.50	8.50	—
1984J Proof	64,000	Value: 2.00				
1985D	2,600,000	—	—	—	2.00	—
1985D Proof	56,000	Value: 2.25				
1985F	3,000,000	—	—	—	1.75	—
1985F Proof	54,000	Value: 2.25				
1985G	1,730,000	—	—	—	1.75	—
1985G Proof	55,000	Value: 2.25				
1985J	2,670,000	—	—	—	1.75	—
1985J Proof	54,000	Value: 2.25				
1986D	2,600,000	—	—	—	1.75	—
1986D Proof	44,000	Value: 2.25				
1986F	3,000,000	—	—	—	1.75	—
1986F Proof	44,000	Value: 2.25				
1986G	1,730,000	—	—	—	1.75	—
1986G Proof	44,000	Value: 2.25				
1986J	2,670,000	—	—	—	1.75	—
1986J Proof	44,000	Value: 2.25				
1987D	4,420,000	—	—	—	1.75	—
1987D Proof	45,000	Value: 2.25				
1987F	5,100,000	—	—	—	1.75	—
1987F Proof	45,000	Value: 2.25				
1987G	2,940,000	—	—	—	1.75	—
1987G Proof	45,000	Value: 2.25				
1987J	4,540,000	—	—	—	1.75	—
1987J Proof	45,000	Value: 2.25				

KM# A127 2 MARK

7.0000 g., Copper-Nickel Clad Nickel, 26.75 mm. **Subject:** Theodor Heuss **Obv:** Imperial eagle above denomination **Rev:** Head left, dates below

Date	Mintage	F	VF	XF	Unc	BU
1970D	7,317,000	—	—	1.50	3.00	—

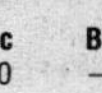

Date	Mintage	F	VF	XF	Unc	BU
1970F	8,426,000	—	—	1.50	3.00	—
1970G	4,844,000	—	—	1.50	3.00	—
1970J	7,476,000	—	—	1.50	3.00	—
1971D	7,280,000	—	—	1.50	3.00	—
1971F	8,403,000	—	—	1.50	3.00	—
1971G	4,841,000	—	—	1.50	3.00	—
1971J	7,476,000	—	—	1.50	3.00	—
1972D	7,288,000	—	—	1.50	3.00	—
1972D Proof	8,000	Value: 4.50				
1972F	8,401,000	—	—	1.50	3.00	—
1972F Proof	8,000	Value: 4.50				
1972G	4,859,000	—	—	1.50	3.00	—
1972G Proof	10,000	Value: 4.50				
1972J	7,476,000	—	—	1.50	3.00	—
1972J Proof	8,000	Value: 4.50				
1973D	10,379,000	—	—	1.50	3.00	—
1973D Proof	9,000	Value: 4.50				
1973F	11,018,000	—	—	1.50	3.00	—
1973F Proof	9,000	Value: 4.50				
1973G	8,975,000	—	—	1.50	3.00	—
1973G Proof	9,000	Value: 4.50				
1973J	12,360,000	—	—	1.50	3.00	—
1973J Proof	9,000	Value: 4.50				
1974D	5,147,000	—	—	1.50	3.00	—
1974D Proof	35,000	Value: 2.00				
1974F	5,899,000	—	—	1.50	3.00	—
1974F Proof	35,000	Value: 2.00				
1974G	3,820,000	—	—	1.50	3.00	—
1974G Proof	35,000	Value: 2.00				
1974J	5,280,000	—	—	1.50	3.00	—
1974J Proof	35,000	Value: 2.00				
1975D	4,623,000	—	—	1.50	2.00	—
1975D Proof	43,000	Value: 2.00				
1975F	5,251,000	—	—	1.50	2.00	—
1975F Proof	43,000	Value: 2.00				
1975G	3,034,000	—	—	1.50	2.00	—
1975G Proof	43,000	Value: 2.00				
1975J	4,675,000	—	—	1.50	2.00	—
1975J Proof	43,000	Value: 2.00				
1976D	4,546,000	—	—	1.50	2.00	—
1976D Proof	43,000	Value: 2.00				
1976F	5,259,000	—	—	1.50	2.00	—
1976F Proof	43,000	Value: 2.00				
1976G	3,028,000	—	—	1.50	2.00	—
1976G Proof	43,000	Value: 2.00				
1976J	4,681,000	—	—	1.50	2.00	—
1976J Proof	43,000	Value: 2.00				
1977D	5,857,000	—	—	1.50	2.00	—
1977D Proof	51,000	Value: 1.75				
1977F	6,752,000	—	—	1.50	2.00	—
1977F Proof	51,000	Value: 1.75				
1977G	3,892,000	—	—	1.50	2.00	—
1977G Proof	51,000	Value: 1.75				
1977J	6,009,000	—	—	1.50	2.00	—
1977J Proof	51,000	Value: 1.75				
1978D	3,804,000	—	—	1.50	2.00	—
Note: Errors without edge inscription exist						
1978D Proof	54,000	Value: 1.75				
1978F	3,804,000	—	—	1.50	2.00	—
1978F Proof	54,000	Value: 1.75				
1978G	2,217,000	—	—	1.50	2.00	—
1978G Proof	54,000	Value: 1.75				
1978J	3,392,000	—	—	1.50	2.00	—
1978J Proof	54,000	Value: 1.75				
1979D	3,209,000	—	—	1.50	2.00	—
1979D Proof	89,000	Value: 1.75				
1979F	3,689,000	—	—	1.50	2.00	—
1979F Proof	89,000	Value: 1.75				
1979G	2,165,000	—	—	1.50	2.00	—
1979G Proof	89,000	Value: 1.75				
1979J	3,293,000	—	—	1.50	2.00	—
1979J Proof	89,000	Value: 1.75				
1980D	2,000,000	—	—	1.50	1.75	—
1980D Proof	110,000	Value: 1.75				
1980F	2,300,000	—	—	1.50	1.75	—
1980F Proof	110,000	Value: 1.75				
1980G	1,300,000	—	—	1.50	1.75	—
1980G Proof	110,000	Value: 1.75				
1980J	2,000,000	—	—	1.50	1.75	—
1980J Proof	110,000	Value: 1.75				
1981D	2,000,000	—	—	1.50	1.75	—
1981D Proof	91,000	Value: 1.75				
1981F	2,300,000	—	—	1.50	1.75	—
1981F Proof	91,000	Value: 1.75				
1981G	1,300,000	—	—	1.50	1.75	—
1981G Proof	91,000	Value: 1.75				
1981J	2,000,000	—	—	1.50	1.75	—
1981J Proof	91,000	Value: 1.75				
1982D	3,100,000	—	—	1.50	1.75	—
1982D Proof	78,000	Value: 1.75				
1982F	3,600,000	—	—	1.50	1.75	—
1982F Proof	78,000	Value: 1.75				
1982G	2,100,000	—	—	1.50	1.75	—
1982G Proof	78,000	Value: 1.75				
1982J	3,200,000	—	—	1.50	1.75	—
1982J Proof	78,000	Value: 1.75				
1983D	1,560,000	—	—	1.50	1.75	—
1983D Proof	75,000	Value: 1.75				
1983F	1,800,000	—	—	1.50	1.75	—
1983F Proof	75,000	Value: 1.75				
1983G	1,030,000	—	—	1.50	1.75	—
1983G Proof	75,000	Value: 1.75				
1983J	1,600,000	—	—	1.50	1.75	—
1983J Proof	75,000	Value: 1.75				
1984D	52,000	—	2.00	4.50	8.50	—
1984D Proof	64,000	Value: 2.00				
1984F	60,000	—	2.00	4.50	8.50	—
1984F Proof	64,000	Value: 2.00				
1984G	35,000	—	3.00	6.00	11.50	—
1984G Proof	64,000	Value: 2.00				
1984J	53,000	—	2.00	4.50	8.50	—
1984J Proof	64,000	Value: 2.00				
1985D	2,600,000	—	—	—	1.75	—
1985D Proof	56,000	Value: 2.25				
1985F	3,000,000	—	—	—	1.75	—
1985F Proof	54,000	Value: 2.25				
1985G	1,730,000	—	—	—	1.75	—
1985G Proof	55,000	Value: 2.25				
1985J	2,670,000	—	—	—	1.75	—
1985J Proof	54,000	Value: 2.25				
1986D	2,600,000	—	—	—	1.75	—
1986D Proof	44,000	Value: 2.25				
1986F	3,000,000	—	—	—	1.75	—
1986F Proof	44,000	Value: 2.25				
1986G	1,730,000	—	—	—	1.75	—
1986G Proof	44,000	Value: 2.25				
1986J	2,670,000	—	—	—	1.75	—
1986J Proof	44,000	Value: 2.25				
1987D	4,420,000	—	—	—	1.75	—
1987D Proof	45,000	Value: 2.25				
1987F	5,100,000	—	—	—	1.75	—
1987F Proof	45,000	Value: 2.25				
1987G	2,940,000	—	—	—	1.75	—
1987G Proof	45,000	Value: 2.25				
1987J	4,540,000	—	—	—	1.75	—
1987J Proof	45,000	Value: 2.25				

KM# 149 2 MARK

7.0000 g., Copper-Nickel Clad Nickel, 26.75 mm. **Subject:** Dr. Kurt Schumacher **Obv:** Imperial above denomination **Rev:** Head 3/4 left divides dates

Date	Mintage	F	VF	XF	Unc	BU
1979D	3,209,000	—	—	1.50	2.00	—
1979D Proof	89,000	Value: 1.75				
1979F	3,689,000	—	—	1.50	2.00	—
1979F Proof	89,000	Value: 1.75				
1979G	2,165,000	—	—	1.50	2.00	—
1979G Proof	89,000	Value: 1.75				
1979J	3,293,000	—	—	1.50	2.00	—
1979J Proof	89,000	Value: 1.75				
1980D	2,000,000	—	—	1.50	2.00	—
1980D Proof	110,000	Value: 1.75				
1980F	2,300,000	—	—	1.50	2.00	—
1980F Proof	110,000	Value: 1.75				
1980G	1,300,000	—	—	1.50	2.00	—
1980G Proof	110,000	Value: 1.75				
1980J	2,000,000	—	—	1.50	2.00	—
1980J Proof	110,000	Value: 1.75				
1981D	2,000,000	—	—	1.50	2.00	—
1981D Proof	91,000	Value: 1.75				
1981F	2,000,000	—	—	1.50	2.00	—
Note: Errors without edge inscription exist						
1981F Proof	91,000	Value: 1.75				
1981G	1,300,000	—	—	1.50	2.00	—
1981G Proof	91,000	Value: 1.75				
1981J	2,000,000	—	—	1.50	2.00	—
1981J Proof	91,000	Value: 1.75				
1982D	3,100,000	—	—	1.50	2.00	—
1982D Proof	78,000	Value: 1.75				
1982F	3,600,000	—	—	1.50	2.00	—
1982F Proof	78,000	Value: 1.75				
1982G	2,100,000	—	—	1.50	2.00	—
1982G Proof	78,000	Value: 1.75				
1982J	3,200,000	—	—	1.50	2.00	—
1982J Proof	78,000	Value: 1.75				
1983D	1,560,000	—	—	1.50	2.00	—
1983D Proof	75,000	Value: 1.75				
1983F	1,800,000	—	—	1.50	2.00	—
1983F Proof	75,000	Value: 1.75				
1983G	1,030,000	—	—	1.50	2.00	—
1983G Proof	75,000	Value: 1.75				
1983J	1,600,000	—	—	1.50	2.00	—
1983J Proof	75,000	Value: 1.75				
1984D	52,000	—	2.00	4.50	8.50	—
1984D Proof	64,000	Value: 1.75				
1984F	60,000	—	2.00	4.50	8.50	—
1984F Proof	64,000	Value: 1.75				
1984G	35,000	—	3.00	6.00	11.50	—
1984G Proof	64,000	Value: 1.75				
1984J	53,000	—	2.00	4.50	8.50	—
1984J Proof	64,000	Value: 1.75				
1985D	2,600,000	—	—	—	1.75	—
1985D Proof	56,000	Value: 2.25				
1985F	3,000,000	—	—	—	1.75	—
1985F Proof	54,000	Value: 2.25				
1985G	1,730,000	—	—	—	1.75	—
1985G Proof	55,000	Value: 2.25				
1985J	2,670,000	—	—	—	1.75	—
1985J Proof	54,000	Value: 2.25				
1986D	2,600,000	—	—	—	1.75	—
1986D Proof	44,000	Value: 2.25				
1986F	3,000,000	—	—	—	1.75	—
1986F Proof	44,000	Value: 2.25				
1986G	1,730,000	—	—	—	1.75	—
1986G Proof	44,000	Value: 2.25				
1986J	2,670,000	—	—	—	1.75	—
1986J Proof	44,000	Value: 2.25				
1987D	4,420,000	—	—	—	1.75	—
1987D Proof	45,000	Value: 2.25				
1987F	5,100,000	—	—	—	1.75	—
1987F Proof	45,000	Value: 2.25				
1987G	2,940,000	—	—	—	1.75	—
1987G Proof	45,000	Value: 2.25				
1987J	4,540,000	—	—	—	1.75	—
1987J Proof	45,000	Value: 2.25				
1988D	5,850,000	—	—	—	1.75	—
1988D Proof	45,000	Value: 2.25				
1988F	6,750,000	—	—	—	1.75	—
1988F Proof	45,000	Value: 2.25				
1988G	3,890,000	—	—	—	1.75	—
1988G Proof	45,000	Value: 2.25				
1988J	6,010,000	—	—	—	1.75	—
1988J Proof	45,000	Value: 2.25				
1989D	10,400,000	—	—	—	1.75	—
1989D Proof	45,000	Value: 2.25				
1989F	12,000,000	—	—	—	1.75	—
1989F Proof	45,000	Value: 2.25				
1989G	6,920,000	—	—	—	1.75	—
1989G Proof	45,000	Value: 2.25				
1989J	10,680,000	—	—	—	1.75	—
1989J Proof	45,000	Value: 2.25				
1990D	18,370,000	—	—	—	1.75	—
1990D Proof	45,000	Value: 2.25				
1990F	21,200,000	—	—	—	1.75	—
1990F Proof	45,000	Value: 2.25				
1990G	12,220,000	—	—	—	1.75	—
1990G Proof	45,000	Value: 2.25				
1990J	18,870,000	—	—	—	1.75	—
1990J Proof	45,000	Value: 2.25				
1991A	4,000,000	—	—	—	1.75	—
1991A Proof	45,000	Value: 2.25				
1991D	4,200,000	—	—	—	1.75	—
1991D Proof	45,000	Value: 2.25				
1991F	4,800,000	—	—	—	1.75	—
1991F Proof	45,000	Value: 2.25				
1991G	2,800,000	—	—	—	1.75	—
1991G Proof	45,000	Value: 2.25				
1991J	4,200,000	—	—	—	1.75	—
1991J Proof	45,000	Value: 2.25				
1992A	7,330,000	—	—	—	1.75	—
1992A Proof	45,000	Value: 2.25				
1992D	7,700,000	—	—	—	1.75	—
1992D Proof	45,000	Value: 2.25				
1992F	8,800,000	—	—	—	1.75	—
1992F Proof	45,000	Value: 2.25				
1992G	5,130,000	—	—	—	1.75	—
1992G Proof	45,000	Value: 2.25				
1992J	7,700,000	—	—	—	1.75	—
1992J Proof	45,000	Value: 2.25				
1993A	600,000	—	—	3.00	7.00	—
1993A Proof	45,000	Value: 2.25				
1993D	630,000	—	—	3.00	7.00	—
1993D Proof	45,000	Value: 2.25				
1993F	720,000	—	—	3.00	7.00	—
1993F Proof	45,000	Value: 2.25				
1993G	420,000	—	—	4.00	10.00	—
1993G Proof	45,000	Value: 2.25				
1993J	630,000	—	—	3.00	7.00	—
1993J Proof	45,000	Value: 2.25				

KM# 170 2 MARK

7.0000 g., Copper-Nickel Clad Nickel, 26.75 mm. **Subject:** Ludwig Erhard **Obv:** Imperial eagle above denomination **Rev:** Head facing divides dates

Date	Mintage	F	VF	XF	Unc	BU
1988D	5,850,000	—	—	—	1.65	—
1988D Proof	45,000	Value: 2.00				
1988F	6,750,000	—	—	—	1.65	—
1988F Proof	45,000	Value: 2.00				
1988G	3,890,000	—	—	—	1.65	—
1988G Proof	45,000	Value: 2.00				
1988J	6,010,000	—	—	—	1.65	—
1988J Proof	45,000	Value: 2.00				
1989D	10,400,000	—	—	—	1.65	—

Date	Mintage	F	VF	XF	Unc	BU
1989D Proof	45,000	Value: 2.00				
1989F	12,000,000	—	—	—	1.65	—
1989F Proof	45,000	Value: 2.00				
1989G	6,920,000	—	—	—	1.65	—
1989G Proof	45,000	Value: 2.00				
1989J	10,680,000	—	—	—	1.65	—
1989J Proof	45,000	Value: 2.00				
1990D	18,370,000	—	—	—	1.65	—
1990D Proof	45,000	Value: 2.00				
1990F	21,200,000	—	—	—	1.65	—
1990F Proof	45,000	Value: 2.00				
1990G	12,220,000	—	—	—	1.65	—
1990G Proof	45,000	Value: 2.00				
1990J	18,870,000	—	—	—	1.65	—
1990J Proof	45,000	Value: 2.00				
1991A	4,000,000	—	—	—	1.65	—
1991A Proof	45,000	Value: 2.00				
1991D	4,200,000	—	—	—	1.65	—
1991D Proof	45,000	Value: 2.00				
1991F	4,800,000	—	—	—	1.65	—
1991F Proof	45,000	Value: 2.00				
1991G	2,800,000	—	—	—	1.65	—
Note: Errors without edge inscription exist						
1991G Proof	45,000	Value: 2.00				
1991J	4,200,000	—	—	—	1.65	—
1991J Proof	45,000	Value: 2.00				
1992A	7,330,000	—	—	—	1.75	—
1992A Proof	45,000	Value: 2.25				
1992D	7,700,000	—	—	—	1.75	—
1992D Proof	45,000	Value: 2.25				
1992F	8,800,000	—	—	—	1.75	—
1992F Proof	45,000	Value: 2.25				
1992G	5,130,000	—	—	—	1.75	—
1992G Proof	45,000	Value: 2.25				
1992J	7,700,000	—	—	—	1.75	—
1992J Proof	45,000	Value: 2.25				
1993A	600,000	—	—	3.00	7.00	—
1993A Proof	45,000	Value: 2.25				
1993D	630,000	—	—	3.00	7.00	—
1993D Proof	45,000	Value: 2.25				
1993F	720,000	—	—	3.00	7.00	—
1993F Proof	45,000	Value: 2.25				
1993G	420,000	—	—	4.00	10.00	—
1993G Proof	45,000	Value: 2.25				
1993J	630,000	—	—	3.00	7.00	—
1993J Proof	45,000	Value: 2.25				
1994A	5,000,000	—	—	—	1.75	—
1994A Proof	45,000	Value: 2.25				
1994D	5,250,000	—	—	—	1.75	—
1994D Proof	45,000	Value: 2.25				
1994F	6,000,000	—	—	—	1.75	—
1994F Proof	45,000	Value: 2.25				
1994G	3,500,000	—	—	—	1.75	—
1994G Proof	45,000	Value: 2.25				
1994J	5,250,000	—	—	—	1.75	—
1994J Proof	45,000	Value: 2.25				
1995A	1,595,000	—	—	—	3.50	—
1995A Proof	45,000	Value: 17.50				
1995D	20,000	—	—	—	60.00	—
Note: In sets only						
1995D Proof	45,000	Value: 17.50				
1995F	20,000	—	—	—	60.00	—
Note: In sets only						
1995F Proof	45,000	Value: 17.50				
1995G	920,000	—	—	—	6.00	—
1995G Proof	45,000	Value: 17.50				
1995J	20,000	—	—	—	60.00	—
Note: In sets only						
1995J Proof	45,000	Value: 17.50				
1996A	—	—	—	—	5.00	—
1996A Proof	45,000	Value: 6.00				
1996D	—	—	—	—	5.00	—
1996D Proof	45,000	Value: 6.00				
1996F	—	—	—	—	5.00	—
1996F Proof	45,000	Value: 6.00				
1996G	—	—	—	—	5.00	—
1996G Proof	45,000	Value: 6.00				
1996J	—	—	—	—	5.00	—
1996J Proof	45,000	Value: 6.00				
1997A	70,000	—	—	—	4.25	—
Note: In sets only						
1997A Proof	45,000	Value: 5.00				
1997D	70,000	—	—	—	4.25	—
Note: In sets only						
1997D Proof	45,000	Value: 5.00				
1997F	70,000	—	—	—	4.25	—
Note: In sets only						
1997F Proof	45,000	Value: 5.00				
1997G	70,000	—	—	—	4.25	—
Note: In sets only						
1997G Proof	45,000	Value: 5.00				
1997J	70,000	—	—	—	4.25	—
Note: In sets only						
1997J Proof	45,000	Value: 5.00				
1998A	70,000	—	—	—	4.25	—
Note: In sets only						
1998A Proof	45,000	Value: 5.00				
1998D	70,000	—	—	—	4.25	—
Note: In sets only						
1998D Proof	45,000	Value: 5.00				
1998F	70,000	—	—	—	4.25	—
Note: In sets only						
1998F Proof	45,000	Value: 5.00				
1998G	70,000	—	—	—	4.25	—
Note: In sets only						
1998G Proof	45,000	Value: 5.00				
1998J	70,000	—	—	—	4.25	—
Note: In sets only						
1998J Proof	45,000	Value: 5.00				
1999A	70,000	—	—	—	4.25	—
Note: In sets only						
1999A Proof	45,000	Value: 5.00				
1999D	70,000	—	—	—	4.25	—
Note: In sets only						
1999D Proof	45,000	Value: 5.00				
1999F	70,000	—	—	—	4.25	—
Note: In sets only						
1999F Proof	45,000	Value: 5.00				
1999G	70,000	—	—	—	4.75	—
Note: In sets only						
1999G Proof	45,000	Value: 5.00				
1999J	70,000	—	—	—	4.75	—
Note: In sets only						
1999J Proof	45,000	Value: 5.00				
2000A	70,000	—	—	—	5.00	—
Note: In sets only						
2000A Proof	45,000	Value: 5.00				
2000D	70,000	—	—	—	5.00	—
Note: In sets only						
2000D Proof	45,000	Value: 5.00				
2000F	70,000	—	—	—	5.00	—
Note: In sets only						
2000F Proof	45,000	Value: 5.00				
2000G	70,000	—	—	—	5.00	—
Note: In sets only						
2000G Proof	45,000	Value: 5.00				
2000J	70,000	—	—	—	5.00	—
Note: In sets only						
2000J Proof	45,000	Value: 5.00				

KM# 175 2 MARK

7.0000 g., Copper-Nickel Clad Nickel, 26.75 mm. **Subject:** Franz Joseph Strauss **Obv:** Imperial eagle above denomination **Rev:** Head left divides dates

Date	Mintage	F	VF	XF	Unc	BU
1990D	18,370,000	—	—	—	1.75	—
1990D Proof	45,000	Value: 2.25				
1990F	21,200,000	—	—	—	1.75	—
1990F Proof	45,000	Value: 2.25				
1990G	12,220,000	—	—	—	1.75	—
1990G Proof	45,000	Value: 2.25				
1990J	18,870,000	—	—	—	1.75	—
1990J Proof	45,000	Value: 2.25				
1991A	4,000,000	—	—	—	1.75	—
1991A Proof	45,000	Value: 2.25				
1991D	4,200,000	—	—	—	1.75	—
1991D Proof	45,000	Value: 2.25				
1991F	4,800,000	—	—	—	1.75	—
1991F Proof	45,000	Value: 2.25				
1991G	2,800,000	—	—	—	1.75	—
1991G Proof	45,000	Value: 2.25				
1991J	4,200,000	—	—	—	1.75	—
1991J Proof	45,000	Value: 2.25				
1992A	7,330,000	—	—	—	1.75	—
1992A Proof	45,000	Value: 2.25				
1992D	7,700,000	—	—	—	1.75	—
1992D Proof	45,000	Value: 2.25				
1992F	8,800,000	—	—	—	1.75	—
1992F Proof	45,000	Value: 2.25				
1992G	5,130,000	—	—	—	1.75	—
1992G Proof	45,000	Value: 2.25				
1992J	7,700,000	—	—	—	1.75	—
1992J Proof	45,000	Value: 2.25				
1993A	600,000	—	—	3.00	7.00	—
1993A Proof	45,000	Value: 2.25				
1993D	630,000	—	—	3.00	7.00	—
1993D Proof	45,000	Value: 2.25				
1993F	720,000	—	—	3.00	7.00	—
1993F Proof	45,000	Value: 2.25				
1993G	420,000	—	—	4.00	10.00	—
1993G Proof	45,000	Value: 2.25				
1993J	630,000	—	—	3.00	7.00	—
1993J Proof	45,000	Value: 2.25				
1994A	5,000,000	—	—	—	1.75	—
1994A Proof	45,000	Value: 2.25				
1994D	5,250,000	—	—	—	1.75	—
1994D Proof	45,000	Value: 2.25				
1994F	6,000,000	—	—	—	1.75	—
1994F Proof	45,000	Value: 2.25				
1994G	3,500,000	—	—	—	1.75	—
1994G Proof	45,000	Value: 2.25				
1994J	5,250,000	—	—	—	1.75	—
1994J Proof	45,000	Value: 2.25				
1995A	1,595,000	—	—	—	3.50	—
1995A Proof	45,000	Value: 17.50				
1995D	20,000	—	—	—	60.00	—
Note: In sets only						
1995D Proof	45,000	Value: 17.50				
1995F	20,000	—	—	—	60.00	—
Note: In sets only						
1995F Proof	45,000	Value: 17.50				
1995G	620,000	—	—	—	7.00	—
1995G Proof	45,000	Value: 17.50				
1995J	20,000	—	—	—	60.00	—
Note: In sets only						
1995J Proof	45,000	Value: 17.50				
1996A	—	—	—	—	5.00	—
1996A Proof	45,000	Value: 6.00				
1996D	—	—	—	—	5.00	—
1996D Proof	45,000	Value: 6.00				
1996F	—	—	—	—	5.00	—
1996F Proof	45,000	Value: 6.00				
1996G	—	—	—	—	5.00	—
1996G Proof	45,000	Value: 6.00				
1996J	—	—	—	—	5.00	—
1996J Proof	45,000	Value: 6.00				
1997A	70,000	—	—	—	4.25	—
Note: In sets only						
1997A Proof	45,000	Value: 5.00				
1997D	70,000	—	—	—	4.25	—
Note: In sets only						
1997D Proof	45,000	Value: 5.00				
1997F	70,000	—	—	—	4.25	—
Note: In sets only						
1997F Proof	45,000	Value: 5.00				
1997G	70,000	—	—	—	4.25	—
Note: In sets only						
1997G Proof	45,000	Value: 5.00				
1997J	70,000	—	—	—	4.25	—
Note: In sets only						
1997J Proof	45,000	Value: 5.00				
1998A	70,000	—	—	—	4.25	—
Note: In sets only						
1998A Proof	45,000	Value: 5.00				
1998D	70,000	—	—	—	4.25	—
Note: In sets only						
1998D Proof	45,000	Value: 5.00				
1998F	70,000	—	—	—	4.25	—
Note: In sets only						
1998F Proof	45,000	Value: 5.00				
1998G	70,000	—	—	—	4.25	—
Note: In sets only						
1998G Proof	45,000	Value: 5.00				
1998J	70,000	—	—	—	4.25	—
Note: In sets only						
1998J Proof	45,000	Value: 5.00				
1999A	70,000	—	—	—	4.25	—
Note: In sets only						
1999A Proof	45,000	Value: 5.00				
1999D	70,000	—	—	—	4.25	—
Note: In sets only						
1999D Proof	45,000	Value: 5.00				
1999F	70,000	—	—	—	4.25	—
Note: In sets only						
1999F Proof	45,000	Value: 5.00				
1999G	70,000	—	—	—	4.25	—
Note: In sets only						
1999G Proof	45,000	Value: 5.00				
1999J	70,000	—	—	—	4.25	—
Note: In sets only						
1999J Proof	45,000	Value: 5.00				
2000A	70,000	—	—	—	5.00	—
Note: In sets only						
2000A Proof	45,000	Value: 5.00				
2000D	70,000	—	—	—	5.00	—
Note: In sets only						
2000D Proof	45,000	Value: 5.00				
2000F	70,000	—	—	—	5.00	—
Note: In sets only						
2000F Proof	45,000	Value: 5.00				
2000G	70,000	—	—	—	5.00	—
Note: In sets only						
2000G Proof	45,000	Value: 5.00				
2000J	70,000	—	—	—	5.00	—
Note: In sets only						
2000J Proof	45,000	Value: 5.00				

KM# 183 2 MARK

7.0000 g., Copper-Nickel Clad Nickel, 26.75 mm. **Subject:** Willy Brandt **Obv:** Imperial eagle above denomination **Rev:** Head facing divides dates

Date	Mintage	F	VF	XF	Unc	BU
1994A	5,000,000	—	—	—	2.00	—
1994A Proof	45,000	Value: 2.50				
1994D	5,250,000	—	—	—	2.00	—
1994D Proof	45,000	Value: 2.50				
1994F	6,000,000	—	—	—	2.00	—
1994F Proof	45,000	Value: 2.50				
1994G	3,600,000	—	—	—	2.00	—
1994G Proof	45,000	Value: 2.50				
1994J	5,250,000	—	—	—	2.00	—
1994J Proof	45,000	Value: 2.50				
1995A	1,595,000	—	—	—	3.50	—
1995A Proof	45,000	Value: 17.50				
1995D	20,000	—	—	—	65.00	—
Note: In sets only						
1995D Proof	45,000	Value: 17.50				
1995F	20,000	—	—	—	65.00	—
Note: In sets only						
1995F Proof	45,000	Value: 17.50				
1995G	1,220,000	—	—	—	4.50	—
1995G Proof	45,000	Value: 17.50				
1995J	75,000	—	—	—	30.00	—
1995J Proof	45,000	Value: 17.50				
1996A	—	—	—	—	5.50	—
1996A Proof	45,000	Value: 6.50				
1996D	—	—	—	—	5.50	—
1996D Proof	45,000	Value: 6.50				
1996F	—	—	—	—	5.50	—
1996F Proof	45,000	Value: 6.50				
1996G	—	—	—	—	5.50	—
1996G Proof	45,000	Value: 6.50				
1996J	—	—	—	—	5.50	—
1996J Proof	45,000	Value: 6.50				
1997A	70,000	—	—	—	4.25	—
Note: In sets only						
1997A Proof	45,000	Value: 5.00				
1997D	70,000	—	—	—	4.25	—
Note: In sets only						
1997D Proof	45,000	Value: 5.00				
1997F	70,000	—	—	—	4.25	—
Note: In sets only						
1997F Proof	45,000	Value: 5.00				
1997G	70,000	—	—	—	4.25	—
Note: In sets only						
1997G Proof	45,000	Value: 5.00				
1997J	70,000	—	—	—	4.25	—
Note: In sets only						
1997J Proof	45,000	Value: 5.00				
1998A	70,000	—	—	—	4.25	—
Note: In sets only						
1998A Proof	45,000	Value: 5.00				
1998D	70,000	—	—	—	4.25	—
Note: In sets only						
1998D Proof	45,000	Value: 5.00				
1998F	70,000	—	—	—	4.25	—
Note: In sets only						
1998F Proof	45,000	Value: 5.00				
1998G	70,000	—	—	—	4.25	—
Note: In sets only						
1998G Proof	45,000	Value: 5.00				
1998J	70,000	—	—	—	4.25	—
Note: In sets only						
1998J Proof	45,000	Value: 5.00				
1999A	70,000	—	—	—	4.25	—
Note: In sets only						
1999A Proof	45,000	Value: 5.00				
1999D	70,000	—	—	—	4.25	—
Note: In sets only						
1999D Proof	45,000	Value: 5.00				
1999F	70,000	—	—	—	4.25	—
Note: In sets only						
1999F Proof	45,000	Value: 5.00				
1999G	70,000	—	—	—	4.25	—
Note: In sets only						
1999G Proof	45,000	Value: 5.00				
1999J	70,000	—	—	—	4.25	—
Note: In sets only						
1999J Proof	45,000	Value: 5.00				
2000A	70,000	—	—	—	5.00	—
Note: In sets only						
2000A Proof	45,000	Value: 5.00				
2000D	70,000	—	—	—	5.00	—
Note: In sets only						
2000D Proof	45,000	Value: 5.00				
2000F	70,000	—	—	—	5.00	—
Note: In sets only						
2000F Proof	45,000	Value: 5.00				
2000G	70,000	—	—	—	5.00	—
Note: In sets only						
2000G Proof	45,000	Value: 5.00				
2000J	70,000	—	—	—	5.00	—
Note: In sets only						
2000J Proof	45,000	Value: 5.00				

KM# 112.1 5 MARK

11.2000 g., 0.6250 Silver .2250 oz. ASW, 29 mm. **Obv:** Denomination above date **Rev:** Large imperial eagle

Date	Mintage	F	VF	XF	Unc	BU
1951D	20,600,000	—	4.00	15.00	65.00	—
1951D Proof	—	Value: 425				
1951F	24,000,000	—	4.00	15.00	75.00	—
1951F Proof	280	Value: 350				
1951G	13,840,000	—	4.00	20.00	125	—
1951G Proof	—	Value: 950				
1951J	21,360,000	—	4.00	15.00	60.00	—
1951J Proof	—	Value: 245				
1956D	1,092,000	2.00	15.00	60.00	275	—
1956D Proof	—	Value: 1,500				
1956F	1,200,000	—	10.00	75.00	475	—
1956F Proof	23	Value: 2,500				
1956J	1,068,000	—	10.00	50.00	250	—
1956J Proof	—	Value: 2,750				
1957D	566,000	—	10.00	65.00	300	—
1957D Proof	—	—	—	—	—	—
1957F	2,100,000	—	7.50	50.00	300	—
1957F Proof	—	Value: 2,500				
1957G	692,000	—	10.00	75.00	650	—
1957G Proof	—	Value: 3,500				
1957J	1,630,000	—	7.50	35.00	225	—
1957J Proof	—	—	—	—	—	—
1958D	1,226,000	—	7.50	30.00	150	—
1958D Proof	—	—	—	—	—	—
1958F	600,000	2.00	20.00	145	800	—
1958F Proof	100	Value: 1,350				
1958G	1,557,000	—	7.50	28.00	140	—
1958G Proof	—	—	—	—	—	—
1958J	60,000	—	1,100	2,500	4,250	—
1958J Proof	—	Value: 7,000				
1959D	496,000	—	10.00	45.00	325	—
1959D Proof	—	Value: 1,250				
1959G	692,000	—	15.00	45.00	285	—
1959G Proof	—	Value: 1,500				
1959J	713,000	—	8.00	40.00	300	—
1959J Proof	—	Value: 2,000				
1960D	1,040,000	—	7.00	20.00	110	—
1960D Proof	—	Value: 1,250				
1960F	1,576,000	—	7.00	20.00	135	—
1960F Proof	50	Value: 1,250				
1960G	692,000	—	7.00	22.00	125	—
1960G Proof	—	Value: 750				
1960J	1,618,000	—	7.00	18.00	90.00	—
1960J Proof	—	—	—	—	—	—
1961D	1,040,000	—	4.50	20.00	100	—
1961D Proof	—	Value: 450				
1961F	824,000	—	4.50	22.00	200	—
1961F Proof	—	Value: 2,200				
1961J	518,000	—	6.00	28.00	165	—
1961J Proof	—	Value: 3,000				
1963D	2,080,000	—	4.50	15.00	60.00	—
1963D Proof	—	—	—	—	—	—
1963F	1,254,000	—	4.50	18.00	75.00	—
1963F Proof	—	Value: 2,500				
1963G	600,000	—	7.50	20.00	90.00	—
1963G Proof	Est. 100	Value: 500				
1963J	2,136,000	—	4.50	15.00	60.00	—
1963J Proof	—	Value: 3,000				
1964D	456,000	—	15.00	50.00	175	—
1964D Proof	—	Value: 3,250				
1964F	2,646,000	—	4.50	15.00	60.00	—
1964F Proof	—	Value: 2,500				
1964G	1,649,000	—	4.50	15.00	60.00	—
1964G Proof	Est. 600	Value: 450				
1964J	1,335,000	—	4.00	15.00	65.00	—
1964J Proof	—	Value: 2,750				
1965D	4,354,000	—	4.00	12.50	30.00	—
1965D Proof	—	Value: 4,000				
1965F	4,050,000	—	4.00	8.00	30.00	—
1965F Proof	Est. 80	Value: 1,000				
1965G	2,335,000	—	4.00	7.00	25.00	—
1965G Proof	8,233	Value: 50.00				
1965J	3,605,000	—	4.00	7.00	25.00	—
1965J Proof	—	Value: 3,250				
1966D	5,200,000	—	4.00	7.00	22.50	—
1966D Proof	—	Value: 4,000				
1966F	6,000,000	—	4.00	7.00	22.50	—
1966F Proof	100	Value: 1,000				
1966G	3,460,000	—	4.00	7.00	22.50	—
1966G Proof	3,070	Value: 50.00				
1966J	5,340,000	—	4.00	7.00	22.50	—
1966J Proof	1,000	Value: 125				
1967D	3,120,000	—	4.00	7.00	22.50	—
1967D Proof	—	Value: 4,000				
1967F	3,598,000	—	4.00	7.00	22.50	—
1967F Proof	1,500	Value: 110				
1967G	1,406,000	—	4.00	7.00	25.00	—
1967G Proof	4,500	Value: 40.00				
1967J	3,204,000	—	4.00	7.00	22.50	—
Note: Errors exist with coin alignment						
1967J Proof	1,500	Value: 100				
1968D	1,300,000	—	4.00	10.00	35.00	—
1968D Proof	—	Value: 4,000				
1968F	1,497,000	—	4.00	10.00	35.00	—
1968F Proof	3,000	Value: 125				
1968G	1,535,000	—	4.00	10.00	35.00	—
1968G Proof	6,023	Value: 50.00				
1968J	1,335,000	—	4.00	10.00	35.00	—
1968J Proof	2,000	Value: 125				
1969D	2,080,000	—	4.00	7.00	20.00	—
1969D Proof	—	Value: 35.00				
1969F	2,395,000	—	4.00	7.00	20.00	—
1969F Proof	5,000	Value: 35.00				
1969G	3,484,000	—	4.00	7.00	20.00	—
1969G Proof	8,700	Value: 30.00				
1969J	2,136,000	—	4.00	7.00	20.00	—
1969J Proof	5,000	Value: 30.00				
1970D	2,000,000	—	4.00	7.00	20.00	—
1970D Proof	—	Value: 30.00				
1970F	1,995,000	—	4.00	7.00	20.00	—
1970F Proof	5,140	Value: 25.00				
1970G	6,000,000	—	3.50	4.50	10.00	—
1970G Proof	10,200	Value: 22.00				
1970J	4,000,000	—	3.50	4.50	10.00	—
1970J Proof	5,000	Value: 25.00				
1971D	4,000,000	—	3.50	4.50	10.00	—
1971D Proof	8,000	Value: 22.00				
1971F	3,993,000	—	3.50	4.50	10.00	—
1971F Proof	8,000	Value: 22.00				
1971G	6,010,000	—	3.50	4.50	10.00	—
1971G Proof	10,000	Value: 22.00				
1971J	6,000,000	—	3.50	4.50	10.00	—
1971J Proof	8,000	Value: 22.00				
1972D	3,000,000	—	3.50	4.50	12.00	—
1972D Proof	8,000	Value: 22.00				
1972F	8,992,000	—	3.50	4.50	10.00	—
1972F Proof	8,100	Value: 22.00				
1972G	4,999,000	—	3.50	4.50	10.00	—
1972G Proof	10,000	Value: 22.00				
1972J	6,000,000	—	3.50	4.50	10.00	—
1972J Proof	8,000	Value: 22.00				
1973D	3,380,000	—	3.50	4.50	10.00	—
1973D Proof	9,000	Value: 22.00				
1973F	3,891,000	—	3.50	4.50	8.50	—
1973F Proof	9,100	Value: 22.00				
1973G	2,240,000	—	3.50	4.50	8.50	—
1973G Proof	9,000	Value: 22.00				
1973J	5,571,000	—	3.50	4.50	8.50	—
1973J Proof	9,000	Value: 22.00				
1974D	4,594,000	—	3.50	4.50	8.50	—
1974D Proof	35,000	Value: 22.00				
1974F	6,514,000	—	3.50	4.50	8.50	—
1974F Proof	35,000	Value: 22.00				
1974G	3,708,000	—	3.50	4.50	8.50	—
1974G Proof	35,000	Value: 22.00				
1974J	2,968,000	—	3.50	4.50	8.50	—
1974J Proof	35,000	Value: 22.00				

KM# 112.2 5 MARK

11.2000 g., 0.6250 Silver .2250 oz. ASW, 29 mm. **Obv:** Denomination **Rev:** Large imperial eagle **Note:** Uninscribed plain edge errors.

Date	Mintage	F	VF	XF	Unc	BU
1959D	Inc. above	—	65.00	125	200	—
1959J	Inc. above	—	65.00	125	200	—
1963J	Inc. above	—	65.00	125	200	—
1964F	Inc. above	—	65.00	125	200	—
1964G	Inc. above	—	—	—	—	—
1965F	Inc. above	—	65.00	125	200	—
1965J	Inc. above	—	—	—	—	—
1965G	Inc. above	—	65.00	125	200	—
1966F	Inc. above	—	125	250	350	—
1966G	Inc. above	—	65.00	125	200	—
Note: Errors without edge inscription exist with coin alignment						
1967D	Inc. above	—	125	250	350	—
1967G	Inc. above	—	65.00	125	200	—
1969F	Inc. above	—	—	—	—	—
1970F	Inc. above	—	—	—	—	—
1970G	Inc. above	—	—	—	—	—
1971F	Inc. above	—	—	—	—	—
1972F	Inc. above	—	—	—	—	—
1973F	Inc. above	—	—	—	—	—
1974F	Inc. above	—	—	—	—	—

KM# 112.3 5 MARK

11.2000 g., 0.6250 Silver .2250 oz. ASW, 29 mm. **Obv:** Denomination **Rev:** Large imperial eagle **Note:** Error. With edge lettering: GRUSS DICH DEUTSCHLAND AUS HERZENSGRUND.

Date	Mintage	F	VF	XF	Unc	BU
1957J	Inc. above	—	1,250	1,650	2,400	—

KM# 112.4 5 MARK

11.2000 g., 0.6250 Silver .2250 oz. ASW, 29 mm. **Obv:** Denomination **Rev:** Large imperial eagle **Note:** Error. With edge lettering: ALLE MENSCHEN WERDEN BRUDER.

Date	Mintage	F	VF	XF	Unc	BU
1970F	—	—	1,250	1,650	2,400	—

KM# 140.3 5 MARK

10.0000 g., Copper-Nickel Clad Nickel, 29 mm. **Obv:** Denomination within rounded square **Rev:** Imperial eagle **Note:** Errors without edge inscription.

Date	Mintage	F	VF	XF	Unc	BU
1975D	—	—	—	—	—	—
1975F	—	—	—	—	—	—

KM# 140.1 5 MARK

10.0000 g., Copper-Nickel Clad Nickel, 29 mm. **Obv:** Denomination within rounded square **Rev:** Imperial eagle above date

Date	Mintage	F	VF	XF	Unc	BU
1975D	65,663,000	—	—	3.50	4.50	—
Note: Error strikes exist without edge inscription						
1975D Proof	43,000	Value: 7.00				
1975F	75,002,000	—	—	3.50	4.50	—
Note: Error strikes exist without edge inscription						
1975F Proof	43,000	Value: 7.00				
1975G	43,297,000	—	—	3.50	4.50	—
1975G Proof	43,000	Value: 7.00				
1975J	67,372,000	—	—	3.50	4.50	—
1975J Proof	43,000	Value: 7.00				
1976D	7,821,000	—	—	3.50	5.00	—
1976D Proof	43,000	Value: 7.00				
1976F	9,072,000	—	—	3.50	5.00	—
1976F Proof	43,000	Value: 7.00				
1976G	5,784,000	—	—	3.50	5.00	—
1976G Proof	43,000	Value: 7.00				
1976J	8,068,000	—	—	3.50	5.00	—
1976J Proof	43,000	Value: 7.00				
1977D	8,321,000	—	—	3.50	5.00	—
1977D Proof	51,000	Value: 6.00				
1977F	9,612,000	—	—	3.50	5.00	—
1977F Proof	51,000	Value: 6.00				
1977G	5,746,000	—	—	3.50	5.00	—
1977G Proof	51,000	Value: 6.00				
1977J	8,577,000	—	—	3.50	5.00	—
1977J Proof	51,000	Value: 6.00				
1978D	7,854,000	—	—	3.50	5.00	—
1978D Proof	54,000	Value: 6.00				
1978F	9,054,000	—	—	3.50	5.00	—
1978F Proof	54,000	Value: 6.00				
1978G	5,244,000	—	—	3.50	5.00	—
1978G Proof	54,000	Value: 6.00				
1978J	8,064,000	—	—	3.50	5.00	—
1978J Proof	54,000	Value: 6.00				
1979D	7,889,000	—	—	3.50	5.00	—
1979D Proof	89,000	Value: 6.00				
1979F	9,089,000	—	—	3.50	5.00	—
1979F Proof	89,000	Value: 6.00				
1979G	5,279,000	—	—	3.50	5.00	—
1979G Proof	89,000	Value: 6.00				
1979J	8,099,000	—	—	3.50	5.00	—
1979J Proof	89,000	Value: 6.00				
1980D	8,300,000	—	—	3.50	5.00	—
1980D Proof	110,000	Value: 6.00				
1980F	9,640,000	—	—	3.50	5.00	—
1980F Proof	110,000	Value: 6.00				
1980G	5,500,000	—	—	3.50	5.00	—
1980G Proof	110,000	Value: 6.00				
1980J	8,500,000	—	—	3.50	5.00	—
1980J Proof	110,000	Value: 6.00				
1981D	8,300,000	—	—	3.50	5.00	—
1981D Proof	91,000	Value: 7.00				
1981F	9,600,000	—	—	3.50	5.00	—
1981F Proof	91,000	Value: 7.00				
1981G	5,500,000	—	—	3.50	5.00	—
1981G Proof	91,000	Value: 7.00				
1981J	8,500,000	—	—	3.50	5.00	—
1981J Proof	91,000	Value: 7.00				
1982D	8,900,000	—	—	3.50	5.00	—
1982D Proof	78,000	Value: 7.00				
1982F	10,300,000	—	—	3.50	5.00	—
1982F Proof	78,000	Value: 7.00				
1982G	5,990,000	—	—	3.50	5.00	—
1982G Proof	78,000	Value: 7.00				
1982J	9,100,000	—	—	3.50	5.00	—
1982J Proof	78,000	Value: 7.00				
1983D	6,240,000	—	—	3.50	5.00	—
1983D Proof	75,000	Value: 9.00				
1983F	7,200,000	—	—	3.50	5.00	—
1983F Proof	75,000	Value: 9.00				
1983G	4,152,000	—	—	3.50	5.00	—
1983G Proof	75,000	Value: 9.00				
1983J	6,408,000	—	—	3.50	5.00	—
1983J Proof	75,000	Value: 9.00				
1984D	6,000,000	—	—	3.50	5.00	—
1984D Proof	64,000	Value: 9.00				
1984F	6,900,000	—	—	3.50	5.00	—
1984F Proof	64,000	Value: 9.00				
1984G	4,000,000	—	—	3.50	5.00	—
1984G Proof	64,000	Value: 9.00				
1984J	6,100,000	—	—	3.50	5.00	—
1984J Proof	64,000	Value: 9.00				
1985D	4,900,000	—	—	3.50	6.00	—
1985D Proof	56,000	Value: 10.00				
1985F	5,700,000	—	—	3.50	6.00	—
1985F Proof	54,000	Value: 10.00				
1985G	3,300,000	—	—	3.50	6.00	—
1985G Proof	55,000	Value: 10.00				
1985J	5,100,000	—	—	3.50	6.00	—
1985J Proof	54,000	Value: 10.00				
1986D	4,900,000	—	—	3.50	7.00	—
1986D Proof	44,000	Value: 20.00				
1986F	5,700,000	—	—	3.50	7.00	—
1986F Proof	44,000	Value: 20.00				
1986G	3,300,000	—	—	3.50	7.00	—
1986G Proof	44,000	Value: 25.00				
1986J	5,100,000	—	—	3.50	7.00	—
1986J Proof	44,000	Value: 20.00				
1987D	6,760,000	—	—	3.50	6.00	—
1987D Proof	45,000	Value: 10.00				
1987F	7,800,000	—	—	3.50	6.00	—
1987F Proof	45,000	Value: 10.00				
1987G	4,500,000	—	—	3.50	6.00	—
1987G Proof	45,000	Value: 10.00				
1987J	6,940,000	—	—	3.50	6.00	—
1987J Proof	45,000	Value: 10.00				
1988D	11,960,000	—	—	—	5.00	—
1988D Proof	45,000	Value: 12.00				
1988F	13,800,000	—	—	—	5.00	—
1988F Proof	45,000	Value: 12.00				
1988G	7,960,000	—	—	—	5.00	—
1988G Proof	45,000	Value: 12.00				
1988J	12,280,000	—	—	—	5.00	—
1988J Proof	45,000	Value: 12.00				
1989D	17,160,000	—	—	—	5.00	—
1989D Proof	45,000	Value: 12.00				
1989F	19,800,000	—	—	—	5.00	—
1989F Proof	45,000	Value: 12.00				
1989G	11,420,000	—	—	—	5.00	—
1989G Proof	45,000	Value: 12.00				
1989J	17,620,000	—	—	—	5.00	—
1989J Proof	45,000	Value: 12.00				
1990D	20,900,000	—	—	—	5.00	—
1990D Proof	45,000	Value: 10.00				
1990F	24,120,000	—	—	—	5.00	—
1990F Proof	45,000	Value: 10.00				
1990G	13,910,000	—	—	—	5.00	—
1990G Proof	45,000	Value: 10.00				
1990J	21,470,000	—	—	—	5.00	—
1990J Proof	45,000	Value: 10.00				
1991A	18,000,000	—	—	—	5.00	—
1991A Proof	45,000	Value: 7.00				
1991D	18,900,000	—	—	—	5.00	—
1991D Proof	45,000	Value: 7.00				
1991F	21,600,000	—	—	—	5.00	—
1991F Proof	45,000	Value: 7.00				
1991G	12,600,000	—	—	—	5.00	—
1991G Proof	45,000	Value: 7.00				
1991J	18,900,000	—	—	—	5.00	—
1991J Proof	45,000	Value: 7.00				
1992A	16,000,000	—	—	—	5.00	—
1992A Proof	45,000	Value: 7.00				
1992D	16,800,000	—	—	—	5.00	—
1992D Proof	45,000	Value: 7.00				
1992F	19,200,000	—	—	—	5.00	—
1992F Proof	45,000	Value: 7.00				
1992G	11,200,000	—	—	—	5.00	—
1992G Proof	45,000	Value: 7.00				
1992J	16,800,000	—	—	—	5.00	—
1992J Proof	45,000	Value: 7.00				
1993A	3,200,000	—	—	—	6.00	—
1993A Proof	45,000	Value: 10.00				
1993D	3,380,000	—	—	—	6.00	—
1993D Proof	45,000	Value: 10.00				
1993F	3,840,000	—	—	—	6.00	—
1993F Proof	45,000	Value: 10.00				
1993G	2,240,000	—	—	—	6.00	—
1993G Proof	45,000	Value: 10.00				
1993J	3,360,000	—	—	—	6.00	—
1993J Proof	45,000	Value: 10.00				
1994A	4,000,000	—	—	—	5.00	—
1994A Proof	45,000	Value: 10.00				
1994D	4,200,000	—	—	—	5.00	—
1994D Proof	45,000	Value: 10.00				
1994F	4,800,000	—	—	—	5.00	—
1994F Proof	45,000	Value: 10.00				
1994G	2,800,000	—	—	—	5.00	—
1994G Proof	45,000	Value: 10.00				
1994J	4,200,000	—	—	—	5.00	—
1994J Proof	45,000	Value: 10.00				
1995A	20,000	—	—	—	80.00	—
Note: In sets only						
1995A Proof	45,000	Value: 30.00				
1995D	20,000	—	—	—	80.00	—
Note: In sets only						
1995D Proof	45,000	Value: 30.00				
1995F	20,000	—	—	—	80.00	—
Note: In sets only						
1995F Proof	45,000	Value: 30.00				
1995G	20,000	—	—	—	80.00	—
Note: In sets only						
1995G Proof	45,000	Value: 30.00				
1995J	20,000	—	—	—	80.00	—
Note: In sets only						
1995J Proof	45,000	Value: 30.00				
1996A	50,000	—	—	—	15.00	—
Note: In sets only						
1996A Proof	45,000	Value: 17.50				
1996D	50,000	—	—	—	15.00	—
Note: In sets only						
1996D Proof	45,000	Value: 17.50				
1996F	50,000	—	—	—	15.00	—
Note: In sets only						
1996F Proof	45,000	Value: 17.50				
1996G	50,000	—	—	—	15.00	—
Note: In sets only						
1996G Proof	45,000	Value: 17.50				
1996J	50,000	—	—	—	15.00	—
Note: In sets only						
1996J Proof	45,000	Value: 17.50				
1997A	70,000	—	—	—	6.00	—
Note: In sets only						
1997A Proof	45,000	Value: 7.00				
1997D	70,000	—	—	—	6.00	—
Note: In sets only						
1997D Proof	45,000	Value: 7.00				
1997F	70,000	—	—	—	6.00	—
Note: In sets only						
1997F Proof	45,000	Value: 7.00				
1997G	70,000	—	—	—	6.00	—
Note: In sets only						
1997G Proof	45,000	Value: 7.00				
1997J	70,000	—	—	—	6.00	—
Note: In sets only						
1997J Proof	45,000	Value: 7.00				
1998A	70,000	—	—	—	6.00	—
Note: In sets only						
1998A Proof	45,000	Value: 7.00				
1998D	70,000	—	—	—	6.00	—
Note: In sets only						
1998D Proof	45,000	Value: 7.00				
1998F	70,000	—	—	—	6.00	—
Note: In sets only						
1998F Proof	45,000	Value: 7.00				
1998G	70,000	—	—	—	6.00	—
Note: In sets only						
1998G Proof	45,000	Value: 7.00				
1998J	70,000	—	—	—	6.00	—
Note: In sets only						
1998J Proof	45,000	Value: 7.00				
1999A	70,000	—	—	—	6.00	—
Note: In sets only						
1999A Proof	45,000	Value: 7.00				
1999D	70,000	—	—	—	6.00	—
Note: In sets only						
1999D Proof	45,000	Value: 7.00				
1999F	70,000	—	—	—	6.00	—
Note: In sets only						
1999F Proof	45,000	Value: 7.00				
1999G	70,000	—	—	—	6.00	—
Note: In sets only						
1999G Proof	45,000	Value: 7.00				
1999J	70,000	—	—	—	6.00	—
Note: In sets only						
1999J Proof	45,000	Value: 7.00				
2000A	70,000	—	—	—	15.00	—
Note: In sets only						
2000A Proof	45,000	Value: 15.00				
2000D	70,000	—	—	—	15.00	—
Note: In sets only						
2000D Proof	45,000	Value: 15.00				
2000F	70,000	—	—	—	15.00	—
Note: In sets only						
2000F Proof	45,000	Value: 15.00				
2000G	70,000	—	—	—	15.00	—
Note: In sets only						
2000G Proof	45,000	Value: 15.00				
2000J	70,000	—	—	—	15.00	—
Note: In sets only						
2000J Proof	45,000	Value: 15.00				

KM# 140.2 5 MARK

5.4400 g., Copper-Nickel Clad Nickel, 29 mm. **Obv:** Denomination within rounded square **Rev:** Imperial eagle **Note:** Thin variety.

Date	Mintage	F	VF	XF	Unc	BU
1975J	—	—	—	90.00	150	—
Note: Illegally produced by a German Mint official						

COMMEMORATIVE COINAGE

KM# 113 5 MARK

11.2000 g., 0.6250 Silver .2250 oz. ASW, 29 mm. **Subject:** Centenary - Nurnberg Museum **Obv:** Imperial eagle below legend **Rev:** Mosaic eagle divides dates

Date	Mintage	F	VF	XF	Unc	BU
1952D	199,000	—	500	700	800	1,200

Date	Mintage	F	VF	XF	Unc	BU
1952D Proof	1,345	Value: 4,000				

KM# 114 5 MARK

11.2000 g., 0.6250 Silver .2250 oz. ASW, 29 mm. **Subject:** 150th Anniversary - Death of Friedrich von Schiller **Obv:** Imperial eagle above denomination **Rev:** Head with high collar right **Edge Lettering:** SE10 EIN16 EIN16 EIN16

Date	Mintage	F	VF	XF	Unc	BU
1955F	199,000	—	260	400	700	800
1955F Proof	1,217	Value: 1,850				

KM# 115 5 MARK

11.2000 g., 0.6250 Silver .2250 oz. ASW, 29 mm. **Subject:** 300th Anniversary - Birth of Ludwig von Baden **Obv:** Imperial eagle above denomination, date below **Rev:** Bust, right

Date	Mintage	F	VF	XF	Unc	BU
1955G	198,000	—	260	400	600	600
1955G Proof	Est. 2,000	Value: 1,750				

Note: This coin was restruck without authorization by a mint official using genuine dies - quantity unknown

KM# 117 5 MARK

11.2000 g., 0.6250 Silver .2250 oz. ASW, 29 mm. **Subject:** Centenary - Death of Joseph Freiherr von Eichendorff **Obv:** Imperial eagle divides date at top, denomination below **Rev:** Head with high collar left, dates below

Date	Mintage	F	VF	XF	Unc	BU
1957J	198,000	—	200	380	500	600
1957J Proof	2,000	Value: 1,800				

KM# 118.1 5 MARK

11.2000 g., 0.6250 Silver .2250 oz. ASW, 29 mm. **Subject:** 150th Anniversary - Death of Johann Gottlieb Fichte, philosopher **Obv:** Imperial eagle divides date above denomination **Rev:** Head with high collar left, dates below

Date	Mintage	F	VF	XF	Unc	BU
1964J	495,000	—	50.00	75.00	125	—
1964J Proof	5,000	Value: 800				

KM# 118.2 5 MARK

11.2000 g., 0.6250 Silver .2250 oz. ASW, 29 mm. **Obv:** Imperial eagle above denomination **Rev:** Head with high collar left **Note:** Error. Plain edge.

Date	Mintage	F	VF	XF	Unc	BU
1964J	—	—	250	500	900	—

KM# 119.1 5 MARK

11.2000 g., 0.6250 Silver .2250 oz. ASW, 29 mm. **Subject:** 250th Anniversary - Death of Gottfried Wilhelm Leibniz, philosopher **Obv:** Imperial eagle divides date above, denomination below **Rev:** Head 3/4 facing, dates below

Date	Mintage	F	VF	XF	Unc	BU
1966D	1,940,000	—	7.00	12.00	15.00	20.00
1966D Proof	60,000	Value: 110				

KM# 119.2 5 MARK

11.2000 g., 0.6250 Silver .2250 oz. ASW, 29 mm. **Obv:** Imperial eagle divides date, denomination below **Rev:** Head 3/4 facing, dates **Note:** Error. Plain edge.

Date	Mintage	F	VF	XF	Unc	BU
1966D	—	—	225	425	700	—

KM# 120.1 5 MARK

11.2000 g., 0.6250 Silver .2250 oz. ASW, 29 mm. **Subject:** Wilhelm and Alexander von Humboldt **Obv:** Imperial eagle above denomination dividing date **Rev:** Conjoined heads; one left and one facing

Date	Mintage	F	VF	XF	Unc	BU
1967F	2,000,000	—	9.00	12.00	15.00	20.00
1967F Proof	60,000	Value: 140				

KM# 120.2 5 MARK

11.2000 g., 0.6250 Silver .2250 oz. ASW, 29 mm. **Obv:** Imperial eagle **Rev:** Conjoined heads; one left and one facing **Note:** Error. Plain edge.

Date	Mintage	F	VF	XF	Unc	BU
1967F	—	—	225	425	700	—

KM# 121 5 MARK

11.2000 g., 0.6250 Silver .2250 oz. ASW, 29 mm. **Subject:** 150th Anniversary - Birth of Friedrich Raiffeisen **Obv:** Imperial eagle above denomination and date **Rev:** Bust 3/4 facing, dates below

Date	Mintage	F	VF	XF	Unc	BU
1968J	3,860,000	—	3.00	4.50	6.00	8.00
1968J Proof	140,000	Value: 40.00				

KM# 122 5 MARK

11.2000 g., 0.6250 Silver .2250 oz. ASW, 29 mm. **Subject:** 500th Anniversary - Death of Johannes Gutenberg **Obv:** Denomination divides date, imperial eagle above **Rev:** Bust 3/4 right, dates below

Date	Mintage	F	VF	XF	Unc	BU
1968G	2,900,000	—	3.50	7.00	9.00	11.00
1968G Proof	100,000	Value: 70.00				

KM# 123.1 5 MARK

11.2000 g., 0.6250 Silver .2250 oz. ASW, 29 mm. **Subject:** 150th Anniversary - Birth of Max von Pettenkofer **Obv:** Stylized imperial eagle, denomination above **Rev:** Face 3/4 left, dates below

Date	Mintage	F	VF	XF	Unc	BU
1968D	2,900,000	—	3.50	7.00	9.00	11.00
1968D Proof	100,000	Value: 50.00				

KM# 123.2 5 MARK

11.2000 g., 0.6250 Silver .2250 oz. ASW, 29 mm. **Obv:** Stylized imperial eagle, denomination above **Rev:** Face 3/4 left **Note:** Polished devices.

Date	Mintage	F	VF	XF	Unc	BU
1968D Proof	—	Value: 300				

KM# 125.1 5 MARK

11.2000 g., 0.6250 Silver .2250 oz. ASW, 29 mm. **Subject:** 150th Anniversary - Birth of Theodor Fontane, writer, poet **Obv:** Imperial eagle divides date, denomination below **Rev:** Head left

Date	Mintage	F	VF	XF	Unc	BU
1969G	2,830,000	—	3.50	7.00	9.00	11.00
1969G Proof	170,000	Value: 35.00				

KM# 125.2 5 MARK

11.2000 g., 0.6250 Silver .2250 oz. ASW, 29 mm. **Obv:** Imperial eagle divides date, denomination below **Rev:** Head left **Note:** Error. Incomplete nose and hair.

Date	Mintage	F	VF	XF	Unc	BU
1969G Proof	—	Value: 140				

KM# 126.1 5 MARK

11.2000 g., 0.6250 Silver .2250 oz. ASW, 29 mm. **Subject:** 375th Anniversary - Death of Gerhard Mercator **Obv:** Imperial eagle, denomination divides date below **Rev:** Bust with long beard 3/4 right

Date	Mintage	F	VF	XF	Unc	BU
1969F	5,004,000	—	—	—	5.00	6.00
1969F Proof	200,000	Value: 20.00				

KM# 126.2 5 MARK

11.2000 g., 0.6250 Silver .2250 oz. ASW, 29 mm. **Obv:** Imperial eagle, denomination divides date below **Rev:** Bust with long beard 3/4 right **Note:** Error. Plain edge.

Date	Mintage	F	VF	XF	Unc	BU
1969F	—	—	250	450	750	—

KM# 126.3 5 MARK

11.2000 g., 0.6250 Silver .2250 oz. ASW, 29 mm. **Obv:** Imperial eagle, denomination divides date below **Rev:** Bust with long beard 3/4 right **Note:** Error. With edge lettering: Einigkeit und Recht und Freiheit.

Date	Mintage	F	VF	XF	Unc	BU
1969F	—	—	600	1,000	1,600	—

KM# 126.4 5 MARK

11.2000 g., 0.6250 Silver .2250 oz. ASW, 29 mm. **Obv:** Imperial eagle, denomination divides date below **Rev:** Bust with long beard 3/4 right **Note:** Error. With long "R" in "MERCATOR".

Date	Mintage	F	VF	XF	Unc	BU
1969F	—	—	25.00	55.00	100	—

KM# 127 5 MARK
11.2000 g., 0.6250 Silver .2250 oz. ASW, 29 mm. **Subject:** 200th Anniversary - Birth of Ludwig van Beethoven, composer **Obv:** Imperial eagle, denomination divides date below **Rev:** Head left, dates below

Date	Mintage	F	VF	XF	Unc	BU
1970F	5,000,000	—	—	3.50	6.00	7.00
1970F Proof	200,000	Value: 18.00				

KM# 129 5 MARK
11.2000 g., 0.6250 Silver .2250 oz. ASW, 29 mm. **Subject:** 500th Anniversary - Birth of Albrecht Durer **Obv:** Imperial eagle above inscription, date and denomination below **Rev:** Initials above name and dates

Date	Mintage	F	VF	XF	Unc	BU
1971D	8,000,000	—	—	—	4.00	6.00
1971D Proof	200,000	Value: 27.50				

KM# 128.1 5 MARK
11.2000 g., 0.6250 Silver .2250 oz. ASW, 29 mm. **Subject:** Foundation of German Reich 1871 **Obv:** Imperial eagle divides date above legend, denomination below **Rev:** Domed building

Date	Mintage	F	VF	XF	Unc	BU
1971G	5,000,000	—	3.50	5.00	6.00	7.00
1971G Proof	200,000	Value: 20.00				

KM# 128.2 5 MARK
11.2000 g., 0.6250 Silver .2250 oz. ASW, 29 mm. **Obv:** Imperial eagle divides date above legend **Rev:** Domed building **Note:** Error. With weak window details.

Date	Mintage	F	VF	XF	Unc	BU
1971F Proof	—	Value: 100				

KM# 136 5 MARK
11.2000 g., 0.6250 Silver .2250 oz. ASW, 29 mm. **Subject:** 500th Anniversary - Birth of Nicholas Copernicus **Obv:** Imperial eagle in grid form, denomination divides date below **Rev:** Sun at center of rings, planet names descend from top towards center

Date	Mintage	F	VF	XF	Unc	BU
1973J	8,000,000	—	—	—	6.00	7.00
1973J Proof	250,000	Value: 12.00				

KM# 137 5 MARK
11.2000 g., 0.6250 Silver .2250 oz. ASW, 29 mm. **Subject:** 125th Anniversary - Frankfurt Parliament **Obv:** Denomination below stylized imperial eagle divides date **Rev:** Date at center of Parliament building

Date	Mintage	F	VF	XF	Unc	BU
1973G	8,000,000	—	—	—	6.00	7.00
1973G Proof	250,000	Value: 12.00				

KM# 138 5 MARK
11.2000 g., 0.6250 Silver .2250 oz. ASW, 29 mm. **Subject:** 25th Anniversary - Constitutional Law **Obv:** Fat imperial eagle above date divided by denomination **Rev:** Symbol divides dates

Date	Mintage	F	VF	XF	Unc	BU
1974F	8,000,000	—	—	—	6.00	7.00
1974F Proof	250,000	Value: 12.00				

KM# 139 5 MARK
11.2000 g., 0.6250 Silver .2250 oz. ASW, 29 mm. **Subject:** 250th Anniversary - Birth of Immanuel Kant, philosopher **Obv:** Legend divides imperial eagle and denmination **Rev:** Bust at left facing right, name and dates at right

Date	Mintage	F	VF	XF	Unc	BU
1974D	8,000,000	—	—	—	6.00	7.00
1974D Proof	250,000	Value: 14.00				

KM# 143 5 MARK
5.3000 g., 0.6250 Silver .2250 oz. ASW, 29 mm. **Subject:** Centenary - Birth of Albert Schweitzer **Obv:** Imperial eagle above denomination **Rev:** Head facing, dates at right

Date	Mintage	F	VF	XF	Unc	BU
1975G	8,000,000	—	—	—	6.00	7.00
1975G Proof	250,000	Value: 14.00				

KM# 141 5 MARK
11.2000 g., 0.6250 Silver .2250 oz. ASW, 29 mm. **Subject:** 50th Anniversary - Death of Friedrich Ebert **Obv:** Imperial eagle above denomination, date at right **Rev:** Head left, dates at left

Date	Mintage	F	VF	XF	Unc	BU
1975J	8,000,000	—	—	—	6.00	7.00
1975J Proof	250,000	Value: 14.00				

KM# 142.1 5 MARK
11.2000 g., 0.6250 Silver .2250 oz. ASW, 29 mm. **Subject:** European Monument Protection Year **Obv:** Imperial eagle divides date at top, denomination below **Rev:** Patterned designs and two line inscription with date **Note:** 2.1 mm thick.

Date	Mintage	F	VF	XF	Unc	BU
1975F	8,000,000	—	—	—	6.00	7.00
1975F Proof	250,000	Value: 12.00				

KM# 142.2 5 MARK
5.3000 g., 0.6250 Silver .2250 oz. ASW, 29 mm. **Obv:** Imperial eagle divides date at top **Rev:** Patterned design **Note:** 1.4 mm thick.

Date	Mintage	F	VF	XF	Unc	BU
1975F	Inc. above	—	—	—	10.00	11.00

KM# 144 5 MARK
5.3000 g., 0.6250 Silver .2250 oz. ASW, 29 mm. **Subject:** 300th Anniversary - Death of von Grimmelshausen **Obv:** Imperial eagle above denomination, date at left **Rev:** Mythic figure with book left, dates divided above

Date	Mintage	F	VF	XF	Unc	BU
1976D	8,000,000	—	—	—	6.00	7.00
1976D Proof	250,000	Value: 18.00				

KM# 145 5 MARK
5.3000 g., 0.6250 Silver .2250 oz. ASW, 29 mm. **Subject:** 200th Anniversary - Birth of Carl Friedrich Gauss **Obv:** Imperial eagle above date and denomination **Rev:** Head 3/4 facing, dates at right

Date	Mintage	F	VF	XF	Unc	BU
1977J	8,000,000	—	—	—	6.00	7.00
1977J Proof	250,000	Value: 18.00				

KM# 146 5 MARK
5.3000 g., 0.6250 Silver .2250 oz. ASW, 29 mm. **Subject:** 200th Anniversary - Birth of Heinrich von Kleist **Obv:** Imperial eagle above denomination **Rev:** Bust 3/4 left, dates below

Date	Mintage	F	VF	XF	Unc	BU
1977G	8,000,000	—	—	—	6.00	7.00
1977G Proof	250,000	Value: 16.00				

KM# 147 5 MARK
5.3000 g., 0.6250 Silver .2250 oz. ASW, 29 mm. **Subject:** 100th Anniversary - Birth of Gustav Stresemann **Obv:** Imperial eagle above denomination **Rev:** Head left, dates at left

Date	Mintage	F	VF	XF	Unc	BU
1978D	8,000,000	—	—	—	6.00	7.00
1978D Proof	250,000	Value: 14.00				

KM# 148 5 MARK
5.3000 g., 0.6250 Silver .2250 oz. ASW, 29 mm. **Subject:** 225th Anniversary - Death of Balthasar Neumann **Obv:** Imperial eagle above denomination **Rev:** Interior of Vierzehnheiligen

Date	Mintage	F	VF	XF	Unc	BU
1978F	8,000,000	—	—	—	6.00	7.00
1978F Proof	259,000	Value: 12.00				

KM# 150 5 MARK
5.3000 g., 0.6250 Silver .2250 oz. ASW, 29 mm. **Subject:** 150th Anniversary - German Archaeological Institute **Obv:** Denomination divides date, imperial eagle above

Date	Mintage	F	VF	XF	Unc	BU
1979J	8,000,000	—	—	—	6.00	7.00
1979J Proof	250,000	Value: 14.00				

KM# 151 5 MARK
10.0000 g., Copper-Nickel Clad Nickel, 29 mm. **Subject:** 100th Anniversary - Birth of Otto Hahn **Obv:** Stylized eagle above legend **Rev:** Symbols of Hahn's studies in chemistry, name and dates below

Date	Mintage	F	VF	XF	Unc	BU
1979G	5,000,000	—	—	3.50	5.00	6.00
1979G Proof	350,000	Value: 11.00				

KM# 151a 5 MARK
11.2000 g., 0.6250 Silver .2250 oz. ASW, 29 mm. **Obv:** Stylized eagle above legend **Rev:** Chemistry symbols, name and date below

Date	Mintage	F	VF	XF	Unc	BU
1979G	18	—	—	—	22,500	—

KM# 152 5 MARK
10.0000 g., Copper-Nickel Clad Nickel, 29 mm. **Subject:** 750th Anniversary - Death of von der Vogelweide **Obv:** Imperial eagle in statue form above date divided by denomination **Rev:** Sleeping half figure with paper, dates below

Date	Mintage	F	VF	XF	Unc	BU
1980D	5,000,000	—	—	3.50	5.00	6.00
1980D Proof	350,000	Value: 11.50				

KM# 153 5 MARK
10.0000 g., Copper-Nickel Clad Nickel, 29 mm. **Subject:** 100th Anniversary - Cologne Cathedral **Obv:** Imperial eagle, narrow design **Rev:** Cathedral

Date	Mintage	F	VF	XF	Unc	BU
1980F	5,000,000	—	—	4.00	5.00	6.00
1980F Proof	350,000	Value: 13.50				

KM# 154 5 MARK
10.0000 g., Copper-Nickel Clad Nickel, 29 mm. **Subject:** 200th Anniversary - Death of Gotthold Ephraim Lessing **Obv:** Denomination divides date below imperial eagle **Rev:** Bust in silhouette left

Date	Mintage	F	VF	XF	Unc	BU
1981J	6,500,000	—	—	—	4.00	5.00
1981J Proof	350,000	Value: 10.00				

KM# 155 5 MARK
10.0000 g., Copper-Nickel Clad Nickel, 29 mm. **Subject:** 150th Anniversary - Death of Carl vom Stein **Obv:** Imperial eagle in relief, denomination divides date below **Rev:** Bust 3/4 facing, dates at right

Date	Mintage	F	VF	XF	Unc	BU
1981G	6,500,000	—	—	—	4.00	5.00
1981G Proof	350,000	Value: 10.00				

KM# 156 5 MARK
10.0000 g., Copper-Nickel Clad Nickel, 29 mm. **Subject:** 150th Anniversary - Death of Johann Wolfgang von Goethe **Obv:** Imperial eagle above denomination, date at right **Rev:** Head right, dates below

Date	Mintage	F	VF	XF	Unc	BU
1982D	8,000,000	—	—	—	4.00	5.00
1982D Proof	350,000	Value: 11.50				

KM# 157 5 MARK
10.0000 g., Copper-Nickel Clad Nickel, 29 mm. **Subject:** 10th Anniversary - U.N. Environmental Conference **Obv:** Imperial eagle above denomination **Rev:** Stylized figure in center of design, date above

Date	Mintage	F	VF	XF	Unc	BU
1982F	8,000,000	—	—	—	4.00	5.00
1982F Proof	350,000	Value: 10.00				

KM# 158 5 MARK
10.0000 g., Copper-Nickel Clad Nickel, 29 mm. **Subject:** 100th Anniversary - Death of Karl Marx **Obv:** Imperial eagle in relief above denomination **Rev:** Head 3/4 facing, dates below

Date	Mintage	F	VF	XF	Unc	BU
1983J	8,000,000	—	—	—	4.00	5.00
1983J Proof	350,000	Value: 10.00				

KM# 159 5 MARK
10.0000 g., Copper-Nickel Clad Nickel, 29 mm. **Subject:** 500th Anniversary - Birth of Martin Luther **Obv:** Imperial eagle, denomination below divides date **Rev:** Inscription covers head 3/4 right

Date	Mintage	F	VF	XF	Unc	BU
1983G	8,000,000	—	—	—	4.00	5.00
1983G Proof	350,000	Value: 12.00				

KM# 160 5 MARK
10.0000 g., Copper-Nickel Clad Nickel, 29 mm. **Subject:** 150th Anniversary - German Customs Union **Obv:** Imperial eagle, denomination divides date below **Rev:** Horses and carriage

Date	Mintage	F	VF	XF	Unc	BU
1984D	8,000,000	—	—	—	4.00	5.00
1984D Proof	350,000	Value: 11.50				

KM# 161 5 MARK
10.0000 g., Copper-Nickel Clad Nickel, 29 mm. **Subject:** 175th Anniversary - Birth of Felix Bartholdy **Obv:** Imperial eagle above denomination **Rev:** 3/4 figure looking left, left hand on hip, music score in background

Date	Mintage	F	VF	XF	Unc	BU
1984J	8,000,000	—	—	—	4.00	5.00
1984J Proof	350,000	Value: 12.50				

KM# 162 5 MARK
10.0000 g., Copper-Nickel Clad Nickel, 29 mm. **Subject:** European Year of Music **Obv:** Stylized imperial eagle in circle at left, denomination at right, date above **Rev:** Circle at left holds stars and outline of face in harp, music notes at right

Date	Mintage	F	VF	XF	Unc	BU
1985F	8,000,000	—	—	—	4.00	5.00
1985F Proof	350,000	Value: 11.50				

KM# 163 5 MARK
10.0000 g., Copper-Nickel Clad Nickel, 29 mm. **Subject:** 150th Anniversary - German Railroad **Obv:** Stylized imperial eagle above denomination **Rev:** Spoked design

Date	Mintage	F	VF	XF	Unc	BU
1985G	8,000,000	—	—	—	4.00	5.00
1985G Proof	350,000	Value: 10.00				

KM# 164 5 MARK
10.0000 g., Copper-Nickel Clad Nickel, 29 mm. **Subject:** 600th Anniversary - Heidelberg University **Obv:** Denomination divides date below imperial eagle **Rev:** Crowned rampant lion left within legend

Date	Mintage	F	VF	XF	Unc	BU
1986D	8,000,000	—	—	—	4.00	5.00
1986D Proof	350,000	Value: 10.00				

KM# 165 5 MARK
10.0000 g., Copper-Nickel Clad Nickel, 29 mm. **Subject:** 200th Anniversary - Death of Frederick the Great **Obv:** Imperial eagle above denomination **Rev:** Uniformed bust left, dates below

Date	Mintage	F	VF	XF	Unc	BU
1986F	8,000,000	—	—	—	4.00	5.00
1986F Proof	350,000	Value: 12.50				

KM# 130 10 MARK
15.5000 g., 0.6250 Silver .3115 oz. ASW, 33 mm. **Series:** Munich Olympics **Obv:** Artistic imperial eagle, denomination below **Rev:** "In Deutschland" with spiraling symbol

Date	Mintage	F	VF	XF	Unc	BU
1972D	2,500,000	—	—	—	7.50	10.00
1972D Proof	125,000	Value: 26.00				
1972F	2,375,000	—	—	—	7.50	10.00
1972F Proof	125,000	Value: 26.00				
1972G	2,500,000	—	—	—	7.50	10.00
1972G Proof	125,000	Value: 26.00				
1972J	2,500,000	—	—	—	7.50	10.00
1972J Proof	125,000	Value: 26.00				

KM# 131 10 MARK
15.5000 g., 0.6250 Silver .3115 oz. ASW, 33 mm. **Series:** Munich Olympics **Obv:** Imperial eagle above denomination **Rev:** Schleife (knot)

Date	Mintage	F	VF	XF	Unc	BU
1972D	5,000,000	—	—	—	7.50	10.00
1972D Proof	125,000	Value: 20.00				
1972F	4,875,000	—	—	—	7.50	10.00
1972F Proof	125,000	Value: 20.00				
1972G	5,000,000	—	—	—	7.50	10.00
1972G Proof	125,000	Value: 20.00				
1972J	5,000,000	—	—	—	7.50	10.00
1972J Proof	125,000	Value: 20.00				

KM# 132 10 MARK
15.5000 g., 0.6250 Silver .3115 oz. ASW, 33 mm. **Series:** Munich Olympics **Obv:** Imperial eagle above denomination **Rev:** Athletes kneeling

Date	Mintage	F	VF	XF	Unc	BU
1972D	5,000,000	—	—	—	7.00	9.00
1972D Proof	150,000	Value: 16.00				
1972F	4,850,000	—	—	—	7.00	9.00
1972F Proof	150,000	Value: 16.00				
1972G	5,000,000	—	—	—	7.00	9.00
1972G Proof	150,000	Value: 16.00				
1972J	5,000,000	—	—	—	7.00	9.00
1972J Proof	150,000	Value: 16.00				

KM# 133 10 MARK
15.5000 g., 0.6250 Silver .3115 oz. ASW, 33 mm. **Series:** Munich Olympics **Obv:** Imperial eagle above denomination **Rev:** Stadium - aerial view

Date	Mintage	F	VF	XF	Unc	BU
1972D	5,000,000	—	—	—	7.00	9.00
1972D Proof	150,000	Value: 16.00				
1972F	4,850,000	—	—	—	7.00	9.00
1972F Proof	150,000	Value: 16.00				
1972G	5,000,000	—	—	—	7.00	9.00
1972G Proof	150,000	Value: 16.00				
1972J	5,000,000	—	—	—	7.00	9.00
1972J Proof	150,000	Value: 16.00				

KM# 134.1 10 MARK
15.5000 g., 0.6250 Silver .3115 oz. ASW, 33 mm. **Series:** Munich Olympics **Obv:** Imperial eagle above denomination **Rev:** "In Munchen" - with spiral symbol **Edge:** Lettering separated by periods

Date	Mintage	F	VF	XF	Unc	BU
1972D	2,500,000	—	—	—	7.50	10.00
1972D Proof	150,000	Value: 20.00				
1972F	2,350,000	—	—	—	7.50	10.00
1972F Proof	150,000	Value: 20.00				
1972G	2,500,000	—	—	—	7.50	10.00
1972G Proof	150,000	Value: 20.00				
1972J	2,500,000	—	—	—	7.50	10.00
1972J Proof	150,000	Value: 20.00				

KM# 134.2 10 MARK
15.5000 g., 0.6250 Silver .3115 oz. ASW, 33 mm. **Obv:** Imperial eagle above denomination **Rev:** Spiral design **Edge:** Lettering separated by arabesques **Note:** Error.

Date	Mintage	F	VF	XF	Unc	BU
1972D	—	—	—	—	2,760	—
1972F	—	—	—	—	2,760	—
1972G	—	—	—	—	2,760	—
1972J	600	—	200	300	550	—

KM# 135 10 MARK
15.5000 g., 0.6250 Silver .3115 oz. ASW, 33 mm. **Series:** Munich Olympics **Obv:** Imperial eagle above denomination **Rev:** Olympic Flame, spiral symbol above, rings divide date below

Date	Mintage	F	VF	XF	Unc	BU
1972D	5,000,000	—	—	—	7.00	9.00
1972D Proof	150,000	Value: 16.00				
1972F	4,850,000	—	—	—	7.00	9.00
1972F Proof	150,000	Value: 16.00				
1972G	5,000,000	—	—	—	7.00	9.00
1972G Proof	150,000	Value: 16.00				
1972J	5,000,000	—	—	—	7.00	9.00
1972J Proof	150,000	Value: 16.00				

KM# 166 10 MARK
15.5000 g., 0.6250 Silver .3115 oz. ASW, 33 mm. **Subject:** 750th Anniversary - Berlin **Obv:** Imperial eagle above denomination **Rev:** Bear at right holding circular shield

Date	Mintage	F	VF	XF	Unc	BU
1987J	8,000,000	—	—	—	9.00	11.00
1987J Proof	350,000	Value: 70.00				

KM# 167 10 MARK
15.5000 g., 0.6250 Silver .3115 oz. ASW, 33 mm. **Subject:** 30 Years of European Unity **Obv:** Imperial eagle above denomination **Rev:** Horses pulling 30 year symbol, dates at right

Date	Mintage	F	VF	XF	Unc	BU
1987G	8,000,000	—	—	—	7.00	9.00
1987G Proof	350,000	Value: 40.00				

KM# 168 10 MARK
15.5000 g., 0.6250 Silver .3115 oz. ASW, 33 mm. **Subject:** 200th Anniversary - Birth of Arthur Schopenhauer **Obv:** Imperial eagle above denomination **Rev:** Head facing, dates below left

Date	Mintage	F	VF	XF	Unc	BU
1988D	8,000,000	—	—	—	7.00	9.00
1988D Proof	350,000	Value: 30.00				

KM# 169 10 MARK
15.5000 g., 0.6250 Silver .3115 oz. ASW, 33 mm. **Subject:** 100th Anniversary - Death of Carl Zeiss **Obv:** Imperial eagle above denomination **Rev:** Head at left, looking right

Date	Mintage	F	VF	XF	Unc	BU
1988F	8,000,000	—	—	—	7.00	9.00
1988F Proof	350,000	Value: 30.00				

KM# 171 10 MARK
15.5000 g., 0.6250 Silver .3115 oz. ASW, 33 mm. **Subject:** 800th Year - Port of Hamburg **Obv:** Small imperial eagle above denomination **Rev:** Three towered gated building, waves in front

Date	Mintage	F	VF	XF	Unc	BU
1989J	8,000,000	—	—	—	7.00	9.00
1989J Proof	350,000	Value: 25.00				

KM# 172 10 MARK
15.5000 g., 0.6250 Silver .3115 oz. ASW, 33 mm. **Subject:** 2000th Anniversary - City of Bonn **Obv:** Imperial eagle above denomination **Rev:** Building left of sun design

Date	Mintage	F	VF	XF	Unc	BU
1989D	8,000,000	—	—	—	7.00	9.00
1989D Proof	350,000	Value: 25.00				

KM# 173 10 MARK
15.5000 g., 0.6250 Silver .3115 oz. ASW, 33 mm. **Subject:** 40th Anniversary - Republic **Obv:** Lines make up imperial eagle above date and denomination **Rev:** Eleven shields form a circle

Date	Mintage	F	VF	XF	Unc	BU
1989G	8,000,000	—	—	—	7.00	9.00
1989G Proof	350,000	Value: 30.00				

KM# 174 10 MARK
15.5000 g., 0.6250 Silver .3115 oz. ASW, 33 mm. **Subject:** 800th Anniversary - Death of Kaiser Friedrich Barbarossa **Obv:** Imperial eagle above denomination **Rev:** Crowned figure with royal orb and scepter rising above castle walls, dates below

Date	Mintage	F	VF	XF	Unc	BU
1990F	7,850,000	—	—	—	7.00	9.00
1990F Proof	400,000	Value: 20.00				

KM# 176 10 MARK
15.5000 g., 0.6250 Silver .3115 oz. ASW, 33 mm. **Subject:** 800th Anniversary - The Teutonic Order **Obv:** Imperial eagle above denomination **Rev:** Wrinkled page with Madonna and child pictured, shield upper left

Date	Mintage	F	VF	XF	Unc	BU
1990J	8,850,000	—	—	—	7.00	9.00
1990J Proof	450,000	Value: 12.50				

KM# 177 10 MARK
15.5000 g., 0.6250 Silver .3115 oz. ASW, 33 mm. **Subject:** German Unity **Obv:** Imperial eagle above denomination **Rev:** Brandenburg Gate in Berlin

Date	Mintage	F	VF	XF	Unc	BU
1991A	8,850,000	—	—	—	7.00	9.00
1991A Proof	450,000	Value: 17.50				

KM# 178 10 MARK
15.5000 g., 0.6250 Silver .3115 oz. ASW, 33 mm. **Subject:** 125th Anniversary - Birth of Kathe Kollwitz - Artist and Sculptor **Obv:** Denomination divides date below imperial eagle **Rev:** Figure at easel drawing, dates below

Date	Mintage	F	VF	XF	Unc	BU
1992G	8,450,000	—	—	—	7.00	9.00
1992G Proof	450,000	Value: 12.00				

KM# 179 10 MARK
15.5000 g., 0.6250 Silver .3115 oz. ASW, 33 mm. **Subject:** 150th Anniversary - Civil Pour-le-Merite Order **Obv:** Imperial eagle above denomination, date at left **Rev:** Alexander von Humbolt, 1st chancellor of the Order

Date	Mintage	F	VF	XF	Unc	BU
1992D	8,450,000	—	—	—	7.00	9.00
1992D Proof	450,000	Value: 12.00				

KM# 180 10 MARK
15.5000 g., 0.6250 Silver .3115 oz. ASW, 33 mm. **Subject:** 1000th Anniversary - Potsdam **Obv:** Imperial eagle above denomination, date at left **Rev:** Palace of Sanssouci and Nicolai Church

Date	Mintage	F	VF	XF	Unc	BU
1993F	7,950,000	—	—	—	7.00	9.00
1993F Proof	450,000	Value: 12.00				

KM# 181 10 MARK
15.5000 g., 0.6250 Silver .3115 oz. ASW, 33 mm. **Subject:** 150th Birth Anniversary of Robert Koch **Obv:** Imperial eagle above denomination **Rev:** Head 3/4 facing

Date	Mintage	F	VF	XF	Unc	BU
1993J	7,450,000	—	—	—	7.00	9.00
1993J Proof	450,000	Value: 12.00				

KM# 182 10 MARK
15.5000 g., 0.6250 Silver .3115 oz. ASW, 33 mm. **Subject:** Attempt on Hitler's Life, July 20, 1944 **Obv:** Imperial eagle above denomination **Rev:** Wing with chain surrounding, date below

Date	Mintage	F	VF	XF	Unc	BU
1994A	7,450,000	—	—	—	7.00	9.00
1994A Proof	450,000	Value: 20.00				

KM# 184 10 MARK
15.5000 g., 0.6250 Silver .3115 oz. ASW, 33 mm. **Subject:** 250th Birth Anniversary- Johann Gottfried Herder **Obv:** Imperial eagle, denomination at left and below **Rev:** Head looking right, shadow head behind

Date	Mintage	F	VF	XF	Unc	BU
1994G	7,450,000	—	—	—	7.00	9.00
1994G Proof	450,000	Value: 12.00				

KM# 185 10 MARK
15.5000 g., 0.6250 Silver .3115 oz. ASW, 33 mm. **Subject:** 50th Anniversary of Peace and Reconciliation **Obv:** Imperial eagle

above denomination and date **Rev:** Ruins of Frauen Kirche in Dresden **Edge Lettering:** STEINERNE GLOCKE SYMBOL FUER TOLERANZ

Date	Mintage	F	VF	XF	Unc	BU
1995J	7,450,000	—	—	—	7.00	9.00
1995J Proof	450,000	Value: 12.00				

KM# 186 10 MARK

15.5000 g., 0.6250 Silver .3115 oz. ASW, 33 mm. **Subject:** 500th Anniversary of death - Henry the Lion **Obv:** Thin imperial eagle divides date and denomination **Rev:** Artistic rampant lion, left **Edge Lettering:** HEINRICH DER LOEWE AUS KAISERLICHEM STAMM

Date	Mintage	F	VF	XF	Unc	BU
1995F	7,450,000	—	—	—	7.00	9.00
1995F Proof	450,000	Value: 12.00				

KM# 187 10 MARK

15.5000 g., 0.6250 Silver .3115 oz. ASW, 33 mm. **Subject:** 150th Birth Anniversary - Wilhelm Conrad Rontgen; 100th Anniversary of x-ray **Obv:** Imperial eagle divides date and denomination **Rev:** Hand and X-rayed hand **Edge Lettering:** ERSTER NOBEL PREIS FUER PHYSIK

Date	Mintage	F	VF	XF	Unc	BU
1995D	6,900,000	—	—	—	7.00	9.00
1995D Proof	450,000	Value: 12.00				

KM# 188 10 MARK

15.5000 g., 0.6250 Silver .3115 oz. ASW, 33 mm. **Subject:** 150th Anniversary of founding - Kolpingwerk **Obv:** Sectioned imperial eagle, denomination at left and below **Rev:** Globe in background, face in triangle at right, three pictures in rectangle at left **Edge Lettering:** TAETIGE LIEBE HEILT ALLE WUNDEN

Date	Mintage	F	VF	XF	Unc	BU
1996A	5,600,000	—	—	—	7.00	9.00
1996A Proof	400,000	Value: 12.00				

KM# 189.1 10 MARK

15.5000 g., 0.6250 Silver .3115 oz. ASW, 33 mm. **Subject:** 500th Birth Anniversary - Philipp Melanchthon **Obv:** Stylized eagle above denomination **Rev:** Bust left, dates at right

Date	Mintage	F	VF	XF	Unc	BU
1997A Proof	150,000	Value: 17.50				
1997D Proof	150,000	Value: 17.50				
1997F Proof	150,000	Value: 17.50				
1997G Proof	150,000	Value: 17.50				
1997J	3,000,000	—	—	—	9.00	11.00
1997J Proof	150,000	Value: 17.50				

KM# 189.2 10 MARK

15.5000 g., 0.6250 Silver .3115 oz. ASW, 33 mm. **Subject:** 500th Birth Anniversary - Philipp Melanchthon **Obv:** Stylized eagle, denomination **Rev:** Different forelock on portrait

Date	Mintage	F	VF	XF	Unc	BU
1997J	—	—	—	—	9.00	11.00
1997J Proof	—	Value: 20.00				

KM# 190 10 MARK

15.5000 g., 0.6250 Silver .3115 oz. ASW, 33 mm. **Subject:** 200th Birth Anniversary - Heinrich Heine **Obv:** Stylized eagle, denomination below **Rev:** Half figure 3/4 left with handwritten text in background **Edge Lettering:** DEUTSCHLAND DASSIND WIR SELBER **Designer:** Reinhart Heinsdorff

Date	Mintage	F	VF	XF	Unc	BU
1997A Proof	150,000	Value: 22.50				
1997D	3,000,000	—	—	—	9.00	—
1997D Proof	750,000	Value: 22.50				
1997F Proof	150,000	Value: 22.50				
1997G Proof	150,000	Value: 22.50				
1997J Proof	150,000	Value: 22.50				

KM# 192 10 MARK

15.5000 g., 0.6250 Silver .3115 oz. ASW, 33 mm. **Subject:** Diesel Engine Centennial **Obv:** Stylized eagle above denomination **Rev:** First diesel engine

Date	Mintage	F	VF	XF	Unc	BU
1997A Proof	150,000	Value: 16.00				
1997D Proof	150,000	Value: 16.00				
1997F	3,000,000	—	—	—	9.00	11.00
1997F Proof	150,000	Value: 16.00				
1997G Proof	150,000	Value: 16.00				
1997J Proof	150,000	Value: 16.00				

KM# 191 10 MARK

15.5000 g., 0.9250 Silver .4610 oz. ASW, 33 mm. **Subject:** 300th Anniversary end of 30 Years War - Peace of Westphalia **Obv:** Stylized eagle above denomination **Rev:** Clasped hands, dove and quill

Date	Mintage	F	VF	XF	Unc	BU
1998A Proof	200,000	Value: 16.00				
1998D Proof	200,000	Value: 16.00				
1998F Proof	200,000	Value: 16.00				
1998G Proof	200,000	Value: 16.00				
1998J	3,500,000	—	—	—	9.00	11.00
1998J Proof	200,000	Value: 16.00				

Note: A 1997 strike of this coin does not exist

KM# 193 10 MARK

0.9250 Silver, 33 mm. **Subject:** 900th Anniversary - Birth of Hildegard von Bingen (1098-1178AD), abbess and scholar **Obv:** Stylized eagle above denomination **Rev:** Seated figure writing, small hand above left **Edge Lettering:** WISSE DIE WEGE DES HERRN

Date	Mintage	F	VF	XF	Unc	BU
1998A Proof	200,000	Value: 16.00				
1998D Proof	200,000	Value: 16.00				
1998F Proof	200,000	Value: 16.00				
1998G	3,500,000	—	—	—	9.00	11.00
1998G Proof	200,000	Value: 16.00				
1998J Proof	200,000	Value: 16.00				

KM# 194 10 MARK

15.5000 g., 0.9000 Silver .5345 oz. ASW, 33 mm. **Subject:** 300th Anniversary Franckesche Charitable Endowment

Date	Mintage	F	VF	XF	Unc	BU
1998A	—	—	—	—	9.00	11.00
1998A Proof	—	Value: 16.00				
1998D Proof	—	Value: 16.00				
1998F Proof	—	Value: 16.00				
1998G Proof	—	Value: 16.00				
1998J Proof	—	Value: 16.00				

KM# 195 10 MARK

15.5000 g., 0.9250 Silver .4610 oz. ASW, 33 mm. **Subject:** 50 Years of German Deutsch Mark **Obv:** Denomination above eagle **Rev:** Seven coin designs **Edge Lettering:** EINIGKEIT UND RECHT UND FREIHEIT

Date	Mintage	F	VF	XF	Unc	BU
1998A Proof	—	Value: 17.50				
1998D Proof	—	Value: 17.50				
1998F	—	—	—	—	9.00	11.00
1998F Proof	—	Value: 17.50				
1998G Proof	—	Value: 17.50				
1998J Proof	—	Value: 17.50				

KM# 196 10 MARK

15.5000 g., 0.9250 Silver .4610 oz. ASW, 33 mm. **Subject:** 50th Anniversary - Bundes Republic Constitution **Obv:** Small imperial eagle above denomination **Rev:** German constitution **Edge Lettering:** FUR DAS GESAMTE DEUTSCH VOLK

Date	Mintage	F	VF	XF	Unc	BU
1999A Proof	—	Value: 16.00				
1999D	—	—	—	—	9.00	11.00
1999D Proof	—	Value: 16.00				
1999F Proof	—	Value: 16.00				
1999G Proof	—	Value: 16.00				
1999J Proof	—	Value: 16.00				

KM# 197 10 MARK

15.5000 g., 0.9250 Silver .4610 oz. ASW, 33 mm. **Subject:** 250th Anniversary - Birth of J.W. von Goethe **Obv:** Imperial eagle above denomination **Rev:** Bust at left facing inscribed field right **Edge Lettering:** WIRKE GUT SO WIRKST DU LANGER

Date	Mintage	F	VF	XF	Unc	BU
1999A Proof	—	Value: 16.00				
1999D Proof	—	Value: 16.00				
1999F	—	—	—	—	9.00	11.00
1999F Proof	—	Value: 16.00				
1999G Proof	—	Value: 16.00				
1999J Proof	—	Value: 16.00				

KM# 198 10 MARK
15.5000 g., 0.9250 Silver .4610 oz. ASW, 33 mm. **Subject:** Charity for children without parents all over the world **Obv:** Stylized imperial eagle, denomination divides date below **Rev:** Stylized globe, children playing **Edge Lettering:** SOS - KINDERDORFER - EINE IDEE FUR DIE WELT **Designer:** Mathias Farthmair

Date	Mintage	F	VF	XF	Unc	BU
1999A Proof	—	Value: 16.00				
1999D Proof	—	Value: 16.00				
1999F Proof	—	Value: 16.00				
1999G Proof	—	Value: 16.00				
1999J	—	—	—	—	9.00	11.00
1999J Proof	—	Value: 16.00				

Note: NOTE: A 1997 strike of this coin does not exist.

KM# 199 10 MARK
15.5000 g., 0.9250 Silver .4610 oz. ASW, 33 mm. **Subject:** Expo 2000 **Obv:** Stylized eagle **Rev:** Childlike drawing of human balance scale **Edge Lettering:** WELTAUSSTELLUNG EXPO 2000 HANNOVER

Date	Mintage	F	VF	XF	Unc	BU
2000A	3,000,000	—	—	—	9.00	11.00
2000A Proof	160,000	Value: 16.00				
2000D Proof	160,000	Value: 16.00				
2000F Proof	160,000	Value: 16.00				
2000G Proof	160,000	Value: 16.00				
2000J Proof	160,000	Value: 16.00				

KM# 200 10 MARK
15.5000 g., 0.9250 Silver .4610 oz. ASW, 33 mm. **Subject:** Founding the Church in Aachen 1200 Years Ago by Charlemagne **Obv:** Stylized eagle **Rev:** Charlemagne handing church model to Madonna and child **Edge Lettering:** URBS AQUENSIS - URBS REGALIS

Date	Mintage	F	VF	XF	Unc	BU
2000A Proof	160,000	Value: 16.00				
2000D Proof	160,000	Value: 16.00				
2000F Proof	160,000	Value: 16.00				
2000G	3,000,000	—	—	—	9.00	11.00
2000G Proof	160,000	Value: 16.00				
2000J Proof	160,000	Value: 16.00				

KM# 201 10 MARK
15.5000 g., 0.9250 Silver .4610 oz. ASW, 33 mm. **Subject:** 10th Anniversary of Reunification **Obv:** Eagle and denomination **Rev:** Parliament building **Edge Lettering:** "WIR SIND DAS VOLK WIR SIND EIN VOLK"

Date	Mintage	F	VF	XF	Unc	BU
2000A Proof	—	Value: 16.00				
2000D	—	—	—	—	9.00	11.00
2000D Proof	—	Value: 16.00				
2000F Proof	—	Value: 16.00				
2000G Proof	—	Value: 16.00				
2000J Proof	—	Value: 16.00				

KM# 202 10 MARK
15.5000 g., 0.9250 Silver .4610 oz. ASW, 33 mm. **Obv:** Imperial eagle above denomination **Rev:** Face on inscribed background, dates below **Edge Lettering:** "JOHANN SEBASTIAN BACH 250 TODESTAG"

Date	Mintage	F	VF	XF	Unc	BU
2000A Proof	—	Value: 16.00				
2000D Proof	—	Value: 16.00				
2000F	—	—	—	—	9.00	11.00
2000F Proof	—	Value: 16.00				
2000G Proof	—	Value: 16.00				
2000J Proof	—	Value: 16.00				

PATTERNS

Including off metal strikes

KM#	Date	Mintage	Identification	Mkt Val
Pn397	1950D	—	2 Mark. Copper-Nickel. With Hole, PN#400.	—
Pn398	1951D	—	2 Mark. Copper-Nickel. Max Planck.	—
Pn399	1951F	—	2 Mark. Copper-Nickel. Max Planck.	—
Pn400	1955J	—	2 Mark.	—
Pn401	1959F	—	2 Pfennig. Brass.	—
Pn402	1960F	—	2 Pfennig. Zinc.	—

TRIAL STRIKES

KM#	Date	Mintage	Identification	Mkt Val
TS1	NDJ	—	10 Pfennig. KM#4. Uniface.	—
TS2	NDJ	—	2 Mark. Silver. Pn400. Uniface.	—
TS3	1950J	—	2 Mark. Silver. Pn400. Uniface.	—
TS4	NDJ	—	2 Mark. Lead. Pn400. Uniface.	—
TS5	1950J	—	2 Mark. Lead. Pn400. Uniface.	—
TS6	1951F	—	2 Mark. Lead. Max Planck. Uniface.	—
TS7	NDF	—	2 Mark. Lead. Max Planck. Uniface.	—
TS8	1951J	—	2 Mark. Iron. Max Planck. Uniface.	—
TS9	NDJ	—	2 Mark. Iron. Max Planck. Uniface.	—
TS10	1951J	—	2 Mark. Lead. Max Planck. Uniface.	—
TS11	NDJ	—	2 Mark. Lead. Max Planck. Uniface.	—

MINT SETS

KM#	Date	Mintage	Identification	Issue Price	Mkt Val
MS1	1974D (9)	20,000	KM#105, 106a, 107-108, 109.2, 110, 112.1, 124, A127	—	45.00
MS2	1974F (9)	20,000	KM#105, 106a, 107-108, 109.2, 110, 112.1, 124, A127	—	45.00
MS3	1974G (9)	20,000	KM#105, 106a, 107-108, 109.2, 110, 112.1, 124, A127	—	45.00
MS4	1974J (9)	20,000	KM#105, 106a, 107-108, 109.2, 110, 112.1, 124, A127	—	45.00
MS5	1975D (9)	26,000	KM#105, 106a, 107-108, 109.2, 110, 124, A127, 140.1	—	28.00
MS6	1975F (9)	26,000	KM#105, 106a, 107-108, 109.2, 110, 124, A127, 140.1	—	28.00
MS7	1975G (9)	26,000	KM#105, 106a, 107-108, 109.2, 110, 124, A127, 140.1	—	28.00
MS8	1975J (9)	26,000	KM#105, 106a, 107-108, 109.2, 110, 124, A127, 140.1	—	28.00
MS9	1976D (9)	26,000	KM#105, 106a, 107-108, 109.2, 110, 124, A127, 140.1	—	28.00
MS10	1976F (9)	26,000	KM#105, 106a, 107-108, 1092., 110, 124, A127, 140.1	—	28.00
MS11	1976G (9)	26,000	KM#105, 106a, 107-108, 109.2, 110, 124, A127, 140.1	—	28.00
MS12	1976J (9)	26,000	KM#105, 106a, 107-108, 109.2, 110, 124, A127, 140.1	—	28.00
MS13	1977D (9)	29,000	KM#105, 106a, 107-108, 109.2, 110, 124, A127, 140.1	—	20.00
MS14	1977F (9)	29,000	KM#105, 106a, 107-108, 109.2, 110, 124, A127, 140.1	—	20.00
MS15	1977G (9)	29,000	KM#105, 106a, 107-108, 109.2, 110, 124, A127, 140.1	—	20.00
MS16	1977J (9)	29,000	KM#105, 106a, 107-108, 109.2, 110, 124, A127, 140.1	—	20.00
MS17	1978D (9)	30,000	KM#105, 106a, 107-108, 109.2, 110, 124, A127, 140.1	—	20.00
MS18	1978F (9)	30,000	KM#105, 106a, 107-108, 109.2, 110, 124, A127, 140.1	—	20.00
MS19	1978g (9)	30,000	KM#105, 106a, 107-108, 109.2, 110, 124, A127, 140.1	—	20.00
MS20	1978J (9)	30,000	KM#105, 106a, 107-108, 109.2, 110, 124, A127, 140.1	—	20.00
MS21	1979D (10)	34,000	KM105, 106a, 107-108, 109.2, 110, 124, A127, 140.1, 149	11.00	20.00
MS22	1979F (10)	34,000	KM105, 106a, 107-108, 109.2, 110, 124, A127, 140.1, 149	11.00	20.00
MS23	1979G (10)	34,000	KM105, 106a, 107-108, 109.2, 110, 124, A127, 140.1, 149	11.00	20.00
MS24	1979J (10)	34,000	KM105, 106a, 107-108, 109.2, 110, 124, A127, 140.1, 149	11.00	20.00
MS25	1980D (10)	36,000	KM105, 106a, 107-108, 109.2, 110, 124, A127, 140.1, 149	11.00	20.00
MS26	1980F (10)	36,000	KM105, 106a, 107-108, 109.2, 110, 124, A127, 140.1, 149	11.00	20.00
MS27	1980G (10)	36,000	KM105, 106a, 107-108, 109.2, 110, 124, A127, 140.1, 149	11.00	20.00
MS28	1980J (10)	36,000	KM105, 106a, 107-108, 109.2, 110, 124, A127, 140.1, 149	11.00	20.00
MS29	1981D (10)	38,000	KM105, 106a, 107-108, 109.2, 110, 124, A127, 140.1, 149	11.00	20.00
MS30	1981F (10)	38,000	KM105, 106a, 107-108, 109.2, 110, 124, A127, 140.1, 149	11.00	20.00
MS31	1981G (10)	38,000	KM105, 106a, 107-108, 109.2, 110, 124, A127, 140.1, 149	11.00	20.00
MS32	1981J (10)	38,000	KM105, 106a, 107-108, 109.2, 110, 124, A127, 140.1, 149	11.00	20.00
MS33	1982D (10)	33,000	KM105, 106a, 107-108, 109.2, 110, 124, A127, 140.1, 149	11.00	20.00
MS34	1982F (10)	33,000	KM105, 106a, 107-108, 109.2, 110, 124, A127, 140.1, 149	11.00	20.00
MS35	1982G (10)	33,000	KM105, 106a, 107-108, 109.2, 110, 124, A127, 140.1, 149	11.00	20.00
MS36	1982J (10)	33,000	KM105, 106a, 107-108, 109.2, 110, 124, A127, 140.1, 149	11.00	20.00
MS37	1983D (10)	31,000	KM105, 106a, 107-108, 109.2, 110, 124, A127, 140.1, 149	11.00	20.00
MS38	1983F (10)	31,000	KM105, 106a, 107-108, 109.2, 110, 124, A127, 140.1, 149	11.00	20.00
MS39	1983G (10)	31,000	KM105, 106a, 107-108, 109.2, 110, 124, A127, 140.1, 149	11.00	20.00
MS40	1983J (10)	31,000	KM105, 106a, 107-108, 109.2, 110, 124, A127, 140.1, 149	11.00	20.00
MS41	1984D (10)	25,000	KM105, 106a, 107-108, 109.2, 110, 124, A127, 140.1, 149	11.00	50.00
MS42	1984F (10)	25,000	KM105, 106a, 107-108, 109.2, 110, 124, A127, 140.1, 149	11.00	50.00
MS43	1984G (10)	25,000	KM105, 106a, 107-108, 109.2, 110, 124, A127, 140.1, 149	11.00	50.00
MS44	1984J (10)	25,000	KM105, 106a, 107-108, 109.2, 110, 124, A127, 140.1, 149	11.00	50.00
MS45	1985D (10)	23,000	KM105, 106a, 107-108, 109.2, 110, 124, A127, 140.1, 149	11.00	20.00
MS46	1985F (10)	23,000	KM105, 106a, 107-108, 109.2, 110, 124, A127, 140.1, 149	11.00	20.00
MS47	1985G (10)	23,000	KM105, 106a, 107-108, 109.2, 110, 124, A127, 140.1, 149	11.00	20.00
MS48	1985J (10)	23,000	KM105, 106a, 107-108, 109.2, 110, 124, A127, 140.1, 149	11.00	20.00
MS49	1986D (10)	15,000	KM105, 106a, 107-108, 109.2, 110, 124, A127, 140.1, 149	11.00	100
MS50	1986F (10)	15,000	KM105, 106a, 107-108, 109.2, 110, 124, A127, 140.1, 149	11.00	100
MS51	1986G (10)	15,000	KM105, 106a, 107-108, 109.2, 110, 124, A127, 140.1, 149	11.00	100
MS52	1986J (10)	15,000	KM105, 106a, 107-108, 109.2, 110, 124, A127, 140.1, 149	11.00	100
MS53	1987D (10)	18,000	KM105, 106a, 107-108, 109.2, 110, 124, A127, 140.1, 149	11.00	45.00
MS54	1987F (10)	18,000	KM105, 106a, 107-108, 109.2, 110, 124, A127, 140.1, 149	11.00	45.00
MS55	1987G (10)	18,000	KM105, 106a, 107-108, 109.2, 110, 124, A127, 140.1, 149	11.00	45.00
MS56	1987J (10)	18,000	KM105, 106a, 107-108, 109.2, 110, 124, A127, 140:1, 149	11.00	45.00
MS57	1988D (9)	18,000	KM105, 106a, 107-108, 109.2, 110, 140.1, 149, 170	—	27.50
MS58	1988F (9)	18,000	KM105, 106a, 107-108, 109.2, 110, 140.1, 149, 170	—	27.50
MS59	1988G (9)	18,000	KM105, 106a, 107-108, 109.2, 110, 140.1, 149, 170	—	27.50
MS60	1988J (9)	18,000	KM105, 106a, 107-108, 109.2, 110, 140.1, 149, 170	—	27.50
MS61	1989D (9)	18,000	KM105, 106a, 107-108, 109.2, 110, 140.1, 149, 170	—	27.50
MS62	1989F (9)	18,000	KM105, 106a, 107-108, 109.2, 110, 140.1, 149, 170	—	27.50

KM#	Date	Mintage	Identification	Issue Price	Mkt Val
MS63	1989G (9)	18,000	KM105, 106a, 107-108, 109.2, 110, 140.1, 149, 170	—	27.50
MS64	1989J (9)	18,000	KM105, 106a, 107-108, 109.2, 110, 140.1, 149, 170	—	27.50
MS65	1990D (10)	20,000	KM105, 106a, 107-108, 109.2, 110, 140.1, 149, 170, 175	—	25.00
MS66	1990F (10)	20,000	KM105, 106a, 107-108, 109.2, 110, 140.1, 149, 170, 175	—	25.00
MS67	1990G (10)	20,000	KM105, 106a, 107-108, 109.2, 110, 140.1, 149, 170, 175	—	25.00
MS68	1990J (10)	20,000	KM105, 106a, 107-108, 109.2, 110, 140.1, 149, 170, 175	—	25.00
MS69	1991A (10)	20,000	KM105, 106a, 107-108, 109.2, 110, 140.1, 149, 170, 175	—	30.00
MS70	1991D (10)	20,000	KM105, 106a, 107-108, 109.2, 110, 140.1, 149, 170, 175	—	30.00
MS71	1991F (10)	20,000	KM105, 106a, 107-108, 109.2, 110, 140.1, 149, 170, 175	—	30.00
MS72	1991G (10)	20,000	KM105, 106a, 107-108, 109.2, 110, 140.1, 149, 170, 175	—	30.00
MS73	1991J (10)	20,000	KM105, 106a, 107-108, 109.2, 110, 140.1, 149, 170, 175	—	30.00
MS74	1992A (10)	20,000	KM105, 106a, 107-108, 109.2, 110, 140.1, 149, 170, 175	—	30.00
MS75	1992D (10)	20,000	KM105, 106a, 107-108, 109.2, 110, 140.1, 149, 170, 175	—	30.00
MS76	1992F (10)	20,000	KM105, 106a, 107-108, 109.2, 110, 140.1, 149, 170, 175	—	30.00
MS77	1992G (10)	20,000	KM105, 106a, 107-108, 109.2, 110, 140.1, 149, 170, 175	—	30.00
MS78	1992J (10)	20,000	KM105, 106a, 107-108, 109.2, 110, 140.1, 149, 170, 175	—	30.00
MS79	1993A (10)	20,000	KM105, 106a, 107-108, 109.2, 110, 140.1, 149, 170, 175	—	40.00
MS80	1993D (10)	20,000	KM105, 106a, 107-108, 109.2, 110, 140.1, 149, 170, 175	—	40.00
MS81	1993F (10)	20,000	KM105, 106a, 107-108, 109.2, 110, 140.1, 149, 170, 175	—	40.00
MS82	1993G (10)	20,000	KM105, 106a, 107-108, 109.2, 110, 140.1, 149, 170, 175	—	40.00
MS83	1993J (10)	20,000	KM105, 106a, 107-108, 109.2, 110, 140.1, 149, 170, 175	—	40.00
MS84	1994A (10)	10,000	KM105, 106A, 107-108, 109.2, 110, 140.1, 170, 175, 183	—	30.00
MS85	1994D (10)	20,000	KM105, 106a, 107-108, 109.2, 110, 140.1, 170, 175, 183	—	30.00
MS86	1994F (10)	20,000	KM105, 106a, 107-108, 109.2, 110, 140.1, 170, 175, 183	—	30.00
MS87	1994G (10)	20,000	KM105, 106a, 107-108, 109.2, 110, 140.1, 170, 175, 183	—	30.00
MS88	1994J (10)	20,000	KM105, 106a, 107-108, 109.2, 110, 140.1, 170, 175, 183	—	30.00
MS89	1995A (10)	20,000	KM105, 106a, 107-108, 109.2, 110, 140.1, 170, 175, 183	—	300
MS90	1995D (10)	20,000	KM105, 106a, 107-108, 109.2, 110, 140.1, 170, 175, 183	—	300
MS91	1995F (10)	20,000	KM105, 106a, 107-108, 109.2, 110, 140.1, 170, 175, 183	—	300
MS92	1995G (10)	20,000	KM105, 106a, 107-108, 109.2, 110, 140.1, 170, 175, 183	—	300
MS93	1995J (10)	20,000	KM105, 106A, 107-108, 109.2, 110, 140.1, 170, 175, 183	—	300
MS94	1996A (10)	50,000	KM105, 106a, 107-108, 109.2, 110, 140.1, 170, 175, 183	—	50.00
MS95	1996D (10)	50,000	KM105, 106a, 107-108, 109.2, 110, 140.1, 170, 175, 183	—	50.00
MS96	1996F (10)	50,000	KM105, 106a, 107-108, 109.2, 110, 140.1, 170, 175, 183	—	50.00
MS97	1996G (10)	50,000	KM105, 106a, 107-108, 109.2, 110, 140.1, 170, 175, 183	—	50.00
MS98	1996J (10)	50,000	KM105, 106a, 107-108, 109.2, 110, 140.1, 170, 175, 183	—	50.00
MS99	1997A (9)	70,000	KM105, 106a, 108, 109.2, 110, 140.1, 170, 175, 183	—	30.00
MS100	1997D (10)	70,000	KM105, 106a, 107-108, 109.2, 110, 140.1, 170, 175, 183	—	30.00
MS101	1997F (10)	70,000	KM105, 106a, 107-108, 109.2, 110, 140.1, 170, 175, 183	—	30.00
MS102	1997G (10)	70,000	KM105, 106a, 107-108, 109.2, 110, 140.1, 170, 175, 183	—	30.00
MS103	1997J (10)	70,000	KM105, 106a, 107-108, 109.2, 110, 140.1, 170, 175, 183	—	30.00
MS104	1998A (10)	70,000	KM105, 106a, 107-108, 109.2, 110, 140.1, 170, 175, 183	—	30.00
MS105	1998D (10)	70,000	KM105, 106a, 107-108, 109.2, 110, 140.1, 170, 175, 183	—	30.00
MS106	1998F (10)	70,000	KM105, 106a, 107-108, 109.2, 110, 140.1, 170, 175, 183	—	30.00
MS107	1998G (10)	70,000	KM105, 106a, 107-108, 109.2, 110, 140.1, 170, 175, 183	—	30.00
MS108	1998J (10)	70,000	KM105, 106a, 107-108, 109.2, 110, 140.1, 170, 175, 183	—	30.00
MS109	1999A (10)	70,000	KM105, 106a, 107-108, 109.2, 110, 140.1, 170, 175, 183	—	30.00
MS110	1999D (10)	70,000	km105, 106A, 107-108, 109.2, 110, 140.1, 170, 175, 183	—	30.00
MS112	1999G (10)	70,000	KM105, 106a, 107-108, 109.2, 110, 140.1, 170, 175, 183	—	30.00
MS114	1999J (10)	70,000	KM105, 106a, 107-108, 109.2, 110, 140.1, 170, 175, 183	—	30.00
MS115	2000D (10)	20,000	KM105, 106a, 107-108, 109.2, 110, 140.1, 170, 175, 183	—	45.00
MS116	2000F (10)	20,000	KM105, 160a, 107-108, 109.2, 110, 140.1, 170, 175, 183	—	45.00
MS117	2000G (10)	20,000	KM105, 106a, 107-108, 109.2, 110, 140.1, 170, 175, 183	—	45.00
MS118	2000J (10)	20,000	KM105, 106a, 107-108, 109.2, 110, 140.1, 170, 175, 183	—	45.00

PROOF SETS

KM#	Date	Mintage	Identification	Issue Price	Mkt Val
PS1	1950-64G (8)	600	KM105-108, 109.1, 110, 112.1, 116	—	1,500
PS2	1950-65F (8)	300	KM105-108, 109.1, 110, 112.1, 116	—	3,500
PS3	1950-65G (8)	8,233	KM105-108, 109.1, 110, 112.1, 116	—	200
PS4	1966F (8)	450	KM105-108, 109.1, 110, 112.1, 116	—	3,500
PS5	1966G (8)	3,070	KM105-108, 109.1, 110, 112.1, 116	—	550
PS6	1966J (8)	1,000	KM105-108, 109.1, 110, 112.1, 116	—	900
PS9	1967G (8)	520	KM105, 106a*, 107-108, 109.1, 110, 112.1, 116	—	3,500
PS7	1967F (8)	1,600	KM105-108, 109.1, 110, 112.1, 116	—	600
PS8	1967G (8)	3,630	KM105-108, 109.1, 110, 112.1, 116	—	400
PS10	1967J (8)	1,500	KM105, 106a, 107-108, 109.1, 110, 112.1, 116	—	800
PS11	1968F (8)	3,000	KM105, 106a, 107-108, 109.1, 110, 112.1, 116	—	550
PS12	1968G (8)	3,651	KM105, 106, 107-108, 109.1, 110, 112.1, 116	—	325
PS12a	1968G (8)	2,372	KM105, 106a, 107-108, 109.1, 110, 112.1, 116	—	400
PS13	1968J (8)	2,000	KM105, 106a, 107-108, 109.1, 110, 112.1, 116	—	550
PS14	1969F (8)	5,000	KM105, 106a, 107-108, 109.1, 110, 112.1, 116	—	100
PS15	1969G (8)	8,700	KM105, 106a, 107-108, 109.1, 110, 112.1, 116	—	100
PS16	1969J (8)	5,000	KM105, 106a, 107-108, 109.1, 110, 112.1, 116	—	100
PS17	1970F (8)	5,140	KM105, 106a, 107-108, 109.1, 110, 112.1, 116	—	140
PS18	1970G (8)	10,200	KM105, 106a, 107-108, 109.1, 110, 112.1, 116	—	100
PS19	1970J (8)	5,000	KM105, 106a, 107-108, 109.1, 110, 112.1, 116	—	100
PS20	1971D (8)	8,000	KM105, 106a, 107-108, 109.1, 110, 112.1, 116	—	95.00
PS21	1971F (8)	8,000	KM105, 106a, 107-108, 109.1, 110, 112.1, 116	—	95.00
PS22	1971G (8)	10,200	KM105, 106a, 107-108, 109.1, 110, 112.1, 116	—	95.00
PS23	1971J (8)	8,000	KM105, 106a, 107-108, 109.1, 110, 112.1, 116	—	95.00
PS24	1972D (9)	8,000	KM105, 106a, 107-108, 109.2, 110, 112.1, 124, A127	—	95.00
PS25	1972F (9)	8,000	KM105, 106a, 107-108, 109.2, 110, 112.1, 124, A127	—	95.00
PS26	1972G (9)	10,000	KM105, 106a, 107-108, 109.2, 110, 112.1, 124, A127	—	95.00
PS27	1972J (9)	8,000	KM105, 106a, 107-108, 109.2, 110, 112.1, 124, A127	—	95.00
PS28	1973D (9)	9,000	KM105, 106a, 107-108, 109.2, 110, 112.1, 124, A127	—	95.00
PS29	1973F (9)	9,000	KM105, 106a, 107-108, 109.2, 110, 112.1, 124, A127	—	95.00
PS30	1973G (9)	9,000	KM105, 106a, 107-108, 109.2, 110, 112.1, 124, A127	—	95.00
PS31	1973J (9)	9,000	KM105, 106a, 107-108, 109.2, 110, 112.1, 124, A127	—	95.00
PS32	1974D (9)	35,000	KM105, 106a, 107-108, 109.2, 110,112.1, 124, A127	10.00	40.00
PS33	1974F (9)	35,000	KM105, 106a, 107-108, 109.2, 110, 112.1, 124, A127	10.00	40.00
PS34	1974G (9)	35,000	KM105, 106a, 107-108, 109.2, 110, 112.1, 124, A127	10.00	40.00
PS35	1974J (9)	35,000	KM105, 106a, 107-108, 109.2, 110, 112.1, 124, A127	10.00	40.00
PS36	1975D (9)	43,120	KM105, 106a, 107-108, 109.2, 110, 124, A127, 140.1	10.00	22.00
PS37	1975F (9)	43,100	KM105, 106a, 107-108, 109.2, 110, 124, A127, 140.1	10.00	22.00
PS38	1975G (9)	43,100	KM105, 106a, 107-108, 109.2, 110, 124, A127, 140.1	10.00	22.00
PS39	1975J (9)	43,120	KM105, 106a, 107-108, 109.2, 110, 124, A127, 140.1	10.00	22.00
PS40	1976D (9)	43,120	KM105, 106a, 107-108, 109.2, 110, 124, A127,140.1	10.00	22.00
PS41	1976F (9)	43,100	KM105, 106a, 107-108, 109.2, 110, 124, A127, 140.1	10.00	22.00
PS42	1976G (9)	43,100	KM105, 106a, 107-108, 109.2, 110, 124, A127, 140.1	10.00	22.00
PS43	1976J (9)	43,120	KM105, 106a, 107-108, 109.2, 110, 124, A127, 140.1	10.00	22.00
PS44	1977D (9)	50,620	KM105, 106a, 107-108, 109.2, 110, 124, A127, 140.1	12.50	22.00
PS45	1977F (9)	50,600	KM105, 106a, 107-108, 109.2, 110, 124, A127, 140.1	12.50	22.00
PS46	1977G (9)	50,600	KM105, 106a, 107-108, 109.2, 110, 124, A127, 140.1	12.50	22.00
PS47	1977J (9)	50,620	KM105, 106a, 107-108, 109.2, 110, 124, A127, 140.1	12.50	22.00
PS48	1978D (9)	54,000	KM105, 106A, 107-108, 109.2, 110, 124, A127, 140.1	13.00	22.00
PS49	1978F (9)	54,000	KM105, 106a, 107-108, 109.2, 110, 124, A127, 140.1	13.00	22.00
PS50	1978G (9)	54,000	KM105, 106a, 107-108, 109.2, 110, 124, A127, 140.1	13.00	22.00
PS51	1978J (9)	54,000	KM105, 106a, 107-108, 109.2, 110, 124, A127, 140.1	13.00	22.00
PS52	1979D (10)	89,000	KM105, 106a, 107-108, 109.2, 110, 124, A127, 140.1, 149	15.00	22.00
PS53	1979F (10)	89,000	KM105, 106A, 107-108, 109.2, 110, 124, A127, 140.1, 149	15.00	22.00
PS54	1979G (10)	89,000	KM105, 106a, 107-108, 109.2, 110, 124, A127, 140.1, 149	15.00	22.00
PS55	1979J (10)	89,000	KM105, 106a, 107-108, 109.2, 110, 124, A127, 140.1, 149	15.00	22.00
PS56	1980D (10)	60,000	KM105, 106a, 107-108, 109.2, 110, 124, A127, 140.1, 149	15.00	22.00
PS57	1980F (10)	60,000	KM105, 106a, 107-108, 109.2, 110, 124, A127, 140.1, 149	15.00	22.00
PS58	1980G (10)	60,000	KM105, 106a, 107-108, 109.2, 110, 124, A127, 140.1, 149	15.00	22.00
PS59	1980J (10)	60,000	KM105, 106a, 107-108, 109.2, 110, 124, A127, 140.1, 149	15.00	22.00
PS60	1981D (10)	60,000	KM105, 106a, 107-108, 109.2, 110, 124, A127, 140.1, 149	15.00	22.00
PS61	1981F (10)	91,000	KM105, 106a, 107-108, 109.2, 110, 124, A127, 140.1, 149	15.00	22.00
PS62	1981G (10)	91,000	KM105, 106a, 107-108, 109.2, 110, 124, A127, 140.1, 149	15.00	22.00

KM#	Date	Mintage	Identification	Issue Price	Mkt Val
PS63	1981J (10)	78,000	KM105, 106a, 107-108, 109.2, 110, 124, A127, 140.1, 149	15.00	22.00
PS64	1982D (10)	78,000	KM105, 106a, 107-108, 109.2, 110, 124, A127, 140.1, 149	15.00	22.00
PS65	1982F (10)	78,000	KM105, 106a,107-108, 109.2, 110, 124, A127, 140.1, 149	15.00	22.00
PS66	1982G (10)	78,000	KM105, 106a, 107-108, 109.2, 110, 124, A127, 140.1, 149	15.00	22.00
PS67	1982J (10)	78,000	KM105, 106a, 107-108, 109.2, 110, 124, A127, 140.1, 149	15.00	22.00
PS68	1983D (10)	75,000	KM105, 106a, 107-108, 109.2, 110, 124, A127, 140.1, 149	15.00	22.00
PS69	1983F (10)	75,000	KM105, 106a, 107-108, 109.2, 110, 124, A127, 140.1, 149	15.00	22.00
PS70	1983G (10)	75,000	KM105, 106a, 107-108, 109.2, 110, 124, A127, 140.1, 149	15.00	22.00
PS71	1983J (10)	75,000	KM105, 106a, 107-108, 109.2, 110, 124, A127, 140.1, 149	15.00	22.00
PS72	1984D (10)	64,000	KM105, 106a, 107-108, 109.2, 110, 124, A127, 140.1, 149	15.00	26.50
PS73	1984F (10)	64,000	KM105, 106a, 107-108, 109.2, 110, 124, A127, 140.1, 149	15.00	26.50
PS74	1984G (10)	64,000	KM105, 106a, 107-108, 109.2, 110, 124, A127, 140.1, 149	15.00	26.50
PS75	1985D (10)	56,000	KM105, 106a, 107-108, 109.2, 110, 124, A127, 140.1, 149	15.00	26.50
PS76	1985D	56,000	MK#105, 106a, 107-108, 109.2, 110, 124, A127, 140.1, 149	15.00	25.00
PS77	1985F (10)	54,000	KM105, 106a, 107-108, 109.2, 110, 124, A127, 140.1, 149	15.00	25.00
PS78	1985G (10)	55,000	KM105, 106a, 107-108, 109.2, 110, 124, A127, 140.1, 149	15.00	25.00
PS79	1985J (10)	54,000	KM105, 106a, 107-108, 109.2, 110, 124, A127, 140.1, 149	15.00	25.00
PS80	1986D (10)	44,000	KM105, 106a, 107-108, 109.2, 110, 124, A127, 140.1, 149	15.00	27.50
PS81	1986F (10)	44,000	KM105, 106a, 107-108, 109.2, 110, 124, A127, 140.1, 149	15.00	27.50
PS82	1986G (10)	44,000	KM105, 106a, 107-108, 109.2, 110, 124, A127, 140.1, 149	15.00	27.50
PS83	1986J (10)	44,000	KM105, 106a, 107-108, 109.2, 110, 124, A127, 140.1, 149	15.00	27.50
PS84	1987D (10)	45,000	KM105, 106a, 107-108, 109.2, 110, 124, A127, 140.1, 149	15.00	35.00
PS85	1987F (10)	45,000	KM105, 106a, 107-108, 109.2, 110, 124, A127, 140.1, 149	15.00	35.00
PS86	1987G (10)	45,000	KM105, 106a, 107-108, 109.2, 110, 124, A127, 140.1, 149	15.00	35.00
PS87	1987J (10)	45,000	KM105, 106a, 107-108, 109.2, 110, 124, A127, 140.1, 149	15.00	35.00
PS88	1988D (9)	45,000	KM105, 106a, 107-108, 109.2, 110, 140.1, 149, 170	—	25.00
PS89	1988F (9)	45,000	KM105, 106a, 107-108, 109.2, 110, 140.1, 149, 170	—	25.00
PS90	1988G (9)	45,000	KM105, 106a, 107-108, 109.2, 110, 140.1, 149, 170	—	25.00
PS91	1988J (9)	45,000	KM105, 106a, 107-108, 109.2, 110, 140.1, 149, 170	—	25.00
PS92	1989D (9)	45,000	KM105, 106a, 107-108, 109.2, 110, 140.1, 149, 170	—	25.00
PS93	1989F (9)	45,000	KM105, 106a, 107-108, 109.2, 110, 140.1, 149, 170	—	25.00
PS94	1989G (9)	45,000	KM105-106a, 107-108, 109.2, 110, 140.1, 149, 170	—	25.00
PS95	1989J (9)	45,000	KM105-106a, 107-108, 109.2, 110, 140.1, 149, 170	—	25.00
PS96	1990D (10)	45,000	KM105, 106a, 107-108, 109.2, 110, 140.1, 149, 170, 175	—	25.00
PS97	1990F (10)	45,000	KM105, 106a, 107-108, 109.2, 110, 140.1, 149, 170, 175	—	25.00
PS98	1990G (10)	45,000	KM105,106a,107-180,109.2,110,140.1,149,170,175	—	25.00
PS99	1990J (10)	45,000	KM105,106a,107-108,109.2,110,140.1,149,170,175	—	25.00
PS100	1991A (10)	45,000	KM105,106a,107-108,109.2,110,140.1,149,170,175	—	27.50
PS101	1991D (10)	45,000	KM105,106a,107-108,109.2,110,140.1,149,170,175	—	27.50
PS102	1991F (10)	45,000	KM105,106a,107-108,109.2,110,140.1,149,170,175	—	27.50
PS103	1991G (10)	45,000	KM105,106a,107-108,109.2,110,140.1,149,170,175	—	27.50
PS104	1991J (10)	45,000	KM105,106a,107-108,109.2,110,140.1,149,170,175	—	27.50
PS105	1992A (10)	45,000	KM105,106a,107-108,109.2,110,140.1,149,170,175	—	27.50
PS106	1992D (10)	45,000	KM105,106a,107-108,109.2,110,140.1,149,170,175	—	27.50
PS107	1992F (10)	45,000	KM105,106a,107-108,109.2,110,140.1,149,170,175	—	27.50
PS108	1992G (10)	45,000	KM105,106a,107,108,109.2,110,140.1,149,170,175	—	27.50
PS109	1992J (10)	45,000	KM105,106a,107-108,109.2,110,140.1,149,170,175	—	27.50
PS110	1993A (10)	45,000	KM105,106a,107-108,109.2,110,140.1,149,170,175	—	35.00
PS111	1993D (10)	45,000	KM105,106a,107-108,109.2,110,140.1,149,170,175	—	35.00
PS112	1993F (10)	45,000	KM105,106a,107-108,109.2,110,140.1,149,170,175	—	35.00
PS113	1993J (10)	45,000	KM105,106a,107-108,109.2,110,140.1,149,170,175	—	35.00
PS114	1993J	45,000	KM105,106a,107-108,109.2,110,140.1,149,170,175	—	35.00
PS115	1994A (10)	45,000	KM105,106a,107-108,109.2,110,140.1,170,175,183	—	25.00
PS116	1994D (10)	45,000	KM105,106a,107-108,109.2,110,140.1,170,175,183	—	25.00
PS117	1994F (10)	45,000	KM105,106a,107-108,109.2,110,140,1,170,175,183	—	25.00
PS118	1994G (10)	45,000	KM105,106a,107-108,109.2,110,140.1,170,175,183	—	25.00
PS119	1994J (10)	45,000	KM105,106a,107-108,109.2,110,140.1,170,175,183	—	25.00
PS120	1995A (10)	45,000	KM105,106a,107-108,109.2,110,140.1,170,175,183	—	225
PS121	1995D (10)	45,000	KM105,106a,107-108,109.2,110,140.1,170,175,183	—	225
PS123	1995G (10)	45,000	KM105,106a,107-108,109.2,110,140.1,170,175,183	—	225
PS122	1995F (10)	45,000	KM105,106a,107-108,109.2,110,140.1,170,175,183	—	225
PS124	1995J (10)	45,000	KM105,106a,107-108,109.2,110,140.1,170,175,183	—	225
PS125	1996A (10)	45,000	KM105,106a,107-108,109.2,110,140.1,170,175,183	—	50.00
PS126	1996D (10)	45,000	KM105,106a,107-108,109.2,110,140.1,170,175,183	—	50.00
PS127	1996F (10)	45,000	KM105,106a,107-108,109.2,110,140.1,170,175,183	—	50.00
PS128	1996G (10)	45,000	KM105,106a,107-108,109.2,110,140.1,170,175,183	—	50.00
PS129	1996J (10)	45,000	KM105,106a,107-108,109.2,110,140.1,170,175,183	—	50.00
PS130	1997A (10)	45,000	KM105,106a,107-108,109.2,110,140.1,170,175,183	—	30.00
PS131	1997D (10)	45,000	KM105,106a,107-108,109.2,110,140.1,170,175,183	—	30.00
PS132	1997F (10)	45,000	KM105,106a,107-108,109.2,11o,140.1,170,175,183	—	30.00
PS133	1997G (10)	45,000	KM105,106a,107-108,109.2,110,140.1,170,175,183	—	30.00
PS134	1997J (10)	45,000	KM105,106a,107-108,109.2,110,140.1,170,175,183	—	30.00
PS135	1998A (10)	45,000	KM105,106a,107-108,109.2,110,140.1,170,175,183	—	30.00
PS136	1998D (10)	45,000	KM105,106a,107-108,109.2,110,140.1,170,175,183	—	37.50
PS137	1998F (10)	45,000	KM105,106a,107-108,109.2,110,140.1,170,175,183	—	37.50
PS142	1999F (10)	45,000	KM105,106a,107-108,109.2,110,140.1,170,175,183	—	30.00
PS138	1998G (10)	45,000	KM105,106a,107-108,109.2,110,140.1,170,175,183	—	37.50
PS139	1998J (10)	45,000	KM105,106a,107-108,109.2,110,140.1,170,175,183	—	30.00
PS144	1999J (10)	45,000	KM105,106a,107-108,109.2,110,140.1,170,175,183	—	30.00
PS140	1999A (10)	45,000	KM105,106a,107-108,109.2,110,140.1,170,175,183	—	30.00
PS141	1999D (10)	45,000	KM105,106a,107-108,109.2,110,140.1,170,175,183	—	30.00
PS143	1999G (10)	45,000	KM105,106a,107-108,109.2,110,140.1,170,175,183	—	30.00
PS145	2000A (10)	45,000	KM105,106a,107-108,109.2,110,140.1,170,175,183	—	55.00
PS146	2000D (10)	45,000	KM105,106a,107-108,109.2,110,140.1,170,175,183	—	55.00
PS147	2000F (10)	45,000	KM105,106a,107,108,109.2,110,140.1,170,175,183	—	55.00
PS148	2000G (10)	45,000	KM105,106a,107-108,109.2,110,140.1,170,175,183	—	55.00
PS149	2000J (10)	45,000	KM105,106a,107-108,109.2,110,140.1,170,175,183	—	55.00

1949-1990

The German Democratic Republic, formerly East Germany, was located on the great north European plain, had an area of 41,768 sq. mi. (108,330 sq. km.) and a population of 16.6 million. The figures included East Berlin, which had been incorporated into the G.D.R. Capital: East Berlin. The economy was highly industrialized. Machinery, transport equipment chemicals, and lignite were exported.

During the closing days of World War II in Europe, Soviet troops advancing into Germany from the east occupied the German provinces of Mecklenburg, Brandenburg, Lusatia, Saxony and Thuringia. These five provinces comprised the occupation zone administered by the Soviet Union after the cessation of hostilities. The other three zones were administered by the U.S., Great Britain and France. Under the Potsdam agreement, questions affecting Germany as a whole were to be settled by the commanders of the occupation zones acting jointly and by unanimous decision. When Soviet intransigence rendered the quadripartite commission inoperable, the three western zones were united to form the Federal Republic of Germany, May 23, 1949. Thereupon the Soviet Union dissolved its occupation zone and established it as the Democratic Republic of Germany, Oct. 7, 1949.

The post-WW II division of Germany was ended Oct. 3,1990, when the German Democratic Republic (East Germany) ceased to exist and its five constituent provinces were formally admitted to the Federal Republic of Germany. An election Dec. 2, 1990, chose representatives to the united federal parliament (Bundestag), which then conducted its opening session in Berlin in the old Reichstag building.

MARKS

A - Berlin

E - Muldenhutten

MONETARY SYSTEM

100 Pfennig = 1 Mark

DEMOCRATIC REPUBLIC

STANDARD COINAGE

KM# 1 PFENNIG

Aluminum **Obv:** Denomination **Rev:** Cogwheel back of grain sprig

Date	Mintage	F	VF	XF	Unc	BU
1948A	243,000,000	—	1.00	9.00	40.00	70.00
1949A	Inc. above	—	1.00	8.00	35.00	45.00
1949E	55,200,000	—	11.50	50.00	250	325
1950A	—	—	1.00	8.00	35.00	45.00
1950E	—	—	6.00	20.00	75.00	100

KM# 5 PFENNIG

Aluminum **Obv:** Denomination **Rev:** Grain sprigs back of hammer and protractor

Date	Mintage	F	VF	XF	Unc	BU
1952A	297,213,000	—	0.50	3.00	7.00	9.00
1952E	49,296,000	—	5.00	10.00	40.00	55.00
1953A	114,002,000	—	1.00	3.00	8.00	12.00
1953E	50,876,000	—	4.00	15.00	50.00	65.00

KM# 8.1 PFENNIG

Aluminum, 17 mm. **Obv:** State emblem **Rev:** Denomination flanked by oak leaves, date below

Date	Mintage	F	VF	XF	Unc	BU
1960A	101,808,000	—	0.25	0.75	3.00	4.00
1961A	101,776,000	—	0.25	0.75	3.00	4.00
1962A	81,459,000	—	0.25	0.75	3.00	4.00
1963A	101,402,000	—	0.25	0.75	3.00	4.00
1964A	98,967,000	—	0.25	0.75	3.00	4.00
1965A	38,585,000	—	3.00	15.00	40.00	60.00
1968A	813,680,000	—	0.25	0.80	2.50	3.00
1972A	4,801,000	—	3.00	10.00	20.00	25.00
1973A	5,518,000	—	3.00	8.00	20.00	25.00
1975A	202,752,000	—	0.25	0.75	2.50	3.00

KM# 8.2 PFENNIG

0.7000 g., Aluminum, 17 mm. **Obv:** State emblem, smaller design features **Rev:** Denomination flanked by leaves, smaller design features

Date	Mintage	F	VF	XF	Unc	BU
1977A	61,560,000	—	0.10	0.25	2.00	3.00
1978A	200,050,000	—	0.10	0.20	1.00	2.00
1979A	100,640,000	—	0.10	0.20	1.00	2.00
1979A Proof	—	Value: 45.00				
1980A	153,000,000	—	0.10	0.20	1.00	2.00
1980A Proof	—	Value: 45.00				
1981A	200,436,000	—	0.10	0.20	1.00	2.00
1981A Proof	40	—	—	—	1.00	2.00
1982A	99,200,000	—	0.10	0.20	1.00	2.00
1982A Proof	2,500	Value: 10.00				
1983A	150,000,000	—	0.10	0.20	1.00	2.00
1983A Proof	2,550	Value: 18.00				
1984A	137,600,000	—	0.10	0.20	1.00	2.00
1984A Proof	3,015	Value: 4.50				
1985A	125,060,000	—	0.10	0.20	1.00	2.00
1985A Proof	2,816	Value: 4.50				
1986A	73,900,000	—	0.10	0.20	1.00	2.00
1986A Proof	2,800	Value: 4.50				
1987A	50,015,000	—	0.10	0.20	1.00	2.00
1987A Proof	2,345	Value: 4.50				
1988A	75,450,000	—	0.10	0.20	1.00	2.00
1988A Proof	2,300	Value: 4.50				
1989A	84,410,000	—	0.10	0.20	1.00	2.00
1989A Proof	2,300	Value: 4.50				
1990A	15,670,000	—	0.10	2.00	5.00	10.00

KM# 2 5 PFENNIG

Aluminum **Obv:** Denomination **Rev:** Cogwheel back of grain sprig

Date	Mintage	F	VF	XF	Unc	BU
1948A	205,072,000	—	2.50	6.00	50.00	75.00
1949A	Inc. above	—	2.50	6.00	60.00	100
1950A	Inc. above	—	2.50	6.00	40.00	65.00

KM# 6 5 PFENNIG

Aluminum **Obv:** Denomination **Rev:** Grain sprigs flank hammer and protractor, date below

Date	Mintage	F	VF	XF	Unc	BU
1952A	113,397,000	—	2.00	5.00	10.00	13.00
1952E	24,024,000	—	3.50	9.00	35.00	45.00
1953A	40,994,000	—	2.00	6.50	15.00	20.00
1953E	28,665,000	—	5.00	17.50	90.00	120

KM# 9.1 5 PFENNIG

Aluminum, 19 mm. **Obv:** State emblem **Rev:** Denomination flanked by oak leaves, date below

Date	Mintage	F	VF	XF	Unc	BU
1968A	282,303,000	—	0.50	1.00	2.50	3.00
1972A	51,462,000	—	0.50	1.00	2.00	3.00
1975A	84,710,000	—	0.50	1.00	2.00	3.00

KM# 9.2 5 PFENNIG

1.0000 g., Aluminum, 19 mm. **Obv:** State emblem, smaller design features **Rev:** Denomination flanked by oak leaves, smaller design features **Note:** Varieties exist.

Date	Mintage	F	VF	XF	Unc	BU
1976A 2 known	—	—	—	—	—	—
1978A	43,257,000	—	0.15	0.25	1.00	2.00
1979A	46,194,000	—	0.15	0.25	1.00	2.00
1979A Proof	—	Value: 45.00				
1980A	31,977,000	—	0.15	0.25	1.00	2.00
1980A Proof	—	Value: 45.00				
1981A	33,101,999	—	0.15	0.25	1.00	2.00
1981A Proof	40	—	—	—	—	—
1982A	916,000	—	10.00	35.00	25.00	35.00
1982A Proof	2,500	Value: 10.00				
1983A	100,890,000	—	0.15	0.25	1.00	2.00
1983A Proof	2,550	Value: 18.00				
1984A	Est. 6,000	—	—	—	30.00	40.00
1984A Proof	3,015	Value: 4.50				
1985A	1,000,000	—	1.50	6.50	15.00	18.00
1985A Proof	2,816	Value: 4.50				
1986A	1,000,000	—	1.50	6.50	10.00	15.00
1986A Proof	2,800	Value: 4.50				
1987A	Est. 20,000	—	—	—	12.50	16.00
1987A Proof	2,345	Value: 4.50				
1988A	35,930,000	—	0.15	0.25	1.00	2.00
1988A Proof	2,300	Value: 4.50				
1989A	21,550,000	—	0.15	0.25	1.00	2.00
1989A Proof	2,300	Value: 4.50				
1990A	50,640,000	—	0.15	0.25	1.00	2.00

KM# 3 10 PFENNIG

Aluminum **Obv:** Denomination **Rev:** Cogwheel back of grain sprigs **Note:** Also exists with medallic die rotation (1950E).

Date	Mintage	F	VF	XF	Unc	BU
1948A	216,537,000	—	2.50	19.00	75.00	100
1949A	Inc. above	—	2.50	15.00	70.00	90.00
1950A	Inc. above	—	2.50	10.00	70.00	90.00
1950E	16,000,000	—	15.00	150	800	1,000

KM# 7 10 PFENNIG

Aluminum **Obv:** Denomination **Rev:** Grain sprigs flank hammer and protractor, date below

Date	Mintage	F	VF	XF	Unc	BU
1952A	70,427,000	—	2.00	12.00	60.00	80.00
1952E	21,498,000	—	10.00	30.00	300	400
1953A	18,611,000	—	3.50	18.00	75.00	100
1953E	11,500,000	—	15.00	70.00	400	550

KM# 10 10 PFENNIG

1.5000 g., Aluminum, 21 mm. **Obv:** State emblem **Rev:** Denomination divides leaf and date

Date	Mintage	F	VF	XF	Unc	BU
1963A	21,063,000	—	7.00	30.00	60.00	80.00
1965A	55,313,000	—	1.00	2.00	3.00	4.00
1967A	96,955,000	—	0.15	1.00	3.00	4.00
1968A	207,461,000	—	0.15	1.00	2.00	3.00
1970A	13,387,000	—	0.15	1.00	3.00	5.00
1971A	66,617,999	—	0.15	1.00	2.00	3.00
1972A	5,702,000	—	0.50	3.00	8.00	10.00
1973A	11,257,000	—	0.15	1.00	3.00	4.00
1978A	40,000,000	—	0.15	1.00	2.00	3.00
1979A	54,665,000	—	0.15	1.00	2.00	3.00
1979A Proof	—	Value: 45.00				
1980A	20,664,000	—	0.15	1.00	3.00	4.00
1980A Proof	—	Value: 45.00				
1981A	40,704,000	—	0.15	1.00	2.00	3.00
1981A Proof	40	—	—	—	—	—
1982A	40,212,000	—	0.15	1.00	3.00	4.00
1982A Proof	2,500	Value: 10.00				
1983A	40,699,000	—	0.15	10.00	50.00	75.00
1983A Proof	2,550	Value: 20.00				
1984A	Est. 12,000	—	—	10.00	25.00	35.00
Note: Issued in sets only, remainder unaccountable						
1984A Proof	3,015	Value: 4.50				
1985A	1,010,000	—	0.35	4.50	12.00	15.00
1985A Proof	2,816	Value: 4.50				
1986A	1,000,000	—	0.35	4.50	12.00	15.00
1986A Proof	2,800	Value: 4.50				
1987A	Est. 20,000	—	—	7.00	12.00	15.00
Note: Issued in sets only, remainder unaccountable						
1987A Proof	2,345	Value: 4.50				
1988A	10,705,000	—	0.15	1.00	2.00	3.00

Date	Mintage	F	VF	XF	Unc	BU
1988A Proof	2,300	Value: 4.50				
1989A	37,640,000	—	0.15	1.00	2.00	3.00
1989A Proof	2,300	Value: 4.50				
1990A	Est. 14,000	—	—	—	17.00	25.00

Note: Issued in sets only, remainder unaccountable

KM# 11 20 PFENNIG

5.4000 g., Brass, 22.3 mm. **Obv:** State emblem **Rev:** Denomination above date **Note:** Ribbon width varieties exist.

Date	Mintage	F	VF	XF	Unc	BU
1969	167,168,000	—	0.25	2.00	5.00	7.00
1971	24,563,000	—	0.25	3.00	6.00	7.00
1972A	5,007,000	—	1.00	4.00	10.00	12.00
1973A	2,524,000	—	1.00	4.50	10.00	12.00
1974A	7,458,000	—	1.00	2.50	8.00	10.00
1979A	293,000	—	1.00	3.00	7.50	9.00
1979A Proof	—	Value: 50.00				
1980A	2,190,000	—	1.00	3.00	20.00	30.00
1980A Proof	—	Value: 50.00				
1981A	983,000	—	1.00	4.00	9.00	12.00
1981A Proof	40	—	—	—	—	—
1982A	10,458,000	—	1.00	4.00	9.00	12.00
1982A Proof	2,500	Value: 12.50				
1983A	25,809,000	—	1.00	2.00	3.00	5.00
1983A Proof	2,550	Value: 25.00				
1984A	25,009,000	—	1.00	2.00	3.00	5.00
1984A Proof	3,015	Value: 5.50				
1985A	1,559,000	—	1.00	3.00	8.00	12.00
1985A Proof	2,816	Value: 5.50				
1986A	1,147,000	—	1.00	4.00	10.00	15.00
1986A Proof	2,800	Value: 5.50				
1987A	Est. 20,000	—	4.00	6.00	10.00	15.00
Note: Issued in sets only, remainder unaccountable						
1987A Proof	2,345	Value: 5.50				
1988A	Est. 15,000	—	4.00	6.00	10.00	15.00
Note: Issued in sets only, remainder unaccountable						
1988A Proof	2,300	Value: 5.50				
1989A	14,690,000	—	0.20	1.00	2.00	3.00
1989A Proof	2,300	Value: 5.50				
1990A	Est. 14,000	—	—	—	15.00	20.00

Note: Issued in sets only, remainder unaccountable

KM# 4 50 PFENNIG

Aluminum-Bronze **Obv:** Denomination above date **Rev:** Man and cart in front of buildings with tall stacks

Date	Mintage	F	VF	XF	Unc	BU
1949A	Inc. below	—	—	7,500	8,000	10,000
1950A	67,703,000	—	3.50	10.00	70.00	300

Note: Some authorities believe the 1949-dated piece is a pattern

KM# 12.1 50 PFENNIG

Aluminum, 23 mm. **Obv:** Small state emblem

Date	Mintage	F	VF	XF	Unc	BU
1958A	101,606,000	—	1.00	3.00	8.00	10.00

KM# 12.2 50 PFENNIG

1.9000 g., Aluminum, 23 mm. **Obv:** State emblem **Rev:** Denomination divides date and leaf **Note:** Inscription varieties exist.

Date	Mintage	F	VF	XF	Unc	BU
1968A	19,860,000	—	1.00	2.00	4.00	5.00
1971A	35,829,000	—	1.00	2.00	3.00	4.00
1972A	8,117,000	—	1.00	2.00	4.50	5.50
1973A	6,530,000	—	1.00	2.00	6.00	8.00
1979A	1,026,999	—	1.00	2.00	6.00	8.00
1979A Proof	—	—	—	—	—	—
1980A	1,118,000	—	5.00	10.00	15.00	20.00
1980A Proof	—	—	—	—	—	—
1981A	10,546,000	—	1.00	3.00	5.00	7.00
1981A Proof	40	—	—	—	—	—
1982A	79,832,000	—	0.35	0.75	2.50	3.00
1982A Proof	2,500	Value: 12.50				
1983A	1,309,000	—	1.00	3.00	8.00	12.00
1983A Proof	2,550	Value: 25.00				

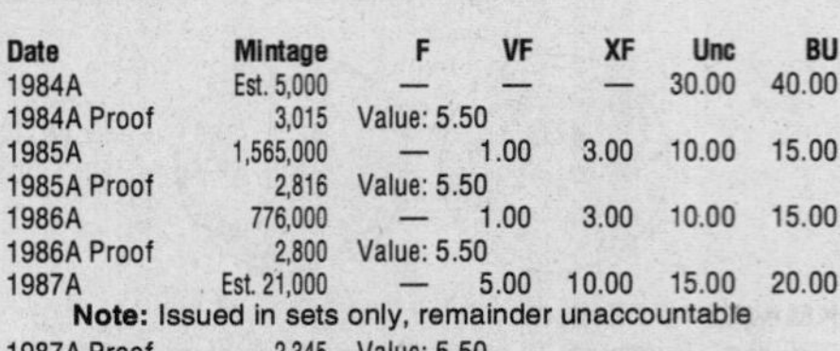

Date	Mintage	F	VF	XF	Unc	BU
1984A	Est. 5,000	—	—	—	30.00	40.00
1984A Proof	3,015	Value: 5.50				
1985A	1,565,000	—	1.00	3.00	10.00	15.00
1985A Proof	2,816	Value: 5.50				
1986A	776,000	—	1.00	3.00	10.00	15.00
1986A Proof	2,800	Value: 5.50				
1987A	Est. 21,000	—	5.00	10.00	15.00	20.00
Note: Issued in sets only, remainder unaccountable						
1987A Proof	2,345	Value: 5.50				
1988A	Est. 15,000	—	6.00	12.00	15.00	20.00
Note: Issued in sets only, remainder unaccountable						
1988A Proof	2,300	Value: 5.50				
1989A	31,000	—	1.00	3.00	8.00	12.00
1989A Proof	2,300	Value: 5.50				
1990A	Est. 14,000	—	—	—	15.00	20.00

Note: Issued in sets only, remainder unaccountable

KM# 13 MARK

Aluminum **Obv:** State emblem **Rev:** Large, thick denomination flanked by leaves, date below

Date	Mintage	F	VF	XF	Unc	BU
1956A	112,108,000	—	1.00	3.00	9.00	12.00
1962A	45,920,000	—	1.00	4.00	8.00	12.00
1963A	31,910,000	—	1.00	2.50	8.00	12.00

KM# 35.1 MARK

Aluminum **Obv:** State emblem **Rev:** Large 1 flanked by oak leaves

Date	Mintage	F	VF	XF	Unc	BU
1972A	30,288,000	—	1.00	4.00	5.00	8.00

KM# 35.2 MARK

2.4000 g., Aluminum, 25 mm. **Obv:** State emblem **Rev:** Large, thick denomination flanked by leaves, small date below

Date	Mintage	F	VF	XF	Unc	BU
1973A	6,972,000	—	1.00	4.00	10.00	12.00
1975A	32,094,000	—	1.00	2.00	5.00	7.00
1977A	119,813,000	—	0.50	1.00	2.00	3.00
1978A	18,824,000	—	0.50	1.00	2.00	3.00
1979A	1,002,999	—	1.00	2.00	7.50	10.00
1979A Proof	—	—	—	—	—	—
1980A	1,069,000	—	5.00	10.00	15.00	20.00
1980A Proof	—	—	—	—	—	—
1981A	1,006,000	—	1.00	3.00	7.50	10.00
1981A Proof	40	—	—	—	—	—
1982A	51,619,000	—	0.50	1.00	2.00	3.00
1982A Proof	2,500	Value: 25.00				
1983A	1,065,000	—	1.00	2.00	7.50	10.00
1983A Proof	2,550	Value: 30.00				
1984A	Est. 5,000	—	—	—	40.00	50.00
1984A Proof	3,015	Value: 7.50				
1985A	1,128,000	—	1.00	2.00	7.50	10.00
1985A Proof	2,816	Value: 7.50				
1986A	1,000,000	—	1.00	2.00	7.50	10.00
1986A Proof	2,800	Value: 7.50				
1987A	Est. 21,000	—	8.00	12.00	18.00	22.00
Note: Issued in sets only, remainder unaccountable						
1987A Proof	2,345	Value: 7.50				
1988A	Est. 15,000	—	—	—	15.00	20.00
Note: Issued in sets only, remainder unaccountable						
1988A Proof	2,300	Value: 7.50				
1989A	33,000	—	2.00	10.00	15.00	20.00
1989A Proof	2,300	Value: 7.50				
1990A	Est. 14,000	—	—	—	20.00	25.00

Note: Issued in sets only, remainder unaccountable

KM# 14 2 MARK

Aluminum **Obv:** State emblem **Rev:** Large denomination flanked by leaves, date below

Date	Mintage	F	VF	XF	Unc	BU
1957A	77,961,000	—	2.00	4.00	8.00	10.00

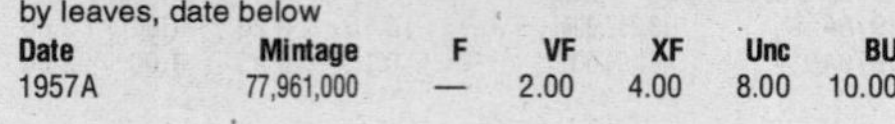

KM# 48 2 MARK

3.0000 g., Aluminum, 27 mm. **Obv:** State emblem **Rev:** Large denomination flanked by leaves, date below

Date	Mintage	F	VF	XF	Unc	BU
1972A	—	—	—	—	—	—
Note: 3 pieces known						
1974A	5,790,000	—	2.00	5.00	12.00	15.00
1975A	32,464,000	—	2.00	2.00	9.00	10.00
1977A	27,859,000	—	2.00	5.00	8.00	10.00
1978A	23,415,000	—	2.00	5.00	8.00	10.00
1979A	985,000	—	2.00	5.00	8.00	10.00
1979A Proof	—	—	—	—	—	—
1980A	1,018,999	—	2.00	5.00	9.00	12.00
1980A Proof	—	—	—	—	—	—
1981A	939,000	—	2.00	5.00	8.00	10.00
1981A Proof	40	—	—	—	—	—
1982A	60,488,000	—	1.00	2.00	3.00	4.00
1982A Proof	2,500	Value: 55.00				
1983A	1,030,000	—	1.00	2.00	6.00	8.00
1983A Proof	2,550	Value: 75.00				
1984A	Est. 6,000	—	—	—	30.00	40.00
1984A Proof	3,015	Value: 20.00				
1985A	1,310,000	—	3.00	6.00	10.00	15.00
1985A Proof	2,816	Value: 20.00				
1986A	1,000,000	—	3.00	6.00	10.00	15.00
1986A Proof	2,800	Value: 20.00				
1987A	Est. 30,000	—	8.00	12.00	18.00	22.00
Note: Issued in sets only, remainder unaccountable						
1987A Proof	2,345	Value: 20.00				
1988A	Est. 15,000	—	8.00	12.00	18.00	22.00
Note: Issued in sets only, remainder unaccountable						
1988A Proof	2,300	Value: 20.00				
1989A	46,000	—	5.00	10.00	15.00	20.00
1989A Proof	2,300	Value: 20.00				
1990A	Est. 14,000	—	—	—	30.00	40.00

Note: Issued in sets only, remainder unaccountable

KM# 19.1 5 MARK

9.7000 g., Copper-Nickel, 29 mm. **Subject:** 125th Anniversary of Birth of Robert Koch, doctor **Obv:** State emblem **Rev:** Head left

Date	Mintage	F	VF	XF	Unc	BU
1968	100,000	—	—	10.00	20.00	30.00

KM# 19.2 5 MARK

9.7000 g., Copper-Nickel, 29 mm. **Obv:** State emblem **Rev:** Head left **Note:** Error: plain edge.

Date	Mintage	F	VF	XF	Unc	BU
1968	—	—	—	—	400	450

KM# 23 5 MARK

9.7000 g., Copper-Nickel, 29 mm. **Subject:** Heinrich Hertz, physicist **Obv:** State emblem, denomination **Rev:** Head right, dates below

Date	Mintage	F	VF	XF	Unc	BU
1969	100,000	—	—	20.00	35.00	50.00

KM# 22.1 5 MARK

Nickel-Bronze, 29 mm. **Subject:** 20th Anniversary D.D.R **Obv:** State emblem **Rev:** Denomination, date at left

Date	Mintage	F	VF	XF	Unc	BU
1969	50,222,000	—	—	3.00	4.50	7.50

Note: 10% nickel and 90% copper

KM# 22.1a 5 MARK

Copper-Nickel, 29 mm. **Obv:** State emblem **Rev:** Denomination, date at left

Date	Mintage	F	VF	XF	Unc	BU
1969	12,741	—	50.00	60.00	70.00	80.00

Note: 25% nickel and 75% copper

KM# 22.2 5 MARK

Nickel-Bronze, 29 mm. **Obv:** State emblem **Rev:** Denomination, date at left **Note:** Error: plain edge.

Date	Mintage	F	VF	XF	Unc	BU
1969	—	—	—	—	120	150

KM# 22.3 5 MARK

Nickel-Bronze, 29 mm. **Obv:** State emblem **Rev:** Denomination, date at left **Note:** Error: Mongolian inscription and dates on edge.

Date	Mintage	F	VF	XF	Unc	BU
1969	—	—	—	—	—	—

KM# 26 5 MARK

9.7000 g., Copper-Nickel, 29 mm. **Subject:** Wilhelm Conrad Rontgen, physicist

Date	Mintage	F	VF	XF	Unc	BU
1970	100,000	—	—	15.00	20.00	25.00

KM# 29 5 MARK

9.7000 g., Copper-Nickel, 29 mm. **Subject:** Brandenburg Gate

Date	Mintage	F	VF	XF	Unc	BU
1971A	4,000,000	—	—	3.00	10.00	20.00
1979A	32,000	—	—	10.00	25.00	35.00
1979A Proof	2,500	—	—	—	—	—
1980A	30,000	—	—	10.00	15.00	20.00
1980A Proof	2,500	—	—	—	—	—
1981A	30,000	—	—	10.00	15.00	20.00

Date	Mintage	F	VF	XF	Unc	BU
1981A Proof	2,500	—	—	—	—	—
1982A	28,000	—	—	10.00	15.00	25.00
1982A Proof	2,500	Value: 200				
1983A	3,000	—	—	—	900	1,100
1984A	28,000	—	—	25.00	40.00	60.00
1984A Proof	3,015	Value: 120				
1985A	3,000	—	—	—	900	1,100
1986A	28,000	—	—	50.00	110	125
1986A Proof	2,800	Value: 140				
1987A	220,000	—	—	10.00	15.00	20.00
1987A Proof	6,424	Value: 80.00				
1988A	28,000	—	—	12.00	15.00	35.00
1988A Proof	2,300	Value: 125				
1989A	28,000	—	—	121	25.00	35.00
1989A Proof	2,405	Value: 125				
1990A	50,000	—	—	12.00	25.00	35.00

KM# 30 5 MARK

9.7000 g., Copper-Nickel, 29 mm. **Subject:** Johannes Kepler, scientist

Date	Mintage	F	VF	XF	Unc	BU
1971	100,000	—	—	15.00	20.00	25.00

KM# 37 5 MARK

9.7000 g., Copper-Nickel, 29 mm. **Subject:** City of Meissen **Obv:** State emblem, denomination **Rev:** City scene

Date	Mintage	F	VF	XF	Unc	BU
1972A	3,500,000	—	—	4.00	10.00	12.00
1981A Proof	40	Value: 2,750				
1983A	28,000	—	—	150	180	200
1983A Proof	2,550	Value: 400				

KM# 36.1 5 MARK

9.7000 g., Copper-Nickel, 29 mm. **Subject:** 75th Anniversary - Death of Johannes Brahms **Obv:** State emblem, denomination **Rev:** Name, musical score, dates

Date	Mintage	F	VF	XF	Unc	BU
1972	55,000	—	—	15.00	20.00	25.00

KM# 36.2 5 MARK

9.7000 g., Copper-Nickel, 29 mm. **Obv:** State emblem, denomination **Rev:** Musical score, name and dates **Note:** Error: Double edge inscription.

Date	Mintage	F	VF	XF	Unc	BU
1972	—	—	—	—	475	575

KM# 43 5 MARK

9.7000 g., Copper-Nickel, 29 mm. **Subject:** 125th Anniversary - Birth of Otto Lilienthal, aviation pioneer **Obv:** State emblem, denomination **Rev:** Plane divides dates

Date	Mintage	F	VF	XF	Unc	BU
1973	100,000	—	—	40.00	50.00	60.00

KM# 49 5 MARK

9.7000 g., Copper-Nickel, 29 mm. **Subject:** Centenary - Death of Philipp Reis, physicist, telephone inventor **Obv:** State emblem, denomination **Rev:** Telephone and telegraph divided by name, dates at bottom

Date	Mintage	F	VF	XF	Unc	BU
1974	100,000	—	—	—	20.00	30.00

KM# 54 5 MARK

9.7000 g., Copper-Nickel, 29 mm. **Subject:** 100th Anniversary - Birth of Thomas Mann, writer **Obv:** State emblem, denomination **Rev:** Head left, dates below

Date	Mintage	F	VF	XF	Unc	BU
1975	100,000	—	—	15.00	20.00	25.00

KM# 55 5 MARK

9.7000 g., Copper-Nickel, 29 mm. **Subject:** International Women's Year **Obv:** State emblem, denomination **Rev:** Profiles of three women right

Date	Mintage	F	VF	XF	Unc	BU
1975	250,000	—	—	15.00	20.00	25.00

KM# 60 5 MARK

9.7000 g., Copper-Nickel, 29 mm. **Subject:** 200th Anniversary - Birth of Ferdinand von Schill, military officer **Obv:** State emblem, denomination **Rev:** Hat divides dates above sword and name

Date	Mintage	F	VF	XF	Unc	BU
1976	100,000	—	—	20.00	28.00	35.00

KM# 64 5 MARK

9.7000 g., Copper-Nickel, 29 mm. **Subject:** 125th Anniversary - Death of Friedrich Ludwig Jahn, father of German gymnastics **Obv:** State emblem, denomination **Rev:** Bust 3/4 facing, dates below

Date	Mintage	F	VF	XF	Unc	BU
1977	90,000	—	—	30.00	40.00	50.00
1977 Proof	10,000	Value: 80.00				

KM# 67 5 MARK

9.7000 g., Copper-Nickel, 29 mm. **Subject:** 175th Anniversary - Death of Friedrich Klopstock, poet **Obv:** State emblem, denomination **Rev:** Bust left

Date	Mintage	F	VF	XF	Unc	BU
1978	96,000	—	—	30.00	40.00	50.00
1978 Proof	4,500	Value: 100				

KM# 68 5 MARK

9.7000 g., Copper-Nickel, 29 mm. **Subject:** Anti-Apartheid Year **Obv:** Denomination, date below small state emblem at left **Rev:** Raised clenched fist

Date	Mintage	F	VF	XF	Unc	BU
1978A	196,000	—	—	20.00	25.00	30.00
1978A Proof	4,000	Value: 110				

KM# 72 5 MARK

9.7000 g., Copper-Nickel, 29 mm. **Subject:** 100th Anniversary - Birth of Albert Einstein, physicist **Obv:** State emblem, denomination **Rev:** Head 3/4 right

Date	Mintage	F	VF	XF	Unc	BU
1979	56,000	—	—	55.00	80.00	95.00
1979 Proof	4,500	Value: 120				

KM# 76 5 MARK

9.7000 g., Copper-Nickel, 29 mm. **Subject:** 75th Anniversary - Death of Adolph von Menzel **Obv:** State emblem, denomination **Rev:** Bust left divides dates

Date	Mintage	F	VF	XF	Unc	BU
1980	55,000	—	—	35.00	50.00	60.00
1980 Proof	5,500	Value: 110				

KM# 79 5 MARK

9.7000 g., Copper-Nickel, 29 mm. **Subject:** 450th Anniversary - Death of Tilman Riemenschneider, sculptor **Obv:** State emblem, denomination **Rev:** Bust 3/4 facing, divides dates

Date	Mintage	F	VF	XF	Unc	BU
1981	55,000	—	—	40.00	60.00	70.00
1981 Proof	5,500	Value: 110				

KM# 84 5 MARK

9.7000 g., Copper-Nickel, 29 mm. **Subject:** 200th Anniversary - Birth of Friedrich Frobel **Obv:** State emblem, denomination **Rev:** Three children with building blocks, dates below

Date	Mintage	F	VF	XF	Unc	BU
1982	55,000	—	—	40.00	60.00	75.00
1982 Proof	5,500	Value: 100				

KM# 85 5 MARK
9.7000 g., Copper-Nickel-Zinc, 29 mm. **Subject:** Goethe's Weimar Cottage **Obv:** Small state emblem, denomination **Rev:** Cottage

Date	Mintage	F	VF	XF	Unc	BU
1982A	245,000	—	—	25.00	35.00	42.00
1982A Proof	5,500	Value: 100				
Note: House and trees frosted						
1982A Proof	210	Value: 3,000				
Note: House only frosted						

KM# 86 5 MARK
9.7000 g., Copper-Nickel-Zinc, 29 mm. **Subject:** Wartburg Castle **Obv:** State emblem, denomination **Rev:** Castle **Designer:** Heinz Rodewald

Date	Mintage	F	VF	XF	Unc	BU
1982A	245,000	—	—	25.00	40.00	45.00
1982A Proof	5,500	Value: 90.00				
1983A	10,000	—	—	—	400	450

KM# 89 5 MARK
9.7000 g., Copper-Nickel, 29 mm. **Subject:** Wittenberg Church **Obv:** Small state emblem, denomination **Rev:** Church **Designer:** Heinz Rodewald

Date	Mintage	F	VF	XF	Unc	BU
1983A	245,000	—	—	25.00	40.00	50.00
1983A Proof	5,500	Value: 80.00				

KM# 90 5 MARK
9.7000 g., Copper-Nickel, 29 mm. **Subject:** Martin Luther's birthplace **Obv:** State emblem, denomination **Rev:** House **Designer:** Heinz Rodewald

Date	Mintage	F	VF	XF	Unc	BU
1983A	245,000	—	—	25.00	40.00	50.00
1983A Proof	5,500	Value: 90.00				

KM# 91 5 MARK
Copper-Nickel-Zinc, 29 mm. **Subject:** 125th Anniversary - Birth of Max Planck **Obv:** State emblem, denomination **Rev:** Head right, dates below **Rev. Designer:** Dietrich Dorfstedoer

Date	Mintage	F	VF	XF	Unc	BU
1983	56,000	—	—	32.00	45.00	55.00
1983 Proof	4,200	Value: 100				

KM# 96 5 MARK
9.7000 g., Copper-Nickel, 29 mm. **Subject:** Leipzig Old City Hall **Obv:** State emblem, denomination **Rev:** City hall building

Date	Mintage	F	VF	XF	Unc	BU
1984A	245,000	—	—	25.00	40.00	50.00
1984A Proof	5,500	Value: 70.00				

KM# 97 5 MARK
9.7000 g., Copper-Nickel, 29 mm. **Subject:** Thomas Church of Leipzig **Obv:** State emblem, denomination **Rev:** Church

Date	Mintage	F	VF	XF	Unc	BU
1984A	245,000	—	—	25.00	40.00	50.00
1984A Proof	5,500	Value: 70.00				

KM# 98 5 MARK
9.7000 g., Copper-Nickel, 29 mm. **Subject:** 150th Anniversary - Death of Adolf Freiherr von Lutzow **Obv:** State emblem, denomination **Rev:** Three uniformed figures on horses

Date	Mintage	F	VF	XF	Unc	BU
1984A	55,000	—	—	55.00	70.00	80.00
1984A Proof	5,000	Value: 110				

KM# 102 5 MARK
9.7000 g., Copper-Nickel, 29 mm. **Subject:** Restoration of Dresden Women's Church **Obv:** State emblem divides date above six line inscription, denomination below **Rev:** Church buildings, date above

Date	Mintage	F	VF	XF	Unc	BU
1985A	245,000	—	—	25.00	35.00	40.00
1985A Proof	8,476	Value: 70.00				

KM# 103 5 MARK
9.7000 g., Copper-Nickel, 29 mm. **Subject:** Restoration of Dresden Zwinger **Obv:** State emblem, denomination **Rev:** Building

Date	Mintage	F	VF	XF	Unc	BU
1985A	245,000	—	—	25.00	35.00	45.00
1985A Proof	5,500	Value: 70.00				

KM# 104 5 MARK
9.7000 g., Copper-Nickel, 29 mm. **Subject:** 225th Anniversary - Death of Caroline Neuber **Obv:** State emblem, denomination **Rev:** Caroline on stage, 1697-1760

Date	Mintage	F	VF	XF	Unc	BU
1985A	56,000	—	—	75.00	90.00	100
1985A Proof	4,000	Value: 150				

KM# 110 5 MARK
9.7000 g., Copper-Nickel, 29 mm. **Subject:** Potsdam - Sanssouci Palace **Obv:** State emblem, denomination **Rev:** Palace

Date	Mintage	F	VF	XF	Unc	BU
1986A	296,000	—	—	9.00	12.00	17.50
1986A Proof	4,200	Value: 100				

KM# 111 5 MARK
9.7000 g., Copper-Nickel, 29 mm. **Subject:** Potsdam - New Palace **Obv:** State emblem, denomination **Rev:** Palace buildings

Date	Mintage	F	VF	XF	Unc	BU
1986A	296,000	—	—	9.00	12.00	17.50
1986A Proof	4,200	Value: 100				

KM# 112 5 MARK
9.7000 g., Copper-Nickel, 29 mm. **Subject:** 175th Anniversary - Death of Heinrich von Kleist **Obv:** State emblem, denomination **Rev:** Bust left looking forward divides dates

Date	Mintage	F	VF	XF	Unc	BU
1986A	56,000	—	—	130	150	180
1986A Proof	4,000	Value: 200				

KM# 114 5 MARK
9.7000 g., Copper-Zinc-Nickel, 29 mm. **Subject:** Berlin - Nikolai Quarter **Obv:** State emblem, denomination **Rev:** Buildings with two towers

Date	Mintage	F	VF	XF	Unc	BU
1987A	496,000	—	—	8.00	12.00	15.00
1987A Proof	4,200	Value: 75.00				

KM# 115 5 MARK
9.7000 g., Copper-Zinc-Nickel, 29 mm. **Subject:** Berlin - Red City Hall **Obv:** State emblem, denomination **Rev:** City hall building

Date	Mintage	F	VF	XF	Unc	BU
1987A	496,000	—	—	8.00	12.00	15.00
1987A Proof	4,200	Value: 75.00				

KM# 116 5 MARK
9.7000 g., Copper-Zinc-Nickel, 29 mm. **Subject:** Berlin - Universal Time Clock **Obv:** State emblem, denomination **Rev:** Universal clock

Date	Mintage	F	VF	XF	Unc	BU
1987A	496,000	—	—	8.00	12.00	15.00
1987A Proof	4,200	Value: 75.00				

KM# 120 5 MARK
9.7000 g., Copper-Nickel, 29 mm. **Subject:** Germany's First Railroad **Obv:** State emblem, denomination **Rev:** Train engine, tower in background

Date	Mintage	F	VF	XF	Unc	BU
1988A	496,000	—	—	8.00	9.00	12.50
1988A Proof	4,200	Value: 130				

KM# 121 5 MARK
9.7000 g., Copper-Nickel, 29 mm. **Subject:** Port City of Rostock **Obv:** State emblem, denomination **Rev:** Ships in port

Date	Mintage	F	VF	XF	Unc	BU
1988A	496,000	—	—	8.00	9.00	12.50
1988A Proof	4,200	Value: 120				

KM# 122 5 MARK
9.7000 g., Copper-Nickel, 29 mm. **Subject:** 50th Anniversary - Death of Ernst Barlach **Obv:** State emblem, denomination **Rev:** Full-length figure playing horn, dates at right

Date	Mintage	F	VF	XF	Unc	BU
1988A	56,000	—	—	50.00	65.00	80.00
1988A Proof	4,000	Value: 175				

KM# 129 5 MARK
9.7000 g., Copper-Zinc-Nickel, 29 mm. **Subject:** Katharinen Kirche in Zwickau **Obv:** State emblem, denomination **Rev:** Church **Rev. Designer:** Wilfried Klink

Date	Mintage	F	VF	XF	Unc	BU
1989A	496,000	—	—	7.00	9.00	11.50
1989A Proof	4,200	Value: 110				

KM# 130 5 MARK
9.7000 g., Copper-Zinc-Nickel, 29 mm. **Subject:** Marien Kirche in Muhlhausen **Obv:** State emblem, denomination **Rev:** Church and city scene **Rev. Designer:** Heinz Rodewald

Date	Mintage	F	VF	XF	Unc	BU
1989A	496,000	—	—	7.00	9.00	11.50
1989A Proof	4,200	Value: 110				

KM# 131 5 MARK
9.7000 g., Copper-Zinc-Nickel, 29 mm. **Subject:** 100th Anniversary - Birth of Carl von Ossietzky **Obv:** State emblem, denomination **Rev:** Bust left, dates at right

Date	Mintage	F	VF	XF	Unc	BU
1989A	56,000	—	—	60.00	75.00	90.00
1989A Proof	4,000	Value: 200				

KM# 135 5 MARK
9.7000 g., Copper-Zinc-Nickel, 29 mm. **Subject:** Zeughaus Museum **Obv:** State emblem, denomination **Rev:** Museum

Date	Mintage	F	VF	XF	Unc	BU
1990A	496,000	—	—	7.00	8.00	10.00
1990A Proof	4,200	Value: 100				

KM# 133 5 MARK
9.7000 g., Copper-Zinc-Nickel, 29 mm. **Subject:** 100th Anniversary - Birth of Kurt Tucholsky **Obv:** State emblem, denomination **Rev:** Head facing, dates below

Date	Mintage	F	VF	XF	Unc	BU
1990A	51,000	—	—	40.00	60.00	70.00
1990A Proof	4,000	Value: 125				

KM# 134 5 MARK
9.7000 g., Copper-Zinc-Nickel, 29 mm. **Subject:** 500 Years of Postal Service **Obv:** State emblem, denomination **Rev:** Antique car

Date	Mintage	F	VF	XF	Unc	BU
1990A	496,000	—	—	7.00	9.00	11.00
1990A Proof	4,200	Value: 100				

KM# 15.1 10 MARK
17.0000 g., 0.8000 Silver .4373 oz. ASW, 31 mm. **Subject:** 125th Anniversary - Death of Karl Friedrich Schinkel, artist, painter **Obv:** State emblem, denomination **Rev:** Head right, dates below **Edge Lettering:** 10 MARK DER DEUTSCHEN NOTEN BANK

Date	Mintage	F	VF	XF	Unc	BU
1966	50,000	—	—	325	400	425
1966 Proof, extremely rare	—	—	—	—	—	—

KM# 15.2 10 MARK
17.0000 g., 0.8000 Silver .4373 oz. ASW, 31 mm. **Obv:** State emblem, denomination **Rev:** Head right, dates below **Note:** Error: Plain edge.

Date	Mintage	F	VF	XF	Unc	BU
1966	—	—	—	—	—	—

KM# 17.1 10 MARK
17.0000 g., 0.8000 Silver .4373 oz. ASW, 31 mm. **Subject:** 100th Anniversary - Birth of Kathe Kollwitz, artist **Obv:** State emblem, denomination **Rev:** Head left, dates below **Rev. Designer:** Rommel **Edge Lettering:** 10 MARK DER DEUTSCHEN NOTENBANK

Date	Mintage	F	VF	XF	Unc	BU
1967	97,000	—	—	60.00	70.00	90.00
1967 Proof, extrememly rare	—	—	—	—	—	—

KM# 17.2 10 MARK
17.0000 g., 0.8000 Silver .4373 oz. ASW, 31 mm. **Subject:** 100th Anniversary - Birth of Kathe Kollwitz **Obv:** State emblem, denomination **Rev:** Head left, dates below **Note:** Error, edge: 10 MARK*10 MARK*10 MARK*

Date	Mintage	F	VF	XF	Unc	BU
1967	3,000	—	—	—	200	250

KM# 20.1 10 MARK
17.0000 g., 0.6250 Silver .3416 oz. ASW, 31 mm. **Subject:** 500th Anniversary - Death of Johann Gutenberg

Date	Mintage	F	VF	XF	Unc	BU
1968	100,000	—	—	55.00	65.00	85.00

KM# 20.2 10 MARK
17.0000 g., 0.6250 Silver .3416 oz. ASW, 31 mm. **Subject:** 500th Anniversary - Death of Johann Gutenberg **Note:** Error: Plain edge.

Date	Mintage	F	VF	XF	Unc	BU
1968	—	—	—	—	700	800

KM# 24 10 MARK
17.0000 g., 0.6250 Silver .3416 oz. ASW, 31 mm. **Subject:** 250th Anniversary - Death of Johann Friedrich Bottger **Obv:** State emblem, denomination **Rev:** Pitcher, dates divided above

Date	Mintage	F	VF	XF	Unc	BU
1969	100,000	—	—	50.00	60.00	75.00

KM# 27.1 10 MARK
17.0000 g., 0.6250 Silver .3416 oz. ASW, 31 mm. **Subject:** Ludwig Van Beethoven, composer **Obv:** State emblem, denomination **Rev:** Head left, dates below

Date	Mintage	F	VF	XF	Unc	BU
1970	100,000	—	—	50.00	60.00	70.00
1970 Proof, extremely rare	—	—	—	—	—	—

KM# 27.2 10 MARK

17.0000 g., 0.6250 Silver .3416 oz. ASW, 31 mm. **Obv:** State emblem, denomination **Rev:** Head left **Note:** Error: Plain edge.

Date	Mintage	F	VF	XF	Unc	BU
1970	—	—	—	—	—	600

KM# 27.2 10 MARK

17.0000 g., 0.6250 Silver .3416 oz. ASW, 31 mm. **Obv:** State emblem, denomination **Rev:** Head left **Note:** Error: Plain edge.

Date	Mintage	F	VF	XF	Unc	BU
1970	—	—	—	—	—	600

KM# 31 10 MARK

17.0000 g., 0.6250 Silver .3416 oz. ASW, 31 mm. **Subject:** Albrecht Durer, artist **Obv:** State emblem, denomination **Rev:** Durer's monogram

Date	Mintage	F	VF	XF	Unc	BU
1971	100,000	—	—	50.00	60.00	75.00
1971 Proof, extremely rare	—	—	—	—	—	—

KM# 38 10 MARK

Copper-Nickel, 31 mm. **Subject:** Buchenwald Memorial **Obv:** State emblem, denomination **Rev:** Monument

Date	Mintage	F	VF	XF	Unc	BU
1972A	2,500,000	—	—	—	8.00	10.00
1972A Prooflike	—	—	—	—	20.00	30.00

KM# 39 10 MARK

17.0000 g., 0.6250 Silver .3416 oz. ASW, 31 mm. **Subject:** 175th Anniversary - Birth of Heinrich Heine, poet **Obv:** Hammer and protractor within wreath, (state emblem), denomination and date below **Rev:** Bust 3/4 left, divides dates

Date	Mintage	F	VF	XF	Unc	BU
1972	100,000	—	—	55.00	65.00	80.00

KM# 44 10 MARK

Copper-Nickel, 31 mm. **Subject:** 10th Youth Festival Games **Obv:** State emblem below date and denomination **Rev:** Games symbol

Date	Mintage	F	VF	XF	Unc	BU
1973A	1,500,000	—	—	—	5.00	12.00
1973A Prooflike	—	—	—	—	15.00	20.00

KM# 45 10 MARK

17.0000 g., 0.6250 Silver .3416 oz. ASW, 31 mm. **Subject:** 75th Anniversary - Birth of Bertolt Brecht, poet **Obv:** State emblem, denomination **Rev:** Head left, dates below

Date	Mintage	F	VF	XF	Unc	BU
1973	100,000	—	—	50.00	60.00	80.00
1973 Proof, extremely rare	—	—	—	—	—	—

KM# 50 10 MARK

Copper-Nickel, 31 mm. **Subject:** 25th Anniversary (with state motto) **Obv:** Date and denomination below legend **Rev:** Dates above state emblem

Date	Mintage	F	VF	XF	Unc	BU
1974A	3,000,000	—	—	—	6.00	14.00
1974A Prooflike	—	—	—	—	15.00	20.00

KM# 51 10 MARK

17.0000 g., 0.6250 Silver .3416 oz. ASW, 31 mm. **Subject:** 25th Anniversary D.D.R. **Obv:** State emblem, denomination **Rev:** City scene

Date	Mintage	F	VF	XF	Unc	BU
1974	70,000	—	—	50.00	60.00	80.00
1974 Proof	200	Value: 5,000				

KM# 52 10 MARK

17.0000 g., 0.6250 Silver .3416 oz. ASW, 31 mm. **Subject:** 200th Anniversary - Birth of Caspar David Friedrich, painter **Obv:** State emblem, denomination **Rev:** Bust right within inner circle, dates below

Date	Mintage	F	VF	XF	Unc	BU
1974	75,000	—	—	50.00	60.00	75.00
1974 Proof	—	Value: 7,000				

KM# 56 10 MARK

17.0000 g., 0.6250 Silver .3416 oz. ASW, 31 mm. **Subject:** Centenary - Birth of Albert Schweitzer, doctor and philosopher **Obv:** State emblem, denomination **Rev:** Head left, dates below

Date	Mintage	F	VF	XF	Unc	BU
1975	99,000	—	—	50.00	60.00	80.00
1975 Proof	1,040	Value: 1,700				

KM# 57 10 MARK

17.0000 g., 0.5000 Silver .2733 oz. ASW, 31 mm. **Subject:** Mule **Obv:** State emblem below denomination, date **Rev:** Head left, dates below **Edge:** Plain

Date	Mintage	F	VF	XF	Unc	BU
1975A	6,700	—	—	—	—	180

KM# 58 10 MARK

Copper-Nickel, 31 mm. **Subject:** 20th Anniversary - Warsaw Pact **Obv:** State emblem below denomination, date **Rev:** Roman numerals, 'XX' divide seven shields

Date	Mintage	F	VF	XF	Unc	BU
1975A	2,500,000	—	—	7.00	10.00	15.00
1974A Prooflike	—	—	—	—	20.00	30.00

KM# 61 10 MARK

Copper-Nickel, 31 mm. **Subject:** 20th Anniversary - National People's Army **Obv:** State emblem below denomination, date **Rev:** Bust of soldier 3/4 facing

Date	Mintage	F	VF	XF	Unc	BU
1976A	750,000	—	—	10.00	15.00	20.00
1976A Prooflike	—	—	—	—	30.00	40.00

KM# 62 10 MARK

17.0000 g., 0.5000 Silver .2733 oz. ASW, 31 mm. **Subject:** 150th Anniversary - Death of Carl Maria von Weber, composer **Obv:** State emblem, denomination **Rev:** Bust right divides dates

Date	Mintage	F	VF	XF	Unc	BU
1976	94,000	—	—	70.00	80.00	95.00
1976 Proof	6,037	Value: 125				

KM# 65 10 MARK

17.0000 g., 0.5000 Silver .2733 oz. ASW, 31 mm. **Subject:** 375th Anniversary - Birth of Otto von Guericke **Obv:** State emblem, denomination **Rev:** Vacuum pump below and castle above divide dates

Date	Mintage	F	VF	XF	Unc	BU
1977	69,000	—	—	100	115	125
1977 Proof	6,000	Value: 160				

KM# 69 10 MARK
17.0000 g., 0.5000 Silver .2733 oz. ASW, 31 mm. **Subject:** 175th Anniversary - Birth of Justus von Liebig, chemist **Obv:** State emblem, denomination **Rev:** Bust 3/4 facing, dates at left

Date	Mintage	F	VF	XF	Unc	BU
1978	71,000	—	—	80.00	115	130
1978 Proof	4,500	Value: 150				

KM# 70 10 MARK
Copper-Nickel, 31 mm. **Subject:** Joint USSR-DDR Orbital Flight **Obv:** State emblem below denomination, date

Date	Mintage	F	VF	XF	Unc	BU
1978A	748,000	—	—	20.00	30.00	40.00
1978A Proof	2,200	Value: 600				

KM# 73 10 MARK
17.0000 g., 0.5000 Silver .2733 oz. ASW, 31 mm. **Subject:** 175th Anniversary - Birth of Ludwig Feuerbach, philosopher **Obv:** State emblem below denomination, date **Rev:** Bust 3/4 right, dates and name below

Date	Mintage	F	VF	XF	Unc	BU
1979	51,000	—	—	150	175	190
1979 Proof	4,500	Value: 225				

KM# 77 10 MARK
17.0000 g., 0.5000 Silver .2733 oz. ASW, 31 mm. **Subject:** 225th Anniversary - Birth of Gerhard von Scharnhorst **Obv:** State emblem below denomination, date **Rev:** Bust left divides dates

Date	Mintage	F	VF	XF	Unc	BU
1980	55,000	—	—	40.00	50.00	60.00
1980 Proof	5,500	Value: 95.00				

KM# 80 10 MARK
Copper-Nickel, 31 mm. **Subject:** 25th Anniversary - National People's Army **Obv:** State emblem and denomination divide date **Rev:** Plane above ship at center, tank below, dates at sides

Date	Mintage	F	VF	XF	Unc	BU
1981A	745,000	—	—	12.00	22.00	25.00
1981A Proof	5,500	Value: 80.00				

KM# 81 10 MARK
17.0000 g., 0.5000 Silver .2733 oz. ASW, 31 mm. **Subject:** 150th Anniversary - Death of Georg Hegel, philosopher **Obv:** Date and denomination above legend, state emblem below **Rev:** Head right divides dates

Date	Mintage	F	VF	XF	Unc	BU
1981	50,000	—	—	45.00	55.00	65.00
1981 Proof	5,500	Value: 95.00				

KM# 82 10 MARK
Copper-Nickel, 31 mm. **Subject:** 700th Anniversary - Berlin Mint **Obv:** State emblem and denomination divide date **Rev:** Ancient coin at center

Date	Mintage	F	VF	XF	Unc	BU
1981	55,000	—	—	40.00	45.00	55.00
1981 Proof	5,500	Value: 95.00				

KM# 87 10 MARK
17.0000 g., 0.5000 Silver .2733 oz. ASW, 31 mm. **Subject:** Leipzig Gewandhaus **Obv:** Legend divides denomination and state emblem **Rev:** Design above building

Date	Mintage	F	VF	XF	Unc	BU
1982	50,000	—	—	50.00	60.00	70.00
1982 Proof	5,500	Value: 95.00				

KM# 92 10 MARK
17.1100 g., 0.5000 Silver .2751 oz. ASW, 31 mm. **Subject:** 100th Anniversary - Death of Richard Wagner **Obv:** Legend divides state emblem and denomination **Rev:** Group of people, dates below

Date	Mintage	F	VF	XF	Unc	BU
1983	44,000	—	—	50.00	60.00	70.00
1983 Proof	5,500	Value: 95.00				

KM# 93 10 MARK
Copper-Nickel-Zinc, 31 mm. **Subject:** 30th Anniversary - Worker's Militia **Obv:** Legend divides state emblem and denomination **Rev:** Worker and soldier facing left **Designer:** Evely Nitzche-Hartnick and Dietrich Dorfstecker

Date	Mintage	F	VF	XF	Unc	BU
1983A	495,000	—	—	12.00	20.00	30.00
1983A Proof	5,000	Value: 90.00				

KM# 99 10 MARK
17.0000 g., 0.5000 Silver .2733 oz. ASW, 31 mm. **Subject:** 100th Anniversary - Death of Alfred Brehm **Obv:** State emblem, denomination **Rev:** Marabou stork left

Date	Mintage	F	VF	XF	Unc	BU
1984A	50,000	—	—	65.00	85.00	100
1984A Proof	5,000	Value: 135				

KM# 101 10 MARK
17.0000 g., 0.5000 Silver .2733 oz. ASW, 31 mm. **Subject:** Restoration of Semper Opera in Dresden **Obv:** Legend divides state emblem and denomination **Rev:** Opera House

Date	Mintage	F	VF	XF	Unc	BU
1985A	50,000	—	—	60.00	70.00	85.00
1985A Proof	5,000	Value: 120				

KM# 106 10 MARK
Copper-Nickel-Zinc, 31 mm. **Subject:** 40th Anniversary - Liberation from Fascism **Obv:** State emblem, denomination **Rev:** Statue divides inscription

Date	Mintage	F	VF	XF	Unc	BU
1985A	745,000	—	—	10.00	20.00	25.00
1985A Proof	5,500	Value: 90.00				

KM# 107 10 MARK
17.0000 g., 0.5000 Silver 0.2733 oz. ASW, 31 mm. **Subject:** 175th Anniversary - Humboldt University **Obv:** Legend divides state emblem and denomination **Rev:** Seated statues in front of building

Date	Mintage	F	VF	XF	Unc	BU
1985A	51,000	—	—	75.00	90.00	100
1985A Proof	4,000	Value: 125				

KM# 109 10 MARK
Copper-Nickel, 31 mm. **Subject:** 100th Anniversary - Birth of Ernst Thalmann **Obv:** State emblem below denomination, date **Rev:** People behind front figure with right fist raised

Date	Mintage	F	VF	XF	Unc	BU
1986A	746,000	—	—	10.00	17.50	25.00
1986A Proof	4,000	Value: 110				

KM# 113 10 MARK
17.0000 g., 0.5000 Silver .2733 oz. ASW, 31 mm. **Subject:** Charite - Berlin **Obv:** State emblem divides date below legend, denomination above **Rev:** Building

Date	Mintage	F	VF	XF	Unc	BU
1986A	51,000	—	—	70.00	80.00	90.00
1986A Proof	4,000	Value: 125				

KM# 118 10 MARK
17.0000 g., 0.5000 Silver .2733 oz. ASW, 31 mm. **Subject:** Berlin - Theater **Obv:** State emblem and denomination divide date **Rev:** Theater building

Date	Mintage	F	VF	XF	Unc	BU
1987A	51,000	—	—	60.00	70.00	85.00
1987A Proof	4,000	Value: 125				

KM# 123 10 MARK
17.0000 g., 0.5000 Silver .2733 oz. ASW, 31 mm. **Subject:** 500th Anniversary - Birth of Ulrich von Hutten **Obv:** State emblem, denomination **Rev:** Half figure left divides dates

Date	Mintage	F	VF	XF	Unc	BU
1988A	52,000	—	—	70.00	90.00	110
1988A Proof	3,500	Value: 250				

KM# 125 10 MARK
Copper-Nickel, 31 mm. **Subject:** East German Sports **Obv:** State emblem, denomination **Rev:** Three women running left, dates below

Date	Mintage	F	VF	XF	Unc	BU
1988A	747,000	—	—	10.00	20.00	28.00
1988A Proof	3,200	Value: 175				

KM# 126 10 MARK
Copper-Nickel, 31 mm. **Subject:** Council of Mutual Economic Aid **Obv:** State emblem, denomination **Rev:** Tall building, dates at right **Designer:** Heinz Rodewald and Lorelies Ziemainz

Date	Mintage	F	VF	XF	Unc	BU
1989A	—	—	—	30.00	50.00	60.00
1989A Proof	3,000	Value: 300				

KM# 128 10 MARK
17.0000 g., 0.5000 Silver .2733 oz. ASW, 31 mm. **Subject:** 225th Anniversary - Birth of Johann Gottfried Schadow **Obv:** State emblem, denomination **Rev:** Winged figure in chariot, dates below

Date	Mintage	F	VF	XF	Unc	BU
1989A	51,000	—	—	95.00	120	150
1989A Proof	4,000	Value: 350				

KM# 132 10 MARK
Copper-Nickel-Zinc, 31 mm. **Subject:** 40th Anniversary - East German Government **Obv:** State emblem divides dates above inscription, denomination below **Rev:** Fifteen shields on right, legend at left **Edge Lettering:** 10 MARK (repeated)

Date	Mintage	F	VF	XF	Unc	BU
1989A	746,000	—	—	12.00	15.00	20.00
1989A Proof	3,080	Value: 250				

KM# 136 10 MARK
Copper-Nickel-Zinc, 31 mm. **Subject:** International Labor Day **Obv:** State emblem below date and denomination **Rev:** Stylized lettering divides dates **Edge Lettering:** 10 MARK (repeated)

Date	Mintage	F	VF	XF	Unc	BU
1990A	747,000	—	—	4.00	7.00	10.00
1990A Proof	4,367	Value: 120				

KM# 137 10 MARK
17.0000 g., 0.5000 Silver .2733 oz. ASW, 31 mm. **Subject:** Johann Gottlieb Fichte **Obv:** State emblem, denomination **Rev:** Figure at lectern facing left

Date	Mintage	F	VF	XF	Unc	BU
1990A	37,000	—	—	70.00	90.00	110
1990A Proof	4,900	Value: 175				

KM# 16.1 20 MARK
20.9000 g., 0.8000 Silver .5376 oz. ASW, 33 mm. **Subject:** 250th Anniversary - Death of Gottfried Wilhelm Leibniz **Obv:** State emblem, denomination **Rev:** Bust right, dates below **Edge Lettering:** 20 MARK DER DEUTSCHEN NOTEN BANK

Date	Mintage	F	VF	XF	Unc	BU
1966	50,000	—	—	175	225	275
1966 Proof, extremely rare	—	—	—	—	—	—

KM# 16.2 20 MARK
20.9000 g., 0.8000 Silver .5376 oz. ASW, 33 mm. **Obv:** State emblem, denomination **Rev:** Bust right **Edge:** Error: In inscription **Edge Lettering:** 10 MARK DER DEUTSCHEN NOTEN BANK

Date	Mintage	F	VF	XF	Unc	BU
1966	—	—	—	—	—	—

KM# 18.1 20 MARK
20.9000 g., 0.8000 Silver .5376 oz. ASW, 33 mm. **Subject:** 200th Anniversary - Birth of Wilhelm von Humboldt **Obv:** State emblem, denomination **Rev:** Head with high collar left, dates below **Edge Lettering:** 20 MARK DER DEUTSCHEN NOTENBANK **Designer:** Rommel

Date	Mintage	F	VF	XF	Unc	BU
1967	97,000	—	—	160	180	210
1967 Proof, extremely rare	—	—	—	—	—	—

KM# 18.2 20 MARK
20.9000 g., 0.8000 Silver .5376 oz. ASW, 33 mm. **Obv:** State emblem, denomination **Rev:** Head with high collar left, dates below **Edge:** Error: In inscription **Edge Lettering:** 20 MARK*20 MARK*20 MARK*20 MARK

Date	Mintage	F	VF	XF	Unc	BU
1967	3,000	—	—	—	—	275

KM# 21 20 MARK
20.9000 g., 0.8000 Silver .5376 oz. ASW, 33 mm. **Subject:** 150th Anniversary - Birth of Karl Marx **Obv:** State emblem, denomination **Rev:** Head left, dates below **Designer:** Rommel

Date	Mintage	F	VF	XF	Unc	BU
1968	100,000	—	—	80.00	100	120
1968 Proof, extremely rare	—	—	—	—	—	—

KM# 25 20 MARK
20.9000 g., 0.6250 Silver .4200 oz. ASW, 33 mm. **Subject:** 240th Birth Anniversary - Johann Wolfgang von Goethe, poet **Obv:** State emblem, denomination **Rev:** Head left, dates below

Date	Mintage	F	VF	XF	Unc	BU
1969	100,000	—	—	140	160	180
1969 Proof, extremely rare	—	—	—	—	—	—

KM# 28 20 MARK
20.9000 g., 0.6250 Silver .4200 oz. ASW, 33 mm. **Subject:** 150th Anniversary - Birth of Friedrich Engels **Obv:** State emblem, denomination **Rev:** Head left, dates at right

Date	Mintage	F	VF	XF	Unc	BU
1970	100,000	—	—	85.00	100	120
1970 Proof, extremely rare	—	—	—	—	—	—

KM# 32 20 MARK
20.9000 g., 0.6250 Silver .4200 oz. ASW, 33 mm. **Subject:** Karl Kiebknecht - Rosa Luxemburg **Obv:** State emblem, denomination **Rev:** Jugate busts left, dates below **Edge Lettering:** 20 MARK (repeated)

Date	Mintage	F	VF	XF	Unc	BU
1971	100,000	—	—	75.00	90.00	100
1971 Proof, extremely rare	—	—	—	—	—	—

KM# 33 20 MARK
Copper-Nickel, 33 mm. **Subject:** 100th Anniversary - Birth of Heinrich Mann, writer **Obv:** State emblem, denomination **Rev:** Head left, dates below **Edge Lettering:** 20 MARK (repeated)

Date	Mintage	F	VF	XF	Unc	BU
1971	2,000,000	—	—	4.00	6.50	28.00

KM# 34 20 MARK
Copper-Nickel, 33 mm. **Subject:** 85th Birthday of Ernst Thalmann **Obv:** State emblem, denomination **Rev:** Head left, dates below **Edge Lettering:** 20 MARK (repeated) **Note:** Edge varieties exist.

Date	Mintage	F	VF	XF	Unc	BU
1971A	2,500,000	—	—	4.00	5.50	20.00
1971A Prooflike	—	—	—	—	25.00	35.00

KM# 40 20 MARK
Copper-Nickel, 33 mm. **Subject:** Friedrich von Schiller, poet **Obv:** State emblem, denomination **Rev:** Head right divides dates

Date	Mintage	F	VF	XF	Unc	BU
1972A	3,000,000	—	—	4.00	15.00	18.00
1972A Prooflike	—	—	—	—	35.00	45.00

KM# 41 20 MARK
20.9000 g., 0.6250 Silver .4200 oz. ASW, 33 mm. **Subject:** 500th Anniversary - Birth of Lucas Cranach, painter **Obv:** State emblem, denomination **Rev:** Crowned snake with ring and wings, wings divide dates above **Edge Lettering:** 20 MARK (repeated)

Date	Mintage	F	VF	XF	Unc	BU
1972	100,000	—	—	60.00	90.00	110
1972 Proof, extremely rare	—	—	—	—	—	—

KM# 42 20 MARK
Copper-Nickel, 33 mm. **Subject:** Wilhelm Pieck **Obv:** State emblem, denomination **Rev:** Head left, dates below

Date	Mintage	F	VF	XF	Unc	BU
1972A	2,500,000	—	—	4.00	15.00	20.00
1972A Prooflike	—	—	—	—	35.00	45.00

KM# 46 20 MARK
20.9000 g., 0.6250 Silver .4200 oz. ASW, 33 mm. **Subject:** 60th Anniversary - Death of August Bebel **Obv:** State emblem, denomination **Rev:** Bust half facing, dates at left

Date	Mintage	F	VF	XF	Unc	BU
1973	100,000	—	—	60.00	70.00	90.00
1973 Proof, extremely rare	—	—	—	—	—	—

KM# 47 20 MARK
Copper-Nickel, 33 mm. **Subject:** Otto Grotewohl **Obv:** State emblem, denomination **Rev:** Head left, dates below **Edge Lettering:** 20 MARK (repeated)

Date	Mintage	F	VF	XF	Unc	BU
1973A	2,500,000	—	—	5.00	10.00	15.00
1973A Prooflike	—	—	—	—	20.00	30.00

KM# 53 20 MARK
20.9000 g., 0.6250 Silver .4200 oz. ASW, 33 mm. **Subject:** 250th Anniversary - Death of Immanuel Kant, philosopher **Obv:** State emblem, denomination **Rev:** Bust 3/4 facing, dates at left

Date	Mintage	F	VF	XF	Unc	BU
1974	96,000	—	—	60.00	85.00	150
1974 Proof	4,221	Value: 210				

KM# 59 20 MARK
20.9000 g., 0.6250 Silver .4200 oz. ASW, 33 mm. **Subject:** 225th Anniversary - Death of Johann Sebastian Bach, composer **Obv:** State emblem, denomination **Rev:** Musical score, dates upper left

Date	Mintage	F	VF	XF	Unc	BU
1975	100,000	—	—	100	125	145
1975 Proof	Inc. above	Value: 3,500				

KM# 63 20 MARK
20.9000 g., 0.6250 Silver .4200 oz. ASW, 33 mm. **Subject:** 150th Anniversary - Birth of Wilhelm Liebknecht **Obv:** State emblem, denomination **Rev:** Bust 3/4 left divides dates

Date	Mintage	F	VF	XF	Unc	BU
1976	96,000	—	—	60.00	70.00	90.00
1976 Proof	4,000	Value: 195				

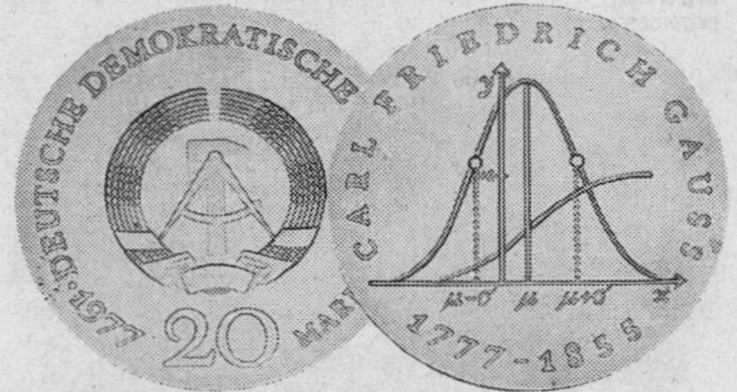

KM# 66 20 MARK
20.9000 g., 0.5000 Silver .3360 oz. ASW, 33 mm. **Subject:** 200th Anniversary - Birth of Carl Friedrich Gauss, scientist **Obv:** State emblem, denomination **Rev:** Lines and arrows form graph, dates below

Date	Mintage	F	VF	XF	Unc	BU
1977	55,000	—	—	90.00	110	125

KM# 71 20 MARK
20.9000 g., 0.5000 Silver .3360 oz. ASW, 33 mm. **Subject:** 175th Anniversary - Death of Johann von Herder, philosopher **Obv:** State emblem, denomination **Rev:** Head 3/4 left, dates at right

Date	Mintage	F	VF	XF	Unc	BU
1978	51,000	—	—	90.00	100	120
1978 Proof	4,500	Value: 175				

KM# 74 20 MARK
20.9000 g., 0.5000 Silver .3360 oz. ASW, 33 mm. **Subject:** 250th Anniversary - Birth of Gotthold Ephraim Lessing, poet **Obv:** State emblem, denomination **Rev:** Three figures and two palm trees, dates above

Date	Mintage	F	VF	XF	Unc	BU
1979	41,000	—	—	100	130	150
1979 Proof	4,500	Value: 200				

KM# 75 20 MARK
Copper-Nickel, 33 mm. **Subject:** 30th Anniversary - East German Regime **Obv:** Large denomination above date, state emblem below **Rev:** Two jugate heads; front head facing, back head left, building at left

Date	Mintage	F	VF	XF	Unc	BU
1979A	1,000,000	—	—	—	15.00	25.00
1979A Prooflike	—	—	—	—	20.00	30.00

KM# 78 20 MARK
20.9200 g., 0.5000 Silver .3360 oz. ASW, 33 mm. **Subject:** 75th Anniversary - Death of Ernst Abbe, physicist **Obv:** Legend divides state emblem and denomination **Rev:** Early optical instrument, dates below

Date	Mintage	F	VF	XF	Unc	BU
1980	40,000	—	—	70.00	90.00	110
1980 Proof	5,500	Value: 145				

KM# 83 20 MARK
20.9200 g., 0.5000 Silver .3360 oz. ASW, 33 mm. **Subject:** 150th Anniversary - Death of vom Stein **Obv:** Legend divides state emblem and denomination **Rev:** Small bust half left below name

Date	Mintage	F	VF	XF	Unc	BU
1981	40,000	—	—	60.00	70.00	90.00
1981 Proof	5,500	Value: 135				

KM# 88 20 MARK
20.9200 g., 0.5000 Silver .3360 oz. ASW, 33 mm. **Subject:** 125th Anniversary - Birth of Clara Zetkin **Obv:** State emblem, denomination **Rev:** Bust 3/4 left, dates at left

Date	Mintage	F	VF	XF	Unc	BU
1982	40,000	—	—	65.00	80.00	100
1982 Proof	5,500	Value: 125				

KM# 94 20 MARK
20.9200 g., 0.5000 Silver .3360 oz. ASW, 33 mm. **Subject:** 500th Anniversary - Birth of Martin Luther **Obv:** State emblem divides date, denomination below **Rev:** Bust holding bible looking left **Designer:** Heinz Rodewald

Date	Mintage	F	VF	XF	Unc	BU
1983	45,000	—	—	600	700	750
1983 Proof	5,000	Value: 750				

KM# 95 20 MARK
Copper-Nickel, 33 mm. **Subject:** 100th Anniversary - Death of Karl Marx **Obv:** State emblem above inscription, date and denomination below **Rev:** Head 3/4 facing, name and dates below

Date	Mintage	F	VF	XF	Unc	BU
1983A	995,000	—	—	12.00	20.00	30.00
1983A Proof	5,000	Value: 65.00				

KM# 100 20 MARK
20.9200 g., 0.5000 Silver .3360 oz. ASW, 33 mm. **Subject:** 225th Anniversary - Death of Georg Friedrich Handel **Obv:** State emblem, denomination **Rev:** Bust looking right, dates below **Designer:** Heinz Rodewald

Date	Mintage	F	VF	XF	Unc	BU
1984A	41,000	—	—	160	190	220
1984A Proof	4,500	Value: 240				

KM# 105 20 MARK
20.9200 g., 0.5000 Silver .3360 oz. ASW, 33 mm. **Subject:** 125th Anniversary - Death of Ernst Moritz Arndt **Obv:** State emblem, denomination **Rev:** Bust 3/4 right divides dates

Date	Mintage	F	VF	XF	Unc	BU
1985A	41,000	—	—	130	150	175
1985A Proof	4,000	Value: 225				

KM# 108 20 MARK
20.9000 g., 0.6250 Silver .4200 oz. ASW, 33 mm. **Subject:** 200th Anniversary - Birth of Jacob and Wilhelm Grimm **Obv:** State emblem, denomination **Rev:** "Puss 'n Boots" divides dates

Date	Mintage	F	VF	XF	Unc	BU
1986A	37,000	—	—	245	300	350
1986A Proof	3,500	Value: 475				

KM# 119.1 20 MARK
20.9000 g., 0.6250 Silver .4200 oz. ASW, 33 mm. **Subject:**

Berlin - City Seal **Obv:** State emblem, denomination **Rev:** Helmeted shield with supporters within circle

Date	Mintage	F	VF	XF	Unc	BU
1987A	42,000	—	—	425	500	575
1987A Proof	2,100	Value: 1,500				

Note: Seal on reverse totally frosted on proof coins

KM# 119.2 20 MARK

20.9000 g., 0.6250 Silver .4200 oz. ASW, 33 mm. **Obv:** State emblem, denomination **Rev:** Fields in seal polished

Date	Mintage	F	VF	XF	Unc	BU
1987A Proof	2,100	Value: 1,500				

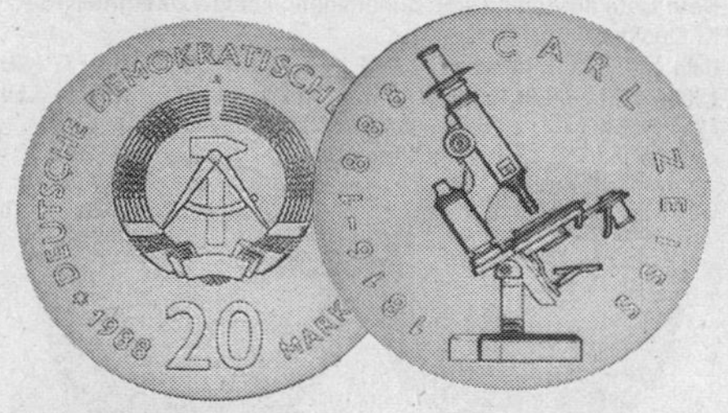

KM# 124 20 MARK

20.9000 g., 0.6250 Silver .4200 oz. ASW, 33 mm. **Subject:** 100th Anniversary - Death of Carl Zeiss **Obv:** State emblem, denomination **Rev:** Microscope, dates at left

Date	Mintage	F	VF	XF	Unc	BU
1988A	37,000	—	—	225	250	300
1988A Proof	3,500	Value: 450				

KM# 127 20 MARK

20.9000 g., 0.6250 Silver .4200 oz. ASW, 33 mm. **Subject:** 500th Anniversary - Birth of Thomas Muntzer **Obv:** State emblem, denomination **Rev:** Head left divides dates **Designer:** Gunter Gnauk

Date	Mintage	F	VF	XF	Unc	BU
1989A	37,000	—	—	80.00	95.00	110
1989A Proof	3,500	Value: 295				

KM# 138 20 MARK

20.9000 g., 0.6250 Silver .4200 oz. ASW, 33 mm. **Subject:** Andreas Schluter **Obv:** State emblem, denomination **Rev:** Head right on decorative shield divides dates

Date	Mintage	F	VF	XF	Unc	BU
1990A	37,000	—	—	90.00	130	160
1990A Proof	3,500	Value: 285				

KM# 139 20 MARK

Copper-Nickel, 33 mm. **Subject:** Opening of Brandenburg Gate **Obv:** State emblem, denomination **Rev:** Brandenburg Gate

Date	Mintage	F	VF	XF	Unc	BU
1990A	300,000	—	—	7.00	10.00	15.00

KM# 139a 20 MARK

18.2000 g., 0.9990 Silver .5852 oz. ASW, 33 mm. **Subject:** Opening of Brandenburg Gate **Obv:** State emblem, denomination

Date	Mintage	F	VF	XF	Unc	BU
1990A	145,000	—	—	16.00	20.00	25.00
1990A Proof	5,000	Value: 125				

PIEFORTS

KM#	Date	Mintage	Identification	Mkt Val
P1	ND(1985)	—	5 Mark. Copper-Zinc-Nickel. KM#110, Unc.	—

PROBAS

KM#	Date	Mintage	Identification	Mkt Val
PR1	1948A	—	Pfennig. Zinc.	1,750
PR2	ND	—	Pfennig. Aluminum. Mule - obv: obv. of KM#8.1, rev: obverse of KM#5.	—
PR3	ND(1967)	—	10 Mark. Silver. Neubauer.	3,750
PR4	1968A	—	5 Pfennig. Brass. KM#9.1.	—
PR5	1968A	—	10 Pfennig. Brass Plated Steel. KM#10.1	375
PR6	1968A	—	50 Pfennig. Brass. KM#12.	450
PR7	1968	—	20 Mark. 0.9990 Gold. KM#21.	—
PR8	ND(1969)	—	20 Pfennig. Brass. Mule - 2 obverses of KM#11.	—
PR9	1969	—	20 Pfennig. Nickel. KM#11.	—
PR10	1969	12,741	5 Mark. Copper-Nickel-Zinc. PROBE.	500
PR11	1972A	—	10 Pfennig. Steel. KM#10.1.	—
PRA12	1972A	—	2 Mark. Aluminum. KM#48.	—
PR12	1973A	—	10 Mark. Copper-Nickel. Edge: 10 MARK* 10 MARK * 10 MARK *, KM#44	700
PR13	1974A	1,500	10 Mark. 0.5000 Silver. KM#50.	1,500
PR14	1974A	100	10 Mark. 0.6250 Silver. Mintage numbered on lead seal, PROBE, KM#52.	7,500
PR15	1975A	—	5 Pfennig. Nickel. KM#9.1,	—
PR16	1975	10,261	20 Mark. Silver. Incuse notes, Unc, KM#59.	160
PR17	1975	I.A.	20 Mark. Silver. Incuse notes, matte fields, proof, KM#59.	4,500
PR18	1975	8,810	10 Mark. Silver. PROBE, KM#57.	160
PRA19	1976A	—	5 Pfennig. Aluminum. KM#9.2.	—
PR19	ND(1977)	6,000	10 Mark. Silver. State emblem, denomination. Ancient vacuum pump above horses, dates below. Guericke.	500
PR20	1978A	100	10 Mark. Silver. KM#70.	—
PR21	1979A	—	20 Mark. Copper-Nickel-Zinc. Obverse: PROBA instead of date, KM#75.	—
PR22	1979A	10,000	20 Mark. Copper-Nickel-Zinc. Large denomination above state emblem. Dates above split leaf design.	150
PR23	1981		10 Mark. 0.5000 Silver. State emblem divides date, denomination below. Shields within inner circle form cross. PROBE on obverse, Unc.	2,000
PR24	1981	2,250	10 Mark. 0.5000 Silver. PROBE on obverse, Proof.	1,300
PR25	1982A	—	5 Pfennig. Aluminum. Reeded edge, PROBA, KM#9.2.	350
PR26	1982A	—	20 Pfennig. Brass Plated Steel. KM#11.	500
PR27	1982A	210	5 Mark. Copper-Zinc-Nickel. House frosted on reverse, K#85, Proof.	6,000
PR28	1982	90	20 Mark. Silver. State emblem, denomination. Head 1/4 right, dates at right. Countermark number of issue right of date, KM#88, Unc.	8,500
PRA29	1983A	—	5 Pfennig. Nickel. KM#9.2.	—
PR29	1983A	100	10 Mark. Copper-Zinc-Nickel. Countermark PROBE and number on obverse, KM#93, Unc.	2,000
PR30	1983	100	20 Mark. Copper-Zinc-Nickel. PROBE and number below date, KM#94, Unc.	3,500
PR31	1983	100	20 Mark. Copper-Zinc-Nickel. PROBE and issue number left and right of denomination, KM#95, Unc.	—
PR33	1985A	112	10 Mark. Silver. Denomination above state emblem. Building within circle.	8,000
PR32	ND(1985)	300	5 Mark. Copper-Zinc-Nickel. Incusely numbered, PROBA, Unc.	—
PR34	1985A	50	10 Mark. Copper-Zinc-Nickel. Reverse large design size, KM#106, Unc.	5,000
PR35	1985A	—	10 Mark. 0.5000 Silver. KM#106, Unc.	—
PR36	1985A	—	10 Mark. 0.5000 Silver. KM#106, Proof.	12,500
PR37	1985A	266	10 Mark. 0.3330 Gold. Alloyed with silver, KM#16, Proof.	5,500
PR38	1986A	—	Mark. Copper-Zinc-Nickel. PROBE, KM#35.	—
PR39	1986A	—	2 Mark. Copper-Zinc-Nickel. PROBE, KM#48.	—
PR40	1986A	110	5 Mark. Copper-Zinc-Nickel. P below tower, Unc.	—
PR41	1986A	107	10 Mark. 0.5000 Silver. P next to state emblem, KM#109, Unc.	3,000
PR42	1988A	1,000	10 Mark. 0.5000 Silver. P below value, KM#125, Proof.	1,200
PR43	1988A	15	20 Mark. Silver. PROBE, large inscription, KM#124, Unc.	9,500
PR44	1989A	—	10 Mark. 0.5000 Silver. KM#132, Proof.	11,500

TRIAL STRIKES

KM#	Date	Mintage	Identification	Mkt Val
TS1	ND(1966)	300	10 Mark. Aluminum. Uniface, Reverse of KM#15.	230
TS2	ND(1966)	300	20 Mark. Aluminum. Uniface, Reverse of KM#16.	270
TS3	ND(1967)	400	10 Mark. Aluminum. Uniface, Reverse of KM#17.	230
TS4	ND(1967)	400	20 Mark. Aluminum. Uniface, Reverse of KM#18.	270
TS5	1968A	350	5 Mark. Aluminum. Uniface, Reverse of KM#19.	235
TS6	ND(1968)	300	10 Mark. Aluminum. Uniface, Reverse of KM#20.	250
TS7	ND(1968)	300	20 Mark. Aluminum. Uniface, Reverse of KM#21.	270
TS8	ND(1969)	—	5 Mark. Nickel-Bronze. Uniface, obverse of KM#14, edge 5 MARK * 5 MARK * 5 MARK *	—
TS9	ND(1969)	350	5 Mark. Aluminum. Uniface, reverse of KM#23.	235
TS10	ND(1969)	300	10 Mark. Aluminum. Uniface, reverse of KM#24.	250
TS11	ND(1969)	300	20 Mark. Aluminum. Uniface, reverse of KM#25.	260
TS12	ND(1970)	350	5 Mark. Aluminum. Uniface, reverse of KM#26.	235
TS13	ND(1970)	300	10 Mark. Aluminum. Uniface, reverse of KM#27.	250
TS14	ND(1970)	330	20 Mark. Aluminum. Uniface, reverse of KM#28.	260
TS15	ND(1971)	450	5 Mark. Aluminum. Uniface, reverse of KM#30.	235
TS16	ND(1971)	300	10 Mark. Aluminum. Uniface, reverse of KM#31.	250

KM#	Date	Mintage	Identification	Mkt Val
TS17	ND(1971)	410	20 Mark. Aluminum. Uniface, reverse of KM#32.	250
TS18	ND(1972)	300	5 Mark. Aluminum. Uniface, reverse of KM#36.	235
TS19	ND(1972)	300	10 Mark. Aluminum. Uniface, reverse of KM#39.	250
TS20	ND(1972)	300	20 Mark. Aluminum. Uniface, reverse of KM#41.	260
TS21	ND(1973)	300	5 Mark. Aluminum. Uniface, reverse of KM#43.	235
TS22	ND(1973)	—	20 Mark. Copper-Zinc-Nickel. Uniface, reverse of KM#47.	—
TS23	ND(1973)	—	20 Mark. Copper-Zinc-Nickel. Uniface, reverse with portrait within circular legend, KM#47.	—
TS24	ND(1975)	306	10 Mark. Aluminum. Uniface, reverse of KM#56.	220
TS25	1979	—	20 Mark. Copper-Zinc-Nickel. Uniface, reverse of PR22.	—

MINT SETS

KM#	Date	Mintage	Identification	Issue Price	Mkt Val
MS1	1979A (8)	26,000	KM#8.2-10, 11-12.2, 29, 35.2, 48	—	80.00
MS2	1980A (8)	25,000	KM#8.2-10, 11-12.2, 35.2, 48	—	100
MS3	1981 (8)	25,000	KM#8.2-10, 11-12.2, 29, 35.2, 48	—	70.00
MS4	1982 (8)	21,000	KM#8.2-10, 11-12.2, 29, 35.2, 48	—	100
MS5	1982 (7)	4,500	KM#8.2-10, 11-12.2, 35.2, 48	—	150
MS6	1983 (8)	19,000	KM#8.2-10, 11-12.2, 35.2, 37, 48	—	225
MS7	1983 (7)	4,500	KM#8.2-10, 11-12.2, 35.2, 48	—	200
MS8	1984 (8)	19,000	KM#8.2-10, 11-12.2, 29, 35.2, 48	—	175
MS9	1984 (7)	4,500	KM#8.2-10, 11-12.2, 35.2, 48	—	150
MS10	1985 (8)	6,000	KM#8.2-10, 11-12.2, 35.2, 48, 102	—	70.00
MS11	1985 (7)	4,500	KM#8.2-10, 11-12.2, 35.2, 48	—	70.00
MS12	1986 (8)	7,000	KM#8.2-10, 11-12, 29, 35.2, 48	—	130
MS13	1986 (7)	4,500	KM#8.2-10, 11-12.2, 35.2, 48	—	85.00
MSA16	1987 (4)	—	KM#29, 114-116	—	60.00
MS14	1987 (8)	8,000	KM#8.2-10, 11-12.2, 29, 35.2, 48	—	75.00
MS15	1987 (7)	4,500	KM#8.2-10, 11-12.2, 35.2, 48	—	85.00
MS16	1988 (8)	11,000	KM#8.2-10, 11-12.2, 29, 35.2, 48	—	75.00
MS17	1988 (7)	4,500	KM#8.2-10, 11-12.2, 35.2, 48	—	85.00
MS18	1989 (8)	11,000	KM8.2-10, 11-12.2, 29, 35.2, 48	—	75.00
MS19	1989 (7)	4,500	KM#8.2-10, 11-12.2, 35.2,48	—	85.00
MS20	1990 (8)	11,000	KM#8.2-10, 11-12.2, 29, 35.2, 48	—	180
MS21	1990 (7)	4,500	KM#8.2-10, 11-12.2, 35.2, 48	—	180

PROOF SETS

KM#	Date	Mintage	Identification	Issue Price	Mkt Val
PS2	1981 (8)	20	KM#8.2-10, 11-12.2, 35.2, 37, 48	—	—
PS1	1981 (8)	20	KM#8.2-10, 11-12.2, 35.2, 48, 79	—	—
PS3	1982 (8)	2,500	KM#8.2-10, 11-12.2, 29, 35.2, 48	—	500
PS4	1983 (8)	2,550	KM#8.2-10, 11-12.2, 35.2, 37, 48	—	450
PS5	1984 (8)	3,015	KM#8.2-10, 11-12.2, 29, 35.2, 48	—	200
PS6	1985 (8)	2,816	KM#8.2-10, 11-12.2, 35.2, 48, 102	—	125
PS7	1986 (8)	2,800	KM#8.2-10, 11-12.2, 29, 35.2, 48	—	200
PS8	1987 (8)	2,345	KM#8.2-10, 11-12.2, 29, 35.2, 48	—	150
PS9	1988 (8)	2,300	KM#8.2-10, 11-12.2, 28, 35.2, 48	—	180
PS10	1989 (8)	2,300	KM#8.2-10, 11-12.2, 28, 35.2, 48	—	250

GHANA

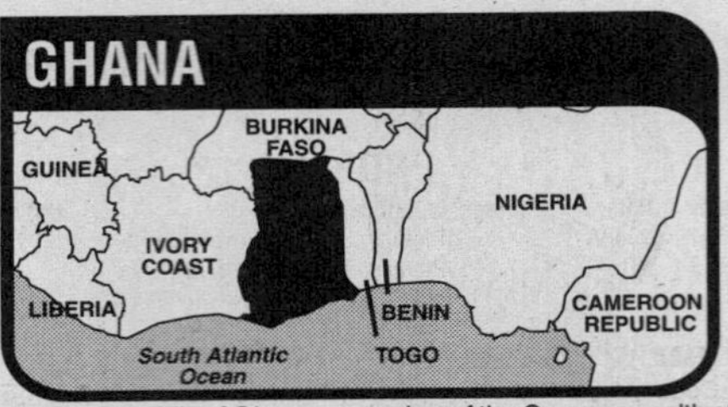

The Republic of Ghana, a member of the Commonwealth of Nations situated on the West Coast of Africa between Ivory Coast and Togo, has an area of 92,100 sq. mi. (238,540 sq. km.) and a population of 14 million, almost entirely African. Capital: Accra. Cocoa (the major crop), coconuts, palm kernels and coffee are exported. Mining, second in importance to agriculture, is concentrated on gold, manganese and industrial diamonds.

The state of Ghana, comprising the Gold Coast and British Togoland, obtained independence on March 6, 1957, becoming the first Negro African colony to do so. On July l, 1960, Ghana adopted a republican constitution, changing from a ministerial to a presidential form of government. The government was overthrown, the constitution suspended and the National Assembly dissolved by the Ghanaian army and police on Feb. 24, 1966. The government was returned to civilian authority in Oct. 1969, but was again seized by military officers in a bloodless coup on Jan. 13, 1972, but 3 further coups occurred in 1978, 1979 and 1981. The latter 2 coups were followed by suspension of the constitution and banning of political parties. A new constitution, which allowed multiparty politics, was approved in April 1992.

Ghana's monetary denomination of Cedi' is derived from the word 'sedie' meaning cowrie, a shell money commonly employed by coastal tribes.

MONETARY SYSTEM
12 Pence = 1 Shilling

REPUBLIC

STANDARD COINAGE

KM# 1 1/2 PENNY
Bronze **Obv:** Dr. Kwame Nkrumah head right **Rev:** Date divided by star, denomination below **Designer:** P. K. K. Quaidoo

Date	Mintage	F	VF	XF	Unc	BU
1958	32,200,000	—	0.10	0.25	0.50	1.50
1958 Proof	20,000	Value: 0.75				

KM# 2 PENNY
Bronze **Obv:** Dr. Kwame Nkrumah head right **Rev:** Date divided by star, denomination below **Designer:** P. K. K. Quaidoo

Date	Mintage	F	VF	XF	Unc	BU
1958	60,000,000	—	0.15	0.35	0.75	1.75
1958 Proof	20,000	Value: 1.00				

KM# 3 3 PENCE
Copper Nickel, 19.5 mm. **Obv:** Dr. Kwame Nkrumah head right **Rev:** Date divided by star, denomination below **Shape:** Scalloped **Designer:** P. K. K. Quaidoo

Date	Mintage	F	VF	XF	Unc	BU
1958	25,200,000	—	0.20	0.45	1.00	2.00
1958 Proof	20,000	Value: 1.50				

KM# 4 6 PENCE
Copper Nickel **Obv:** Dr. Kwame Nkrumah head right **Rev:** Date divided by star, denomination below **Designer:** P. K. K. Quaidoo

Date	Mintage	F	VF	XF	Unc	BU
1958	15,200,000	—	0.20	0.45	1.00	2.00
1958 Proof	—	Value: 1.50				

KM# 5 SHILLING
Copper Nickel, 21 mm. **Obv:** Dr. Kwame Nkrumah head right **Rev:** Date divided by star, denomination below **Designer:** P. K. K. Quaidoo

Date	Mintage	F	VF	XF	Unc	BU
1958	34,400,000	—	0.25	0.50	1.75	3.50
1958 Proof	20,000	Value: 2.50				

KM# 6 2 SHILLING
Copper Nickel, 26.5 mm. **Obv:** Dr. Kwame Nkrumah head right **Rev:** Date divided by star, denomination below **Designer:** P. K. K. Quaidoo

Date	Mintage	F	VF	XF	Unc	BU
1958	72,700,000	—	0.35	0.75	2.25	4.50
1958 Proof	20,000	Value: 3.50				

KM# 7 10 SHILLING
28.2800 g., 0.9250 Silver .8411 oz. ASW, 38 mm. **Obv:** Dr. Kwame Nkrumah head right **Rev:** Date divided by star, denomination below **Edge Lettering:** 6 MARCH 1957 - INDEPENDENCE OF GHANA **Designer:** P. K. K. Quaidoo

Date	Mintage	F	VF	XF	Unc	BU
1958 Proof	11,000	Value: 13.50				

DECIMAL COINAGE

KM# 12 1/2 PESEWA
Bronze, 20.3 mm. **Obv:** Bush drums **Rev:** Star divides date and denomination

Date	Mintage	F	VF	XF	Unc	BU
1967	30,000,000	—	0.10	0.20	0.50	0.75
1967 Proof	2,000	Value: 1.00				

KM# 13 PESEWA
Bronze, 25.5 mm. **Obv:** Bush drums **Rev:** Star divides date and denomination

Date	Mintage	F	VF	XF	Unc	BU
1967	30,000,000	—	0.15	0.25	0.60	0.85
1967 Proof	2,000	Value: 1.25				
1975	50,250,000	—	0.10	0.20	0.50	0.75
1979	50,000,000	—	0.10	0.20	0.50	0.75

KM# 14 2-1/2 PESEWAS
Copper-Nickel, 19.5 mm. **Obv:** Cocoa beans within circle **Rev:** Rampant lion at center of quartered shield dividing date and denomination **Shape:** Scalloped

Date	Mintage	F	VF	XF	Unc	BU
1967	6,000,000	—	0.10	0.20	0.75	1.25
1967 Proof	2,000	Value: 1.50				

KM# 8 5 PESEWAS
Copper-Nickel **Obv:** Dr. Kwame Nkrumah head right **Rev:** Star divides date and denomination **Shape:** Scalloped

Date	Mintage	F	VF	XF	Unc	BU
1965	30,000,000	—	0.20	0.35	1.25	2.25

KM# 15 5 PESEWAS
Copper-Nickel, 19.5 mm. **Obv:** Cocoa beans within circle **Rev:** Rampant lion at center of quartered shield dividing date and denomination

Date	Mintage	F	VF	XF	Unc	BU
1967	30,000,000	—	0.15	0.25	0.75	1.25
1967 Proof	2,000	Value: 2.00				
1973	8,000,000	—	0.15	0.25	0.75	1.25
1975	20,000,000	—	0.15	0.25	0.75	1.25

KM# 9 10 PESEWAS
Copper-Nickel **Obv:** Dr. Kwame Nkrumah head right **Rev:** Star divides date and denomination

Date	Mintage	F	VF	XF	Unc	BU
1965	50,000,000	—	0.25	0.50	1.25	2.00

KM# 16 10 PESEWAS
Copper-Nickel, 13.5 mm. **Obv:** Cocoa beans within circle **Rev:** Rampant lion at center of quartered shield dividing date and denomination

Date	Mintage	F	VF	XF	Unc	BU
1967	13,200,000	—	0.20	0.40	1.50	2.00
1967 Proof	2,000	Value: 2.50				
1975	20,000,000	—	0.20	0.40	1.25	1.75
1979	5,500,000	—	0.20	0.40	1.25	1.75

KM# 17 20 PESEWAS
Copper-Nickel, 28.5 mm. **Obv:** Cocoa beans within circle **Rev:** Rampant lion at center of quartered shield dividing date and denomination

Date	Mintage	F	VF	XF	Unc	BU
1967	25,800,000	—	0.25	0.50	1.75	2.50
1967 Proof	2,000	Value: 3.00				
1979	5,000,000	—	0.25	0.50	1.75	2.50

KM# 10 25 PESEWAS
Copper-Nickel **Obv:** Dr. Kwame Nkrumah head right **Rev:** Star divides date and denomination

Date	Mintage	F	VF	XF	Unc	BU
1965	60,100,000	—	0.35	0.75	2.00	3.50

KM# 11 50 PESEWAS
Copper-Nickel **Obv:** Dr. Kwame Nkrumah head right **Rev:** Star divides date and denomination

Date	Mintage	F	VF	XF	Unc	BU
1965	18,200,000	—	0.75	1.50	3.50	5.00

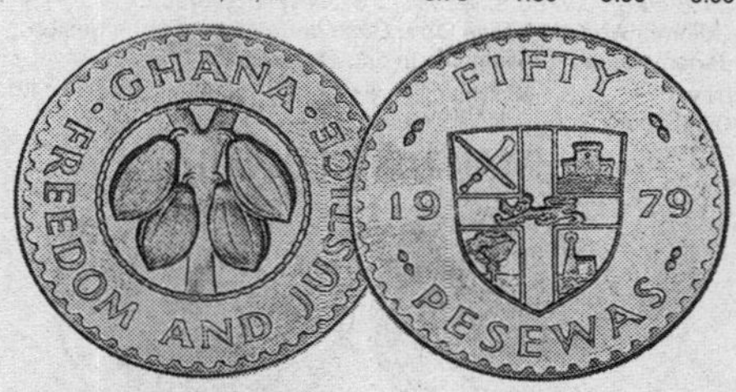

KM# 18 50 PESEWAS
Brass **Series:** F.A.O. **Obv:** Cocoa beans within circle **Rev:** Rampant lion at center of quartered shield dividing date and denomination

Date	Mintage	F	VF	XF	Unc	BU
1979	60,000,000	—	0.45	0.75	2.25	3.50

KM# 24 50 PESEWAS
Brass **Obv:** Cocoa beans within circle **Rev:** Rampant lion at center of quartered shield dividing date and denomination

Date	Mintage	F	VF	XF	Unc	BU
1984	10,000,000	—	0.10	0.25	0.60	1.00

KM# 19 CEDI
Brass, 30 mm. **Series:** F.A.O. **Obv:** Cowrie shell **Rev:** Rampant lion at center of quartered shield dividing date and denomination

Date	Mintage	F	VF	XF	Unc	BU
1979	160,000,000	—	0.35	0.85	3.00	5.00

KM# 25 CEDI
Brass **Obv:** Cowrie shell **Rev:** Rampant lion at center of quartered shield dividing date and denomination

Date	Mintage	F	VF	XF	Unc	BU
1984	40,000,000	—	0.10	0.25	1.50	2.50

KM# 26 5 CEDIS
Brass **Obv:** Bush drums **Rev:** Rampant lion at center of quartered shield dividing date and denomination

Date	Mintage	F	VF	XF	Unc	BU
1984	88,920,000	—	0.10	0.20	0.50	0.75

KM# 33 5 CEDIS
Brass Plated Steel **Obv:** Bush drums **Rev:** Rampant lion at center of quartered shield dividing date and denomination

Date	Mintage	F	VF	XF	Unc	BU
1991	—	—	0.10	0.20	0.50	0.75

KM# 29 10 CEDIS
3.5000 g., Nickel Clad Steel, 21.8 mm. **Obv:** Cocoa beans within circle **Rev:** Rampant lion at center of quartered shield dividing date and denomination **Shape:** 7-sided

Date	Mintage	F	VF	XF	Unc	BU
1991	—	—	—	0.35	0.75	1.25

KM# 30 20 CEDIS
5.4000 g., Nickel Clad Steel, 24.5 mm. **Obv:** Cowrie shell **Rev:** Rampant lion at center of quartered shield dividing date and denomination

Date	Mintage	F	VF	XF	Unc	BU
1991	—	—	—	0.35	1.50	2.50
1995	—	—	—	0.35	1.50	2.50

KM# 20 50 CEDIS
28.2800 g., 0.9250 Silver .8411 oz. ASW **Subject:** International Year of Disabled Persons **Obv:** Triangular symbol within wreath, date above **Rev:** Person in wheelchair divides dates, denomination below

Date	Mintage	F	VF	XF	Unc	BU
1981	10,000	—	—	—	25.00	28.00
1981 Proof	10,000	Value: 35.00				

KM# 21 50 CEDIS
Copper Nickel **Series:** F.A.O. **Subject:** World Fisheries Conference **Obv:** Bush drums **Rev:** People in boat on water, denomination **Rev. Designer:** Stuart Devlin

Date	Mintage	F	VF	XF	Unc	BU
ND(1984)	100,000	—	—	—	6.50	8.50

KM# 21a 50 CEDIS
28.2800 g., 0.9250 Silver .8411 oz. ASW **Series:** F.A.O. **Subject:** World Fisheries Conference **Obv:** Bust drums **Rev:** People in boat on water, denomination

Date	Mintage	F	VF	XF	Unc	BU
ND(1984) Proof	21,000	Value: 55.00				

KM# 21b 50 CEDIS
47.5400 g., 0.9170 Gold 1.4017 oz. AGW **Series:** F.A.O. **Subject:** World Fisheries Conference **Obv:** Bush drums **Rev:** People in boat on water, denomination

Date	Mintage	F	VF	XF	Unc	BU
ND(1984) Proof	105	Value: 2,000				

KM# 22 50 CEDIS
28.2800 g., 0.9250 Silver .8411 oz. ASW **Subject:** Year of the Scout **Obv:** Rampant lion at center of quartered shield, denomination below, rope encircles **Rev:** Two scouts planting trees, dates at left

Date	Mintage	F	VF	XF	Unc	BU
ND(1984)	10,000	—	—	—	40.00	—
ND(1984) Proof	Inc. above	Value: 85.00				

KM# 31 50 CEDIS
Copper-Nickel, 27.4 mm. **Obv:** Bush drums **Rev:** Rampant lion at center of quartered shield dividing date and denomination

Date	Mintage	F	VF	XF	Unc	BU
1991	—	—	—	1.00	2.25	3.50
1995	—	—	—	1.00	2.25	3.50
1997	—	—	—	1.00	2.25	3.50
1999	—	—	—	1.00	2.25	3.50

KM# 31a 50 CEDIS
7.4000 g., Nickel Plated Steel, 27.4 mm. **Obv:** Bush drums **Rev:** Rampant lion at center of quartered shield dividing date and denomination

Date	Mintage	F	VF	XF	Unc	BU
1995	—	—	—	1.00	2.25	3.50
1997	—	—	—	1.00	2.25	3.50
1999	—	—	—	1.00	2.25	3.50

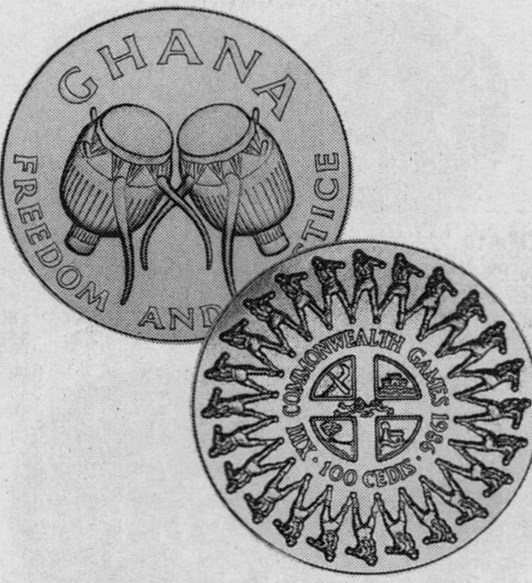

KM# 27 100 CEDIS
28.2800 g., 0.5000 Silver .4546 oz. ASW **Subject:** Commonwealth Games **Obv:** Bush drums **Rev:** Game design, denomination and date within ring of boxers

Date	Mintage	F	VF	XF	Unc	BU
1986	50,000	—	—	—	16.50	20.00

KM# 27a 100 CEDIS
28.2800 g., 0.9250 Silver .8411 oz. ASW **Subject:** Commonwealth Games **Obv:** Bush drums **Rev:** Game design, denomination and date within ring of boxers

Date	Mintage	F	VF	XF	Unc	BU
1986 Proof	20,000	Value: 28.00				

KM# 32 100 CEDIS
6.9000 g., Bi-Metallic Brass center in Copper-Nickel ring, 25 mm. **Obv:** Cocoa beans within circle **Rev:** Rampant lion at center of quartered shield dividing date and denomination, circle surrounds

Date	Mintage	F	VF	XF	Unc	BU
1991	—	—	—	1.75	3.50	4.75
1997	—	—	—	1.50	3.25	4.50
1998	—	—	—	1.50	3.25	4.50

KM# 35 200 CEDIS
Nickel Plated Steel **Obv:** Cowrie shell **Rev:** Rampant lion at center of quartered shield dividing date and denomination **Shape:** 7-sided

Date	Mintage	F	VF	XF	Unc	BU
1996	—	—	—	—	4.00	5.00
1998	—	—	—	—	4.00	5.00

Note: Fields frosted but not center design

KM# 28 500 CEDIS
15.9800 g., 0.9170 Gold .4711 oz. AGW **Subject:** International Year of Disabled Persons **Obv:** Triangular symbol within wreath, date above **Rev:** Bust 3/4 left divides dates, denomination below

Date	Mintage	F	VF	XF	Unc	BU
1981	—	—	—	—	335	350
1981 Proof	—	Value: 400				

KM# 23 500 CEDIS
15.9800 g., 0.9170 Gold .4711 oz. AGW **Subject:** Year of the Scout **Obv:** Rampant lion at center of quartered shield, denomination below, rope encircles **Rev:** Scouting symbol within rope, dates below

Date	Mintage	F	VF	XF	Unc	BU
ND(1984)	2,000	—	—	—	315	335
ND(1984) Proof	2,000	Value: 375				

KM# 34 500 CEDIS
Nickel-Brass **Obv:** Bush drums **Rev:** Rampant lion at center of quartered shield dividing date and denomination

Date	Mintage	F	VF	XF	Unc	BU
1996	—	—	—	—	4.75	5.50
1998	—	—	—	—	4.75	5.50

PIEFORTS

KM#	Date	Mintage	Identification	Issue Price	Mkt Val
P1	1981	1,050	50 Cedis. Silver. KM20.	—	65.00
P2	1981	—	500 Cedis. Gold. KM28.	—	800
P3	ND(1984)	520	50 Cedis. Silver. KM21a.	—	80.00

PROOF SETS

KM#	Date	Mintage	Identification	Issue Price	Mkt Val
PS1	1958 (7)	6,431	KM1-7	—	23.50
PS2	1967 (6)	100	KM12-17	8.53	11.50

GIBRALTAR

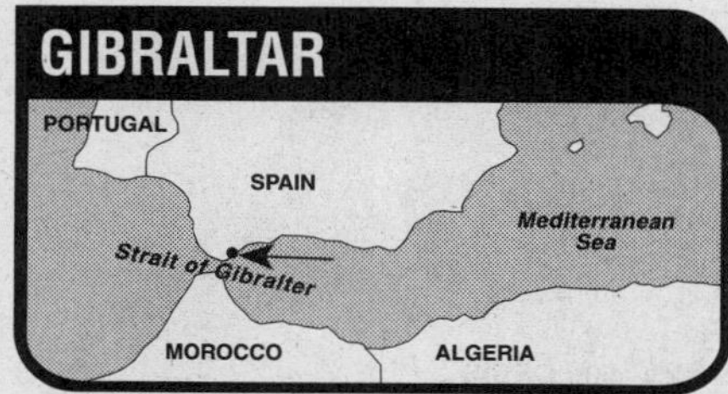

The British Colony of Gibraltar, located at the southernmost point of the Iberian Peninsula, has an area of 2.25 sq. mi. (6.5 sq. km.) and a population of 29,651. Capital (and only town): Gibraltar. Aside from its strategic importance as guardian of the western entrance to the Mediterranean Sea, Gibraltar is also a free port and a British naval base.

Gibraltar, rooted in Greek mythology as one of the Pillars of Hercules, has long been a coveted stronghold. Moslems took it from Spain and fortified it in 711. Spain retook it in 1309, lost it again to the Moors in 1333 and retook it in 1462. After 1540 Spain strengthened its defenses and held it until the War of the Spanish Succession when it was captured by a combined British and Dutch force in 1704. Britain held it against the Franco-Spanish attacks of 1704-05 and through the historic Great Siege of 1779-83.Recently Spain has attempted to discourage British occupancy by harassment and economic devices. In 1967, Gibraltar's inhabitants voted 12,138 to 44 to remain under British rule.

Gibraltar's celebrated Barbary Ape, the last monkey to be found in a wild state in Europe, is featured on the colony's first decimal crown, released in 1972.

RULERS
British

MINT MARKS
PM - Pobjoy Mint

MINT PRIVY MARKS
U - Unc finish

DIE MARKS
1988: AA-AE
1989: AA-AF
1990: AA-AB
1991: AA
1992: AA-BB
1993: AA-BB
1994-1999: AA

MONETARY SYSTEM
4 Farthings = 1 Penny
12 Pence = 1 Shilling
2 Shillings = 1 Crown
5 Shillings = 1 Crown
20 Shillings = 1 Pound

BRITISH COLONY

CROWN COINAGE

1967-1970

KM# 4 CROWN

Copper-Nickel, 38.5 mm. **Ruler:** Elizabeth II **Obv:** Young bust right **Obv. Designer:** Arnold Machin **Rev:** Key below castle divides date, denomination below

Date	Mintage	F	VF	XF	Unc	BU
1967	125,000	—	1.00	2.00	5.00	—
1968	40,000	—	1.25	2.50	6.00	—
1969	40,000	—	1.25	2.50	6.00	—
1970	45,000	—	1.25	2.50	6.00	—

KM# 4a CROWN

28.2800 g., 0.5000 Silver .4546 oz. ASW, 38.5 mm. **Ruler:** Elizabeth II **Obv:** Young bust right **Rev:** Key below castle divides date

Date	Mintage	F	VF	XF	Unc	BU
1967 Frosted Proof	50	Value: 200				
1967 Proof	10,000	Value: 12.50				

DECIMAL COINAGE

KM# 20 PENNY

Bronze, 20.5 mm. **Ruler:** Elizabeth II **Obv:** Crowned head right **Obv. Designer:** Raphael Maklouf **Rev:** Barbary partridge divides denomination **Rev. Designer:** Alfred Ryman

Date	Mintage	F	VF	XF	Unc	BU
1988 AA	—	—	—	—	0.35	0.50
1988 AB	—	—	—	—	0.35	0.50
1988 AC	—	—	—	—	0.35	0.50
1988 AD	—	—	—	—	0.35	0.50
1988 AE	—	—	—	—	0.35	0.50
1989 AA	—	—	—	—	0.35	0.50
1989 AB	—	—	—	—	0.35	0.50
1989 AC	—	—	—	—	0.35	0.50
1989 AD	—	—	—	—	0.35	0.50
1989 AE	—	—	—	—	0.35	0.50
1989 AF	—	—	—	—	0.35	0.50
1990 AA	—	—	—	—	0.35	0.50
1990 AB	—	—	—	—	0.35	0.50
1991 AA	—	—	—	—	0.35	0.50
1992 AA	—	—	—	—	0.35	0.50
1992 BB	—	—	—	—	0.35	0.50
1993 AA	—	—	—	—	0.35	0.50
1993 BB	—	—	—	—	0.35	0.50
1994 AA	—	—	—	—	0.35	0.50
1995 AB	—	—	—	—	0.35	0.50
1995 AA	—	—	—	—	0.35	0.50

KM# 20a PENNY

Bronze Plated Steel, 20.5 mm. **Ruler:** Elizabeth II **Obv:** Crowned head right **Rev:** Barbary partridge left divides denomination

Date	Mintage	F	VF	XF	Unc	BU
1995PM AB	—	—	—	—	0.35	0.50
1995 AA	—	—	—	—	0.35	0.50
1996 AA	—	—	—	—	0.35	0.50
1997 AA	—	—	—	—	0.35	0.50

KM# 773 PENNY

Bronze Plated Steel, 20.5 mm. **Ruler:** Elizabeth II **Obv:** Head with tiara right **Obv. Designer:** Ian Rank-Broadley **Rev:** Barbary partridge left divides denomination

Date	Mintage	F	VF	XF	Unc	BU
1998 AA	—	—	—	—	0.35	0.50
1999 AA	—	—	—	—	0.35	0.50
2000PM AA	—	—	—	—	0.35	0.50

KM# 21 2 PENCE

Bronze, 26 mm. **Ruler:** Elizabeth II **Obv:** Crowned head right **Obv. Designer:** Raphael Maklouf **Rev:** Lighthouse on Europa Point, denomination **Rev. Designer:** Alfred Ryman

Date	Mintage	F	VF	XF	Unc	BU
1988 AA	—	—	—	—	0.50	0.75
1988 AB	—	—	—	—	0.50	0.75
1988 AC	—	—	—	—	0.50	0.75
1988 AD	—	—	—	—	0.50	0.75
1988 AE	—	—	—	—	0.50	0.75
1989 AA	—	—	—	—	0.50	0.75
1989 AB	—	—	—	—	0.50	0.75
1989 AC	—	—	—	—	0.50	0.75
1989 AD	—	—	—	—	0.50	0.75
1989 AE	—	—	—	—	0.50	0.75
1989 AF	—	—	—	—	0.50	0.75
1990 AA	—	—	—	—	0.50	0.75
1990 AB	—	—	—	—	0.50	0.75
1991 AA	—	—	—	—	0.50	0.75
1991 AB	—	—	—	—	0.50	0.75
1992 AA	—	—	—	—	0.50	0.75
1992 BB	—	—	—	—	0.50	0.75
1993 AA	—	—	—	—	0.50	0.75
1993 BB	—	—	—	—	0.50	0.75
1994 AA	—	—	—	—	0.50	0.75
1995 AA	—	—	—	—	0.50	0.75

KM# 21a 2 PENCE

Bronze Plated Steel, 26 mm. **Ruler:** Elizabeth II **Obv:** Crowned head right **Rev:** Lighthouse on Europa Point, denomination

Date	Mintage	F	VF	XF	Unc	BU
1995 AA	—	—	—	—	0.50	0.75
1995 AB	—	—	—	—	0.50	0.65
1996 AA	—	—	—	—	0.50	0.75
1997 AA	—	—	—	—	0.50	0.75

KM# 774 2 PENCE

Bronze Plated Steel, 26 mm. **Ruler:** Elizabeth II **Obv:** Head with tiara right **Obv. Designer:** Ian Rank-Broadley

Date	Mintage	F	VF	XF	Unc	BU
1998 AA	—	—	—	—	0.50	0.85
1999 AA	—	—	—	—	0.50	0.85
2000 AA	—	—	—	—	0.50	0.85

KM# 22 5 PENCE

Copper-Nickel, 23.6 mm. **Ruler:** Elizabeth II **Obv:** Crowned head right **Obv. Designer:** Raphael Maklouf **Rev:** Barbary ape divides denomination **Rev. Designer:** Alfred Ryman

Date	Mintage	F	VF	XF	Unc	BU
1988 AA	—	—	—	—	0.85	1.50
1989 AA	—	—	—	—	0.85	1.50
1989 AB	—	—	—	—	0.85	1.50
1990 AA	—	—	—	—	0.85	1.50
1990 AB	—	—	—	—	0.85	1.50

KM# 22a 5 PENCE

3.1000 g., Copper-Nickel, 18 mm. **Ruler:** Elizabeth II **Obv:** Crowned head right **Rev:** Barbary ape divides denomination **Note:** Reduced size.

Date	Mintage	F	VF	XF	Unc	BU
1990 AA	—	—	—	—	0.60	1.00
1990 AB	—	—	—	—	0.60	1.00
1991 AA	—	—	—	—	0.60	1.00
1992 AA	—	—	—	—	0.60	1.00
1992 AB	—	—	—	—	0.60	1.00
1993 AA	—	—	—	—	0.60	1.00
1993 AB	—	—	—	—	0.60	1.00
1994 AA	—	—	—	—	0.60	1.00
1995 AA	—	—	—	—	0.60	1.00
1996 AA	—	—	—	—	0.60	1.00
1997 AA	—	—	—	—	0.60	1.00

KM# 22b 5 PENCE

3.2500 g., 0.9250 Silver .0966 oz. ASW, 18 mm. **Ruler:** Elizabeth II **Obv:** Crowned head right **Rev:** Barbary ape left divides denomination

Date	Mintage	F	VF	XF	Unc	BU
1990 Proof	5,000	Value: 25.00				

KM# 22c 5 PENCE

3.2500 g., 0.9170 Gold .0958 oz. AGW, 18 mm. **Ruler:** Elizabeth II **Obv:** Crowned head right **Rev:** Barbary ape left divides denomination

Date	Mintage	F	VF	XF	Unc	BU
1990 Proof	1,000	Value: 125				

KM# 775 5 PENCE

3.1000 g., Copper-Nickel, 18 mm. **Ruler:** Elizabeth II **Obv:** Head with tiara right **Obv. Designer:** Ian Rank-Broadley **Rev:** Barbary Ape left divides denomination

Date	Mintage	F	VF	XF	Unc	BU
1998 AA	—	—	—	—	0.60	0.75
1999 AA	—	—	—	—	0.60	0.75
2000	—	—	—	—	0.60	0.75

KM# 23.1 10 PENCE

11.5000 g., Copper-Nickel, 28.5 mm. **Ruler:** Elizabeth II **Obv:** Crowned head right **Obv. Designer:** Raphael Maklouf **Rev:** Moorish castle, denomination **Rev. Designer:** Alfred Ryman

Date	Mintage	F	VF	XF	Unc	BU
1988 AA	—	—	—	—	1.00	1.25
1988 AB	—	—	—	—	1.00	1.25
1989 AA	—	—	—	—	1.00	1.25
1989PM AB	—	—	—	—	1.00	1.25
1989PM AC	—	—	—	—	1.00	1.25
1989PM AD	—	—	—	—	1.00	1.25
1990 AA	—	—	—	—	1.00	1.25
1990 AB	—	—	—	—	1.00	1.25
1990 AC	—	—	—	—	1.00	1.25
1991 AA	—	—	—	—	1.00	1.25
1991 AB	—	—	—	—	1.00	1.25

KM# 112 10 PENCE

6.5000 g., Copper-Nickel, 24.5 mm. **Ruler:** Elizabeth II **Obv:** Crowned head right **Obv. Designer:** Raphael Maklouf **Rev:** Europort

Date	Mintage	F	VF	XF	Unc	BU
1992 AA	—	—	—	—	0.75	1.00
1993 AA	—	—	—	—	0.75	1.00
1995 AA	—	—	—	—	0.75	1.00
1996 AA	—	—	—	—	0.75	1.00
1996PM BB	—	—	—	—	0.75	1.00
1997 AA	—	—	—	—	0.75	1.00

KM# 112a 10 PENCE

6.5000 g., 0.9250 Silver .1933 oz. ASW, 24.5 mm. **Ruler:** Elizabeth II **Obv:** Crowned head right **Rev:** Europort

Date	Mintage	F	VF	XF	Unc	BU
1992 Proof	25,000	Value: 25.00				

KM# 112b 10 PENCE

6.5000 g., 0.9170 Gold .1916 oz. AGW **Ruler:** Elizabeth II **Obv:** Crowned head right **Rev:** Europort

Date	Mintage	F	VF	XF	Unc	BU
1992 Proof	3,500	Value: 165				

KM# 112c 10 PENCE

6.5000 g., 0.9500 Platinum .1985 oz. APW **Ruler:** Elizabeth II **Obv:** Crowned head right **Rev:** Europort

Date	Mintage	F	VF	XF	Unc	BU
1992 Proof	3,500	Value: 300				

KM# 23.2 10 PENCE

6.5000 g., Copper-Nickel, 24.5 mm. **Ruler:** Elizabeth II **Obv:** Crowned head right **Obv. Designer:** Raphael Maklouf **Rev:** Moorish castle, denomination **Rev. Designer:** Alfred Ryman **Edge:** Reeded **Note:** Reduced size.

Date	Mintage	F	VF	XF	Unc	BU
1994 AA	—	—	—	—	1.00	1.25

KM# 776 10 PENCE

6.5000 g., Copper-Nickel, 24.5 mm. **Ruler:** Elizabeth II **Obv:** Head with tiara right, date below **Obv. Designer:** Ian Rank-Broadley **Rev:** Denomination below building

Date	Mintage	F	VF	XF	Unc	BU
1998 AA	—	—	—	—	1.00	1.25
1999 AA	—	—	—	—	1.00	1.25
2000	—	—	—	—	1.00	1.25

KM# 16 20 PENCE

5.0000 g., Copper-Nickel, 21.4 mm. **Ruler:** Elizabeth II **Obv:** Crowned head right **Obv. Designer:** Raphael Maklouf **Rev:** Our Lady of Europa, a polychrome wood statue, two-feet tall, from the 16th century **Rev. Designer:** Alfred Ryman **Shape:** 7-sided

Date	Mintage	F	VF	XF	Unc	BU
1988 AA	—	—	—	—	1.50	2.00
1988 AB	—	—	—	—	1.50	2.00
1988 AC	—	—	—	—	1.50	2.00
1988 AA Proof	—	—	—	—	—	—
1989 AA	—	—	—	—	1.50	2.00
1990 AA	—	—	—	—	1.50	2.00
1991 AA	—	—	—	—	1.50	2.00
1992 AA	—	—	—	—	1.50	2.00
1993 AA	—	—	—	—	1.50	2.00
1994 AA	—	—	—	—	1.50	2.00
1995 AA	—	—	—	—	1.50	2.00
1995 AA Proof	—	—	—	—	—	—
1996 AA	—	—	—	—	1.50	2.00
1997 AA	—	—	—	—	1.50	2.00

KM# 777 20 PENCE

5.0000 g., Copper-Nickel, 21.4 mm. **Ruler:** Elizabeth II **Obv:** Head with tiara right, date below **Obv. Designer:** Ian Rank-Broadley **Rev:** Our Lady of Europa, denomination below and right **Rev. Designer:** Alfred Ryman **Shape:** 7-sided

Date	Mintage	F	VF	XF	Unc	BU
1998 AA	—	—	—	—	1.50	2.00
1999 AA	—	—	—	—	1.50	2.00
2000 AA	—	—	—	—	1.50	2.00

KM# 5 25 NEW PENCE

Copper-Nickel, 38.5 mm. **Ruler:** Elizabeth II **Obv:** Young bust right, date below **Obv. Designer:** Arnold Machin **Rev:** Barbary ape left, denomination below **Rev. Designer:** Christopher Ironside

Date	Mintage	F	VF	XF	Unc	BU
1971	75,000	—	—	2.00	6.00	12.00

KM# 5a 25 NEW PENCE

28.2800 g., 0.5000 Silver .4546 oz. ASW, 38.5 mm. **Ruler:** Elizabeth II **Obv:** Young bust right, date below **Rev:** Barbary ape left, denomination

Date	Mintage	F	VF	XF	Unc	BU
1971 Proof	20,000	Value: 15.00				
1971 Frosted Proof	50	Value: 200				

KM# 6 25 NEW PENCE

Copper-Nickel, 38.5 mm. **Ruler:** Elizabeth II **Subject:** 25th Wedding Anniversary **Obv:** Young bust right **Obv. Designer:** Arnold Machin **Rev:** Arms of Queen Elizabeth II and Prince Philip, date and denomination below **Rev. Designer:** Stuart Devlin

Date	Mintage	F	VF	XF	Unc	BU
1972	70,000	—	—	1.50	3.50	5.00

KM# 6a 25 NEW PENCE

28.2800 g., 0.9250 Silver .8411 oz. ASW, 38.5 mm. **Ruler:** Elizabeth II **Subject:** 25th Wedding Anniversary **Obv:** Young bust right

Date	Mintage	F	VF	XF	Unc	BU
1972 Proof	15,000	Value: 14.50				

KM# 10 25 NEW PENCE

Copper-Nickel, 38.5 mm. **Ruler:** Elizabeth II **Subject:** Queen's Silver Jubilee **Obv:** Young bust right **Obv. Designer:** Arnold Machin **Rev:** Shield within wreath of apes and laurel, denomination below

Date	Mintage	F	VF	XF	Unc	BU
1977	65,000	—	—	1.50	3.50	5.00

KM# 10a 25 NEW PENCE

28.2800 g., 0.9250 Silver .8411 oz. ASW, 38.5 mm. **Ruler:** Elizabeth II **Subject:** Queen's Silver Jubilee **Obv:** Young bust right

Date	Mintage	F	VF	XF	Unc	BU
1977 Proof	24,000	Value: 14.50				

KM# 17 50 PENCE

13.4000 g., Copper-Nickel, 30 mm. **Ruler:** Elizabeth II **Obv:** Crowned head right **Obv. Designer:** Raphael Maklouf **Rev:** Denomination in wreath of Candytuft flowers (Iberis Gibraltarica) **Rev. Designer:** Alfred Ryman **Shape:** 7-sided

Date	Mintage	F	VF	XF	Unc	BU
1988 AA	30,000	—	—	—	2.00	2.50
1988 AB	—	—	—	—	2.00	2.50
1989 AA	—	—	—	—	2.00	2.50
1989 AB	—	—	—	—	2.00	2.50

KM# 19 50 PENCE

13.4000 g., Copper-Nickel, 30 mm. **Ruler:** Elizabeth II **Subject:** Christmas **Obv:** Crowned head right **Obv. Designer:** Raphael Maklouf **Rev:** The Three Wise Men

Date	Mintage	F	VF	XF	Unc	BU
1988	—	—	—	—	4.00	5.00
1988 Proof	Est. 30,000	Value: 15.00				

KM# 19a 50 PENCE

15.5000 g., 0.9250 Silver .4610 oz. ASW, 30 mm. **Ruler:** Elizabeth II **Subject:** Christmas **Obv:** Crowned head right **Rev:** The Three Wise Men

Date	Mintage	F	VF	XF	Unc	BU
1988 Proof	Est. 5,000	Value: 15.00				

KM# 19b 50 PENCE

26.0000 g., 0.9170 Gold .7665 oz. AGW, 30 mm. **Ruler:** Elizabeth II **Subject:** Christmas **Obv:** Crowned head right **Rev:** The Three Wise Men

Date	Mintage	F	VF	XF	Unc	BU
1988 Proof	250	Value: 550				

KM# 19c 50 PENCE

30.4000 g., 0.9950 Platinum .9725 oz. APW, 30 mm. **Ruler:** Elizabeth II **Subject:** Christmas **Obv:** Crowned head right **Rev:** The Three Wise Men

Date	Mintage	F	VF	XF	Unc	BU
1988 Proof	50	Value: 1,450				

KM# 31 50 PENCE
13.4000 g., Copper-Nickel, 30 mm. **Ruler:** Elizabeth II **Subject:** Christmas **Obv:** Crowned head right **Obv. Designer:** Raphael Maklouf **Rev:** Choir boy, denomination below **Shape:** 7-sided

Date	Mintage	F	VF	XF	Unc	BU
1989 AA	—	—	—	—	4.00	5.00
1989 AA Proof	Est. 30,000	Value: 7.50				

KM# 31a 50 PENCE
15.5000 g., 0.9250 Silver .4610 oz. ASW, 30 mm. **Ruler:** Elizabeth II **Subject:** Christmas **Obv:** Crowned head right **Rev:** Choir boy

Date	Mintage	F	VF	XF	Unc	BU
1989 Proof	Est. 5,000	Value: 45.00				

KM# 31b 50 PENCE
26.0000 g., 0.9170 Gold .7665 oz. AGW, 30 mm. **Ruler:** Elizabeth II **Subject:** Christmas **Obv:** Crowned head right **Rev:** Choir boy

Date	Mintage	F	VF	XF	Unc	BU
1989 Proof	Est. 250	Value: 750				

KM# 31c 50 PENCE
30.4000 g., 0.9950 Platinum .9628 oz. APW, 30 mm. **Ruler:** Elizabeth II **Subject:** Christmas **Obv:** Crowned head right **Rev:** Choir boy

Date	Mintage	F	VF	XF	Unc	BU
1989 Proof	Est. 50	Value: 1,450				

KM# 39 50 PENCE
13.4000 g., Copper-Nickel, 30 mm. **Ruler:** Elizabeth II **Obv:** Crowned head right **Obv. Designer:** Raphael Maklouf **Rev:** Dolphins surround denomination **Shape:** 7-sided

Date	Mintage	F	VF	XF	Unc	BU
1990 AA	—	—	—	—	4.50	5.50
1991 AA	—	—	—	—	4.50	5.50
1992 AA	—	—	—	—	4.50	5.50
1993 AA	—	—	—	—	4.50	5.50
1994 AA	—	—	—	—	4.50	5.50
1995 AA	—	—	—	—	4.50	5.50
1996 AA	—	—	—	—	4.50	5.50
1997	—	—	—	—	4.00	5.50

KM# 39a 50 PENCE
15.5000 g., 0.9250 Silver .4610 oz. ASW **Ruler:** Elizabeth II **Obv:** Crowned head right **Rev:** Dolphins **Shape:** 7-sided

Date	Mintage	F	VF	XF	Unc	BU
1990 Proof	2,500	Value: 47.50				
1993 Proof	—	Value: 50.00				

KM# 39b 50 PENCE
26.0000 g., 0.9170 Gold .7665 oz. AGW, 30 mm. **Ruler:** Elizabeth II **Obv:** Crowned head right **Rev:** Dolphins

Date	Mintage	F	VF	XF	Unc	BU
1990 Proof	250	Value: 800				

KM# 47 50 PENCE
13.4000 g., Copper-Nickel, 30 mm. **Ruler:** Elizabeth II **Subject:** Christmas **Obv:** Crowned head right **Obv. Designer:** Raphael Maklouf **Rev:** Mary and Joseph with child, denomination below **Shape:** 7-sided

Date	Mintage	F	VF	XF	Unc	BU
1990 AA	—	—	—	—	—	—
1990 Proof	Est. 30,000	Value: 8.00				

KM# 47a 50 PENCE
15.5000 g., 0.9250 Silver .4610 oz. ASW, 30 mm. **Ruler:** Elizabeth II **Subject:** Christmas **Obv:** Crowned head right **Rev:** Mary and Joseph with child **Shape:** 7-sided

Date	Mintage	F	VF	XF	Unc	BU
1990 Proof	5,000	Value: 45.00				

KM# 47b 50 PENCE
26.0000 g., 0.9170 Gold .7665 oz. AGW, 30 mm. **Ruler:** Elizabeth II **Subject:** Christmas **Obv:** Crowned head right **Rev:** Mary and Joseph with child **Shape:** 7-sided

Date	Mintage	F	VF	XF	Unc	BU
1990 Proof	250	Value: 700				

KM# 47c 50 PENCE
30.4000 g., 0.9950 Platinum .9723 oz. APW, 30 mm. **Ruler:** Elizabeth II **Subject:** Christmas **Obv:** Crowned head right **Rev:** Mary and Joseph with child **Shape:** 7-sided

Date	Mintage	F	VF	XF	Unc	BU
1990 Proof	50	Value: 1,450				

KM# 83 50 PENCE
13.4000 g., Copper-Nickel, 30 mm. **Ruler:** Elizabeth II **Subject:** Christmas **Obv:** Crowned head right **Obv. Designer:** Raphael Maklouf **Rev:** Family caroling, denomination below **Shape:** 7-sided

Date	Mintage	F	VF	XF	Unc	BU
1991 AA	—	—	—	—	4.00	5.00
1991 AA Proof	Est. 30,000	Value: 7.50				

KM# 83a 50 PENCE
15.5000 g., 0.9250 Silver .4610 oz. ASW, 30 mm. **Ruler:** Elizabeth II **Subject:** Christmas **Obv:** Crowned head right **Rev:** Family caroling **Shape:** 7-sided

Date	Mintage	F	VF	XF	Unc	BU
1991 Proof	Est. 5,000	Value: 40.00				

KM# 83b 50 PENCE
26.0000 g., 0.9170 Gold .7665 oz. AGW, 30 mm. **Ruler:** Elizabeth II **Subject:** Christmas **Obv:** Crowned head right **Rev:** Family caroling **Shape:** 7-sided

Date	Mintage	F	VF	XF	Unc	BU
1991 Proof	250	Value: 685				

KM# 83c 50 PENCE
30.4000 g., 0.9500 Platinum .9286 oz. APW, 30 mm. **Ruler:** Elizabeth II **Subject:** Christmas **Obv:** Crowned head right **Rev:** Family caroling **Shape:** 7-sided

Date	Mintage	F	VF	XF	Unc	BU
1991 Proof	50	Value: 1,375				

KM# 108 50 PENCE
13.4000 g., Copper-Nickel, 30 mm. **Ruler:** Elizabeth II **Subject:** Christmas **Obv:** Crowned head right **Obv. Designer:** Raphael Maklouf **Rev:** Bust of Santa facing, denomination below **Shape:** 7-sided

Date	Mintage	F	VF	XF	Unc	BU
1992 AA Proof	—	Value: 6.50				
1992 AA	Est. 30,000	—	—	—	3.50	4.50

KM# 108a 50 PENCE
15.5000 g., 0.9250 Silver .4610 oz. ASW, 30 mm. **Ruler:** Elizabeth II **Subject:** Christmas **Obv:** Crowned head right **Rev:** Bust of Santa facing **Shape:** 7-sided

Date	Mintage	F	VF	XF	Unc	BU
1992 Proof	Est. 5,000	Value: 40.00				

KM# 108b 50 PENCE
26.0000 g., 0.9170 Gold .7665 oz. AGW, 30 mm. **Ruler:** Elizabeth II **Subject:** Christmas **Obv:** Crowned head right **Rev:** Bust of Santa facing **Shape:** 7-sided

Date	Mintage	F	VF	XF	Unc	BU
1992 Proof	250	Value: 685				

KM# 108c 50 PENCE
30.4000 g., 0.9950 Platinum .9725 oz. APW, 30 mm. **Ruler:** Elizabeth II **Subject:** Christmas **Obv:** Crowned head right **Rev:** Bust of Santa facing **Shape:** 7-sided

Date	Mintage	F	VF	XF	Unc	BU
1992 Proof	50	Value: 1,450				

KM# 190 50 PENCE
13.4000 g., Copper-Nickel, 30 mm. **Ruler:** Elizabeth II **Subject:** Christmas **Obv:** Crowned head right **Obv. Designer:** Raphael Maklouf **Rev:** Santa in automobile, denomination below **Shape:** 7-sided

Date	Mintage	F	VF	XF	Unc	BU
1993 AA	30,000	—	—	—	3.50	4.50

KM# 190a 50 PENCE
15.5000 g., 0.9250 Silver .4610 oz. ASW, 30 mm. **Ruler:** Elizabeth II **Subject:** Christmas **Obv:** Crowned head right **Rev:** Santa in automobile **Shape:** 7-sided

Date	Mintage	F	VF	XF	Unc	BU
1993 Proof	Est. 5,000	Value: 40.00				

KM# 190b 50 PENCE
26.0000 g., 0.9170 Gold .7665 oz. AGW, 30 mm. **Ruler:** Elizabeth II **Subject:** Christmas **Obv:** Crowned head right **Rev:** Santa in automobile **Shape:** 7-sided

Date	Mintage	F	VF	XF	Unc	BU
1993 Proof	Est. 250	Value: 685				

KM# 190c 50 PENCE
30.4000 g., 0.9500 Platinum .9286 oz. APW, 30 mm. **Ruler:** Elizabeth II **Subject:** Christmas **Obv:** Crowned head right **Rev:** Santa in automobile **Shape:** 7-sided

Date	Mintage	F	VF	XF	Unc	BU
1993 Proof	Est. 50	Value: 1,375				

KM# 294 50 PENCE
13.4000 g., Copper-Nickel, 30 mm. **Ruler:** Elizabeth II **Subject:** Christmas **Obv:** Crowned head right **Obv. Designer:** Raphael Maklouf **Rev:** Santa with sack and hot air balloon **Shape:** 7-sided

Date	Mintage	F	VF	XF	Unc	BU
1994 AA	30,000	—	—	—	3.50	4.50
1994PM Prooflike	—	—	—	—	—	6.00

KM# 294a 50 PENCE
15.5000 g., 0.9250 Silver .4610 oz. ASW **Ruler:** Elizabeth II **Subject:** Christmas **Obv:** Crowned head right **Rev:** Santa with sack and hot air balloon **Shape:** 7-sided

Date	Mintage	F	VF	XF	Unc	BU
1994 Proof	Est. 5,000	Value: 40.00				

KM# 294b 50 PENCE
26.0000 g., 0.9170 Gold .7665 oz. AGW, 30 mm. **Ruler:** Elizabeth II **Subject:** Christmas **Obv:** Crowned head right **Rev:** Santa with sack and hot air balloon **Shape:** 7-sided

Date	Mintage	F	VF	XF	Unc	BU
1994 Proof	Est. 250	Value: 700				

KM# 294c 50 PENCE
30.4000 g., 0.9500 Platinum .9286 oz. APW, 30 mm. **Ruler:** Elizabeth II **Subject:** Christmas **Obv:** Crowned head right **Rev:** Santa with sack and hot air balloon **Shape:** 7-sided

Date	Mintage	F	VF	XF	Unc	BU
1994 Proof	Est. 50	Value: 1,375				

KM# 336 50 PENCE
13.4000 g., Copper-Nickel, 30 mm. **Ruler:** Elizabeth II **Subject:** Christmas **Obv:** Crowned head right **Obv. Designer:** Raphael Maklouf **Rev:** Penguins parading, denomination below **Shape:** 7-sided

Date	Mintage	F	VF	XF	Unc	BU
1995 AA	Est. 30,000	—	—	—	4.00	5.00

KM# 336a 50 PENCE
15.5000 g., 0.9250 Silver .4610 oz. ASW, 30 mm. **Ruler:** Elizabeth II **Subject:** Christmas **Obv:** Crowned head right **Rev:** Penguins parading **Shape:** 7-sided

Date	Mintage	F	VF	XF	Unc	BU
1995 Proof	Est. 5,000	Value: 40.00				

KM# 336b 50 PENCE
26.0000 g., 0.9170 Gold .7665 oz. AGW, 30 mm. **Ruler:** Elizabeth II **Subject:** Christmas **Obv:** Crowned head right **Rev:** Penguins parading **Shape:** 7-sided

Date	Mintage	F	VF	XF	Unc	BU
1995 Proof	Est. 250	Value: 700				

KM# 336c 50 PENCE
30.4000 g., 0.9950 Platinum .9769 oz. APW, 30 mm. **Ruler:** Elizabeth II **Subject:** Christmas **Obv:** Crowned head right **Rev:** Penguins parading **Shape:** 7-sided

Date	Mintage	F	VF	XF	Unc	BU
1995 Proof	50	Value: 1,450				

KM# 453 50 PENCE
Copper-Nickel, 30 mm. **Ruler:** Elizabeth II **Subject:** Christmas **Obv:** Crowned head right **Obv. Designer:** Raphael Maklouf **Rev:** Santa Claus and biplane **Shape:** 7-sided

Date	Mintage	F	VF	XF	Unc	BU
1996 No die letters	—	—	—	—	—	—
1996 AA	Est. 30,000	—	—	—	4.00	5.00

KM# 453a 50 PENCE
15.0000 g., 0.9250 Silver .4610 oz. ASW, 30 mm. **Ruler:** Elizabeth II **Subject:** Christmas **Obv:** Crowned head right **Rev:** Santa Claus and biplane **Shape:** 7-sided

Date	Mintage	F	VF	XF	Unc	BU
1996 Proof	Est. 5,000	Value: 35.00				

KM# 453b 50 PENCE
26.0000 g., 0.9170 Gold .7665 oz. AGW, 30 mm. **Ruler:** Elizabeth II **Subject:** Christmas **Obv:** Crowned head right **Rev:** Santa Claus and biplane **Shape:** 7-sided

Date	Mintage	F	VF	XF	Unc	BU
1996 Proof	Est. 250	Value: 645				

KM# 606 50 PENCE
Copper-Nickel, 27.3 mm. **Ruler:** Elizabeth II **Subject:** Christmas **Obv:** Crowned head right **Obv. Designer:** Raphael Maklouf **Rev:** Santa Claus in sleigh **Shape:** 7-sided

Date	Mintage	F	VF	XF	Unc	BU
1997	Est. 30,000	—	—	—	4.00	5.00

KM# 606a 50 PENCE
8.0000 g., 0.9250 Silver .2379 oz. ASW, 27.3 mm. **Ruler:** Elizabeth II **Subject:** Christmas **Obv:** Crowned head right **Rev:** Santa Claus in sleigh **Shape:** 7-sided

Date	Mintage	F	VF	XF	Unc	BU
1997 Proof	Est. 5,000	Value: 35.00				

KM# 606b 50 PENCE
8.0000 g., 0.9170 Gold .2359 oz. AGW, 27.3 mm. **Ruler:** Elizabeth II **Subject:** Christmas **Obv:** Crowned head right **Rev:** Santa in sleigh **Shape:** 7-sided

Date	Mintage	F	VF	XF	Unc	BU
1997 Proof	Est. 250	Value: 550				

KM# 39.1 50 PENCE
8.0000 g., Copper-Nickel, 27.3 mm. **Ruler:** Elizabeth II **Obv:** Crowned head right **Rev:** Dolphins surround denomination **Shape:** 7-sided

Date	Mintage	F	VF	XF	Unc	BU
1997 AA	—	—	—	—	4.50	5.00

KM# 39.1a 50 PENCE
8.0000 g., 0.9250 Silver .2379 oz. ASW, 27.3 mm. **Ruler:** Elizabeth II **Obv:** Crowned head right **Rev:** Dolphins surround denomination **Shape:** 7-sided

Date	Mintage	F	VF	XF	Unc	BU
1997 Proof	Est. 5,000	Value: 35.00				

KM# 39.1b 50 PENCE
8.0000 g., 0.9999 Gold .2569 oz. AGW, 27.3 mm. **Ruler:** Elizabeth II **Obv:** Crowned head right **Rev:** Dolphins surround denomination **Shape:** 7-sided

Date	Mintage	F	VF	XF	Unc	BU
1997 Proof	Est. 250	Value: 400				

KM# 778 50 PENCE
8.0000 g., Copper-Nickel, 27.3 mm. **Ruler:** Elizabeth II **Obv:** Head with tiara right **Obv. Designer:** Ian Rank-Broadley **Rev:** Dolphins surround denomination **Edge:** Plain **Shape:** 7-sided

Date	Mintage	F	VF	XF	Unc	BU
1998PM AA	—	—	—	—	4.50	5.50
1999PM AA	—	—	—	—	4.50	5.50
2000PM AA	—	—	—	—	4.50	5.50

KM# 769 50 PENCE
Copper-Nickel, 27.3 mm. **Ruler:** Elizabeth II **Obv:** Head with tiara right, date below **Obv. Designer:** Ian Rank-Broadley **Rev:** Santa Claus in chimney **Shape:** 7-sided

Date	Mintage	F	VF	XF	Unc	BU
1998	Est. 30,000	—	—	—	4.00	5.00

KM# 769a 50 PENCE
8.0000 g., 0.9250 Silver .2379 oz. ASW, 27.3 mm. **Ruler:** Elizabeth II **Obv:** Head with tiara right **Rev:** Santa Claus in chimney **Shape:** 7-sided

Date	Mintage	F	VF	XF	Unc	BU
1998 Proof	Est. 5,000	Value: 35.00				

KM# 769b 50 PENCE
8.0000 g., 0.9170 Gold .2359 oz. AGW, 27.3 mm. **Ruler:** Elizabeth II **Obv:** Head with tiara right **Rev:** Santa Claus in chimney **Shape:** 7-sided

Date	Mintage	F	VF	XF	Unc	BU
1998 Proof	Est. 250	Value: 550				

KM# 866 50 PENCE
Copper-Nickel, 27.3 mm. **Ruler:** Elizabeth II **Obv:** Head with tiara right, date below **Obv. Designer:** Ian Rank-Broadley **Rev:** Santa with pair of monkeys **Shape:** 7-sided

Date	Mintage	F	VF	XF	Unc	BU
1999 BB	Est. 30,000	—	—	—	4.00	—
1999 BB Prooflike	Est. 30,000	—	—	—	4.00	5.00

KM# 866a 50 PENCE
8.0000 g., 0.9250 Silver .2379 oz. ASW, 27.3 mm. **Ruler:** Elizabeth II **Obv:** Head with tiara right **Rev:** Santa with pair of monkeys **Shape:** 7-sided

Date	Mintage	F	VF	XF	Unc	BU
1999 Proof	Est. 5,000	Value: 35.00				

KM# 866b 50 PENCE
8.0000 g., 0.9170 Gold .2359 oz. AGW, 27.3 mm. **Ruler:** Elizabeth II **Obv:** Head with tiara right **Rev:** Santa with pair of monkeys **Shape:** 7-sided

Date	Mintage	F	VF	XF	Unc	BU
1999 Proof	Est. 250	Value: 550				

KM# 887 50 PENCE
8.0000 g., Copper-Nickel, 27.3 mm. **Ruler:** Elizabeth II **Subject:** Christmas **Obv:** Head with tiara right, date below **Obv. Designer:** Ian Rank-Broadley **Rev:** Madonna and child with angels **Edge:** Plain **Shape:** 7-sided

Date	Mintage	F	VF	XF	Unc	BU
2000 AA	30,000	—	—	—	4.00	5.00

KM# 887a 50 PENCE
8.0000 g., 0.9250 Silver .2379 oz. ASW, 27.3 mm. **Ruler:** Elizabeth II **Subject:** Christmas **Obv:** Head with tiara right **Rev:** Madonna and child with angels **Shape:** 7-sided

Date	Mintage	F	VF	XF	Unc	BU
2000 Proof	5,000	Value: 35.00				

KM# 887b 50 PENCE
8.0000 g., 0.9160 Gold .2356 oz. AGW, 27.3 mm. **Ruler:** Elizabeth II **Subject:** Christmas **Obv:** Head with tiara **Rev:** Madonna and child with angels **Shape:** 7-sided **Note:** KM#310-317 previously listed here do not exist and have been removed.

Date	Mintage	F	VF	XF	Unc	BU
2000 Proof	250	Value: 550				

KM# 310 1/25 CROWN
1.2440 g., 0.9990 Gold 0.04 oz. AGW, 13.9 mm. **Ruler:** Elizabeth II **Subject:** Barcelona Olympics **Obv:** Crowned bust right **Rev:** Ancient discus thrower within circle, denomination below **Edge:** Reeded

Date	Mintage	F	VF	XF	Unc	BU
1991 Proof	—	Value: 45.00				

KM# 311 1/25 CROWN
1.2440 g., 0.9990 Gold 0.04 oz. AGW, 13.9 mm. **Ruler:** Elizabeth II **Subject:** Barcelona Olympics **Obv:** Crowned bust right **Rev:** Ancient chariot racers within circle, denomination below **Edge:** Reeded

Date	Mintage	F	VF	XF	Unc	BU
1991 Proof	—	Value: 45.00				

KM# 312 1/25 CROWN
1.2440 g., 0.9990 Gold 0.04 oz. AGW, 13.9 mm. **Ruler:** Elizabeth II **Subject:** Barcelona Olympics **Obv:** Crowned bust right **Rev:** Ancient runners within circle, denomination below **Edge:** Reeded

Date	Mintage	F	VF	XF	Unc	BU
1991 Proof	—	Value: 45.00				

KM# 313 1/25 CROWN
1.2440 g., 0.9990 Gold 0.04 oz. AGW, 13.9 mm. **Ruler:** Elizabeth II **Subject:** Barcelona Olympics **Obv:** Crowned bust right **Rev:** Ancient javelin thrower within circle, denomination below **Edge:** Reeded

Date	Mintage	F	VF	XF	Unc	BU
1991 Proof	—	Value: 45.00				

KM# 314 1/25 CROWN
1.2440 g., 0.9990 Gold 0.04 oz. AGW, 13.9 mm. **Ruler:** Elizabeth II **Subject:** Barcelona Olympics **Obv:** Crowned bust right **Rev:** Ancient wrestlers, head at left looking right, circle surrounds **Edge:** Reeded

Date	Mintage	F	VF	XF	Unc	BU
1991 Proof	—	Value: 45.00				

KM# 315 1/25 CROWN
1.2440 g., 0.9990 Gold 0.04 oz. AGW, 13.9 mm. **Ruler:** Elizabeth II **Subject:** Barcelona Olympics **Obv:** Crowned bust right **Rev:** Ancient boxer within circle, denomination below **Edge:** Reeded

Date	Mintage	F	VF	XF	Unc	BU
1991 Proof	—	Value: 45.00				

KM# 316 1/25 CROWN
1.2440 g., 0.9990 Gold 0.04 oz. AGW, 13.9 mm. **Ruler:** Elizabeth II **Subject:** Barcelona Olympics **Obv:** Crowned bust right **Rev:** Long jumper within circle, denomination below **Edge:** Reeded

Date	Mintage	F	VF	XF	Unc	BU
1991 Proof	—	Value: 45.00				

KM# 317 1/25 CROWN
1.2440 g., 0.9990 Gold 0.04 oz. AGW, 13.9 mm. **Ruler:** Elizabeth II **Subject:** Barcelona Olympics **Obv:** Crowned bust right **Rev:** Ancient victor wearing laurels, denomination below **Edge:** Reeded

Date	Mintage	F	VF	XF	Unc	BU
1991 Proof	—	Value: 45.00				

KM# 124 1/25 CROWN
1.2440 g., 0.9999 Gold .0400 oz. AGW, 13.9 mm. **Ruler:** Elizabeth II **Rev:** Japanese Royal Wedding

Date	Mintage	F	VF	XF	Unc	BU
1993 Proof	Est. 25,000	Value: 50.00				

KM# 183 1/25 CROWN
1.2440 g., 0.9990 Gold 0.04 oz. AGW, 13.9 mm. **Ruler:** Elizabeth II **Obv:** Crowned bust right **Rev:** Stylized panda **Edge:** Reeded

Date	Mintage	F	VF	XF	Unc	BU
1993 Proof	—	Value: 50.00				

KM# 187 1/25 CROWN
1.2440 g., 0.9990 Gold 0.04 oz. AGW, 13.9 mm. **Ruler:** Elizabeth II **Obv:** Crowned bust right **Rev:** Natural panda amongst bamboo shoots **Edge:** Reeded

Date	Mintage	F	VF	XF	Unc	BU
1993 Proof	—	Value: 50.00				

KM# 202 1/25 CROWN
1.2440 g., 0.9999 Gold .0400 oz. AGW, 13.9 mm. **Ruler:** Elizabeth II **Series:** Peter Rabbit Centennial **Subject:** The Tale of Peter Rabbit **Obv:** Crowned bust right **Rev:** Peter Rabbit eating carrots

Date	Mintage	F	VF	XF	Unc	BU
1993 Proof	Est. 25,000	Value: 40.00				

KM# 202a 1/25 CROWN
1.2440 g., 0.9950 Platinum .0400 oz. APW, 13.9 mm. **Ruler:** Elizabeth II **Series:** Peter Rabbit Centennial **Subject:** The Tale of Peter Rabbit **Obv:** Crowned bust right **Rev:** Peter Rabbit eating carrots

Date	Mintage	F	VF	XF	Unc	BU
1993 Proof	7,500	Value: 65.00				

KM# 206 1/25 CROWN
1.2440 g., 0.9999 Gold .0400 oz. AGW, 13.9 mm. **Ruler:** Elizabeth II **Series:** Peter Rabbit Centennial **Subject:** The Tale of Peter Rabbit **Obv:** Crowned bust right **Rev:** Mrs. Tiggy-Winkel ironing

Date	Mintage	F	VF	XF	Unc	BU
1993 Proof	Est. 25,000	Value: 40.00				

KM# 210 1/25 CROWN
1.2440 g., 0.9999 Gold .0400 oz. AGW, 13.9 mm. **Ruler:** Elizabeth II **Series:** Peter Rabbit Centennial **Subject:** The Tale of Peter Rabbit **Obv:** Crowned bust right **Rev:** Jeremy Fisher fishing

Date	Mintage	F	VF	XF	Unc	BU
1993 Proof	Est. 25,000	Value: 40.00				

KM# 214 1/25 CROWN
1.2440 g., 0.9999 Gold .0400 oz. AGW, 13.9 mm. **Ruler:** Elizabeth II **Series:** Peter Rabbit Centennial **Subject:** The Tale of Peter Rabbit **Obv:** Crowned bust right **Rev:** Tom Kitten with mother cat

Date	Mintage	F	VF	XF	Unc	BU
1993 Proof	Est. 25,000	Value: 40.00				

KM# 218 1/25 CROWN
1.2440 g., 0.9999 Gold .0400 oz. AGW, 13.9 mm. **Ruler:** Elizabeth II **Series:** Peter Rabbit Centennial **Subject:** The Tale of Peter Rabbit **Obv:** Crowned bust right **Rev:** Benjamin Bunny wearing hat and holding coat

Date	Mintage	F	VF	XF	Unc	BU
1993 Proof	Est. 25,000	Value: 40.00				

KM# 222 1/25 CROWN
1.2440 g., 0.9999 Gold .0400 oz. AGW, 13.9 mm. **Ruler:** Elizabeth II **Series:** Peter Rabbit Centennial **Subject:** The Tale of Peter Rabbit **Obv:** Crowned bust right **Rev:** Jemima Puddle Duck talking with fox

Date	Mintage	F	VF	XF	Unc	BU
1993 Proof	Est. 25,000	Value: 40.00				

KM# 437 1/25 CROWN
1.2440 g., 0.9999 Gold .0400 oz. AGW, 13.9 mm. **Ruler:** Elizabeth II **Series:** Peter Rabbit Centennial **Subject:** The Tale of Peter Rabbit **Obv:** Crowned bust right **Rev:** Mother and bunnies

Date	Mintage	F	VF	XF	Unc	BU
1994 Proof	25,000	Value: 45.00				

KM# 437a 1/25 CROWN
1.2440 g., 0.9950 Platinum .0400 oz. APW, 13.9 mm. **Ruler:** Elizabeth II **Series:** Peter Rabbit Centennial **Subject:** The Tale of Peter Rabbit **Obv:** Crowned bust right **Rev:** Mother and bunnies

Date	Mintage	F	VF	XF	Unc	BU
1994 Proof	Est. 7,500	Value: 65.00				

KM# 368 1/25 CROWN
1.2441 g., 0.9999 Gold .0400 oz. AGW, 13.9 mm. **Ruler:** Elizabeth II **Obv:** Crowned bust right **Rev:** Roses

Date	Mintage	F	VF	XF	Unc	BU
1996 Proof	Est. 25,000	Value: 45.00				

KM# 375 1/25 CROWN
1.2441 g., 0.9999 Gold .0400 oz. AGW, 13.9 mm. **Ruler:** Elizabeth II **Series:** Peter Rabbit Centennial **Subject:** The Tale of Peter Rabbit **Obv:** Crowned bust right **Rev:** Rabbit escaping the garden

Date	Mintage	F	VF	XF	Unc	BU
1996 Proof	Est. 25,000	Value: 45.00				

KM# 375a 1/25 CROWN
1.2500 g., 0.9950 Platinum .0400 oz. APW, 13.9 mm. **Ruler:** Elizabeth II **Series:** Peter Rabbit Centennial **Subject:** The Tale of Peter Rabbit **Obv:** Crowned bust right **Rev:** Rabbit escaping the garden

Date	Mintage	F	VF	XF	Unc	BU
1996 Proof	Est. 7,500	Value: 65.00				

KM# 390 1/25 CROWN
1.2441 g., 0.9999 Gold .0400 oz. AGW, 13.9 mm. **Ruler:** Elizabeth II **Series:** Centenary of the Cinema **Subject:** Grace Kelly - actress, 1929-82 **Obv:** Crowned bust right **Rev:** Bust 3/4 facing, denomination

Date	Mintage	F	VF	XF	Unc	BU
1996 Proof	Est. 25,000	Value: 45.00				

KM# 395 1/25 CROWN
1.2441 g., 0.9999 Gold .0400 oz. AGW, 13.9 mm. **Ruler:** Elizabeth II **Series:** Centenary of the Cinema **Subject:** James Dean **Obv:** Crowned bust right **Rev:** Standing central figure, dates at right

Date	Mintage	F	VF	XF	Unc	BU
1996 Proof	Est. 25,000	Value: 45.00				

KM# 400 1/25 CROWN
1.2441 g., 0.9999 Gold .0400 oz. AGW, 13.9 mm. **Ruler:** Elizabeth II **Series:** Centenary of the Cinema **Subject:** Marilyn Monroe - actress, 1926-62 **Obv:** Crowned bust right **Rev:** Bust looking back over shoulder

Date	Mintage	F	VF	XF	Unc	BU
1996 Proof	Est. 25,000	Value: 45.00				

KM# 405 1/25 CROWN
1.2441 g., 0.9999 Gold .0400 oz. AGW, 13.9 mm. **Ruler:** Elizabeth II **Series:** Centenary of the Cinema **Subject:** Audrey Hepburn - actress, 1929-93 **Obv:** Crowned bust right **Rev:** Head 3/4 facing

Date	Mintage	F	VF	XF	Unc	BU
1996 Proof	25,000	Value: 45.00				

KM# 405a 1/25 CROWN
1.2500 g., 0.9950 Platinum .0400 oz. APW, 13.9 mm. **Ruler:** Elizabeth II **Series:** Centenary of the Cinema **Subject:** Audrey Hepburn - actress, 1929-93 **Obv:** Crowned bust right **Rev:** Head 3/4 facing

Date	Mintage	F	VF	XF	Unc	BU
1996 Proof	Est. 1,000	Value: 75.00				

KM# 410 1/25 CROWN
1.2441 g., 0.9999 Gold .0400 oz. AGW, 13.9 mm. **Ruler:** Elizabeth II **Series:** Centenary of the Cinema **Subject:** Bruce Lee - actor, 1940-73 **Obv:** Crowned bust right **Rev:** Kickboxer and chinese dragon

Date	Mintage	F	VF	XF	Unc	BU
1996 Proof	Est. 25,000	Value: 55.00				

KM# 415 1/25 CROWN
1.2441 g., 0.9999 Gold .0400 oz. AGW, 13.9 mm. **Ruler:** Elizabeth II **Series:** Centenary of the Cinema **Subject:** Charlie Chaplan - actor, 1889-1977 **Obv:** Crowned bust right **Rev:** Standing central figure with cane, dates

Date	Mintage	F	VF	XF	Unc	BU
1996 Proof	Est. 25,000	Value: 55.00				

KM# 420 1/25 CROWN
1.2441 g., 0.9999 Gold .0400 oz. AGW, 13.9 mm. **Ruler:** Elizabeth II **Series:** Centenary of the Cinema **Subject:** Gone With The Wind **Obv:** Crowned bust right **Rev:** Rhett Butler and Scarlett O'Hara

Date	Mintage	F	VF	XF	Unc	BU
1996 Proof	Est. 25,000	Value: 55.00				

KM# 425 1/25 CROWN
1.2441 g., 0.9999 Gold .0400 oz. AGW, 13.9 mm. **Ruler:** Elizabeth II **Series:** Centenary of the Cinema **Obv:** Crowned bust right **Rev:** The Flintstones

Date	Mintage	F	VF	XF	Unc	BU
1996 Proof	Est. 25,000	Value: 55.00				

KM# 452 1/25 CROWN
1.2441 g., 0.9999 Gold .0400 oz. AGW, 13.9 mm. **Ruler:** Elizabeth II **Series:** Centenary of the Cinema **Subject:** James Dean - actor, 1931-55 **Obv:** Crowned bust right **Rev:** Standing central figure, dates

Date	Mintage	F	VF	XF	Unc	BU
1996 Proof	Est. 25,000	Value: 60.00				

KM# 454 1/25 CROWN
1.2441 g., 0.9999 Gold .0400 oz. AGW, 13.9 mm. **Ruler:** Elizabeth II **Series:** Centenary of the Cinema **Subject:** Wizard of Oz **Obv:** Crowned bust right **Rev:** Characters of Oz

Date	Mintage	F	VF	XF	Unc	BU
1996 Proof	Est. 25,000	Value: 45.00				

KM# 458 1/25 CROWN
1.2441 g., 0.9999 Gold .0400 oz. AGW, 13.9 mm. **Ruler:** Elizabeth II **Series:** Centenary of the Cinema **Subject:** The Marx Brothers - actors **Obv:** Crowned bust right **Rev:** Three busts 3/4 left

Date	Mintage	F	VF	XF	Unc	BU
1996 Proof	Est. 25,000	Value: 45.00				

KM# 462 1/25 CROWN
1.2441 g., 0.9999 Gold .0400 oz. AGW, 13.9 mm. **Ruler:** Elizabeth II **Series:** Centenary of the Cinema **Subject:** Elvis Presley - actor/entertainer, 1935-77 **Obv:** Crowned bust right **Rev:** Guitar beneath and behind bust 3/4 left

Date	Mintage	F	VF	XF	Unc	BU
1996 Proof	Est. 25,000	Value: 45.00				

KM# 466 1/25 CROWN
1.2441 g., 0.9999 Gold .0400 oz. AGW, 13.9 mm. **Ruler:** Elizabeth II **Series:** Centenary of the Cinema **Subject:** Casablanca **Obv:** Crowned bust right **Rev:** Bogart and Bergman

Date	Mintage	F	VF	XF	Unc	BU
1996 Proof	Est. 25,000	Value: 45.00				

KM# 470 1/25 CROWN
1.2441 g., 0.9999 Gold .0400 oz. AGW, 13.9 mm. **Ruler:** Elizabeth II **Series:** Centenary of the Cinema **Obv:** Crowned bust right **Rev:** E.T.

Date	Mintage	F	VF	XF	Unc	BU
1996 Proof	Est. 25,000	Value: 45.00				

KM# 474 1/25 CROWN
1.2441 g., 0.9999 Gold .0400 oz. AGW, 13.9 mm. **Ruler:** Elizabeth II **Series:** Centenary of the Cinema **Subject:** Alfred Hitchcock - Producer/Director, 1899-1980 **Obv:** Crowned bust right **Rev:** Bust facing looking at bird on left shoulder

Date	Mintage	F	VF	XF	Unc	BU
1996 Proof	Est. 25,000	Value: 45.00				

KM# 518 1/25 CROWN
1.2441 g., 0.9999 Gold .0400 oz. AGW, 13.9 mm. **Ruler:** Elizabeth II **Subject:** The Tale of Peter Rabbit **Obv:** Crowned bust right **Rev:** Standing rabbit

Date	Mintage	F	VF	XF	Unc	BU
1997 Proof	Est. 25,000	Value: 45.00				

KM# 518a 1/25 CROWN
1.2504 g., 0.9950 Platinum .0400 oz. APW, 13.9 mm. **Ruler:** Elizabeth II **Subject:** The Tale of Peter Rabbit **Obv:** Crowned bust right **Rev:** Standing rabbit

Date	Mintage	F	VF	XF	Unc	BU
1997 Proof	Est. 7,500	Value: 65.00				

KM# 537 1/25 CROWN
1.2440 g., 0.9999 Gold .0400 oz. AGW, 13.9 mm. **Ruler:** Elizabeth II **Obv:** Crowned bust right **Rev:** Peonies

Date	Mintage	F	VF	XF	Unc	BU
1997 Proof	Est. 25,000	Value: 45.00				

KM# 541 1/25 CROWN
1.2440 g., 0.9999 Gold .0400 oz. AGW, 13.9 mm. **Ruler:** Elizabeth II **Subject:** Nefertiti **Obv:** Crowned bust right **Rev:** Head right

Date	Mintage	F	VF	XF	Unc	BU
1997 Proof	Est. 10,000	Value: 45.00				

KM# 545 1/25 CROWN
1.2440 g., 0.9999 Gold .0400 oz. AGW, 13.9 mm. **Ruler:** Elizabeth II **Subject:** Cleopatra **Obv:** Crowned bust right **Rev:** Head facing

Date	Mintage	F	VF	XF	Unc	BU
1997 Proof	Est. 10,000	Value: 45.00				

KM# 549 1/25 CROWN
1.2440 g., 0.9999 Gold .0400 oz. AGW, 13.9 mm. **Ruler:** Elizabeth II **Subject:** Europa **Obv:** Crowned bust right **Rev:** Head 1/4 left

Date	Mintage	F	VF	XF	Unc	BU
1997 Proof	Est. 10,000	Value: 45.00				

KM# 553 1/25 CROWN
1.2440 g., 0.9999 Gold .0400 oz. AGW, 13.9 mm. **Ruler:** Elizabeth II **Subject:** Liberty **Obv:** Crowned bust right **Rev:** Laureate head right

Date	Mintage	F	VF	XF	Unc	BU
1997 Proof	Est. 10,000	Value: 45.00				

KM# 581 1/25 CROWN
1.2440 g., 0.9999 Gold .0400 oz. AGW, 13.9 mm. **Ruler:** Elizabeth II **Series:** Evolution of Mankind **Subject:** Egypt **Obv:** Crowned bust right **Rev:** Three ancient Egyptians, pyramids, hieroglyphics

Date	Mintage	F	VF	XF	Unc	BU
1997 Proof	Est. 15,000	Value: 40.00				

KM# 583 1/25 CROWN
1.2440 g., 0.9999 Gold .0400 oz. AGW, 13.9 mm. **Ruler:** Elizabeth II **Series:** Evolution of Mankind **Subject:** Israel **Obv:** Crowned bust right **Rev:** Star of David, Moses and Temple of Solomon

Date	Mintage	F	VF	XF	Unc	BU
1997 Proof	Est. 15,000	Value: 40.00				

KM# 585 1/25 CROWN
1.2440 g., 0.9999 Gold .0400 oz. AGW, 13.9 mm. **Ruler:** Elizabeth II **Series:** Evolution of Mankind **Subject:** China **Obv:** Crowned bust right **Rev:** Emperor and the Great Wall

Date	Mintage	F	VF	XF	Unc	BU
1997 Proof	Est. 15,000	Value: 40.00				

KM# 587 1/25 CROWN
1.2440 g., 0.9999 Gold .0400 oz. AGW, 13.9 mm. **Ruler:** Elizabeth II **Series:** Evolution of Mankind **Subject:** Greece **Obv:** Crowned bust right **Rev:** Aristotle, classic Greek building

Date	Mintage	F	VF	XF	Unc	BU
1997 Proof	Est. 15,000	Value: 40.00				

KM# 589 1/25 CROWN
1.2440 g., 0.9999 Gold .0400 oz. AGW, 13.9 mm. **Ruler:** Elizabeth II **Series:** Evolution of Mankind **Subject:** Rome **Obv:** Crowned bust right **Rev:** Julius Caesar and Stonehenge

Date	Mintage	F	VF	XF	Unc	BU
1997 Proof	Est. 15,000	Value: 40.00				

KM# 591 1/25 CROWN
1.2440 g., 0.9999 Gold .0400 oz. AGW, 13.9 mm. **Ruler:** Elizabeth II **Series:** Evolution of Mankind **Subject:** India **Obv:** Crowned bust right **Rev:** Krishna playing flute by a temple

Date	Mintage	F	VF	XF	Unc	BU
1997 Proof	Est. 15,000	Value: 40.00				

KM# 593 1/25 CROWN
1.2440 g., 0.9999 Gold .0400 oz. AGW, 13.9 mm. **Ruler:** Elizabeth II **Series:** Evolution of Mankind **Subject:** Holy Roman Empire **Obv:** Crowned bust right **Rev:** Charlemagne and soldiers on horseback

Date	Mintage	F	VF	XF	Unc	BU
1997 Proof	Est. 15,000	Value: 40.00				

KM# 595 1/25 CROWN
1.2440 g., 0.9999 Gold .0400 oz. AGW, 13.9 mm. **Ruler:** Elizabeth II **Series:** Evolution of Mankind **Subject:** Macedonia **Obv:** Crowned bust right **Rev:** Alexander the Great on horseback

Date	Mintage	F	VF	XF	Unc	BU
1997 Proof	Est. 15,000	Value: 40.00				

KM# 597 1/25 CROWN
1.2440 g., 0.9999 Gold .0400 oz. AGW, 13.9 mm. **Ruler:** Elizabeth II **Series:** Evolution of Mankind **Subject:** Native America **Obv:** Crowned bust right **Rev:** Native american on horseback, totem pole at left

Date	Mintage	F	VF	XF	Unc	BU
1997 Proof	Est. 15,000	Value: 40.00				

KM# 599 1/25 CROWN
1.2440 g., 0.9999 Gold .0400 oz. AGW, 13.9 mm. **Ruler:** Elizabeth II **Series:** Evolution of Mankind **Subject:** Asia **Obv:** Crowned bust right **Rev:** Buddha and temple

Date	Mintage	F	VF	XF	Unc	BU
1997 Proof	Est. 15,000	Value: 40.00				

KM# 601 1/25 CROWN
1.2440 g., 0.9999 Gold .0400 oz. AGW, 13.9 mm. **Ruler:** Elizabeth II **Series:** Evolution of Mankind **Subject:** Inca Empire **Obv:** Crowned bust right **Rev:** Incan Emperor and Machu Picchu

Date	Mintage	F	VF	XF	Unc	BU
1997 Proof	Est. 15,000	Value: 40.00				

KM# 603 1/25 CROWN
1.2440 g., 0.9999 Gold .0400 oz. AGW, 13.9 mm. **Ruler:** Elizabeth II **Series:** Evolution of Mankind **Subject:** Islamic Civilization **Obv:** Crowned bust right **Rev:** General Tariq Ibn Ziyad and building

Date	Mintage	F	VF	XF	Unc	BU
1997 Proof	Est. 15,000	Value: 40.00				

KM# 608 1/25 CROWN
1.2440 g., 0.9999 Gold .0400 oz. AGW, 13.9 mm. **Ruler:** Elizabeth II **Series:** Traders of the World **Subject:** Sir Francis Drake **Obv:** Crowned bust right **Rev:** Bust at right, ship and beach

Date	Mintage	F	VF	XF	Unc	BU
1997 Proof	Est. 15,000	Value: 45.00				

KM# 610 1/25 CROWN
1.2440 g., 0.9999 Gold .0400 oz. AGW, 13.9 mm. **Ruler:** Elizabeth II **Series:** Traders of the World **Subject:** Romans **Obv:** Crowned bust right **Rev:** Lion, lioness, ship, map

Date	Mintage	F	VF	XF	Unc	BU
1997 Proof	Est. 15,000	Value: 45.00				

KM# 612 1/25 CROWN
1.2440 g., 0.9999 Gold .0400 oz. AGW, 13.9 mm. **Ruler:** Elizabeth II **Series:** Traders of the World **Subject:** Venetians **Obv:** Crowned bust right **Rev:** Pair of oysters with pearls, Venetian canal scene

Date	Mintage	F	VF	XF	Unc	BU
1997 Proof	Est. 15,000	Value: 45.00				

KM# 614 1/25 CROWN
1.2440 g., 0.9999 Gold .0400 oz. AGW, 13.9 mm. **Ruler:** Elizabeth II **Series:** Traders of the World **Subject:** Portuguese **Obv:** Crowned bust right **Rev:** Gold ingots and Portuguese ship

Date	Mintage	F	VF	XF	Unc	BU
1997 Proof	Est. 15,000	Value: 45.00				

KM# 616 1/25 CROWN

1.2440 g., 0.9999 Gold .0400 oz. AGW, 13.9 mm. **Ruler:** Elizabeth II **Series:** Traders of the World **Subject:** Spanish **Obv:** Crowned bust right **Rev:** Tobacco leaves, ship, map and gems

Date	Mintage	F	VF	XF	Unc	BU
1997 Proof	Est. 15,000	Value: 45.00				

KM# 618 1/25 CROWN

1.2440 g., 0.9999 Gold .0400 oz. AGW, 13.9 mm. **Ruler:** Elizabeth II **Series:** Traders of the World **Subject:** English **Obv:** Crowned bust right **Rev:** Profile of Queen above fighting ships

Date	Mintage	F	VF	XF	Unc	BU
1997 Proof	Est. 15,000	Value: 45.00				

KM# 620 1/25 CROWN

1.2440 g., 0.9999 Gold .0400 oz. AGW, 13.9 mm. **Ruler:** Elizabeth II **Series:** Traders of the World **Subject:** Captain Bligh **Obv:** Crowned bust right **Rev:** Figure sitting on rock on beach, ship in background

Date	Mintage	F	VF	XF	Unc	BU
1997 Proof	Est. 15,000	Value: 45.00				

KM# 622 1/25 CROWN

1.2440 g., 0.9999 Gold .0400 oz. AGW **Series:** Traders of the World **Subject:** Captain Cook **Obv:** Crowned bust right **Rev:** Beaver on rock, ship, bust in background

Date	Mintage	F	VF	XF	Unc	BU
1997 Proof	Est. 15,000	Value: 45.00				

KM# 649 1/25 CROWN

1.2440 g., 0.9999 Gold .0400 oz. AGW, 13.9 mm. **Ruler:** Elizabeth II **Subject:** The Tale of Peter Rabbit **Obv:** Crowned bust right **Rev:** Standing rabbit facing

Date	Mintage	F	VF	XF	Unc	BU
1998 Proof	Est. 25,000	Value: 45.00				

KM# 649a 1/25 CROWN

1.2441 g., 0.9950 Platinum .0398 oz. APW, 13.9 mm. **Ruler:** Elizabeth II **Subject:** The Tale of Peter Rabbit **Obv:** Crowned bust right **Rev:** Standing rabbit facing

Date	Mintage	F	VF	XF	Unc	BU
1998 Proof	Est. 7,500	Value: 65.00				

KM# 657 1/25 CROWN

1.2441 g., 0.9999 Gold .0400 oz. AGW, 13.9 mm. **Ruler:** Elizabeth II **Subject:** Chrysanthemum **Obv:** Crowned bust right **Rev:** Three blossoms

Date	Mintage	F	VF	XF	Unc	BU
1998 Proof	Est. 25,000	Value: 45.00				

KM# 662 1/25 CROWN

1.2441 g., 0.9999 Gold .0400 oz. AGW, 13.9 mm. **Ruler:** Elizabeth II **Subject:** Britannia **Obv:** Crowned bust right **Rev:** Helmeted head right

Date	Mintage	F	VF	XF	Unc	BU
1998 Proof	Est. 10,000	Value: 45.00				

KM# 663 1/25 CROWN

1.2441 g., 0.9999 Gold .0400 oz. AGW, 13.9 mm. **Ruler:** Elizabeth II **Subject:** Juno **Obv:** Crowned bust right **Rev:** Head facing

Date	Mintage	F	VF	XF	Unc	BU
1998 Proof	Est. 10,000	Value: 45.00				

KM# 664 1/25 CROWN

1.2441 g., 0.9999 Gold .0400 oz. AGW, 13.9 mm. **Ruler:** Elizabeth II **Subject:** Athena **Obv:** Crowned bust right **Rev:** Helmeted head right

Date	Mintage	F	VF	XF	Unc	BU
1998 Proof	Est. 10,000	Value: 45.00				

KM# 665 1/25 CROWN

1.2441 g., 0.9999 Gold .0400 oz. AGW, 13.9 mm. **Subject:** Arethusa **Obv:** Crowned bust right **Rev:** Head left with dolphins

Date	Mintage	F	VF	XF	Unc	BU
1998 Proof	Est. 10,000	Value: 45.00				

KM# 678 1/25 CROWN

1.2441 g., 0.9999 Gold .0400 oz. AGW, 13.9 mm. **Ruler:** Elizabeth II **Obv:** Crowned bust right **Rev:** Paddington with suitcase

Date	Mintage	F	VF	XF	Unc	BU
1998 Proof	Est. 7,500	Value: 45.00				

KM# 678a 1/25 CROWN

1.2440 g., 0.9950 Platinum .0400 oz. APW, 13.9 mm. **Ruler:** Elizabeth II **Obv:** Crowned bust right **Rev:** Paddington with suitcase

Date	Mintage	F	VF	XF	Unc	BU
1998 Proof	Est. 5,000	Value: 65.00				

KM# 691 1/25 CROWN

1.2440 g., 0.9999 Gold .0400 oz. AGW, 13.9 mm. **Ruler:** Elizabeth II **Series:** Traders of the World **Subject:** Phoenecians, 200BC-600AD **Obv:** Crowned bust right **Rev:** Phoenician Galley, shells below

Date	Mintage	F	VF	XF	Unc	BU
1998 Proof	Est. 10,000	Value: 45.00				

KM# 693 1/25 CROWN

1.2440 g., 0.9999 Gold .0400 oz. AGW, 13.9 mm. **Ruler:** Elizabeth II **Series:** Traders of the World **Subject:** Vikings **Obv:** Crowned bust right **Rev:** Viking ship (900 AD), pair of fish

Date	Mintage	F	VF	XF	Unc	BU
1998 Proof	Est. 10,000	Value: 45.00				

KM# 695 1/25 CROWN

1.2440 g., 0.9999 Gold .0400 oz. AGW, 13.9 mm. **Ruler:** Elizabeth II **Series:** Traders of the World **Subject:** Marco Polo, 1254-1324 **Obv:** Crowned bust right **Rev:** Bust at right facing, ship at left

Date	Mintage	F	VF	XF	Unc	BU
1998 Proof	Est. 10,000	Value: 45.00				

KM# 697 1/25 CROWN

1.2440 g., 0.9999 Gold .0400 oz. AGW, 13.9 mm. **Ruler:** Elizabeth II **Series:** Traders of the World **Subject:** Hanseatic League Nations **Obv:** Crowned bust right **Rev:** Hanseatic Kogge (circa 1350), coins above ship

Date	Mintage	F	VF	XF	Unc	BU
1998 Proof	Est. 10,000	Value: 45.00				

KM# 699 1/25 CROWN

1.2440 g., 0.9999 Gold .0400 oz. AGW, 13.9 mm. **Ruler:** Elizabeth II **Series:** Traders of the World **Subject:** Chinese **Obv:** Crowned bust right **Rev:** Chinese Junk (1400s)

Date	Mintage	F	VF	XF	Unc	BU
1998 Proof	Est. 10,000	Value: 45.00				

KM# 701 1/25 CROWN

1.2440 g., 0.9999 Gold .0400 oz. AGW, 13.9 mm. **Ruler:** Elizabeth II **Series:** Traders of the World **Subject:** Christopher Columbus, 1451-1506 **Obv:** Crowned bust right **Rev:** Bust at left looking right and ship

Date	Mintage	F	VF	XF	Unc	BU
1998 Proof	Est. 10,000	Value: 45.00				

KM# 703 1/25 CROWN

1.2440 g., 0.9999 Gold .0400 oz. AGW, 13.9 mm. **Ruler:** Elizabeth II **Series:** Traders of the World **Subject:** Sir Walter Raleigh, 1552-1618 **Obv:** Crowned bust right **Rev:** Figure standing on beach, ship in background

Date	Mintage	F	VF	XF	Unc	BU
1998 Proof	Est. 10,000	Value: 45.00				

KM# 705 1/25 CROWN

1.2440 g., 0.9999 Gold .0400 oz. AGW, 13.9 mm. **Ruler:** Elizabeth II **Series:** Traders of the World **Obv:** Crowned bust right **Rev:** Sinking ships at the Boston Tea Party (1773), tea leaf

Date	Mintage	F	VF	XF	Unc	BU
1998 Proof	Est. 10,000	Value: 45.00				

KM# 707 1/25 CROWN

1.2440 g., 0.9999 Gold .0400 oz. AGW **Ruler:** Elizabeth II **Series:** Evolution of Mankind **Subject:** Australopithecus - Lucy **Obv:** Crowned head right **Rev:** Upright figure left, brain depiction at left

Date	Mintage	F	VF	XF	Unc	BU
1998 Proof	Est. 15,000	Value: 45.00				

KM# 709 1/25 CROWN

1.2440 g., 0.9999 Gold .0400 oz. AGW, 13.9 mm. **Ruler:** Elizabeth II **Series:** Traders of the World **Subject:** Homo Habilis **Obv:** Crowned head right **Rev:** Squatting figure using tools

Date	Mintage	F	VF	XF	Unc	BU
1998 Proof	Est. 15,000	Value: 45.00				

KM# 711 1/25 CROWN

1.2440 g., 0.9999 Gold .0400 oz. AGW, 13.9 mm. **Ruler:** Elizabeth II **Series:** Traders of the World **Subject:** Homo Erectus **Obv:** Crowned bust right **Rev:** Cave people using fire

Date	Mintage	F	VF	XF	Unc	BU
1998 Proof	Est. 15,000	Value: 45.00				

KM# 713 1/25 CROWN

1.2440 g., 0.9999 Gold .0400 oz. AGW, 13.9 mm. **Ruler:** Elizabeth II **Series:** Evolution of Mankind **Subject:** Gibraltar Skull **Obv:** Crowned bust right **Rev:** Caveman, skull and 'the rock'

Date	Mintage	F	VF	XF	Unc	BU
1998 Proof	Est. 15,000	Value: 45.00				

KM# 715 1/25 CROWN

1.2440 g., 0.9999 Gold .0400 oz. AGW, 13.9 mm. **Ruler:** Elizabeth II **Series:** Evolution of Mankind **Subject:** Neanderthal Man **Obv:** Crowned bust right **Rev:** Early man at burial scene, skull

Date	Mintage	F	VF	XF	Unc	BU
1998 Proof	Est. 15,000	Value: 45.00				

KM# 717 1/25 CROWN

1.2440 g., 0.9999 Gold .0400 oz. AGW, 13.9 mm. **Ruler:** Elizabeth II **Series:** Evolution of Mankind **Subject:** Homo Sapiens **Obv:** Crowned bust right **Rev:** Early man doing cave painting

Date	Mintage	F	VF	XF	Unc	BU
1998 Proof	Est. 15,000	Value: 45.00				

KM# 719 1/25 CROWN

1.2440 g., 0.9999 Gold .0400 oz. AGW, 13.9 mm. **Ruler:** Elizabeth II **Series:** Evolution of Mankind **Subject:** Homo Sapiens Hunting Mammoth **Obv:** Crowned bust right **Rev:** Figures spearing mammoth

Date	Mintage	F	VF	XF	Unc	BU
1998 Proof	Est. 15,000	Value: 45.00				

KM# 722 1/25 CROWN

1.2440 g., 0.9999 Gold .0400 oz. AGW, 13.9 mm. **Ruler:** Elizabeth II **Series:** Evolution of Mankind **Subject:** Theory of Evolution **Obv:** Crowned bust right **Rev:** Illustrated theory of evolution

Date	Mintage	F	VF	XF	Unc	BU
1998 Proof	Est. 15,000	Value: 45.00				

KM# 723 1/25 CROWN

1.2440 g., 0.9999 Gold .0400 oz. AGW, 13.9 mm. **Ruler:** Elizabeth II **Series:** Evolution of Mankind **Subject:** The Common Ancestry of Man and Ape **Obv:** Crowned bust right **Rev:** Human and primate mothers with young

Date	Mintage	F	VF	XF	Unc	BU
1998 Proof	Est. 15,000	Value: 45.00				

KM# 725 1/25 CROWN

1.2440 g., 0.9999 Gold .0400 oz. AGW, 13.9 mm. **Ruler:** Elizabeth II **Series:** Evolution of Mankind **Subject:** Charles Darwin **Obv:** Crowned bust right **Rev:** Bust facing, neanderthal and space shuttle

Date	Mintage	F	VF	XF	Unc	BU
1998 Proof	Est. 15,000	Value: 45.00				

KM# 727 1/25 CROWN

1.2440 g., 0.9999 Gold .0400 oz. AGW, 13.9 mm. **Ruler:** Elizabeth II **Series:** Evolution of Mankind **Subject:** Raymond Dart **Obv:** Crowned bust right **Rev:** Bust at left looking at skull on right

Date	Mintage	F	VF	XF	Unc	BU
1998 Proof	Est. 15,000	Value: 45.00				

KM# 729 1/25 CROWN

1.2440 g., 0.9999 Gold .0400 oz. AGW, 13.9 mm. **Ruler:** Elizabeth II **Series:** Evolution of Mankind **Subject:** 20th Century Homo Sapiens **Obv:** Crowned bust right **Rev:** Five depictions of evolution

Date	Mintage	F	VF	XF	Unc	BU
1998 Proof	Est. 15,000	Value: 45.00				

KM# 779.1 1/25 CROWN

1.2440 g., 0.9999 Gold .0400 oz. AGW, 13.9 mm. **Ruler:** Elizabeth II **Subject:** 1999 The Year of the Rabbit **Obv:** Crowned bust right **Rev:** Rabbit reading, sparrow and chinese characters

Date	Mintage	F	VF	XF	Unc	BU
1999 Proof	Est. 5,000	Value: 45.00				

KM# 779.1a 1/25 CROWN

1.2400 g., 0.9950 Platinum .0400 oz. APW, 13.9 mm. **Ruler:** Elizabeth II **Subject:** 1999 The Year of the Rabbit **Obv:** Crowned bust right **Rev:** Rabbit reading, sparrow and chinese characters

Date	Mintage	F	VF	XF	Unc	BU
1999 Proof	Est. 3,000	Value: 70.00				

KM# 779.2 1/25 CROWN

1.2440 g., 0.9999 Gold .0400 oz. AGW, 13.9 mm. **Ruler:** Elizabeth II **Subject:** The Year of the Rabbit **Obv:** Crowned bust right **Rev:** Rabbit reading, sparrow; without Chinese characters

Date	Mintage	F	VF	XF	Unc	BU
1999 Proof	Inc. above	Value: 45.00				

KM# 779.2a 1/25 CROWN

1.2400 g., 0.9950 Platinum .0400 oz. APW **Ruler:** Elizabeth II **Subject:** The Year of the Rabbit **Obv:** Crowned bust right **Rev:** Rabbit reading, sparrow; without Chinese characters

Date	Mintage	F	VF	XF	Unc	BU
1999 Proof	Inc. above	Value: 70.00				

KM# 50 1/10 CROWN

3.1100 g., 0.9999 Gold .1000 oz. AGW, 17.95 mm. **Ruler:** Elizabeth II **Series:** Barcelona Olympics **Obv:** Crowned bust right **Rev:** Discus thrower

Date	Mintage	F	VF	XF	Unc	BU
1991 Proof	Est. 20,000	Value: 80.00				
1992 Proof	Est. 20,000	Value: 90.00				

KM# 51 1/10 CROWN

3.1100 g., 0.9999 Gold .1000 oz. AGW, 17.95 mm. **Ruler:** Elizabeth II **Series:** Barcelona Olympics **Obv:** Crowned bust right **Rev:** Chariot racing

Date	Mintage	F	VF	XF	Unc	BU
1991 Proof	Est. 20,000	Value: 80.00				
1992 Proof	Est. 20,000	Value: 90.00				

KM# 52 1/10 CROWN

3.1100 g., 0.9999 Gold .1000 oz. AGW, 17.95 mm. **Ruler:** Elizabeth II **Series:** Barcelona Olympics **Obv:** Crowned bust right **Rev:** Runners

Date	Mintage	F	VF	XF	Unc	BU
1991 Proof	Est. 20,000	Value: 80.00				
1992 Proof	Est. 20,000	Value: 90.00				

KM# 53 1/10 CROWN

3.1100 g., 0.9999 Gold .1000 oz. AGW, 17.95 mm. **Ruler:** Elizabeth II **Series:** Barcelona Olympics **Obv:** Crowned bust right **Rev:** Javelin thrower

Date	Mintage	F	VF	XF	Unc	BU
1991 Proof	Est. 20,000	Value: 80.00				
1992 Proof	Est. 20,000	Value: 90.00				

KM# 54 1/10 CROWN

3.1100 g., 0.9999 Gold .1000 oz. AGW, 17.95 mm. **Ruler:** Elizabeth II **Series:** Barcelona Olympics **Obv:** Crowned bust right **Rev:** Wrestlers

Date	Mintage	F	VF	XF	Unc	BU
1991 Proof	Est. 20,000	Value: 80.00				
1992 Proof	Est. 20,000	Value: 90.00				

KM# 55 1/10 CROWN

3.1100 g., 0.9999 Gold .1000 oz. AGW, 17.95 mm. **Ruler:** Elizabeth II **Series:** Barcelona Olympics **Obv:** Crowned bust right **Rev:** Boxers

Date	Mintage	F	VF	XF	Unc	BU
1991 Proof	Est. 20,000	Value: 80.00				
1992 Proof	Est. 20,000	Value: 90.00				

KM# 56 1/10 CROWN

3.1100 g., 0.9999 Gold .1000 oz. AGW, 17.95 mm. **Ruler:** Elizabeth II **Series:** Barcelona Olympics **Obv:** Crowned bust right **Rev:** Long jumper

Date	Mintage	F	VF	XF	Unc	BU
1991 Proof	Est. 20,000	Value: 80.00				
1992 Proof	Est. 20,000	Value: 90.00				

KM# 57 1/10 CROWN

3.1100 g., 0.9999 Gold .1000 oz. AGW, 17.95 mm. **Ruler:** Elizabeth II **Series:** Barcelona Olympics **Obv:** Crowned bust right **Rev:** Olympic victor

Date	Mintage	F	VF	XF	Unc	BU
1991 Proof	Est. 20,000	Value: 80.00				
1992 Proof	Est. 20,000	Value: 90.00				

KM# 125 1/10 CROWN

3.1100 g., 0.9999 Gold .1000 oz. AGW, 17.95 mm. **Ruler:** Elizabeth II **Subject:** Japanese Royal Wedding

Date	Mintage	F	VF	XF	Unc	BU
1993 Proof	Est. 10,000	Value: 95.00				

KM# 203 1/10 CROWN
3.1100 g., 0.9999 Gold .1000 oz. AGW, 17.95 mm. **Ruler:** Elizabeth II **Series:** Peter Rabbit Centennial **Subject:** The Tale of Peter Rabbit **Obv:** Crowned bust right **Rev:** Rabbit eating carrots, sparrow on handle

Date	Mintage	F	VF	XF	Unc	BU
1993 Proof	Est. 20,000	Value: 85.00				

KM# 203a 1/10 CROWN
3.1100 g., 0.9990 Platinum .1000 oz. APW **Ruler:** Elizabeth II **Series:** Peter Rabbit Centennial **Subject:** The Tale of Peter Rabbit **Obv:** Crowned bust right **Rev:** Rabbit eating carrots, sparrow on handle

Date	Mintage	F	VF	XF	Unc	BU
1993 Proof	Est. 5,000	Value: 145				

KM# 207 1/10 CROWN
3.1100 g., 0.9990 Platinum .1000 oz. APW **Ruler:** Elizabeth II **Series:** Peter Rabbit Centennial **Subject:** The Tale of Peter Rabbit **Obv:** Crowned bust right **Rev:** Mrs. Tiggy-Winkel ironing

Date	Mintage	F	VF	XF	Unc	BU
1993 Proof	Est. 20,000	Value: 145				

KM# 211 1/10 CROWN
3.1100 g., 0.9990 Platinum .1000 oz. APW **Ruler:** Elizabeth II **Series:** Peter Rabbit Centennial **Subject:** The Tale of Peter Rabbit **Obv:** Crowned bust right **Rev:** Jeremy Fisher fishing

Date	Mintage	F	VF	XF	Unc	BU
1993 Proof	Est. 20,000	Value: 145				

KM# 215 1/10 CROWN
3.1100 g., 0.9990 Platinum .1000 oz. APW **Ruler:** Elizabeth II **Series:** Peter Rabbit Centennial **Subject:** The Tale of Peter Rabbit **Obv:** Crowned bust right **Rev:** Tom Kitten with mother cat

Date	Mintage	F	VF	XF	Unc	BU
1993 Proof	Est. 20,000	Value: 145				

KM# 219 1/10 CROWN
3.1100 g., 0.9990 Platinum .1000 oz. APW **Ruler:** Elizabeth II **Series:** Peter Rabbit Centennial **Subject:** The Tale of Peter Rabbit **Obv:** Crowned bust right **Rev:** Benjamin Bunny wearing hat and holding coat

Date	Mintage	F	VF	XF	Unc	BU
1993 Proof	Est. 20,000	Value: 145				

KM# 223 1/10 CROWN
3.1100 g., 0.9990 Platinum .1000 oz. APW **Ruler:** Elizabeth II **Series:** Peter Rabbit Centennial **Subject:** The Tale of Peter Rabbit **Obv:** Crowned bust right **Rev:** Jemima Puddle Duck talking with fox

Date	Mintage	F	VF	XF	Unc	BU
1993 Proof	Est. 20,000	Value: 145				

KM# 439 1/10 CROWN
3.1100 g., 0.9990 Platinum .1000 oz. APW **Ruler:** Elizabeth II **Series:** Peter Rabbit Centennial **Subject:** The Tale of Peter Rabbit **Obv:** Crowned bust right **Rev:** Mother Rabbit and bunnies

Date	Mintage	F	VF	XF	Unc	BU
1994 Proof	Est. 20,000	Value: 145				

KM# 439a 1/10 CROWN
3.1103 g., 0.9950 Platinum .1000 oz. APW **Ruler:** Elizabeth II **Series:** Peter Rabbit Centennial **Obv:** Crowned bust right **Rev:** Mother Rabbit and bunnies

Date	Mintage	F	VF	XF	Unc	BU
1994 Proof	Est. 5,000	Value: 150				

KM# 369 1/10 CROWN
3.1103 g., 0.9999 Gold .1000 oz. AGW, 17.95 mm. **Ruler:** Elizabeth II **Subject:** Roses **Obv:** Crowned bust right

Date	Mintage	F	VF	XF	Unc	BU
1996 Proof	Est. 20,000	Value: 85.00				

KM# 377 1/10 CROWN
3.1103 g., 0.9999 Gold .1000 oz. AGW, 17.95 mm. **Ruler:** Elizabeth II **Series:** Peter Rabbit Centennial **Subject:** The Tale of Peter Rabbit **Obv:** Crowned bust right **Rev:** Rabbit escaping the garden

Date	Mintage	F	VF	XF	Unc	BU
1996 Proof	Est. 20,000	Value: 85.00				

KM# 377a 1/10 CROWN
3.1259 g., 0.9950 Platinum .1000 oz. APW **Ruler:** Elizabeth II **Series:** Peter Rabbit Centennial **Subject:** The Tale of Peter Rabbit **Obv:** Crowned bust right **Rev:** Rabbit escaping the garden

Date	Mintage	F	VF	XF	Unc	BU
1996 Proof	Est. 10,000	Value: 145				

KM# 391 1/10 CROWN
3.1103 g., 0.9999 Gold .1000 oz. AGW, 17.95 mm. **Ruler:** Elizabeth II **Series:** Centenary of the Cinema **Subject:** Grace Kelly - actress, 1929-82 **Obv:** Crowned bust right **Rev:** Bust 3/4 facing, dates

Date	Mintage	F	VF	XF	Unc	BU
1996 Proof	Est. 20,000	Value: 85.00				

KM# 396 1/10 CROWN
3.1103 g., 0.9999 Gold .1000 oz. AGW, 17.95 mm. **Ruler:** Elizabeth II **Series:** Centenary of the Cinema **Subject:** James Dean - actor, 1931-55 **Obv:** Crowned bust right **Rev:** Bust facing, dates

Date	Mintage	F	VF	XF	Unc	BU
1996 Proof	20,000	Value: 95.00				

KM# 401 1/10 CROWN
3.1103 g., 0.9999 Gold .1000 oz. AGW, 17.95 mm. **Ruler:** Elizabeth II **Series:** Centenary of the Cinema **Subject:** Marilyn Monroe - actress, 1926-62 **Obv:** Crowned bust right **Rev:** Bust looking back over shoulder, dates

Date	Mintage	F	VF	XF	Unc	BU
1996 Proof	Est. 20,000	Value: 85.00				

KM# 406 1/10 CROWN
3.1103 g., 0.9999 Gold .1000 oz. AGW, 17.95 mm. **Ruler:** Elizabeth II **Series:** Centenary of the Cinema **Subject:** Audrey Hepburn - actress, 1929-93 **Obv:** Crowned bust right **Rev:** Bust facing, dates

Date	Mintage	F	VF	XF	Unc	BU
1996 Proof	Est. 20,000	Value: 85.00				

KM# 406a 1/10 CROWN
3.1103 g., 0.9950 Platinum .1000 oz. APW **Ruler:** Elizabeth II **Series:** Centenary of the Cinema **Subject:** Audrey Hepburn - actress, 1929-93 **Obv:** Crowned bust right **Rev:** Bust facing, dates

Date	Mintage	F	VF	XF	Unc	BU
1996 Proof	Est. 1,000	Value: 155				

KM# 411 1/10 CROWN
3.1103 g., 0.9999 Gold .1000 oz. AGW, 17.95 mm. **Ruler:** Elizabeth II **Series:** Centenary of the Cinema **Subject:** Bruce Lee **Obv:** Crowned bust right **Rev:** Kickboxer and chinese dragon

Date	Mintage	F	VF	XF	Unc	BU
1996 Proof	Est. 20,000	Value: 85.00				

KM# 416 1/10 CROWN
3.1103 g., 0.9999 Gold .1000 oz. AGW, 17.95 mm. **Ruler:** Elizabeth II **Series:** Centenary of the Cinema **Subject:** Charlie Chaplan - actor, 1889-1977 **Obv:** Crowned bust right **Rev:** Standing central figure with cane, dates

Date	Mintage	F	VF	XF	Unc	BU
1996 Proof	Est. 20,000	Value: 80.00				

KM# 421 1/10 CROWN
3.1103 g., 0.9999 Gold .1000 oz. AGW, 17.95 mm. **Ruler:** Elizabeth II **Series:** Centenary of the Cinema **Subject:** Gone With The Wind **Obv:** Crowned bust right **Rev:** Rhett Butler and Scarlett O'Hara

Date	Mintage	F	VF	XF	Unc	BU
1996 Proof	Est. 20,000	Value: 85.00				

KM# 426 1/10 CROWN
3.1103 g., 0.9999 Gold .1000 oz. AGW, 17.95 mm. **Ruler:** Elizabeth II **Series:** Centenary of the Cinema **Obv:** Crowned bust right **Rev:** The Flintstones

Date	Mintage	F	VF	XF	Unc	BU
1996 Proof	Est. 20,000	Value: 85.00				

KM# 446 1/10 CROWN
3.1103 g., 0.9999 Gold .1000 oz. AGW, 17.95 mm. **Ruler:** Elizabeth II **Subject:** Lord Buddha **Rev:** Seated figure facing

Date	Mintage	F	VF	XF	Unc	BU
1996 Proof	Est. 10,000	Value: 95.00				

KM# 455 1/10 CROWN
3.1103 g., 0.9999 Gold .1000 oz. AGW, 17.95 mm. **Ruler:** Elizabeth II **Series:** Centenary of the Cinema **Subject:** Wizard of Oz **Obv:** Crowned bust right **Rev:** Wizard of Oz characters

Date	Mintage	F	VF	XF	Unc	BU
1996 Proof	Est. 20,000	Value: 85.00				

KM# 459 1/10 CROWN
3.1103 g., 0.9999 Gold .1000 oz. AGW, 17.95 mm. **Ruler:** Elizabeth II **Series:** Centenary of the Cinema **Subject:** Marx Brothers **Obv:** Crowned bust right **Rev:** Three busts left

Date	Mintage	F	VF	XF	Unc	BU
1996 Proof	Est. 20,000	Value: 85.00				

KM# 463 1/10 CROWN
3.1103 g., 0.9999 Gold .1000 oz. AGW, 17.95 mm. **Ruler:** Elizabeth II **Series:** Centenary of the Cinema **Subject:** Elvis Presley **Obv:** Crowned bust right **Rev:** Guitar beneath and behind bust 3/4 left

Date	Mintage	F	VF	XF	Unc	BU
1996 Proof	Est. 20,000	Value: 85.00				

KM# 467 1/10 CROWN
3.1103 g., 0.9999 Gold .1000 oz. AGW, 17.95 mm. **Ruler:** Elizabeth II **Series:** Centenary of the Cinema **Subject:** Casablanca **Obv:** Crowned bust right **Rev:** Bogart and Bergman

Date	Mintage	F	VF	XF	Unc	BU
1996 Proof	Est. 20,000	Value: 85.00				

KM# 471 1/10 CROWN
3.1103 g., 0.9999 Gold .1000 oz. AGW, 17.95 mm. **Ruler:** Elizabeth II **Series:** Centenary of the Cinema **Obv:** Crowned bust right **Rev:** E.T.

Date	Mintage	F	VF	XF	Unc	BU
1996 Proof	Est. 20,000	Value: 85.00				

KM# 475 1/10 CROWN
3.1103 g., 0.9999 Gold .1000 oz. AGW, 17.95 mm. **Ruler:** Elizabeth II **Series:** Centenary of the Cinema **Subject:** Alfred Hitchcock - Producer/Director, 1899-1980 **Obv:** Crowned bust right **Rev:** Bust facing looking at bird on left shoulder

Date	Mintage	F	VF	XF	Unc	BU
1996 Proof	Est. 20,000	Value: 85.00				

KM# 520 1/10 CROWN
3.1103 g., 0.9999 Gold .1000 oz. AGW, 17.95 mm. **Ruler:** Elizabeth II **Subject:** Tale of Peter Rabbit **Obv:** Crowned bust right **Rev:** Standing rabbit facing

Date	Mintage	F	VF	XF	Unc	BU
1997 Proof	Est. 20,000	Value: 85.00				

KM# 520a 1/10 CROWN
3.1259 g., 0.9950 Platinum .1000 oz. APW **Ruler:** Elizabeth II **Subject:** Tale of Peter Rabbit **Obv:** Crowned bust right **Rev:** Standing rabbit facing

Date	Mintage	F	VF	XF	Unc	BU
1997 Proof	Est. 5,000	Value: 155				

KM# 538 1/10 CROWN
3.1100 g., 0.9999 Gold .1000 oz. AGW, 17.95 mm. **Obv:** Crowned bust right **Rev:** Peonies

Date	Mintage	F	VF	XF	Unc	BU
1997 Proof	Est. 20,000	Value: 80.00				

KM# 542 1/10 CROWN
3.1100 g., 0.9999 Gold .1000 oz. AGW, 17.95 mm. **Ruler:** Elizabeth II **Subject:** Nefertiti **Obv:** Crowned bust right **Rev:** Head right

Date	Mintage	F	VF	XF	Unc	BU
1997 Proof	Est. 7,500	Value: 80.00				

KM# 546 1/10 CROWN
3.1100 g., 0.9999 Gold .1000 oz. AGW, 17.95 mm. **Ruler:** Elizabeth II **Subject:** Cleopatra **Obv:** Crowned bust right **Rev:** Head facing

Date	Mintage	F	VF	XF	Unc	BU
1997 Proof	Est. 7,500	Value: 80.00				

KM# 550 1/10 CROWN
3.1100 g., 0.9999 Gold .1000 oz. AGW, 17.95 mm. **Ruler:** Elizabeth II **Subject:** Europa **Obv:** Crowned bust right **Rev:** Head 3/4 left

Date	Mintage	F	VF	XF	Unc	BU
1997 Proof	Est. 7,500	Value: 80.00				

KM# 554 1/10 CROWN
3.1100 g., 0.9999 Gold .1000 oz. AGW, 17.95 mm. **Ruler:** Elizabeth II **Subject:** Liberty **Obv:** Crowned bust right **Rev:** Laureate head right

Date	Mintage	F	VF	XF	Unc	BU
1997 Proof	Est. 7,500	Value: 80.00				

KM# 651 1/10 CROWN
3.1100 g., 0.9999 Gold .1000 oz. AGW, 17.95 mm. **Ruler:** Elizabeth II **Subject:** Tale of Peter Rabbit **Obv:** Crowned bust right **Rev:** Standing rabbit facing, sparrow

Date	Mintage	F	VF	XF	Unc	BU
1998 Proof	Est. 20,000	Value: 90.00				

KM# 651a 1/10 CROWN
3.1103 g., 0.9950 Platinum .1000 oz. APW **Ruler:** Elizabeth II **Subject:** Tale of Peter Rabbit **Obv:** Crowned bust right **Rev:** Standing rabbit facing, sparrow

Date	Mintage	F	VF	XF	Unc	BU
1998 Proof	Est. 5,000	Value: 145				

KM# 658 1/10 CROWN
3.1100 g., 0.9999 Gold .1000 oz. AGW, 17.95 mm. **Ruler:** Elizabeth II **Subject:** Chrysanthemum **Obv:** Crowned bust right **Rev:** Three blossoms

Date	Mintage	F	VF	XF	Unc	BU
1998 Proof	Est. 20,000	Value: 90.00				

KM# 666 1/10 CROWN
3.1100 g., 0.9999 Gold .1000 oz. AGW, 17.95 mm. **Ruler:** Elizabeth II **Subject:** Brittania **Obv:** Crowned bust right **Rev:** Helmeted head right

Date	Mintage	F	VF	XF	Unc	BU
1998 Proof	Est. 7,500	Value: 90.00				

KM# 667 1/10 CROWN
3.1100 g., 0.9999 Gold .1000 oz. AGW, 17.95 mm. **Ruler:** Elizabeth II **Subject:** Juno **Obv:** Crowned bust right **Rev:** Head 3/4 facing

Date	Mintage	F	VF	XF	Unc	BU
1998 Proof	Est. 7,500	Value: 90.00				

KM# 668 1/10 CROWN
3.1100 g., 0.9999 Gold .1000 oz. AGW, 17.95 mm. **Ruler:** Elizabeth II **Subject:** Athena **Obv:** Crowned bust right **Rev:** Helmeted head right

Date	Mintage	F	VF	XF	Unc	BU
1998 Proof	Est. 7,500	Value: 90.00				

KM# 669 1/10 CROWN
3.1100 g., 0.9999 Gold .1000 oz. AGW, 17.95 mm. **Ruler:** Elizabeth II **Subject:** Arethusa **Obv:** Crowned bust right **Rev:** Head left with dolphins

Date	Mintage	F	VF	XF	Unc	BU
1998 Proof	Est. 7,500	Value: 90.00				

KM# 679 1/10 CROWN
3.1100 g., 0.9999 Gold .1000 oz. AGW, 17.95 mm. **Ruler:** Elizabeth II **Subject:** Paddington Bear **Obv:** Crowned bust right **Rev:** Bear with suitcase

Date	Mintage	F	VF	XF	Unc	BU
1998 Proof	Est. 7,500	Value: 90.00				

KM# 679a 1/10 CROWN
3.1103 g., 0.9950 Platinum .1000 oz. APW **Ruler:** Elizabeth II **Subject:** Paddington Bear **Obv:** Crowned bust right **Rev:** Bear with suitcase

Date	Mintage	F	VF	XF	Unc	BU
1998 Proof	Est. 5,000	Value: 145				

KM# 48 1/5 CROWN
6.2200 g., 0.9990 Gold .2000 oz. AGW, 22 mm. **Ruler:**

Elizabeth II **Series:** 150th Anniversary of the First Adhesive Postage Stamp **Subject:** Penny Black Stamp **Obv:** Crowned bust right **Rev:** Heads flank stamp design

Date	Mintage	F	VF	XF	Unc	BU
1990 Proof	Est. 5,000	Value: 215				

KM# 76 1/5 CROWN

6.2200 g., 0.9990 Gold .2000 oz. AGW, 22 mm. **Ruler:** Elizabeth II **Series:** World Cup Soccer **Obv:** Crowned bust right **Rev:** Italian flag

Date	Mintage	F	VF	XF	Unc	BU
1990 Proof	Est. 5,000	Value: 215				

KM# 76a 1/5 CROWN

6.2200 g., 0.9950 Platinum .2000 oz. APW **Ruler:** Elizabeth II **Series:** World Cup Soccer **Obv:** Crowned bust right **Rev:** Italian flag

Date	Mintage	F	VF	XF	Unc	BU
1990 Proof	Est. 1,000	Value: 325				

KM# 77 1/5 CROWN

6.2200 g., 0.9999 Gold .2000 oz. AGW, 22 mm. **Ruler:** Elizabeth II **Series:** World Cup Soccer **Obv:** Crowned bust right **Rev:** Map of Italy

Date	Mintage	F	VF	XF	Unc	BU
1990 Proof	Est. 5,000	Value: 215				

KM# 77a 1/5 CROWN

6.2200 g., 0.9950 Platinum .2000 oz. APW, 22 mm. **Ruler:** Elizabeth II **Series:** World Cup Soccer **Obv:** Crowned bust right **Rev:** Map of Italy

Date	Mintage	F	VF	XF	Unc	BU
1990 Proof	Est. 1,000	Value: 325				

KM# 78 1/5 CROWN

6.2200 g., 0.9999 Gold .2000 oz. AGW, 22 mm. **Ruler:** Elizabeth II **Series:** World Cup Soccer **Obv:** Crowned bust right **Rev:** Goalie catching ball

Date	Mintage	F	VF	XF	Unc	BU
1990 Proof	Est. 5,000	Value: 215				

KM# 78a 1/5 CROWN

6.2200 g., 0.9950 Platinum .2000 oz. APW **Ruler:** Elizabeth II **Series:** World Cup Soccer **Obv:** Crowned bust right **Rev:** Goalie catching ball

Date	Mintage	F	VF	XF	Unc	BU
1990 Proof	Est. 1,000	Value: 325				

KM# 79 1/5 CROWN

6.2200 g., 0.9999 Gold .2000 oz. AGW, 22 mm. **Ruler:** Elizabeth II **Series:** World Cup Soccer **Obv:** Crowned bust right **Rev:** One player

Date	Mintage	F	VF	XF	Unc	BU
1990 Proof	Est. 5,000	Value: 215				

KM# 79a 1/5 CROWN

6.2200 g., 0.9950 Platinum .2000 oz. APW **Ruler:** Elizabeth II **Series:** World Cup Soccer **Obv:** Crowned bust right **Rev:** One player

Date	Mintage	F	VF	XF	Unc	BU
1990 Proof	Est. 1,000	Value: 325				

KM# 80 1/5 CROWN

6.2200 g., 0.9999 Gold .2000 oz. AGW, 22 mm. **Ruler:** Elizabeth II **Series:** World Cup Soccer **Obv:** Crowned bust right **Rev:** Two players

Date	Mintage	F	VF	XF	Unc	BU
1990 Proof	Est. 5,000	Value: 215				

KM# 80a 1/5 CROWN

6.2200 g., 0.9950 Platinum .2000 oz. APW **Ruler:** Elizabeth II **Series:** World Cup Soccer **Obv:** Crowned bust right **Rev:** Two players

Date	Mintage	F	VF	XF	Unc	BU
1990 Proof	Est. 1,000	Value: 325				

KM# 81 1/5 CROWN

6.2200 g., 0.9999 Gold .2000 oz. AGW, 22 mm. **Ruler:** Elizabeth II **Series:** World Cup Soccer **Obv:** Crowned bust right **Rev:** Three players

Date	Mintage	F	VF	XF	Unc	BU
1990 Proof	Est. 5,000	Value: 215				

KM# 81a 1/5 CROWN

6.2200 g., 0.9950 Platinum .2000 oz. APW **Ruler:** Elizabeth II **Series:** World Cup Soccer **Obv:** Crowned bust right **Rev:** Three players

Date	Mintage	F	VF	XF	Unc	BU
1990 Proof	Est. 1,000	Value: 325				

KM# 58 1/5 CROWN

6.2200 g., 0.9999 Gold .2000 oz. AGW, 22 mm. **Ruler:** Elizabeth II **Series:** Barcelona Olympics **Obv:** Crowned bust right **Rev:** Discus thrower

Date	Mintage	F	VF	XF	Unc	BU
1991 Proof	Est. 5,000	Value: 165				
1992 Proof	Est. 5,000	Value: 165				

KM# 58a 1/5 CROWN

6.2200 g., 0.9950 Platinum .2000 oz. APW **Ruler:** Elizabeth II **Series:** Barcelona Olympics **Obv:** Crowned bust right **Rev:** Discus thrower

Date	Mintage	F	VF	XF	Unc	BU
1991 Proof	Est. 1,000	Value: 300				

KM# 59 1/5 CROWN

6.2200 g., 0.9999 Gold .2000 oz. AGW, 22 mm. **Ruler:** Elizabeth II **Series:** Barcelona Olympics **Obv:** Crowned bust right **Rev:** Chariot racing

Date	Mintage	F	VF	XF	Unc	BU
1991 Proof	Est. 5,000	Value: 165				
1992 Proof	Est. 5,000	Value: 165				

KM# 59a 1/5 CROWN

6.2200 g., 0.9950 Platinum .2000 oz. APW **Ruler:** Elizabeth II **Series:** Barcelona Olympics **Obv:** Crowned bust right **Rev:** Chariot racing

Date	Mintage	F	VF	XF	Unc	BU
1991 Proof	Est. 1,000	Value: 300				

KM# 60 1/5 CROWN

6.2200 g., 0.9999 Gold .2000 oz. AGW, 22 mm. **Ruler:** Elizabeth II **Series:** Barcelona Olympics **Obv:** Crowned bust right **Rev:** Runners

Date	Mintage	F	VF	XF	Unc	BU
1991 Proof	Est. 5,000	Value: 165				
1992 Proof	Est. 5,000	Value: 165				

KM# 60a 1/5 CROWN

6.2200 g., 0.9950 Platinum .2000 oz. APW **Ruler:** Elizabeth II **Series:** Barcelona Olympics **Obv:** Crowned bust right **Rev:** Runners

Date	Mintage	F	VF	XF	Unc	BU
1991 Proof	Est. 1,000	Value: 300				

KM# 61 1/5 CROWN

6.2200 g., 0.9999 Gold .2000 oz. AGW, 22 mm. **Ruler:** Elizabeth II **Series:** Barcelona Olympics **Obv:** Crowned bust right **Rev:** Javelin thrower

Date	Mintage	F	VF	XF	Unc	BU
1991 Proof	Est. 5,000	Value: 165				
1992 Proof	Est. 5,000	Value: 165				

KM# 61a 1/5 CROWN

6.2200 g., 0.9950 Platinum .2000 oz. APW **Ruler:** Elizabeth II **Series:** Barcelona Olympics **Obv:** Crowned bust right **Rev:** Javelin thrower

Date	Mintage	F	VF	XF	Unc	BU
1991 Proof	Est. 1,000	Value: 300				

KM# 62 1/5 CROWN

6.2200 g., 0.9999 Gold .2000 oz. AGW, 22 mm. **Ruler:** Elizabeth II **Series:** Barcelona Olympics **Obv:** Crowned bust right **Rev:** Wrestlers

Date	Mintage	F	VF	XF	Unc	BU
1991 Proof	Est. 5,000	Value: 165				
1992 Proof	Est. 5,000	Value: 165				

KM# 62a 1/5 CROWN

6.2200 g., 0.9950 Platinum .2000 oz. APW **Ruler:** Elizabeth II **Series:** Barcelona Olympics **Obv:** Crowned bust right **Rev:** Wrestlers

Date	Mintage	F	VF	XF	Unc	BU
1991 Proof	Est. 1,000	Value: 300				

KM# 63 1/5 CROWN

6.2200 g., 0.9999 Gold .2000 oz. AGW, 22 mm. **Ruler:** Elizabeth II **Series:** Barcelona Olympics **Obv:** Crowned bust right **Rev:** Boxers

Date	Mintage	F	VF	XF	Unc	BU
1991 Proof	Est. 5,000	Value: 165				
1992 Proof	Est. 5,000	Value: 165				

KM# 63a 1/5 CROWN

6.2200 g., 0.9950 Platinum .2000 oz. APW **Ruler:** Elizabeth II **Series:** Barcelona Olympics **Obv:** Crowned bust right **Rev:** Boxers

Date	Mintage	F	VF	XF	Unc	BU
1991 Proof	Est. 1,000	Value: 300				

KM# 64 1/5 CROWN

6.2200 g., 0.9999 Gold .2000 oz. AGW, 22 mm. **Ruler:** Elizabeth II **Series:** Barcelona Olympics **Obv:** Crowned bust right **Rev:** Long jumper

Date	Mintage	F	VF	XF	Unc	BU
1991 Proof	Est. 5,000	Value: 165				
1992 Proof	Est. 5,000	Value: 165				

KM# 64a 1/5 CROWN

6.2200 g., 0.9950 Platinum .2000 oz. APW **Ruler:** Elizabeth II **Series:** Barcelona Olympics **Obv:** Crowned bust right **Rev:** Long jumper

Date	Mintage	F	VF	XF	Unc	BU
1991 Proof	Est. 1,000	Value: 300				

KM# 65 1/5 CROWN

6.2200 g., 0.9999 Gold .2000 oz. AGW, 22 mm. **Ruler:** Elizabeth II **Series:** Barcelona Olympics **Obv:** Crowned bust right **Rev:** Olympic victor

Date	Mintage	F	VF	XF	Unc	BU
1991 Proof	Est. 5,000	Value: 165				
1992 Proof	—	Value: 165				

KM# 65a 1/5 CROWN

6.2200 g., 0.9950 Platinum .2000 oz. APW **Ruler:** Elizabeth II **Series:** Barcelona Olympics **Obv:** Crowned bust right **Rev:** Olympic victor

Date	Mintage	F	VF	XF	Unc	BU
1991 Proof	Est. 1,000	Value: 300				

KM# 126 1/5 CROWN

6.2200 g., 0.9999 Gold .2000 oz. AGW, 22 mm. **Ruler:** Elizabeth II **Rev:** Japanese Royal Wedding **Note:** Similar to 1/2 Crown, KM#127.

Date	Mintage	F	VF	XF	Unc	BU
1993 Proof	Est. 10,000	Value: 145				

KM# 150 1/5 CROWN

6.2200 g., 0.9999 Gold .2000 oz. AGW **Ruler:** Elizabeth II **Series:** Preserve Planet Earth **Subject:** Cetiosaurus **Obv:** Crowned bust right **Rev:** Long-necked dinosaur

Date	Mintage	F	VF	XF	Unc	BU
1993 Proof	Est. 5,000	Value: 145				

KM# 152 1/5 CROWN

6.2200 g., 0.9999 Gold .2000 oz. AGW, 22 mm. **Ruler:** Elizabeth II **Series:** Preserve Planet Earth **Subject:** Stegosaurus **Obv:** Crowned bust right **Rev:** Dinosaur with pointed plates along spine

Date	Mintage	F	VF	XF	Unc	BU
1993 Proof	Est. 5,000	Value: 145				

KM# 153 1/5 CROWN

6.2200 g., 0.9999 Gold .2000 oz. AGW, 22 mm. **Ruler:** Elizabeth II **Series:** WWII Warships **Obv:** Crowned bust right **Rev:** USS Philadelphia

Date	Mintage	F	VF	XF	Unc	BU
1993 Proof	Est. 5,000	Value: 165				

KM# 154 1/5 CROWN

6.2200 g., 0.9999 Gold .2000 oz. AGW, 22 mm. **Ruler:** Elizabeth II **Series:** WWII Warships **Obv:** Crowned bust right **Rev:** USS McLanahan

Date	Mintage	F	VF	XF	Unc	BU
1993 Proof	Est. 5,000	Value: 165				

KM# 155 1/5 CROWN

6.2200 g., 0.9999 Gold .2000 oz. AGW, 22 mm. **Ruler:** Elizabeth II **Series:** WWII Warships **Obv:** Crowned bust right **Rev:** HNLMS Isaac Sweers

Date	Mintage	F	VF	XF	Unc	BU
1993 Proof	Est. 5,000	Value: 165				

KM# 156 1/5 CROWN

6.2200 g., 0.9999 Gold .2000 oz. AGW, 22 mm. **Ruler:** Elizabeth II **Series:** WWII Warships **Obv:** Crowned bust right **Rev:** USS Weehawken

Date	Mintage	F	VF	XF	Unc	BU
1993 Proof	Est. 5,000	Value: 165				

KM# 157 1/5 CROWN

6.2200 g., 0.9999 Gold .2000 oz. AGW, 22 mm. **Ruler:** Elizabeth II **Series:** WWII Warships **Obv:** Crowned bust right **Rev:** HMS Warspite

Date	Mintage	F	VF	XF	Unc	BU
1993 Proof	Est. 5,000	Value: 165				

KM# 158 1/5 CROWN

6.2200 g., 0.9999 Gold .2000 oz. AGW, 22 mm. **Ruler:** Elizabeth II **Series:** WWII Warships **Obv:** Crowned bust right **Rev:** HMS Hood

Date	Mintage	F	VF	XF	Unc	BU
1993 Proof	Est. 5,000	Value: 165				

KM# 159 1/5 CROWN

6.2200 g., 0.9999 Gold .2000 oz. AGW, 22 mm. **Ruler:** Elizabeth II **Series:** WWII Warships **Obv:** Crowned bust right **Rev:** HMS Penelope

Date	Mintage	F	VF	XF	Unc	BU
1993 Proof	Est. 5,000	Value: 165				

KM# 160 1/5 CROWN
6.2200 g., 0.9999 Gold .2000 oz. AGW, 22 mm. **Ruler:** Elizabeth II **Series:** WWII Warships **Obv:** Crowned bust right **Rev:** HMCS Prescott

Date	Mintage	F	VF	XF	Unc	BU
1993 Proof	Est. 5,000	Value: 165				

KM# 161 1/5 CROWN
6.2200 g., 0.9999 Gold .2000 oz. AGW, 22 mm. **Ruler:** Elizabeth II **Series:** WWII Warships **Obv:** Crowned bust right **Rev:** HMS Ark Royal

Date	Mintage	F	VF	XF	Unc	BU
1993 Proof	Est. 5,000	Value: 165				

KM# 162 1/5 CROWN
6.2200 g., 0.9999 Gold .2000 oz. AGW, 22 mm. **Ruler:** Elizabeth II **Series:** WWII Warships **Obv:** Crowned bust right **Rev:** USS Gleaves

Date	Mintage	F	VF	XF	Unc	BU
1993 Proof	Est. 5,000	Value: 165				

KM# 163 1/5 CROWN
6.2200 g., 0.9999 Gold .2000 oz. AGW, 22 mm. **Ruler:** Elizabeth II **Series:** WWII Warships **Obv:** Crowned bust right **Rev:** HMAS Waterhen

Date	Mintage	F	VF	XF	Unc	BU
1993 Proof	Est. 5,000	Value: 165				

KM# 164 1/5 CROWN
6.2200 g., 0.9999 Gold .2000 oz. AGW, 22 mm. **Ruler:** Elizabeth II **Series:** WWII Warships **Obv:** Crowned bust right **Rev:** FSS Savorgnan de Brazza

Date	Mintage	F	VF	XF	Unc	BU
1993 Proof	Est. 5,000	Value: 165				

KM# 165 1/5 CROWN
6.2200 g., 0.9999 Gold .2000 oz. AGW, 22 mm. **Ruler:** Elizabeth II **Series:** House of - Stuart **Subject:** Queen Anne, 1702-1714 **Obv:** Young bust right **Rev:** Bust left

Date	Mintage	F	VF	XF	Unc	BU
1993 Proof	Est. 5,000	Value: 160				

KM# 166 1/5 CROWN
6.2200 g., 0.9999 Gold .2000 oz. AGW, 22 mm. **Ruler:** Elizabeth II **Series:** House of - Hanover **Subject:** King George I, 1714-1727 **Obv:** Young bust right **Rev:** Laureate bust right

Date	Mintage	F	VF	XF	Unc	BU
1993 Proof	Est. 5,000	Value: 160				

KM# 167 1/5 CROWN
6.2200 g., 0.9999 Gold .2000 oz. AGW, 22 mm. **Ruler:** Elizabeth II **Series:** House of - Hanover **Subject:** King George II, 1727-1760 **Obv:** Young bust right **Rev:** Bust left

Date	Mintage	F	VF	XF	Unc	BU
1993 Proof	Est. 5,000	Value: 160				

KM# 168 1/5 CROWN
6.2200 g., 0.9999 Gold .2000 oz. AGW, 22 mm. **Ruler:** Elizabeth II **Series:** House of - Hanover **Subject:** King George III, 1760-1820 **Obv:** Young bust right **Rev:** Bust right

Date	Mintage	F	VF	XF	Unc	BU
1993 Proof	Est. 5,000	Value: 160				

KM# 169 1/5 CROWN
6.2200 g., 0.9999 Gold .2000 oz. AGW, 22 mm. **Ruler:** Elizabeth II **Series:** House of - Hanover **Subject:** King George IV, 1820-1830 **Obv:** Young bust right **Rev:** Bust left

Date	Mintage	F	VF	XF	Unc	BU
1993 Proof	Est. 5,000	Value: 160				

KM# 170 1/5 CROWN
6.2200 g., 0.9999 Gold .2000 oz. AGW, 22 mm. **Ruler:** Elizabeth II **Series:** House of - Hanover **Subject:** King William IV, 1830-1837 **Obv:** Young bust right **Rev:** Bust right

Date	Mintage	F	VF	XF	Unc	BU
1993 Proof	Est. 5,000	Value: 160				

KM# 171 1/5 CROWN
6.2200 g., 0.9999 Gold .2000 oz. AGW, 22 mm. **Ruler:** Elizabeth II **Series:** House of - Hanover **Subject:** Queen Victoria, 1837-1901 **Obv:** Young bust right **Rev:** Bust left

Date	Mintage	F	VF	XF	Unc	BU
1993 Proof	Est. 5,000	Value: 160				

KM# 172 1/5 CROWN
6.2200 g., 0.9999 Gold .2000 oz. AGW, 22 mm. **Ruler:** Elizabeth II **Series:** House of - Saxe-Coburg **Subject:** King Edward VII, 1901-1910 **Obv:** Young bust right **Rev:** Uniformed bust right

Date	Mintage	F	VF	XF	Unc	BU
1993 Proof	Est. 5,000	Value: 160				

KM# 173 1/5 CROWN
6.2200 g., 0.9999 Gold .2000 oz. AGW, 22 mm. **Ruler:** Elizabeth II **Series:** House of - Windsor **Subject:** King George V, 1910-1936 **Obv:** Young bust right **Rev:** Uniformed bust left

Date	Mintage	F	VF	XF	Unc	BU
1993 Proof	Est. 5,000	Value: 160				

KM# 174 1/5 CROWN
6.2200 g., 0.9999 Gold .2000 oz. AGW, 22 mm. **Ruler:** Elizabeth II **Series:** House of - Windsor **Subject:** King Edward VIII, 1936 **Obv:** Young bust right **Rev:** Bust left

Date	Mintage	F	VF	XF	Unc	BU
1993 Proof	Est. 5,000	Value: 160				

KM# 175 1/5 CROWN
6.2200 g., 0.9999 Gold .2000 oz. AGW, 22 mm. **Ruler:** Elizabeth II **Series:** House of - Windsor **Subject:** King George VI, 1936-1952 **Obv:** Young bust right **Rev:** Bust left

Date	Mintage	F	VF	XF	Unc	BU
1993 Proof	Est. 5,000	Value: 160				

KM# 176 1/5 CROWN
6.2200 g., 0.9999 Gold .2000 oz. AGW, 22 mm. **Ruler:** Elizabeth II **Obv:** Crowned bust right **Rev:** Queen Elizabeth II bust left

Date	Mintage	F	VF	XF	Unc	BU
1993 Proof	Est. 5,000	Value: 160				

KM# 181 1/5 CROWN
6.2200 g., 0.9999 Gold .2000 oz. AGW, 22 mm. **Ruler:** Elizabeth II **Series:** International Friendship **Obv:** Crowned bust right **Rev:** Stylized panda

Date	Mintage	F	VF	XF	Unc	BU
1993 Proof	Est. 5,000	Value: 165				

KM# 185 1/5 CROWN
6.2200 g., 0.9999 Gold .2000 oz. AGW, 22 mm. **Ruler:** Elizabeth II **Series:** International Friendship **Obv:** Crowned bust right **Rev:** Natural panda

Date	Mintage	F	VF	XF	Unc	BU
1993 Proof	Est. 5,000	Value: 165				

KM# 189 1/5 CROWN
6.2200 g., 0.9999 Gold .2000 oz. AGW **Ruler:** Elizabeth II **Series:** International Friendship **Obv:** Crowned bust right **Rev:** General Sikarski portrait above B-24 bomber with Rock of Gibraltar in background

Date	Mintage	F	VF	XF	Unc	BU
1993 Proof	Est. 5,000	Value: 165				

KM# 199 1/5 CROWN
6.2143 g., 0.9999 Gold .1998 oz. AGW **Ruler:** Elizabeth II **Subject:** Dependent Territories Conference **Obv:** Crowned bust right **Rev:** 7 shields, 2 in center, 5 around with rope loops

Date	Mintage	F	VF	XF	Unc	BU
1993 Proof	Est. 5,000	Value: 160				

KM# 204 1/5 CROWN
6.2200 g., 0.9999 Gold .2000 oz. AGW, 22 mm. **Ruler:** Elizabeth II **Series:** Peter Rabbit Centennial **Subject:** The Tale of Peter Rabbit **Obv:** Crowned bust right **Rev:** Rabbit eating carrots, sparrow on handle

Date	Mintage	F	VF	XF	Unc	BU
1993 Proof	Est. 5,000	Value: 160				

KM# 204a 1/5 CROWN
6.2200 g., 0.9950 Platinum .2000 oz. APW **Ruler:** Elizabeth II **Series:** Peter Rabbit Centennial **Subject:** The Tale of Peter Rabbit **Obv:** Crowned bust right **Rev:** Rabbit eating carrots, sparrow on handle

Date	Mintage	F	VF	XF	Unc	BU
1993 Proof	Est. 5,000	Value: 300				

KM# 208 1/5 CROWN
6.2200 g., 0.9999 Gold .2000 oz. AGW, 22 mm. **Ruler:** Elizabeth II **Series:** Peter Rabbit Centennial **Subject:** The Tale of Peter Rabbit **Obv:** Crowned bust right **Rev:** Mrs. Tiggy-Winkel ironing

Date	Mintage	F	VF	XF	Unc	BU
1993 Proof	Est. 5,000	Value: 160				

KM# 212 1/5 CROWN
6.2200 g., 0.9999 Gold .2000 oz. AGW, 22 mm. **Ruler:** Elizabeth II **Series:** Peter Rabbit Centennial **Subject:** The Tale of Peter Rabbit **Obv:** Crowned bust right **Rev:** Jeremy Fisher fishing

Date	Mintage	F	VF	XF	Unc	BU
1993 Proof	Est. 5,000	Value: 160				

KM# 216 1/5 CROWN
6.2200 g., 0.9999 Gold .2000 oz. AGW, 22 mm. **Ruler:** Elizabeth II **Series:** Peter Rabbit Centennial **Subject:** The Tale of Peter Rabbit **Obv:** Crowned bust right **Rev:** Tom Kitten with mother cat

Date	Mintage	F	VF	XF	Unc	BU
1993 Proof	Est. 5,000	Value: 160				

KM# 220 1/5 CROWN
6.2200 g., 0.9999 Gold .2000 oz. AGW, 22 mm. **Ruler:** Elizabeth II **Series:** Peter Rabbit Centennial **Subject:** The Tale of Peter Rabbit **Obv:** Crowned bust right **Rev:** Benjamin Bunny wearing hat and holding coat

Date	Mintage	F	VF	XF	Unc	BU
1993 Proof	Est. 5,000	Value: 160				

KM# 224 1/5 CROWN
6.2200 g., 0.9999 Gold .2000 oz. AGW, 22 mm. **Ruler:** Elizabeth II **Series:** Peter Rabbit Centennial **Subject:** The Tale of Peter Rabbit **Obv:** Crowned bust right **Rev:** Jemima Puddle-Duck talking with fox

Date	Mintage	F	VF	XF	Unc	BU
1993 Proof	Est. 5,000	Value: 160				

KM# 643 1/5 CROWN
6.2200 g., 0.9999 Gold .2000 oz. AGW, 22 mm. **Series:** XVII Winter Olympics **Obv:** Crowned bust right **Rev:** Figure skaters

Date	Mintage	F	VF	XF	Unc	BU
1993 Proof	Est. 5,000	Value: 185				

KM# 644 1/5 CROWN
6.2200 g., 0.9999 Gold .2000 oz. AGW, 22 mm. **Ruler:** Elizabeth II **Series:** XVII Winter Olympics **Obv:** Crowned bust right **Rev:** Ice hockey

Date	Mintage	F	VF	XF	Unc	BU
1993 Proof	Est. 5,000	Value: 185				

KM# 645 1/5 CROWN
6.2200 g., 0.9999 Gold .2000 oz. AGW, 22 mm. **Ruler:** Elizabeth II **Series:** XVII Winter Olympics **Obv:** Crowned bust right **Rev:** Bobsledding

Date	Mintage	F	VF	XF	Unc	BU
1993 Proof	Est. 5,000	Value: 185				

KM# 646 1/5 CROWN
6.2200 g., 0.9999 Gold .2000 oz. AGW, 22 mm. **Ruler:** Elizabeth II **Series:** XVII Winter Olympics **Obv:** Crowned bust right **Rev:** Skiers

Date	Mintage	F	VF	XF	Unc	BU
1993 Proof	Est. 5,000	Value: 185				

KM# 226 1/5 CROWN
6.2200 g., 0.9999 Gold .2000 oz. AGW, 22 mm. **Ruler:** Elizabeth II **Series:** World Cup Soccer **Obv:** Crowned bust right **Rev:** 3 players kicking ball up field

Date	Mintage	F	VF	XF	Unc	BU
1994 Proof	Est. 5,000	Value: 160				

KM# 228 1/5 CROWN
6.2200 g., 0.9999 Gold .2000 oz. AGW, 22 mm. **Ruler:** Elizabeth II **Series:** World Cup Soccer **Obv:** Crowned bust right **Rev:** 2 players facing; 1 kicking and 1 defending

Date	Mintage	F	VF	XF	Unc	BU
1994 Proof	Est. 5,000	Value: 160				

KM# 230 1/5 CROWN
6.2200 g., 0.9999 Gold .2000 oz. AGW, 22 mm. **Ruler:** Elizabeth II **Series:** World Cup Soccer **Obv:** Crowned bust right **Rev:** 2 players; 1 goalie and 1 player trying to score

Date	Mintage	F	VF	XF	Unc	BU
1994 Proof	Est. 5,000	Value: 160				

KM# 232 1/5 CROWN
6.2200 g., 0.9999 Gold .2000 oz. AGW, 22 mm. **Ruler:** Elizabeth II **Series:** World Cup Soccer **Obv:** Crowned bust right **Rev:** 1 player looking up

Date	Mintage	F	VF	XF	Unc	BU
1994 Proof	Est. 5,000	Value: 160				

KM# 234 1/5 CROWN
6.2200 g., 0.9999 Gold .2000 oz. AGW, 22 mm. **Ruler:** Elizabeth II **Series:** World Cup Soccer **Obv:** Crowned bust right **Rev:** 1 player kicking, 1 player running forward

Date	Mintage	F	VF	XF	Unc	BU
1994 Proof	Est. 5,000	Value: 160				

KM# 236 1/5 CROWN
6.2200 g., 0.9999 Gold .2000 oz. AGW, 22 mm. **Ruler:** Elizabeth II **Series:** World Cup Soccer **Obv:** Crowned bust right **Rev:** Player in foreground heading ball to player

Date	Mintage	F	VF	XF	Unc	BU
1994 Proof	Est. 5,000	Value: 160				

KM# 238 1/5 CROWN
6.2200 g., 0.9999 Gold .2000 oz. AGW, 22 mm. **Ruler:** Elizabeth II **Series:** Preserve Planet Earth **Obv:** Crowned bust right **Rev:** Sabre Tooth Tiger

Date	Mintage	F	VF	XF	Unc	BU
1994 Proof	Est. 5,000	Value: 165				

KM# 240 1/5 CROWN
6.2200 g., 0.9999 Gold .2000 oz. AGW, 22 mm. **Ruler:** Elizabeth II **Series:** Preserve Planet Earth **Obv:** Crowned bust right **Rev:** Spanish Eagle flying above island

Date	Mintage	F	VF	XF	Unc	BU
1994 Proof	Est. 5,000	Value: 165				

KM# 242 1/5 CROWN
6.2200 g., 0.9999 Gold .2000 oz. AGW, 22 mm. **Ruler:** Elizabeth II **Series:** Preserve Planet Earth **Obv:** Crowned bust right **Rev:** Three Striped Dolphins

Date	Mintage	F	VF	XF	Unc	BU
1994 Proof	Est. 5,000	Value: 165				

KM# 244 1/5 CROWN
6.2200 g., 0.9999 Gold .2000 oz. AGW, 22 mm. **Ruler:** Elizabeth II **Series:** Preserve Planet Earth **Obv:** Crowned bust right **Rev:** Mother and baby elephants

Date	Mintage	F	VF	XF	Unc	BU
1994 Proof	Est. 5,000	Value: 165				

KM# 253 1/5 CROWN
6.2200 g., 0.9999 Gold .2000 oz. AGW, 22 mm. **Ruler:** Elizabeth II **Series:** World War II **Obv:** Crowned bust right **Rev:** Maltese convoy of ships

Date	Mintage	F	VF	XF	Unc	BU
1994 Proof	Est. 5,000	Value: 165				

KM# 254 1/5 CROWN
6.2200 g., 0.9999 Gold .2000 oz. AGW, 22 mm. **Ruler:** Elizabeth II **Series:** World War II **Obv:** Crowned bust right **Rev:** Squadron 202 flying, Rock of Gibraltar in background

Date	Mintage	F	VF	XF	Unc	BU
1994 Proof	Est. 5,000	Value: 165				

KM# 255 1/5 CROWN
6.2200 g., 0.9999 Gold .2000 oz. AGW, 22 mm. **Ruler:** Elizabeth II **Series:** World War II **Obv:** Crowned bust right **Rev:** Admiral Somerville, ship in background

Date	Mintage	F	VF	XF	Unc	BU
1994 Proof	Est. 5,000	Value: 165				

KM# 256 1/5 CROWN
6.2200 g., 0.9999 Gold .2000 oz. AGW, 22 mm. **Ruler:** Elizabeth II **Series:** World War II **Obv:** Crowned bust right **Rev:** Glen Miller and band

Date	Mintage	F	VF	XF	Unc	BU
1994 Proof	Est. 5,000	Value: 165				

KM# 257 1/5 CROWN
6.2200 g., 0.9999 Gold .2000 oz. AGW, 22 mm. **Ruler:** Elizabeth II **Series:** World War II **Obv:** Crowned bust right **Rev:** King George VI congratulating pilots

Date	Mintage	F	VF	XF	Unc	BU
1994 Proof	Est. 5,000	Value: 165				

KM# 258 1/5 CROWN
6.2200 g., 0.9999 Gold .2000 oz. AGW, 22 mm. **Ruler:** Elizabeth II **Series:** World War II **Obv:** Crowned bust right **Rev:** General Eisenhower, planes and ships in background

Date	Mintage	F	VF	XF	Unc	BU
1994 Proof	Est. 5,000	Value: 165				

KM# 265 1/5 CROWN
6.2200 g., 0.9999 Gold .2000 oz. AGW, 22 mm. **Ruler:** Elizabeth II **Series:** First Man on Moon **Obv:** Crowned bust right **Rev:** Dr. Wernher von Braun with replica of rocket

Date	Mintage	F	VF	XF	Unc	BU
1994 Proof	Est. 5,000	Value: 165				

KM# 266 1/5 CROWN
6.2200 g., 0.9999 Gold .2000 oz. AGW, 22 mm. **Ruler:** Elizabeth II **Series:** First Man on Moon **Obv:** Crowned bust right **Rev:** Rocket on pad before lift-off

Date	Mintage	F	VF	XF	Unc	BU
1994 Proof	Est. 5,000	Value: 165				

KM# 267 1/5 CROWN
6.2200 g., 0.9999 Gold .2000 oz. AGW, 22 mm. **Ruler:** Elizabeth II **Series:** First Man on Moon **Obv:** Crowned bust right **Rev:** Recovering space capsule after splashdown

Date	Mintage	F	VF	XF	Unc	BU
1994 Proof	Est. 5,000	Value: 165				

KM# 268 1/5 CROWN
6.2200 g., 0.9999 Gold .2000 oz. AGW, 22 mm. **Ruler:** Elizabeth II **Series:** First Man on Moon **Obv:** Crowned bust right **Rev:** Lunar Module landing on the moon

Date	Mintage	F	VF	XF	Unc	BU
1994 Proof	Est. 5,000	Value: 165				

KM# 269 1/5 CROWN
6.2200 g., 0.9999 Gold .2000 oz. AGW, 22 mm. **Ruler:** Elizabeth II **Series:** First Man on Moon **Obv:** Crowned bust right **Rev:** Astronaut stepping on the moon

Date	Mintage	F	VF	XF	Unc	BU
1994 Proof	Est. 5,000	Value: 165				

KM# 270 1/5 CROWN
6.2200 g., 0.9999 Gold .2000 oz. AGW, 22 mm. **Ruler:** Elizabeth II **Series:** First Man on Moon **Obv:** Crowned bust right **Rev:** Astronaut setting up flag on the moon

Date	Mintage	F	VF	XF	Unc	BU
1994 Proof	Est. 5,000	Value: 165				

KM# 277 1/5 CROWN
6.2200 g., 0.9999 Gold .2000 oz. AGW, 22 mm. **Ruler:** Elizabeth II **Series:** Sherlock Holmes **Obv:** Crowned bust right **Rev:** Holmes sitting with pipe in hand

Date	Mintage	F	VF	XF	Unc	BU
1994 Proof	Est. 5,000	Value: 165				

KM# 278 1/5 CROWN
6.2200 g., 0.9999 Gold .2000 oz. AGW, 22 mm. **Ruler:** Elizabeth II **Series:** Sherlock Holmes **Obv:** Crowned bust right **Rev:** Holmes playing violin, Dr. Watson watching

Date	Mintage	F	VF	XF	Unc	BU
1994 Proof	Est. 5,000	Value: 165				

KM# 279 1/5 CROWN
6.2200 g., 0.9999 Gold .2000 oz. AGW, 22 mm. **Ruler:** Elizabeth II **Series:** Sherlock Holmes **Obv:** Crowned bust right **Rev:** People talking before 221 B Baker St.

Date	Mintage	F	VF	XF	Unc	BU
1994 Proof	Est. 5,000	Value: 165				

KM# 280 1/5 CROWN
6.2200 g., 0.9999 Gold .2000 oz. AGW, 22 mm. **Ruler:** Elizabeth II **Series:** Sherlock Holmes **Obv:** Crowned bust right **Rev:** Scene from book "The Empty House"

Date	Mintage	F	VF	XF	Unc	BU
1994 Proof	Est. 5,000	Value: 165				

KM# 281 1/5 CROWN
6.2200 g., 0.9999 Gold .2000 oz. AGW, 22 mm. **Ruler:** Elizabeth II **Series:** Sherlock Holmes **Obv:** Crowned bust right **Rev:** Sailing ship "Mary Celeste"

Date	Mintage	F	VF	XF	Unc	BU
1994 Proof	Est. 5,000	Value: 175				

KM# 282 1/5 CROWN
6.2200 g., 0.9999 Gold .2000 oz. AGW, 22 mm. **Ruler:** Elizabeth II **Series:** Sherlock Holmes **Obv:** Crowned bust right **Rev:** Scene from the "Hound of the Baskervilles"

Date	Mintage	F	VF	XF	Unc	BU
1994 Proof	Est. 5,000	Value: 170				

KM# 283 1/5 CROWN
6.2200 g., 0.9999 Gold .2000 oz. AGW, 22 mm. **Ruler:** Elizabeth II **Series:** Sherlock Holmes **Obv:** Crowned bust right **Rev:** Scene from the "Three Garriders"

Date	Mintage	F	VF	XF	Unc	BU
1994 Proof	Est. 5,000	Value: 165				

KM# 284 1/5 CROWN
6.2200 g., 0.9999 Gold .2000 oz. AGW, 22 mm. **Ruler:** Elizabeth II **Series:** Sherlock Holmes **Obv:** Crowned bust right **Rev:** Scene from the "Final Problem"

Date	Mintage	F	VF	XF	Unc	BU
1994 Proof	Est. 5,000	Value: 165				

KM# 441 1/5 CROWN
6.2200 g., 0.9999 Gold .2000 oz. AGW, 22 mm. **Ruler:** Elizabeth II **Subject:** The Tale of Peter Rabbit **Obv:** Crowned bust right **Rev:** Peter rabbit with four little bunnies

Date	Mintage	F	VF	XF	Unc	BU
1994 Proof	Est. 10,000	Value: 185				

KM# 442 1/5 CROWN
6.2200 g., 0.9950 Platinum .2000 oz. APW, 22 mm. **Ruler:** Elizabeth II

Date	Mintage	F	VF	XF	Unc	BU
1994 Proof	Est. 2,500	Value: 295				

KM# 295 1/5 CROWN
6.2200 g., 0.9999 Gold .2000 oz. AGW, 22 mm. **Ruler:** Elizabeth II **Series:** Atlanta Olympics **Obv:** Crowned bust right **Rev:** Long jumpers

Date	Mintage	F	VF	XF	Unc	BU
1995 Proof	Est. 5,000	Value: 160				

KM# 296 1/5 CROWN
6.2200 g., 0.9999 Gold .2000 oz. AGW, 22 mm. **Ruler:** Elizabeth II **Series:** Atlanta Olympics **Obv:** Crowned bust right **Rev:** Discus throwers

Date	Mintage	F	VF	XF	Unc	BU
1995 Proof	Est. 5,000	Value: 160				

KM# 297 1/5 CROWN
6.2200 g., 0.9999 Gold .2000 oz. AGW, 22 mm. **Ruler:** Elizabeth II **Series:** Atlanta Olympics **Obv:** Crowned bust right **Rev:** Relay racers

Date	Mintage	F	VF	XF	Unc	BU
1995 Proof	Est. 5,000	Value: 160				

KM# 298 1/5 CROWN
6.2200 g., 0.9999 Gold .2000 oz. AGW, 22 mm. **Ruler:** Elizabeth II **Series:** Atlanta Olympics **Obv:** Crowned bust right **Rev:** Javelin throwers

Date	Mintage	F	VF	XF	Unc	BU
1995 Proof	Est. 5,000	Value: 160				

KM# 303 1/5 CROWN
6.2200 g., 0.9999 Gold .2000 oz. AGW, 22 mm. **Ruler:** Elizabeth II **Obv:** Crowned bust right **Rev:** Rock of Gibraltar and rising sun

Date	Mintage	F	VF	XF	Unc	BU
1995 Proof	Est. 5,000	Value: 165				

KM# 326 1/5 CROWN
6.2200 g., 0.9999 Gold .2000 oz. AGW, 22 mm. **Ruler:** Elizabeth II **Subject:** The Tale of Peter Rabbit **Obv:** Crowned bust right **Rev:** Peter Rabbit running right

Date	Mintage	F	VF	XF	Unc	BU
1995 Proof	Est. 5,000	Value: 165				

KM# 326a 1/5 CROWN
6.2200 g., 0.9950 Platinum .2000 oz. APW **Ruler:** Elizabeth II **Subject:** The Tale of Peter Rabbit **Obv:** Crowned bust right **Rev:** Peter rabbit running right

Date	Mintage	F	VF	XF	Unc	BU
1995 Proof	Est. 2,500	Value: 295				

KM# 328 1/5 CROWN
6.2200 g., 0.9999 Gold .2000 oz. AGW, 22 mm. **Ruler:** Elizabeth II **Series:** Island Games **Obv:** Crowned bust right **Rev:** Circle of athletes with shield at center

Date	Mintage	F	VF	XF	Unc	BU
1995 Proof	Est. 5,000	Value: 160				

KM# 330 1/5 CROWN
6.2200 g., 0.9999 Gold .2000 oz. AGW, 22 mm. **Ruler:** Elizabeth II **Series:** Island Games **Obv:** Crowned bust right **Rev:** Circle of athletes with shield at center

Date	Mintage	F	VF	XF	Unc	BU
1995 Proof	Est. 5,000	Value: 160				

KM# 342 1/5 CROWN
6.2200 g., 0.9999 Gold .2000 oz. AGW, 22 mm. **Ruler:** Elizabeth II **Series:** Olympics **Obv:** Crowned bust right **Rev:** Tennis player

Date	Mintage	F	VF	XF	Unc	BU
1996 Proof	Est. 5,000	Value: 165				

KM# 343 1/5 CROWN
6.2200 g., 0.9999 Gold .2000 oz. AGW, 22 mm. **Ruler:** Elizabeth II **Series:** Olympics **Obv:** Crowned bust right **Rev:** Wrestlers

Date	Mintage	F	VF	XF	Unc	BU
1996 Proof	Est. 5,000	Value: 165				

KM# 344 1/5 CROWN
6.2200 g., 0.9999 Gold .2000 oz. AGW, 22 mm. **Ruler:** Elizabeth II **Series:** Olympics **Obv:** Crowned bust right **Rev:** Baseball players

Date	Mintage	F	VF	XF	Unc	BU
1996 Proof	Est. 5,000	Value: 165				

KM# 345 1/5 CROWN
6.2200 g., 0.9999 Gold .2000 oz. AGW, 22 mm. **Ruler:** Elizabeth II **Series:** Olympics **Obv:** Crowned bust right **Rev:** Flame

Date	Mintage	F	VF	XF	Unc	BU
1996 Proof	Est. 5,000	Value: 165				

KM# 346 1/5 CROWN
6.2200 g., 0.9999 Gold .2000 oz. AGW, 22 mm. **Ruler:** Elizabeth II **Series:** Olympics **Obv:** Crowned bust right **Rev:** Volleyball game

Date	Mintage	F	VF	XF	Unc	BU
1996 Proof	Est. 5,000	Value: 165				

KM# 347 1/5 CROWN
6.2200 g., 0.9999 Gold .2000 oz. AGW, 22 mm. **Ruler:** Elizabeth II **Series:** Olympics **Obv:** Crowned bust right **Rev:** Basketball game

Date	Mintage	F	VF	XF	Unc	BU
1996 Proof	Est. 5,000	Value: 165				

KM# 357 1/5 CROWN
6.2200 g., 0.9999 Gold .2000 oz. AGW, 22 mm. **Ruler:** Elizabeth II **Subject:** Nefusat Yehuda Synagogue Renovation **Obv:** Crowned bust right **Rev:** Hebrew symbol, rock, arms and building

Date	Mintage	F	VF	XF	Unc	BU
1996 Proof	Est. 5,000	Value: 165				

KM# 360 1/5 CROWN
6.2200 g., 0.9999 Gold .2000 oz. AGW, 22 mm. **Ruler:** Elizabeth II **Series:** Euro 96 **Rev:** England

Date	Mintage	F	VF	XF	Unc	BU
1996 Proof	Est. 5,000	Value: 175				

KM# 370 1/5 CROWN
6.2200 g., 0.9999 Gold .2000 oz. AGW, 22 mm. **Ruler:** Elizabeth II **Obv:** Crowned bust right **Rev:** Roses

Date	Mintage	F	VF	XF	Unc	BU
1996 Proof	Est. 5,000	Value: 165				

KM# 370a 1/5 CROWN
6.2518 g., 0.9950 Platinum .2000 oz. APW **Ruler:** Elizabeth II **Obv:** Crowned bust right **Rev:** Roses

Date	Mintage	F	VF	XF	Unc	BU
1996 Proof	Est. 1,000	Value: 300				

KM# 379 1/5 CROWN
6.2207 g., 0.9999 Gold .2000 oz. AGW, 22 mm. **Ruler:** Elizabeth II **Series:** Peter Rabbit Centennial **Subject:** The Tale of Peter Rabbit **Obv:** Crowned bust right **Rev:** Peter Rabbit escaping garden

Date	Mintage	F	VF	XF	Unc	BU
1996 Proof	Est. 7,500	Value: 165				

KM# 379a 1/5 CROWN
6.2200 g., 0.9950 Platinum .2000 oz. APW **Ruler:** Elizabeth II **Series:** Peter Rabbit Centennial **Subject:** The Tale of Peter Rabbit **Obv:** Crowned bust right **Rev:** Peter Rabbit escaping garden

Date	Mintage	F	VF	XF	Unc	BU
1996 Proof	Est. 5,000	Value: 295				

KM# 384 1/5 CROWN
6.2207 g., 0.9999 Gold .2000 oz. AGW, 22 mm. **Ruler:** Elizabeth II **Series:** Preserve Planet Earth **Obv:** Crowned bust right **Rev:** Shag Birds

Date	Mintage	F	VF	XF	Unc	BU
1996 Proof	Est. 5,000	Value: 165				

KM# 385 1/5 CROWN
6.2207 g., 0.9999 Gold .2000 oz. AGW, 22 mm. **Ruler:** Elizabeth II **Series:** Preserve Planet Earth **Obv:** Crowned bust right **Rev:** Puffins

Date	Mintage	F	VF	XF	Unc	BU
1996 Proof	Est. 5,000	Value: 165				

KM# 392 1/5 CROWN
6.2207 g., 0.9999 Gold .2000 oz. AGW, 22 mm. **Ruler:** Elizabeth II **Series:** Cinema Centennial **Subject:** Grace Kelly - actress, 1929-82 **Obv:** Crowned bust right **Rev:** Bust 3/4 facing, dates

Date	Mintage	F	VF	XF	Unc	BU
1996 Proof	Est. 5,000	Value: 165				

KM# 392a 1/5 CROWN
6.2200 g., 0.9950 Platinum .2000 oz. APW **Ruler:** Elizabeth II **Series:** Cinema Centennial **Subject:** Grace Kelly - actress, 1929-82 **Obv:** Crowned bust right **Rev:** Bust 3/4 facing

Date	Mintage	F	VF	XF	Unc	BU
1996 Proof	Est. 1,000	Value: 300				

KM# 397 1/5 CROWN
6.2207 g., 0.9999 Gold .2000 oz. AGW, 22 mm. **Ruler:** Elizabeth II **Series:** Centenary of the Cinema **Subject:** James Dean - actor, 1931-55 **Obv:** Crowned bust right **Rev:** Standing central figure, dates

Date	Mintage	F	VF	XF	Unc	BU
1996 Proof	Est. 5,000	Value: 165				

KM# 397a 1/5 CROWN
6.2200 g., 0.9950 Platinum .2000 oz. APW **Ruler:** Elizabeth II **Series:** Centenary of the Cinema **Subject:** James Dean - actor, 1931-55 **Obv:** Crowned bust right **Rev:** Standing central figure, dates

Date	Mintage	F	VF	XF	Unc	BU
1996 Proof	Est. 1,000	Value: 300				

KM# 402 1/5 CROWN
6.2207 g., 0.9999 Gold .2000 oz. AGW, 22 mm. **Ruler:** Elizabeth II **Series:** Centenary of the Cinema **Subject:** Marilyn Monroe - actress, 1926-62 **Obv:** Crowned bust right **Rev:** Bust looking back over shoulder

Date	Mintage	F	VF	XF	Unc	BU
1996 Proof	Est. 5,000	Value: 165				

KM# 402a 1/5 CROWN
6.2200 g., 0.9950 Platinum .2000 oz. APW **Ruler:** Elizabeth II **Series:** Centenary of the Cinema **Subject:** Marilyn Monroe - actress, 1926-62 **Obv:** Crowned bust right **Rev:** Bust looking back over shoulder

Date	Mintage	F	VF	XF	Unc	BU
1996 Proof	Est. 1,000	Value: 300				

KM# 407 1/5 CROWN
6.2207 g., 0.9999 Gold .2000 oz. AGW, 22 mm. **Ruler:** Elizabeth II **Series:** Centenary of the Cinema **Subject:** Audrey Hepburn - actress, 1929-93 **Obv:** Crowned bust right **Rev:** Bust 3/4 facing, dates

Date	Mintage	F	VF	XF	Unc	BU
1996 Proof	Est. 5,000	Value: 165				

KM# 407a 1/5 CROWN
6.2200 g., 0.9950 Platinum .2000 oz. APW **Ruler:** Elizabeth II **Series:** Centenary of the Cinema **Subject:** Audrey Hepburn - actress, 1929-93 **Obv:** Crowned bust right **Rev:** Bust 3/4 facing, dates

Date	Mintage	F	VF	XF	Unc	BU
1996 Proof	Est. 1,000	Value: 300				

KM# 412 1/5 CROWN
6.2207 g., 0.9999 Gold .2000 oz. AGW, 22 mm. **Ruler:** Elizabeth II **Series:** Centenary of the Cinema **Subject:** Bruce Lee - actor, 1940-73 **Obv:** Crowned bust right **Rev:** Kickboxer and chinese dragon, dates

Date	Mintage	F	VF	XF	Unc	BU
1996 Proof	Est. 5,000	Value: 165				

KM# 417 1/5 CROWN
6.2207 g., 0.9999 Gold .2000 oz. AGW, 22 mm. **Ruler:** Elizabeth II **Series:** Centenary of the Cinema **Subject:** Charlie Chaplan - actor, 1889-1977 **Obv:** Crowned bust right **Rev:** Standing central figure with cane, dates

Date	Mintage	F	VF	XF	Unc	BU
1996 Proof	Est. 5,000	Value: 165				

KM# 422 1/5 CROWN
6.2207 g., 0.9999 Gold .2000 oz. AGW, 22 mm. **Ruler:** Elizabeth II **Series:** Centenary of the Cinema **Subject:** Gone With the Wind **Obv:** Crowned bust right **Rev:** Rhett Butler and Scarlett O'Hara

Date	Mintage	F	VF	XF	Unc	BU
1996 Proof	Est. 5,000	Value: 165				

KM# 427 1/5 CROWN
6.2207 g., 0.9999 Gold .2000 oz. AGW, 22 mm. **Ruler:** Elizabeth II **Series:** Centenary of the Cinema **Obv:** Crowned bust right **Rev:** The Flintstones

Date	Mintage	F	VF	XF	Unc	BU
1996 Proof	Est. 5,000	Value: 165				

KM# 431 1/5 CROWN
6.2207 g., 0.9999 Gold .2000 oz. AGW, 22 mm. **Ruler:** Elizabeth II **Series:** Duke of Edinburgh Awards Scheme **Obv:** Crowned bust right **Rev:** 7 Events surround central crowned arms

Date	Mintage	F	VF	XF	Unc	BU
1996 Proof	Est. 5,000	Value: 165				

KM# 434 1/5 CROWN
6.2207 g., 0.9999 Gold .2000 oz. AGW, 22 mm. **Ruler:** Elizabeth II **Series:** Duke of Edinburgh Awards Scheme **Obv:** Crowned bust right **Rev:** Cameo above team of horses pulling wagon

Date	Mintage	F	VF	XF	Unc	BU
1996 Proof	Est. 5,000	Value: 165				

KM# 447 1/5 CROWN
6.2207 g., 0.9999 Gold .2000 oz. AGW, 22 mm. **Ruler:** Elizabeth II **Subject:** Lord Buddha **Obv:** Crowned bust right **Rev:** Seated facing figure

Date	Mintage	F	VF	XF	Unc	BU
1996 Proof	Est. 8,000	Value: 185				

KM# 456 1/5 CROWN
6.2207 g., 0.9999 Gold .2000 oz. AGW, 22 mm. **Ruler:** Elizabeth II **Series:** Centenary of the Cinema **Subject:** Wizard of Oz **Obv:** Crowned bust right **Rev:** Wizard of Oz characters

Date	Mintage	F	VF	XF	Unc	BU
1996 Proof	Est. 5,000	Value: 165				

KM# 460 1/5 CROWN
6.2207 g., 0.9999 Gold .2000 oz. AGW, 22 mm. **Ruler:** Elizabeth II **Series:** Centenary of the Cinema **Subject:** Marx Brothers **Obv:** Crowned bust right **Rev:** Three busts 3/4 left

Date	Mintage	F	VF	XF	Unc	BU
1996 Proof	Est. 5,000	Value: 165				

KM# 464 1/5 CROWN
6.2207 g., 0.9999 Gold .2000 oz. AGW, 22 mm. **Ruler:** Elizabeth II **Series:** Centenary of the Cinema **Subject:** Elvis Presley - actor/entertainer, 1935-77 **Obv:** Crowned bust right **Rev:** Guitar below and behind bust 3/4 left, dates

Date	Mintage	F	VF	XF	Unc	BU
1996 Proof	Est. 5,000	Value: 165				

KM# 468 1/5 CROWN
6.2207 g., 0.9999 Gold .2000 oz. AGW, 22 mm. **Ruler:** Elizabeth II **Series:** Centenary of the Cinema **Subject:** Casablanca **Obv:** Crowned bust right **Rev:** Bogart and Bergman

Date	Mintage	F	VF	XF	Unc	BU
1996 Proof	Est. 5,000	Value: 165				

KM# 472 1/5 CROWN
6.2207 g., 0.9999 Gold .2000 oz. AGW, 22 mm. **Ruler:** Elizabeth II **Series:** Centenary of the Cinema **Obv:** Crowned bust right **Rev:** E.T.

Date	Mintage	F	VF	XF	Unc	BU
1996 Proof	Est. 5,000	Value: 165				

KM# 476 1/5 CROWN
6.2207 g., 0.9999 Gold .2000 oz. AGW, 22 mm. **Ruler:** Elizabeth II **Series:** Centenary of the Cinema **Subject:** Alfred Hitchcock - Producer/Director, 1899-1980 **Obv:** Crowned bust right **Rev:** Bust facing looking at bird on left shoulder

Date	Mintage	F	VF	XF	Unc	BU
1996 Proof	Est. 5,000	Value: 165				

KM# 513 1/5 CROWN
6.2207 g., 0.9999 Gold .2000 oz. AGW, 22 mm. **Ruler:** Elizabeth II **Obv:** Crowned bust right **Rev:** Peacocks, one with tail spread

Date	Mintage	F	VF	XF	Unc	BU
1997 Proof	Est. 5,000	Value: 185				

KM# 522 1/5 CROWN
6.2207 g., 0.9999 Gold .2000 oz. AGW, 22 mm. **Ruler:** Elizabeth II **Subject:** The Tale of Peter Rabbit **Obv:** Crowned bust right **Rev:** Standing rabbit 3/4 right

Date	Mintage	F	VF	XF	Unc	BU
1997 Proof	Est. 10,000	Value: 165				

KM# 522a 1/5 CROWN

6.2518 g., 0.9950 Platinum .2000 oz. APW **Ruler:** Elizabeth II **Subject:** The Tale of Peter Rabbit **Obv:** Crowned bust right **Rev:** Standing rabbit 3/4 right

Date	Mintage	F	VF	XF	Unc	BU
1997 Proof	Est. 2,500	Value: 295				

KM# 529 1/5 CROWN

6.2207 g., 0.9999 Gold .2000 oz. AGW, 22 mm. **Ruler:** Elizabeth II **Series:** Golden Wedding Anniversary **Subject:** Queen Elizabeth and Prince Philip **Obv:** Crowned bust right **Rev:** Engagement portrait

Date	Mintage	F	VF	XF	Unc	BU
1997 Proof	Est. 3,500	Value: 160				

KM# 531 1/5 CROWN

6.2207 g., 0.9999 Gold .2000 oz. AGW, 22 mm. **Ruler:** Elizabeth II **Series:** Golden Wedding Anniversary **Subject:** Queen Elizabeth and Prince Philip **Obv:** Crowned bust right **Rev:** Queen with her first born, Prince Charles

Date	Mintage	F	VF	XF	Unc	BU
1997 Proof	Est. 3,500	Value: 160				

KM# 533 1/5 CROWN

6.2207 g., 0.9999 Gold .2000 oz. AGW, 22 mm. **Ruler:** Elizabeth II **Series:** Golden Wedding Anniversary **Subject:** Queen Elizabeth and Prince Philip **Obv:** Crowned bust right **Rev:** the Queen, two children and a monkey

Date	Mintage	F	VF	XF	Unc	BU
1997 Proof	Est. 3,500	Value: 160				

KM# 535 1/5 CROWN

6.2207 g., 0.9999 Gold .2000 oz. AGW, 22 mm. **Ruler:** Elizabeth II **Series:** Golden Wedding Anniversary **Subject:** Queen Elizabeth and Prince Philip **Obv:** Crowned bust right **Rev:** Queen and adoring crowd

Date	Mintage	F	VF	XF	Unc	BU
1997 Proof	Est. 3,500	Value: 160				

KM# 539 1/5 CROWN

6.2207 g., 0.9999 Gold .2000 oz. AGW, 22 mm. **Ruler:** Elizabeth II **Obv:** Crowned bust right **Rev:** Peonies

Date	Mintage	F	VF	XF	Unc	BU
1997 Proof	Est. 5,000	Value: 160				

KM# 539a 1/5 CROWN

6.2200 g., 0.9950 Platinum .1990 oz. APW **Ruler:** Elizabeth II **Obv:** Crowned bust right **Rev:** Peonies

Date	Mintage	F	VF	XF	Unc	BU
1997 Proof	Est. 1,000	Value: 295				

KM# 543 1/5 CROWN

6.2200 g., 0.9999 Gold .2000 oz. AGW, 22 mm. **Ruler:** Elizabeth II **Subject:** Nefertiti **Obv:** Crowned bust right **Rev:** Head right

Date	Mintage	F	VF	XF	Unc	BU
1997 Proof	Est. 5,000	Value: 160				

KM# 543a 1/5 CROWN

6.2200 g., 0.9950 Platinum .1990 oz. APW **Ruler:** Elizabeth II **Subject:** Nefertiti **Obv:** Crowned bust right **Rev:** Head right

Date	Mintage	F	VF	XF	Unc	BU
1997 Proof	Est. 1,000	Value: 295				

KM# 547 1/5 CROWN

6.2200 g., 0.9999 Gold .2000 oz. AGW, 22 mm. **Ruler:** Elizabeth II **Subject:** Cleopatra **Obv:** Crowned bust right **Rev:** Head facing

Date	Mintage	F	VF	XF	Unc	BU
1997 Proof	Est. 5,000	Value: 160				

KM# 547a 1/5 CROWN

6.2200 g., 0.9950 Platinum .1990 oz. APW **Ruler:** Elizabeth II **Subject:** Cleopatra **Obv:** Crowned bust right **Rev:** Head facing

Date	Mintage	F	VF	XF	Unc	BU
1997 Proof	Est. 1,000	Value: 295				

KM# 551 1/5 CROWN

6.2200 g., 0.9999 Gold .2000 oz. AGW, 22 mm. **Ruler:** Elizabeth II **Subject:** Europa **Obv:** Crowned bust right **Rev:** Head 3/4 left

Date	Mintage	F	VF	XF	Unc	BU
1997 Proof	Est. 5,000	Value: 160				

KM# 551a 1/5 CROWN

6.2200 g., 0.9950 Platinum .1990 oz. APW **Ruler:** Elizabeth II **Subject:** Europa **Obv:** Crowned bust right **Rev:** Head 3/4 left

Date	Mintage	F	VF	XF	Unc	BU
1997 Proof	Est. 1,000	Value: 295				

KM# 555 1/5 CROWN

6.2200 g., 0.9999 Gold .2000 oz. AGW, 22 mm. **Ruler:** Elizabeth II **Subject:** Liberty **Obv:** Crowned bust right **Rev:** Laureate head right

Date	Mintage	F	VF	XF	Unc	BU
1997 Proof	Est. 5,000	Value: 160				

KM# 555a 1/5 CROWN

6.2200 g., 0.9950 Platinum .1990 oz. APW **Ruler:** Elizabeth II **Subject:** Liberty **Obv:** Crowned bust right **Rev:** Laureate head right

Date	Mintage	F	VF	XF	Unc	BU
1997 Proof	Est. 1,000	Value: 295				

KM# 562 1/5 CROWN

6.2200 g., 0.9999 Gold .2000 oz. AGW, 22 mm. **Ruler:** Elizabeth II **Series:** Queen's Birthday **Obv:** Crowned bust right **Rev:** Queen on horseback left

Date	Mintage	F	VF	XF	Unc	BU
1997 Proof	Est. 5,000	Value: 165				

KM# 563 1/5 CROWN

6.2200 g., 0.9999 Gold .2000 oz. AGW, 22 mm. **Ruler:** Elizabeth II **Series:** Queen's Birthday **Obv:** Crowned bust right **Rev:** Queen on horseback returning salute

Date	Mintage	F	VF	XF	Unc	BU
1997 Proof	Est. 5,000	Value: 165				

KM# 564 1/5 CROWN

6.2200 g., 0.9999 Gold .2000 oz. AGW, 22 mm. **Ruler:** Elizabeth II **Series:** Queen's Birthday **Obv:** Crowned bust right **Rev:** Trooping the Colors scene, cameo above

Date	Mintage	F	VF	XF	Unc	BU
1997 Proof	Est. 5,000	Value: 165				

KM# 565 1/5 CROWN

6.2200 g., 0.9999 Gold .2000 oz. AGW, 22 mm. **Ruler:** Elizabeth II **Series:** Queen's Birthday **Obv:** Crowned bust right **Rev:** Gurkha troops with dragons

Date	Mintage	F	VF	XF	Unc	BU
1997 Proof	Est. 5,000	Value: 165				

KM# 570 1/5 CROWN

6.2200 g., 0.9999 Gold .2000 oz. AGW, 22 mm. **Ruler:** Elizabeth II **Subject:** The New Mosque **Obv:** Crowned bust right **Rev:** Two cavalry riders with mosque in background

Date	Mintage	F	VF	XF	Unc	BU
1997 Proof	Est. 5,000	Value: 165				

KM# 635 1/5 CROWN

6.2200 g., 0.9999 Gold .2000 oz. AGW, 22 mm. **Ruler:** Elizabeth II **Subject:** Winter Olympics Japan **Obv:** Crowned bust right **Rev:** Speed skater and "Bullet Train"

Date	Mintage	F	VF	XF	Unc	BU
1998 Proof	Est. 5,000	Value: 165				

KM# 637 1/5 CROWN

6.2200 g., 0.9999 Gold .2000 oz. AGW, 22 mm. **Ruler:** Elizabeth II **Series:** Winter Olympics Japan **Obv:** Crowned bust right **Rev:** Ski jumper and Buddha

Date	Mintage	F	VF	XF	Unc	BU
1998 Proof	Est. 5,000	Value: 165				

KM# 639 1/5 CROWN

6.2200 g., 0.9999 Gold .2000 oz. AGW, 22 mm. **Ruler:** Elizabeth II **Series:** Winter Olympics Japan **Obv:** Crowned bust right **Rev:** Cross-country skiers

Date	Mintage	F	VF	XF	Unc	BU
1998 Proof	Est. 5,000	Value: 165				

KM# 641 1/5 CROWN

6.2200 g., 0.9999 Gold .2000 oz. AGW, 22 mm. **Ruler:** Elizabeth II **Series:** Winter Olympics Japan **Obv:** Crowned bust right **Rev:** Slalom skier and Zenkoji temple

Date	Mintage	F	VF	XF	Unc	BU
1998 Proof	Est. 5,000	Value: 165				

KM# 653 1/5 CROWN

6.2200 g., 0.9999 Gold .2000 oz. AGW, 22 mm. **Ruler:** Elizabeth II **Subject:** The Tale of Peter Rabbit **Obv:** Crowned bust right **Rev:** Standing rabbit facing with sparrow at left

Date	Mintage	F	VF	XF	Unc	BU
1998 Proof	Est. 10,000	Value: 165				

KM# 653a 1/5 CROWN

6.2200 g., 0.9950 Platinum .2000 oz. APW **Ruler:** Elizabeth II **Subject:** The Tale of Peter Rabbit **Obv:** Crowned bust right **Rev:** Standing rabbit facing with sparrow at left

Date	Mintage	F	VF	XF	Unc	BU
1998 Proof	Est. 2,500	Value: 295				

KM# 659 1/5 CROWN

6.2200 g., 0.9999 Gold .2000 oz. AGW, 22 mm. **Ruler:** Elizabeth II **Obv:** Crowned bust right **Rev:** Chrysanthemum

Date	Mintage	F	VF	XF	Unc	BU
1998 Proof	Est. 5,000	Value: 165				

KM# 659a 1/5 CROWN

6.2200 g., 0.9950 Platinum .2000 oz. APW **Ruler:** Elizabeth II **Obv:** Crowned bust right **Rev:** Chrysanthemum

Date	Mintage	F	VF	XF	Unc	BU
1998 Proof	Est. 1,000	Value: 295				

KM# 671 1/5 CROWN

6.2200 g., 0.9999 Gold .2000 oz. AGW, 22 mm. **Ruler:** Elizabeth II **Subject:** Juno **Obv:** Crowned bust right **Rev:** Head 3/4 facing

Date	Mintage	F	VF	XF	Unc	BU
1998 Proof	Est. 5,000	Value: 165				

KM# 671a 1/5 CROWN

6.2200 g., 0.9950 Platinum .2000 oz. APW **Ruler:** Elizabeth II **Subject:** Juno **Obv:** Crowned bust right **Rev:** Head 3/4 facing

Date	Mintage	F	VF	XF	Unc	BU
1998 Proof	Est. 1,000	Value: 295				

KM# 672 1/5 CROWN

6.2200 g., 0.9999 Gold .2000 oz. AGW, 22 mm. **Ruler:** Elizabeth II **Subject:** Athena **Obv:** Crowned bust right **Rev:** Helmeted head right

Date	Mintage	F	VF	XF	Unc	BU
1998 Proof	Est. 5,000	Value: 165				

KM# 672a 1/5 CROWN

6.2200 g., 0.9950 Platinum .2000 oz. APW **Subject:** Athena **Obv:** Crowned bust right **Rev:** Helmeted head right

Date	Mintage	F	VF	XF	Unc	BU
1998 Proof	Est. 1,000	Value: 295				

KM# 673 1/5 CROWN

6.2200 g., 0.9999 Gold .2000 oz. AGW, 22 mm. **Ruler:** Elizabeth II **Subject:** Arethusa **Obv:** Crowned bust right **Rev:** Head left with dolphins

Date	Mintage	F	VF	XF	Unc	BU
1998 Proof	Est. 5,000	Value: 165				

KM# 673a 1/5 CROWN

6.2200 g., 0.9950 Platinum .2000 oz. APW **Ruler:** Elizabeth II **Subject:** Arethusa **Obv:** Crowned bust right **Rev:** Head left with dolphins

Date	Mintage	F	VF	XF	Unc	BU
1998 Proof	Est. 1,000	Value: 295				

KM# 680 1/5 CROWN

6.2200 g., 0.9999 Gold .2000 oz. AGW, 22 mm. **Ruler:** Elizabeth II **Subject:** Paddington Bear **Obv:** Crowned bust right **Rev:** Bear with suitcase

Date	Mintage	F	VF	XF	Unc	BU
1998 Proof	Est. 5,000	Value: 165				

KM# 680a 1/5 CROWN

6.2200 g., 0.9950 Platinum .2000 oz. APW **Ruler:** Elizabeth II **Subject:** Paddington Bear **Obv:** Crowned bust right **Rev:** Bear with suitcase

Date	Mintage	F	VF	XF	Unc	BU
1998 Proof	Est. 2,000	Value: 295				

KM# 683 1/5 CROWN

6.2200 g., 0.9999 Gold .2000 oz. AGW, 22 mm. **Ruler:** Elizabeth II **Subject:** World Cup France 1998 **Obv:** Crowned bust right **Rev:** Goalie, map of Europe

Date	Mintage	F	VF	XF	Unc	BU
1998 Proof	Est. 5,000	Value: 165				

KM# 684 1/5 CROWN

6.2200 g., 0.9999 Gold .2000 oz. AGW, 22 mm. **Ruler:** Elizabeth II **Subject:** World Cup France 1998 **Obv:** Crowned bust right **Rev:** Player kicking to left

Date	Mintage	F	VF	XF	Unc	BU
1998 Proof	Est. 5,000	Value: 165				

KM# 685 1/5 CROWN

6.2200 g., 0.9999 Gold .2000 oz. AGW, 22 mm. **Ruler:** Elizabeth II **Subject:** World Cup France 1998 **Obv:** Crowned bust right **Rev:** Player dribbling ball

Date	Mintage	F	VF	XF	Unc	BU
1998 Proof	Est. 5,000	Value: 165				

KM# 686 1/5 CROWN

6.2200 g., 0.9999 Gold .2000 oz. AGW, 22 mm. **Ruler:** Elizabeth II **Subject:** World Cup France 1998 **Obv:** Crowned bust right **Rev:** Two players, map of Europe

Date	Mintage	F	VF	XF	Unc	BU
1998 Proof	Est. 5,000	Value: 165				

KM# 731 1/5 CROWN

6.2200 g., 0.9999 Gold .2000 oz. AGW, 22 mm. **Ruler:** Elizabeth II **Obv:** Crowned bust right **Rev:** Cupid with hologram heart

Date	Mintage	F	VF	XF	Unc	BU
1998 Proof	Est. 5,000	Value: 165				

KM# 741 1/5 CROWN

6.2200 g., 0.9999 Gold .2000 oz. AGW, 22 mm. **Ruler:** Elizabeth II **Subject:** Year of the Ocean **Obv:** Crowned bust right **Rev:** Polar bear and walrus

Date	Mintage	F	VF	XF	Unc	BU
1998 Proof	Est. 5,000	Value: 170				

KM# 742 1/5 CROWN

6.2200 g., 0.9999 Gold .2000 oz. AGW, 22 mm. **Ruler:** Elizabeth II **Subject:** Year of the Ocean **Obv:** Crowned bust right **Rev:** Seals and penguins

Date	Mintage	F	VF	XF	Unc	BU
1998 Proof	Est. 5,000	Value: 170				

KM# 743 1/5 CROWN

6.2200 g., 0.9999 Gold .2000 oz. AGW, 22 mm. **Ruler:** Elizabeth II **Subject:** Year of the Ocean **Obv:** Crowned bust right **Rev:** Sea cow with calf

Date	Mintage	F	VF	XF	Unc	BU
1998 Proof	Est. 5,000	Value: 170				

KM# 744 1/5 CROWN

6.2200 g., 0.9999 Gold .2000 oz. AGW, 22 mm. **Ruler:**

Elizabeth II **Subject:** Year of the Ocean **Obv:** Crowned bust right **Rev:** Surfer

Date	Mintage	F	VF	XF	Unc	BU
1998 Proof	Est. 5,000	Value: 165				

KM# 767 1/5 CROWN

6.2200 g., 0.9999 Gold .2000 oz. AGW, 22 mm. **Ruler:** Elizabeth II **Subject:** Gibraltar Regiment New Colours **Obv:** Crowned bust right **Rev:** Soldiers presenting keys

Date	Mintage	F	VF	XF	Unc	BU
1998 Proof	Est. 5,000	Value: 165				

KM# 798 1/5 CROWN

6.2200 g., 0.9999 Gold .2000 oz. AGW, 22 mm. **Ruler:** Elizabeth II **Series:** The World At War **Subject:** General D.D. Eisenhower **Obv:** Crowned bust right **Rev:** Bust facing and North African invasion scene

Date	Mintage	F	VF	XF	Unc	BU
1998 Proof	Est. 5,000	Value: 165				

KM# 781.1 1/5 CROWN

6.2200 g., 0.9999 Gold .2000 oz. AGW, 22 mm. **Ruler:** Elizabeth II **Subject:** 1999 Year of the Rabbit **Obv:** Crowned bust right **Rev:** Rabbit reading, sparrow, Chinese characters

Date	Mintage	F	VF	XF	Unc	BU
1999 Proof	Est. 3,500	Value: 165				

KM# 781.1a 1/5 CROWN

6.2200 g., 0.9950 Platinum .2000 oz. APW **Ruler:** Elizabeth II **Subject:** 1999 Year of the Rabbit **Obv:** Crowned bust right **Rev:** Rabbit reading, sparrow, Chinese characters

Date	Mintage	F	VF	XF	Unc	BU
1999 Proof	Est. 1,500	Value: 295				

KM# 781.2 1/5 CROWN

6.2200 g., 0.9999 Gold .2000 oz. AGW, 22 mm. **Ruler:** Elizabeth II **Obv:** Crowned bust right **Rev:** Rabbit reading, sparrow, without Chinese characters

Date	Mintage	F	VF	XF	Unc	BU
1999 Proof	Inc. above	Value: 165				

KM# 781.2a 1/5 CROWN

6.2200 g., 0.9950 Platinum .2000 oz. APW **Ruler:** Elizabeth II **Obv:** Crowned bust right **Rev:** Rabbit reading, sparrow; without Chinese characters

Date	Mintage	F	VF	XF	Unc	BU
1999 Proof	Inc. above	Value: 295				

KM# 784 1/5 CROWN

6.2200 g., 0.9999 Gold .2000 oz. AGW, 22 mm. **Ruler:** Elizabeth II **Series:** Summer Olympics - Sydney **Obv:** Crowned bust right **Rev:** Broad jumper with kangaroo

Date	Mintage	F	VF	XF	Unc	BU
1999 Proof	Est. 5,000	Value: 165				

KM# 786 1/5 CROWN

6.2200 g., 0.9999 Gold .2000 oz. AGW, 22 mm. **Ruler:** Elizabeth II **Series:** Summer Olympics - Sydney **Obv:** Crowned bust right **Rev:** Sailboats and platypus

Date	Mintage	F	VF	XF	Unc	BU
1999 Proof	Est. 5,000	Value: 165				

KM# 788 1/5 CROWN

6.2200 g., 0.9999 Gold .2000 oz. AGW, 22 mm. **Ruler:** Elizabeth II **Series:** Summer Olympics - Sydney **Obv:** Crowned bust right **Rev:** Swimmer and koala bear

Date	Mintage	F	VF	XF	Unc	BU
1999 Proof	Est. 5,000	Value: 165				

KM# 790 1/5 CROWN

6.2200 g., 0.9999 Gold .2000 oz. AGW, 22 mm. **Ruler:** Elizabeth II **Series:** Summer Olympics - Sydney **Obv:** Crowned bust right **Rev:** Two oarsmen and cockatoos

Date	Mintage	F	VF	XF	Unc	BU
1999 Proof	Est. 5,000	Value: 165				

KM# 792 1/5 CROWN

6.2200 g., 0.9999 Gold .2000 oz. AGW, 22 mm. **Ruler:** Elizabeth II **Series:** Summer Olympics - Sydney **Obv:** Crowned bust right **Rev:** Man with torch and dog

Date	Mintage	F	VF	XF	Unc	BU
1999 Proof	Est. 5,000	Value: 165				

KM# 794 1/5 CROWN

6.2200 g., 0.9999 Gold .2000 oz. AGW, 22 mm. **Ruler:** Elizabeth II **Series:** Summer Olympics - Sydney **Obv:** Crowned bust right **Rev:** Torch runner, portrait of Aborigini and Ayers Rock

Date	Mintage	F	VF	XF	Unc	BU
1999 Proof	Est. 5,000	Value: 165				

KM# 796 1/5 CROWN

6.2200 g., 0.9999 Gold .2000 oz. AGW, 22 mm. **Ruler:** Elizabeth II **Subject:** Millennium 2000 **Obv:** Head with tiara right **Rev:** Sundial, digital clock face, candle and traditional clock face

Date	Mintage	F	VF	XF	Unc	BU
1999 Proof	Est. 5,000	Value: 165				

KM# 800 1/5 CROWN

6.2200 g., 0.9999 Gold .2000 oz. AGW, 22 mm. **Ruler:** Elizabeth II **Subject:** King Alfred the Great, 871-899 **Obv:** Crowned bust right **Rev:** Crowned bust left

Date	Mintage	F	VF	XF	Unc	BU
1999 Proof	Est. 5,000	Value: 165				

KM# 802 1/5 CROWN

6.2200 g., 0.9999 Gold .2000 oz. AGW, 22 mm. **Ruler:** Elizabeth II **Subject:** King Canute, 1016-1035 **Obv:** Crowned bust right **Rev:** Crowned bust left

Date	Mintage	F	VF	XF	Unc	BU
1999 Proof	Est. 5,000	Value: 165				

KM# 804 1/5 CROWN

6.2200 g., 0.9999 Gold .2000 oz. AGW, 22 mm. **Ruler:** Elizabeth II **Subject:** King Edward the Confessor, 1042-1066 **Obv:** Crowned bust right **Rev:** Crowned bust left

Date	Mintage	F	VF	XF	Unc	BU
1999 Proof	Est. 5,000	Value: 165				

KM# 806 1/5 CROWN

6.2200 g., 0.9999 Gold .2000 oz. AGW, 22 mm. **Ruler:** Elizabeth II **Series:** House of - Normandy **Subject:** King William I, 1066-1087 **Obv:** Crowned bust right **Rev:** Crowned bust left

Date	Mintage	F	VF	XF	Unc	BU
1999 Proof	Est. 5,000	Value: 165				

KM# 808 1/5 CROWN

6.2200 g., 0.9999 Gold .2000 oz. AGW, 22 mm. **Ruler:** Elizabeth II **Series:** House of - Plantagenet **Subject:** King Richard I, 1189-1199 **Obv:** Crowned bust right **Rev:** Crowned bust right

Date	Mintage	F	VF	XF	Unc	BU
1999 Proof	Est. 5,000	Value: 165				

KM# 810 1/5 CROWN

6.2200 g., 0.9999 Gold .2000 oz. AGW, 22 mm. **Ruler:** Elizabeth II **Series:** House of - Plantagenet **Subject:** King John, 1199-1216 **Obv:** Crowned bust right **Rev:** Crowned bust left

Date	Mintage	F	VF	XF	Unc	BU
1999 Proof	Est. 5,000	Value: 165				

KM# 812 1/5 CROWN

6.2200 g., 0.9999 Gold .2000 oz. AGW, 22 mm. **Ruler:** Elizabeth II **Series:** House of - Lancaster **Subject:** King Henry V, 1413-1422 **Obv:** Crowned bust right **Rev:** Bust right

Date	Mintage	F	VF	XF	Unc	BU
1999 Proof	Est. 5,000	Value: 165				

KM# 814 1/5 CROWN

6.2200 g., 0.9999 Gold .2000 oz. AGW, 22 mm. **Ruler:** Elizabeth II **Series:** House of - York **Subject:** King Richard III, 1483-1485 **Obv:** Crowned bust right **Rev:** Bust with hat right

Date	Mintage	F	VF	XF	Unc	BU
1999 Proof	Est. 5,000	Value: 165				

KM# 816 1/5 CROWN

6.2200 g., 0.9999 Gold .2000 oz. AGW, 22 mm. **Ruler:** Elizabeth II **Series:** House of - Tudor **Subject:** King Henry VIII, 1509-1547 **Obv:** Crowned bust right **Rev:** Bust with hat right

Date	Mintage	F	VF	XF	Unc	BU
1999 Proof	Est. 5,000	Value: 165				

KM# 818 1/5 CROWN

6.2200 g., 0.9999 Gold .2000 oz. AGW, 22 mm. **Ruler:** Elizabeth II **Series:** House of - Tudor **Subject:** Queen Elizabeth, 1558-1603 **Obv:** Crowned bust right **Rev:** Crowned bust with high ruffled collar left

Date	Mintage	F	VF	XF	Unc	BU
1999 Proof	Est. 5,000	Value: 165				

KM# 820 1/5 CROWN

6.2200 g., 0.9999 Gold .2000 oz. AGW, 22 mm. **Ruler:** Elizabeth II **Series:** House of - Stuart **Subject:** King Charles I, 1625-1649 **Obv:** Crowned bust right **Rev:** Bust right

Date	Mintage	F	VF	XF	Unc	BU
1999 Proof	Est. 5,000	Value: 165				

KM# 822 1/5 CROWN

6.2200 g., 0.9999 Gold .2000 oz. AGW, 22 mm. **Ruler:** Elizabeth II **Series:** House of - Stuart **Subject:** King Charles II, 1660-1685 **Obv:** Crowned bust right **Rev:** Laureate bust right

Date	Mintage	F	VF	XF	Unc	BU
1999 Proof	Est. 5,000	Value: 165				

KM# 824 1/5 CROWN

6.2200 g., 0.9999 Gold .2000 oz. AGW, 22 mm. **Ruler:** Elizabeth II **Subject:** The Wedding of Prince Edward and Miss Sophie Rhys-Jones **Obv:** Crowned bust right **Rev:** Heads facing above banner and wedding bells

Date	Mintage	F	VF	XF	Unc	BU
1999 Proof	Est. 5,000	Value: 165				

KM# 826.1 1/5 CROWN

6.2200 g., 0.9999 Gold .2000 oz. AGW, 22 mm. **Ruler:** Elizabeth II **Subject:** The Wedding of Prince Edward and Miss Sophie Rhys-Jones **Obv:** Crowned bust right **Rev:** St. George's Chapel

Date	Mintage	F	VF	XF	Unc	BU
1999 Proof	Est. 5,000	Value: 165				

KM# 834 1/5 CROWN

6.2200 g., 0.9999 Gold .2000 oz. AGW, 22 mm. **Ruler:** Elizabeth II **Subject:** The Life of Queen Elizabeth **Obv:** Crowned bust right **Rev:** 1905 portrait of Queen Mother as a girl

Date	Mintage	F	VF	XF	Unc	BU
1999 Proof	Est. 5,000	Value: 165				

KM# 836 1/5 CROWN

6.2200 g., 0.9999 Gold .2000 oz. AGW, 22 mm. **Ruler:** Elizabeth II **Subject:** The Life of Queen Elizabeth **Obv:** Crowned bust right **Rev:** 1918 portrait of Queen Mother with wounded veteran

Date	Mintage	F	VF	XF	Unc	BU
1999 Proof	Est. 5,000	Value: 165				

KM# 838 1/5 CROWN

6.2200 g., 0.9999 Gold .2000 oz. AGW, 22 mm. **Ruler:** Elizabeth II **Subject:** The Life of Queen Elizabeth **Obv:** Crowned bust right **Rev:** 1923 wedding portrait

Date	Mintage	F	VF	XF	Unc	BU
1999 Proof	Est. 5,000	Value: 165				

KM# 840 1/5 CROWN

6.2200 g., 0.9999 Gold .2000 oz. AGW, 22 mm. **Ruler:** Elizabeth II **Subject:** The Life of Queen Elizabeth **Obv:** Crowned bust right **Rev:** 1936 family portrait

Date	Mintage	F	VF	XF	Unc	BU
1999 Proof	Est. 5,000	Value: 165				

KM# 843 1/5 CROWN

6.2200 g., 0.9999 Gold .2000 oz. AGW, 22 mm. **Ruler:** Elizabeth II **Series:** The World At War **Subject:** Franklin D. Roosevelt **Obv:** Crowned bust right **Rev:** Bust writing at left, Zero fighter at right

Date	Mintage	F	VF	XF	Unc	BU
1999 Proof	—	Value: 165				

KM# 844 1/5 CROWN

6.2200 g., 0.9999 Gold .2000 oz. AGW, 22 mm. **Ruler:** Elizabeth II **Subject:** The World At War **Obv:** Crowned bust right **Rev:** Bomber dropping food packets

Date	Mintage	F	VF	XF	Unc	BU
1999 Proof	Est. 5,000	Value: 165				

KM# 847 1/5 CROWN

6.2200 g., 0.9999 Gold .2000 oz. AGW, 22 mm. **Ruler:** Elizabeth II **Subject:** The World At War **Obv:** Crowned bust right **Rev:** B-29, mushroom cloud and bust at right

Date	Mintage	F	VF	XF	Unc	BU
1999 Proof	Est. 5,000	Value: 165				

KM# 848 1/5 CROWN

6.2200 g., 0.9999 Gold .2000 oz. AGW, 22 mm. **Ruler:** Elizabeth II **Subject:** The World At War **Obv:** Crowned bust right **Rev:** Bust at left reading, bomber above dam

Date	Mintage	F	VF	XF	Unc	BU
1999 Proof	Est. 5,000	Value: 165				

KM# 850 1/5 CROWN

6.2200 g., 0.9999 Gold .2000 oz. AGW, 22 mm. **Ruler:** Elizabeth II **Subject:** The World At War **Obv:** Crowned bust right **Rev:** Bust at left facing, planes in combat

Date	Mintage	F	VF	XF	Unc	BU
1999 Proof	Est. 5,000	Value: 165				

KM# 852 1/5 CROWN

6.2200 g., 0.9999 Gold .2000 oz. AGW, 22 mm. **Ruler:** Elizabeth II **Subject:** Winston Churchill **Obv:** Crowned bust right **Rev:** Bust with hand showing 'V' sign, crowd in background

Date	Mintage	F	VF	XF	Unc	BU
1999 Proof	Est. 5,000	Value: 165				

KM# 854 1/5 CROWN

6.2200 g., 0.9999 Gold .2000 oz. AGW, 22 mm. **Ruler:** Elizabeth II **Subject:** Tirpitz **Obv:** Crowned bust right **Rev:** Battleship and sailor

Date	Mintage	F	VF	XF	Unc	BU
1999 Proof	Est. 5,000	Value: 165				

KM# 856 1/5 CROWN

6.2200 g., 0.9999 Gold .2000 oz. AGW, 22 mm. **Ruler:** Elizabeth II **Subject:** War Babies **Obv:** Crowned bust right **Rev:** Soldier kissing child

Date	Mintage	F	VF	XF	Unc	BU
1999 Proof	Est. 5,000	Value: 165				

KM# 858 1/5 CROWN

6.2200 g., 0.9999 Gold .2000 oz. AGW, 22 mm. **Ruler:** Elizabeth II **Subject:** The World At War **Obv:** Crowned bust right **Rev:** 2 firemen in action after air raid

Date	Mintage	F	VF	XF	Unc	BU
1999 Proof	Est. 5,000	Value: 165				

KM# 860 1/5 CROWN

6.2200 g., 0.9999 Gold .2000 oz. AGW, 22 mm. **Ruler:** Elizabeth II **Subject:** The World At War **Obv:** Crowned bust right **Rev:** Landing scene

Date	Mintage	F	VF	XF	Unc	BU
1999 Proof	Est. 5,000	Value: 165				

KM# 862 1/5 CROWN
6.2200 g., 0.9999 Gold .2000 oz. AGW, 22 mm. **Ruler:** Elizabeth II **Subject:** The World At War **Obv:** Crowned bust right **Rev:** Military skier

Date	Mintage	F	VF	XF	Unc	BU
1999 Proof	Est. 5,000	Value: 165				

KM# 864 1/5 CROWN
6.2200 g., 0.9999 Gold .2000 oz. AGW, 22 mm. **Ruler:** Elizabeth II **Subject:** The World At War **Obv:** Crowned bust right **Rev:** German tanks in Russia

Date	Mintage	F	VF	XF	Unc	BU
1999 Proof	Est. 5,000	Value: 165				

KM# 870 1/5 CROWN
6.2200 g., 0.9999 Gold .2000 oz. AGW, 22 mm. **Ruler:** Elizabeth II **Series:** Queen Mother **Obv:** Head with tiara right **Rev:** 1937 Coronation scene

Date	Mintage	F	VF	XF	Unc	BU
2000 Proof	5,000	Value: 175				

KM# 872 1/5 CROWN
6.2200 g., 0.9999 Gold .2000 oz. AGW, 22 mm. **Ruler:** Elizabeth II **Series:** Queen Mother **Obv:** Crowned bust right **Rev:** 1938 Visit to France

Date	Mintage	F	VF	XF	Unc	BU
2000 Proof	5,000	Value: 175				

KM# 874 1/5 CROWN
6.2200 g., 0.9999 Gold .2000 oz. AGW, 22 mm. **Ruler:** Elizabeth II **Series:** Queen Mother **Obv:** Crowned bust right **Rev:** 1940 Bomb damage

Date	Mintage	F	VF	XF	Unc	BU
2000 Proof	5,000	Value: 175				

KM# 876 1/5 CROWN
6.2200 g., 0.9999 Gold .2000 oz. AGW, 22 mm. **Ruler:** Elizabeth II **Series:** Queen Mother **Obv:** Crowned bust right

Date	Mintage	F	VF	XF	Unc	BU
2000 Proof	5,000	Value: 175				

KM# 879 1/5 CROWN
6.2200 g., 0.9999 Gold .2000 oz. AGW, 22 mm. **Ruler:** Elizabeth II **Subject:** 18th Birthday of Prince William **Obv:** Crowned bust right **Rev:** Bust facing **Edge:** Reeded

Date	Mintage	F	VF	XF	Unc	BU
2000 Proof	5,000	Value: 175				

KM# 881 1/5 CROWN
6.2200 g., 0.9999 Gold .2000 oz. AGW, 22 mm. **Ruler:** Elizabeth II **Series:** 100th Birthday of the Queen Mother **Obv:** Crowned bust right **Rev:** Bust facing **Note:** Queen Mother's portrait has a real diamond chip (.015) set in her crown.

Date	Mintage	F	VF	XF	Unc	BU
2000 Proof	2,000	Value: 175				

KM# 868.1 1/4 CROWN
7.7800 g., 0.9250 Silver .2314 oz. ASW **Ruler:** Elizabeth II **Subject:** 1999 The Year of the Rabbit **Obv:** Crowned bust right **Rev:** Peter Rabbit reading, sparrow, Chinese characters

Date	Mintage	F	VF	XF	Unc	BU
1999 Proof	Est. 25,000	Value: 35.00				

KM# 868.2 1/4 CROWN
7.7800 g., 0.9250 Silver .2314 oz. ASW **Ruler:** Elizabeth II **Obv:** Crowned bust right **Rev:** Rabbit reading, sparrow; without Chinese characters

Date	Mintage	F	VF	XF	Unc	BU
1999 Proof	Inc. above	Value: 35.00				

KM# 886 1/2 CROWN
15.5500 g., 0.9999 Gold .5000 oz. AGW, 30 mm. **Ruler:** Elizabeth II **Subject:** Rotary Club of Gibraltar

Date	Mintage	F	VF	XF	Unc	BU
1991 Proof	5,000	Value: 500				

KM# 127 1/2 CROWN
15.5500 g., 0.9999 Gold .5000 oz. AGW, 30 mm. **Ruler:** Elizabeth II **Subject:** Japanese Royal Wedding **Obv:** Crowned bust right **Rev:** Peacocks

Date	Mintage	F	VF	XF	Unc	BU
1993 Proof	5,000	Value: 350				

KM# 177 1/2 CROWN
15.5500 g., 0.9990 Silver .5000 oz. ASW **Ruler:** Elizabeth II **Series:** WWII Warships **Obv:** Crowned bust right **Rev:** HMS Hood

Date	Mintage	F	VF	XF	Unc	BU
1993	Est. 30,000	—	—	—	35.00	—

KM# 198 1/2 CROWN
15.5500 g., 0.9990 Silver .5000 oz. ASW **Ruler:** Elizabeth II **Subject:** King Edward VIII, House of Windsor **Obv:** Young bust right **Rev:** Bust left

Date	Mintage	F	VF	XF	Unc	BU
1993 Proof	Est. 30,000	Value: 27.50				

KM# 443 1/2 CROWN
15.5500 g., 0.9999 Gold .5000 oz. AGW, 30 mm. **Ruler:** Elizabeth II **Series:** Peter Rabbit Centennial **Subject:** The Tale of Peter Rabbit **Obv:** Crowned bust right **Rev:** Mother and bunnies

Date	Mintage	F	VF	XF	Unc	BU
1994 Proof	Est. 5,000	Value: 375				

KM# 572 1/2 CROWN
15.5500 g., 0.9990 Silver .5000 oz. ASW **Ruler:** Elizabeth II **Obv:** Crowned bust right **Rev:** Sherlock Holmes smoking pipe left

Date	Mintage	F	VF	XF	Unc	BU
1994 Proof	Est. 30,000	Value: 22.50				

KM# 372 1/2 CROWN
15.5500 g., 0.9999 Gold .5000 oz. AGW, 30 mm. **Ruler:** Elizabeth II **Obv:** Crowned bust right **Rev:** Roses

Date	Mintage	F	VF	XF	Unc	BU
1996 Proof	Est. 3,000	Value: 365				

KM# 381 1/2 CROWN
15.5500 g., 0.9999 Gold .5000 oz. AGW, 30 mm. **Ruler:** Elizabeth II **Series:** Peter Rabbit Centennial **Subject:** The Tale of Peter Rabbit **Obv:** Crowned bust right **Rev:** Peter Rabbit escaping garden

Date	Mintage	F	VF	XF	Unc	BU
1996 Proof	Est. 5,000	Value: 375				

KM# 448 1/2 CROWN
15.5500 g., 0.9999 Gold .5000 oz. AGW, 30 mm. **Ruler:** Elizabeth II **Subject:** Lord Buddha **Obv:** Crowned bust right **Rev:** Seated figure facing

Date	Mintage	F	VF	XF	Unc	BU
1996 Proof	Est. 5,000	Value: 365				

KM# 524 1/2 CROWN
15.5500 g., 0.9999 Gold .5000 oz. AGW, 30 mm. **Ruler:** Elizabeth II **Subject:** The Tale of Peter Rabbit **Obv:** Crowned bust right **Rev:** Standing rabbit 3/4 right

Date	Mintage	F	VF	XF	Unc	BU
1997 Proof	Est. 2,500	Value: 375				

KM# 647 1/2 CROWN
15.5500 g., 0.9999 Gold .5000 oz. AGW, 30 mm. **Ruler:** Elizabeth II **Obv:** Crowned bust right **Rev:** Cupid with hologram heart

Date	Mintage	F	VF	XF	Unc	BU
1998 Proof	Est. 3,500	Value: 350				

KM# 655 1/2 CROWN
15.5500 g., 0.9999 Gold .5000 oz. AGW, 30 mm. **Ruler:** Elizabeth II **Subject:** The Tale of Peter Rabbit **Obv:** Crowned bust right **Rev:** Standing rabbit facing, sparrow at left

Date	Mintage	F	VF	XF	Unc	BU
1998 Proof	Est. 2,500	Value: 375				

KM# 681 1/2 CROWN
15.5500 g., 0.9999 Gold .5000 oz. AGW, 30 mm. **Ruler:** Elizabeth II **Subject:** Paddington Bear **Obv:** Crowned bust right **Rev:** Bear with suitcase

Date	Mintage	F	VF	XF	Unc	BU
1998 Proof	Est. 2,500	Value: 365				

KM# 732 1/2 CROWN
15.5500 g., 0.9999 Gold .5000 oz. AGW, 30 mm. **Ruler:** Elizabeth II **Subject:** Peacocks **Obv:** Crowned bust right **Rev:** Pair of peacocks, one with full display in hologram, denomination below

Date	Mintage	F	VF	XF	Unc	BU
1998 Proof	Est. 3,500	Value: 385				

KM# 895 1/2 CROWN
15.7800 g., 0.9990 Silver .5068 oz. ASW, 32.25 mm. **Ruler:** Elizabeth II **Subject:** Cupid **Obv:** Crowned bust right **Rev:** Cupid with multicolor holographic heart similar to 1/2 crown KM#-647 but without the metal content statement, denomination below **Edge:** Reeded

Date	Mintage	F	VF	XF	Unc	BU
1998 Proof	10,000	Value: 50.00				

KM# 782.1 1/2 CROWN
15.5500 g., 0.9999 Gold .5000 oz. AGW, 30 mm. **Ruler:** Elizabeth II **Subject:** 1999 The Year of the Rabbit **Obv:** Crowned bust right **Rev:** Rabbit reading, sparrow, Chinese characters

Date	Mintage	F	VF	XF	Unc	BU
1999 Proof	Est. 1,000	Value: 350				

KM# 782.2 1/2 CROWN
15.5500 g., 0.9999 Gold .5000 oz. AGW, 30 mm. **Ruler:** Elizabeth II **Obv:** Crowned bust right **Rev:** Rabbit reading, sparrow; without Chinese characters

Date	Mintage	F	VF	XF	Unc	BU
1999	Inc. above	—	—	—	345	—

KM# 883 1/2 CROWN
Ring Weight: 9.0000 g. **Ring Composition:** 0.9990 Gold .2893 oz. AGW **Center Composition:** Titanium **Ruler:** Elizabeth II **Subject:** 160th Anniversary of the Uniform Penny Post **Obv:** Crowned bust right **Rev:** Postage stamp design **Edge:** Reeded

Date	Mintage	F	VF	XF	Unc	BU
2000 Proof	5,000	Value: 210				

KM# 894 1/2 CROWN
15.5517 g., 0.9990 Gold .5000 oz. AGW, 30 mm. **Ruler:** Elizabeth II **Obv:** Crowned bust right **Rev:** Postage stamp design **Edge:** Reeded

Date	Mintage	F	VF	XF	Unc	BU
2000 Proof	999	Value: 350				

KM# 11 CROWN
Copper-Nickel, 38.8 mm. **Ruler:** Elizabeth II **Subject:** 80th Birthday of Queen Mother **Rev:** Bust left, mountain and water in background

Date	Mintage	F	VF	XF	Unc	BU
1980	—	—	—	1.50	3.00	4.00

KM# 11a CROWN
28.2800 g., 0.9250 Silver .8411 oz. ASW, 38.8 mm. **Ruler:** Elizabeth II **Subject:** 80th Birthday of Queen Mother **Rev:** Bust left, mountains and water in background

Date	Mintage	F	VF	XF	Unc	BU
1980 Proof	Est. 25,000	Value: 13.50				

KM# 12 CROWN
Copper-Nickel, 38.8 mm. **Ruler:** Elizabeth II **Subject:** 175th Anniversary - Death of Nelson **Obv:** Young bust right **Rev:** Head at right looking left, ship in background

Date	Mintage	F	VF	XF	Unc	BU
1980	Est. 100,000	—	—	2.00	4.00	6.50

KM# 12a CROWN
28.2800 g., 0.9250 Silver .8411 oz. ASW, 38.8 mm. **Ruler:** Elizabeth II **Subject:** 175th Anniversary - Death of Nelson **Obv:** Bust right

Date	Mintage	F	VF	XF	Unc	BU
1980 Proof	Est. 15,000	Value: 22.50				

KM# 14 CROWN
Copper-Nickel, 38.8 mm. **Ruler:** Elizabeth II **Subject:** Wedding of Prince Charles and Lady Diana **Rev:** The royal couple facing

Date	Mintage	F	VF	XF	Unc	BU
1981	—	—	—	1.00	2.50	3.50

KM# 14a CROWN
28.2800 g., 0.9250 Silver .8411 oz. ASW, 38.8 mm. **Ruler:** Elizabeth II **Subject:** The Wedding of Prince Charles and Lady Diana **Rev:** The royal couple facing

Date	Mintage	F	VF	XF	Unc	BU
1981 Proof	Est. 30,000	Value: 12.50				

KM# 49 CROWN
Copper-Nickel, 38.8 mm. **Ruler:** Elizabeth II **Series:** 150th Anniversary of the First Adhesive Postage Stamp **Subject:** Penny Black Stamp **Obv:** Crowned bust right **Rev:** Heads flank stamp design

Date	Mintage	F	VF	XF	Unc	BU
1990 Proof	Est. 50,000	Value: 18.00				
1990	—	—	—	—	7.50	9.00

KM# 33 CROWN
Copper-Nickel, 38.8 mm. **Ruler:** Elizabeth II **Series:** World Cup Soccer **Obv:** Crowned bust right **Rev:** Italian flag, soccer player and globe

Date	Mintage	F	VF	XF	Unc	BU
1990	—	—	—	—	3.50	5.00

KM# 33a CROWN
28.2800 g., 0.9250 Silver .8411 oz. ASW, 38.8 mm. **Ruler:** Elizabeth II **Series:** World Cup Soccer **Obv:** Crowned bust right **Rev:** Italian flag, soccer player and globe

Date	Mintage	F	VF	XF	Unc	BU
1990 Proof	Est. 30,000	Value: 32.50				

KM# 34 CROWN
Copper-Nickel, 38.8 mm. **Ruler:** Elizabeth II **Series:** World Cup Soccer **Obv:** Crowned bust right **Rev:** Map of Italy on soccer ball background

Date	Mintage	F	VF	XF	Unc	BU
1990	—	—	—	—	3.50	5.00

KM# 34a CROWN
28.2800 g., 0.9250 Silver .8411 oz. ASW, 38.8 mm. **Ruler:** Elizabeth II **Series:** World Cup Soccer **Obv:** Crowned bust right **Rev:** Map of Italy on soccer ball background

Date	Mintage	F	VF	XF	Unc	BU
1990 Proof	Est. 30,000	Value: 32.50				

KM# 35 CROWN
Copper-Nickel, 38.8 mm. **Ruler:** Elizabeth II **Series:** World Cup Soccer **Obv:** Crowned bust right **Rev:** Goalie catching ball

Date	Mintage	F	VF	XF	Unc	BU
1990	—	—	—	—	3.50	5.00

KM# 35a CROWN
28.2800 g., 0.9250 Silver .8411 oz. ASW, 38.8 mm. **Ruler:** Elizabeth II **Series:** World Cup Soccer **Obv:** Crowned bust right **Rev:** Goalie catching ball

Date	Mintage	F	VF	XF	Unc	BU
1990 Proof	Est. 30,000	Value: 32.50				

KM# 36 CROWN
Copper-Nickel, 38.8 mm. **Ruler:** Elizabeth II **Series:** World Cup Soccer **Obv:** Crowned bust right **Rev:** Ball at head

Date	Mintage	F	VF	XF	Unc	BU
1990	—	—	—	—	3.50	5.00

KM# 36a CROWN
28.2800 g., 0.9250 Silver .8411 oz. ASW, 38.8 mm. **Ruler:** Elizabeth II **Series:** World Cup Soccer **Obv:** Crowned bust right **Rev:** Ball at head

Date	Mintage	F	VF	XF	Unc	BU
1990 Proof	Est. 30,000	Value: 32.50				

KM# 37 CROWN
Copper-Nickel, 38.8 mm. **Ruler:** Elizabeth II **Series:** World Cup Soccer **Obv:** Crowned bust right **Rev:** Ball at feet

Date	Mintage	F	VF	XF	Unc	BU
1990	—	—	—	—	3.50	5.00

KM# 37a CROWN
28.2800 g., 0.9250 Silver .8411 oz. ASW, 38.8 mm. **Ruler:** Elizabeth II **Series:** World Cup Soccer **Obv:** Crowned bust right **Rev:** Ball at feet

Date	Mintage	F	VF	XF	Unc	BU
1990 Proof	Est. 30,000	Value: 32.50				

KM# 38 CROWN
Copper-Nickel, 38.8 mm. **Ruler:** Elizabeth II **Series:** World Cup Soccer **Obv:** Crowned bust right **Rev:** Three players

Date	Mintage	F	VF	XF	Unc	BU
1990	—	—	—	—	3.50	5.00

KM# 38a CROWN
28.2800 g., 0.9250 Silver .8411 oz. ASW, 38.8 mm. **Ruler:** Elizabeth II **Series:** World Cup Soccer **Obv:** Crowned bust right **Rev:** Three players

Date	Mintage	F	VF	XF	Unc	BU
1990 Proof	Est. 30,000	Value: 32.50				

KM# 40 CROWN
Copper-Nickel, 38.8 mm. **Ruler:** Elizabeth II **Subject:** 21st Anniversary - Constitution **Obv:** Crowned bust right **Rev:** Standing figure with key, shield and spear

Date	Mintage	F	VF	XF	Unc	BU
1990	—	—	—	—	6.50	8.50

KM# 40a CROWN
28.2800 g., 0.9250 Silver .8411 oz. ASW, 38.8 mm. **Ruler:** Elizabeth II **Subject:** 21st Anniversary - Constitution **Obv:** Crowned bust right **Rev:** Standing figure with key, spear and shield

Date	Mintage	F	VF	XF	Unc	BU
1990 Proof	Est. 30,000	Value: 50.00				

KM# 46 CROWN
Copper-Nickel, 38.6 mm. **Ruler:** Elizabeth II **Obv:** Crowned bust right **Rev:** Head 3/4 left divides dates

Date	Mintage	F	VF	XF	Unc	BU
1990	—	—	—	—	4.50	6.00

KM# 46a CROWN
28.2800 g., 0.9250 Silver .8411 oz. ASW, 38.6 mm. **Ruler:** Elizabeth II **Obv:** Crowned bust right **Rev:** Head 3/4 left divides dates

Date	Mintage	F	VF	XF	Unc	BU
1990 Proof	Est. 30,000	Value: 17.50				

KM# 46b CROWN
6.2200 g., 0.9999 Gold .2000 oz. AGW **Ruler:** Elizabeth II **Obv:** Crowned bust right **Rev:** Head 3/4 left divides date

Date	Mintage	F	VF	XF	Unc	BU
1990 Proof	Est. 5,000	Value: 175				

KM# 46c CROWN
6.2200 g., 0.9950 Platinum .2000 oz. APW **Ruler:** Elizabeth II **Obv:** Crowned bust right **Rev:** Head 3/4 left divides dates

Date	Mintage	F	VF	XF	Unc	BU
1990 Proof	Est. 1,000	Value: 300				

KM# 49a CROWN
28.2800 g., 0.9250 Silver .8411 oz. ASW **Ruler:** Elizabeth II **Series:** 150th Anniversary of the First Adhesive Postage Stamp **Subject:** Penny Black Stamp **Obv:** Crowned bust right **Rev:** Heads flank stamp design

Date	Mintage	F	VF	XF	Unc	BU
1990 Proof	Est. 30,000	Value: 45.00				

KM# 49b CROWN
31.1000 g., 0.9999 Gold .9999 oz. AGW **Ruler:** Elizabeth II **Series:** 150th Anniversary of the First Adhesive Postage Stamp **Subject:** Penny Black Stamp **Obv:** Crowned bust right **Rev:** Heads flank stamp design

Date	Mintage	F	VF	XF	Unc	BU
1990 Proof	Est. 1,000	Value: 1,100				

KM# 49c CROWN
15.5500 g., 0.9999 Gold .4999 oz. AGW **Ruler:** Elizabeth II **Series:** 150th Anniversary of the First Adhesive Postage Stamp **Subject:** Penny Black Stamp **Obv:** Crowned bust right **Rev:** Heads flank stamp design

Date	Mintage	F	VF	XF	Unc	BU
1990 Proof	Est. 2,500	Value: 500				

KM# 66 CROWN
Copper-Nickel, 38.8 mm. **Ruler:** Elizabeth II **Series:** Barcelona Olympics **Obv:** Crowned bust right **Rev:** Discus thrower

Date	Mintage	F	VF	XF	Unc	BU
1991 Proof	Est. 8,000	Value: 22.50				
1991	—	—	—	—	4.50	5.50
1992	—	—	—	—	5.00	6.00

KM# 67 CROWN
Copper-Nickel, 38.8 mm. **Ruler:** Elizabeth II **Series:** Barcelona Olympics **Obv:** Crowned bust right **Rev:** Chariot racing

Date	Mintage	F	VF	XF	Unc	BU
1991 Proof	Est. 8,000	Value: 22.50				
1991	—	—	—	—	5.00	6.00
1992	—	—	—	—	5.00	6.00

KM# 68 CROWN
Copper-Nickel, 38.8 mm. **Ruler:** Elizabeth II **Series:** Barcelona Olympics **Obv:** Crowned bust right **Rev:** Runners

Date	Mintage	F	VF	XF	Unc	BU
1991 Proof	Est. 8,000	Value: 22.50				
1991	—	—	—	—	4.50	5.50
1992	—	—	—	—	5.00	6.00

KM# 69 CROWN
Copper-Nickel, 38.8 mm. **Ruler:** Elizabeth II **Series:** Barcelona Olympics **Obv:** Crowned bust right **Rev:** Javelin thrower

Date	Mintage	F	VF	XF	Unc	BU
1991 Proof	Est. 8,000	Value: 22.50				
1991	—	—	—	—	4.50	5.50
1992	—	—	—	—	5.00	6.00

KM# 70 CROWN
Copper-Nickel, 38.8 mm. **Ruler:** Elizabeth II **Series:** Barcelona Olympics **Obv:** Crowned bust right **Rev:** Head facing at left, wrestlers at right

Date	Mintage	F	VF	XF	Unc	BU
1991 Proof	Est. 8,000	Value: 22.50				
1991	—	—	—	—	4.50	5.50
1992	—	—	—	—	5.00	6.00

KM# 71 CROWN

Copper-Nickel, 38.8 mm. **Ruler:** Elizabeth II **Series:** Barcelona Olympics **Obv:** Crowned bust right **Rev:** Seated figure at left, boxers at right

Date	Mintage	F	VF	XF	Unc	BU
1991 Proof	Est. 8,000	Value: 22.50				
1991	—	—	—	—	4.50	5.50
1992	—	—	—	—	5.00	6.00

KM# 72 CROWN

Copper-Nickel, 38.8 mm. **Ruler:** Elizabeth II **Series:** Barcelona Olympics **Obv:** Crowned bust right **Rev:** Long jumper

Date	Mintage	F	VF	XF	Unc	BU
1991	—	—	—	—	4.50	5.50
1991 Proof	Est. 8,000	Value: 22.50				
1992	—	—	—	—	5.00	6.00

KM# 73 CROWN

Copper-Nickel **Ruler:** Elizabeth II **Series:** Barcelona Olympics **Obv:** Crowned bust right **Rev:** Olympic victor

Date	Mintage	F	VF	XF	Unc	BU
1991	—	—	—	—	4.50	5.50
1991 Proof	Est. 8,000	Value: 22.50				
1992	—	—	—	—	5.00	6.00

KM# 66a CROWN

28.2800 g., 0.9250 Silver .8411 oz. ASW **Ruler:** Elizabeth II **Series:** Barcelona Olympics **Obv:** Crowned bust right **Rev:** Discus thrower

Date	Mintage	F	VF	XF	Unc	BU
1991 Proof	Est. 30,000	Value: 27.50				
1992 Proof	—	Value: 100				

KM# 67a CROWN

28.2800 g., 0.9250 Silver .8411 oz. ASW, 38.8 mm. **Ruler:** Elizabeth II **Series:** Barcelona Olympics **Obv:** Crowned bust right **Rev:** Chariot racing

Date	Mintage	F	VF	XF	Unc	BU
1991 Proof	Est. 30,000	Value: 27.50				

KM# 68a CROWN

28.2800 g., 0.9250 Silver .8411 oz. ASW, 38.8 mm. **Ruler:** Elizabeth II **Series:** Barcelona Olympics **Obv:** Crowned bust right **Rev:** Runners

Date	Mintage	F	VF	XF	Unc	BU
1991 Proof	Est. 30,000	Value: 27.50				

KM# 69a CROWN

28.2800 g., 0.9250 Silver .8411 oz. ASW, 38.8 mm. **Ruler:** Elizabeth II **Series:** Barcelona Olympics **Obv:** Crowned bust right **Rev:** Javelin thrower

Date	Mintage	F	VF	XF	Unc	BU
1991 Proof	Est. 30,000	Value: 27.50				
1992 Proof	—	Value: 65.00				

KM# 70a CROWN

28.2800 g., 0.9250 Silver .8411 oz. ASW, 38.8 mm. **Ruler:** Elizabeth II **Series:** Barcelona Olympics **Obv:** Crowned bust right **Rev:** Head facing at left, wrestlers at right

Date	Mintage	F	VF	XF	Unc	BU
1991 Proof	Est. 30,000	Value: 27.50				

KM# 71a CROWN

28.2800 g., 0.9250 Silver .8411 oz. ASW, 38.8 mm. **Ruler:** Elizabeth II **Series:** Barcelona Olympics **Obv:** Crowned bust right **Rev:** Seated figure at left, boxers at right

Date	Mintage	F	VF	XF	Unc	BU
1991 Proof	Est. 30,000	Value: 27.50				

KM# 72a CROWN

28.2800 g., 0.9250 Silver .8411 oz. ASW, 38.8 mm. **Ruler:** Elizabeth II **Series:** Barcelona Olympics **Obv:** Crowned bust right **Rev:** Long jumper

Date	Mintage	F	VF	XF	Unc	BU
1991 Proof	Est. 30,000	Value: 27.50				

KM# 73a CROWN

28.2800 g., 0.9250 Silver .8411 oz. ASW, 38.8 mm. **Ruler:** Elizabeth II **Series:** Barcelona Olympics **Obv:** Crowned bust right **Rev:** Olympic victor

Date	Mintage	F	VF	XF	Unc	BU
1991 Proof	Est. 30,000	Value: 27.50				

KM# 74 CROWN

Copper-Nickel, 38.8 mm. **Ruler:** Elizabeth II **Subject:** Rotary Club of Gibraltar **Obv:** Crowned bust right **Rev:** Cogwheel design on globe

Date	Mintage	F	VF	XF	Unc	BU
1991	—	—	—	—	5.00	7.00

KM# 74a CROWN

28.2800 g., 0.9250 Silver .8411 oz. ASW, 38.8 mm. **Ruler:** Elizabeth II **Subject:** Rotary Club of Gibraltar **Obv:** Crowned bust right **Rev:** Cogwheel design on globe

Date	Mintage	F	VF	XF	Unc	BU
1991 Proof	Est. 30,000	Value: 22.50				

KM# 74b CROWN

15.5500 g., 0.9990 Gold 0.4994 oz. AGW, 32.25 mm. **Ruler:** Elizabeth II **Subject:** Rotary Club of Gibraltar **Obv:** Crowned bust right **Rev:** Cogwheel design on globe

Date	Mintage	F	VF	XF	Unc	BU
1991 Proof	5,000	Value: 650				

KM# 84 CROWN

Copper-Nickel, 38.5 mm. **Ruler:** Elizabeth II **Series:** 10th Wedding Anniversary **Subject:** Prince Charles **Rev:** Head 3/4 left

Date	Mintage	F	VF	XF	Unc	BU
1991	—	—	—	—	4.00	5.00

KM# 84a CROWN

28.2800 g., 0.9250 Silver .8411 oz. ASW, 38.5 mm. **Ruler:** Elizabeth II **Series:** 10th Wedding Anniversary **Subject:** Prince Charles **Rev:** Head 3/4 left

Date	Mintage	F	VF	XF	Unc	BU
1991 Proof	Est. 30,000	Value: 35.00				

KM# 84b CROWN

6.2200 g., 0.9999 Gold .2000 oz. AGW **Ruler:** Elizabeth II **Series:** 10th Wedding Anniversary **Subject:** Prince Charles **Rev:** Head 3/4 left

Date	Mintage	F	VF	XF	Unc	BU
1991 Proof	Est. 5,000	Value: 185				

KM# 85 CROWN

Copper-Nickel, 38.5 mm. **Ruler:** Elizabeth II **Series:** 10th Wedding Anniversary **Subject:** Princess Diana **Rev:** Head 3/4 right

Date	Mintage	F	VF	XF	Unc	BU
1991	—	—	—	—	4.00	5.00

KM# 85a CROWN

28.2800 g., 0.9250 Silver .8411 oz. ASW, 38.5 mm. **Ruler:** Elizabeth II **Series:** 10th Wedding Anniversary **Subject:** Princess Diana **Rev:** Head 3/4 right

Date	Mintage	F	VF	XF	Unc	BU
1991 Proof	—	Value: 37.50				

KM# 85b CROWN

6.2200 g., 0.9999 Gold .2000 oz. AGW **Ruler:** Elizabeth II **Series:** 10th Wedding Anniversary **Subject:** Princess Diana **Rev:** Head 3/4 right

Date	Mintage	F	VF	XF	Unc	BU
1991 Proof	—	Value: 185				

KM# 86 CROWN

Copper-Nickel, 38.5 mm. **Ruler:** Elizabeth II **Series:** 10th Wedding Anniversary **Subject:** Royal Yacht 'Brittannia' **Rev:** Luxury liner at sea

Date	Mintage	F	VF	XF	Unc	BU
1991	—	—	—	—	4.00	5.00

KM# 86a CROWN

28.2800 g., 0.9250 Silver .8411 oz. ASW, 38.5 mm. **Ruler:** Elizabeth II **Series:** 10th Wedding Anniversary **Subject:** Royal Yacht 'Britannia' **Rev:** Luxury liner at sea

Date	Mintage	F	VF	XF	Unc	BU
1991 Proof	Est. 30,000	Value: 35.00				

KM# 86b CROWN

6.2200 g., 0.9999 Gold .2000 oz. AGW **Ruler:** Elizabeth II **Series:** 10th Wedding Anniversary **Subject:** Royal Yacht 'Britannia' **Rev:** Luxury liner at sea

Date	Mintage	F	VF	XF	Unc	BU
1991 Proof	Est. 5,000	Value: 185				

KM# 95 CROWN

Copper-Nickel, 38.8 mm. **Ruler:** Elizabeth II **Obv:** Crowned bust right **Rev:** Corgi

Date	Mintage	F	VF	XF	Unc	BU
1991	—	—	—	—	12.50	15.00

KM# 95a CROWN

31.1030 g., 0.9990 Silver 1.0000 oz. ASW, 38.8 mm. **Ruler:** Elizabeth II **Obv:** Crowned bust right **Rev:** Corgi

Date	Mintage	F	VF	XF	Unc	BU
1991 Proof	Est. 50,000	Value: 35.00				

KM# 103 CROWN

Copper-Nickel, 38.8 mm. **Ruler:** Elizabeth II **Obv:** Crowned bust right **Rev:** Cocker Spaniel

Date	Mintage	F	VF	XF	Unc	BU
1992	—	—	—	—	12.50	15.00

KM# 103a CROWN

28.2800 g., 0.9250 Silver .8411 oz. ASW, 38.8 mm. **Ruler:** Elizabeth II **Obv:** Crowned bust right **Rev:** Cocker Spaniel

Date	Mintage	F	VF	XF	Unc	BU
1992	—	—	—	—	30.00	35.00

KM# 178 CROWN

Copper-Nickel, 38.8 mm. **Ruler:** Elizabeth II **Subject:** Gibraltar City Charter **Obv:** Crowned bust right **Rev:** Bust left at right, building at left

Date	Mintage	F	VF	XF	Unc	BU
1992	—	—	—	—	5.00	6.50

KM# 178a CROWN

28.2800 g., 0.9250 Silver .8411 oz. ASW, 38.8 mm. **Ruler:** Elizabeth II **Subject:** Gibraltar City Charter **Obv:** Crowned bust right **Rev:** Bust left at right, building at left

Date	Mintage	F	VF	XF	Unc	BU
1992 Proof	Est. 30,000	Value: 35.00				

KM# 113 CROWN

Copper-Nickel, 38.8 mm. **Ruler:** Elizabeth II **Series:** WWII Warships **Obv:** Crowned bust right **Rev:** USS Philadelphia

Date	Mintage	F	VF	XF	Unc	BU
1993	—	—	—	—	4.00	5.00

KM# 113a CROWN

28.2800 g., 0.9250 Silver .8411 oz. ASW, 38.8 mm. **Ruler:** Elizabeth II **Series:** WWII Warships **Obv:** Crowned bust right **Rev:** USS Philadelphia

Date	Mintage	F	VF	XF	Unc	BU
1993 Proof	Est. 30,000	Value: 26.50				

KM# 114 CROWN

Copper-Nickel, 38.8 mm. **Ruler:** Elizabeth II **Series:** WWII Warships **Obv:** Crowned bust right **Rev:** USS McLanahan

Date	Mintage	F	VF	XF	Unc	BU
1993	—	—	—	—	4.00	5.00

KM# 114a CROWN

28.2800 g., 0.9250 Silver .8411 oz. ASW, 38.8 mm. **Ruler:** Elizabeth II **Series:** WWII Warships **Obv:** Crowned bust right **Rev:** USS McLanahan

Date	Mintage	F	VF	XF	Unc	BU
1993 Proof	Est. 30,000	Value: 26.50				

KM# 115 CROWN

Copper-Nickel, 38.8 mm. **Ruler:** Elizabeth II **Series:** WWII Warships **Obv:** Crowned bust right **Rev:** HNLMS Isaac Sweers

Date	Mintage	F	VF	XF	Unc	BU
1993	—	—	—	—	4.00	5.00

KM# 115a CROWN

28.2800 g., 0.9250 Silver .8411 oz. ASW, 38.8 mm. **Ruler:** Elizabeth II **Series:** WWII Warships **Obv:** Crowned bust right **Rev:** HNLMS Isaac Sweers

Date	Mintage	F	VF	XF	Unc	BU
1993 Proof	Est. 30,000	Value: 26.50				

KM# 116 CROWN

Copper-Nickel, 38.8 mm. **Ruler:** Elizabeth II **Series:** WWII Warships **Obv:** Crowned bust right **Rev:** USS Weehawken

Date	Mintage	F	VF	XF	Unc	BU
1993	—	—	—	—	4.00	5.00

KM# 116a CROWN

28.2800 g., 0.9250 Silver .8411 oz. ASW, 38.8 mm. **Ruler:** Elizabeth II **Series:** WWII Warships **Obv:** Crowned bust right **Rev:** USS Weehawken

Date	Mintage	F	VF	XF	Unc	BU
1993 Proof	Est. 30,000	Value: 26.50				

KM# 117 CROWN

Copper-Nickel, 38.8 mm. **Ruler:** Elizabeth II **Series:** WWII Warships **Obv:** Crowned bust right **Rev:** HMS Warspite

Date	Mintage	F	VF	XF	Unc	BU
1993	—	—	—	—	4.00	5.00

KM# 117a CROWN

28.2800 g., 0.9250 Silver .8411 oz. ASW, 38.8 mm. **Ruler:** Elizabeth II **Series:** WWII Warships **Obv:** Crowned bust right **Rev:** HMS Warspite

Date	Mintage	F	VF	XF	Unc	BU
1993 Proof	Est. 30,000	Value: 26.50				

KM# 118 CROWN

Copper-Nickel, 38.8 mm. **Ruler:** Elizabeth II **Series:** WWII Warships **Obv:** Crowned bust right **Rev:** HMS Hood

Date	Mintage	F	VF	XF	Unc	BU
1993	—	—	—	—	4.00	5.00

KM# 118a CROWN

28.2800 g., 0.9250 Silver .8411 oz. ASW, 38.8 mm. **Ruler:** Elizabeth II **Series:** WWII Warships **Obv:** Crowned bust right **Rev:** HMS Hood

Date	Mintage	F	VF	XF	Unc	BU
1993 Proof	Est. 30,000	Value: 26.50				

KM# 119 CROWN

Copper-Nickel, 38.8 mm. **Ruler:** Elizabeth II **Series:** WWII Warships **Obv:** Crowned bust right **Rev:** HMS Penelope

Date	Mintage	F	VF	XF	Unc	BU
1993	—	—	—	—	4.00	5.00

KM# 119a CROWN

28.2800 g., 0.9250 Silver .8411 oz. ASW, 38.8 mm. **Ruler:** Elizabeth II **Series:** WWII Warships **Obv:** Crowned bust right **Rev:** HMS Penelope

Date	Mintage	F	VF	XF	Unc	BU
1993 Proof	Est. 30,000	Value: 26.50				

KM# 120 CROWN

Copper-Nickel, 38.8 mm. **Ruler:** Elizabeth II **Series:** WWII Warships **Obv:** Crowned bust right **Rev:** HMCS Prescott

Date	Mintage	F	VF	XF	Unc	BU
1993	—	—	—	—	4.00	5.00

KM# 120a CROWN

28.2800 g., 0.9250 Silver .8411 oz. ASW, 38.8 mm. **Ruler:** Elizabeth II **Series:** WWII Warships **Obv:** Crowned bust right **Rev:** HMCS Prescott

Date	Mintage	F	VF	XF	Unc	BU
1993 Proof	Est. 30,000	Value: 26.50				

KM# 121 CROWN

Copper-Nickel, 38.8 mm. **Ruler:** Elizabeth II **Series:** WWII Warships **Obv:** Crowned bust right **Rev:** HMS Ark Royal

Date	Mintage	F	VF	XF	Unc	BU
1993	—	—	—	—	4.00	5.00

KM# 121a CROWN

28.2800 g., 0.9250 Silver .8411 oz. ASW, 38.8 mm. **Ruler:** Elizabeth II **Series:** WWII Warships **Obv:** Crowned bust right **Rev:** HMS Ark Royal

Date	Mintage	F	VF	XF	Unc	BU
1993 Proof	Est. 30,000	Value: 26.50				

KM# 122 CROWN

Copper-Nickel, 38.8 mm. **Ruler:** Elizabeth II **Series:** WWII Warships **Obv:** Crowned bust right **Rev:** USS Gleaves

Date	Mintage	F	VF	XF	Unc	BU
1993	—	—	—	—	4.00	5.00

KM# 122a CROWN

28.2800 g., 0.9250 Silver .8411 oz. ASW, 38.8 mm. **Ruler:** Elizabeth II **Series:** WWII Warships **Obv:** Crowned bust right **Rev:** USS Gleaves

Date	Mintage	F	VF	XF	Unc	BU
1993 Proof	Est. 30,000	Value: 26.50				

KM# 123 CROWN

Copper-Nickel, 38.8 mm. **Ruler:** Elizabeth II **Series:** WWII Warships **Obv:** Crowned bust right **Rev:** HMAS Waterhen

Date	Mintage	F	VF	XF	Unc	BU
1993	—	—	—	—	4.00	5.00

KM# 123a CROWN

28.2800 g., 0.9250 Silver .8411 oz. ASW, 38.8 mm. **Ruler:** Elizabeth II **Series:** WWII Warships **Obv:** Crowned bust right **Rev:** HMAS Waterhen

Date	Mintage	F	VF	XF	Unc	BU
1993 Proof	Est. 30,000	Value: 26.50				

KM# 132 CROWN

Copper-Nickel, 38.8 mm. **Ruler:** Elizabeth II **Series:** House of - Stuart **Subject:** Queen Anne, 1702-1714 **Obv:** Young bust right **Rev:** Bust left

Date	Mintage	F	VF	XF	Unc	BU
1993 Prooflike	—	—	—	—	4.00	5.00

KM# 132a CROWN

28.2800 g., 0.9250 Silver .8411 oz. ASW, 38.8 mm. **Ruler:** Elizabeth II **Series:** House of - Stuart **Subject:** Queen Anne, 1702-1714 **Obv:** Young bust right **Rev:** Bust left

Date	Mintage	F	VF	XF	Unc	BU
1993 Proof	Est. 30,000	Value: 35.00				

KM# 133 CROWN

Copper-Nickel, 38.8 mm. **Ruler:** Elizabeth II **Series:** House of - Hanover **Subject:** King GeorgeI, 1714-1727 **Obv:** Young bust right **Rev:** Laureate bust right

Date	Mintage	F	VF	XF	Unc	BU
1993 Prooflike	—	—	—	—	4.00	5.00

KM# 133a CROWN

28.2800 g., 0.9250 Silver .8411 oz. ASW, 38.8 mm. **Ruler:** Elizabeth II **Series:** House of - Hanover **Subject:** King George I, 1714-1727 **Obv:** Young bust right **Rev:** Laureate bust right

Date	Mintage	F	VF	XF	Unc	BU
1993 Proof	Est. 30,000	Value: 35.00				

KM# 134 CROWN

Copper-Nickel, 38.8 mm. **Ruler:** Elizabeth II **Series:** House of - Hanover **Subject:** King George II, 1727-1760 **Obv:** Young bust right **Rev:** Uniformed bust left

Date	Mintage	F	VF	XF	Unc	BU
1993 Prooflike	—	—	—	—	4.00	5.00

KM# 134a CROWN

28.2800 g., 0.9250 Silver .8411 oz. ASW, 38.8 mm. **Ruler:** Elizabeth II **Series:** House of - Hanover **Subject:** King George II, 1727-1760 **Obv:** Young bust right **Rev:** Uniformed bust left

Date	Mintage	F	VF	XF	Unc	BU
1993 Proof	Est. 30,000	Value: 32.50				

KM# 135 CROWN

Copper-Nickel, 38.8 mm. **Ruler:** Elizabeth II **Series:** House of - Hanover **Subject:** King George III, 1760-1820 **Obv:** Young bust right **Rev:** Bust right

Date	Mintage	F	VF	XF	Unc	BU
1993 Prooflike	—	—	—	—	4.00	5.00

KM# 135a CROWN

28.2800 g., 0.9250 Silver .8411 oz. ASW, 38.8 mm. **Ruler:** Elizabeth II **Series:** House of - Hanover **Subject:** King George III, 1760-1820 **Obv:** Young bust right **Rev:** Bust right

Date	Mintage	F	VF	XF	Unc	BU
1993 Proof	Est. 30,000	Value: 32.50				

KM# 136 CROWN

Copper-Nickel, 38.8 mm. **Ruler:** Elizabeth II **Series:** House of - Hanover **Subject:** King George IV, 1820-1830 **Obv:** Young bust right **Rev:** Bust left

Date	Mintage	F	VF	XF	Unc	BU
1993 Prooflike	—	—	—	—	4.00	5.00

KM# 136a CROWN

28.2800 g., 0.9250 Silver .8411 oz. ASW, 38.8 mm. **Ruler:** Elizabeth II **Series:** House of - Hanover **Subject:** King George IV, 1820-1830 **Obv:** Young bust right **Rev:** Bust left

Date	Mintage	F	VF	XF	Unc	BU
1993 Proof	Est. 30,000	Value: 35.00				

KM# 137 CROWN

Copper-Nickel, 38.8 mm. **Ruler:** Elizabeth II **Series:** House of - Hanover **Subject:** King William IV, 1830-1837 **Obv:** Young bust right **Rev:** Bust right

Date	Mintage	F	VF	XF	Unc	BU
1993 Prooflike	—	—	—	—	4.00	5.00

KM# 137a CROWN

28.2800 g., 0.9250 Silver .8411 oz. ASW, 38.8 mm. **Ruler:** Elizabeth II **Series:** House of - Hanover **Subject:** King William IV, 1830-1837 **Obv:** Young bust right **Rev:** Bust right

Date	Mintage	F	VF	XF	Unc	BU
1993 Proof	Est. 30,000	Value: 35.00				

KM# 138 CROWN

Copper-Nickel, 38.8 mm. **Ruler:** Elizabeth II **Series:** House of - Hanover **Subject:** Queen Victoria, 1837-1901 **Obv:** Young bust right **Rev:** Bust left

Date	Mintage	F	VF	XF	Unc	BU
1993 Prooflike	—	—	—	—	4.00	5.00

KM# 138a CROWN

28.2800 g., 0.9250 Silver .8411 oz. ASW, 38.8 mm. **Ruler:** Elizabeth II **Series:** House of - Hanover **Subject:** Queen Victoria, 1837-1901 **Obv:** Young bust right **Rev:** Bust left

Date	Mintage	F	VF	XF	Unc	BU
1993 Proof	Est. 30,000	Value: 35.00				

KM# 139 CROWN

Copper-Nickel, 38.8 mm. **Ruler:** Elizabeth II **Series:** House of - Saxe-Coburg **Subject:** King Edward VII, 1901-1910 **Obv:** Young bust right **Rev:** Uniformed bust right

Date	Mintage	F	VF	XF	Unc	BU
1993 Prooflike	—	—	—	—	4.00	5.00

KM# 139a CROWN

28.2800 g., 0.9250 Silver .8411 oz. ASW, 38.8 mm. **Ruler:** Elizabeth II **Series:** House of - Saxe-Coburg **Subject:** King Edward VII, 1901-1910 **Obv:** Young bust right **Rev:** Uniformed bust right

Date	Mintage	F	VF	XF	Unc	BU
1993 Proof	Est. 30,000	Value: 37.50				

KM# 140 CROWN

Copper-Nickel, 38.8 mm. **Ruler:** Elizabeth II **Series:** House of - Windsor **Subject:** King George V, 1910-1936 **Obv:** Young bust right **Rev:** Uniformed bust left

Date	Mintage	F	VF	XF	Unc	BU
1993 Prooflike	—	—	—	—	4.00	5.00

KM# 140a CROWN

28.2800 g., 0.9250 Silver .8411 oz. ASW, 38.8 mm. **Ruler:** Elizabeth II **Series:** House of - Windsor **Subject:** King George V, 1910-1936 **Obv:** Young bust right **Rev:** Uniformed bust left

Date	Mintage	F	VF	XF	Unc	BU
1993 Proof	Est. 30,000	Value: 35.00				

KM# 141 CROWN

Copper-Nickel, 38.8 mm. **Ruler:** Elizabeth II **Series:** House of - Windsor **Subject:** King Edward VIII, 1936 **Obv:** Young bust right **Rev:** Bust left

Date	Mintage	F	VF	XF	Unc	BU
1993 Prooflike	—	—	—	—	4.00	5.00

KM# 141a CROWN

28.2800 g., 0.9250 Silver .8411 oz. ASW, 38.8 mm. **Ruler:** Elizabeth II **Series:** House of - Windsor **Subject:** King Edward VIII, 1936 **Obv:** Young bust right **Rev:** Bust left

Date	Mintage	F	VF	XF	Unc	BU
1993 Proof	Est. 30,000	Value: 35.00				

KM# 142 CROWN

Copper-Nickel, 38.8 mm. **Ruler:** Elizabeth II **Series:** House of - Windsor **Subject:** King George VI, 1936-1952 **Obv:** Young bust right **Rev:** Bust left

Date	Mintage	F	VF	XF	Unc	BU
1993 Prooflike	—	—	—	—	4.00	5.00

KM# 142a CROWN

28.2800 g., 0.9250 Silver .8411 oz. ASW, 38.8 mm. **Ruler:** Elizabeth II **Series:** House of - Windsor **Subject:** King George VI, 1936-1952 **Obv:** Young bust right **Rev:** Bust left

Date	Mintage	F	VF	XF	Unc	BU
1993 Proof	Est. 30,000	Value: 35.00				

KM# 143 CROWN

Copper-Nickel, 38.8 mm. **Ruler:** Elizabeth II **Subject:** Coronation of Queen Elizabeth II **Rev:** Crowned half figure left with scepter divides dates

Date	Mintage	F	VF	XF	Unc	BU
1993	—	—	—	—	4.00	5.00

KM# 143a CROWN

28.2800 g., 0.9250 Silver .8411 oz. ASW **Subject:** Coronation of Queen Elizabeth II **Rev:** Crowned half figure left with scepter divides dates

Date	Mintage	F	VF	XF	Unc	BU
1993 Proof	Est. 30,000	Value: 35.00				

KM# 144 CROWN

Copper-Nickel, 38.8 mm. **Ruler:** Elizabeth II **Series:** WWII Warships **Obv:** Crowned bust right **Rev:** FSS Savorgnan de Brazza

Date	Mintage	F	VF	XF	Unc	BU
1993	—	—	—	—	4.00	5.00

KM# 144a CROWN

28.2800 g., 0.9250 Silver .8411 oz. ASW, 38.8 mm. **Ruler:** Elizabeth II **Subject:** WWII Warships **Obv:** Crowned bust right **Rev:** FSS Savorgnan de Brazza

Date	Mintage	F	VF	XF	Unc	BU
1993 Proof	Est. 30,000	Value: 26.50				

KM# 145 CROWN

Copper-Nickel, 38.8 mm. **Ruler:** Elizabeth II **Series:** XVII Winter Olympics **Rev:** Skaters

Date	Mintage	F	VF	XF	Unc	BU
1993 Proof	—	Value: 5.00				

KM# 145a CROWN

28.2800 g., 0.9250 Silver .8411 oz. ASW, 38.8 mm. **Ruler:** Elizabeth II **Series:** XVII Winter Olympics **Rev:** Skaters

Date	Mintage	F	VF	XF	Unc	BU
1993 Proof	Est. 30,000	Value: 35.00				

KM# 145b CROWN

6.2200 g., 0.9999 Gold .2000 oz. AGW **Ruler:** Elizabeth II **Series:** XVII Winter Olympics **Rev:** Skaters

Date	Mintage	F	VF	XF	Unc	BU
1993 Proof	Est. 5,000	Value: 200				

KM# 146 CROWN

Copper-Nickel, 38.8 mm. **Ruler:** Elizabeth II **Series:** XVII Winter Olympics **Rev:** Ice hockey

Date	Mintage	F	VF	XF	Unc	BU
1993 Proof	—	Value: 5.00				

KM# 146a CROWN

28.2800 g., 0.9250 Silver .8411 oz. ASW, 38.8 mm. **Ruler:** Elizabeth II **Series:** XVII Winter Olympics **Rev:** Ice hockey

Date	Mintage	F	VF	XF	Unc	BU
1993 Proof	Est. 30,000	Value: 35.00				

KM# 146b CROWN

6.2200 g., 0.9999 Gold .2000 oz. AGW **Ruler:** Elizabeth II **Series:** XVII Winter Olympics **Rev:** Ice hockey

Date	Mintage	F	VF	XF	Unc	BU
1993 Proof	Est. 5,000	Value: 200				

KM# 147 CROWN

Copper-Nickel, 38.8 mm. **Ruler:** Elizabeth II **Series:** XVII Winter Olympics **Rev:** Bobsledding

Date	Mintage	F	VF	XF	Unc	BU
1993 Proof	—	Value: 5.00				

KM# 147a CROWN

28.2800 g., 0.9250 Silver .8411 oz. ASW, 38.8 mm. **Ruler:** Elizabeth II **Series:** XVII Winter Olympics **Rev:** Bobsledding

Date	Mintage	F	VF	XF	Unc	BU
1993 Proof	Est. 30,000	Value: 35.00				

KM# 147b CROWN

6.2200 g., 0.9999 Gold .2000 oz. AGW **Ruler:** Elizabeth II **Series:** XVII Winter Olympics **Rev:** Bobsledding

Date	Mintage	F	VF	XF	Unc	BU
1993 Proof	Est. 5,000	Value: 200				

KM# 148 CROWN

Copper-Nickel, 38.8 mm. **Ruler:** Elizabeth II **Series:** XVII Winter Olympics **Rev:** Skiers

Date	Mintage	F	VF	XF	Unc	BU
1993 Proof	—	Value: 5.00				

KM# 148a CROWN

28.2800 g., 0.9250 Silver .8411 oz. ASW, 38.8 mm. **Ruler:** Elizabeth II **Series:** XVII Winter Olympics **Rev:** Skiers

Date	Mintage	F	VF	XF	Unc	BU
1993 Proof	Est. 30,000	Value: 35.00				

KM# 148b CROWN

6.2200 g., 0.9999 Gold .2000 oz. AGW **Ruler:** Elizabeth II **Rev:** XVII Winter Olympics

Date	Mintage	F	VF	XF	Unc	BU
1993 Proof	Est. 5,000	Value: 200				

KM# 149 CROWN

Copper-Nickel, 38.8 mm. **Ruler:** Elizabeth II **Series:** Preserve Planet Earth **Obv:** Crowned bust right **Rev:** Cetiosaurus

Date	Mintage	F	VF	XF	Unc	BU
1993	—	—	—	—	10.00	12.00

KM# 149a CROWN

28.2800 g., 0.9250 Silver .8411 oz. ASW, 38.8 mm. **Ruler:** Elizabeth II **Series:** Preserve Planet Earth **Obv:** Crowned bust right **Rev:** Cetiosaurus

Date	Mintage	F	VF	XF	Unc	BU
1993 Proof	Est. 30,000	Value: 35.00				

KM# 151 CROWN

Copper-Nickel, 38.8 mm. **Ruler:** Elizabeth II **Series:** Preserve Planet Earth **Obv:** Crowned bust right **Rev:** Stegosaurus

Date	Mintage	F	VF	XF	Unc	BU
1993	—	—	—	—	10.00	12.00

KM# 151a CROWN

28.2800 g., 0.9250 Silver .8411 oz. ASW, 38.8 mm. **Ruler:** Elizabeth II **Series:** Preserve Planet Earth **Obv:** Crowned bust right **Rev:** Stegosaurus

Date	Mintage	F	VF	XF	Unc	BU
1993 Proof	Est. 30,000	Value: 35.00				

KM# 180 CROWN

Copper-Nickel, 38.8 mm. **Ruler:** Elizabeth II **Series:** International Friendship **Obv:** Crowned bust right **Rev:** Stylized panda

Date	Mintage	F	VF	XF	Unc	BU
1993	—	—	—	—	8.50	12.00

KM# 180a CROWN

28.2800 g., 0.9250 Silver .8411 oz. ASW, 38.8 mm. **Ruler:** Elizabeth II **Series:** International Friendship **Obv:** Crowned bust right **Rev:** Stylized panda

Date	Mintage	F	VF	XF	Unc	BU
1993 Proof	Est. 30,000	Value: 35.00				

KM# 184 CROWN

Copper-Nickel, 38.8 mm. **Ruler:** Elizabeth II **Series:** International Friendship **Obv:** Crowned bust right **Rev:** Natural panda

Date	Mintage	F	VF	XF	Unc	BU
1993	—	—	—	—	8.50	12.00

KM# 184a CROWN

28.2800 g., 0.9250 Silver .8411 oz. ASW, 38.8 mm. **Ruler:** Elizabeth II **Series:** International Friendship **Obv:** Crowned bust right **Rev:** Natural panda

Date	Mintage	F	VF	XF	Unc	BU
1993 Proof	Est. 30,000	Value: 35.00				

KM# 188 CROWN

Copper-Nickel, 38.8 mm. **Ruler:** Elizabeth II **Series:** International Friendship **Subject:** General Sikorski **Obv:** Crowned bust right **Rev:** Uniformed bust above plane, mountains in background

Date	Mintage	F	VF	XF	Unc	BU
1993	—	—	—	—	5.00	6.50

KM# 188a CROWN

28.2800 g., 0.9250 Silver .8411 oz. ASW, 38.8 mm. **Ruler:** Elizabeth II **Series:** International Friendship **Subject:** General Sikorski **Obv:** Crowned bust right **Rev:** Uniformed bust above plane, mountains in background

Date	Mintage	F	VF	XF	Unc	BU
1993 Proof	Est. 30,000	Value: 35.00				

KM# 192.1 CROWN

Copper-Nickel, 38.8 mm. **Ruler:** Elizabeth II **Obv:** Crowned bust right **Rev:** Long-haired Dachshund

Date	Mintage	F	VF	XF	Unc	BU
1993	—	—	—	—	10.00	15.00

KM# 192.1a CROWN

31.1030 g., 0.9250 Silver 1.0000 oz. ASW **Ruler:** Elizabeth II **Obv:** Crowned bust right **Rev:** Long-haired Dachshund

Date	Mintage	F	VF	XF	Unc	BU
1993 Proof	Est. 50,000	Value: 30.00				

KM# 192.2 CROWN

Copper-Nickel, 38.8 mm. **Ruler:** Elizabeth II **Obv:** Crowned bust right **Rev:** Long-haired Dachshund, mint mark left of dog

Date	Mintage	F	VF	XF	Unc	BU
1993(c)	—	—	—	—	10.00	14.00

KM# 192.2a CROWN

28.2800 g., 0.9250 Silver .8411 oz. ASW **Ruler:** Elizabeth II **Obv:** Crowned bust right **Rev:** Mint mark left of dog

Date	Mintage	F	VF	XF	Unc	BU
1993	—	—	—	—	27.50	30.00

KM# 200 CROWN

Copper-Nickel, 38.8 mm. **Ruler:** Elizabeth II **Subject:** Dependent Territories Conference **Obv:** Crowned bust right **Rev:** Two shields at center surrounded by five shields

Date	Mintage	F	VF	XF	Unc	BU
1993	—	—	—	—	5.50	7.00

KM# 200a CROWN

28.2800 g., 0.9250 Silver .8411 oz. ASW, 38.8 mm. **Ruler:** Elizabeth II **Subject:** Dependent Territories Conference **Obv:** Crowned bust right **Rev:** Two center shields surrounded by five shields

Date	Mintage	F	VF	XF	Unc	BU
1993 Proof	Est. 30,000	Value: 35.00				

KM# 201 CROWN

Copper-Nickel, 38.8 mm. **Ruler:** Elizabeth II **Series:** Peter Rabbit Centennial **Subject:** The Tale of Peter Rabbit **Obv:** Crowned bust right **Rev:** Peter Rabbit, sparrow on handle

Date	Mintage	F	VF	XF	Unc	BU
1993	—	—	—	—	7.50	9.00

KM# 201a CROWN

28.2800 g., 0.9250 Silver .8411 oz. ASW, 38.8 mm. **Ruler:** Elizabeth II **Series:** Peter Rabbit Centennial **Subject:** The Tale of Peter Rabbit **Obv:** Crowned bust right **Rev:** Peter Rabbit, sparrow on handle

Date	Mintage	F	VF	XF	Unc	BU
1993 Proof	Est. 30,000	Value: 37.50				

KM# 205 CROWN

Copper-Nickel, 38.8 mm. **Ruler:** Elizabeth II **Series:** Peter Rabbit Centennial **Subject:** The Tale of Peter Rabbit **Obv:** Crowned bust right **Rev:** Mrs. Tiggy-Winkel ironing

Date	Mintage	F	VF	XF	Unc	BU
1993	—	—	—	—	7.50	9.00

KM# 205a CROWN

28.2800 g., 0.9250 Silver .8411 oz. ASW, 38.8 mm. **Ruler:** Elizabeth II **Series:** Peter Rabbit Centennial **Subject:** The Tale of Peter Rabbit **Obv:** Crowned bust right **Rev:** Mrs. Tiggy-Winkel ironing

Date	Mintage	F	VF	XF	Unc	BU
1993 Proof	Est. 30,000	Value: 25.00				

KM# 209 CROWN

Copper-Nickel, 38.8 mm. **Ruler:** Elizabeth II **Series:** Peter Rabbit Centennial **Subject:** The Tale of Peter Rabbit **Obv:** Crowned bust right **Rev:** Jeremy Fisher fishing

Date	Mintage	F	VF	XF	Unc	BU
1993	—	—	—	—	7.50	9.00

KM# 209a CROWN

28.2800 g., 0.9250 Silver .8411 oz. ASW, 38.8 mm. **Ruler:** Elizabeth II **Series:** Peter Rabbit Centennial **Subject:** The Tale of Peter Rabbit **Obv:** Crowned bust right **Rev:** Jeremy Fisher fishing

Date	Mintage	F	VF	XF	Unc	BU
1993 Proof	Est. 30,000	Value: 25.00				

KM# 213 CROWN

Copper-Nickel, 38.8 mm. **Ruler:** Elizabeth II **Series:** Peter Rabbit Centennial **Subject:** The Tale of Peter Rabbit **Obv:** Crowned bust right **Rev:** Tom Kitten with mother cat

Date	Mintage	F	VF	XF	Unc	BU
1993	—	—	—	—	7.50	9.00

KM# 213a CROWN

28.2800 g., 0.9250 Silver .8411 oz. ASW, 38.8 mm. **Ruler:** Elizabeth II **Series:** Peter Rabbit Centennial **Subject:** The Tale of Peter Rabbit **Obv:** Crowned bust right **Rev:** Tom Kitten with mother cat

Date	Mintage	F	VF	XF	Unc	BU
1993 Proof	Est. 30,000	Value: 25.00				

KM# 217 CROWN

Copper-Nickel, 38.8 mm. **Ruler:** Elizabeth II **Series:** Peter Rabbit Centennial **Subject:** The Tale of Peter Rabbit **Obv:** Crowned bust right **Rev:** Benjamin Bunny with hat, holding coat

Date	Mintage	F	VF	XF	Unc	BU
1993	—	—	—	—	7.50	9.00

KM# 217a CROWN

28.2800 g., 0.9250 Silver .8411 oz. ASW, 38.8 mm. **Ruler:** Elizabeth II **Series:** Peter Rabbit Centennial **Subject:** The Tale of Peter Rabbit **Obv:** Crowned bust right **Rev:** Benjamin Bunny with hat holding coat

Date	Mintage	F	VF	XF	Unc	BU
1993 Proof	Est. 30,000	Value: 25.00				

KM# 221 CROWN

Copper-Nickel, 38.8 mm. **Ruler:** Elizabeth II **Series:** Peter Rabbit Centennial **Subject:** The Tale of Peter Rabbit **Obv:** Crowned bust right **Rev:** Jemima Puddle-Duck talking to fox

Date	Mintage	F	VF	XF	Unc	BU
1993	—	—	—	—	7.50	9.00

KM# 221a CROWN

28.2800 g., 0.9250 Silver .8411 oz. ASW, 38.8 mm. **Ruler:** Elizabeth II **Series:** Peter Rabbit Centennial **Subject:** The Tale of Peter Rabbit **Obv:** Crowned bust right **Rev:** Jemima Puddle-Duck talking to fox

Date	Mintage	F	VF	XF	Unc	BU
1993 Proof	Est. 30,000	Value: 25.00				

KM# 342C CROWN

Copper-Nickel, 38.8 mm. **Ruler:** Elizabeth II **Subject:** Year of the Cockerel **Obv:** Crowned bust right **Rev:** Cockerel (rooster)

Date	Mintage	F	VF	XF	Unc	BU
1993	—	—	—	—	9.00	—

KM# 225 CROWN

Copper-Nickel, 38.8 mm. **Ruler:** Elizabeth II **Subject:** World Cup Soccer **Obv:** Crowned bust right **Rev:** Three players

Date	Mintage	F	VF	XF	Unc	BU
1994	—	—	—	—	4.75	6.00

KM# 225a CROWN

28.2800 g., 0.9250 Silver .8411 oz. ASW, 38.8 mm. **Ruler:** Elizabeth II **Subject:** World Cup Soccer **Obv:** Crowned bust right **Rev:** Three players

Date	Mintage	F	VF	XF	Unc	BU
1994 Proof	Est. 30,000	Value: 30.00				

KM# 227 CROWN

Copper-Nickel, 38.8 mm. **Ruler:** Elizabeth II **Subject:** World Cup Soccer **Obv:** Crowned bust right **Rev:** Two players

Date	Mintage	F	VF	XF	Unc	BU
1994	—	—	—	—	4.75	6.00

KM# 227a CROWN

28.2800 g., 0.9250 Silver .8411 oz. ASW, 38.8 mm. **Ruler:** Elizabeth II **Subject:** World Cup Soccer **Obv:** Crowned bust right **Rev:** Two players facing

Date	Mintage	F	VF	XF	Unc	BU
1994 Proof	Est. 30,000	Value: 30.00				

KM# 229 CROWN

Copper-Nickel, 38.8 mm. **Ruler:** Elizabeth II **Subject:** World Cup Soccer **Obv:** Crowned bust right **Rev:** Goalie and scorer

Date	Mintage	F	VF	XF	Unc	BU
1994	—	—	—	—	4.75	6.00

KM# 229a CROWN

28.2800 g., 0.9250 Silver .8411 oz. ASW, 38.8 mm. **Ruler:** Elizabeth II **Subject:** World Cup Soccer **Obv:** Crowned bust right **Rev:** Goalie and scorer

Date	Mintage	F	VF	XF	Unc	BU
1994 Proof	Est. 30,000	Value: 30.00				

KM# 231 CROWN

Copper-Nickel, 38.8 mm. **Ruler:** Elizabeth II **Subject:** World Cup Soccer **Obv:** Crowned bust right **Rev:** One player

Date	Mintage	F	VF	XF	Unc	BU
1994	—	—	—	—	4.75	6.00

KM# 231a CROWN

28.2800 g., 0.9250 Silver .8411 oz. ASW, 38.8 mm. **Ruler:** Elizabeth II **Subject:** World Cup Soccer **Obv:** Crowned bust right **Rev:** One player

Date	Mintage	F	VF	XF	Unc	BU
1994	Est. 30,000	Value: 30.00				

KM# 233 CROWN

Copper-Nickel, 38.8 mm. **Ruler:** Elizabeth II **Subject:** World Cup Soccer **Obv:** Crowned bust right **Rev:** Two players, one kicking

Date	Mintage	F	VF	XF	Unc	BU
1994	—	—	—	—	4.75	6.00

KM# 233a CROWN

28.2800 g., 0.9250 Silver .8411 oz. ASW, 38.8 mm. **Ruler:** Elizabeth II **Subject:** World Cup Soccer **Obv:** Crowned bust right **Rev:** Two players, one kicking

Date	Mintage	F	VF	XF	Unc	BU
1994 Proof	Est. 30,000	Value: 30.00				

KM# 235 CROWN

Copper-Nickel, 38.8 mm. **Ruler:** Elizabeth II **Subject:** World Cup Soccer **Obv:** Crowned bust right **Rev:** Two players sideways

Date	Mintage	F	VF	XF	Unc	BU
1994	—	—	—	—	4.75	6.00

KM# 235a CROWN

28.2800 g., 0.9250 Silver .8411 oz. ASW, 38.8 mm. **Ruler:** Elizabeth II **Subject:** World Cup Soccer **Obv:** Crowned bust right **Rev:** Two players sideways

Date	Mintage	F	VF	XF	Unc	BU
1994 Proof	Est. 30,000	Value: 30.00				

KM# 239 CROWN

Copper-Nickel, 38.8 mm. **Ruler:** Elizabeth II **Series:** Preserve Planet Earth **Obv:** Crowned bust right **Rev:** Sabre-tooth Tiger

Date	Mintage	F	VF	XF	Unc	BU
1994	—	—	—	—	7.00	9.00

KM# 239a CROWN

28.2800 g., 0.9250 Silver .8411 oz. ASW, 38.8 mm. **Ruler:** Elizabeth II **Series:** Preserve Planet Earth **Obv:** Crowned bust right **Rev:** Sabre-tooth Tiger

Date	Mintage	F	VF	XF	Unc	BU
1994 Proof	Est. 30,000	Value: 35.00				

KM# 241 CROWN

Copper-Nickel, 38.8 mm. **Ruler:** Elizabeth II **Series:** Preserve Planet Earth **Obv:** Crowned bust right **Rev:** Spanish Eagle

Date	Mintage	F	VF	XF	Unc	BU
1994	—	—	—	—	9.00	12.00

KM# 241a CROWN

28.2800 g., 0.9250 Silver .8411 oz. ASW **Series:** Preserve Planet Earth **Obv:** Crowned bust right **Rev:** Spanish Eagle

Date	Mintage	F	VF	XF	Unc	BU
1994 Proof	Est. 30,000	Value: 37.50				

KM# 243 CROWN

Copper-Nickel, 38.8 mm. **Ruler:** Elizabeth II **Series:** Preserve Planet Earth **Obv:** Crowned bust right **Rev:** Striped Dolphins

Date	Mintage	F	VF	XF	Unc	BU
1994	—	—	—	—	9.00	12.00

KM# 243a CROWN

28.2800 g., 0.9250 Silver .8411 oz. ASW, 38.8 mm. **Ruler:** Elizabeth II **Series:** Preserve Planet Earth **Obv:** Crowned bust right **Rev:** Striped Dolphins

Date	Mintage	F	VF	XF	Unc	BU
1994 Proof	Est. 30,000	Value: 37.50				

KM# 245 CROWN

Copper-Nickel, 38.8 mm. **Ruler:** Elizabeth II **Series:** Preserve Planet Earth **Obv:** Crowned bust right **Rev:** African Elephants

Date	Mintage	F	VF	XF	Unc	BU
1994	—	—	—	—	9.00	12.00

KM# 245a CROWN

28.2800 g., 0.9250 Silver .8411 oz. ASW, 38.8 mm. **Ruler:** Elizabeth II **Series:** Preserve Planet Earth **Obv:** Crowned bust right **Rev:** African Elephants

Date	Mintage	F	VF	XF	Unc	BU
1994 Proof	Est. 30,000	Value: 37.50				

KM# 259 CROWN

Copper-Nickel, 38.8 mm. **Ruler:** Elizabeth II **Series:** World War II **Obv:** Crowned bust right **Rev:** Maltese convoy

Date	Mintage	F	VF	XF	Unc	BU
1994	—	—	—	—	6.00	8.00

KM# 259a CROWN

28.2800 g., 0.9250 Silver .8411 oz. ASW, 38.8 mm. **Ruler:** Elizabeth II **Series:** World War II **Obv:** Crowned bust right **Rev:** Maltese convoy

Date	Mintage	F	VF	XF	Unc	BU
1994 Proof	Est. 30,000	Value: 32.50				

KM# 260 CROWN

Copper-Nickel, 38.8 mm. **Ruler:** Elizabeth II **Series:** World War II **Obv:** Crowned bust right **Rev:** Squadron 202 in Gibraltar

Date	Mintage	F	VF	XF	Unc	BU
1994	—	—	—	—	6.00	8.00

KM# 260a CROWN

28.2800 g., 0.9250 Silver .8411 oz. ASW, 38.8 mm. **Ruler:** Elizabeth II **Series:** World War II **Obv:** Crowned bust right **Rev:** Squadron 202 in Gibraltar

Date	Mintage	F	VF	XF	Unc	BU
1994 Proof	Est. 30,000	Value: 32.50				

KM# 261 CROWN

Copper-Nickel, 38.8 mm. **Ruler:** Elizabeth II **Series:** World War II **Obv:** Crowned bust right **Rev:** Admiral Somerville

Date	Mintage	F	VF	XF	Unc	BU
1994	—	—	—	—	6.00	8.00

KM# 261a CROWN

28.2800 g., 0.9250 Silver .8411 oz. ASW, 38.8 mm. **Ruler:** Elizabeth II **Series:** World War II **Obv:** Crowned bust right **Rev:** Admiral Somerville

Date	Mintage	F	VF	XF	Unc	BU
1994 Proof	Est. 30,000	Value: 32.50				

KM# 262 CROWN

Copper-Nickel, 38.8 mm. **Ruler:** Elizabeth II **Series:** World War II **Obv:** Crowned bust right **Rev:** Glen Miller and band

Date	Mintage	F	VF	XF	Unc	BU
1994	—	—	—	—	6.00	8.00

KM# 262a CROWN

28.2800 g., 0.9250 Silver .8411 oz. ASW, 38.8 mm. **Ruler:** Elizabeth II **Series:** World War II **Obv:** Crowned bust right **Rev:** Glen Miller and band

Date	Mintage	F	VF	XF	Unc	BU
1994 Proof	Est. 30,000	Value: 30.00				

KM# 263 CROWN

Copper-Nickel, 38.8 mm. **Ruler:** Elizabeth II **Series:** World War II **Obv:** Crowned bust right **Rev:** King George VI and pilots

Date	Mintage	F	VF	XF	Unc	BU
1994	—	—	—	—	6.00	8.00

KM# 263a CROWN

28.2800 g., 0.9250 Silver .8411 oz. ASW, 38.8 mm. **Ruler:** Elizabeth II **Series:** World War II **Obv:** Crowned bust right **Rev:** King George VI and pilots

Date	Mintage	F	VF	XF	Unc	BU
1994 Proof	Est. 30,000	Value: 35.00				

KM# 264 CROWN

Copper-Nickel, 38.8 mm. **Ruler:** Elizabeth II **Series:** World War II **Obv:** Crowned bust right **Rev:** General Eisenhower

Date	Mintage	F	VF	XF	Unc	BU
1994	—	—	—	—	6.00	8.00

KM# 264a CROWN

28.2800 g., 0.9250 Silver .8411 oz. ASW, 38.8 mm. **Ruler:** Elizabeth II **Series:** World War II **Obv:** Crowned bust right **Rev:** General Eisenhower

Date	Mintage	F	VF	XF	Unc	BU
1994 Proof	—	Value: 35.00				

KM# 271 CROWN

Copper-Nickel, 38.8 mm. **Ruler:** Elizabeth II **Series:** First Man on Moon **Obv:** Crowned bust right **Rev:** Dr. Wernher von Braun with model of shuttle

Date	Mintage	F	VF	XF	Unc	BU
1994	—	—	—	—	5.75	6.50

KM# 271a CROWN

28.2800 g., 0.9250 Silver .8411 oz. ASW, 38.8 mm. **Ruler:** Elizabeth II **Series:** First Man on Moon **Obv:** Crowned bust right **Rev:** Dr. Wernher von Braun with model of shuttle

Date	Mintage	F	VF	XF	Unc	BU
1994 Proof	Est. 30,000	Value: 22.00				

KM# 272 CROWN

Copper-Nickel, 38.8 mm. **Ruler:** Elizabeth II **Series:** First Man on Moon **Obv:** Crowned bust right **Rev:** Rocket launching

Date	Mintage	F	VF	XF	Unc	BU
1994	—	—	—	—	5.75	6.50

KM# 272a CROWN

28.2800 g., 0.9250 Silver .8411 oz. ASW, 38.8 mm. **Ruler:** Elizabeth II **Series:** First Man on Moon **Obv:** Crowned bust right **Rev:** Rocket launching

Date	Mintage	F	VF	XF	Unc	BU
1994 Proof	Est. 30,000	Value: 22.00				

KM# 273 CROWN

Copper-Nickel, 38.8 mm. **Ruler:** Elizabeth II **Series:** First Man on Moon **Obv:** Crowned bust right **Rev:** Space capsule recovery

Date	Mintage	F	VF	XF	Unc	BU
1994	—	—	—	—	5.75	6.50

KM# 273a CROWN

28.2800 g., 0.9250 Silver .8411 oz. ASW, 38.8 mm. **Ruler:** Elizabeth II **Series:** First Man on Moon **Obv:** Crowned bust right **Rev:** Space capsule recovery

Date	Mintage	F	VF	XF	Unc	BU
1994 Proof	Est. 30,000	Value: 20.00				

KM# 274 CROWN

Copper-Nickel, 38.8 mm. **Ruler:** Elizabeth II **Series:** First Man on Moon **Obv:** Crowned bust right **Rev:** First manned lunar landing

Date	Mintage	F	VF	XF	Unc	BU
1994	—	—	—	—	5.75	6.50

KM# 274a CROWN

28.2800 g., 0.9250 Silver .8411 oz. ASW, 38.8 mm. **Ruler:** Elizabeth II **Series:** First Man on Moon **Obv:** Crowned bust right **Rev:** First manned lunar landing

Date	Mintage	F	VF	XF	Unc	BU
1994 Proof	Est. 30,000	Value: 22.00				

KM# 275 CROWN

Copper-Nickel, 38.8 mm. **Ruler:** Elizabeth II **Series:** First Man on Moon **Obv:** Crowned bust right **Rev:** First step on moon

Date	Mintage	F	VF	XF	Unc	BU
1994	—	—	—	—	5.75	6.50

KM# 275a CROWN

28.2800 g., 0.9250 Silver .8411 oz. ASW, 38.8 mm. **Ruler:** Elizabeth II **Series:** First Man on Moon **Obv:** Crowned bust right **Rev:** First step on moon

Date	Mintage	F	VF	XF	Unc	BU
1994 Proof	Est. 30,000	Value: 20.00				

KM# 276 CROWN

Copper-Nickel, 38.8 mm. **Ruler:** Elizabeth II **Series:** First Man on Moon **Obv:** Crowned bust right **Rev:** First flag planted on moon

Date	Mintage	F	VF	XF	Unc	BU
1994	—	—	—	—	5.75	6.50

KM# 276a CROWN

28.2800 g., 0.9250 Silver .8411 oz. ASW, 38.8 mm. **Ruler:** Elizabeth II **Series:** First Man on Moon **Obv:** Crowned bust right **Rev:** First flag planted on moon

Date	Mintage	F	VF	XF	Unc	BU
1994 Proof	Est. 30,000	Value: 20.00				

KM# 285 CROWN

Copper-Nickel, 38.8 mm. **Ruler:** Elizabeth II **Series:** 100th Anniversary of The Return of Sherlock Holmes **Subject:** Sherlock Holmes **Obv:** Crowned bust right **Rev:** Bust with pipe left

Date	Mintage	F	VF	XF	Unc	BU
1994	—	—	—	—	8.00	9.00

KM# 285a CROWN

28.2800 g., 0.9250 Silver .8411 oz. ASW, 38.8 mm. **Ruler:** Elizabeth II **Series:** 100th Anniversary of The Return of Sherlock Holmes **Subject:** Sherlock Holmes **Obv:** Crowned bust right **Rev:** Bust with pipe left

Date	Mintage	F	VF	XF	Unc	BU
1994 Proof	Est. 30,000	Value: 27.50				

KM# 286 CROWN

Copper-Nickel, 38.8 mm. **Ruler:** Elizabeth II **Series:** 100th Anniversary of The Return of Sherlock Holmes **Obv:** Crowned bust right **Rev:** Sherlock Holmes playing violin for Dr. Watson

Date	Mintage	F	VF	XF	Unc	BU
1994	—	—	—	—	8.00	9.00

KM# 286a CROWN

28.2800 g., 0.9250 Silver .8411 oz. ASW, 38.8 mm. **Ruler:** Elizabeth II **Series:** 100th Anniversary of The Return of Sherlock Holmes **Obv:** Crowned bust right **Rev:** Sherlock Holmes playing violin for Dr. Watson

Date	Mintage	F	VF	XF	Unc	BU
1994 Proof	Est. 30,000	Value: 27.50				

KM# 287 CROWN

Copper-Nickel, 38.8 mm. **Ruler:** Elizabeth II **Series:** 100th Anniversary of The Return of Sherlock Holmes **Subject:** 221 B Baker Street **Obv:** Crowned bust right **Rev:** Figures in front of building

Date	Mintage	F	VF	XF	Unc	BU
1994	—	—	—	—	8.00	9.00

KM# 287a CROWN

28.2800 g., 0.9250 Silver .8411 oz. ASW, 38.8 mm. **Ruler:** Elizabeth II **Series:** 100th Anniversary of The Return of Sherlock Holmes **Subject:** 221 B Baker Street **Obv:** Crowned bust right **Rev:** Figures in front of building

Date	Mintage	F	VF	XF	Unc	BU
1994 Proof	Est. 30,000	Value: 22.50				

KM# 288 CROWN

Copper-Nickel, 38.8 mm. **Ruler:** Elizabeth II **Series:** 100th Anniversary of The Return of Sherlock Holmes **Subject:** The Empty House **Obv:** Crowned bust right **Rev:** Three figures

Date	Mintage	F	VF	XF	Unc	BU
1994	—	—	—	—	8.00	9.00

KM# 288a CROWN

28.2800 g., 0.9250 Silver .8411 oz. ASW, 38.8 mm. **Ruler:** Elizabeth II **Series:** 100th Anniversary of The Return of Sherlock Holmes **Subject:** The Empty House **Obv:** Crowned bust right **Rev:** Three figures

Date	Mintage	F	VF	XF	Unc	BU
1994 Proof	Est. 30,000	Value: 22.50				

KM# 289 CROWN

Copper-Nickel, 38.8 mm. **Ruler:** Elizabeth II **Series:** 100th Anniversary of The Return of Sherlock Holmes **Subject:** The Mary Celeste **Obv:** Crowned bust right **Rev:** Cameo left of masted ship at sea

Date	Mintage	F	VF	XF	Unc	BU
1994	—	—	—	—	8.00	9.00

KM# 289a CROWN

28.2800 g., 0.9250 Silver .8411 oz. ASW, 38.8 mm. **Ruler:** Elizabeth II **Series:** 100th Anniversary of The Return of Sherlock Holmes **Subject:** The Mary Celeste **Obv:** Crowned bust right **Rev:** Cameo left of masted ship at sea

Date	Mintage	F	VF	XF	Unc	BU
1994 Proof	Est. 30,000	Value: 37.50				

KM# 290 CROWN

Copper-Nickel, 38.8 mm. **Ruler:** Elizabeth II **Series:** 100th Anniversary of The Return of Sherlock Holmes **Subject:** The Hound of the Baskervilles **Obv:** Crowned bust right **Rev:** Two figures back and right of large dog at front

Date	Mintage	F	VF	XF	Unc	BU
1994	—	—	—	—	8.00	9.00

KM# 290a CROWN

28.2800 g., 0.9250 Silver .8411 oz. ASW, 38.8 mm. **Ruler:** Elizabeth II **Series:** 100th Anniversary of The Return of Sherlock Holmes **Subject:** The Hound of the Baskervilles **Obv:** Crowned bust right **Rev:** Two figures back and right of large dog at front

Date	Mintage	F	VF	XF	Unc	BU
1994 Proof	Est. 30,000	Value: 35.00				

KM# 291 CROWN

Copper-Nickel, 38.8 mm. **Ruler:** Elizabeth II **Series:** 100th Anniversary of The Return of Sherlock Holmes **Subject:** The Three Garriders **Obv:** Crowned bust right **Rev:** Two seated figures **Note:** Variety exists with spelling error: GARRIDEBS.

Date	Mintage	F	VF	XF	Unc	BU
1994	—	—	—	—	8.00	9.00

KM# 291a CROWN

28.2800 g., 0.9250 Silver .8411 oz. ASW, 38.8 mm. **Ruler:** Elizabeth II **Series:** 100th Anniversary of The Return of Sherlock Holmes **Subject:** The Three Garriders **Obv:** Crowned bust right **Rev:** Two seated figures

Date	Mintage	F	VF	XF	Unc	BU
1994 Proof	Est. 30,000	Value: 20.00				

KM# 292 CROWN

Copper-Nickel, 38.8 mm. **Ruler:** Elizabeth II **Series:** 100th Anniversary of The Return of Sherlock Holmes **Subject:** The Final Problem **Obv:** Crowned bust right **Rev:** Two figures and waterfall

Date	Mintage	F	VF	XF	Unc	BU
1994	—	—	—	—	8.00	9.00

KM# 292a CROWN

28.2800 g., 0.9250 Silver .8411 oz. ASW, 38.8 mm. **Ruler:** Elizabeth II **Series:** 100th Anniversary of The Return of Sherlock Holmes **Subject:** The Final Problem **Obv:** Crowned bust right **Rev:** Two figures and waterfall

Date	Mintage	F	VF	XF	Unc	BU
1994 Proof	Est. 30,000	Value: 20.00				

KM# 444 CROWN

Copper-Nickel, 38.8 mm. **Ruler:** Elizabeth II **Subject:** The Tale of Peter Rabbit **Obv:** Crowned bust right **Rev:** Mother rabbit with bunnies

Date	Mintage	F	VF	XF	Unc	BU
1994	—	—	—	—	7.50	10.00

KM# 444a CROWN

28.2800 g., 0.9250 Silver .8411 oz. ASW, 38.8 mm. **Ruler:** Elizabeth II **Subject:** The Tale of Peter Rabbit **Obv:** Crowned bust right **Rev:** Mother rabbit with bunnies

Date	Mintage	F	VF	XF	Unc	BU
1994 Proof	Est. 30,000	Value: 40.00				

KM# 299 CROWN

Copper-Nickel, 38.8 mm. **Ruler:** Elizabeth II **Series:** Atlanta Olympics **Obv:** Crowned bust right **Rev:** Long jumper

Date	Mintage	F	VF	XF	Unc	BU
1995 Proof	—	Value: 6.00				

KM# 299a CROWN

28.2800 g., 0.9250 Silver .8411 oz. ASW, 38.8 mm. **Ruler:** Elizabeth II **Series:** Atlanta Olympics **Obv:** Crowned bust right **Rev:** Long jumper

Date	Mintage	F	VF	XF	Unc	BU
1995 Proof	Est. 30,000	Value: 27.50				

KM# 300 CROWN

Copper-Nickel, 38.8 mm. **Ruler:** Elizabeth II **Series:** Atlanta Olympics **Obv:** Crowned bust right **Rev:** Discus thrower

Date	Mintage	F	VF	XF	Unc	BU
1995	—	—	—	—	5.50	6.00

KM# 300a CROWN

28.2800 g., 0.9250 Silver .8411 oz. ASW, 38.8 mm. **Ruler:** Elizabeth II **Series:** Atlanta Olympics **Obv:** Crowned bust right **Rev:** Discus thrower

Date	Mintage	F	VF	XF	Unc	BU
1995 Proof	Est. 30,000	Value: 27.50				

KM# 301 CROWN

Copper-Nickel, 38.8 mm. **Ruler:** Elizabeth II **Obv:** Crowned bust right **Rev:** Relay runners

Date	Mintage	F	VF	XF	Unc	BU
1995	—	—	—	—	5.50	6.00

KM# 301a CROWN

28.2800 g., 0.9250 Silver .8411 oz. ASW, 38.8 mm. **Ruler:** Elizabeth II **Obv:** Crowned bust right **Rev:** Relay runners

Date	Mintage	F	VF	XF	Unc	BU
1995 Proof	Est. 30,000	Value: 27.50				

KM# 302 CROWN

Copper-Nickel, 38.8 mm. **Ruler:** Elizabeth II **Series:** Atlanta Olympics **Obv:** Crowned bust right **Rev:** Javelin throwers

Date	Mintage	F	VF	XF	Unc	BU
1995	—	—	—	—	5.50	6.00

KM# 302a CROWN

28.2800 g., 0.9250 Silver .8411 oz. ASW, 38.8 mm. **Ruler:** Elizabeth II **Series:** Atlanta Olympics **Obv:** Crowned bust right **Rev:** Javelin throwers

Date	Mintage	F	VF	XF	Unc	BU
1995 Proof	Est. 30,000	Value: 27.50				

KM# 304 CROWN

Copper-Nickel, 38.8 mm. **Ruler:** Elizabeth II **Obv:** Crowned bust right **Rev:** Sun rising over Rock of Gibraltar

Date	Mintage	F	VF	XF	Unc	BU
1995	—	—	—	—	6.50	7.50

KM# 304a CROWN

28.2800 g., 0.9250 Silver .8411 oz. ASW, 38.8 mm. **Ruler:** Elizabeth II **Obv:** Crowned bust right **Rev:** Sun rising over Rock of Gibraltar

Date	Mintage	F	VF	XF	Unc	BU
1995 Proof	Est. 30,000	Value: 40.00				

KM# 306 CROWN

Copper-Nickel, 38.8 mm. **Ruler:** Elizabeth II **Series:** Preserve Planet Earth **Obv:** Crowned bust right **Rev:** Monkeys

Date	Mintage	F	VF	XF	Unc	BU
1995	—	—	—	—	9.00	12.00

KM# 306a CROWN

28.2800 g., 0.9250 Silver .8411 oz. ASW, 38.8 mm. **Series:** Preserve Planet Earth **Obv:** Crowned bust right **Rev:** Monkeys

Date	Mintage	F	VF	XF	Unc	BU
1995 Proof	Est. 30,000	Value: 40.00				

KM# 308 CROWN

Copper-Nickel, 38.8 mm. **Ruler:** Elizabeth II **Series:** Preserve Planet Earth **Obv:** Crowned bust right **Rev:** Sperm whale

Date	Mintage	F	VF	XF	Unc	BU
1995	—	—	—	—	9.00	12.00

KM# 308a CROWN

28.2800 g., 0.9250 Silver .8411 oz. ASW, 38.8 mm. **Ruler:** Elizabeth II **Series:** Preserve Planet Earth **Obv:** Crowned bust right **Rev:** Sperm whale

Date	Mintage	F	VF	XF	Unc	BU
1995 Proof	Est. 30,000	Value: 42.50				

KM# 327 CROWN

Copper-Nickel, 38.8 mm. **Ruler:** Elizabeth II **Subject:** The Tale of Peter Rabbit **Obv:** Crowned bust right **Rev:** Rabbit running right

Date	Mintage	F	VF	XF	Unc	BU
1995	—	—	—	—	6.50	8.00

KM# 327a CROWN

28.2800 g., 0.9250 Silver .8411 oz. ASW, 38.8 mm. **Ruler:** Elizabeth II **Subject:** The Tale of Peter Rabbit **Obv:** Crowned bust right **Rev:** Rabbit running right

Date	Mintage	F	VF	XF	Unc	BU
1995 Proof	Est. 30,000	Value: 37.50				

KM# 329 CROWN

Copper-Nickel, 38.8 mm. **Ruler:** Elizabeth II **Series:** Island Games **Obv:** Crowned bust right **Rev:** Various athletes around shield

Date	Mintage	F	VF	XF	Unc	BU
1995	—	—	—	—	6.00	7.50

KM# 329a CROWN

28.2800 g., 0.9250 Silver .8411 oz. ASW, 38.8 mm. **Ruler:** Elizabeth II **Series:** Island Games **Obv:** Crowned bust right **Rev:** Various athletes around shield

Date	Mintage	F	VF	XF	Unc	BU
1995 Proof	Est. 30,000	Value: 35.00				

KM# 331 CROWN

Copper-Nickel, 38.8 mm. **Ruler:** Elizabeth II **Series:** Island Games **Obv:** Crowned bust right **Rev:** Various athletes around shield

Date	Mintage	F	VF	XF	Unc	BU
1995	—	—	—	—	6.00	7.50

KM# 331a CROWN

28.2800 g., 0.9250 Silver .8411 oz. ASW, 38.8 mm. **Ruler:** Elizabeth II **Series:** Island Games **Obv:** Crowned bust right **Rev:** Various athletes around shield

Date	Mintage	F	VF	XF	Unc	BU
1995 Proof	Est. 30,000	Value: 35.00				

KM# 408a CROWN

28.2800 g., 0.9250 Silver .8411 oz. ASW, 38.8 mm. **Ruler:** Elizabeth II **Series:** Centenary of the Cinema **Subject:** Audrey Hepburn - actress, 1929-93 **Obv:** Crowned bust right **Rev:** Bust 3/4 facing, dates

Date	Mintage	F	VF	XF	Unc	BU
1996 Proof	Est. 30,000	Value: 37.50				

KM# 348 CROWN

Copper-Nickel, 38.8 mm. **Ruler:** Elizabeth II **Series:** Atlanta Olympics **Obv:** Crowned bust right **Rev:** Tennis player

Date	Mintage	F	VF	XF	Unc	BU
1996	—	—	—	—	6.00	7.50

KM# 348a CROWN

28.2800 g., 0.9250 Silver .8411 oz. ASW, 38.8 mm. **Ruler:** Elizabeth II **Series:** Atlanta Olympics **Obv:** Crowned bust right **Rev:** Tennis player

Date	Mintage	F	VF	XF	Unc	BU
1996 Proof	Est. 30,000	Value: 42.50				

KM# 349 CROWN

28.2800 g., 0.9250 Silver .8411 oz. ASW, 38.8 mm. **Ruler:** Elizabeth II **Series:** 1996 Atlanta Olympics **Obv:** Crowned bust right **Rev:** Wrestlers

Date	Mintage	F	VF	XF	Unc	BU
1996	—	—	—	—	6.00	7.50

KM# 349a CROWN

28.2800 g., 0.9250 Silver .8411 oz. ASW, 38.8 mm. **Ruler:** Elizabeth II **Series:** 1996 Atlanta Olympics **Obv:** Crowned bust right **Rev:** Wrestlers

Date	Mintage	F	VF	XF	Unc	BU
1996 Proof	Est. 30,000	Value: 42.50				

KM# 350 CROWN

Copper-Nickel, 38.8 mm. **Ruler:** Elizabeth II **Series:** 1996 Atlanta Olympics **Obv:** Crowned bust right **Rev:** Flag at center of baseball game

Date	Mintage	F	VF	XF	Unc	BU
1996	—	—	—	—	6.00	7.50

KM# 350a CROWN

28.2800 g., 0.9250 Silver .8411 oz. ASW, 38.8 mm. **Ruler:** Elizabeth II **Series:** 1996 Atlanta Olympics **Obv:** Crowned bust right **Rev:** Flag at center of baseball game

Date	Mintage	F	VF	XF	Unc	BU
1996 Proof	Est. 30,000	Value: 42.50				

KM# 351 CROWN

Copper-Nickel, 38.8 mm. **Ruler:** Elizabeth II **Series:** 1996 Atlanta Olympics **Obv:** Crowned bust right **Rev:** Olympic Flame

Date	Mintage	F	VF	XF	Unc	BU
1996	—	—	—	—	6.00	7.50

KM# 351a CROWN

28.2800 g., 0.9250 Silver .8411 oz. ASW, 38.8 mm. **Ruler:** Elizabeth II **Series:** 1996 Atlanta Olympics **Obv:** Crowned bust right **Rev:** Olympic Flame

Date	Mintage	F	VF	XF	Unc	BU
1996 Proof	Est. 30,000	Value: 42.50				

KM# 352 CROWN

Copper-Nickel, 38.8 mm. **Ruler:** Elizabeth II **Series:** 1996 Atlanta Olympics **Obv:** Crowned bust right **Rev:** Volleyball game

Date	Mintage	F	VF	XF	Unc	BU
1996	—	—	—	—	6.00	7.50

KM# 352a CROWN

28.2800 g., 0.9250 Silver .8411 oz. ASW, 38.8 mm. **Ruler:** Elizabeth II **Series:** 1996 Atlanta Olympics **Obv:** Crowned bust right **Rev:** Volleyball game

Date	Mintage	F	VF	XF	Unc	BU
1996 Proof	Est. 30,000	Value: 42.50				

KM# 353 CROWN

Copper-Nickel, 38.8 mm. **Ruler:** Elizabeth II **Series:** 1996 Atlanta Olympics **Obv:** Crowned bust right **Rev:** Basketball game

Date	Mintage	F	VF	XF	Unc	BU
1996	—	—	—	—	6.00	7.50

KM# 353a CROWN

28.2800 g., 0.9250 Silver .8411 oz. ASW, 38.8 mm. **Ruler:** Elizabeth II **Series:** 1996 Atlanta Olympics **Obv:** Crowned bust right **Rev:** Basketball game

Date	Mintage	F	VF	XF	Unc	BU
1996 Proof	Est. 30,000	Value: 42.50				

KM# 358 CROWN

Copper-Nickel, 38.8 mm. **Ruler:** Elizabeth II **Obv:** Crowned bust right **Rev:** Nefusot Yehuda Synagogue Renovation, denomination below

Date	Mintage	F	VF	XF	Unc	BU
1996	—	—	—	—	7.00	9.00

KM# 358a CROWN

28.2800 g., 0.9250 Silver .8411 oz. ASW, 38.8 mm. **Ruler:** Elizabeth II **Obv:** Crowned bust right **Rev:** Nefusot Yehuda Synagogue Renovation

Date	Mintage	F	VF	XF	Unc	BU
1996 Proof	Est. 30,000	Value: 40.00				

KM# 359 CROWN
Copper-Nickel, 38.8 mm. **Ruler:** Elizabeth II **Subject:** Euro Soccer 96 **Obv:** Crowned bust right **Rev:** Net and soccer player

Date	Mintage	F	VF	XF	Unc	BU
1996	—	—	—	—	8.00	9.50

KM# 359a CROWN
28.2800 g., 0.9250 Silver .8411 oz. ASW, 38.8 mm. **Ruler:** Elizabeth II **Subject:** Euro Soccer 96 **Obv:** Crowned bust right **Rev:** Soccer player and net

Date	Mintage	F	VF	XF	Unc	BU
1996 Proof	Est. 30,000	Value: 45.00				

KM# 373 CROWN
Copper-Nickel, 38.8 mm. **Ruler:** Elizabeth II **Obv:** Crowned bust right **Rev:** Roses

Date	Mintage	F	VF	XF	Unc	BU
1996	—	—	—	—	8.00	9.50

KM# 373a CROWN
28.2800 g., 0.9250 Silver .8411 oz. ASW, 38.8 mm. **Ruler:** Elizabeth II **Obv:** Crowned bust right **Rev:** Roses

Date	Mintage	F	VF	XF	Unc	BU
1996 Proof	Est. 30,000	Value: 40.00				

KM# 382 CROWN
Copper-Nickel, 38.8 mm. **Ruler:** Elizabeth II **Subject:** The Tale of Peter Rabbit **Obv:** Crowned bust right **Rev:** Rabbit escaping the garden

Date	Mintage	F	VF	XF	Unc	BU
1996	—	—	—	—	6.50	8.00

KM# 382a CROWN
28.2800 g., 0.9250 Silver .8411 oz. ASW, 38.8 mm. **Ruler:** Elizabeth II **Subject:** The Tale of Peter Rabbit **Obv:** Crowned bust right **Rev:** Rabbit escaping the garden

Date	Mintage	F	VF	XF	Unc	BU
1996 Proof	Est. 30,000	Value: 40.00				

KM# 386 CROWN
Copper-Nickel, 38.8 mm. **Ruler:** Elizabeth II **Series:** Preserve Planet Earth **Obv:** Crowned bust right **Rev:** Shag Birds

Date	Mintage	F	VF	XF	Unc	BU
1996	—	—	—	—	9.00	12.00

KM# 386a CROWN
28.2800 g., 0.9250 Silver .8411 oz. ASW, 38.8 mm. **Ruler:** Elizabeth II **Series:** Preserve Planet Earth **Obv:** Crowned bust right **Rev:** Shag Birds

Date	Mintage	F	VF	XF	Unc	BU
1996 Proof	Est. 30,000	Value: 40.00				

KM# 387 CROWN
Copper-Nickel, 38.8 mm. **Ruler:** Elizabeth II **Series:** Preserve Planet Earth **Obv:** Crowned bust right **Rev:** Atlantic Puffins

Date	Mintage	F	VF	XF	Unc	BU
1996	—	—	—	—	9.00	12.00

KM# 387a CROWN
28.2800 g., 0.9250 Silver .8411 oz. ASW, 38.8 mm. **Ruler:** Elizabeth II **Series:** Preserve Planet Earth **Obv:** Crowned bust right **Rev:** Atlantic Puffins

Date	Mintage	F	VF	XF	Unc	BU
1996 Proof	Est. 30,000	Value: 40.00				

KM# 393 CROWN
Copper-Nickel, 38.8 mm. **Ruler:** Elizabeth II **Series:** Centenary of the Cinema **Subject:** Grace Kelly - actress, 1929-82 **Obv:** Crowned bust right **Rev:** Bust 3/4 facing, dates

Date	Mintage	F	VF	XF	Unc	BU
1996	—	—	—	—	8.00	9.50

KM# 393a CROWN
28.2800 g., 0.9250 Silver .8411 oz. ASW, 38.8 mm. **Ruler:** Elizabeth II **Series:** Centenary of the Cinema **Subject:** Grace Kelly - actress, 1929-82 **Obv:** Crowned bust right **Rev:** Bust 3/4 facing, dates

Date	Mintage	F	VF	XF	Unc	BU
1996 Proof	Est. 30,000	Value: 37.50				

KM# 398 CROWN
Copper-Nickel, 38.8 mm. **Ruler:** Elizabeth II **Series:** Centenary of the Cinema **Subject:** James Dean - actor, 1931-55 **Obv:** Crowned bust right **Rev:** Standing central figure, dates

Date	Mintage	F	VF	XF	Unc	BU
1996	—	—	—	—	8.00	9.50

KM# 398a CROWN
28.2800 g., 0.9250 Silver .8411 oz. ASW, 38.8 mm. **Ruler:** Elizabeth II **Series:** Centenary of the Cinema **Subject:** James Dean - actor, 1931-55 **Obv:** Crowned bust right **Rev:** Standing central figure, dates

Date	Mintage	F	VF	XF	Unc	BU
1996 Proof	Est. 30,000	Value: 40.00				

KM# 403 CROWN
Copper-Nickel, 38.8 mm. **Ruler:** Elizabeth II **Series:** Centenary of the Cinema **Subject:** Marilyn Monroe - actress, 1926-62 **Obv:** Crowned bust right **Rev:** Bust looking back over shoulder, dates

Date	Mintage	F	VF	XF	Unc	BU
1996	—	—	—	—	8.00	9.50

KM# 403a CROWN
28.2800 g., 0.9250 Silver .8411 oz. ASW, 38.8 mm. **Ruler:** Elizabeth II **Series:** Centenary of the Cinema **Subject:** Marilyn Monroe - actress, 1926-62 **Obv:** Crowned bust right **Rev:** Bust looking back over shoulder, dates

Date	Mintage	F	VF	XF	Unc	BU
1996 Proof	—	Value: 40.00				

KM# 408 CROWN
Copper-Nickel, 38.8 mm. **Ruler:** Elizabeth II **Series:** Centenary of the Cinema **Subject:** Audrey Hepburn - actress, 1929-93 **Obv:** Crowned bust right **Rev:** Bust 3/4 facing, dates

Date	Mintage	F	VF	XF	Unc	BU
1996	—	—	—	—	8.00	9.50

KM# 413 CROWN
Copper-Nickel, 38.8 mm. **Ruler:** Elizabeth II **Series:** Centenary of the Cinema **Subject:** Bruce Lee - actor, 1940-73 **Obv:** Crowned bust right **Rev:** Kickboxer and chinese dragon

Date	Mintage	F	VF	XF	Unc	BU
1996	—	—	—	—	8.00	9.50

KM# 413a CROWN
28.2800 g., 0.9250 Silver .8411 oz. ASW, 38.8 mm. **Ruler:** Elizabeth II **Series:** Centenary of the Cinema **Subject:** Bruce Lee - actor, 1940-73 **Obv:** Crowned bust right **Rev:** Kickboxer and chinese dragon

Date	Mintage	F	VF	XF	Unc	BU
1996 Proof	Est. 30,000	Value: 40.00				

KM# 418 CROWN
Copper-Nickel, 38.8 mm. **Ruler:** Elizabeth II **Series:** Centenary of the Cinema **Subject:** Charlie Chaplan - actor, 1889-1977 **Obv:** Crowned bust right **Rev:** Standing central figure with cane, dates

Date	Mintage	F	VF	XF	Unc	BU
1996	—	—	—	—	8.00	9.50

KM# 418a CROWN
28.2800 g., 0.9250 Silver .8411 oz. ASW, 38.8 mm. **Ruler:** Elizabeth II **Series:** Centenary of the Cinema **Subject:** Charlie Chaplan - actor, 1889-1977 **Obv:** Crowned bust right **Rev:** Standing central figure with cane, dates

Date	Mintage	F	VF	XF	Unc	BU
1996 Proof	Est. 30,000	Value: 37.50				

KM# 423 CROWN
Copper-Nickel, 38.8 mm. **Ruler:** Elizabeth II **Series:** Centenary of the Cinema **Subject:** Gone With The Wind **Obv:** Crowned bust right **Rev:** Rhett Butler and Scarlett O'Hara

Date	Mintage	F	VF	XF	Unc	BU
1996	—	—	—	—	8.00	9.50

KM# 423a CROWN
28.2800 g., 0.9250 Silver .8411 oz. ASW, 38.8 mm. **Ruler:** Elizabeth II **Series:** Centenary of the Cinema **Subject:** Gone With The Wind **Obv:** Crowned bust right **Rev:** Rhett Butler and Scarlett O'Hara

Date	Mintage	F	VF	XF	Unc	BU
1996 Proof	Est. 30,000	Value: 40.00				

KM# 428 CROWN
Copper-Nickel, 38.8 mm. **Ruler:** Elizabeth II **Series:** Centenary of the Cinema **Obv:** Crowned bust right **Rev:** The Flintstones

Date	Mintage	F	VF	XF	Unc	BU
1996	—	—	—	—	8.00	9.50

KM# 428a CROWN
28.2800 g., 0.9250 Silver .8411 oz. ASW, 38.8 mm. **Ruler:** Elizabeth II **Series:** Centenary of the Cinema **Obv:** Crowned bust right **Rev:** The Flintstones

Date	Mintage	F	VF	XF	Unc	BU
1996 Proof	Est. 30,000	Value: 40.00				

KM# 430 CROWN
28.2800 g., 0.9250 Silver .8411 oz. ASW, 38.8 mm. **Ruler:** Elizabeth II **Series:** European Football Championship **Subject:** Goliath **Obv:** Crowned bust right **Rev:** Cartoon lion with football

Date	Mintage	F	VF	XF	Unc	BU
1996 Proof	Est. 10,000	Value: 32.50				

KM# 432 CROWN
Copper-Nickel, 38.8 mm. **Ruler:** Elizabeth II **Series:** Duke of Edinburgh Awards Scheme **Obv:** Crowned bust right **Rev:** 7 scenes surround center crowned arms

Date	Mintage	F	VF	XF	Unc	BU
1996	—	—	—	—	8.00	9.00

KM# 432a CROWN
28.2800 g., 0.9250 Silver .8411 oz. ASW, 38.8 mm. **Ruler:** Elizabeth II **Series:** Duke of Edinburgh Awards Scheme **Obv:** Crowned bust right **Rev:** 7 scenes surround center crowned arms

Date	Mintage	F	VF	XF	Unc	BU
1996 Proof	Est. 30,000	Value: 40.00				

KM# 435 CROWN
Copper-Nickel, 38.8 mm. **Ruler:** Elizabeth II **Series:** Duke of Edinburgh Awards Scheme **Obv:** Crowned bust right **Rev:** Cameo above team of horses pulling wagon

Date	Mintage	F	VF	XF	Unc	BU
1996	—	—	—	—	8.00	9.00

KM# 435a CROWN
28.2800 g., 0.9250 Silver .8411 oz. ASW, 38.8 mm. **Ruler:** Elizabeth II **Series:** Duke of Edinburgh Awards Scheme **Obv:** Duke of Edinburgh Awards Scheme **Rev:** Cameo above team of horses pulling wagon

Date	Mintage	F	VF	XF	Unc	BU
1996 Proof	Est. 30,000	Value: 40.00				

KM# 449 CROWN

Copper-Nickel, 38.8 mm. **Ruler:** Elizabeth II **Subject:** Lord Buddha **Obv:** Crowned bust right **Rev:** Seated figure facing

Date	Mintage	F	VF	XF	Unc	BU
1996	—	—	—	—	7.50	8.50

KM# 449a CROWN

28.2800 g., 0.9250 Silver .8411 oz. ASW, 38.8 mm. **Ruler:** Elizabeth II **Subject:** Lord Buddha **Obv:** Crowned bust right **Rev:** Seated figure facing

Date	Mintage	F	VF	XF	Unc	BU
1996 Proof	Est. 15,000	Value: 25.00				

KM# 457 CROWN

Copper-Nickel, 38.8 mm. **Ruler:** Elizabeth II **Series:** Centenary of the Cinema **Subject:** Wizard of Oz **Obv:** Crowned bust right **Rev:** Characters of Oz

Date	Mintage	F	VF	XF	Unc	BU
1996	—	—	—	—	7.75	9.00

KM# 457a CROWN

28.2800 g., 0.9250 Silver .8411 oz. ASW, 38.8 mm. **Ruler:** Elizabeth II **Series:** Centenary of the Cinema **Subject:** Wizard of Oz **Obv:** Crowned bust right **Rev:** Characters of Oz

Date	Mintage	F	VF	XF	Unc	BU
1996 Proof	Est. 30,000	Value: 40.00				

KM# 461 CROWN

Copper-Nickel, 38.8 mm. **Ruler:** Elizabeth II **Series:** Centenary of the Cinema **Subject:** The Marx Brothers **Obv:** Crowned bust right **Rev:** Three busts 3/4 left

Date	Mintage	F	VF	XF	Unc	BU
1996	—	—	—	—	7.75	9.00

KM# 461a CROWN

28.2800 g., 0.9250 Silver .8411 oz. ASW, 38.8 mm. **Ruler:** Elizabeth II **Series:** Centenary of the Cinema **Subject:** The Marx Brothers **Obv:** Crowned bust right **Rev:** Three busts 3/4 left

Date	Mintage	F	VF	XF	Unc	BU
1996 Proof	Est. 30,000	Value: 37.50				

KM# 465 CROWN

Copper-Nickel, 38.8 mm. **Ruler:** Elizabeth II **Series:** Centenary of the Cinema **Subject:** Elvis Presley - actor/entertainer, 1935-77 **Obv:** Crowned bust right **Rev:** Guitar beneath and behind bust 3/4 left

Date	Mintage	F	VF	XF	Unc	BU
1996	—	—	—	—	7.75	9.00

KM# 465a CROWN

28.0000 g., 0.9250 Silver .8411 oz. ASW, 38.8 mm. **Ruler:** Elizabeth II **Series:** Centenary of the Cinema **Subject:** Elvis Presley - actor/entertainer, 1935-77 **Obv:** Crowned bust right **Rev:** Guitar beneath and behind bust 3/4 left

Date	Mintage	F	VF	XF	Unc	BU
1996 Proof	Est. 30,000	Value: 40.00				

KM# 469 CROWN

Copper-Nickel, 38.8 mm. **Ruler:** Elizabeth II **Series:** Centenary of the Cinema **Subject:** Casablanca **Obv:** Crowned bust right **Rev:** Bogart and Bergman

Date	Mintage	F	VF	XF	Unc	BU
1996	—	—	—	—	7.75	9.00

KM# 469a CROWN

28.0000 g., 0.9250 Silver .8411 oz. ASW, 38.8 mm. **Ruler:** Elizabeth II **Series:** Centenary of the Cinema **Subject:** Casablanca **Obv:** Crowned bust right **Rev:** Bogart and Bergman

Date	Mintage	F	VF	XF	Unc	BU
1996 Proof	Est. 30,000	Value: 37.50				

KM# 473 CROWN

Copper-Nickel, 38.8 mm. **Ruler:** Elizabeth II **Series:** Centenary of the Cinema **Obv:** Crowned bust right **Rev:** E.T.

Date	Mintage	F	VF	XF	Unc	BU
1996	—	—	—	—	7.75	9.00

KM# 473a CROWN

28.0000 g., 0.9250 Silver .8411 oz. ASW, 38.8 mm. **Ruler:** Elizabeth II **Series:** Centenary of the Cinema **Obv:** Crowned bust right **Rev:** E.T.

Date	Mintage	F	VF	XF	Unc	BU
1996 Proof	Est. 30,000	Value: 37.50				

KM# 477 CROWN

Copper-Nickel, 38.8 mm. **Ruler:** Elizabeth II **Series:** Centenary of the Cinema **Subject:** Alfred Hitchcock - Director/Producer, 1899-1980 **Obv:** Crowned bust right **Rev:** Bust facing looking at bird on left shoulder

Date	Mintage	F	VF	XF	Unc	BU
1996	—	—	—	—	7.75	9.00

KM# 477a CROWN

28.0000 g., 0.9250 Silver .8411 oz. ASW, 38.8 mm. **Ruler:** Elizabeth II **Series:** Centenary of the Cinema **Subject:** Alfred Hitchcock - Director/Producer, 1899-1980 **Obv:** Crowned bust right **Rev:** Bust facing looking at bird on left shoulder

Date	Mintage	F	VF	XF	Unc	BU
1996 Proof	Est. 30,000	Value: 37.50				

KM# 586a CROWN

28.3400 g., Copper-Nickel, 38.5 mm. **Ruler:** Elizabeth II **Obv:** Crowned bust right **Rev:** Chinese Emperor Shih Huang Ti and Great Wall **Edge:** Reeded

Date	Mintage	F	VF	XF	Unc	BU
1997	—	—	—	—	10.00	14.00

KM# 514 CROWN

Copper-Nickel, 38.8 mm. **Ruler:** Elizabeth II **Obv:** Crowned bust right **Rev:** Two peacocks, one with tail spread

Date	Mintage	F	VF	XF	Unc	BU
1997	—	—	—	—	12.00	15.00

KM# 514a CROWN

28.2800 g., 0.9250 Silver .8411 oz. ASW, 38.8 mm. **Ruler:** Elizabeth II **Obv:** Crowned bust right **Rev:** Two peacocks, one with tail spread

Date	Mintage	F	VF	XF	Unc	BU
1997	Est. 30,000	Value: 40.00				

KM# 525 CROWN

Copper-Nickel, 38.8 mm. **Ruler:** Elizabeth II **Subject:** The Tale of Peter Rabbit **Obv:** Crowned bust right **Rev:** Rabbit standing 3/4 right

Date	Mintage	F	VF	XF	Unc	BU
1997	—	—	—	—	10.00	12.00

KM# 526 CROWN

28.2800 g., 0.9250 Silver .8411 oz. ASW, 38.8 mm. **Ruler:** Elizabeth II

Date	Mintage	F	VF	XF	Unc	BU
1997 Proof	Est. 30,000	Value: 40.00				

KM# 530 CROWN

Copper-Nickel, 38.8 mm. **Ruler:** Elizabeth II **Series:** Golden Wedding Anniversary **Subject:** Queen Elizabeth and Prince Phillip **Obv:** Crowned bust right **Rev:** Royal couple facing

Date	Mintage	F	VF	XF	Unc	BU
1997	—	—	—	—	7.50	9.00

KM# 530a CROWN

28.2800 g., 0.9250 Gold Clad Silver .8411 oz., 38.8 mm. **Ruler:** Elizabeth II **Series:** Golden Wedding Anniversary **Subject:** Queen Elizabeth and Prince Phillip **Obv:** Crowned bust right **Rev:** Royal couple facing

Date	Mintage	F	VF	XF	Unc	BU
1997 Proof	Est. 10,000	Value: 45.00				

KM# 532 CROWN

Copper-Nickel, 38.8 mm. **Ruler:** Elizabeth II **Series:** Golden Wedding Anniversary **Subject:** Queen Elizabeth and Prince Philip **Obv:** Crowned bust right **Rev:** The Queen with her first-born, Prince Charles

Date	Mintage	F	VF	XF	Unc	BU
1997	—	—	—	—	7.50	9.00

KM# 532a CROWN

28.2800 g., 0.9250 Gold Clad Silver .8411 oz., 38.8 mm. **Ruler:** Elizabeth II **Series:** Golden Wedding Anniversary **Subject:** Queen Elizabeth and Prince Philip **Obv:** Crowned bust right **Rev:** The Queen with her first-born, Prince Charles

Date	Mintage	F	VF	XF	Unc	BU
1997 Proof	Est. 10,000	Value: 45.00				

KM# 534 CROWN

Copper-Nickel, 38.8 mm. **Ruler:** Elizabeth II **Series:** Golden Wedding Anniversary **Subject:** Queen Elizabeth and Prince Philip **Obv:** Crowned bust right **Rev:** The Queen, two children and a monkey

Date	Mintage	F	VF	XF	Unc	BU
1997	—	—	—	—	7.50	9.00

KM# 534a CROWN

28.2800 g., 0.9250 Gold Clad Silver .8411 oz., 38.8 mm. **Ruler:** Elizabeth II **Series:** Golden Wedding Anniversary **Subject:** Queen Elizabeth and Prince Philip **Obv:** Crowned bust right **Rev:** The Queen, two children and a monkey

Date	Mintage	F	VF	XF	Unc	BU
1997 Proof	Est. 10,000	Value: 45.00				

KM# 536 CROWN

Copper-Nickel, 38.8 mm. **Ruler:** Elizabeth II **Series:** Golden Wedding Anniversary **Subject:** Queen Elizabeth and Prince Philip **Obv:** Crowned bust right **Rev:** The Queen and adoring crowd

Date	Mintage	F	VF	XF	Unc	BU
1997	—	—	—	—	7.50	9.00

KM# 536a CROWN

28.2800 g., 0.9250 Gold Clad Silver .8411 oz., 38.8 mm. **Ruler:** Elizabeth II **Series:** Golden Wedding Anniversary **Subject:** Queen Elizabeth and Prince Philip **Obv:** Crowned bust right **Rev:** The Queen and adoring crowd

Date	Mintage	F	VF	XF	Unc	BU
1997 Proof	Est. 10,000	Value: 45.00				

KM# 540 CROWN

Copper-Nickel, 38.8 mm. **Ruler:** Elizabeth II **Obv:** Crowned bust right **Rev:** Peonies

Date	Mintage	F	VF	XF	Unc	BU
1997	—	—	—	—	8.00	9.00

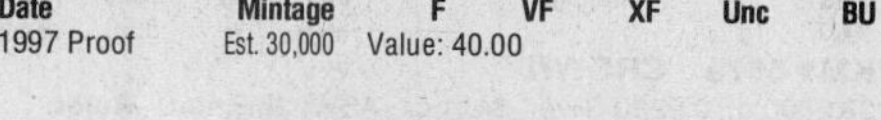

KM# 540a CROWN

28.2800 g., 0.9250 Silver .8411 oz. ASW, 38.8 mm. **Ruler:** Elizabeth II **Obv:** Crowned bust right **Rev:** Peonies

Date	Mintage	F	VF	XF	Unc	BU
1997 Proof	Est. 30,000	Value: 40.00				

KM# 544 CROWN

28.2800 g., 0.9250 Silver .8411 oz. ASW, 38.8 mm. **Ruler:** Elizabeth II **Subject:** Nefertiti **Obv:** Crowned bust right **Rev:** Head right

Date	Mintage	F	VF	XF	Unc	BU
1997 Proof	Est. 10,000	Value: 40.00				

KM# 548 CROWN

28.2800 g., 0.9250 Silver .8411 oz. ASW, 38.8 mm. **Ruler:** Elizabeth II **Subject:** Cleopatra **Obv:** Crowned bust right **Rev:** Head facing

Date	Mintage	F	VF	XF	Unc	BU
1997 Proof	Est. 10,000	Value: 40.00				

KM# 552 CROWN

28.2800 g., 0.9250 Silver .8411 oz. ASW, 38.8 mm. **Ruler:** Elizabeth II **Subject:** Europa **Obv:** Crowned bust right **Rev:** Head 3/4 left

Date	Mintage	F	VF	XF	Unc	BU
1997 Proof	Est. 10,000	Value: 40.00				

KM# 556 CROWN

28.2800 g., 0.9250 Silver .8411 oz. ASW, 38.8 mm. **Ruler:** Elizabeth II **Subject:** Liberty **Obv:** Crowned bust right **Rev:** Laureate head right

Date	Mintage	F	VF	XF	Unc	BU
1997 Proof	Est. 10,000	Value: 40.00				

KM# 561 CROWN

Copper-Nickel, 38.8 mm. **Ruler:** Elizabeth II **Subject:** Yorkshire Terrier **Obv:** Crowned bust right

Date	Mintage	F	VF	XF	Unc	BU
1997	—	—	—	—	10.00	12.00

KM# 566 CROWN

Copper-Nickel, 38.8 mm. **Ruler:** Elizabeth II **Series:** Queen's Birthday **Obv:** Crowned bust right **Rev:** Queen on horseback, Rock of Gibraltar in background

Date	Mintage	F	VF	XF	Unc	BU
1997	—	—	—	—	8.50	9.50

KM# 566a CROWN

28.2800 g., 0.9250 Silver .8411 oz. ASW, 38.8 mm. **Ruler:** Elizabeth II **Series:** Queen's Birthday **Obv:** Crowned bust right **Rev:** Queen on horseback, Rock of Gibraltar in background

Date	Mintage	F	VF	XF	Unc	BU
1997 Proof	Est. 30,000	Value: 40.00				

KM# 567 CROWN

Copper-Nickel, 38.8 mm. **Ruler:** Elizabeth II **Series:** Queen's Birthday **Obv:** Crowned bust right **Rev:** Queen on horseback returning salute

Date	Mintage	F	VF	XF	Unc	BU
1997	—	—	—	—	8.50	9.50

KM# 567a CROWN

28.2800 g., 0.9250 Silver .8411 oz. ASW, 38.8 mm. **Ruler:** Elizabeth II **Series:** Queen's Birthday **Obv:** Crowned bust right **Rev:** Queen on horseback returning salute

Date	Mintage	F	VF	XF	Unc	BU
1997 Proof	Est. 30,000	Value: 40.00				

KM# 568 CROWN

Copper-Nickel, 38.8 mm. **Ruler:** Elizabeth II **Series:** Queen's Birthday **Obv:** Crowned bust right **Rev:** Cameo above Trooping the Colors scene

Date	Mintage	F	VF	XF	Unc	BU
1997	—	—	—	—	8.50	9.50

KM# 568a CROWN

28.2800 g., 0.9250 Silver .8411 oz. ASW, 38.8 mm. **Ruler:** Elizabeth II **Series:** Queen's Birthday **Obv:** Crowned bust right **Rev:** Cameo above Trooping the Colors scene

Date	Mintage	F	VF	XF	Unc	BU
1997 Proof	Est. 30,000	Value: 40.00				

KM# 569 CROWN

Copper-Nickel, 38.8 mm. **Ruler:** Elizabeth II **Series:** Queen's Birthday **Obv:** Crowned bust right **Rev:** Gurkha troops with dragons

Date	Mintage	F	VF	XF	Unc	BU
1997	—	—	—	—	8.50	9.50

KM# 569a CROWN

28.2800 g., 0.9250 Silver .8411 oz. ASW, 38.8 mm. **Ruler:** Elizabeth II **Series:** Queen's Birthday **Obv:** Crowned bust right **Rev:** Gurkha troops with dragons

Date	Mintage	F	VF	XF	Unc	BU
1997 Proof	—	Value: 40.00				

KM# 571 CROWN

Copper-Nickel, 38.8 mm. **Ruler:** Elizabeth II **Subject:** The New Mosque **Obv:** Crowned bust right **Rev:** Two Moorish cavalry riders with mosque in background

Date	Mintage	F	VF	XF	Unc	BU
1997	—	—	—	—	8.00	9.00

KM# 571a CROWN

28.2800 g., 0.9250 Silver .8411 oz. ASW, 38.8 mm. **Ruler:** Elizabeth II **Subject:** The New Mosque **Obv:** Crowned bust right **Rev:** Two Moorish cavalry riders with mosque in background

Date	Mintage	F	VF	XF	Unc	BU
1997 Proof	Est. 30,000	Value: 40.00				

KM# 573 CROWN

28.2800 g., 0.9250 Silver .8411 oz. ASW, 38.8 mm. **Ruler:** Elizabeth II **Series:** Wonders of the World **Subject:** Mausoleum at Halicarnassus **Obv:** Crowned bust right **Rev:** Gold coin design inset on mausoleum

Date	Mintage	F	VF	XF	Unc	BU
1997 Proof	Est. 7,500	Value: 50.00				

KM# 574 CROWN

28.2800 g., 0.9250 Silver .8411 oz. ASW, 38.8 mm. **Ruler:** Elizabeth II **Series:** Wonders of the World **Subject:** Statue of Zeus at Olympia **Obv:** Crowned bust right **Rev:** Gold coin design inset on statue of Zeus

Date	Mintage	F	VF	XF	Unc	BU
1997 Proof	Est. 7,500	Value: 50.00				

KM# 575 CROWN

28.2800 g., 0.9250 Silver .8411 oz. ASW, 38.8 mm. **Ruler:** Elizabeth II **Series:** Wonders of the World **Subject:** The Pharos of Alexandria **Obv:** Crowned bust right **Rev:** Gold coin design inset on lighthouse

Date	Mintage	F	VF	XF	Unc	BU
1997 Proof	Est. 7,500	Value: 50.00				

KM# 576 CROWN

28.2800 g., 0.9250 Silver .8411 oz. ASW, 38.8 mm. **Ruler:** Elizabeth II **Series:** Wonders of the World **Subject:** The Pillars of Hercules **Obv:** Crowned bust right **Rev:** Gold coin design inset on the Rock of Gibraltar

Date	Mintage	F	VF	XF	Unc	BU
1997 Proof	Est. 7,500	Value: 50.00				

KM# 577 CROWN

28.2800 g., 0.9250 Silver .8411 oz. ASW, 38.8 mm. **Ruler:** Elizabeth II **Series:** Wonders of the World **Subject:** The Colossus of Rhodes **Obv:** Crowned bust right **Rev:** Gold coin design inset on large statue

Date	Mintage	F	VF	XF	Unc	BU
1997 Proof	Est. 7,500	Value: 50.00				

KM# 578 CROWN

28.2800 g., 0.9250 Silver .8411 oz. ASW, 38.8 mm. **Ruler:** Elizabeth II **Series:** Wonders of the World **Subject:** The Pyramids of Egypt **Obv:** Crowned bust right **Rev:** Gold coin design inset on pyramids

Date	Mintage	F	VF	XF	Unc	BU
1997 Proof	Est. 7,500	Value: 50.00				

KM# 579 CROWN

28.2800 g., 0.9250 Silver .8411 oz. ASW, 38.8 mm. **Ruler:** Elizabeth II **Series:** Wonders of the World **Subject:** The Hanging Gardens of Babylon **Obv:** Crowned bust right **Rev:** Gold coin design inset on an overgrown building

Date	Mintage	F	VF	XF	Unc	BU
1997 Proof	Est. 7,500	Value: 50.00				

KM# 580 CROWN

28.2800 g., 0.9250 Silver .8411 oz. ASW, 38.8 mm. **Ruler:** Elizabeth II **Series:** Wonders of the World **Subject:** The Temple of Artemis at Ephesus **Obv:** Crowned bust right **Rev:** Gold coin design inset on classic Greek building

Date	Mintage	F	VF	XF	Unc	BU
1997	Est. 7,500	Value: 50.00				

KM# 582 CROWN

28.2800 g., 0.9250 Silver .8411 oz. ASW, 38.8 mm. **Ruler:** Elizabeth II **Series:** Evolution of Mankind **Subject:** Egypt **Obv:** Crowned bust right **Rev:** Three ancient Egyptians, pyramids, hieroglyphics

Date	Mintage	F	VF	XF	Unc	BU
1997 Proof	Est. 10,000	Value: 40.00				

KM# 584 CROWN

28.2800 g., 0.9250 Silver .8411 oz. ASW, 38.8 mm. **Ruler:** Elizabeth II **Series:** Evolution of Mankind **Subject:** Israel **Obv:** Crowned bust right **Rev:** Star of David, Moses and Temple of Solomon

Date	Mintage	F	VF	XF	Unc	BU
1997 Proof	Est. 10,000	Value: 40.00				

KM# 586 CROWN

28.2800 g., 0.9250 Silver .8411 oz. ASW, 38.8 mm. **Ruler:** Elizabeth II **Series:** Evolution of Mankind **Subject:** China **Obv:** Crowned bust right **Rev:** Emperor and the Great Wall

Date	Mintage	F	VF	XF	Unc	BU
1997 Proof	Est. 10,000	Value: 40.00				

KM# 588 CROWN

28.2800 g., 0.9250 Silver .8411 oz. ASW, 38.8 mm. **Ruler:** Elizabeth II **Series:** Evolution of Mankind **Subject:** Greece **Obv:** Crowned bust right **Rev:** Aristotle, classic Greek building

Date	Mintage	F	VF	XF	Unc	BU
1997 Proof	Est. 10,000	Value: 40.00				

KM# 590 CROWN

28.2800 g., 0.9250 Silver .8411 oz. ASW, 38.8 mm. **Ruler:** Elizabeth II **Series:** Evolution of Mankind **Subject:** Rome **Obv:** Crowned bust right **Rev:** Julius Caesar and Stonehenge

Date	Mintage	F	VF	XF	Unc	BU
1997 Proof	Est. 10,000	Value: 40.00				

KM# 592 CROWN

28.2800 g., 0.9250 Silver .8411 oz. ASW, 38.8 mm. **Ruler:** Elizabeth II **Series:** Evolution of Mankind **Subject:** India **Obv:** Crowned bust right **Rev:** Krishna playing flute by a temple

Date	Mintage	F	VF	XF	Unc	BU
1997 Proof	Est. 10,000	Value: 40.00				

KM# 594 CROWN

28.2800 g., 0.9250 Silver .8411 oz. ASW, 38.8 mm. **Ruler:** Elizabeth II **Series:** Evolution of Mankind **Subject:** Holy Roman Empire **Obv:** Crowned bust right **Rev:** Charlemagne and soldiers on horseback

Date	Mintage	F	VF	XF	Unc	BU
1997 Proof	Est. 10,000	Value: 40.00				

KM# 596 CROWN

28.2800 g., 0.9250 Silver .8411 oz. ASW, 38.8 mm. **Ruler:** Elizabeth II **Series:** Evolution of Mankind **Subject:** Macedonia **Obv:** Crowned bust right **Rev:** Alexander the Great on horseback

Date	Mintage	F	VF	XF	Unc	BU
1997 Proof	Est. 10,000	Value: 40.00				

KM# 598 CROWN

28.2800 g., 0.9250 Silver .8411 oz. ASW, 38.8 mm. **Ruler:** Elizabeth II **Series:** Evolution of Mankind **Subject:** Native America **Obv:** Crowned bust right **Rev:** North American native on horseback and totem pole

Date	Mintage	F	VF	XF	Unc	BU
1997 Proof	Est. 10,000	Value: 40.00				

KM# 600 CROWN

28.2800 g., 0.9250 Silver .8411 oz. ASW, 38.8 mm. **Ruler:** Elizabeth II **Series:** Evolution of Mankind **Subject:** Asia **Obv:** Crowned bust right **Rev:** Buddha and temple

Date	Mintage	F	VF	XF	Unc	BU
1997 Proof	Est. 10,000	Value: 40.00				

KM# 602 CROWN

28.2800 g., 0.9250 Silver .8411 oz. ASW, 38.8 mm. **Ruler:** Elizabeth II **Series:** Evolution of Mankind **Subject:** Inca Empire **Obv:** Crowned bust right **Rev:** Incan Emperor and Machu Picchu

Date	Mintage	F	VF	XF	Unc	BU
1997 Proof	Est. 10,000	Value: 40.00				

KM# 604 CROWN

28.2800 g., 0.9250 Silver .8411 oz. ASW, 38.8 mm. **Ruler:** Elizabeth II **Series:** Evolution of Mankind **Subject:** Islamic Civilization **Obv:** Crowned bust right **Rev:** General Tariq Ibn Ziyad and building

Date	Mintage	F	VF	XF	Unc	BU
1997 Proof	Est. 10,000	Value: 40.00				

KM# 609 CROWN

28.2800 g., 0.9250 Silver .8410 oz. ASW, 38.8 mm. **Ruler:** Elizabeth II **Series:** Traders of the World **Subject:** Sir Francis Drake **Obv:** Crowned bust right **Rev:** Sir Francis Drake, ship and beach

Date	Mintage	F	VF	XF	Unc	BU
1997 Proof	Est. 10,000	Value: 45.00				

KM# 611 CROWN

28.2800 g., 0.9250 Silver .8410 oz. ASW, 38.8 mm. **Ruler:** Elizabeth II **Series:** Traders of the World **Subject:** Romans **Obv:** Crowned bust right **Rev:** Lion, lioness, ship and map

Date	Mintage	F	VF	XF	Unc	BU
1997 Proof	Est. 10,000	Value: 45.00				

KM# 613 CROWN

28.2800 g., 0.9250 Silver .8410 oz. ASW, 38.8 mm. **Ruler:** Elizabeth II **Series:** Traders of the World **Subject:** Venetians **Obv:** Crowned bust right **Rev:** Pair of oysters with pearls, Venetian canal scene

Date	Mintage	F	VF	XF	Unc	BU
1997 Proof	Est. 10,000	Value: 45.00				

KM# 615 CROWN

28.2800 g., 0.9250 Silver .8410 oz. ASW, 38.8 mm. **Ruler:** Elizabeth II **Series:** Traders of the World **Subject:** Portuguese **Obv:** Crowned bust right **Rev:** Gold ingots and Portuguese ship

Date	Mintage	F	VF	XF	Unc	BU
1997 Proof	Est. 10,000	Value: 45.00				

KM# 617 CROWN

28.2800 g., 0.9250 Silver .8410 oz. ASW, 38.8 mm. **Ruler:** Elizabeth II **Series:** Traders of the World **Subject:** Spanish **Obv:** Crowned bust right **Rev:** Tobacco leaves, ship, map, gems

Date	Mintage	F	VF	XF	Unc	BU
1997 Proof	Est. 10,000	Value: 45.00				

KM# 619 CROWN

28.2800 g., 0.9250 Silver .8410 oz. ASW, 38.8 mm. **Ruler:** Elizabeth II **Series:** Traders of the World **Subject:** English **Obv:** Crowned bust right **Rev:** Profile of Queen Elizabeth I above fighting ships

Date	Mintage	F	VF	XF	Unc	BU
1997 Proof	Est. 10,000	Value: 45.00				

KM# 621 CROWN

28.2800 g., 0.9250 Silver .8410 oz. ASW, 38.8 mm. **Ruler:** Elizabeth II **Series:** Traders of the World **Subject:** Captain Bligh **Obv:** Queen's portrait **Rev:** Figure seated on rock, ship at right

Date	Mintage	F	VF	XF	Unc	BU
1997 Proof	Est. 10,000	Value: 45.00				

KM# 623 CROWN

28.2800 g., 0.9250 Silver .8410 oz. ASW, 38.8 mm. **Ruler:** Elizabeth II **Series:** Traders of the World **Subject:** Captain Cook **Obv:** Crowned bust right **Rev:** Beaver on rock, ship at right, bust facing in background

Date	Mintage	F	VF	XF	Unc	BU
1997 Proof	Est. 10,000	Value: 45.00				

KM# 720 CROWN

Copper-Nickel, 38.8 mm. **Ruler:** Elizabeth II **Series:** Evolution of Mankind **Subject:** Homo Sapiens Hunting Mammoth **Obv:** Crowned bust right **Rev:** Figures spearing mammoth

Date	Mintage	F	VF	XF	Unc	BU
1998	—	—	—	—	10.00	15.00

KM# 636 CROWN

Copper-Nickel, 38.8 mm. **Ruler:** Elizabeth II **Series:** Winter Olympics - Japan **Obv:** Crowned bust right **Rev:** Speed skater and Bullet Train

Date	Mintage	F	VF	XF	Unc	BU
1998	—	—	—	—	8.00	10.00

KM# 636a CROWN

28.2800 g., 0.9250 Silver .8410 oz. ASW, 38.8 mm. **Ruler:** Elizabeth II **Series:** Winter Olympics - Japan **Obv:** Crowned bust right **Rev:** Speed skater and Bullet Train

Date	Mintage	F	VF	XF	Unc	BU
1998 Proof	Est. 30,000	Value: 45.00				

KM# 638 CROWN

Copper-Nickel, 38.8 mm. **Ruler:** Elizabeth II **Series:** Winter Olympics - Japan **Obv:** Crowned bust right **Rev:** Ski jumper and Buddha

Date	Mintage	F	VF	XF	Unc	BU
1998	—	—	—	—	8.00	10.00

KM# 638a CROWN

28.2800 g., 0.9250 Silver .8410 oz. ASW, 38.8 mm. **Ruler:** Elizabeth II **Subject:** Winter Olympics - Japan **Obv:** Crowned bust right **Rev:** Ski jumper and Buddha

Date	Mintage	F	VF	XF	Unc	BU
1998 Proof	Est. 30,000	Value: 45.00				

KM# 640 CROWN

Copper-Nickel, 38.8 mm. **Ruler:** Elizabeth II **Series:** Winter Olympics - Japan **Obv:** Crowned bust right **Rev:** Cross-country skiers

Date	Mintage	F	VF	XF	Unc	BU
1998	—	—	—	—	8.00	10.00

KM# 640a CROWN

28.2800 g., 0.9250 Silver .8410 oz. ASW, 38.8 mm. **Ruler:** Elizabeth II **Series:** Winter Olympics - Japan **Obv:** Crowned bust right **Rev:** Cross-country skiers

Date	Mintage	F	VF	XF	Unc	BU
1998 Proof	Est. 30,000	Value: 45.00				

KM# 642 CROWN

Copper-Nickel, 38.8 mm. **Ruler:** Elizabeth II **Series:** Winter Olympics - Japan **Obv:** Crowned bust right **Rev:** Slalom skier, Zenkoji temple

Date	Mintage	F	VF	XF	Unc	BU
1998	—	—	—	—	8.00	10.00

KM# 642a CROWN

28.2800 g., 0.9250 Silver .8410 oz. ASW, 38.8 mm. **Ruler:** Elizabeth II **Series:** Winter Olympics - Japan **Obv:** Crowned bust right **Rev:** Slalom skier, Zenkoji temple

Date	Mintage	F	VF	XF	Unc	BU
1998 Proof	Est. 30,000	Value: 45.00				

KM# 656 CROWN

Copper-Nickel, 38.8 mm. **Ruler:** Elizabeth II **Subject:** The Tale of Peter Rabbit **Obv:** Crowned bust right **Rev:** Standing rabbit facing, sparrow at left

Date	Mintage	F	VF	XF	Unc	BU
1998	—	—	—	—	10.00	12.00

KM# 656a CROWN

28.2800 g., 0.9250 Silver .8411 oz. ASW, 38.8 mm. **Ruler:** Elizabeth II **Subject:** The Tale of Peter Rabbit **Obv:** Crowned bust right **Rev:** Standing rabbit facing, sparrow at left

Date	Mintage	F	VF	XF	Unc	BU
1998 Proof	Est. 30,000	Value: 50.00				

KM# 661 CROWN

Copper-Nickel, 38.8 mm. **Ruler:** Elizabeth II **Subject:** Chrysanthemum **Obv:** Crowned bust right **Rev:** Three blossoms

Date	Mintage	F	VF	XF	Unc	BU
1998	—	—	—	—	8.50	9.50

KM# 661a CROWN

28.2800 g., 0.9250 Silver .8411 oz. ASW, 38.8 mm. **Ruler:** Elizabeth II **Subject:** Chrysanthemum **Obv:** Crowned bust right **Rev:** Three blossoms

Date	Mintage	F	VF	XF	Unc	BU
1998 Proof	Est. 30,000	Value: 50.00				

KM# 674 CROWN

28.2800 g., 0.9250 Silver .8411 oz. ASW, 38.8 mm. **Ruler:** Elizabeth II **Subject:** Britannia **Obv:** Crowned bust right **Rev:** Helmeted head right

Date	Mintage	F	VF	XF	Unc	BU
1998 Proof	Est. 10,000	Value: 50.00				

KM# 675 CROWN

28.2800 g., 0.9250 Silver .8411 oz. ASW, 38.8 mm. **Ruler:** Elizabeth II **Subject:** Juno **Obv:** Crowned bust right **Rev:** Head 3/4 facing

Date	Mintage	F	VF	XF	Unc	BU
1998 Proof	Est. 10,000	Value: 50.00				

KM# 676 CROWN

28.2800 g., 0.9250 Silver .8411 oz. ASW, 38.8 mm. **Ruler:** Elizabeth II **Subject:** Athena **Obv:** Crowned bust right **Rev:** Helmeted head right

Date	Mintage	F	VF	XF	Unc	BU
1998 Proof	Est. 10,000	Value: 50.00				

KM# 677 CROWN

28.2800 g., 0.9250 Silver .8411 oz. ASW, 38.8 mm. **Ruler:** Elizabeth II **Subject:** Arethusa **Obv:** Crowned bust right **Rev:** Head left with dolphins

Date	Mintage	F	VF	XF	Unc	BU
1998 Proof	Est. 10,000	Value: 50.00				

KM# 682 CROWN

Copper-Nickel, 38.8 mm. **Ruler:** Elizabeth II **Subject:** Paddington Bear **Obv:** Crowned bust right **Rev:** Bear with suitcase

Date	Mintage	F	VF	XF	Unc	BU
1998	—	—	—	—	10.00	12.00

KM# 682a CROWN
28.2800 g., 0.9250 Silver .8410 oz. ASW, 38.8 mm. **Ruler:** Elizabeth II **Subject:** Paddington Bear **Obv:** Crowned bust right **Rev:** Bear with suitcase

Date	Mintage	F	VF	XF	Unc	BU
1998 Proof	Est. 30,000	Value: 50.00				

KM# 687 CROWN
Copper-Nickel, 38.8 mm. **Ruler:** Elizabeth II **Series:** World Cup France 1998 **Obv:** Crowned bust right **Rev:** Goalie

Date	Mintage	F	VF	XF	Unc	BU
1998	—	—	—	—	8.00	9.00

KM# 687a CROWN
28.2800 g., 0.9250 Silver .8410 oz. ASW, 38.8 mm. **Ruler:** Elizabeth II **Series:** World Cup France 1998 **Obv:** Crowned bust right **Rev:** Goalie

Date	Mintage	F	VF	XF	Unc	BU
1998 Proof	Est. 30,000	Value: 50.00				

KM# 688 CROWN
Copper-Nickel, 38.8 mm. **Ruler:** Elizabeth II **Series:** World Cup France 1998 **Obv:** Crowned bust right **Rev:** Player kicking to the left

Date	Mintage	F	VF	XF	Unc	BU
1998	—	—	—	—	8.00	9.00

KM# 688a CROWN
28.2800 g., 0.9250 Silver .8410 oz. ASW, 38.8 mm. **Ruler:** Elizabeth II **Series:** World Cup France 1998 **Obv. Inscription:** Crowned bust right **Rev:** Player kicking to the left

Date	Mintage	F	VF	XF	Unc	BU
1998 Proof	Est. 30,000	Value: 50.00				

KM# 689 CROWN
Copper-Nickel, 38.8 mm. **Ruler:** Elizabeth II **Series:** World Cup France 1998 **Obv:** Crowned bust right **Rev:** Player advancing ball

Date	Mintage	F	VF	XF	Unc	BU
1998	—	—	—	—	8.00	9.00

KM# 689a CROWN
28.2800 g., 0.9250 Silver .8410 oz. ASW, 38.8 mm. **Ruler:** Elizabeth II **Series:** World Cup France 1998 **Obv:** Crowned bust right **Rev:** Player advancing ball

Date	Mintage	F	VF	XF	Unc	BU
1998 Proof	Est. 30,000	Value: 50.00				

KM# 690 CROWN
Copper-Nickel, 38.8 mm. **Ruler:** Elizabeth II **Series:** World Cup France 1998 **Obv:** Crowned bust right **Rev:** Two players

Date	Mintage	F	VF	XF	Unc	BU
1998	—	—	—	—	8.00	9.00

KM# 690a CROWN
28.2800 g., 0.9250 Silver .8410 oz. ASW, 38.8 mm. **Ruler:** Elizabeth II **Series:** World Cup France 1998 **Obv:** Crowned bust right **Rev:** Two players

Date	Mintage	F	VF	XF	Unc	BU
1998 Proof	Est. 30,000	Value: 50.00				

KM# 692 CROWN
28.2800 g., 0.9250 Silver .8410 oz. ASW, 38.8 mm. **Ruler:** Elizabeth II **Series:** Traders of the World **Subject:** Phoenecians **Obv:** Crowned bust right **Rev:** Galley (200BC-600AD) above shells

Date	Mintage	F	VF	XF	Unc	BU
1998 Proof	Est. 10,000	Value: 50.00				

KM# 694 CROWN
28.2800 g., 0.9250 Silver .8410 oz. ASW, 38.8 mm. **Ruler:** Elizabeth II **Series:** Traders of the World **Subject:** Vikings, 900AD **Obv:** Crowned bust right **Rev:** Ship (900AD), pair of fish and walrus tusks

Date	Mintage	F	VF	XF	Unc	BU
1998 Proof	Est. 10,000	Value: 50.00				

KM# 696 CROWN
28.2800 g., 0.9250 Silver .8410 oz. ASW, 38.8 mm. **Ruler:** Elizabeth II **Series:** Traders of the World **Subject:** Marco Polo, 1254-1324 **Obv:** Crowned bust right **Rev:** Chopsticks with noodles below bust at right, ship at left

Date	Mintage	F	VF	XF	Unc	BU
1998 Proof	Est. 10,000	Value: 50.00				

KM# 698 CROWN
28.2800 g., 0.9250 Silver .8410 oz. ASW, 38.8 mm. **Ruler:** Elizabeth II **Series:** Traders of the World **Subject:** Hanseatic League Nations **Obv:** Queen's portrait **Rev:** Coins of the nations above Hanseatic Kogge (circa 1350), map at right

Date	Mintage	F	VF	XF	Unc	BU
1998 Proof	Est. 10,000	Value: 50.00				

KM# 700 CROWN
28.2800 g., 0.9250 Silver .8410 oz. ASW, 38.8 mm. **Ruler:** Elizabeth II **Series:** Traders of the World **Subject:** Chinese **Obv:** Crowned bust right **Rev:** Chinese Junk (1400s), silk worm and pottery

Date	Mintage	F	VF	XF	Unc	BU
1998 Proof	Est. 10,000	Value: 50.00				

KM# 702 CROWN
28.2800 g., 0.9250 Silver .8410 oz. ASW, 38.8 mm. **Ruler:** Elizabeth II **Series:** Traders of the World **Subject:** Christopher Columbus, 1451-1506 **Obv:** Crowned bust right **Rev:** Bust at left looking right, ship at right

Date	Mintage	F	VF	XF	Unc	BU
1998 Proof	Est. 10,000	Value: 50.00				

KM# 704 CROWN
Copper-Nickel, 38.8 mm. **Ruler:** Elizabeth II **Series:** Traders of the World **Subject:** Sir Walter Raleigh, 1552-1618 **Obv:** Crowned bust right **Rev:** Standing figure, ship in background

Date	Mintage	F	VF	XF	Unc	BU
1998	—	—	—	—	10.00	14.00

KM# 704a CROWN
28.2800 g., 0.9250 Silver .8410 oz. ASW, 38.8 mm. **Ruler:** Elizabeth II **Series:** Traders of the World **Subject:** Sir Walter Raleigh, 1552-1618 **Obv:** Crowned bust right **Rev:** Standing figure, ship in background

Date	Mintage	F	VF	XF	Unc	BU
1998 Proof	Est. 10,000	Value: 50.00				

KM# 706 CROWN
28.2800 g., 0.9250 Silver .8410 oz. ASW, 38.8 mm. **Ruler:** Elizabeth II **Series:** Traders of the World **Obv:** Crowned bust right **Rev:** Boston Tea Party (1773) scene, tea leaf above

Date	Mintage	F	VF	XF	Unc	BU
1998 Proof	Est. 10,000	Value: 50.00				

KM# 708 CROWN
Copper-Nickel, 38.8 mm. **Ruler:** Elizabeth II **Series:** Evolution of Mankind **Subject:** Australopithecus, Lucy **Obv:** Crowned bust right **Rev:** Upright figure left, brain depiction at left

Date	Mintage	F	VF	XF	Unc	BU
1998	—	—	—	—	12.00	15.00

KM# 708a CROWN
28.2800 g., 0.9250 Silver .8410 oz. ASW, 38.8 mm. **Ruler:** Elizabeth II **Series:** Evolution of Mankind **Subject:** Australopithecus, Lucy **Obv:** Crowned bust right **Rev:** Upright figure left, brain depiction at left

Date	Mintage	F	VF	XF	Unc	BU
1998 Proof	Est. 10,000	Value: 50.00				

KM# 710 CROWN
Copper-Nickel, 38.8 mm. **Ruler:** Elizabeth II **Series:** Evolution of Mankind **Subject:** Homo Habilis **Obv:** Crowned bust right **Rev:** Squatted figure right using tools

Date	Mintage	F	VF	XF	Unc	BU
1998	—	—	—	—	12.00	15.00

KM# 710a CROWN
28.2800 g., 0.9250 Silver .8410 oz. ASW, 38.8 mm. **Ruler:** Elizabeth II **Series:** Evolution of Mankind **Subject:** Homo Habilis **Obv:** Crowned bust right **Rev:** Squatted figure right using tools

Date	Mintage	F	VF	XF	Unc	BU
1998 Proof	Est. 10,000	Value: 50.00				

KM# 712 CROWN
Copper-Nickel, 38.8 mm. **Ruler:** Elizabeth II **Series:** Evolution of Mankind **Subject:** Homo Erectus **Obv:** Crowned bust right **Rev:** Three figures with fire

Date	Mintage	F	VF	XF	Unc	BU
1998	—	—	—	—	12.00	15.00

KM# 712a CROWN
28.2800 g., 0.9250 Silver .8410 oz. ASW, 38.8 mm. **Ruler:** Elizabeth II **Series:** Evolution of Mankind **Subject:** Homo Erectus **Obv:** Crowned bust right **Rev:** Three figures with fire

Date	Mintage	F	VF	XF	Unc	BU
1998 Proof	Est. 10,000	Value: 50.00				

KM# 714 CROWN
Copper-Nickel, 38.8 mm. **Ruler:** Elizabeth II **Series:** Evolution of Mankind **Subject:** Gibraltar Skull **Obv:** Crowned bust right **Rev:** Skull, rock and caveman

Date	Mintage	F	VF	XF	Unc	BU
1998	—	—	—	—	12.00	15.00

KM# 714a CROWN
28.2800 g., 0.9250 Silver .8410 oz. ASW, 38.8 mm. **Ruler:** Elizabeth II **Series:** Evolution of Mankind **Subject:** Gibraltar Skull **Obv:** Crowned bust right **Rev:** Skull, rock and caveman

Date	Mintage	F	VF	XF	Unc	BU
1998 Proof	Est. 10,000	Value: 50.00				

KM# 716 CROWN
Copper-Nickel, 38.8 mm. **Ruler:** Elizabeth II **Series:** Evolution of Mankind **Subject:** Neanderthal Man **Obv:** Crowned bust right **Rev:** Skull left of burial scene

Date	Mintage	F	VF	XF	Unc	BU
1998	—	—	—	—	12.00	15.00

KM# 716a CROWN
28.2800 g., 0.9250 Silver .8410 oz. ASW, 38.8 mm. **Ruler:** Elizabeth II **Series:** Evolution of Mankind **Subject:** Neanderthal Man **Obv:** Crowned bust right **Rev:** Skull left of burial scene

Date	Mintage	F	VF	XF	Unc	BU
1998 Proof	Est. 10,000	Value: 50.00				

KM# 718 CROWN
Copper-Nickel, 38.8 mm. **Ruler:** Elizabeth II **Series:** Evolution of Mankind **Subject:** Homo Sapiens **Obv:** Crowned bust right **Rev:** Figure doing cave painting

Date	Mintage	F	VF	XF	Unc	BU
1998	—	—	—	—	12.00	15.00

KM# 718a CROWN
28.2800 g., 0.9250 Silver .8410 oz. ASW, 38.8 mm. **Ruler:** Elizabeth II **Series:** Evolution of Mankind **Subject:** Homo Sapiens **Obv:** Crowned bust right **Rev:** Figure doing cave painting

Date	Mintage	F	VF	XF	Unc	BU
1998 Proof	Est. 10,000	Value: 50.00				

KM# 720a CROWN
28.2800 g., 0.9250 Silver .8410 oz. ASW, 38.8 mm. **Ruler:** Elizabeth II **Series:** Evolution of Mankind **Subject:** Homo Sapiens Hunting Mammoth **Obv:** Crowned bust right **Rev:** Figures spearing mammoth

Date	Mintage	F	VF	XF	Unc	BU
1998 Proof	Est. 10,000	Value: 50.00				

KM# 722a CROWN
28.2800 g., 0.9250 Silver .8410 oz. ASW, 38.8 mm. **Ruler:** Elizabeth II **Series:** Evolution of Mankind **Obv:** Queen's portrait **Rev:** Illustrated theory of evolution

Date	Mintage	F	VF	XF	Unc	BU
1998 Proof	Est. 10,000	Value: 50.00				

KM# 722.1 CROWN
Copper-Nickel, 38.8 mm. **Ruler:** Elizabeth II **Series:** Evolution of Mankind **Obv:** Queen's portrait **Rev:** Pictorial representation of theory of evolution, denomination below

Date	Mintage	F	VF	XF	Unc	BU
1998	—	—	—	—	12.00	15.00

KM# 724 CROWN
Copper-Nickel, 38.8 mm. **Ruler:** Elizabeth II **Series:** Evolution of Mankind **Subject:** The Common Ancestry of Ape and Man **Obv:** Crowned bust right **Rev:** Human and primate mothers with young

Date	Mintage	F	VF	XF	Unc	BU
1998	—	—	—	—	12.00	15.00

KM# 724a CROWN
28.2800 g., 0.9250 Silver .8410 oz. ASW, 38.8 mm. **Ruler:** Elizabeth II **Series:** Evolution of Mankind **Subject:** The Common Ancestry of Ape and Man **Obv:** Crowned bust right **Rev:** Human and primate mothers with young

Date	Mintage	F	VF	XF	Unc	BU
1998 Proof	Est. 10,000	Value: 50.00				

KM# 726 CROWN
Copper-Nickel, 38.8 mm. **Ruler:** Elizabeth II **Series:** Evolution of Mankind **Subject:** Charles Darwin, 1809-1882 **Obv:** Homo Sapiens Hunting Mammoth **Rev:** Bust facing, caveman and space shuttle at right

Date	Mintage	F	VF	XF	Unc	BU
1998	—	—	—	—	12.00	15.00

KM# 726a CROWN
28.2800 g., 0.9250 Silver .8410 oz. ASW, 38.8 mm. **Ruler:** Elizabeth II **Series:** Evolution of Mankind **Subject:** Charles Darwin, 1809-1882 **Obv:** Crowned bust right **Rev:** Bust facing, caveman and space shuttle at right

Date	Mintage	F	VF	XF	Unc	BU
1998 Proof	Est. 10,000	Value: 50.00				

KM# 728 CROWN
Copper-Nickel, 38.8 mm. **Ruler:** Elizabeth II **Series:** Evolution of Mankind **Subject:** Raymond Dart **Obv:** Crowned bust right **Rev:** Bust at left looking at skull

Date	Mintage	F	VF	XF	Unc	BU
1998	—	—	—	—	12.00	15.00

KM# 728a CROWN
28.2800 g., 0.9250 Silver .8410 oz. ASW, 38.8 mm. **Ruler:** Elizabeth II **Series:** Evolution of Mankind **Subject:** Raymond Dart **Obv:** Crowned bust right **Rev:** Bust at left looking at skull on right

Date	Mintage	F	VF	XF	Unc	BU
1998 Proof	Est. 10,000	Value: 50.00				

KM# 730 CROWN
Copper-Nickel, 38.8 mm. **Ruler:** Elizabeth II **Series:** Evolution of Mankind **Subject:** 20th Century Homo Sapiens **Obv:** Crowned bust right **Rev:** Five depictions of evolution

Date	Mintage	F	VF	XF	Unc	BU
1998	—	—	—	—	12.00	15.00

KM# 730a CROWN
28.2800 g., 0.9250 Silver .8410 oz. ASW, 38.8 mm. **Ruler:** Elizabeth II **Series:** Evolution of Mankind **Subject:** 20th Century Homo Sapiens **Obv:** Crowned bust right **Rev:** Five depictions of evolution

Date	Mintage	F	VF	XF	Unc	BU
1998 Proof	Est. 10,000	Value: 50.00				

KM# 733 CROWN
28.2800 g., 0.9250 Silver .8410 oz. ASW, 38.8 mm. **Ruler:** Elizabeth II **Series:** Wonders of the World **Subject:** Guilin Hills, China **Obv:** Crowned bust right **Rev:** Chinese coin design inlay below hill scene

Date	Mintage	F	VF	XF	Unc	BU
1998 Proof	Est. 7,500	Value: 60.00				

KM# 734 CROWN
28.2800 g., 0.9250 Silver .8410 oz. ASW, 38.8 mm. **Ruler:** Elizabeth II **Series:** Wonders of the World **Subject:** Victoria Falls, Africa **Obv:** Crowned bust right **Rev:** South African coin design inlay below falls scene

Date	Mintage	F	VF	XF	Unc	BU
1998 Proof	Est. 7,500	Value: 60.00				

KM# 735 CROWN
28.2800 g., 0.9250 Silver .8410 oz. ASW, 38.8 mm. **Ruler:** Elizabeth II **Series:** Wonders of the World **Subject:** The Materhorn, Switzerland, Italy **Obv:** Crowned bust right **Rev:** Swiss coin design inlay below mountain

Date	Mintage	F	VF	XF	Unc	BU
1998 Proof	Est. 7,500	Value: 60.00				

KM# 736 CROWN
28.2800 g., 0.9250 Silver .8410 oz. ASW, 38.8 mm. **Ruler:** Elizabeth II **Series:** Wonders of the World **Subject:** Taroko Gorge, Taiwan **Obv:** Crowned bust right **Rev:** Taiwanese coin design inlay below gorge scene

Date	Mintage	F	VF	XF	Unc	BU
1998 Proof	Est. 7,500	Value: 60.00				

KM# 737 CROWN
28.2800 g., 0.9250 Silver .8410 oz. ASW, 38.8 mm. **Ruler:** Elizabeth II **Series:** Wonders of the World **Subject:** Niagara Falls, Canada, USA **Obv:** Crowned bust right **Rev:** American coin design inlay below falls scene

Date	Mintage	F	VF	XF	Unc	BU
1998 Proof	Est. 7,500	Value: 60.00				

KM# 738 CROWN
28.2800 g., 0.9250 Silver .8410 oz. ASW, 38.8 mm. **Ruler:** Elizabeth II **Series:** Wonders of the World **Subject:** Mount Fuji, Japan **Obv:** Crowned bust right **Rev:** Japanese coin design inlay below plants and mountain

Date	Mintage	F	VF	XF	Unc	BU
1998 Proof	Est. 7,500	Value: 60.00				

KM# 739 CROWN
28.2800 g., 0.9250 Silver .8410 oz. ASW, 38.8 mm. **Ruler:** Elizabeth II **Series:** Wonders of the World **Subject:** Uluru, Australia **Obv:** Crowned bust right **Rev:** Australian coin design inlay below mountain

Date	Mintage	F	VF	XF	Unc	BU
1998 Proof	Est. 7,500	Value: 60.00				

KM# 745 CROWN
Copper-Nickel, 38.8 mm. **Ruler:** Elizabeth II **Series:** Year of the Ocean **Obv:** Crowned bust right **Rev:** Mermaid and dolphin

Date	Mintage	F	VF	XF	Unc	BU
1998	—	—	—	—	10.00	12.50

KM# 745a CROWN
28.2800 g., 0.9250 Silver .8410 oz. ASW, 38.8 mm. **Ruler:** Elizabeth II **Series:** Year of the Ocean **Obv:** Crowned bust right **Rev:** Mermaid and dolphin

Date	Mintage	F	VF	XF	Unc	BU
1998 Proof	Est. 30,000	Value: 50.00				

KM# 746 CROWN
Copper-Nickel, 38.8 mm. **Ruler:** Elizabeth II **Series:** Year of the Ocean **Obv:** Crowned bust right **Rev:** Octopus, fish and coral

Date	Mintage	F	VF	XF	Unc	BU
1998	—	—	—	—	10.00	12.50

KM# 746a CROWN
28.2800 g., 0.9250 Silver .8410 oz. ASW, 38.8 mm. **Ruler:** Elizabeth II **Series:** Year of the Ocean **Obv:** Crowned bust right **Rev:** Octopus, fish and coral

Date	Mintage	F	VF	XF	Unc	BU
1998 Proof	Est. 30,000	Value: 50.00				

KM# 747 CROWN
Copper-Nickel, 38.8 mm. **Ruler:** Elizabeth II **Series:** Year of the Ocean **Obv:** Crowned bust right **Rev:** Jellyfish, stingray and fish

Date	Mintage	F	VF	XF	Unc	BU
1998	—	—	—	—	10.00	12.50

KM# 747a CROWN
28.2800 g., 0.9250 Silver .8410 oz. ASW, 38.8 mm. **Ruler:** Elizabeth II **Series:** Year of the Ocean **Obv:** Crowned bust right **Rev:** Jellyfish, stingray and fish

Date	Mintage	F	VF	XF	Unc	BU
1998 Proof	Est. 30,000	Value: 60.00				

KM# 748 CROWN
Copper-Nickel, 38.8 mm. **Ruler:** Elizabeth II **Series:** Year of the Ocean **Obv:** Crowned bust right **Rev:** Two wind surfers

Date	Mintage	F	VF	XF	Unc	BU
1998	—	—	—	—	9.50	12.00

KM# 748a CROWN
28.2800 g., 0.9250 Silver .8410 oz. ASW, 38.8 mm. **Ruler:** Elizabeth II **Series:** Year of the Ocean **Obv:** Crowned bust right **Rev:** Two wind surfers

Date	Mintage	F	VF	XF	Unc	BU
1998 Proof	Est. 30,000	Value: 60.00				

KM# 768 CROWN
Copper-Nickel, 38.8 mm. **Ruler:** Elizabeth II **Subject:** The Gibraltar Regiment New Colors **Obv:** Crowned bust right **Rev:** Soldier presenting keys, flags and crowned arms

Date	Mintage	F	VF	XF	Unc	BU
1998	—	—	—	—	10.00	12.50

KM# 768a CROWN
28.2800 g., 0.9250 Silver .8410 oz. ASW, 38.8 mm. **Ruler:** Elizabeth II **Subject:** The Gibraltar Regiment New Colors **Obv:** Crowned bust right **Rev:** Soldier presenting keys, flags and crowned arms

Date	Mintage	F	VF	XF	Unc	BU
1998 Proof	Est. 30,000	Value: 50.00				

KM# 799 CROWN
Copper-Nickel, 38.8 mm. **Ruler:** Elizabeth II **Series:** The World At War **Subject:** General D.D. Eisenhower **Obv:** Crowned bust right **Rev:** North African invasion scene

Date	Mintage	F	VF	XF	Unc	BU
1998	—	—	—	—	8.00	10.00

KM# 799a CROWN
28.2800 g., 0.9250 Silver .8410 oz. ASW, 38.8 mm. **Ruler:** Elizabeth II **Series:** The World At War **Subject:** General D.D. Eisenhower **Obv:** Crowned bust right **Rev:** North African invasion scene

Date	Mintage	F	VF	XF	Unc	BU
1998 Proof	Est. 10,000	Value: 50.00				

KM# 791 CROWN
28.2800 g., Copper-Nickel, 38.8 mm. **Ruler:** Elizabeth II **Series:** Summer Olympics - Sydney **Obv:** Crowned bust right **Rev:** Two oarsmen below cockatoos

Date	Mintage	F	VF	XF	Unc	BU
1999	—	—	—	—	8.00	10.00
2000PM	—	—	—	—	8.00	10.00

KM# 785 CROWN
28.2800 g., Copper-Nickel, 38.8 mm. **Ruler:** Elizabeth II **Series:** Summer Olympics - Sydney **Obv:** Crowned bust right **Rev:** Broad jumper and kangaroo

Date	Mintage	F	VF	XF	Unc	BU
1999	—	—	—	—	8.00	10.00
2000PM	—	—	—	—	8.00	10.00

KM# 787 CROWN
28.2800 g., Copper-Nickel, 38.8 mm. **Ruler:** Elizabeth II **Series:** Summer Olympics - Sydney **Obv:** Crowned bust right **Rev:** Sailboats and platypus

Date	Mintage	F	VF	XF	Unc	BU
1999	—	—	—	—	8.00	10.00
2000PM	—	—	—	—	8.00	10.00

KM# 789 CROWN
28.2800 g., Copper-Nickel, 38.8 mm. **Ruler:** Elizabeth II **Series:** Summer Olympics - Sydney **Obv:** Crowned bust right **Rev:** Swimmer and koala bear

Date	Mintage	F	VF	XF	Unc	BU
1999	—	—	—	—	8.00	10.00
2000PM	—	—	—	—	8.00	10.00

KM# 793 CROWN
28.2800 g., Copper-Nickel, 38.8 mm. **Ruler:** Elizabeth II **Series:** Summer Olympics - Sydney **Obv:** Crowned bust right **Rev:** Man with torch and dingo, denomination below

Date	Mintage	F	VF	XF	Unc	BU
1999	—	—	—	—	8.00	10.00
2000PM	—	—	—	—	8.00	10.00

KM# 859 CROWN
Copper-Nickel, 38.8 mm. **Ruler:** Elizabeth II **Series:** The World At War **Subject:** The Blitz **Obv:** Crowned bust right **Rev:** Firefighters in action after air raid

Date	Mintage	F	VF	XF	Unc	BU
1999	—	—	—	—	10.00	12.00

KM# 795 CROWN
28.2800 g., Copper-Nickel, 38.8 mm. **Ruler:** Elizabeth II **Series:** Summer Olympics - Sydney **Obv:** Crowned bust right **Rev:** Runner with torch, Aboriginal portrait and Ayer's Rock

Date	Mintage	F	VF	XF	Unc	BU
1999	—	—	—	—	8.00	10.00
2000PM	—	—	—	—	8.00	10.00

KM# 783.1 CROWN
Copper-Nickel, 38.8 mm. **Ruler:** Elizabeth II **Subject:** 1999 The Year of the Rabbit **Obv:** Cronwned bust right **Rev:** Rabbit reading, sparrow, Chinese characters

Date	Mintage	F	VF	XF	Unc	BU
1999	—	—	—	—	10.00	12.00

KM# 783.1a CROWN
28.2800 g., 0.9250 Silver .8410 oz. ASW, 38.8 mm. **Ruler:** Elizabeth II **Subject:** 1999 The Year of the Rabbit **Obv:** Crowned bust right **Rev:** Rabbit reading, sparrow, Chinese characters

Date	Mintage	F	VF	XF	Unc	BU
1999 Proof	Est. 10,000	Value: 50.00				

KM# 783.2 CROWN
Copper-Nickel, 38.8 mm. **Ruler:** Elizabeth II **Obv:** Crowned bust right **Rev:** Rabbit reading, sparrow; without Chinese characters

Date	Mintage	F	VF	XF	Unc	BU
1999	Inc. above	—	—	—	10.00	12.00

KM# 783.2a CROWN
28.2800 g., 0.9250 Silver .8410 oz. ASW, 38.8 mm. **Ruler:** Elizabeth II **Obv:** Crowned bust right **Rev:** Rabbit reading, sparrow; without Chinese characters

Date	Mintage	F	VF	XF	Unc	BU
1999 Proof	Inc. above	Value: 50.00				

KM# 785a CROWN
28.2800 g., 0.9250 Silver .8410 oz. ASW, 38.8 mm. **Ruler:** Elizabeth II **Series:** Summer Olympics - Sydney **Obv:** Crowned bust right **Rev:** Broad jumper and kangaroo

Date	Mintage	F	VF	XF	Unc	BU
1999 Proof	Est. 30,000	Value: 50.00				

KM# 787a CROWN
28.2800 g., 0.9250 Silver .8410 oz. ASW, 38.8 mm. **Ruler:** Elizabeth II **Series:** Summer Olympics - Sydney **Obv:** Crowned bust right **Rev:** Sailboats and platypus

Date	Mintage	F	VF	XF	Unc	BU
1999 Proof	Est. 30,000	Value: 50.00				

KM# 789a CROWN
28.2800 g., 0.9250 Silver .8410 oz. ASW, 38.8 mm. **Ruler:** Elizabeth II **Series:** Summer Olympics - Sydney **Obv:** Crowned bust right **Rev:** Swimmer and koala bear

Date	Mintage	F	VF	XF	Unc	BU
1999 Proof	Est. 30,000	Value: 50.00				

KM# 791a CROWN
28.2800 g., 0.9250 Silver .8410 oz. ASW, 38.8 mm. **Ruler:** Elizabeth II **Series:** Summer Olympics - Sydney **Obv:** Crowned bust right **Rev:** Two oarsmen below cockatoos **Note:** Prev. KM791.1

Date	Mintage	F	VF	XF	Unc	BU
1999 Proof	Est. 30,000	Value: 50.00				

KM# 793a CROWN
28.2800 g., 0.9250 Silver .8410 oz. ASW, 38.8 mm. **Ruler:** Elizabeth II **Series:** Summer Olympics - Sydney **Obv:** Crowned bust right **Rev:** Man with torch and dingo

Date	Mintage	F	VF	XF	Unc	BU
1999 Proof	Est. 30,000	Value: 50.00				

KM# 795a CROWN
28.2800 g., 0.9250 Silver .8410 oz. ASW, 38.8 mm. **Ruler:** Elizabeth II **Series:** Summer Olympics - Sydney **Obv:** Crowned bust right **Rev:** Runner with torch, Aboriginal portrait and Ayer's Rock

Date	Mintage	F	VF	XF	Unc	BU
1999 Proof	Est. 30,000	Value: 50.00				

KM# 796.1 CROWN
6.2200 g., 0.9999 Gold .2000 oz. AGW **Ruler:** Elizabeth II **Subject:** Millennium 2000 **Obv:** Head with tiara right **Obv. Designer:** Rank-Broadley **Rev:** Sundial, digital clock face, candle and traditional clock face

Date	Mintage	F	VF	XF	Unc	BU
1999 Proof	5,000	Value: 175				

KM# 801 CROWN
Copper-Nickel, 38.8 mm. **Ruler:** Elizabeth II **Subject:** King Alfred the Great, 871-899 **Obv:** Crowned bust right **Rev:** Crowned bust left, dates

Date	Mintage	F	VF	XF	Unc	BU
1999	—	—	—	—	7.50	9.00

KM# 801a CROWN
28.2800 g., 0.9250 Silver .8410 oz. ASW, 38.8 mm. **Ruler:** Elizabeth II **Subject:** King Alfred the Great, 871-899 **Obv:** Crowned bust right **Rev:** Crowned bust left, dates

Date	Mintage	F	VF	XF	Unc	BU
1999 Proof	Est. 10,000	Value: 45.00				

KM# 803 CROWN
Copper-Nickel, 38.8 mm. **Ruler:** Elizabeth II **Subject:** King Canute, 1016-1035 **Obv:** Crowned bust right **Rev:** Crowned bust left, dates

Date	Mintage	F	VF	XF	Unc	BU
1999	—	—	—	—	7.50	9.00

KM# 803a CROWN
28.2800 g., 0.9250 Silver .8410 oz. ASW, 38.8 mm. **Ruler:** Elizabeth II **Subject:** King Canute, 1016-1035 **Obv:** Crowned bust right **Rev:** Crowned bust left, dates

Date	Mintage	F	VF	XF	Unc	BU
1999 Proof	Est. 10,000	Value: 45.00				

KM# 805 CROWN
Copper-Nickel, 38.8 mm. **Ruler:** Elizabeth II **Subject:** King Edward the Confessor, 1042-1066 **Obv:** Crowned bust right **Rev:** Crowned bust left, dates

Date	Mintage	F	VF	XF	Unc	BU
1999	—	—	—	—	7.50	9.00

KM# 805a CROWN
28.2800 g., 0.9250 Silver .8410 oz. ASW, 38.8 mm. **Ruler:** Elizabeth II **Subject:** King Edward the Confessor, 1042-1066 **Obv:** Crowned bust right **Rev:** Crowned bust left, dates

Date	Mintage	F	VF	XF	Unc	BU
1999 Proof	Est. 10,000	Value: 45.00				

KM# 807 CROWN
Copper-Nickel, 38.8 mm. **Ruler:** Elizabeth II **Series:** House - Normandy **Subject:** King William I, 1066-1087 **Obv:** Crowned bust right **Rev:** Crowned bust left, dates

Date	Mintage	F	VF	XF	Unc	BU
1999	—	—	—	—	7.50	9.00

KM# 807a CROWN
28.2800 g., 0.9250 Silver .8410 oz. ASW, 38.8 mm. **Ruler:** Elizabeth II **Series:** House of - Normandy **Subject:** King William I, 1066-1087 **Obv:** Crowned bust right **Rev:** Crowned bust left, dates

Date	Mintage	F	VF	XF	Unc	BU
1999 Proof	Est. 10,000	Value: 45.00				

KM# 809 CROWN
Copper-Nickel, 38.8 mm. **Ruler:** Elizabeth II **Series:** House of - Plantagenet **Subject:** King Richard I, 1189-1199 **Obv:** Crowned bust right **Rev:** Crowned bust right, dates

Date	Mintage	F	VF	XF	Unc	BU
1999	—	—	—	—	7.50	9.00

KM# 809a CROWN
28.2800 g., 0.9250 Silver .8410 oz. ASW, 38.8 mm. **Ruler:** Elizabeth II **Series:** House of - Plantagenet **Subject:** King Richard I, 1189-1199 **Obv:** Crowned bust right **Rev:** Crowned bust right, dates

Date	Mintage	F	VF	XF	Unc	BU
1999 Proof	Est. 10,000	Value: 50.00				

KM# 811 CROWN
Copper-Nickel, 38.8 mm. **Ruler:** Elizabeth II **Series:** House of - Plantagenet **Subject:** King John, 1199-1216 **Obv:** Crowned bust right **Rev:** Crowned bust left, dates

Date	Mintage	F	VF	XF	Unc	BU
1999	—	—	—	—	7.50	9.00

KM# 811a CROWN
28.2800 g., 0.9250 Silver .8410 oz. ASW, 38.8 mm. **Ruler:** Elizabeth II **Series:** House of - Plantagenet **Subject:** King John, 1199-1216 **Obv:** Crowned bust right **Rev:** Crowned bust left, dates

Date	Mintage	F	VF	XF	Unc	BU
1999 Proof	Est. 10,000	Value: 45.00				

KM# 813 CROWN
Copper-Nickel, 38.8 mm. **Ruler:** Elizabeth II **Series:** House of - Lancaster **Subject:** King Henry V, 1413-1422 **Obv:** Crowned bust right **Rev:** Bust right, dates

Date	Mintage	F	VF	XF	Unc	BU
1999	—	—	—	—	7.50	9.00

KM# 813a CROWN
28.2800 g., 0.9250 Silver .8410 oz. ASW, 38.8 mm. **Ruler:** Elizabeth II **Series:** House of - Lancaster **Subject:** King Henry V, 1413-1422 **Obv:** Crowned bust right **Rev:** Bust right, dates

Date	Mintage	F	VF	XF	Unc	BU
1999 Proof	Est. 10,000	Value: 45.00				

KM# 815 CROWN
Copper-Nickel, 38.8 mm. **Ruler:** Elizabeth II **Series:** House of - York **Subject:** King Richard III, 1483-1485 **Obv:** Crowned bust right **Rev:** Bust with hat right, dates

Date	Mintage	F	VF	XF	Unc	BU
1999	—	—	—	—	7.50	9.00

KM# 815a CROWN
28.2800 g., 0.9250 Silver .8410 oz. ASW, 38.8 mm. **Ruler:** Elizabeth II **Series:** House of - York **Subject:** King Richard III, 1483-1485 **Obv:** Crowned bust right **Rev:** Bust with hat right, dates

Date	Mintage	F	VF	XF	Unc	BU
1999 Proof	Est. 10,000	Value: 45.00				

KM# 817 CROWN
Copper-Nickel, 38.8 mm. **Ruler:** Elizabeth II **Series:** House of - Tudor **Subject:** King Henry VIII, 1509-1547 **Obv:** Crowned bust right **Rev:** Bust with flat hat right, dates

Date	Mintage	F	VF	XF	Unc	BU
1999	—	—	—	—	7.50	9.00

KM# 817a CROWN
28.2800 g., 0.9250 Silver .8410 oz. ASW, 38.8 mm. **Ruler:** Elizabeth II **Series:** House of - Tudor **Subject:** King Henry VIII, 1509-1547 **Obv:** Crowned bust right **Rev:** Bust with flat hat right, dates

Date	Mintage	F	VF	XF	Unc	BU
1999 Proof	Est. 10,000	Value: 45.00				

KM# 819 CROWN
Copper-Nickel, 38.8 mm. **Ruler:** Elizabeth II **Series:** Tudor **Subject:** Queen Elizabeth I, 1558-1603 **Obv:** Crowned bust right **Rev:** Crowned bust with high ruffled collar left, dates

Date	Mintage	F	VF	XF	Unc	BU
1999	—	—	—	—	7.50	9.00

KM# 819a CROWN
28.2800 g., 0.9250 Silver .8410 oz. ASW, 38.8 mm. **Ruler:** Elizabeth II **Series:** House of - Tudor **Subject:** Queen Elizabeth I, 1558-1603 **Obv:** Crowned bust right **Rev:** Crowned bust with high ruffled collar left, dates

Date	Mintage	F	VF	XF	Unc	BU
1999 Proof	Est. 10,000	Value: 45.00				

KM# 821 CROWN
Copper-Nickel, 38.8 mm. **Ruler:** Elizabeth II **Series:** House of - Stuart **Subject:** King Charles I, 1625-1649 **Obv:** Crowned bust right **Rev:** Bust right, dates

Date	Mintage	F	VF	XF	Unc	BU
1999	—	—	—	—	7.50	9.00

KM# 821a CROWN
28.2800 g., 0.9250 Silver .8410 oz. ASW, 38.8 mm. **Ruler:** Elizabeth II **Series:** House of - Stuart **Subject:** King Charles I, 1625-1649 **Obv:** Crowned bust right **Rev:** Bust right, dates

Date	Mintage	F	VF	XF	Unc	BU
1999 Proof	Est. 10,000	Value: 45.00				

KM# 823 CROWN
Copper-Nickel, 38.8 mm. **Ruler:** Elizabeth II **Series:** House of - Stuart **Subject:** King Charles II, 1660-1685 **Obv:** Crowned bust right **Rev:** Laureate bust right, dates

Date	Mintage	F	VF	XF	Unc	BU
1999	—	—	—	—	7.50	9.00

KM# 823a CROWN
28.2800 g., 0.9250 Silver .8410 oz. ASW, 38.8 mm. **Ruler:** Elizabeth II **Series:** House of - Stuart **Subject:** King Charles II, 1660-1685 **Obv:** Crowned bust right **Rev:** Laureate bust right, dates

Date	Mintage	F	VF	XF	Unc	BU
1999 Proof	Est. 10,000	Value: 45.00				

KM# 826a CROWN
28.2800 g., 0.9250 Silver .8410 oz. ASW, 38.8 mm. **Ruler:** Elizabeth II **Subject:** The Wedding of Prince Edward and Miss Sophie Rhys-Jones **Obv:** Crowned bust right **Rev:** St. George's Chapel

Date	Mintage	F	VF	XF	Unc	BU
1999 Proof	10,000	Value: 50.00				

KM# 826.2 CROWN

Copper-Nickel, 38.8 mm. **Ruler:** Elizabeth II **Subject:** The Wedding of Prince Edward and Miss Sophie Rhys-Jones **Obv:** Crowned bust right **Rev:** Two heads facing above banner and wedding bells **Note:** Prev. KM#826.1.

Date	Mintage	F	VF	XF	Unc	BU
1999	—	—	—	—	8.00	9.50

KM# 827 CROWN

Copper-Nickel, 38.8 mm. **Ruler:** Elizabeth II **Subject:** The Wedding of Prince Edward and Miss Sophie Rhys-Jones **Obv:** Crowned bust right **Rev:** St. George's Chapel

Date	Mintage	F	VF	XF	Unc	BU
1999	—	—	—	—	8.00	9.50

KM# 827a CROWN

28.2800 g., 0.9250 Silver .8410 oz. ASW, 38.8 mm. **Ruler:** Elizabeth II **Subject:** The Wedding of Prince Edward and Miss Sophie Rhys-Jones **Obv:** Crowned bust right **Rev:** St. George's Chapel

Date	Mintage	F	VF	XF	Unc	BU
1999 Proof	Est. 10,000	Value: 50.00				

KM# 835 CROWN

Copper-Nickel, 38.8 mm. **Ruler:** Elizabeth II **Series:** The Life Of Queen Elizabeth The Queen Mother **Subject:** Queen's childhood **Obv:** Crowned bust right **Rev:** 1903 portrait of Queen Mother as a girl

Date	Mintage	F	VF	XF	Unc	BU
1999	—	—	—	—	8.00	9.50

KM# 835a CROWN

28.2800 g., 0.9250 Silver .8410 oz. ASW, 38.8 mm. **Ruler:** Elizabeth II **Series:** The Life Of Queen Elizabeth The Queen Mother **Subject:** Queen's childhood **Obv:** Crowned bust right **Rev:** 1903 portrait of Queen Mother as a girl

Date	Mintage	F	VF	XF	Unc	BU
1999 Proof	Est. 10,000	Value: 50.00				

KM# 835b CROWN

28.4600 g., 0.9250 Gilt Silver 0.8464 oz., 38.5 mm. **Ruler:** Elizabeth II **Series:** The Life Of Queen Elizabeth The Queen Mother **Subject:** Queen's childhood **Obv:** Crowned bust right **Rev:** Queen Mother as a young girl **Edge:** Reeded

Date	Mintage	F	VF	XF	Unc	BU
1999PM Proof	—	Value: 50.00				

KM# 837 CROWN

Copper-Nickel, 38.8 mm. **Ruler:** Elizabeth II **Series:** The Life Of Queen Elizabeth The Queen Mother **Subject:** World War I - Glamis **Obv:** Crowned bust right **Rev:** 1918 portrait with wounded soldier

Date	Mintage	F	VF	XF	Unc	BU
1999	—	—	—	—	8.00	9.50

KM# 837a CROWN

28.2800 g., 0.9250 Silver .8410 oz. ASW, 38.8 mm. **Ruler:** Elizabeth II **Series:** The Life Of Queen Elizabeth The Queen Mother **Subject:** World War I - Glamis **Obv:** Crowned bust right **Rev:** 1918 portrait with wounded soldier

Date	Mintage	F	VF	XF	Unc	BU
1999 Proof	Est. 10,000	Value: 50.00				

KM# 837b CROWN

28.4600 g., 0.9250 Gilt Silver 0.8464 oz., 38.5 mm. **Ruler:** Elizabeth II **Series:** The Life Of Queen Elizabeth The Queen Mother **Subject:** World War I - Glamis **Obv:** Crowned bust right **Rev:** Queen Mother with wounded soldier in 1918 **Edge:** Reeded

Date	Mintage	F	VF	XF	Unc	BU
1999PM Proof	—	Value: 50.00				

KM# 839 CROWN

Copper-Nickel, 38.8 mm. **Ruler:** Elizabeth II **Series:** The Life Of Queen Elizabeth The Queen Mother **Subject:** A Royal Marriage Mother **Obv:** Crowned bust right **Rev:** 1923 wedding portrait

Date	Mintage	F	VF	XF	Unc	BU
1999	—	—	—	—	8.00	9.50

KM# 839a CROWN

28.2800 g., 0.9250 Silver .8410 oz. ASW, 38.8 mm. **Ruler:** Elizabeth II **Series:** The Life Of Queen Elizabeth The Queen Mother **Subject:** A Royal Marriage **Obv:** Crowned bust right **Rev:** 1923 wedding portrait

Date	Mintage	F	VF	XF	Unc	BU
1999 Proof	Est. 10,000	Value: 50.00				

KM# 839b CROWN

28.4600 g., 0.9250 Gilt Silver 0.8464 oz., 38.5 mm. **Ruler:** Elizabeth II **Series:** The Life Of Queen Elizabeth The Queen Mother **Subject:** A Royal Marriage **Obv:** Crowned bust right **Rev:** Queen Mother's 1923 wedding portrait **Edge:** Reeded

Date	Mintage	F	VF	XF	Unc	BU
1999PM Proof	—	Value: 50.00				

KM# 841 CROWN

Copper-Nickel, 38.8 mm. **Ruler:** Elizabeth II **Series:** The Life Of Queen Elizabeth The Queen Mother **Subject:** A Royal Family **Obv:** Crowned bust right **Rev:** 1936 family portrait

Date	Mintage	F	VF	XF	Unc	BU
1999	—	—	—	—	8.00	9.50

KM# 841a CROWN

28.2800 g., 0.9250 Silver .8410 oz. ASW, 38.8 mm. **Ruler:** Elizabeth II **Series:** The Life Of Queen Elizabeth The Queen Mother **Subject:** A Royal Family **Obv:** Crowned bust right **Rev:** 1936 family portrait

Date	Mintage	F	VF	XF	Unc	BU
1999 Proof	Est. 10,000	Value: 50.00				

KM# 841b CROWN

28.4600 g., 0.9250 Gilt Silver 0.8464 oz., 38.5 mm. **Ruler:** Elizabeth II **Series:** The Life Of Queen Elizabeth The Queen Mother **Subject:** A Royal Family **Obv:** Crowned bust right **Rev:** 1936 Queen Mother's family portrait **Edge:** Reeded

Date	Mintage	F	VF	XF	Unc	BU
1999PM Proof	—	Value: 50.00				

KM# 843a CROWN

28.2800 g., 0.9250 Silver .8410 oz. ASW, 38.8 mm. **Ruler:** Elizabeth II **Series:** The World At War **Subject:** Franklin D. Roosevelt **Obv:** Crowned bust right **Rev:** Bust writing at left, Zero fighter plane at right

Date	Mintage	F	VF	XF	Unc	BU
1999 Proof	Est. 10,000	Value: 50.00				

KM# 843.1 CROWN

28.2800 g., 0.9250 Silver .8410 oz. ASW **Subject:** The World at War **Obv:** Queen's portrait **Rev:** Franklin Roosevelt and Zero fighter

Date	Mintage	F	VF	XF	Unc	BU
1999	—	—	—	—	10.00	12.00

KM# 845 CROWN

Copper-Nickel, 38.8 mm. **Ruler:** Elizabeth II **Series:** The World At War **Subject:** Operation Manna **Obv:** Crowned bust right **Rev:** Bomber dropping food packets

Date	Mintage	F	VF	XF	Unc	BU
1999	—	—	—	—	10.00	12.00

KM# 845a CROWN

28.2800 g., 0.9250 Silver .8410 oz. ASW, 38.8 mm. **Ruler:** Elizabeth II **Series:** The World At War **Subject:** Operation Manna **Obv:** Crowned bust right **Rev:** Bomber dropping food packets

Date	Mintage	F	VF	XF	Unc	BU
1999 Proof	Est. 10,000	Value: 50.00				

KM# 847.1 CROWN

Copper-Nickel, 38.8 mm. **Ruler:** Elizabeth II **Series:** The World At War **Subject:** J. Robert Oppenheimer **Obv:** Crowned bust right **Rev:** Bust at right looking left, B-29 and mushroom cloud

Date	Mintage	F	VF	XF	Unc	BU
1999	—	—	—	—	10.00	12.00

KM# 847a CROWN

28.2800 g., 0.9250 Silver .8410 oz. ASW, 38.8 mm. **Ruler:** Elizabeth II **Series:** The World At War **Subject:** J. Robert Oppenheimer **Obv:** Crowned bust right **Rev:** Bust at right looking left, B-29 and mushroom cloud

Date	Mintage	F	VF	XF	Unc	BU
1999 Proof	Est. 10,000	Value: 50.00				

KM# 849 CROWN

Copper-Nickel, 38.8 mm. **Ruler:** Elizabeth II **Series:** The World At War **Subject:** Barnes Wallis **Obv:** Crowned bust right **Rev:** Seated figure at left reading, bomber above dam at right

Date	Mintage	F	VF	XF	Unc	BU
1999	—	—	—	—	10.00	12.00

KM# 849a CROWN

28.2800 g., 0.9250 Silver .8410 oz. ASW, 38.8 mm. **Ruler:** Elizabeth II **Series:** The World At War **Subject:** Barnes Wallis **Obv:** Crowned bust right **Rev:** Seated figure at left reading, bomber above dam at right

Date	Mintage	F	VF	XF	Unc	BU
1999 Proof	Est. 10,000	Value: 50.00				

KM# 851 CROWN

Copper-Nickel, 38.8 mm. **Ruler:** Elizabeth II **Series:** The World At War **Subject:** Douglas Bader **Obv:** Crowned bust right **Rev:** Bust facing at left, planes in combat

Date	Mintage	F	VF	XF	Unc	BU
1999	—	—	—	—	10.00	12.00

KM# 851a CROWN

28.2800 g., 0.9250 Silver .8410 oz. ASW, 38.8 mm. **Ruler:** Elizabeth II **Series:** The World At War **Subject:** Douglas Bader **Obv:** Crowned bust right **Rev:** Bust facing at left, planes in combat

Date	Mintage	F	VF	XF	Unc	BU
1999 Proof	Est. 10,000	Value: 50.00				

KM# 853 CROWN

Copper-Nickel, 38.8 mm. **Ruler:** Elizabeth II **Series:** The World At War **Subject:** Winston Churchill **Obv:** Crowned bust right **Rev:** Bust facing with hand raised in "V" sign and crowd

Date	Mintage	F	VF	XF	Unc	BU
1999	—	—	—	—	10.00	12.00

KM# 853a CROWN

28.2800 g., 0.9250 Silver .8410 oz. ASW, 38.8 mm. **Ruler:** Elizabeth II **Series:** The World At War **Subject:** Winston Churchill **Obv:** Crowned bust right **Rev:** Bust facing with hand raised in "V" sign and crowd

Date	Mintage	F	VF	XF	Unc	BU
1999 Proof	Est. 10,000	Value: 50.00				

KM# 855 CROWN

Copper-Nickel, 38.8 mm. **Ruler:** Elizabeth II **Series:** The World At War **Subject:** Tirpitz **Obv:** Crowned bust right **Rev:** Battleship and sailor

Date	Mintage	F	VF	XF	Unc	BU
1999	—	—	—	—	10.00	12.00

KM# 855a CROWN

28.2800 g., 0.9250 Silver .8410 oz. ASW, 38.8 mm. **Ruler:** Elizabeth II **Series:** The World At War **Subject:** Tirpitz **Obv:** Crowned bust right **Rev:** Battleship and sailor

Date	Mintage	F	VF	XF	Unc	BU
1999 Proof	Est. 10,000	Value: 50.00				

KM# 857 CROWN

Copper-Nickel, 38.8 mm. **Ruler:** Elizabeth II **Series:** The World At War **Subject:** War Babies **Obv:** Crowned bust right **Rev:** Soldier kissing child

Date	Mintage	F	VF	XF	Unc	BU
1999	—	—	—	—	10.00	12.00

KM# 857a CROWN

28.2800 g., 0.9250 Silver .8410 oz. ASW, 38.8 mm. **Ruler:** Elizabeth II **Series:** The World At War **Subject:** War Babies **Obv:** Crowned bust right **Rev:** Soldier kissing child

Date	Mintage	F	VF	XF	Unc	BU
1999 Proof	Est. 10,000	Value: 50.00				

KM# 859a CROWN

28.2800 g., 0.9250 Silver .8410 oz. ASW, 38.8 mm. **Ruler:** Elizabeth II **Series:** The World At War **Subject:** The Blitz **Obv:** Crowned bust right **Rev:** Firefighters in action after air raid

Date	Mintage	F	VF	XF	Unc	BU
1999 Proof	Est. 10,000	Value: 50.00				

KM# 861 CROWN

Copper-Nickel, 38.8 mm. **Ruler:** Elizabeth II **Series:** The World At War **Subject:** D-Day **Obv:** Crowned bust right **Rev:** D-Day landing scene

Date	Mintage	F	VF	XF	Unc	BU
1999	—	—	—	—	10.00	12.00

KM# 861a CROWN

28.2800 g., 0.9250 Silver .8410 oz. ASW, 38.8 mm. **Ruler:** Elizabeth II **Series:** The World At War **Subject:** D-Day **Obv:** Crowned bust right **Rev:** D-Day landing scene

Date	Mintage	F	VF	XF	Unc	BU
1999 Proof	Est. 10,000	Value: 50.00				

KM# 863 CROWN

Copper-Nickel, 38.8 mm. **Ruler:** Elizabeth II **Series:** The World At War **Subject:** Operation Heavywater **Obv:** Crowned bust right **Rev:** Military skier

Date	Mintage	F	VF	XF	Unc	BU
1999	—	—	—	—	10.00	12.00

KM# 863a CROWN

28.2800 g., 0.9250 Silver .8410 oz. ASW, 38.8 mm. **Ruler:** Elizabeth II **Series:** The World At War **Subject:** Operation Heavywater **Obv:** Crowned bust right **Rev:** Military skier

Date	Mintage	F	VF	XF	Unc	BU
1999 Proof	Est. 10,000	Value: 50.00				

KM# 865 CROWN

Copper-Nickel, 38.8 mm. **Ruler:** Elizabeth II **Series:** The World At War **Subject:** Barbarossa **Obv:** Crowned bust right **Rev:** German tanks in Russia

Date	Mintage	F	VF	XF	Unc	BU
1999	—	—	—	—	10.00	12.00

KM# 865a CROWN

28.2800 g., 0.9250 Silver .8410 oz. ASW, 38.8 mm. **Ruler:** Elizabeth II **Series:** The World At War **Subject:** Barbarossa **Obv:** Crowned bust right **Rev:** German tanks in Russia

Date	Mintage	F	VF	XF	Unc	BU
1999 Proof	Est. 10,000	Value: 50.00				

KM# 871 CROWN

28.2800 g., Copper-Nickel, 38.8 mm. **Ruler:** Elizabeth II **Series:** The Life Of Queen Elizabeth The Queen Mother **Subject:** Crowned Queen Consort **Obv:** Head with tiara right **Rev:** 1937 crowning of the Queen consort

Date	Mintage	F	VF	XF	Unc	BU
2000	—	—	—	—	10.00	12.00

KM# 871a CROWN

28.2800 g., 0.9250 Silver .8410 oz. ASW, 38.8 mm. **Ruler:** Elizabeth II **Series:** The Life Of Queen Elizabeth The Queen Mother **Subject:** Crowned Queen Consort **Obv:** Head with tiara right **Rev:** 1937 coronation scene

Date	Mintage	F	VF	XF	Unc	BU
2000 Proof	10,000	Value: 50.00				

KM# 873 CROWN

Copper-Nickel, 38.8 mm. **Ruler:** Elizabeth II **Series:** The Life Of Queen Elizabeth The Queen Mother **Subject:** State Visit To France **Obv:** Crowned bust right **Rev:** Seated figure looking left

Date	Mintage	F	VF	XF	Unc	BU
2000	—	—	—	—	10.00	12.00

KM# 873a CROWN

28.2800 g., 0.9250 Silver .8410 oz. ASW, 38.8 mm. **Ruler:** Elizabeth II **Series:** The Life Of Queen Elizabeth The Queen Mother **Subject:** State Visit To France **Obv:** Crowned bust right **Rev:** Seated figure looking left

Date	Mintage	F	VF	XF	Unc	BU
2000 Proof	10,000	Value: 50.00				

KM# 875 CROWN

Copper-Nickel, 38.8 mm. **Ruler:** Elizabeth II **Series:** The Life Of Queen Elizabeth The Queen Mother **Subject:** London Bombings **Obv:** Crowned bust right **Rev:** Royals looking at bomb damage

Date	Mintage	F	VF	XF	Unc	BU
2000	—	—	—	—	10.00	12.00

KM# 875a CROWN

28.2800 g., 0.9250 Silver .8410 oz. ASW, 38.8 mm. **Ruler:** Elizabeth II **Series:** The Life Of Queen Elizabeth The Queen Mother **Subject:** London Bombings **Obv:** Crowned bust right **Rev:** Royals looking at bomb damage

Date	Mintage	F	VF	XF	Unc	BU
2000 Proof	10,000	Value: 50.00				

KM# 877 CROWN

Copper-Nickel, 38.8 mm. **Ruler:** Elizabeth II **Series:** The Life Of Queen Elizabeth The Queen Mother **Subject:** Victory **Obv:** Crowned bust right **Rev:** Portrait of royal family

Date	Mintage	F	VF	XF	Unc	BU
2000	—	—	—	—	10.00	12.00

KM# 877a CROWN

28.2800 g., 0.9250 Silver .8410 oz. ASW, 38.8 mm. **Ruler:** Elizabeth II **Series:** The Life Of Queen Elizabeth The Queen Mother **Subject:** Victory **Obv:** Crowned bust right **Rev:** Portrait of royal family

Date	Mintage	F	VF	XF	Unc	BU
2000 Proof	10,000	Value: 50.00				

KM# 880 CROWN

28.2800 g., Copper-Nickel, 38.8 mm. **Ruler:** Elizabeth II **Subject:** 18th Birthday - H.R.H. The Prince William **Obv:** Crowned bust right **Rev:** Bust 3/4 right

Date	Mintage	F	VF	XF	Unc	BU
2000	—	—	—	—	10.00	12.00

KM# 880a CROWN

28.2800 g., 0.9250 Silver .8410 oz. ASW, 38.8 mm. **Ruler:** Elizabeth II **Subject:** 18th Birthday - H.R.H. The Prince William **Obv:** Crowned bust right **Rev:** Bust 3/4 right

Date	Mintage	F	VF	XF	Unc	BU
2000 Proof	10,000	Value: 50.00				

KM# 882 CROWN

Copper-Nickel, 38.8 mm. **Ruler:** Elizabeth II **Subject:** Queen Mother **Obv:** Queen's portrait **Rev:** Queen Mother's portrait

Date	Mintage	F	VF	XF	Unc	BU
2000	—	—	—	—	10.00	12.00

KM# 882a CROWN

28.2800 g., 0.9250 Silver .8410 oz. ASW, 38.8 mm. **Ruler:** Elizabeth II **Obv:** Queen's portrait

Date	Mintage	F	VF	XF	Unc	BU
2000 Proof	10,000	Value: 50.00				

KM# 884 CROWN

Bi-Metallic Titanium center in Gold ring, 38.8 mm. **Ruler:** Elizabeth II **Subject:** 160th Anniversary - Uniform Penny Post **Obv:** Queen's portrait **Rev:** Postage stamp design **Edge:** Reeded

Date	Mintage	F	VF	XF	Unc	BU
2000 Proof	999	Value: 625				

KM# 128 2 CROWN

62.2070 g., 0.9990 Silver 2.0000 oz. ASW **Ruler:** Elizabeth II **Subject:** Japanese Royal Wedding **Obv:** Crowned bust right **Rev:** Pair of peacocks

Date	Mintage	F	VF	XF	Unc	BU
1993 Proof	Est. 20,000	Value: 65.00				

KM# 128a 2 CROWN

62.2070 g., 0.9999 Gold 2.0000 oz. AGW **Ruler:** Elizabeth II **Subject:** Japanese Royal Wedding **Obv:** Crowned bust right **Rev:** Pair of peacocks

Date	Mintage	F	VF	XF	Unc	BU
1993 Proof	Est. 2,500	Value: 1,450				

KM# 129 2 CROWN

62.2070 g., 0.9990 Silver 2.0000 oz. ASW **Ruler:** Elizabeth II **Subject:** Japanese Royal Wedding **Obv:** Crowned bust right **Rev:** Two peacocks, one in full display

Date	Mintage	F	VF	XF	Unc	BU
1993 Proof	Est. 20,000	Value: 45.00				

KM# 129a 2 CROWN

62.2070 g., 0.9999 Gold 2.0000 oz. AGW **Ruler:** Elizabeth II **Subject:** Japanese Royal Wedding **Obv:** Crowned bust right **Rev:** Two peacocks, one in full display

Date	Mintage	F	VF	XF	Unc	BU
1993 Proof	Est. 2,500	Value: 1,500				

KM# 106 5 CROWN

155.9230 g., 0.9990 Silver 5.0000 oz. ASW, 65 mm. **Ruler:** Elizabeth II **Series:** Olympics - Barcelona **Obv:** Crowned bust right **Rev:** Discus thrower **Note:** Illustration reduced.

Date	Mintage	F	VF	XF	Unc	BU
1991 Proof	Est. 1,000	Value: 225				

KM# 451 5 CROWN

155.5175 g., 0.9999 Gold 5.0000 oz. AGW **Ruler:** Elizabeth II **Subject:** Lord Buddha **Rev:** Seated figure facing

Date	Mintage	F	VF	XF	Unc	BU
1996 Proof	Est. 250	Value: 3,500				

KM# 107 10 CROWN

311.8460 g., 0.9990 Silver 10.0000 oz. ASW, 73 mm. **Ruler:** Elizabeth II **Series:** Olympics - Barcelona **Obv:** Crowned bust right **Rev:** Ancient runners **Note:** Illustration reduced.

Date	Mintage	F	VF	XF	Unc	BU
1991 Proof	Est. 1,000	Value: 300				

KM# 130 10 CROWN

311.8460 g., 0.9990 Silver 10.0000 oz. ASW, 73 mm. **Ruler:** Elizabeth II **Subject:** Japanese Royal Wedding **Obv:** Crowned bust right **Rev:** Pair of peacocks

Date	Mintage	F	VF	XF	Unc	BU
1993 Proof	Est. 5,000	Value: 285				

KM# 131 32 CROWNS

1000.0000 g., 0.9990 Silver 32.15 oz. ASW, 85 mm. **Ruler:** Elizabeth II **Subject:** Japanese Royal Wedding **Obv:** Crowned bust right **Rev:** Two peacocks, one in full display

Date	Mintage	F	VF	XF	Unc	BU
1993 Proof	Est. 1,000	Value: 600				

KM# 333 40 CROWN

1244.1400 g., 0.9990 Silver 40.0000 oz. ASW, 100 mm. **Ruler:** Elizabeth II **Rev:** Rock of Gibraltar and rising sun **Note:** Illustration reduced.

Date	Mintage	F	VF	XF	Unc	BU
1994 Proof	Est. 1,500	Value: 595				

KM# 18 POUND

9.5000 g., Nickel-Brass, 22.5 mm. **Ruler:** Elizabeth II **Obv:** Crowned head right **Obv. Designer:** Raphael Maklouf **Rev:** Gibraltar castle and key **Rev. Designer:** Alfred Ryman

Date	Mintage	F	VF	XF	Unc	BU
1988 AA	—	—	—	—	3.50	4.50
1988PM AB	—	—	—	—	3.50	4.50
1990 AA	—	—	—	—	3.50	4.50
1991 AA	—	—	—	—	3.50	4.50
1991 AC	—	—	—	—	3.50	4.50
1992 AA	—	—	—	—	3.50	4.50
1993 AA	—	—	—	—	3.50	4.50
1996 AA	—	—	—	—	3.50	4.50
1997 AA	—	—	—	—	3.50	4.50

KM# 18a POUND

9.5000 g., 0.9250 Silver .2825 oz. ASW, 22.5 mm. **Ruler:** Elizabeth II **Obv:** Crowned head right **Rev:** Gibraltar castle and key

Date	Mintage	F	VF	XF	Unc	BU
1988 Proof	—	Value: 15.00				

KM# 18b POUND

9.5000 g., 0.9170 Gold .2801 oz. AGW, 22.5 mm. **Ruler:** Elizabeth II **Obv:** Crowned head right **Rev:** Gibraltar castle and key

Date	Mintage	F	VF	XF	Unc	BU
1988 Proof	—	Value: 350				

KM# 32 POUND

9.5000 g., Nickel-Brass, 22.5 mm. **Ruler:** Elizabeth II **Subject:** 150th Anniversary of Gibraltar Coinage **Obv:** Crowned head right **Obv. Designer:** Raphael Maklouf **Rev:** Gibraltar castle and key within circle

Date	Mintage	F	VF	XF	Unc	BU
1989 AA	—	—	—	—	4.00	5.00

KM# 32a POUND

9.5000 g., 0.9250 Silver .2826 oz. ASW, 22.5 mm. **Ruler:** Elizabeth II **Subject:** 150th Anniversary of Gibraltar Coinage **Obv:** Crowned head right **Rev:** Gibraltar castle and key

Date	Mintage	F	VF	XF	Unc	BU
1989 Proof	Est. 2,500	Value: 35.00				

KM# 32b POUND

9.5000 g., 0.9170 Gold .2801 oz. AGW, 22.5 mm. **Ruler:** Elizabeth II **Subject:** 150th Anniversary of Gibraltar Coinage **Obv:** Crowned head right **Rev:** Gibraltar castle and key

Date	Mintage	F	VF	XF	Unc	BU
1989 Proof	150	Value: 350				

KM# 32c POUND

9.0000 g., 0.9500 Platinum .2749 oz. APW, 22.5 mm. **Ruler:** Elizabeth II **Obv:** Crowned head right **Rev:** Gibraltar castle and key

Date	Mintage	F	VF	XF	Unc	BU
1989 Proof	100	Value: 420				

KM# 191 POUND
Nickel-Brass, 22.5 mm. **Ruler:** Elizabeth II **Subject:** Referendum of 1967 **Obv:** Crowned head right **Obv. Designer:** Raphael Maklouf **Rev:** Gibraltar arms above Rock of Gibraltar with Union Jack background

Date	Mintage	F	VF	XF	Unc	BU
1993 AA	—	—	—	—	4.50	5.50

KM# 191a POUND
9.5000 g., 0.9250 Silver .2825 oz. ASW, 22.5 mm. **Ruler:** Elizabeth II **Subject:** Referendum of 1967 **Obv:** Crowned head right **Rev:** Gibraltar arms above Rock of Gibraltar with Union Jack background

Date	Mintage	F	VF	XF	Unc	BU
1993 Proof	Est. 5,000	Value: 35.00				

KM# 191b POUND
9.5000 g., 0.9170 Gold .2801 oz. AGW, 22.5 mm. **Ruler:** Elizabeth II **Subject:** Referendum of 1967 **Obv:** Crowned head right **Rev:** Gibraltar arms above Rock of Gibraltar with Union Jack background

Date	Mintage	F	VF	XF	Unc	BU
1993 Proof	Est. 3,500	Value: 350				

KM# 324 POUND
9.5000 g., Nickel-Brass, 22.5 mm. **Ruler:** Elizabeth II **Subject:** 40th Anniversary - Queen Elizabeth II's 1st Royal Visit to Gibraltar **Obv:** Crowned head right **Obv. Designer:** Raphael Maklouf **Rev:** Luxury liner at sea

Date	Mintage	F	VF	XF	Unc	BU
1994 AA	—	—	—	—	7.50	9.00

KM# 340 POUND
9.5000 g., Nickel-Brass, 22.5 mm. **Ruler:** Elizabeth II **Subject:** National Day, 50th Anniversary of the U.N. **Obv:** Crowned head right **Obv. Designer:** Raphael Maklouf **Rev:** Rock of Gibraltar

Date	Mintage	F	VF	XF	Unc	BU
1995 AA	—	—	—	—	3.50	5.00

KM# 340a POUND
9.5000 g., 0.9250 Silver .2825 oz. ASW, 22.5 mm. **Ruler:** Elizabeth II **Obv:** Crowned head right **Rev:** Rock of Gibraltar

Date	Mintage	F	VF	XF	Unc	BU
1995 Proof	3,500	Value: 35.00				

KM# 869 POUND
9.5000 g., Nickel-Brass, 22.5 mm. **Ruler:** Elizabeth II **Obv:** Crowned head right **Obv. Designer:** Ian Rank-Broadley **Rev:** Gibraltar castle and key

Date	Mintage	F	VF	XF	Unc	BU
1998 AA	—	—	—	—	3.50	4.50
1999 AA	—	—	—	—	3.50	4.50
2000 AA	—	—	—	—	3.50	4.50

KM# 24 2 POUNDS
Virenium **Ruler:** Elizabeth II **Obv:** Crowned head right **Obv. Designer:** Raphael Maklouf **Rev:** Cannon in fortress tunnel **Rev. Designer:** Alfred Ryman

Date	Mintage	F	VF	XF	Unc	BU
1988 AA	—	—	—	—	7.50	8.50
1989 AA	—	—	—	—	7.50	8.50
1990 AA	—	—	—	—	7.50	8.50
1991 AA	—	—	—	—	7.50	8.50
1993 AA	—	—	—	—	7.50	8.50
1995 AA	—	—	—	—	7.50	8.50
1995 AB	—	—	—	—	7.50	8.50

Date	Mintage	F	VF	XF	Unc	BU
1995 AC	—	—	—	—	7.50	8.50
1996 AA	—	—	—	—	7.50	8.50

KM# 98 2 POUNDS
Virenium **Ruler:** Elizabeth II **Obv:** Crowned head right **Obv. Designer:** Raphael Maklouf **Rev:** Columbus and ship

Date	Mintage	F	VF	XF	Unc	BU
1992 AA	—	—	—	—	6.50	7.50

KM# 98a 2 POUNDS
9.3000 g., 0.9250 Silver .2766 oz. ASW **Ruler:** Elizabeth II **Obv:** Crowned head right **Rev:** Columbus and ship

Date	Mintage	F	VF	XF	Unc	BU
1992 Proof	Est. 5,000	Value: 40.00				

KM# 98b 2 POUNDS
15.9400 g., 0.9170 Gold .4700 oz. AGW **Ruler:** Elizabeth II **Obv:** Crowned head right **Rev:** Columbus and ship

Date	Mintage	F	VF	XF	Unc	BU
1992 Proof	Est. 5,000	Value: 335				

KM# 98c 2 POUNDS
18.0000 g., 0.9500 Platinum .5498 oz. APW **Ruler:** Elizabeth II **Obv:** Crowned head right **Rev:** Columbus and ship

Date	Mintage	F	VF	XF	Unc	BU
1992 Proof	Est. 1,000	Value: 800				

KM# 325 2 POUNDS
Virenium **Ruler:** Elizabeth II **Subject:** 40th Anniversary - Queen Elizabeth II's 1st Royal Visit to Gibraltar **Obv:** Crowned head right **Obv. Designer:** Raphael Maklouf **Rev:** Luxury liner at sea

Date	Mintage	F	VF	XF	Unc	BU
1994 AA	Est. 5,000	—	—	—	6.50	7.50

KM# 755 2 POUNDS
Ring Composition: Brass **Center Composition:** Copper-Nickel, 28.4 mm. **Ruler:** Elizabeth II **Subject:** The Labours of Hercules **Obv:** Crowned head right **Obv. Designer:** Raphael Maklouf **Rev:** Hercules wrestling the Nimean Lion

Date	Mintage	F	VF	XF	Unc	BU
1997 AA	—	—	—	—	7.50	9.00
1997	—	—	—	—	7.50	9.00

KM# 755a 2 POUNDS
12.0000 g., 0.9990 Gold Plated Silver .999 oz. ASW AGW **Ruler:** Elizabeth II **Subject:** The Labours of Hercules **Obv:** Crowned head right **Rev:** Hercules wrestling the Nimean Lion

Date	Mintage	F	VF	XF	Unc	BU
1997 Proof	Est. 7,500	Value: 60.00				

KM# 758a 2 POUNDS
0.9990 Gold Plated Silver .999 oz. ASW AGW **Ruler:** Elizabeth II **Subject:** The Labours of Hercules **Obv:** Crowned head right **Rev:** Hercules wrestles the Erymanthian Boar

Date	Mintage	F	VF	XF	Unc	BU
1997 Proof	7,500	Value: 60.00				

KM# 756a 2 POUNDS
12.0000 g., 0.9990 Gold Plated Silver .999 oz. ASW AGW **Ruler:** Elizabeth II **Subject:** The Labours of Hercules **Obv:** Crowned head right **Rev:** Hercules fighting the Hydra

Date	Mintage	F	VF	XF	Unc	BU
1997 Proof	Est. 7,500	Value: 60.00				

KM# 757a 2 POUNDS
12.0000 g., 0.9990 Gold Plated Silver .999 oz. ASW AGW **Ruler:** Elizabeth II **Subject:** The Labours of Hercules **Obv:** Crowned head right **Rev:** Hercules and the Ceryneian Hind

Date	Mintage	F	VF	XF	Unc	BU
1997 Proof	Est. 7,500	Value: 60.00				

KM# 758 2 POUNDS
Bi-Metallic Copper-nickel center in Brass ring, 28.4 mm. **Ruler:** Elizabeth II **Subject:** The Labours of Hercules **Obv:** Crowned head right **Rev:** Hercules wrestles the Erymanthian Boar

Date	Mintage	F	VF	XF	Unc	BU
1998 AA	—	—	—	—	7.50	9.00

KM# 757 2 POUNDS
Bi-Metallic Copper-nickel center in Brass ring, 28.4 mm. **Ruler:** Elizabeth II **Subject:** The Labours of Hercules **Obv:** Crowned head right **Rev:** Hercules and the Ceryneian Hind

Date	Mintage	F	VF	XF	Unc	BU
1998 AA	—	—	—	—	7.50	9.00

KM# 756 2 POUNDS
Bi-Metallic Copper-nickel center in Brass ring, 28.4 mm. **Ruler:** Elizabeth II **Subject:** The Labours of Hercules **Obv:** Crowned head right **Obv. Designer:** Rank-Broadley **Rev:** Hercules fighting the Hydra

Date	Mintage	F	VF	XF	Unc	BU
1998 AA	—	—	—	—	7.50	9.00

KM# 759 2 POUNDS
12.0000 g., Bi-Metallic Copper-Nickel center in Brass ring, 28.4 mm. **Ruler:** Elizabeth II **Subject:** The Labours of Hercules **Obv:** Crowned head right **Rev:** Hercules and the Augean Stables

Date	Mintage	F	VF	XF	Unc	BU
1999 AA	—	—	—	—	7.50	9.00

KM# 759a 2 POUNDS
10.0000 g., 0.9990 Gold Plated Silver .999 oz. ASW AGW **Ruler:** Elizabeth II **Subject:** The Labours of Hercules **Obv:** Crowned head right **Rev:** Hercules and the Augean Stables

Date	Mintage	F	VF	XF	Unc	BU
1999 Proof	Est. 25,000	Value: 60.00				

KM# 760 2 POUNDS
Copper-Nickel, 28.4 mm. **Ruler:** Elizabeth II **Subject:** The Labours of Hercules **Obv:** Crowned head right **Rev:** Hercules and the Cretan Bull

Date	Mintage	F	VF	XF	Unc	BU
1999 AA	—	—	—	—	7.50	9.00
1999 No die letters	—	—	—	—	7.50	9.00

KM# 760a 2 POUNDS
10.0000 g., 0.9990 Gold Plated Silver .999 oz. ASW AGW **Subject:** The Labours of Hercules **Obv:** Crowned head right **Rev:** Hercules and the Cretan Bull

Date	Mintage	F	VF	XF	Unc	BU
1999 Proof	Est. 25,000	Value: 60.00				

KM# 761 2 POUNDS
Bi-Metallic Copper-nickel center in Brass ring, 28.4 mm. **Ruler:** Elizabeth II **Subject:** The Labours of Hercules **Obv:** Crowned head right **Rev:** Hercules and the Stymphalian Birds

Date	Mintage	F	VF	XF	Unc	BU
1999 AA	—	—	—	—	8.00	10.00

KM# 761a 2 POUNDS
10.0000 g., 0.9990 Gold Plated Silver .999 oz. ASW AGW **Ruler:** Elizabeth II **Subject:** The Labours of Hercules **Obv:** Crowned head right **Rev:** Hercules and the Stymphalian Birds

Date	Mintage	F	VF	XF	Unc	BU
1999 Proof	Est. 25,000	Value: 60.00				

KM# 762 2 POUNDS
Bi-Metallic Copper-nickel center in Brass ring, 28.4 mm. **Ruler:** Elizabeth II **Subject:** The Labours of Hercules **Obv:** Crowned head right **Rev:** Hercules and the Mares of Diomedes

Date	Mintage	F	VF	XF	Unc	BU
1999 AA	—	—	—	—	8.00	10.00
1999 No die letters	—	—	—	—	7.50	9.00

KM# 762a 2 POUNDS
10.0000 g., 0.9990 Gold Plated Silver .999 oz. ASW AGW **Ruler:** Elizabeth II **Subject:** The Labours of Hercules **Obv:** Crowned head right **Rev:** Hercules and the Mares of Diomedes

Date	Mintage	F	VF	XF	Unc	BU
1999 Proof	Est. 25,000	Value: 60.00				

KM# 765 2 POUNDS
Bi-Metallic Copper-nickel center in Brass ring, 28.4 mm. **Ruler:** Elizabeth II **Subject:** The Labours of Hercules **Obv:** Head with tiara right **Obv. Designer:** Ian Rank-Broadley **Rev:** Hercules carrying the world while facing a man with a bushel of apples **Edge:** Reeded

Date	Mintage	F	VF	XF	Unc	BU
2000 AA	—	—	—	—	7.50	—
2000 No die letters	—	—	—	—	7.50	9.00
2000 AA	—	—	—	—	7.50	9.00

KM# 766 2 POUNDS
Bi-Metallic Copper-nickel center in Brass ring, 28.4 mm. **Ruler:** Elizabeth II **Subject:** The Labours of Hercules **Obv:** Head with tiara right **Obv. Designer:** Ian Rank-Broadley **Rev:** Hercules chaining Cerberus

Date	Mintage	F	VF	XF	Unc	BU
2000 AA	—	—	—	—	7.50	—

Date	Mintage	F	VF	XF	Unc	BU
2000 No die letters	—	—	—	—	7.50	9.00
2000 AA	—	—	—	—	8.00	10.00

KM# 763 2 POUNDS

Bi-Metallic Copper-nickel center in Brass ring, 28.4 mm. **Ruler:** Elizabeth II **Subject:** The Labours of Hercules **Obv:** Head with tiara right **Obv. Designer:** Ian Rank-Broadley **Rev:** Hercules and Hippolyta's Girdle **Edge:** Reeded

Date	Mintage	F	VF	XF	Unc	BU
2000 AA	Est. 2,000	—	—	—	7.50	9.00
2000 No die letters	—	—	—	—	7.50	9.00

KM# 764 2 POUNDS

12.0000 g., Bi-Metallic Copper-nickel center in Brass ring, 28.4 mm. **Ruler:** Elizabeth II **Subject:** The Labours of Hercules - Geryon's Cattle **Obv:** Head with tiara right **Obv. Designer:** Ian Rank-Broadley **Rev:** Hercules with cow and three devils shot by one arrow **Edge:** Reeded

Date	Mintage	F	VF	XF	Unc	BU
2000 No die letters	—	—	—	—	7.50	9.00
2000 AA	—	—	—	—	8.00	10.00

KM# 763a 2 POUNDS

12.0000 g., 0.9990 Silver .3854 oz. ASW, 28.4 mm. **Ruler:** Elizabeth II **Subject:** The Labours of Hercules **Obv:** Crowned head right **Rev:** Hercules and Hippolyta's Girdle **Edge:** Reeded **Note:** Partially gold plated.

Date	Mintage	F	VF	XF	Unc	BU
2000 Proof	7,500	Value: 60.00				

KM# 764a 2 POUNDS

12.0000 g., 0.9990 Silver .3854 oz. ASW, 28.4 mm. **Ruler:** Elizabeth II **Subject:** The Labours of Hercules **Obv:** Head with tiara right **Rev:** Hercules with cow and three devils shot by one arrow **Edge:** Reeded **Note:** Partially gold plated.

Date	Mintage	F	VF	XF	Unc	BU
2000 Proof	7,500	Value: 60.00				

KM# 765a 2 POUNDS

12.0000 g., 0.9990 Silver .3854 oz. ASW, 28.4 mm. **Ruler:** Elizabeth II **Subject:** The Labours of Hercules **Obv:** Head with tiara right **Rev:** Hercules carrying the world while facing a man with a bushel of apples **Edge:** Reeded **Note:** Partially gold plated.

Date	Mintage	F	VF	XF	Unc	BU
2000 Proof	7,500	Value: 60.00				

KM# 766a 2 POUNDS

12.0000 g., 0.9990 Silver .3854 oz. ASW, 28.4 mm. **Ruler:** Elizabeth II **Subject:** The Labours of Hercules **Obv:** Head with tiara right **Rev:** Hercules chaining Cerberus **Note:** Partially gold plated.

Date	Mintage	F	VF	XF	Unc	BU
2000 Proof	7,500	Value: 60.00				

KM# 25 5 POUNDS

Virenium, 36 mm. **Ruler:** Elizabeth II **Obv:** Crowned head right **Obv. Designer:** Raphael Maklouf **Rev:** Hercules statue standing **Rev. Designer:** Alfred Ryman

Date	Mintage	F	VF	XF	Unc	BU
1988 AA	—	—	—	—	14.00	16.00
1989 AA	—	—	—	—	14.00	16.00
1989 No die letters	—	—	—	—	14.00	16.00
1990 AA	—	—	—	—	14.00	16.00
1991 AA	—	—	—	—	14.00	16.00
1992 AA	—	—	—	—	14.00	16.00
1993 AA	—	—	—	—	14.00	16.00

KM# 309 5 POUNDS

Virenium, 36 mm. **Ruler:** Elizabeth II **Obv:** Crowned bust right **Rev:** D-Day - Soldier, sailor and pilot above tank, plane, and ship

Date	Mintage	F	VF	XF	Unc	BU
1994	—	—	—	—	16.50	18.00
1994 Proof	Est. 5,000	Value: 20.00				

KM# 309a 5 POUNDS

23.5000 g., 0.9250 Silver .6989 oz. ASW, 36 mm. **Ruler:** Elizabeth II **Obv:** Crowned bust right **Rev:** D-Day - Soldier, sailor and pilot above tank, plane, and ship

Date	Mintage	F	VF	XF	Unc	BU
1994 Proof	Est. 5,000	Value: 40.00				

KM# 309b 5 POUNDS

39.8300 g., 0.9170 Gold 1.1743 oz. AGW, 36 mm. **Ruler:** Elizabeth II **Obv:** Crowned bust right **Rev:** D-Day - Soldier, sailor and pilot above tank, plane, and ship

Date	Mintage	F	VF	XF	Unc	BU
1994 Proof	Est. 850	Value: 840				

KM# 332 5 POUNDS

Virenium, 36 mm. **Ruler:** Elizabeth II **Obv:** Crowned head right **Rev:** 50th Anniversary - VE Day

Date	Mintage	F	VF	XF	Unc	BU
1995	—	—	—	—	16.50	18.50
1995 Proof	Est. 5,000	Value: 22.00				

KM# 332a 5 POUNDS

23.5000 g., 0.9250 Silver .6989 oz. ASW, 36 mm. **Ruler:** Elizabeth II **Obv:** Crowned head right **Rev:** 50th Anniversary - VE Day

Date	Mintage	F	VF	XF	Unc	BU
1995 Proof	Est. 5,000	Value: 40.00				

KM# 332b 5 POUNDS

39.8300 g., 0.9170 Gold 1.1743 oz. AGW, 36 mm. **Ruler:** Elizabeth II **Obv:** Crowned head right **Rev:** 50th Anniversary - VE Day

Date	Mintage	F	VF	XF	Unc	BU
1995 Proof	Est. 850	Value: 850				

KM# 334 5 POUNDS

Virenium, 36 mm. **Ruler:** Elizabeth II **Obv:** Crowned head right **Rev:** Queen Mother viewing bomb-damaged Buckingham Palace

Date	Mintage	F	VF	XF	Unc	BU
1995	—	—	—	—	15.00	17.00

KM# 334a 5 POUNDS

25.5000 g., 0.9250 Silver .6980 oz. ASW, 36 mm. **Ruler:** Elizabeth II **Obv:** Crowned head right **Rev:** Queen Mother viewing bomb-damaged Buckingham Palace

Date	Mintage	F	VF	XF	Unc	BU
1995 Proof	Est. 5,000	Value: 40.00				

KM# 334b 5 POUNDS

39.8300 g., 0.9170 Gold 1.1743 oz. AGW, 36 mm. **Ruler:** Elizabeth II **Obv:** Crowned head right **Rev:** Queen Mother viewing bom- damaged Buckingham Palace

Date	Mintage	F	VF	XF	Unc	BU
1995 Proof	Est. 850	Value: 840				

KM# 335 5 POUNDS

Virenium, 36 mm. **Ruler:** Elizabeth II **Obv:** Crowned head right **Rev:** VJ Day - Flag Raising

Date	Mintage	F	VF	XF	Unc	BU
1995 AA	—	—	—	—	16.50	18.50
1995 Proof	Est. 5,000	Value: 22.00				

KM# 335a 5 POUNDS

23.5000 g., 0.9250 Silver .6989 oz. ASW, 36 mm. **Ruler:** Elizabeth II **Obv:** Crowned head right **Rev:** VJ Day - Flag Raising

Date	Mintage	F	VF	XF	Unc	BU
1995 Proof	Est. 5,000	Value: 40.00				

KM# 335b 5 POUNDS

39.8300 g., 0.9170 Gold 1.1743 oz. AGW, 36 mm. **Ruler:** Elizabeth II **Obv:** Crowned head right **Rev:** VJ Day - Flag Raising

Date	Mintage	F	VF	XF	Unc	BU
1995 Proof	Est. 850	Value: 850				

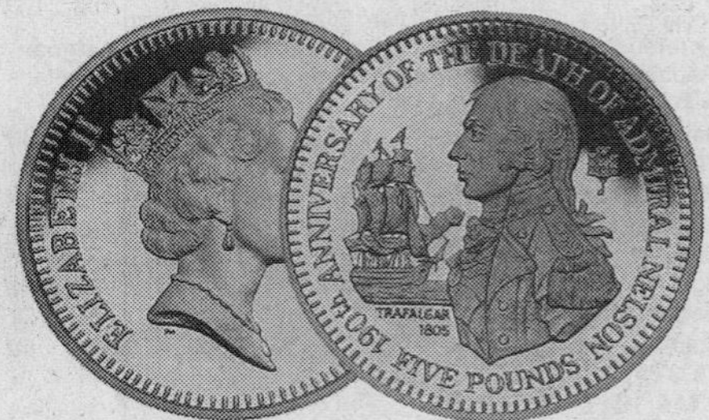

KM# 341 5 POUNDS

Virenium, 36 mm. **Ruler:** Elizabeth II **Subject:** 190th Anniversary - Death Of Admiral Nelson **Obv:** Crowned head right **Rev:** Bust at right facing left, ship at left

Date	Mintage	F	VF	XF	Unc	BU
1995 AA	—	—	—	—	15.00	17.00

KM# 341a 5 POUNDS

23.5000 g., 0.9250 Silver .6989 oz. ASW, 36 mm. **Ruler:** Elizabeth II **Subject:** 190th Anniversary - Death of Admiral Nelson **Obv:** Crowned head right **Rev:** Bust at right facing left, ship at left

Date	Mintage	F	VF	XF	Unc	BU
1995 Proof	Est. 5,000	Value: 40.00				

KM# 341b 5 POUNDS

39.0830 g., 0.9170 Gold 1.1743 oz. AGW, 36 mm. **Ruler:** Elizabeth II **Subject:** 190th Anniversary - Death of Admiral Nelson **Obv:** Crowned head right **Rev:** Bust at right facing left, ship at left

Date	Mintage	F	VF	XF	Unc	BU
1995 Proof	Est. 850	Value: 900				

KM# 354 5 POUNDS

Virenium, 36 mm. **Ruler:** Elizabeth II **Subject:** 70th Birthday of Queen Elizabeth II **Obv:** Crowned head right **Rev:** Monogram and castle within ribbon

Date	Mintage	F	VF	XF	Unc	BU
1996 AA	—	—	—	—	16.50	18.50

KM# 354a 5 POUNDS

23.5000 g., 0.9250 Silver .6989 oz. ASW, 36 mm. **Ruler:** Elizabeth II **Subject:** 70th Birthday of Queen Elizabeth II **Obv:** Crowned head right **Rev:** Monogram and castle within ribbon

Date	Mintage	F	VF	XF	Unc	BU
1996 Proof	Est. 5,000	Value: 40.00				

KM# 354b 5 POUNDS

39.8300 g., 0.9170 Gold 1.1743 oz. AGW, 36 mm. **Ruler:** Elizabeth II **Subject:** 70th Birthday of Queen Elizabeth II **Obv:** Crowned head right **Rev:** Monogram and castle within ribbon

Date	Mintage	F	VF	XF	Unc	BU
1996 Proof	Est. 850	Value: 835				

KM# 355 5 POUNDS

Virenium, 36 mm. **Ruler:** Elizabeth II **Subject:** Centennial Olympics **Obv:** Crowned head right **Rev:** Zeus on Throne, various athletes flank

Date	Mintage	F	VF	XF	Unc	BU
1996	—	—	—	—	16.50	18.50

KM# 355a 5 POUNDS

23.5000 g., 0.9250 Silver .3989 oz. ASW, 36 mm. **Ruler:** Elizabeth II **Subject:** Centennial Olympics **Obv:** Crowned head right **Rev:** Zeus on Throne, various athletes flank

Date	Mintage	F	VF	XF	Unc	BU
1996 Proof	Est. 5,000	Value: 40.00				

KM# 355b 5 POUNDS

39.8300 g., 0.9170 Gold 1.1743 oz. AGW, 36 mm. **Ruler:** Elizabeth II **Subject:** Centennial Olympics **Obv:** Crowned head right **Rev:** Zeus on Throne, various athletes flank

Date	Mintage	F	VF	XF	Unc	BU
1996 Proof	850	Value: 840				

KM# 527 5 POUNDS

Virenium, 36 mm. **Ruler:** Elizabeth II **Subject:** Queen Elizabeth II's Golden Wedding Anniversary **Obv:** Crowned head right **Rev:** Two hands within wreath of ribbon

Date	Mintage	F	VF	XF	Unc	BU
1997 AA	—	—	—	—	17.50	20.00

KM# 527a 5 POUNDS

25.5000 g., 0.9250 Silver .6989 oz. ASW, 36 mm. **Ruler:** Elizabeth II **Subject:** Queen Elizabeth II's Golden Wedding Anniversary **Obv:** Crowned head right **Rev:** Two hands within wreath of ribbon

Date	Mintage	F	VF	XF	Unc	BU
1997 Proof	Est. 10,000	Value: 40.00				

KM# 527b 5 POUNDS

39.8300 g., 0.9170 Gold 1.1743 oz. AGW, 36 mm. **Ruler:** Elizabeth II **Subject:** Queen Elizabeth II's Golden Wedding Anniversary **Obv:** Crowned head right **Rev:** Two hands within wreath of ribbon

Date	Mintage	F	VF	XF	Unc	BU
1997 Proof	Est. 850	Value: 840				

KM# 605 5 POUNDS

Virenium, 36 mm. **Ruler:** Elizabeth II **Subject:** Bicentennial - Arrival of Commodore Nelson **Obv:** Crowned head right **Rev:** Cameo left of full masted ship

Date	Mintage	F	VF	XF	Unc	BU
1997 AA	—	—	—	—	16.50	18.50

KM# 605a 5 POUNDS

23.5000 g., 0.9250 Silver .6989 oz. ASW, 36 mm. **Ruler:** Elizabeth II **Subject:** Bicentennial - Arrival of Commodore Nelson **Obv:** Crowned head right **Rev:** Cameo left of full masted ship

Date	Mintage	F	VF	XF	Unc	BU
1997 Proof	Est. 10,000	Value: 40.00				

KM# 605b 5 POUNDS

39.8300 g., 0.9170 Gold 1.1743 oz. AGW, 36 mm. **Ruler:** Elizabeth II **Subject:** Bicentennial - Arrival of Commodore Nelson **Obv:** Crowned head right **Rev:** Cameo left of full masted ship

Date	Mintage	F	VF	XF	Unc	BU
1997 Proof	Est. 850	Value: 850				

KM# 607 5 POUNDS

Virenium, 36 mm. **Ruler:** Elizabeth II **Subject:** Last Voyage of Britannia **Obv:** Crowned head right **Rev:** Ship sailing past Gibraltar

Date	Mintage	F	VF	XF	Unc	BU
1997 AA	—	—	—	—	16.50	18.50

KM# 607a 5 POUNDS

23.5000 g., 0.9250 Silver .6989 oz. ASW, 36 mm. **Ruler:** Elizabeth II **Subject:** Last Voyage of Britannia **Obv:** Crowned head right **Rev:** Ship sailing past Gibraltar

Date	Mintage	F	VF	XF	Unc	BU
1997 Proof	Est. 5,000	Value: 50.00				

KM# 607b 5 POUNDS

39.8300 g., 0.9170 Gold 1.1743 oz. AGW, 36 mm. **Ruler:** Elizabeth II **Subject:** Last Voyage of Britannia **Obv:** Crowned head right **Rev:** Ship sailing past Gibraltar

Date	Mintage	F	VF	XF	Unc	BU
1997 Proof	Est. 850	Value: 850				

KM# 740 5 POUNDS

Virenium, 36 mm. **Ruler:** Elizabeth II **Subject:** 40th Anniversary of Radio Gibraltar **Obv:** Head with tiara right **Obv. Designer:** Ian Rank-Broadley **Rev:** Radio broadcaster, rock in background

Date	Mintage	F	VF	XF	Unc	BU
1998 AA	—	—	—	—	16.00	18.00

KM# 740a 5 POUNDS

23.5000 g., 0.9250 Silver .6989 oz. ASW, 36 mm. **Ruler:** Elizabeth II **Subject:** 40th Anniversary of Radio Gibraltar **Obv:** Head with tiara right **Rev:** Radio broadcaster, rock in background

Date	Mintage	F	VF	XF	Unc	BU
1998 Proof	Est. 5,000	Value: 40.00				

KM# 740b 5 POUNDS

39.8300 g., 0.9170 Gold 1.1743 oz. AGW, 36 mm. **Ruler:** Elizabeth II **Subject:** 40th Anniversary of Radio Gibraltar **Obv:** Head with tiara right **Rev:** Radio broadcaster, rock in background

Date	Mintage	F	VF	XF	Unc	BU
1998 Proof	Est. 850	Value: 850				

KM# 770 5 POUNDS

Virenium, 36 mm. **Ruler:** Elizabeth II **Subject:** 80th Anniversary of the RAF **Obv:** Crowned head right **Rev:** Eurofighter over map

Date	Mintage	F	VF	XF	Unc	BU
1998	—	—	—	—	16.00	18.00

KM# 770a 5 POUNDS

23.5000 g., 0.9250 Silver .6989 oz. ASW, 36 mm. **Ruler:** Elizabeth II **Subject:** 80th Anniversary of the RAF **Obv:** Crowned head right **Rev:** Eurofighter over map

Date	Mintage	F	VF	XF	Unc	BU
1998 Proof	Est. 5,000	Value: 50.00				

KM# 770b 5 POUNDS

39.8300 g., 0.9170 Gold 1.1743 oz. AGW, 36 mm. **Ruler:** Elizabeth II **Subject:** 80th Anniversary of the RAF **Obv:** Crowned head right **Rev:** Eurofighter over map

Date	Mintage	F	VF	XF	Unc	BU
1998 Proof	Est. 850	Value: 850				

KM# 771 5 POUNDS

Virenium, 36 mm. **Ruler:** Elizabeth II **Subject:** Millennium 2000 **Obv:** Head with tiara right **Rev:** Landmarks of London

Date	Mintage	F	VF	XF	Unc	BU
1998 AA	—	—	—	—	16.00	18.00

KM# 771a 5 POUNDS

23.5000 g., 0.9250 Silver .6989 oz. ASW, 36 mm. **Ruler:** Elizabeth II **Subject:** Millennium 2000 **Obv:** Head with tiara right **Rev:** Landmarks of London

Date	Mintage	F	VF	XF	Unc	BU
1998 Proof	Est. 5,000	Value: 50.00				

KM# 771b 5 POUNDS

39.8300 g., 0.9170 Gold 1.1743 oz. AGW, 36 mm. **Ruler:** Elizabeth II **Obv:** Head with tiara right **Rev:** Millennium 2000

Date	Mintage	F	VF	XF	Unc	BU
1998 Proof	850	Value: 875				

KM# 772 5 POUNDS

Virenium, 36 mm. **Ruler:** Elizabeth II **Subject:** 50th Birthday of Prince Charles **Obv:** Crowned head right **Rev:** Heads of Prince Charles and sons William and Harry left

Date	Mintage	F	VF	XF	Unc	BU
1998 AA	—	—	—	—	16.00	18.00

KM# 772a 5 POUNDS

23.5000 g., 0.9250 Silver .6989 oz. ASW, 36 mm. **Ruler:** Elizabeth II **Subject:** 50th Birthday of Prince Charles **Obv:** Crowned head right **Rev:** Heads of Prince Charles and sons William and Harry

Date	Mintage	F	VF	XF	Unc	BU
1998 Proof	5,000	Value: 50.00				

KM# 772b 5 POUNDS

39.8300 g., 0.9170 Gold 1.1743 oz. AGW, 36 mm. **Ruler:** Elizabeth II **Subject:** 50th Birthday of Prince Charles **Obv:** Crowned head right **Rev:** Heads of Prince Charles and sons William and Harry

Date	Mintage	F	VF	XF	Unc	BU
1998 Proof	850	Value: 875				

KM# 797 5 POUNDS

Virenium, 36 mm. **Ruler:** Elizabeth II **Subject:** Millennium 2000 **Obv:** Head with tiara right **Obv. Designer:** Ian Rank-Broadley **Rev:** Sundial, digital clock face, candle and traditional clock face

Date	Mintage	F	VF	XF	Unc	BU
1999	—	—	—	—	16.00	18.00

KM# 797a 5 POUNDS

Titanium **Ruler:** Elizabeth II **Subject:** Millennium 2000 **Obv:** Head with tiara right **Obv. Designer:** Rank-Broadley **Rev:** Sundial, digital clock face, candle and traditional clock face

Date	Mintage	F	VF	XF	Unc	BU
1999	Est. 25,000	—	—	—	35.00	40.00

KM# 797b 5 POUNDS

28.2800 g., 0.9250 Silver .8410 oz. ASW, 36 mm. **Ruler:** Elizabeth II **Subject:** Millennium 2000 **Obv:** Head with tiara right **Obv. Designer:** Rank-Broadley **Rev:** Sundial, digital clock face, candle and traditional clock face

Date	Mintage	F	VF	XF	Unc	BU
1999 Proof	Est. 5,000	Value: 65.00				

KM# 867 5 POUNDS

Virenium, 36 mm. **Ruler:** Elizabeth II **Subject:** Mediterranean Rowing Club **Obv:** Head with tiara right **Obv. Designer:** Ian Rank-Broadley **Rev:** A one-man and a four-man row boat

Date	Mintage	F	VF	XF	Unc	BU
1999	—	—	—	—	16.00	18.00

KM# 867a 5 POUNDS

23.5000 g., 0.9250 Silver, 36 mm. **Ruler:** Elizabeth II **Subject:** Mediterranean Rowing Club **Obv:** Head with tiara right **Obv. Designer:** Rank-Broadley **Rev:** A one-man and a four-man row boat

Date	Mintage	F	VF	XF	Unc	BU
1999 Proof	Est. 5,000	Value: 65.00				

KM# 867b 5 POUNDS

39.8300 g., 0.9170 Gold 1.1743 oz. AGW, 36 mm. **Ruler:** Elizabeth II **Subject:** Mediterranean Rowing Club **Obv:** Head with tiara right **Obv. Designer:** Rank-Broadley **Rev:** A one-man and a four-man row boat

Date	Mintage	F	VF	XF	Unc	BU
1999 Proof	Est. 850	Value: 885				

KM# 878 5 POUNDS
Virenium, 36 mm. **Ruler:** Elizabeth II **Subject:** Battle of Britain **Obv:** Head with tiara right **Rev:** Spitfire in flight

Date	Mintage	F	VF	XF	Unc	BU
2000 AA	—	—	—	—	15.00	17.00

KM# 878a 5 POUNDS
23.5000 g., 0.9250 Silver 69.89 oz. ASW, 36 mm. **Ruler:** Elizabeth II **Subject:** Battle of Britain **Obv:** Head with tiara right **Rev:** Spitfire in flight

Date	Mintage	F	VF	XF	Unc	BU
2000 Proof	Est. 10,000	Value: 50.00				

KM# 878b 5 POUNDS
39.8300 g., 0.9160 Gold 1.1738 oz. AGW, 36 mm. **Ruler:** Elizabeth II **Subject:** Battle of Britain **Obv:** Head with tiara right **Rev:** Spitfire in flight

Date	Mintage	F	VF	XF	Unc	BU
2000 Proof	Est. 850	Value: 885				

KM# 885 5 POUNDS
10.0000 g., Titanium **Ruler:** Elizabeth II **Subject:** 160th Anniversary - Uniform Penny Post **Obv:** Head with tiara right **Rev:** Postage stamp design **Edge:** Reeded

Date	Mintage	F	VF	XF	Unc	BU
2000 Proof	15,000	Value: 35.00				

KM# 7 25 POUNDS
7.7700 g., 0.9170 Gold .2291 oz. AGW **Ruler:** Elizabeth II **Subject:** 250th Anniversary - Introduction of British Sterling **Obv:** Young bust right **Obv. Designer:** Arnold Machin **Rev:** Lion and key **Rev. Designer:** Michael Rizzello

Date	Mintage	F	VF	XF	Unc	BU
1975	2,395	—	—	—	165	175
1975 Proof	750	Value: 200				

KM# 8 50 POUNDS
15.5500 g., 0.9170 Gold .4585 oz. AGW **Ruler:** Elizabeth II **Subject:** 250th Anniversary - Introduction of British Sterling **Obv:** Young bust right **Obv. Designer:** Arnold Machin **Rev:** Our Lady of Europa **Rev. Designer:** Michael Rizzello

Date	Mintage	F	VF	XF	Unc	BU
1975	1,625	—	—	—	325	335
1975 Proof	750	Value: 350				

KM# 13 50 POUNDS
15.9760 g., 0.9170 Gold .4711 oz. AGW **Ruler:** Elizabeth II **Subject:** 175th Anniversary - Death of Admiral Nelson **Obv:** Young bust right **Obv. Designer:** Arnold Machin **Rev:** Bust right of ship at left looking left

Date	Mintage	F	VF	XF	Unc	BU
1980	Est. 7,500	—	—	—	320	330
1980 Proof	Est. 5,000	Value: 340				

KM# 15 50 POUNDS
15.9760 g., 0.9170 Gold .4711 oz. AGW **Ruler:** Elizabeth II **Subject:** Wedding of Prince Charles and Lady Diana **Obv. Designer:** Arnold Machin **Rev:** The royal couple

Date	Mintage	F	VF	XF	Unc	BU
1981	—	—	—	—	320	330
1981 Proof	Est. 2,500	Value: 340				

KM# 9 100 POUNDS
31.1000 g., 0.9170 Gold .9170 oz. AGW **Ruler:** Elizabeth II **Subject:** 250th Anniversary - Introduction of British Sterling **Obv. Designer:** Arnold Machin **Rev:** Coat of arms **Rev. Designer:** Michael Rizzello

Date	Mintage	F	VF	XF	Unc	BU
1975	1,625	—	—	—	—	665
1975 Proof	750	Value: 685				

SOVEREIGN COINAGE

KM# 26 1/4 SOVEREIGN
1.9900 g., 0.9170 Gold .0587 oz. AGW **Ruler:** Elizabeth II **Subject:** 150th Anniversary of Regal Coinage **Obv:** Crowned bust right **Obv. Designer:** Raphael Maklouf **Rev:** Queen and lion left

Date	Mintage	F	VF	XF	Unc	BU
1989 U	—	—	—	—	—	—
1989 Proof	Est. 1,989	Value: 70.00				

KM# 41 1/4 SOVEREIGN
1.9900 g., 0.9170 Gold .0587 oz. AGW **Ruler:** Elizabeth II **Subject:** 21st Anniversary - Constitution **Obv:** Crowned bust right **Obv. Designer:** Raphael Maklouf **Rev:** Standing figure with key and trident, shield lower right

Date	Mintage	F	VF	XF	Unc	BU
1990 Proof	Est. 1,000	Value: 65.00				

KM# 515 1/4 SOVEREIGN
1.2241 g., 0.9999 Gold .0400 oz. AGW **Ruler:** Elizabeth II **Obv:** Crowned bust right **Obv. Designer:** Raphael Maklouf **Rev:** Queen and lion left

Date	Mintage	F	VF	XF	Unc	BU
1997 Proof	—	Value: 50.00				

KM# 27 1/2 SOVEREIGN
3.9800 g., 0.9170 Gold .1173 oz. AGW **Ruler:** Elizabeth II **Subject:** 150th Anniversary of Regal Coinage **Obv:** Crowned bust right **Obv. Designer:** Raphael Maklouf **Rev:** Queen and lion left

Date	Mintage	F	VF	XF	Unc	BU
1989 U	—	—	—	—	—	—
1989 Proof	Est. 1,989	Value: 135				

KM# 42 1/2 SOVEREIGN
3.9800 g., 0.9170 Gold .1173 oz. AGW **Ruler:** Elizabeth II **Subject:** 21st Anniversary - Constitution **Obv:** Crowned bust right **Obv. Designer:** Raphael Maklouf **Rev:** Standing figure with key and trident, shield lower right

Date	Mintage	F	VF	XF	Unc	BU
1990 Proof	1,000	Value: 125				

KM# 516 1/2 SOVEREIGN
3.1103 g., 0.9999 Gold .10000 oz. AGW **Ruler:** Elizabeth II **Obv:** Crowned bust right **Obv. Designer:** Raphael Maklouf **Rev:** Queen and lion left

Date	Mintage	F	VF	XF	Unc	BU
1997 Proof	—	Value: 95.00				

KM# 28 SOVEREIGN
7.9600 g., 0.9170 Gold .2347 oz. AGW **Ruler:** Elizabeth II **Subject:** 150th Anniversary of Regal Coinage **Obv:** Crowned bust right **Obv. Designer:** Raphael Maklouf **Rev:** Queen and lion left

Date	Mintage	F	VF	XF	Unc	BU
1989 U	—	—	—	—	—	—
1989 Proof	Est. 1,989	Value: 265				

KM# 43 SOVEREIGN
7.9600 g., 0.9170 Gold .2347 oz. AGW **Ruler:** Elizabeth II **Subject:** 21st Anniversary - Constitution **Obv:** Crowned bust right **Obv. Designer:** Raphael Maklouf **Rev:** Standing figure with key and trident, shield at lower right

Date	Mintage	F	VF	XF	Unc	BU
1990 Proof	Est. 1,000	Value: 250				

KM# 517 SOVEREIGN
6.2207 g., 0.9999 Gold .2000 oz. AGW **Ruler:** Elizabeth II **Obv:** Crowned bust right **Obv. Designer:** Raphael Maklouf **Rev:** Queen and lion left

Date	Mintage	F	VF	XF	Unc	BU
1997 Proof	—	Value: 185				

KM# 29 2 SOVEREIGNS
15.9400 g., 0.9170 Gold .4700 oz. AGW **Ruler:** Elizabeth II **Subject:** 150th Anniversary of Regal Coinage **Obv:** Crowned bust right **Obv. Designer:** Raphael Maklouf **Rev:** Queen and lion left

Date	Mintage	F	VF	XF	Unc	BU
1989 Proof	1,989	Value: 550				

KM# 44 2 SOVEREIGNS
15.9400 g., 0.9170 Gold .4700 oz. AGW **Ruler:** Elizabeth II **Subject:** 21st Anniversary - Constitution **Obv:** Crowned bust right **Obv. Designer:** Raphael Maklouf **Rev:** Standing figure with key and trident, shield lower right

Date	Mintage	F	VF	XF	Unc	BU
1990 Proof	1,000	Value: 525				

KM# 30 5 SOVEREIGNS
39.8300 g., 0.9170 Gold 1.1743 oz. AGW **Ruler:** Elizabeth II **Subject:** 150th Anniversary of Regal Coinage **Obv:** Crowned bust right **Obv. Designer:** Raphael Maklouf **Rev:** Queen and lion left

Date	Mintage	F	VF	XF	Unc	BU
1989 Proof	1,989	Value: 1,100				

KM# 45 5 SOVEREIGNS
39.8300 g., 0.9170 Gold 1.1743 oz. AGW **Ruler:** Elizabeth II **Subject:** 21st Anniversary - Constitution **Obv:** Crowned bust right **Obv. Designer:** Raphael Maklouf **Rev:** Standing figure with key and trident, shield lower right

Date	Mintage	F	VF	XF	Unc	BU
1990 Proof	Est. 1,000	Value: 975				

ROYAL COINAGE

KM# 91 1/25 ROYAL
1.2400 g., 0.9999 Gold .0400 oz. AGW **Ruler:** Elizabeth II **Subject:** Dogs **Obv:** Crowned bust right **Rev:** Corgi

Date	Mintage	F	VF	XF	Unc	BU
1991	—	—	—	—	75.00	—
1991 Proof	Est. 1,000	Value: 76.50				

KM# 99 1/25 ROYAL
1.2400 g., 0.9999 Gold .0400 oz. AGW **Ruler:** Elizabeth II **Subject:** Dogs **Obv:** Crowned bust right **Rev:** Cocker Spaniel

Date	Mintage	F	VF	XF	Unc	BU
1992	—	—	—	—	40.00	—
1992 Proof	Est. 1,000	Value: 42.50				

KM# 193 1/25 ROYAL
1.2400 g., 0.9999 Gold .0400 oz. AGW **Ruler:** Elizabeth II **Subject:** Dogs **Obv:** Crowned bust right **Rev:** Long-haired Dachshund

Date	Mintage	F	VF	XF	Unc	BU
1993	—	—	—	—	40.00	—
1993 Proof	Est. 1,000	Value: 42.50				

KM# 248 1/25 ROYAL
1.2400 g., 0.9999 Gold .0400 oz. AGW **Ruler:** Elizabeth II **Subject:** Dogs **Obv:** Crowned bust right **Rev:** Pekingese

Date	Mintage	F	VF	XF	Unc	BU
1994	—	—	—	—	40.00	—
1994 Proof	Est. 1,000	Value: 42.50				

KM# 319 1/25 ROYAL
1.2400 g., 0.9999 Gold .0400 oz. AGW **Ruler:** Elizabeth II **Subject:** Crowned bust right **Obv:** Crowned bust right **Rev:** Collie

Date	Mintage	F	VF	XF	Unc	BU
1995 Proof	Est. 1,000	Value: 42.50				
1995	—	—	—	—	40.00	—

KM# 361 1/25 ROYAL
1.2400 g., 0.9999 Gold .0400 oz. AGW **Ruler:** Elizabeth II **Subject:** Dogs **Obv:** Crowned bust right **Rev:** Bulldog

Date	Mintage	F	VF	XF	Unc	BU
1996	—	—	—	—	40.00	—
1996 Proof	Est. 1,000	Value: 42.50				

KM# 557 1/25 ROYAL
1.2400 g., 0.9999 Gold .0400 oz. AGW **Ruler:** Elizabeth II **Subject:** Dogs **Obv:** Crowned bust right **Rev:** Yorkshire Terrier

Date	Mintage	F	VF	XF	Unc	BU
1997	—	—	—	—	50.00	—
1997 Proof	Est. 1,000	Value: 52.00				

KM# 749 1/25 ROYAL

1.2400 g., 0.9999 Gold .0400 oz. AGW **Ruler:** Elizabeth II **Obv:** Crowned bust right **Obv. Designer:** Raphael Maklouf **Rev:** Kissing cherubs

Date	Mintage	F	VF	XF	Unc	BU
1998	—	—	—	—	50.00	—
1998 Proof	Est. 1,000	Value: 52.00				

KM# 749a 1/25 ROYAL

1.2400 g., 0.9950 Platinum .0400 oz. APW **Ruler:** Elizabeth II **Obv:** Crowned bust right **Rev:** Kissing cherubs

Date	Mintage	F	VF	XF	Unc	BU
1998 Proof	—	Value: 75.00				

KM# 828 1/25 ROYAL

1.2400 g., 0.9990 Gold .0400 oz. AGW **Ruler:** Elizabeth II **Obv:** Crowned bust right **Rev:** Cherub

Date	Mintage	F	VF	XF	Unc	BU
1999 U	—	—	—	—	35.00	—
1999 U Y2K	Est. 20,000	—	—	—	35.00	—
1999 Proof	Est. 1,000	Value: 40.00				

KM# 828a 1/25 ROYAL

1.2400 g., 0.9950 Platinum .0400 oz. APW **Ruler:** Elizabeth II **Obv:** Crowned bust right **Rev:** One cherub

Date	Mintage	F	VF	XF	Unc	BU
1999 Proof	Est. 1,000	Value: 75.00				

KM# 888 1/25 ROYAL

1.2441 g., 0.9990 Gold .0400 oz. AGW, 13.92 mm. **Ruler:** Elizabeth II **Subject:** Bullion **Obv:** Crowned bust right **Rev:** 2 cherubs **Edge:** Reeded

Date	Mintage	F	VF	XF	Unc	BU
2000	—	—	—	—	35.00	—
2000	1,000	Value: 40.00				

Note: In proof sets only

KM# 92 1/10 ROYAL

3.1100 g., 0.9999 Gold .1000 oz. AGW **Ruler:** Elizabeth II **Subject:** Dogs **Obv:** Crowned bust right **Rev:** Corgi

Date	Mintage	F	VF	XF	Unc	BU
1991	—	—	—	—	77.50	—
1991 Proof	Est. 1,000	Value: 80.00				

KM# 100 1/10 ROYAL

3.1100 g., 0.9999 Gold .1000 oz. AGW **Ruler:** Elizabeth II **Subject:** Dogs **Obv:** Crowned bust right **Rev:** Cocker Spaniel

Date	Mintage	F	VF	XF	Unc	BU
1992	—	—	—	—	77.50	—
1992 Proof	Est. 1,000	Value: 80.00				

KM# 194 1/10 ROYAL

3.1100 g., 0.9999 Gold .1000 oz. AGW **Ruler:** Elizabeth II **Obv:** Crowned bust right **Rev:** Long-haired Dachshund

Date	Mintage	F	VF	XF	Unc	BU
1993	—	—	—	—	70.00	—
1993 Proof	Est. 1,000	Value: 72.50				

KM# 249 1/10 ROYAL

3.1100 g., 0.9999 Gold .1000 oz. AGW **Ruler:** Elizabeth II **Subject:** Dogs **Obv:** Crowned bust right **Rev:** Pekingese

Date	Mintage	F	VF	XF	Unc	BU
1994	—	—	—	—	70.00	—
1994 Proof	Est. 1,000	Value: 72.50				

KM# 320 1/10 ROYAL

3.1100 g., 0.9999 Gold .1000 oz. AGW **Ruler:** Elizabeth II **Subject:** Dogs **Obv:** Crowned bust right **Rev:** Collie

Date	Mintage	F	VF	XF	Unc	BU
1995	—	—	—	—	70.00	—
1995 Proof	Est. 1,000	Value: 72.50				

KM# 362 1/10 ROYAL

3.1100 g., 0.9999 Gold .1000 oz. AGW **Ruler:** Elizabeth II **Subject:** Dogs **Obv:** Crowned bust right **Rev:** Bulldog

Date	Mintage	F	VF	XF	Unc	BU
1996	—	—	—	—	70.00	—
1996 Proof	Est. 1,000	Value: 72.50				

KM# 558 1/10 ROYAL

3.1100 g., 0.9999 Gold .1000 oz. AGW **Ruler:** Elizabeth II **Subject:** Dogs **Obv:** Crowned bust right **Rev:** Yorkshire Terrier

Date	Mintage	F	VF	XF	Unc	BU
1997	—	—	—	—	75.00	—
1997 Proof	Est. 1,000	Value: 76.50				

KM# 750 1/10 ROYAL

3.1100 g., 0.9999 Gold .1000 oz. AGW **Ruler:** Elizabeth II **Obv:** Crowned bust right **Rev:** Kissing cherubs

Date	Mintage	F	VF	XF	Unc	BU
1998	—	—	—	—	75.00	—
1998 Proof	Est. 1,000	Value: 76.50				

KM# 829 1/10 ROYAL

3.1100 g., 0.9999 Gold .1000 oz. AGW **Ruler:** Elizabeth II **Obv:** Crowned bust right **Rev:** Cherub

Date	Mintage	F	VF	XF	Unc	BU
1999 U	—	—	—	—	68.00	—
1999 U Y2K	Est. 10,000	—	—	—	68.00	—
1999 Proof	—	Value: 70.00				

KM# 829a 1/10 ROYAL

3.1100 g., 0.9950 Platinum .0999 oz. APW **Ruler:** Elizabeth II **Obv:** Crowned bust right **Rev:** Cherub

Date	Mintage	F	VF	XF	Unc	BU
1999 Proof	Est. 1,000	Value: 145				

KM# 889 1/10 ROYAL

3.1100 g., 0.9990 Gold .1000 oz. AGW **Ruler:** Elizabeth II **Obv:** Crowned bust right **Rev:** Two cherubs **Edge:** Reeded

Date	Mintage	F	VF	XF	Unc	BU
2000	—	—	—	—	75.00	—
2000 Proof	1,000	Value: 76.50				

KM# 93 1/5 ROYAL

6.2200 g., 0.9999 Gold .20000 oz. AGW **Ruler:** Elizabeth II **Subject:** Dogs **Obv:** Crowned bust right **Rev:** Corgi

Date	Mintage	F	VF	XF	Unc	BU
1991	—	—	—	—	175	—
1991 Proof	Est. 1,000	Value: 177				

KM# 101 1/5 ROYAL

6.2200 g., 0.9999 Gold .20000 oz. AGW **Ruler:** Elizabeth II **Subject:** Dogs **Obv:** Crowned bust right **Rev:** Cocker Spaniel

Date	Mintage	F	VF	XF	Unc	BU
1992	—	—	—	—	145	—
1992 Proof	Est. 1,000	Value: 150				

KM# 195 1/5 ROYAL

6.2200 g., 0.9999 Gold .20000 oz. AGW **Ruler:** Elizabeth II **Subject:** Dogs **Obv:** Crowned bust right **Rev:** Long-haired Dachshund

Date	Mintage	F	VF	XF	Unc	BU
1993	—	—	—	—	145	—
1993 Proof	Est. 1,000	Value: 150				

KM# 250 1/5 ROYAL

6.2200 g., 0.9999 Gold .20000 oz. AGW **Ruler:** Elizabeth II **Subject:** Dogs **Obv:** Crowned bust right **Rev:** Pekingese

Date	Mintage	F	VF	XF	Unc	BU
1994	—	—	—	—	145	—
1994 Proof	Est. 1,000	Value: 150				

KM# 321 1/5 ROYAL

6.2200 g., 0.9999 Gold .20000 oz. AGW **Ruler:** Elizabeth II **Subject:** Dogs **Obv:** Crowned bust right **Rev:** Collie

Date	Mintage	F	VF	XF	Unc	BU
1995	—	—	—	—	145	—
1995 Proof	Est. 1,000	Value: 150				

KM# 363 1/5 ROYAL

6.2200 g., 0.9999 Gold .20000 oz. AGW **Ruler:** Elizabeth II **Subject:** Dogs **Obv:** Crowned bust right **Rev:** Bulldog

Date	Mintage	F	VF	XF	Unc	BU
1996	—	—	—	—	145	—
1996 Proof	Est. 1,000	Value: 150				

KM# 559 1/5 ROYAL

6.2200 g., 0.9999 Gold .20000 oz. AGW **Ruler:** Elizabeth II **Subject:** Dogs **Obv:** Crowned bust right **Rev:** Yorkshire Terrier

Date	Mintage	F	VF	XF	Unc	BU
1997	—	—	—	—	150	—
1997 Proof	Est. 1,000	Value: 152				

KM# 751 1/5 ROYAL

6.2200 g., 0.9999 Gold .20000 oz. AGW **Ruler:** Elizabeth II **Obv:** Crowned bust right **Rev:** Kissing cherubs

Date	Mintage	F	VF	XF	Unc	BU
1998	—	—	—	—	145	—
1998 Proof	Est. 1,000	Value: 150				

KM# 830 1/5 ROYAL

6.2200 g., 0.9999 Gold .2000 oz. AGW **Ruler:** Elizabeth II **Obv:** Crowned bust right **Rev:** Four cherubs

Date	Mintage	F	VF	XF	Unc	BU
1999 U Y2K	Est. 5,000	—	—	—	140	—
1999 Proof	—	Value: 145				
1999 U	—	—	—	—	140	—

KM# 830a 1/5 ROYAL

6.2200 g., 0.9950 Platinum .2000 oz. APW **Ruler:** Elizabeth II **Obv:** Crowned bust right **Rev:** Four cherubs

Date	Mintage	F	VF	XF	Unc	BU
1999 Proof	Est. 1,000	Value: 300				

KM# 890 1/5 ROYAL

6.2200 g., 0.9990 Gold .2000 oz. AGW **Ruler:** Elizabeth II **Obv:** Crowned bust right **Rev:** 2 cherubs **Edge:** Reeded

Date	Mintage	F	VF	XF	Unc	BU
2000	—	—	—	—	140	—
2000 Proof	1,000	Value: 185				

KM# 94 1/2 ROYAL

15.5500 g., 0.9999 Gold .5000 oz. AGW **Ruler:** Elizabeth II **Subject:** Dogs **Obv:** Crowned bust right **Rev:** Corgi

Date	Mintage	F	VF	XF	Unc	BU
1991	—	—	—	—	375	385
1991 Proof	Est. 1,000	Value: 390				

KM# 102 1/2 ROYAL

15.5500 g., 0.9999 Gold .5000 oz. AGW **Ruler:** Elizabeth II **Subject:** Dogs **Obv:** Crowned bust right **Rev:** Cocker Spaniel

Date	Mintage	F	VF	XF	Unc	BU
1992	—	—	—	—	345	365
1992 Proof	Est. 1,000	Value: 375				

KM# 196 1/2 ROYAL

15.5500 g., 0.9999 Gold .5000 oz. AGW **Ruler:** Elizabeth II **Subject:** Dogs **Obv:** Crowned bust right **Rev:** Long-haired Dachshund

Date	Mintage	F	VF	XF	Unc	BU
1993	—	—	—	—	345	365
1993 Proof	Est. 1,000	Value: 375				

KM# 251 1/2 ROYAL

15.5500 g., 0.9999 Gold .5000 oz. AGW **Ruler:** Elizabeth II **Subject:** Dogs **Obv:** Crowned bust right **Rev:** Pekingese

Date	Mintage	F	VF	XF	Unc	BU
1994	—	—	—	—	345	365
1994 Proof	Est. 1,000	Value: 375				

KM# 322 1/2 ROYAL

15.5500 g., 0.9999 Gold .5000 oz. AGW **Ruler:** Elizabeth II **Subject:** Dogs **Obv:** Crowned bust right **Rev:** Collie

Date	Mintage	F	VF	XF	Unc	BU
1995	—	—	—	—	345	365
1995 Proof	Est. 1,000	Value: 375				

KM# 364 1/2 ROYAL

15.5500 g., 0.9999 Gold .5000 oz. AGW **Ruler:** Elizabeth II **Subject:** Dogs **Obv:** Crowned bust right **Rev:** Bulldog

Date	Mintage	F	VF	XF	Unc	BU
1996	—	—	—	—	345	365
1996 Proof	Est. 1,000	Value: 375				

KM# 560 1/2 ROYAL

15.5500 g., 0.9999 Gold .5000 oz. AGW **Ruler:** Elizabeth II **Subject:** Dogs **Obv:** Crowned bust right **Rev:** Yorkshire Terrier

Date	Mintage	F	VF	XF	Unc	BU
1997	—	—	—	—	345	365
1997 Proof	Est. 1,000	Value: 375				

KM# 752 1/2 ROYAL

15.5500 g., 0.9999 Gold .5000 oz. AGW **Ruler:** Elizabeth II **Obv:** Crowned bust right **Rev:** Kissing cherubs

Date	Mintage	F	VF	XF	Unc	BU
1998	—	—	—	—	340	350
1998 Proof	Est. 1,000	Value: 305				

KM# 831 1/2 ROYAL

15.5500 g., 0.9999 Gold .5000 oz. AGW **Ruler:** Elizabeth II **Obv:** Crowned bust right **Rev:** Four cherubs

Date	Mintage	F	VF	XF	Unc	BU
1999	—	—	—	—	340	350
1999 Proof	—	Value: 360				

KM# 891 1/2 ROYAL
15.5500 g., 0.9999 Gold .5000 oz. AGW **Ruler:** Elizabeth II
Obv: Crowned bust right **Rev:** Two cherubs **Edge:** Reeded

Date	Mintage	F	VF	XF	Unc	BU
2000	—	—	—	—	340	350
2000 Proof	1,000	Value: 360				

KM# 97 ROYAL
31.1030 g., 0.9999 Gold 1.0000 oz. AGW **Ruler:** Elizabeth II
Obv: Crowned bust right **Rev:** Corgi

Date	Mintage	F	VF	XF	Unc	BU
1991 Proof	Est. 1,000	Value: 675				
1991	—	—	—	—	685	700

KM# 105 ROYAL
31.1030 g., 0.9999 Gold 1.0000 oz. AGW **Ruler:** Elizabeth II
Obv: Crowned bust right **Rev:** Cocker Spaniel

Date	Mintage	F	VF	XF	Unc	BU
1992	—	—	—	—	685	700
1992 Proof	Est. 1,000	Value: 675				

KM# 197 ROYAL
31.1030 g., 0.9999 Gold 1.0000 oz. AGW **Ruler:** Elizabeth II
Obv: Crowned bust right **Rev:** Long-haired Dachshund

Date	Mintage	F	VF	XF	Unc	BU
1993	—	—	—	—	685	700
1993 Proof	Est. 1,000	Value: 675				

KM# 246 ROYAL
Copper-Nickel **Ruler:** Elizabeth II **Subject:** Dogs **Obv:** Crowned bust right **Rev:** Pekingese Dog

Date	Mintage	F	VF	XF	Unc	BU
1994PM Proof	250	Value: 25.00				
1994	—	—	—	—	7.00	12.00

KM# 252 ROYAL
31.1000 g., 0.9990 Silver .9989 oz. ASW **Ruler:** Elizabeth II
Subject: Dogs **Obv:** Crowned bust right **Rev:** Pekingese

Date	Mintage	F	VF	XF	Unc	BU
1994 Proof	Est. 50,000	Value: 35.00				

KM# 252a ROYAL
31.1030 g., 0.9999 Gold 1.0000 oz. AGW **Ruler:** Elizabeth II
Subject: Dogs **Obv:** Crowned bust right **Rev:** Pekingese

Date	Mintage	F	VF	XF	Unc	BU
1994	—	—	—	—	665	685
1994 Proof	Est. 1,000	Value: 675				

KM# 318 ROYAL
28.6200 g., Copper-Nickel, 38.8 mm. **Ruler:** Elizabeth II **Subject:** Collie **Obv:** Crowned bust right **Rev:** Collie **Edge:** Reeded

Date	Mintage	F	VF	XF	Unc	BU
1995	—	—	—	—	12.00	14.00

KM# 318b ROYAL
31.1030 g., 0.9999 Gold 1.0000 oz. AGW **Ruler:** Elizabeth II
Subject: Dogs **Obv:** Crowned bust right **Rev:** Collie

Date	Mintage	F	VF	XF	Unc	BU
1995	—	—	—	—	665	685
1995 Proof	Est. 1,000	Value: 675				

KM# 318a ROYAL
31.1030 g., 0.9990 Silver 1.0000 oz. ASW **Ruler:** Elizabeth II
Subject: Dogs **Obv:** Crowned bust right **Rev:** Collie

Date	Mintage	F	VF	XF	Unc	BU
1995 Proof	Est. 50,000	Value: 35.00				

KM# 365 ROYAL
31.1030 g., 0.9990 Silver 1.0000 oz. ASW **Ruler:** Elizabeth II
Subject: Dogs **Obv:** Crowned bust right **Rev:** Bulldog

Date	Mintage	F	VF	XF	Unc	BU
1996 Proof	Est. 50,000	Value: 40.00				

KM# 365b ROYAL
31.1030 g., 0.9999 Gold 1.0000 oz. AGW **Ruler:** Elizabeth II
Subject: Dogs **Obv:** Crowned bust right **Rev:** Bulldog

Date	Mintage	F	VF	XF	Unc	BU
1996	—	—	—	—	665	685
1996 Proof	Est. 1,000	Value: 675				

KM# 561a ROYAL
31.1035 g., 0.9990 Silver 1.0000 oz. ASW **Ruler:** Elizabeth II
Subject: Dogs **Obv:** Crowned bust right **Rev:** Yorkshire terrier

Date	Mintage	F	VF	XF	Unc	BU
1997 Proof	Est. 50,000	Value: 35.00				

KM# 561b ROYAL
31.1035 g., 0.9999 Gold 1.0000 oz. AGW **Ruler:** Elizabeth II
Subject: Dogs **Obv:** Crowned bust right **Rev:** Yorkshire terrier

Date	Mintage	F	VF	XF	Unc	BU
1997	—	—	—	—	665	685
1997 Proof	Est. 1,000	Value: 675				

KM# 561a.1 ROYAL
31.3000 g., 0.9990 Silver 1.0053 oz. ASW, 38.5 mm. **Ruler:** Elizabeth II **Subject:** Dogs **Obv:** Crowned bust right **Rev:** Gold-plated Yorkshire Terrier **Edge:** Reeded

Date	Mintage	F	VF	XF	Unc	BU
1997 Proof	—	—	—	—	50.00	55.00

KM# 753 ROYAL
Copper-Nickel **Ruler:** Elizabeth II **Obv:** Crowned bust right **Rev:** Kissing cherubs

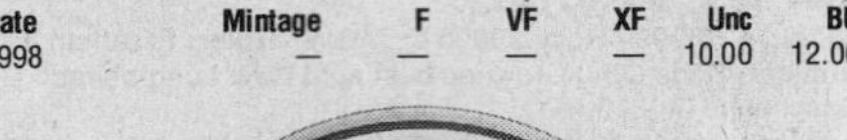

Date	Mintage	F	VF	XF	Unc	BU
1998	—	—	—	—	10.00	12.00

KM# 753a ROYAL
28.2800 g., 0.9990 Silver 1.0000 oz. ASW **Ruler:** Elizabeth II
Obv: Crowned bust right **Rev:** Kissing cherubs

Date	Mintage	F	VF	XF	Unc	BU
1998 Proof	Est. 20,000	Value: 45.00				

KM# 754 ROYAL
31.1030 g., 0.9999 Gold 1.0000 oz. AGW **Ruler:** Elizabeth II
Obv: Crowned bust right **Rev:** Kissing cherubs

Date	Mintage	F	VF	XF	Unc	BU
1998	—	—	—	—	665	685
1998 Proof	Est. 1,000	Value: 675				

KM# 832 ROYAL
Copper-Nickel **Ruler:** Elizabeth II **Obv:** Crowned bust right **Rev:** Four cherubs

Date	Mintage	F	VF	XF	Unc	BU
1999	—	—	—	—	10.00	12.00

KM# 832a ROYAL
31.1035 g., 0.9990 Silver 1.0000 oz. ASW **Ruler:** Elizabeth II
Obv: Crowned bust right **Rev:** Four cherubs

Date	Mintage	F	VF	XF	Unc	BU
1999 Proof	Est. 50,000	Value: 50.00				

KM# 833 ROYAL
31.1030 g., 0.9999 Gold 1.0000 oz. AGW **Ruler:** Elizabeth II
Obv: Crowned bust right **Rev:** Four cherubs

Date	Mintage	F	VF	XF	Unc	BU
1999 U	—	—	—	—	665	685
1999 Proof	—	Value: 675				

KM# 892 ROYAL
28.2800 g., Copper-Nickel **Ruler:** Elizabeth II **Obv:** Crowned bust right **Rev:** 2 cherubs **Edge:** Reeded

Date	Mintage	F	VF	XF	Unc	BU
2000	—	—	—	—	10.00	12.00

KM# 892a ROYAL
31.1035 g., 0.9990 Silver 1.0000 oz. ASW **Ruler:** Elizabeth II
Obv: Crowned bust right **Rev:** 2 cherubs **Edge:** Reeded

Date	Mintage	F	VF	XF	Unc	BU
2000 Proof	10,000	Value: 50.00				

KM# 893 ROYAL
31.1035 g., 0.9990 Gold 1.0000 oz. AGW **Ruler:** Elizabeth II
Obv: Crowned bust right **Rev:** Two cherubs **Edge:** Reeded

Date	Mintage	F	VF	XF	Unc	BU
2000	—	—	—	—	665	685
2000	1,000	Value: 675				

Note: In proof sets only

EUROPEAN CURRENCY UNITS

Dual Denomination Coinage

KM# 293 2.8 ECUS - 2 POUNDS
Copper-Nickel **Ruler:** Elizabeth II **Obv:** Crowned bust right **Rev:** Knight on horseback jumping left, stars encircle

Date	Mintage	F	VF	XF	Unc	BU
1992	—	—	—	—	12.50	14.50

KM# 87 14 ECUS - 10 POUNDS
10.0000 g., 0.9250 Silver .2974 oz. ASW **Ruler:** Elizabeth II
Subject: European Currency Unit **Obv:** Crowned bust right **Rev:** Knight on horseback jumping left, stars encircle

Date	Mintage	F	VF	XF	Unc	BU
1991 Proof	Est. 10,000	Value: 20.00				
1992 Proof	Est. 5,000	Value: 30.00				
1993	—	—	—	—	75.00	80.00
1994	—	—	—	—	75.00	80.00

KM# 109 14 ECUS - 10 POUNDS
10.0000 g., 0.9250 Silver .2974 oz. ASW **Ruler:** Elizabeth II
Obv: Uncouped portrait **Rev:** Mounted rider right

Date	Mintage	F	VF	XF	Unc	BU
1992	—	—	—	—	15.00	17.50
1992 Proof	—	Value: 30.00				
1993 Proof	—	Value: 35.00				

KM# 624 14 ECUS - 10 POUNDS
10.0000 g., 0.9250 Silver .2974 oz. ASW **Ruler:** Elizabeth II
Obv: Crowned bust right **Rev:** Knight on horseback jumping left, stars encircle

Date	Mintage	F	VF	XF	Unc	BU
1992 Proof	Est. 2,500	Value: 25.00				

KM# 89 14 ECUS - 10 POUNDS
10.0000 g., 0.9250 Silver .2974 oz. ASW **Ruler:** Elizabeth II
Obv: Crowned bust right **Rev:** Knight on horse jumping right

Date	Mintage	F	VF	XF	Unc	BU
1992A Matte	—	—	—	—	20.00	22.50

KM# 337 14 ECUS - 10 POUNDS
10.0000 g., 0.9250 Silver .2974 oz. ASW **Ruler:** Elizabeth II
Obv: Crowned bust right **Rev:** Torch shield

Date	Mintage	F	VF	XF	Unc	BU
1992 Proof	2,500	Value: 25.00				

KM# 627 14 ECUS - 10 POUNDS

10.0000 g., 0.9250 Silver .2974 oz. ASW **Ruler:** Elizabeth II **Obv:** Crowned bust right **Rev:** Knight on horseback jumping right, stars encircle

Date	Mintage	F	VF	XF	Unc	BU
1993 Proof	Est. 2,500	Value: 25.00				

KM# 88 35 ECUS - 25 POUNDS

28.2800 g., 0.9250 Silver .8411 oz. ASW **Ruler:** Elizabeth II **Obv:** Crowned bust right **Rev:** Knight on horseback jumping left, stars encircle

Date	Mintage	F	VF	XF	Unc	BU
1991 Proof	Est. 10,000	Value: 60.00				
1992	—	—	—	—	40.00	45.00
1992 Proof	Est. 15,000	Value: 60.00				

KM# 110 35 ECUS - 25 POUNDS

28.2800 g., 0.9250 Silver .8411 oz. ASW **Ruler:** Elizabeth II **Obv:** Crowned bust right **Rev:** Knight on horseback jumping right, stars encircle

Date	Mintage	F	VF	XF	Unc	BU
1992 Proof	Est. 15,000	Value: 50.00				
1993 Proof	—	Value: 70.00				

KM# 338 35 ECUS - 25 POUNDS

28.2800 g., 0.9250 Silver .8411 oz. ASW **Ruler:** Elizabeth II **Obv:** Crowned bust right **Rev:** Knight on horseback jumping left, stars encircle

Date	Mintage	F	VF	XF	Unc	BU
1992 Proof	Est. 2,000	Value: 85.00				

KM# 625 35 ECUS - 25 POUNDS

28.2800 g., 0.9250 Silver .8411 oz. ASW **Ruler:** Elizabeth II **Obv:** Crowned bust right **Rev:** Knight on horseback jumping left, stars encircle

Date	Mintage	F	VF	XF	Unc	BU
1992 Proof	Est. 2,000	Value: 100				

KM# 628 35 ECUS - 25 POUNDS

28.2800 g., 0.9250 Silver .8411 oz. ASW **Ruler:** Elizabeth II **Obv:** Crowned bust right **Rev:** Knight on horseback jumping right, three lions on shield

Date	Mintage	F	VF	XF	Unc	BU
1993 Proof	Est. 2,000	Value: 75.00				

KM# 75 70 ECUS - 50 POUNDS

6.1200 g., 0.5000 Gold .1000 oz. AGW **Ruler:** Elizabeth II **Obv:** Crowned bust right **Rev:** Knight on horseback jumping left, stars encircle

Date	Mintage	F	VF	XF	Unc	BU
1991 Proof	Est. 5,000	Value: 200				
1991	—	—	—	—	85.00	90.00
1992	—	—	—	—	85.00	90.00
1992 Proof	Est. 2,000	Value: 225				
1994	—	—	—	—	250	270

KM# 111 70 ECUS - 50 POUNDS

6.1200 g., 0.5000 Gold .1000 oz. AGW **Ruler:** Elizabeth II **Obv:** Crowned bust right **Rev:** Knight on horseback jumping right, stars encircle

Date	Mintage	F	VF	XF	Unc	BU
1992 Proof	Est. 2,000	Value: 175				
1993 Proof	Est. 1,000	Value: 200				

KM# 339 70 ECUS - 50 POUNDS

6.1200 g., 0.5000 Gold .1000 oz. AGW **Ruler:** Elizabeth II **Obv:** Crowned bust right **Rev:** Knight on horseback jumping left, stars encircle

Date	Mintage	F	VF	XF	Unc	BU
1992 Proof	Est. 1,000	Value: 200				

KM# 626 70 ECUS - 50 POUNDS

6.1200 g., 0.5000 Gold .1000 oz. AGW **Ruler:** Elizabeth II **Obv:** Crowned bust right **Rev:** Knight on horseback jumping left, stars encircle

Date	Mintage	F	VF	XF	Unc	BU
1992 Proof	Est. 1,000	Value: 200				

KM# 629 70 ECUS - 50 POUNDS

6.1200 g., 0.5000 Gold .1000 oz. AGW **Ruler:** Elizabeth II **Obv:** Crowned bust right **Rev:** Knight on horseback jumping right, stars encircle

Date	Mintage	F	VF	XF	Unc	BU
1993 Proof	Est. 1,000	Value: 150				

STERLING ECU

KM# 478 2.8 ECUS

Copper-Nickel **Ruler:** Elizabeth II **Subject:** Euro Tunnel **Obv:** Crowned bust right **Rev:** Train exiting tunnel

Date	Mintage	F	VF	XF	Unc	BU
1993	—	—	—	—	9.50	11.50

KM# 630 2.8 ECUS

Copper-Nickel **Ruler:** Elizabeth II **Subject:** A'riane - European Space Programme **Obv:** Crowned bust right **Rev:** Rocket orbiting earth

Date	Mintage	F	VF	XF	Unc	BU
1993	—	—	—	—	7.50	9.00

KM# 484 2.8 ECUS

Copper-Nickel **Ruler:** Elizabeth II **Subject:** Euro Tunnel **Obv:** Crowned bust right **Rev:** Clasping hands

Date	Mintage	F	VF	XF	Unc	BU
1994	—	—	—	—	9.00	11.00

KM# 489 2.8 ECUS

Copper-Nickel **Ruler:** Elizabeth II **Subject:** Mythology **Obv:** Crowned bust right **Rev:** Winged Victory above chariot

Date	Mintage	F	VF	XF	Unc	BU
1994	—	—	—	—	8.50	10.00

KM# 1022 2.8 ECUS

Copper Nickel **Ruler:** Elizabeth II **Obv:** Crowned bust right **Rev:** Europa sowing seeds

Date	Mintage	F	VF	XF	Unc	BU
1994	—	—	—	—	9.00	11.00

KM# 494 2.8 ECUS

Copper-Nickel **Ruler:** Elizabeth II **Subject:** 190th Anniversary of Admiral Nelson's Death **Obv:** Crowned bust right **Rev:** Bust at right of ship looking left

Date	Mintage	F	VF	XF	Unc	BU
1995	—	—	—	—	8.50	10.00

KM# 508 2.8 ECUS

Copper-Nickel **Ruler:** Elizabeth II **Obv:** Crowned bust right **Rev:** Austrian knight on rearing horse within circle of shields and stars

Date	Mintage	F	VF	XF	Unc	BU
1996	—	—	—	—	8.50	10.00

KM# 1033 4.2 ECUS

Bi-Metallic Brass center in Copper-nickel ring, 26 mm. **Ruler:** Elizabeth II **Obv:** Crowned bust right **Rev:** Knight on horseback jumping left, stars encircle

Date	Mintage	F	VF	XF	Unc	BU
1994 Prooflike	10,000	—	—	—	11.50	14.50

KM# 479 14 ECUS

10.0000 g., 0.9250 Silver .2974 oz. ASW **Ruler:** Elizabeth II **Subject:** Euro Tunnel **Obv:** Crowned bust right **Rev:** Train exiting tunnel

Date	Mintage	F	VF	XF	Unc	BU
1993 Proof	30,000	Value: 13.50				

KM# 631 14 ECUS

10.0000 g., 0.9250 Silver .2974 oz. ASW **Ruler:** Elizabeth II **Subject:** Sir Winston Churchill **Obv:** Crowned bust right **Rev:** Uniformed bust at left looking right

Date	Mintage	F	VF	XF	Unc	BU
1993 Proof	Est. 20,000	Value: 15.00				

KM# 483 14 ECUS

10.0000 g., 0.9250 Silver .2974 oz. ASW **Ruler:** Elizabeth II **Subject:** International Aid for Europe **Obv:** Crowned bust right **Rev:** Two faces facing each other

Date	Mintage	F	VF	XF	Unc	BU
1994 Proof	Est. 30,000	Value: 18.50				

KM# 485 14 ECUS

10.0000 g., 0.9250 Silver .2974 oz. ASW **Ruler:** Elizabeth II **Subject:** Euro Tunnel **Obv:** Crowned bust right **Rev:** Train exiting tunnel

Date	Mintage	F	VF	XF	Unc	BU
1994 Proof	Est. 30,000	Value: 20.00				

KM# 490 14 ECUS

10.0000 g., 0.9250 Silver .2974 oz. ASW **Ruler:** Elizabeth II **Obv:** Crowned bust right **Rev:** Parthenon and Brandenburg Gate

Date	Mintage	F	VF	XF	Unc	BU
1994 Proof	Est. 30,000	Value: 14.50				

KM# 495 14 ECUS

10.0000 g., 0.9250 Silver .2974 oz. ASW **Ruler:** Elizabeth II **Obv:** Crowned bust right **Rev:** L'Arc de Triumph, Ceres

Date	Mintage	F	VF	XF	Unc	BU
1995 Proof	Est. 30,000	Value: 17.50				

KM# 496 14 ECUS

10.0000 g., 0.9250 Silver .2974 oz. ASW **Ruler:** Elizabeth II **Obv:** Crowned bust right **Rev:** Richard the Lionheart

Date	Mintage	F	VF	XF	Unc	BU
1995 Proof	Est. 30,000	Value: 17.50				

KM# 509 14 ECUS

10.0000 g., 0.9250 Silver .2974 oz. ASW **Ruler:** Elizabeth II **Obv:** Crowned bust right **Rev:** Napoleon Above European Battle Site

Date	Mintage	F	VF	XF	Unc	BU
1996 Proof	Est. 30,000	Value: 16.50				

KM# 510 14 ECUS
10.0000 g., 0.9250 Silver .2974 oz. ASW **Ruler:** Elizabeth II **Obv:** Crowned bust right **Rev:** Leaning Tower of Pisa, Irish Harp

Date	Mintage	F	VF	XF	Unc	BU
1996 Proof	Est. 30,000	Value: 16.50				

KM# 497 15 ECUS
1.2400 g., 0.9999 Gold .0399 oz. AGW **Ruler:** Elizabeth II **Obv:** Crowned bust right **Rev:** Knight with shield and banner

Date	Mintage	F	VF	XF	Unc	BU
1995 Proof	15,000	Value: 32.50				

KM# 504 15 ECUS
1.2400 g., 0.9999 Gold .0399 oz. AGW **Ruler:** Elizabeth II **Obv:** Crowned bust right **Rev:** Sir Francis Drake's ship "Golden Hind"

Date	Mintage	F	VF	XF	Unc	BU
1996 Proof	Est. 1,500	Value: 40.00				

KM# 480 21 ECUS
19.2000 g., 0.9250 Silver .5710 oz. ASW **Ruler:** Elizabeth II **Subject:** Euro Tunnel **Obv:** Crowned bust right **Rev:** Trains exiting tunnel

Date	Mintage	F	VF	XF	Unc	BU
1993 Proof	Est. 15,000	Value: 35.00				

KM# 482 21 ECUS
19.2000 g., 0.9250 Silver .5710 oz. ASW **Ruler:** Elizabeth II **Subject:** Euro Tunnel **Obv:** Crowned bust right **Rev:** Tunnel view and Napoleon

Date	Mintage	F	VF	XF	Unc	BU
1993 Proof	Est. 15,000	Value: 22.50				

KM# 632 21 ECUS
19.2000 g., 0.9250 Silver .5710 oz. ASW **Ruler:** Elizabeth II **Subject:** European Economic Community **Obv:** Crowned bust right **Rev:** European coins within circle

Date	Mintage	F	VF	XF	Unc	BU
1993 Proof	Est. 15,000	Value: 27.50				

KM# 486 21 ECUS
19.2000 g., 0.9250 Silver .5710 oz. ASW **Ruler:** Elizabeth II **Subject:** Euro Tunnel **Obv:** Crowned bust right **Rev:** Two trains and motor vehicle

Date	Mintage	F	VF	XF	Unc	BU
1994 Proof	Est. 15,000	Value: 27.50				

KM# 491 21 ECUS
19.2000 g., 0.9250 Silver .5710 oz. ASW **Ruler:** Elizabeth II **Subject:** 21 Years - European Community Membership **Obv:** Crowned bust right **Rev:** Europa on bull holding starred rope

Date	Mintage	F	VF	XF	Unc	BU
1994 Proof	Est. 15,000	Value: 32.50				

KM# 498 21 ECUS
19.2000 g., 0.9250 Silver .5710 oz. ASW **Ruler:** Elizabeth II **Obv:** Crowned bust right **Rev:** Europa with Shields of Austria, Sweden and Finland

Date	Mintage	F	VF	XF	Unc	BU
1995 Proof	Est. 15,000	Value: 35.00				

KM# 499 21 ECUS
19.2000 g., 0.9250 Silver .5710 oz. ASW **Ruler:** Elizabeth II **Subject:** Agreement of Cooperation between Russia and the European Union **Obv:** Crowned bust right **Rev:** European landmark buildings and arrows

Date	Mintage	F	VF	XF	Unc	BU
1995 Proof	Est. 15,000	Value: 35.00				

KM# 505 35 ECUS
3.1100 g., 0.9999 Gold .1000 oz. AGW **Ruler:** Elizabeth II **Obv:** Crowned bust right **Rev:** Ship "Hanseatic Kogge"

Date	Mintage	F	VF	XF	Unc	BU
1996 Proof	Est. 1,500	Value: 80.00				

KM# 633 70 ECUS
155.5175 g., 0.9990 Silver 5.0000 oz. ASW **Ruler:** Elizabeth II **Subject:** Ariane - European Space Programme **Obv:** Crowned bust right **Rev:** Rocket orbiting Earth

Date	Mintage	F	VF	XF	Unc	BU
1993 Proof	Est. 2,000	Value: 165				

KM# 634 70 ECUS
6.2200 g., 0.9999 Gold .2000 oz. AGW **Ruler:** Elizabeth II **Subject:** Ariane - European Space Programme **Obv:** Crowned bust right **Rev:** Rocket orbiting Earth, stars encircle

Date	Mintage	F	VF	XF	Unc	BU
1993 Proof	Est. 2,000	Value: 175				
1994 Proof	Est. 1,000	Value: 180				

KM# 1023 70 ECUS
155.5175 g., 0.9990 Silver 4.995 oz. ASW **Ruler:** Elizabeth II **Obv:** Crowned bust right **Rev:** European coins

Date	Mintage	F	VF	XF	Unc	BU
1993 Proof	Est. 2,000	Value: 125				

KM# 1024 70 ECUS
155.5175 g., 0.9990 Silver 4.995 oz. ASW **Ruler:** Elizabeth II **Obv:** Crowned bust right **Rev:** Train exiting tunnel

Date	Mintage	F	VF	XF	Unc	BU
1994 Proof	—	Value: 165				

KM# 487 70 ECUS
155.5175 g., 0.9990 Silver 5.0000 oz. ASW, 65 mm. **Ruler:** Elizabeth II **Subject:** Euro Tunnel **Obv:** Crowned bust right **Rev:** Tunnel view and Napoleon bust **Note:** Illustration reduced.

Date	Mintage	F	VF	XF	Unc	BU
1994 Proof	Est. 2,000	Value: 135				

KM# 492 70 ECUS
155.5175 g., 0.9990 Silver 5.0000 oz. ASW, 65 mm. **Ruler:** Elizabeth II **Subject:** European Unity **Obv:** Crowned bust right **Rev:** Goddess with quadriga **Note:** Illustration reduced.

Date	Mintage	F	VF	XF	Unc	BU
1994 Proof	Est. 2,000	Value: 135				

KM# 488 70 ECUS
6.2200 g., 0.9999 Gold .2000 oz. AGW **Ruler:** Elizabeth II **Subject:** Euro Tunnel **Obv:** Crowned bust right **Rev:** Outreached hands above English Channel

Date	Mintage	F	VF	XF	Unc	BU
1994 Proof	Est. 2,000	Value: 150				

KM# 493 70 ECUS
6.2200 g., 0.9999 Gold .2000 oz. AGW **Ruler:** Elizabeth II **Subject:** Mythology **Obv:** Crowned bust right **Rev:** Europa sowing seeds

Date	Mintage	F	VF	XF	Unc	BU
1994 Proof	Est. 2,000	Value: 150				

KM# 501 70 ECUS
155.9200 g., 0.9990 Silver 5.0079 oz. ASW **Ruler:** Elizabeth II **Obv:** Crowned bust right **Rev:** Liberty and Brittania seated above Euro Tunnel

Date	Mintage	F	VF	XF	Unc	BU
1995 Proof	Est. 2,000	Value: 165				

KM# 502 70 ECUS
6.2200 g., 0.9999 Gold .2000 oz. AGW **Ruler:** Elizabeth II **Obv:** Crowned bust right **Rev:** Mercury above ship

Date	Mintage	F	VF	XF	Unc	BU
1995 Proof	Est. 2,000	Value: 170				

KM# 503 70 ECUS
6.2200 g., 0.9999 Gold .2000 oz. AGW **Ruler:** Elizabeth II **Obv:** Crowned bust right **Rev:** Richard the Lionheart

Date	Mintage	F	VF	XF	Unc	BU
1995 Proof	Est. 2,000	Value: 170				

KM# 500 70 ECUS
155.9200 g., 0.9990 Silver 5.0079 oz. ASW, 65 mm. **Ruler:** Elizabeth II **Subject:** 190th Anniversary of Admiral Nelson's Death **Obv:** Crowned bust right **Rev:** Admiral Nelson and HMS Victory **Note:** Illustration reduced.

Date	Mintage	F	VF	XF	Unc	BU
1995 Proof	2,000	Value: 165				

KM# 506 70 ECUS
6.2200 g., 0.9999 Gold .2000 oz. AGW **Ruler:** Elizabeth II **Obv:** Crowned bust right **Rev:** HMS Victory

Date	Mintage	F	VF	XF	Unc	BU
1996 Proof	Est. 1,500	Value: 170				

KM# 511 70 ECUS
155.5175 g., 0.9990 Silver 5.000 oz. ASW **Ruler:** Elizabeth II **Obv:** Crowned bust right **Rev:** Sir Francis Drake and "Golden Hind"

Date	Mintage	F	VF	XF	Unc	BU
1996 Proof	Est. 2,000	Value: 165				

KM# 512 70 ECUS
6.2200 g., 0.9999 Gold .2000 oz. AGW **Ruler:** Elizabeth II **Obv:** Crowned bust right **Rev:** Austrian Knight within circle of stars and shields

Date	Mintage	F	VF	XF	Unc	BU
1996 Proof	2,000	Value: 170				

KM# 528 75 ECUS
3.8880 g., 0.9995 Bi-Metallic Platinum center in Gold ring .1250 oz. **Ruler:** Elizabeth II **Subject:** Austrian Centennial **Obv:** Crowned bust right **Rev:** Standing allegorical figure with shield and trident

Date	Mintage	F	VF	XF	Unc	BU
1996 Proof	1,500	Value: 250				

KM# 507 140 ECUS
15.5500 g., 0.9999 Gold .4999 oz. AGW **Ruler:** Elizabeth II **Obv:** Crowned bust right **Rev:** Viking Longship

Date	Mintage	F	VF	XF	Unc	BU
1996	Est. 1,500	—	—	—	385	—

Note: In Proof sets only

PATTERNS

Including off metal strikes

KM#	Date	Mintage	Identification	Mkt Val
Pn4	1989	—	1/4 Sovereign. Gold. Similar to Pn8.	—
Pn5	1989	—	1/2 Sovereign. Gold. Similar to Pn8.	—
Pn6	1989	—	Sovereign. Gold. Similar to Pn8.	—
Pn7	1989	—	2 Sovereigns. Gold. Similar to Pn8.	—
Pn8	1989	—	5 Sovereigns. Gold. Una and the lion with the Rock of Gibraltar in background.	—

PIEFORTS

KM#	Date	Mintage	Identification	Mkt Val
P1	1990	5,000	5 Pence. 0.9250 Silver. 6.0000 g. KM#22b.	70.00
P2	1990	1,000	5 Pence. 0.9160 Gold. 6.0000 g. KM#22c.	—
P3	1993	5,000	14 Ecus. 0.9250 Silver. KM#631.	60.00

MINT SETS

KM#	Date	Mintage	Identification	Issue Price	Mkt Val
MS1	1975 (3)	1,625	KM#7-9	—	1,150
MS2	1988 (9)	—	KM#16-18, 20-25	21.00	32.00
MS3	1989 (9)	—	KM#16-17, 20-25, 32	—	35.00
MS4	1990 (9)	—	km#16, 18, 20-21, 22A, 23-25, 39	25.00	35.00
MS5	1991 (9)	—	KM#16, 18, 20-21, 22a, 23-25, 39	25.00	35.00
MS6	1993-1998 (6)	5,000	KM#201, 327, 382, 444, 525, 656, mixed dates	—	45.00
MS7	1995 (9)	—	KM#16, 20-21, 22A, 24, 39, 112, 334, 340	—	35.00
MS8	1996 (9)	—	KM#16, 18, 20-21, 22, 24, 39, 112, 355	—	35.00
MS9	1997 (9)	—	KM#16, 18, 20-21, 22a, 24, 39, 113, 355	—	35.00
MS10	1998 (9)	—	KM#777, 869, 773-75, 778, 776, 756 & 740	—	35.00
MS11	1999 (9)	—	KM#777, 869, 773-75, 778, 776, 759 & 797	—	35.00

PROOF SETS

KM#	Date	Mintage	Identification	Issue Price	Mkt Val
PS1	1975 (3)	750	KM#7-9	875	1,150
PS2	1989 (5)	—	KM#26-30	—	2,250
PS3	1989 (2)	—	KM#29-30	—	1,700
PS4	1990 (6)	500	KM#76-81	—	1,500
PS5	1990 (6)	250	KM#76a-81a	—	2,100
PS6	1990 (5)	1,000	KM#41-45	1,800	1,975
PS7	1991 (8)	20,000	KM#50-57	—	650
PS8	1991 (8)	5,000	KM#58-65	—	1,350
PS9	1991 (8)	1,000	KM#58a-65a	—	2,300
PS10	1991 (8)	50	KM#66-73	120	120
PS11	1991 (5)	1,000	KM#91-94, 97	—	1,450
PS12	1992 (5)	1,000	KM#99-102, 105	—	1,250
PS13	1993 (5)	1,000	KM#193-197	—	1,200
PS14	1993 (5)	300	KM#124-128	—	675
PS15	1994 (5)	1,000	KM#248-251, 252a	—	1,200
PS16	1994-95 (3)	5,000	KM#309, 332, 335	—	60.00
PS17	1994-95 (3)	3,000	KM#309a, 332a, 335a	—	120
PS18	1994-95 (3)	3,000	KM#309, 332, 335	—	120
PS19	1995 (5)	1,000	KM#319-323	—	1,200
PS21	1996 (5)	1,000	KM#361-364, 365b	—	1,200
PS22	1996 (4)	1,500	KM#504-507	—	650
PS23	1997 (5)	1,000	KM#557-560, 561b	—	1,200
PS24	1998 (5)	1,000	KM#749-752, 754	1,310	1,200
PS25	1999 (5)	1,000	KM#828-831, 833	1,310	1,200
PS26	2000 (5)	1,000	KM#888-891, 893	—	1,200

PROOF-LIKE SETS (PL)

KM#	Date	Mintage	Identification	Issue Price	Mkt Val
PL1	1992 (8)	—	KM#66-73	—	100

facing left **Obv. Legend:** EDWARD • VIII • KING • & • EMPEROR **Rev:** Supported arms **Note:** Prev. X#2.

Date	Mintage	F	VF	XF	Unc	BU
1936 Proof	—	Value: 125				

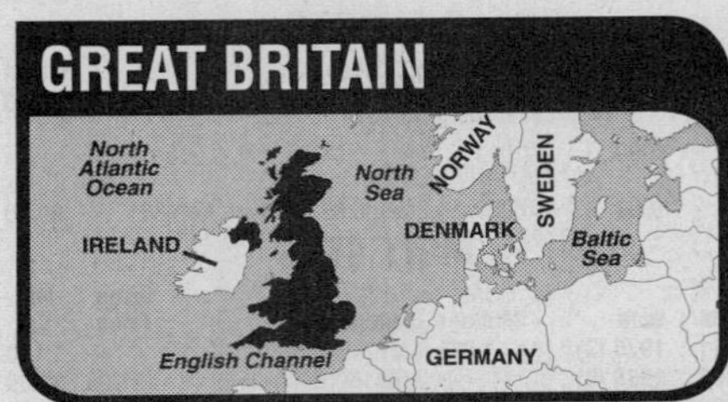

The United Kingdom of Great Britain and Northern Ireland, located off the northwest coast of the European continent, has an area of 94,227 sq. mi. (244,820 sq. km.) and a population of 54 million. Capital: London. The economy is based on industrial activity and trading. Machinery, motor vehicles, chemicals, and textile yarns and fabrics are exported.

After the departure of the Romans, who brought Britain into a more active relationship with Europe, it fell prey to invaders from Scandinavia and the Low Countries who drove the original Britons into Scotland and Wales, and established a profusion of kingdoms that finally united in the 11th century under the Danish King Canute. Norman rule, following the conquest of 1066, stimulated the development of those institutions, which have since distinguished British life. Henry VIII (1509-47) turned Britain from continental adventuring and faced it to the sea - a decision that made Britain a world power during the reign of Elizabeth I (1558-1603). Strengthened by the Industrial Revolution and the defeat of Napoleon, 19th century Britain turned to the remote parts of the world and established a colonial empire of such extent and prosperity that the world has never seen its like. World Wars I and II sealed the fate of the Empire and relegated Britain to a lesser role in world affairs by draining her resources and inaugurating a worldwide movement toward national self-determination in her former colonies.

By the mid-20th century, most of the territories formerly comprising the British Empire had gained independence, and the empire had evolved into the Commonwealth of Nations, an association of equal and autonomous states, which enjoy special trade interests. The Commonwealth is presently composed of 54 member nations, including the United Kingdom. All recognize the British monarch as head of the Commonwealth. Sixteen continue to recognize the British monarch as Head of State. They are: United Kingdom, Antigua and Barbuda, Australia, Bahamas, Barbados, Belize, Canada, Grenada, Jamaica, New Zealand, Papua New Guinea, St. Christopher & Nevis, Saint Lucia, Saint Vincent and the Grenadines, Solomon Islands, and Tuvalu. Elizabeth II is personally, and separately, the Queen of the sovereign, independent countries just mentioned. There is no other British connection between the several individual, national sovereignties, except that High Commissioners represent them each instead of ambassadors in each others' countries.

RULERS

Victoria, 1837-1901
Edward VII, 1901-1910
George V, 1910-1936
Edward VIII, 1936
George VI, 1936-1952
Elizabeth II, 1952--

MINT MARKS

H - Heaton
KN - King's Norton

MONETARY SYSTEM

Colloquial Denomination Terms

Ha'penny = 1/2 Penny
Tanner = 6 Pence
Bob = 1 Shilling
Half a Crown (Half a Dollar) = 2 Shillings 6 Pence
Dollar = 5 Shillings
Half a quid = 10 Shillings
Quid = 1 Pound
Tenner = 10 Pounds
Pony = 20 Pounds

(Until 1970)

4 Farthings = 1 Penny
12 Pence = 1 Shilling
2 Shillings = 1 Florin
5 Shillings = 1 Crown
20 Shillings = 1 Pound (Sovereign)
21 Shillings = 1 Guinea
½ Sovereign = 10 Shillings (i.e. ½ Pound)
1 Sovereign = 1 Pound

NOTE: Proofs exist for many dates of British coins in the 19th and early 20th centuries and for virtually all coins between 1926 and 1964. Those not specifically listed here are extremely rare.

NOTE: Pound Coinage - Strictly red, original mint luster coins in the copper series command premiums.

KINGDOM

Resumed

POUND COINAGE

KM# 791 1/3 FARTHING

0.9500 g., Bronze **Ruler:** Edward VII **Obv:** Head right **Rev:** Denomination and date within crowned oak wreath **Note:** Homeland style struck for Malta.

Date	Mintage	F	VF	XF	Unc	BU
1902	288,000	2.50	5.00	10.00	35.00	—

KM# 823 1/3 FARTHING

0.9500 g., Bronze **Ruler:** George V **Obv:** Head left **Rev:** Crowned value within oak wreath **Note:** Homeland style struck for Malta.

Date	Mintage	F	VF	XF	Unc	BU
1913	288,000	2.50	5.00	10.00	35.00	—

KM# 788.2 FARTHING

2.8000 g., Bronze, 20 mm. **Ruler:** Victoria **Obv:** Veiled bust left **Obv. Designer:** Thomas Brock **Rev:** Britannia seated right **Note:** Blackened finish.

Date	Mintage	F	VF	XF	Unc	BU
1901	8,016,000	0.30	0.50	2.00	17.00	—

KM# 792 FARTHING

Bronze, 20 mm. **Ruler:** Edward VII **Obv:** Head right **Rev:** Britannia seated right

Date	Mintage	F	VF	XF	Unc	BU
1902	5,125,000	0.50	1.50	5.00	25.00	—
1903	5,331,000	0.50	1.50	5.50	25.00	—
1903 Proof	—	Value: 1,000				
Note: Shield heraldically colored						
1904	3,629,000	1.50	2.50	8.00	30.00	—
1905	4,077,000	0.50	1.25	5.50	25.00	—
1906	5,340,000	0.50	1.25	5.50	25.00	—
1907	4,399,000	0.50	1.25	5.50	25.00	—
1908	4,265,000	0.50	1.25	5.50	25.00	—
1909	8,852,000	0.50	1.25	5.50	25.00	—
1910	2,598,000	1.00	3.00	8.00	25.00	—

KM# 808.1 FARTHING

Bronze, 20 mm. **Ruler:** George V **Obv:** Head left **Obv. Designer:** Bertram MacKennal **Rev:** Britannia seated right

Date	Mintage	F	VF	XF	Unc	BU
1911	5,197,000	0.60	1.00	3.00	12.00	—
1912	7,670,000	0.35	0.75	2.25	10.00	—
1913	4,184,000	0.50	0.75	2.25	10.00	—
1914	6,127,000	0.35	0.75	2.25	10.00	—
1915	7,129,000	0.50	0.75	4.50	15.00	—
1916	10,993,000	0.35	0.75	2.00	10.00	—
1917	21,435,000	0.15	0.35	1.50	10.00	—
1918	19,363,000	0.75	1.50	9.50	27.00	—

KM# 808.2 FARTHING

Bronze, 20 mm. **Ruler:** George V **Obv:** Head left **Obv. Designer:** Bertram MacKennal **Rev:** Britannia seated right **Note:** Bright finish.

Date	Mintage	F	VF	XF	Unc	BU
1918	Inc. above	0.20	0.40	1.00	7.50	—
1919	15,089,000	0.20	0.40	1.00	7.50	—
1920	11,481,000	0.20	0.40	1.00	7.50	—
1921	9,469,000	0.20	0.40	1.00	8.00	—
1922	9,957,000	0.20	0.40	1.00	8.00	—
1923	8,034,000	0.20	0.40	1.00	8.00	—
1924	8,733,000	0.20	0.40	1.00	8.00	—
1924 Specimen	2	—	—	—	—	1,000
1925	12,635,000	0.20	0.40	1.00	8.00	—

KM# 825 FARTHING

Bronze, 20 mm. **Ruler:** George V **Obv:** Head left, modified effigy **Obv. Designer:** Bertram MacKennal **Rev:** Britannia seated right

Date	Mintage	F	VF	XF	Unc	BU
1926	9,792,000	0.15	0.40	1.00	6.50	—
1926 Proof	—	Value: 600				
1927	7,868,000	0.15	0.40	1.00	6.50	—
1927 Proof	—	Value: 450				
1928	11,626,000	0.15	0.35	1.00	6.50	—
1928 Proof	—	Value: 350				
1929	8,419,000	0.15	0.35	1.00	6.50	—
1929 Proof	—	Value: 350				
1930	4,195,000	0.25	0.50	1.00	6.50	—
1930 Proof	—	Value: 350				
1931	6,595,000	0.15	0.35	1.00	6.50	—
1931 Proof	—	Value: 350				
1932	9,293,000	0.15	0.35	1.00	6.50	—
1932 Proof	—	Value: 350				
1933	4,560,000	0.15	0.35	1.00	6.50	—
1933 Proof	—	Value: 350				
1934	3,053,000	0.35	0.75	2.00	10.00	—
1934 Proof	—	Value: 350				
1935	2,227,000	1.00	2.00	3.00	7.50	—
1935 Proof	—	Value: 350				
1936	9,734,000	0.15	0.35	1.00	5.00	—
1936 Proof	—	Value: 350				

KM# 843 FARTHING

Bronze, 20 mm. **Ruler:** George VI **Obv:** Head left **Obv. Designer:** T. H. Paget **Rev:** Wren left

Date	Mintage	F	VF	XF	Unc	BU
1937	8,131,000	0.15	0.25	0.50	5.00	—
1937 Matte Proof	—	Value: 1,500				
Note: There are reportedly 3-4 pieces known of this variety struck specifically for use in photographs						
1937 Proof	26,000	Value: 11.00				
1938	7,450,000	0.15	0.30	0.60	7.50	—
1938 Proof	—	Value: 350				
1939	31,440,000	0.10	0.25	0.50	5.00	—
1939 Proof	—	Value: 350				
1940	18,360,000	0.10	0.25	0.50	5.00	—
1940 Proof	—	Value: 350				
1941	27,312,000	0.10	0.25	0.50	4.50	—
1941 Proof	—	Value: 350				
1942	28,858,000	0.10	0.20	0.50	4.50	—
1942 Proof	—	Value: 350				
1943	33,345,999	0.10	0.15	0.50	4.50	—
1943 Proof	—	Value: 400				
1944	25,138,000	0.10	0.15	0.50	4.50	—
1944 Proof	—	Value: 400				
1945	23,736,000	0.10	0.20	0.50	4.50	—
1945 Proof	—	Value: 350				
1946	24,365,000	0.10	0.20	0.50	4.50	—
1946 Proof	—	Value: 350				
1947	14,746,000	0.10	0.20	0.50	4.50	—
1947 Proof	—	Value: 350				
1948	16,622,000	0.10	0.20	0.50	4.50	—
1948 Proof	—	Value: 350				

KM# 867 FARTHING

Bronze, 20 mm. **Ruler:** George VI **Obv:** Head left **Obv. Legend:** Without IND IMP **Obv. Designer:** T. H. Paget **Rev:** Wren left

Date	Mintage	F	VF	XF	Unc	BU
1949	8,424,000	0.10	0.20	0.50	6.50	—
1949 Proof	—	Value: 350				
1950	10,325,000	0.10	0.20	0.50	6.50	—
1950 Matte Proof	—	Value: 900				
Note: There are reportedly 3-4 known of this variety, struck specifically for use in photographs						
1950 Proof	18,000	Value: 13.00				
1951	14,016,000	0.10	0.20	0.50	7.00	—
1951 Matte Proof	—	Value: 900				

Date	Mintage	F	VF	XF	Unc	BU

Note: There are reportedly 3-4 known of this variety, struck specifically for use in photographs

Date	Mintage	F	VF	XF	Unc	BU
1951 Proof	20,000	Value: 20.00				
1952	5,251,000	0.10	0.20	0.50	6.00	—
1952 Proof	—	Value: 350				

KM# 881 FARTHING

Bronze, 20 mm. **Ruler:** Elizabeth II **Obv:** Laureate bust right **Obv. Designer:** Mary Gillick **Rev:** Wren left

Date	Mintage	F	VF	XF	Unc	BU
1953	6,131,000	0.15	0.25	0.50	3.00	—
1953 Proof	40,000	Value: 8.00				
1953 Matte Proof	—	Value: 800				

Note: There are reportedly 1-2 known of this variety, struck specifically for use in photographs

KM# 895 FARTHING

Bronze, 20 mm. **Ruler:** Elizabeth II **Obv:** Laureate bust right **Obv. Legend:** Without BRITT OMN **Obv. Designer:** Mark Gillick **Rev:** Wren left

Date	Mintage	F	VF	XF	Unc	BU
1954	6,566,000	0.10	0.15	0.50	5.00	—
1954 Proof	—	Value: 250				
1955	5,779,000	0.10	0.15	0.50	5.00	—
1955 Proof	—	Value: 250				
1956	1,997,000	0.25	0.50	3.00	7.50	—
1956 Proof	—	Value: 250				

KM# 789 1/2 PENNY

5.7000 g., Bronze, 25.5 mm. **Ruler:** Victoria **Obv:** Veiled bust left **Obv. Designer:** Thomas Brock **Rev:** Britannia seated right

Date	Mintage	F	VF	XF	Unc	BU
1901	11,127,000	1.50	3.00	12.00	30.00	—
1901 Proof	—	Value: 600				

KM# 793.1 1/2 PENNY

Bronze, 25.5 mm. **Ruler:** Edward VII **Obv:** Head right **Rev:** Britannia seated right, low horizon line

Date	Mintage	F	VF	XF	Unc	BU
1902	13,673,000	10.00	30.00	75.00	180	—

KM# 793.2 1/2 PENNY

Bronze, 25.5 mm. **Ruler:** Edward VII **Obv:** Head right **Rev:** Britannia seated right, high horizon line

Date	Mintage	F	VF	XF	Unc	BU
1902	Inc. above	0.50	1.25	5.00	25.00	—
1903	11,451,000	0.75	2.25	10.00	35.00	—
1904	8,131,000	1.00	3.00	11.00	40.00	—
1905	10,125,000	0.75	2.50	10.00	35.00	—
1906	11,101,000	0.75	2.00	10.00	30.00	—
1907	16,849,000	0.75	1.50	8.00	25.00	—
1908	16,620,999	0.75	1.50	8.00	25.00	—
1909	8,279,000	0.75	2.50	10.00	35.00	—
1910	10,770,000	0.75	2.50	10.00	30.00	—

KM# 809 1/2 PENNY

Bronze, 25.5 mm. **Ruler:** George V **Obv:** Head left **Obv. Designer:** Bertram MacKennal **Rev:** Britannia seated right

Date	Mintage	F	VF	XF	Unc	BU
1911	12,571,000	0.75	1.50	9.00	25.00	—
1912	21,186,000	0.50	1.25	9.00	35.00	—
1913	17,476,000	0.75	1.75	12.00	35.00	—
1914	20,289,000	0.75	1.50	9.00	35.00	—
1915	21,563,000	0.75	1.50	9.00	35.00	—
1916	39,386,000	0.75	1.50	5.00	35.00	—
1917	38,245,000	0.75	1.50	5.00	35.00	—
1918	22,321,000	0.75	1.50	5.00	35.00	—
1919	28,104,000	0.50	1.50	5.00	35.00	—
1920	35,147,000	0.50	1.50	5.00	35.00	—
1921	28,027,000	0.75	1.50	5.00	35.00	—
1922	10,735,000	1.00	2.00	7.00	35.00	—
1923	12,266,000	0.50	1.50	5.00	35.00	—
1924	13,971,000	0.75	2.00	5.00	35.00	—
1924 Specimen	2	—	—	—	—	1,250
1925	12,216,000	1.00	2.00	5.00	35.00	—

KM# 824 1/2 PENNY

Bronze, 25.5 mm. **Ruler:** George V **Obv:** Head left, modified effigy **Obv. Designer:** Bertram MacKennal **Rev:** Britannia seated right

Date	Mintage	F	VF	XF	Unc	BU
1925	Inc. above	1.50	4.00	8.00	60.00	—
1926	6,712,000	1.50	3.00	6.00	35.00	—
1926 Proof	—	Value: 800				
1927	15,590,000	0.75	1.50	5.00	35.00	—
1927 Proof	—	Value: 550				

KM# 837 1/2 PENNY

Bronze, 25.5 mm. **Ruler:** George V **Obv:** Smaller head left **Obv. Designer:** Bertram MacKennal **Rev:** Britannia seated right

Date	Mintage	F	VF	XF	Unc	BU
1928	20,935,000	0.25	0.50	2.50	25.00	—
1928 Proof	—	Value: 425				
1929	25,680,000	0.25	0.50	2.50	25.00	—
1929 Proof	—	Value: 425				
1930	12,533,000	0.25	0.50	2.50	25.00	—
1930 Proof	—	Value: 425				
1931	16,138,000	0.25	0.50	2.50	25.00	—
1931 Proof	—	Value: 425				
1932	14,448,000	0.25	0.50	2.50	25.00	—
1932 Proof	—	Value: 425				
1933	10,560,000	0.25	0.50	2.50	25.00	—
1933 Proof	—	Value: 425				
1934	7,704,000	0.50	1.00	4.00	25.00	—
1934 Proof	—	Value: 450				
1935	12,180,000	0.25	0.50	2.50	25.00	—
1935 Proof	—	Value: 400				
1936	23,009,000	0.25	0.50	2.50	19.00	—
1936 Proof	—	Value: 400				

KM# 844 1/2 PENNY

Bronze, 25.5 mm. **Ruler:** George VI **Obv:** Head left **Rev:** The Golden Hind **Designer:** T. H. Paget

Date	Mintage	F	VF	XF	Unc	BU
1937	24,504,000	0.25	0.35	0.50	7.00	—
1937 Proof	26,000	Value: 11.00				
1937 Matte Proof	Est. 4	Value: 800				
1938	40,320,000	0.25	0.50	1.00	10.00	—
1938 Proof	—	Value: 350				
1939	28,925,000	0.25	0.50	2.00	12.00	—
1939 Proof	—	Value: 350				
1940	32,162,000	0.25	0.50	3.00	14.00	—
1940 Proof	—	Value: 350				
1941	45,120,000	0.20	0.50	1.00	7.50	—
1941 Proof	—	Value: 350				
1942	71,909,000	0.10	0.20	0.60	7.50	—
1942 Proof	—	Value: 350				
1943	76,200,000	0.10	0.25	0.75	7.50	—
1943 Proof	—	Value: 400				
1944	81,840,000	0.10	0.25	0.75	7.50	—
1944 Proof	—	Value: 400				
1945	57,000,000	0.10	0.25	1.00	9.00	—
1945 Proof	—	Value: 400				
1946	22,726,000	0.20	0.50	2.50	12.00	—
1946 Proof	—	Value: 400				
1947	21,266,000	0.10	0.25	1.50	10.00	—
1947 Proof	—	Value: 350				
1948	26,947,000	0.10	0.25	0.90	7.50	—
1948 Proof	—	Value: 375				

KM# 868 1/2 PENNY

Bronze, 25.5 mm. **Ruler:** George VI **Obv:** Head left **Obv. Legend:** Without IND IMP **Rev:** The Golden Hind **Designer:** T. H. Paget

Date	Mintage	F	VF	XF	Unc	BU
1949	24,744,000	0.10	0.25	4.00	15.00	—
1949 Proof	—	Value: 350				
1950	24,154,000	0.10	0.25	3.00	12.00	—
1950 Proof	18,000	Value: 12.00				
1950 Matte Proof	—	Value: 900				

Note: There are reportedly 1-2 known of this variety, struck specifically for use in photographs

Date	Mintage	F	VF	XF	Unc	BU
1951	14,868,000	0.25	0.50	5.00	24.00	—
1951 Proof	20,000	Value: 15.00				
1951 Matte Proof	—	Value: 900				

Note: There are reportedly 1-2 known of this variety, struck specifically for use in photographs

Date	Mintage	F	VF	XF	Unc	BU
1952	33,278,000	0.10	0.25	1.00	10.00	—
1952 Proof	—	Value: 350				

KM# 882 1/2 PENNY

Bronze, 25.5 mm. **Ruler:** Elizabeth II **Obv:** Laureate bust right **Obv. Designer:** Mary Gillick **Rev:** The Golden Hind **Rev. Designer:** T. H. Paget

Date	Mintage	F	VF	XF	Unc	BU
1953	8,926,000	0.20	0.40	1.00	5.00	—
1953 Proof	40,000	Value: 13.00				
1953 Matte Proof	—	Value: 900				

Note: There are reportedly 1-2 known of this variety, struck specifically for use in photographs

KM# 896 1/2 PENNY

Bronze, 25.5 mm. **Ruler:** Elizabeth II **Obv:** Laureate bust right **Obv. Legend:** Without BRITT OMN **Rev:** The Golden Hind

Date	Mintage	F	VF	XF	Unc	BU
1954	19,375,000	0.10	0.25	1.50	4.00	—
1954 Proof	—	Value: 300				
1955	18,799,000	0.10	0.25	1.25	3.50	—
1955 Proof	—	Value: 300				
1956	21,799,000	0.15	0.50	1.25	3.50	—
1956 Proof	—	Value: 300				
1957	43,684,000	0.10	0.25	0.50	3.50	—
1957 Proof	—	Value: 300				
1958	62,318,000	—	0.10	0.20	2.00	—
1958 Proof	—	Value: 300				
1959	79,176,000	—	0.10	0.15	1.25	—
1959 Proof	—	Value: 300				
1960	41,340,000	—	0.10	0.15	1.00	—
1960 Proof	—	Value: 300				
1962	41,779,000	—	—	0.10	1.00	—

Date	Mintage	F	VF	XF	Unc	BU
1962 Proof	—	Value: 300				
1963	45,036,000	—	—	0.10	1.00	—
1963 Proof	—	Value: 300				
1964	78,583,000	—	—	0.10	1.00	—
1964 Proof	—	Value: 300				
1965	98,083,000	—	—	—	1.00	—
1965 Proof	—	—	—	—	—	—
Note: Reported, not confirmed						
1966	95,289,000	—	—	—	0.55	—
1966 Proof	—	—	—	—	—	—
Note: Reported, not confirmed						
1967	146,491,000	—	—	—	0.55	—
1967 Proof	—	—	—	—	—	—
Note: Reported, not confirmed						
1970 Proof	750,000	Value: 3.50				

KM# 775 PENNY

0.4713 g., 0.9250 Silver .0140 oz. ASW **Ruler:** Victoria **Obv:** Veiled bust left **Obv. Designer:** Thomas Brock **Rev:** Crowned denomination divides date within oak wreath

Date	Mintage	F	VF	XF	Unc	BU
1901 Prooflike	18,000	—	—	—	20.00	35.00

KM# 790 PENNY

9.4500 g., Bronze, 30.8 mm. **Ruler:** Victoria **Obv:** Veiled bust left **Obv. Designer:** Thomas Brock **Rev:** Britannia seated right

Date	Mintage	F	VF	XF	Unc	BU
1901	22,206,000	0.30	1.00	10.00	25.00	—
1901 Proof	—	—	—	—	—	—

KM# 794.1 PENNY

9.4500 g., Bronze, 30.8 mm. **Ruler:** Edward VII **Obv:** Head right **Rev:** Britannia seated right, low sea level

Date	Mintage	F	VF	XF	Unc	BU
1902	26,977,000	5.00	20.00	75.00	180	—

KM# 794.2 PENNY

Bronze, 30.8 mm. **Ruler:** Edward VII **Obv:** Head right **Rev:** Britannia seated right, high sea level

Date	Mintage	F	VF	XF	Unc	BU
1902	Inc. above	0.50	1.50	5.00	30.00	—
1903	21,415,000	0.50	2.25	12.00	40.00	—
1904	12,913,000	1.00	5.00	30.00	120	—
1905	17,784,000	0.50	4.00	25.00	90.00	—
1906	37,990,000	0.50	3.00	12.00	65.00	—
1907	47,322,000	0.50	4.00	15.00	75.00	—
1908	31,506,000	0.50	3.00	12.00	65.00	—
1908 Matte Proof; Rare	3	—	—	—	—	—
1909	19,617,000	0.50	4.00	15.00	75.00	—
1910	29,549,000	0.35	2.00	10.00	50.00	—

KM# 795 PENNY

0.4713 g., 0.9250 Silver .0140 oz. ASW **Ruler:** Edward VII **Obv:** Head right **Rev:** Crowned denomination divides date within oak wreath

Date	Mintage	F	VF	XF	Unc	BU
1902 Prooflike	21,000	—	—	—	25.00	40.00
1903 Prooflike	17,000	—	—	—	25.00	40.00
1904 Prooflike	19,000	—	—	—	25.00	40.00
1905 Prooflike	18,000	—	—	—	25.00	40.00
1906 Prooflike	19,000	—	—	—	25.00	40.00
1907 Prooflike	18,000	—	—	—	25.00	40.00
1908 Prooflike	18,000	—	—	—	25.00	40.00
1909 Prooflike	2,948	—	—	—	35.00	60.00
1910 Prooflike	3,392	—	—	—	40.00	65.00

KM# 811 PENNY

0.4713 g., 0.9250 Silver .0140 oz. ASW **Ruler:** George V **Obv:** Head left **Obv. Designer:** Bertram MacKennal **Rev:** Crowned denomination divides date within oak wreath

Date	Mintage	F	VF	XF	Unc	BU
1911 Prooflike	1,913	—	—	—	35.00	45.00
1912 Prooflike	1,616	—	—	—	35.00	45.00
1913 Prooflike	1,590	—	—	—	35.00	45.00
1914 Prooflike	1,818	—	—	—	35.00	45.00
1915 Prooflike	2,072	—	—	—	35.00	45.00
1916 Prooflike	1,647	—	—	—	35.00	45.00
1917 Prooflike	1,820	—	—	—	35.00	45.00
1918 Prooflike	1,911	—	—	—	35.00	45.00
1919 Prooflike	1,699	—	—	—	35.00	45.00
1920 Prooflike	1,715	—	—	—	35.00	45.00

KM# 811a PENNY

0.4713 g., 0.5000 Silver .0076 oz. ASW **Ruler:** George V **Obv:** Head left **Obv. Designer:** Bertram MacKennal **Rev:** Crowned denomination divides date within oak wreath

Date	Mintage	F	VF	XF	Unc	BU
1921 Prooflike	1,847	—	—	—	35.00	45.00
1922 Prooflike	1,758	—	—	—	35.00	45.00
1923 Prooflike	1,840	—	—	—	35.00	45.00
1924 Prooflike	1,619	—	—	—	35.00	45.00
1925 Prooflike	1,890	—	—	—	35.00	45.00
1926 Prooflike	2,180	—	—	—	35.00	45.00
1927 Prooflike	1,647	—	—	—	35.00	45.00

KM# 810 PENNY

9.4500 g., Bronze, 30.8 mm. **Ruler:** George V **Obv:** Head left **Obv. Legend:** GEORGIVS V DEI GRA: BRITT: OMN: REX FID: DEF: IND: IMP: **Obv. Designer:** Bertram MacKennal **Rev:** Britannia seated right **Note:** Fully struck and orginal mint lustre coins command a premium.

Date	Mintage	F	VF	XF	Unc	BU
1911	23,079,000	0.40	1.25	8.00	35.00	—
1912	48,306,000	0.35	1.00	10.00	45.00	—
1912H	16,800,000	1.00	8.00	75.00	230	—
1913	65,497,000	0.40	2.00	15.00	50.00	—
1914	50,821,000	0.35	1.00	10.00	45.00	—
1915	47,311,000	0.50	1.25	10.00	45.00	—
1916	86,411,000	0.35	1.00	10.00	45.00	—
1917	107,905,000	0.35	1.00	10.00	45.00	—
1918	84,227,000	0.35	1.00	10.00	45.00	—
1918H	2,573,000	2.00	15.00	175	600	—
1918KN	Inc. above	3.00	27.50	375	1,000	—
1919	113,761,000	0.50	1.00	10.00	45.00	—
1919H	4,526,000	1.25	15.00	275	700	—
1919KN	Inc. above	4.00	30.00	400	1,250	—
1920	124,693,000	0.50	1.50	10.00	45.00	—
1921	129,717,999	0.30	1.00	10.00	45.00	—
1922	16,347,000	0.75	4.00	20.00	50.00	—
1922	—	—	—	—	3,000	—
Note: Reverse of 1927						
1922 Specimen	2	—	—	—	—	15,000
Note: Reverse of 1927						
1926	4,499,000	2.50	7.00	30.00	100	—
1926 Proof	—	Value: 1,250				

KM# 826 PENNY

Bronze, 30.8 mm. **Ruler:** George V **Obv:** Modified head left **Obv. Designer:** Bertram MacKennal **Rev:** Britannia seated right

Date	Mintage	F	VF	XF	Unc	BU
1926	—	20.00	125	800	2,500	—
1926 Proof	—	—	—	—	—	—
Note: Reported, not confirmed						
1927	60,990,000	0.35	0.75	8.00	30.00	—
1927 Proof	—	Value: 1,000				

KM# 838 PENNY

Bronze, 30.8 mm. **Ruler:** George V **Obv:** Smaller head left **Obv. Designer:** Bertram MacKennal **Rev:** Britannia seated right

Date	Mintage	F	VF	XF	Unc	BU
1928	50,178,000	0.25	0.50	8.00	30.00	—
1928 Proof	—	Value: 1,000				
1929	49,133,000	0.25	0.50	8.00	30.00	—
1929 Proof	—	Value: 1,000				
1930	29,098,000	0.25	1.00	10.00	35.00	—
1930 Proof	—	Value: 1,000				
1931	19,843,000	0.25	1.00	10.00	35.00	—
1931 Proof	—	Value: 1,000				
1932	8,278,000	1.00	4.50	20.00	70.00	—
1932 Proof	—	Value: 1,250				
1933 Rare	—	—	—	—	—	—
1933 Proof	—	—	—	—	—	—
1934	13,966,000	0.50	4.00	20.00	60.00	—
1934 Proof	—	Value: 1,250				
1935	56,070,000	0.25	0.50	5.00	30.00	—
1935 Proof	—	Value: 850				
1936	154,296,000	0.25	0.40	5.00	25.00	—
1936 Proof	—	Value: 850				

KM# 839 PENNY

0.4713 g., 0.5000 Silver .0076 oz. ASW **Ruler:** George V **Obv:** Modified head left **Obv. Designer:** Bertram MacKennal **Rev:** Crowned denomination divides date within oak wreath

Date	Mintage	F	VF	XF	Unc	BU
1928 Prooflike	1,846	—	—	—	45.00	50.00
1929 Prooflike	1,837	—	—	—	45.00	50.00
1930 Prooflike	1,724	—	—	—	45.00	50.00
1931 Prooflike	1,759	—	—	—	45.00	50.00
1932 Prooflike	1,835	—	—	—	45.00	50.00
1933 Prooflike	1,872	—	—	—	45.00	50.00
1934 Prooflike	1,919	—	—	—	45.00	50.00
1935 Prooflike	1,975	—	—	—	45.00	50.00
1936 Prooflike	1,329	—	—	—	50.00	55.00

KM# 845 PENNY

9.4500 g., Bronze, 30.8 mm. **Ruler:** George VI **Obv:** Head left **Obv. Designer:** T. H. Paget **Rev:** Britannia seated right

Date	Mintage	F	VF	XF	Unc	BU
1937	88,896,000	0.20	0.35	1.00	7.50	—
1937 Proof	26,000	Value: 19.00				
1937 Matte Proof	Est. 4	Value: 2,000				
1938	121,560,000	0.20	0.35	1.00	10.00	—
1938 Proof	—	Value: 750				
1939	55,560,000	0.25	0.50	4.00	15.00	—
1939 Proof	—	Value: 750				
1940	42,284,000	0.25	0.50	10.00	40.00	—
1940 Proof	—	Value: 750				
1944	42,600,000	0.25	0.50	6.00	20.00	—
1944 Proof	—	Value: 800				
1945	79,531,000	0.20	0.35	5.00	19.00	—
1945 Proof	—	Value: 800				
1946	66,855,999	0.20	0.35	5.00	19.00	—
1946 Proof	—	Value: 800				
1947	52,220,000	0.15	0.25	0.75	7.50	—
1947 Proof	—	Value: 700				
1948	63,961,000	0.15	0.25	0.75	7.50	—
1948 Proof	—	Value: 700				

KM# 846 PENNY

0.4713 g., 0.5000 Silver .0076 oz. ASW **Ruler:** George VI **Obv:** Head left **Obv. Designer:** T. H. Paget **Rev:** Crowned denomination divides date within oak wreath

Date	Mintage	F	VF	XF	Unc	BU
1937 Prooflike	1,329	—	—	—	35.00	40.00
1938 Prooflike	1,275	—	—	—	40.00	45.00
1939 Prooflike	1,253	—	—	—	40.00	45.00
1940 Prooflike	1,375	—	—	—	40.00	45.00
1941 Prooflike	1,255	—	—	—	40.00	45.00
1942 Prooflike	1,243	—	—	—	40.00	45.00
1943 Prooflike	1,347	—	—	—	40.00	45.00
1944 Prooflike	1,259	—	—	—	40.00	45.00
1945 Prooflike	1,367	—	—	—	40.00	45.00
1946 Prooflike	1,479	—	—	—	40.00	45.00

KM# 846a PENNY

0.4713 g., 0.9250 Silver .0140 oz. ASW **Ruler:** George VI **Obv:** Head left **Obv. Designer:** T. H. Paget **Rev:** Crowned denomination divides date within oak wreath

Date	Mintage	F	VF	XF	Unc	BU
1947 Prooflike	1,387	—	—	—	40.00	45.00
1948 Prooflike	1,397	—	—	—	40.00	45.00

KM# 869 PENNY

Bronze, 30.8 mm. **Ruler:** George VI **Obv:** Head left **Obv. Legend:** without IND: IMP: **Obv. Designer:** T. H. Paget **Rev:** Britannia seated right

Date	Mintage	F	VF	XF	Unc	BU
1949	14,324,000	0.20	0.35	0.75	7.50	—
1949 Proof	—	Value: 700				
1950	240,000	2.00	6.00	20.00	55.00	—
1950 Matte Proof	—	Value: 2,000				
Note: There are reportedly 1-2 known of this variety, struck specifically for use in photography						
1950 Proof	18,000	Value: 40.00				
1951	120,000	2.00	15.00	35.00	60.00	—
1951 Matte Proof	—	Value: 2,000				
Note: There are reportedly 1-2 known of this variety, struck specifically for use in photography						
1951 Proof	20,000	Value: 50.00				
1952 Unique	—	—	—	—	—	—

KM# 870 PENNY

0.4713 g., 0.9250 Silver .0140 oz. ASW **Ruler:** George VI **Obv:** Head left **Obv. Legend:** without IND: IMP: **Obv. Designer:** T. H. Paget **Rev:** Crowned denomination divides date within oak wreath

Date	Mintage	F	VF	XF	Unc	BU
1949 Prooflike	1,407	—	—	—	40.00	45.00
1950 Prooflike	1,527	—	—	—	40.00	45.00
1951 Prooflike	1,480	—	—	—	40.00	45.00
1952 Prooflike	1,024	—	—	—	50.00	55.00

KM# 883 PENNY

Bronze, 30.8 mm. **Ruler:** Elizabeth II **Obv:** Laureate bust right **Rev:** Britannia seated right

Date	Mintage	F	VF	XF	Unc	BU
1953	1,308,000	0.75	1.25	5.00	18.00	—
1953 Proof	40,000	Value: 20.00				
1953 Matte Proof; Rare	—	Value: 2,000				
Note: There are reportedly 1-2 known of this variety, struck specifically for use in photography						

KM# 884 PENNY

0.4713 g., 0.9250 Silver .0140 oz. ASW **Ruler:** Elizabeth II **Obv:** Laureate bust right **Obv. Designer:** Mary Gillick **Rev:** Britannia seated right

Date	Mintage	F	VF	XF	Unc	BU
1953 Prooflike	1,050	—	—	—	170	185

KM# 897 PENNY

Bronze, 30.8 mm. **Ruler:** Elizabeth II **Obv:** Laureate bust right **Obv. Legend:** without BRITT: OMN: **Rev:** Britannia seated right

Date	Mintage	F	VF	XF	Unc	BU
1954 1 Known	—	—	—	—	—	—
1961	48,313,000	—	0.10	0.15	2.00	—
1961 Proof	—	Value: 500				
1962	143,309,000	—	—	0.10	1.00	—
1962 Proof	—	Value: 500				
1963	125,236,000	—	—	0.10	1.00	—
1963 Proof	—	Value: 500				
1964	153,294,000	—	—	—	0.55	—
1964 Proof	—	Value: 500				
1965	121,310,000	—	—	—	0.55	—
1966	165,739,000	—	—	—	0.55	—
1967	654,564,000	—	—	—	0.30	—
1970 Proof	750,000	Value: 5.00				

KM# 898 PENNY

0.4713 g., 0.9250 Silver .0140 oz. ASW **Ruler:** Elizabeth II **Obv:** Laureate bust right **Obv. Designer:** Mary Gillick **Rev:** Crowned denomination divides date within wreath

Date	Mintage	F	VF	XF	Unc	BU
1954 Prooflike	1,088	—	—	—	35.00	40.00
1955 Prooflike	1,036	—	—	—	35.00	40.00
1956 Prooflike	1,100	—	—	—	35.00	40.00
1957 Prooflike	1,168	—	—	—	35.00	40.00
1958 Prooflike	1,112	—	—	—	35.00	40.00
1959 Prooflike	1,118	—	—	—	35.00	40.00
1960 Prooflike	1,124	—	—	—	35.00	40.00
1961 Prooflike	1,200	—	—	—	35.00	40.00
1962 Prooflike	1,127	—	—	—	35.00	40.00
1963 Prooflike	1,133	—	—	—	35.00	40.00
1964 Prooflike	1,215	—	—	—	35.00	40.00
1965 Prooflike	1,143	—	—	—	35.00	40.00
1966 Prooflike	1,206	—	—	—	35.00	40.00
1967 Prooflike	1,068	—	—	—	38.00	45.00
1968 Prooflike	964	—	—	—	38.00	45.00
1969 Prooflike	1,002	—	—	—	38.00	45.00
1970 Prooflike	980	—	—	—	38.00	45.00
1971 Prooflike	1,108	—	—	—	38.00	45.00
1972 Prooflike	1,026	—	—	—	38.00	45.00
1973 Prooflike	1,004	—	—	—	38.00	45.00
1974 Prooflike	1,138	—	—	—	38.00	45.00
1975 Prooflike	1,050	—	—	—	38.00	45.00
1976 Prooflike	1,158	—	—	—	38.00	45.00
1977 Prooflike	1,240	—	—	—	38.00	45.00
1978 Prooflike	1,178	—	—	—	38.00	45.00
1979 Prooflike	1,188	—	—	—	38.00	45.00
1980 Prooflike	1,198	—	—	—	38.00	45.00
1981 Prooflike	1,288	—	—	—	38.00	45.00
1982 Prooflike	1,218	—	—	—	38.00	45.00
1983 Prooflike	1,228	—	—	—	38.00	45.00
1984 Prooflike	1,354	—	—	—	38.00	45.00
1985 Prooflike	1,248	—	—	—	38.00	45.00
1986 Prooflike	1,378	—	—	—	38.00	45.00
1987 Prooflike	1,512	—	—	—	38.00	45.00
1988 Prooflike	1,402	—	—	—	38.00	45.00
1989 Prooflike	1,353	—	—	—	38.00	45.00
1990 Prooflike	1,523	—	—	—	40.00	45.00
1991 Prooflike	1,514	—	—	—	40.00	45.00
1992 Prooflike	1,556	—	—	—	40.00	45.00
1993 Prooflike	1,440	—	—	—	40.00	45.00
1994 Prooflike	1,443	—	—	—	40.00	45.00
1995 Prooflike	1,466	—	—	—	40.00	45.00
1996 Prooflike	1,629	—	—	—	42.00	48.00
1997 Prooflike	1,786	—	—	—	42.00	48.00
1998 Prooflike	1,654	—	—	—	42.00	48.00
1999 Prooflike	1,676	—	—	—	42.00	48.00
2000 Prooflike	1,686	—	—	—	50.00	55.00

KM# 776 2 PENCE

0.9426 g., 0.9250 Silver .0280 oz. ASW **Ruler:** Victoria **Obv:** Veiled bust left **Obv. Designer:** Thomas Brock **Rev:** Crowned denomination divides date within oak wreath

Date	Mintage	F	VF	XF	Unc	BU
1901 Prooflike	14,000	—	—	—	20.00	35.00

KM# 796 2 PENCE

0.9426 g., 0.9250 Silver .0280 oz. ASW **Ruler:** Edward VII **Obv:** Head right **Rev:** Crowned denomination divides date within oak wreath

Date	Mintage	F	VF	XF	Unc	BU
1902 Prooflike	14,000	—	—	—	25.00	40.00
1903 Prooflike	13,000	—	—	—	25.00	40.00
1904 Prooflike	14,000	—	—	—	25.00	40.00
1905 Prooflike	11,000	—	—	—	25.00	40.00
1906 Prooflike	11,000	—	—	—	25.00	40.00
1907 Prooflike	8,760	—	—	—	25.00	40.00
1908 Prooflike	15,000	—	—	—	25.00	40.00
1909 Prooflike	2,695	—	—	—	35.00	60.00
1910 Prooflike	2,998	—	—	—	40.00	65.00

KM# 812 2 PENCE

0.9426 g., 0.9250 Silver .0280 oz. ASW **Ruler:** George V **Obv:** Head left **Obv. Designer:** Bertram MacKennal **Rev:** Crowned denomination divides date within oak wreath

Date	Mintage	F	VF	XF	Unc	BU
1911 Prooflike	1,635	—	—	—	45.00	50.00
1912 Prooflike	1,678	—	—	—	45.00	50.00
1913 Prooflike	1,880	—	—	—	45.00	50.00
1914 Prooflike	1,659	—	—	—	45.00	50.00
1915 Prooflike	1,465	—	—	—	45.00	50.00
1916 Prooflike	1,509	—	—	—	45.00	50.00
1917 Prooflike	1,506	—	—	—	45.00	50.00
1918 Prooflike	1,547	—	—	—	45.00	50.00
1919 Prooflike	1,567	—	—	—	45.00	50.00
1920 Prooflike	1,630	—	—	—	45.00	50.00

KM# 812a 2 PENCE

0.9426 g., 0.5000 Silver .0152 oz. ASW **Ruler:** George V **Obv:** Head left **Obv. Designer:** Bertram MacKennal **Rev:** Crowned denomination divides date within oak wreath

Date	Mintage	F	VF	XF	Unc	BU
1921 Prooflike	1,794	—	—	—	45.00	50.00
1922 Prooflike	3,074	—	—	—	45.00	50.00
1923 Prooflike	1,527	—	—	—	45.00	50.00
1924 Prooflike	1,602	—	—	—	45.00	50.00
1925 Prooflike	1,670	—	—	—	45.00	50.00
1926 Prooflike	1,902	—	—	—	45.00	50.00
1927 Prooflike	1,766	—	—	—	45.00	50.00

KM# 840 2 PENCE

0.9426 g., 0.5000 Silver .0152 oz. ASW **Ruler:** George V **Obv:** Modified head left **Obv. Designer:** Bertram MacKennal **Rev:** Crowned denomination divides date within oak wreath

Date	Mintage	F	VF	XF	Unc	BU
1928 Prooflike	1,706	—	—	—	50.00	60.00
1929 Prooflike	1,862	—	—	—	50.00	60.00
1930 Prooflike	1,901	—	—	—	50.00	60.00
1931 Prooflike	1,897	—	—	—	50.00	60.00
1932 Prooflike	1,960	—	—	—	50.00	60.00
1933 Prooflike	2,066	—	—	—	50.00	60.00
1934 Prooflike	1,927	—	—	—	50.00	60.00
1935 Prooflike	1,928	—	—	—	50.00	60.00
1936 Prooflike	1,365	—	—	—	55.00	65.00

KM# 847 2 PENCE

0.9426 g., 0.5000 Silver .0152 oz. ASW **Ruler:** George VI **Obv:** Head left **Obv. Designer:** T. H. Paget **Rev:** Crowned denomination divides date within oak wreath

Date	Mintage	F	VF	XF	Unc	BU
1937 Prooflike	1,472	—	—	—	35.00	40.00
1938 Prooflike	1,374	—	—	—	40.00	45.00
1939 Prooflike	1,436	—	—	—	40.00	45.00
1940 Prooflike	1,277	—	—	—	40.00	45.00
1941 Prooflike	1,345	—	—	—	40.00	45.00
1942 Prooflike	1,231	—	—	—	40.00	45.00
1943 Prooflike	1,239	—	—	—	40.00	45.00
1944 Prooflike	1,345	—	—	—	40.00	45.00
1945 Prooflike	1,355	—	—	—	40.00	45.00
1946 Prooflike	1,365	—	—	—	40.00	45.00

KM# 847a 2 PENCE

0.9426 g., 0.9250 Silver .0280 oz. ASW **Ruler:** George VI **Obv:** Head left **Obv. Designer:** T. H. Paget **Rev:** Crowned denomination divides date within oak wreath

Date	Mintage	F	VF	XF	Unc	BU
1947 Prooflike	1,479	—	—	—	40.00	45.00
1948 Prooflike	1,385	—	—	—	40.00	45.00

KM# 871 2 PENCE

0.9426 g., 0.9250 Silver .0280 oz. ASW **Ruler:** George VI **Obv:** Head left **Obv. Legend:** without IND IMP **Obv. Designer:** T. H. Paget **Rev:** Crowned denomination divides date within oak wreath

Date	Mintage	F	VF	XF	Unc	BU
1949 Prooflike	1,395	—	—	—	40.00	45.00
1950 Prooflike	1,405	—	—	—	40.00	45.00
1951 Prooflike	1,580	—	—	—	40.00	45.00
1952 Prooflike	1,064	—	—	—	50.00	55.00

KM# 885 2 PENCE

0.9426 g., 0.9250 Silver .0280 oz. ASW **Ruler:** Elizabeth II **Obv:** Laureate bust right **Obv. Designer:** Mary Gillick **Rev:** Crowned denomination divides date within oak wreath

Date	Mintage	F	VF	XF	Unc	BU
1953 Prooflike	1,025	—	—	—	170	185

KM# 899 2 PENCE

0.9426 g., 0.9250 Silver .0280 oz. ASW **Ruler:** Elizabeth II **Obv:** Laureate bust right **Obv. Legend:** Without BRITT OMN **Obv. Designer:** Mary Gillick **Rev:** Crowned denomination divides date within wreath

Date	Mintage	F	VF	XF	Unc	BU
1954 Prooflike	1,020	—	—	—	35.00	40.00
1955 Prooflike	1,082	—	—	—	35.00	40.00
1956 Prooflike	1,088	—	—	—	35.00	40.00
1957 Prooflike	1,094	—	—	—	35.00	40.00
1958 Prooflike	1,164	—	—	—	35.00	40.00
1959 Prooflike	1,106	—	—	—	35.00	40.00
1960 Prooflike	1,112	—	—	—	35.00	40.00
1961 Prooflike	1,118	—	—	—	35.00	40.00
1962 Prooflike	1,197	—	—	—	35.00	40.00
1963 Prooflike	1,131	—	—	—	35.00	40.00
1964 Prooflike	1,137	—	—	—	35.00	40.00
1965 Prooflike	1,221	—	—	—	35.00	40.00
1966 Prooflike	1,206	—	—	—	35.00	40.00
1967 Prooflike	986	—	—	—	38.00	45.00
1968 Prooflike	1,048	—	—	—	38.00	45.00
1969 Prooflike	1,002	—	—	—	38.00	45.00
1970 Prooflike	980	—	—	—	38.00	45.00
1971 Prooflike	1,018	—	—	—	38.00	45.00
1972 Prooflike	1,026	—	—	—	38.00	45.00
1973 Prooflike	1,004	—	—	—	38.00	45.00
1974 Prooflike	1,042	—	—	—	38.00	45.00
1975 Prooflike	1,148	—	—	—	38.00	45.00
1976 Prooflike	1,158	—	—	—	38.00	45.00
1977 Prooflike	1,138	—	—	—	38.00	45.00
1978 Prooflike	1,282	—	—	—	38.00	45.00
1979 Prooflike	1,188	—	—	—	38.00	45.00
1980 Prooflike	1,198	—	—	—	38.00	45.00
1981 Prooflike	1,178	—	—	—	38.00	45.00
1982 Prooflike	1,330	—	—	—	38.00	45.00
1983 Prooflike	1,228	—	—	—	38.00	45.00
1984 Prooflike	1,238	—	—	—	38.00	45.00
1985 Prooflike	1,366	—	—	—	38.00	45.00
1986 Prooflike	1,378	—	—	—	38.00	45.00
1987 Prooflike	1,390	—	—	—	38.00	45.00
1988 Prooflike	1,526	—	—	—	38.00	45.00
1989 Prooflike	1,353	—	—	—	38.00	45.00
1990 Prooflike	1,523	—	—	—	40.00	45.00
1991 Prooflike	1,384	—	—	—	40.00	45.00
1992 Prooflike	1,424	—	—	—	40.00	45.00
1993 Prooflike	1,440	—	—	—	40.00	45.00
1994 Prooflike	1,443	—	—	—	40.00	45.00
1995 Prooflike	1,466	—	—	—	40.00	45.00
1996 Prooflike	1,629	—	—	—	42.00	48.00
1997 Prooflike	1,786	—	—	—	42.00	48.00
1998 Prooflike	1,654	—	—	—	42.00	48.00
1999 Prooflike	1,676	—	—	—	42.00	48.00
2000 Prooflike	1,686	—	—	—	55.00	60.00

KM# 777 3 PENCE

1.4138 g., 0.9250 Silver .0420 oz. ASW, 16 mm. **Ruler:** Victoria **Obv:** Veiled bust left **Obv. Designer:** Thomas Brock **Rev:** Crowned denomination divides date within oak wreath

Date	Mintage	F	VF	XF	Unc	BU
1901	6,100,000	1.00	2.00	6.00	20.00	—
1901 Prooflike	8,976	—	—	—	40.00	60.00

Small ball on 3

KM# 797.1 3 PENCE

1.4138 g., 0.9250 Silver .0420 oz. ASW, 16 mm. **Ruler:** Edward VII **Obv:** Head right **Rev:** Crowned denomination divides date within oak wreath **Note:** The prooflike coins come with a mirror or satin finish.

Date	Mintage	F	VF	XF	Unc	BU
1902	8,287,000	1.00	4.00	8.00	18.00	—
1902 Prooflike	8,976	—	—	—	35.00	50.00
1902 Matte Proof	15,000	Value: 50.00				
1903	5,235,000	2.00	7.00	25.00	70.00	—
1903 Prooflike	8,976	—	—	—	35.00	50.00
1904	3,630,000	5.00	12.00	45.00	200	—
1904 Prooflike	8,876	—	—	—	35.00	50.00

Large ball on 3

KM# 797.2 3 PENCE

1.4138 g., 0.9250 Silver .0420 oz. ASW, 16 mm. **Ruler:** Edward VII **Obv:** Head right **Rev:** Crowned denomination divides date within oak wreath **Note:** The below Prooflike listings can be of mirror or satin-like finish, which are more difficult to separate from the currency strikes, especially for the years 1903-1906.

Date	Mintage	F	VF	XF	Unc	BU
1904	Inc. above	4.00	8.50	35.00	90.00	—
1905	3,563,000	2.50	7.50	28.00	75.00	—
1905 Prooflike	8,976	—	—	—	35.00	50.00
1906	3,174,000	3.00	8.50	35.00	125	—
1906 Prooflike	8,800	—	—	—	35.00	50.00
1907	4,841,000	1.50	7.00	28.00	50.00	—
1907 Prooflike	11,000	—	—	—	35.00	50.00
1908	8,176,000	1.50	3.00	12.50	35.00	—
1908 Prooflike	8,760	—	—	—	35.00	50.00
1909	4,054,999	1.50	7.00	27.00	45.00	—
1909 Prooflike	1,983	—	—	—	45.00	75.00
1910	4,565,000	0.75	1.50	10.00	30.00	—
1910 Prooflike	1,140	—	—	—	50.00	80.00

KM# 813 3 PENCE

1.4138 g., 0.9250 Silver .0420 oz. ASW, 16 mm. **Ruler:** George V **Obv:** Head left **Obv. Designer:** Bertram MacKennal **Rev:** Crowned denomination divides date within oak wreath

Date	Mintage	F	VF	XF	Unc	BU
1911	5,843,000	0.75	1.25	5.00	15.00	—
1911 Prooflike	1,991	—	—	—	60.00	70.00
1911 Proof	6,007	Value: 65.00				
1912	8,934,000	0.75	1.25	5.00	15.00	—
1912 Prooflike	1,246	—	—	—	60.00	70.00
1913	7,144,000	0.75	1.25	5.00	15.00	—
1913 Prooflike	1,228	—	—	—	60.00	70.00
1914	6,735,000	0.75	1.25	5.00	15.00	—
1914 Prooflike	982	—	—	—	60.00	70.00
1915	5,452,000	0.75	1.25	5.00	20.00	—
1915 Prooflike	1,293	—	—	—	60.00	70.00
1916	18,556,000	0.65	1.00	3.00	15.00	—
1916 Prooflike	1,128	—	—	—	60.00	70.00
1917	21,664,000	0.65	1.00	3.00	15.00	—
1917 Prooflike	1,237	—	—	—	60.00	70.00
1918	20,632,000	0.65	1.00	3.00	15.00	—
1918 Prooflike	1,375	—	—	—	60.00	70.00
1919	16,846,000	0.65	1.00	3.00	15.00	—
1919 Prooflike	1,258	—	—	—	60.00	70.00
1920	16,704,999	0.65	1.00	3.00	20.00	—
1920 Prooflike	1,399	—	—	—	60.00	70.00

KM# 813a 3 PENCE

1.4138 g., 0.5000 Silver .0227 oz. ASW, 16 mm. **Ruler:** George V **Obv:** Head left **Obv. Designer:** Bertram MacKennal **Rev:** Crowned denomination divides date within oak wreath

Date	Mintage	F	VF	XF	Unc	BU
1920	Inc. above	—	1.00	3.00	18.00	—
1921	8,751,000	—	1.00	3.00	20.00	—
1921 Prooflike	1,386	—	—	—	50.00	60.00
1922	7,981,000	—	1.00	10.00	22.50	—
1922 Prooflike	1,373	—	—	—	50.00	60.00
1923 Prooflike	1,430	—	—	—	50.00	60.00
1924 Prooflike	1,515	—	—	—	50.00	60.00
1924 Satin specimen	2	—	—	—	—	2,000
1925	3,733,000	0.75	2.00	14.00	32.50	—
1925 Prooflike	1,438	—	—	—	50.00	60.00
1926	4,109,000	1.25	4.00	16.50	45.00	—
1926 Prooflike	1,504	—	—	—	50.00	60.00
1927 Prooflike	1,690	—	—	—	50.00	60.00

KM# 827 3 PENCE

1.4138 g., 0.5000 Silver .0227 oz. ASW, 16 mm. **Ruler:** George V **Obv:** Modified head left **Obv. Designer:** Bertram MacKennal **Rev:** Crowned denomination divides date within oak wreath

Date	Mintage	F	VF	XF	Unc	BU
1926	Inc. above	0.75	1.75	8.00	50.00	—
1928 Prooflike	1,835	—	—	—	45.00	50.00
1929 Prooflike	1,761	—	—	—	45.00	50.00
1930 Prooflike	1,948	—	—	—	45.00	50.00
1931 Prooflike	1,818	—	—	—	45.00	50.00
1932 Prooflike	2,042	—	—	—	45.00	50.00
1933 Prooflike	1,920	—	—	—	45.00	50.00
1934 Prooflike	1,887	—	—	—	45.00	50.00
1935 Prooflike	2,007	—	—	—	45.00	50.00
1936 Prooflike	1,307	—	—	—	50.00	55.00

KM# 831 3 PENCE

1.4138 g., 0.5000 Silver .0227 oz. ASW, 16 mm. **Ruler:** George V **Obv:** Head left **Obv. Designer:** Bertram MacKennal **Rev:** Three oak leaves and acorns divided

Date	Mintage	F	VF	XF	Unc	BU
1927 Proof	15,000	Value: 50.00				
1928	1,302,000	1.75	3.50	14.50	45.00	—
1928 Proof	—	Value: 450				
1930	1,319,000	1.50	3.00	14.00	45.00	—
1930 Proof	—	Value: 500				
1931	6,252,000	BV	0.50	1.25	12.00	—
1931 Proof	—	Value: 450				
1932	5,887,000	BV	0.60	1.75	12.50	—
1932 Proof	—	Value: 450				
1933	5,579,000	BV	0.60	1.75	12.50	—
1933 Proof	—	Value: 450				
1934	7,406,000	BV	0.50	1.25	12.00	—
1934 Proof	—	Value: 450				
1935	7,028,000	BV	0.50	1.25	12.00	—
1935 Proof	—	Value: 450				
1936	3,239,000	BV	0.60	1.75	13.00	—
1936 Proof	—	Value: 450				

KM# 848 3 PENCE

1.4138 g., 0.5000 Silver .0227 oz. ASW, 16 mm. **Ruler:** George VI **Obv:** Head left **Obv. Designer:** T. H. Paget **Rev:** St. George shield on Tudor rose divides date **Rev. Designer:** George Krueger-Gray

Date	Mintage	F	VF	XF	Unc	BU
1937	8,148,000	BV	0.50	1.25	10.00	—
1937 Proof	26,000	Value: 15.00				
1937 Matte Proof; Rare	—	—	—	—	—	—

Note: There are reportedly 2-4 known of this variety, struck specifically for use in photography

Date	Mintage	F	VF	XF	Unc	BU
1938	6,402,000	BV	0.50	1.25	10.00	—
1938 Proof	—	Value: 400				
1939	1,356,000	BV	1.00	7.00	15.00	—
1939 Proof	—	Value: 425				
1940	7,914,000	BV	0.60	3.00	14.00	—
1940 Proof	—	Value: 400				
1941	7,979,000	BV	0.60	6.00	20.00	—
1941 Proof	—	Value: 400				
1942	4,144,000	BV	5.00	15.00	50.00	—
1942 Proof	—	Value: 400				
1943	1,379,000	BV	5.00	15.00	60.00	—
1943 Proof	—	Value: 450				
1944	2,005,999	1.50	10.00	25.00	80.00	—
1944 Proof	—	Value: 500				
1945 Rare	320,000	—	—	—	—	—

Note: Issue melted, only one known

KM# 849 3 PENCE

Nickel-Brass **Ruler:** George VI **Obv:** Head left **Obv. Designer:** T. H. Paget **Rev:** Thrift plant (allium porrum) **Rev. Designer:** Frances Madge Kitchener **Shape:** 12-sided

Date	Mintage	F	VF	XF	Unc	BU
1937	45,708,000	0.25	0.40	2.00	12.00	—

Date	Mintage	F	VF	XF	Unc	BU
1937 Proof	26,000	Value: 17.50				
1937 Matte Proof ; Rare	—	—	—	—	—	—

Note: There are reportedly 2-4 known of this variety, struck specifically for use in photography

Date	Mintage	F	VF	XF	Unc	BU
1938	14,532,000	0.40	0.80	6.00	25.00	—
1938 Proof	—	Value: 350				
1939	5,603,000	0.40	1.50	10.00	50.00	—
1939 Proof	—	Value: 350				
1940	12,636,000	0.25	0.50	6.00	20.00	—
1940 Proof	—	Value: 350				
1941	60,239,000	0.25	0.40	3.00	12.00	—
1941 Proof	—	Value: 350				
1942	103,214,000	0.25	0.40	3.00	12.00	—
1942 Proof	—	—	—	—	—	—
1943	101,702,000	0.25	0.40	3.00	12.00	—
1943 Proof	—	—	—	—	—	—
1944	69,760,000	0.25	0.40	3.00	12.00	—
1944 Proof	—	—	—	—	—	—
1945	33,942,000	0.25	0.50	5.00	18.00	—
1945 Proof	—	—	—	—	—	—
1946	621,000	4.00	17.50	75.00	350	—
1946 Proof	—	Value: 700				
1948	4,230,000	0.60	1.50	8.00	55.00	—
1948 Proof	—	—	—	—	—	—

KM# 850 3 PENCE
1.4138 g., 0.5000 Silver .0227 oz. ASW, 16 mm. **Ruler:** George VI **Obv:** Head left **Obv. Designer:** T. H. Paget **Rev:** Crowned denomination divides date within oak wreath

Date	Mintage	F	VF	XF	Unc	BU
1937 Prooflike	1,351	—	—	—	45.00	50.00
1938 Prooflike	1,350	—	—	—	50.00	55.00
1939 Prooflike	1,234	—	—	—	50.00	55.00
1940 Prooflike	1,290	—	—	—	50.00	55.00
1941 Prooflike	1,253	—	—	—	50.00	55.00
1942 Prooflike	1,325	—	—	—	50.00	55.00
1943 Prooflike	1,335	—	—	—	50.00	55.00
1944 Prooflike	1,345	—	—	—	50.00	55.00
1945 Prooflike	1,355	—	—	—	50.00	55.00
1946 Prooflike	1,365	—	—	—	50.00	55.00

KM# 850a 3 PENCE
1.4138 g., 0.9250 Silver .0420 oz. ASW, 16 mm. **Ruler:** George VI **Obv:** Head left **Obv. Designer:** T. H. Paget **Rev:** Crowned denomination divides date within oak wreath

Date	Mintage	F	VF	XF	Unc	BU
1947 Prooflike	1,375	—	—	—	50.00	55.00
1948 Prooflike	1,491	—	—	—	50.00	55.00

KM# 872 3 PENCE
1.4138 g., 0.9250 Silver .0420 oz. ASW, 16 mm. **Ruler:** George VI **Obv:** Head left **Obv. Legend:** without IND IMP **Obv. Designer:** T. H. Paget **Rev:** Crowned denomination divides date within oak wreath

Date	Mintage	F	VF	XF	Unc	BU
1949 Prooflike	1,395	—	—	—	50.00	55.00
1950 Prooflike	1,405	—	—	—	50.00	55.00
1951 Prooflike	1,468	—	—	—	50.00	55.00
1952 Prooflike	1,012	—	—	—	55.00	60.00

KM# 873 3 PENCE
Nickel-Brass **Ruler:** George VI **Obv:** Head left **Obv. Legend:** without IND IMP **Obv. Designer:** T. H. Paget **Rev:** Thrift plant (allium porrum) **Rev. Designer:** Frances Madge Kitchener

Date	Mintage	F	VF	XF	Unc	BU
1949	464,000	4.00	17.50	75.00	375	—
1949 Proof	—	Value: 750				
1950	1,600,000	1.00	3.00	15.00	75.00	—
1950 Proof	18,000	Value: 35.00				
1950 Matte Proof; Rare	—	—	—	—	—	—

Note: There are reportedly 2-4 known of this variety, struck specifically for use in photography

Date	Mintage	F	VF	XF	Unc	BU
1951	1,184,000	1.00	3.00	20.00	110	—
1951 Proof	20,000	Value: 40.00				
1951 Matte Proof; Rare	—	—	—	—	—	—

Note: There are reportedly 2-4 known of this variety, struck specifically for use in photography

Date	Mintage	F	VF	XF	Unc	BU
1952	25,494,000	0.25	0.50	5.00	19.00	—
1952 Proof	—	Value: 450				

KM# 886 3 PENCE
Nickel-Brass **Ruler:** Elizabeth II **Obv:** Laureate bust right **Obv. Designer:** Mary Gillick **Rev:** Crowned portcullis **Rev. Designer:** William Gardner

Date	Mintage	F	VF	XF	Unc	BU
1953	30,618,000	0.25	0.50	0.75	6.00	—
1953 Proof	40,000	Value: 12.00				
1953 Matte Proof; Rare	—	—	—	—	—	—

Note: There are reportedly 2-4 known of this variety, struck specifically for use in photography

KM# 887 3 PENCE
1.4138 g., 0.9250 Silver .0420 oz. ASW **Ruler:** Elizabeth II **Obv:** Laureate bust right **Obv. Designer:** Mary Gillick **Rev:** Crowned portcullis

Date	Mintage	F	VF	XF	Unc	BU
1953 Prooflike	1,078	—	—	—	180	200

KM# 900 3 PENCE
Nickel-Brass **Ruler:** Elizabeth II **Obv:** Laureate bust right **Obv. Legend:** without BRITT OMN **Obv. Designer:** Mary Gillick **Rev:** Crowned portcullis **Rev. Designer:** William Gardner **Shape:** 12-sided

Date	Mintage	F	VF	XF	Unc	BU
1954	41,720,000	—	0.25	0.50	10.00	—
1954 Proof	—	Value: 300				
1955	41,075,000	—	—	0.75	10.00	—
1955 Proof	—	Value: 300				
1956	36,902,000	—	—	0.75	10.00	—
1956 Proof	—	Value: 300				
1957	24,294,000	—	—	0.50	5.00	—
1957 Proof	—	Value: 300				
1958	20,504,000	—	0.25	0.50	8.00	—
1958 Proof	—	Value: 300				
1959	28,499,000	—	—	0.50	6.50	—
1959 Proof	—	Value: 300				
1960	83,078,000	—	—	0.40	6.50	—
1960 Proof	—	Value: 300				
1961	41,102,000	—	—	0.25	2.50	—
1961 Proof	—	Value: 300				
1962	47,242,000	—	—	0.25	1.00	—
1962 Proof	—	Value: 300				
1963	35,280,000	—	—	0.25	1.00	—
1963 Proof	—	Value: 300				
1964	47,440,000	—	—	0.25	1.00	—
1964 Proof	—	—	—	—	—	—
1965	23,907,000	—	—	0.25	1.00	—
1965 Proof	—	—	—	—	—	—
1966	55,320,000	—	—	0.25	0.50	—
1966 Proof	—	—	—	—	—	—
1967	49,000,000	—	0.15	0.25	0.50	—
1967 Proof	—	—	—	—	—	—
1970 Proof	750,000	Value: 3.50				

KM# 901 3 PENCE
1.4138 g., 0.9250 Silver .0420 oz. ASW **Ruler:** Elizabeth II **Obv:** Laureate bust right **Obv. Legend:** without BRITT OMN **Obv. Designer:** Mary Gillick **Rev:** Crowned denomination divides date within wreath

Date	Mintage	F	VF	XF	Unc	BU
1954 Prooflike	1,076	—	—	—	45.00	50.00
1955 Prooflike	1,082	—	—	—	45.00	50.00
1956 Prooflike	1,088	—	—	—	45.00	50.00
1957 Prooflike	1,094	—	—	—	45.00	50.00
1958 Prooflike	1,100	—	—	—	45.00	50.00
1959 Prooflike	1,172	—	—	—	45.00	50.00
1960 Prooflike	1,112	—	—	—	45.00	50.00
1961 Prooflike	1,118	—	—	—	45.00	50.00
1962 Prooflike	1,125	—	—	—	45.00	50.00
1963 Prooflike	1,205	—	—	—	45.00	50.00
1964 Prooflike	1,213	—	—	—	45.00	50.00
1965 Prooflike	1,221	—	—	—	45.00	50.00
1966 Prooflike	1,206	—	—	—	45.00	50.00
1967 Prooflike	986	—	—	—	48.00	55.00
1968 Prooflike	964	—	—	—	48.00	55.00
1969 Prooflike	1,088	—	—	—	48.00	55.00
1970 Prooflike	980	—	—	—	48.00	55.00
1971 Prooflike	1,018	—	—	—	48.00	55.00
1972 Prooflike	1,026	—	—	—	48.00	55.00
1973 Prooflike	1,098	—	—	—	48.00	55.00
1974 Prooflike	1,138	—	—	—	48.00	55.00
1975 Prooflike	1,148	—	—	—	48.00	55.00
1976 Prooflike	1,158	—	—	—	48.00	55.00
1977 Prooflike	1,138	—	—	—	48.00	55.00
1978 Prooflike	1,178	—	—	—	48.00	55.00
1979 Prooflike	1,294	—	—	—	48.00	55.00
1980 Prooflike	1,198	—	—	—	48.00	55.00
1981 Prooflike	1,178	—	—	—	48.00	55.00
1982 Prooflike	1,218	—	—	—	48.00	55.00
1983 Prooflike	1,342	—	—	—	48.00	55.00
1984 Prooflike	1,354	—	—	—	48.00	55.00
1985 Prooflike	1,366	—	—	—	48.00	55.00
1986 Prooflike	1,378	—	—	—	48.00	55.00
1987 Prooflike	1,390	—	—	—	48.00	55.00
1988 Prooflike	1,528	—	—	—	48.00	55.00
1989 Prooflike	1,353	—	—	—	48.00	55.00
1990 Prooflike	1,523	—	—	—	50.00	55.00
1991 Prooflike	1,384	—	—	—	50.00	55.00
1992 Prooflike	1,424	—	—	—	50.00	55.00
1993 Prooflike	1,440	—	—	—	50.00	55.00
1994 Prooflike	1,433	—	—	—	50.00	55.00
1995 Prooflike	1,466	—	—	—	50.00	55.00
1996 Prooflike	1,629	—	—	—	55.00	60.00
1997 Prooflike	1,786	—	—	—	55.00	60.00
1998 Prooflike	1,654	—	—	—	55.00	60.00
1999 Prooflike	1,676	—	—	—	55.00	60.00
2000 Prooflike	1,686	—	—	—	58.00	62.00

KM# 778 4 PENCE (Groat)
1.8851 g., 0.9250 Silver .0561 oz. ASW **Ruler:** Victoria **Obv:** Veiled bust left **Obv. Designer:** Thomas Brock **Rev:** Crowned denomination divides date within oak wreath

Date	Mintage	F	VF	XF	Unc	BU
1901 Prooflike	12,000	—	—	—	30.00	50.00

KM# 798 4 PENCE (Groat)
1.8851 g., 0.9250 Silver .0561 oz. ASW **Ruler:** Edward VII **Obv:** Head left **Rev:** Crowned denomination divides date within oak wreath

Date	Mintage	F	VF	XF	Unc	BU
1902 Prooflike	10,000	—	—	—	30.00	45.00
1903 Prooflike	9,729	—	—	—	30.00	45.00
1904 Prooflike	12,000	—	—	—	30.00	45.00
1905 Prooflike	11,000	—	—	—	30.00	45.00
1906 Prooflike	11,000	—	—	—	30.00	45.00
1907 Prooflike	11,000	—	—	—	30.00	45.00
1908 Prooflike	9,929	—	—	—	30.00	45.00
1909 Prooflike	2,428	—	—	—	40.00	70.00
1910 Prooflike	2,755	—	—	—	45.00	75.00

KM# 814 4 PENCE (Groat)
1.8851 g., 0.9250 Silver .0561 oz. ASW **Ruler:** George V **Obv:** Head left **Obv. Designer:** Bertram MacKennal **Rev:** Crowned denomination divides date within oak wreath

Date	Mintage	F	VF	XF	Unc	BU
1911 Prooflike	1,768	—	—	—	45.00	50.00
1912 Prooflike	1,700	—	—	—	45.00	50.00
1913 Prooflike	1,798	—	—	—	45.00	50.00
1914 Prooflike	1,651	—	—	—	45.00	50.00
1915 Prooflike	1,441	—	—	—	45.00	50.00
1916 Prooflike	1,499	—	—	—	45.00	50.00
1917 Prooflike	1,478	—	—	—	45.00	50.00
1918 Prooflike	1,479	—	—	—	45.00	50.00
1919 Prooflike	1,524	—	—	—	45.00	50.00
1920 Prooflike	1,460	—	—	—	45.00	50.00

KM# 814a 4 PENCE (Groat)
1.8851 g., 0.5000 Silver .0303 oz. ASW **Ruler:** George V **Obv:** Head left **Obv. Designer:** Bertram MacKennal **Rev:** Crowned denomination divides date within oak wreath

Date	Mintage	F	VF	XF	Unc	BU
1921 Prooflike	1,542	—	—	—	45.00	50.00
1922 Prooflike	1,609	—	—	—	45.00	50.00
1923 Prooflike	1,635	—	—	—	45.00	50.00
1924 Prooflike	1,665	—	—	—	45.00	50.00
1925 Prooflike	1,786	—	—	—	45.00	50.00

Date	Mintage	F	VF	XF	Unc	BU
1926 Prooflike	1,762	—	—	—	45.00	50.00
1927 Prooflike	1,681	—	—	—	45.00	50.00

KM# 841 4 PENCE (Groat)

1.8851 g., 0.5000 Silver .0303 oz. ASW **Ruler:** George V **Obv:** Modified head left **Rev:** Crowned denomination divides date within oak wreath **Rev. Designer:** Bertram MacKennal

Date	Mintage	F	VF	XF	Unc	BU
1928 Prooflike	1,642	—	—	—	45.00	50.00
1929 Prooflike	1,969	—	—	—	45.00	50.00
1930 Prooflike	1,744	—	—	—	45.00	50.00
1931 Prooflike	1,915	—	—	—	45.00	50.00
1932 Prooflike	1,937	—	—	—	45.00	50.00
1933 Prooflike	1,931	—	—	—	45.00	50.00
1934 Prooflike	1,893	—	—	—	45.00	50.00
1935 Prooflike	1,995	—	—	—	45.00	50.00
1936 Prooflike	1,323	—	—	—	50.00	55.00

KM# 851 4 PENCE (Groat)

1.8851 g., 0.5000 Silver .0303 oz. ASW **Ruler:** George VI **Obv:** Head left **Obv. Designer:** T. H. Paget **Rev:** Crowned denomination divides date within oak wreath

Date	Mintage	F	VF	XF	Unc	BU
1937 Prooflike	1,325	—	—	—	45.00	50.00
1938 Prooflike	1,424	—	—	—	50.00	55.00
1939 Prooflike	1,332	—	—	—	50.00	55.00
1940 Prooflike	1,367	—	—	—	50.00	55.00
1941 Prooflike	1,345	—	—	—	50.00	55.00
1942 Prooflike	1,325	—	—	—	50.00	55.00
1943 Prooflike	1,335	—	—	—	50.00	55.00
1944 Prooflike	1,345	—	—	—	50.00	55.00
1945 Prooflike	1,355	—	—	—	50.00	55.00
1946 Prooflike	1,365	—	—	—	50.00	55.00

KM# 851a 4 PENCE (Groat)

1.8851 g., 0.9250 Silver .0561 oz. ASW **Ruler:** George VI **Obv:** Head left **Obv. Designer:** T. H. Paget **Rev:** Crowned denomination divides date within oak wreath

Date	Mintage	F	VF	XF	Unc	BU
1947 Prooflike	1,375	—	—	—	50.00	55.00
1948 Prooflike	1,385	—	—	—	50.00	55.00

KM# 874 4 PENCE (Groat)

1.8851 g., 0.9250 Silver .0561 oz. ASW **Ruler:** George VI **Obv:** Head left **Obv. Legend:** without IND IMP **Obv. Designer:** T. H. Paget **Rev:** Crowned denomination divides date within oak wreath

Date	Mintage	F	VF	XF	Unc	BU
1949 Prooflike	1,503	—	—	—	50.00	55.00
1950 Prooflike	1,515	—	—	—	50.00	55.00
1951 Prooflike	1,580	—	—	—	50.00	55.00
1952 Prooflike	1,064	—	—	—	55.00	60.00

KM# 888 4 PENCE (Groat)

1.8851 g., 0.9250 Silver .0561 oz. ASW **Ruler:** Elizabeth II **Obv:** Bust right **Obv. Designer:** Mary Gillick **Rev:** Crowned denomination divides date within oak wreath

Date	Mintage	F	VF	XF	Unc	BU
1953 Prooflike	1,078	—	—	—	180	200

KM# 902 4 PENCE (Groat)

1.8851 g., 0.9250 Silver .0561 oz. ASW **Ruler:** Elizabeth II **Obv:** Laureate bust right **Obv. Inscription:** without BRITT OMN **Rev:** Crowned denomination divides date within wreath

Date	Mintage	F	VF	XF	Unc	BU
1954 Prooflike	1,076	—	—	—	45.00	50.00
1955 Prooflike	1,082	—	—	—	45.00	50.00
1956 Prooflike	1,088	—	—	—	45.00	50.00
1957 Prooflike	1,094	—	—	—	45.00	50.00
1958 Prooflike	1,100	—	—	—	45.00	50.00
1959 Prooflike	1,106	—	—	—	45.00	50.00
1960 Prooflike	1,180	—	—	—	45.00	50.00
1961 Prooflike	1,118	—	—	—	45.00	50.00
1962 Prooflike	1,197	—	—	—	45.00	50.00
1963 Prooflike	1,205	—	—	—	45.00	50.00

Date	Mintage	F	VF	XF	Unc	BU
1964 Prooflike	1,213	—	—	—	45.00	50.00
1965 Prooflike	1,221	—	—	—	45.00	50.00
1966 Prooflike	1,206	—	—	—	45.00	50.00
1967 Prooflike	986	—	—	—	48.00	55.00
1968 Prooflike	964	—	—	—	48.00	55.00
1969 Prooflike	1,002	—	—	—	48.00	55.00
1970 Prooflike	1,068	—	—	—	48.00	55.00
1971 Prooflike	1,108	—	—	—	48.00	55.00
1972 Prooflike	1,118	—	—	—	48.00	55.00
1973 Prooflike	1,098	—	—	—	48.00	55.00
1974 Prooflike	1,138	—	—	—	48.00	55.00
1975 Prooflike	1,148	—	—	—	48.00	55.00
1976 Prooflike	1,158	—	—	—	48.00	55.00
1977 Prooflike	1,138	—	—	—	48.00	55.00
1978 Prooflike	1,178	—	—	—	48.00	55.00
1979 Prooflike	1,188	—	—	—	48.00	55.00
1980 Prooflike	1,306	—	—	—	48.00	55.00
1981 Prooflike	1,288	—	—	—	48.00	55.00
1982 Prooflike	1,330	—	—	—	48.00	55.00
1983 Prooflike	1,342	—	—	—	48.00	55.00
1984 Prooflike	1,354	—	—	—	48.00	55.00
1985 Prooflike	1,366	—	—	—	48.00	55.00
1986 Prooflike	1,378	—	—	—	48.00	55.00
1987 Prooflike	1,390	—	—	—	48.00	55.00
1988 Prooflike	1,402	—	—	—	48.00	55.00
1989 Prooflike	1,353	—	—	—	48.00	55.00
1990 Prooflike	1,523	—	—	—	50.00	55.00
1991 Prooflike	1,514	—	—	—	50.00	55.00
1992 Prooflike	1,556	—	—	—	50.00	55.00
1993 Prooflike	1,440	—	—	—	50.00	55.00
1994 Prooflike	1,433	—	—	—	50.00	55.00
1995 Prooflike	1,466	—	—	—	50.00	55.00
1996 Prooflike	1,629	—	—	—	55.00	60.00
1997 Prooflike	1,786	—	—	—	55.00	60.00
1998 Prooflike	1,654	—	—	—	55.00	60.00
1999 Prooflike	1,676	—	—	—	55.00	60.00
2000 Prooflike	1,686	—	—	—	58.00	62.00

KM# 779 6 PENCE

3.0100 g., 0.9250 Silver .0895 oz. ASW, 19.5 mm. **Ruler:** Victoria **Obv:** Veiled bust left **Obv. Designer:** Thomas Brock **Rev:** Crowned denomination within oak wreath

Date	Mintage	F	VF	XF	Unc	BU
1901	5,109,000	4.00	8.00	25.00	50.00	—

KM# 799 6 PENCE

3.0100 g., 0.9250 Silver .0895 oz. ASW, 19.5 mm. **Ruler:** Edward VII **Obv:** Head right **Rev:** Crowned denomination within oak wreath, date below

Date	Mintage	F	VF	XF	Unc	BU
1902	6,356,000	5.00	10.00	30.00	50.00	—
1902 Matte Proof	15,000	Value: 50.00				
1903	5,411,000	4.00	10.00	30.00	100	—
1904	4,487,000	6.00	15.00	45.00	200	—
1905	4,236,000	5.00	12.00	35.00	135	—
1906	7,641,000	4.00	10.00	30.00	100	—
1907	8,734,000	5.00	10.00	35.00	100	—
1908	6,739,000	5.00	12.00	40.00	160	—
1909	6,584,000	4.00	10.00	35.00	100	—
1910	12,491,000	3.00	5.00	25.00	65.00	—

KM# 815 6 PENCE

3.0100 g., 0.9250 Silver .0895 oz. ASW, 19.5 mm. **Ruler:** George V **Obv:** Head left **Obv. Designer:** Bertram MacKennal **Rev:** Lion atop crown dividing date

Date	Mintage	F	VF	XF	Unc	BU
1911	9,165,000	2.00	8.00	15.00	30.00	—
1911 Proof	6,007	Value: 50.00				
1912	10,984,000	4.00	10.00	25.00	50.00	—
1913	7,500,000	5.00	12.00	30.00	75.00	—
1914	22,715,000	2.00	8.00	15.00	35.00	—
1915	15,695,000	2.00	8.00	15.00	35.00	—
1916	22,207,000	2.00	8.00	15.00	35.00	—
1917	7,725,000	5.00	15.00	30.00	85.00	—
1918	27,559,000	2.00	8.00	15.00	35.00	—
1919	13,375,000	4.00	10.00	20.00	42.50	—
1920	14,136,000	4.00	10.00	25.00	45.00	—

KM# 815a.1 6 PENCE

2.8276 g., 0.5000 Silver .0455 oz. ASW, 19.5 mm. **Ruler:** George V **Obv:** Head left **Obv. Designer:** Bertram MacKennal **Rev:** Lion atop crown dividing date **Note:** Narrow rim.

Date	Mintage	F	VF	XF	Unc	BU
1920	Inc. above	2.00	4.00	12.00	32.00	—
1921	30,340,000	2.00	4.00	12.00	32.00	—
1922	16,879,000	2.00	5.00	15.00	38.00	—
1923	6,383,000	3.00	6.00	20.00	90.00	—
1924	17,444,000	2.00	4.00	12.00	30.00	—
1924 Satin specimen	2	—	—	—	—	1,500
1925	12,721,000	2.00	4.00	15.00	35.00	—

KM# 815a.2 6 PENCE

2.8276 g., 0.5000 Silver .0455 oz. ASW, 19.5 mm. **Ruler:** George V **Obv:** Head left **Obv. Designer:** Bertram MacKennal **Rev:** Lion atop crown dividing date **Note:** Wide rim.

Date	Mintage	F	VF	XF	Unc	BU
1925	Inc. above	2.00	4.00	12.00	35.00	—
1926	21,810,000	2.00	4.00	15.00	35.00	—

KM# 828 6 PENCE

2.8276 g., 0.5000 Silver .0455 oz. ASW, 19.5 mm. **Ruler:** George V **Obv:** Modified head left **Obv. Designer:** Bertram MacKennal **Rev:** Lion atop crown divides date

Date	Mintage	F	VF	XF	Unc	BU
1926	Inc. above	BV	3.00	10.00	22.50	—
1927	8,925,000	2.00	4.00	15.00	25.00	—
1927 Proof	—	Value: 1,000				

KM# 832 6 PENCE

2.8276 g., 0.5000 Silver .0455 oz. ASW, 19.5 mm. **Ruler:** George V **Obv:** Head left **Obv. Designer:** Bertram MacKennal **Rev:** Six oak leaves and acorns divided **Note:** Varieties in edge milling exist.

Date	Mintage	F	VF	XF	Unc	BU
1927 Proof	15,000	Value: 35.00				
1927 Matte Proof; Rare	—	—	—	—	—	—
Note: There are reportedly 3-4 known of this variety, struck specifically for use in photographs						
1928	23,123,000	BV	2.00	5.00	20.00	—
1928 Proof	—	Value: 450				
1929	28,319,000	BV	2.00	4.50	22.00	—
1929 Proof	—	Value: 500				
1930	16,990,000	BV	2.00	4.50	25.00	—
1930 Proof	—	Value: 450				
1931	16,873,000	2.00	3.00	8.00	30.00	—
1931 Proof	—	Value: 450				
1932	9,406,000	2.00	4.00	17.00	50.00	—
1932 Proof	—	Value: 450				
1933	22,185,000	2.00	3.00	8.00	25.00	—
1933 Proof	—	Value: 450				
1934	9,304,000	2.00	3.00	10.00	35.00	—
1934 Proof	—	Value: 450				
1935	13,996,000	BV	2.00	6.00	18.00	—
1935 Proof	—	Value: 450				
1936	24,380,000	BV	2.00	5.00	15.00	—
1936 Proof	—	Value: 450				

KM# 852 6 PENCE

2.8276 g., 0.5000 Silver .0455 oz. ASW, 19.5 mm. **Ruler:** George VI **Obv:** Head left **Obv. Designer:** T. H. Paget **Rev:** Crowned monogram divides date **Rev. Designer:** George Krueger-Gray

Date	Mintage	F	VF	XF	Unc	BU
1937	22,303,000	—	BV	1.00	10.00	—
1937 Proof	26,000	Value: 18.00				
1937 Matte Proof; Rare	—	—	—	—	—	—
Note: There are reportedly 3-4 known of this variety, struck specifically for use in photographs						
1938	13,403,000	BV	1.25	7.00	23.00	—
1938 Proof	—	Value: 400				
1939	28,670,000	—	BV	2.50	15.00	—
1939 Proof	—	Value: 400				
1940	20,875,000	—	BV	2.50	15.00	—
1940 Proof	—	Value: 400				
1941	23,087,000	—	BV	2.00	10.00	—

Date	Mintage	F	VF	XF	Unc	BU
1941 Proof	—	Value: 400				
1942	44,943,000	—	BV	1.00	10.00	—
1942 Proof	—	Value: 400				
1943	46,927,000	—	BV	1.00	10.00	—
1943 Proof	—	Value: 400				
1944	36,953,000	—	BV	1.00	10.00	—
1944 Proof	—	Value: 450				
1945	39,939,000	—	BV	1.00	10.00	—
1945 Proof	—	Value: 500				
1946	43,466,000	—	BV	1.00	10.00	—
1946 Proof	—	Value: 500				

KM# 862 6 PENCE

Copper-Nickel, 19.5 mm. **Ruler:** George VI **Obv:** Head left **Obv. Designer:** T. H. Paget **Rev:** Crowned monogram divides date **Rev. Designer:** George Krueger-Gray

Date	Mintage	F	VF	XF	Unc	BU
1947	29,993,000	—	0.20	0.50	6.00	—
1947 Proof	—	Value: 400				
1948	88,324,000	—	0.20	0.50	5.00	—
1948 Proof	—	Value: 400				

KM# 875 6 PENCE

Copper-Nickel, 19.5 mm. **Ruler:** George VI **Obv:** Head left **Rev:** Crowned monogram divides date **Rev. Legend:** without IND IMP **Rev. Designer:** T. H. Paget

Date	Mintage	F	VF	XF	Unc	BU
1949	41,336,000	—	0.20	1.00	10.00	—
1949 Proof	—	Value: 400				
1950	32,741,999	—	0.20	1.00	10.00	—
1950 Proof	18,000	Value: 15.00				
1950 Matte Proof; Rare	—	—	—	—	—	—

Note: There are reportedly 3-4 known of this variety, struck specifically for use in photographs

Date	Mintage	F	VF	XF	Unc	BU
1951	40,399,000	—	0.20	5.00	19.00	—
1951 Proof	20,000	Value: 16.00				
1951 Matte Proof; Rare	—	—	—	—	—	—

Note: There are reportedly 3-4 known of this variety, struck specifically for use in photographs

Date	Mintage	F	VF	XF	Unc	BU
1952	1,012,999	1.25	5.00	20.00	75.00	—
1952 Proof	—	Value: 1,200				

KM# 889 6 PENCE

Copper-Nickel, 19.5 mm. **Ruler:** Elizabeth II **Obv:** Laureate bust right **Obv. Designer:** Mary Gillick **Rev:** Flora; leek, rose, thistle and shamrock **Rev. Designer:** F. G. Fuller and Cecil Thomas

Date	Mintage	F	VF	XF	Unc	BU
1953	70,324,000	—	0.15	0.50	2.50	—
1953 Proof	40,000	Value: 7.50				
1953 Matte Proof; Rare	—	—	—	—	—	—

Note: There are reportedly 3-4 known of this variety, struck specifically for use in photographs

KM# 903 6 PENCE

Copper-Nickel, 19.5 mm. **Ruler:** Elizabeth II **Obv:** Laureate bust right **Obv. Legend:** Without BRITT OMN **Obv. Designer:** Mary Gillick **Rev:** Flora; leek, rose, thistle and shamrock **Rev. Designer:** F. G. Fuller and Cecil Thomas

Date	Mintage	F	VF	XF	Unc	BU
1954	105,241,000	—	0.15	0.50	6.00	—
1954 Proof	—	Value: 350				
1955	109,930,000	—	0.15	0.35	4.00	—
1955 Proof	—	Value: 350				
1956	109,842,000	—	0.15	0.35	4.00	—
1956 Proof	—	Value: 350				
1957	105,654,000	—	0.15	0.35	3.50	—
1957 Proof	—	Value: 350				
1958	123,519,000	—	0.15	0.35	3.00	—
1958 Proof	—	Value: 350				
1959	93,089,000	—	0.15	0.35	2.50	—
1959 Proof	—	Value: 350				
1960	103,283,000	—	0.15	0.35	3.00	—
1960 Proof	—	Value: 350				
1961	115,052,000	—	0.15	0.35	2.00	—
1961 Proof	—	Value: 350				
1962	166,484,000	—	0.15	0.35	1.75	—
1962 Proof	—	Value: 350				
1963	120,056,000	—	0.15	0.30	1.50	—
1963 Proof	—	Value: 350				
1964	152,336,000	—	0.15	0.25	1.50	—
1964 Proof	—	—	—	—	—	—

Note: Reported, not confirmed

Date	Mintage	F	VF	XF	Unc	BU
1965	129,644,000	—	0.10	0.20	1.00	—
1965 Proof	—	—	—	—	—	—

Note: Reported, not confirmed

Date	Mintage	F	VF	XF	Unc	BU
1966	175,676,000	—	0.10	0.20	1.00	—
1966 Proof	—	—	—	—	—	—

Note: Reported, not confirmed

Date	Mintage	F	VF	XF	Unc	BU
1967	240,788,000	—	0.10	0.20	1.00	—
1967 Proof	—	—	—	—	—	—

Note: Reported, not confirmed

Date	Mintage	F	VF	XF	Unc	BU
1970 Proof	750,000	Value: 3.50				

KM# 780 SHILLING

5.6552 g., 0.9250 Silver .1682 oz. ASW, 23.5 mm. **Ruler:** Victoria **Obv:** Veiled bust left **Obv. Designer:** Thomas Brock **Rev:** Crowned shields of England, Scotland and Ireland **Rev. Designer:** Edward Paynter

Date	Mintage	F	VF	XF	Unc	BU
1901	3,426,000	4.00	10.00	35.00	75.00	—

KM# 800 SHILLING

5.6552 g., 0.9250 Silver .1682 oz. ASW, 23.5 mm. **Ruler:** Edward VII **Obv:** Head right **Rev:** Lion atop crown dividing date

Date	Mintage	F	VF	XF	Unc	BU
1902	7,890,000	5.00	15.00	50.00	80.00	—
1902 Matte Proof	15,000	Value: 90.00				
1903	2,061,999	8.00	20.00	95.00	350	—
1904	2,040,000	8.00	15.00	90.00	300	—
1905	488,000	50.00	150	650	2,000	—
1906	10,791,000	5.00	11.00	55.00	200	—
1907	14,083,000	5.00	11.00	60.00	225	—
1908	3,807,000	10.00	21.00	90.00	650	—
1909	5,665,000	10.00	21.00	90.00	500	—
1910	26,547,000	3.00	10.00	45.00	150	—

KM# 816 SHILLING

5.6552 g., 0.9250 Silver .1682 oz. ASW, 23.5 mm. **Ruler:** George V **Obv:** Head left **Obv. Designer:** Bertram MacKennal **Rev:** Lion atop crown dividing date **Note:** Fully struck 1914-1918 pieces command a premium.

Date	Mintage	F	VF	XF	Unc	BU
1911	20,066,000	2.50	4.50	20.00	75.00	—
1911 Proof	6,007	Value: 90.00				
1912	15,594,000	3.00	6.00	30.00	100	—
1913	9,002,000	4.00	8.00	45.00	125	—
1914	23,416,000	2.50	4.00	25.00	45.00	—
1915	39,279,000	2.50	3.50	20.00	45.00	—
1916	35,862,000	2.50	3.50	20.00	40.00	—
1917	22,203,000	2.50	4.00	25.00	50.00	—
1918	34,916,000	2.50	3.50	20.00	40.00	—
1919	10,824,000	3.00	6.00	30.00	65.00	—

KM# 816a SHILLING

5.6552 g., 0.5000 Silver .0909 oz. ASW, 23.5 mm. **Ruler:** George V **Obv:** Head left **Obv. Designer:** Bertram MacKennal **Rev:** Lion atop crown dividing date

Date	Mintage	F	VF	XF	Unc	BU
1920	22,825,000	2.00	4.00	25.00	50.00	—
1921	22,649,000	2.50	6.00	30.00	70.00	—
1922	27,216,000	2.00	4.00	25.00	60.00	—
1923	14,575,000	2.00	3.50	25.00	50.00	—
1924	9,250,000	2.00	5.00	30.00	70.00	—
1924	2	—	—	—	—	2,500

Note: Satin specimen

Date	Mintage	F	VF	XF	Unc	BU
1925	5,419,000	4.00	8.00	45.00	110	—
1926	22,516,000	2.00	5.00	21.00	50.00	—

KM# 829 SHILLING

5.6552 g., 0.5000 Silver .0909 oz. ASW, 23.5 mm. **Ruler:** George V **Obv:** Modified head left **Obv. Designer:** Bertram MacKennal **Rev:** Lion atop crown dividing date

Date	Mintage	F	VF	XF	Unc	BU
1926	Inc. above	1.50	3.50	18.00	50.00	—
1927	9,262,000	1.50	4.00	25.00	50.00	—

KM# 833 SHILLING

5.6552 g., 0.5000 Silver .0909 oz. ASW, 23.5 mm. **Ruler:** George V **Obv:** Head left **Obv. Designer:** Bertram MacKennal **Rev:** Lion atop crown

Date	Mintage	F	VF	XF	Unc	BU
1927	Inc. above	1.50	3.00	15.00	50.00	—
1927 Proof	15,000	Value: 50.00				
1927 Matte Proof	—	Value: 2,500				

Note: There are reportedly 1-2 of this variety, struck specifically for use in photographs

Date	Mintage	F	VF	XF	Unc	BU
1928	18,137,000	BV	2.00	11.00	30.00	—
1928 Proof	—	Value: 750				
1929	19,343,000	BV	2.00	10.00	30.00	—
1929 Proof	—	Value: 750				
1930	3,137,000	2.50	6.00	23.00	70.00	—
1930 Proof	—	Value: 800				
1931	6,994,000	2.00	3.50	11.00	25.00	—
1931 Proof	—	Value: 750				
1932	12,168,000	2.00	3.50	11.00	25.00	—
1932 Proof	—	Value: 750				
1933	11,512,000	1.50	3.00	10.00	25.00	—
1933 Proof	—	Value: 750				
1934	6,138,000	2.00	5.50	18.00	55.00	—
1934 Proof	—	Value: 800				
1935	9,183,000	1.50	3.00	10.00	25.00	—
1935 Proof	—	Value: 750				
1936	11,911,000	1.50	2.50	8.00	25.00	—
1936 Proof	—	Value: 750				

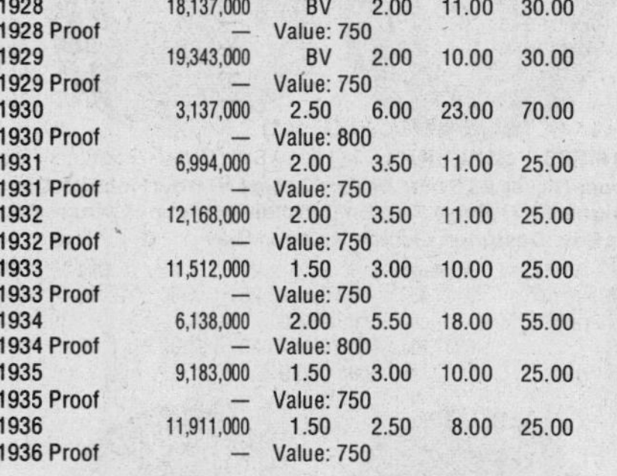

KM# 853 SHILLING

5.6552 g., 0.5000 Silver .0909 oz. ASW, 23.5 mm. **Ruler:** George VI **Obv:** Head left **Obv. Designer:** T. H. Paget **Rev:** Lion atop crown dividing date **Rev. Designer:** George Krueger-Gray

Date	Mintage	F	VF	XF	Unc	BU
1937	8,359,000	—	BV	2.50	8.00	—
1937 Proof	26,000	Value: 15.00				
1937 Matte Proof	—	Value: 2,000				

Note: There are reportedly 1-2 known of this variety, struck specifically for use in photographs

Date	Mintage	F	VF	XF	Unc	BU
1938	4,833,000	—	BV	5.00	35.00	—
1938 Proof	—	Value: 650				
1939	11,053,000	—	BV	3.00	17.50	—
1939 Proof	—	Value: 600				
1940	11,099,000	—	BV	2.50	13.00	—
1940 Proof	—	Value: 600				
1941	11,392,000	—	BV	2.00	13.00	—
1941 Proof	—	Value: 600				
1942	17,454,000	—	BV	2.00	13.00	—
1942 Proof	—	Value: 600				
1943	11,404,000	—	BV	2.00	13.00	—
1943 Proof	—	Value: 600				
1944	11,587,000	—	BV	2.00	13.00	—
1944 Proof	—	Value: 650				
1945	15,143,000	—	BV	1.50	8.50	—
1945 Proof	—	Value: 750				
1946	18,664,000	—	BV	1.50	8.00	—
1946 Proof	—	Value: 750				

KM# 854 SHILLING

5.6552 g., 0.5000 Silver .0909 oz. ASW, 23.5 mm. **Ruler:** George VI **Obv:** Head left **Obv. Designer:** T. H. Paget **Rev:** Scottish crest; lion seated atop crown holding sword and scepter divides date, shields flank **Rev. Designer:** George Krueger-Gray

Date	Mintage	F	VF	XF	Unc	BU
1937	6,749,000	—	BV	1.75	8.00	—
1937 Proof	26,000	Value: 15.00				
1937 Matte Proof	—	Value: 2,000				
Note: There are reportedly 1-2 known of this variety, struck specifically for use in photographs						
1938	4,798,000	—	BV	4.00	35.00	—
1938 Proof	—	Value: 650				
1939	10,264,000	—	BV	3.00	17.00	—
1939 Proof	—	Value: 600				
1940	9,913,000	—	BV	2.50	13.00	—
1940 Proof	—	Value: 600				
1941	8,086,000	—	BV	2.00	13.00	—
1941 Proof	—	Value: 600				
1942	13,677,000	—	BV	2.00	13.00	—
1942 Proof	—	Value: 600				
1943	9,824,000	—	BV	2.00	13.00	—
1943 Proof	—	Value: 650				
1944	10,990,000	—	BV	2.00	13.00	—
1944 Proof	—	Value: 650				
1945	15,106,000	—	BV	1.50	8.00	—
1945 Proof	—	Value: 750				
1946	16,382,000	—	BV	1.50	8.00	—
1946 Proof	—	Value: 750				

KM# 863 SHILLING

Copper-Nickel, 23.5 mm. **Ruler:** George VI **Obv:** Head left **Obv. Designer:** T. H. Paget **Rev:** English crest; lion atop crown dividing date **Rev. Designer:** George Krueger-Gray

Date	Mintage	F	VF	XF	Unc	BU
1947	12,121,000	0.10	0.25	1.00	10.00	—
1947 Proof	—	Value: 550				
1948	45,577,000	0.10	0.20	1.00	6.00	—
1948 Proof	—	Value: 550				

KM# 864 SHILLING

Copper-Nickel, 23.5 mm. **Ruler:** George VI **Obv:** Head left **Obv. Designer:** T. H. Paget **Rev:** Scottish crest; lion seated atop crown holding sword and scepter divides date, shields flank **Rev. Designer:** George Krueger-Gray

Date	Mintage	F	VF	XF	Unc	BU
1947	12,283,000	0.10	0.25	1.00	10.00	—
1947 Proof	—	Value: 550				
1948	45,352,000	0.10	0.20	1.00	6.00	—
1948 Proof	—	Value: 550				

KM# 876 SHILLING

Copper-Nickel, 23.5 mm. **Ruler:** George VI **Obv:** Head left **Obv. Designer:** T. H. Paget **Rev:** English crest; lion atop crown dividing date **Rev. Designer:** George Krueger-Gray

Date	Mintage	F	VF	XF	Unc	BU
1949	19,328,000	0.10	0.25	1.50	15.00	—
1949 Proof	—	Value: 600				
1950	19,244,000	0.10	0.25	1.50	19.00	—
1950 Proof	18,000	Value: 19.00				
1950 Matte Proof	—	Value: 1,500				
Note: There are reportedly 1-2 known of this variety, struck specifically for use in photographs						
1951	9,957,000	0.10	0.25	3.50	24.00	—
1951 Proof	20,000	Value: 20.00				
1951 Matte Proof	—	Value: 1,500				
Note: There are reportedly 1-2 known of this variety, struck specifically for use in photographs						
1952 Proof; Rare	—	—	—	—	—	—
Note: There are reportedly 1-2 known of this variety, struck specifically for use in photographs						

KM# 877 SHILLING

Copper-Nickel, 23.5 mm. **Ruler:** George VI **Obv:** Head left **Obv. Designer:** T. H. Paget **Rev:** Scottish crest; lion seated atop crown holding sword and scepter divides date, shields flank **Rev. Designer:** George Krueger-Gray

Date	Mintage	F	VF	XF	Unc	BU
1949	21,243,000	0.10	0.25	1.50	19.00	—
1949 Proof	—	Value: 500				
1950	14,300,000	0.10	0.25	1.50	19.00	—
1950 Proof	18,000	Value: 19.00				
1950 Matte Proof	—	Value: 1,500				
Note: There are reportedly 1-2 known of this variety, struck specifically for use in photographs						
1951	10,961,000	0.10	0.25	3.50	24.00	—
1951 Proof	20,000	Value: 18.00				
1951 Matte Proof	—	Value: 1,500				
Note: There are reportedly 1-2 known of this variety, struck specifically for use in photographs						

KM# 890 SHILLING

Copper-Nickel, 23.5 mm. **Ruler:** Elizabeth II **Obv:** Laureate bust right **Obv. Designer:** Mary Gillick **Rev:** Crowned English shield divides date **Rev. Designer:** William Gardner

Date	Mintage	F	VF	XF	Unc	BU
1953	41,943,000	—	0.15	0.50	4.50	—
1953 Proof	40,000	Value: 8.00				
1953 Matte Proof	—	Value: 1,500				
Note: There are reportedly 1-2 known of this variety, struck specifically for use in photographs						

KM# 891 SHILLING

Copper-Nickel, 23.5 mm. **Ruler:** Elizabeth II **Obv:** Laureate bust right **Obv. Designer:** Mary Gillick **Rev:** Crowned Scottish shield divides date **Rev. Designer:** William Gardner

Date	Mintage	F	VF	XF	Unc	BU
1953	20,664,000	—	0.15	0.50	5.00	—
1953 Proof	40,000	Value: 8.00				
1953 Matte Proof	—	Value: 1,500				
Note: There are reportedly 1-2 known of this variety, struck specifically for use in photographs						

KM# 904 SHILLING

Copper-Nickel, 23.5 mm. **Ruler:** Elizabeth II **Obv:** Laureate bust right **Obv. Legend:** without BRITT OMN **Obv. Designer:** Mary Gillick **Rev:** Crowned English shield divides date **Rev. Designer:** William Gardner

Date	Mintage	F	VF	XF	Unc	BU
1954	30,162,000	—	0.15	0.50	6.50	—
1954 Proof	—	Value: 500				
1955	45,260,000	—	0.15	0.50	6.50	—
1955 Proof	—	Value: 500				
1956	44,970,000	—	0.15	0.50	10.00	—
1956 Proof	—	Value: 500				
1957	42,774,000	—	0.15	0.50	5.00	—
1957 Proof	—	Value: 500				
1958	14,392,000	0.25	0.50	3.00	22.50	—
1958 Proof	—	Value: 550				
1959	19,443,000	—	0.15	0.40	4.00	—
1959 Proof	—	Value: 500				
1960	27,028,000	—	0.15	0.35	4.00	—
1960 Proof	—	Value: 500				
1961	39,817,000	—	0.15	0.35	2.50	—
1961 Proof	—	Value: 475				
1962	36,704,000	—	0.15	0.25	1.75	—
1962 Proof	—	Value: 475				
1963	49,434,000	—	—	0.25	1.25	—
1963 Proof	—	Value: 475				
1964	8,591,000	—	—	0.25	1.25	—
1964 Proof	—	—	—	—	—	—
Note: Reported, not confirmed						
1965	9,216,000	—	—	0.25	1.25	—
1965 Proof	—	—	—	—	—	—
Note: Reported, not confirmed						
1966	15,002,000	—	—	0.25	1.25	—
1966 Proof	—	—	—	—	—	—
Note: Reported, not confirmed						
1970 Proof	750,000	Value: 5.00				

KM# 905 SHILLING

Copper-Nickel, 23.5 mm. **Ruler:** Elizabeth II **Obv:** Laureate bust right **Obv. Designer:** Mary Gillick **Rev:** Crowned Scottish shield divides date **Rev. Designer:** William Gardner

Date	Mintage	F	VF	XF	Unc	BU
1954	26,772,000	—	0.15	0.25	6.50	—
1954 Proof	—	Value: 500				
1954 Matte Proof; Rare	Est. 2	—	—	—	—	—
1955	27,951,000	—	0.15	0.35	8.00	—
1955 Proof	—	Value: 500				
1956	42,854,000	—	0.15	1.00	12.00	—
1956 Proof	—	Value: 500				
1957	17,960,000	—	0.25	3.50	25.00	—
1957 Proof	—	Value: 550				
1958	40,823,000	—	0.15	0.50	3.25	—
1958 Proof	—	Value: 500				
1959	1,012,999	0.50	1.00	3.50	25.00	—
1959 Proof	—	Value: 550				
1960	14,376,000	—	0.15	0.50	5.00	—
1960 Proof	—	Value: 500				
1961	2,763,000	—	0.20	1.00	8.00	—
1961 Proof	—	Value: 500				
1962	17,475,000	—	0.15	0.25	4.50	—
1962 Proof	—	Value: 475				
1963	32,299,999	—	0.15	0.25	1.25	—
1963 Proof	—	Value: 475				
1964	5,239,000	—	0.15	0.25	2.00	—
1964 Proof	—	—	—	—	—	—
Note: Reported, not confirmed						
1965	2,774,000	—	0.15	0.25	1.75	—
1965 Proof	—	—	—	—	—	—
Note: Reported, not confirmed						
1966	15,604,000	—	0.15	0.25	1.25	—
1966 Proof	—	—	—	—	—	—
Note: Reported, not confirmed						
1970 Proof	750,000	Value: 3.00				

KM# 781 FLORIN (Two Shillings)

11.3104 g., 0.9250 Silver .3364 oz. ASW, 28.3 mm. **Ruler:** Victoria **Obv:** Veiled bust left **Obv. Designer:** Thomas Brock **Rev:** Crown above shields of England, Scotland and Ireland

Date	Mintage	F	VF	XF	Unc	BU
1901	2,649,000	6.00	12.00	60.00	125	—

KM# 801 FLORIN (Two Shillings)

11.3104 g., 0.9250 Silver .3364 oz. ASW, 28.3 mm. **Ruler:** Edward VII **Obv:** Head right **Rev:** Britannia standing looking right

Date	Mintage	F	VF	XF	Unc	BU
1902	2,190,000	8.00	20.00	60.00	120	—
1902 Matte Proof	15,000	Value: 120				
1903	995,000	10.00	28.00	90.00	400	—
1904	2,770,000	12.00	35.00	125	450	—
1905	1,188,000	75.00	150	600	1,400	—
1906	6,910,000	10.00	25.00	100	350	—
1907	5,948,000	10.00	30.00	125	375	—
1908	3,280,000	15.00	40.00	200	600	—
1909	3,483,000	15.00	40.00	150	600	—
1910	5,651,000	10.00	20.00	90.00	300	—

KM# 817 FLORIN (Two Shillings)

11.3104 g., 0.9250 Silver .3364 oz. ASW, 28.3 mm. **Ruler:** George V **Obv:** Head left **Obv. Designer:** Bertram MacKennal **Rev:** Cross of crowned shield, sceptres in angles

Date	Mintage	F	VF	XF	Unc	BU
1911	5,951,000	5.00	10.00	40.00	100	—
1911 Proof	6,007	Value: 110				
1912	8,572,000	5.00	12.00	55.00	110	—
1913	4,545,000	6.50	15.00	75.00	150	—
1914	21,253,000	BV	6.00	25.00	60.00	—
1915	12,358,000	4.75	8.00	45.00	110	—
1916	21,064,000	BV	6.00	28.00	70.00	—
1917	11,182,000	4.75	7.00	30.00	85.00	—
1918	29,212,000	BV	6.00	28.00	65.00	—
1919	9,469,000	5.00	12.00	30.00	100	—

KM# 817a FLORIN (Two Shillings)

11.3104 g., 0.5000 Silver .1818 oz. ASW, 28.3 mm. **Ruler:** George V **Obv:** Head left **Obv. Designer:** Bertram MacKennal **Rev:** Cross of crowned shields, sceptres in angles

Date	Mintage	F	VF	XF	Unc	BU
1920	15,388,000	2.75	6.00	35.00	110	—
1921	34,864,000	2.75	5.50	30.00	60.00	—
1922	23,861,000	2.65	4.50	28.00	55.00	—
1923	21,547,000	2.50	4.00	23.00	45.00	—
1924	4,582,000	3.50	7.00	45.00	85.00	—
1924 Satin specimen	2	—	—	—	—	2,000
1925	1,404,000	20.00	40.00	125	300	—
1926	5,125,000	3.00	8.50	40.00	100	—

KM# 834 FLORIN (Two Shillings)

11.3104 g., 0.5000 Silver .1818 oz. ASW, 28.3 mm. **Ruler:** George V **Obv:** Head left **Obv. Designer:** Bertram MacKennal **Rev:** Cross of crowned sceptres, shields in angles

Date	Mintage	F	VF	XF	Unc	BU
1927 Proof	15,000	Value: 75.00				
1928	11,088,000	BV	3.00	11.50	25.00	—
1928 Proof	—	Value: 700				
1929	16,397,000	BV	3.00	11.50	25.00	—
1929 Proof	—	Value: 800				
1930	5,734,000	BV	5.00	12.50	37.50	—
1930 Proof	—	Value: 1,200				
1931	6,556,000	BV	5.00	11.50	45.00	—
1931 Proof	—	Value: 700				
1932	717,000	20.00	50.00	150	600	—
1932 Proof	—	Value: 2,000				
1933	8,685,000	BV	3.00	11.50	30.00	—
1933 Proof	—	Value: 700				
1935	7,541,000	BV	3.00	11.50	25.00	—
1935 Proof	—	Value: 700				
1936	9,897,000	BV	2.75	11.50	25.00	—
1936 Proof	—	Value: 700				

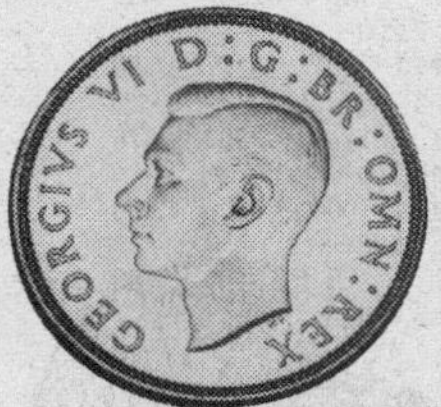

KM# 855 FLORIN (Two Shillings)

11.3104 g., 0.5000 Silver .1818 oz. ASW, 28.3 mm. **Ruler:** George VI **Obv:** Head left **Obv. Designer:** T. H. Paget **Rev:** Crowned tudor rose, thistle, letter 'G', and shamrock, letter 'R' flanking **Rev. Designer:** George Krueger-Gray

Date	Mintage	F	VF	XF	Unc	BU
1937	13,007,000	—	BV	3.00	13.00	—
1937 Proof	26,000	Value: 18.00				
1937 Matte Proof; Rare	—	—	—	—	—	—

Note: There are reportedly 1-2 known of this variety, struck specifically for use in photographs

Date	Mintage	F	VF	XF	Unc	BU
1938	7,909,000	BV	2.75	10.00	30.00	—
1938 Proof	—	Value: 550				
1939	20,851,000	—	BV	4.50	12.00	—
1939 Proof	—	Value: 500				
1940	18,700,000	—	BV	4.50	12.00	—
1940 Proof	—	Value: 500				
1941	24,451,000	—	BV	4.50	12.00	—
1941 Proof	—	Value: 500				
1942	39,895,000	—	BV	3.00	10.00	—
1942 Proof	—	Value: 500				
1943	26,712,000	—	BV	3.00	10.00	—
1943 Proof	—	Value: 500				
1944	27,560,000	—	BV	3.00	10.00	—
1944 Proof	—	Value: 600				
1945	25,858,000	—	BV	3.00	10.00	—
1945 Proof	—	Value: 700				
1946	22,300,000	—	BV	3.00	10.00	—
1946 Proof	—	Value: 700				

KM# 865 FLORIN (Two Shillings)

Copper-Nickel, 28.3 mm. **Ruler:** George VI **Obv:** Head left **Obv. Designer:** T. H. Paget **Rev:** Crowned tudor rose, thistle, letter 'G', and shamrock, letter 'R' flanking **Rev. Designer:** George Krueger-Gray

Date	Mintage	F	VF	XF	Unc	BU
1947	22,910,000	0.20	0.35	1.00	10.00	—
1947 Proof	—	Value: 450				
1948	67,554,000	0.20	0.35	1.00	10.00	—
1948 Proof	—	Value: 450				

KM# 878 FLORIN (Two Shillings)

Copper-Nickel, 28.3 mm. **Ruler:** George VI **Obv:** Head left **Obv. Legend:** without IND IMP **Obv. Designer:** T. H. Paget **Rev:** Crowned tudor rose, thistle, letter 'G', and shamrock, letter 'R' flanking **Rev. Designer:** George Krueger-Gray

Date	Mintage	F	VF	XF	Unc	BU
1949	28,615,000	0.20	0.35	1.00	18.00	—
1949 Proof	—	Value: 450				
1950	24,357,000	0.20	0.35	1.00	20.00	—
1950 Proof	18,000	Value: 25.00				
1950 Matte Proof; Rare	—	—	—	—	—	—

Note: There are reportedly 1-2 known of this variety, struck specifically for use in photographs

Date	Mintage	F	VF	XF	Unc	BU
1951	27,412,000	0.20	0.75	4.00	25.00	—
1951 Proof	20,000	Value: 30.00				
1951 Matte Proof; Rare	—	—	—	—	—	—

Note: There are reportedly 1-2 known of this variety, struck specifically for use in photographs

KM# 892 FLORIN (Two Shillings)

Copper-Nickel, 28.3 mm. **Ruler:** Elizabeth II **Obv:** Laureate bust right **Obv. Designer:** Mary Gillick **Rev:** Tudor rose at center, thistle and shamrock wreath surround **Rev. Designer:** F. G. Fuller and Cecil Thomas

Date	Mintage	F	VF	XF	Unc	BU
1953	11,959,000	0.25	0.50	1.00	8.00	—
1953 Proof	40,000	Value: 10.00				
1953 Matte Proof; Rare	—	—	—	—	—	—

Note: There are reportedly 1-2 known of this variety, struck specifically for use in photographs

KM# 906 FLORIN (Two Shillings)

Copper-Nickel, 28.3 mm. **Ruler:** Elizabeth II **Obv:** Laureate bust right **Obv. Legend:** without BRITT OMN **Obv. Designer:** Mary Gillick **Rev:** Tudor rose at center, thistle and shamrock wreath surround **Rev. Designer:** F. G. Fuller and Cecil Thomas

Date	Mintage	F	VF	XF	Unc	BU
1954	13,085,000	0.20	0.50	5.50	45.00	—
1954 Proof	—	Value: 450				
1955	25,887,000	0.20	0.50	2.00	6.00	—
1955 Proof	—	Value: 425				
1956	47,824,000	0.20	0.30	1.00	6.00	—
1956 Proof	—	Value: 400				
1957	33,070,999	0.20	0.40	5.00	45.00	—
1957 Proof	—	Value: 525				
1958	9,565,000	0.25	1.25	5.00	30.00	—
1958 Proof	—	Value: 525				
1959	14,080,000	0.25	0.50	5.00	40.00	—
1959 Proof	—	Value: 450				
1960	13,832,000	—	0.20	1.25	6.00	—
1960 Proof	—	Value: 400				
1961	37,735,000	—	0.20	1.00	5.00	—
1961 Proof	—	Value: 400				
1962	35,148,000	—	0.20	0.75	5.00	—
1962 Proof	—	Value: 400				
1963	26,471,000	—	0.20	0.75	5.00	—
1963 Proof	—	Value: 400				
1964	16,539,000	—	0.20	0.50	5.00	—
1965	48,163,000	—	0.20	0.50	4.50	—
1966	83,999,000	—	0.20	0.30	2.50	—
1967	39,718,000	—	0.20	0.30	2.00	—
1970 Proof	750,000	Value: 6.50				

KM# 782 1/2 CROWN

14.1380 g., 0.9250 Silver .4205 oz. ASW, 32.3 mm. **Ruler:** Victoria **Obv:** Veiled bust left **Obv. Designer:** Thomas Brock **Rev:** Crowned and quartered spade shield within wreath

Date	Mintage	F	VF	XF	Unc	BU
1901	1,577,000	16.00	27.00	65.00	150	—

KM# 802 1/2 CROWN

14.1380 g., 0.9250 Silver .4205 oz. ASW, 32.3 mm. **Ruler:** Edward VII **Obv:** Head right **Rev:** Crowned and quartered shield within Garter band **Note:** Particular attention should be given to quality of detail in hair and beard on obverse.

Date	Mintage	F	VF	XF	Unc	BU
1902	1,316,000	15.00	35.00	60.00	150	—
1902 Matte Proof	15,000	Value: 160				
1903	275,000	65.00	250	725	2,500	—
1904	710,000	50.00	200	450	1,800	—
1905	166,000	175	450	1,200	4,500	—
1906	2,886,000	20.00	45.00	200	650	—
1907	3,694,000	20.00	45.00	200	700	—
1908	1,759,000	25.00	50.00	325	1,100	—
1909	3,052,000	20.00	45.00	275	825	—
1910	2,558,000	15.00	35.00	175	500	—

KM# 818.1 1/2 CROWN

14.1380 g., 0.9250 Silver .4205 oz. ASW, 32.3 mm. **Ruler:** George V **Obv:** Head left **Obv. Designer:** Bertram MacKennal **Rev:** Crowned and quartered shield within Garter band **Note:** Fully struck World War I (1914-1918) specimens command a premium.

Date	Mintage	F	VF	XF	Unc	BU
1911	2,915,000	6.00	18.00	40.00	125	—
1911 Proof	6,007	Value: 125				
1912	4,701,000	7.00	25.00	65.00	150	—
1913	4,090,000	8.50	30.00	75.00	150	—
1914	18,333,000	BV	10.00	28.00	65.00	—
1915	32,433,000	BV	10.00	28.00	65.00	—
1916	29,530,000	BV	10.00	28.00	65.00	—
1917	11,172,000	6.00	15.00	45.00	85.00	—
1918	29,080,000	BV	10.00	28.00	65.00	—
1919	10,267,000	6.00	15.00	45.00	85.00	—

KM# 818.1a 1/2 CROWN

14.1380 g., 0.5000 Silver .2273 oz. ASW, 32.3 mm. **Ruler:** George V **Obv:** Head left **Obv. Designer:** Bertram MacKennal **Rev:** Crowned shield within Garter rose, crown touches shield **Note:** Fully struck coins command a premium.

Date	Mintage	F	VF	XF	Unc	BU
1920	17,983,000	5.00	8.00	25.00	75.00	—
1921	23,678,000	6.00	10.00	30.00	85.00	—
1922	16,396,999	5.50	8.00	35.00	100	—

KM# 818.2 1/2 CROWN

14.1380 g., 0.5000 Silver .2273 oz. ASW, 32.3 mm. **Ruler:** George V **Obv:** Head left **Obv. Designer:** Bertram MacKennal **Rev:** Crowned shield within Garter band, groove between crown and shield **Note:** Fully struck coins command a premium.

Date	Mintage	F	VF	XF	Unc	BU
1922	Inc. above	4.00	8.00	25.00	100	—
1923	26,309,000	3.50	5.00	15.00	50.00	—
1924	5,866,000	6.00	10.00	35.00	100	—
1924	2	—	—	—	—	3,500

Note: Satin specimen

Date	Mintage	F	VF	XF	Unc	BU
1925	1,413,000	23.00	50.00	175	550	—
1926	4,474,000	5.00	10.00	35.00	150	—

KM# 830 1/2 CROWN
14.1380 g., 0.5000 Silver .2273 oz. ASW, 32.3 mm. **Ruler:** George V **Obv:** Modified head left, larger beads **Obv. Designer:** Bertram MacKennal **Rev:** Crowned shield within Garter band

Date	Mintage	F	VF	XF	Unc	BU
1926	Inc. above	5.00	10.00	45.00	125	—
1927	6,838,000	4.50	7.00	28.00	70.00	—

KM# 835 1/2 CROWN
14.1380 g., 0.5000 Silver .2273 oz. ASW, 32.3 mm. **Ruler:** George V **Obv:** Head left **Obv. Designer:** Bertram MacKennal **Rev:** Quartered shield flanked by crowned monograms

Date	Mintage	F	VF	XF	Unc	BU
1927 Proof	15,000	Value: 60.00				
1927 Matte Proof; Rare	—	—	—	—	—	—

Note: There are reportedly 1-2 known of this variety, struck specifically for use in photographs

Date	Mintage	F	VF	XF	Unc	BU
1928	18,763,000	BV	5.00	11.00	35.00	—
1928 Proof	—	Value: 700				
1929	17,633,000	BV	5.00	11.00	35.00	—
1929 Proof	—	Value: 700				
1930	810,000	10.00	25.00	100	550	—
1930 Proof	—	Value: 1,200				
1931	11,264,000	BV	5.00	11.00	35.00	—
1931 Proof	—	Value: 700				
1932	4,794,000	4.00	8.00	17.50	75.00	—
1932 Proof	—	Value: 850				
1933	10,311,000	BV	5.00	11.00	35.00	—
1933 Proof	—	Value: 700				
1934	2,422,000	4.50	10.00	25.00	100	—
1934 Proof	—	Value: 850				
1935	7,022,000	BV	5.00	11.00	28.00	—
1935 Proof	—	Value: 700				
1936	7,039,000	BV	3.25	9.00	25.00	—
1936 Proof	—	Value: 700				

KM# 856 1/2 CROWN
14.1380 g., 0.5000 Silver .2273 oz. ASW, 32.3 mm. **Ruler:** George VI **Obv:** Head left **Obv. Designer:** T. H. Paget **Rev:** Quartered shield flanked by crowned monograms **Rev. Designer:** George Krueger-Gray

Date	Mintage	F	VF	XF	Unc	BU
1937	9,106,000	—	BV	4.50	19.00	—
1937 Proof	26,000	Value: 20.00				
1937 Matte Proof; Rare	—	—	—	—	—	—

Note: There are reportedly 1-2 known of this variety, struck specifically for use in photographs

Date	Mintage	F	VF	XF	Unc	BU
1938	6,426,000	—	BV	10.00	35.00	—
1938 Proof	—	Value: 850				
1939	15,479,000	—	BV	5.50	19.00	—
1939 Proof	—	Value: 650				
1940	17,948,000	—	BV	5.50	19.00	—
1940 Proof	—	Value: 650				
1941	15,774,000	—	BV	5.50	19.00	—
1941 Proof	—	Value: 600				
1942	31,220,000	—	BV	3.50	10.00	—
1942 Proof	—	Value: 600				
1943	15,463,000	—	BV	3.50	19.00	—
1943 Proof	—	Value: 600				
1944	15,255,000	—	BV	3.50	10.00	—
1944 Proof	—	Value: 700				
1945	19,849,000	—	BV	3.50	10.00	—
1945 Proof	—	Value: 800				
1946	22,725,000	—	BV	3.50	10.00	—
1946 Proof	—	Value: 800				

KM# 866 1/2 CROWN
Copper-Nickel, 32.3 mm. **Ruler:** George VI **Obv:** Head left **Obv. Designer:** T. H. Paget **Rev:** Quartered shield flanked by crowned monograms **Rev. Designer:** George Krueger-Gray

Date	Mintage	F	VF	XF	Unc	BU
1947	21,910,000	0.25	0.50	1.00	10.00	—
1947 Proof	—	Value: 600				
1948	71,165,000	0.25	0.50	1.00	10.00	—
1948 Proof	—	Value: 650				

KM# 879 1/2 CROWN
Copper-Nickel, 32.3 mm. **Ruler:** George VI **Obv:** Head left **Obv. Designer:** T. H. Paget **Rev:** Quartered shield flanked by crowned monograms **Rev. Legend:** without IND IMP **Rev. Designer:** George Krueger-Gray

Date	Mintage	F	VF	XF	Unc	BU
1949	28,273,000	0.25	0.50	1.25	10.00	—
1949 Proof	—	Value: 600				
1950	28,336,000	0.25	0.50	3.00	22.50	—
1950 Proof	18,000	Value: 25.00				
1950 Matte Proof; Rare	—	—	—	—	—	—

Note: There are reportedly 1-2 known of this variety, struck specifically for use in photographs

Date	Mintage	F	VF	XF	Unc	BU
1951	9,004,000	0.50	0.75	1.50	35.00	—
1951 Proof	20,000	Value: 30.00				
1951 Matte Proof; Rare	—	—	—	—	—	—

Note: There are reportedly 1-2 known of this variety, struck specifically for use in photographs

Date	Mintage	F	VF	XF	Unc	BU
1952	Est. 1	—	40,000	—	—	—
1952 Proof	Est. 1	Value: 60,000				

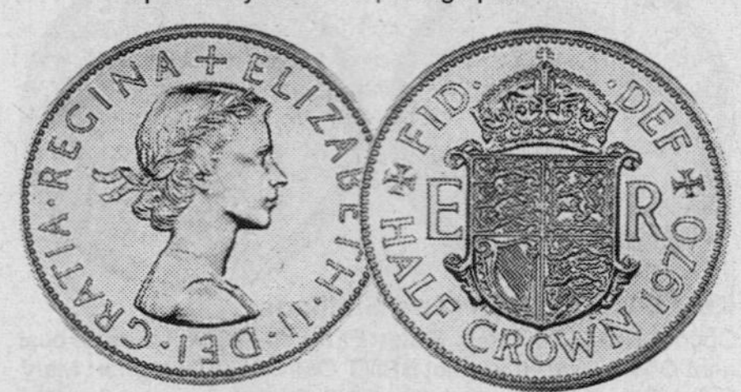

KM# 893 1/2 CROWN
Copper-Nickel, 32.3 mm. **Ruler:** Elizabeth II **Obv:** Laureate bust right **Obv. Designer:** Mary Gillick **Rev:** Crowned quartered shield flanked by initials, 'ER' **Rev. Designer:** F. G. Fuller and Cecil Thomas

Date	Mintage	F	VF	XF	Unc	BU
1953	4,333,000	0.50	0.75	1.75	10.50	—
1953 Proof	40,000	Value: 15.00				
1953 Matte Proof; Rare	—	—	—	—	—	—

Note: There are reportedly 1-2 known of this variety, struck specifically for use in photographs

KM# 907 1/2 CROWN
Copper-Nickel, 32.3 mm. **Ruler:** Elizabeth II **Obv:** Laureate bust right **Obv. Legend:** without BRITT OMN **Obv. Designer:** Mary Gillick **Rev:** Crowned quartered shield flanked by initials, 'ER' **Rev. Designer:** F. G. Fuller and Cecil Thomas

Date	Mintage	F	VF	XF	Unc	BU
1954	11,615,000	0.50	0.75	4.00	30.00	—
1954 Proof	—	Value: 500				
1955	23,629,000	0.25	0.50	1.00	10.00	—
1955 Proof	—	Value: 500				
1956	33,935,000	0.25	0.50	0.75	13.00	—
1956 Proof	—	Value: 500				
1957	34,201,000	0.25	0.50	0.75	5.50	—
1957 Proof	—	Value: 500				
1958	15,746,000	0.25	0.75	3.50	20.00	—
1958 Proof	—	Value: 600				
1959	9,029,000	0.75	1.25	6.00	35.00	—
1959 Proof	—	Value: 600				
1960	19,929,000	0.25	0.50	0.75	7.00	—
1960 Proof	—	Value: 600				
1961	25,888,000	0.25	0.50	0.75	5.00	—
1961 Prooflike	—	—	—	—	15.00	—
1961 Proof	—	—	—	—	—	—
1962	24,013,000	0.25	0.50	0.75	5.00	—
1962 Proof	—	—	—	—	—	—
1963	17,625,000	0.25	0.50	0.75	5.00	—
1963 Proof	—	—	—	—	—	—
1964	5,974,000	0.25	0.50	0.75	6.00	—
1965	9,778,000	0.20	0.30	0.50	5.00	—
1966	13,375,000	0.20	0.30	0.50	1.50	—
1967	33,058,000	0.20	0.30	0.50	1.50	—
1970 Proof	750,000	Value: 6.50				

KM# 803 CROWN
28.2759 g., 0.9250 Silver .8409 oz. ASW, 38.5 mm. **Ruler:** Edward VII **Obv:** Head right **Rev:** St. George slaying the dragon

Date	Mintage	F	VF	XF	Unc	BU
1902	256,000	50.00	75.00	125	250	—
1902 Matte Proof	15,000	Value: 250				

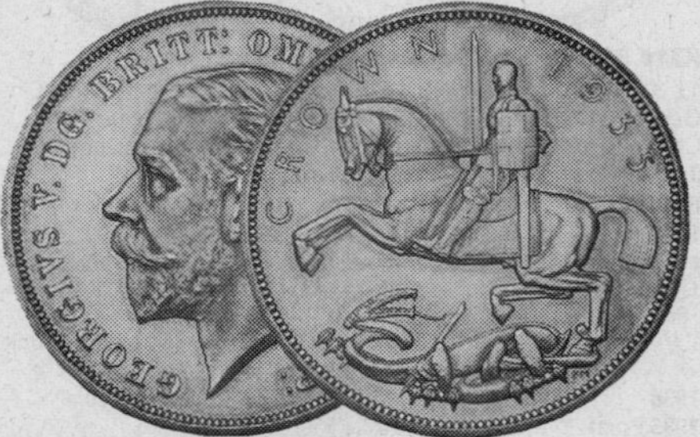

KM# 836 CROWN
28.2759 g., 0.5000 Silver .4546 oz. ASW, 38.5 mm. **Ruler:** George V **Obv:** Head left **Obv. Designer:** Bertram MacKennal **Rev:** Date divided above crown within wreath

Date	Mintage	F	VF	XF	Unc	BU
1927 Proof	15,000	Value: 275				
1928	9,034	50.00	125	200	350	—
1928 Proof	—	Value: 2,500				
1929	4,994	60.00	125	200	375	—
1929 Proof	—	Value: 2,500				
1930	4,847	70.00	125	225	375	—
1930 Proof	—	Value: 2,400				
1931	4,056	70.00	150	250	400	—
1931 Proof	—	Value: 2,200				
1932	2,395	100	200	325	750	—
1932 Proof	—	Value: 3,000				
1933	7,132	60.00	125	200	375	—
1933 Proof	—	Value: 2,200				
1934	932	700	100	1,800	4,000	—
1934 Proof	—	Value: 5,000				
1936	2,473	100	200	325	750	—
1936 Proof	—	Value: 3,000				

KM# 842 CROWN
28.2759 g., 0.5000 Silver .4546 oz. ASW, 38.5 mm. **Ruler:** George V **Subject:** Silver Jubilee **Obv:** Head left **Obv. Designer:** Bertram MacKennal **Rev:** St. George slaying the dragon **Rev. Designer:** Percy Metcalfe

Date	Mintage	F	VF	XF	Unc	BU
1935	715,000	10.00	15.00	20.00	50.00	—

Note: Incused edge lettering

Date	Mintage	F	VF	XF	Unc	BU
1935 Proof	—	Value: 1,500				
1935	—	—	—	—	85.00	—

Note: Specimen in box of issue

Date	Mintage	F	VF	XF	Unc	BU
1935	Inc. above	—	250	500	1,000	—

Note: (Error) Edge lettering: MEN.ANNO-REGNIXXV

KM# 842a CROWN
0.9250 Silver, 38.5 mm. **Ruler:** George V **Subject:** Silver Jubilee **Obv:** Head left **Obv. Designer:** Bertram MacKennal **Rev:** St. George slaying the dragon

Date	Mintage	F	VF	XF	Unc	BU
1935	2,500	Value: 400				

Note: Raised edge lettering

Date	Mintage	F	VF	XF	Unc	BU
1935 Proof	—	Value: 1,500				

Note: (Error) Edge lettering: DECUS ANNO REGNI TUTAMEN•XXV•

KM# 842b CROWN
47.8300 g., 0.9170 Gold 1.4096 oz. AGW, 38.5 mm. **Ruler:** George V **Subject:** Silver Jubilee **Obv:** Head left **Rev:** St. George slaying the dragon

Date	Mintage	F	VF	XF	Unc	BU
1935 Proof	28	Value: 14,500				

KM# 857 CROWN
0.5000 Silver, 38.5 mm. **Ruler:** George VI **Obv:** Head left **Obv. Designer:** T. H. Paget **Rev:** Crowned, quartered shield with supporters **Rev. Designer:** George Krueger-Gray

Date	Mintage	F	VF	XF	Unc	BU
1937	419,000	8.00	12.00	25.00	50.00	—
1937 Proof	26,000	Value: 60.00				
1937 Proof	—	Value: 600				

Note: Frosted cameo relief; V.I.P. issue

Date	Mintage	F	VF	XF	Unc	BU
1937 Matte Proof; Rare	—	—	—	—	—	—

Note: 1-2 pieces known

KM# 880 CROWN
Copper-Nickel, 38.5 mm. **Ruler:** George VI **Subject:** Festival of Britain **Obv:** Head left **Obv. Designer:** T. H. Paget **Rev:** St. George slaying the dragon **Rev. Designer:** Pistrucci

Date	Mintage	F	VF	XF	Unc	BU
1951 Prooflike	2,004,000	—	—	—	22.50	—
1951 Proof	—	Value: 25.00				
1951 Proof	—	Value: 650				

Note: Frosted cameo relief; V.I.P. issue; 30-50 pieces known

Date	Mintage	F	VF	XF	Unc	BU
1951 Matte Proof	—	Value: 3,000				

Note: 1-2 pieces known

KM# 894 CROWN
Copper-Nickel, 38.5 mm. **Ruler:** Elizabeth II **Subject:** Coronation of Queen Elizabeth II **Obv:** Queen on horseback left, crowned monograms flank **Obv. Designer:** Gilbert Ledward **Rev:** Crown at center of cross formed by Rose, shamrock, leek and thistle, shields in angles **Rev. Designer:** F. G. Fuller and Cecil Thomas **Edge Lettering:** FAITH AND TRUTH I WILL BEAR UNTO YOU

Date	Mintage	F	VF	XF	Unc	BU
1953	5,963,000	—	—	7.50	15.00	—
1953 Proof	40,000	Value: 45.00				
1953 Proof	—	Value: 550				

Note: 20-30 pieces; V.I.P. issue

Date	Mintage	F	VF	XF	Unc	BU
1953 Matte Proof	—	Value: 3,000				

Note: 1-2 pieces

KM# 909 CROWN
Copper-Nickel, 38.5 mm. **Ruler:** Elizabeth II **Subject:** British Exhibition in New York **Obv:** Laureate bust right **Obv. Designer:** Mary Gillick **Rev:** Crown at center of cross formed by Rose, shamrock, leek and thistle, shields in angles **Rev. Designer:** F. G. Fuller and Cecil Thomas

Date	Mintage	F	VF	XF	Unc	BU
1960	1,024,000	—	—	6.00	12.00	—
1960 Prooflike	70,000	—	—	—	35.00	—
1960 Proof	—	Value: 600				

Note: V.I.P. issue; 30-50 pieces

KM# 910 CROWN
Copper-Nickel, 38.5 mm. **Ruler:** Elizabeth II **Subject:** Winston Churchill **Obv:** Laureate bust right **Obv. Designer:** Mary Gillick **Rev:** Head right **Rev. Designer:** Oscar Neman

Date	Mintage	F	VF	XF	Unc	BU
1965	9,640,000	—	—	0.65	2.00	—
1965 Specimen	—	—	—	—	850	—

Note: Satin finish

SOVEREIGN COINAGE

KM# 784 1/2 SOVEREIGN
3.9940 g., 0.9170 Gold .1177 oz. AGW **Ruler:** Victoria **Obv:** Veiled bust left **Obv. Designer:** Thomas Brock **Rev:** St. George slaying the dragon

Date	Mintage	F	VF	XF	Unc	BU
1901	2,037,999	—	BV	90.00	150	—

KM# 804 1/2 SOVEREIGN
3.9940 g., 0.9170 Gold .1177 oz. AGW **Ruler:** Edward VII **Obv:** Head right **Rev:** St. George slaying the dragon

Date	Mintage	F	VF	XF	Unc	BU
1902	4,244,000	—	80.00	90.00	120	—
1902 Proof	15,000	Value: 225				
1903	2,522,000	—	BV	90.00	120	—
1904	1,717,000	—	BV	90.00	120	—
1905	3,024,000	—	BV	90.00	120	—
1906	4,245,000	—	BV	90.00	120	—
1907	4,233,000	—	BV	90.00	120	—
1908	3,997,000	—	BV	90.00	120	—
1909	4,011,000	—	BV	90.00	120	—
1910	5,024,000	—	BV	90.00	120	—

KM# 819 1/2 SOVEREIGN
3.9940 g., 0.9170 Gold .1177 oz. AGW **Ruler:** George V **Obv:** Head left **Obv. Designer:** Bertram MacKennal **Rev:** St. George slaying the dragon

Date	Mintage	F	VF	XF	Unc	BU
1911	6,104,000	—	BV	90.00	120	—
1911 Proof	3,764	Value: 350				
1912	6,224,000	—	BV	90.00	120	—
1913	6,094,000	—	BV	90.00	120	—
1914	7,251,000	—	BV	90.00	120	—
1915	2,043,000	—	BV	90.00	120	—

KM# 858 1/2 SOVEREIGN
3.9940 g., 0.9170 Gold .1177 oz. AGW **Ruler:** George VI **Obv:** Head left **Obv. Designer:** T. H. Paget **Rev:** St. George slaying the dragon

Date	Mintage	F	VF	XF	Unc	BU
1937 Proof	5,500	Value: 400				
1937 Matte Proof; Unique	—	—	—	—	—	—

KM# 922 1/2 SOVEREIGN
3.9900 g., 0.9170 Gold .1176 oz. AGW **Ruler:** Elizabeth II **Obv:** Young bust right **Obv. Designer:** Arnold Machin **Rev:** St. George slaying the dragon

Date	Mintage	F	VF	XF	Unc	BU
1980 Proof	10,000	Value: 110				
1982	2,500,000	—	—	—	90.00	—
1982 Proof	23,000	Value: 100				
1983 Proof	22,000	Value: 100				
1984 Proof	22,000	Value: 100				

KM# 942 1/2 SOVEREIGN

3.9900 g., 0.9170 Gold .1176 oz. AGW **Ruler:** Elizabeth II **Obv:** Crowned head right **Obv. Designer:** Raphael Maklouf **Rev:** St. George slaying the dragon

Date	Mintage	F	VF	XF	Unc	BU
1985 Proof	25,000	Value: 100				
1986 Proof	25,000	Value: 100				
1987 Proof	23,000	Value: 100				
1988 Proof	Est. 23,000	Value: 100				
1990 Proof	Est. 20,000	Value: 125				
1991 Proof	Est. 9,000	Value: 125				
1992 Proof	7,500	Value: 150				
1993 Proof	7,500	Value: 150				
1994 Proof	Est. 7,500	Value: 150				
1995 Proof	4,900	Value: 150				
1996 Proof	5,730	Value: 150				
1997 Proof	7,500	Value: 150				

KM# 955 1/2 SOVEREIGN

3.9900 g., 0.9170 Gold .1176 oz. AGW **Ruler:** Elizabeth II **Subject:** 500th Anniversary of the Gold Sovereign **Obv:** Elizabeth II seated on the Coronation throne **Rev:** Crowned and quartered shield on tudor rose **Designer:** Bernard R. Sindall

Date	Mintage	F	VF	XF	Unc	BU
ND(1989) Proof	Est. 25,000	Value: 200				

KM# 1001 1/2 SOVEREIGN

3.9900 g., 0.9170 Gold .1176 oz. AGW **Ruler:** Elizabeth II **Obv:** Head with tiara right **Obv. Designer:** Ian Rank-Broadley **Rev:** St. George slaying the dragon

Date	Mintage	F	VF	XF	Unc	BU
1998 Proof	6,144	Value: 150				
1999 Proof	7,500	Value: 175				
2000	146,542	—	—	—	90.00	—
2000 Proof	7,500	Value: 150				

KM# 785 SOVEREIGN

7.9881 g., 0.9170 Gold .2354 oz. AGW **Ruler:** Victoria **Obv:** Veiled bust left **Obv. Designer:** Thomas Brock **Rev:** St. George slaying the dragon

Date	Mintage	F	VF	XF	Unc	BU
1901	1,579,000	—	—	BV	175	—

KM# 805 SOVEREIGN

7.9881 g., 0.9170 Gold .2354 oz. AGW **Ruler:** Edward VII **Obv:** Head right **Rev:** St. George slaying the dragon

Date	Mintage	F	VF	XF	Unc	BU
1902	4,738,000	—	—	BV	170	—
1902 Proof	15,000	Value: 350				
1903	8,889,000	—	—	BV	170	—
1904	10,041,000	—	—	BV	170	—
1905	5,910,000	—	—	BV	170	—
1906	10,467,000	—	—	BV	170	—
1907	18,459,000	—	—	BV	170	—
1908	11,729,000	—	—	BV	170	—
1909	12,157,000	—	—	BV	170	—
1910	22,380,000	—	—	BV	170	—

KM# 820 SOVEREIGN

7.9881 g., 0.9170 Gold .2354 oz. AGW **Ruler:** George V **Obv:** Head left **Obv. Designer:** Bertram MacKennal **Rev:** St. George slaying the dragon

Date	Mintage	F	VF	XF	Unc	BU
1911	30,044,000	—	—	BV	170	—
1911 Proof	3,764	Value: 800				
1912	30,318,000	—	—	BV	170	—
1913	24,540,000	—	—	BV	170	—
1914	11,501,000	—	—	BV	170	—
1915	20,295,000	—	—	BV	170	—
1916	1,554,000	—	—	BV	185	—
1917	1,014,999	3,000	3,500	6,500	12,000	—
1925	4,406,000	—	—	BV	170	—

KM# 859 SOVEREIGN

7.9881 g., 0.9170 Gold .2354 oz. AGW **Ruler:** George VI **Obv:** Head left **Obv. Designer:** T. H. Paget **Rev:** St. George slaying the dragon

Date	Mintage	F	VF	XF	Unc	BU
1937 Proof	5,500	Value: 2,000				
1937 Matte Proof; Unique	—	—	—	—	—	—

KM# 908 SOVEREIGN

7.9881 g., 0.9170 Gold .2354 oz. AGW **Ruler:** Elizabeth II **Obv:** Laureate bust right **Obv. Designer:** Mary Gillick **Rev:** St. George slaying the dragon

Date	Mintage	F	VF	XF	Unc	BU
1957	2,072,000	—	—	BV	165	—
1957 Proof	—	—	—	—	—	—
1958	8,700,000	—	—	BV	165	—
1958 Proof	—	—	—	—	—	—
1959	1,358,000	—	—	BV	165	—
1959 Proof	—	—	—	—	—	—
1962	3,000,000	—	—	BV	165	—
1962 Proof	—	—	—	—	—	—
1963	7,400,000	—	—	BV	165	—
1963 Proof	—	—	—	—	—	—
1964	3,000,000	—	—	BV	165	—
1965	3,800,000	—	—	BV	165	—
1966	7,050,000	—	—	BV	165	—
1967	5,000,000	—	—	BV	165	—
1968	4,203,000	—	—	BV	165	—

KM# 919 SOVEREIGN

7.9881 g., 0.9170 Gold .2354 oz. AGW **Ruler:** Elizabeth II **Obv:** Young bust right **Obv. Designer:** Arnold Machin **Rev:** St. George slaying the dragon

Date	Mintage	F	VF	XF	Unc	BU
1974	5,003,000	—	—	BV	165	—
1976	4,150,000	—	—	BV	165	—
1978	6,550,000	—	—	BV	165	—
1979	9,100,000	—	—	BV	165	—
1979 Proof	50,000	Value: 175				
1980	5,100,000	—	—	BV	165	—
1980 Proof	91,000	Value: 175				
1981	5,000,000	—	—	BV	165	—
1981 Proof	33,000	Value: 175				
1982	2,950,000	—	—	BV	165	—
1982 Proof	23,000	Value: 175				
1983 Proof	21,000	Value: 175				
1984 Proof	20,000	Value: 175				

KM# 943 SOVEREIGN

7.9881 g., 0.9170 Gold .2354 oz. AGW **Ruler:** Elizabeth II **Obv:** Crowned head right **Obv. Designer:** Raphael Maklouf **Rev:** St. George slaying the dragon

Date	Mintage	F	VF	XF	Unc	BU
1985 Proof	17,000	Value: 225				
1986 Proof	25,000	Value: 225				
1987 Proof	22,000	Value: 225				
1988 Proof	Est. 25,000	Value: 225				
1990 Proof	Est. 20,000	Value: 225				
1991 Proof	Est. 9,000	Value: 250				
1992 Proof	7,500	Value: 250				
1993 Proof	7,500	Value: 250				
1994 Proof	Est. 7,500	Value: 250				
1995 Proof	7,500	Value: 250				
1996 Proof	7,500	Value: 250				
1997 Proof	7,500	Value: 250				

KM# 956 SOVEREIGN

7.9881 g., 0.9170 Gold .2354 oz. AGW **Ruler:** Elizabeth II **Subject:** 500th Anniversary of the Gold Sovereign **Obv:** Elizabeth II seated on coronation throne **Rev:** Crowned and quartered shield on tudor rose **Designer:** Bernard R. Sindall

Date	Mintage	F	VF	XF	Unc	BU
ND(1989) Proof	Est. 28,000	Value: 300				

KM# 1002 SOVEREIGN

7.9881 g., 0.9170 Gold .2354 oz. AGW **Ruler:** Elizabeth II **Obv:** Head with tiara right **Obv. Designer:** Ian Rank-Broadley **Rev:** St. George slaying the dragon

Date	Mintage	F	VF	XF	Unc	BU
1998 Proof	10,000	Value: 250				
1999 Proof	10,000	Value: 350				
2000	129,069	—	—	—	200	—
2000 Proof	10,000	Value: 225				

KM# 806 2 POUNDS

15.9761 g., 0.9170 Gold .4708 oz. AGW **Ruler:** Edward VII **Obv:** Head right **Rev:** St. George slaying the dragon

Date	Mintage	F	VF	XF	Unc	BU
1902	46,000	BV	325	400	700	—
1902 Proof	8,066	Value: 750				

Note: Proof issues with mint mark S below right rear hoof of horse were struck at Sydney, refer to Australia listings

KM# 821 2 POUNDS

15.9761 g., 0.9170 Gold .4708 oz. AGW **Ruler:** George V **Obv:** Head left **Obv. Designer:** Bertram MacKennal **Rev:** St. George slaying the dragon

Date	Mintage	F	VF	XF	Unc	BU
1911 Proof	2,812	Value: 1,100				

KM# 860 2 POUNDS

15.9761 g., 0.9170 Gold .4708 oz. AGW **Ruler:** George VI **Obv:** Head left **Obv. Designer:** T. H. Paget **Rev:** St. George slaying the dragon

Date	Mintage	F	VF	XF	Unc	BU
1937 Proof	5,500	Value: 1,100				
1937 Matte Proof; Unique	—	—	—	—	—	—

KM# 923 2 POUNDS

15.9200 g., 0.9170 Gold .4694 oz. AGW **Ruler:** Elizabeth II **Obv:** Young bust right **Obv. Designer:** Arnold Machin

Date	Mintage	F	VF	XF	Unc	BU
1980 Proof	10,000	Value: 350				
1982 Proof	2,500	Value: 350				
1983 Proof	13,000	Value: 325				

KM# 944 2 POUNDS
15.9200 g., 0.9170 Gold .4694 oz. AGW **Ruler:** Elizabeth II **Obv:** Crowned head right **Obv. Designer:** Raphael Maklouf **Rev:** St. George slaying the dragon

Date	Mintage	F	VF	XF	Unc	BU
1985 Proof	5,849	Value: 350				
1987 Proof	14,000	Value: 350				
1988 Proof	15,000	Value: 350				
1990 Proof	Est. 12,000	Value: 375				
1991 Proof	Est. 5,000	Value: 375				
1992 Proof	3,000	Value: 375				
1993 Proof	3,000	Value: 375				
1999 Proof	—	Value: 500				

KM# 957 2 POUNDS
15.9800 g., 0.9170 Gold .4708 oz. AGW **Ruler:** Elizabeth II **Subject:** 500th Anniversary of the Gold Sovereign **Obv:** Elizabeth II seated on Coronation throne **Rev:** Crowned and quartered shield on tudor rose **Designer:** Bernard R. Sindall

Date	Mintage	F	VF	XF	Unc	BU
ND(1989) Proof	Est. 17,000	Value: 350				

KM# 807 5 POUNDS
39.9403 g., 0.9170 Gold 1.1773 oz. AGW **Ruler:** Edward VII **Obv:** Head right **Rev:** St. George slaying the dragon

Date	Mintage	F	VF	XF	Unc	BU
1902	Est. 35,000	—	BV	800	1,500	—
Note: 27,000 pieces were melted						
1902 Proof	8,066	Value: 1,400				
Note: Proof issues with mint mark S below right rear hoof of horse were struck at Sydney, refer to Australia listings						

KM# 822 5 POUNDS
39.9403 g., 0.9170 Gold 1.1773 oz. AGW **Ruler:** George V **Obv:** Head left **Obv. Designer:** Bertram MacKennal **Rev:** St. George slaying the dragon

Date	Mintage	F	VF	XF	Unc	BU
1911 Proof	2,812	Value: 2,750				

KM# 861 5 POUNDS
39.9403 g., 0.9170 Gold 1.1773 oz. AGW **Ruler:** George V **Obv:** Head left **Obv. Designer:** T. H. Paget **Rev:** St. George slaying the dragon

Date	Mintage	F	VF	XF	Unc	BU
1937 Proof	5,500	Value: 1,500				
Note: Impaired and blemished proofs of the 1937 issue are common and trade at much lower values; The value listed here is for blemish-free examples						
1937 Matte Proof; Unique	—	—	—	—	—	—

KM# 924 5 POUNDS
39.9400 g., 0.9170 Gold 1.1775 oz. AGW **Ruler:** Elizabeth II **Obv:** Young bust right **Obv. Designer:** Arnold Machin **Rev:** St. George slaying the dragon

Date	Mintage	F	VF	XF	Unc	BU
1980 Proof	10,000	Value: 820				
1981 Proof	5,400	Value: 845				
1982 Proof	2,500	Value: 845				
1984	25,000	—	—	—	845	—
1984 Proof	8,000	Value: 850				

KM# 945 5 POUNDS
39.9400 g., 0.9170 Gold 1.1775 oz. AGW **Ruler:** Elizabeth II **Obv:** Crowned head right **Obv. Designer:** Raphael Maklouf **Rev:** St. George slaying the dragon

Date	Mintage	F	VF	XF	Unc	BU
1985	14,000	—	—	—	820	—
1985 Proof	13,000	Value: 845				
1986	7,723	—	—	—	820	—
1990	1,226	—	—	—	845	—
1990 Proof	Est. 2,500	Value: 845				
1991	976	—	—	—	845	—
1991 Proof	Est. 1,500	Value: 865				
1992 Proof	1,250	Value: 865				
1992	797	—	—	—	845	—
1993	906	—	—	—	845	—
1994 Proof	Est. 1,250	Value: 865				
1995 Proof	Est. 1,000	Value: 865				
1995 Proof	Est. 1,250	Value: 865				
1996	901	—	—	—	845	—
1997	802	—	—	—	845	—

KM# 949 5 POUNDS
39.9400 g., 0.9170 Gold 1.1775 oz. AGW **Ruler:** Elizabeth II **Obv:** Crowned head right **Obv. Designer:** Raphael Maklouf **Rev:** St. George slaying the dragon

Date	Mintage	F	VF	XF	Unc	BU
1987	10,000	—	—	—	820	—
1988	Est. 10,000	—	—	—	820	—

KM# 958 5 POUNDS
39.9400 g., 0.9170 Gold 1.1775 oz. AGW **Ruler:** Elizabeth II **Subject:** 500th Anniversary of the Gold Sovereign **Obv:** Elizabeth II seated on Coronation throne **Rev:** Crowned and quartered shield on tudor rose **Designer:** Bernard R. Sindall

Date	Mintage	F	VF	XF	Unc	BU
1989	10,000	—	—	—	820	—
1989 Proof	Est. 5,000	Value: 845				

KM# 1003 5 POUNDS
39.9400 g., 0.9170 Gold 1.1775 oz. AGW, 36 mm. **Ruler:** Elizabeth II **Obv:** Head with tiara right **Obv. Designer:** Ian Rank-Broadley **Rev:** St. George slaying dragon **Edge:** Reeded

Date	Mintage	F	VF	XF	Unc	BU
1999 Proof	—	Value: 975				
2000	10,000	—	—	—	865	—

DECIMAL COINAGE

1971-1981, 100 New Pence = 1 Pound; 1982, 100 Pence = 1 Pound

KM# 914 1/2 NEW PENNY
1.7820 g., Bronze, 17.14 mm. **Ruler:** Elizabeth II **Obv:** Young bust right **Obv. Designer:** Arnold Machin **Rev:** Crown **Rev. Designer:** Christopher Ironside

Date	Mintage	F	VF	XF	Unc	BU
1971	1,394,188,000	—	—	0.10	0.20	—
1971 Proof	350,000	Value: 1.00				
1972 Proof	150,000	Value: 3.00				
1973	365,680,000	—	—	0.15	0.40	—
1973 Proof	100,000	Value: 1.00				
1974	365,448,000	—	—	0.15	0.35	—
1974 Proof	100,000	Value: 1.00				
1975	197,600,000	—	—	0.15	0.45	—
1975 Proof	100,000	Value: 1.00				
1976	412,172,000	—	—	0.15	0.35	—
1976 Proof	100,000	Value: 1.00				
1977	66,368,000	—	—	0.15	0.20	—
1977 Proof	194,000	Value: 1.00				
1978	59,532,000	—	—	0.15	0.20	—
1978 Proof	88,000	Value: 1.00				
1979	219,132,000	—	—	0.15	0.20	—
1979 Proof	81,000	Value: 1.00				
1980	202,788,000	—	—	0.15	0.20	—
1980 Proof	143,000	Value: 1.00				
1981	46,748,000	—	—	0.15	0.40	—
1981 Proof	100,000	Value: 1.00				

KM# 926 1/2 PENNY

1.7820 g., Bronze, 17.14 mm. **Ruler:** Elizabeth II **Obv:** Bust right **Obv. Designer:** Arnold Machin **Rev:** "HALF PENNY" above crown and fraction **Rev. Designer:** Christopher Ironside **Note:** Denomination now demonetized.

Date	Mintage	F	VF	XF	Unc	BU
1982	190,752,000	—	—	0.15	0.20	—
1982 Proof	107,000	Value: 1.00				
1983	7,600,000	—	—	0.25	0.55	—
1983 Proof	108,000	Value: 1.50				
1984	Est. 159,000	—	—	—	2.00	—
Note: In sets only						
1984 Proof	107,000	Value: 2.50				

KM# 915 NEW PENNY

3.5600 g., Bronze, 20.32 mm. **Ruler:** Elizabeth II **Obv:** Young bust right **Obv. Designer:** Arnold Machin **Rev:** Crowned portocullis **Rev. Designer:** Christopher Ironside

Date	Mintage	F	VF	XF	Unc	BU
1971	1,521,666,000	—	—	0.15	0.20	—
1971 Proof	350,000	Value: 1.25				
1972 Proof	150,000	Value: 3.00				
1973	280,196,000	—	—	0.15	0.40	—
1973 Proof	100,000	Value: 1.25				
1974	330,892,000	—	—	0.15	0.40	—
1974 Proof	100,000	Value: 1.25				
1975	221,604,000	—	—	0.15	0.50	—
1975 Proof	100,000	Value: 1.25				
1976	300,160,000	—	—	0.15	0.30	—
1976 Proof	100,000	Value: 1.25				
1977	285,430,000	—	—	0.15	0.20	—
1977 Proof	194,000	Value: 1.25				
1978	292,770,000	—	—	0.15	0.45	—
1978 Proof	88,000	Value: 1.25				
1979	459,000,000	—	—	0.15	0.20	—
1979 Proof	81,000	Value: 1.25				
1980	416,304,000	—	—	0.15	0.20	—
1980 Proof	143,000	Value: 1.25				
1981	301,800,000	—	—	0.15	0.25	—
1981 Proof	100,000	Value: 1.25				

KM# 927 PENNY

3.5600 g., Bronze, 20.32 mm. **Ruler:** Elizabeth II **Obv:** Young bust right **Obv. Designer:** Arnold Machin **Rev:** Crowned portcullis **Rev. Designer:** Christopher Ironside

Date	Mintage	F	VF	XF	Unc	BU
1982	100,292,000	—	—	0.15	0.20	—
1982 Proof	107,000	Value: 1.25				
1983	243,002,000	—	—	0.15	0.40	—
1983 Proof	108,000	Value: 1.25				
1984	154,760,000	—	—	0.20	1.25	—
1984 Proof	107,000	Value: 1.25				

KM# 935 PENNY

3.5600 g., Bronze, 20.32 mm. **Ruler:** Elizabeth II **Obv:** Crowned head right **Obv. Designer:** Raphael Maklouf **Rev:** Crowned portcullis **Rev. Designer:** Christopher Ironside **Note:** Queen's head reduced size.

Date	Mintage	F	VF	XF	Unc	BU
1985	200,605,000	—	—	0.15	0.35	—
1985 Proof	102,000	Value: 1.25				
1986	369,989,000	—	—	0.15	0.35	—
1986 Proof	125,000	Value: 1.25				
1987	499,946,000	—	—	0.15	0.25	—
1987 Proof	89,000	Value: 1.25				
1988	793,492,000	—	—	0.15	0.25	—
1988 Proof	125,000	Value: 1.25				
1989	658,142,000	—	—	0.15	0.25	—
1989 Proof	100,000	Value: 1.25				
1990	529,048,000	—	—	0.15	0.25	—
1990 Proof	100,000	Value: 1.25				
1991	206,458,000	—	—	0.15	0.25	—
1991 Proof	—	Value: 1.25				
1992	—	—	—	—	0.50	—
Note: In sets only						
1992 Proof	—	Value: 1.75				
Note: In sets only						

KM# 935a PENNY

Copper Plated Steel, 20.32 mm. **Ruler:** Elizabeth II **Obv:** Crowned head right **Obv. Designer:** Raphael Maklouf **Rev:** Crowned portcullis **Rev. Designer:** Christopher Ironside

Date	Mintage	F	VF	XF	Unc	BU
1992	253,867,000	—	—	0.15	0.25	—
1993	602,590,000	—	—	0.15	0.25	—
1993 Proof	—	Value: 1.25				
1994	843,834,000	—	—	0.15	0.25	—
1994 Proof	—	Value: 1.25				
1995	303,314,000	—	—	0.15	0.25	—
1995 Proof	—	Value: 1.25				
1996	723,840,000	—	—	—	0.25	—
1996 Proof	—	Value: 1.25				
1997	396,874,000	—	—	—	0.25	—
1997 Proof	—	Value: 1.25				

KM# 935b PENNY

0.9250 Silver, 20.32 mm. **Ruler:** Elizabeth II **Obv:** Crowned head right **Obv. Designer:** Raphael Maklouf **Rev:** Crowned portcullis **Rev. Designer:** Christopher Ironside

Date	Mintage	F	VF	XF	Unc	BU
1996 Proof	—	Value: 16.50				

KM# 986 PENNY

Copper Plated Steel, 20.32 mm. **Ruler:** Elizabeth II **Obv:** Head with tiara right **Obv. Designer:** Ian Rank-Broadley **Rev:** Crowned portcullis **Rev. Designer:** Christopher Ironside

Date	Mintage	F	VF	XF	Unc	BU
1998	739,770,000	—	—	—	0.20	—
1998 Proof	Est. 100,000	Value: 3.25				
1999	891,392,000	—	—	—	0.20	—
2000	1,060,364,000	—	—	—	0.20	—

KM# 986a PENNY

Bronze, 20.3 mm. **Ruler:** Elizabeth II **Obv:** Head with tiara right **Rev:** Crowned portcullis **Edge:** Plain **Note:** Issued in sets only

Date	Mintage	F	VF	XF	Unc	BU
1999	916,000,000	—	—	—	0.20	—
1999 Proof	79,401	Value: 2.50				

KM# 986b PENNY

3.5600 g., 0.9250 Silver 0.1059 oz. ASW, 20.3 mm. **Ruler:** Elizabeth II **Obv:** Head with tiara right **Obv. Designer:** Ian Rank-Broadley **Rev:** Crowned portcullis **Rev. Designer:** Christopher Ironside **Edge:** Plain

Date	Mintage	F	VF	XF	Unc	BU
2000 Proof	15,000	Value: 16.50				

KM# 916 2 NEW PENCE

7.1200 g., Bronze, 25.91 mm. **Ruler:** Elizabeth II **Obv:** Young bust right **Obv. Designer:** Arnold Machin **Rev:** Welsh plumes and crown **Rev. Designer:** Christopher Ironside

Date	Mintage	F	VF	XF	Unc	BU
1971	1,454,856,000	—	—	0.10	0.20	—
1971 Proof	350,000	Value: 1.50				
1972 Proof	150,000	Value: 3.50				
1973 Proof	100,000	Value: 3.50				
1974 Proof	100,000	Value: 3.50				
1975	145,545,000	—	—	0.15	0.40	—
1975 Proof	100,000	Value: 1.50				
1976	181,379,000	—	—	0.15	0.30	—
1976 Proof	100,000	Value: 1.50				
1977	109,281,000	—	—	0.15	0.20	—
1977 Proof	194,000	Value: 1.50				
1978	189,658,000	—	—	0.15	0.40	—
1978 Proof	88,000	Value: 1.50				
1979	260,200,000	—	—	0.15	0.25	—
1979 Proof	81,000	Value: 1.50				
1980	408,527,000	—	—	0.15	0.25	—
1980 Proof	143,000	Value: 1.50				
1981	353,191,000	—	—	0.15	0.25	—
1981 Proof	100,000	Value: 1.50				

KM# 928 2 PENCE

7.1200 g., Bronze, 25.91 mm. **Ruler:** Elizabeth II **Obv:** Young bust right **Obv. Designer:** Arnold Machin **Rev:** Welsh plumes and crown **Rev. Designer:** Christopher Ironside

Date	Mintage	F	VF	XF	Unc	BU
1982	205,000	—	—	—	1.00	—
Note: In sets only						
1982 Proof	107,000	Value: 1.50				
1983	631,000	—	—	—	1.00	—
Note: In sets only						
1983 Proof	108,000	Value: 1.50				
1984	159,000	—	—	—	1.50	—
Note: In sets only						
1984 Proof	107,000	Value: 1.50				

KM# 936 2 PENCE

7.1200 g., Bronze, 25.91 mm. **Ruler:** Elizabeth II **Obv:** Crowned head right **Obv. Designer:** Raphael Maklouf **Rev:** Welsh plumes and crown **Rev. Designer:** Christopher Ironside

Date	Mintage	F	VF	XF	Unc	BU
1985	107,113,000	—	—	0.15	0.25	—
1985 Proof	102,000	Value: 1.50				
1986	168,968,000	—	—	0.15	0.50	—
1986 Proof	125,000	Value: 1.50				
1987	218,101,000	—	—	0.15	0.25	—
1987 Proof	89,000	Value: 1.50				
1988	419,889,000	—	—	0.15	0.25	—
1988 Proof	125,000	Value: 1.50				
1989	359,226,000	—	—	0.15	0.25	—
1989 Proof	100,000	Value: 1.50				
1990	204,500,000	—	—	0.15	0.25	—
1990 Proof	100,000	Value: 1.50				
1991	86,625,000	—	—	0.15	0.25	—
1991 Proof	—	Value: 1.50				
1992	—	—	—	—	0.50	—
Note: In sets only						
1992 Proof	—	Value: 2.00				

KM# 936a 2 PENCE

Copper Plated Steel, 25.91 mm. **Ruler:** Elizabeth II **Obv:** Crowned head right **Obv. Designer:** Raphael Maklouf **Rev:** Welsh plumes and crown **Rev. Designer:** Christopher Ironside

Date	Mintage	F	VF	XF	Unc	BU
1992	102,247,000	—	—	0.15	0.25	—
1993	235,674,000	—	—	0.15	0.25	—
1993 Proof	—	Value: 1.50				
1994	531,628,000	—	—	0.10	0.25	—
1994 Proof	—	Value: 1.50				
1995	124,482,000	—	—	0.10	0.25	—
1995 Proof	—	Value: 1.50				
1996	296,278,000	—	—	0.10	0.25	—
1996 Proof	—	Value: 1.50				
1997	496,116,000	—	—	0.10	0.25	—
1997 Proof	—	Value: 1.50				

KM# 936b 2 PENCE

0.9250 Silver, 25.91 mm. **Ruler:** Elizabeth II **Obv:** Crowned head right **Obv. Designer:** Raphael Maklouf **Rev:** Welsh plumes and crown **Rev. Designer:** Christopher Ironside

Date	Mintage	F	VF	XF	Unc	BU
1996 Proof	—	Value: 17.50				

KM# 987 2 PENCE

Copper Plated Steel, 25.91 mm. **Ruler:** Elizabeth II **Obv:** Head with tiara right **Obv. Designer:** Ian Rank-Broadley **Rev:** Welsh plumes and crown **Rev. Designer:** Christopher Ironside

Date	Mintage	F	VF	XF	Unc	BU
1998	115,154,000	—	—	—	0.25	—
1998 Proof	Est. 100,000	Value: 3.25				
1999	353,816,000	—	—	—	0.25	—
1999 Proof	—	Value: 3.25				
2000	536,643,000	—	—	—	0.25	—

KM# 987a 2 PENCE

Bronze, 25.91 mm. **Ruler:** Elizabeth II **Obv:** Head with tiara right **Obv. Designer:** Ian Rank-Broadley **Rev:** Welsh plumes and crown **Rev. Designer:** Christopher Ironside

Date	Mintage	F	VF	XF	Unc	BU
1998	98,676,000	—	—	—	0.25	—
1999	460,000,000	—	—	—	0.25	—
1999 Proof	79,401	Value: 2.50				
Note: In sets only						
2000 Proof	—	—	—	—	—	—

KM# 987b 2 PENCE

7.1200 g., 0.9250 Silver 0.2117 oz. ASW, 25.9 mm. **Ruler:** Elizabeth II **Obv:** Head with tiara right **Obv. Designer:** Ian Rank-Broadley **Rev:** Welsh plumes and crown **Rev. Designer:** Christopher Ironside **Edge:** Plain

Date	Mintage	F	VF	XF	Unc	BU
2000 Proof	15,000	Value: 17.50				

KM# 911 5 NEW PENCE

5.6500 g., Copper-Nickel, 23.59 mm. **Ruler:** Elizabeth II **Obv:** Young bust right **Obv. Designer:** Arnold Machin **Rev:** Crowned thistle **Rev. Designer:** Christopher Ironside

Date	Mintage	F	VF	XF	Unc	BU
1968	98,868,000	—	—	0.15	0.30	—
1969	120,270,000	—	—	0.15	0.40	—
1970	225,949,000	—	—	0.15	0.40	—
1971	81,783,000	—	—	0.15	0.45	—
1971 Proof	350,000	Value: 1.75				
1972 Proof	150,000	Value: 3.50				
1973 Proof	100,000	Value: 3.50				
1974 Proof	100,000	Value: 3.50				
1975	141,539,000	—	—	0.15	0.30	—
1975 Proof	100,000	Value: 1.50				
1976 Proof	100,000	Value: 3.50				
1977	24,308,000	—	—	0.15	0.35	—
1977 Proof	194,000	Value: 1.50				
1978	61,094,000	—	—	0.15	0.50	—
1978 Proof	88,000	Value: 1.50				
1979	155,456,000	—	—	0.15	0.30	—
1979 Proof	81,000	Value: 1.50				
1980	220,566,000	—	—	0.15	0.30	—
1980 Proof	143,000	Value: 1.50				
1981 Proof	100,000	Value: 1.75				

KM# 929 5 PENCE

5.6500 g., Copper-Nickel, 23.59 mm. **Ruler:** Elizabeth II **Obv:** Young bust right **Obv. Designer:** Arnold Machin **Rev:** Crowned thistle **Rev. Designer:** Christopher Ironside

Date	Mintage	F	VF	XF	Unc	BU
1982	205,000	—	—	—	2.25	—
Note: In sets only						
1982 Proof	107,000	Value: 1.75				
1983	637,000	—	—	—	1.75	—
Note: In sets only						
1983 Proof	108,000	Value: 1.75				
1984	159,000	—	—	—	1.75	—
Note: In sets only						
1984 Proof	107,000	Value: 1.50				

KM# 937 5 PENCE

5.6500 g., Copper-Nickel, 23.59 mm. **Ruler:** Elizabeth II **Obv:** Crowned head right **Obv. Designer:** Raphael Maklouf **Rev:** Modified design, Five Pence is away from the edge **Rev. Designer:** Christopher Ironside

Date	Mintage	F	VF	XF	Unc	BU
1985	178,000	—	—	—	2.00	—
Note: In sets only						
1985 Proof	102,000	Value: 1.50				
1986	167,000	—	—	—	1.00	—
Note: In sets only						
1986 Proof	125,000	Value: 1.50				
1987	48,220,000	—	—	0.15	0.30	—
1987 Proof	89,000	Value: 1.75				
1988	120,745,000	—	—	0.15	0.30	—
1988 Proof	125,000	Value: 1.75				
1989	101,406,000	—	—	0.15	0.30	—
1989 Proof	100,000	Value: 1.75				
1990	—	—	—	—	2.50	—
Note: In sets only						
1990 Proof	—	Value: 2.75				

KM# 937a 5 PENCE

5.6000 g., 0.9250 Silver .1683 oz. ASW, 23.59 mm. **Ruler:** Elizabeth II **Obv:** Crowned head right **Obv. Designer:** Raphael Maklouf **Rev:** Crowned thistle **Rev. Designer:** Christopher Ironside

Date	Mintage	F	VF	XF	Unc	BU
1990 Proof	35,000	Value: 22.00				

KM# 937c 5 PENCE

3.2500 g., 0.9250 Silver .0967 oz. ASW, 18 mm. **Ruler:** Elizabeth II **Obv:** Crowned head right **Obv. Designer:** Ralphael Maklouf **Rev:** Crowned thistle **Rev. Designer:** Christopher Ironside

Date	Mintage	F	VF	XF	Unc	BU
1990 Proof	35,000	Value: 20.00				
1996 Proof	—	Value: 20.00				

KM# 937d 5 PENCE

6.5000 g., 0.9250 Silver .1933 oz. ASW, 18 mm. **Ruler:** Elizabeth II **Obv:** Crowned head right **Obv. Designer:** Raphael Maklouf **Rev:** Crowned thistle **Rev. Designer:** Christopher Ironside **Note:** Piefort.

Date	Mintage	F	VF	XF	Unc	BU
1990 Proof	20,000	Value: 25.00				

KM# 937b 5 PENCE

3.2500 g., Copper-Nickel, 18 mm. **Ruler:** Elizabeth II **Obv:** Crowned head right **Obv. Designer:** Raphael Maklouf **Rev:** Crowned thistle **Rev. Designer:** Christopher Ironside **Note:** Reduced size. Varieties in thickness and edge milling exist.

Date	Mintage	F	VF	XF	Unc	BU
1990	1,634,976,000	—	—	—	0.35	—
1990 Proof	—	Value: 2.00				
1991	724,979,000	—	—	—	0.35	—
1991 Proof	—	Value: 2.00				
1992	453,174,000	—	—	—	0.35	—
1992 Proof	—	Value: 2.00				
1993	56,945	—	—	—	1.25	—
Note: In sets only						
1993 Proof	—	Value: 2.00				
1994	93,602,000	—	—	—	0.35	—
1994 Proof	—	Value: 2.00				
1995	183,384,000	—	—	—	0.35	—
1995 Proof	—	Value: 2.00				
1996	302,902,000	—	—	—	0.35	—
1996 Proof	—	Value: 2.00				
1997	236,596,000	—	—	—	0.35	—
1997 Proof	—	Value: 2.00				

KM# 988 5 PENCE

Copper-Nickel, 18 mm. **Ruler:** Elizabeth II **Obv:** Head with tiara right **Obv. Designer:** Ian Rank-Broadley **Rev:** Crowned thistle

Date	Mintage	F	VF	XF	Unc	BU
1998	217,376,000	—	—	—	0.30	—
1998 Proof	Est. 100,000	Value: 3.25				
1999	195,490,000	—	—	—	0.30	—
1999 Proof	79,401	Value: 3.00				
2000	388,506,000	—	—	—	0.30	—
2000 Proof	Est. 100,000	Value: 3.00				

KM# 988a 5 PENCE

3.2500 g., 0.9250 Silver 0.0967 oz. ASW, 18 mm. **Ruler:** Elizabeth II **Obv:** Head with tiara right **Obv. Designer:** Ian Rank-Broadley **Rev:** Crowned thistle **Rev. Designer:** Christopher Ironside **Edge:** Reeded

Date	Mintage	F	VF	XF	Unc	BU
2000 Proof	15,000	Value: 20.00				

KM# 912 10 NEW PENCE

11.3100 g., Copper-Nickel, 28.5 mm. **Ruler:** Elizabeth II **Obv:** Young bust right **Obv. Designer:** Arnold Machin **Rev:** Crowned lion prancing left

Date	Mintage	F	VF	XF	Unc	BU
1968	336,143,000	—	—	0.25	0.50	—
1969	314,008,000	—	—	0.25	0.55	—
1970	133,571,000	—	—	0.25	0.65	—
1971	63,205,000	—	—	0.25	0.90	—
1971 Proof	350,000	Value: 1.75				
1972 Proof	150,000	Value: 3.75				
1973	152,174,000	—	—	0.25	0.50	—
1973 Proof	100,000	Value: 1.75				
1974	92,741,000	—	—	0.25	0.50	—
1974 Proof	100,000	Value: 1.75				
1975	181,559,000	—	—	0.25	0.50	—
1975 Proof	100,000	Value: 1.75				
1976	228,220,000	—	—	0.25	0.50	—
1976 Proof	100,000	Value: 1.75				
1977	59,323,000	—	—	0.25	0.60	—
1977 Proof	194,000	Value: 1.75				
1978 Proof	88,000	Value: 5.25				
1979	115,457,000	—	—	0.25	0.60	—
1979 Proof	81,000	Value: 1.75				
1980	88,650,000	—	—	0.25	0.65	—
1980 Proof	143,000	Value: 1.75				
1981	3,487,000	—	0.25	0.50	1.75	—
1981 Proof	100,000	Value: 1.75				

KM# 930 10 PENCE

11.3100 g., Copper-Nickel, 28.5 mm. **Ruler:** Elizabeth II **Obv:** Young bust right **Obv. Designer:** Arnold Machin **Rev:** Crowned lion prancing left **Rev. Designer:** Christopher Ironside

Date	Mintage	F	VF	XF	Unc	BU
1982	205,000	—	—	—	2.75	—
Note: In sets only						
1982 Proof	107,000	Value: 1.75				
1983	637,000	—	—	—	2.75	—
Note: In sets only						
1983 Proof	108,000	Value: 1.75				
1984	159,000	—	—	—	2.00	—
Note: In sets only						
1984 Proof	107,000	Value: 1.75				

KM# 938 10 PENCE

11.3100 g., Copper-Nickel, 28.5 mm. **Ruler:** Elizabeth II **Obv:** Crowned head right **Obv. Designer:** Raphael Maklouf **Rev:** Modified design, Ten Pence is away from the edge **Rev. Designer:** Christopher Ironside

Date	Mintage	F	VF	XF	Unc	BU
1985	178,000	—	—	—	2.75	—
Note: In sets only						
1985 Proof	102,000	Value: 1.75				
1986	167,000	—	—	—	1.75	—
Note: In sets only						
1986 Proof	125,000	Value: 1.75				
1987	172,000	—	—	—	2.75	—
Note: In sets only						
1987 Proof	89,000	Value: 2.75				
1988	134,000	—	—	—	2.75	—
Note: In sets only						
1988 Proof	125,000	Value: 2.75				
1989	78,000	—	—	—	3.50	—
Note: In sets only						
1989 Proof	100,000	Value: 2.75				
1990	—	—	—	—	3.50	—
Note: In sets only						
1990 Proof	100,000	Value: 2.75				
1991	—	—	—	—	3.50	—
Note: In sets only						
1991 Proof	—	Value: 2.75				
1992	—	—	—	—	2.75	—
Note: In sets only						
1992 Proof	—	Value: 3.50				

KM# 938c 10 PENCE

6.5000 g., 0.9250 Silver .1933 oz. ASW, 28.5 mm. **Ruler:** Elizabeth II **Obv:** Crowned head right **Obv. Designer:** Raphael Maklouf **Rev:** Crowned lion prancing left **Rev. Designer:** Christopher Ironside

Date	Mintage	F	VF	XF	Unc	BU
1992 Proof	35,000	Value: 17.50				
1996 Proof	—	Value: 17.50				

KM# 938b 10 PENCE

6.5000 g., Copper-Nickel, 24.5 mm. **Ruler:** Elizabeth II **Obv:** Crowned head right **Rev:** Crowned lion prancing left **Note:** Reduced size. Varieties in thickness and edge milling exist.

Date	Mintage	F	VF	XF	Unc	BU
1992	1,413,455,000	—	—	0.25	0.50	—
1992 Proof	—	Value: 2.75				
1993	—	—	—	—	1.00	—
Note: In sets only						
1993 Proof	—	Value: 1.75				
1994	—	—	—	—	1.00	—
Note: In sets only						
1994 Proof	—	Value: 1.75				
1995	43,259,000	—	—	—	1.00	—
1995 Proof	—	Value: 1.75				
1996	118,738,000	—	—	—	1.00	—
1996 Proof	—	Value: 1.75				
1997	99,196,000	—	—	—	1.00	—
1997 Proof	—	Value: 1.75				

KM# 938a 10 PENCE

11.3100 g., 0.9250 Silver .3363 oz. ASW, 28.5 mm. **Ruler:** Elizabeth II **Obv:** Crowned head right **Rev:** Crowned lion prancing left **Note:** Date varieties exist.

Date	Mintage	F	VF	XF	Unc	BU
1992 Proof	35,000	Value: 25.00				

KM# 989 10 PENCE

Copper-Nickel, 24.5 mm. **Ruler:** Elizabeth II **Obv:** Head with tiara right **Obv. Designer:** Ian Rank-Broadley **Rev:** Crowned lion prancing left **Rev. Designer:** Christopher Ironside

Date	Mintage	F	VF	XF	Unc	BU
1998	—	—	—	—	1.25	—
Note: In sets only						
1998 Proof	—	Value: 4.50				
Note: In sets only						
1999	136,492	—	—	—	1.25	—
Note: In sets only						
1999 Proof	79,401	Value: 3.25				
Note: In sets only						
2000	134,727,000	—	—	—	0.40	—
2000 Proof	Est. 100,000	Value: 3.25				

KM# 989a 10 PENCE

6.5000 g., 0.9250 Silver 0.1933 oz. ASW, 24.5 mm. **Ruler:** Elizabeth II **Obv:** Head with tiara right **Obv. Designer:** Ian Rank-Broadley **Rev:** Crowned lion prancing left **Rev. Designer:** Christopher Ironside **Edge:** Reeded

Date	Mintage	F	VF	XF	Unc	BU
2000 Proof	15,000	Value: 17.50				

KM# 931 20 PENCE

5.0000 g., Copper-Nickel, 21.4 mm. **Ruler:** Elizabeth II **Obv:** Young bust right **Obv. Designer:** Arnold Machin **Rev:** Crowned rose **Rev. Designer:** William Gardner **Shape:** 7-sided

Date	Mintage	F	VF	XF	Unc	BU
1982	740,815,000	—	—	0.45	0.65	—
1982 Proof	107,000	Value: 4.50				
1983	158,463,000	—	—	0.45	0.65	—
1983 Proof	108,000	Value: 2.25				
1984	65,351,000	—	—	0.45	0.65	—
1984 Proof	107,000	Value: 2.25				

KM# 939 20 PENCE

5.0000 g., Copper-Nickel, 21.4 mm. **Ruler:** Elizabeth II **Obv:** Crowned head right **Obv. Designer:** Raphael Maklouf **Rev:** Crowned rose **Rev. Designer:** William Gardner **Shape:** 7-sided

Date	Mintage	F	VF	XF	Unc	BU
1985	74,274,000	—	—	0.45	0.75	—
1985 Proof	102,000	Value: 4.50				
1986	167,000	—	—	—	1.00	—
Note: In sets only						
1986 Proof	125,000	Value: 4.50				
1987	137,450,000	—	—	0.45	0.75	—
1987 Proof	89,000	Value: 4.50				
1988	38,038,000	—	—	0.45	0.75	—
1988 Proof	125,000	Value: 5.00				
1989	132,014,000	—	—	0.45	0.75	—
1989 Proof	100,000	Value: 5.00				
1990	88,098,000	—	—	0.45	0.75	—
1990 Proof	100,000	Value: 5.00				
1991	35,901,000	—	—	0.45	1.00	—
1991 Proof	—	Value: 5.00				
1992	31,205,000	—	—	0.45	1.00	—
1992 Proof	—	Value: 5.00				
1993	123,124,000	—	—	0.45	0.75	—
1993 Proof	—	Value: 5.00				
1994	67,131,000	—	—	0.45	1.00	—
1994 Proof	—	Value: 5.00				
1995	102,005,000	—	—	0.45	0.75	—
1995 Proof	—	Value: 5.00				
1996	83,164,000	—	—	0.45	0.75	—
1996 Proof	—	Value: 5.00				
1997	89,519,000	—	—	0.45	0.75	—
Note: Variations in portrait exist						
1997 Proof	—	Value: 5.00				

KM# 939a 20 PENCE

0.9250 Silver, 21.4 mm. **Ruler:** Elizabeth II **Obv:** Crowned head right **Obv. Designer:** Raphael Maklouf **Rev:** Crowned rose **Rev. Designer:** William Gardner **Shape:** 7-sided

Date	Mintage	F	VF	XF	Unc	BU
1996 Proof	—	Value: 18.50				

KM# 990 20 PENCE

5.0000 g., Copper-Nickel, 21.4 mm. **Ruler:** Elizabeth II **Obv:** Head with tiara right **Obv. Designer:** Ian Rank-Broadley **Rev:** Crowned rose **Rev. Designer:** William Gardner **Shape:** 7-sided

Date	Mintage	F	VF	XF	Unc	BU
1998	76,965,000	—	—	—	0.60	—
1998 Proof	Est. 100,000	Value: 3.50				
1999	73,478,750	—	—	—	0.60	—
1999 Proof	79,401	Value: 3.00				
2000	136,418,750	—	—	—	0.60	—
2000 Proof	Est. 100,000	Value: 3.25				

KM# 990a 20 PENCE

5.0000 g., 0.9250 Silver 0.1487 oz. ASW, 21.4 mm. **Ruler:** Elizabeth II **Obv:** Head with tiara right **Obv. Designer:** Ian Rank-Broadley **Rev:** Crowned rose **Rev. Designer:** William Gardner **Edge:** Plain **Shape:** 7-sided

Date	Mintage	F	VF	XF	Unc	BU
2000 Proof	15,000	Value: 18.50				

KM# 917 25 NEW PENCE

Copper-Nickel, 38.5 mm. **Ruler:** Elizabeth II **Subject:** Royal Silver Wedding Anniversary **Obv:** Young bust right **Obv. Designer:** Arnold Machin **Rev:** Crowned EP monogram **Rev. Designer:** Arnold Machin

Date	Mintage	F	VF	XF	Unc	BU
ND(1972)	7,452,000	—	—	0.65	2.50	—
ND(1972) Proof	150,000	Value: 7.50				

KM# 917a 25 NEW PENCE

28.2759 g., 0.9250 Silver .8409 oz. ASW, 38.5 mm. **Ruler:** Elizabeth II **Obv:** Young bust right **Rev:** Crowned EP monogram

Date	Mintage	F	VF	XF	Unc	BU
ND(1972) Proof	100,000	Value: 25.00				

KM# 920 25 NEW PENCE

Copper-Nickel, 38.5 mm. **Ruler:** Elizabeth II **Subject:** Silver Jubilee of Reign **Obv:** Queen on horseback left **Rev:** Eagle over spoon within circle, crown above **Designer:** Arnold Machin

Date	Mintage	F	VF	XF	Unc	BU
1977	37,061,000	—	—	0.65	1.50	—
1977 Proof	194,000	Value: 6.00				
1977 (RMF)	—	—	—	—	4.00	—
Note: Seated in Royal Mint Folder and First Day Covers						
1981 (RMF)	—	—	—	—	—	—
Note: Reported, not confirmed						

KM# 920a 25 NEW PENCE

28.2759 g., 0.9250 Silver .8409 oz. ASW, 38.5 mm. **Ruler:** Elizabeth II **Obv:** Queen on horseback left **Rev:** Eagle over spoon within circle, crown above

Date	Mintage	F	VF	XF	Unc	BU
1977 Proof	377,000	Value: 20.00				

KM# 921 25 NEW PENCE

Copper-Nickel, 38.5 mm. **Ruler:** Elizabeth II **Subject:** 80th Birthday of Queen Mother **Obv:** Young bust right **Obv. Designer:** Arnold Machin **Rev:** Queen Mother's profile left within circle of rampant lions and banners **Rev. Designer:** Richard Guyatt

Date	Mintage	F	VF	XF	Unc	BU
ND(1980)	9,306,000	—	—	0.65	2.50	—

KM# 921a 25 NEW PENCE

28.2759 g., 0.9250 Silver .8409 oz. ASW, 38.5 mm. **Ruler:** Elizabeth II **Obv:** Young bust right **Rev:** Queen Mother's profile left in circle of rampant lions and banners

Date	Mintage	F	VF	XF	Unc	BU
ND(1980) Proof	84,000	Value: 55.00				

KM# 925 25 NEW PENCE
Copper-Nickel, 38.5 mm. **Ruler:** Elizabeth II **Subject:** Wedding of Prince Charles and Lady Diana **Obv:** Young bust right **Obv. Designer:** Arnold Machin **Rev:** Jugate heads left **Rev. Designer:** Philip Nathan

Date	Mintage	F	VF	XF	Unc	BU
1981	26,773,000	—	—	0.65	2.50	—

KM# 925a 25 NEW PENCE
28.2759 g., 0.9250 Silver .8409 oz. ASW, 38.5 mm. **Ruler:** Elizabeth II **Subject:** Wedding of Prince Charles and Lady Diana **Obv:** Young bust right **Rev:** Jugate heads left

Date	Mintage	F	VF	XF	Unc	BU
1981 Proof	218,000	Value: 27.50				

KM# 913 50 NEW PENCE
13.5000 g., Copper-Nickel, 30 mm. **Ruler:** Elizabeth II **Obv:** Young bust right **Obv. Designer:** Arnold Machin **Rev:** Britannia seated right **Rev. Designer:** Christopher Ironside **Shape:** 7-sided

Date	Mintage	F	VF	XF	Unc	BU
1969	188,400,000	—	—	1.25	2.50	—
1970	19,461,000	—	—	1.25	3.50	—
1971 Proof	350,000	Value: 3.50				
1972 Proof	150,000	Value: 6.50				
1974 Proof	100,000	Value: 3.00				
1975 Proof	100,000	Value: 3.00				
1976	43,747,000	—	—	1.75	3.50	—
1976 Proof	100,000	Value: 2.50				
1977	49,536,000	—	—	1.75	3.50	—
1977 Proof	194,000	Value: 2.50				
1978	72,005,000	—	—	1.75	3.50	—
1978 Proof	88,000	Value: 2.75				
1979	58,680,000	—	—	1.75	2.25	—
1979 Proof	81,000	Value: 2.75				
1980	89,086,000	—	—	1.75	2.25	—
1980 Proof	143,000	Value: 2.50				
1981	74,003,000	—	—	1.75	2.25	—
1981 Proof	100,000	Value: 2.50				

KM# 918 50 PENCE
13.5000 g., Copper-Nickel, 30 mm. **Ruler:** Elizabeth II **Subject:** Britain's entry into E.E.C **Obv:** Young bust right **Obv. Designer:** Arnold Machin **Rev:** Denomination and date at center of nine clasped hands **Rev. Designer:** David Wynne **Shape:** 7-sided

Date	Mintage	F	VF	XF	Unc	BU
1973	89,775,000	—	—	1.25	2.00	—
1973 Proof	357,000	Value: 5.50				

KM# 932 50 PENCE
13.5000 g., Copper-Nickel, 30 mm. **Ruler:** Elizabeth II **Obv:** Young bust right **Obv. Designer:** Arnold Machin **Rev:** Britannia seated right **Rev. Designer:** Christopher Ironside **Shape:** 7-sided

Date	Mintage	F	VF	XF	Unc	BU
1982	51,312,000	—	—	1.25	1.75	—
1982 Proof	107,000	Value: 2.50				
1983	62,825,000	—	—	1.25	2.00	—
1983 Proof	125,000	Value: 2.50				
1984	Est. 107,000	—	—	—	2.75	—
Note: In sets only						
1984 Proof	125,000	Value: 2.50				

KM# 940.1 50 PENCE
13.5000 g., Copper-Nickel, 30 mm. **Ruler:** Elizabeth II **Obv:** Crowned head right **Obv. Designer:** Raphael Maklouf **Rev:** Britannia seated right **Rev. Designer:** Christopher Ironside **Shape:** 7-sided

Date	Mintage	F	VF	XF	Unc	BU
1985	682,100	—	—	1.25	5.50	—
1985 Proof	102,000	Value: 2.75				
1986	167,000	—	—	—	2.75	—
Note: In sets only						
1986 Proof	125,000	Value: 2.75				
1987	172,000	—	—	—	2.75	—
Note: In sets only						
1987 Proof	89,000	Value: 2.75				
1988	134,000	—	—	—	2.75	—
Note: In sets only						
1988 Proof	125,000	Value: 3.50				
1989	78,000	—	—	—	3.50	—
Note: In sets only						
1989 Proof	100,000	Value: 2.75				
1990	—	—	—	—	3.50	—
Note: In sets only						
1990 Proof	100,000	Value: 6.00				
1991	—	—	—	—	3.50	—
Note: In sets only						
1991 Proof	—	Value: 6.50				
1992	—	—	—	—	3.50	—
Note: In sets only						
1992 Proof	—	Value: 6.50				
1993	—	—	—	—	3.50	—
Note: In sets only						
1993 Proof	—	Value: 3.50				
1995	—	—	—	—	2.75	—
Note: In sets only						
1995 Proof	—	Value: 3.50				
1996	—	—	—	—	2.75	—
Note: In sets only						
1996 Proof	—	Value: 3.50				
1997	—	—	—	—	2.75	—
Note: In sets only						
1997 Proof	—	Value: 3.50				

KM# 963 50 PENCE
13.5000 g., Copper-Nickel, 30 mm. **Ruler:** Elizabeth II **Subject:** British Presidency of European Council of Ministers **Obv:** Crowned head right **Obv. Designer:** Raphael Maklouf **Rev:** Stars on conference table **Shape:** 7-sided

Date	Mintage	F	VF	XF	Unc	BU
ND(1992)	109,000	—	—	—	5.75	—
ND(1992) Proof	Est. 100,000	Value: 13.50				

KM# 963a 50 PENCE
13.5000 g., 0.9250 Silver .4014 oz. ASW, 30 mm. **Ruler:** Elizabeth II **Obv:** Crowned head right **Rev:** Stars on conference table

Date	Mintage	F	VF	XF	Unc	BU
ND(1992) Proof	Est. 35,000	Value: 30.00				

KM# 963b 50 PENCE
26.3200 g., 0.9170 Gold .7757 oz. AGW, 30 mm. **Ruler:** Elizabeth II **Subject:** British Presidency of European Council of Ministers **Obv:** Crowned head right **Rev:** Stars on conference table

Date	Mintage	F	VF	XF	Unc	BU
ND(1992) Proof	Est. 2,500	Value: 550				

KM# 966 50 PENCE
13.5000 g., Copper-Nickel, 30 mm. **Ruler:** Elizabeth II **Subject:** 50th Anniversary of Normandy Invasion **Obv:** Crowned head right **Obv. Designer:** Raphael Maklouf **Rev:** Boats and planes **Rev. Designer:** John Mills **Shape:** 7-sided

Date	Mintage	F	VF	XF	Unc	BU
1994	6,706,000	—	—	—	2.50	—
1994 Proof	—	Value: 11.50				

KM# 966a 50 PENCE
13.5000 g., 0.9250 Silver .4014 oz. ASW, 30 mm. **Ruler:** Elizabeth II **Obv:** Crowned head right **Rev:** Boats and planes

Date	Mintage	F	VF	XF	Unc	BU
1994 Proof	—	Value: 45.00				

KM# 966b 50 PENCE
26.3200 g., 0.9170 Gold .7757 oz. AGW, 30 mm. **Ruler:** Elizabeth II **Obv:** Crowned head right **Rev:** Boats and planes

Date	Mintage	F	VF	XF	Unc	BU
1994 Proof	—	Value: 575				

KM# 940.1a 50 PENCE
Silver, 30 mm. **Ruler:** Elizabeth II **Obv:** Crowned head right **Rev:** Britannia seated

Date	Mintage	F	VF	XF	Unc	BU
1996 Proof	—	Value: 30.00				

KM# 940.2 50 PENCE
8.0000 g., Copper-Nickel, 27.3 mm. **Ruler:** Elizabeth II **Obv:** Crowned head right **Obv. Designer:** Raphael Maklouf **Rev:** Britannia seated right **Rev. Designer:** Christopher Ironside **Shape:** 7-sided **Note:** Reduced size.

Date	Mintage	F	VF	XF	Unc	BU
1997	456,364,000	—	—	—	2.50	—
1997 Proof	—	Value: 3.50				

KM# 991 50 PENCE
Copper-Nickel, 27.3 mm. **Ruler:** Elizabeth II **Obv:** Head with tiara right **Obv. Designer:** Ian Rank-Broadley **Rev:** Britannia seated right **Rev. Designer:** Christopher Ironside **Shape:** 7-sided

Date	Mintage	F	VF	XF	Unc	BU
1998	74,350,500	—	—	—	1.75	—
1998 Proof	Est. 100,000	Value: 2.50				
1999	29,905,000	—	—	—	1.75	—
1999 Proof	79,401	Value: 2.50				
2000	39,172,000	—	—	—	1.75	—
2000 Proof	Est. 100,000	Value: 2.50				

KM# 992 50 PENCE
8.0000 g., Copper-Nickel, 27.3 mm. **Ruler:** Elizabeth II **Subject:** 25th Anniversary - Britain in the Common Market **Obv:** Head with tiara right **Obv. Designer:** Ian Rank-Broadley **Rev:** Bouquet of stars **Rev. Designer:** John Mills **Shape:** 7-sided

Date	Mintage	F	VF	XF	Unc	BU
1998	4,967,000	—	—	—	2.75	—
1998 Proof	Est. 100,000	Value: 9.50				

KM# 992a 50 PENCE
8.0000 g., 0.9250 Silver .2379 oz. ASW, 27.3 mm. **Ruler:** Elizabeth II **Obv:** Head with tiara right **Rev:** Bouquet of stars

Date	Mintage	F	VF	XF	Unc	BU
1998 Proof	—	Value: 45.00				

KM# 996 50 PENCE
8.0000 g., Copper-Nickel, 27.3 mm. **Ruler:** Elizabeth II **Subject:** National Health Service **Obv:** Head with tiara right **Obv. Designer:** Ian Rank-Broadley **Rev:** Radiant hands within circle **Rev. Designer:** David Cornell **Shape:** 7-sided

Date	Mintage	F	VF	XF	Unc	BU
1998	5,001,000	—	—	—	2.75	—
1998	—	—	—	—	7.00	—
Note: In folder						
1998 Proof	—	Value: 12.00				

KM# 996a 50 PENCE
8.0000 g., 0.9250 Silver .2379 oz. ASW, 27.3 mm. **Ruler:** Elizabeth II **Subject:** National Health Service **Obv:** Head with tiara right **Obv. Designer:** Ian Rank-Broadley **Rev:** Radiant hands **Shape:** 7-sided

Date	Mintage	F	VF	XF	Unc	BU
1998 Proof	Est. 25,000	Value: 45.00				

KM# 996b 50 PENCE
15.5000 g., 0.9167 Gold .4568 oz. AGW, 27.3 mm. **Ruler:** Elizabeth II **Subject:** National Health Service **Obv:** Head with tiara right **Obv. Designer:** Rank-Broadley **Rev:** Radiant hands **Shape:** 7-sided

Date	Mintage	F	VF	XF	Unc	BU
1998 Proof	Est. 1,500	Value: 475				

KM# 1004 50 PENCE
8.0000 g., Copper-Nickel, 27.3 mm. **Ruler:** Elizabeth II **Subject:** Public Library **Obv:** Head with tiara right **Obv. Designer:** Ian Rank-Broadley **Rev:** Open book above building, CDs in pediment **Edge:** Plain edge **Shape:** 7-sided

Date	Mintage	F	VF	XF	Unc	BU
2000	Est. 5,000,000	—	—	—	2.75	—
2000 Proof	100,000	Value: 12.50				

KM# 991a 50 PENCE
8.0000 g., 0.9250 Silver 0.2379 oz. ASW, 27.3 mm. **Ruler:** Elizabeth II **Obv:** Head with tiara right **Obv. Designer:** Ian Rank-Broadley **Rev:** Britannia seated **Rev. Designer:** Christopher Ironside **Edge:** Plain **Shape:** 7-sided

Date	Mintage	F	VF	XF	Unc	BU
2000 Proof	15,000	Value: 25.00				

KM# 933 POUND
9.5000 g., Nickel-Brass, 22.5 mm. **Ruler:** Elizabeth II **Obv:** Young bust right **Obv. Designer:** Arnold Machin **Rev:** Shield of Great Britain within the Garter, crowned and supported **Rev. Designer:** Eric Sewell **Edge Lettering:** DECUS ET TUTAMEN

Date	Mintage	F	VF	XF	Unc	BU
1983	443,054,000	—	—	2.25	4.00	5.50
1983 Proof	108,000	Value: 6.00				

KM# 933a POUND
9.5000 g., 0.9250 Silver .2825 oz. ASW, 22.5 mm. **Ruler:** Elizabeth II **Obv:** Young bust right **Rev:** Shield of Great Britain within the Garter, crowned and supported

Date	Mintage	F	VF	XF	Unc	BU
1983 Proof	50,000	Value: 27.50				

KM# 934 POUND
9.5000 g., Nickel-Brass, 22.5 mm. **Ruler:** Elizabeth II **Obv:** Young bust right **Obv. Designer:** Arnold Machin **Rev:** Scottish thistle **Rev. Designer:** Leslie Durbin **Edge Lettering:** NEMO ME IMPUNE LACESSIT

Date	Mintage	F	VF	XF	Unc	BU
1984	146,257,000	—	—	2.25	4.00	5.50
1984 Proof	107,000	Value: 6.00				

KM# 934a POUND
9.5000 g., 0.9250 Silver .2825 oz. ASW, 22.5 mm. **Ruler:** Elizabeth II **Obv:** Young bust right **Rev:** Scottish thistle

Date	Mintage	F	VF	XF	Unc	BU
1984 Proof	45,000	Value: 27.50				

KM# 941 POUND
9.5000 g., Nickel-Brass, 22.5 mm. **Ruler:** Elizabeth II **Obv:** Crowned head right **Obv. Designer:** Raphael Maklouf **Rev:** Welsh leek, crown encircles **Rev. Designer:** Leslie Durbin **Edge Lettering:** PLEIDIOL WYF I'M GWLAD

Date	Mintage	F	VF	XF	Unc	BU
1985	228,431,000	—	—	2.00	3.50	5.00
1985 Proof	102,000	Value: 6.00				
1990	97,269,000	—	—	2.00	4.00	5.50
1990 Proof	100,000	Value: 6.00				

KM# 941a POUND
9.5000 g., 0.9250 Silver .2825 oz. ASW, 22.5 mm. **Ruler:** Elizabeth II **Obv:** Crowned head right **Obv. Designer:** Raphael Maklouf **Rev:** Welsh leek, crown encircles **Rev. Designer:** Leslie Durbin

Date	Mintage	F	VF	XF	Unc	BU
1985 Proof	50,000	Value: 27.50				
1990 Proof	Est. 25,000	Value: 36.50				

KM# 946 POUND
9.5000 g., Nickel-Brass, 22.5 mm. **Ruler:** Elizabeth II **Obv:** Crowned head right **Obv. Designer:** Raphael Maklouf **Rev:** Northern Ireland - Blooming flax, crown encircles **Rev. Designer:** Leslie Durbin **Edge Lettering:** DECUS ET TUTAMEN

Date	Mintage	F	VF	XF	Unc	BU
1986	10,410,000	—	—	2.00	4.00	5.50
1986 Proof	125,000	Value: 6.00				
1991	38,444,000	—	—	2.00	4.00	5.50
1991 Proof	—	Value: 6.00				

KM# 946a POUND
9.5000 g., 0.9250 Silver .2825 oz. ASW, 22.5 mm. **Ruler:** Elizabeth II **Obv:** Crowned head right **Obv. Designer:** Raphael Maklouf **Rev:** Northern Ireland - Blooming flax, crown encircles **Rev. Designer:** Leslie Durbin

Date	Mintage	F	VF	XF	Unc	BU
1986 Proof	50,000	Value: 27.50				
1991 Proof	Est. 25,000	Value: 35.00				

KM# 948 POUND
9.5000 g., Nickel-Brass, 22.5 mm. **Ruler:** Elizabeth II **Obv:** Crowned head right **Obv. Designer:** Raphael Maklouf **Rev:** Oak tree, crown encircles **Rev. Designer:** Leslie Durbin **Edge Lettering:** DECUS ET TUTAMEN

Date	Mintage	F	VF	XF	Unc	BU
1987	39,299,000	—	—	—	3.50	5.00
1987 Proof	125,000	Value: 6.00				
1992	36,320,000	—	—	—	4.00	5.50
1992 Proof	—	Value: 6.00				

KM# 948a POUND
9.5000 g., 0.9250 Silver .2825 oz. ASW, 22.5 mm. **Ruler:** Elizabeth II **Obv:** Crowned head right **Obv. Designer:** Raphael Maklouf **Rev:** Oak tree, crown encircles **Rev. Designer:** Leslie Durbin

Date	Mintage	F	VF	XF	Unc	BU
1987 Proof	50,000	Value: 27.50				
1992 Proof	Est. 25,000	Value: 36.50				

KM# 954 POUND
9.5000 g., Nickel-Brass, 22.5 mm. **Ruler:** Elizabeth II **Obv:** Crowned head right **Obv. Designer:** Raphael Maklouf **Rev:** Crowned shield of the United Kingdom **Rev. Designer:** Derek Carringe **Edge Lettering:** DECUS ET TUTAMEN

Date	Mintage	F	VF	XF	Unc	BU
1988	7,119,000	—	—	—	4.00	5.50
1988 Proof	Est. 125,000	Value: 7.00				

KM# 954a POUND
9.5000 g., 0.9250 Silver .2825 oz. ASW, 22.5 mm. **Ruler:** Elizabeth II **Obv:** Crowned head right **Obv. Designer:** Raphael Maklouf **Rev:** Crowned shield of the United Kingdom **Rev. Designer:** Derek Carringe

Date	Mintage	F	VF	XF	Unc	BU
1988 Proof	Est. 50,000	Value: 40.00				

KM# 959 POUND
9.5000 g., Nickel-Brass, 22.5 mm. **Ruler:** Elizabeth II **Obv:** Crowned head right **Obv. Designer:** Raphael Maklouf **Rev:** Scottish thistle, crown encircles **Rev. Designer:** Leslie Durbin **Edge Lettering:** NEMO ME IMPUNE LACESSIT

Date	Mintage	F	VF	XF	Unc	BU
1989	70,581,000	—	—	—	4.00	5.50
1989 Proof	100,000	Value: 6.00				

KM# 959a POUND
9.5000 g., 0.9250 Silver .2825 oz. ASW, 22.5 mm. **Ruler:** Elizabeth II **Obv:** Crowned head right **Obv. Designer:** Raphael Maklouf **Rev:** Scottish thistle, crown encircles **Rev. Designer:** Leslie Durbin

Date	Mintage	F	VF	XF	Unc	BU
1989 Proof	Est. 25,000	Value: 32.50				

KM# 964 POUND
9.5000 g., Nickel-Brass, 22.5 mm. **Ruler:** Elizabeth II **Obv:** Crowned head right **Obv. Designer:** Raphael Maklouf **Rev:** Shield of Great Britain with Garter, crowned and supported **Rev. Designer:** Eric Sewell **Edge Lettering:** DECUS ET TUTAMEN

Date	Mintage	F	VF	XF	Unc	BU
1993	114,745,000	—	—	—	4.00	5.50
1993 Proof	—	Value: 6.00				

KM# 964a POUND
9.5000 g., 0.9250 Silver .2825 oz. ASW, 22.5 mm. **Ruler:** Elizabeth II **Obv:** Crowned head right **Obv. Designer:** Raphael Maklouf **Rev:** Shield of Great Britain within Garter, crowned and supported **Rev. Designer:** Eric Sewell

Date	Mintage	F	VF	XF	Unc	BU
1993 Proof	Est. 25,000	Value: 40.00				

KM# 967 POUND
9.5000 g., Nickel-Brass, 22.5 mm. **Ruler:** Elizabeth II **Obv:** Crowned head right **Obv. Designer:** Raphael Maklouf **Rev:** Scottish arms; rampant lion left within circle **Rev. Designer:** Norman Sillman **Edge Lettering:** NEMO ME IMPUNE LACESSIT

Date	Mintage	F	VF	XF	Unc	BU
1994	29,753,000	—	—	2.00	3.50	6.00
1994 Proof	—	Value: 6.00				

KM# 967a POUND

9.5000 g., 0.9250 Silver .2825 oz. ASW, 22.5 mm. **Ruler:** Elizabeth II **Obv:** Crowned head right **Obv. Designer:** Raphael Maklouf **Rev:** Scottish arms; rampant lion left within circle **Rev. Designer:** Norman Sillman

Date	Mintage	F	VF	XF	Unc	BU
1994 Proof	Est. 25,000	Value: 60.00				

KM# 969 POUND

9.5000 g., Nickel-Brass, 22.5 mm. **Ruler:** Elizabeth II **Obv:** Crowned head right **Obv. Designer:** Raphael Maklouf **Rev:** Welsh Dragon left **Rev. Designer:** Norman Sillman **Edge Lettering:** PLEIDIOL WYF I'M GWLAD

Date	Mintage	F	VF	XF	Unc	BU
1995	34,504,000	—	—	2.50	5.50	7.00
1995 Proof	100,000	Value: 7.00				

KM# 969a POUND

9.5000 g., 0.9250 Silver .2825 oz. ASW, 22.5 mm. **Ruler:** Elizabeth II **Obv:** Crowned head right **Obv. Designer:** Raphael Maklouf **Rev:** Welsh dragon left **Rev. Designer:** Norman Sillman

Date	Mintage	F	VF	XF	Unc	BU
1995 Proof	27,000	Value: 37.50				

KM# 972 POUND

9.5000 g., Nickel-Brass, 22.5 mm. **Ruler:** Elizabeth II **Obv:** Crowned head right **Obv. Designer:** Raphael Maklouf **Rev:** Celtic Cross **Rev. Designer:** Norman Sillman **Edge Lettering:** DECUS ET TUTAMEN

Date	Mintage	F	VF	XF	Unc	BU
1996	89,886,000	—	—	—	3.50	5.00
1996 Proof	Est. 100,000	Value: 6.00				

KM# 972a POUND

9.5000 g., 0.9250 Silver .2825 oz. ASW, 22.5 mm. **Ruler:** Elizabeth II **Obv:** Crowned head right **Obv. Designer:** Raphael Maklouf **Rev:** Celtic cross **Rev. Designer:** Norman Sillman

Date	Mintage	F	VF	XF	Unc	BU
1996 Proof	40,000	Value: 37.50				

KM# 975 POUND

9.5000 g., Nickel-Brass, 22.5 mm. **Ruler:** Elizabeth II **Obv:** Crowned head right **Obv. Designer:** Raphael Maklouf **Rev:** Plantagenet lions **Rev. Designer:** Norman Sillman **Edge Lettering:** DECUS ET TUTAMEN

Date	Mintage	F	VF	XF	Unc	BU
1996	—	—	—	—	—	—
Note: Counterfeit date						
1997	57,117,450	—	—	—	3.50	5.50
1997 Proof	Est. 100,000	Value: 6.00				

KM# 975a POUND

9.5000 g., 0.9250 Silver .2825 oz. ASW, 22.5 mm. **Ruler:** Elizabeth II **Obv:** Crowned head right **Obv. Designer:** Raphael Maklouf **Rev:** Plantagenet lions **Rev. Designer:** Norman Sillman **Edge Lettering:** DECUS ET TUTAMEN

Date	Mintage	F	VF	XF	Unc	BU
1997 Proof	30,000	Value: 40.00				

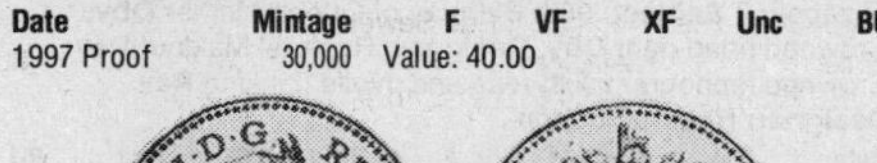

KM# 993 POUND

9.5000 g., Nickel-Brass, 22.5 mm. **Ruler:** Elizabeth II **Obv:** Head with tiara right **Obv. Designer:** Ian Rank-Broadley **Rev:** Shield of Great Britain within Garter, crowned and supported **Rev. Designer:** Eric Sewell **Edge Lettering:** DECUS ET TUTAMEN

Date	Mintage	F	VF	XF	Unc	BU
1998	Est. 100,000	—	—	—	8.50	10.00
Note: In sets only						

KM# 993a POUND

9.5000 g., 0.9250 Silver .2825 oz. ASW, 22.5 mm. **Ruler:** Elizabeth II **Obv:** Head with tiara right **Obv. Designer:** Ian Rank-Broadley **Rev:** Shield of Great Britain within Garter, crowned and supported **Rev. Designer:** Eric Sewell

Date	Mintage	F	VF	XF	Unc	BU
1998	13,863	—	—	—	40.00	—

KM# 998 POUND

9.5000 g., Nickel-Brass, 22.5 mm. **Ruler:** Elizabeth II **Obv:** Head with tiara right **Obv. Designer:** Ian Rank-Broadley **Rev:** Scottish lion within circle **Rev. Designer:** Norman Sillman **Edge Lettering:** NEMO ME IMPUNE LACESSTT

Date	Mintage	F	VF	XF	Unc	BU
1999	—	—	—	2.00	3.50	6.00
Note: In sets only						
1999 Proof	Est. 100,000	Value: 6.00				

KM# 998a POUND

9.5000 g., 0.9250 Silver .2825 oz. ASW, 22.5 mm. **Ruler:** Elizabeth II **Obv:** Head with tiara right **Obv. Designer:** Ian Rank-Broadley **Rev:** Scottish lion within circle **Rev. Designer:** Eric Sewell

Date	Mintage	F	VF	XF	Unc	BU
1999 Proof	23,000	Value: 40.00				
1999 Proof	Est. 2,000	—	—	—	—	—
Note: Frosted reverse						

KM# 1005 POUND

9.5000 g., Nickel-Brass, 22.5 mm. **Ruler:** Elizabeth II **Obv:** Head with tiara right **Obv. Designer:** Ian Rank-Broadley **Rev:** Welsh dragon left **Rev. Designer:** Norman Sillman **Edge:** Reeded and lettered **Edge Lettering:** PLEIDOL WYF I'M GWLAD

Date	Mintage	F	VF	XF	Unc	BU
2000	109,496,500	—	—	—	3.50	7.00
2000 Proof	Est. 100,000	Value: 6.00				

KM# 1005a POUND

9.5000 g., 0.9250 Silver 0.2825 oz. ASW, 22.5 mm. **Ruler:** Elizabeth II **Subject:** Wales **Obv:** Head with tiara right **Obv. Designer:** Ian Rank-Broadley **Rev:** Welsh dragon left **Rev. Designer:** Norman Silllman **Edge:** Reeded **Edge Lettering:** PLEIDIOL WYF I'M GWLAD

Date	Mintage	F	VF	XF	Unc	BU
2000 Proof	15,865	Value: 40.00				

KM# 947 2 POUNDS

15.9800 g., Nickel-Brass, 28.4 mm. **Ruler:** Elizabeth II **Subject:** Commonwealth Games **Obv:** Crowned head right **Obv. Designer:** Raphael Maklouf **Rev:** Thistle on St. Andrew's Cross **Rev. Designer:** Norman Sillman **Edge Lettering:** XIII COMMONWEALTH GAMES SCOTLAND 1986

Date	Mintage	F	VF	XF	Unc	BU
1986	8,212,000	—	—	4.50	6.50	10.00
1986 Proof	125,000	Value: 11.50				

KM# 947a 2 POUNDS

15.9800 g., 0.5000 Silver .2569 oz. ASW, 28.4 mm. **Ruler:** Elizabeth II **Subject:** Commonwealth Games **Obv:** Crowned head right **Obv. Designer:** Raphael Maklouf **Rev:** Thistle on St. Andrew's cross **Rev. Designer:** Norman Sillman

Date	Mintage	F	VF	XF	Unc	BU
1986	125,000	—	—	—	15.00	20.00

KM# 947b 2 POUNDS

15.9800 g., 0.9250 Silver .4752 oz. ASW, 28.4 mm. **Ruler:** Elizabeth II **Subject:** Commonwealth Games **Obv:** Crowned head right **Obv. Designer:** Raphael Maklouf **Rev:** Thistle on St. Andrew's Cross **Rev. Designer:** Norman Sillman

Date	Mintage	F	VF	XF	Unc	BU
1986 Proof	75,000	Value: 25.00				

KM# 947c 2 POUNDS

15.9800 g., 0.9170 Gold .4710 oz. AGW, 28.4 mm. **Ruler:** Elizabeth II **Subject:** Commonwealth Games **Obv:** Crowned head right **Obv. Designer:** Raphael Maklouf **Rev:** Thistle on St. Andrew's Cross **Rev. Designer:** Norman Sillman

Date	Mintage	F	VF	XF	Unc	BU
1986 Proof	18,000	Value: 350				

KM# 960 2 POUNDS

15.9800 g., Nickel-Brass, 28.4 mm. **Ruler:** Elizabeth II **Subject:** Tercentenary - Bill of Rights **Obv:** Crowned head right **Obv. Designer:** Raphael Maklouf **Rev:** St. Edward's crown above sceptre and WM monogram **Rev. Designer:** John Lobban

Date	Mintage	F	VF	XF	Unc	BU
ND(1989)	4,397,000	—	—	—	6.50	10.00
ND(1989) Proof	100,000	Value: 11.50				

KM# 960a 2 POUNDS

15.9800 g., 0.9250 Silver .4752 oz. ASW, 28.4 mm. **Ruler:** Elizabeth II **Subject:** Tercentenary - Bill of Rights **Obv:** Crowned head right **Obv. Designer:** Raphael Maklouf **Rev:** St. Edward's crowned above sceptre and WM monogram **Rev. Designer:** John Lobban

Date	Mintage	F	VF	XF	Unc	BU
ND(1989) Proof	25,000	Value: 25.00				

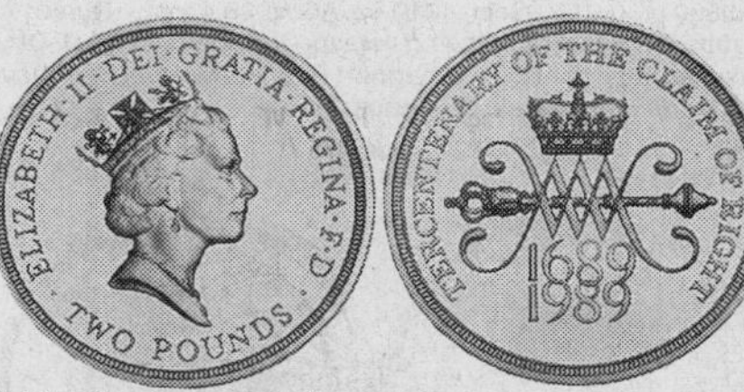

KM# 961 2 POUNDS

15.9800 g., Nickel-Brass, 28.4 mm. **Ruler:** Elizabeth II **Subject:** Tercentenary - Bill of Rights **Obv:** Crowned head right **Obv. Designer:** Raphael Maklouf **Rev:** Crown of Scotland above sceptre and WM monogram **Rev. Designer:** John Lobban

Date	Mintage	F	VF	XF	Unc	BU
ND(1989)	346,000	—	—	—	9.00	15.00
ND(1989) Proof	100,000	Value: 17.50				

KM# 961a 2 POUNDS

15.9800 g., 0.9250 Silver .4752 oz. ASW, 28.4 mm. **Ruler:** Elizabeth II **Subject:** Tercentenary - Bill of Rights **Obv:** Crowned head right **Obv. Designer:** Raphael Maklouf **Rev:** Crown of Scotland above sceptre and WM monogram **Rev. Designer:** John Lobban

Date	Mintage	F	VF	XF	Unc	BU
ND(1989) Proof	25,000	Value: 25.00				

KM# 968 2 POUNDS

15.9800 g., Nickel-Brass, 28.4 mm. **Ruler:** Elizabeth II **Subject:** 300th Anniversary - Bank of England **Obv:** Crowned head right **Obv. Designer:** Raphael Maklouf **Rev:** Britiannia seated within oval divides dates, crowned WM monogram above **Edge Lettering:** SIC VOS NON VOBIS

Date	Mintage	F	VF	XF	Unc	BU
ND(1994)	1,443,000	—	—	—	5.50	9.00
ND(1994) Proof	—	Value: 10.00				

KM# 968a 2 POUNDS

15.9800 g., 0.9250 Silver .4752 oz. ASW, 28.4 mm. **Ruler:** Elizabeth II **Subject:** 300th Anniversary - Bank of England **Obv:** Crowned head right **Obv. Designer:** Raphael Maklouf **Rev:** Britiannia seated within oval, Crowned WM monogram above

Date	Mintage	F	VF	XF	Unc	BU
ND(1994) Proof	Est. 40,000	Value: 40.00				

KM# 968c 2 POUNDS

15.9800 g., 0.9170 Gold .4710 oz. AGW, 28.4 mm. **Ruler:** Elizabeth II **Subject:** 300th Anniversary - Bank of England **Obv:** Crowned head right **Obv. Designer:** Raphael Maklouf **Rev:** Britiannia seated within oval, Crowned WM monogram above

Date	Mintage	F	VF	XF	Unc	BU
ND(1994) Proof	Est. 3,500	Value: 470				

KM# 1012 2 POUNDS

15.9800 g., 0.9170 Gold .4710 oz. AGW, 28.4 mm. **Ruler:** Elizabeth II **Obv:** Crowned head right **Rev:** Britiannia seated within oval, crowned WM monogram above **Note:** Muled die error.

Date	Mintage	F	VF	XF	Unc	BU
ND(1994)	—	—	—	—	600	—

KM# 970 2 POUNDS

15.9800 g., Nickel-Brass, 28.4 mm. **Ruler:** Elizabeth II **Subject:** 50th Anniversary - End of World War II **Obv:** Crowned head right **Obv. Designer:** Raphael Maklouf **Rev:** Large dove with laurel branch **Rev. Designer:** John Mills **Edge Lettering:** 1945 IN PEACE GOODWILL 1995

Date	Mintage	F	VF	XF	Unc	BU
ND(1995)	6,057,000	—	—	—	6.00	10.00
ND(1995) Proof	100,000	Value: 12.00				

KM# 970a 2 POUNDS

15.9800 g., 0.9250 Silver .4752 oz. ASW, 28.4 mm. **Ruler:** Elizabeth II **Subject:** 50th Anniversary - End of World War II **Obv:** Crowned head right **Obv. Designer:** Raphael Maklouf **Rev:** Dove with laurel branch **Rev. Designer:** John Mills

Date	Mintage	F	VF	XF	Unc	BU
ND(1995) Proof	50,000	Value: 40.00				

KM# 970c 2 POUNDS

15.9800 g., 0.9170 Gold .4710 oz. AGW, 28.4 mm. **Ruler:** Elizabeth II **Subject:** 50th Anniversary - End of World War II **Obv:** Crowned head right **Obv. Designer:** Raphael Maklouf **Rev:** Dove with laurel branch **Rev. Designer:** John Mills

Date	Mintage	F	VF	XF	Unc	BU
ND(1995) Proof	2,500	Value: 475				

KM# 971 2 POUNDS

15.9800 g., Nickel-Brass, 28.4 mm. **Ruler:** Elizabeth II **Subject:** 50th Anniversary - United Nations **Obv:** Crowned head right **Obv. Designer:** Raphael Maklouf **Rev:** Flags and UN Logo **Rev. Designer:** Michael Rizzello **Note:** Mintage included with KM#970.

Date	Mintage	F	VF	XF	Unc	BU
ND(1995)	Inc. above	—	—	—	6.00	9.00

KM# 971a 2 POUNDS

15.9760 g., 0.9250 Silver .4751 oz. ASW, 28.4 mm. **Ruler:** Elizabeth II **Subject:** 50th Anniversary - United Nations **Obv:** Crowned head right **Obv. Designer:** Raphael Maklouf **Rev:** Flags and UN Logo **Rev. Designer:** Michael Rizzello

Date	Mintage	F	VF	XF	Unc	BU
ND(1995) Proof	Est. 175,000	Value: 40.00				

KM# 971c 2 POUNDS

15.9760 g., 0.9170 Gold .4708 oz. AGW, 28.4 mm. **Ruler:** Elizabeth II **Subject:** 50th Anniversary - United Nations **Obv:** Crowned head right **Obv. Designer:** Raphael Maklouf **Rev:** Flags and UN Logo **Rev. Designer:** Michael Rizzello

Date	Mintage	F	VF	XF	Unc	BU
ND(1995) Proof	Est. 5,000	Value: 450				

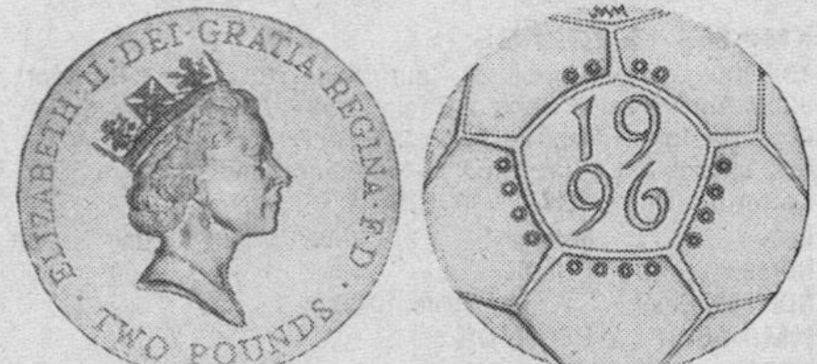

KM# 973 2 POUNDS

15.9800 g., Nickel-Brass, 28.4 mm. **Ruler:** Elizabeth II **Obv:** Crowned head right **Obv. Designer:** Raphael Maklouf **Rev:** Soccer ball, date in center **Rev. Designer:** John Mills **Edge Lettering:** TENTH EUROPEAN CHAMPIONSHIP

Date	Mintage	F	VF	XF	Unc	BU
1996	5,141,000	—	—	—	6.50	10.00
1996 Proof	Est. 100,000	Value: 11.50				

KM# 973a 2 POUNDS

15.9760 g., 0.9250 Silver .4751 oz. ASW, 28.4 mm. **Ruler:** Elizabeth II **Obv:** Crowned head right **Obv. Designer:** Raphael Maklouf **Rev:** Soccer ball, date at center **Rev. Designer:** John Mills

Date	Mintage	F	VF	XF	Unc	BU
1996 Proof	—	Value: 40.00				

KM# 976 2 POUNDS

12.0000 g., Bi-Metallic Copper-Nickel center in Nickel-Brass ring, 28.35 mm. **Ruler:** Elizabeth II **Obv:** Crowned head right **Obv. Designer:** Raphael Maklouf **Rev:** Celtic designs within circle **Rev. Designer:** Bruce Rushin **Edge Lettering:** STANDING ON THE SHOULDERS OF GIANTS

Date	Mintage	F	VF	XF	Unc	BU
1997	13,735,000	—	—	—	7.50	12.50
1997 Proof	Est. 100,000	Value: 13.00				

KM# 976a 2 POUNDS

12.0000 g., 0.9250 Silver .3568 oz. ASW, 28.35 mm. **Ruler:** Elizabeth II **Obv:** Crowned head right **Obv. Designer:** Raphael Maklouf **Rev:** Celtic designs within circle **Rev. Designer:** Bruce Rushin **Note:** Gold plated silver ring, silver center.

Date	Mintage	F	VF	XF	Unc	BU
1997 Proof	Est. 40,000	Value: 45.00				

KM# 976b 2 POUNDS

15.9800 g., 0.9170 Gold .4710 oz. AGW, 28.35 mm. **Ruler:** Elizabeth II **Obv:** Crowned head right **Obv. Designer:** Raphael Maklouf **Rev:** Celtic design within circle **Rev. Designer:** Bruce Rushin **Note:** Red gold ring, yellow gold center.

Date	Mintage	F	VF	XF	Unc	BU
1997 Proof	Est. 2,500	Value: 600				

KM# 994a 2 POUNDS

12.0000 g., 0.9250 Silver .3568 oz. ASW, 28.35 mm. **Ruler:** Elizabeth II **Obv:** Head with tiara right within circle **Obv. Designer:** Ian Rank-Broadley **Rev:** Celtic design within circle **Rev. Designer:** Bruce Rushin **Note:** Gold plated silver ring, silver center.

Date	Mintage	F	VF	XF	Unc	BU
1998 Proof	7,646	Value: 50.00				
2000 Proof	15,000	—	—	—	—	—

KM# 994 2 POUNDS

12.0000 g., Bi-Metallic Copper-Nickel center in Nickel-Brass ring, 28.35 mm. **Ruler:** Elizabeth II **Obv:** Head with tiara right within circle **Obv. Designer:** Ian Rank-Broadley **Rev:** Celtic design within circle **Rev. Designer:** Bruce Rushin **Edge Lettering:** STANDING ON THE SHOULDERS OF GIANTS

Date	Mintage	F	VF	XF	Unc	BU
1998	91,110,375	—	—	—	6.00	8.50
1998 Proof	Est. 100,000	Value: 10.00				
1999	38,652,000	—	—	—	6.00	8.50
1999 Proof	—	Value: 10.00				
2000	25,770,000	—	—	—	6.00	8.50
2000 Proof	—	Value: 10.00				

KM# 994b 2 POUNDS

12.0000 g., 0.9250 Silver .3568 oz. ASW, 28.35 mm. **Ruler:** Elizabeth II **Obv:** Head with tiara right within circle **Obv. Designer:** Ian Rank-Broadley **Rev:** Celtic design within circle **Rev. Designer:** Bruce Rushin **Note:** Without gold plating.

Date	Mintage	F	VF	XF	Unc	BU
1998 Proof	19,978	Value: 40.00				

KM# 994c 2 POUNDS

15.9800 g., 0.9167 Gold 0.471 oz. AGW, 28.35 mm. **Ruler:** Elizabeth II **Obv:** Head with tiara right within circle **Obv. Designer:** Ian Rank-Broadley **Rev:** Celtic design within circle **Rev. Designer:** Bruce Rushin

Date	Mintage	F	VF	XF	Unc	BU
2000	1,250	—	—	—	—	—

KM# 999 2 POUNDS

12.0000 g., Bi-Metallic Copper-Nickel center in Nickel-Brass ring, 28.35 mm. **Ruler:** Elizabeth II **Subject:** Rugby World Cup **Obv:** Head with tiara right **Rev:** 2-tone rugby design **Rev. Designer:** Ron Dutton **Edge Lettering:** RUGBY WORLD CUP 1999 **Note:** Varieties exist.

Date	Mintage	F	VF	XF	Unc	BU
1999	5,000,000	—	—	—	7.00	9.00
1999 Proof	Est. 100,000	Value: 11.50				

KM# 999a 2 POUNDS

12.0000 g., 0.9250 Silver .3569 oz. ASW, 28.35 mm. **Ruler:** Elizabeth II **Subject:** Rugby World Cup **Obv:** Head with tiara right **Obv. Designer:** Ian Rank-Broadley **Rev:** 2-tone rugby design **Rev. Designer:** Ron Dutton **Edge:** Reeded, lettered edge **Note:** Gold plated ring.

Date	Mintage	F	VF	XF	Unc	BU
1999 Proof	Est. 25,000	Value: 47.50				

KM# 999b 2 POUNDS

15.9800 g., 0.9170 Gold .4710 oz. AGW, 28.35 mm. **Ruler:** Elizabeth II **Subject:** Rugby World Cup **Obv:** Head with tiara right **Obv. Designer:** Ian Rank-Broadley **Rev:** 2-tone rugby design **Rev. Designer:** Ron Dutton

Date	Mintage	F	VF	XF	Unc	BU
1999 Proof	4,250	Value: 500				

KM# 999c 2 POUNDS

24.0000 g., 0.9250 Silver .7137 oz. ASW, 28.35 mm. **Ruler:** Elizabeth II **Obv:** Head with tiara right within gold-plated ring **Rev:** Multicolor hologram center within gold-plated ring **Edge:** Reeded, lettered edge

Date	Mintage	F	VF	XF	Unc	BU
1999 Proof	10,000	Value: 75.00				

KM# 962 5 POUNDS

28.2800 g., Copper-Nickel, 38.61 mm. **Ruler:** Elizabeth II **Subject:** 90th Birthday of Queen Mother **Obv:** Crowned head right **Obv. Designer:** Raphael Maklouf **Rev:** Crowned monogram with rose and thistle flanking **Rev. Designer:** Robert Elderton

Date	Mintage	F	VF	XF	Unc	BU
ND(1990)	2,761,000	—	—	—	15.00	17.00

KM# 962a 5 POUNDS

28.2800 g., 0.9250 Silver .8411 oz. ASW, 38.61 mm. **Ruler:** Elizabeth II **Subject:** 90th Birthday of Queen Mother **Obv:** Crowned head right **Obv. Designer:** Raphael Maklouf **Rev:** Crowned monogram with rose and thistle flanking **Rev. Designer:** Robert Elderton

Date	Mintage	F	VF	XF	Unc	BU
ND(1990) Proof	Est. 150,000	Value: 40.00				

KM# 962b 5 POUNDS

39.9400 g., 0.9170 Gold 1.1775 oz. AGW, 38.61 mm. **Ruler:** Elizabeth II **Subject:** 90th Birthday of Queen Mother **Obv:** Crowned head right **Obv. Designer:** Raphael Maklouf **Rev:** Crowned monogram with rose and thistle flanking **Rev. Designer:** Robert Elderton

Date	Mintage	F	VF	XF	Unc	BU
ND(1990) Proof	Est. 2,500	Value: 845				

KM# 965 5 POUNDS

28.2800 g., Copper-Nickel, 38.61 mm. **Ruler:** Elizabeth II **Subject:** 40th Anniversary of Reign **Obv:** Laureate head, right within circle of bugling horsemen **Obv. Designer:** Mary Gillick and Robert Elderton **Rev:** Crown within circle **Rev. Designer:** Robert Elderton

Date	Mintage	F	VF	XF	Unc	BU
ND(1993)	1,835,000	—	—	—	13.50	15.00
ND(1993) Proof	Est. 100,000	Value: 18.50				

KM# 965a 5 POUNDS

28.2800 g., 0.9250 Silver .8411 oz. ASW, 38.61 mm. **Ruler:** Elizabeth II **Subject:** 40th Anniversary of Reign **Obv:** Laureate head right within circle of bugling horsemen **Obv. Designer:** Mary Gillick and Robert Elderton **Rev:** Crown within circle **Rev. Designer:** Robert Elderton

Date	Mintage	F	VF	XF	Unc	BU
ND(1993) Proof	Est. 100,000	Value: 45.00				

KM# 965b 5 POUNDS

39.9400 g., 0.9170 Gold 1.1775 oz. AGW, 38.61 mm. **Ruler:** Elizabeth II **Subject:** 40th Anniversary of Reign **Obv:** Laureate head right with circle of bugling horsemen **Obv. Designer:** Mary Gillick and Robert Elderton **Rev:** Crown within circle **Rev. Designer:** Robert Elderton

Date	Mintage	F	VF	XF	Unc	BU
ND(1993) Proof	Est. 2,500	Value: 900				

KM# 974 5 POUNDS

28.2800 g., Copper-Nickel, 38.61 mm. **Ruler:** Elizabeth II **Subject:** 70th Birthday of Queen Elizabeth II **Obv:** Crowned head right **Rev:** Five banners above Windsor Castle **Rev. Designer:** Avril Vaughan **Edge Lettering:** VIVAT REGINA ELIZABETHA

Date	Mintage	F	VF	XF	Unc	BU
ND(1996)	2,936,000	—	—	—	14.00	16.00
ND(1996) Proof	—	Value: 22.00				

KM# 974a 5 POUNDS

28.2800 g., 0.9250 Silver .8411 oz. ASW, 38.61 mm. **Ruler:** Elizabeth II **Subject:** 70th Birthday of Queen Elizabeth II **Obv:** Crowned head right **Rev:** Five banners above Windsor Castle **Rev. Designer:** Avril Vaughan

Date	Mintage	F	VF	XF	Unc	BU
ND(1996) Proof	Est. 70,000	Value: 45.00				

KM# 974b 5 POUNDS

39.9400 g., 0.9170 Gold 1.1775 oz. AGW, 38.61 mm. **Ruler:** Elizabeth II **Subject:** 70th Birthday of Queen Elizabeth II **Obv:** Crowned head right **Rev:** Five banners above Windsor Castle **Rev. Designer:** Avril Vaughan

Date	Mintage	F	VF	XF	Unc	BU
ND(1996) Proof	Est. 2,750	Value: 900				

KM# 977 5 POUNDS

28.2800 g., Copper-Nickel, 38.61 mm. **Ruler:** Elizabeth II **Subject:** Queen Elizabeth II and Prince Philip - Golden Wedding Anniversary **Obv:** Jugate busts right **Rev:** Crown above two shields, anchor below

Date	Mintage	F	VF	XF	Unc	BU
ND(1997)	1,733,000	—	—	—	15.00	17.00
ND(1997) Proof	—	Value: 22.00				

KM# 977a 5 POUNDS

28.2800 g., 0.9250 Silver .8411 oz. ASW, 38.61 mm. **Ruler:** Elizabeth II **Subject:** Queen Elizabeth II and Prince Philip - Golden Wedding Anniversary **Obv:** Jugate busts right **Rev:** Crown above two shields, anchor below

Date	Mintage	F	VF	XF	Unc	BU
ND(1997) Proof	Est. 70,000	Value: 50.00				

KM# 977b 5 POUNDS

39.9400 g., 0.9170 Gold 1.1775 oz. AGW, 38.61 mm. **Ruler:** Elizabeth II **Subject:** Queen Elizabeth II and Prince Philip - Golden Wedding Anniversary **Obv:** Jugate busts right **Rev:** Crown above two shields, anchor below

Date	Mintage	F	VF	XF	Unc	BU
ND(1997) Proof	Est. 2,750	Value: 900				

KM# 995 5 POUNDS

28.2800 g., Copper-Nickel, 38.61 mm. **Ruler:** Elizabeth II **Subject:** 50th Birthday - Prince Charles **Obv:** Head with tiara right **Obv. Designer:** Ian Rank-Broadley **Rev:** Portrait of Prince Charles

Date	Mintage	F	VF	XF	Unc	BU
1998	1,407,000	—	—	—	15.00	—
1998 Proof	Est. 100,000	Value: 20.00				

KM# 995a 5 POUNDS

28.2800 g., 0.9250 Silver .8411 oz. ASW, 38.61 mm. **Ruler:** Elizabeth II **Subject:** 50th Birthday - Prince Charles **Obv:** Head right **Rev:** Portrait of Prince Charles

Date	Mintage	F	VF	XF	Unc	BU
1998 Proof	13,379	Value: 50.00				

KM# 995b 5 POUNDS

39.9400 g., 0.9167 Gold 1.1771 oz. AGW, 38.61 mm. **Ruler:** Elizabeth II **Subject:** 50th Birthday - Prince Charles **Obv:** Head with tiara right **Obv. Designer:** Ian Rank-Broadley **Rev:** Portrait of Prince Charles

Date	Mintage	F	VF	XF	Unc	BU
1998 Proof	773	Value: 900				

KM# 997 5 POUNDS

Copper-Nickel, 38.61 mm. **Ruler:** Elizabeth II **Subject:** In Memory of Diana - Princess of Wales **Obv:** Head with tiara right **Obv. Designer:** Ian Rank-Broadley **Rev:** Head right, dates **Rev. Designer:** David Cornell

Date	Mintage	F	VF	XF	Unc	BU
1999	5,000,000	—	—	—	16.00	18.00
1999 Proof	Est. 100,000	Value: 22.00				

KM# 997a 5 POUNDS

28.2800 g., 0.9250 Silver .8410 oz. ASW, 38.61 mm. **Ruler:** Elizabeth II **Subject:** In Memory of Diana - Princess of Wales **Obv:** Head with tiara right **Obv. Designer:** Ian Rank-Broadley **Rev:** Head right, dates **Rev. Designer:** David Cornell

Date	Mintage	F	VF	XF	Unc	BU
1999 Proof	Est. 49,545	Value: 50.00				

KM# 997b 5 POUNDS

39.9400 g., 0.9170 Gold 1.1775 oz. AGW, 38.61 mm. **Ruler:** Elizabeth II **Subject:** In Memory of Diana - Princess of Wales **Obv:** Head with tiara right **Obv. Designer:** Ian Rank-Broadley **Rev:** Head right, dates **Rev. Designer:** David Cornell

Date	Mintage	F	VF	XF	Unc	BU
1999 Proof	Est. 7,500	Value: 875				

KM# 1006 5 POUNDS

28.2800 g., Copper-Nickel, 38.61 mm. **Ruler:** Elizabeth II **Obv:** Head with tiara right **Rev:** Map with Greenwich Meridian **Rev. Designer:** Jeffrey Matthews **Edge Lettering:** WHAT'S PAST IS PROLOGUE

Date	Mintage	F	VF	XF	Unc	BU
1999 Proof	—	Value: 20.00				
1999	5,396,300	—	—	—	14.00	16.00
2000	3,147,010	—	—	—	14.00	16.00
2000 Proof	Est. 100,000	Value: 20.00				

Note: Gold overlay on the British Isles

KM# 1006a 5 POUNDS

28.2800 g., 0.9250 Silver .8410 oz. ASW, 38.61 mm. **Ruler:** Elizabeth II **Obv:** Head with tiara right **Rev:** Map with Greenwich Meridian **Rev. Designer:** Jeffrey Matthews

Date	Mintage	F	VF	XF	Unc	BU
1999 Proof	75,000	Value: 55.00				
2000 Proof	50,000	Value: 55.00				

KM# 1006b 5 POUNDS

39.9400 g., 0.9170 Gold 1.1771 oz. AGW, 38.61 mm. **Ruler:** Elizabeth II **Obv:** Head with tiara right **Rev:** Map with Greenwich Meridian **Rev. Designer:** Jeffrey Matthews

Date	Mintage	F	VF	XF	Unc	BU
1999 Proof	2,500	Value: 900				
2000 Proof	2,500	Value: 900				

KM# 1006c 5 POUNDS

28.2800 g., 0.9990 Silver 0.9083 oz. ASW, 38.61 mm. **Ruler:** Elizabeth II **Obv:** Head with tiara right **Rev:** Map with Greenwich Meridian **Rev. Designer:** Jeffrey Matthews **Note:** With gold-plated British map.

Date	Mintage	F	VF	XF	Unc	BU
2000 Proof	15,000	Value: 65.00				

KM# 1006.1 5 POUNDS

28.2800 g., Copper-Nickel, 38.61 mm. **Ruler:** Elizabeth II **Obv:** Head with tiara right **Rev:** Map with Greenwich Meridian, world globe at 3 o'clock in inner circle **Rev. Designer:** Jeffrey Matthews

Date	Mintage	F	VF	XF	Unc	BU
2000	—	—	—	—	20.00	22.00

KM# 1007 5 POUNDS
Copper-Nickel **Ruler:** Elizabeth II **Subject:** 100th Birthday - Queen Elizabeth, The Queen Mother **Obv:** Head with tiara right **Rev:** Head left, signature below **Edge:** Reeded **Designer:** Ian Rank-Broadley

Date	Mintage	F	VF	XF	Unc	BU
2000	3,147,092	—	—	—	15.00	17.00

KM# 1007a 5 POUNDS
28.2800 g., 0.9250 Silver .8410 oz. ASW, 38.61 mm. **Ruler:** Elizabeth II **Subject:** Queen Mother's Centennial **Obv:** Head with tiara right **Rev:** Head left with signature below **Edge:** Reeded **Designer:** Ian Rank-Broadley

Date	Mintage	F	VF	XF	Unc	BU
2000 Proof	100,000	Value: 55.00				

KM# 1007b 5 POUNDS
39.9400 g., 0.9167 Gold 1.0003 oz. AGW, 38.61 mm. **Ruler:** Elizabeth II **Subject:** Queen Mother's Centennial **Obv:** Head with tiara right **Rev:** Head left with signature below **Designer:** Ian Rank-Broadley

Date	Mintage	F	VF	XF	Unc	BU
2000 Proof	3,000	Value: 900				

BULLION COINAGE

Until 1990, .917 Gold was commonly alloyed with copper by the British Royal Mint.

All proof issues have designers name as P. Nathan. The uncirculated issues use only Nathan.

KM# 978 20 PENCE
3.2400 g., 0.9580 Silver .0998 oz. ASW **Ruler:** Elizabeth II **Obv:** Crowned head right **Rev:** Britannia in chariot

Date	Mintage	F	VF	XF	Unc	BU
1997 Proof	8,686	Value: 25.00				

KM# 979 50 PENCE
8.1100 g., 0.9580 Silver .2498 oz. ASW, 27.3 mm. **Ruler:** Elizabeth II **Obv:** Crowned head right **Rev:** Britannia in chariot

Date	Mintage	F	VF	XF	Unc	BU
1997	Est. 15,000	Value: 25.00				

Note: In proof sets only

KM# 980 POUND
16.2200 g., 0.9580 Silver .4996 oz. ASW **Ruler:** Elizabeth II **Obv:** Crowned head right **Rev:** Britannia in chariot

Date	Mintage	F	VF	XF	Unc	BU
1997 Proof	Est. 15,000	Value: 40.00				

KM# 981 2 POUNDS
32.5400 g., 0.9580 Silver .9995 oz. ASW **Ruler:** Elizabeth II **Obv:** Crowned head right **Obv. Designer:** Raphael Maklouf **Rev:** Britannia in chariot **Rev. Designer:** Philip Nathan

Date	Mintage	F	VF	XF	Unc	BU
1997 Proof	Est. 35,000	Value: 50.00				

KM# 1029 2 POUNDS
32.5400 g., 0.9580 Silver .9995 oz. ASW, 40 mm. **Ruler:** Elizabeth II **Obv:** Head with tiara right **Obv. Designer:** Ian Rank-Broadley **Rev:** Standing Britannia **Edge:** Reeded

Date	Mintage	F	VF	XF	Unc	BU
1998	88,909	—	—	—	20.00	22.00
1998 Proof	2,168	Value: 50.00				
2000	81,301	—	—	—	20.00	22.00

KM# 1000 2 POUNDS
32.5400 g., 0.9580 Silver .9995 oz. ASW **Ruler:** Elizabeth II **Obv:** Head with tiara right **Obv. Designer:** Rank-Broadley **Rev:** Britannia in chariot

Date	Mintage	F	VF	XF	Unc	BU
1999 Proof	Est. 100,000	Value: 45.00				

KM# 950 10 POUNDS (1/10 Ounce - Britannia)
3.4120 g., 0.9170 Gold .1000 oz. AGW **Ruler:** Elizabeth II **Obv:** Crowned head right **Rev:** Britannia standing **Note:** Copper alloy.

Date	Mintage	F	VF	XF	Unc	BU
1987	—	—	—	—	BV+16%	—
1987 Proof	3,500	Value: 80.00				
1988	—	—	—	—	BV+16%	—
1988 Proof	2,694	Value: 80.00				
1989	—	—	—	—	BV+16%	—
1989 Proof	1,609	Value: 80.00				

KM# 950a 10 POUNDS (1/10 Ounce - Britannia)
3.4120 g., 0.9170 Gold .1000 oz. AGW **Ruler:** Elizabeth II **Obv:** Crowned head right **Rev:** Britannia standing **Note:** Silver alloy.

Date	Mintage	F	VF	XF	Unc	BU
1990 Proof	1,571	Value: 80.00				
1991 Proof	954	Value: 125				
1992 Proof	1,000	Value: 125				
1993 Proof	997	Value: 125				
1994 Proof	994	Value: 110				
1995 Proof	1,500	Value: 110				
1996 Proof	2,379	Value: 110				
1999 Proof	Est. 5,750	Value: 100				

KM# 982 10 POUNDS (1/10 Ounce - Britannia)
3.4100 g., 0.9167 Gold .1005 oz. AGW **Ruler:** Elizabeth II **Obv:** Crowned head right **Rev:** Britannia in chariot

Date	Mintage	F	VF	XF	Unc	BU
1997 Proof	11,821	Value: 120				

KM# 1008 10 POUNDS (1/10 Ounce - Britannia)
3.4100 g., 0.9167 Gold .1005 oz. AGW **Ruler:** Elizabeth II **Obv:** Head with tiara right **Rev:** Britannia standing **Edge:** Reeded

Date	Mintage	F	VF	XF	Unc	BU
1999 Proof	1,058	Value: 115				
2000 Proof	659	Value: 100				

KM# 951 25 POUNDS (1/4 Ounce - Britannia)
8.5130 g., 0.9170 Gold .2500 oz. AGW **Ruler:** Elizabeth II **Obv:** Crowned head right **Rev:** Britannia standing **Note:** Copper alloy.

Date	Mintage	F	VF	XF	Unc	BU
1987	—	—	—	—	BV+10%	—
1987 Proof	3,500	Value: 185				
1988	—	—	—	—	BV+10%	—
1988 Proof	Est. 14,000	Value: 185				
1989	—	—	—	—	BV+10%	—
1989 Proof	Est. 4,000	Value: 185				

KM# 951a 25 POUNDS (1/4 Ounce - Britannia)
8.5130 g., 0.9170 Gold .2500 oz. AGW **Ruler:** Elizabeth II **Obv:** Crowned head right **Rev:** Britannia standing **Note:** Silver alloy.

Date	Mintage	F	VF	XF	Unc	BU
1990 Proof	Est. 2,500	Value: 195				
1991 Proof	750	Value: 225				
1992 Proof	500	Value: 225				
1993 Proof	Est. 500	Value: 225				
1994 Proof	500	Value: 215				
1995 Proof	500	Value: 215				
1996 Proof	2,500	Value: 215				
1999 Proof	1,750	Value: 215				

KM# 983 25 POUNDS (1/4 Ounce - Britannia)
8.5100 g., 0.9167 Gold .2508 oz. AGW **Ruler:** Elizabeth II **Obv:** Crowned head right **Rev:** Britannia in chariot

Date	Mintage	F	VF	XF	Unc	BU
1997 Proof	Est. 4,000	Value: 215				

KM# 1009 25 POUNDS (1/4 Ounce - Britannia)
8.5100 g., 0.9167 Gold .2508 oz. AGW **Ruler:** Elizabeth II **Obv:** Head with tiara right **Rev:** Britannia standing **Edge:** Reeded

Date	Mintage	F	VF	XF	Unc	BU
1999 Proof	1,000	Value: 220				
2000 Proof	Est. 500	Value: 200				

KM# 952 50 POUNDS (1/2 Ounce - Britannia)
17.0250 g., 0.9170 Gold .5000 oz. AGW **Ruler:** Elizabeth II **Obv:** Crowned head right **Rev:** Britannia standing **Note:** Copper alloy.

Date	Mintage	F	VF	XF	Unc	BU
1987	—	—	—	—	BV+10%	—
1987 Proof	2,486	Value: 375				
1988	—	—	—	—	BV+10%	—
1988 Proof	626	Value: 375				
1989	—	—	—	—	BV+10%	—
1989 Proof	338	Value: 375				

KM# 952a 50 POUNDS (1/2 Ounce - Britannia)
17.0250 g., 0.9170 Gold .5000 oz. AGW **Ruler:** Elizabeth II **Obv:** Crowned head right **Rev:** Britannia standing **Note:** Silver alloy.

Date	Mintage	F	VF	XF	Unc	BU
1990 Proof	527	Value: 375				
1991 Proof	509	Value: 400				
1992 Proof	500	Value: 425				
1993 Proof	462	—	—	—	—	—
1994 Proof	435	Value: 425				
1995 Proof	500	Value: 425				
1996 Proof	483	Value: 400				
1999 Proof	740	Value: 450				

KM# 984 50 POUNDS (1/2 Ounce - Britannia)
17.0300 g., 0.9167 Gold .5019 oz. AGW **Ruler:** Elizabeth II **Obv:** Crowned head right **Rev:** Britannia in chariot

Date	Mintage	F	VF	XF	Unc	BU
1997 Proof	Est. 1,500	Value: 400				

KM# 1010 50 POUNDS (1/2 Ounce - Britannia)
17.0300 g., 0.9167 Gold .5019 oz. AGW **Ruler:** Elizabeth II **Obv:** Head with tiara right **Rev:** Britannia standing **Edge:** Reeded

Date	Mintage	F	VF	XF	Unc	BU
1999 Proof	—	Value: 425				
2000 Proof	750	Value: 425				

KM# 953 100 POUNDS (1 Ounce - Britannia)
34.0500 g., 0.9170 Gold 1.0000 oz. AGW **Ruler:** Elizabeth II **Obv:** Crowned head right **Rev:** Britannia standing **Note:** Copper alloy.

Date	Mintage	F	VF	XF	Unc	BU
1987	—	—	—	—	BV+12%	—
1987 Proof	13,000	Value: 765				
1988	—	—	—	—	BV+12%	—
1988 Proof	Est. 8,500	Value: 765				
1989	—	—	—	—	BV+12%	—
1989 Proof	Est. 2,600	Value: 765				

KM# 953a 100 POUNDS (1 Ounce - Britannia)
34.0500 g., 0.9170 Gold 1.0000 oz. AGW **Ruler:** Elizabeth II **Obv:** Crowned head right **Rev:** Britannia standing **Note:** Silver alloy.

Date	Mintage	F	VF	XF	Unc	BU
1990 Proof	262	Value: 800				
1991 Proof	143	Value: 850				
1992 Proof	500	Value: 875				
1993 Proof	Est. 500	Value: 875				
1994 Proof	Est. 500	Value: 850				
1995 Proof	Est. 500	Value: 900				
1996 Proof	2,500	Value: 800				
1999 Proof	Est. 750	Value: 845				

KM# 985 100 POUNDS (1 Ounce - Britannia)
34.0500 g., 0.9167 Gold 1.0035 oz. AGW **Ruler:** Elizabeth II
Obv: Crowned head right **Rev:** Britannia in chariot

Date	Mintage	F	VF	XF	Unc	BU
1997	—	—	—	—	BV+15%	—
1997 Proof	164	Value: 865				

KM# 1011 100 POUNDS (1 Ounce - Britannia)
34.0500 g., 0.9167 Gold 1.0035 oz. AGW **Ruler:** Elizabeth II
Obv: Head with tiara right **Rev:** Britannia standing **Edge:** Reeded

Date	Mintage	F	VF	XF	Unc	BU
1999 Proof	—	Value: 875				
2000 Proof	750	Value: 875				

TRADE COINAGE

Britannia Issues

Issued to facilitate British trade in the Orient, the reverse design incorporated the denomination in Chinese characters and Malay script.

This issue was struck at the Bombay (B) and Calcutta (C) Mints in India, except for 1925 and 1930 issues which were struck at London. Through error the mint marks did not appear on some early (1895-1900) issues as indicated.

KM# T5 DOLLAR
26.9568 g., 0.9000 Silver .7800 oz. ASW **Obv:** Britannia standing
Rev: Oriental designs on cross **Designer:** G. W. de Saulles

Date	Mintage	F	VF	XF	Unc	BU
1901/0B	25,680,000	40.00	60.00	100	200	—
1901B	Inc. above	15.00	20.00	25.00	60.00	—
1901B Proof	Inc. above	Value: 800				
1901C	1,514,000	25.00	45.00	100	200	—
1902B	30,404,000	15.00	20.00	25.00	60.00	—
1902B Proof	Inc. above	Value: 800				
1902C	1,267,000	25.00	45.00	80.00	175	—
1902C Proof	Inc. above	Value: 800				
1903/2B	3,956,000	12.00	25.00	40.00	75.00	—
1903B	Inc. above	12.00	20.00	—	60.00	—
1903B Proof	Inc. above	Value: 800				
1904/898B	649,000	50.00	80.00	125	200	—
1904/3B	Inc. above	30.00	50.00	100	225	—
1904/0B	Inc. above	80.00	125	175	300	—
1904B	Inc. above	40.00	60.00	100	250	—
1904B Proof	Inc. above	Value: 700				
1907B	1,946,000	12.00	20.00	25.00	60.00	—
1908/3B	6,871,000	40.00	60.00	100	175	—
1908/7B	Inc. above	35.00	50.00	90.00	125	—
1908B	Inc. above	12.00	20.00	25.00	60.00	—
1908B Proof	Inc. above	Value: 700				
1909/8B	5,954,000	30.00	45.00	80.00	125	—
1909B	Inc. above	12.00	20.00	25.00	60.00	—
1910/00B	553,000	40.00	60.00	100	175	—
1910B	Inc. above	12.00	20.00	25.00	60.00	—
1911/00B	—	30.00	50.00	100	150	—
1911B	37,471,000	12.00	20.00	25.00	60.00	—
1912B	5,672,000	12.00	20.00	25.00	60.00	—
1912B Proof	Inc. above	Value: 800				
1913/2B	—	100	150	250	700	—
1913B	1,567,000	30.00	60.00	125	300	—
1913B Proof	Inc. above	Value: 800				
1921B	5	—	—	—	15,000	—

Note: Original mintage 50,211

Date	Mintage	F	VF	XF	Unc	BU
1921B Proof; restrike	—	Value: 4,500				
1925	6,870,000	15.00	20.00	25.00	70.00	—
1929/1B	5,100,000	30.00	50.00	80.00	200	—
1929B	Inc. above	12.00	20.00	25.00	60.00	—
1929B Proof	Inc. above	Value: 800				
1930B	10,400,000	12.00	20.00	25.00	60.00	—
1930B Proof	Inc. above	Value: 800				
1930	666,000	12.00	20.00	25.00	60.00	—
1934B	17,335,000	75.00	150	200	500	—
1934B Proof	Inc. above	Value: 3,500				
1934B Proof; restrike	20	Value: 3,000				
1935B	Est. 25	1,000	1,500	2,500	15,000	—

Note: Original mintage 6,811,995

Date	Mintage	F	VF	XF	Unc	BU
1935B Proof	20	Value: 7,500				
1935B Proof; restrike	20	Value: 4,000				

KM# T5a DOLLAR
Gold **Obv:** Britannia standing **Rev:** Oriental design on cross
Designer: G. W. de Saulies

Date	Mintage	F	VF	XF	Unc	BU
1901B Proof; restrike	—	Value: 7,500				
1902B Proof; restrike	—	Value: 7,500				

PIEFORTS

KM#	Date	Mintage	Identification	Mkt Val
P1	1973	—	50 Pence. 0.9250 Silver.	1,250
P2	1982	—	20 Pence. 0.9250 Silver.	50.00
P3	1983	10,000	Pound. 0.9250 Silver. KM#933.	125
P4	1984	15,000	Pound. 0.9250 Silver. KM#934.	50.00
P5	1985	15,000	Pound. 0.9250 Silver. KM#941.	45.00
P6	1986	15,000	Pound. 0.9250 Silver. KM#946.	45.00
P7	1987	15,000	Pound. 0.9250 Silver. KM#948.	45.00
P8	1988	15,000	Pound. 0.9250 Silver. KM#954.	45.00
P9	1989	15,000	Pound. 0.9250 Silver. KM#959.	45.00
P10	1989	25,000	2 Pounds. 0.9250 Silver. KM#960a.	47.50
P11	1989	10,000	2 Pounds. 0.9250 Silver. KM#961a.	47.50
P12	1990	20,000	5 Pence. 0.9250 Silver. KM#937c.	25.00
P13	1992	15,000	10 Pence. 0.9250 Silver. KM#938b.	50.00
P15	1992	—	50 Pence. 0.9250 Silver. KM#963a.	70.00
P16	1993	—	Pound. 0.9250 Silver. KM#964.	47.50
P17	1994	—	50 Pence. 0.9250 Silver. KM#966b.	65.00
P18	1994	—	Pound. 0.9250 Silver. KM#967.	70.00
P19	1994	—	2 Pounds. 0.9250 Silver. KM#968a.	80.00
P20	1995	8,458	Pound. 0.9250 Silver. KM#969.	65.00
P21	1995	—	2 Pounds. 0.9250 Silver. KM#970a.	70.00
P22	1995	—	2 Pounds. 0.9250 Silver. KM#971a.	70.00
P23	1996	10,000	Pound. 0.9250 Silver. KM#972.	60.00
P24	1997	—	50 Pence. 0.9250 Silver. KM#963.	70.00
P26	1998	—	Pound. 0.9250 Silver. KM#993a.	—
P27	1997	—	2 Pounds. 0.9250 Silver. KM#976a.	75.00
P25	1997	—	Pound. 0.9250 Silver. KM#975.	70.00
P29	1998	—	50 Pence. 0.9250 Silver. KM#996a.	70.00
P28	1998	—	50 Pence. 0.9250 Silver. KM#992a.	70.00
P30	1998	—	2 Pounds. 0.9250 Silver. KM#994a.	75.00
P31	1999	—	Pound. 0.9250 Silver. KM998a	—

TRIAL STRIKES

KM#	Date	Mintage	Identification	Mkt Val
TS1	1926	—	3 Pence. Silver. MODEL. Thistle.	1,000
TS2	1926	—	6 Pence. Silver. MODEL.	1,000
TS3	1926	—	Shilling. Silver. MODEL. Lion on crown.	1,250
TS4	1926	—	2 Shilling. Silver. MODEL. Stemmed rose.	1,350
TS5	1926	—	1/2 Crown. Silver. MODEL. Crown over heraldic shield.	3,000
TSA6	1926	—	Crown. Silver. MODEL.	5,000

Note: A complete set of silver plated copper electro types officially prepared for the designer has been recorded; Market value $2,000

KM#	Date	Mintage	Identification	Mkt Val
TS6	1926	—	Crown. Silver. Britannia reclining. Blank. (MCMXXVI) Unique	10,000
TS7	1963	—	1/4 New Penny. Aluminum. Rose. Uniface.	—
TS8	1963	—	1/2 New Penny. Bronze. Winged animal. Uniface.	—
TS9	1963	—	New Penny. Bronze. Uniface.	—
TS10	1963	—	2 New Pence. Bronze. Britannia seated right. Uniface.	—
TS11	1963	—	5 New Pence. Silver. Three crowns. Uniface.	—
TS12	1963	—	10 New Pence. Silver. Uniface.	—
TS13	1963	—	20 New Pence. Silver. Uniface.	—
TS14	1963	—	20 New Pence. Silver. Helmeted and supported arms. Uniface.	—

PATTERNS

Including off metal strikes

KM#	Date	Mintage	Identification	Mkt Val
PnA121	1922	—	Florin. Gold. KM817a	15,000
PnB121	1923	—	3 Pence. Nickel. KM#813a.	3,500
PnC121	1923	—	Shilling. Nickel. KM816a	1,400
PnD121	1924	1	3 Pence. Gold. KM813a	10,000
pnE121	1924	3	6 Pence. Gold. KM#815a.1	10,000
PnF121	1924	—	Shilling. Nickel. 5.0000 g. KM816a	1,400
Pn121	1924	—	Shilling. Nickel. KM816a	1,400
PnA122	1925	—	3 Pence. Nickel. Modified effigy. KM#831.	1,500
PnB122	1925	—	3 Pence. Silver. MODEL. Matte proof; KM#831.	1,500
PnC122	1925	—	6 Pence: Nickel. Modified effigy. KM#832.	1,500
PnD122	1925	—	6 Pence. Silver. MODEL. Matte proof; KM#832.	1,500
PnE122	1925	—	Shilling. Nickel. Modified effigy. KM#833.	2,500
PnF122	1925	—	Shilling. Silver. MODEL. Matte proof; KM#833.	2,500
PnG122	1926	—	1/2 Crown. Silver. MODEL. Matte proof; KM#835.	—
PnH122	1926	—	Crown. Silver. MODEL. Matte proof; KM#836.	—
PnI122	1927	—	6 Pence. Nickel. KM#828	1,200
PnJ122A	1927	—	Shilling. Silver. MODEL. Unique.	—
PnJ122	1927	—	Florin. Silver. MODEL. Matte proof, KM#834.	2,500
PnK122	1927	—	1/2 Crown. Nickel. Modified effigy. KM830	—
PnL122	1927	—	1/2 Crown. Gold. Modified Effigy. KM830	—
PnM122	1935	—	Crown. Gold. Similar to KM842.	18,000

KM#	Date	Mintage	Identification	Mkt Val
Pn123	1937	18,000	1/2 Penny. Bronze. Edward VIII.	—
Pn124	1937	25,000	Penny. Bronze. Head left. Edward VIII.	—
Pn125	1937	—	3 Pence. Nickel-Brass. Edward VIII.	—
Pn126	1937	—	3 Pence. Nickel-Brass. Head left. Thrift Plant. Edward VIII.	45,000
Pn127	1937	18,000	6 Pence. 0.5000 Silver. Head left. Six joined rings form design. Edward VIII.	—
Pn128	1937	25,000	Shilling. 0.5000 Silver. Head left. Scottish Crest. Edward VIII.	37,000
Pn129	1937	35,000	Florin. 0.5000 Silver. Edward VIII.	—
Pn130	1937	60,000	1/2 Crown. 0.5000 Silver. Head left. Quartered flag divides crowned monograms. Edward VIII.	—
Pn131	1937	120,000	Crown. 0.5000 Silver. Head left. Crowned and quartered shield with supporters. Edward VIII.	100,000
Pn132	1937	6	Sovereign. 0.9160 Gold. Head left. St. George slaying the dragon. Edward VIII.	120,000
Pn122	1937	18,000	Farthing. Bronze. Head left. Wren left. Edward VIII.	—
Pn133	1946	—	6 Pence. Copper-Nickel. KM# 852.	—
PnA133	1946	—	Shilling. Copper-Nickel. KM# 853.	2,000
PnB133	1946	—	2 Shilling. Copper-Nickel. KM# 855.	2,000
PnC133	1946	—	1/2 Crown. Copper-Nickel. KM# 856.	—
PnA134	1950	—	4 Shilling. Copper-Nickel.	—
PnB134	1952	—	Shilling. Nickel. KM#876.	—
Pn134	1953	—	Penny. Bronze. Dentilated border.	—
PnA135	1953	—	Crown. Copper-Nickel. Matte, KM#894.	—
Pn135	1953	—	1/2 Sovereign. 0.9160 Gold.	—
Pn136	1953	—	Sovereign. 0.9160 Gold. Y#137.	40,000
Pn137	1953	—	2 Pounds. 0.9160 Gold.	—
Pn138	1953	—	5 Pounds. 0.9160 Gold.	—
Pn142	1961	—	10 Cents. Copper-Nickel.	—
Pn143	1961	—	20 Cents. Copper-Nickel. Britannia, standing facing.	—
Pn144	1961	—	50 Cents. Silver. Una and lion.	—
Pn141	1961	—	5 Cents. Copper-Nickel. Lion on crown.	—
Pn139	1961	—	Cent. Bronze.	—
Pn140	1961	—	2 Cents. Bronze.	—
Pn145	1963	—	1/2 Penny. Bronze. Decimal.	—
Pn146	1963	—	Penny. Bronze. Decimal.	—

MAUNDY SETS

KM#	Date	Mintage	Identification	Issue Price	Mkt Val
MDS157	1901 (4)	8,976	KM#775-778	—	150
MDS158	1902 (4)	8,976	KM#795-796, 797.1-798	—	125
MDS159	1902 (4)	—	KM#795-796, 797.1-798 Proof	—	150
MDS160	1903 (4)	8,976	KM#795-796; 797.1-798	—	125
MDS161	1904 (4)	8,976	KM#795-796, 797.1-798	—	150
MDS162	1905 (4)	8,976	KM#795-796, 797.2-798	—	150
MDS163	1906 (4)	8,800	KM#795-796, 797.2-798	—	125
MDS164	1907 (4)	8,760	KM#795-796, 797.2-798	—	125
MDS165	1908 (4)	8,760	KM#795-796, 797.2-798	—	125
MDS166	1909 (4)	1,983	KM#795-796, 797.2-798	—	225
MDS167	1910 (4)	1,440	KM#795-796, 797.2-798	—	245
MDS168	1911 (4)	1,768	KM#811-814	—	195
MDS169	1911 (4)	6,007	KM#811-814 Proof	—	195
MDS170	1912 (4)	1,246	KM#811-814	—	195
MDS171	1913 (4)	1,228	KM#811-814	—	195
MDS172	1914 (4)	982	KM#811-814	—	215
MDS173	1915 (4)	1,293	KM#811-814	—	195
MDS174	1916 (4)	1,128	KM#811-814	—	185
MDS175	1917 (4)	1,237	KM#811-814	—	195
MDS176	1918 (4)	1,375	KM#811-814	—	185
MDS177	1919 (4)	1,258	KM#811-814	—	195
MDS178	1920 (4)	1,399	KM#811-814	—	195
MDS179	1921 (4)	1,386	KM#811a-814a	—	200
MDS180	1922 (4)	1,373	KM#811a-814a	—	195
MDS181	1923 (4)	1,430	KM#811a-814a	—	200
MDS182	1924 (4)	1,515	KM#811a-814a	—	200
MDS183	1925 (4)	1,438	KM#811a-814a	—	185
MDS184	1926 (4)	1,504	KM#811a-814a	—	185
MDS185	1927 (4)	1,647	KM#811a-814a	—	195
MDS186	1928 (4)	1,642	KM#827, 839-841	—	195
MDS187	1929 (4)	1,761	KM#827, 839-841	—	200
MDS188	1930 (4)	1,724	KM#827, 839-841	—	185
MDS189	1931 (4)	1,759	KM#827, 839-841	—	185
MDS190	1932 (4)	1,835	KM#827, 839-841	—	185
MDS191	1933 (4)	1,872	KM#827, 839-841	—	185
MDS192	1934 (4)	1,887	KM#827, 839-841	—	185
MDS193	1935 (4)	1,926	KM#827, 839-841	—	210
MDS194	1936 (4)	1,323	KM#827, 839-841	—	225
MDS195	1937 (4)	1,325	KM#846-847, 850-851	—	160
MDS196	1937 (4)	26,000	KM#846-847, 850-851 Proof	—	160
MDS197	1938 (4)	1,275	KM#846-847, 850-851	—	185
MDS198	1939 (4)	1,234	KM#846-847, 850-851	—	185
MDS199	1940 (4)	1,277	KM#846-847, 850-851	—	185
MDS200	1941 (4)	1,253	KM#846-847, 850-851	—	195
MDS201	1942 (4)	1,231	KM#846-847, 850-851	—	185
MDS202	1943 (4)	1,239	KM#846-847, 850-851	—	185
MDS203	1944 (4)	1,259	KM#846-847, 850-851	—	185
MDS204	1945 (4)	1,355	KM#846-847, 850-851	—	185
MDS205	1946 (4)	1,365	KM#846-847, 850-851	—	185
MDS206	1947 (4)	1,375	KM#846a-847a, 850a-851a	—	195
MDS207	1948 (4)	1,385	KM#846a-847a, 850a-851a	—	195
MDS208	1949 (4)	1,395	KM#870-872, 874	—	195
MDS209	1950 (4)	1,405	KM#870-872, 874	—	195
MDS210	1951 (4)	1,468	KM#870-872, 874	—	195
MDS211	1952 (4)	1,012	KM#870-872, 874	—	225
MDS212	1953 (4)	1,025	KM#884-885, 887-888	—	750
MDS213	1954 (4)	1,020	KM#898-899, 901-902	—	165
MDS214	1955 (4)	1,036	KM#898-899, 901-902	—	165
MDS215	1956 (4)	1,088	KM#898-899, 901-902	—	165
MDS216	1957 (4)	1,094	KM#898-899, 901-902	—	165
MDS217	1958 (4)	1,100	KM#898-899, 901-902	—	165
MDS218	1959 (4)	1,106	KM#898-899, 901-902	—	165
MDS219	1960 (4)	1,112	KM#898-899, 901-902	—	165
MDS220	1961 (4)	—	KM#898-899, 901-902	—	165
MDS221	1962 (4)	1,125	KM#898-899, 901-902	—	165
MDS222	1963 (4)	1,131	KM#898-899, 901-902	—	165
MDS223	1964 (4)	1,137	KM#898-899, 901-902	—	165
MDS224	1965 (4)	1,143	KM#898-899, 901-902	—	165
MDS225	1966 (4)	1,206	KM#898-899, 901-902	—	165
MDS226	1967 (4)	986	KM#898-899, 901-902	—	175
MDS227	1968 (4)	964	KM#898-899, 901-902	—	175
MDS228	1969 (4)	1,002	KM#898-899, 901-902	—	175
MDS229	1970 (4)	980	KM#898-899, 901-902	—	175
MDS230	1971 (4)	1,018	KM#898-899, 901-902 Tewkesbury Abbey	—	175
MDS231	1972 (4)	1,026	KM#898-899, 901-902 York Minster Abbey	—	185
MDS232	1973 (4)	1,004	KM#898-899, 901-902 Westminster Abbey	—	175
MDS233	1974 (4)	1,042	KM#898-899, 901-902 Salisbury Cathedral	—	175
MDS234	1975 (4)	1,050	KM#898-899, 901-902 Peterborough Cathedral	—	175
MDS235	1976 (4)	1,257	KM#898-899, 901-902 Hereford Cathedral	—	175
MDS236	1977 (4)	1,248	KM#898-899, 901-902 Westminster Abbey	—	185
MDS237	1978 (4)	1,179	KM#898-899, 901-902 Carlisle Cathedral	—	175
MDS238	1979 (4)	1,180	KM#898-899, 901-902 Winchester Cathedral	—	175
MDS239	1980 (4)	1,148	KM#898-899, 901-902 Worcester Cathedral	—	175
MDS240	1981 (4)	1,398	KM#898-899, 901-902 Westminster Abbey	—	175
MDS241	1982 (4)	1,220	KM#898-899, 901-902 St. David's Cathedral	—	175
MDS242	1983 (4)	1,228	KM#898-899, 901-902 Exeter Cathedral	—	175
MDS243	1984 (4)	1,238	KM#898-899, 901-902 Southwell Minster	—	175
MDS244	1985 (4)	1,248	KM#898-899, 901-902 Ripon Cathedral	—	175
MDS245	1986 (4)	1,378	KM#898-899, 901-902 Chichester Cathedral	—	175
MDS246	1987 (4)	1,390	KM#898-899, 901-902 Ely Cathedral	—	185
MDS247	1988 (4)	1,402	KM#898-899, 901-902 Lichfield Cathedral	—	185
MDS248	1989 (4)	1,353	KM#898-899, 901-902 Birmingham Cathedral	—	185
MDS249	1990 (4)	1,523	KM#898-899, 901-902 Newcastle Cathedral	—	190
MDS250	1991 (4)	1,384	KM#898-899, 901-902 Westminster Abbey	—	190

KM#	Date	Mintage	Identification	Issue Price	Mkt Val
MDS251	1992 (4)	1,424	KM#898-899, 901-902 Chester Cathedral	—	190
MDS252	1993 (4)	1,440	KM#898-899, 901-902 Wells Cathedral	—	190
MDS253	1994 (4)	1,433	KM#898-899, 901-902 Truro Cathedral	—	190
MDS254	1995 (4)	1,466	KM#898-899, 901-902 Coventry Cathedral	—	195
MDS255	1996 (4)	1,629	KM#898-899, 901-902 Norwich Cathedral	—	200
MDS256	1997 (4)	1,786	KM#898-899, 901-902 Birmingham Cathedral	—	200
MDS257	1998 (4)	1,654	KM#898-899, 901-902 Portsmouth Cathedral	—	200
MDS258	1999 (4)	1,676	KM#898-899, 901-902 Bristol Cathedral	—	200
MDS259	2000 (4)	1,686	KM#898-899, 901-902 Lincoln Cathedral	—	225

MINT SETS

KM#	Date	Mintage	Identification	Issue Price	Mkt Val
MS101	1953 (9)	—	KM#881-883, 886, 889-893	1.25	30.00
MS102	1968/71 (5)	—	KM#911-912 (1968), 914-916 (1971), blue wallet	0.50	2.00
MS103	1982 (7)	205,000	KM#926-932	6.00	12.50
MS104	1983 (8)	637,100	KM#926-933	8.75	22.00
MS105	1984 (8)	158,820	KM#926-932, 934	8.75	19.00
MS106	1985 (7)	178,375	KM#935-940.1, 941	8.75	15.00
MS107	1986 (8)	167,224	KM#935-940.1, 946-947	9.75	20.00
MS108	1987 (7)	172,425	KM#935-940.1, 948	9.00	21.50
MS109	1988 (7)	134,067	KM#935-940.1, 954	9.00	17.50
MS110	1989 (7)	77,569	KM#935-940.1, 959	10.00	26.00
MS111	1989 (2)	—	KM#960-961	11.00	17.00
MS112	1990 (8)	102,606	KM#935-936, 937, 936b, 938-940.1, 941	15.00	23.50
MS113	1991 (7)	74,975	KM#935-936, 937b, 938-940.1, 946	15.00	20.00
MS114	1991 (7)	—	KM#935-936, 937b, 938-940.1, 946 Baby Pack	18.50	22.50
MS115	1992 (9)	78,421	KM#935-936, 937b, 938, 938b, 939-940.1, 948, 963	17.50	20.00
MS116	1992 (9)	—	KM#935-936, 937b, 938, 938b, 939-940.1, 948, 963 Baby Pack	22.50	20.00
MS117	1993 (8)	56,945	KM#935a-936a, 937b, 938b, 939-940.1, 963-964	22.50	22.50
MS118	1994 (8)	177,971	KM#935a-936a, 937b, 938b, 939, 966-968	22.50	20.00
MS119	1995 (8)	105,647	KM#935a-936a, 937b-938b, 939-940.1, 969-970	—	20.00
MS120	1996 (8)	86,501	KM#935a-936a, 937b-938b, 939-940.1, 972-973	18.50	20.00
MS121	1997 (9)	109,557	KM#935a, 936a, 937b, 938b, 939-940.1, 940.2, 975-976	—	20.00
MS122	1998 (9)	16,192	KM#986-994	25.00	15.00
MS124	1998 (2)	96,149	KM#991-992	15.00	9.50
MS125	1999 (8)	136,492	KM#986a-987a, 988-991, 998-999	20.00	18.00
MS126	2000 (9)	—	KM#986-991, 994, 1004, 1005 Wedding Collection	20.00	20.00
MS127	2000 (9)	117,750	KM#986-991, 994, 1004, 1005	25.00	25.00
MS128	2000 (9)	—	M#986-991, 994, 1004, 1005 Baby Gift Set	25.00	25.00

PROOF SETS

KM#	Date	Mintage	Identification	Issue Price	Mkt Val
PS15	1902 (13)	8,066	KM#795-797.1, 798-807	—	2,500
PS16	1902 (11)	7,057	KM#795-797.1, 798-805	—	900
PS17	1911 (12)	2,812	KM#811-818.1, 819-822	—	4,000
PS18	1911 (10)	952	KM#811-818.1, 819-820	—	1,150
PS19	1911 (8)	2,241	KM#811-818.1	—	600
PS20	1927 (6)	15,030	KM#831-836	—	375
PSA20	1927 (6)	—	KM#831-836 Matte Proof; Rare	—	15,000
PS21	1937 (15)	26,402	KM#843-857	—	350
PSA21	1937 (15)	—	KM#843-857 Matte Proof; Rare	—	—
PS22	1937 (4)	5,500	KM#858-861	—	4,500
PSA22	1937 (4)	1	KM#858-861 Matte Proof; Unique	—	25,000
PS23	1950 (9)	17,513	KM#867-869, 873, 875-879	2.50	125
PSA23	1950 (9)	3	KM#867-869, 873, 875-879; Rare, matte proof	—	10,000
PS24	1951 (10)	20,000	KM#867-869, 873, 875-880	2.80	150
PSA24	1951 (10)	3	KM#867-869, 873, 875-880; Rare, matte proof	—	10,000
PS25	1953 (10)	40,000	KM#881-883, 886, 889-894	3.50	100
PSA25	1953 (10)	3	KM#881-883, 886, 889-894; Rare, matte proof	—	10,000
PS26	1970 (8)	750,000	KM#896-897, 900, 903-907 (Issued 1971)	8.75	20.00
PS27	1971 (6)	350,000	KM#911-916 (Issued 1973)	8.85	14.50
PS28	1972 (7)	150,000	KM#911-917 (Issued 1976)	13.00	19.00
PS29	1973 (6)	100,000	KM#911-912, 914-916, 918 (Issued 1976)	13.00	17.50
PS30	1974 (6)	100,000	KM#911-916 (Issued 1976)	13.00	13.50
PS31	1975 (6)	100,000	KM#911-916 (Issued 1976)	13.00	13.50
PS32	1976 (6)	100,000	KM#911-916	13.00	14.00
PS33	1977 (7)	193,800	KM#911-916, 920	17.00	17.50
PS34	1978 (6)	88,100	KM#911-916	15.00	19.50
PS35	1979 (6)	81,000	KM#911-916	15.00	16.00
PS36	1980 (6)	143,400	KM#911-916	23.00	15.50
PS37	1980 (4)	10,000	KM#919, 922-924	2,650	1,150
PS38	1981 (2)	2,500	KM#919, 925a	—	160
PS39	1981 (6)	—	KM#911-916	26.00	15.50
PS40	1981 (9)	5,000	KM#911-916, 919, 924, 925a	—	935
PS41	1982 (7)	—	KM#926-932	21.60	16.00
PS42	1982 (4)	2,500	KM#919, 922-924	—	1,350
PS43	1983 (8)	125,000	KM#926-933	29.95	25.00
PS44	1983 (3)	—	KM#919, 922-923	775	535
PS45	1984 (8)	125,000	KM#926-932, 934	29.95	23.50
PS46	1984 (3)	—	KM#919, 922, 924	1,275	910
PS47	1985 (7)	125,000	KM#935-940.1, 941	29.75	23.50
PS48	1985 (4)	12,500	KM#942-945	1,395	1,175
PS49	1986 (8)	125,000	KM#935-940.1, 946-947	29.75	28.50
PS50	1986 (3)	12,500	KM#942-943, 947c	675	535
PS51	1987 (7)	125,000	KM#935-940.1, 948	29.75	25.00
PS52	1987 (4)	10,000	KM#950-953	1,595	1,000
PS53	1987 (3)	12,500	KM#942-944	675	535
PS54	1987 (2)	12,500	KM#950-951	325	190
PS55	1988 (7)	125,000	KM#935-940.1, 954	29.75	27.50
PS56	1988 (4)	6,500	KM#950-953	1,595	1,000
PS57	1988 (3)	—	KM#942-944	775	510
PS58	1988 (2)	7,500	KM#950-951	340	190
PS59	1989 (9)	100,000	KM#935-940.1, 959-961	34.95	46.00
PS60	1989 (4)	2,500	KM#950-953	1,595	1,000
PS61	1989 (4)	5,000	KM#955-958	1,595	1,600
PS62	1989 (3)	15,000	KM#955-957	775	675
PS63	1989 (2)	1,500	KM#950-951	340	200
PS64	1989 (2)	—	KM#960a-961a	—	55.00
PS65	1989 (2)	—	KM#960b-961b	—	95.00
PS66	1990 (8)	100,000	KM#935-937, 937b, 938-940.1, 941 Leatherette Case	35.00	36.00
PS67	1990 (8)	I.A.	KM#935-937, 937b, 938-940.1, 941 Leather Case	45.00	35.00
PS68	1990 (4)	2,500	KM#942-944, 949	1,595	1,400
PS69	1990 (4)	2,500	KM#950a-953a	1,595	1,000
PS70	1990 (3)	7,500	KM#942-944	775	570
PS71	1990 (2)	35,000	KM#937a-937c	47.50	39.00
PS72	1991 (7)	10,000	KM#935-936, 937b, 938-940.1, 946 Leatherette Case	38.50	22.50
PS73	1991 (7)	10,000	KM#935-936, 937b, 938-940.1, 946 Leather Case	48.50	27.50
PS74	1991 (4)	1,500	KM#942-944, 949	1,750	1,500
PS75	1991 (4)	750	KM#950a-953a	1,750	1,500
PS76	1991 (3)	2,500	KM#942-944	895	665
PS77	1992 (9)	100,000	KM#935-936, 937b, 938, 938b, 939-94.1, 948, 963 Leatherette Case	44.50	46.00
PS78	1992 (9)	100,000	KM#935-936, 937b, 938, 938b, 939-940.1, 948, 963 Leather Case	44.50	40.00
PS79	1992 (4)	1,250	KM#942-945	1,750	1,450
PS80	1992 (4)	1,000	KM#938b, 938c, 948a, 963a	122	125
PS81	1992 (3)	1,250	KM#942-944	895	710
PS82	1992 (2)	—	KM#938a-938c	59.45	46.00
PS83	1993 (8)	100,000	KM#935a-936a, 937b, 938b, 939-940.1, 964-965 Standard Case	50.00	47.00
PS84	1993 (8)	I.A.	KM#935a-936a, 937b, 938b, 939-940.1, 964-965 Deluxe Case	60.00	55.00
PS85	1993 (4)	500	KM#950a-953a	1,755	1,600
PS86	1993 (4)	1,250	KM#942-945	1,560	1,530
PS87	1993 (3)	1,250	KM#942-944	800	670
PS88	1994 (8)	100,000	KM#935a-936a, 937b, 938b, 939, 966-968 Standard Case	45.00	34.00
PS89	1994 (8)	I.A.	KM#935a-936a, 937b, 938b, 939, 966-968 Deluxe Case	55.00	50.00
PS90	1994 (4)	500	KM#950a-953a	1,499	1,500
PS91	1994 (4)	1,250	KM#942-943, 945, 968c	—	1,550
PS92	1994 (3)	1,250	KM#942-943, 968c	—	760
PS93	1995 (8)	42,842	KM#935a-936a, 937b-938b, 939-940.1, 969-970	—	41.50
PS94	1995 (8)	17,797	KM#935a-936a, 937b-938b, 939-940.1, 969-970 Deluxe Case	—	60.00
PS95	1995 (4)	1,250	KM#942-943, 945, 971c	—	1,675
PS96	1995 (4)	500	KM#950a-953a	1,500	1,500
PS97	1995 (3)	1,250	KM#942-943, 945	—	860
PS98	1996 (9)	100,000	KM#935a-936a, 937b-938b, 939-940.1, 972-973	44.75	42.50
PS99	1996 (9)	—	KM#935a-936a, 937b-938b, 939-940.1, 972-973 Deluxe Case	56.00	55.00
PS100	1996 (4)	2,500,000	KM#950a-953a	1,600	1,500
PS101	1996 (7)	—	KM#935b, 936b, 937c, 938c, 939a, 940.1a, 972a	—	155
PS102	1997 (10)	70,000	KM#935a, 936a, 937b, 938b, 939, 940.1, 940.2, 975-976, 977a	—	50.00
PS103	1997 (4)	15,000	KM#978-981	145	135
PS104	1997 (4)	1,500	KM#982-985	1,600	1,650
PS105	1998 (10)	100,000	KM#986,987a, 988-995	55.00	50.00
PSA105	1998 (2)	10,000	Piefort versions of KM#992a, 996a	—	140
PS106	1999 (9)	100,000	KM#986a-987a, 988-991, 997-999	50.00	50.00
PS107	1999 (4)	1,000	KM#999a, 1001-1003	1,725	1,725
PS108	1999 (3)	1,250	KM#1001-1003	—	955
PS109	1999 (4)	750	KM#950a-953a	1,495	1,500
PS110	1999 (4)	—	KM#1008-1011	1,595	—
PS111	2000 (10)	90,000	KM#986-991, 994, 1004-1006 Standard Set	50.00	50.00
PS112	2000 (10)	10,000	KM#986-991, 994, 1004-1006 Deluxe Set	65.00	65.00
PS113	2000 (10)	15,000	KM#986-991, 994, 1004-1006 Executive Set	115	115
PS114	2000 (4)	750	KM#1008-1011	1,495	1,498
PS115	2000 (13)	15,000	KM#898, 899, 901, 902, 986b, 987b, 988a, 989a, 990a, 991a, 994a, 1005a, 1006a	—	375
PSA115	2000 (3)	1,250	KM#994c, 1001, 1002	—	—
PSB115	2000 (13)	15,000	KM#898, 899, 901, 902, 986b, 987b, 988a-991a, 994a, 1005a	—	—

The Hellenic (Greek) Republic is situated in southeastern Europe on the southern tip of the Balkan Peninsula. The republic includes many islands, the most important of which are Crete and the Ionian Islands. Greece (including islands) has an area of 50,944 sq. mi. (131,940 sq. km.) and a population of 10.3 million. Capital: Athens. Greece is still largely agricultural. Tobacco, cotton, fruit and wool are exported.

Greece, the Mother of Western civilization, attained the peak of its culture in the 5th century B.C., when it contributed more to government, drama, art and architecture than any other people to this time. Greece fell under Roman domination in the 2nd and 1st centuries B.C., becoming part of the Byzantine Empire until Constantinople fell to the Crusaders in 1202. With the fall of Constantinople to the Turks in 1453, Greece became part of the Ottoman Empire. Independence from Turkey was won with the revolution of 1821-27. In 1833, Greece was established as a monarchy, with sovereignty guaranteed by Britain, France and Russia. After a lengthy power struggle between the monarchist forces and democratic factions, Greece was proclaimed a republic in 1925. The monarchy was restored in 1935 and reconfirmed by a plebiscite in 1946. The Italians invaded Greece via Albania on Oct. 28, 1940 but were driven back well within the Albanian border. Germany began their invasion in April 1941 and quickly overran the entire country and drove off a British Expeditionary force by the end of April. King George II and his new government went into exile. The German-Italian occupation of Greece lasted until Oct. 1944 after which only German troops remained until the end of the occupation. On April 21, 1967, a military junta took control of the government and suspended the constitution. King Constantine II made an unsuccessful attempt against the junta in the fall of 1968 and consequently fled to Italy. The monarchy was formally abolished by plebiscite, Dec. 8, 1974, and Greece was established as the Hellenic Republic, the third republic in Greek history.

RULERS

George I, 1863-1913
Constantine I, 1913-1917, 1920-1922
Alexander I, 1917-1920
George II, 1922-1923, 1935-1947
Paul I, 1947-1964
Constantine II, 1964-1973

MINT MARKS

(a) - Paris, privy marks only
A - Paris
B - Vienna
BB - Strassburg
H - Heaton, Birmingham
K - Bordeaux
KN - King's Norton
(p) - Poissy – Thunderbolt
Anthemion – Greek National Mint, Athens

MONETARY SYSTEM

Commencing 1831
100 Lepta = 1 Drachma

KINGDOM

DECIMAL COINAGE

KM# 62 5 LEPTA

Nickel **Ruler:** George I **Obv:** Crown right of center hole **Rev:** Owl on amphora left of center hole **Rev. Designer:** Ch. Pillet

Date	Mintage	F	VF	XF	Unc	BU
1912(a)	25,053,000	0.75	2.50	7.50	65.00	175

KM# 63 10 LEPTA

Nickel, 21 mm. **Ruler:** George I **Obv:** Crown right of center hole **Rev:** Owl on amphora left of center hole **Rev. Designer:** Ch. Pillet

Date	Mintage	F	VF	XF	Unc	BU
1912(a)	28,973,000	0.75	2.50	7.50	65.00	125

KM# 66.1 10 LEPTA

1.5200 g., Aluminum **Ruler:** George II **Obv:** Crown above date **Rev:** Olive branch, denomination **Note:** 1.77mm thick.

Date	Mintage	F	VF	XF	Unc	BU
1922(p)	120,000,000	1.00	2.00	9.00	40.00	60.00

KM# 66.2 10 LEPTA

1.6500 g., Aluminum **Ruler:** Constantine I **Obv:** Crown above date **Rev:** Olive branch, denomination **Note:** 2.2mm thick.

Date	Mintage	F	VF	XF	Unc	BU
1922(p)	—	3.00	10.00	20.00	75.00	150

KM# 64 20 LEPTA

Nickel **Ruler:** George I **Obv:** Crowned, mantled shield right of center hole **Rev:** Athena standing at left of center hole, olive branch at right

Date	Mintage	F	VF	XF	Unc	BU
1912(a)	10,145,000	0.75	2.00	8.50	75.00	125

KM# 65 50 LEPTA

Copper-Nickel **Ruler:** Constantine I **Obv:** Crowned, mantled shield right of center hole **Rev:** Olive branch below center hole **Designer:** George Jakobicles **Note:** Most of these were melted and only 30 - 40 of each piece are known to exist.

Date	Mintage	F	VF	XF	Unc	BU
1921H	1,000,000	—	1,500	3,500	7,500	10,000
1921KN	1,524,000	—	4,000	7,000	12,000	20,000

KM# 60 DRACHMA

5.0000 g., 0.8350 Silver .1342 oz. ASW **Ruler:** George I **Obv:** Head left **Rev:** Mythological figure Thetis with shield of Achilles, seated on sea horse

Date	Mintage	F	VF	XF	Unc	BU
1910(a)	4,570,000	7.50	15.00	45.00	200	300
1911(a)	1,881,000	9.00	20.00	55.00	300	500

KM# 61 2 DRACHMAI

10.0000 g., 0.8350 Silver .2684 oz. ASW **Ruler:** George I **Obv:** Head left **Rev:** Mythological figure Thetis with shield of Achilles seated on sea horse

Date	Mintage	F	VF	XF	Unc	BU
1911(a)	1,500,000	10.00	30.00	80.00	1,500	2,500

REPUBLIC

DECIMAL COINAGE

KM# 67 20 LEPTA

Copper-Nickel **Obv:** Denomination above date **Rev:** Athena head left

Date	Mintage	F	VF	XF	Unc	BU
1926	20,000,000	0.75	1.50	5.00	20.00	60.00

KM# 68 50 LEPTA

Copper-Nickel **Obv:** Denomination above date **Rev:** Athena head left

Date	Mintage	F	VF	XF	Unc	BU
1926	20,000,000	0.45	1.00	4.50	20.00	60.00
1926B (1930)	20,000,000	0.45	1.00	4.50	20.00	60.00

KM# 69 DRACHMA

Copper-Nickel, 23 mm. **Obv:** Denomination above date **Rev:** Athena head left

Date	Mintage	F	VF	XF	Unc	BU
1926	15,000,000	0.45	1.00	5.00	35.00	75.00
1926B	20,000,000	0.45	1.00	5.00	50.00	100

KM# 70 2 DRACHMAI

Copper-Nickel, 27 mm. **Obv:** Denomination above date **Rev:** Athena head left

Date	Mintage	F	VF	XF	Unc	BU
1926	22,000,000	1.00	2.00	9.00	50.00	100

KM# 71.1 5 DRACHMAI

Nickel **Obv:** Phoenix and flames **Rev:** Denomination within wreath **Note:** LONDON MINT: In second set of berries on left only 1 berry will have a dot on it.

Date	Mintage	F	VF	XF	Unc	BU
1930	23,500,000	0.75	1.50	8.00	75.00	150
1930 Proof	—	Value: 2,500				

KM# 71.2 5 DRACHMAI

Nickel **Obv:** Phoenix and flames **Rev:** Denomination within wreath **Note:** BRUSSELLS MINT: 2 berries will have dots.

Date	Mintage	F	VF	XF	Unc	BU
1930	1,500,000	1.50	3.50	20.00	125	275

KM# 72 10 DRACHMAI
7.0000 g., 0.5000 Silver .1125 oz. ASW **Obv:** Grain sprig divides denomination **Rev:** Demeter head left

Date	Mintage	F	VF	XF	Unc	BU
1930	7,500,000	5.00	10.00	30.00	350	600
1930 Proof	—	Value: 3,000				

KM# 73 20 DRACHMAI
11.3100 g., 0.5000 Silver .1818 oz. ASW **Obv:** Prow of ancient ship **Rev:** Neptune head right

Date	Mintage	F	VF	XF	Unc	BU
1930	11,500,000	6.00	12.50	28.00	210	300
1930 Proof	—	Value: 3,000				

KINGDOM

DECIMAL COINAGE

KM# 77 5 LEPTA
Aluminum, 20.5 mm. **Obv:** Center hole within crowned wreath **Rev:** Grain sprigs left of center hole

Date	Mintage	F	VF	XF	Unc	BU
1954	15,000,000	—	0.20	0.50	4.00	10.00
1971	1,002,000	0.20	0.50	1.00	5.00	10.00

Note: 1971 dated coins have smaller hole at center

KM# 78 10 LEPTA
Aluminum **Obv:** Center hole within crowned wreath **Rev:** Olives above center hole, double denomination below

Date	Mintage	F	VF	XF	Unc	BU
1954	48,000,000	—	0.15	0.45	4.00	10.00
1959	20,000,000	—	0.15	0.45	4.00	10.00
1964	12,000,000	—	0.15	0.45	4.00	7.00
1965	—	—	—	—	6.50	—
Note: In sets only						
1965 Proof	4,987	Value: 10.00				
1966	20,000,000	—	0.15	0.45	4.00	7.00
1969	20,000,000	—	0.15	0.45	4.00	7.00
1971	5,922,000	—	0.35	1.00	5.00	8.00

Note: Small center hole

KM# 102 10 LEPTA
Aluminum **Obv:** Soldier and Phoenix **Rev:** Trident between two dolphins

Date	Mintage	F	VF	XF	Unc	BU
1973	2,742,000	—	0.20	1.00	5.00	7.00

KM# 79 20 LEPTA
Aluminum, 24 mm. **Obv:** Center hole within crowned wreath **Rev:** Olive branch left of center hole

Date	Mintage	F	VF	XF	Unc	BU
1954	24,000,000	—	0.15	0.50	4.00	10.00
1959	20,000,000	—	0.15	0.50	4.00	10.00
1964	8,000,000	—	0.15	0.50	3.50	6.50
1966	15,000,000	—	0.15	0.50	3.50	6.50
1969	20,000,000	—	0.15	0.50	3.50	6.50
1971	4,108,000	—	0.35	1.00	4.00	7.00

Note: Small center hole

KM# 104 20 LEPTA
Aluminum **Obv:** Soldier in front of phoenix, anniversary date below **Rev:** Olive branch, denomination

Date	Mintage	F	VF	XF	Unc	BU
1973	2,718,000	—	0.20	0.60	5.00	7.00

KM# 80 50 LEPTA
Copper-Nickel, 18 mm. **Ruler:** Paul I **Obv:** Head left **Rev:** Crowned arms with supporters

Date	Mintage	F	VF	XF	Unc	BU
1954	37,228,000	0.15	0.25	1.25	30.00	85.00
1957	5,108,000	1.00	5.00	50.00	200	450
1957 Proof	—	Value: 2,000				
1959	10,160,000	0.15	0.25	5.00	60.00	150
1962	20,500,000	0.15	0.25	1.50	8.00	75.00
Note: Plain edge						
1962	Inc. above	0.15	0.25	1.50	8.00	75.00
Note: Serrated edge						
1964	20,000,000	0.15	0.25	1.50	8.00	75.00
1965	—	—	—	—	6.50	—
Note: In sets only						
1965 Proof	4,987	Value: 12.50				

KM# 88 50 LEPTA
Copper-Nickel, 18 mm. **Ruler:** Constantine II **Obv:** Head left **Rev:** Crowned arms with supporters **Designer:** Vassos Phalireas

Date	Mintage	F	VF	XF	Unc	BU
1966	30,000,000	0.20	0.50	1.00	5.50	25.00
1966 Proof	—	Value: 1,500				
1970	10,160,000	0.30	0.60	1.50	6.00	27.50

KM# 97.1 50 LEPTA
Copper-Nickel **Ruler:** Constantine II **Obv:** Small head left **Rev:** Soldier in front of Phoenix **Designer:** Vassos Philareas

Date	Mintage	F	VF	XF	Unc	BU
1971	10,999,000	—	0.10	0.15	4.00	20.00
1973	9,342,000	—	0.20	0.50	5.00	22.00

KM# 97.2 50 LEPTA
Copper-Nickel **Ruler:** Constantine II **Obv:** Large head left **Rev:** Soldier in front of Phoenix **Designer:** Vassos Philareas

Date	Mintage	F	VF	XF	Unc	BU
1973	Inc. above	—	0.20	0.50	5.00	15.00

KM# 81 DRACHMA
Copper-Nickel, 20.8 mm. **Ruler:** Paul I **Obv:** Head left **Rev:** Crowned arms with supporters

Date	Mintage	F	VF	XF	Unc	BU
1954	24,091,000	0.15	0.25	0.75	40.00	90.00
1957	8,151,000	1.00	5.00	50.00	150	500
1957 Proof	—	Value: 2,500				
1959	10,180,000	0.15	0.25	2.00	40.00	150
1962	20,060,000	0.25	1.00	2.00	8.00	100
1965	—	—	—	—	6.50	—
Note: In sets only						
1965 Proof	4,987	Value: 12.50				

KM# 89 DRACHMA
Copper-Nickel **Ruler:** Constantine II **Obv:** Head left **Rev:** Crowned arms with supporters **Designer:** Vassos Philareas

Date	Mintage	F	VF	XF	Unc	BU
1966	20,000,000	—	0.15	0.45	4.50	12.00
1966 Proof	—	Value: 1,250				
1967	20,000,000	—	0.15	0.45	4.50	12.00
1970	7,001,000	—	0.50	1.00	7.00	16.00
1970 Proof	—	Value: 1,500				

KM# 98 DRACHMA
Copper-Nickel **Ruler:** Constantine II **Obv:** Head left **Rev:** Soldier in front of Phoenix **Designer:** Vassos Phalireas

Date	Mintage	F	VF	XF	Unc	BU
1971	11,985,000	—	0.20	0.75	4.50	12.00
1973	8,196,000	—	0.25	1.00	5.50	14.00

KM# 82 2 DRACHMAI
Copper-Nickel **Ruler:** Paul I **Obv:** Head left **Rev:** Crowned arms with supporters

Date	Mintage	F	VF	XF	Unc	BU
1954	12,609,000	0.50	0.75	1.50	7.00	100
1957	10,171,000	1.00	5.00	50.00	200	500
1957 Proof	—	Value: 3,000				
1959	5,000,000	1.00	2.00	25.00	300	1,000
1962	10,096,000	0.50	0.75	2.50	10.00	100
1965	—	—	—	—	5.50	—
Note: In sets only						
1965 Proof	4,987	Value: 12.50				

KM# 90 2 DRACHMAI
Copper-Nickel **Ruler:** Constantine II **Obv:** Head left **Rev:** Crowned arms with supporters **Designer:** Vassos Phalireas

Date	Mintage	F	VF	XF	Unc	BU
1966	10,000,000	0.15	0.25	0.50	4.50	12.00
1966 Proof	—	Value: 1,400				
1967	10,000,000	0.15	0.25	0.50	4.50	12.00
1970	7,000,000	0.50	1.00	2.00	8.00	18.00
1970 Proof	—	Value: 2,000				

KM# 99 2 DRACHMAI
Copper-Nickel, 22.9 mm. **Ruler:** Constantine II **Obv:** Head left **Rev:** Soldier in front of Phoenix **Designer:** Vassos Phalireas

Date	Mintage	F	VF	XF	Unc	BU
1971	9,998,000	0.15	0.25	0.75	4.50	12.00
1973	7,972,000	0.20	0.50	1.50	5.50	14.00

KM# 83 5 DRACHMAI
Copper-Nickel **Ruler:** Paul I

Date	Mintage	F	VF	XF	Unc	BU
1954	21,000,000	0.25	0.50	1.50	25.00	50.00
1965	—	—	—	—	5.50	—
Note: In sets only						
1965 Proof	4,987	Value: 15.00				

KM# 91 5 DRACHMAI
Copper-Nickel, 27.5 mm. **Ruler:** Constantine II **Obv:** Head left **Rev:** Crowned arms with supporters **Designer:** Vassos Phalireas

Date	Mintage	F	VF	XF	Unc	BU
1966	12,000,000	0.15	0.25	1.00	6.00	22.00
1966	—	Value: 1,250				
1970	5,000,000	0.50	1.00	3.00	10.00	25.00

KM# 100 5 DRACHMAI
Copper-Nickel **Ruler:** Constantine II **Obv:** Head left **Rev:** Soldier in front of Phoenix **Designer:** Vassos Phalireas

Date	Mintage	F	VF	XF	Unc	BU
1971	4,014,000	0.25	0.50	2.00	6.00	15.00
1973	3,166,000	0.25	0.50	1.50	5.50	15.00

KM# 84 10 DRACHMAI
Nickel, 30 mm. **Ruler:** Paul I **Obv:** Head left **Rev:** Crowned arms with supporters

Date	Mintage	F	VF	XF	Unc	BU
1959	20,000,000	0.30	0.50	2.00	16.00	50.00
1959 Proof	—	Value: 2,000				
1965	—	—	—	—	5.50	—
Note: In sets only						
1965 Proof	4,987	Value: 15.00				

KM# 96 10 DRACHMAI
Copper-Nickel **Ruler:** Constantine II **Obv:** Head left **Rev:** Crowned arms with supporters **Designer:** Vassos Phalireas

Date	Mintage	F	VF	XF	Unc	BU
1968	40,000,000	0.25	0.50	0.75	5.50	15.00

KM# 101 10 DRACHMAI
Copper-Nickel, 29.9 mm. **Ruler:** Constantine II **Obv:** Head left **Rev:** Soldier in front of Phoenix **Designer:** Vassos Phalireas

Date	Mintage	F	VF	XF	Unc	BU
1971	502,000	0.25	0.50	1.00	7.50	16.00
1973	541,000	0.50	1.00	2.50	8.00	18.00

KM# 74 20 DRACHMAI
6.4516 g., 0.9000 Gold .1867 oz. AGW, 22 mm. **Ruler:** George II **Subject:** 5th Anniversary - Restoration of Monarchy **Obv:** Head left **Rev:** Denomination within crowned wreath

Date	Mintage	F	VF	XF	Unc	BU
ND(1940) Proof	200	Value: 15,000				

KM# 85 20 DRACHMAI
7.5000 g., 0.8350 Silver .2013 oz. ASW, 26.2 mm. **Ruler:** Paul I **Obv:** Head left **Rev:** Selene, moon goddess

Date	Mintage	F	VF	XF	Unc	BU
1960	20,000,000	—	—	BV	7.00	16.00
1960 Proof	—	Value: 2,000				
1965	—	—	—	—	8.00	18.00
1965 Proof	4,987	Value: 18.00				

KM# 92 20 DRACHMAI
6.4516 g., 0.9000 Gold .1867 oz. AGW **Ruler:** Constantine II **Subject:** Commemorative of the April 21, 1967 revolution **Obv:** Crowned shield with supporters **Rev:** Soldier in front of Phoenix

Date	Mintage	F	VF	XF	Unc	BU
ND (1970)	20,000	—	—	—	350	450

KM# 111.3 20 DRACHMAI
Copper-Nickel **Ruler:** Constantine II **Obv:** Soldier in front of Phoenix **Rev:** Selene, wide rim with continuous wave design at rear hoof

Date	Mintage	F	VF	XF	Unc	BU
1973	Inc. above	0.50	1.00	2.00	10.00	15.00

KM# 111 20 DRACHMAI
Copper-Nickel **Ruler:** Constantine II **Obv:** Soldier in front of Phoenix **Rev:** Selene, narrow rim with faint veil or no veil **Note:** Possible varieties exist; narrow rim with faint veil or no veil / wide rim with heavy veil and broken wave design at rear hoof.

Date	Mintage	F	VF	XF	Unc	BU
1973	3,092,000	0.50	1.00	2.00	8.50	11.50

KM# 86 30 DRACHMAI
18.0000 g., 0.8350 Silver .4832 oz. ASW, 34 mm. **Ruler:** Paul I **Subject:** Centennial - Five Greek Kings **Edge Lettering:** Greek text

Date	Mintage	F	VF	XF	Unc	BU
ND(1963)	3,000,000	—	BV	7.50	10.00	12.00

KM# 87 30 DRACHMAI
12.0000 g., 0.8350 Silver .3221 oz. ASW, 30.3 mm. **Ruler:** Constantine II **Subject:** Constantine and Anne-Marie Wedding **Edge Lettering:** Greek text

Date	Mintage	F	VF	XF	Unc	BU
1964	1,000,000	—	BV	5.00	9.00	12.00
Note: Berne: small edge lettering, BØ below epaulette						
1964	1,000,000	—	BV	5.00	8.00	12.00
Note: Kongsberg: large edge lettering, BØ on top of shoulder						
1964 Proof	—	Value: 3,500				

KM# 93 50 DRACHMAI
12.5000 g., 0.8350 Silver .3355 oz. ASW **Ruler:** Constantine II **Subject:** April 21, 1967 Revolution **Obv:** Crowned shield with supporters **Rev:** Soldier in front of Phoenix

Date	Mintage	F	VF	XF	Unc	BU
1967(1970)	100,000	—	—	25.00	75.00	100

KM# 75 100 DRACHMAI
25.0000 g., 0.9000 Silver .7235 oz. ASW, 38 mm. **Ruler:** George II **Subject:** 5th Anniversary - Restoration of Monarchy **Obv:** Head left **Rev:** Crowned and mantled arms

Date	Mintage	F	VF	XF	Unc	BU
ND (1940) Proof	500	Value: 2,500				

KM# 76 100 DRACHMAI
32.2580 g., 0.9000 Gold .9335 oz. AGW, 38 mm. **Ruler:** George II **Obv:** Head left **Rev:** Denomination within crowned wreath

Date	Mintage	F	VF	XF	Unc	BU
ND (1940) Proof	140	Value: 25,000				

KM# 94 100 DRACHMAI
25.0000 g., 0.8350 Silver .6712 oz. ASW **Ruler:** Constantine II **Subject:** April 21, 1967 Revolution

Date	Mintage	F	VF	XF	Unc	BU
ND (1970)	30,000	—	—	35.00	100	150

KM# 95 100 DRACHMAI
32.2580 g., 0.9000 Gold .9335 oz. AGW **Ruler:** Constantine II **Subject:** April 21, 1967 Revolution **Obv:** Crowned arms with supporters **Rev:** Soldier in front of Phoenix

Date	Mintage	F	VF	XF	Unc	BU
ND (1970)	10,000	—	—	—	950	1,250
ND(1970)	10,000	—	—	—	950	1,250

REPUBLIC

DECIMAL COINAGE

KM# 103 10 LEPTA
Aluminum **Obv:** Phoenix above flame **Rev:** Pair of dolphins flank trident

Date	Mintage	F	VF	XF	Unc	BU
1973	15,134,472	—	0.10	0.50	2.00	5.00

KM# 113 10 LEPTA
Aluminum **Obv:** Arms within wreath **Rev:** Charging bull right

Date	Mintage	F	VF	XF	Unc	BU
1976	2,043,000	—	0.10	0.30	2.00	5.00
1978	791,000	0.50	1.00	2.50	5.00	10.00
1978 Proof	20,000	Value: 5.00				

KM# 105 20 LEPTA
Aluminum **Obv:** Soldier in front of Phoenix **Rev:** Olive branch, denomination

Date	Mintage	F	VF	XF	Unc	BU
1973	15,265,797	—	0.20	0.50	2.50	5.00

KM# 114 20 LEPTA
Aluminum **Obv:** Arms within wreath **Rev:** Stallion's head left

Date	Mintage	F	VF	XF	Unc	BU
1976	2,506,000	—	0.15	0.40	2.50	5.00
1978	803,000	0.45	1.00	2.50	5.00	10.00
1978 Proof	20,000	Value: 5.00				

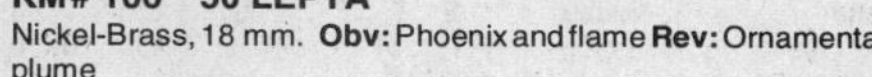

KM# 106 50 LEPTA
Nickel-Brass, 18 mm. **Obv:** Phoenix and flame **Rev:** Ornamental plume

Date	Mintage	F	VF	XF	Unc	BU
1973	55,231,898	—	—	0.15	1.00	3.00

KM# 115 50 LEPTA
Nickel-Brass, 18 mm. **Subject:** Markos Botsaris **Obv:** Denomination **Rev:** Bust left

Date	Mintage	F	VF	XF	Unc	BU
1976	51,016,000	—	—	0.15	1.00	—
1978	12,010,000	—	—	0.15	1.00	—
1978 Proof	20,000	Value: 8.00				
1980	6,682,000	—	—	0.15	1.25	—
1982	3,365,000	—	—	0.15	1.25	—
1984	1,208,000	—	—	0.15	1.25	—
1986	—	—	—	0.15	1.25	—

KM# 107 DRACHMA
Nickel-Brass, 21 mm. **Obv:** Phoenix and flame **Rev:** Owl left of denomination

Date	Mintage	F	VF	XF	Unc	BU
1973	45,218,431	—	0.50	1.00	3.00	5.00

KM# 116 DRACHMA
Nickel-Brass, 21 mm. **Subject:** Konstantinos Kanaris **Obv:** Full masted ship at sea **Rev:** Bust left

Date	Mintage	F	VF	XF	Unc	BU
1976	102,060,000	—	—	0.15	1.00	3.00
Note: Varieties exist						
1978	21,200,000	—	—	0.15	1.00	2.00
1978 Proof	20,000	Value: 8.00				
1980	52,503,000	—	—	0.15	1.00	2.00
1982	54,186,000	—	—	0.15	1.00	2.00
1984	33,665,000	—	—	0.15	1.00	2.00
1986	17,901,000	—	—	0.15	1.00	3.00

KM# 150 DRACHMA
2.8000 g., Copper, 18 mm. **Subject:** Lascarina Bouboulina, 1783-1825 **Obv:** Full masted ship at sea **Rev:** Bust left

Date	Mintage	F	VF	XF	Unc	BU
1988(an)	36,707,000	—	—	—	0.50	1.00
1990(an)	—	—	—	—	0.50	1.00
1992	—	—	—	—	0.50	1.00
1993	—	—	—	—	10.00	15.00
Note: In sets only						
1993 Proof	—	Value: 45.00				
1994	—	—	—	—	0.50	1.00
1998	—	—	—	—	0.50	1.00
2000	—	—	—	—	0.50	1.00

KM# 189 DRACHMA
8.5000 g., 0.9167 Gold 0.2505 oz. AGW **Obv:** Sailing ship **Rev:** Bouboulina, heroine, bust left

Date	Mintage	F	VF	XF	Unc	BU
2000 Proof	—	Value: 400				

KM# 108 2 DRACHMAI
Nickel-Brass **Obv:** Phoenix and flame **Rev:** Owl left of denomination

Date	Mintage	F	VF	XF	Unc	BU
1973	51,163,812	—	0.50	1.25	4.00	6.00

KM# 117 2 DRACHMAI
Nickel-Brass, 24 mm. **Subject:** Georgios Karaiskakis **Obv:** Crossed rifles with branch **Rev:** Bust left

Date	Mintage	F	VF	XF	Unc	BU
1976	92,401,000	—	—	0.25	1.00	2.00
1978	16,772,000	—	—	0.25	1.00	2.00
1978 Proof	20,000	Value: 8.00				
1980	45,955,000	—	—	0.25	1.00	2.00

KM# 130 2 DRACHMES
Nickel-Brass, 24 mm. **Subject:** Georgios Karaiskakis **Obv:** Crossed rifles and branch **Rev:** Bust left

Date	Mintage	F	VF	XF	Unc	BU
1982	64,414,000	—	—	0.20	1.00	2.00
1984	37,861,000	—	—	0.20	1.00	2.00
1986	21,019,000	—	—	0.20	1.00	2.00

KM# 151 2 DRACHMES
3.8000 g., Copper, 21 mm. **Subject:** Manto Mavrogenous, 1797-1840 - independence hero **Obv:** Ship's wheel, scope and anchor **Rev:** Bust facing looking right

Date	Mintage	F	VF	XF	Unc	BU
1988(an)	36,707,000	—	—	—	0.50	1.00
1990	—	—	—	—	0.50	1.00
1992	—	—	—	—	0.50	1.00
1993	—	—	—	—	10.00	15.00
Note: In sets only						
1993 Proof	—	Value: 45.00				
1994	—	—	—	—	0.50	1.00
1998	—	—	—	—	0.50	1.00
2000	—	—	—	—	0.50	1.00

KM# 109.1 5 DRACHMAI
Copper-Nickel, 25 mm. **Obv:** Phoenix and flame **Rev:** Pegasus rearing right **Note:** Denomination spelling ends with I.

Date	Mintage	F	VF	XF	Unc	BU
1973	33,957,473	0.75	1.25	2.00	4.00	10.00

KM# 109.2 5 DRACHMAI
Copper-Nickel, 25 mm. **Obv:** Phoenix and flame **Rev:** Pegasus rearing right **Note:** Denomination spelling ends with A.

Date	Mintage	F	VF	XF	Unc	BU
1973	Inc. above	1.00	2.00	4.00	10.00	15.00

KM# 118 5 DRACHMAI
Copper-Nickel, 22.5 mm. **Subject:** Aristotle **Obv:** Denomination **Rev:** Head left

Date	Mintage	F	VF	XF	Unc	BU
1976	85,187,000	—	0.20	0.35	1.00	2.00
1978	17,404,000	—	0.20	0.35	1.00	3.00
1978 Proof	20,000	Value: 8.00				
1980	33,701,000	—	0.20	0.35	1.00	2.00

KM# 131 5 DRACHMES
5.5000 g., Copper-Nickel, 22.5 mm. **Subject:** Aristotle **Obv:** Denomination **Rev:** Head left

Date	Mintage	F	VF	XF	Unc	BU
1982	42,647,000	—	0.20	0.35	1.00	2.00
1984	29,778,000	—	0.20	0.35	1.00	2.00
1986	16,730,000	—	0.20	0.35	1.00	2.00
1988	30,273,000	—	—	0.30	0.75	1.50
1990	—	—	—	0.30	0.75	1.50
1992	—	—	—	0.30	0.75	1.50
1993	—	—	—	—	10.00	15.00
Note: In sets only						
1993 Proof	—	Value: 50.00				
1994	—	—	—	—	0.75	1.50
1998	—	—	—	—	0.75	1.50
1999	—	—	—	—	0.75	1.50
2000	—	—	—	—	0.75	1.50

KM# 110 10 DRACHMAI
Copper-Nickel **Obv:** Phoenix and flame **Rev:** Pegasus rearing right

Date	Mintage	F	VF	XF	Unc	BU
1973	22,599,848	1.00	1.50	2.50	6.00	10.00

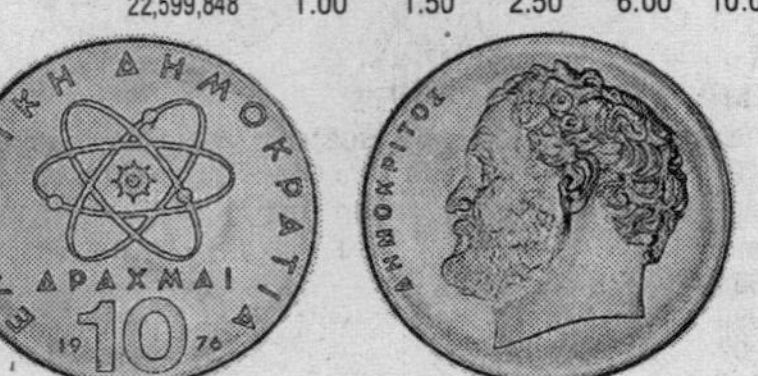

KM# 119 10 DRACHMAI
Copper-Nickel, 25.6 mm. **Subject:** Democritus **Obv:** Atom design **Rev:** Head left

Date	Mintage	F	VF	XF	Unc	BU
1976	76,816,000	—	0.25	0.50	1.00	5.00
1978	14,637,000	—	0.25	0.50	1.00	5.00
1978 Proof	20,000	Value: 10.00				
1980	28,733,000	—	0.25	0.50	1.00	5.00

KM# 132 10 DRACHMES
7.6000 g., Copper-Nickel, 26 mm. **Obv:** Atom design **Rev:** Head left

Date	Mintage	F	VF	XF	Unc	BU
1982	35,539,000	—	0.25	0.50	1.00	2.00
1984	23,802,000	—	0.25	0.50	1.00	2.00
1986	24,441,000	—	0.25	0.50	1.00	2.00
1988	16,869,000	—	0.20	0.45	1.00	2.00
1990	—	—	0.20	0.45	1.00	2.00
1992	—	—	0.20	0.45	1.00	2.00
1993	—	—	—	—	15.00	20.00
Note: In sets only						
1993 Proof	—	Value: 60.00				
1994	—	—	0.20	0.45	1.00	2.00
1998	—	—	0.20	0.45	1.00	2.00
2000	—	—	—	—	1.00	2.00

KM# 112 20 DRACHMAI
Copper-Nickel, 29 mm. **Subject:** Athena **Obv:** Phoenix and flame **Rev:** Helmeted head left

Date	Mintage	F	VF	XF	Unc	BU
1973	20,650,087	0.35	0.50	1.00	2.00	5.00

KM# 120 20 DRACHMAI
Copper-Nickel, 29 mm. **Subject:** Pericles **Obv:** The Parthenon **Rev:** Helmeted head left **Edge Lettering:** In Greek

Date	Mintage	F	VF	XF	Unc	BU
1976	53,167,500	—	0.30	0.50	1.25	5.00
1978	65,353,000	—	0.30	0.50	1.50	5.00
1978 Proof	20,000	Value: 10.00				
1980	17,562,000	—	0.30	0.50	1.25	5.00

KM# 133 20 DRACHMES
Copper-Nickel, 28.8 mm. **Subject:** Pericles **Obv:** The Parthenon **Rev:** Helmeted head left **Edge Lettering:** In Greek

Date	Mintage	F	VF	XF	Unc	BU
1982	24,299,000	—	0.30	0.50	1.00	3.00
1984	13,412,000	—	0.30	0.50	1.25	3.50
1986	10,553,000	—	0.30	0.50	1.00	3.00
1988	16,196,000	—	—	0.50	1.00	3.00

KM# 154 20 DRACHMES
7.0000 g., Nickel-Bronze, 24.5 mm. **Subject:** Dionysios Solomos, composer of National Anthem **Obv:** Olive branch right of lined field **Rev:** Bust looking right

Date	Mintage	F	VF	XF	Unc	BU
1990(an)	—	—	—	—	1.25	2.50
1992	—	—	—	—	1.25	2.50
1993	—	—	—	—	15.00	20.00
Note: In sets only						
1993 Proof	—	Value: 85.00				
1994	—	—	—	—	1.25	2.50
1998(an)	—	—	—	—	1.25	2.50
2000	—	—	—	—	1.25	2.50

KM# 124 50 DRACHMAI
Copper-Nickel **Subject:** Solon the Archon of Athens **Obv:** Denomination above waves and date **Rev:** Head left

Date	Mintage	F	VF	XF	Unc	BU
1980(an)	32,250,999	0.50	0.75	1.50	3.50	6.00

KM# 134 50 DRACHMES
Copper-Nickel, 31 mm. **Subject:** Solon the Archon of Athens **Obv:** Denomination above waves and date **Rev:** Head left **Note:** Obv: Denomination in modern Greek

Date	Mintage	F	VF	XF	Unc	BU
1982(an)	18,899,000	0.40	0.60	1.00	1.50	3.00
1984(an)	11,411,000	0.40	0.60	1.00	1.50	3.00

KM# 147 50 DRACHMES
9.2000 g., Nickel-Brass, 27.6 mm. **Subject:** Homer **Obv:** Ancient sailing boat **Rev:** Head left

Date	Mintage	F	VF	XF	Unc	BU
1986(an)	12,078,000	—	0.50	1.00	2.50	5.00
1988(an)	23,589,000	—	—	0.75	1.50	3.00
1990(an)	—	—	—	0.75	1.75	3.50
1992	—	—	—	0.75	1.75	3.50
1993	—	—	—	—	20.00	25.00
Note: In sets only						
1993 Proof	—	Value: 70.00				
1994	—	—	—	0.75	1.75	3.50
1998	—	—	—	—	1.75	3.50
1999	—	—	—	—	1.75	3.50
2000	—	—	—	—	1.75	3.50

KM# 164 50 DRACHMES
Brass, 27 mm. **Series:** 150th Anniversary of the Constitution **Subject:** Dimitrios Kallergis **Obv:** Bust 3/4 left **Rev:** Center of Parliament Building

Date	Mintage	F	VF	XF	Unc	BU
ND(1994)(an)	7,500,000	—	—	—	3.00	5.00

KM# 168 50 DRACHMES
Brass, 27 mm. **Series:** 150th Anniversary of the Constitution **Subject:** Makrygiannis **Obv:** Bust 3/4 left **Rev:** Center of Parliament Building

Date	Mintage	F	VF	XF	Unc	BU
ND(1994)(an)	7,500,000	—	—	—	3.00	5.00

KM# 171 50 DRACHMES
Brass **Subject:** Rigas Feraios **Obv:** Arms within wreath **Rev:** Bust 3/4 right divides dates

Date	Mintage	F	VF	XF	Unc	BU
ND (1998)	—	—	—	—	3.50	5.50

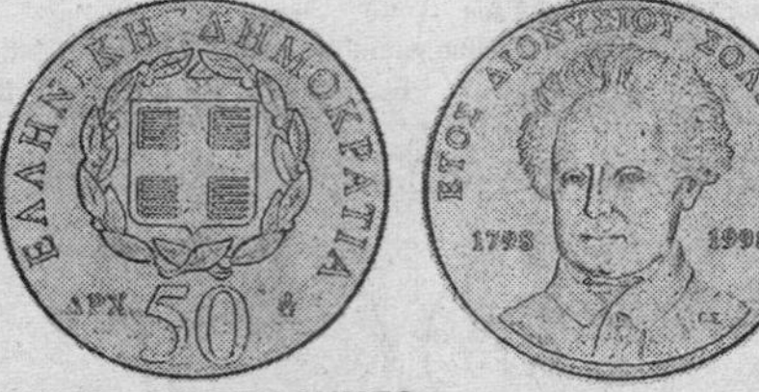

KM# 172 50 DRACHMES
Brass **Subject:** Dionysios Solomos **Obv:** Arms within wreath **Rev:** Bust 3/4 facing divides dates

Date	Mintage	F	VF	XF	Unc	BU
ND (1998)	—	—	—	—	3.50	5.50

KM# 121 100 DRACHMAI
13.0000 g., 0.6500 Silver .2717 oz. ASW **Subject:** 50th Anniversary - Bank of Greece **Obv:** Denomination **Rev:** Athena seated right

Date	Mintage	F	VF	XF	Unc	BU
1978 Proof	25,000	Value: 150				

KM# 125 100 DRACHMAI
5.7800 g., 0.9000 Silver .1672 oz. ASW **Subject:** Pan-European Games **Obv:** Arms within wreath **Rev:** Ancient olympic broad jump

Date	Mintage	F	VF	XF	Unc	BU
1981	150,000	—	—	—	8.00	10.00
1981 Proof	150,000	Value: 15.00				

KM# 135 100 DRACHMAI
5.7800 g., 0.9000 Silver .1672 oz. ASW **Subject:** Pan-European Games **Obv:** Arms within wreath **Rev:** Olympic high jump

Date	Mintage	F	VF	XF	Unc	BU
1982	150,000	—	—	—	8.00	10.00
1982 Proof	Inc. above	Value: 15.00				

KM# 136 100 DRACHMAI
5.7800 g., 0.9000 Silver .1672 oz. ASW **Subject:** Pan-European Games **Obv:** Arms within wreath **Rev:** Pole vault

Date	Mintage	F	VF	XF	Unc	BU
1982	150,000	—	—	—	8.00	10.00
1982 Proof	Inc. above	Value: 15.00				

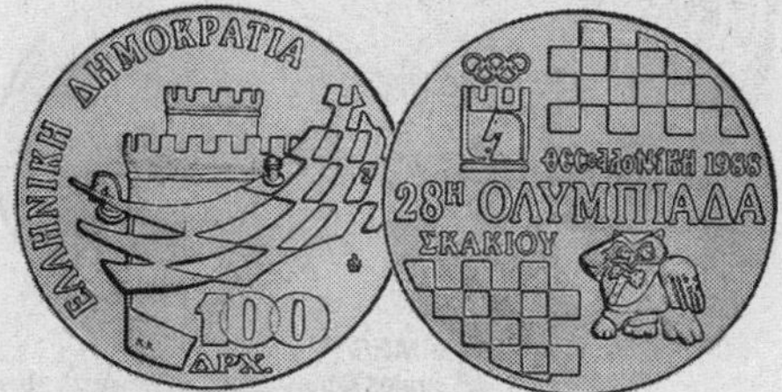

KM# 152 100 DRACHMES
Copper-Nickel **Subject:** 28th Chess Olympics **Obv:** Castle towers and stylized chessboard **Rev:** Legend divides block design, shield at left and owl at right

Date	Mintage	F	VF	XF	Unc	BU
1988(an)	30,000	—	—	—	12.00	15.00

KM# 159 100 DRACHMES
10.2000 g., Brass, 29.3 mm. **Subject:** Macedonia - Alexander the Great **Obv:** Radiant design within circle **Rev:** Head right

Date	Mintage	F	VF	XF	Unc	BU
1990(an)	—	—	—	—	2.35	4.50
1992	—	—	—	—	2.35	4.50
1993	—	—	—	—	20.00	25.00
Note: In sets only						
1993 Proof	—	Value: 85.00				
1994	—	—	—	—	2.35	4.50
1998	—	—	—	—	2.35	4.50
2000	—	—	—	—	2.35	4.50

KM# 169 100 DRACHMES
Brass **Subject:** VI Universal Track Championship Games **Obv:** Ancient city view and track **Rev:** Runner and track

Date	Mintage	F	VF	XF	Unc	BU
1997(an)	5,000,000	—	—	—	2.75	5.00

KM# 170 100 DRACHMES
Brass **Subject:** 13th World Basketball Championships **Obv:** Cup in ball design **Rev:** Four basketball players in action

Date	Mintage	F	VF	XF	Unc	BU
1998(an)	—	—	—	—	4.50	6.50

KM# 173 100 DRACHMES
10.0000 g., Brass, 29.4 mm. **Obv:** Ancient wrestlers **Rev:** Modern wrestlers **Edge:** Reeded and plain sections

Date	Mintage	F	VF	XF	Unc	BU
1999	—	—	—	—	3.50	5.50

KM# 174 100 DRACHMES
10.0000 g., Brass, 29.4 mm. **Obv:** Statue of Atlas **Rev:** Weight lifter **Edge:** Reeded and plain sections

Date	Mintage	F	VF	XF	Unc	BU
1999	—	—	—	—	3.50	5.50

KM# 126 250 DRACHMAI
14.4400 g., 0.9000 Silver .4178 oz. ASW **Subject:** Pan-European Games **Obv:** Arms within wreath **Rev:** Ancient Olympic javelin throwing

Date	Mintage	F	VF	XF	Unc	BU
1981	150,000	—	—	—	12.50	14.50
1981 Proof	150,000	Value: 20.00				

KM# 137 250 DRACHMAI
14.4400 g., 0.9000 Silver .4178 oz. ASW **Subject:** Pan-European Games **Obv:** Arms within wreath **Rev:** 1896 Olympic discus throwing

Date	Mintage	F	VF	XF	Unc	BU
1982	150,000	—	—	—	12.50	14.50
1982 Proof	Inc. above	Value: 20.00				

KM# 138 250 DRACHMAI
14.4400 g., 0.9000 Silver .4178 oz. ASW **Subject:** Pan-European Games **Obv:** Arms within wreath **Rev:** Shot put

Date	Mintage	F	VF	XF	Unc	BU
1982	150,000	—	—	—	12.50	14.50
1982 Proof	Inc. above	Value: 20.00				

KM# 127 500 DRACHMAI
28.8800 g., 0.9000 Silver .8357 oz. ASW **Subject:** Pan-European Games **Obv:** Arms within wreath **Rev:** Ancient Olympic relay race

Date	Mintage	F	VF	XF	Unc	BU
1981	150,000	—	—	—	20.00	22.50
1981 Proof	150,000	Value: 27.50				

KM# 139 500 DRACHMAI
28.8800 g., 0.9000 Silver .8357 oz. ASW **Subject:** Pan-European Games **Obv:** Arms within wreath **Rev:** 1896 Olympic racers at starting blocks

Date	Mintage	F	VF	XF	Unc	BU
1982	150,000	—	—	—	20.00	22.50
1982 Proof	Inc. above	Value: 27.50				

KM# 140 500 DRACHMAI
28.8800 g., 0.9000 Silver .8357 oz. ASW **Subject:** Pan-European Games **Obv:** Arms within wreath **Rev:** Racers

Date	Mintage	F	VF	XF	Unc	BU
1982	150,000	—	—	—	20.00	22.50
1982 Proof	Inc. above	Value: 27.50				

KM# 122 500 DRACHMES
13.0000 g., 0.9000 Silver .3762 oz. ASW **Subject:** Common Market Membership **Obv:** Inscription above denomination **Rev:** Figure in tree

Date	Mintage	F	VF	XF	Unc	BU
ND (1979)	—	—	—	—	—	—
ND (1979) Proof	18,000	Value: 200				

KM# 145 500 DRACHMES
18.0000 g., 0.9000 Silver .5209 oz. ASW **Subject:** Olympics **Obv:** Arms within wreath, torch at right **Rev:** Runner with torch

Date	Mintage	F	VF	XF	Unc	BU
1984	25,000	—	—	—	75.00	90.00
1984 Proof	25,000	Value: 150				

KM# 153 500 DRACHMES
18.1100 g., 0.9000 Silver .5240 oz. ASW **Subject:** 28th Chess Olympics **Obv:** Ancient figures playing chess **Rev:** Legend divides block design, shield at left and owl at right

Date	Mintage	F	VF	XF	Unc	BU
1988 Proof	3,000	Value: 300				

KM# 157 500 DRACHMES
18.0000 g., 0.9000 Silver .5208 oz. ASW **Subject:** XI Mediterranean Games **Obv:** Design and denomination **Rev:** Fish wearing hat, logo at right

Date	Mintage	F	VF	XF	Unc	BU
1991 Proof	10,000	Value: 60.00				

KM# 160 500 DRACHMES
17.0000 g., 0.9250 Silver .5056 oz. ASW **Subject:** 2500th Anniversary of Democracy **Obv:** Head on old coin right **Rev:** One seated and one standing figure within square

Date	Mintage	F	VF	XF	Unc	BU
1993 Proof	Est. 30,000	Value: 300				

KM# 162 500 DRACHMES
17.0000 g., 0.9250 Silver .5056 oz. ASW **Subject:** Volleyball Centennial **Rev:** Players in rectangle, date at corners

Date	Mintage	F	VF	XF	Unc	BU
1994 Proof	1,750	Value: 125				

KM# 175 500 DRACHMES
9.5400 g., Copper-Nickel, 28 mm. **Series:** 2004 Olympics **Obv:** Laurel wreath within square, games logo below **Rev:** Arched entry to ancient Olympic stadium **Edge:** Plain

Date	Mintage	F	VF	XF	Unc	BU
2000	—	—	—	—	4.50	6.00

KM# 176 500 DRACHMES
9.5400 g., Copper-Nickel, 28 mm. **Series:** 2004 Olympics **Obv:** Laurel wreath within square, games logo below **Rev:** Runner receiving Olympic torch **Edge:** Plain

Date	Mintage	F	VF	XF	Unc	BU
2000	—	—	—	—	4.50	6.00

KM# 177 500 DRACHMES
9.5400 g., Copper-Nickel, 28 mm. **Series:** 2004 Olympics **Obv:** Laurel wreath within square, games logo below **Rev:** Ancient winner Diagoras being carried **Edge:** Plain

Date	Mintage	F	VF	XF	Unc	BU
2000	—	—	—	—	4.50	6.00

KM# 178 500 DRACHMES
9.5400 g., Copper-Nickel, 28 mm. **Series:** 2004 Olympics **Subject:** President Vikelas and Baron Couberten **Obv:** Laurel wreath within square, games logo below **Rev:** Jugate busts; one left and one facing **Edge:** Plain

Date	Mintage	F	VF	XF	Unc	BU
2000	—	—	—	—	4.50	6.00

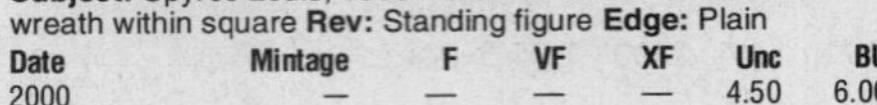

KM# 179 500 DRACHMES
9.5400 g., Copper-Nickel, 28 mm. **Series:** 2004 Olympics **Subject:** Spyros Louis, 1896 marathon winner **Obv:** Laurel wreath within square **Rev:** Standing figure **Edge:** Plain

Date	Mintage	F	VF	XF	Unc	BU
2000	—	—	—	—	4.50	6.00

KM# 180 500 DRACHMES
9.5400 g., Copper-Nickel, 28 mm. **Series:** 2004 Olympics **Obv:** Laurel wreath within square, games logo below **Rev:** 1896 Olympic gold medal design **Edge:** Plain

Date	Mintage	F	VF	XF	Unc	BU
2000	—	—	—	—	4.50	6.00

KM# 148 1000 DRACHMES
23.3300 g., 0.9250 Silver .6939 oz. ASW **Subject:** Decade For Women **Rev:** Statue of women figures with arms raised

Date	Mintage	F	VF	XF	Unc	BU
1985 Proof	3,660	Value: 125				

KM# 155 1000 DRACHMES
18.0000 g., 0.9000 Silver .5208 oz. ASW **Subject:** 50th Anniversary - Italian Invasion of Greece **Obv:** Arms within wreath **Rev:** Soldiers and horse

Date	Mintage	F	VF	XF	Unc	BU
1990 Proof	7,000	Value: 150				

KM# 165 1000 DRACHMES
33.6300 g., 0.9250 Silver 1.001 oz. ASW **Subject:** Olympics **Obv:** Track field **Rev:** 4 ancient runners **Edge Lettering:** CITIUS ALTIUS FORTIUS

Date	Mintage	F	VF	XF	Unc	BU
1996 Proof	100,000	Value: 50.00				

KM# 166 1000 DRACHMES
33.6300 g., 0.9250 Silver 1.001 oz. ASW **Subject:** Olympics **Rev:** 2 ancient wrestlers **Edge Lettering:** CITIUS ALTIUS FORTIUS

Date	Mintage	F	VF	XF	Unc	BU
1996 Proof	100,000	Value: 50.00				

KM# 128 2500 DRACHMAI
6.4500 g., 0.9000 Gold .1866 oz. AGW **Series:** Pan-European Games **Subject:** Ancient Olympics, Agon **Obv:** Arms within wreath **Rev:** Winged figure holding rings

Date	Mintage	F	VF	XF	Unc	BU
1981 Proof	75,000	Value: 155				

KM# 141 2500 DRACHMAI
6.4500 g., 0.9000 Gold .1866 oz. AGW **Series:** Pan-European Games **Subject:** 1896 Olympics, Spiros **Obv:** Arms within wreath **Rev:** Half figure holding wreath

Date	Mintage	F	VF	XF	Unc	BU
1982 Proof	50,000	Value: 150				

KM# 142 2500 DRACHMAI
6.4500 g., 0.9000 Gold .1866 oz. AGW **Series:** Pan-European Games **Obv:** Arms within wreath **Rev:** Winged statue

Date	Mintage	F	VF	XF	Unc	BU
1982 Proof	50,000	Value: 155				

KM# 129 5000 DRACHMAI
12.5000 g., 0.9000 Gold .3617 oz. AGW **Series:** Pan-European Games **Subject:** Ancient Olympics, Zeus **Obv:** Arms within wreath **Rev:** Laureate head left

Date	Mintage	F	VF	XF	Unc	BU
1981 Proof	75,000	Value: 265				

KM# 143 5000 DRACHMAI
12.5000 g., 0.9000 Gold .3617 oz. AGW **Series:** Pan-European Games **Subject:** 1896 Olympics, Pierre de Coubertin **Obv:** Arms within wreath **Rev:** Head 3/4 facing

Date	Mintage	F	VF	XF	Unc	BU
1982 Proof	50,000	Value: 265				

KM# 144 5000 DRACHMAI
12.5000 g., 0.9000 Gold .3617 oz. AGW **Series:** Pan-European Games **Obv:** Arms within wreath **Rev:** Birds flying

Date	Mintage	F	VF	XF	Unc	BU
1982 Proof	50,000	Value: 265				

KM# 146 5000 DRACHMES
8.0000 g., 0.9000 Gold .2315 oz. AGW **Subject:** Olympics **Obv:** Arms at left, torch at right **Rev:** Apollo

Date	Mintage	F	VF	XF	Unc	BU
1984 Proof	15,000	Value: 400				

KM# 123 10000 DRACHMES
20.0000 g., 0.9000 Gold .5787 oz. AGW **Subject:** Common Market Membership **Obv:** Inscription above denomination **Rev:** Seated figure left

Date	Mintage	F	VF	XF	Unc	BU
ND (1979) Proof	—	Value: 550				

KM# 149 10000 DRACHMES
7.1300 g., 0.9000 Gold .2063 oz. AGW **Subject:** Decade For Women **Obv:** Arms within wreath **Rev:** Standing figure

Date	Mintage	F	VF	XF	Unc	BU
1985 Proof	2,835	Value: 800				

KM# 158 10000 DRACHMES
8.0000 g., 0.9000 Gold .2315 oz. AGW **Subject:** XI Mediterranean Games **Obv:** Design, denomination **Rev:** Fish wearing hat, logo at right

Date	Mintage	F	VF	XF	Unc	BU
1991 Proof	2,000	Value: 400				

KM# 161 10000 DRACHMES
8.5000 g., 0.9170 Gold .2506 oz. AGW **Subject:** 2500th Anniversary of Democracy **Obv:** Statue **Rev:** Head left

Date	Mintage	F	VF	XF	Unc	BU
1993 Proof	Est. 10,000	Value: 450				

KM# 163 10000 DRACHMES
8.5000 g., 0.9170 Gold .2506 oz. AGW **Subject:** Volleyball Centennial **Obv:** Ancient coin divides date

Date	Mintage	F	VF	XF	Unc	BU
1994 Proof	669	Value: 1,500				

KM# 156 20000 DRACHMES
8.0000 g., 0.9000 Gold .2315 oz. AGW **Subject:** 50th Anniversary - Italian Invasion of Greece **Rev:** Soldiers and horse

Date	Mintage	F	VF	XF	Unc	BU
1990 Proof	1,000	Value: 2,000				

KM# 167 20000 DRACHMES
16.9700 g., 0.9170 Gold .5001 oz. AGW **Subject:** Olympics **Obv:** Track field **Rev:** Ancient javelin throwers **Edge Lettering:** CITIUS ALTIUS FORTIUS

Date	Mintage	F	VF	XF	Unc	BU
1996 Proof	60,000	Value: 500				

ESSAIS

KM#	Date	Mintage	Identification	Mkt Val
E23	1911	4	2 Drachmai. Silver. 1868 2 Drachmai. ESSAI to right of denomination.	8,500
EA23	1911	2	2 Drachmai. Silver. Without mintmark, ESSAI to right of sea-horse.	10,000
E24	1912	—	5 Lepta. Nickel. Crown right of center hole. Owl left of center hole. ESSAI, plain edge, without mintmark	2,500
E25	1912	—	5 Lepta. Zinc. ESSAI	3,000
E26	1912	—	10 Lepta. Nickel. Crown right of center hole. Owl left of center hole. ESSAI, plain edge, without mintmark.	2,500
E27	1912	—	10 Lepta. Zinc. ESSAI.	3,000
E28	1912	—	10 Lepta. Nickel. ESSAI, with mintmark	4,000

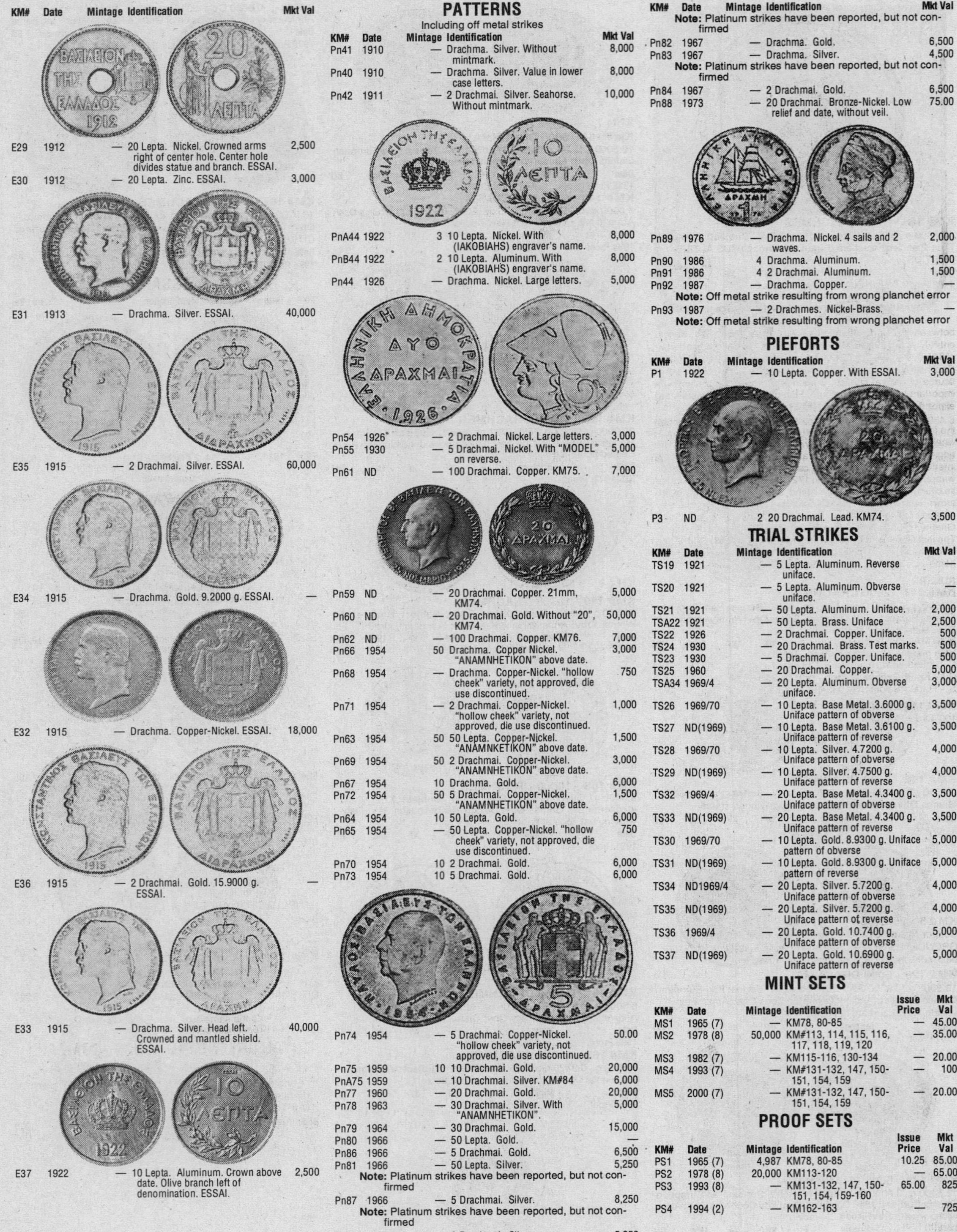

KM#	Date	Mintage	Identification	Mkt Val
E29	1912	—	20 Lepta. Nickel. Crowned arms right of center hole. Center hole divides statue and branch. ESSAI.	2,500
E30	1912	—	20 Lepta. Zinc. ESSAI.	3,000
E31	1913	—	Drachma. Silver. ESSAI.	40,000
E35	1915	—	2 Drachmai. Silver. ESSAI.	60,000
E34	1915	—	Drachma. Gold. 9.2000 g. ESSAI.	—
E32	1915	—	Drachma. Copper-Nickel. ESSAI.	18,000
E36	1915	—	2 Drachmai. Gold. 15.9000 g. ESSAI.	—
E33	1915	—	Drachma. Silver. Head left. Crowned and mantled shield. ESSAI.	40,000
E37	1922	—	10 Lepta. Aluminum. Crown above date. Olive branch left of denomination. ESSAI.	2,500

PATTERNS

Including off metal strikes

KM#	Date	Mintage	Identification	Mkt Val
Pn41	1910	—	Drachma. Silver. Without mintmark.	8,000
Pn40	1910	—	Drachma. Silver. Value in lower case letters.	8,000
Pn42	1911	—	2 Drachmai. Silver. Seahorse. Without mintmark.	10,000
PnA44	1922	3	10 Lepta. Nickel. With (IAKOBIAHS) engraver's name.	8,000
PnB44	1922	2	10 Lepta. Aluminum. With (IAKOBIAHS) engraver's name.	8,000
Pn44	1926	—	Drachma. Nickel. Large letters.	5,000
Pn54	1926	—	2 Drachmai. Nickel. Large letters.	3,000
Pn55	1930	—	5 Drachmai. Nickel. With "MODEL" on reverse.	5,000
Pn61	ND	—	100 Drachmai. Copper. KM75.	7,000
Pn59	ND	—	20 Drachmai. Copper. 21mm, KM74.	5,000
Pn60	ND	—	20 Drachmai. Gold. Without "20", KM74.	50,000
Pn62	ND	—	100 Drachmai. Copper. KM76.	7,000
Pn66	1954	50	Drachma. Copper Nickel. "ANAMNHETIKON" above date.	3,000
Pn68	1954	—	Drachma. Copper-Nickel. "hollow cheek" variety, not approved, die use discontinued.	750
Pn71	1954	—	2 Drachmai. Copper-Nickel. "hollow cheek" variety, not approved, die use discontinued.	1,000
Pn63	1954	50	50 Lepta. Copper-Nickel. "ANAMNKETIKON" above date.	1,500
Pn69	1954	50	2 Drachmai. Copper-Nickel. "ANAMNHETIKON" above date.	3,000
Pn67	1954	10	Drachma. Gold.	6,000
Pn72	1954	50	5 Drachmai. Copper-Nickel. "ANAMNHETIKON" above date.	1,500
Pn64	1954	10	50 Lepta. Gold.	6,000
Pn65	1954	—	50 Lepta. Copper-Nickel. "hollow cheek" variety, not approved, die use discontinued.	750
Pn70	1954	10	2 Drachmai. Gold.	6,000
Pn73	1954	10	5 Drachmai. Gold.	6,000
Pn74	1954	—	5 Drachmai. Copper-Nickel. "hollow cheek" variety, not approved, die use discontinued.	50.00
Pn75	1959	10	10 Drachmai. Gold.	20,000
PnA75	1959	—	10 Drachmai. Silver. KM#84	6,000
Pn77	1960	—	20 Drachmai. Gold.	20,000
Pn78	1963	—	30 Drachmai. Silver. With "ANAMNHETIKON".	5,000
Pn79	1964	—	30 Drachmai. Gold.	15,000
Pn80	1966	—	50 Lepta. Gold.	—
Pn86	1966	—	5 Drachmai. Gold.	6,500
Pn81	1966	—	50 Lepta. Silver.	5,250

Note: Platinum strikes have been reported, but not confirmed

KM#	Date	Mintage	Identification	Mkt Val
Pn87	1966	—	5 Drachmai. Silver.	8,250

Note: Platinum strikes have been reported, but not confirmed

KM#	Date	Mintage	Identification	Mkt Val
Pn85	1967	—	2 Drachmai. Silver.	5,250

Note: Platinum strikes have been reported, but not confirmed

KM#	Date	Mintage	Identification	Mkt Val
Pn82	1967	—	Drachma. Gold.	6,500
Pn83	1967	—	Drachma. Silver.	4,500

Note: Platinum strikes have been reported, but not confirmed

KM#	Date	Mintage	Identification	Mkt Val
Pn84	1967	—	2 Drachmai. Gold.	6,500
Pn88	1973	—	20 Drachmai. Bronze-Nickel. Low relief and date, without veil.	75.00
Pn89	1976	—	Drachma. Nickel. 4 sails and 2 waves.	2,000
Pn90	1986	4	Drachma. Aluminum.	1,500
Pn91	1986	4	2 Drachmai. Aluminum.	1,500
Pn92	1987	—	Drachma. Copper.	—

Note: Off metal strike resulting from wrong planchet error

KM#	Date	Mintage	Identification	Mkt Val
Pn93	1987	—	2 Drachmes. Nickel-Brass.	—

Note: Off metal strike resulting from wrong planchet error

PIEFORTS

KM#	Date	Mintage	Identification	Mkt Val
P1	1922	—	10 Lepta. Copper. With ESSAI.	3,000
P3	ND	2	20 Drachmai. Lead. KM74.	3,500

TRIAL STRIKES

KM#	Date	Mintage	Identification	Mkt Val
TS19	1921	—	5 Lepta. Aluminum. Reverse uniface.	—
TS20	1921	—	5 Lepta. Aluminum. Obverse uniface.	—
TS21	1921	—	50 Lepta. Aluminum. Uniface.	2,000
TSA22	1921	—	50 Lepta. Brass. Uniface	2,500
TS22	1926	—	2 Drachmai. Copper. Uniface.	500
TS24	1930	—	20 Drachmai. Brass. Test marks.	500
TS23	1930	—	5 Drachmai. Copper. Uniface.	500
TS25	1960	—	20 Drachmai. Copper.	5,000
TSA34	1969/4	—	20 Lepta. Aluminum. Obverse uniface.	3,000
TS26	1969/70	—	10 Lepta. Base Metal. 3.6000 g. Uniface pattern of obverse	3,500
TS27	ND(1969)	—	10 Lepta. Base Metal. 3.6100 g. Uniface pattern of reverse	3,500
TS28	1969/70	—	10 Lepta. Silver. 4.7200 g. Uniface pattern of obverse	4,000
TS29	ND(1969)	—	10 Lepta. Silver. 4.7500 g. Uniface pattern of reverse	4,000
TS32	1969/4	—	20 Lepta. Base Metal. 4.3400 g. Uniface pattern of obverse	3,500
TS33	ND(1969)	—	20 Lepta. Base Metal. 4.3400 g. Uniface pattern of reverse	3,500
TS30	1969/70	—	10 Lepta. Gold. 8.9300 g. Uniface pattern of obverse	5,000
TS31	ND(1969)	—	10 Lepta. Gold. 8.9300 g. Uniface pattern of reverse	5,000
TS34	ND1969/4	—	20 Lepta. Silver. 5.7200 g. Uniface pattern of obverse	4,000
TS35	ND(1969)	—	20 Lepta. Silver. 5.7200 g. Uniface pattern of reverse	4,000
TS36	1969/4	—	20 Lepta. Gold. 10.7400 g. Uniface pattern of obverse	5,000
TS37	ND(1969)	—	20 Lepta. Gold. 10.6900 g. Uniface pattern of reverse	5,000

MINT SETS

KM#	Date	Mintage	Identification	Issue Price	Mkt Val
MS1	1965 (7)	—	KM78, 80-85	—	45.00
MS2	1978 (8)	50,000	KM#113, 114, 115, 116, 117, 118, 119, 120	—	35.00
MS3	1982 (7)	—	KM115-116, 130-134	—	20.00
MS4	1993 (7)	—	KM#131-132, 147, 150-151, 154, 159	—	100
MS5	2000 (7)	—	KM#131-132, 147, 150-151, 154, 159	—	20.00

PROOF SETS

KM#	Date	Mintage	Identification	Issue Price	Mkt Val
PS1	1965 (7)	4,987	KM78, 80-85	10.25	85.00
PS2	1978 (8)	20,000	KM113-120	—	65.00
PS3	1993 (8)	—	KM131-132, 147, 150-151, 154, 159-160	65.00	825
PS4	1994 (2)	—	KM162-163	—	725

GREENLAND

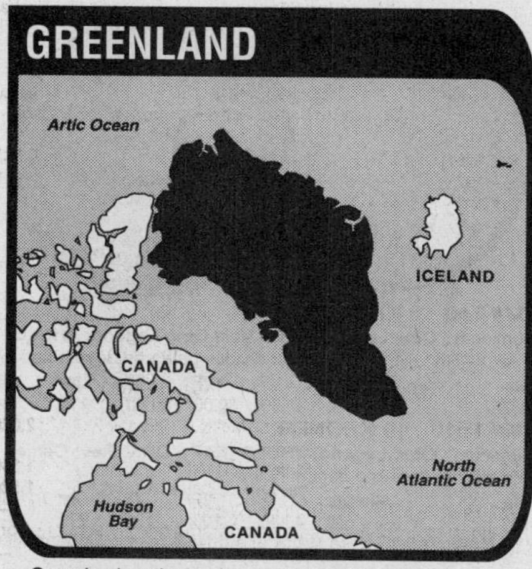

Greenland, an integral part of the Danish realm is situated between the North Atlantic Ocean and the Polar Sea, almost entirely within the Arctic Circle. An island nation, it has an area of 840,000 sq. mi. (2,175,600 sq. km.) and a population of 57,000. Capital: Nuuk (formerly Godthaab). Greenland is the world's only source of natural cryolite, a fluoride of sodium and aluminum, important in making aluminum. Fish products and minerals are exported.

Eric the Red discovered Greenland in 982 and established the first settlement in 986. Greenland was a republic until 1261, when the sovereignty of Norway was extended to the island. The original colony was abandoned about 1400 when increasing cold interfered with the breeding of cattle. Successful recolonization was undertaken by Denmark in 1721. In 1921 Denmark extended its claim to include the entire island, and made it a colony of the crown in 1924. The island's colonial status was abolished by amendment to the Danish constitution on June 5, 1953, and Greenland became an integral part of the Kingdom of Denmark. The last Greenlandic coins were withdrawn on July 1, 1967, and since then, Danish coins have been used. Greenland has had home rule since May 1, 1979.

RULERS
Danish

MINT MARKS
Heart (h) Copenhagen (Kobenhavn)

MINTMASTERS' INITIALS
HCN - Hans Christian Nielsen, 1919-1927
C - Alfred Kristian Frederik Christiansen, 1956-1971
GJ - Knud Gunnar Jensen, 1901-1933
S - Harald Salomon, 1933-1968

MONETARY SYSTEM
100 Øre = 1 Krone

DANISH COLONY

MILLED COINAGE

KM# 5 25 ORE
Copper-Nickel **Obv:** Crowned arms of Denmark **Obv. Legend:** GRØNLANDS STYRELSE **Rev:** Polar bear walking left, date below divided by 'GS', denomination above

Date	Mintage	F	VF	XF	Unc	BU
1926(h) HCN GJ	310,000	4.00	7.00	12.50	37.50	50.00

Note: This coin was withdrawn from circulation during 1940 and sent to the United States to be holed to avoid confusion with the Danish 1 Krone coin

KM# 6 25 ORE
Copper-Nickel **Obv:** Crowned arms of Denmark **Rev:** Hole at center of polar bear, left, denomination above, date below divided by 'GS' **Note:** Center hole added to KM#5.

Date	Mintage	F	VF	XF	Unc	BU
1926(h) HCN GJ	31,716	20.00	40.00	75.00	125	—

Note: The hole was added 1940/41 in New York to avoid confusion with the 1 Krone coins of Denmark

KM# 7 50 ORE
Aluminum-Bronze **Obv:** Crowned arms of Denmark **Obv. Legend:** GRØNLANDS STYRELSE **Rev:** Polar bear walking left, denomination above, date below divided by 'GS'

Date	Mintage	F	VF	XF	Unc	BU
1926(h) HCN CJ	195,837	6.00	9.50	15.00	37.50	55.00

KM# 8 KRONE
Aluminum-Bronze **Obv:** Crowned arms of Denmark **Obv. Legend:** GRØNLANDS STYRELSE **Rev:** Polar bear walking left, denomination above, date below divided by 'GS'

Date	Mintage	F	VF	XF	Unc	BU
1926(h) HCN CJ	286,982	4.50	10.00	18.00	56.50	67.50

KM# 9 5 KRONER
Brass **Obv:** Crowned arms of Denmark **Obv. Legend:** GRØNLANDS STYRELSE **Rev:** Polar bear walking left, denomination above, date below divides by "GS" **Rev. Designer:** Gilroy Roberts **Note:** Mainly struck for use by American forces in Greenland during WWII, when 5 Kroner was equal to one U.S. dollar.

Date	Mintage	F	VF	XF	Unc	BU
1944	100,000	40.00	60.00	80.00	125	150

Note: Struck at the Philadelphia Mint; Without mintmark

TOKEN ISSUES - GREENLAND MINING LTD.

Josvas (Innatsiaq)

A place in southwest Greenland, where the Gronlandsk Minedrifts Aktieselskab ran a copper mine from 1907-1914 yielding little more than 60 tons of copper, as a minor bonus, over 50 kg of silver and half a kg of gold.

KM# Tn1 10 ORE
Nickel Plated Zinc **Obv:** Date within legend **Obv. Legend:** GRØNLANDSK MINEDRIFTS-AKTIESELSKAB **Rev:** Crossed hammers over denomination **Note:** Struck at L. Chr. Lauer, Nürnberg, Germany.

Date	Mintage	VG	F	VF	XF	Unc
1911	5,000	—	10.00	16.00	32.00	—

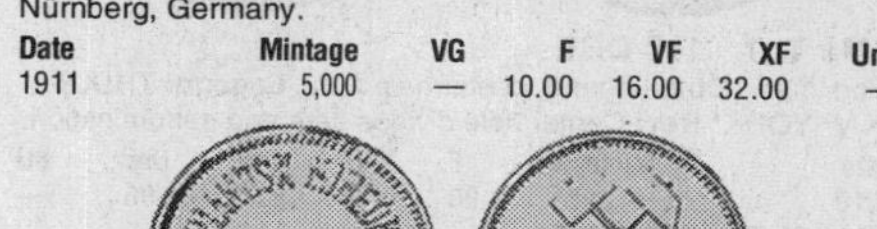

KM# Tn2 25 ORE
Nickel Plated Zinc **Obv:** Date within legend **Obv. Legend:** GRØNLANDSK MINEDRIFTS-AKTIESELSKAB **Rev:** Crossed hammers over denomination **Note:** Struck at L. Chr. Lauer, Nürnberg, Germany.

Date	Mintage	VG	F	VF	XF	Unc
1911	5,000	—	10.00	16.00	32.00	—

KM# Tn3 100 ORE
Nickel Plated Zinc **Obv:** Date within legend **Obv. Legend:** GRØNLANDSK MINEDRIFTS-AKTIESELSKAB **Rev:** Crossed hammers over denomination **Note:** Struck at L. Chr. Lauer, Nürnberg, Germany.

Date	Mintage	VG	F	VF	XF	Unc
1911	5,000	—	10.00	16.00	35.00	—

IVIGTUT CRYOLITE MINING & TRADING CO.

Series IV, 1922

KM# Tn46 10 ORE
Copper-Nickel **Obv:** Seated polar bear on helmeted shield, mining tools flank **Obv. Legend:** IVIGTUT KRYOLITHBRUD **Rev:** Denomination at center **Rev. Legend:** KRYOLITH MINE OG HANDELS SELSKABET

Date	Mintage	VG	F	VF	XF	Unc
1922	10,018	5.00	12.00	15.00	32.50	50.00

KM# Tn47 50 ORE
Copper-Nickel **Obv:** Seated polar bear on helmeted shield, mining tools flank **Obv. Legend:** IVIGTUT KRYOLITHBRUD **Rev. Legend:** KRYOLITH MINE OG HANDELS SELSKABET

Date	Mintage	VG	F	VF	XF	Unc
1922	4,018	16.00	35.00	60.00	100	150

KM# Tn48 2 KRONER
Copper-Nickel **Obv:** Seated polar bear on helmeted shield, mining tools flank **Obv. Legend:** IVIGTUT KRYOLITHBRUD **Rev:** Rosettes flank denomination **Rev. Legend:** KRYOLITH MINE OG HANDELS SELSKABET

Date	Mintage	VG	F	VF	XF	Unc
1922	4,018	15.00	35.00	70.00	100	165

KM# Tn49 10 KRONER
Copper-Nickel **Obv:** Seated polar bear on shield **Obv. Legend:** IVIGTUT KRYOLITHBRUD **Rev. Legend:** KRYOLITH MINE OG HANDELS SELSKABET **Edge:** Reeded

Date	Mintage	VG	F	VF	XF	Unc
1922	10,706	20.00	55.00	85.00	140	200

Note: Struck in 1926 using 1922 dies

KM# Tn49a 10 KRONER
Aluminum-Bronze **Obv:** Polar bear on shield **Edge:** Plain

Date	Mintage	VG	F	VF	XF	Unc
1922	7,018	—	—	800	1,125	1,550

Note: This token was removed from circulation because it had the same size, weight and color of Denmark's 2 Kroner, issued in 1924.

ROYAL GREENLAND TRADE (COMPANY)

(Den Kongelige Grønlandske Handel)

Located on Angmagssalik Island off the east coast of Greenland just below the Arctic Circle.

KM# Tn25 500 ORE
Aluminum **Note:** Uniface

Date	Mintage	VG	F	VF	XF	Unc
ND(1905)	200	50.00	100	200	300	—

DANISH STATE
1953-1979
MILLED COINAGE

KM# 10 KRONE
Aluminum-Bronze, 27.3 mm. **Issuer:** Royal Greenland Trade Company **Obv:** Crowned arms of Denmark and Greenland, date below **Obv. Legend:** DEN KONGELIGE GRØNLANDSKE HANDEL **Rev:** Denomination within flower spray

Date	Mintage	F	VF	XF	Unc	BU
1957(h) C S	100,209	8.00	12.50	22.50	55.00	70.00

KM# 10a KRONE
Copper-Nickel, 27.3 mm. **Issuer:** Royal Greenland Trade Company **Obv:** Crowned arms of Denmark and Greenland **Rev:** Denomination within floral wreath

Date	Mintage	F	VF	XF	Unc	BU
1960(h) C S	108,500	3.75	7.50	12.50	22.50	—
1964(h) C S	110,000	8.00	15.00	20.00	30.00	—

TRIAL STRIKES

Angmagssalik - Royal Greenland Trade (Company)

KM#	Date	Mintage Identification	Mkt Val

TS1	ND(1905)	— Ore. Aluminum. 27 mm.	—

TS2	ND(1905)	— 5 Ore. Aluminum. 30 mm.	—

TS3	ND(1905)	— 10 Ore. Aluminum. 34 mm.	—

TS4	ND(1905)	— 25 Ore. Aluminum. 34 mm.	—

KM#	Date	Mintage Identification	Mkt Val

TS5	ND(1905)	— 50 Ore. Aluminum. 38 mm.	—
TS6	ND(1905)	— 100 Ore. Aluminum. 39 mm.	—

THULE-KAP YORK

The Thule (gaanaaq)-Cape York Arctic trading station located in northwestern Greenland on the coast of the Hayes Peninsula north of Cap York was established in 1910 by polar explorer Knud Rasmussen. U.S. military bases are currently there.

THULE KAP YORK
TOKEN COINAGE

KM# Tn5.1 5 ORE
Aluminum **Obv:** Legend, center hole **Obv. Legend:** THULE *KAP YORK* **Rev:** Center hole divides denomination and date

Date	Mintage	F	VF	XF	Unc	BU
1910	5,000	2.00	4.50	8.00	17.50	—

KM# Tn5.2 5 ORE
Aluminum **Obv:** Legend **Obv. Legend:** THULE *KAP YORK* **Rev:** Denomination above date **Note:** Error - struck without center hole.

Date	Mintage	F	VF	XF	Unc	BU
1910 Rare	—	—	—	—	—	—

KM# Tn6 25 ORE
Aluminum **Obv:** Legend, center hole **Obv. Legend:** THULE *KAP YORK* **Rev:** Center hole divides date and denomination

Date	Mintage	F	VF	XF	Unc	BU
1910	5,000	2.00	5.00	8.00	17.50	—

KM# Tn7 100 ORE
Aluminum **Obv:** Legend, center hole **Obv. Legend:** THULE *KAP YORK* **Rev:** Center hole divides date and denomination

Date	Mintage	F	VF	XF	Unc	BU
1910	2,000	4.00	10.00	18.00	38.00	—

KM# Tn8 500 ORE
Aluminum **Obv:** Legend, center hole **Obv. Legend:** THULE *KAP YORK* **Rev:** Center hole divides date and denomination

Date	Mintage	F	VF	XF	Unc	BU
1910	2,000	6.00	18.00	25.00	55.00	—

Note: Tn5-8 were struck at L. Chr. Lauer, Nürnberg, Germany, in 1913

KM# Tn9 5 KRONER
Aluminum **Obv:** Legend, center hole **Obv. Legend:** THULE *KAP YORK* **Rev:** Center hole divides date and denomination

Date	Mintage	F	VF	XF	Unc	BU
1932	500	15.00	30.00	60.00	112	—

KM# Tn10 10 KRONER
Aluminum **Obv. Legend:** THULE *KAP YORK* **Rev:** Center hole divides date and denomination

Date	Mintage	F	VF	XF	Unc	BU
1932	500	40.00	100	165	275	—

Note: Tn9-10 were struck at a private mint in Copenhagen

GRENADA

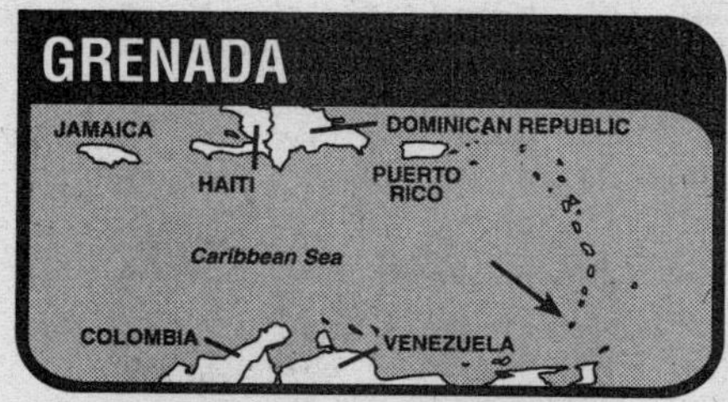

The State of Grenada, located in the Windward Islands of the Caribbean Sea 90 miles (145 km.) north of Trinidad, has(with Carriacou and Petit Martinique) an area of 133 sq. mi. (344 sq. km.) and a population of 94,000. Capital: St.George's. Grenada is the smallest independent nation in the Western Hemisphere. The economy is based on agriculture and tourism. Sugar, coconuts, nutmeg, cocoa and bananas are exported.

Columbus discovered Grenada in 1498 during his third voyage to the Americas. Spain failed to colonize the island, and in 1627 granted it to the British who sold it to the French who colonized it in 1650. Grenada was captured by the British in 1763, retaken by the French in 1779, and finally ceded to the British in 1783. In 1958 Grenada joined the Federation of the West Indies, which was dissolved in 1962. In 1967 it became an internally self-governing British associated state. Full independence was attained on Feb. 4, 1974. Grenada is a member of the Commonwealth of Nations. The prime minister is the Head of Government. Elizabeth II is Head of State as Queen of Grenada.

The early coinage of Grenada consists of cut and countermarked pieces of Spanish or Spanish Colonial Reales, which were valued at 11 Bits. In 1787 8 Reales coins were cut into 11 triangular pieces and countermarked with an incuse G. Later in 1814 large denomination cut pieces were issued being 1/2, 1/3 or 1/6 cuts and countermarked with a TR, incuse G and a number 6, 4,2, or 1 indicating the value in bitts.

RULERS
British

INDEPENDENT STATE
Commonwealth of Nations
MODERN COINAGE

KM# 15 4 DOLLARS
Copper-Nickel, 38.5 mm. **Series:** F.A.O. **Obv:** Cocoa beans within oval **Rev:** Sugar cane and banana tree branch

Date	Mintage	F	VF	XF	Unc	BU
1970	13,000	—	6.00	10.00	20.00	30.00
1970 Proof	2,000	Value: 35.00				

KM# 16 10 DOLLARS
Copper-Nickel **Subject:** Royal Visit **Obv:** Crowned bust right **Rev:** Arms with supporters within circle

Date	Mintage	F	VF	XF	Unc	BU
1985	Est. 100,000	—	—	4.50	9.00	—

KM# 16a 10 DOLLARS
28.2800 g., 0.9250 Silver .8411 oz. ASW **Subject:** Royal Visit **Obv:** Crowned bust right **Rev:** Arms with supporters within circle

Date	Mintage	F	VF	XF	Unc	BU
1985 Proof	Est. 5,000	Value: 55.00				

KM# 16b 10 DOLLARS
47.5400 g., 0.9170 Gold 1.4013 oz. AGW **Subject:** Royal Visit **Obv:** Crowned bust right **Rev:** Arms with supporters within circle

Date	Mintage	F	VF	XF	Unc	BU
1985 Proof	Est. 250	Value: 1,350				

KM# 17 100 DOLLARS
129.5900 g., 0.9250 Silver 3.8543 oz. ASW, 63 mm. **Subject:** Tropical Birds - Grenada Dove **Obv:** Arms within in circle, country name above **Note:** Illustration reduced.

Date	Mintage	F	VF	XF	Unc	BU
1988 Proof	Est. 10,000	Value: 125				

GUADELOUPE

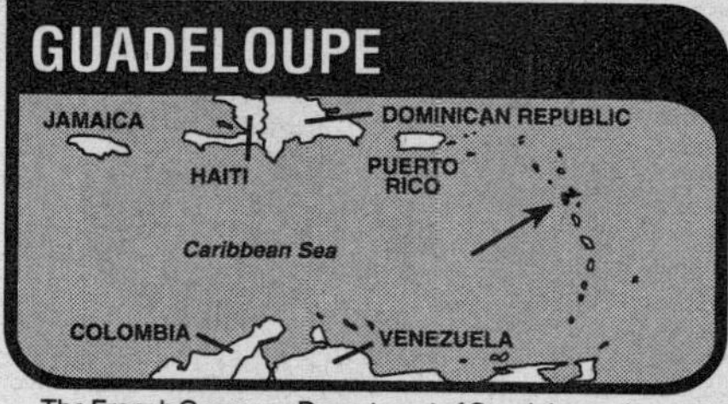

The French Overseas Department of Guadeloupe, located in the Leeward Islands of the West Indies about 300 miles (493 km.) southeast of Puerto Rico, has an area of 687 sq. mi. (1,780 sq. km.) and a population of 306,000. Actually it is two islands separated by a narrow saltwater stream: volcanic Basse-Terre to the west and the flatter limestone formation of Grande-Terre to the east. Capital: Basse-Terre, on the island of that name. The principal industries are agriculture, the distillation of liquors, and tourism. Sugar, bananas, and rum are exported.

Guadeloupe was discovered by Columbus in 1493 and settled in 1635 by two Frenchmen, L'Olive and Duplessis, who took possession in the name of the French Company of the Islands of America. When repeated efforts by private companies to colonize the island failed, it was relinquished to the French crown in 1674, and established as a dependency of Martinique. The British occupied the island on two occasions, 1759-63 and 1810-16, before it passed permanently to France. A colony until 1946 Guadeloupe was then made an overseas territory of the FrenchUnion. In 1958 it voted to become an Overseas Department within the new French Community.

The well-known R.F. in garland oval countermark of the French Government is only legitimate if on a French Colonies 12 deniers 1767 C#4. Two other similar but incuse RF countermarks are on cut pieces in the values of 1 and 4 escalins. Contemporary and modern counterfeits are known of both these types.

RULERS
French 1816-

MONETARY SYSTEM
100 Centimes = 1 Franc

FRENCH COLONY
MODERN COINAGE

KM# 45 50 CENTIMES
Copper-Nickel **Obv:** Armored head left within circle **Obv. Designer:** A. Patay **Rev:** Sugar cane stalk divides date and denomination **Shape:** 18-sided

Date	Mintage	F	VF	XF	Unc	BU
1903	600,000	16.00	35.00	85.00	240	500
1921	600,000	12.00	30.00	75.00	185	400

KM# 46 FRANC
Copper-Nickel **Obv:** Armored head left within circle **Obv. Designer:** A. Patay **Rev:** Sugar cane stalk divides date and denomination **Note:** 20-sided.

Date	Mintage	F	VF	XF	Unc	BU
1903	700,000	20.00	40.00	90.00	250	550
1921	700,000	15.00	30.00	80.00	200	450

ESSAIS

KM#	Date	Mintage	Identification	Mkt Val
E1	1903	—	50 Centimes. Copper-Nickel.	180
E2	1903	—	50 Centimes. Silver.	400
E3	1903	—	Franc. Copper-Nickel.	250
E4	1903	—	Franc. Silver.	600
E5	19(21)	—	Franc. Bronze.	160

PIEFORTS

KM#	Date	Mintage	Identification	Mkt Val
P1	1903	—	50 Centimes. Copper-Nickel. Armored head left within circle. Sugar cane stalk divides date and denomination.	400

KM#	Date	Mintage	Identification	Mkt Val
P2	1903	—	Franc. Copper-Nickel.	500

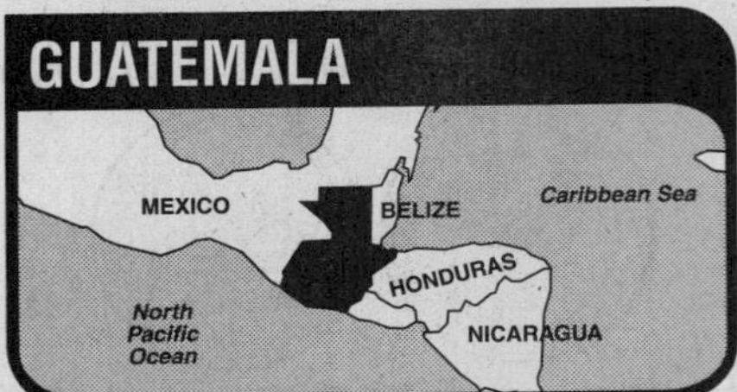

The Republic of Guatemala, the northernmost of the five Central American republics, has an area of 42,042 sq. mi. (108,890 sq. km.) and a population of 10.7 million. Capital: Guatemala City. The economy of Guatemala is heavily dependent on agriculture, however, the country is rich in nickel resources which are being developed. Coffee, cotton and bananas are exported.

Guatemala, once the site of an ancient Mayan civilization, was conquered by Pedro de Alvarado, the resourceful lieutenant of Cortes who undertook the conquest from Mexico. Cruel but strategically skillful, he progressed rapidly along the Pacific coastal lowlands to the highland plain of Quetzaltenango where the decisive battle for Guatemala was fought. After routing the Indian forces, he established the city of Guatemala in 1524. The Spanish Captaincy-General of Guatemala included all Central America but Panama. Guatemala declared its independence of Spain in 1821 and was absorbed into the Mexican empire of Augustin Iturbide (1822-23). From 1823 to 1839 Guatemala was a constituent state of the Central American Republic. Upon dissolution of that confederation, Guatemala proclaimed itself an independent republic. Like El Salvador, Guatemala suffered from internal strife between right-wing, US-backed military government and leftist indigenous peoples from ca. 1954 to ca. 1997.

MINT MARKS

H, (H) - Heaton, Birmingham
(KN) – Birmingham, King's Norton Mint
(L) – London, Royal Mint
(P) – Philadelphia, USA
NG - ??? 1992
(S) – San Francisco, USA

REPUBLIC

STANDARD COINAGE

8 Reales = 1 Peso

KM# 175 1/4 REAL

Copper-Nickel **Obv:** Sun above three hills, date below **Rev:** Denomination within wreath, 5 stars below **Note:** Medal rotation.

Date	Mintage	F	VF	XF	Unc	BU
1901H	5,056,000	0.25	0.45	1.00	2.50	—

KM# 176 1/2 REAL (Medio)

Copper-Nickel **Obv:** Seated figure left **Note:** Medal rotation.

Date	Mintage	F	VF	XF	Unc	BU
1901(H)	6,652,000	0.35	0.65	1.25	2.75	—

KM# 177 REAL

Copper-Nickel, 21 mm. **Obv:** Seated figure left **Rev:** National arms, thick wreath **Note:** Medal rotation.

Date	Mintage	F	VF	XF	Unc	BU
1901(H)	7,388,000	0.20	0.35	1.20	4.00	—
1910H	4,000,000	0.25	0.40	1.25	5.00	—
1911(H)	2,000,000	0.25	0.45	1.35	5.00	—
1912(H)	8,000,000	0.20	0.35	1.00	3.00	—

PROVISIONAL COINAGE

1915-1923

KM# 230 12-1/2 CENTAVOS

Copper **Obv:** Word at center divides flower **Rev:** Denomination within circle

Date	Mintage	F	VF	XF	Unc	BU
1915	6,000,000	0.75	1.25	3.50	12.50	—

KM# 231 25 CENTAVOS

Copper **Obv:** Word at center divides flower **Rev:** Denomination within circle

Date	Mintage	F	VF	XF	Unc	BU
1915	4,000,000	0.75	1.25	5.00	15.00	—

KM# 232.1 50 CENTAVOS

Aluminum-Bronze **Obv:** Flower design **Rev:** Denomination within circle **Note:** Thin numerals in denomination.

Date	Mintage	F	VF	XF	Unc	BU
1922	3,803,000	0.80	1.50	5.50	17.50	—

KM# 232.2 50 CENTAVOS

Aluminum-Bronze **Obv:** Flower design **Rev:** Denomination within circle **Note:** Thick numerals in denomination.

Date	Mintage	F	VF	XF	Unc	BU
1922	Inc. above	0.80	1.50	5.50	17.50	—

KM# 233 PESO

Aluminum-Bronze **Subject:** Miguel Garcia Granados **Obv:** Bust left **Rev:** Denomination

Date	Mintage	F	VF	XF	Unc	BU
1923	1,477,000	1.50	2.50	8.50	28.00	—

KM# 234 5 PESOS

Aluminum-Bronze **Subject:** Justo Rufino Barrios **Obv:** Bust right **Rev:** Denomination

Date	Mintage	F	VF	XF	Unc	BU
1923	440,000	2.00	4.00	16.00	48.00	—

KM# 234a 5 PESOS

Copper **Subject:** Justo Rufino Barrios **Obv:** Bust right **Rev:** Denomination

Date	Mintage	F	VF	XF	Unc	BU
1923	Inc. above	2.00	4.00	16.00	48.00	—

REFORM COINAGE

100 Centavos = 1 Quetzal

KM# 248 1/2 CENTAVO (Medio)

Brass **Obv:** National arms **Rev:** Denomination

Date	Mintage	F	VF	XF	Unc	BU
1932(L)	6,000,000	0.15	0.50	2.00	5.00	—
1932(L) Proof	—	Value: 200				
1946	640,000	0.75	1.75	3.75	15.00	—

KM# 237 CENTAVO (Un)

Copper **Obv:** Incuse legend on scroll **Rev:** Denomination

Date	Mintage	F	VF	XF	Unc	BU
1925	357,000	4.50	7.50	20.00	40.00	—

KM# 237a CENTAVO (Un)

Bronze **Obv:** National arms **Rev:** Denomination

Date	Mintage	F	VF	XF	Unc	BU
1925	Inc. above	5.00	8.00	15.00	40.00	—

KM# 247 CENTAVO (Un)

Copper **Obv:** National arms **Rev:** Denomination

Date	Mintage	F	VF	XF	Unc	BU
1929(L)	500,000	2.00	3.00	8.00	25.00	—
1929(L) Proof	—	—	—	—	—	—

KM# 249 CENTAVO (Un)

Brass, 20.3 mm. **Obv:** National arms **Rev:** Denomination

Date	Mintage	F	VF	XF	Unc	BU
1932(L)	3,000,000	0.40	1.00	350	11.50	—
1932(L) Proof	—	—	—	—	—	—
1933(L)	1,500,000	0.60	1.50	4.50	12.50	—
1933(L) Proof	—	—	—	—	—	—
1934(L)	1,000,000	0.50	1.25	4.50	12.50	—
1934(L) Proof	—	—	—	—	—	—
1936(L)	1,500,000	0.40	1.00	4.50	12.50	—
1936(L) Proof	—	—	—	—	—	—
1938/7(L)	1,000,000	0.40	1.00	5.00	14.00	—
1938(L)	Inc. above	0.40	1.00	4.50	12.50	—
1938(L) Proof	—	—	—	—	—	—
1939(L)	1,500,000	0.50	1.25	4.50	10.00	—
1939(L) Proof	—	—	—	—	—	—
1946	539,000	—	0.15	0.75	6.00	—
1947	1,121,000	—	0.15	0.35	3.50	—
1948	1,651,000	—	0.15	0.35	4.50	—
1949	1,022,000	—	0.15	0.45	5.00	—

KM# 251 CENTAVO (Un)

3.0000 g., Brass, 20 mm. **Obv:** Bird with shield above date **Rev:** Branch right of denomination

Date	Mintage	F	VF	XF	Unc	BU
1943(P)	450,000	3.00	6.00	10.00	30.00	—
1944(S)	2,049,999	0.50	1.25	2.50	8.00	—

KM# 254 CENTAVO (Un)

Brass, 22 mm. **Subject:** Fray Bartolome de las Casas **Obv:** National arms **Rev:** Bust left

Date	Mintage	F	VF	XF	Unc	BU
1949	1,091,000	—	0.15	0.35	5.00	—
1950	3,663,000	—	0.15	0.25	1.75	—
1951	3,586,000	—	0.25	5.00	25.00	—
1952	1,445,000	—	0.15	0.30	20.00	—
1953	2,214,000	—	0.15	0.25	5.00	—
1954	1,455,000	—	0.15	0.30	2.25	—

KM# 259 CENTAVO (Un)

Nickel-Brass, 21 mm. **Subject:** Fray Bartolome de las Casas **Obv:** National arms **Rev:** Larger bust left

Date	Mintage	F	VF	XF	Unc	BU
1954(KN)	10,000,000	—	—	0.15	3.00	—
1957(KN)	1,600,000	—	0.15	0.25	1.00	—
1958(KN)	2,000,000	—	0.15	0.25	2.00	—

KM# 260 CENTAVO (Un)
Brass, 21 mm. **Subject:** Fray Bartolome de las Casas **Obv:** National arms **Rev:** Bust left **Note:** Larger obverse lettering

Date	Mintage	F	VF	XF	Unc	BU
1958	10,001,000	—	—	0.15	2.00	—
1961	1,826,000	—	—	0.15	1.00	—
1963	4,926,000	—	—	0.15	1.00	—
1964	4,280,000	—	—	0.15	1.00	—

KM# 265 CENTAVO (Un)
Brass, 19 mm. **Subject:** Fray Bartolome de las Casas **Obv:** National arms **Rev:** Bust left **Note:** Size reduced. Varieties in size and style of date exist.

Date	Mintage	F	VF	XF	Unc	BU
1965	3,845,000	—	—	0.15	1.00	—
1966	6,100,000	—	—	0.15	1.00	—
1967	6,400,000	—	—	0.15	1.00	—
1968	2,590,000	—	—	0.15	1.00	—
1969	13,780,000	—	—	0.15	1.00	—
1970	10,511,000	—	—	0.15	1.00	—

KM# 273 CENTAVO (Un)
Brass **Subject:** Fray Bartolome de las Casas **Obv:** National arms **Rev:** Bust left **Note:** Smaller date and lettering.

Date	Mintage	F	VF	XF	Unc	BU
1972	11,500,000	—	—	0.15	0.25	—
1973	12,000,000	—	—	0.15	0.25	—

KM# 275.1 CENTAVO (Un)
Brass **Subject:** Fray Bartolome de las Casas **Obv:** National arms **Rev:** Bust left, larger head **Note:** Larger date and lettering; no dots left and right of date.

Date	Mintage	F	VF	XF	Unc	BU
1974	10,000,000	—	—	0.15	0.25	—
1975	15,000,000	—	—	0.15	0.25	—
1976	15,230,000	—	—	0.15	0.25	—
1977	30,000,000	—	—	0.15	0.25	—
1978	30,000,000	—	—	0.15	0.25	—
1979	30,000,000	—	—	0.15	0.25	—

KM# 275.2 CENTAVO (Un)
Brass, 18 mm. **Obv:** National arms **Rev:** Bust left, smaller head **Note:** Smaller legend and date. Dots left and right of date

Date	Mintage	F	VF	XF	Unc	BU
1979	Inc. above	—	—	0.15	0.25	—
1980	20,000,000	—	—	0.15	0.25	—
1984	20,000,000	—	—	0.15	0.25	—

KM# 275.4 CENTAVO (Un)
Brass **Obv:** National arms, legend on scroll in relief **Rev:** Bust left **Note:** Varieties exist.

Date	Mintage	F	VF	XF	Unc	BU
1981	30,000,000	—	—	0.15	0.25	—
1982	30,000,000	—	—	0.15	0.25	—

KM# 275.3 CENTAVO (Un)
Brass, 19 mm. **Rev:** Fray Bartolome de las Casas, smaller head **Note:** Smaller legend and date. Dots left and right of date.

Date	Mintage	F	VF	XF	Unc	BU
1985	—	—	—	0.15	0.25	—
1986	—	—	—	0.15	0.25	—
1987	50,000,000	—	—	0.15	0.25	—
1988	51,400,000	—	—	0.15	0.25	—
1989	—	—	—	0.15	0.25	—
1990	—	—	—	0.15	0.25	—
1991	—	—	—	0.15	0.25	—
1992	—	—	—	0.15	0.25	—

KM# 275.5 CENTAVO (Un)
Brass **Subject:** Fray Bartolome de las Casas **Obv:** National arms **Rev:** Head left, modified portrait

Date	Mintage	F	VF	XF	Unc	BU
1993	—	—	—	0.15	0.25	—
1994	—	—	—	0.15	0.25	—
1995	—	—	—	0.15	0.25	—

KM# 282 CENTAVO (Un)
0.8000 g., Aluminum **Subject:** Fray Bartolome de las Casas **Obv:** National arms **Rev:** Bust left **Edge:** Plain **Shape:** 7-sided

Date	Mintage	F	VF	XF	Unc	BU
1999	—	—	—	0.15	0.25	—

KM# 250 2 CENTAVOS (Dos)
Brass **Obv:** National arms **Rev:** Denomination

Date	Mintage	F	VF	XF	Unc	BU
1932(L)	3,000,000	0.50	1.25	10.00	35.00	—
1932(L) Proof	—	—	—	—	—	—

KM# 252 2 CENTAVOS (Dos)
6.0000 g., Brass **Obv:** Bird with shield above date **Rev:** Branch right of denomination

Date	Mintage	F	VF	XF	Unc	BU
1943(P)	150,000	3.50	7.50	15.00	45.00	—
1944(S)	1,100,000	0.60	2.00	8.00	25.00	—

KM# 238.1 5 CENTAVOS
1.6667 g., 0.7200 Silver .0386 oz. ASW **Obv:** National arms **Rev:** Bird on pillar, engraver's initials 'JAC' below "Centavos"

Date	Mintage	F	VF	XF	Unc	BU
1925	573,000	3.00	5.75	15.00	35.00	—
1944	1,026,000	BV	1.25	5.00	15.00	—
1945	4,026,000	BV	0.75	4.00	10.00	—
1947	1,834,000	BV	1.00	4.00	10.00	—
1948	1,103,000	BV	1.00	5.00	12.00	—
1949	551,000	0.65	1.50	10.00	25.00	—

KM# 238.1a 5 CENTAVOS
2.5000 g., 0.9000 Gold .0723 oz. AGW **Obv:** National arms **Rev:** Bird on pillar

Date	Mintage	F	VF	XF	Unc	BU
1925	8	—	—	750	950	—

KM# 238.2 5 CENTAVOS
1.6667 g., 0.7200 Silver .0386 oz. ASW **Obv:** National arms, short-tailed quetzal **Rev:** Bird on pillar, without engraver's initials

Date	Mintage	F	VF	XF	Unc	BU
1928(L)	1,000,000	BV	1.00	10.00	35.00	—
1928(L) Proof	—	Value: 400				
1929(L)	1,000,000	BV	1.00	4.00	12.00	—
1929(L) Proof	—	—	—	—	—	—
1932(L)	2,000,000	BV	1.00	4.00	10.00	—
1932(L) Proof	—	—	—	—	—	—
1933(L)	600,000	BV	1.00	5.00	15.00	—
1933(L) Proof	—	—	—	—	—	—
1934(L)	1,200,000	BV	1.00	4.00	10.00	—
1934(L) Proof	—	—	—	—	—	—
1937(L)	400,000	BV	1.00	4.00	10.00	—
1937(L) Proof	—	—	—	—	—	—
1938(L)	300,000	0.65	1.50	5.00	15.00	—
1938(L) Proof	—	—	—	—	—	—
1943(P)	900,000	BV	0.75	4.00	10.00	—

KM# 255 5 CENTAVOS
1.6667 g., 0.7200 Silver .0386 oz. ASW **Obv:** National arms **Rev:** Kapok tree **Note:** Varieties exist with and without dashes.

Date	Mintage	F	VF	XF	Unc	BU
1949	305,000	0.65	1.50	7.00	25.00	—

KM# 257.1 5 CENTAVOS
1.6667 g., 0.7200 Silver .0386 oz. ASW **Obv:** National arms **Rev:** Kapok tree

Date	Mintage	F	VF	XF	Unc	BU
1950	453,000	BV	1.00	4.00	10.00	—
1951	1,032,000	BV	1.00	2.00	8.00	—
1952	913,000	BV	1.00	2.00	7.00	—
1953	447,000	BV	1.00	2.00	7.00	—
1954	520,000	BV	1.00	3.00	9.00	—
1955	2,061,999	BV	1.00	1.50	3.00	—
1956	1,301,000	BV	1.00	1.50	3.00	—
1957	2,941,000	BV	1.00	1.50	2.50	—

KM# 257.1a 5 CENTAVOS
2.7300 g., 0.6200 Gold .0544 oz. AGW **Obv:** National arms **Rev:** Kapok tree **Note:** Distributed among delegates.

Date	Mintage	F	VF	XF	Unc	BU
1953	25	—	—	—	550	—

Small date

Large date

KM# 257.2 5 CENTAVOS
1.6670 g., 0.7200 Silver .0386 oz. ASW **Obv:** National arms **Rev:** Kapok tree **Note:** Small crude date and large crude dates.

Date	Mintage	F	VF	XF	Unc	BU
1958 Small date	3,025,000	BV	0.75	1.00	2.50	—
1958 Large date	Inc. above	BV	1.00	1.75	3.50	—
1959	232,000	BV	1.00	1.50	2.00	—

KM# 257.3 5 CENTAVOS
1.6670 g., 0.7200 Silver .0386 oz. ASW **Obv:** National arm, short-tailed quetzal **Obv. Legend:** Kapok tree

Date	Mintage	F	VF	XF	Unc	BU
1958 Small date	—	BV	1.00	1.75	3.50	—
1958 Large date	—	BV	1.00	1.75	3.50	—

KM# 261 5 CENTAVOS
1.6670 g., 0.7200 Silver .0386 oz. ASW **Obv:** National arms **Rev:** Kapok tree, level ground

Date	Mintage	F	VF	XF	Unc	BU
1960	4,770,000	—	BV	0.65	1.25	—
1961	6,756,000	—	BV	0.65	1.25	—
1964	1,529,000	—	BV	0.65	1.25	—

KM# 266 5 CENTAVOS
Copper-Nickel, 16 mm. **Obv:** National arms **Rev:** Kapok tree **Note:** Dates for 1965 and 1966 are smaller with curved tails in the "9" & "6", while dates for 1967-1970 have straight tails in the "9" & "6".

Date	Mintage	F	VF	XF	Unc	BU
1965 Small date	1,642,000	—	0.15	0.50	4.00	—
1966 Small date	3,600,000	—	—	0.15	0.35	—
1967 Large date	2,800,000	—	—	0.15	0.35	—
1968 Large date	4,030,000	—	—	0.15	0.35	—

Date	Mintage	F	VF	XF	Unc	BU
1969 Large date	7,210,000	—	—	0.15	0.35	—
1970 Large date	8,121,000	—	—	0.15	0.35	—

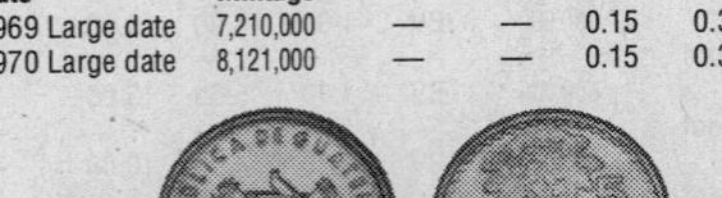

KM# 270 5 CENTAVOS

Copper-Nickel, 16 mm. **Obv:** Legend on scroll incuse, small shield and quetzal **Obv. Legend:** Kapok tree

Date	Mintage	F	VF	XF	Unc	BU
1971	8,270,000	—	—	0.15	0.35	—
1974	10,575,000	—	—	0.15	0.35	—
1975	10,000,000	—	—	0.15	0.35	—
1976	6,000,000	—	—	0.15	0.35	—
1977	20,000,000	—	—	0.15	0.35	—

KM# 276.1 5 CENTAVOS

Copper-Nickel, 16 mm. **Obv:** National arms, large shield and quetzal **Rev:** Kapok tree

Date	Mintage	F	VF	XF	Unc	BU
1977	Inc. above	—	—	0.15	0.35	—
1978	15,000,000	—	—	0.15	0.30	—
1979	12,000,000	—	—	0.15	0.30	—

KM# 276.2 5 CENTAVOS

Copper-Nickel, 16 mm. **Obv:** Legend on scroll in relief **Rev:** Kapok tree

Date	Mintage	F	VF	XF	Unc	BU
1980	8,000,000	—	—	0.15	0.30	—

KM# 276.3 5 CENTAVOS

Copper-Nickel, 16 mm. **Obv:** National arms **Rev:** Kapok tee modified

Date	Mintage	F	VF	XF	Unc	BU
1981	8,000,000	—	—	0.15	0.30	—
1985	—	—	—	0.15	0.30	—

KM# 276.4 5 CENTAVOS

Copper-Nickel, 16 mm. **Obv:** National arms, legend on scroll incuse **Rev:** Kapok tree smaller, less ground below **Note:** Varieties exist.

Date	Mintage	F	VF	XF	Unc	BU
1985	—	—	—	0.15	0.30	—
1986 Large date	—	—	—	0.15	0.30	—
1986 Small date	—	—	—	—	—	—
1987	25,000,000	—	—	0.15	0.30	—
1988	21,800,000	—	—	0.15	0.30	—
1989	—	—	—	0.15	0.30	—
1990	—	—	—	0.15	0.30	—
1991	—	—	—	0.15	0.30	—
1992	—	—	—	0.15	0.30	—
1993	—	—	—	0.15	0.30	—
1994	—	—	—	0.15	0.30	—
1996	—	—	—	0.15	0.30	—
1998	—	—	—	0.15	0.30	—

KM# 276.5 5 CENTAVOS

Copper-Nickel, 16 mm. **Obv:** National arms, smaller lettering **Rev:** Kapok tree

Date	Mintage	F	VF	XF	Unc	BU
1995	—	—	—	0.15	0.30	—

KM# 276.6 5 CENTAVOS

Copper-Nickel, 16 mm. **Obv:** National arms, smaller sized emblem **Obv. Legend:** Kapok tree **Note:** Varieties exist.

Date	Mintage	F	VF	XF	Unc	BU
1997	—	—	—	0.15	0.30	—
1998	—	—	—	0.15	0.30	—
2000	—	—	—	0.15	0.30	—

KM# 239.1 10 CENTAVOS

3.3333 g., 0.7200 Silver .0772 oz. ASW **Obv:** National arms **Rev:** Bird on engraved pillar, engraver's initials below "CENTAVOS" **Note:** Varieties exist.

Date	Mintage	F	VF	XF	Unc	BU
1925	573,000	3.50	6.50	15.00	35.00	—
1944	155,000	1.25	3.50	10.00	20.00	—
1945	1,499,000	BV	1.25	2.00	5.00	—
1947	471,000	BV	1.50	3.00	10.00	—
1948	324,000	BV	1.50	2.00	7.00	—
1949	145,000	BV	2.00	4.50	10.00	—

KM# 239.1a 10 CENTAVOS

5.0000 g., 0.9000 Gold .1446 oz. AGW **Obv:** National arms **Rev:** Long-tailed quetzal on pillar

Date	Mintage	F	VF	XF	Unc	BU
1925 Rare	8	—	—	—	—	—

KM# 239.2 10 CENTAVOS

3.3333 g., 0.7200 Silver .0772 oz. ASW **Obv:** National arms, short-tailed quetzal **Rev:** Bird on engraved pillar, without engraver's initials

Date	Mintage	F	VF	XF	Unc	BU
1928(L)	500,000	BV	2.50	5.00	30.00	—
1928(L) Proof	—	Value: 250				
1929(L)	500,000	BV	2.00	3.50	25.00	—
1929(L) Proof	—	—	—	—	—	—
1932(L)	500,000	BV	2.00	3.50	15.00	—
1932(L) Proof	—	—	—	—	—	—
1933(L)	650,000	BV	1.75	3.00	18.00	—
1933(L) Proof	—	—	—	—	—	—
1934(L)	300,000	BV	1.75	3.00	18.00	—
1934(L) Proof	—	—	—	—	—	—
1936(L)	200,000	BV	2.50	6.00	20.00	—
1936(L) Proof	—	—	—	—	—	—
1938(L)	150,000	1.25	3.00	6.00	18.00	—
1938(L) Proof	—	—	—	—	—	—
1943(P)	600,000	BV	1.25	3.00	10.00	—

KM# 239.3 10 CENTAVOS

3.3333 g., 0.7200 Silver .0772 oz. ASW **Obv:** National arms **Rev:** Quetzal on pillar, with engraver's initials **Note:** Mintage included above, in KM#239.1. Varieties exist.

Date	Mintage	F	VF	XF	Unc	BU
1947	—	BV	3.00	4.00	10.00	—

KM# 256.1 10 CENTAVOS

3.3333 g., 0.7200 Silver .0772 oz. ASW **Obv:** National arms **Rev:** Small monolith

Date	Mintage	F	VF	XF	Unc	BU
1949	281,000	BV	2.50	5.00	15.00	—
1950	550,000	BV	1.50	3.00	7.00	—
1951	263,000	BV	2.50	5.00	15.00	—
1952	307,000	BV	1.50	3.00	7.00	—
1953	388,000	BV	1.50	3.00	7.00	—
1955	896,000	BV	1.50	3.00	7.00	—
1956	501,000	BV	1.50	5.00	15.00	—
1958	1,528,000	BV	1.50	3.00	8.00	—

KM# 256.2 10 CENTAVOS

3.3333 g., 0.7200 Silver .0772 oz. ASW **Obv:** National arms **Rev:** Larger monolith

Date	Mintage	F	VF	XF	Unc	BU
1957	1,123,000	BV	1.25	2.00	3.00	—
1958	Inc. above	BV	1.50	2.50	5.00	—
1958	Inc. above	6.00	12.00	22.50	40.00	—

Note: Medallic die alignment

KM# 256.3 10 CENTAVOS

3.3333 g., 0.7200 Silver .0772 oz. ASW **Obv:** National arms **Rev:** Small monolith

Date	Mintage	F	VF	XF	Unc	BU
1958	Inc. above	BV	1.25	2.00	3.00	—
1959	461,000	BV	1.25	2.00	3.00	—
1959	Inc. above	6.00	12.00	22.50	37.50	—

Note: Medallic die alignment

KM# 262 10 CENTAVOS

3.3333 g., 0.7200 Silver .0772 oz. ASW **Obv:** National arms **Rev:** Monolith

Date	Mintage	F	VF	XF	Unc	BU
1960	1,743,000	BV	1.50	2.00	2.50	—
1961	2,647,000	BV	1.50	2.00	2.50	—
1964	965,000	BV	1.50	2.00	2.50	—

KM# 267 10 CENTAVOS

Copper-Nickel, 21 mm. **Obv:** National arms **Rev:** Monolith **Note:** Varieties of curved and straight "9" in date exist.

Date	Mintage	F	VF	XF	Unc	BU
1965	2,227,000	—	0.15	0.25	0.75	—
1966	1,550,000	—	0.15	0.35	0.85	—
1967	3,120,000	—	0.15	0.25	0.75	—
1968	3,220,000	—	0.15	0.25	0.75	—
1969	3,530,000	—	0.15	0.25	0.75	—
1970	4,153,000	—	0.15	0.25	0.75	—

KM# 271.1 10 CENTAVOS

Copper-Nickel, 21 mm. **Obv:** National arms, small wreath **Rev:** Monolith

Date	Mintage	F	VF	XF	Unc	BU
1971	4,580,000	—	0.15	0.25	0.75	—

KM# 271.2 10 CENTAVOS

Copper-Nickel, 21 mm. **Obv:** National arms, large wreath **Rev:** Monolith

Date	Mintage	F	VF	XF	Unc	BU
1971	Inc. above	—	0.15	0.25	0.75	—
1973	—	—	0.15	0.25	0.75	—

KM# 274 10 CENTAVOS

Copper-Nickel, 21 mm. **Obv:** National arms **Rev:** Monolith

Date	Mintage	F	VF	XF	Unc	BU
1974	3,500,000	—	0.15	0.25	0.75	—
1975 Dots flank date	6,000,000	—	0.15	0.25	0.75	—

KM# 277.1 10 CENTAVOS

Copper-Nickel, 21 mm. **Obv:** National arms **Rev:** Monolith **Note:** Wide rim toothed border.

Date	Mintage	F	VF	XF	Unc	BU
1976	2,000,000	—	0.15	0.25	0.75	—
1977	5,000,000	—	0.15	0.25	0.75	—

KM# 277.2 10 CENTAVOS

Copper-Nickel, 21 mm. **Obv:** National arms **Rev:** Monolith **Note:** Round beads instead of toothed border.

Date	Mintage	F	VF	XF	Unc	BU
1978	8,500,000	—	0.15	0.25	0.75	—
1979	11,000,000	—	0.15	0.25	0.75	—

KM# 277.3 10 CENTAVOS

Copper-Nickel, 21 mm. **Obv:** Legend on scroll in relief, quetzal in silhouette **Rev:** Monolith, front view

Date	Mintage	F	VF	XF	Unc	BU
1980	5,000,000	—	0.15	0.25	0.75	—
1981	4,000,000	—	0.15	0.25	0.75	—

KM# 277.4 10 CENTAVOS

Copper-Nickel, 21 mm. **Obv:** Quetzal is solid **Rev:** Monolith, larger

Date	Mintage	F	VF	XF	Unc	BU
1983	20,000,000	—	0.15	0.25	0.75	—
1986	—	—	0.15	0.25	0.75	—

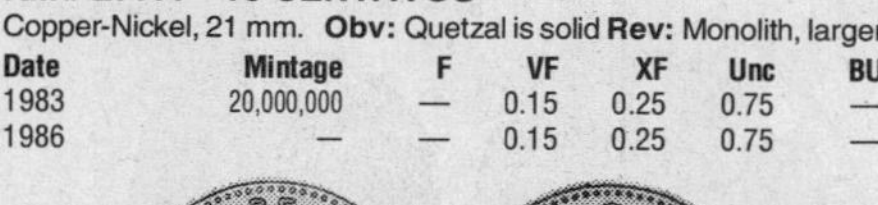

KM# 277.5 10 CENTAVOS

Copper-Nickel, 21 mm. **Obv:** National arms **Rev:** Monolith, larger **Note:** Varieties exist with fine and course characters.

Date	Mintage	F	VF	XF	Unc	BU
1986	—	—	0.15	0.25	0.75	—
1987	17,000,000	—	0.15	0.25	0.75	—
1988	13,250,000	—	0.15	0.25	0.75	—
1989	—	—	0.15	0.25	0.75	—
1990	—	—	0.15	0.25	0.75	—
1991	—	—	0.15	0.25	0.75	—
1992	—	—	0.15	0.25	0.75	—
1993	—	—	0.15	0.25	0.75	—
1994	—	—	0.15	0.25	0.75	—

KM# 277.6 10 CENTAVOS

Copper-Nickel, 21 mm. **Obv:** National arms **Obv. Legend:** Smaller letters in REPUBLICA DE GUATEMALA **Rev:** Monolith **Note:** Varieties exist.

Date	Mintage	F	VF	XF	Unc	BU
1995	—	—	0.15	0.25	0.75	—
1996	—	—	0.15	0.25	0.75	—
1997	—	—	0.15	0.25	0.75	—
1998	—	—	0.15	0.25	0.75	—
2000	—	—	0.15	0.25	0.75	—

KM# 240.1 1/4 QUETZAL

8.3333 g., 0.7200 Silver .1929 oz. ASW **Obv:** National arms **Rev:** Quetzal on pillar **Edge:** Lettered

Date	Mintage	F	VF	XF	Unc	BU
1925(P)	1,160,000	4.50	9.00	25.00	50.00	75.00

KM# 240.2 1/4 QUETZAL

8.3333 g., 0.7200 Silver .1929 oz. ASW **Obv:** National arms, without NOBLES below scroll **Rev:** Quetzal atop engraved pillar

Date	Mintage	F	VF	XF	Unc	BU
1925 (P)	Inc. above	37.50	75.00	175	400	—

KM# 240a 1/4 QUETZAL

0.9000 Gold **Obv:** National arms **Rev:** Quetzal on pillar

Date	Mintage	F	VF	XF	Unc	BU
1925 (P) Rare	8	—	—	—	—	—

KM# 243.1 1/4 QUETZAL

8.3333 g., 0.7200 Silver .1929 oz. ASW, 27 mm. **Obv:** National arms **Rev:** Quetzal on pillar, larger design **Edge Lettering:** REPUBLICA DE GUATEMALA AMERICA CENTRAL

Date	Mintage	F	VF	XF	Unc	BU
1926(L)	2,000,000	3.00	6.00	15.00	65.00	—
1926(L) Proof	—	—	—	—	—	—
1928(L)	400,000	3.50	5.50	10.00	55.00	70.00
1928(L) Proof	—	—	—	—	—	—
1929(L)	400,000	3.50	6.00	12.50	45.00	55.00
1929(L) Proof	—	—	—	—	—	—

KM# 243.2 1/4 QUETZAL

8.3333 g., 0.7200 Silver .1929 oz. ASW, 27 mm. **Obv:** National arms **Rev:** Quetzal atop engraved pillar **Edge:** Reeded

Date	Mintage	F	VF	XF	Unc	BU
1946	203,000	3.50	6.50	13.50	22.00	30.00
1947	134,000	4.00	8.00	12.50	20.00	30.00
1948	129,000	4.00	7.50	12.00	20.00	30.00
1949/8	25,000	5.25	10.00	16.50	30.00	40.00
1949	Inc. above	12.50	27.50	55.00	100	—

KM# 253 25 CENTAVOS

8.3333 g., 0.7200 Silver .1929 oz. ASW, 27 mm. **Obv:** Quetzal and map of the state **Rev:** Government buildings

Date	Mintage	F	VF	XF	Unc	BU
1943(P)	900,000	3.00	6.00	12.00	45.00	55.00

Note: 150,000 of total mintage struck in 1943, remainder struck in 1944

KM# 258 25 CENTAVOS

8.3333 g., 0.7200 Silver .1929 oz. ASW, 27 mm. **Obv:** National arms **Rev:** Head left **Note:** Denticulated rims.

Date	Mintage	F	VF	XF	Unc	BU
1950	81,000	3.50	6.00	12.00	30.00	40.00
1951	11,000	8.50	17.50	27.50	70.00	80.00
1952	112,000	BV	3.50	7.00	15.00	25.00
1954	246,000	BV	3.50	6.00	12.00	17.50
1955	409,000	BV	3.50	6.00	12.00	17.50
1956	342,000	BV	3.50	6.00	12.00	17.50
1957	257,000	BV	3.25	5.50	10.00	14.00
1958	394,000	BV	3.25	5.50	10.00	14.00
1959/8	277,000	BV	3.25	5.50	10.00	14.00
1959	Inc. above	BV	3.50	6.50	12.50	20.00

KM# 263 25 CENTAVOS

8.3333 g., 0.7200 Silver .1929 oz. ASW, 27 mm.

Date	Mintage	F	VF	XF	Unc	BU
1960	560,000	BV	2.75	3.25	6.00	—
1960	Inc. above	20.00	50.00	100	175	—

Note: Planchet size and weight vary in 1960 type as well as density of reeding; Medallic die alignment

Date	Mintage	F	VF	XF	Unc	BU
1961	750,000	BV	2.75	3.25	6.00	—
1962	—	—	BV	3.25	6.00	—
1963	1,100,000	—	BV	3.00	5.50	—
1964	299,000	BV	2.75	3.25	6.00	—

KM# 268 25 CENTAVOS

Copper-Nickel, 27 mm. **Obv:** National arms **Rev:** Head left **Edge Lettering:** REPUBLICA DE GUATEMALA C. A.

Date	Mintage	F	VF	XF	Unc	BU
1965	1,178,000	0.15	0.25	0.60	1.75	—
1966	910,000	0.15	0.25	0.60	1.75	—

KM# 269 25 CENTAVOS

Copper-Nickel, 27 mm. **Obv:** National arms **Rev:** Head left, modified design **Edge Lettering:** REPUBLICA DE GUATEMALA C. A.

Date	Mintage	F	VF	XF	Unc	BU
1967	1,140,000	0.15	0.25	0.60	1.75	—
1968	1,540,000	0.15	0.25	0.60	1.50	—
1969 Large date	2,069,000	0.15	0.25	0.60	1.50	—
1970	2,501,000	0.15	0.25	0.60	1.50	—

KM# 272 25 CENTAVOS

Copper-Nickel, 27 mm. **Obv:** Smaller arms, legend on scroll incuse **Rev:** Head left

Date	Mintage	F	VF	XF	Unc	BU
1971	2,850,000	0.15	0.25	0.50	1.00	—
1975	1,592,000	0.15	0.25	0.50	1.00	—
1976	2,000,000	0.15	0.25	0.50	1.00	—

KM# 278.1 25 CENTAVOS

Copper-Nickel, 27 mm. **Obv:** National arms **Rev:** Large head left

Date	Mintage	F	VF	XF	Unc	BU
1977	2,000,000	0.15	0.25	0.65	1.25	—
1978	4,400,000	0.15	0.25	0.45	1.00	—
1979	5,400,000	0.15	0.25	0.45	1.00	—

KM# 278.2 25 CENTAVOS

Copper-Nickel, 27 mm. **Obv:** National arms, legend on scroll in relief **Rev:** Small head left **Note:** Wide rim

Date	Mintage	F	VF	XF	Unc	BU
1981	1,600,000	0.15	0.25	0.50	1.00	—

KM# 278.4 25 CENTAVOS

Copper-Nickel, 27 mm. **Obv:** National arms, quetzal is solid **Rev:** Head left **Note:** Narrow rim.

Date	Mintage	F	VF	XF	Unc	BU
1982	2,000,000	0.15	0.25	0.50	1.00	—

KM# 278.3 25 CENTAVOS

Copper-Nickel, 27 mm. **Obv:** National arms, legend on scroll incuse **Rev:** Small head left

Date	Mintage	F	VF	XF	Unc	BU
1984	2,000,000	0.15	0.25	0.50	1.00	—

KM# 278.5 25 CENTAVOS
Copper-Nickel, 27 mm. **Obv:** National arms **Rev:** Large head left **Edge Lettering:** REPUBLICA DE GUATEMALA C. A. **Note:** Varieties exist in number of wing feathers and details on head.

Date	Mintage	F	VF	XF	Unc	BU
1985	—	0.15	0.25	0.35	0.85	—
1986	—	0.15	0.25	0.35	0.85	—
1987	13,316,000	0.15	0.25	0.35	0.85	—
1988	6,600,000	0.15	0.25	0.35	0.85	—
1989	—	0.15	0.25	0.35	0.85	—
1990	—	0.15	0.25	0.35	0.85	—
1991	—	0.15	0.25	0.35	0.85	—
1992	—	0.15	0.25	0.35	0.85	—
1993	—	0.15	0.25	0.35	0.85	—
1994	—	0.15	0.25	0.35	0.85	—
1995	—	0.15	0.25	0.35	0.85	—

KM# 278.6 25 CENTAVOS
Copper-Nickel, 27 mm. **Obv:** Smaller design with wider rims **Rev:** Head left, smaller design with wider rims **Edge Lettering:** REPUBLICA DE GUATEMALA CA **Note:** Varieties exist.

Date	Mintage	F	VF	XF	Unc	BU
1996	—	0.15	0.25	0.35	0.85	—
1997	—	0.15	0.25	0.35	0.85	—
1998	—	0.15	0.25	0.35	0.85	—

KM# 264 50 CENTAVOS
12.0000 g., 0.7200 Silver .2777 oz. ASW, 30.5 mm. **Obv:** National arms **Rev:** Whitenun orchid (lycaste skinneri var. alba)

Date	Mintage	F	VF	XF	Unc	BU
1962	1,983,000	—	BV	3.00	6.00	9.00
1963/2	350,000	3.50	7.50	12.50	20.00	25.00
1963	Inc. above	—	—	3.00	6.00	9.00

KM# 283 50 CENTAVOS
5.5400 g., Brass, 24.2 mm. **Obv:** National arms **Rev:** Whitenun orchid (lycaste skinneri var. alba) **Edge:** Reeded

Date	Mintage	F	VF	XF	Unc	BU
1998	—	—	—	0.50	1.25	1.75

KM# 241.1 1/2 QUETZAL
16.6667 g., 0.7200 Silver .3858 oz. ASW **Obv:** National arms **Rev:** Quetzal on engraved pillar

Date	Mintage	F	VF	XF	Unc	BU
1925(P)	400,000	18.50	30.00	65.00	225	300

KM# 241.2 1/2 QUETZAL
16.6667 g., 0.7200 Silver .3858 oz. ASW **Obv:** Without NOBLES below scroll **Rev:** Quetzal on pillar

Date	Mintage	F	VF	XF	Unc	BU
1925 (P)	Inc. above	70.00	120	250	550	—

KM# 242 QUETZAL
33.3333 g., 0.7200 Silver .7716 oz. ASW **Obv:** National arms **Rev:** Quetzal on engraved pillar

Date	Mintage	F	VF	XF	Unc	BU
1925(P)	Est. 10,000	475	675	1,150	2,200	—

Note: 7,000 pieces were withdrawn and remelted in 1927 and 1928. Of those remaining, an additonal unknown quantity was melted in 1932, leaving somewhat less than 3000 survivors of this type.

KM# 279 QUETZAL
27.0000 g., 0.9250 Silver .8030 oz. ASW **Subject:** Carlos Merida **Obv:** National arms **Rev:** Heads facing and right

Date	Mintage	F	VF	XF	Unc	BU
1992NG Proof	—	Value: 50.00				

KM# 280 QUETZAL
27.0000 g., 0.9250 Silver .8030 oz. ASW **Subject:** Environmental Protection **Rev:** Horned Guan

Date	Mintage	F	VF	XF	Unc	BU
1994 Proof	20,000	Value: 45.00				

KM# 281 QUETZAL
27.0000 g., 0.9250 Silver .8030 oz. ASW **Subject:** 50th Anniversary - National Bank of Guatemala **Obv:** Coin designs around national emblem **Rev:** Pre-Columbian artisans

Date	Mintage	F	VF	XF	Unc	BU
1996 Proof	—	Value: 50.00				

KM# 284 QUETZAL
11.1000 g., Brass, 28.9 mm. **Obv:** National arms **Rev:** PAX above stylized dove **Edge:** Reeded

Date	Mintage	F	VF	XF	Unc	BU
1999	—	—	—	1.00	2.50	3.00
2000 Small letters	—	—	—	1.00	2.50	3.00

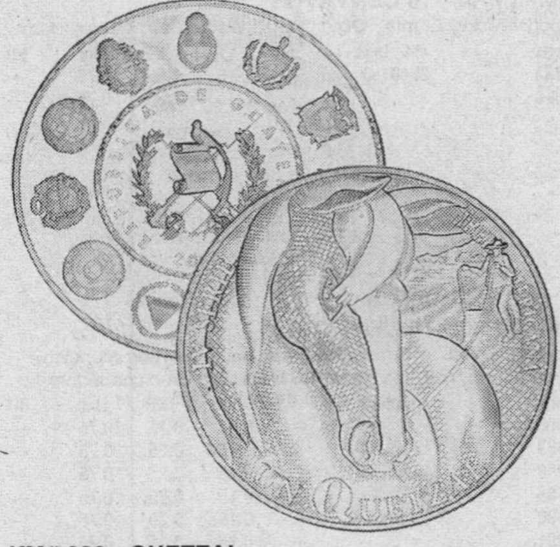

KM# 286 QUETZAL
27.0000 g., 0.9250 Silver 0.803 oz. ASW, 40 mm. **Subject:** Ibero-America Series **Obv:** National arms in circle of arms **Rev:** Horse pulling a walk-behind plow **Edge:** Reeded

Date	Mintage	F	VF	XF	Unc	BU
2000 Proof	—	Value: 100				

KM# 244 5 QUETZALES
8.3592 g., 0.9000 Gold .2419 oz. AGW **Obv:** National arms **Rev:** Quetzal atop engraved pillar

Date	Mintage	F	VF	XF	Unc	BU
1926(P)	48,000	BV	210	275	350	—

KM# 245 10 QUETZALES
16.7185 g., 0.9000 Gold .4838 oz. AGW **Obv:** National arms **Rev:** Quetzal atop engraved pillar

Date	Mintage	F	VF	XF	Unc	BU
1926(P)	18,000	BV	345	450	750	—

KM# 246 20 QUETZALES
33.4370 g., 0.9000 Gold .9676 oz. AGW **Obv:** National arms **Rev:** Quetzal atop engraved pillar

Date	Mintage	F	VF	XF	Unc	BU
1926(P)	49,000	650	675	750	1,000	—

TRIAL STRIKES

KM#	Date	Mintage	Identification	Mkt Val
TS1	1945	—	10 Centavos. Copper Nickel.	150

PATTERNS

Including off metal strikes

KM#	Date	Mintage	Identification	Mkt Val
Pn17	ND(ca.19 20-22)	—	2 Pesos. Porcelain. 25.26 mm. QUATEMALA/*PESOS*/large 2 in center. Arms of Quatemala within triangle; coffee tree leaf to each side; below: Meissen mint mark (crossed swords) separates two stars. Arms in triangle; made at state porcelain works, Meissen, Germany.	2,000
Pn18	1921	—	Peso. Copper-Nickel. 5.1000 g. 25 mm. Plain edge. MONEDA NACIONAL NIQUEL.	—
Pn19	1922	—	5 Pesos. Silver. 3/4 facing bust of Barrios.	—
Pn20	1922	—	5 Pesos. Aluminum-Brass. 3/4 facing bust of Barrios.	—
Pn21	1923	—	5 Pesos. Gold. KM234	—
Pn22	1949	20	Centavo. Brass. large bust.	450
Pn23	1949	20	5 Centavos. 0.7200 Silver.	475
Pn24	1949	20	10 Centavos. 0.7200 Silver.	525
Pn25	1949	20	25 Centavos. 0.7200 Silver.	575
Pn26	1960	—	25 Centavos. Aluminum. Plain edge. KM#263.	—
Pn27	1995	100	Quetzal. Brass center. Silver ring. 22.4300 g. 38 mm. National arms. Humming bird flying above lake. Reeded edge. Brass center in Silver ring within Brass ring.	100
Pn28	1995	100	Quetzal. Brass center. Silver ring. 22.2400 g. 38 mm. National arms. Parrot on branch, buildings in back. Reeded edge. Brass center in Silver ring within Brass ring.	100

GUERNSEY

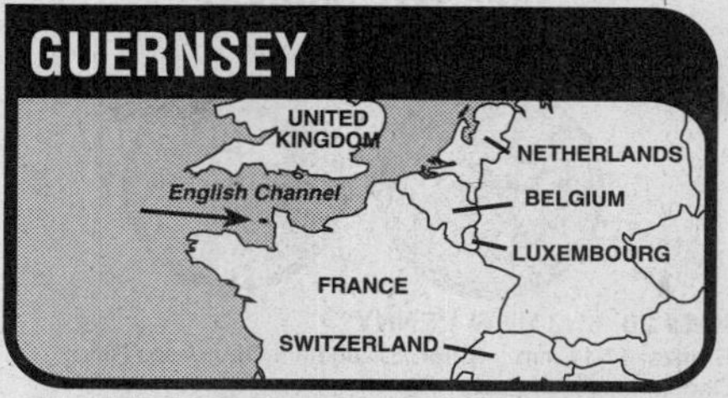

The Bailiwick of Guernsey, a British crown dependency located in the English Channel 30 miles (48 km.) west of Normandy, France, has an area of 30 sq. mi. (194 sq. km.)(including the isles of Alderney, Jethou, Herm, Brechou, and Sark), and a population of 54,000. Capital: St. Peter Port. Agriculture and cattle breeding are the main occupations.

Militant monks from the duchy of Normandy established the first permanent settlements on Guernsey prior to the Norman invasion of England, but the prevalence of prehistoric monuments suggests an earlier occupancy. The island, the only part of the duchy of Normandy belonging to the British crown, has been a possession of Britain since the Norman Conquest of 1066. During the Anglo-French wars, the harbors of Guernsey were employed in the building and out-fitting of ships for the English privateers preying on French shipping. Guernsey is administered by its own laws and customs. Unless the island is mentioned specifically, acts passed by the British Parliament are not applicable to Guernsey. During World War II, German troops occupied the island from June 30, 1940 till May 9,1945.

RULERS
British

MINT MARKS
H - Heaton, Birmingham

MONETARY SYSTEM
8 Doubles = 1 Penny
12 Pence = 1 Shilling
5 Shillings = 1 Crown
20 Shillings = 1 Pound

1 Stem

3 Stems

BRITISH DEPENDENCY

STANDARD COINAGE

KM# 10 DOUBLE

Bronze **Obv:** Arms **Rev:** Denomination above date

Date	Mintage	F	VF	XF	Unc	BU
1902H	84,000	0.25	0.60	2.50	6.00	—
1902H Proof	—	Value: 250				
1903H	112,000	0.25	0.50	2.25	5.00	—
1911H	45,000	0.50	1.50	4.00	12.00	—

KM# 11 DOUBLE

Bronze **Obv:** Arms **Rev:** Denomination above date

Date	Mintage	F	VF	XF	Unc	BU
1911H	90,000	0.30	1.20	3.00	10.00	—
1914H	45,000	1.50	3.00	6.00	12.00	—
1929H	79,000	0.30	0.85	2.50	5.50	—
1933H	96,000	0.30	0.85	2.50	5.50	—
1938H	96,000	0.30	0.85	2.50	5.50	—

KM# 9 2 DOUBLES

Bronze **Obv:** Arms **Rev:** Denomination above date

Date	Mintage	F	VF	XF	Unc	BU
1902H	18,000	4.50	9.00	18.00	30.00	—
1902H Proof	—	Value: 250				
1903H	18,000	6.00	12.50	22.00	35.00	—
1906H	18,000	6.00	12.50	22.00	35.00	—
1908H	18,000	6.00	12.50	22.00	35.00	—
1911H	29,000	4.50	9.00	15.00	27.50	—

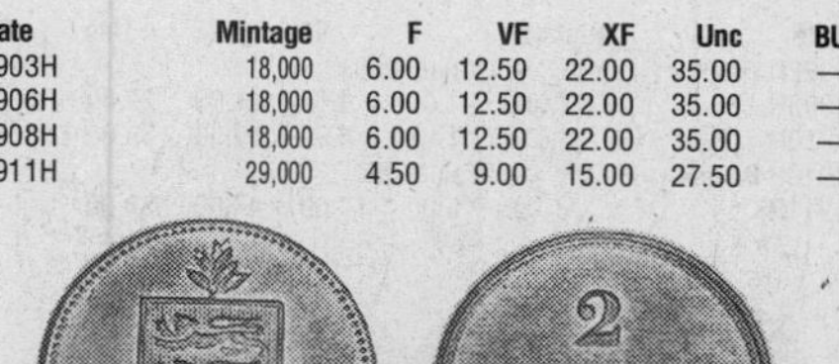

KM# 12 2 DOUBLES

Bronzed Copper **Obv:** Arms **Rev:** Denomination above date

Date	Mintage	F	VF	XF	Unc	BU
1914H	29,000	4.50	9.00	18.50	27.50	—
1914H Proof	—	Value: 125				
1917H	15,000	20.00	35.00	70.00	155	—
1918H	57,000	1.25	2.50	9.00	15.00	—
1920H	57,000	1.25	2.50	9.00	15.00	—
1929H	79,000	0.35	1.25	6.00	10.00	—

KM# 5 4 DOUBLES

Bronze **Obv:** Arms **Rev:** Denomination above date **Note:** Varieties exist.

Date	Mintage	F	VF	XF	Unc	BU
1902H	105,000	1.50	3.00	5.00	22.00	—
1902H Proof	—	Value: 250				
1903H	52,000	1.50	3.00	9.00	25.00	—
1906H	52,000	1.50	3.00	9.00	25.00	—
1908H	26,000	3.00	7.50	15.00	30.00	—
1910H	52,000	1.50	3.00	9.00	25.00	—
1910H Proof	—	Value: 250				
1911H	52,000	2.25	4.50	13.50	27.50	—

KM# 13 4 DOUBLES

Bronze **Obv:** Arms **Rev:** Denomination above date

Date	Mintage	F	VF	XF	Unc	BU
1914H	209,000	0.75	1.50	4.50	24.00	—
1918H	157,000	0.75	1.50	6.00	27.00	—
1920H	157,000	0.45	1.25	4.50	18.00	—
1945H	96,000	0.45	1.25	4.50	10.00	—
1949H	19,000	1.50	3.00	12.00	20.00	—

KM# 15 4 DOUBLES

Bronze **Obv:** Arms **Rev:** Guernsey lily

Date	Mintage	F	VF	XF	Unc	BU
1956	240,000	0.25	0.45	0.75	2.00	3.50
1956 Proof	2,100	Value: 4.00				
1966 Proof	10,000	Value: 2.00				

KM# 7 8 DOUBLES

Bronze **Obv:** Arms within wreath **Rev:** Denomination and date within wreath

Date	Mintage	F	VF	XF	Unc	BU
1902H	235,000	2.50	4.50	12.00	29.00	—

Date	Mintage	F	VF	XF	Unc	BU
1902H Proof	—	Value: 250				
1903H	118,000	1.00	4.00	11.00	27.00	—
1910H	91,000	1.25	4.00	12.50	35.00	—
1910H Proof	—	Value: 250				
1911H	78,000	6.00	17.00	40.00	80.00	—

KM# 14 8 DOUBLES

Bronze **Obv:** Arms within wreath **Rev:** Denomination and date within wreath

Date	Mintage	F	VF	XF	Unc	BU
1914H	157,000	1.00	3.00	8.00	23.00	—
1914H Proof	—	Value: 150				
1918H	157,000	1.50	4.00	11.00	27.00	—
1920H	157,000	1.00	2.00	6.00	15.00	—
1920H Proof	—	Value: 150				
1934H	124,000	1.00	2.00	6.00	18.00	—
1934H Proof	500	Value: 175				
1938H	120,000	0.50	1.50	4.00	9.00	—
1938H Proof	—	Value: 250				
1945H	192,000	0.40	0.85	2.00	5.50	—
1947H	240,000	0.30	0.60	2.25	5.00	—
1949H	230,000	0.30	0.60	2.25	5.00	—

KM# 16 8 DOUBLES

Bronze **Ruler:** Elizabeth II **Obv:** Arms **Rev:** Three flowered lily

Date	Mintage	F	VF	XF	Unc	BU
1956	500,000	0.10	0.20	0.50	1.25	2.50
1956 Proof	2,100	Value: 4.00				
1959	500,000	0.10	0.20	0.50	1.25	2.50
1959 Proof	—	—	—	—	—	—
1966 Proof	10,000	Value: 3.50				

KM# 17 3 PENCE

Copper Nickel, 21 mm. **Ruler:** Elizabeth II **Obv:** Arms **Rev:** Guernsey cow (bos primigenius taurus) right **Shape:** Scalloped **Note:** Thin flan.

Date	Mintage	F	VF	XF	Unc	BU
1956	500,000	0.10	0.20	0.50	1.50	2.00
1956 Proof	2,100	Value: 4.00				

KM# 18 3 PENCE

Copper Nickel, 21 mm. **Ruler:** Elizabeth II **Obv:** Arms **Rev:** Guernsey cow (bos primigenius taurus) right **Shape:** Scalloped **Note:** Thick flan.

Date	Mintage	F	VF	XF	Unc	BU
1959	500,000	0.10	0.20	0.50	1.50	2.00
1959 Proof	—	Value: 150				
1966 Proof	10,000	Value: 2.00				

KM# 19 10 SHILLING

Copper Nickel **Ruler:** Elizabeth II **Series:** 90th Anniversary - Norman Conquest **Subject:** William I **Obv:** Young bust right **Rev:** Crowned bust left **Shape:** 4-sided **Designer:** Arnold Machin

Date	Mintage	F	VF	XF	Unc	BU
1966	300,000	—	1.00	1.25	1.75	—
1966 Proof	10,000	Value: 3.00				

DECIMAL COINAGE

100 Pence = 1 Pound

KM# 20 1/2 NEW PENNY

Bronze, 17.14 mm. **Ruler:** Elizabeth II **Obv:** Arms **Rev:** Denomination and date

Date	Mintage	F	VF	XF	Unc	BU
1971	2,066,000	—	—	0.15	0.30	0.50
1971 Proof	10,000	Value: 1.00				

KM# 33 1/2 PENNY

Bronze, 17.14 mm. **Ruler:** Elizabeth II **Obv:** Arms **Rev:** Denomination and date

Date	Mintage	F	VF	XF	Unc	BU
1979 Proof	20,000	Value: 1.00				

KM# 21 NEW PENNY

3.5500 g., Bronze, 20.3 mm. **Ruler:** Elizabeth II **Obv:** Arms **Rev:** Gannet in flight

Date	Mintage	F	VF	XF	Unc	BU
1971	1,922,000	—	—	0.15	0.45	0.75
1971 Proof	10,000	Value: 1.00				

KM# 27 PENNY

3.5500 g., Bronze, 20.3 mm. **Ruler:** Elizabeth II **Obv:** Arms **Rev:** Gannet in flight

Date	Mintage	F	VF	XF	Unc	BU
1977	640,000	—	—	0.15	0.45	0.75
1979	2,400,000	—	—	0.15	0.45	0.65
1979 Proof	20,000	Value: 1.00				
1981 Proof	10,000	Value: 2.00				

KM# 40 PENNY

3.5500 g., Bronze, 20.3 mm. **Ruler:** Elizabeth II **Obv:** Crowned head right, small arms at left **Rev:** Edible crab **Rev. Designer:** Robert Elderton

Date	Mintage	F	VF	XF	Unc	BU
1985	60,000	—	—	0.15	0.50	0.75
1985 Proof	2,500	Value: 2.00				
1986	1,010,000	—	—	0.15	0.50	0.75
1986 Proof	2,500	Value: 2.00				
1987	5,000	—	—	0.15	0.50	0.75
1987 Proof	2,500	Value: 2.00				
1988	500,000	—	—	0.15	0.50	0.75
1988 Proof	2,500	Value: 2.00				
1989	1,000,000	—	—	0.15	0.50	0.75
1989 Proof	2,500	Value: 2.00				
1990	5,000	—	—	0.15	0.50	0.75
1990 Proof	700	Value: 4.00				

KM# 40a PENNY

3.5500 g., Copper Plated Steel, 20.3 mm. **Ruler:** Elizabeth II **Obv:** Crowned head right, small arms at left **Rev:** Chancre crab **Rev. Designer:** Robert Elderton

Date	Mintage	F	VF	XF	Unc	BU
1992	—	—	—	—	0.35	0.75
Note: In sets only						
1992 Proof	—	Value: 5.00				
1994	750,000	—	—	—	0.35	0.75
1997	2,000,000	—	—	—	0.35	0.75
1997 Proof	—	Value: 5.00				

KM# 89 PENNY

3.5500 g., Copper Plated Steel, 20.3 mm. **Ruler:** Elizabeth II **Obv:** Head with tiara right **Obv. Designer:** Rank-Broadley **Rev:** Edible crab **Rev. Designer:** Robert Elderton

Date	Mintage	F	VF	XF	Unc	BU
1998	—	—	—	—	0.50	0.75

KM# 22 2 NEW PENCE

7.1000 g., Bronze, 25.9 mm. **Ruler:** Elizabeth II **Obv:** Arms **Rev:** Windmill from Sark

Date	Mintage	F	VF	XF	Unc	BU
1971	1,680,000	—	—	0.15	0.35	0.50
1971 Proof	10,000	Value: 1.00				

KM# 28 2 PENCE

7.1000 g., Bronze, 25.9 mm. **Ruler:** Elizabeth II **Obv:** Arms **Rev:** Windmill from Sark

Date	Mintage	F	VF	XF	Unc	BU
1977	700,000	—	—	0.15	0.25	0.45
1979	2,400,000	—	—	0.15	0.25	0.45
1979 Proof	20,000	Value: 1.00				
1981 Proof	10,000	Value: 2.00				

KM# 41 2 PENCE

7.1000 g., Bronze, 25.9 mm. **Ruler:** Elizabeth II **Obv:** Crowned head right, small arms at left **Rev:** Guernsey cows **Rev. Designer:** Robert Elderton

Date	Mintage	F	VF	XF	Unc	BU
1985	60,000	—	—	0.20	0.75	1.50
1985 Proof	2,500	Value: 2.00				
1986	510,000	—	—	0.20	0.75	1.50
1986 Proof	2,500	Value: 2.00				
1987	5,000	—	—	0.20	0.75	1.50
1987 Proof	2,500	Value: 2.00				
1988	500,000	—	—	0.20	0.75	1.50
1988 Proof	2,500	Value: 2.00				
1989	500,000	—	—	0.20	0.75	1.50
1989 Proof	2,500	Value: 2.00				
1990	380,000	—	—	0.20	0.75	1.50
1990 Proof	700	Value: 4.00				

KM# 41a 2 PENCE

7.2000 g., Copper Plated Steel, 25.9 mm. **Ruler:** Elizabeth II **Obv:** Crowned head right, small arms at left **Rev:** Guernsey cows **Rev. Designer:** Robert Elderton **Edge:** Plain

Date	Mintage	F	VF	XF	Unc	BU
1992	—	—	—	—	0.30	0.75
Note: In sets only						
1992 Proof	—	Value: 5.00				
1996	500,000	—	—	—	0.30	0.75
1997	—	—	—	—	0.30	0.75
Note: In sets only						
1997 Proof	—	Value: 5.00				

KM# 96 2 PENCE
7.2000 g., Copper Plated Steel, 25.9 mm. **Ruler:** Elizabeth II **Obv:** Head with tiara, shield at left **Obv. Designer:** Rank-Broadley **Rev:** Guernsey cows **Rev. Designer:** Robert Elderton **Edge:** Plain

Date	Mintage	F	VF	XF	Unc	BU
1999	600,000	—	—	—	0.50	1.00

KM# 23 5 NEW PENCE
5.6500 g., Copper-Nickel, 23.6 mm. **Ruler:** Elizabeth II **Obv:** Arms **Rev:** Guernsey lily **Rev. Designer:** Arnold Machin

Date	Mintage	F	VF	XF	Unc	BU
1968	800,000	—	0.15	0.25	0.45	0.65
1971 Proof	10,000	Value: 2.00				

KM# 29 5 PENCE
5.6500 g., Copper-Nickel, 23.6 mm. **Ruler:** Elizabeth II **Obv:** Arms **Rev:** Guernsey lily **Rev. Designer:** Arnold Machin

Date	Mintage	F	VF	XF	Unc	BU
1977	250,000	—	—	0.20	0.45	0.65
1979	200,000	—	—	0.20	0.45	0.65
1979 Proof	20,000	Value: 2.00				
1981 Proof	10,000	Value: 3.00				
1982	200,000	—	—	0.20	0.45	0.65

KM# 42.1 5 PENCE
5.6500 g., Copper-Nickel, 23.6 mm. **Ruler:** Elizabeth II **Obv:** Crowned head right, small arms at left **Rev:** Sailboats **Rev. Designer:** Robert Elderton

Date	Mintage	F	VF	XF	Unc	BU
1985	35,000	—	—	0.20	0.45	0.65
1985 Proof	2,500	Value: 2.50				
1986	100,000	—	—	0.20	0.45	0.65
1986 Proof	2,500	Value: 2.50				
1987	300,000	—	—	0.20	0.45	0.65
1987 Proof	2,500	Value: 2.50				
1988	405,000	—	—	0.20	0.45	0.65
1988 Proof	2,500	Value: 2.50				
1989	5,000	—	—	0.20	0.50	0.75
1989 Proof	2,500	Value: 2.50				
1990	Est. 2,520	—	—	—	0.60	0.85
Note: In sets only						
1990 Proof	700	Value: 5.00				

KM# 42.2 5 PENCE
3.2600 g., Copper-Nickel, 18 mm. **Obv:** Crowned head right, small arms at left **Rev:** Sailboats **Rev. Designer:** Robert Elderton **Note:** Reduced size

Date	Mintage	F	VF	XF	Unc	BU
1990	2,400,000	—	—	0.20	0.45	0.65
1990 Proof	700	Value: 5.00				
1992	1,300,000	—	—	—	0.50	0.75
1997	—	—	—	—	0.50	0.75
1997 Proof	—	Value: 5.00				

KM# 97 5 PENCE
3.2600 g., Copper-Nickel, 18 mm. **Ruler:** Elizabeth II **Obv:** Head with tiara right **Obv. Designer:** Rank-Broadley **Rev:** Sailboat **Rev. Designer:** Robert Elderton **Edge:** Reeded

Date	Mintage	F	VF	XF	Unc	BU
1999	1,700,000	—	—	—	0.45	0.65

KM# 24 10 NEW PENCE
11.3000 g., Copper-Nickel, 28.5 mm. **Ruler:** Elizabeth II **Obv:** Arms **Rev:** Guernsey cow **Rev. Designer:** Arnold Machin

Date	Mintage	F	VF	XF	Unc	BU
1968	600,000	—	0.20	0.40	1.50	1.75
1970	300,000	—	0.20	0.40	1.50	1.75
1971 Proof	10,000	Value: 2.00				

KM# 30 10 PENCE
11.3000 g., Copper-Nickel, 28.5 mm. **Ruler:** Elizabeth II **Obv:** Arms **Rev:** Guernsey cow **Rev. Designer:** Arnold Machin

Date	Mintage	F	VF	XF	Unc	BU
1977	480,000	—	—	0.25	1.00	1.50
1979	659,000	—	—	0.25	1.00	1.50
1979 Proof	20,000	Value: 2.00				
1981 Proof	10,000	Value: 3.00				
1982	200,000	—	—	0.35	1.25	1.75
1984	400,000	—	—	0.25	1.00	1.50

KM# 43.1 10 PENCE
11.3000 g., Copper-Nickel, 28.5 mm. **Ruler:** Elizabeth II **Obv:** Crowned head right, small arms at left **Rev:** Tomato plant **Rev. Designer:** Robert Elderton

Date	Mintage	F	VF	XF	Unc	BU
1985	110,000	—	—	0.25	0.60	0.85
1985 Proof	2,500	Value: 2.50				
1986	300,000	—	—	0.25	0.60	0.85
1986 Proof	2,500	Value: 6.00				
1987	250,000	—	—	0.25	0.60	0.85
1987 Proof	2,500	Value: 2.50				
1988	300,000	—	—	0.25	0.60	0.85
1988 Proof	2,500	Value: 2.50				
1989	200,000	—	—	0.25	0.60	0.85
1989 Proof	2,500	Value: 2.50				
1990	3,500	—	—	0.25	0.60	0.85
1990 Proof	700	Value: 5.00				

KM# 43.2 10 PENCE
Copper-Nickel, 24.5 mm. **Obv:** Crowned head right, small arms at left **Rev:** Tomato plant **Rev. Designer:** Robert Elderton **Note:** Reduced size.

Date	Mintage	F	VF	XF	Unc	BU
1992	3,500,000	—	—	—	0.60	0.85
1992 Proof	—	Value: 6.00				
1997	—	—	—	—	0.60	0.85
Note: In sets only						
1997 Proof	—	Value: 6.00				

KM# 38 20 PENCE
5.1000 g., Copper-Nickel, 21.4 mm. **Ruler:** Elizabeth II **Obv:** Arms **Rev:** Guernsey milk can **Shape:** 7-sided

Date	Mintage	F	VF	XF	Unc	BU
1982	500,000	—	—	0.45	0.90	1.25
1983	500,000	—	—	0.45	0.90	1.25

KM# 44 20 PENCE
5.1000 g., Copper-Nickel, 21.4 mm. **Ruler:** Elizabeth II **Obv:** Crowned head right, small arms at left **Rev:** Island map within cogwheel **Rev. Designer:** Robert Elderton **Shape:** 7-sided

Date	Mintage	F	VF	XF	Unc	BU
1985	35,000	—	—	0.45	0.85	1.20
1985 Proof	2,500	Value: 3.00				
1986	10,000	—	—	0.45	0.85	1.20
1986 Proof	2,500	Value: 3.00				
1987	5,000	—	—	0.45	0.85	1.20
1987 Proof	2,500	Value: 3.00				
1988	5,000	—	—	0.45	0.85	1.20
1988 Proof	2,500	Value: 3.00				
1989	93,000	—	—	0.45	0.85	1.20
1989 Proof	2,500	Value: 3.00				
1990	113,000	—	—	0.45	0.85	1.20
1990 Proof	700	Value: 6.00				
1992	800,000	—	—	—	1.00	1.50
1992 Proof	—	Value: 7.00				
1997	—	—	—	—	1.00	1.50
1997 Proof	—	Value: 3.00				

KM# 90 20 PENCE
5.1000 g., Copper-Nickel, 21.4 mm. **Ruler:** Elizabeth II **Obv:** Head with tiara right, small arms at left **Obv. Designer:** Rank-Broadley **Rev:** Island map within cogwheel **Rev. Designer:** Robert Elderton **Shape:** 7-sided

Date	Mintage	F	VF	XF	Unc	BU
1999	800,000	—	—	—	0.90	1.25
1999 Proof	—	Value: 3.00				

KM# 26 25 PENCE
Copper-Nickel, 38.5 mm. **Ruler:** Elizabeth II **Subject:** 25th Wedding Anniversary - Elizabeth and Philip **Obv:** Arms **Rev:** Standing cupid right

Date	Mintage	F	VF	XF	Unc	BU
1972	56,000	—	—	2.50	5.50	7.00

KM# 26a 25 PENCE
28.2759 g., 0.9250 Silver .8410 oz. ASW, 38.5 mm. **Ruler:** Elizabeth II **Subject:** 25th Wedding Anniversary - Elizabeth and Philip **Obv:** Arms **Rev:** Standing cupid right

Date	Mintage	F	VF	XF	Unc	BU
1972 Proof	15,000	Value: 14.00				

KM# 31 25 PENCE
Copper-Nickel, 38.5 mm. **Ruler:** Elizabeth II **Subject:** Queen's Silver Jubilee **Obv:** Young bust right **Rev:** Scene from above **Designer:** Arnold Machin

Date	Mintage	F	VF	XF	Unc	BU
ND(1977)	207,000	—	—	1.25	2.25	3.50

KM# 31a 25 PENCE
28.2759 g., 0.9250 Silver .8410 oz. ASW, 38.5 mm. **Ruler:** Elizabeth II **Subject:** Queen's Silver Jubilee **Obv:** Young bust right **Rev:** Scene from above

Date	Mintage	F	VF	XF	Unc	BU
ND(1977) Proof	25,000	Value: 12.50				

KM# 32 25 PENCE
Copper-Nickel, 38.5 mm. **Ruler:** Elizabeth II **Subject:** Royal Visit **Obv:** Young bust right **Obv. Designer:** Arnold Machin **Rev:** Arms

Date	Mintage	F	VF	XF	Unc	BU
1978	105,000	—	—	1.25	2.50	3.75

KM# 32a 25 PENCE
28.2759 g., 0.9250 Silver .8410 oz. ASW, 38.5 mm. **Ruler:** Elizabeth II **Subject:** Royal Visit **Obv:** Young bust right **Obv. Designer:** Arnold Machin **Rev:** Arms

Date	Mintage	F	VF	XF	Unc	BU
1978 Proof	25,000	Value: 13.50				

KM# 35 25 PENCE
Copper-Nickel, 38.5 mm. **Ruler:** Elizabeth II **Subject:** Queen Mother's 80th Birthday **Obv:** Young bust right **Obv. Designer:** Arnold Machin **Rev:** Bust left

Date	Mintage	F	VF	XF	Unc	BU
ND(1980)	150,000	—	—	1.25	2.50	3.75

KM# 35a 25 PENCE
28.2759 g., 0.9250 Silver .8410 oz. ASW, 38.5 mm. **Ruler:** Elizabeth II **Subject:** Queen Mother's 80th Birthday **Obv:** Young bust right **Obv. Designer:** Arnold Machin **Rev:** Bust left

Date	Mintage	F	VF	XF	Unc	BU
ND(1980) Proof	25,000	Value: 14.50				

KM# 36 25 PENCE
Copper-Nickel, 38.5 mm. **Ruler:** Elizabeth II **Subject:** Wedding of Prince Charles and Lady Diana **Obv:** Young bust right **Rev:** Arms divided by royal couple **Designer:** Arnold Machin

Date	Mintage	F	VF	XF	Unc	BU
1981	114,000	—	—	1.50	2.75	4.00

KM# 36a 25 PENCE
28.2759 g., 0.9250 Silver .8410 oz. ASW, 38.5 mm. **Ruler:** Elizabeth II **Subject:** Wedding of Prince Charles and Lady Diana **Obv:** Young bust right **Rev:** Royal couple divide arms **Designer:** Arnold Machin

Date	Mintage	F	VF	XF	Unc	BU
1981 Proof	12,000	Value: 16.50				

KM# 25 50 NEW PENCE
13.5000 g., Copper-Nickel, 30 mm. **Obv:** Arms **Rev:** Ducal cap of the Duke of Normandy **Shape:** 7-sided

Date	Mintage	F	VF	XF	Unc	BU
1969	200,000	—	1.00	1.50	2.50	3.50
1970	200,000	—	1.00	1.50	2.50	3.50
1971 Proof	10,000	Value: 4.00				

KM# 34 50 PENCE
13.5000 g., Copper-Nickel, 30 mm. **Ruler:** Elizabeth II **Obv:** Arms **Rev:** Ducal cap of the Duke of Normandy **Shape:** 7-sided

Date	Mintage	F	VF	XF	Unc	BU
1979 Proof	20,000	Value: 4.50				
1981	200,000	—	—	0.90	1.45	2.25
1981 Proof	10,000	Value: 5.50				
1982	150,000	—	—	0.90	1.45	2.25
1983	200,000	—	—	0.90	1.45	2.25
1984	200,000	—	—	0.90	1.45	2.25

KM# 45.1 50 PENCE
13.5000 g., Copper-Nickel, 30 mm. **Ruler:** Elizabeth II **Obv:** Crowned head right, small shield at left **Rev:** Freesia flowers **Rev. Designer:** Robert Elderton **Shape:** 7-sided

Date	Mintage	F	VF	XF	Unc	BU
1985	35,000	—	—	0.90	1.45	2.25
1985 Proof	2,500	Value: 4.00				
1986	10,000	—	—	0.90	1.45	2.25
1986 Proof	2,500	Value: 4.00				
1987	5,000	—	—	0.90	1.45	2.25
1987 Proof	2,500	Value: 4.50				
1988	6,000	—	—	0.90	1.45	2.25
1988 Proof	2,500	Value: 4.50				
1989	55,000	—	—	0.90	1.45	2.25
1989 Proof	2,500	Value: 4.50				
1990	80,000	—	—	0.90	1.45	2.25

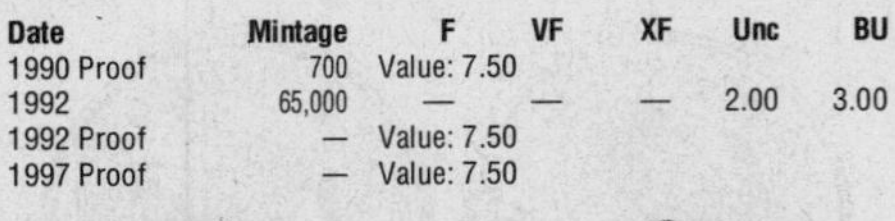

Date	Mintage	F	VF	XF	Unc	BU
1990 Proof	700	Value: 7.50				
1992	65,000	—	—	—	2.00	3.00
1992 Proof	—	Value: 7.50				
1997 Proof	—	Value: 7.50				

KM# 45.2 50 PENCE
Copper-Nickel, 27.3 mm. **Ruler:** Elizabeth II **Obv:** Crowned head right, small shield at left **Rev:** Freesia flowers **Rev. Designer:** Robert Elderton **Shape:** 7-sided

Date	Mintage	F	VF	XF	Unc	BU
1997	1,000,000	—	—	—	1.75	2.75
1997 Proof	—	Value: 8.50				

KM# 105 50 PENCE
7.9700 g., Copper-Nickel, 27.3 mm. **Ruler:** Elizabeth II **Subject:** 60th Anniversary - Battle of Britain **Obv:** Head with tiara right **Rev:** Pilot and fighter plane **Edge:** Plain **Shape:** 7-sided

Date	Mintage	F	VF	XF	Unc	BU
2000	10,000	—	—	—	1.50	2.50

KM# 105a 50 PENCE
8.1000 g., 0.9250 Silver .2409 oz. ASW, 27.3 mm. **Ruler:** Elizabeth II **Obv:** Head with tiara right **Rev:** Pilot and fighter plane **Shape:** 7-sided

Date	Mintage	F	VF	XF	Unc	BU
2000 Proof	15,000	Value: 25.00				

KM# 105b 50 PENCE
15.5000 g., 0.9170 Gold .4570 oz. AGW, 27.3 mm. **Ruler:** Elizabeth II **Obv:** Head with tiara right **Rev:** Pilot and fighter plane **Edge:** Plain **Shape:** 7-sided

Date	Mintage	F	VF	XF	Unc	BU
2000 Proof	1,500	Value: 345				

KM# 37 POUND
7.9000 g., Nickel-Brass, 22 mm. **Ruler:** Elizabeth II **Obv:** Arms **Rev:** Guernsey lily

Date	Mintage	F	VF	XF	Unc	BU
1981	200,000	—	1.80	2.00	3.50	4.50
1981 Proof	10,000	Value: 5.00				

KM# 37a POUND
8.0000 g., 0.9170 Gold .2358 oz. AGW, 22 mm. **Ruler:** Elizabeth II **Obv:** Arms **Rev:** Guernsey lily

Date	Mintage	F	VF	XF	Unc	BU
1981 Proof	4,500	Value: 170				

KM# 39 POUND
Nickel-Brass, 22.5 mm. **Ruler:** Elizabeth II **Obv:** Arms **Rev:** H.M.S. Crescent

Date	Mintage	F	VF	XF	Unc	BU
1983	269,000	—	1.80	2.00	3.50	4.50

KM# 46 POUND
Nickel-Brass, 22.5 mm. **Ruler:** Elizabeth II **Obv:** Crowned head right, small shield at left **Rev:** Design divides denomination

Date	Mintage	F	VF	XF	Unc	BU
1985	35,000	—	—	1.75	2.50	3.50
1985 Proof	2,500	Value: 6.50				
1986	10,000	—	—	1.75	2.50	3.50
1986 Proof	2,500	Value: 6.50				
1987	5,000	—	—	1.75	2.50	3.50
1987 Proof	2,500	Value: 6.50				
1988	5,000	—	—	1.75	2.50	3.50
1988 Proof	2,500	Value: 6.50				
1989	5,000	—	—	1.75	2.50	3.50
1989 Proof	2,500	Value: 6.50				
1990	3,500	—	—	1.75	2.50	3.50
1990 Proof	700	Value: 10.00				
1992	—	—	—	—	3.50	5.00
Note: In sets only						
1992 Proof	—	Value: 12.50				
1997	—	—	—	—	3.50	5.00
Note: In sets only						
1997 Proof	—	Value: 12.50				

KM# 77 POUND
9.5000 g., 0.9250 Silver .2825 oz. ASW, 22.5 mm. **Ruler:** Elizabeth II **Subject:** Queen Elizabeth the Queen Mother **Rev:** Bust facing, flowers flank

Date	Mintage	F	VF	XF	Unc	BU
1995 Proof	—	Value: 27.50				

KM# 78 POUND
9.5000 g., 0.9250 Silver .2825 oz. ASW, 22.5 mm. **Ruler:** Elizabeth II **Subject:** 70th Birthday of Queen Elizabeth II **Obv:** Crowned head right **Rev:** Queen Mother at left, arms above rock at right

Date	Mintage	F	VF	XF	Unc	BU
1996 Proof	—	Value: 20.00				

KM# 70 POUND
9.5000 g., 0.9250 Silver .2825 oz. ASW, 22.5 mm. **Ruler:** Elizabeth II **Subject:** Golden Wedding Anniversary **Obv:** Crowned head right **Rev:** Queen Elizabeth II and Prince Philip, monogrammed shield, Westminster Abbey

Date	Mintage	F	VF	XF	Unc	BU
1997 Proof	Est. 50,000	Value: 20.00				

KM# 73 POUND
9.5000 g., 0.9250 Silver .2825 oz. ASW, 22.5 mm. **Ruler:** Elizabeth II **Series:** Castle **Subject:** Tower of London

Date	Mintage	F	VF	XF	Unc	BU
1997 Proof	15,000	Value: 32.50				

KM# 84 POUND
9.5000 g., 0.9250 Silver .2825 oz. ASW, 22.5 mm. **Ruler:** Elizabeth II **Subject:** 80th Anniversary - Royal Air Force **Obv:** Head with tiara right **Obv. Designer:** Rank-Broadley **Rev:** Three Spitfires and RAF Benevolent Fund Crest

Date	Mintage	F	VF	XF	Unc	BU
1998 Proof	Est. 30,000	Value: 45.00				

KM# 95 POUND
9.5000 g., 0.9250 Silver .2825 oz. ASW, 22.5 mm. **Ruler:** Elizabeth II **Subject:** Prince Edward's Wedding **Obv:** Queen's portrait **Rev:** Portraits of Edward and Sophie **Edge:** Reeded

Date	Mintage	F	VF	XF	Unc	BU
1999 Proof	50,000	Value: 30.00				

KM# 120 POUND
9.5000 g., 0.9250 Silver 0.2825 oz. ASW, 22.4 mm. **Ruler:** Elizabeth II **Subject:** Queen Mother **Obv:** Head with tiara right **Rev:** Bust 3/4 right **Edge:** Reeded

Date	Mintage	F	VF	XF	Unc	BU
1999 Proof	—	Value: 35.00				

KM# 133 POUND
9.5000 g., 0.9250 Silver 0.2825 oz. ASW, 22.5 mm. **Ruler:** Elizabeth II **Subject:** Queen Mother **Obv:** Head with tiara right **Rev:** Bust 3/4 right **Edge:** Reeded

Date	Mintage	F	VF	XF	Unc	BU
1999 Proof	50,000	Value: 30.00				

KM# 109 POUND
9.5000 g., 0.9250 Silver .2825 oz. ASW, 22.5 mm. **Ruler:** Elizabeth II **Subject:** Winston Churchill **Obv:** Queen's portrait **Rev:** Churchill's portrait **Edge:** Reeded

Date	Mintage	F	VF	XF	Unc	BU
1999 Proof	30,000	Value: 25.00				

KM# 87 POUND
9.5000 g., 0.9250 Gold Plated Silver .2825 oz. ASW AGW, 22.5 mm. **Ruler:** Elizabeth II **Subject:** Year 2000 **Obv:** Head with tiara right **Rev:** Hands holding planet Earth, **Note:** Millennium insert for 5 pounds, KM#86.

Date	Mintage	F	VF	XF	Unc	BU
2000 Proof	Est. 50,000	Value: 45.00				

KM# 99 POUND
9.5000 g., 0.9250 Silver .2825 oz. ASW, 22.5 mm. **Ruler:** Elizabeth II **Subject:** Queen Mother's 100th Birthday **Obv:** Head with tiara right **Rev:** Head facing, flowers and age at right **Edge:** Reeded

Date	Mintage	F	VF	XF	Unc	BU
2000 Proof	50,000	Value: 25.00				

KM# 47 2 POUNDS
Copper-Nickel, 38.61 mm. **Ruler:** Elizabeth II **Subject:** 40th Anniversary - Liberation from Germany **Obv:** Crowned head right, small arms at left **Rev:** Pair of doves sharing laurel branch **Rev. Designer:** John Savage

Date	Mintage	F	VF	XF	Unc	BU
ND(1985)	75,000	—	—	3.50	6.00	7.50
ND(1985) Proof	2,500	Value: 9.00				

KM# 47a 2 POUNDS
28.2800 g., 0.9250 Silver .8411 oz. ASW, 38.61 mm. **Ruler:** Elizabeth II **Subject:** 40th Anniversary - Liberation from Germany **Obv:** Crowned head right, small arms at left **Rev:** Pair of doves sharing laurel branch

Date	Mintage	F	VF	XF	Unc	BU
ND (1985) Proof	2,500	Value: 30.00				

KM# 48 2 POUNDS
Copper-Nickel, 38.61 mm. **Ruler:** Elizabeth II **Subject:** Commonwealth Games **Rev:** Eight shields of athletes surround arms **Rev. Designer:** Stuart Devlin

Date	Mintage	F	VF	XF	Unc	BU
1986	18,000	—	—	—	6.00	7.00
1986	Est. 2,500	Value: 10.00				
Note: In proof sets only						

KM# 48a 2 POUNDS
28.2800 g., 0.5000 Silver .4547 oz. ASW, 38.61 mm. **Ruler:** Elizabeth II **Subject:** Commonwealth Games **Rev:** Eight shields of athletes surround arms

Date	Mintage	F	VF	XF	Unc	BU
1986	Est. 50,000	—	—	—	13.50	15.00

KM# 48b 2 POUNDS
28.2800 g., 0.9250 Silver .8411 oz. ASW, 38.61 mm. **Ruler:** Elizabeth II **Subject:** Commonwealth Games **Rev:** Eight shields of athletes surround arms

Date	Mintage	F	VF	XF	Unc	BU
1986 Proof	Est. 20,000	Value: 22.50				

KM# 49 2 POUNDS
Copper-Nickel, 38.5 mm. **Ruler:** Elizabeth II **Subject:** 900th Anniversary - Death of William the Conqueror **Obv:** Crowned head right, small arms at left **Rev:** Crowned bust left **Rev. Designer:** Arnold Machin

Date	Mintage	F	VF	XF	Unc	BU
ND(1987)	18,000	—	—	—	6.50	7.50
ND(1987) Proof	Est. 2,500	Value: 10.00				

KM# 49a 2 POUNDS
28.2800 g., 0.9250 Silver .8411 oz. ASW, 38.5 mm. **Ruler:** Elizabeth II **Subject:** 900th Anniversary - Death of William the Conqueror **Obv:** Crowned head right, small arms at left **Rev:** Crowned bust left

Date	Mintage	F	VF	XF	Unc	BU
ND(1987) Proof	2,500	Value: 30.00				

KM# 49b 2 POUNDS
47.5400 g., 0.9170 Gold 1.4012 oz. AGW, 38.5 mm. **Ruler:** Elizabeth II **Subject:** 900th Anniversary - Death of William the Conqueror **Obv:** Crowned head right, small arms at left **Rev:** Crowned bust left

Date	Mintage	F	VF	XF	Unc	BU
ND(1987) Proof	90	Value: 1,250				

KM# 50 2 POUNDS
Copper-Nickel, 38.5 mm. **Ruler:** Elizabeth II **Subject:** William II, 1087-1100 **Obv:** Crowned head right, small arms at left **Rev:** Bust facing **Rev. Designer:** Robert Elderton

Date	Mintage	F	VF	XF	Unc	BU
1988	7,500	—	—	—	6.50	7.50
1988 Proof	2,500	Value: 10.00				

KM# 50a 2 POUNDS
28.2800 g., 0.9250 Silver .8411 oz. ASW, 38.5 mm. **Ruler:** Elizabeth II **Subject:** William II, 1087-1100 **Obv:** Crowned head right, small arms at left **Rev:** Bust facing

Date	Mintage	F	VF	XF	Unc	BU
1988 Proof	2,500	Value: 28.00				

KM# 51 2 POUNDS
Copper-Nickel, 38.5 mm. **Ruler:** Elizabeth II **Subject:** Henry I, 1100-1135 **Obv:** Crowned head right, small arms at left **Rev:** Crowned bust right

Date	Mintage	F	VF	XF	Unc	BU
1989	10,000	—	—	—	6.50	7.50
1989 Proof	Est. 2,500	Value: 10.00				

KM# 51a 2 POUNDS
28.2800 g., 0.9250 Silver .8411 oz. ASW, 38.5 mm. **Ruler:** Elizabeth II **Subject:** Henry I, 1100-1135 **Obv:** Crowned head right, small arms at left **Rev:** Crowned bust right

Date	Mintage	F	VF	XF	Unc	BU
1989 Proof	Est. 2,500	Value: 28.00				

KM# 52 2 POUNDS
Copper-Nickel, 38.5 mm. **Ruler:** Elizabeth II **Subject:** Royal Visit **Obv:** Crowned bust right **Rev:** Royal Yacht "Britannia"

Date	Mintage	F	VF	XF	Unc	BU
1989	5,000	—	—	—	8.00	10.00

KM# 52a 2 POUNDS
28.2800 g., 0.9250 Silver .8411 oz. ASW, 38.5 mm. **Ruler:** Elizabeth II **Subject:** Royal Visit **Obv:** Crowned bust right **Rev:** Royal yacht, "Britannia"

Date	Mintage	F	VF	XF	Unc	BU
1989 Proof	5,000	Value: 35.00				

KM# 53 2 POUNDS
Copper-Nickel, 38.5 mm. **Ruler:** Elizabeth II **Subject:** 90th Birthday of Queen Mother **Obv:** Crowned bust right **Rev:** Crowned monogram flanked by flowers **Rev. Designer:** Robert Elderton

Date	Mintage	F	VF	XF	Unc	BU
ND(1990)	9,000	—	—	—	7.00	8.00

KM# 53a 2 POUNDS
28.2800 g., 0.9250 Silver .8411 oz. ASW, 38.5 mm. **Ruler:** Elizabeth II **Subject:** 90th Birthday of Queen Mother **Obv:** Crowned bust right **Rev:** Crowned monogram flanked by flowers

Date	Mintage	F	VF	XF	Unc	BU
ND(1990) Proof	1,302	Value: 50.00				

KM# 54 2 POUNDS
Copper-Nickel, 38.5 mm. **Ruler:** Elizabeth II **Subject:** Henry II, 1154-1189 **Obv:** Crowned head right, small arms at left **Rev:** Crowned bust half left

Date	Mintage	F	VF	XF	Unc	BU
1991	1,200	—	—	—	6.50	7.50

KM# 54a 2 POUNDS
28.2800 g., 0.9250 Silver .8411 oz. ASW, 38.5 mm. **Ruler:** Elizabeth II **Subject:** Henry II, 1154-1189 **Obv:** Crowned head right, small arms at left **Rev:** Crowned half left

Date	Mintage	F	VF	XF	Unc	BU
1991 Proof	Est. 2,500	Value: 50.00				

KM# 55 2 POUNDS
Copper-Nickel, 38.5 mm. **Ruler:** Elizabeth II **Subject:** 40th Anniversary of Coronation **Obv:** Crowned bust right **Rev:** Crowned, ribbon monogram with date on field of vines and flowers

Date	Mintage	F	VF	XF	Unc	BU
ND(1993)	13,000	—	—	—	6.50	7.50

KM# 55a 2 POUNDS
28.2800 g., 0.9250 Silver .8411 oz. ASW, 38.5 mm. **Ruler:** Elizabeth II **Subject:** 40th Anniversary of Coronation **Obv:** Crowned bust right **Rev:** Crowned, ribbon monogram with date on field of vines and flowers

Date	Mintage	F	VF	XF	Unc	BU
ND(1993) Proof	Est. 10,000	Value: 45.00				

KM# 56 2 POUNDS
Copper-Nickel, 38.5 mm. **Ruler:** Elizabeth II **Subject:** 50th Anniversary - Normandy Landing **Obv:** Crowned head right, small arms at left **Rev:** Cameo portrait above invasion scene

Date	Mintage	F	VF	XF	Unc	BU
ND(1994)	49,000	—	—	—	7.50	9.00

KM# 56a 2 POUNDS
28.2800 g., 0.9250 Silver .8411 oz. ASW, 38.5 mm. **Ruler:** Elizabeth II **Subject:** 50th Anniversary - Normandy Landing **Obv:** Crowned head right, small arms at left **Rev:** Cameo portrait above invasion scene

Date	Mintage	F	VF	XF	Unc	BU
ND(1994) Proof	Est. 10,000	Value: 35.00				

KM# 61 2 POUNDS
Copper-Nickel, 38.5 mm. **Ruler:** Elizabeth II **Subject:** 50th Anniversary of Liberation **Obv:** Crowned head right, small arms at left **Rev:** Soldiers and ship

Date	Mintage	F	VF	XF	Unc	BU
ND(1995)	42,000	—	—	—	7.50	9.00

KM# 61a 2 POUNDS
28.2800 g., 0.9250 Silver .8411 oz. ASW, 38.5 mm. **Ruler:** Elizabeth II **Subject:** 50th Anniversary of Liberation **Obv:** Crowned head right, small arms at left **Rev:** Soldiers and ship

Date	Mintage	F	VF	XF	Unc	BU
ND(1995) Proof	7,000	Value: 35.00				

KM# 61b 2 POUNDS
56.5600 g., 0.9250 Silver 1.6822 oz. ASW, 38.5 mm. **Ruler:** Elizabeth II **Subject:** 50th Anniversary of Liberation **Obv:** Crowned head right, small arms at left **Rev:** Soldiers and ship

Date	Mintage	F	VF	XF	Unc	BU
ND(1995) Proof	800	Value: 60.00				

KM# 80 2 POUNDS
Copper-Nickel, 38.5 mm. **Ruler:** Elizabeth II **Subject:** WWF Conserving Nature **Obv:** Crowned head right **Rev:** Emperor Moth **Rev. Designer:** Willem Vis

Date	Mintage	F	VF	XF	Unc	BU
1997	—	—	—	—	9.00	12.00

KM# 80a 2 POUNDS
28.2800 g., 0.9250 Silver .841 oz. ASW, 38.5 mm. **Ruler:** Elizabeth II **Subject:** WWF Conserving Nature **Obv:** Crowned head right **Rev:** Emperor moth

Date	Mintage	F	VF	XF	Unc	BU
1997 Proof	Est. 15,000	Value: 50.00				

KM# 88 2 POUNDS
12.0000 g., Bi-Metallic Copper-Nickel center in Nickel-Brass ring, 28.35 mm. **Ruler:** Elizabeth II **Obv:** Crowned head right **Rev:** Latent image arms on cross design **Edge:** Bailiwick of Guernsey

Date	Mintage	F	VF	XF	Unc	BU
1997	—	—	—	—	8.50	10.00
Note: In sets only						
1997 Proof	—	Value: 12.00				
Note: In sets only						

KM# 81 2 POUNDS
Copper-Nickel, 38.5 mm. **Ruler:** Elizabeth II **Subject:** WWF Conserving Nature **Obv:** Crowned head right **Rev:** Brimstone butterfly **Rev. Designer:** Willem Vis

Date	Mintage	F	VF	XF	Unc	BU
1998	—	—	—	—	8.00	12.00

KM# 83 2 POUNDS
12.0000 g., Bi-Metallic Copper-Nickel center in Nickel-Brass ring, 28.35 mm. **Ruler:** Elizabeth II **Obv:** Head with tiara right **Obv. Designer:** Rank-Broadley **Rev:** Latent image arms on cross **Edge:** Bailiwick of Guernsey

Date	Mintage	F	VF	XF	Unc	BU
1998	Est. 150,000	—	—	—	8.50	10.00

KM# 66 5 POUNDS
Copper-Nickel, 38.5 mm. **Ruler:** Elizabeth II **Subject:** Queen Elizabeth the Queen Mother **Obv:** Crowned head right **Rev:** Bust facing, flowers flank

Date	Mintage	F	VF	XF	Unc	BU
1995	56,000	—	—	—	15.00	16.50

KM# 66a 5 POUNDS
28.2800 g., 0.9250 Silver .8411 oz. ASW, 38.5 mm. **Ruler:** Elizabeth II **Subject:** Queen Elizabeth The Queen Mother **Obv:** Crowned head right **Rev:** Bust facing, flowers flank

Date	Mintage	F	VF	XF	Unc	BU
1995 Proof	Est. 40,000	Value: 50.00				

KM# 67 5 POUNDS
7.8100 g., 0.9990 Gold .2508 oz. AGW **Ruler:** Elizabeth II **Obv:** Crowned head right **Rev:** Queen Mother

Date	Mintage	F	VF	XF	Unc	BU
1995 Proof	Est. 2,500	Value: 225				

KM# 68 5 POUNDS
Copper-Nickel, 38.5 mm. **Ruler:** Elizabeth II **Subject:** European Football **Rev:** Soccer ball and European map

Date	Mintage	F	VF	XF	Unc	BU
1996	—	—	—	—	15.00	16.50

KM# 68a 5 POUNDS
28.2800 g., 0.9250 Silver .8411 oz. ASW, 38.5 mm. **Ruler:** Elizabeth II **Subject:** European Football **Rev:** Soccer ball and European map

Date	Mintage	F	VF	XF	Unc	BU
1996 Proof	Est. 20,000	Value: 65.00				

KM# 79 5 POUNDS
Copper-Nickel, 38.5 mm. **Ruler:** Elizabeth II **Subject:** 70th Birthday of Queen Elizabeth II **Obv:** Crowned head right **Rev:** Bust at left looking right, ship and arms at right

Date	Mintage	F	VF	XF	Unc	BU
1996	—	—	—	—	15.00	16.50

KM# 79a 5 POUNDS
28.2800 g., 0.9250 Silver .8411 oz. ASW, 38.5 mm. **Ruler:** Elizabeth II **Subject:** 70th Birthday of Queen Elizabeth II **Obv:** Crowned head right **Rev:** Bust at left looking right, arms and ship at right

Date	Mintage	F	VF	XF	Unc	BU
1996 Proof	—	Value: 45.00				

KM# 71 5 POUNDS
Copper-Nickel, 38.5 mm. **Ruler:** Elizabeth II **Subject:** Queen Elizabeth II's Golden Wedding Anniversary **Obv:** Crowned head right **Rev:** Queen Elizabeth II and Prince Philip, monogrammed shield and Westminster Abbey

Date	Mintage	F	VF	XF	Unc	BU
1997	22,000	—	—	—	12.50	14.00

KM# 71a 5 POUNDS
28.2800 g., 0.9250 Silver .8411 oz. ASW, 38.5 mm. **Ruler:** Elizabeth II **Subject:** Queen Elizabeth II's Golden Wedding Anniversary **Obv:** Crowned head right **Rev:** Queen Elizabeth II and Prince Philip, monogrammed shield and Westminster Abbey

Date	Mintage	F	VF	XF	Unc	BU
1997 Proof	Est. 20,000	Value: 65.00				

KM# 74 5 POUNDS
Copper-Nickel, 38.5 mm. **Ruler:** Elizabeth II **Subject:** Castle Cornet **Obv:** Crowned head right **Rev:** Castle

Date	Mintage	F	VF	XF	Unc	BU
1997	—	—	—	—	10.00	12.00

KM# 74a 5 POUNDS
28.2800 g., 0.9250 Silver .8411 oz. ASW, 38.5 mm. **Ruler:** Elizabeth II **Subject:** Castle Cornet **Obv:** Crowned head right **Rev:** Castle

Date	Mintage	F	VF	XF	Unc	BU
1997 Proof	Est. 10,000	Value: 60.00				

KM# 75 5 POUNDS
28.2800 g., 0.9250 Silver .8411 oz. ASW, 38.5 mm. **Ruler:** Elizabeth II **Subject:** Castle Caernarfon **Obv:** Crowned head right **Rev:** Castle

Date	Mintage	F	VF	XF	Unc	BU
1997 Proof	Est. 10,000	Value: 60.00				

KM# 76 5 POUNDS
28.2800 g., 0.9250 Silver .8411 oz. ASW, 38.5 mm. **Ruler:** Elizabeth II **Subject:** Castle Leeds **Obv:** Crowned head right **Rev:** Castle

Date	Mintage	F	VF	XF	Unc	BU
1997 Proof	Est. 10,000	Value: 60.00				

KM# 98 5 POUNDS
1.2000 g., 0.9167 Gold .0354 oz. AGW, 9 mm. **Ruler:** Elizabeth II **Subject:** Queen's 50th Wedding Anniversary **Rev:** Royal couple, shield and church **Edge:** Reeded

Date	Mintage	F	VF	XF	Unc	BU
1997 Proof	—	Value: 40.00				

KM# 82 5 POUNDS
Copper-Nickel, 38.5 mm. **Ruler:** Elizabeth II **Subject:** 80th Anniversary of the Royal Air Force **Obv:** Head with tiara right **Obv. Designer:** Rank-Broadley **Rev:** Three Spitfires and an oval crest

Date	Mintage	F	VF	XF	Unc	BU
1998	—	—	—	—	12.50	14.50

KM# 82a 5 POUNDS
28.2800 g., 0.9250 Silver .8410 oz. ASW, 38.5 mm. **Ruler:** Elizabeth II **Subject:** 80th Anniversary of the Royal Air Force **Obv:** Head with tiara right **Obv. Designer:** Rank-Broadley **Rev:** Three Spitfires and an oval crest

Date	Mintage	F	VF	XF	Unc	BU
1998 Proof	15,000	Value: 55.00				

KM# 86 5 POUNDS
28.2800 g., 0.9250 Silver .8410 oz. ASW, 38.5 mm. **Ruler:** Elizabeth II **Subject:** Millennium 2000 **Obv:** Head with tiara right below center hole **Rev:** Rising sun design surrounds center hole

Date	Mintage	F	VF	XF	Unc	BU
1999 Proof	Est. 50,000	Value: 40.00				

KM# 91 5 POUNDS
Bi-Metallic Brass center in Copper-Nickel ring, 38.5 mm. **Ruler:** Elizabeth II **Subject:** Millennium 2000 **Obv:** Head with tiara right at center and below **Rev:** Hands holding planet earth in center, rising sun design surrounds

Date	Mintage	F	VF	XF	Unc	BU
1999	22,000	—	—	—	18.00	20.00

KM# 92 5 POUNDS
27.7100 g., Copper Nickel, 38.6 mm. **Ruler:** Elizabeth II **Subject:** Prince Edward's Marriage **Obv:** Head with tiara right **Rev:** Conjoined heads of Edward and Sophie left **Edge:** Reeded

Date	Mintage	F	VF	XF	Unc	BU
1999	19,000	—	—	—	15.00	16.50

KM# 92a 5 POUNDS
28.2800 g., 0.9250 Silver .8410 oz. ASW, 38.6 mm. **Ruler:** Elizabeth II **Subject:** Prince Edward's Marriage **Obv:** Head with tiara right **Rev:** Conjoined heads left of Edward and Sophie left

Date	Mintage	F	VF	XF	Unc	BU
1999 Proof	—	Value: 37.50				

KM# 93 5 POUNDS
27.7100 g., Copper-Nickel, 38.5 mm. **Ruler:** Elizabeth II **Subject:** Queen Mother **Obv:** Head with tiara right **Rev:** Bust 3/4 right

Date	Mintage	F	VF	XF	Unc	BU
1999	5,000	—	—	—	16.50	18.00

KM# 94 5 POUNDS
27.7100 g., Copper-Nickel, 38.5 mm. **Ruler:** Elizabeth II **Subject:** Winston Churchill **Obv:** Head with tiara right **Obv. Designer:** Rank-Broadley **Rev:** Head right **Edge:** Reeded

Date	Mintage	F	VF	XF	Unc	BU
1999	5,000	—	—	—	16.50	18.00

KM# 94a 5 POUNDS
28.2800 g., 0.9250 Silver 0.841 oz. ASW, 38.5 mm. **Ruler:** Elizabeth II **Obv:** Head with tiara right **Obv. Designer:** Rank-Broadley **Rev:** Head right **Rev. Inscription:** Winston Spencer Churchill

Date	Mintage	F	VF	XF	Unc	BU
1999 Proof	—	Value: 47.50				

KM# 94b 5 POUNDS
47.5400 g., 0.9166 Gold 1.4011 oz. AGW, 38.5 mm. **Ruler:** Elizabeth II **Subject:** Winston Churchill **Obv:** Head with tiara right **Obv. Designer:** Rank-Broadley **Rev:** Head right **Edge:** Reeded

Date	Mintage	F	VF	XF	Unc	BU
1999 Proof	125,000	Value: 975				

KM# 134 5 POUNDS
1.2440 g., 0.9990 Gold 0.04 oz. AGW, 13.9 mm. **Ruler:** Elizabeth II **Subject:** Queen Mother **Obv:** Head with tiara right **Rev:** Queen Mother's portrait **Edge:** Reeded

Date	Mintage	F	VF	XF	Unc	BU
1999	20,000	—	—	—	65.00	75.00

KM# 100 5 POUNDS
28.2800 g., Copper-Nickel, 38.6 mm. **Ruler:** Elizabeth II **Obv:** Head with tiara right **Rev:** Queen Mother's portrait **Edge:** Reeded

Date	Mintage	F	VF	XF	Unc	BU
2000	2,000	—	—	—	7.50	8.50

KM# 100a 5 POUNDS
28.2800 g., 0.9250 Silver .8410 oz. ASW, 38.6 mm. **Ruler:** Elizabeth II **Subject:** Queen Mother's 100th Birthday **Obv:** Head with tiara right with gold-plated "100" **Rev:** Queen Mother's portrait **Edge:** Reeded

Date	Mintage	F	VF	XF	Unc	BU
2000 Proof	20,000	Value: 47.50				

KM# 101 5 POUNDS
1.1300 g., 0.9170 Gold .0333 oz. AGW, 13.9 mm. **Ruler:** Elizabeth II **Subject:** Queen Mother's 100th Birthday **Obv:** Head with tiara right **Rev:** Queen Mother's portrait **Edge:** Reeded

Date	Mintage	F	VF	XF	Unc	BU
2000 Proof	20,000	Value: 65.00				

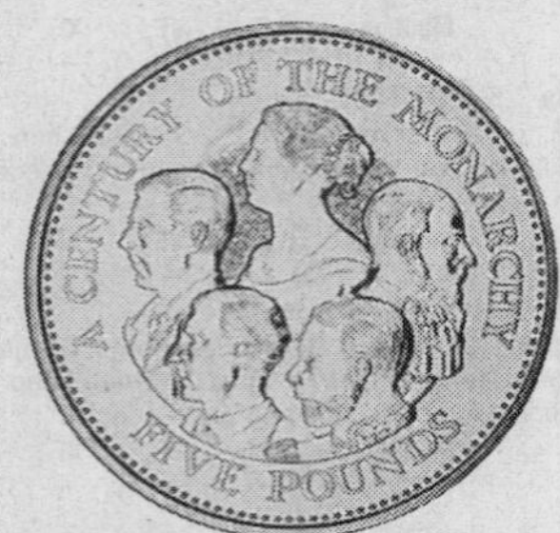

KM# 102 5 POUNDS
27.9500 g., Copper-Nickel, 38.4 mm. **Ruler:** Elizabeth II **Subject:** Century of Monarchy **Obv:** Head with tiara right **Obv. Designer:** Rank-Broadley **Rev:** Portraits of past five sovereigns **Edge:** Reeded

Date	Mintage	F	VF	XF	Unc	BU
2000	10,246	—	—	—	11.00	12.50

KM# 102a 5 POUNDS
28.2800 g., 0.9250 Silver .8410 oz. ASW, 38.6 mm. **Ruler:** Elizabeth II **Subject:** Century of Monarchy **Obv:** Head with tiara right **Obv. Designer:** Rank-Broadley **Rev:** Portraits of past five sovereigns **Edge:** Reeded

Date	Mintage	F	VF	XF	Unc	BU
2000 Proof	10,000	Value: 47.50				

KM# 113 5 POUNDS
1.1300 g., 0.9170 Gold .0333 oz. AGW, 13.9 mm. **Ruler:** Elizabeth II **Subject:** 20th Century Monarchy **Obv:** Head with tiara right **Obv. Designer:** Rank-Broadley **Rev:** Portraits of past five sovereigns **Edge:** Reeded

Date	Mintage	F	VF	XF	Unc	BU
2000 Proof	—	Value: 65.00				

KM# 102b 5 POUNDS
39.9400 g., 0.9166 Gold 1.177 oz. AGW, 38.6 mm. **Ruler:** Elizabeth II **Subject:** Century of Monarchy **Obv:** Head with tiara right **Obv. Designer:** Rank-Broadley **Rev:** Portraits of past five sovereigns **Edge:** Reeded

Date	Mintage	F	VF	XF	Unc	BU
2000 Proof	200	Value: 925				

KM# 57 10 POUNDS
3.1300 g., 0.9990 Gold .1005 oz. AGW **Ruler:** Elizabeth II **Subject:** 50th Anniversary - Normandy Invasion **Rev:** Soldiers and tank

Date	Mintage	F	VF	XF	Unc	BU
ND(1994)	Est. 500	Value: 85.00				

Note: Sold only in sets

KM# 62 10 POUNDS
3.1300 g., 0.9990 Gold .1005 oz. AGW **Ruler:** Elizabeth II **Subject:** 50th Anniversary of Liberation **Rev:** Uniformed figure giving speech

Date	Mintage	F	VF	XF	Unc	BU
ND(1995) Proof	Est. 500	Value: 85.00				

Note: Sold only in sets

KM# 157 10 POUNDS
163.2000 g., 0.9250 Silver with Gold insert 4.8535 oz. ASW, 64.9 mm. **Ruler:** Elizabeth II **Subject:** Queen's Golden Wedding Anniversary **Obv:** Crowned head right **Rev:** Elizabeth and Philip, gold insert shield and cathedral **Edge:** Reeded **Note:** Photo reduced.

Date	Mintage	F	VF	XF	Unc	BU
1997 Proof	—	Value: 250				

KM# 138 10 POUNDS
13.6600 g., 0.9990 Gold 0.4387 oz. AGW, 19.35 mm. **Ruler:** Elizabeth II **Subject:** Millennium **Obv:** Head with tiara right **Rev:** Hands holding planet **Edge:** Reeded

Date	Mintage	F	VF	XF	Unc	BU
2000	7,500	—	—	—	550	—

KM# 104 10 POUNDS
141.7500 g., 0.9990 Silver 4.5528 oz. ASW, 65 mm. **Ruler:** Elizabeth II **Subject:** Century of Monarchy **Obv:** Head with tiara right **Rev:** Portraits of past five sovereigns **Edge:** Reeded

Date	Mintage	F	VF	XF	Unc	BU
2000 Proof	950	Value: 200				

KM# 58 25 POUNDS
7.8100 g., 0.9990 Gold .2509 oz. AGW **Ruler:** Elizabeth II **Subject:** 50th Anniversary - Normandy Invasion **Rev:** Uniformed figure standing at right, invasion scene in background

Date	Mintage	F	VF	XF	Unc	BU
ND(1994)	Est. 500	—	—	—	200	—
ND(1994) Proof	Est. 500	Value: 200				

Note: Sold only in sets

KM# 63 25 POUNDS
7.8100 g., 0.9990 Gold .2509 oz. AGW **Ruler:** Elizabeth II **Subject:** 50th Anniversary of Liberation **Obv:** Crowned head right, small arms at left **Rev:** Supply worker and ship

Date	Mintage	F	VF	XF	Unc	BU
ND(1995) In proof sets only	Est. 500	Value: 200				

KM# 69 25 POUNDS
7.8100 g., 0.9990 Gold .2509 oz. AGW **Ruler:** Elizabeth II **Subject:** European Football **Rev:** Soccer ball and European map

Date	Mintage	F	VF	XF	Unc	BU
1996 Proof	1,500	Value: 185				

KM# 72 25 POUNDS
7.8100 g., 0.9990 Gold .2509 oz. AGW **Ruler:** Elizabeth II **Subject:** Queen Elizabeth II's Golden Wedding Anniversary **Obv:** Crowned head right **Rev:** Queen Elizabeth II and Prince Philip, monogrammed shield and Westminster Abbey

Date	Mintage	F	VF	XF	Unc	BU
1997 Proof	Est. 5,000	Value: 275				

KM# 85 25 POUNDS
7.8100 g., 0.9990 Gold .2509 oz. AGW **Ruler:** Elizabeth II **Subject:** 80th Anniversary - Royal Air Force **Obv:** Head with tiara right **Rev:** Three Spitfires and RAF Benevolent Fund Crest

Date	Mintage	F	VF	XF	Unc	BU
1998 Proof	Est. 2,500	Value: 185				

KM# 132 25 POUNDS
7.8100 g., 0.9990 Gold 0.2508 oz. AGW, 22 mm. **Ruler:** Elizabeth II **Subject:** Winston Churchill **Obv:** Head with tiara right **Rev:** Head right **Edge:** Reeded

Date	Mintage	F	VF	XF	Unc	BU
1999 Proof	2,500	Value: 250				

KM# 135 25 POUNDS
7.8100 g., 0.9990 Gold 0.2508 oz. AGW, 22 mm. **Ruler:** Elizabeth II **Subject:** Queen Mother **Obv:** Head with tiara right **Rev:** Queen Mother's portrait **Edge:** Reeded

Date	Mintage	F	VF	XF	Unc	BU
1999 Proof	5,000	Value: 250				

KM# 137 25 POUNDS
7.8100 g., 0.9990 Gold 0.2508 oz. AGW, 22 mm. **Ruler:** Elizabeth II **Subject:** Prince Edward's Marriage **Obv:** Head with tiara right **Rev:** Jugate heads left of Edward and Sophie left **Edge:** Reeded

Date	Mintage	F	VF	XF	Unc	BU
1999 Proof	5,000	Value: 250				

KM# 103 25 POUNDS
7.8100 g., 0.9170 Gold .2303 oz. AGW, 22 mm. **Ruler:** Elizabeth II **Subject:** Queen Mother's 100th Birthday **Obv:** Head with tiara right **Rev:** Queen Mother's portrait **Edge:** Reeded

Date	Mintage	F	VF	XF	Unc	BU
2000 Proof	5,000	Value: 235				

KM# 59 50 POUNDS
15.6100 g., 0.9990 Gold .5014 oz. AGW **Ruler:** Elizabeth II **Subject:** 50th Anniversary - Normandy Invasion **Rev:** Parachuters

Date	Mintage	F	VF	XF	Unc	BU
ND(1994)	Est. 500	Value: 385				

Note: In sets only

KM# 64 50 POUNDS
15.6100 g., 0.9990 Gold .5014 oz. AGW **Ruler:** Elizabeth II **Subject:** 50th Anniversary of Liberation **Rev:** Uniformed figure signing document, ship in background

Date	Mintage	F	VF	XF	Unc	BU
ND(1995)	Est. 500	Value: 385				

Note: In sets only

KM# 136 50 POUNDS
15.5517 g., 0.9990 Gold 0.4995 oz. AGW, 27 mm. **Ruler:** Elizabeth II **Subject:** Queen Mother **Obv:** Head with tiara right **Rev:** Queen Mother's portrait **Edge:** Reeded

Date	Mintage	F	VF	XF	Unc	BU
1999 Proof	1,250	Value: 575				

KM# 60 100 POUNDS
31.2100 g., 0.9990 Gold 1.0025 oz. AGW **Ruler:** Elizabeth II **Subject:** 50th Anniversary - Normandy Invasion **Obv:** Crowned head right, small arms at left **Rev:** Cameo portrait above invasion scene

Date	Mintage	F	VF	XF	Unc	BU
ND(1994)	Est. 500	Value: 745				

Note: In sets only

KM# 65 100 POUNDS
31.2100 g., 0.9990 Gold 1.0025 oz. AGW **Ruler:** Elizabeth II **Subject:** 50th Anniversary of Liberation **Rev:** Soldiers and ship

Date	Mintage	F	VF	XF	Unc	BU
ND(1995)	Est. 500	Value: 745				

Note: In sets only

PIEFORTS

KM#	Date	Mintage	Identification	Mkt Val
P1	1981	500	Pound. 16.0000 g. KM#37a.	265
P2	2000	10,000	50 Pence. 0.9250 Silver. 16.2000 g. KM#105a.	55.00

MINT SETS

KM#	Date	Mintage	Identification	Issue Price	Mkt Val
MS1	1985 (8)	10,000	KM40-41, 42.1, 43-47	8.75	12.50
MS2	1985 (7)	—	KM40-41, 42.1, 43-46	—	—
MS3	1986 (7)	5,000	KM40-46	8.75	6.50
MS4	1987 (7)	7,500	KM40-46	11.00	6.50
MS5	1988 (7)	5,000	KM40-46	13.00	15.00
MS6	1989 (7)	5,000	KM40-46	17.00	16.50
MS7	1990 (8)	2,520	KM40-41, 42.1-42.2, 43-46	16.00	20.00
MS8	1992 (7)	1,500	KM40-41, 42.2, 43-46	22.50	25.00
MS9	1997 (8)	—	KM 40a, 41a, 42.2, 43.2, 44, 45.2, 46, 88	—	25.00

PROOF SETS

KM#	Date	Mintage	Identification	Issue Price	Mkt Val
PS3	1902H (4)	—	KM5, 7-8, 10	—	1,000
PS4	1910H (2)	—	KM5, 7	—	500
PS5	1956 (6)	1,050	KM15-17 double set	—	22.50
PS6	1966 (4)	10,000	KM15-16, 18, 19	—	8.50
PS7	1971 (6)	10,000	KM20-25	16.00	9.50
PS8	1979 (6)	4,963	KM27-30, 33-34	25.00	11.50
PS9	1981 (6)	10,000	KM27-30, 34, 37	29.00	20.00
PS10	1985 (8)	2,500	KM40-47	29.75	30.00
PS11	1986 (8)	2,500	KM40-46, 48	35.00	32.00
PS12	1987 (8)	2,500	KM40-46, 49	33.00	32.00
PS13	1988 (8)	2,500	KM40-46, 50	45.00	32.00
PS14	1989 (8)	2,500	KM40-46, 51	45.00	32.00
PS15	1990 (9)	700	KM40-41, 42.1-42.2, 43-46	46.00	46.00
PS16	1992 (7)	500	KM40-41, 42.2, 43.2, 44-46	52.50	55.00
PS17	1994 (4)	500	KM57-60	1,595	1,400
PS18	ND (1995) (4)	500	KM62-65	1,600	1,400
PS19	1996 (2)	1,500	KM68a, 69	—	275
PS20	1997 (3)	—	KM70, 71a, 72	—	420
PS21	1997 (4)	—	KM73, 74a, 75-76	181	215
PS22	1997 (9)	—	KM#40a, 41a, 42.2, 43.2, 44, 45.1, 45.2, 46, 88	—	—

The Republic of Guinea, situated on the Atlantic Coast of Africa between Sierra Leone and Guinea-Bissau, has an area of 94,964 sq. mi. (245,860 sq. km.) and a population of 6.4 million. Capital: Conakry. Although Guinea contains one-third of the world's reserves of bauxite and significant deposits of iron ore, gold and diamonds, the economy is still dependent on agriculture, aluminum, bananas, copra and coffee are exported.

The coast of Guinea was known to Portuguese navigators of the 15th century but was seldom visited by European traders of the 16th-18th centuries because of its dangerous coastal waters. French penetration of the area began in the mid-19th century with the entering into of protectorate treaties with several of the coastal chiefs. After a long struggle with Guinea's native leader Samory Toure, France secured the area and until 1890 administered it as a part of Senegal. In 1895 the colony (Guinee Francais) became an autonomous part of the federation of French West Africa. The inhabitants were extended French citizenship in 1946 when the colony became an overseas territory of the French Union. Guinea became an independent republic on Oct. 2, 1958, when it declined to enter the new French Community.

MONETARY SYSTEM
100 Centimes = 1 Franc

REPUBLIC

DECIMAL COINAGE

KM# 4 FRANC
Copper-Nickel **Obv:** Head of Ahmed Sekou Toure left **Rev:** Feathers flank denomination within wreath

Date	Mintage	F	VF	XF	Unc	BU
1962	—	1.25	2.00	3.50	7.00	15.00
1962 Proof	—	Value: 50.00				

KM# 1 5 FRANCS
Aluminum-Bronze **Obv:** Head of Ahmed Sekou Toure right **Rev:** Palm trees flank denomination

Date	Mintage	F	VF	XF	Unc	BU
1959	—	2.75	4.75	9.00	22.50	—

KM# 5 5 FRANCS
Copper-Nickel, 20 mm. **Obv:** Head right **Rev:** Denomination within wreath, coconuts below **Note:** Mules with two obverses exist.

Date	Mintage	F	VF	XF	Unc	BU
1962	—	1.25	2.00	3.00	6.50	12.50
1962 Proof	—	Value: 70.00				

KM# 2 10 FRANCS
Aluminum-Bronze **Obv:** Head of Ahmed Sekou Toure left **Rev:** Denomination above spray

Date	Mintage	F	VF	XF	Unc	BU
1959	—	5.00	20.00	50.00	90.00	—

KM# 6 10 FRANCS

Copper-Nickel, 22 mm. **Obv:** Head of Ahmed Sekou Toure left **Rev:** Denomination within wreath

Date	Mintage	F	VF	XF	Unc	BU
1962	—	1.75	2.75	6.00	12.00	25.00
1962 Proof	—	Value: 85.00				

KM# 3 25 FRANCS

Aluminum-Bronze **Obv:** Head of Ahmed Sekou Toure right **Rev:** Palm trees flank denomination

Date	Mintage	F	VF	XF	Unc	BU
1959	—	10.00	50.00	110	200	—

KM# 7 25 FRANCS

Copper-Nickel **Obv:** Head of Ahmed Sekou Toure right **Rev:** Denomination within wreath

Date	Mintage	F	VF	XF	Unc	BU
1962	—	2.50	4.00	7.50	15.00	30.00
1962 Proof	—	Value: 120				

KM# 8 50 FRANCS

Copper-Nickel **Obv:** Head of Ahmed Sekou Toure left **Rev:** Denomination within wreath **Note:** Not released into circulation.

Date	Mintage	F	VF	XF	Unc	BU
1969	4,000	—	—	35.00	55.00	85.00

KM# 9 100 FRANCS

5.6500 g., 0.9990 Silver .1816 oz. ASW **Series:** 10th Anniversary of Independence **Subject:** Martin Luther King **Rev:** National arms

Date	Mintage	F	VF	XF	Unc	BU
1969 Proof	9,700	Value: 7.50				
1970 Proof	Inc. above	Value: 7.50				

KM# 41 100 FRANCS

Copper-Nickel **Obv:** Head of Ahmed Sekou Toure right **Rev:** Denomination within wreath **Note:** Not released into circulation.

Date	Mintage	F	VF	XF	Unc	BU
1971	2,585,000	—	—	22.50	45.00	75.00

KM# 10 200 FRANCS

11.7000 g., 0.9990 Silver .3761 oz. ASW **Series:** 10th Anniversary of Independence **Subject:** John and Robert Kennedy **Obv:** Conjoined heads right **Rev:** National arms

Date	Mintage	F	VF	XF	Unc	BU
1969 Proof	10,000	Value: 15.00				
1970 Proof	Inc. above	Value: 15.00				

KM# 11 200 FRANCS

11.7000 g., 0.9990 Silver .3761 oz. ASW **Series:** 10th Anniversary of Independence **Subject:** Almamy Samory Toure **Obv:** Bust facing divides dates **Rev:** National arms

Date	Mintage	F	VF	XF	Unc	BU
1969 Proof	6,100	Value: 16.50				
1970 Proof	Inc. above	Value: 16.50				

KM# 12 250 FRANCS

14.5300 g., 0.9990 Silver .4671 oz. ASW **Series:** 10th Anniversary of Independence **Subject:** Lunar Landing **Obv:** Planets bound together, astronaut and space shuttle **Rev:** National arms

Date	Mintage	F	VF	XF	Unc	BU
1969 Proof	26,000	Value: 18.00				
1970 Proof	Inc. above	Value: 18.00				

KM# 13 250 FRANCS

14.5300 g., 0.9990 Silver .4671 oz. ASW **Series:** 10th Anniversary of Independence **Subject:** Alpha Yaya Diallo **Obv:** Bust with spear facing **Rev:** National arms

Date	Mintage	F	VF	XF	Unc	BU
1969 Proof	6,100	Value: 20.00				
1970 Proof	Inc. above	Value: 20.00				

KM# 14 250 FRANCS

14.5300 g., 0.9990 Silver .4671 oz. ASW **Series:** 10th Anniversary of Independence **Subject:** Apollo XIII **Obv:** Radiant planet back of three charging horses **Rev:** National arms

Date	Mintage	F	VF	XF	Unc	BU
1969 Proof	4,450	Value: 22.50				
1970 Proof	Inc. above	Value: 22.50				

KM# 21 250 FRANCS

14.5300 g., 0.9990 Silver .4671 oz. ASW **Series:** 10th Anniversary of Independence **Subject:** Spacecraft Soyuz **Obv:** Spacecraft in flight **Rev:** National arms

Date	Mintage	F	VF	XF	Unc	BU
1970 Proof	3,500	Value: 20.00				

KM# 15 500 FRANCS

29.0800 g., 0.9990 Silver .9349 oz. ASW **Series:** 10th Anniversary of Independence **Subject:** Munich Olympics **Obv:** Medals of the Olympics in Helsinki 1952; Melbourne 1956; Rome 1968; Tokyo 1964; Mexico City 1968 **Rev:** National arms

Date	Mintage	F	VF	XF	Unc	BU
1969 Proof	7,200	Value: 35.00				
1970 Proof	1,900	Value: 45.00				

KM# 16 500 FRANCS

29.0800 g., 0.9990 Silver .9349 oz. ASW **Series:** 10th Anniversary of Independence **Subject:** Oiseaux Dancers **Obv:** Dancers and hut **Rev:** National arms

Date	Mintage	F	VF	XF	Unc	BU
1969 Proof	7,150	Value: 37.50				
1970 Proof	—	Value: 47.50				

KM# 22 500 FRANCS

29.0800 g., 0.9990 Silver .9349 oz. ASW **Series:** 10th Anniversary of Independence **Subject:** Ikhnaton **Obv:** Head 3/4 facing **Rev:** National arms

Date	Mintage	F	VF	XF	Unc	BU
1970 Proof	4,180	Value: 32.50				

KM# 23 500 FRANCS

29.0800 g., 0.9990 Silver .9349 oz. ASW **Series:** 10th Anniversary of Independence **Subject:** Chephren **Obv:** Head with parrot right **Rev:** National arms

Date	Mintage	F	VF	XF	Unc	BU
1970 Proof	4,600	Value: 32.50				

KM# 24 500 FRANCS

29.0800 g., 0.9990 Silver .9349 oz. ASW **Series:** 10th Anniversary of Independence **Subject:** Cleopatra **Obv:** Head left **Rev:** National arms

Date	Mintage	F	VF	XF	Unc	BU
1970 Proof	5,250	Value: 35.00				

KM# 25 500 FRANCS

29.0800 g., 0.9990 Silver .9349 oz. ASW **Series:** 10th Anniversary of Independence **Subject:** Nefertiti, 1372-1350BC **Obv:** Head left **Rev:** National arms

Date	Mintage	F	VF	XF	Unc	BU
1970 Proof	4,610	Value: 35.00				

KM# 26 500 FRANCS

29.0800 g., 0.9990 Silver .9349 oz. ASW **Series:** 10th Anniversary of Independence **Subject:** Ramses III **Obv:** Head right **Rev:** National arms

Date	Mintage	F	VF	XF	Unc	BU
1970 Proof	4,330	Value: 35.00				

KM# 27 500 FRANCS

29.0800 g., 0.9990 Silver .9349 oz. ASW **Series:** 10th Anniversary of Independence **Subject:** Tutankhamen **Obv:** Bust facing **Rev:** National arms

Date	Mintage	F	VF	XF	Unc	BU
1970 Proof	4,280	Value: 40.00				

KM# 28 500 FRANCS

29.0800 g., 0.9990 Silver .9349 oz. ASW **Series:** 10th Anniversary of Independence **Subject:** Queen Teyi, mother of Pharoah Amenophis IV (Ichnation), reigned 1352-1336BC **Obv:** Head right **Rev:** National arms

Date	Mintage	F	VF	XF	Unc	BU
1970 Proof	4,120	Value: 32.50				

KM# 29 500 FRANCS

29.0800 g., 0.9990 Silver .9349 oz. ASW **Series:** 10th Anniversary of Independence **Subject:** Gamal Abdel Nasser **Obv:** Head right **Rev:** National arms

Date	Mintage	F	VF	XF	Unc	BU
1970 Proof	950	Value: 125				

KM# 17 1000 FRANCS

4.0000 g., 0.9000 Gold .1157 oz. AGW **Series:** 10th Anniversary of Independence **Subject:** John and Robert Kennedy **Obv:** Jugate heads right **Rev:** National arms

Date	Mintage	F	VF	XF	Unc	BU
1969 Proof	6,600	Value: 85.00				
1970 Proof	Inc. above	Value: 85.00				

KM# 18 2000 FRANCS

8.0000 g., 0.9000 Gold .2315 oz. AGW **Series:** 10th Anniversary of Independence **Subject:** Lunar Landing **Obv:** Planets bound together, space shuttle and astronaut **Rev:** National arms

Date	Mintage	F	VF	XF	Unc	BU
1969 Proof	15,000	Value: 165				

KM# 30 2000 FRANCS

8.0000 g., 0.9000 Gold .2315 oz. AGW **Series:** 10th Anniversary of Independence **Subject:** Apollo XIII **Obv:** Radiant planet back of three charging horses **Rev:** National arms

Date	Mintage	F	VF	XF	Unc	BU
1970 Proof	1,775	Value: 185				

KM# 31 2000 FRANCS

8.0000 g., 0.9000 Gold .2315 oz. AGW **Series:** 10th Anniversary of Independence **Subject:** Spacecraft Soyuz **Obv:** Spacecraft in flight **Rev:** National arms

Date	Mintage	F	VF	XF	Unc	BU
1970 Proof	2,840	Value: 170				

KM# 32 5000 FRANCS

20.0000 g., 0.9000 Gold .5787 oz. AGW **Series:** 10th Anniversary of Independence **Subject:** Munich Olympics **Obv:** Medals of the Olympics in Helsinki 1952; Melbourne 1956; Rome 1968; Tokyo 1964; Mexico City 1968 **Rev:** National arms

Date	Mintage	F	VF	XF	Unc	BU
1969 Proof	2,740	Value: 425				
1970 Proof	500	Value: 475				

KM# 19 5000 FRANCS

20.0000 g., 0.9000 Gold .5787 oz. AGW **Series:** 10th Anniversary of Independence **Subject:** Gamel Abdel Nasser **Obv:** Head right **Rev:** National arms

Date	Mintage	F	VF	XF	Unc	BU
1970 Proof	4,000	Value: 450				

KM# 33 5000 FRANCS

20.0000 g., 0.9000 Gold .5787 oz. AGW **Series:** 10th Anniversary of Independence **Subject:** Ikhnaton **Obv:** Head 3/4 facing **Rev:** National arms

Date	Mintage	F	VF	XF	Unc	BU
1970 Proof	685	Value: 500				

KM# 34 5000 FRANCS

20.0000 g., 0.9000 Gold .5787 oz. AGW **Series:** 10th Anniversary of Independence **Subject:** Chephren **Obv:** Head with parrot right **Rev:** National arms

Date	Mintage	F	VF	XF	Unc	BU
1970 Proof	675	Value: 500				

KM# 35 5000 FRANCS

20.0000 g., 0.9000 Gold .5787 oz. AGW **Series:** 10th Anniversary of Independence **Subject:** Cleopatra **Obv:** Head left **Rev:** National arms

Date	Mintage	F	VF	XF	Unc	BU
1970 Proof	789	Value: 500				

KM# 36 5000 FRANCS

20.0000 g., 0.9000 Gold .5787 oz. AGW **Series:** 10th Anniversary of Independence **Subject:** Queen Nefertiti, 1372-1350BC **Obv:** Head left **Rev:** National arms

Date	Mintage	F	VF	XF	Unc	BU
1970 Proof	774	Value: 500				

KM# 37 5000 FRANCS

20.0000 g., 0.9000 Gold .5787 oz. AGW **Series:** 10th Anniversary of Independence **Subject:** Ramses III **Obv:** Head right **Rev:** National arms

Date	Mintage	F	VF	XF	Unc	BU
1970 Proof	695	Value: 500				

KM# 38 5000 FRANCS

20.0000 g., 0.9000 Gold .5787 oz. AGW **Series:** 10th Anniversary of Independence **Subject:** Tutankhamen **Obv:** Bust facing **Rev:** National arms

Date	Mintage	F	VF	XF	Unc	BU
1970 Proof	675	Value: 500				

KM# 39 5000 FRANCS

20.0000 g., 0.9000 Gold .5787 oz. AGW **Series:** 10th Anniversary of Independence **Subject:** Queen Teyi, mother of Pharoah Amenophis IV (Ichnaton), reigned 1352-1336BC **Obv:** Head right **Rev:** National arms

Date	Mintage	F	VF	XF	Unc	BU
1970 Proof	685	Value: 500				

KM# 20 10000 FRANCS
40.0000 g., 0.9000 Gold 1.1575 oz. AGW **Series:** 10th Anniversary of Independence **Subject:** Ahmed Sekou Toure **Obv:** Head left **Rev:** National arms

Date	Mintage	F	VF	XF	Unc	BU
1969 Proof	2,300	Value: 800				
1970 Proof	—	Value: 975				

DECIMAL COINAGE

100 Cauris = 1 Syli

KM# 42 50 CAURIS
Aluminum **Obv:** Cowrie shell **Rev:** Denomination within wreath **Note:** Nkrumah

Date	Mintage	F	VF	XF	Unc	BU
1971	—	1.00	2.00	3.50	6.00	—

KM# 43 SYLI
Aluminum **Obv:** Bust facing **Rev:** Denomination within wreath

Date	Mintage	F	VF	XF	Unc	BU
1971	—	2.00	3.00	5.50	12.50	—

KM# 44 2 SYLIS
Aluminum **Obv:** Head left **Rev:** Denomination within wreath

Date	Mintage	F	VF	XF	Unc	BU
1971	—	1.00	2.00	5.00	10.00	—

KM# 45 5 SYLIS
Aluminum **Obv:** Head left **Rev:** Denomination within wreath

Date	Mintage	F	VF	XF	Unc	BU
1971	—	1.25	2.25	5.50	11.50	—

KM# 46 500 SYLI
40.0000 g., 0.9250 Silver 1.1897 oz. ASW **Subject:** Miriam Makeba, South African singer in exile **Obv:** Bust right divides people at lower right and left **Rev:** National arms

Date	Mintage	F	VF	XF	Unc	BU
1977	500	—	—	—	130	—
1977 Proof	500	Value: 200				

KM# 47 500 SYLI
40.0000 g., 0.9250 Silver 1.1897 oz. ASW **Subject:** Patrice Lumumba **Obv:** Bust facing **Rev:** National arms

Date	Mintage	F	VF	XF	Unc	BU
1977	250	—	—	—	180	—
1977 Proof	150	Value: 275				

KM# 48 1000 SYLI
2.9300 g., 0.9000 Gold .0847 oz. AGW **Subject:** Miriam Makeba, South African singer in exile **Obv:** Bust right divides people at lower right and left **Rev:** National arms

Date	Mintage	F	VF	XF	Unc	BU
1977	300	—	—	—	90.00	100
1977 Proof	250	Value: 125				

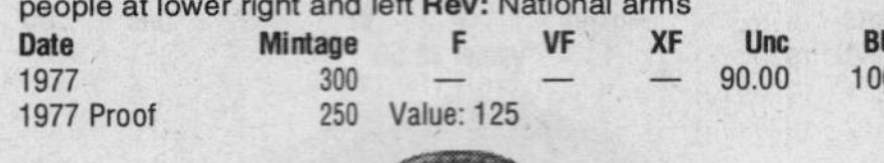

KM# 49 1000 SYLI
2.9300 g., 0.9000 Gold .0847 oz. AGW **Subject:** Nkrumah **Obv:** Bust right **Rev:** National arms

Date	Mintage	F	VF	XF	Unc	BU
1977	150	—	—	—	110	125
1977 Proof	150	Value: 135				

KM# 50 2000 SYLI
5.8700 g., 0.9000 Gold .1698 oz. AGW **Subject:** Mao Tse Tung **Obv:** Bust facing **Rev:** National arms

Date	Mintage	F	VF	XF	Unc	BU
1977	200	—	—	—	200	225
1977 Proof	200	Value: 250				

KM# 51 2000 SYLI
5.8700 g., 0.9000 Gold .1698 oz. AGW **Subject:** Ahmen Sekou Toure **Obv:** Bust left **Rev:** National arms

Date	Mintage	F	VF	XF	Unc	BU
1977	100	—	—	—	225	250
1977 Proof	50	Value: 325				

REFORM COINAGE

KM# 56 FRANC
1.4000 g., Brass Clad Steel, 15 mm. **Obv:** Shield with rifle and sword crossed on branch held by bird above **Rev:** Palm branch right of denomination

Date	Mintage	F	VF	XF	Unc	BU
1985	—	0.10	0.20	0.40	1.00	—

KM# 53 5 FRANCS
2.0000 g., Brass Clad Steel, 17.5 mm. **Obv:** Shield with rifle and sword crossed on branch held by bird above **Rev:** Palm branch right of denomination

Date	Mintage	F	VF	XF	Unc	BU
1985	—	0.10	0.20	0.40	1.00	—

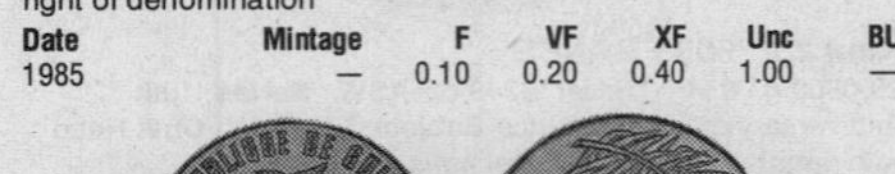

KM# 52 10 FRANCS
2.9500 g., Brass Clad Steel, 20.4 mm. **Obv:** Shield with rifle and sword crossed on branch held by bird above **Rev:** Palm branch right of denomination

Date	Mintage	F	VF	XF	Unc	BU
1985	—	0.20	0.40	0.80	1.25	—

KM# 60 25 FRANCS
4.9500 g., Brass, 22.5 mm. **Obv:** Shield with rifle and sword crossed on branch held by bird above **Rev:** Palm branch right of denomination

Date	Mintage	F	VF	XF	Unc	BU
1987	—	0.20	0.40	0.85	1.75	—

KM# 63 50 FRANCS
Copper-Nickel **Obv:** Without sword and rifle **Rev:** Leaves right of denomination

Date	Mintage	F	VF	XF	Unc	BU
1994	—	0.30	0.60	1.25	2.75	—

KM# 57 100 FRANCS
16.0000 g., 0.9990 Silver .5144 oz. ASW **Subject:** 1992 Olympics **Obv:** Shield with rifle and sword crossed on branch held by bird above **Rev:** Discus thrower, lady with parasol and shield at left

Date	Mintage	F	VF	XF	Unc	BU
1988 Matte	Est. 5,000	—	—	—	75.00	—

KM# 58 200 FRANCS
16.0000 g., 0.9990 Silver .5144 oz. ASW **Subject:** 1992 Olympics **Obv:** Shield with rifle and sword crossed on branch held by bird above **Rev:** Basketball players, lady with parasol and shield at left

Date	Mintage	F	VF	XF	Unc	BU
1988 Matte	Est. 5,000	—	—	—	85.00	—

KM# 59 300 FRANCS
16.0000 g., 0.9990 Silver .5144 oz. ASW **Subject:** 1992 Olympics **Obv:** Shield with rifle and sword crossed on branch held by bird above **Rev:** Stadium, lady with parasol and shield above

Date	Mintage	F	VF	XF	Unc	BU
1988	Est. 5,000	—	—	—	95.00	—

KM# 61 10000 FRANCS
25.0000 g., 0.9990 Silver .8038 oz. ASW **Subject:** 30th Anniversary of Currency **Obv:** Shield with rifle and sword crossed on branch held by bird above **Rev:** Palm branch and denomination

Date	Mintage	F	VF	XF	Unc	BU
ND(1990) Proof	1,000	Value: 75.00				

KM# 62 10000 FRANCS
15.9760 g., 0.9170 Gold .4708 oz. AGW **Subject:** 30th Anniversary of Currency **Obv:** Arms with dates on each side **Rev:** Palm branches and denomination

Date	Mintage	F	VF	XF	Unc	BU
1990 Proof	Est. 200	Value: 500				

KM# 64 20000 FRANCS
31.4700 g., 0.9250 Silver .9359 oz. ASW **Subject:** 35th Anniversary of Guinea Franc **Obv:** Without sword and rifle **Rev:** Woman planting palm tree

Date	Mintage	F	VF	XF	Unc	BU
ND(1995) Proof	Est. 5,000	Value: 40.00				

TRIAL STRIKES

KM#	Date	Mintage	Identification	Mkt Val
TS1	ND(1969)	—	100 Francs. KM#9.	45.00
TS2	ND(1969)	—	200 Francs. KM#11.	45.00
TS3	ND(1969)	—	250 Francs. KM#13.	50.00
TS4	ND(1969)	—	500 Francs. KM#16.	60.00

KM#	Date	Mintage	Identification	Mkt Val
TS5	ND(1969)	—	1000 Francs. Goldine. Jugate heads right.	100

MINT SETS

KM#	Date	Mintage	Identification	Issue Price	Mkt Val
MS1	1977 (6)	—	KM46-51	—	830
MS2	1988 (3)	5,000	KM57-59	150	250

PROOF SETS

KM#	Date	Mintage	Identification	Issue Price	Mkt Val
PS1	1969 (7)	5,000	KM#9-13, 15-16	62.50	145
PS2	1969 (8)	—	KM9, 11, 13, 16-18, 20, 32	—	1,825
PS3	1969 (4)	—	KM#17-20	—	1,310
PS4	1969 (4)	4,000	KM#17, 18, 20, 32	223	1,235
PS5	1969-70 (17)	—	KM#9-21, 29-32	1,326	2,192
PS6	1969-70 (6)	—	KM#12, 14, 18, 21, 30-31	318	530
PS7	1970 (3)	900	KM12, 14, 21	30.00	60.00
PS8	1970 (7)	300	KM#9-13, 15-16	62.50	165
PS9	1970 (7)	750	KM#22-28	201	245
PS10	1970 (7)	—	KM#33-39	440	3,325
PS11	1970 (10)	—	KM#9-16, 21, 29	220	292
PS12	1970 (14)	—	KM#22-28, 33-39	1,650	3,570

GUINEA-BISSAU

The Republic of Guinea-Bissau, formerly Portuguese Guinea, an overseas province on the west coast of Africa between Senegal and Guinea, has an area of 13,948 sq. mi. (36,120sq. km.) and a population of 1.1 million. Capital: Bissau. The country has undeveloped deposits of oil and bauxite. Peanuts, oil-palm kernels and hides are exported.

Portuguese Guinea was discovered by Portuguese navigator, Nuno Tristao, in 1446. Trading rights in the area were granted to Cape Verde islanders but few prominent posts were established before 1851, and they were principally coastal installations. The chief export of this colony's early period was slaves for South America, a practice that adversely affected trade with the native people and retarded subjection of the interior. Territorial disputes with France delayed final demarcation of the colony's frontiers until 1905.

The African Party for the Independence of Guinea-Bissau was founded in 1956, and several years later began a guerrilla warfare that grew in effectiveness until 1974,when the rebels controlled most of the colony. Portugal's costly overseas wars in her African territories resulted in a military coup in Portugal in April 1974, which appreciably brightened the prospects for freedom for Guinea-Bissau. In August 1974, the Lisbon government signed an agreement granting independence to Portuguese Guinea effective Sept. 10, 1974. The new republic took the name of Guinea-Bissau.

RULERS
Portuguese until 1974

PORTUGUESE GUINEA

DECIMAL COINAGE

KM# 1 5 CENTAVOS
Bronze **Obv:** Denomination above date **Rev:** Liberty head left

Date	Mintage	F	VF	XF	Unc	BU
1933	100,000	30.00	60.00	90.00	165	—

KM# 2 10 CENTAVOS
Bronze **Obv:** Denomination above date **Rev:** Liberty head left

Date	Mintage	F	VF	XF	Unc	BU
1933	250,000	28.00	85.00	500	1,000	—

KM# 12 10 CENTAVOS
Aluminum **Obv:** Denomination above date **Rev:** Divided shield with crowned towers and small shields above on lined circle

Date	Mintage	F	VF	XF	Unc	BU
1973	100,000	4.00	8.00	15.00	30.00	40.00

KM# 3 20 CENTAVOS
Bronze **Obv:** Denomination above date **Rev:** Liberty head left

Date	Mintage	F	VF	XF	Unc	BU
1933	350,000	4.00	8.50	35.00	65.00	100

KM# 13 20 CENTAVOS
Bronze **Obv:** Denomination above date **Rev:** Crowned towers and small shields above divided shield on lined circle

Date	Mintage	F	VF	XF	Unc	BU
1973	100,000	3.00	6.00	15.00	30.00	40.00

KM# 4 50 CENTAVOS
Nickel-Bronze **Obv:** Laureate head right **Rev:** Shield on lined circle within wreath

Date	Mintage	F	VF	XF	Unc	BU
1933	600,000	15.00	50.00	200	450	—

KM# 6 50 CENTAVOS
Bronze, 23 mm. **Subject:** 500th Anniversary of Discovery **Obv:** Denomination within circle, dates below **Rev:** Crowned towers above divided shield on lined circle

Date	Mintage	F	VF	XF	Unc	BU
ND(1946)	2,000,000	1.00	3.00	15.00	30.00	40.00

KM# 8 50 CENTAVOS
Bronze **Obv:** Denomination **Rev:** Towers above divided shield on lined circle

Date	Mintage	F	VF	XF	Unc	BU
1952	10,000,000	0.35	0.75	2.00	5.00	8.00

KM# 5 ESCUDO
Nickel-Bronze **Obv:** Laureate head right **Rev:** Shield on lined circle within wreath

Date	Mintage	F	VF	XF	Unc	BU
1933	800,000	7.50	22.50	200	450	—

KM# 7 ESCUDO
Bronze, 27 mm. **Subject:** 500th Anniversary of Discovery **Obv:** Denomination within circle **Rev:** Crowned towers and small shields above divided shield on lined circle

Date	Mintage	F	VF	XF	Unc	BU
ND(1946)	2,000,000	0.75	2.00	6.00	16.00	28.00

KM# 14 ESCUDO
Bronze **Obv:** Denomination **Rev:** Crowned towers and small shields above divided shield on lined circle

Date	Mintage	F	VF	XF	Unc	BU
1973	250,000	6.50	12.50	22.50	40.00	55.00

KM# 9 2-1/2 ESCUDOS
Copper-Nickel **Obv:** Shield on lined circle at center of cross **Rev:** Crowned towers and small shields above divided shield on lined circle

Date	Mintage	F	VF	XF	Unc	BU
1952	3,010,000	0.50	1.50	3.00	7.00	10.00

KM# 15 5 ESCUDOS
Copper-Nickel **Obv:** Shield on lined circle at center of cross **Rev:** Crowned towers and small shields above divided shield on lined circle

Date	Mintage	F	VF	XF	Unc	BU
1973	800,000	2.50	5.00	10.00	20.00	28.00

KM# 10 10 ESCUDOS
5.0000 g., 0.7200 Silver .1157 oz. ASW **Obv:** Shield on lined circle at center of cross **Rev:** Crowned towers and small shields above divided shield on lined circle

Date	Mintage	F	VF	XF	Unc	BU
1952	1,200,000	4.00	18.00	70.00	140	180

KM# 16 10 ESCUDOS
Copper-Nickel **Obv:** Shield on lined circle at center of cross **Rev:** Crowned towers and small shields above divided shield on lined circle

Date	Mintage	F	VF	XF	Unc	BU
1973	1,700,000	3.00	10.00	20.00	40.00	55.00

KM# 11 20 ESCUDOS
10.0000 g., 0.7200 Silver .2315 oz. ASW **Obv:** Shield on lined circle at center of cross, date below **Rev:** Crowned towers and small shields above divided shield on lined circle

Date	Mintage	F	VF	XF	Unc	BU
1952	750,000	6.00	15.00	45.00	90.00	—

REPUBLIC

DECIMAL COINAGE

KM# 17 50 CENTAVOS
Aluminum **Series:** F.A.O. **Obv:** National arms **Rev:** Palm tree left of denomination

Date	Mintage	F	VF	XF	Unc	BU
1977	6,000,000	2.00	3.00	4.50	8.00	10.00

KM# 17a 50 CENTAVOS
6.0000 g., Aluminum-Bronze, 25 mm. **Obv:** National arms **Rev:** Palm tree left of denomination **Note:** Struck on KM#19 planchet.

Date	Mintage	F	VF	XF	Unc	BU
1977	—	—	—	—	—	—

KM# 18 PESO
Aluminum-Bronze **Series:** F.A.O. **Obv:** National arms **Rev:** Denomination below bouquet

Date	Mintage	F	VF	XF	Unc	BU
1977	7,000,000	2.25	3.50	5.50	9.00	12.00

KM# 19 2-1/2 PESOS
Aluminum-Bronze **Series:** F.A.O. **Obv:** National arms **Rev:** Tree divides denomination

Date	Mintage	F	VF	XF	Unc	BU
1977	4,000,000	2.25	4.50	6.50	10.00	15.00

KM# 20 5 PESOS
Copper-Nickel **Series:** F.A.O. **Obv:** National arms **Rev:** Denomination above bouquet

Date	Mintage	F	VF	XF	Unc	BU
1977	6,000,000	2.50	5.00	7.00	11.50	16.00

KM# 21 20 PESOS
Copper-Nickel **Series:** F.A.O. **Obv:** National arms **Rev:** Plants left of denomination

Date	Mintage	F	VF	XF	Unc	BU
1977	2,500,000	4.00	6.50	11.50	18.00	25.00

KM# 28 2000 PESOS
Nickel Plated Steel **Subject:** Olympics **Obv:** National arms **Rev:** Handball player, stylized date in background

Date	Mintage	F	VF	XF	Unc	BU
1991	5,000	—	—	—	17.50	20.00

KM# 38 2000 PESOS
Nickel Plated Steel **Subject:** 50th Anniversary - FAO **Obv:** National arms **Rev:** Pineapple harvest

Date	Mintage	F	VF	XF	Unc	BU
ND(1995)	—	—	—	—	17.50	20.00

KM# 27 10000 PESOS
16.0000 g., 0.9990 Silver .5144 oz. ASW **Subject:** Nuno Tristao - Discovery of Guinea-Bissau **Obv:** National arms **Rev:** Ships landing

Date	Mintage	F	VF	XF	Unc	BU
1991 Proof	—	Value: 35.00				

KM# 29 10000 PESOS
11.9700 g., 0.9990 Silver .3848 oz. ASW **Obv:** National arms **Rev:** Soccer player

Date	Mintage	F	VF	XF	Unc	BU
1991	—	—	—	—	32.00	—

KM# 30 10000 PESOS
19.6700 g., 0.9990 Silver .6324 oz. ASW **Subject:** XXV Olympics **Obv:** National arms **Rev:** Floor exercise, date below

Date	Mintage	F	VF	XF	Unc	BU
1992 Proof	Est. 10,000	Value: 25.00				

KM# 39 10000 PESOS
20.0000 g., 0.9990 Silver 0.6424 oz. ASW **Subject:** European Soccer '94

Date	Mintage	F	VF	XF	Unc	BU
1992 Proof	—	Value: 27.50				

KM# 31 10000 PESOS
15.0000 g., 0.9990 Silver .4823 oz. ASW **Obv:** National arms **Rev:** Elephant standing on Africa

Date	Mintage	F	VF	XF	Unc	BU
1993 Proof	—	Value: 25.00				

KM# 32 10000 PESOS
15.0000 g., 0.9990 Silver .4823 oz. ASW **Subject:** Prehistoric Life **Obv:** National arms **Rev:** Stegosaurus

Date	Mintage	F	VF	XF	Unc	BU
1993 Proof	—	Value: 30.00				

KM# 35 10000 PESOS
16.1000 g., 0.9990 Silver .5177 oz. ASW **Subject:** Prehistoric Life **Obv:** National arms **Rev:** Vulcanodon

Date	Mintage	F	VF	XF	Unc	BU
1994 Proof	—	Value: 45.00				

KM# 25 20000 PESOS
25.0000 g., 0.9990 Silver .8039 oz. ASW **Obv:** Stylized national arms **Rev:** Bust 3/4 right **Rev. Legend:** II CONGRESSO EXTRAORDINARIO

Date	Mintage	F	VF	XF	Unc	BU
ND(1990)	2,000	—	—	—	42.50	—

KM# 26 20000 PESOS
25.0000 g., 0.9990 Silver .8039 oz. ASW **Subject:** 10th Anniversary - L. Cabral Deposed **Obv:** National arms **Rev:** Figure giving speech, soldiers in background

Date	Mintage	F	VF	XF	Unc	BU
1990 Proof	Est. 2,500	Value: 47.50				

KM# 33 20000 PESOS
20.0000 g., 0.9990 Silver .6430 oz. ASW **Subject:** Defense of Nature **Obv:** National arms **Rev:** Elephant

Date	Mintage	F	VF	XF	Unc	BU
1993 Proof	—	Value: 37.50				

KM# 34 20000 PESOS
20.1000 g., 0.9990 Silver .6456 oz. ASW **Obv:** National arms **Rev:** Sailing ship - Passat

Date	Mintage	F	VF	XF	Unc	BU
1993	100	—	—	—	275	—
1993 Proof	—	Value: 37.50				

KM# 36 50000 PESOS
31.4700 g., 0.9250 Silver .9359 oz. ASW **Obv:** National arms **Rev:** Female hippopotamus and calf

Date	Mintage	F	VF	XF	Unc	BU
1996 Proof	Est. 15,000	Value: 60.00				

KM# 37 50000 PESOS
31.4700 g., 0.9250 Silver .9359 oz. ASW **Obv:** National arms **Rev:** Sailing ship - Alvise Da Cadamosto

Date	Mintage	F	VF	XF	Unc	BU
1996 Proof	Est. 10,000	Value: 50.00				

PATTERNS

KM#	Date	Mintage	Identification	Mkt Val
Pn1	1977	—	2-1/2 Pesos. Aluminum. KM#19.	—

PROVAS

Standard metals; stamped

KM#	Date	Mintage	Identification	Issue Price	Mkt Val
Pr1	1933	—	5 Centavos. Bronze. KM#1.	—	30.00
Pr2	1933	—	10 Centavos. Bronze. KM#2.	—	30.00
Pr3	1933	—	20 Centavos. Bronze. KM#3.	—	30.00
Pr4	1933	—	50 Centavos. Nickel-Bronze. KM#4.	—	40.00
Pr5	1933	—	Escudo. Nickel-Bronze. KM#5.	—	45.00
Pr6	1946	—	50 Centavos. Bronze. KM#6.	—	15.00
Pr7	1946	—	Escudo. Bronze. KM#7.	—	15.00
Pr8	1952	—	50 Centavos. Bronze. KM#8.	—	15.00
Pr9	1952	—	2-1/2 Escudos. Copper-Nickel. KM#9.	—	20.00
Pr10	1952	—	10 Escudos. Silver center. KM#10.	—	45.00
Pr11	1952	—	20 Escudos. Silver. KM#11.	—	50.00
Pr12	1973	—	Escudo. Bronze. KM#14.	—	20.00
Pr13	1973	—	10 Escudos. Copper-Nickel. KM#16.	—	25.00

The Cooperative Republic of Guyana, is situated on the northeast coast of South America, has an area of 83,000 sq. mi. (214,970 sq. km.) and a population of 729,000. Capital: Georgetown. The economy is basically agrarian. Sugar, rice and bauxite are exported.

The original area of Essequibo and Demerary, which included present-day Suriname, French Guiana, and parts of Brazil and Venezuela was sighted by Columbus in 1498. The first European settlement was made late in the 16th century by the Dutch, however, the region was claimed for the British by Sir Walter Raleigh during the reign of Elizabeth I. For the next 150 years, possession alternated between the Dutch and the British, with a short interval of French control. The British exercised de facto control after 1796 over the Dutch colonies of Essequibo, Demerary and Berbice. They were not ceded to them by the Dutch until 1814. From 1803 to 1831, Essequibo and Demerary were administered separately from Berbice. The three colonies were united in the British Crown Colony of British Guiana in 1831. British Guiana won internal self-government in 1952 and full independence, under the traditional name of Guyana, on May 26,1966. Guyana became a republic on Feb. 23, 1970. It is a member of the Commonwealth of Nations. The president is the Chief of State. The prime minister is the Head of Government. Guyana is a member of the Caribbean Community and Common Market (CARICOM).

RULERS

British, until 1966

***NOTE**: From 1975-1985 the Franklin Mint produced coinage in up to 3 different qualities. Qualities of issue are designated in ( ) after each date and are defined as follows:

(M) MATTE - Normal circulation strike or a dull finish produced by sandblasting special uncirculated (polish finish) or proof quality dies.

(U) SPECIAL UNCIRCULATED - Polished or proof-like in appearance without any frosted features.

(P) PROOF - The highest quality obtainable having mirror-like fields and frosted features.

BRITISH GUIANA AND WEST INDIES

STERLING COINAGE

KM# 26 4 PENCE
1.8851 g., 0.9250 Silver .0560 oz. ASW **Obv:** Head left **Rev:** Crowned denomination within wreath

Date	Mintage	F	VF	XF	Unc	BU
1901	60,000	3.00	7.50	22.50	55.00	70.00

KM# 27 4 PENCE
1.8851 g., 0.9250 Silver .0560 oz. ASW **Obv:** Crowned bust right **Obv. Designer:** G.W. DeSaulles **Rev:** Crowned denomination within wreath

Date	Mintage	F	VF	XF	Unc	BU
1903	60,000	3.00	7.50	22.50	55.00	70.00
1903 Matte proof	—	Value: 450				
1908	30,000	5.00	12.50	40.00	90.00	100
1909	36,000	5.00	12.50	40.00	90.00	100
1910	66,000	5.00	10.00	40.00	85.00	100

KM# 28 4 PENCE
1.8851 g., 0.9250 Silver .0560 oz. ASW **Obv:** Crowned bust left **Obv. Designer:** E.B. MacKennal **Rev:** Crowned denomination within wreath

Date	Mintage	F	VF	XF	Unc	BU
1911	30,000	8.00	25.00	70.00	115	130
1913	30,000	8.00	25.00	70.00	115	130
1916	30,000	8.00	25.00	70.00	115	130

BRITISH GUIANA

STERLING COINAGE

KM# 29 4 PENCE
1.8851 g., 0.9250 Silver .0560 oz. ASW **Obv:** Crowned bust left **Obv. Designer:** E.B. MacKennal **Rev:** Crowned denomination within wreath

Date	Mintage	F	VF	XF	Unc	BU
1917	72,000	5.00	12.50	40.00	90.00	100
1917 Matte proof	—	Value: 450				
1918	210,000	1.25	3.50	15.00	55.00	65.00
1921	90,000	5.00	10.00	27.50	70.00	85.00
1923	12,000	20.00	45.00	85.00	160	180
1925	30,000	8.00	20.00	50.00	100	125
1926	30,000	8.00	20.00	50.00	100	125
1931	15,000	10.00	25.00	60.00	120	140
1931 Proof	—	Value: 175				
1935	36,000	3.00	12.50	50.00	175	200
1935 Proof	—	Value: 175				
1936	63,000	1.75	2.50	10.00	30.00	45.00
1936 Proof	—	Value: 225				

KM# 30 4 PENCE
1.8851 g., 0.9250 Silver .0560 oz. ASW **Obv:** Crowned head left **Obv. Designer:** Percy Metcalf **Rev:** Crowned denomination within wreath

Date	Mintage	F	VF	XF	Unc	BU
1938	30,000	8.00	20.00	50.00	100	125
1938 Proof	—	Value: 175				
1939	48,000	1.75	2.50	7.50	20.00	30.00
1939 Proof	—	Value: 175				
1940	90,000	1.25	2.00	3.50	18.50	25.00
1940 Proof	—	Value: 175				
1941	120,000	1.25	1.75	3.00	12.50	17.50
1941 Proof	—	Value: 175				
1942	180,000	1.25	1.75	3.00	12.50	17.50
1942 Proof	—	Value: 175				
1943	240,000	1.25	1.75	2.50	8.00	12.00
1943 Proof	—	Value: 400				

KM# 30a 4 PENCE
1.8851 g., 0.5000 Silver .0303 oz. ASW **Obv:** Head left **Obv. Designer:** Percy Metcalf **Rev:** Crowned denomination within wreath

Date	Mintage	F	VF	XF	Unc	BU
1944	90,000	0.85	1.25	2.50	8.00	10.00
1945	120,000	0.65	1.00	2.00	7.00	9.00
1945 Proof	—	Value: 200				

REPUBLIC

DECIMAL COINAGE

KM# 31 CENT
Nickel-Brass **Obv:** Denomination within circle **Rev:** Stylized lotus flower

Date	Mintage	F	VF	XF	Unc	BU
1967	6,000,000	—	—	0.10	0.25	0.35
1967 Proof	5,100	Value: 2.00				
1969	4,000,000	—	—	0.10	0.25	0.35
1970	6,000,000	—	—	0.10	0.25	0.35
1971	4,000,000	—	—	0.10	0.25	0.35
1972	4,000,000	—	—	0.10	0.25	0.35
1973	4,000,000	—	—	0.10	0.25	0.35
1974	11,000,000	—	—	0.10	0.20	0.30
1975	—	—	—	0.10	0.25	0.35
1976	—	—	—	0.10	0.25	0.35
1977	16,000,000	—	—	0.10	0.20	0.30
1978	10,450,000	—	—	0.10	0.20	0.30
1979	—	—	—	0.10	0.20	0.30
1980	12,000,000	—	—	0.10	0.20	0.30
1981	10,000,000	—	—	0.10	0.20	0.30
1982	8,000,000	—	—	0.10	0.20	0.30
1983	12,000,000	—	—	0.10	0.20	0.30
1985	8,000,000	—	—	0.10	0.20	0.30

Date	Mintage	F	VF	XF	Unc	BU
1987	6,000,000	—	—	0.10	0.20	0.30
1988	80,000	—	—	0.15	0.50	0.75
1989	—	—	—	0.10	0.20	0.30
1991	—	—	—	0.10	0.20	0.30
1992	—	—	—	0.10	0.20	0.30

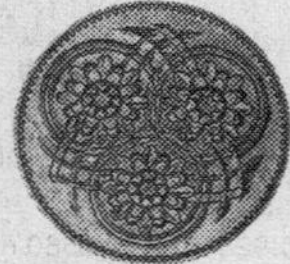

KM# 37 CENT

Nickel-Brass, 16 mm. **Subject:** 10th Anniversary of Independence **Obv:** Helmeted and supported arms **Rev:** Manatee

Date	Mintage	F	VF	XF	Unc	BU
1976FM (M)	15,000	—	—	0.15	1.00	3.00
1976FM (U)	50	—	—	—	—	—
1976FM (P)	28,000	Value: 1.50				
1977FM (M)	—	—	—	—	3.00	4.50
1977FM (U)	15,000	—	—	0.20	1.00	3.00
1977FM (P)	7,215	Value: 1.50				
1978FM (M)	—	—	—	—	3.00	4.50
1978FM (U)	15,000	—	—	0.20	1.00	3.00
1978FM (P)	5,044	Value: 1.50				
1979FM (U)	15,000	—	—	0.20	1.00	3.00
1979FM (P)	3,547	Value: 1.50				
1980FM (U)	30,000	—	—	0.20	1.00	3.00
1980FM (P)	2,763	Value: 1.75				

KM# 32 5 CENTS

Nickel-Brass, 19.5 mm. **Obv:** Denomination within circle **Rev:** Stylized lotus flower **Note:** Varieties exist.

Date	Mintage	F	VF	XF	Unc	BU
1967	4,600,000	—	—	0.10	0.30	0.40
1967 Proof	5,100	Value: 2.00				
1972	1,200,000	—	—	0.10	0.35	0.45
1974	3,000,000	—	—	0.10	0.35	0.45
1975	—	—	—	0.10	0.35	0.45
1976	—	—	—	0.10	0.35	0.45
1977	1,500,000	—	—	0.10	0.35	0.45
1978	2,000	—	—	1.25	4.00	6.00
1979	—	—	—	0.30	1.00	1.50
1980	1,000,000	—	—	0.10	0.35	0.45
1981	1,000,000	—	—	0.10	0.35	0.45
1982	2,000,000	—	—	0.10	0.30	0.40
1985	3,000,000	—	—	0.10	0.30	0.40
1986	4,000,000	—	—	0.10	0.30	0.40
1987	3,000,000	—	—	0.10	0.30	0.40
1988	2,000,000	—	—	0.10	0.30	0.40
1989	—	—	—	0.10	0.30	0.40
1990	—	—	—	0.10	0.30	0.40
1991	—	—	—	0.10	0.30	0.40
1992	—	—	—	0.10	0.30	0.40

KM# 38 5 CENTS

Nickel-Brass, 19.5 mm. **Subject:** 10th Anniversary of Independence **Obv:** Helmeted and supported arms **Rev:** Jaguar (panthera onca)

Date	Mintage	F	VF	XF	Unc	BU
1976FM (M)	15,000	—	—	0.20	1.75	5.00
1976FM (U)	50	—	—	—	—	—
1976FM (P)	28,000	Value: 1.75				
1977FM (M)	—	—	—	—	3.00	5.00
1977FM (U)	15,000	—	—	0.20	1.75	5.00
1977FM (P)	7,215	Value: 2.00				
1978FM (M)	—	—	—	—	5.00	6.50
1978FM (U)	15,000	—	—	0.20	1.75	5.00
1978FM (P)	5,044	Value: 2.00				
1979FM (U)	15,000	—	—	0.20	1.75	5.00
1979FM (P)	3,547	Value: 2.25				
1980FM (U)	30,000	—	—	0.20	1.75	5.00
1980FM (P)	2,763	Value: 2.50				

KM# 33 10 CENTS

Copper-Nickel **Obv:** Denomination within circle **Rev:** Helmeted and supported arms

Date	Mintage	F	VF	XF	Unc	BU
1967	4,000,000	—	0.10	0.20	0.35	0.50
1967 Proof	5,100	Value: 2.50				
1973	1,500,000	—	0.10	0.20	0.40	0.60
1974	1,700,000	—	0.10	0.20	0.40	0.60
1976	—	—	0.10	0.20	0.40	0.60
1977	4,000,000	—	0.10	0.20	0.40	0.60
1978	2,010,000	—	0.10	0.20	0.40	0.60
1979	—	—	0.10	0.20	0.40	0.60
1980	1,000,000	—	0.10	0.20	0.40	0.60
1981	1,000,000	—	0.10	0.20	0.40	0.60
1982	2,000,000	—	0.10	0.20	0.35	0.50
1985	3,000,000	—	0.10	0.20	0.35	0.50
1986	4,000,000	—	0.10	0.20	0.35	0.50
1987	3,000,000	—	0.10	0.20	0.35	0.50
1988	2,000,000	—	0.10	0.20	0.35	0.50
1989	—	—	0.10	0.20	0.35	0.50
1990	—	—	0.10	0.20	0.35	0.50
1991	—	—	0.10	0.20	0.35	0.50
1992	—	—	0.10	0.20	0.35	0.50

KM# 39 10 CENTS

Copper-Nickel, 18 mm. **Subject:** 10th Anniversary of Independence **Obv:** Helmeted and supported arms **Rev:** Squirrel Monkey

Date	Mintage	F	VF	XF	Unc	BU
1976	2,006,000	—	—	0.25	1.50	3.00
1976FM (M)	10,000	—	—	0.25	1.50	3.00
1976FM (U)	50	—	—	—	—	—
1976FM (P)	28,000	Value: 3.00				
1977	1,500,000	—	—	0.25	1.50	3.00
1977FM (M)	—	—	—	—	8.00	10.00
1977FM (U)	10,000	—	—	0.25	1.50	3.00
1977FM (P)	7,215	Value: 3.00				
1978FM (M)	—	—	—	—	8.00	10.00
1978FM (U)	10,000	—	—	0.25	1.50	3.00
1978FM (P)	5,044	Value: 3.00				
1979FM (U)	10,000	—	—	0.25	1.50	3.00
1979FM (P)	3,547	Value: 3.00				
1980FM (U)	20,000	—	—	0.25	1.50	3.00
1980FM (P)	2,763	Value: 4.00				

KM# 34 25 CENTS

Copper-Nickel **Obv:** Denomination within circle **Rev:** Helmeted and supported arms

Date	Mintage	F	VF	XF	Unc	BU
1967	3,500,000	—	0.15	0.25	0.60	0.75
1967 Proof	5,100	Value: 2.50				
1972	1,000,000	—	0.15	0.25	0.65	0.85
1974	4,000,000	—	0.15	0.25	0.65	0.85
1975	—	—	0.15	0.25	0.65	0.85
1976	—	—	0.15	0.25	0.65	0.85
1977	4,000,000	—	0.15	0.25	0.65	0.85
1978	2,006,000	—	0.15	0.25	0.65	0.85
1981	1,000,000	—	0.15	0.25	0.65	0.85
1982	1,500,000	—	0.15	0.25	0.65	0.85
1984	1,000,000	—	0.15	0.25	0.65	0.85
1985	2,000,000	—	0.15	0.25	0.60	0.75
1986	4,000,000	—	0.15	0.25	0.60	0.75
1987	3,000,000	—	0.15	0.25	0.60	0.75
1988	4,000,000	—	0.15	0.25	0.60	0.75
1989	—	—	0.15	0.25	0.60	0.75
1990	—	—	0.15	0.25	0.60	0.75
1991	—	—	0.15	0.25	0.60	0.75
1992	—	—	0.15	0.25	0.60	0.75

KM# 40 25 CENTS

Copper-Nickel, 21.5 mm. **Subject:** 10th Anniversary of Independence **Obv:** Helmeted and supported arms **Rev:** Harpy Eagle

Date	Mintage	F	VF	XF	Unc	BU
1976FM (M)	4,000	—	—	0.30	2.50	3.50
1976FM (U)	50	—	—	—	—	—
1976FM (P)	28,000	Value: 3.00				
1977	2,000,000	—	0.15	0.25	2.00	3.50
1977FM (M)	—	—	—	—	10.00	12.00
1977FM (U)	4,000	—	—	0.30	4.00	5.00
1977FM (P)	7,215	Value: 3.00				
1978FM (M)	—	—	—	—	10.00	12.00
1978FM (U)	4,000	—	—	0.30	4.00	5.00
1978FM (P)	5,044	Value: 3.50				
1979FM (U)	4,000	—	—	0.30	4.00	5.00
1979FM (P)	3,547	Value: 3.50				
1980FM (U)	8,437	—	—	0.30	4.00	5.00
1980FM (P)	2,763	Value: 4.50				

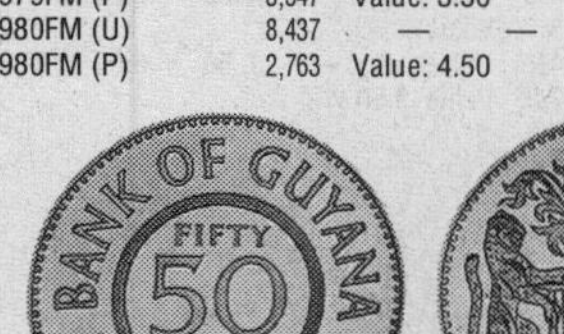

KM# 35 50 CENTS

Copper-Nickel **Obv:** Denomination within circle **Rev:** Helmeted and supported arms

Date	Mintage	F	VF	XF	Unc	BU
1967	1,000,000	—	0.25	0.35	0.75	1.25
1967 Proof	5,100	Value: 3.50				

KM# 41 50 CENTS

Copper-Nickel, 25 mm. **Subject:** 10th Anniversary of Independence **Obv:** Helmeted and supported arms **Rev:** Hoatzin

Date	Mintage	F	VF	XF	Unc	BU
1976FM (M)	2,000	—	—	0.40	5.00	6.00
1976FM (U)	50	—	—	—	—	—
1976FM (P)	28,000	Value: 4.00				
1977FM (M)	—	—	—	—	20.00	22.50
1977FM (U)	2,000	—	—	0.40	5.00	6.00
1977FM (P)	7,215	Value: 4.00				
1978FM (M)	—	—	—	—	20.00	22.50
1978FM (U)	2,000	—	—	0.40	5.00	6.00
1978FM (P)	5,044	Value: 4.50				
1979FM (U)	2,000	—	—	0.40	5.00	6.00
1979FM (P)	3,547	Value: 4.50				
1980FM (U)	4,437	—	—	0.40	3.50	5.00
1980FM (P)	2,763	Value: 5.50				

KM# 36 DOLLAR

Copper-Nickel, 35.5 mm. **Series:** F.A.O. **Obv:** Bulls head left of denomination **Rev:** Head left **Rev. Designer:** Patrick Munroe **Note:** Cuffy, slave who organized a revolt on 23 Feb. 1763, which was the first step towards independence.

Date	Mintage	F	VF	XF	Unc	BU
1970	500,000	—	0.50	1.75	4.00	5.00
1970 Proof	5,000	Value: 6.00				

KM# 42 DOLLAR

Copper-Nickel, 35.5 mm. **Series:** F.A.O. **Subject:** 10th Anniversary of Independence **Obv:** Helmeted and supported arms **Rev:** Common Caiman

Date	Mintage	F	VF	XF	Unc	BU
1976FM (M)	600	—	—	0.50	6.00	7.00
1976FM (U)	50	—	—	—	—	—
1976FM (P)	28,000	Value: 7.00				
1977FM (M)	—	—	—	—	30.00	32.50
1977FM (U)	500	—	—	0.50	6.00	7.00
1977FM (P)	7,215	Value: 7.50				

Date	Mintage	F	VF	XF	Unc	BU
1978FM (M)	—	—	—	—	30.00	32.50
1978FM (U)	500	—	—	0.50	6.00	7.00
1978FM (P)	5,044	Value: 8.00				
1979FM (U)	500	—	—	0.50	6.00	7.00
1979FM (P)	3,547	Value: 8.00				
1980FM (U)	1,437	—	—	0.50	6.00	7.00
1980FM (P)	2,763	Value: 8.50				

KM# 50 DOLLAR
2.4000 g., Copper Plated Steel, 17 mm. **Obv:** Helmeted and supported arms **Rev:** Hand gathering rice **Rev. Designer:** Jean Thomas

Date	Mintage	F	VF	XF	Unc	BU
1996	—	—	—	—	0.50	0.65

KM# 43 5 DOLLARS
Copper-Nickel **Subject:** 10th Anniversary of Independence **Obv:** Helmeted and supported arms **Rev:** Head at right facing

Date	Mintage	F	VF	XF	Unc	BU
1976FM (M)	400	—	—	—	15.00	17.50
1976FM (U)	150	—	—	—	17.50	20.00
1977FM (M)	—	—	—	—	45.00	50.00
1977FM (U)	100	—	—	—	25.00	27.50
1978FM (M)	—	—	—	—	45.00	50.00
1978FM (U)	100	—	—	—	25.00	27.50
1979FM (U)	100	—	—	—	25.00	27.50
1980FM (U)	200	—	—	—	15.00	17.50

KM# 43a 5 DOLLARS
37.3000 g., 0.5000 Silver .5996 oz. ASW **Obv:** Helmeted and supported arms **Rev:** Head at right facing

Date	Mintage	F	VF	XF	Unc	BU
1976FM (P)	18,000	Value: 9.00				
1977FM (P)	5,685	Value: 10.00				
1978FM (P)	3,825	Value: 12.00				
1979FM (P)	2,665	Value: 15.00				
1980FM (P)	2,763	Value: 15.00				

KM# 51 5 DOLLARS
3.7500 g., Copper Plated Steel, 20.5 mm. **Obv:** Helmeted and supported arms **Rev:** Sugar cane **Rev. Designer:** Selayn Cambridge

Date	Mintage	F	VF	XF	Unc	BU
1996	—	—	—	—	0.75	1.00

KM# 44 10 DOLLARS
Copper-Nickel **Subject:** 10th Anniversary of Independence **Obv:** Helmeted and supported arms **Rev:** Head at left looking right

Date	Mintage	F	VF	XF	Unc	BU
1976FM (M)	300	—	—	—	30.00	40.00
1976FM (U)	300	—	—	—	30.00	40.00
1977FM (M)	—	—	—	—	80.00	100
1977FM (U)	100	—	—	—	50.00	60.00
1978FM (M)	—	—	—	—	80.00	90.00
1978FM (U)	100	—	—	—	50.00	60.00
1979FM (U)	100	—	—	—	50.00	60.00
1980FM (U)	200	—	—	—	40.00	50.00

KM# 44a 10 DOLLARS
43.2300 g., 0.9250 Silver 1.2856 oz. ASW **Subject:** 10th Anniversary of Independence **Obv:** Helmeted and supported arms **Rev:** Head at left looking right

Date	Mintage	F	VF	XF	Unc	BU
1976FM (P)	18,000	Value: 18.50				
1977FM (P)	5,685	Value: 20.00				
1978FM (P)	3,825	Value: 22.50				
1979FM (P)	2,665	Value: 25.00				
1980FM (P)	2,763	Value: 25.00				

KM# 52 10 DOLLARS
5.0000 g., Nickel Plated Steel, 23 mm. **Obv:** Helmeted and supported arms **Rev:** Gold mining scene **Rev. Designer:** Ignatias Adams **Edge:** Plain **Shape:** 7-sided

Date	Mintage	F	VF	XF	Unc	BU
1996	—	—	—	—	1.25	1.50

KM# 45 50 DOLLARS
48.3000 g., 0.9250 Silver 1.4365 oz. ASW **Subject:** 10th Anniversary of Independence **Rev:** Enmoe Martyrs

Date	Mintage	F	VF	XF	Unc	BU
1976FM (U)	100	—	—	—	100	120
1976FM (P)	1,001	Value: 70.00				

KM# 48 50 DOLLARS
28.2800 g., 0.9250 Silver .8411 oz. ASW **Subject:** Royal Visit **Rev:** Small portraits of royals above people welcoming the royal ship

Date	Mintage	F	VF	XF	Unc	BU
1994 Proof	—	Value: 50.00				

KM# 46 100 DOLLARS
5.7400 g., 0.5000 Gold .0923 oz. AGW **Subject:** 10th Anniversary of Independence **Obv:** Helmeted and supported arms **Rev:** Arawak Indian

Date	Mintage	F	VF	XF	Unc	BU
1976FM (U)	100	—	—	—	95.00	110
1976FM (P)	21,000	Value: 75.00				

KM# 47 100 DOLLARS
5.5800 g., 0.5000 Gold .0897 oz. AGW **Obv:** Helmeted and supported arms **Rev:** Legendary Golden Man

Date	Mintage	F	VF	XF	Unc	BU
1977FM (U)	100	—	—	—	100	115
1977FM (P)	7,635	Value: 80.00				

KM# 49 500 DOLLARS
47.5400 g., 0.9170 Gold 1.4017 oz. AGW **Subject:** Royal Visit **Obv:** Small portraits left of royals above people welcoming the royal ship

Date	Mintage	F	VF	XF	Unc	BU
1994 Proof	100	Value: 1,100				

KM# 53 2000 DOLLARS
28.5000 g., 0.9250 Silver, 38.6 mm. **Subject:** Millennium **Obv:** Helmeted and supported arms **Rev:** World globe and radiant sun within circle **Edge:** Plain **Shape:** 12-sided

Date	Mintage	F	VF	XF	Unc	BU
ND(1999) Proof	Est. 30,000	Value: 45.00				

KM# 53a 2000 DOLLARS
28.5000 g., Copper-Nickel, 38.6 mm. **Subject:** Millennium **Obv:** National arms **Rev:** World globe and radiant sun **Edge:** Plain **Shape:** 12-sided

Date	Mintage	F	VF	XF	Unc	BU
ND(1999)	—	—	—	—	15.00	—

PATTERNS

Including off metal strikes

KM#	Date	Mintage	Identification	Mkt Val
Pn1	1967	—	5 Cents. Silver. KM#32.	—

MINT SETS

KM#	Date	Mintage	Identification	Issue Price	Mkt Val
MS1	1977 (8)	—	KM#37-44	—	150
MS2	1978 (8)	—	KM#37-44	—	150

PROOF SETS

KM#	Date	Mintage	Identification	Issue Price	Mkt Val
PS1	1967 (5)	5,100	KM#31-35	10.50	9.00
PS2	1976 (8)	17,536	KM#37-42, 43a, 44a	45.00	37.50
PS3	1976 (6)	10,302	KM#37-42	15.00	17.00
PS4	1977 (8)	5,685	KM#37-42, 43a, 44a	45.00	42.00
PS5	1977 (6)	1,530	KM#37-42	15.00	20.00
PS6	1978 (8)	3,825	KM#37-42, 43a, 44a	47.50	47.50
PS7	1978 (6)	1,219	KM#37-42	16.00	20.00
PS8	1979 (8)	2,665	KM#37-42, 43a, 44a	47.50	52.00
PS9	1979 (6)	882	KM#37-42	16.00	20.00
PS10	1980 (8)	1,900	KM#37-42, 43a, 44a	100	58.00
PS11	1980 (6)	863	KM#37-42	19.00	22.50

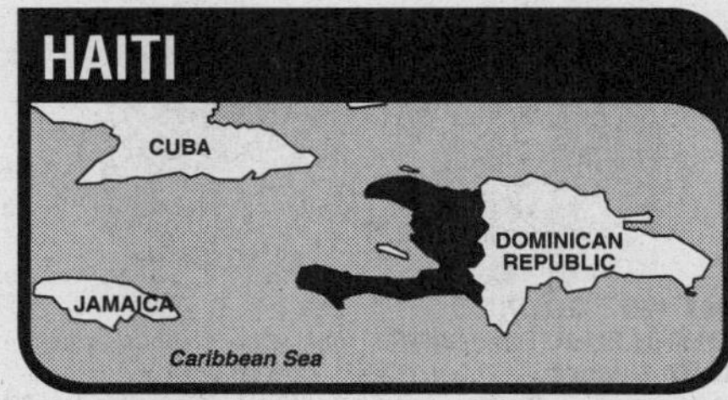

The Republic of Haiti, which occupies the western one-third of the island of Hispaniola in the Caribbean Sea between Puerto Rico and Cuba, has an area of 10,714 sq. mi. (27,750 sq. km.) and a population of 6.5 million. Capital: Port-au-Prince. The economy is based on agriculture; but light manufacturing and tourism are increasingly important. Coffee, bauxite, sugar, essential oils and handicrafts are exported.

Columbus discovered Hispaniola in 1492. Spain colonized the island, making Santo Domingo the base for exploration of the Western Hemisphere. The area that is now Haiti was ceded to France by Spain in 1697. Slaves brought from Africa to work the coffee and sugar cane plantations made it one of the richest colonies of the French Empire. A slave revolt in the 1790's led to the establishment of the Republic of Haiti in 1804, making it the oldest Black republic in the world and the second oldest republic (after the United States) in the Western Hemisphere.

The French language is used on Haitian coins although it is spoken by only about 10% of the populace. A form of Creole is the language of the Haitians.

MINT MARKS

A - Paris
(a) - Paris, privy marks only
HEATON - Birmingham
R - Rome
(w) = Waterbury (Connecticut, USA) (Scoville Mfg. Co.)
(p) – Philadelphia (U.S.A. mint)

MONETARY SYSTEM

100 Centimes = 1 Gourde

REPUBLIC
1863 -
DECIMAL COINAGE

100 Centimes = 1 Gourde

KM# 53 5 CENTIMES

Copper-Nickel **Obv:** President Pierre Nord Alexis left **Rev:** National arms

Date	Mintage	F	VF	XF	Unc	BU
1904(w)	2,000,000	1.00	4.00	10.00	25.00	30.00
1904(w) Proof	—	Value: 90.00				
1905(w)	20,000,000	0.75	3.00	10.00	25.00	30.00
1905(w) Proof	—	Value: 100				

KM# 52 5 CENTIMES

Copper-Nickel **Obv:** National arms **Rev:** Denomination above date **Note:** Struck at the Scovill Mfg. Co., Waterbury, Connecticut; design incorporates Paris privy and mint director's marks.

Date	Mintage	F	VF	XF	Unc	BU
1904(w)	—	3.00	10.00	20.00	55.00	65.00
1904(w) Proof	—	Value: 120				

KM# 57 5 CENTIMES

Copper-Nickel **Obv:** President Dumarsais Estime left **Rev:** National arms

Date	Mintage	F	VF	XF	Unc	BU
1949(p)	10,000,000	0.25	0.75	2.00	6.00	7.50

KM# 59 5 CENTIMES

Nickel-Silver **Obv:** President Paul Eugene Magloire left

Date	Mintage	F	VF	XF	Unc	BU
1953(p)	3,000,000	0.25	0.35	0.65	1.50	2.00

KM# 62 5 CENTIMES

Copper-Nickel, 20 mm. **Obv:** President Francois Duvalier left **Rev:** National arms **Designer:** Gilroy Roberts

Date	Mintage	F	VF	XF	Unc	BU
1958(p)	15,000,000	—	—	0.10	0.25	0.50
1970	5,000,000	—	—	0.10	0.20	0.45

KM# 119 5 CENTIMES

Copper-Nickel **Series:** F.A.O. **Obv:** President Jean-Claude Duvalier left **Rev:** National arms

Date	Mintage	F	VF	XF	Unc	BU
1975	16,000,000	—	—	0.10	0.20	0.45

KM# 145 5 CENTIMES

Copper-Nickel **Series:** F.A.O. **Obv:** Head right, small logo at left **Rev:** Woman and child **Note:** Denomination as 0.05 Gourdes.

Date	Mintage	F	VF	XF	Unc	BU
1981R	15,000	—	0.10	0.75	1.00	1.50

KM# 154 5 CENTIMES

3.1000 g., Nickel-Plated Steel, 19.9 mm. **Subject:** Charlemagne Peralte, national hero **Obv:** Bust facing **Rev:** National arms

Date	Mintage	F	VF	XF	Unc	BU
1995	—	—	—	—	0.25	0.40

KM# 154a 5 CENTIMES

Nickel Plated Steel **Subject:** Charlemagne Peralte, national hero **Obv:** Bust facing **Rev:** National arms

Date	Mintage	F	VF	XF	Unc	BU
1995	—	—	—	—	0.35	0.50
1997	—	—	—	—	0.35	0.50

KM# 54 10 CENTIMES

Copper-Nickel **Obv:** President Pierre Nord Alexis left **Rev:** National arms

Date	Mintage	F	VF	XF	Unc	BU
1906(w)	10,000,000	1.00	3.00	7.00	20.00	25.00
1906(w) Proof	—	Value: 100				

KM# 58 10 CENTIMES

Copper-Nickel **Obv:** President Dumarsais Estime left **Rev:** National arms

Date	Mintage	F	VF	XF	Unc	BU
1949(p)	5,000,000	0.50	2.00	6.00	15.00	17.50

KM# 60 10 CENTIMES

Nickel-Silver **Obv:** President Paul Eugene Magloire left **Rev:** National arms

Date	Mintage	F	VF	XF	Unc	BU
1953(p)	1,500,000	—	0.25	1.00	5.00	7.50

KM# 63 10 CENTIMES

Copper-Nickel, 22.5 mm. **Obv:** President Francois Duvalier left **Rev:** National arms **Designer:** Gilroy Roberts

Date	Mintage	F	VF	XF	Unc	BU
1958(p)	7,500,000	—	0.10	0.15	0.35	0.50
1970	2,500,000	—	—	0.10	0.20	0.40

KM# 120 10 CENTIMES

Copper-Nickel **Series:** F.A.O. **Obv:** President Jean-Claude Duvalier left **Rev:** National arms

Date	Mintage	F	VF	XF	Unc	BU
1975	12,000,000	—	—	0.10	0.20	0.40
1983	2,000,000	—	—	0.10	0.30	0.50

KM# 146 10 CENTIMES

Copper-Nickel **Series:** F.A.O. **Obv:** Head right, small logo at left **Rev:** Sun above farmer in field on tractor **Note:** Denomination as 0.10 Gourdes.

Date	Mintage	F	VF	XF	Unc	BU
1981R	15,000	—	0.10	0.35	1.00	1.25

KM# 55 20 CENTIMES

Copper-Nickel **Obv:** President Pierre Nord Alexis left **Rev:** National arms

Date	Mintage	F	VF	XF	Unc	BU
1907(w)	5,000,000	2.00	6.00	15.00	35.00	40.00
1907(w) Proof	—	Value: 125				
1908(w)	—	—	—	—	—	—

Note: Reported, not confirmed

KM# 61 20 CENTIMES

Nickel-Silver **Obv:** President Paul Eugene Magliore left **Rev:** National arms

Date	Mintage	F	VF	XF	Unc	BU
1956(p)	2,500,000	0.60	1.00	2.00	5.00	6.50

KM# 77 20 CENTIMES

Nickel-Silver **Obv:** President Francois Duvalier left **Rev:** National arms

Date	Mintage	F	VF	XF	Unc	BU
1970	1,000,000	—	0.25	0.35	0.85	1.00

KM# 100 20 CENTIMES

Copper-Nickel, 26 mm. **Series:** F.A.O. **Obv:** President Jean-Claude Duvalier left **Rev:** National arms

Date	Mintage	F	VF	XF	Unc	BU
1972	1,500,000	—	0.10	0.25	1.00	1.25
1975	4,000,000	—	0.10	0.20	0.85	1.00
1983	1,500,000	—	0.10	0.20	0.85	1.00

KM# 147 20 CENTIMES

Copper-Nickel, 26.2 mm. **Series:** F.A.O. **Obv:** Head right, small logo at left **Rev:** Harvesters **Note:** Denomination as 0.20 Gourdes.

Date	Mintage	F	VF	XF	Unc	BU
1981R	15,000	—	0.10	0.45	1.25	1.40

KM# 152 20 CENTIMES

Copper-Nickel, 26.2 mm. **Subject:** Charlemagne Peralte, national hero **Obv:** Bust facing **Rev:** National arms **Note:** No accent marks on obverse legend.

Date	Mintage	F	VF	XF	Unc	BU
1986	2,500,000	—	0.10	0.20	0.65	0.95
1989	—	—	0.10	0.20	0.65	0.95
1991	—	—	0.10	0.20	0.65	0.95

KM# 152a 20 CENTIMES

Nickel Plated Steel, 26.2 mm. **Subject:** Charlemagne Peralte, national hero **Obv:** Bust facing **Rev:** National arms **Note:** Accent marks on E and Is in obverse legend.

Date	Mintage	F	VF	XF	Unc	BU
1995	—	—	—	—	0.75	1.00
2000	—	—	—	—	0.75	1.00

KM# 56 50 CENTIMES

Copper-Nickel, 29 mm. **Obv:** President Pierre Nord Alexis left **Rev:** National arms

Date	Mintage	F	VF	XF	Unc	BU
1907(w)	2,000,000	1.00	5.50	15.00	45.00	50.00
1907(w) Proof	—	Value: 250				
1908(w)	800,000	1.25	6.00	15.00	45.00	50.00
1908(w) Proof	—	Value: 300				

KM# 101 50 CENTIMES

Copper-Nickel **Series:** F.A.O. **Obv:** President Jean-Claude Duvalier left **Rev:** National arms

Date	Mintage	F	VF	XF	Unc	BU
1972	600,000	—	0.10	0.25	1.50	2.00

KM# 101a 50 CENTIMES

Copper-Nickel-Zinc **Obv:** Head left **Rev:** National arms **Note:** Varieties exist.

Date	Mintage	F	VF	XF	Unc	BU
1975	1,200,000	—	0.10	0.20	1.00	1.50
1979	2,000,000	—	0.10	0.20	1.00	1.50
1983	1,000,000	—	0.10	0.20	1.00	1.50
1985	—	—	—	—	0.75	1.00

KM# 148 50 CENTIMES

Copper-Nickel **Series:** F.A.O. **Obv:** Head right, small logo at left **Rev:** Plants **Note:** Denomination as 0.50 Gourdes.

Date	Mintage	F	VF	XF	Unc	BU
1981R	15,000	—	0.15	0.65	1.75	2.00

KM# 153 50 CENTIMES

8.4000 g., Copper-Nickel, 29 mm. **Subject:** Charlemagne Peralte, national hero **Obv:** Bust facing **Rev:** National arms **Note:** No accent marks on obverse legend.

Date	Mintage	F	VF	XF	Unc	BU
1986	2,000,000	—	0.10	0.25	1.00	1.50
1989	—	—	0.10	0.25	1.00	1.50
1991	—	—	0.10	0.25	1.00	1.50

RÉPUBLIQUE D'HAÏTI 1995 LIBERTÉ · ÉGALITÉ · FRATERNITÉ 50

KM# 153a 50 CENTIMES

Nickel Plated Steel, 29 mm. **Subject:** Charlemagne Peralte, national hero **Obv:** Bust facing **Rev:** National arms **Note:** Accent marks on obverse legend.

Date	Mintage	F	VF	XF	Unc	BU
1995	—	—	0.10	0.25	1.25	1.50
1999	—	—	0.10	0.25	1.25	1.50

KM# 155 GOURDE

6.3000 g., Brass Plated Steel, 23 mm. **Obv:** National arms **Shape:** 7-sided

Date	Mintage	F	VF	XF	Unc	BU
1995	—	—	—	—	1.75	2.00

KM# 64.1 5 GOURDES

23.5200 g., 0.9990 Silver .7555 oz. ASW **Series:** 10th Anniversary of Revolution **Subject:** Columbus Discovers America **Obv:** Three ships and map **Rev:** National arms

Date	Mintage	F	VF	XF	Unc	BU
1967 IC Proof	4,650	Value: 11.50				
1968 IC Proof	5,750	Value: 11.50				
1969 IC Proof	1,175	Value: 20.00				
1970 IC Proof	2,060	Value: 18.00				

KM# 64.2 5 GOURDES

23.5200 g., 0.9990 Silver .7555 oz. ASW **Series:** 10th Anniversary of the Revolution **Subject:** Columbus Discovers America **Obv:** Three ships and map **Rev:** Additional "1 AR" countermark at 8 o'clock

Date	Mintage	F	VF	XF	Unc	BU
1970 Proof	—	Value: 25.00				

KM# 78 5 GOURDES

23.5200 g., 0.9990 Silver .7555 oz. ASW **Rev:** Haitienne paradise

Date	Mintage	F	VF	XF	Unc	BU
1971 IC Proof	1,585	Value: 60.00				

KM# 156 5 GOURDES

9.2000 g., Brass Plated Steel, 28 mm. **Obv:** Four portraits in circle of Haitian statesmen top: Gen. Tonsaint Louverture, Left: Henri Christophe, Right: Jean Jacques Dessalines, Bottom: Alexandre Petion, date below **Rev:** National arms **Shape:** 7-sided

Date	Mintage	F	VF	XF	Unc	BU
1995	—	—	—	—	2.75	3.00

KM# 65.1 10 GOURDES

47.0500 g., 0.9990 Silver 1.5113 oz. ASW **Series:** 10th Anniversary of Revolution **Subject:** General Toussaint L'Overture **Obv:** Figure on rearing horse left **Rev:** National arms

Date	Mintage	F	VF	XF	Unc	BU
1967 IC Proof	6,750	Value: 22.00				
1968 IC Proof	5,725	Value: 22.00				
1969 IC Proof	1,100	Value: 30.00				
1970 IC Proof	1,500	Value: 30.00				

KM# 65.2 10 GOURDES

47.0500 g., 0.9990 Silver 1.5113 oz. ASW **Series:** 10th Anniversary of the Revolution **Subject:** General Toussaint L'Overture **Obv:** Figure on rearing horse left **Rev:** National arms **Note:** Rev; Additional"1 AR" countermark left of the initials "IC"

Date	Mintage	F	VF	XF	Unc	BU
1970 IC Proof	—	Value: 65.50				

KM# 79 10 GOURDES

47.0500 g., 0.9990 Silver 1.5113 oz. ASW **Obv:** Seminole Chief - Osceola facing **Rev:** National arms

Date	Mintage	F	VF	XF	Unc	BU
1971 IC Proof	3,535	Value: 35.00				

KM# 80 10 GOURDES

47.0500 g., 0.9990 Silver 1.5113 oz. ASW **Obv:** Sioux Chief - Sitting Bull **Rev:** National arms

Date	Mintage	F	VF	XF	Unc	BU
1971 IC Proof	3,185	Value: 35.00				

KM# 81 10 GOURDES

47.0500 g., 0.9990 Silver 1.5113 oz. ASW **Obv:** Fox Chief - Playing Fox **Rev:** National arms

Date	Mintage	F	VF	XF	Unc	BU
1971 IC Proof	3,035	Value: 35.00				

KM# 82 10 GOURDES

47.0500 g., 0.9990 Silver 1.5113 oz. ASW **Obv:** Chiricahua Chief - Geronimo **Rev:** National arms

Date	Mintage	F	VF	XF	Unc	BU
1971 IC Proof	3,285	Value: 35.00				

KM# 83 10 GOURDES

47.0500 g., 0.9990 Silver 1.5113 oz. ASW **Obv:** Seminole Chief - Billy Bowlegs **Rev:** National arms

Date	Mintage	F	VF	XF	Unc	BU
1971 IC Proof	3,735	Value: 35.00				

KM# 84 10 GOURDES

47.0500 g., 0.9990 Silver 1.5113 oz. ASW **Obv:** Nez Perce Chief - Joseph **Rev:** National arms

Date	Mintage	F	VF	XF	Unc	BU
1971 IC Proof	3,235	Value: 35.00				

KM# 85 10 GOURDES

47.0500 g., 0.9990 Silver 1.5113 oz. ASW **Obv:** Yankton Sioux Chief - War Eagle **Rev:** National arms

Date	Mintage	F	VF	XF	Unc	BU
1971 IC Proof	3,135	Value: 35.00				

KM# 86 10 GOURDES

47.0500 g., 0.9990 Silver 1.5113 oz. ASW **Obv:** Oglala Sioux Chief - Red Cloud **Rev:** National arms

Date	Mintage	F	VF	XF	Unc	BU
1971 IC Proof	3,235	Value: 35.00				

KM# 87 10 GOURDES

47.0500 g., 0.9990 Silver 1.5113 oz. ASW **Obv:** Cherokee Chief - Stalking Turkey **Rev:** National arms

Date	Mintage	F	VF	XF	Unc	BU
1971 IC Proof	3,185	Value: 35.00				

KM# 66 20 GOURDES

3.9500 g., 0.9000 Gold .1143 oz. AGW **Series:** 10th Anniversary of Revolution **Obv:** Native left with knife in left hand **Rev:** National arms **Note:** Mackandal

Date	Mintage	F	VF	XF	Unc	BU
1967 IC Proof	10,351	Value: 82.50				
1968 IC Proof	—	Value: 82.50				
1969 IC Proof	—	Value: 90.00				
1970 IC Proof	—	Value: 95.00				

KM# 67.1 25 GOURDES

117.6000 g., 0.9990 Silver 3.7809 oz. ASW, 60 mm. **Subject:** 10th Anniversary of Revolution **Obv:** Art objects **Rev:** National arms

Date	Mintage	F	VF	XF	Unc	BU
1967 IC Proof	4,650	Value: 55.00				
1968 IC Proof	5,810	Value: 55.00				

Date	Mintage	F	VF	XF	Unc	BU
1969 IC Proof	1,115	Value: 75.00				
1970 IC Proof	1,000	Value: 75.00				

KM# 67.2 25 GOURDES

117.6000 g., 0.9990 Silver 3.7809 oz. ASW, 60 mm. **Obv:** Art objects **Rev:** National arms with additional "1 AR" countermark at 8 o'clock

Date	Mintage	F	VF	XF	Unc	BU
1970 Proof	—	Value: 165				

KM# 88 25 GOURDES

117.6000 g., 0.9990 Silver 3.7809 oz. ASW, 60 mm. **Obv:** International airport **Rev:** National arms

Date	Mintage	F	VF	XF	Unc	BU
1971 IC Proof	1,935	Value: 85.00				

KM# 102 25 GOURDES

10.0000 g., 0.9250 Silver .2973 oz. ASW **Obv:** Bust facing **Rev:** National arms

Date	Mintage	F	VF	XF	Unc	BU
1973	6,100	—	—	—	6.50	8.00
1973 Proof	5,470	Value: 9.00				
1974 Proof	—	Value: 30.00				

KM# 103 25 GOURDES

10.0000 g., 0.9250 Silver .2973 oz. ASW **Subject:** World Soccer Championship Games **Obv:** Games logo **Rev:** National arms

Date	Mintage	F	VF	XF	Unc	BU
1973	57,000	—	—	—	6.00	7.50
1973 Proof	6,430	Value: 9.00				
1974 Proof	—	Value: 30.00				

KM# 112.1 25 GOURDES

8.3750 g., 0.9250 Silver .2491 oz. ASW **Series:** United States Bicentennial **Obv:** Soldiers with cannon **Rev:** National arms

Date	Mintage	F	VF	XF	Unc	BU
1974	25,000	—	—	—	6.50	8.00
1974 Proof	600	Value: 20.00				
1975 Proof	—	Value: 35.00				
1976 Proof	10,000	Value: 12.50				

KM# 112.2 25 GOURDES

8.3750 g., 0.9250 Silver .2491 oz. ASW **Obv:** Soldiers with cannon, error; without country name at top **Rev:** National arms

Date	Mintage	F	VF	XF	Unc	BU
1974	25,000	—	—	—	40.00	45.00

KM# 121 25 GOURDES

8.3750 g., 0.9250 Silver .2491 oz. ASW **Series:** International Women's Year **Obv:** Women with raised arms, inscription **Rev:** National arms

Date	Mintage	F	VF	XF	Unc	BU
1975	7,180	—	—	—	20.00	30.00
1975 Proof	1,440	Value: 40.00				

KM# 72 30 GOURDES

9.1100 g., 0.8580 Gold .1713 oz. AGW **Series:** 10th Anniversary of Revolution **Obv:** Citadel of Saint Christopher **Rev:** National arms

Date	Mintage	F	VF	XF	Unc	BU
1969 IC Proof	1,185	Value: 135				
1970 IC Proof	Inc. above	Value: 165				

KM# 73 40 GOURDES

12.1500 g., 0.5850 Gold .2285 oz. AGW **Series:** 10th Anniversary of Revolution **Subject:** J.J. Dessalines **Obv:** Uniformed bust facing divides dates **Rev:** National arms

Date	Mintage	F	VF	XF	Unc	BU
1969 Proof	1,005	Value: 215				
1970 Proof	Inc. above	Value: 230				

KM# 68 50 GOURDES

9.8700 g., 0.9000 Gold .2856 oz. AGW **Series:** 10th Anniversary of Revolution **Obv:** Dancer **Rev:** National arms

Date	Mintage	F	VF	XF	Unc	BU
1967 IC Proof	8,681	Value: 210				
1968 IC Proof	—	Value: 220				
1969 IC Proof	—	Value: 230				
1970 IC Proof	—	Value: 250				

KM# 89 50 GOURDES

9.8700 g., 0.9000 Gold .2856 oz. AGW **Series:** 10th Anniversary of Revolution **Obv:** Soldiers **Rev:** National arms **Note:** Heros de Vertieres

Date	Mintage	F	VF	XF	Unc	BU
1971 IC Proof	485	Value: 300				

KM# 104.2 50 GOURDES

16.4500 g., 0.9250 Silver 0.4892 oz. ASW, 37.9 mm. **Obv:** Woman on beach **Rev:** National arms, fineness stamp right of value **Edge:** Reeded

Date	Mintage	F	VF	XF	Unc	BU
1973 Proof	—	Value: 50.00				

KM# 104.1 50 GOURDES

20.0000 g., 0.9250 Silver .5949 oz. ASW **Obv:** Woman on the beach **Rev:** National arms, fineness mark left of value

Date	Mintage	F	VF	XF	Unc	BU
1973	8,685	—	—	—	16.50	18.00
1973 Proof	5,973	Value: 20.00				
1974 Proof	—	Value: 45.00				

KM# 105 50 GOURDES

20.0000 g., 0.9250 Silver .5949 oz. ASW **Obv:** Woman and child **Rev:** National arms

Date	Mintage	F	VF	XF	Unc	BU
1973	7,300	—	—	—	13.50	15.00
1973 Proof	5,853	Value: 16.50				
1974	—	—	—	—	37.50	40.00
1974 Proof	—	Value: 45.00				

KM# 106 50 GOURDES

16.7500 g., 0.9250 Silver .4982 oz. ASW **Series:** World Soccer Championship Games **Obv:** Games logo **Rev:** National arms

Date	Mintage	F	VF	XF	Unc	BU
1973 Proof	12,000	Value: 15.00				

KM# 113 50 GOURDES

16.7500 g., 0.9250 Silver .4982 oz. ASW **Series:** 1976 Montreal Olympiad **Obv:** Half-figure with torch above Olympic flame flanked by athletes **Rev:** National arms

Date	Mintage	F	VF	XF	Unc	BU
1974	21,000	—	—	—	15.00	20.00
1974 Proof	2,358	Value: 22.00				
1975 Proof	—	Value: 27.50				
1976	—	—	—	—	—	—

Date	Mintage	F	VF	XF	Unc	BU
1976 Thin 6; Proof	8,000	Value: 25.00				
1976 Thick 6; Proof	Inc. above	Value: 30.00				

KM# 114 50 GOURDES
16.7500 g., 0.9250 Silver .4982 oz. ASW **Obv:** Half-figure with torch above Olympic flame, athletes flank **Rev:** National arms, smaller 4 in date

Date	Mintage	F	VF	XF	Unc	BU
1974	—	—	—	—	20.00	25.00
1974 Proof	—	Value: 30.00				

KM# 123 50 GOURDES
16.7500 g., 0.9250 Silver .4982 oz. ASW **Subject:** Holy Year **Obv:** Pope Paul and Praying hands above St. Peter's Square **Rev:** National arms

Date	Mintage	F	VF	XF	Unc	BU
1974	—	—	—	—	12.50	15.00
1974 Proof	960	Value: 25.00				
1975	—	—	—	—	35.00	40.00
1976 Proof	6,000	Value: 25.00				

KM# 129 50 GOURDES
21.3000 g., 0.9250 Silver .6334 oz. ASW **Series:** 1980 Moscow Olympics **Obv:** Olympic flame above date, athletes flank **Rev:** National arms

Date	Mintage	F	VF	XF	Unc	BU
1977	3,969	—	—	—	22.50	25.00
1977 Proof	3,720	Value: 27.50				
1978 Proof	Est. 350	Value: 225				

KM# 130.1 50 GOURDES
21.3000 g., 0.9250 Silver .6334 oz. ASW **Series:** 20th Anniversary of European Market **Obv:** Map of Europe on globe design **Rev:** National arms

Date	Mintage	F	VF	XF	Unc	BU
1977	421	—	—	—	65.00	70.00
1977 Proof	364	Value: 80.00				
1978	—	—	—	—	65.00	70.00

KM# 130.2 50 GOURDES
21.3000 g., 0.9250 Silver .6334 oz. ASW **Obv:** Map of Europe on globe design, entire area within circle frosted **Rev:** National arms

Date	Mintage	F	VF	XF	Unc	BU
1978	—	—	—	—	75.00	80.00
1978 Proof	—	Value: 90.00				

KM# 127 50 GOURDES
21.3000 g., 0.9250 Silver .6334 oz. ASW **Series:** World Soccer Championship Games **Obv:** Soccer ball with date at center **Rev:** National arms

Date	Mintage	F	VF	XF	Unc	BU
1977	11,000	—	—	—	22.50	25.00
1977 Proof	9,000	Value: 28.00				

KM# 128 50 GOURDES
21.3000 g., 0.9250 Silver .6334 oz. ASW **Subject:** Human Rights **Obv:** Kneeling figure with broken chains **Rev:** National arms

Date	Mintage	F	VF	XF	Unc	BU
1977	800	—	—	—	27.50	30.00
1977 Proof	545	Value: 35.00				

KM# 131 50 GOURDES
21.3000 g., 0.9250 Silver .6334 oz. ASW **Obv:** Queen of the Sugar left **Rev:** National arms

Date	Mintage	F	VF	XF	Unc	BU
1977	321	—	—	—	30.00	35.00
1977 Proof	602	Value: 37.50				

KM# 149 50 GOURDES
20.0000 g., 0.9250 Silver .5948 oz. ASW **Series:** F.A.O. **Obv:** Head left **Rev:** Plants

Date	Mintage	F	VF	XF	Unc	BU
1981R	Est. 14,000	—	—	—	30.00	35.00
1981R Proof	—	Value: 55.00				

KM# 150 50 GOURDES
20.0000 g., 0.9250 Silver .5948 oz. ASW **Subject:** Holy Year **Obv:** National arms **Rev:** Buildings

Date	Mintage	F	VF	XF	Unc	BU
1983R Proof	1,000	Value: 85.00				

KM# 74 60 GOURDES
18.2200 g., 0.5850 Gold .3427 oz. AGW **Series:** 10th Anniversary of the Revolution **Obv:** Alexandre Petion **Rev:** National arms

Date	Mintage	F	VF	XF	Unc	BU
1969 IC Proof	935	Value: 245				
1970 IC Proof	Inc. above	Value: 385				

KM# 69 100 GOURDES
19.7500 g., 0.9000 Gold .5715 oz. AGW **Series:** 10th Anniversary of the Revolution **Subject:** Marie Jeanne **Obv:** Half-figure left with knife in right hand **Rev:** National arms

Date	Mintage	F	VF	XF	Unc	BU
1967 IC Proof	Est. 8,682	Value: 400				
1968 IC Proof	—	Value: 420				
1969 IC Proof	—	Value: 420				
1970 IC Proof	—	Value: 450				

KM# 90 100 GOURDES
19.7500 g., 0.9000 Gold .5715 oz. AGW **Obv:** Seminole Tribal Chief - Osceola **Rev:** National arms

Date	Mintage	F	VF	XF	Unc	BU
1971 IC Proof	435	Value: 425				

KM# 91 100 GOURDES
19.7500 g., 0.9000 Gold .5715 oz. AGW **Obv:** Sioux Chief - Sitting Bull **Rev:** National arms

Date	Mintage	F	VF	XF	Unc	BU
1971 IC Proof	475	Value: 425				

KM# 92 100 GOURDES
19.7500 g., 0.9000 Gold .5715 oz. AGW **Obv:** Fox Chief - Playing Fox **Rev:** National arms

Date	Mintage	F	VF	XF	Unc	BU
1971 IC Proof	425	Value: 385				

KM# 93 100 GOURDES
19.7500 g., 0.9000 Gold .5715 oz. AGW **Obv:** Chiricahua Chief - Geronimo **Rev:** National arms

Date	Mintage	F	VF	XF	Unc	BU
1971 IC Proof	520	Value: 425				

KM# 94 100 GOURDES
19.7500 g., 0.9000 Gold .5715 oz. AGW **Obv:** Seminole Chiel - Billy Bowlegs **Rev:** National arms

Date	Mintage	F	VF	XF	Unc	BU
1971 IC Proof	425	Value: 425				

KM# 95 100 GOURDES
19.7500 g., 0.9000 Gold .5715 oz. AGW **Obv:** Nez Perce Chief - Joseph **Rev:** National arms

Date	Mintage	F	VF	XF	Unc	BU
1971 IC Proof	455	Value: 425				

KM# 96 100 GOURDES
19.7500 g., 0.9000 Gold .5715 oz. AGW **Obv:** Yankton Sioux Chief - War Eagle **Rev:** National arms

Date	Mintage	F	VF	XF	Unc	BU
1971 IC Proof	455	Value: 425				

KM# 97 100 GOURDES
19.7500 g., 0.9000 Gold .5715 oz. AGW **Obv:** Oglala Sioux Chief - Red Cloud **Rev:** National arms

Date	Mintage	F	VF	XF	Unc	BU
1971 IC Proof	455	Value: 425				

KM# 98 100 GOURDES
19.7500 g., 0.9000 Gold .5715 oz. AGW **Obv:** Cherokee Chief - Stalking Turkey **Rev:** National arms

Date	Mintage	F	VF	XF	Unc	BU
1971 IC Proof	425	Value: 425				

KM# 107 100 GOURDES
1.4500 g., 0.9000 Gold .0419 oz. AGW **Subject:** Christopher Columbus **Obv:** Bust facing **Rev:** National arms

Date	Mintage	F	VF	XF	Unc	BU
1973	3,233	—	—	—	40.00	45.00
1973 Proof	915	Value: 55.00				

KM# 132 100 GOURDES
43.0000 g., 0.9250 Silver 1.2789 oz. ASW **Subject:** Presidents Sadat and Begin **Obv:** Profiles facing each other, Dove of Peace above **Rev:** National arms

Date	Mintage	F	VF	XF	Unc	BU
1977	550	—	—	—	55.00	60.00
1977 Proof	500	Value: 80.00				

KM# 133 100 GOURDES
43.0000 g., 0.9250 Silver 1.2789 oz. ASW **Subject:** 20th Anniversary of European Market **Obv:** Ships wheel and sailboat **Rev:** National arms

Date	Mintage	F	VF	XF	Unc	BU
1977	321	—	—	—	85.00	90.00
1977 Proof	214	Value: 100				

KM# 134 100 GOURDES
43.0000 g., 0.9250 Silver 1.2789 oz. ASW **Subject:** 50th Anniversary of Lindbergh's New York to Paris Flight **Obv:** Portrait of Lindbergh in flier's cap above "Spirit of St. Louis" **Rev:** National arms

Date	Mintage	F	VF	XF	Unc	BU
1977	321	—	—	—	80.00	85.00
1977 Proof	214	Value: 125				

KM# 135 100 GOURDES
43.0000 g., 0.9250 Silver 1.2789 oz. ASW **Obv:** Statue of Liberty **Rev:** National arms

Date	Mintage	F	VF	XF	Unc	BU
1977	321	—	—	—	80.00	85.00
1977 Proof	214	Value: 125				

KM# 158 100 GOURDES
40.0000 g., 0.9250 Silver 1.1896 oz. ASW **Subject:** 10th Anniversary of the Presidency of Jean Claude Duvalier **Obv:** Head right without FAO **Rev:** Woman and child

Date	Mintage	F	VF	XF	Unc	BU
1981R Proof	—	Value: 150				

KM# 159 100 GOURDES
40.0000 g., 0.9250 Silver 1.1896 oz. ASW **Subject:** 10th

Anniversary of the Presidency of Jean Claude Duvalier **Obv:** Head right without FAO **Rev:** Infants on open book

Date	Mintage	F	VF	XF	Unc	BU
1981R Proof	—	Value: 150				

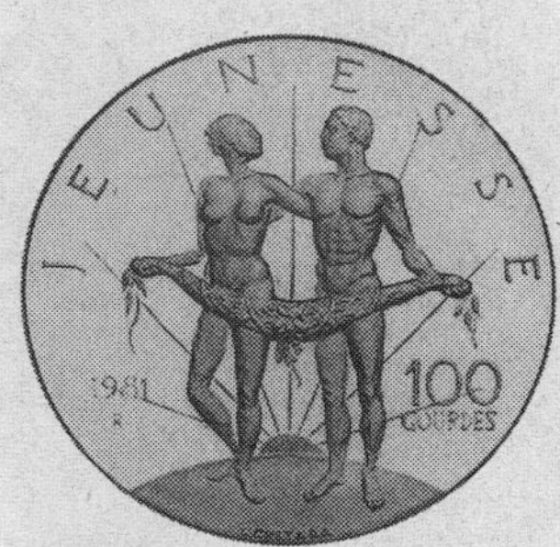

KM# 160 100 GOURDES

40.0000 g., 0.9250 Silver 1.1896 oz. ASW **Subject:** 10th Anniversary of the Presidency of Jean Claude Duvalier **Obv:** Head right without FAO **Rev:** Nude woman and man

Date	Mintage	F	VF	XF	Unc	BU
1981R Proof	—	Value: 175				

KM# 70 200 GOURDES

39.4900 g., 0.9000 Gold 1.1427 oz. AGW **Subject:** Revolt of Santo Domingo **Obv:** Native running with weapons **Rev:** National arms

Date	Mintage	F	VF	XF	Unc	BU
1967 IC Proof	Est. 4,199	Value: 800				
1968 IC Proof	—	Value: 825				
1969 IC Proof	—	Value: 825				
1970 IC Proof	—	Value: 850				

KM# 99 200 GOURDES

39.4900 g., 0.9000 Gold 1.1427 oz. AGW **Obv:** Revolutionist from Santo Domingo **Rev:** National arms

Date	Mintage	F	VF	XF	Unc	BU
1971 IC Proof	235	Value: 900				

KM# 108 200 GOURDES

2.9100 g., 0.9000 Gold .0842 oz. AGW **Series:** World Soccer Championship Games **Obv:** Games logo **Rev:** National arms

Date	Mintage	F	VF	XF	Unc	BU
1973	5,167	—	—	—	60.00	65.00
1973 Proof	915	Value: 85.00				

KM# 115 200 GOURDES

2.9100 g., 0.9000 Gold .0842 oz. AGW **Subject:** Holy Year **Obv:** Pope Paul and Praying hands above St. Peter's Square **Rev:** National arms, fineness stamped on hexagonal mound

Date	Mintage	F	VF	XF	Unc	BU
1974	4,965	—	—	—	65.00	70.00
1974 Proof	660	Value: 100				

KM# 124 200 GOURDES

2.9100 g., 0.9000 Gold .0842 oz. AGW **Subject:** Holy Year **Obv:** Pope Paul and Praying hands above St. Peter's Square **Rev:** National arms, fineness stamped on oval mound

Date	Mintage	F	VF	XF	Unc	BU
1975 Proof	—	Value: 90.00				

KM# 125 200 GOURDES

2.9100 g., 0.9000 Gold .0842 oz. AGW **Series:** International Women's Year **Obv:** Two women with arms upraised **Rev:** National arms

Date	Mintage	F	VF	XF	Unc	BU
1975	2,260	—	—	—	65.00	70.00
1975 Proof	840	Value: 125				

KM# 75 250 GOURDES

75.9500 g., 0.5850 Gold 1.4286 oz. AGW **Series:** 10th Anniversary of Revolution **Obv:** King H. Christophe **Rev:** National arms

Date	Mintage	F	VF	XF	Unc	BU
1969 IC Proof	470	Value: 975				
1970 IC Proof	—	Value: 1,100				

KM# 136 250 GOURDES

4.2500 g., 0.9000 Gold .1229 oz. AGW **Subject:** Human Rights **Obv:** Kneeling figure with broken chains **Rev:** National arms

Date	Mintage	F	VF	XF	Unc	BU
1977	282	—	—	—	125	140
1977 Proof	288	Value: 145				

KM# 137 250 GOURDES

4.2500 g., 0.9000 Gold .1229 oz. AGW **Subject:** Presidents Sadat and Begin **Obv:** Profiles facing each other, Dove of Peace above **Rev:** National arms

Date	Mintage	F	VF	XF	Unc	BU
1977	270	—	—	—	110	120
1977 Proof	520	Value: 100				

KM# 138 250 GOURDES

4.2500 g., 0.9000 Gold .1229 oz. AGW **Subject:** 20th Anniversary of European Market **Obv:** Ships wheel and sailboat **Rev:** National arms

Date	Mintage	F	VF	XF	Unc	BU
1977	107	—	—	—	175	200
1977 Proof	107	Value: 210				

KM# 139 250 GOURDES

4.2500 g., 0.9000 Gold .1229 oz. AGW **Subject:** 50th Anniversary of Lindbergh's New York to Paris Flight **Obv:** Portrait of Lindbergh in flier's cap above "Spirit of St. Louis" **Rev:** National arms

Date	Mintage	F	VF	XF	Unc	BU
1977	107	—	—	—	225	245
1977 Proof	107	Value: 250				

KM# 76 500 GOURDES

151.9000 g., 0.5850 Gold 2.8572 oz. AGW, 68 mm. **Series:** 10th Anniversary of Revolution **Obv:** Haitian native art **Rev:** National arms **Note:** Photo reduced.

Date	Mintage	F	VF	XF	Unc	BU
1969 IC Proof	435	Value: 2,000				
1970 IC Proof	—	Value: 2,500				

KM# 109 500 GOURDES

7.2800 g., 0.9000 Gold .2106 oz. AGW **Obv:** Woman with shell right **Rev:** National arms

Date	Mintage	F	VF	XF	Unc	BU
1973	2,380	—	—	—	155	165
1973 Proof	915	Value: 185				

KM# 110 500 GOURDES

7.2800 g., 0.9000 Gold .2106 oz. AGW **Obv:** Woman with child **Rev:** National arms

Date	Mintage	F	VF	XF	Unc	BU
1973	2,265	—	—	—	150	160
1973 Proof	915	Value: 175				

KM# 116 500 GOURDES

6.5000 g., 0.9000 Gold .1881 oz. AGW **Obv:** Battle scene **Rev:** National arms

Date	Mintage	F	VF	XF	Unc	BU
1974 Proof	—	Value: 165				

KM# 117 500 GOURDES
6.5000 g., 0.9000 Gold .1881 oz. AGW **Series:** 1976 Montreal Olympics **Obv:** Half-figure with torch above Olympic flame, athletes flank **Rev:** National arms, fineness stamped on hexagonal mound

Date	Mintage	F	VF	XF	Unc	BU
1974	3,489	—	—	—	135	150
1974 Proof	1,140	Value: 165				

KM# 126 500 GOURDES
6.5000 g., 0.9000 Gold .1881 oz. AGW **Series:** 1976 Montreal Olympics **Obv:** Half-figure with torch above Olympic flame, athletes flank **Rev:** National arms, fineness stamped on hexagonal mound

Date	Mintage	F	VF	XF	Unc	BU
1975	120	—	—	—	450	500

KM# 140 500 GOURDES
8.5000 g., 0.9000 Gold .2459 oz. AGW **Series:** World Soccer Championship Games **Obv:** Soccer ball with date in center **Rev:** National arms

Date	Mintage	F	VF	XF	Unc	BU
1977	450	—	—	—	185	200
1977 Proof	200	Value: 250				

KM# 141 500 GOURDES
8.5000 g., 0.9000 Gold .2459 oz. AGW **Series:** 1980 Moscow Olympics **Rev:** National arms

Date	Mintage	F	VF	XF	Unc	BU
1977	695	—	—	—	180	200
1977 Proof	504	Value: 210				
1978 Proof	Est. 350	Value: 350				

KM# 142 500 GOURDES
8.5000 g., 0.9000 Gold .2459 oz. AGW **Subject:** 20th Anniversary of European Common Market **Obv:** Map of Europe **Rev:** National arms

Date	Mintage	F	VF	XF	Unc	BU
1977	207	—	—	—	225	250
1977 Proof	257	Value: 265				
1978	—	—	—	—	275	300
1978 Proof	150	Value: 350				

KM# 143 500 GOURDES
8.5000 g., 0.9000 Gold .2459 oz. AGW **Subject:** Economic Connections **Rev:** National arms

Date	Mintage	F	VF	XF	Unc	BU
1977	107	—	—	—	235	260
1977 Proof	107	Value: 300				

KM# 144 500 GOURDES
8.5000 g., 0.9000 Gold .2459 oz. AGW **Obv:** Jean-Claude Duvalier **Rev:** National arms

Date	Mintage	F	VF	XF	Unc	BU
1977	107	—	—	—	235	250
1977 Proof	328	Value: 200				

KM# 161 500 GOURDES
7.0000 g., 0.9000 Gold .2025 oz. AGW **Subject:** 10th Anniversary of the Presidency of Jean Claude Duvalier **Obv:** Head right without FAO **Rev:** Sun above farmer on tractor in field

Date	Mintage	F	VF	XF	Unc	BU
1981R Proof	—	Value: 650				

KM# 162 500 GOURDES
7.0000 g., 0.9000 Gold .2025 oz. AGW **Subject:** 10th Anniversary of the Presidency of Jean Claude Duvalier **Obv:** Head right without FAO **Rev:** Plants

Date	Mintage	F	VF	XF	Unc	BU
1981R Proof	—	Value: 650				

KM# 163 500 GOURDES
7.0000 g., 0.9000 Gold .2025 oz. AGW **Subject:** 10th Anniversary of the Presidency of Jean Claude Duvalier **Obv:** Head right without FAO **Rev:** Harvesters

Date	Mintage	F	VF	XF	Unc	BU
1981R Proof	—	Value: 650				

KM# 151 500 GOURDES
10.5000 g., 0.9000 Gold .3038 oz. AGW **Subject:** Papal Visit **Obv:** National arms **Rev:** Bust left above people

Date	Mintage	F	VF	XF	Unc	BU
1983R Proof	1,000	Value: 225				

KM# 165 500 GOURDES
28.2300 g., 0.9250 Silver 0.8395 oz. ASW, 38.5 mm. **Subject:** Millennium **Obv:** Multicolor and gold-plated national arms **Rev:** Dove and partially gold-plated sun rays **Edge:** Reeded

Date	Mintage	F	VF	XF	Unc	BU
ND(1999) Proof	—	Value: 100				

KM# 71 1000 GOURDES
197.4800 g., 0.9000 Gold 5.7148 oz. AGW **Series:** 10th Anniversary of Revolution **Obv:** Dr. Francois Duvalier **Rev:** National arms

Date	Mintage	F	VF	XF	Unc	BU
1967 IC Proof	Est. 2,950	Value: 3,900				
1968 IC Proof	—	Value: 3,950				
1969 IC Proof	—	Value: 4,000				
1970 IC Proof	—	Value: 4,100				

KM# 111 1000 GOURDES
14.5600 g., 0.9000 Gold .4213 oz. AGW **Obv:** President Jean Claude Duvalier left **Rev:** National arms

Date	Mintage	F	VF	XF	Unc	BU
1973	—	—	—	—	300	320
1973 Proof	915	Value: 345				

KM# 118.1 1000 GOURDES
13.0000 g., 0.9000 Gold .3762 oz. AGW **Series:** United States Bicentennial **Obv:** Battle scene **Rev:** National arms

Date	Mintage	F	VF	XF	Unc	BU
1974	3,040	—	—	—	230	250
1974 Proof	480	Value: 325				
1975 Proof	—	Value: 600				

KM# 118.2 1000 GOURDES
13.0000 g., 0.9000 Gold .3762 oz. AGW **Obv:** Error; without country name at top **Rev:** National arms

Date	Mintage	F	VF	XF	Unc	BU
1974	—	—	—	—	650	700

KM# 164 1000 GOURDES
14.0000 g., 0.9000 Gold .4051 oz. AGW **Subject:** 10th Anniversary of the Presidency of Jean Claude Duvalier **Obv:** Head right without FAO **Rev:** Three nudes and flag

Date	Mintage	F	VF	XF	Unc	BU
1981R Proof	—	Value: 1,150				

PATTERNS

Including off metal strikes

KM#	Date	Mintage	Identification	Mkt Val
Pn87	1974	—	25 Gourdes. 0.9250 Silver. KM#112	—

TRIAL STRIKES

KM#	Date	Mintage	Identification	Mkt Val
TS1	ND(1971)	—	100 Gourdes. Gilt Bronze. Bust in headdress facing. Blank. KM#93	100

MINT SETS

KM#	Date	Mintage	Identification	Issue Price	Mkt Val
MS1	1973 (8)	8,000	KM#102, 104-105, 107-111,	490	600
MS2	1973 (8)	—	KM#102, 104, 105, 107-111	60.00	37.50
MS3	1974 (2)	—	KM#115, 123	—	70.00
MS4	1975 (2)	—	KM#121, 125	50.25	65.00
MS5	1976 (2)	—	KM#113, 117	—	—
MS6	1995 (5)	—	KM#152a-156a	—	10.00

PROOF SETS

KM#	Date	Mintage	Identification	Issue Price	Mkt Val
PSA1	1967 (8)	—	KM#64.1, 65-71	—	3,500
PS1	1967 (5)	2,525	KM#66, 68-71	722	3,900
PS2	1967 (3)	4,650	KM#64.1, 65.1, 67.1	47.00	90.00
PS3	1968 (5)	475	KM#66, 68-71	823	4,200
PS4	1968 (3)	5,725	KM#64, 65, 67	53.50	100
PS5	1969 (5)	435	KM#72-76	475	3,750
PS6	1969 (5)	140	KM#66, 68-71	823	4,650
PS7	1969 (3)	1,100	KM#64, 65, 67	53.50	145
PS8	1970 (5)	—	KM#66, 68-71	823	5,000
PSA9	1970 (3)	1,000	KM#64, 65, 67	53.50	145
PS9	1970 (3)	—	KM#64.2, 65.2, 67.2	—	265
PSA10	1970-71 (5)	—	KM#64.1, 65.1, 67.1, 78, 88	265	—
PS10	1971 (9)	—	KM#79-87	135	325
PSA11	1971 (18)	—	KM#79-87, 90-98	—	3,900
PS11	1971 (9)	—	KM#90-98	—	3,500
PS12	1973 (8)	1,250	KM#102-105, 107-109, 111	830	600
PS13	1973 (4)	3,500	KM#102-105	60.00	50.00
PS14	1974 (4)	—	KM#102-105	—	145
PS15	1975 (2)	—	KM#121, 125	67.25	160
PS17	1976 (3)	—	KM#112, 113, 123 Although the insert information card in #PS17 state B.U., this issue is considered to be of proof quality.	—	65.00
PS18	1978 (2)	350	KM#129, 141	—	475
PS19	1978 (2)	—	KM#130.2, 142	—	450
PS20	1981R (7)	10	KM#158-164	—	3,650

HEJAZ

Hejaz, a province of Saudi Arabia and a former vilayet of the Ottoman Empire, occupies an 800-mile long (1,287km.) coastal strip between Nejd and the Red Sea. The province was a Turkish dependency until freed in World War I. Husain Ibn Ali, Amir of Mecca, opposed the Turkish control and, with the aid of Lawrence of Arabia, wrested much of Hejaz from the Turks and in 1916 assumed the title of King of Hejaz. Abd Al-Aziz Bin Sa'ud, of Nejd conquered Hejaz in 1925, and in 1926 combined it and Nejd into a single kingdom.

TITLES

Hal-Hejaz

RULERS

al Husain Ibn Ali, AH1334-42/1916-24AD
Abd Al-Aziz Bin Sa'ud, AH1343-1373/1925-1953AD

MONETARY SYSTEM

40 Para = 1 Piastre (Ghirsh)
20 Piastres = 1 Riyal
100 Piastres = 1 Dinar

KINGDOM

COUNTERMARKED COINAGE

Minor Coins

Following the defeat of the Ottomans in 1916, Turkish 10, 20 and 40 Para coins of Muhammed V and 40 Para coins of Muhammed VI were countermarked al-Hejaz in Arabic. The countermark was applied to the obverse side effacing the Ottoman Sultan's toughra, and thus refuting Turkish rule in Hejaz.

Countermarks on the reverse are rare errors. The 10 Para of Muhammed V and 10 and 20 Para (billon) of Abdul Mejid and Mahmud II exist with a smaller, 6-milimeter countermark. These are probably unofficial. Other host coins are considered controversial.

KM# 2 10 PARA

Nickel **Countermark:** Hejaz **Obv:** Reshat **Note:** Large countermark on Turkey 10 Para, KM#760. Accession date: 1327.

CM Date	Host Date	Good	VG	F	VF	XF
ND(AH1327)	AH1327//7 Rare	—	—	—	—	—
ND(1327)	AH1327//2-7 Rare	—	—	—	—	—

KM# 3 20 PARA

Nickel **Countermark:** "Hejaz" **Note:** Countermark on Turkey 20 Para, KM#761. Accession date: 1327.

CM Date	Host Date	Good	VG	F	VF	XF
ND(1327)	AH1327//2	5.00	9.00	20.00	40.00	—
ND(1327)	AH1327//3	4.00	7.00	15.00	30.00	—
ND(1327)	AH1327//4	3.00	6.00	12.00	25.00	—
ND(1327)	AH1327//5	3.00	6.00	12.00	25.00	—
ND(1327)	AH1327//6	3.00	6.00	12.00	25.00	—
ND(1327)	AH1327//x p.y. obliterated	2.00	5.00	10.00	20.00	—

KM# 4 40 PARA

Nickel **Countermark:** "Hejaz" **Obv:** El Ghazi **Note:** Countermark on Turkey 40 Para, KM#766. Accession date: 1327.

CM Date	Host Date	Good	VG	F	VF	XF
ND(1327)	AH1327//3	6.00	10.00	20.00	40.00	—
ND(1327)	AH1327//4	3.00	6.00	12.00	25.00	—
ND(1327)	AH1327//5	3.00	6.00	12.00	25.00	—
ND(1327)	AH1327//x p.y. obliterated	2.00	5.00	10.00	20.00	—

KM# 5 40 PARA

Copper-Nickel **Countermark:** "Hejaz" **Note:** Countermark on Turkey 40 Para, KM#779. Accession date: 1327.

CM Date	Host Date	Good	VG	F	VF	XF
ND(1327)	AH1327//8	4.00	6.00	12.00	25.00	—
ND(1327)	AH1327//9	20.00	30.00	75.00	150	—
ND(1327)	AH1327//x p.y. obliterated	3.00	6.00	10.00	20.00	—

KM# 6 40 PARA

Copper-Nickel **Countermark:** "Hejaz" **Note:** Countermark on Turkey 40 Para, KM#828. Accession date: 1336.

CM Date	Host Date	Good	VG	F	VF	XF
ND(1326)	AH1336//4	50.00	75.00	150	250	—
ND(1326)	AH1336//x	40.00	50.00	100	200	—

COUNTERMARKED COINAGE

Silver Coins

Silver coins of various sizes were also countermarked al-Hejaz. The most common host coins include the Maria Theresa Thaler of Austria, and 5, 10, and 20 Kurush or Qirsh of Turkey and Egypt. The countermark occurs in various sizes and styles of script. These countermarks may have been applied by local silversmiths to discourage re-exportation of the badly needed hard currency and silver of known fineness.

Some crown-sized examples exist with both the al-Hejaz and Nejd countermarks. The authenticity of the silver countermarked coins has long been discussed, and it is likely that most were privately produced. Other host coins are considered controversial.

KM# 10 5 PIASTRES

Silver **Countermark:** "Hejaz" **Note:** Countermark on Turkey 5 Kurush, KM#750. Accession date: 1327.

CM Date	Host Date	Good	VG	F	VF	XF
(1916-20)	ND(AH1327// 1-7)	100	125	200	400	—

KM# 11 5 PIASTRES

Silver **Countermark:** "Hejaz" **Note:** Countermark on Turkey 5 Kurush, KM#771. Accession date: 1327.

CM Date	Host Date	Good	VG	F	VF	XF
(1916-20)	ND(AH1327// 7-9)	100	125	200	400	—

KM# 12 5 PIASTRES

Silver **Countermark:** "Hejaz" **Note:** Countermark on Egypt 5 Qirsh, KM#308. Accession date: 1327.

CM Date	Host Date	Good	VG	F	VF	XF
(1916-20)	ND(AH1327// 2H-4H, 6H)	100	125	200	400	—

KM# 13 10 PIASTRES

Silver **Countermark:** "Hejaz" **Note:** Countermark on Turkey 10 Kurush, KM#751. Accession date: 1327.

CM Date	Host Date	Good	VG	F	VF	XF
(1916-20)	ND(AH1327// 1-7)	125	200	300	500	—

KM# 14 10 PIASTRES

Silver **Countermark:** "Hejaz" **Note:** Countermark on Turkey 10 Kurush, KM#772. Accession date: 1327.

CM Date	Host Date	Good	VG	F	VF	XF
(1916-20)	ND(AH1327// 7-10)	125	200	300	500	—

KM# 15 10 PIASTRES

Silver **Countermark:** "Hejaz" **Note:** Countermark on Egypt 10 Qirsh, KM#309. Accession date: 1327.

CM Date	Host Date	Good	VG	F	VF	XF
(1916-20)	ND(AH1327// 2H-4H, 6H)	125	200	300	500	—

KM# 16 20 PIASTRES

Silver **Countermark:** "Hejaz" **Note:** Countermark on Egypt 20 Qirsh, KM#310. Accession date: 1327.

CM Date	Host Date	Good	VG	F	VF	XF
(1916-20)	ND(AH1327// 2H-4H, 6H)	125	200	300	500	—

KM# 17 20 PIASTRES

Silver **Countermark:** "Hejaz" **Note:** Countermark on Turkey 20 Kurush, KM#780. Accession date: 1327.

CM Date	Host Date	Good	VG	F	VF	XF
(1916-20)	ND(AH1327// 8-10)	125	200	300	500	—

KM# 18 20 PIASTRES

Silver **Countermark:** "Hejaz" **Note:** Countermark on Austria Maria Theresa Thaler, KM#T1. Accession date: 1327.

CM Date	Host Date	Good	VG	F	VF	XF
ND(1916-20)	1780	100	150	250	400	—

REGULAR COINAGE

All the regular coins of Hejaz bear the accessional date AH1334 of Al-Husain Ibn Ali, plus the regnal year. Many of the bronze coins occur with a light silver wash mostly on thicker specimens. A variety of planchet thicknesses exist.

KM# 21 1/8 PIASTRE

Bronze, 12-13 mm. **Note:** Reeded and plain edge varieties exist. Size varies.

Date	Mintage	Good	VG	F	VF	XF
AH1334//5	—	—	125	200	300	600

KM# 22 1/4 PIASTRE

1.1400 g., Bronze, 16 mm. **Note:** Reeded and plain edge varieties exist.

Date	Mintage	Good	VG	F	VF	XF
AH1334//5	—	—	8.00	15.00	35.00	65.00
AH1334//6/5	—	—	75.00	300	600	1,200
AH1334//6	—	—	400	750	1,500	2,500

KM# 25 1/4 PIASTRE

Bronze, 17 mm. **Edge:** Plain

Date	Mintage	Good	VG	F	VF	XF
AH1334//8	—	—	10.00	20.00	40.00	75.00

KM# 23 1/2 PIASTRE

Bronze, 18-19 mm. **Note:** Reeded and plain edge varieties exist. Size varies.

Date	Mintage	Good	VG	F	VF	XF
AH1334//5	—	—	10.00	20.00	35.00	75.00

KM# 26 1/2 PIASTRE

3.1400 g., Bronze, 19 mm. **Note:** Similar to 1/4 Piastre, KM#25. Most known specimens were overstruck as "Hejaz & Nejd" KM#1.

Date	Mintage	Good	VG	F	VF	XF
AH1334//8 Rare	—	—	—	—	—	—

KM# 24 PIASTRE

Bronze, 21-22 mm. **Edge:** Reeded **Note:** Size varies.

Date	Mintage	Good	VG	F	VF	XF
AH1334//5	—	—	10.00	20.00	40.00	75.00
AH1334//6/5	—	—	100	200	400	750

KM# 27 PIASTRE

Bronze, 21 mm. **Edge:** Plain

Date	Mintage	Good	VG	F	VF	XF
AH1334//8	—	—	60.00	125	200	325

KM# 28 5 PIASTRES

6.1000 g., 0.9170 Silver .1798 oz. ASW, 24 mm.

Date	Mintage	Good	VG	F	VF	XF
AH1334//8	—	—	50.00	90.00	175	300

KM# 29 10 PIASTRES

12.0500 g., 0.9170 Silver .3552 oz. ASW, 28 mm.

Date	Mintage	Good	VG	F	VF	XF
AH1334//8	—	—	250	400	750	1,200

KM# 30 20 PIASTRES (1 Riyal)

24.1000 g., 0.9170 Silver .7105 oz. ASW, 37 mm.

Date	Mintage	Good	VG	F	VF	XF
AH1334//8	—	—	40.00	75.00	125	200
AH1334//9	—	—	125	200	300	500

KM# 31 DINAR HASHIMI

Gold

Date	Mintage	VG	F	VF	XF	Unc
AH1334-8	—	—	250	400	600	1,000

PATTERNS

Including off metal strikes

KM#	Date	Mintage	Identification	Mkt Val
Pn1	AH1340//1	—	20 Piastres. Bronze. Struck at the Heaton Mint (not to be confused with the modern copies listed in Unusual World Coins; struck in various metals, including bronze, nickel and silver).	—
PnA1	AH1340/1	—	10 Piastres. Bronze. Struck at the Heaton Mint.	—

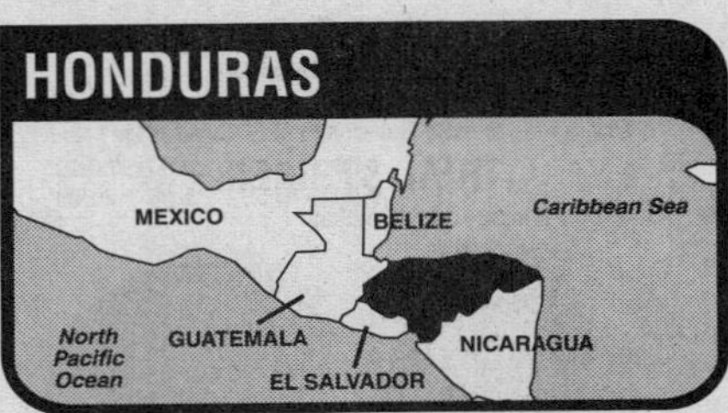

The Republic of Honduras, situated in Central America alongside El Salvador, between Nicaragua and Guatemala, has an area of 43,277sq. mi. (112,090 sq. km.) and a population of 5.6 million. Capital: Tegucigalpa. Agriculture, mining (gold and silver), and logging are the major economic activities, with increasing tourism and emerging petroleum resource discoveries. Precious metals, bananas, timber and coffee are exported.

The eastern part of Honduras was part of the ancient Mayan Empire; however, the largest Indian community in Honduras was the not too well known Lencas. Columbus claimed Honduras for Spain in 1502, during his last voyage to the Americas. Cristobal de Olid established the first settlement under orders from Hernando Cortes, then in Mexico. The area, regarded as one of the most promising sources of gold and silver in the New World, was a part of the Captaincy General of Guatemala throughout the colonial period. After declaring its independence from Spain on September 15, 1821, Honduras fell under the Mexican empire of Augustin de Iturbide, and then joined the Central American Republic (1823-39). Upon the effective dissolution of that federation (ca. 1840), Honduras reclaimed its independence as a self-standing republic. Honduras forces played a major part in permanently ending the threat of William Walker to establish a slave holding empire in Central America based on his self engineered elections to the Presidency of Nicaragua. Thrice expelled from Central America, Walker was shot by a Honduran firing squad in 1860. 1876 to 1933 saw a period of instability and for some months U.S. Marine Corp military occupation. From 1933 to 1940 General Tiburcio Carias Andino was dictator president of the Republic. Since 1990 democratic practices have become more consistent.

RULERS

Spanish, until 1821

Augustin Iturbide (Emperor of Mexico), 1822-1823

MINT MARKS

A - Paris, 1869-1871

P-Y - Provincia Yoro (?)

T - Tegucigalpa, 1825-1862

T.G. - Yoro

T.L. – Comayagua

NOTE: Extensive die varieties exist for coins struck in Honduras with almost endless date and overdate varieties. Federation style coinage continued to be struck until 1861. (See Central American Republic listings.)

MONETARY SYSTEM

16 Reales = 1 Escudo

100 Centavos = 1 Peso

REPUBLIC

DECIMAL COINAGE

100 Centavos = 1 Peso

KM# 46 CENTAVO

4.5000 g., Bronze **Obv:** Towers front pyramid within circle **Rev:** Denomination and date within wreath **Edge:** Plain, reeded, and plain and reeded **Note:** Varieties exist.

Date	Mintage	VG	F	VF	XF	Unc
1901/0	98,000	6.50	20.00	42.50	60.00	—
1901	Inc. above	6.50	20.00	42.50	60.00	—
1902 large 0	—	5.00	15.00	27.50	50.00	125
1902 small 0	—	5.00	15.00	27.50	50.00	125
1903/2/0	—	6.00	16.50	32.50	55.00	—
1903/2/1/0	—	40.00	80.00	145	—	—
Note: 5 known						
1904	—	4.50	13.50	30.00	52.50	—
1907/4	234,000	8.00	20.00	35.00	60.00	—
1907	Inc. above	6.50	16.50	30.00	55.00	—

KM# 59 CENTAVO

4.5000 g., Bronze **Obv:** Towers front pyramid within circle **Rev:** Denomination within thick circle **Note:** Varieties exist.

Date	Mintage	VG	F	VF	XF	Unc
1907 large UN	—	0.50	2.00	4.00	10.00	25.00

Date	Mintage	VG	F	VF	XF	Unc
Note: Mintage included in KM#46						
1907 small UN	—	0.50	2.00	4.00	10.00	25.00
Note: Mintage included in KM#46						
1908/7	263,000	9.00	16.50	35.00	80.00	—
1908	—	9.00	16.50	35.00	80.00	—

KM# 61 CENTAVO

4.5000 g., Bronze **Obv:** Towers front pyramid within inner circle, wreath surrounds outer circle **Rev:** Denomination within thick circle **Note:** The 1890, 1891 and 1908 dates are found with a die-cutting error or broken die that reads REPLBLICA. Other differences exist.

Date	Mintage	VG	F	VF	XF	Unc
1908	—	6.50	14.50	28.00	55.00	—

KM# 65 CENTAVO

2.1200 g., Bronze **Obv:** Towers front pyramid within circle **Rev:** Denomination and date within wreath **Note:** Varieties exist.

Date	Mintage	VG	F	VF	XF	Unc
1910/1884	—	12.50	25.00	40.00	70.00	—
1910/5	410,000	10.00	22.00	35.00	60.00	—
1910 large 0	410,000	8.50	20.00	32.50	50.00	—
1911/811	62,000	6.00	18.00	28.00	45.00	—
Note: Struck over 1/2 centavo KM45 or simply the re-use of a recut 1/2 Centavo die						
1911/885	Inc. above	6.00	18.00	28.00	45.00	—
Note: Struck over 1/2 centavo KM45 or simply the re-use of a recut 1/2 Centavo die						
1911/886	Inc. above	6.00	18.00	28.00	45.00	—
Note: Struck over 1/2 centavo KM45 or simply the re-use of a recut 1/2 Centavo die						
1911 CENTAVO	Inc. above	6.00	15.00	25.00	40.00	—
1911 CENTAVOS	Inc. above	150	—	—	—	—

KM# 66 CENTAVO

2.1200 g., Bronze **Obv:** Towers front pyramid within circle **Rev:** Altered KM#45

Date	Mintage	VG	F	VF	XF	Unc
1910	Inc. above	9.00	25.00	45.00	90.00	—
1610 error, inverted 9	Inc. above	65.00	125	225	350	—
1910 error, second 1 inverted	Inc. above	12.00	27.50	50.00	100	—

KM# 67 CENTAVO

2.1200 g., Bronze **Obv:** Towers front pyramid within inner circle, wreath surrounds outer circle **Rev:** Denomination within wreath

Date	Mintage	VG	F	VF	XF	Unc
1910	Inc. above	4.00	8.00	17.00	40.00	—

KM# 68 CENTAVO

2.1200 g., Bronze **Obv:** Towers front pyramid within inner circle **Rev:** Denomination within wreath

Date	Mintage	VG	F	VF	XF	Unc
1910	Inc. above	22.50	45.00	85.00	170	—

KM# 70 CENTAVO

2.1200 g., Bronze **Obv:** Towers front pyramid within circle **Rev:** Denomination and date within wreath, CENTAVO omitted

Date	Mintage	VG	F	VF	XF	Unc
1919	168,000	1.50	3.00	6.50	25.00	—
1920	30,000	3.00	6.50	15.00	37.50	—

KM# 64 2 CENTAVOS

4.2500 g., Bronze **Obv:** Towers front pyramid within circle **Rev:** Denomination within thick circle

Date	Mintage	VG	F	VF	XF	Unc
1907 Rare	Inc. below	—	—	—	—	—
1908/7	Inc. below	50.00	100	200	400	—
1908	Inc. below	40.00	80.00	150	300	—

KM# 69 2 CENTAVOS

Bronze **Obv:** Towers front pyramid within circle **Rev:** Denomination and date within wreath **Note:** Reverse dies often very crudely recut, especially 1910 and 1911. Some coins of 1910 appear to be struck over earlier 1 or 2 Centavos, probably 1907 or 1908.

Date	Mintage	VG	F	VF	XF	Unc
1910	435,000	1.25	4.00	10.00	20.00	45.00
1911	68,000	6.50	18.50	40.00	85.00	—
1912 CENTAVOS	88,000	1.00	4.50	15.00	35.00	—
1912 CENTAVO	Inc. above	3.00	6.00	14.50	35.00	—
1913	258,000	1.00	2.50	6.00	18.50	—

KM# 71 2 CENTAVOS

4.2500 g., Bronze **Obv:** Towers front pyramid within circle **Rev:** Denomination and date within wreath, CENTAVOS omitted **Note:** Varieties exist.

Date	Mintage	VG	F	VF	XF	Unc
1919	117,000	2.50	9.00	18.00	55.00	—
1920	283,000	0.65	3.00	15.00	50.00	—
1920 Dot divides date	Inc. above	5.00	10.00	20.00	60.00	—

KM# 48 5 CENTAVOS

1.2500 g., 0.8350 Silver .0336 oz. ASW **Obv:** Towers front pyramid within inner circle, wreath surrounds outer circle **Rev:** Denomination within wreath

Date	Mintage	VG	F	VF	XF	Unc
1902	—	35.00	75.00	125	200	—

KM# 50a 25 CENTAVOS

6.2500 g., 0.8350 Silver .1678 oz. ASW **Note:** Varieties exist.

Date	Mintage	VG	F	VF	XF	Unc
1901/801	54,000	4.00	8.00	15.00	45.00	—
1901/11	Inc. above	6.00	12.50	30.00	60.00	—
1901/0	—	7.00	15.00	35.00	65.00	—
1901 Large first 1	Inc. above	3.00	5.00	9.00	20.00	—
1902/801	—	10.00	17.50	25.00	50.00	—
1902/802	—	10.00	17.50	25.00	50.00	—
1902/812	—	10.00	17.50	25.00	50.00	—
1902/891	—	10.00	17.50	25.00	50.00	—
1902/1 F	—	3.75	6.00	10.00	20.00	125
1902 F	—	4.00	7.50	13.50	25.00	—
1904	—	20.00	40.00	65.00	125	—
1907/4	14,000	7.00	15.00	35.00	60.00	—
1907	Inc. above	7.50	17.50	37.50	65.00	—
1912 .835/.900	7,168	12.50	22.50	45.00	95.00	—
1913/0	52,000	25.00	50.00	100	200	—
1913/2	Inc. above	—	—	—	—	—
1913	Inc. above	10.00	18.50	30.00	55.00	—

KM# 51a 50 CENTAVOS

12.5000 g., Silver .3355 oz. ASW **Obv:** Towers front pyramid within inner circle, crowned and flagged decorative mantle behind **Rev:** Seated Liberty figure with flag and tablet, Neptunes symbols flank **Note:** Fineness can be .835 or .900.

Date	Mintage	VG	F	VF	XF	Unc
1908/897	447	35.00	65.00	165	275	—
1908	Inc. above	30.00	55.00	115	225	—

KM# 51 50 CENTAVOS

12.5000 g., 0.9000 Silver .3617 oz. ASW **Obv:** Towers front pyramid within inner circle, crowned and flagged decorative mantle behind **Rev:** Seated Liberty figure with flag and tablet, Neptunes symbols flank

Date	Mintage	VG	F	VF	XF	Unc
1910	602	500	900	—	—	—

KM# 56 PESO

1.6120 g., 0.9000 Gold .0467 oz. AGW **Obv:** Towers front pyramid within inner circle, bouquets flank outer circle **Rev:** Liberty head left, crossed caduceus and trident flank

Date	Mintage	F	VF	XF	Unc	BU
1901	—	150	300	600	1,150	—
1902	—	140	300	500	1,000	—
1907	—	140	250	450	900	—
1914/882	—	275	450	650	1,200	—
1914/03	—	275	450	600	1,150	—
1919	—	150	300	550	1,100	—
1920	—	150	300	550	1,100	—
1922	—	140	250	450	900	—
ND(ca.1922-25)	—	—	—	—	—	—

KM# 52 PESO

25.0000 g., 0.9000 Silver .7234 oz. ASW **Obv:** Towers front pyramid within inner circle, crowned and flagged mantle behind **Rev:** Seated Liberty figure with flag and tablet, Neptunes symbols flank, large CENTRO-AMERICA **Note:** Overdates and recut dies are prevalent.

Date	Mintage	VG	F	VF	XF	Unc
1902	—	27.50	50.00	80.00	135	—
1903 flat-top 3	—	27.50	45.00	70.00	125	—
1903 round-top 3	—	30.00	55.00	90.00	165	—
1904	20,000	30.00	55.00	90.00	165	—
1914	—	200	500	900	1,500	—

KM# 53 5 PESOS

8.0645 g., 0.9000 Gold .2333 oz. AGW **Obv:** Towers front pyramid within inner circle, bouquets flank outer circle **Rev:** Liberty head left, crossed trident and caduceus flank

Date	Mintage	F	VF	XF	Unc	BU
1902	—	450	650	1,000	2,500	—
1908/888	—	450	650	1,000	2,500	—
1913	1,200	450	650	1,000	2,500	—

KM# 57 20 PESOS

32.2580 g., 0.9000 Gold .9335 oz. AGW **Obv:** Towers front pyramid within inner circle, bouquets flank outer circle **Rev:** Liberty head left, crossed caduceus and trident flank

Date	Mintage	F	VF	XF	Unc	BU
1908/888 Rare	—	—	—	—	—	—
1908/897 Rare	—	—	—	—	—	—
Note: Stack's Hammel sale 9-82 VF 1908/897 realized $12,000. Ponterio & Associates NYINC. sale 12-86 choice XF realized $30,800. Superior Casterline sale 5-89 choice XF realized $28,600.						
1908 Rare	—	—	—	—	—	—

REFORM COINAGE

100 Centavos = 1 Lempira

KM# 77.1 CENTAVO

2.0000 g., Bronze, 15 mm. **Obv:** National arms **Rev:** Denomination within circle, wreath surrounds **Note:** Thick planchet.

Date	Mintage	F	VF	XF	Unc	BU
1935(P)	2,000,000	0.25	1.00	5.00	15.00	—
1939(P)	2,000,000	0.25	0.75	3.00	10.00	—
1949(P)	4,000,000	0.10	0.50	2.00	4.00	—

KM# 77.2 CENTAVO
1.5000 g., Bronze, 15 mm. **Obv:** National arms **Rev:** Denomination within circle, wreath surrounds **Note:** Thin planchet.

Date	Mintage	F	VF	XF	Unc	BU
1954	3,500,000	0.10	0.15	1.00	3.00	—
1956	2,000,000	0.10	0.15	0.75	2.00	—
1957/6	28,000,000	—	—	—	—	—
1957	Inc. above	—	0.10	0.15	0.30	—

KM# 77a CENTAVO
Copper Clad Steel, 15 mm. **Obv:** National arms, without clouds behind pyramids **Rev:** Denomination within circle, wreath surrounds

Date	Mintage	F	VF	XF	Unc	BU
1974	—	—	0.10	0.15	0.25	—
1985	—	—	0.10	0.15	0.25	—
1992	—	—	0.10	0.15	0.25	—
1994	—	—	0.10	0.15	0.25	—
1998	—	—	0.10	0.15	0.25	—

KM# 77b CENTAVO
Copper Plated Steel, 15 mm. **Obv:** National arms, clouds behind pyramids **Rev:** Denomination within circle, wreath surrounds

Date	Mintage	F	VF	XF	Unc	BU
1988	50,000,000	—	0.10	0.15	0.25	—

KM# 78 2 CENTAVOS
3.0000 g., Bronze, 21 mm. **Obv:** National arms **Rev:** Denomination within circle, wreath surrounds

Date	Mintage	F	VF	XF	Unc	BU
1939(P)	2,000,000	0.25	1.00	3.00	9.00	—
1949(P)	3,000,000	0.10	0.50	2.00	6.00	—
1954	2,000,000	0.10	0.25	1.00	3.00	—
1956	20,000,000	—	0.10	0.25	1.00	—

KM# 78a 2 CENTAVOS
2.7000 g., Bronze Clad Steel, 21 mm. **Obv:** National arms **Rev:** Denomination within circle, wreath surrounds

Date	Mintage	F	VF	XF	Unc	BU
1974	—	—	0.10	0.15	0.25	—

KM# 72.1 5 CENTAVOS
5.0000 g., Copper-Nickel, 21 mm. **Obv:** National arms **Rev:** Denomination within circle, wreath surrounds **Note:** Dentilated border.

Date	Mintage	F	VF	XF	Unc	BU
1931(P)	2,000,000	0.50	2.00	7.00	20.00	—
1932(P)	1,000,000	0.35	0.75	4.00	14.00	—
1949(P)	2,000,000	0.20	0.50	3.00	9.00	—
1956(P)	10,070,000	—	0.15	0.25	0.60	—
1972	5,000,000	—	0.10	0.15	0.35	—

KM# 72.2 5 CENTAVOS
5.0000 g., Copper-Nickel, 21 mm. **Obv:** National arms **Rev:** Denomination within circle, wreath surrounds **Note:** Beaded border.

Date	Mintage	F	VF	XF	Unc	BU
1954	1,400,000	0.15	0.25	1.00	3.00	—
1980	20,000,000	—	0.10	0.50	1.00	—

KM# 72.2a 5 CENTAVOS
Brass, 21 mm. **Obv:** National arms, without clouds behind pyramids **Rev:** Denomination within circle, wreath surrounds

Date	Mintage	F	VF	XF	Unc	BU
1975	20,000,000	—	0.10	0.15	0.35	—
1989	—	—	0.10	0.15	0.35	—

KM# 72.3 5 CENTAVOS
Brass, 21 mm. **Obv:** National arms, with clouds behind pyramids **Rev:** Denomination within circle, wreath surrounds

Date	Mintage	F	VF	XF	Unc	BU
1993	—	—	0.10	0.15	0.35	—
1994	—	—	0.10	0.15	0.35	—

KM# 72.4 5 CENTAVOS
Brass, 21 mm. **Obv:** National arms, without clouds behind pyramids **Rev:** Denomination within circle, wreath surrounds

Date	Mintage	F	VF	XF	Unc	BU
1995	—	—	0.10	0.15	0.35	—
1998	—	—	0.10	0.15	0.35	—
1999	—	—	0.10	0.15	0.35	—

KM# 76.1 10 CENTAVOS
7.0000 g., Copper-Nickel, 26 mm. **Obv:** National arms **Rev:** Denomination within circle, wreath surrounds **Note:** Dentilated border.

Date	Mintage	F	VF	XF	Unc	BU
1932(P)	1,500,000	1.00	2.50	10.00	35.00	—
1951(P)	1,000,000	0.50	1.00	4.00	12.00	—
1956(P)	7,560,000	0.10	0.25	0.50	1.00	—

KM# 76.2 10 CENTAVOS
7.0000 g., Copper-Nickel, 26 mm. **Obv:** National arms **Rev:** Denomination within circle, wreath surrounds **Note:** Beaded border.

Date	Mintage	F	VF	XF	Unc	BU
1954	1,200,000	0.10	0.25	1.00	7.00	—
1967	—	0.10	0.25	0.50	2.00	—
1980	15,000,000	0.10	0.25	0.50	2.00	—
1993	—	0.10	0.25	0.50	2.00	—

KM# 76.1a 10 CENTAVOS
Brass, 26 mm. **Obv:** Large letters and national arms **Rev:** Denomination within circle, wreath surrounds **Note:** Dentilated border.

Date	Mintage	F	VF	XF	Unc	BU
1976	—	0.10	0.15	0.25	0.60	—
1989	—	0.10	0.15	0.25	0.60	—

KM# 76.2a 10 CENTAVOS
Brass, 26 mm. **Obv:** Small letters and national arms, without clouds behind pyramids **Rev:** Denomination within circle, wreath surrounds **Note:** Beaded border.

Date	Mintage	F	VF	XF	Unc	BU
1993	—	—	0.10	0.20	0.45	—
1994	—	—	0.10	0.20	0.45	—
1995	—	—	0.10	0.20	0.45	—
1995 Small date	—	—	0.10	0.20	0.45	—

KM# 76.3 10 CENTAVOS
Brass, 26 mm. **Obv:** National arms, with clouds behind pyramid **Rev:** Denomination within circle, wreath surrounds

Date	Mintage	F	VF	XF	Unc	BU
1995	—	—	0.10	0.20	0.45	—
1999 Small date	—	—	0.10	0.20	0.45	—

KM# 73 20 CENTAVOS
2.5000 g., 0.9000 Silver .0723 oz. ASW, 18 mm. **Obv:** National arms **Rev:** Chief Lempira left within circle

Date	Mintage	F	VF	XF	Unc	BU
1931(P)	1,000,000	1.25	3.50	9.00	30.00	—
1932(P)	750,000	1.25	3.50	8.00	22.50	—
1951(P)	1,500,000	BV	1.25	3.00	8.00	—
1952	2,500,000	BV	1.25	2.50	7.00	—
1958	2,000,000	BV	1.25	2.00	6.00	—

KM# 79 20 CENTAVOS
2.2000 g., Copper-Nickel, 18 mm. **Obv:** National arms **Rev:** Chief Lempira left within circle

Date	Mintage	F	VF	XF	Unc	BU
1967	12,000,000	—	0.10	0.35	1.00	1.50

KM# 81 20 CENTAVOS
2.2000 g., Copper-Nickel, 18 mm. **Obv:** National arms, date below **Rev:** Chief Lempira left within circle **Note:** Different style lettering.

Date	Mintage	F	VF	XF	Unc	BU
1973	15,000,000	—	0.10	0.20	0.60	1.00

KM# 83.1 20 CENTAVOS
2.2000 g., Copper-Nickel, 18 mm. **Obv:** National arms **Rev:** Head left within circle

Date	Mintage	F	VF	XF	Unc	BU
1978	30,000,000	—	0.10	0.20	0.60	1.00
1990	—	—	0.10	0.20	0.60	1.00

KM# 83.1a 20 CENTAVOS
Nickel Plated Steel, 18 mm. **Obv:** Small arms and legend, with clouds behind pyramid **Rev:** Head left within circle

Date	Mintage	F	VF	XF	Unc	BU
1991	—	—	0.10	0.20	0.60	1.00
1993	—	—	0.10	0.20	0.60	1.00
1994	—	—	0.10	0.20	0.60	1.00

KM# 83.2a 20 CENTAVOS
Nickel Plated Steel, 18 mm. **Obv:** National arms, without clouds **Rev:** Head left within circle

Date	Mintage	F	VF	XF	Unc	BU
1995	—	—	0.10	0.20	0.60	1.00
1996	—	—	0.10	0.20	0.60	1.00
1999	—	—	0.10	0.20	0.60	1.00

KM# 74 50 CENTAVOS
6.2500 g., 0.9000 Silver .1808 oz. ASW, 23.8 mm. **Obv:** National arms **Rev:** Chiefs head left within circle

Date	Mintage	F	VF	XF	Unc	BU
1931(P)	500,000	3.25	7.00	15.00	40.00	—
1932(P)	1,100,000	2.75	5.00	10.00	35.00	—
1937(P)	1,000,000	2.75	5.00	10.00	35.00	—
1951(P)	500,000	2.75	4.00	9.00	30.00	—

KM# 80 50 CENTAVOS
5.7000 g., Copper-Nickel, 24 mm. **Obv:** National arms **Rev:** Chief Lempira left within circle

Date	Mintage	F	VF	XF	Unc	BU
1967	4,800,000	—	0.25	0.35	1.25	2.00

KM# 82 50 CENTAVOS
5.7000 g., Copper-Nickel, 24 mm. **Series:** F.A.O. **Obv:** National arms **Rev:** Chief Lempira left within circle

Date	Mintage	F	VF	XF	Unc	BU
1973	4,400,000	—	0.25	0.35	1.25	2.00

KM# 84 50 CENTAVOS
5.7000 g., Copper-Nickel, 24 mm. **Obv:** National arms, with clouds behind pyramid **Rev:** Head left within circle

Date	Mintage	F	VF	XF	Unc	BU
1978	12,000,000	—	0.25	0.35	1.00	1.50
1990	—	—	0.25	0.35	1.00	1.50

KM# 84.a1 50 CENTAVOS
Nickel Plated Steel, 24 mm. **Obv:** National arms **Rev:** Head left within circle

Date	Mintage	F	VF	XF	Unc	BU
1991	—	—	0.25	0.35	1.00	1.50
1994	—	—	0.25	0.35	1.00	1.50

KM# 88 50 CENTAVOS
Nickel Plated Steel, 24 mm. **Subject:** 50th Anniversary F.A.O. **Obv:** National arms **Rev:** Head left within circle, logo below

Date	Mintage	F	VF	XF	Unc	BU
1994	2,000,000	—	—	—	1.50	2.00

KM# 84.a2 50 CENTAVOS
Nickel Plated Steel, 24 mm. **Obv:** National arms, no clouds behind pyramid **Rev:** Head left within circle

Date	Mintage	F	VF	XF	Unc	BU
1995	—	—	0.25	0.35	1.00	1.50
1996	—	—	0.25	0.35	1.00	1.50

KM# 75 LEMPIRA
12.5000 g., 0.9000 Silver .3617 oz. ASW, 31 mm. **Obv:** National arms **Rev:** Chiefs head left within circle

Date	Mintage	F	VF	XF	Unc	BU
1931(P)	550,000	6.00	9.00	20.00	75.00	—
1932(P)	1,000,000	5.00	7.50	16.00	65.00	—
1933(P)	400,000	BV	6.50	10.00	45.00	—
1934(P)	600,000	BV	6.00	9.00	40.00	—
1935(P)	1,000,000	—	BV	9.00	40.00	—
1937(P)	4,000,000	—	BV	7.00	25.00	—

KM# 89 LEMPIRA
33.6250 g., 0.9250 Silver 1.0000 oz. ASW, 38 mm. **Subject:** Central Bank's 50th Anniversary **Obv:** National arms within beaded circle **Rev:** Bank building with n beaded circle, wreath surrounds **Edge:** Plain

Date	Mintage	F	VF	XF	Unc	BU
ND(2000) Proof	3,000	Value: 65.00				

KM# 90 LEMPIRA
7.7750 g., 0.9990 Gold .2497 oz. AGW, 24 mm. **Subject:** Central Bank's 50th Anniversary **Obv:** National arms within beaded circle **Rev:** Bank building within beaded circle, wreath surrounds **Edge:** Reeded

Date	Mintage	F	VF	XF	Unc	BU
ND(2000) Proof	1,200	Value: 215				

KM# 85 100 LEMPIRAS
27.0000 g., 0.9250 Silver .8030 oz. ASW **Subject:** 500th Anniversary - Discovery of America **Rev:** Ship approaching curved wall

Date	Mintage	F	VF	XF	Unc	BU
1992 Proof	5,000,000	Value: 60.00				

KM# 86 200 LEMPIRAS
6.5000 g., 0.9000 Gold .1881 oz. AGW, 20 mm. **Subject:** Bicentenary of Birth - Gen. Francisco Morazan **Obv:** Emblem within legend **Rev:** Head left

Date	Mintage	F	VF	XF	Unc	BU
1992 Proof	1,500,000	Value: 175				

KM# 87 500 LEMPIRAS
12.5000 g., 0.9000 Gold .3617 oz. AGW, 26 mm. **Subject:** Bicentenary of Birth - Gen. Francisco Morazan

Date	Mintage	F	VF	XF	Unc	BU
1992	1,500,000	Value: 280				

PATTERNS

Including off metal strikes

Rosettes separate legends on Pn1-Pn5a.

KM#	Date	Mintage	Identification	Mkt Val
Pn22	1909	—	Centavo. Copper.	150
Pn23	1919	—	Peso. Copper. KM#56.	100

HONG KONG

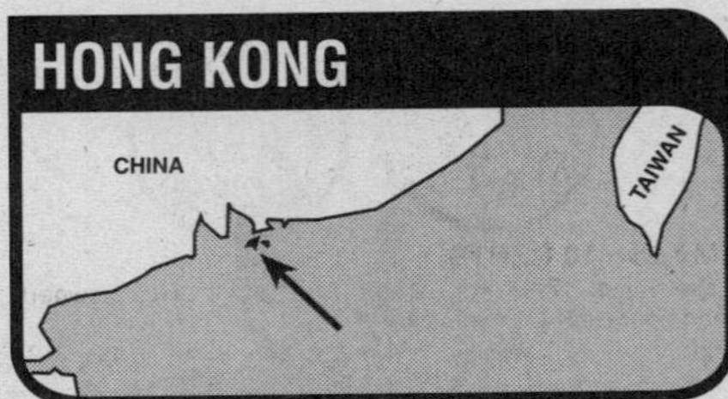

Hong Kong, a former British colony, reverted to control of the People's Republic of China on July 1, 1997 as a Special Administrative Region. It is situated at the mouth of the Canton or Pearl River 90 miles (145 km.) southeast of Canton, has an area of 403 sq. mi. (1,040 sq. km.) and an estimated population of 6.3 million. Capital: Victoria. The free port of Hong Kong, the commercial center of the Far East, is a trans-shipment point for goods destined for China and the countries of the Pacific Rim. Light manufacturing and tourism are important components of the economy.

Long a haven for fishermen-pirates and opium smugglers, the island of Hong Kong was ceded to Britain at the conclusion of the first Opium War, 1839-1842. The acquisition of a 'barren rock' was ridiculed by London and English merchants operating in the Far East. The Kowloon Peninsula and Stonecutter's Island were ceded in 1860, and the so-called New Territories, comprising most of the mainland of the colony, were leased to Britain for 99 years in 1898.

The legends on Hong Kong coinage are bilingual: English and Chinese. The rare 1941 cent was dispatched to Hong Kong in several shipments. One fell into Japanese hands, while another was melted down by the British and a third was sunk during enemy action.

RULERS

British 1842-1997

MINT MARKS

H - Heaton

KN - King's Norton

MONETARY SYSTEM

10 Mils (Wen, Ch'ien) = 1 Cent (Hsien)

10 Cents = 1 Chiao

100 Cents = 10 Chiao = 1 Dollar (Yuan)

BRITISH COLONY

DECIMAL COINAGE

KM# 4.3 CENT

Bronze, 27.6 mm. **Ruler:** Victoria **Obv:** Crowned bust left, five pearls in center of crown **Rev:** English around central Chinese legend

Date	Mintage	F	VF	XF	Unc	BU
1901	5,000,000	2.50	5.50	16.00	80.00	—
1901H	10,000,000	2.50	5.50	16.00	70.00	—

KM# 11 CENT

Bronze, 27.6 mm. **Ruler:** Edward VII **Obv:** Crowned bust right **Rev:** English around central Chinese legend

Date	Mintage	F	VF	XF	Unc	BU
1902	5,000,000	2.50	4.50	10.00	80.00	—
1903	5,000,000	2.50	4.50	10.00	80.00	—
1904H	10,000,000	1.75	3.50	10.00	60.00	—
1905	2,500,000	3.75	7.50	15.00	125	—
1905H	12,500,000	2.50	4.50	10.00	60.00	—

KM# 16 CENT

Bronze, 27.6 mm. **Ruler:** George V **Obv:** Crowned bust left **Rev:** English around central Chinese legend

Date	Mintage	F	VF	XF	Unc	BU
1919H	2,500,000	2.00	4.00	10.00	40.00	—
1923	2,500,000	1.50	3.00	7.50	50.00	—
1924	5,000,000	1.25	2.50	4.50	20.00	—
1925	2,500,000	1.25	2.50	4.50	20.00	—
1926	2,500,000	1.25	2.50	4.50	20.00	—
1926 Proof	—	Value: 350				

KM# 17 CENT

Bronze, 22 mm. **Ruler:** George V **Obv:** Crowned bust left **Rev:** English around central Chinese legend

Date	Mintage	F	VF	XF	Unc	BU
1931	5,000,000	0.75	1.00	2.00	5.50	—
1931 Proof	—	Value: 250				
1933	6,500,000	0.75	1.00	2.00	5.50	—
1933 Proof	—	Value: 250				
1934	5,000,000	0.75	1.00	2.00	5.50	—
1934 Proof	—	Value: 250				

KM# 24 CENT

Bronze **Ruler:** George VI **Obv:** Crowned head left **Rev:** English around central Chinese legend

Date	Mintage	F	VF	XF	Unc	BU
1941	5,000,000	1,100	2,000	4,000	7,500	—
1941 Proof	—	Value: 10,000				

KM# 5 5 CENTS

1.3577 g., 0.8000 Silver .0349 oz. ASW **Ruler:** Victoria **Obv:** Head left **Rev:** English around central Chinese legend **Note:** Coins dated 1866-1868 struck at the Hong Kong Mint; coins without mintmarks dated 1872-1901, were struck at the British Royal Mint.

Date	Mintage	F	VF	XF	Unc	BU
1901	10,000,000	1.25	2.50	5.00	20.00	—

KM# 12 5 CENTS

1.3577 g., 0.8000 Silver .0349 oz. ASW **Ruler:** Edward VII **Obv:** Crowned bust right **Rev:** English around central Chinese legend

Date	Mintage	F	VF	XF	Unc	BU
1903	6,000,000	1.00	2.00	4.00	12.50	—
1903 Proof	—	Value: 225				
1904	8,000,000	1.00	2.00	4.00	12.50	—
1904 Proof	—	Value: 200				
1905	1,000,000	1.25	3.00	6.50	17.50	—
1905H	7,000,000	1.00	2.00	4.00	12.50	—

KM# 18 5 CENTS

1.3577 g., 0.8000 Silver .0349 oz. ASW **Ruler:** George V **Obv:** Crowned bust left **Rev:** English around central Chinese legend

Date	Mintage	F	VF	XF	Unc	BU
1932	3,000,000	1.00	1.50	4.00	10.00	—
1932 Proof	—	Value: 165				
1933	2,000,000	1.00	1.50	3.25	10.00	—
1933 Proof	—	Value: 165				

KM# 18a 5 CENTS

Copper-Nickel **Ruler:** George V **Obv:** Crowned bust left **Rev:** English around central Chinese legend

Date	Mintage	F	VF	XF	Unc	BU
1935	1,000,000	1.00	2.00	4.50	16.50	—
1935 Proof	—	Value: 115				

KM# 20 5 CENTS

Nickel **Ruler:** George VI **Obv:** Crowned head left **Rev:** English around central Chinese legend

Date	Mintage	F	VF	XF	Unc	BU
1937	3,000,000	0.75	1.25	2.25	7.50	—
1937 Proof	—	Value: 85.00				

KM# 22 5 CENTS

Nickel, 16.5 mm. **Ruler:** George VI **Obv:** Crowned head left **Rev:** English around central Chinese legend

Date	Mintage	F	VF	XF	Unc	BU
1938	3,000,000	0.50	1.00	2.00	6.50	—
1938 Proof	—	Value: 125				
1939H	3,090,000	0.50	1.00	2.00	6.50	—
1939H Proof	—	Value: 125				
1939KN	4,710,000	0.50	1.00	2.00	6.50	—
1941H	777,000	350	750	1,400	3,150	—
1941KN	1,075,000	150	300	600	1,200	—

KM# 26 5 CENTS

Nickel-Brass, 16.5 mm. **Ruler:** George VI **Obv:** Crowned head left **Rev:** English around central Chinese legend

Date	Mintage	F	VF	XF	Unc	BU
1949	15,000,000	0.25	0.50	1.25	7.50	—
1949 Proof	—	Value: 125				
1950	20,400,000	0.25	0.50	1.25	7.50	—
1950 Proof	—	Value: 125				

KM# 29.1 5 CENTS

Nickel-Brass, 16.5 mm. **Ruler:** Elizabeth II **Obv:** Crowned head right **Rev:** English around central Chinese legend **Edge:** Reeded and security

Date	Mintage	F	VF	XF	Unc	BU
1958H	5,000,000	—	0.25	0.75	4.50	—
1960	5,000,000	—	0.15	0.50	3.50	—
1960 Proof	—	Value: 65.00				
1963	7,000,000	—	0.15	0.50	3.50	—
1963 Proof	—	Value: 65.00				
1964H	—	50.00	85.00	150	550	—
1965	18,000,000	—	0.10	0.40	2.00	—
1967	10,000,000	—	0.10	0.40	2.00	—

KM# 29.2 5 CENTS

Nickel-Brass, 16.5 mm. **Ruler:** Elizabeth II **Obv:** Crowned head right **Rev:** English around central Chinese legend **Edge:** Reeded **Note:** Error.

Date	Mintage	F	VF	XF	Unc	BU
1958H	Inc. above	2.50	5.00	9.00	20.00	—
1960	Inc. above	2.50	5.00	9.00	20.00	—

KM# 29.3 5 CENTS

2.6000 g., Nickel-Brass, 16.5 mm. **Ruler:** Elizabeth II **Obv:** Crowned head right **Rev:** English around central Chinese legend **Edge:** Reeded

Date	Mintage	F	VF	XF	Unc	BU
1971KN	14,000,000	—	—	0.25	0.50	—
1971H	6,000,000	—	—	0.25	0.50	—
1972H	14,000,000	—	—	0.25	0.50	—
1977	6,000,000	—	—	0.25	0.50	—
1978	10,000,000	—	—	0.25	0.50	—
1979	4,000,000	—	—	0.25	0.50	—
1980 Not issued	50,000,000	—	—	—	—	—

KM# 61 5 CENTS

2.6000 g., Nickel-Brass, 16.5 mm. **Ruler:** Elizabeth II **Obv:** Crowned head right **Rev:** English around central Chinese legend

Date	Mintage	F	VF	XF	Unc	BU
1988	50,000	—	—	—	4.00	—
1988 Proof	25,000	Value: 5.00				

KM# 6.3 10 CENTS

2.7154 g., 0.8000 Silver .0698 oz. ASW **Ruler:** Victoria **Obv:** Crowned bust left, five pearls in center of crown **Rev:** English around central Chinese legend **Note:** Coins dated 1866-1868 struck at the Hong Kong Mint; coins without mintmarks dated 1869-1901, struck at the British Royal Mint.

Date	Mintage	F	VF	XF	Unc	BU
1901	25,000,000	1.25	2.25	4.50	18.50	—

KM# 13 10 CENTS

2.7154 g., 0.8000 Silver .0698 oz. ASW **Ruler:** Edward VII **Obv:** Crowned bust right **Rev:** English around central Chinese legend

Date	Mintage	F	VF	XF	Unc	BU
1902	18,000,000	1.25	2.25	4.50	30.00	—
1902 Proof	—	Value: 200				
1903	25,000,000	1.25	2.25	4.50	30.00	—
1903 Proof	—	Value: 200				
1904	30,000,000	1.25	2.25	4.50	30.00	—
1904 Proof	—	Value: 165				
1905	33,487,000	225	400	650	1,800	—
1905 Proof	—	Value: 2,000				

KM# 19 10 CENTS

Copper-Nickel, 20.5 mm. **Ruler:** George V **Obv:** Crowned bust left **Rev:** English around central Chinese legend

Date	Mintage	F	VF	XF	Unc	BU
1935	10,000,000	0.50	1.00	3.50	15.00	—
1935 Proof	—	Value: 75.00				
1936	5,000,000	0.50	1.00	3.50	15.00	—
1936 Proof	—	Value: 75.00				

KM# 21 10 CENTS

Nickel, 20.5 mm. **Ruler:** George VI **Obv:** Crowned head left **Rev:** English around central Chinese legend

Date	Mintage	F	VF	XF	Unc	BU
1937	17,500,000	0.50	0.80	1.50	6.50	—
1937 Proof	—	Value: 85.00				

KM# 23 10 CENTS

Nickel, 20.5 mm. **Ruler:** George VI **Obv:** Crowned head left **Rev:** English around central Chinese legend

Date	Mintage	F	VF	XF	Unc	BU
1938	7,500,000	0.65	1.00	2.25	7.50	—
1938 Proof	—	Value: 85.00				
1939H	5,000,000	0.65	1.00	2.25	7.50	—
1939KN	5,000,000	0.65	1.00	2.25	7.50	—
1939KN Proof	—	Value: 85.00				

KM# 25 10 CENTS

Nickel-Brass, 20.5 mm. **Ruler:** George VI **Obv:** Crowned head left **Rev:** English around central Chinese legend **Edge:** Reeded and security

Date	Mintage	F	VF	XF	Unc	BU
1948	30,000,000	0.25	0.50	1.25	6.50	—
1948 Proof	—	Value: 65.00				
1949	35,000,000	0.25	0.50	1.25	6.50	—
1949 Proof	—	Value: 65.00				
1950	20,000,000	0.25	0.50	1.25	6.50	—
1950 Proof	—	Value: 65.00				
1951	5,000,000	0.50	1.00	3.00	22.50	—
1951 Proof	—	Value: 85.00				

KM# 25a 10 CENTS

Nickel-Brass, 20.5 mm. **Ruler:** George VI **Obv:** Crowned head left **Rev:** English around central Chinese legend **Edge:** Reeded **Note:** Error.

Date	Mintage	F	VF	XF	Unc	BU
1950	Inc. above	3.50	6.50	12.50	25.00	—

KM# 28.1 10 CENTS

Nickel-Brass, 20.5 mm. **Ruler:** Elizabeth II **Obv:** Crowned head right **Rev:** English around central Chinese legend **Edge:** Reeded with security

Date	Mintage	F	VF	XF	Unc	BU
1955	10,000,000	0.15	0.25	0.50	5.50	—
1955 Proof	—	Value: 50.00				
1956	3,110,000	0.25	0.50	1.25	15.00	—
1956 Proof	—	Value: 50.00				
1956H	4,488,000	0.15	0.25	1.00	10.00	—
1956KN	2,500,000	0.25	0.50	2.00	16.50	—
1957H	5,250,000	0.15	0.25	0.50	10.00	—
1957KN	2,800,000	0.15	0.25	1.00	15.00	—
1958KN	10,000,000	0.15	0.25	0.50	10.00	—
1959H	20,000,000	0.10	0.15	0.25	6.00	—
1960	12,500,000	0.10	0.15	0.25	6.00	—
1960 Proof	—	Value: 50.00				
1960H	10,000,000	0.10	0.15	0.25	6.00	—
1961	20,000,000	0.10	0.15	0.25	4.00	—
1961 Proof	—	Value: 50.00				
1961H	5,000,000	0.15	0.25	0.50	5.00	—
1961KN	5,000,000	0.15	0.25	0.50	5.00	—
1963	27,000,000	0.10	0.15	0.25	4.00	—
1963 Proof	—	Value: 50.00				
1963H	3,000,000	0.20	0.30	0.50	4.00	—
1963KN	Inc. above	0.10	0.15	0.25	3.50	—
1964	9,000,000	0.10	0.15	0.25	2.00	—
1964H	21,000,000	0.10	0.15	0.25	2.00	—
1965	40,000,000	0.10	0.15	0.25	2.00	—
1965H	8,000,000	0.10	0.15	0.25	2.50	—
1965KN	Inc. above	0.10	0.15	0.25	2.50	—
1967	10,000,000	0.10	0.15	0.25	2.00	—
1968H	15,000,000	0.10	0.15	0.25	2.00	—

KM# 28.2 10 CENTS

Nickel-Brass, 20.5 mm. **Ruler:** Elizabeth II **Obv:** Crowned head right **Rev:** English around central Chinese legend **Edge:** Reeded **Note:** Error.

Date	Mintage	F	VF	XF	Unc	BU
1956	Inc. above	2.25	4.50	8.50	25.00	—
1963	—	2.25	4.50	8.50	25.00	—

KM# 28.3 10 CENTS

Nickel-Brass, 20.5 mm. **Ruler:** Elizabeth II **Obv:** Crowned head right **Rev:** English around central Chinese legend **Edge:** Reeded

Date	Mintage	F	VF	XF	Unc	BU
1971H	22,000,000	—	0.10	0.15	0.65	—
1972KN	20,000,000	—	0.10	0.15	0.65	—
1973	2,250,000	0.15	0.25	0.65	3.50	—
1974	4,600,000	—	0.10	0.15	0.65	—
1975	44,840,000	—	0.10	0.15	0.65	—
1978	57,500,000	—	0.10	0.15	0.65	—
1979	101,500,000	—	0.10	0.15	0.65	—
1980	24,000,000	—	7.00	15.00	35.00	—

Note: Few pieces were released for circulation in 1980, but large numbers have found their way onto the market in subsequent years. About 3,500 are known to exist.

KM# 49 10 CENTS

2.0000 g., Nickel-Brass, 17.55 mm. **Ruler:** Elizabeth II **Obv:** Young bust right **Rev:** Denomination

Date	Mintage	F	VF	XF	Unc	BU
1982	—	—	0.10	0.15	0.25	—
1983	110,016,000	—	0.10	0.15	0.25	—
1984	30,016,000	—	0.10	0.15	0.25	—

KM# 55 10 CENTS

Nickel-Brass, 17.55 mm. **Ruler:** Elizabeth II **Obv:** Crowned head right **Rev:** Denomination

Date	Mintage	F	VF	XF	Unc	BU
1985	34,016,000	—	0.10	0.15	0.25	—
1986	40,000,000	—	0.10	0.15	0.25	—
1987	—	—	0.10	0.15	0.25	—
1988	30,000,000	—	0.10	0.15	0.25	—
1988 Proof	20,000	Value: 5.00				
1989	40,000,000	—	0.10	0.15	0.25	—
1990	—	—	0.10	0.15	0.25	—
1991	—	—	0.10	0.15	0.25	—
1992	24,000,000	—	0.10	0.15	0.25	—

KM# 66 10 CENTS

Brass Plated Steel, 17.55 mm. **Ruler:** Elizabeth II **Obv:** Bauhinia flower **Rev:** Denomination

Date	Mintage	F	VF	XF	Unc	BU
1993	—	—	0.10	0.15	0.30	—
1993 Proof	—	Value: 2.50				
1994	—	—	0.10	0.15	0.30	—
1995	—	—	0.10	0.15	0.30	—
1996	—	—	0.10	0.15	0.30	—
1997	—	—	0.10	0.15	0.30	—
1998	—	—	0.10	0.15	0.30	—

KM# 14 20 CENTS

5.4308 g., 0.8000 Silver .1397 oz. ASW **Ruler:** Edward VII **Obv:** Crowned bust right **Rev:** English around central Chinese legend

Date	Mintage	F	VF	XF	Unc	BU
1902	250,000	20.00	40.00	90.00	500	—
1902 Proof	—	Value: 1,200				
1904	250,000	20.00	40.00	90.00	500	—
1905	750,000	300	600	1,200	3,000	—
1905 Proof	—	Value: 6,500				

KM# 36 20 CENTS

2.6000 g., Nickel-Brass, 19 mm. **Ruler:** Elizabeth II **Obv:** Young bust right **Rev:** English around central Chinese legend **Shape:** Scalloped

Date	Mintage	F	VF	XF	Unc	BU
1975	71,000,000	—	0.10	0.20	0.35	—
1976	42,000,000	—	0.10	0.20	0.35	—
1977	Inc. above	—	0.10	0.20	0.35	—
1978	86,000,000	—	0.10	0.20	0.35	—
1979	94,500,000	—	0.10	0.20	0.35	—
1980	65,000,000	—	0.10	0.20	0.35	—
1982	30,000,000	—	0.10	0.20	0.35	—
1983	15,000,000	—	0.10	0.20	0.35	—

KM# 59 20 CENTS

2.6000 g., Brass, 19 mm. **Ruler:** Elizabeth II **Obv:** Crowned head right **Rev:** English around central Chinese legend **Shape:** Scalloped

Date	Mintage	F	VF	XF	Unc	BU
1985	10,000,000	—	0.10	0.20	0.35	—
1988	Est. 40,000	—	0.10	0.20	0.35	—
1988 Proof	Est. 20,000	Value: 5.00				
1989	17,000,000	—	0.10	0.20	0.35	—
1990	—	—	0.10	0.20	0.35	—
1991	131,000,000	—	0.10	0.20	0.35	—

KM# 67 20 CENTS
2.6000 g., Nickel-Brass, 19 mm. **Ruler:** Elizabeth II **Obv:** Bauhinia flower **Rev:** Denomination **Shape:** Scalloped

Date	Mintage	F	VF	XF	Unc	BU
1993	—	—	0.10	0.20	0.40	—
1993 Proof	—	Value: 2.50				
1994	—	—	0.10	0.20	0.40	—
1995	—	—	0.10	0.20	0.40	—
1997	—	—	0.10	0.20	0.40	—
1998	—	—	0.10	0.20	0.40	—

KM# 15 50 CENTS
13.5769 g., 0.8000 Silver .3492 oz. ASW **Ruler:** Edward VII **Obv:** Crowned bust right **Rev:** English and Chinese legend, denomination at center

Date	Mintage	F	VF	XF	Unc	BU
1902	100,000	25.00	35.00	55.00	150	—
1902 Proof	—	Value: 650				
1904	100,000	25.00	35.00	60.00	200	—
1904 Proof	—	Value: 650				
1905	300,000	20.00	25.00	50.00	110	—
1905 Proof	—	Value: 650				

KM# 27.1 50 CENTS
Copper-Nickel, 23.5 mm. **Ruler:** George VI **Obv:** Crowned head left **Rev:** English around central Chinese legend **Edge:** Reeded and security

Date	Mintage	F	VF	XF	Unc	BU
1951	15,000,000	1.00	2.00	3.50	12.00	—
1951 Proof	—	Value: 250				

KM# 27.2 50 CENTS
Copper-Nickel, 23.5 mm. **Ruler:** George VI **Obv:** Crowned head left **Rev:** English around central Chinese legend **Edge:** Reeded **Note:** Error.

Date	Mintage	F	VF	XF	Unc	BU
1951	Inc. above	3.00	5.00	10.00	22.00	—

KM# 30.1 50 CENTS
Copper-Nickel, 23.5 mm. **Ruler:** Elizabeth II **Obv:** Crowned head right **Rev:** English around central Chinese legend **Edge:** Reeded and security

Date	Mintage	F	VF	XF	Unc	BU
1958H	4,000,000	—	0.50	1.25	4.50	—
1960	4,000,000	—	0.40	1.00	4.00	—
1960 Proof	—	Value: 100				
1961	6,000,000	—	0.40	1.00	3.50	—
1961 Proof	—	Value: 100				
1963H	10,000,000	—	0.40	1.00	3.50	—
1964	5,000,000	—	0.40	1.00	3.50	—
1965KN	8,000,000	—	0.40	1.00	3.00	—
1966	5,000,000	—	0.40	1.00	3.50	—
1967	12,000,000	—	0.40	1.00	3.00	—
1968H	12,000,000	—	0.40	1.00	3.00	—
1970H	4,600,000	—	0.40	1.00	3.00	—

KM# 30.2 50 CENTS
Copper-Nickel, 23.5 mm. **Ruler:** Elizabeth II **Obv:** Crowned head right **Rev:** English around central Chinese legend **Edge:** Reeded **Note:** Error.

Date	Mintage	F	VF	XF	Unc	BU
1958H	Inc. above	2.00	4.00	8.00	20.00	—

KM# 34 50 CENTS
Copper-Nickel, 23.5 mm. **Ruler:** Victoria **Obv:** Crowned head right **Rev:** English around central Chinese legend **Edge:** Reeded

Date	Mintage	F	VF	XF	Unc	BU
1971KN	—	—	0.20	0.40	1.50	—
1972	30,000,000	—	0.20	0.40	1.50	—
1973	36,800,000	—	0.20	0.40	1.50	—
1974	6,000,000	—	0.20	0.40	1.50	—
1975	8,000,000	—	0.20	0.40	1.50	—

KM# 41 50 CENTS
4.9000 g., Nickel-Brass, 22.5 mm. **Ruler:** Elizabeth II **Obv:** Young bust right **Rev:** English around central Chinese legend

Date	Mintage	F	VF	XF	Unc	BU
1977	60,001,000	—	0.20	0.30	0.80	—
1978	70,000,000	—	0.20	0.30	0.80	—
1979	60,640,000	—	0.20	0.30	0.80	—
1980	120,000,000	—	0.20	0.30	0.80	—

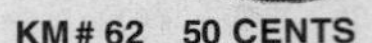

KM# 62 50 CENTS
4.9000 g., Nickel-Brass, 22.5 mm. **Ruler:** Elizabeth II **Obv:** Crowned head right **Rev:** English around central Chinese legend

Date	Mintage	F	VF	XF	Unc	BU
1988	50,000	—	—	—	8.00	—
1988 Proof	25,000	Value: 10.00				
1990	27,000	—	0.20	0.30	0.80	—

KM# 68 50 CENTS
Brass Plated Steel, 22.5 mm. **Ruler:** Elizabeth II **Obv:** Bauhinia flower **Rev:** Denomination

Date	Mintage	F	VF	XF	Unc	BU
1993	—	—	0.20	0.30	0.80	—
1993 Proof	—	Value: 5.50				
1994	—	—	0.20	0.30	0.80	—
1995	—	—	0.20	0.30	0.80	—
1997	—	—	0.20	0.30	0.80	—
1998	—	—	0.20	0.30	0.80	—

KM# 31.1 DOLLAR
Copper-Nickel, 29.8 mm. **Ruler:** Elizabeth II **Obv:** Crowned head right **Rev:** Upright crowned 3/4 lion with orb left **Note:** Mint mark is below "LL" of "DOLLAR".

Date	Mintage	F	VF	XF	Unc	BU
1960H	40,000,000	—	0.60	1.75	5.50	—
1960H Proof	—	Value: 3,350				
1960KN	40,000,000	—	0.60	1.75	5.50	—
1970H	15,000,000	—	0.60	1.25	4.50	—

KM# 31.2 DOLLAR
Copper-Nickel, 29.8 mm. **Ruler:** Elizabeth II **Obv:** Crowned head right **Rev:** Upright crowned 3/4 lion with orb left **Edge:** Reeded **Note:** Error. Mint mark is below "LL" of "DOLLAR"

Date	Mintage	F	VF	XF	Unc	BU
1960H	Inc. above	4.00	7.00	15.00	30.00	—

KM# 35 DOLLAR
Copper-Nickel, 29.8 mm. **Ruler:** Elizabeth II **Obv:** Crowned head right **Rev:** Upright crowned 3/4 lion with orb left **Edge:** Reeded

Date	Mintage	F	VF	XF	Unc	BU
1971H	8,000,000	—	0.60	1.25	4.50	—
1972	20,000,000	—	0.60	1.25	3.50	—
1973	8,125,000	—	0.60	1.25	4.50	—
1974	26,000,000	—	0.60	1.25	3.50	—
1975	22,500,000	—	0.60	1.25	3.50	—

KM# 43 DOLLAR
7.1000 g., Copper-Nickel, 25.5 mm. **Ruler:** Elizabeth II **Obv:** Young bust right **Rev:** Upright crowned 3/4 lion with orb left

Date	Mintage	F	VF	XF	Unc	BU
1978	120,000,000	—	0.40	0.70	1.50	—
1979	104,908,000	—	0.40	0.70	1.50	—
1980	100,000,000	—	0.40	0.70	1.50	—

KM# 63 DOLLAR
7.1000 g., Copper-Nickel, 25.5 mm. **Ruler:** Elizabeth II **Obv:** Crowned head right **Rev:** Upright crowned 3/4 lion with orb left

Date	Mintage	F	VF	XF	Unc	BU
1987	—	—	0.30	0.50	1.00	—
1988	20,000,000	—	0.30	0.50	1.00	—
1988 Proof	20,000	Value: 20.00				
1989	20,000,000	—	0.30	0.50	1.00	—
1990	—	—	0.30	0.50	1.00	—
1991	—	—	0.30	0.50	1.00	—
1992	25,000,000	—	0.30	0.50	1.00	—

KM# 69 DOLLAR
7.1000 g., Nickel Plated Steel, 25.5 mm. **Ruler:** Elizabeth II **Obv:** Bauhinia flower **Rev:** Denomination, large numeral

Date	Mintage	F	VF	XF	Unc	BU
1993	—	—	0.30	0.50	1.00	—
1993 Proof	—	Value: 10.00				

KM# 69a DOLLAR
7.1000 g., Copper-Nickel, 25.5 mm. **Ruler:** Elizabeth II **Obv:** Bauhinia flower **Rev:** Denomination, large numeral

Date	Mintage	F	VF	XF	Unc	BU
1994	—	—	0.30	0.50	1.00	—
1995	—	—	0.30	0.50	1.00	—
1996	—	—	0.30	0.50	1.00	—
1997	—	—	0.30	0.50	1.00	—
1998	—	—	0.30	0.50	1.00	—

KM# 37 2 DOLLARS

8.4000 g., Copper-Nickel, 28 mm. **Ruler:** Elizabeth II **Obv:** Young bust right **Rev:** Upright crowned 3/4 lion with orb left **Shape:** Scalloped

Date	Mintage	F	VF	XF	Unc	BU
1975	60,000,000	—	0.45	0.85	1.75	—
1978	504,000	—	0.45	1.00	10.00	—
1979	9,032,000	—	0.45	0.85	1.75	—
1980	30,000,000	—	0.45	0.85	1.75	—
1981	30,000,000	—	0.45	0.85	1.75	—
1982	30,000,000	—	0.45	0.85	1.75	—
1983	7,002,000	—	0.45	0.85	1.75	—
1984	22,002,000	—	0.45	0.85	1.75	—

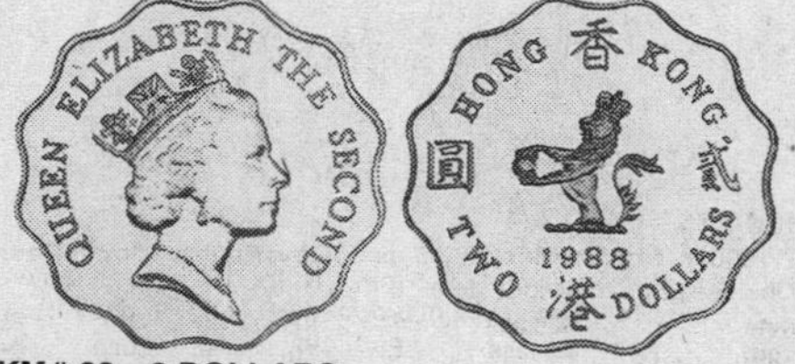

KM# 60 2 DOLLARS

8.4000 g., Copper-Nickel, 28 mm. **Ruler:** Elizabeth II **Obv:** Crowned head right **Rev:** Upright crowned 3/4 lion with orb left **Shape:** Scalloped

Date	Mintage	F	VF	XF	Unc	BU
1985	10,002,000	—	0.45	0.65	1.25	—
1986	15,000,000	—	0.45	0.65	1.25	—
1987	—	—	0.45	2.00	10.00	—
1988	5,000,000	—	0.45	0.65	1.25	—
1988 Proof	20,000	Value: 35.00				
1989	33,000,000	—	0.45	0.65	1.25	—
1990	—	—	0.45	0.65	1.25	—
1992	4,370,000	—	0.45	2.00	10.00	—

KM# 64 2 DOLLARS

8.4000 g., Copper-Nickel, 28 mm. **Ruler:** Elizabeth II **Obv:** Bauhinia flower **Rev:** Denomination, large numeral **Shape:** Scalloped

Date	Mintage	F	VF	XF	Unc	BU
1993	—	—	0.45	0.65	1.25	—
1993 Proof	—	Value: 12.50				
1994	—	—	0.45	0.65	1.25	—
1995	—	—	0.45	0.65	1.25	—
1997	—	—	0.45	0.65	1.25	—
1998	—	—	0.45	0.65	1.25	—

KM# 39 5 DOLLARS

Copper-Nickel, 30.8 mm. **Ruler:** Elizabeth II **Obv:** Young bust right **Rev:** Upright crowned 3/4 lion with orb left **Shape:** 10-sided

Date	Mintage	F	VF	XF	Unc	BU
1976	30,000,000	—	1.00	3.00	10.00	—
1978	10,000,000	—	1.00	3.00	15.00	—
1979	12,000,000	—	1.00	3.00	12.00	—

KM# 46 5 DOLLARS

13.4000 g., Copper-Nickel, 27 mm. **Ruler:** Elizabeth II **Obv:** Young bust right **Rev:** Denomination, large numeral

Date	Mintage	F	VF	XF	Unc	BU
1980	40,000,000	—	1.00	1.50	6.00	—
1981	20,000,000	—	1.00	1.50	6.00	—
1982	10,000,000	—	1.00	1.50	6.00	—
1983	4,000,000	—	1.00	1.50	10.00	—
1984	4,500,000	—	1.00	1.50	10.00	—

KM# 56 5 DOLLARS

13.4000 g., Copper-Nickel, 27 mm. **Ruler:** Elizabeth II **Obv:** Crowned head right **Rev:** Denomination, large numeral

Date	Mintage	F	VF	XF	Unc	BU
1985	6,000,000	—	0.75	1.25	6.00	—
1986	8,000,000	—	0.75	1.25	6.00	—
1987	—	—	0.75	1.25	6.00	—
1988	16,000,000	—	0.75	1.25	6.00	—
1988 Proof	25,000	Value: 45.00				
1989	37,000,000	—	0.75	1.25	6.00	—

KM# 65 5 DOLLARS

13.4000 g., Copper-Nickel, 27 mm. **Ruler:** Elizabeth II **Obv:** Bauhinia flower **Rev:** Denomination, large numeral **Edge Lettering:** in Chinese: HONG KONG FIVE DOLLARS

Date	Mintage	F	VF	XF	Unc	BU
1993	—	—	0.75	1.25	2.25	—
1993 Proof	—	Value: 20.00				
1995	—	—	0.75	1.25	2.25	—
1997	—	—	0.75	1.25	2.25	—
1998	—	—	0.75	1.25	2.25	—

KM# 70 10 DOLLARS

Bi-Metallic Nickel-Brass center in Copper-Nickel ring, 24 mm. **Ruler:** Elizabeth II **Obv:** Bauhinia flower **Rev:** Numerals 10 and denomination in Chinese and English

Date	Mintage	F	VF	XF	Unc	BU
1993	—	—	2.50	4.50	10.00	—
1993 Proof	Est. 30,000	Value: 20.00				
1994	—	—	1.50	2.50	5.00	—
1995	—	—	1.50	2.50	5.00	—

KM# 70a 10 DOLLARS

Ring Composition: 0.3750 Gold **Center Weight:** 18.3000 g. **Center Composition:** 0.9170 Gold .3826 oz. AGW , 24 mm. **Ruler:** Elizabeth II **Obv:** Bauhinia flower **Rev:** Numerals 10 and denomination in Chinese and English

Date	Mintage	F	VF	XF	Unc	BU
1994	20,000	—	—	—	260	280

KM# 38 1000 DOLLARS

15.9700 g., 0.9170 Gold .4708 oz. AGW **Ruler:** Elizabeth II **Subject:** Visit of Queen Elizabeth **Obv:** Young bust right **Rev:** Arms with supporters **Rev. Designer:** Leslie Durbin

Date	Mintage	F	VF	XF	Unc	BU
1975	15,000	—	—	—	300	350
1975 Proof	5,005	Value: 1,150				

KM# 40 1000 DOLLARS

15.9700 g., 0.9170 Gold .4708 oz. AGW **Ruler:** Elizabeth II **Subject:** Year of the Dragon **Obv:** Young bust right **Rev:** Dragon left **Rev. Designer:** Elizabeth Haddon-Care

Date	Mintage	F	VF	XF	Unc	BU
1976	20,000	—	—	—	465	500
1976 Proof	6,911	Value: 1,000				

KM# 42 1000 DOLLARS

15.9700 g., 0.9170 Gold .4708 oz. AGW **Ruler:** Elizabeth II **Subject:** Year of the Snake **Obv:** Young bust right **Rev:** Snake **Rev. Designer:** Elizabeth Haddon-Care

Date	Mintage	F	VF	XF	Unc	BU
1977	20,000	—	—	—	320	365
1977 Proof	10,000	Value: 475				

KM# 44 1000 DOLLARS

15.9700 g., 0.9170 Gold .4708 oz. AGW **Ruler:** Elizabeth II **Subject:** Year of the Horse **Obv:** Young bust right **Rev:** Horse left **Rev. Designer:** Elizabeth Haddon-Care

Date	Mintage	F	VF	XF	Unc	BU
1978	20,000	—	—	—	320	350
1978 Proof	10,000	Value: 450				

KM# 45 1000 DOLLARS

15.9700 g., 0.9170 Gold .4708 oz. AGW **Ruler:** Elizabeth II **Subject:** Year of the Goat **Obv:** Young bust right **Rev:** Goat left **Rev. Designer:** Elizabeth Haddon-Care

Date	Mintage	F	VF	XF	Unc	BU
1979	30,000	—	—	—	320	350
1979 Proof	15,000	Value: 350				

KM# 47 1000 DOLLARS

15.9700 g., 0.9170 Gold .4708 oz. AGW **Ruler:** Elizabeth II **Subject:** Year of the Monkey **Obv:** Young bust right **Rev:** Monkey seated right **Rev. Designer:** Elizabeth Haddon-Care

Date	Mintage	F	VF	XF	Unc	BU
1980	31,000	—	—	—	320	350
1980 Proof	18,000	Value: 375				

KM# 48 1000 DOLLARS

15.9700 g., 0.9170 Gold .4708 oz. AGW **Ruler:** Elizabeth II **Subject:** Year of the Cockerel **Obv:** Young bust right **Rev:** Rooster right **Rev. Designer:** Elizabeth Haddon-Care

Date	Mintage	F	VF	XF	Unc	BU
1981	33,000	—	—	—	320	350
1981 Proof	22,000	Value: 375				

KM# 50 1000 DOLLARS

15.9700 g., 0.9170 Gold .4708 oz. AGW **Ruler:** Elizabeth II **Subject:** Year of the Dog **Obv:** Young bust right **Rev:** Dog right **Rev. Designer:** Elizabeth Haddon-Care

Date	Mintage	F	VF	XF	Unc	BU
1982	33,000	—	—	—	320	350
1982 Proof	22,000	Value: 375				

KM# 51 1000 DOLLARS

15.9700 g., 0.9170 Gold .4708 oz. AGW **Ruler:** Elizabeth II **Subject:** Year of the Pig **Obv:** Young bust right **Rev:** Pig right **Rev. Designer:** Elizabeth Haddon-Care

Date	Mintage	F	VF	XF	Unc	BU
1983	33,000	—	—	—	375	450
1983 Proof	22,000	Value: 650				

KM# 52 1000 DOLLARS

15.9700 g., 0.9170 Gold .4708 oz. AGW **Ruler:** Elizabeth II **Subject:** Year of the Rat **Obv:** Young bust right **Rev:** Rat left **Rev. Designer:** Elizabeth Haddon-Care

Date	Mintage	F	VF	XF	Unc	BU
1984	20,000	—	—	—	350	400
1984 Proof	10,000	Value: 525				

KM# 53 1000 DOLLARS

15.9700 g., 0.9170 Gold .4708 oz. AGW **Ruler:** Elizabeth II **Subject:** Year of the Ox **Obv:** Young bust right **Rev:** Ox left **Rev. Designer:** Elizabeth Haddon-Care

Date	Mintage	F	VF	XF	Unc	BU
1985	30,000	—	—	—	325	375
1985 Proof	10,000	Value: 525				

KM# 54 1000 DOLLARS

15.9700 g., 0.9170 Gold .4708 oz. AGW **Ruler:** Elizabeth II **Subject:** Year of the Tiger **Obv:** Young bust right **Rev:** Tiger **Rev. Designer:** Elizabeth Haddon-Care

Date	Mintage	F	VF	XF	Unc	BU
1986	20,000	—	—	—	320	345
1986 Proof	10,000	Value: 475				

KM# 57 1000 DOLLARS

15.9700 g., 0.9170 Gold .4708 oz. AGW **Ruler:** Elizabeth II **Subject:** Royal visit of Queen Elizabeth II **Obv:** Crowned head right **Rev:** Arms with supporters **Rev. Designer:** Leslie Durbin

Date	Mintage	F	VF	XF	Unc	BU
1986	20,000	—	—	—	320	345
1986 Proof	12,000	Value: 375				

KM# 58 1000 DOLLARS

15.9700 g., 0.9170 Gold .4708 oz. AGW **Ruler:** Elizabeth II **Subject:** Year of the Rabbit **Obv:** Young bust right **Rev:** Rabbit left **Rev. Designer:** Elizabeth Haddon-Care

Date	Mintage	F	VF	XF	Unc	BU
1987	20,000	—	—	—	325	345
1987 Proof	12,000	Value: 375				

SPECIAL ADMINISTRATION REGION (S.A.R.)

DECIMAL COINAGE

KM# 72 10 CENTS

Brass Plated Steel, 17.55 mm. **Obv:** Bauhinia flower **Rev:** Sailing junk

Date	Mintage	F	VF	XF	Unc	BU
1997	—	—	0.10	0.15	0.30	0.45
1997 Proof	Est. 97,000	Value: 1.50				

KM# 73 20 CENTS

Nickel-Brass, 19 mm. **Obv:** Bauhinia flower **Rev:** Butterfly kites

Date	Mintage	F	VF	XF	Unc	BU
1997	—	—	0.10	0.20	0.40	0.60
1997 Proof	—	Value: 1.50				
1998	—	—	0.10	0.20	0.40	0.60

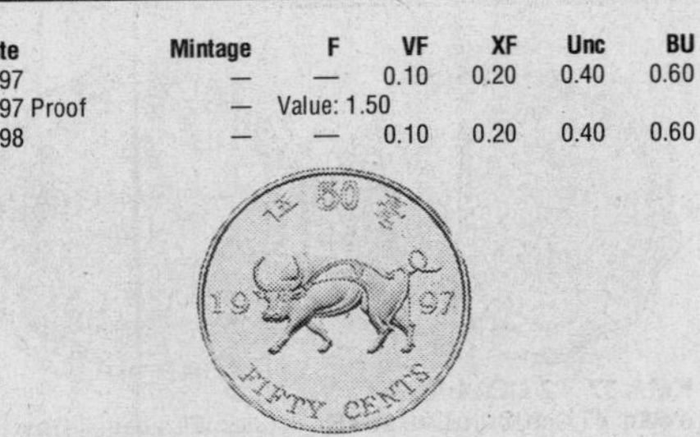

KM# 74 50 CENTS

Brass Plated Steel, 22.5 mm. **Obv:** Bauhinia flower **Rev:** Ox left divides date

Date	Mintage	F	VF	XF	Unc	BU
1997	—	—	0.20	0.30	0.80	1.00
1997 Proof	Est. 97,000	Value: 2.50				
1998	—	—	0.20	0.30	0.80	1.00

KM# 75 DOLLAR

7.1000 g., Copper-Nickel, 25.5 mm. **Obv:** Bauhinia flower **Rev:** Chinese unicorn divides date

Date	Mintage	F	VF	XF	Unc	BU
1997	—	—	0.30	0.50	1.00	1.25
1997 Proof	—	Value: 5.50				

KM# 76 2 DOLLARS

8.4000 g., Copper-Nickel, 28 mm. **Obv:** Bauhinia flower **Rev:** Ho Ho brothers divide date **Shape:** Scalloped

Date	Mintage	F	VF	XF	Unc	BU
1997	—	—	0.45	0.65	1.25	1.50
1997 Proof	Est. 97,000	Value: 8.00				

KM# 77 5 DOLLARS

13.4000 g., Copper-Nickel, 27 mm. **Obv:** Bauhinia flower **Rev:** Shou character divides date **Edge Lettering:** in Chinese: HONG KONG FIVE DOLLARS

Date	Mintage	F	VF	XF	Unc	BU
1997	—	—	0.75	1.25	2.25	2.50
1997 Proof	Est. 97,000	Value: 12.50				

KM# 78 10 DOLLARS

Bi-Metallic Nickel-Brass center in Copper-Nickel ring, 24 mm. **Obv:** Bauhinia flower **Rev:** Suspension bridge

Date	Mintage	F	VF	XF	Unc	BU
1997	—	—	1.75	3.50	6.50	7.00
1997 Proof	Est. 97,000	Value: 13.50				

KM# 71 1000 DOLLARS
15.9700 g., 0.9170 Gold .4708 oz. AGW **Subject:** Return of Hong Kong to China **Obv:** Bauhinia flower **Rev:** Skyline view

Date	Mintage	F	VF	XF	Unc	BU
1997 Proof	97,000	Value: 330				

KM# 79 1000 DOLLARS
15.9700 g., 0.9170 Gold .4708 oz. AGW **Subject:** Hong Kong International Airport **Obv:** Bauhinia flower **Rev:** Stylized airplane lifting off from runway

Date	Mintage	F	VF	XF	Unc	BU
1998 Proof	15,000	Value: 450				

MINT SETS

KM#	Date	Mintage	Identification	Issue Price	Mkt Val
MS1	1988 (7)	50,000	KM55-56, 59-63	13.00	30.00
MS2	1993 (7)	—	KM64-70	20.00	20.00
MS3	1997 (7)	—	KM72-78	30.00	12.50

PROOF SETS

KM#	Date	Mintage	Identification	Issue Price	Mkt Val
PS4	1988 (7)	25,000	KM55-56, 59-63	39.75	60.00
PS5	1993 (7)	30,000	KM64-70	50.00	40.00
PS6	1997 (7)	97,000	KM72-78	—	30.00

The Republic of Hungary, located in central Europe, has an area of 35,929 sq. mi. (93,030 sq. km.) and a population of 10.7 million. Capital: Budapest. The economy is based on agriculture, bauxite and a rapidly expanding industrial sector. Machinery, chemicals, iron and steel, and fruits and vegetables are exported.

The ancient kingdom of Hungary, founded by the Magyars in the 9th century, achieved its greatest extension in the mid-14th century when its dominions touched the Baltic, Black and Mediterranean Seas. After suffering repeated Turkish invasions, Hungary accepted Habsburg rule to escape Turkish occupation, regaining independence in 1867 with the Emperor of Austria as king of a dual Austro-Hungarian monarchy.

After World War I, Hungary lost 2/3 of its territory and 1/2 of its population and underwent a period of drastic political revision. The short-lived republic of 1918 was followed by a chaotic interval of communist rule, 1919, and the restoration of the monarchy in 1920 with Admiral Horthy as regent of the kingdom. Although a German ally in World War II, Hungary was occupied by German troops who imposed a pro-Nazi dictatorship, 1944. Soviet armies drove out the Germans in 1945 and assisted the communist minority in seizing power. A revised constitution published on Aug. 20, 1949, established Hungary as a People's Republic of the Soviet type. On October 23, 1989, Hungary was pro-claimed the Republic of Hungary.

RULERS
Franz Joseph I, 1848-1916
Karl I, 1916-1918

MINT MARKS
B, K, KB - Kremnitz (Kormoczbanya)
BP - Budapest

MONETARY SYSTEM

1892-1925
100 Filler = 1 Korona

1926-1945
100 Filler = 1 Pengo

Commencing 1946
100 Filler = 1 Forint

NOTE: Many coins of Hungary through 1948, especially 1925-1945, have been restruck in recent times. These may be identified by a rosette in the vicinity of the mintmark. Restrike mintages for KM#440-449, 451-458, 468-469, 475-477, 480-483, 494, 496-498 are usually about 1000 pieces, later date mintages are not known.

KINGDOM

REFORM COINAGE

100 Filler = 1 Korona

KM# 480 FILLER
Bronze **Ruler:** Franz Joseph I **Obv:** Crown of St. Stephen **Rev:** Denomination within wreath

Date	Mintage	F	VF	XF	Unc	BU
1901KB	5,994,000	4.00	8.00	17.00	32.50	—
1902KB	16,299,000	0.20	0.50	1.25	4.00	—
1903KB	2,291,000	12.00	25.00	65.00	110	—
1906KB	61,000	65.00	160	350	600	—
1914KB	—	65.00	130	280	380	—
1914KB Proof	—	Value: 350				

KM# 481 2 FILLER
Bronze **Ruler:** Franz Joseph I **Obv:** Crown of St. Stephen **Rev:** Denomination within wreath

Date	Mintage	F	VF	XF	Unc	BU
1901KB	25,805,000	0.50	1.00	2.50	5.00	—
1902KB	6,937,000	5.50	8.50	13.50	20.00	—
1903KB	4,052,000	12.00	20.00	65.00	130	—
1904KB	4,203,000	6.00	12.00	25.00	70.00	—
1905KB	9,335,000	0.70	1.75	3.00	6.00	—
1906KB	3,140,000	1.75	2.50	5.00	7.50	—
1907KB	9,943,000	5.50	9.00	12.00	17.50	—
1908KB	16,486,000	0.50	1.00	2.50	5.00	—
1909KB	19,075,000	0.50	1.00	2.50	5.00	—
1910KB	5,338,000	4.50	7.50	10.00	15.00	—
1910KB Proof, restrike with rosette	—	Value: 10.00				
1914KB	4,106,000	0.50	1.00	2.50	5.00	—
1915KB	1,294,000	1.50	2.00	4.00	7.00	—

KM# 497 2 FILLER
Iron **Ruler:** Karl I **Obv:** Crown of St. Stephen **Rev:** Denomination above sprays **Note:** Varieties in planchet thickness exist for 1917.

Date	Mintage	F	VF	XF	Unc	BU
1916	—	6.00	10.00	15.00	25.00	—
1917	—	1.00	2.50	6.00	12.00	—
1918	—	2.00	4.50	9.00	15.00	—

KM# 482 10 FILLER
Nickel **Ruler:** Franz Joseph I **Obv:** Crown of St. Stephen **Rev:** Denomination within wreath **Note:** Edge varieties exist.

Date	Mintage	F	VF	XF	Unc	BU
1906KB	56,000	75.00	175	250	325	—
1908KB	6,819,000	0.25	0.50	1.50	4.00	—
1909KB	17,204,000	0.30	0.60	2.00	4.00	—
1914KB	—	—	175	275	550	900

KM# 494 10 FILLER
Copper-Nickel-Zinc **Ruler:** Franz Joseph I **Obv:** Crown of St. Stephen **Rev:** Denomination above sprays **Note:** Varieties exist.

Date	Mintage	F	VF	XF	Unc	BU
1914	4,400,000	—	200	300	500	900
1915	Inc. above	0.30	0.60	1.50	4.00	—
1915 Proof	Inc. above	Value: 4.00				
Note: Restrike with rosette						
1916	Inc. above	0.50	1.25	2.50	5.00	—

KM# 496 10 FILLER
Iron **Ruler:** Karl I **Obv:** Crown of St. Stephen **Rev:** Denomination above sprays **Note:** Varieties exist.

Date	Mintage	F	VF	XF	Unc	BU
1915	11,500,000	9.00	20.00	80.00	140	—
1916 Rare	Inc. above	—	—	—	—	—
1918	Inc. above	15.00	30.00	55.00	85.00	—
1918 Proof, restrike	—	Value: 18.00				
1920	3,275,000	4.50	19.00	50.00	85.00	—
1920 Proof, restrike	—	Value: 18.00				

KM# 483 20 FILLER
Nickel **Ruler:** Franz Joseph I **Obv:** Crown of St. Stephen **Rev:** Denomination within wreath **Note:** Edge varieties exist.

Date	Mintage	F	VF	XF	Unc	BU
1906KB	67,000	275	400	600	1,250	—
1907KB	1,248,000	3.00	6.00	12.00	24.00	—
1908KB	10,770,000	0.75	1.75	3.75	7.50	—
1914KB	5,387,000	3.75	6.50	10.00	15.00	—
1914KB Restrike; proof	—	Value: 12.50				

KM# 498 20 FILLER
Iron **Obv:** Crown of St. Stephen **Rev:** Denomination within wreath **Note:** Edge varieties exist.

Date	Mintage	F	VF	XF	Unc	BU
1914	18,826,000	18.00	32.50	45.00	70.00	—
1916	Inc. above	0.50	1.25	2.50	7.00	—
1917	Inc. above	0.75	1.75	3.50	8.00	—
1918	Inc. above	0.75	1.75	3.50	8.00	—
1918 Proof, restrike	—	Value: 6.00				
1920	12,000,000	2.50	5.00	9.00	18.00	—
1921	Inc. above	18.00	32.50	45.00	70.00	—
1921 Proof, restrike	—	Value: 12.00				
1922 Rare	—	—	—	—	—	—
1922 Proof, restrike	—	Value: 12.00				

KM# 498a 20 FILLER
Brass **Obv:** Crown of St. Stephen **Rev:** Denomination above sprays

Date	Mintage	F	VF	XF	Unc	BU
1922	400	—	—	—	—	—
1922 Proof, restrike	—	Value: 30.00				

KM# 484 KORONA
5.0000 g., 0.8350 Silver .1342 oz. ASW **Ruler:** Franz Joseph I **Obv:** Laureate head right **Rev:** Crown of St. Stephen within wreath **Note:** Obverse varieties exist.

Date	Mintage	F	VF	XF	Unc	BU
1906KB	24,000	150	200	300	425	—

KM# 492 KORONA
5.0000 g., 0.8350 Silver .1342 oz. ASW **Ruler:** Franz Joseph I **Obv:** Laureate head right **Obv. Legend:** Crown of St. Stephen within wreath

Date	Mintage	F	VF	XF	Unc	BU
1912	4,004,000	2.50	5.00	10.00	15.00	—
1913	5,214	50.00	80.00	140	200	—
1914	5,886,000	BV	3.75	6.50	10.00	—
1915	3,934,000	BV	3.00	4.50	6.00	—
1916	—	BV	3.50	6.00	8.00	—

KM# 493 2 KORONA
10.0000 g., 0.8350 Silver .2685 oz. ASW **Ruler:** Franz Joseph I **Obv:** Laureate head right **Rev:** Crown of St. Stephen supported by two angels, spray below

Date	Mintage	F	VF	XF	Unc	BU
1912KB	4,000,000	BV	4.50	6.50	13.50	—
1913KB	3,000,000	BV	4.50	6.50	13.50	—
1914KB	500,000	20.00	30.00	50.00	80.00	—

KM# 488 5 KORONA
24.0000 g., 0.9000 Silver .6944 oz. ASW **Ruler:** Franz Joseph I **Obv:** Laureate head right **Rev:** Crown of St. Stephen supported by two angels, spray below

Date	Mintage	F	VF	XF	Unc	BU
1906KB	1,263	1,000	1,500	2,000	2,500	—
1907KB	500,000	14.00	20.00	40.00	85.00	—
1908KB	1,742,000	12.00	18.00	40.00	75.00	—
1909KB	1,299,000	12.00	18.00	40.00	90.00	—
1909KB U.P. Proof, restrike	—	Value: 35.00				

KM# 489 5 KORONA
24.0000 g., 0.9000 Silver .6944 oz. ASW, 36 mm. **Ruler:** Franz Joseph I **Subject:** 40th Anniversary - Coronation of Franz Josef **Obv:** Laureate head right **Rev:** Coronation scene **Edge Lettering:** BIZALMAM AZ OSI ERÈNYBEN **Designer:** Karoly Gerl

Date	Mintage	F	VF	XF	Unc	BU
1907	300,000	15.00	22.00	35.00	55.00	—
1907 Proof, restrike	—	Value: 30.00				
1907 U.P. Proof, restrike	—	Value: 30.00				

KM# 485 10 KORONA
3.3875 g., 0.9000 Gold .0980 oz. AGW **Ruler:** Franz Joseph I **Obv:** Emperor standing **Rev:** Crowned shield with angel supporters

Date	Mintage	F	VF	XF	Unc	BU
1901KB	230,000	—	BV	65.00	85.00	—
1902KB	243,000	—	BV	70.00	90.00	—
1903KB	228,000	—	BV	70.00	90.00	—
1904KB	1,531,000	—	BV	70.00	90.00	—
1905KB	869,000	—	BV	70.00	90.00	—
1906KB	748,000	—	BV	70.00	90.00	—
1907KB	752,000	—	BV	70.00	90.00	—
1908KB	509,000	—	BV	70.00	90.00	—
1909KB	574,000	—	BV	70.00	90.00	—
1910KB	1,362,000	—	BV	70.00	90.00	—
1911KB	1,828,000	—	BV	70.00	90.00	—
1912KB	739,000	BV	75.00	130	220	—
1913KB	137,000	BV	100	220	300	—
1914KB	115,000	BV	200	450	500	—
1915KB	54,000	1,000	2,000	3,000	4,000	—

KM# 486 20 KORONA
6.7750 g., 0.9000 Gold .1960 oz. AGW **Ruler:** Franz Joseph I **Obv:** Emperor standing **Rev:** Crowned shield with angel supporters

Date	Mintage	F	VF	XF	Unc	BU
1901KB	510,000	—	BV	135	150	—
1901KB	510,000	—	BV	95.00	150	—
1902KB	523,000	—	BV	135	150	—
1903KB	505,000	—	BV	135	150	—
1904KB	572,000	—	BV	135	150	—
1905KB	526,000	—	BV	135	150	—
1906KB	353,000	—	BV	135	150	—
1907KB	194,000	BV	150	175	200	—
1908KB	138,000	—	BV	135	150	—
1909KB	459,000	—	BV	135	150	—
1910KB	85,000	135	175	250	300	—
1911KB	63,000	—	BV	135	150	—
1912KB	211,000	—	BV	135	150	—
1913KB	320,000	BV	140	165	200	—
1914KB	176,000	—	BV	135	150	—
1915KB	690,000	BV	140	165	200	—

KM# 495 20 KORONA
6.7750 g., 0.9000 Gold .1960 oz. AGW **Ruler:** Franz Joseph I **Obv:** Emperor standing **Rev:** Crowned shield (Bosnian arms added) with angel supporters

Date	Mintage	F	VF	XF	Unc	BU
1914	—	—	BV	135	155	—
1915	—	—	—	—	—	—
1916	—	BV	175	275	400	—

KM# 500 20 KORONA
6.7750 g., 0.9000 Gold .1960 oz. AGW **Ruler:** Karl I **Obv. Legend:** KAROLY...

Date	Mintage	F	VF	XF	Unc	BU
1918 Rare	—	—	—	—	—	—

KM# 490 100 KORONA
33.8753 g., 0.9000 Gold .9802 oz. AGW, 36 mm. **Ruler:** Franz Joseph I **Subject:** 40th Anniversary - Coronation of Franz Josef **Obv:** Laureate head right **Rev:** Coronation scene **Edge Lettering:** BIZALMAM AZ ÖSI ERÈNYBEN **Designer:** Karoly Gerl

Date	Mintage	F	VF	XF	Unc	BU
1907KB	11,000	BV	675	950	1,350	—
1907KB U.P. Restrike	—	—	—	—	825	—

KM# 491 100 KORONA
33.8753 g., 0.9000 Gold .9802 oz. AGW **Ruler:** Franz Joseph I **Obv:** Emperor standing **Rev:** Crowned shield with angel supporters

Date	Mintage	F	VF	XF	Unc	BU
1907	1,088	BV	1,100	1,450	1,900	—
1907 U.P. Restrike	—	—	—	—	700	—
1908	4,038	BV	850	1,250	1,800	—
1908 U.P Restrike	—	—	—	—	700	—

REGENCY COINAGE

1926 - 1945

KM# 505 FILLER
Bronze **Obv:** Crown of St. Stephen **Rev:** Denomination

Date	Mintage	F	VF	XF	Unc	BU
1926BP	6,471,000	0.50	1.00	2.00	4.00	—
1927BP	16,529,000	0.10	0.20	0.50	3.00	—
1928BP	7,000,000	0.25	0.50	1.00	3.75	—
1929BP	418,000	5.00	10.00	20.00	35.00	—
1930BP	3,734,000	0.30	0.60	1.50	5.00	—
1931BP	10,849,000	0.10	0.20	0.60	3.00	—

Date	Mintage	F	VF	XF	Unc	BU
1932BP	5,000,000	0.25	0.50	1.00	4.00	—
1932BP Proof, restrike	—	Value: 3.75				
1933BP	5,000,000	0.25	0.50	1.00	4.00	—
1934BP	3,111,000	0.30	0.60	1.20	4.50	—
1935BP	6,889,000	0.25	0.50	1.00	4.00	—
1936BP	10,000,000	0.10	0.20	0.60	2.50	—
1938BP	10,575,000	0.10	0.20	0.60	2.50	—
1939BP	10,425,000	0.10	0.20	0.60	2.50	—

KM# 506 2 FILLER

Bronze **Obv:** Crown of St. Stephen **Rev:** Denomination

Date	Mintage	F	VF	XF	Unc	BU
1926BP	17,777,000	0.10	0.20	0.40	2.00	—
1927BP	44,836,000	0.10	0.20	0.40	2.00	—
1928BP	11,448,000	0.10	0.20	0.40	2.00	—
1929BP	8,995,000	0.10	0.25	0.50	2.50	—
1930BP	6,943,000	0.10	0.25	0.50	2.50	—
1931BP	826,000	0.40	0.90	2.50	6.50	—
1932BP	4,174,000	4.00	8.00	15.00	25.00	—
1933BP	501,000	3.00	6.00	10.00	18.00	—
1934BP	9,499,000	0.10	0.20	0.40	2.00	—
1935BP	10,000,000	0.10	0.20	0.40	2.00	—
1936BP	2,049,000	0.15	0.30	0.75	4.00	—
1937BP	7,951,000	0.10	0.25	0.50	2.00	—
1938BP	14,125,000	0.10	0.20	0.40	1.50	—
1939BP	16,875,000	0.10	0.20	0.40	1.50	—
1940BP	7,000,000	0.10	0.25	0.50	1.50	—

KM# 518.1 2 FILLER

Steel **Obv:** Crown of St. Stephen **Rev:** Denomination

Date	Mintage	F	VF	XF	Unc	BU
1940	64,500,000	1.00	2.00	5.00	10.00	—

KM# 518.2 2 FILLER

Steel **Obv:** Crown of St. Stephen **Rev:** Denomination

Date	Mintage	F	VF	XF	Unc	BU
1940	78,000,000	0.50	1.00	2.00	4.50	—
1941	12,000,000	30.00	65.00	125	200	—
1942	13,000,000	0.50	1.00	2.00	4.50	—
1942 Proof, restrike	—	Value: 6.50				

KM# 519 2 FILLER

Zinc, 17 mm. **Obv:** Crown of St. Stephen **Rev:** Denomination **Note:** Variations in planchets exist.

Date	Mintage	F	VF	XF	Unc	BU
1943	37,000,000	0.10	0.20	0.70	3.00	—
1943 Proof, restrike	—	Value: 6.50				
1944	55,159,000	0.10	0.20	0.70	2.50	—

KM# 507 10 FILLER

Copper-Nickel **Obv:** Crown of St. Stephen within small circle on radiant background **Rev:** Denomination

Date	Mintage	F	VF	XF	Unc	BU
1926BP	20,001,000	0.50	1.50	3.00	10.00	—
1927BP	12,255,000	0.50	1.50	3.00	7.00	—
1935BP	4,740,000	0.50	1.50	3.00	4.50	—
1936BP	3,005,000	0.50	1.50	3.00	4.50	—
1938BP	6,700,000	0.50	1.50	3.00	4.50	—
1939BP	4,460,000	3.00	5.00	10.00	20.00	—
1940BP	960,000	15.00	30.00	50.00	75.00	—

KM# 507a 10 FILLER

Steel **Obv:** Crown of St. Stephen within small circle on radiant background **Rev:** Denomination

Date	Mintage	F	VF	XF	Unc	BU
1940	45,927,000	0.10	0.20	0.80	3.50	—
1941	24,963,000	0.10	0.20	0.80	3.50	—
1942	44,110,000	0.10	0.20	0.80	3.50	—

KM# 508 20 FILLER

Copper-Nickel **Obv:** Crown of St. Stephen within small circle on radiant background **Rev:** Denomination

Date	Mintage	F	VF	XF	Unc	BU
1926BP	25,000,000	1.50	3.50	10.00	15.00	—
1927BP	830,000	10.00	30.00	60.00	100	—
1938BP	20,150,000	0.10	0.25	1.00	2.50	—
1939BP	2,020,000	6.50	10.00	20.00	35.00	—
1940BP	2,470,000	4.00	7.50	18.00	30.00	—

KM# 520 20 FILLER

Steel **Obv:** Crown of St. Stephen above center hole **Rev:** Center hole divides denomination

Date	Mintage	F	VF	XF	Unc	BU
1941	75,007,000	0.10	0.20	0.90	4.00	—
1943	7,500,000	0.10	0.20	0.90	4.00	—
1944	25,000,000	0.10	0.20	0.90	4.00	—
1944 Proof, restrike	—	Value: 7.00				

KM# 509 50 FILLER

Copper-Nickel **Obv:** Crown of St. Stephen **Rev:** Denomination

Date	Mintage	F	VF	XF	Unc	BU
1926BP	14,921,000	0.75	2.00	3.50	6.00	—
1938BP	20,079,000	0.20	0.40	1.00	3.00	—
1939BP	2,770,000	6.50	15.00	30.00	50.00	—
1939BP Proof, restrike	—	Value: 20.00				
1940BP	6,230,000	4.00	7.50	18.00	30.00	—

KM# 510 PENGO

5.0000 g., 0.6400 Silver .1029 oz. ASW **Obv:** Crowned shield within branches **Rev:** Denomination within wreath

Date	Mintage	F	VF	XF	Unc	BU
1926BP	15,000,000	BV	2.50	6.50	20.00	—
1927BP	18,000,000	BV	175	4.50	12.00	—
1937BP	4,000,000	BV	1.65	2.50	6.00	—
1938BP	5,000,000	BV	1.65	2.50	6.00	—
1939BP	13,000,000	—	BV	2.00	5.00	—

KM# 521 PENGO

Aluminum **Obv:** Crowned shield **Rev:** Denomination and date divide wreath

Date	Mintage	F	VF	XF	Unc	BU
1941	80,000,000	0.10	0.20	0.50	1.00	—
1942	19,000,000	0.10	0.20	0.50	1.00	—
1943	2,000,000	1.00	4.00	8.00	15.00	—
1944	16,000,000	0.10	0.20	0.50	1.00	—

KM# 511 2 PENGO

10.0000 g., 0.6400 Silver .2058 oz. ASW, 27 mm. **Obv:** Angels flank crowned shield above spray **Rev:** Hungarian Madonna

Date	Mintage	F	VF	XF	Unc	BU
1929BP	5,000,000	BV	3.50	6.50	12.50	—
1931BP	110,000	10.00	25.00	45.00	90.00	—
1932BP	602,000	BV	4.00	8.00	15.00	—
1933BP	1,051,000	BV	3.50	6.00	12.50	—
1935BP	50,000	25.00	65.00	120	250	—
1936BP	711,000	BV	5.00	10.00	20.00	—
1937BP	1,500,000	BV	3.25	—	8.50	—
1938BP	6,417,000	BV	3.25	4.75	8.50	—
1939BP	2,103,000	BV	3.25	4.75	8.50	—

KM# 513 2 PENGO

10.0000 g., 0.6400 Silver .2058 oz. ASW, 27 mm. **Subject:** Tercentenary - Founding of Pazmany University **Obv:** Crowned, ornate shield **Rev:** Cardinal Peter Pazmany with two others **Designer:** Lajos Beran

Date	Mintage	F	VF	XF	Unc	BU
1935	50,000	3.50	6.50	10.00	20.00	—
1935 Proof	—	Value: 22.50				

Note: Restrike not marked

KM# 514 2 PENGO

10.0000 g., 0.6400 Silver .2058 oz. ASW, 27 mm. **Subject:** Bicentennial - Death of Rakoczi, Prince of Hungary and Transylvania **Obv:** Ornaments surround crowned shield **Rev:** Bust right **Designer:** Lajos Beran

Date	Mintage	F	VF	XF	Unc	BU
1935	100,000	3.00	4.50	6.50	10.00	—
1935 Proof	—	Value: 22.50				

Note: Restrike not marked

KM# 515 2 PENGO

10.0000 g., 0.6400 Silver .2058 oz. ASW, 27 mm. **Subject:** 50th Anniversary - Death of Franz von Liszt **Obv:** Crowned shield within wreath **Rev:** Head right **Designer:** Lajos Beran

Date	Mintage	F	VF	XF	Unc	BU
1936	200,000	BV	3.00	4.50	8.00	—
1936 Proof	—	Value: 18.00				

Note: Restrike not marked

KM# 522.1 2 PENGO

Aluminum, 27 mm. **Obv:** Crowned shield within circle **Rev:** Denomination within circle, wreath surrounds

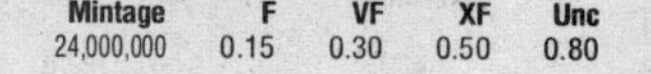

Date	Mintage	F	VF	XF	Unc	BU
1941	24,000,000	0.15	0.30	0.50	0.80	—

Date	Mintage	F	VF	XF	Unc	BU
1942	8,000,000	0.15	0.30	0.50	0.80	—
1943	10,000,000	0.15	0.30	0.50	0.80	—

KM# 522.2 2 PENGO

Aluminum, 27 mm. **Obv:** Crowned shield within circle **Rev:** Denomination within circle, wreath surrounds, base of 2 is wavy

Date	Mintage	F	VF	XF	Unc	BU
1941	40,000	10.00	20.00	35.00	65.00	—
1941 Restrike, rose	—	—	—	—	—	—

KM# 512.1 5 PENGO

25.0000 g., 0.6400 Silver .5213 oz. ASW, 36 mm. **Subject:** 10th Anniversary - Regency of Admiral Horthy **Obv:** Bust right **Rev:** Crowned shield with standing angel supporters **Edge:** Raised, sharp reeding **Designer:** Lojos Beran

Date	Mintage	F	VF	XF	Unc	BU
1930BP	3,650,000	7.50	9.00	12.00	17.50	—

KM# 512.2 5 PENGO

25.3300 g., 0.6400 Silver .5145 oz. ASW, 36 mm. **Subject:** 10th Anniversary - Regency of Admiral Horthy **Obv:** Bust right **Rev:** Crowned shield with standing angel supporters

Date	Mintage	F	VF	XF	Unc	BU
1930 Proof, restrike	—	Value: 18.50				

KM# 516 5 PENGO

25.0000 g., 0.6400 Silver .5145 oz. ASW, 36 mm. **Subject:** 900th Anniversary - Death of St. Stephan **Obv:** Sword and scepter between crown and shield **Rev:** Crowned bust right **Designer:** Lojos Beran

Date	Mintage	F	VF	XF	Unc	BU
1938	600,000	7.50	9.00	12.50	25.00	—
1938 Proof, restrike not marked	—	Value: 28.50				

KM# 517 5 PENGO

25.0000 g., 0.6400 Silver .5145 oz. ASW, 36 mm. **Subject:** Admiral Miklos Horthy **Obv:** Uniformed bust left **Rev:** Crowned shield with standing angel supporters **Edge:** Smooth, ornamented **Designer:** Lojos Beran

Date	Mintage	F	VF	XF	Unc	BU
1938	60	—	—	—	800	—
1939	408,000	7.50	9.00	12.50	25.00	—

KM# 523 5 PENGO

Aluminum, 36 mm. **Subject:** 75th Birthday of Admiral Horthy **Obv:** Uniformed bust left **Rev:** Crowned shield with standing angel supporters **Designer:** Lojos Beran

Date	Mintage	F	VF	XF	Unc	BU
1943	2,000,000	0.50	1.00	2.00	4.00	—
1943 Proof, restrike	—	Value: 6.00				

PROVISIONAL GOVERNMENT
1944-1946
DECIMAL COINAGE

KM# 525 5 PENGO

Aluminum **Obv:** Parliament Building **Rev:** Crowned shield flanked by grain, fruit and leaves

Date	Mintage	F	VF	XF	Unc	BU
1945BP	5,002,000	0.50	1.00	3.00	6.50	—
1945BP PROBAVERET Proof, restrike	—	Value: 17.50				

FIRST REPUBLIC
1946-1949
DECIMAL COINAGE

KM# 529 2 FILLER

3.0000 g., Bronze **Obv:** Arms of the Republic **Rev:** Grain stalk divides denomination

Date	Mintage	F	VF	XF	Unc	BU
1946BP	13,665,000	0.25	0.50	1.00	2.00	—
1947BP	23,865,000	0.25	0.50	1.00	2.50	—
1947BP Proof, restrike	—	Value: 6.50				

KM# 535 5 FILLER

6.0000 g., Aluminum **Obv:** Head left **Rev:** Denomination within wreath

Date	Mintage	F	VF	XF	Unc	BU
1948BP	24,000,000	0.40	1.00	2.00	5.00	—
1951BP	15,000,000	0.40	0.75	1.75	5.00	—

KM# 530 10 FILLER

3.0000 g., Aluminum-Bronze **Obv:** Dove with branch **Rev:** Denomination

Date	Mintage	F	VF	XF	Unc	BU
1946BP	23,565,000	0.15	0.30	0.70	2.00	—
1947BP	29,580,000	0.15	0.30	0.70	2.00	—
1947BP Proof, restrike	—	Value: 7.50				
1948BP	4,885,000	2.00	3.00	4.00	8.00	—
1950BP	8,000,000	1.00	2.00	3.50	7.50	—

KM# 530a 10 FILLER

1.0000 g., Aluminum **Obv:** Dove with branch **Rev:** Denomination

Date	Mintage	F	VF	XF	Unc	BU
1950	—	20.00	30.00	40.00	60.00	—

KM# 531 20 FILLER

4.0000 g., Aluminum-Bronze **Obv:** Three wheat ears divide date **Rev:** Denomination

Date	Mintage	F	VF	XF	Unc	BU
1946BP	16,560,000	0.40	0.80	1.50	3.00	—
1946BP Proof, restrike	—	Value: 8.00				
1947BP	18,260,000	0.50	1.00	2.00	4.00	—
1948BP	5,180,000	2.00	4.00	8.00	12.00	—
1950BP	6,000,000	1.00	2.00	4.00	10.00	—

KM# 536 50 FILLER

1.4000 g., Aluminum **Obv:** Blacksmith sitting on anvil **Rev:** Denomination within wreath

Date	Mintage	F	VF	XF	Unc	BU
1948BP	15,000,000	50.00	70.00	120	—	—
1948BP Proof, restrike	—	—	—	—	—	—

KM# 532 FORINT

1.5000 g., Aluminum **Obv:** Arms of the Republic **Rev:** Denomination flanked by leaves

Date	Mintage	F	VF	XF	Unc	BU
1946BP	38,900,000	1.00	2.00	4.00	10.00	—
1947BP	2,600,000	4.00	8.00	15.00	25.00	—
1949BP	17,000,000	2.50	5.00	10.00	20.00	—

KM# 533 2 FORINT

2.8000 g., Aluminum **Obv:** Shield within wreath, star at top **Rev:** Denomination, large numeral

Date	Mintage	F	VF	XF	Unc	BU
1946BP	10,000,000	2.00	5.00	10.00	20.00	—
1947BP	3,500,000	3.00	7.50	15.00	30.00	—

KM# 534 5 FORINT

20.0000 g., 0.8350 Silver .5369 oz. ASW **Subject:** Lajos Kossuth **Obv:** Arms of the Republic **Rev:** Head right **Edge Lettering:** MUNKA A NEMZETI **Note:** Thick planchet.

Date	Mintage	F	VF	XF	Unc	BU
1946BP	39,802	7.50	10.00	15.00	30.00	—

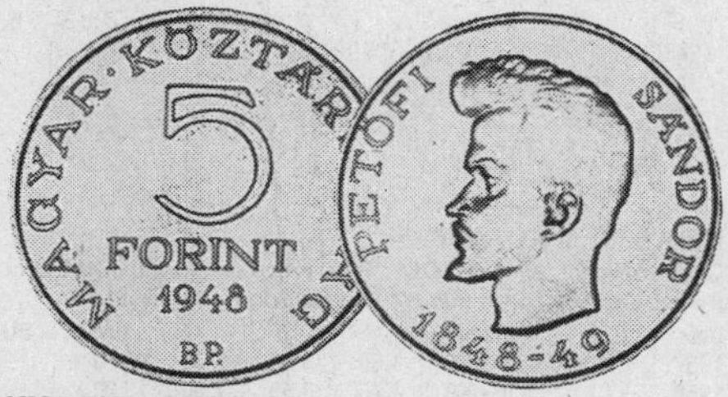

KM# 534a 5 FORINT

12.0000 g., 0.5000 Silver .1929 oz. ASW, 32 mm. **Subject:** Lajos Kossuth **Obv:** Arms of the Republic **Rev:** Head right **Note:** 1.7mm thin planchet.

Date	Mintage	F	VF	XF	Unc	BU
1947	10,004,252	—	BV	3.00	5.00	—
1947 Proof, restrike	—	Value: 12.00				

KM# 537 5 FORINT

12.0000 g., 0.5000 Silver .1929 oz. ASW, 32 mm. **Subject:** Centenary of 1848 Revolution - Sandor Petofi **Obv:** Denomination above date **Rev:** Head left **Designer:** Jòzsef Remenyi

Date	Mintage	F	VF	XF	Unc	BU
1948	100,000	BV	3.00	6.00	10.00	—
1948 Proof, restrike	—	Value: 15.00				

KM# 538 10 FORINT

20.0000 g., 0.5000 Silver .3215 oz. ASW, 36 mm. **Subject:** Centenary of 1848 Revolution **Obv:** Denomination **Rev:** Istvan Szechenyi **Designer:** Jozsef Remenyi

Date	Mintage	F	VF	XF	Unc	BU
1948BP	100,000	BV	5.00	7.50	15.00	—
1948BP Proof, restrike	—	Value: 22.50				

KM# 539 20 FORINT

28.0000 g., 0.5000 Silver .4501 oz. ASW, 40 mm. **Subject:** Centenary of 1848 Revolution **Obv:** Arms of the Republic **Rev:** Mihaly Tancsics **Designer:** Istvan Ivan

Date	Mintage	F	VF	XF	Unc	BU
1948BP	50,000	6.50	9.50	17.50	30.00	—
1948BP Proof, restrike	—	Value: 40.00				

PEOPLES REPUBLIC

1949-1989

DECIMAL COINAGE

KM# 546 2 FILLER

0.6500 g., Aluminum, 18 mm. **Obv:** Legend and wreath surround center hole **Rev:** Center hole divides denomination within wreath

Date	Mintage	F	VF	XF	Unc	BU
1950BP	24,990,000	—	0.10	0.20	0.50	—
1952BP	5,600,000	—	0.10	0.30	1.00	—
1953BP	9,400,000	—	0.10	0.20	0.50	—
1954BP	10,000,000	—	0.10	0.20	0.50	—
1955BP	6,029,000	—	0.10	0.25	0.75	—
1956BP	4,000,000	—	0.15	0.30	1.00	—
1957BP	5,000,000	—	0.10	0.25	0.50	—
1960BP	3,000,000	0.10	0.15	0.30	0.60	—
1961BP	2,000,000	0.20	0.40	0.60	1.00	—
1962BP	3,000,000	0.10	0.15	0.30	0.60	—
1963BP	2,082,000	0.10	0.20	0.35	0.70	—
1965BP	540,000	—	4.00	8.00	16.00	—
1971BP	1,041,000	0.10	0.15	0.30	0.60	—
1972BP	1,000,000	0.10	0.15	0.30	0.60	—
1973BP	2,820,000	0.10	0.15	0.30	0.60	—
1974BP	50,000	—	0.40	0.80	1.50	—
1975BP	50,000	—	0.40	0.80	1.50	—
1976BP	50,000	—	0.40	0.80	1.50	—
1977BP	60,000	—	0.40	0.80	1.50	—
1978BP	50,000	—	0.40	0.80	1.50	—
1979BP	30,000	—	0.75	1.25	2.50	—
1980BP	30,000	—	0.75	1.25	2.50	—
1981BP	30,000	—	0.75	1.25	2.50	—
1982BP	30,000	—	0.75	1.25	2.50	—
1983BP	30,000	—	0.75	1.25	2.50	—
1984BP	30,000	—	0.75	1.25	2.50	—
1985BP	30,000	—	0.75	1.25	2.50	—
1986BP	30,000	—	0.75	1.25	2.50	—
1987BP	30,000	—	0.75	1.25	2.50	—
1988BP	30,000	—	0.75	1.25	2.50	—
1989BP	30,000	—	0.75	1.25	2.50	—

KM# 546a 2 FILLER

0.6500 g., Copper-Nickel, 17 mm. **Obv:** Legend and wreath surround center hole **Rev:** Center hole divides denomination within wreath

Date	Mintage	F	VF	XF	Unc	BU
1966 Proof	5,000	Value: 4.00				
1967 Proof	5,000	Value: 4.00				

KM# 549 5 FILLER

0.6000 g., Aluminum, 17 mm. **Obv:** Head left **Rev:** Denomination within wreath

Date	Mintage	F	VF	XF	Unc	BU
1953BP	10,000,000	0.10	0.15	0.30	0.50	—
1955BP	6,005,000	0.15	0.20	0.50	1.00	—
1956BP	6,012,000	0.15	0.20	0.50	1.00	—
1957BP	5,000,000	0.20	0.30	0.60	1.20	—
1959BP	8,000,000	0.15	0.20	0.50	1.00	—
1960BP	7,000,000	0.15	0.20	0.50	1.00	—
1961BP	4,410,000	0.20	0.30	0.60	1.20	—
1962BP	5,590,000	0.20	0.30	0.60	1.20	—
1963BP	4,020,000	0.20	0.30	0.60	1.20	—
1964BP	3,600,000	0.20	0.30	0.60	1.20	—
1965BP	6,000,000	0.20	0.30	0.60	1.20	—
1970BP	3,900,000	—	2.50	5.00	10.00	—
1971BP	100,000	—	0.25	0.50	1.00	—
1972BP	50,000	—	0.25	0.50	1.00	—
1973BP	105,000	—	0.25	0.50	1.00	—
1974BP	60,000	—	0.25	0.50	1.00	—
1975BP	60,000	—	0.25	0.50	1.00	—
1976BP	50,000	—	0.25	0.50	1.00	—
1977BP	60,000	—	0.25	0.50	1.00	—
1978BP	50,000	—	0.25	0.50	1.00	—
1979BP	30,000	—	0.50	1.00	2.00	—
1980BP	30,000	—	0.50	1.00	2.00	—
1981BP	30,000	—	0.50	1.00	2.00	—
1982BP	30,000	—	0.50	1.00	2.00	—
1983BP	30,000	—	0.50	1.00	2.00	—
1984BP	30,000	—	0.50	1.00	2.00	—
1985BP	30,000	—	0.50	1.00	2.00	—
1986BP	30,000	—	0.50	1.00	2.00	—
1987BP	30,000	—	0.50	1.00	2.00	—
1988BP	30,000	—	0.50	1.00	2.00	—
1989BP	30,000	—	0.50	1.00	2.00	—

KM# 549a 5 FILLER

Copper-Nickel, 17 mm. **Obv:** Head left **Rev:** Denomination within wreath

Date	Mintage	F	VF	XF	Unc	BU
1966 Proof	5,000	Value: 5.00				
1967 Proof	5,000	Value: 5.00				

KM# 547 10 FILLER

Aluminum **Obv:** Dove with branch **Rev:** Denomination

Date	Mintage	F	VF	XF	Unc	BU
1950BP	5,040,000	10.00	20.00	30.00	50.00	—
1951BP	80,950,000	1.50	3.00	5.00	10.00	—
1955BP	10,019,000	2.00	4.00	7.00	15.00	—
1957BP	13,000,000	2.00	4.00	7.00	15.00	—
1958BP	12,015,000	2.00	4.00	7.00	15.00	—
1959BP	15,000,000	2.00	4.00	7.00	15.00	—
1960BP	5,000,000	2.50	5.00	8.00	17.00	—
1961BP	13,000,000	2.00	4.00	7.00	15.00	—
1962BP	4,000,000	2.50	5.00	9.00	18.00	—
1963BP	8,000,000	2.50	5.00	8.00	17.00	—
1964BP	17,008,000	2.00	4.00	7.00	15.00	—
1965BP	21,880,000	2.00	4.00	7.00	15.00	—
1966BP	8,120,000	2.50	5.00	8.00	17.00	—

KM# 547a 10 FILLER

Copper-Nickel **Obv:** Dove with branch **Rev:** Denomination

Date	Mintage	F	VF	XF	Unc	BU
1966 Proof	5,000	Value: 6.00				
1967 Proof	5,000	Value: 6.00				

KM# 572 10 FILLER

0.6000 g., Aluminum, 18.5 mm. **Obv:** Dove with branch **Rev:** Denomination **Note:** Reduced size.

Date	Mintage	F	VF	XF	Unc	BU
1967	5,000	5.00	10.00	20.00	45.00	—
1968	16,000,000	0.50	1.00	2.50	5.00	—
1969	50,760,000	0.50	1.00	2.50	5.00	—
1970	28,470,000	0.50	1.00	2.50	5.00	—
1971	28,800,000	—	0.50	1.25	2.50	—
1972	17,220,000	—	0.50	1.25	2.50	—
1973	33,720,000	—	0.50	1.25	2.50	—
1974	24,930,000	—	0.50	1.25	2.50	—
1975	30,000,000	—	0.50	1.25	2.50	—
1976	20,025,000	—	0.50	1.25	2.50	—
1977	30,075,000	—	0.50	1.25	2.50	—
1978	36,005,000	—	0.40	1.00	2.00	—
1979	36,060,000	—	0.40	1.00	2.00	—
1980	36,010,000	—	0.40	1.00	2.00	—
1981	36,000,000	—	0.40	1.00	2.00	—
1982	45,015,000	—	0.30	0.75	1.50	—
1983	45,030,000	—	0.30	0.75	1.50	—
1984	42,075,000	—	0.30	0.75	1.50	—
1985	40,035,000	—	0.30	0.75	1.50	—
1986	48,075,000	—	0.30	0.75	1.50	—
1987	45,000,000	—	0.30	0.75	1.50	—
1988	48,015,000	—	0.30	0.75	1.50	—
1989	55,515,000	—	0.25	0.65	1.50	—

KM# 550 20 FILLER

Aluminum **Obv:** Three wheat ears divide date **Rev:** Lines divide denomination

Date	Mintage	F	VF	XF	Unc	BU
1953BP	45,000,000	1.00	2.00	4.00	8.00	—
1955BP	10,023,000	1.25	2.50	5.00	10.00	—
1957BP	5,000,000	1.75	3.50	7.00	15.00	—
1958BP	10,000,000	1.25	2.50	5.00	10.00	—
1959BP	13,000,000	1.25	2.50	5.00	10.00	—
1961BP	9,000,000	1.25	2.50	5.00	10.00	—
1963BP	7,000,000	1.50	3.00	6.00	12.00	—
1964BP	10,400,000	1.25	2.50	5.00	10.00	—
1965BP	15,000,000	1.25	2.50	5.00	10.00	—
1966BP	5,000,000	1.50	3.00	6.50	12.50	—

KM# 550a 20 FILLER

Copper-Nickel **Obv:** Three wheat ears divide date **Rev:** Lines divide denomination

Date	Mintage	F	VF	XF	Unc	BU
1966 Proof	5,000	Value: 8.00				
1967 Proof	5,000	Value: 8.00				

KM# 573 20 FILLER
0.9000 g., Aluminum, 20.4 mm. **Obv:** Three wheat ears divide date **Rev:** Lines divide denomination **Note:** Reduced size.

Date	Mintage	F	VF	XF	Unc	BU
1967	10,000,000	0.25	0.75	2.50	6.00	—
1968	56,500,000	0.10	0.40	1.25	3.00	—
1969	28,550,000	0.15	0.45	1.50	4.00	—
1970	19,960,000	0.20	0.60	2.00	5.00	—
1971	31,090,000	0.10	0.20	0.75	2.00	—
7971 Error	11,000	3.50	7.50	15.00	30.00	—
1972	21,070,000	0.15	0.30	0.75	1.50	—
1973	22,970,000	0.15	0.30	0.75	1.50	—
1974	35,010,000	0.15	0.30	0.75	1.50	—
1975	30,010,000	0.15	0.30	0.75	1.50	—
1976	30,010,000	0.15	0.30	0.75	1.50	—
1977	30,050,000	0.15	0.30	0.75	1.50	—
1978	30,140,000	0.15	0.30	0.75	1.50	—
1979	32,010,000	0.15	0.30	0.75	1.50	—
1980	45,010,000	0.10	0.20	0.50	1.00	—
1981	34,030,000	0.10	0.20	0.50	1.00	—
1982	35,010,000	0.10	0.20	0.50	1.00	—
1983	43,210,000	0.10	0.20	0.50	1.00	—
1984	42,270,000	0.10	0.20	0.50	1.00	—
1985	40,440,000	0.10	0.20	0.50	1.00	—
1986	48,000,000	0.10	0.20	0.50	1.00	—
1987	55,000,000	0.10	0.20	0.50	1.00	—
1988	48,010,000	0.10	0.20	0.50	1.00	—
1989	64,660,000	—	—	0.10	0.50	—

KM# 627 20 FILLER
0.9000 g., Aluminum, 20.4 mm. **Series:** F.A.O. **Obv:** Three wheat ears above banner **Rev:** Lines divide denomination

Date	Mintage	F	VF	XF	Unc	BU
1983	50,000	—	0.50	1.00	2.50	—

KM# 551 50 FILLER
Aluminum **Obv:** Blacksmith seated on anvil **Rev:** Denomination within wreath

Date	Mintage	F	VF	XF	Unc	BU
1953BP	10,017,000	1.50	3.00	6.00	12.00	—
1965BP	3,005,000	1.25	2.50	5.00	10.00	—
1966BP	1,500,000	1.75	3.50	7.00	15.00	—

KM# 551a 50 FILLER
Copper-Nickel **Obv:** Blacksmith seated on anvil **Rev:** Denomination within wreath

Date	Mintage	F	VF	XF	Unc	BU
1966 Proof	5,000	Value: 10.00				
1967 Proof	5,000	Value: 10.00				

KM# 574 50 FILLER
1.2000 g., Aluminum, 21.5 mm. **Subject:** Elizabeth Bridge in Budapest **Obv:** Bridge **Rev:** Denomination above date

Date	Mintage	F	VF	XF	Unc	BU
1967	20,000,000	0.50	1.00	2.00	4.00	—
1968	13,861,000	0.60	1.25	2.50	5.00	—
1969	10,085,000	0.60	1.25	2.50	5.00	—
1971	50,000	0.30	0.60	1.25	2.50	—
1972	470,000	0.20	0.50	1.00	2.00	—
1973	7,600,000	0.20	0.50	1.00	2.00	—
1974	5,000,000	0.20	0.50	1.00	2.00	—
1975	10,160,000	0.10	0.30	0.75	1.50	—
1976	15,130,000	0.10	0.30	0.75	1.50	—
1977	10,050,000	0.10	0.30	0.75	1.50	—
1978	10,110,000	0.10	0.30	0.75	1.50	—
1979	10,070,000	0.10	0.30	0.75	1.50	—
1980	15,000,000	0.10	0.30	0.75	1.50	—
1981	10,030,000	0.10	0.30	0.75	1.50	—
1982	10,000,000	0.10	0.30	0.75	1.50	—
1983	10,070,000	0.10	0.30	0.75	1.50	—
1984	14,060,000	0.10	0.30	0.75	1.50	—
1985	12,020,000	0.10	0.30	0.75	1.50	—
1986	17,140,000	0.10	0.30	0.75	1.50	—
1987	23,000,000	—	0.10	0.50	1.00	—
1988	18,050,000	—	0.10	0.50	1.00	—
1989	18,200,000	—	0.10	0.50	1.00	—

KM# 545 FORINT
Aluminum **Obv:** Wreath surrounds wheat ear and hammer on radiant background below star **Rev:** Leaves flank denomination

Date	Mintage	F	VF	XF	Unc	BU
1949BP	19,440,000	1.50	3.00	6.00	12.00	—
1950BP	39,060,000	2.25	4.50	9.00	18.00	—
1952BP	63,018,000	2.00	4.00	8.00	16.00	—

KM# 555 FORINT
1.4000 g., Aluminum, 22.8 mm. **Obv:** Star above shield within wreath **Rev:** Leaves flank denomination

Date	Mintage	F	VF	XF	Unc	BU
1957	7,500,000	2.00	4.00	8.00	16.00	—
1958	5,070,000	1.50	3.00	6.00	12.00	—
1960	5,000,000	1.25	2.50	5.00	10.00	—
1961	5,000,000	1.25	2.50	5.00	10.00	—
1963	3,000,000	1.50	3.00	6.50	12.50	—
1964	6,080,000	1.00	2.00	4.00	8.00	—
1965	9,810,000	1.00	2.00	4.00	8.00	—
1966	5,680,000	1.75	3.50	7.50	15.00	—

KM# 555a FORINT
5.8500 g., 0.8350 Silver .0570 oz. ASW, 22.8 mm. **Obv:** Star above shield within wreath **Rev:** Leaves flank denomination

Date	Mintage	F	VF	XF	Unc	BU
1966 Proof	5,000	Value: 12.00				
1967 Proof	5,000	Value: 12.00				

KM# 575 FORINT
1.4000 g., Aluminum, 22.8 mm. **Obv:** Star above shield within wreath **Rev:** Leaves flank denomination

Date	Mintage	F	VF	XF	Unc	BU
1967	60,000,000	0.65	1.25	2.50	5.00	—
1968	53,230,000	0.65	1.25	2.50	6.00	—
1969	27,664,000	1.00	2.00	4.00	8.00	—
1970	11,290,000	1.00	2.00	4.00	10.00	—
1971	100,000	0.10	0.20	0.50	1.00	—
1972	110,000	0.25	0.50	1.00	2.00	—
1973	1,990,000	0.10	0.20	0.50	1.00	—
1974	4,990,000	0.10	0.20	0.50	1.00	—
1975	10,000,000	0.10	0.20	0.40	0.80	—
1976	15,000,000	0.10	0.20	0.40	0.80	—
1977	10,050,000	0.10	0.20	0.40	0.80	—
1978	50,000	0.20	0.40	0.85	1.75	—
1979	10,070,000	0.10	0.20	0.35	0.70	—
1980	20,040,000	0.10	0.20	0.35	0.70	—
1981	25,040,000	0.10	0.20	0.35	0.70	—
1982	10,000,000	0.10	0.20	0.35	0.70	—
1983	20,140,000	0.10	0.20	0.35	0.70	—
1984	6,010,000	0.15	0.30	0.60	1.20	—
1985	30,000	0.25	0.50	1.00	2.00	—
1986	30,000	0.25	0.50	1.00	2.00	—
1987	13,000,000	0.10	0.20	0.50	1.00	—
1988	20,080,000	0.10	0.20	0.35	0.75	—
1989	115,920,000	—	0.15	0.30	0.60	—

KM# 548 2 FORINT
Copper-Nickel **Obv:** Wreath surrounds hammer and wheat ear on radiant background with star above **Rev:** Denomination within 3/4 wreath

Date	Mintage	F	VF	XF	Unc	BU
1950BP	18,500,000	1.75	3.50	7.00	15.00	—
1951BP	4,000,000	2.00	4.00	8.00	16.00	—
1952BP	4,530,000	2.00	4.00	8.00	16.00	—

KM# 556 2 FORINT
Copper-Nickel, 25 mm. **Obv:** Star above shield within wreath **Rev:** Denomination within 3/4 wreath **Edge:** Flora vines

Date	Mintage	F	VF	XF	Unc	BU
1957	5,000,000	1.50	3.00	6.00	12.50	—
1958	1,033,000	1.75	3.50	7.00	15.00	—
1960	4,000,000	1.50	3.00	6.00	12.50	—
1961	690,000	2.00	4.00	8.00	16.00	—
1962	1,190,000	1.50	3.00	6.00	12.50	—

KM# 556a 2 FORINT
Copper-Nickel-Zinc **Obv:** Star above shield within wreath **Rev:** Denomination within 3/4 wreath

Date	Mintage	F	VF	XF	Unc	BU
1962	1,210,000	1.25	2.50	5.00	10.00	—
1963	3,100,000	1.25	2.50	5.00	10.00	—
1964	3,250,000	1.25	2.50	5.00	10.00	—
1965	4,395,000	1.25	2.50	5.00	10.00	—
1966	6,630,000	1.25	2.50	5.00	10.00	—

KM# 556b 2 FORINT
6.1200 g., 0.8350 Silver .1643 oz. ASW **Obv:** Star above shield within wreath **Rev:** Denomination within 3/4 wreath

Date	Mintage	F	VF	XF	Unc	BU
1966 Proof	5,000	Value: 14.00				
1967 Proof	5,000	Value: 14.00				

KM# 591 2 FORINT
4.4400 g., Brass, 22.4 mm. **Rev:** Denomination divides date

Date	Mintage	F	VF	XF	Unc	BU
1970	49,195,000	0.50	1.00	2.00	4.00	—
1971	10,830,000	0.10	0.50	1.00	2.00	—
1972	10,015,000	0.10	0.50	1.00	2.00	—
1973	820,000	1.00	2.00	4.00	8.00	—
1974	10,000,000	0.25	0.75	1.50	3.00	—
1975	20,030,000	0.25	0.75	1.50	3.00	—
1976	15,000,000	0.25	0.75	1.50	3.00	—
1977	10,115,000	0.25	0.75	1.50	3.00	—
1978	12,000,000	0.25	0.75	1.50	3.00	—
1979	10,127,000	0.25	0.75	1.50	3.00	—
1980	12,005,000	0.25	0.75	1.50	3.00	—
1981	10,010,000	0.25	0.75	1.50	3.00	—
1982	10,005,000	0.25	0.75	1.50	3.00	—
1983	20,160,000	0.25	0.75	1.50	3.00	—
1984	5,000,000	0.75	1.50	3.00	6.00	—
1985	10,675,000	0.25	0.75	1.50	3.00	—
1986	30,000	1.50	3.00	6.00	12.00	—
1987	5,030,000	0.50	1.00	2.00	4.00	—
1988	5,035,000	0.50	1.00	2.00	4.00	—
1989	79,223,000	0.10	0.25	0.50	1.00	—

KM# 576 5 FORINT
Copper-Nickel, 27 mm. **Subject:** Lajos Kossuth **Obv:** Star above shield within wreath **Rev:** Head right

Date	Mintage	F	VF	XF	Unc	BU
1967BP	20,000,000	0.50	1.00	2.50	5.00	—
1968BP	29,000	5.00	10.00	20.00	35.00	—

KM# 594 5 FORINT
5.7300 g., Nickel, 24.3 mm. **Obv:** Head right **Rev:** Small shield above denomination

Date	Mintage	F	VF	XF	Unc	BU
1971	20,004,000	0.20	0.35	0.75	1.50	—
1972	5,000,000	0.25	0.50	1.00	2.00	—
1973	100,000	0.35	0.75	1.50	3.00	—
1974	50,000	0.35	0.75	1.50	3.00	—
1975	50,000	0.35	0.75	1.50	3.00	—
1976	5,090,000	0.25	0.50	1.00	2.00	—
1977	50,000	0.35	0.75	1.50	3.00	—
1978	6,000,000	0.25	0.50	1.00	2.00	—
1979	10,000,000	0.25	0.50	1.00	2.00	—
1980	6,002,000	0.25	0.50	1.00	2.00	—
1981	5,002,000	0.25	0.50	1.00	2.00	—
1982	936,000	0.30	0.60	1.25	2.50	—

KM# 628 5 FORINT
Nickel **Series:** F.A.O. **Obv:** Flower holds logo within circle **Rev:** Small shield above denomination **Designer:** György Bognar

Date	Mintage	F	VF	XF	Unc	BU
1983	50,000	—	1.00	2.00	3.50	—

KM# 635 5 FORINT
Copper-Nickel **Subject:** Lajos Kossuth **Obv:** Head right **Rev:** Small shield above denomination

Date	Mintage	F	VF	XF	Unc	BU
1983	15,240,000	0.15	0.25	0.50	1.00	—
1984	25,018,000	0.15	0.25	0.50	1.00	—
1985	25,286,000	0.15	0.25	0.50	1.00	—
1986	1,030,000	0.20	0.35	0.75	1.50	—
1987	30,000	0.30	0.60	1.25	2.50	—
1988	4,050,000	0.20	0.35	0.75	1.50	—
1989	39,014,000	0.15	0.25	0.50	1.00	—

KM# 552 10 FORINT
12.5000 g., 0.8000 Silver .3215 oz. ASW, 30 mm. **Subject:** 10th Anniversary of Forint **Obv:** National Museum in Budapest **Rev:** Leaves back of denomination, small shield above **Designer:** Ivan Istvan

Date	Mintage	F	VF	XF	Unc	BU
1956BP	22,000	BV	5.50	8.00	16.00	—

KM# 595 10 FORINT
8.8300 g., Nickel, 28 mm. **Obv:** Strobl Monument **Rev:** Small shield below denomination

Date	Mintage	F	VF	XF	Unc	BU
1971	24,998,000	0.35	0.75	1.50	3.00	4.50
1972	25,078,000	0.35	0.75	1.50	3.00	4.50
1973	78,000	0.60	1.25	2.50	5.00	7.50
1974	50,000	0.60	1.25	2.50	5.00	7.50
1975	50,000	0.60	1.25	2.50	5.00	7.50
1976	3,568,000	0.50	1.00	2.00	4.00	5.50
1977	4,618,000	0.50	1.00	2.00	4.00	5.50
1978	50,000	0.60	1.25	2.50	5.00	7.50
1979	5,000,000	0.50	1.00	2.00	4.00	5.50
1980	2,550,000	0.50	1.00	2.00	4.00	5.50
1982	30,000	0.60	1.25	2.50	5.00	7.50

KM# 620 10 FORINT
8.8300 g., Nickel, 28 mm. **Series:** F.A.O. **Obv:** Strobl Monument **Rev:** Small shield below denomination

Date	Mintage	F	VF	XF	Unc	BU
1981	60,000	—	—	2.50	5.00	7.50

KM# 629 10 FORINT
8.8300 g., Nickel, 28 mm. **Series:** F.A.O. **Obv:** Logo at right of figure with large jar and bowl **Rev:** Small shield below denomination **Designer:** Gyorgi Bognar

Date	Mintage	F	VF	XF	Unc	BU
1983	50,000	—	—	2.50	5.00	—

KM# 636 10 FORINT
Aluminum-Bronze, 28 mm. **Obv:** Strobl Monument **Rev:** Small shield below denomination **Note:** Circulation coinage.

Date	Mintage	F	VF	XF	Unc	BU
1983	11,004,000	0.25	0.50	1.00	2.00	3.00
1984	7,578,000	0.25	0.50	1.00	2.00	3.00
1985	27,648,000	0.25	0.50	1.00	2.00	3.00
1986	15,006,000	0.25	0.50	1.00	2.00	3.00
1987	10,000,000	0.25	0.50	1.00	2.00	3.00
1988	5,000,000	0.25	0.50	1.00	2.00	3.00
1989	37,094,000	0.25	0.50	1.00	2.00	3.00

KM# 553 20 FORINT
17.5000 g., 0.8000 Silver .4501 oz. ASW, 32 mm. **Subject:** 10th Anniversary of Forint **Obv:** Szechenyi suspension bridge in Budapest **Rev:** Shield on ornamental background **Designer:** Ivan Istvan

Date	Mintage	F	VF	XF	Unc	BU
1956BP	22,000	6.50	8.00	12.00	20.00	—

KM# 630 20 FORINT
Copper-Nickel, 26.5 mm. **Subject:** György Dózsa **Obv:** Head looking left **Rev:** Small shield above denomination

Date	Mintage	F	VF	XF	Unc	BU
1982	13,404,000	0.25	0.50	0.80	1.60	—
1983	18,006,000	0.25	0.50	0.80	1.60	—
1984	31,016,000	0.25	0.50	0.80	1.60	—
1985	20,122,000	0.25	0.50	0.80	1.60	—
1986	6,000,000	0.35	0.65	1.25	2.25	—
1987	30,000	0.40	0.75	1.50	3.00	—
1988	30,000	0.40	0.75	1.50	3.00	—
1989	31,890,000	0.25	0.50	0.80	1.60	—

KM# 637 20 FORINT
Copper-Nickel **Subject:** Forestry for Development **Obv:** Leaf within globe above denomination **Rev:** Stylized tree within patterned archway

Date	Mintage	F	VF	XF	Unc	BU
1984	15,000	—	—	—	3.00	—
1984 Proof	5,000	Value: 7.00				

KM# 653 20 FORINT
Copper-Nickel **Series:** F.A.O. **Obv:** Logos with dates within box above stylized denomination **Rev:** Wheat ear divides fish and leaf, lined background

Date	Mintage	F	VF	XF	Unc	BU
1985	25,000	—	—	—	3.00	—
1985 Proof	—	Value: 6.50				

KM# 554 25 FORINT (Huszonot)
20.0000 g., 0.8000 Silver .5144 oz. ASW, 34 mm. **Subject:** 10th Anniversary Forint **Obv:** Parliament Building in Budapest **Rev:** Leaves within cogwheel, arms above **Designer:** Ivan Istvan

Date	Mintage	F	VF	XF	Unc	BU
1956BP	22,000	7.50	10.00	15.00	20.00	—

KM# 557 25 FORINT (Huszonot)
17.5000 g., 0.7500 Silver .4220 oz. ASW **Subject:** 150th Anniversary - Birth of Liszt, Musician **Obv:** Harp **Rev:** Head right

Date	Mintage	F	VF	XF	Unc	BU
1961 Proof	15,000	Value: 15.50				

KM# 558 25 FORINT (Huszonot)
17.5000 g., 0.7500 Silver .4220 oz. ASW **Subject:** 80th Anniversary - Birth of Bartok, Composer **Obv:** Small harp above denomination **Rev:** Head left

Date	Mintage	F	VF	XF	Unc	BU
1961 Proof	15,000	Value: 16.50				

KM# 567 25 FORINT (Huszonot)
12.0000 g., 0.6400 Silver .2469 oz. ASW **Subject:** 40th Anniversary - Death of Zrinyi **Obv:** Monument **Rev:** Head 3/4 right

Date	Mintage	F	VF	XF	Unc	BU
1966 Proof	11,000	Value: 20.00				

KM# 577 25 FORINT (Huszonot)
12.0000 g., 0.7500 Silver .2893 oz. ASW **Subject:** 85th Birthday of Kodaly, Composer **Obv:** Peacock above denomination **Rev:** Bust 3/4 left

Date	Mintage	F	VF	XF	Unc	BU
1967	15,000	—	—	—	10.00	—
1967 Proof	—	Value: 12.50				

KM# 559 50 FORINT (Otven)
20.0000 g., 0.7500 Silver .4922 oz. ASW **Subject:** 150th Anniversary - Birth of Liszt, Musician **Obv:** Harp below denomination **Rev:** Head right

Date	Mintage	F	VF	XF	Unc	BU
1961BP Proof	15,000	Value: 20.00				

KM# 560 50 FORINT (Otven)
3.8380 g., 0.9860 Gold .1217 oz. AGW **Subject:** 150th Anniversary - Birth of Liszt, Musician **Obv:** Harp below denomination **Rev:** Head right

Date	Mintage	F	VF	XF	Unc	BU
1961 Proof	2,503	Value: 90.00				

KM# 561 50 FORINT (Otven)
20.0000 g., 0.7500 Silver .4822 oz. ASW **Subject:** 80th Anniversary - Birth of Bartok, Composer **Obv:** Small harp above denomination **Rev:** Head left

Date	Mintage	F	VF	XF	Unc	BU
1961 Proof	15,000	Value: 20.00				

KM# 562 50 FORINT (Otven)
3.8380 g., 0.9860 Gold .1217 oz. AGW **Subject:** 80th Anniversary - Birth of Bartok, Composer **Obv:** Small harp above denomination **Rev:** Head left

Date	Mintage	F	VF	XF	Unc	BU
1961 Proof	2,503	Value: 95.00				

KM# 568 50 FORINT (Otven)
20.0000 g., 0.6400 Silver .4115 oz. ASW **Subject:** 400th Anniversary - Death of Zrinyi **Obv:** Monument **Rev:** Head 3/4 right

Date	Mintage	F	VF	XF	Unc	BU
1966BP Proof	11,000	Value: 25.00				

KM# 578 50 FORINT (Otven)
20.0000 g., 0.7500 Silver .4822 oz. ASW **Subject:** 85th Birthday of Kodaly, Composer **Obv:** Peacock above denomination **Rev:** Bust 3/4 left

Date	Mintage	F	VF	XF	Unc	BU
1967	15,000	—	—	—	10.00	11.50
1967 Proof	—	Value: 12.50				

KM# 582 50 FORINT (Otven)
20.0000 g., 0.6400 Silver .4115 oz. ASW **Subject:** 150th Anniversary - Birth of Semmelweis **Obv:** Head right **Rev:** Star above shield on radiant background, wreath surrounds

Date	Mintage	F	VF	XF	Unc	BU
1968	20,000	—	—	—	10.00	11.50
1968 Proof	4,750	Value: 12.50				

KM# 583 50 FORINT (Otven)
4.2050 g., 0.9000 Gold .1217 oz. AGW **Subject:** 150th Anniversary - Birth of Semmelweis **Obv:** Head right **Rev:** Star above shield within wreath

Date	Mintage	F	VF	XF	Unc	BU
1968 Proof	25,000	Value: 85.00				

KM# 589 50 FORINT (Otven)
16.0000 g., 0.6400 Silver .3292 oz. ASW **Subject:** 50th Anniversary - Republic of Councils **Obv:** Small arms above denomination **Rev:** Half figure with arms spread

Date	Mintage	F	VF	XF	Unc	BU
1969	12,000	—	—	—	8.00	10.00
1969 Proof	3,000	Value: 15.00				

KM# 592 50 FORINT (Otven)
16.0000 g., 0.6400 Silver .3292 oz. ASW **Subject:** 25th Anniversary of Liberation **Obv:** Strobl monument **Rev:** Small shield below denomination **Designer:** D. Kovacs

Date	Mintage	F	VF	XF	Unc	BU
1970	20,000	—	—	—	7.00	9.00
1970 Proof	5,000	Value: 12.50				

KM# 596 50 FORINT (Otven)
16.0000 g., 0.6400 Silver .3292 oz. ASW **Subject:** 1000th Anniversary - Birth of St. Stephen **Obv:** Denomination below central design **Obv. Designer:** Jozsef Garanyi **Rev:** St. Stephan on horseback **Rev. Designer:** Andras Kiss-Nagy

Date	Mintage	F	VF	XF	Unc	BU
1972	24,000	—	—	—	10.00	12.00
1972 Proof	6,000	Value: 15.00				

KM# 599 50 FORINT (Otven)
16.0000 g., 0.6400 Silver .3292 oz. ASW **Subject:** 150th Anniversary - Birth of Sandor Petofi, Poet **Obv:** Ribbon above denomination **Obv. Designer:** Jozsef Garanyi **Rev:** Bust 3/4 facing, upper right **Rev. Designer:** Tamas Vigh

Date	Mintage	F	VF	XF	Unc	BU
1973	24,000	—	—	—	8.00	10.00
1973 Proof	6,000	Value: 12.00				

KM# 601 50 FORINT (Otven)
16.0000 g., 0.6400 Silver .3292 oz. ASW **Subject:** 50th Anniversary of National Bank **Obv:** Small shield left of denomination **Obv. Designer:** Jozsef Garanyi **Rev:** Bank building **Rev. Designer:** Viktoria Csucs

Date	Mintage	F	VF	XF	Unc	BU
1974	24,000	—	—	—	7.00	8.50
1974 Proof	6,000	Value: 10.00				

KM# 663 50 FORINT (Otven)
Copper-Nickel **Subject:** 25th Anniversary of World Wildlife Foundation **Obv:** Star above shield within wreath **Rev:** Red-footed Falcon

Date	Mintage	F	VF	XF	Unc	BU
1988	45,000	—	—	—	6.50	8.00

KM# 563 100 FORINT (Szaz)
7.6760 g., 0.9860 Gold .2431 oz. AGW **Subject:** 150th Anniversary - Birth of Liszt, Musician **Obv:** Head right **Rev:** Harp below denomination

Date	Mintage	F	VF	XF	Unc	BU
1961BP Proof	2,500	Value: 175				

KM# 564 100 FORINT (Szaz)
7.6760 g., 0.9860 Gold .2431 oz. AGW **Subject:** 80th Anniversary - Birth of Bartok, Composer **Obv:** Head left **Rev:** Small harp above denomination

Date	Mintage	F	VF	XF	Unc	BU
1961 Proof	2,500	Value: 175				

KM# 569 100 FORINT (Szaz)
8.4100 g., 0.9000 Gold .2433 oz. AGW **Subject:** 400th Anniversary - Death of Zrinyi **Obv:** Monument **Rev:** Head 3/4 right

Date	Mintage	F	VF	XF	Unc	BU
1966 Proof	3,300	Value: 175				

KM# 579 100 FORINT (Szaz)
28.0000 g., 0.7500 Silver .6752 oz. ASW **Subject:** 85th Birthday of Kodaly, Composer **Obv:** Peacock above denomination **Rev:** Bust 3/4 left

Date	Mintage	F	VF	XF	Unc	BU
1967BP	10,000	—	—	—	25.00	28.00
1967BP Proof	—	Value: 40.00				

KM# 584 100 FORINT (Szaz)
28.0000 g., 0.6400 Silver .5762 oz. ASW **Subject:** 150th Anniversary - Birth of Semmelweis **Obv:** Head right **Rev:** Star above shield within wreath

Date	Mintage	F	VF	XF	Unc	BU
1968	20,000	—	—	—	9.00	11.00
1968 Proof	4,750	Value: 17.50				

KM# 585 100 FORINT (Szaz)
8.4100 g., 0.9000 Gold .2433 oz. AGW **Subject:** 150th Anniversary - Birth of Semmelweis **Obv:** Head right **Rev:** Star above shield within wreath

Date	Mintage	F	VF	XF	Unc	BU
1968 Proof	23,000	Value: 170				

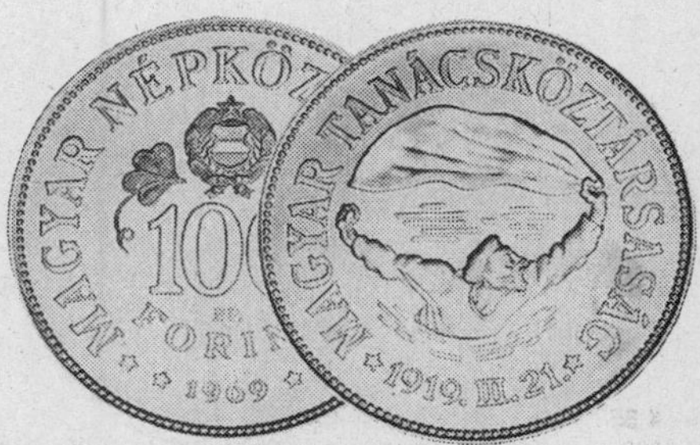

KM# 590 100 FORINT (Szaz)
22.0000 g., 0.6400 Silver .4527 oz. ASW **Subject:** 50th Anniversary - Republic of Councils **Obv:** Denomination below small arms flanked by clovers **Rev:** Half figure with arms spread

Date	Mintage	F	VF	XF	Unc	BU
1969	12,000	—	—	—	10.00	12.00
1969 Proof	3,000	Value: 15.00				

KM# 593 100 FORINT (Szaz)
22.0000 g., 0.6400 Silver .4527 oz. ASW **Subject:** 25th Anniversary of Liberation **Obv:** Strobl monument **Obv. Designer:** D. Kovacs **Rev:** Star above shield within wreath

Date	Mintage	F	VF	XF	Unc	BU
1970	20,000	—	—	—	9.00	11.00
1970 Proof	5,000	Value: 14.00				

KM# 597 100 FORINT (Szaz)
22.0000 g., 0.6400 Silver .4527 oz. ASW **Subject:** 1000th Anniversary - Birth of St. Stephen **Obv:** St. Stephen's monogram **Rev:** Crowned bust facing

Date	Mintage	F	VF	XF	Unc	BU
1972	24,000	—	—	—	10.00	12.00
1972 Proof	6,000	Value: 15.00				

KM# 598 100 FORINT (Szaz)
22.0000 g., 0.6400 Silver .4527 oz. ASW **Subject:** Buda and Pest Union Centennial **Obv:** Star above shield within wreath **Rev:** Design depicting union, roman numerals below **Designer:** Tomas Asszonyi

Date	Mintage	F	VF	XF	Unc	BU
1972	25,000	—	—	—	10.00	12.00
1972 Proof	6,000	Value: 15.00				

KM# 600 100 FORINT (Szaz)
22.0000 g., 0.6400 Silver .4527 oz. ASW **Subject:** 150th Anniversary - Birth of Sandor Petofi, Poet **Obv:** Star above shield within wreath divides date **Obv. Designer:** Viktoria Csucs **Rev:** Head 3/4 facing below inscription **Rev. Designer:** Tomas Vigh

Date	Mintage	F	VF	XF	Unc	BU
1973	24,000	—	—	—	8.50	10.00
1973 Proof	6,000	Value: 12.50				

KM# 602 100 FORINT (Szaz)
22.0000 g., 0.6400 Silver .4527 oz. ASW **Subject:** 25th Anniversary of KGST **Obv:** Star above shield within wreath **Rev:** Coins of Hungary, Russia, Romania, East Germany, Mongolia, Poland, Cuba, Czechslovakia and Bulgaria

Date	Mintage	F	VF	XF	Unc	BU
1974	20,000	—	—	—	8.50	9.50
1974 Proof	5,000	Value: 11.50				

KM# 603 100 FORINT (Szaz)
22.0000 g., 0.6400 Silver .4527 oz. ASW **Subject:** 50th Anniversary of National Bank **Obv:** Small shield at upper left **Obv. Designer:** Jòzsef Garanyi **Rev:** Depictions of symbols of various professions **Rev. Designer:** Viktoria Csucs

Date	Mintage	F	VF	XF	Unc	BU
1974	24,000	—	—	—	7.50	8.50
1974 Proof	6,000	Value: 10.00				

KM# 617 100 FORINT (Szaz)
Nickel, 32 mm. **Subject:** 1st Soviet-Hungarian Space Flight **Obv:** Star above shield within wreath **Rev:** Astronauts above globe, shuttle lower right

Date	Mintage	F	VF	XF	Unc	BU
1980	180,000	—	—	—	4.00	6.00
1980 Proof	20,000	Value: 8.00				

KM# 621 100 FORINT (Szaz)
Nickel, 32 mm. **Subject:** World Food Day **Obv:** Grain stalks **Rev:** Kneeling figure

Date	Mintage	F	VF	XF	Unc	BU
1981	80,000	—	—	—	7.00	—
1981 Proof	20,000	Value: 10.00				

KM# 622 100 FORINT (Szaz)
Copper-Nickel-Zinc, 32 mm. **Subject:** 1300th Anniversary of Bulgarian Statehood **Obv:** Star above shield within wreath, grain stalks flank **Rev:** Sword handle and feather divide heads of Sàndor Petofi and Khristro Botev

Date	Mintage	F	VF	XF	Unc	BU
1981 Proof	50,000	Value: 8.00				

KM# 626 100 FORINT (Szaz)
Copper-Nickel, 38.5 mm. **Subject:** World Football Championship **Obv:** Star above shield within wreath **Rev:** Soccer players

Date	Mintage	F	VF	XF	Unc	BU
1982	150,000	—	—	—	2.50	4.00

KM# 631 100 FORINT (Szaz)
Copper-Nickel, 38.5 mm. **Series:** F.A.O. **Obv:** Denomination and date right of logo on lined background **Rev:** Small hearts below stylized design

Date	Mintage	F	VF	XF	Unc	BU
1983	50,000	—	—	—	3.50	4.50
1983 Proof	10,000	Value: 5.50				

KM# 632 100 FORINT (Szaz)
Copper-Nickel-Zinc, 32 mm. **Subject:** 200th Anniversary - Birth of Simon Bolivar **Obv:** Andean Condor **Rev:** Grain sprigs form collar below head 3/4 left, map at left

Date	Mintage	F	VF	XF	Unc	BU
1983	20,000	—	—	—	6.50	7.50
1983 Proof	10,000	Value: 9.50				

KM# 633 100 FORINT (Szaz)
Copper-Nickel-Zinc, 32 mm. **Subject:** Count Istvàn Szèchenyi **Obv:** Small shield above denomination **Rev:** Bust at left, three shields at right

Date	Mintage	F	VF	XF	Unc	BU
1983	30,000	—	—	—	6.00	7.00
1983 Proof	20,000	Value: 9.00				

KM# 634 100 FORINT (Szaz)
Copper-Nickel-Zinc, 32 mm. **Subject:** 100th Anniversary - Birth of Bèla Czobel, Painter **Obv:** Denomination within wreath **Rev:** Head 3/4 facing

Date	Mintage	F	VF	XF	Unc	BU
1983	20,000	—	—	—	6.00	7.00
1983 Proof	10,000	Value: 10.00				

KM# 638 100 FORINT (Szaz)
Copper-Nickel-Zinc **Subject:** 200th Anniversary - Birth of Sàndor Kórósicsoma **Obv:** Design divides date and denomination **Rev:** Half figure and dates left **Designer:** Kutas

Date	Mintage	F	VF	XF	Unc	BU
1984	20,000	—	—	—	6.00	7.00
1984 Proof	10,000	Value: 10.00				

KM# 639 100 FORINT (Szaz)
Copper-Nickel-Zinc, 32 mm. **Subject:** Forestry for Development **Obv:** Tree at center of globe **Rev:** Stumps and seedlings

Date	Mintage	F	VF	XF	Unc	BU
1984	15,000	—	—	—	6.00	7.00
1984 Proof	5,000	Value: 10.00				

KM# 644 100 FORINT (Szaz)
Copper-Nickel-Zinc, 32 mm. **Subject:** Wildlife Preservation **Obv:** Dates within side circles, divided by artistic denomination and legend within box **Rev:** Pond Turtle within square

Date	Mintage	F	VF	XF	Unc	BU
1985	20,000	—	—	—	10.00	12.50

KM# 645 100 FORINT (Szaz)
Copper-Nickel-Zinc, 32 mm. **Subject:** Wildlife Preservation **Obv:** Dates within side circles, divided by artistic denomination and legend within box **Rev:** European Otter

Date	Mintage	F	VF	XF	Unc	BU
1985	20,000	—	—	—	10.00	12.50

KM# 646 100 FORINT (Szaz)
Copper-Nickel-Zinc, 32 mm. **Subject:** Wildlife Preservation **Obv:** Dates within side circles, divided by artistic denomination and legend within box **Rev:** Wildcat

Date	Mintage	F	VF	XF	Unc	BU
1985	20,000	—	—	—	10.00	12.50

KM# 647 100 FORINT (Szaz)
Copper-Nickel-Zinc, 38.5 mm. **Subject:** World Football **Obv:** Soccer ball and globe form zeros of denomination **Rev:** Map of Mexico

Date	Mintage	F	VF	XF	Unc	BU
1985	30,000	—	—	—	7.50	9.00

KM# 648 100 FORINT (Szaz)
Copper-Nickel-Zinc, 38.5 mm. **Subject:** World Football **Obv:** Soccer ball and globe form zeros of denomination **Rev:** Native Mexican artifacts

Date	Mintage	F	VF	XF	Unc	BU
1985	30,000	—	—	—	7.50	9.00

KM# 651 100 FORINT (Szaz)
Copper-Nickel-Zinc, 32 mm. **Subject:** Budapest Cultural Forum **Obv:** Denomination **Rev:** Inscription within window, plant on sill

Date	Mintage	F	VF	XF	Unc	BU
1985	40,000	—	—	—	5.00	6.00
1985 Proof	—	Value: 8.00				

KM# 654 100 FORINT (Szaz)
Copper-Nickel-Zinc, 32 mm. **Series:** F.A.O. **Obv:** Logo and dates within box above denomination **Rev:** Grain sprigs divide fish in water and tree

Date	Mintage	F	VF	XF	Unc	BU
1985	20,000	—	—	—	6.00	7.00
1985 Proof	5,000	Value: 8.00				

KM# 655 100 FORINT (Szaz)
Copper-Nickel-Zinc, 32 mm. **Subject:** 200th Anniversary - Birth of Andras Fay **Obv:** Denomination and date above legend, fly below **Rev:** Bust at right looking left

Date	Mintage	F	VF	XF	Unc	BU
1986	42,000	—	—	—	5.00	6.00
1986 Proof	8,000	Value: 8.00				

KM# 664 100 FORINT (Szaz)
Copper-Nickel, 38.5 mm. **Subject:** 1990 World Cup Soccer **Obv:** Denomination **Rev:** Soccer players **Designer:** Kutas

Date	Mintage	F	VF	XF	Unc	BU
1988	23,000	—	—	—	9.00	10.00

KM# 665 100 FORINT (Szaz)
Copper-Nickel-Zinc, 38.5 mm. **Subject:** Europe Football Championship **Obv:** Flag and maps on globes make up denomination numerals **Rev:** Soccer player and net within television screen

Date	Mintage	F	VF	XF	Unc	BU
1988	20,000	—	—	—	9.00	10.00

KM# 668 100 FORINT (Szaz)
Copper-Nickel, 38.5 mm. **Subject:** 1990 World Cup Soccer **Obv:** Denomination **Rev:** Players with pennants shaking hands **Designer:** Kutas

Date	Mintage	F	VF	XF	Unc	BU
1989	23,000	—	—	—	9.00	10.00

KM# 586 200 FORINT (Ketszaz)
16.8210 g., 0.9000 Gold .4867 oz. AGW **Subject:** 150th Anniversary - Birth of Ignac Semmelweis **Obv:** Head right **Rev:** Star above shield within wreath

Date	Mintage	F	VF	XF	Unc	BU
1968BP Proof	14,000	Value: 345				

KM# 604 200 FORINT (Ketszaz)
28.0000 g., 0.6400 Silver .5762 oz. ASW **Subject:** 30th Anniversary of Liberation **Obv:** Small shield divides date, denomination below **Rev:** Dove above legend and bridge **Designer:** Robert Csikszentmihalya

Date	Mintage	F	VF	XF	Unc	BU
1975BP	20,000	—	—	—	9.00	10.00
1975BP Proof	10,000	Value: 12.50				

KM# 605 200 FORINT (Ketszaz)
28.0000 g., 0.6400 Silver .5762 oz. ASW **Subject:** 150th Anniversary - Academy of Science **Obv:** Denomination, legend **Rev:** Legend on building at center divides dates

Date	Mintage	F	VF	XF	Unc	BU
1975	20,000	—	—	—	9.00	10.00
1975 Proof	10,000	Value: 12.50				

KM# 606 200 FORINT (Ketszaz)
28.0000 g., 0.6400 Silver .5762 oz. ASW **Subject:** 300th Anniversary - Birth of Ferencz Rakoczi II **Obv:** Shield within wreath divides denomination and date **Rev:** Figure on horseback and soldiers

Date	Mintage	F	VF	XF	Unc	BU
1976	25,000	—	—	—	9.00	10.00
1976 Proof	5,000	Value: 13.50				

KM# 607 200 FORINT (Ketszaz)
28.0000 g., 0.6400 Silver .5762 oz. ASW **Obv:** Quartered design with arms and denomination opposite each other **Rev:** Mihaly Munkacsy, painter

Date	Mintage	F	VF	XF	Unc	BU
1976	25,000	—	—	—	9.00	10.00
1976 Proof	5,000	Value: 12.50				

KM# 608 200 FORINT (Ketszaz)
28.0000 g., 0.6400 Silver .5762 oz. ASW **Obv:** Quartered design with arms and denomination opposite each other **Rev:** Pal Szinyei Merse, painter

Date	Mintage	F	VF	XF	Unc	BU
1976	25,000	—	—	—	9.00	10.00
1976 Proof	5,000	Value: 12.50				

KM# 609 200 FORINT (Ketszaz)
28.0000 g., 0.6400 Silver .5762 oz. ASW **Obv:** Quartered design with arms and denomination opposite each other **Rev:** Gyula Derkovits, painter

Date	Mintage	F	VF	XF	Unc	BU
1976	25,000	—	—	—	9.00	10.00
1976 Proof	5,000	Value: 12.50				

KM# 610 200 FORINT (Ketszaz)
28.0000 g., 0.6400 Silver .5762 oz. ASW **Obv:** Quartered design with arms and denomination opposite each other **Rev:** Adam Manyoki, painter

Date	Mintage	F	VF	XF	Unc	BU
1977	25,000	—	—	—	9.00	10.00
1977 Proof	5,000	Value: 12.50				

KM# 611 200 FORINT (Ketszaz)
28.0000 g., 0.6400 Silver .5762 oz. ASW **Obv:** Quartered design with arms and denomination opposite each other **Rev:** Tivadar CS. Kosztka, painter

Date	Mintage	F	VF	XF	Unc	BU
1977	25,000	—	—	—	9.00	10.00
1977 Proof	5,000	Value: 12.50				

KM# 612 200 FORINT (Ketszaz)
28.0000 g., 0.6400 Silver .5762 oz. ASW **Obv:** Quartered design with arms and denomination opposite each other **Rev:** Jozsef Rippl-Ronai, painter

Date	Mintage	F	VF	XF	Unc	BU
1977	25,000	—	—	—	9.00	10.00
1977 Proof	5,000	Value: 12.50				

KM# 613 200 FORINT (Ketszaz)
28.0000 g., 0.6400 Silver .5762 oz. ASW **Subject:** 175th Anniversary of National Museum **Obv:** Denomination within building, date below **Rev:** Stylized bird with condors flanking

Date	Mintage	F	VF	XF	Unc	BU
1977	25,000	—	—	—	10.00	12.00
1977 Proof	5,000	Value: 16.00				

KM# 614 200 FORINT (Ketszaz)
28.0000 g., 0.6400 Silver .5762 oz. ASW **Subject:** First Hungarian Gold Forint **Obv:** Artistic fleur design **Rev:** Figure and shield within design

Date	Mintage	F	VF	XF	Unc	BU
1978	25,000	—	—	—	10.00	12.00
1978 Proof	5,000	Value: 16.00				

KM# 615 200 FORINT (Ketszaz)
28.0000 g., 0.6400 Silver .5762 oz. ASW, 37 mm. **Subject:** International Year of the Child **Obv:** Logo **Rev:** Depictions of childrens artwork

Date	Mintage	F	VF	XF	Unc	BU
1979	9,000	—	—	—	10.00	12.00
1979 Proof	21,000	Value: 14.00				

KM# 616 200 FORINT (Ketszaz)
22.0000 g., 0.6400 Silver .4527 oz. ASW, 37 mm. **Subject:** 350th Anniversary - Death of Gabor Bethlen **Obv:** Crowned shield at center, legend within circle surrounds **Rev:** Half-figure at left looking right

Date	Mintage	F	VF	XF	Unc	BU
1979	15,000	—	—	—	13.50	16.00
1979 Proof	5,000	Value: 18.50				

KM# 618 200 FORINT (Ketszaz)
16.0000 g., 0.6400 Silver .3292 oz. ASW, 36 mm. **Series:** XIII Winter Olympics - Lake Placid **Obv:** Two figure skaters and denomination **Rev:** Olympic logo

Date	Mintage	F	VF	XF	Unc	BU
1980 Proof	15,000	Value: 10.00				

KM# 643 200 FORINT (Ketszaz)
16.0000 g., 0.6400 Silver .3292 oz. ASW **Subject:** Wildlife Preservation **Obv:** Dates within side circles, divided by artistic denomination and legend within box **Rev:** Otter within square

Date	Mintage	F	VF	XF	Unc	BU
1985	13,000	—	—	—	12.50	15.00
1985 Proof	2,000	Value: 17.50				

KM# 649 200 FORINT (Ketszaz)
16.0000 g., 0.6400 Silver .3292 oz. ASW **Subject:** Wildlife Preservation **Obv:** Date within side circles divided by artistic denomination and legend within box **Rev:** Pond turtle within square

Date	Mintage	F	VF	XF	Unc	BU
1985	13,000	—	—	—	12.50	15.00
1985 Proof	2,000	Value: 17.50				

KM# 650 200 FORINT (Ketszaz)
16.0000 g., 0.6400 Silver .3292 oz. ASW **Subject:** Wildlife Preservation **Obv:** Date within side circles, divided by artistic denomination and legend within box **Rev:** Wildcat within square

Date	Mintage	F	VF	XF	Unc	BU
1985	13,000	—	—	—	12.50	15.00
1985 Proof	2,000	Value: 17.50				

KM# 565 500 FORINT (Otszaz)
38.3800 g., 0.9860 Gold 1.2168 oz. AGW **Subject:** 150th Anniversary - Birth of Ferenc Liszt **Obv:** Harp below denomination **Rev:** Head right

Date	Mintage	F	VF	XF	Unc	BU
1961BP	2,503	Value: 875				

KM# 566 500 FORINT (Otszaz)
38.3800 g., 0.9860 Gold 1.2168 oz. AGW **Subject:** 80th Anniversary - Birth of Bela Bartok, Composer **Obv:** Small harp above denomination **Rev:** Head left

Date	Mintage	F	VF	XF	Unc	BU
1961	2,503	Value: 875				

KM# 570 500 FORINT (Otszaz)
42.0522 g., 0.9000 Gold 1.2169 oz. AGW **Subject:** 400th Anniversary - Death of Miklos Zrinyi **Obv:** Monument **Rev:** Head right

Date	Mintage	F	VF	XF	Unc	BU
1966 Proof	1,100	Value: 925				

KM# 580 500 FORINT (Otszaz)
42.0522 g., 0.9000 Gold 1.2169 oz. AGW **Subject:** 85th Birthday of Zoltan Kodaly, Composer **Obv:** Peacock above denomination **Rev:** Bust 3/4 left

Date	Mintage	F	VF	XF	Unc	BU
1967	—	—	—	—	875	900
1967 Proof	1,000	Value: 950				

KM# 587 500 FORINT (Otszaz)
42.0522 g., 0.9000 Gold 1.2169 oz. AGW **Subject:** 150th Anniversary - Birth of Ignacz Semmelweis **Obv:** Head right **Rev:** Star above shield within wreath

Date	Mintage	F	VF	XF	Unc	BU
1968 Proof	9,000	Value: 875				

KM# 619 500 FORINT (Otszaz)
39.0000 g., 0.6400 Silver .8025 oz. ASW, 46 mm. **Series:** XIII Winter Olympics - Lake Placid **Obv:** Two figure skaters **Rev:** Olympic logo

Date	Mintage	F	VF	XF	Unc	BU
1980BP Proof	13,000	Value: 55.00				

KM# 623 500 FORINT (Otszaz)
25.0000 g., 0.6400 Silver .5144 oz. ASW **Subject:** Centennial - Birth of Bela Bartok, Composer **Obv:** Musical score, statue and denomination **Rev:** Head left, map in background

Date	Mintage	F	VF	XF	Unc	BU
1981	13,000	—	—	—	16.50	18.00
1981 Proof	13,000	Value: 20.00				

KM# 624 500 FORINT (Otszaz)
28.0000 g., 0.6400 Silver .5762 oz. ASW **Subject:** World Football Championship **Obv:** Soccer player **Rev:** Soccer field, soccer ball on shield at lower left

Date	Mintage	F	VF	XF	Unc	BU
1981	6,000	—	—	—	20.00	25.00
1981 Proof	40,000	Value: 16.50				

KM# 625 500 FORINT (Otszaz)
28.0000 g., 0.6400 Silver .5762 oz. ASW **Subject:** World Football Championship **Obv:** Soccer ball on shield within lined design **Rev:** Soccer players

Date	Mintage	F	VF	XF	Unc	BU
1981	6,000	—	—	—	20.00	25.00
1981 Proof	40,000	Value: 16.50				

KM# 640 500 FORINT (Otszaz)
28.0000 g., 0.6400 Silver .5762 oz. ASW **Subject:** Decade for Women **Obv:** Ankh on shaded stylized dove **Rev:** Kneeling woman

Date	Mintage	F	VF	XF	Unc	BU
1984	8,000	—	—	—	18.50	—
1984 Proof	20,000	Value: 22.50				

KM# 641 500 FORINT (Otszaz)
28.0000 g., 0.6400 Silver .5762 oz. ASW **Series:** Winter Olympics - Sarajevo **Obv:** Olympic flame, snowflakes and denomination **Rev:** Cross-country skiers

Date	Mintage	F	VF	XF	Unc	BU
1984	8,000	—	—	—	10.00	11.50
1984 Proof	12,000	Value: 12.50				

KM# 642 500 FORINT (Otszaz)
28.0000 g., 0.6400 Silver .5762 oz. ASW **Subject:** Los Angeles Olympics **Obv:** Denomination, torch at left **Rev:** Gymnast

Date	Mintage	F	VF	XF	Unc	BU
1984	8,000	—	—	—	10.00	11.50
1984 Proof	12,000	Value: 12.50				

KM# 652 500 FORINT (Otszaz)
28.0000 g., 0.6400 Silver .5762 oz. ASW **Subject:** Budapest Cultural Forum **Obv:** Denomination **Rev:** Bird, right of shield within ornamental design, legend within column below

Date	Mintage	F	VF	XF	Unc	BU
1985	15,000	—	—	—	10.00	11.50
1985 Proof	10,000	Value: 17.50				

KM# 656 500 FORINT (Otszaz)
28.0000 g., 0.6400 Silver .5762 oz. ASW **Subject:** World Football Championship **Obv:** Soccer ball and globe make up zeros of denomination **Rev:** Football players

Date	Mintage	F	VF	XF	Unc	BU
1986	8,000	—	—	—	14.00	16.00
1986 Proof	17,000	Value: 12.50				

KM# 657 500 FORINT (Otszaz)
28.0000 g., 0.6400 Silver .5762 oz. ASW **Subject:** World Football Championship **Obv:** Denomination **Rev:** Stadium

Date	Mintage	F	VF	XF	Unc	BU
1986	8,000	—	—	—	14.00	16.00
1986 Proof	17,000	Value: 12.50				

KM# 658 500 FORINT (Otszaz)
28.0000 g., 0.9000 Silver .8102 oz. ASW **Subject:** 300th Anniversary - Repossession of Buda from the Turks **Obv:** Sword crosses top of denomination **Rev:** Village scene

Date	Mintage	F	VF	XF	Unc	BU
1986	20,000	—	—	—	20.00	22.00
1986 Proof	10,000	Value: 25.00				

KM# 659 500 FORINT (Otszaz)
28.0000 g., 0.9000 Silver .8102 oz. ASW **Series:** Winter Olympics - Calgary 1988 **Obv:** Snowflake designs on flames **Rev:** Speed skater

Date	Mintage	F	VF	XF	Unc	BU
1986	15,000	—	—	—	12.50	14.00
1986 Proof	15,000	Value: 15.00				

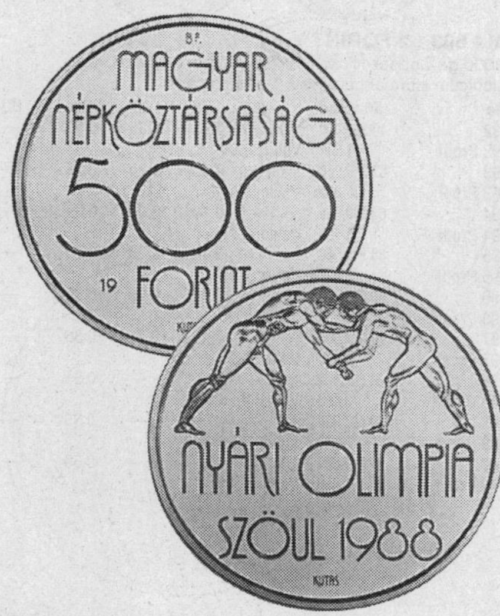

KM# 660 500 FORINT (Otszaz)
28.0000 g., 0.9000 Silver .8102 oz. ASW **Subject:** Seoul Olympics **Obv:** Denomination **Rev:** Wrestlers

Date	Mintage	F	VF	XF	Unc	BU
1987	15,000	—	—	—	14.50	16.50
1987 Proof	15,000	Value: 22.50				

KM# 661 500 FORINT (Otszaz)
28.0000 g., 0.9000 Silver .8102 oz. ASW **Subject:** World Wildlife Fund **Obv:** Denomination **Rev:** Montagu's Harrier

Date	Mintage	F	VF	XF	Unc	BU
1988	10,000	—	—	—	22.50	25.00
1988 Proof	25,000	Value: 25.00				

KM# 662 500 FORINT (Otszaz)
28.0000 g., 0.9000 Silver .8102 oz. ASW **Subject:** 950th Anniversary - Death of St. Stephan **Obv:** Ancient coin designs above denomination **Rev:** Figure of King Stephen at left and Queen Gisela of Bavaria at right

Date	Mintage	F	VF	XF	Unc	BU
1988	5,000	—	—	—	38.00	42.00
1988 Proof	15,000	Value: 25.00				

KM# 666 500 FORINT (Otszaz)
28.0000 g., 0.9000 Silver .8102 oz. ASW **Subject:** Europe Football Championship **Obv:** Stenciled denomination **Rev:** Soccer player behind net

Date	Mintage	F	VF	XF	Unc	BU
1988	8,000	—	—	—	17.50	18.50
1988 Proof	12,000	Value: 16.50				

KM# 667 500 FORINT (Otszaz)
28.0000 g., 0.9000 Silver .8102 oz. ASW **Subject:** World Football Championship **Obv:** Denomination **Rev:** Soccer players

Date	Mintage	F	VF	XF	Unc	BU
1988	7,000	—	—	—	18.50	20.00
1988 Proof	15,000	Value: 17.50				

KM# 669 500 FORINT (Otszaz)
28.0000 g., 0.9000 Silver .8102 oz. ASW **Subject:** World Football Championship **Obv:** Denomination **Rev:** Two players

Date	Mintage	F	VF	XF	Unc	BU
1989	7,000	—	—	—	18.50	20.00
1989 Proof	15,000	Value: 17.50				

KM# 670 500 FORINT (Otszaz)
28.0000 g., 0.9000 Silver .8102 oz. ASW **Subject:** Save the Children Fund **Obv:** Denomination below figure and lined design **Rev:** Seedling within outline of child

Date	Mintage	F	VF	XF	Unc	BU
1989	10,000	—	—	—	22.50	25.00
1989 Proof	20,000	Value: 22.50				

KM# 671 500 FORINT (Otszaz)

28.0000 g., 0.9000 Silver .8102 oz. ASW **Series:** 1992 Barcelona Olympics **Obv:** Denomination within lined design **Rev:** Torch bearer lighting the flame

Date	Mintage	F	VF	XF	Unc	BU
1989	15,000	—	—	—	22.50	25.00
1989 Proof	15,000	Value: 27.50				

KM# 571 1000 FORINT (Ezer)

84.1040 g., 0.9000 Gold 2.4339 oz. AGW **Subject:** 400th Anniversary - Death of Miklos Zrinyi **Obv:** Monument **Rev:** Head 3/4 right

Date	Mintage	F	VF	XF	Unc	BU
1966 Proof	330	Value: 1,900				

KM# 581 1000 FORINT (Ezer)

84.1040 g., 0.9000 Gold 2.4339 oz. AGW **Subject:** 85th Birthday of Zoltan Kodaly, Composer **Obv:** Peacock above denomination **Rev:** Bust 3/4 left

Date	Mintage	F	VF	XF	Unc	BU
1967 Proof	500	Value: 1,800				

KM# 588 1000 FORINT (Ezer)

84.1040 g., 0.9000 Gold 2.4339 oz. AGW **Subject:** 150th Anniversary - Birth of Ignacz Semmelweis **Rev:** Star above shield within wreath

Date	Mintage	F	VF	XF	Unc	BU
1968	7,000	Value: 1,675				

TRANSITIONAL COINAGE

KM# 736 FORINT

Aluminum **Obv:** Star above shield within wreath **Rev:** Leaves flank denomination **Note:** Communist design type with New Republic legends

Date	Mintage	F	VF	XF	Unc	BU
1990	10,000	—	—	—	10.00	12.00

KM# 737 2 FORINT

Brass **Obv:** Star above shield within wreath **Rev:** Large denomination divides date **Note:** Communist design type with New Republic legends

Date	Mintage	F	VF	XF	Unc	BU
1990	10,000	—	—	—	15.00	17.00

KM# 738 5 FORINT

Copper-Nickel **Subject:** Lajos Kossuth **Obv. Inscription:** Head right **Rev:** Small shield divides date above denomination **Note:** Communist design with New Republic legends

Date	Mintage	F	VF	XF	Unc	BU
1990	10,000	—	—	—	20.00	22.00

KM# 739 10 FORINT

Aluminum-Bronze **Obv:** Strobl Monument **Rev:** Small shield below denomination

Date	Mintage	F	VF	XF	Unc	BU
1990	10,000	—	—	—	25.00	30.00

KM# 740 20 FORINT

Copper-Nickel **Subject:** György Dózsa **Obv:** Head looking left **Rev:** Grain sprigs flank denomination, small shield above

Date	Mintage	F	VF	XF	Unc	BU
1990	10,000	—	—	—	30.00	35.00

SECOND REPUBLIC

1989-present

DECIMAL COINAGE

KM# 673 2 FILLER

6.5000 g., Aluminum **Obv:** Wreath surrounds center hole **Rev:** Center hole divides denomination within wreath

Date	Mintage	F	VF	XF	Unc	BU
1990BP	10,000	—	—	—	2.00	—
1991BP	10,000	—	—	—	3.00	—
1992BP	30,000	—	—	—	3.00	—

KM# 674 5 FILLER

6.0000 g., Aluminum **Obv:** Head left **Rev:** Denomination within wreath

Date	Mintage	F	VF	XF	Unc	BU
1990BP	10,000	—	—	—	2.00	—
1991BP	10,000	—	—	—	3.00	—
1992BP	30,000	—	—	—	3.00	—

KM# 675 10 FILLER

6.0000 g., Aluminum **Obv:** Dove with branch **Rev:** Denomination

Date	Mintage	F	VF	XF	Unc	BU
1990BP	46,515,000	0.10	0.15	0.20	0.35	—
1991BP	2,370,000	0.25	0.40	0.55	0.75	—
1992BP	15,828,000	0.15	0.25	0.35	0.50	—
1993BP	30,000	—	—	—	1.00	—
1994BP	30,000	—	—	—	1.00	—
1995BP	30,000	—	—	—	1.00	—
1996BP	20,000	—	—	—	1.20	—

KM# 676 20 FILLER

0.9000 g., Aluminum **Obv:** Three wheat ears divide date **Rev:** Lines divide denomination

Date	Mintage	F	VF	XF	Unc	BU
1990BP	59,360,000	0.10	0.15	0.20	0.35	—
1991BP	20,210,000	0.20	0.35	0.50	0.75	—
1992BP	30,000	—	—	—	1.00	—
1993BP	30,000	—	—	—	1.00	—
1994BP	30,000	—	—	—	1.00	—
1995BP	30,000	—	—	—	1.00	—
1996BP	20,000	—	—	—	1.25	—

KM# 677 50 FILLER

1.2000 g., Aluminum **Obv:** Erzsebet Bridge **Rev:** Denomination

Date	Mintage	F	VF	XF	Unc	BU
1990BP	20,550,000	—	0.10	0.20	0.30	—
1991BP	31,250,000	—	—	0.10	0.25	—
1992BP	440,000	—	—	—	0.85	—
1993BP	30,000	—	—	—	1.20	—
1994BP	30,000	—	—	—	1.20	—
1995BP	30,000	—	—	—	1.20	—
1996BP	20,000	—	—	—	1.60	—
1997BP	10,000	—	—	—	2.50	—
1998BP	10,000	—	—	—	2.50	—
1999BP	10,000	—	—	—	2.50	—

KM# 692 FORINT

2.0500 g., Brass, 16.5 mm. **Obv:** Crowned shield **Rev:** Denomination

Date	Mintage	F	VF	XF	Unc	BU
1992	23,890,100	—	0.10	0.25	0.35	—
1992 Proof	1,000	Value: 6.00				
1993	75,100,000	—	—	0.10	0.25	—
1993 Proof	30,000	Value: 1.00				
1994	66,605,005	—	—	0.10	0.25	—
1994 Proof	15,000	Value: 1.20				
1995	50,535,000	—	—	0.10	0.25	—
1995 Proof	15,000	Value: 1.20				
1996	67,000,010	—	—	0.10	0.25	—
1996 Proof	10,000	Value: 1.40				
1997	—	—	—	0.10	0.25	—
1997 Proof	3,000	Value: 3.75				
1998	—	—	—	0.10	0.25	—
1998 Proof	3,000	Value: 3.75				
1999	—	—	—	0.10	0.25	—
1999 Proof	3,000	Value: 3.75				
2000	—	—	—	0.10	0.25	—
2000 Proof	3,000	Value: 3.75				

KM# 693 2 FORINT

3.1000 g., Copper-Nickel, 19 mm. **Obv:** Native flower: Colchicum Hungaricum **Rev:** Denomination

Date	Mintage	F	VF	XF	Unc	BU
1992	10,380,100	0.10	0.25	0.35	0.50	—
1992 Proof	1,000	Value: 6.00				
1993	82,915,000	—	0.10	0.25	0.35	—
1993 Proof	30,000	Value: 1.50				
1994	68,370,005	—	0.10	0.25	0.35	—
1994 Proof	15,000	Value: 1.75				
1995	60,945,000	—	0.10	0.25	0.35	—
1995 Proof	15,000	Value: 1.75				
1996	50,010,000	—	0.10	0.25	0.35	—
1996 Proof	10,000	Value: 1.95				
1997	70,007,000	—	0.10	0.20	0.35	—
1997 Proof	3,000	Value: 4.25				
1998	20,007,000	—	—	—	0.35	—
1998 Proof	3,000	Value: 4.25				
1999	50,007,000	—	—	—	0.35	—
1999 Proof	3,000	Value: 4.25				
2000	55,007,000	—	—	—	0.35	—
2000 Proof	3,000	Value: 4.25				

KM# 694 5 FORINT
4.2000 g., Brass, 21.5 mm. **Obv:** Great White Egret **Rev:** Denomination

Date	Mintage	F	VF	XF	Unc	BU
1992	1,145,300	0.15	0.30	0.60	1.00	—
1992 Proof	1,000	Value: 7.00				
1993	37,180,000	0.10	0.25	0.45	1.00	—
1993 Proof	30,000	Value: 2.00				
1994	53,615,000	0.10	0.20	0.30	1.00	—
1994 Proof	15,000	Value: 2.50				
1995	24,670,000	0.15	0.30	0.40	1.00	—
1995 Proof	15,000	Value: 2.50				
1996	6,010,000	0.25	0.50	0.65	1.00	—
1996 Proof	10,000	Value: 3.00				
1997	20,007,000	0.15	0.30	0.40	1.00	—
1997 Proof	3,000	Value: 5.00				
1998	7,000	—	—	—	3.00	—
1998 Proof	3,000	Value: 5.00				
1999	25,007,000	0.15	0.30	0.40	1.00	—
1999 Proof	3,000	Value: 5.00				
2000	30,007,000	0.10	0.25	0.35	1.00	—
2000 Proof	3,000	Value: 5.00				

KM# 695 10 FORINT
6.1000 g., Copper-Nickel Clad Brass, 25 mm. **Obv:** Crowned shield **Rev:** Denomination

Date	Mintage	F	VF	XF	Unc	BU
1992	2,000	—	—	—	6.00	—
1992 Proof	1,000	Value: 8.00				
1993	35,565,000	0.10	0.25	0.45	1.00	—
1993 Proof	30,000	Value: 2.50				
1994	69,078,000	—	0.15	0.35	0.85	—
1994 Proof	15,000	Value: 3.00				
1995	40,910,000	0.10	0.25	0.45	1.00	—
1995 Proof	15,000	Value: 3.00				
1996	13,010,000	0.15	0.30	0.50	1.00	—
1996 Proof	10,000	Value: 3.50				
1997	8,007,000	0.20	0.35	0.55	1.00	—
1997 Proof	3,000	Value: 5.50				
1998	7,000	—	—	—	2.50	—
1998 Proof	3,000	Value: 5.50				
1999	7,000	—	—	—	2.50	—
1999 Proof	3,000	Value: 5.50				
2000	7,000	—	—	—	2.50	—
2000 Proof	3,000	Value: 5.50				

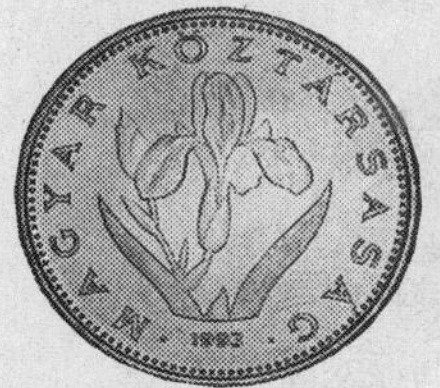

KM# 696 20 FORINT
6.9000 g., Nickel-Brass, 26.3 mm. **Obv:** Hungarian Iris **Rev:** Denomination

Date	Mintage	F	VF	XF	Unc	BU
1992	2,000	—	—	—	7.00	—
1992 Proof	1,000	Value: 9.00				
1993	42,965,000	0.20	0.30	0.60	1.50	2.00
1993 Proof	30,000	Value: 3.50				
1994	68,965,005	0.15	0.25	0.50	1.25	1.75
1994 Proof	15,000	Value: 4.00				
1995	53,395,000	0.15	0.25	0.50	1.25	1.75
1995 Proof	15,000	Value: 4.00				
1996	6,010,000	0.20	0.35	0.70	1.50	2.00
1996 Proof	10,000	Value: 4.00				
1997	7,000	—	—	—	5.00	6.00
1997 Proof	3,000	Value: 6.00				
1998	7,000	—	—	—	3.50	4.00
1998 Proof	3,000	Value: 6.00				
1999	7,000	—	—	—	3.50	4.00
1999 Proof	3,000	Value: 6.00				
2000	7,000	—	—	—	3.50	4.00
2000 Proof	3,000	Value: 6.00				

KM# 697 50 FORINT
7.7000 g., Copper-Nickel Clad Brass, 27.5 mm. **Obv:** Saker falcon **Rev:** Denomination

Date	Mintage	F	VF	XF	Unc	BU
1992	2,000	—	—	—	10.00	—
1992 Proof	1,000	Value: 12.00				
1993	860,500	0.50	0.65	1.25	3.00	3.50
1993 Proof	30,000	Value: 5.00				
1994	8,397,005	0.25	0.45	0.85	3.00	3.50
1994 Proof	15,000	Value: 5.00				
1995	36,985,000	—	0.25	0.50	2.50	3.00
1995 Proof	15,000	Value: 5.00				
1996	7,010,000	0.30	0.50	1.00	3.00	3.50
1996 Proof	10,000	Value: 5.00				
1997	12,007,000	—	—	—	3.00	3.50
1997 Proof	3,000	Value: 6.50				
1998	7,000	—	—	—	5.50	6.50
1998 Proof	3,000	Value: 6.50				
1999	7,000	—	—	—	5.50	6.50
1999 Proof	3,000	Value: 6.50				
2000	7,000	—	—	—	5.50	6.50
2000 Proof	3,000	Value: 6.50				

KM# 734 75 FORINT
31.4600 g., 0.9250 Silver .9356 oz. ASW **Subject:** 75th Anniversary - Hungarian National Bank **Obv:** Crowned shield above denomination **Rev:** Goddess Juno

Date	Mintage	F	VF	XF	Unc	BU
1999	Est. 3,000	—	—	—	32.50	35.00
1999 Proof	Est. 4,500	Value: 40.00				

KM# 760 100 FORINT
8.0000 g., Bi-Metallic Stainless Steel center in Brass plated Steel ring, 23.7 mm. **Subject:** Lajos Kossuth **Obv:** Head right within circle **Rev:** Denomination within circle **Edge:** Reeded

Date	Mintage	F	VF	XF	Unc	BU
2002	990,000	—	—	—	2.00	—

KM# 678 100 FORINT (Szaz)
12.0000 g., Copper-Nickel-Zinc, 32 mm. **Subject:** Adreas Fay **Obv:** Fly below legend, denomination and date above **Rev:** Bust 3/4 left **Edge:** Reeded

Date	Mintage	F	VF	XF	Unc	BU
1990BP	20,000	—	—	—	5.00	—
1990BP Proof	10,000	Value: 7.00				

KM# 700 100 FORINT (Szaz)
12.0000 g., Copper-Nickel **Subject:** S.O.S. Gyermekfalu, Children's Village **Obv:** Children and flower within box divide date above denomination **Rev:** Mother protecting child

Date	Mintage	F	VF	XF	Unc	BU
1990 Proof	50,000	Value: 12.00				

KM# 701 100 FORINT (Szaz)
12.0000 g., Copper-Nickel **Subject:** Hungarian Theatre **Obv:** Denomination divides date within wreath **Rev:** Theatre scene

Date	Mintage	F	VF	XF	Unc	BU
1990	5,000	—	—	—	10.00	—
1990 Proof	5,000	Value: 12.00				

KM# 682 100 FORINT (Szaz)
12.0000 g., Copper-Nickel-Zinc **Subject:** Papal Visit **Obv:** Arms of the Republic **Rev:** Pope John Paul II

Date	Mintage	F	VF	XF	Unc	BU
1991	30,000	—	—	—	3.00	—
1991 Proof	30,000	Value: 6.00				

KM# 698 100 FORINT (Szaz)
9.4000 g., Brass **Obv:** Crowned shield **Rev:** Denomination

Date	Mintage	F	VF	XF	Unc	BU
1992	2,000	—	—	—	12.00	—
1992 Proof	1,000	Value: 15.00				
1993	924,500	—	—	—	3.00	—
1993 Proof	30,000	Value: 6.00				
1994	7,861,005	—	—	—	2.50	—
1994 Proof	15,000	Value: 6.00				
1995	27,485,000	—	—	—	2.50	—
1995 Proof	15,000	Value: 6.00				
1996	6,210,000	—	—	—	2.50	—
1996 Proof	10,000	Value: 6.00				
1997	7,000	—	—	—	6.00	—
1997 Proof	3,000	Value: 8.00				
1998	7,000	—	—	—	6.00	—
1998 Proof	3,000	Value: 8.00				

KM# 721 100 FORINT (Szaz)
Bi-Metallic Brass plated Steel center in Stainless Steel ring, 23.6 mm. **Obv:** Crowned shield **Rev:** Denomination

Date	Mintage	F	VF	XF	Unc	BU
1996	35,001,000	—	—	—	4.50	—
1996 Proof	1,000	Value: 12.00				
1997	60,007,000	—	—	—	4.50	—
1997 Proof	3,000	Value: 8.00				
1998	60,007,000	—	—	—	4.50	—
1998 Proof	3,000	Value: 8.00				
1999	7,000	—	—	—	6.50	—
1999 Proof	3,000	Value: 8.00				
2000	7,000	—	—	—	6.50	—
2000 Proof	3,000	Value: 8.00				

KM# 726 100 FORINT (Szaz)
9.4000 g., Bronze **Subject:** Revolution of 1848 **Obv:** Hungarian Order of Military Merit (1848-1849) II Class **Rev:** Revolutionary ribbon badge above poetry verse

Date	Mintage	F	VF	XF	Unc	BU
1998	15,000	—	—	—	7.00	—
1998 Proof	15,000	Value: 9.00				

KM# 688 200 FORINT
10.0000 g., 0.5000 Silver .1608 oz. ASW **Obv:** Crowned shield below globe **Rev:** White storks

Date	Mintage	F	VF	XF	Unc	BU
1992BP	20,000	—	—	—	10.00	12.50
1992BP Proof	80,000	Value: 15.00				

KM# 689 200 FORINT
12.0000 g., 0.5000 Silver .1929 oz. ASW **Obv:** Erzsebet Bridge, crowned shield divides date above **Rev:** National Bank

Date	Mintage	F	VF	XF	Unc	BU
1992	3,514,023	—	—	—	6.00	7.00
1992 Proof	29,998	Value: 9.00				
1993	2,540,993	—	—	—	6.00	7.00
1993 Proof	30,000	Value: 9.00				

KM# 707 200 FORINT
12.0000 g., 0.5000 Silver .1929 oz. ASW **Obv:** Erzsebet Bridge **Rev:** Ferenc Deak

Date	Mintage	F	VF	XF	Unc	BU
1994	5,000,000	—	—	—	6.50	—
1994 Proof	15,000	Value: 10.00				
1995	85,000	—	—	—	7.50	—
1995 Proof	15,000	Value: 10.00				
1997	7,000	—	—	—	10.00	—
1997 Proof	3,000	Value: 12.00				
1998	7,000	—	—	—	10.00	—
1998 Proof	3,000	Value: 12.00				

KM# 745 200 FORINT
9.5600 g., Brass **Subject:** Millennium **Obv:** Crowned shield above denomination **Rev:** Rodin's "The Thinker" statue and solar system **Edge:** Plain

Date	Mintage	F	VF	XF	Unc	BU
2000	15,000	—	—	—	4.50	—
2000 Proof	10,000	Value: 6.00				

KM# 672 500 FORINT (Otszaz)
28.0000 g., 0.9000 Silver .8102 oz. ASW **Series:** Albertville Olympics 1992 **Obv:** Denomination, date below **Rev:** Hockey players

Date	Mintage	F	VF	XF	Unc	BU
1989BP	15,000	—	—	—	27.50	30.00
1989BP Proof	15,000	Value: 32.50				

KM# 679 500 FORINT (Otszaz)
28.0000 g., 0.9000 Silver .8102 oz. ASW **Obv:** King Mathias on horse left **Rev:** Busts of King Mathias and Queen Beatrix facing each other

Date	Mintage	F	VF	XF	Unc	BU
1990BP	15,000	—	—	—	32.50	35.00
1990BP Proof	15,000	Value: 37.50				

KM# 680 500 FORINT (Otszaz)
28.0000 g., 0.9000 Silver .8102 oz. ASW **Obv:** Denomination, legend and date within decorative outline **Rev:** Two capital cities of King Mathias

Date	Mintage	F	VF	XF	Unc	BU
1990	15,000	—	—	—	32.50	35.00
1990 Proof	15,000	Value: 37.50				

KM# 699 500 FORINT (Otszaz)
28.0000 g., 0.9000 Silver .8102 oz. ASW **Subject:** 200th Anniversary - Birth of Ferenc Kolcsey **Obv:** Crowned arms and denomination **Rev:** Ferenc Kölcsey

Date	Mintage	F	VF	XF	Unc	BU
1990BP	10,000	—	—	—	40.00	42.50
1990BP Proof	5,000	Value: 50.00				

KM# 683 500 FORINT (Otszaz)
28.0000 g., 0.9000 Silver .8102 oz. ASW **Subject:** Papal Visit **Obv:** Arms of the Republic **Rev:** Pope John Paul II

Date	Mintage	F	VF	XF	Unc	BU
1991BP	10,000	—	—	—	22.50	25.00
1991BP Proof	20,000	Value: 28.50				

KM# 685 500 FORINT (Otszaz)
28.0000 g., 0.9000 Silver .8102 oz. ASW **Subject:** 200th Anniversary - Birth of Count Szechenyi **Obv:** Locomotive and value **Rev:** Istvan Szechenyi

Date	Mintage	F	VF	XF	Unc	BU
1991BP	15,000	—	—	—	25.00	27.50
1991BP Proof	15,000	Value: 32.50				

KM# 686 500 FORINT (Otszaz)

28.0000 g., 0.9000 Silver .8102 oz. ASW **Obv:** Denomination **Rev:** Anjou Liliom **Rev. Legend:** Karoly Robert Emlekere

Date	Mintage	F	VF	XF	Unc	BU
1992BP	10,000	—	—	—	22.50	25.00
1992BP Proof	20,000	Value: 30.00				

KM# 687 500 FORINT (Otszaz)

28.0000 g., 0.9000 Silver .8102 oz. ASW **Subject:** Canonization of King Ladislaus **Obv:** Ladislaus Denar (obv. and rev.) and denomination **Rev:** King Ladislaus

Date	Mintage	F	VF	XF	Unc	BU
1992BP	10,000	—	—	—	25.00	27.50
1992BP Proof	20,000	Value: 32.50				

KM# 690 500 FORINT (Otszaz)

31.4600 g., 0.9250 Silver .9356 oz. ASW **Obv:** Crowned shield and denomination **Rev:** Telstar I satellite above globe

Date	Mintage	F	VF	XF	Unc	BU
1992BP	Est. 5,000	—	—	—	22.50	25.00
1992BP Proof	Est. 15,000	Value: 27.50				

KM# 702 500 FORINT (Otszaz)

31.4600 g., 0.9250 Silver .9356 oz. ASW **Obv:** Denomination above crowned arms **Rev:** Old Danube Ship "Arpad"

Date	Mintage	F	VF	XF	Unc	BU
1993BP	10,000	—	—	—	15.00	16.50
1993BP Proof	15,000	Value: 17.50				

KM# 704 500 FORINT (Otszaz)

31.4600 g., 0.9250 Silver .9357 oz. ASW **Obv:** Crowned arms divide date above denomination **Rev:** European Currency Union

Date	Mintage	F	VF	XF	Unc	BU
1993BP	10,000	—	—	—	18.50	20.00
1993BP Proof	30,000	Value: 22.00				

KM# 705 500 FORINT (Otszaz)

31.4600 g., 0.9250 Silver .9357 oz. ASW **Subject:** Expo '96 **Obv:** Logo above denomination **Rev:** Ship sailing on sea of letters

Date	Mintage	F	VF	XF	Unc	BU
1993	20,000	—	—	—	17.50	20.00
1993 Proof	80,000	Value: 20.00				

KM# 708 500 FORINT (Otszaz)

31.4600 g., 0.9250 Silver .9357 oz. ASW **Obv:** Denomination above crowned arms **Rev:** Old Danube Ship "Carolina"

Date	Mintage	F	VF	XF	Unc	BU
1994	10,000	—	—	—	18.00	20.00
1994 Proof	15,000	Value: 22.00				

KM# 709 500 FORINT (Otszaz)

31.4600 g., 0.9250 Silver .9357 oz. ASW **Subject:** Death of Lajos Kossuth **Obv:** Denomination within shield outline **Rev:** Bust 3/4 right

Date	Mintage	F	VF	XF	Unc	BU
1994	10,000	—	—	—	23.50	25.00
1994 Proof	10,000	Value: 28.50				

KM# 710 500 FORINT (Otszaz)

31.4600 g., 0.9250 Silver .9357 oz. ASW **Subject:** International European Union **Obv:** Crowned arms divide date above denomination **Rev:** St. Istvan and Halaszbastya

Date	Mintage	F	VF	XF	Unc	BU
1994	10,000	—	—	—	22.50	25.00
1994 Proof	30,000	Value: 27.50				

KM# 723 750 FORINT

10.0000 g., 0.5000 Silver .1607 oz. ASW **Subject:** Soccer **Obv:** Denomination in goal **Rev:** Ball in net above the Eiffel Tower

Date	Mintage	F	VF	XF	Unc	BU
1997	3,000	—	—	—	25.00	30.00
1997 Proof	17,000	Value: 20.00				

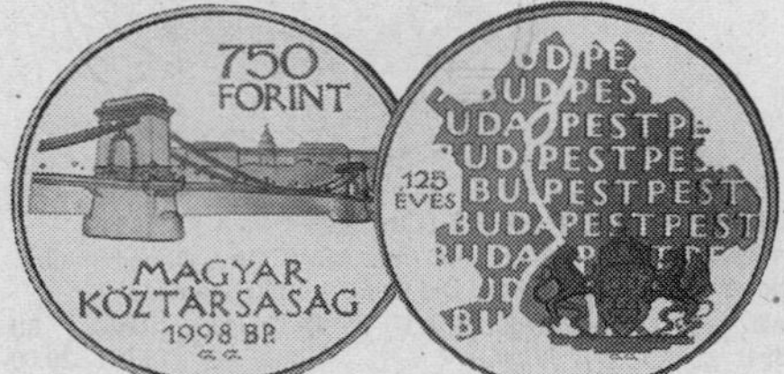

KM# 725 750 FORINT

10.0000 g., 0.5000 Silver .1607 oz. ASW **Subject:** 125th Anniversary - Budapest **Obv:** Lanc Bridge **Rev:** City map and arms

Date	Mintage	F	VF	XF	Unc	BU
1998	3,000	—	—	—	30.00	35.00
1998 Proof	12,000	Value: 20.00				

KM# 706 1000 FORINT

31.4600 g., 0.9250 Silver .9357 oz. ASW **Subject:** World Cup Soccer **Obv:** Small crowned arms above denomination **Rev:** Goalie

Date	Mintage	F	VF	XF	Unc	BU
1993BP	10,000	—	—	—	23.50	25.00
1993BP Proof	15,000	Value: 27.50				

KM# 712 1000 FORINT

31.4600 g., 0.9250 Silver .9357 oz. ASW **Series:** Atlanta Olympics **Obv:** Olympic flame in bowl above denomination **Rev:** Swimmers

Date	Mintage	F	VF	XF	Unc	BU
1994	10,000	—	—	—	20.00	22.50
1994 Proof	40,000	Value: 24.00				

KM# 713 1000 FORINT

31.4600 g., 0.9250 Silver .9357 oz. ASW **Subject:** Protect Our World **Obv:** Stylized bird right below denomination **Rev:** Globe in trunk

Date	Mintage	F	VF	XF	Unc	BU
1994	10,000	—	—	—	25.00	27.50
1994 Proof	10,000	Value: 30.00				

KM# 714 1000 FORINT

31.4600 g., 0.9250 Silver .9357 oz. ASW **Obv:** Crowned shield below denomination **Rev:** Old Danube Ship "Hableany"

Date	Mintage	F	VF	XF	Unc	BU
1995	10,000	—	—	—	25.00	27.50
1995 Proof	20,000	Value: 28.00				

KM# 715 1000 FORINT

31.4600 g., 0.9250 Silver .9357 oz. ASW **Obv:** Abbot's seal impression and value **Rev:** Pannonhalma ruins

Date	Mintage	F	VF	XF	Unc	BU
1995	10,000	—	—	—	28.00	30.00
1995 Proof	10,000	Value: 32.50				

KM# 716 1000 FORINT

31.4600 g., 0.9250 Silver .9357 oz. ASW **Series:** Atlanta Olympics **Obv:** Denomination **Rev:** Fencing match

Date	Mintage	F	VF	XF	Unc	BU
1995	5,000	—	—	—	30.00	35.00
1995 Proof	25,000	Value: 27.50				

KM# 720 1000 FORINT

31.4600 g., 0.9250 Silver .9357 oz. ASW **Subject:** European Union **Obv:** Crowned arms divide date **Rev:** Hungarian Parliament building, "ecu"

Date	Mintage	F	VF	XF	Unc	BU
1995	5,000	—	—	—	32.50	37.50
1995 Proof	18,000	Value: 30.00				

KM# 717 2000 FORINT

31.4600 g., 0.9250 Silver .9357 oz. ASW **Subject:** 50th Anniversary Forint Rebirth **Obv:** Anjou Lilium below fold of material, crowned arms above **Rev:** 13 coin designs

Date	Mintage	F	VF	XF	Unc	BU
1996	5,000	—	—	—	35.00	40.00
1996 Proof	5,000	Value: 45.00				

KM# 718 2000 FORINT

31.4600 g., 0.9250 Silver .9357 oz. ASW **Subject:** 1100th Anniversary of Hungarian Nationhood **Obv:** Date and denomination below shield of designs **Rev:** Three equestrian archers above old shield

Date	Mintage	F	VF	XF	Unc	BU
1996	10,000	—	—	—	35.00	40.00
1996 Proof	10,000	Value: 45.00				

KM# 722 2000 FORINT
31.4600 g., 0.9250 Silver .9357 oz. ASW **Obv:** Lake Balaton view above denomination **Rev:** Steam ships "Helka" and "Kelen"

Date	Mintage	F	VF	XF	Unc	BU
1997	5,000	—	—	—	38.00	42.00
1997 Proof	15,000	Value: 35.00				

KM# 724 2000 FORINT
31.1035 g., 0.9250 Silver .9250 oz. ASW **Subject:** European Union **Obv:** Crowned shield divides date above denomination **Rev:** Royal Palace of Budapest

Date	Mintage	F	VF	XF	Unc	BU
1997	3,000	—	—	—	38.00	42.00
1997 Proof	27,000	Value: 35.00				

KM# 727 2000 FORINT
31.4600 g., 0.9250 Silver .9356 oz. ASW **Subject:** Revolution of 1848 **Obv:** Hungarian Order of Military Merit (1848-1849) I Class **Rev:** Hungarian military flag over European map

Date	Mintage	F	VF	XF	Unc	BU
1998	5,000	—	—	—	38.00	42.00
1998 Proof	10,000	Value: 35.00				

KM# 729 2000 FORINT
31.4600 g., 0.9250 Silver .9356 oz. ASW **Subject:** UNICEF - For the Children of the World **Obv:** UNICEF logo above denomination **Rev:** Child's drawing of a princess

Date	Mintage	F	VF	XF	Unc	BU
1998 Proof	Est. 28,000	Value: 47.50				

KM# 730 2000 FORINT
31.4600 g., 0.9250 Silver .9356 oz. ASW **Subject:** World Wildlife Fund **Obv:** World Wildlife Fund logo above arms **Rev:** Fork-tailed barn swallows

Date	Mintage	F	VF	XF	Unc	BU
1998 Proof	Est. 18,000	Value: 50.00				

KM# 731 2000 FORINT
31.4600 g., 0.9250 Silver .9356 oz. ASW **Obv:** Sailboats on Lake Balaton **Rev:** The "Phoenix" under full sail

Date	Mintage	F	VF	XF	Unc	BU
1998	Est. 5,000	—	—	—	37.50	40.00
1998 Proof	Est. 10,000	Value: 32.50				

KM# 732 2000 FORINT
31.4600 g., 0.9250 Silver .9356 oz. ASW **Subject:** 150th Birthday - Lorand Eotvos **Obv:** Denomination **Rev:** Framed portrait and scientific instrument

Date	Mintage	F	VF	XF	Unc	BU
1998	3,000	—	—	—	40.00	42.50
1998 Proof	3,000	Value: 45.00				

KM# 733 2000 FORINT
31.4600 g., 0.9250 Silver .9356 oz. ASW **Subject:** European Union **Obv:** National arms **Rev:** Monuments, Euro logo

Date	Mintage	F	VF	XF	Unc	BU
1998	3,000	—	—	—	40.00	45.00
1998 Proof	12,000	Value: 50.00				

KM# 743 2000 FORINT
20.0000 g., 0.9250 Silver .5948 oz. ASW **Subject:** Millennium **Obv:** Crowned shield divides date, denomination below **Rev:** Rodin's "The Thinker" and solar system **Edge:** Plain **Shape:** 7-sided

Date	Mintage	F	VF	XF	Unc	BU
1999	5,000	—	—	—	32.00	35.00
1999 Proof	15,000	Value: 37.50				

KM# 744 2000 FORINT
20.0000 g., 0.9250 Silver .5948 oz. ASW **Subject:** Olympics **Obv:** Crowned shield above denomination **Rev:** Hammer throw

Date	Mintage	F	VF	XF	Unc	BU
1999	5,000	—	—	—	27.50	30.00
1999 Proof	15,000	Value: 32.50				

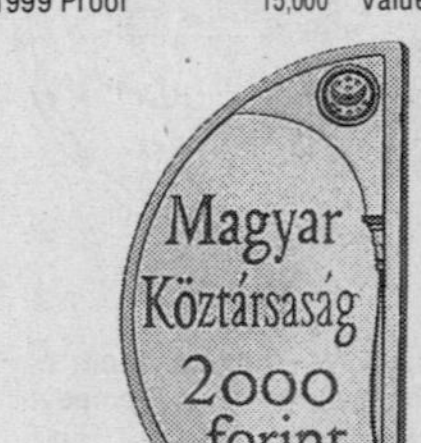

KM# 747 2000 FORINT
15.7240 g., 0.9250 Silver .4676 oz. ASW, 19.3 x 38.4 mm. **Obv:** Denomination and date **Rev:** Angel in wreath **Rev. Inscription:** Koll./ Sàrospatak/ • 1531 • **Edge:** Reeded and plain sections **Shape:** Half circle

Date	Mintage	F	VF	XF	Unc	BU
2000	3,000	—	—	—	20.00	22.50
2000 Proof	3,000	Value: 25.00				

KM# 748 2000 FORINT
15.7240 g., 0.9250 Silver .4676 oz. ASW **Obv:** Country name, denomination and date **Rev:** Seal and dates **Rev. Inscription:** Loránttfy/ Zsuzsanna/ 1600-1660 **Shape:** Half circle

Date	Mintage	F	VF	XF	Unc	BU
2000	Est. 3,000	—	—	—	20.00	22.50
2000 Proof	3,000	Value: 25.00				

KM# 735 3000 FORINT
31.4600 g., 0.9250 Silver .9356 oz. ASW **Subject:** European Union **Obv:** Crowned arms above denomination **Rev:** Statue and Euro logo

Date	Mintage	F	VF	XF	Unc	BU
1999	3,000	—	—	—	35.00	40.00
1999 Proof	17,000	Value: 42.50				

KM# 741 3000 FORINT
31.4600 g., 0.9250 Silver .9356 oz. ASW **Subject:** Hungarian Millennium **Obv:** Crown above denomination within circle, date below **Rev:** Round window design **Edge:** Plain **Note:** Gold-plated center.

Date	Mintage	F	VF	XF	Unc	BU
1999	Est. 5,000	—	—	—	40.00	42.50
1999 Proof	5,000	Value: 50.00				

KM# 746 3000 FORINT
31.4600 g., 0.9250 Silver .9356 oz. ASW **Obv:** Denomination **Rev:** Beaver **Edge:** Reeded

Date	Mintage	F	VF	XF	Unc	BU
2000	3,000	—	—	—	42.50	45.00
2000 Proof	7,000	Value: 50.00				

KM# 749 3000 FORINT
31.4600 g., 0.9250 Silver .9356 oz. ASW **Subject:** Hologram inventor - Dènes Gábor **Obv:** Hologram initials in center **Rev:** Bust of Dènes Gábor right **Edge:** Reeded

Date	Mintage	F	VF	XF	Unc	BU
2000	Est. 3,000	—	—	—	47.50	50.00
2000 Proof	3,000	Value: 57.50				

KM# 750 3000 FORINT
31.4600 g., 0.9250 Silver .9356 oz. ASW **Subject:** 125th Anniversary - Franz Liszt Music Academy **Obv:** Half-length Franz Liszt right **Rev:** Academy entrance **Edge:** Reeded

Date	Mintage	F	VF	XF	Unc	BU
2000	Est. 3,000	—	—	—	47.50	50.00
2000 Proof	3,000	Value: 57.50				

KM# 681 5000 FORINT
6.9820 g., 0.9860 Gold .2213 oz. AGW **Subject:** 500th Anniversary - Death of Mathias I **Obv:** Hunyadi coat of arms **Rev:** Seated King Mathias with scepter and orb

Date	Mintage	F	VF	XF	Unc	BU
1990BP Proof	10,000	Value: 160				

KM# 711 5000 FORINT
7.7700 g., 0.5840 Gold .1459 oz. AGW **Obv:** Denomination and date **Rev:** Great Bustard Bird

Date	Mintage	F	VF	XF	Unc	BU
1994 Proof	5,000	Value: 120				

KM# 684 10000 FORINT (Tizezer)
6.9820 g., 0.9860 Gold .2213 oz. AGW **Subject:** Papal Visit **Obv:** Crowned shield within beaded circle **Rev:** Madonna and child

Date	Mintage	F	VF	XF	Unc	BU
1991BP Proof	10,000	Value: 170				

KM# 691 10000 FORINT (Tizezer)
6.9820 g., 0.9860 Gold .2213 oz. AGW **Subject:** 650th Anniversary - Death of King Karoly Robert **Obv:** Denomination **Rev:** Crowned head 3/4 right

Date	Mintage	F	VF	XF	Unc	BU
1992 Proof	10,000	Value: 165				

KM# 703 10000 FORINT (Tizezer)
6.9820 g., 0.9860 Gold .2213 oz. AGW **Subject:** Centennial - Death of Ferenc Erkel **Obv:** Denomination and date **Rev:** Bust 3/4 left

Date	Mintage	F	VF	XF	Unc	BU
1993 Proof	5,000	Value: 175				

KM# 719 20000 FORINT
6.9820 g., 0.9860 Gold .2213 oz. AGW **Subject:** 1100th Anniversary of Hungarian Nationhood **Obv:** Denomination and date above designs at bottom **Rev:** Two equestrian archers right

Date	Mintage	F	VF	XF	Unc	BU
1996 Proof	5,000	Value: 225				

KM# 728 20000 FORINT
6.9820 g., 0.9860 Gold .2213 oz. AGW **Subject:** Revolution of 1848 **Obv:** Hungarian Order of Military Merit III Class **Rev:** Portrait of Lajos Batthyany

Date	Mintage	F	VF	XF	Unc	BU
1998 Proof	Est. 5,000	Value: 225				

KM# 742 20000 FORINT
6.9820 g., 0.9860 Gold .2213 oz. AGW **Subject:** Hungarian State Millennium **Obv:** Portrait of St. Michael the Archangel **Rev:** Crown of St. Stephen **Edge:** Plain

Date	Mintage	F	VF	XF	Unc	BU
1999 Proof	Est. 3,000	Value: 250				

PATTERNS

Including off metal strikes

KM#	Date	Mintage	Identification	Mkt Val
Pn126	1910	—	2 Korona. Lead. KM#493.	—
Pn127	1913	—	2 Korona. Aluminum. KM#493.	—
Pn128	1914	—	Filler. Steel. KM#480.	—
Pn129	1914	—	10 Filler. Silver. KM#482.	800
Pn130	1914	—	2 Korona. Aluminum. KM#493.	—
Pn131	1915	—	2 Filler. New Silver. KM#481	130
Pn132	1915	—	10 Filler. Nickel. KM#494.	—
Pn133	1915	—	10 Filler. Nickel. KM#496.	—
Pn134	1915	—	20 Filler. Iron. KM#498.	250
Pn135	1915	—	20 Filler. Iron. Circle around crown.	—
Pn136	1915	—	20 Filler. Silver. KM#483.	1,000
Pn137	1915	—	1/2 Korona. Silver. Franz Joseph I bust right. Value in wreath.	1,000
Pn138	1916	—	2 Heller. Lead. One side.	—
Pn139	1916	—	2 Filler. Iron. KM#481	350
Pn140	1916	—	2 Filler. Iron. 2 in square.	—
Pn141	1916	—	2 Filler. Iron. Circle around crown.	—
Pn142	ND(1916)	—	2 Filler. Lead. Ornaments around 2, without legend.	—
Pn143	1916KB	—	10 Filler. Iron. KM#496	—
Pn144	1916	—	20 Filler. Lead. KM#498.	—
Pn145	1917	—	20 Filler. Zinc.	—
Pn146	1917	—	2 Filler. Steel. With rosette.	—
Pn147	1917	—	10 Filler. Iron. Crown above sceptor and sword. Value between wheat.	—
Pn148	1917	—	10 Filler. Zinc.	—
Pn149	1917	—	10 Filler. New Silver.	—
Pn150	1918	—	2 Filler. Aluminum. KM#497	—
Pn151	1918	—	50 Filler. Iron. Large crown.	—
Pn152	1918	—	50 Filler. Lead.	—
Pn153	NDBP	—	10 Korona. Silver.	—
Pn154	NDBP	3	10 Korona. Bronze.	—
Pn155	1922	—	20 Filler. Bronze.	—
Pn156	1922	—	20 Filler. New Silver.	—
Pn157	1922	—	20 Filler. Nickel.	—
Pn158	1922	—	5 Korona. Aluminum.	—
Pn159	1922	—	5 Korona. Brass.	—
Pn160	1926	—	10 Filler. Lead. KM#507	—
Pn161	1927	—	10 Pengo. Brass. Fr#100	—
Pn162	1927	—	10 Pengo. Gold.	—
Pn163	1927	—	20 Pengo. Brass. Denomination in grape-wheat ear wreath. Fr#99.	—
Pn164	1927	—	20 Pengo. Brass. Denomination in wreath. Fr#99.	—
Pn165	1927	—	20 Pengo. Gold. Denomination in grape-wheat ear wreath.	—
Pn166	1927	—	20 Pengo. Gold. Denomination in laurel wreath.	2,700
Pn167	1928BP	—	10 Pengo. Gold. Fr#100	2,700
Pn168	1928	—	20 Pengo. Brass. Smaller arms. Fr#99a.	—
Pn169	1928BP	—	20 Pengo. Gold. Fr#99.	2,700
Pn170	1929	—	5 Pengo. Lead.	—
Pn171	1929	—	5 Pengo. Silver.	—
Pn172	1929BP	—	20 Pengo. Gold. Fr#99a.	2,700
Pn173	1930	—	5 Pengo. Y#44	—
Pn174	1935	—	2 Filler. Nickel. KM#506.	—
Pn175	1935BP	—	2 Pengo.	—
Pn176	1938	—	50 Filler. Aluminum. KM#509.	—
Pn177	1939	—	Filler. Aluminum. KM#505.	—
Pn178	1940	—	Filler. Iron. KM#505.	—
Pn179	1940	—	10 Filler. Lead. KM#507.	—
Pn180	1941	—	50 Filler. Iron. KM#509.	—
Pn181	1943	—	2 Filler. Aluminum. KM#519.	—

PIEFORTS

KM#	Date	Mintage	Identification	Mkt Val
P22	1979	2,500	200 Forint. Silver. 0.6400 g. KM#615	100
P23	1979	2,500	200 Forint. Silver. 0.6400 g. KM#616	40.00
P24	1980	3,000	100 Forint. Nickel. KM#617	30.00
P25	1980	3,000	200 Forint. Silver. 0.6400 g. KM#618	27.50
P26	1980	1,500	500 Forint. Silver. 0.6400 g. KM#619	125

PROBA

KM#	Date	Mintage	Identification	Mkt Val
Pr1	1986	—	500 Forint. Silver. KM#656. Soccer players.	325
Pr2	1986	—	500 Forint. Silver. KM#657. Stadium.	325
Pr3	1988	—	100 Forint. Copper-Nickel. KM#664. Soccer players.	—
Pr4	1988	—	100 Forint. Copper-Nickel. KM#665. Soccer goalie in net.	—
Pr5	1989	—	100 Forint. Copper-Nickel. KM#668. Soccer players shaking hands.	—

TRIAL STRIKES

KM#	Date	Mintage	Identification	Mkt Val
TS39	1907	—	100 Korona. Bronze. KM#491.	—
TS40	1907	—	100 Korona. Bronze. KM#490. Without legend.	—
TS41	1910	—	2 Korona. Lead. KM#493.	—
TS42	1913	—	2 Korona. Aluminum. KM#493.	—
TS43	1914KB	—	Filler. Iron. KM#480.	—
TS44	1914KB	—	2 Filler. Nickel. KM#481.	—
TS45	1914KB	—	10 Filler. Copper-Zinc. KM#482.	—
TS46	1914	—	10 Filler. Silver Plated Copper-Nickel-Zinc.	—
TS47	1914KB	—	10 Filler. Silver. KM#482.	—
TS48	1914KB	—	20 Filler. Iron. KM#483.	—
TS49	1914	—	2 Korona. Aluminum. KM#493.	—
TS50	1914	—	2 Korona. Bronze. KM#486.	—
TS51	1915KB	—	2 Filler. Iron. KM#481.	—
TS52	1915KB	—	10 Filler. Nickel. KM#496.	—
TS53	1915KB	—	20 Filler. Silver. KM#483.	1,200
TS54	1916	—	20 Filler. Lead. KM#498.	—
TS55	1916KB	—	1/2 Korona. Silver.	1,200
TS56	1917KB	—	10 Filler. Lead.	—
TS57	1917KB	—	10 Filler. Zinc.	—
TS58	1917KB	—	10 Filler. Copper-Nickel-Zinc.	—
TS59	1918KB	—	50 Filler. Lead.	—
TS60	1918	—	20 Korona. Lead. KM#486.	—
TS61	1920	—	10 Filler. Copper-Nickel-Zinc. KM#496.	—
TS62	1922	—	20 Filler. Nickel. KM#498.	—
TS63	1922	—	20 Filler. Bronze. KM#498.	—
TS64	1922	—	20 Filler. Brass. KM#498.	—
TS65	1922	—	20 Filler. Copper-Nickel-Zinc. KM#498.	—
TS66	1930	—	5 Pengo. Lead. Obverse only, KM#512.	—
TS67	1930	—	5 Pengo. Lead. Reverse only, KM#512.	—
TS68	1935	—	2 Filler. Nickel. KM#506	—
TS69	1935	—	2 Pengo. Lead. Reverse only, KM#514.	—
TS70	1936	—	2 Pengo. Lead. Obverse only, KM#515.	—
TS71	1938	—	5 Pengo. Copper-Zinc. KM#517.	—
TS72	1938	—	5 Pengo. Copper-Zinc. KM#516.	—
TS73	1938	—	5 Pengo. Lead. Obverse only, KM#516.	—
TS74	1938	—	5 Pengo. Lead. Reverse only, KM#516.	—
TS75	1939	—	Filler. Aluminum. KM#505.	—
TS76	1939	—	50 Filler. Aluminum. KM#509.	—
TS77	1941	—	50 Filler. Iron. KM#509.	—
TS78	1943	—	2 Filler. Aluminum. KM#519.	—
TS79	1943	—	5 Pengo. Copper-Zinc. KM#523.	—

MINT SETS

KM#	Date	Mintage	Identification	Issue Price	Mkt Val
MS-A1	1956 (3)	—	KM#552, 553, 554	—	55.00
MS1	1971 (9)	—	KM#546, 549, 572-575, 591, 594, 595	—	20.00
MS2	1972 (9)	—	KM#546, 549, 572-575, 591, 594, 595	—	20.00
MS3	1973 (9)	—	KM#546, 549, 572-575, 591, 594, 595	—	20.00
MS4	1974 (9)	—	KM#546, 549, 572-575, 591, 594, 595	—	20.00
MS5	1975 (9)	—	KM#546, 549, 572-575, 591, 594, 595	—	20.00
MS6	1976 (9)	—	KM#546, 549, 572-575, 591, 594, 595	—	20.00
MS7	1977 (9)	—	KM#546, 549, 572-575, 591, 594, 595	—	20.00
MSA7	1977 (3)	—	KM#610-612	—	35.00
MS8	1978 (9)	—	KM#546, 549, 572-575, 591, 594, 595	—	20.00
MS9	1979 (9)	—	KM#546, 549, 572-575, 591, 594, 595	—	20.00
MS10	1980 (9)	—	KM#546, 549, 572-575, 591, 594, 595	—	20.00
MS11	1981 (9)	—	KM#546, 549, 572-575, 591, 594, 620	—	20.00
MS12	1982 (9)	—	KM#546, 549, 572-575, 591, 594, 595	—	20.00
MS13	1983 (10)	—	KM#546, 549, 572-575, 591, 630, 635, 636	—	22.00
MSA13	1983 (3)	—	KM#627, 628, 629	—	15.00
MS14	1984 (10)	—	KM#546, 549, 572-575, 591, 630, 635, 636	—	22.00
MS15	1985 (10)	—	KM#546, 549, 572-575, 591, 630, 635, 636	—	22.00
MS16	1986 (10)	—	KM#546, 549, 572-575, 591, 630, 635, 636	—	22.00
MS17	1987 (10)	—	KM#546, 549, 572-575, 591, 630, 635, 636	—	22.00
MS18	1988 (10)	—	KM#546, 549, 572-575, 591, 630, 635, 636	—	22.00
MS19	1989 (10)	—	KM#546, 549, 572-575, 591, 630, 635, 636	—	22.00
MS20	1990 (5)	—	KM673-677	—	15.00
MS21	1991 (5)	—	KM673-677	—	18.00
MS22	1992 (8)	—	KM689, 692-698	—	30.00
MSA22	1992 (5)	—	KM673-677	—	20.00
MS23	1993 (11)	—	KM675-677, 689, 692-698	—	25.00
MS24	1994 (11)	—	KM675-677, 692-698, 707	—	22.00
MS25	1995 (10)	—	KM675-677, 692-698	—	15.00
MS26	1995 (11)	—	KM675-677, 692-698, 707	17.50	25.00
MS27	1996 (10)	—	KM675-677, 692-698	—	15.00
MS28	1997 (10)	7,000	KM677, 692-698, 707, 721	18.50	22.00
MS29	1998 (11)	—	KM677, 692-698, 707, 721, 726	22.50	30.00
MS30	1999 (8)	—	KM677, 692-697, 721	—	17.50
MS31	2000 (8)	—	KM692-697, 721, 745	—	16.50

PROOF SETS

KM#	Date	Mintage	Identification	Issue Price	Mkt Val
PSA1	1948 (3)	—	KM537-539	70.00	70.00
PS1	1961 (6)	2,500	KM560, 562-566	—	2,200
PS2	1961 (4)	—	KM557-559, 561	—	80.00
PS3	1966 (8)	2,000	KM534b, 546a, 547a, 549a-551a, 555a, 556b	15.00	48.00
PS4	1966 (3)	330	KM569-571	430	2,850
PS5	1966 (2)	11,000	KM567-568	7.50	45.00
PS6	1967 (8)	5,000	KM534b, 546a, 547a, 549a-551a, 555a, 556b	15.00	55.00
PS7	1967 (2)	500	KM580, 581	—	2,450
PS8	1968 (5)	7,000	KM583, 585-588	—	2,850
PS9	1968 (2)	4,750	KM582, 584	35.00	90.00
PS10	1969 (2)	3,000	KM589, 590	35.00	30.00
PS11	1970 (2)	4,000	KM592, 593	25.00	25.00
PS12	1972 (2)	6,000	KM596, 597	25.00	32.50
PS13	1973 (2)	6,000	KM599, 600	—	27.50
PS14	1974 (2)	—	KM601, 603	—	25.00
PS15	1976 (3)	5,000	KM607-609	—	50.00
PS16	1977 (3)	—	KM610-612	—	50.00
PS17	1992 (8)	1,000	KM689, 692-698	—	80.00
PS18	1993 (8)	—	KM 689, 692-698	—	47.50
PSA19	1993/4 (2)	—	KM704, 710	—	52.50
PS19	1994 (8)	—	KM692-698, 707	—	47.50
PS20	1995 (8)	—	KM692-698, 707	24.50	47.50
PS21	1997 (8)	3,000	KM692-698, 707, 721	29.50	50.00
PS22	1998 (3)	5,000	KM726-728	268	275
PS23	1999 (7)	—	KM692-697, 721	—	32.50
PS24	1999 (2)	—	KM741, 742	240	310
PS25	2000 (8)	—	KM692-697, 721, 745	—	40.00

SPECIMEN SETS (SS)

KM#	Date	Mintage	Identification	Issue Price	Mkt Val
SS1	1977 (9)	—	KM546, 549, 572-575, 591, 594-595	—	10.00
SS2	1978 (9)	—	KM546, 549, 572-575, 591, 594-595	—	10.00
SS3	1979 (9)	—	KM546, 549, 572-575, 591, 594-595	—	10.00
SS4	1981 (9)	—	KM546, 549, 572-575, 591, 594, 620	—	10.00
SS5	1989 (10)	—	KM546, 549, 572-575, 591, 630, 635, 636	—	9.00

ICELAND

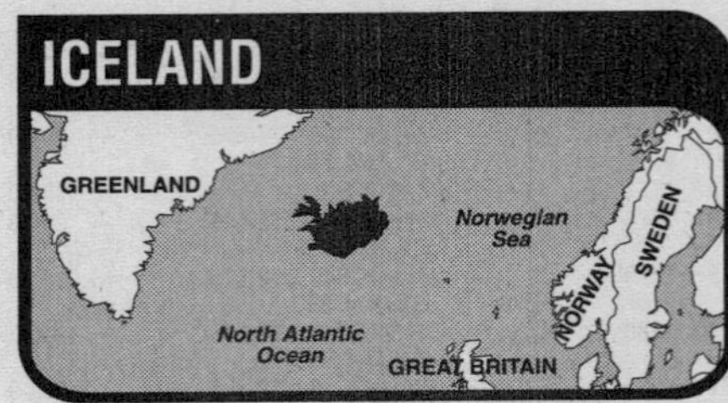

The Republic of Iceland, an island of recent volcanic origin in the North Atlantic east of Greenland and immediately south of the Arctic Circle, has an area of 39,768sq. mi. (103,000 sq. km.) and a population of just over 300,000. Capital: Reykjavik. Fishing is the chief industry and accounts for a little less than 60 percent of the exports.

Iceland was settled by Norwegians in the 9th century and established as an independent republic in 930. The Icelandic assembly called the Althingi', also established in 930, is the oldest parliament in the world. Iceland came under Norwegian sovereignty in 1262, and passed to Denmark when Norway and Denmark were united under the Danish crown in 1380. In 1918 it was established as a virtually independent kingdom in union with Denmark. On June 17, 1944, while Denmark was still under occupation by troops of the Third Reich, Iceland was established by plebiscite as an independent republic.

RULERS
Christian X, 1912-1944

MINT MARKS
Heart (h) - Copenhagen

MINTMASTERS' INITIALS
HCN - Hans Christian Nielsen, 1919-1927 (for Iceland, 1922-1926)
N - Niels Peter Nielsen, 1927-1955 (for Iceland, 1929-1940)

MONEYERS' INITIALS
GJ - Knud Gunnar Jensen, 1901-1933

MONETARY SYSTEM
100 Aurar = 1 Krona

KINGDOM

DECIMAL COINAGE

KM# 5.1 EYRIR
Bronze **Ruler:** Christian X **Obv:** Crown divides date above monogram **Rev:** Large denomination

Date	Mintage	F	VF	XF	Unc	BU
1926(h) HCN-GJ	405,000	1.50	3.00	7.50	30.00	—
1931(h) N-GJ	462,000	1.00	2.50	6.00	27.50	—
1937(h) N-GJ Wide date	211,000	2.00	4.00	8.00	35.00	—
1938(h) N-GJ	279,000	1.00	2.00	4.00	13.50	—
1938(h) N-GJ Large 3 over small 3	—	1.00	2.00	3.50	12.50	—
1939(h) N-GJ Large 3	305,000	1.00	2.00	3.50	12.50	—
1939(h) N-GJ Small 3	Inc. above	1.00	2.00	3.50	12.50	—
1939(h) N-GJ Large 3 / small 3	Inc. above	1.00	2.00	3.50	12.50	—

KM# 5.2 EYRIR
Bronze **Ruler:** Christian X **Obv:** Crown divides date above monogram **Rev:** Large denomination, ornaments flank

Date	Mintage	F	VF	XF	Unc	BU
1940	1,000,000	0.25	0.50	1.00	2.50	—
1940 Proof	—	Value: 240				
1942	2,000,000	0.25	0.40	0.75	2.00	—

KM# 6.1 2 AURAR
Bronze **Ruler:** Christian X **Obv:** Crown divides date above monogram **Rev:** Large denomination, ornaments flank **Note:** Varieties exist in the appearance of the numeral 8 in 1938 dated coins. As the die slowly deteriorated, "globs" were added to the upper loop and later to the lower loop.

Date	Mintage	F	VF	XF	Unc	BU
1926(h) HCN-GJ	498,000	1.50	3.00	8.00	40.00	—
1931(h) N-GJ	446,000	1.00	2.50	7.00	30.00	—
1938(h) N-GJ	206,000	6.00	12.00	17.50	55.00	—
1940(h) N-GJ	257,000	5.00	10.00	15.00	37.50	—

KM# 6.2 2 AURAR
Bronze **Ruler:** Christian X **Obv:** Crown divides date above monogram **Rev:** Large denomination, ornaments flank

Date	Mintage	F	VF	XF	Unc	BU
1940	1,000,000	0.40	0.75	1.50	3.00	—
1940 Proof	—	Value: 280				
1942	2,000,000	0.20	0.50	1.00	2.00	—

KM# 7.1 5 AURAR
Bronze **Ruler:** Christian X **Obv:** Crown divides date above monogram **Rev:** Large denomination, ornaments flank

Date	Mintage	F	VF	XF	Unc	BU
1926(h) HCN-GJ	355,000	5.00	10.00	25.00	85.00	—
1931(h) N-GJ	311,000	5.00	10.00	25.00	85.00	—

KM# 7.2 5 AURAR
Bronze **Ruler:** Christian X **Obv:** Crown divides date above monogram **Rev:** Large denomination, ornaments flank

Date	Mintage	F	VF	XF	Unc	BU
1940	1,000,000	0.60	1.25	2.50	5.00	—
1940 Proof	—	Value: 300				
1942	2,000,000	0.35	0.85	1.50	3.00	—

KM# 1.1 10 AURAR
Copper-Nickel **Ruler:** Christian X **Obv:** Ornaments flank denomination **Rev:** Crowned arms divide monogram

Date	Mintage	F	VF	XF	Unc	BU
1922(h) HCN GJ	300,000	2.00	3.50	7.00	38.50	—
1923(h) HCN GJ	302,000	3.00	4.50	9.00	46.50	—
1925(h) HCN GJ	321,000	15.00	25.00	40.00	110	—
1929(h) N-GJ	176,000	15.00	25.00	45.00	120	—
1933(h) N-GJ	157,000	10.00	20.00	30.00	87.50	—
1936(h) N-GJ	213,000	3.00	6.00	10.00	35.00	—
1939/6(h) N-GJ	208,000	5.00	10.00	15.00	42.50	—
1939(h) N-GJ	Inc. above	4.00	8.00	12.00	32.50	—

KM# 1.2 10 AURAR
Copper-Nickel **Ruler:** Christian X **Obv:** Ornaments flank denomination **Rev:** Crowned arms divide monogram

Date	Mintage	F	VF	XF	Unc	BU
1940	1,500,000	0.35	0.75	1.50	4.50	—
1940 Proof	—	Value: 240				

KM# 1a 10 AURAR
Zinc **Ruler:** Christian X **Obv:** Ornaments flank denomination **Rev:** Crowned arms divide monogram

Date	Mintage	F	VF	XF	Unc	BU
1942	2,000,000	1.50	3.00	6.00	30.00	—
1942 Prooflike	—	—	—	—	—	—

KM# 2.1 25 AURAR
Copper-Nickel **Ruler:** Christian X **Obv:** Ornaments flank denomination **Rev:** Crowned arms divide monogram

Date	Mintage	F	VF	XF	Unc	BU
1922(h) HCN GJ	300,000	1.00	2.50	4.00	35.50	—
1923(h) HCN GJ	304,000	1.00	2.50	4.00	35.50	—
1925(h) HCN GJ	207,000	2.50	4.50	10.00	50.00	—
1933(h) N-GJ	104,000	10.00	15.00	25.00	100	—
1937(h) N-GJ Near 7	201,000	3.00	5.00	9.00	40.00	—
1937(h) N-GJ Far 7	Inc. above	3.00	5.00	9.00	40.00	—

KM# 2.2 25 AURAR
Copper-Nickel **Ruler:** Christian X **Obv:** Ornaments flank denomination **Rev:** Crowned arms divide monogram

Date	Mintage	F	VF	XF	Unc	BU
1940	1,500,000	0.25	0.50	1.00	2.50	—
1940 Proof	—	Value: 260				

KM# 2a 25 AURAR
Zinc **Ruler:** Christian X **Obv:** Ornaments flank denomination **Rev:** Crowned arms divide monogram

Date	Mintage	F	VF	XF	Unc	BU
1942	2,000,000	1.00	2.50	5.00	28.50	—
1942 Prooflike	—	—	—	—	—	—

KM# 3.1 KRONA
Aluminum-Bronze **Ruler:** Christian X **Obv:** Ornaments flank denomination **Rev:** Crowned arms divide monogram

Date	Mintage	F	VF	XF	Unc	BU
1925(h) HCN GJ	252,000	3.00	6.00	25.00	185	—
1929(h) N-GJ	154,000	5.00	10.00	32.00	220	—
1940(h) N-GJ	209,000	1.50	2.50	5.00	15.00	—

KM# 3.2 KRONA
Aluminum-Bronze **Ruler:** Christian X **Obv:** Ornaments flank denomination **Rev:** Crowned arms divide monogram

Date	Mintage	F	VF	XF	Unc	BU
1940	715,000	1.00	2.00	4.00	10.00	—
1940 Proof; rare	—	—	—	—	—	—

KM# 4.1 2 KRONUR
Aluminum-Bronze **Ruler:** Christian X **Obv:** Ornaments flank denomination **Rev:** Crowned arms divide monogram

Date	Mintage	F	VF	XF	Unc	BU
1925(h) HCN GJ	126,000	7.50	12.50	41.50	235	—
1929(h) N-GJ	77,000	10.00	20.00	67.50	350	—

KM# 4.2 2 KRONUR
Aluminum-Bronze **Ruler:** Christian X **Obv:** Ornaments flank denomination **Rev:** Crowned arms divide monogram

Date	Mintage	F	VF	XF	Unc	BU
1940	546,000	0.75	1.50	3.50	10.00	—
1940 Proof; rare	—	—	—	—	—	—

TOKEN COINAGE

N. Chr. Gram.

Thingeyri

KM# Tn3 10 ORE
Bronze **Issuer:** N. Chr. Gram., Thingeyri **Note:** Similar to 25 Ore, KM#Tn4.

Date	Mintage	VG	F	VF	XF	Unc
ND(1902) Rare	—	—	—	—	—	—

KM# Tn4 25 ORE
Bronze **Issuer:** N. Chr. Gram., Thingeyri

Date	Mintage	VG	F	VF	XF	Unc
ND(1902) Rare	—	—	—	—	—	—

KM# Tn23 50 ORE

Bronze **Issuer:** N. Chr. Gram., Thingeyri **Note:** Similar to 25 Ore, KM#Tn4.

Date	Mintage	VG	F	VF	XF	Unc
ND(1902) Rare	—	—	—	—	—	—

P.J. Thorsteinsson

Bildudal

KM# Tn12 10 AURAR

1.7000 g., Brass **Issuer:** P.J. Thorsteinsson, Bildudal **Note:** Similar to 100 Aurar, KM#Tn21. Struck by L. Chr. Lauer of Nurnberg.

Date	Mintage	VG	F	VF	XF	Unc
ND(1901)	—	12.00	25.00	50.00	135	—

KM# Tn15 25 AURAR

1.7000 g., Brass **Issuer:** P.J. Thorsteinsson, Bildudal **Note:** Similar to 100 Aurar, KM#Tn21. Struck by L. Chr. Lauer of Nurnberg.

Date	Mintage	VG	F	VF	XF	Unc
ND(1901)	—	6.00	12.00	25.00	60.00	—

KM# Tn18 50 AURAR

2.2000 g., Brass **Issuer:** P.J. Thorsteinsson, Bildudal **Note:** Similar to 100 Aurar, KM#Tn21. Struck by L. Chr. Lauer of Nurnberg.

Date	Mintage	VG	F	VF	XF	Unc
ND(1901)	—	6.00	12.00	25.00	60.00	—

KM# Tn21 100 AURAR

1.1000 g., Aluminum **Issuer:** P.J. Thorsteinsson, Bildudal **Note:** Struck by L. Chr. Lauer of Nurnberg.

Date	Mintage	VG	F	VF	XF	Unc
ND(1901) Rare	—	—	—	—	—	—

KM# Tn22 500 AURAR

1.1000 g., Aluminum **Issuer:** P.J. Thorsteinsson, Bildudal **Note:** Similar to 100 Aurar, KM#Tn21. Struck by L. Chr. Lauer of Nurnberg.

Date	Mintage	VG	F	VF	XF	Unc
ND(1901)	—	7.00	15.00	30.00	75.00	—

REPUBLIC

DECIMAL COINAGE

KM# 8 EYRIR

Bronze **Obv:** Leaves flank denomination **Rev:** Arms within wreath **Note:** Values for the 1953-59 proof issues are for impaired proofs. Brilliant proofs may bring 3 to 4 times these figures.

Date	Mintage	F	VF	XF	Unc	BU
1946	4,000,000	0.10	0.15	0.50	1.00	—
1946 Proof	—	Value: 270				
1953	4,000,000	0.10	0.15	0.40	0.75	—
1953 Proof	—	Value: 67.50				
1956	2,000,000	0.10	0.15	0.40	0.75	—
1956 Proof	—	Value: 67.50				
1957	2,000,000	0.10	0.15	0.40	0.75	—
1957 Proof	—	Value: 67.50				
1958	2,000,000	0.10	0.15	0.40	0.75	—
1958 Proof	—	Value: 67.50				
1959	1,600,000	0.10	0.15	0.40	0.75	—
1959 Proof	—	Value: 67.50				
1966	1,000,000	0.10	0.15	0.40	0.75	—
1966 Proof	15,000	Value: 3.25				

KM# 9 5 AURAR

Bronze **Obv:** Leaves flank denomination **Rev:** Arms within wreath **Note:** Values for the 1958-63 proof issues are for impaired proofs. Brilliant proofs may bring 3 to 4 times these figures.

Date	Mintage	F	VF	XF	Unc	BU
1946	4,000,000	0.10	0.25	0.50	1.25	—
1946 Proof	—	Value: 425				
1958	400,000	0.50	2.00	3.50	5.00	—
1958 Proof	—	Value: 100				
1959	600,000	0.50	2.00	3.00	4.50	—
1959 Proof	—	Value: 100				
1960	1,200,000	0.15	0.40	1.00	1.75	—
1960 Proof	—	Value: 100				
1961	1,200,000	0.15	0.40	1.00	1.75	—
1961 Proof	—	Value: 100				
1963	1,200,000	0.10	0.30	0.75	1.50	—
1963 Proof	—	Value: 100				
1965	800,000	0.10	0.20	0.50	1.00	—
1966	1,000,000	0.10	0.20	0.50	1.00	—
1966 Proof	15,000	Value: 3.25				

KM# 10 10 AURAR

Copper-Nickel **Obv:** Leaves flank denomination **Rev:** Arms within wreath **Note:** Values for the 1953-63 proof issues are for impaired proofs. Brilliant proofs may bring 3 to 4 times these figures.

Date	Mintage	F	VF	XF	Unc	BU
1946	4,000,000	—	0.10	0.20	0.60	—
1946 Proof	—	Value: 425				
1953	4,000,000	—	0.10	0.20	0.50	—
1953 Proof	—	Value: 67.50				
1957	1,200,000	0.25	0.75	2.00	5.00	—
1957 Proof	—	Value: 67.50				
1958	500,000	0.20	0.50	1.00	2.00	—
1958 Proof	—	Value: 67.50				
1959	3,000,000	0.20	0.50	1.50	4.00	—
1959 Proof	—	Value: 67.50				
1960	1,000,000	0.10	0.20	0.40	1.00	—
1960 Proof	—	Value: 67.50				
1961	2,000,000	—	—	0.10	0.30	—
1961 Proof	—	Value: 67.50				
1962	3,000,000	—	—	0.10	0.20	—
1962 Proof	—	Value: 67.50				
1963	4,000,000	—	—	0.10	0.20	—
1963 Proof	—	Value: 67.50				
1965	2,000,000	—	—	0.10	0.20	—
1966	4,000,000	—	—	0.10	0.20	—
1967	2,000,000	—	—	0.10	0.20	—
1969	3,200,000	—	—	0.10	0.20	—
Note: Coarse edge reeding						
1969	Inc. above	—	—	0.10	0.20	—
Note: Fine edge reeding						

KM# 10a 10 AURAR

Aluminum, 15 mm. **Obv:** Leaves flank denomination **Rev:** Arms within wreath

Date	Mintage	F	VF	XF	Unc	BU
1970	4,800,000	—	—	0.10	0.20	—
1971	11,200,000	—	—	0.10	0.20	—
1973	4,800,000	—	—	0.10	0.20	—
1974	4,800,000	—	—	0.10	0.20	—
1974 Proof	15,000	Value: 3.25				

KM# 11 25 AURAR

Copper-Nickel **Obv:** Leaves flank denomination **Rev:** Arms within wreath **Note:** Values for the 1951-63 proof issues are for impaired proofs. Brilliant proofs may bring 3 to 4 times these figures.

Date	Mintage	F	VF	XF	Unc	BU
1946	2,000,000	0.10	0.15	0.35	1.25	—
1946 Proof	—	Value: 430				
1951	2,000,000	0.10	0.15	0.35	0.75	—
1951 Proof	—	Value: 77.50				
1954	2,000,000	0.10	0.15	0.35	0.75	—
1954 Proof	—	Value: 77.50				
1957	1,000,000	0.20	0.50	1.50	3.50	—
1957 Proof	—	Value: 77.50				
1958	500,000	0.20	0.40	0.60	1.00	—
1958 Proof	—	Value: 77.50				
1959	2,000,000	0.20	0.50	1.50	3.00	—
1959 Proof	—	Value: 77.50				
1960	1,000,000	—	—	0.10	0.30	—
1960 Proof	—	Value: 77.50				
1961	1,200,000	—	—	0.10	0.30	—
1961 Proof	—	Value: 77.50				
1962	2,000,000	—	—	0.10	0.25	—
1962 Proof	—	Value: 77.50				
1963	3,000,000	—	—	0.10	0.25	—
1963 Proof	—	Value: 77.50				
1965	4,000,000	—	—	0.10	0.25	—
1966	2,000,000	—	—	0.10	0.25	—
1967	3,000,000	—	—	0.10	0.25	—
1967 Proof	15,000	Value: 3.25				

KM# 17 50 AURAR

Nickel-Brass **Obv:** Leaves flank denomination **Rev:** Arms within wreath

Date	Mintage	F	VF	XF	Unc	BU
1969	2,000,000	—	—	0.10	0.30	—
1970	2,000,000	—	—	0.10	0.30	—
1971	2,000,000	—	—	0.10	0.30	—
1973	1,000,000	—	—	0.10	0.30	—
1974	2,000,000	—	—	0.10	0.30	—
1974 Proof	15,000	Value: 3.25				

KM# 12 KRONA

Aluminum-Bronze **Obv:** Leaves flank denomination **Rev:** Arms with supporters

Date	Mintage	F	VF	XF	Unc	BU
1946	2,175,000	—	0.10	0.40	1.50	—
1946 Proof	—	Value: 425				

KM# 12a KRONA

Nickel-Brass **Obv:** Denomination, leaves flank **Rev:** Shield with supporters, date below **Note:** Values for the 1957-63 proof issues are for impaired proofs. Brilliant proofs may bring 3 to 4 times these figures.

Date	Mintage	F	VF	XF	Unc	BU
1957	1,000,000	0.10	0.15	0.40	1.50	—
1957 Proof	—	Value: 90.00				
1959	500,000	0.10	0.20	0.75	2.00	—
1959 Proof	—	Value: 90.00				
1961	500,000	0.10	0.20	0.75	2.00	—
1961 Proof	—	Value: 90.00				
1962	1,000,000	0.10	0.15	0.20	0.60	—
1962 Proof	—	Value: 90.00				
1963	1,500,000	—	0.10	0.15	0.50	—
1963 Proof	—	Value: 90.00				
1965	2,000,000	—	—	0.10	0.50	—
1966	2,000,000	—	—	0.10	0.50	—
1969	2,000,000	—	—	0.10	0.25	—
1970	3,000,000	—	—	0.10	0.25	—
1971	2,500,000	—	—	0.10	0.25	—
1973 Large round-knob 3	2,500,000	—	—	0.10	0.50	—
1973 Thin, sharp-end 3	3,500,000	—	—	0.10	0.25	—
1974	5,000,000	—	—	0.10	0.25	—
1975	10,500,000	—	—	0.10	0.25	—
1975 Proof	15,000	Value: 3.25				

KM# 23 KRONA

Aluminum, 17 mm. **Obv:** Leaves flank denomination **Rev:** Arms with supporters

Date	Mintage	F	VF	XF	Unc	BU
1976	10,000,000	—	—	0.10	0.20	—
1977	10,000,000	—	—	0.10	0.20	—
1978	13,000,000	—	—	0.10	0.20	—
1980	7,225,000	—	—	0.10	0.20	—
1980 Proof	15,000	Value: 3.25				

KM# 13 2 KRONUR

Aluminum-Bronze **Obv:** Leaves flank denomination **Rev:** Arms with supporters

Date	Mintage	F	VF	XF	Unc	BU
1946	1,086,000	0.20	0.40	0.80	3.50	—
1946 Proof	—	Value: 475				

KM# 13a.1 2 KRONUR

Nickel-Brass, 28 mm. **Obv:** Leaves flank denomination **Rev:** Arms with supporters **Note:** Values for the 1958-63 proof issues are for impaired proofs. Brilliant proofs may bring 3 to 4 times these figures.

Date	Mintage	F	VF	XF	Unc	BU
1958	500,000	0.20	0.50	1.00	3.00	—
1958 Proof	—	Value: 120				
1962	500,000	0.20	0.50	1.00	3.00	—
1962 Proof	—	Value: 120				
1963	750,000	0.15	0.30	0.60	2.00	—
1963 Proof	—	Value: 120				
1966	1,000,000	0.10	0.20	0.40	1.50	—
1966 Proof	15,000	Value: 3.25				

KM# 13a.2 2 KRONUR

11.5000 g., Nickel-Brass **Obv:** Leaves flank denomination **Rev:** Arms with supporters **Note:** Thick planchet.

Date	Mintage	F	VF	XF	Unc	BU
1966	300	—	—	360	475	—

KM# 18 5 KRONUR

Copper-Nickel **Obv:** Leaves flank denomination **Rev:** Arms with supporters

Date	Mintage	F	VF	XF	Unc	BU
1969	2,000,000	—	0.15	0.25	0.50	—
1970	1,000,000	—	0.15	0.25	0.50	—
1971	500,000	0.10	0.20	0.50	1.00	—
1973	1,100,000	—	0.10	0.20	0.40	—
1974	1,200,000	—	0.10	0.15	0.25	—
1975	1,500,000	—	0.10	0.15	0.25	—
1976	500,000	—	0.10	0.20	0.40	—
1977	1,000,000	—	0.10	0.15	0.25	—
1978	4,672,000	—	0.10	0.15	0.25	—
1980	2,400,000	—	0.10	0.15	0.25	—
1980 Proof	15,000	Value: 3.25				

KM# 15 10 KRONUR

Copper-Nickel, 25 mm. **Obv:** Leaves flank denomination **Rev:** Arms with supporters

Date	Mintage	F	VF	XF	Unc	BU
1967	1,000,000	0.15	0.25	0.50	1.50	—
1969	500,000	0.15	0.30	0.75	2.00	—
1970	1,500,000	—	0.15	0.30	0.75	—
1971	1,500,000	—	0.15	0.30	0.75	—
1973	1,500,000	—	0.15	0.30	0.75	—
1974	2,000,000	—	0.10	0.25	0.60	—
1975	2,500,000	—	0.10	0.25	0.60	—
1976	2,500,000	—	0.10	0.25	0.60	—
1977	2,000,000	—	0.10	0.25	0.60	—
1978	10,500,000	—	0.10	0.25	0.60	—
1980	4,600,000	—	0.10	0.25	0.60	—
1980 Proof	15,000	Value: 3.25				

KM# 16 50 KRONUR

Nickel **Subject:** 50th Anniversary of Sovereignty **Obv:** Denomination **Rev:** Parliament Building in Reyjavik **Designer:** Magnusson Sigurdsson

Date	Mintage	F	VF	XF	Unc	BU
1968	100,000	1.50	2.50	4.00	7.00	—

KM# 19 50 KRONUR

Copper-Nickel, 30 mm. **Obv:** Denomination **Rev:** Parliament Building in Reykjavic **Designer:** Magnusson Sigurdsson

Date	Mintage	F	VF	XF	Unc	BU
1970	800,000	0.25	0.50	1.00	2.00	—
1971	500,000	0.25	0.50	1.00	2.50	—
1973	50,000	1.00	1.50	2.50	4.00	—
1974	200,000	0.25	0.50	1.00	2.00	—
1975	500,000	0.20	0.35	0.75	1.50	—
1976	500,000	0.20	0.35	0.75	1.50	—
1977	200,000	0.20	0.35	0.75	1.50	—
1978	2,040,000	0.20	0.35	0.50	1.00	—
1980	1,500,000	0.20	0.35	0.50	1.00	—
1980 Proof	15,000	Value: 3.25				

KM# 14 500 KRONUR

8.9604 g., 0.9000 Gold .2593 oz. AGW **Subject:** Jon Sigurdsson Sesquicentennial **Obv:** Arms with supporters **Rev:** Head right

Date	Mintage	F	VF	XF	Unc	BU
ND(1961)	10,000	—	—	—	200	—
ND(1961) Proof	—	Value: 825				

KM# 20 500 KRONUR

20.0000 g., 0.9250 Silver .5968 oz. ASW **Subject:** 1100th Anniversary - 1st Settlement **Obv:** Quartered design of eagle, dragon, bull and giant **Rev:** Female and cow **Designer:** Throstur Magnusson

Date	Mintage	F	VF	XF	Unc	BU
ND(1974)	70,000	—	—	—	10.00	13.00
ND(1974) Proof	Est. 58,000	Value: 16.50				

Note: 17,000 proof coins were remelted

KM# 21 1000 KRONUR

30.0000 g., 0.9250 Silver .8923 oz. ASW **Subject:** 1100th Anniversary - 1st Settlement **Obv:** Quartered design of eagle, dragon, bull and giant **Rev:** Two Vikings and fire **Designer:** Throstur Magnusson

Date	Mintage	F	VF	XF	Unc	BU
ND(1974)	70,000	—	—	—	13.50	16.00
ND(1974) Proof	Est. 58,000	Value: 18.50				

Note: 17,000 proof coins were remelted

KM# 22 10000 KRONUR

15.5000 g., 0.9000 Gold .4485 oz. AGW **Subject:** 1100th Anniversary - 1st Settlement **Obv:** Quartered design of eagle, dragon, bull, giant **Rev:** Ingulfur Arnason getting ready to throw his home posts on the beach **Designer:** Throstur Magnusson

Date	Mintage	F	VF	XF	Unc	BU
ND(1974)	12,000	—	—	—	320	—
ND(1974) Proof	8,000	Value: 340				

REFORM COINAGE

100 Old Kronur = 1 New Krona

KM# 24 5 AURAR

Bronze, 15 mm. **Obv:** Eagle with upraised wing **Rev:** Denomination on Skate

Date	Mintage	F	VF	XF	Unc	BU
1981	15,000,000	—	—	—	0.35	0.75
1981 Proof	15,000	Value: 3.50				

KM# 25 10 AURAR

Bronze, 17 mm. **Obv:** Bulls head facing **Rev:** Flying squid

Date	Mintage	F	VF	XF	Unc	BU
1981	50,000,000	—	—	—	0.45	1.00
1981 Proof	15,000	Value: 5.00				

KM# 26 50 AURAR

Bronze, 20 mm. **Obv:** Dragons head right **Rev:** Northern shrimp

Date	Mintage	F	VF	XF	Unc	BU
1981	10,000,000	—	—	0.10	0.50	1.00
1981 Proof	15,000	Value: 6.00				

KM# 26a 50 AURAR

Bronze Coated Steel, 20 mm. **Obv:** Dragons head right **Rev:** Northern shrimp

Date	Mintage	F	VF	XF	Unc	BU
1986	2,144,000	—	—	—	0.50	1.00

KM# 27 KRONA

4.5000 g., Copper-Nickel, 21.5 mm. **Obv:** Giant facing **Rev:** Cod **Edge:** Reeded

Date	Mintage	F	VF	XF	Unc	BU
1981	18,000,000	—	—	0.15	0.75	1.25
1981 Proof	15,000	Value: 8.00				
1984	7,000,000	—	—	0.15	0.75	1.25
1987	7,500,000	—	—	0.15	0.75	1.25

KM# 27a KRONA

4.0000 g., Nickel Coated Steel, 21.5 mm. **Obv:** Giant facing **Rev:** Cod **Edge:** Reeded

Date	Mintage	F	VF	XF	Unc	BU
1989	5,000,000	—	—	—	0.75	1.25
1991	5,180,000	—	—	—	0.75	1.25
1992	5,000,000	—	—	—	0.75	1.25
1994	5,000,000	—	—	—	0.75	1.25
1996	6,000,000	—	—	—	0.75	1.25
1999	10,000,000	—	—	—	0.75	1.25
2000	10,000	—	—	—	1.50	2.00

KM# 28 5 KRONUR

6.5000 g., Copper-Nickel, 24.5 mm. **Obv:** Quartered design of Eagle, dragon, bull and giant **Rev:** Two dolphins leaping left **Edge:** Reeded

Date	Mintage	F	VF	XF	Unc	BU
1981	4,350,000	—	—	0.25	1.50	2.00
1981 Proof	15,000	Value: 10.00				
1984	1,000,000	—	—	0.25	1.50	2.00
1987	3,000,000	—	—	0.25	1.50	2.00
1992	2,000,000	—	—	0.25	1.50	2.00

KM# 28a 5 KRONUR

5.6000 g., Nickel Clad Steel, 24.5 mm. **Obv:** Quartered design of Eagle, dragon, bull and giant **Rev:** Two dolphins leaping left **Edge:** Reeded

Date	Mintage	F	VF	XF	Unc	BU
1996	1,500,000	—	—	—	1.50	2.00
1999	2,000,000	—	—	—	1.50	2.00
2000	10,000	—	—	—	2.00	3.00

KM# 29.1 10 KRONUR

Copper-Nickel, 27.5 mm. **Obv:** Quartered design of Eagle, dragon, bull and giant **Rev:** Four capelins left **Edge:** Reeded

Date	Mintage	F	VF	XF	Unc	BU
1984	10,000,000	—	—	0.35	1.75	2.50
1987	7,500,000	—	—	0.35	1.75	2.50
1994	2,500,000	—	—	0.35	1.75	2.50

KM# 29.2 10 KRONUR

8.0000 g., Nickel Clad Steel, 24.5 mm. **Obv:** Quartered design of Eagle, dragon, bull and giant **Rev:** Four capelins left **Edge:** Reeded **Note:** Struck on flan of Indian Rupee in error.

Date	Mintage	F	VF	XF	Unc	BU
1984	Inc. above	—	—	100	150	—

KM# 29.1a 10 KRONUR

8.0000 g., Nickel Clad Steel, 27.5 mm. **Obv:** Quartered design of Eagle, dragon, bull and giant **Rev:** Four capelins left **Edge:** Reeded

Date	Mintage	F	VF	XF	Unc	BU
1996	4,000,000	—	—	—	1.75	2.50
2000	10,000	—	—	—	2.50	3.50

KM# 31 50 KRONUR

8.2500 g., Nickel-Brass, 23 mm. **Obv:** Quartered design of eagle, dragon, bull and giant **Rev:** Crab **Edge:** Reeded

Date	Mintage	F	VF	XF	Unc	BU
1987	4,000,000	—	—	—	4.00	5.00
1992	2,000,000	—	—	—	4.00	5.00
2000	10,000	—	—	—	5.00	7.00

KM# 35 100 KRONUR

8.5000 g., Nickel-Brass, 25.5 mm. **Obv:** Quartered design of Eagle, dragon, bull and giant **Rev:** Lumpfish left **Edge:** Reeded

Date	Mintage	F	VF	XF	Unc	BU
1995	6,000,000	—	—	—	6.00	7.00
2000	10,000	—	—	—	7.00	10.00

KM# 30 500 KRONUR

20.0000 g., 0.5000 Silver .3215 oz. ASW **Subject:** 100th Anniversary of Icelandic Banknotes **Obv:** Fishing vessel **Rev:** Seated figure with sword and shield **Designer:** Throstur Magnusson

Date	Mintage	F	VF	XF	Unc	BU
ND(1986)	15,000	—	—	—	55.00	65.00

KM# 30a 500 KRONUR

20.0000 g., 0.9250 Silver .5968 oz. ASW **Subject:** 100th Anniversary of Icelandic Banknotes **Obv:** Fishing vessel **Rev:** Seated figure with sword and shield

Date	Mintage	F	VF	XF	Unc	BU
ND(1986) Proof	5,000	Value: 70.00				

KM# 32 1000 KRONUR

30.0000 g., 0.9250 Silver .8922 oz. ASW **Subject:** 50th Anniversary of Icelandic Republic - Sveinn Bjornsson **Obv:** Arms with supporters **Rev:** Head left **Designer:** Throstur Magnusson **Note:** In sets only.

Date	Mintage	F	VF	XF	Unc	BU
ND(1994)	6,000	—	—	—	55.00	62.50
ND(1994) Proof	3,000	Value: 95.00				

KM# 33 1000 KRONUR

30.0000 g., 0.9250 Silver .8922 oz. ASW **Subject:** Asgeir Asgeirsson **Obv:** Arms with supporters **Rev:** Head left **Designer:** Throstur Magnusson **Note:** In sets only.

Date	Mintage	F	VF	XF	Unc	BU
ND(1994)	6,000	—	—	—	55.00	62.50
ND(1994) Proof	3,000	Value: 95.00				

KM# 34 1000 KRONUR

30.0000 g., 0.9250 Silver .8922 oz. ASW **Subject:** Kristjan Eldjarn **Obv:** Arms with supporters **Rev:** Head left **Designer:** Throstur Magnusson **Note:** In sets only.

Date	Mintage	F	VF	XF	Unc	BU
ND(1994)	6,000	—	—	—	55.00	62.50
ND(1994) Proof	3,000	Value: 90.00				

KM# 37 1000 KRONUR

27.7300 g., 0.9000 Silver .7720 oz. ASW **Subject:** Leif Ericsson Millennium

Date	Mintage	F	VF	XF	Unc	BU
ND(2000) Proof	150,000	Value: 65.00				

KM# 36 10000 KRONUR

8.6500 g., 0.9000 Gold .2503 oz. AGW **Subject:** 1000 Years of Christianity **Obv:** Arms with supporters **Rev:** Old crosier top

Date	Mintage	F	VF	XF	Unc	BU
ND(2000) Proof	3,000	Value: 285				

MINT SETS

KM#	Date	Mintage	Identification	Issue Price	Mkt Val
MS1	1930 (3)	10,000	KM#M1-M3	—	365
MS2	1970 (6)	—	KM#10a, 12a, 15, 17-19	—	11.50
MS3	1971 (6)	—	KM#10a, 12a, 15, 17-19	—	10.00
MS4	1973 (6)	—	KM#10a, 12a (knob 3), 15, 17-19	3.25	9.00
MS5	1974 (6)	—	KM#10a, 12a, 15, 17-19	3.25	7.50
MS6	1974 (2)	70,000	KM#20-21	30.00	26.50
MS7	1975 (4)	—	KM#12a, 15, 18-19	—	5.50
MS8	1976 (4)	—	KM#15, 18-19, 23	—	5.50
MS9	1977 (4)	—	KM#15, 18-19, 23	—	5.50
MS10	1978 (4)	—	KM#15, 18-19, 23	—	5.50
MS11	1980 (4)	—	KM#15, 18-19, 23	—	5.50
MS12	1981 (5)	—	KM#24-28	—	5.50
MS13	1981-1996 (8)	—	1981: KM#24-25; 1986: KM#26a; 1992: KM#31; 1995: KM#35; 1996: KM#27a, 28a, 29.1a	—	12.50
MS14	1994 (3)	6,000	KM#32-34	110	185
MS15	2000 (5)	10,000	KM#27a, 28a, 29.1a, 31, 35	—	18.50

PROOF SETS

KM#	Date	Mintage	Identification	Issue Price	Mkt Val
PS1	1974 (3)	8,000	KM#20-22	272	350
PS2	1974 (2)	58,000	KM#20-21	38.00	32.00
PS3	1966-1980 (11)	15,000	1966: KM#8-9, 13a.1; 1967: KM#11; 1974: KM#10a, 17; 1975: KM#12a; 1980: KM#15, 18-19, 23	40.00	37.50
PS4	1981 (5)	15,000	KM#24-28	32.00	37.50
PS5	1994 (3)	3,000	KM#32-34	155	325
PS6	2000 (2)	150,000	KM#37 and US Ericson Dollar	68.00	110

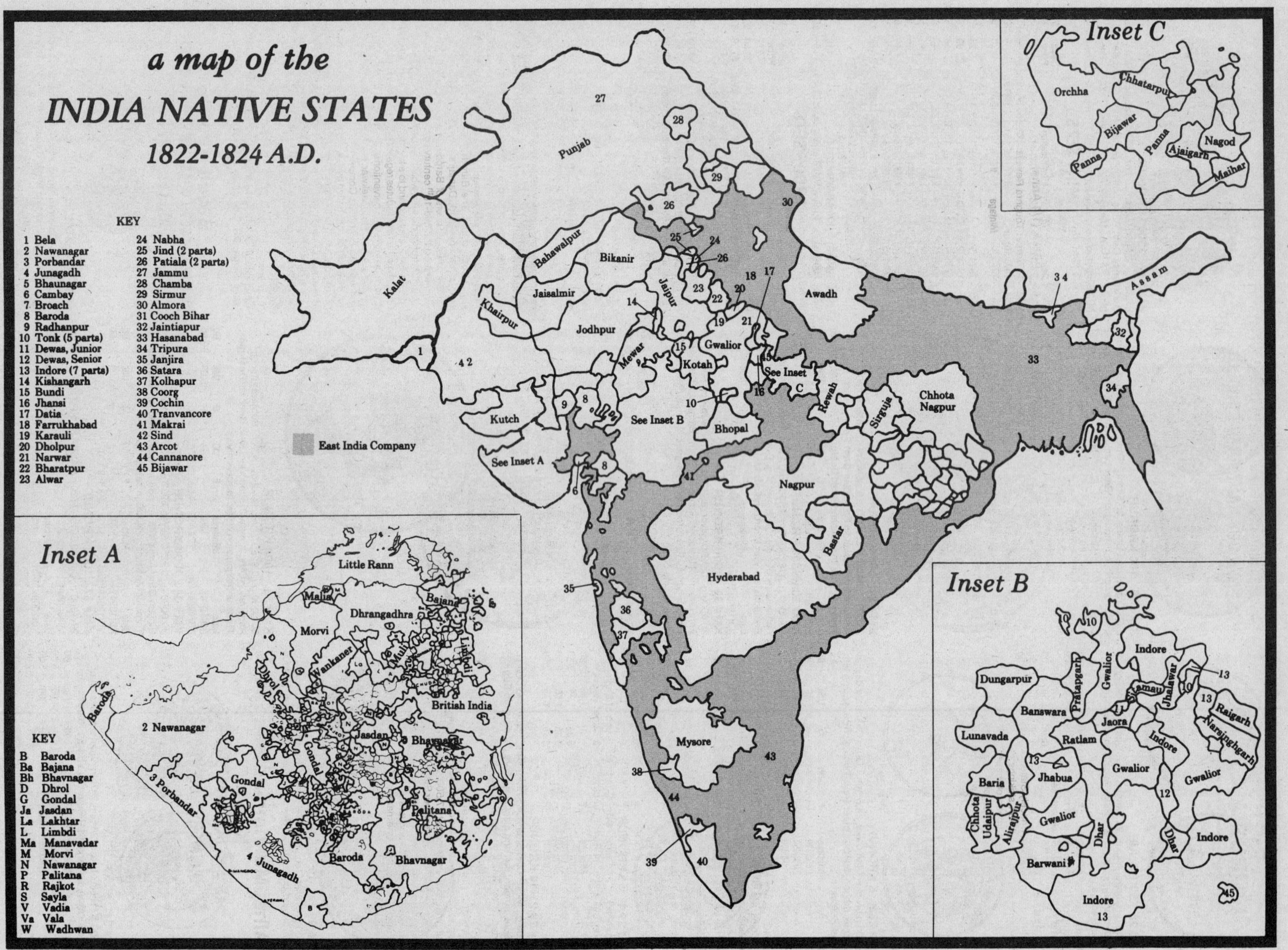

a map of the
INDIA NATIVE STATES
1822-1824 A.D.
KEY
1 Bela
2 Nawanagar
3 Porbandar
4 Junagadh
5 Bhaunagar
6 Cambay
7 Broach
8 Baroda
9 Radhanpur
10 Tonk (5 parts)
11 Dewas, Junior
12 Dewas, Senior
13 Indore (7 parts)
14 Kishangarh
15 Bundi
16 Jhansi
17 Datia
18 Farrukhabad
19 Karauli
20 Dholpur
21 Narwar
22 Bharatpur
23 Alwar
24 Nabha
25 Jind (2 parts)
26 Patiala (2 parts)
27 Jammu
28 Chamba
29 Sirmur
30 Almora
31 Cooch Bihar
32 Jaintiapur
33 Hasanabad
34 Tripura
35 Janjira
36 Satara
37 Kolhapur
38 Coorg
39 Cochin
40 Tranvancore
41 Makrai
42 Sind
43 Arcot
44 Cannanore
45 Bijawar
East India Company
Kalat
Punjab
Bahawalpur
Bikanir
Jaisalmir
Khairpur
Jodhpur
Jaipur
Mewar
Gwalior
Kotah
Awadh
Assam
See Inset C
Rewah
Sirguja
Chhota Nagpur
Kutch
See Inset A
See Inset B
Bhopal
Nagpur
Bastar
Hyderabad
Mysore
Inset C
Orchha
Chhatarpur
Bijawar
Panna
Ajaigarh
Nagod
Maihar
Inset A
Little Rann
Malia
Dhrangadhra
Bajana
Morvi
Wankaner
Muli
Limbdi
Dhrol
British India
Jasdan
Bhavnagar
2 Nawanagar
Gondal
Baroda
3 Porbandar
Palitana
4 Junagadh
KEY
B Baroda
Ba Bajana
Bh Bhavnagar
D Dhrol
G Gondal
Ja Jasdan
La Lakhtar
L Limbdi
Ma Manavadar
M Morvi
N Nawanagar
P Palitana
R Rajkot
S Sayla
V Vadia
Va Vala
W Wadhwan
Inset B
Dungarpur
Pratapgarh
Indore
Jhalawar
Banswara
Jaora
Raigarh
Narsinghgarh
Lunavada
Ratlam
Jhabua
Baria
Chhota Udaipur
Alirajpur
Dhar
Barwani

INDIA - PRINCELY STATES

MONETARY SYSTEMS

In each state, local rates of exchange prevailed. There was no fixed rate between copper, silver or gold coin, but the rates varied in accordance with the values of the metal and by the edict of the local authority.

Within the subcontinent, different regions used distinctive coinage standards. In North India and the Deccan, the silver rupee (11.6 g) and gold mohur (11.0 g) predominated. In Gujarat, the silver kori (4.7 g) and gold kori (6.4 g) were the main currency. In South India the silver fanam (0.7-1.0 g) and gold hun or Pagoda (3.4 g) were current. Copper coins in all parts of India were produced to a myriad of local metrologies with seemingly endless varieties.

NAZARANA ISSUES

Throughout the Indian Princely States listings are Nazarana designations for special full flan strikings of copper, silver and some gold coinage. The purpose of these issues was for presentation to the local monarch to gain favor. For example if one had an audience with one's ruler he would exchange goods, currency notes or the cruder struck circulating coinage for Nazarana pieces which he would present to the ruler as a gift. The borderline between true Nazarana pieces and well struck regular issues is often indistinct. The Nazaranas sometimes circulated alongside the cruder "dump" issues.

PRICING

As the demand for Indian Princely coinage develops, and more dealers handle the material, sale records and price lists enable a firmer basis for pricing most series. For scarcer types adequate sale records are often not available, and prices must be regarded as tentative. Inasmuch as date collectors of Princely States series are few, dates known to be scarce are usually worth little more than common ones. Coins of a dated type, which do not show the full date on their flans should be valued at about 70 per cent of the prices indicated.

DATING

Coins are dated in several eras. Arabic and Devanagari numerals are used in conjunction with the Hejira era (AH), the Vikrama Samvat (VS), Saka Samvat (Saka), Fasli era (FE) Mauludi era (AM), and Malabar era (ME), as well as the Christian era (AD).

GRADING

Copper coins are rarely found in high grade, as they were the workhorse of coinage circulation, and were everywhere used for day-to-day transactions. Moreover, they were carelessly struck and even when 'new', can often only be distinguished from VF coins with difficulty, if at all.

Silver coins were often hoarded and not infrequently, turn up in nearly as-struck condition. The silver coins of Hyderabad (dump coins) are common in high grades, and the rupees of some states are scarcer 'used' than 'new'. Great caution must be exercised in determining the value or scarcity of high grade dump coins.

Dump gold was rarely circulated, and usually occurs in high grades, or is found made into jewelry.

BAHAWALPUR

The Amirs of Bahawalpur established their independence from Afghan control towards the close of the 18th century. In the 1830's the state's independence under British suzerainty became guaranteed by treaty. With the creation of Pakistan in 1947 Bahawalpur, with an area of almost 17,500 square miles, became its premier Princely State. Bahawalpur State, named after its capital, stretched for almost three hundred miles along the left bank of the Sutlej, Panjnad and Indus rivers.

For earlier issues in the names of the Durrani rulers, see Afghanistan.

RULERS

Amirs

Alhaj Muhammad Bahawal Khan V, AH1317-1325/1899-1907AD

Sir Sadiq Muhammad Khan V, AH1325-1365/1907-1947AD

MINTS

Bahawalpur

Alhaj Muhammad Bahawal Khan V

AH1317-1325 / 1899-1907AD

HAMMERED COINAGE

Y# 6 PAISA

Copper **Obverse:** Legend in Persian **Obv. Legend:** Muhammad Bahawal ... **Mint:** Bahawalpur **Note:** For anonymous Paisas struck during the years of his reign, see Y#2.1, 2.2.

Date	Mintage	Good	VG	F	VF	XF
AH1324	—	3.50	6.00	8.00	12.50	20.00
AH1325	—	3.50	6.00	8.00	12.50	20.00

Anonymous

(Alhaj Muhammad Bahawal Khan V) 1899-1907

ANONYMOUS HAMMERED COINAGE

Y# 2.1 PAISA

Copper **Obverse:** Star above cresent, flanked by sprigs **Reverse:** Inscription divides date above **Shape:** Irregular or square **Mint:** Bahawalpur

Date	Mintage	Good	VG	F	VF	XF
AH1321	—	4.75	7.00	9.00	12.50	20.00
AH1325	—	4.75	7.00	9.00	12.50	20.00

Y# 2.2a PAISA

Brass **Shape:** Irregular or square **Mint:** Bahawalpur

Date	Mintage	Good	VG	F	VF	XF
ND(ca.1909)	—	6.00	12.00	17.50	25.00	—

Y# 2.2 PAISA

Copper **Shape:** Irregular or square **Mint:** Bahawalpur **Note:** Contemporary ND imitations exist.

Date	Mintage	Good	VG	F	VF	XF
ND(ca. 1909)	—	4.00	7.50	12.00	20.00	32.50

Sir Sadiq Muhammad Khan V

AH1325-1365 / 1907-1947AD

HAMMERED COINAGE

Y# 7.1 PAISA

Copper **Obverse:** Legend in Persian **Obv. Legend:** Sadiq Muhammad ... **Mint:** Bahawalpur

Date	Mintage	Good	VG	F	VF	XF
AH1326	—	3.50	6.00	9.00	12.50	20.00
AH1327	—	3.50	6.00	9.00	12.50	20.00

Y# 7.2 PAISA

Copper **Obverse:** Legend in Persian **Obv. Legend:** Sadiq Muhammad ... **Reverse:** Without date **Mint:** Bahawalpur

Date	Mintage	Good	VG	F	VF	XF
ND(c. 1910)	—	4.00	7.50	12.50	20.00	32.50

Y# 7.3 PAISA

Copper **Obverse:** Legend in Persian **Obv. Legend:** Sadiq Muhammad ... **Reverse:** Without date or star **Mint:** Bahawalpur

Date	Mintage	Good	VG	F	VF	XF
ND(c. 1910)	—	5.50	9.00	13.50	20.00	32.50

Y# 8 PAISA

Copper **Obverse:** Toughra **Mint:** Bahawalpur

Date	Mintage	Good	VG	F	VF	XF
AH1342	—	7.50	11.00	15.00	20.00	32.50
AH1343	—	7.50	11.00	15.00	20.00	32.50

MILLED COINAGE

Y# 12 1/2 PICE

Copper **Obverse:** Bust of Muhammad Bahawal Khan V left **Reverse:** Toughra **Mint:** Bahawalpur

Date	Mintage	VG	F	VF	XF	Unc
AH1359	—	0.15	0.35	0.75	1.25	2.00
AH1359 Proof	—	—	—	—	—	—

Y# 9 PAISA (1/4 Anna)

Copper Or Bronze **Obverse:** Toughra **Reverse:** Three branches in square **Mint:** Bahawalpur

Date	Mintage	VG	F	VF	XF	Unc
AH1343	—	4.50	11.50	17.50	25.00	40.00

Y# 9a PAISA (1/4 Anna)

Brass **Obverse:** Toughra **Reverse:** Three branches in square **Mint:** Bahawalpur

Date	Mintage	VG	F	VF	XF	Unc
AH1343	—	—	11.50	17.50	25.00	40.00

Y# 13 PAISA (1/4 Anna)

Copper **Obverse:** Bust of Muhammad Bahawal Khan V left **Reverse:** Toughra **Mint:** Bahawalpur

Date	Mintage	VG	F	VF	XF	Unc
AH1359	—	0.30	0.75	1.25	2.00	3.00
AH1359 Proof	—	—	—	—	—	—

Y# 14 RUPEE

6.5000 g., Silver .9167 oz. ASW **Obverse:** Toughra **Mint:** Bahawalpur

Date	Mintage	VG	F	VF	XF	Unc
AH1343	—	8.50	13.50	22.50	37.50	100

BARODA

Maratha state located in western India. The ruling line was descended from Damaji, a Maratha soldier, who received the title of "Distinguished Swordsman" in 1721 (hence the scimitar on most Baroda coins). The Baroda title "Gaikwara" comes from "gaikwar" or cow herd, Damaji's father's occupation.

The Maratha rulers of Baroda, the Gaekwar family rose to prominence in the mid-18th century by carving out for themselves a dominion from territories, which were previously under the control of the Poona Marathas, and to a lesser extent, of the Raja of Jodhpur. Chronic internal disputes regarding the succession to the masnad culminated in the intervention of British troops in support of one candidate, Anand Rao Gaekwar, in 1800. Then, in 1802, an agreement with the East India Company released the Baroda princes from their fear of domination by the Maratha Peshwa of Poona but subordinated them to Company interests. Nevertheless, for almost the next century and a half Baroda maintained a good relationship with the British and continued as a major Princely State right up to 1947, when it acceded to the Indian Union.

RULERS

Gaekwars

Sayaji Rao III, AH1292-1357/VS1932-1995/1875-1938AD

Pratap Singh, VS1995-2008/1938-1951AD

Sayaji Rao IIII

AH1292-1357 / VS1932-95 / 1875-1938AD

MILLED COINAGE

Y# 37 1/6 MOHUR

Gold, 14.5 mm. **Obverse:** Crowned bust, right **Reverse:** Inscription, scimitar, date within wreath **Mint:** Baroda **Note:** 1.04-1.18 grams.

Date	Mintage	VG	F	VF	XF	Unc
VS1959 (1902)	—	—	175	225	275	350

Y# 38 1/3 MOHUR

Gold, 16 mm. **Obverse:** Bust of Sayaji Rao III right **Mint:** Baroda **Note:** Weight varies: 2.07-2.39 grams.

Date	Mintage	VG	F	VF	XF	Unc
VS1959 (1902)	—	—	225	275	350	450

Y# 39 MOHUR

Gold, 21 mm. **Obverse:** Crowned bust, right **Reverse:** Inscription, scimitar, date within wreath **Mint:** Baroda **Note:** Weight varies: 6.20-6.40 grams.

Date	Mintage	VG	F	VF	XF	Unc
VS1959 (1902)	—	—	265	350	475	650

BHAUNAGAR

State located in northwest India on the west shore of the Gulf of Cambay.

The Thakurs of Bhaunagar, as the rulers were titled, were Gohel Rajputs. They traced their control of the area back to the 13th century. Under the umbrella of British paramountcy, the Thakurs of Bhaunagar were regarded as relatively enlightened rulers. The State was absorbed into Saurashtra in February 1948.

Anonymous Types: Bearing the distinguishing Nagari legend *Bahadur* in addition to the Mughal legends.

MONETARY SYSTEM

2 Trambiyo = 1 Dokda

1-1/2 Dokda = 1 Dhingla

Thakurs of Bhaunagar

Gohel Rajputs

ANONYMOUS HAMMERED COINAGE

KM# 1 DOKDA

Copper

Date	Mintage	Good	VG	F	VF	XF
VS2004(1947)	—	4.00	6.00	10.00	15.00	—

BUNDI

State in Rajputana in northwest India.

Bundi was founded in 1342 by a Chauhan Rajput, Rao Dewa (Deoraj). Until the Maratha defeat early in the 19th century, Bundi was greatly harassed by the forces of Holkar and Sindhia. In 1818 it came under British protection and control and remained so until 1947.In 1948 the State was absorbed into Rajasthan.

RULERS

Raghubir Singh VS1946-1984/1889-1927AD

Ishwari Singh VS1984-2004/1927-1947AD

MINT

	PERSO-ARABIC	DEVANAGARI
Bundi	بندي	बुन्दी

بوندي

Mint name: Bundi

Victoria

1837-1901AD

HAMMERED COINAGE

Regal Style

Y# 10 NAZARANA RUPEE

Silver **Obverse:** Seated figure holding katar **Obv. Legend:** VICTORIA QUEEN **Shape:** Square **Note:** Weight varies: 10.60-11.00 grams.

Date	Mintage	Good	VG	F	VF	XF
VS1958 (1901)	—	18.50	37.50	55.00	90.00	145

Edward VII

1901-1910AD

HAMMERED COINAGE

Regal Style

Y# A12 1/2 PAISA

Copper **Obverse:** Katar **Obv. Legend:** EDWARD VII EMPEROR **Note:** Weight varies: 4.70-5.10 grams.

Date	Mintage	Good	VG	F	VF	XF
NDVS1963 (1906)	—	6.50	9.00	12.50	17.50	—
VS1965 (1908)	—	6.50	9.00	12.50	17.50	—
VS1966 (1909)	—	6.50	9.00	12.50	17.50	—
VS1967 (1910)	—	6.50	9.00	12.50	17.50	—
VS1973 (1916)	—	6.50	9.00	12.50	17.50	—
VS1974 (1917)	—	6.50	9.00	12.50	17.50	—
VS1976 (1918)	—	6.50	9.00	12.50	17.50	—

Y# B11 1/4 RUPEE

Silver **Obverse:** Seated figure holding katar **Obv. Legend:** EMPEROR-EDWARD VII **Note:** Weight varies: 2.65-2.70 grams.

Date	Mintage	Good	VG	F	VF	XF
VS1958 (1901)	—	3.50	8.50	21.50	30.00	40.00
VS1959 (1902)	—	3.50	8.50	21.50	30.00	40.00
VS1961 (1904)	—	3.50	8.50	21.50	30.00	40.00
VS1962 (1905)	—	3.50	8.50	21.50	30.00	40.00

Y# 12 1/4 RUPEE

Silver **Obverse:** Katar **Obv. Legend:** EDWARD VII EMPEROR **Note:** Weight varies: 2.65-2.70 grams.

Date	Mintage	Good	VG	F	VF	XF
VS1963 (1906)	—	1.25	2.75	6.50	9.00	14.50
VS1964 (1907)	—	1.25	2.75	6.50	9.00	14.50
VS1965 (1908)	—	1.25	2.75	6.50	9.00	14.50
VS1966 (1909)	—	1.25	2.75	6.50	9.00	14.50

Y# A11 1/2 RUPEE

Silver, 16-18 mm. **Obverse:** Seated figure holding katar **Obv. Legend:** EMPEROR-EDWARD VII **Note:** Weight varies: 5.30-5.40 grams.

Date	Mintage	Good	VG	F	VF	XF
VS1958 (1901)	—	4.00	10.00	21.50	30.00	42.50

Y# 13 1/2 RUPEE

Silver, 16-18 mm. **Obverse:** Katar **Obv. Legend:** EDWARD VII EMPEROR **Note:** Weight varies: 5.30-5.40 grams.

Date	Mintage	Good	VG	F	VF	XF
VS1963 (1906)	—	1.75	4.50	8.50	12.50	18.50
VS1964 (1907)	—	1.50	3.75	7.50	10.00	16.00
VS1965 (1908)	—	1.50	3.75	7.50	10.00	16.00
VS1966 (1909)	—	1.50	3.75	7.50	10.00	16.00

Y# 11 RUPEE

Silver, 21-25 mm. **Obverse:** Seated figure holding katar **Obv. Legend:** EMPEROR-EDWARD VII **Note:** Weight varies: 10.60-10.70 grams. Size varies.

Date	Mintage	Good	VG	F	VF	XF
VS1958 (1901)	—	4.75	7.00	12.00	16.00	24.00
VS1959 (1902)	—	4.75	7.00	12.00	16.00	24.00
VS1960 (1903)	—	4.75	7.00	12.00	16.00	24.00
VS1961 (1904)	—	4.75	7.00	12.00	16.00	24.00
VS1962 (1905)	—	4.75	7.00	12.00	16.00	24.00
VS1963 (1906)	—	4.75	7.00	12.00	16.00	24.00

Y# 14 RUPEE

Silver, 18-21 mm. **Obverse:** Katar **Obv. Legend:** EDWARD VII EMPEROR **Note:** Weight varies: 10.60-10.70 grams. Size varies.

Date	Mintage	Good	VG	F	VF	XF
VS1963 (1906)	—	4.50	6.50	10.00	15.00	23.50
VS1964 (1907)	—	4.50	6.50	10.00	15.00	23.50
VS1965 (1908)	—	4.50	6.50	10.00	15.00	23.50
VS1966 (1909)	—	4.50	6.50	10.00	15.00	23.50
VS1967 (1910)	—	4.50	6.50	10.00	15.00	23.50
VS1968 (1911)	—	4.50	6.50	10.00	15.00	23.50
VS1969 (1912)	—	4.50	6.50	10.00	15.00	23.50

Y# 11a NAZARANA RUPEE

Silver **Obverse:** Seated figure holding katar **Obv. Legend:** EMPEROR-EDWARD VII **Shape:** Broad, square flan **Note:** Weight varies: 10.60-10.70 grams.

Date	Mintage	Good	VG	F	VF	XF
VS1962 (1906)	—	20.00	40.00	65.00	120	175

Y# 14a NAZARANA RUPEE

Silver **Obverse:** Katar **Obv. Legend:** EDWARD VII EMPEROR **Note:** Weight varies: 10.60-10.70 grams.

Date	Mintage	Good	VG	F	VF	XF
VS1965 (1908)	—	17.50	35.00	55.00	110	150
VS1966 (1909)	—	17.50	35.00	55.00	110	150
VS1967 (1910)	—	17.50	35.00	55.00	110	150
VS1968 (1911)	—	17.50	35.00	55.00	110	150
VS1969 (1912)	—	17.50	35.00	55.00	110	150
VS1970 (1913)	—	17.50	35.00	55.00	110	150

Y# 14b NAZARANA RUPEE

Silver, 26 mm. **Obverse:** Katar **Obv. Legend:** EDWARD VII EMPEROR **Shape:** Round flan **Note:** Weight varies: 10.60-10.70 grams.

Date	Mintage	Good	VG	F	VF	XF
VS1966 (1909)	—	6.50	12.50	20.00	35.00	60.00
VS1967 (1910)	—	6.50	12.50	20.00	35.00	60.00
VS1968 (1911)	—	6.50	12.50	20.00	35.00	60.00
VS1969 (1912)	—	7.00	15.00	21.50	30.00	40.00
VS1970 (1913)	—	7.00	15.00	21.50	30.00	40.00

George V

1910-1936AD

HAMMERED COINAGE

Regal Style

Y# 15.1 1/2 PAISA

Copper **Obverse:** Katar **Obv. Legend:** EMPEROR-GEORGE V **Shape:** Rectangular or square **Note:** Weight varies: 5.00-5.35 grams.

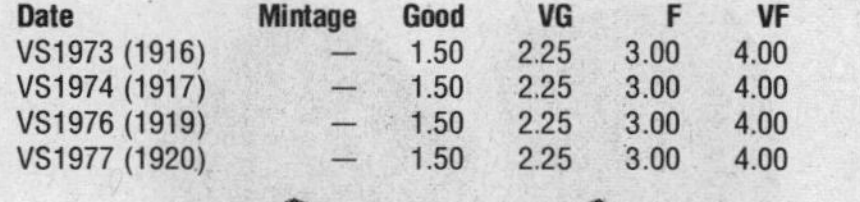

Date	Mintage	Good	VG	F	VF	XF
VS1973 (1916)	—	1.50	2.25	3.00	4.00	—
VS1974 (1917)	—	1.50	2.25	3.00	4.00	—
VS1976 (1919)	—	1.50	2.25	3.00	4.00	—
VS1977 (1920)	—	1.50	2.25	3.00	4.00	—

Y# 15.2 1/2 PAISA

Copper **Obverse:** Katar **Obv. Legend:** GEORGE V EMPEROR **Shape:** Rectangular or square **Note:** Weight varies: 5.00-5.35 grams. Size varies.

Date	Mintage	Good	VG	F	VF	XF
VS1980 (1923)	—	1.50	2.25	3.00	4.00	—
VS1981 (1924)	—	1.50	2.25	3.00	4.00	—
VS1982 (1925)	—	1.50	2.25	3.00	4.00	—
VS1983 (1926)	—	1.50	2.25	3.00	4.00	—
VS1984 (1927)	—	1.50	2.25	3.00	4.00	—
VS1986 (1929)	—	2.00	3.00	4.00	5.00	—
VS1987 (1930)	—	2.00	3.00	4.00	5.00	—
VS1988 (1931)	—	3.00	4.00	5.50	7.50	—
VS1990 (1933)	—	3.00	4.00	5.50	7.50	—
VS1991 (1934)	—	3.00	4.00	5.50	7.50	—
VS1992 (1935)	—	3.00	4.00	5.50	7.50	—

Y# 16.1 1/4 RUPEE

Silver **Obverse:** Katar **Obv. Legend:** EMPEROR-GEORGE V **Note:** Weight varies: 2.60-2.70 grams.

Date	Mintage	Good	VG	F	VF	XF
VS1972 (1915)	—	0.85	2.00	5.00	7.50	12.00
VS1973 (1916)	—	0.85	2.00	5.00	7.50	12.00
VS1974 (1917)	—	0.85	2.00	5.00	7.50	12.00

Y# 16.2 1/4 RUPEE

Silver **Obverse:** Katar **Obv. Legend:** GEORGE V EMPEROR **Note:** Weight varies: 2.60-2.70 grams.

Date	Mintage	Good	VG	F	VF	XF
VS1980 (1923)	—	0.85	2.00	5.00	7.50	12.00
VS1981 (1924)	—	0.85	2.00	5.00	7.50	12.00
VS1982 (1925)	—	0.85	2.00	5.00	7.50	12.00

Y# A19 1/4 RUPEE

Silver, 13 mm. **Obverse:** Date 1925 at center **Obv. Legend:** EMPEROR GEORGE V **Note:** Weight varies: 2.60-2.70 grams.

Date	Mintage	Good	VG	F	VF	XF
VS1915 (1925)	—	6.00	15.00	31.50	42.50	60.00

Y# 17.1 1/2 RUPEE

Silver **Note:** Weight varies: 5.30-5.40 grams.

Date	Mintage	Good	VG	F	VF	XF
VS1972 (1915)	—	1.50	3.75	7.00	10.00	15.00
VS1973 (1916)	—	1.50	3.75	7.00	10.00	15.00
VS1974 (1917)	—	1.25	3.00	6.00	9.00	13.50
VS1979 (1922)	—	1.25	3.00	6.00	9.00	13.50

Y# 17.2 1/2 RUPEE

Silver **Obverse:** Legend arranged differently **Note:** Weight varies: 5.30-5.40 grams.

Date	Mintage	Good	VG	F	VF	XF
VS1979 (1922)	—	1.75	3.00	6.00	9.00	13.50
VS1980 (1923)	—	1.75	3.00	6.00	9.00	13.50
VS1981 (1924)	—	1.75	3.00	6.00	9.00	13.50
VS1982 (1925)	—	1.75	3.00	6.00	9.00	13.50
VS1983 (1926)	—	1.75	3.00	6.00	9.00	13.50
VS1984 (1927)	—	1.75	3.00	6.00	9.00	13.50

Y# 19 1/2 RUPEE

Silver **Obverse:** Date 1925 at center **Obv. Legend:** EMPEROR GEORGE V **Note:** Weight varies: 5.30-5.40 grams.

Date	Mintage	Good	VG	F	VF	XF
VS1915 (1925)	—	8.00	20.00	38.50	55.00	80.00

Y# 18.1 RUPEE

Silver **Obverse:** Katar **Obv. Legend:** EMPEROR GEORGE V **Note:** Weight varies: 10.60-10.70 grams.

Date	Mintage	Good	VG	F	VF	XF
VS1972 (1915)	—	4.50	6.00	9.00	13.50	20.00
VS1973 (1916)	—	4.50	6.00	9.00	13.50	20.00
VS1974 (1917)	—	4.50	6.00	9.00	13.50	20.00
VS1975 (1918)	—	4.50	6.00	9.00	13.50	20.00
VS1979 (1922)	—	4.50	6.00	9.00	13.50	20.00

Y# 18.2 RUPEE

Silver **Obverse:** Katar **Obv. Legend:** GEORGE V EMPEROR **Note:** Weight varies: 10.60-10.70 grams.

Date	Mintage	Good	VG	F	VF	XF
VS1979 (1922)	—	4.50	6.00	9.00	13.50	20.00
VS1980 (1923)	—	4.50	6.00	9.00	13.50	20.00
VS1981 (1924)	—	4.50	6.00	9.00	13.50	20.00
VS1982 (1925)	—	4.50	6.00	9.00	13.50	20.00
VS1983 (1926)	—	4.50	6.00	9.00	13.50	20.00
VS1984 (1927)	—	4.50	6.00	9.00	13.50	20.00
VS1985 (1928)	—	4.50	6.00	9.00	13.50	20.00
VS1987 (1930)	—	4.50	6.00	9.00	13.50	20.00
VS1989 (1932)	—	4.50	6.00	9.00	13.50	20.00

Y# 20 RUPEE

Silver **Obverse:** Date "1925" at center **Obv. Legend:** EMPEROR GEORGE V **Note:** Weight varies: 10.60-10.70 grams.

Date	Mintage	Good	VG	F	VF	XF
VS1915 (1925)	—	14.00	35.00	70.00	100	140

Y# 18a.1 NAZARANA RUPEE

Silver **Obverse:** Katar **Obv. Legend:** EMPEROR GEORGE V **Shape:** Square **Note:** Weight varies: 10.55-10.80 grams.

Date	Mintage	Good	VG	F	VF	XF
VS1965 (1908)	—	13.50	27.50	45.00	75.00	125
VS1971 (1914)	—	13.50	27.50	45.00	75.00	125
VS1974 (1917)	—	13.50	27.50	45.00	75.00	125
VS1975 (1918)	—	13.50	27.50	45.00	75.00	125
VS1977 (1920)	—	13.50	27.50	45.00	75.00	125

Y# 18a.2 NAZARANA RUPEE

Silver **Obverse:** Katar **Obv. Legend:** GEORGE V **Shape:** Square **Note:** Weight varies: 10.55-10.80 grams.

Date	Mintage	Good	VG	F	VF	XF
VS1979 (1922)	—	13.50	27.50	45.00	75.00	125
VS1980 (1923)	—	13.50	27.50	45.00	75.00	125
VS1981 (1924)	—	13.50	27.50	45.00	75.00	125
VS1983 (1926)	—	13.50	27.50	45.00	75.00	125
VS1984 (1927)	—	13.50	27.50	45.00	75.00	125
VS1987 (1930)	—	13.50	27.50	45.00	75.00	125

Y# 20a NAZARANA RUPEE

Silver **Obverse:** Date "1925" at center **Obv. Legend:** EMPEROR GEORGE V **Shape:** Square **Note:** Weight varies: 10.55-10.80 grams.

Date	Mintage	Good	VG	F	VF	XF
VS1915 (1925)	—	22.50	45.00	75.00	110	150

CAMBAY

Khanbayat

Although of very ancient origins as a port, located at the head of the Gulf of Cambay in West India, Cambay did not come into existence as a separate state until about 1730 after the break-down of Mughal authority in Delhi. The nawabs of Cambay traced their ancestry to Momin Khan II, the last of the Muslim governors of Gujerat. The State came under British control after two decades of Maratha rule.

RULERS

Ja'far Ali Khan, AH1297-1333/VS1937-1972/1880-1915AD

MINT

Khanbayat

Jafar Ali Khan
1880-1915AD

ANONYMOUS HAMMERED COINAGE

Y# 5 1/2 PAISA

Copper **Obverse:** Persian inscription **Obv. Inscription:** Cambay **Reverse:** Denomination in words **Note:** Varieties in countermark exist.

Date	Mintage	Good	VG	F	VF	XF
VS1963(1906)	—	3.50	6.50	9.00	12.50	—
VS1964(1907)	—	3.50	6.50	9.00	12.50	—

Y# 5a 1/2 PAISA

Copper **Obverse:** Persian inscription **Obv. Inscription:** Cambay **Reverse:** Denomination in numerals

Date	Mintage	Good	VG	F	VF	XF
VS1964(1907)	—	3.00	5.00	7.50	10.00	—
VS1965(1908)	—	3.00	5.00	7.50	10.00	—
VS1966(1909)	—	3.00	5.00	7.50	10.00	—

Y# 6 PAISA

Copper **Obverse:** Persian inscription **Obv. Inscription:** Cambay **Note:** Varieties exist.

Date	Mintage	Good	VG	F	VF	XF
VS1962(1905)	—	1.00	1.50	2.00	3.50	—
VS1963(1906)	—	1.00	1.50	2.00	3.50	—
VS1964(1907)	—	1.25	1.75	2.50	4.25	—
VS1965(1908)	—	1.00	1.50	2.00	3.50	—
VS1966(1909)	—	1.00	1.50	2.00	3.50	—
VS1968(1911)	—	1.00	1.50	2.00	3.50	—
VS1970(1913)	—	1.65	2.50	4.00	5.00	—

HAMMERED COINAGE

Y# 10 RUPEE

Silver, 19-20 mm. **Obverse:** Persian inscription **Obv. Inscription:** Ja'afar Ali Khan **Reverse:** Mint name **Mint:** Cambay **Note:** Weight varies, 10.70-11.60 grams. Size varies.

Date	Mintage	Good	VG	F	VF	XF
AH1319//23(1901-1902)	—	18.00	30.00	50.00	80.00	125

COUNTERMARKED COINAGE

Y# 2 1/4 PAISA

Copper **Countermark:** Persian "Shah" **Shape:** Round flan **Note:** Varieties in countermark exist.

CM Date	Host Date	Good	VG	F	VF	XF
ND	ND	3.00	5.50	7.50	10.00	—

Y# 3 1/2 PAISA

Copper **Countermark:** Persian "Shah" **Shape:** Round and square flans **Note:** Varieties in countermark exist.

CM Date	Host Date	Good	VG	F	VF	XF
ND	ND	3.00	5.50	7.50	10.00	—

DATIA

State located in north-central India, governed by Maharajas. Datia was founded in 1735 by Bhagwan Das, son of Narsingh Dev of the Orchha royal house. In 1804 the State concluded its first treaty with the East India Company and thereafter came under British protection and control.

RULERS
Bhawani Singh, AH1274-1325/1857-1907AD
Govind Singh, AH1325-1368/1907-1948AD

MINT

Dalipnagar

Gaja Shahi Series

Struck for more than 100 years, with the AH date on the obverse and the regnal year on the reverse bearing little relationship to each other. These are close copies of Orchha C#24-32 and can only be distinguished by the symbols, which are always different from those of Orchha, except for the Gaja (mace):

Gaja always on reverse

On obverse (Datia Mint Symbol)

On reverse

BRITISH PROTECTORATE

Bhawani Singh
AH1274-1325 / 1857-1907AD

HAMMERED COINAGE

Gaja Shahi Series

C# 22 1/2 PAISA

6.0000 g., Copper **Note:** Weight varies 6.00-6.50 grams. Posthumous regnal years of Muhammad Akbar II.

Date	Mintage	Good	VG	F	VF	XF
AH1320(1902)	—	3.00	4.50	6.50	10.00	—

DEWAS

A Maratha state located in west-central India. The raja, the brother of the raja of Dewas Senior Branch had a palace in Dewas City. They descended from two brothers, Tukoji and Jiwaji who were given Dewas City in 1726 by Peshwa Baji Rao as a reward for army services.

Largely due to its geographical location Dewas suffered much at the hands of the armies of Holkar and Sindhia,and from Pindari incursions. In 1818 the State came under British protection.

LOCAL RULERS
Vikrama Simha Rao, 1937-1948AD

BRITISH PROTECTORATE

Senior Branch

Narayan Rao

HAMMERED COINAGE

KM# 10 PAISA

Copper **Reverse:** Heart, cross **Mint:** Allote **Note:** Weight varies 10.50-12.77 grams; varieteis exist.

Date	Mintage	VG	F	VF	XF	Unc
ND (c.1850-1904)	—	7.50	12.50	20.00	—	—

Vikrama Simha Rao
VS1994-2005 / 1937-1948AD

MILLED COINAGE

Regal Style

KM# 13 PAISA

Copper **Obverse:** Bust of Vikrama Simha Rao right **Reverse:** Arms **Mint:** Allote

Date	Mintage	VG	F	VF	XF	Unc
2000/1944	—	11.50	27.50	55.00	90.00	150
2001/1944	—	11.50	22.50	45.00	75.00	125

DUNGARPUR

A district in northwest India which became part of Rajasthan in 1948.

The maharawals of Dungarpur were descended from the Mewar chieftains of the 12th century. In 1527 the upper Mahi basin was bifurcated to form the Princely States of Dungarpur and Banswara. Thereafter Dungarpur came successively under Mughal and Maratha control until in 1818 it came under British protection.

RULERS
Bijey Singh, VS1955-1975/1898-1918AD
Lakshman Singh, VS1975-2005/1918-1948AD

INSCRIPTION:
Rajya Dungarpur

BRITISH PROTECTORATE

Lakshman Singh
VS1975-2005 / 1918-1948AD

HAMMERED COINAGE

KM# 9 NAZARANA MOHUR

11.0000 g., Gold **Obverse:** Sword and "jhar" to right **Rev. Inscription:** Rajya/Dungarpur

Date	Mintage	Good	VG	F	VF	XF
VS1996 (1939)	—	—	1,000	1,500	2,000	3,500

WW II EMERGENCY COINAGE

KM# 7 PAISA

Copper **Reverse:** 2 bars above 'P' in "Paisa"

Date	Mintage	Good	VG	F	VF	XF
VS2001(1944)	—	7.50	18.50	30.00	50.00	75.00

KM# 8 PAISA

Copper **Reverse:** One bar above 'P' in "Paisa"

Date	Mintage	Good	VG	F	VF	XF
VS2001(1944)	—	3.50	9.00	15.00	25.00	37.50

GWALIOR

Sindhia

State located in central India. Capital originally was Ujjain (= Daru-l-fath), but was later transferred to Gwalior in 1810. The Gwalior ruling family, the Sindhias, were descendants of the Maratha chief Ranoji Sindhia (d.1750). His youngest son, Mahadji Sindhia (d.1794) was anxious to establish his independence from the overlordship of the Peshwas of Poona. Unable to achieve this alone, it was the Peshwa's crushing defeat by Ahmad Shah Durrani at Panipat in 1761, which helped realize his ambitions. Largely in the interests of sustaining this autonomy, but partly as a result of a defeat at East India Company hands in 1781, Mahadji concluded an alliance with the British in 1782. In 1785, he reinstalled the fallen Mughal Emperor, Shah Alam, on the throne at Dehli. Very early in the 19th century, Gwalior's relationship with the British began to deteriorate, a situation which culminated in the Anglo-Maratha War of 1803. Gwalior's forces under Daulat Rao were defeated. In consequence, and by the terms of the peace treaty which followed, his territory was truncated. In 1818, Gwalior suffered a further loss of land at British hands. In the years that ensued, as the East India Company's possessions became transformed into empire and as the Pax Britannica swept across the subcontinent, the Sindhia family's relationship with their British overlords steadily improved.

RULERS
Madho Rao, VS1943-1982/1886-1925AD
Jivaji Rao, VS1982-2005/1925-1948AD

MINT

Gwalior Fort

KINGDOM

Madho Rao
VS1943-1982 / 1886-1925AD

MILLED COINAGE

KM# 164 1/2 PICE

Copper, 20 mm. **Obverse:** Cobra above crossed spear and trident **Mint:** Gwalior Fort

Date	Mintage	Good	VG	F	VF	XF
VS1958 (1901)	—	—	0.25	0.65	2.00	4.00

KM# 169 1/4 ANNA

Copper **Obverse:** Cobra above crossed spear and trident

Date	Mintage	VG	F	VF	XF	Unc
VS1958 (1901)	—	0.30	0.75	2.25	4.50	11.00

KM# 170 1/4 ANNA

6.6000 g., Copper **Obverse:** Bust of Madho Rao right **Reverse:** Arms **Note:** Thick planchet, 2.2mm.

Date	Mintage	VG	F	VF	XF	Unc
VS1970 (1913)	—	0.10	0.25	0.75	1.50	3.00

KM# 171 1/4 ANNA

5.1000 g., Copper **Obverse:** Bust of Madho Rao right **Reverse:** Arms **Note:** Thin planchet, 1.6mm.

Date	Mintage	VG	F	VF	XF	Unc
VS1970 (1913)	—	0.50	1.25	3.50	5.00	7.00
VS1974 (1917)	—	0.10	0.25	0.75	1.50	3.00

KM# 172 1/4 ANNA

Copper **Obverse:** Bust of Madho Rao right, continuous legend around portrait **Reverse:** Arms

Date	Mintage	VG	F	VF	XF	Unc
VS1974 (1917)	—	1.50	4.00	6.00	9.00	12.50

KM# 175 1/3 MOHUR

3.4500 g., Gold **Obverse:** Bust of Madho Rao right **Reverse:** Arms

Date	Mintage	VG	F	VF	XF	Unc
VS1959 (1902)	—	—	275	550	1,150	2,000

Jivaji Rao
VS1985-2005 / 1925-1948AD
MILLED COINAGE

KM# 177 1/4 ANNA

Copper **Obverse:** Crude style bust of Jivaji Rao left **Reverse:** Arms **Note:** Thin planchet. 3.00-3.15 grams.

Date	Mintage	VG	F	VF	XF	Unc
VS1986 (1929)	—	0.30	0.75	2.50	3.50	6.00
VS1999 (1942)	—	0.40	1.00	3.50	5.00	7.50

KM# 176.1 1/4 ANNA

Copper **Obverse:** Fine style bust of Jivaji Rao left **Reverse:** Arms **Note:** Thick planchet. 4.65-5.15 grams.

Date	Mintage	VG	F	VF	XF	Unc
VS1986 (1929)	—	0.10	0.25	0.75	1.50	3.00

KM# 176.2 1/4 ANNA

Copper **Obverse:** Crude style "pug-nose" bust of Jivaji Rao left **Reverse:** Arms

Date	Mintage	VG	F	VF	XF	Unc
VS1986 (1929)	—	0.10	0.25	0.75	1.50	3.00

KM# 178.1 1/4 ANNA

Copper **Obverse:** Facing coiled cobras below bust of Jivaji Rao left **Reverse:** Arms, without inscription on side

Date	Mintage	VG	F	VF	XF	Unc
VS1999 (1942)	—	0.10	0.20	0.60	1.00	2.00

KM# 178.2 1/4 ANNA

Copper **Obverse:** Without facing coiled cobras below bust of Jivaji Rao left **Reverse:** Arms

Date	Mintage	VG	F	VF	XF	Unc
VS1999 (1942)	—	0.10	0.20	0.60	1.00	2.00

KM# 179 1/2 ANNA

Brass **Obverse:** Bust of Jivaji Rao left **Reverse:** Arms

Date	Mintage	VG	F	VF	XF	Unc
VS1999 (1942)	—	0.10	0.20	0.60	1.00	2.00
VS1999 (1942) Proof	—	Value: 50.00				

PATTERNS

Including off metal strikes

KM#	Date	Mintage	Identification	Mkt Val
Pn1	VS1977(1920)	—	4 Anna. Silver.	—

HYDERABAD

Haidarabad

Hyderabad State, the largest Indian State and the last remnant of Mughal suzerainty in South or Central India, traced its foundation to Nizam-ul Mulk, the Mughal viceroy in the Deccan. From about 1724 the first nizam, as the rulers of Hyderabad came to be called, took advantage of Mughal decline in the North to assert an all but ceremonial independence of the emperor. The East India Company defeated Hyderabad's natural enemies, the Muslim rulers of Mysore and the Marathas, with the help of troops furnished under alliances between them and the Nizam. This formed the beginning of a relationship, which persisted for a century and a half until India's Independence. Hyderabad was the premier Princely State, with a population (in 1935) of fourteen and a half million. It was not absorbed into the Indian Union until 1948. Hyderabad City is located beside Golkonda, the citadel of the Qutb Shahi sultans until they were overthrown by Aurangzeb in 1687. A beautifully located city on the bank of the Musi river, the mint epithet was appropriately Farkhanda Bunyad, "of happy foundation".

Hyderabad exercised authority over a number of feudatories or samasthans. Some of these, such as Gadwal and Shorapur, paid tribute to both the Nizam and the Marathas. These feudatories were generally in the hands of local rajas whose ancestry predated the establishment of Hyderabad State. There were also many mints in the State, both private and government. There was little or no standardization of the purity of silver coinage until the 20th century. At least one banker, Pestonji Meherji by name, was distinguished by minting his own coins.

RULERS

Mir Mahbub Ali Khan II, AH1285-1329/1869-1911AD
Mir Usman Ali Khan, AH1329-1367/1911-1948AD

MINT

فرخنده بنیاد حیدراباد

Haidarabad
Mintname: Farkhanda Bunyad Haidarabad

NIZAMATE
Mir Mahbub Ali Khan II
AH1285-1329 / 1869-1911AD
HAMMERED COINAGE

Y# 13 1/16 RUPEE

0.6980 g., 0.8180 Silver .0183 oz. ASW **Obverse:** Persian letter "M" for Mahbub above "k" of "Mulk" **Obv. Inscription:** "Asaf Jah, Nizam al-Mulk" **Mint:** Haidarabad (Farkhanda Bunyad)

Date	Mintage	Good	VG	F	VF	XF
AH1321//37	—	0.50	1.00	1.75	2.50	4.00

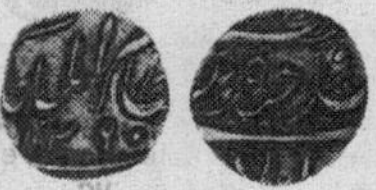

Y# 14 1/8 RUPEE

1.3970 g., 0.8180 Silver .0367 oz. ASW **Obverse:** Persian letter "M" for Mahbub above "k" of "Mulk" **Obv. Inscription:** "Asaf Jah, Nizam al-Mulk" **Mint:** Haidarabad (Farkhanda Bunyad)

Date	Mintage	Good	VG	F	VF	XF
AH1321//37	—	1.00	1.75	2.25	3.00	4.50

Y# 15 1/4 RUPEE

2.7940 g., 0.8180 Silver .0735 oz. ASW **Obverse:** Persian letter "M" for Mahbub above "k" of "Mulk" **Obv. Inscription:** "Asaf Jah, Nizam al-Mulk" **Mint:** Haidarabad (Farkhanda Bunyad)

Date	Mintage	Good	VG	F	VF	XF
AH1321//37	—	1.25	2.00	2.75	4.50	7.00

Y# 18 1/16 ASHRAFI

0.6980 g., 0.9100 Gold **Obverse:** Persian letter "M" for Mahbub above "k" of "Mulk" **Obv. Inscription:** "Asaf Jah, Nizam al-Mulk" **Mint:** Haidarabad (Farkhanda Bunyad)

Date	Mintage	Good	VG	F	VF	XF
AH1321//37	—	15.00	22.00	32.00	40.00	60.00

Y# 19 1/8 ASHRAFI

1.3970 g., 0.9100 Gold .0408 oz. AGW **Obverse:** Persian letter "M" for Mahbub above "k" of "Mulk" **Obv. Inscription:** "Asaf Jah, Nizam al-Mulk" **Mint:** Haidarabad (Farkhanda Bunyad)

Date	Mintage	Good	VG	F	VF	XF
AH1320	—	BV	30.00	45.00	60.00	80.00
AH1321	—	BV	30.00	45.00	60.00	80.00

Y# 20 1/4 ASHRAFI

2.7940 g., 0.9100 Gold .0817 oz. AGW **Obverse:** Persian letter "M" for Mahbub above "k" of "Mulk" **Obv. Inscription:** "Asaf Jah, Nizam al-Mulk" **Mint:** Haidarabad (Farkhanda Bunyad)

Date	Mintage	Good	VG	F	VF	XF
AH1319//35	—	—	BV	65.00	85.00	110
AH1318//35 (sic)	—	—	BV	65.00	85.00	110

Y# 21 1/2 ASHRAFI

5.5890 g., 0.9100 Gold .1635 oz. AGW **Obverse:** Persian letter "M" for Mahbub above "k" of "Mulk" **Obv. Inscription:** "Asaf Jah, Nizam al-Mulk" **Mint:** Haidarabad (Farkhanda Bunyad)

Date	Mintage	Good	VG	F	VF	XF
AH1320	—	—	135	150	175	225
AH1321	—	—	135	150	175	225

Y# 22 ASHRAFI

11.1780 g., 0.9100 Gold .3270 oz. AGW **Obverse:** Persian letter "M" for Mahbub above "k" of "Mulk" **Obv. Inscription:** "Asaf Jah, Nizam al-Mulk" **Mint:** Haidarabad (Farkhanda Bunyad)

Date	Mintage	Good	VG	F	VF	XF
AH1319	—	—	BV	235	250	300
AH1320	—	—	BV	235	250	300
AH1321	—	—	BV	235	250	300

MILLED COINAGE

Provisional Series

Y# 29 2 ANNAS

1.3970 g., 0.8180 Silver **Obverse:** Persian letter "M" for Mahbub above "k" of "Mulk" **Obv. Inscription:** "Asaf Jah, Nizam al-Mulk", (Founder of the Nizami line) **Mint:** Haidarabad (Farkhanda Bunyad)

Date	Mintage	VG	F	VF	XF	Unc
AH1318//35 (sic)	—	10.00	17.50	27.50	37.50	—

Y# 30 4 ANNAS

2.7940 g., 0.8180 Silver **Obverse:** Persian letter "M" for Mahbub above "k" of "Mulk" **Obv. Inscription:** "Asaf Jah, Nizam al-Mulk" **Mint:** Haidarabad (Farkhanda Bunyad)

Date	Mintage	VG	F	VF	XF	Unc
AH1318//35 (sic)	—	8.50	16.50	25.00	35.00	—

Y# 31 8 ANNAS

5.5890 g., 0.8180 Silver **Obverse:** Persian letter "M" for Mahbub above "k" of "Mulk" **Obv. Inscription:** "Asaf Jah, Nizam al-Mulk" **Mint:** Haidarabad (Farkhanda Bunyad)

Date	Mintage	VG	F	VF	XF	Unc
AH1318//35 (sic)	—	10.00	20.00	30.00	40.00	—

MILLED COINAGE

Standard Series

Y# 34 PAI

Copper **Obverse:** Toughra **Mint:** Haidarabad (Farkhanda Bunyad)

Date	Mintage	VG	F	VF	XF	Unc
AH1326//42	—	1.50	4.00	6.00	9.00	15.00
AH1327//42	—	1.50	4.00	6.00	9.00	15.00

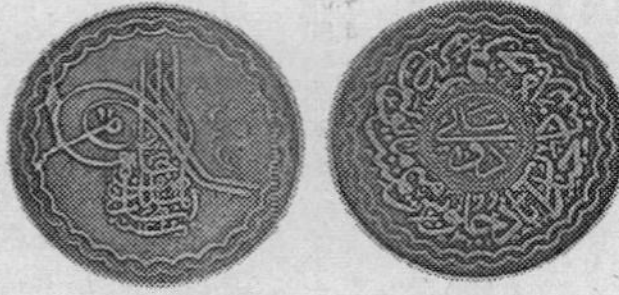

Y# 35 2 PAI

Copper **Obverse:** Toughra **Mint:** Haidarabad (Farkhanda Bunyad)

Date	Mintage	VG	F	VF	XF	Unc
AH1322//37	—	0.40	1.00	1.25	1.75	3.00
AH1322//38	—	0.30	0.75	1.00	1.50	2.50
AH1322//39 (sic)	—	0.40	1.00	1.25	1.75	3.00
AH1322//42	—	0.40	1.00	1.25	1.75	2.00
AH1323//38	—	0.40	1.00	1.25	1.75	3.00
AH1323//39	—	0.25	0.60	0.75	1.00	3.00
AH1323//40 (sic)	—	0.30	0.75	1.00	1.50	2.50
AH1323//41(sic)	—	0.30	0.75	1.00	1.50	2.50
AH1324//39	—	0.40	1.00	1.25	1.75	3.00
AH1324//40	—	0.25	0.60	0.85	1.25	2.25
AH1324//41 (sic)	—	0.30	0.75	1.00	1.50	2.50
AH1325//40	—	0.40	1.00	1.25	1.75	3.00
AH1325//41	—	0.30	0.75	1.00	1.50	2.50
AH1328//42	—	0.30	0.75	1.00	1.50	2.50
AH1329//43 (sic)	—	0.20	0.50	0.65	1.00	2.00
AH1329//44	—	0.20	0.50	0.65	1.00	2.00
AH1329//45 (sic)	—	0.20	0.50	0.65	1.00	2.00

Y# 36 1/2 ANNA

Copper **Obverse:** Toughra **Mint:** Haidarabad (Farkhanda Bunyad)

Date	Mintage	VG	F	VF	XF	Unc
AH1324//38 (sic)	—	1.00	2.50	4.00	7.00	12.00
AH1324//40	—	0.60	1.50	2.25	3.00	5.00
AH1325//40	—	0.80	2.00	3.25	3.75	6.00
AH1325//41 (sic)	—	0.80	2.00	3.25	3.75	5.50
AH1324//41	—	0.90	2.25	3.00	3.50	6.00
AH1326//41	—	1.00	2.50	3.75	4.50	7.00
AH1329//44	—	0.60	1.50	2.50	3.00	5.00

Y# 37 2 ANNAS

1.3900 g., 0.8180 Silver .0367 oz. ASW, 15 mm. **Obverse:** Chahar Minar gateway **Mint:** Haidarabad (Farkhanda Bunyad)

Date	Mintage	VG	F	VF	XF	Unc
AH1323//34	—	1.25	1.75	3.50	6.00	10.00
Note: R.Y. '34' error for '39'						
AH1323//39	—	1.00	1.35	1.85	3.00	6.00

Y# 38.1 4 ANNAS

2.7940 g., 0.8180 Silver .0735 oz. ASW, 20 mm. **Obverse:** Chahar Minar gateway, signature variety Type I between minarets **Mint:** Haidarabad (Farkhanda Bunyad)

Date	Mintage	VG	F	VF	XF	Unc
AH1323//39	—	2.00	3.50	5.50	7.50	12.50
AH1326//43 (sic)	—	3.50	8.50	16.50	25.00	40.00

Y# 38.2 4 ANNAS

2.7940 g., 0.8180 Silver .0735 oz. ASW, 20 mm. **Obverse:** Chahar Minar gateway, signature variety Type I between minarets **Mint:** Haidarabad (Farkhanda Bunyad) **Note:** Struck with dies of 1/2 Ashrafi.

Date	Mintage	VG	F	VF	XF	Unc
AH1324//40 Rare	—	—	—	—	—	—

Y# 38.3 4 ANNAS

2.7940 g., 0.8180 Silver .0735 oz. ASW, 20 mm. **Obverse:** Chahar Minar gateway, signature variety Type II between minarets **Mint:** Haidarabad (Farkhanda Bunyad)

Date	Mintage	VG	F	VF	XF	Unc
AH1328//43	—	2.00	4.00	5.00	6.50	11.50
AH1329//44	—	2.00	4.00	5.00	6.00	10.00

Y# 39.1 8 ANNAS

5.5890 g., 0.8180 Silver .1470 oz. ASW, 24 mm. **Obverse:** Chahar Minar gateway, signature variety Type I **Mint:** Haidarabad (Farkhanda Bunyad)

Date	Mintage	VG	F	VF	XF	Unc
AH1322//38	—	—	—	—	—	—

Y# 39.2 8 ANNAS

5.5890 g., 0.8180 Silver .1470 oz. ASW, 24 mm. **Obverse:** Chahar Minar gateway, signature variety Type II between minarets **Mint:** Haidarabad (Farkhanda Bunyad)

Date	Mintage	VG	F	VF	XF	Unc
AH1328//43	—	4.00	5.50	7.50	10.00	16.50
AH1329//44	—	4.00	5.50	7.50	10.00	16.50

Y# 40.1 RUPEE

11.1780 g., 0.8180 Silver .2940 oz. ASW, 30 mm. **Obverse:** Chahar Minar gateway, signature variety Type I between minarets **Mint:** Haidarabad (Farkhanda Bunyad)

Date	Mintage	VG	F	VF	XF	Unc
AH1319//35	—	6.50	10.00	13.50	18.50	30.00
AH1321//37	—	6.50	10.00	13.50	18.50	30.00
AH1322//38 (sic)	—	6.00	9.00	12.50	15.00	25.00
AH1321//38	—	6.00	9.00	12.50	15.00	25.00
AH1323//39 (sic)	—	6.00	9.00	12.50	15.00	25.00
AH1322//39	—	6.00	9.00	12.50	15.00	25.00
AH1324//40	—	6.00	9.00	12.50	15.00	25.00
AH1325//41	—	6.00	9.00	12.50	15.00	25.00
AH1326//41	—	6.00	9.00	12.50	15.00	25.00

Y# 40.2 RUPEE

11.1780 g., 0.8180 Silver .2940 oz. ASW, 30 mm. **Obverse:** Chahar Minar gateway, signature variety Type II between minarets **Mint:** Haidarabad (Farkhanda Bunyad)

Date	Mintage	VG	F	VF	XF	Unc
AH1328//43	—	6.00	9.00	12.50	15.00	25.00
AH1329//44	—	6.00	9.00	12.50	15.00	25.00

Y# 41.1 1/8 ASHRAFI

1.3940 g., 0.9100 Gold **Obverse:** Chahar Minar gateway, signature variety Type I between minarets **Mint:** Haidarabad (Farkhanda Bunyad)

Date	Mintage	VG	F	VF	XF	Unc
AH1325//41	—	30.00	38.00	55.00	75.00	100

Y# 41.2 1/8 ASHRAFI

1.3940 g., 0.9100 Gold **Obverse:** Chahar Minar gateway, signature variety Type II between minarets **Mint:** Haidarabad (Farkhanda Bunyad)

Date	Mintage	VG	F	VF	XF	Unc
AH1329//44	—	30.00	38.00	55.00	75.00	100

Y# 42.1 1/4 ASHRAFI

2.7940 g., 0.9100 Gold **Obverse:** Chahar Minar gateway, signature variety Type I between minarets **Mint:** Haidarabad (Farkhanda Bunyad)

Date	Mintage	VG	F	VF	XF	Unc
AH1325//41	—	60.00	70.00	85.00	110	150

Y# 42.2 1/4 ASHRAFI

2.7940 g., 0.9100 Gold **Obverse:** Chahar Minar gateway, signature variety Type II between minarets **Mint:** Haidarabad (Farkhanda Bunyad)

Date	Mintage	VG	F	VF	XF	Unc
AH1328//43	—	60.00	70.00	85.00	100	150
AH1329//44	—	60.00	70.00	85.00	100	150

Y# 43.1 1/2 ASHRAFI

5.5890 g., 0.9100 Gold **Obverse:** Chahar Minar gateway, signature variety Type I between minarets **Mint:** Haidarabad (Farkhanda Bunyad)

Date	Mintage	VG	F	VF	XF	Unc
AH1325//41	—	120	135	160	185	275
AH1326//41	—	120	135	160	185	275

Y# 43.2 1/2 ASHRAFI

5.5890 g., 0.9100 Gold **Obverse:** Chahar Minar gateway, signature variety Type II between minarets **Mint:** Haidarabad (Farkhanda Bunyad)

Date	Mintage	VG	F	VF	XF	Unc
AH1328//43	—	120	135	160	185	275
AH1329//44	—	120	135	160	185	275

Y# 44.1 ASHRAFI

11.1780 g., 0.9100 Gold **Obverse:** Chahar Minar gateway, signature variety Type I between minarets **Mint:** Haidarabad (Farkhanda Bunyad)

Date	Mintage	VG	F	VF	XF	Unc
AH1325//41	—	225	250	275	325	400

Y# 44.2 ASHRAFI

11.1780 g., 0.9100 Gold **Obverse:** Chahar Minar gateway, signature variety Type II between minarets **Mint:** Haidarabad (Farkhanda Bunyad)

Date	Mintage	VG	F	VF	XF	Unc
AH1328//43	—	225	250	275	325	400
AH1329//44	—	225	250	275	325	400

Mir Usman Ali Khan
AH1329-1367 / 1911-1948AD

MILLED COINAGE
First Series

Y# 45 PAI

Bronze **Obverse:** Toughra **Mint:** Haidarabad (Farkhanda Bunyad)

Date	Mintage	VG	F	VF	XF	Unc
AH1338	—	0.60	1.50	2.00	2.50	4.00
AH1344//15	—	0.25	0.60	0.75	1.00	2.00
AH1349//20	—	0.25	0.60	0.75	1.00	2.00
AH1352//23	—	0.40	1.00	1.25	1.50	3.00
AH1352//24	—	0.40	1.00	1.25	1.50	3.00
AH1353//23 (sic)	—	0.40	1.00	1.25	1.50	2.25
AH1353//24	—	0.30	0.70	0.85	1.10	3.00

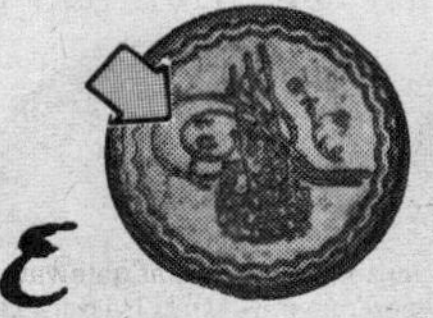
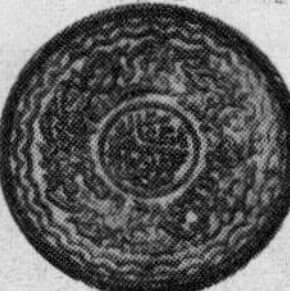

Y# 46a 2 PAI

Bronze **Obverse:** Full "Ain" in toughra **Mint:** Haidarabad (Farkhanda Bunyad)

Date	Mintage	VG	F	VF	XF	Unc
AH1330//1	—	0.60	1.50	2.00	2.50	5.00
AH1331//2	—	0.15	0.35	0.50	0.65	1.25
AH1330//2	—	0.15	0.35	0.50	0.65	1.25
AH1332//3	—	0.15	0.35	0.50	0.65	1.25
AH1331//3	—	0.20	0.50	0.65	0.75	1.25
AH1333//3 (sic)	—	0.25	0.60	0.75	1.00	2.00
AH1332//4	—	0.25	0.60	0.75	1.00	2.00
AH1333//4	—	0.15	0.35	0.50	0.65	1.25
AH1334//3 (sic)	—	0.25	0.60	0.75	1.00	2.50
AH1333//5	—	0.30	0.75	1.00	1.25	2.00
AH1335//6	—	0.15	0.35	0.50	0.65	1.25
AH1336//7	—	0.15	0.35	0.50	0.65	1.25
AH1335//7	—	0.15	0.35	0.50	0.65	1.25
AH1337//7	—	0.30	0.75	1.00	1.25	1.65
AH1336//8	—	0.20	0.50	0.65	0.80	2.50
AH1337//8	—	0.25	0.60	0.75	1.00	2.00
AH1338//8	—	0.30	0.75	1.00	1.25	2.50
AH1338//9	—	0.15	0.35	0.50	0.65	1.25
AH1339//10	—	0.30	0.75	1.00	1.25	2.00
AH1338//11 (sic)	—	0.20	0.50	0.75	1.00	2.50
AH1339//11	—	0.30	0.75	1.00	1.25	2.50
AH1342//13	—	0.25	0.60	0.75	1.00	2.00
AH1343//14	—	0.15	0.35	0.50	0.65	1.25
AH1342//14	—	0.15	0.35	0.50	0.65	1.25
AH1344//15	—	0.20	0.50	0.65	0.80	1.50
AH1343//15	—	0.25	0.40	0.60	0.75	1.65
AH1345//16	—	0.15	0.35	0.50	0.65	1.25
AH1347//18	—	0.30	0.75	1.00	1.25	2.50
AH1348//19	—	0.15	0.35	0.50	0.65	2.50
AH1347//19	—	0.30	0.75	1.00	1.25	1.25
AH1349//20	—	0.15	0.35	0.50	0.65	1.25

Y# 46 2 PAI

Bronze **Obverse:** Short "Ain" in toughra **Mint:** Haidarabad (Farkhanda Bunyad) **Note:** See also 1 Rupee, Y#53 and Y#53a.

Date	Mintage	VG	F	VF	XF	Unc
AH1330//1	—	3.25	8.00	12.50	20.00	40.00
AH1329//1	—	—	4.00	10.00	15.00	22.50

Y# 47 1/2 ANNA

Bronze **Obverse:** Toughra **Mint:** Haidarabad (Farkhanda Bunyad)

Date	Mintage	VG	F	VF	XF	Unc
AH1332//2 (sic)	—	0.30	0.75	1.00	1.50	3.00
AH1332//3	—	0.30	0.75	1.00	1.50	3.00
AH1334//4 (sic)	—	0.50	1.25	1.50	2.50	5.00
AH1344//15	—	0.50	1.25	1.50	2.50	5.00
AH1348//20	—	0.40	1.00	1.35	2.00	4.00

Y# 48 ANNA

Copper-Nickel **Obverse:** Toughra **Mint:** Haidarabad (Farkhanda Bunyad) **Note:** Round flan.

Date	Mintage	VG	F	VF	XF	Unc
AH1338	—	0.20	0.50	0.75	1.00	2.00
AH1339	—	0.40	1.00	1.35	1.75	3.50
AH1340	—	0.25	0.60	0.85	1.25	2.50
AH1341	—	0.30	0.75	1.00	1.35	2.75
AH1344	—	0.20	0.50	0.75	1.00	2.00
AH1347	—	0.20	0.50	0.75	1.00	2.00
AH1348	—	0.25	0.60	0.85	1.25	2.50
AH1349	—	0.20	0.50	0.75	1.00	2.00
AH1351	—	0.20	0.50	0.75	1.00	2.00
AH1352	—	0.40	1.00	1.35	1.75	3.50
AH1353	—	0.20	0.50	0.75	1.00	2.00
AH1354	—	0.20	0.50	0.75	1.00	2.00

Y# 49 ANNA

Copper-Nickel **Obverse:** Toughra **Mint:** Haidarabad (Farkhanda Bunyad) **Note:** Square flan.

Date	Mintage	VG	F	VF	XF	Unc
AH1356	—	0.15	0.35	0.50	0.65	1.25
AH1357	—	0.20	0.50	0.65	0.85	1.75
AH1358	—	0.15	0.35	0.50	0.65	1.25
AH1359	—	0.30	0.75	1.00	1.25	2.50
AH1360	—	0.30	0.75	1.00	1.25	2.50
AH1361	—	0.30	0.75	1.00	1.25	2.50

Y# 50 2 ANNAS

1.3970 g., 0.8180 Silver .0367 oz. ASW **Obverse:** Chahar Minar gateway **Mint:** Haidarabad (Farkhanda Bunyad)

Date	Mintage	VG	F	VF	XF	Unc
AH1335//6	—	0.75	1.25	1.75	2.50	5.00
AH1337//9	—	0.65	1.00	1.50	2.50	5.00
AH1338//10	—	0.65	1.00	1.50	2.50	5.00
AH1340//11	—	0.65	1.00	1.50	2.50	5.00
AH1341//13	—	0.65	1.00	1.50	2.50	5.00
AH1342//13	—	0.75	1.00	1.50	2.50	6.00
AH1341//14 (sic)	—	0.65	1.25	2.00	3.00	5.00
AH1343//14	—	0.65	1.00	1.50	2.25	4.50
AH1343//15	—	0.65	1.00	1.50	2.25	4.50
AH1347	—	0.75	1.25	2.00	3.00	6.00
AH1348//19	—	0.65	1.00	1.50	2.25	4.50
AH1351//22	—	0.65	1.00	1.50	2.50	5.00
AH1355//26	—	0.65	1.00	1.50	2.50	5.00

Y# 51 4 ANNAS

2.7940 g., 0.8180 Silver .0735 oz. ASW **Obverse:** Chahar Minar gateway **Mint:** Haidarabad (Farkhanda Bunyad)

Date	Mintage	VG	F	VF	XF	Unc
AH1337//9	—	1.25	1.75	3.00	4.50	7.50
AH1340//11	—	1.25	1.75	3.00	4.50	7.50
AH1342//13	—	1.25	1.75	3.00	4.50	7.50
AH1342//14	—	1.25	1.75	3.00	4.50	7.50
AH1348//19	—	1.25	1.75	3.00	4.50	7.50
AH1351//22	—	1.25	1.75	3.00	4.50	7.50
AH1354//25	—	1.25	1.75	3.00	4.50	7.50
AH1358//30	—	1.25	1.75	3.00	4.50	7.50

Y# 52 8 ANNAS

5.5890 g., 0.8180 Silver .1470 oz. ASW **Obverse:** Chahar Minar gateway **Mint:** Haidarabad (Farkhanda Bunyad)

Date	Mintage	VG	F	VF	XF	Unc
AH1337//9	—	2.25	3.50	5.00	8.00	13.50
AH1342//13	—	2.25	3.50	5.00	8.00	13.50
AH1343//13 (sic)	—	2.25	3.50	5.00	8.00	13.50
AH1354//25	—	2.25	3.50	5.00	8.00	13.50

Y# 53 RUPEE

11.1780 g., 0.8180 Silver .2940 oz. ASW **Obverse:** Chahar Minar gateway with short initials "Ain" in doorway **Mint:** Haidarabad (Farkhanda Bunyad)

Date	Mintage	VG	F	VF	XF	Unc
AH1330//1	—	4.50	6.50	10.00	16.00	26.50

Y# 53a RUPEE

11.1780 g., 0.8180 Silver .2940 oz. ASW **Obverse:** Chahar Minar gateway with full "Ain" in doorway **Mint:** Haidarabad (Farkhanda Bunyad)

Date	Mintage	VG	F	VF	XF	Unc
AH1330//1	—	4.50	7.00	10.00	16.00	26.50
AH1331//2	—	4.50	7.00	10.00	12.50	26.50
AH1330//2	—	4.50	6.50	8.50	16.00	20.00
AH1332//3	—	4.50	6.00	8.00	12.50	20.00
AH1331//3	—	4.50	6.00	8.00	12.50	20.00
AH1334//6	—	4.50	6.00	8.00	12.50	20.00
AH1335//6	—	4.50	6.00	8.00	12.50	20.00
AH1335//7	—	4.50	6.00	8.00	12.50	20.00
AH1336//7	—	4.50	6.00	8.00	12.50	20.00
AH1337//8	—	4.50	6.00	8.00	12.50	20.00
AH1338//9	—	4.50	6.00	8.00	12.50	32.50
AH1337//9	—	5.00	8.50	13.50	20.00	20.00
AH1339//9 (sic)	—	4.50	6.00	8.00	12.50	20.00
AH1340//11	—	4.50	6.00	8.00	12.50	20.00
AH1341//12	—	4.50	6.00	8.00	12.50	20.00
AH1342//13	—	4.50	6.00	8.00	12.50	20.00
AH1343//14	—	4.50	6.00	8.00	12.50	20.00

Y# 54.1 1/8 ASHRAFI

1.3940 g., 0.9100 Gold .0408 oz. AGW **Obverse:** Chahar Minar gateway with short "Ain" in doorway **Mint:** Haidarabad (Farkhanda Bunyad)

Date	Mintage	VG	F	VF	XF	Unc
AH1329//1 Rare	—	—	—	—	—	—

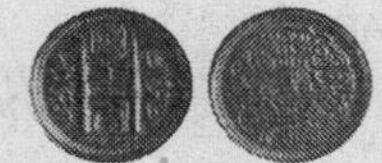

Y# 54.2 1/8 ASHRAFI

1.3940 g., 0.9100 Gold .0408 oz. AGW **Obverse:** Chahar Minar gateway with full "Ain" in doorway **Mint:** Haidarabad (Farkhanda Bunyad)

Date	Mintage	VG	F	VF	XF	Unc
AH1337//8	—	—	32.50	42.50	50.00	80.00
AH1340//11	—	—	32.50	42.50	50.00	80.00
AH1343	—	—	32.50	42.50	50.00	80.00

Date	Mintage	VG	F	VF	XF	Unc
AH1344//15	—	—	32.50	42.50	50.00	80.00
AH1353	—	—	32.50	42.50	50.00	80.00
AH1354//25	—	—	32.50	42.50	50.00	80.00
AH1356//27	—	—	32.50	42.50	50.00	80.00
AH1360	—	—	32.50	42.50	50.00	80.00
AH1366//37	—	—	32.50	42.50	50.00	80.00
AH1368//39	—	—	32.50	42.50	50.00	80.00

Y# 55 1/4 ASHRAFI

2.7940 g., 0.9100 Gold .0817 oz. AGW **Obverse:** Chahar Minar gateway **Mint:** Haidarabad (Farkhanda Bunyad)

Date	Mintage	VG	F	VF	XF	Unc
AH1337//8	—	—	60.00	75.00	90.00	135
AH1342//13	—	—	60.00	75.00	90.00	135
AH1342//14	—	—	60.00	75.00	90.00	135
AH1349//20	—	—	60.00	75.00	90.00	135
AH1353//23 (sic)	—	—	60.00	75.00	90.00	135
AH1354//25	—	—	60.00	75.00	90.00	135
AH1357	—	—	60.00	75.00	90.00	135
AH1360//31	—	—	60.00	75.00	90.00	135
AH1367//38	—	—	60.00	75.00	90.00	135

Y# 56.1 1/2 ASHRAFI

5.5890 g., 0.9100 Gold .1635 oz. AGW **Obverse:** Chahar Minar gateway with short "Ain" in doorway **Mint:** Haidarabad (Farkhanda Bunyad)

Date	Mintage	VG	F	VF	XF	Unc
AH1329//1	—	—	100	135	185	300

Y# 56.2 1/2 ASHRAFI

5.5890 g., 0.9100 Gold .1635 oz. AGW **Obverse:** Chahar Minar gateway with full "Ain" in doorway **Mint:** Haidarabad (Farkhanda Bunyad)

Date	Mintage	VG	F	VF	XF	Unc
AH1337//8	—	—	120	150	175	250
AH1342//14	—	—	120	150	175	250
AH1343//14	—	—	120	150	175	250
AH1344//14 (sic)	—	—	120	150	175	250
AH1345//16	—	—	120	150	175	250
AH1349//20	—	—	120	150	175	250
AH1354//25	—	—	120	150	175	250
AH1357//29	—	—	120	150	175	250
AH1366//37	—	—	120	150	175	250
AH1367//38	—	—	120	150	175	250

Y# 57 ASHRAFI

11.1780 g., 0.9100 Gold .3270 oz. AGW **Obverse:** Chahar Minar gateway with short initial "Ain" in doorway **Mint:** Haidarabad (Farkhanda Bunyad)

Date	Mintage	VG	F	VF	XF	Unc
AH1330//1	—	—	235	300	350	500
AH1329//1	—	—	235	300	350	500

Y# 57a ASHRAFI

11.1780 g., 0.9100 Gold .3270 oz. AGW **Obverse:** Chahar Minar gateway with full initial "Ain" in doorway **Mint:** Haidarabad (Farkhanda Bunyad)

Date	Mintage	VG	F	VF	XF	Unc
AH1331//3	—	—	225	285	325	450
AH1333//4	—	—	225	285	325	450
AH1337//8	—	—	225	285	325	450
AH1338//9	—	—	225	285	325	450
AH1337//9	—	—	225	285	325	450
AH1340//11	—	—	225	285	325	450
AH1343//14	—	—	225	285	325	450
AH1342//14	—	—	225	285	325	450

Date	Mintage	VG	F	VF	XF	Unc
AH1344//15	—	—	225	285	325	450
AH1348//19	—	—	225	285	325	450
AH1349//20	—	—	225	285	325	450
AH1354//25	—	—	225	285	325	450
AH1358//30	—	—	225	285	325	450
AH1360//31	—	—	225	285	325	450
AH1362//34	—	—	225	285	325	450

MILLED COINAGE

Second Series

Y# 58 2 PAI

Bronze **Mint:** Haidarabad (Farkhanda Bunyad)

Date	Mintage	VG	F	VF	XF	Unc
AH1362//33	—	0.10	0.25	0.35	0.50	1.00
AH1363//34	—	0.10	0.25	0.35	0.50	1.00
AH1363//35	—	0.10	0.20	0.25	0.50	1.00
AH1364//35	—	0.10	0.20	0.25	0.50	1.00
AH1365//36	—	0.10	0.20	0.25	0.50	1.00
AH1366//37	—	0.10	0.20	0.25	0.50	1.00
AH1368//39	—	0.10	0.20	0.25	0.50	1.00

Y# 59 ANNA

Bronze **Obverse:** Toughra **Mint:** Haidarabad (Farkhanda Bunyad) **Note:** Square flan.

Date	Mintage	VG	F	VF	XF	Unc
AH1361	—	0.15	0.40	0.50	0.75	1.50
AH1362	—	0.15	0.40	0.50	0.75	1.50
AH1364	—	0.15	0.40	0.50	0.75	1.50
AH1365	—	0.15	0.40	0.50	0.75	1.50
AH1366	—	0.15	0.40	0.50	0.75	1.50
AH1368	—	0.15	0.40	0.50	0.75	1.50

Y# 60 2 ANNAS

1.3970 g., 0.8180 Silver .0367 oz. ASW, 15 mm. **Mint:** Haidarabad (Farkhanda Bunyad)

Date	Mintage	VG	F	VF	XF	Unc
AH1362//33	—	0.65	0.75	0.85	1.25	2.50

Y# 64 2 ANNAS

Nickel **Mint:** Haidarabad (Farkhanda Bunyad)

Date	Mintage	VG	F	VF	XF	Unc
AH1366//37	—	0.10	0.15	0.25	0.35	0.75
AH1368//39	—	0.10	0.25	0.35	0.45	0.85

Y# 61 4 ANNAS

2.7940 g., 0.8180 Silver .0735 oz. ASW, 20 mm. **Mint:** Haidarabad (Farkhanda Bunyad)

Date	Mintage	VG	F	VF	XF	Unc
AH1362//33	—	1.25	1.50	1.85	2.25	3.50
AH1362//34	—	1.25	1.50	1.85	2.25	3.50
AH1364//33 (sic)	—	1.25	1.50	1.85	2.25	3.50
AH1364//35	—	1.25	1.50	1.85	2.25	3.50
AH1364//36	—	1.25	1.50	1.85	2.25	3.50
AH1365//36	—	1.25	1.50	1.85	2.25	3.50

Y# 65 4 ANNAS

Nickel **Mint:** Haidarabad (Farkhanda Bunyad)

Date	Mintage	VG	F	VF	XF	Unc
AH1366//37	—	0.15	0.40	0.50	0.75	1.50
AH1368//37	—	—	—	—	—	—
AH1368//39	—	0.15	0.40	0.50	0.75	1.50

Y# 62 8 ANNAS

5.5890 g., 0.8180 Silver .1470 oz. ASW, 24 mm. **Mint:** Haidarabad (Farkhanda Bunyad)

Date	Mintage	VG	F	VF	XF	Unc
AH1363//34	—	2.50	4.00	7.00	11.50	16.50

Y# 66 8 ANNAS

Nickel **Mint:** Haidarabad (Farkhanda Bunyad)

Date	Mintage	VG	F	VF	XF	Unc
AH1366//37	—	0.25	0.60	0.80	1.00	2.00

Y# 63 RUPEE

11.1780 g., Silver .2940 oz. ASW, 30 mm. **Mint:** Haidarabad (Farkhanda Bunyad)

Date	Mintage	VG	F	VF	XF	Unc
AH1361//31	—	4.50	6.00	8.50	13.50	20.00
AH1361//32	—	4.50	6.00	8.50	13.50	20.00
AH1362//34	—	4.50	6.00	8.50	13.50	20.00
AH1364//35	—	4.50	6.00	8.50	13.50	20.00
AH1364//36	—	4.50	6.00	8.50	13.50	20.00
AH1365//36	—	4.50	6.00	8.50	13.50	20.00

Y# 67 ASHRAFI

11.1780 g., 0.9100 Gold .3270 oz. AGW **Mint:** Haidarabad (Farkhanda Bunyad)

Date	Mintage	VG	F	VF	XF	Unc
AH1368//39	—	—	—	—	—	—

PATTERNS

Including off metal strikes

KM#	Date	Mintage	Identification	Mkt Val
Pn10	AH1319//35	—	Rupee. Silver. . Y#53a.	—
Pn11	AH1324//40	—	1/2 Ashrafi. Silver. Y#43.	—
Pn12	AH1324//40	—	Ashrafi. Silver. . Y#44.	—
Pn13	AH1362/33	—	2 Annas. Copper. 1.3800 g. Copper, Y#60.	—
Pn14	AH1366/37	—	2 Pai. Bronze. 0.8100 g. Small, thin flan, larger hole, Y#58.	—

INDORE

The Holkars were one of the three dominant Maratha powers (with the Peshwas and Sindhias), with major landholdings in Central India.

Indore State originated in 1728 with a grant of land north of the Narbada river by the Maratha Peshwa of Poona to Malhar Rao Holkar, a cavalry commander in his service. After Holkar's death (ca.1765) his daughter-in-law, Ahalya Bai, assumed the position of Queen Regent. Together with Tukoji Rao she effectively ruled the State until her death thirty years later. But it was left to Tukoji's son, Jaswant Rao, to challenge the dominance of the Poona Marathas in the Maratha Confederacy, eventually defeating the

Peshwa's army in 1802. But at this point the fortunes of the Holkars suffered a serious reverse. Although Jaswant Rao had initially defeated a small British force under Col. William Monson, he was badly beaten by a contingent under Lord Lake. As a result Holkar was forced to cede a considerable portion of his territory and from this time until India's independence in 1947, the residual State of Indore was obliged to accept British protection.

For more detailed data on the Indore series, see *A Study of Holkar State Coinage*, by P.K.Sethi, S.K. Bhatt and R. Holkar (1976).

HOLKAR RULERS

Shivaji Rao, VS1943-1960/FE1296-1313/1886-1903AD
Tukoji Rao III, VS1960-1983/1903-1926AD
Yashwant Rao, VS1983-2005/1926-1948AD

HONORIFIC TITLE

Bahadur

MINT

اندور or इंदौर

Indore

INDORE MINT

Coins issued intermittently from 1772-1935AD.

BRITISH PROTECTORATE

Shivaji Rao

VS1943-1960 / FE1296-1313 / 1886-1903AD

MILLED COINAGE

KM# 33.3 1/4 ANNA

Copper, 27 mm. **Obverse:** Continuous legend around reclining bull **Obv. Legend:** Shivaji Rao...Bahadur **Reverse:** "Indore" above denomination and date **Mint:** Indore **Note:** Floral border varieties exist. Weight varies 6.026-6.674 grams.

Date	Mintage	Good	VG	F	VF	XF
VS1958(1901)	—	0.65	1.25	1.75	3.50	7.00
VS1959(1902)	—	0.65	1.25	1.75	3.50	7.00

KM# 35.3 1/2 ANNA

Copper, 31 mm. **Obverse:** Continuous legend around reclining bull **Obv. Legend:** Shivaji Rao **Reverse:** "Indore" above denomination and date **Mint:** Indore

Date	Mintage	Good	VG	F	VF	XF
VS1958(1901)	—	1.00	1.50	2.00	4.00	8.00
VS1959(1902)	—	1.00	1.50	2.00	4.00	8.00

MILLED COINAGE

Third Series

This series was introduced in 1898 to counteract counterfeiting of the second series which had begun to proliferate as a result of a sharp fall in the price of silver. Idle minting machines were reactivated for this purpose, but the series was short-lived.

KM# 47.2 RUPEE

11.2000 g., Silver **Obverse:** Bust facing; continuous legend **Reverse:** Arms **Mint:** Indore

Date	Mintage	VG	F	VF	XF	Unc
VS1958(1901)	—	70.00	140	200	275	450

Yashwant Rao

VS1983-2005 / 1926-1948AD

MILLED COINAGE

Fourth Series

KM# 49 1/4 ANNA

Copper **Obverse:** Bust facing 3/4 right **Mint:** Indore

Date	Mintage	VG	F	VF	XF	Unc
VS1992(1935)	—	0.40	1.00	2.25	4.50	7.50

KM# 50 1/2 ANNA

Copper **Obverse:** Bust facing **Mint:** Indore

Date	Mintage	VG	F	VF	XF	Unc
VS1992(1935)	—	0.50	1.25	2.50	5.00	8.50

JAIPUR

Tradition has it that the region of Jaipur, located in northwest India, once belonged to an ancient Kachwaha Rajput dynasty which claimed descent from Kush, one of the sons of Rama, King of Ayodhya. But the Princely State of Jaipur originated in the 12th century. Comparatively small in size, the State remained largely unnoticed until after the 16th century when the Jaipur royal house became famous for its military skills and thereafter supplied the Mughals with some of their more distinguished generals. The city of Jaipur was founded about 1728 by Maharaja Jai Singh II who was well known for his knowledge of mathematics and astronomy. The late 18th and early 19th centuries were difficult times for Jaipur. They were marked by internal rivalry, exacerbated by Maratha or Pindari incursions. In 1818 this culminated with a treaty whereby Jaipur came under British protection and oversight.

RULERS

Madho Singh II, 1880-1922AD
Man Singh II, 1922-1949AD

MINT NAMES

Coins were struck at two mints, which bear the following characteristic marks on the reverse:
Sawai Jaipur
Sawai Madhopur

JAIPUR MINT

In the names of Queen Victoria

كوين وكٹوريا

مادهو سنگه

And Madho Singh II

Years 1-43/1880-1922AD

NOTE: Queen Victoria's name was retained on Madho Singh II's coinage until 1922AD. No coins were struck with Edward VII's name by Madho Singh II.

Madho Singh

1880-1922AD

HAMMERED COINAGE

Regal Style

To distinguish coins betweenRam Singh and his son/successor Madho Singh II, note that the coins of Ram Singh have a small slanting cross or dagger between the Ram and Singh symbols, whereas the coins of Singh II do not.

KM# 130 PAISA

Copper **Obverse:** Inscription: Queen Victoria... **Reverse:** Jhar, inscription **Rev. Inscription:** "Madho Singh II" **Mint:** Sawai Jaipur **Note:** Weight varies 6.15-6.30g .

Date	Mintage	Good	VG	F	VF	XF
ND//22 (1901)	—	0.30	0.65	1.35	2.00	—
ND//23 (1902)	—	0.30	0.65	1.35	2.00	—
ND//24 (1903)	—	0.30	0.65	1.35	2.00	—
ND//25 (1904)	—	0.30	0.65	1.35	2.00	—
ND//25 (1904)	—	0.30	0.65	1.35	2.00	—
ND//27 (1906)	—	0.30	0.65	1.35	2.00	—
ND//28 (1907)	—	0.30	0.65	1.35	2.00	—
ND//29 (1908)	—	0.30	0.65	1.35	2.00	—
ND//37 (1916)	—	0.30	0.65	1.35	2.00	—
ND//38 (1917)	—	0.30	0.65	1.35	2.00	—
ND//39 (1918)	—	0.30	0.65	1.35	2.00	—
ND//41 (1920)	—	0.30	0.65	1.35	2.00	—

KM# 135 1/16 RUPEE

Silver **Obv. Inscription:** Victoria... **Reverse:** Jhar **Rev. Inscription:** "Madho Singh II" **Mint:** Sawai Jaipur **Note:** Weight varies 0.67-0.72g.

Date	Mintage	Good	VG	F	VF	XF
ND//23 (1912)	—	2.00	5.00	7.00	10.00	15.00

KM# 137 1/8 RUPEE

Silver **Obv. Inscription:** Victoria... **Reverse:** Jhar **Rev. Inscription:** "Madho Singh II" **Mint:** Sawai Jaipur **Note:** Weight varies 1.34-1.45g.

Date	Mintage	Good	VG	F	VF	XF
ND//22 (1901)	—	1.20	2.50	3.50	5.00	8.00
ND//23 (1902)	—	1.20	2.50	3.50	5.00	8.00
ND//26 (1905)	—	1.20	2.50	3.50	5.00	8.00
ND//27 (1906)	—	1.20	2.50	3.50	5.00	8.00
ND//28 (1907)	—	2.25	2.50	3.50	5.00	8.00
ND//29 (1908)	—	2.25	2.50	3.50	5.00	8.00
ND//41 (1920)	—	2.25	2.50	3.50	5.00	8.00
ND//42 (1921)	—	2.25	2.50	3.50	5.00	8.00
ND(1933)/4	—	2.50	3.50	5.00	8.00	—

KM# 137 1/8 RUPEE

Silver **Obv. Inscription:** Victoria... **Reverse:** Jhar **Rev. Inscription:** "Madho Singh II" **Mint:** Sawai Jaipur **Note:** Weight varies 1.34-1.45g.

Date	Mintage	VG	F	VF	XF	Unc
ND//22 (1901)	—	1.20	2.50	3.50	5.00	8.00
ND//23 (1902)	—	1.20	2.50	3.50	5.00	8.00
ND//26 (1905)	—	1.20	2.50	3.50	5.00	8.00
ND//27 (1906)	—	1.20	2.50	3.50	5.00	8.00
ND//28 (1907)	—	2.25	2.50	3.50	5.00	8.00
ND//29 (1908)	—	2.25	2.50	3.50	5.00	8.00
ND//41 (1920)	—	2.25	2.50	3.50	5.00	8.00
ND//42 (1921)	—	2.25	2.50	3.50	5.00	8.00
ND(1933)/4	—	2.50	3.50	5.00	8.00	—

KM# 139 1/4 RUPEE

Silver **Obv. Inscription:** Victoria... **Reverse:** Jhar **Rev. Inscription:** "Madho Singh II" **Mint:** Sawai Jaipur **Note:** Weight varies 2.68-2.90g.

Date	Mintage	Good	VG	F	VF	XF
ND//22 (1901)	—	1.50	3.00	4.50	6.50	10.00
ND//23 (1902)	—	1.50	3.00	4.50	6.50	10.00
ND//24 (1903)	—	1.50	3.00	4.50	6.50	10.00
ND//26 (1905)	—	1.50	3.00	4.50	6.50	10.00
ND//27 (1906)	—	1.50	3.00	4.50	6.50	10.00
ND//28 (1907)	—	1.50	3.00	4.50	6.50	10.00
ND//29 (1908)	—	1.50	3.00	4.50	6.50	10.00
ND//30 (1909)	—	1.50	3.00	4.50	6.50	10.00
ND//34 (1913)	—	1.50	3.00	4.50	6.50	10.00
ND//37 (1916)	—	1.50	3.00	4.50	6.50	10.00
ND//38 (1917)	—	1.50	3.00	4.50	6.50	10.00
ND//42 (1921)	—	1.50	3.00	4.50	6.50	10.00

KM# 142 1/2 RUPEE

Silver **Obv. Inscription:** Victoria... **Reverse:** Jhar **Rev. Inscription:** "Madho Singh II" **Mint:** Sawai Jaipur **Note:** Weight varies 5.35-5.80g.

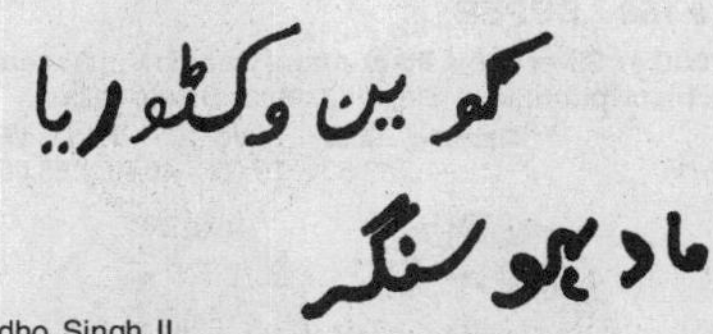

Date	Mintage	Good	VG	F	VF	XF
ND//22 (1901)	—	2.25	3.50	5.00	7.50	12.50
ND//23 (1902)	—	2.25	3.50	5.00	7.50	12.50
ND//25 (1904)	—	2.25	3.50	5.00	7.50	12.50
ND//26 (1905)	—	2.25	3.50	5.00	7.50	12.50
ND//27 (1906)	—	2.25	3.50	5.00	7.50	12.50
ND//28 (1907)	—	2.25	3.50	5.00	7.50	12.50
ND//29 (1908)	—	2.25	3.50	5.00	7.50	12.50
ND//30 (1909)	—	2.25	3.50	5.00	7.50	12.50
ND//34 (1913)	—	2.25	3.50	5.00	7.50	12.50
ND//37 (1916)	—	2.25	3.50	5.00	7.50	12.50

KM# 145 RUPEE

Silver **Obv. Inscription:** Victoria... **Reverse:** Jhar **Rev. Inscription:** "Madho Singh II" **Mint:** Sawai Jaipur **Note:** Weight varies 10.70-11.60g.

Date	Mintage	Good	VG	F	VF	XF
ND//23 (1902)	—	4.50	6.00	8.00	11.00	15.00
ND//24 (1903)	—	4.50	6.00	8.00	11.00	15.00
ND//25 (1904)	—	4.50	6.00	8.00	11.00	15.00
ND//26 (1905)	—	4.50	6.00	8.00	11.00	15.00
ND//27 (1906)	—	4.50	6.00	8.00	11.00	15.00
ND//29 (1908)	—	4.50	6.00	8.00	11.00	15.00
ND//30 (1909)	—	4.50	6.00	8.00	11.00	15.00
ND//31 (1910)	—	4.50	6.00	8.00	11.00	15.00
ND//33 (1912)	—	4.50	6.00	8.00	11.00	15.00
ND//37 (1916)	—	4.50	6.00	8.00	11.00	15.00
191(8)//39	—	4.50	6.00	8.00	11.00	15.00
ND//40 (1919)	—	4.50	6.00	8.00	11.00	15.00
ND//42 (1921)	—	4.50	6.00	8.00	11.00	15.00
1922//43	—	4.50	6.00	8.00	11.00	15.00

KM# 150 MOHUR

Gold **Obv. Inscription:** Victoria.... **Reverse:** Jhar **Rev. Inscription:** "Madho Singh II" **Mint:** Sawai Jaipur **Note:** Weight varies 10.70-11.40 g.

Date	Mintage	Good	VG	F	VF	XF
ND//24 (1904)	—	—	225	250	275	325
ND//37 (1916)	—	—	225	250	275	325
ND//37 (1916)	—	—	225	250	275	325
ND//40 (1919)	—	—	225	250	275	325
ND//41 (1920)	—	—	225	250	275	325

MILLED COINAGE

KM# 132 NAZARANA NEW PAISA

Copper, 32-36 mm. **Obv. Inscription:** Victoria... **Reverse:** Jhar **Rev. Inscription:** "Madho Singh II" **Mint:** Sawai Jaipur **Note:** Size varies. Well-centered issues on thin planchets may be restrikes.

Date	Mintage	VG	F	VF	XF
1901//22	—	4.00	10.00	17.50	25.00	40.00
1902//23	—	4.00	10.00	17.50	25.00	40.00
1903//24	—	4.00	10.00	17.50	25.00	40.00
1904//25	—	4.00	10.00	17.50	25.00	40.00
1905//26	—	4.00	10.00	17.50	25.00	40.00
1906//27	—	4.00	10.00	17.50	25.00	40.00
1907//28	—	4.00	10.00	17.50	25.00	40.00
1908//29	—	4.00	10.00	17.50	25.00	40.00
1909//30	—	4.00	10.00	17.50	25.00	40.00
1910//31	—	4.00	10.00	17.50	25.00	40.00
1911//32	—	4.00	10.00	17.50	25.00	40.00
1912//33	—	4.00	10.00	17.50	25.00	40.00
1913//34	—	4.00	10.00	17.50	25.00	40.00
1914//35	—	4.00	10.00	17.50	25.00	40.00
1915//36	—	4.00	10.00	17.50	25.00	40.00
1916//37	—	4.00	10.00	17.50	25.00	40.00
1917//38	—	4.00	10.00	17.50	25.00	40.00

KM# 147 NAZARANA RUPEE

Silver **Obv. Inscription:** Victoria... **Reverse:** Jhar **Rev. Inscription:** "Madho Singh II" **Mint:** Sawai Jaipur **Note:** Size varies 36-37mm.

Date	Mintage	Good	VG	F	VF	XF
1901//22	—	10.00	25.00	40.00	52.50	75.00
1903//24	—	10.00	25.00	40.00	52.50	75.00
1904//25	—	10.00	25.00	40.00	52.50	75.00
1906//27	—	10.00	25.00	40.00	52.50	75.00
1908//29	—	10.00	25.00	40.00	52.50	75.00
1909//30	—	10.00	25.00	40.00	52.50	75.00
1910//31	—	10.00	25.00	40.00	52.50	75.00
1911//32	—	10.00	25.00	40.00	52.50	75.00
1912//33	—	10.00	25.00	40.00	52.50	75.00
1913//34	—	10.00	25.00	40.00	52.50	75.00
1914//35	—	10.00	25.00	40.00	52.50	75.00
1915//36	—	10.00	25.00	40.00	52.50	75.00
1916//37	—	10.00	25.00	40.00	52.50	75.00
1917//38	—	10.00	25.00	40.00	52.50	75.00
1918//39	—	10.00	25.00	40.00	52.50	75.00
1919//40	—	10.00	25.00	40.00	52.50	75.00
1920//41	—	10.00	25.00	40.00	52.50	75.00
1921//42	—	10.00	25.00	40.00	52.50	75.00

Man Singh II

1922-1949AD

HAMMERED COINAGE

Regal Style

To distinguish coins betweenRam Singh and his son/successor Madho Singh II, note that the coins of Ram Singh have a small slanting cross or dagger between the Ram and Singh symbols, whereas the coins of Singh II do not.

KM# 175 1/2 PAISA

Copper, 21-23 mm. **Obv. Inscription:** George VI... **Reverse:** Jhar **Rev. Inscription:** Man Singh (II)... **Mint:** Sawai Jaipur **Note:** Size varies.

Date	Mintage	Good	VG	F	VF	XF
ND//21 (1942)	—	0.40	1.00	1.75	2.50	4.50

KM# 158 RUPEE

10.7000 g., Silver **Obv. Inscription:** George V... **Reverse:** Jhar **Rev. Inscription:** Man Singh II... **Mint:** Sawai Jaipur

Date	Mintage	Good	VG	F	VF	XF
1922//1	—	12.50	25.00	40.00	65.00	90.00

KM# 163 MOHUR

Gold **Obv. Inscription:** George V... **Reverse:** Jhar **Rev. Inscription:** Man Singh II... **Mint:** Sawai Jaipur **Note:** Weight varies 10.70-11.40 g.

Date	Mintage	Good	VG	F	VF	XF
ND//2 (1923)	—	—	235	265	300	425
1(924)//3	—	—	235	265	300	425
1925//4	—	—	235	265	300	425
19(28)//7	—	—	235	265	300	425

KM# 200 MOHUR

Gold **Obv. Inscription:** George (VI)... **Rev. Inscription:** Man Singh (II)... **Mint:** Sawai Jaipur **Note:** Weight varies 10.70-11.40 g.

Date	Mintage	Good	VG	F	VF	XF
ND//20 (1941)	—	—	225	250	275	325
ND//22 (1943)	—	—	225	250	275	325
ND//26 (1947)	—	—	225	250	275	325
ND//27 (1948)	—	—	225	250	275	325
1949//28	—	—	225	250	275	325

MILLED COINAGE

KM# 185 ANNA

Brass **Obverse:** Jhar **Mint:** Sawai Jaipur

Date	Mintage	Good	VG	F	VF	XF
1943	—	0.10	0.20	0.40	0.60	1.00
Note: Lg. and sm. denomination						
1944/3	—	0.15	0.40	0.80	1.20	2.00
1944	—	0.10	0.20	0.40	0.60	1.00

KM# 186 ANNA

5.1700 g., Brass **Obverse:** Jhar **Mint:** Sawai Jaipur **Note:** Thick planchet.

Date	Mintage	Good	VG	F	VF	XF
1943	—	0.10	0.25	0.50	0.80	1.50

KM# 187 ANNA

2.7800 g., Brass **Obverse:** Jhar **Mint:** Sawai Jaipur **Note:** Thin planchet.

Date	Mintage	Good	VG	F	VF	XF
1943	—	0.10	0.20	0.40	0.60	1.00

KM# 188 ANNA

Brass **Obverse:** Bust of Man Singh II right **Reverse:** Jhar **Mint:** Sawai Jaipur

Date	Mintage	Good	VG	F	VF	XF
1944	—	0.10	0.20	0.40	0.60	1.00
1944 Proof; Rare	—	—	—	—	—	—

KM# 190 2 ANNA

Brass **Reverse:** Jhar **Mint:** Sawai Jaipur **Note:** Square flan.

Date	Mintage	Good	VG	F	VF	XF
1942//21	—	1.50	3.50	5.00	7.00	11.50

KM# 176 1/2 PAISA

Copper, 21-23 mm. **Obverse:** George VI **Reverse:** Jhar **Rev. Inscription:** Man Singh (II)... **Mint:** Sawai Jaipur **Note:** Crude struck in collar. Size varies.

Date	Mintage	Good	VG	F	VF	XF
ND//22 (1943)	—	0.40	1.00	1.75	2.50	4.50
ND//23 (1944)	—	0.40	1.00	1.75	2.50	4.50

KM# 155 NAZARANA PAISA

Copper **Obv. Inscription:** George V... **Reverse:** Jhar **Rev. Inscription:** Man Singh II... **Mint:** Sawai Jaipur

Date	Mintage	Good	VG	F	VF	XF
1922//1	—	6.00	15.00	25.00	40.00	60.00
1923//2	—	6.00	15.00	25.00	40.00	60.00
1924//3	—	6.00	15.00	25.00	40.00	60.00
1924//4	—	6.00	15.00	25.00	40.00	60.00
1925//4	—	6.00	15.00	25.00	40.00	60.00
1926//5	—	6.00	15.00	25.00	40.00	60.00
1927//5	—	6.00	15.00	25.00	40.00	60.00
1927//6	—	6.00	15.00	25.00	40.00	60.00
1928//7	—	6.00	15.00	25.00	40.00	60.00
1929//8	—	6.00	15.00	25.00	40.00	60.00
1930//9	—	6.00	15.00	25.00	40.00	60.00
19(30)//10	—	6.00	15.00	25.00	40.00	60.00
1931//10	—	6.00	15.00	25.00	40.00	60.00
1932//11	—	6.00	15.00	25.00	40.00	60.00
1933//12	—	6.00	15.00	25.00	40.00	60.00
1934//13	—	6.00	15.00	25.00	40.00	60.00
1935//14	—	6.00	15.00	25.00	40.00	60.00

KM# 167 NAZARANA PAISA

6.4400 g., Copper **Obv. Inscription:** Edward (VIII)... **Reverse:** Jhar **Rev. Inscription:** Man Singh (II)... **Mint:** Sawai Jaipur

Date	Mintage	Good	VG	F	VF	XF
1936//15	—	60.00	150	250	325	400

KM# 180 NAZARANA PAISA

Copper **Obv. Inscription:** George VI... **Reverse:** Jhar **Rev. Inscription:** Man Singh (II)... **Mint:** Sawai Jaipur

Date	Mintage	Good	VG	F	VF	XF
1937//16	—	4.00	10.00	17.50	25.00	40.00
1938//17	—	4.00	10.00	17.50	25.00	40.00
1939//18	—	4.00	10.00	17.50	25.00	40.00
1940//19	—	4.00	10.00	17.50	25.00	40.00
1941//19	—	4.00	10.00	17.50	25.00	40.00
1941//20	—	4.00	10.00	17.50	25.00	40.00
1942//21	—	4.00	10.00	17.50	25.00	40.00
1943//22	—	4.00	10.00	17.50	25.00	40.00
1944//23	—	4.00	10.00	17.50	25.00	40.00
1945//24	—	4.00	10.00	17.50	25.00	40.00
1946//25	—	4.00	10.00	17.50	25.00	40.00
1947//26	—	4.00	10.00	17.50	25.00	40.00
1947//27	—	4.00	10.00	17.50	25.00	40.00
1948//27	—	4.00	10.00	17.50	25.00	40.00
1949//28	—	4.00	10.00	17.50	25.00	40.00

KM# 159 NAZARANA RUPEE

10.7000 g., Silver **Obv. Inscription:** George V... **Reverse:** Jhar **Rev. Inscription:** Man Singh II... **Mint:** Sawai Jaipur

Date	Mintage	Good	VG	F	VF	XF
1924//3	—	15.00	40.00	62.50	85.00	120
1928//7	—	15.00	40.00	62.50	85.00	120
1932//11	—	15.00	40.00	62.50	85.00	120

KM# 170 NAZARANA RUPEE

10.7000 g., Silver **Obv. Inscription:** Edward (VIII)... **Reverse:** Jhar **Rev. Inscription:** Man Singh (II)... **Mint:** Sawai Jaipur

Date	Mintage	VG	F	VF	XF	Unc
1936//15 Rare	—	—	—	—	—	—

KM# 196 NAZARANA RUPEE

Silver, 37-38 mm. **Obv. Inscription:** George (VI)... **Rev. Inscription:** Man Singh (II).... **Mint:** Sawai Jaipur **Note:** Size varies. Similar rupees approximately 30mm in diameter are modern forgeries.

Date	Mintage	Good	VG	F	VF	XF
1938//20	—	11.00	27.50	42.50	70.00	100
1939//18	—	5.00	10.00	16.50	28.50	40.00
1941//20	—	5.00	10.00	16.50	28.50	40.00
1943//22	—	5.00	10.00	16.50	28.50	40.00
1945//24	—	5.00	10.00	16.50	28.50	40.00
1948//27	—	5.00	10.00	16.50	28.50	40.00
1949//28	—	5.00	10.00	16.50	28.50	40.00

KM# 195 NAZARANA RUPEE

Silver **Obv. Inscription:** George (VI)... **Rev. Inscription:** Madho Singh (II)... **Mint:** Sawai Jaipur **Note:** Weight varies 10.70-11.60 g.

Date	Mintage	Good	VG	F	VF	XF
1949//3	—	8.00	20.00	32.50	55.00	80.00

KM# 201 NAZARANA MOHUR

Gold **Obv. Inscription:** George (VI)... **Rev. Inscription:** Man Singh (II)... **Mint:** Sawai Jaipur

Date	Mintage	Good	VG	F	VF	XF
ND1949//28 Rare	—	—	—	—	—	—

JODHPUR

Jodhpur, also known as Marwar, located in northwest India, was the largest Princely State in the Rajputana Agency. Its population in 1941 exceeded two and a half million. The "Maharajadhirajas" ("Great Kings of Kings") of Jodhpur were Rathor Rajputs who claimed an extremely ancient ancestry from Rama, king of Ayodhya. With the collapse of the Rathor rulers of Kanauj in 1194 the family entered Marwar where they laid the foundation of the new state. The city of Jodhpur was built by Rao Jodha in 1459, and the city and the state were named after him. In 1561 the Mughal Emperor Akbar invaded Jodhpur, forcing its submission. In 1679 Emperor Aurangzeb sacked the city, an experience which stimulated the Rajput royal house to forge a new unity among themselves in order to extricate themselves from Mughal hegemony. Internal dissension once again asserted itself and Rajput unity, which had both benefited from and accelerated Mughal decline, fell apart before the Marathas. In 1818 Jodhpur came under British protection and control and after Indian independence in 1947 the State was merged into Rajasthan. Jodhpur is best known for its particular style of riding breeches (jodpurs) which became very popular in the West in the late 19th century.

RULERS

Sardar Singh, VS1952-1968/1895-1911AD
Sumer Singh, VS1968-1975/1911-1918AD
Umaid Singh, VS1975-2004/1918-1947AD
Hanwant Singh, as Titular Ruler, VS2004-2009/1947-1949AD

MINTS

جودهپور

Jodhpur

جود پور

Jodpur

دارالمنصور

Dar-al-Mansur

MINT MARKS

Before 1858AD

Sojat, always on reverse. (KM#226)
Sojat, sometimes on obverse. (KM#226)
Pali, (KM#227)
Pali, Sojat
Nagor, (on reverse of KM#177.2)
Usually on obverse.
Jodhpur, on obverse. (KM#47)

Issues of 1858-1873AD

After 1858AD, the mint marks vary, and are given for each listing, wherever there is a difference.

All gold coins struck at Jodhpur Mint. All mints except Jodhpur closed by or before 1893AD. All copper coins were probably struck at the Jodhpur Mint, but if struck elsewhere, they bear no distinguishing marks.

In addition to the mint marks indicating the mint cities, there are also the marks of the Darogas (mint overseers), which are very useful in identifying the mints, especially when the city marks are missing or off the flan. These are given by cat.# and mint: (Only one of the marks appears on any one coin, always on the obverse.)

Issues of Edward VII and George V and Sardar Singh and Sumer Singh

म

Jodhpur (KM#91-95, 98-100, 109, 113-115)
Jodhpur (KM#120)

Issues of George V and Sumer Singh

द

Jodhpur (KM#111-112)

Issues of George V and Umaid Singh

ॐ

Jodhpur (KM#128 & 129)

श्री

Jodhpur (KM#129)

Issues of Edward VIII and Umaid Singh

रं

Jodhpur all

Issues of George VI and Umaid Singh

रं

Jodhpur (KM#141-143)

Jodhpur (KM#144- 147, 150-151)

Issues of George VI and Hanwant Singh

जो

Jodhpur all

The Daroga's marks generally consist of a symbol or a single Nagari letter, sometimes inverted, and even lying on its side. Some letters are found on more than one series, so that the mark is not a positive identification, but taken together with the city mark and the style of the coin, will provide a correct attribution.

JODHPUR MINT

Operative between 1761AD (AH1175) and 1945AD (VS2002). There are a number of mules of late Jodhpur types struck in 1945 and later for collectors.

KINGDOM

Sardar Singh

VS1952-1968 / 1895-1911AD

HAMMERED COINAGE

KM# 91.1 1/4 ANNA

10.5000 g., Copper, 18 mm. **Obv. Inscription:** Edward (VII)... **Reverse:** Inscription; date at top **Rev. Inscription:** Sardar Singh... **Mint:** Jodhpur **Note:** Other blundered dates may exist. Y#20.

Date	Mintage	Good	VG	F	VF	XF
1901	—	1.50	2.50	3.75	5.50	—
1902	—	1.50	2.50	3.75	5.50	—
1903	—	1.50	2.50	3.75	5.50	—
1904	—	1.50	2.50	3.75	5.50	—
1905	—	1.50	2.50	3.75	5.50	—
1906	—	0.50	1.00	1.75	2.50	—
1609 Error	—	1.50	2.50	3.75	5.50	—
1907	—	1.00	2.00	3.25	4.50	—
1908	—	1.00	2.00	3.25	4.50	—
1909	—	1.00	2.00	3.25	4.50	—
1910	—	1.00	2.00	3.25	4.50	—
1290(1910) Error	—	1.25	2.25	3.00	4.00	—
1291(1910) Error	—	0.75	1.50	2.25	3.25	—
1292(1910) Error	—	—	—	—	—	—
1967(1910) Error	—	1.25	2.25	3.00	4.00	—
2091(1910) Error	—	1.25	2.25	3.00	4.00	—
5201(1910) Error	—	1.25	2.25	3.00	4.00	—
5291(1910) Error	—	—	—	—	—	—
0292 (1910) Error	—	—	—	—	—	—
192 (1910) Error	—	—	—	—	—	—
0192 (1910) Error	—	—	—	—	—	—
1091 (1910) Error	—	—	—	—	—	—
0196 (1910) Error	—	—	—	—	—	—
1291 (1910) Retrograde 9	—	—	—	—	—	—
1067 (1910) Error	—	—	—	—	—	—
1291 (1910) 2 engraved over 1	—	—	—	—	—	—

KM# 91.2 1/4 ANNA

10.5000 g., Copper, 16 mm. **Obv. Inscription:** Edward (VII)... **Reverse:** Inscription; date at bottom **Rev. Inscription:** Sardar Singh... **Mint:** Jodhpur **Note:** Y#20.

Date	Mintage	Good	VG	F	VF	XF
1906	—	—	—	—	—	—

KM# 92.1 1/2 ANNA

Copper **Obv. Inscription:** Edward (VII)... **Rev. Inscription:** Sardar Singh... **Mint:** Jodhpur **Note:** 20.00-21.00 grams. Y#21.

Date	Mintage	Good	VG	F	VF	XF
1906	—	3.50	5.00	7.50	11.50	—

KM# 92.2 1/2 ANNA

Copper **Obv. Inscription:** Edward (VII)... **Reverse:** Legend without Bahadur **Rev. Inscription:** Sardar Singh... **Mint:** Jodhpur **Note:** Y#21.

Date	Mintage	Good	VG	F	VF	XF
1906	—	3.50	5.00	7.50	11.50	—
1908	—	3.50	5.00	7.50	11.50	—

KM# 93 1/8 RUPEE

1.4000 g., Silver **Obv. Inscription:** Edward (VII)... **Rev. Inscription:** Sardar Singh... **Mint:** Jodhpur

Date	Mintage	Good	VG	F	VF	XF
ND(1908)	—	7.00	17.50	25.00	35.00	50.00

KM# 94 1/4 RUPEE

2.8000 g., Silver, 19 mm. **Obv. Inscription:** Edward (VII)... **Rev. Inscription:** Sardar Singh... **Mint:** Jodhpur **Note:** Y#22.

Date	Mintage	Good	VG	F	VF	XF
VS1965	—	7.50	18.50	26.50	37.50	55.00

KM# 95 1/2 RUPEE

5.6000 g., Silver, 13 mm. **Obv. Inscription:** Edward (VII)... **Rev. Inscription:** Sardar Singh... **Mint:** Jodhpur

Date	Mintage	Good	VG	F	VF	XF
ND(1908)	—	10.00	20.00	31.50	42.50	60.00

KM# 98 1/4 MOHUR

2.8000 g., Gold **Obv. Inscription:** Edward (VII)... **Rev. Inscription:** Sardar Singh... **Mint:** Jodhpur **Note:** Y#23.

Date	Mintage	Good	VG	F	VF	XF
ND(1906)	—	—	65.00	85.00	110	165

KM# 99 1/2 MOHUR

5.5000 g., Gold, 18 mm. **Obv. Inscription:** Edward (VII)... **Rev. Inscription:** Sardar Singh... **Mint:** Jodhpur **Note:** Y#24.

Date	Mintage	Good	VG	F	VF	XF
ND(1906)	—	—	125	165	225	300

KM# 100.1 MOHUR

11.0000 g., Gold, 20 mm. **Obverse:** "Ma." **Obv. Inscription:** Edward (VII)... **Rev. Inscription:** Sardar Singh... **Mint:** Jodhpur **Note:** Y#25.

Date	Mintage	Good	VG	F	VF	XF
1906	—	—	225	285	375	550

KM# 100.2 MOHUR

11.0000 g., Gold, 20 mm. **Obverse:** "Sa." **Obv. Inscription:** Edward (VII)... **Rev. Inscription:** Sardar Singh... **Mint:** Jodhpur **Note:** Y#25.

Date	Mintage	Good	VG	F	VF	XF
1906	—	—	225	285	375	550

Sumar Singh

HAMMERED COINAGE

KM# 110 1/4 ANNA

10.5000 g., Copper, 16-18 mm. **Obv. Inscription:** George V, "Emperor"... **Rev. Inscription:** Sumar Singh... **Mint:** Jodhpur **Note:** Y#27. Size varies.

Date	Mintage	Good	VG	F	VF	XF
1914	—	6.50	9.00	12.50	17.50	—

KM# 111 1/4 ANNA

10.5000 g., Copper, 16-18 mm. **Obv. Inscription:** George V, "Shah"... **Rev. Inscription:** Sumar Singh... **Mint:** Jodhpur **Note:** Y#27. Size varies.

Date	Mintage	Good	VG	F	VF	XF
1914	—	—	—	—	—	—

KM# 112.1 1/2 ANNA

21.0000 g., Copper, 25 mm. **Obv. Inscription:** George V, "Emperor"... **Rev. Inscription:** Sumar Singh... **Mint:** Jodhpur **Note:** Y#28.

Date	Mintage	Good	VG	F	VF	XF
1914	—	5.00	8.50	12.50	20.00	—

KM# 112.2 1/2 ANNA

21.0000 g., Copper, 25 mm. **Obv. Inscription:** George V, "Shah"... **Rev. Inscription:** Sumar Singh... **Mint:** Jodhpur **Note:** Y#28.

Date	Mintage	Good	VG	F	VF	XF
1914	—	5.00	8.50	12.50	20.00	—

KM# 113 1/8 RUPEE

1.4000 g., Silver, 13 mm. **Obv. Inscription:** George V, "Shah"... **Rev. Inscription:** Sumar Singh... **Mint:** Jodhpur **Note:** Y#29.

Date	Mintage	Good	VG	F	VF	XF
ND(1911-18)	—	6.50	13.50	21.50	30.00	45.00

KM# 114 1/4 RUPEE

2.8000 g., Silver, 14 mm. **Mint:** Jodhpur **Note:** Y#30.

Date	Mintage	Good	VG	F	VF	XF
ND(1911-18)	—	6.50	13.50	21.50	30.00	45.00

KM# 115 1/2 RUPEE

5.6000 g., Silver, 18 mm. **Mint:** Jodhpur **Note:** Y#31.

Date	Mintage	Good	VG	F	VF	XF
ND(1911-18)	—	6.50	13.50	21.50	30.00	45.00

KM# 116 RUPEE

11.2000 g., Silver, 21 mm. **Mint:** Jodhpur **Note:** Y#32.

Date	Mintage	Good	VG	F	VF	XF
ND(1911-18)	—	7.00	15.00	26.50	37.50	55.00

KM# 119 1/2 MOHUR

5.5000 g., Gold, 19 mm. **Obv. Inscription:** "Ha" **Mint:** Jodhpur **Note:** Y#26.

Date	Mintage	Good	VG	F	VF	XF
ND(1911-18)	—	—	120	150	190	250

KM# 120.1 MOHUR

11.0000 g., Gold, 18 mm. **Obverse:** "Ma." **Mint:** Jodhpur **Note:** Y#33.

Date	Mintage	Good	VG	F	VF	XF
ND(1911-18)	—	—	225	285	375	550

KM# 120.2 MOHUR

11.0000 g., Gold, 18 mm. **Obv. Inscription:** "Ha" **Mint:** Jodhpur **Note:** Y#33.

Date	Mintage	Good	VG	F	VF	XF
ND(1911-18)	—	—	225	300	400	600

Umaid Singh

HAMMERED COINAGE

KM# 132 1/4 ANNA

10.5000 g., Copper **Obverse:** Large Persian "8" left of Daroga's mark **Obv. Inscription:** Edward (VIII)... **Rev. Inscription:** Umaid Singh... **Mint:** Jodhpur **Note:** Varieties include 2 dots replacing the Persian "8" in the inscription and are quite common.

Date	Mintage	Good	VG	F	VF	XF
1936	—	1.75	2.75	4.00	6.50	—

Note: Blundered legend varieties also exist

KM# 133 1/4 ANNA

10.5000 g., Copper **Obverse:** Small Persian "8" left of Daroga's mark **Obv. Inscription:** Edward (VIII)... **Rev. Inscription:** Umaid Singh... **Mint:** Jodhpur **Note:** Varieties include 2 dots replacing the Persian "8" in the inscription and are quite common.

Date	Mintage	Good	VG	F	VF	XF
1936	—	1.75	2.75	4.00	6.50	—

KM# 131 1/4 ANNA

10.5000 g., Copper **Obverse:** Without Persian "8" left of Daroga's mark **Obv. Inscription:** Edward (VIII)... **Rev. Inscription:** Umaid Singh... **Mint:** Jodhpur **Note:** Y#39.

Date	Mintage	Good	VG	F	VF	XF
1936	—	1.75	2.75	4.00	6.50	—

KM# 141 1/4 ANNA

Copper **Obv. Inscription:** George (VI)... **Reverse:** Inscription; date at top **Rev. Inscription:** Umaid Singh... **Mint:** Jodhpur **Note:** Thick, 10.50-10.70 grams. Y#40.

Date	Mintage	Good	VG	F	VF	XF
1937	—	1.25	1.75	2.50	3.50	—
1938	—	1.25	1.75	2.50	3.50	—
1939	—	1.25	1.75	2.50	3.50	—

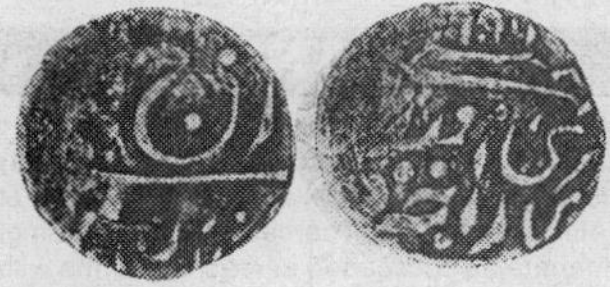

KM# 142 1/4 ANNA

Copper **Obv. Inscription:** George (VI)... **Rev. Inscription:** Umaid Singh... **Mint:** Jodhpur

Date	Mintage	Good	VG	F	VF	XF
VS1996	—	2.00	3.00	4.00	6.00	—

KM# 143 1/4 ANNA

Copper, 19-20 mm. **Obv. Inscription:** George (VI)... **Rev. Inscription:** Umaid Singh... **Mint:** Jodhpur **Note:** Size varies.

Date	Mintage	Good	VG	F	VF	XF
ND	—	3.00	4.50	6.50	10.00	—

KM# 124 1/4 RUPEE

3.1000 g., Silver **Obv. Inscription:** George (V)... **Rev. Inscription:** Umaid Singh... **Mint:** Jodhpur **Note:** Y#35.

Date	Mintage	Good	VG	F	VF	XF
ND(1918-35)	—	7.50	18.50	26.50	37.50	55.00

KM# 125 1/2 RUPEE

Silver **Obv. Inscription:** George (V)... **Rev. Inscription:** Umaid Singh... **Shape:** Round **Mint:** Jodhpur

Date	Mintage	Good	VG	F	VF	XF
ND(1918-35)	—	—	—	—	—	—

KM# 125a 1/2 RUPEE

Silver **Obv. Inscription:** George (V)... **Rev. Inscription:** Umaid Singh... **Mint:** Jodhpur **Note:** Square flan.

Date	Mintage	Good	VG	F	VF	XF
ND(1918-35)	—	—	—	—	—	—

KM# 126 RUPEE

Silver **Obv. Inscription:** George (V)... **Rev. Inscription:** Umaid Singh... **Mint:** Jodhpur

Date	Mintage	Good	VG	F	VF	XF
ND(1918-35)	—	—	—	—	—	—

KM# 127.1 1/4 MOHUR

2.7000 g., Gold, 16 mm. **Obverse:** "OM" **Obv. Inscription:** George (V)... **Rev. Inscription:** Umaid Singh... **Mint:** Jodhpur **Note:** Y#36.

Date	Mintage	Good	VG	F	VF	XF
ND(1918-35)	—	—	70.00	90.00	120	175

KM# 127.2 1/4 MOHUR

2.7000 g., Gold, 16 mm. **Obverse:** "Shri" **Obv. Inscription:** George (V)... **Rev. Inscription:** Umaid Singh... **Mint:** Jodhpur **Note:** Y#36.

Date	Mintage	Good	VG	F	VF	XF
ND(1918-35)	—	—	70.00	90.00	120	175

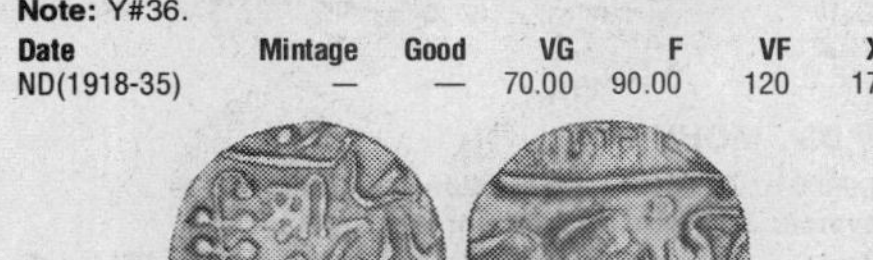

KM# 128 1/2 MOHUR

5.5000 g., Gold, 18 mm. **Obv. Inscription:** "George (V)..." **Rev. Inscription:** "Umaid Singh..." **Mint:** Jodhpur **Note:** Y#37.

Date	Mintage	Good	VG	F	VF	XF
ND(1918-35)	—	—	120	165	220	300

KM# 129 MOHUR

11.0000 g., Gold, 18-20 mm. **Obverse:** "Om" **Obv. Inscription:** "George (V)..." **Rev. Inscription:** "Umaid Singh..." **Mint:** Jodhpur **Note:** Y#38. Size varies.

Date	Mintage	Good	VG	F	VF	XF
19x8	—	—	225	285	375	550

KM# 130 MOHUR

11.0000 g., Gold, 18-20 mm. **Obverse:** "Shri" **Obv. Inscription:** "George (V)..." **Rev. Inscription:** "Umaid Singh..." **Mint:** Jodhpur **Note:** Y#38. Size varies.

Date	Mintage	Good	VG	F	VF	XF
ND(1918-35)	—	—	225	265	325	450

KM# 140 MOHUR

11.0100 g., Gold **Obv. Inscription:** Edward VIII **Mint:** Jodhpur

Date	Mintage	Good	VG	F	VF	XF
1936	—	—	—	—	—	—

KM# 150 MOHUR

11.0000 g., Gold, 18 mm. **Obverse:** Large legend, Persian "6" after "George" **Obv. Inscription:** "George (VI)..." **Reverse:** Large legend, Persian "6" after "George" **Rev. Inscription:** "Umaid Singh..." **Mint:** Jodhpur **Note:** Y#42.

Date	Mintage	Good	VG	F	VF	XF
VS1997 (1940)	—	—	—	—	—	—
ND(1943)	—	—	250	325	450	650

KM# 151.1 MOHUR

11.0200 g., Gold **Obverse:** Small legend, without Persian "6" **Obv. Inscription:** "George (VI)..." **Reverse:** Small legend, without Persian "6" **Rev. Inscription:** "Umaid Singh..." **Mint:** Jodhpur

Date	Mintage	Good	VG	F	VF	XF
VS1999	—	—	250	325	450	650
ND(1942)	—	—	250	325	450	650
VS2000	—	—	250	325	450	650

KM# 151.2 MOHUR

11.0200 g., Gold **Obverse:** With Persian "6" below Daroga's mark **Obv. Inscription:** George (VI)... **Rev. Inscription:** Umaid Singh ... **Mint:** Jodhpur **Note:** Varieties exist.

Date	Mintage	Good	VG	F	VF	XF
VS2001 (1944)	—	—	250	325	450	650

MILLED COINAGE

KM# 144 1/4 ANNA

3.0000 g., Copper **Obverse:** Without Persian "6" below Daroga's mark **Obv. Inscription:** George (VI)... **Rev. Inscription:** Umaid Singh... **Mint:** Jodhpur **Note:** Thin flan. Y#41.

Date	Mintage	Good	VG	F	VF	XF
ND Date off flan	—	0.20	0.30	0.50	1.00	—
VS2000	—	1.75	2.75	4.00	5.50	—

KM# 147 1/4 ANNA

2.6000 g., Copper **Obverse:** Cock with wings raised facing left, legend around **Obv. Inscription:** George (VI)... **Reverse:** Date and "Rajya Marwar" **Rev. Inscription:** Umaid Singh... **Mint:** Jodhpur

Date	Mintage	Good	VG	F	VF	XF
VS2000 Rare	—	—	—	—	—	—

KM# 145 1/4 ANNA

2.6000 g., Copper **Obverse:** Persian "6" below Daroga's mark **Obv. Inscription:** George (VI)... **Rev. Inscription:** Umaid Singh... **Mint:** Jodhpur **Note:** Varieties exist.

Date	Mintage	Good	VG	F	VF	XF
VS2001	—	1.75	2.75	4.00	5.50	—
VS2002	—	1.75	2.75	4.00	5.50	—

KM# 146 1/4 ANNA

2.6000 g., Copper **Obverse:** Persian 2 (error for 6) below Daroga's mark **Obv. Inscription:** George (VI)... **Rev. Inscription:** Umaid Singh... **Mint:** Jodhpur

Date	Mintage	Good	VG	F	VF	XF
VS	—	—	—	—	—	—

Hanwant Singh
as Titular Ruler
HAMMERED COINAGE

KM# 152 1/4 ANNA

4.2000 g., Copper **Obv. Inscription:** George (VI)... **Rev. Inscription:** Hanwant Singh... **Mint:** Jodhpur **Note:** Y#43.

Date	Mintage	Good	VG	F	VF	XF
VS(2004)	—	12.50	20.00	32.50	50.00	—

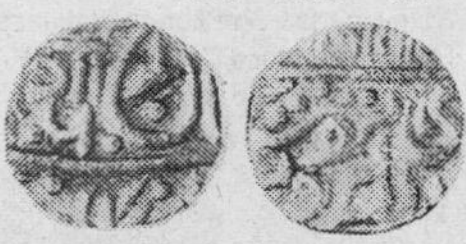

KM# 158 1/4 MOHUR

2.7000 g., Gold **Obv. Inscription:** "George (VI)..." **Rev. Inscription:** "Hanwant Singh..." **Mint:** Jodhpur

Date	Mintage	Good	VG	F	VF	XF
VS(2004) Rare	—	—	—	—	—	—

KM# 160 MOHUR

11.0000 g., Gold **Obv. Inscription:** "George (VI)..." **Rev. Inscription:** "Hanwant Singh..." **Mint:** Jodhpur

Date	Mintage	Good	VG	F	VF	XF
VS(2004)	—	—	250	350	500	650

JUNAGADH

A state located in the Kathiawar peninsula of Western India was originally a petty Rajput kingdom until conquered by the Sultan of Ahmadabad in 1472. It became a Mughal dependency under the Emperor Akbar, administered by the Ahmadabad Subah. In 1735, when the empire began to disintegrate, a Mughal officer and military adventurer, Sher Khan Babi, expelled the Mughal governor and asserted his independence. From that time until Indian independence his descendents ruled the state as nawabs. In 1947 the Nawab of Junagadh tried to acceed to the new nation of Pakistan but the Hindu majority in the state objected and Junagadh was absorbed by the Republic of India.

Junagadh first entered into treaty relations with the British in 1807 and maintained a close and friendly association with the Raj. In 1924 this relationship was formalized when Junagadh was placed under an Agent to the Governor General in the western India States. In 1935 the state comprised 3,337 square miles with a population of 545,152, four-fifths of whom were Hindus.

RULERS

Rasul Muhammad Khan, AH1309-1329/VS1948-1968/1891-1911AD

Mahabat Khan III, AH1329-1368/VS1968-2005/1911-1948AD

KINGDOM

Rasul Muhammad Khan

AH1309-1329 / VS1948-1968 / 1891-1911AD

MILLED COINAGE

KM# 43 DOKDO

Copper **Obv. Inscription:** Perso-Arabic "Ek paisa Junagadh Riiyaasat (government)" **Rev. Inscription:** "Devanagari-Shri Sorath Sarkaar" **Mint:** Junagadh

Date	Mintage	Good	VG	F	VF	XF
AH1325/VS1963	—	4.50	6.50	10.00	15.00	—

KM# 44.1 DOKDO

Copper **Obv. Inscription:** Perso-Arabic Ek paisa Junagadh Riiyaasat (government) **Reverse:** Inscription; date without rosettes **Rev. Inscription:** Devanagari-Shri Sorath Sarkaar **Mint:** Junagadh

Date	Mintage	Good	VG	F	VF	XF
VS1963(1906)	—	1.25	2.00	3.00	4.50	—
VS1964(1907)	—	—	—	—	—	—

KM# 44.2 DOKDO

Copper **Obv. Inscription:** Perso-Arabic Ek paisa Junagadh Riiyaasat (government) **Reverse:** Inscription; date with annulets **Rev. Inscription:** Devanagari-Shri Sorath Sarkaar **Mint:** Junagadh

Date	Mintage	Good	VG	F	VF	XF
VS1964(1907)	—	1.25	2.00	3.00	4.50	—

KM# 44.3 DOKDO

Copper **Obv. Inscription:** Perso-Arabic Ek paisa Junagadh Riiyaasat (government) **Reverse:** Inscription; date between solid stars **Rev. Inscription:** Devanagari-Shri Sorath Sarkaar **Mint:** Junagadh

Date	Mintage	Good	VG	F	VF	XF
VS1964(1907)	—	1.25	2.00	3.00	4.50	—

KM# 44.5 DOKDO

Copper **Obv. Inscription:** Perso-Arabic Ek paisa Junagadh Riiyaasat (government) **Reverse:** Inscription; solid star only to left of date **Rev. Inscription:** Devanagari-Shri Sorath Sarkaar **Mint:** Junagadh **Note:** Prev. KM#44.3a.

Date	Mintage	Good	VG	F	VF	XF
VS1964(1907)	—	2.50	4.00	6.00	10.00	—

KM# 44.4 DOKDO

Copper **Obv. Inscription:** Perso-Arabic Ek paisa Junagadh Riiyaasat (government) **Reverse:** Date with outlined stars **Rev. Inscription:** Devanagari-Shri Sorath Sarkaar **Mint:** Junagadh

Date	Mintage	Good	VG	F	VF	XF
VS1964(1907)	—	1.25	2.00	3.00	4.50	7.50

KM# 45.1 DOKDO

Copper **Obv. Inscription:** Perso-Arabic Ek paisa Junagadh Riiyaasat (government) **Reverse:** Date between rosettes **Rev. Inscription:** Devanagari-Shri Sorath Sarkaar **Mint:** Junagadh

Date	Mintage	Good	VG	F	VF	XF
VS1964(1907)	—	0.50	0.85	1.25	1.75	—
VS1965(1908)	—	0.50	0.85	1.25	1.75	—
VS1966(1909)	—	0.50	0.85	1.25	1.75	—
VS1967(1910)	—	0.75	0.50	2.50	3.50	—

KM# 45.2 DOKDO

Copper **Obv. Inscription:** Perso-Arabic Ek paisa Junagadh Riiyaasat (government) **Reverse:** Date divided by space in legend **Rev. Inscription:** Devanagari-Shri Sorath Sarkaar **Mint:** Junagadh

Date	Mintage	Good	VG	F	VF	XF
VS1966(1909)	—	0.75	1.50	2.50	3.50	—

KM# 45.3 DOKDO

Copper **Obv. Inscription:** Perso-Arabic Ek paisa Junagadh Riiyaasat (government) **Reverse:** Date at top in legend **Rev. Inscription:** Devanagari-Shri Sorath Sarkaar **Mint:** Junagadh

Date	Mintage	Good	VG	F	VF	XF
VS1966(1909)	—	1.75	2.75	4.00	6.50	—

KM# 46.1 DOKDO

Copper **Obv. Inscription:** Perso-Arabic Ek paisa Junagadh Riiyaasat (government) **Rev. Inscription:** Devanagari-Shri Sorath Sarkaar **Mint:** Junagadh

Date	Mintage	Good	VG	F	VF	XF
ND(1909)	—	1.75	2.75	4.00	6.50	—

KM# 46.2 DOKDO

Copper **Obv. Inscription:** Perso-Arabic Ek paisa Junagadh Riiyaasat (government) **Reverse:** Stars between inscriptions **Rev. Inscription:** Devanagari-Shri Sorath Sarkaar **Mint:** Junagadh

Date	Mintage	Good	VG	F	VF	XF
ND(1909)	—	1.75	2.75	4.00	6.50	—

KM# 48 2 DOKDA

Copper **Obv. Inscription:** Perso-Arabic Ek paisa Junagadh Riiyaasat (government) **Rev. Inscription:** Devanagari-Shri Sorath Sarkaar **Mint:** Junagadh

Date	Mintage	Good	VG	F	VF	XF
VS1964(1907)	—	7.50	12.50	20.00	30.00	—

KM# 52 KORI

4.6000 g., Silver, 15 mm. **Mint:** Junagadh

Date	Mintage	VG	F	VF	XF	Unc
VS1966(1909)	—	17.50	25.00	35.00	50.00	—

KM# 58 GOLD KORI

Gold **Obverse:** Perso-Arabic inscription **Obv. Inscription:** "Nawab Bahadur Muhammad Khanji" **Reverse:** Date, mint name **Mint:** Junagadh **Note:** Weight varies: 4.02-4.77 grams.

Date	Mintage	VG	F	VF	XF	Unc
AH1325/VS1963 (1908)	—	—	—	500	850	1,250

KM# 60 MOHUR

11.5400 g., Gold **Obverse:** Perso-Arabic inscription **Obv. Inscription:** "Nawab Bahadur Muhammad Khanji" **Reverse:** Date, mint name **Mint:** Junagadh

Date	Mintage	VG	F	VF	XF	Unc
AH1325/VS1963 (1908)	—	—	—	—	2,000	2,800

KM# 61 MOHUR

11.5400 g., Gold **Obverse:** "Shri Divan" in Devanagari below **Mint:** Junagadh

Date	Mintage	Good	VG	F	VF	XF
AH1325(1907) Rare	—	—	—	—	—	—

Mahabat Khan III

AH1329-1368 / VS1968-2005 / 1911-1948AD

MILLED COINAGE

KM# 63 DOKDO

Copper

Date	Mintage	Good	VG	F	VF	XF
VS1985(1928)	—	10.00	16.50	25.00	40.00	—
VS1990(1933)	—	10.00	16.50	25.00	40.00	—

KISHANGARH

The maharajas of Kishangarh, a small state in northwest India, in the vicinity of Ajmer, belonged to the Rathor Rajputs. The town of Kishangarh, which gave its name to the state, was founded in 1611 and was itself named after Kishen Singh, the first ruler. The maharajas succeeded in reaching terms with Akbar in the late 16th century, and again in 1818 with the British. In 1949 the state was merged into Rajasthan.

RULERS

Sardul Singh, VS1936-1957/1879-1900AD
Madan Singh, VS1957-1983/1900-1926AD
Yaghyanarayan Singh, VS1983-1995/1926-1938AD
Sumer Singh, VS1995-2000/1938-1949AD

MINT

Kishangarh

MINT MARK

Symbol on reverse: Jhar

KINGDOM

HAMMERED COINAGE

Regal Style
1900-1926

Y# B3 1/4 RUPEE

2.7000 g., Silver **Obv. Inscription:** Edward (VII)... **Reverse:** Jhar **Rev. Inscription:** Madan Singh...

Date	Mintage	Good	VG	F	VF	XF
ND//24 (sic) (1902)	—	5.00	12.50	20.00	30.00	50.00

Y# A3 1/2 RUPEE

5.4000 g., Silver **Obv. Inscription:** Empress Victoria... **Reverse:** Jhar **Rev. Inscription:** Madan Singh...

Date	Mintage	Good	VG	F	VF	XF
ND (1900-01)	—	20.00	40.00	65.00	100	145

Y# 3 1/2 RUPEE

5.4000 g., Silver **Obv. Inscription:** Edward (VII)... **Reverse:** Jhar **Rev. Inscription:** Madan Singh...

Date	Mintage	Good	VG	F	VF	XF
1902//24	—	5.00	12.50	20.00	30.00	50.00

Y# C3 RUPEE

10.8000 g., Silver **Obv. Inscription:** Empress Victoria... **Reverse:** Jhar **Rev. Inscription:** Madan Singh...

Date	Mintage	Good	VG	F	VF	XF
ND (1900-01)	—	—	—	—	—	—

Y# D3 MOHUR

10.9000 g., Gold **Obv. Inscription:** Empress Victoria... **Reverse:** Jhar **Rev. Inscription:** Madan Singh...

Date	Mintage	Good	VG	F	VF	XF
ND (1900-01)	—	120	200	300	550	900

HAMMERED COINAGE

1926-1938

Y# 4 1/4 RUPEE

2.7000 g., Silver **Obv. Inscription:** George (V)... **Reverse:** Jhar **Rev. Inscription:** Yaghyanarayan...

Date	Mintage	Good	VG	F	VF	XF
ND//24 (sic) (1926-38)	—	5.00	12.50	20.00	30.00	50.00

Y# 5 1/2 RUPEE

5.4000 g., Silver **Obv. Inscription:** George (V)... **Reverse:** Jhar **Rev. Inscription:** Yaghyanarayan...

Date	Mintage	Good	VG	F	VF	XF
ND//24 (sic) (1926-38)	—	5.00	12.50	20.00	30.00	50.00

Y# 6 RUPEE

10.8000 g., Silver **Obv. Inscription:** George (V)... **Reverse:** Jhar **Rev. Inscription:** Yaghyanarayan...

Date	Mintage	Good	VG	F	VF	XF
ND//24 (sic) (1926-38)	—	7.50	18.50	31.50	45.00	65.00

Y# 6a NAZARANA RUPEE

Silver **Obv. Inscription:** George (V)... **Reverse:** Jhar **Rev. Inscription:** Yaghyanarayan... **Note:** Weight varies: 10.70-10.80 grams.

Date	Mintage	Good	VG	F	VF	XF
ND(1926-38)	—	30.00	60.00	100	160	225

Y# 7 1/2 MOHUR

Gold, 18 mm. **Obv. Inscription:** George (V)... **Reverse:** Jhar **Rev. Inscription:** Yaghyanarayan... **Note:** Approximately 5.50 grams.

Date	Mintage	Good	VG	F	VF	XF
ND//24 (sic) (1926-38)	—	—	145	225	550	850

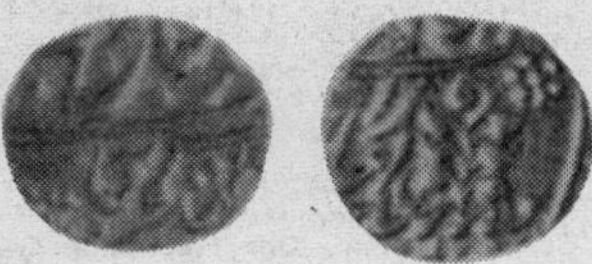

Y# 8 MOHUR

Gold, 19 mm. **Obv. Inscription:** George (V)... **Reverse:** Jhar **Rev. Inscription:** Yaghyanarayan... **Note:** Approximately 11.00 grams.

Date	Mintage	Good	VG	F	VF	XF
ND//24 (sic) (1926-38)	—	—	225	300	500	800

ANONYMOUS HAMMERED "DUMP" COINAGE

First Series

Y# 9 1/8 RUPEE

1.3500 g., Silver, 12 mm. **Obv. Inscription:** Nagari "Chadi" (silver) **Reverse:** Jhar

Date	Mintage	Good	VG	F	VF	XF
ND//24 (sic) (ca.1902-38)	—	20.00	40.00	65.00	100	150

Y# 10 1/4 RUPEE

2.7000 g., Silver, 15 mm. **Obv. Inscription:** Nagari "Chadi" (silver) **Reverse:** Jhar

Date	Mintage	Good	VG	F	VF	XF
ND//24 (sic) (ca.1902-38)	—	20.00	40.00	65.00	100	150

Y# 11 1/2 RUPEE

5.4000 g., Silver, 17-18 mm. **Obv. Inscription:** Nagari "Chadi" (silver) **Reverse:** Jhar **Note:** Size varies.

Date	Mintage	Good	VG	F	VF	XF
ND(ca.1902-38)	—	20.00	40.00	65.00	100	150
ND(ca.1902-38)	—	40.00	65.00	100	150	—
ND//24 (sic) (ca. 1902-38)	—	20.00	40.00	65.00	100	150

Y# A11 1/2 RUPEE

(No Composition) **Obverse:** As #Y11. **Obv. Inscription:** Nagari "Chadi" (Silver) **Reverse:** As #Y5. **Rev. Inscription:** Maharajah Yaghyanarayan... **Note:** Mule.

Date	Mintage	VG	F	VF	XF	Unc
ND(1902-38) Rare	—	—	—	—	—	—

Y# 12 RUPEE

Silver, 20-24 mm. **Obv. Inscription:** Nagari "Chadi" (silver) **Reverse:** Jhar **Note:** Weight varies: 10.85-11.05 grams. Size varies.

Date	Mintage	Good	VG	F	VF	XF
ND//24 (sic) (ca.1902-38)	—	12.50	25.00	40.00	65.00	100

ANONYMOUS HAMMERED "DUMP" COINAGE

Second Series

Denominations in Nagari, Persian and 'merchants numerals', in Annas on obverse.

Y# 13 2 ANNAS

1.3200 g., Silver, 11 mm. **Reverse:** Jhar

Date	Mintage	Good	VG	F	VF	XF
ND//24 (sic) (ca.1902-38)	—	6.00	15.00	25.00	40.00	60.00

Y# 14 4 ANNAS

2.6200 g., Silver, 12-13 mm. **Reverse:** Jhar **Note:** Size varies.

Date	Mintage	Good	VG	F	VF	XF
ND//24 (sic) (ca.1902-38)	—	5.00	12.50	20.00	30.00	50.00

Y# 15 8 ANNAS

5.3500 g., Silver, 16 mm. **Reverse:** Jhar

Date	Mintage	Good	VG	F	VF	XF
ND//24 (sic) (ca.1902-38)	—	6.00	15.00	25.00	40.00	60.00

KOTAH

Kotah State, located in northwest India was subdivided out of Bundi early in the 17th century when it was given to a younger son of the Bundi raja by the Mughal emperor. The ruler, or maharao, was a Chauhan Rajput. During the years of Maratha ascendancy Kotah fell on hard times, especially from the depredations of Holkar. In 1817 the State came under treaty with the British.

RULERS

Ram Singh II,
VS1885-1923/1828-1866AD
Chattar Singh,
VS1923-1946/1866-1889AD
Umed Singh II,
VS1946-1992/1889-1935AD

MINT

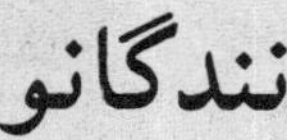

Mint name: *Nandgaon*

نندگانو عرف کوته

Kotah urf Nandgaon
or *Nandgaon urf Kotah* on earliest issues.

MINT MARKS

Mint mark #1 appears beneath #4 on most Kotah coins, and serves to distinguish coins of Kotah from similar issues of Bundi in the pre-Victoria period.

C#28 has mint mark #2 on obv., #1, 3 and 4 on rev. All later issues have #1 on obv., #1, 5 and 4 on rev.

BRITISH PROTECTORATE

HAMMERED COINAGE

Regal Style

Y# 6 RUPEE

11.2000 g., Silver, 18-20 mm. **Obv. Inscription:** "Badshah Zaman Inglistan... (Victoria)" **Note:** Size varies.

Date	Mintage	Good	VG	F	VF	XF
ND//44 (1901)	—	4.50	6.00	9.00	15.00	25.00

Y# 6a NAZARANA RUPEE

11.2000 g., Silver, 26-30 mm. **Obv. Inscription:** "Badshah Zaman Inglistan... (Victoria)" **Note:** Size varies.

Date	Mintage	Good	VG	F	VF	XF
ND//44 (1901)	—	17.50	32.50	45.00	75.00	125

Y# 8 MOHUR

10.7000 g., Gold, 18 mm. **Obv. Inscription:** "Badshah Zaman Inglistan... (Victoria)"

Date	Mintage	Good	VG	F	VF	XF
ND//44 (1901)	—	—	250	300	400	600

KUTCH

State located in northwest India, consisting of a peninsula north of the Gulf of Kutch.

The rulers of Kutch were Jareja Rajputs who, coming from Tatta in Sind, conquered Kutch in the 14th or 15th centuries. The capital city of Bhuj is thought to date from the mid-16th century. In 1617, after Akbar's conquest of Gujerat and the fall of the Gujerat sultans, the Kutch ruler, Rao Bharmal I (1586-1632) visited Jahangir and established a relationship which was sufficiently warm as to leave Kutch virtually independent throughout the Mughal period. Early in the 19th century internal disorder and the existence of rival claimants to the throne resulted in British intrusion into the state's affairs. Rao Bharmalji II was deposed in favor of Rao Desalji II who proved much more amenable to the Government of India's wishes. He and his successors continued to rule in a manner considered by the British to be most enlightened and, as a result, Maharao Khengarji III was created a Knight Grand Commander of the Indian Empire. In view of its geographical isolation Kutch came under the direct control of the Central Government at India's independence.

First coinage was struck in 1617AD.

RULERS

Khengarji III, VS1932-1999/1875-1942AD

M(a)-ha-ra-o Sri Khen-ga-r-ji

मादाराउ खेंगारजी

Ma-ha-ra-o Khen-ga-r-ji

मा दा राजा हिराज मिरजा मदाराओ

Ma-ha-ra-ja Dhi-ra-j Mi-r-ja M(a)-ha-ra-o Sri

खेंगारजी बहादर कछभुज

Khen-ga-r-ji B(a)-ha-du-r K(a)-chh-bhu-j

मिरजामहाराओश्री खेंगारजी

Mi-r-jan M(a)-ha-ra-o Sri Khen-ga-r-ji

महाराओश्री खेंगारजी

M(a)-ha-ra-o Sri Khen-ga-r-ji

महाराजाधिराजमिरजा महाराउ

M(a)-ha-ra-ja Dhi-ra-j Mi-r-jan M(a)-ha-ra-o

श्री खेंगारजीबहादुर

Sri-Khen-ga-r-ji B(a)-ha-du-r

श्री खेंगारजीसवाई बहादुर

Sri Khen-ga-r-ji Sa-va-i B(a)-ha-du-r

महाराउश्री खेंगारजी कच्छभुज

M(a)-ha-ra-o Sri Khen-ga-r-ji K(a)-chchh-bhu-j
Vijayarajji, VS1999-2004/1942-1947AD

विजयराजजी

Vi-j(a)-y(a)-ra-j-ji

महाराओश्री विजयराजजी

M(a)-ha-ra-o Sri Vi-j(a)-y(a)-ra-j-ji K(a)-chchh 2000
Madanasinhji, VS2004-- /1947-1948AD

मदनसिंहजी

M(a)-d(a)-n(a)-sin-h-ji
Pragmalji III & Maharani Pritidevi, VS2048-/1991AD-

MINT

भुज or بهج

Bhuj (Devanagari) (Persian)

KINGDOM

Khengarji III
VS1932-98 / 1875-1942AD

MILLED COINAGE
Regal Issues - Second Series

Y# 35.1 KORI

4.7000 g., 0.6100 Silver .0921 oz. ASW **Obv. Inscription:** "Victoria, Empress of India" **Reverse:** Open crescent

Date	Mintage	Good	VG	F	VF	XF
1901//VS1957	—	1.50	3.00	4.50	6.50	10.00

Y# 37.6 5 KORI

13.8700 g., 0.9370 Silver .4178 oz. ASW
Obv. Inscription: "Victoria, Empress of India"

Date	Mintage	Good	VG	F	VF	XF
1901//VS1957	—	7.00	17.50	25.00	35.00	50.00

MILLED COINAGE
Regal Issues - Third Series

Y# 38 TRAMBIYO

4.0000 g., Copper, 16 mm. **Obv. Legend:** Edward VII...

Date	Mintage	Good	VG	F	VF	XF
1908/VS1965	—	0.60	1.50	2.50	3.50	4.50
1909/VS1965	—	0.25	0.60	1.00	1.50	2.50
1909/VS1966	—	0.25	0.60	1.00	1.50	2.00
1910/VS1966	—	0.85	1.65	2.75	4.25	6.00

Y# 39 DOKDO

8.0000 g., Copper, 20.5 mm. **Obv. Legend:** Edward VII...

Date	Mintage	Good	VG	F	VF	XF
1909/VS1965	—	0.30	0.75	1.25	1.50	2.00
1909/VS1966	—	0.30	0.75	1.25	1.50	2.00

Y# 40 1-1/2 DOKDA

12.0000 g., Copper, 23 mm. **Obv. Legend:** Edward VII...

Date	Mintage	Good	VG	F	VF	XF
1909/VS1965	—	30.00	60.00	100	115	150

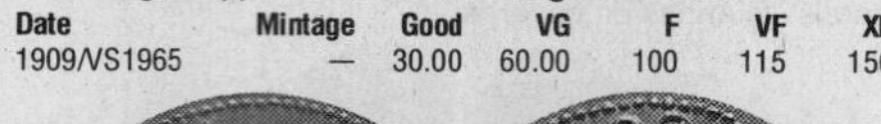

Y# 41 3 DOKDA

24.0000 g., Copper **Obv. Legend:** Edward VII...

Date	Mintage	Good	VG	F	VF	XF
1909/VS1965	—	30.00	60.00	100	115	150

Y# 45 5 KORI

13.8700 g., 0.9370 Silver .4178 oz. ASW **Obv. Legend:** Edward VII...

Date	Mintage	Good	VG	F	VF	XF
1902/VS1959	—	60.00	120	185	250	375
1903/VS1960	—	60.00	120	185	250	375
1904/VS1961	—	60.00	120	185	250	375
1905/VS1962	—	60.00	120	185	250	375
1906/VS1963	—	60.00	120	185	250	375
1907VS1964	—	60.00	120	185	250	375
1908/VS1965	—	50.00	100	150	235	350
1909/VS1966	—	50.00	100	150	235	350

MILLED COINAGE
Regal Issues - Fourth Series

Y# 46 TRAMBIYO

4.0000 g., Copper, 16 mm. **Obv. Inscription:** George V...

Date	Mintage	Good	VG	F	VF	XF
1919/VS1976	—	0.10	0.30	0.50	0.75	1.00
1920/VS1976	—	0.10	0.30	0.50	0.75	1.50
1920/VS1977	—	0.10	0.30	0.50	0.75	1.50

Y# 54 TRAMBIYO

4.0000 g., Copper, 16 mm. **Obv. Inscription:** George V...

Date	Mintage	Good	VG	F	VF	XF
1928/VS1984	—	0.25	0.60	1.00	2.00	3.00
1928/VS1985	—	0.10	0.30	0.50	0.75	1.00

Y# 47 DOKDO

8.0000 g., Copper, 21 mm. **Obv. Inscription:** George V...

Date	Mintage	Good	VG	F	VF	XF
1920/VS1976	—	0.25	0.60	1.00	1.25	2.00
1920/VS1977	—	0.25	0.60	1.00	1.25	2.00

Y# 55 DOKDO

8.0000 g., Copper, 21 mm. **Obv. Inscription:** George V...

Date	Mintage	Good	VG	F	VF	XF
1922/VS1982 (sic)	—	0.50	1.25	1.75	2.50	3.50
1928/VS1984	—	0.25	0.60	1.00	1.25	1.50
1929/VS1985	—	0.25	0.60	1.00	1.25	1.50

Y# 48 1-1/2 DOKDA

12.0000 g., Copper, 23.5 mm. **Obv. Inscription:** George V...

Date	Mintage	Good	VG	F	VF	XF
1926/VS1982	—	0.35	0.90	1.50	2.50	3.00

Y# 56 1-1/2 DOKDA

12.0000 g., Copper, 23 mm. **Obv. Inscription:** George V...

Date	Mintage	Good	VG	F	VF	XF
1928/VS1985	—	0.20	0.50	0.75	1.00	1.50
1929/VS1985	—	0.20	0.50	0.75	1.00	1.50
1929/VS1986	—	0.20	0.50	0.75	1.00	1.50
1931/VS1987	—	0.20	0.50	0.75	1.00	1.50
1931/VS1988	—	0.20	0.50	0.75	1.00	1.50
1932/VS1988	—	0.40	1.00	1.50	2.50	4.00
1932/VS1989	—	0.20	0.50	0.75	1.00	1.50

Y# 49 3 DOKDA

24.0000 g., Copper, 33 mm. **Obv. Inscription:** George V...

Date	Mintage	Good	VG	F	VF	XF
1926/VS1982	—	0.60	1.50	2.50	3.50	4.50

Y# 57 3 DOKDA

24.0000 g., Copper, 33 mm. **Obv. Inscription:** George V...

Date	Mintage	Good	VG	F	VF	XF
1928/VS1985	—	0.25	0.60	1.00	1.50	2.25
1929/VS1985	—	0.25	0.60	1.00	1.50	2.25
1929/VS1986	—	0.25	0.60	1.00	1.50	2.25
1930/VS1987	—	0.25	0.60	1.00	1.50	2.25
1931/VS1987	—	0.25	0.60	1.00	1.50	2.25
1934/VS1990	—	0.25	0.60	1.00	1.50	2.25
1934/VS1991	—	0.25	0.60	1.00	1.50	2.25
1935/VS1992	—	0.25	0.60	1.00	1.50	2.25

Y# 58 1/2 KORI

2.3500 g., 0.6010 Silver .0460 oz. ASW, 14 mm.
Obv. Inscription: George V...

Date	Mintage	Good	VG	F	VF	XF
1928/VS1985	—	0.75	2.00	3.00	4.00	7.00

Y# 51 KORI

4.7000 g., 0.6010 Silver .0921 oz. ASW **Obv. Inscription:** George V...

Date	Mintage	VG	F	VF	XF	Unc
1913/VS1970	—	1.50	2.00	3.00	4.00	7.00
1923/VS1979	—	1.50	2.00	3.00	4.00	7.00
1923/VS1980	—	1.50	2.00	3.00	4.00	7.00
1927/VS1984	—	1.75	2.50	3.50	5.00	8.00

Y# 59 KORI

4.7000 g., 0.6010 Silver .0921 oz. ASW, 17 mm. **Obv. Legend:** George V...

Date	Mintage	VG	F	VF	XF	Unc
1928/VS1985	—	1.50	2.50	3.50	5.00	8.00
1929/VS1985	—	1.50	2.50	3.50	5.00	8.00
1931/VS1987	—	2.75	6.50	10.00	15.00	22.50
1931/VS1988	—	1.50	2.50	3.00	5.00	8.00
1932/VS1988	—	1.50	2.50	3.00	5.00	8.00
1932/VS1989	—	1.50	2.50	3.00	5.00	8.00
1933/VS1989	—	1.50	2.50	3.00	5.00	8.00
1933/VS1990	—	1.50	2.50	3.00	5.00	8.00
1934/VS1990	—	1.50	2.50	3.00	5.00	8.00
1934/VS1991	—	1.50	2.50	3.00	5.00	8.00
1935/VS1991	—	1.50	2.50	3.00	5.00	8.00
1935/VS1992	—	1.50	2.50	3.00	5.00	8.00
1936/VS1992	—	1.75	3.00	4.50	6.50	10.00

Y# 52 2-1/2 KORI

6.9350 g., 0.9370 Silver .2089 oz. ASW **Obv. Inscription:** George V...

Date	Mintage	VG	F	VF	XF	Unc
1916/VS1973	—	3.00	4.00	6.00	9.00	13.50
1917/VS1973	—	3.00	4.00	6.00	9.00	13.50
1917/VS1974	—	3.00	4.00	6.00	9.00	13.50
1918/VS1974	—	3.00	4.00	6.00	9.00	13.50
1919/VS1975	—	3.00	4.00	6.00	9.00	13.50
1922/VS1978	—	3.00	4.00	6.00	9.00	13.50
1922/VS1979	—	3.00	4.00	6.00	9.00	13.50
1924/VS1981	—	3.00	4.00	6.00	9.00	13.50
1926/VS1983	—	3.00	4.00	6.00	9.00	13.50

Y# 52a 2-1/2 KORI

6.9350 g., 0.9370 Silver .2089 oz. ASW **Obv. Inscription:** George V... **Reverse:** Smaller legend

Date	Mintage	VG	F	VF	XF	Unc
1927/VS1984	—	3.00	5.00	7.00	10.00	15.00
1928/VS1985	—	3.00	4.00	6.00	9.00	13.50
1930/VS1986	—	3.00	4.00	6.00	9.00	13.50
1930/VS1987	—	3.00	4.00	6.00	9.00	13.50
1932/VS1988	—	3.00	4.00	6.00	9.00	13.50
1932/VS1989	—	3.00	4.00	6.00	9.00	13.50
1933/VS1989	—	3.00	4.00	6.00	9.00	13.50
1933/VS1990	—	3.00	4.00	6.00	9.00	13.50
1934/VS1990	—	3.00	4.00	6.00	9.00	13.50
1934/VS1991	—	3.00	4.00	6.00	9.00	13.50
1935/VS1991	—	3.00	4.00	6.00	9.00	13.50
1935/VS1992	—	3.00	4.00	6.00	9.00	13.50

Y# 53 5 KORI

13.8700 g., 0.9370 Silver .4178 oz. ASW **Obv. Inscription:** George V... **Note:** 5 Kori coins were issued with reeded edges until 1928AD, which is when the security edge was introduced. Due to counterfeiting, the government recalled pieces and added lettering as a mark of authentication.

Date	Mintage	VG	F	VF	XF	Unc
1913/VS1970	—	6.00	7.50	10.00	15.00	22.50
1915/VS1972	—	6.00	7.50	10.00	15.00	22.50
1916/VS1973	—	6.00	7.50	10.00	15.00	22.50
1916/VS1975 (Sic)	—	6.50	12.50	18.50	25.00	35.00
1917/VS1973	—	6.00	7.50	10.00	15.00	22.50
1917/VS1974	—	6.00	7.50	10.00	15.00	22.50
1918/VS1974	—	6.00	7.50	10.00	15.00	22.50
1918/VS1975	—	6.00	7.50	10.00	15.00	22.50
1919/VS1975	—	6.00	7.50	10.00	15.00	22.50
1919/VS1976	—	12.50	25.00	37.50	50.00	70.00
1920/VS1977	—	6.50	8.00	11.50	16.50	25.00
1921/VS1977	—	6.00	7.50	10.00	15.00	22.50
1921/VS1978	—	6.00	7.50	10.00	15.00	22.50
1922/VS1974 (Sic)	—	—	—	—	—	—
1922/VS1978	—	6.00	7.50	10.00	15.00	22.50
1922/VS1979	—	6.00	7.50	10.00	15.00	22.50
1922/VS1982 (Sic)	—	6.00	7.50	12.50	18.50	27.50
1923/VS1979	—	6.00	7.50	10.00	15.00	22.50
1924/VS1978 (Sic)	—	10.00	20.00	31.50	42.50	60.00
1924/VS1980	—	6.00	7.50	10.00	15.00	22.50
1924/VS1981	—	6.00	7.50	10.00	15.00	22.50
1925/VS1982	—	6.00	7.50	10.00	15.00	22.50
1926/VS1978 (Sic)	—	6.50	12.50	18.50	25.00	35.00
1926/VS1982	—	6.00	7.50	10.00	15.00	22.50
1926/VS1893	—	6.00	7.50	10.00	15.00	22.50
1927/VS1984	—	7.00	17.50	25.00	35.00	50.00
1927/VS1984 Proof	—	Value: 275				

Y# 53a 5 KORI

13.8700 g., 0.9370 Silver .4178 oz. ASW **Obverse:** Smaller legend **Obv. Inscription:** George V... **Reverse:** Smaller legend

Date	Mintage	VG	F	VF	XF	Unc
1928/VS1985	—	6.50	15.00	21.50	30.00	40.00
1929/VS1986	—	6.00	7.50	10.00	15.00	22.50
1930/VS1986	—	6.00	7.50	10.00	15.00	22.50
1930/VS1987	—	6.00	7.50	10.00	15.00	22.50
1931/VS1987	—	6.00	7.50	10.00	15.00	22.50
1931/VS1988	—	6.00	7.50	10.00	15.00	22.50
1932/VS1988	—	6.00	7.50	10.00	15.00	22.50
1932/VS1989	—	6.00	7.50	10.00	15.00	22.50
1933/VS1989	—	6.00	7.50	10.00	15.00	22.50
1933/VS1990	—	6.00	7.50	10.00	15.00	22.50
1934/VS1990	—	6.00	7.50	10.00	15.00	22.50
1934/VS1991	—	6.00	7.50	10.00	15.00	22.50
1935/VS1991	—	6.00	7.50	10.00	15.00	22.50
1935/VS1992	—	6.00	7.50	10.00	15.00	22.50
1936/VS1992	—	6.00	7.50	10.00	15.00	22.50

MILLED COINAGE

Regal Issues - Fifth Series

Y# 63 3 DOKDA

24.0000 g., Copper **Obv. Legend:** Edward VIII...

Date	Mintage	Good	VG	F	VF	XF
1936/VS1993	—	1.25	3.00	5.00	7.50	10.00

Y# 65 KORI

4.7000 g., 0.6010 Silver .0921 oz. ASW **Obv. Legend:** Edward VIII...

Date	Mintage	VG	F	VF	XF	Unc
1936/VS1992	—	1.50	3.00	4.50	6.50	10.00
1936/VS1993	—	1.50	3.00	4.50	6.50	10.00

Y# 66 2-1/2 KORI

6.9350 g., 0.9370 Silver .2089 oz. ASW **Obv. Inscription:** Edward VIII...

Date	Mintage	VG	F	VF	XF	Unc
1936/VS1992	—	4.00	11.50	17.50	23.50	32.50
1936/VS1993	—	4.00	11.50	17.50	23.50	32.50

Y# 67 5 KORI

13.8700 g., 0.9370 Silver .4178 oz. ASW **Obv. Inscription:** Edward VIII...

Date	Mintage	VG	F	VF	XF	Unc
1936/VS1992	—	6.00	7.00	8.00	11.50	17.50
1936/VS1993	—	6.00	7.00	8.00	11.50	17.50

MILLED COINAGE

Regal Issues - Sixth Series

Y# 71 3 DOKDA

24.0000 g., Copper **Obv. Legend:** George VI

Date	Mintage	VG	F	VF	XF	Unc
1937/VS1993	—	0.90	1.50	2.00	3.00	5.50

Y# 73 KORI

4.7000 g., 0.6010 Silver .0921 oz. ASW **Obv. Legend:** George VI

Date	Mintage	VG	F	VF	XF	Unc
1937/VS1993	—	1.50	3.00	4.50	6.50	10.00
1937/VS1994	—	1.50	3.00	4.50	6.50	10.00
1938/VS1995	—	1.50	3.00	4.50	6.50	10.00
1939/VS1995	—	1.50	3.00	4.50	6.50	10.00
1939/VS1996	—	1.50	3.00	4.50	6.50	10.00
1940/VS1996	—	1.50	3.00	4.50	6.50	10.00

Y# 74 2-1/2 KORI

6.9350 g., 0.9370 Silver .2089 oz. ASW **Obv. Inscription:** George VI

Date	Mintage	VG	F	VF	XF	Unc
1937/VS1993	—	3.00	5.00	7.00	10.00	15.00

Y# 75 5 KORI

13.8700 g., 0.9370 Silver .4178 oz. ASW **Obv. Inscription:** George VI

Date	Mintage	VG	F	VF	XF	Unc
1936/VS1993	—	6.50	8.50	11.50	16.50	25.00
1937/VS1993	—	6.00	7.50	10.00	15.00	22.50
1937/VS1994	—	6.00	7.50	10.00	15.00	22.50
1938/VS1994	—	6.00	7.50	10.00	15.00	22.50
1938/VS1995	—	6.00	7.50	10.00	15.00	22.50
1941/VS1997	—	7.00	10.00	15.00	21.50	30.00
1941/VS1998	—	6.00	7.50	10.00	15.00	22.50

Vijayarajji

VS1998-2004 / 1942-1947AD

MILLED COINAGE

Regal Issues - Sixth Series

Y# 76 TRAMBIYO

Copper **Obv. Legend:** George VI

Date	Mintage	VG	F	VF	XF	Unc
1943/VS2000	—	0.10	0.25	0.50	1.00	1.50
1944/VS2000	—	0.10	0.25	0.50	1.00	1.50

Y# 78 DHABU (1/8 Kori = 3 Dokda)

Copper, 23 mm. **Obv. Legend:** George VI

Date	Mintage	VG	F	VF	XF	Unc
1943/VS1999	—	0.10	0.25	0.40	0.65	1.00
1943/VS2000	—	0.10	0.25	0.40	0.65	1.00
1944/VS2000	—	0.10	0.25	0.40	0.65	1.00
1947/VS2004	—	0.10	0.25	0.40	0.65	1.00

Y# 77 DHINGLO (1/16 Kori = 1-1/2 Dokda)

Copper, 21 mm. **Obv. Legend:** George VI

Date	Mintage	VG	F	VF	XF	Unc
1943/VS2000	—	0.10	0.25	0.40	0.65	1.00
1944/VS2000	—	0.10	0.25	0.40	0.65	1.00
1947/VS2004	—	0.10	0.25	0.40	0.65	1.00
1948/VS2004	—	0.20	0.50	1.00	2.00	3.50

Y# 79 PAYALO (1/4 Kori)

Copper, 27 mm. **Obv. Legend:** George VI

Date	Mintage	VG	F	VF	XF	Unc
1943/VS1999	—	0.30	0.75	1.00	1.50	2.50
1943/VS2000	—	0.30	0.75	1.00	1.50	2.50
1944/VS2000	—	0.30	0.75	1.00	1.50	2.50
1944/VS2001	—	0.30	0.75	1.00	1.50	2.50
1945/VS2001	—	0.15	0.35	0.50	0.75	1.25
1945/VS2002	—	0.15	0.35	0.50	0.75	1.25
1946/VS2002	—	0.15	0.35	0.50	0.75	1.25
1946/VS2003	—	0.15	0.35	0.50	0.75	1.25
1947/VS2003	—	0.30	0.75	1.00	1.50	2.50

Y# 80 ADHIO (1/2 Kori)

Copper, 36 mm. **Obv. Legend:** George VI

Date	Mintage	VG	F	VF	XF	Unc
1943/VS1999	—	0.60	1.50	1.75	2.00	3.50
1943/VS2000	—	0.60	1.50	1.75	2.00	3.50
1944/VS2001	—	0.60	1.25	1.50	1.75	3.00
1945/VS2001	—	0.60	1.50	1.75	2.00	3.50
1945/VS2002	—	0.60	1.50	1.75	2.00	3.50
1946/VS2002	—	0.60	1.50	1.75	2.00	3.50

Y# A81 KORI

4.6600 g., Silver **Obv. Legend:** George VI **Note:** Similar to Y#51.

Date	Mintage	VG	F	VF	XF	Unc
1942/VS1998 Rare	—	—	—	—	—	—

Y# 81 KORI

4.7000 g., 0.6010 Silver .0921 oz. ASW **Obv. Legend:** George VI

Date	Mintage	VG	F	VF	XF	Unc
1942/VS1999	—	1.50	2.50	3.50	5.00	8.00
1943/VS1999	—	1.50	2.50	3.50	5.00	8.00
1943/VS2000	—	1.50	2.50	3.50	5.00	8.00
1944/VS2000	—	1.50	2.50	3.50	5.00	8.00
1944/VS2001	—	1.50	2.50	3.50	5.00	8.00

Y# 82 5 KORI

13.8700 g., 0.9370 Silver .4178 oz. ASW **Obv. Inscription:** George VI

Date	Mintage	VG	F	VF	XF	Unc
1942/VS1998	—	6.00	7.50	10.00	15.00	22.50
1942/VS1999	—	6.00	7.50	10.00	15.00	22.50
1943/VS1998 Reported, not confirmed	—	—	—	—	—	—

Y# 82A 10 KORI

17.3900 g., Silver **Obv. Inscription:** George VI

Date	Mintage	VG	F	VF	XF	Unc
1943/VS1999 Rare	—	—	—	—	—	—

Madanasinghji

VS2004-2005 / 1947-1948AD

MILLED COINAGE

Regal Issues - Sixth Series

Y# 83 DHABU (1/8 Kori)

Copper **Subject:** Victory for Indian Independence

Date	Mintage	VG	F	VF	XF	Unc
VS2004/1947	—	0.30	0.75	1.25	1.75	3.00

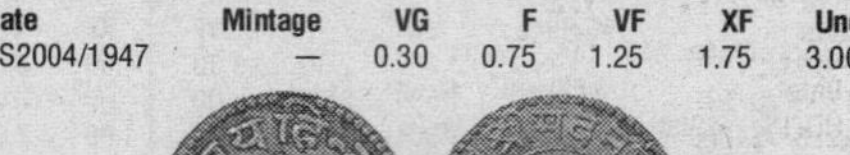

Y# 84 KORI

4.7000 g., 0.6010 Silver .0921 oz. ASW **Subject:** Victory for Indian Independence

Date	Mintage	VG	F	VF	XF	Unc
VS2004/1947	—	1.75	5.00	7.00	10.00	15.00

Y# 85 5 KORI

13.8700 g., 0.9370 Silver .4178 oz. ASW **Subject:** Victory for Indian Independence

Date	Mintage	VG	F	VF	XF	Unc
VS2004/1947	—	35.00	80.00	125	185	275

LUNAVADA

This small state in the Panch Mahal district of western India was ruled by Solanki Rajputs who claimed descent from Sidraj Jaisingh, the ruler of Anhalwara Patan and Gujerat. The rulers, or maharanas, traced their sovereignty to the early decades of the 15th century. At different times the State was feudatory to either Baroda or Sindhia.

Wakhat Singhji
VS1924-1986/1867-1929AD
HAMMERED COINAGE

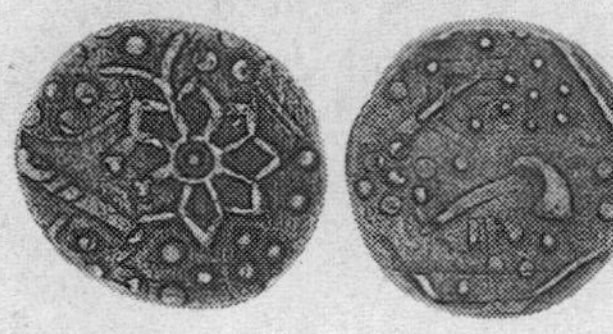

KM# 12 PAISA

Copper **Obverse:** Lotus Blossom **Reverse:** Persian legend **Shape:** Round **Note:** Weight varies: 6.50-8.30 grams.

Date	Mintage	Good	VG	F	VF	XF
VS1968(1911)	—	2.75	4.50	6.00	9.00	—
ND(ca.1911)	—	2.75	4.50	6.00	9.00	—

MALER KOTLA

State located in the Punjab in northwest India, founded by the Maler Kotla family who were Sherwani Afghans who had travelled to India from Kabul in 1467 as officials of the Delhi emperors.

Coins are rupees of Ahmad Shah Durrani, and except for the last ruler, contain the chief's initial on the reverse. The chiefs were called Ra'is until 1821, Nawabs thereafter.

For similar issues see Jind, Nabha and Patiala.

RULERS:
Ibrahim Ali Khan, AH1288-1326/1871-1908AD
Ahmad ali Khan, AH1326/1908AD

Ibrahim Ali Khan
AH1288-1326 / 1871-1908 AD
HAMMERED COINAGE

Y# 4 1/4 RUPEE

Silver **Note:** 2.68-290 grams.

Date	Mintage	Good	VG	F	VF	XF
ND(1871-1908)	—	16.00	40.00	65.00	100	150

Y# 5 1/2 RUPEE

Silver, 16mm. **Note:** 5.35-5.80 grams.

Date	Mintage	Good	VG	F	VF	XF
ND(1871-1908)	—	18.00	45.00	75.00	120	170

Ahmad Ali Khan
AH1326- / 1908- AD
HAMMERED COINAGE

Y# 7 1/2 PAISA

Copper **Obverse:** Persian inscription **Obv. Inscription:** Ahmad Ali Khan ...

Date	Mintage	Good	VG	F	VF	XF
AH1326 (1908)	—	7.00	11.00	16.50	25.00	—

Y# 8 PAISA

Copper **Obverse:** Persian inscription **Obv. Inscription:** Ahmad Ali Khan ...

Date	Mintage	Good	VG	F	VF	XF
AH1326(1908-09)	—	17.50	25.00	35.00	50.00	—

Y# A9 RUPEE

10.7700 g., Silver, 18.5 mm. **Obv. Inscription:** Persian "Ahmad Ali Kahn..." **Rev. Inscription:** "Nawab" tc left of "S" in "Julus" **Edge:** Plain

Y# 9 RUPEE

Silver **Obverse:** Persian inscription **Obv. Inscription:** Ahmad Ali Khan ... **Note:** Weight varies: 10.70-11.60 grams.

Date	Mintage	Good	VG	F	VF	XF
ND(1908-09)	—	4.50	6.50	10.00	15.00	25.00

Y# 10 NAZARANA 2 RUPEE

22.0000 g., Silver **Obverse:** Persian inscription **Obv. Inscription:** Ahmad Ali Khan ...

Date	Mintage	Good	VG	F	VF	XF
AH1326(1908-09) Rare	—	—	—	—	—	—

Y# 11 1/2 MOHUR

5.9400 g., Gold **Obverse:** Persian inscription **Obv. Inscription:** Ahmad Ali Khan ...

Date	Mintage	F	VF	XF	Unc
AH1326 (1908-09)	—	—	—	—	—

MEWAR

State located in Rajputana, northwest India. Capital:Udaipur.

The rulers of Mewar were universally regarded as the highest ranking Rajput house in India. The maharana of Mewar was looked upon as the representative of Rama, the ancient king of Ayodhya - and the family who were Sescdia Rajputs of the Gehlot clan, traced its descent through Rama to Kanak Sen who ruled in the 2nd century. The clan is believed to have migrated to Chitor from Gujarat sometime in the 8th century.

None of the indigenous rulers of India resisted the Muslim invasions into India with greater tenacity than the Rajputs of Mewar. It was their proud boast that they had never permitted a daughter to go into the Mughal harem. Three times the fortress and town of Chitor had fallen to Muslim invaders, to Alauddin Khilji (1303), to Bahadur Shah of Gujarat (1534) and to Akbar (1568). Each time Chitor gradually recovered but the last was the most traumatic experience of all. Rather than to submit to the Mughal onslaught, the women burned themselves on funeral pyres in a fearful rite called jauhar, and the men fell on the swords of the invaders.

After the sacking of Chitor the rana, Udai Singh, retired to the Aravali hills where he founded Udaipur, the capital after 1570. Udai Singh's son, Partab, refused to submit to the Mughal and recovered most of the territory lost in 1568. In the early 19th century Mewar suffered much at the hands of Marathas - Holkar, Sindhia and the Pindaris - until, in 1818, the State came under British supervision. In April 1948 Mewar was merged into Rajasthan and the maharana became governor Maharaj pramukh of the new province.

RULERS
Fatteh Singh, VS1941-1986/1884-1929AD
Bhupal Singh, VS1987-2005/1930-1948AD

MINTS

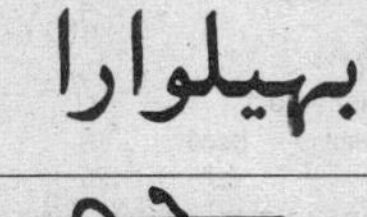

Bhilwara

चितोड़

Chitor

चित्रकूट

Chitarkot

उदयपुर

Udaipur

NOTE: All Mewar coinage is struck without ruler's name, and is largely undated. Certain types were generally struck over several reigns.

BRITISH PROTECTORATE
HAMMERED COINAGE

Y# 7.1 1/16 RUPEE

0.6500 g., Silver **Series:** Swarupshahi **Obv. Inscription:** Chitarkot/Udaipur **Rev. Inscription:** "Dosti Lundhun - Friendship With London" **Shape:** Round **Mint:** Udaipur

Date	Mintage	Good	VG	F	VF	XF
ND(1858-1920)	—	1.00	2.50	3.50	5.00	8.00

Y# 7.2 1/16 RUPEE

0.6500 g., Silver, 8-10 mm. **Obv. Inscription:** Chitarkot/Udaipur **Rev. Inscription:** "Dosti Lundhun - Friendship With London" **Shape:** Irregular **Mint:** Udaipur

Date	Mintage	Good	VG	F	VF	XF
ND(1858-1920)	—	1.25	3.00	4.50	6.50	10.00

Y# 8 1/8 RUPEE

1.3000 g., Silver, 11-12 mm. **Series:** Swarupshahi **Obv. Inscription:** Chitarkot/Udaipur **Rev. Inscription:** "Dosti Lundhun - Friendship With London" **Mint:** Udaipur

Date	Mintage	Good	VG	F	VF	XF
ND(1858-1920)	—	1.25	3.00	4.50	6.50	10.00

Y# 9 1/4 RUPEE

2.6000 g., Silver, 14-15 mm. **Series:** Swarupshahi **Obv. Inscription:** Chitarkot/Udaipur **Rev. Inscription:** "Dosti Lundhun - Friendship With London" **Mint:** Udaipur **Note:** Size varies.

Date	Mintage	Good	VG	F	VF	XF
ND(1858-1920)	—	1.25	2.50	3.50	5.00	8.00

Y# 10 1/2 RUPEE

Silver **Series:** Swarupshahi **Obv. Inscription:** Chitarkot/Udaipur **Rev. Inscription:** "Dosti Lundhun - Friendship With London" **Mint:** Udaipur **Note:** Weight varies: 5.20-5.40 grams.

Date	Mintage	Good	VG	F	VF	XF
ND(1858-1920)	—	2.25	3.00	4.50	6.50	10.00

Y# 11 RUPEE

Silver **Series:** Swarupshahi **Obv. Inscription:** Chitarkot/Udaipur **Rev. Inscription:** "Dosti Lundhun - Friendship With London" **Mint:** Udaipur **Note:** Weight varies: 10.75-10.85 grams.

Date	Mintage	Good	VG	F	VF	XF
ND(1858-1920)	—	4.25	5.00	6.00	9.00	14.00

Y# B12 1/8 MOHUR

1.3500 g., Gold **Series:** Swarupshahi **Obv. Inscription:** Chitarkot/Udaipur **Mint:** Udaipur

Date	Mintage	VG	F	VF	XF	Unc
ND(1858-1920)	—	—	150	225	400	600

Y# A12 1/4 MOHUR

Gold **Series:** Swarupshahi **Obv. Inscription:** Chitarkot/Udaipur **Mint:** Udaipur **Note:** Weight varies: 2.70-2.75 grams.

Date	Mintage	VG	F	VF	XF	Unc
ND(1858-1920)	—	—	150	300	500	750

Y# C12 1/2 MOHUR

5.4000 g., Gold **Series:** Swarupshahi **Obv. Inscription:** Chitarkot/Udaipur **Mint:** Udaipur

Date	Mintage	VG	F	VF	XF	Unc
ND(1858-1920)	—	—	150	300	500	750

Y# 12 MOHUR

10.9500 g., Gold, 23-24 mm. **Series:** Swarupshahi **Obv. Inscription:** Chitarkot/Udaipur **Mint:** Udaipur **Note:** Size varies.

Date	Mintage	VG	F	VF	XF	Unc
ND(1858-1920)	—	—	BV	250	350	525

Fatteh Singh
VS1941-1986 / 1884-1929AD

MILLED COINAGE

VS1985 ie. 1928AD, but actually struck at the Alipore Mint in Calcutta between 1931-1932AD, the Y#22 rupee in 1931, the rest in 1932

Y# 13 PIE

2.5000 g., Copper, 16 mm. **Obverse:** Inscription and date **Obv. Inscription:** Chitor, date **Rev. Inscription:** Udaipur **Mint:** Udaipur

Date	Mintage	Good	VG	F	VF	XF
VS1975(1918)	—	7.50	12.50	18.50	27.50	—

Y# 14 PIE

2.1000 g., Copper **Obverse:** Inscription and date **Obv. Inscription:** Chitor, date **Rev. Inscription:** Udaipur **Mint:** Udaipur

Date	Mintage	Good	VG	F	VF	XF
VS1978(1921)	—	6.00	10.00	15.00	22.50	—

Y# 18 1/16 RUPEE

0.9500 g., Silver, 12 mm. **Obv. Inscription:** "Chitarkot/Udaipur" **Rev. Inscription:** "Dosti Lundhun (Friendship with London)"

Date	Mintage	VG	F	VF	XF	Unc
VS1985(1928)	3,262,000	1.00	2.00	3.00	5.00	7.00

Y# 19 1/8 RUPEE

1.3600 g., Silver, 15 mm. **Obv. Inscription:** "Chitarkot/Udaipur" **Rev. Inscription:** "Dosti Lundhun (Friendship with London)"

Date	Mintage	VG	F	VF	XF	Unc
VS1985(1928)	800,000	1.25	2.50	3.50	6.00	8.00

Y# 20 1/4 RUPEE

2.7200 g., Silver, 19 mm. **Obv. Inscription:** "Chitarkot/Udaipur" **Rev. Inscription:** "Dosti Lundhun (Friendship with London)"

Date	Mintage	VG	F	VF	XF	Unc
VS1985(1928)	839,000	1.50	3.00	4.00	7.50	10.00

Y# 21 1/2 RUPEE

5.4600 g., Silver, 24 mm. **Obv. Inscription:** "Chitarkot/Udaipur" **Rev. Inscription:** "Dosti Lundhun (Friendship with London)"

Date	Mintage	VG	F	VF	XF	Unc
VS1985(1928)	648,000	2.25	4.00	6.00	9.00	15.00

Y# 21a 1/2 RUPEE

Gold, 24 mm. **Obv. Inscription:** "Chitarkot/Udaipur" **Rev. Inscription:** "Dosti Lundhun (Friendship with London)" **Note:** Weight varies: 5.35-5.70 grams.

Date	Mintage	VG	F	VF	XF	Unc
VS1985(1928) Proof	—	Value: 1,500				

Y# 22.1 RUPEE

10.8600 g., Silver, 30 mm. **Obv. Inscription:** Thin characters, Chitarkot/Udaipur **Rev. Inscription:** Dosti Lundhun (Friendship with London)

Date	Mintage	VG	F	VF	XF	Unc
VS1985(1928)	14,906,000	4.50	5.50	7.50	10.00	15.00

Y# 22.2 RUPEE

10.8600 g., Silver, 30 mm. **Obv. Inscription:** Thick characters, Chitarkot/Udaipur **Rev. Inscription:** Dosti Lundhun (Friendship with London)

Date	Mintage	VG	F	VF	XF	Unc
VS1985(1928)	Inc. above	6.00	15.00	20.00	30.00	45.00

Y# 22a RUPEE

Gold, 30 mm. **Obv. Inscription:** Chitarkot/Udaipur **Rev. Inscription:** Dosti Lundhun (Friendship with London)

Date	Mintage	VG	F	VF	XF	Unc
VS1985(1928) Proof	—	Value: 2,500				

Bhupal Singh
VS1987-2005 / 1930-1948AD

HAMMERED COINAGE

Umarda Local Issues

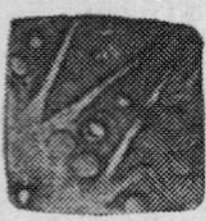

Y# 24 1/2 PAISA

Copper **Note:** Varieties exist.

Date	Mintage	Good	VG	F	VF	XF
ND(1938-1941)	—	0.75	1.25	1.75	2.50	—

MILLED COINAGE

VS1985 ie. 1928AD, but actually struck at the Alipore Mint in Calcutta between 1931-1932AD, the Y#22 rupee in 1931, the rest in 1932

Y# 15 1/4 ANNA

2.2000 g., Copper **Obv. Inscription:** "Chitarkot/Udaipur"

Date	Mintage	VG	F	VF	XF	Unc
VS1999	—	0.20	0.50	0.85	1.25	2.00

Y# 16.1 1/2 ANNA

3.5000 g., Copper **Obv. Inscription:** Large characters, Chitarkot/Udaipur

Date	Mintage	VG	F	VF	XF	Unc
VS1999	—	0.20	0.50	0.85	1.25	2.00

Y# 16.2 1/2 ANNA

3.5000 g., Copper **Obverse:** Small characters in inscription **Obv. Inscription:** Chitarkot/Udaipur

Date	Mintage	VG	F	VF	XF	Unc
VS1999	—	0.20	0.50	0.85	1.25	2.00

Y# 17 ANNA

4.3000 g., Copper **Obv. Inscription:** "Chitarkot/Udaipur" **Note:** Variations with 3 or 4 brushes exist.

Date	Mintage	VG	F	VF	XF	Unc
VS2000	—	0.25	0.60	1.00	1.25	2.50

PATTERNS

Including off metal strikes

KM#	Date	Mintage	Identification	Mkt Val
Pn1	VS1985(1928)	—	1/16 Rupee. Silver.	—
Pn2	VS1985 (1928)	—	1/16 Rupee. Gold.	—

KM#	Date	Mintage	Identification	Mkt Val
Pn3	VS1985(1928)	—	1/8 Rupee. Silver.	—
Pn4	VS1985 (1928)	—	1/8 Rupee. Gold.	—
Pn5	VS1985(1928)	—	1/4 Rupee. Silver.	—
Pn6	VS1985(1928)	—	1/4 Rupee. Gold. KM20.	750

KM#	Date	Mintage	Identification	Mkt Val
Pn7	VS1985(1928)	—	1/2 Rupee. Silver.	—
Pn8	VS1985 (1928)	—	1/2 Rupee. Gold.	—
Pn9	VS1985 (1928)	—	Rupee. Silver.	—
Pn10	VS1985 (1928)	—	Rupee. Gold.	—

PATIALA

State located in the Punjab in northwest India. In the mid-18th century the Raja was given his title and mint right by Ahmad Shah Durrani of Afghanistan, whose coin he copied.

The rulers became Maharajas in 1810AD. The maharaja of Patiala was also recognized as the leader of the Phulkean tribe. Unlike others, Patiala's Sikh rulers had never hesitated to seek British assistance at those times when they felt threatened by their co-religionist neighbors. In 1857, Patiala's forces were immediately made available on the side of the British.

RULERS:

Bhupindar Singh, VS1958-1994/1900-1937AD
Yadvindar Singh, VS1994-2005/1937-1948AD

PRINCELY STATE

Bhupindar Singh
VS1958-1994 / 1900-1937AD
HAMMERED COINAGE

KM# 28 RUPEE

Silver **Obverse:** Persian inscription **Obv. Inscription:** Guru Govind Singh **Reverse:** Dagger at left **Note:** Weight varies: 11.10-11.20 grams. Prev. Y#A3.

Date	Mintage	VG	F	VF	XF	Unc
VS1958 (1901)	—	—	—	—	—	—

Y# 14 1/6 MOHUR

1.7500 g., Gold **Obverse:** Persian inscription **Obv. Inscription:** "Ahmad Shah Durrani" **Reverse:** Dagger at left

Date	Mintage	VG	F	VF	XF	Unc
VS(19)58	—	—	85.00	100	125	175
VS(19)90	—	—	—	—	—	—

KM# 15 1/3 MOHUR

3.5000 g., Gold **Obverse:** Persian inscription **Obv. Inscription:** "Ahmad Shah Durrani" **Reverse:** Dagger at left

Date	Mintage	VG	F	VF	XF	Unc
VS(19)58	—	—	100	120	140	200

Y# 16 2/3 MOHUR

7.0000 g., Gold **Obverse:** Persian inscription **Obv. Inscription:** "Ahmad Shah Durrani" **Reverse:** Dagger at left

Date	Mintage	VG	F	VF	XF	Unc
VS(19)58	—	—	165	200	250	325

Y# 17 MOHUR

10.5000 g., Gold **Obverse:** Persian inscription **Obv. Inscription:** "Ahmad Shah Durrani" **Reverse:** Dagger at left

Date	Mintage	VG	F	VF	XF	Unc
VS(19)58	—	—	225	265	325	400

Yadvindar Singh
VS1994-2005 / 1937-1948AD
HAMMERED COINAGE

KM# 27 1/4 RUPEE

Silver **Obverse:** Persian inscription **Obv. Inscription:** Guru Govind Singh **Reverse:** Bayoneted rifle at left **Note:** Weight varies: 11.10-11.20 grams. Prev. Y#A1.

Date	Mintage	VG	F	VF	XF	Unc
VS1994 (1937)	—	—	—	—	—	—

KM# 29 1/6 MOHUR

1.7500 g., Gold **Obverse:** Persian inscription **Obv. Inscription:** "Ahmad Shah Durrani" **Reverse:** Bayoneted rifle at left **Note:** Prev. Y#19.

Date	Mintage	VG	F	VF	XF	Unc
VS(19)94 /(1937)	—	—	75.00	100	125	175

KM# 30 1/3 MOHUR

3.5000 g., Gold **Obverse:** Persian inscription **Obv. Inscription:** "Ahmad Shah Durrani" **Reverse:** Bayoneted rifle at left **Note:** Prev. KM#20.

Date	Mintage	VG	F	VF	XF	Unc
VS(19)94 /(1937AD)	—	—	100	120	140	200

KM# 31 2/3 MOHUR

7.0000 g., Gold **Obverse:** Persian inscription **Obv. Inscription:** "Ahmad Shah Durrani" **Reverse:** Bayoneted rifle at left **Note:** Prev. Y#21.

Date	Mintage	VG	F	VF	XF	Unc
VS(19)94/(1937AD)	—	—	165	200	250	325

SAILANA

This small state in west-central India, of slightly over one hundred square miles had once been part of Ratlam, but about 1709 it asserted its independence under the leadership of Pratab Singh, the second son of Chhatrasal. The town of Sailana was founded in 1730 by Jai Singh's successor, and from that date the state was named after it. Due to its small size and vulnerability, Sailana was obliged to become tributary to Sindhia to ensure its survival. In 1819 this payment was limited to one-third of the state's revenues. Later, under agreements of 1840 and 1860, the tribute went to the British for the support of British Indian troops in the region. Barmawal was feudatory to Sailana.

LOCAL RULERS

Jaswant Singh, 1895-1919AD
Dilip Singh Bahadur, 1919-1948

Jaswant Singh
1890-1919AD
MILLED COINAGE

Regal Series

KM# 15 1/4 ANNA

Copper **Obverse:** Bust of King Edward VII right **Obv. Designer:** G.W. DeSaulles

Date	Mintage	VG	F	VF	XF	Unc
1908 Proof	—	Value: 175				
1908	224,000	5.00	12.50	25.00	50.00	100

KM# 16 1/4 ANNA

Copper **Obverse:** Crowned bust of King George V left **Obv. Designer:** E.B. MacKennal

Date	Mintage	VG	F	VF	XF	Unc
1912	224,000	1.25	3.50	6.50	12.50	25.00
1912 Proof	—	Value: 175				

SUNTH

Located 15 miles east of Lunawada with an area of 394 sq. miles, (1,020 sq. km.). This state was ruled by a Maharana who was a member of the Pramara Rajput clan. The state capital was Rampur.

RULERS

Shivsinghji, 1774-1819
Kalyan Singhji, 1819-1835
Bhawan Singhji, 1835-1871
Pratap Singhji, 1871-1896
Jarawar Singhji, 1896-?

KINGDOM
HAMMERED COINAGE

KM# 1 1/2 PAISA

Copper **Obverse:** Open hand in square **Rev. Legend:** "Rampura" **Note:** Weight varies: 3.00-4.00 grams.

Date	Mintage	Good	VG	F	VF	XF
ND(c.1870-1920)	—	2.50	6.50	10.00	15.00	—

KM# 2 1/2 PAISA

Copper **Obverse:** Sunbursts **Rev. Legend:** "Rampura" **Note:** Weight varies: 3.00-4.00 grams.

Date	Mintage	Good	VG	F	VF	XF
ND(c.1870-1920)	—	3.50	9.00	13.00	20.00	—

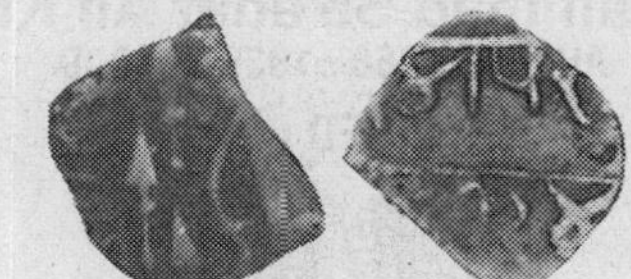

KM# 5 PAISA

8.5000 g., Copper **Obverse:** Spears **Rev. Legend:** "Rampura" **Shape:** Round, rectangular, or square

Date	Mintage	Good	VG	F	VF	XF
ND(c.1870-1920)	—	1.25	3.25	5.00	8.50	—

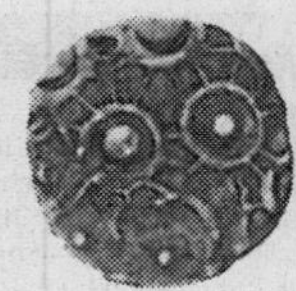

KM# 6.1 PAISA

Copper **Obverse:** Sunbursts **Rev. Legend:** "Rampura"

Date	Mintage	Good	VG	F	VF	XF
ND(c.1870-1920)	—	1.25	3.25	5.00	8.50	—

KM# 6.2 PAISA

Copper **Obverse:** Sunburst with serrated rays **Rev. Legend:** "Rampura" **Shape:** Odd, rectangular, or square

Date	Mintage	Good	VG	F	VF	XF
ND(c.1870-1920)	—	2.50	6.00	9.00	14.00	—

KM# 9 PAISA

Copper **Obverse:** Open hands **Reverse:** "Rampur" **Shape:** Rectangular or square

Date	Mintage	Good	VG	F	VF	XF
ND(c.1870-1920)	—	2.50	6.00	9.00	14.00	—

KM# 8 PAISA

Copper **Obverse:** Spears **Reverse:** Persian legend **Shape:** Odd **Note:** Attribution uncertain.

Date	Mintage	Good	VG	F	VF	XF
ND(c.1870-1920)	—	1.25	3.25	5.00	8.50	—

KM# 3 PAISA

Copper **Obverse:** Sunbursts **Rev. Legend:** "Rampura" **Shape:** Rectangular or square **Note:** Weight varies: 1.90-4.30 grams.

Date	Mintage	Good	VG	F	VF	XF
ND(c.1870-1920)	—	1.25	3.25	5.00	8.50	—

KM# 4 PAISA

Copper **Obverse:** Spears **Reverse:** Spears **Shape:** Rectangular or square **Note:** Weight varies: 1.90-4.30 grams. Attribution uncertain.

Date	Mintage	Good	VG	F	VF	XF
ND(c.1870-1920)	—	1.25	3.25	5.00	8.50	—

KM# 7 PAISA

Copper **Obverse:** Solar symbol **Rev. Legend:** "Rampura" **Shape:** Odd or square **Note:** Weight varies: 7.50-8.30 grams.

Date	Mintage	Good	VG	F	VF	XF
ND(c.1870-1920)	—	2.50	6.00	9.00	14.00	—

TONK

Tunk

State located partially in Rajputana and in central India. Tonk was founded in 1806 by Amir Khan (d. 1834), the Pathan Pindari leader who received the territory from Holkar. Amir Khan caused great havoc in Central India by his lightning raids into neighboring states. In 1817 he was forced into submission by the East India Company and remained under British control until India's independence. In March 1948 Tonk was incorporated into Rajasthan.

RULERS

Muhammad Ibrahim Ali Khan, AH1284-1349/1868-1930AD
Muhammad Sa'adat Ali Khan, AH1349-1368/1930-1949AD

MINT MARKS

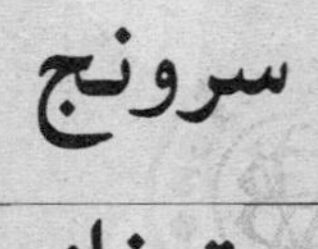

Sironj

تونك

Tonk

Flower (on all)

Leaf (several forms)

Beginning with the reign of Muhammad Ibrahim Ali Khan, most coins have both AD and AH dates. Coins with both dates fully legible are worth about 20% more than listed prices. Coins with one date fully legible are worth prices shown. Coins with both dates off are of little value.

There are many minor and major variations of type, varying with location of date, orientation of leaf, arrangement of legend. Although these fall into easily distinguished patterns, they are strictly for the specialist and are omitted here.

The Tonk rupee was known as the "Chanwarshahi".

BRITISH PROTECTORATE

Muhammad Ibrahim Ali Khan

AH1284-1349 / 1868-1930AD

HAMMERED COINAGE

Y# A24 1/2 PAISA

5.4000 g., Copper **Obv. Inscription:** George V...
Rev. Inscription: Muhammad Ibrahim Ali Khan... **Mint:** Tonk

Date	Mintage	Good	VG	F	VF	XF
AH13(46)//1928	—	3.00	6.00	10.00	15.00	—

Y# 24.1 PAISA

7.3000 g., Copper **Obv. Inscription:** George V...
Rev. Inscription: Muhammad Ibrahim Ali Khan... **Mint:** Tonk

Date	Mintage	Good	VG	F	VF	XF
AH1329//1911	—	1.25	2.25	3.50	5.50	—
AH1329(sic)//1329	—	1.25	2.25	3.50	5.50	—
1911(sic)	—	1.25	2.25	3.50	5.50	—
AH1330//1911	—	1.25	2.25	3.50	5.50	—

Y# 24.2 PAISA

5.0000 g., Copper **Obv. Inscription:** George V...
Rev. Inscription: Muhammad Ibrahim Ali Khan... **Mint:** Tonk
Note: Reduced weight.

Date	Mintage	Good	VG	F	VF	XF
AH1335//1917	—	1.25	2.25	3.50	5.50	—
AH(13)38//1924	—	1.25	2.25	3.50	5.50	—
AH1342//1924	—	1.00	1.75	2.50	4.50	—
AH1344//1925	—	1.00	1.75	2.50	4.50	—

Date	Mintage	Good	VG	F	VF	XF
AH1344//1926	—	1.00	1.75	2.50	4.50	—
AH1345//1927	—	1.00	1.75	2.50	4.50	—
AH134x//1928	—	1.00	1.75	2.50	4.50	—

Y# A25.1 1/4 ANNA

8.3000 g., Copper **Obv. Inscription:** George V...
Rev. Inscription: Muhammad Ibrahim Ali Khan... **Mint:** Tonk

Date	Mintage	Good	VG	F	VF	XF
AH1335//1917	—	1.25	2.25	3.50	5.50	—
AH1336//1917	—	1.25	2.25	3.50	5.50	—

Y# A25.2 1/4 ANNA

5.4000 g., Copper **Obv. Inscription:** George V...
Rev. Inscription: Muhammad Ibrahim Ali Khan... **Mint:** Tonk
Note: Reduced weight.

Date	Mintage	Good	VG	F	VF	XF
AH1336//1917	—	1.00	1.75	2.50	4.50	—

Y# 25 1/8 RUPEE

Silver **Obv. Inscription:** George V... **Rev. Inscription:** Muhammad Ibrahim Ali Khan... **Mint:** Tonk **Note:** Weight varies: 1.34-1.45 grams.

Date	Mintage	Good	VG	F	VF	XF
AH1340//1922	—	2.75	6.50	10.00	16.50	25.00
AH1346//1928	—	2.75	6.50	10.00	16.50	25.00

Y# 26 1/4 RUPEE

Silver **Obv. Inscription:** George V... **Rev. Inscription:** Muhammad Ibrahim Ali Khan... **Mint:** Tonk **Note:** Weight varies: 2.68-2.90 grams.

Date	Mintage	Good	VG	F	VF	XF
AH1346//1928	—	2.75	6.50	10.00	15.00	25.00

Y# 27 1/2 RUPEE

Silver **Obv. Inscription:** George V... **Rev. Inscription:** Muhammad Ibrahim Ali Khan... **Mint:** Tonk **Note:** Weight varies: 5.35-5.80 grams.

Date	Mintage	Good	VG	F	VF	XF
AH1346//1928	—	4.75	11.50	17.50	25.00	37.50

Y# 28 RUPEE

Silver **Obv. Inscription:** George V... **Rev. Inscription:** Muhammad Ibrahim Ali Khan... **Mint:** Tonk **Note:** Weight varies: 10.70-11.60 grams.

Date	Mintage	Good	VG	F	VF	XF
AH1329//1911	—	4.50	6.00	8.50	13.50	20.00
AH1330//1912	—	4.50	6.00	8.50	13.50	20.00
AH1341//1923	—	4.50	6.00	8.50	13.50	20.00
AH1342//1923	—	4.50	6.00	8.50	13.50	20.00
AH1342//1924	—	4.50	6.00	8.50	13.50	20.00
AH1343//1924	—	4.50	6.00	8.50	13.50	20.00
AH1343//1925	—	4.50	6.00	8.50	13.50	20.00
AH1344//1925	—	4.50	6.00	8.50	13.50	20.00
AH1344//1926	—	4.50	6.00	8.50	13.50	20.00
AH1345//1926	—	4.50	6.00	8.50	13.50	20.00
AH1346//1926	—	4.50	6.00	8.50	13.50	20.00
AH1346//1927	—	4.50	6.00	8.50	13.50	20.00
AH1347//1928	—	4.50	6.00	8.50	13.50	20.00
AH1348//1928	—	4.50	6.00	8.50	13.50	20.00
AH1348//1929	—	4.50	6.00	8.50	13.50	20.00
AH134x//1930	—	4.50	6.00	8.50	13.50	20.00

Muhammad Sa'adat Ali Khan

AH1349-1368 / 1930-1949AD

HAMMERED COINAGE

Y# 30 1/8 RUPEE

Silver **Obv. Inscription:** George V... **Rev. Inscription:** Muhammad Sa'adat Ali Khan... **Mint:** Tonk **Note:** Weight varies: 1.34-1.45 grams.

Date	Mintage	Good	VG	F	VF	XF
AH1351//1932	—	1.50	4.00	6.50	10.00	16.50
AH1352//1933	—	1.50	4.00	6.50	10.00	18.50
AH1353//1934	—	1.50	4.00	6.50	10.00	18.50

MILLED COINAGE

KM# 29 PICE (Paisa)

Copper, 26 mm. **Obverse:** Arms **Reverse:** Leaf

Date	Mintage	VG	F	VF	XF	Unc
AH1350//1932	640,000	0.20	0.50	1.00	2.00	3.50

KM# 29a PICE (Paisa)

Copper, 21 mm. **Obverse:** Arms **Reverse:** Leaf

Date	Mintage	VG	F	VF	XF	Unc
AH1350//1932	640,000	—	0.25	0.50	1.00	1.75

TRAVANCORE

State located in extreme southwest India. A mint was established in ME965/1789-1790AD.

The region of Travancore had a lengthy history before being annexed by the Vijayanagar kingdom. With Vijayanagar's defeat at the battle of Talikota in 1565, Travancore passed under Muslim control until the late 18th century, when it merged as a state in its own right under Raja Martanda Varma. At this time the raja allied himself with British interests as a protection against the Muslim dynasty of Mysore. In 1795 the raja of Travancore officially accepted a subsidiary alliance with the East India Company, and remained within the orbit of British influence from then until India's independence.

RULERS

Rama Varma VI, ME1062-1101/1885-1924AD
Bala Rama Varma II, ME1101-1126/1924-1949AD

DATING

ME dates are of the Malabar Era. Add 824 or 825 to the ME date for the AD date. (i.e., ME1112 plus 824-825 = 1936-1937AD).

KINGDOM

Rama Varma VI

ME1062-1101 / 1885-1924AD

MILLED COINAGE

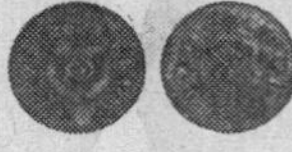

KM# 40 CASH

0.6500 g., Copper **Obv. Legend:** CASH 1

Date	Mintage	VG	F	VF	XF	Unc
ND(1901)	—	4.00	9.00	15.00	22.50	35.00

KM# 46 CASH

0.6500 g., Copper **Obverse:** Sankha (conch shell) in 8-pointed star **Note:** Thick

Date	Mintage	VG	F	VF	XF	Unc
ND(1901-10)	—	0.15	0.50	0.70	1.00	1.50

Note: Refer to Bala Rama Varma II listings for thin variety, KM#57

KM# 41 4 CASH

Copper **Obverse:** RV monogram **Obv. Legend:** CASH FOUR
Reverse: Sankha (conch shell) in sprays

Date	Mintage	VG	F	VF	XF	Unc
ND(1901-10)	—	1.25	3.00	5.00	8.00	13.50

KM# 47 4 CASH

Copper **Obverse:** RV monogram **Obv. Legend:** FOUR CASH **Reverse:** Malayalam "Oru Kasu" (One Cash)

Date	Mintage	VG	F	VF	XF	Unc
ND(1906-35)	—	0.40	1.00	1.75	2.50	4.25
ND(1906-35) Proof	—	Value: 65.00				

KM# 42 8 CASH

Copper **Obverse:** RV monogram **Obv. Legend:** CASH EIGHT **Reverse:** Sankha (conch shell) in sprays

Date	Mintage	VG	F	VF	XF	Unc
ND(1901-10)	—	1.75	4.50	7.00	10.00	17.50

KM# 48 8 CASH

Copper **Obverse:** RV monogram **Obv. Legend:** EIGHT CASH **Reverse:** Sankha (conch shell) in sprays

Date	Mintage	VG	F	VF	XF	Unc
ND(1906-35)	—	0.50	1.35	2.25	3.00	5.00
ND(1906-35) Proof	—	Value: 75.00				

KM# 43 CHUCKRAM

Copper **Obverse:** RV monogram **Obv. Legend:** CHUCKRAM ONE **Reverse:** Sankha (conch shell) in sprays

Date	Mintage	VG	F	VF	XF	Unc
ND(1901-10)	—	1.75	4.50	7.00	10.00	17.50

KM# 49 CHUCKRAM

Copper **Obverse:** RV monogram **Obv. Legend:** ONE CHUCKRAM **Reverse:** Sankha (conch shell) in sprays

Date	Mintage	VG	F	VF	XF	Unc
ND(1906-35)	—	0.50	1.35	2.25	3.00	5.50

KM# 44 2 CHUCKRAMS

Silver, 10 mm. **Obverse:** RV monogram **Obv. Legend:** CHS. 2 **Reverse:** Sankha (conch shell) in sprays

Date	Mintage	VG	F	VF	XF	Unc
ND(1901)	—	2.00	4.50	7.00	10.00	17.50

KM# 50 2 CHUCKRAMS

Silver **Obverse:** RV monogram **Obv. Legend:** 2 CHS. **Reverse:** Sankha (conch shell) in sprays

Date	Mintage	VG	F	VF	XF	Unc
ND(1906-28)	—	1.00	2.00	3.50	5.00	9.00

KM# 45 FANAM

Silver **Obverse:** RV monogram **Obv. Legend:** FANAM ONE **Reverse:** Sankha (conch shell) in sprays **Edge:** Plain

Date	Mintage	VG	F	VF	XF	Unc
ND(1901)	—	1.75	3.50	6.00	8.50	15.00

KM# 51 FANAM

0.9500 Silver **Reverse:** Sankha (conch shell) in sprays

Date	Mintage	VG	F	VF	XF	Unc
ME1087(1911)	1,100,000	1.25	3.00	5.00	7.00	10.00
ME1096 (1920)	350,000	1.50	3.50	6.00	8.50	15.00
ME1087 (1911)	—	1.25	3.00	5.00	7.00	12.50
ME1096(1911)	350,000	1.35	3.50	6.00	8.50	12.00
ME1099 (1923)	350,000	1.50	3.50	6.00	8.50	15.00
ME1100 (1924)	700,000	1.50	3.50	6.00	8.50	15.00
ME1103 (1927)	700,000	1.50	3.50	6.00	8.50	15.00

KM# 54 FANAM

Silver **Obverse:** RV monogram **Obv. Legend:** ONE FANAM **Reverse:** Sankha (conch shell) in sprays **Edge:** Plain

Date	Mintage	VG	F	VF	XF	Unc
ND(1911)	—	4.00	10.00	17.50	25.00	40.00

KM# 55 FANAM

Silver **Obverse:** RV monogram **Obv. Legend:** FANAM ONE **Reverse:** Sankha (conch shell) in sprays **Edge:** Reeded

Date	Mintage	VG	F	VF	XF	Unc
ND(1911)	—	1.50	3.00	5.00	7.00	12.50

KM# 52 1/4 RUPEE

2.7200 g., 0.9500 Silver .0831 oz. ASW **Obv. Legend:** RAMA VURMA-TRAVENCORE **Reverse:** Sankha (conch shell) in sprays

Date	Mintage	VG	F	VF	XF	Unc
ME1082 (1906)	—	2.50	6.00	10.00	16.50	25.00
ME1083 (1907)	—	2.50	6.00	10.00	16.50	25.00
ME1085 (1909)	—	2.50	6.00	10.00	16.50	25.00
ME1086 (1910)	—	2.50	6.00	10.00	16.50	25.00
ME1087 (1911)	400,000	2.00	4.50	7.00	12.00	20.00
ME1096 (1920)	—	1.50	3.00	5.00	8.50	15.00
ME1099 (1923)	—	1.50	3.00	5.00	8.50	15.00
ME1100 (1924)	—	1.50	3.00	5.00	8.50	15.00
ME1103 (1927)	200,000	1.50	3.00	5.00	8.50	15.00
ME1106 (1930)	200,000	1.50	3.00	5.00	8,50	15.00

KM# 53 1/2 RUPEE

5.4400 g., 0.9500 Silver .1662 oz. ASW **Reverse:** Legend shorter on bottom

Date	Mintage	VG	F	VF	XF	Unc
ME1084 (1908)	—	3.50	8.50	14.00	20.00	32.50
ME1085 (1909)	—	3.50	8.50	14.00	20.00	32.50
ME1086 (1911)	—	3.50	8.50	14.00	20.00	32.50
ME1087 (1911)	300,000	2.50	6.00	10.00	15.00	25.00
ME1103 (1927)	100,000	3.00	7.50	12.50	18.50	28.50
ME1106 (1930)	100,000	3.00	7.50	12.50	18.50	28.50
ME1106 (1930) Proof; Rare	—	—	—	—	—	—
ME1107 (1931)	800,000	2.50	6.00	10.00	14.00	20.00

Bala Rama Varma II

ME1101-1126 / 1924-1949AD

MILLED COINAGE

KM# 57 CASH

0.4800 g., Copper **Obverse:** Sankha (conch shell) in 8-pointed star **Reverse:** Malayalam "Oru Kasu" (one cash) **Note:** Thin .8mm planchet.

Date	Mintage	VG	F	VF	XF	Unc
ND(1928-49)	—	—	0.15	0.25	0.35	0.60

Note: Refer to Rama Varma VI listings for thick variety, KM#46

KM# 58 4 CASH

Bronze **Obverse:** RV monogram **Reverse:** Sankha (conch shell) in sprays

Date	Mintage	VG	F	VF	XF	Unc
ND(1938-49)	—	0.25	0.60	1.00	1.50	2.50

KM# 59 8 CASH

Bronze **Obverse:** BRV monogram **Reverse:** Sankha (conch shell) in sprays

Date	Mintage	VG	F	VF	XF	Unc
ND(1938-49)	—	0.35	0.85	1.50	2.25	3.75

KM# 60 CHUCKRAM

Bronze **Obverse:** Bust of Bala Rama Barma II right **Reverse:** Sankha (conch shell) in sprays

Date	Mintage	VG	F	VF	XF	Unc
ME1114(1938)	—	0.50	1.25	2.25	3.50	5.50
ND(1939-49)	—	0.25	0.60	1.00	1.50	2.50

KM# 60a CHUCKRAM

Gold **Obverse:** Bust of Bala Rama Barma II right **Reverse:** Sankha (conch shell) in sprays

Date	Mintage	VG	F	VF	XF	Unc
ND(1939-49) Prooflike; restrike	—	—	—	—	—	5,000

KM# 61 FANAM

0.9500 g., Silver **Obv. Legend:** BALA RAMA VARMA-TRAVANCORE **Reverse:** Sankha (conch shell) in sprays

Date	Mintage	VG	F	VF	XF	Unc
ME1112(1937)	350,000	1.50	3.00	5.00	7.00	12.50

KM# 65 FANAM

1.5100 g., 0.5000 Silver .0243 oz. ASW **Obv. Legend:** BALA RAMA VARMA-TRAVANCORE **Reverse:** Sankha (conch shell) in sprays

Date	Mintage	VG	F	VF.	XF	Unc
ME1116(1941)	2,096,000	0.45	0.90	1.50	2.00	5.00
ME1118(1942)	4,157,000	0.45	0.90	1.50	2.00	3.50
ME1119(1946)	1,925,000	0.60	1.25	2.25	3.50	6.00

KM# 62 1/4 RUPEE

0.9500 g., Silver **Obv. Legend:** BALA RAMA VARMA-TRAVANCORE

Date	Mintage	VG	F	VF	XF	Unc
ME1112(1937)	200,000	2.00	4.50	7.00	10.00	17.50

KM# 66 1/4 RUPEE

2.6600 g., 0.5000 Silver .0428 oz. ASW **Obv. Legend:** BALA RAMA VARMA-TRAVANCORE

Date	Mintage	VG	F	VF	XF	Unc
ME1116(1941)	126,000	1.25	2.25	3.75	5.50	9.00
ME1116(1941) Proof	—	Value: 65.00				
ME1118(1942)	—	2.00	4.00	7.00	10.00	17.50

KM# 63 1/2 RUPEE

0.9500 g., Silver **Obv. Legend:** BALA RAMA VARMA-TRAVENCORE

Date	Mintage	VG	F	VF	XF	Unc
ME1112(1937)	200,000	4.00	8.50	14.00	20.00	35.00

KM# 64 1/2 CHITRA RUPEE

Silver **Obv. Legend:** BALA RAMA VARMA-TRAVENCORE **Edge:** Reeded

Date	Mintage	VG	F	VF	XF	Unc
ME1114 (1938-39)	—	3.00	6.00	10.00	15.00	25.00

KM# 67 1/2 CHITRA RUPEE

5.3100 g., 0.5000 Silver .0852 oz. ASW **Obv. Legend:** BALA RAMA VARMA-TRAVENCORE **Edge:** Security

Date	Mintage	VG	F	VF	XF	Unc
ME1116(1941)	1,600,000	1.50	3.00	5.00	7.00	12.00
ME1118/6(1942)	1,111,000	2.00	4.00	7.00	10.00	17.50
ME1118(1942)	Inc. above	1.50	3.00	5.00	7.00	12.00
ME1121(1946)	200,000	1.50	3.00	5.00	7.00	12.00

PATTERNS

Including off metal strikes

KM#	Date	Mintage	Identification	Mkt Val
Pn3	ME1086(1909)	—	1/4 Rupee. Bronze. KM#52	90.00

EUROPEAN INFLUENCES IN INDIA

Vasco da Gama, the Portuguese explorer, first visited India in 1498. Portugal seized control of a number of islands and small enclaves on the west coast of India, and for the next hundred years enjoyed a monopoly on trade. With the arrival of powerful Dutch and English fleets in the first half of the 17th century, Portuguese power in the area declined until virtually all of India that remained under Portuguese control were the west coast enclaves of Goa, Damao and Diu. They were forcibly annexed by India in 1962.

RULERS

Portuguese, until 1961

DENOMINATION

The denomination of most copper coins appears in numerals on the reverse, though 30 Reis is often given as "1/2 T," and 60 Reis as "T" (T = Tanga). The silver coins have the denomination in words, usually on the obverse until 1850, then on the reverse.

MONETARY SYSTEM

960 Reis = 16 Tanga = 1 Rupia

PORTUGUESE ADMINISTRATION

Kingdom of Portugal

MILLED COINAGE

KM# 13 1/12 TANGA

Bronze **Obv:** Head of Carlos I right **Rev:** Crowned shield **Note:** Roman numeral dating.

Date	Mintage	F	VF	XF	Unc	BU
1901	960,000	6.00	12.00	28.00	55.00	—
1901 Prooflike	—	—	—	—	—	—
1903	960,000	6.00	12.00	28.00	55.00	—

KM# 14 1/8 TANGA

Bronze **Obv:** Head of Carlos I right **Rev:** Crowned shield **Note:** Roman numeral dating

Date	Mintage	F	VF	XF	Unc	BU
1901	960,000	7.00	15.00	32.00	70.00	—
1901 Prooflike	—	—	—	—	—	—
1903	960,000	7.00	15.00	32.00	70.00	—

KM# 15 1/4 TANGA (15 Reis)

Bronze **Obv:** Head of Carlos I right **Rev:** Crowned shield **Note:** Roman numeral dating.

Date	Mintage	F	VF	XF	Unc	BU
1901	800,000	7.50	16.00	35.00	75.00	—
1901 Prooflike	—	—	—	—	200	—
1903	800,000	7.50	16.00	35.00	75.00	—

KM# 16 1/2 TANGA (30 Reis)

Bronze **Obv:** Head of Carlos I right **Note:** Roman numeral dating.

Date	Mintage	F	VF	XF	Unc	BU
1901	800,000	8.00	17.50	37.50	80.00	—
1901 Prooflike	—	—	—	—	225	—
1903	800,000	8.00	17.50	37.50	80.00	—

KM# 17 RUPIA

11.6600 g., 0.9170 Silver .3438 oz. ASW **Obv:** Head of Carlos I right **Rev:** Crowned shield within wreath

Date	Mintage	F	VF	XF	Unc	BU
1903	200,000	8.00	16.00	32.00	65.00	—
1904	100,000	9.00	18.00	35.00	70.00	—

Republic of Portugal

MILLED COINAGE

KM# 19 TANGA (60 Reis)
Bronze **Obv:** Divided shield **Rev:** Five shields on shield

Date	Mintage	F	VF	XF	Unc	BU
1934	100,000	25.00	70.00	245	500	—

KM# 24 TANGA (60 Reis)
Bronze, 25 mm. **Obv:** Denomination **Rev:** Tiny towers and shields above divided shield on lined circle

Date	Mintage	F	VF	XF	Unc	BU
1947	1,000,000	2.00	7.00	15.00	30.00	—

KM# 28 TANGA (60 Reis)
Bronze, 20 mm. **Obv:** Denomination **Rev:** Tiny towers and shields above divided shield on lined circle

Date	Mintage	F	VF	XF	Unc	BU
1952	9,600,000	1.00	4.00	9.00	20.00	—

KM# 20 2 TANGAS
Copper-Nickel

Date	Mintage	F	VF	XF	Unc	BU
1934	150,000	10.00	20.00	185	400	—

KM# 21 4 TANGAS
Copper-Nickel **Obv:** Divided shield **Rev:** Five shields on shield

Date	Mintage	F	VF	XF	Unc	BU
1934	100,000	20.00	60.00	210	450	—

KM# 25 1/4 RUPIA
Copper-Nickel **Obv:** Denomination **Rev:** Tiny towers and shields above divided shield on lined circle

Date	Mintage	F	VF	XF	Unc	BU
1947	800,000	5.00	10.00	20.00	40.00	—
1952	4,000,000	2.00	4.00	12.00	25.00	—

KM# 23 1/2 RUPIA
6.0000 g., 0.8350 Silver .1610 oz. ASW **Obv:** Shield on lined circle at center of Maltese Cross **Rev:** Divided shield

Date	Mintage	F	VF	XF	Unc	BU
1936	100,000	16.00	28.00	45.00	90.00	—

KM# 26 1/2 RUPIA
Copper-Nickel **Obv:** Denomination **Rev:** Tiny towers and shields above divided shield on lined circle

Date	Mintage	F	VF	XF	Unc	BU
1947	600,000	7.00	15.00	30.00	60.00	—
1952	2,000,000	2.00	5.00	12.00	25.00	—

1912/1

KM# 18 RUPIA
11.6600 g., 0.9170 Silver .3438 oz. ASW **Obv:** Liberty head left **Rev:** Denomination within wreath

Date	Mintage	F	VF	XF	Unc	BU
1912/1	300,000	75.00	150	285	500	—
1912/1 Proof	—	Value: 1,250				
1912	Inc. above	35.00	75.00	150	285	—

KM# 22 RUPIA
12.0000 g., 0.9170 Silver .3536 oz. ASW **Obv:** Shield on lined circle at center of Maltese Cross **Rev:** Divided shield

Date	Mintage	F	VF	XF	Unc	BU
1935	300,000	7.50	15.00	30.00	55.00	—

KM# 27 RUPIA
12.0000 g., 0.5000 Silver .1929 oz. ASW **Obv:** Shield on lined circle at center of Maltese Cross **Rev:** Tiny towers and shields above divided shield on lined circle

Date	Mintage	F	VF	XF	Unc	BU
1947	900,000	7.50	15.00	30.00	60.00	—

KM# 29 RUPIA
Copper-Nickel **Obv:** Shield on lined circle at center of Maltese cross **Rev:** Tiny towers and shields above divided shield on lined circle

Date	Mintage	F	VF	XF	Unc	BU
1952	1,000,000	7.50	15.00	30.00	60.00	—

DECIMAL COINAGE

100 Centavos = 1 Escudo

KM# 30 10 CENTAVOS
Bronze, 18 mm. **Obv:** Denomination **Rev:** Tiny towers and shields above divided shield on lined circle

Date	Mintage	F	VF	XF	Unc	BU
1958	5,000,000	1.00	3.00	7.00	16.00	—
1959	Inc. above	1.00	3.00	7.00	16.00	—
1961	1,000,000	0.50	1.00	1.50	3.00	—

KM# 31 30 CENTAVOS
Bronze **Obv:** Denomination **Rev:** Tiny towers and shields above divided shield on lined circle

Date	Mintage	F	VF	XF	Unc	BU
1958	5,000,000	0.75	2.50	7.00	16.00	—
1959	Inc. above	2.50	7.00	15.00	30.00	—

KM# 32 60 CENTAVOS
Copper-Nickel **Obv:** Shield on lined circle at center of Maltese Cross **Rev:** Tiny towers and shields above divided shield on lined circle

Date	Mintage	F	VF	XF	Unc	BU
1958	5,000,000	2.00	4.00	10.00	20.00	—
1959	Inc. above	1.25	2.50	6.50	13.50	—

KM# 33 ESCUDO
Copper-Nickel **Obv:** Shield on lined circle at center of Maltese Cross **Rev:** Tiny towers and shields above divided shield on lined circle

Date	Mintage	F	VF	XF	Unc	BU
1958	6,000,000	1.25	2.50	7.50	16.00	—
1959	Inc. above	1.25	2.50	6.50	13.50	—

KM# 34 3 ESCUDOS
Copper-Nickel **Obv:** Shield on lined circle at center of Maltese Cross **Rev:** Tiny towers and shields above divided shield on lined circle

Date	Mintage	F	VF	XF	Unc	BU
1958	5,000,000	2.50	5.00	12.00	22.00	—
1959	Inc. above	2.50	4.50	9.00	18.00	—

KM# 35 6 ESCUDOS
Copper-Nickel **Obv:** Shield on lined circle at center of Maltese Cross **Rev:** Tiny towers and shields above divided shield on lined circle

Date	Mintage	F	VF	XF	Unc	BU
1959	4,000,000	2.50	4.50	9.00	20.00	—

PATTERNS

Including off metal strikes

KM#	Date	Mintage	Identification	Mkt Val
Pn28	1901	—	1/2 Tanga. Aluminum. KM#13	150
Pn29	1901	—	1/8 Tanga. Aluminum. KM#14	150
Pn30	1901	—	1/4 Tanga. Aluminum. KM#15	150
Pn31	1911	—	Rupia. Silver. KM#18	—
Pn32	1911	—	Rupia. Copper. KM#18	750

PROVAS

Standard metals unless otherwise noted; Stamped

KM#	Date	Mintage	Identification	Issue Price	Mkt Val
Pr1	1934	—	Tanga. Bronze. KM#19	—	325
Pr2	1934	—	2 Tangas. Copper-Nickel. KM#20	—	335
Pr3	1934	—	4 Tangas. Copper-Nickel. KM#21	—	340
Pr4	1935	—	Rupia. Silver. KM#22	—	140
Pr5	1936	—	1/2 Rupia. Silver. KM#23	—	95.00
Pr6	1947	—	1/4 Rupia. Copper-Nickel. KM#25	—	50.00
Pr7	1947	—	1/2 Rupia. Copper-Nickel. KM#26	—	50.00
Pr8	1947	—	Tanga. Bronze. KM#24	—	50.00
Pr9	1947	—	Rupia. Silver. KM#27	—	85.00
Pr10	1952	—	1/4 Rupia. Copper-Nickel. KM#25	—	50.00
Pr11	1952	—	1/2 Rupia. Copper-Nickel. KM#26	—	40.00
Pr12	1952	—	Tanga. Bronze. KM#28	—	40.00
Pr13	1952	—	Rupia. Copper-Nickel. KM#29	—	50.00
Pr14	1954	—	Rupia. Copper-Nickel. KM#29	—	250
Pr15	1958	—	10 Centavos. Bronze. KM#30	—	30.00
Pr16	1958	—	30 Centavos. Bronze. KM#31	—	40.00
Pr17	1958	—	60 Centavos. Copper-Nickel. KM#32	—	40.00
Pr18	1958	—	Escudo. Copper-Nickel. KM#33	—	45.00
Pr19	1958	—	3 Escudos. Copper-Nickel. KM#34	—	45.00
Pr20	1959	—	10 Centavos. Bronze. KM#30	—	40.00
Pr21	1959	—	30 Centavos. Bronze. KM#31	—	40.00
Pr22	1959	—	60 Centavos. Copper-Nickel. KM#32	—	40.00
Pr23	1959	—	Escudo. Copper-Nickel. KM#33	—	40.00
Pr24	1959	—	3 Escudos. Copper-Nickel. KM#34	—	40.00
Pr25	1959	—	6 Escudos. Copper-Nickel. KM#35	—	40.00
Pr26	1961	—	10 Centavos. Bronze. KM#30	—	35.00
Pr27	1961	—	10 Centavos. Nickel-Brass. Incuse N; KM#30	—	45.00

INDIA-BRITISH

The civilization of India, which began about 2500 B.C., flourished under a succession of empires - notably those of the Mauryas, the Kushans, the Guptas, the Delhi Sultans and the Mughals – until undermined in the 18th and 19th centuries by European colonial powers.

The Portuguese were the first to arrive, off Calicut in May 1498. It wasn't until 1612, after the Portuguese and Spanish power had begun to wane, that the British East India Company established its initial settlement at Surat. Britain could not have chosen a more propitious time as the central girdle of petty states, and the southern Vijayanagar Empire were crumbling and ripe for foreign exploitation. By the end of the century, English traders were firmly established in Bombay, Madras, Calcutta and lesser places elsewhere, and Britain was implementing its announced policy to create such civil and military institutions as may be the foundation of secure English domination for all time'. By 1757, following the successful conclusion of a war of colonial rivalry with France during which the military victories of Robert Clive, a young officer with the British East India Company, made him a powerful man in India, the British were firmly settled in India not only as traders but as conquerors. During the next 60 years, the British East India Company acquired dominion over most of India by bribery and force, and governed it directly or through puppet princelings.

As a result of the Sepoy Mutiny of 1857-58, a large-scale mutiny among Indian soldiers of the Bengal army, control of the government of India was transferred from the East India Company to the British Crown. At this point in world history, India was the brightest jewel in the British imperial diadem, but even then a movement for greater Indian representation in government presaged the Indian Empire's twilight hour less than a century later- it would pass into history on Aug. 15, 1947.

COLONIAL COINAGE

This section lists the coins of British India from the reign of William IV (1835) to the reign of George VI (1947). The issues are divided into two main parts:

Coins struck under the authority of the East India Company (E.I.C.) from 1835 until the trading monopoly of the E.I.C. was abolished in 1853. From August 2, 1858 the property and powers of the Company were transferred to the British Crown. From November 1, 1858 to November 1, 1862 the coins continued to bear the design and inscription of the Company.

Coins struck under the authority of the Crown (Regal issues) from 1862 until 1947.

The first regal issues bear the date 1862 and were struck with the date 1862 unchanged until 1874. From then onward all coins bear the year date.

The copper coins dated 1862 have been tentatively attributed by their size to the mint of issue. The silver coins dated 1862 have been attributed to various years of issue by their characteristic marks according to mint records.

In 1877 Queen Victoria was proclaimed Empress of India and the title of the obverse legend was changed accordingly.

For a detailed account of the work of the various mints and the numerous die varieties the general collector and specialist should refer to *The Coins of the British Commonwealth of Nations*, to the end of the reign of King George VI – 1952, Part 4, India, Vol. 1 and 2, by F. Pridmore, Spink, 1980.

RULERS

British until 1947

MINT MARKS

The coins of British India were struck at the following mints, indicated in the catalogue by either capital letters after the date when the actual letter appears on the coins or small letters in () designating the mint of issue. Plain dates indicate Royal Mint strikes.

B – Mumbai (Bombay), 1835-1947, (dot on coin)
C or CM – Calcutta, 1835-1947, (no mint mark on coin)
I – Mumbai (Bombay), 1918-1919
L – Lahore, 1943-1945
P – Pretoria, South Africa, 1943-1944

In 1947 British rule came to an end and India was divided into two self-governing countries, India and Pakistan. In 1971 Bangladash seceded from Pakistan. All are now independent republics and although they are still members of the British Commonwealth of Nations, their coinages do not belong to the British India series.

MONETARY SYSTEM

3 Pies = 1 Pice (Paisa)
4 Pice = 1 Anna
16 Annas = 1 Rupee
15 Rupees = 1 Mohur

The transition from the coins of the Moslem monetary system began with the silver pattern Rupees of William IV, 1834, issued by the East India Company, with the value on the reverse, given in English, Bengali, Persian and Nagari characters. This coinage was struck for several years, as dated, except for the currency, Rupee, which was struck from 1835-1840, all dated 1835.

The portrait coins issued by the East India Company for Victoria show two different head designs on the obverse, which are called Type I and Type II. The coins with Type I head have a continuous obverse legend and were struck from 1840 to 1851. The coins with the Type II head have a divided obverse legend and were struck from 1850 (Calcutta) until 1862. The date on the coins remained unchanged: The Rupee, 1/2 Rupee and 1/4 Rupee are dated 1840. Noticeable differences in the ribbon designs of the English vs. Indian obverses exist.

Type I coins have on the reverse a dot after the date those of Type II have no dot, except for some rare 1/4 Rupees and 2 Annas. The latter are mules, struck from reverse dies of the preceding issue.

KING GEORGE VI: First and Second Heads

While King George VI's First Head is engraved in somewhat higher relief than his second head on all denominations from the 1/12 Anna to the Rupee, an easier way of distinguishing between the two types is that on the First Head the two *fleurs de lis* on the royal crown are larger and extend upward to touch the beaded crest at the top of the crown, while the two *fleurs de lis* on the crown of the Second Head are smaller and extend upward to touch only the line on the crown below the beaded crest.

ENGRAVER INITIALS

The following initials appear on the obverse on the truncation:

S incuse (Type I).
WW raised or incuse (Type II).
WWS or SWW (Type II).
WWB raised (Type II).

Proof and Prooflike restrikes

Original proofs are similar to early English Specimen strikes with wire edges and matte finish busts, arms, etc. Restrikes of most of the coins minted from the period 1835 were regularly supplied until this practice was discontinued on July 1, 1970.

Early proof restrikes are found with slight hairlines from polishing of the old dies. Bust, field, arms, etc. are of even smoothness.

Modern proof-like (P/L) restrikes usually have many hairlines from excessive polishing of the old dies and have a glassy, varnished or proof-like appearance. Many are common while some are quite scarce including some unusual mulings. These listings are indicated by **P/L-R** after the date and mint mark, for example; "1907(s) P/L R".

DISTINGUISHING FEATURES

Pice

NOTE: There are three types of the crown, which is on the obverse at the top. These are shown below and are designated as (RC) Round Crown, (HC) High Crown, and (FC) Flat Crown. Calcutta Mint issues have no mint mark. The issues from the other mints have the mint mark below the date as following: Lahore, raised "L"; Pretoria, small round dot; Mumbai (Bombay), diamond dot or "large" round dot. On the Mumbai (Bombay) issues dated 1944 the mint mark appears to be a large dot over a diamond.

Round Crown (RC)

High Crown (HC)

Flat Crown (FC)

½ Anna

The Calcutta Mint continued to issue this denomination with the dot before and after INDIA in 1946 and 1947. Mumbai (Bombay) also struck in 1946 and 1947, the 1946 issue denoted by a small dot in the center of the dashes before and after the date on the reverse (as well as a dot before and after INDIA, like Calcutta); the characteristics of the 1947 Bombay issue have not been determined but are thought also to resemble the 1946 issue. This denomination is also reported to have been struck in a quantity of 50,829,000 pieces in 1946 at the new Lahore Mint but no way of distinguishing this issue has been found. The proof issue in 1946 was struck by Mumbai (Bombay), not Calcutta. Source: Pridmore.

¼ Rupee

BUST A - Front of dress has 4 panels. The bottom panel has 3 leaves at left and a small flower at upper right.

BUST B - Front of dress has 3-1/2 panels. The bottom incomplete panel has only 3 leaf tops.

REVERSE I - Large top flower; 2 large petals above the base of the top flower are long and curved downward.

REVERSE II - Small top flower; 2 large petals above the base of the top flower are short and horizontal.

First Head
Small head, high relief, small denticles

Second Head
Small head, low relief, large denticles

Second Head
Large head, low relief, small denticles

From 1942 to 1945 the reverse designs of the silver coins change slightly every year. However, a distinct reverse variety occurs on Rupees and 1/4 Rupees dated 1943-44 and on the half Rupee dated 1944, all struck at Mumbai (Bombay). This variety may be distinguished from the other coins by the design of the center bottom flower as illustrated, and is designated as Reverse B.

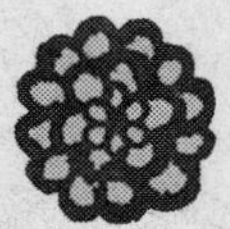

On the normal common varieties dated 1943-44 the three "scalloped circles" are not connected to each other and the bead in the center is not attached to the nearest circle.

Obv: First head, reeded edge

Calcutta Mint issues have no mint mark. Mumbai (Bombay) coins have a small bead below the lotus flower at the bottom on the reverse, except those dated 1943-1944 with reverse B which has a diamond. Lahore Mint issues have a small "L" in the same position. The nickel coins have a diamond below the date on the reverse.

Rupee
Obverse Dies

Type I **Type II**

Type I - Obv. die w/elephant with pig-like feet and short tail. Nicknamed "pig rupee".

Type II - Obv. die w/redesigned elephant with outlined ear, heavy feet and long tail.

The Rupees, dated 1911, were rejected by the public because the elephant, on the Order of the Indian Empire shown on the King's robe, was thought to resemble a pig, an animal considered unclean by most Indians. Out of a total of 9.4 million pieces struck at both mints, only 700,000 were issued, and many of these were withdrawn and melted with un-issued pieces. The issues dated 1912 and later have a re-designed elephant.

COLONY

MILLED COINAGE

Regal Style

KM# 483 1/12 ANNA (1 Pie)

Copper, 17.5 mm. **Ruler:** Victoria **Obv:** Crowned bust left **Obv. Legend:** VICTORIA EMPRESS **Rev:** Value and date within beaded circle and wreath

Date	Mintage	F	VF	XF	Unc	BU
1901(c)	21,345,000	0.35	0.75	1.75	4.00	—
1901(c) Proof	—	Value: 175				
1901(c) P/L; Restrike	—	—	—	—	90.00	—

KM# 483b 1/12 ANNA (1 Pie)

Silver **Ruler:** Victoria **Obv:** Crowned bust left **Rev:** Value and date within beaded circle and wreath

Date	Mintage	F	VF	XF	Unc	BU
1901(c) P/L; Restrike	—	—	—	—	250	—

KM# 483c 1/12 ANNA (1 Pie)

Gold **Ruler:** Victoria **Obv:** Crowned bust left **Rev:** Value and date within beaded circle and wreath **Note:** All dates of this type are prooflike restrikes.

Date	Mintage	F	VF	XF	Unc	BU
1901(c)	—	—	—	—	725	—

KM# 497 1/12 ANNA (1 Pie)

Copper, 17.5 mm. **Ruler:** Edward VII **Obv:** Head right **Obv. Legend:** EDWARD VII KING & EMPEROR **Rev:** Date and denomination within circle, wreath surrounds **Note:** Thick planchet.

Date	Mintage	F	VF	XF	Unc	BU
1903(c)	7,883,000	0.35	1.25	6.00	15.00	—
1903(c) Proof	—	Value: 180				
1903(c) P/L; Restrike	—	—	—	—	80.00	—
1904(c)	16,506,000	0.25	1.00	4.00	12.00	—
1904(c) Proof	—	Value: 180				
1904(c) P/L; Restrike	—	—	—	—	80.00	—
1905(c)	13,060,000	0.25	1.00	4.00	12.00	—
1905(c) P/L; Restrike	—	—	—	—	80.00	—
1906(c)	9,072,000	0.25	1.00	4.00	12.00	—
1906(c) Proof	—	Value: 180				
1906(c) P/L; Restrike	—	—	—	—	80.00	—

KM# 497a 1/12 ANNA (1 Pie)

Silver **Ruler:** Edward VII **Obv:** Head right **Rev:** Date and denomination within circle, wreath surrounds

Date	Mintage	F	VF	XF	Unc	BU
1904(c) P/L; Restrike	—	—	—	—	200	—
1905(c) P/L; Restrike	—	—	—	—	200	—

KM# 498 1/12 ANNA (1 Pie)

Bronze, 17.5 mm. **Ruler:** Edward VII **Obv:** Head right **Obv. Legend:** EDWARD VII KING & EMPEROR **Rev:** Date and denomination within circle, wreath surrounds **Note:** Thin planchet.

Date	Mintage	F	VF	XF	Unc	BU
1906(c)	2,184,000	0.35	0.75	5.00	15.00	—
1906(c) Proof	—	Value: 150				
1907(c)	20,985,000	0.25	0.50	3.00	9.00	—
1907(c) Proof	—	Value: 150				
1907(c) P/L; Restrike	—	—	—	—	80.00	—
1908(c)	22,036,000	0.25	0.50	3.00	9.00	—
1908(c) Proof	—	Value: 150				
1908(c) P/L; Restrike	—	—	—	—	80.00	—
1909(c)	12,316,000	0.25	0.50	3.00	9.00	—
1909(c) P/L; Restrike	—	—	—	—	80.00	—
1910(c)	23,520,000	0.25	0.50	3.00	9.00	—
1910(c) P/L; Restrike	—	—	—	—	80.00	—

KM# 498a 1/12 ANNA (1 Pie)

Aluminum, 17.5 mm. **Ruler:** Edward VII **Obv:** Head right **Rev:** Date and denomination within circle, wreath surrounds

Date	Mintage	F	VF	XF	Unc	BU
1909(c) Proof	—	Value: 200				

KM# 509 1/12 ANNA (1 Pie)

Bronze, 17.5 mm. **Ruler:** George V **Obv:** Crowned bust left **Obv. Legend:** GEORGE V KING EMPEROR **Rev:** Date and denomination within circle, wreath surrounds

Date	Mintage	F	VF	XF	Unc	BU
1912(c)	25,938,000	0.50	0.75	1.50	4.50	—
1912(c) Proof	—	Value: 150				
1912(c) P/L; Restrike	—	—	—	—	80.00	—
1913(c)	16,149,000	0.25	0.50	1.00	3.00	—
1913(c) Proof	—	Value: 120				
1913(c) P/L; Restrike	—	—	—	—	80.00	—
1914(c)	19,814,000	0.25	0.50	0.75	2.00	—
1914(c) Proof	—	Value: 120				
1914(c) P/L; Restrike	—	—	—	—	80.00	—
1915(c)	20,563,000	0.25	0.50	0.75	2.00	—
1915(c) Proof	—	Value: 120				
1915(c) P/L; Restrike	—	—	—	—	80.00	—
1916(c)	14,438,000	0.25	0.50	0.75	2.00	—
1916(c) Proof	—	Value: 120				
1916(c) P/L; Restrike	—	—	—	—	80.00	—
1917(c)	35,174,000	0.25	0.50	0.75	2.00	—
1917(c) Proof	—	Value: 120				
1917(c) P/L; Restrike	—	—	—	—	80.00	—
1918(c)	24,192,000	0.25	0.50	0.75	2.00	—
1918(c) Proof	—	Value: 120				
1918(c) P/L; Restrike	—	—	—	—	80.00	—
1919(c)	17,472,000	0.25	0.50	0.75	2.00	—
1919(c) Proof	—	Value: 120				
1919(c) P/L; Restrike	—	—	—	—	80.00	—
1920(c)	39,878,000	0.25	0.50	0.75	2.00	—
1920(c) Proof	—	Value: 120				
1920(c) P/L; Restrike	—	—	—	—	80.00	—
1921(c)	19,334,000	0.25	0.50	0.75	2.00	—
1921(c) Proof	—	Value: 120				
1921(c) P/L; Restrike	—	—	—	—	80.00	—
1923(c)	8,429,000	0.25	0.50	0.75	2.00	—
1923(c) Proof	—	Value: 120				
1923(b)	8,717,000	0.25	0.50	0.75	2.00	—
1923(b) Proof	—	Value: 120				
1924(c)	7,200,000	0.50	0.75	1.50	4.50	—
1924(c) Proof	—	Value: 120				
1924(b)	9,869,000	0.25	0.50	0.75	2.00	—
1924(b) Proof	—	Value: 120				
1924(b) P/L; Restrike	—	—	—	—	80.00	—
1925(c)	5,818,000	0.50	0.75	1.50	4.50	—
1925(c) Proof	—	Value: 120				
1925(b)	6,415,000	0.50	0.75	1.50	4.50	—
1925(b) Proof	—	Value: 120				
1925(b) P/L; Restrike	—	—	—	—	80.00	—
1926(c)	4,147,000	0.50	0.75	1.50	4.50	—
1926(c) Proof	—	Value: 120				
1926(b)	15,464,000	0.25	0.50	0.75	2.00	—
1926(b) Proof	—	Value: 120				
1926(b) P/L; Restrike	—	—	—	—	80.00	—
1927(c)	6,662,000	0.50	0.75	1.50	4.50	—
1927(c) Proof	—	Value: 120				
1927(b)	6,788,000	0.50	0.75	1.50	4.50	—
1927(b) Proof	—	Value: 120				
1927(b) P/L; Restrike	—	—	—	—	80.00	—
1928(c)	8,064,000	0.25	0.50	0.75	2.00	—
1928(c) Proof	—	Value: 120				
1928(b)	6,135,000	0.50	0.75	1.50	4.50	—
1928(b) Proof	—	Value: 120				
1928(b) P/L; Restrike	—	—	—	—	80.00	—
1929(c)	15,130,000	0.25	0.50	0.75	2.00	—
1929(c) Proof	—	Value: 120				
1929(c) P/L; Restrike	—	—	—	—	80.00	—
1930(c)	13,498,000	0.25	0.50	0.75	2.00	—
1930(c) Proof	—	Value: 120				
1930(c) P/L; Restrike	—	—	—	—	80.00	—
1931(c)	18,278,000	0.25	0.50	0.75	2.00	—
1931(c) Proof	—	Value: 120				
1931(c) P/L; Restrike	—	—	—	—	80.00	—
1932(c)	23,213,000	0.25	0.50	0.75	2.00	—
1932(c) Proof	—	Value: 120				
1932(c) P/L; Restrike	—	—	—	—	80.00	—
1933(c)	16,896,000	0.25	0.50	0.75	2.00	—
1933(c) Proof	—	Value: 120				
1933(c) P/L; Restrike	—	—	—	—	80.00	—
1934(c)	17,146,000	0.25	0.50	0.75	2.00	—
1934(c) Proof	—	Value: 120				
1934(c) P/L; Restrike	—	—	—	—	80.00	—
1935(c)	19,142,000	0.25	0.50	0.75	2.00	—
1935(c) Proof	—	Value: 120				
1935(c) P/L; Restrike	—	—	—	—	80.00	—
1936(c)	23,213,000	0.25	0.50	0.75	2.00	—
1936(b)	12,887,000	0.25	0.50	0.75	2.00	—
1936(b) P/L; Restrike	—	—	—	—	80.00	—

KM# 526 1/12 ANNA (1 Pie)

Bronze, 17.5 mm. **Ruler:** George VI **Obv:** Crowned head left **Obv. Legend:** GEORGE VI KING EMPEROR **Rev:** Date and denomination within circle, wreath surrounds **Note:** First head.

Date	Mintage	F	VF	XF	Unc	BU
1938(c) Proof	—	Value: 120				
1939(c)	3,571,000	0.50	0.75	1.50	4.50	—
1939(b)	17,407,000	0.25	0.50	1.00	2.50	—

KM# 527 1/12 ANNA (1 Pie)

Bronze, 17.5 mm. **Ruler:** George VI **Obv:** Crowned head left **Obv. Legend:** GEORGE VI KING EMPEROR **Rev:** Date and denomination within circle, wreath surrounds **Note:** Second head.

Date	Mintage	F	VF	XF	Unc	BU
1938(c) P/L; Restrike	—	—	—	—	80.00	—
1939(c)	5,245,000	0.25	0.50	1.00	2.50	—
1939(c) Proof	—	Value: 120				

Date	Mintage	F	VF	XF	Unc	BU
1939(b)	31,306,000	0.25	0.50	0.75	2.00	—
1939(b) Proof	—	Value: 120				
1939(b) P/L; Restrike	—	—	—	—	80.00	—
1941(b)	6,137,000	0.25	0.50	0.75	2.00	—
1942(b)	6,124,000	0.50	0.75	1.50	4.50	—
1942(b) Proof	—	Value: 120				
1942(b) P/L; Restrike	—	—	—	—	80.00	—

KM# 484 1/2 PICE

Copper **Ruler:** Victoria **Obv:** Crowned bust left **Obv. Legend:** VICTORIA EMPRESS **Rev:** Value and date within beaded circle and wreath

Date	Mintage	F	VF	XF	Unc	BU
1901(c)	16,057,000	1.00	1.75	3.50	8.50	—
1901(c) Proof	—	Value: 175				
1901(c) P/L; Restrike	—	—	—	—	90.00	—

KM# 484b 1/2 PICE

Silver **Ruler:** Victoria **Obv:** Crowned bust left **Rev:** Value and date within beaded circle and wreath

Date	Mintage	F	VF	XF	Unc	BU
1901(c) P/L; Restrike	—	—	—	—	250	—

KM# 484c 1/2 PICE

Gold **Ruler:** Victoria **Obv:** Crowned bust left **Rev:** Value and date within beaded circle and wreath **Note:** All dates of this type are prooflike restrikes.

Date	Mintage	F	VF	XF	Unc	BU
1901(c)	—	—	—	—	950	—

KM# 500c 1/2 PICE

Silver **Ruler:** Edward VII

Date	Mintage	F	VF	XF	Unc	BU
1903(c) P/L; Restrike	—	—	—	—	200	—
1904(c) P/L; Restrike	—	—	—	—	200	—
1905(c) P/L; Restrike	—	—	—	—	200	—

KM# 499 1/2 PICE

Copper **Ruler:** Edward VII **Obv:** Head right **Obv. Legend:** EDWARD VII KING & EMPEROR **Rev:** Date and denomination within circle, wreath surrounds

Date	Mintage	F	VF	XF	Unc	BU
1903(c)	5,376,000	0.75	1.50	5.00	15.00	—
1903(c) Proof	—	Value: 135				
1903(c) P/L; Restrike	—	—	—	—	80.00	—
1904(c)	8,464,000	0.75	1.50	5.00	15.00	—
1904(c) Proof	—	Value: 135				
1904(c) P/L; Restrike	—	—	—	—	80.00	—
1905(c)	8,922,000	0.75	1.50	5.00	15.00	—
1905(c) P/L; Restrike	—	—	—	—	80.00	—
1906(c)	6,346,000	0.75	1.50	5.00	15.00	—
1906(c) Proof	—	Value: 135				
1906(c) P/L; Restrike	—	—	—	—	80.00	—

KM# 500 1/2 PICE

Bronze **Ruler:** Edward VII **Obv. Legend:** EDWARD VII KING & EMPEROR **Note:** Thinner planchets.

Date	Mintage	F	VF	XF	Unc	BU
1904(c) Proof	—	Value: 135				
1906(c)	5,860,000	0.75	1.50	4.50	12.50	—
1906(c) Proof	—	Value: 135				
1907(c)	8,060,000	0.75	1.50	4.50	12.50	—
1907(c) Proof	—	Value: 135				
1907(c) P/L; Restrike	—	—	—	—	80.00	—
1908(c)	10,035,000	0.75	1.50	4.50	12.50	—
1908(c) Proof	—	Value: 135				
1908(c) P/L; Restrike	—	—	—	—	80.00	—
1909(c)	8,493,000	0.75	1.50	4.50	12.50	—
1909(c) P/L; Restrike	—	—	—	—	80.00	—
1910(c)	17,408,000	0.75	1.50	4.50	12.50	—

KM# 500a 1/2 PICE

Aluminum **Ruler:** Edward VII

Date	Mintage	F	VF	XF	Unc	BU
1909(c) Proof	—	Value: 300				

KM# 500b 1/2 PICE

Nickel **Ruler:** Edward VII

Date	Mintage	F	VF	XF	Unc	BU
1904(c) Proof	—	Value: 300				

KM# 510 1/2 PICE

Bronze **Ruler:** George V **Obv:** Crowned bust left **Obv. Legend:** GEORGE V KING EMPEROR **Rev:** Date and denomination within circle, wreath surrounds

Date	Mintage	F	VF	XF	Unc	BU
1912(c)	12,911,000	0.25	0.50	0.75	3.00	—
1912(c) Proof	—	Value: 120				
1912(c) P/L; Restrike	—	—	—	—	80.00	—
1913(c)	10,897,000	0.25	0.50	0.75	3.00	—
1913(c) Proof	—	Value: 120				
1913(c) P/L; Restrike	—	—	—	—	80.00	—
1914(c)	4,877,000	0.15	0.30	0.50	2.50	—
1914(c) Proof	—	Value: 120				
1914(c) P/L; Restrike	—	—	—	—	80.00	—
1915(c)	9,830,000	0.15	0.30	0.50	2.50	—
1915(c) Proof	—	Value: 120				
1915(c) P/L; Restrike	—	—	—	—	80.00	—
1916(c)	5,734,000	0.15	0.30	0.50	2.50	—
1916(c) Proof	—	Value: 120				
1916(c) P/L; Restrike	—	—	—	—	80.00	—
1917(c)	15,296,000	0.15	0.30	0.50	2.50	—
1917(c) Proof	—	Value: 120				
1917(c) P/L; Restrike	—	—	—	—	80.00	—
1918(c)	6,244,000	0.15	0.30	0.50	2.50	—
1918(c) Proof	—	Value: 120				
1918(c) P/L; Restrike	—	—	—	—	80.00	—
1919(c)	11,162,000	0.15	0.30	0.50	2.50	—
1919(c) Proof	—	Value: 120				
1919(c) P/L; Restrike	—	—	—	—	80.00	—
1920(c)	4,493,000	0.15	0.30	0.50	2.50	—
1920(c) Proof	—	Value: 120				
1920(c) P/L; Restrike	—	—	—	—	80.00	—
1921(c)	6,234,000	0.15	0.30	0.50	2.50	—
1921(c) Proof	—	Value: 120				
1921(c) P/L; Restrike	—	—	—	—	80.00	—
1922(c)	6,336,000	0.15	0.30	0.50	2.50	—
1922(c) Proof	—	Value: 120				
1922(c) P/L; Restrike	—	—	—	—	80.00	—
1923(c)	7,411,000	0.15	0.30	0.50	2.50	—
1923(c) Proof	—	Value: 120				
1923(c) P/L; Restrike	—	—	—	—	80.00	—
1924(c)	9,523,000	0.15	0.30	0.50	2.50	—
1924(c) Proof	—	Value: 120				
1924(c) P/L; Restrike	—	—	—	—	80.00	—
1925(c)	3,981,000	0.50	0.75	1.50	4.50	—
1925(c) Proof	—	Value: 120				
1925(c) P/L; Restrike	—	—	—	—	80.00	—
1926(c)	7,885,000	0.15	0.30	0.50	2.50	—
1926(c) Proof	—	Value: 120				
1926(c) P/L; Restrike	—	—	—	—	80.00	—
1927(c)	5,888,000	0.15	0.30	0.50	2.50	—
1927(c) Proof	—	Value: 120				
1927(c) P/L; Restrike	—	—	—	—	80.00	—
1928(c)	5,456,000	0.15	0.30	0.50	2.50	—
1928(c) Proof	—	Value: 120				
1928(c) P/L; Restrike	—	—	—	—	80.00	—
1929(c)	7,654,000	0.15	0.30	0.50	2.50	—
1929(c) Proof	—	Value: 120				
1929(c) P/L; Restrike	—	—	—	—	80.00	—
1930(c)	7,181,000	0.15	0.30	0.50	2.50	—
1930(c) Proof	—	Value: 120				
1930(c) P/L; Restrike	—	—	—	—	80.00	—
1931(c)	8,794,000	0.15	0.30	0.50	2.50	—
1931(c) Proof	—	Value: 120				
1931(c) P/L; Restrike	—	—	—	—	80.00	—
1932(c)	5,440,000	0.15	0.30	0.50	2.50	—
1932(c) Proof	—	Value: 120				
1932(c) P/L; Restrike	—	—	—	—	80.00	—
1933(c)	9,242,000	0.15	0.30	0.50	2.50	—
1933(c) Proof	—	Value: 120				
1933(c) P/L; Restrike	—	—	—	—	80.00	—
1934(c)	8,947,000	0.15	0.30	0.50	2.50	—
1934(c) Proof	—	Value: 120				
1934(c) P/L; Restrike	—	—	—	—	80.00	—
1935(c)	15,501,000	0.15	0.30	0.50	2.50	—
1935(c) Proof	—	Value: 120				
1935(c) P/L; Restrike	—	—	—	—	80.00	—
1936(c)	26,726,000	0.10	0.25	0.40	1.25	—
1936(c) P/L; Restrike	—	—	—	—	80.00	—

KM# 528 1/2 PICE

Bronze **Ruler:** George VI **Obv:** First head; high relief **Obv. Legend:** GEORGE VI KING EMPEROR **Rev:** Date and denomination within circle, wreath surrounds **Note:** Calcutta Mint issues have no mint mark. Mumbai (Bombay) Mint issues have a small dot below the date.

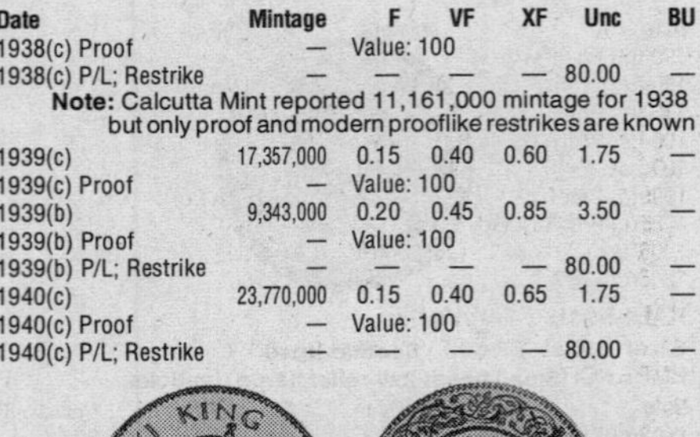

Date	Mintage	F	VF	XF	Unc	BU
1938(c) Proof	—	Value: 100				
1938(c) P/L; Restrike	—	—	—	—	80.00	—

Note: Calcutta Mint reported 11,161,000 mintage for 1938 but only proof and modern prooflike restrikes are known

Date	Mintage	F	VF	XF	Unc	BU
1939(c)	17,357,000	0.15	0.40	0.60	1.75	—
1939(c) Proof	—	Value: 100				
1939(b)	9,343,000	0.20	0.45	0.85	3.50	—
1939(b) Proof	—	Value: 100				
1939(b) P/L; Restrike	—	—	—	—	80.00	—
1940(c)	23,770,000	0.15	0.40	0.65	1.75	—
1940(c) Proof	—	Value: 100				
1940(c) P/L; Restrike	—	—	—	—	80.00	—

KM# 529 1/2 PICE

Bronze **Ruler:** George VI **Obv:** Second head; low relief **Obv. Legend:** GEORGE VI KING EMPEROR **Rev:** Date and denomination within circle, wreath surrounds

Date	Mintage	F	VF	XF	Unc	BU
1942(b) Proof	—	Value: 150				
1942(b) P/L; Restrike	—	—	—	—	100	—

KM# 532 PICE

Bronze **Ruler:** George VI **Obv:** Small date, small legends

Date	Mintage	F	VF	XF	Unc	BU
1943(b) (RC) diamond	164,659	0.30	0.50	1.00	3.50	—

KM# 533 PICE

Bronze **Ruler:** George VI **Obv:** Center hole, large date, large legends **Rev:** Wreath surrounds center hole

Date	Mintage	F	VF	XF	Unc	BU
1943(b) (HC) large dot	—	0.15	0.35	0.65	1.25	—
1943(p) (HC) small dot	98,997,000	0.15	0.35	0.65	1.25	—
1944(c) (HC)	—	0.15	0.35	0.65	1.25	—
1944(c) (HC) Proof	—	Value: 100				
1944(b) (HC) large dot	195,354,000	0.15	0.35	0.65	1.25	—
1944(b) (HC) diamond	—	0.20	0.40	0.75	2.00	—
1944(b) (FC) large dot	—	0.20	0.40	0.75	2.00	—
1944(b) P/L; Restrike	—	—	—	—	80.00	—
1944(p) (HC) small dot	141,003,000	0.20	0.40	0.75	2.00	—
1944L (HC)	29,802,000	0.20	0.40	0.80	3.50	—
1945(c) (FC)	156,322,000	0.15	0.35	0.65	1.25	—
1945(b) (FC) diamond	237,197,000	0.15	0.35	0.65	1.25	—
1945(b) (FC) large dot	Inc. above	0.15	0.35	0.65	1.25	—
1945(b) P/L; Restrike	—	—	—	—	80.00	—
1945L (FC)	238,825,000	0.15	0.35	0.65	1.25	—
1947(c) (HC)	153,702,000	0.15	0.35	0.65	1.25	—
1947(b) (HC) diamond	43,654,000	0.20	0.40	0.80	3.50	—
1947(b) Proof	—	Value: 100				
1947 P/L; Restrike	—	—	—	—	80.00	—

KM# 486 1/4 ANNA

Copper **Ruler:** Victoria **Obv:** Crowned bust left **Obv. Legend:** VICTORIA EMPRESS **Rev:** Value and date within beaded circle and wreath

Date	Mintage	F	VF	XF	Unc	BU
1901(c)	136,091,000	0.35	0.75	1.50	4.50	—
1901(c) Proof	—	Value: 250				
1901(c) P/L; Restrike	—	—	—	—	125	—

KM# 486b 1/4 ANNA

Silver **Ruler:** Victoria **Obv:** Crowned bust left **Rev:** Value and date within beaded circle and wreath

Date	Mintage	F	VF	XF	Unc	BU
1901(c) P/L; Restrike	—	—	—	—	275	—

KM# 486c 1/4 ANNA

Gold **Ruler:** Victoria **Obv:** Crowned bust left **Rev:** Value and date within beaded circle and wreath **Note:** All dates of this type are Prooflike Restrikes.

Date	Mintage	F	VF	XF	Unc	BU
1901(c) P/L; Restrike	—	—	—	—	1,150	—

KM# 501 1/4 ANNA

Copper **Ruler:** Edward VII **Obv. Legend:** EDWARD VII KING & EMPEROR

Date	Mintage	F	VF	XF	Unc	BU
1903(c)	105,974,000	0.35	1.75	7.50	35.00	—
1903(c) Proof	—	Value: 150				

Date	Mintage	F	VF	XF	Unc	BU
1903(c) P/L; Restrike	—	—	—	—	85.00	—
1904(c)	104,595,000	0.35	1.75	7.50	35.00	—
1904(c) Proof	—	Value: 150				
1904(c) P/L; Restrike	—	—	—	—	85.00	—
1905(c)	130,058,000	0.35	1.75	7.50	35.00	—
1905(c) Proof	—	Value: 150				
1905(c) P/L; Restrike	—	—	—	—	85.00	—
1906(c)	47,229,000	0.35	1.75	7.50	35.00	—
1906(c) Proof	—	Value: 150				

KM# 501b 1/4 ANNA

Silver **Ruler:** Edward VII **Obv. Legend:** EDWARD VII KING & EMPEROR

Date	Mintage	F	VF	XF	Unc	BU
1903(c) P/L; Restrike	—	—	—	—	300	—
1904(c) P/L; Restrike	—	—	—	—	300	—
1905(c) P/L; Restrike	—	—	—	—	300	—

KM# 501a 1/4 ANNA

Nickel **Ruler:** Edward VII **Obv. Legend:** EDWARD VII KING & EMPEROR

Date	Mintage	F	VF	XF	Unc	BU
1906(c) Proof	—	Value: 450				

KM# 502 1/4 ANNA

Bronze, 25.5 mm. **Ruler:** Edward VII **Obv:** Head right **Obv. Legend:** EDWARD VII KING & EMPEROR **Rev:** Date and denomination within circle, wreath surrounds **Note:** Thinner planchet.

Date	Mintage	F	VF	XF	Unc	BU
1906(c)	115,786,000	0.35	1.25	6.50	30.00	—
1906(c) Proof	—	Value: 120				
1907(c)	234,682,000	0.35	1.25	6.50	30.00	—
1907(c) Proof	—	Value: 120				
1907(c) P/L; Restrike	—	—	—	—	80.00	—
1908(c)	58,066,000	0.35	1.25	6.50	30.00	—
1908(c) Proof	—	Value: 120				
1908(c) P/L; Restrike	—	—	—	—	80.00	—
1909(c)	29,966,000	0.35	1.25	6.50	30.00	—
1909(c) Proof	—	Value: 120				
1909(c) P/L; Restrike	—	—	—	—	80.00	—
1910(c)	47,265,000	0.35	1.25	6.50	30.00	—
1910(c) P/L; Restrike	—	—	—	—	80.00	—

KM# 502a 1/4 ANNA

Aluminum **Ruler:** Edward VII **Obv:** Head right **Obv. Legend:** EDWARD VII KING & EMPEROR **Rev:** Date and denomination within circle, wreath surrounds

Date	Mintage	VG	F	VF	XF	Unc
1908(c) Proof	—	Value: 450				

KM# 511 1/4 ANNA

Bronze **Ruler:** George V **Obv:** Type I **Obv. Legend:** GEORGE V KING EMPEROR **Note:** Calcutta Mint issues have no mint mark. Mumbai (Bombay) Mint issues have a small dot below the date. The pieces dated 1911, like the other coins with that date, show the "Pig" elephant.

Date	Mintage	F	VF	XF	Unc	BU
1911(c)	55,918,000	0.75	2.00	5.00	20.00	—
1911(c) Proof	—	Value: 175				
1911(c) P/L; Restrike	—	—	—	—	80.00	—

KM# 512 1/4 ANNA

Bronze **Ruler:** George V **Obv:** Crowned bust left, type II **Obv. Legend:** GEORGE V KING EMPEROR **Rev:** Date and denomination within circle, wreath surrounds

Date	Mintage	F	VF	XF	Unc	BU
1912(c)	107,456,000	0.20	0.40	1.00	4.00	—
1912(c) Proof	—	Value: 120				
1912(c) P/L; Restrike	—	—	—	—	80.00	—
1913(c)	82,061,000	0.25	0.50	1.25	4.50	—
1913(c) Proof	—	Value: 120				
1913(c) P/L; Restrike	—	—	—	—	80.00	—
1914(c)	40,576,000	0.50	0.75	1.50	3.50	—
1914(c) Proof	—	Value: 120				
1914(c) P/L; Restrike	—	—	—	—	80.00	—
1916(c)	1,632,000	3.50	7.00	12.00	25.00	—
1916(c) Proof	—	Value: 150				
1917(c)	69,370,000	0.20	0.40	0.80	3.50	—
1917(c) Proof	—	Value: 120				
1917(c) P/L; Restrike	—	—	—	—	80.00	—
1918(c)	84,045,000	0.20	0.40	0.80	3.50	—
1918(c) Proof	—	Value: 120				
1918(c) P/L; Restrike	—	—	—	—	80.00	—

Date	Mintage	F	VF	XF	Unc	BU
1919(c)	212,467,000	0.20	0.40	0.80	3.50	—
1919(c) Proof	—	Value: 120				
1919(c) P/L; Restrike	—	—	—	—	80.00	—
1920(c)	96,019,000	0.20	0.40	0.80	3.50	—
1920(c) Proof	—	Value: 120				
1920(c) P/L; Restrike	—	—	—	—	80.00	—
1921(c) Proof	—	Value: 120				
1924(b)	16,322,000	0.20	0.40	0.80	3.50	—
1924(b) Proof	—	Value: 120				
1925(c)	14,598,000	0.20	0.40	0.80	3.50	—
1925(b)	14,588,000	0.20	0.40	0.80	3.50	—
1925(b) Proof	—	Value: 120				
1926(c)	17,389,000	0.20	0.40	0.80	3.50	—
1926(c) Proof	—	Value: 120				
1926(b)	16,073,000	0.20	0.40	0.80	3.50	—
1926(b) Proof	—	Value: 120				
1926(b) P/L; Restrike	—	—	—	—	80.00	—
1927(c)	6,925,000	0.50	0.75	1.50	4.50	—
1927(c) Proof	—	Value: 120				
1927(b)	12,440,000	0.20	0.40	0.80	3.50	—
1927(b) Proof	—	Value: 120				
1927(b) P/L; Restrike	—	—	—	—	80.00	—
1928(c)	257,779,000	0.20	0.40	0.80	3.50	—
1928(c) Proof	—	Value: 120				
1928(b)	10,057,000	0.20	0.40	0.80	3.50	—
1928(b) Proof	—	Value: 120				
1928(b) P/L; Restrike	—	—	—	—	80.00	—
1929(c)	61,542,000	0.20	0.40	0.80	3.50	—
1929(c) Proof	—	Value: 120				
1929(c) P/L; Restrike	—	—	—	—	80.00	—
1930(c)	40,698,000	0.20	0.40	0.80	3.50	—
1930(c) Proof	—	Value: 120				
1930(b)	9,646,000	0.50	0.75	1.50	4.50	—
1930(b) Proof	—	Value: 120				
1930(b) P/L; Restrike	—	—	—	—	80.00	—
1931(c)	6,835,000	0.50	0.75	1.50	4.50	—
1931(c) Proof	—	Value: 120				
1931(c) P/L; Restrike	—	—	—	—	80.00	—
1933(c)	40,230,000	0.20	0.40	0.80	3.50	—
1933(c) Proof	—	Value: 120				
1933(c) P/L; Restrike	—	—	—	—	80.00	—
1934(c)	80,506,000	0.20	0.40	0.80	3.50	—
1934(c) Proof	—	Value: 120				
1934(c) P/L; Restrike	—	—	—	—	80.00	—
1935(c)	92,595,000	0.20	0.40	0.80	3.50	—
1935(c) Proof	—	Value: 120				
1935(c) P/L; Restrike	—	—	—	—	80.00	—
1936(c)	227,501,000	0.20	0.40	0.80	3.50	—
1936(b)	61,926,000	0.20	0.40	0.80	3.50	—
1936(b) Proof	—	Value: 120				
1936(b) P/L; Restrike	—	—	—	—	80.00	—

KM# 530 1/4 ANNA

Bronze **Ruler:** George VI **Obv:** First head; high relief **Obv. Legend:** GEORGE VI KING EMPEROR **Rev:** Date and denomination within circle, wreath surrounds

Date	Mintage	F	VF	XF	Unc	BU
1938(c)	33,792,000	0.25	0.40	0.75	2.00	—
1938(c) Proof	—	Value: 120				
1938(b)	16,796,000	0.50	0.75	1.50	4.50	—
1938(b) P/L; Restrike	—	—	—	—	100	—
1939(c)	78,279,000	0.30	0.50	1.00	2.50	—
1939(c) Proof	—	Value: 120				
1939(b)	60,171,000	0.30	0.50	1.00	3.50	—
1939(b) Proof	—	Value: 120				
1939(b) P/L; Restrike	—	—	—	—	100	—
1940(b)	116,721,000	0.35	0.75	1.50	3.50	—

KM# 531 1/4 ANNA

Bronze **Ruler:** George VI **Obv:** Second head; low relief **Obv. Legend:** GEORGE VI KING EMPEROR **Rev:** Denomination and date within wreath

Date	Mintage	F	VF	XF	Unc	BU
1940(c)	140,410,000	0.30	0.50	1.00	3.50	—
1940(c) Proof	—	Value: 120				
1940(b)	—	0.30	0.50	1.00	3.50	—
Note: Mintage included in KM#530						
1940(b) P/L; Restrike	—	—	—	—	100	—
1941(c)	121,107,000	0.30	0.50	1.00	3.50	—
1941(c) P/L; Restrike	—	—	—	—	100	—
1941(b)	1,446,000	0.40	0.90	2.00	6.00	—

Date	Mintage	F	VF	XF	Unc	BU
1942(c)	34,298,000	0.30	0.50	1.00	3.50	—
1942(b)	8,768,000	0.30	0.50	1.00	3.50	—
1942(b) P/L; Restrike	—	—	—	—	100	—

KM# 503 1/2 ANNA

Copper **Ruler:** Edward VII **Obv:** Head of Edward VII **Rev:** Value and date within beaded circle and wreath

Date	Mintage	F	VF	XF	Unc	BU
1904(c) Proof	—	Value: 2,200				

KM# 534 1/2 ANNA

Copper-Nickel **Ruler:** George VI **Obv:** Crowned head left **Obv. Legend:** GEORGE VI KING EMPEROR **Rev:** Denomination and date within decorative outline **Rev. Legend:** • INDIA • **Shape:** 4-sided

Date	Mintage	F	VF	XF	Unc	BU
1940(c) Proof	—	Value: 650				
1940(c) P/L; Restrike	—	—	—	—	150	—

KM# 534a 1/2 ANNA

Gold **Ruler:** George VI **Obv:** Crowned head left **Rev:** Denomination and date within decorative outline

Date	Mintage	F	VF	XF	Unc	BU
1940(c)	—	—	—	—	550	—
Note: Prooflike; Restrike						

KM# 534b.2 1/2 ANNA

Nickel-Brass **Ruler:** George VI **Obv:** Crowned head left **Rev:** Denomination and date within decorative outline **Rev. Legend:** • INDIA •

Date	Mintage	F	VF	XF	Unc	BU
1942(c)	159,000,000	0.10	0.25	0.50	2.00	—
1942(c) Proof	—	Value: 100				
1943(c)	437,760,000	0.10	0.25	0.50	2.00	—
1943(c) Proof	—	Value: 120				
1944(c)	514,800,000	0.10	0.25	0.50	2.00	—
1944(c) Proof	—	Value: 120				
1945(c)	215,732,000	0.10	0.25	0.50	2.00	—
1945(c) Proof	—	Value: 120				

KM# 534b.1 1/2 ANNA

Nickel-Brass **Ruler:** George VI **Obv:** Crowned head left, second head **Obv. Legend:** GEORGE VI KING EMPEROR **Rev:** Denomination and date within decorative outline **Rev. Legend:** INDIA (without dots) **Note:** Bombay Mint issues dated 1942-1945 are without a dot before and after India.

Date	Mintage	F	VF	XF	Unc	BU
1942(b)	7,945,000	0.30	0.50	1.00	3.50	—
1942(b) P/L; Restrike	—	—	—	—	120	—
1943(b) P/L; Restrike	—	—	—	—	120	—
1944(b) P/L; Restrike	—	—	—	—	120	—
1945(b) P/L; Restrike	—	—	—	—	100	—

KM# 535.1 1/2 ANNA

Copper-Nickel **Ruler:** George VI **Obv:** Crowned head left **Rev:** Denomination and date within decorative outline **Shape:** 4-sided

Date	Mintage	F	VF	XF	Unc	BU
1946(b)	48,744,000	0.10	0.25	0.50	2.00	—
1946(b) Proof	—	Value: 120				
1946(b) P/L; Restrike	—	—	—	—	100	—
1947(b) P/L; Restrike	—	—	—	—	150	—

KM# 535.2 1/2 ANNA

Copper-Nickel **Ruler:** George VI **Obv:** Crowned head left **Rev:** Denomination and date within decorative outline **Shape:** 4-sided

Date	Mintage	F	VF	XF	Unc	BU
1946(c)	75,159,000	0.15	0.30	0.50	2.50	—
1947(c)	126,392,000	0.10	0.20	0.45	1.25	—
1947(c) Proof	—	Value: 120				
1947(c) P/L; Restrike	—	—	—	—	100	—

KM# 504 ANNA

Copper-Nickel **Ruler:** Edward VII **Obv:** Crowned bust right **Obv. Legend:** EDWARD VII KING & EMPEROR **Rev:** Denomination and date within decorative outline **Shape:** Scalloped **Note:** Struck only at the Mumbai (Bombay) Mint. Small incuse "B" mint mark in the space below the cross pattee of the crown on the obverse.

Date	Mintage	F	VF	XF	Unc	BU
1906B	200,000	20.00	50.00	125	300	—
1907B	37,256,000	0.50	1.25	2.00	5.00	—
1907B Proof	—	Value: 60.00				
1908B	22,536,000	0.50	1.25	2.00	5.00	—
1908B Proof	—	Value: 60.00				
1909B	24,800,000	0.50	1.25	2.00	5.00	—
1909B Proof	—	Value: 60.00				
1910B	40,200,000	0.50	1.25	2.00	5.00	—
1910B Proof	—	Value: 60.00				

KM# 513 ANNA

Copper-Nickel **Ruler:** George VI **Obv:** Crowned bust left **Obv. Legend:** GEORGE VI KING EMPEROR **Rev:** Denomination and date within decorative outline **Shape:** Scalloped **Note:** Until 1920, all were struck at the Mumbai (Bombay) Mint without mint mark. From 1923 on, the Mumbai (Bombay) Mint issues have a small, raised bead or dot below the date. Calcutta Mint issues have no mint mark.

Date	Mintage	F	VF	XF	Unc	BU
1912(b)	39,400,000	0.40	1.00	2.50	6.00	—
1912 Proof	—	Value: 150				
1913(b)	39,776,000	0.40	1.00	2.50	6.00	—
1913 Proof	—	Value: 150				
1914(b)	48,000,000	0.25	0.50	1.75	4.00	—
1914 Proof	—	Value: 150				
1915(b)	7,670,000	0.40	1.00	2.50	6.00	—
1915 Proof	—	Value: 150				
1916(b)	39,087,000	0.25	0.50	1.75	4.00	—
1917(b)	58,067,000	0.25	0.50	1.75	4.00	—
1917 Proof	—	Value: 150				
1918(b)	80,692,000	0.25	0.50	1.75	4.00	—
1918(b) Proof	—	Value: 150				
1919(b)	122,795,000	0.25	0.50	1.75	4.00	—
1919(b) Proof	—	Value: 150				
1919(c) Proof	—	Value: 150				
1920(b)	9,264,000	0.25	0.50	1.75	4.50	—
1920(b) Proof	—	Value: 150				
1923(b)	7,125,000	0.25	0.50	1.75	4.50	—
1923(b) Proof	—	Value: 150				
1924(c)	16,640,000	0.25	0.50	1.75	4.00	—
1924(c) Proof	—	Value: 150				
1924(b)	17,285,000	0.25	0.50	2.00	5.00	—
1924(b) Proof	—	Value: 150				
1924(b) P/L; Restrike	—	—	—	—	80.00	—
1925(c)	22,388,000	0.25	0.50	2.00	5.00	—
1925(c) Proof	—	Value: 150				
1925(b)	11,763,000	0.25	0.50	2.00	5.00	—
1925(b) Proof	—	Value: 150				
1925(b) P/L; Restrike	—	—	—	—	80.00	—
1926(c)	13,440,000	0.25	0.50	2.00	5.00	—
1926(c) Proof	—	Value: 150				
1926(b)	8,088,000	0.25	0.50	2.00	5.00	—
1926(b) Proof	—	Value: 150				
1926(b) P/L; Restrike	—	—	—	—	80.00	—
1927(c)	6,296,000	0.40	1.00	2.50	6.00	—
1927(c) Proof	—	Value: 150				
1927(b)	12,953,000	0.25	0.50	2.00	5.00	—
1927(b) Proof	—	Value: 150				
1927(b) P/L; Restrike	—	—	—	—	80.00	—
1928(c)	29,568,000	1.00	1.75	3.50	8.50	—
1928(c) Proof	—	Value: 150				
1928(b)	4,832,000	0.25	0.50	2.00	5.00	—
1928(b) Proof	—	Value: 150				
1928(b) P/L; Restrike	—	—	—	—	80.00	—
1929(c)	42,200,000	0.25	0.50	2.00	5.00	—
1929(c) Proof	—	Value: 150				
1929(c) P/L; Restrike	—	—	—	—	80.00	—
1930(c)	22,816,000	0.25	0.50	2.00	5.00	—
1930(c) Proof	—	Value: 150				
1930(c) P/L; Restrike	—	—	—	—	80.00	—
1933(c)	17,432,000	0.25	0.50	2.00	5.00	—
1933(c) Proof	—	Value: 150				
1933(c) P/L; Restrike	—	—	—	—	80.00	—
1934(c)	34,216,000	0.25	0.40	1.50	4.00	—
1934(c) Proof	—	Value: 150				
1934(c) P/L; Restrike	—	—	—	—	80.00	—
1935(c)	12,952,000	0.25	0.40	1.50	4.00	—
1935(c) Proof	—	Value: 150				
1935(b)	41,112,000	0.25	0.40	1.50	4.00	—
1935(b) Proof	—	Value: 150				
1935(b) P/L; Restrike	—	—	—	—	80.00	—
1936(c)	21,592,000	0.25	0.40	1.50	4.00	—
1936(b)	107,136,000	0.20	0.35	1.25	3.00	—
1936(b) Proof	—	Value: 150				

KM# 536 ANNA

Copper-Nickel **Ruler:** George VI **Obv:** First head, high relief **Obv. Legend:** GEORGE VI KING EMPEROR **Rev:** Denomination and date within decorative outline **Shape:** Scalloped **Note:** Calcutta Mint issues have no mint mark. Bombay Mint issues have a small dot below the date.

Date	Mintage	VG	F	VF	XF	Unc
1938(c)	7,128,000	—	0.30	0.75	1.50	5.00
1938(c) Proof	—	Value: 120				
1938(b)	3,126,000	—	0.40	1.00	2.00	5.00
1938(b) P/L; Restrike	—	—	—	—	—	80.00
1939(c)	18,192,000	—	0.30	0.75	1.50	3.00
1939(b)	36,157,000	—	0.30	0.75	1.50	3.00
1939(b) P/L; Restrike	—	—	—	—	—	80.00
1940(c)	60,945,000	—	0.30	0.75	1.50	3.00
1940(c) P/L; Restrike	—	—	—	—	—	80.00
1940(b)	—	—	1.00	2.00	4.00	10.00

KM# 537 ANNA

Copper-Nickel **Ruler:** George VI **Obv:** Second head, low relief, large crown **Obv. Legend:** GEORGE VI KING EMPEROR **Rev:** Large denomination and date within decorative outline **Shape:** Scalloped

Date	Mintage	VG	F	VF	XF	Unc
1940(c)	76,392,000	—	0.10	0.25	0.50	2.00
1940(c) P/L; Restrike	—	—	—	—	—	100
1940(b)	144,712,000	—	0.10	0.25	0.50	2.00
1940(b) P/L; Restrike	—	—	—	—	—	80.00
1941(c)	62,480,000	—	0.10	0.25	0.50	2.00
1941(b)	40,170,000	—	0.15	0.40	1.00	1.50
1941(b) P/L; Restrike	—	—	—	—	—	100

KM# 537a ANNA

Nickel-Brass **Ruler:** George VI **Obv:** Second head, low relief, large crown **Obv. Legend:** GEORGE VI KING EMPEROR **Rev:** Large denomination and date within decorative outline **Shape:** Scalloped

Date	Mintage	VG	F	VF	XF	Unc
1942(c)	194,056,000	—	0.10	0.25	0.50	2.00
1942(c) Proof	—	Value: 120				
1942(b)	103,240,000	—	0.15	0.40	1.00	2.50
1942(b) P/L; Restrike	—	—	—	—	—	80.00
1943(c)	352,256,000	—	0.10	0.25	0.50	2.00
1943(c) Proof	—	Value: 120				
1943(b)	134,500,000	—	0.10	0.25	0.50	2.00
1943(b) P/L; Restrike	—	—	—	—	—	80.00
1944(c)	457,608,000	—	0.10	0.25	0.50	2.00
1944(c) Proof	—	Value: 120				
1944(b)	175,208,000	—	0.10	0.25	0.50	2.00
1944(b) P/L; Restrike	—	—	—	—	—	80.00
1945(c)	278,360,000	—	0.10	0.25	0.50	2.00
1945(b)	61,228,000	—	0.20	0.40	0.80	3.50

KM# 539 ANNA

Nickel-Brass, 21 mm. **Ruler:** George VI **Obv:** Second head, low relief, small crown **Obv. Legend:** GEORGE VI KING EMPEROR **Rev:** Denomination and date within decorative outline **Shape:** Scalloped

Date	Mintage	VG	F	VF	XF	Unc
1945(c)	278,360,000	—	0.10	0.25	0.75	2.00
1945(c) Proof	—	Value: 120				
1945(b)	61,228,000	—	0.10	0.25	0.75	2.00
1945(b) P/L; Restrike	—	—	—	—	—	100

KM# 538 ANNA

Copper-Nickel **Ruler:** George VI **Obv:** Second head, low relief, small crown **Obv. Legend:** GEORGE VI KING EMPEROR **Rev:** Denomination and date within decorative outline **Shape:** Scalloped

Date	Mintage	F	VF	XF	Unc	BU
1946(c)	100,820,000	0.10	0.15	0.35	1.50	—
1946(b)	82,052,000	0.10	0.15	0.35	1.50	—
1946(b) Proof	—	Value: 120				
1946(b) P/L; Restrike	—	—	—	—	100	—
1947(c)	148,656,000	0.10	0.25	0.35	1.50	—
1947(c) Proof	—	Value: 120				
1947(b)	50,096,000	0.10	0.25	0.50	2.00	—
1947(b) Proof	—	Value: 120				

KM# 488 2 ANNAS

1.4600 g., 0.9170 Silver .0430 oz. ASW **Ruler:** Victoria **Obv:** Crowned bust left **Obv. Legend:** VICTORIA EMPRESS **Rev:** Value and date within wreath

Date	Mintage	F	VF	XF	Unc	BU
1901C Incuse	8,944,000	1.25	2.50	5.00	10.00	—
Note: Type B Bust, Type II Reverse						
1901C Proof	Inc. above	Value: 35.00				
1901B Incuse	—	2.50	5.00	10.00	20.00	—
Note: Type B Bust, Type I Reverse						
1901B Incuse	1,706,000	1.25	2.50	5.00	10.00	—
Note: Type B Bust, Type II Reverse						
1901B Proof	—	Value: 125				
1901B P/L; Restrike	—	—	—	—	30.00	—
1901B Raised	—	2.50	5.00	10.00	20.00	—
Note: Type B Bust, Type I Reverse						
1901B Raised	Inc. above	1.25	2.50	5.00	10.00	—
Note: Type B Bust, Type II Reverse						

KM# 505 2 ANNAS

1.4600 g., 0.9170 Silver .0430 oz. ASW **Ruler:** Edward VII **Obv:** Head right **Obv. Legend:** EDWARD VII KING AND EMPEROR **Rev:** Crown above denomination, sprays flank **Note:** Mule.

Date	Mintage	F	VF	XF	Unc	BU
1903(c)	4,434,000	1.75	3.50	7.00	14.00	—
1903(c) Proof	—	Value: 200				
1903(c) P/L; Restrike	—	—	—	—	100	—
1904(c)	14,632,000	1.50	3.00	6.00	12.00	—
1904(c) Proof	—	Value: 200				
1904(c) P/L; Restrike	—	—	—	—	100	—
1905(c)	19,303,000	1.50	3.00	6.00	12.00	—
1905(c) P/L; Restrike	—	—	—	—	100	—
1906(c)	13,031,000	1.50	3.00	6.00	12.00	—
1906(c) P/L; Restrike	—	—	—	—	100	—
1907(c)	22,145,000	1.50	3.00	6.00	12.00	—
1907(c) Proof	—	Value: 200				
1908(c)	21,600,000	1.50	3.00	6.00	12.00	—
1908(c) Proof	—	Value: 200				
1908(c) P/L; Restrike	—	—	—	—	100	—
1909(c)	6,769,000	1.75	3.50	7.00	14.00	—
1909(c) Proof	—	Value: 200				
1909(c) P/L; Restrike	—	—	—	—	100	—
1910(c)	1,604,000	1.75	3.50	7.00	14.00	—
1910(c) Proof	—	Value: 200				
1910(c) P/L; Restrike	—	—	—	—	100	—

KM# 505a 2 ANNAS

Gold **Ruler:** Edward VII **Obv:** Head right **Obv. Legend:** EDWARD VII KING AND EMPEROR **Rev:** Crown above denomination, sprays flank **Note:** All dates of this type are prooflike restrikes.

Date	Mintage	F	VF	XF	Unc	BU
1904(c)	—	—	—	—	900	—
1906(c)	—	—	—	—	900	—
1910(c)	—	—	—	—	900	—

KM# 514 2 ANNAS

1.4600 g., 0.9170 Silver .0430 oz. ASW **Ruler:** George V **Obv:** Crowned bust left, type I **Obv. Legend:** GEORGE V KING EMPEROR **Rev:** Denomination within wreath

Date	Mintage	F	VF	XF	Unc	BU
1911(c)	16,760,000	1.50	3.00	6.00	12.00	—
1911(c) Proof	—	Value: 200				
1911(c) P/L; Restrike	—	—	—	—	150	—

KM# 515 2 ANNAS

1.4600 g., 0.9170 Silver .0430 oz. ASW **Ruler:** George V **Obv:** Crowned bust left, type II **Obv. Legend:** GEORGE V KING EMPEROR **Rev:** Denomination within wreath

Date	Mintage	F	VF	XF	Unc	BU
1912(c)	7,724,000	1.25	2.50	5.00	10.00	—
1912(c) Proof	—	Value: 150				
1912(b)	2,462,000	1.50	3.00	6.00	12.00	—
1912(b) Proof	—	Value: 150				
1912(b) P/L; Restrike	—	—	—	—	100	—
1913(c)	13,959,000	1.25	2.50	5.00	10.00	—
1913(c) Proof	—	Value: 150				
1913(b)	5,461,000	1.25	2.50	5.00	10.00	—
1913(b) Proof	—	Value: 150				
1913(b) P/L; Restrike	—	—	—	—	100	—
1914(c)	13,622,000	1.25	2.50	5.00	10.00	—
1914(c) Proof	—	Value: 150				
1914(b)	8,579,000	1.25	2.50	5.00	10.00	—
1914(b) P/L; Restrike	—	—	—	—	100	—
1915(c)	5,892,000	1.25	2.50	5.00	10.00	—
1915(c) Proof	—	Value: 150				
1915(b)	5,943,000	1.25	2.50	5.00	10.00	—
1915(b) P/L; Restrike	—	—	—	—	100	—
1916(c)	197,878,000	1.25	2.00	4.00	8.00	—
1916(c) Proof	—	Value: 150				
1916(c) P/L; Restrike	—	—	—	—	100	—
1917(c)	25,560,000	1.25	2.00	4.00	8.00	—
1917(c) Proof	—	Value: 150				
1917(c) P/L; Restrike	—	—	—	—	100	—

KM# 516 2 ANNAS

Copper-Nickel **Ruler:** George V **Obv:** Crowned bust left within circle **Obv. Legend:** GEORGE V KING EMPEROR **Rev:** Large denomination within square **Shape:** 4-sided **Note:** Calcutta Mint issues have no mint mark. Bombay Mint issues have a small raised dot on the reverse at the bottom near the rim.

Date	Mintage	F	VF	XF	Unc	BU
1918(c)	53,412,000	1.25	1.75	4.00	10.00	—
1918(c) Proof	—	Value: 250				
1918(b)	9,191,000	1.25	1.75	4.00	10.00	—
1918(b) Proof	—	Value: 250				
1918(b) P/L; Restrike	—	—	—	—	150	—
1919(c)	89,040,000	1.25	1.75	4.00	10.00	—
1919(c) Proof	—	Value: 250				
1919(c) P/L; Restrike	—	—	—	—	150	—
1920(b) Proof	—	Value: 350				
1920(c)	13,520,000	1.25	1.75	4.00	10.00	—
1920(c) Proof	—	Value: 250				
1921(c) P/L; Restrike	—	1.25	1.75	4.00	10.00	—
1923(c)	7,656,000	1.25	1.75	4.00	10.00	—
1923(c) Proof	—	Value: 250				
1923(b)	6,431,000	1.25	1.75	4.00	10.00	—
1923(b) Proof	—	Value: 250				
1923(b) P/L; Restrike	—	—	—	—	150	—
1924(c)	8,384,000	1.25	1.75	4.00	10.00	—
1924(c) Proof	—	Value: 250				
1924(b)	4,818,000	1.50	3.00	6.00	12.00	—
1924(b) Proof	—	Value: 250				
1924(b) P/L; Restrike	—	—	—	—	150	—
1925(c)	10,848,000	1.25	1.75	4.00	10.00	—
1925(c) Proof	—	Value: 250				
1925(b)	8,348,000	1.25	1.75	4.00	10.00	—
1925(b) Proof	—	Value: 250				
1925(b) P/L; Restrike	—	—	—	—	150	—
1926(c)	8,352,000	1.25	1.75	4.00	10.00	—
1926(c) Proof	—	Value: 250				
1926(b)	2,927,000	1.75	3.50	7.00	14.00	—
1926(b) Proof	—	Value: 250				
1926(b) P/L; Restrike	—	—	—	—	150	—
1927(c)	6,424,000	1.25	1,375	4.00	10.00	—
1927(c) Proof	—	Value: 250				
1927(b)	4,835,000	1.50	3.00	6.00	12.00	—
1927(b) Proof	—	Value: 250				
1927(b) P/L; Restrike	—	—	—	—	150	—
1928(c)	7,352,000	1.25	1.75	4.00	10.00	—
1928(c) Proof	—	Value: 250				
1928(b)	4,876,000	1.50	3.00	6.00	12.00	—
1928(b) Proof	—	Value: 250				
1928(b) P/L; Restrike	—	—	—	—	150	—
1929(c)	13,408,000	1.25	1.75	4.00	10.00	—
1929(c) Proof	—	Value: 250				
1929(c) P/L; Restrike	—	—	—	—	150	—
1930(c)	8,888,000	1.25	1.75	4.00	10.00	—
1930(c) Proof	—	Value: 250				
1930(c) P/L; Restrike	—	—	—	—	150	—
1930(b)	—	1.25	1.75	4.00	10.00	—
1933(c)	4,300,000	1.50	3.00	6.00	12.00	—
1933(c) Proof	—	Value: 250				
1933(c) P/L; Restrike	—	—	—	—	150	—
1934(c)	7,016,000	1.25	1.75	4.00	10.00	—
1934(c) Proof	—	Value: 250				
1934(c) P/L; Restrike	—	—	—	—	150	—
1935(c)	12,344,000	1.25	1.75	4.00	10.00	—
1935(b)	21,017,000	1.00	1.50	3.00	8.00	—
1935(b) Proof	—	Value: 250				
1935(b) P/L; Restrike	—	—	—	—	150	—
1936(b)	36,295,000	1.00	1.50	3.00	8.00	—
1936(b) Proof	—	Value: 250				

KM# 540 2 ANNAS

Copper-Nickel, 25 mm. **Ruler:** George VI **Obv:** First head, high relief **Obv. Legend:** GEORGE VI KING EMPEROR **Rev:** Denomination and date within decorative cutlines **Shape:** Square **Note:** Calcutta Mint issues have no mint mark. Mumbai (Bombay) Mint issues have a small dot before and after the date.

Date	Mintage	F	VF	XF	Unc	BU
1939(c)	4,148,000	1.25	3.00	6.00	15.00	—
1939(b)	3,392,000	2.00	5.00	10.00	25.00	—

KM# 541 2 ANNAS

Copper-Nickel, 25 mm. **Ruler:** George VI **Obv:** Second head, low relief, large crown **Obv. Legend:** GEORGE VI KING EMPEROR **Rev:** Denomination and date within decorative outlines **Shape:** 4-sided

Date	Mintage	F	VF	XF	Unc	BU
1939(c)	Inc. above	1.25	2.00	2.50	4.00	—
1939(c) Proof	—	Value: 185				
1939(b)	Inc. above	0.20	0.30	0.50	1.50	—
1939(b) Proof	—	Value: 185				
1939(b) P/L; Restrike	—	—	—	—	125	—
1940(c)	37,636,000	0.20	0.30	0.50	2.00	—
1940(c) Proof	—	Value: 185				
1940(b)	50,599,000	0.20	0.30	0.50	2.00	—
1940(b) P/L; Restrike	—	—	—	—	125	—
1941(c)	63,456,000	0.20	0.30	0.50	1.50	—
1941(b)	10,760,000	1.25	2.00	2.50	4.00	—
1941(b) Proof	—	Value: 185				
1941(b) P/L; Restrike	—	—	—	—	125	—

KM# 541a 2 ANNAS

Nickel-Brass, 25 mm. **Ruler:** George VI **Obv:** Second head, low relief, large crown **Obv. Legend:** GEORGE VI KING EMPEROR **Rev:** Denomination and date within decorative outlines **Shape:** 4-sided

Date	Mintage	F	VF	XF	Unc	BU
1942(b) Small 4	133,000,000	0.25	0.35	0.50	2.25	—
1942(b) Large 4	Inc. above	0.20	0.35	0.50	2.25	—
1943(b)	343,680,000	0.25	0.35	0.50	2.25	—
1944L	6,352,000	0.50	1.25	2.00	5.00	—

Note: On 1944 Lahore issues, a tiny L replaces the decorative stroke in the four quatrefoil angles.

Date	Mintage	F	VF	XF	Unc	BU
1944(b) Small 4	219,700,000	0.25	0.35	0.50	2.25	—
1944(b) Large 4	Inc. above	0.25	0.35	0.50	2.25	—

KM# 543 2 ANNAS

Nickel-Brass **Ruler:** George VI **Obv:** Second head, low relief, large crown **Obv. Legend:** GEORGE VI KING EMPEROR **Rev:** Small "2" **Shape:** Square

Date	Mintage	F	VF	XF	Unc	BU
1945(c)	24,260,000	0.25	0.75	1.25	2.75	—
1945(c) Proof	—	Value: 185				
1945(b)	136,688,000	0.25	0.35	0.50	1.50	—
1945(b) P/L; Restrike	—	—	—	—	125	—

KM# 542 2 ANNAS

Copper-Nickel **Ruler:** George VI **Obv:** Second head, low relief, small crown **Obv. Legend:** GEORGE VI KING EMPEROR **Rev:** Denomination and date within decorative outlines **Shape:** Square

Date	Mintage	F	VF	XF	Unc	BU
1946(c)	67,267,000	0.20	0.30	0.50	2.25	—
1946(b)	52,500,000	0.20	0.30	0.50	2.25	—
1946(b) Proof	—	Value: 185				
1946(b) P/L; Restrike	—	—	—	—	125	—
1946(l)	25,480,000	0.20	0.30	0.50	2.25	—

Note: Without "L" mintmark but with small diamond-shaped mark left of "I" on reverse

Date	Mintage	F	VF	XF	Unc	BU
1947(c)	57,428,000	0.20	0.30	0.50	2.25	—
1947(b)	38,908,000	0.20	0.30	0.50	2.25	—
1947(b) Proof	—	Value: 185				
1947(b) P/L; Restrike	—	—	—	—	125	—

KM# 519 4 ANNAS

Copper-Nickel **Ruler:** George V **Obv:** Crowned bust left within circle **Obv. Legend:** GEORGE V KING EMPEROR • INDIA • **Rev:** Denomination within square **Shape:** Scalloped **Note:** Calcutta Mint issues have no mint mark. Bombay Mint issues have a small raised dot on the reverse at the bottom near the rim.

Date	Mintage	F	VF	XF	Unc	BU
1919(c)	18,632,000	2.50	5.00	10.00	20.00	—
1919(c) Proof	—	Value: 550				
1919(b)	7,672,000	3.25	6.50	12.50	25.00	—
1919 P/L; Restrike	—	—	—	—	125	—
1920(c)	18,191,000	2.50	5.00	10.00	20.00	—
1920(c) Proof	—	Value: 550				
1920(b)	1,666,000	3.25	6.50	12.50	25.00	—
1920(b) Proof	—	Value: 550				
1920(b) P/L; Restrike	—	—	—	—	125	—
1921(c) Proof	—	Value: 550				
1921(c) P/L; Restrike	—	—	—	—	125	—
1921(b)	1,219,000	3.75	7.50	15.00	30.00	—
1921(b) Proof	—	Value: 550				

KM# 520 8 ANNAS

Copper-Nickel **Ruler:** George V **Obv:** Crowned bust left **Obv. Legend:** GEORGE V KING EMPEROR **Rev:** Denomination and date within scallop, square surrounds **Note:** Calcutta Mint issues have no mint mark. Mumbai (Bombay) Mint issues have a small raised dot on the reverse at the bottom near the rim.

Date	Mintage	F	VF	XF	Unc	BU
1919(c)	2,980,000	3.75	7.50	15.00	30.00	—
1919(c) Proof	—	Value: 550				
1919(b)	1,400,000	4.00	8.50	17.50	35.00	—
1919(b) P/L; Restrike	—	—	—	—	150	—
1920(c) Proof	—	Value: 550				
1920(c) P/L; Restrike	—	—	—	—	350	—

Date	Mintage	F	VF	XF	Unc	BU
1920(b)	1,000,000	12.50	25.00	50.00	100	—
1920(b) Proof	—	Value: 550				
1920(b) P/L; Restrike	—	—	—	—	150	—

KM# 490 1/4 RUPEE
2.9200 g., 0.9170 Silver .0860 oz. ASW **Ruler:** Victoria **Obv:** Crowned bust left **Obv. Legend:** VICTORIA EMPRESS **Rev:** Value and date within wreath **Note:** Mule.

Date	Mintage	F	VF	XF	Unc	BU
1901C Incuse	4,476,000	2.00	3.00	6.00	15.00	—
Note: Type C Bust, Type II Reverse						
1901C Proof	—	Value: 600				
1901C P/L; Restrike	—	—	—	—	175	—

KM# 506 1/4 RUPEE
2.9200 g., 0.9170 Silver .0860 oz. ASW **Ruler:** Edward VII **Obv:** Head right **Obv. Legend:** EDWARD VII KING AND EMPEROR **Rev:** Crown above denomination, sprays flank

Date	Mintage	F	VF	XF	Unc	BU
1903(c)	7,060,000	1.75	3.50	8.00	20.00	—
1903(c) Proof	—	Value: 400				
1903(c) P/L; Restrike	—	—	—	—	150	—
1904(c)	10,026,000	1.75	3.50	8.00	20.00	—
1904(c) Proof	—	Value: 400				
1904(c) P/L; Restrike	—	—	—	—	150	—
1905(c)	6,300,000	1.75	3.50	8.00	20.00	—
1905(c) Proof	—	Value: 400				
1905(c) P/L; Restrike	—	—	—	—	150	—
1906(c)	10,672,000	1.75	3.50	8.00	20.00	—
1906(c) P/L; Restrike	—	—	—	—	150	—
1907(c)	11,464,000	1.75	3.50	8.00	20.00	—
1907(c) Proof	—	Value: 400				
1907(c) P/L; Restrike	—	—	—	—	150	—
1908(c)	7,084,000	1.75	3.50	8.00	20.00	—
1908(c) Proof	—	Value: 400				
1908(c) P/L; Restrike	—	—	—	—	150	—
1909(c) Proof	—	Value: 500				
1909(c) P/L; Restrike	—	—	—	—	150	—
1910(c)	8,024,000	1.75	3.50	8.00	20.00	—
1910(c) Proof	—	Value: 400				
1910(c) P/L; Restrike	—	—	—	—	150	—

KM# 506a 1/4 RUPEE
Gold **Ruler:** Edward VII **Obv:** Head right **Rev:** Crown above denomination, sprays flank

Date	Mintage	F	VF	XF	Unc	BU
1910(c)	—	—	—	—	1,000	—
Note: Prooflike; Restrike						

KM# 517 1/4 RUPEE
2.9200 g., 0.9170 Silver .0860 oz. ASW **Ruler:** George V **Obv:** Type I **Obv. Legend:** GEORGE V KING EMPEROR

Date	Mintage	F	VF	XF	Unc	BU
1911(c)	2,245,000	2.00	4.00	8.00	8.00	—
1911(c) Proof	—	Value: 350				
1911(c) P/L; Restrike	—	—	—	—	300	—

KM# 518 1/4 RUPEE
2.9200 g., 0.9170 Silver .0860 oz. ASW **Ruler:** George V **Obv:** Crowned bust left, type II **Obv. Legend:** GEORGE V KING EMPEROR **Rev:** Denomination and date within circle, wreath surrounds

Date	Mintage	F	VF	XF	Unc	BU
1912(c)	9,587,000	2.00	3.00	5.00	12.00	—
1912(c) Proof	—	Value: 250				
1912(b)	2,200,000	2.00	3.00	5.00	12.00	—
1912(b) Proof	—	Value: 250				
1912(b) P/L; Restrike	—	—	—	—	120	—
1913(c)	12,686,000	2.00	3.00	5.00	12.00	—
1913(c) Proof	—	Value: 250				
1913(b)	2,276,000	2.00	3.00	5.00	12.00	—
1913(b) Proof	—	Value: 250				
1913(b) P/L; Restrike	—	—	—	—	120	—
1914(c)	1,423,000	2.00	3.00	5.00	12.00	—
1914(c) Proof	—	Value: 250				
1914(b)	7,949,000	2.00	3.00	5.00	10.00	—
1914(b) P/L; Restrike	—	—	—	—	120	—
1915(c)	851,000	2.25	4.00	10.00	35.00	—
1915(c) Proof	—	Value: 250				
1915(b)	2,096,000	2.00	3.00	5.00	12.00	—
1915(c) P/L; Restrike	—	—	—	—	—	—
1915(b) P/L; Restrike	—	—	—	—	120	—
1916(c)	13,178,000	2.00	3.00	5.00	12.00	—
1916(c) Proof	—	Value: 250				
1916(c) P/L; Restrike	—	—	—	—	120	—
1917(c)	21,072,000	2.00	3.00	5.00	12.00	—
1917(c) Proof	—	Value: 250				
1917(c) P/L; Restrike	—	—	—	—	120	—
1918(c)	50,575,000	2.00	3.00	5.00	12.00	—
1918(c) Proof	—	Value: 250				
1919(b)	—	3.50	7.50	15.00	30.00	—
1919(c)	26,135,000	2.00	3.00	5.00	12.00	—
1919(c) Proof	—	Value: 250				
1920(b)	—	3.25	6.50	12.50	25.00	—
1925(b)	4,007,000	2.00	3.00	5.00	12.00	—
1925(b) Proof	—	Value: 250				
1925(b) P/L; Restrike	—	—	—	—	120	—
1926(c)	8,169,000	2.00	3.00	5.00	12.00	—
1926(c) Proof	—	Value: 250				
1926(c) P/L; Restrike	—	—	—	—	120	—
1928(b)	4,023,000	2.00	3.00	5.00	12.00	—
1928(b) Proof	—	Value: 250				
1929(c)	4,013,000	2.00	3.00	5.00	12.00	—
1929(c) Proof	—	Value: 250				
1929(c) P/L; Restrike	—	—	—	—	120	—
1930(c)	3,222,000	2.00	3.00	5.00	12.00	—
1930(c) Proof	—	Value: 250				
1930(c) P/L; Restrike	—	—	—	—	120	—
1934(c)	3,946,000	2.00	3.00	5.00	10.00	—
1936(c)	25,744,000	1.50	2.50	4.00	8.00	—
1936(b)	9,864,000	1.50	2.50	4.00	8.00	—
1936(b) P/L; Restrike	—	—	—	—	120	—

KM# 544 1/4 RUPEE
2.9200 g., 0.9170 Silver .0860 oz. ASW **Ruler:** George VI **Obv:** Crowned head left **Obv. Legend:** GEORGE VI KING EMPEROR **Rev:** Denomination and date within circle, wreath surrounds

Date	Mintage	F	VF	XF	Unc	BU
1938(c) Proof	—	Value: 250				
1938(c) P/L; Restrike	—	—	—	—	125	—
1939(c)	3,072,000	2.00	3.50	6.00	12.00	—
1939(c) Proof	—	Value: 250				
1939(b)	6,770,000	2.00	3.50	5.00	10.00	—
1939(b) P/L; Restrike	—	—	—	—	125	—

KM# 544a 1/4 RUPEE
2.9200 g., 0.5000 Silver .0469 oz. ASW **Ruler:** George VI **Obv:** Crowned head left **Obv. Legend:** GEORGE VI KING EMPEROR **Rev:** Denomination and date within circle, wreath surrounds

Date	Mintage	F	VF	XF	Unc	BU
1940(b)	24,635,000	2.00	3.50	5.00	10.00	—

KM# 545 1/4 RUPEE
2.9200 g., 0.5000 Silver .0469 oz. ASW **Ruler:** George VI **Obv:** Large second head, small rim decoration **Obv. Legend:** GEORGE VI KING EMPEROR **Rev:** Denomination and date within circle, wreath surrounds **Edge:** Reeded

Date	Mintage	VG	F	VF	XF	Unc
1940(c)	68,675,000	—	BV	1.50	2.50	6.00
1940(c) Proof	—	Value: 250				
1940(b)	28,947,000	—	BV	1.50	2.50	6.00

KM# 546 1/4 RUPEE
2.9200 g., 0.5000 Silver .0469 oz. ASW **Ruler:** George VI **Obv:** Small second head, large rim decoration **Obv. Legend:** GEORGE VI KING EMPEROR **Rev:** Denomination and date within circle, wreath surrounds **Edge:** Reeded

Date	Mintage	F	VF	XF	Unc	BU
1942(c)	88,096,000	BV	1.50	2.25	4.50	—
1943(c)	90,994,000	BV	1.50	2.25	4.50	—

KM# 547 1/4 RUPEE
2.9200 g., 0.5000 Silver .0469 oz. ASW **Ruler:** George VI **Obv:** Small second head, large rim decoration **Obv. Legend:** GEORGE VI KING EMPEROR **Rev:** Denomination and date within circle, wreath surrounds **Edge:** Security

Date	Mintage	F	VF	XF	Unc	BU
1943B	95,200,000	BV	1.50	2.25	4.50	—
1943B Proof	—	Value: 250				
1943B Reverse B	Inc. above	BV	1.50	2.25	4.50	—
1943L	23,700,000	BV	1.50	2.25	4.50	—
1944B	170,504,000	BV	1.50	2.25	4.50	—
1944B Reverse B	Inc. above	BV	1.50	2.25	4.50	—
1944L	86,400,000	BV	1.50	2.25	4.50	—
1945(b) Small 5	181,648,000	BV	1.50	2.25	4.50	—
1945(b) Large 5	Inc. above	10.00	15.00	25.00	40.00	—
1945L Small 5	29,751,000	BV	1.50	2.25	4.50	—
1945L Large 5	Inc. above	BV	1.00	2.00	5.00	—

KM# 548 1/4 RUPEE
Nickel **Ruler:** George VI **Obv:** Crowned head left **Obv. Legend:** GEORGE VI KING EMPEROR **Rev:** Indian tiger (panthera tigris) **Edge:** Reeded

Date	Mintage	F	VF	XF	Unc	BU
1946(b)	83,600,000	0.40	0.75	2.50	7.50	10.00
1947(b)	109,948,000	0.40	0.75	2.50	7.50	10.00
1947(b) Proof	—	Value: 200				

KM# 507 1/2 RUPEE
5.8300 g., 0.9170 Silver .1719 oz. ASW **Ruler:** Edward VII **Obv:** Head right **Obv. Legend:** EDWARD VII KING AND EMPEROR **Rev:** Crown above denomination, sprays flank **Note:** Calcutta Mint issues have no mint mark. Mumbai (Bombay) Mint issues have a small incuse "B" in the space below the cross pattee of the crown on the reverse.

Date	Mintage	F	VF	XF	Unc	BU
1904(c) Proof	—	Value: 500				
1904(c) P/L; Restrike	—	—	—	—	175	—
1905(c)	823,000	3.50	10.00	25.00	50.00	—
1905(c) P/L; Restrike	—	—	—	—	175	—
1906(c)	3,036,000	3.50	10.00	25.00	50.00	—
1906B	400,000	3.75	12.50	30.00	60.00	—
1906B P/L; Restrike	—	—	—	—	175	—
1907(c)	2,786,000	3.50	10.00	25.00	50.00	—
1907(c) Proof	—	Value: 450				
1907B	1,856,000	3.50	10.00	25.00	50.00	—
1907B Proof	—	Value: 450				
1907B P/L; Restrike	—	—	—	—	175	—
1908(c)	1,577,000	3.50	10.00	25.00	50.00	—
1908(c) Proof	—	Value: 450				
1908(c) P/L; Restrike	—	—	—	—	175	—
1909(c)	1,569,000	3.50	10.00	25.00	50.00	—
1909(c) Proof	—	Value: 450				
1909(c) P/L; Restrike	—	—	—	—	175	—
1909B Proof	—	Value: 750				
1909B P/L; Restrike	—	—	—	—	350	—
1910(c)	3,413,000	3.50	10.00	25.00	50.00	—
1910(c) Proof	—	Value: 450				
1910B	809,000	3.50	10.00	25.00	50.00	—
1910B "B" raised	—	10.00	15.00	30.00	55.00	—
1910B Proof	—	Value: 450				
1910B P/L; Restrike	—	—	—	—	175	—

KM# 521 1/2 RUPEE
5.8300 g., 0.9170 Silver .1719 oz. ASW **Ruler:** George V **Obv:** Crowned bust left, type I **Obv. Legend:** GEORGE V KING EMPEROR **Rev:** Denomination and date within circle, wreath

surrounds **Note:** Calcutta Mint issues have no mint mark. Mumbai (Bombay) Mint issues have a small raised bead or dot in the space below the lotus flower at the bottom of the reverse. The half Rupee dated 1911 like the Rupee and all the other issues of that year has the "Pig" elephant. It was struck only at the Calcutta Mint.

Date	Mintage	F	VF	XF	Unc	BU
1911(c)	2,293,000	2.75	6.00	12.50	30.00	—
1911(c) Proof	—	Value: 500				
1911(c) P/L; Restrike	—	—	—	—	250	—

KM# 522 1/2 RUPEE

5.8300 g., 0.9170 Silver .1719 oz. ASW **Ruler:** George V **Obv:** Crowned bust left, type II **Obv. Legend:** GEORGE V KING EMPEROR **Rev:** Denomination and date within circle, wreath surrounds

Date	Mintage	F	VF	XF	Unc	BU
1912(c)	3,390,000	2.75	6.00	12.00	28.00	—
1912(c) Proof	—	Value: 500				
1912(b)	1,505,000	2.75	6.00	12.00	28.00	—
1912(b) Proof	—	Value: 500				
1912(b) P/L; Restrike	—	—	—	—	150	—
1913(c)	2,723,000	2.75	6.00	12.00	28.00	—
1913(c) Proof	—	Value: 500				
1913(b)	1,825,000	2.75	6.00	12.00	28.00	—
1913(b) Proof	—	Value: 500				
1913(b) P/L; Restrike	—	—	—	—	150	—
1914(c)	1,400,000	2.75	6.00	12.00	28.00	—
1914(c) Proof	—	Value: 500				
1914(b)	903,000	2.75	6.00	12.50	30.00	—
1914(b) P/L; Restrike	—	—	—	—	150	—
1915(c)	2,804,000	2.75	6.00	12.00	28.00	—
1915(c) Proof	—	Value: 500				
1915(c) P/L; Restrike	—	2.75	6.00	12.00	28.00	—
1916(c)	3,644,000	2.75	6.00	12.00	28.00	—
1916(c) Proof	—	Value: 500				
1916(b)	5,880,000	2.75	6.00	12.00	28.00	—
1917(c) Proof	—	Value: 500				
1917(b)	8,822,000	2.75	6.00	12.00	28.00	—
1917(b) Proof	—	Value: 500				
1918(c) P/L; Restrike	—	—	—	—	150	—
1918(b) P/L; Restrike	—	—	—	—	150	—
1918(b)	10,325,000	2.75	6.00	12.00	28.00	—
1919(b)	8,958,000	2.75	6.00	12.00	28.00	—
1919(b) Proof	—	Value: 500				
1919(b) P/L; Restrike	—	—	—	—	150	—
1919(c) P/L; Restrike	—	—	—	—	150	—
1921(c)	5,804,000	2.75	6.00	12.00	28.00	—
1921(c) Proof	—	Value: 500				
1921(c) P/L; Restrike	—	—	—	—	150	—
1922(c)	5,551,000	2.75	6.00	12.00	28.00	—
1922(c) Proof	—	Value: 500				
1922(b)	1,037,000	2.75	6.00	12.00	28.00	—
1922(b) Proof	—	Value: 500				
1922(b) P/L; Restrike	—	—	—	—	150	—
1923(c)	3,925,000	2.75	6.00	12.00	28.00	—
1923(c) P/L; Restrike	—	—	—	—	150	—
1923(b)	2,076,000	2.75	6.00	12.00	28.00	—
1923(b) Proof	—	Value: 500				
1923(b) P/L; Restrike	—	—	—	—	150	—
1924(c)	4,007,000	2.75	6.00	12.00	28.00	—
1924(c) Proof	—	Value: 500				
1924(b)	2,664,000	2.75	6.00	12.00	28.00	—
1924(b) Proof	—	Value: 500				
1924(b) P/L; Restrike	—	—	—	—	150	—
1925(c)	4,119,000	2.75	6.00	12.00	28.00	—
1925(c) Proof	—	Value: 500				
1925(b)	1,627,000	2.75	6.00	12.00	28.00	—
1925(b) Proof	—	Value: 500				
1925(b) P/L; Restrike	—	—	—	—	150	—
1926(c)	4,027,000	2.75	6.00	12.00	28.00	—
1926(c) Proof	—	Value: 500				
1926(b)	2,011,000	2.75	6.00	12.00	28.00	—
1926(b) Proof	—	Value: 500				
1926(b) P/L; Restrike	—	—	—	—	150	—
1927(c)	2,032,000	2.75	6.00	12.00	28.00	—
1927(c) Proof	—	Value: 500				
1927(c) P/L; Restrike	—	—	—	—	150	—
1928(b)	2,466,000	2.75	6.00	12.00	28.00	—
1928(b) Proof	—	Value: 500				
1929(c)	4,050,000	2.75	6.00	12.00	28.00	—
1929(c) Proof	—	Value: 500				
1929(c) P/L; Restrike	—	—	—	—	150	—
1930(c)	2,036,000	2.75	6.00	12.00	28.00	—
1930(c) Proof	—	Value: 500				
1930(c) P/L; Restrike	—	—	—	—	150	—
1933/2(c)	4,056,000	5.00	10.00	25.00	50.00	—
1933(c)	Inc. above	2.75	6.00	12.00	28.00	—
1933(c) Proof	—	Value: 300				
1933(c) P/L; Restrike	—	—	—	—	150	—
1934(c)	4,056,000	2.75	6.00	12.00	28.00	—
1934(c) Proof	—	Value: 500				
1934(c) P/L; Restrike	—	—	—	—	150	—
1936(c)	16,919,000	2.75	6.00	12.00	28.00	—
1936(b)	6,693,000	2.75	6.00	12.00	28.00	—
1936(b) P/L; Restrike	—	—	—	—	150	—

KM# 549 1/2 RUPEE

5.8300 g., 0.9170 Silver .1719 oz. ASW **Ruler:** George VI **Obv:** Crowned head left, first head **Obv. Legend:** GEORGE VI KING EMPEROR **Rev:** Denomination and date within circle, wreath surrounds **Edge:** Reeded

Date	Mintage	F	VF	XF	Unc	BU
1938(c) Proof	—	Value: 400				
1938(b)	2,200,000	BV	3.00	7.50	15.00	—
1938(b) P/L; Restrike	—	—	—	—	150	—
1939(c)	3,300,000	BV	3.00	7.50	15.00	—
1939(c) Proof	—	Value: 300				
1939(b)	10,096,000	BV	3.00	7.50	15.00	—
1939(b) Proof	—	Value: 300				
1939(b) P/L; Restrike	—	—	—	—	150	—

KM# A553 1/2 RUPEE

Copper-Nickel **Ruler:** George VI **Obv:** Crowned head left **Obv. Legend:** GEORGE VI KING EMPEROR **Rev:** Denomination and date within circle, wreath surrounds **Note:** Mule.

Date	Mintage	F	VF	XF	Unc	BU
1938(c) P/L; Restrike	—	—	—	—	—	—

KM# 550 1/2 RUPEE

5.8300 g., 0.9170 Silver .1719 oz. ASW **Ruler:** George VI **Obv:** Large second head, small rim decoration **Obv. Legend:** GEORGE VI KING EMPEROR **Rev:** Denomination and date within circle, wreath surrounds **Edge:** Reeded

Date	Mintage	VG	F	VF	XF	Unc
1939(c)	Inc. above	—	BV	3.00	6.50	15.00
1939(b)	Inc. above	—	BV	3.00	6.50	13.50

KM# 550a 1/2 RUPEE

5.8300 g., 0.5000 Silver .0937 oz. ASW **Ruler:** George VI **Obv:** Large second head, small rim decoration **Obv. Legend:** GEORGE VI KING EMPEROR **Rev:** Denomination and date within circle, wreath surrounds

Date	Mintage	F	VF	XF	Unc	BU
1940(c)	32,898,000	BV	3.00	6.00	12.00	—
1940(c) Proof	—	Value: 300				
1940(b)	17,811,000	BV	3.00	6.50	13.50	—
1940(b) P/L; Restrike	—	—	—	—	150	—

KM# 551 1/2 RUPEE

5.8300 g., 0.5000 Silver .0937 oz. ASW **Ruler:** George VI **Obv:** Large second head, small rim decoration **Obv. Legend:** GEORGE VI KING EMPEROR **Rev:** Denomination and date within circle, wreath surrounds **Edge:** Security

Date	Mintage	VG	F	VF	XF	Unc
1941(b)	26,100,000	—	BV	2.00	5.00	12.50
1942(b)	61,600,000	—	BV	2.00	5.00	12.50

NOTE: Example of large 5 in date 1945.

KM# 552 1/2 RUPEE

5.8300 g., 0.5000 Silver .0937 oz. ASW **Ruler:** George VI **Obv:** Small second head, large rim decoration **Obv. Legend:** GEORGE VI KING EMPEROR **Rev:** Denomination and inner circle smaller **Edge:** Security

Date	Mintage	F	VF	XF	Unc	BU
1942(b)	Inc. above	BV	2.00	4.50	9.00	—
1943(b) Dot	90,400,000	BV	2.00	4.50	9.00	—
1943(b) Proof	—	Value: 300				
1943(b) Diamond	—	BV	2.00	4.50	9.00	—
1943L	9,000,000	BV	2.00	4.50	9.00	—
1943L Proof	—	Value: 300				
1944(b) Dot	46,200,000	BV	2.00	4.50	9.00	—
1944(b) Diamond	Inc. above	BV	2.00	4.50	9.00	—
1944L	79,100,000	BV	2.00	4.50	9.00	—
1944L Proof	—	Value: 300				
1945(b) Small 5	32,722,000	BV	2.00	4.50	9.00	—
1945(b) Large 5	—	20.00	25.00	35.00	50.00	—
1945L Small dot	79,192,000	BV	2.00	4.50	9.00	—
1945L Proof	—	Value: 300				
1945L Large dot	Inc. above	2.50	5.00	10.00	20.00	—

KM# 553 1/2 RUPEE

Nickel **Ruler:** George VI **Obv:** Crowned head left **Obv. Legend:** GEORGE VI KING EMPEROR **Rev:** Indian tiger (panthera tigris) **Edge:** Reeded

Date	Mintage	F	VF	XF	Unc	BU
1946(b)	47,500,000	0.50	1.00	2.50	7.50	12.00
1947(b)	62,724,000	0.50	1.00	2.50	7.50	12.00
1947(b) Proof	—	Value: 275				

KM# 492 RUPEE

11.6600 g., 0.9170 Silver .3438 oz. ASW **Ruler:** Victoria **Obv:** Crowned bust left **Obv. Legend:** VICTORIA EMPRESS **Rev:** Value and date within wreath

Date	Mintage	F	VF	XF	Unc	BU
1901C C/I, "C" incuse	72,017,000	6.00	8.00	12.00	25.00	—
1901C Proof	Inc. above	Value: 725				
1901B A/I, "B" incuse	130,258,000	6.00	8.00	12.00	25.00	—
1901B Proof	—	Value: 725				
1901B P/L; Restrike	—	—	—	—	250	—
1901B C/I, "B" incuse	Inc. above	6.00	8.00	12.00	25.00	—

KM# 508 RUPEE

11.6600 g., 0.9170 Silver .3438 oz. ASW **Ruler:** Edward VII **Obv:** Head right **Obv. Legend:** EDWARD VII KING & EMPEROR **Rev:** Crown above denomination, sprays flank **Note:** Calcutta Mint issues have no mint mark. Mumbai (Bombay) Mint issues have a small incuse "B" in the space below the cross pattee of the crown on the reverse.

Date	Mintage	F	VF	XF	Unc	BU
1903(c)	49,403,000	6.00	9.00	13.50	28.00	—
1903(c) Proof	—	Value: 700				
1903B In relief	52,969	6.00	9.00	13.50	28.00	—
1903B Proof	—	Value: 700				
1903B Incuse	Inc. above	6.00	9.00	13.50	28.00	—
1903B P/L; Restrike	—	—	—	—	200	—
1904(c)	58,339,000	6.00	9.00	13.50	28.00	—
1904(c) Proof	—	Value: 700				
1904B	101,949,000	6.00	9.00	13.50	28.00	—
1904B Proof	—	Value: 700				
1904B P/L; Restrike	—	—	—	—	200	—
1905(c)	51,258,000	6.00	9.00	13.50	28.00	—
1905(c) Proof	—	Value: 700				
1905B	76,202,000	6.00	9.00	13.50	28.00	—
1905B Proof	—	Value: 700				
1905B P/L; Restrike	—	—	—	—	200	—
1906(c)	104,797,000	6.00	9.00	15.00	30.00	—
1906B	158,953,000	6.00	9.00	15.00	30.00	—
1906B Proof	—	Value: 700				

Date	Mintage	F	VF	XF	Unc	BU
1906B P/L; Restrike	—	—	—	—	200	—
1907(c)	81,338,000	6.00	9.00	15.00	30.00	—
1907(c) Proof	—	Value: 700				
1907B	170,912,000	6.00	9.00	15.00	30.00	—
1907B Proof	—	Value: 700				
1907B P/L; Restrike	—	—	—	—	200	—
1908(c)	20,218,000	6.00	9.00	15.00	30.00	—
1908(c) Proof	—	Value: 700				
1908B	10,715,000	8.50	15.00	30.00	60.00	—
1908B Proof	—	Value: 700				
1908B P/L; Restrike	—	—	—	—	200	—
1909(c)	12,759,000	6.00	9.00	15.00	30.00	—
1909(c) Proof	—	Value: 700				
1909B	9,539,000	8.50	15.00	30.00	60.00	—
1909B Proof	—	Value: 700				
1909B P/L; Restrike	—	—	—	—	200	—
1910(c)	12,627,000	6.00	9.00	15.00	30.00	—
1910(c) Proof	—	Value: 700				
1910B	10,885,000	6.00	9.00	15.00	30.00	—
1910B Proof	—	Value: 700				
1910B P/L; Restrike	—	—	—	—	200	—

KM# 523 RUPEE
11.6600 g., 0.9170 Silver .3438 oz. ASW **Ruler:** George V **Obv:** Type I **Obv. Legend:** GEORGE V KING EMPEROR

Date	Mintage	F	VF	XF	Unc	BU
1911(c)	4,300,000	10.00	20.00	40.00	100	—
1911(c) Proof	—	Value: 1,200				
1911(b)	5,143,000	10.00	20.00	40.00	100	—
1911(b) P/L; Restrike	—	—	—	—	350	—

KM# 524 RUPEE
11.6600 g., 0.9170 Silver .3438 oz. ASW **Ruler:** George V **Obv:** Crowned bust left, type II **Obv. Legend:** GEORGE V KING EMPEROR **Rev:** Denomination and date within circle, wreath surrounds

Date	Mintage	F	VF	XF	Unc	BU
1912(c)	45,122,000	6.00	9.50	15.00	35.00	—
1912(c) Proof	—	Value: 1,000				
1912(b)	79,067,000	5.50	8.00	12.50	25.00	—
1912(b) Proof	—	Value: 1,000				
1912B P/L; Restrike	—	—	—	—	225	—
1913(c)	75,800,000	5.50	8.00	12.50	25.00	—
1913(c) Proof	—	Value: 1,000				
1913(b)	87,466,000	5.50	8.00	12.50	25.00	—
1913(b) Proof	—	Value: 1,000				
1913(b) P/L; Restrike	—	—	—	—	225	—
1914(c)	33,100,000	5.50	8.00	12.50	25.00	—
1914(c) Proof	—	Value: 1,000				
1914(b)	15,270,000	5.50	8.00	12.50	25.00	—
1914(b) Proof	—	Value: 1,000				
1914(b) P/L; Restrike	—	—	—	—	225	—
1915(c)	9,900,000	8.50	15.00	30.00	60.00	—
1915(c) Proof	—	Value: 1,000				
1915(b)	5,372,000	10.00	20.00	40.00	80.00	—
1915(b) Proof	—	Value: 1,000				
1915(b) P/L; Restrike	—	—	—	—	225	—
1916(c)	115,000,000	5.50	8.00	12.50	20.00	—
1916(c) Proof	—	Value: 1,000				
1916(b)	97,900,000	5.50	8.00	12.50	20.00	—
1916(b) Proof	—	—	—	—	—	—
1916(b) P/L; Restrike	—	—	—	—	225	—
1917(c)	114,974,000	5.50	8.00	12.50	20.00	—
1917(c) Proof	—	Value: 1,000				
1917(b)	151,583,000	5.50	8.00	12.50	20.00	—
1917(b) Proof	—	Value: 1,000				
1917(b) P/L; Restrike	—	—	—	—	225	—
1918(c)	205,420,000	5.50	8.00	12.50	20.00	—
1918(c) Proof	—	Value: 1,000				
1918(b)	210,550,000	5.50	8.00	12.50	20.00	—
1918(b) Proof	—	Value: 1,000				
1918(b) P/L; Restrike	—	—	—	—	225	—
1919(c)	211,206,000	5.50	8.00	12.50	20.00	—
1919(c) Proof	—	Value: 1,000				
1919(b)	226,706,000	5.50	8.00	12.50	20.00	—
1919(b) Proof	—	Value: 1,000				
1919(b) P/L; Restrike	—	—	—	—	225	—
1920(c)	50,500,000	5.50	8.00	12.50	20.00	—
1920(c) Proof	—	Value: 1,000				
1920(b)	55,937,000	5.50	8.00	12.50	20.00	—
1920(b) Proof	—	Value: 1,000				
1921(b)	5,115,000	10.00	20.00	40.00	85.00	—
1921(b) Proof	—	Value: 1,000				
1922(b)	2,051,000	10.00	20.00	40.00	85.00	—
1922(b) Proof	—	Value: 1,000				
1935(c) Proof	—	Value: 1,000				
1935(c) P/L; Restrike	—	—	—	—	225	—
1936(c) Proof	—	Value: 1,000				

KM# 554 RUPEE
11.6600 g., 0.9170 Silver .3438 oz. ASW **Ruler:** George VI **Obv:** Crowned head left, first head **Obv. Legend:** GEORGE VI KING EMPEROR **Rev:** Denomination and date within circle, wreath surrounds **Edge:** Reeded

Date	Mintage	F	VF	XF	Unc	BU
1938(c) Proof	—	Value: 550				
1939(c) Proof	—	Value: 700				

KM# 555 RUPEE
11.6600 g., 0.9170 Silver .3438 oz. ASW **Ruler:** George VI **Obv:** Second head, small rim decoration **Obv. Legend:** GEORGE VI KING EMPEROR **Rev:** Denomination and date within circle, wreath surrounds **Edge:** Reeded

Date	Mintage	F	VF	XF	Unc	BU
1938(b) Without dot	7,352,000	7.50	11.50	16.50	27.50	—
1938(b) Dot	Inc. above	7.50	11.50	16.50	27.50	—
1938(b) P/L; Restrike	—	—	—	—	375	—
1939(b) Dot	2,450,000	150	300	600	1,200	—

KM# A559 RUPEE
Copper-Nickel **Ruler:** George VI **Obv:** Small second head, large rim decoration **Obv. Legend:** GEORGE VI KING EMPEROR **Rev:** Denomination and date within circle, wreath surrounds **Note:** Mule

Date	Mintage	F	VF	XF	Unc	BU
1938(c) P/L; Restrike	—	—	—	—	750	—

KM# A556 RUPEE
Copper-Nickel **Ruler:** George VI **Obv:** Small second head, large rim decoration **Obv. Legend:** GEORGE VI KING EMPEROR **Rev:** Denomination and date within circle, wreath surrounds **Note:** Mule.

Date	Mintage	F	VF	XF	Unc	BU
1938(c) P/L; Restrike	—	—	—	—	150	—

KM# 556 RUPEE
11.6600 g., 0.5000 Silver .3438 oz. ASW **Ruler:** George VI **Obv:** Crowned head left **Obv. Legend:** GEORGE VI KING EMPEROR **Rev:** Denomination and date within circle, wreath surrounds **Edge:** Security

Date	Mintage	F	VF	XF	Unc	BU
1939(b)	—	200	400	800	1,500	—
1940(b)	153,120,000	BV	6.00	10.00	20.00	—
1941(b)	111,480,000	BV	6.00	10.00	20.00	—
1943(b)	—	BV	6.00	10.00	20.00	—

Note: 1943(b) mintage included with KM#557.1.

KM# 557.1 RUPEE
11.6600 g., 0.5000 Silver .1874 oz. ASW, 30.5 mm. **Ruler:** George VI **Obv:** Small second head, large rim decoration **Obv. Legend:** GEORGE VI KING EMPEROR **Rev:** Denomination and date within circle, wreath surrounds **Edge:** Security

Date	Mintage	F	VF	XF	Unc	BU
1942(b) Without dot	7,352,000	BV	4.50	10.00	20.00	—
1943(b)	65,995,000	BV	4.50	10.00	20.00	—
1943(b) Reverse B	Inc. above	BV	4.50	10.00	20.00	—
1944(b) Reverse B	146,206,000	BV	4.50	10.00	20.00	—
1944(b)	Inc. above	BV	4.50	10.00	20.00	—
1944L Small L	91,400,000	BV	4.50	10.00	20.00	—
1944L Large L	Inc. above	BV	4.50	10.00	20.00	—
1945(b) Small 5	142,666,000	BV	3.50	6.00	12.50	—
1945(b) Large 5	Inc. above	30.00	35.00	45.00	60.00	—
1945(b) Proof	—	—	—	—	—	—
1945L	118,126,000	BV	3.50	6.00	12.50	—

KM# 557a RUPEE
Copper-Nickel, 30.5 mm. **Ruler:** George VI **Obv:** Crowned head left **Obv. Legend:** GEORGE VI KING EMPEROR **Rev:** Denomination and date within circle, wreath surrounds

Date	Mintage	F	VF	XF	Unc	BU
1943(b) P/L; Restrike	—	—	—	—	650	—

KM# 557.2 RUPEE
11.6600 g., 0.9170 Silver 0.3438 oz. ASW **Ruler:** George VI **Obv:** Crowned head left **Rev:** Denomination and date within circle, wreath surrounds **Note:** Reeded edge (error). Prev. KM#558.

Date	Mintage	F	VF	XF	Unc	BU
1944(b)	—	—	—	—	—	—
1945(b)	—	—	—	—	—	—

KM# 559 RUPEE
Nickel **Ruler:** George VI **Obv:** Crowned head left **Rev:** Indian tiger (panthera tigris) **Edge:** Security

Date	Mintage	F	VF	XF	Unc	BU
1947(b)	118,028,000	1.50	2.50	5.00	12.00	15.00
1947B Proof	—	Value: 375				

Note: Mumbai (Bombay) issue has diamond mark below date

Date	Mintage	F	VF	XF	Unc	BU
1947(l)	41,911,000	1.50	3.00	6.00	15.00	20.00

Note: Lahore issue without privy mark

KM# 525 15 RUPEES
7.9881 g., 0.9170 Gold .2354 oz. AGW **Ruler:** George V **Obv:** Crowned bust left **Obv. Legend:** GEORGE V KING EMPEROR **Rev:** Denomination and date within circle, wreath surrounds **Note:** This issue is equal in weight and fineness to the British sovereign.

Date	Mintage	F	VF	XF	Unc	BU
1918(b)	2,110,000	275	350	500	750	—
1918(b) Proof	12	Value: 7,000				
1918(b) P/L; Restrike	—	—	—	—	800	—

TRADE COINAGE

The Mansfield Commission of 1868 allowed for the admission of British and Australian sovereigns (see Australian section; sovereigns with shield reverse were struck for export to India) as payment for sums due.

The fifth branch of the Royal Mint was established in a section of the Mumbai (Bombay) Mint as of December 21, 1917. This was a war-time measure, its purpose being to strike into sovereigns the gold blanks supplied by the Mumbai and other Indian mints. The Mumbai sovereigns bear the mint mark 'I' and were struck from August 15, 1918, to April 22, 1919. The branch mint was closed in May 1919.

KM# 525A SOVEREIGN
7.9881 g., 0.9170 Gold .2354 oz. AGW **Ruler:** George V **Obv:** Head left **Rev:** St. George slaying the dragon **Note:** Mint mark "I".

Date	Mintage	F	VF	XF	Unc	BU
1918	1,295,000	—	BV	170	200	—
1918 Proof	—	—	—	—	—	—
1918 P/L; Restrike	—	—	—	—	850	—

BULLION COINAGE

Private bullion issues have been recorded in weights of 1/4, 1/2, 1, 5, 10, 20 and 25 Tolas in gold and silver. The actual weight of the Tola is based on the obsolete English Guinea.

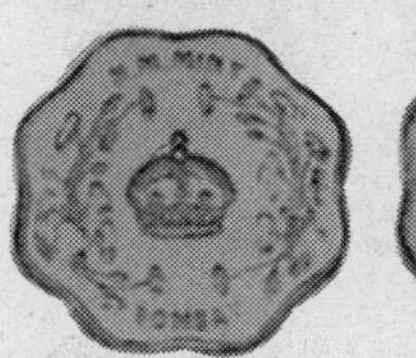

KM# A496 TOLA
11.7000 g., 0.9960 Gold .3747 oz. AGW **Ruler:** George V
Obv: Crown within wreath **Rev:** Denomination and weight
Shape: Scalloped **Note:** Prev. KM#496A.

Date	Mintage	VG	F	VF	XF	Unc
ND(1931)	—	—	—	BV	265	285

KM# B496 5 TOLAS
58.5000 g., 0.9957 Gold 1.8727 oz. AGW **Ruler:** George V
Obv: Building **Rev:** Denomination and weight **Shape:** Square
Note: Prev. KM#496B.

Date	Mintage	VG	F	VF	XF	Unc
ND(1931)	—	—	—	BV	1,275	1,350

KM# C496 10 TOLAS
117.0000 g., 0.9956 Gold 3.7451 oz. AGW **Ruler:** George V
Obv: Legend, crown, weight and denomination
Shape: Rectangular **Note:** Uniface. Prev. KM#496C.

Date	Mintage	VG	F	VF	XF	Unc
ND(1921)	—	—	—	BV	2,550	2,700

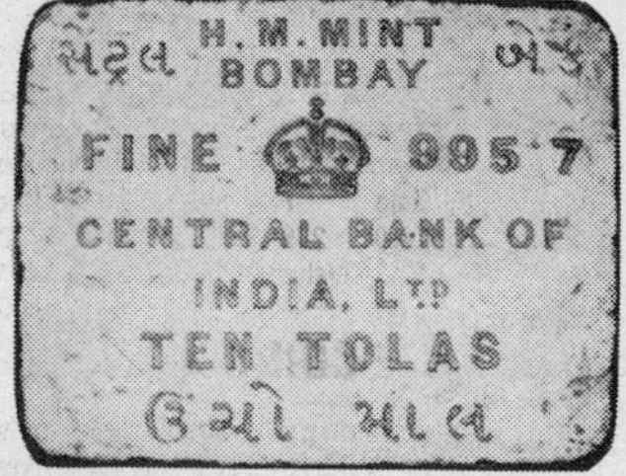

KM# D496 10 TOLAS
0.9957 Gold **Ruler:** George V **Obv:** Legend, crown, denomination and weight **Shape:** Rectangular **Note:** Prev. KM#496D.

Date	Mintage	VG	F	VF	XF	Unc
ND(1922)	—	—	—	BV	2,550	2,700

PATTERNS

Including off metal strikes

P# are in reference to The Coins of the British Commonwealth of Nations Part 4, India, Vol. 1 and 2 by F. Pridmore (Spink and Son Ltd., London 1980).

KM#	Date	Mintage	Identification	Mkt Val
Pn66	1901(c)	—	Rupee. Silver. Prid.#1045	1,750
Pn67	1901(c)	—	Rupee. Silver. Prid.#1046	1,750
Pn68	1903(c)	—	1/4 Rupee. Silver. With "718.93" countermark. Prid.#1074	—
Pn69	1903(c)	—	Anna. Nickel. Prid.#1053	450
Pn70	1904(c)	—	1/4 Anna. Copper. Prid.#1051	750

KM#	Date	Mintage	Identification	Mkt Val
Pn71	1904(c)	—	Anna. Copper-Nickel. Prid.#1054.	350
Pn72	1904(c)	—	Anna. Tin. 22 mm. Prid.#1055	450
Pn73	1904(c)	—	Anna. Copper-Nickel. 21 mm. Prid.#1056	350
Pn74	1904(c)	—	Anna. Copper-Nickel. Prid.#1058	350
Pn75	1904(c)	—	Anna. Copper-Nickel. Prid.#1059	350
Pn76	1904(c)	—	Anna. Copper-Nickel. Prid.#1060	350
Pn77	1904(c)	—	Anna. White Metal. Prid.#1061	350
Pn78	1904(c)	—	Anna. Copper-Nickel. Prid.#1062	350
Pn79	1904(c)	—	Anna. Copper-Nickel. Prid.#1063	350
Pn80	1904(c)	—	1/4 Rupee. Nickel. Prid.#1075	350
PnA80	1904(c)	—	1/4 Rupee. Copper. 3.9000 g. as Prid.#1075	350
Pn80a	1904C	—	1/4 Rupee. Bronze. 3.8600 g. 21.2 mm. Edward VII. Denomination. Scalloped edge.	—
Pn81	1905(c)	—	Anna. Copper-Nickel. Prid.#924	—

KM#	Date	Mintage	Identification	Mkt Val
Pn82	1905(c)	—	Anna. White Metal. Prid.#1057	350
Pn83	1905(c)	—	Anna.	350
Pn84	1905(c)	—	Anna. White Metal. Low relief bust; Prid.#1066	350
Pn85	1905(c)	—	Anna. White Metal. High relief bust; Prid.#1067	350
Pn86	1905(c)	—	Anna. Copper. High relief bust; Prid.#1069	350
Pn87	1905(c)	—	Anna. Silver. High relief bust; Prid.#1068	350

KM#	Date	Mintage	Identification	Mkt Val
Pn88	1905(c)	—	Anna. White Metal. Without dot border. Prid.#1070A	350
Pn89	1905	—	Anna. Copper-Nickel.	—
Pn90	1905(c)	—	Anna. Silver. Without dot border. Prid.#1070B	350
Pn91	1906(c)	—	Anna. White Metal. Raised bar edge. Prid.#1064	350
Pn92	1906(c)	—	Anna. White Metal. Double raised bar edge. Prid.#1065	350
Pn93	1906(c)	—	Anna. Copper-Nickel. Scalloped planchet; Prid.#1071	350
Pn94	1906(c)	—	Rupee. Copper-Nickel. "SPECIMEN" divided by crown. Lettered edge. Prid.#1047	1,000
Pn95	1907(b)	—	Rupee. Silver. Prid.#1048	—
Pn96	1908	—	1/2 Anna. Copper-Nickel.	350
Pn97	1908(c)	—	1/2 Anna. White Metal. Prid.#1073	500
Pn98	1909	—	1/2 Pice. Aluminum.	175
Pn99	1910(c)	—	Rupee. Silver. Prid.#1049	1,750
Pn100	1910(c)	—	Rupee. Gold. Prid.#1050	—
Pn101	ND(c)	—	2 Annas. Tin. Prid.#1052	—
Pn102	1917(c)	—	2 Annas. Copper-Nickel. Round; Prid.#1078	—
Pn103	1917(c)	—	2 Annas. Copper-Nickel. Square; Prid.#1079	—
Pn104	1918(c)	—	4 Annas. Copper-Nickel. Round with center hole; Prid.#1076	—
Pn105	1919(c)	—	2 Annas. Copper-Nickel. Eight-lobed planchet; Prid.#1087	—
Pn106	1919(c)	—	4 Annas. Copper-Nickel. Triangle; Prid.#1077	—
Pn107	1921(c)	—	Anna. Copper-Nickel. Prid.#1080	250
Pn108	1921(c)	—	Anna. Copper. Prid.#1081	250
Pn109	1921(c)	—	Anna. Gold. Prid.#1082	—
Pn110	1929(c)	—	Anna. Copper-Nickel. Prid.#1083	400
Pn111	1929(c)	—	Anna. Copper-Nickel. Wide border; Prid.#1084	400

KM#	Date	Mintage	Identification	Mkt Val
Pn112	1937(c)	—	2 Annas. Copper-Nickel. Prid.#1093	800
Pn113	1937(c)	—	2 Annas. Copper-Nickel. Serrated circular border. Prid.#1094	800
Pn115	1938(c)	—	1/2 Anna. Nickel. Prid.#1095	—
Pn114	1938(b)	—	1/4 Anna. Bronze. Head of George V	—
Pn116	1938(b)	—	Rupee. Silver. Head of George V	—
Pn117	1941(c)	—	Dollar. Silver. Prid.#1088A	2,500
Pn118	1941(c)	—	Dollar. Silver. Fine milled edge.	750
Pn119	1941(b)	—	Dollar. Silver. "S" in "RUPEES" 1/2 to left of large "1"; Prid.#1088B	—
Pn120	1941(c)	—	Dollar. Silver. Prid.#1089	2,500
Pn121	1943(c)	—	Pice. Bronze. Prid.#1091	450
Pn122	1945(c)	—	Pie. Bronze. Prid.#1092	—
Pn123	1946(c)	—	Pie. Bronze. Tiger left. Prid.#1090.	—

PROOF SETS

KM#	Date	Mintage	Identification	Issue Price	Mkt Val
PS3	1904 (5)	—	KM#497, 499, 503, Pn70(2)	—	3,000
PS4	1904 (3)	—	KM#497, 499, 501(bronze) with "1" countermark on reverse	—	3,000
PS5	1911(c) (4)	—	KM#514, 517, 521, 523	—	400
PS6	1919(c) (8)	—	KM#513, 516, 519-520 (2 each - V.I.P.)	—	1,500
PS7	1938(c) (6)	—	KM#527-528, 530, 536, 544, 555	—	350
PS8	1947(b) (7)	—	KM#533, 535, 538, 542, 548, 553, 559	—	300

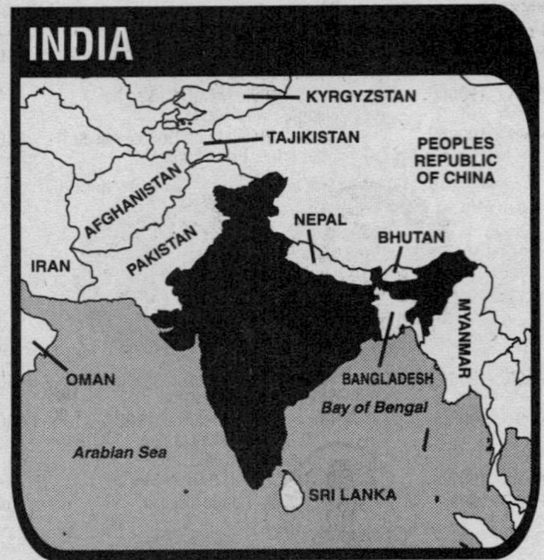

The Republic of India, a subcontinent jutting southward from the mainland of Asia, has an area of 1,269,346 sq. mi. (3,287,590 sq. km.) and a population of over 900 million, second only to that of the People's Republic of China. Capital: New Delhi. India's economy is based on agriculture and industrial activity. Engineering goods, cotton apparel and fabrics, handicrafts, tea, iron and steel are exported.

The Indian Mutiny (called the first War of Independence by Indian Nationalists) of 1857-58, begun by Indian troops in the service of the British East India Company, revealed the intensity of the growing resentment against British domination. The widespread rebellion against British rule was unsuccessful, but resulted in the transfer of government from the company to the British crown, and was a source of inspiration, to later Indian nationalists. Agitation for representation in the government continued.

Following World War I, in which India sent six million troops to fight at the side of the Allies, Indian nationalism intensified under the banner of the Indian National Congress and the leadership of Mohandas Karamchand Gandhi, who called for non-violent revolt against British authority. The Government of India Act of 1935 proposed a federal status linking the British Indian provinces with the many princely states; in addition, provincial legislatures were to be created. The federal status was never implemented, but the legislatures were created after the election of 1937, with the National Congress winning majorities in most of the provinces.

When Britain declared war on Germany in Sept. 1939, the Viceroy declared India also to be at war with a common enemy. The Congress, however, demanded independence as a condition for cooperation; Britain refused. But as the Japanese advanced into Asia, Britain offered to transfer to Indians power over all but military affairs during the war, and set forth a plan for postwar independence. Congress was willing to accept the wartime transfer of power, but both Congress and the Muslim League rejected Britain's plan for independence; Congress because it did not sufficiently safeguard Indian unity, the Muslims (who wanted a separate Muslim state) because of fears of what would happen to Muslims within a united India.

Early in 1947, Prime Minister Clement Attlee announced that Britain would leave India "by a date not later than June 1948," even though the Hindus and Muslims could not agree among themselves on a plan for self-government. The National Congress, aware that the Muslim League would revolt rather than accept an all-India government, reluctantly agreed to the formation of a separate Muslim state. The Muslim-majority provinces of the North West Frontier, Sindh and West Punjab in the west, and East Bengal in the east were separated from India to form the Muslim state of Pakistan, which became independent on Aug. 14, 1947. India became independent on the following day. Because British India coins dated 1947 were struck until 1950, they can be considered the first coins of Independent India. India became a republic on Jan. 26, 1950.

The Republic of India is a member of the Commonwealth of Nations. The president is the Chief of State. The prime minister is the Head of Government.

MINT MARKS

(Mint marks usually appear directly below the date.)

B - Mumbai (Bombay), proof issues only
(B) - Mumbai (Bombay), diamond
C – Ottawa (1985 25 Paise; 1988 10, 25 & 50 Paise)
(C) - Calcutta, no mint mark
H - Birmingham (1985 Rupee only)
(H) - Hyderabad, star (1963)
(Hd) - Hyderabad, diamond split vertically (1953-1960)
(Hy) - Hyderabad, incuse dot in diamond (1960-1968)
(K) - Kremnica, Slovakia, MK in circle
(L) - London, diamond below first date digit
M - Mumbai (Bombay), proof only after 1996
(M) - Mexico City, M beneath O
(N) - Noida, dot
(P) - Pretoria, M in oval
(R) – Moscow, MMD in oval
(T) - Taegu (Korea), star below first date digit

From 1950 through 1964 the Republic of India proof coins carry the regular diamond mint mark and can be distinguished from circulation issues only by their proof-like finish. From 1969 proofs carry the capital "B" mint mark. Some Bombay issues after1969 have a "proof-like" appearance although bearing the diamond mint mark of circulation issues. Beginning in 1972 proofs of the larger denominations - 10, 20 and 100 rupees -were partly frosted on their main features, including numerals. From 1975 all proofs were similarly frosted, from the 1 paisa to 100 rupees. Proof-like issues are often erroneously offered as proofs.

MONETARY SYSTEM

(Until 1957)

4 Pice = 1 Anna
16 Annas = 1 Rupee

REPUBLIC

STANDARD COINAGE

KM# 1.1 PICE

Bronze **Obv:** Asoka lion pedestal **Rev:** Horse (equus caballus equidae) **Note:** 1.6mm thick, 0.3mm edge rim.

Date	Mintage	F	VF	XF	Unc	BU
1950(B)	32,080,000	—	1.00	2.00	3.00	5.00

KM# 1.2 PICE

Bronze **Obv:** Asoka lion pedestal **Rev:** Horse left **Note:** 1.6mm thick, 1.0mm edge rim.

Date	Mintage	F	VF	XF	Unc	BU
1950(B)	Inc. above	—	0.40	0.80	1.50	2.00
1950(B) Proof	—	Value: 2.50				
1950C	14,000,000	—	0.50	1.00	1.75	2.25

KM# 1.3 PICE

Bronze **Obv:** Asoka lion pedestal **Rev:** Horse left **Note:** 1.2mm thick, 0.8mm edge rim.

Date	Mintage	F	VF	XF	Unc	BU
1951(B)	104,626,000	—	0.20	0.40	0.75	1.50
1951(C)	127,300,000	—	0.20	0.40	0.75	1.50

KM# 1.4 PICE

Bronze, 21 mm. **Obv:** Asoka lion pedestal **Rev:** Horse left **Note:** Larger date, 2mm thick, 0.8mm edge rim.

Date	Mintage	F	VF	XF	Unc	BU
1952(B)	213,830,000	—	0.25	0.40	0.80	1.50
1953(B)	242,358,000	—	0.25	0.50	1.00	1.50
1953(C)	111,000,000	—	—	—	—	—
1953(Hd)	Inc. above	—	15.00	20.00	—	—
1954(B)	136,758,000	—	0.25	0.50	1.00	1.50
1954(B) Proof	Inc. above	Value: 5.00				
1954(C)	52,600,000	—	0.35	0.70	1.25	2.00
1954(Hd)	Inc. above	—	10.00	15.00	—	—
1955(B)	24,423,000	—	0.50	1.25	2.00	2.50
1955(Hd)	Inc. above	—	15.00	20.00	—	—

KM# 2.1 1/2 ANNA

Copper-Nickel **Obv:** Asoka lion pedestal **Rev:** Zebu **Shape:** 4-sided

Date	Mintage	F	VF	XF	Unc	BU
1950(B)	26,076,000	—	0.20	0.40	1.00	—
1950(B) Proof	—	Value: 3.00				
1950(C)	3,100,000	—	1.25	2.00	3.25	—

KM# 2.2 1/2 ANNA

Copper-Nickel **Obv:** Asoka lion pedestal **Rev:** Zebu, larger date **Shape:** Square

Date	Mintage	F	VF	XF	Unc	BU
1954(B)	14,000,000	—	0.40	0.65	1.25	—
1954(B) Proof	—	Value: 5.00				
1954(C)	20,800,000	—	0.30	0.50	1.00	—
1955(B)	22,488,000	—	0.40	0.65	1.25	—

KM# 3.1 ANNA

Copper-Nickel **Obv:** Asoka lion pedestal **Rev:** Zebu **Shape:** Scalloped **Note:** A similar shaped Independence commemorative issued in 1947, bearing a map of India, circulated to some degree as an Anna coin.

Date	Mintage	F	VF	XF	Unc	BU
1950(B)	9,944,000	—	0.45	0.75	1.50	—
1950(B) Proof	—	Value: 4.00				

KM# 3.2 ANNA

Copper-Nickel **Obv:** Asoka lion pedestal **Rev:** Zebu, larger date, first Hindi letter varieties **Shape:** Scalloped

Date	Mintage	F	VF	XF	Unc	BU
1954(B)	20,388,000	—	0.35	0.60	1.25	—
1954(B) Proof	—	Value: 6.50				
1955(B)	—	—	15.00	20.00	30.00	—

KM# 4.1 2 ANNAS

Copper-Nickel **Obv:** Asoka lion pedestal **Rev:** Zebu **Note:** A similar shaped Independence commemorative issued in 1947, bearing a map of India, circulated to some degree as a 2 Anna coin.

Date	Mintage	F	VF	XF	Unc	BU
1950(B)	7,536,000	—	0.75	1.50	2.50	—
1950(B) Proof	—	Value: 5.00				

KM# 4.2 2 ANNAS

Copper-Nickel **Obv:** Asoka lion pedestal **Rev:** Zebu **Note:** Larger date.

Date	Mintage	F	VF	XF	Unc	BU
1954(B)	10,548,000	—	0.75	1.50	2.50	—
1954(B) Proof	—	Value: 8.00				
1955(B)	—	—	15.00	20.00	30.00	—

KM# 5.1 1/4 RUPEE

Nickel **Obv:** Asoka lion pedestal **Rev:** Grain sprigs flank denomination **Note:** Large lion.

Date	Mintage	F	VF	XF	Unc	BU
1950(B)	7,650,000	—	0.60	1.50	2.50	—
1950(B) Proof	—	Value: 5.00				
1950(C)	7,800,000	—	0.60	1.50	2.50	—
1951(B)	41,439,000	—	0.45	1.00	2.00	—
1951(C)	13,500,000	—	0.55	1.00	2.00	—

KM# 5.3 1/4 RUPEE

Nickel **Obv:** Asoka lion pedestal **Rev:** Grain sprigs flank denomination **Note:** Small lion.

Date	Mintage	F	VF	XF	Unc	BU
1954(C)	Inc. above	—	0.40	1.00	1.75	—
1955(C)	28,900,000	—	0.40	1.00	1.75	—
1956(C)	22,000,000	—	0.70	1.25	2.00	—

KM# 5.2 1/4 RUPEE

Nickel **Obv:** Asoka lion pedestal **Rev:** Grain sprigs flank denomination **Note:** Larger date, large lion.

Date	Mintage	F	VF	XF	Unc	BU
1954(C)	58,300,000	—	0.65	1.50	2.50	—
1954(B) Proof	Inc. above	Value: 6.00				
1955(B)	57,936,000	—	2.00	4.00	6.00	—

KM# 6.1 1/2 RUPEE

Nickel **Obv:** Asoka lion pedestal **Rev:** Grain sprigs flank denomination **Note:** Large lion.

Date	Mintage	F	VF	XF	Unc	BU
1950(B)	12,352,000	—	0.75	1.25	2.50	—
1950(B) Proof	—	Value: 5.50				
1950(C)	1,100,000	—	1.25	2.00	5.00	—
1951(B)	9,239,000	—	1.00	1.50	3.50	—

KM# 6.2 1/2 RUPEE

Nickel **Obv:** Asoka lion pedestal **Rev:** Grain sprigs flank denomination **Note:** Larger date.

Date	Mintage	F	VF	XF	Unc	BU
1954(B) Proof	—	Value: 8.00				
1954(C)	36,300,000	—	0.50	1.00	2.50	—
1955(B)	18,977,000	—	0.75	1.50	4.50	—

KM# 6.3 1/2 RUPEE

Nickel **Obv:** Asoka lion pedestal within circle, dots missing between words **Rev:** Grain sprigs flank denomination **Note:** Small lion.

Date	Mintage	F	VF	XF	Unc	BU
1956(C)	24,900,000	—	0.50	1.00	2.50	—

KM# 7.1 RUPEE

Nickel **Obv:** Asoka lion pedestal **Rev:** Grain sprigs flank denomination, thick numeral

Date	Mintage	F	VF	XF	Unc	BU
1950(B)	19,412,000	—	1.50	2.50	4.50	—
1950(B) Proof	—	Value: 7.00				

KM# 7.2 RUPEE

Nickel **Obv:** Asoka lion pedestal **Rev:** Thick numeral, first Hindi letter varieties

Date	Mintage	F	VF	XF	Unc	BU
1954(B)	Inc. above	—	2.00	3.00	5.50	—
1954(B) Proof	—	Value: 10.00				

DECIMAL COINAGE

100 Naye Paise = 1 Rupee (1957-63); 100 Paise = 1 Rupee (1964-)

NOTE: The Paisa was at first called Naya Paisa (= New Paisa), so that people would distinguish from the old non-decimal Paisa (or Pice, equal to 1/64 Rupee). After 7 years, the word new was dropped, and the coin was simply called a Paisa.

NOTE: Many of the Paisa standard types come with three obverse varieties.

1957-1989

TYPE 1: Side lions toothless with 2 to 3 fur rows, short squat D in INDIA.

1967-1994

TYPE 2: Asoka lion pedestal more imposing. Side lions with 3 or 4 fur rows, more elegant D in INDIA. The shape of the D in INDIA is the easiest way to distinguish this obverse.

1979-

TYPE 3: Similar to Type I but 2 teeth, 4 to 5 fur rows, bull fatter.

NOTE: Paisa standard pieces with mint mark B, 1969 to date, were struck only in proof.

NOTE: Indian mintage figures are not divided by mint, and often include dates other than the year in which struck. They should be regarded with reserve.

KM# 8 NAYA PAISA

Bronze **Obv:** Asoka lion pedestal **Rev:** Denomination and date

Date	Mintage	F	VF	XF	Unc	BU
1957(B)	618,630,000	—	0.30	0.50	0.85	—
1957(C)	Inc. above	—	0.30	0.50	0.85	—
1957(Hd)	Inc. above	—	0.30	0.50	0.85	—
1958(B)	468,630,000	—	0.45	0.75	1.50	—
1958(Hd)	Inc. above	—	0.45	0.75	1.50	—
1959(B)	351,120,000	—	0.30	0.50	0.85	—
1959(C)	Inc. above	—	0.30	0.50	0.85	—
1959(Hd)	Inc. above	—	0.30	0.50	0.85	—
1960(B)	357,940,000	—	0.30	0.50	0.85	—
1960(B) Proof	—	Value: 2.00				
1960(C)	Inc. above	—	2.25	3.50	5.00	—
1960(Hd)	Inc. above	—	3.25	4.00	5.00	—
1961(B)	573,170,000	—	0.30	0.50	0.85	—
1961(B) Proof	—	Value: 2.00				
1961(C)	Inc. above	—	0.30	0.50	0.85	—
1961(Hy)	Inc. above	—	0.50	0.75	1.25	—
1962(B)	—	—	—	—	—	—

Note: 1962(B) has only been found in some of the 1962 uncirculated mint sets; varieties of the split diamond have been reported.

KM# 8a NAYA PAISA

Nickel-Brass **Obv:** Asoka lion pedestal **Rev:** Denomination and date

Date	Mintage	F	VF	XF	Unc	BU
1962(B)	235,103,000	—	0.20	0.35	0.70	—
1962(B) Proof	—	Value: 1.50				
1962(C)	Inc. above	—	0.20	0.35	0.70	—
1962(Hy)	Inc. above	—	0.50	0.75	1.25	—
1963(B)	343,313,000	—	0.20	0.35	0.70	—
1963(B) Proof	—	Value: 1.50				
1963(C)	Inc. above	—	0.25	0.50	1.00	—
1963(H)	Inc. above	—	0.25	0.40	0.80	—

KM# 9 PAISA

Nickel-Brass **Obv:** Asoka lion pedestal **Rev:** Denomination and date **Note:** Type I.

Date	Mintage	F	VF	XF	Unc	BU
1964(B)	539,068,000	—	0.20	0.45	1.00	—
1964(C)	Inc. above	—	0.20	0.45	1.00	—
1964(H)	Inc. above	—	0.20	0.45	1.00	—

KM# 9a PAISA

Bronze **Obv:** Asoka lion pedestal **Rev:** Denomination and date **Note:** Included in mintage of KM#9.

Date	Mintage	F	VF	XF	Unc	BU
1964(H)	Inc. above	—	0.20	0.45	1.00	—

KM# 10.1 PAISA

Aluminum, 17 mm. **Obv:** Asoka lion pedestal **Rev:** Denomination and date **Shape:** 4-sided **Note:** Type I.

Date	Mintage	F	VF	XF	Unc	BU
1965(B)	223,480,000	—	0.40	0.65	1.00	—
1965(Hy)	Inc. above	—	0.40	0.65	1.00	—
1966(B)	404,200,000	—	0.20	0.30	0.50	—
1966(C)	Inc. above	—	0.30	0.50	1.00	—
1966(Hy)	Inc. above	—	0.20	0.30	0.50	—
1967(B)	450,433,000	—	0.20	0.30	0.50	—
1967(C)	Inc. above	—	0.20	0.30	0.50	—
1967(Hy)	Inc. above	—	0.20	0.30	0.50	—
1968(B)	302,720,000	—	0.20	0.30	0.50	—
1968(C)	Inc. above	—	0.20	0.30	0.50	—
1968(Hy)	Inc. above	—	0.20	0.30	0.50	—
1969(B)	125,930,000	—	1.50	2.25	3.00	—
1969B Proof	9,147	Value: 1.50				
1969(H)	Inc. above	—	3.00	4.00	5.00	—
1970(B)	15,800,000	—	2.00	2.50	5.00	—

Note: 1970(B) is found only in the uncirculated sets of that year. It has a mirror-like surface.

Date	Mintage	F	VF	XF	Unc	BU
1970B Proof	3,046	Value: 1.00				
1971B Proof	4,375	Value: 1.00				
1971(H)	112,100,000	—	0.20	0.30	0.50	—
1972(B)	62,090,000	—	0.20	0.30	0.50	—
1972B Proof	7,895	Value: 1.00				
1972(H)	Inc. above	—	0.20	0.30	0.50	—
1973B Proof	7,562	Value: 1.00				
1974B Proof	—	Value: 1.00				
1975B Proof	—	Value: 1.00				
1976B Proof	—	Value: 1.00				
1977B Proof	—	Value: 1.00				
1978B Proof	—	Value: 1.00				
1979B Proof	—	Value: 1.00				
1980B Proof	—	Value: 1.00				
1981B Proof	—	Value: 1.00				

KM# 10.2 PAISA

Aluminum **Obv:** Asoka lion pedestal **Rev:** Denomination and date **Shape:** 4-sided **Note:** Type II.

Date	Mintage	F	VF	XF	Unc	BU
1969(C)	Inc. above	—	2.50	3.00	4.00	—
1970(C)	Inc. above	—	0.40	0.65	1.00	—

KM# 11 2 NAYE PAISE

Copper-Nickel **Obv:** Asoka lion pedestal **Rev:** Denomination and date **Shape:** Scalloped

Date	Mintage	F	VF	XF	Unc	BU
1957(B)	406,230,000	—	0.15	0.40	0.80	—
1957(C)	Inc. above	—	0.15	0.40	0.80	—
1958(B)	245,660,000	—	0.15	0.40	0.80	—
1958(C)	Inc. above	—	0.15	0.40	0.80	—
1959(B)	171,445,000	—	0.15	0.40	0.80	—
1959(C)	Inc. above	—	0.15	0.40	0.80	—
1960(B)	121,820,000	—	0.15	0.40	0.80	—
1960(B) Proof	—	Value: 2.00				
1960(C)	Inc. above	—	0.20	0.40	0.80	—
1961(B)	190,610,000	—	0.20	0.40	0.80	—
1961(B) Proof	—	Value: 2.00				
1961(C)	Inc. above	—	0.20	0.40	0.80	—
1962(B)	318,181,000	—	0.20	0.40	0.80	—
1962(B) Proof	—	Value: 1.50				
1962(C)	Inc. above	—	0.20	0.40	0.80	—
1963(B)	372,380,000	—	0.20	0.40	0.80	—
1963(B) Proof	—	Value: 1.50				
1963(C)	Inc. above	—	0.20	0.40	0.80	—

KM# 12 2 PAISE

Copper-Nickel **Obv:** Asoka lion pedestal **Rev:** Denomination and date **Shape:** Scalloped **Note:** Type I.

Date	Mintage	F	VF	XF	Unc	BU
1964(B)	323,504,000	—	0.20	0.40	0.80	—
1964(C)	Inc. above	—	0.20	0.40	0.80	—

KM# 13.1 2 PAISE

Aluminum **Obv:** Asoka lion pedestal **Rev:** Denomination and date, 10mm "2" **Shape:** Scalloped **Note:** Type I. Obv. 1

Date	Mintage	F	VF	XF	Unc	BU
1965(B)	175,770,000	—	0.20	0.40	0.80	—
1965(C)	Inc. above	—	0.40	0.65	1.00	—
1966(B)	386,795,000	—	0.20	0.30	0.50	—
1966(C)	Inc. above	—	0.20	0.30	0.50	—
1967(B)	454,593,000	—	0.20	0.30	0.50	—

KM# 13.2 2 PAISE

Aluminum **Obv:** Asoka lion pedestal **Rev:** Denomination and date, 10-1/2mm "2" **Note:** Type 1.

Date	Mintage	F	VF	XF	Unc	BU
1967(C)	Inc. above	—	0.40	0.65	1.25	—

KM# 13.3 2 PAISE

Aluminum **Obv:** Asoka lion pedestal **Rev:** Denomination and date, 10mm "2" **Note:** Type 2.

Date	Mintage	F	VF	XF	Unc	BU
1967(B)	—	—	3.00	5.00	8.00	—

KM# 13.4 2 PAISE

Aluminum **Obv:** Asoka lion pedestal **Rev:** Denomination and date, 11mm "2" **Note:** Type 1.

Date	Mintage	F	VF	XF	Unc	BU
1968(C)	—	—	6.00	8.00	10.00	—
1977(B)	—	—	0.60	1.00	1.50	—
1978(B)	—	—	0.40	0.65	1.00	—

KM# 13.5 2 PAISE

Aluminum **Obv:** Asoka lion pedestal **Rev:** Denomination and date, 11mm "2" **Shape:** Scalloped **Note:** Type 2.

Date	Mintage	F	VF	XF	Unc	BU
1968(C)	Inc. above	—	0.20	0.30	0.50	—
1968(B)	305,205,000	—	0.10	0.25	0.50	—
1969(B)	5,335,000	—	2.00	3.00	5.00	—
1969B Proof	9,147	Value: 1.00				
1970(B)	—	—	—	—	5.00	—

Note: 1970(B) is found only in the uncirculated sets of that year; It has a mirror-like surface.

Date	Mintage	F	VF	XF	Unc	BU
1970B Proof	3,046	Value: 1.00				
1970(C)	79,100,000	—	0.20	0.30	0.50	—
1971B Proof	4,375	Value: 1.00				
1971(C)	207,900,000	—	0.20	0.30	0.50	—

KM# 13.6 2 PAISE

Aluminum **Obv:** Asoka lion pedestal **Rev:** Denomination and small date **Note:** Varieties of date size exist. Type 2.

Date	Mintage	F	VF	XF	Unc	BU
1972B Proof	7,895	Value: 1.00				
1972(C)	261,270,000	—	0.20	0.30	0.50	—
1972(H)	Inc. above	—	0.20	0.30	0.50	—
1973B Proof	7,562	Value: 1.00				
1973(C)	—	—	0.15	0.25	0.50	—
1973(H)	—	—	0.15	0.25	0.50	—
1974B Proof	—	Value: 1.00				
1974(C)	—	—	0.15	0.25	0.50	—
1974(H)	—	—	0.15	0.25	0.50	—
1975B Proof	—	Value: 1.00				
1975(C)	184,500,000	—	0.40	0.65	1.00	—
1975(H)	Inc. above	—	0.15	0.25	0.50	—
1976(B)	68,140,000	—	0.15	0.25	0.50	—
1976B Proof	—	Value: 1.00				
1976(H)	—	—	1.50	2.25	3.00	—
1977(B)	251,955,000	—	0.25	0.40	0.70	—
1977B Proof	—	Value: 1.00				
1977(H)	Inc. above	—	0.15	0.25	0.50	—
1978B Proof	—	Value: 1.00				
1978(H)	144,010,000	—	0.15	0.25	0.50	—
1979B Proof	—	Value: 1.00				
1979(H)	—	—	0.65	1.00	1.50	—
1980B Proof	—	Value: 1.00				
1981B Proof	—	Value: 1.00				

KM# 14.1 3 PAISE

Aluminum **Obv:** Asoka lion pedestal **Rev:** Denomination and date **Shape:** 6-sided **Note:** Type 1.

Date	Mintage	F	VF	XF	Unc	BU
1964(B)	138,890,000	—	0.20	0.40	0.70	—
1964(C)	Inc. above	—	0.20	0.40	0.70	—
1965(B)	459,825,000	—	0.20	0.30	0.60	—
1965(C)	Inc. above	—	0.20	0.30	0.60	—
1966(B)	390,440,000	—	0.20	0.30	0.60	—
1966(C)	Inc. above	—	0.20	0.30	0.60	—
1966(Hy)	Inc. above	—	0.20	0.30	0.60	—
1967(B)	167,018,000	—	0.20	0.30	0.60	—
1967(C)	Inc. above	—	0.20	0.30	0.60	—
1967(H)	Inc. above	—	0.75	1.25	2.00	—
1968(B)	—	—	3.00	4.00	6.00	—
1968(H)	—	—	—	—	—	—

KM# 14.2 3 PAISE

Aluminum **Obv:** Asoka lion pedestal **Rev:** Denomination and date **Shape:** 6-sided **Note:** Type 2.

Date	Mintage	F	VF	XF	Unc	BU
1967(C)	—	—	4.00	6.00	8.00	—
1967(H)	Inc. above	—	4.00	6.00	8.00	—
1968(B)	246,390,000	—	—	0.25	0.50	—
1968(C)	Inc. above	—	0.10	0.25	0.50	—
1968(H)	Inc. above	—	0.20	0.35	0.60	—
1969(B)	—	—	0.10	0.25	0.50	—
1969B Proof	9,147	Value: 1.00				
1969(C)	7,025,000	—	0.20	0.30	0.50	—
1969(H)	Inc. above	—	1.75	2.50	4.00	—
1970(B)	—	—	—	—	5.00	—

Note: 1970(B) is found only in the uncirculated sets of that year; It has a mirror-like surface.

Date	Mintage	F	VF	XF	Unc	BU
1970B Proof	3,046	Value: 1.00				
1970(C)	15,300,000	—	0.10	0.25	0.50	—
1971B Proof	4,375	Value: 1.00				
1971(C)	203,100,000	—	—	0.25	0.50	—
1971(H)	Inc. above	—	—	0.25	0.50	—

KM# 15 3 PAISE

Aluminum **Obv:** Asoka lion pedestal **Rev:** Denomination and date **Shape:** 6-sided **Note:** Type 2.

Date	Mintage	F	VF	XF	Unc	BU
1972B Proof	7,895	Value: 1.00				
1973B Proof	7,562	Value: 1.00				
1974B Proof	—	Value: 1.00				
1975B Proof	—	Value: 1.00				
1976B Proof	—	Value: 1.00				
1977B Proof	—	Value: 1.00				
1978B Proof	—	Value: 1.00				
1979B Proof	—	Value: 1.00				
1980B Proof	—	Value: 1.00				
1981B Proof	—	Value: 1.00				

KM# 16 5 NAYE PAISE

Copper-Nickel, 22 mm. **Obv:** Asoka lion pedestal **Rev:** Denomination and date **Shape:** Rounded square

Date	Mintage	F	VF	XF	Unc	BU
1957(B)	227,210,000	—	0.25	0.45	1.00	—
1957(C)	Inc. above	—	0.25	0.45	1.00	—
1958(B)	214,320,000	—	0.25	0.45	1.00	—
1958(C)	Inc. above	—	0.25	0.45	1.00	—
1959(B)	137,105,000	—	0.25	0.45	1.00	—
1959(C)	Inc. above	—	2.50	4.00	7.00	—
1960(B)	93,345,000	—	0.25	0.45	1.00	—
1960(B) Proof	—	Value: 2.00				
1960(C)	Inc. above	—	0.25	0.45	1.00	—
1960(Hy)	Inc. above	—	6.00	10.00	—	—
1961(B)	197,620,000	—	0.25	0.45	1.00	—
1961(B) Proof	—	Value: 2.00				
1961(C)	Inc. above	—	0.35	0.60	1.00	—
1961(Hy)	Inc. above	—	6.00	10.00	—	—
1962(B)	224,277,000	—	0.25	0.45	1.00	—
1962(B) Proof	—	Value: 1.50				
1962(C)	Inc. above	—	0.25	0.45	1.00	—
1962(Hy)	Inc. above	—	2.00	3.25	7.00	—
1963(B)	332,600,000	—	0.20	0.35	0.80	—
1963(B) Proof	—	Value: 1.50				
1963(C)	Inc. above	—	2.00	3.00	6.00	—
1963(H)	Inc. above	—	2.00	3.25	7.00	—

KM# 17 5 PAISE

Copper-Nickel **Obv:** Asoka lion pedestal **Rev:** Denomination and date **Shape:** Rounded square **Note:** Type 1.

Date	Mintage	F	VF	XF	Unc	BU
1964(B)	156,000,000	—	0.40	0.60	1.00	—
1964(C)	Inc. above	—	0.40	0.60	1.00	—
1964(H)	Inc. above	—	6.00	10.00	—	—
1965(B)	203,855,000	—	0.25	0.45	0.75	—
1965(C)	Inc. above	—	0.40	0.60	1.00	—
1965(H)	Inc. above	—	6.00	10.00	—	—
1966(B)	101,395,000	—	0.75	1.25	2.00	—
1966(C)	Inc. above	—	0.40	0.60	1.00	—

KM# 18.1 5 PAISE

Aluminum **Obv:** Asoka lion pedestal **Rev:** Denomination and date, 6mm, short 5 **Shape:** 4-sided **Note:** Type 1.

Date	Mintage	F	VF	XF	Unc	BU
1967(B)	608,533,000	—	0.35	0.60	1.00	—

KM# 18.2 5 PAISE

Aluminum **Obv:** Asoka lion pedestal **Rev:** Denomination and date, 7mm, tall 5 **Note:** Type 1.

Date	Mintage	F	VF	XF	Unc	BU
1967(C)	Inc. above	—	0.15	0.25	0.50	—
1967(H)	Inc. above	—	0.15	0.25	0.50	—
1967(B)	Inc. above	—	0.15	0.25	0.50	—
1968(B)	—	—	3.50	5.00	8.50	—
1968(C)	—	—	3.50	5.00	8.50	—
1968(H)	666,750,000	—	0.75	1.25	2.00	—
1971(H)	499,200,000	—	0.10	0.25	0.50	—

KM# 18.3 5 PAISE

Aluminum **Obv:** Asoka lion pedestal **Rev:** Denomination and date **Note:** Type 2.

Date	Mintage	F	VF	XF	Unc	BU
1967(H)	—	—	4.50	7.00	10.00	—
1968(B)	—	—	0.15	0.25	0.50	—

Note: Mintage included in KM18.2

Date	Mintage	F	VF	XF	Unc	BU
1968(C)	—	—	0.15	0.25	0.50	—

Note: Mintage included in KM18.2

Date	Mintage	F	VF	XF	Unc	BU
1968(H)	—	—	0.40	0.60	1.00	—

Note: Mintage included in KM18.2

Date	Mintage	F	VF	XF	Unc	BU
1969(B)	3,740,000	—	2.00	3.50	5.00	—
1969B Proof	9,147	Value: 1.00				
1970(B)	39,900,000	—	1.25	2.00	3.50	—
1970B Proof	3,046	Value: 1.00				
1970(C)	Inc. above	—	0.25	0.35	0.60	—
1970(H)	Inc. above	—	0.25	0.40	0.75	—
1971(B)	—	—	0.10	0.15	0.50	—

Note: Included with 1971(H) of KM18.2

Date	Mintage	F	VF	XF	Unc	BU
1971B Proof	4,375	Value: 1.00				

Date	Mintage	F	VF	XF	Unc	BU
1971(C)	Inc. above	—	0.10	0.15	0.50	—
1971(H)	—	—	0.25	0.45	0.75	—

KM# 18.4 5 PAISE

Aluminum **Obv:** Asoka lion pedestal **Rev:** Denomination and date **Note:** Type 1, new reverse.

Date	Mintage	F	VF	XF	Unc	BU
1972(H)	512,430,000	—	0.35	0.60	1.00	—

KM# 18.5 5 PAISE

Aluminum **Obv:** Asoka lion pedestal **Rev:** Denomination and date, larger 5 **Note:** Type 1.

Date	Mintage	F	VF	XF	Unc	BU
1973(H)	—	—	2.50	3.50	5.50	—
1977(B)	—	—	2.00	3.00	5.00	—
1978(B)	—	—	0.75	1.25	2.00	—

KM# 18.6 5 PAISE

Aluminum **Obv:** Asoka lion pedestal **Rev:** Denomination and date **Shape:** Rounded-off square **Note:** Type 2.

Date	Mintage	F	VF	XF	Unc	BU
1972(B)	—	—	0.10	0.15	0.50	—
Note: Mintage included in KM18.4						
1972B Proof	7,895	Value: 1.00				
1972(C)	—	—	0.10	0.15	0.50	—
Note: Mintage included in KM18.4						
1972(H)	—	—	3.50	5.00	7.00	—
1973(B)	—	—	0.10	0.15	0.50	—
1973B Proof	7,562	Value: 1.00				
1973(C)	—	—	0.20	0.30	0.60	—
1973(H)	—	—	0.10	0.15	0.50	—
1974B Proof	—	Value: 1.00				
1974(B)	—	—	0.10	0.15	0.50	—
1974(C)	—	—	0.10	0.15	0.50	—
1974(H)	—	—	0.10	0.15	0.50	—
1975(B)	—	—	0.10	0.15	0.50	—
1975B Proof	—	Value: 1.00				
1975(C)	289,080,000	—	0.20	0.30	0.60	—
1975(H)	Inc. above	—	0.10	0.15	0.50	—
1976(B)	53,205,000	—	0.10	0.15	0.50	—
1976(C)	—	—	—	0.10	0.20	—
1976(H)	—	—	0.10	0.15	0.50	—
1977(B)	257,899,999	—	0.10	0.15	0.50	—
1977(C)	Inc. above	—	0.10	0.15	0.50	—
1977(H)	Inc. above	—	0.10	0.15	0.50	—
1978(C)	—	—	0.10	0.15	0.50	—
1978(H)	—	—	0.10	0.15	0.50	—
1979(B)	—	—	0.10	0.15	0.50	—
1979(C)	—	—	0.20	0.35	0.80	—
1979(H)	—	—	0.10	0.15	0.50	—
1980(B)	21,440,000	—	0.10	0.15	0.50	—
1980B Proof	—	Value: 1.00				
1980(C)	Inc. above	—	0.20	0.30	0.60	—
1980(H)	Inc. above	—	0.10	0.15	0.50	—
1981B Proof	—	Value: 1.00				
1981(C)	4,365,000	—	0.10	0.15	0.50	—
1981(H)	Inc. above	—	0.10	0.15	0.50	—
Note: Due to faulty dies, 1981(H) often resembles the non-existent 1981(B).						
1982B Proof	3,499,000	Value: 1.00				
1982(C)	Inc. above	—	0.10	0.15	0.50	—
1982(H)	Inc. above	—	0.10	0.15	0.50	—
1983(C)	3,110,000	—	0.25	0.50	1.00	—
1983(H)	Inc. above	—	0.10	0.15	0.50	—
1984(C)	—	—	0.25	0.50	1.00	—
1984(H)	Inc. above	—	0.10	0.15	0.50	—

KM# 19 5 PAISE

Aluminum **Series:** F.A.O. **Subject:** Food and Work For All **Obv:** Asoka lion pedestal **Rev:** Figure on tractor, utility pole and buildings in background **Shape:** Rounded-off square

Date	Mintage	F	VF	XF	Unc	BU
1976(B)	34,680,000	—	0.35	0.50	1.00	—
1976B Proof	—	Value: 1.00				
1976(C)	60,040,000	—	0.35	0.50	1.00	—
1976(H)	60,290,000	—	0.35	1.00	2.00	—

KM# 20 5 PAISE

Aluminum **Series:** F.A.O. **Subject:** Save For Development **Obv:** Asoka lion pedestal **Rev:** Symbols and date **Shape:** Square

Date	Mintage	F	VF	XF	Unc	BU
1977(B)	20,100,000	—	0.30	0.50	1.00	—
1977B Proof	2,224	Value: 1.25				
1977(C)	40,470,000	—	0.30	0.50	1.00	—
1977(H)	20,380,000	—	2.25	3.50	5.00	—

KM# 21 5 PAISE

Aluminum **Series:** F.A.O. **Subject:** Food and Shelter For All **Obv:** Asoka lion pedestal **Rev:** Building, grain sprig and road within circle **Shape:** Square

Date	Mintage	F	VF	XF	Unc	BU
1978(B)	28,440,000	—	0.35	0.50	1.00	—
1978B Proof	—	Value: 1.25				
1978(C)	30,870,000	—	0.50	1.00	2.00	—
1978(H)	21,100,000	—	1.00	1.50	2.25	—

KM# 22 5 PAISE

Aluminum **Series:** International Year of the Child **Obv:** Asoka lion pedestal **Rev:** Logo within circle, wreath surrounds **Shape:** Square

Date	Mintage	F	VF	XF	Unc	BU
1979(B)	39,860,000	—	0.35	0.50	1.00	—
1979B Proof	—	Value: 1.25				
1979(C)	80,370,000	—	0.35	0.50	1.00	—
1979(H)	1,100,000	—	1.50	2.00	2.50	—

KM# 23 5 PAISE

Aluminum **Obv:** Asoka lion pedestal **Rev:** Denomination and date **Shape:** Square **Note:** Weight reduced.

Date	Mintage	F	VF	XF	Unc	BU
1984(C)	—	—	6.00	8.00	10.00	—
1985(B)	54,860,000	—	6.00	8.00	10.00	—
1985(C)	Inc. above	—	10.00	15.00	20.00	—
1985(H)	Inc. above	—	0.50	0.75	1.00	—
1986(C)	—	—	0.50	0.75	1.00	—
1986(H)	—	—	0.50	0.75	1.00	—
1987(C)	—	—	0.50	0.75	1.00	—
1987(H)	—	—	0.75	1.00	2.00	—
1988(C)	—	—	0.25	0.50	1.00	—
1988(H)	—	—	0.50	1.00	2.00	—
1989(C)	—	—	0.50	1.00	2.00	—
1989(H)	—	—	0.50	1.00	2.00	—
1990(B)	—	—	2.00	4.00	6.00	—
1990(C)	—	—	1.00	1.50	2.50	—
1990(H)	—	—	1.00	1.50	2.50	—
1991(C)	—	—	0.50	0.75	1.25	—
1991(H)	—	—	0.25	0.50	1.00	—
1992(B)	—	—	1.00	1.50	2.50	—
1992(H)	—	—	0.25	0.50	1.00	—
1993(C)	—	—	1.00	1.50	2.50	—
1993(H)	—	—	0.25	0.50	1.00	—
1994(H)	—	—	0.25	0.50	1.00	—

KM# 24.1 10 NAYE PAISE

Copper-Nickel, 23 mm. **Obv:** Asoka lion pedestal **Rev:** Denomination and date, 6.5mm "10" **Shape:** Scalloped

Date	Mintage	F	VF	XF	Unc	BU
1957(B)	139,655,000	—	0.25	0.50	1.00	—
1957(C)	Inc. above	—	0.25	0.50	1.00	—

KM# 24.2 10 NAYE PAISE

Copper-Nickel, 23 mm. **Obv:** Asoka lion pedestal **Rev:** Denomination and date, 7mm "10"

Date	Mintage	F	VF	XF	Unc	BU
1958(B)	123,160,000	—	0.25	0.50	1.00	—
1958(C)	Inc. above	—	0.25	0.50	1.00	—
1959(B)	148,570,000	—	0.25	0.50	1.00	—
1959(C)	Inc. above	—	0.25	0.50	1.00	—
1960(B)	52,335,000	—	0.35	0.75	2.00	—
1960(B) Proof	—	Value: 2.00				
1961(B)	172,545,000	—	0.25	0.50	1.00	—
1961(B) Proof	—	Value: 2.00				
1961(C)	Inc. above	—	0.25	0.50	1.00	—
1961(Hy)	Inc. above	—	3.50	6.50	11.50	—
1962(B)	172,777,000	—	0.25	0.50	1.00	—
1962(B) Proof	—	Value: 1.50				
1962(C)	Inc. above	—	0.25	0.50	1.00	—
1962(Hy)	Inc. above	—	3.25	5.00	9.00	—
1963(B)	182,834,000	—	0.25	0.50	1.00	—
1963(B) Proof	—	Value: 1.50				
1963(C)	Inc. above	—	0.25	0.50	1.00	—
1963(H)	Inc. above	—	1.00	2.50	5.00	—

KM# 25 10 PAISE

Copper-Nickel, 23 mm. **Obv:** Asoka lion pedestal **Rev:** Denomination and date, 6.5mm "10" **Shape:** Scalloped **Note:** Type 1.

Date	Mintage	F	VF	XF	Unc	BU
1964(B) Open 4	84,112,000	—	0.20	0.50	1.00	—
1964(B) Closed 4	Inc. above	—	5.00	7.00	10.00	—
1964(C)	Inc. above	—	0.20	0.50	1.00	—
1964(H)	Inc. above	—	3.00	5.00	7.00	—
1965(B)	253,430,000	—	0.20	0.50	1.00	—
1965(C)	Inc. above	—	0.20	0.50	1.00	—
1965(Hy)	Inc. above	—	4.00	6.00	8.00	—
1965(H)	Inc. above	—	3.00	5.00	7.00	—
1966(B)	326,990,000	—	0.20	0.50	1.00	—
1966(C)	Inc. above	—	0.20	1.00	1.00	—
1966(Hy)	Inc. above	—	0.40	0.75	1.25	—
1967(B)	59,443,000	—	0.40	0.75	1.25	—
1967(C)	Inc. above	—	0.40	0.75	1.25	—
1967(H)	Inc. above	—	3.00	5.00	7.00	—

KM# 26.1 10 PAISE

Nickel-Brass, 23 mm. **Obv:** Asoka lion pedestal **Rev:** Denomination and date **Note:** Type 1.

Date	Mintage	F	VF	XF	Unc	BU
1968(H)	55,940,000	—	30.00	50.00	80.00	—

KM# 26.2 10 PAISE

Nickel-Brass, 23 mm. **Obv:** Asoka lion pedestal **Rev:** Denomination and date, 6.5mm "10" **Shape:** Scalloped **Note:** Type 2. Mintage included in KM26.1.

Date	Mintage	F	VF	XF	Unc	BU
1968(B)	—	—	0.20	0.50	1.00	—
1968(C)	—	—	0.20	0.50	1.00	—
1968(H)	—	—	0.20	0.50	1.00	—

KM# 26.3 10 PAISE

Nickel-Brass, 23 mm. **Obv:** Asoka lion pedestal **Rev:** Denomination and date, 7mm "10" **Shape:** Scalloped **Note:** Type 2.

Date	Mintage	F	VF	XF	Unc	BU
1969(B)	65,405,000	—	0.20	0.50	1.00	—
1969B Proof	9,147	Value: 1.50				
1969(C)	Inc. above	—	0.20	0.50	1.00	—

Date	Mintage	F	VF	XF	Unc	BU
1969(H)	Inc. above	—	0.20	0.50	1.00	—
1970(B)	48,400,000	—	0.20	0.50	1.00	—
1970B Proof	3,046	Value: 1.50				
1970(C)	Inc. above	—	0.20	0.50	1.00	—
1971(B)	88,800,000	—	0.20	0.50	1.00	—
1971B Proof	4,375	Value: 1.30				

KM# 27.1 10 PAISE

Aluminum, 26 mm. **Obv:** Asoka lion pedestal within beaded circle, wreath surrounds **Rev:** Denomination and date within beaded circle, wreath surrounds, 9mm "10" **Shape:** Scalloped **Note:** Type 2.

Date	Mintage	F	VF	XF	Unc	BU
1971(B)	146,100,000	—	0.20	0.50	1.00	—
1971(C)	Inc. above	—	0.20	0.50	1.00	—
1971(H)	Inc. above	—	0.50	1.00	2.00	—
1972(B)	735,090,000	—	0.20	0.35	1.00	—
1972B Proof	7,895	Value: 1.30				
1972(C)	Inc. above	—	0.20	0.50	1.00	—
1973(B)	—	—	0.20	0.50	1.00	—
1973B Proof	7,567	Value: 1.30				
1973(C)	—	—	0.20	0.50	1.00	—
1973(H)	—	—	0.20	0.50	1.00	—
1974(B)	—	—	0.20	0.50	1.00	—
1974(C)	—	—	0.20	0.50	1.00	—
1974(H)	—	—	2.00	3.00	5.00	—
1975(B)	—	—	1.00	2.00	3.00	—
1975(C)	298,830,000	—	1.00	2.00	3.00	—
1976(C)	Inc. above	—	2.00	3.00	5.00	—
1977(B)	25,288,000	—	1.00	2.00	3.00	—
1977(C)	Inc. above	—	0.25	0.50	1.00	—
1978(B)	48,215,000	—	0.15	0.30	1.00	—
1978(C)	Inc. above	—	0.15	0.30	1.00	—
1978(H)	Inc. above	—	0.15	0.30	1.00	—

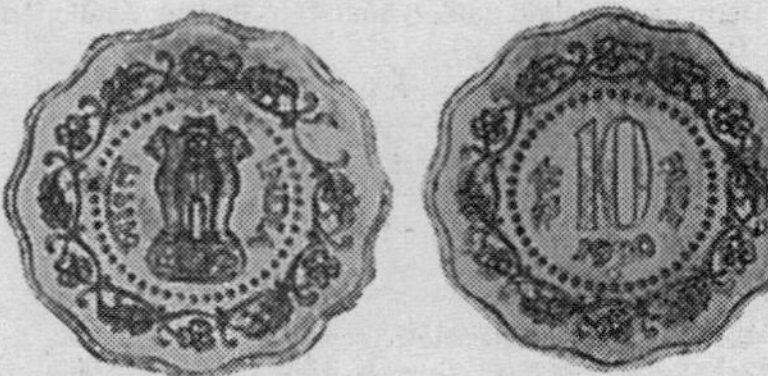

KM# 27.2 10 PAISE

Aluminum, 26 mm. **Obv:** Asoka lion pedestal within beaded circle, wreath surrounds **Rev:** Denomination and date within beaded circle, wreath surrounds, 8mm 10 **Shape:** Scalloped **Note:** Type 1

Date	Mintage	F	VF	XF	Unc	BU
1979(B)	—	—	0.50	1.00	2.00	—
1979(C)	—	—	0.50	1.50	3.00	—
1979(H)	—	—	0.50	1.00	2.00	—
1980(C)	—	—	10.00	12.00	15.00	—

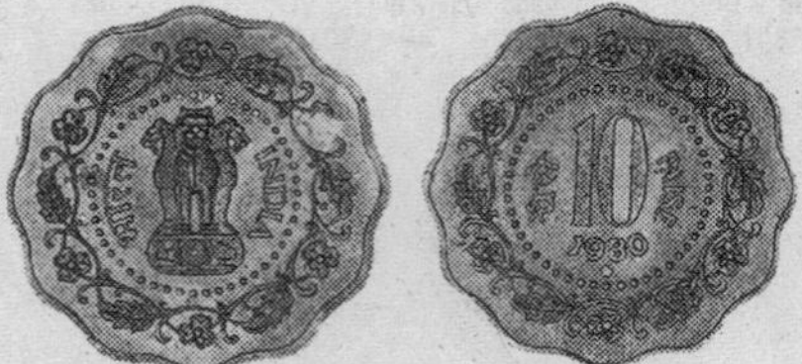

KM# 27.3 10 PAISE

Aluminum, 26 mm. **Obv:** Asoka lion pedestal within beaded circle, wreath surrounds **Rev:** Denomination and date within beaded circle, wreath surrounds **Note:** Type 3.

Date	Mintage	F	VF	XF	Unc	BU
1980(B)	—	—	0.20	0.50	1.00	—
1980(C)	—	—	0.20	0.50	1.00	—
1980(H)	—	—	0.20	0.50	1.00	—
1981(B)	—	—	0.20	0.50	1.00	—
1981(C)	—	—	0.20	0.50	1.00	—
1982(C)	—	—	0.20	0.50	1.00	—
1982(H)	—	—	0.20	0.50	1.00	—

KM# 28 10 PAISE

Aluminum, 26 mm. **Series:** F.A.O. **Obv:** Asoka lion pedestal **Rev:** Family above date within triangle, grain sprigs flank **Shape:** Scalloped

Date	Mintage	F	VF	XF	Unc	BU
1974(B)	146,070,000	—	0.30	0.50	1.00	—
1974B Proof	—	Value: 1.00				
1974(C)	168,500,000	—	0.50	1.00	2.00	—
1974(H)	10,010,000	—	3.00	4.00	6.00	—

KM# 29 10 PAISE

Aluminum, 26 mm. **Series:** F.A.O. **Subject:** Women's Year **Obv:** Asoka lion pedestal **Rev:** Bust at left looking right, grain sprig at right **Shape:** Scalloped **Designer:** N. B. Sabannavar **Note:** Mint mark is below wheat stalk.

Date	Mintage	F	VF	XF	Unc	BU
1975(B)	69,160,000	—	0.30	0.50	1.00	—
1975B Proof	—	Value: 1.00				
1975(C)	84,820,000	—	0.30	0.60	1.00	—

KM# 30 10 PAISE

Aluminum, 26 mm. **Series:** F.A.O. **Subject:** Food and Work For All **Obv:** Asoka lion pedestal **Rev:** Figure on tractor, utility pole and buildings in background **Shape:** Scalloped

Date	Mintage	F	VF	XF	Unc	BU
1976(B)	36,040,000	—	1.00	1.50	2.00	—
1976B Proof	—	Value: 3.00				
1976(C)	26,180,000	—	2.00	3.00	5.00	—

KM# 31 10 PAISE

Aluminum, 26 mm. **Series:** F.A.O. **Subject:** Save For Development **Obv:** Asoka lion pedestal **Rev:** Symbols and date **Shape:** Scalloped

Date	Mintage	F	VF	XF	Unc	BU
1977(B)	17,040,000	—	0.25	0.50	1.00	—
1977B Proof	2,224	Value: 1.00				
1977(C)	8,020,000	—	2.00	3.00	5.00	—

KM# 32 10 PAISE

Aluminum, 26 mm. **Series:** F.A.O. **Subject:** Food and Shelter For All **Obv:** Asoka lion pedestal **Rev:** Building, grain sprig and road within circle **Shape:** Scalloped

Date	Mintage	F	VF	XF	Unc	BU
1978(B)	24,470,000	—	0.25	0.50	1.00	—
1978B Proof	—	Value: 1.00				
1978(C)	26,160,000	—	1.00	1.50	2.00	—
1978(H)	12,100,000	—	1.00	1.50	2.00	—

KM# 33 10 PAISE

Aluminum, 26 mm. **Series:** International Year of the Child **Obv:** Asoka lion pedestal **Rev:** Logo on square within circle, wreath surrounds **Shape:** Scalloped

Date	Mintage	F	VF	XF	Unc	BU
1979(B)	39,270,000	—	0.25	0.50	1.00	—
1979B Proof	—	Value: 1.00				
1979(C)	61,700,000	—	0.50	1.00	2.50	—
1979(H)	2,250,000	—	0.60	1.00	2.50	—

KM# 34 10 PAISE

Aluminum, 26 mm. **Obv:** Asoka lion pedestal, denomination below **Rev:** Emblem on square, within circle, wreath surrounds, date below **Note:** Mule.

Date	Mintage	F	VF	XF	Unc	BU
1979(B)	—	—	5.00	7.50	10.00	—

KM# 35 10 PAISE

Aluminum, 26 mm. **Subject:** Rural Women's Advancement **Obv:** Asoka lion pedestal **Rev:** Woman grinding wheat within circle **Shape:** Scalloped

Date	Mintage	F	VF	XF	Unc	BU
1980(B)	38,080,000	—	0.25	0.40	1.00	—
1980B Proof	—	Value: 1.00				
1980(C)	42,830,000	—	0.25	0.50	1.00	—
1980(H)	11,070,000	—	0.50	1.00	1.50	—

KM# 36 10 PAISE

2.3000 g., Aluminum, 26 mm. **Subject:** World Food Day **Obv:** Asoka lion pedestal **Rev:** Man and woman, man carrying sheaf **Shape:** Scalloped

Date	Mintage	F	VF	XF	Unc	BU
1981(B)	83,280,000	—	0.25	0.40	1.00	—
1981B Proof	—	Value: 1.00				
1981(C)	33,930,000	—	0.25	0.50	1.00	—

KM# 37 10 PAISE

2.3000 g., Aluminum, 26 mm. **Subject:** IX Asian Games **Obv:** Asoka lion pedestal **Rev:** Sun above symbol **Shape:** Scalloped

Date	Mintage	F	VF	XF	Unc	BU
1982(B)	—	—	0.25	0.45	0.75	—
1982B Proof	—	Value: 1.00				
1982(C)	30,560,000	—	0.25	0.45	0.75	—
1982(H)	17,080,000	—	0.25	0.50	1.00	—

KM# 38 10 PAISE

2.3000 g., Aluminum, 26 mm. **Subject:** World Food Day **Obv:** Asoka lion pedestal **Rev:** Grain sprig within stylized sun design **Shape:** Scalloped

Date	Mintage	F	VF	XF	Unc	BU
1982(C)	2,970,000	—	2.50	3.50	5.00	—
1982(B)	—	—	—	—	—	—
1982(H)	11,690,000	—	0.50	1.00	2.00	—

KM# 39 10 PAISE

2.3000 g., Aluminum, 26 mm. **Obv:** Asoka lion pedestal **Rev:** Denomination and date **Shape:** Scalloped

Date	Mintage	F	VF	XF	Unc	BU
1983(B)	—	—	0.10	0.25	0.50	—
1983(C)	—	—	0.10	0.25	0.50	—

Date	Mintage	F	VF	XF	Unc	BU
1983(H)	—	—	0.10	0.25	0.50	—
1984(B)	112,050,000	—	0.10	0.25	0.50	—
1984(C)	Inc. above	—	0.25	0.50	1.00	—
1984(H)	Inc. above	—	0.10	0.25	0.50	—
1985(B)	184,655,000	—	0.20	0.30	0.50	—
1985(C)	Inc. above	—	0.20	0.30	0.50	—
1985(H)	Inc. above	—	0.20	0.30	0.50	—
1986(B)	298,525,000	—	0.10	0.15	0.30	—
1986(C)	Inc. above	—	0.20	0.30	0.50	—
1986(H)	Inc. above	—	0.50	1.00	1.50	—
1987(C)	299,460,000	—	0.15	0.25	0.45	—
1987(H)	Inc. above	—	0.15	0.25	0.45	—
1988(B)	264,510,000	—	0.10	0.15	0.30	—
1988(C)	Inc. above	—	0.10	0.15	0.30	—
1988(H)	Inc. above	—	1.00	1.50	2.00	—
1989(B)	—	—	0.15	0.25	0.45	—
1989(C)	—	—	0.15	0.25	0.45	—
1989(H)	—	—	0.15	0.25	0.45	—
1990(B)	—	—	0.50	0.75	1.25	—
1991(B)	—	—	0.15	0.25	0.45	—
1991(C)	—	—	0.15	0.25	0.45	—
1991(H)	—	—	0.15	0.25	0.45	—
1993(C)	—	—	0.15	0.30	0.60	—
1993(H)	—	—	0.30	0.50	0.75	—

KM# 40.1 10 PAISE
Stainless Steel **Obv:** Asoka lion pedestal **Obv. Legend:** BHARAT **Rev:** Denomination and date

Date	Mintage	F	VF	XF	Unc	BU
1988C	183,040,000	—	0.10	0.15	0.25	—
1988(B)	4,040,000	—	0.25	0.40	0.75	—
1988(C)	—	—	5.00	7.00	10.00	—
1988(H)	Inc. above	—	3.00	5.00	8.00	—
1988(N)	—	—	0.15	0.25	0.40	—
1989(B)	—	—	0.60	1.00	1.50	—
1989(C)	—	—	0.40	0.70	1.00	—
1989(H)	—	—	0.20	0.30	0.50	—
1989(N)	—	—	0.25	0.40	0.75	—
1990(B)	—	—	0.15	0.30	0.50	—
1990(C)	—	—	0.40	0.70	1.00	—
1990(H)	—	—	0.20	0.30	0.50	—
1990(N) Small mm	—	—	0.15	0.30	0.50	—
1990(N) Large mm	—	—	1.25	1.75	2.50	—
1991(C)	—	—	0.15	0.30	0.50	—
1991(H)	—	—	0.15	0.30	0.50	—
1991(N)	—	—	0.15	0.30	0.50	—
1992(N)	—	—	0.30	0.60	1.00	—
1992(B)	—	—	1.00	1.50	2.50	—
1993(H)	—	—	0.15	0.30	0.50	—
1996(C)	—	—	0.15	0.30	0.50	—
1996(B)	—	—	1.50	2.50	5.00	—
1996(N)	—	—	0.15	0.30	0.50	—
1997(C)	—	—	0.15	0.30	0.50	—
1997(B)	—	—	1.50	2.50	5.00	—
1997(H)	—	—	0.20	0.30	0.50	—
1998(B)	—	—	0.25	0.40	0.70	—
1998(C)	—	—	0.25	0.40	0.70	—

KM# 40.2 10 PAISE
Stainless Steel **Obv:** Error: MARAT for BHARAT
Rev: Denomination and date

Date	Mintage	F	VF	XF	Unc	BU
1988(C)	—	—	1.25	2.00	3.00	—
1989(C)	—	—	7.00	10.00	15.00	—

KM# 41 20 PAISE
Nickel-Brass **Obv:** Asoka lion pedestal **Rev:** Lotus blossom
Note: Varieties of high and low date exist.

Date	Mintage	F	VF	XF	Unc	BU
1968(B)	10,585,000	—	0.50	1.00	1.50	—
1968(C)	Inc. above	—	0.50	1.00	1.50	—
1969(B)	197,940,000	—	0.40	0.85	1.50	—
1969(C)	—	—	0.40	0.85	1.50	—
1970(B)	Inc. above	—	0.30	0.60	1.00	—
1970(C)	Inc. above	—	0.30	0.60	1.00	—
1970(H)	Inc. above	—	0.30	0.60	1.00	—
1971(B)	124,200,000	—	0.30	0.60	1.00	—

KM# 42.1 20 PAISE
Aluminum-Bronze **Subject:** Centennial - Birth of Mahatma Gandhi **Obv:** Asoka lion pedestal **Obv. Legend:** .7-.9 from rims **Rev:** Head left

Date	Mintage	F	VF	XF	Unc	BU
ND(1969)(B)	45,010	—	0.40	0.65	1.00	—
ND(1969)B Proof	9,147	Value: 2.00				
ND(1969)(C)	45,070,000	—	0.50	0.80	1.50	—
ND(1969)(H)	3,000,000	—	0.75	1.50	2.50	—

KM# 42.2 20 PAISE
Aluminum-Bronze **Obv:** Asoka lion pedestal
Obv. Legend: 1.2mm from rim **Rev:** Head left

Date	Mintage	F	VF	XF	Unc	BU
ND(1969)(B)	—	—	2.00	3.00	5.00	—
ND(1969)(C)	—	—	3.00	5.00	8.00	—

KM# 42.3 20 PAISE
Aluminum-Bronze **Obv:** Asoka lion pedestal **Rev:** Head left
Note: Eyes, mustache recut, legends 1.2mm from rim.

Date	Mintage	F	VF	XF	Unc	BU
ND(1969)(B)	—	—	0.60	1.00	1.50	—

Note: The KM 42 subtypes were struck during 1969 and 1970

KM# 43.1 20 PAISE
Aluminum-Bronze **Series:** F.A.O. **Subject:** Food For All **Obv:** Asoka lion pedestal **Rev:** Sun above floating lotus **Note:** Wide rims.

Date	Mintage	F	VF	XF	Unc	BU
1970(B)	5,160,000	—	0.75	1.25	2.00	—
1970B Proof	3,046	Value: 2.00				
1970(C)	5,010,000	—	0.75	1.25	2.00	—

KM# 43.2 20 PAISE
Aluminum-Bronze **Obv:** Asoka lion pedestal **Rev:** Sun above floating lotus **Note:** Narrow rims, lion's fur recut.

Date	Mintage	F	VF	XF	Unc	BU
1971(B)	60,000	—	0.70	0.90	1.25	—
1971B Proof	4,375	Value: 2.00				

KM# 44 20 PAISE
2.1500 g., Aluminum, 26 mm. **Obv:** Asoka lion pedestal **Rev:** Denomination and date within decorative wreath **Shape:** 6-sided

Date	Mintage	F	VF	XF	Unc	BU
1982(B)	—	—	0.25	0.40	1.00	—
1982(H)	—	—	0.25	0.40	1.00	—
1982(H) Without mm	—	—	0.25	0.40	1.00	—
1983(C)	28,505,000	—	0.25	0.40	1.00	—
1983(H)	Inc. above	—	0.25	0.40	1.00	—
1984(B)	—	—	0.25	0.40	1.00	—
1984(C)	Inc. above	—	0.25	0.40	1.00	—
1984(H)	Inc. above	—	0.25	0.40	1.00	—
1985(B)	84,495,000	—	0.25	0.40	1.00	—
1985(C)	Inc. above	—	0.25	0.40	1.00	—
1985(H)	Inc. above	—	0.25	0.40	1.00	—
1986(B)	155,610,000	—	0.25	0.40	0.75	—
1986(C)	Inc. above	—	0.15	0.30	0.75	—
1986(H)	Inc. above	—	0.15	0.30	0.75	—
1987(C)	—	—	0.15	0.30	0.75	—
1987(H)	153,073,000	—	0.15	0.30	0.75	—
1988(B)	125,048,000	—	0.15	0.30	0.75	—
1988(C)	Inc. above	—	0.15	0.30	0.75	—
1988(H)	Inc. above	—	0.35	0.60	1.00	—
1989(C)	—	—	0.35	0.60	1.00	—
1989(H)	—	—	0.15	0.25	0.75	—
1990(C)	—	—	0.35	0.60	1.00	—
1990(H)	—	—	0.15	0.25	0.75	—
1991(C)	—	—	0.15	0.25	0.75	—
1991(H)	—	—	0.15	0.25	0.75	—
1992(H)	—	—	0.15	0.25	0.75	—
1994(H)	—	—	0.15	0.25	0.75	—
1996(H)	—	—	1.00	2.00	4.00	—
1997(H)	—	—	3.00	5.00	10.00	—

KM# 45 20 PAISE
Aluminum **Series:** F.A.O. **Obv:** Asoka lion pedestal **Rev:** Grain sprig within stylized sun design **Shape:** 6-sided

Date	Mintage	F	VF	XF	Unc	BU
1982(C)	—	—	2.00	3.25	5.00	—
1982(H)	—	—	1.00	1.50	2.50	—

KM# 46 20 PAISE
2.1500 g., Aluminum, 26 mm. **Series:** F.A.O. **Subject:** Fisheries **Obv:** Asoka lion pedestal **Rev:** People with fishing nets **Shape:** 6-sided

Date	Mintage	F	VF	XF	Unc	BU
1983(C)	—	—	1.00	1.50	2.50	—
Note: Mintage included in KM44						
1983(H)	—	—	1.00	1.50	2.50	—
Note: Mintage included in KM44						

KM# 47.1 25 NAYE PAISE
Nickel **Obv:** Asoka lion pedestal **Rev:** Denomination and date

Date	Mintage	F	VF	XF	Unc	BU
1957(B)	5,640,000	—	0.75	1.25	2.00	—
1957(C)	Inc. above	—	0.75	1.25	2.00	—
1959(B)	43,080,000	—	0.45	0.75	1.25	—
1959(C)	Inc. above	—	0.45	0.75	1.25	—
1960(B)	115,320,000	—	0.30	0.60	1.00	—
1960(B) Proof	—	Value: 2.00				
1960(C)	Inc. above	—	0.30	0.60	1.00	—

KM# 47.2 25 NAYE PAISE
2.5000 g., Nickel, 19 mm. **Obv:** Asoka lion pedestal
Rev: Denomination and date, large 25

Date	Mintage	F	VF	XF	Unc	BU
1961(B)	109,008,000	—	0.30	0.60	1.00	—
1961(B) Proof	—	Value: 2.00				
1961(C)	Inc. above	—	0.30	0.60	1.00	—
1962(B)	79,242,000	—	0.30	0.60	1.00	—
1962(B) Proof	—	Value: 2.00				
1962(C)	Inc. above	—	0.30	0.60	1.00	—
1963(B)	101,565,000	—	0.30	0.60	1.00	—
1963(B) Proof	—	Value: 2.00				
1963(C)	Inc. above	—	0.30	0.60	1.00	—

KM# 48.1 25 PAISE
Nickel, 19 mm. **Obv:** Asoka lion pedestal **Rev:** Denomination and date **Note:** Type 1.

Date	Mintage	F	VF	XF	Unc	BU
1964(B)	85,321,000	—	0.30	0.60	1.25	—
1964(C)	Inc. above	—	0.30	0.60	1.25	—

KM# 48.2 25 PAISE
Nickel, 19 mm. **Obv:** Asoka lion pedestal **Rev:** Smaller date and denomination **Note:** Type 1

Date	Mintage	F	VF	XF	Unc	BU
1965(B)	143,662,000	—	0.30	0.60	1.00	—
1965(C)	Inc. above	—	0.30	0.60	1.00	—
1966(B)	59,040,000	—	0.30	0.60	1.00	—
1966(C)	Inc. above	—	0.30	0.60	1.00	—
1967(B)	30,027,000	—	4.50	6.00	8.00	—

KM# 48.3 25 PAISE

Nickel, 19 mm. **Obv:** Asoka lion pedestal **Rev:** Denomination and date **Note:** Type 2. Mintage included in KM48.2.

Date	Mintage	F	VF	XF	Unc	BU
1967(C)	—	—	0.30	0.70	1.50	—
1968(C)	—	—	1.50	2.25	3.50	—

KM# 49.1 25 PAISE

2.5000 g., Copper-Nickel, 19 mm. **Obv:** Asoka lion pedestal **Rev:** Denomination and date **Note:** Type 1, lion with whiskers, faces and wheel redesigned. 1984-86 have edges rounded (local blanks) or flat (Korean blanks).

Date	Mintage	F	VF	XF	Unc	BU
1972(B)	367,640,000	—	0.20	0.40	0.70	—
1972B Proof	7,895	Value: 1.00				
1972(H)	Inc. above	—	0.45	1.00	2.00	—
1973(B)	—	—	0.20	0.40	0.70	—
1973B Proof	7,567	Value: 1.00				
1973(H)	—	—	0.35	0.60	1.00	—
1974(B)	—	—	0.20	0.40	0.70	—
1974B Proof	—	Value: 1.00				
1974(H)	—	—	0.45	0.75	1.25	—
1975(B)	559,980,000	—	0.20	0.40	0.70	—
1975B Proof	—	Value: 1.00				
1975(H)	Inc. above	—	3.00	4.00	5.00	—
1976(B)	30,016,000	—	0.60	1.00	1.50	—
1976B Proof	Inc. above	Value: 1.00				
1976(H)	Inc. above	—	0.60	1.00	1.50	—
1977(B)	270,520,000	—	0.20	0.40	0.70	—
1977(C)	Inc. above	—	0.35	0.60	1.00	—
1977(H)	Inc. above	—	0.35	0.60	1.00	—
1978B Proof	—	Value: 1.00				
1978(C)	131,632,000	—	0.25	0.40	0.70	—
1978(H)	—	—	0.25	0.40	0.70	—
1979(C)	—	—	0.50	1.00	1.50	—
1979(H)	—	—	0.50	1.00	1.50	—
1980(C)	6,175,000	—	0.25	0.40	0.70	—
1980(H)	Inc. above	—	0.25	0.40	0.70	—
1981(B)	11,048,000	—	0.25	0.40	0.70	—
1981(C)	Inc. above	—	1.50	2.00	2.50	—
1981(H)	Inc. above	—	0.45	0.75	1.25	—
1982(C)	38,288,000	—	0.45	0.75	1.25	—
1983(C)	137,488,000	—	0.45	0.75	1.25	—
1984(B)	98,740,000	—	0.45	0.75	1.25	—
1984(C)	Inc. above	—	0.45	0.75	1.25	—
1985(B)	113,872,000	—	0.45	0.75	1.25	—
1985C	Inc. above	—	0.15	0.25	0.50	—
1985(C)	Inc. above	—	0.45	0.75	1.25	—
1985(H)	Inc. above	—	0.45	0.75	1.25	—
1986(B)	362,624,000	—	0.60	0.90	1.50	—
1986(C)	Inc. above	—	0.60	0.90	1.50	—
1986(H)	Inc. above	—	0.60	0.90	1.50	—
1987(C)	341,160,000	—	0.60	0.90	1.50	—
1987(H)	Inc. above	—	0.60	0.90	1.50	—
1988(H)	303,252,000	—	0.60	0.90	1.50	—

KM# 49.2 25 PAISE

Copper-Nickel, 19 mm. **Obv:** Asoka lion pedestal **Rev:** Denomination and date **Note:** Type 2, 9mm between lions' nose tips, 15mm across field.

Date	Mintage	F	VF	XF	Unc	BU
1972(C)	—	—	0.35	0.60	1.00	—
1977(B)	—	—	0.35	0.60	1.00	—
Note: Mintage included in KM49.1						
1977B Proof	—	Value: 1.50				
Note: Mintage included in KM49.1						
1978(B)	—	—	3.25	5.00	7.00	—
Note: Mintage included in KM49.1						
1979B Proof	—	Value: 1.50				

KM# 49.3 25 PAISE

Copper-Nickel, 19 mm. **Obv:** Asoka lion pedestal **Rev:** Denomination and date **Note:** Type 2, 10mm between lion nosetips, 16-16.3mm across field. Bull has three legs.

Date	Mintage	F	VF	XF	Unc	BU
1972(C)	—	—	2.50	3.50	5.00	—
Note: Mintage included in KM49.1						
1973(C)	—	—	0.85	1.25	2.00	—
1974(C)	—	—	0.85	1.25	2.00	—

KM# 49.4 25 PAISE

Copper-Nickel, 19 mm. **Obv:** Asoka lion pedestal **Rev:** Denomination and date **Note:** Type 1, central lion, bull and horse re-engraved.

Date	Mintage	F	VF	XF	Unc	BU
1974(B)	—	—	2.00	5.00	6.50	—
1975(B)	—	—	5.00	7.00	12.00	—
1975(H)	—	—	1.00	3.00	5.00	—
1976(H)	—	—	6.00	8.00	15.00	—
1977(B)	—	—	2.00	4.00	8.00	—
1978(B)	—	—	2.00	3.00	5.00	—
1979(B)	—	—	2.50	5.00	7.00	—
1981(B)	—	—	4.00	6.00	8.00	—

KM# 49.5 25 PAISE

2.5000 g., Copper-Nickel, 19 mm. **Obv:** Asoka lion pedestal **Rev:** Denomination and date **Note:** Type 3.

Date	Mintage	F	VF	XF	Unc	BU
1986(B)	—	—	0.15	0.30	1.00	—
1986(C)	—	—	0.45	0.75	1.25	—
1986(H)	—	—	0.45	0.75	1.25	—
1987(B)	—	—	0.15	0.30	1.00	—
1987(C)	—	—	0.25	0.40	1.50	—
1987(C) Long 7	—	—	0.25	0.40	1.50	—
1988(B)	—	—	0.20	0.35	1.25	—
1988(C) 8's 1.3mm tall	—	—	0.45	0.75	2.00	—
1988(C) 8's 1.8mm tall	—	—	0.45	0.75	2.00	—
1988(H)	—	—	0.45	1.00	1.75	—
1989(B)	—	—	0.45	1.00	1.75	—
1989(C)	—	—	2.00	2.50	3.00	—
1990(B)	—	—	2.00	3.50	7.00	—
1990(C)	—	—	2.00	3.50	7.00	—

KM# 49.6 25 PAISE

Copper-Nickel, 19 mm. **Obv:** Asoka lion pedestal **Rev:** Denomination and date **Note:** 9-1/2mm between lions' nose tips. Bull has four legs. Type 1.

Date	Mintage	F	VF	XF	Unc	BU
1974(C)	—	—	0.85	1.25	2.00	—
1975(C)	—	—	0.85	1.25	2.00	—
1976(C)	—	—	2.00	3.50	5.00	—

KM# 49.7 25 PAISE

Nickel, 19 mm. **Obv:** Asoka lion pedestal **Rev:** Denomination and date, large 25 **Note:** Type 1, lion without whiskers.

Date	Mintage	F	VF	XF	Unc	BU
1972(B)	—	—	8.00	14.00	20.00	—

KM# 50 25 PAISE

Copper-Nickel, 19 mm. **Subject:** Rural Women's Advancement **Obv:** Asoka lion pedestal **Rev:** Woman grinding wheat

Date	Mintage	F	VF	XF	Unc	BU
1980(B)	15,050,000	—	0.30	0.50	1.00	—
1980B Proof	—	Value: 1.00				
1980(C)	8,520,000	—	0.50	1.00	1.50	—
1980(H)	10,380,000	—	1.00	1.50	2.00	—

KM# 51 25 PAISE

Copper-Nickel, 19 mm. **Subject:** World Food Day **Obv:** Asoka lion pedestal **Rev:** Man and woman, man carrying sheaf

Date	Mintage	F	VF	XF	Unc	BU
1981(B)	2,170,000	—	1.00	1.50	2.00	—
1981B Proof	—	Value: 2.00				
1981(C)	4,500,000	—	1.00	1.50	2.00	—
1981(H)	9,340,000	—	1.50	2.00	3.00	—

KM# 52 25 PAISE

Copper-Nickel, 19 mm. **Subject:** IX Asian Games **Obv:** Asoka lion pedestal **Rev:** Sun above symbol

Date	Mintage	F	VF	XF	Unc	BU
1982(B)	12,000,000	—	0.30	0.50	1.00	—
1982B Proof	—	Value: 1.00				
1982(C)	12,000,000	—	0.30	0.50	1.00	—
1982(H)	330,000	—	2.50	3.50	5.00	—

KM# 53.1 25 PAISE

Copper-Nickel, 19 mm. **Subject:** Forestry **Obv:** Asoka lion pedestal **Rev:** Central tree divides squatting figure and stag **Edge:** Rounded

Date	Mintage	F	VF	XF	Unc	BU
1985(B)	—	—	1.50	2.00	2.75	—
Note: Mintage included in KM49.1						
1985(H)	—	—	5.00	7.00	10.00	—
Note: Mintage included in KM49.1						

KM# 53.2 25 PAISE

Copper-Nickel, 19 mm. **Obv:** Asoka lion pedestal **Rev:** Central tree divides squatting figure and stag **Edge:** Flat

Date	Mintage	F	VF	XF	Unc	BU
1985(B)	—	—	5.00	7.00	10.00	—
1985(C)	—	—	3.00	5.00	7.00	—

KM# 54 25 PAISE

Stainless Steel, 19 mm. **Obv:** Small Asoka lion pedestal **Rev:** Rhinoceros left **Note:** Varieties of date size exist.

Date	Mintage	F	VF	XF	Unc	BU
1988C	305,280,000	—	0.10	0.20	1.00	—
1988(B)	—	—	0.45	0.75	1.25	—
1988(C)	18,920,000	—	3.50	5.00	8.00	—
1988(H)	—	—	6.00	8.00	10.00	—
1988(N)	Inc. above	—	0.45	0.75	1.25	—
1989(B)	—	—	0.65	1.00	1.50	—
1989(C)	—	—	0.65	1.00	1.50	—
1989(H)	—	—	1.00	2.00	3.00	—
1989(N)	—	—	0.15	0.30	0.60	—
1990(B)	—	—	0.25	0.50	1.00	—
1990(C)	—	—	0.25	0.50	1.00	—
1990(H)	—	—	0.25	0.40	1.00	—
1990(N) Small mm	—	—	0.40	0.65	1.00	—
1991(B)	—	—	0.25	0.40	1.00	—
1991(C)	—	—	0.25	0.40	1.00	—
1991(H)	—	—	0.25	0.40	1.00	—
1991(N)	—	—	0.25	0.40	1.00	—
1992(B)	—	—	0.25	0.40	1.00	—
1992(C)	—	—	1.00	2.00	3.00	—
1992(H)	—	—	1.00	2.00	3.00	—
1992(N)	—	—	0.50	1.00	2.00	—
1993(B)	—	—	0.50	1.00	2.00	—
1993(C)	—	—	0.50	1.00	2.00	—
1993(H)	—	—	2.00	3.00	5.00	—
1993(N)	—	—	0.50	0.70	1.00	—
1994(B)	—	—	0.15	0.30	1.00	—
1994(C)	—	—	0.10	0.20	1.00	—
1994(H)	—	—	0.10	0.20	1.00	—
1994(N)	—	—	0.10	0.20	1.00	—
1995(B)	—	—	0.10	0.20	1.00	—
1995(C)	—	—	0.25	0.50	1.00	—
1995(H)	—	—	0.10	0.20	1.00	—
1995(N)	—	—	0.10	0.20	1.00	—
1996(B)	—	—	0.10	0.20	1.00	—
1996(C)	—	—	0.10	0.20	1.00	—
1996(H)	—	—	0.10	0.20	1.00	—
1996(N)	—	—	0.10	0.20	1.00	—
1997(B)	—	—	0.10	0.20	1.00	—
1997(C)	—	—	0.10	0.20	1.00	—
1997(H)	—	—	0.50	1.00	2.00	—
1997(N)	—	—	0.10	0.20	1.00	—
1998(B)	—	—	0.10	0.20	1.00	—
1998(C)	—	—	0.10	0.20	1.00	—
1998(H)	—	—	0.10	0.20	1.00	—
1998(N)	—	—	0.10	0.20	1.00	—
1999(B)	—	—	0.10	0.20	1.00	—
1999(C)	—	—	0.10	0.20	1.00	—
1999(H)	—	—	0.10	0.20	1.00	—
1999(N)	—	—	0.10	0.20	1.00	—
2000(B)	—	—	0.10	0.20	1.00	—
2000(C)	—	—	0.10	0.20	1.00	—
2000(H)	—	—	0.10	0.20	1.00	—
2000(N)	—	—	0.10	0.20	1.00	—

KM# 55 50 NAYE PAISE

Nickel **Obv:** Asoka lion pedestal **Rev:** Denomination and date

Date	Mintage	F	VF	XF	Unc	BU
1960(B)	11,224,000	—	1.00	1.50	2.50	—
1960(B) Proof	—	Value: 3.00				
1960(C)	Inc. above	—	0.50	1.25	2.00	—
1961(B)	45,992,000	—	0.25	0.60	1.25	—
1961(B) Proof	—	Value: 3.00				
1961(C)	Inc. above	—	0.25	0.60	1.25	—
1962(B)	64,227,999	—	0.25	0.60	1.25	—
1962(B) Proof	—	Value: 3.00				
1962(C)	Inc. above	—	0.25	0.60	1.25	—
1963(B)	58,168,000	—	0.25	0.60	1.25	—
1963(B) Proof	—	Value: 3.00				
1963(C)	Inc. above	—	1.00	1.50	2.50	—

KM# 58.3 50 PAISE
Nickel **Obv:** Asoka lion pedestal, type 1 **Rev:** Denomination and date, smaller 50

Date	Mintage	F	VF	XF	Unc	BU
1970(B)	—	—	1.00	2.00	3.00	—
Note: Mintage included with 1969						
1970B Proof	3,046	Value: 2.00				
1971B Proof	4,375	Value: 2.00				

KM# 56 50 PAISE
Nickel **Subject:** Death of Jawaharlal Nehru **Obv:** Asoka lion pedestal **Rev:** Head left **Rev. Legend:** English **Note:** Struck from 1964 through 1967.

Date	Mintage	F	VF	XF	Unc	BU
ND(1964)(B)	21,900,000	—	0.40	0.65	1.00	—
ND(1964)B Proof	—	Value: 2.50				
ND(1964)(C)	7,160,000	—	0.75	1.50	2.75	—

KM# 57 50 PAISE
Nickel **Subject:** Death of Jawaharlal Nehru **Obv:** Asoka lion pedestal **Rev:** Head left **Rev. Legend:** Hindi **Note:** Struck from 1964 until 1967.

Date	Mintage	F	VF	XF	Unc	BU
ND(1964)(B)	36,190,000	—	0.40	0.65	1.00	—
ND(1964)(C)	28,350,000	—	0.40	0.65	1.00	—

KM# 58.1 50 PAISE
Nickel **Obv:** Asoka lion pedestal **Rev:** Denomination and date **Note:** Type 1.

Date	Mintage	F	VF	XF	Unc	BU
1964(C)	23,361,000	—	0.50	1.00	1.75	—
1967(B)	19,267,000	—	0.50	1.00	1.75	—
Note: Varieties of 1967(B) reverse edges exist, half teeth and the scarce full teeth						

KM# 58.2 50 PAISE
Nickel **Obv:** Asoka lion pedestal **Rev:** Denomination and date, smaller 50 **Note:** Type 2.

Date	Mintage	F	VF	XF	Unc	BU
1967(C)	—	—	0.60	1.00	1.50	—
1968(B)	28,076,000	—	0.25	0.60	1.00	—
Note: A scarce 1968(B) variety exists with crude obverse, no whiskers, thick horsetail						
1968(C)	Inc. above	—	0.25	0.60	1.00	—
1969(B)	59,388,000	—	0.25	0.60	1.00	—
1969(C)	Inc. above	—	0.35	0.75	1.25	—
1970(B)	Inc. above	—	0.35	0.75	1.25	—
1970(C)	Inc. above	—	0.25	0.60	1.00	—
1971(C)	57,900,000	—	0.25	0.50	0.85	—

KM# 59 50 PAISE
Nickel, 24 mm. **Subject:** Centennial - Birth of Mahatma Gandhi **Obv:** Asoka lion pedestal **Rev:** Head left **Note:** Struck during 1969 and 1970.

Date	Mintage	F	VF	XF	Unc	BU
ND(1969)(B)	10,260,000	—	0.25	0.50	1.00	—
ND(1969)B Proof	9,147	Value: 2.00				
ND(1969)(C)	12,100,000	—	0.25	0.50	1.00	—

KM# 61 50 PAISE
Copper-Nickel, 24 mm. **Obv:** Asoka lion pedestal **Rev:** Denomination above date, lettering spaced out **Note:** Type 2.

Date	Mintage	F	VF	XF	Unc	BU
1972(C)	—	—	0.35	0.60	1.00	—
1972(B)	—	—	0.35	0.60	1.00	—
1973(B)	—	—	0.35	0.60	1.00	—
1973(C)	—	—	2.00	3.50	6.00	—

KM# 60 50 PAISE
Copper-Nickel, 24 mm. **Subject:** 25th Anniversary of Independence **Obv:** Asoka lion pedestal **Rev:** Figures with flag, building in background **Designer:** P. B. Chitnis

Date	Mintage	F	VF	XF	Unc	BU
ND(1972)(B)	43,800,000	—	0.30	0.50	1.00	—
ND(1972)B Proof	7,895	Value: 2.00				
ND(1972)(C)	40,080,000	—	0.45	0.75	1.50	—

KM# 62 50 PAISE
Copper-Nickel, 24 mm. **Series:** F.A.O. **Subject:** Grow More Food **Obv:** Asoka lion pedestal **Rev:** Inscription on shield within grain sprigs

Date	Mintage	F	VF	XF	Unc	BU
1973(B)	28,720,000	—	0.30	0.50	1.00	—
1973B Proof	11,000	Value: 2.00				
1973(C)	40,100,000	—	0.30	0.50	1.00	—

KM# 63 50 PAISE
Copper-Nickel, 24 mm. **Obv:** Asoka lion pedestal **Rev:** Denomination above date, lettering close **Note:** Type 2.

Date	Mintage	F	VF	XF	Unc	BU
1974(B)	—	—	0.25	0.50	1.00	—
1974B Proof	—	Value: 2.00				
1974(C)	—	—	0.35	0.75	1.50	—
1975(B)	225,880,000	—	0.25	0.50	1.00	—
1975B Proof	—	Value: 2.00				
1975(C)	Inc. above	—	0.25	0.50	1.00	—
1975(H)	—	—	0.75	1.25	2.00	—
1976(B)	99,564,000	—	0.25	0.50	1.00	—
1976B Proof	Inc. above	Value: 2.00				
1976(C)	Inc. above	—	0.35	0.75	1.50	—
1976(H)	Inc. above	—	0.75	1.25	2.00	—
1977(B)	97,272,000	—	0.25	0.50	1.00	—
1977B Proof	Inc. above	Value: 2.00				
1977(C)	Inc. above	—	0.40	0.75	1.50	—
1977(H)	Inc. above	—	0.40	0.75	1.50	—
1978B Proof	25,648,000	Value: 2.00				
1978(C)	—	—	0.25	0.50	1.00	—
1979B Proof	—	Value: 2.00				
1980(B)	—	—	0.25	0.50	1.00	—
1980B Proof	—	Value: 2.00				
1980(C)	—	—	5.00	8.00	12.00	—
1981B Proof	—	Value: 2.00				
1983(C)	62,634,000	—	5.00	8.00	12.00	—

KM# 64 50 PAISE
Copper-Nickel, 24 mm. **Subject:** National Integration **Obv:** Asoka lion pedestal **Rev:** Flag on map

Date	Mintage	F	VF	XF	Unc	BU
1982(B)	9,804,000	—	0.40	0.75	1.25	—
1982B Proof	—	Value: 3.00				
1982(C)	Inc. above	—	10.00	15.00	20.00	—

KM# 65 50 PAISE
Copper-Nickel, 24 mm. **Obv:** Asoka lion pedestal, ornaments surround **Rev:** Denomination and date, ornaments surround **Note:** Type 3.

Date	Mintage	F	VF	XF	Unc	BU
1984(B)	61,548,000	—	0.25	0.50	0.85	—
1984(C)	Inc. above	—	1.00	1.50	2.50	—
1984(H)	—	—	2.00	3.00	5.00	—
1985(B)	210,964,000	—	0.25	0.50	0.85	—
1985(C)	Inc. above	—	0.25	0.50	0.85	—
1985(H)	Inc. above	—	1.00	1.50	3.00	—
1985(T)	Inc. above	—	0.20	0.30	0.65	—
1986(C)	117,576,000	—	0.50	1.00	2.00	—
1987(B)	—	—	0.25	0.50	0.85	—
1987(C)	145,140,000	—	0.25	0.50	0.85	—
1987(H)	Inc. above	—	0.40	0.75	1.50	—
1988(B)	149,092,000	—	0.25	0.50	0.85	—
1988(C)	Inc. above	—	1.00	1.50	3.00	—
1988(H)	Inc. above	—	1.00	1.50	2.50	—
1989(B)	—	—	0.50	1.00	2.00	—
1989(C)	—	—	0.50	1.00	2.00	—
1990(B)	—	—	2.00	4.00	7.00	—

KM# 66 50 PAISE
Copper-Nickel, 24 mm. **Subject:** Golden Jubilee of Reserve Bank of India **Obv:** Asoka lion pedestal **Rev:** Lion beneath trees

Date	Mintage	F	VF	XF	Unc	BU
ND(1985)(B)	—	—	0.50	1.00	4.50	—
Note: Mintage included in KM65						
ND(1985)B Proof	—	Value: 15.00				
Note: Mintage included in KM680						
ND(1985)(C)	—	—	2.00	3.00	6.00	—
ND(1985)(H)	—	—	0.75	1.25	4.00	—
Note: Mintage included in KM65						

KM# 67.1 50 PAISE
Copper-Nickel, 24 mm. **Subject:** Death of Indira Gandhi - statesperson, 1917-1984 **Obv:** Asoka lion pedestal **Rev:** Head right

Date	Mintage	F	VF	XF	Unc	BU
ND(1985)(B)	—	—	0.20	0.40	1.00	—
Note: Mintage included in KM65						
ND(1985)B Proof	—	Value: 17.50				
Note: Mintage included in KM65						
ND(1985)(C)	—	—	0.20	0.40	1.00	—
Note: Mintage included in KM65						
ND(1985)(H)	—	—	0.65	1.00	1.50	—
Note: Mintage included in KM65						

KM# 67.2 50 PAISE
Copper-Nickel, 24 mm. **Subject:** Death of Indira Gandhi, 1917-1984 statesperson **Obv:** Asoka lion pedestal **Rev:** Head right **Note:** Mule.

Date	Mintage	F	VF	XF	Unc	BU
ND(1985)(C)	—	—	35.00	50.00	80.00	—

KM# 68.1 50 PAISE

Copper-Nickel, 24 mm. **Series:** F.A.O. **Subject:** Fisheries **Obv:** Asoka lion pedestal **Rev:** People with fishing nets

Date	Mintage	F	VF	XF	Unc	BU
1986(B)	—	—	0.30	0.50	1.00	—
Note: Mintage included in KM65						
1986B Proof	—	Value: 15.00				
Note: Mintage included in KM65						
1986(C)	—	—	2.00	3.00	5.00	—
1986(H)	—	—	2.00	3.00	5.00	—
Note: Mintage included in KM65						

KM# 68.2 50 PAISE

Copper-Nickel, 24 mm. **Obv:** Asoka lion pedestal **Rev:** People with fishing nets **Note:** Mule.

Date	Mintage	F	VF	XF	Unc	BU
1986(C)	—	—	50.00	70.00	100	—

KM# 69 50 PAISE

3.8000 g., Stainless Steel, 22 mm. **Subject:** Parliament Building in New Delhi **Obv:** Denomination **Rev:** Building

Date	Mintage	F	VF	XF	Unc	BU
1988C	272,160,000	—	0.20	0.30	0.50	—
1988(B)	—	—	0.20	0.40	0.75	—
1988(C)	2,195,000	—	6.00	9.00	14.00	—
1988(H)	Inc. above	—	6.00	9.00	14.00	—
1988(N)	—	—	0.20	0.40	0.75	—
1989(B)	—	—	0.20	0.40	0.75	—
1989(C)	—	—	1.50	3.00	5.00	—
1989(H)	—	—	0.50	1.00	2.00	—
1989(N)	—	—	0.15	0.50	1.00	—
1990(B)	—	—	0.15	0.50	1.00	—
1990(C)	—	—	0.50	1.00	2.00	—
1990(H)	—	—	0.15	0.50	1.00	—
1990(N) Small mm	—	—	0.15	0.50	1.00	—
1990(N) Large mm	—	—	0.15	0.50	1.00	—
1991(B)	—	—	0.15	0.50	1.00	—
1991(C)	—	—	0.15	0.50	1.00	—
1991(H)	—	—	0.15	0.25	0.50	—
1991(N)	—	—	0.10	0.35	0.60	—
1992(B)	—	—	0.10	0.35	0.60	—
1992(C)	—	—	0.50	1.00	2.00	—
1992(H)	—	—	0.10	0.35	0.60	—
1992(N)	—	—	0.10	0.35	0.60	—
1993(C)	—	—	0.50	1.00	2.00	—
1993(N)	—	—	0.10	0.35	0.60	—
1994(B)	—	—	0.10	0.35	0.60	—
1994(C)	—	—	0.50	1.00	2.00	—
1994(H)	—	—	0.10	0.35	0.60	—
1994(N)	—	—	0.10	0.35	0.60	—
1995(B)	—	—	0.10	0.20	0.35	—
1995(C)	—	—	0.50	1.00	2.00	—
1995(H)	—	—	0.20	0.30	0.50	—
1995(N)	—	—	0.10	0.20	0.35	—
1996(B)	—	—	0.10	0.20	0.35	—
1996(C)	—	—	0.10	0.20	0.35	—
1996(H)	—	—	0.10	0.20	0.35	—
1996(N)	—	—	0.10	0.20	0.35	—
1997(B)	—	—	0.10	0.20	0.35	—
1997(C)	—	—	0.10	0.20	0.35	—
1997(H)	—	—	2.00	3.00	5.00	—
1997(N)	—	—	0.10	0.20	0.35	—
1998(B)	—	—	0.10	0.20	0.35	—
1998(C)	—	—	0.10	0.20	0.35	—
1998(H)	—	—	1.00	1.50	3.00	—
1998(N)	—	—	0.10	0.20	0.35	—
1999(B)	—	—	0.15	0.25	0.50	—
1999(C)	—	—	0.15	0.25	0.50	—
1999(H)	—	—	0.15	0.25	0.50	—
1999(N)	—	—	0.15	0.25	0.50	—
2000(B)	—	—	0.15	0.25	0.50	—
2000(C)	—	—	0.15	0.25	0.50	—
2000(H)	—	—	0.15	0.25	0.50	—
2000(N)	—	—	0.15	0.25	0.50	—

KM# 70 50 PAISE

Stainless Steel **Subject:** 50th Anniversary of Independence **Obv:** Small Asoka lion pedestal above denomination **Rev:** Line of people

Date	Mintage	F	VF	XF	Unc	BU
1997(B)	—	—	0.25	0.40	0.75	—
1997(C)	—	—	0.25	0.40	0.75	—
1997(H)	—	—	0.25	0.40	0.75	—
1997(M) Proof	—	Value: 15.00				
1997(N)	—	—	0.25	0.40	0.75	—

KM# 75.1 RUPEE

10.0000 g., Nickel, 28 mm. **Obv:** Asoka lion pedestal **Rev:** Denomination and date, grain ears flank **Note:** Type 1.

Date	Mintage	F	VF	XF	Unc	BU
1962(B) Proof	—	—	—	—	—	—
1962(C)	3,689,000	—	1.00	2.00	3.00	—

KM# 75.2 RUPEE

10.0000 g., Nickel, 28 mm. **Obv:** Asoka lion pedestal **Rev:** Smaller date and denomination **Note:** Type 1.

Date	Mintage	F	VF	XF	Unc	BU
1970(B)	Inc. above	—	3.50	5.00	7.00	—
1970B Proof	3,046	Value: 3.00				
1971B Proof	4,375	Value: 3.00				
1972B Proof	7,895,000	Value: 2.50				
1973B Proof	7,567	Value: 2.50				
1974B Proof	—	Value: 2.50				

KM# 76 RUPEE

10.0000 g., Nickel, 28 mm. **Subject:** Death of Jawaharlal Nehru **Obv:** Small Asoka lion pedestal **Rev:** Head left **Note:** Struck from 1964 through 1967.

Date	Mintage	F	VF	XF	Unc	BU
ND(1964)(B)	10,010,000	—	0.65	1.00	2.00	—
ND(1964)B Proof	—	Value: 5.00				
ND(1964)(C)	10,020,000	—	0.65	1.00	2.00	—

KM# 77 RUPEE

10.0000 g., Nickel, 28 mm. **Subject:** Centennial - Birth of Mahatma Gandhi **Obv:** Asoka lion pedestal **Rev:** Head left **Note:** Struck during 1969 and 1970.

Date	Mintage	F	VF	XF	Unc	BU
ND(1969)(B)	5,180,000	—	0.70	1.25	2.00	—
ND(1969)B Proof	9,147	Value: 3.00				
ND(1969)(C)	6,690,000	—	1.00	1.50	2.50	—

KM# 78.1 RUPEE

8.0000 g., Copper-Nickel, 28 mm. **Obv:** Asoka lion pedestal **Rev:** Denomination and date, grain ears flank **Note:** Type 1.

Date	Mintage	F	VF	XF	Unc	BU
1975(B)	98,850,000	—	0.40	0.85	1.50	—
1975B Proof	—	Value: 2.50				
1975(C)	—	—	6.50	8.00	10.00	—
1976(B)	161,895,000	—	0.35	0.75	1.50	—
1976B Proof	Inc. above	Value: 2.50				
1977(B)	177,105,000	—	0.35	0.75	1.50	—
1977B Proof	Inc. above	Value: 2.50				
1978(B)	127,348,000	—	0.40	0.80	1.50	—
1978B Proof	Inc. above	Value: 2.50				
1978(C)	Inc. above	—	0.50	1.00	1.75	—
1979(C)	—	—	8.00	11.00	15.00	—

KM# 78.2 RUPEE

8.0000 g., Copper-Nickel, 28 mm. **Obv:** Asoka lion pedestal **Rev:** Denomination and date, grain ears flank **Note:** Type 2.

Date	Mintage	F	VF	XF	Unc	BU
1975(C)	—	—	0.40	0.85	1.50	—
Note: Mintage included in KM78.1						
1976(C)	—	—	0.50	1.25	2.25	—
Note: Mintage included in KM78.1						

KM# 78.3 RUPEE

8.0000 g., Copper-Nickel, 28 mm. **Obv:** Asoka lion pedestal **Rev:** Denomination and date, grain ears flank **Note:** Type 3. Border varieties of long vs. short teeth on 1981 reverse and 1982 obverse.

Date	Mintage	F	VF	XF	Unc	BU
1979(B)	—	—	0.35	0.60	1.00	—
1979B Proof	—	Value: 2.50				
1979(C)	—	—	0.40	0.75	1.50	—
1980(B)	84,768,000	—	0.35	0.60	1.00	—
1980B Proof	—	Value: 2.50				
1980(C)	Inc. above	—	0.40	0.75	1.25	—
1981(B)	82,458,000	—	0.35	0.60	1.00	—
1981B Proof	—	Value: 2.50				
1981(C)	Inc. above	—	0.40	0.75	1.25	—
1982(B)	116,811,000	—	0.40	0.75	1.25	—

KM# 79.1 RUPEE

6.0000 g., Copper-Nickel, 26 mm. **Obv:** Asoka lion pedestal within seven sided beaded outline **Rev:** Denomination and date, grain ears flank, seven-sided outline surrounds **Edge:** Security **Note:** Type 3. Lions' hair and ears on 1984(B)-1989(B) issues vary from others.

Date	Mintage	F	VF	XF	Unc	BU
1983(B)	32,490,000	—	0.30	0.50	1.00	—
1983(C)	Inc. above	—	0.30	0.50	1.00	—
1984(B)	152,378,000	—	0.25	0.40	0.75	—
1984(C)	Inc. above	—	0.25	0.40	0.75	—
1984(H)	Inc. above	—	1.50	2.25	3.00	—
1985(B)	444,516,000	—	0.25	0.40	0.75	—
1985(C)	Inc. above	—	0.25	0.40	0.75	—
1985H	Inc. above	—	0.25	0.40	0.75	—
1985(L)	Inc. above	—	0.25	0.40	0.75	—
1986(B)	1,396,074,000	—	0.25	0.40	0.75	—
1986(C)	Inc. above	—	0.25	0.40	0.75	—
1986(H)	Inc. above	—	1.50	2.25	3.00	—
1987(B)	685,502,000	—	0.25	0.40	0.75	—
1987(C)	Inc. above	—	0.25	0.40	0.75	—
1987(H)	Inc. above	—	0.25	0.40	0.75	—
1988(B)	240,447,000	—	0.75	1.25	2.00	—
1988(C)	Inc. above	—	0.25	0.40	0.75	—
1988(H)	Inc. above	—	0.40	0.75	1.25	—
1989(B)	—	—	1.50	2.25	3.00	—
1989(C)	—	—	0.25	0.45	0.75	—
1989(H)	—	—	0.25	0.45	0.75	—
1990(C)	—	—	1.50	2.25	3.00	—
1990(H)	—	—	0.25	0.45	0.75	—

KM# 79.2 RUPEE

6.0000 g., Copper-Nickel, 26 mm. **Obv:** Horse in pedestal shorter, more detailed, 7-sided beaded outline surrounds **Rev:** Denomination and date, grain ears flank, within 7-sided beaded outline

Date	Mintage	F	VF	XF	Unc	BU
1988(B)	—	—	1.00	1.50	2.50	—
1989(N)	—	—	1.00	1.50	2.50	—
1990(N)	—	—	1.00	1.50	2.50	—

KM# 79.3 RUPEE

6.0000 g., Copper-Nickel, 26 mm. **Obv:** Lions' chest hairs restyled, 7-sided beaded outline surrounds **Rev:** Denomination and date, grain ears flank, 7-sided beaded outline surrounds

Date	Mintage	F	VF	XF	Unc	BU
1988(B)	—	—	0.25	0.50	1.00	—
1989(B)	—	—	0.25	0.50	1.00	—
1990(B)	—	—	0.25	0.50	1.00	—

KM# 79.4 RUPEE

6.0000 g., Copper-Nickel, 26 mm. **Obv:** Asoka lion pedestal, within 7-sided beaded outline, similar to 79.1 **Rev:** Denomination and date, grain ears flank, 7-sided beaded outline surrounds **Edge:** Milled **Note:** Traces of security edge and/or mostly smooth edges are frequently encountered, especially for 1989. 1989-1991(c) is a variety with bulging eyes on side lions and irregular straight hair on central lion.

Date	Mintage	F	VF	XF	Unc	BU
1989(B)	—	—	10.00	15.00	20.00	—
1989(C)	—	—	5.00	7.00	11.00	—
1989(H)	—	—	10.00	15.00	20.00	—
1990(C)	—	—	0.35	0.50	1.00	—
1990(H)	—	—	0.50	0.75	1.50	—
1991(C)	—	—	0.35	0.50	1.00	—

KM# 79.5 RUPEE

6.0000 g., Copper-Nickel, 26 mm. **Obv:** Lions' chest hairs restyled, 7-sided beaded outline surrounds **Rev:** Denomination and date, grain ears flank, 7-sided beaded outline surrounds

Date	Mintage	F	VF	XF	Unc	BU
1990(C)	—	—	0.50	1.00	2.00	—
1990(B)	—	—	0.35	0.60	1.00	—
1991(B)	—	—	0.20	0.35	0.85	—
1991(H)	—	—	0.35	0.60	1.00	—

KM# 80 RUPEE

6.0000 g., Copper-Nickel, 26 mm. **Subject:** Youth Year **Obv:** Small asoka lion pedestal above denomination **Rev:** Three outlined profiles between dove and laurel branch **Edge:** Security

Date	Mintage	F	VF	XF	Unc	BU
1985(B)	—	—	0.35	0.60	1.25	—
Note: Mintage included in KM79.1						
1985(C)	—	—	0.50	1.00	2.00	—
Note: Mintage included in KM79.1						
1985(C) Proof	—	Value: 10.00				
Note: Mintage included in KM79.1						
1985(H)	—	—	2.00	3.00	5.00	—

KM# 81 RUPEE

6.0000 g., Copper-Nickel, 26 mm. **Series:** F.A.O. **Obv:** Asoka lion pedestal **Rev:** Two figures working in field

Date	Mintage	F	VF	XF	Unc	BU
1987(B)	234,223,000	—	0.35	0.60	1.25	—
1987B Proof	—	Value: 5.00				
1987(C)	Inc. above	—	0.50	1.00	2.00	—
1987(H)	191,120,000	—	1.50	3.00	4.00	—

KM# 82 RUPEE

6.0000 g., Copper-Nickel, 26 mm. **Series:** F.A.O. **Subject:** Rainfed farming **Obv:** Asoka lion pedestal **Rev:** Figure with flowers, rain cloud in background

Date	Mintage	F	VF	XF	Unc	BU
1988(B)	—	—	1.00	1.50	3.00	—
Note: Mintage included in KM79.1						
1988(C)	—	—	1.00	2.00	4.00	—
1988(H)	—	—	3.00	5.00	8.00	—

KM# 83.2 RUPEE

Copper-Nickel, 26 mm. **Obv:** Asoka lion pedestal **Rev:** Head right

Date	Mintage	F	VF	XF	Unc	BU
1989(B)	—	—	20.00	50.00	80.00	—

KM# A85 RUPEE

Copper-Nickel, 26 mm. **Subject:** Rajiv Gandhi **Obv:** Asoka lion pedestal above denomination **Rev:** Bust looking left **Note:** Mule.

Date	Mintage	F	VF	XF	Unc	BU
1989(B)	—	—	1.50	4.00	10.00	—

KM# 84 RUPEE

6.0000 g., Copper-Nickel, 26 mm. **Series:** F.A.O. **Subject:** Food and Environment **Obv:** Asoka lion pedestal **Rev:** Sun above wheat stalks

Date	Mintage	F	VF	XF	Unc	BU
1989(N)	—	—	1.00	2.00	3.50	—
1989(H)	—	—	5.00	8.00	10.00	—
1989(B)	—	—	1.00	2.00	3.50	—

KM# 83.1 RUPEE

6.0000 g., Copper-Nickel, 26 mm. **Subject:** 100th Anniversary of Nehru's Birth **Obv:** Asoka lion pedestal **Rev:** Head right **Note:** Mule.

Date	Mintage	F	VF	XF	Unc	BU
1989B Proof	—	Value: 5.00				
1989(C)	—	—	1.00	2.00	3.00	—
1989(B)	—	—	0.25	0.50	1.00	—
1989(H)	—	—	1.00	2.00	3.00	—

KM# 87.1 RUPEE

6.0000 g., Copper-Nickel, 26 mm. **Subject:** SAARC Year - Care for the Girl Child **Obv:** Asoka lion pedestal **Rev:** Girl cutout below sun, symbol at left **Edge:** Security

Date	Mintage	F	VF	XF	Unc	BU
1990(B)	—	—	0.40	0.80	2.00	—

KM# 87.2 RUPEE

6.0000 g., Copper-Nickel, 26 mm. **Subject:** SAARC Year - Care for the Girl Child **Obv:** Asoka lion pedestal, denomination below **Rev:** Girl cutout below sun, symbol at left **Edge:** Milled **Note:** Edge varieties exist.

Date	Mintage	F	VF	XF	Unc	BU
1990(B)	—	—	0.50	1.25	3.00	—
1990(H)	—	—	0.50	1.25	3.00	—

KM# 85 RUPEE

6.0000 g., Copper-Nickel, 26 mm. **Subject:** Dr. Ambedkar **Obv:** Asoka lion pedestal, denomination below **Rev:** Bust looking right

Date	Mintage	F	VF	XF	Unc	BU
1990(B)	—	—	0.20	0.75	1.50	—
1990(H)	—	—	0.40	1.25	2.50	—

KM# 86 RUPEE

6.0000 g., Copper-Nickel, 26 mm. **Subject:** 15th Anniversary of I.C.D.S. **Obv:** Asoka lion pedestal, denomination below **Rev:** Seated figure holding child, radiant design surrounds

Date	Mintage	F	VF	XF	Unc	BU
ND(1990)(B)	—	—	0.20	0.75	1.50	—
ND(1990)(H)	—	—	0.40	1.25	2.50	—

KM# 88 RUPEE

6.0000 g., Copper-Nickel, 26 mm. **Series:** F.A.O. **Obv:** Asoka lion pedestal, denomination below **Rev:** Farming scene

Date	Mintage	F	VF	XF	Unc	BU
1990(C)	—	—	3.00	5.00	8.00	—
Note: 1990(C) is seldom well struck						
1990(H)	—	—	5.00	7.00	10.00	—

KM# 89 RUPEE

6.0000 g., Copper-Nickel, 26 mm. **Subject:** Rajiv Gandhi **Obv:** Asoka lion pedestal, denomination below **Rev:** Head looking left **Note:** Edge varieties exist.

Date	Mintage	F	VF	XF	Unc	BU
ND(1991)(B)	—	—	0.35	0.75	1.50	—
Note: The Mumbai (Bombay) mint mark occasionally resembles the Noida mintmark						
ND(1991)(H)	—	—	0.40	1.00	2.00	—

KM# 90 RUPEE

6.0000 g., Copper-Nickel, 26 mm. **Subject:** Commonwealth Parliamentary Conference **Obv:** Asoka lion pedestal, denomination below **Rev:** Building

Date	Mintage	F	VF	XF	Unc	BU
1991(B)	—	—	0.35	0.75	1.50	—
1991(B) Prooflike	—	—	—	—	3.00	—
1991B Proof	—	Value: 5.00				

KM# 91 RUPEE

6.0000 g., Copper-Nickel, 26 mm. **Subject:** Tourism Year **Obv:** Asoka lion pedestal above denomination **Rev:** Stylized peacock

Date	Mintage	F	VF	XF	Unc	BU
1991(B)	—	—	0.35	0.75	1.50	—
1991(H)	—	—	0.60	1.25	2.50	—
1991(B) Prooflike	—	—	—	—	3.00	—
1991B Proof	—	Value: 5.00				

KM# 92.2 RUPEE
4.8500 g., Stainless Steel, 25 mm. **Obv:** Asoka lion pedestal **Rev:** Denomination and date, grain ears flank **Edge:** Plain

Date	Mintage	F	VF	XF	Unc	BU
1995(B)	—	—	1.00	1.50	2.50	—
1995(H)	—	—	1.00	1.50	2.50	—
1995(N)	—	—	1.00	1.50	2.50	—
1996(B)	—	—	0.15	0.35	0.60	—
1996(C)	—	—	0.15	0.35	0.60	—
1996(H)	—	—	0.15	0.35	0.60	—
1996(N)	—	—	0.15	0.35	0.60	—
1997(B)	—	—	0.15	0.35	0.60	—
1997(C)	—	—	0.15	0.35	0.60	—
1997(H)	—	—	1.50	2.00	3.00	—
1997(M)	—	—	0.15	0.35	0.50	—
1997(N)	—	—	0.15	0.35	0.50	—
1998(B)	—	—	0.15	0.35	0.50	—
1998(P)	—	—	0.15	0.30	0.45	—
1998(C)	—	—	0.15	0.35	0.50	—
1998(H)	—	—	0.15	0.35	0.50	—
1998(K)	—	—	0.15	0.35	0.50	—
1998(N)	—	—	0.15	0.35	0.50	—
1999(B)	—	—	0.15	0.35	0.50	—
1999(K)	—	—	0.15	0.30	0.45	—
1999(P)	—	—	0.15	0.30	0.45	—
1999(N)	—	—	0.15	0.30	0.45	—
1999(C)	—	—	0.15	0.35	0.50	—
1999(H)	—	—	0.15	0.35	0.50	—
2000(B)	—	—	0.15	0.30	0.45	—
2000(K)	—	—	0.15	0.30	0.45	—
2000(C)	—	—	0.15	0.30	0.45	—
2000(H)	—	—	0.15	0.30	0.45	—
2000(N)	—	—	0.15	0.30	0.45	—

KM# 92.1 RUPEE
4.8500 g., Stainless Steel, 25 mm. **Obv:** Asoka lion pedestal **Rev:** Denomination and date, grain ears flank **Edge:** Milled **Note:** Edge sometimes faint.

Date	Mintage	F	VF	XF	Unc	BU
1992(H)	—	—	0.20	0.30	0.60	—
1992(B)	—	—	0.20	0.30	0.60	—
1993(B)	—	—	0.20	0.30	0.60	—
Note: Two mintmark shapes exist						
1993(C)	—	—	0.20	0.30	0.60	—
1993(H)	—	—	0.20	0.30	0.60	—
1993(N)	—	—	0.20	0.30	0.60	—
1994(B)	—	—	0.15	0.25	0.50	—
Note: Two mintmark shapes exist						
1994(C)	—	—	0.15	0.25	0.50	—
1994(H)	—	—	0.15	0.25	0.50	—
1994(N)	—	—	0.15	0.25	0.50	—
1995(B)	—	—	0.15	0.25	0.50	—
1995(C)	—	—	0.15	0.25	0.50	—
1995(H)	—	—	0.15	0.25	0.50	—
1995(N)	—	—	0.15	0.25	0.50	—
1996(H)	—	—	1.00	1.50	2.50	—

KM# 93 RUPEE
Copper-Nickel **Subject:** Quit India **Obv:** Asoka lion pedestal, denomination below **Rev:** Monument **Edge:** Milled

Date	Mintage	F	VF	XF	Unc	BU
ND(1992)(C)	—	—	1.00	3.00	6.00	—
ND(1992)(H)	—	—	2.00	3.50	8.00	—
ND(1992)(B)	—	—	0.50	1.00	2.00	—

KM# 94 RUPEE.
Copper-Nickel **Series:** World Food Day **Obv:** Asoka lion pedestal, denomination below **Rev:** Food items left of grain stalks

Date	Mintage	F	VF	XF	Unc	BU
1992(C)	—	—	1.50	2.50	4.50	—

KM# 95 RUPEE
Copper-Nickel **Subject:** Inter Parliamentary Union Conference **Obv:** Asoka lion pedestal, denomination below **Rev:** Small building and date within wreath below curved building

Date	Mintage	F	VF	XF	Unc	BU
1993(B)	—	—	0.50	1.25	3.00	—

KM# 96 RUPEE
Stainless Steel **Subject:** International Year of the Family **Obv:** Asoka lion pedestal, denomination below **Rev:** Family group forms circular design at center

Date	Mintage	F	VF	XF	Unc	BU
1994(B)	—	—	0.40	0.75	2.00	—
1994(N)	—	—	1.00	1.50	2.50	—

KM# 97.1 RUPEE
Stainless Steel **Subject:** Eighth World Tamil Conference **Obv:** Asoka lion pedestal, denomination below **Rev:** St. Thiruvalluvar **Edge:** Milled

Date	Mintage	F	VF	XF	Unc	BU
1995(B)	—	—	0.50	1.00	1.50	—
1995(H)	—	—	0.70	1.25	2.00	—
1995(N)	—	—	0.50	1.00	1.75	—

KM# 97.2 RUPEE
Stainless Steel **Obv:** Asoka lion pedestal, denomination below **Rev:** St. Thiruvalluvar **Edge:** Plain

Date	Mintage	F	VF	XF	Unc	BU
1995(H)	—	—	4.00	7.00	10.00	—
1995(N)	—	—	4.00	7.00	10.00	—

KM# 98 RUPEE
Stainless Steel **Obv:** Asoka lion pedestal, denomination below **Rev:** Cellular jail, Port Blair **Note:** Varieties exist.

Date	Mintage	F	VF	XF	Unc	BU
1997(B)	—	—	0.30	0.50	0.80	—
1997(C)	—	—	0.30	0.50	0.80	—
1997(H)	—	—	0.30	0.50	0.80	—
1997(N)	—	—	0.40	0.60	1.00	—

KM# 295.2 RUPEE
5.0000 g., Stainless Steel **Subject:** St. Dnyaneshwar **Obv:** Asoka lion pedestal, denomination below **Rev:** Seated figure **Note:** Asoka column 13.8mm tall.

Date	Mintage	F	VF	XF	Unc	BU
1999(B)	—	—	0.40	0.60	1.00	—
1999(N)	—	—	1.00	1.50	2.50	—

KM# 295.3 RUPEE
5.0000 g., Stainless Steel **Obv:** Asoka lion pedestal, denominaton below **Rev:** Seated figure **Note:** Asoka column 14.5mm tall.

Date	Mintage	F	VF	XF	Unc	BU
1999(N)	—	—	1.50	2.50	4.00	—

KM# 295.1 RUPEE
5.0000 g., Stainless Steel **Subject:** St. Dnyaneshwar **Obv:** Asoka lion pedestal, denomination below **Rev:** Seated figure **Note:** Asoka column 13.2mm tall.

Date	Mintage	F	VF	XF	Unc	BU
1999(B)	—	—	1.75	3.00	5.00	—
1999(C)	—	—	0.60	0.90	1.50	—

2 RUPEES

2 Rupee Obverses

A. Asoka column 15mm tall. 5 fur rows on right lion. No lion whiskers, circle in central wheel.

B. Asoka column 14mm tall. 3 fur rows on right lion. 5 lion whiskers, no circle in central wheel.

C. Asoka column 13mm tall. 4 fur rows on right lion. No dot in central wheel.

D. Asoka column 13mm tall. 4 fur rows. Recut chest on central lion. Dot in central wheel.

E. Asoka column 13mm tall. No fur rows on right lion. 2 whiskers on central lion.

NOTE: Obverses C and D include both 4.5 x 5mm and 5 x 5.5mm numeral 2 varieties.

KM# 120 2 RUPEES
Copper-Nickel **Subject:** IX Asian Games **Obv:** Asoka lion pedestal, denomination below **Rev:** Sun above logo

Date	Mintage	F	VF	XF	Unc	BU
1982(B)	12,720,000	—	0.35	0.50	1.25	—
1982B Proof	Inc. above	Value: 2.50				
1982(C)	Inc. above	—	0.35	0.50	1.25	—

KM# 121.1 2 RUPEES
Copper-Nickel **Subject:** National Integration **Obv:** Type B **Rev:** Flag on map

Date	Mintage	F	VF	XF	Unc	BU
1982B Proof	—	Value: 3.50				
1982(C)	—	—	0.30	1.00	2.25	—

Date	Mintage	F	VF	XF	Unc	BU
Note: Mintage included in KM120						
1982(B)	—	—	0.30	1.00	1.75	—
Note: Mintage included in KM120						

KM# 121.2 2 RUPEES

Copper-Nickel **Obv:** Type A **Rev:** Flag on map

Date	Mintage	F	VF	XF	Unc	BU
1990(B)	—	—	0.40	1.00	2.25	—
1990(C)	—	—	0.40	1.00	2.25	—
1990(H)	—	—	0.80	3.00	5.00	—

KM# 121.3 2 RUPEES

Copper-Nickel, 26 mm. **Obv:** Type A **Rev:** Flag on map **Shape:** 11-sided **Note:** Reduced size.

Date	Mintage	F	VF	XF	Unc	BU
1992(B)	—	—	2.50	4.00	7.00	—
1992(C)	—	—	0.30	0.50	1.00	—
1992(H)	—	—	0.40	1.00	1.50	—
1993(C)	—	—	0.40	1.25	2.00	—
1993(H)	—	—	0.35	0.60	1.25	—
1994(C)	—	—	0.40	1.25	2.00	—
1994(H)	—	—	0.35	0.80	1.50	—
1995(B)	—	—	2.50	4.00	7.00	—
1995(C)	—	—	0.30	0.50	1.00	—
1995(H)	—	—	0.30	0.50	1.00	—
1996(C)	—	—	0.30	0.50	1.00	—
1996(H)	—	—	0.30	0.50	1.00	—
1997(C)	—	—	0.30	0.50	1.00	—
1997(H)	—	—	0.30	0.50	1.00	—
1998(C)	—	—	0.30	0.50	1.00	—
1999(C)	—	—	0.30	0.50	1.00	—
2000(C)	—	—	0.30	0.50	1.00	—

KM# 121.4 2 RUPEES

Copper-Nickel **Obv:** Type B **Rev:** Flag on map **Shape:** 11-sided

Date	Mintage	F	VF	XF	Unc	BU
1992(B)	—	—	0.30	0.50	1.00	—
1993(B)	—	—	0.30	0.50	1.00	—
1994(B)	—	—	0.30	0.50	1.00	—
1994(H)	—	—	2.75	5.00	6.50	—
1994(N)	—	—	2.75	5.00	6.50	—
1995(B)	—	—	0.30	0.50	1.00	—
1995(H)	—	—	3.00	5.50	8.00	—
1995(N)	—	—	0.30	0.50	1.00	—
1996(B)	—	—	2.50	4.00	6.00	—
1996(B-H)	—	—	5.00	10.00	15.00	—
1996(N)	—	—	0.30	0.50	1.00	—
1997(B)	—	—	0.30	0.50	1.00	—
1998(N)	—	—	0.30	0.50	1.00	—
1999(N)	—	—	0.30	0.50	1.00	—

KM# 121.5 2 RUPEES

Copper-Nickel **Obv:** Type C **Rev:** Flag on map

Date	Mintage	F	VF	XF	Unc	BU
1995(B)	—	—	2.50	4.00	6.00	—
1996(B)	—	—	0.30	0.50	1.00	—
1996(H)	—	—	0.30	0.50	1.00	—
1997(B)	—	—	0.30	0.50	1.00	—
1997(H)	—	—	0.30	0.50	1.00	—
1997(T)	—	—	0.30	0.50	1.00	—
1998(B)	—	—	0.30	0.50	1.00	—
1998(H)	—	—	0.30	0.50	1.00	—
1998(P)	—	—	0.30	0.50	1.00	—
1998(T)	—	—	0.30	0.50	1.00	—
1999(B)	—	—	0.30	0.50	1.00	—
1999(H)	—	—	0.30	0.50	1.00	—
1999(Ld)	—	—	0.30	0.50	1.00	—
1999(N)	—	—	0.30	0.50	1.00	—
1999(C)	—	—	0.30	0.50	1.00	—
2000(B)	—	—	0.30	0.50	1.00	—
2000(C)	—	—	0.30	0.50	1.00	—
2000(H)	—	—	0.30	0.50	1.00	—
2000(N)	—	—	0.30	0.50	1.00	—
2000(R)	—	—	0.30	0.50	1.00	—

KM# 122 2 RUPEES

Copper-Nickel **Subject:** Golden Jubilee of Reserve Bank of India **Obv:** Asoka lion pedestal, denomination below **Rev:** Lion in front of tree

Date	Mintage	F	VF	XF	Unc	BU
ND(1985)(B) Proof	—	Value: 60.00				

KM# 123 2 RUPEES

Copper-Nickel **Subject:** Tourism Year **Obv:** Asoka lion pedestal above denomination **Rev:** Stylized design

Date	Mintage	F	VF	XF	Unc	BU
1991 Prooflike	—	—	—	—	8.00	—
1991 Proof	—	Value: 12.00				

KM# 323 2 RUPEES

5.7500 g., Copper-Nickel, 26.4 mm. **Subject:** National Land Conservation **Obv:** Asoka lion pedestal above denomination **Rev:** Tree above wavy lines **Edge:** Plain **Shape:** Eleven sided

Date	Mintage	F	VF	XF	Unc	BU
1992 (1993)	—	—	—	—	—	—

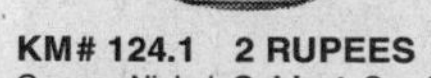

KM# 124.1 2 RUPEES

Copper-Nickel **Subject:** Small Family Happy Family **Obv:** Type B **Rev:** Family scene

Date	Mintage	F	VF	XF	Unc	BU
1993(B)	—	—	0.50	0.90	1.50	—

KM# 124.2 2 RUPEES

Copper-Nickel **Obv:** Type A **Rev:** Family scene

Date	Mintage	F	VF	XF	Unc	BU
1993(H)	—	—	2.00	3.00	5.00	—

KM# 125.1 2 RUPEES

Copper-Nickel **Series:** World Food Day **Subject:** Bio Diversity **Obv:** Type B **Rev:** Mountains, trees and fish

Date	Mintage	F	VF	XF	Unc	BU
1993(B)	—	—	0.50	0.90	1.50	—

KM# 125.2 2 RUPEES

Copper-Nickel **Obv:** Type A **Rev:** Mountains, trees and fish

Date	Mintage	F	VF	XF	Unc	BU
1993(H)	—	—	2.00	3.00	5.00	—

KM# 126.1 2 RUPEES

Copper-Nickel **Series:** F.A.O. **Subject:** Water For Life **Obv:** Type A **Rev:** Large teardrop above water

Date	Mintage	F	VF	XF	Unc	BU
1994(B)	—	—	0.60	1.10	2.00	—
1994(C)	—	—	1.00	2.00	4.00	—
1994(H)	—	—	2.00	4.50	11.00	—

KM# 126.2 2 RUPEES

Copper-Nickel **Obv:** Type B **Rev:** Large teardrop above water

Date	Mintage	F	VF	XF	Unc	BU
1994(B)	—	20.00	35.00	50.00	75.00	—

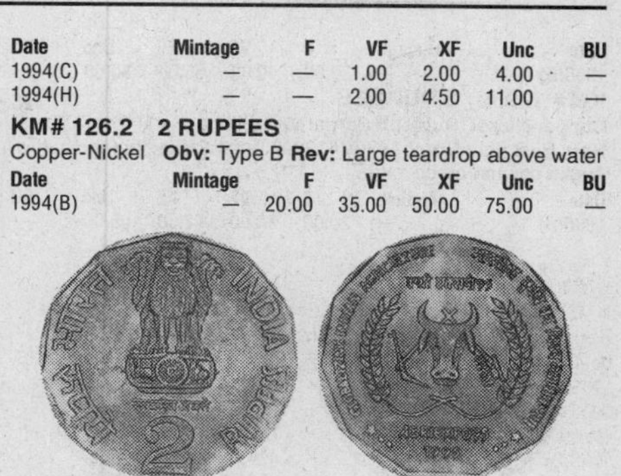

KM# 127.1 2 RUPEES

Copper-Nickel **Subject:** Globalizing Indian Agriculture - Agriexpo 95 **Obv:** Type A **Rev:** Steer head within wreath of two stalks of wheat

Date	Mintage	F	VF	XF	Unc	BU
1995(B)	—	—	0.60	1.25	2.00	—
1995(C)	—	—	1.00	3.00	6.00	—

KM# 127.2 2 RUPEES

Copper-Nickel **Obv:** Type B **Rev:** Steer head within wreath of two stalks of wheat

Date	Mintage	F	VF	XF	Unc	BU
1995(B)	—	20.00	30.00	50.00	75.00	—

KM# 127.3 2 RUPEES

Copper-Nickel **Obv:** Type C **Rev:** Steer head within wreath of two stalks of wheat

Date	Mintage	F	VF	XF	Unc	BU
1995(B)	—	30.00	50.00	75.00	100	—

KM# 128 2 RUPEES

Copper-Nickel **Subject:** Eighth World Tamil Conference **Obv:** Type C, Asoka column 13mm tall **Rev:** St. Thiruvalluvar

Date	Mintage	F	VF	XF	Unc	BU
1995(B)	—	—	0.60	1.00	1.75	—

KM# 129.1 2 RUPEES

Copper-Nickel **Subject:** Sardar Vallabhbhai Patel **Obv:** Type A **Rev:** Bust right

Date	Mintage	F	VF	XF	Unc	BU
1995(B)	—	—	2.50	4.00	7.00	—
1996M Proof	—	Value: 8.00				
1996(C)	—	—	2.50	4.00	7.00	—

KM# 129.2 2 RUPEES

Copper-Nickel **Subject:** Sardar Vallabhbhai Patel **Obv:** Type B **Rev:** Bust right

Date	Mintage	F	VF	XF	Unc	BU
1996(N)	—	—	1.00	1.50	3.00	—

KM# 129.3 2 RUPEES

Copper-Nickel **Subject:** Sardar Vallabhbhai Patel **Obv:** Type C **Rev:** Bust right

Date	Mintage	F	VF	XF	Unc	BU
1996(B)	—	—	2.00	3.00	5.00	—
1996(H)	—	—	0.40	0.70	1.25	—

KM# 129.4 2 RUPEES

Copper-Nickel **Subject:** Sardar Vallabhbhai Patel **Obv:** Type D **Rev:** Bust right

Date	Mintage	F	VF	XF	Unc	BU
1996(B)	—	—	0.40	0.70	1.25	—
1996(C)	—	—	0.30	0.60	1.00	—

KM# 129.5 2 RUPEES

Copper-Nickel **Subject:** Sardar Vallabhbhai Patel **Obv:** Type E **Rev:** Bust right

Date	Mintage	F	VF	XF	Unc	BU
1996(B)	—	30.00	40.00	55.00	80.00	—

KM# 129.6 2 RUPEES

Copper-Nickel **Subject:** Sardar Vallabhbhai Patel **Obv:** Type E **Rev:** Bust right **Note:** As KM#129.5, but with die damage below Asoka column on obverse.

Date	Mintage	F	VF	XF	Unc	BU
1996(B)	—	20.00	30.00	42.50	65.00	—

KM# 130.1 2 RUPEES

Copper-Nickel **Subject:** Subhas Chandra Bose **Obv:** Type C **Rev:** Bust left

Date	Mintage	F	VF	XF	Unc	BU
1996(C)	—	—	10.00	12.00	15.00	—
1997(B)	—	—	0.60	0.90	1.25	—
1997(C)	—	—	0.60	0.90	1.25	—
1997(H)	—	—	1.50	2.50	4.00	—
1997(M) Proof	—	Value: 3.25				

KM# 130.2 2 RUPEES

Copper-Nickel **Subject:** Subhas Chandra Bose **Obv:** Type B **Rev:** Bust left

Date	Mintage	F	VF	XF	Unc	BU
1997(N)	—	—	1.00	2.00	3.50	—
1997(H)	—	—	0.60	0.90	1.25	—

KM# 131.1 2 RUPEES

Copper-Nickel **Subject:** Sri Aurobindo **Obv:** Type C **Rev:** Head 3/4 facing

Date	Mintage	F	VF	XF	Unc	BU
1998(B)	—	—	0.60	0.90	1.50	—
1998(N)	—	—	1.00	1.50	3.00	—
1998(C)	—	—	1.00	1.50	3.00	—
1998(M) Proof	—	Value: 3.50				
1999(C)	—	—	1.00	1.50	3.00	—
1999(H)	—	—	1.00	1.50	3.00	—

KM# 121.6 2 RUPEES

Copper-Nickel **Obv:** Type D **Rev:** Flag on map

Date	Mintage	F	VF	XF	Unc	BU
1998(B)	—	—	0.30	0.50	1.00	—
1998(H)	—	—	0.30	0.50	1.00	—
1999(B)	—	—	0.75	1.00	1.50	—
2000(B)	—	—	0.75	1.00	1.50	—

KM# 296.5 2 RUPEES

Copper-Nickel **Obv:** Type C **Rev:** Head facing **Note:** 3-5mm, edge flat.

Date	Mintage	F	VF	XF	Unc	BU
1998(N)	—	—	2.00	3.00	5.00	—
1998(C)	—	—	3.00	4.00	6.00	—

KM# 131.2 2 RUPEES

Copper-Nickel **Subject:** Sri Aurobindo **Obv:** Type D **Rev:** Head 3/4 facing

Date	Mintage	F	VF	XF	Unc	BU
1998(B)	—	—	3.00	5.00	8.00	—

KM# 296.1 2 RUPEES

Copper-Nickel **Subject:** Deshbandhu Chittaranjan Das **Obv:** Type A **Rev:** Head facing

Date	Mintage	F	VF	XF	Unc	BU
1998(C)	—	—	10.00	15.00	25.00	—

KM# 296.2 2 RUPEES

Copper-Nickel **Subject:** Deshbandhu Chittaranjan Das **Obv:** Type B **Rev:** Head facing

Date	Mintage	F	VF	XF	Unc	BU
1998(N)	—	—	3.00	4.00	6.00	—

KM# 296.3 2 RUPEES

Copper-Nickel **Subject:** Deshbandhu Chittaranjan Das **Obv:** Type C **Rev:** Head facing **Note:** 7mm, edge flat.

Date	Mintage	F	VF	XF	Unc	BU
1998(C)	—	—	4.00	6.00	8.00	—

KM# 296.4 2 RUPEES

Copper-Nickel **Obv:** Type C **Rev:** Head facing **Note:** 5-6mm, edge flat.

Date	Mintage	F	VF	XF	Unc	BU
1998(C)	—	—	6.00	8.00	12.00	—

KM# 296.6 2 RUPEES

Copper-Nickel **Subject:** Deshbandhu Chittaranjan Das **Obv:** Type D **Rev:** Head facing **Note:** 3-5mm, edge flat.

Date	Mintage	F	VF	XF	Unc	BU
1998(C)	—	—	0.75	1.25	2.00	—

KM# 290 2 RUPEES

Copper-Nickel **Subject:** Chhatrapati Shivaji **Obv:** Type C **Rev:** Turbaned bust right

Date	Mintage	F	VF	XF	Unc	BU
1999(B)	—	—	0.75	1.25	2.00	—
1999(N)	—	—	0.75	1.25	2.00	—
1999(C)	—	—	0.75	1.25	2.00	—
1999(H)	—	—	1.00	1.75	3.00	—

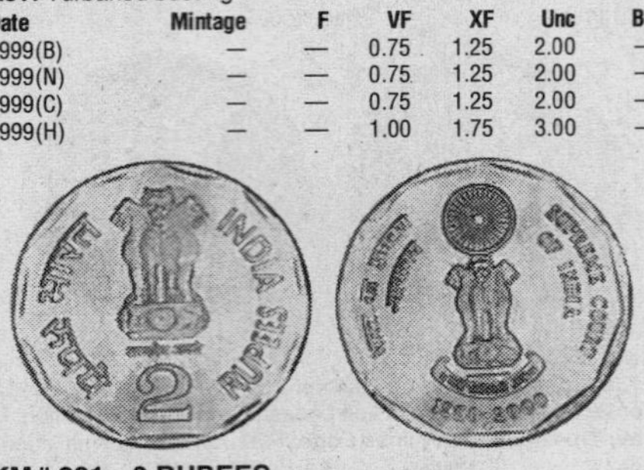

KM# 291 2 RUPEES

6.0000 g., Copper-Nickel **Subject:** Supreme Court: 50 Years **Obv:** Type C **Rev:** Wheel above asoka lion pedestal **Edge:** Plain

Date	Mintage	F	VF	XF	Unc	BU
2000(B)	—	—	0.75	1.25	2.00	—
2000(C)	—	—	0.75	1.25	2.00	—

KM# 150 5 RUPEES

Copper-Nickel **Subject:** Death of Indira Gandi - statesperson, 1917-1984 **Obv:** Asoka lion pedestal, denomination below **Rev:** Bust right

Date	Mintage	F	VF	XF	Unc	BU
ND(1985)(B)	59,288,000	—	0.75	1.50	3.00	—
ND(1985)B Proof	Inc. above	Value: 27.50				
ND(1985)(H)	Inc. above	—	3.50	6.00	15.00	—

KM# 151 5 RUPEES

Copper-Nickel **Subject:** Centennial - Nehru's Birth **Obv:** Asoka lion pedestal, denomination below **Rev:** Head right

Date	Mintage	F	VF	XF	Unc	BU
1989(B)	—	—	1.00	2.00	3.00	—
Note: Short rim teeth.						
1989(B)	—	—	2.00	3.00	4.50	—
Note: Long rim teeth.						
1989B Proof	—	Value: 25.00				
1989(H)	—	—	3.50	6.00	15.00	—

KM# 152 5 RUPEES

Copper-Nickel **Subject:** Commonwealth Parliamentary Conference **Obv:** Asoka lion pedestal, denomination below **Rev:** Building

Date	Mintage	F	VF	XF	Unc	BU
1991(B) Prooflike	—	—	—	—	10.00	—
1991B Proof	—	Value: 20.00				

KM# 153 5 RUPEES

Copper-Nickel **Subject:** Tourism **Obv:** Asoka lion pedestal, denomination below **Rev:** Stylized design

Date	Mintage	F	VF	XF	Unc	BU
1991(B) Prooflike	—	—	—	—	10.00	—
1991B Proof	—	Value: 20.00				

KM# 154.1 5 RUPEES

Copper-Nickel, 23 mm. **Obv:** Asoka lion pedestal **Rev:** Denomination flanked by flowers **Note:** (C) - Calcutta mint has issued 2 distinctly different security edge varieties every year 1992-2003.

Date	Mintage	F	VF	XF	Unc	BU
1992(B)	—	—	0.20	0.75	1.50	—
1992(C)	—	—	0.20	0.75	1.50	—
1992(H)	—	—	0.20	0.75	1.50	—
1993(B)	—	—	0.20	0.75	1.50	—
1993(C)	—	—	0.20	0.75	1.50	—
1994(B)	—	—	0.20	0.75	1.50	—
1994(C)	—	—	0.20	0.75	1.50	—
1994(H)	—	—	0.20	0.75	1.50	—
1995(B)	—	—	0.20	0.75	1.50	—
1995(C)	—	—	0.20	0.75	1.50	—
1995(H)	—	—	0.20	0.75	1.50	—
1995(N)	—	—	0.20	0.75	1.50	—
1996(B)	—	—	0.20	0.50	1.00	—
1996(C)	—	—	0.20	0.50	1.00	—
1996(H)	—	—	0.20	0.50	1.00	—
1996(N)	—	—	0.20	0.50	1.00	—
1997(B)	—	—	0.20	0.50	1.00	—
1997(C)	—	—	0.20	0.50	1.00	—
1997(H)	—	—	0.20	0.50	1.00	—
1997(N)	—	—	0.20	0.50	1.00	—
1998(B)	—	—	0.20	0.50	1.00	—
1998(C)	—	—	0.20	0.50	1.00	—
1998(H)	—	—	0.25	0.50	1.00	—
1998(N)	—	—	0.25	0.50	1.00	—
1999(B)	—	—	0.50	0.25	1.00	—
1999M	—	—	0.25	0.50	1.00	—
1999(C)	—	—	0.25	0.50	1.00	—
1999(H)	—	—	0.25	0.50	1.00	—
1999(N)	—	—	0.25	0.50	1.00	—
1999(R)	—	—	0.25	0.50	1.00	—
2000(B)	—	—	0.50	0.25	1.00	—
2000(C)	—	—	0.25	0.50	1.00	—
2000(H)	—	—	0.50	1.00	2.00	—
2000(R)	—	—	0.25	0.50	1.00	—
2000(N)	—	—	0.25	0.50	1.00	—

KM# 154.2 5 RUPEES

Copper-Nickel, 23 mm. **Obv:** Asoka lion pedestal **Rev:** Denomination flanked by flowers **Edge:** Milled

Date	Mintage	F	VF	XF	Unc	BU
1996(C)	—	—	8.00	10.00	15.00	—
1997(C)	—	—	8.00	10.00	15.00	—
1997(H)	—	—	8.00	10.00	15.00	—
1998(H)	—	—	8.00	10.00	15.00	—
1998(C)	—	—	8.00	10.00	15.00	—
1999(C)	—	—	8.00	10.00	15.00	—
1999(H)	—	—	8.00	10.00	15.00	—
2000(C)	—	—	8.00	10.00	15.00	—

KM# 154.3 5 RUPEES

Copper-Nickel, 23 mm. **Obv:** Asoka lion pedestal **Rev:** Denomination flanked by flowers **Edge:** Plain

Date	Mintage	F	VF	XF	Unc	BU
1998(H) Error	—	—	5.00	10.00	15.00	—

KM# 154.4 5 RUPEES

Copper-Nickel, 23 mm. **Obv:** Asoka lion pedestal **Rev:** Denomination flanked by flowers

Date	Mintage	F	VF	XF	Unc	BU
1998(B)	—	—	0.25	0.50	1.00	—
1999(B)	—	—	0.25	0.50	1.00	—
2000(B)	—	—	0.25	0.50	1.00	—

KM# 155 5 RUPEES

Copper-Nickel, 23 mm. **Subject:** World of Work **Obv:** Asoka lion pedestal, denomination below **Rev:** Denomination within broken dentil circle, wreath surrounds **Edge:** Security

Date	Mintage	F	VF	XF	Unc	BU
ND(1994)(B)	—	—	0.75	1.00	1.75	—
ND(1994)B Proof	—	Value: 5.00				
ND(1994)(H)	—	—	1.50	2.25	4.00	—
ND(1994)(N)	—	—	1.00	1.50	3.00	—

KM# 156 5 RUPEES
Copper-Nickel, 23 mm. **Series:** 50 Years - United Nations **Obv:** Asoka lion pedestal, denomination below **Rev:** Date above UN logo

Date	Mintage	F	VF	XF	Unc	BU
1995(B)	—	—	0.75	1.00	1.75	—
1995(N)	—	—	1.00	1.50	3.00	—

KM# 157 5 RUPEES
Copper-Nickel, 23 mm. **Series:** 50th Anniversary - F.A.O. **Obv:** Asoka lion pedestal, denomination below **Rev:** Hand clutching stalks of wheat

Date	Mintage	F	VF	XF	Unc	BU
1995(B)	—	—	0.75	1.00	1.75	—
1995(H)	—	—	1.50	3.00	5.00	—
1995(N)	—	—	1.00	1.50	3.00	—

KM# 158 5 RUPEES
Copper-Nickel, 23 mm. **Subject:** Eighth World Tamil Conference **Obv:** Asoka lion pedestal, denomination below **Rev:** St. Thiruvalluvar

Date	Mintage	F	VF	XF	Unc	BU
1995(B)	—	—	0.75	1.00	1.75	—

KM# 159 5 RUPEES
Copper-Nickel, 23 mm. **Subject:** Mother's Health is Child's Health

Date	Mintage	F	VF	XF	Unc	BU
1996(B)	—	—	0.75	1.00	1.50	—
1996(H)	—	—	0.75	1.00	1.50	—
1996(N)	—	—	1.00	1.50	2.25	—

KM# 160 5 RUPEES
Copper-Nickel, 23 mm. **Subject:** 2nd International Crop Science Conference **Obv:** Asoka lion pedestal, denomination below **Rev:** Plants on globe, spray below, braid above **Note:** This conference was never held.

Date	Mintage	F	VF	XF	Unc	BU
1996(C)	11,000	—	15.00	17.00	20.00	—

KM# 185 10 RUPEES
15.0000 g., 0.8000 Silver .3858 oz. ASW **Subject:** Centennial - Mahatma Gandhi's Birth **Obv:** Asoka lion pedestal, denomination below **Rev:** Head left **Note:** Struck during 1969 and 1970.

Date	Mintage	F	VF	XF	Unc	BU
ND(1969)(B)	3,160,000	—	—	6.00	9.00	—
ND(1969)B Proof	9,147	Value: 10.00				
ND(1969)(C)	100,000	—	—	7.00	10.00	—

KM# 186 10 RUPEES
15.0000 g., 0.8000 Silver .3858 oz. ASW **Series:** F.A.O. **Obv:** Asoka lion pedestal **Rev:** Floating lotus flower below sun

Date	Mintage	F	VF	XF	Unc	BU
1970(B)	300,000	—	—	6.00	9.00	—
1970B Proof	3,046	Value: 9.00				
1970(C)	100,000	—	—	7.00	10.00	—
1971(B)	—	—	—	7.00	10.00	—
1971B Proof	1,594	Value: 10.00				

KM# 187 10 RUPEES
22.5000 g., 0.5000 Silver .3617 oz. ASW **Subject:** 25th Anniversary of Independence **Obv:** Asoka lion pedestal **Rev:** Figures holding flag, building in background **Designer:** P. B. Chitnis

Date	Mintage	F	VF	XF	Unc	BU
ND(1972)(B)	1,000,000	—	—	—	7.50	—
ND(1972)B Proof	7,895	Value: 9.50				

KM# 187a 10 RUPEES
Copper-Nickel **Obv:** Asoka lion pedestal **Rev:** Figures holding flag, building in background

Date	Mintage	F	VF	XF	Unc	BU
ND(1972)(B)	—	—	—	—	6.00	—
ND(1972)(C)	—	—	—	—	6.00	—

Note: Rim thinner, inner flag circle missing on Calcutta issues

KM# 188 10 RUPEES
22.3000 g., 0.5000 Silver .3585 oz. ASW **Series:** F.A.O. **Obv:** Asoka lion pedestal **Rev:** Inscription on shield within grain stalks

Date	Mintage	F	VF	XF	Unc	BU
1973(B)	64,000	—	—	—	7.00	—
1973B Proof	15,000	Value: 9.50				

KM# 189 10 RUPEES
Copper-Nickel **Series:** F.A.O. **Obv:** Asoka lion pedestal **Rev:** Family within triangle, grain ears flank

Date	Mintage	F	VF	XF	Unc	BU
1974(B)	65,000	—	—	2.00	4.50	—
1974B Proof	12,000	Value: 7.00				

KM# 190 10 RUPEES
Copper-Nickel **Series:** F.A.O. **Subject:** Women's Year **Obv:** Asoka lion pedestal **Rev:** Bust at left looking right, grain ear at right **Designer:** N. B. Sabannavar

Date	Mintage	F	VF	XF	Unc	BU
1975(B)	49,000	—	—	2.00	4.50	—
1975B Proof	2,531	Value: 8.50				

KM# 191 10 RUPEES
Copper-Nickel **Series:** F.A.O. **Subject:** Food and Work For All **Obv:** Asoka lion pedestal **Rev:** Figure on tractor, utility pole and buildings in background

Date	Mintage	F	VF	XF	Unc	BU
1976(B)	49,000	—	—	2.00	4.50	—
1976B Proof	3,400	Value: 8.50				

KM# 192 10 RUPEES
Copper-Nickel **Series:** F.A.O. **Subject:** Save For Development
Obv: Asoka lion pedestal **Rev:** Symbols of development

Date	Mintage	F	VF	XF	Unc	BU
1977(B)	20,000	—	—	2.00	4.50	—
1977B Proof	5,969	Value: 8.50				

KM# 193 10 RUPEES
Copper-Nickel **Series:** F.A.O. **Subject:** Food and Shelter For All **Obv:** Asoka lion pedestal **Rev:** Grain sprig, house and road within circle

Date	Mintage	F	VF	XF	Unc	BU
1978(B)	25,000	—	—	2.00	4.50	—
1978B Proof	—	Value: 8.50				

KM# 194 10 RUPEES
Copper-Nickel **Series:** International Year of the Child
Obv: Asoka lion pedestal, denomination below **Rev:** Logo on square within circle, wreath surrounds

Date	Mintage	F	VF	XF	Unc	BU
1979(B)	—	—	—	2.50	5.00	—
1979B Proof	—	Value: 9.50				

KM# 195 10 RUPEES
Copper-Nickel **Subject:** Rural Women's Advancement
Obv: Asoka lion pedestal, denomination below **Rev:** Woman grinding wheat

Date	Mintage	F	VF	XF	Unc	BU
1980(B)	—	—	—	2.50	5.00	—
1980B Proof	—	Value: 9.50				

KM# 196 10 RUPEES
Copper-Nickel **Series:** World Food Day **Obv:** Asoka lion pedestal **Rev:** Man and woman, man carrying sheaf

Date	Mintage	F	VF	XF	Unc	BU
1981(B)	—	—	—	2.50	5.00	—
1981B Proof	—	Value: 9.50				

KM# 197 10 RUPEES
Copper-Nickel **Subject:** IX Asian Games

Date	Mintage	F	VF	XF	Unc	BU
1982(B)	—	—	—	2.50	5.00	—
1982B Proof	—	Value: 9.50				

KM# 198 10 RUPEES
Copper-Nickel **Subject:** National Integration **Obv:** Asoka lion pedestal **Rev:** Flag on map

Date	Mintage	F	VF	XF	Unc	BU
1982(B)	—	—	—	—	6.00	—
1982B Proof	—	Value: 10.00				

KM# 199 10 RUPEES
Copper-Nickel **Subject:** Golden Jubilee - Reserve Bank of India
Obv: Asoka lion pedestal **Rev:** Lion in front of tree

Date	Mintage	F	VF	XF	Unc	BU
ND(1985)(B)	—	—	—	—	70.00	—
ND(1985)B Proof	—	Value: 80.00				

KM# 200 10 RUPEES
Copper-Nickel **Subject:** Youth Year **Obv:** Small asoka pedestal above denomination **Rev:** Three outlined profiles between dove and laurel branch

Date	Mintage	F	VF	XF	Unc	BU
1985(C)	—	—	—	—	10.00	—
1985(C) Proof	—	Value: 30.00				

KM# 201 10 RUPEES
Copper-Nickel **Subject:** Commonwealth Parliamentary Conference **Obv:** Asoka lion pedestal above denomination **Rev:** Building

Date	Mintage	F	VF	XF	Unc	BU
1991(B) Prooflike	—	—	—	—	10.00	—
1991B Proof	—	Value: 20.00				

KM# 202 10 RUPEES
Copper-Nickel **Subject:** India **Obv:** Asoka lion pedestal above denomination **Rev:** Monument

Date	Mintage	F	VF	XF	Unc	BU
1992(B) Proof	—	Value: 10.00				

KM# 203 10 RUPEES
Copper-Nickel **Subject:** 100th Anniversary - Birth of Patel
Obv: Type A **Rev:** Head right

Date	Mintage	F	VF	XF	Unc	BU
1996(B)	—	—	—	—	8.00	—
1996M Proof	—	Value: 12.00				

KM# 204 10 RUPEES
Copper-Nickel **Subject:** Subhas Chandra Bose **Obv:** Type C
Rev: Bust left

Date	Mintage	F	VF	XF	Unc	BU
1997(C)	—	—	—	—	8.00	—
1997M Proof	—	Value: 12.00				

KM# 205 10 RUPEES
Copper-Nickel **Subject:** Sri Aurobindo **Obv:** Type C **Rev:** Head 3/4 facing

Date	Mintage	F	VF	XF	Unc	BU
1998(B)	—	—	—	—	8.00	—
1998M Proof	—	Value: 12.00				

KM# 297 10 RUPEES
12.5000 g., Copper-Nickel, 31 mm. **Subject:** Deshbandhu Chittaranjan Das **Obv:** Asoka lion pedestal above denomination **Rev:** Bust facing **Edge:** Reeded

Date	Mintage	F	VF	XF	Unc	BU
1998(C)	—	—	—	—	7.50	—
1998(C) Proof	—	Value: 12.00				

KM# 240 20 RUPEES
30.0000 g., 0.5000 Silver .4823 oz. ASW **Series:** F.A.O.
Obv: Asoka lion pedestal, denomination below **Rev:** Inscription on shield, grain stalks flank

Date	Mintage	F	VF	XF	Unc	BU
1973(B)	64,000	—	—	—	8.50	—
1973B Proof	12,000	Value: 12.50				

KM# 241 20 RUPEES

Copper-Nickel **Subject:** Death of Indira Gandhi - statesperson, 1917-1984 **Rev:** Head right

Date	Mintage	F	VF	XF	Unc	BU
ND(1985)(B)	—	—	—	—	12.50	—
ND(1985)B Proof	—	Value: 50.00				

KM# 242 20 RUPEES

Copper-Nickel **Series:** F.A.O. **Subject:** Fisheries **Obv:** Asoka lion pedestal, denomination below **Rev:** People with fishing nets

Date	Mintage	F	VF	XF	Unc	BU
1986(B)	—	—	—	—	10.00	—
1986B Proof	—	Value: 20.00				

KM# 243 20 RUPEES

Copper-Nickel **Series:** F.A.O. **Subject:** Small Farmers **Obv:** Asoka lion pedestal, denomination below **Rev:** Farmers planting

Date	Mintage	F	VF	XF	Unc	BU
1987(B)	—	—	—	—	10.00	—
1987B Proof	—	Value: 20.00				

KM# 244 20 RUPEES

Copper-Nickel **Subject:** 100th Anniversary of Nehru's Birth **Obv:** Asoka lion pedestal, denomination below **Rev:** Head right

Date	Mintage	F	VF	XF	Unc	BU
1989(B)	—	—	—	—	10.00	—
1989B Proof	—	Value: 20.00				

KM# 255 50 RUPEES

34.7000 g., 0.5000 Silver .5578 oz. ASW **Series:** F.A.O. **Obv:** Asoka lion pedestal, denomination below **Rev:** Family within triangle, grain ears flank

Date	Mintage	F	VF	XF	Unc	BU
1974(B)	82,000	—	—	—	9.50	—
1974B Proof	13,000	Value: 12.50				

KM# 256 50 RUPEES

34.7000 g., 0.5000 Silver .5578 oz. ASW **Series:** F.A.O. **Subject:** Women's Year **Obv:** Asoka lion pedestal, denomination below **Rev:** Bust at left looking right, grain sprig at right **Designer:** N. B. Sabannavar

Date	Mintage	F	VF	XF	Unc	BU
1975(B)	65,000	—	—	—	11.50	—
1975B Proof	2,691	Value: 20.00				

KM# 257 50 RUPEES

34.7000 g., 0.5000 Silver .5578 oz. ASW **Series:** F.A.O. **Subject:** Food and Work For All **Obv:** Asoka lion pedestal, denomination below **Rev:** Figure on tractor, utility pole and buildings in background

Date	Mintage	F	VF	XF	Unc	BU
1976(B)	42,000	—	—	—	12.50	—
1976B Proof	3,385	Value: 20.00				

KM# 258 50 RUPEES

34.7000 g., 0.5000 Silver .5578 oz. ASW **Series:** F.A.O. **Subject:** Save For Development **Obv:** Asoka lion pedestal, denomination below **Rev:** Symbols of development

Date	Mintage	F	VF	XF	Unc	BU
1977(B)	26,000	—	—	—	12.50	—
1977B Proof	2,544	Value: 20.00				

KM# 259 50 RUPEES

34.7000 g., 0.5000 Silver .5578 oz. ASW **Series:** F.A.O. **Subject:** Food and Shelter For All **Obv:** Asoka lion pedestal, denomination below **Rev:** Grain stalk, house and road within circle

Date	Mintage	F	VF	XF	Unc	BU
1978(B)	25,000	—	—	—	12.50	—
1978B Proof	—	Value: 20.00				

KM# 260 50 RUPEES

34.7000 g., 0.5000 Silver .5578 oz. ASW **Series:** International Year of the Child **Obv:** Asoka lion pedestal, denomination below **Rev:** Emblem on square within circle, wreath surrounds

Date	Mintage	F	VF	XF	Unc	BU
1979(B)	—	—	—	—	12.50	—
1979B Proof	—	Value: 20.00				

KM# 261 50 RUPEES
Copper-Nickel **Subject:** India **Obv:** Asoka lion pedestal, denomination below **Rev:** Monument

Date	Mintage	F	VF	XF	Unc	BU
1992(B)	—	—	—	—	12.50	—

KM# 262 50 RUPEES
Copper-Nickel **Subject:** International Labor Organizations **Obv:** Asoka lion pedestal, denomination below **Rev:** Denomination within broken dentil circle, wreath surrounds

Date	Mintage	F	VF	XF	Unc	BU
ND(1994)	—	—	—	—	15.00	—
ND(1994) Proof	—	Value: 20.00				

KM# 263 50 RUPEES
Copper-Nickel **Subject:** 100th Anniversary - BIrth of Patel **Obv:** Type A **Rev:** Head right

Date	Mintage	F	VF	XF	Unc	BU
1996(B)	—	—	—	—	15.00	—
1996M Proof	—	Value: 30.00				

KM# 264 50 RUPEES
Copper-Nickel **Subject:** Subhas Chandra Bose **Obv:** Type C **Rev:** Bust left

Date	Mintage	F	VF	XF	Unc	BU
1997(C)	—	—	—	—	15.00	—
1997(C) Proof	—	Value: 45.00				

KM# 265 50 RUPEES
22.5000 g., 0.5000 Silver .3617 oz. ASW **Subject:** 50th Anniversary of Independence **Obv:** Small Asoka lion pedestal above large denomination **Rev:** Line of people

Date	Mintage	F	VF	XF	Unc	BU
1997(B)	—	—	—	—	35.00	—
1997M Proof	—	Value: 60.00				

KM# 266 50 RUPEES
22.5000 g., 0.5000 Silver .3617 oz. ASW **Subject:** Sri Aurobindo **Obv:** Type C **Rev:** Head 3/4 facing

Date	Mintage	F	VF	XF	Unc	BU
1998(B)	—	—	—	—	15.00	—
1998M Proof	—	Value: 30.00				

KM# 298 50 RUPEES
30.0000 g., Copper-Nickel, 39 mm. **Subject:** Deshbandhu Chittaranjan Das **Obv:** Type C **Rev:** Bust facing **Edge:** Reeded

Date	Mintage	F	VF	XF	Unc	BU
1998(C)	—	—	—	—	15.00	—
1998 Proof	—	Value: 30.00				

KM# 300 50 RUPEES
30.0000 g., Copper-Nickel, 39 mm. **Subject:** Chhatrapati Shivaji **Obv:** Asoka lion pedestal above denomination **Rev:** Turbaned bust right **Edge:** Reeded

Date	Mintage	F	VF	XF	Unc	BU
1999	—	—	—	—	16.50	—

KM# 293 50 RUPEES
Copper-Nickel **Subject:** Supreme Court - 50 Years **Obv:** Type C **Rev:** Wheel above asoka lion pedestal

Date	Mintage	F	VF	XF	Unc	BU
2000(B)	—	—	—	—	15.00	—
2000(C)	—	—	—	—	15.00	—

KM# 275 100 RUPEES
35.0000 g., 0.5000 Silver .5627 oz. ASW **Subject:** Rural Women's Advancement **Obv:** Asoka lion pedestal above denomination **Rev:** Woman grinding wheat

Date	Mintage	F	VF	XF	Unc	BU
1980(B)	21,000	—	—	—	18.50	—
1980B Proof	5,811	Value: 27.50				

KM# 276 100 RUPEES
35.0000 g., 0.5000 Silver .5627 oz. ASW **Series:** World Food Day

Date	Mintage	F	VF	XF	Unc	BU
1981(B)	22,000	—	—	—	18.50	—
1981B Proof	2,950	Value: 28.50				

KM# 277 100 RUPEES
29.1600 g., 0.9250 Silver .8673 oz. ASW **Series:** International Year of the Child **Obv:** Asoka lion pedestal, denomination below **Rev:** Native musicians and dancer

Date	Mintage	F	VF	XF	Unc	BU
1981 (1983)B Proof	—	Value: 25.00				

KM# 278 100 RUPEES
35.0000 g., 0.5000 Silver .5627 oz. ASW **Subject:** IX Asian Games

Date	Mintage	F	VF	XF	Unc	BU
1982(B)	—	—	—	—	17.50	—
1982B Proof	—	Value: 27.50				

KM# 279 100 RUPEES
35.0000 g., 0.5000 Silver .5627 oz. ASW **Subject:** National Integration **Obv:** Asoka lion pedestal above denomination **Rev:** Flag on map

Date	Mintage	F	VF	XF	Unc	BU
1982(B)	—	—	—	—	25.00	—
1982B Proof	—	Value: 35.00				

KM# 280 100 RUPEES
35.0000 g., 0.5000 Silver .5627 oz. ASW **Subject:** Golden Jubilee - Reserve Bank of India

Date	Mintage	F	VF	XF	Unc	BU
1985(B)	—	—	—	—	75.00	—
1985B Proof	—	Value: 85.00				

KM# 281 100 RUPEES
35.0000 g., 0.5000 Silver .5627 oz. ASW **Subject:** Death of Indira Gandhi - statesperson, 1917-1984 **Obv:** Asoka lion pedestal above denomination **Rev:** Bust right

Date	Mintage	F	VF	XF	Unc	BU
ND(1985)(B)	—	—	—	—	30.00	—
ND(1985)B Proof	—	Value: 70.00				

KM# 282 100 RUPEES
35.0000 g., 0.5000 Silver .5627 oz. ASW **Subject:** Youth Year **Obv:** Small Asoka lion pedestal, denomination below **Rev:** Three outlined profiles between dove and laurel branch

Date	Mintage	F	VF	XF	Unc	BU
1985(C)	16,000	—	—	—	30.00	—
1985(C) Proof	6,267	Value: 50.00				

KM# 283 100 RUPEES
35.0000 g., 0.5000 Silver .5627 oz. ASW **Series:** F.A.O. **Subject:** Fisheries **Obv:** Asoka lion pedestal, denomination below **Rev:** People with fishing nets

Date	Mintage	F	VF	XF	Unc	BU
1986(B)	—	—	—	—	30.00	—
1986B Proof	—	Value: 50.00				

KM# 284 100 RUPEES
35.0000 g., 0.5000 Silver .5627 oz. ASW **Series:** F.A.O. **Subject:** Small Farmers **Obv:** Asoka lion pedestal, denomination below **Rev:** Farmers planting

Date	Mintage	F	VF	XF	Unc	BU
1987(B)	—	—	—	—	30.00	—
1987B Proof	—	Value: 50.00				

KM# 285 100 RUPEES

35.0000 g., 0.5000 Silver .5627 oz. ASW **Subject:** 100th Anniversary of Nehru's Birth **Obv:** Asoka lion pedestal, denomination below **Rev:** Head right

Date	Mintage	F	VF	XF	Unc	BU
1989(B)	—	—	—	—	30.00	—
1989B Proof	—	Value: 50.00				

KM# 286 100 RUPEES

35.0000 g., 0.5000 Silver .5627 oz. ASW **Subject:** India **Obv:** Asoka lion pedestal, denomination below **Rev:** Monument

Date	Mintage	F	VF	XF	Unc	BU
1992(B)	—	—	—	—	25.00	—

KM# 287 100 RUPEES

35.0000 g., 0.5000 Silver .5627 oz. ASW **Subject:** World of Work **Obv:** Asoka lion pedestal, denomination below **Rev:** Denomination within broken dentil circle, wreath surrounds

Date	Mintage	F	VF	XF	Unc	BU
ND(1994)	—	—	—	—	25.00	—
ND(1994) Proof	—	Value: 40.00				

KM# 288 100 RUPEES

35.0000 g., 0.5000 Silver .5627 oz. ASW **Subject:** 100th Anniversary - Birth of Patel **Obv:** Type A **Rev:** Head right

Date	Mintage	F	VF	XF	Unc	BU
1996(B)	—	—	—	—	50.00	—
1996M Proof	—	Value: 70.00				

KM# 289 100 RUPEES

35.0000 g., 0.5000 Silver .5627 oz. ASW **Subject:** Subhas Chandra Bose **Obv:** Type C **Rev:** Bust left

Date	Mintage	F	VF	XF	Unc	BU
1997(C)	—	—	—	—	35.00	—

KM# 299 100 RUPEES

35.0000 g., 0.5000 Silver 0.5626 oz. ASW, 44 mm. **Subject:** Deshbandhu Chittaranjan Das **Obv:** Asoka lion pedestal, denomination below **Rev:** Bust facing **Edge:** Reeded

Date	Mintage	F	VF	XF	Unc	BU
1998(C)	—	—	—	—	30.00	—
1998(C) Proof	—	Value: 50.00				

KM# 292 100 RUPEES

35.0000 g., 0.5000 Silver .5627 oz. ASW **Subject:** Sri Aurobindo **Obv:** Type C **Rev:** Head 3/4 facing

Date	Mintage	F	VF	XF	Unc	BU
1998(B)	—	—	—	—	30.00	—
1998M Proof	—	Value: 50.00				

KM# 301 100 RUPEES

35.0000 g., 0.5000 Silver 0.5626 oz. ASW, 44 mm. **Subject:** Chhatrapati Shivaji **Obv:** Asoka lion pedestal, denomination below **Rev:** Turbaned bust right **Edge:** Reeded

Date	Mintage	F	VF	XF	Unc	BU
1999(C)	—	—	—	—	30.00	—
1999(C) Proof	—	Value: 50.00				

KM# 302 100 RUPEES

35.0000 g., 0.5000 Silver 0.5626 oz. ASW, 44 mm. **Subject:** St. Dnyanneshwar **Obv:** Asoka lion pedestal, denomination below **Rev:** Seated figure **Edge:** Reeded

Date	Mintage	F	VF	XF	Unc	BU
1999(C)	—	—	—	—	30.00	—
1999(C) Proof	—	Value: 50.00				

PATTERNS

Including off metal strikes

KM#	Date	Mintage	Identification	Mkt Val
Pn1	1946(B)	—	1/4 Rupee. Nickel. KM#548.	—
Pn2	1946(B)	—	1/2 Rupee. Nickel. KM#553.	—

KM#	Date	Mintage	Identification	Mkt Val
Pn3	1946(B)	—	Rupee. Nickel. KM#559.	—
Pn4	1947(B)	—	1/4 Rupee. Copper-Nickel.	—
Pn5	1947(B)	—	1/2 Rupee. Copper-Nickel.	—
Pn6	1947(B)	—	Rupee. Copper-Nickel.	—
Pn7	1947(B)	—	Rupee. Nickel. Set of Pn1-3.	1,500
Pn8	1949	—	Pice. Bronze.	—
Pn9	1949	—	Anna. Copper-Nickel.	—
Pn10	1949	—	2 Annas. Copper-Nickel. Profile peacock left.	—
Pn11	1949	—	2 Annas. Copper-Nickel. Facing displayed peacock.	—
PnA12	1949	—	2 Annas. Brass. Proof	—
Pn12	1949	—	1/4 Rupee. Nickel.	—
Pn13	1949	—	1/2 Rupee. Nickel. Worker with finished background.	—
Pn14	1949	—	1/2 Rupee. Nickel. Worker with plain background.	—
Pn15	1949	—	Rupee. Nickel. Standing figure.	—
Pn16	1949	—	Rupee. Nickel. Similar to Pn9.	—
Pn17	1964(C)	—	Paisa. Copper. Half thickness and weight.	—
Pn18	1992(C)	—	2 Rupees.	—

PIEFORTS

KM#	Date	Mintage	Identification	Mkt Val
P1	1981	—	100 Rupees. Silver. KM#277	250

MINT SETS

KM#	Date	Mintage	Identification	Issue Price	Mkt Val
MS3	1962(B) (6)	—	KM#8a, 11, 16, 24.2, 47.2, 55	1.50	5.00
MS4	1962(B) (7)	—	KM#8a, 11, 16, 24.2, 47.2, 55, 75.1(C)	3.60	8.00
MS5	ND(1964)(B) (2)	—	KM#56, 76	1.00	3.75
MS6	1967(B) (8)	—	KM#10.1, 13.1, 14.1, 18.1, 25, 48.2, 58.1, 75.1 (1962 dated Rupee)	1.00	15.00
MS8	1970(B) (8)	—	KM#10.1, 13.5, 14.2, 18.3, 26.3, 41, 58.2, 75.2 Brown vinyl case	1.00	18.00
MS7	ND(1969)(B) (4)	25,281	KM#42.1, 59, 77, 185 Blue plastic case	2.50	10.00
MS9	1970(B) (2)	22,999	KM#43.1, 186	2.00	9.00
MS10	1971(B) (2)	9,987	KM#43.2, 186	—	8.50
MS11	1972(B) (2)	43,121	KM#60, 187	2.00	7.00
MS11a	1972(B (2)	—	KM#60, 187a	2.00	7.50
MS12	1973(B) (2)	48,670	KM#188, 240	—	15.00
MS13	1974(B) (2)	50,219	KM#189, 255	10.00	12.50
MS14	1975(B) (2)	40,279	KM#190, 256	12.00	13.50
MS15	1976(B) (2)	25,105	KM#191, 257	12.00	16.00
MS16	1977(B) (2)	17,071	KM#192, 258	12.00	16.00
MS17	1978(B) (2)	15,041	KM#193, 259	10.00	16.00
MS18	1979(B) (2)	—	KM#194, 260	—	16.50
MS19	1980(B) (2)	—	KM#195, 275	—	21.50
MS20	1981(B) (2)	—	KM#196, 276	—	21.50
MS21	1982(B) (2)	—	KM#197, 278	—	21.50
MS22	1985(B) (2)	—	KM#199, 280	48.00	140
MS23	ND(1985)(B) (2)	—	KM#241, 281	43.00	100
MS24	ND(1985)(C) (2)	—	KM#200, 282	—	40.00
MS25	1986 (2)	—	KM#242, 283	45.00	100
MS26	1987(B) (2)	—	KM#243, 284	45.00	40.00
MS27	1989(B) (2)	—	KM#244, 285	40.00	40.00
MS28	1989(B) (2)	—	KM#83, 285	50.00	45.00

KM#	Date	Mintage	Identification	Issue Price	Mkt Val
MS29	1991(B) (2)	—	KM#152, 201	—	18.00
MS30	1991(B) (3)	—	KM#90, 152, 201	—	20.00
MS31	1991(B) (2)	—	KM#123, 153	—	20.00
MS32	1991(B) (3)	—	KM#91, 123, 153	—	22.00
MS33	1992(B) (4)	—	KM#92.1, 202, 261, 286	—	45.00
MS34	1994(B) (3)	—	KM#155, 262, 287	—	45.00
MS35	1996(M) (3)	—	KM#203, 263, 288	—	50.00
MS36	1996(M) (2)	—	KM#263, 288	65.00	45.00
MS37	1997(C) (3)	—	KM#204, 264, 289	—	50.00
MS38	1997(B) (2)	—	KM#70, 265	50.00	40.00
MS39	1998(B) (4)	—	KM#131.1, 205, 266, 292	—	55.00
MS40	1998(C) (3)	—	KM#297, 298, 299	—	50.00
MS41	1999(C) (2)	—	KM#295, 302	—	40.00
MS42	1999(B) (3)	—	KM#290, 300, 301	—	50.00
MS43	2000(B) (2)	—	KM#291, 293	—	40.00

PROOF SETS

KM#	Date	Mintage	Identification	Issue Price	Mkt Val
PS1	1950(B) (7)	—	KM#1.2, 2.1, 3.1, 4, 5.1, 6.1, 7.1	8.40	30.00
PS2	1954(B) (7)	—	KM#1.3, 2.2, 3.2, 4, 5.1, 6.1, 7.2	8.40	50.00
PS3	1960(B) (6)	—	KM#8, 11, 16, 24.2, 47.1, 55	7.00	30.00
PS4	1961(B) (6)	—	KM#8, 11, 16, 24.2, 47.2, 55	7.00	40.00
PS5	1962(B) (7)	—	KM#8, 11, 16, 24.2, 47.2, 55, 75.1	8.40	40.00
PS6	1962(B) (7)	—	KM#8a, 11, 16, 24.1, 47.2, 55, 75.1	8.40	35.00
PS7	1963(B) (6)	—	KM#8a, 11, 16, 24.2, 47.2, 55, 75.1	7.00	30.00
PS8	1963(B) (7)	—	KM#8a, 11, 16, 24.2, 47.2, 55, 75.1	8.40	25.00
PS9	ND(1964)(B) (2)	—	KM#56, 76	5.00	7.50
PS10	1969B (9)	9,097	KM#10.1, 13.5, 14.2, 18.3, 26.3, 42.1, 59, 77, 185	15.25	15.00
PS11	1970B (9)	2,900	KM#10.1, 13.5, 14.2, 18.3, 26.3, 43.1, 58.3, 75.2, 186	15.25	15.00
PS12	1971B (9)	4,161	KM#10.1, 13.5, 14.2, 18.3, 26.3, 43.2, 58.3, 75.2, 186	15.25	15.00
PS13	1972B (9)	7,701	KM#10.1, 13.6, 15, 18.6, 27.1, 49.1, 60, 75.2, 187	15.25	15.00
PS14	1973B (10)	7,563	KM#10.1, 13.5, 15, 18.6, 27.1, 49.1, 62, 75.1, 188, 240	26.00	25.00
PS15	1973B (9)	3,326	KM#10.1, 13.6, 15, 18.6, 27.1, 49.1, 62, 75.2, 188	15.25	15.00
PS16	1973B (2)	2,408	KM#188, 240	17.50	22.00
PS17	1974B (10)	9,138	KM#10.1, 13.6, 15, 18.6, 28, 49.1, 63, 75.2, 189, 255	29.00	22.00
PS18	1974B (2)	1,712	KM#189, 255	7.50	20.00
PS19	1975B (10)	2,370	KM#10.1, 13.6, 15, 18.6, 29, 49.1, 63, 78.1	35.00	30.00
PS20	1975B (2)	160	KM#190, 256	22.00	27.50
PS21	1976B (10)	3,209	KM#10.1, 13.6, 15, 19, 30, 49.1, 63, 78.1, 191, 257	35.00	30.00
PS22	1976B (2)	190	KM#191, 257	22.00	27.50
PS23	1977B (10)	2,222	KM#10.1, 13.6, 15, 20, 31, 63, 78.1, 192, 258	35.00	30.00
PS24	1977B (2)	—	KM#192, 258	—	27.50
PS25	1978B (10)	1,390	KM#10.1, 13.6, 15, 21, 32, 49.1, 63, 78.1, 193, 259	35.00	30.00
PS26	1978B (2)	—	KM#193, 259	—	27.50
PS27	1979B (10)	—	KM#10.1, 13.6, 15, 22, 33, 49.2, 63, 78.3, 194, 260	—	35.00
PS28	1979B (2)	—	KM#194, 260	—	28.00
PS29	1980B (4)	—	KM#35, 50, 195, 275	—	40.00
PS30	1980B (2)	—	KM#195, 275	—	35.00
PS31	1981B (4)	—	KM#36, 51, 196, 276	—	40.00
PS32	1981B (2)	—	KM#196, 276	—	35.00
PS-A33	1982B (4)	—	KM#64, 121.1, 198, 279	—	52.50
PS33	1982B (4)	—	KM#52, 120, 197, 278	48.00	40.00
PS-A34	1982B (2)	—	KM#198, 279	—	45.00
PS34	1982B (2)	—	KM#197, 278	38.00	35.00
PS35	1985B (4)	—	KM#66, 122, 199, 280	98.00	235
PS36	1985B (2)	—	KM#199, 280	58.00	160
PS37	ND(1985)B (4)	—	KM#67.1, 150, 241-2, 281	88.00	150
PS38	ND(1985)B (2)	—	KM#241, 281	48.00	120
PS39	1985(C) (3)	—	KM#80, 200, 282	—	70.00
PS40	1986B (3)	—	KM#68.1, 242, 283	70.00	130
PS41	1986B (2)	—	KM#242, 283	50.00	120
PS42	1987B (3)	—	KM#81, 243, 284	65.00	75.00
PS43	1987B (2)	—	KM#243, 284	60.00	70.00
PS44	1989B (4)	—	KM#83, 151, 244, 285	90.00	100
PS45	1989B (2)	—	KM#244, 285	65.00	70.00
PS46	1991(B) (3)	—	KM#90, 152, 201	—	45.00
PS47	1991(B) (3)	—	KM#91, 123, 153	—	35.00
PS48	ND(1994) (3)	—	KM#155, 262, 287	18.75	55.00
PS49	ND(1994) (2)	—	KM#262, 287	18.05	50.00
PS50	1996M (4)	—	KM#129, 203, 263, 288	110	85.00
PS51	1996M (2)	—	KM#263, 288	100	75.00
PS52	1997(C) (3)	—	KM#24, 264, 289	—	75.00
PS53	1997M (2)	—	KM#70, 265	75.00	60.00
PS54	1998M (4)	—	KM#131.1, 205, 266, 290	—	85.00
PS55	1998(C) (4)	—	KM#296.3, 298, 299, 297	—	85.00

The Republic of Indonesia, the world's largest archipelago, extends for more than 3,000 miles (4,827 km.) along the equator from the mainland of southeast Asia to Australia. The 17,508 islands comprising the archipelago have a combined area of 788,425 sq. mi. (1,919,440 sq.km.) and a population of 205 million, including East Timor. On August 30, 1999, the Timorese majority voted for independence. The Inter FET (International Forces for East Timor) is now in charge of controlling the chaotic situation. Capitol: Jakarta. Petroleum, timber, rubber, and coffee are exported.

Had Columbus succeeded in reaching the fabled Spice Islands, he would have found advanced civilizations a millennium old, and temples still ranking among the finest examples of ancient art. During the opening centuries of the Christian era, the islands were influenced by Hindu priests and traders who spread their culture and religion. Moslem invasions began in the 13th century, fragmenting the island kingdoms into small states which were unable to resist Western colonial infiltration. Portuguese traders established posts in the 16th century, but they were soon outnumbered by the Dutch who arrived in 1596 and gradually asserted control over the islands comprising present-day Indonesia. Dutch dominance, interrupted by British incursions during the Napoleonic Wars, established the Netherlands East Indies as one of the richest colonial possessions in the world.

The Indonesian independence movement, which began between the two world wars, was encouraged by the Japanese during their 3 1/2-year occupation during World War II. Indonesia proclaimed its independence on Aug. 17,1945, three days after the surrender of Japan and full sovereignty. On Dec. 27, 1949, after four years of guerilla warfare including two large-scale campaigns by the Dutch in an effort to reassert control, complete independence was established. Rebellions in Bandung and on the Molluccan Islands occurred in 1950. During the reign of President Mohammad Achmad Sukarno (1950-67) the new Republic not only held together but started to develop. West Irian, formerly Netherlands New Guinea, came under the administration of Indonesia on May 1, 1963. In 1965, the army staged an anti-communist coup in which thousands perished.

On November 28, 1975, the Portuguese Province of Timor, an overseas province occupying the eastern half of the East Indian island of Timor, attained independence as the People's Democratic Republic of East Timor. On December 5, 1975, the government of the People's Democratic Republic was seized by a guerrilla faction sympathetic to the Indonesian territorial claim to East Timor which ousted the constitutional government and replaced it with the Provisional Government of East Timor. On July 17, 1976, the Provisional Government enacted a law that dissolved the free republic and made East Timor the 27th province of Indonesia.

The VOC (United East India Company) struck coins and emergency issues for the Indonesian Archipelago and for the islands at various mints in the Netherlands and the islands. In 1798 the VOC was subsumed by the Dutch government, which issued VOC type transitional and regal types during the Batavian Republic and the Kingdom of the Netherlands until independence. The British issued a coinage during the various occupations by the British East Indian Company, 1811-24. Modern coinage issued by the Republic of Indonesia includes separate series for West Irian and for the Riau Archipelago, an area of small islands between Singapore and Sumatra.

MONETARY SYSTEM

100 Sen = 1 Rupiah

REPUBLIC

STANDARD COINAGE

100 Sen = 1 Rupiah

KM# 7 SEN

Aluminum **Obv:** Rice stalk surrounds center hole **Rev:** Text around center hole

Date	Mintage	F	VF	XF	Unc	BU
1952(u)	100,000	—	0.20	0.40	0.75	1.50

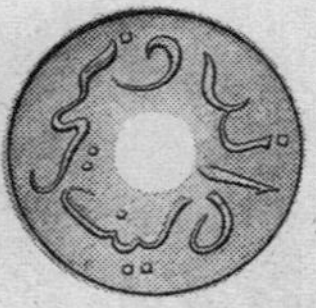

KM# 5 5 SEN

Aluminum **Obv:** Rice stalk surrounds center hole **Rev:** Text around center hole

Date	Mintage	F	VF	XF	Unc	BU
1951(u)	—	—	0.10	0.25	0.50	1.00
1954	—	—	0.10	0.25	0.50	1.00

KM# 6 10 SEN

Aluminum **Obv:** Denomination within scalloped design, ornaments flank date below **Rev:** National emblem

Date	Mintage	F	VF	XF	Unc	BU
1951(u)	—	—	0.10	0.20	0.35	0.65
1954	50,000,000	—	0.10	0.20	0.35	0.75

KM# 12 10 SEN

Aluminum **Obv:** Denomination within scalloped design, ornaments flank date below **Rev:** National emblem

Date	Mintage	F	VF	XF	Unc	BU
1957	50,224,000	—	0.20	0.40	0.75	1.25

KM# 8 25 SEN

Aluminum **Obv:** Denomination within scalloped design, ornaments flank date below **Rev:** National emblem

Date	Mintage	F	VF	XF	Unc	BU
1952(u)	200,000,000	—	0.10	0.20	0.25	0.45

KM# 11 25 SEN

Aluminum **Obv:** Denomination within scalloped design, ornaments flank date below **Rev:** National emblem

Date	Mintage	F	VF	XF	Unc	BU
1955	25,767,000	—	0.10	0.20	0.35	0.65
1957	99,752,926	—	0.10	0.20	0.35	0.50

KM# 9 50 SEN

Copper-Nickel **Obv:** Denomination within scalloped design, ornaments flank date below **Rev:** Turbaned head left

Date	Mintage	F	VF	XF	Unc	BU
1952(u)	100,000,000	—	0.10	0.20	0.35	0.50

KM# 10.1 50 SEN

Copper-Nickel **Obv:** Denomination within scalloped design, ornaments flank date below **Rev:** Turbaned head left

Date	Mintage	F	VF	XF	Unc	BU
1954	1,290,000	—	1.00	2.25	4.50	—
1955	15,000,000	—	0.10	0.20	0.35	0.75

KM# 10.2 50 SEN

Copper-Nickel **Obv:** Denomination within scalloped design, ornaments flank date below **Rev:** Different head, larger lettering

Date	Mintage	F	VF	XF	Unc	BU
1957	26,267,313	—	0.10	0.20	0.35	0.65

KM# 13 50 SEN

Aluminum **Obv:** Denomination within inner circle, ornaments flank date below **Rev:** National emblem

Date	Mintage	F	VF	XF	Unc	BU
1958	33,740,000	—	0.10	0.20	0.40	0.75

KM# 14 50 SEN

Aluminum, 29 mm. **Obv:** Denomination within inner circle, ornaments flank date below **Rev:** National emblem, modified eagle

Date	Mintage	F	VF	XF	Unc	BU
1959	100,009,000	—	0.10	0.20	0.40	0.65
1961	150,000,000	—	0.10	0.20	0.40	0.65

KM# 20 RUPIAH

1.4000 g., Aluminum, 22 mm. **Rev:** Fantail flycatcher

Date	Mintage	F	VF	XF	Unc	BU
1970	136,010,000	—	—	0.15	0.50	0.75

KM# 21 2 RUPIAH

2.3000 g., Aluminum, 26 mm. **Obv:** Stars flank date below denomination **Rev:** Rice and cotton stalks

Date	Mintage	F	VF	XF	Unc	BU
1970	139,230,000	—	—	0.15	0.25	0.40

KM# 22 5 RUPIAH

Aluminum **Obv:** Stars flank date below denomination **Rev:** Black drongo

Date	Mintage	F	VF	XF	Unc	BU
1970	448,000,000	—	0.15	0.30	0.75	1.00

KM# 37 5 RUPIAH

Aluminum, 28.6 mm. **Subject:** Family Planning Program **Obv:** Stars flank date below denomination **Rev:** The ideal family within rice and cotton stalk wreath

Date	Mintage	F	VF	XF	Unc	BU
1974	447,910,000	—	0.10	0.15	0.25	0.35

KM# 43 5 RUPIAH

1.4000 g., Aluminum, 23 mm. **Subject:** Family Planning Program **Obv:** Stars flank date below denomination, inner circle surrounds **Rev:** The ideal family within rice and cotton stalk wreath, inner circle surrounds

Date	Mintage	F	VF	XF	Unc	BU
1979	413,200,000	—	0.10	0.15	0.25	0.35
1995	6,420,000	—	0.20	0.30	0.60	1.00
1996	—	—	0.20	0.30	0.60	1.00

KM# 33 10 RUPIAH

Copper-Nickel **Series:** F.A.O. **Rev:** Rice and cotton stalks

Date	Mintage	F	VF	XF	Unc	BU
1971	286,360,000	—	0.10	0.25	0.50	0.75

KM# 38 10 RUPIAH

Brass-Clad Steel, 22 mm. **Subject:** National Saving Program **Obv:** Stars flank date below denomination **Rev:** Rice and cotton stalks form wreath around teapot design

Date	Mintage	F	VF	XF	Unc	BU
1974	222,910,000	—	0.10	0.25	0.75	1.25

KM# 44 10 RUPIAH

1.9000 g., Aluminum, 25 mm. **Series:** F.A.O. **Obv:** Stars flank date below denomination **Rev:** Rice and cotton stalks form wreath around teapot design

Date	Mintage	F	VF	XF	Unc	BU
1979	285,670,000	—	0.10	0.20	0.40	0.65

KM# 34 25 RUPIAH

3.5000 g., Copper-Nickel, 28 mm. **Obv:** Stars flank date below denomination **Rev:** Victoria crowned pigeon

Date	Mintage	F	VF	XF	Unc	BU
1971	1,221,610,000	—	0.10	0.20	0.40	0.75

KM# 55 25 RUPIAH

Aluminum **Obv:** National emblem **Rev:** Nutmeg plant

Date	Mintage	F	VF	XF	Unc	BU
1991	30,000,000	—	—	0.40	0.75	1.25
1992	64,000,000	—	—	0.40	0.75	1.25
1993	20,000,000	—	—	0.40	0.75	1.25
1994	250,000,000	—	—	0.25	0.50	0.75
1995	184,480,000	—	—	0.25	0.50	0.75
1996	—	—	—	0.25	0.50	0.75

KM# 35 50 RUPIAH

6.0000 g., Copper-Nickel, 24 mm. **Obv:** Stars flank date below denomination **Rev:** Greater Bird of Paradise

Date	Mintage	F	VF	XF	Unc	BU
1971	1,035,435,000	—	0.15	0.30	0.65	0.85

KM# 52 50 RUPIAH

Aluminum-Bronze **Obv:** National emblem **Rev:** Komodo dragon lizard

Date	Mintage	F	VF	XF	Unc	BU
1991	67,000,000	—	0.10	0.20	0.50	1.00
1992	70,000,000	—	0.10	0.20	0.50	1.00
1993	120,000,000	—	0.10	0.20	0.50	1.00
1994	300,000,000	—	0.10	0.20	0.50	1.00
1995	591,880,000	—	0.10	0.20	0.50	1.00
1996	—	—	0.10	0.25	0.60	1.20
1997	150,000	—	0.10	0.25	0.60	1.20
1998	150,000	—	0.10	0.25	0.60	1.20

KM# 60 50 RUPIAH

Aluminum **Obv:** National emblem **Rev:** Black-naped Oriole

Date	Mintage	F	VF	XF	Unc	BU
1999	—	—	—	—	0.40	0.75

KM# 36 100 RUPIAH

Copper-Nickel **Obv:** Stars flank date below denomination **Rev:** Minangkabu house

Date	Mintage	F	VF	XF	Unc	BU
1973	252,868,000	—	0.35	0.75	1.50	3.00

KM# 42 100 RUPIAH

7.0000 g., Copper-Nickel, 28.5 mm. **Subject:** Forestry for prosperity **Obv:** Minangkabu house **Rev:** Legendary tree of life

Date	Mintage	F	VF	XF	Unc	BU
1978	907,773,000	—	0.25	0.50	1.50	3.00

KM# 53 100 RUPIAH

Aluminum-Bronze, 22 mm. **Subject:** Buffalo racing **Obv:** National emblem **Rev:** Buffalo racers

Date	Mintage	F	VF	XF	Unc	BU
1991	94,000,000	—	0.15	0.30	0.60	1.00
1992	120,000,000	—	0.15	0.30	0.60	1.00
1993	300,000,000	—	0.15	0.30	0.60	1.00
1994	550,000,000	—	0.15	0.30	0.60	1.00
1995	798,100,000	—	0.15	0.30	0.60	1.00
1996	41,000,000	—	0.15	0.30	0.65	1.00
1997	150,000,000	—	0.15	0.30	0.65	1.00
1998	59,000,000	—	0.15	0.30	0.65	1.00

KM# 61 100 RUPIAH

Aluminum, 23 mm. **Obv:** National emblem **Rev:** Palm Cockatoo

Date	Mintage	F	VF	XF	Unc	BU
1999	—	—	—	—	0.75	1.50
2000	—	—	—	—	0.75	1.50

KM# 23 200 RUPIAH

8.0000 g., 0.9990 Silver .2569 oz. ASW **Subject:** 25th anniversary of independence **Obv:** Great Bird of Paradise (paradisea apoda- Paradisaeidae) **Rev:** National emblem

Date	Mintage	F	VF	XF	Unc	BU
1970 Proof	5,100	Value: 17.50				

KM# 24 250 RUPIAH

10.0000 g., 0.9990 Silver .3212 oz. ASW **Subject:** 25th anniversary of independence **Obv:** Manjusri statue from Temple of Tumpang **Rev:** National emblem

Date	Mintage	F	VF	XF	Unc	BU
1970 Proof	5,000	Value: 18.50				

KM# 25 500 RUPIAH

20.0000 g., 0.9990 Silver .6424 oz. ASW **Subject:** 25th Anniversary of Independence **Obv:** Wayang dancer **Rev:** National emblem

Date	Mintage	F	VF	XF	Unc	BU
1970 Proof	4,800	Value: 30.00				

KM# 54 500 RUPIAH

Aluminum-Bronze, 24 mm. **Obv:** National emblem **Rev:** Jasmine

Date	Mintage	F	VF	XF	Unc	BU
1991	71,000,000	—	—	1.25	2.50	3.00
1992	100,000,000	—	—	1.25	2.50	3.00
1993	—	—	—	1.25	2.50	3.00
1994	—	—	—	1.25	2.50	3.00

KM# 59 500 RUPIAH

Aluminum-Bronze **Obv:** National emblem **Rev:** Denomination

Date	Mintage	F	VF	XF	Unc	BU
1997	—	—	—	—	2.00	2.50
1999	—	—	—	—	2.00	2.50
2000	—	—	—	—	2.00	2.50

KM# 26 750 RUPIAH

30.0000 g., 0.9990 Silver .9636 oz. ASW **Subject:** 25th Anniversary of Independence **Obv:** Garuda bird **Rev:** National emblem

Date	Mintage	F	VF	XF	Unc	BU
1970 Proof	4,950	Value: 45.00				

KM# 27 1000 RUPIAH

40.0000 g., 0.9990 Silver 1.2848 oz. ASW **Subject:** 25th Anniversary of Independence - Gen. Sudirman **Obv:** Bust 3/4 facing **Rev:** National emblem

Date	Mintage	F	VF	XF	Unc	BU
1970 Proof	4,250	Value: 60.00				

KM# 56 1000 RUPIAH

Bi-Metallic Brass center in Copper-Nickel ring **Obv:** National emblem within inner circle **Rev:** Palm tree within inner circle

Date	Mintage	F	VF	XF	Unc	BU
1993	5,000,000	—	—	—	3.50	4.50
1994	6,000,000	—	—	—	3.50	4.50
1995	19,900,000	—	—	—	3.50	4.50
1996	—	—	—	—	3.50	4.50
1997	—	—	—	—	3.50	4.50
2000	—	—	—	—	3.50	4.50

KM# 28 2000 RUPIAH

4.9300 g., 0.9000 Gold .1426 oz. AGW **Subject:** 25th Anniversary of Independence **Obv:** Great Bird of Paradise **Rev:** National emblem

Date	Mintage	F	VF	XF	Unc	BU
1970 Proof	2,970	Value: 125				

KM# 39 2000 RUPIAH

25.6500 g., 0.5000 Silver .4123 oz. ASW **Subject:** Conservation series **Obv:** National emblem **Rev:** Javan tiger (panthera tigris-felidae) **Rev. Designer:** Leslie Durbin

Date	Mintage	F	VF	XF	Unc	BU
1974	43,000	—	—	—	15.00	17.50

KM# 39a 2000 RUPIAH

28.2800 g., 0.9250 Silver .8411 oz. ASW **Subject:** Conservation series **Obv:** National emblem **Rev:** Javan tiger (panthera tigris-felidae)

Date	Mintage	F	VF	XF	Unc	BU
1974 Proof	18,000	Value: 25.00				

KM# 29 5000 RUPIAH

12.3400 g., 0.9000 Gold .3571 oz. AGW **Subject:** 25th Anniversary of Independence **Obv:** Manjusri statue from Temple of Tumpang **Rev:** National emblem

Date	Mintage	F	VF	XF	Unc	BU
1970 Proof	2,150	Value: 260				

KM# 40 5000 RUPIAH

32.0000 g., 0.5000 Silver .5144 oz. ASW **Series:** Conservation **Obv:** National emblem **Rev:** Orangutan (pongo pygmaeus Pongidae) **Rev. Designer:** Leslie Durbin

Date	Mintage	F	VF	XF	Unc	BU
1974	43,000	—	—	—	15.00	17.50

KM# 40a 5000 RUPIAH
35.0000 g., 0.9250 Silver 1.0409 oz. ASW **Series:** Conservation **Obv:** National emblem **Rev:** Orangutan

Date	Mintage	F	VF	XF	Unc	BU
1974 Proof	17,000	Value: 25.00				

KM# 30 10000 RUPIAH
24.6800 g., 0.9000 Gold .7142 oz. AGW **Subject:** 25th Anniversary of Independence **Obv:** Wayang dancer **Rev:** National emblem

Date	Mintage	F	VF	XF	Unc	BU
1970 Proof	1,440	Value: 550				

KM# 45 10000 RUPIAH
19.4400 g., 0.9250 Silver .5782 oz. ASW **Subject:** Wildlife **Obv:** National emblem **Rev:** Babi rusa (wild pig)

Date	Mintage	F	VF	XF	Unc	BU
1987 Proof	25,000	Value: 35.00				

KM# 50 10000 RUPIAH
19.4400 g., 0.9250 Silver .5782 oz. ASW **Series:** Save the Child **Obv:** National emblem **Rev:** Playing badminton

Date	Mintage	F	VF	XF	Unc	BU
1990 Proof	20,000	Value: 50.00				

KM# 62 10000 RUPIAH
28.2800 g., 0.9250 Silver 0.841 oz. ASW, 38.61 mm. **Obv:** National emblem; UNICEF logo at left **Rev:** Two girl scouts planting a tree **Edge:** Milled **Note:** Struck at Hungarian Mint.

Date	Mintage	F	VF	XF	Unc	BU
1999 Proof	—	Value: 40.00				

KM# 31 20000 RUPIAH
49.3700 g., 0.9000 Gold 1.4391 oz. AGW **Subject:** 25th Anniversary of Independence **Obv:** Garuda bird **Rev:** National emblem

Date	Mintage	F	VF	XF	Unc	BU
1970 Proof	1,285	—	—	—	1,150	—

KM# 32 25000 RUPIAH
61.7100 g., 0.9000 Gold 1.7858 oz. AGW **Subject:** 25th Anniversary of Independence - Gen. Sudirman **Obv:** Bust facing **Rev:** National Emblem

Date	Mintage	F	VF	XF	Unc	BU
1970 Proof	970	Value: 1,350				

KM# 41 100000 RUPIAH
33.4370 g., 0.9000 Gold .9676 oz. AGW **Series:** Conservation **Obv:** National emblem **Rev:** Komodo dragon lizard (varanus komodensis) **Rev. Designer:** Leslie Durbin

Date	Mintage	F	VF	XF	Unc	BU
1974	5,333	—	—	—	675	—
1974 Proof	1,369	Value: 725				

KM# 47 125000 RUPIAH
8.0000 g., 0.9580 Gold .2465 oz. AGW **Subject:** Museum of Struggle '45 **Obv:** National emblem **Rev:** Museum

Date	Mintage	F	VF	XF	Unc	BU
1990 Proof	16,000	Value: 175				

KM# 63 150000 RUPIAH
6.2200 g., 0.9990 Gold .1998 oz. AGW, 22 mm. **Subject:** UNICEF - For the Children of the World **Obv:** National emblem; UNICEF logo at left **Rev:** Young boy riding a horse **Edge:** Milled.

Date	Mintage	F	VF	XF	Unc	BU
1999 Proof	—	Value: 220				

KM# 46 200000 RUPIAH
10.0000 g., 0.9170 Gold .2947 oz. AGW **Subject:** Wildlife **Obv:** National emblem **Rev:** Javan rhinoceros right

Date	Mintage	F	VF	XF	Unc	BU
1987 Proof	5,000	Value: 300				

KM# 51 200000 RUPIAH
10.0000 g., 0.9170 Gold .2947 oz. AGW **Series:** Save the Children **Obv:** National emblem **Rev:** Balinese dancer

Date	Mintage	F	VF	XF	Unc	BU
1990 Proof	3,000	Value: 300				

KM# 48 250000 RUPIAH
17.0000 g., 0.9580 Gold .5238 oz. AGW **Subject:** 45 years - Indonesian Independence **Obv:** National emblem **Rev:** Map, dates and denomination below

Date	Mintage	F	VF	XF	Unc	BU
1990 Proof	16,000	Value: 375				

KM# 57 300000 RUPIAH
17.0000 g., 0.9583 Gold .5238 oz. AGW **Subject:** 50th Anniversary of Independence **Obv:** National emblem **Rev:** Presidential talk show

Date	Mintage	F	VF	XF	Unc	BU
1995 Sets only	3,000	—	—	—	800	—

KM# 49 750000 RUPIAH
45.0000 g., 0.9580 Gold 1.3866 oz. AGW **Subject:** 45 Years - Arms of Generation 1945 **Obv:** National emblem **Rev:** National emblem within wreath of rice and cotton stalks

Date	Mintage	F	VF	XF	Unc	BU
1990 Proof	16,000	—	—	—	975	—

KM# 58 850000 RUPIAH

50.0000 g., 0.9583 Gold 1.5405 oz. AGW **Subject:** 50th Anniversary of Independence - President Soeharto **Obv:** National emblem **Rev:** Bust facing

Date	Mintage	F	VF	XF	Unc	BU
1995 Sets only	3,000	—	—	—	2,200	—

PATTERNS

Including off metal strikes

KM#	Date	Mintage	Identification	Mkt Val
Pn1	1951	—	25 Sen. Aluminum.	275
Pn2	1955	—	50 Sen. Raised SPECIMEN.	325

KM#	Date	Mintage	Identification	Mkt Val
Pn3	1963	—	2-1/2 Rupiah. Aluminum.	185
PnA4	1965	—	50 Sen. Aluminum. Sukarno. Arms.	185
Pn4	1970	—	Rupiah. Bronze. KM20.	160
Pn5	1970	—	2 Rupiah. Copper. KM21.	160
Pn6	1970	—	2 Rupiah. Bronze. KM20.	160
Pn7	1970	—	25 Rupiah. Bronze.	—
Pn8	1973	—	100 Rupiah. Aluminum.	250
Pn9	1979	—	10 Rupiah. Copper-Nickel.	—
Pn10	1990	—	125000 Rupiah. Gold. Gold-plated base metal. KM#47.	—
Pn11	1990	—	250000 Rupiah. Gold. Gold-plated base metal. KM#48.	—
Pn12	1990	—	750000 Rupiah. Gold. Gold-plated base metal. KM#49.	—
Pn13	1991	—	500 Rupiah. Copper-Nickel.	—
Pn14	1992	—	500 Rupiah. Bronze.	—
Pn15	1993	—	50 Rupiah. Copper-Nickel.	—
Pn16	1993	—	100 Rupiah. Copper-Nickel.	—

MINT SETS

KM#	Date	Mintage	Identification	Issue Price	Mkt Val
MS1	Mixed dates (14)	—	KM5-6 (1951, 1954), 7-9 (1952), 10.1 (1955), 10.2 (1957), 11 (1955, 1957), 12 (1957), 14 (1961)	—	18.00
MS2	Mixed dates (9)	—	KM20-21 (1970), 33-35 (1971), 36 (1973), 37-38 (1974), 42 (1978)	2.40	6.50
MS3	1970 (3)	—	KM20-22	—	1.50
MS4	1971 (3)	—	KM33-35	—	1.50

PROOF SETS

KM#	Date	Mintage	Identification	Issue Price	Mkt Val
PS1	1970 (10)	970	KM23-32	490	3,400
PS2	1970 (5)	4,250	KM23-27	50.00	170
PS3	1974 (2)	30,000	KM39a-40a	50.00	36.00
PS4	1990 (3)	15,750	KM47-49	755	1,525
PS5	1990 (2)	—	KM50-51	—	350
PS6	1995 (2)	3,000	KM57-58	2,975	3,000

IRIAN BARAT

(West Irian, Irian Jaya, Netherlands New Guinea)

A province of Indonesia comprising the western half of the island of New Guinea. A special set of coins dated 1962 were issued in 1964, were recalled December 31, 1971, and are no longer legal tender.

INDONESIAN PROVINCE

STANDARD COINAGE

No inscription on edge

KM# 5 SEN

Aluminum **Subject:** Mohammed Ahmad Sukarno **Obv:** Head left **Rev:** Denomination within wreath of cotton and rice stalks **Edge:** Plain

Date	Mintage	F	VF	XF	Unc	BU
1962	—	0.25	0.50	1.00	2.00	—

KM# 6 5 SEN

Aluminum **Subject:** Mohammed Ahmad Sukarno **Obv:** Head left **Rev:** Denomination within wreath of cotton and rice stalks **Edge:** Plain

Date	Mintage	F	VF	XF	Unc	BU
1962	—	0.25	0.50	1.25	2.00	—

KM# 7 10 SEN

Aluminum **Subject:** Mohammed Ahmad Sukarno **Obv:** Head left **Rev:** Denomination within rice and cotton stalks **Edge:** Plain

Date	Mintage	F	VF	XF	Unc	BU
1962	—	0.25	0.50	1.25	2.50	—

KM# 8.1 25 SEN

Aluminum **Subject:** Mohammed Ahmad Sukarno **Obv:** Head left **Rev:** Denomination within wreath of cotton and rice stalks **Edge:** Reeded

Date	Mintage	F	VF	XF	Unc	BU
1962	—	—	—	—	—	—

KM# 8.2 25 SEN

Aluminum **Obv:** Head left **Rev:** Denomination within wreath of cotton and rice stalks

Date	Mintage	F	VF	XF	Unc	BU
1962	—	0.75	1.50	2.50	4.00	—

KM# 9 50 SEN

Aluminum **Subject:** Mohammed Ahmad Sukarno **Obv:** Head left **Rev:** Denomination within wreath of cotton and rice stalks **Edge:** Reeded

Date	Mintage	F	VF	XF	Unc	BU
1962	—	0.85	1.60	3.00	5.00	—

PATTERNS

Including off metal strikes

KM#	Date	Mintage	Identification	Mkt Val
Pn2	1963	—	2-1/2 Rupiah.	100
Pn3	1965	—	25 Sen. Aluminum. Plain edge. KM#8.2	100
Pn4	1965	—	50 Sen. Aluminum center. Reeded edge. KM#9	100
Pn5	1965	—	50 Sen. Aluminum. Plain edge. KM#9	100

KM#	Date	Mintage	Identification	Mkt Val
Pn6	1965//1962	—	50 Sen. Aluminum. As KM#9.	150

RIAU ARCHIPELAGO

A group of 3,214 islands off the tip of the Malay Peninsula. Coins were issued near the end of 1963 (although dated 1962) and recalled as worthless on Sept. 30, 1964. They were legal tender from Oct. 15, 1963 to July 1, 1964.

INSCRIPTION ON EDGE
KEPULAUAN RIAU

INDONESIAN PROVINCE

STANDARD COINAGE

Inscription on edge: "Kepulauan Riau"

KM# 5 SEN

Aluminum **Obv:** Head left **Rev:** Denomination within wreath of cotton and rice stalks

Date	Mintage	F	VF	XF	Unc	BU
1962	—	0.35	0.75	1.25	2.00	—

KM# 6 5 SEN

Aluminum **Obv:** Head left **Rev:** Denomination within wreath of cotton and rice stalks

Date	Mintage	F	VF	XF	Unc	BU
1962	—	0.30	0.60	1.50	2.00	—

KM# 7 10 SEN

Aluminum **Subject:** Mohammed Ahmad Sukarno **Obv:** Head left **Rev:** Denomination within wreath of cotton and rice stalks

Date	Mintage	F	VF	XF	Unc	BU
1962	—	0.35	0.70	1.75	2.75	—

KM# 8.1 25 SEN

Aluminum **Obv:** Head left **Rev:** Denomination within wreath of cotton and rice stalks

Date	Mintage	F	VF	XF	Unc	BU
1962	—	—	—	—	—	—

KM# 8.2 25 SEN

Aluminum **Subject:** Mohammed Ahmad Sukarno **Obv:** Head left **Rev:** Denomination within wreath of cotton and rice stalks

Date	Mintage	F	VF	XF	Unc	BU
1962	—	0.85	1.60	2.75	4.50	—

KM# 9 50 SEN

Aluminum **Subject:** Mohammed Ahmad Sukarno **Obv:** Bust left **Rev:** Denomination within wreath of cotton and rice stalks

Date	Mintage	F	VF	XF	Unc	BU
1962	—	1.00	2.00	3.50	5.50	—

IRAN

The Islamic Republic of Iran, located between the Caspian Sea and the Persian Gulf in southwestern Asia, has an area of 636,296 sq. mi. (1,648,000 sq. km.) and a population of 40 million. Capital: Tehran. Although predominantly an agricultural state, Iran depends heavily on oil fcr foreign exchange. Crude oil, carpets and agricultural products are exported.

Iran (historically known as Persia until 1931AD) is one of the world's most ancient and resilient nations. Strategically astride the lower land gate to Asia, it has been conqueror and conquered, sovereign nation and vassal state, ever emerging from its periods of glory or travail with its culture and political individuality intact. Iran (Persia) was a powerful empire under Cyrus the Great (600-529 B.C.), its borders extending from the Indus to the Nile. It has also been conquered by the predatory empires of antique and recent times - Assyrian, Medean, Macedonian, Seljuq, Turk, Mongol - and more recently been coveted by Russia, the Third Reich and Great Britain. Revolts against the absolute power of the Persian shahs resulted in the establishment of a constitutional monarchy in 1906.

With 4,000 troops, Reza Khan marched on the capital arriving in Tehran in the early morning of Feb. 22,1921. The government was taken over with hardly a shot and Zia ad-Din was set up as premier, but the real power was with Reza Khan, although he was officially only the minister of war. In 1923, Reza Khan appointed himself prime minister and summoned the "majlis." Who eventually gave him military powers and he became independent of the shah's authority. In 1925 Reza Khan Pahlavi was elected Shah of Persia. A few weeks later his eldest son, Shahpur Mohammed Reza was appointed Crown Prince and was crowned on April 25, 1926.

In 1931 the Kingdom of Persia became known as the Kingdom of Iran. In 1979 the monarchy was toppled and an Islamic Republic proclaimed.

TITLES

دار الخلافة

Dar al-Khilafat

RULERS

Qajar Dynasty

مظفرالدين

Muzaffar al-Din Shah, AH1313-1324/1896-1907AD

Muhammad Ali Shah, AH1324-1327/1907-1909AD

سلطان احمد

Sultan Ahmad Shah, AH1327-1344/1909-1925AD

Pahlavi Dynasty

رضا

Reza Shah, as prime minister, SH1302-1304/1923-1925AD
as Shah, SH1304-1320/1925-1941AD

محمد رضا

Mohammad Reza Pahlavi, Shah SH1320-1358/1941-1979AD

جمهوری اسلامی ایران

Islamic Republic, SH1358-/1979-AD

MINT NAMES

طهران

Tehran

تفليس

Tiflis

MINT MARKS

H - Heaton (Birmingham)
L - Leningrad (St. Petersburg)

COIN DATING

Iranian coins were dated according to the Moslem lunar calendar until March 21, 1925 (AD), when dating was switched to a new calendar based on the solar year, indicated by the notation SH. The monarchial calendar system was adopted in 1976 = MS2535 and was abandoned in 1978 = MS2537. The previously used solar year calendar was restored at that time.

MONETARY SYSTEM

1825-1931
(AH1241-1344, SH1304-09)

50 Dinars = 1 Shahi
20 Shahis = 1 Kran (Qiran)
10 Krans = 1 Toman

NOTE: From AD1830-34 (AH1245-50) the gold Toman was known as a 'Keshwarsetan.'

1932-Date (SH1310-Date)

5 Dinars = 1 Shahi
20 Shahis = 1 Rial (100 Dinars)
10 Rials = 1 Toman

NOTE: The Toman ceased to be an official unit in 1932, but continues to be applied in popular usage. Thus, 135 Rials' is always expressed as 13 Toman, 5 Rials'. The term Rial' is often used in conversation, as well as either Kran' or Ezar' (short for Hazar = 1000) is used.

NOTE: The Law of 18 March 1930 fixed the gold Pahlavi at 20 Rials. No gold coins were struck. The Law of 13 March1932 divided the Pahlavi into 100 Rials, instead of 20. The Rial's weight was reduced from 0.3661 grams of pure gold to 0.0732. Since 1937 gold has been allowed to float and the Pahlavi is quoted daily in Rials in the marketplaces.

KINGDOM

NOTE: Other mints also produced local Falus, for which examples were not available to illustrate. Still other mints operated only or largely at earlier dates. These include Damavand, Damghan, Darabjird, Fa'Farafad, Kangan, Ra', Semnan, Tus, Tuy and others.

SILVER AND GOLD COINAGE

The precious metal monetary system of Qajar Persia prior to the reforms of 1878 was the direct descendant of the Mongol system introduced by Ghazan Mahmud in 1297AD, and was the last example of a medieval islamic coinage. It is not a modern system, and cannot be understood as such. It is not possible to list types, dates, and mints as for other countries, both because of the nature of the coinage, and because very little research has been done on the series. The following comments should help elucidate its nature.

STANDARDS: The weight of the primary silver and gold coins was set by law and was expressed in terms of the Mesqal (about 4.61 g) and the Nokhod (24 Nokhod = 1 Mesqal). The primary silver coin was the Rupee from AH1211-1212, the Riyal from AH1212-1241, and the Gheran from AH1241-1344. The standard gold coin was the Toman. Currently the price of gold is quoted in Mesqals.

DENOMINATIONS: In addition to the primary denominations, noted in the last paragraph, fractional pieces were coined, valued at one-eighth, one-fourth, and one-half the primary denomination, usually in much smaller quantities. These were ordinarily struck from the same dies as the larger pieces, sometimes on broad, thin flans, sometimes on thick, dumpy flans. On the smaller coins, the denomination can best be determined only by weighing the coin. The denomination is almost never expressed on the coin!

DEVALUATIONS: From time to time, the standard for silver and gold was reduced, and the old coin recalled and replaced with lighter coin, the difference going to the government coffers. The effect was that of a devaluation of the primary silver and gold coins, or inversely regarded, an increase in the price of silver and gold. The durations of each standard varied from about 2 to 20 years. The standards are given for each ruler, as the denomination can only be determined when the standard is known.

LIGHTWEIGHT AND ALLOYED PIECES: Most of the smaller denomination coins were issued at lighter weights than those prescribed by law, with the difference going to the pockets of the mintmasters. Other mints, notably Hamadan, added excessive amounts of alloy to the coins, and some mintmasters lost their heads as a result. Discrepancies in weight of as much as 15 percent and more are observed, with the result that it is often quite impossible to determine the denomination of a coin!

OVERSIZE COINS: Occasionally, multiples of the primary denominations were produced, usually on special occasions for presentation by the Shah to his favorites. These 'coins' did not circulate (except as bullion), and were usually worn as ornaments. They were the 'NCLT's' of their day.

MINTS & EPITHETS: Qajar coinage was struck at 34 mints (plus at least a dozen others striking only copper Falus), which are listed previously, with drawings of the mintnames in Persian, as they appear on the coins. However, the Persian script admits of infinite variation and stylistic whimsy, so the forms given are only guides, and not absolute. Only a knowledge of the script will assure correct reading. In addition to the city name, most mintnames were given identifying epithets, which occasionally appear in lieu of the mintname, particularly at Iravan and Mashhad.

TYPES: There were no types in the modern sense, but the arrangement of the legends and the ornamental borders were frequently changed. These changes do not coincide with changes in standards, and cannot be used to determine the mint, which must be found by actually reading the reverse inscriptions.

ARRANGEMENT

The following listings are arranged first by ruler, with various standards explained. Then, the coins are listed by denomination within each reign. For each denomination, one or more pieces, when available, are illustrated, with the mint and date noted beneath each photo. For each type, a date range is given, but this range indicates the years during which the particular type was current, and does not imply that every year of the interval is known on actual coins. Because dates were carelessly engraved, and old dies were used until they wore out or broke, we occasionally find coins of a particular type dated before or after the indicated interval. Such coins command no premium. No attempt has been made to determine which mints actually exist for which types.

KRAN STANDARD
AH1293-1344, SH1304-1309,
1876-1931AD
50 Dinars = 1 Shahi
1000 Dinars = 20 Shahis = 1 Kran (Qiron)
10 Krans = 1 Toman

Special Gold Issue
AH1337/1918-1919AD
1 Ashrafi (= 1 Toman)
SH1305-1309/1927-1931AD

Toman replaced by Pahlavi (light standard). Relationship of Pahlavi to Kran not known.

NOTE: Dated reverse dies lacking the ruler's name were not discarded at the end of a reign (especially from Nasir al-Din to Muzaffar al-Din), but remained in use until broken or worn out. Sometimes the old date was scratched out or changed, but often the die was used with the old date unaltered. Some dies with date below wreath retained the old date but had the new date engraved among the lion's legs.

SHAHI SEFID
(White Shahi)

Called the White (i.e. silver) Shahi to distinguish it from the Black or Copper Shahi, the Shahi Sefid was actually worth 3 Shahis (150 Dinars) or 3 1/8 Shahis (156 ¼ Dinars). It was used primarily for distribution on New Year's Day (now RUZ) as good-luck gifts. Since 1926 special privately struck tokens, having no monetary value, have been used instead of coins. The Shahi Sefid was broader, but much thinner than the ¼ Kran (Rob'l), worth 250 Dinars.

Milled Gold Coinage:

Modern imitations exist of many types, particularly the small 1/5, 1/2, and 1 Toman coins. These are usually underweight (or rarely overweight), and are sold in the bazaars at a small premium over bullion. They are usually crude and probably not intended to deceive collectors, but some are sold for jewelry and some are dated outside the reign of the ruler whose name or portrait they bear. A few deceptive counterfeits are known of the large 10 Toman pieces.

KINGDOM

Muzaffar al-Din Shah
AH1313-1324 / 1896-1907AD

MILLED COINAGE

KM# 961 50 DINARS

Copper-Nickel **Obverse:** Legend within beaded circle with crown on top **Reverse:** Radiant lion holding sword within wreath **Mint:** Tehran

Date	Mintage	F	VF	XF	Unc
AH1319	12,000,000	1.00	3.50	7.00	10.00
AH1321	10,000,000	0.75	1.50	4.00	8.00
AH1326	8,000,000	4.00	10.00	20.00	30.00
AH1332	6,000,000	1.00	2.00	5.00	12.50
AH1337	7,000,000	1.50	4.00	8.00	12.00

KM# 965 SHAHI SEFID (White Shahi)

0.0691 g., 0.9000 Silver .0200 oz. ASW **Obverse:** Legend and value within circle and wreath **Obv. Legend:** "Muzaffar al-Din Shah" **Reverse:** Crown above lion and sun within wreath **Mint:** Tehran

Date	Mintage	F	VF	XF	Unc
AH1319	—	15.00	30.00	60.00	120
AH1039	—	25.00	50.00	100	200
Note: Error for 1319					
AH1320	150,000	15.00	30.00	60.00	120

KM# 966 SHAHI SEFID (White Shahi)

0.0691 g., 0.9000 Silver .0200 oz. ASW **Obverse:** Legend within circle and wreath **Reverse:** Radiant lion holding sword within crowned wreath **Mint:** Tehran

Date	Mintage	F	VF	XF	Unc
ND (1901)	—	50.00	80.00	165	300

Date	Mintage	F	VF	XF	Unc
AH1319 (1901) Rare	—	—	—	—	—

Note: A number of varieties and mulings of KM#965 and KM#966 with other denominations, especially 1/4 Krans and 500 Dinar pieces, are reported; these command a premium over others of the same types; a total of 58,000 pieces were reported struck in AH1322, 1323 and 1324, but none are known with those dates; the specimens were either struck from old dies or were undated types.

KM# 967 SHAHI SEFID (White Shahi)

0.0691 g., 0.9000 Silver .0200 oz. ASW **Obverse:** Legend within center circle of wreath **Obv. Legend:** "Muzaffar al-Din Shah" **Reverse:** Legend within center circle of wreath **Rev. Legend:** "Sahib al-Zaman" **Mint:** Tehran **Note:** Thick and thin lettering varieties exist.

Date	Mintage	F	VF	XF	Unc
ND (1903)	—	50.00	85.00	165	300

KM# 962 100 DINARS (2 Shahi)

Copper-Nickel **Obverse:** Legend within beaded circle and crowned wreath **Reverse:** Radiant lion holding sword within crowned wreath

Date	Mintage	F	VF	XF	Unc
AH1319	9,000,000	2.50	5.00	10.00	20.00
AH1321/19	5,000,000	6.00	12.00	30.00	50.00
AH1321	Inc. above	0.75	1.50	4.00	8.00
AH1326	6,000,000	1.50	2.50	6.00	15.00
AH1332	5,000,000	1.00	2.00	5.00	12.50
AH1337	6,500,000	2.00	5.00	10.00	15.00

KM# 968 1/4 KRAN (Robi = 5 Shahis)

1.1513 g., 0.9000 Silver .0333 oz. ASW **Obverse:** Legend and value within circle and wreath **Obv. Legend:** "Muzaffar al-din Shah" **Reverse:** Crown above lion and sun within wreath **Mint:** Tehran **Note:** 300 specimens reportedly struck in AH1322, but none known to exist.

Date	Mintage	F	VF	XF	Unc
AH1319	—	20.00	35.00	65.00	130

Forms of the denomination:

500 DINARS: ۵۰۰ دینار
or
پانصد دینار
ده شاهی

KM# 969 500 DINARS (10 Shahis = 1/2 Kran)

2.3025 g., 0.9000 Silver .0666 oz. ASW **Obverse:** Legend and value within circle and wreath **Obv. Legend:** "Muzaffar al-din", 500 Dinars **Reverse:** Crown above lion and sun within wreath **Mint:** Tehran **Note:** Some reverse dies were previously used under Nasir al-Din and show traces of old date beneath wreath on reverse.

Date	Mintage	F	VF	XF	Unc
AH1319	—	20.00	40.00	100	200
AH1322	—	20.00	30.00	50.00	100

KM# 977 500 DINARS (10 Shahis = 1/2 Kran)

2.3025 g., 0.9000 Silver .0666 oz. ASW **Obverse:** Uniformed bust 1/4 right **Reverse:** Radiant lion holding sword within crowned wreath **Mint:** Tehran

Date	Mintage	F	VF	XF	Unc
AH1323 (1905)	130,000	20.00	35.00	80.00	160

Forms of the denomination:

1000 DINARS: یکهزار دینار

1 KRAN: یکقران

KM# 972 1000 DINARS (Kran, Qiran)

4.6050 g., 0.9000 Silver .1332 oz. ASW **Obverse:** Legend and value within circle and wreath **Reverse:** Crown above lion and sun within wreath **Mint:** Tehran

Date	Mintage	F	VF	XF	Unc
AH1319	—	150	225	350	500
AH1322	—	100	175	250	350

KM# 978 1000 DINARS (Kran, Qiran)

4.6050 g., 0.9000 Silver .1332 oz. ASW **Obverse:** Uniformed bust 1/4 right **Reverse:** Radiant lion holding sword within crowned wreath **Mint:** Tehran

Date	Mintage	F	VF	XF	Unc
AH1323 (1905)	125,000	20.00	30.00	65.00	125

KM# 974 2000 DINARS (2 Kran)

9.2100 g., 0.9000 Silver .2665 oz. ASW **Obverse:** Legend and value within wreath, star above **Reverse:** Crown above lion and sun within wreath **Mint:** Tehran **Note:** Blundered dates exist.

Date	Mintage	F	VF	XF	Unc
AH1319	—	10.00	20.00	35.00	90.00
AH1320	13,959,000	10.00	20.00	35.00	75.00

KM# 975 2000 DINARS (2 Kran)

9.2100 g., 0.9000 Silver .2665 oz. ASW **Obverse:** Legend within circle and wreath **Reverse:** Radiant lion holding sword within crowned wreath **Rev. Legend:** 2 Krans **Mint:** Tehran

Date	Mintage	F	VF	XF	Unc
AH1320 (1902)	Inc. above	12.50	20.00	40.00	100
AH1321 (1903)	18,108,000	15.00	22.50	45.00	100
Note: In blundered form as 13201					
AH1322 (1904)	8,640,000	8.00	15.00	30.00	80.00

KM# 979 2000 DINARS (2 Kran)

9.2100 g., 0.9000 Silver .2665 oz. ASW **Obverse:** Uniformed bust 1/4 right within wreath **Reverse:** Radiant lion holding sword within crowned wreath **Mint:** Tehran

Date	Mintage	F	VF	XF	Unc
AH1323 (1905)	—	15.00	30.00	60.00	120

Note: Mintage inluded in AH1323 above

Date	Mintage	F	VF	XF	Unc
AH'13' (1905)	—	60.00	100	200	400

Note: 23 of 1323 filled in or never punched

Date	Mintage	F	VF	XF	Unc
AH13233 (1905)	—	45.00	85.00	190	380

Note: Error

KM# 976 5000 DINARS (5 Kran)

23.0251 g., 0.9000 Silver .6662 oz. ASW **Obverse:** Legend within crowned wreath **Obv. Legend:** "Muzaffar al-din Shah" **Reverse:** Radiant lion holding sword within crowned wreath **Note:** Dav.#288.

Date	Mintage	F	VF	XF	Unc
AH1320 (1902)	250,000	12.00	16.00	32.00	60.00

Note: Actual mintage must be considerably greater

KM# 980 5000 DINARS (5 Kran)

23.0251 g., 0.9000 Silver .6662 oz. ASW, 36 mm. **Subject:** Royal Birthday **Obverse:** Uniformed bust 1/4 right within wreath **Reverse:** Radiant lion holding sword within crowned wreath **Note:** Dav.#287.

Date	Mintage	F	VF	XF	Unc
AH1322 (1904)	—	400	550	800	1,200

KM# 981 5000 DINARS (5 Kran)

23.0251 g., 0.9000 Silver .6662 oz. ASW, 36 mm. **Obverse:** Uniformed bust 1/4 right within wreath **Reverse:** Radiant lion holding sword within crowned wreath **Note:** Dav.#289. Without additional inscription flanking head

Date	Mintage	F	VF	XF	Unc
AH1324 (1906)	3,040	1,000	2,000	3,000	4,000

KM# 986 2000 DINARS (1/5 Toman)

0.6520 g., 0.9000 Gold .0188 oz. AGW **Obv. Legend:** "Mazaffar-al-Din Shah" **Reverse:** Crown above lion and sun within wreath

Date	Mintage	F	VF	XF	Unc
AH9301 Error for 1319	—	200	300	500	750

KM# 991 2000 DINARS (1/5 Toman)

0.5749 g., 0.9000 Gold .0166 oz. AGW **Obverse:** Uniformed bust left **Reverse:** Legend and value within circle and wreath

Date	Mintage	F	VF	XF	Unc
ND	—	200	300	400	500

KM# 922 2000 DINARS (1/5 Toman)

0.6520 g., 0.9000 Gold .0188 oz. AGW **Reverse:** Legend and value within circle and wreath **Note:** Mule. Reverse: KM#923, reverse: KM#991.

Date	Mintage	VG	F	VF	XF	Unc
AH1295 (sic)	—	—	—	—	—	—

KM# 992 2000 DINARS (1/5 Toman)

0.5749 g., 0.9000 Gold .0166 oz. AGW **Obverse:** Date and denomination added

Date	Mintage	F	VF	XF	Unc
AH1319 (1901)	—	50.00	100	150	250
AH1322 (1904)	—	50.00	100	150	250

Date	Mintage	F	VF	XF	Unc
AH1323 (1905)	—	100	200	300	400
AH1324 (1906)	—	100	200	300	400

KM# 994.1 5000 DINARS (1/2 Toman)

1.4372 g., 0.9000 Gold .0416 oz. AGW **Obverse:** Uniformed bust 3/4 right **Reverse:** Legend and value within cirlce and wreath **Note:** Prev. KM#994.

Date	Mintage	F	VF	XF	Unc
AH1319	—	100	200	300	400
AH1320	—	35.00	60.00	100	200
AH1321	—	35.00	60.00	100	200
AH1322	—	35.00	60.00	100	200
AH1324	—	100	200	300	400

KM# 994.2 5000 DINARS (1/2 Toman)

1.4372 g., 0.9000 Gold .0416 oz. AGW **Obverse:** Bust with headdress 3/4 right divides date **Reverse:** Legend within circle and wreath

Date	Mintage	F	VF	XF	Unc
AH1323	—	100	200	300	400

KM# 995 TOMAN

2.8744 g., 0.9000 Gold .0832 oz. AGW, 19 mm. **Obverse:** Uniformed bust 3/4 right, accession date, AH1314 above left **Reverse:** Legend and value within circle and wreath

Date	Mintage	F	VF	XF	Unc
AH1319	—	60.00	100	160	250
AH1321	—	100	200	300	400

KM# 996 2 TOMAN

5.7488 g., 0.9000 Gold .1663 oz. AGW, 19 mm. **Obverse:** Uniformed bust 3/4 left, date at left **Reverse:** Legend within circle and wreath **Rev. Legend:** "Muzaffer al-Din Shah"

Date	Mintage	F	VF	XF	Unc
AH1322 (1904)	—	250	400	750	1,500

KM# 997 2 TOMAN

5.7488 g., 0.9000 Gold .1663 oz. AGW, 19 mm. **Subject:** Royal Birthday **Obverse:** Uniformed bust 3/4 left divides legend **Reverse:** Legend within circle and wreath **Rev. Legend:** "Muzaffer al-Din Shah"

Date	Mintage	F	VF	XF	Unc
AH1322 (1904)	—	250	500	1,000	1,500

Muhammad Ali Shah

AH1324-1327 / 1907-1909AD

MILLED COINAGE

KM# 1006 SHAHI SEFID (White Shahi)

0.0691 g., 0.9000 Silver .0200 oz. ASW, 17 mm. **Obverse:** Legend within circle and wreath **Obv. Legend:** "Muhammad Ali Shah" **Reverse:** Radiant lion holding sword within crowned wreath **Mint:** Tehran

Date	Mintage	F	VF	XF	Unc
AH1325 (1907)	—	30.00	60.00	110	200
AH1326 (1908)	—	25.00	40.00	90.00	180
AH1327 (1909)	—	20.00	40.00	80.00	160

KM# 1007 SHAHI SEFID (White Shahi)

0.0691 g., 0.9000 Silver .0200 oz. ASW **Obverse:** Legend within circle and wreath **Obv. Legend:** "Sahib al-Zaman" **Reverse:** Radiant lion holding sword within crowned wreath **Mint:** Tehran

Date	Mintage	F	VF	XF	Unc
AH1326 (1908)	—	60.00	125	175	325

KM# 1008 SHAHI SEFID (White Shahi)

0.0691 g., 0.9000 Silver .0200 oz. ASW **Obverse:** Legend within circle and wreath **Reverse:** Radiant lion holding sword within crowned wreath **Mint:** Tehran

Date	Mintage	F	VF	XF	Unc
ND (1909)	—	50.00	80.00	150	300

KM# 1009 1/4 KRAN (Robi = 5 Shahis)

1.1513 g., 0.9000 Silver .0333 oz. ASW, 15 mm. **Obverse:** Legend within circle and wreath **Obv. Legend:** "Muhammad Ali Shah" **Reverse:** Radiant lion holding sword within crowned wreath **Mint:** Tehran

Date	Mintage	F	VF	XF	Unc
AH1325 (1907)	—	30.00	50.00	100	200
AH1326 (1908)	—	15.00	27.50	40.00	80.00
AH1327 (1909)	—	10.00	20.00	35.00	70.00

KM# 1010 500 DINARS (10 Shahis = 1/2 Kran)

2.3025 g., 0.9000 Silver .0666 oz. ASW, 18 mm. **Obverse:** Legend within circle and wreath **Obv. Legend:** "Muhammad Ali Shah" **Reverse:** Radiant lion holding sword within crowned wreath **Mint:** Tehran

Date	Mintage	F	VF	XF	Unc
AH1325 (1907)	218,000	40.00	75.00	160	300
AH1326 (1908)	218,000	25.00	50.00	110	225
AH1336 (1908) Error for 1326	Inc. above	35.00	60.00	125	250

KM# 1014 500 DINARS (10 Shahis = 1/2 Kran)

2.3025 g., 0.9000 Silver .0666 oz. ASW **Obverse:** Uniformed bust 3/4 left within wreath, date **Reverse:** Crown above lion and sun within wreath, date **Mint:** Tehran

Date	Mintage	F	VF	XF	Unc
AH1325 (1907)	—	125	175	320	500
AH1326 (1908)	—	100	150	240	400

KM# 1013 500 DINARS (10 Shahis = 1/2 Kran)

2.3025 g., 0.9000 Silver .0666 oz. ASW **Obverse:** Uniformed bust 1/4 left within sprigs **Reverse:** Radiant lion holding sword within crowned wreath **Mint:** Tehran

Date	Mintage	F	VF	XF	Unc
AH1326 (1908)	—	40.00	85.00	150	300

Note: Mintage included in KM#1010

Date	Mintage	F	VF	XF	Unc
AH1327 (1909)	—	40.00	85.00	150	300

KM# 1011 1000 DINARS (Kran, Qiran)

4.6050 g., 0.9000 Silver .1332 oz. ASW, 23 mm. **Obverse:** Legend within circle and crowned wreath **Obv. Legend:** "Muhammad Ali Shah" **Reverse:** Radiant lion holding sword within crowned wreath **Mint:** Tehran

Date	Mintage	F	VF	XF	Unc
AH1325 (1907)	289,000	150	300	600	800
AH1326 (1908)	289,000	150	300	600	800

KM# 1015 1000 DINARS (Kran, Qiran)

4.6050 g., 0.9000 Silver .1332 oz. ASW **Obverse:** Uniformed bust 3/4 left within wreath, date below **Reverse:** Radiant lion holding sword within crowned wreath **Mint:** Tehran

Date	Mintage	F	VF	XF	Unc
AH1326 (1908)	—	45.00	70.00	150	375

Note: Mintage included in KM#1011

Date	Mintage	F	VF	XF	Unc
AH1327/6 (1909)	—	40.00	60.00	125	350
AH1327 (1909)	—	40.00	60.00	125	350

KM# 1016 1000 DINARS (Kran, Qiran)

4.6050 g., 0.9000 Silver .1332 oz. ASW **Obverse:** Uniformed bust 3/4 left within wreath, date **Reverse:** Radiant lion holding sword within crowned wreath, date **Mint:** Tehran

Date	Mintage	F	VF	XF	Unc
AH1326 (1908)	—	125	200	350	500

Note: Mintage included in KM#1011

KM# 1012 2000 DINARS (2 Kran)

9.2100 g., 0.9000 Silver .2665 oz. ASW, 28 mm. **Obverse:** Legend within circle and crowned wreath **Obv. Legend:** "Muhammad Ali Shah" **Reverse:** Radiant lion holding sword within crowned wreath **Mint:** Tehran

Date	Mintage	F	VF	XF	Unc
AH1325 (1907)	3,076,000	15.00	25.00	50.00	100
AH1326 (1908)	3,069,000	7.50	11.50	20.00	50.00
AH1327 (1909)	—	7.50	11.50	20.00	50.00

KM# 1017 2000 DINARS (2 Kran)

9.2100 g., 0.9000 Silver .2665 oz. ASW **Obverse:** Uniformed bust 3/4 left within wreath, date below **Reverse:** Radiant lion holding sword within crowned wreath **Mint:** Tehran

Date	Mintage	F	VF	XF	Unc
AH1326 (1908)	—	500	1,000	1,500	2,500

Note: Mintage included in KM#1012

KM# 1018 5000 DINARS (5 Kran)

23.0251 g., 0.9000 Silver .6662 oz. ASW **Obverse:** Uniformed bust 3/4 left within wreath **Reverse:** Crown above lion and sun within wreath **Note:** Dav.#290.

Date	Mintage	F	VF	XF	Unc
AH1327 (1909)	—	250	500	1,000	1,500

Note: Obverse always weakly struck with little detail in head and face

KM# 1024 2000 DINARS (1/5 Toman)

0.5749 g., 0.9000 Gold .0166 oz. AGW **Obverse:** Uniformed bust 3/4 left within wreath **Reverse:** Legend in wreath

Date	Mintage	F	VF	XF	Unc
AH1326 (1908)	—	75.00	100	150	275
AH1327 (1909)	—	75.00	100	150	275

KM# 1021 5000 DINARS (1/2 Toman)

1.4372 g., 0.9000 Gold .0416 oz. AGW, 17 mm. **Obverse:** Legend within circle and wreath **Obv. Legend:** Muhammad Ali Shah **Reverse:** Radiant lion holding sword within crowned wreath

Date	Mintage	F	VF	XF	Unc
AH1324 (1906)	—	75.00	100	150	275
AH1325 (1907)	—	75.00	100	150	275

KM# 1025 5000 DINARS (1/2 Toman)

1.4372 g., 0.9000 Gold .0416 oz. AGW, 17 mm. **Obverse:** Uniformed bust 3/4 left divides date **Reverse:** Legend within circle and wreath **Rev. Legend:** "Muhammad Ali Shah"

Date	Mintage	F	VF	XF	Unc
AH1326 (1908)	—	75.00	100	150	275
AH1362 (1908) Error for 1326	—	75.00	100	150	275
AH1327 (1909)	—	75.00	100	150	275

KM# 1022 TOMAN

2.8744 g., 0.9000 Gold .0832 oz. AGW, 19 mm. **Obverse:** Legend within circle and wreath **Obv. Legend:** "Muhammad Ali Shah" **Reverse:** Radiant lion holding sword within crowned wreath

Date	Mintage	F	VF	XF	Unc
AH1324 (1906)	—	90.00	150	300	500

KM# 1026 TOMAN

2.8744 g., 0.9000 Gold .0832 oz. AGW **Obverse:** Uniformed bust 3/4 left divides date **Reverse:** Legend within circle and closed wreath **Rev. Legend:** "Muhammad Ali Shah"

Date	Mintage	F	VF	XF	Unc
AH1327 (1909)	—	90.00	150	300	500

MILLED COINAGE

Silver Kran Standard

KM# 891 SHAHI SEFID (White Shahi)

Copper-Nickel Clad Brass **Obv. Legend:** "Nasir al-Din" (KM#889) **Rev. Legend:** "Shahib al-zaman" (obverse of KM#1007) **Mint:** Tehran **Note:** Mule using old obverse die.

Date	Mintage	F	VF	XF	Unc
ND	—	50.00	75.00	125	250

Sultan Ahmad Shah

AH1327-1344 / 1909-1925AD

MILLED COINAGE

KM# 1031 SHAHI SEFID (White Shahi)

0.0691 g., 0.9000 Silver .0200 oz. ASW **Obverse:** Legend within circle and wreath **Obv. Legend:** "Ahmad Shah" **Reverse:** Radiant lion holding sword within crowned wreath **Mint:** Tehran

Date	Mintage	F	VF	XF	Unc
AH1328 (1910)	—	5.00	10.00	20.00	40.00
AH1329 (1911)	—	6.00	12.00	25.00	50.00
AH1330 (1911)	189,000	4.00	10.00	20.00	40.00

KM# 1032 SHAHI SEFID (White Shahi)

0.0691 g., 0.9000 Silver .0200 oz. ASW **Obverse:** Legend within circle and wreath **Reverse:** Radiant lion holding sword within crowned wreath **Mint:** Tehran

Date	Mintage	F	VF	XF	Unc
AH1332 (1913)	10,000	30.00	50.00	85.00	150

KM# 1033 SHAHI SEFID (White Shahi)

0.0691 g., 0.9000 Silver .0200 oz. ASW **Obverse:** Legend within circle and wreath **Obv. Legend:** "Ahmad Shah" **Reverse:** Legend within circle and wreath **Rev. Legend:** "Sahib-al-Zaman" **Mint:** Tehran

Date	Mintage	F	VF	XF	Unc
ND (1913)	—	60.00	125	200	400

KM# 1049 SHAHI SEFID (White Shahi)

0.0691 g., 0.9000 Silver .0200 oz. ASW **Obverse:** Legend within circle and wreath **Reverse:** Radiant lion holding sword within crowned wreath **Rev. Legend:** "Sahib-al-Zaman" **Mint:** Tehran

Date	Mintage	F	VF	XF	Unc
ND (1913)	—	10.00	20.00	40.00	75.00
AH1332 (1913)	—	10.00	18.00	35.00	80.00
Note: Included in KM#1032					
AH1333 (1914)	—	10.00	20.00	40.00	80.00
Note: Included in KM#1047					
AH1337 (1918)	—	10.00	20.00	40.00	80.00
Note: Included in KM#1047					
AH1341 (1922)	3,000	15.00	25.00	50.00	100
AH1342 (1923)	—	15.00	25.00	50.00	100
Note: Included in KM#1047					

KM# 1047 SHAHI SEFID (White Shahi)

0.0691 g., 0.9000 Silver .0200 oz. ASW **Obverse:** Legend within circle and wreath, date below **Reverse:** Radiant lion holding sword within crowned wreath **Mint:** Tehran **Note:** Varieties exist.

Date	Mintage	F	VF	XF	Unc
AH1333 (1914)	78,000	5.00	10.00	20.00	40.00
AH1334 (1915)	6,000	12.00	20.00	40.00	80.00
AH1335 (1916)	73,000	8.00	15.00	30.00	60.00
AH1335//1337 (1918)	Inc. above	40.00	80.00	165	250
AH1337 (1918)	76,000	8.00	15.00	30.00	60.00
AH1337//1337 (1918)	—	40.00	75.00	150	280
AH1339 (1920)	10,000	12.00	20.00	40.00	80.00
AH1342 (1923)	20,000	12.00	20.00	40.00	80.00

KM# 1048 SHAHI SEFID (White Shahi)

0.0691 g., 0.9000 Silver .0200 oz. ASW **Obverse:** Legend within circle and wreath **Reverse:** Legend within circle and wreath, date below **Rev. Legend:** "Sahib-al-Zaman" **Mint:** Tehran

Date	Mintage	F	VF	XF	Unc
AH1335 (1916)	—	50.00	80.00	150	300

Note: Mintage included in KM#1047 of AH1335

KM# 1050 SHAHI SEFID (White Shahi)

0.6908 g., 0.9000 Silver .0200 oz. ASW **Obverse:** Legend within circle and wreath, dated AH1339 **Reverse:** Radiant lion with sword within crowned wreath with AH1341 between lion's legs, AH1327 below wreath **Mint:** Tehran

Date	Mintage	F	VF	XF	Unc
AH1339//1341 & 1327 (1922)	—	50.00	80.00	150	300

Note: Numerous silver Nouruz tokens, some with dates SH1328-1346, are available in Tehran for a fraction of the price of true Shahis

KM# 1035 1/4 KRAN (Robi = 5 Shahis)

1.1513 g., 0.9000 Silver .0333 oz. ASW, 15 mm. **Obverse:** Legend within circle and wreath **Obv. Legend:** "Ahmad Shah" **Reverse:** Radiant lion holding sword within crowned wreath **Mint:** Tehran

Date	Mintage	F	VF	XF	Unc
AH1327 (1909)	—	5.00	10.00	20.00	40.00
AH1328 (1910)	—	4.00	7.50	15.00	30.00
AH1329 (1911)	130,000	12.50	20.00	40.00	80.00
AH1330 (1911)	156,000	4.00	7.50	15.00	30.00
AH1331 (1912)	30,000	—	—	—	—
Note: Reported, not confirmed.					
AH1313 (1912) Error for 1331	Inc. above	—	—	—	—
Note: Reported, not confirmed.					

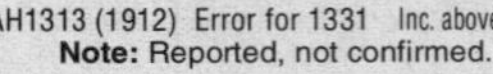

KM# 1052 1/4 KRAN (Robi = 5 Shahis)

1.1513 g., 0.9000 Silver .0333 oz. ASW **Obverse:** Legend within circle and wreath, date below **Obv. Legend:** "Ahmad Shah" **Reverse:** Radiant lion holding sword within crowned wreath **Mint:** Tehran **Note:** Mule.

Date	Mintage	F	VF	XF	Unc
ND (1909)	—	45.00	65.00	125	200
AH1327 (1909)	—	65.00	135	185	300

KM# 1051 1/4 KRAN (Robi = 5 Shahis)

1.1513 g., 0.9000 Silver .0333 oz. ASW **Obverse:** Legend within circle and wreath **Obv. Legend:** "Ahmad Shah" **Reverse:** Radiant lion holding sword within crowned wreath **Mint:** Tehran

Date	Mintage	F	VF	XF	Unc
AH1332 (1913)	252,000	5.00	10.00	20.00	40.00
AH1333 (1914)	Inc. above	6.00	12.00	25.00	50.00
AH1334 (1915)	70,000	10.00	20.00	50.00	100
AH1335 (1916)	260,000	4.00	8.00	15.00	30.00
AH1336 (1917)	160,000	4.00	8.00	15.00	30.00
AH1337 (1918)	80,000	6.00	12.00	25.00	50.00
AH1339 (1920)	28,000	9.00	15.00	30.00	60.00
AH1341 (1922)	22,000	12.00	20.00	40.00	80.00
AH1342 (1923)	110,000	6.00	12.00	25.00	50.00
AH1343 (1924)	186,000	4.00	8.00	15.00	30.00

KM# 1053 1/4 KRAN (Robi = 5 Shahis)

1.1513 g., 0.9000 Silver .0333 oz. ASW **Obverse:** Legend within circle and wreath **Reverse:** Radiant lion holding sword within crowned wreath **Mint:** Tehran

Date	Mintage	F	VF	XF	Unc
AH1334 (1915)	—	35.00	75.00	150	250

Note: Mintage included with KM#1051

KM# 1036 500 DINARS (10 Shahis = 1/2 Kran)

2.3025 g., 0.9000 Silver .0666 oz. ASW, 18 mm. **Obverse:** Legend within circle and wreath **Obv. Legend:** "Ahmad Shah" **Reverse:** Radiant lion holding sword within crowned wreath **Mint:** Tehran

Date	Mintage	F	VF	XF	Unc
AH1327 (1909)	—	8.00	15.00	30.00	50.00
AH1328 (1910)	—	5.00	12.50	20.00	40.00
AH1329 (1911)	44,000	10.00	20.00	40.00	80.00
AH1330 (1911)	627,000	8.00	15.00	30.00	50.00

KM# 1054 500 DINARS (10 Shahis = 1/2 Kran)

2.3025 g., 0.9000 Silver .0666 oz. ASW **Obverse:** Uniformed bust 1/4 left within wreath, date below **Reverse:** Radiant lion holding sword within crowned wreath **Mint:** Tehran

Date	Mintage	F	VF	XF	Unc
AH1331 (1912)	—	8.00	15.00	30.00	50.00
Note: Mintage included in AH1330 above					
AH1332 (1913)	560,000	8.00	15.00	30.00	50.00
AH1333 (1914)	292,000	5.00	10.00	15.00	30.00
AH1334 (1915)	65,000	5.00	10.00	15.00	30.00
AH1335 (1916)	150,000	8.00	15.00	30.00	60.00
AH1336 (1917)	240,000	4.00	8.00	20.00	40.00
AH1339 (1920)	—	17.50	25.00	40.00	80.00
AH1343 (1924)	160,000	6.00	10.00	25.00	50.00

Note: 10,000 reported struck in AH1337 probably dated AH1336

KM# 1055 500 DINARS (10 Shahis = 1/2 Kran)

2.3025 g., 0.9000 Silver .0666 oz. ASW **Obverse:** Uniformed bust 1/4 left within wreath, date below **Reverse:** Radiant lion holding sword within crowned wreath **Mint:** Tehran

Date	Mintage	F	VF	XF	Unc
AH1332 (1913)	—	30.00	50.00	90.00	200

Note: Mintage included in KM#1054

KM# 1038 1000 DINARS (Kran, Qiran)

4.6050 g., 0.9000 Silver .1332 oz. ASW, 23 mm. **Obverse:** Legend within circle and wreath **Obv. Legend:** "Sultan Ahmad Shah" **Reverse:** Radiant lion holding sword within crowned wreath **Mint:** Tehran

Date	Mintage	F	VF	XF	Unc
AH1327 (1909)	—	7.50	15.00	30.00	60.00
AH1328 (1910)	—	6.50	12.50	25.00	50.00
AH1329 (1911)	3,000,000	6.50	12.50	25.00	50.00
AH1330 (1911)	—	6.50	12.50	25.00	50.00

KM# 1037 1000 DINARS (Kran, Qiran)

4.6050 g., 0.9000 Silver .1332 oz. ASW **Obverse:** Legend within circle and wreath **Reverse:** Radiant lion holding sword within crowned wreath **Mint:** Tehran **Note:** Mule.

Date	Mintage	F	VF	XF	Unc
AH1336 (1909)	—	—	—	100	200

KM# 1056 1000 DINARS (Kran, Qiran)

4.6050 g., 0.9000 Silver .1332 oz. ASW **Obverse:** Uniformed bust 1/4 left within wreath, date below **Reverse:** Radiant lion holding sword within crowned wreath **Mint:** Tehran

Date	Mintage	F	VF	XF	Unc
AH1331 (1912)	1,310,000	5.00	8.00	25.00	40.00
AH1332 (1913)	1,891,000	3.00	5.00	12.50	30.00
AH1333 (1914)	2,179,000	7.50	12.00	25.00	40.00
AH1334 (1915)	1,273,000	3.00	5.00	12.50	25.00
AH1335 (1916)	2,162,000	3.00	5.00	12.50	25.00
AH1336 (1917)	1,412,000	3.50	6.00	15.00	30.00
AH1337 (1918)	3,330,000	3.00	5.00	12.50	25.00
AH1339 (1920)	35,000	12.50	25.00	55.00	90.00
AH1330 (1921) Error for 1340	—	30.00	65.00	125	175
AH1340 (1921)	28,000	15.00	30.00	60.00	100
AH1341 (1922)	170,000	8.00	15.00	35.00	60.00
AH1342 (1923)	255,000	3.00	6.00	20.00	30.00
AH1343 (1924)	1,345,000	3.00	6.00	20.00	30.00
AH1344 (1925)	2,978,000	4.00	6.00	20.00	35.00

KM# 1059 1000 DINARS (Kran, Qiran)

4.6050 g., 0.9000 Silver .1332 oz. ASW, 23 mm. **Subject:** 10th Year of Reign **Obverse:** Uniformed bust 1/4 left within wreath, date below **Reverse:** Radiant lion holding sword within crowned wreath **Mint:** Tehran

Date	Mintage	F	VF	XF	Unc
AH1337 (1918)	975,000	35.00	75.00	125	250

KM# 1040 2000 DINARS (2 Kran)

9.2100 g., 0.9000 Silver .2665 oz. ASW, 28 mm. **Obverse:** Legend within circle and crowned wreath **Obv. Legend:** "Ahmad Shah" **Reverse:** Radiant lion holding sword within crowned wreath **Mint:** Tehran

Date	Mintage	F	VF	XF	Unc
AH1327 (1909)	—	7.50	15.00	30.00	50.00
Note: Mintage included in KM#1328					
AH1328 (1910)	30,000,000	5.00	10.00	20.00	40.00
AH1329 (1911)	29,250,000	5.00	10.00	20.00	40.00

KM# 1041 2000 DINARS (2 Kran)

9.2100 g., 0.9000 Silver .2665 oz. ASW **Obverse:** Legend within circle and crowned wreath **Reverse:** Radiant lion holding sword within crowned wreath **Mint:** Tehran

Date	Mintage	F	VF	XF	Unc
AH1330 (1911)	2,901,000	7.50	15.00	30.00	60.00

KM# 1043 2000 DINARS (2 Kran)

9.2100 g., 0.9000 Silver .2665 oz. ASW **Obverse:** Legend within circle and crowned wreath **Obv. Legend:** "Ahmad Shah" **Reverse:** Radiant lion holding sword within crowned wreath **Mint:** Tehran

Date	Mintage	F	VF	XF	Unc
AH1330 (1911)	—	7.50	15.00	30.00	60.00
Note: Mintage included in KM#1041					
AH1331 (1912)	13,412,000	7.50	15.00	30.00	60.00

KM# 1057 2000 DINARS (2 Kran)

9.2100 g., 0.9000 Silver .2665 oz. ASW **Obverse:** Uniformed bust 1/4 left within wreath, date below **Reverse:** Radiant lion holding sword within crowned wreath **Mint:** Tehran

Date	Mintage	F	VF	XF	Unc
AH1331 (1912)	—	6.00	12.50	25.00	50.00
Note: Mintage included in KM#1043					
AH1332 (1913)	12,926,000	5.00	7.50	15.00	30.00
AH1333 (1914)	Inc. above	5.00	7.50	15.00	30.00
AH1334 (1915)	4,299,000	5.00	7.50	15.00	30.00
AH1335 (1916)	9,777,000	5.00	7.50	15.00	30.00
AH1336 (1917)	5,401,000	5.00	7.50	15.00	30.00
AH1337 (1918)	2,951,000	5.00	7.50	15.00	30.00
AH1339 (1920)	1,085,000	6.00	12.50	25.00	50.00
AH1330 (1921) Error for 1340	—	50.00	100	150	250
Note: Mintage included in KM#1043					
AH1340 (1921)	254,000	9.00	15.00	30.00	65.00
AH1341 (1922)	4,460,000	5.00	7.50	15.00	30.00
AH1342 (1923)	2,245,000	5.00	8.00	20.00	35.00
AH1343 (1924)	5,205,000	5.00	8.00	20.00	35.00
AH1344/34 (1925)	12,354	7.00	12.00	25.00	55.00
AH1344 (1925)	Inc. above	6.00	10.00	20.00	40.00

KM# 1060 2000 DINARS (2 Kran)

9.2100 g., 0.9000 Silver .2665 oz. ASW, 28 mm. **Subject:** 10th Anniversary of Reign **Obverse:** Uniformed bust 1/4 left within wreath **Reverse:** Radiant lion with sword within crowned wreath **Mint:** Tehran

Date	Mintage	F	VF	XF	Unc
AH1337 (1918)	3,503,000	60.00	100	150	300

KM# 1058 5000 DINARS (5 Kran)

23.0251 g., 0.9000 Silver .6662 oz. ASW **Obverse:** Uniformed bust 1/4 left within wreath, date below **Reverse:** Radiant lion holding sword within crowned wreath **Note:** Dav.#291.

Date	Mintage	F	VF	XF	Unc
AH1331 (1912)	—	60.00	150	250	500
AH1332 (1913)	3,000,000	10.00	14.00	30.00	85.00
AH1333 (1914)	667,000	12.00	16.00	35.00	90.00
AH1334 (1915)	443,000	12.00	16.00	35.00	90.00
AH1335 (1916)	1,884,000	12.00	16.00	35.00	90.00
AH1337 (1918)	165,000	14.00	25.00	55.00	110
AH1339 (1920)	90,000	20.00	30.00	65.00	125
AH1340 (1921)	303,000	14.00	25.00	55.00	110
AH1341 (1922)	757,000	12.00	16.00	35.00	90.00
AH1342/32 (1923)	546,000	12.00	16.00	35.00	90.00
AH1342 (1923)	Inc. above	12.00	16.00	35.00	90.00
AH1343 (1924)	935,000	12.00	16.00	35.00	90.00
AH1344/34 (1925)	2,284,000	12.00	16.00	30.00	85.00
AH1344 (1925)	Inc. above	15.00	20.00	40.00	95.00

Note: Beware of altered date AH1331 specimens. 9,000 reported minted in AH1336, probably dated earlier

KM# 1066 2000 DINARS (1/5 Toman)

0.5749 g., 0.9000 Gold .0166 oz. AGW, 14 mm. **Obverse:** Legend within circle and wreath **Obv. Legend:** "Ahmad Shah" **Reverse:** Radiant lion holding sword within crowned wreath

Date	Mintage	F	VF	XF	Unc
AH1328 (1910)	—	100	175	250	500
AH1329 (1911)	—	250	550	750	900
AH1330 (1911)	—	100	175	250	500

KM# 1070 2000 DINARS (1/5 Toman)

0.5749 g., 0.9000 Gold .0166 oz. AGW, 14 mm. **Obverse:** Uniformed bust 1/4 left divides date **Reverse:** Legend within circle and wreath **Rev. Legend:** "Ahmad Shah"

Date	Mintage	F	VF	XF	Unc
AH1332 (1913)	—	22.50	40.00	60.00	130
AH1333 (1914)	—	18.50	35.00	60.00	125
AH1334 (1915)	—	25.00	50.00	100	200
AH1335 (1916)	—	16.50	30.00	40.00	60.00
AH1337 (1918)	—	16.50	30.00	40.00	100
AH1339 (1920)	—	18.50	35.00	50.00	100
AH1340 (1921)	—	18.50	40.00	60.00	120
AH1341 (1922)	—	18.50	35.00	50.00	100
AH1342 (1923)	—	18.50	35.00	50.00	100
AH1343/33 (1924)	—	50.00	100	200	400
AH1343 (1924)	—	25.00	50.00	100	200

KM# 1067 5000 DINARS (1/2 Toman)

1.4372 g., 0.9000 Gold .0416 oz. AGW **Obverse:** Legend within circle and wreath **Obv. Legend:** "Ahmad Shah" **Reverse:** Radiant lion holding sword within crowned wreath

Date	Mintage	F	VF	XF	Unc
AH1328 (1910)	—	60.00	125	200	275
AH1329 (1911)	—	175	400	600	750
AH1330 (1911)	—	175	400	600	750

KM# 1071 5000 DINARS (1/2 Toman)

1.4372 g., 0.9000 Gold .0416 oz. AGW, 17 mm. **Obverse:** Uniformed bust 1/4 left divides date **Reverse:** Legend within circle and wreath **Rev. Legend:** "Ahmad Shah"

Date	Mintage	F	VF	XF	Unc
AH1331 (1912)	—	50.00	100	150	300
AH1332 (1913)	—	40.00	60.00	100	150
AH1333 (1914)	—	50.00	100	200	300
AH1334 (1915)	—	50.00	100	200	300
AH1335 (1916)	—	50.00	100	200	300
AH1336 (1917)	—	35.00	40.00	50.00	90.00
AH1337 (1918)	—	50.00	100	200	300
AH1339 (1920)	—	60.00	125	250	350
AH1340 (1921)	—	35.00	40.00	60.00	110
AH1341 (1922)	—	35.00	40.00	50.00	90.00
AH1342 (1923)	—	35.00	40.00	50.00	90.00
AH1343/33 (1924)	—	100	200	400	600
AH1343 (1924)	—	50.00	100	200	300

KM# 1072 5000 DINARS (1/2 Toman)

1.4372 g., 0.9000 Gold .0416 oz. AGW **Obverse:** Bust with headdress 1/4 left within sprigs **Rev. Legend:** "Sahib al-Zaman"

Date	Mintage	F	VF	XF	Unc
AH1339 (1920)	—	100	150	250	600
AH1340 (1921)	—	100	150	250	600

KM# 1068 TOMAN

2.8744 g., 0.9000 Gold .0832 oz. AGW **Obv. Legend:** "Ahmad Shah", AH1328-1332 **Reverse:** Lion and sun

Date	Mintage	F	VF	XF	Unc
AH1329 (1911)	—	200	300	500	750

KM# 1074 TOMAN

2.8744 g., 0.9000 Gold .0832 oz. AGW, 19 mm. **Obverse:** Uniformed bust 1/4 left divides date **Reverse:** Legend within circle and wreath **Rev. Legend:** "Ahmad Shah"

Date	Mintage	F	VF	XF	Unc
AH1332 (1913)	—	75.00	150	250	500
AH1333 (1914)	—	500	750	1,000	1,250
AH1334 (1915)	—	65.00	125	175	300
AH1335 (1916)	—	65.00	125	175	300
AH1337 (1918)	—	BV	60.00	100	175
AH1339 (1920)	—	BV	70.00	100	175
AH1340 (1921)	—	100	200	300	400
AH1341 (1922)	—	BV	60.00	90.00	150
AH1342 (1923)	—	BV	60.00	90.00	150
AH1343 (1924)	—	BV	60.00	90.00	150

KM# 1073 TOMAN

2.8744 g., 0.9000 Gold .0832 oz. AGW, 19 mm. **Obverse:** Bust with headdress 1/4 left **Reverse:** Ahmad Shah Pattern 2 Toman **Note:** The reverse die used was of an unadopted pattern.

Date	Mintage	F	VF	XF	Unc
AH1332 (1913)	—	300	600	900	1,500
AH1333 (1914)	—	350	650	1,000	1,750

KM# 1075 5 TOMAN

14.3720 g., 0.9000 Gold .4159 oz. AGW, 30 mm. **Obverse:** Legend within beaded circle and wreath **Obv. Legend:** "Ahmad Shah" **Reverse:** Radiant lion holding sword within wreath

Date	Mintage	F	VF	XF	Unc
AH1332/1 (1913)	—	3,500	4,500	6,000	8,000
AH1334/2/1 (1915)	—	1,100	1,600	2,000	2,700

Note: A number of gold medals of 5 Toman weight were struck between 1297 and 1326; These bear a couplet which clearly indicates that they are medals awarded by the Shah for bravery

KM# 1076 10 TOMAN

28.7440 g., 0.9000 Gold .8317 oz. AGW, 37 mm. **Obverse:** Uniformed bust 1/4 left within wreath, date below **Obv. Legend:** "Ahmad Shah" **Reverse:** Legend within circle and wreath

Date	Mintage	F	VF	XF	Unc
AH1331 (1912)	—	2,400	4,350	6,500	8,500
AH1334 (1915) Rare	—	—	—	—	—
AH1337//1334 (1918)	—	—	—	6,500	8,500

Note: The date on the AH1334 reverse die was not changed for use as the reverse to the 1337 issue

KM# 1077 10 TOMAN

28.7440 g., 0.9000 Gold .8317 oz. AGW **Obverse:** Uniformed bust 1/4 left within wreath, date **Reverse:** Radiant lion holding sword within wreath

Date	Mintage	F	VF	XF	Unc
AH1337 (1918)	—	1,850	3,000	4,500	5,500

KM# 1080 ASHRAFI

Gold **Obverse:** Bust of Ahmad Shah **Reverse:** Lion and sun within crowned wreath

Date	Mintage	F	VF	XF	Unc
AH1337 (1918)	—	—	125	250	375

KM# A1081 2 ASHRAFI

Gold **Obverse:** Uniformed bust 1/4 left within wreath **Reverse:** Crown above lion and sun within wreath

Date	Mintage	F	VF	XF	Unc
AH1337 (1918)	—	—	250	500	750

KM# 1081 5 ASHRAFI

Gold **Obverse:** Uniformed bust 1/4 left within wreath **Reverse:** Lion and sun within crowned wreath

Date	Mintage	F	VF	XF	Unc
AH1337 (1918)	—	—	500	750	1,000

KM# 1082 10 ASHRAFI

Gold **Obverse:** Uniformed bust 1/4 left within wreath **Reverse:** Lion and sun within crowned wreath

Date	Mintage	F	VF	XF	Unc
AH1337 (1918)	—	500	1,000	1,500	2,000

CLANDESTINE COINAGE

KM# 1039 1000 DINARS (Kran, Qiran)

Silver **Obverse:** Legend within beaded circle and wreath **Reverse:** Radiant lion holding sword within crowned wreath **Mint:** Tehran

Date	Mintage	F	VF	XF	Unc
AH1330 (sic) (1915)	—	12.00	25.00	50.00	75.00
AH1330 (sic) (1915) Proof, rare	—	—	—	—	—

Note: KM#1039 differs from KM#1038 in that it is about 1 millimeter broader and has a much thicker rim and more clearly defined denticles. Struck in Germany, without Iranian authorization, for circulation in western Iran during World War I. Also, the lion lacks the triangular face and fierce expression of KM#1038 and the point of the Talwar (scimitar) does not touch the sunburst as it does on Tehran issues.

KM# 1042 2000 DINARS (2 Kran)

Silver **Reverse:** Lion's face has friendly expression **Mint:** Tehran

Date	Mintage	F	VF	XF	Unc
AH1330 (sic) (1915)	—	12.00	25.00	50.00	75.00

Note: See general note for KM#1039

Reza Shah

AH1344-1360 / 1925-1941AD

MILLED COINAGE

KM# 1091 50 DINARS

Copper-Nickel **Obverse:** Legend within circle and crowned wreath **Reverse:** Radiant lion holding sword within crowned wreath **Mint:** Tehran

Date	Mintage	F	VF	XF	Unc
SH1305 (1926)	11,000,000	2.50	5.00	10.00	20.00
SH1307 (1928)	2,500,000	2.50	5.00	10.00	20.00

KM# 1092 100 DINARS (2 Shahi)

Copper-Nickel **Obverse:** Legend within circle and crowned wreath **Reverse:** Radiant lion holding sword within crowned wreath

Date	Mintage	F	VF	XF	Unc
SH1305 (1926)	4,500,000	2.50	5.00	10.00	20.00
SH1307 (1928)	3,750,000	2.50	5.00	10.00	20.00

KM# 1093 1/4 KRAN (Robi = 5 Shahis)

1.1513 g., 0.9000 Silver .0333 oz. ASW **Obverse:** Legend within circle and wreath **Reverse:** Crown above lion and sun within wreath **Mint:** Tehran **Note:** 8,000 reported struck in SH1305, but that year not yet found and presumed not to exist.

Date	Mintage	F	VF	XF	Unc
SH1304 (1925)	Est. 24,000	20.00	50.00	85.00	160

Note: For similar looking coins dated SH1315, see 1/4 Rial, KM#1127.

KM# 1094 500 DINARS (10 Shahis = 1/2 Kran)

2.3025 g., 0.9000 Silver .0666 oz. ASW **Obverse:** Legend within circle and wreath **Reverse:** Radiant lion holding sword within crowned wreath **Mint:** Tehran

Date	Mintage	F	VF	XF	Unc
SH1304 (1925) Rare		—	—	—	—

KM# 1098 500 DINARS (10 Shahis = 1/2 Kran)

2.3025 g., 0.9000 Silver .0666 oz. ASW **Obverse:** Legend within wreath **Obv. Legend:** "Reza Shah" **Reverse:** Lion and sun within wreath **Mint:** Tehran

Date	Mintage	F	VF	XF	Unc
SH1305 (1926)	10,000	150	250	500	750

KM# 1102 500 DINARS (10 Shahis = 1/2 Kran)

2.3025 g., 0.9000 Silver .0666 oz. ASW **Obverse:** Uniformed bust 3/4 right within wreath divides date **Reverse:** Radiant lion holding sword within crowned wreath **Mint:** Tehran

Date	Mintage	F	VF	XF	Unc
SH1306 (1927)	5,000	50.00	100	150	250
SH1307 (1928)	46,000	10.00	15.00	30.00	60.00
SH1308 (1929)	464,000	10.00	15.00	30.00	60.00

Note: Some of the coins reported in SH1308 were dated 1307

KM# 1095 1000 DINARS (Kran, Qiran)

4.6050 g., 0.9000 Silver .1332 oz. ASW **Obverse:** Legend within circle and wreath **Reverse:** Radiant lion holding sword within crowned wreath **Mint:** Tehran

Date	Mintage	F	VF	XF	Unc
SH1304 (1925)	2,573,000	10.00	20.00	30.00	50.00
SH1305 (1926)	2,265,000	10.00	20.00	30.00	50.00

KM# 1099 1000 DINARS (Kran, Qiran)

4.6050 g., 0.9000 Silver .1332 oz. ASW **Obverse:** Legend within circle and wreath **Obv. Legend:** "Reza Shah" **Reverse:** Radiant lion holding sword within crowned wreath **Mint:** Tehran

Date	Mintage	F	VF	XF	Unc
SH1305 (1926)	—	10.00	20.00	30.00	50.00
Note: Mintage included in KM#1095					
SH1306/5 (1927)	3,130,000	5.00	8.00	15.00	25.00
SH1306 (1927)	Inc. above	10.00	20.00	30.00	50.00

KM# 1103 1000 DINARS (Kran, Qiran)

4.6050 g., 0.9000 Silver .1332 oz. ASW **Obverse:** Uniformed bust 3/4 right within wreath divides date of Ascession in SH1304 **Reverse:** Lion and sun within crowned wreath **Mint:** Tehran

Date	Mintage	F	VF	XF	Unc
SH1306 (1927)	—	10.00	20.00	30.00	60.00
Note: Mintage included in KM#1099					
SH1307 (1928)	4,300,000	10.00	20.00	30.00	50.00
SH1308 (1929)	603,000	10.00	20.00	30.00	50.00

KM# 1096 2000 DINARS (2 Kran)

9.2100 g., 0.9000 Silver .2665 oz. ASW **Obverse:** Legend within circle and wreath **Reverse:** Date below lion **Mint:** Tehran

Date	Mintage	F	VF	XF	Unc
SH1304 (1925)	11,920,000	15.00	30.00	50.00	75.00
SH1305 (1926)	9,785,000	15.00	30.00	50.00	75.00

KM# 1100 2000 DINARS (2 Kran)

9.2100 g., 0.9000 Silver .2665 oz. ASW **Obverse:** Legend within circle and wreath **Obv. Legend:** "Reza Shah" **Reverse:** Radiant lion holding sword within crowned wreath **Mint:** Tehran

Date	Mintage	F	VF	XF	Unc
SH1305 (1926)	—	15.00	30.00	50.00	75.00
SH1306 (1927)	9,380,000	4.50	7.50	12.50	25.00

KM# 1104 2000 DINARS (2 Kran)

9.2100 g., 0.9000 Silver .2665 oz. ASW **Obverse:** Uniformed bust 3/4 right within wreath divides date of Ascession in SH1304 **Reverse:** Radiant lion holding sword within crowned wreath

Date	Mintage	F	VF	XF	Unc
SH1306 (1927)	—	5.00	10.00	25.00	50.00
Note: Mintage included in KM#1100					
SH1306 (1927) H	11,714,000	5.00	10.00	25.00	50.00
SH1306 (1927) L	7,500,000	5.00	10.00	25.00	50.00
SH1306 (1927) H Proof	—	Value: 375			
SH1307 (1928)	11,146,000	5.00	10.00	25.00	50.00
SH1308 (1929)	1,611,000	5.00	10.00	25.00	50.00

KM# 1105 2000 DINARS (2 Kran)

9.2100 g., 0.9000 Silver .2665 oz. ASW **Obverse:** Uniformed bust 3/4 right within wreath **Reverse:** Crown above lion and sun within wreath **Mint:** Tehran **Note:** Mule.

Date	Mintage	F	VF	XF	Unc
SH1306 (1927)	—	—	—	50.00	100

KM# 1097 5000 DINARS (5 Kran)

23.0251 g., 0.9000 Silver .6662 oz. ASW **Obverse:** Legend within crowned wreath **Reverse:** Radiant lion holding sword within wreath **Note:** Dav.#292.

Date	Mintage	F	VF	XF	Unc
SH1304 (1925)	500,000	16.00	40.00	75.00	150
SH1305 (1926)	1,363,000	16.00	40.00	75.00	150

KM# 1101 5000 DINARS (5 Kran)

23.0251 g., 0.9000 Silver .6662 oz. ASW **Obverse:** Legend within crowned wreath **Obv. Legend:** "Reza Shah" **Reverse:** Radiant lion holding sword within wreath **Note:** Dav.#293.

Date	Mintage	F	VF	XF	Unc
SH1305 (1926)	—	35.00	70.00	100	150
Note: Mintage included in KM#1097					
SH1306 (1927)	3,186,000	35.00	70.00	100	150

KM# 1106 5000 DINARS (5 Kran)

23.0251 g., 0.9000 Silver .6662 oz. ASW **Obverse:** Uniformed bust 3/4 right within wreath divides date of Ascession in SH1304 **Reverse:** Crown above lion and sun within wreath **Note:** Dav.#294. Mint marks located as on 2000 Dinars, KM#1104.

Date	Mintage	F	VF	XF	Unc
SH1306 (1927)	—	12.00	25.00	50.00	100
Note: Mintage including in KM#1101					
SH1306 (1927) Proof	—	Value: 400			
SH1306 (1927) H	4,711,000	12.00	25.00	50.00	100
SH1306 (1927) L	3,000,000	12.00	25.00	50.00	100
SH1307 (1928)	3,928,000	15.00	35.00	75.00	150
SH1308 (1929)	584,000	15.00	35.00	75.00	150

KM# 1107 5000 DINARS (5 Kran)

23.0251 g., 0.9000 Silver .6662 oz. ASW **Obverse:** Uniformed bust 3/4 right within wreath **Reverse:** Crown above lion and sun within wreath **Note:** Mule.

Date	Mintage	F	VF	XF	Unc
SH1306 (1927)	—	—	—	75.00	150

KM# 1108 TOMAN

2.8744 g., Gold .0832 oz. AGW, 19 mm. **Subject:** Reza's First New Year Celebration **Obverse:** Reza type legend **Reverse:** Radiant lion holding sword within crowned wreath

Date	Mintage	F	VF	XF	Unc
SH1305 (1926)	—	200	300	500	750

KM# 1111 PAHLAVI

1.9180 g., Gold .0555 oz. AGW **Obverse:** Legend within crowned wreath **Reverse:** Radiant lion holding sword within crowned wreath

Date	Mintage	F	VF	XF	Unc
SH1305 (1926)	5,000	125	250	400	600

KM# 1114 PAHLAVI

2.8744 g., Gold .0832 oz. AGW **Obverse:** Uniformed bust right above sprays **Reverse:** Value and legend within beaded circle and crowned wreath

Date	Mintage	F	VF	XF	Unc
SH1306 (1927)	21,000	BV	65.00	85.00	125
SH1307 (1928)	5,000	65.00	90.00	125	185
SH1308 (1929)	989	80.00	100	160	275

KM# 1112 2 PAHLAVI

3.8360 g., Gold .1110 oz. AGW **Obverse:** Legend within crowned wreath **Reverse:** Radiant lion holding sword within crowned wreath

Date	Mintage	F	VF	XF	Unc
SH1305 (1926)	1,134	250	400	750	1,250

KM# 1115 2 PAHLAVI

3.8360 g., Gold .1110 oz. AGW **Obverse:** Uniformed bust right above sprays **Reverse:** Value and legend within beaded circle and crowned wreath

Date	Mintage	F	VF	XF	Unc
SH1306 (1927)	2,494	80.00	100	150	250
SH1307 (1928)	7,000	80.00	100	150	230
SH1308 (1929)	789	90.00	115	200	285

KM# 1113 5 PAHLAVI

9.5900 g., Gold .2775 oz. AGW **Obverse:** Legend within crowned wreath **Reverse:** Radiant lion holding sword within crowned wreath

Date	Mintage	F	VF	XF	Unc
SH1305 (1926)	271	500	700	950	2,000

KM# 1116 5 PAHLAVI

9.5900 g., Gold .2775 oz. AGW **Obverse:** Uniformed bust right above sprays **Reverse:** Legend and value within beaded circle and crowned wreath

Date	Mintage	F	VF	XF	Unc
SH1306 (1927)	909	600	1,000	1,500	2,000
SH1307 (1928)	785	600	1,000	1,500	2,000
SH1308 (1929)	121	750	1,250	2,000	2,500

REFORM COINAGE

KM# 1126.1 2-1/2 ABBASI (10 Shahi)

Copper, 24.5 mm. **Obverse:** Radiant lion holding sword within crowned wreath **Reverse:** Legend within beaded heart-shaped circle within designed crowned wreath **Edge:** Reeded

Date		Mintage	F	VF	XF	Unc
SH1314 (1935)	Small date	15,714,000	3.00	4.00	12.50	30.00
SH1314 (1935)	Large date	Inc. above	3.00	4.00	12.50	30.00

KM# 1126.2 2-1/2 ABBASI (10 Shahi)

Copper, 24.5 mm. **Obverse:** Radiant lion holding sword within crowned wreath **Reverse:** Legend within beaded heart shaped circle within designed crowned wreath **Edge:** Plain

Date	Mintage	F	VF	XF	Unc
SH1314 (1935)	Inc. above	5.00	7.00	15.00	40.00

KM# 1121 DINAR

Bronze **Obverse:** Radiant lion holding sword within crowned wreath **Reverse:** Value within large flowered wreath

Date	Mintage	F	VF	XF	Unc
SH1310 (1931)	10,000,000	30.00	50.00	75.00	175

KM# 1122 2 DINARS

Bronze **Obverse:** Radiant lion holding sword within crowned wreath **Reverse:** Value within large flowered wreath

Date	Mintage	F	VF	XF	Unc
SH1310 (1931)	5,000,000	30.00	50.00	75.00	175

KM# 1123 5 DINARS

Copper-Nickel, 18.5 mm. **Obverse:** Radiant lion holding sword within crowned wreath **Reverse:** Value within beaded circle and designed crowned wreath

Date	Mintage	F	VF	XF	Unc
SH1310 (1931)	3,750,000	20.00	40.00	100	275

KM# 1123a 5 DINARS

Copper **Obverse:** Radiant lion holding sword within crowned wreath **Reverse:** Value within beaded circle and crowned designed wreath

Date	Mintage	F	VF	XF	Unc
SH1314	480,000	150	250	400	—

KM# 1138 5 DINARS

Aluminum-Bronze, 16 mm. **Obverse:** Radiant lion holding sword within crowned wreath **Reverse:** Value within large flowered wreath

Date	Mintage	F	VF	XF	Unc
SH1315 (1936)	5,665,000	2.50	4.00	10.00	20.00
SH1316 (1937)	Inc. above	0.40	0.75	1.50	5.00
SH1317 (1938)	13,025,000	0.40	0.75	1.50	5.00
SH1318 (1939)	—	0.40	0.75	1.50	5.00
SH1319 (1940)	—	0.40	0.75	1.50	5.00
SH1320 (1941)	—	0.40	0.75	1.50	4.00
SH1321 (1942)	—	0.40	0.75	1.50	5.00

KM# 1124 10 DINARS

4.0000 g., Copper-Nickel, 21 mm. **Obverse:** Radiant lion holding sword within crowned wreath **Reverse:** Value within beaded circle and crowned designed wreath **Note:** Struck at Berlin.

Date	Mintage	F	VF	XF	Unc
SH1310 (1931)	3,750,000	10.00	30.00	75.00	250

KM# 1124a 10 DINARS

3.2000 g., Copper **Obverse:** Radiant lion holding sword within crowned wreath **Reverse:** Value within beaded circle and crowned designed wreath **Mint:** Tehran **Note:** Struck at Tehran.

Date	Mintage	F	VF	XF	Unc
SH1314 (1935)	11,350,000	11.50	20.00	45.00	125

KM# 1139 10 DINARS

Aluminum-Bronze, 18 mm. **Obverse:** Radiant lion holding sword within crowned wreath **Reverse:** Value within wreath

Date	Mintage	F	VF	XF	Unc
SH1315 (1936)	6,195,000	2.00	5.00	15.00	25.00
SH1316 (1937)	Inc. above	0.80	1.50	4.00	10.00
SH1317 (1938)	17,120,000	0.40	0.80	2.00	6.00
SH1318 (1939)	—	0.40	0.80	2.00	6.00
SH1319 (1940)	—	0.40	0.80	2.00	6.00
SH1320 (1941)	—	0.40	0.80	2.00	6.00
SH1321 (1942)	—	0.45	1.00	2.50	6.00

KM# 1125 25 DINARS

Copper-Nickel, 24 mm. **Obverse:** Radiant lion holding sword within crowned wreath **Reverse:** Value within beaded circle and crowned designed wreath

Date	Mintage	F	VF	XF	Unc
SH1310 (1931)	750,000	25.00	60.00	150	300

KM# 1125a 25 DINARS

Copper **Obverse:** Radiant lion holding sword within crowned wreath **Reverse:** Value within beaded circle and crowned designed wreath

Date	Mintage	F	VF	XF	Unc
SH1314 (1935)	1,152,000	25.00	50.00	75.00	125

KM# 1142 50 DINARS

Aluminum-Bronze, 20 mm. **Obverse:** Radiant lion holding sword within crowned wreath **Reverse:** Value within wreath

Date	Mintage	F	VF	XF	Unc
SH1315 (1936)	15,968,000	3.00	4.50	10.00	35.00
SH1316 (1937)	34,200,000	1.25	2.50	6.00	20.00
SH1317 (1938)	17,314,000	0.60	1.50	4.00	15.00
SH1318 (1939)	—	0.60	1.50	4.00	15.00
SH1319 (1940)	—	1.50	2.50	6.00	20.00
SH1320 (1941)	—	0.75	1.50	3.00	10.00
SH1321/0 (1942)	—	0.75	1.50	3.00	15.00
SH1322/10 (1943)	—	0.75	1.50	3.00	15.00
SH1322/12 (1943)	—	0.75	1.50	3.00	10.00
SH1322/0 (1943)	—	0.75	1.50	3.00	10.00
SH1322/1 (1943)	—	0.75	1.50	3.00	10.00
SH1331 (1952)	8,162,000	3.50	4.50	10.00	25.00
SH1332 (1953)	22,892,000	2.00	3.00	5.00	10.00

KM# 1142a 50 DINARS

Copper **Obverse:** Radiant lion holding sword within crowned wreath **Reverse:** Value within wreath

Date	Mintage	F	VF	XF	Unc
SH1322 (1943)	—	2.00	4.00	7.00	12.00

Date	Mintage	F	VF	XF	Unc
SH1322/0 (1943)	—	2.00	6.00	9.00	15.00

KM# 1127 1/4 RIAL

1.2500 g., 0.8280 Silver .0332 oz. ASW **Obverse:** Value within circle and wreath **Reverse:** Radiant lion holding sword within crowned wreath

Date	Mintage	F	VF	XF	Unc
SH1315	600,000	1.50	2.50	5.00	10.00

Note: The second "1" is often short, so that the date looks like 1305

KM# 1128 1/2 RIAL

2.5000 g., 0.8280 Silver .0665 oz. ASW, 18 mm. **Obverse:** Value within crowned wreath **Obv. Legend:** "Reza Shah" **Reverse:** Radiant lion holding sword within crowned wreath **Note:** All 1/2 Rials dated SH1311-1315 are recut dies, usually from SH1310.

Date	Mintage	F	VF	XF	Unc
SH1310 (1931)	2,000,000	2.50	5.00	10.00	20.00
SH1311 (1932)	—	50.00	100	150	200
SH1312 (1933)	—	2.50	5.00	10.00	20.00
SH1313 (1934)	1,945,000	2.50	5.00	10.00	20.00
SH1314 (1935)	100,000	2.50	5.00	10.00	20.00
SH1315 (1936)	800,000	5.00	10.00	20.00	30.00

KM# 1129 RIAL

5.0000 g., 0.8280 Silver 0.1331 oz. ASW, 22.5 mm. **Obverse:** Value within crowned wreath **Reverse:** Radiant lion holding sword within crowned wreath

Date	Mintage	F	VF	XF	Unc
SH1310	2,190,000	100	20.00	25.00	35.00
AH1311	10,256,000	20.00	30.00	50.00	75.00
AH1312	25,768,000	20.00	30.00	50.00	75.00
AH1313	6,670,000	20.00	30.00	50.00	75.00

KM# 1130 2 RIALS

10.0000 g., 0.8280 Silver .2662 oz. ASW, 26 mm. **Obverse:** Value within crowned wreath **Obv. Legend:** "Reza Shah" **Reverse:** Radiant lion holding sword within crowned wreath **Note:** All coins dated SH1311-13 cut or punched over SH1310.

Date	Mintage	F	VF	XF	Unc
SH1310 (1931)	6,145,000	10.00	20.00	25.00	35.00
SH1311 (1932)	8,838,000	20.00	30.00	50.00	75.00
SH1312 (1933)	19,175,000	10.00	15.00	25.00	35.00
SH1313 (1934)	4,015,000	20.00	30.00	50.00	75.00

KM# 1131 5 RIALS

25.0000 g., 0.8280 Silver .6655 oz. ASW, 37 mm. **Obverse:** Value within crowned wreath **Obv. Legend:** "Reza Shah" **Reverse:** Radiant lion holding sword within crowned wreath **Note:** Most coins dated SH1311-13 are cut or punched over SH1310.

Date	Mintage	F	VF	XF	Unc
SH1310 (1931)	5,471,000	12.00	18.00	25.00	50.00
SH1311 (1932)	4,527,000	12.00	18.00	25.00	50.00
SH1312/0 (1933)	5,502,000	15.00	20.00	30.00	60.00
SH1312 (1933)	Inc. above	12.00	18.00	25.00	50.00
SH1313 (1934)	1,208,000	15.00	20.00	30.00	60.00

KM# 1132 1/2 PAHLAVI

4.0680 g., 0.9000 Gold .1177 oz. AGW **Obverse:** Uniformed bust left **Reverse:** Radiant lion holding sword within crowned wreath

Date	Mintage	F	VF	XF	Unc
SH1310 (1931)	696	BV	150	275	375
SH1311 (1932)	286	BV	175	300	400
SH1312 (1933)	892	BV	150	250	350
SH1313 (1934)	531	BV	175	300	400
SH1314 (1935)	—	BV	175	300	400
SH1315 (1936)	1,042	BV	175	275	375

KM# 1133 PAHLAVI

8.1360 g., 0.9000 Gold .2354 oz. AGW **Obverse:** Uniformed bust left **Reverse:** Radiant lion holding sword within crowned wreath

Date	Mintage	F	VF	XF	Unc
SH1310 (1931)	304	1,500	3,000	4,000	5,000

Muhammad Reza Pahlavi Shah

SH1320-1358 / 1941-1979AD

REFORM COINAGE

KM# 1140 25 DINARS

Aluminum-Bronze, 19 mm. **Obverse:** Radiant lion holding sword within crowned wreath **Reverse:** Value within wreath

Date	Mintage	F	VF	XF	Unc
SH1326 (1947)	—	20.00	30.00	60.00	125
SH1327 (1948)	—	25.00	50.00	100	150
SH1329 (1950)	—	25.00	50.00	100	150

KM# 1141 25 DINARS

Aluminum-Bronze **Obverse:** Value within wreath **Reverse:** Radiant lion holding sword within crowned wreath **Note:** Mule

Date	Mintage	F	VF	XF	Unc
SH1329 (1950)	—	500	750	1,000	1,500

KM# 1156 50 DINARS

Aluminum-Bronze **Obverse:** Radiant lion holding sword within crowned wreath **Reverse:** Value within wreath **Note:** Reduced thickness = 1mm; wide and narrow rim varieties exist for some dates.

Date	Mintage	F	VF	XF	Unc
SH1332 (1953)	—	25.00	30.00	40.00	50.00
SH1333 (1954)	4,036,000	0.75	1.50	2.50	8.00
SH1334 (1955)	1,370,000	0.75	1.50	4.00	10.00
SH1335 (1956)	926,000	0.75	1.50	2.50	8.00
SH1336 (1957)	—	1.00	1.25	2.00	8.00
Note: Mint reports record 126,500 in SH1337 and 20,000 in SH1338; these were probably dated SH1336					
SH1342 (1963)	800,000	0.60	1.00	1.75	6.00
SH1343 (1964)	1,400,000	0.60	1.00	1.75	6.00
SH1344 (1965)	1,600,000	0.35	0.65	1.25	5.00
SH1345 (1966)	1,690,000	0.35	0.65	1.25	5.00
SH1346 (1967)	—	0.20	0.25	0.50	2.00
Note: Mintage report seems excessive for this and all SH1346 coinage					
SH1347 (1968)	2,000,000	0.20	0.25	0.50	2.00
SH1348 (1969)	1,500,000	0.20	0.25	0.50	2.00
SH1349 (1970)	360,000	2.00	3.00	4.50	12.50
SH1350 (1971)	—	0.30	0.50	0.75	2.00
SH1351 (1972)	—	0.30	0.50	0.75	2.00
SH1353 (1974)	60,000	0.30	0.50	0.75	2.00
SH1354 (1975)	16,000	0.75	1.25	2.00	5.00

KM# 1156a 50 DINARS

Brass-Coated Steel **Obverse:** Radiant lion holding sword within wreath **Reverse:** Value within wreath

Date	Mintage	F	VF	XF	Unc
MS2535 (1976)	27,000	5.00	10.00	20.00	30.00
MS2536 (1977)	—	5.00	10.00	20.00	30.00
MS2537 (1978)	—	5.00	10.00	20.00	30.00
SH1357 (1978)	—	5.00	10.00	20.00	30.00
SH1358 (1979)	—	10.00	20.00	30.00	40.00

KM# 1143 RIAL

1.6000 g., 0.6000 Silver .0308 oz. ASW, 18 mm. **Obverse:** Value within crowned wreath **Obv. Legend:** "Muhammad Reza Shah Pahlavi" **Reverse:** Radiant lion holding sword within crowned wreath

Date	Mintage	F	VF	XF	Unc
SH1322 (1943)	—	0.60	1.00	2.00	5.00
SH1323/3 (1944)	—	—	—	—	—
SH1323 (1944)	—	0.60	1.00	2.00	5.00
SH1324/3 (1945)	—	—	—	—	—
SH1324 (1945)	—	0.60	1.00	2.00	5.00
SH1424 (1945) Error for 1324	—	—	—	—	—
SH1325 (1946)	—	0.75	1.50	2.00	5.00
SH1326 (1947)	567,000	35.00	40.00	50.00	100
SH1327 (1948)	5,795,000	1.50	2.50	4.00	8.00
SH1328 (1949)	1,565,000	1.50	2.50	4.00	8.00
SH1329 (1950)	144,000	50.00	100	150	200
SH1330 (1951)	—	2.00	3.00	5.00	15.00

KM# 1157 RIAL

Copper-Nickel, 18.5 mm. **Obverse:** Value within wreath **Obv. Legend:** "Muhammad Reza Shah Pahlavi" **Reverse:** Radiant lion holding sword within crowned wreath

Date	Mintage	F	VF	XF	Unc
SH(13)31 (1952)	4,735,000	1.00	2.00	5.00	15.00
SH(13)32 (1953)	3	4.00	8.00	15.00	30.00
SH(13)33 (1954)	16,405,000	0.60	1.00	2.00	5.00
SH(13)34 (1955)	8,980,000	0.60	1.00	2.00	5.00
SH(13)35 (1956)	8,910,000	0.50	1.00	1.00	5.00
SH(13)36 (1957)	4,450,000	1.00	2.00	8.00	20.00

KM# 1171 RIAL

2.0000 g., Copper-Nickel **Obverse:** Value within crowned wreath **Obv. Legend:** "Muhammad Reza Pahlavi" **Reverse:** Radiant lion holding sword within crowned wreath

Date	Mintage	F	VF	XF	Unc
SH1337 (1958)	8,005,000	0.50	1.00	2.00	5.00

KM# 1171a RIAL

1.7500 g., Copper-Nickel, 18.3 mm. **Obverse:** Value within crowned wreath **Reverse:** Radiant lion holding sword within crowned wreath **Note:** Date varieties exist.

Date	Mintage	F	VF	XF	Unc
SH1338 (1959)	14,940,000	0.10	0.20	0.40	3.00
SH1339 (1960)	8,400,000	0.25	0.50	1.00	4.00
SH1340 (1961)	8,490,000	0.25	0.50	1.00	4.00
SH1341 (1962)	8,680,000	0.25	0.50	1.00	4.00
SH1342 (1963)	13,332,000	0.10	0.20	0.40	3.00
SH1343 (1964)	14,746,000	0.10	0.15	0.25	2.00
SH1344 (1965)	12,050,000	0.10	0.20	0.50	3.50
SH1345 (1966)	13,786,000	0.10	0.15	0.20	2.00
SH1346 (1967)	155,321,000	0.10	0.15	0.20	2.00
SH1347 (1968)	20,664,000	0.10	0.15	0.25	3.00

Date	Mintage	F	VF	XF	Unc
SH1348 (1969)	22,960,000	0.10	0.15	0.20	2.00
SH1349 (1970)	19,918,000	0.10	0.15	0.20	2.00
SH1350 (1971)	24,248,000	0.10	0.20	0.65	2.00
SH1351/0 (1972)	21,825,000	0.10	0.25	0.40	3.00
SH1351 (1972)	Inc. above	0.10	0.15	0.20	2.00
SH1352 (1973)	31,449,000	0.10	0.15	0.20	2.00
SH1353 (1974) Large date	33,700,000	0.10	0.20	0.25	3.00
SH1353 (1974) Small date	Inc. above	0.10	0.15	0.20	2.00
SH1354 (1975)	—	3.00	6.00	8.00	10.00
MS2536 (1977)	—	3.00	6.00	8.00	10.00

KM# 1183 RIAL

Copper-Nickel **Series:** F.A.O. **Obverse:** Head left divides date **Obv. Legend:** "Muhammad Reza Shah Pahlavi" **Reverse:** Crown above lion and sun within wreath

Date	Mintage	F	VF	XF	Unc
SH1350 (1971)	2,770,000	3.00	6.00	8.00	10.00
SH1351 (1972)	8,605,000	3.00	6.00	8.00	10.00
SH1353 (1974)	2,000,000	3.00	6.00	8.00	10.00
SH1354 (1975)	1,000,000	3.00	6.00	8.00	10.00

KM# 1205 RIAL

Copper-Nickel, 18.3 mm. **Subject:** 50th Anniversary of Pahlavi Rule **Obverse:** Value within crowned wreath **Reverse:** Radiant lion holding sword within crowned wreath

Date	Mintage	F	VF	XF	Unc
MS2535 (1976)	61,945,000	3.00	6.00	8.00	10.00

KM# 1172 RIAL

Copper-Nickel **Obverse:** Value within crowned wreath, "Aryamehr" added to legend **Reverse:** Radiant lion holding sword within crowned wreath

Date	Mintage	F	VF	XF	Unc
MS2536 (1977)	71,150,000	3.00	6.00	8.00	10.00
MS2537 (1978)	—	3.00	6.00	8.00	10.00
MS2537/6537 (1978) Error 2/6	—	—	—	—	6.00
SH1357/6 (1978)	—	3.00	6.00	8.00	10.00
SH1357 (1978)	—	2.50	5.00	10.00	15.00

KM# 1144 2 RIALS

3.2000 g., 0.6000 Silver .0617 oz. ASW, 22 mm. **Obverse:** Value within crowned wreath **Obv. Legend:** "Muhammad Reza Shah Pahlavi" **Reverse:** Radiant lion holding sword within crowned wreath

Date	Mintage	F	VF	XF	Unc
SH1322 (1943)	—	1.00	1.50	3.50	7.00
SH1323/2 (1944)	—	10.00	20.00	30.00	50.00
SH1323 (1944)	—	1.00	1.50	3.00	6.00
SH1324 (1945)	—	2.50	5.00	10.00	15.00
SH1325 (1946)	—	5.00	10.00	15.00	25.00
SH1326 (1947)	187,000	5.00	10.00	25.00	50.00
SH1327 (1948)	3,140,000	1.50	3.00	5.00	12.50
SH1328 (1949)	1,198,000	2.50	4.50	7.50	16.00
SH1329 (1950)	—	100	200	300	400
SH1330 (1951)	—	5.00	8.00	12.50	30.00

KM# 1158 2 RIALS

Copper-Nickel, 22.5 mm. **Obverse:** Value above sprigs **Obv. Legend:** "Muhammad Reza Shah Pahlavi" **Reverse:** Crown above radiant lion holding sword within wreath

Date	Mintage	F	VF	XF	Unc
SH1331 (1952)	5,335,000	1.25	3.00	7.00	20.00
SH1332 (1953)	6,870,000	1.00	2.00	4.00	8.00
SH1333 (1954)	13,668,000	0.15	0.75	2.00	7.00
SH1334 (1955)	7,185,000	0.15	0.75	2.00	7.00
SH1335 (1956)	2,400,000	0.15	0.75	3.00	12.50
SH1336 (1957)	325,000	25.00	50.00	75.00	100

KM# 1173 2 RIALS

Copper-Nickel **Obverse:** Value within crowned wreath **Obv. Legend:** "Muhammad Reza Pahlavi" **Reverse:** Radiant lion holding sword within crowned wreath

Date	Mintage	F	VF	XF	Unc
SH1338 (1959)	17,610,000	0.10	0.25	0.75	4.00
SH1339 (1960)	8,575,000	0.10	0.25	0.50	4.00
SH1340 (1961)	5,668,000	0.10	0.25	0.50	4.00
SH1341 (1962)	5,820,000	0.10	0.25	0.75	4.00
SH1342 (1963)	8,570,000	0.10	0.25	0.50	4.00
SH1343 (1964)	11,250,000	0.10	0.25	0.50	3.00
SH1344 (1965)	5,155,000	0.10	0.25	0.50	4.00
SH1345 (1966)	2,267,000	0.15	0.30	1.00	5.00
SH1346 (1967)	92,792,000	—	0.10	0.20	4.00
SH1347 (1968)	10,300,000	—	0.10	1.00	6.00
SH1348 (1969)	9,319,000	0.20	0.45	1.10	4.00
SH1349 (1970)	9,895,000	0.20	0.40	1.00	4.00
SH1350 (1971)	9,545,000	0.15	0.35	1.00	4.00
SH1351 (1972)	13,305,000	0.15	0.35	1.00	3.00
SH1352 (1973)	15,910,000	—	0.10	0.20	3.00
SH1353 (1974)	28,477,000	—	0.10	0.20	3.00
SH1354/3 (1975)	—	0.20	0.40	1.00	5.00
SH1354 (1975)	41,700,000	—	0.10	0.20	3.00
MS2536 (1977)	54,725,000	—	0.10	0.20	3.00

KM# 1206 2 RIALS

Copper-Nickel **Subject:** 50th Anniversary of Pahlavi Rule **Obverse:** Value within crowned wreath **Reverse:** Radiant lion holding sword within crowned wreath

Date	Mintage	F	VF	XF	Unc
MS2535 (1976)	59,568,000	2.50	5.00	10.00	15.00

KM# 1174 2 RIALS

Copper-Nickel **Obverse:** Value within crowned wreath **Obv. Legend:** "Muhammad Reza Pahlavi","Aryamehr" added **Reverse:** Radiant lion holding sword within crowned wreath

Date	Mintage	F	VF	XF	Unc
MS2536 (1977)	Inc. above	0.50	1.00	2.50	5.00
MS2537 (1978)	—	0.50	1.00	2.50	5.00
SH1357 (1978)	—	2.50	5.00	10.00	20.00

KM# 1145 5 RIALS

8.0000 g., 0.6000 Silver .1543 oz. ASW, 26 mm. **Obverse:** Value within crowned wreath **Obv. Legend:** "Muhammad Reza Shah Pahlavi" **Reverse:** Radiant lion holding sword within crowned wreath

Date	Mintage	F	VF	XF	Unc
SH1322 (1943)	—	BV	2.50	3.50	6.00
SH1323 (1944)	—	BV	2.50	3.50	6.00
SH1324 (1945)	—	BV	2.75	4.50	10.00
SH1325 (1946)	—	BV	2.50	3.50	6.00
SH1326 (1947)	61,000	5.00	10.00	25.00	50.00
SH1327 (1948)	836,000	2.50	5.00	7.50	20.00
SH1328 (1949)	282,000	3.50	10.00	20.00	40.00
SH1329 (1950)	—	85.00	125	200	350

KM# 1159 5 RIALS

Copper-Nickel, 26 mm. **Obverse:** Value above sprigs, date below **Obv. Legend:** "Muhammad Reza Shah Pahlavi" **Reverse:** Crown above radiant lion holding sword within wreath

Date	Mintage	F	VF	XF	Unc
SH1331 (1952)	3,660,000	2.50	5.00	10.00	20.00
SH1332 (1953)	16,350,000	1.00	2.50	5.00	10.00
SH1333 (1954)	6,582,000	1.00	2.50	5.00	10.00
SH1334 (1955)	300,000	15.00	25.00	50.00	75.00
SH1336 (1957)	1,410,000	15.00	25.00	50.00	75.00

KM# 1175 5 RIALS

7.0000 g., Copper-Nickel, 25.5 mm. **Obverse:** Value within crowned wreath **Obv. Legend:** "Muhammad Reza Shah Pahlavi" **Reverse:** Radiant lion holding sword within crowned wreath

Date	Mintage	F	VF	XF	Unc
SH1337 (1958)	3,660,000	1.00	2.50	7.50	22.50
SH1338 (1959)	10,467,000	0.50	2.50	8.00	20.00

KM# 1175a 5 RIALS

5.0000 g., Copper-Nickel, 25.6 mm. **Obverse:** Value within crowned wreath **Reverse:** Radiant lion holding sword within crowned wreath

Date	Mintage	F	VF	XF	Unc
SH1338 (1959)	Inc. above	0.25	0.40	1.50	5.00
SH1339 (1960)	3,980,000	0.25	0.40	1.50	5.00
SH1340 (1961)	3,814,000	0.25	0.40	1.50	5.00
SH1341 (1962)	2,332,000	0.25	0.40	1.50	5.00
SH1342 (1963)	7,838,000	0.25	0.40	1.00	4.00
SH1343 (1964)	9,484,000	0.25	0.40	1.00	4.00
SH1344 (1965)	3,468,000	0.25	0.40	1.00	4.00
SH1345 (1966)	6,092,000	0.25	0.40	1.00	4.00
SH1346/36 (1967)	74,781,000	0.25	0.40	1.50	5.00
SH1346 (1967)	Inc. above	0.25	0.40	1.00	4.00

KM# 1176 5 RIALS

4.6000 g., Copper-Nickel **Obverse:** Value and legend within crowned wreath, "Aryamehr" added to legend **Reverse:** Radiant lion holding sword within crowned wreath

Date	Mintage	F	VF	XF	Unc
SH1347 (1968)	7,745,000	0.50	0.85	1.50	4.00
SH1348 (1969)	9,193,000	0.50	0.75	1.25	4.00
SH1349 (1970)	7,300,000	0.50	0.75	1.25	4.00
SH1350 (1971)	10,160,000	0.35	0.75	1.25	3.50
SH1351 (1972)	20,582,000	0.25	0.75	1.25	3.50
SH1352 (1973)	23,590,000	0.25	0.75	1.25	3.50
SH1353 (1974)	28,367,000	0.25	0.75	1.25	3.50
SH1353 (1974) Large date	Inc. above	0.25	0.75	1.25	3.50
SH1354 (1975)	27,294,000	0.25	0.75	1.25	3.50
MS2536 (1977)	47,906,000	0.20	0.50	1.25	3.50
MS2537 (1978)	—	0.35	0.65	1.25	3.50
SH1357 (1978)	—	2.50	5.00	10.00	20.00

KM# 1207 5 RIALS

Copper-Nickel **Subject:** 50th Anniversary of Pahlavi Rule

Date	Mintage	F	VF	XF	Unc
MS2535 (1976)	37,144,000	1.00	2.50	5.00	10.00

KM# 1146 10 RIALS

16.0000 g., 0.6000 Silver .3086 oz. ASW, 32 mm. **Obverse:** Value and legend within crowned wreath **Obv. Legend:** "Muhammad Reza Shah Pahlavi" **Reverse:** Radiant lion holding sword within crowned wreath **Note:** Counterfeits are known dated SH1322.

Date	Mintage	F	VF	XF	Unc
SH1323/2 (1944)	—	—	4.50	7.50	20.00
SH1323 (1944)	—	—	BV	5.00	12.00
SH1324 (1945)	—	—	BV	5.50	15.00
SH1325 (1946)	—	—	BV	6.00	17.50
SH1326 (1947)	—	5.50	15.00	35.00	75.00

KM# 1177 10 RIALS

12.0000 g., Copper-Nickel **Obverse:** Crown above value and legend within wreath **Obv. Legend:** "Muhammad Reza Shah Pahlavi" **Reverse:** Crown above lion and sun within wreath

Date	Mintage	F	VF	XF	Unc
SH1333 (1954)	—	—	—	—	—
SH1335 (1956)	6,225,000	0.50	2.00	4.00	9.00
SH1336 (1957)	4,415,000	5.00	10.00	15.00	25.00
SH1337 (1958)	715,000	3.00	6.00	9.00	20.00
SH1338 (1959)	1,210,000	0.50	2.00	6.00	14.00
SH1339 (1960)	2,775,000	0.50	2.00	4.00	9.00
SH1340 (1961)	3,660,000	0.50	2.00	4.00	9.00
SH1341 (1962)	744,000	20.00	35.00	50.00	75.00
SH1343 (1963)	6,874,000	0.50	2.00	4.00	9.00

KM# 1177a 10 RIALS

9.0000 g., Copper-Nickel **Obverse:** Crown above value and legend wtihin wreath **Reverse:** Crown above radiant lion holding sword within wreath **Note:** Thin flan.

Date	Mintage	F	VF	XF	Unc
SH1341 (1962)	—	0.35	1.00	2.50	5.00
Note: Mintage included in KM#1177					
SH1342 (1963)	3,763,000	0.35	1.00	2.00	4.00
SH1343 (1964)	—	0.35	0.75	1.50	2.50
Note: Mintage included in KM#1177					
SH1344 (1965)	1,627,000	0.35	0.75	1.50	2.50

KM# 1178 10 RIALS

Copper-Nickel **Obverse:** Head left, legend above, date below **Obv. Legend:** "Muhammad Reza Shah Pahlavi" **Reverse:** Crown above radiant lion holding sword within wreath

Date	Mintage	F	VF	XF	Unc
SH1345 (1966)	1,699,000	0.50	0.60	2.00	5.00
SH1346 (1967)	38,897,000	0.40	0.50	1.00	4.00
SH1347 (1968)	8,220,000	0.40	0.65	1.50	8.00
SH1348 (1969)	7,156,000	0.40	0.50	1.00	4.00
SH1349 (1970)	7,397,000	0.40	0.50	1.00	4.00
SH1350 (1971)	8,972,000	0.40	0.50	1.00	4.00
SH1351 (1972)	9,912,000	0.40	0.50	1.00	4.00
SH1352 (1973)	28,776,000	0.50	2.00	4.50	7.00

KM# 1182 10 RIALS

Copper-Nickel **Series:** F.A.O. **Obverse:** Head left, legend above **Reverse:** Crown above radiant lion holding sword within wreath, dates and F.A.O

Date	Mintage	F	VF	XF	Unc
SH1348 (1969)	150,000	1.00	2.50	5.00	10.00

KM# 1179 10 RIALS

Copper-Nickel **Obverse:** Head left, legend above, date below **Reverse:** Crown above lion, sun and numeral value within wreath

Date	Mintage	F	VF	XF	Unc
SH1352 (1973)	Inc. above	0.30	0.60	1.00	4.00
SH1353 (1974)	22,234,000	0.30	0.60	1.00	3.00
SH1354 (1975)	23,482,000	0.30	0.60	1.00	4.00
MS2536 (1977)	24,324,000	0.30	0.60	1.00	3.00
MS2537 (1978)	—	0.30	0.60	1.00	4.00
SH1357 (1978)	—	10.00	15.00	20.00	25.00

KM# 1208 10 RIALS

Copper-Nickel **Subject:** 50th Anniversary of Pahlavi Rule **Obverse:** Head left, legend above, date below **Reverse:** Crown above lion, sun and numeral value within wreath

Date	Mintage	F	VF	XF	Unc
MS2535 (1976)	29,859,000	0.50	1.00	2.50	5.00

KM# 1180 20 RIALS

Copper-Nickel **Obverse:** Head left, legend above, date below **Obv. Legend:** "Muhammad Reza Shah Pahlavi" **Reverse:** Crown above lion, sun and written value within wreath

Date	Mintage	F	VF	XF	Unc
SH1350 (1971)	2,349,000	0.25	1.00	3.00	6.00
SH1351 (1972)	11,416,000	0.25	0.85	1.00	3.00
SH1352 (1973)	7,172,000	0.25	0.85	1.25	5.00

KM# 1181 20 RIALS

Copper-Nickel, 30 mm. **Obverse:** Head left, legend above, date below **Reverse:** Crown above lion, sun and numeral value within wreath **Note:** Varieties exist in date size.

Date	Mintage	F	VF	XF	Unc
SH1352 (1973)	—	0.25	0.75	1.00	3.50
Note: Mintage included in KM#1180					
SH1353 (1974)	12,601,000	0.25	0.75	1.00	3.75
SH1354 (1975)	16,246,000	0.25	0.75	1.00	4.00
MS2536 (1977)	—	0.40	0.75	1.00	4.00
MS2537 (1978)	—	0.50	0.75	1.00	4.00
SH1357 (1978)	—	5.00	10.00	15.00	25.00

KM# 1196 20 RIALS

Copper-Nickel **Subject:** 7th Asian Games **Obverse:** Head left, legend above **Reverse:** Star design within entwined circles and written words

Date	Mintage	F	VF	XF	Unc
SH1353 (1974)	Inc. above	5.00	10.00	15.00	25.00

KM# 1209 20 RIALS

Copper-Nickel **Subject:** 50th Anniversary of Pahlavi Rule **Obverse:** Head left, legend above, date below **Reverse:** Crown above lion, sun and numeral value within wreath

Date	Mintage	F	VF	XF	Unc
MS2535 (1976)	—	3.00	7.50	12.00	15.00

KM# 1211 20 RIALS

Copper-Nickel **Series:** F.A.O. **Obverse:** Head left, legend above **Reverse:** Crown above lion, sun and numeral value within wreath

Date	Mintage	F	VF	XF	Unc
MS2535-1976	10,000,000	3.00	7.50	12.00	15.00
MS2536-1977	23,370,000	3.00	7.50	12.00	15.00

KM# 1215 20 RIALS

Copper-Nickel **Series:** F.A.O. **Obverse:** Head left, legend above **Reverse:** Crown above lion, sun, numeral value, dates and F.A.O. within wreath

Date	Mintage	F	VF	XF	Unc
SH1357-1978	5,000,000	3.00	7.50	12.00	15.00

KM# 1214 20 RIALS

Copper-Nickel **Subject:** 50th Anniversary of Bank Melli **Obverse:** Head left, legend above and below **Reverse:** Head left, legend above and below

Date	Mintage	F	VF	XF	Unc
SH1357 (1978)	—	5.00	10.00	20.00	30.00

KM# 1184 25 RIALS

7.5000 g., 0.9990 Silver .2409 oz. ASW **Subject:** 2500th Anniversary of Persian Empire **Obverse:** Small crown over lion and sun above value within circle of crowns **Reverse:** Conjoined column heads **Note:** Column head from Artaxerxes' Palace in Susa. With "1 AR" and 1000 assayer's marks

Date	Mintage	F	VF	XF	Unc
SH1350-1971 Proof	18,000	Value: 12.00			

KM# 1185 50 RIALS

15.0000 g., 0.9990 Silver .4818 oz. ASW **Subject:** 2500th Anniversary of Persian Empire **Obverse:** Small crown over lion and sun above value and dates within circle of crowns **Reverse:** Winged griffin with ram antlers **Note:** With "1 AR" and 1000 assayer's marks

Date	Mintage	F	VF	XF	Unc
SH1350-1971 Proof	18,000	Value: 16.50			

KM# 1186 75 RIALS

22.5000 g., 0.9990 Silver .7227 oz. ASW **Subject:** 2500th Anniversary of Persian Empire **Obverse:** Small crown above radiant lion holding sword above value and dates within circle of crowns **Reverse:** Arms above Stone of Cyrus II and inscription, wreath of crowns surrounds **Note:** With "1 AR" and 1000 assayer's marks

Date	Mintage	F	VF	XF	Unc
SH1350-1971 Proof	18,000	Value: 18.50			

KM# 1187.1 100 RIALS

30.0000 g., 0.9990 Silver .9636 oz. ASW **Subject:** 2500th Anniversary of Persian Empire **Obverse:** Small crown over lion and sun, value and date below **Reverse:** Polished field below pillared palace

Date	Mintage	F	VF	XF	Unc
SH1350-1971 Proof	18,000	Value: 27.50			

KM# 1187.2 100 RIALS

30.0000 g., 0.9990 Silver .9636 oz. ASW **Obverse:** Small crown over lion and sun above value and dates within circle of crowns **Reverse:** Frosted field below pillared palace **Note:** Countermarked with "1 AR" and "1000" on reverse.

Date	Mintage	F	VF	XF	Unc
SH1350-1971 Proof	Inc. above	Value: 27.50			

KM# 1188 200 RIALS

60.0000 g., 0.9990 Silver 1.9273 oz. ASW **Subject:** 2500th Anniversary of Persian Empire **Obverse:** Conjoined busts left **Reverse:** Polished field below pillared palace **Note:** Countermarked with "1 AR" and "1000" on reverse.

Date	Mintage	F	VF	XF	Unc
SH1350-1971 Proof	23,000	Value: 45.00			

KM# 1189 500 RIALS

6.5100 g., 0.9000 Gold .1883 oz. AGW **Subject:** 2500th Anniversary of Persian Empire **Obverse:** Small crown over lion and sun above value and dates within circle of crowns **Reverse:** Walking griffin with ram antlers

Date	Mintage	F	VF	XF	Unc
SH1350-1971 Proof	11,000	Value: 140			

KM# 1190 750 RIALS

9.7700 g., 0.9000 Gold .2827 oz. AGW **Subject:** 2500th Anniversary of Persian Empire **Obverse:** Small crown above lion and sun, value and date below **Reverse:** Arms above Stone of Cyrus II and inscription within wreath of crowns

Date	Mintage	F	VF	XF	Unc
SH1350-1971 Proof	10,000	Value: 200			

KM# 1191.1 1000 RIALS

13.0300 g., 0.9000 Gold .3770 oz. AGW **Subject:** 2500th Anniversary of Persian Empire **Obverse:** Small crown over lion and sun above value and dates within circle of crowns **Reverse:** Polished fields below pillared palace

Date	Mintage	F	VF	XF	Unc
SH1350-1971 Proof	10,000	Value: 275			

KM# 1191.2 1000 RIALS

13.0300 g., 0.9000 Gold .3770 oz. AGW **Subject:** 2500th Anniversary of Persian Empire **Obverse:** Small crown over lion and sun above value and dates within circle of crowns **Reverse:** Polished fields below pillared palace

Date	Mintage	F	VF	XF	Unc
SH1350-1971 Proof	Inc. above	Value: 275			

KM# 1192 2000 RIALS

26.0600 g., 0.9000 Gold .7541 oz. AGW **Subject:** 2500th Anniversary of Persian Empire **Obverse:** Conjoined busts left **Reverse:** Small crown over lion and sun above value and dates within circle of crowns

Date	Mintage	F	VF	XF	Unc
SH1350-1971 Proof	9,805	Value: 550			

KM# 1160 1/4 PAHLAVI

2.0340 g., 0.9000 Gold .0589 oz. AGW, 14 mm. **Obverse:** Head left, legend above, date below **Reverse:** Crown over lion and sun above value within wreath

Date	Mintage	F	VF	XF	Unc
SH1332 (1953)	41,000	BV	50.00	100	125
SH1333 (1954)	7,000	50.00	60.00	125	175
SH1334 (1955)	—	—	BV	45.00	60.00
SH1335 (1956)	41,000	BV	50.00	100	125
SH1336 (1957)	—	BV	50.00	100	175

KM# 1160a 1/4 PAHLAVI

2.0340 g., 0.9000 Gold .0589 oz. AGW, 16 mm. **Obverse:** Head left, legend above, date below **Reverse:** Crown above lion holding sword within wreath **Note:** Thinner and broader.

Date	Mintage	F	VF	XF	Unc
SH1336 (1957)	7,000	—	45.00	75.00	125
SH1337 (1958)	33,000	—	—	BV	50.00
SH1338 (1959)	136,000	—	—	BV	50.00
SH1339 (1960)	156,000	—	—	BV	50.00
SH1340 (1961)	60,000	—	—	BV	50.00

Date	Mintage	F	VF	XF	Unc
SH1342 (1963)	80,000	—	—	BV	50.00
SH1344 (1965)	30,000	—	60.00	90.00	125
SH1345 (1966)	40,000	—	—	BV	50.00
SH1346 (1967)	30,000	—	—	BV	50.00
SH1347 (1968)	60,000	—	—	BV	50.00
SH1348 (1969)	60,000	—	—	BV	50.00
SH1349 (1970)	80,000	—	—	BV	50.00
SH1350 (1971)	80,000	—	—	BV	50.00
SH1351 (1972)	103,000	—	—	BV	50.00
SH1353 (1974)	—	—	—	BV	50.00

KM# 1198 1/4 PAHLAVI

2.0340 g., 0.9000 Gold .0589 oz. AGW **Obverse:** Head left, legend above, date below, "Aryamehr" added to legend **Reverse:** Crown above lion and sun within wreath

Date	Mintage	F	VF	XF	Unc
SH1354 (1975)	106,000	—	—	BV	45.00
SH1355 (1976)	186,000	—	—	BV	45.00
MS2536 (1977)	—	—	—	BV	45.00
MS2537 (1978)	—	—	—	BV	45.00
SH1358 (1979)	—	200	300	400	500

KM# 1147 1/2 PAHLAVI

4.0680 g., 0.9000 Gold .1177 oz. AGW **Obverse:** Legend **Obv. Legend:** "Muhammad Reza Shah" **Reverse:** Crown above radiant lion holding sword within wreath

Date	Mintage	F	VF	XF	Unc
SH1320 (1941)	—	1,000	2,000	2,500	3,000
SH1321 (1942)	—	—	100	200	300
SH1322 (1943)	—	—	—	BV	85.00
SH1323 (1944)	76,000	—	—	BV	85.00

KM# 1149 1/2 PAHLAVI

4.0680 g., 0.9000 Gold .1177 oz. AGW **Obverse:** High relief head left, legend above and date below **Reverse:** Crown above radiant lion holding sword within wreath

Date	Mintage	F	VF	XF	Unc
SH1324 (1945)	—	—	—	BV	85.00
SH1325 (1946)	—	—	—	BV	85.00
SH1326 (1947)	36,000	—	BV	85.00	110
SH1327 (1948)	36,000	—	BV	85.00	110
SH1328 (1949)	—	—	BV	85.00	130
SH1329 (1950)	75	—	275	475	750
SH1330 (1951)	98,000	—	175	300	500

KM# 1161 1/2 PAHLAVI

4.0680 g., 0.9000 Gold .1177 oz. AGW **Obverse:** Low relief head left, legend above with date below **Reverse:** Crown above radiant lion holding sword within wreath

Date	Mintage	F	VF	XF	Unc
SH1330 (1951)	—	—	—	BV	85.00
Note: Mintage included in KM#1149					
SH1332 (1952)	—	—	1,250	2,000	2,500
SH1333 (1954)	—	BV	200	250	300
SH1334 (1955)	—	—	200	250	300
SH1335 (1956)	—	—	—	BV	85.00
SH1336 (1957)	132,000	—	—	BV	85.00
SH1337 (1958)	102,000	—	—	BV	85.00
SH1338 (1959)	140,000	—	—	BV	85.00
SH1339 (1960)	142,000	—	—	BV	85.00
SH1340 (1961)	439,000	—	—	BV	85.00
SH1342 (1963)	40,000	—	—	BV	85.00
SH1344 (1965)	30,000	BV	200	250	300
SH1345 (1966)	40,000	—	—	BV	85.00
SH1346 (1967)	40,000	—	—	BV	85.00
SH1347 (1968)	50,000	—	—	BV	85.00
SH1348 (1969)	40,000	—	—	BV	85.00
SH1349 (1970)	80,000	—	—	BV	85.00
SH1350 (1971)	80,000	—	—	BV	85.00
SH1351 (1972)	103,000	—	—	BV	85.00

Date	Mintage	F	VF	XF	Unc
SH1352 (1973)	67,000	—	—	BV	85.00
SH1353 (1974)	—	—	—	BV	85.00

KM# 1199 1/2 PAHLAVI

4.0680 g., 0.9000 Gold .1177 oz. AGW **Obverse:** Head left, legend above and date below, "Aryamehr" added to legend **Reverse:** Crown above radiant lion holding sword within wreath

Date	Mintage	F	VF	XF	Unc
SH1354 (1975)	37,000	—	—	BV	85.00
SH1355 (1976)	153,000	—	—	BV	85.00
MS2536 (1977)	—	—	—	BV	85.00
MS2537 (1978)	—	—	—	BV	85.00
SH1358 (1979)	—	300	500	1,000	1,500

KM# 1148 PAHLAVI

8.1360 g., 0.9000 Gold .2354 oz. AGW **Obverse:** Legend and date **Obv. Legend:** "Muhammad Reza Shah" **Reverse:** Crown above radiant lion holding sword within wreath

Date	Mintage	F	VF	XF	Unc
SH1320 (1941)	—	100	2,000	3,000	4,000
Note: Possibly a pattern					
SH1321 (1942)	—	1,000	2,000	3,000	4,000
Note: Possibly a pattern					
SH1322 (1943)	—	—	—	BV	165
SH1323 (1944)	311,000	—	—	BV	165
SH1324 (1945)	—	—	—	BV	165

KM# 1150 PAHLAVI

8.1360 g., 0.9000 Gold .2354 oz. AGW **Obverse:** High relief head left, legend above and date below **Reverse:** Crown above radiant lion holding sword within wreath

Date	Mintage	F	VF	XF	Unc
SH1324 (1945)	—	—	—	BV	165
SH1325 (1946)	—	—	—	BV	165
SH1326 (1947)	151,000	—	—	BV	165
SH1327 (1948)	20,000	—	—	BV	165
SH1328 (1949)	4,000	—	BV	185	260
SH1329 (1950)	4,000	—	300	500	750
SH1330 (1951)	48,000	—	200	300	400

KM# 1162 PAHLAVI

8.1360 g., 0.9000 Gold .2354 oz. AGW **Obverse:** Low relief head left, legend above and date below **Reverse:** Crown above radiant lion holding sword within wreath

Date	Mintage	F	VF	XF	Unc
SH1330 (1951)	—	—	—	BV	165
SH1331 (1952)	—	2,000	3,000	3,500	3,750
SH1332 (1953)	—	2,000	3,000	3,500	3,750
SH1333 (1954)	—	BV	200	250	350
SH1334 (1955)	—	BV	200	250	350
SH1335 (1956)	—	—	—	BV	165
SH1336 (1957)	453,000	—	—	BV	165
SH1337 (1958)	665,000	—	—	BV	165
SH1338 (1959)	776,000	—	—	BV	165
SH1339 (1960)	847,000	—	—	BV	165
SH1340 (1961)	528,000	—	—	BV	165
SH1342 (1963)	20,000	—	—	BV	165
SH1344 (1965)	—	BV	200	250	350
SH1345 (1966)	20,000	—	—	BV	165
SH1346 (1967)	30,000	—	—	BV	165
SH1347 (1968)	40,000	—	—	BV	165
SH1348 (1969)	70,000	—	—	BV	165
SH1349 (1970)	70,000	—	—	BV	165
SH1350 (1971)	60,000	—	—	BV	165
SH1351 (1972)	100,000	—	—	BV	165

Date	Mintage	F	VF	XF	Unc
SH1352 (1973)	320,000	—	—	BV	165
SH1353 (1974)	—	—	—	BV	165

KM# 1200 PAHLAVI

8.1360 g., 0.9000 Gold .2354 oz. AGW **Obverse:** Head left, legend above, date below, "Aryamehr" added to legend **Reverse:** Crown above radiant lion holding sword within wreath

Date	Mintage	F	VF	XF	Unc
SH1354 (1975)	21,000	—	—	BV	165
SH1355 (1976)	203,000	—	—	BV	165
MS2536 (1977)	—	—	—	BV	165
MS2537 (1978)	—	—	—	BV	165
SH1358 (1979)	—	300	500	1,000	1,500

KM# A1163 2-1/2 PAHLAVI

20.3400 g., 0.9000 Gold .5885 oz. AGW **Obverse:** Head left, legend above **Reverse:** Inscription and date

Date	Mintage	F	VF	XF	Unc
SH1338 (1959)	—	—	BV	425	450

KM# 1163 2-1/2 PAHLAVI

20.3400 g., 0.9000 Gold .5885 oz. AGW **Obverse:** Head left, legend above **Reverse:** Crown above lion, sun and value within wreath

Date	Mintage	F	VF	XF	Unc
SH1339 (1960)	1,682	—	—	—	420
SH1340 (1961)	2,788	—	—	BV	420
SH1342 (1963)	30	—	—	—	—
SH1348 (1969)	3,000	—	—	BV	420
SH1350 (1971)	2,000	—	—	BV	420
SH1351 (1972)	2,500	—	—	BV	420
SH1352 (1973)	3,000	—	—	BV	420
SH1353 (1974)	—	—	—	BV	420

KM# 1201 2-1/2 PAHLAVI

20.3400 g., 0.9000 Gold .5885 oz. AGW, 30 mm. **Obverse:** Head left, legend above, date below, "Aryamehr" added to legend **Reverse:** Crown above radiant lion holding sword within wreath **Edge:** Reeded

Date	Mintage	F	VF	XF	Unc
SH1354 (1975)	18,000	—	—	BV	420
SH1355 (1976)	16,000	—	—	BV	420
MS2536 (1977)	—	—	—	BV	420
MS2537 (1978)	—	—	—	BV	420
SH1358 (1979) Rare	—	—	—	—	750
MS2538 (1979) Rare	—	—	—	—	750

KM# 1164 5 PAHLAVI

40.6799 g., 0.9000 Gold 1.1772 oz. AGW **Obverse:** Head left, legend above **Reverse:** Crown above lion and sun within wreath

Date	Mintage	F	VF	XF	Unc
SH1339 (1960)	2,225	—	—	BV	825
SH1340 (1961)	2,430	—	—	BV	825
SH1342 (1963)	20	—	—	2,500	4,000
SH1348 (1969)	2,000	—	—	BV	825
SH1350 (1971)	2,000	—	—	BV	825
SH1351 (1972)	2,500	—	—	BV	825
SH1352 (1973)	2,100	—	—	BV	825
SH1353 (1974)	—	—	—	BV	825

KM# 1202 5 PAHLAVI

40.6799 g., 0.9000 Gold 1.1772 oz. AGW **Obverse:** Head left, legend above, date below, "Aryamehr" added to legend **Reverse:** Crown above radiant lion holding sword within wreath

Date	Mintage	F	VF	XF	Unc
SH1354 (1975)	10,000	—	—	BV	825
SH1355 (1976)	17,000	—	—	BV	825
MS2536 (1977)	—	—	—	BV	825
MS2537 (1978)	—	—	—	BV	825
SH1358 (1979)	—	—	1,250	1,500	1,750

KM# 1210 10 PAHLAVI

81.3598 g., 0.9000 Gold 2.3544 oz. AGW **Subject:** 50th Anniversary of Pahlavi Rule **Obverse:** Conjoined busts left **Reverse:** Crown, inscription and date at center circle of circle wreaths

Date	Mintage	F	VF	XF	Unc
MS2535 (1976)	—	—	—	BV	1,650

KM# 1212 10 PAHLAVI

81.3598 g., 0.9000 Gold 2.3544 oz. AGW **Subject:** Centenary of Reza Shah's Birth **Obverse:** Conjoined busts left **Reverse:** Crown above inscription and date within wreath

Date	Mintage	F	VF	XF	Unc
MS2536 (1977)	—	—	—	BV	1,650

KM# 1213 10 PAHLAVI

81.3598 g., 0.9000 Gold 2.3544 oz. AGW **Obverse:** Head left, legend above, date below, "Aryamehr" added to legend **Reverse:** Crown above radiant lion holding sword within wreath

Date	Mintage	F	VF	XF	Unc
MS2537 (1978)	—	—	—	BV	1,650
SH1358 (1979)	—	—	—	4,000	5,000

ISLAMIC REPUBLIC

MILLED COINAGE

KM# 1231 50 DINARS

Brass Clad Steel **Obverse:** Radiant lion holding sword within wreath **Reverse:** Value within flowered wreath

Date	Mintage	F	VF	XF	Unc
SH1358 (1979)	—	10.00	20.00	30.00	40.00

KM# 1232 RIAL

Copper-Nickel **Obverse:** Inscription within wreath **Reverse:** Value and date within wreath

Date	Mintage	F	VF	XF	Unc
SH1358 (1979)	—	—	0.25	0.75	1.75
SH1359 (1980)	—	—	0.25	0.75	1.75
SH1360 (1981)	—	—	0.25	0.75	1.75
SH1361 (1982)	—	—	0.25	0.75	1.75
SH1362 (1983)	—	—	0.25	0.75	1.75
SH1363 (1984)	—	—	0.25	0.75	1.75
SH1364 (1985)	—	—	0.25	0.75	1.75
SH1365 (1986)	—	—	0.15	0.65	1.25
SH1366 (1987)	—	—	0.15	0.65	1.25
SH1367 (1988)	—	—	0.15	0.65	1.25

KM# 1245 RIAL

Bronze Clad Steel, 20 mm. **Subject:** World Jerusalem Day **Obverse:** Value flanked by tulips **Reverse:** Mosque above date

Date	Mintage	F	VF	XF	Unc
SH1359 (1980)	—	—	1.00	2.50	5.00

KM# 1263 RIAL

Brass **Obverse:** Value and date divides inscription and flower sprig within beaded circle **Reverse:** Mountain within beaded circle

Date	Mintage	F	VF	XF	Unc
SH1371 (1992)	—	—	10.00	20.00	30.00
SH1372 (1993)	—	—	10.00	10.00	15.00
SH1373 (1994)	—	—	10.00	20.00	30.00
SH1374 (1995)	—	—	10.00	20.00	30.00

KM# 1233 2 RIALS

Copper-Nickel **Obverse:** Inscription within tulip wreath **Reverse:** Value and date within wreath

Date	Mintage	F	VF	XF	Unc
SH1358 (1979)	—	—	0.60	1.25	3.50
SH1359 (1980)	—	—	0.50	1.25	3.50
SH1360 (1981)	—	—	0.50	1.25	3.50
SH1361 (1982)	—	—	0.50	1.00	3.00
SH1362 (1983)	—	—	0.35	0.75	2.75
SH1363 (1984)	—	—	0.50	1.00	3.00
SH1364 (1985)	—	—	0.35	0.75	2.75
SH1365 (1986)	—	—	0.25	0.75	2.50
SH1366 (1987)	—	—	0.25	0.75	2.50
SH1367 (1988)	—	—	0.25	0.75	2.50

KM# 1234 5 RIALS

Copper-Nickel, 25 mm. **Obverse:** Inscription within tulip wreath **Reverse:** Value and date within wreath **Note:** Date varieties exist.

Date	Mintage	F	VF	XF	Unc
SH1358 (1979)	—	—	0.75	1.25	3.50
SH1359 (1980)	—	—	0.75	1.25	3.50
SH1360 (1981)	—	—	0.75	1.25	3.50
SH1361 (1982)	—	—	0.75	1.25	3.50
SH1362 (1983)	—	—	0.75	1.25	3.50
SH1363 (1984)	—	—	0.75	1.25	3.50
SH1364 (1985)	—	—	0.75	1.25	3.50
SH1365 (1986)	—	—	0.75	1.25	3.50
SH1366 (1987)	—	—	0.75	1.25	3.50

Date	Mintage	F	VF	XF	Unc
SH1367 (1988)	—	—	0.75	1.25	3.50
SH1368 (1989)	—	—	0.75	1.25	3.50

KM# 1258 5 RIALS

Brass, 19.5 mm. **Obverse:** Value and date divides inscription and flower sprig within beaded circle **Reverse:** Tomb within beaded circle

Date	Mintage	F	VF	XF	Unc
SH1371 (1992)	—	—	0.50	1.25	3.00
SH1372 (1993)	—	—	0.50	1.25	3.00
SH1373 (1994)	—	—	0.50	1.25	3.00
SH1375 (1996)	—	—	0.50	1.25	3.00
SH1376 (1997)	—	—	0.50	1.25	3.00
SH1378 (1999)	—	—	—	2.00	5.00

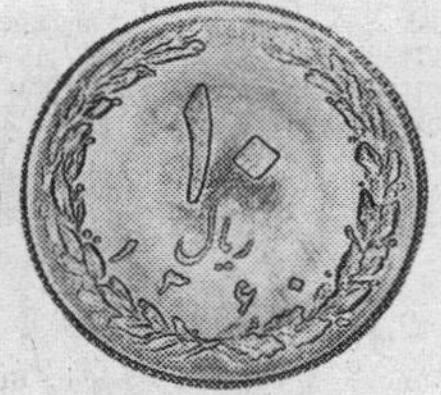

KM# 1235.1 10 RIALS

Copper-Nickel, 28 mm. **Obverse:** Inscription and value within tulip wreath **Reverse:** Value and date within wreath

Date	Mintage	F	VF	XF	Unc
SH1358 (1979)	—	—	1.00	2.50	4.50
SH1358 (1979) Large date	—	—	1.00	2.50	4.50
SH1359 (1980)	—	—	1.00	2.50	4.50
SH1360 (1981)	—	—	1.00	2.50	4.50
SH1361 (1982)	—	—	1.00	2.00	4.00

KM# 1243 10 RIALS

Copper-Nickel, 28 mm. **Subject:** 1st Anniversary of Revolution **Obverse:** Value and inscription within wreath **Reverse:** Tulips in center of inscription, dates and value

Date	Mintage	F	VF	XF	Unc
SH1358 (1979)	—	—	5.00	10.00	15.00

KM# 1249 10 RIALS

6.9700 g., Copper-Nickel, 28 mm. **Subject:** Moslem Unity **Obverse:** Capitol building flanked by dates **Reverse:** Kaaba at Mecca, date with value below **Edge:** Reeded

Date	Mintage	F	VF	XF	Unc
SH1361-AH1402 (1982)	—	—	5.00	10.00	15.00

KM# 1235.2 10 RIALS

Copper-Nickel, 28 mm. **Obverse:** Inscription and value within tulip wreath **Reverse:** Value and date within wreath **Note:** Date varieties exist.

Date	Mintage	F	VF	XF	Unc
SH1361 (1982)	—	—	1.00	2.00	4.00
SH1362 (1983)	—	—	1.00	2.00	4.00
SH1363 (1984)	—	—	1.00	2.00	4.00
SH1364 (1985)	—	—	0.90	1.50	4.00
SH1365 (1986)	—	—	0.90	1.50	4.00
SH1366 (1987)	—	—	0.90	1.50	4.00
SH1366 (1987) Small date	—	—	0.90	1.50	4.00
SH1367 (1988)	—	—	0.65	1.50	3.00

KM# 1253.1 10 RIALS

3.0200 g., Copper-Nickel, 21.2 mm. **Subject:** World Jerusalem Day **Obverse:** Capitol building divides date **Reverse:** Kaaba at Mecca divides date with value below **Edge:** Plain

Date	Mintage	F	VF	XF	Unc
SH1368 (1989)	—	—	1.50	3.00	6.00

KM# 1253.2 10 RIALS

3.0200 g., Copper-Nickel, 21.2 mm. **Obverse:** Capitol building divides dates **Reverse:** Kaaba at Mecca divides dates with value below

Date	Mintage	F	VF	XF	Unc
SH1368 (1989)	—	—	1.50	3.00	6.00

KM# 1259 10 RIALS

Aluminum-Bronze, 21 mm. **Subject:** Tomb of Ferdousi **Obverse:** Value and date divides inscription and flower sprig within beaded circle **Reverse:** Tomb within beaded circle

Date	Mintage	F	VF	XF	Unc
SH1371 (1992)	—	—	1.00	2.00	3.75
SH1372 (1993)	—	—	1.00	2.00	3.75
SH1373 (1994)	—	—	1.00	2.00	3.75
SH1374 (1995)	—	—	1.00	2.00	3.75
SH1375 (1996)	—	—	1.00	2.00	3.75
SH1376 (1996)	—	—	1.00	2.00	3.75

KM# 1244 20 RIALS

Copper-Nickel, 31 mm. **Subject:** 1400th Anniversary of Mohammed's Flight **Obverse:** Value and inscription within wreath **Reverse:** Inscription within banner on top of world globe under radiant sun

Date	Mintage	F	VF	XF	Unc
SH1358-AH1400 (1979)	—	—	5.00	10.00	15.00

KM# 1236 20 RIALS

Copper-Nickel, 31 mm. **Obverse:** Inscription within tulip wreath **Reverse:** Value and date within wreath **Note:** Date varieties exist.

Date	Mintage	F	VF	XF	Unc
SH1358 (1979)	—	—	1.00	1.75	4.50
SH1359 (1980)	—	—	1.00	1.75	4.50
SH1360 (1981)	—	—	1.00	1.75	4.50
SH1361 (1982)	—	—	1.00	1.75	4.50
SH1362 (1983)	—	—	1.00	1.75	4.50
SH1363 (1984)	—	—	1.00	1.75	4.50
SH1364 (1985)	—	—	1.00	1.75	4.50
SH1365 (1986)	—	—	1.00	1.75	4.50
SH1366 (1987)	—	—	1.00	1.75	4.50
SH1367 (1988)	—	—	1.00	1.75	4.50

KM# 1246 20 RIALS

Copper-Nickel, 31 mm. **Subject:** 2nd Anniversary of Islamic Revolution **Obverse:** Value flanked by tulips and inscription with date below **Reverse:** Legend

Date	Mintage	F	VF	XF	Unc
SH1359 (1980)	—	—	5.00	10.00	15.00

KM# 1247 20 RIALS

Copper-Nickel, 31 mm. **Subject:** 3rd Anniversary of Islamic Revolution **Obverse:** Artistic tulip design within circle **Reverse:** Inscription within artistic design

Date	Mintage	F	VF	XF	Unc
SH1360 (1981)	—	—	5.00	10.00	15.00

KM# 1251 20 RIALS

Copper-Nickel, 31 mm. **Subject:** Islamic Banking Week **Obverse:** Inscription within tulip wreath **Reverse:** Building within 1/2 wreath and gear design

Date	Mintage	F	VF	XF	Unc
SH1367 (1988)	—	—	5.00	10.00	15.00

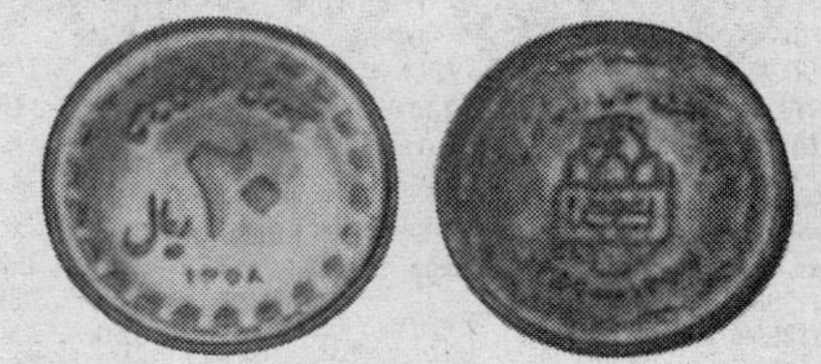

KM# 1254.1 20 RIALS

Copper-Nickel, 24 mm. **Subject:** 8 Years of Sacred Defense **Obverse:** Value and date within circle of small crowns **Reverse:** Shield divides dates and inscription within wreath **Note:** 2.0mm thick.

Date	Mintage	F	VF	XF	Unc
SH1368 (1989)	—	—	3.00	5.00	10.00

KM# 1254.2 20 RIALS

Copper-Nickel, 24 mm. **Obverse:** Value, date and inscription within circle of small crowns **Reverse:** Shield divides inscription and dates within wreath **Note:** 1.70mm thick.

Date	Mintage	F	VF	XF	Unc
SH1368 (1989)	—	—	3.00	5.00	10.00

KM# 1254.3 20 RIALS

Copper-Nickel, 24 mm. **Obverse:** Inscription, value and date within circle on small crowns **Reverse:** Shield divides inscription and dates within wreath

Date	Mintage	F	VF	XF	Unc
SH1368 (1989)	—	—	3.00	5.00	10.00

KM# 1237.1 50 RIALS

Aluminum-Bronze, 26 mm. **Subject:** Oil and Agriculture **Obverse:** Value at upper left of towers within 1/2 gear and oat sprigs **Reverse:** Map in relief **Edge:** Lettered in Arabic **Note:** Two varieties of edge lettering exist.

Date	Mintage	F	VF	XF	Unc
SH1359 (1980)	—	—	2.00	3.50	8.00
SH1360 (1981)	—	—	2.00	3.50	8.00
SH1361 (1982)	—	—	2.00	3.50	8.00
SH1362 (1983)	—	—	2.00	3.50	8.00
SH1364 (1985)	—	—	2.00	3.50	8.00
SH1365 (1986)	—	—	2.00	3.50	8.00

KM# 1237.2 50 RIALS

Aluminum-Bronze, 26 mm. **Obverse:** Value at upper left of towers within 1/2 gear and oat sprigs **Reverse:** Map incuse **Edge:** Lettered in Arabic

Date	Mintage	F	VF	XF	Unc
SH1366 (1987)	—	—	4.00	6.00	9.00
SH1367 (1988)	—	—	—	4.50	7.00
SH1368 (1989)	—	—	—	4.50	7.00

KM# 1252 50 RIALS

Copper-Nickel **Subject:** 10th Anniversary of Revolution **Obverse:** Value at upper left of towers within 1/2 gear and oat sprigs **Reverse:** Flower-like design above inscription and date within designed border

Date	Mintage	F	VF	XF	Unc
SH1367 (1988)	—	—	5.00	10.00	15.00

KM# 1237.1a 50 RIALS

Copper-Nickel **Obverse:** Value at upper left of towers within 1/2 gear and oat sprigs **Reverse:** Map in relief **Edge:** Lettered in Arabic

Date	Mintage	F	VF	XF	Unc
SH1368 (1989)	—	—	2.00	3.50	7.50
SH1369 (1990)	—	—	2.00	3.50	7.50
SH1370 (1991)	—	—	2.00	3.50	7.50

KM# 1260 50 RIALS

Copper-Nickel, 26 mm. **Subject:** Shrine of Hazrat Masumah **Obverse:** Value and date **Reverse:** Shrine within beaded circle **Edge:** Reeded

Date	Mintage	F	VF	XF	Unc
SH1371 (1992)	—	—	2.50	3.50	5.00
SH1372 (1993)	—	—	2.50	3.50	5.00
SH1373 (1994)	—	—	2.50	3.50	5.00
SH1374 (1995)	—	—	2.50	3.50	5.00
SH1375 (1996)	—	—	2.50	3.50	5.00
SH1376 (1997)	—	—	2.50	3.50	5.00
SH1377 (1998)	—	—	2.50	3.50	5.00
SH1378 (1999)	—	—	2.50	3.50	5.00

KM# 1261.1 100 RIALS

Copper-Nickel **Subject:** Shrine of Imam Reza **Obverse:** Value and date divides inscription and flower sprig within beaded border **Reverse:** Shrine within designed border **Note:** Thin denomination and numerals

Date	Mintage	F	VF	XF	Unc
SH1371 (1992)	—	—	—	—	6.50

KM# 1261.2 100 RIALS

Copper-Nickel, 29 mm. **Obverse:** Value and date **Reverse:** Shrine within designed border **Note:** Thick denomination and numerals

Date	Mintage	F	VF	XF	Unc
SH1372 (1993)	—	—	—	—	6.50
SH1373 (1994)	—	—	—	—	6.50
SH1375 (1996)	—	—	—	—	6.50
SH1376 (1997)	—	—	—	—	6.50
SH1377 (1998)	—	—	—	—	6.50
SH1378 (1999)	—	—	—	—	6.50
SH1379 (2000)	—	—	—	—	6.50

KM# 1262 250 RIALS

Bi-Metallic Copper-Nickel center in Brass ring, 28 mm. **Obverse:** Value within circle, inscription and date divide wreath **Reverse:** Stylized flower within circle and wreath

Date	Mintage	F	VF	XF	Unc
SH1372 (1993)	—	—	—	—	7.50
SH1373 (1994)	—	—	—	—	7.50
SH1374 (1995)	—	—	—	—	7.50
SH1375 (1996)	—	—	—	—	7.50
SH1376 (1997)	—	—	—	—	7.50
SH1377 (1998)	—	—	—	—	7.50
SH1378 (1999)	—	—	—	—	7.50
SH1379 (2000)	—	—	—	—	7.50

BULLION COINAGE

Issued by the National Bank of Iran

KM# 1238 1/4 AZADI

2.0339 g., 0.9000 Gold .0588 oz. AGW **Obverse:** Mosque within circle **Obv. Legend:** "1st Spring of Freedom" **Reverse:** Artistic design within hexagon and designed border

Date	Mintage	F	VF	XF	Unc
SH1358 (1979)	—	—	—	—	300

KM# 1265 1/4 AZADI

2.0339 g., 0.9000 Gold 0.0589 oz. AGW **Obv. Legend:** "Spring of Freedom"

Date	Mintage	F	VF	XF	Unc
SH1366 (1987)	—	—	—	—	300
SH1368 (1989)	—	—	—	—	300
SH1369 (1990)	—	—	—	—	300
SH1370 (1991)	—	—	—	—	300

KM# 1239 1/2 AZADI

4.0680 g., 0.9000 Gold .1177 oz. AGW **Obverse:** Mosque within circle **Obv. Legend:** "1st Spring of Freedom" **Reverse:** Artistic design within hexagon and designed border

Date	Mintage	F	VF	XF	Unc
SH1358 (1979)	—	—	—	—	100

KM# 1250.1 1/2 AZADI

4.0680 g., 0.9000 Gold .1177 oz. AGW **Obverse:** Legend shortened **Obv. Legend:** "Spring of Freedom"

Date	Mintage	F	VF	XF	Unc
SH1363 (1984)	—	—	—	—	200

KM# 1250.2 1/2 AZADI

4.0680 g., 0.9000 Gold .1177 oz. AGW **Obverse:** Legend larger **Obv. Legend:** "Spring of Freedom"

Date	Mintage	F	VF	XF	Unc
SH1366 (1987)	—	—	—	—	200
SH1368 (1989)	—	—	—	—	200
SH1370 (1991)	—	—	—	—	150

KM# 1240 AZADI

8.1360 g., 0.9000 Gold .2354 oz. AGW **Obverse:** Mosque within circle **Obv. Legend:** "1st Spring of Freedom" **Reverse:** Artistic design within hexagon and designed border

Date	Mintage	F	VF	XF	Unc
SH1358 (1979)	—	—	—	BV	170

KM# 1248.1 AZADI

8.1360 g., 0.9000 Gold .2354 oz. AGW **Obverse:** Mosque within circle **Obv. Legend:** "Spring of Freedom" **Reverse:** Artistic design within hexagon and designed border **Note:** Legend shortened

Date	Mintage	F	VF	XF	Unc
SH1363 (1984)	—	—	—	BV	170

KM# 1248.2 AZADI

8.1360 g., 0.9000 Gold .2354 oz. AGW **Obverse:** Mosque within circle **Obv. Legend:** "Spring of Freedom" **Reverse:** Artistic design within hexagon and designed border **Note:** Larger legend

Date	Mintage	F	VF	XF	Unc
SH1364 (1985)	—	—	—	BV	170
SH1365 (1986)	—	—	—	BV	170
SH1366 (1987)	—	—	—	BV	170
SH1367 (1988)	—	—	—	BV	170
SH1368 (1989)	—	—	—	BV	170
SH1369 (1990)	—	—	—	BV	170
SH1370 (1991)	—	—	—	BV	170

KM# 1264 AZADI

8.1360 g., 0.9000 Gold .2354 oz. AGW **Subject:** Central Bank of Islamic Republic of Iran **Obverse:** Bank within circle **Reverse:** Head 3/4 right above date

Date	Mintage	F	VF	XF	Unc
SH1370 (1991)	—	—	—	BV	170
SH1373 (1994)	—	—	—	BV	170
SH1374 (1995)	—	—	—	BV	170
SH1375 (1996)	—	—	—	BV	170

KM# A1264 AZADI

8.1360 g., 0.9000 Gold 0.2354 oz. AGW, 23.7 mm.
Obverse: Mosque within circle **Reverse:** Head left above date
Edge: Reeded **Mint:** Tehran

Date	Mintage	F	VF	XF	Unc
SH1370 (1991)	—	—	—	BV	170

KM# 1241 2-1/2 AZADI

20.3400 g., 0.9000 Gold .5885 oz. AGW **Obverse:** Mosque within circle **Obv. Legend:** "1st Spring of Freedom"
Reverse: Artistic design within hexagon within designed border

Date	Mintage	F	VF	XF	Unc
SH1358 (1979)	6	—	—	—	1,500

Note: A mintage of 6 pieces is reported, but more exist

KM# 1242 5 AZADI

40.6800 g., 0.9000 Gold 1.1770 oz. AGW **Obverse:** Mosque within circle **Obv. Legend:** "1st Spring of Freedom" **Reverse:** Artistic design within hexagon within designed border

Date	Mintage	F	VF	XF	Unc
SH1358 (1979)	—	—	—	—	3,500

PATTERNS

Including off metal strikes

KM#	Date	Mintage	Identification	Mkt Val
Pn26	SH1319H	—	1/4 Kran.	—
Pn27	SH1319	—	250 Dinars. Silver. Plain edge. Struck at Brussels Mint. Mouzaffer profile.	550
Pn28	SH1319	—	500 Dinars. Silver. Plain edge. Struck at Brussels Mint.	700

KM#	Date	Mintage	Identification	Mkt Val
Pn29	SH1319	—	1000 Dinars. Silver. Plain edge. Struck at Brussels Mint.	700
Pn30	SH1319	—	2000 Dinars. Silver. Plain edge. Struck at Brussels Mint.	800
Pn31	SH1319	—	5000 Dinars. Silver. Plain edge. Struck at Brussels Mint.	1,750
Pn32	SH1319	—	1/4 Toman.	300
Pn33	SH1326	—	2000 Dinars. Gold. KM#1024	1,000
Pn33a	SH1326	—	2000 Dinars. Gold. Mule. Obv. KM#1024, Rev. KM#1070.	2,500
Pn34	SH1326	—	5000 Dinars. Gold. Legend in open wreath. KM#1025	1,500
Pn34a	SH1326	—	5000 Dinars. Gold. Mule. Obv. KM#1025, Rev. KM#1071.	3,000
Pn35	SH1326	—	Toman. Gold. Legend in open wreath. KM#1026	375
Pn36	SH1326	—	2 Ashrafi. . Legend in open wreath.	2,500
PnA37	SH1330	—	2000 Dinars. Nickel. Struck at Berlin.	—
Pn37	SH1331	—	Toman. Gilt Bronze.	1,000
Pn37a	SH1331	—	5000 Dinars. Gold. Mule. Obv. KM#1070, Rev. KM#1024.	2,500
Pn38	SH1331	—	2 Toman. Gilt Bronze. Portrait of Ahmed Shah.	1,000

KM#	Date	Mintage	Identification	Mkt Val
Pn39	SH1332	—	5 Krans. Silver. Plain edge.	1,000
Pn40	SH1332	—	2000 Dinars. Gold.	—
Pn40a	SH1331	—	2000 Dinars. Gold. Mule. Obv. KM#1071, Rev. KM#1025.	3,000
Pn41	SH1337	—	2 Toman. Gold. KM#1080; "2 Ashrafi"	—

KM#	Date	Mintage	Identification	Mkt Val
Pn42	SH1337	—	2000 Dinars. Gold. 14.0000 g.	2,000

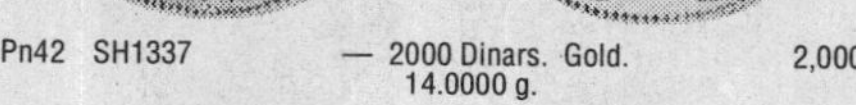

KM#	Date	Mintage	Identification	Mkt Val
Pn43	SH1337	—	2000 Dinars. Gold. 14.0000 g.	2,000
Pn44	SH1337	—	5 Toman. Gold. KM#1081; "5 Ashrafi"	3,500
Pn45	SH1337	—	10 Toman. Gold. KM#1082	—
Pn46	SH1305	—	2000 Dinars. Silver. Reeded edge.	6,500
Pn47	SH1305	—	5000 Dinars. Silver. Reeded edge.	9,500

KM#	Date	Mintage	Identification	Mkt Val
Pn48	SHMS2537 (1978)	—	10 Pahlavi. Silver. 51.5100 g. 48.95 mm. . Reeded edge. 48.95mm. KM#1213.	—

MINT SETS

KM#	Date	Mintage	Identification	Issue Price	Mkt Val
MS1	SH1342(1963) (4)	—	KM#1171a, 1173, 1175a, 1177a	2.00	15.00
MSA3	SH1342-1343 (1963-64) (4)	—	KM#1171a, 1173, 1175a, 1177a	—	—
MS2	SH1343(1964) (4)	—	KM#1171a, 1173, 1175a, 1177a	2.00	11.50
MS3	SH1348(1969) (5)	—	KM#1156, 1171a, 1173, 1176, 1178	2.00	17.00
MS4	SH1350(1971) (5)	—	KM#1156, 1171a, 1173, 1176, 1178	2.00	17.00
MS5	SH1353(1974) (6)	—	KM#1156, 1171a, 1173, 1176, 1179, 1181	2.00	19.00
MS6	SH1354(1975) (6)	—	KM#1156, 1171a, 1173, 1176, 1179, 1181	2.00	22.00
MS7	MS2535(1976) (6)	—	KM#1156a, 1205-1209	2.50	21.50
MS8	MS2536(1977) (6)	—	KM#1156a, 1172-1173, 1176, 1179, 1181	2.50	20.00
MS9	SH1358(1989) (8)	—	KM#1243-1244 dated 1358; 1246 dated 1359; 1247 dated 1360; 1252 dated 1367; 1253.1, 1253.2, 1254.1 dated 1368	—	40.00
MS10	SH1366(1989) (7)	—	KM#1232-1234, 1236 dated 1366; 1235.2, 1237.2 dated 1367; 1237.1a dated 1368	—	60.00
MS11	SH1371(1993) (5)	—	KM#1258-1262	—	60.00
MS12	SH1372, 1375, 1378 (1993, 1996, 1999) (6)	—	KM#1258-1260, 1261.2, 1262, 1263	—	100
MS13	SH1373, 1375, 1378 (1994, 1996, 1999) (6)	—	KM#1258-1260, 1261.2, 1262, 1263	—	100

PROOF SETS

KM#	Date	Mintage	Identification	Issue Price	Mkt Val
PS1	SH1306(1927) (2)	20	KM#1104, 1106	—	1,700
PS2	SH1350(1971) (9)	9,805	KM#1184-1192	262	825
PS3	SH1350(1971) (5)	18,100	KM#1184-1188	59.50	85.00

IRAQ

The Republic of Iraq, historically known as Mesopotamia, is located in the Near East and is bordered by Kuwait, Iran, Turkey, Syria, Jordan and Saudi Arabia. It has area of 167,925 sq. mi. (434,920 sq. km.) and a population of 14 million. Capital: Baghdad. The economy of Iraq is based on agriculture and petroleum. Crude oil accounted for 94 percent of the exports before the war with Iran began in 1980.

Mesopotamia was the site of a number of flourishing civilizations of antiquity - Sumeria, Assyria, Babylonia, Parthia, Persia and the Biblical cities of Ur, Nineveh and Babylon. Desired because of its favored location, which embraced the fertile alluvial plains of the Tigris and Euphrates Rivers, Mesopotamia - 'land between the rivers'- was conquered by Cyrus the Great of Persia, Alexander of Macedonia and by Arabs who made the legendary city of Baghdad the capital of the ruling caliphate. Suleiman the Magnificent conquered Mesopotamia for Turkey in1534, and it formed part of the Ottoman Empire until 1623, and from 1638 to 1917. Great Britain, given a League of Nations mandate over the territory in 1920, recognized Iraq as a kingdom in 1922. Iraq became an independent constitutional monarchy presided over by the Hashemite family, direct descendants of the prophet Mohammed, in 1932. In 1958, the army-led revolution of July 14 overthrew the monarchy and proclaimed a republic.

NOTE: The 'I' mintmark on 1938 and 1943 issues appears on the obverse near the point of the bust. Some of the issues of 1938 have a dot to denote a composition change from nickel to copper-nickel.

RULERS

Ottoman, until 1917
British, 1921-1922
Faisal I, 1921-1933
Ghazi I, 1933-1939
Faisal II, Regency, 1939-1953
As King, 1953-1958

MINT MARK

I – Bombay

MONETARY SYSTEM

Falus, Fulus   Fals, Fils   Falsan

50 Fils = 1 Dirham
200 Fils = 1 Riyal
1000 Fils = 1 Dinar (Pound)

TITLES

العراق

Al-Iraq

المملكة العراقية

SAl-Mamlaka(t) al-Iraqiya(t)

الجمهورية العرقية

Al-Jumhuriya(t) al-Iraqiya(t)

KINGDOM OF IRAQ

Faisal I
1921-1933AD
DECIMAL COINAGE

KM# 95 FILS

2.5000 g., Bronze, 19.5 mm. **Obv:** Head right **Rev:** Value in center circle flanked by dates

Date	Mintage	F	VF	XF	Unc
1931	4,000,000	1.00	3.00	10.00	25.00
AH1349 Proof	—	—	—	—	—
1931 Proof	—	—	—	—	—
1933	6,000,000	1.00	3.00	10.00	25.00
1933 Proof	—	—	—	—	—

KM# 96 2 FILS

5.0000 g., Bronze, 24 mm. **Obv:** Head right **Rev:** Value in center circle flanked by dates

Date	Mintage	F	VF	XF	Unc
1931	2,500,000	1.25	3.50	10.00	25.00
1931	2,500,000	1.25	3.50	10.00	25.00
1931 Proof	—	—	—	—	—
1933	1,000,000	1.50	4.00	15.00	35.00
1933 Proof	—	—	—	—	—

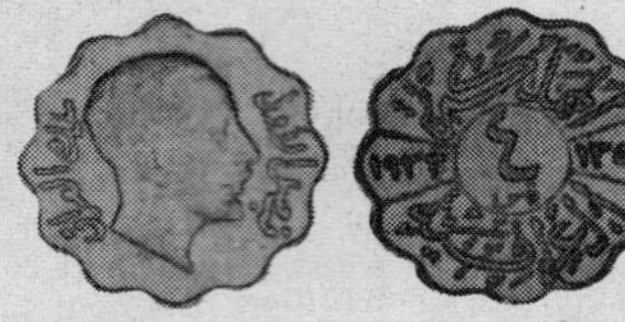

KM# 97 4 FILS

4.0000 g., Nickel, 21 mm. **Obv:** Head right **Rev:** Value in center circle flanked by dates **Shape:** Scalloped

Date	Mintage	F	VF	XF	Unc
1931	4,500,000	1.50	4.00	15.00	50.00
1931 Proof	—	—	—	—	—
1933	6,500,000	1.50	4.00	15.00	50.00
1933 Proof	—	—	—	—	—

KM# 98 10 FILS

6.7500 g., Nickel, 25 mm. **Obv:** Head right **Rev:** Value within center circle flanked by dates **Shape:** Scalloped

Date	Mintage	F	VF	XF	Unc
1931	2,400,000	2.00	5.00	16.50	50.00
1931 Proof	—	—	—	—	—
1933	2,200,000	2.00	5.00	16.50	50.00
1933 Proof	—	—	—	—	—

KM# 99 20 FILS

3.6000 g., 0.5000 Silver .0579 oz. ASW, 20.5 mm. **Obv:** Head right **Rev:** Value in center circle flanked by dates

Date	Mintage	F	VF	XF	Unc
1931	1,500,000	2.50	9.00	25.00	75.00
1931 Proof	—	—	—	—	—
1933	1,100,000	2.50	9.00	25.00	75.00
1933 Proof	—	—	—	—	—
1933 (error) 1252	Inc. above	20.00	60.00	100	200

KM# 100 50 FILS

9.0000 g., 0.5000 Silver .1447 oz. ASW, 26.5 mm. **Obv:** Head right **Rev:** Value in center circle flanked by dates

Date	Mintage	F	VF	XF	Unc
1931	8,800,000	3.50	10.00	28.00	80.00
1931 Proof	—	—	—	—	—
1933	800,000	6.00	15.00	35.00	100
1933 Proof	—	—	—	—	—

KM# 101 RIYAL (200 Fils)

20.0000 g., 0.5000 Silver .3215 oz. ASW, 34 mm. **Obv:** Head right **Rev:** Value in center circle flanked by dates **Note:** Dav. #255.

Date	Mintage	F	VF	XF	Unc
1932	500,000	7.50	15.00	35.00	350
1932 Proof	Est. 20	Value: 1,600			

Ghazi I
1933-1939AD
DECIMAL COINAGE

KM# 102 FILS

2.5000 g., Bronze, 19.5 mm. **Obv:** Head left **Rev:** Value in center circle flanked by dates **Note:** Struck at Royal and Bombay Mint.

Date	Mintage	F	VF	XF	Unc
1936	3,000,000	1.25	4.00	10.00	25.00
1936 Proof	—	—	—	—	—
1938	36,000,000	0.25	0.50	1.00	3.00
1938 Proof	—	—	—	—	—
1938 -I	3,000,000	0.50	2.00	5.00	15.00

KM# 105 4 FILS

4.0000 g., Nickel, 21 mm. **Obv:** Head left **Rev:** Value within center circle flanked by dates **Shape:** Scalloped

Date	Mintage	F	VF	XF	Unc
1938	1,000,000	1.00	2.00	6.00	15.00
1938 Proof	—	—	—	—	—
1939	1,000,000	1.25	2.50	10.00	30.00
1939 Proof	—	—	—	—	—

KM# 105a 4 FILS

21.0000 g., Copper-Nickel, 21 mm. **Obv:** Head left **Rev:** Value within center circle flanked by dates **Shape:** Scalloped **Note:** Struck at Royal and Bombay Mint.

Date	Mintage	F	VF	XF	Unc
1938	2,750,000	0.75	1.00	2.00	6.00
1938 Proof	—	—	—	—	—
1938 -I	2,500,000	1.00	2.00	7.50	15.00

KM# 105b 4 FILS

4.0000 g., Bronze, 21 mm. **Obv:** Head left **Rev:** Value in center circle flanked by dates **Shape:** Scalloped

Date	Mintage	F	VF	XF	Unc
1938	8,000,000	0.50	1.00	2.00	6.00
1938 Proof	—	—	—	—	—

KM# 103 10 FILS

6.7500 g., Nickel, 25 mm. **Obv:** Head left **Rev:** Value in center circle flanked by dates **Shape:** Scalloped

Date	Mintage	F	VF	XF	Unc
1937	400,000	3.00	5.00	16.50	50.00
1937 Proof	—	—	—	—	—
1938	600,000	2.50	4.00	10.00	35.00
1938 Proof	—	—	—	—	—

KM# 103a 10 FILS

6.7500 g., Copper-Nickel, 25 mm. **Obv:** Head left **Rev:** Value within center circle flanked by dates **Shape:** Scalloped **Note:** Struck at Royal and Bombay Mint.

Date	Mintage	F	VF	XF	Unc
1938	1,100,000	1.00	2.00	4.00	10.00
1938 Proof	—	—	—	—	—
1938 -I	1,500,000	1.50	2.50	6.00	15.00

KM# 103b 10 FILS

6.7500 g., Bronze, 25 mm. **Obv:** Head left **Rev:** Value within center circle flanked by dates **Shape:** Scalloped

Date	Mintage	F	VF	XF	Unc
1938	8,250,000	0.50	1.00	2.50	6.50
1938 Proof	—	—	—	—	—

KM# 106 20 FILS

3.6000 g., 0.5000 Silver .0579 oz. ASW, 20.5 mm. **Obv:** Head left **Rev:** Value in center circle flanked by dates

Date	Mintage	F	VF	XF	Unc
1938	1,200,000	2.00	3.50	8.00	22.00
1938 -I	1,350,000	2.00	4.00	9.00	26.00

KM# 104 50 FILS

9.0000 g., 0.5000 Silver .1447 oz. ASW, 26.5 mm. **Obv:** Head left **Rev:** Value in center circle flanked by dates **Note:** Struck at Royal and Bombay Mint.

Date	Mintage	F	VF	XF	Unc
1937	1,200,000	3.00	7.00	10.00	30.00
1937 Proof	—	—	—	—	—
1938	5,300,000	2.50	4.00	8.00	25.00
1938 Proof	—	—	—	—	—
1938 -I	7,500,000	2.50	4.00	8.00	25.00

Faisal II - Regency

1939-1953AD

DECIMAL COINAGE

KM# 107 4 FILS

4.0000 g., Bronze, 21 mm. **Obv:** Head right **Rev:** Value in center circle flanked by dates **Shape:** Scalloped

Date	Mintage	F	VF	XF	Unc
1943 -I	1,500,000	2.00	3.00	7.00	15.00

KM# 111 4 FILS

4.0000 g., Copper-Nickel, 21 mm. **Obv:** Head right **Rev:** Value in center circle flanked by dates **Shape:** Scalloped

Date	Mintage	F	VF	XF	Unc
1953	20,750,000	0.50	0.75	1.00	2.50
1953 Proof	200	Value: 75.00			

KM# 108 10 FILS

6.7500 g., Bronze, 25 mm. **Obv:** Head right **Rev:** Value in center circle flanked by dates **Shape:** Scalloped

Date	Mintage	F	VF	XF	Unc
1943 -I	1,500,000	3.00	7.00	20.00	50.00

KM# 112 10 FILS

6.7500 g., Copper-Nickel, 25 mm. **Obv:** Head right **Rev:** Value in center circle flanked by dates **Shape:** Scalloped

Date	Mintage	F	VF	XF	Unc
1953	11,400,000	0.50	0.75	1.00	2.50
1953 Proof	200	Value: 75.00			

Faisal II - King

1953-1958AD

DECIMAL COINAGE

KM# 109 FILS

Bronze **Obv:** Head right **Rev:** Value in center circle flanked by dates

Date	Mintage	F	VF	XF	Unc
1953	41,000,000	0.25	0.40	0.60	1.00
1953 Proof	200	Value: 75.00			

KM# 110 2 FILS

Bronze **Obv:** Head right **Rev:** Value in center circle flanked by dates

Date	Mintage	F	VF	XF	Unc
1953	500,000	0.50	1.00	3.00	12.50
1953 Proof	200	Value: 100			

KM# 113 20 FILS

3.6000 g., 0.5000 Silver .0579 oz. ASW, 20.5 mm. **Obv:** Head right **Rev:** Value in center circle flanked by dates

Date	Mintage	F	VF	XF	Unc
1953	250,000	25.00	45.00	70.00	140
1953 Proof	200	Value: 300			

KM# 116 20 FILS

2.8000 g., 0.5000 Silver .0450 oz. ASW, 19 mm. **Obv:** Head right **Rev:** Value in center circle, date above sprigs, legend above

Date	Mintage	F	VF	XF	Unc
1955	4,000,000	1.50	3.00	5.00	10.00
1955 Proof	—	Value: 80.00			

KM# 114 50 FILS

9.0000 g., 0.5000 Silver .1447 oz. ASW, 26.5 mm. **Obv:** Head right **Rev:** Value in center circle flanked by dates

Date	Mintage	F	VF	XF	Unc
1953	560,000	50.00	100	150	250
1953 Proof	200	Value: 450			

KM# 117 50 FILS

7.0000 g., 0.5000 Silver .1126 oz. ASW, 26 mm. **Obv:** Head right **Rev:** Value in center circle, date above sprigs, legend above

Date	Mintage	F	VF	XF	Unc
1955	12,000,000	2.50	4.00	6.00	11.50
1955 Proof	—	Value: 80.00			

KM# 115 100 FILS

10.0000 g., 0.9000 Silver .2893 oz. ASW, 29 mm. **Obv:** Head right **Rev:** Value in center circle flanked by dates

Date	Mintage	F	VF	XF	Unc
1953	1,200,000	5.00	7.50	20.00	50.00
1953 Proof	200	Value: 250			

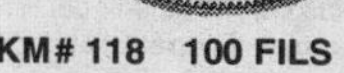

KM# 118 100 FILS

10.0000 g., 0.5000 Silver .1607 oz. ASW, 29 mm. **Obv:** Head right **Rev:** Value in center circle flanked by dates

Date	Mintage	F	VF	XF	Unc
1955	1,000,000	—	700	1,000	1,500
1955 Proof	—	Value: 300			

REPUBLIC

DECIMAL COINAGE

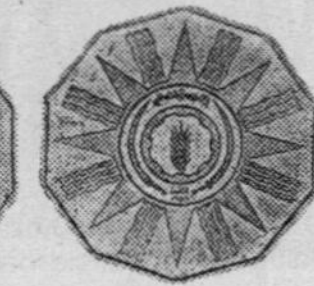

KM# 119 FILS

2.5000 g., Bronze, 19 mm. **Obv:** Value in center circle, dates above sprig, legend above **Rev:** Oat sprig within center circle of star design **Shape:** 10-sided

Date	Mintage	F	VF	XF	Unc
1959	72,000,000	0.15	0.25	0.50	1.00
1959 Proof	400	Value: 30.00			

KM# 120 5 FILS

5.0000 g., Copper-Nickel, 22 mm. **Obv:** Value in center circle above dates and sprigs, legend above **Rev:** Oat sprig within center circle of star design **Shape:** Scalloped

Date	Mintage	F	VF	XF	Unc
1959	30,000,000	0.15	0.25	0.50	1.00
1959 Proof	400	Value: 30.00			

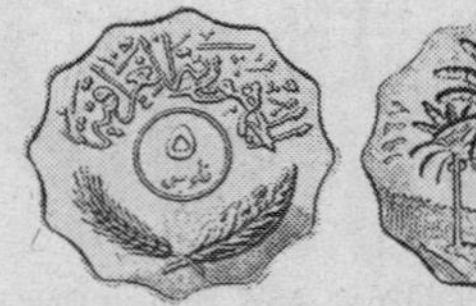

KM# 125 5 FILS

Copper-Nickel **Obv:** Value in center circle above oat sprigs, legend above **Rev:** Palm trees divide dates **Shape:** Scalloped

Date	Mintage	F	VF	XF	Unc
1967	17,000,000	0.15	0.25	0.35	0.50
1971	15,000,000	0.15	0.25	0.35	0.50

KM# 125a 5 FILS

Stainless Steel **Obv:** Value in center circle above oat sprigs, legend above **Rev:** Palm trees divide dates

Date	Mintage	F	VF	XF	Unc
1971	2,000,000	0.20	0.30	0.50	0.75
1974	15,000,000	0.10	0.15	0.25	0.35
1975	94,800,000	0.10	0.15	0.25	0.35
1980	20,160,000	0.10	0.15	0.25	0.35
1981	29,840,000	0.10	0.15	0.25	0.35

Note: Non-magnetic

KM# 141 5 FILS

Stainless Steel **Series:** F.A.O. **Obv:** Value in center circle divides legend **Rev:** Palm trees divide date **Shape:** Scalloped

Date	Mintage	F	VF	XF	Unc
1975	2,000,000	0.10	0.15	0.25	0.50

KM# 159 5 FILS

Stainless Steel **Subject:** Babylon-Ruins **Obv:** Value in center circle divides legend **Rev:** Dates above ruins **Shape:** Scalloped

Date	Mintage	F	VF	XF	Unc
1982	—	0.10	0.15	0.25	0.50

KM# 159a 5 FILS

Copper-Nickel **Subject:** Babylon-Ruins **Obv:** Value in center circle divides legend **Rev:** Dates above ruins

Date	Mintage	F	VF	XF	Unc
1982 Proof	—	Value: 3.00			

KM# 121 10 FILS

6.7500 g., Copper-Nickel, 26 mm. **Obv:** Value in center circle above dates and sprigs, legend above **Rev:** Oat sprig within center circle of star-like design **Shape:** Scalloped

Date	Mintage	F	VF	XF	Unc
1959	24,000,000	0.25	0.35	0.65	1.50
1959 Proof	400	Value: 30.00			

KM# 126 10 FILS

Copper-Nickel, 26 mm. **Obv:** Value in center circle above oat sprigs, legend above **Rev:** Palm trees divide dates **Shape:** Scalloped

Date	Mintage	F	VF	XF	Unc
1967	13,400,000	0.20	0.30	0.60	1.25
1971	12,000,000	0.20	0.30	0.60	1.25

KM# 126a 10 FILS

Stainless Steel, 26 mm. **Obv:** Value in center circle above sprigs, legend above **Rev:** Palm trees divide dates

Date	Mintage	F	VF	XF	Unc
1971	1,550,000	0.25	0.35	0.65	1.50
1974	12,000,000	0.20	0.30	0.50	1.00
1975	52,456,000	0.20	0.30	0.50	1.00
1979	13,800,000	0.20	0.30	0.50	1.00
1980	11,264,000	0.20	0.30	0.50	1.00
1981	63,736,000	0.20	0.30	0.50	1.00

Note: Non-magnetic

KM# 142 10 FILS

Stainless Steel, 26 mm. **Series:** F.A.O. **Obv:** Value within circle divides legend **Rev:** Palm trees divide dates **Shape:** Scalloped

Date	Mintage	F	VF	XF	Unc
1975	1,000,000	0.15	0.25	0.50	0.75

KM# 160 10 FILS

Stainless Steel, 26 mm. **Obv:** Value within circle divides legends **Rev:** Dates above ruins **Rev. Legend:** Babylon - Ishtar Gate **Shape:** Scalloped

Date	Mintage	F	VF	XF	Unc
1982	—	—	—	—	0.75

KM# 160a 10 FILS

Copper-Nickel **Obv:** Value within circle divides legends **Rev:** Dates above ruins **Rev. Legend:** Babylon - Ishtar Gate **Shape:** Scalloped

Date	Mintage	F	VF	XF	Unc
1982 Proof	—	Value: 3.00			

KM# 122 25 FILS

2.5000 g., 0.5000 Silver .0401 oz. ASW, 20 mm. **Obv:** Value within circle above dates and sprigs, legend above **Rev:** Oat sprig within center circle of star-like design

Date	Mintage	F	VF	XF	Unc
1959	12,000,000	0.65	0.85	1.50	3.00
1959 Proof	400	Value: 40.00			

KM# 127 25 FILS

Copper-Nickel, 20 mm. **Obv:** Value in center circle above sprigs, legend above **Rev:** Palm trees divide dates

Date	Mintage	F	VF	XF	Unc
1969	6,000,000	0.20	0.30	0.50	1.00
1970	6,000,000	0.20	0.30	0.50	1.00
1972	12,000,000	0.20	0.30	0.50	1.00
1975	48,000,000	0.20	0.30	0.50	1.00
1981	60,000,000	0.20	0.30	0.50	1.00

KM# 161 25 FILS

Copper-Nickel, 20 mm. **Obv:** Value in center circle divides legend **Rev:** Dates above lion

Date	Mintage	F	VF	XF	Unc
1982 Proof	—	Value: 4.00			
1982	—	—	—	—	1.25

KM# 123 50 FILS

5.0000 g., 0.5000 Silver .0803 oz. ASW, 23 mm. **Obv:** Value in center circle above dates and sprigs, legend above **Rev:** Oat sprig within center circle of star-like design

Date	Mintage	F	VF	XF	Unc
1959	24,000,000	1.25	1.50	2.50	5.00
1959 Proof	400	Value: 80.00			

KM# 128 50 FILS

Copper-Nickel, 23 mm. **Obv:** Value within circle above sprigs, legend above **Rev:** Palm trees divide dates

Date	Mintage	F	VF	XF	Unc
1969	12,000,000	0.25	0.35	0.65	1.25
1970	12,000,000	0.25	0.35	0.65	1.25
1972	12,000,000	0.25	0.35	0.65	1.25
1975	36,000,000	0.25	0.35	0.65	1.25
1979	1,500,000	0.25	0.35	0.65	1.75
1980	23,520,000	0.25	0.35	0.65	1.25
1981	138,995,000	0.25	0.35	0.65	1.00
1990	—	0.25	0.35	0.65	1.00

KM# 162 50 FILS

Copper-Nickel, 23 mm. **Obv:** Value in center circle divides legend **Rev:** Horse right

Date	Mintage	F	VF	XF	Unc
1982	—	0.25	0.50	0.75	2.50
1982 Proof	—	Value: 6.00			

KM# 124 100 FILS

10.0000 g., 0.5000 Silver .1607 oz. ASW, 29 mm. **Obv:** Value within circle above dates and sprigs, legend above **Rev:** Oat sprig within center circle of star-like design

Date	Mintage	F	VF	XF	Unc
1959	6,000,000	2.75	3.75	6.00	10.00
1959 Proof	400	Value: 150			

KM# 129 100 FILS

Copper-Nickel **Obv:** Value within circle above sprigs, legend above **Rev:** Palm trees divide dates

Date	Mintage	F	VF	XF	Unc
1970	6,000,000	0.35	0.50	0.75	1.50
1972	6,000,000	0.35	0.50	0.75	1.50
1975	12,000,000	0.35	0.50	0.75	1.50
1979	1,000,000	0.35	0.75	1.50	3.00

KM# 130 250 FILS

Nickel **Series:** F.A.O. **Subject:** Agrarian Reform Day **Obv:** Value within circle above sprigs, legend above **Rev:** Palm trees divide dates

Date	Mintage	F	VF	XF	Unc
1970	500,000	—	1.50	3.00	6.00
1970 Proof	1,000	Value: 14.50			

Note: Varieties with edge inscription w/FAO-250-repeated three times in relief have been reported

KM# 131 250 FILS

Nickel **Subject:** 1st Anniversary Peace with Kurds **Obv:** Value within circle above dates and sprigs, legend above **Rev:** Value, design and dove within circle, outer circle consists of 1/2 gear and 1/2 sprigs

Date	Mintage	F	VF	XF	Unc
1971	500,000	—	1.50	3.00	6.00
1971 Proof	1,000	Value: 14.50			

KM# 135 250 FILS

Nickel **Subject:** Silver Jublilee of Al Baath Party **Obv:** Value within circle above dates, legend above and below **Rev:** Palm trees divide dates

Date	Mintage	F	VF	XF	Unc
1972	250,000	—	1.50	3.00	6.00

KM# 136 250 FILS

Nickel **Subject:** 25th Anniversary of Central Bank **Obv:** Value within circle above dates, legend above and below **Rev:** Palm trees divide dates

Date	Mintage	F	VF	XF	Unc
1972	250,000	—	1.50	3.00	6.00

KM# 138 250 FILS

Nickel **Subject:** Oil Nationalization **Obv:** Value within circle above dates, legend above and below **Rev:** Torch divides oil rig tower and pump, flanked by dates

Date	Mintage	F	VF	XF	Unc
1973 Proof	5,000	Value: 12.00			
1973	260,000	—	1.50	3.00	6.50

KM# 144 250 FILS

Nickel **Subject:** International Year of the Child **Obv:** Value within circle divides legends and emblems **Rev:** Child's laureate head right within circle

Date	Mintage	F	VF	XF	Unc
1979 Proof	10,000	Value: 8.00			

KM# 146 250 FILS

Copper-Nickel **Subject:** 1st Anniversary of Hussein as President **Obv:** Value within center circle flanked by dates, legend above and below **Rev:** Bust 1/4 left

Date	Mintage	F	VF	XF	Unc
1980	—	—	3.00	6.00	12.00

KM# 147 250 FILS

Copper-Nickel, 29.8 mm. **Obv:** Value within circle above sprigs, legend above **Rev:** Palm trees divide dates **Shape:** Octagon

Date	Mintage	F	VF	XF	Unc
1980	—	—	1.00	2.00	5.00
1981	25,568,000	—	1.00	2.00	5.00
1990	—	—	1.00	2.00	5.00

KM# 152 250 FILS

Copper-Nickel **Subject:** World Food Day **Obv:** F.A.O logo below value flanked by designs, legend above and below **Rev:** Design within circle divides dates **Shape:** Octagon

Date	Mintage	F	VF	XF	Unc
1981	46,432,000	—	1.00	2.00	4.00

KM# 155 250 FILS

Copper-Nickel **Subject:** Nonaligned Nations Baghdad Conference **Obv:** Value within circle, legend above and below **Rev:** Stylized tree divides dates above legend **Shape:** Octagon

Date	Mintage	F	VF	XF	Unc
1982	—	—	1.00	2.00	5.00

KM# 163 250 FILS

Copper-Nickel **Obv:** Value within circle, legend above and below **Rev:** Monument flanked by dates **Shape:** Octagon

Date	Mintage	F	VF	XF	Unc
1982	—	—	1.00	2.00	4.50
1982 Proof	—	Value: 8.00			

KM# 132 500 FILS

Nickel **Subject:** 50th Anniversary of Iraqi Army **Obv:** Value in circle flanked by designs , legend above and below **Rev:** Conjoined armored busts divide dates

Date	Mintage	F	VF	XF	Unc
1971	100,000	—	2.50	4.50	10.00
1971 Proof	5,000	Value: 15.00			

KM# 139 500 FILS

Nickel **Subject:** Oil Nationalization **Obv:** Value within circle, date below, legend above and below **Rev:** Oil rig divides dates

Date	Mintage	F	VF	XF	Unc
1973	260,000	—	2.50	4.50	10.00
1973 Proof	5,000	Value: 17.50			

KM# 165 500 FILS

9.0800 g., Nickel **Obv:** Value within circle above sprigs, "500 Fals" **Rev:** Palm trees divide dates **Shape:** Square

Date	Mintage	F	VF	XF	Unc
1982	—	—	2.50	4.00	7.00

KM# 165a 500 FILS

8.9800 g., Nickel **Obv:** Value within circle above sprigs, "500 Falsan" **Rev:** Palm trees divide dates **Shape:** Square **Note:** Reduced weight.

Date	Mintage	F	VF	XF	Unc
1982	—	—	20.00	35.00	85.00

KM# 168 500 FILS

9.0800 g., Nickel **Obv:** Value within circle divides legend, "500 Fals" **Rev:** Lion of Babylon flanked by dates **Shape:** Square

Date	Mintage	F	VF	XF	Unc
1982	—	—	2.00	3.50	8.00
1982 Proof	—	Value: 12.50			

KM# 168a 500 FILS

9.0800 g., Nickel **Obv:** Value within circle divides legend, "500 Falsan" **Rev:** Lion of Babylon flanked by dates **Shape:** Square

Date	Mintage	F	VF	XF	Unc
1982	—	—	15.00	25.00	75.00

KM# 133 DINAR

31.0000 g., 0.9000 Silver .8971 oz. ASW **Subject:** 50th Anniversary of Iraqi Army **Obv:** Value within circle flanked by designs, legend above and below **Rev:** Conjoined armored busts divide dates

Date	Mintage	F	VF	XF	Unc
1971	20,000	—	—	—	22.50
1971 Proof	—	Value: 40.00			

KM# 137 DINAR

31.0000 g., 0.5000 Silver .4983 oz. ASW **Subject:** 25th Anniversary of Central Bank **Obv:** Value within circle flanked by designs, legend above and below **Rev:** Palm trees divide dates

Date	Mintage	F	VF	XF	Unc
1972	50,000	—	—	—	20.00
1972 Proof	—	Value: 35.00			

KM# 140 DINAR

31.0000 g., 0.5000 Silver .4983 oz. ASW **Subject:** Oil Nationalization **Obv:** Value within circle flanked by designs, legend above and below **Rev:** Half radiant sun divides dates above long ship

Date	Mintage	F	VF	XF	Unc
1973	60,000	—	—	—	20.00
1973 Proof	5,000	Value: 37.50			

KM# 143 DINAR

31.0000 g., 0.9000 Silver .8971 oz. ASW **Subject:** Inauguaration of Tharthat-Euphrates Canal **Obv:** Value within circle flanked by designs, legend above and below **Rev:** Dam with inscription above and dates below

Date	Mintage	F	VF	XF	Unc
1977 Proof	7,000	Value: 40.00			

KM# 145 DINAR

31.0000 g., 0.9000 Silver .8971 oz. ASW **Subject:** International Year of the Child **Obv:** Value within circle flanked by designs, legend above and below **Rev:** Child's laureate head right within circle **Note:** KM#145 is commonly found impaired. Value listed is for unimpaired Proof.

Date	Mintage	F	VF	XF	Unc
1979 Proof	5,000	Value: 47.50			

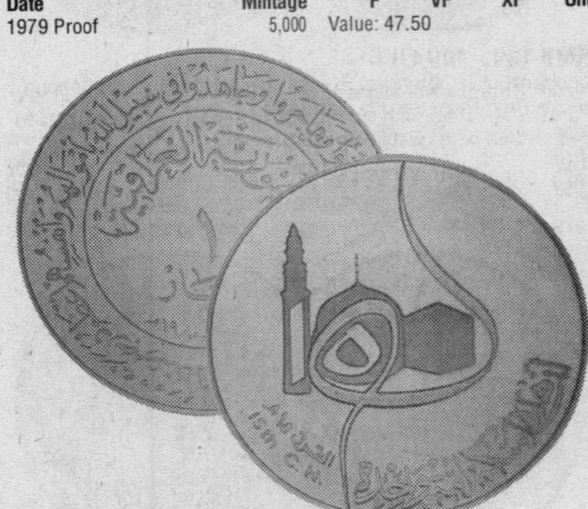

KM# 148 DINAR

30.5300 g., 0.9000 Silver .8835 oz. ASW **Subject:** 15th Century of Hegira **Obv:** Value and dates within circle with legend around border **Rev:** Stylized value within Mosque **Note:** KM#148 is commonly found impaired. Value listed is for unimpaired Proof.

Date	Mintage	F	VF	XF	Unc
1980 Proof	25,000	Value: 50.00			

KM# 149 DINAR

Nickel **Subject:** Battle of Qadissyiat **Obv:** Value within circle flanked by dates, legends and map **Rev:** Bust 1/4 left in front of battle scene **Shape:** 10-sided

Date	Mintage	F	VF	XF	Unc
1980	—	—	—	7.50	15.00
1980 Proof	—	Value: 35.00			

KM# 153 DINAR

Nickel **Subject:** 50th Anniversary of Iraq Air Force **Obv:** Value within circle with legend above and dates and legend below **Rev:** Bust left divides dates, planes above with banner, sprigs below **Shape:** 10-sided

Date	Mintage	F	VF	XF	Unc
1981	—	—	—	10.00	20.00

KM# 170 DINAR

Nickel **Subject:** Circulation Coinage **Obv:** Value within circle above sprigs, legend above **Rev:** Palm trees divide dates **Shape:** 10-sided

Date	Mintage	F	VF	XF	Unc
1981	—	—	—	—	6.50

KM# 156 DINAR

Nickel **Subject:** Nonaligned Nations Baghdad Conference **Obv:** Value within circle with legend above and below **Rev:** Stylized tree divides dates within legend **Shape:** 10-sided

Date	Mintage	F	VF	XF	Unc
1982	—	—	—	3.50	8.00

KM# 164 DINAR

Nickel **Obv:** Value within circle divides legend **Rev:** Tower of Babylon flanked by dates **Shape:** 10-sided

Date	Mintage	F	VF	XF	Unc
1982	—	—	—	3.50	8.00
1982 Proof	—	Value: 12.50			

KM# 134 5 DINARS

13.5700 g., 0.9170 Gold .4001 oz. AGW **Subject:** 50th Anniversary of Iraqi Army **Obv:** Value within circle flanked by designs with legend above and below **Rev:** Conjoined armored busts divide dates

Date	Mintage	F	VF	XF	Unc
1971	20,000	—	—	—	BV
1971 Proof	—	Value: 325			

KM# 171 5 DINARS

Bronze, 28 mm. **Obv:** Denomination and legend **Rev:** Two swords arched above palm tree

Date	Mintage	F	VF	XF	Unc
1990	—	—	—	—	5.00

Note: Not released to circulation

KM# 172 10 DINARS

Bronze **Obv:** Denomination and legend **Rev:** Two swords arched above palm tree

Date	Mintage	F	VF	XF	Unc
1990	—	—	—	—	10.00

Note: Not released to circulation

KM# 166 50 DINARS

13.7000 g., 0.9170 Gold .4037 oz. AGW **Subject:** International Year of the Child **Obv:** Value within circle flanked designs with legend above and below **Rev:** Child's laureate head right within circle

Date	Mintage	F	VF	XF	Unc
1979 Proof	10,000	Value: 350			
1979 Impaired Proof	Inc. above	BV+10%			

KM# 150 50 DINARS

13.0000 g., 0.9170 Gold .3832 oz. AGW **Subject:** 15th Century of Hegira **Obv:** Value and inscription within center circle of legend **Rev:** Stylized value within Mosque

Date	Mintage	F	VF	XF	Unc
1980 Proof	13,000	Value: 275			
1980 Impaired Proof	Inc. above	BV+10%			

KM# 173 50 DINARS

16.9650 g., 0.9170 Gold .5002 oz. AGW **Subject:** 1st Anniversary of Hussein as President

Date	Mintage	F	VF	XF	Unc
1980 Proof	—	Value: 385			

KM# 157 50 DINARS

13.7000 g., 0.9170 Gold .4040 oz. AGW **Subject:** Nonaligned Nations Baghdad Conference

Date	Mintage	F	VF	XF	Unc
1982 Proof	10,000	Value: 295			

KM# 167 100 DINARS

26.0000 g., 0.9170 Gold .7665 oz. AGW **Subject:** International Year of the Child **Obv:** Value within circle flanked by designs, legend above and below **Rev:** Child's laureate head right within circle

Date	Mintage	F	VF	XF	Unc
1979 Proof	10,000	Value: 575			
1979 Impaired Proof	Inc. above	BV+10%			

KM# 151 100 DINARS

26.0000 g., 0.9170 Gold .7665 oz. AGW **Subject:** 15th Century of Hegira **Obv:** Inscription and value within center circle of legend **Rev:** Stylized value within Mosque

Date	Mintage	F	VF	XF	Unc
1980 Proof	14,000	Value: 525			
1980 Impaired Proof	Inc. above	BV+10%			

KM# 174 100 DINARS

33.9300 g., 0.9170 Gold 1.0003 oz. AGW **Subject:** 1st Anniversary of Hussein as President

Date	Mintage	F	VF	XF	Unc
1980 Proof	—	Value: 765			

KM# 158 100 DINARS

33.9300 g., 0.9170 Gold 1.0003 oz. AGW **Subject:** Nonaligned Nations Baghdad Conference **Obv:** Value within circle with legend above and below **Rev:** Stylized tree divides dates

Date	Mintage	F	VF	XF	Unc
1982 Proof	10,000	Value: 700			

PATTERNS

Including off metal strikes

KM#	Date	Mintage	Identification	Mkt Val
Pn1	1935	—	20 Fils. Silver center. . KM106.	450
Pn2	1935	—	50 Fils. Silver. . KM104.	450
Pn3	1936	—	2 Fils. Bronze. . KM96.	250
Pn4	1936	—	4 Fils. Nickel. . KM105.	275
Pn5	1936	—	10 Fils. Nickel. . KM103.	325
Pn6	1936	—	20 Fils. Silver center. . KM106.	425
Pn7	1936	—	50 Fils. Silver. . KM104.	450

PROOF SETS

KM#	Date	Mintage	Identification	Issue Price	Mkt Val
PS1	1953 (7)	200	KM109-115	—	1,325
PS2	1955 (3)	—	KM116-118	—	500
PS3	1959 (6)	400	KM119-124	—	360
PS4	1959 (7)	—	KM119-124, plus medallic crown (M1)	—	400
PS5	1973 (3)	5,000	KM138-140	—	62.00
PS6	1982 (7)	—	KM159a-160a, 161-164, 168	—	50.00

IRELAND REPUBLIC

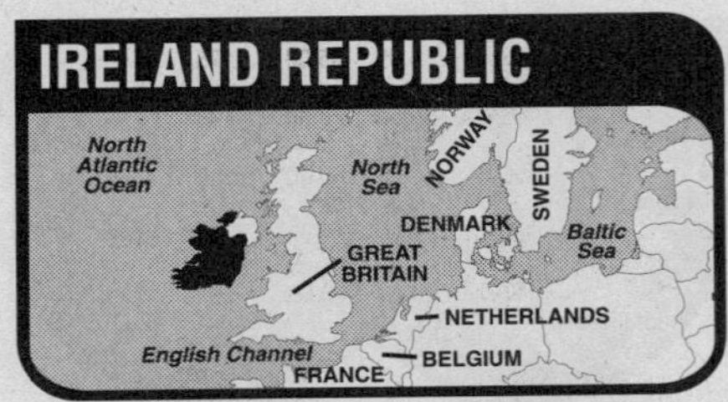

The Republic of Ireland, which occupies five-sixths of the island of Ireland located in the Atlantic Ocean west of Great Britain, has an area of 27,136 sq. mi. (70,280 sq. km.) and a population of 4.3 million. Capital: Dublin. Agriculture and dairy farming are the principal industries. Meat, livestock, dairy products and textiles are exported.

A race of tall, red-haired Celts from Gaul arrived in Ireland about 400 B.C., assimilated the native Erainn and Picts, and established a Gaelic civilization. After the arrival of St. Patrick in 432AD, Ireland evolved into a center of Latin learning, which sent missionaries to Europe and possibly North America. In 1154, Pope Adrian IV gave all of Ireland to English King Henry II to administer as a Papal fief. Because of the enactment of anti-Catholic laws and the awarding of vast tracts of Irish land to Protestant absentee landowners, English control did not become reasonably absolute until 1800 when England and Ireland became the 'United Kingdom of Great Britain and Ireland'. Religious freedom was restored to the Irish in 1829, but agitation for political autonomy continued until the Irish Free State was established as a dominion on Dec. 6, 1921 until 1937 when it became Éire. Ireland proclaimed itself a republic on April 18, 1949. The government, however, does not use the term 'Republic of Ireland,' which tacitly acknowledges the partitioning of the island into Ireland and Northern Ireland, but refers to the country simply as 'Ireland.'

RULERS

British, until 1921

MONETARY SYSTEM

(1928-1971)

4 Farthings = 1 Penny
12 Pence = 1 Shilling
2 Shillings = 1 Florin
20 Shillings = 1 Pound

NOTE: This section has been renumbered to segregate the coinage of the Irish Free State from the earlier crown coinage of Ireland.

REPUBLIC

STERLING COINAGE

KM# 1 FARTHING

2.8300 g., Bronze, 20.3 mm. **Obv:** Irish harp divides date **Obv. Legend:** SAORSTAT EIREANN (Irish Free State) **Rev:** Woodcock below value **Edge:** Plain **Designer:** Percy Metcalfe

Date	Mintage	F	VF	XF	Unc	BU
1928	300,000	0.50	1.50	4.50	10.00	—
1928 Proof	6,001	Value: 15.00				
1930	288,000	0.75	1.50	4.50	16.50	—
1930 Proof; Rare	—	—	—	—	—	—
1931	192,000	4.50	8.00	15.00	35.00	—
1931 Proof	—	—	—	—	—	—
1932	192,000	5.00	10.00	18.00	45.00	—
1932 Proof; Rare	—	—	—	—	—	—
1933	480,000	0.75	1.50	4.00	16.50	—
1933 Proof; Rare	—	—	—	—	—	—
1935	192,000	5.00	8.00	15.00	35.00	—
1935 Proof; Rare	—	—	—	—	—	—
1936	192,000	5.00	8.00	16.50	37.50	—
1936 Proof; Rare	—	—	—	—	—	—
1937	480,000	0.50	1.50	3.00	14.50	—
1937 Proof; Rare	—	—	—	—	—	—

KM# 9 FARTHING

2.8300 g., Bronze, 20.3 mm. **Obv:** Irish harp divides date **Obv. Legend:** EIRE (Ireland) **Rev:** Woodcock below value **Edge:** Plain **Designer:** Percy Metcalfe

Date	Mintage	F	VF	XF	Unc	BU
1939	786,000	0.50	1.00	2.00	7.50	—
1939 Proof	—	Value: 815				
1940	192,000	2.00	4.00	8.00	20.00	—
1940 Proof; Rare	—	—	—	—	—	—
1941	480,000	0.50	0.75	2.00	6.50	—
1941 Proof; Rare	—	—	—	—	—	—
1943	480,000	0.50	0.75	2.00	6.50	15.00
1944	480,000	0.75	1.25	3.00	10.00	—
1946	480,000	0.50	0.75	2.00	6.00	12.50
1946 Proof	—	—	—	—	—	—
1949	192,000	0.75	3.00	6.00	18.00	—
1949 Proof	—	Value: 300				
1953	192,000	0.25	0.50	1.25	3.00	7.50
1953 Proof	—	Value: 300				
1959	192,000	0.25	0.50	1.25	3.00	—
1959 Proof; Rare	—	—	—	—	—	—
1966	96,000	0.35	0.75	1.50	3.50	8.00

KM# 2 1/2 PENNY

5.6700 g., Bronze, 25.5 mm. **Obv:** Irish harp divides date **Obv. Legend:** SAORSTAT EIREANN (Irish Free State) **Rev:** Sow with piglets below value **Edge:** Plain **Designer:** Percy Metcalfe

Date	Mintage	F	VF	XF	Unc	BU
1928	2,880,000	0.75	2.00	5.00	14.00	—
1928 Proof	6,001	Value: 15.00				
1933	720,000	5.00	15.00	80.00	450	—
1933 Proof; Rare	—	—	—	—	—	—
1935	960,000	2.00	6.00	50.00	275	—
1935 Proof; Rare	—	—	—	—	—	—
1937	960,000	1.00	3.00	15.00	35.00	—

KM# 10 1/2 PENNY

5.6700 g., Bronze, 25.5 mm. **Obv:** Irish harp **Obv. Legend:** EIRE (Ireland) **Rev:** Sow with piglets below value **Edge:** Plain **Designer:** Percy Metcalfe

Date	Mintage	F	VF	XF	Unc	BU
1939	240,000	10.00	17.50	60.00	200	—
1939 Proof	—	Value: 1,000				
1940	1,680,000	1.00	4.50	40.00	150	—
1940 Proof; Rare	—	—	—	—	—	—
1941	2,400,000	0.20	0.50	2.50	20.00	—
1941 Proof; Rare	—	—	—	—	—	—
1942	6,931,000	0.10	0.25	1.50	8.00	—
1943	2,669,000	0.20	0.50	3.00	22.00	35.00
1946	720,000	1.00	2.50	15.00	60.00	—
1946 Proof; Rare	—	—	—	—	—	—
1949	1,344,000	0.10	0.25	1.50	12.50	—
1949 Proof; Rare	—	—	—	—	—	—
1953	2,400,000	0.10	0.15	0.25	1.50	5.00
1953 Proof	—	Value: 400				
1964	2,160,000	0.10	0.15	0.25	1.50	2.50
1964 Proof; Rare	—	—	—	—	—	—
1965	1,440,000	0.10	0.15	0.75	2.50	3.50
1966	1,680,000	0.10	0.15	0.25	1.50	2.50
1967	1,200,000	0.10	0.15	0.25	1.50	5.00

KM# 3 PENNY

9.4500 g., Bronze, 30.9 mm. **Obv:** Irish harp divides date **Obv. Legend:** SAORSTAT EIREANN (Irish Free State) **Rev:** Hen with chicks **Edge:** Plain **Designer:** Percy Metcalfe

Date	Mintage	F	VF	XF	Unc	BU
1928	9,000,000	0.50	1.00	4.00	20.00	—
1928 Proof	6,001	Value: 18.50				
1931	2,400,000	1.00	2.00	12.00	50.00	—
1931 Proof	—	Value: 1,500				
1933	1,680,000	1.00	2.50	20.00	125	—
1933 Proof; Rare	—	—	—	—	—	—
1935	5,472,000	0.50	1.00	8.00	32.00	—
1935 Proof; Rare	—	—	—	—	—	—
1937	5,400,000	0.50	1.00	15.00	70.00	—
1937 Proof	—	Value: 1,250				

KM# 11 PENNY

9.4500 g., Bronze, 30.9 mm. **Obv:** Irish harp **Obv. Legend:** EIRE (Ireland) **Rev:** Hen with chicks **Edge:** Plain **Designer:** Percy Metcalfe **Note:** Varieties exist.

Date	Mintage	F	VF	XF	Unc	BU
1940	312,000	3.00	10.00	65.00	325	—
1940 Proof; Rare	—	—	—	—	—	—
1941	4,680,000	0.25	0.50	8.00	50.00	—
1941 Proof; Rare	—	—	—	—	—	—
1942	17,520,000	0.25	0.50	2.00	11.50	—
1942 Proof; Rare	—	—	—	—	—	—
1943	3,360,000	0.75	1.50	7.50	45.00	—
1946	4,800,000	0.25	0.50	3.00	20.00	30.00
1946 Proof; Rare	—	—	—	—	—	—
1948	4,800,000	0.25	0.50	3.00	8.00	—
1948 Proof; Rare	—	—	—	—	—	—
1949	4,080,000	0.25	0.50	3.00	8.00	—
1949 Proof	—	Value: 600				
1950	2,400,000	0.25	0.50	3.50	12.50	—
1950 Proof	—	Value: 600				
1952	2,400,000	0.25	0.50	2.00	6.00	—
1952 Proof; Rare	—	—	—	—	—	—
1962	1,200,000	0.75	2.50	3.50	12.50	—
1962 Proof	—	Value: 175				
1963	9,600,000	0.20	0.40	0.75	2.00	—
1963 Proof	—	Value: 175				
1964	6,000,000	0.20	0.40	0.75	1.50	—
1964 Proof	—	—	—	—	—	—
1965	11,160,000	0.20	0.40	0.75	1.50	—
1966	6,000,000	0.20	0.40	0.75	1.50	—
1967	2,400,000	0.20	0.40	0.75	1.50	—
1968	21,000,000	0.20	0.40	0.75	1.50	3.00
1968 Proof	—	Value: 350				

KM# 4 3 PENCE

3.2400 g., Nickel, 17.6 mm. **Obv:** Irish harp divides date **Obv. Legend:** SAORSTAT EIREANN (Irish Free State) **Rev:** Rabbit **Edge:** Plain **Designer:** Percy Metcalfe

Date	Mintage	F	VF	XF	Unc	BU
1928	1,500,000	0.50	1.00	3.50	10.00	—
1928 Proof	6,001	Value: 20.00				
1933	320,000	3.00	10.00	75.00	350	—
1933 Proof; Rare	—	—	—	—	—	—
1934	800,000	1.00	2.00	12.50	70.00	—
1934 Proof; Rare	—	—	—	—	—	—
1935	240,000	3.00	8.00	35.00	225	—
1935 Proof; Rare	—	—	—	—	—	—

KM# 12 3 PENCE

3.2400 g., Nickel, 17.6 mm. **Obv:** Irish harp **Obv. Legend:** EIRE (Ireland) **Rev:** Rabbit **Edge:** Plain **Designer:** Percy Metcalfe

Date	Mintage	F	VF	XF	Unc	BU
1939	64,000	10.00	20.00	70.00	525	—
1939 Proof	—	Value: 1,500				
1940	720,000	1.50	3.00	12.50	50.00	—
1940 Proof; Rare	—	—	—	—	—	—

KM# 12a 3 PENCE

3.2400 g., Copper-Nickel, 18 mm. **Obv:** Irish harp **Obv. Legend:** EIRE (Ireland) **Rev:** Rabbit **Edge:** Plain **Designer:** Percy Metcalfe

Date	Mintage	F	VF	XF	Unc	BU
1942	4,000,000	0.25	0.75	6.00	30.00	—
1942 Proof	—	Value: 350				
1943	1,360,000	0.50	2.00	15.00	80.00	—
1943 Proof	—	—	—	—	—	—
1946	800,000	1.00	2.00	10.00	45.00	—
1946 Proof	—	Value: 200				
1948	1,600,000	1.00	2.00	35.00	125	—
1948 Proof; Rare	—	—	—	—	—	—
1949	1,200,000	0.25	0.50	3.00	25.00	—
1949 Proof	—	Value: 200				
1950	1,600,000	0.25	0.50	3.00	20.00	—
1950 Proof	—	Value: 400				
1953	1,600,000	0.25	0.50	2.00	10.00	—
1953 Proof; Rare	—	—	—	—	—	—
1956	1,200,000	0.25	0.50	2.00	8.00	15.00
1956 Proof; Rare	—	—	—	—	—	—
1961	2,400,000	0.15	0.25	0.50	6.00	—
1961 Proof; Rare	—	—	—	—	—	—
1962	3,200,000	0.15	0.25	0.50	8.00	—
1962 Proof; Rare	—	—	—	—	—	—
1963	4,000,000	0.15	0.25	0.50	2.50	—
1963 Proof; Rare	—	—	—	—	—	—
1964	4,000,000	0.10	0.15	0.25	1.50	3.00
1965	3,600,000	0.10	0.15	0.25	1.50	—
1966	4,000,000	0.10	0.15	0.25	1.50	3.00
1967	2,400,000	0.10	0.15	0.25	1.50	—

Date	Mintage	F	VF	XF	Unc	BU
1968	4,000,000	0.10	0.15	0.25	1.50	—
1968 Proof	—	—	—	—	—	—

KM# 5 6 PENCE
4.5400 g., Nickel, 20.8 mm. **Obv:** Irish harp divides date **Obv. Legend:** SAORSTAT EIREANN (Irish Free State) **Rev:** Irish Wolfhound **Edge:** Plain **Designer:** Percy Metcalfe

Date	Mintage	F	VF	XF	Unc	BU
1928	3,201,000	0.50	1.00	5.00	17.50	—
1928 Proof	6,001	Value: 25.00				
1933 Proof; Rare	—	—	—	—	—	—
1934	600,000	1.00	2.00	18.00	120	—
1934 Proof; Rare	—	—	—	—	—	—
1935	520,000	1.00	3.00	30.00	320	—
1935 Proof; Rare	—	—	—	—	—	—

KM# 13 6 PENCE
4.5400 g., Nickel, 20.8 mm. **Obv:** Irish harp **Obv. Legend:** EIRE (Ireland) **Rev:** Irish Wolfhound **Edge:** Plain **Designer:** Percy Metcalfe

Date	Mintage	F	VF	XF	Unc	BU
1939	876,000	0.75	2.00	8.00	55.00	—
1939 Proof	—	Value: 1,150				
1940	1,120,000	0.75	2.00	6.00	45.00	—
1940 Proof; Rare	—	—	—	—	—	—

KM# 13a 6 PENCE
4.5400 g., Copper-Nickel, 20.8 mm. **Obv:** Irish harp **Obv. Legend:** EIRE (Ireland) **Rev:** Irish Wolfhound **Edge:** Plain **Designer:** Percy Metcalfe

Date	Mintage	F	VF	XF	Unc	BU
1942	1,320,000	0.50	1.00	5.00	40.00	—
1942 Proof; Rare	—	—	—	—	—	—
1945	400,000	2.00	8.00	50.00	160	—
1945 Proof; Rare	—	—	—	—	—	—
1946	720,000	2.00	10.00	75.00	350	—
1946 Proof; Rare	—	—	—	—	—	—
1947	800,000	1.00	12.00	30.00	70.00	—
1947 Proof; Rare	—	—	—	—	—	—
1948	800,000	1.00	1.50	10.00	55.00	—
1948 Proof; Rare	—	—	—	—	—	—
1949	600,000	1.50	3.50	15.00	65.00	—
1949 Proof; Rare	—	—	—	—	—	—
1950	800,000	1.00	3.00	12.00	60.00	—
1950 Proof; Rare	—	—	—	—	—	—
1952	800,000	0.50	1.00	5.00	20.00	—
1952 Proof	—	Value: 175				
1953	800,000	0.50	1.00	5.00	18.00	—
1953 Proof; Rare	—	—	—	—	—	—
1955	600,000	1.00	2.50	8.00	20.00	—
1955 Proof; Rare	—	—	—	—	—	—
1956	600,000	0.75	2.00	4.00	15.00	—
1956 Proof; Rare	—	—	—	—	—	—
1958	600,000	1.00	2.50	6.00	65.00	—
1958	—	Value: 350				
1959	2,000,000	0.25	0.50	3.00	15.00	—
1959 Proof; Rare	—	—	—	—	—	—
1960	2,020,000	0.25	0.50	2.00	12.00	—
1960 Proof; Rare	—	—	—	—	—	—
1961	3,000,000	0.25	0.25	1.00	6.50	—
1961 Proof; Rare	—	—	—	—	—	—
1962	4,000,000	0.25	0.75	4.00	60.00	—
1962 Proof; Rare	—	—	—	—	—	—
1963	4,000,000	0.15	0.25	0.50	3.00	—
1963 Proof; Rare	—	—	—	—	—	—
1964	6,000,000	0.15	0.25	0.50	3.00	—
1966	2,000,000	0.15	0.25	0.50	3.00	—
1967	4,000,000	0.15	0.25	0.50	3.00	—
1968	8,000,000	0.15	0.25	0.50	3.00	—
1969	2,000,000	0.15	0.25	0.50	3.00	—

KM# 6 SHILLING
5.6552 g., 0.7500 Silver .1364 oz. ASW, 23.6 mm. **Obv:** Irish harp divides date **Obv. Legend:** SAORSTAT EIREANN (Irish Free State) **Rev:** Bull **Edge:** Reeded **Designer:** Percy Metcalfe

Date	Mintage	F	VF	XF	Unc	BU
1928	2,700,000	2.00	5.00	10.00	30.00	—
1928 Proof	6,001	Value: 27.50				
1930	460,000	6.00	25.00	100	450	—
1930 Proof	—	Value: 1,200				
1931	400,000	4.50	18.00	90.00	275	—
1931 Proof; Rare	—	—	—	—	—	—
1933	300,000	5.00	20.00	100	325	—
1933 Proof; Rare	—	—	—	—	—	—
1935	400,000	3.00	7.00	25.00	85.00	—
1935 Proof; Rare	—	—	—	—	—	—
1937	100,000	12.00	65.00	500	2,000	—
1937 Proof; Rare	—	—	—	—	—	—

KM# 14 SHILLING
5.6552 g., 0.7500 Silver .1364 oz. ASW, 23.6 mm. **Obv:** Irish harp **Obv. Legend:** EIRE (Ireland) **Rev:** Bull **Edge:** Reeded **Designer:** Percy Metcalfe

Date	Mintage	F	VF	XF	Unc	BU
1939 Proof	—	Value: 775				
1939	1,140,000	2.50	4.50	12.50	40.00	—
1940	580,000	3.00	5.00	15.00	45.00	—
1940 Proof; Rare	—	—	—	—	—	—
1941	300,000	4.00	12.00	22.50	50.00	—
1941 Proof; Rare	—	—	—	—	—	—
1942	286,000	4.00	7.50	15.00	40.00	60.00
1942 Proof; Rare	—	—	—	—	—	—

KM# 14a SHILLING
5.6600 g., Copper-Nickel, 23.6 mm. **Obv:** Irish harp **Obv. Legend:** EIRE (Ireland) **Rev:** Bull **Edge:** Reeded **Designer:** Percy Metcalfe

Date	Mintage	F	VF	XF	Unc	BU
1951	2,000,000	0.25	0.50	2.50	15.00	—
1951 Proof	—	Value: 500				
1954	3,000,000	0.25	0.50	2.50	11.50	—
1954 Proof	—	—	—	—	—	—
1955	1,000,000	1.00	2.00	5.00	15.00	—
1955 Proof	—	—	—	—	—	—
1959	2,000,000	0.25	0.50	4.00	35.00	—
1959 Proof; Rare	—	—	—	—	—	—
1962	4,000,000	0.25	0.50	1.00	7.00	—
1962 Proof; Rare	—	—	—	—	—	—
1963	4,000,000	0.25	0.50	1.00	3.00	7.50
1963 Proof; Rare	—	—	—	—	—	—
1964	4,000,000	0.25	0.50	1.00	2.50	—
1966	3,000,000	0.25	0.50	1.00	2.50	5.00
1968	4,000,000	0.25	0.50	1.00	2.50	—

KM# 7 FLORIN
11.3104 g., 0.7500 Silver .2727 oz. ASW, 28.5 mm. **Obv:** Irish harp divides date **Obv. Legend:** SAORSTAT EIREANN (Irish Free State) **Rev:** Salmon **Edge:** Reeded **Designer:** Percy Metcalfe

Date	Mintage	F	VF	XF	Unc	BU
1928	2,025,000	4.00	7.00	15.00	40.00	—
1928 Proof	6,001	Value: 42.50				
1930	330,000	6.50	25.00	135	400	—
1930 Proof; Rare	—	—	—	—	—	—

Date	Mintage	F	VF	XF	Unc	BU
1931	200,000	8.00	35.00	175	500	—
1931 Proof; Rare	—	—	—	—	—	—
1933	300,000	6.50	27.50	195	575	—
1933 Proof; Rare	—	—	—	—	—	—
1934	150,000	10.00	60.00	250	750	—
1934 Proof	—	Value: 2,750				
1935	390,000	5.00	17.50	65.00	185	—
1935 Proof; Rare	—	—	—	—	—	—
1937	150,000	10.00	35.00	210	750	—
1937 Proof; Rare	—	—	—	—	—	—

KM# 15 FLORIN
11.3104 g., 0.7500 Silver .2727 oz. ASW, 28.5 mm. **Obv:** Irish harp **Obv. Legend:** EIRE (Ireland) **Rev:** Salmon **Edge:** Reeded **Designer:** Percy Metcalfe

Date	Mintage	F	VF	XF	Unc	BU
1939	1,080,000	4.00	7.00	18.00	45.00	—
1939 Proof	—	Value: 800				
1940	670,000	4.00	7.50	20.00	50.00	—
1940 Proof; Rare	—	—	—	—	—	—
1941	400,000	4.00	8.50	22.50	60.00	—
1941 Proof	—	Value: 800				
1942	109,000	5.00	15.00	25.00	55.00	—
1943	—	1,200	2,000	4,000	8,000	—

Note: Approximately 35 known

KM# 15a FLORIN
11.3100 g., Copper-Nickel, 28.5 mm. **Obv:** Irish harp **Obv. Legend:** EIRE (Ireland) **Rev:** Salmon **Edge:** Reeded **Designer:** Percy Metcalfe

Date	Mintage	F	VF	XF	Unc	BU
1951	1,000,000	1.00	2.00	6.00	16.00	—
1951 Proof	—	Value: 600				
1954	1,000,000	1.00	2.00	6.00	18.00	—
1954 Proof	—	Value: 450				
1955	1,000,000	1.00	2.00	5.00	15.00	—
1955 Proof	—	Value: 450				
1959	2,000,000	0.50	1.00	2.50	10.00	—
1959 Proof; Rare	—	—	—	—	—	—
1961	2,000,000	0.50	1.00	7.00	22.00	—
1961 Proof; Rare	—	—	—	—	—	—
1962	2,400,000	0.50	1.00	2.00	10.00	—
1962 Proof; Rare	—	—	—	—	—	—
1963	3,000,000	0.25	0.50	0.75	4.00	15.00
1963 Proof; Rare	—	—	—	—	—	—
1964	4,000,000	0.25	0.50	0.75	2.00	8.00
1965	2,000,000	0.25	0.50	0.75	2.00	—
1966	3,625,000	0.25	0.50	0.75	2.00	4.00
1968	1,000,000	0.25	0.35	1.00	4.50	—
1969	—	0.25	0.35	1.00	4.50	—

KM# 8 1/2 CROWN
14.1380 g., 0.7500 Silver .3409 oz. ASW, 32.3 mm. **Obv:** Irish harp divides date **Obv. Legend:** SAORSTAT EIREANN (Irish Free State) **Rev:** Horse **Rev. Designer:** Percy Metcalfe **Edge:** Reeded **Note:** Close O and I in COROIN. 8 tufts in horse's tail, with 156 beads.

Date	Mintage	F	VF	XF	Unc	BU
1928 Proof	6,001	Value: 55.00				
1928	2,160,000	5.00	10.00	20.00	50.00	—
1930	352,000	7.00	20.00	125	400	—
1930 Proof; Rare	—	—	—	—	—	—
1931	160,000	10.00	30.00	250	650	—
1931 Proof; Rare	—	—	—	—	—	—
1933	336,000	7.00	20.00	125	400	—

Date	Mintage	F	VF	XF	Unc	BU
1933 Proof; Rare	—	—	—	—	—	—
1934	480,000	6.00	15.00	40.00	175	—
1934 Proof; Rare	—	—	—	—	—	—
1937	40,000	65.00	150	750	1,750	—
1937 Proof; Rare	—	—	—	—	—	—

KM# 16 1/2 CROWN

14.1380 g., 0.7500 Silver .3409 oz. ASW, 32.3 mm. **Obv:** Irish harp **Obv. Legend:** EIRE (Ireland) **Rev:** Horse **Edge:** Reeded **Designer:** Percy Metcalfe **Note:** Normal spacing between O and I in COROIN, 7 tufts in horse's tail, with 151 beads in border.

Date	Mintage	F	VF	XF	Unc	BU
1939	888,000	5.00	9.50	17.50	55.00	—
1939 Proof	—	Value: 800				
1940	752,000	5.00	9.00	15.00	50.00	—
1940 Proof; Rare	—	—	—	—	—	—
1941	320,000	5.50	12.50	30.00	75.00	—
1941 Proof; Rare	—	—	—	—	—	—
1942	286,000	5.50	12.50	25.00	50.00	—
1943	Est. 1,000	250	500	1,350	2,500	—

Note: Approximately 500 known

KM# 16a 1/2 CROWN

14.1400 g., Copper-Nickel, 32.3 mm. **Obv:** Irish harp **Obv. Legend:** EIRE (Ireland) **Rev:** Horse **Edge:** Reeded **Designer:** Percy Metcalfe **Note:** Normal spacing between O and I on "COROIN", 7 tufts in horse's tail, with 151 beads in border.

Date	Mintage	F	VF	XF	Unc	BU
1951	800,000	1.50	3.00	10.00	35.00	—
1951 Proof	—	Value: 600				
1954	400,000	2.00	4.00	15.00	50.00	—
1954 Proof	—	Value: 500				
1955	1,080,000	1.00	2.00	6.00	25.00	—
1955 Proof	—	Value: 200				
1959	1,600,000	1.00	1.75	3.00	12.50	—
1959 Proof; Rare	—	—	—	—	—	—
1961	1,600,000	1.00	1.75	3.50	20.00	—
1961 Proof	—	—	—	—	—	—
1962	3,200,000	0.50	1.00	2.50	12.50	—
1962 Proof	—	—	—	—	—	—
1963	2,400,000	0.50	1.00	2.00	7.50	10.00
1963 Proof; Rare	—	—	—	—	—	—
1964	3,200,000	0.50	1.00	2.00	7.50	—
1966	700,000	0.75	1.50	3.00	7.50	—
1967	2,000,000	0.50	1.00	2.00	7.50	—

Note: 1967 exists struck with a polished reverse die; Estimated value is $15.00 in Uncirculated

KM# 17 1/2 CROWN

Copper-Nickel **Obv:** Irish harp **Rev:** Horse **Note:** Mule. Distinguishing charactoristics: 2s6d the d is open, PM the P is not under the hoof.

Date	Mintage	VG	F	VF	XF	Unc
1961	Inc. above	—	8.00	25.00	200	—

KM# 18 10 SHILLING

18.1400 g., 0.8333 Silver .4858 oz. ASW, 30.5 mm. **Subject:** 50th Anniversary - Irish Uprising of Easter, 1916 **Obv:** Bust right **Rev:** Monument **Rev. Designer:** Cuchulainn modified by T.H. Paget **Edge Lettering:** EIRI AMAC NA CASCA 1916

Date	Mintage	F	VF	XF	Unc	BU
1966	Est. 2,000,000	—	—	10.00	20.00	—

Date	Mintage	F	VF	XF	Unc	BU

Note: Approximately 1,270,000 melted down

Date	Mintage	F	VF	XF	Unc	BU
1966 Proof	20,000	Value: 25.00				

DECIMAL COINAGE

100 Pence = 1 Pound (Punt)

KM# 19 1/2 PENNY

1.7800 g., Bronze, 17.1 mm. **Subject:** Stylized bird adapted from an illumination in a celtic manuscript from Cologne Cathedral **Obv:** Irish harp **Rev:** Stylized bird and value **Rev. Designer:** G. Hayes **Edge:** Plain **Note:** This mintage figure represents a surplus of coins minted for Polished Standard Specimen Sets (proof sets) later released into circulation. The entire surplus was presumably remelted due to demonitization of this denomination Jan. 1, 1987

Date	Mintage	F	VF	XF	Unc	BU
1971	100,500,000	—	—	0.10	0.30	0.50
1971 Proof	50,000	Value: 1.00				
1975	10,500,000	—	—	0.10	0.30	0.50
1976	5,464,000	—	—	0.10	0.30	0.50
1978	20,302,000	—	—	—	0.25	0.50
1980	20,616,000	—	—	—	0.25	0.50
1982	9,660,000	—	—	—	0.30	0.50
1985	2,784,000	—	—	—	—	—
1986 Proof	6,750	Value: 12.50				
1986	Est. 12,250	—	—	—	—	—

Note: This mintage figure represents a surplus of coins minted for Polished Standard Specimen Sets (Proof Sets) later released into circulation. The entire surplus was presumably remelted due to demonitization of this denomination Jan. 1, 1987.

KM# 20 PENNY

3.5600 g., Bronze, 20.3 mm. **Obv:** Irish harp **Rev:** Stylized bird **Rev. Designer:** G. Hayes **Edge:** Plain **Note:** Stylized bird adapted form an ornamental detail in the book of Kells

Date	Mintage	F	VF	XF	Unc	BU
1971	100,500,000	—	—	0.10	0.30	0.75
1971 Proof	50,000	Value: 1.25				
1974	10,000,000	—	—	0.10	0.35	0.75
1975	10,000,000	—	—	0.10	0.35	0.75
1976	38,164,000	—	—	0.10	0.30	0.75
1978	25,746,000	—	—	0.10	0.30	0.75
1979	21,766,000	—	—	0.10	0.30	0.75
1980	86,712,000	—	—	0.10	0.30	0.75
1982	54,189,000	—	—	0.10	0.30	0.75
1985	19,242,000	—	—	0.10	0.30	0.75
1986	36,584,000	—	—	0.10	0.30	0.75
1986 Proof	6,750	Value: 1.25				
1988	56,772,000	—	—	0.10	0.30	0.75

KM# 20a PENNY

3.5600 g., Copper Plated Steel, 20.3 mm. **Subject:** Styilized bird adapted from an ornamental detail in the book of Kells **Obv:** Irish harp **Rev:** Stylized bird **Edge:** Plain

Date	Mintage	F	VF	XF	Unc	BU
1988	Inc. above	—	—	—	—	—
1990	65,099,000	—	—	0.10	0.15	0.50
1992	25,643,000	—	—	0.10	0.15	0.50
1993	10,000,000	—	—	0.10	0.15	0.50
1994	45,800,000	—	—	0.10	0.15	0.50
1995	70,836,000	—	—	0.10	0.15	0.50
1996	190,092,000	—	—	0.10	0.15	0.50
1998	40,744,000	—	—	0.10	0.15	0.50
2000	133,760,000	—	—	0.10	0.15	0.50

KM# 21 2 PENCE

7.1200 g., Bronze, 25.9 mm. **Subject:** Styilized bird detail from the Second Bible of Charles the Bald **Obv:** Irish harp **Rev:** Stylized bird **Rev. Designer:** G. Hayes **Edge:** Plain

Date	Mintage	F	VF	XF	Unc	BU
1971	75,500,000	—	—	0.10	1.00	1.20
1971 Proof	50,000	Value: 1.50				
1975	20,010,000	—	—	0.10	0.50	0.75
1976	5,414,000	—	—	0.10	0.60	0.85
1978	12,000,000	—	—	0.10	0.50	0.75
1979	32,373,000	—	—	0.10	0.50	0.75
1980	59,828,000	—	—	0.10	0.50	0.75
1982	30,435,000	—	—	0.10	0.50	0.75
1985	14,469,000	—	—	0.10	0.50	0.75
1986	23,865,000	—	—	0.10	0.50	0.75
1986 Proof	6,750	Value: 1.50				
1988	35,868,000	—	—	0.10	0.50	0.75

KM# 21a 2 PENCE

7.1200 g., Copper Plated Steel, 25.9 mm. **Subject:** Styilized bird detail from the Second Bible of Charles the Bald **Obv:** Irish harp **Rev:** Stylized bird **Edge:** Plain

Date	Mintage	F	VF	XF	Unc	BU
1988	Inc. above	—	—	—	—	—
1990	34,284,000	—	—	0.10	0.25	0.50
1992	10,215,000	—	—	0.10	0.25	0.50
1995	55,459,000	—	—	0.10	0.25	0.50
1996	69,342,000	—	—	0.10	0.25	0.50
1998	33,688,000	—	—	0.10	0.25	0.50
2000	66,960,000	—	—	0.10	0.25	0.50

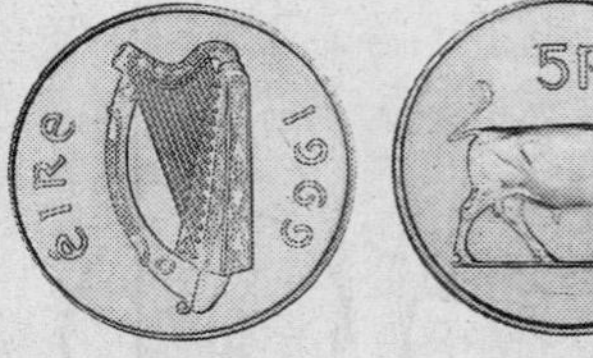

KM# 22 5 PENCE

5.6600 g., Copper-Nickel, 23.6 mm. **Obv:** Irish harp **Rev:** Bull right **Edge:** Reeded **Designer:** Percy Metcalfe

Date	Mintage	F	VF	XF	Unc	BU
1969	5,000,000	—	0.10	0.15	1.00	1.25
1970	10,000,000	—	—	0.10	0.75	1.20
1971	8,000,000	—	—	0.10	0.75	1.25
1971 Proof	50,000	Value: 2.00				
1974	7,000,000	—	—	0.10	0.75	1.25
1975	10,000,000	—	—	0.10	0.75	1.25
1976	20,616,000	—	—	0.10	0.75	1.25
1978	28,536,000	—	—	0.10	0.75	1.25
1980	22,190,000	—	—	0.10	0.75	1.25
1982	24,404,000	—	—	0.10	0.75	1.20
1985	4,202,000	—	—	0.10	0.75	1.20
1986	15,298,000	—	0.10	0.15	1.00	1.25
1986 Proof	6,750	Value: 2.00				
1990	7,547,000	—	—	0.10	0.75	1.20

KM# 28 5 PENCE

3.2500 g., Copper-Nickel, 18.5 mm. **Obv:** Irish harp **Rev:** Bull left **Edge:** Reeded **Designer:** Percy Metcalfe **Note:** Reduced size: 18.5mm. Varieties exist.

Date	Mintage	F	VF	XF	Unc	BU
1992	74,526,000	—	—	0.10	0.50	0.75
1993	89,109,000	—	—	0.10	0.50	0.75
1994	31,058,000	—	—	0.10	0.50	0.75
1995	14,667,000	—	—	0.10	0.50	0.75
1996	158,546,000	—	—	0.10	0.50	0.75
1998	63,247,000	—	—	0.10	0.50	0.75
2000	58,000,000	—	—	0.10	0.50	0.75

KM# 23 10 PENCE

11.3200 g., Copper-Nickel, 28.5 mm. **Obv:** Irish harp **Rev:** Salmon **Edge:** Reeded **Designer:** Percy Metcalfe

Date	Mintage	F	VF	XF	Unc	BU
1969	27,000,000	—	—	0.40	1.25	2.00
1971	4,000,000	—	—	0.40	1.25	2.00
1971 Proof	50,000	Value: 2.50				
1973	2,500,000	—	—	0.40	1.50	2.25
1974	7,500,000	—	—	0.35	1.25	2.00
1975	15,000,000	—	—	0.35	1.25	2.00
1976	9,433,000	—	—	0.35	1.25	2.00
1978	30,905,000	—	—	0.25	1.00	1.75
1980	44,605,000	—	—	0.25	1.00	1.75
1982	7,374,000	—	—	0.25	1.00	1.75
1985	4,099,999	—	—	0.25	1.25	2.00
1986 Proof	6,750	Value: 16.50				
1986	Est. 4,250	—	2.00	5.00	16.50	—

Note: This mintage figure represents a surplus of coins minted for Polished Standard Specimen Sets (Proof Sets), later released into circulation.

KM# 29 10 PENCE

5.4500 g., Copper-Nickel, 22 mm. **Obv:** Irish harp **Rev:** Salmon **Edge:** Reeded **Designer:** Percy Metcalfe **Note:** Reduced size.

Date	Mintage	F	VF	XF	Unc	BU
1993	80,061,000	—	—	—	0.75	1.25
1994	58,510,000	—	—	—	0.75	1.25
1995	15,781,000	—	—	—	0.75	1.25
1996	18,402,000	—	—	—	0.75	1.25
1997	10,033,000	—	—	—	0.75	1.25
1998	10,000,000	—	—	—	0.75	1.25
1999	24,500,000	—	—	—	0.75	1.25
2000	45,679,000	—	—	—	0.75	1.25

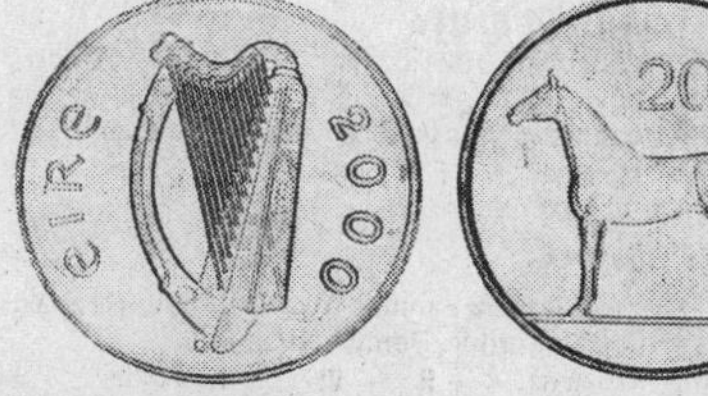

KM# 25 20 PENCE

8.4700 g., Nickel-Bronze, 27.1 mm. **Obv:** Irish harp **Rev:** Horse **Edge:** Alternating plain and reeded **Designer:** Percy Metcalfe

Date	Mintage	F	VF	XF	Unc	BU
1986 Proof	6,750	Value: 3.50				
1986	50,430,000	—	—	0.50	1.75	3.00
1988	20,661,000	—	—	0.50	1.75	3.00
1992	14,761,000	—	—	0.50	1.75	3.00
1994	11,086,000	—	—	0.50	1.75	3.00
1995	18,160,000	—	—	0.50	1.75	3.00
1998	25,024,000	—	—	0.50	1.75	3.00
1999	11,000,000	—	—	0.50	1.75	3.00
2000	28,500,000	—	—	0.50	1.75	3.00

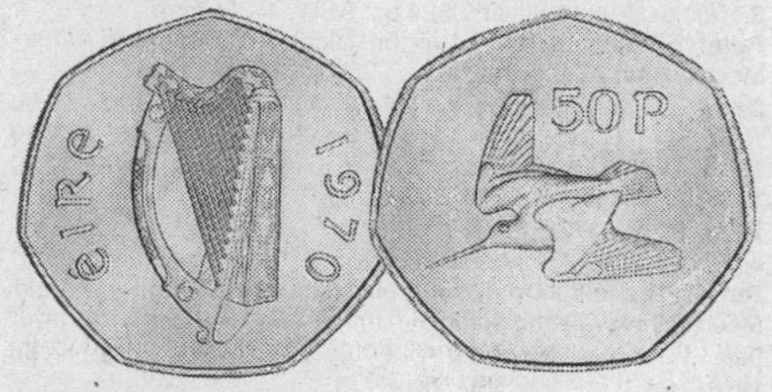

KM# 24 50 PENCE

13.3000 g., Copper-Nickel, 30 mm. **Obv:** Irish harp **Rev:** Woodcock **Edge:** Plain **Shape:** 7 curved sides **Designer:** Percy Metcalfe

Date	Mintage	F	VF	XF	Unc	BU
1970	9,000,000	—	—	1.50	4.00	5.00
1971	600,000	—	1.00	2.00	6.00	8.00
1971 Proof	50,000	Value: 3.50				
1974	1,000,000	—	1.00	2.00	7.00	9.00
1975	2,000,000	—	—	1.50	4.00	5.00
1976	3,000,000	—	—	1.25	3.00	4.00
1977	4,800,000	—	—	1.25	3.00	4.00
1978	4,500,000	—	—	1.25	3.00	4.00
1979	4,000,000	—	—	1.25	3.00	4.00
1981	6,000,000	—	—	1.00	2.00	3.50
1982	2,000,000	—	—	1.25	3.00	4.00
1983	7,000,000	—	—	1.00	2.00	3.50
1984	—	—	—	—	—	—
1986	3,250	—	3.00	6.00	18.50	—

Note: This circulation mintage figure represents a surplus of coins minted for Polished Standard Specimen Sets (Proof Sets), later released into circulation

Date	Mintage	F	VF	XF	Unc	BU
1986 Proof	6,750	Value: 18.50				
1988	Est. 7,000,500	—	—	1.00	2.00	3.50
1996	6,000,000	—	—	1.00	2.00	3.50
1997	6,000,000	—	—	1.00	2.00	3.50
1998	13,825,000	—	—	1.00	2.00	3.50
1999	7,000,000	—	—	1.00	2.00	3.50
2000	15,600,000	—	—	1.00	2.00	3.50

KM# 26 50 PENCE

13.5000 g., Copper-Nickel, 30 mm. **Subject:** Dublin Millennium **Obv:** Irish harp **Rev:** Sheild above banner with value above **Rev. Designer:** Thomas Ryan

Date	Mintage	F	VF	XF	Unc	BU
1988 Proof	50,000	Value: 15.00				
1988	5,000,000	—	—	—	2.50	3.50

KM# 27 PUNT (Pound)

10.0000 g., Copper-Nickel, 31.1 mm. **Obv:** Irish harp **Rev:** Irish Red Deer left **Rev. Designer:** Thomas Ryan **Note:** The normal KM27 was struck with an milled and engrailed edge. Examples with plain edge, or partial engrailing command a premium of approximately four times the values listed here.

Date	Mintage	F	VF	XF	Unc	BU
1990	62,292,000	2.00	3.00	5.50	7.00	8.00
1990 Proof	42,000	Value: 27.50				
1994	14,925,000	2.00	3.00	5.50	7.50	8.50
1995	10,215,000	2.00	3.00	5.50	7.50	8.50
1996	9,230,000	2.00	3.00	5.50	7.50	8.50
1998	22,955,000	2.00	3.00	5.50	7.50	8.50
1999	10,000,000	2.00	3.00	5.50	7.50	8.50
2000	31,913,000	2.00	3.00	5.50	7.50	8.50

KM# 30 PUNT (Pound)

28.2800 g., 0.9250 Silver .8328 oz. ASW, 38.6 mm. **Subject:** 50th Anniversary - United Nations **Obv:** Irish harp above dates **Rev:** Dove holding banner with dates to left of U.N. logo and numeral 50 **Rev. Inscription:** NATIONS UNITED FOR PEACE **Edge:** Milled **Designer:** David McGrail

Date	Mintage	F	VF	XF	Unc	BU
ND(1995) Proof	—	Value: 100				

KM# 31 PUNT (Pound)

10.0000 g., Copper-Nickel **Subject:** Millennium **Obv:** Irish harp **Rev:** Cross within stylized ancient ship **Edge:** Milled and engrailed **Designer:** Alan Ardiff and Garret Stokes **Note:** Struck at Sandyford.

Date	Mintage	F	VF	XF	Unc	BU
2000	5,000,000	—	—	—	7.50	8.50

PATTERNS

Including off metal strikes

KM#	Date	Mintage	Identification	Mkt Val
Pn1	1938	2	Penny. Bronze. KM11.	15,000
Pn2	1938	—	1/2 Crown. 0.7500 Silver. KM16. Unique.	—
Pn3	1985	—	20 Pence. Nickel-Bronze. KM#25.	—

PROVAS

Publio Morbiducci Series

KM#	Date	Mintage	Identification	Mkt Val
Pr1	1927	—	Farthing.	—
Pr2	1927	—	1/2 Penny.	—

KM#	Date	Mintage	Identification	Mkt Val
Pr3	1927	—	Penny. Silvered Bronze. Irish harp. Hen with chicks.	8,000

KM#	Date	Mintage	Identification	Mkt Val
Pr4	1927	4	3 Pence. Nickel. Irish harp. Rabbit.	5,000

KM#	Date	Mintage	Identification	Mkt Val
Pr5	1927	4	6 Pence. Nickel. Irish harp. Rabbit.	5,000

KM#	Date	Mintage	Identification	Mkt Val
Pr6	1927	5	Shilling. Silver. Irish harp. Bull with head down.	5,000

KM#	Date	Mintage	Identification	Mkt Val
Pr7	1927	4	Florin. Silver. Irish harp. Fish.	6,500

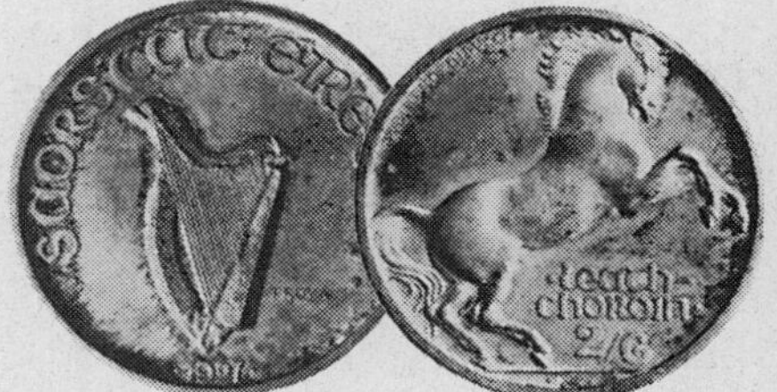

KM#	Date	Mintage	Identification	Mkt Val
Pr8	1927	5	1/2 Crown. Silver. Irish harp. Rearing horse.	8,500
Pr8a	1927	—	1/2 Crown. Copper. Irish harp. Rearing horse.	—

Note: This series exists in other than standard metals

PIEFORTS

KM#	Date	Mintage	Identification	Mkt Val
P1	2000	—	Punt. Silver. 20.0000 g. Stylized ancient ship. as KM#31	35.00

MINT SETS

KM#	Date	Mintage	Identification	Issue Price	Mkt Val
MS1	1928 (8)	—	KM#1-8	—	—
MS2	1966 (8)	96,000	KM9-11, 12a-16a	—	25.00

KM#	Date	Mintage	Identification	Issue Price	Mkt Val
MS3	1969-1971 (6)	—	KM19-21(1971), 22 (1970), 23(1969), 24(1970), mixed dates	—	6.50
MS4	1971 (6)	—	KM19-24	1.50	9.00
MS5	1978 (6)	—	KM19-24	—	5.00
MS6	1982 (6)	—	KM19-24	—	5.00
MS7	1996 (7)	—	KM20a-21a, 24-25, 27-29	—	30.00
MS8	1998 (7)	—	KM20a-21a, 25-25, 27-29	—	30.00
MS9	2000 (7)	—	KM20a-21a, 24-25, 28-29, 31	—	100
MS10	2002 (8)	20,000	KM#32,33,34,35,36,37,38,39	10.00	200
MS11	2003 (8)	30,000	KM#32-39	10.00	75.00
MS12	2003 (9)	—	KM#32-40 Special Olympics	—	90.00
MS13	2004 (8)	—	KM#32-39	—	45.00
MS14	2005 (8)	—	KM#32-39	—	45.00
MS15	2006 (8)	—	KM#32-39	—	45.00
MS16	2006 (8)	—	KM#32-39 Boy Baby Set	—	—
MS17	2006 (8)	—	KM#32-39 Girl Baby Set	—	—

PROOF SETS

KM#	Date	Mintage	Identification	Issue Price	Mkt Val
PS1	1928 (8)	6,001	KM1-8	—	400
PS2	1966 (2)	1,000	KM18(2)	—	75.00
PS3	1971 (6)	50,000	KM19-24	4.40	15.00
PS4	1986 (7)	6,750	KM19-25	—	800
PS5	1990 (3)	—	KMM1-M3	—	500
PS6	2006 (8)	5,000	KM#32-39	125	150
PS7	2006 (2)	—	KM#45-46	—	110

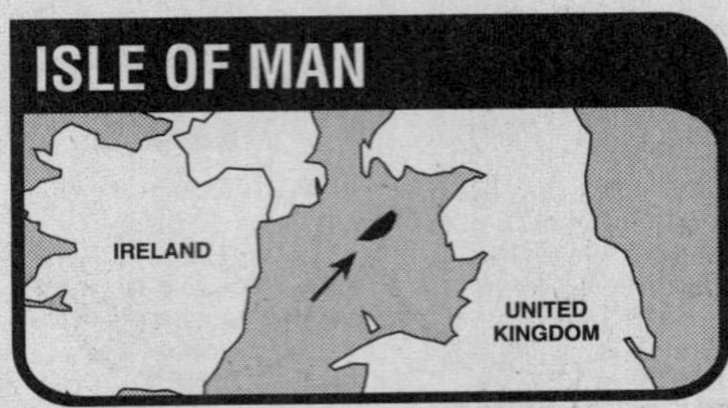

The Isle of Man, a dependency of the British Crown located in the Irish Sea equidistant from Ireland, Scotland and England, has an area of 227 sq. mi. (588 sq. km.) and a population of 68,000. Capital: Douglas. Agriculture, dairy farming, fishing and tourism are the chief industries.

The prevalence of prehistoric artifacts and monuments on the island give evidence that its' mild, almost sub-tropical climate was enjoyed by mankind before the dawn of history. Vikings came to the Isle of Man during the 9th century and remained until ejected by the Scottish in 1266. The island came under the protection of the British Crown in 1288, and in 1406 was granted, in perpetuity, to the earls of Derby, from whom it was inherited, 1736, by the Duke of Atholl. The British Crown purchased the rights and title in 1765; the remaining privileges of the Atholl family were transferred to the crown in 1829. The Isle of Man is ruled by its own legislative council and the House of Keys, the oldest, continuous legislative assembly in the world. Acts of Parliament passed in London do not affect the island unless it is specifically mentioned.

RULERS

James Murray, Duke of Atholl, 1736-1765
British Commencing 1765

MINT MARK

PM - Pobjoy Mint

PRIVY MARKS

(a) - Big Apple - 1988
(at) - Angel Blowing Trumpet – 1997

(b) - Baby Crib - 1982
(ba) - Basel Bugle - 1990
(bb) - Big Ben - 1987-1988
(br) - Brooklyn Bridge - 1989
(bs) - Teddy Bear in Stocking - 1996
(c) - Chicago Water Tower CICF - 1990-1991
(cc) - Christmas cracker - 1991
(d) - St. Paul's Cathedral - 1989
(f) - FUN logo - 1988
(fl) - Fleur de Lis - 1990
(fr) - Frauenkirche - Munich Numismata - 1990-1991
(fw) - Fairy w/magic wand - 1999
(h) - Horse - Hong Kong Int. - 1990
(l) - Statue of Liberty - 1987
(lc) - Lion crowned - 1989
(m) - Queen mother's portrait - 1980
(ma) - Maple leaf - CNA - 1990
(mt) - Mistletoe - Christmas - 1987, 1989
(ns) - North Star - 1994
(p) - Carrier Pigeon - Basel - 1988-1989
(pi) - Pine tree - 1986
(pt) - Partridge in a pear tree - 1988
(py) - Poppy - 1995
(s) - Bridge - SINPEX - 1987
(sb) - Soccer ball - 1982
(sc) - Santa Claus - 1995
(sg) - Sleigh - Christmas - 1990
(SL) - St. Louis Arch - 1987
(ss) - Sailing Ship - Sydney - 1988
(t) - Stylized triskelion - 1979
(tb) - Tower Bridge - 1990
(ti) - TICC logo - Tokyo - 1990
(v) - Viking ship - 1980
(vw) - Viking ship in wreath - 1986
(w) - Stylized triskelion - 1985
(x) - Snowman - 1998

PRIVY LETTERS

A - ANA - 1985-1992
C - Coinex, London - 1985-1989
D.M.I.H.E. - Ideal Home Exhibit, London, 1980
D.M.I.H.E.N. - Ideal Home Exhibit, Manchester, 1980
F - FUN - 1987
H - Hong Kong Expo - 1985
L - Long Beach - 1985-1987
T - Torex, Toronto - 1986
U - Uncirculated - 1988, 1990, 1994, 1995
X - Ameripex - 1986

BRITISH DEPENDENCY

DECIMAL COINAGE

5 New Pence = 1 Shilling; 25 New Pence = 1 Crown; 100 New Pence = 1 Pound

KM# 19 1/2 NEW PENNY

Bronze, 17.14 mm. **Ruler:** Elizabeth II **Obv:** Young bust right **Obv. Designer:** Arnold Machin **Rev:** Flowered weed **Rev. Designer:** Christopher Ironside

Date	Mintage	F	VF	XF	Unc	BU
1971	495,000	—	—	0.15	0.35	0.75
1971 Proof	10,000	Value: 1.50				
1972	1,000	—	—	—	18.00	20.00
1973	1,000	—	—	—	18.00	20.00
1974	1,000	—	—	—	18.00	20.00
1975	825,000	—	—	0.15	0.25	0.65

KM# 19a 1/2 NEW PENNY

2.1000 g., 0.9250 Silver .0624 oz. ASW, 17.4 mm. **Ruler:** Elizabeth II **Obv:** Young bust right **Obv. Designer:** Arnold Machin **Rev:** Flowered weed **Rev. Designer:** Christopher Ironside

Date	Mintage	F	VF	XF	Unc	BU
1975	20,000	—	—	—	2.50	3.00

KM# 19b 1/2 NEW PENNY

4.0000 g., 0.9500 Platinum .1221 oz. APW, 17.4 mm. **Ruler:** Elizabeth II **Obv:** Young bust right **Obv. Designer:** Arnold Machin **Rev:** Flowered weed **Rev. Designer:** Christopher Ironside

Date	Mintage	F	VF	XF	Unc	BU
1975 Proof	600	Value: 175				

KM# 32 1/2 PENNY

Bronze, 17.4 mm. **Ruler:** Elizabeth II **Obv:** Young bust right **Obv. Designer:** Arnold Machin **Rev:** Atlantic herring

Date	Mintage	F	VF	XF	Unc	BU
1976	600,000	—	—	0.20	0.45	1.00
1978	—	—	—	0.20	0.45	1.00
1978 Proof	—	Value: 1.25				
1979(t) AA	—	—	—	0.20	0.45	1.00
1979(t) AB	—	—	—	0.20	0.45	1.00

KM# 32a 1/2 PENNY

2.1000 g., 0.9250 Silver .0624 oz. ASW, 17.14 mm. **Ruler:** Elizabeth II **Obv:** Young bust right **Obv. Designer:** Arnold Machin **Rev:** Atlantic herring

Date	Mintage	F	VF	XF	Unc	BU
1976	20,000	—	—	—	2.00	2.50
1978	10,000	—	—	—	2.00	2.50
1979 (t) Proof	10,000	Value: 2.50				

KM# 32b 1/2 PENNY

4.0000 g., 0.9500 Platinum .1221 oz. APW, 17.14 mm. **Ruler:** Elizabeth II **Obv:** Young bust right **Obv. Designer:** Arnold Machin **Rev:** Atlantic herring

Date	Mintage	F	VF	XF	Unc	BU
1976 Proof	600	Value: 175				
1978 Proof	600	Value: 175				
1979 (t) Proof	500	Value: 175				

KM# 40 1/2 PENNY

Bronze, 17.14 mm. **Ruler:** Elizabeth II **Series:** F.A.O. **Obv:** Young bust right **Obv. Designer:** Arnold Machin **Rev:** Atlantic herring

Date	Mintage	F	VF	XF	Unc	BU
1977	700,000	—	—	0.20	0.45	1.00
Note: PM on reverse						
1977	Inc. above	—	—	—	5.00	6.00
Note: Without PM on reverse						

KM# 40a 1/2 PENNY

2.1000 g., 0.9250 Silver .0624 oz. ASW, 17.14 mm. **Ruler:** Elizabeth II **Obv:** Young bust right **Obv. Designer:** Arnold Machin **Rev:** Atlantic herring

Date	Mintage	F	VF	XF	Unc	BU
1977 Proof	10,000	Value: 4.00				

KM# 58 1/2 PENNY

Bronze, 17.14 mm. **Ruler:** Elizabeth II **Obv:** Young bust right **Obv. Designer:** Arnold Machin **Rev:** Atlantic herring within net **Rev. Designer:** Leslie Lindsay

Date	Mintage	F	VF	XF	Unc	BU
1980 AA	—	—	—	0.15	0.35	0.75
1980 AB	—	—	—	0.15	0.35	0.75
1980PM DD Proof	—	Value: 1.00				
1981 AA	—	—	—	0.15	0.35	0.75

Date	Mintage	F	VF	XF	Unc	BU
1981 DD Proof	—	Value: 1.00				
1982 AA	—	—	—	0.15	0.35	0.75
1982 (b)	—	—	—	0.15	0.35	0.75
1982 (b) Proof	25,000	Value: 1.00				
1983 AA	—	—	—	0.15	0.35	0.75

KM# 58b 1/2 PENNY

2.1000 g., 0.9250 Silver .0624 oz. ASW, 17.14 mm. **Ruler:** Elizabeth II **Obv:** Young bust right **Obv. Designer:** Arnold Machin **Rev:** Atlantic herring within net **Rev. Designer:** Leslie Lindsay

Date	Mintage	F	VF	XF	Unc	BU
1982 Proof	10,000	Value: 4.00				
1983 Proof	5,000	Value: 5.00				

KM# 58c 1/2 PENNY

3.5500 g., 0.9170 Gold .1046 oz. AGW, 17.14 mm. **Ruler:** Elizabeth II **Obv:** Young bust right **Obv. Designer:** Arnold Machin **Rev:** Atlantic herring within net **Rev. Designer:** Leslie Lindsay

Date	Mintage	F	VF	XF	Unc	BU
1980 Proof	—	Value: 80.00				
1982 (b) Proof	500	Value: 80.00				
1983 Proof	—	Value: 80.00				

KM# 58d 1/2 PENNY

4.0000 g., 0.9500 Platinum .1221 oz. APW, 17.14 mm. **Ruler:** Elizabeth II **Obv:** Young bust right **Obv. Designer:** Arnold Machin **Rev:** Atlantic herring within net **Rev. Designer:** Leslie Lindsay

Date	Mintage	F	VF	XF	Unc	BU
1980 Proof	500	Value: 180				
1982 (b) Proof	500	Value: 180				
1983 Proof	—	Value: 180				

KM# 58a 1/2 PENNY

2.1000 g., 0.5000 Silver .0337 oz. ASW, 17.14 mm. **Ruler:** Elizabeth II **Obv:** Young bust right **Obv. Designer:** Arnold Machin **Rev:** Atlantic herring within net **Rev. Designer:** Leslie Lindsay

Date	Mintage	F	VF	XF	Unc	BU
1980 Proof	10,000	Value: 4.00				

KM# 72.1 1/2 PENNY

4.0000 g., 0.9500 Bronze .1221 oz., 17.14 mm. **Ruler:** Elizabeth II **Series:** F.A.O. **Obv:** Young bust right **Obv. Designer:** Arnold Machin **Rev:** Atlantic herring

Date	Mintage	F	VF	XF	Unc	BU
1981	—	—	—	—	0.50	1.00

KM# 72.2 1/2 PENNY

4.0000 g., 0.9500 Bronze .1221 oz., 17.14 mm. **Ruler:** Elizabeth II **Obv:** Young bust right **Obv. Designer:** Arnold Machin **Rev:** Atlantic herring

Date	Mintage	F	VF	XF	Unc	BU
1981	10,000	—	2.00	5.00	10.00	12.50

KM# 111 1/2 PENNY

4.0000 g., 0.9500 Bronze .1221 oz., 17.14 mm. **Ruler:** Elizabeth II **Subject:** Quincentenary of the College of Arms **Obv:** Young bust right **Obv. Designer:** Arnold Machin **Rev:** Fuchsia blossom on garnished and scrolled shield **Rev. Designer:** Leslie Lindsay

Date	Mintage	F	VF	XF	Unc	BU
1984 AA	—	—	—	—	0.15	0.25

KM# 111a 1/2 PENNY

2.1000 g., 0.9250 Silver .0625 oz. ASW, 17.14 mm. **Ruler:** Elizabeth II **Obv:** Young bust right **Obv. Designer:** Arnold Machin **Rev:** Fuchsia blossom on garnished and scrolled shield **Rev. Designer:** Leslie Lindsay

Date	Mintage	F	VF	XF	Unc	BU
1984 Proof	—	Value: 5.00				

KM# 111b 1/2 PENNY

3.5500 g., 0.9170 Gold .1046 oz. AGW, 17.14 mm. **Ruler:** Elizabeth II **Obv:** Young bust right **Obv. Designer:** Arnold Machin **Rev:** Fuchsia blossom on garnished and scrolled shield **Rev. Designer:** Leslie Lindsay

Date	Mintage	F	VF	XF	Unc	BU
1984 Proof	150	Value: 125				

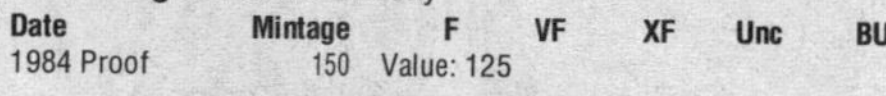

KM# 142 1/2 PENNY

Bronze, 17.14 mm. **Ruler:** Elizabeth II **Obv:** Crowned head right **Obv. Designer:** Raphael Maklouf **Rev:** Fuchsia blossom on garnished and scrolled shield **Rev. Designer:** Leslie Lindsay

Date	Mintage	F	VF	XF	Unc	BU
1985(w) AA	—	—	—	—	0.15	0.25
1985 Proof	50,000	Value: 2.00				

KM# 142a 1/2 PENNY

, 17.14 mm. **Ruler:** Elizabeth II **Obv:** Crowned head right **Obv. Designer:** Raphael Maklouf **Rev:** Fuchsia blossom on garnished and scrolled shield **Rev. Designer:** Leslie Lindsay

Date	Mintage	F	VF	XF	Unc	BU
1985 Proof	10,000	Value: 3.00				

KM# 142b 1/2 PENNY

3.5500 g., 0.9170 Gold .1046 oz. AGW, 17.14 mm. **Ruler:** Elizabeth II **Obv:** Crowned head right **Obv. Designer:** Raphael Maklouf **Rev:** Fuchsia blossom on garnished and scrolled shield **Rev. Designer:** Leslie Lindsay

Date	Mintage	F	VF	XF	Unc	BU
1985 Proof	300	Value: 85.00				

KM# 142c 1/2 PENNY

4.0000 g., 0.9500 Platinum .1221 oz. APW, 17.14 mm. **Ruler:** Elizabeth II **Obv:** Crowned head right **Obv. Designer:** Raphael Maklouf **Rev:** Fuchsia blossom on garnished and scrolled shield **Rev. Designer:** Leslie Lindsay

Date	Mintage	F	VF	XF	Unc	BU
1985 Proof	200	Value: 180				

KM# 20 NEW PENNY

3.5500 g., Bronze, 20.32 mm. **Ruler:** Elizabeth II **Obv:** Young bust right **Obv. Designer:** Arnold Machin **Rev:** Celtic cross **Rev. Designer:** Christopher Ironside

Date	Mintage	F	VF	XF	Unc	BU
1971	100,000	—	—	0.10	0.35	0.65
1971 Proof	10,000	Value: 2.00				
1972	1,000	—	—	—	18.00	20.00
1973	1,000	—	—	—	18.00	20.00
1974	1,000	—	—	—	18.00	20.00
1975	855,000	—	—	0.10	0.20	0.40

KM# 20a NEW PENNY

4.2000 g., 0.9250 Silver .1249 oz. ASW, 20.32 mm. **Ruler:** Elizabeth II **Obv:** Young bust right **Obv. Designer:** Arnold Machin **Rev:** Celtic cross **Rev. Designer:** Christopher Ironside

Date	Mintage	F	VF	XF	Unc	BU
1975	20,000	—	—	—	5.00	6.50

KM# 20b NEW PENNY

8.0000 g., 0.9500 Platinum .2443 oz. APW, 20.32 mm. **Ruler:** Elizabeth II **Obv:** Young bust right **Obv. Designer:** Arnold Machin **Rev:** Celtic cross **Rev. Designer:** Christopher Ironside

Date	Mintage	F	VF	XF	Unc	BU
1975 Proof	600	Value: 365				

KM# 33 PENNY

3.5500 g., Bronze, 20.32 mm. **Ruler:** Elizabeth II **Obv:** Young bust right **Obv. Designer:** Arnold Machin **Rev:** Loaghtyn sheep

Date	Mintage	F	VF	XF	Unc	BU
1976	900,000	—	—	0.25	0.75	1.25
1977	1,000,000	—	—	0.25	0.75	1.25
1978	—	—	—	0.25	0.75	1.25
1978 Proof	—	Value: 1.50				
1979 AA(t)	—	—	—	0.25	0.75	1.25
1979 AB(t)	—	—	—	0.25	0.75	1.25
1979 AC(t)	—	—	—	0.25	0.75	1.25
1979 AD(t)	—	—	—	0.25	0.75	1.25
1979 AE(t)	—	—	—	0.25	0.75	1.25

KM# 33a PENNY

4.2000 g., 0.9250 Silver .1249 oz. ASW, 20.32 mm. **Ruler:** Elizabeth II **Obv:** Young bust right **Obv. Designer:** Arnold Machin **Rev:** Loaghtyn sheep

Date	Mintage	F	VF	XF	Unc	BU
1976	20,000	—	—	—	4.00	4.50
1977 Proof	10,000	Value: 5.00				
1978	10,000	—	—	—	4.00	4.50
1979 (t) Proof	10,000	Value: 5.00				

KM# 33b PENNY

8.0000 g., 0.9500 Platinum .2443 oz. APW, 20.32 mm. **Ruler:** Elizabeth II **Obv:** Young bust right **Obv. Designer:** Arnold Machin **Rev:** Loaghtyn sheep

Date	Mintage	F	VF	XF	Unc	BU
1976 Proof	600	Value: 365				
1978 Proof	600	Value: 365				
1979 (t) Proof	500	Value: 365				

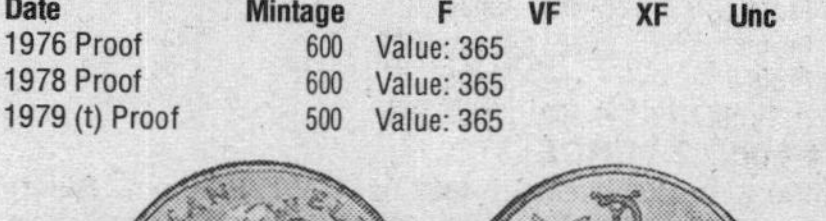

KM# 59 PENNY

3.5500 g., Bronze, 20.32 mm. **Ruler:** Elizabeth II **Obv:** Young bust right **Obv. Designer:** Arnold Machin **Rev:** Manx cat **Rev. Designer:** Leslie Lindsay

Date	Mintage	F	VF	XF	Unc	BU
1980 AA	—	—	—	0.25	1.00	2.50
1980 AB	—	—	—	0.25	1.00	2.50
1980 AC	—	—	—	0.25	1.00	2.50
1980PM DD Proof	—	Value: 2.75				
1981 AA	—	—	—	0.25	1.00	2.50
1981 DD Proof	—	Value: 2.75				
1982 AA	—	—	—	0.25	1.00	2.50
1982 (b)	—	—	—	0.25	1.00	2.50
1982 (b) Proof	25,000	Value: 2.75				
1983 AA	—	—	—	0.25	1.00	2.50
1983 AC	—	—	—	0.25	1.00	2.50
1983 AB	—	—	—	0.25	1.00	2.50

KM# 59a PENNY

4.2000 g., 0.5000 Silver .0675 oz. ASW, 20.32 mm. **Ruler:** Elizabeth II **Obv:** Young bust right **Obv. Designer:** Arnold Machin **Rev:** Manx cat **Rev. Designer:** Leslie Lindsay

Date	Mintage	F	VF	XF	Unc	BU
1980 Proof	10,000	Value: 6.00				

KM# 59b PENNY

4.2000 g., 0.9250 Silver .0675 oz. ASW, 20.32 mm. **Ruler:** Elizabeth II **Obv:** Young bust right **Obv. Designer:** Arnold Machin **Rev:** Manx cat **Rev. Designer:** Leslie Lindsay

Date	Mintage	F	VF	XF	Unc	BU
1981 Proof	—	Value: 6.00				
1982 (b) Proof	10,000	Value: 6.00				
1983 Proof	5,000	Value: 6.00				

KM# 59c PENNY

7.1000 g., 0.9170 Gold .2093 oz. AGW, 20.32 mm. **Ruler:** Elizabeth II **Obv:** Young bust right **Obv. Designer:** Arnold Machin **Rev:** Manx cat **Rev. Designer:** Leslie Lindsay

Date	Mintage	F	VF	XF	Unc	BU
1980 Proof	300	Value: 165				
1982 (b) Proof	500	Value: 165				
1983 Proof	—	Value: 165				

KM# 59d PENNY

8.0000 g., 0.9500 Platinum .2443 oz. APW, 20.32 mm. **Ruler:** Elizabeth II **Obv:** Young bust right **Obv. Designer:** Arnold Machin **Rev:** Manx cat **Rev. Designer:** Leslie Lindsay

Date	Mintage	F	VF	XF	Unc	BU
1980 Proof	500	Value: 365				
1982 (b) Proof	500	Value: 365				
1983 Proof	—	Value: 365				

KM# 112 PENNY

3.5500 g., Bronze, 20.32 mm. **Ruler:** Elizabeth II **Subject:** Quincentenary of the College of Arms **Obv:** Young bust right **Obv. Designer:** Arnold Machin **Rev:** Shag bird on tilting shield **Rev. Designer:** Leslie Lindsay

Date	Mintage	F	VF	XF	Unc	BU
1984 AA	—	—	—	0.25	0.50	1.00

KM# 112a PENNY

4.2000 g., 0.9250 Silver .0675 oz. ASW, 20.32 mm. **Ruler:** Elizabeth II **Obv:** Young bust right **Obv. Designer:** Arnold Machin **Rev:** Shag bird on tilting shield **Rev. Designer:** Leslie Lindsay

Date	Mintage	F	VF	XF	Unc	BU
1984 Proof	—	Value: 5.00				

KM# 112b PENNY

7.1000 g., 0.9170 Gold .2093 oz. AGW, 20.32 mm. **Ruler:** Elizabeth II **Obv:** Young bust right **Obv. Designer:** Arnold Machin **Rev:** Shag bird on tilting shield **Rev. Designer:** Leslie Lindsay

Date	Mintage	F	VF	XF	Unc	BU
1984 Proof	150	Value: 250				

KM# 143 PENNY

3.5500 g., Bronze, 20.32 mm. **Ruler:** Elizabeth II **Obv:** Crowned head right **Obv. Designer:** Raphael Maklouf **Rev:** Shag bird on tilting shield **Rev. Designer:** Leslie Lindsay

Date	Mintage	F	VF	XF	Unc	BU
1985 AA(w)	—	—	—	0.10	0.50	1.00
1985 Proof	50,000	Value: 2.00				
1986 AA	—	—	—	0.10	0.50	1.00
1987 AA	—	—	—	0.10	0.50	1.00
1987 AB	—	—	—	0.10	0.50	1.00
1987 AC	—	—	—	0.10	0.50	1.00

KM# 143a PENNY

4.2000 g., 0.9250 Silver .0675 oz. ASW, 20.32 mm. **Ruler:** Elizabeth II **Obv:** Raphael Maklouf **Rev:** Shag bird on tilting shield **Rev. Designer:** Leslie Lindsay

Date	Mintage	F	VF	XF	Unc	BU
1985 Proof	10,000	Value: 3.00				

KM# 143b PENNY

7.1000 g., 0.9170 Gold .2093 oz. AGW, 20.32 mm.
Ruler: Elizabeth II **Obv:** Crowned head right
Obv. Designer: Raphael Maklouf **Rev:** Shag bird on tilting shield
Rev. Designer: Leslie Lindsay

Date	Mintage	F	VF	XF	Unc	BU
1985 Proof	300	Value: 175				

KM# 143c PENNY

8.0000 g., 0.9500 Platinum .2443 oz. APW, 20.32 mm.
Ruler: Elizabeth II **Obv:** Crowned head right
Obv. Designer: Raphael Maklouf **Rev:** Shag bird on tilting shield
Rev. Designer: Leslie Lindsay

Date	Mintage	F	VF	XF	Unc	BU
1985 Proof	200	Value: 365				

KM# 207 PENNY

3.5500 g., Bronze, 20.32 mm. **Ruler:** Elizabeth II **Obv:** Crowned head right **Obv. Designer:** Raphael Maklouf **Rev:** Precision lathe superimposed on a cog wheel

Date	Mintage	F	VF	XF	Unc	BU
1988 AA	—	—	—	—	0.20	0.35
1988 AB	—	—	—	0.10	0.30	0.50
1988 AC	—	—	—	0.10	0.30	0.50
1988 AD	—	—	—	0.10	0.30	0.50
1989 AA	—	—	—	—	0.20	0.35
1989 AB	—	—	—	0.10	0.30	0.50
1989 AC	—	—	—	0.10	0.30	0.50
1989 AD	—	—	—	0.10	0.30	0.50
1989 AE	—	—	—	0.10	0.30	0.50
1990 AA	—	—	—	—	0.20	0.35
1991 AA	—	—	—	—	0.20	0.35
1991 AB	—	—	—	—	0.20	0.35
1991 AC	—	—	—	—	0.20	0.35
1991 AD	—	—	—	—	0.20	0.35
1991 AE	—	—	—	—	0.20	0.35
1992 AA	—	—	—	—	0.20	0.35
1993 AA	—	—	—	—	0.20	0.35
1994 AA	—	—	—	—	0.20	0.35
1995 AA	—	—	—	—	0.20	0.35

KM# 588 PENNY

Bronze-Plated Steel, 20.32 mm. **Ruler:** Elizabeth II
Subject: Sports **Obv:** Crowned head right **Obv. Designer:** Raphael Maklouf **Rev:** Rugby ball within 3/4 square and wreath

Date	Mintage	F	VF	XF	Unc	BU
1996 AA	—	—	—	—	0.20	0.35
1997 AA	—	—	—	—	0.20	0.35
1998 AA	—	—	—	—	0.20	0.35

KM# 588a PENNY

4.2000 g., 0.9250 Silver .0675 oz. ASW, 20.32 mm.
Ruler: Elizabeth II **Subject:** Sports **Obv:** Crowned head right **Obv. Designer:** Raphael Maklouf **Rev:** Rugby ball within 3/4 square and wreath

Date	Mintage	F	VF	XF	Unc	BU
1996 Proof	—	Value: 10.00				

KM# 823.2 PENNY

Bronze-Plated Steel, 20.32 mm. **Ruler:** Elizabeth II **Obv:** Head with tiara right with small triskeles dividing legend **Obv. Designer:** Ian Rank-Broadley **Rev:** Rugby ball within 3/4 square and wreath

Date	Mintage	F	VF	XF	Unc	BU
1998PM AA	—	—	—	—	0.20	0.35
1999PM AA	—	—	—	—	0.20	0.35

KM# 823.1 PENNY

Bronze-Plated Steel, 20.32 mm. **Ruler:** Elizabeth II **Obv:** Head with tiara right **Obv. Designer:** Ian Rank-Broadley **Rev:** Rugby ball within 3/4 square and wreath

Date	Mintage	F	VF	XF	Unc	BU
1998 AA	—	—	—	—	0.20	0.35

KM# 1036 PENNY

3.5300 g., Bronze-Plated Steel, 20.32 mm. **Ruler:** Elizabeth II
Obv: Head with tiara right with small triskeles dividing legend
Obv. Designer: Ian Rank-Broadley **Rev:** Ruins **Edge:** Plain

Date	Mintage	F	VF	XF	Unc	BU
2000 AA	—	—	—	—	0.25	0.45

KM# 21 2 NEW PENCE

7.0000 g., Bronze, 25.91 mm. **Ruler:** Elizabeth II **Obv:** Young bust right **Obv. Designer:** Arnold Machin **Rev:** Falcons

Date	Mintage	F	VF	XF	Unc	BU
1971	100,000	—	—	0.25	1.00	2.00
1971 Proof	10,000	Value: 2.50				
1972	1,000	—	—	—	18.00	20.00
1973	1,000	—	—	—	18.00	20.00
1974	1,000	—	—	—	18.00	20.00
1975	725,000	—	—	0.25	1.00	1.50

KM# 21a 2 NEW PENCE

8.4000 g., 0.9250 Silver .2498 oz. ASW, 25.91 mm.
Ruler: Elizabeth II **Obv:** Young bust right **Obv. Designer:** Arnold Machin **Rev:** Falcons

Date	Mintage	F	VF	XF	Unc	BU
1975	20,000	—	—	—	7.50	8.50

KM# 21b 2 NEW PENCE

16.0000 g., 0.9500 Platinum .4887 oz. APW, 25.91 mm.
Ruler: Elizabeth II **Obv:** Young bust right **Obv. Designer:** Arnold Machin **Rev:** Falcons

Date	Mintage	F	VF	XF	Unc	BU
1975 Proof	600	Value: 725				

KM# 34 2 PENCE

7.0000 g., Bronze, 25.91 mm. **Ruler:** Elizabeth II **Obv:** Young bust right **Obv. Designer:** Arnold Machin **Rev:** Bird in flight over map

Date	Mintage	F	VF	XF	Unc	BU
1976	800,000	—	—	0.20	0.50	1.00
1977	1,000,000	—	—	0.20	0.50	1.00
1978	—	—	—	—	0.50	1.00
1978 Proof	—	Value: 1.25				
1979 AA(t)	10,000	—	—	0.20	0.50	1.00
1979 AB(t)	—	—	—	0.20	0.50	1.00
1979 AC(t)	—	—	—	0.20	0.50	1.00
1979 AD(t)	—	—	—	0.20	0.50	1.00
1979 AE(t)	—	—	—	0.20	0.50	1.00
1979 AF(t)	—	—	—	0.20	0.50	1.00
1979 AG(t)	—	—	—	0.20	0.50	1.00
1979 AH(t)	—	—	—	0.20	0.50	1.00

KM# 34a 2 PENCE

8.4000 g., 0.9250 Silver .2498 oz. ASW, 25.91 mm.
Ruler: Elizabeth II **Obv:** Young bust right **Obv. Designer:** Arnold Machin **Rev:** Bird in flight over map

Date	Mintage	F	VF	XF	Unc	BU
1976	20,000	—	—	—	4.50	5.00
1977 Proof	10,000	Value: 6.00				
1978	10,000	—	—	—	5.50	6.00
1979 (t) Proof	10,000	Value: 6.00				

KM# 34b 2 PENCE

16.0000 g., 0.9500 Platinum .4887 oz. APW, 25.91 mm.
Ruler: Elizabeth II **Obv:** Young bust right **Obv. Designer:** Arnold Machin **Rev:** Bird in flight over map

Date	Mintage	F	VF	XF	Unc	BU
1976 Proof	600	Value: 725				
1977 Proof	600	Value: 725				
1978 Proof	—	Value: 725				
1979 (t) Proof	500	Value: 725				

KM# 60d 2 PENCE

16.0000 g., 0.9500 Platinum .4887 oz. APW, 25.91 mm. **Ruler:** Elizabeth II **Obv:** Young bust right **Obv. Designer:** Arnold Machin **Rev:** Bird in center of design **Rev. Designer:** Leslie Lindsay

Date	Mintage	F	VF	XF	Unc	BU
1980 Proof	500	Value: 725				
1982 (b) Proof	500	Value: 725				
1983 Proof	—	Value: 725				

KM# 60c 2 PENCE

14.2000 g., 0.9170 Gold .4186 oz. AGW, 25.91 mm. **Ruler:** Elizabeth II **Obv:** Young bust right **Obv. Designer:** Arnold Machin **Rev:** Bird in center of design **Rev. Designer:** Leslie Lindsay

Date	Mintage	F	VF	XF	Unc	BU
1980 Proof	300	Value: 300				
1982 (b) Proof	500	Value: 300				
1983 Proof	—	Value: 300				

KM# 60b 2 PENCE

8.4000 g., 0.9250 Silver .2498 oz. ASW, 25.91 mm. **Ruler:** Elizabeth II **Obv:** Young bust right **Obv. Designer:** Arnold Machin **Rev:** Bird in center of design **Rev. Designer:** Leslie Lindsay

Date	Mintage	F	VF	XF	Unc	BU
1981 Proof	—	—	—	—	—	—
1982 (b) Proof	10,000	Value: 5.00				
1983 Proof	5,000	Value: 7.00				

KM# 60 2 PENCE

7.0000 g., Bronze, 25.91 mm. **Ruler:** Elizabeth II **Obv:** Young bust right **Obv. Designer:** Arnold Machin **Rev:** Bird in center of design **Rev. Designer:** Leslie Lindsay

Date	Mintage	F	VF	XF	Unc	BU
1980 AA	—	—	—	0.25	0.60	1.50
1980 AB	—	—	—	0.25	0.60	1.50
1980 AC	—	—	—	0.25	0.60	1.50
1980 AD	—	—	—	0.25	0.60	1.50
1980PM DD Proof	—	Value: 1.75				
1981 AA	—	—	—	0.25	0.60	1.50
1981 AB	—	—	—	0.25	0.60	1.50
1981 DD Proof	—	Value: 1.75				
1982 AA	—	—	—	0.25	0.60	1.50
1982 (b)	—	—	—	0.25	0.60	1.50
1982 (b) Proof	25,000	Value: 1.75				
1983 AA	—	—	—	0.25	0.60	1.50
1983 AB	—	—	—	0.25	0.60	1.50
1983 AC	—	—	—	0.25	0.60	1.50
1983 AD	—	—	—	0.25	0.60	1.50
1983 AE	—	—	—	0.25	0.60	1.50

KM# 60a 2 PENCE

8.4000 g., 0.5000 Silver .1350 oz. ASW, 25.91 mm. **Ruler:** Elizabeth II **Obv:** Young bust right **Obv. Designer:** Arnold Machin **Rev:** Bird in center of design **Rev. Designer:** Leslie Lindsay

Date	Mintage	F	VF	XF	Unc	BU
1980 Proof	10,000	Value: 5.00				

KM# 113 2 PENCE

7.0000 g., Bronze, 25.91 mm. **Ruler:** Elizabeth II
Subject: Quincentenary of the College of Arms **Obv:** Young bust right **Obv. Designer:** Arnold Machin **Rev:** Falcon on ornamented shield **Rev. Designer:** Leslie Lindsay

Date	Mintage	F	VF	XF	Unc	BU
1984 AA	—	—	—	0.20	1.00	2.50

KM# 113a 2 PENCE

8.4000 g., 0.9250 Silver .2498 oz. ASW, 25.91 mm. **Ruler:** Elizabeth II **Obv:** Young bust right **Obv. Designer:** Arnold Machin **Rev:** Falcon on ornamented shield **Rev. Designer:** Leslie Lindsay

Date	Mintage	F	VF	XF	Unc	BU
1984 Proof	—	Value: 6.00				

KM# 113b 2 PENCE

14.2000 g., 0.9170 Gold .4185 oz. AGW, 25.91 mm. **Ruler:** Elizabeth II **Obv:** Young bust right **Obv. Designer:** Arnold Machin **Rev:** Falcon on ornamented shield **Rev. Designer:** Leslie Lindsay

Date	Mintage	F	VF	XF	Unc	BU
1984 Proof	150	Value: 450				

KM# 144 2 PENCE

7.0000 g., Bronze, 25.91 mm. **Ruler:** Elizabeth II **Obv:** Crowned head right **Obv. Designer:** Raphael Maklouf **Rev:** Falcon on ornamented shield **Rev. Designer:** Leslie Lindsay

Date	Mintage	F	VF	XF	Unc	BU
1985(w) AA	—	—	—	0.20	1.25	2.50
1985(w) AB	—	—	—	0.20	1.25	2.50
1985 Proof	50,000	Value: 3.00				
1986 AA	—	—	—	0.20	1.25	2.50
1986 AB	—	—	—	0.20	1.25	2.50
1986 AC	—	—	—	0.20	1.25	2.50

Date	Mintage	F	VF	XF	Unc	BU
1986 AD	—	—	—	0.20	1.25	2.50
1987 AA	—	—	—	0.20	1.25	2.50
1987 AB	—	—	—	0.20	1.25	2.50
1987 AC	—	—	—	0.20	1.25	2.50
1987 AD	—	—	—	0.20	1.25	2.50

KM# 144a 2 PENCE

8.4000 g., 0.9250 Silver .2498 oz. ASW, 25.91 mm.
Ruler: Elizabeth II **Obv:** Crowned head right
Obv. Designer: Raphael Maklouf **Rev:** Falcon on ornamented shield **Rev. Designer:** Leslie Lindsay

Date	Mintage	F	VF	XF	Unc	BU
1985 Proof	10,000	Value: 12.00				

KM# 144b 2 PENCE

14.2000 g., 0.9170 Gold .4185 oz. AGW, 25.91 mm.
Ruler: Elizabeth II **Obv:** Crowned head right
Obv. Designer: Raphael Maklouf **Rev:** Falcon on ornamented shield **Rev. Designer:** Leslie Lindsay

Date	Mintage	F	VF	XF	Unc	BU
1985 Proof	300	Value: 325				

KM# 144c 2 PENCE

16.0000 g., 0.9500 Platinum .4887 oz. APW, 25.91 mm.
Ruler: Elizabeth II **Obv:** Crowned head right
Obv. Designer: Raphael Maklouf **Rev:** Falcon on ornamented shield **Rev. Designer:** Leslie Lindsay

Date	Mintage	F	VF	XF	Unc	BU
1985 Proof	200	Value: 725				

KM# 208 2 PENCE

7.0000 g., Bronze, 25.91 mm. **Ruler:** Elizabeth II **Obv:** Crowned head right **Obv. Designer:** Raphael Maklouf **Rev:** Assorted designs within celtic cross within circle

Date	Mintage	F	VF	XF	Unc	BU
1988 AA	—	—	—	—	0.30	0.50
1988 AB	—	—	—	0.10	0.30	0.50
1988 AC	—	—	—	0.10	0.30	0.50
1988 AD	—	—	—	0.10	0.30	0.50
1989 AA	—	—	—	—	0.30	0.50
1989 AB	—	—	—	0.10	0.30	0.50
1989 AC	—	—	—	0.10	0.30	0.50
1989 AD	—	—	—	0.10	0.30	0.50
1989 AE	—	—	—	0.10	0.30	0.50
1990 AA	—	—	—	—	0.30	0.50
1991 AA	—	—	—	—	0.30	0.50
1992 AA	—	—	—	—	0.30	0.50
1993 AA	—	—	—	—	0.30	0.50
1994 AA	—	—	—	—	0.30	0.50
1995 AA	—	—	—	—	0.30	0.50

KM# 589 2 PENCE

Bronze-Clad Steel, 25.91 mm. **Ruler:** Elizabeth II
Subject: Sports **Obv:** Crowned head right
Obv. Designer: Raphael Maklouf **Rev:** Bicyclists within sprigs

Date	Mintage	F	VF	XF	Unc	BU
1996 AA	—	—	—	—	0.20	0.40
1997 AA	—	—	—	—	0.20	0.40

KM# 901.1 2 PENCE

Bronze-Clad Steel, 25.91 mm. **Ruler:** Elizabeth II **Obv:** Head with tiara right **Obv. Designer:** Ian Rank-Broadley **Rev:** Two bicyclists within sprigs

Date	Mintage	F	VF	XF	Unc	BU
1998 AA	—	—	—	—	0.20	0.40
1998PM AA	—	—	—	—	0.20	0.40
1999PM AA	—	—	—	—	0.50	0.75

KM# 901.2 2 PENCE

Bronze Plated Steel, 25.91 mm. **Ruler:** Elizabeth II **Obv:** Head with tiara right with small triskeles dividing legend **Obv. Designer:** Ian Rank-Broadley **Rev:** Two bicyclists within sprigs

Date	Mintage	F	VF	XF	Unc	BU
1998PM AA Reported not confirmed	—	—	—	—	—	—
1999PM AA Reported not confirmed	—	—	—	—	—	—

KM# 1037 2 PENCE

7.1000 g., Brass-Plated Steel, 25.91 mm. **Ruler:** Elizabeth II **Obv:** Head with tiara right **Obv. Designer:** Ian Rank-Broadley **Rev:** Sailboat **Edge:** Plain

Date	Mintage	F	VF	XF	Unc	BU
2000PM AA	—	—	—	—	0.40	0.60

KM# 22 5 NEW PENCE

5.6500 g., Copper-Nickel, 23.59 mm. **Ruler:** Elizabeth II **Obv:** Young bust right **Obv. Designer:** Arnold Machin **Rev:** Towers on hill **Rev. Designer:** Christopher Ironside

Date	Mintage	F	VF	XF	Unc	BU
1971	100,000	—	—	0.10	0.50	1.00
1971 Proof	10,000	Value: 2.50				
1972	1,000	—	—	—	20.00	22.50
1973	1,000	—	—	—	20.00	22.50
1974	1,000	—	—	—	20.00	22.50
1975	1,400,000	—	—	0.10	0.25	0.50

KM# 22a 5 NEW PENCE

6.5000 g., 0.9250 Silver .1933 oz. ASW, 23.59 mm.
Ruler: Elizabeth II **Obv:** Young bust right **Obv. Designer:** Arnold Machin **Rev:** Towers on hill **Rev. Designer:** Christopher Ironside

Date	Mintage	F	VF	XF	Unc	BU
1975	20,000	—	—	—	5.00	5.50

KM# 22b 5 NEW PENCE

12.5000 g., 0.9500 Platinum .3818 oz. APW, 23.59 mm.
Ruler: Elizabeth II **Obv:** Young bust right **Obv. Designer:** Arnold Machin **Rev:** Towers on hill **Rev. Designer:** Christopher Ironside

Date	Mintage	F	VF	XF	Unc	BU
1975 Proof	600	Value: 550				

KM# 35.1 5 PENCE

5.6500 g., Copper-Nickel, 23.59 mm. **Ruler:** Elizabeth II **Obv:** Young bust right **Obv. Designer:** Arnold Machin **Rev:** Laxey wheel
Note: Lady Isabella; Mint mark: PM on obverse and reverse.

Date	Mintage	F	VF	XF	Unc	BU
1976	800,000	—	—	0.10	0.60	0.85
1977	—	—	—	0.10	0.60	0.85
1978	—	—	—	0.10	0.60	0.85
1978 Proof	—	Value: 1.50				
1979(t) AA	—	—	—	0.10	0.60	0.85

KM# 35.1a 5 PENCE

6.5000 g., 0.9250 Silver .1933 oz. ASW, 23.59 mm.
Ruler: Elizabeth II **Obv:** Young bust right **Obv. Designer:** Arnold Machin **Rev:** Laxey wheel

Date	Mintage	F	VF	XF	Unc	BU
1976	20,000	—	—	—	5.00	5.50
1977 Proof	10,000	Value: 5.50				
1978	10,000	—	—	—	5.00	5.50
1979(t) AA Proof	10,000	Value: 5.50				

KM# 35.1b 5 PENCE

12.5000 g., 0.9500 Platinum .3818 oz. APW, 23.59 mm.
Ruler: Elizabeth II **Obv:** Young bust right **Obv. Designer:** Arnold Machin **Rev:** Laxey wheel

Date	Mintage	F	VF	XF	Unc	BU
1976 Proof	600	Value: 565				
1978 Proof	600	Value: 565				
1979 Proof	500	Value: 565				

KM# 35.2 5 PENCE

5.6500 g., Copper-Nickel, 23.59 mm. **Ruler:** Elizabeth II **Obv:** Young bust right **Obv. Designer:** Arnold Machin **Rev:** Laxey wheel **Note:** Mint mark: PM on obverse only.

Date	Mintage	F	VF	XF	Unc	BU
1976	Inc. above	—	—	0.15	0.75	1.00

KM# 61 5 PENCE

5.6500 g., Copper-Nickel, 23.59 mm. **Ruler:** Elizabeth II **Obv:** Young bust right **Obv. Designer:** Arnold Machin **Rev:** Stylized Loagthyn sheep **Rev. Designer:** Leslie Lindsay

Date	Mintage	F	VF	XF	Unc	BU
1979 AA	—	—	—	0.15	0.75	1.00
1979 AA	—	—	—	0.15	0.75	1.25
1979 AB	—	—	—	0.15	0.75	1.25
1980 AB	—	—	—	0.15	0.75	1.00
1980 AC	—	—	—	0.15	0.75	1.00
1980 AA	—	—	—	0.15	0.75	1.00
1980PM DD Proof	—	Value: 1.50				
1980 AA	—	—	—	0.15	0.75	1.25
1980 AB	—	—	—	0.15	0.75	1.25
1980 AC	—	—	—	0.15	0.75	1.25
1981 AA	—	—	—	0.15	0.75	1.25
1981 AA	—	—	—	0.15	0.75	1.00
1981 DD Proof	—	Value: 1.50				
1982 (b)	—	—	—	0.15	0.75	1.00
1982 (b) Proof	25,000	Value: 1.50				
1982 AA	—	—	—	0.15	0.75	1.00
1982 AA	—	—	—	0.15	0.75	1.25
1982 (b)	—	—	—	0.15	0.75	1.25
1982 (b) Proof	—	Value: 1.50				
1983 AA	—	—	—	0.15	1.50	2.00
1983 AA	—	—	—	0.15	0.75	1.00

KM# 61a 5 PENCE

6.5000 g., 0.5000 Silver .1045 oz. ASW, 23.59 mm. **Ruler:** Elizabeth II **Obv:** Young bust right **Obv. Designer:** Arnold Machin **Rev:** Stylized Loagthyn sheep **Rev. Designer:** Leslie Lindsay

Date	Mintage	F	VF	XF	Unc	BU
1980 Proof	10,000	Value: 5.00				

KM# 61b 5 PENCE

6.5000 g., 0.9250 Silver .1933 oz. ASW, 23.59 mm. **Ruler:** Elizabeth II **Obv:** Young bust right **Obv. Designer:** Arnold Machin **Rev:** Stylized Loagthyn sheep **Rev. Designer:** Leslie Lindsay

Date	Mintage	F	VF	XF	Unc	BU
1981 Proof	—	Value: 5.00				
1982 Proof	10,000	Value: 5.00				
1983 Proof	5,000	Value: 5.00				

KM# 61c 5 PENCE

11.0000 g., 0.9170 Gold .3243 oz. AGW, 23.59 mm. **Ruler:** Elizabeth II **Obv:** Young bust right **Obv. Designer:** Arnold Machin **Rev:** Stylized Loagthyn sheep **Rev. Designer:** Leslie Lindsay

Date	Mintage	F	VF	XF	Unc	BU
1980 Proof	300	Value: 235				
1982 (b) Proof	500	Value: 235				
1983 Proof	—	Value: 235				

KM# 61d 5 PENCE

12.5000 g., 0.9500 Platinum .3818 oz. APW, 23.59 mm. **Ruler:** Elizabeth II **Obv:** Young bust right **Obv. Designer:** Arnold Machin **Rev:** Stylized Loagthyn sheep **Rev. Designer:** Leslie Lindsay

Date	Mintage	F	VF	XF	Unc	BU
1980 Proof	500	Value: 565				
1982 Proof	500	Value: 565				
1983 Proof	—	Value: 565				

KM# 114 5 PENCE

5.6500 g., Copper-Nickel, 23.59 mm. **Ruler:** Elizabeth II
Subject: Quincentenary of the College of Arms **Obv:** Young bust right **Obv. Designer:** Arnold Machin **Rev:** Cushag within design **Rev. Designer:** Leslie Lindsay

Date	Mintage	F	VF	XF	Unc	BU
1984 AA	—	—	—	0.10	0.50	0.75

KM# 114a 5 PENCE

6.5000 g., 0.9250 Silver .1933 oz. ASW, 23.59 mm. **Ruler:** Elizabeth II **Obv:** Young bust right **Obv. Designer:** Arnold Machin **Rev:** Cushag within design **Rev. Designer:** Leslie Lindsay

Date	Mintage	F	VF	XF	Unc	BU
1984 Proof	—	Value: 5.00				

KM# 114b 5 PENCE

11.0000 g., 0.9170 Gold .3242 oz. AGW, 23.59 mm. **Ruler:** Elizabeth II **Obv:** Young bust right **Obv. Designer:** Arnold Machin **Rev:** Cushag within design **Rev. Designer:** Leslie Lindsay

Date	Mintage	F	VF	XF	Unc	BU
1984 Proof	150	Value: 400				

KM# 145 5 PENCE
5.6500 g., Copper-Nickel, 23.59 mm. **Ruler:** Elizabeth II **Obv:** Crowned head right **Obv. Designer:** Raphael Maklouf **Rev:** Cushag within design **Rev. Designer:** Leslie Lindsay

Date	Mintage	F	VF	XF	Unc	BU
1985(w) AA	—	—	—	0.10	0.50	0.75
1985 Proof	50,000	Value: 3.00				
1986 AA	—	—	—	0.10	0.50	0.75
1986 AB	—	—	—	0.10	0.50	0.75
1986 AC	—	—	—	0.10	0.50	0.75
1986 AD	—	—	—	0.10	0.50	0.75
1987 AA	—	—	—	0.10	0.50	0.75

KM# 145a 5 PENCE
6.5000 g., 0.9250 Silver .1933 oz. ASW, 23.59 mm. **Ruler:** Elizabeth II **Obv:** Crowned head right **Obv. Designer:** Raphael Maklouf **Rev:** Cushag within design **Rev. Designer:** Leslie Lindsay

Date	Mintage	F	VF	XF	Unc	BU
1985 Proof	10,000	Value: 8.00				

KM# 145b 5 PENCE
11.0000 g., 0.9170 Gold .3242 oz. AGW, 23.59 mm. **Ruler:** Elizabeth II **Obv:** Crowned head right **Obv. Designer:** Raphael Maklouf **Rev:** Cushag within design **Rev. Designer:** Leslie Lindsay

Date	Mintage	F	VF	XF	Unc	BU
1985 Proof	300	Value: 235				

KM# 145c 5 PENCE
12.5000 g., 0.9500 Platinum .3818 oz. APW, 23.59 mm. **Ruler:** Elizabeth II **Obv:** Crowned head right **Obv. Designer:** Raphael Maklouf **Rev:** Cushag within design **Rev. Designer:** Leslie Lindsay

Date	Mintage	F	VF	XF	Unc	BU
1985 Proof	200	Value: 565				

KM# 209.1 5 PENCE
5.6500 g., Copper-Nickel, 23.59 mm. **Ruler:** Elizabeth II **Obv:** Crowned head right **Obv. Designer:** Raphael Maklouf **Rev:** Windsurfing

Date	Mintage	F	VF	XF	Unc	BU
1988 AA	—	—	—	—	0.50	0.75
1989 AA	—	—	—	—	0.50	0.75
1990	—	—	—	—	0.50	0.75

KM# 209.2 5 PENCE
Copper-Nickel, 18 mm. **Ruler:** Elizabeth II **Obv:** Crowned head right **Obv. Designer:** Raphael Maklouf **Rev:** Windsurfing **Note:** Reduced size.

Date	Mintage	F	VF	XF	Unc	BU
1990 AA	—	—	—	—	0.50	0.75
1991 AA	—	—	—	—	0.50	0.75
1991 AB	—	—	—	—	0.50	0.75
1992 AA	—	—	—	—	0.50	0.75
1993 AA	—	—	—	—	0.50	0.75

KM# 392 5 PENCE
Copper-Nickel, 18 mm. **Ruler:** Elizabeth II **Obv:** Crowned head right **Obv. Designer:** Raphael Maklouf **Rev:** Golf clubs and ball

Date	Mintage	F	VF	XF	Unc	BU
1994 AA	—	—	—	—	0.50	0.75
1995 AA	—	—	—	—	0.50	0.75

KM# 392a 5 PENCE
3.2500 g., 0.9250 Silver .0967 oz. ASW, 18 mm. **Ruler:** Elizabeth II **Obv:** Crowned head right **Obv. Designer:** Raphael Maklouf **Rev:** Golf clubs and ball

Date	Mintage	F	VF	XF	Unc	BU
1994 Proof	Est. 25,000	Value: 10.00				

KM# 392b 5 PENCE
3.2500 g., 0.9170 Gold .0958 oz. AGW, 18 mm. **Ruler:** Elizabeth II **Obv:** Crowned head right **Obv. Designer:** Raphael Maklouf **Rev:** Golf clubs and ball

Date	Mintage	F	VF	XF	Unc	BU
1994 Proof	10,000	Value: 75.00				

KM# 392c 5 PENCE
3.2500 g., 0.9500 Platinum .0992 oz. APW, 18 mm. **Ruler:** Elizabeth II **Obv:** Crowned head right **Obv. Designer:** Raphael Maklouf **Rev:** Golf clubs and ball

Date	Mintage	F	VF	XF	Unc	BU
1994 Proof	3,500	Value: 150				

KM# 590 5 PENCE
Copper-Nickel, 18 mm. **Ruler:** Elizabeth II **Subject:** Sports **Obv:** Crowned head right **Obv. Designer:** Raphael Maklouf **Rev:** Golfer within sprigs

Date	Mintage	F	VF	XF	Unc	BU
1996 AA	—	—	—	—	0.50	0.75
1997 AA	—	—	—	—	0.50	0.75

KM# 590a 5 PENCE
3.2500 g., 0.9250 Silver .0967 oz. ASW, 18 mm. **Ruler:** Elizabeth II **Subject:** Sports **Obv:** Crowned head right **Obv. Designer:** Raphael Maklouf **Rev:** Golfer within sprigs

Date	Mintage	F	VF	XF	Unc	BU
1996 Proof	—	Value: 10.00				

KM# 902.1 5 PENCE
Copper-Nickel, 18 mm. **Ruler:** Elizabeth II **Obv:** Head with tiara right **Obv. Designer:** Ian Rank-Broadley **Rev:** Golfer within sprigs

Date	Mintage	F	VF	XF	Unc	BU
1998 AA	—	—	—	—	0.50	0.75

KM# 902.2 5 NEW PENCE
Copper Nickel, 18 mm. **Ruler:** Elizabeth II **Obv:** Head with tiara right with small triskeles dividing legend **Obv. Designer:** Ian Rank-Broadley **Rev:** Golpher within sprigs

Date	Mintage	F	VF	XF	Unc	BU
1998PM AA	—	—	—	—	0.50	—
1999PM AA	—	—	—	—	0.50	—

KM# 1038 5 PENCE
3.2400 g., Copper-Nickel, 18 mm. **Ruler:** Elizabeth II **Obv:** Head with tiara right **Obv. Designer:** Ian Rank-Broadley **Rev:** Gaut's Cross **Edge:** Reeded

Date	Mintage	F	VF	XF	Unc	BU
2000 AA	—	—	—	—	0.75	1.00
2000 AB	—	—	—	—	0.75	1.00
2000 AC	—	—	—	—	0.75	1.00

KM# 23 10 NEW PENCE
11.5000 g., Copper-Nickel, 28.5 mm. **Ruler:** Elizabeth II **Obv:** Young bust right **Obv. Designer:** Arnold Machin **Rev:** Triskeles **Rev. Designer:** Christopher Ironside

Date	Mintage	F	VF	XF	Unc	BU
1971	100,000	—	—	0.20	0.50	1.00
1971 Proof	10,000	Value: 3.50				
1972	1,000	—	—	—	20.00	22.50
1973	1,000	—	—	—	20.00	22.50
1974	1,000	—	—	—	20.00	22.50
1975	1,500,000	—	—	0.20	0.40	0.75

KM# 23a 10 NEW PENCE
13.0000 g., 0.9250 Silver .3866 oz. ASW, 28.5 mm. **Ruler:** Elizabeth II **Obv:** Young bust right **Obv. Designer:** Arnold Machin **Rev:** Triskeles **Rev. Designer:** Christopher Ironside

Date	Mintage	F	VF	XF	Unc	BU
1975	20,000	—	—	—	9.00	10.00

KM# 23b 10 NEW PENCE
25.0000 g., 0.9500 Platinum .7636 oz. APW, 28.5 mm. **Ruler:** Elizabeth II **Obv:** Young bust right **Obv. Designer:** Arnold Machin **Rev:** Triskeles **Rev. Designer:** Christopher Ironside

Date	Mintage	F	VF	XF	Unc	BU
1975 Proof	600	Value: 1,000				

KM# 36.1a 10 PENCE
13.0000 g., 0.9250 Silver .3866 oz. ASW, 28.5 mm. **Ruler:** Elizabeth II **Obv:** Young bust right **Obv. Designer:** Arnold Machin **Rev:** Triskeles on map **Rev. Designer:** Christopher Ironside

Date	Mintage	F	VF	XF	Unc	BU
1976	20,000	—	—	—	9.00	10.00
1977 Proof	10,000	Value: 10.00				
1978	10,000	—	—	—	9.00	10.00
1979 (t) Proof	10,000	Value: 10.00				

KM# 36.1b 10 PENCE
25.0000 g., 0.9500 Platinum .7636 oz. APW, 28.5 mm. **Ruler:** Elizabeth II **Obv:** Young bust right **Obv. Designer:** Arnold Machin **Rev:** Triskeles on map **Rev. Designer:** Christopher Ironside

Date	Mintage	F	VF	XF	Unc	BU
1976 Proof	600	Value: 1,000				
1978 Proof	600	Value: 1,000				
1979 (t) Proof	500	Value: 1,000				

KM# 36.1 10 PENCE
11.5000 g., Copper-Nickel, 28.5 mm. **Ruler:** Elizabeth II **Obv:** Young bust right **Obv. Designer:** Arnold Machin **Rev:** Triskeles on map **Rev. Designer:** Christopher Ironside **Note:** Mintmark: PM on obverse and reverse.

Date	Mintage	F	VF	XF	Unc	BU
1976	2,800,000	—	—	0.20	0.80	1.00
1977	—	—	—	0.20	0.80	1.00
1978	—	—	—	0.20	0.80	1.00
1978 Proof	—	Value: 2.00				
1979(t) AA	—	—	—	0.20	0.80	1.00
1979(t) AB	—	—	—	0.20	0.80	1.00

KM# 36.2 10 PENCE
Copper-Nickel, 28.5 mm. **Ruler:** Elizabeth II **Obv:** Young bust right **Obv. Designer:** Arnold Machin **Rev:** Triskeles on map **Rev. Designer:** Christopher Ironside **Note:** Mintmark: PM on obverse only.

Date	Mintage	F	VF	XF	Unc	BU
1976	Inc. above	—	—	0.20	1.00	1.25
1977	—	—	—	0.20	1.00	1.25

KM# 62 10 PENCE
11.5000 g., Copper-Nickel, 28.5 mm. **Ruler:** Elizabeth II **Obv:** Young bust right **Obv. Designer:** Arnold Machin **Rev:** Falcon within design **Rev. Designer:** Leslie Lindsay

Date	Mintage	F	VF	XF	Unc	BU
1980 AA	—	—	—	0.25	1.00	2.00
1980 AB	—	—	—	0.25	1.00	2.00
1980PM DD Proof	—	Value: 2.50				
1981 AA	—	—	—	0.25	1.00	2.00
1981 DD Proof	—	Value: 2.50				
1982 AA	—	—	—	0.25	1.00	2.00
1982 AB	—	—	—	0.25	1.00	2.00
1982 AB(b)	—	—	—	0.25	1.00	2.00
1982 AC	—	—	—	0.25	1.00	2.00
1982 AD	—	—	—	0.25	1.00	2.00
1982 (b) Proof	25,000	Value: 2.50				
1983 AA	—	—	—	0.25	1.00	2.00
1983 AB	—	—	—	0.25	1.00	2.00
1983 AC	—	—	—	0.25	1.00	2.00
1983 AD	—	—	—	0.25	1.00	2.00

KM# 62a 10 PENCE
13.0000 g., 0.5000 Silver .2090 oz. ASW, 28.5 mm. **Ruler:** Elizabeth II **Obv:** Young bust right **Obv. Designer:** Arnold Machin **Rev:** Falcon within design **Rev. Designer:** Leslie Lindsay

Date	Mintage	F	VF	XF	Unc	BU
1980 Proof	10,000	Value: 10.00				

KM# 62b 10 PENCE
13.0000 g., 0.9250 Silver .3866 oz. ASW, 28.5 mm. **Ruler:** Elizabeth II **Obv:** Young bust right **Obv. Designer:** Arnold Machin **Rev:** Falcon within design **Rev. Designer:** Leslie Lindsay

Date	Mintage	F	VF	XF	Unc	BU
1981 Proof	—	Value: 10.00				
1982 Proof	10,000	Value: 10.00				
1983 Proof	5,000	Value: 12.50				

KM# 62c 10 PENCE
22.0000 g., 0.9170 Gold .6486 oz. AGW, 28.5 mm. **Ruler:** Elizabeth II **Obv:** Young bust right **Obv. Designer:** Arnold Machin **Rev:** Falcon within design **Rev. Designer:** Leslie Lindsay

Date	Mintage	F	VF	XF	Unc	BU
1980 Proof	300	Value: 465				
1982 (b) Proof	500	Value: 465				
1983 Proof	—	Value: 465				

KM# 62d 10 PENCE

25.0000 g., 0.9500 Platinum .7636 oz. APW, 28.5 mm. **Ruler:** Elizabeth II **Obv:** Young bust right **Obv. Designer:** Arnold Machin **Rev:** Falcon within design **Rev. Designer:** Leslie Lindsay

Date	Mintage	F	VF	XF	Unc	BU
1980 Proof	500	Value: 1,000				
1982 (b) Proof	500	Value: 1,000				
1983 Proof	—	Value: 1,000				

KM# 115 10 PENCE

11.5000 g., Copper-Nickel, 28.5 mm. **Ruler:** Elizabeth II **Subject:** Quincentenary of the College of Arms **Obv:** Young bust right **Obv. Designer:** Arnold Machin **Rev:** Loagthyn ram within shield **Rev. Designer:** Leslie Lindsay

Date	Mintage	F	VF	XF	Unc	BU
1984 AA	—	—	—	0.25	1.00	1.25
1984 AB	—	—	—	0.25	1.00	1.25
1984 AC	—	—	—	0.25	1.00	1.25
1984 AD	—	—	—	0.25	1.00	1.25
1984 AE	—	—	—	0.25	1.00	1.25
1984 AF	—	—	—	0.25	1.00	1.25
1984 AG	—	—	—	0.25	1.00	1.25

KM# 115a 10 PENCE

Silver, 28.5 mm. **Ruler:** Elizabeth II **Obv:** Young bust right **Obv. Designer:** Arnold Machin **Rev:** Loagthyn ram within shield **Rev. Designer:** Leslie Lindsay

Date	Mintage	F	VF	XF	Unc	BU
1984 Proof	—	Value: 10.00				

KM# 115b 10 PENCE

22.0000 g., 0.9170 Gold .6484 oz. AGW, 28.5 mm. **Ruler:** Elizabeth II **Obv:** Young bust right **Obv. Designer:** Arnold Machin **Rev:** Loagthyn ram within shield **Rev. Designer:** Leslie Lindsay

Date	Mintage	F	VF	XF	Unc	BU
1984 Proof	150	Value: 700				

KM# 146 10 PENCE

11.5000 g., Copper-Nickel, 28.5 mm. **Ruler:** Elizabeth II **Obv:** Crowned head right **Obv. Designer:** Raphael Maklouf **Rev:** Loagthyn ram within designed shield **Rev. Designer:** Leslie Lindsay

Date	Mintage	F	VF	XF	Unc	BU
1985(w) AA	—	—	—	0.20	0.80	1.00
1985(w) AB	—	—	—	0.20	0.80	1.00
1985 Proof	50,000	Value: 3.00				
1986 AA	—	—	—	0.20	0.80	1.00
1987 AA	—	—	—	0.20	0.80	1.00

KM# 146a 10 PENCE

13.0000 g., 0.9250 Silver .3866 oz. ASW, 28.5 mm. **Ruler:** Elizabeth II **Obv:** Crowned head right **Obv. Designer:** Raphael Maklouf **Rev:** Loagthyn ram within designed shield **Rev. Designer:** Leslie Lindsay

Date	Mintage	F	VF	XF	Unc	BU
1985 Proof	10,000	Value: 18.00				

KM# 146b 10 PENCE

22.0000 g., 0.9170 Gold .6484 oz. AGW, 28.5 mm. **Ruler:** Elizabeth II **Obv:** Crowned head right **Obv. Designer:** Raphael Maklouf **Rev:** Loagthyn ram within designed shield **Rev. Designer:** Leslie Lindsay

Date	Mintage	F	VF	XF	Unc	BU
1985 Proof	300	Value: 500				

KM# 146c 10 PENCE

25.0000 g., 0.9500 Platinum .7636 oz. APW, 28.5 mm. **Ruler:** Elizabeth II **Obv:** Crowned head right **Obv. Designer:** Raphael Maklouf **Rev:** Loagthyn ram within designed shield **Rev. Designer:** Leslie Lindsay

Date	Mintage	F	VF	XF	Unc	BU
1985 Proof	200	Value: 1,000				

KM# 210 10 PENCE

11.5000 g., Copper-Nickel, 28.5 mm. **Ruler:** Elizabeth II **Obv:** Crowned head right **Obv. Designer:** Raphael Maklouf **Rev:** Island and portcullis on globe

Date	Mintage	F	VF	XF	Unc	BU
1988 AA	—	—	—	—	0.75	1.00
1989 AA	—	—	—	—	0.75	1.00
1990 AA	—	—	—	—	0.75	1.00
1991 AA	—	—	—	—	0.75	1.00
1991 AB	—	—	—	—	0.75	1.00
1991 AC	—	—	—	—	0.75	1.00
1992 AA	—	—	—	—	0.75	1.00

KM# 337 10 PENCE

Copper-Nickel, 24.5 mm. **Ruler:** Elizabeth II **Obv:** Crowned head right **Obv. Designer:** Raphael Maklouf **Rev:** Triskeles and value **Note:** Varieties exist.

Date	Mintage	F	VF	XF	Unc	BU
1992PM AA	—	—	—	—	0.75	1.00
1992PM AB	—	—	—	—	0.75	1.00
1992PM AC	—	—	—	—	0.75	1.00
1992PM AD	—	—	—	—	0.75	1.00
1992PM AE	—	—	—	—	1.00	1.25
1993PM AA	—	—	—	—	0.75	1.00
1994PM AA	—	—	—	—	0.75	1.00
1995PM AA	—	—	—	—	0.75	1.00

KM# 337a 10 PENCE

8.0457 g., 0.9250 Silver .2392 oz. ASW, 24.5 mm. **Ruler:** Elizabeth II **Obv:** Crowned head right **Obv. Designer:** Raphael Maklouf **Rev:** Triskeles and value

Date	Mintage	F	VF	XF	Unc	BU
1992PM D Proof	—	Value: 13.50				

KM# 337b 10 PENCE

13.6158 g., 0.9170 Gold .4013 oz. AGW, 24.5 mm. **Ruler:** Elizabeth II **Obv:** Crowned head right **Obv. Designer:** Raphael Maklouf **Rev:** Triskeles and value

Date	Mintage	F	VF	XF	Unc	BU
1992 Proof	—	Value: 285				

KM# 337c 10 PENCE

15.4725 g., 0.9500 Platinum .4725 oz. APW, 24.5 mm. **Ruler:** Elizabeth II **Obv:** Crowned head right **Obv. Designer:** Raphael Maklouf **Rev:** Triskeles and value

Date	Mintage	F	VF	XF	Unc	BU
1992 Proof	—	Value: 625				

KM# 591 10 PENCE

Copper-Nickel, 24.5 mm. **Ruler:** Elizabeth II **Subject:** Sports **Obv:** Crowned head right **Obv. Designer:** Raphael Maklouf **Rev:** Sailboat divides wreath

Date	Mintage	F	VF	XF	Unc	BU
1996 AA	—	—	—	—	1.00	1.50
1997 AA	—	—	—	—	1.00	1.50

KM# 591a 10 PENCE

8.0457 g., 0.9250 Silver .2392 oz. ASW, 24.5 mm. **Ruler:** Elizabeth II **Subject:** Sports **Obv:** Crowned head right **Obv. Designer:** Raphael Maklouf **Rev:** Sailboat divides wreath

Date	Mintage	F	VF	XF	Unc	BU
1996 Proof	—	Value: 22.50				

KM# 903.2 10 PENCE

Copper-Nickel, 24.5 mm. **Ruler:** Elizabeth II **Obv:** Head with tiara right with small triskeles dividing legend **Obv. Designer:** Ian Rank-Broadley **Rev:** Sailboat divides wreath

Date	Mintage	F	VF	XF	Unc	BU
1998PM AA	—	—	—	—	1.00	1.50
1999PM AA	—	—	—	—	1.00	1.50

KM# 903.1 10 PENCE

Copper-Nickel, 24.5 mm. **Ruler:** Elizabeth II **Obv:** Head with tiara right **Obv. Designer:** Ian Rank-Broadley **Rev:** Sailboat divides wreath

Date	Mintage	F	VF	XF	Unc	BU
1998PM AA	—	—	—	—	1.00	1.50

KM# 1039 10 PENCE

3.2500 g., Copper-Nickel, 24.5 mm. **Ruler:** Elizabeth II **Obv:** Head with tiara right **Obv. Designer:** Ian Rank-Broadley **Rev:** Cathedral **Edge:** Reeded

Date	Mintage	F	VF	XF	Unc	BU
2000PM AA	—	—	—	—	1.00	1.50

KM# 90 20 PENCE

5.0000 g., Copper-Nickel, 21.4 mm. **Ruler:** Elizabeth II **Subject:** Medieval Norse History **Obv:** Young bust right **Obv. Designer:** Arnold Machin **Rev:** Ship within small circle within artistic design with viking helmet above **Rev. Designer:** Leslie Lindsay **Shape:** 7-sided

Date	Mintage	F	VF	XF	Unc	BU
1982 AA	30,000	—	—	0.35	1.00	1.50
1982 AB	—	—	—	0.35	1.00	1.50
1982 AB(b)	—	—	0.50	1.00	5.00	—
1982 AC	—	—	—	0.35	1.00	1.50
1982 AD	—	—	—	0.35	1.00	1.50
1982 (b) Proof	25,000	Value: 6.00				
1982 BB Proof	—	Value: 1.50				
1982 BC Proof	—	Value: 1.50				
1983 AA	—	—	—	0.35	1.00	1.50

KM# 90a 20 PENCE

6.0000 g., 0.9250 Silver .1784 oz. ASW, 21.4 mm. **Ruler:** Elizabeth II **Subject:** Medieval Norse History **Obv:** Young bust right **Obv. Designer:** Arnold Machin **Rev:** Ship within small circle of design with Viking helmet above **Rev. Designer:** Leslie Lindsay **Shape:** 7-sided

Date	Mintage	F	VF	XF	Unc	BU
1982 Proof	15,000	Value: 10.00				
1982 (b) Proof	10,000	Value: 10.00				
1983 Proof	5,000	Value: 15.00				

KM# 90b 20 PENCE

10.00 g., 0.9170 Gold .2948 oz. AGW, 21.4 mm. **Ruler:** Elizabeth II **Subject:** Medieval Norse History **Obv:** Young bust right **Obv. Designer:** Arnold Machin **Rev:** Ship within small circle of design with Viking helmet above **Rev. Designer:** Leslie Lindsay **Shape:** 7-sided

Date	Mintage	F	VF	XF	Unc	BU
1982 Proof	1,500	Value: 210				
1982 (b) Proof	500	Value: 225				
1983 Proof	—	Value: 225				

KM# 90c 20 PENCE

11.30 g., 0.9500 Platinum .3452 oz. APW, 21.4 mm. **Ruler:** Elizabeth II **Subject:** Medieval Norse History **Obv:** Young bust right **Obv. Designer:** Arnold Machin **Rev:** Ship within small circle of design with Viking helmet above **Rev. Designer:** Leslie Lindsay **Shape:** 7-sided

Date	Mintage	F	VF	XF	Unc	BU
1982 Proof	250	Value: 500				
1982 (b) Proof	500	Value: 500				
1983 Proof	—	Value: 500				

KM# 116 20 PENCE

5.0000 g., Copper-Nickel, 21.4 mm. **Ruler:** Elizabeth II **Subject:** Quincentenary of the College of Arms **Obv:** Young bust right **Obv. Designer:** Arnold Machin **Rev:** Atlantic herring within designed shield **Rev. Designer:** Leslie Lindsay **Shape:** 7-sided

Date	Mintage	F	VF	XF	Unc	BU
1984 AA	—	—	—	0.35	1.00	1.50

KM# 116a 20 PENCE

Silver, 21.4 mm. **Ruler:** Elizabeth II **Subject:** Quincentenary of the College of Arms **Obv:** Young bust right **Obv. Designer:** Arnold Machin **Rev:** Atlantic herring within designed shield **Rev. Designer:** Leslie Lindsay **Shape:** 7-sided

Date	Mintage	F	VF	XF	Unc	BU
1984 Proof	—	Value: 20.00				

KM# 116b 20 PENCE

5.0000 g., 0.9170 Gold .1474 oz. AGW, 21.4 mm. **Ruler:** Elizabeth II **Subject:** Quincentenary of the College of Arms **Obv:** Young bust right **Obv. Designer:** Arnold Machin **Rev:** Atlantic herring within designed shield **Rev. Designer:** Leslie Lindsay **Shape:** 7-sided

Date	Mintage	F	VF	XF	Unc	BU
1984 Proof	150	Value: 175				

KM# 147 20 PENCE

5.0000 g., Copper-Nickel, 21.4 mm. **Ruler:** Elizabeth II **Obv:** Crowned head right **Obv. Designer:** Raphael Maklouf **Rev:** Atlantic herring within designed shield **Rev. Designer:** Leslie Lindsay **Shape:** 7-sided

Date	Mintage	F	VF	XF	Unc	BU
1985(w) AA	—	—	—	0.35	1.00	1.50
1985 Proof	50,000	Value: 3.00				
1986 AA	—	—	—	0.35	1.00	1.50
1986 AB	—	—	—	0.35	1.00	1.50
1986 AC	—	—	—	0.35	1.00	1.50
1987 AA	—	—	—	0.35	1.00	1.50

KM# 147a 20 PENCE

5.0000 g., 0.9250 Silver .1487 oz. ASW, 21.4 mm. **Ruler:** Elizabeth II **Obv:** Crowned head right **Obv. Designer:** Raphael Maklouf **Rev:** Atlantic herring within designed shield **Rev. Designer:** Leslie Lindsay **Shape:** 7-sided

Date	Mintage	F	VF	XF	Unc	BU
1985 Proof	10,000	Value: 8.00				

KM# 147b 20 PENCE

5.0000 g., 0.9170 Gold .1474 oz. AGW, 21.4 mm. **Ruler:** Elizabeth II **Obv:** Crowned head right **Obv. Designer:** Raphael Maklouf **Rev:** Atlantic herring within designed shield **Rev. Designer:** Leslie Lindsay **Shape:** 7-sided

Date	Mintage	F	VF	XF	Unc	BU
1985 Proof	300	Value: 120				

KM# 147c 20 PENCE

5.0000 g., 0.9500 Platinum .1527 oz. APW, 21.4 mm. **Ruler:** Elizabeth II **Obv:** Crowned head right **Obv. Designer:** Raphael Maklouf **Rev:** Atlantic herring within designed shield **Rev. Designer:** Leslie Lindsay **Shape:** 7-sided

Date	Mintage	F	VF	XF	Unc	BU
1985 Proof	200	Value: 225				

KM# 211 20 PENCE

5.0000 g., Copper-Nickel, 21.4 mm. **Ruler:** Elizabeth II **Obv:** Crowned head right **Obv. Designer:** Raphael Maklouf **Rev:** Combine within sprigs **Shape:** 7-sided

Date	Mintage	F	VF	XF	Unc	BU
1988 AA	—	—	—	—	1.00	1.50
1989 AA	—	—	—	—	1.00	1.50
1990 AA	—	—	—	—	1.00	1.50
1991 AA	—	—	—	—	1.00	1.50
1992 AA	—	—	—	—	1.00	1.50

KM# 391 20 PENCE

5.0000 g., Copper-Nickel, 21.4 mm. **Ruler:** Elizabeth II **Obv:** Crowned head right **Obv. Designer:** Raphael Maklouf **Rev:** Combine within sprigs **Shape:** 7-sided **Note:** Obverse and reverse design revised with border.

Date	Mintage	F	VF	XF	Unc	BU
1993 AA	—	—	—	—	1.00	1.50
1994 AA	—	—	—	—	1.00	1.50
1995 AA	—	—	—	—	1.00	1.50

KM# 592 20 PENCE

5.0000 g., Copper-Nickel, 21.4 mm. **Ruler:** Elizabeth II **Subject:** Sports **Obv:** Crowned head right **Obv. Designer:** Raphael Maklouf **Rev:** Race cars within sprigs **Shape:** 7-sided

Date	Mintage	F	VF	XF	Unc	BU
1996 AA	—	—	—	—	1.25	1.75
1997 AA	—	—	—	—	1.25	1.75

KM# 904.1 20 PENCE

5.0000 g., Copper-Nickel, 21.4 mm. **Ruler:** Elizabeth II **Obv:** Head with tiara right with small triskeles dividing legend **Obv. Legend:** "ELIZABETH II" **Obv. Designer:** Ian Rank-Broadley **Rev:** Race cars above sprigs **Shape:** 7-sided **Note:** Prev. KM#904.

Date	Mintage	F	VF	XF	Unc	BU
1998PM AA	—	—	—	—	1.25	1.75
1999PM AA	—	—	—	—	1.25	1.75

KM# 904.2 20 PENCE

5.0000 g., Copper Nickel, 21.4 mm. **Ruler:** Elizabeth II **Obv:** Head with tiara right with small triskeles dividing legend **Obv. Legend:** ISLE OF MAN **Obv. Designer:** Ian Rank-Broadley **Rev:** Race cars above sprigs

Date	Mintage	F	VF	XF	Unc	BU
1999PM AA	—	—	—	—	1.25	1.75

KM# 1040 20 PENCE

5.0000 g., Copper-Nickel, 21.4 mm. **Ruler:** Elizabeth II **Subject:** Rushen Abbey **Obv:** Head with tiara right **Obv. Designer:** Ian Rank-Broadley **Rev:** Monk writing **Edge:** Plain **Shape:** 7-sided

Date	Mintage	F	VF	XF	Unc	BU
2000 AA	—	—	—	—	1.50	2.00

KM# 25 25 PENCE

Copper-Nickel, 38.5 mm. **Ruler:** Elizabeth II **Subject:** 25th Wedding Anniversary **Obv:** Young bust right **Obv. Designer:** Arnold Machin **Rev:** Tilted shields divide date within rope wreath **Rev. Designer:** Stuart Devlin **Note:** Struck at the Royal Canadian Mint.

Date	Mintage	F	VF	XF	Unc	BU
1972	70,000	—	—	—	4.50	5.00

KM# 25a 25 PENCE

28.2800 g., 0.9250 Silver .8411 oz. ASW, 38.5 mm. **Ruler:** Elizabeth II **Obv:** Young bust right **Obv. Designer:** Arnold Machin **Rev:** Tilted shields divide dates within rope wreath **Rev. Designer:** Stuart Devlin **Note:** Struck at the Royal Canadian Mint.

Date	Mintage	F	VF	XF	Unc	BU
1972 Proof	15,000	Value: 12.50				

KM# 31 25 PENCE

Copper-Nickel, 38.5 mm. **Ruler:** Elizabeth II **Obv:** Young bust right **Obv. Designer:** Arnold Machin **Rev:** Manx cat **Rev. Designer:** Christopher Ironside

Date	Mintage	F	VF	XF	Unc	BU
1975	35,000	—	—	—	6.00	7.50

KM# 31a 25 PENCE

28.2800 g., 0.9250 Silver .8411 oz. ASW, 38.5 mm. **Ruler:** Elizabeth II **Obv:** Young bust right **Obv. Designer:** Arnold Machin **Rev:** Manx cat **Rev. Designer:** Christopher Ironside

Date	Mintage	F	VF	XF	Unc	BU
1975	—	—	—	—	12.50	13.50
1975 Proof	30,000	Value: 15.00				

KM# 24 50 NEW PENCE

13.5000 g., Copper-Nickel, 30 mm. **Ruler:** Elizabeth II **Obv:** Young bust right **Obv. Designer:** Arnold Machin **Rev:** Sailing Viking ship **Rev. Designer:** Christopher Ironside **Shape:** 7-sided

Date	Mintage	F	VF	XF	Unc	BU
1971	100,000	—	—	1.00	5.00	7.50
1971 Proof	10,000	Value: 8.00				
1972	1,000	—	—	—	27.50	32.50
1973	1,000	—	—	—	27.50	32.50
1974	1,000	—	—	—	27.50	32.50
1975	227,000	—	—	1.00	5.00	7.50

KM# 24a 50 NEW PENCE

15.5000 g., 0.9250 Silver .4610 oz. ASW, 30 mm. **Ruler:** Elizabeth II **Obv:** Young bust right **Obv. Designer:** Arnold Machin **Rev:** Sailing Viking ship **Rev. Designer:** Christopher Ironside **Shape:** 7-sided

Date	Mintage	F	VF	XF	Unc	BU
1975	20,000	—	—	—	12.00	13.00

KM# 24b 50 NEW PENCE

30.4000 g., 0.9500 Platinum .9286 oz. APW, 30 mm. **Ruler:** Elizabeth II **Obv:** Young bust right **Obv. Designer:** Arnold Machin **Rev:** Sailing Viking ship **Rev. Designer:** Christopher Ironside **Shape:** 7-sided

Date	Mintage	F	VF	XF	Unc	BU
1975 Proof	600	Value: 1,225				

KM# 39 50 PENCE

13.5000 g., Copper-Nickel, 30 mm. **Ruler:** Elizabeth II **Obv:** Young bust right **Obv. Designer:** Arnold Machin **Rev:** Sailing Viking ship **Shape:** 7-sided

Date	Mintage	F	VF	XF	Unc	BU
1976	250,000	—	—	0.75	2.00	3.00
1977	50,000	—	—	0.75	2.50	3.50
1978	25,000	—	—	0.75	2.50	3.50
1978 Proof	—	Value: 4.50				
1979 (t)AA	—	—	—	0.75	3.00	4.00

KM# 39a 50 PENCE

15.5000 g., 0.9250 Silver .4610 oz. ASW, 30 mm. **Ruler:** Elizabeth II **Obv:** Young bust right **Obv. Designer:** Arnold Machin **Rev:** Sailing Viking ship **Shape:** 7-sided

Date	Mintage	F	VF	XF	Unc	BU
1976	20,000	—	—	—	12.00	13.00
1977 Proof	10,000	Value: 12.50				
1978	10,000	—	—	—	12.00	13.00
1979 (t) Proof	10,000	Value: 12.50				

KM# 39b 50 PENCE

30.4000 g., 0.9500 Platinum .9286 oz. APW, 30 mm. **Ruler:** Elizabeth II **Obv:** Young bust right **Obv. Designer:** Arnold Machin **Rev:** Sailing Viking ship **Shape:** 7-sided

Date	Mintage	F	VF	XF	Unc	BU
1976 Proof	600	Value: 1,225				
1978 Proof	600	Value: 1,225				
1979 (t) Proof	500	Value: 1,225				

KM# 51.1 50 PENCE

13.5000 g., Copper-Nickel, 30 mm. **Ruler:** Elizabeth II **Subject:** Manx Day of Tynwald, July 5 **Obv:** Young bust right **Obv. Designer:** Arnold Machin **Rev:** Viking ship **Edge:** Upright with obverse on top **Edge Lettering:** H.M Q.E-II ROYAL VISIT I.O.M. JULY 1979 **Shape:** 7-sided

Date	Mintage	F	VF	XF	Unc	BU
1979 AA	50,000	—	—	—	4.50	5.00
1979 AB	—	—	—	—	4.50	5.00

KM# 51.2 50 PENCE

13.5000 g., Copper-Nickel, 30 mm. **Ruler:** Elizabeth II **Obv:** Young bust right **Obv. Designer:** Arnold Machin **Rev:** Viking ship **Edge:** Lettering upright with reverse on top **Shape:** 7-sided

Date	Mintage	F	VF	XF	Unc	BU
1979 AA	—	—	—	—	4.50	5.00
1979 AB	—	—	—	—	4.50	5.00

KM# 51.3 50 PENCE

13.5000 g., Copper-Nickel, 30 mm. **Ruler:** Elizabeth II **Obv:** Young bust right **Obv. Designer:** Arnold Machin **Rev:** Viking ship **Note:** Inscription not centered in flat sections.

Date	Mintage	F	VF	XF	Unc	BU
1979 AA	—	—	—	—	4.50	5.00
1979 AB	—	—	—	—	4.50	5.00

KM# 51a 50 PENCE

15.5000 g., 0.9250 Silver .4610 oz. ASW, 30 mm. **Ruler:** Elizabeth II **Obv:** Young bust right **Obv. Designer:** Arnold Machin **Rev:** Viking ship **Shape:** 7-sided

Date	Mintage	F	VF	XF	Unc	BU
1979	10,000	—	—	—	10.00	12.00
1979 D Proof	5,000	Value: 15.00				
1979 E Proof	—	Value: 15.00				
1979 D Proof	5,000	Value: 15.00				

KM# 51b 50 PENCE

30.4000 g., 0.9500 Platinum .9286 oz. APW, 30 mm. **Ruler:** Elizabeth II **Subject:** Manx Millennium of Tynwald **Obv:** Young bust right **Obv. Designer:** Arnold Machin **Rev:** Viking ship **Edge:** H.M.Q.E. II ROYAL VISIT I.O.M. JULY 5, 1979

Date	Mintage	F	VF	XF	Unc	BU
1979 Proof	500	Value: 1,225				

KM# 53 50 PENCE

13.5000 g., Copper-Nickel, 30 mm. **Ruler:** Elizabeth II **Obv:** Young bust right **Obv. Designer:** Arnold Machin **Rev:** Odin's Raven, Point of Ayre lighthouse **Note:** Same as KM#51.1 with no edge lettering.

Date	Mintage	F	VF	XF	Unc	BU
1979 AA	—	—	—	—	3.00	4.00
1979 AB	—	—	—	—	3.00	4.00

KM# 53a 50 PENCE

15.5000 g., 0.9250 Silver .4610 oz. ASW, 30 mm. **Ruler:** Elizabeth II **Obv:** Young bust right **Rev:** Odin's Raven, Point of Ayre lighhouse

Date	Mintage	F	VF	XF	Unc	BU
1979	—	—	—	—	10.00	12.00
1979 Proof	—	Value: 15.00				

KM# 71 50 PENCE

13.5000 g., Copper-Nickel, 30 mm. **Ruler:** Elizabeth II **Subject:** Christmas 1980 **Obv:** Young bust right **Obv. Designer:** Arnold Machin **Rev:** Carriage pulled by horses, ship in background **Shape:** 7-sided

Date	Mintage	F	VF	XF	Unc	BU
1980 AA	30,000	—	—	—	2.50	3.50
1980 AB	—	—	—	—	2.50	3.50
1980 AC	—	—	—	—	2.50	3.50
1980 AD	—	—	—	—	2.50	3.50
1980PM BC	—	—	—	—	2.50	3.50

Note: Pobjoy called this item a "Diamond finish".

KM# 70b 50 PENCE

15.5000 g., 0.9250 Silver .4610 oz. ASW, 30 mm. **Ruler:** Elizabeth II **Obv:** Young bust right **Obv. Designer:** Arnold Machin **Rev:** Viking longship within design **Rev. Designer:** Leslie Lindsay **Shape:** 7-sided

Date	Mintage	F	VF	XF	Unc	BU
1981 Proof	—	Value: 17.50				
1983 Proof	5,000	Value: 17.50				

KM# 57 50 PENCE

15.5000 g., 0.9250 Silver .4610 oz. ASW, 30 mm. **Ruler:** Elizabeth II **Obv:** Young bust right **Obv. Designer:** Arnold Machin **Rev:** Christmas scene with stage coach **Note:** Mule.

Date	Mintage	F	VF	XF	Unc	BU
1980	—	—	—	—	—	—

KM# 70 50 PENCE

13.5000 g., Copper-Nickel, 30 mm. **Ruler:** Elizabeth II **Obv:** Young bust right **Obv. Designer:** Arnold Machin **Rev:** Viking longship within design **Rev. Designer:** Leslie Lindsay **Shape:** 7-sided

Date	Mintage	F	VF	XF	Unc	BU
1980 AA	10,000	—	—	1.00	5.00	7.50
1980PM DD Proof	—	Value: 8.00				
1981 AA	—	—	—	1.00	5.00	7.50
1980 AA	10,000	—	—	1.00	5.00	7.50
1982 (b)	—	—	—	1.00	5.00	7.50
1982 (b) Proof	25,000	Value: 8.00				
1983 AA	—	—	—	1.00	5.00	7.50
1983 AB	—	—	—	1.00	5.00	7.50
1984 AA	—	—	—	1.00	5.00	7.50
1980 AB	—	—	—	1.00	5.00	7.50
1982 AC	—	—	—	1.00	5.00	7.50

KM# 69 50 PENCE

13.5000 g., Copper-Nickel, 30 mm. **Ruler:** Elizabeth II **Obv:** Young bust right **Obv. Designer:** Arnold Machin **Edge Lettering:** ODINS RAVEN VIKING EXHIBN NEW YORK 1980 **Note:** Same as KM#51.1, different edge lettering.

Date	Mintage	F	VF	XF	Unc	BU
1980 AA	20,000	—	—	—	4.00	5.00
1980PM AB	—	—	—	—	4.00	5.00
1980PM AC	—	—	—	—	4.00	5.00

KM# 69a 50 PENCE

15.5000 g., 0.9250 Silver .4610 oz. ASW, 30 mm. **Ruler:** Elizabeth II **Obv:** Young bust right **Obv. Designer:** Arnold Machin

Date	Mintage	F	VF	XF	Unc	BU
1980	—	—	—	—	15.00	17.00
1980 Proof	5,000	Value: 20.00				

KM# 57a 50 PENCE

13.5000 g., Copper Nickel, 30 mm. **Ruler:** Elizabeth II **Subject:** Christmas **Obv:** Young bust right **Obv. Designer:** Arnold Machin **Rev:** Christmas scene with stagecoach **Shape:** 7-sided

Date	Mintage	F	VF	XF	Unc	BU
1980	—	—	—	—	50.00	55.00

KM# 69b 50 PENCE

26.0000 g., 0.9170 Gold .7666 oz. AGW, 30 mm. **Ruler:** Elizabeth II **Obv:** Young bust right **Obv. Designer:** Arnold Machin **Edge Lettering:** ODINS RAVEN VIKING EXHIBN NEW YORK 1980

Date	Mintage	F	VF	XF	Unc	BU
1980	250	—	—	—	600	650

KM# 70a 50 PENCE

15.5000 g., 0.5000 Silver .2491 oz. ASW, 30 mm. **Ruler:** Elizabeth II **Obv:** Young bust right **Obv. Designer:** Arnold Machin **Rev:** Viking longship within design **Shape:** 7-sided

Date	Mintage	F	VF	XF	Unc	BU
1982 (b) Proof	10,000	Value: 15.00				
1980 Proof	10,000	Value: 10.00				

KM# 69c 50 PENCE

30.4000 g., 0.9500 Platinum .9286 oz. APW, 30 mm. **Ruler:** Elizabeth II **Obv:** Young bust right **Obv. Designer:** Arnold Machin

Date	Mintage	F	VF	XF	Unc	BU
1980 Proof	50	Value: 1,275				

KM# 70c 50 PENCE

26.0000 g., 0.9170 Gold .7666 oz. AGW, 30 mm. **Ruler:** Elizabeth II **Obv:** Young bust right **Obv. Designer:** Arnold Machin **Rev:** Viking longship within design **Shape:** 7-sided

Date	Mintage	F	VF	XF	Unc	BU
1982 (b) Proof	500	Value: 550				
1983 Proof	—	Value: 550				
1980 Proof	300	Value: 550				

KM# 71a 50 PENCE

15.5000 g., 0.9250 Silver .4610 oz. ASW, 30 mm. **Ruler:** Elizabeth II **Obv:** Young bust right **Obv. Designer:** Arnold Machin **Rev:** Carriage pulled by horses, ship in background **Shape:** 7-sided

Date	Mintage	F	VF	XF	Unc	BU
1980 D Proof	5,000	Value: 12.50				
1980PM D Proof	5,000	Value: 12.50				

KM# 70d 50 PENCE

30.4000 g., 0.9500 Platinum .9286 oz. APW, 30 mm. **Ruler:** Elizabeth II **Obv:** Young bust right **Obv. Designer:** Arnold Machin **Rev:** Viking longship within design **Shape:** 7-sided

Date	Mintage	F	VF	XF	Unc	BU
1982 (b) Proof	500	Value: 1,225				
1983 Proof	—	Value: 1,225				
1980 Proof	500	Value: 1,225				

KM# 71b 50 PENCE

26.0000 g., 0.9170 Gold .7666 oz. AGW, 30 mm. **Ruler:** Elizabeth II **Subject:** Christmas 1980 **Obv:** Young bust right **Obv. Designer:** Arnold Machin **Rev:** Carriage pulled by horses, ship in background **Shape:** 7-sided

Date	Mintage	F	VF	XF	Unc	BU
1980 Proof	250	Value: 600				

KM# 71c 50 PENCE

30.4000 g., 0.9500 Platinum .9286 oz. APW, 30 mm. **Ruler:** Elizabeth II **Obv:** Young bust right **Obv. Designer:** Arnold Machin **Rev:** Carriage pulled by horses, ship in background **Shape:** 7-sided

Date	Mintage	F	VF	XF	Unc	BU
1980 Proof	50	Value: 1,275				

KM# 84 50 PENCE

13.5000 g., Copper-Nickel, 30 mm. **Ruler:** Elizabeth II **Subject:** Christmas 1981 **Obv:** Young bust right **Obv. Designer:** Arnold Machin **Rev:** Boat, standing figures and value **Shape:** 7-sided

Date	Mintage	F	VF	XF	Unc	BU
1981PM BC Proof	Inc. above	Value: 7.50				
1981PM BB Proof	30,000	Value: 7.50				
1981 AA	30,000	—	—	—	3.00	4.00
1981 AB	Inc. above	—	—	—	3.00	4.00
1981 BB Proof	—	Value: 7.50				

KM# 83 50 PENCE

13.5000 g., Copper-Nickel, 30 mm. **Ruler:** Elizabeth II **Subject:** Tourist Trophy Motorcycle Races **Obv:** Young bust right **Obv. Designer:** Arnold Machin **Rev:** Motorcyclist within sprigs **Shape:** 7-sided

Date	Mintage	F	VF	XF	Unc	BU
1981 AA	30,000	—	—	—	3.00	4.00
1981 AB	Inc. above	—	—	—	3.00	4.00
1981PM BB	—	—	—	—	3.00	4.00

KM# 83a 50 PENCE

15.5000 g., 0.9250 Silver .4610 oz. ASW, 30 mm. **Ruler:** Elizabeth II **Subject:** Tourist Trophy Motorcycle Races **Obv:** Young bust right **Obv. Designer:** Arnold Machin **Rev:** Motorcyclist within sprigs **Shape:** 7-sided

Date	Mintage	F	VF	XF	Unc	BU
1981PM D Proof	5,000	Value: 15.00				

KM# 83b 50 PENCE

26.0000 g., 0.9170 Gold .7666 oz. AGW, 30 mm. **Ruler:** Elizabeth II **Subject:** Tourist Trophy Motorcycle Races **Obv:** Young bust right **Obv. Designer:** Arnold Machin **Rev:** Motorcyclist within sprigs **Shape:** 7-sided

Date	Mintage	F	VF	XF	Unc	BU
1981 Proof	250	Value: 600				

KM# 83c 50 PENCE

30.4000 g., 0.9500 Platinum .9286 oz. APW, 30 mm. **Ruler:** Elizabeth II **Subject:** Tourist Trophy Motorcycle Races **Obv:** Young bust right **Obv. Designer:** Arnold Machin **Rev:** Motorcyclist within sprigs **Shape:** 7-sided

Date	Mintage	F	VF	XF	Unc	BU
1981 Proof	50	Value: 1,275				

KM# 84a 50 PENCE

15.5000 g., 0.9250 Silver .4610 oz. ASW, 30 mm. **Ruler:** Elizabeth II **Subject:** Christmas 1981 **Obv:** Young bust right **Obv. Designer:** Arnold Machin **Rev:** Boat, standing figures and value **Shape:** 7-sided

Date	Mintage	F	VF	XF	Unc	BU
1981PM D Proof	5,000	Value: 12.50				

KM# 84b 50 PENCE

26.0000 g., 0.9170 Gold .7666 oz. AGW, 30 mm. **Ruler:** Elizabeth II **Subject:** Christmas 1981 **Obv:** Young bust right **Obv. Designer:** Arnold Machin **Rev:** Boat, standing figures and value **Shape:** 7-sided

Date	Mintage	F	VF	XF	Unc	BU
1981 Proof	250	Value: 600				

KM# 84c 50 PENCE

30.4000 g., 0.9500 Platinum .9286 oz. APW, 30 mm. **Ruler:** Elizabeth II **Subject:** Christmas 1981 **Obv:** Young bust right **Obv. Designer:** Arnold Machin **Rev:** Boat, standing figures and value **Shape:** 7-sided

Date	Mintage	F	VF	XF	Unc	BU
1981 Proof	—	Value: 1,275				

KM# 101 50 PENCE

13.5000 g., Copper-Nickel, 30 mm. **Ruler:** Elizabeth II **Subject:** Tourist Trophy Motorcycle Races **Obv:** Young bust right **Obv. Designer:** Arnold Machin **Rev:** Motorcyclist within sprigs **Shape:** 7-sided

Date	Mintage	F	VF	XF	Unc	BU
1982 AA	30,000	—	—	—	3.00	4.00
1982 Proof	—	Value: 7.50				

KM# 101a 50 PENCE

15.5000 g., 0.9250 Silver .4610 oz. ASW, 30 mm. **Ruler:** Elizabeth II **Subject:** Tourist Trophy Motorcycle Races **Obv:** Young bust right **Obv. Designer:** Arnold Machin **Rev:** Motorcyclist within sprigs **Shape:** 7-sided

Date	Mintage	F	VF	XF	Unc	BU
1982 Proof	5,000	Value: 15.00				

KM# 101b 50 PENCE

26.0000 g., 0.9170 Gold .7666 oz. AGW, 30 mm. **Ruler:** Elizabeth II **Subject:** Tourist Trophy Motorcycle Races **Obv:** Young bust right **Obv. Designer:** Arnold Machin **Rev:** Motorcyclist within sprigs **Shape:** 7-sided

Date	Mintage	F	VF	XF	Unc	BU
1982 Proof	250	Value: 600				

KM# 101c 50 PENCE

30.4000 g., 0.9500 Platinum .9286 oz. APW, 30 mm. **Ruler:** Elizabeth II **Subject:** Tourist Trophy, Motorcycle Races **Obv:** Young bust right **Obv. Designer:** Arnold Machin **Rev:** Motorcyclist within sprigs **Shape:** 7-sided

Date	Mintage	F	VF	XF	Unc	BU
1982 Proof	50	Value: 1,275				

KM# 102 50 PENCE

13.5000 g., Copper-Nickel, 30 mm. **Ruler:** Elizabeth II **Subject:** Christmas 1982 **Obv:** Young bust right **Obv. Designer:** Arnold Machin **Rev:** Carolers around tree **Shape:** 7-sided

Date	Mintage	F	VF	XF	Unc	BU
1982 AA	30,000	—	—	—	2.50	3.50
1982 AB	Inc. above	—	—	—	2.50	3.50
1982PM BB Proof	30,000	Value: 7.50				

KM# 102a 50 PENCE
15.5000 g., 0.9250 Silver .4610 oz. ASW, 30 mm.
Ruler: Elizabeth II **Subject:** Christmas 1982 **Obv:** Young bust right **Obv. Designer:** Arnold Machin **Rev:** Carolers around tree **Shape:** 7-sided

Date	Mintage	F	VF	XF	Unc	BU
1982PM D Proof	5,000	Value: 12.50				

KM# 102b 50 PENCE
26.0000 g., 0.9170 Gold .7666 oz. AGW, 30 mm. **Ruler:** Elizabeth II **Subject:** Christmas 1982 **Obv:** Young bust right **Obv. Designer:** Arnold Machin **Rev:** Carolers around tree **Shape:** 7-sided

Date	Mintage	F	VF	XF	Unc	BU
1982 Proof	250	Value: 600				

KM# 102c 50 PENCE
30.4000 g., 0.9500 Platinum .9286 oz. APW, 30 mm.
Ruler: Elizabeth II **Subject:** Christmas 1982 **Obv:** Young bust right **Obv. Designer:** Arnold Machin **Rev:** Carolers around tree **Shape:** 7-sided

Date	Mintage	F	VF	XF	Unc	BU
1982 Proof	50	Value: 1,275				

KM# 107 50 PENCE
13.5000 g., Copper-Nickel, 30 mm. **Ruler:** Elizabeth II
Subject: Christmas 1983 **Obv:** Young bust right
Obv. Designer: Arnold Machin **Rev:** Ford Model T driving left
Rev. Designer: Leslie Lindsay **Shape:** 7-sided

Date	Mintage	F	VF	XF	Unc	BU
1983 AA	—	—	—	—	4.00	5.00
1983 AB	—	—	—	—	4.00	5.00
1983 AC	30,000	—	—	—	4.00	5.00
1983 BB	—	—	—	—	4.00	5.00

KM# 107a 50 PENCE
15.5000 g., 0.9250 Silver .4610 oz. ASW, 30 mm.
Ruler: Elizabeth II **Series:** Christmas 1983 **Obv:** Young bust right **Obv. Designer:** Arnold Machin **Rev:** Ford Model T driving left **Shape:** 7-sided

Date	Mintage	F	VF	XF	Unc	BU
1983 Proof	5,000	Value: 12.50				

KM# 107b 50 PENCE
26.0000 g., 0.9170 Gold .7666 oz. AGW, 30 mm.
Ruler: Elizabeth II **Subject:** Christmas 1983 **Obv:** Young bust right **Obv. Designer:** Arnold Machin **Rev:** Ford Model T driving left **Shape:** 7-sided

Date	Mintage	F	VF	XF	Unc	BU
1983 Proof	250	Value: 600				

KM# 107c 50 PENCE
30.4000 g., 0.9500 Platinum .9286 oz. APW, 30 mm.
Ruler: Elizabeth II **Subject:** Christmas 1983 **Obv:** Young bust right **Obv. Designer:** Arnold Machin **Rev:** Ford Model T driving left **Shape:** 7-sided

Date	Mintage	F	VF	XF	Unc	BU
1983 Proof	50	Value: 1,275				

KM# 108 50 PENCE
13.5000 g., Copper-Nickel, 30 mm. **Ruler:** Elizabeth II
Subject: Tourist Trophy Motorcycle Races **Obv:** Young bust right **Obv. Designer:** Arnold Machin **Rev:** Motorcyclist within sprigs **Rev. Designer:** Leslie Lindsay **Shape:** 7-sided

Date	Mintage	F	VF	XF	Unc	BU
1983 AA	30,000	—	—	—	5.00	6.00
1983 AB	Inc. above	—	—	—	5.00	6.00
1983 AC	Inc. above	—	—	—	5.00	6.00
1983 AD	Inc. above	—	—	—	5.00	6.00

KM# 108a 50 PENCE
15.5000 g., 0.9250 Silver .4610 oz. ASW, 30 mm. **Ruler:** Elizabeth II **Obv:** Young bust right **Obv. Designer:** Arnold Machin **Rev:** Motorcyclist within sprigs **Rev. Designer:** Leslie Lindsay **Edge Lettering:** Tourist Trophy Motorcycle Races **Shape:** 7-sided

Date	Mintage	F	VF	XF	Unc	BU
1983 Proof	5,000	Value: 15.00				

KM# 108b 50 PENCE
26.0000 g., 0.9170 Gold .7666 oz. AGW, 30 mm.
Subject: Tourist Trophy Motorcycle Races **Obv:** Young bust right **Obv. Designer:** Arnold Machin **Rev:** Motorcyclist within sprigs **Rev. Designer:** Leslie Lindsay **Shape:** 7-sided

Date	Mintage	F	VF	XF	Unc	BU
1983 Proof	250	Value: 600				

KM# 108c 50 PENCE
30.4000 g., 0.9500 Platinum .9286 oz. APW, 30 mm.
Ruler: Elizabeth II **Subject:** Tourist Trophy Motorcycle Races **Obv:** Young bust right **Obv. Designer:** Arnold Machin **Rev:** Motorcyclist within sprigs **Rev. Designer:** Leslie Lindsay **Shape:** 7-sided

Date	Mintage	F	VF	XF	Unc	BU
1983 Proof	50	Value: 1,275				

KM# 125 50 PENCE
13.5000 g., Copper-Nickel, 30 mm. **Ruler:** Elizabeth II
Subject: Quincentenary of the College of Arms **Obv:** Young bust right **Obv. Designer:** Arnold Machin **Rev:** Viking longship on shield **Shape:** 7-sided

Date	Mintage	F	VF	XF	Unc	BU
1984 AA	—	—	—	—	5.00	6.00
1984 AB	—	—	—	—	5.00	6.00

KM# 125a 50 PENCE
15.5000 g., 0.9250 Silver .4610 oz. ASW, 30 mm.
Ruler: Elizabeth II **Subject:** Quincentenary of the College of Arms **Obv:** Young bust right **Obv. Designer:** Arnold Machin **Rev:** Viking longship on shield **Shape:** 7-sided

Date	Mintage	F	VF	XF	Unc	BU
1984 Proof	—	Value: 15.00				

KM# 125b 50 PENCE
26.0000 g., 0.9170 Gold .7666 oz. AGW, 30 mm.
Ruler: Elizabeth II **Subject:** Quincentenary of the College of Arms **Obv:** Young bust right **Obv. Designer:** Arnold Machin **Rev:** Viking longship on shield **Shape:** 7-sided

Date	Mintage	F	VF	XF	Unc	BU
1984 Proof	150	Value: 550				

KM# 126 50 PENCE
13.5000 g., Copper-Nickel, 30 mm. **Ruler:** Elizabeth II
Subject: Tourist Trophy Motorcycle Races **Obv:** Young bust right **Obv. Designer:** Arnold Machin **Rev:** Motorcyclists within sprigs **Shape:** 7-sided

Date	Mintage	F	VF	XF	Unc	BU
1984 AA	30,000	—	—	—	5.00	6.00

KM# 126a 50 PENCE
15.5000 g., 0.9250 Silver .4610 oz. ASW, 30 mm.
Ruler: Elizabeth II **Subject:** Tourist Trophy Motorcycle Races **Obv:** Young bust right **Obv. Designer:** Arnold Machin **Rev:** Motorcyclists within sprigs **Shape:** 7-sided

Date	Mintage	F	VF	XF	Unc	BU
1984 Proof	5,000	Value: 15.00				

KM# 126b 50 PENCE
26.0000 g., 0.9170 Gold .7666 oz. AGW, 30 mm.
Ruler: Elizabeth II **Subject:** Tourist Trophy Motorcycle Races **Obv:** Young bust right **Obv. Designer:** Arnold Machin **Rev:** Motorcyclists within sprigs **Shape:** 7-sided

Date	Mintage	F	VF	XF	Unc	BU
1984 Proof	250	Value: 550				

KM# 126c 50 PENCE
30.4000 g., 0.9500 Platinum .9286 oz. APW, 30 mm.
Ruler: Elizabeth II **Subject:** Tourist Trophy Motorcycle Races **Obv:** Young bust right **Obv. Designer:** Arnold Machin **Rev:** Motorcyclists within sprigs **Shape:** 7-sided

Date	Mintage	F	VF	XF	Unc	BU
1984 Proof	50	Value: 1,275				

KM# 127 50 PENCE
13.5000 g., Copper-Nickel, 30 mm. **Ruler:** Elizabeth II **Subject:** Christmas 1984 **Obv:** Young bust right **Obv. Designer:** Arnold Machin **Rev:** Train and standing figures **Rev. Designer:** Leslie Lindsay **Shape:** 7-sided

Date	Mintage	F	VF	XF	Unc	BU
1984 AA	—	—	—	—	5.00	6.00
1984 AB	—	—	—	—	5.00	6.00
1984 AC	—	—	—	—	5.00	6.00
1984 AD	—	—	—	—	5.00	6.00
1984 BB Proof	30,000	Value: 8.00				

KM# 127a 50 PENCE
15.5000 g., 0.9250 Silver .4610 oz. ASW, 30 mm.
Ruler: Elizabeth II **Subject:** Christmas 1984 **Obv:** Young bust right **Obv. Designer:** Arnold Machin **Rev:** Train and standing figures **Rev. Designer:** Leslie Lindsay **Shape:** 7-sided

Date	Mintage	F	VF	XF	Unc	BU
1984 Proof	—	Value: 25.00				

KM# 127b 50 PENCE
26.0000 g., 0.9170 Gold .7666 oz. AGW, 30 mm.
Ruler: Elizabeth II **Subject:** Christmas 1984 **Obv:** Young bust right **Obv. Designer:** Arnold Machin **Rev:** Train and standing figures **Rev. Designer:** Leslie Lindsay **Shape:** 7-sided

Date	Mintage	F	VF	XF	Unc	BU
1984 Proof	250	Value: 550				

KM# 127c 50 PENCE
30.4000 g., 0.9500 Platinum .9286 oz. APW **Ruler:** Elizabeth II **Subject:** Christmas 1984 **Obv:** Young bust right **Obv. Designer:** Arnold Machin **Rev:** Train and standing figures **Rev. Designer:** Leslie Lindsay **Shape:** 7-sided

Date	Mintage	F	VF	XF	Unc	BU
1984 Proof	—	Value: 1,275				

KM# 148 50 PENCE
13.5000 g., Copper-Nickel, 30 mm. **Ruler:** Elizabeth II
Obv: Crowned head right **Obv. Designer:** Raphael Maklouf
Rev: Viking longship on shield **Shape:** 7-sided

Date	Mintage	F	VF	XF	Unc	BU
1985(w) AA	—	—	—	—	5.00	6.00
1985(w) AB	—	—	—	—	5.00	6.00
1985 (w) Proof	50,000	Value: 8.00				
1986 AA	—	—	—	—	5.00	6.00
1986 AB	—	—	—	—	5.00	6.00
1987 AA	—	—	—	—	5.00	6.00

KM# 148a 50 PENCE
15.5000 g., 0.9250 Silver .4610 oz. ASW, 30 mm.
Ruler: Elizabeth II **Obv:** Crowned head right **Obv. Designer:** Raphael Maklouf **Rev:** Viking longship on shield **Shape:** 7-sided

Date	Mintage	F	VF	XF	Unc	BU
1985 Proof	Est. 10,000	Value: 15.00				

KM# 148b 50 PENCE
26.0000 g., 0.9170 Gold .7666 oz. AGW, 30 mm.
Ruler: Elizabeth II **Obv:** Crowned head right **Obv. Designer:** Raphael Maklouf **Rev:** Viking longship on shield **Shape:** 7-sided

Date	Mintage	F	VF	XF	Unc	BU
1985 Proof	Est. 300	Value: 550				

KM# 148c 50 PENCE
30.4000 g., 0.9500 Platinum .9286 oz. APW, 30 mm.
Ruler: Elizabeth II **Obv:** Crowned head right **Obv. Designer:** Raphael Maklouf **Rev:** Viking longship on shield **Shape:** 7-sided

Date	Mintage	F	VF	XF	Unc	BU
1985 Proof	Est. 200	Value: 1,275				

KM# 158 50 PENCE
13.5000 g., Copper-Nickel, 30 mm. **Ruler:** Elizabeth II **Subject:** Christmas 1985, commemorates first Christmas air mail of 1935 **Obv:** Crowned head right **Obv. Designer:** Raphael Maklouf **Rev:** Airplanes **Rev. Designer:** Leslie Lindsay **Shape:** 7-sided

Date	Mintage	F	VF	XF	Unc	BU
1985 AA	—	—	—	—	3.50	4.50
1985 AB	—	—	—	—	3.50	4.50
1985 BB	—	—	—	—	3.50	4.50
1985 Proof	—	Value: 9.50				

KM# 158a 50 PENCE
15.5000 g., 0.9250 Silver .4610 oz. ASW, 30 mm.
Ruler: Elizabeth II **Subject:** Christmas 1985 **Obv:** Crowned head right **Obv. Designer:** Raphael Maklouf **Rev:** Airplanes **Rev. Designer:** Leslie Lindsay **Shape:** 7-sided

Date	Mintage	F	VF	XF	Unc	BU
1985 Proof	5,000	Value: 20.00				

KM# 158b 50 PENCE
26.0000 g., 0.9170 Gold .7666 oz. AGW, 30 mm.
Ruler: Elizabeth II **Subject:** Christmas 1985 **Obv:** Crowned head right **Obv. Designer:** Raphael Maklouf **Rev:** Airplanes **Rev. Designer:** Leslie Lindsay **Shape:** 7-sided

Date	Mintage	F	VF	XF	Unc	BU
1985 Proof	Est. 250	Value: 550				

KM# 158c 50 PENCE
30.4000 g., 0.9500 Platinum .9286 oz. APW, 30 mm.
Ruler: Elizabeth II **Subject:** Christmas 1985 **Obv:** Crowned head right **Obv. Designer:** Raphael Maklouf **Rev:** Airplanes **Rev. Designer:** Leslie Lindsay **Shape:** 7-sided

Date	Mintage	F	VF	XF	Unc	BU
1985 Proof	—	Value: 1,275				

KM# 172 50 PENCE
13.5000 g., Copper-Nickel, 30 mm. **Ruler:** Elizabeth II **Subject:** Christmas 1986 **Obv:** Crowned head right **Obv. Designer:** Raphael Maklouf **Rev:** Horse-drawn tram **Shape:** 7-sided

Date	Mintage	F	VF	XF	Unc	BU
1986 AA	—	—	—	—	3.50	4.50

Date	Mintage	F	VF	XF	Unc	BU
1986 AB	—	—	—	—	3.50	4.50
1986 Proof	—	Value: 9.50				

KM# 172a 50 PENCE

15.5000 g., 0.9250 Silver .4610 oz. ASW, 30 mm.
Ruler: Elizabeth II **Subject:** Christmas 1986 **Obv:** Crowned head right **Obv. Designer:** Raphael Maklouf **Rev:** Horse-drawn tram **Shape:** 7-sided

Date	Mintage	F	VF	XF	Unc	BU
1986 Proof	Est. 5,000	Value: 20.00				

KM# 172b 50 PENCE

26.0000 g., 0.9170 Gold .7666 oz. AGW, 30 mm.
Ruler: Elizabeth II **Subject:** Christmas 1986 **Obv:** Crowned head right **Obv. Designer:** Raphael Maklouf **Rev:** Horse-drawn tram **Shape:** 7-sided

Date	Mintage	F	VF	XF	Unc	BU
1986 Proof	—	Value: 550				

KM# 190 50 PENCE

13.5000 g., Copper-Nickel, 30 mm. **Ruler:** Elizabeth II **Subject:** Christmas 1987 **Obv:** Crowned head right **Obv. Designer:** Raphael Maklouf **Rev:** Bus and standing figures **Shape:** 7-sided

Date	Mintage	F	VF	XF	Unc	BU
1987 AA	Est. 30,000	—	—	—	2.50	3.50
1987 D	—	—	—	—	2.50	3.50
1987 Proof	—	Value: 7.50				

KM# 190a 50 PENCE

15.5000 g., 0.9250 Silver .4610 oz. ASW, 30 mm.
Ruler: Elizabeth II **Subject:** Christmas 1987 **Obv:** Crowned head right **Obv. Designer:** Raphael Maklouf **Rev:** Bus and standing figures **Shape:** 7-sided

Date	Mintage	F	VF	XF	Unc	BU
1987 Proof	Est. 5,000	Value: 20.00				

KM# 190b 50 PENCE

26.0000 g., 0.9170 Gold .7666 oz. AGW, 30 mm.
Ruler: Elizabeth II **Subject:** Christmas 1987 **Obv:** Crowned head right **Obv. Designer:** Raphael Maklouf **Rev:** Bus and standing figures **Shape:** 7-sided

Date	Mintage	F	VF	XF	Unc	BU
1987 Proof	Est. 250	Value: 550				

KM# 190c 50 PENCE

30.4000 g., 0.9500 Platinum .9286 oz. APW, 30 mm.
Ruler: Elizabeth II **Subject:** Christmas 1987 **Obv:** Crowned head right **Obv. Designer:** Raphael Maklouf **Rev:** Bus and standing figures **Shape:** 7-sided

Date	Mintage	F	VF	XF	Unc	BU
1987 Proof	Est. 50	Value: 1,275				

KM# 212 50 PENCE

13.5000 g., Copper-Nickel, 30 mm. **Ruler:** Elizabeth II **Obv:** Crowned head right **Obv. Designer:** Raphael Maklouf **Rev:** Computer **Shape:** 7-sided

Date	Mintage	F	VF	XF	Unc	BU
1988 AA	—	—	—	—	5.00	6.00
1989 AA	—	—	—	—	5.00	6.00
1990 AA	—	—	—	—	5.00	6.00
1991 AA	—	—	—	—	5.00	6.00
1992 AA	—	—	—	—	5.00	6.00
1993 AA	—	—	—	—	5.00	6.00
1994 AA	—	—	—	—	5.00	6.00
1995 AA	—	—	—	—	5.00	6.00
1997 AA	—	—	—	—	—	—

KM# 244 50 PENCE

13.5000 g., Copper-Nickel, 30 mm. **Ruler:** Elizabeth II **Subject:** Christmas 1988 **Obv:** Crowned head right **Obv. Designer:** Raphael Maklouf **Rev:** Motorbike and sidecar **Shape:** 7-sided

Date	Mintage	F	VF	XF	Unc	BU
1988 AA	—	—	—	—	2.50	3.50
1988 BA	—	—	—	—	2.50	3.50
1988 BB Proof	—	Value: 6.50				

KM# 244a 50 PENCE

15.5000 g., 0.9250 Silver .4610 oz. ASW, 30 mm.
Ruler: Elizabeth II **Subject:** Christmas 1988 **Obv:** Crowned head right **Obv. Designer:** Raphael Maklouf **Rev:** Motorbike and sidecar **Shape:** 7-sided

Date	Mintage	F	VF	XF	Unc	BU
1988 Proof	—	Value: 20.00				

KM# 244b 50 PENCE

26.0000 g., 0.9170 Gold .7666 oz. AGW, 30 mm.
Ruler: Elizabeth II **Subject:** Christmas 1988 **Obv:** Crowned head right **Obv. Designer:** Raphael Maklouf **Rev:** Motorbike and sidecar **Shape:** 7-sided

Date	Mintage	F	VF	XF	Unc	BU
1988 Proof	—	Value: 550				

KM# 244c 50 PENCE

30.4000 g., 0.9500 Platinum .9286 oz. APW, 30 mm.
Ruler: Elizabeth II **Subject:** Christmas 1988 **Obv:** Crowned head right **Obv. Designer:** Raphael Maklouf **Rev:** Motorbike and sidecar **Shape:** 7-sided

Date	Mintage	F	VF	XF	Unc	BU
1988 Proof	—	Value: 1,275				

KM# 259 50 PENCE

13.5000 g., Copper-Nickel, 30 mm. **Ruler:** Elizabeth II **Subject:** Christmas 1989 **Obv:** Crowned head right **Obv. Designer:** Raphael Maklouf **Rev:** Electric trolley car **Shape:** 7-sided

Date	Mintage	F	VF	XF	Unc	BU
1989 AA	—	—	—	—	2.50	3.50
1989 BB Proof	—	Value: 6.50				

KM# 259a 50 PENCE

15.5000 g., 0.9250 Silver .4610 oz. ASW, 30 mm.
Ruler: Elizabeth II **Subject:** Christmas 1989 **Obv:** Crowned head right **Obv. Designer:** Raphael Maklouf **Rev:** Electric trolly car **Shape:** 7-sided

Date	Mintage	F	VF	XF	Unc	BU
1989 Proof	—	Value: 40.00				

KM# 259b 50 PENCE

26.0000 g., 0.9170 Gold .7666 oz. AGW, 30 mm.
Ruler: Elizabeth II **Subject:** Christmas 1989 **Obv:** Crowned head right **Obv. Designer:** Raphael Maklouf **Rev:** Electric trolley car **Shape:** 7-sided

Date	Mintage	F	VF	XF	Unc	BU
1989 Proof	—	Value: 800				

KM# 259c 50 PENCE

30.4000 g., 0.9500 Platinum .9286 oz. APW, 30 mm.
Ruler: Elizabeth II **Subject:** Christmas 1989 **Obv:** Crowned head right **Obv. Designer:** Raphael Maklouf **Rev:** Electric trolley car **Shape:** 7-sided

Date	Mintage	F	VF	XF	Unc	BU
1989 Proof	—	Value: 1,350				

KM# 282 50 PENCE

13.5000 g., Copper-Nickel, 30 mm. **Ruler:** Elizabeth II **Subject:** Christmas 1990 **Obv:** Crowned head right **Obv. Designer:** Raphael Maklouf **Rev:** Ship and standing figures **Shape:** 7-sided

Date	Mintage	F	VF	XF	Unc	BU
1990 AA	—	—	—	—	2.50	3.50
1990 AB	—	—	—	—	2.50	3.50
1990 Proof	30,000	Value: 6.50				

KM# 282a 50 PENCE

15.5000 g., 0.9250 Silver .4610 oz. ASW, 30 mm.
Ruler: Elizabeth II **Subject:** Christmas 1990 **Obv:** Crowned head right **Obv. Designer:** Raphael Maklouf **Rev:** Ship and standing figures **Shape:** 7-sided

Date	Mintage	F	VF	XF	Unc	BU
1990 Proof	5,000	Value: 40.00				

KM# 282b 50 PENCE

26.0000 g., 0.9170 Gold .7666 oz. AGW, 30 mm.
Ruler: Elizabeth II **Subject:** Christmas 1990 **Obv:** Crowned head right **Obv. Designer:** Raphael Maklouf **Rev:** Ship and standing figures **Shape:** 7-sided

Date	Mintage	F	VF	XF	Unc	BU
1990 Proof	250	Value: 750				

KM# 282c 50 PENCE

30.4000 g., 0.9500 Platinum .9286 oz. APW, 30 mm.
Ruler: Elizabeth II **Subject:** Christmas 1990 **Obv:** Crowned head right **Obv. Designer:** Raphael Maklouf **Rev:** TShip and standing figures **Shape:** 7-sided

Date	Mintage	F	VF	XF	Unc	BU
1990 Proof	50	Value: 1,300				

KM# 303 50 PENCE

13.5000 g., Copper-Nickel, 30 mm. **Ruler:** Elizabeth II **Subject:** Christmas 1991 **Obv:** Crowned head right **Obv. Designer:** Raphael Maklouf **Rev:** Nativity scene **Shape:** 7-sided

Date	Mintage	F	VF	XF	Unc	BU
1991 AA	—	—	—	—	5.00	6.00
1991 Proof	30,000	Value: 8.00				

KM# 303a 50 PENCE

15.5000 g., 0.9250 Silver .4610 oz. ASW, 30 mm.
Ruler: Elizabeth II **Subject:** Christmas 1991 **Obv:** Crowned head right **Obv. Designer:** Raphael Maklouf **Rev:** Nativity scene **Shape:** 7-sided

Date	Mintage	F	VF	XF	Unc	BU
1991 Proof	5,000	Value: 40.00				

KM# 303b 50 PENCE

26.0000 g., 0.9170 Gold .7666 oz. AGW, 30 mm.
Ruler: Elizabeth II **Subject:** Christmas 1991 **Obv:** Crowned head right **Obv. Designer:** Raphael Maklouf **Rev:** Nativity scene **Shape:** 7-sided

Date	Mintage	F	VF	XF	Unc	BU
1991 Proof	250	Value: 685				

KM# 303c 50 PENCE

30.4000 g., 0.9500 Platinum .9286 oz. APW, 30 mm.
Ruler: Elizabeth II **Subject:** Christmas 1991 **Obv:** Crowned head right **Obv. Designer:** Raphael Maklouf **Rev:** Nativity scene **Shape:** 7-sided

Date	Mintage	F	VF	XF	Unc	BU
1991 Proof	50	Value: 1,300				

KM# 335 50 PENCE

13.5000 g., Copper-Nickel, 30 mm. **Ruler:** Elizabeth II **Subject:** Christmas 1992 **Obv:** Crowned head right **Obv. Designer:** Raphael Maklouf **Rev:** Newspaper boy hawking the Manx Mercury **Shape:** 7-sided

Date	Mintage	F	VF	XF	Unc	BU
1992 Proof	—	Value: 6.50				
1992 AA	—	—	—	—	2.50	3.50

KM# 335a 50 PENCE

15.5000 g., 0.9250 Silver .4610 oz. ASW, 30 mm.
Ruler: Elizabeth II **Subject:** Christmas 1992 **Obv:** Crowned head right **Obv. Designer:** Raphael Maklouf **Rev:** Newspaper boy hawking the Manx Mercury **Shape:** 7-sided

Date	Mintage	F	VF	XF	Unc	BU
1992 Proof	5,000	Value: 40.00				

KM# 335b 50 PENCE

26.0000 g., 0.9170 Gold 0.7665 oz. AGW, 30 mm.
Ruler: Elizabeth II **Subject:** Christmas 1992 **Obv:** Crowned head right **Obv. Designer:** Raphael Maklouf **Rev:** Newspaper boy hawking the Manx Mercury **Shape:** 7-sided

Date	Mintage	F	VF	XF	Unc	BU
1992 Proof	250	Value: 685				

KM# 335c 50 PENCE

30.4000 g., 0.9500 Platinum 0.9286 oz. APW, 30 mm.
Ruler: Elizabeth II **Subject:** Christmas 1992 **Obv:** Crowned head right **Obv. Designer:** Raphael Maklouf **Rev:** Newspaper boy hawking the Manx Mercury **Shape:** 7-sided

Date	Mintage	F	VF	XF	Unc	BU
1992 Proof	50	Value: 1,300				

KM# 356 50 PENCE

13.5000 g., Copper-Nickel, 30 mm. **Ruler:** Elizabeth II **Subject:** Christmas 1993 **Obv:** Crowned head right **Obv. Designer:** Raphael Maklouf **Rev:** Framed nativity scene **Shape:** 7-sided

Date	Mintage	F	VF	XF	Unc	BU
1993 AA	—	—	—	—	2.50	3.50
1993 D	—	—	—	—	2.50	3.50
1993 Proof	30,000	Value: 6.50				

KM# 356a 50 PENCE

15.5000 g., 0.9250 Silver .4610 oz. ASW, 30 mm.
Ruler: Elizabeth II **Subject:** Christmas 1993 **Obv:** Crowned head right **Obv. Designer:** Raphael Maklouf **Rev:** Framed nativity scene **Shape:** 7-sided

Date	Mintage	F	VF	XF	Unc	BU
1993 Proof	Est. 5,000	Value: 40.00				

KM# 356b 50 PENCE

26.0000 g., 0.9170 Gold .7666 oz. AGW, 30 mm.
Ruler: Elizabeth II **Subject:** Christmas 1993 **Obv:** Crowned head right **Obv. Designer:** Raphael Maklouf **Rev:** Framed nativity scene **Shape:** 7-sided

Date	Mintage	F	VF	XF	Unc	BU
1993 Proof	Est. 250	Value: 700				

KM# 356c 50 PENCE

30.4000 g., 0.9500 Platinum .9286 oz. APW, 30 mm.
Ruler: Elizabeth II **Subject:** Christmas 1993 **Obv:** Crowned head right **Obv. Designer:** Raphael Maklouf **Rev:** Framed nativity scene **Shape:** 7-sided

Date	Mintage	F	VF	XF	Unc	BU
1993 Proof	Est. 50	Value: 1,300				

KM# 425 50 PENCE

13.5000 g., Copper-Nickel, 30 mm. **Ruler:** Elizabeth II **Subject:** Christmas 1994 **Obv:** Crowned head right **Obv. Designer:** Raphael Maklouf **Rev:** Two young boys with pole **Edge:** Smooth **Shape:** 7-sided

Date	Mintage	F	VF	XF	Unc	BU
1994 AA	—	—	—	—	2.50	3.50

KM# 425a 50 PENCE
15.5000 g., 0.9250 Silver .4610 oz. ASW, 30 mm.
Ruler: Elizabeth II **Subject:** Christmas 1994 **Obv:** Crowned head right **Obv. Designer:** Raphael Maklouf **Rev:** Two young boys with pole **Shape:** 7-sided

Date	Mintage	F	VF	XF	Unc	BU
1994 Proof	—	Value: 40.00				

KM# 456 50 PENCE
13.5000 g., Copper-Nickel, 30 mm. **Ruler:** Elizabeth II **Subject:** Legislative Building Centenary **Obv:** Crowned head right **Obv. Designer:** Raphael Maklouf **Rev:** Building **Edge:** Smooth **Shape:** 7-sided

Date	Mintage	F	VF	XF	Unc	BU
1994 AA	—	—	—	—	3.00	4.00

KM# 456a 50 PENCE
15.5000 g., 0.9250 Silver .4610 oz. ASW, 30 mm.
Ruler: Elizabeth II **Subject:** Legislative Building Centenary **Obv:** Crowned head right **Obv. Designer:** Raphael Maklouf **Rev:** Building **Shape:** 7-sided

Date	Mintage	F	VF	XF	Unc	BU
1994 Proof	—	Value: 40.00				

KM# 521 50 PENCE
13.5000 g., Copper-Nickel, 30 mm. **Ruler:** Elizabeth II **Subject:** Christmas 1995 **Obv:** Crowned head right **Obv. Designer:** Raphael Maklouf **Rev:** Sledding scene **Edge:** Smooth **Shape:** 7-sided

Date	Mintage	F	VF	XF	Unc	BU
1995 AA	Est. 30,000	—	—	—	2.50	3.50

KM# 521a 50 PENCE
15.5000 g., 0.9250 Silver .4610 oz. ASW, 30 mm.
Ruler: Elizabeth II **Subject:** Christmas 1995 **Obv:** Crowned head right **Obv. Designer:** Raphael Maklouf **Rev:** Sledding scene **Shape:** 7-sided

Date	Mintage	F	VF	XF	Unc	BU
1995 Proof	Est. 5,000	Value: 40.00				

KM# 521b 50 PENCE
26.0000 g., 0.9170 Gold .7666 oz. AGW, 30 mm. **Ruler:** Elizabeth II **Subject:** Christmas 1995 **Obv:** Crowned head right **Obv. Designer:** Raphael Maklouf **Rev:** Sledding scene **Shape:** 7-sided

Date	Mintage	F	VF	XF	Unc	BU
1995 Proof	Est. 250	Value: 675				

KM# 593 50 PENCE
13.5000 g., Copper-Nickel, 30 mm. **Ruler:** Elizabeth II **Subject:** Sports **Obv:** Crowned head right **Obv. Designer:** Raphael Maklouf **Rev:** Motorcyclists **Edge:** Smooth

Date	Mintage	F	VF	XF	Unc	BU
1996 AA	—	—	—	—	3.00	4.00
1997 AA	—	—	—	—	3.00	4.00

KM# 694 50 PENCE
13.5000 g., Copper-Nickel, 30 mm. **Ruler:** Elizabeth II **Subject:** Christmas 1996 **Obv:** Crowned head right **Obv. Designer:** Raphael Maklouf **Rev:** Children throwing snowballs in front of church **Edge:** Smooth **Shape:** 7-sided

Date	Mintage	F	VF	XF	Unc	BU
1996 AA	Est. 30,000	—	—	—	5.00	6.00

KM# 694a 50 PENCE
15.5000 g., 0.9250 Silver .4610 oz. ASW, 30 mm.
Ruler: Elizabeth II **Subject:** Christmas 1996 **Obv:** Crowned head right **Obv. Designer:** Raphael Maklouf **Rev:** Children throwing snowballs in front of church **Shape:** 7-sided

Date	Mintage	F	VF	XF	Unc	BU
1996 Proof	Est. 5,000	Value: 40.00				

KM# 694b 50 PENCE
26.0000 g., 0.9170 Gold .7666 oz. AGW, 30 mm.
Ruler: Elizabeth II **Subject:** Christmas 1996 **Obv:** Crowned head right **Obv. Designer:** Raphael Maklouf **Rev:** Children throwing snowballs in front of church **Shape:** 7-sided

Date	Mintage	F	VF	XF	Unc	BU
1996 Proof	Est. 250	Value: 675				

KM# 794 50 PENCE
8.0000 g., Copper-Nickel, 27.3 mm. **Ruler:** Elizabeth II **Subject:** Christmas 1997 **Obv:** Crowned head right **Obv. Designer:** Raphael Maklouf **Rev:** Cameo at lower left of figures on book **Edge:** Smooth **Shape:** 7-sided

Date	Mintage	F	VF	XF	Unc	BU
1997	Est. 30,000	—	—	—	2.75	3.75

KM# 794a 50 PENCE
8.0000 g., 0.9250 Silver .2379 oz. ASW, 27.3 mm.
Ruler: Elizabeth II **Subject:** Christmas 1987 **Obv:** Crowned head right **Obv. Designer:** Raphael Maklouf **Rev:** Cameo at lower left of figures on book **Shape:** 7-sided

Date	Mintage	F	VF	XF	Unc	BU
1997 Proof	Est. 5,000	Value: 40.00				

KM# 794b 50 PENCE
8.0000 g., 0.9160 Gold .2356 oz. AGW, 27.3 mm.
Ruler: Elizabeth II **Subject:** Christmas 1997 **Obv:** Crowned head right **Obv. Designer:** Raphael Maklouf **Rev:** Cameo to lower left of figures on book **Shape:** 7-sided

Date	Mintage	F	VF	XF	Unc	BU
1997 Proof	250	Value: 500				

KM# 806 50 PENCE
8.0000 g., Copper Nickel, 27.3 mm. **Ruler:** Elizabeth II **Obv:** Crowned head right **Obv. Designer:** Raphael Maklouf **Rev:** Two motorcycle racers **Edge:** Plain **Shape:** 7-sided

Date	Mintage	F	VF	XF	Unc	BU
1997PM AA	—	—	—	—	3.00	4.00

KM# 806.1 50 PENCE
8.0000 g., Copper-Nickel, 27.3 mm. **Ruler:** Elizabeth II **Obv:** Crowned head right **Obv. Designer:** Raphael Maklouf **Rev:** Two motorcycle racers **Edge:** Plain **Shape:** 7-sided

Date	Mintage	F	VF	XF	Unc	BU
1997PM	—	—	—	—	3.00	4.00

KM# 806a 50 PENCE
8.0000 g., 0.9250 Silver 0.2379 oz. ASW, 27.3 mm. **Ruler:** Elizabeth II **Obv:** Crowned head right **Obv. Designer:** Raphael Maklouf **Rev:** Two motorcycle racers **Edge:** Plain **Shape:** 7-sided

Date	Mintage	F	VF	XF	Unc	BU
1997PM Proof	5,000	Value: 35.00				

KM# 806b 50 PENCE
8.0000 g., 0.9999 Gold 0.2572 oz. AGW, 27.3 mm. **Ruler:** Elizabeth II **Obv:** Crowned head right **Obv. Designer:** Raphael Maklouf **Rev:** Two motorcycle racers **Edge:** Plain **Shape:** 7-sided

Date	Mintage	F	VF	XF	Unc	BU
1997PM Proof	250	Value: 500				

KM# 905 50 PENCE
8.0000 g., Copper-Nickel, 27.3 mm. **Ruler:** Elizabeth II **Obv:** Head with tiara right **Obv. Designer:** Ian Rank-Broadley **Rev:** Motorcyclists **Edge:** Smooth **Shape:** 7-sided
Note: Varieties with and without triskelions.

Date	Mintage	F	VF	XF	Unc	BU
1998PM AA	—	—	—	—	3.00	4.00
1999PM AA	—	—	—	—	3.00	4.00

KM# 905a 50 PENCE
8.0000 g., 0.9250 Silver .2379 oz. ASW, 27.3 mm.
Ruler: Elizabeth II **Obv:** Head with tiara right **Obv. Designer:** Ian Rank-Broadley **Rev:** Two motorcycle racers **Shape:** 7-sided

Date	Mintage	F	VF	XF	Unc	BU
1998PM Proof	5,000	Value: 35.00				

KM# 905b 50 PENCE
8.0000 g., 0.9999 Gold .2572 oz. AGW, 27.3 mm.
Ruler: Elizabeth II **Obv:** Head with tiara right **Obv. Designer:** Ian Rank-Broadley **Rev:** Two motorcycle racers **Shape:** 7-sided

Date	Mintage	F	VF	XF	Unc	BU
1998PM Proof	Est. 250	Value: 500				

KM# 908 50 PENCE
Copper-Nickel, 27.3 mm. **Ruler:** Elizabeth II **Subject:** Christmas 1998 **Obv:** Head with tiara right **Obv. Designer:** Ian Rank-Broadley **Rev:** Kitchen scene **Edge:** Smooth **Shape:** 7-sided

Date	Mintage	F	VF	XF	Unc	BU
1998PM	Est. 30,000	—	—	—	3.00	4.00

KM# 908a 50 PENCE
8.0000 g., 0.9250 Silver .2379 oz. ASW, 27.3 mm.
Ruler: Elizabeth II **Subject:** Christmas 1998 **Obv:** Head with tiara right **Obv. Designer:** Ian Rank-Broadley **Rev:** Kitchen scene **Shape:** 7-sided

Date	Mintage	F	VF	XF	Unc	BU
1998 Proof	5,000	Value: 35.00				

KM# 908b 50 PENCE
8.0000 g., 0.9167 Gold .2358 oz. AGW, 27.3 mm.
Ruler: Elizabeth II **Subject:** Christmas 1998 **Obv:** Head with tiara right **Obv. Designer:** Ian Rank-Broadley **Rev:** Kitchen scene **Shape:** 7-sided

Date	Mintage	F	VF	XF	Unc	BU
1998 Proof	250	Value: 500				

KM# 993 50 PENCE
Copper-Nickel, 27.3 mm. **Ruler:** Elizabeth II **Obv:** Head with tiara right **Obv. Designer:** Ian Rank-Broadley **Rev:** Motorcyclist within sprigs **Edge:** Smooth **Shape:** 7-sided

Date	Mintage	F	VF	XF	Unc	BU
1999PM AA	—	—	—	—	3.00	4.00

KM# 993a 50 PENCE
8.0000 g., 0.9250 Silver .2379 oz. ASW, 27.3 mm.
Ruler: Elizabeth II **Obv:** Head with tiara right **Obv. Designer:** Rank-Broadley **Rev:** Motorcyclist within sprigs **Shape:** 7-sided

Date	Mintage	F	VF	XF	Unc	BU
1999 Proof	Est. 5,000	Value: 35.00				

KM# 993b 50 PENCE
8.0000 g., 0.9160 Gold .2356 oz. AGW, 27.3 mm.
Ruler: Elizabeth II **Obv:** Head with tiara right **Obv. Designer:** Rank-Broadley **Rev:** Motorcyclist within sprigs **Shape:** 7-sided

Date	Mintage	F	VF	XF	Unc	BU
1999 Proof	Est. 250	Value: 500				

KM# 1011 50 PENCE
8.0000 g., Copper-Nickel, 27.3 mm. **Ruler:** Elizabeth II **Subject:** Christmas 1999 **Obv:** Head with tiara right **Obv. Designer:** Ian Rank-Broadley **Rev:** Tree decorating scene **Edge:** Smooth **Shape:** 7-sided

Date	Mintage	F	VF	XF	Unc	BU
1999 AA	Est. 30,000	—	—	—	3.00	4.00

KM# 1011a 50 PENCE
8.0000 g., 0.9250 Silver .2379 oz. ASW, 27.3 mm.
Ruler: Elizabeth II **Subject:** Christmas 1999 **Obv:** Head with tiara right **Obv. Designer:** Rank-Broadley **Rev:** Tree decorating scene **Shape:** 7-sided

Date	Mintage	F	VF	XF	Unc	BU
1999 Proof	Est. 5,000	Value: 35.00				

KM# 1011b 50 PENCE
8.0000 g., 0.9160 Gold .2356 oz. AGW, 27.3 mm.
Ruler: Elizabeth II **Subject:** Christmas 1999 **Obv:** Head with tiara right **Obv. Designer:** Rank-Broadley. **Rev:** Tree decorating scene **Shape:** 7-sided

Date	Mintage	F	VF	XF	Unc	BU
1999 Proof	Est. 250	Value: 500				

KM# 1041 50 PENCE
8.0000 g., Copper-Nickel, 27.3 mm. **Ruler:** Elizabeth II **Obv:** Head with tiara right **Obv. Designer:** Ian Rank-Broadley **Rev:** Stylized crucifix **Edge:** Plain **Shape:** 7-sided

Date	Mintage	F	VF	XF	Unc	BU
2000PM AA	—	—	—	—	2.25	2.75

KM# 1050 50 PENCE
8.0000 g., Copper-Nickel, 27.3 mm. **Ruler:** Elizabeth II **Obv:** Head with tiara right **Obv. Designer:** Ian Rank-Broadley **Rev:** Seated figure at desk **Edge:** Plain **Shape:** 7-sided

Date	Mintage	F	VF	XF	Unc	BU
2000 BB	30,000	—	—	—	7.00	8.00

KM# 1050a 50 PENCE
8.0000 g., 0.9250 Silver .2379 oz. ASW, 27.3 mm. **Ruler:** Elizabeth II **Obv:** Head with tiara right **Obv. Designer:** Ian Rank-Broadley **Rev:** Seated figure at desk **Edge:** Plain **Shape:** 7-sided

Date	Mintage	F	VF	XF	Unc	BU
2000 Proof	5,000	Value: 35.00				

KM# 1050b 50 PENCE
8.0000 g., 0.9160 Gold .2356 oz. AGW, 27.3 mm. **Ruler:** Elizabeth II **Obv:** Head with tiara right **Obv. Designer:** Ian Rank-Broadley **Rev:** Seated figure at desk **Edge:** Plain **Shape:** 7-sided

Date	Mintage	F	VF	XF	Unc	BU
2000 Proof	250	Value: 500				

KM# 15 1/2 SOVEREIGN (1/2 Pound)
3.9940 g., 0.9170 Gold .1177 oz. AGW **Ruler:** Elizabeth II **Subject:** 200th Anniversary of Acquisition **Obv:** Crowned bust right **Obv. Designer:** T. H. Paget **Rev:** Triskeles on shield within rope wreath **Rev. Designer:** John Nicholson

Date	Mintage	F	VF	XF	Unc	BU
1965	1,500	—	—	—	85.00	95.00

KM# 15a 1/2 SOVEREIGN (1/2 Pound)
4.0000 g., 0.9800 Gold .1260 oz. AGW **Ruler:** Elizabeth II **Subject:** 200th Anniversary of Acquisition **Obv:** Crowned bust right **Obv. Designer:** T. H. Paget **Rev:** Triskeles on shield within rope wreath **Rev. Designer:** John Nicholson

Date	Mintage	F	VF	XF	Unc	BU
1965 Proof	1,000	Value: 95.00				

KM# 26 1/2 SOVEREIGN (1/2 Pound)
3.9813 g., 0.9170 Gold .1173 oz. AGW **Ruler:** Elizabeth II **Obv:** Young bust right **Obv. Designer:** Arnold Machin **Rev:** Armored equestrian

Date	Mintage	F	VF	XF	Unc	BU
1973 A	14,000	—	—	—	85.00	95.00
1973 Proof	1,250	Value: 100				
1974 A	6,566	—	—	—	85.00	95.00
1974 B	Inc. above	—	—	—	85.00	95.00
1974 Proof	2,500	Value: 100				
1975 A	1,956	—	—	—	85.00	95.00
1975 B	Inc. above	—	—	—	85.00	95.00
1975 Proof	—	Value: 100				
1976 A	2,558	—	—	—	85.00	95.00
1976 B	Inc. above	—	—	—	85.00	95.00
1976 Proof	—	Value: 100				
1977 A	—	—	—	—	85.00	95.00
1977 B	—	—	—	—	85.00	95.00
1977 Proof	1,250	Value: 100				
1978 Proof	1,250	Value: 100				
1979 (t) A	8,000	—	—	—	85.00	95.00
1979 (t) B	Inc. above	—	—	—	85.00	95.00
1979 (t) Proof	30,000	Value: 100				
1980 A	—	—	—	—	—	—
1980 B	—	—	—	—	—	—
1980 (m) Proof	7,500	Value: 100				
1980 (v) Proof	—	Value: 100				
1982 (b) Proof	30,000	Value: 100				
1982 (b)	40,000	—	—	—	85.00	95.00

KM# 85 1/2 SOVEREIGN (1/2 Pound)
3.9813 g., 0.9170 Gold .1173 oz. AGW **Ruler:** Elizabeth II **Subject:** Wedding of Prince Charles and Lady Diana **Obv:** Young bust right **Obv. Designer:** Arnold Machin **Rev:** Portraits of Royal Couple, joined shields

Date	Mintage	F	VF	XF	Unc	BU
1981 Proof	30,000	Value: 100				

KM# 260 1/2 SOVEREIGN (1/2 Pound)
3.9813 g., 0.9170 Gold .1173 oz. AGW **Ruler:** Elizabeth II **Obv:** Young bust right **Obv. Designer:** Arnold Machin **Rev:** Four crowned shields

Date	Mintage	F	VF	XF	Unc	BU
1984 Proof	20	Value: 220				
1984	20	—	—	—	200	210

KM# 264 1/2 SOVEREIGN (1/2 Pound)
3.9813 g., 0.9170 Gold .1173 oz. AGW **Ruler:** Elizabeth II **Obv:** Crowned head right **Obv. Designer:** Raphael Maklouf **Rev:** Four crowned shields

Date	Mintage	F	VF	XF	Unc	BU
1988 Proof	5,879	Value: 90.00				

KM# 16 SOVEREIGN (Pound)
7.9881 g., 0.9170 Gold .2355 oz. AGW **Ruler:** Elizabeth II **Subject:** 200th Anniversary of Acquisition **Obv:** Crowned bust right **Obv. Designer:** T. H. Paget **Rev:** Triskeles on shield within rope wreath **Rev. Designer:** John Nicholson

Date	Mintage	F	VF	XF	Unc	BU
1965	2,000	—	—	—	170	180

KM# 16a SOVEREIGN (Pound)
8.0000 g., 0.9800 Gold .2520 oz. AGW **Ruler:** Elizabeth II **Subject:** 200th Anniversary of Acquisition **Obv:** Crowned bust right **Obv. Designer:** T. H. Paget **Rev:** Triskeles on shield within rope wreath **Rev. Designer:** John Nicholson

Date	Mintage	F	VF	XF	Unc	BU
1965 Proof	1,000	Value: 185				

KM# 27 SOVEREIGN (Pound)
7.9627 g., 0.9170 Gold .2347 oz. AGW **Ruler:** Elizabeth II **Obv:** Young bust right **Obv. Designer:** Arnold Machin **Rev:** Armored equestrian

Date	Mintage	F	VF	XF	Unc	BU
1973 A	40,000	—	—	—	165	175
1973 B	Inc. above	—	—	—	165	175
1973 C	Inc. above	—	—	—	165	175
1973 Proof	1,250	Value: 180				
1974 A	8,604	—	—	—	165	175
1974 B	Inc. above	—	—	—	165	175
1974 C	Inc. above	—	—	—	165	175
1974 Proof	2,500	Value: 180				
1975 A	956	—	—	—	165	175
1975 B	Inc. above	—	—	—	165	175
1975 C	Inc. above	—	—	—	165	175
1975 Proof	—	Value: 180				
1976 A	1,238	—	—	—	165	175
1976 B	Inc. above	—	—	—	165	175
1976 C	Inc. above	—	—	—	165	175
1976 Proof	—	Value: 180				
1977 A	—	—	—	—	165	175
1977 B	—	—	—	—	165	175
1977 C	—	—	—	—	165	175
1977 Proof	1,250	Value: 180				
1978 Proof	1,250	Value: 180				
1979 B	—	—	—	—	165	175
1979 C	—	—	—	—	165	175
1979 AA (t)	10,000	—	—	—	165	175
1979 D (t)	—	—	—	—	165	175
1979 (t) Proof	30,000	Value: 180				
1980 D (m) Proof	5,000	Value: 180				
1980 (v) Proof	—	Value: 180				
1982 (b)	30,000	—	—	—	165	175
1982 (b) Proof	40,000	Value: 180				

KM# 44 SOVEREIGN (Pound)
Nickel-Brass **Ruler:** Elizabeth II **Obv:** Young bust right **Obv. Designer:** Arnold Machin **Rev:** Triskeles flanked by designs

Date	Mintage	F	VF	XF	Unc	BU
1978 AA	—	—	—	—	3.00	3.50
1978 AB	—	—	—	—	3.00	3.50
1978 AC	—	—	—	—	2.50	3.00
1978 AD	3,780	—	—	—	7.50	8.50
1978 BB	—	—	—	—	—	—
1978 BC Proof	150,000	Value: 3.50				
1979 AA(t)	—	—	—	—	2.50	3.00
1979 AB(t)	—	—	—	—	2.50	3.00
1979 AC(t)	—	—	—	—	2.50	3.00
1979 BB(t) Proof	—	Value: 3.50				
1979 (t) Crossed oars	—	—	—	—	2.50	3.00
1980 AA DMIHE	30,000	—	—	—	2.50	3.00
1980 AA DMIHEN	—	—	—	—	2.50	3.00
1980 AA TT	—	—	—	—	2.50	3.00
1980 AB DMIHE	—	—	—	—	2.50	3.00
1980 AB DHIHEN	—	—	—	—	2.50	3.00
1980 AB TT	—	—	—	—	5.50	6.50
1980 AC DMIHE	100,000	—	—	—	2.50	3.00
1980PM BB Proof	5,000	Value: 10.00				
1980 AA	—	—	—	—	2.50	3.00
1980 AB	—	—	—	—	2.50	3.00
1980 AC	—	—	—	—	2.50	3.00
1981PM BB Proof	26,000	Value: 10.00				
1981 AA	—	—	—	—	2.50	3.00

KM# 44a SOVEREIGN (Pound)
4.6000 g., 0.9250 Silver .1368 oz. ASW **Ruler:** Elizabeth II **Obv:** Young bust right **Obv. Designer:** Arnold Machin **Rev:** Triskeles flanked by designs **Edge:** Smooth, reeded alternating edge

Date	Mintage	F	VF	XF	Unc	BU
1978PM E Proof	Inc. above	Value: 8.00				
1978 D Proof	100,000	Value: 8.00				
1979PM E Proof	Inc. above	Value: 15.00				
1979 D(t) Proof	75,000	Value: 15.00				
1980 Proof	75,000	Value: 8.00				
1981 Proof	—	Value: 8.00				
1982 (b) Proof	1,000	Value: 35.00				

KM# 44b SOVEREIGN (Pound)
9.0000 g., 0.9500 Platinum .2749 oz. APW **Ruler:** Elizabeth II **Obv:** Young bust right **Obv. Designer:** Arnold Machin **Rev:** Triskeles flanked by designs

Date	Mintage	F	VF	XF	Unc	BU
1978 Proof	1,000	Value: 375				
1979 Proof	—	Value: 375				
1980 Proof	1,000	Value: 375				
1982 (b) Proof	100	Value: 400				

KM# 44c SOVEREIGN (Pound)
7.9627 g., 0.9170 Gold .2347 oz. AGW **Ruler:** Elizabeth II **Obv:** Young bust right **Obv. Designer:** Arnold Machin **Rev:** Triskeles flanked by designs

Date	Mintage	F	VF	XF	Unc	BU
1980 Proof	5,000	Value: 165				
1980 T.T. Proof	300	Value: 225				
1982 (b)	250	—	—	—	225	—
1982 (b) Proof	750	Value: 200				

KM# 44d SOVEREIGN (Pound)
4.6000 g., 0.5000 Silver .0739 oz. ASW **Ruler:** Elizabeth II **Obv:** Young bust right **Obv. Designer:** Arnold Machin **Rev:** Triskeles flanked by designs

Date	Mintage	F	VF	XF	Unc	BU
1980 Proof	10,000	Value: 15.00				

KM# 86 SOVEREIGN (Pound)
7.9627 g., 0.9170 Gold .2347 oz. AGW **Ruler:** Elizabeth II **Subject:** Wedding of Prince Charles and Lady Diana **Obv:** Young bust right **Obv. Designer:** Arnold Machin **Rev:** Portraits of Royal Couple, joined shields

Date	Mintage	F	VF	XF	Unc	BU
1981 Proof	40,000	Value: 165				

KM# 109 SOVEREIGN (Pound)
9.5000 g., Nickel-Brass, 22.5 mm. **Ruler:** Elizabeth II **Obv:** Young bust right **Obv. Designer:** Arnold Machin **Rev:** City view with ships within circle **Rev. Designer:** Leslie Lindsay

Date	Mintage	F	VF	XF	Unc	BU
1983 AA	—	—	—	—	3.50	4.00
1983 AB	—	—	—	—	3.50	4.00

KM# 109a SOVEREIGN (Pound)
4.6000 g., 0.9250 Silver .1368 oz. ASW, 22.5 mm. **Ruler:** Elizabeth II **Obv:** Young bust right **Obv. Designer:** Arnold Machin **Rev:** Peel **Rev. Designer:** Leslie Lindsay **Edge:** Reeded, smooth alternating edge

Date	Mintage	F	VF	XF	Unc	BU
1983 D Proof	—	Value: 20.00				

KM# 109b SOVEREIGN (Pound)
9.5000 g., 0.3740 Gold .1142 oz. AGW, 22.5 mm. **Ruler:** Elizabeth II **Obv:** Young bust right **Obv. Designer:** Arnold Machin **Rev:** City view with ships within circle **Rev. Designer:** Leslie Lindsay

Date	Mintage	F	VF	XF	Unc	BU
1983 Proof	—	Value: 85.00				

KM# 109c SOVEREIGN (Pound)
7.9627 g., 0.9170 Gold .2347 oz. AGW, 22.5 mm. **Ruler:** Elizabeth II **Obv:** Young bust right **Obv. Designer:** Arnold Machin **Rev:** City view with ships within circle **Rev. Designer:** Leslie Lindsay

Date	Mintage	F	VF	XF	Unc	BU
1983 Proof	—	Value: 170				

KM# 109d SOVEREIGN (Pound)
9.0000 g., 0.9500 Platinum .2749 oz. APW, 22.5 mm. **Ruler:** Elizabeth II **Obv:** Young bust right **Obv. Designer:** Arnold Machin **Rev:** City view with ships within circle **Rev. Designer:** Leslie Lindsay

Date	Mintage	F	VF	XF	Unc	BU
1983 Proof	—	Value: 375				

KM# 128 SOVEREIGN (Pound)
9.5000 g., Nickel-Brass, 22.5 mm. **Ruler:** Elizabeth II **Obv:** Young bust right **Obv. Designer:** Arnold Machin **Rev:** Crown flanked by designs above city view within shield **Rev. Designer:** Leslie Lindsay **Edge:** Reeded, smooth alternating edge

Date	Mintage	F	VF	XF	Unc	BU
1984 D	—	—	—	—	4.00	4.50
1984 AA	—	—	—	—	4.00	4.50

KM# 128a SOVEREIGN (Pound)
4.6000 g., 0.9250 Silver .1368 oz. ASW, 22.5 mm. **Ruler:** Elizabeth II **Obv:** Young bust right **Obv. Designer:** Arnold Machin **Rev:** Crown flanked by designs above city view within shield **Rev. Designer:** Leslie Lindsay **Edge:** Reeded, smooth alternating edge

Date	Mintage	F	VF	XF	Unc	BU
1984	—	—	—	—	10.00	12.00
1984 D Proof	—	Value: 20.00				

KM# 128b SOVEREIGN (Pound)
9.5000 g., 0.3740 Gold .1142 oz. AGW, 22.5 mm. **Ruler:** Elizabeth II **Obv:** Young bust right **Obv. Designer:** Arnold Machin **Rev:** Crown flanked by designs above city view within shield **Rev. Designer:** Leslie Lindsay

Date	Mintage	F	VF	XF	Unc	BU
1984 Proof	4,950	Value: 85.00				

KM# 128c SOVEREIGN (Pound)
7.9627 g., 0.9170 Gold .2347 oz. AGW, 22.5 mm.
Ruler: Elizabeth II **Obv:** Young bust right **Obv. Designer:** Arnold Machin **Rev:** Crown flanked by designs above city view within shield **Rev. Designer:** Leslie Lindsay

Date	Mintage	F	VF	XF	Unc	BU
1984 Proof	950	Value: 170				

KM# 128d SOVEREIGN (Pound)
9.0000 g., 0.9500 Platinum .2749 oz. APW, 22.5 mm.
Ruler: Elizabeth II **Obv:** Young bust right **Obv. Designer:** Arnold Machin **Rev:** Crown flanked by designs above city view within shield **Rev. Designer:** Leslie Lindsay

Date	Mintage	F	VF	XF	Unc	BU
1984 Proof	—	Value: 375				

KM# 261 SOVEREIGN (Pound)
7.9627 g., 0.9170 Gold .2347 oz. AGW, 22.5 mm.
Ruler: Elizabeth II **Obv:** Young bust right **Obv. Designer:** Arnold Machin **Rev:** Four crowned shields

Date	Mintage	F	VF	XF	Unc	BU
1984	20	—	—	—	350	375
1984 Proof	20	Value: 450				

KM# 151 SOVEREIGN (Pound)
9.5000 g., Nickel-Brass, 22.5 mm. **Ruler:** Elizabeth II
Obv: Crowned head right **Obv. Designer:** Raphael Maklouf **Rev:** Shield **Rev. Designer:** Leslie Lindsay **Edge:** Smooth, reeded alternating edge

Date	Mintage	F	VF	XF	Unc	BU
1985(w) AA	—	—	—	—	3.50	4.00
1985 AA Proof	25,000	Value: 6.00				
1985 AA	—	—	—	—	3.50	—
1985 AA Proof	25,000	Value: 6.00				

KM# 135 SOVEREIGN (Pound)
4.6000 g., 0.9250 Silver .1368 oz. ASW, 22.5 mm.
Ruler: Elizabeth II **Obv:** Young bust right **Obv. Designer:** Arnold Machin **Rev:** Shield **Rev. Designer:** Leslie Lindsay
Edge: Reeded, smooth alternating edge

Date	Mintage	F	VF	XF	Unc	BU
1985 D	—	—	—	—	10.00	12.00
1985 D Proof	Est. 5,000	Value: 22.50				

KM# 135b SOVEREIGN (Pound)
7.9627 g., 0.9170 Gold .2347 oz. AGW, 22.5 mm.
Ruler: Elizabeth II **Obv:** Young bust right **Obv. Designer:** Arnold Machin **Rev:** Shield **Rev. Designer:** Leslie Lindsay

Date	Mintage	F	VF	XF	Unc	BU
1985 Proof	Est. 150	Value: 185				

KM# 135c SOVEREIGN (Pound)
9.0000 g., 0.9500 Platinum .2749 oz. APW, 22.5 mm.
Ruler: Elizabeth II **Obv:** Young bust right **Obv. Designer:** Arnold Machin **Rev:** Shield **Rev. Designer:** Leslie Lindsay

Date	Mintage	F	VF	XF	Unc	BU
1985 Proof	Est. 550	Value: 380				

KM# 151a SOVEREIGN (Pound)
4.6000 g., 0.9250 Silver .1368 oz. ASW, 22.5 mm.
Ruler: Elizabeth II **Obv:** Crowned head right **Obv. Designer:** Raphael Maklouf **Rev:** Shield **Rev. Designer:** Leslie Lindsay

Date	Mintage	F	VF	XF	Unc	BU
1985 Proof	—	Value: 35.00				

KM# 136 SOVEREIGN (Pound)
4.6000 g., 0.9250 Silver .1368 oz. ASW, 22.5 mm.
Ruler: Elizabeth II **Obv:** Crowned head right **Obv. Designer:** Raphael Maklouf **Rev:** Shield **Rev. Designer:** Leslie Lindsay

Date	Mintage	F	VF	XF	Unc	BU
1986 AA	—	—	—	—	10.00	12.00
1986 D Proof	—	Value: 25.00				

KM# 136b SOVEREIGN (Pound)
7.9627 g., 0.9170 Gold .2347 oz. AGW, 22.5 mm.
Ruler: Elizabeth II **Obv:** Crowned head right **Obv. Designer:** Raphael Maklouf **Rev:** Shield **Rev. Designer:** Leslie Lindsay

Date	Mintage	F	VF	XF	Unc	BU
1986 Proof	—	Value: 170				

KM# 136c SOVEREIGN (Pound)
9.0000 g., 0.9500 Platinum .2749 oz. APW, 22.5 mm.
Ruler: Elizabeth II **Obv:** Crowned head right **Obv. Designer:** Raphael Maklouf **Rev:** Shield **Rev. Designer:** Leslie Lindsay

Date	Mintage	F	VF	XF	Unc	BU
1986 Proof	—	Value: 380				

KM# 175 SOVEREIGN (Pound)
9.5000 g., Nickel-Brass, 22.5 mm. **Ruler:** Elizabeth II
Obv: Crowned head right **Obv. Designer:** Raphael Maklouf
Rev: Shield **Rev. Designer:** Leslie Lindsay

Date	Mintage	F	VF	XF	Unc	BU
1986	—	—	—	—	3.50	4.00
1986 Proof	25,000	Value: 6.00				

KM# 182 SOVEREIGN (Pound)
9.5000 g., Nickel-Brass, 22.5 mm. **Ruler:** Elizabeth II
Obv: Crowned head right **Obv. Designer:** Raphael Maklouf
Rev: Rearing armored equestrian within circle **Edge:** Reeded, smooth alternating edge

Date	Mintage	F	VF	XF	Unc	BU
1987 AA	—	—	—	—	3.50	4.00

KM# 265 SOVEREIGN (Pound)
7.9627 g., 0.9170 Gold .2347 oz. AGW, 22.5 mm.
Ruler: Elizabeth II **Obv:** Crowned head right
Obv. Designer: Raphael Maklouf **Rev:** Four crowned shields

Date	Mintage	F	VF	XF	Unc	BU
1988 Proof	1,600	Value: 170				
1988	5,876	—	—	—	165	—

KM# 213 SOVEREIGN (Pound)
9.5000 g., Nickel-Brass, 22.5 mm. **Ruler:** Elizabeth II
Obv: Crowned head right **Obv. Designer:** Raphael Maklouf
Rev: Cordless phone divides satellite and receiving station
Edge: Reeded, smooth alternating edge

Date	Mintage	F	VF	XF	Unc	BU
1988 AA	—	—	—	—	2.50	3.00
1988 BB	—	—	—	—	2.50	3.00
1988 D	—	—	—	—	2.50	3.00
1989 AA	—	—	—	—	2.50	3.00
1990 AA	—	—	—	—	2.50	3.00
1991 AA	—	—	—	—	2.50	3.00
1992 AB	—	—	—	—	2.50	3.00
1993 AA	—	—	—	—	2.50	3.00
1994 AA	—	—	—	—	2.50	3.00
1995 AA	—	—	—	—	2.50	3.00

KM# 213a SOVEREIGN (Pound)
4.6000 g., 0.9250 Silver .1368 oz. ASW, 22.5 mm. **Ruler:** Elizabeth II **Obv:** Crowned head right **Obv. Designer:** Raphael Maklouf **Rev:** Cordless phone divides satelite and receiving station

Date	Mintage	F	VF	XF	Unc	BU
1988 Proof	—	Value: 10.00				
1989 Proof	—	Value: 10.00				
1990 Proof	—	Value: 10.00				
1991 Proof	—	Value: 10.00				
1992 Proof	—	Value: 10.00				

KM# 594 SOVEREIGN (Pound)
9.5000 g., Nickel-Brass, 22.5 mm. **Ruler:** Elizabeth II
Subject: Sports **Obv:** Crowned head right
Obv. Designer: Raphael Maklouf **Rev:** Cricket equipment

Date	Mintage	F	VF	XF	Unc	BU
1996 AA	—	—	—	—	4.00	4.50
1997 AA	—	—	—	—	4.00	4.50

KM# 594a SOVEREIGN (Pound)
4.6000 g., 0.9250 Silver .1368 oz. ASW, 22.5 mm.
Ruler: Elizabeth II **Subject:** Sports **Obv:** Crowned head right
Obv. Designer: Raphael Maklouf **Rev:** Cricket equipment

Date	Mintage	F	VF	XF	Unc	BU
1996 Proof	—	Value: 25.00				

KM# 655 SOVEREIGN (Pound)
9.5000 g., Nickel-Brass, 22.5 mm. **Ruler:** Elizabeth II **Subject:** Douglas Centenary **Obv:** Crowned head right **Obv. Designer:** Raphael Maklouf **Rev:** City arms **Rev. Designer:** Leslie Lindsay

Date	Mintage	F	VF	XF	Unc	BU
1996 AA	—	—	—	—	4.00	4.50

KM# 655a SOVEREIGN (Pound)
9.5000 g., 0.9250 Silver .2825 oz. ASW, 22.5 mm.
Ruler: Elizabeth II **Subject:** Douglas Centenary **Obv:** Crowned head right **Obv. Designer:** Raphael Maklouf **Rev:** City arms **Rev. Designer:** Leslie Lindsay

Date	Mintage	F	VF	XF	Unc	BU
1996 Proof	25,000	Value: 15.00				

KM# 655b SOVEREIGN (Pound)
9.5000 g., 0.9160 Gold .2798 oz. AGW, 22.5 mm.
Ruler: Elizabeth II **Subject:** Douglas Centenary **Obv:** Crowned head right **Obv. Designer:** Raphael Maklouf **Rev:** City arms **Rev. Designer:** Leslie Lindsay

Date	Mintage	F	VF	XF	Unc	BU
1996 Proof	Est. 10,000	Value: 200				

KM# 665a SOVEREIGN (Pound)
9.5000 g., 0.9250 Silver .2825 oz. ASW, 22.5 mm. **Subject:** Douglas Centenary **Obv:** Head of Queen Elizabeth II right

Date	Mintage	F	VF	XF	Unc	BU
1996 Proof	Est. 25,000 - Value: 15.00					

KM# 906.1 SOVEREIGN (Pound)
9.5000 g., Nickel-Brass, 22.5 mm. **Ruler:** Elizabeth II
Obv: Head with tiara right **Obv. Designer:** Ian Rank-Broadley
Rev: Cricket equipment flanked by sprigs

Date	Mintage	F	VF	XF	Unc	BU
1998 AA	—	—	—	—	4.00	4.50

KM# 906.2 POUND
9.5000 g., Nickel-Brass, 22.5 mm. **Ruler:** Elizabeth II
Obv: Head with tiara right with small triskeles dividing legend
Obv. Designer: Ian Rank-Broadley **Rev:** Cricket equipment

Date	Mintage	F	VF	XF	Unc	BU
1998PM AA	—	—	—	—	4.00	4.50
1999PM AA	—	—	—	—	4.00	4.50

KM# 1042 POUND
9.5000 g., Brass, 22.5 mm. **Ruler:** Elizabeth II
Subject: Millennium Bells **Obv:** Head with tiara right
Obv. Designer: Ian Rank-Broadley **Rev:** Triskeles and three bells **Edge:** Reeded and plain sections

Date	Mintage	F	VF	XF	Unc	BU
2000PM AA	—	—	—	—	4.00	5.00

KM# 28 2 POUNDS
15.9253 g., 0.9170 Gold .4695 oz. AGW **Ruler:** Elizabeth II
Obv: Young bust right **Obv. Designer:** Arnold Machin
Rev: Armored equestrian

Date	Mintage	F	VF	XF	Unc	BU
1973 A	3,612	—	—	—	335	345
1973 Proof	1,250	Value: 360				
1974 A	1,257	—	—	—	335	345
1974 B	Inc. above	—	—	—	335	345
1974 Proof	2,500	Value: 360				
1975 A	456	—	—	—	335	345
1975 B	Inc. above	—	—	—	335	345
1975 Proof	—	Value: 360				
1976 A	578	—	—	—	335	345
1976 B	Inc. above	—	—	—	335	345
1976 Proof	—	Value: 360				
1977 A	—	—	—	—	335	345
1977 B	Inc. above	—	—	—	335	345
1977 Proof	1,250	Value: 360				
1978 Proof	1,250	Value: 360				
1979 (t) A	2,000	—	—	—	335	345
1979 (t) B	Inc. above	—	—	—	335	345
1979 (t) Proof	30,000	Value: 360				
1980 (m) Proof	2,000	Value: 360				
1982 (b) Proof	5,000	Value: 360				
1982 (b)	15,000	—	—	—	335	345

KM# 87 2 POUNDS
15.9253 g., 0.9170 Gold .4695 oz. AGW **Ruler:** Elizabeth II
Subject: Wedding of Prince Charles and Lady Diana **Obv:** Young bust right **Obv. Designer:** Arnold Machin **Rev:** Portraits of Royal Couple, joined shields

Date	Mintage	F	VF	XF	Unc	BU
1981 Proof	5,000	Value: 335				

KM# 129 2 POUNDS
Virenium **Ruler:** Elizabeth II **Obv:** Young bust right
Obv. Designer: Arnold Machin **Rev:** Tower of Refuge and Manx Shearwater in flight **Rev. Designer:** Leslie Lindsay

Date	Mintage	F	VF	XF	Unc	BU
1984PM	—	—	—	—	—	—

Note: Reported, not confirmed

KM# 129a 2 POUNDS
Silver **Ruler:** Elizabeth II **Obv:** Young bust right
Obv. Designer: Arnold Machin **Rev:** Tower of Refuge and Manx Shearwater in flight **Rev. Designer:** Leslie Lindsay

Date	Mintage	F	VF	XF	Unc	BU
1984PM	—	—	—	—	—	—

Note: Reported, not confirmed

KM# 262 2 POUNDS
15.9200 g., 0.9170 Gold .4695 oz. AGW **Ruler:** Elizabeth II **Obv:** Young bust right **Obv. Designer:** Arnold Machin **Rev:** Four crowned shields

Date	Mintage	F	VF	XF	Unc	BU
1984	20	—	—	—	650	—
1984 Proof	20	Value: 800				

KM# 149 2 POUNDS
Virenium **Ruler:** Elizabeth II **Obv:** Crowned head right **Obv. Designer:** Raphael Maklouf **Rev:** Tower of Refuge and Manx Shearwater in flight

Date	Mintage	F	VF	XF	Unc	BU
1985	—	—	—	—	—	—

Note: Reported, not confirmed

KM# 149a 2 POUNDS
Silver **Ruler:** Elizabeth II **Obv:** Crowned head right **Obv. Designer:** Raphael Maklouf **Rev:** Tower of Refuge and Manx Shearwater in flight

Date	Mintage	F	VF	XF	Unc	BU
1985	—	—	—	—	—	—

Note: Reported, not confirmed

KM# 167 2 POUNDS
Virenium **Ruler:** Elizabeth II **Obv:** Crowned head right **Obv. Designer:** Raphael Maklouf **Rev:** Bird above towered building

Date	Mintage	F	VF	XF	Unc	BU
1986 (vw)	—	—	—	—	7.50	8.50
1986 Proof	—	Value: 10.00				
1987 AA	—	—	—	—	7.50	8.50

KM# 214 2 POUNDS
Virenium **Ruler:** Elizabeth II **Obv:** Crowned head right **Obv. Designer:** Raphael Maklouf **Rev:** Airplane

Date	Mintage	F	VF	XF	Unc	BU
1988 D	—	—	—	—	7.50	8.50
1988 AA	—	—	—	—	7.50	8.50
1989	—	—	—	—	7.50	8.50
1990 AA	—	—	—	—	7.50	8.50
1991 AA	—	—	—	—	7.50	8.50
1992 AA	—	—	—	—	7.50	8.50
1993 AA	—	—	—	—	7.50	8.50

KM# 257 2 POUNDS
Virenium **Ruler:** Elizabeth II **Obv:** Crowned head right **Obv. Designer:** Raphael Maklouf **Rev:** Blimp

Date	Mintage	F	VF	XF	Unc	BU
1989 AA	—	—	—	—	—	—

Note: Most recalled by government; Few actually issued

KM# 257a 2 POUNDS
9.3000 g., 0.9250 Silver .2766 oz. ASW **Ruler:** Elizabeth II **Obv:** Crowned head right **Obv. Designer:** Raphael Maklouf **Rev:** Blimp

Date	Mintage	F	VF	XF	Unc	BU
1989	—	—	—	—	—	—

Note: Reported, not confirmed

KM# 257b 2 POUNDS
15.9400 g., 0.9170 Gold .4730 oz. AGW **Ruler:** Elizabeth II **Obv:** Crowned head right **Obv. Designer:** Raphael Maklouf **Rev:** Blimp

Date	Mintage	F	VF	XF	Unc	BU
1989	—	—	—	—	—	—

Note: Reported, not confirmed

KM# 257c 2 POUNDS
18.0000 g., 0.9500 Platinum .5498 oz. APW **Ruler:** Elizabeth II **Obv:** Crowned head right **Obv. Designer:** Raphael Maklouf **Rev:** Blimp **Note:** Reported, not confirmed; most recalled by government; few actually issued

Date	Mintage	F	VF	XF	Unc	BU
1989	—	—	—	—	—	—

Note: Reported, not confirmed

KM# 344 2 POUNDS
Virenium **Ruler:** Elizabeth II **Subject:** World Champion - Nigel Mansell **Obv:** Crowned head right **Obv. Designer:** Raphael Maklouf **Rev:** Racecars

Date	Mintage	F	VF	XF	Unc	BU
1993 AA	—	—	—	—	6.50	—

KM# 398 2 POUNDS
Virenium **Ruler:** Elizabeth II **Subject:** Indycar World Series Champion - Nigel Mansell **Obv:** Crowned head right **Obv. Designer:** Raphael Maklouf **Rev:** Racecars

Date	Mintage	F	VF	XF	Unc	BU
1994 AA	—	—	—	—	8.00	10.00

KM# 465 2 POUNDS
Virenium **Ruler:** Elizabeth II **Subject:** 50th Anniversary - VE and VJ Day **Obv:** Crowned head right **Obv. Designer:** Raphael Maklouf **Rev:** Lion head within crowned circular design within flowered wreath

Date	Mintage	F	VF	XF	Unc	BU
1995	—	—	—	—	7.00	8.00

KM# 595 2 POUNDS
Virenium **Ruler:** Elizabeth II **Subject:** Sports **Obv:** Crowned head right **Obv. Designer:** Raphael Maklouf **Rev:** Racecars within sprigs **Edge:** Reeded, smooth alternating edge

Date	Mintage	F	VF	XF	Unc	BU
1996 AA	—	—	—	—	7.50	8.50
1997 AA	—	—	—	—	7.50	8.50

KM# 844 2 POUNDS
Bi-Metallic Copper-Nickel center in Brass ring **Ruler:** Elizabeth II **Obv:** Crowned head right within beaded circle **Obv. Designer:** Raphael Maklouf **Rev:** Racecars within beaded circle and sprigs **Edge:** Reeded

Date	Mintage	F	VF	XF	Unc	BU
1997 AA	—	—	—	—	8.00	9.00

KM# 858 2 POUNDS
Bi-Metallic Copper-Nickel center in Brass ring **Ruler:** Elizabeth II **Obv:** Head with tiara right within beaded circle **Rev:** Three racecars **Edge:** Reeded **Designer:** Ian Rank-Broadley

Date	Mintage	F	VF	XF	Unc	BU
1998 AA With triskeles in legend	—	—	—	—	8.00	9.00
1998 AA Without triskeles in legend	—	—	—	—	8.00	9.00
1999 AA	—	—	—	—	8.00	9.00

KM# 1043 2 POUNDS
12.0000 g., Bi-Metallic Copper-Nickel center in Brass ring **Ruler:** Elizabeth II **Subject:** Thorwald's Cross **Obv:** Head with tiara right within beaded circle **Obv. Designer:** Ian Rank-Broadley **Rev:** Ancient drawing within circle **Edge:** Reeded

Date	Mintage	F	VF	XF	Unc	BU
2000PM AA	—	—	—	—	6.50	7.50

KM# 17 5 POUNDS
39.9403 g., 0.9170 Gold 1.1776 oz. AGW **Ruler:** Elizabeth II **Subject:** 200th Anniversary of Acquisition **Obv:** Crowned bust right **Obv. Designer:** T. H. Paget **Rev:** Triskeles on shield within rope wreath **Rev. Designer:** John Nicholson

Date	Mintage	F	VF	XF	Unc	BU
1965	500	—	—	—	825	845

KM# 17a 5 POUNDS
39.9500 g., 0.9800 Gold 1.2588 oz. AGW **Ruler:** Elizabeth II **Subject:** 200th Anniversary of Acquisition **Obv:** Crowned bust right **Obv. Designer:** T. H. Paget **Rev:** Triskeles on shield within rope wreath **Rev. Designer:** John Nicholson

Date	Mintage	F	VF	XF	Unc	BU
1965 Proof	1,000	Value: 900				

KM# 29 5 POUNDS
39.8134 g., 0.9170 Gold 1.1739 oz. AGW **Ruler:** Elizabeth II **Obv:** Young bust right **Obv. Designer:** Arnold Machin **Rev:** Rearing armored equestrian

Date	Mintage	F	VF	XF	Unc	BU
1973 A	3,035	—	—	—	810	835
1973 B	Inc. above	—	—	—	810	835
1973 C	Inc. above	—	—	—	810	835
1973 D	Inc. above	—	—	—	810	835
1973 E	Inc. above	—	—	—	810	835
1973 Proof	1,250	Value: 850				
1974 A	481	—	—	—	810	835
1974 B	Inc. above	—	—	—	810	835
1974 Proof	2,500	Value: 850				
1975 A	306	—	—	—	810	835
1975 B	Inc. above	—	—	—	810	835
1975 Proof	—	Value: 850				
1976 A	370	—	—	—	810	835
1976 B	Inc. above	—	—	—	810	835
1976 Proof	—	Value: 850				
1977 A	—	—	—	—	810	835
1977 B	Inc. above	—	—	—	810	835
1977 Proof	1,250	Value: 850				
1978 Proof	1,250	Value: 850				
1979 (t) A	1,000	—	—	—	810	835
1979 (t) B	Inc. above	—	—	—	810	835
1979 (t) Proof	1,000	Value: 850				
1980 (m)	250	—	—	—	810	835
1982 (b)	10,000	—	—	—	810	835
1982 (b) Proof	500	Value: 850				

KM# 29a 5 POUNDS
23.8400 g., 0.9800 Silver 0.7511 oz. ASW, 36.1 mm.
Ruler: Elizabeth II **Obv:** Young bust right **Obv. Designer:** Arnold Machin **Rev:** Rearing armored equestrian **Edge:** Reeded
Note: Subject is a possible pattern.

Date	Mintage	F	VF	XF	Unc	BU
1980(m)PM Proof	—	—	—	—	—	—

KM# 88 5 POUNDS
Virenium, 36.5 mm. **Ruler:** Elizabeth II **Obv:** Young bust right **Obv. Designer:** Arnold Machin **Rev:** Triskeles on map **Rev. Designer:** Leslie Lindsay **Edge:** Reeded, smooth alternating edge

Date	Mintage	F	VF	XF	Unc	BU
1981 AA	—	—	—	—	10.00	12.50
1981 AB	—	—	—	—	10.00	12.50
1981 AC	—	—	—	—	10.00	12.50
1981 AD	—	—	—	—	10.00	12.50
1981PM BB Proof	30,000	Value: 14.00				
1982 Proof	—	Value: 14.00				
1983 AA	—	—	—	—	20.00	22.00
1984 AA	—	—	—	—	20.00	22.00
1984 AB	—	—	—	—	20.00	22.00
1984 AC	—	—	—	—	10.00	12.50

KM# 88a 5 POUNDS
23.5000 g., 0.9250 Silver .6989 oz. ASW, 36.5 mm.
Ruler: Elizabeth II **Obv:** Young bust right **Obv. Designer:** Arnold Machin **Rev:** Triskeles on map **Rev. Designer:** Leslie Lindsay

Date	Mintage	F	VF	XF	Unc	BU
1981 Proof	500	Value: 40.00				
1982 (b) Proof	1,000	Value: 35.00				
1983 Proof	5,000	Value: 25.00				

KM# 88b 5 POUNDS
39.9000 g., 0.9170 Gold 1.1764 oz. AGW, 36.5 mm.
Ruler: Elizabeth II **Obv:** Young bust right **Obv. Designer:** Arnold Machin **Rev:** Triskeles on map **Rev. Designer:** Leslie Lindsay

Date	Mintage	F	VF	XF	Unc	BU
1981 Proof	1,000	Value: 840				
1982 (b) Proof	250	Value: 840				
1982 (b) Proof	750	Value: 840				
1983 Proof	—	Value: 840				

KM# 88c 5 POUNDS
45.5000 g., 0.9500 Platinum 1.3898 oz. APW, 36.5 mm.
Ruler: Elizabeth II **Obv:** Young bust right **Obv. Designer:** Arnold Machin **Rev:** Triskeles on map **Rev. Designer:** Leslie Lindsay

Date	Mintage	F	VF	XF	Unc	BU
1981 Proof	500	Value: 1,850				
1982 (b) Proof	100	Value: 1,850				
1983 Proof	—	Value: 1,850				

KM# 89 5 POUNDS
39.8134 g., 0.9170 Gold 1.1739 oz. AGW **Ruler:** Elizabeth II **Subject:** Wedding of Prince Charles and Lady Diana **Obv:** Young bust right **Obv. Designer:** Arnold Machin **Rev:** Portraits of Royal Couple, joined shields

Date	Mintage	F	VF	XF	Unc	BU
1981 Proof	1,000	Value: 840				

KM# 134 5 POUNDS
Virenium, 36.5 mm. **Ruler:** Elizabeth II **Subject:** Quincentenery of the College of Arms **Obv:** Young bust right **Obv. Designer:** Arnold Machin **Rev:** Mounted knight in armor with sword facing right within circle **Rev. Designer:** Leslie Lindsay

Date	Mintage	F	VF	XF	Unc	BU
1984 AA	—	—	—	—	10.00	12.50
1984 BB	—	—	—	—	10.00	12.50

KM# 134a 5 POUNDS
23.5000 g., 0.9250 Silver .6989 oz. ASW, 36.5 mm.
Ruler: Elizabeth II **Subject:** Quincentenery of the College of Arms **Obv:** Young bust right **Obv. Designer:** Arnold Machin **Rev:** Mounted knight in armor with sword, facing right within circle **Rev. Designer:** Leslie Lindsay

Date	Mintage	F	VF	XF	Unc	BU
1984 Proof	—	Value: 40.00				

KM# 134b 5 POUNDS
39.9000 g., 0.9170 Gold 1.1759 oz. AGW, 36.5 mm.
Ruler: Elizabeth II **Subject:** Quincentenery of the College of Arms **Obv:** Young bust right **Obv. Designer:** Arnold Machin **Rev:** Mounted knight in armor with sword, facing right within circle **Rev. Designer:** Leslie Lindsay

Date	Mintage	F	VF	XF	Unc	BU
1984 Proof	150	Value: 845				

KM# 134c 5 POUNDS
45.5000 g., 0.9500 Platinum 1.3898 oz. APW, 36.5 mm.
Ruler: Elizabeth II **Subject:** Quincentenery of the College of Arms **Obv:** Young bust right **Obv. Designer:** Arnold Machin **Rev:** Mounted knight in armor with sword facing right within circle **Rev. Designer:** Leslie Lindsay

Date	Mintage	F	VF	XF	Unc	BU
1984 Proof	—	Value: 1,850				

KM# 263 5 POUNDS
39.8300 g., 0.9170 Gold 1.1740 oz. AGW **Ruler:** Elizabeth II **Obv:** Young bust right **Obv. Designer:** Arnold Machin **Rev:** Four crowned shields

Date	Mintage	F	VF	XF	Unc	BU
1984	20	—	—	—	1,250	1,350
1984 Proof	20	Value: 1,650				

KM# 150 5 POUNDS
Virenium, 36.5 mm. **Ruler:** Elizabeth II **Obv:** Crowned head right **Obv. Designer:** Raphael Maklouf **Rev:** Similar to KM#134 with additional sports privy mark **Rev. Designer:** Leslie Lindsay **Edge:** Reeded, smooth alternating edge

Date	Mintage	F	VF	XF	Unc	BU
1985 AA(w)	—	—	—	—	10.00	12.50
1985 Proof	25,000	Value: 12.50				
1986 AA	—	—	—	—	10.00	12.50
1987 AA	—	—	—	—	10.00	12.50

KM# 150a 5 POUNDS
23.5000 g., 0.9250 Silver .6989 oz. ASW, 36.5 mm.
Ruler: Elizabeth II **Obv:** Crowned head right **Obv. Designer:** Raphael Maklouf **Rev:** Mounted knight in armor with sword facing right within circle **Rev. Designer:** Leslie Lindsay

Date	Mintage	F	VF	XF	Unc	BU
1985 Proof	Est. 5,000	Value: 40.00				

KM# 150b 5 POUNDS
39.9000 g., 0.9170 Gold 1.1759 oz. AGW, 36.5 mm.
Ruler: Elizabeth II **Obv:** Crowned head right **Obv. Designer:** Raphael Maklouf **Rev:** Mounted knight in armor with sword facing right within circle **Rev. Designer:** Leslie Lindsay

Date	Mintage	F	VF	XF	Unc	BU
1985 Proof	Est. 150	Value: 845				

KM# 150c 5 POUNDS
45.5000 g., 0.9500 Platinum 1.3898 oz. APW, 36.5 mm.
Ruler: Elizabeth II **Obv:** Crowned head right **Obv. Designer:** Raphael Maklouf **Rev:** Mounted knight in armor with sword facing right within circle **Rev. Designer:** Leslie Lindsay

Date	Mintage	F	VF	XF	Unc	BU
1985 Proof	Est. 100	Value: 1,850				

KM# 215 5 POUNDS
Virenium, 36.5 mm. **Ruler:** Elizabeth II **Obv:** Crowned head right **Obv. Designer:** Raphael Maklouf **Rev:** Boat below triskeles within circle **Edge:** Smooth, reeded alternating edge

Date	Mintage	F	VF	XF	Unc	BU
1988 AA	—	—	—	—	10.00	12.50
1989 AA	—	—	—	—	10.00	12.50
1990 AA	—	—	—	—	10.00	12.50
1991 AA	—	—	—	—	10.00	12.50
1992 AA	—	—	—	—	10.00	12.50

KM# 336 5 POUNDS
Virenium, 36.5 mm. **Ruler:** Elizabeth II **Subject:** World Champion - Nigel Mansell **Obv:** Crowned head right **Obv. Designer:** Raphael Maklouf **Rev:** Racecars **Edge:** Reeded, smooth alternating edge

Date	Mintage	F	VF	XF	Unc	BU
1993 AA	—	—	—	—	12.50	16.50

KM# 399 5 POUNDS
Virenium, 36.5 mm. **Ruler:** Elizabeth II **Subject:** Indycar World Series Champion - Nigel Mansell **Obv:** Crowned head right **Obv. Designer:** Raphael Maklouf **Rev:** Two racecars

Date	Mintage	F	VF	XF	Unc	BU
1994 AA	—	—	—	—	15.00	18.50

KM# 466 5 POUNDS
Virenium, 36.5 mm. **Ruler:** Elizabeth II **Subject:** 50th Anniversary - End of World War II **Obv:** Crowned head right **Obv. Designer:** Raphael Maklouf **Rev:** Bust facing giving peace sign

Date	Mintage	F	VF	XF	Unc	BU
1995	—	—	—	—	14.00	17.50

KM# 466a 5 POUNDS
23.5000 g., 0.9250 Silver .6989 oz. ASW, 36.5 mm.
Ruler: Elizabeth II **Subject:** 50th Anniversary - End of World War II **Obv:** Crowned head right **Obv. Designer:** Raphael Maklouf **Rev:** Bust facing giving peace sign

Date	Mintage	F	VF	XF	Unc	BU
1995 Proof	—	Value: 40.00				

KM# 466b 5 POUNDS
39.8300 g., 0.9170 Gold 1.1759 oz. AGW, 36.5 mm.
Ruler: Elizabeth II **Subject:** 50th Anniversary - End of World War II **Obv:** Crowned head right **Obv. Designer:** Raphael Maklouf **Rev:** Bust facing giving peace sign

Date	Mintage	F	VF	XF	Unc	BU
1995 Proof	Est. 850	Value: 850				

KM# 587 5 POUNDS
Virenium, 36.5 mm. **Ruler:** Elizabeth II **Subject:** European Soccer Championships **Obv:** Crowned head right **Obv. Designer:** Raphael Maklouf **Rev:** Soccer players

Date	Mintage	F	VF	XF	Unc	BU
1996 AA	—	—	—	—	16.00	—

KM# 587a 5 POUNDS
23.5000 g., 0.9250 Silver .6989 oz. ASW, 36.5 mm. **Ruler:** Elizabeth II **Subject:** European Soccer Championships **Obv:** Crowned head right **Obv. Designer:** Raphael Maklouf **Rev:** Soccer players

Date	Mintage	F	VF	XF	Unc	BU
1996 Proof	Est. 5,000	Value: 40.00				

KM# 587b 5 POUNDS
39.0830 g., 0.9160 Gold 1.1510 oz. AGW, 36.5 mm. **Ruler:** Elizabeth II **Subject:** European Soccer Championships **Obv:** Crowned head right **Obv. Designer:** Raphael Maklouf **Rev:** Soccer players

Date	Mintage	F	VF	XF	Unc	BU
1996 Proof	Est. 850	Value: 900				

KM# 769 5 POUNDS
Virenium, 36.5 mm. **Ruler:** Elizabeth II **Subject:** 50th Anniversary - Queen Elizabeth and Prince Philip **Obv:** Crowned head right **Obv. Designer:** Raphael Maklouf **Rev:** Current portrait of Queen Elizabeth and Prince Philip **Edge:** Reeded, smooth alternating edge

Date	Mintage	F	VF	XF	Unc	BU
1997 AA	—	—	—	—	17.50	—

KM# 769a 5 POUNDS
23.5000 g., 0.9250 Silver .6989 oz. ASW, 36.5 mm. **Ruler:** Elizabeth II **Subject:** 50th Anniversary - Queen Elizabeth and Prince Philip **Obv:** Crowned head right **Obv. Designer:** Raphael Maklouf **Rev:** Current portrait of Queen Elizabeth and Prince Philip

Date	Mintage	F	VF	XF	Unc	BU
1997 Proof	Est. 5,000	Value: 40.00				

KM# 769b 5 POUNDS
39.8300 g., 0.9167 Gold 1.1740 oz. AGW, 36.5 mm. **Ruler:** Elizabeth II **Subject:** 50th Anniversary - Queen Elizabeth and Prince Philip **Obv:** Crowned head right **Obv. Designer:** Raphael Maklouf **Rev:** Current portrait of Queen Elizabeth and Prince Philip

Date	Mintage	F	VF	XF	Unc	BU
1997 Proof	Est. 850	Value: 900				

KM# 991 5 POUNDS
Virenium, 36.5 mm. **Ruler:** Elizabeth II **Subject:** Soccer **Obv:** Head with tiara right **Obv. Designer:** Ian Rank-Broadley **Rev:** Soccer players flanked by sprigs **Edge:** Reeded, smooth alternating edge

Date	Mintage	F	VF	XF	Unc	BU
1998 AA	—	—	—	—	16.50	18.00
1999 AA	—	—	—	—	16.50	18.00

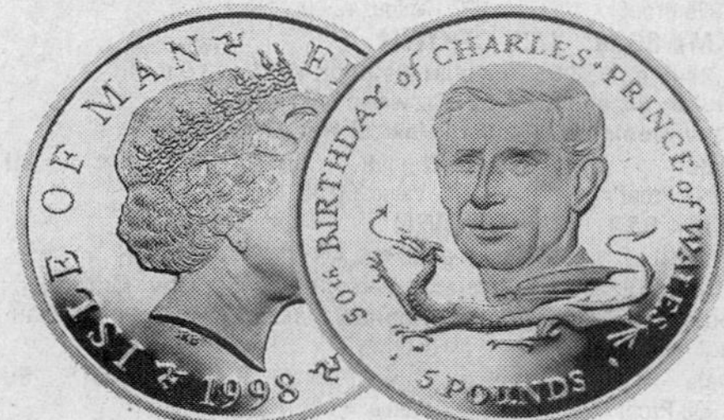

KM# 912 5 POUNDS
Virenium, 36.5 mm. **Ruler:** Elizabeth II **Subject:** 50th Birthday - Prince Charles **Obv:** Head with tiara right **Obv. Designer:** Ian Rank-Broadley **Rev:** Portrait of Prince Charles **Edge:** Reeded, smooth alternating edge

Date	Mintage	F	VF	XF	Unc	BU
1998 AA	—	—	—	—	15.50	17.50

KM# 912a 5 POUNDS
23.5000 g., 0.9250 Silver .6989 oz. ASW, 36.5 mm. **Ruler:** Elizabeth II **Subject:** 50th Birthday - Prince Charles **Obv:** Head with tiara right **Obv. Designer:** Ian Rank-Broadley **Rev:** Portrait of Prince Charles

Date	Mintage	F	VF	XF	Unc	BU
1998 Proof	Est. 5,000	Value: 50.00				

KM# 912b 5 POUNDS
39.8300 g., 0.9167 Gold 1.1740 oz. AGW, 36.5 mm. **Ruler:** Elizabeth II **Subject:** 50th Birthday - Prince Charles **Obv:** Head with tiara right **Obv. Designer:** Ian Rank-Broadley **Rev:** Portrait of Prince Charles

Date	Mintage	F	VF	XF	Unc	BU
1998 Proof	Est. 850	Value: 885				

KM# 943 5 POUNDS
Virenium, 36.5 mm. **Ruler:** Elizabeth II **Subject:** 175th Anniversary of the RN LI **Obv:** Head with tiara right **Obv. Designer:** Ian Rank-Broadley **Rev:** Lifeboat with flag

Date	Mintage	F	VF	XF	Unc	BU
1999	—	—	—	—	15.50	17.50

KM# 943a 5 POUNDS
23.5000 g., 0.9250 Silver .6989 oz. ASW, 36.5 mm. **Ruler:** Elizabeth II **Subject:** 175th Anniversary of the RN LI **Obv:** Head with tiara right **Obv. Designer:** Ian Rank-Broadley **Rev:** Lifeboat with flag

Date	Mintage	F	VF	XF	Unc	BU
1999 Proof	Est. 10,000	Value: 50.00				

KM# 943b 5 POUNDS
39.8300 g., 0.9167 Gold 1.1739 oz. AGW, 36.5 mm. **Ruler:** Elizabeth II **Subject:** 175th Anniversary of the RN LI **Obv:** Head with tiara right **Obv. Designer:** Ian Rank-Broadley **Rev:** Lifeboat with flag

Date	Mintage	F	VF	XF	Unc	BU
1999 Proof	850	Value: 885				

KM# 1044 5 POUNDS
20.1000 g., Virenium, 36.5 mm. **Ruler:** Elizabeth II **Subject:** St. Patrick's Hymn **Obv:** Head with tiara right **Obv. Designer:** Ian Rank-Broadley **Rev:** Stylized cross design **Edge:** Reeded and plain sections

Date	Mintage	F	VF	XF	Unc	BU
2000PM AA	—	—	—	—	15.00	16.50

KM# 345 10 POUNDS
10.0000 g., 0.9250 Silver .2973 oz. ASW **Ruler:** Elizabeth II **Subject:** Indycar World Series Champion - Nigel Mansell **Obv:** Crowned head right **Obv. Designer:** Raphael Maklouf **Rev:** Racecar

Date	Mintage	F	VF	XF	Unc	BU
1993 Proof	Est. 20,000	Value: 35.00				

KM# 400 10 POUNDS
10.0000 g., 0.9250 Silver .2973 oz. ASW **Ruler:** Elizabeth II **Subject:** Indycar World Series Champion - Nigel Mansell **Obv:** Crowned head right **Obv. Designer:** Raphael Maklouf **Rev:** Two racecars

Date	Mintage	F	VF	XF	Unc	BU
1994 Proof	Est. 20,000	Value: 35.00				

KM# 346 25 POUNDS
28.2800 g., 0.9250 Silver .8411 oz. ASW **Ruler:** Elizabeth II **Subject:** World Champion - Nigel Mansell **Obv:** Crowned bust right **Obv. Designer:** Raphael Maklouf **Rev:** Two racecars

Date	Mintage	F	VF	XF	Unc	BU
1993 Proof	Est. 15,000	Value: 50.00				

KM# 347 50 POUNDS
6.2200 g., 0.9990 Gold .2000 oz. AGW **Ruler:** Elizabeth II **Subject:** World Champion - Nigel Mansell **Obv:** Crowned bust right **Obv. Designer:** Raphael Maklouf **Rev:** Two racecars

Date	Mintage	F	VF	XF	Unc	BU
1993 Proof	Est. 5,000	Value: 150				

KM# 401 50 POUNDS
6.2200 g., 0.9990 Gold .2000 oz. AGW **Ruler:** Elizabeth II **Subject:** Indycar World Series Champion - Nigel Mansell **Obv:** Crowned bust right **Obv. Designer:** Raphael Maklouf **Rev:** Two racecars

Date	Mintage	F	VF	XF	Unc	BU
1994 Proof	Est. 5,000	Value: 150				

CROWN SERIES

Pobjoy Mint Key

(M) MATTE - Normal circulation strike

(U) SPECIAL UNCIRCULATED - Polished or prooflike in appearance, slightly frosted features.

(P) PROOF - The highest quality obtainable having mirror-like fields and frosted features.

KM# 235 1/25 CROWN
1.2441 g., 0.9990 Gold .0400 oz. AGW, 13.9 mm. **Ruler:** Elizabeth II **Obv:** Crowned bust right **Obv. Designer:** Raphael Maklouf **Rev:** Manx cat

Date	Mintage	F	VF	XF	Unc	BU
1988	40,000	—	—	—	30.00	—
1988 Proof	5,000	Value: 35.00				

KM# 252 1/25 CROWN
1.2441 g., 0.9990 Gold .0400 oz. AGW, 13.9 mm. **Ruler:** Elizabeth II **Obv:** Crowned bust right **Obv. Designer:** Raphael Maklouf **Rev:** Persian cat

Date	Mintage	F	VF	XF	Unc	BU
1989	—	—	—	—	40.00	—
1989 Proof	—	Value: 45.00				

KM# 467 1/25 CROWN
1.2441 g., 0.9995 Platinum .0400 oz. APW, 13.9 mm. **Ruler:** Elizabeth II **Obv:** Crowned bust right **Obv. Designer:** Raphael Maklouf **Rev:** Persian cat

Date	Mintage	F	VF	XF	Unc	BU
1989	—	—	—	—	50.00	—
1989 Proof	—	Value: 55.00				

KM# 277 1/25 CROWN
1.2441 g., 0.9990 Gold .0400 oz. AGW, 13.9 mm. **Ruler:** Elizabeth II **Obv:** Crowned bust right **Obv. Designer:** Raphael Maklouf **Rev:** Alley cat

Date	Mintage	F	VF	XF	Unc	BU
1990	—	—	—	—	50.00	—
1990 Proof	—	Value: 55.00				

KM# 294 1/25 CROWN
1.2441 g., 0.9990 Gold .0400 oz. AGW, 13.9 mm. **Ruler:** Elizabeth II **Obv:** Crowned bust right **Obv. Designer:** Raphael Maklouf **Rev:** Norwegian cat

Date	Mintage	F	VF	XF	Unc	BU
1991	—	—	—	—	50.00	—
1991 Proof	—	Value: 55.00				

KM# 322 1/25 CROWN
1.2441 g., 0.9990 Gold .0400 oz. AGW, 13.9 mm. **Ruler:** Elizabeth II **Subject:** America's Cup **Obv:** Crowned bust right **Obv. Designer:** Raphael Maklouf **Rev:** Cameo of "Star of India" above two modern sailboats

Date	Mintage	F	VF	XF	Unc	BU
1992 Prooflike	50,000	—	—	—	50.00	—

KM# 328 1/25 CROWN
1.2441 g., 0.9990 Gold .0400 oz. AGW, 13.9 mm. **Ruler:** Elizabeth II **Obv:** Crowned bust right **Obv. Designer:** Raphael Maklouf **Rev:** Siamese cat

Date	Mintage	F	VF	XF	Unc	BU
1992	—	—	—	—	45.00	—
1992 Proof	—	Value: 47.00				

KM# 338 1/25 CROWN
1.2441 g., 0.9990 Gold .0400 oz. AGW, 13.9 mm.
Ruler: Elizabeth II **Subject:** Year of the Cockerel **Obv:** Crowned bust right **Obv. Designer:** Raphael Maklouf **Rev:** Cockerel within circle **Rev. Designer:** Barry Stanton

Date	Mintage	F	VF	XF	Unc	BU
1993 Proof	Est. 25,000	Value: 40.00				

KM# 349 1/25 CROWN
1.2441 g., 0.9990 Gold .0400 oz. AGW, 13.9 mm.
Ruler: Elizabeth II **Obv:** Crowned bust right
Obv. Designer: Raphael Maklouf **Rev:** Maine Coon cat

Date	Mintage	F	VF	XF	Unc	BU
1993	—	—	—	—	45.00	—
1993 Proof	—	Value: 47.00				

KM# 376 1/25 CROWN
1.2441 g., 0.9990 Gold .0400 oz. AGW, 13.9 mm.
Ruler: Elizabeth II **Obv:** Crowned bust right
Obv. Designer: Raphael Maklouf **Rev:** Japanese Bobtail cat

Date	Mintage	F	VF	XF	Unc	BU
1994	—	—	—	—	40.00	—
1994 Proof	—	Value: 42.00				

KM# 402 1/25 CROWN
1.2441 g., 0.9990 Gold .0400 oz. AGW, 13.9 mm.
Ruler: Elizabeth II **Obv:** Crowned bust right
Obv. Designer: Raphael Maklouf **Rev:** Pekingese

Date	Mintage	F	VF	XF	Unc	BU
1994 Proof	Est. 25,000	Value: 50.00				

KM# 473 1/25 CROWN
1.2441 g., 0.9995 Platinum .0400 oz. APW, 13.9 mm.
Ruler: Elizabeth II **Obv:** Crowned bust right
Obv. Designer: Raphael Maklouf **Rev:** Japanese Bobtail cat

Date	Mintage	F	VF	XF	Unc	BU
1994	—	—	—	—	65.00	—
1994 Proof	—	Value: 70.00				

KM# 442 1/25 CROWN
1.2441 g., 0.9990 Gold .0400 oz. AGW, 13.9 mm.
Ruler: Elizabeth II **Obv:** Crowned bust right
Obv. Designer: Raphael Maklouf **Rev:** Turkish cat

Date	Mintage	F	VF	XF	Unc	BU
1995 U	—	—	—	—	40.00	—
1995 Proof	—	Value: 42.00				

KM# 449 1/25 CROWN
1.2441 g., 0.9990 Gold .0400 oz. AGW, 13.9 mm.
Ruler: Elizabeth II **Subject:** Year of the Pig **Obv:** Crowned bust right **Obv. Designer:** Raphael Maklouf **Rev:** Sow with piglets

Date	Mintage	F	VF	XF	Unc	BU
1995 Proof	Est. 25,000	Value: 45.00				

KM# 478 1/25 CROWN
1.2441 g., 0.9995 Platinum .0400 oz. APW, 13.9 mm.
Ruler: Elizabeth II **Obv:** Crowned bust right
Obv. Designer: Raphael Maklouf **Rev:** Turkish cat

Date	Mintage	F	VF	XF	Unc	BU
1995	—	—	—	—	55.00	—
1995 Proof	—	Value: 58.00				

KM# 597 1/25 CROWN
1.2441 g., 0.9990 Gold .0400 oz. AGW, 13.9 mm.
Ruler: Elizabeth II **Series:** Flower Fairies **Obv:** Crowned bust right **Obv. Designer:** Raphael Maklouf **Rev:** Orchis
Rev. Designer: Cecily Mary Barker

Date	Mintage	F	VF	XF	Unc	BU
1996 Proof	Est. 25,000	Value: 40.00				

KM# 598 1/25 CROWN
1.2441 g., 0.9990 Gold .0400 oz. AGW, 13.9 mm.
Ruler: Elizabeth II **Series:** Flower Fairies **Obv:** Crowned bust right **Obv. Designer:** Raphael Maklouf **Rev:** Rose
Rev. Designer: Cecily Mary Barker

Date	Mintage	F	VF	XF	Unc	BU
1996 Proof	Est. 25,000	Value: 40.00				

KM# 599 1/25 CROWN
1.2441 g., 0.9990 Gold .0400 oz. AGW, 13.9 mm.
Ruler: Elizabeth II **Series:** Flower Fairies **Obv:** Crowned bust right **Obv. Designer:** Raphael Maklouf **Rev:** Fuchsia
Rev. Designer: Cecily Mary Barker

Date	Mintage	F	VF	XF	Unc	BU
1996 Proof	Est. 25,000	Value: 40.00				

KM# 600 1/25 CROWN
1.2441 g., 0.9990 Gold .0400 oz. AGW, 13.9 mm.
Ruler: Elizabeth II **Series:** Flower Fairies **Obv:** Crowned bust right **Obv. Designer:** Raphael Maklouf **Rev:** Pinks
Rev. Designer: Cecily Mary Barker

Date	Mintage	F	VF	XF	Unc	BU
1996 Proof	Est. 25,000	Value: 40.00				

KM# 613 1/25 CROWN
1.2441 g., 0.9990 Gold .0400 oz. AGW, 13.9 mm.
Ruler: Elizabeth II **Obv:** Crowned bust right **Obv. Designer:** Raphael Maklouf **Rev:** Burmese cat **Note:** #621a.

Date	Mintage	F	VF	XF	Unc	BU
1996 U	—	—	—	—	40.00	—
1996 Proof	—	Value: 42.00				

KM# 614 1/25 CROWN
1.2441 g., 0.9995 Platinum .0400 oz. APW, 13.9 mm.
Ruler: Elizabeth II **Obv:** Crowned bust right
Obv. Designer: Raphael Maklouf **Rev:** Burmese cat

Date	Mintage	F	VF	XF	Unc	BU
1996	—	—	—	—	65.00	—
1996 Proof	—	Value: 70.00				

KM# 728 1/25 CROWN
1.2441 g., 0.9990 Gold .0400 oz. AGW, 13.9 mm.
Ruler: Elizabeth II **Subject:** Year of the Rat **Obv:** Crowned bust right **Obv. Designer:** Raphael Maklouf **Rev:** Rat

Date	Mintage	F	VF	XF	Unc	BU
1996 Proof	—	—	—	—	—	—

Note: Entire series purchased by one buyer; Mintage, disposition, and market value unknown

KM# 721 1/25 CROWN
1.2441 g., 0.9990 Gold .0400 oz. AGW, 13.9 mm.
Ruler: Elizabeth II **Subject:** Year of the Ox **Obv:** Crowned bust right **Obv. Designer:** Raphael Maklouf **Rev:** Ox laying down

Date	Mintage	F	VF	XF	Unc	BU
1997 Proof	Est. 20,000	Value: 40.00				

KM# 735 1/25 CROWN
1.2441 g., 0.9990 Gold .0400 oz. AGW, 13.9 mm.
Ruler: Elizabeth II **Series:** Flower Fairies **Obv:** Crowned bust right **Obv. Designer:** Raphael Maklouf **Rev:** Candytuft
Rev. Designer: Cecily Mary Barker

Date	Mintage	F	VF	XF	Unc	BU
1997 Proof	Est. 25,000	Value: 40.00				

KM# 735a 1/25 CROWN
1.2504 g., 0.9950 Platinum .0400 oz. APW, 13.9 mm.
Ruler: Elizabeth II **Series:** Flower Fairies **Obv:** Crowned bust right **Obv. Designer:** Raphael Maklouf **Rev:** Candytuft
Rev. Designer: Cecily Mary Barker

Date	Mintage	F	VF	XF	Unc	BU
1997 Proof	Est. 7,500	Value: 60.00				

KM# 736 1/25 CROWN
1.2441 g., 0.9999 Gold .0400 oz. AGW, 13.9 mm.
Ruler: Elizabeth II **Series:** Flower Fairies **Obv:** Crowned bust right **Obv. Designer:** Raphael Maklouf **Rev:** Snowdrop
Rev. Designer: Cecily Mary Barker

Date	Mintage	F	VF	XF	Unc	BU
1997 Proof	Est. 25,000	Value: 40.00				

KM# 736a 1/25 CROWN
1.2504 g., 0.9950 Platinum .0400 oz. APW, 13.9 mm.
Ruler: Elizabeth II **Series:** Flower Fairies **Obv:** Crowned bust right **Obv. Designer:** Raphael Maklouf **Rev:** Snowdrop
Rev. Designer: Cecily Mary Barker

Date	Mintage	F	VF	XF	Unc	BU
1997 Proof	Est. 7,500	Value: 60.00				

KM# 737 1/25 CROWN
1.2441 g., 0.9999 Gold .0400 oz. AGW, 13.9 mm.
Ruler: Elizabeth II **Series:** Flower Fairies **Obv:** Crowned bust right **Obv. Designer:** Raphael Maklouf **Rev:** Tulip
Rev. Designer: Cecily Mary Barker

Date	Mintage	F	VF	XF	Unc	BU
1997 Proof	Est. 25,000	Value: 40.00				

KM# 737a 1/25 CROWN
1.2504 g., 0.9950 Platinum .0400 oz. APW, 13.9 mm.
Ruler: Elizabeth II **Series:** Flower Fairies **Obv:** Crowned bust right **Obv. Designer:** Raphael Maklouf **Rev:** Tulip
Rev. Designer: Cecily Mary Barker

Date	Mintage	F	VF	XF	Unc	BU
1997 Proof	Est. 7,500	Value: 60.00				

KM# 738 1/25 CROWN
1.2441 g., 0.9999 Gold .0400 oz. AGW, 13.9 mm.
Ruler: Elizabeth II **Series:** Flower Fairies **Obv:** Crowned bust right **Obv. Designer:** Raphael Maklouf **Rev:** Jasmine
Rev. Designer: Cecily Mary Barker

Date	Mintage	F	VF	XF	Unc	BU
1997 Proof	Est. 25,000	Value: 40.00				

KM# 738a 1/25 CROWN
1.2504 g., 0.9950 Platinum .0400 oz. APW, 13.9 mm.
Ruler: Elizabeth II **Series:** Flower Fairies **Obv:** Crowned bust right **Obv. Designer:** Raphael Maklouf **Rev:** Jasmine
Rev. Designer: Cecily Mary Barker

Date	Mintage	F	VF	XF	Unc	BU
1997 Proof	Est. 7,500	Value: 60.00				

KM# 770 1/25 CROWN
1.2440 g., 0.9999 Gold .0400 oz. AGW, 13.9 mm.
Ruler: Elizabeth II **Obv:** Crowned bust right
Obv. Designer: Raphael Maklouf **Rev:** Long-haired Smoke cat

Date	Mintage	F	VF	XF	Unc	BU
1997	—	—	—	—	45.00	—
1997 Proof	—	Value: 50.00				

KM# 770a 1/25 CROWN
1.2440 g., 0.9999 Platinum .0400 oz. APW, 13.9 mm.
Ruler: Elizabeth II **Obv:** Crowned bust right **Obv. Designer:** Raphael Maklouf **Rev:** Long-haired Smoke cat

Date	Mintage	F	VF	XF	Unc	BU
1997	—	—	—	—	60.00	—
1997 Proof	—	Value: 65.00				

KM# 789 1/25 CROWN
1.2440 g., 0.9999 Gold .0400 oz. AGW, 13.9 mm. **Ruler:** Elizabeth II **Subject:** History of the Cat **Obv:** Crowned bust right **Obv. Designer:** Raphael Maklouf **Rev:** Cat stalking a spider

Date	Mintage	F	VF	XF	Unc	BU
1997 Proof	Est. 25,000	Value: 45.00				

KM# 812 1/25 CROWN
1.2441 g., 0.9999 Gold .0400 oz. AGW, 13.9 mm.
Ruler: Elizabeth II **Subject:** Year of the Tiger **Obv:** Crowned bust right **Obv. Designer:** Raphael Maklouf **Rev:** Tiger

Date	Mintage	F	VF	XF	Unc	BU
1998 Proof	Est. 20,000	Value: 45.00				

KM# 828 1/25 CROWN
1.2441 g., 0.9999 Gold .0400 oz. AGW, 13.9 mm.
Ruler: Elizabeth II **Series:** Flower Fairies **Obv:** Crowned bust right **Obv. Designer:** Raphael Maklouf **Rev:** Fairy standing, lavender **Rev. Designer:** Cecily Mary Barker

Date	Mintage	F	VF	XF	Unc	BU
1998 Proof	Est. 25,000	Value: 45.00				

KM# 828a 1/25 CROWN
1.2441 g., 0.9995 Platinum .0400 oz. APW, 13.9 mm.
Ruler: Elizabeth II **Series:** Flower Fairies **Obv:** Crowned bust right **Obv. Designer:** Raphael Maklouf **Rev:** Fairy standing, lavender **Rev. Designer:** Cecily Mary Barker

Date	Mintage	F	VF	XF	Unc	BU
1998 Proof	Est. 7,500	Value: 60.00				

KM# 829 1/25 CROWN
1.2441 g., 0.9999 Gold .0400 oz. AGW, 13.9 mm.
Ruler: Elizabeth II **Series:** Flower Fairies **Obv:** Crowned bust right **Obv. Designer:** Raphael Maklouf **Rev:** Two fairies, sweet pea **Rev. Designer:** Cecily Mary Barker

Date	Mintage	F	VF	XF	Unc	BU
1998 Proof	Est. 25,000	Value: 45.00				

KM# 829a 1/25 CROWN
1.2441 g., 0.9995 Platinum .0400 oz. APW, 13.9 mm.
Ruler: Elizabeth II **Series:** Flower Fairies **Obv:** Crowned bust right **Obv. Designer:** Raphael Maklouf **Rev:** Two fairies, sweet pea **Rev. Designer:** Cecily Mary Barker

Date	Mintage	F	VF	XF	Unc	BU
1998 Proof	Est. 7,500	Value: 60.00				

KM# 830 1/25 CROWN
1.2441 g., 0.9999 Gold .0400 oz. AGW, 13.9 mm.
Ruler: Elizabeth II **Series:** Flower Fairies **Obv:** Crowned bust right **Obv. Designer:** Raphael Maklouf **Rev:** Two fairies, sweet pea **Rev. Designer:** Cecily Mary Barker

Date	Mintage	F	VF	XF	Unc	BU
1998 Proof	—	Value: 45.00				

KM# 830a 1/25 CROWN
1.2441 g., 0.9995 Platinum .0400 oz. APW, 13.9 mm.
Ruler: Elizabeth II **Series:** Flower Fairies **Obv:** Crowned bust right **Obv. Designer:** Raphael Maklouf **Rev:** Two fairies, sweet pea **Rev. Designer:** Cecily Mary Barker

Date	Mintage	F	VF	XF	Unc	BU
1998 Proof	Est. 30,000	Value: 60.00				

KM# 831 1/25 CROWN
1.2441 g., 0.9999 Gold .0400 oz. AGW, 13.9 mm.
Ruler: Elizabeth II **Series:** Flower Fairies **Obv:** Crowned bust right **Obv. Designer:** Raphael Maklouf **Rev:** Fairy standing, daffodil **Rev. Designer:** Cecily Mary Barker

Date	Mintage	F	VF	XF	Unc	BU
1998 Proof	Est. 25,000	Value: 45.00				

KM# 831a 1/25 CROWN
1.2441 g., 0.9995 Platinum .0400 oz. APW, 13.9 mm.
Ruler: Elizabeth II **Series:** Flower Fairies **Obv:** Crowned bust right **Obv. Designer:** Raphael Maklouf **Rev:** Fairy standing, daffodil **Rev. Designer:** Cecily Mary Barker

Date	Mintage	F	VF	XF	Unc	BU
1998 Proof	Est. 7,500	Value: 60.00				

KM# 853 1/25 CROWN
1.2440 g., 0.9999 Gold .0400 oz. AGW, 13.9 mm.
Ruler: Elizabeth II **Obv:** Crowned bust right
Obv. Designer: Raphael Maklouf **Rev:** Birman cat

Date	Mintage	F	VF	XF	Unc	BU
1998	—	—	—	—	40.00	—
1998 Proof	1,000	Value: 42.00				

KM# 853a 1/25 CROWN
1.2440 g., 0.9995 Platinum .0400 oz. APW, 13.9 mm.
Ruler: Elizabeth II **Obv:** Crowned bust right
Obv. Designer: Raphael Maklouf **Rev:** Birman cat

Date	Mintage	F	VF	XF	Unc	BU
1998 Proof	—	Value: 60.00				

KM# 859 1/25 CROWN
1.2440 g., 0.9999 Gold .0400 oz. AGW, 13.9 mm.
Ruler: Elizabeth II **Subject:** History of the Cat **Obv:** Crowned bust right **Obv. Designer:** Raphael Maklouf **Rev:** Egyptian Mau cat with earring

Date	Mintage	F	VF	XF	Unc	BU
1998 Proof	Est. 25,000	Value: 45.00				

KM# 948 1/25 CROWN
1.2440 g., 0.9999 Gold .0400 oz. AGW, 13.9 mm.
Ruler: Elizabeth II **Subject:** Year of the Rabbit **Obv:** Crowned bust right **Obv. Designer:** Raphael Maklouf **Rev:** Two rabbits

Date	Mintage	F	VF	XF	Unc	BU
1999 Proof	Est. 20,000	Value: 45.00				

KM# 958 1/25 CROWN
1.2440 g., 0.9999 Gold .0400 oz. AGW, 13.9 mm.
Ruler: Elizabeth II **Obv:** Crowned bust right
Obv. Designer: Raphael Maklouf **Rev:** British Blue cat

Date	Mintage	F	VF	XF	Unc	BU
1999	—	—	—	—	40.00	—
1999 Proof	—	Value: 42.00				
1999 U Y2K	20,000	—	—	—	40.00	—

KM# 958a 1/25 CROWN
1.2441 g., 0.9995 Platinum .0400 oz. APW, 13.9 mm.
Ruler: Elizabeth II **Obv:** Crowned bust right
Obv. Designer: Raphael Maklouf **Rev:** British Blue cat

Date	Mintage	F	VF	XF	Unc	BU
1999 Proof	—	Value: 60.00				

KM# 1052 1/25 CROWN
1.2400 g., 0.9999 Gold .0399 oz. AGW, 13.92 mm.
Ruler: Elizabeth II **Obv:** Crowned bust right **Obv. Designer:** Raphael Maklouf **Rev:** Scottish fold kitten **Edge:** Reeded

Date	Mintage	F	VF	XF	Unc	BU
2000	—	—	—	—	35.00	—
2000 Proof	—	Value: 45.00				

KM# 1052a 1/25 CROWN
1.2441 g., 0.9995 Platinum .0400 oz. APW, 13.9 mm.
Ruler: Elizabeth II **Obv:** Crowned bust right
Obv. Designer: Raphael Maklouf **Rev:** Scottish fold kitten

Date	Mintage	F	VF	XF	Unc	BU
2000	—	—	—	—	42.00	—

KM# 1012 1/25 CROWN
1.2440 g., 0.9999 Gold .0400 oz. AGW, 13.9 mm.
Ruler: Elizabeth II **Subject:** Year of the Dragon **Obv:** Crowned bust right **Obv. Designer:** Raphael Maklouf **Rev:** Dragon, Chinese characters

Date	Mintage	F	VF	XF	Unc	BU
2000 Proof	Est. 20,000	Value: 45.00				

KM# 236 1/10 CROWN
3.1100 g., 0.9990 Gold .1000 oz. AGW **Ruler:** Elizabeth II **Obv:** Crowned bust right **Obv. Designer:** Raphael Maklouf **Rev:** Manx cat

Date	Mintage	F	VF	XF	Unc	BU
1988	12,000	—	—	—	100	—
1988 Proof	5,000	Value: 102				

KM# 253 1/10 CROWN
3.1100 g., 0.9990 Gold .1000 oz. AGW, 17.95 mm.
Ruler: Elizabeth II **Obv:** Crowned bust right
Obv. Designer: Raphael Maklouf **Rev:** Persian cat

Date	Mintage	F	VF	XF	Unc	BU
1989	—	—	—	—	85.00	—
1989 Proof	—	Value: 90.00				

KM# 468 1/10 CROWN
3.1100 g., 0.9995 Platinum .1000 oz. APW, 17.95 mm.
Ruler: Elizabeth II **Obv:** Crowned bust right
Obv. Designer: Raphael Maklouf **Rev:** Persian cat

Date	Mintage	F	VF	XF	Unc	BU
1989	—	—	—	—	125	—
1989 Proof	—	Value: 135				

KM# 278 1/10 CROWN
3.1100 g., 0.9990 Gold .1000 oz. AGW, 17.95 mm.
Ruler: Elizabeth II **Obv:** Crowned bust right
Obv. Designer: Raphael Maklouf **Rev:** Alley cat

Date	Mintage	F	VF	XF	Unc	BU
1990	—	—	—	—	75.00	—
1990 Proof	—	Value: 80.00				

KM# 295 1/10 CROWN
3.1100 g., 0.9990 Gold .1000 oz. AGW, 17.95 mm.
Ruler: Elizabeth II **Obv:** Crowned bust right
Obv. Designer: Raphael Maklouf **Rev:** Norwegian cat

Date	Mintage	F	VF	XF	Unc	BU
1991	—	—	—	—	75.00	—
1991 Proof	—	Value: 80.00				

KM# 323 1/10 CROWN
3.1100 g., 0.9990 Gold .1000 oz. AGW, 17.95 mm.
Ruler: Elizabeth II **Subject:** America's Cup **Obv:** Crowned bust right **Obv. Designer:** Raphael Maklouf **Rev:** Cameo of "Star of India" above two modern sailboats

Date	Mintage	F	VF	XF	Unc	BU
1992 Prooflike	25,000	—	—	—	125	—

KM# 323a 1/10 CROWN
3.1100 g., 0.9995 Platinum .1000 oz. APW, 17.95 mm.
Ruler: Elizabeth II **Subject:** America's Cup **Obv:** Crowned bust right **Obv. Designer:** Raphael Maklouf **Rev:** Sailboat

Date	Mintage	F	VF	XF	Unc	BU
1992 Prooflike	5,000	—	—	—	180	—

KM# 329 1/10 CROWN
3.1100 g., 0.9990 Gold .1000 oz. AGW, 17.95 mm.
Ruler: Elizabeth II **Obv:** Crowned bust right
Obv. Designer: Raphael Maklouf **Rev:** Siamese cat

Date	Mintage	F	VF	XF	Unc	BU
1992	—	—	—	—	72.00	—
1992 Proof	—	Value: 75.00				

KM# 339 1/10 CROWN
3.1100 g., 0.9990 Gold .1000 oz. AGW, 17.95 mm.
Ruler: Elizabeth II **Subject:** Year of the Cockerel **Obv:** Crowned bust right **Obv. Designer:** Raphael Maklouf **Rev:** Cockerel in inner circle **Rev. Designer:** Barry Stanton

Date	Mintage	F	VF	XF	Unc	BU
1993 Proof	Est. 20,000	Value: 85.00				

KM# 350 1/10 CROWN
3.1100 g., 0.9990 Gold .1000 oz. AGW, 17.95 mm.
Ruler: Elizabeth II **Obv:** Crowned bust right
Obv. Designer: Raphael Maklouf **Rev:** Maine Coon cat

Date	Mintage	F	VF	XF	Unc	BU
1993	—	—	—	—	72.00	—
1993 Proof	—	Value: 75.00				

KM# 377 1/10 CROWN
3.1100 g., 0.9990 Gold .1000 oz. AGW, 17.95 mm.
Ruler: Elizabeth II **Obv:** Crowned bust right
Obv. Designer: Raphael Maklouf **Rev:** Japanese Bobtail cat

Date	Mintage	F	VF	XF	Unc	BU
1994	—	—	—	—	72.00	—
1994 Proof	—	Value: 75.00				

KM# 403 1/10 CROWN
3.1100 g., 0.9990 Gold .1000 oz. AGW, 17.95 mm.
Ruler: Elizabeth II **Obv:** Crowned bust right
Obv. Designer: Raphael Maklouf **Rev:** Pekingese dog

Date	Mintage	F	VF	XF	Unc	BU
1994 Proof	20,000	Value: 95.00				

KM# 474 1/10 CROWN
3.1100 g., 0.9995 Platinum .1000 oz. APW, 17.95 mm.
Ruler: Elizabeth II **Obv:** Crowned bust right
Obv. Designer: Raphael Maklouf **Rev:** Japanese Bobtail cat

Date	Mintage	F	VF	XF	Unc	BU
1994	—	—	—	—	125	—
1994 Proof	—	Value: 135				

KM# 443 1/10 CROWN
3.1100 g., 0.9990 Gold .1000 oz. AGW, 17.95 mm.
Ruler: Elizabeth II **Obv:** Crowned bust right
Obv. Designer: Raphael Maklouf **Rev:** Turkish cat

Date	Mintage	F	VF	XF	Unc	BU
1995	—	—	—	—	72.00	—
1995 Proof	—	Value: 75.00				

KM# 450 1/10 CROWN
3.1100 g., 0.9990 Gold .1000 oz. AGW, 17.95 mm.
Ruler: Elizabeth II **Subject:** Year of the Pig **Obv:** Crowned bust right **Obv. Designer:** Raphael Maklouf **Rev:** Sow with piglets

Date	Mintage	F	VF	XF	Unc	BU
1995 Proof	Est. 20,000	Value: 95.00				

KM# 479 1/10 CROWN
3.1100 g., 0.9995 Platinum .1000 oz. APW, 17.95 mm.
Ruler: Elizabeth II **Obv:** Crowned bust right
Obv. Designer: Raphael Maklouf **Rev:** Turkish cat

Date	Mintage	F	VF	XF	Unc	BU
1995	—	—	—	—	125	—
1995 Proof	—	Value: 135				

KM# 601 1/10 CROWN
3.1100 g., 0.9990 Gold .1000 oz. AGW, 17.95 mm.
Ruler: Elizabeth II **Series:** Flower Fairies **Obv:** Crowned bust right **Obv. Designer:** Raphael Maklouf **Rev:** Orchis
Rev. Designer: Cecily Mary Barker

Date	Mintage	F	VF	XF	Unc	BU
1996 Proof	Est. 20,000	Value: 90.00				

KM# 602 1/10 CROWN
3.1100 g., 0.9990 Gold .1000 oz. AGW, 17.95 mm.
Ruler: Elizabeth II **Series:** Flower Fairies **Obv:** Crowned bust right **Obv. Designer:** Raphael Maklouf **Rev:** Rose
Rev. Designer: Cecily Mary Barker

Date	Mintage	F	VF	XF	Unc	BU
1996 Proof	Est. 20,000	Value: 90.00				

KM# 603 1/10 CROWN
3.1100 g., 0.9990 Gold .1000 oz. AGW, 17.95 mm.
Ruler: Elizabeth II **Series:** Flower Fairies **Obv:** Crowned bust right **Obv. Designer:** Raphael Maklouf **Rev:** Fuchsia
Rev. Designer: Cecily Mary Barker

Date	Mintage	F	VF	XF	Unc	BU
1996 Proof	Est. 20,000	Value: 90.00				

KM# 604 1/10 CROWN
3.1100 g., 0.9990 Gold .1000 oz. AGW, 17.95 mm.
Ruler: Elizabeth II **Obv:** Crowned bust right **Obv. Designer:** Raphael Maklouf **Rev:** Pinks **Rev. Designer:** Cecily Mary Barker

Date	Mintage	F	VF	XF	Unc	BU
1996 Proof	Est. 20,000	Value: 90.00				

KM# 615 1/10 CROWN
3.1100 g., 0.9990 Gold .1000 oz. AGW, 17.95 mm.
Ruler: Elizabeth II **Obv:** Crowned bust right
Obv. Designer: Raphael Maklouf **Rev:** Burmese cat

Date	Mintage	F	VF	XF	Unc	BU
1996	—	—	—	—	67.00	—
1996 Proof	—	Value: 70.00				

KM# 616 1/10 CROWN
3.1100 g., 0.9995 Platinum .1000 oz. APW, 17.95 mm.
Ruler: Elizabeth II **Obv:** Crowned bust right
Obv. Designer: Raphael Maklouf **Rev:** Burmese cat

Date	Mintage	F	VF	XF	Unc	BU
1996	—	—	—	—	125	—
1996 Proof	—	Value: 135				

KM# 729 1/10 CROWN
3.1100 g., 0.9990 Gold .1000 oz. AGW, 17.95 mm.
Ruler: Elizabeth II **Subject:** Year of the Rat **Obv:** Crowned bust right **Obv. Designer:** Raphael Maklouf **Rev:** Rat

Date	Mintage	F	VF	XF	Unc	BU
1996 Proof	—	—	—	—	—	—

Note: Entire series purchased by one buyer. Mintage, disposition and market value unknown

KM# 722 1/10 CROWN
3.1100 g., 0.9990 Gold .1000 oz. AGW, 17.95 mm.
Ruler: Elizabeth II **Subject:** Year of the Ox **Obv:** Crowned bust right **Obv. Designer:** Raphael Maklouf **Rev:** Ox laying down

Date	Mintage	F	VF	XF	Unc	BU
1997 Proof	Est. 15,000	Value: 90.00				

KM# 743 1/10 CROWN
3.1100 g., 0.9990 Gold .1000 oz. AGW, 17.95 mm.
Ruler: Elizabeth II **Series:** Flower Fairies **Obv:** Crowned bust right **Obv. Designer:** Raphael Maklouf **Rev:** Candytuft
Rev. Designer: Cecily Mary Barker

Date	Mintage	F	VF	XF	Unc	BU
1997 Proof	Est. 20,000	Value: 80.00				

KM# 743a 1/10 CROWN
3.1259 g., 0.9950 Platinum .1000 oz. APW, 17.95 mm.
Ruler: Elizabeth II **Series:** Flower Fairies **Obv:** Crowned bust right **Obv. Designer:** Raphael Maklouf **Rev:** Candytuft
Rev. Designer: Cecily Mary Barker

Date	Mintage	F	VF	XF	Unc	BU
1997 Proof	Est. 5,000	Value: 125				

KM# 744 1/10 CROWN
3.1103 g., 0.9999 Gold .1000 oz. AGW, 17.95 mm. **Ruler:** Elizabeth II **Obv:** Crowned bust right **Obv. Designer:** Raphael Maklouf **Rev:** Snowdrop **Rev. Designer:** Cecily Mary Barker

Date	Mintage	F	VF	XF	Unc	BU
1997 Proof	Est. 20,000	Value: 80.00				

KM# 744a 1/10 CROWN
3.1259 g., 0.9950 Platinum .1000 oz. APW, 17.95 mm.
Ruler: Elizabeth II **Series:** Flower Fairies **Obv:** Crowned bust right **Obv. Designer:** Raphael Maklouf **Rev:** Snowdrop
Rev. Designer: Cecily Mary Barker

Date	Mintage	F	VF	XF	Unc	BU
1997 Proof	Est. 5,000	Value: 125				

KM# 745 1/10 CROWN
3.1103 g., 0.9999 Gold .1000 oz. AGW, 17.95 mm.
Ruler: Elizabeth II **Series:** Flower Fairies **Obv:** Crowned bust right **Obv. Designer:** Raphael Maklouf **Rev:** Tulip
Rev. Designer: Cecily Mary Barker

Date	Mintage	F	VF	XF	Unc	BU
1997 Proof	Est. 20,000	Value: 80.00				

KM# 745a 1/10 CROWN
3.1259 g., 0.9950 Platinum .1000 oz. APW, 17.95 mm.
Ruler: Elizabeth II **Series:** Flower Fairies **Obv:** Crowned bust right **Obv. Designer:** Raphael Maklouf **Rev:** Tulip
Rev. Designer: Cecily Mary Barker

Date	Mintage	F	VF	XF	Unc	BU
1997 Proof	Est. 5,000	Value: 125				

KM# 746 1/10 CROWN

3.1103 g., 0.9999 Gold .1000 oz. AGW, 17.95 mm.
Ruler: Elizabeth II **Series:** Flower Fairies **Obv:** Crowned bust right **Obv. Designer:** Raphael Maklouf **Rev:** Jasmine **Rev. Designer:** Cecily Mary Barker

Date	Mintage	F	VF	XF	Unc	BU
1997 Proof	Est. 20,000	Value: 80.00				

KM# 746a 1/10 CROWN

3.1259 g., 0.9950 Platinum .1000 oz. APW, 17.95 mm.
Ruler: Elizabeth II **Series:** Flower Fairies **Obv:** Crowned bust right **Obv. Designer:** Raphael Maklouf **Rev:** Jasmine **Rev. Designer:** Cecily Mary Barker

Date	Mintage	F	VF	XF	Unc	BU
1997 Proof	Est. 5,000	Value: 125				

KM# 771 1/10 CROWN

3.1100 g., 0.9999 Gold .1000 oz. AGW, 17.95 mm.
Ruler: Elizabeth II **Obv:** Crowned bust right **Obv. Designer:** Raphael Maklouf **Rev:** Long-haired Smoke cat

Date	Mintage	F	VF	XF	Unc	BU
1997	—	—	—	—	67.00	—
1997 Proof	—	Value: 70.00				

KM# 771a 1/10 CROWN

3.1100 g., 0.9995 Platinum .1000 oz. APW, 17.95 mm.
Ruler: Elizabeth II **Obv:** Crowned bust right **Obv. Designer:** Raphael Maklouf **Rev:** Long-haired Smoke cat

Date	Mintage	F	VF	XF	Unc	BU
1997	—	—	—	—	125	—
1997 Proof	—	Value: 135				

KM# 790 1/10 CROWN

3.1100 g., 0.9999 Gold .1000 oz. AGW, 17.95 mm. **Ruler:** Elizabeth II **Subject:** History of the Cat **Obv:** Crowned bust right **Obv. Designer:** Raphael Maklouf **Rev:** Cat stalking a spider

Date	Mintage	F	VF	XF	Unc	BU
1997 Proof	Est. 20,000	Value: 90.00				

KM# 813 1/10 CROWN

3.1100 g., 0.9999 Gold .1000 oz. AGW, 17.95 mm.
Ruler: Elizabeth II **Subject:** Year of the Tiger **Obv:** Crowned bust right **Obv. Designer:** Raphael Maklouf **Rev:** Tiger

Date	Mintage	F	VF	XF	Unc	BU
1998 Proof	Est. 15,000	Value: 90.00				

KM# 832 1/10 CROWN

3.1100 g., 0.9999 Gold .1000 oz. AGW, 17.95 mm.
Ruler: Elizabeth II **Series:** Flower Fairies **Obv:** Crowned bust right **Obv. Designer:** Raphael Maklouf **Rev:** Standing fairy, lavender **Rev. Designer:** Cecily Mary Barker

Date	Mintage	F	VF	XF	Unc	BU
1998 Proof	Est. 20,000	Value: 90.00				

KM# 832a 1/10 CROWN

3.1100 g., 0.9995 Platinum .1000 oz. APW, 17.95 mm.
Ruler: Elizabeth II **Series:** Flower Fairies **Obv:** Crowned bust right **Obv. Designer:** Raphael Maklouf **Rev:** Standing fairy, lavender **Rev. Designer:** Cecily Mary Barker

Date	Mintage	F	VF	XF	Unc	BU
1998 Proof	Est. 5,000	Value: 125				

KM# 833 1/10 CROWN

3.1100 g., 0.9999 Gold .1000 oz. AGW, 17.95 mm.
Ruler: Elizabeth II **Series:** Flower Fairies **Obv:** Crowned bust right **Obv. Designer:** Raphael Maklouf **Rev:** Two fairies, sweet pea **Rev. Designer:** Cecily Mary Barker

Date	Mintage	F	VF	XF	Unc	BU
1998 Proof	Est. 20,000	Value: 90.00				

KM# 833a 1/10 CROWN

3.1100 g., 0.9995 Platinum .1000 oz. APW, 17.95 mm.
Ruler: Elizabeth II **Series:** Flower Fairies **Obv:** Crowned bust right **Obv. Designer:** Raphael Maklouf **Rev:** Two fairies, sweet pea **Rev. Designer:** Cecily Mary Barker

Date	Mintage	F	VF	XF	Unc	BU
1998 Proof	Est. 5,000	Value: 125				

KM# 834 1/10 CROWN

3.1100 g., 0.9999 Gold .1000 oz. AGW, 17.95 mm.
Ruler: Elizabeth II **Obv:** Crowned bust right **Obv. Designer:** Raphael Maklouf **Rev:** Fairy looking into flower, White Bindweed **Rev. Designer:** Cecily Mary Barker

Date	Mintage	F	VF	XF	Unc	BU
1998 Proof	Est. 20,000	Value: 90.00				

KM# 834a 1/10 CROWN

3.1100 g., 0.9995 Platinum .1000 oz. APW, 17.95 mm.
Ruler: Elizabeth II **Series:** Flower Fairies **Obv:** Crowned bust right **Obv. Designer:** Raphael Maklouf **Rev:** Fairy looking into flower, White Bindweed **Rev. Designer:** Cecily Mary Barker

Date	Mintage	F	VF	XF	Unc	BU
1998 Proof	Est. 5,000	Value: 125				

KM# 835 1/10 CROWN

3.1100 g., 0.9999 Gold .1000 oz. AGW, 17.95 mm.
Ruler: Elizabeth II **Series:** Flower Fairies **Obv:** Crowned bust right **Obv. Designer:** Raphael Maklouf **Rev:** Fairy standing with flower, daffodil **Rev. Designer:** Cecily Mary Barker

Date	Mintage	F	VF	XF	Unc	BU
1998 Proof	Est. 20,000	Value: 90.00				

KM# 835a 1/10 CROWN

3.1100 g., 0.9995 Platinum .1000 oz. APW, 17.95 mm.
Ruler: Elizabeth II **Obv:** Crowned bust right **Obv. Designer:** Raphael Maklouf **Rev:** Fairy standing with flower, daffodil **Rev. Legend:** Flower Fairies **Rev. Designer:** Cecily Mary Barker

Date	Mintage	F	VF	XF	Unc	BU
1998 Proof	Est. 5,000	Value: 125				

KM# 854 1/10 CROWN

3.1100 g., 0.9999 Gold .1000 oz. AGW, 17.95 mm.
Ruler: Elizabeth II **Obv:** Crowned bust right **Obv. Designer:** Raphael Maklouf **Rev:** Birman cat

Date	Mintage	F	VF	XF	Unc	BU
1998	—	—	—	—	70.00	—
1998 Proof	1,000	Value: 72.00				

KM# 854a 1/10 CROWN

3.1100 g., 0.9995 Platinum .1000 oz. APW, 17.95 mm.
Ruler: Elizabeth II **Obv:** Crowned bust right **Obv. Designer:** Raphael Maklouf **Rev:** Birman cat

Date	Mintage	F	VF	XF	Unc	BU
1998 Proof	—	Value: 130				

KM# 860 1/10 CROWN

3.1100 g., 0.9999 Gold .1000 oz. AGW, 17.95 mm.
Ruler: Elizabeth II **Subject:** History of the Cat **Obv:** Crowned bust right **Obv. Designer:** Raphael Maklouf **Rev:** Egyptian Mau cat with earring

Date	Mintage	F	VF	XF	Unc	BU
1998 Proof	Est. 20,000	Value: 90.00				

KM# 949 1/10 CROWN

3.1100 g., 0.9999 Gold .1000 oz. AGW, 17.95 mm.
Ruler: Elizabeth II **Subject:** Year of the Rabbit **Obv:** Crowned bust right **Obv. Designer:** Raphael Maklouf **Rev:** Two rabbits

Date	Mintage	F	VF	XF	Unc	BU
1999 Proof	—	Value: 90.00				

KM# 960 1/10 CROWN

3.1100 g., 0.9999 Gold .1000 oz. AGW, 17.95 mm.
Ruler: Elizabeth II **Obv:** Crowned bust right **Obv. Designer:** Raphael Maklouf **Rev:** British Blue cat cleaning its paw

Date	Mintage	F	VF	XF	Unc	BU
1999	—	—	—	—	75.00	—
1999 Proof	—	Value: 90.00				
1999 U Y2K	10,000	—	—	—	75.00	—

KM# 960a 1/10 CROWN

3.1104 g., 0.9995 Platinum .1000 oz. APW, 17.95 mm.
Ruler: Elizabeth II **Obv:** Crowned bust right **Obv. Designer:** Raphael Maklouf **Rev:** British Blue cat cleaning its paw

Date	Mintage	F	VF	XF	Unc	BU
1999 Proof	—	Value: 125				

KM# 1053 1/10 CROWN

3.1100 g., 0.9999 Gold .1000 oz. AGW, 17.95 mm. **Ruler:** Elizabeth II **Obv:** Crowned bust right **Obv. Designer:** Raphael Maklouf **Rev:** Scottish kitten playing with the world **Edge:** Reeded

Date	Mintage	F	VF	XF	Unc	BU
2000	—	—	—	—	75.00	—
2000 Proof	—	Value: 90.00				

KM# 1053a 1/10 CROWN

3.1104 g., 0.9995 Platinum .1000 oz. APW, 17.95 mm.
Ruler: Elizabeth II **Obv:** Crowned bust right **Obv. Designer:** Raphael Maklouf **Rev:** Scottish kitten playing with the world

Date	Mintage	F	VF	XF	Unc	BU
2000	—	—	—	—	125	—

KM# 1013 1/10 CROWN

3.1100 g., 0.9999 Gold .1000 oz. AGW, 17.95 mm.
Ruler: Elizabeth II **Subject:** Year of the Dragon **Obv:** Crowned bust right **Obv. Designer:** Raphael Maklouf **Rev:** Dragon, Chinese characters

Date	Mintage	F	VF	XF	Unc	BU
2000 Proof	Est. 15,000	Value: 90.00				

KM# 237 1/5 CROWN

6.2200 g., 0.9990 Gold .2000 oz. AGW, 22 mm.
Ruler: Elizabeth II **Obv:** Crowned bust right **Obv. Designer:** Raphael Maklouf **Rev:** Manx cat

Date	Mintage	F	VF	XF	Unc	BU
1988	6,750	—	—	—	175	—
1988 Proof	5,000	Value: 190				

KM# 254 1/5 CROWN

6.2200 g., 0.9990 Gold .2000 oz. AGW, 22 mm.
Ruler: Elizabeth II **Obv:** Crowned bust right **Obv. Designer:** Raphael Maklouf **Rev:** Persian cat

Date	Mintage	F	VF	XF	Unc	BU
1989	—	—	—	—	150	—
1989 Proof	—	Value: 152				

KM# 274 1/5 CROWN

6.2200 g., 0.9990 Gold .2000 oz. AGW, 22 mm.
Ruler: Elizabeth II **Obv:** Crowned bust right **Obv. Designer:** Raphael Maklouf **Rev:** Cameo head facing within circle

Date	Mintage	F	VF	XF	Unc	BU
1989 Proof	Est. 5,000	Value: 180				

KM# 469 1/5 CROWN

6.2200 g., 0.9990 Platinum .2000 oz. APW, 22 mm.
Ruler: Elizabeth II **Obv:** Crowned bust right **Obv. Designer:** Raphael Maklouf **Rev:** Persian cat

Date	Mintage	F	VF	XF	Unc	BU
1989	—	—	—	—	260	—
1989 Proof	—	Value: 265				

KM# 268 1/5 CROWN

6.2200 g., 0.9990 Gold .2000 oz. AGW, 22 mm.
Ruler: Elizabeth II **Subject:** 150th Anniversary of "Penny Black" Stamp **Obv:** Crowned bust right **Obv. Designer:** Raphael Maklouf **Rev:** Penny Black Stamp

Date	Mintage	F	VF	XF	Unc	BU
1990 Proof	Est. 5,000	Value: 210				

KM# 279.1 1/5 CROWN

6.2200 g., 0.9990 Gold .2000 oz. AGW, 22 mm.
Ruler: Elizabeth II **Obv:** Crowned bust right **Obv. Designer:** Raphael Maklouf **Rev:** Alley cat

Date	Mintage	F	VF	XF	Unc	BU
1990	—	—	—	—	150	—
1990 Proof	—	Value: 175				

KM# 279.2 1/5 CROWN

6.2200 g., 0.9990 Gold .2000 oz. AGW, 22 mm.
Ruler: Elizabeth II **Obv:** Crowned bust right **Obv. Designer:** Raphael Maklouf **Rev:** Alley cat **Note:** Error.(Rev) Dies claiming platinum metal content

Date	Mintage	F	VF	XF	Unc	BU
1990	467	—	—	—	400	—

KM# 306 1/5 CROWN

6.2200 g., 0.9990 Gold .2000 oz. AGW, 22 mm.
Ruler: Elizabeth II **Obv:** Crowned bust right **Obv. Designer:** Raphael Maklouf **Rev:** Queen Mother with two daughters

Date	Mintage	F	VF	XF	Unc	BU
1990 Proof	—	Value: 200				

KM# 306a 1/5 CROWN

6.2200 g., 0.9990 Platinum .2000 oz. APW, 22 mm.
Ruler: Elizabeth II **Obv:** Crowned bust right **Obv. Designer:** Raphael Maklouf **Rev:** Queen Mother with two daughters

Date	Mintage	F	VF	XF	Unc	BU
1990 Proof	—	Value: 265				

KM# 472 1/5 CROWN

6.2200 g., 0.9990 Platinum .2000 oz. APW, 22 mm.
Ruler: Elizabeth II **Obv:** Crowned bust right **Obv. Designer:** Raphael Maklouf **Rev:** Alley cat

Date	Mintage	F	VF	XF	Unc	BU
1990	—	—	—	—	265	—
1990 Proof	—	Value: 275				

KM# 819 1/5 CROWN

6.2200 g., 0.9990 Gold .2000 oz. AGW, 22 mm.
Ruler: Elizabeth II **Subject:** Soccer **Obv:** Crowned bust right **Obv. Designer:** Raphael Maklouf **Rev:** Milano

Date	Mintage	F	VF	XF	Unc	BU
1990 Proof	Est. 500	Value: 135				

KM# 819a 1/5 CROWN

6.2200 g., 0.9990 Platinum .2000 oz. APW, 22 mm.
Ruler: Elizabeth II **Subject:** Soccer **Obv:** Crowned bust right **Obv. Designer:** Raphael Maklouf **Rev:** Milano

Date	Mintage	F	VF	XF	Unc	BU
1990 Proof	Est. 250	Value: 275				

KM# 820 1/5 CROWN

6.2200 g., 0.9990 Gold .2000 oz. AGW, 22 mm.
Ruler: Elizabeth II **Subject:** Soccer **Obv:** Crowned bust right **Obv. Designer:** Raphael Maklouf **Rev:** Torino

Date	Mintage	F	VF	XF	Unc	BU
1990 Proof	Est. 500	Value: 135				

KM# 820a 1/5 CROWN

6.2200 g., 0.9990 Platinum .2000 oz. APW, 22 mm.
Ruler: Elizabeth II **Subject:** Soccer **Obv:** Crowned bust right **Obv. Designer:** Raphael Maklouf **Rev:** Torino

Date	Mintage	F	VF	XF	Unc	BU
1990 Proof	Est. 250	Value: 275				

KM# 821 1/5 CROWN

6.2200 g., 0.9990 Gold .2000 oz. AGW, 22 mm.
Ruler: Elizabeth II **Subject:** Soccer **Obv:** Crowned bust right **Obv. Designer:** Raphael Maklouf **Rev:** Bologna

Date	Mintage	F	VF	XF	Unc	BU
1990 Proof	Est. 500	Value: 135				

KM# 821a 1/5 CROWN

6.2200 g., 0.9990 Platinum .2000 oz. APW, 22 mm.
Ruler: Elizabeth II **Subject:** Soccer **Obv:** Crowned bust right **Obv. Designer:** Raphael Maklouf **Rev:** Bologna

Date	Mintage	F	VF	XF	Unc	BU
1990	Est. 250	Value: 275				

KM# 822 1/5 CROWN

6.2200 g., 0.9990 Gold .2000 oz. AGW, 22 mm.
Ruler: Elizabeth II **Subject:** Soccer **Obv:** Crowned bust right **Obv. Designer:** Raphael Maklouf **Rev:** Palermo

Date	Mintage	F	VF	XF	Unc	BU
1990 Proof	Est. 500	Value: 135				

KM# 822a 1/5 CROWN
6.2200 g., 0.9990 Platinum .2000 oz. APW, 22 mm.
Ruler: Elizabeth II **Subject:** Soccer **Obv:** Crowned bust right
Obv. Designer: Raphael Maklouf **Rev:** Palermo

Date	Mintage	F	VF	XF	Unc	BU
1990	Est. 250	Value: 275				

KM# 290 1/5 CROWN
6.2200 g., 0.9990 Gold .2000 oz. AGW, 22 mm.
Ruler: Elizabeth II **Subject:** 100th Anniversary - American Numismatic Association **Obv:** Crowned bust right **Obv. Designer:** Raphael Maklouf **Rev:** Assorted famous world coins

Date	Mintage	F	VF	XF	Unc	BU
1991 Proof	100	Value: 185				

KM# 296 1/5 CROWN
6.2200 g., 0.9990 Gold .2000 oz. AGW, 22 mm.
Ruler: Elizabeth II **Obv:** Crowned bust right
Obv. Designer: Raphael Maklouf **Rev:** Norwegian cat

Date	Mintage	F	VF	XF	Unc	BU
1991	—	—	—	—	145	—
1991 Proof	—	Value: 150				

KM# 302 1/5 CROWN
6.2200 g., 0.9990 Gold .2000 oz. AGW, 22 mm. **Ruler:** Elizabeth II **Subject:** America's Cup **Obv:** Crowned bust right **Obv. Designer:** Raphael Maklouf **Rev:** Cameo above two modern sailboats

Date	Mintage	F	VF	XF	Unc	BU
1991 Proof	Est. 250	Value: 190				

KM# 324 1/5 CROWN
6.2200 g., 0.9990 Gold .2000 oz. AGW, 22 mm. **Ruler:** Elizabeth II **Subject:** America's Cup **Obv:** Crowned bust right **Obv. Designer:** Raphael Maklouf **Rev:** Cameo above two modern sailboats

Date	Mintage	F	VF	XF	Unc	BU
1992 Prooflike	10,000	—	—	—	140	—

KM# 330 1/5 CROWN
6.2200 g., 0.9990 Gold .2000 oz. AGW, 22 mm.
Ruler: Elizabeth II **Obv:** Crowned bust right
Obv. Designer: Raphael Maklouf **Rev:** Siamese cat

Date	Mintage	F	VF	XF	Unc	BU
1992	—	—	—	—	145	—
1992 Proof	—	Value: 150				

KM# 340 1/5 CROWN
6.2200 g., 0.9990 Gold .2000 oz. AGW, 22 mm.
Ruler: Elizabeth II **Subject:** Year of the Cockerel **Obv:** Crowned bust right within circle **Obv. Designer:** Raphael Maklouf **Rev:** Cockerel within circle **Rev. Designer:** Barry Stanton

Date	Mintage	F	VF	XF	Unc	BU
1993 Proof	Est. 10,000	Value: 160				

KM# 351 1/5 CROWN
6.2200 g., 0.9990 Gold .2000 oz. AGW, 22 mm.
Ruler: Elizabeth II **Obv:** Crowned bust right
Obv. Designer: Raphael Maklouf **Rev:** Maine Coon cat

Date	Mintage	F	VF	XF	Unc	BU
1993	—	—	—	—	145	—
1993 Proof	—	Value: 160				

KM# 365 1/5 CROWN
6.2200 g., 0.9990 Gold .2000 oz. AGW, 22 mm.
Ruler: Elizabeth II **Subject:** World Cup Soccer - Type I **Obv:** Crowned bust right **Obv. Designer:** Raphael Maklouf **Rev:** Player in foreground kicking ball

Date	Mintage	F	VF	XF	Unc	BU
1994 Proof	Est. 5,000	Value: 165				

KM# 367 1/5 CROWN
6.2200 g., 0.9990 Gold .2000 oz. AGW, 22 mm. **Ruler:** Elizabeth II **Subject:** World Cup Soccer - Type II **Obv:** Crowned bust right **Obv. Designer:** Raphael Maklouf **Rev:** Three players

Date	Mintage	F	VF	XF	Unc	BU
1994 Proof	Est. 5,000	Value: 165				

KM# 369 1/5 CROWN
6.2200 g., 0.9990 Gold .2000 oz. AGW, 22 mm. **Ruler:** Elizabeth II **Subject:** World Cup Soccer - Type III **Obv:** Crowned bust right **Obv. Designer:** Raphael Maklouf **Rev:** Soccer players

Date	Mintage	F	VF	XF	Unc	BU
1994 Proof	Est. 5,000	Value: 165				

KM# 371 1/5 CROWN
6.2200 g., 0.9990 Gold .2000 oz. AGW, 22 mm. **Ruler:** Elizabeth II **Subject:** World Cup Soccer - Type IV **Obv:** Crowned bust right **Obv. Designer:** Raphael Maklouf **Rev:** Soccer players

Date	Mintage	F	VF	XF	Unc	BU
1994 Proof	Est. 5,000	Value: 165				

KM# 373 1/5 CROWN
6.2200 g., 0.9990 Gold .2000 oz. AGW, 22 mm. **Ruler:** Elizabeth II **Subject:** World Cup Soccer - Type V **Obv:** Crowned bust right **Obv. Designer:** Raphael Maklouf **Rev:** Goalie catching ball in hand

Date	Mintage	F	VF	XF	Unc	BU
1994 Proof	Est. 5,000	Value: 165				

KM# 375 1/5 CROWN
6.2200 g., 0.9990 Gold .2000 oz. AGW, 22 mm. **Ruler:** Elizabeth II **Subject:** World Cup Soccer - Type VI **Obv:** Crowned bust right **Obv. Designer:** Raphael Maklouf **Rev:** Soccer players

Date	Mintage	F	VF	XF	Unc	BU
1994 Proof	Est. 5,000	Value: 165				

KM# 378 1/5 CROWN
6.2200 g., 0.9990 Gold .2000 oz. AGW, 22 mm.
Ruler: Elizabeth II **Obv:** Crowned bust right
Obv. Designer: Raphael Maklouf **Rev:** Japanese Bobtail cat

Date	Mintage	F	VF	XF	Unc	BU
1994	—	—	—	—	145	—
1994 Proof	—	Value: 160				

KM# 383 1/5 CROWN
6.2200 g., 0.9990 Gold .2000 oz. AGW, 22 mm. **Ruler:** Elizabeth II **Series:** Preserve Planet Earth **Obv:** Crowned bust right **Obv. Designer:** Raphael Maklouf **Rev:** Woolly mammoth

Date	Mintage	F	VF	XF	Unc	BU
1994 Proof	Est. 5,000	Value: 165				

KM# 388 1/5 CROWN
6.2200 g., 0.9990 Gold .2000 oz. AGW, 22 mm.
Ruler: Elizabeth II **Series:** Preserve Planet Earth **Obv:** Crowned bust right **Obv. Designer:** Raphael Maklouf **Rev:** Kangaroos

Date	Mintage	F	VF	XF	Unc	BU
1994 Proof	5,000	Value: 165				

KM# 389 1/5 CROWN
6.2200 g., 0.9990 Gold .2000 oz. AGW, 22 mm.
Ruler: Elizabeth II **Series:** Preserve Planet Earth **Obv:** Crowned bust right **Obv. Designer:** Raphael Maklouf **Rev:** Seals

Date	Mintage	F	VF	XF	Unc	BU
1994 Proof	5,000	Value: 165				

KM# 390 1/5 CROWN
6.2200 g., 0.9990 Gold .2000 oz. AGW, 22 mm.
Ruler: Elizabeth II **Series:** Preserve Planet Earth **Obv:** Crowned bust right **Obv. Designer:** Raphael Maklouf **Rev:** Deer

Date	Mintage	F	VF	XF	Unc	BU
1994 Proof	5,000	Value: 165				

KM# 404 1/5 CROWN
6.2200 g., 0.9990 Gold .2000 oz. AGW, 22 mm.
Ruler: Elizabeth II **Obv:** Crowned bust right
Obv. Designer: Raphael Maklouf **Rev:** Pekingese

Date	Mintage	F	VF	XF	Unc	BU
1994 Proof	10,000	Value: 165				

KM# 409 1/5 CROWN
6.2200 g., 0.9990 Gold .2000 oz. AGW, 22 mm.
Ruler: Elizabeth II **Series:** Man in Flight **Obv:** Crowned bust right **Obv. Designer:** Raphael Maklouf **Rev:** Manned glider

Date	Mintage	F	VF	XF	Unc	BU
1994 Proof	Est. 5,000	Value: 170				

KM# 410 1/5 CROWN
6.2200 g., 0.9990 Gold .2000 oz. AGW, 22 mm. **Ruler:** Elizabeth II **Series:** Man in Flight **Obv:** Crowned bust right **Obv. Designer:** Raphael Maklouf **Rev:** Dirigible, Ferdinand von Zeppelin

Date	Mintage	F	VF	XF	Unc	BU
1994 Proof	Est. 5,000	Value: 170				

KM# 411 1/5 CROWN
6.2200 g., 0.9990 Gold .2000 oz. AGW, 22 mm.
Ruler: Elizabeth II **Series:** Man in Flight **Obv:** Crowned bust right **Obv. Designer:** Raphael Maklouf **Rev:** Bust of Louis Bleriot behind plane flying across channel

Date	Mintage	F	VF	XF	Unc	BU
1994 Proof	Est. 5,000	Value: 170				

KM# 412 1/5 CROWN
6.2200 g., 0.9990 Gold .2000 oz. AGW, 22 mm. **Ruler:** Elizabeth II **Series:** Man in Flight **Obv:** Crowned bust right **Obv. Designer:** Raphael Maklouf **Rev:** Plane in flight above ocean

Date	Mintage	F	VF	XF	Unc	BU
1994 Proof	Est. 5,000	Value: 170				

KM# 413 1/5 CROWN
6.2200 g., 0.9990 Gold .2000 oz. AGW, 22 mm.
Ruler: Elizabeth II **Series:** Man in Flight **Subject:** First England to Australia Flight **Obv:** Crowned bust right
Obv. Designer: Raphael Maklouf **Rev:** Biplane flying

Date	Mintage	F	VF	XF	Unc	BU
1994 Proof	Est. 5,000	Value: 170				

KM# 414 1/5 CROWN
6.2200 g., 0.9990 Gold .2000 oz. AGW, 22 mm.
Ruler: Elizabeth II **Series:** Man in Flight **Subject:** 60th Anniversary of Airmail **Obv:** Crowned bust right **Obv. Designer:** Raphael Maklouf **Rev:** Plane flying left above inscription

Date	Mintage	F	VF	XF	Unc	BU
1994 Proof	Est. 5,000	Value: 170				

KM# 415 1/5 CROWN
6.2200 g., 0.9990 Gold .2000 oz. AGW, 22 mm. **Ruler:** Elizabeth II **Series:** Man in Flight **Subject:** 50th Anniversary of International Civil Aviation Organization **Obv:** Crowned bust right **Obv. Designer:** Raphael Maklouf **Rev:** Trademark of ICAO

Date	Mintage	F	VF	XF	Unc	BU
1994 Proof	Est. 5,000	Value: 170				

KM# 416 1/5 CROWN
6.2200 g., 0.9990 Gold .2000 oz. AGW, 22 mm. **Ruler:** Elizabeth II **Series:** Man in Flight **Subject:** First Concorde Flight **Obv:** Crowned bust right **Obv. Designer:** Raphael Maklouf **Rev:** Concorde waiting at airport

Date	Mintage	F	VF	XF	Unc	BU
1994 Proof	Est. 5,000	Value: 170				

KM# 475 1/5 CROWN
6.2200 g., 0.9990 Platinum .2000 oz. APW, 22 mm.
Ruler: Elizabeth II **Obv:** Crowned bust right **Obv. Designer:** Raphael Maklouf **Rev:** Japanese Bobtail cat

Date	Mintage	F	VF	XF	Unc	BU
1994	—	—	—	—	260	—
1994 Proof	—	Value: 270				

KM# 429 1/5 CROWN
6.2200 g., 0.9990 Gold .2000 oz. AGW, 22 mm.
Ruler: Elizabeth II **Series:** Man in Flight **Obv:** Crowned bust right **Obv. Designer:** Raphael Maklouf **Rev:** Airplane in flight

Date	Mintage	F	VF	XF	Unc	BU
1995 Proof	Est. 5,000	Value: 170				

KM# 426 1/5 CROWN
6.2200 g., 0.9990 Gold .2000 oz. AGW, 22 mm.
Ruler: Elizabeth II **Series:** Man in Flight **Obv:** Crowned bust right **Obv. Designer:** Raphael Maklouf **Rev:** Icarus' wings melting

Date	Mintage	F	VF	XF	Unc	BU
1995 Proof	Est. 5,000	Value: 170				

KM# 427 1/5 CROWN
6.2200 g., 0.9990 Gold .2000 oz. AGW, 22 mm. **Ruler:** Elizabeth II **Series:** Man in Flight **Obv:** Crowned bust right **Obv. Designer:** Raphael Maklouf **Rev:** Leonardo Da Vinci and aircraft design

Date	Mintage	F	VF	XF	Unc	BU
1995 Proof	Est. 5,000	Value: 170				

KM# 428 1/5 CROWN
6.2200 g., 0.9990 Gold .2000 oz. AGW, 22 mm.
Ruler: Elizabeth II **Series:** Man in Flight **Obv:** Crowned bust right **Obv. Designer:** Raphael Maklouf **Rev:** Balloon in flight

Date	Mintage	F	VF	XF	Unc	BU
1995 Proof	Est. 5,000	Value: 170				

KM# 430 1/5 CROWN
6.2200 g., 0.9990 Gold .2000 oz. AGW, 22 mm.
Ruler: Elizabeth II **Series:** Man in Flight **Subject:** 1st Flight Tokyo to Paris by Abe and Kawachi **Obv:** Crowned bust right **Obv. Designer:** Raphael Maklouf **Rev:** Busts above airplane

Date	Mintage	F	VF	XF	Unc	BU
1995 Proof	Est. 5,000	Value: 170				

KM# 431 1/5 CROWN
6.2200 g., 0.9990 Gold .2000 oz. AGW, 22 mm.
Ruler: Elizabeth II **Series:** Man in Flight **Subject:** FW109, First Diesel Powered Aircraft **Obv:** Crowned bust right
Obv. Designer: Raphael Maklouf **Rev:** Grounded airplane

Date	Mintage	F	VF	XF	Unc	BU
1995 Proof	Est. 5,000	Value: 170				

KM# 432 1/5 CROWN
6.2200 g., 0.9990 Gold .2000 oz. AGW, 22 mm.
Ruler: Elizabeth II **Series:** Man in Flight **Subject:** ME262, First Jet Aircraft **Obv:** Crowned bust right **Obv. Designer:** Raphael Maklouf **Rev:** Jet flying into clouds

Date	Mintage	F	VF	XF	Unc	BU
1995 Proof	Est. 5,000	Value: 170				

KM# 433 1/5 CROWN
6.2200 g., 0.9990 Gold .2000 oz. AGW, 22 mm.
Ruler: Elizabeth II **Series:** Man in Flight **Subject:** 25th Anniversary of Boeing 747 **Obv:** Crowned bust right
Obv. Designer: Raphael Maklouf **Rev:** Jumbo jet in flight

Date	Mintage	F	VF	XF	Unc	BU
1995 Proof	Est. 5,000	Value: 170				

KM# 444 1/5 CROWN
6.2200 g., 0.9990 Gold .2000 oz. AGW, 22 mm.
Ruler: Elizabeth II **Obv:** Crowned bust right
Obv. Designer: Raphael Maklouf **Rev:** Turkish cat

Date	Mintage	F	VF	XF	Unc	BU
1995	—	—	—	—	150	—
1995 Proof	—	Value: 165				

KM# 451 1/5 CROWN
6.2200 g., 0.9990 Gold .2000 oz. AGW, 22 mm.
Ruler: Elizabeth II **Subject:** Year of the Pig **Obv:** Crowned bust right **Obv. Designer:** Raphael Maklouf **Rev:** Sow and piglets

Date	Mintage	F	VF	XF	Unc	BU
1995 Proof	Est. 10,000	Value: 165				

KM# 457 1/5 CROWN
6.2200 g., 0.9990 Gold .2000 oz. AGW, 22 mm.
Ruler: Elizabeth II **Subject:** 95th Birthday of Queen Mother **Obv:** Crowned bust right **Obv. Designer:** Raphael Maklouf **Rev:** Bust of Queen Mother

Date	Mintage	F	VF	XF	Unc	BU
1995 Proof	Est. 5,000	Value: 170				

KM# 459 1/5 CROWN
6.2200 g., 0.9990 Gold .2000 oz. AGW, 22 mm.
Ruler: Elizabeth II **Series:** Preserve Planet Earth **Obv:** Crowned bust right **Obv. Designer:** Raphael Maklouf **Rev:** Otter

Date	Mintage	F	VF	XF	Unc	BU
1995 Proof	Est. 5,000	Value: 165				

KM# 460 1/5 CROWN
6.2200 g., 0.9990 Gold .2000 oz. AGW, 22 mm.
Ruler: Elizabeth II **Series:** Preserve Planet Earth **Obv:** Crowned bust right **Obv. Designer:** Raphael Maklouf **Rev:** Egret Birds

Date	Mintage	F	VF	XF	Unc	BU
1995 Proof	Est. 5,000	Value: 165				

KM# 480 1/5 CROWN
6.2200 g., 0.9990 Platinum .2000 oz. APW, 22 mm.
Ruler: Elizabeth II **Obv:** Crowned bust right
Obv. Designer: Raphael Maklouf **Rev:** Turkish cat

Date	Mintage	F	VF	XF	Unc	BU
1995	—	—	—	—	255	—
1995 Proof	—	Value: 265				

KM# 483 1/5 CROWN
6.2200 g., 0.9990 Gold .2000 oz. AGW, 22 mm. **Ruler:** Elizabeth II **Series:** Aircraft of World War II **Obv:** Crowned bust right **Obv. Designer:** Raphael Maklouf **Rev:** Hawker Hurricane

Date	Mintage	F	VF	XF	Unc	BU
1995 Proof	Est. 5,000	Value: 185				

KM# 484 1/5 CROWN
6.2200 g., 0.9990 Gold .2000 oz. AGW, 22 mm.
Ruler: Elizabeth II **Series:** Aircraft of World War II **Obv:** Crowned bust right **Obv. Designer:** Raphael Maklouf **Rev:** P-51 Mustang

Date	Mintage	F	VF	XF	Unc	BU
1995 Proof	Est. 5,000	Value: 185				

KM# 485 1/5 CROWN
6.2200 g., 0.9990 Gold .2000 oz. AGW, 22 mm.
Ruler: Elizabeth II **Series:** Aircraft of World War II **Obv:** Crowned bust right **Obv. Designer:** Raphael Maklouf **Rev:** Letrov S328

Date	Mintage	F	VF	XF	Unc	BU
1995 Proof	Est. 5,000	Value: 185				

KM# 486 1/5 CROWN
6.2200 g., 0.9990 Gold .2000 oz. AGW, 22 mm. **Ruler:** Elizabeth II **Series:** Aircraft of World War II **Obv:** Crowned bust right **Obv. Designer:** Raphael Maklouf **Rev:** Messerschmitt ME262

Date	Mintage	F	VF	XF	Unc	BU
1995 Proof	Est. 5,000	Value: 185				

KM# 487 1/5 CROWN
6.2200 g., 0.9990 Gold .2000 oz. AGW, 22 mm.
Ruler: Elizabeth II **Series:** Aircraft of World War II **Obv:** Crowned bust right **Obv. Designer:** Raphael Maklouf **Rev:** JU87 Stuka

Date	Mintage	F	VF	XF	Unc	BU
1995 Proof	Est. 5,000	Value: 185				

KM# 488 1/5 CROWN
6.2200 g., 0.9990 Gold .2000 oz. AGW, 22 mm.
Ruler: Elizabeth II **Series:** Aircraft of World War II **Obv:** Crowned bust right **Obv. Designer:** Raphael Maklouf **Rev:** MIG 3

Date	Mintage	F	VF	XF	Unc	BU
1995 Proof	Est. 5,000	Value: 185				

KM# 489 1/5 CROWN
6.2200 g., 0.9990 Gold .2000 oz. AGW, 22 mm. **Ruler:** Elizabeth II **Series:** Aircraft of World War II **Obv:** Crowned bust right **Obv. Designer:** Raphael Maklouf **Rev:** Nakajima Ki-49 Donryu

Date	Mintage	F	VF	XF	Unc	BU
1995 Proof	Est. 5,000	Value: 185				

KM# 490 1/5 CROWN
6.2200 g., 0.9990 Gold .2000 oz. AGW, 22 mm. **Ruler:** Elizabeth II **Series:** Aircraft of World War II **Obv:** Crowned bust right **Obv. Designer:** Raphael Maklouf **Rev:** Vickers Wellington

Date	Mintage	F	VF	XF	Unc	BU
1995 Proof	Est. 5,000	Value: 185				

KM# 491 1/5 CROWN
6.2200 g., 0.9990 Gold .2000 oz. AGW, 22 mm.
Ruler: Elizabeth II **Series:** Aircraft of World War II **Obv:** Crowned bust right **Obv. Designer:** Raphael Maklouf **Rev:** Spitfire

Date	Mintage	F	VF	XF	Unc	BU
1995 Proof	Est. 5,000	Value: 185				

KM# 492 1/5 CROWN
6.2200 g., 0.9990 Gold .2000 oz. AGW, 22 mm. **Ruler:** Elizabeth II **Series:** Aircraft of World War II **Obv:** Crowned bust right **Obv. Designer:** Raphael Maklouf **Rev:** Fokker G. 1a

Date	Mintage	F	VF	XF	Unc	BU
1995 Proof	Est. 5,000	Value: 185				

KM# 493 1/5 CROWN
6.2200 g., 0.9990 Gold .2000 oz. AGW, 22 mm.
Ruler: Elizabeth II **Series:** Aircraft of World War II **Obv:** Crowned bust right **Obv. Designer:** Raphael Maklouf **Rev:** Commonwealth Boomerang CA-13

Date	Mintage	F	VF	XF	Unc	BU
1995 Proof	Est. 5,000	Value: 185				

KM# 494 1/5 CROWN
6.2200 g., 0.9990 Gold .2000 oz. AGW, 22 mm. **Ruler:** Elizabeth II **Series:** Aircraft of World War II **Obv:** Crowned bust right **Obv. Designer:** Raphael Maklouf **Rev:** Briston Blenheim 142M

Date	Mintage	F	VF	XF	Unc	BU
1995 Proof	Est. 5,000	Value: 185				

KM# 495 1/5 CROWN
6.2200 g., 0.9990 Gold .2000 oz. AGW, 22 mm.
Ruler: Elizabeth II **Series:** Aircraft of World War II **Obv:** Crowned bust right **Obv. Designer:** Raphael Maklouf **Rev:** Mitsubishi Zero

Date	Mintage	F	VF	XF	Unc	BU
1995 Proof	Est. 5,000	Value: 185				

KM# 496 1/5 CROWN
6.2200 g., 0.9990 Gold .2000 oz. AGW, 22 mm.
Ruler: Elizabeth II **Series:** Aircraft of World War II **Obv:** Crowned bust right **Obv. Designer:** Raphael Maklouf **Rev:** Heinkel HE111

Date	Mintage	F	VF	XF	Unc	BU
1995 Proof	Est. 5,000	Value: 185				

KM# 497 1/5 CROWN
6.2200 g., 0.9990 Gold .2000 oz. AGW, 22 mm. **Ruler:** Elizabeth II **Series:** Aircraft of World War II **Obv:** Crowned bust right **Obv. Designer:** Raphael Maklouf **Rev:** Boulton Paul P82 Defiant

Date	Mintage	F	VF	XF	Unc	BU
1995 Proof	Est. 5,000	Value: 185				

KM# 498 1/5 CROWN
6.2200 g., 0.9990 Gold .2000 oz. AGW, 22 mm. **Ruler:** Elizabeth II **Series:** Aircraft of World War II **Obv:** Crowned bust right **Obv. Designer:** Raphael Maklouf **Rev:** Boeing B289 - Enola Gay

Date	Mintage	F	VF	XF	Unc	BU
1995 Proof	Est. 5,000	Value: 185				

KM# 499 1/5 CROWN
6.2200 g., 0.9990 Gold .2000 oz. AGW, 22 mm. **Ruler:** Elizabeth II **Series:** Aircraft of World War II **Obv:** Crowned bust right **Obv. Designer:** Raphael Maklouf **Rev:** Douglas DC-3 (C47)

Date	Mintage	F	VF	XF	Unc	BU
1995 Proof	Est. 5,000	Value: 185				

KM# 500 1/5 CROWN
6.2200 g., 0.9990 Gold .2000 oz. AGW, 22 mm. **Ruler:** Elizabeth II **Series:** Aircraft of World War II **Obv:** Crowned bust right **Obv. Designer:** Raphael Maklouf **Rev:** Fairey Swordfish

Date	Mintage	F	VF	XF	Unc	BU
1995 Proof	Est. 5,000	Value: 185				

KM# 501 1/5 CROWN
6.2200 g., 0.9990 Gold .2000 oz. AGW, 22 mm.
Ruler: Elizabeth II **Series:** Aircraft of World War II **Obv:** Crowned bust right **Obv. Designer:** Raphael Maklouf **Rev:** Curtiss P40

Date	Mintage	F	VF	XF	Unc	BU
1995 Proof	Est. 5,000	Value: 185				

KM# 523 1/5 CROWN
6.2200 g., 0.9990 Gold .2000 oz. AGW, 22 mm.
Ruler: Elizabeth II **Subject:** America's Cup **Obv:** Crowned bust right **Obv. Designer:** Raphael Maklouf **Rev:** Boats

Date	Mintage	F	VF	XF	Unc	BU
1995 Proof	Est. 5,000	Value: 145				

KM# 525 1/5 CROWN
6.2200 g., 0.9999 Gold .2000 oz. AGW, 22 mm.
Ruler: Elizabeth II **Series:** Inventions of the Modern World **Obv:** Crowned bust right **Obv. Designer:** Raphael Maklouf **Rev:** Cameo of Tsai Lun, paper and tree

Date	Mintage	F	VF	XF	Unc	BU
1995 Proof	Est. 5,000	Value: 165				

KM# 527 1/5 CROWN
6.2200 g., 0.9999 Gold .2000 oz. AGW, 22 mm.
Ruler: Elizabeth II **Series:** Inventions of the Modern World **Obv:** Crowned bust right **Obv. Designer:** Raphael Maklouf **Rev:** Cameo of Chang Heng and Seismograph

Date	Mintage	F	VF	XF	Unc	BU
1995 Proof	Est. 5,000	Value: 165				

KM# 529 1/5 CROWN
6.2200 g., 0.9999 Gold .2000 oz. AGW, 22 mm.
Ruler: Elizabeth II **Series:** Inventions of the Modern World **Obv:** Crowned bust right **Obv. Designer:** Raphael Maklouf **Rev:** Cameo of Tsu Chung Chih and compass cart

Date	Mintage	F	VF	XF	Unc	BU
1995 Proof	Est. 5,000	Value: 165				

KM# 531 1/5 CROWN
6.2200 g., 0.9999 Gold .2000 oz. AGW, 22 mm.
Ruler: Elizabeth II **Series:** Inventions of the Modern World **Obv:** Crowned bust right **Obv. Designer:** Raphael Maklouf **Rev:** Cameo bust facing and movable type

Date	Mintage	F	VF	XF	Unc	BU
1995 Proof	Est. 5,000	Value: 165				

KM# 533 1/5 CROWN
6.2200 g., 0.9999 Gold .2000 oz. AGW, 22 mm.
Ruler: Elizabeth II **Series:** Inventions of the Modern World **Obv:** Crowned bust right **Obv. Designer:** Raphael Maklouf **Rev:** Cameo of Charles Babbage and first computer

Date	Mintage	F	VF	XF	Unc	BU
1995 Proof	Est. 5,000	Value: 165				

KM# 535 1/5 CROWN
6.2200 g., 0.9999 Gold .2000 oz. AGW, 22 mm.
Ruler: Elizabeth II **Series:** Inventions of the Modern World **Obv:** Crowned bust right **Obv. Designer:** Raphael Maklouf **Rev:** Cameo of Fox Talbot, photography

Date	Mintage	F	VF	XF	Unc	BU
1995 Proof	Est. 5,000	Value: 165				

KM# 537 1/5 CROWN
6.2200 g., 0.9999 Gold .2000 oz. AGW, 22 mm.
Ruler: Elizabeth II **Series:** Inventions of the Modern World **Obv:** Crowned bust right **Obv. Designer:** Raphael Maklouf **Rev:** Cameo of Rudolf Diesel, diesel engine

Date	Mintage	F	VF	XF	Unc	BU
1995 Proof	Est. 5,000	Value: 165				

KM# 539 1/5 CROWN
6.2200 g., 0.9999 Gold .2000 oz. AGW, 22 mm.
Ruler: Elizabeth II **Series:** Inventions of the Modern World **Obv:** Crowned bust right **Obv. Designer:** Raphael Maklouf **Rev:** Cameo of Wilhelm K. Roentgen and xray of hand

Date	Mintage	F	VF	XF	Unc	BU
1995 Proof	Est. 5,000	Value: 165				

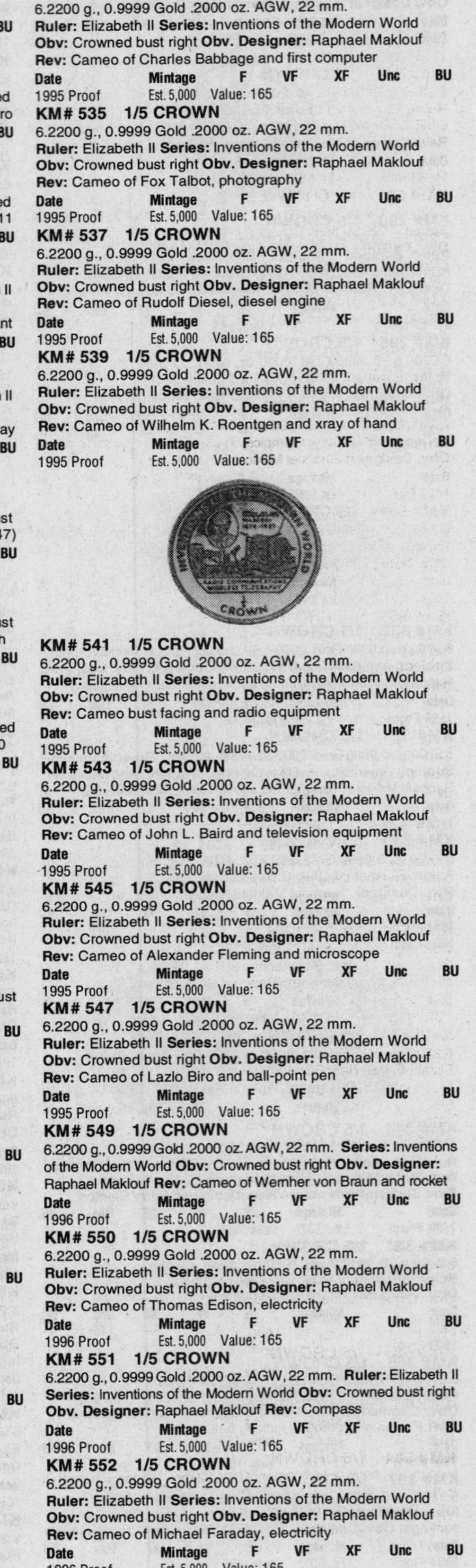

KM# 541 1/5 CROWN
6.2200 g., 0.9999 Gold .2000 oz. AGW, 22 mm.
Ruler: Elizabeth II **Series:** Inventions of the Modern World **Obv:** Crowned bust right **Obv. Designer:** Raphael Maklouf **Rev:** Cameo bust facing and radio equipment

Date	Mintage	F	VF	XF	Unc	BU
1995 Proof	Est. 5,000	Value: 165				

KM# 543 1/5 CROWN
6.2200 g., 0.9999 Gold .2000 oz. AGW, 22 mm.
Ruler: Elizabeth II **Series:** Inventions of the Modern World **Obv:** Crowned bust right **Obv. Designer:** Raphael Maklouf **Rev:** Cameo of John L. Baird and television equipment

Date	Mintage	F	VF	XF	Unc	BU
1995 Proof	Est. 5,000	Value: 165				

KM# 545 1/5 CROWN
6.2200 g., 0.9999 Gold .2000 oz. AGW, 22 mm.
Ruler: Elizabeth II **Series:** Inventions of the Modern World **Obv:** Crowned bust right **Obv. Designer:** Raphael Maklouf **Rev:** Cameo of Alexander Fleming and microscope

Date	Mintage	F	VF	XF	Unc	BU
1995 Proof	Est. 5,000	Value: 165				

KM# 547 1/5 CROWN
6.2200 g., 0.9999 Gold .2000 oz. AGW, 22 mm.
Ruler: Elizabeth II **Series:** Inventions of the Modern World **Obv:** Crowned bust right **Obv. Designer:** Raphael Maklouf **Rev:** Cameo of Lazlo Biro and ball-point pen

Date	Mintage	F	VF	XF	Unc	BU
1995 Proof	Est. 5,000	Value: 165				

KM# 549 1/5 CROWN
6.2200 g., 0.9999 Gold .2000 oz. AGW, 22 mm. **Series:** Inventions of the Modern World **Obv:** Crowned bust right **Obv. Designer:** Raphael Maklouf **Rev:** Cameo of Wernher von Braun and rocket

Date	Mintage	F	VF	XF	Unc	BU
1996 Proof	Est. 5,000	Value: 165				

KM# 550 1/5 CROWN
6.2200 g., 0.9999 Gold .2000 oz. AGW, 22 mm.
Ruler: Elizabeth II **Series:** Inventions of the Modern World **Obv:** Crowned bust right **Obv. Designer:** Raphael Maklouf **Rev:** Cameo of Thomas Edison, electricity

Date	Mintage	F	VF	XF	Unc	BU
1996 Proof	Est. 5,000	Value: 165				

KM# 551 1/5 CROWN
6.2200 g., 0.9999 Gold .2000 oz. AGW, 22 mm. **Ruler:** Elizabeth II **Series:** Inventions of the Modern World **Obv:** Crowned bust right **Obv. Designer:** Raphael Maklouf **Rev:** Compass

Date	Mintage	F	VF	XF	Unc	BU
1996 Proof	Est. 5,000	Value: 165				

KM# 552 1/5 CROWN
6.2200 g., 0.9999 Gold .2000 oz. AGW, 22 mm.
Ruler: Elizabeth II **Series:** Inventions of the Modern World **Obv:** Crowned bust right **Obv. Designer:** Raphael Maklouf **Rev:** Cameo of Michael Faraday, electricity

Date	Mintage	F	VF	XF	Unc	BU
1996 Proof	Est. 5,000	Value: 165				

KM# 553 1/5 CROWN

6.2200 g., 0.9999 Gold .2000 oz. AGW, 22 mm.
Ruler: Elizabeth II **Series:** Inventions of the Modern World
Obv: Crowned bust right **Obv. Designer:** Raphael Maklouf
Rev: Cameo of Emile Berliner and gramophone

Date	Mintage	F	VF	XF	Unc	BU
1996 Proof	Est. 5,000	Value: 165				

KM# 554 1/5 CROWN

6.2200 g., 0.9999 Gold .2000 oz. AGW, 22 mm.
Ruler: Elizabeth II **Series:** Inventions of the Modern World
Obv: Crowned bust right **Obv. Designer:** Raphael Maklouf
Rev: Cameo of Alexander Graham Bell, voice transmission

Date	Mintage	F	VF	XF	Unc	BU
1996 Proof	Est. 5,000	Value: 165				

KM# 561 1/5 CROWN

6.2200 g., 0.9999 Gold .2000 oz. AGW, 22 mm. **Ruler:** Elizabeth II **Series:** 1996 Summer Olympics - Atlanta **Obv:** Crowned bust right **Obv. Designer:** Raphael Maklouf **Rev:** Hurdler

Date	Mintage	F	VF	XF	Unc	BU
1996 Proof	Est. 5,000	Value: 165				

KM# 562 1/5 CROWN

6.2200 g., 0.9999 Gold .2000 oz. AGW, 22 mm. **Ruler:** Elizabeth II **Series:** 1996 Summer Olympics - Atlanta **Obv:** Crowned bust right **Obv. Designer:** Raphael Maklouf **Rev:** Runners

Date	Mintage	F	VF	XF	Unc	BU
1996 Proof	Est. 5,000	Value: 165				

KM# 563 1/5 CROWN

6.2200 g., 0.9999 Gold .2000 oz. AGW, 22 mm. **Ruler:** Elizabeth II **Series:** 1996 Summer Olympics - Atlanta **Obv:** Crowned bust right **Obv. Designer:** Raphael Maklouf **Rev:** Sailing

Date	Mintage	F	VF	XF	Unc	BU
1996 Proof	Est. 5,000	Value: 165				

KM# 564 1/5 CROWN

6.2200 g., 0.9999 Gold .2000 oz. AGW, 22 mm. **Ruler:** Elizabeth II **Series:** 1996 Summer Olympics - Atlanta **Obv:** Crowned bust right **Obv. Designer:** Raphael Maklouf **Rev:** Swimmers

Date	Mintage	F	VF	XF	Unc	BU
1996 Proof	Est. 5,000	Value: 165				

KM# 565 1/5 CROWN

6.2200 g., 0.9999 Gold .2000 oz. AGW, 22 mm. **Ruler:** Elizabeth II **Series:** 1996 Summer Olympics - Atlanta **Obv:** Crowned bust right **Obv. Designer:** Raphael Maklouf **Rev:** Equestrian

Date	Mintage	F	VF	XF	Unc	BU
1996 Proof	Est. 5,000	Value: 165				

KM# 566 1/5 CROWN

6.2200 g., 0.9999 Gold .2000 oz. AGW, 22 mm. **Ruler:** Elizabeth II **Series:** 1996 Summer Olympics - Atlanta **Obv:** Crowned bust right **Obv. Designer:** Raphael Maklouf **Rev:** Cyclists and Nike

Date	Mintage	F	VF	XF	Unc	BU
1996 Proof	Est. 5,000	Value: 165				

KM# 573 1/5 CROWN

6.2200 g., 0.9990 Gold .2000 oz. AGW, 22 mm. **Ruler:** Elizabeth II **Series:** Bicentennial of Robert Burns **Obv:** Crowned bust right **Obv. Designer:** Raphael Maklouf **Rev:** Seated

Date	Mintage	F	VF	XF	Unc	BU
1996 Proof	Est. 5,000	Value: 165				

KM# 574 1/5 CROWN

6.2200 g., 0.9990 Gold .2000 oz. AGW, 22 mm. **Ruler:** Elizabeth II **Series:** Bicentennial of Robert Burns **Obv:** Crowned bust right **Obv. Designer:** Raphael Maklouf **Rev:** Pirate ships

Date	Mintage	F	VF	XF	Unc	BU
1996 Proof	Est. 5,000	Value: 165				

KM# 575 1/5 CROWN

6.2200 g., 0.9990 Gold .2000 oz. AGW, 22 mm. **Ruler:** Elizabeth II **Series:** Bicentennial of Robert Burns **Obv:** Crowned bust right **Obv. Designer:** Raphael Maklouf **Rev:** Auld Lang Syne

Date	Mintage	F	VF	XF	Unc	BU
1996 Proof	Est. 5,000	Value: 165				

KM# 576 1/5 CROWN

6.2200 g., 0.9990 Gold .2000 oz. AGW, 22 mm. **Ruler:** Elizabeth II **Series:** Bicentennial of Robert Burns **Obv:** Crowned bust right **Obv. Designer:** Raphael Maklouf **Rev:** Edinburgh Castle

Date	Mintage	F	VF	XF	Unc	BU
1996 Proof	Est. 5,000	Value: 165				

KM# 581 1/5 CROWN

6.2200 g., 0.9990 Gold .2000 oz. AGW, 22 mm. **Ruler:** Elizabeth II **Subject:** Queen's Birthday **Obv:** Crowned bust right **Obv. Designer:** Raphael Maklouf **Rev:** Flowers

Date	Mintage	F	VF	XF	Unc	BU
1996 Proof	Est. 5,000	Value: 165				

KM# 583 1/5 CROWN

6.2200 g., 0.9990 Gold .2000 oz. AGW, 22 mm. **Ruler:** Elizabeth II **Subject:** Preserve Planet Earth **Obv:** Crowned bust right **Obv. Designer:** Raphael Maklouf **Rev:** Killer whale

Date	Mintage	F	VF	XF	Unc	BU
1996 Proof	Est. 5,000	Value: 165				

KM# 584 1/5 CROWN

6.2200 g., 0.9990 Gold .2000 oz. AGW, 22 mm. **Ruler:** Elizabeth II **Subject:** Preserve Planet Earth **Obv:** Crowned bust right **Obv. Designer:** Raphael Maklouf **Rev:** Razorbill feeding chick

Date	Mintage	F	VF	XF	Unc	BU
1996 Proof	Est. 5,000	Value: 165				

KM# 605 1/5 CROWN

6.2200 g., 0.9990 Gold .2000 oz. AGW, 22 mm. **Ruler:** Elizabeth II **Series:** Flower Fairies **Obv:** Crowned bust right **Obv. Designer:** Raphael Maklouf **Rev:** Orchis **Rev. Designer:** Cecily Mary Barker

Date	Mintage	F	VF	XF	Unc	BU
1996 Proof	Est. 5,000	Value: 170				

KM# 606 1/5 CROWN

6.2200 g., 0.9990 Gold .2000 oz. AGW, 22 mm. **Ruler:** Elizabeth II **Series:** Flower Fairies **Obv:** Crowned bust right **Obv. Designer:** Raphael Maklouf **Rev:** Rose **Rev. Designer:** Cecily Mary Barker

Date	Mintage	F	VF	XF	Unc	BU
1996 Proof	Est. 5,000	Value: 170				

KM# 607 1/5 CROWN

6.2200 g., 0.9990 Gold .2000 oz. AGW, 22 mm. **Ruler:** Elizabeth II **Series:** Flower Fairies **Obv:** Crowned bust right **Obv. Designer:** Raphael Maklouf **Rev:** Fuchsia **Rev. Designer:** Cecily Mary Barker

Date	Mintage	F	VF	XF	Unc	BU
1996 Proof	Est. 5,000	Value: 170				

KM# 608 1/5 CROWN

6.2200 g., 0.9990 Gold .2000 oz. AGW, 22 mm. **Ruler:** Elizabeth II **Series:** Flower Fairies **Obv:** Crowned bust right **Obv. Designer:** Raphael Maklouf **Rev:** Pinks **Rev. Designer:** Cecily Mary Barker

Date	Mintage	F	VF	XF	Unc	BU
1996 Proof	Est. 5,000	Value: 170				

KM# 617 1/5 CROWN

6.2200 g., 0.9990 Gold .2000 oz. AGW, 22 mm.
Ruler: Elizabeth II **Obv:** Crowned bust right
Obv. Designer: Raphael Maklouf **Rev:** Burmese cat

Date	Mintage	F	VF	XF	Unc	BU
1996	—	—	—	—	145	—
1996 Proof	—	Value: 160				

KM# 618 1/5 CROWN

6.2200 g., 0.9990 Platinum .2000 oz. APW, 22 mm.
Ruler: Elizabeth II **Obv:** Crowned bust right **Obv. Designer:** Raphael Maklouf **Rev:** Burmese cat

Date	Mintage	F	VF	XF	Unc	BU
1996	—	—	—	—	260	—
1996 Proof	—	Value: 270				

KM# 625 1/5 CROWN

6.2200 g., 0.9990 Gold .2000 oz. AGW, 22 mm. **Ruler:** Elizabeth II **Obv:** Crowned bust right **Obv. Designer:** Raphael Maklouf **Rev:** Portrait of Ferdinand Magellan, map and ship

Date	Mintage	F	VF	XF	Unc	BU
1996 Proof	Est. 5,000	Value: 165				

KM# 628 1/5 CROWN

6.2200 g., 0.9990 Gold .2000 oz. AGW, 22 mm.
Ruler: Elizabeth II **Obv:** Crowned bust right **Obv. Designer:** Raphael Maklouf **Rev:** Portrait of Sir Francis Drake, map and ship

Date	Mintage	F	VF	XF	Unc	BU
1996 Proof	Est. 5,000	Value: 165				

KM# 631 1/5 CROWN

6.2200 g., 0.9990 Gold .2000 oz. AGW, 22 mm.
Ruler: Elizabeth II **Series:** European Football Championship
Obv: Crowned bust right **Obv. Designer:** Raphael Maklouf
Rev: Romania vs Bulgaria

Date	Mintage	F	VF	XF	Unc	BU
1996 Proof	Est. 5,000	Value: 165				

KM# 634 1/5 CROWN

6.2200 g., 0.9990 Gold .2000 oz. AGW, 22 mm.
Ruler: Elizabeth II **Series:** European Football Championship
Obv: Crowned bust right **Obv. Designer:** Raphael Maklouf
Rev: Czech Republic vs Italy

Date	Mintage	F	VF	XF	Unc	BU
1996 Proof	Est. 5,000	Value: 165				

KM# 637 1/5 CROWN

6.2200 g., 0.9990 Gold .2000 oz. AGW, 22 mm.
Ruler: Elizabeth II **Series:** European Football Championship
Obv: Crowned bust right **Obv. Designer:** Raphael Maklouf
Rev: Germany vs Russia

Date	Mintage	F	VF	XF	Unc	BU
1996 Proof	Est. 5,000	Value: 165				

KM# 640 1/5 CROWN

6.2200 g., 0.9990 Gold .2000 oz. AGW, 22 mm. **Ruler:** Elizabeth II **Series:** European Football Championship **Obv:** Crowned bust right **Obv. Designer:** Raphael Maklouf **Rev:** Spain vs France

Date	Mintage	F	VF	XF	Unc	BU
1996 Proof	Est. 5,000	Value: 165				

KM# 643 1/5 CROWN

6.2200 g., 0.9990 Gold .2000 oz. AGW, 22 mm. **Ruler:** Elizabeth II **Series:** European Football Championship **Obv:** Crowned bust right **Obv. Designer:** Raphael Maklouf **Rev:** Turkey vs Croatia

Date	Mintage	F	VF	XF	Unc	BU
1996 Proof	Est. 5,000	Value: 165				

KM# 646 1/5 CROWN

6.2200 g., 0.9990 Gold .2000 oz. AGW, 22 mm.
Ruler: Elizabeth II **Series:** European Football Championship
Obv: Crowned bust right **Obv. Designer:** Raphael Maklouf
Rev: Denmark vs Portugal

Date	Mintage	F	VF	XF	Unc	BU
1996 Proof	Est. 5,000	Value: 165				

KM# 649 1/5 CROWN

6.2200 g., 0.9990 Gold .2000 oz. AGW, 22 mm.
Ruler: Elizabeth II **Series:** European Football Championship
Obv: Crowned bust right **Obv. Designer:** Raphael Maklouf
Rev: Scotland vs England

Date	Mintage	F	VF	XF	Unc	BU
1996 Proof	Est. 5,000	Value: 165				

KM# 652 1/5 CROWN

6.2200 g., 0.9990 Gold .2000 oz. AGW, 22 mm.
Ruler: Elizabeth II **Series:** European Football Championship
Obv: Crowned bust right **Obv. Designer:** Raphael Maklouf
Rev: Holland vs Switzerland

Date	Mintage	F	VF	XF	Unc	BU
1996 Proof	Est. 5,000	Value: 165				

KM# 656 1/5 CROWN

6.2200 g., 0.9990 Gold .2000 oz. AGW, 22 mm. **Ruler:** Elizabeth II **Series:** European Football Championship **Obv:** Crowned bust right **Obv. Designer:** Raphael Maklouf **Rev:** Winner, Germany

Date	Mintage	F	VF	XF	Unc	BU
1996 Proof	Est. 5,000	Value: 165				

KM# 659 1/5 CROWN

6.2200 g., 0.9990 Gold .2000 oz. AGW, 22 mm. **Ruler:** Elizabeth II **Series:** Legend of King Arthur **Obv:** Crowned bust right **Obv. Designer:** Raphael Maklouf **Rev:** King Arthur with sword, orb

Date	Mintage	F	VF	XF	Unc	BU
1996 Proof	Est. 5,000	Value: 165				

KM# 660 1/5 CROWN

6.2200 g., 0.9990 Gold .2000 oz. AGW, 22 mm.
Ruler: Elizabeth II **Series:** Legend of King Arthur **Obv:** Crowned bust right **Obv. Designer:** Raphael Maklouf **Rev:** 3/4-length figure of Queen Guinevere coming through archway

Date	Mintage	F	VF	XF	Unc	BU
1996 Proof	Est. 5,000	Value: 165				

KM# 661 1/5 CROWN

6.2200 g., 0.9990 Gold .2000 oz. AGW, 22 mm.
Ruler: Elizabeth II **Series:** Legend of King Arthur **Obv:** Crowned bust right **Obv. Designer:** Raphael Maklouf **Rev:** Sir Lancelot

Date	Mintage	F	VF	XF	Unc	BU
1996 Proof	Est. 5,000	Value: 165				

KM# 662 1/5 CROWN

6.2200 g., 0.9990 Gold .2000 oz. APW, 22 mm.
Ruler: Elizabeth II **Series:** Legend of King Arthur **Obv:** Crowned bust right **Obv. Designer:** Raphael Maklouf **Rev:** Merlin

Date	Mintage	F	VF	XF	Unc	BU
1996 Proof	Est. 5,000	Value: 165				

KM# 663 1/5 CROWN

6.2200 g., 0.9990 Gold .2000 oz. AGW, 22 mm. **Ruler:** Elizabeth II **Series:** Legend of King Arthur **Obv:** Crowned bust right **Obv. Designer:** Raphael Maklouf **Rev:** Camelot Castle within circle

Date	Mintage	F	VF	XF	Unc	BU
1996 Proof	Est. 5,000	Value: 165				

KM# 664 1/5 CROWN

6.2200 g., 0.9990 Platinum .2000 oz. APW, 22 mm. **Ruler:** Elizabeth II **Series:** Legend of King Arthur **Obv:** Crowned bust right **Obv. Designer:** Raphael Maklouf **Rev:** King Arthur with sword, orb

Date	Mintage	F	VF	XF	Unc	BU
1996 Proof	Est. 5,000	Value: 255				

KM# 665 1/5 CROWN

6.2200 g., 0.9990 Platinum .2000 oz. APW, 22 mm. **Ruler:** Elizabeth II **Series:** Legend of King Arthur **Obv:** Crowned bust right **Obv. Designer:** Raphael Maklouf **Rev:** Queen Guinevere

Date	Mintage	F	VF	XF	Unc	BU
1996 Proof	Est. 5,000	Value: 255				

KM# 666 1/5 CROWN

6.2200 g., 0.9990 Platinum .2000 oz. APW, 22 mm. **Ruler:** Elizabeth II **Series:** Legend of King Arthur **Obv:** Crowned bust right **Obv. Designer:** Raphael Maklouf **Rev:** Sir Lancelot

Date	Mintage	F	VF	XF	Unc	BU
1996 Proof	Est. 5,000	Value: 255				

KM# 667 1/5 CROWN

6.2200 g., 0.9990 Platinum .2000 oz. APW, 22 mm. **Ruler:** Elizabeth II **Series:** Legend of King Arthur **Obv:** Crowned bust right **Obv. Designer:** Raphael Maklouf **Rev:** Merlin

Date	Mintage	F	VF	XF	Unc	BU
1996 Proof	Est. 5,000	Value: 260				

KM# 668 1/5 CROWN

6.2200 g., 0.9990 Platinum .2000 oz. APW, 22 mm. **Ruler:** Elizabeth II **Series:** Legend of King Arthur **Obv:** Crowned bust right **Obv. Designer:** Raphael Maklouf **Rev:** Camelot Castle

Date	Mintage	F	VF	XF	Unc	BU
1996 Proof	Est. 5,000	Value: 255				

KM# 730 1/5 CROWN

6.2200 g., 0.9990 Gold .2000 oz. AGW, 22 mm. **Ruler:** Elizabeth II **Subject:** Year of the Rat **Obv:** Crowned bust right **Obv. Designer:** Raphael Maklouf **Rev:** Rat

Date	Mintage	F	VF	XF	Unc	BU
1996 Proof	—	—	—	—	—	—

Note: Entire series purchased by one buyer. Mintage, disposition and market value unknown

KM# 766 1/5 CROWN

6.2200 g., 0.9999 Gold .2000 oz. AGW, 22 mm. **Ruler:** Elizabeth II **Subject:** Fridtjof Nansen 1861-1930 **Obv:** Crowned bust right **Obv. Designer:** Raphael Maklouf **Rev:** Portrait, map and ship "The Fram"

Date	Mintage	F	VF	XF	Unc	BU
1997 Proof	Est. 5,000	Value: 175				

KM# 723 1/5 CROWN

6.2200 g., 0.9990 Gold .2000 oz. AGW, 22 mm. **Ruler:** Elizabeth II **Subject:** Year of the Ox **Obv:** Crowned bust right **Obv. Designer:** Raphael Maklouf **Rev:** Ox laying down

Date	Mintage	F	VF	XF	Unc	BU
1997 Proof	Est. 12,000	Value: 170				

KM# 751 1/5 CROWN

6.2200 g., 0.9990 Gold .2000 oz. AGW, 22 mm. **Ruler:** Elizabeth II **Series:** Flower Fairies **Obv:** Crowned bust right **Obv. Designer:** Raphael Maklouf **Rev:** Candytuft **Rev. Designer:** Cecily Mary Barker

Date	Mintage	F	VF	XF	Unc	BU
1997 Proof	Est. 5,000	Value: 165				

KM# 751a 1/5 CROWN

6.2518 g., 0.9950 Platinum .2000 oz. APW, 22 mm. **Ruler:** Elizabeth II **Series:** Flower Fairies **Obv:** Crowned bust right **Obv. Designer:** Raphael Maklouf **Rev:** Candytuft **Rev. Designer:** Cecily Mary Barker

Date	Mintage	F	VF	XF	Unc	BU
1997 Proof	Est. 2,500	Value: 260				

KM# 752 1/5 CROWN

6.2200 g., 0.9999 Gold .2000 oz. AGW, 22 mm. **Ruler:** Elizabeth II **Series:** Flower Fairies **Obv:** Crowned bust right **Obv. Designer:** Raphael Maklouf **Rev:** Snowdrop **Rev. Designer:** Cecily Mary Barker

Date	Mintage	F	VF	XF	Unc	BU
1997 Proof	Est. 5,000	Value: 165				

KM# 752a 1/5 CROWN

6.2518 g., 0.9950 Platinum .2000 oz. APW, 22 mm. **Ruler:** Elizabeth II **Series:** Flower Fairies **Obv:** Crowned bust right **Obv. Designer:** Raphael Maklouf **Rev:** Snowdrop **Rev. Designer:** Cecily Mary Barker

Date	Mintage	F	VF	XF	Unc	BU
1997 Proof	Est. 2,500	Value: 260				

KM# 753 1/5 CROWN

6.2200 g., 0.9999 Gold .2000 oz. AGW, 22 mm. **Ruler:** Elizabeth II **Series:** Flower Fairies **Obv:** Crowned bust right **Obv. Designer:** Raphael Maklouf **Rev:** Tulip **Rev. Designer:** Cecily Mary Barker

Date	Mintage	F	VF	XF	Unc	BU
1997 Proof	Est. 5,000	Value: 165				

KM# 753a 1/5 CROWN

6.2518 g., 0.9950 Platinum .2000 oz. APW, 22 mm. **Ruler:** Elizabeth II **Series:** Flower Fairies **Obv:** Crowned bust right **Obv. Designer:** Raphael Maklouf **Rev:** Tulip **Rev. Designer:** Cecily Mary Barker

Date	Mintage	F	VF	XF	Unc	BU
1997 Proof	Est. 2,500	Value: 260				

KM# 754 1/5 CROWN

6.2200 g., 0.9999 Gold .2000 oz. AGW, 22 mm. **Ruler:** Elizabeth II **Series:** Flower Fairies **Obv:** Crowned bust right **Obv. Designer:** Raphael Maklouf **Rev:** Jasmine **Rev. Designer:** Cecily Mary Barker

Date	Mintage	F	VF	XF	Unc	BU
1997 Proof	Est. 5,000	Value: 165				

KM# 754a 1/5 CROWN

6.2518 g., 0.9950 Platinum .2000 oz. APW, 22 mm. **Ruler:** Elizabeth II **Series:** Flower Fairies **Obv:** Crowned bust right **Obv. Designer:** Raphael Maklouf **Rev:** Jasmine **Rev. Designer:** Cecily Mary Barker

Date	Mintage	F	VF	XF	Unc	BU
1997 Proof	Est. 2,500	Value: 240				

KM# 763 1/5 CROWN

6.2200 g., 0.9999 Gold .2000 oz. AGW, 22 mm. **Ruler:** Elizabeth II **Subject:** Leif Eriksson 999-1001 **Obv:** Crowned bust right **Obv. Designer:** Raphael Maklouf **Rev:** Portrait and Viking ship with map sail

Date	Mintage	F	VF	XF	Unc	BU
1997 Proof	Est. 5,000	Value: 175				

KM# 772 1/5 CROWN

6.2200 g., 0.9999 Gold .2000 oz. AGW, 22 mm. **Ruler:** Elizabeth II **Obv:** Crowned bust right **Obv. Designer:** Raphael Maklouf **Rev:** Long-haired Smoke cat

Date	Mintage	F	VF	XF	Unc	BU
1997	—	—	—	—	145	—
1997 Proof	—	Value: 160				

KM# 772a 1/5 CROWN

6.2200 g., 0.9999 Platinum .2000 oz. APW, 22 mm. **Ruler:** Elizabeth II **Obv:** Crowned bust right **Obv. Designer:** Raphael Maklouf **Rev:** Long-haired Smoke cat

Date	Mintage	F	VF	XF	Unc	BU
1997	—	—	—	—	255	—
1997 Proof	—	Value: 265				

KM# 776 1/5 CROWN

6.2200 g., 0.9999 Gold .2000 oz. AGW, 22 mm. **Ruler:** Elizabeth II **Subject:** History of the Cat **Obv:** Crowned bust right **Obv. Designer:** Raphael Maklouf **Rev:** Cat stalking a spider

Date	Mintage	F	VF	XF	Unc	BU
1997 Proof	Est. 7,500	Value: 165				

KM# 781 1/5 CROWN

6.2200 g., 0.9999 Gold .2000 oz. AGW, 22 mm. **Ruler:** Elizabeth II **Subject:** 90th Anniversary of the TT - 1907 **Obv:** Crowned bust right **Obv. Designer:** Raphael Maklouf **Rev:** 1907 winner Charlie Collier

Date	Mintage	F	VF	XF	Unc	BU
1997 Proof	Est. 5,000	Value: 165				

KM# 783 1/5 CROWN

6.2200 g., 0.9999 Gold .2000 oz. AGW, 22 mm. **Ruler:** Elizabeth II **Subject:** 90th Anniversary of the TT - 1907 **Obv:** Crowned bust right **Obv. Designer:** Raphael Maklouf **Rev:** 1937 winner Omobono Tenni

Date	Mintage	F	VF	XF	Unc	BU
1997 Proof	Est. 5,000	Value: 165				

KM# 785 1/5 CROWN

6.2200 g., 0.9999 Gold .2000 oz. AGW, 22 mm. **Ruler:** Elizabeth II **Subject:** 90th Anniversary of the TT - 1907 **Obv:** Crowned bust right **Obv. Designer:** Raphael Maklouf **Rev:** 1957 winner Bob McIntyre

Date	Mintage	F	VF	XF	Unc	BU
1997 Proof	Est. 5,000	Value: 165				

KM# 787 1/5 CROWN

6.2200 g., 0.9999 Gold .2000 oz. AGW, 22 mm. **Ruler:** Elizabeth II **Subject:** 90th Anniversary of the TT - 1907 **Obv:** Crowned bust right **Obv. Designer:** Raphael Maklouf **Rev:** 1967 winner Mike Hailwood

Date	Mintage	F	VF	XF	Unc	BU
1997 Proof	Est. 5,000	Value: 165				

KM# 792 1/5 CROWN

6.2200 g., 0.9999 Gold .2000 oz. AGW, 22 mm. **Ruler:** Elizabeth II **Subject:** Golden Wedding Anniversary of Queen Elizabeth II and Prince Philip **Obv:** Crowned bust right **Obv. Designer:** Raphael Maklouf **Rev:** Wedding portrait

Date	Mintage	F	VF	XF	Unc	BU
1997 Proof	Est. 3,500	Value: 165				

KM# 798 1/5 CROWN

6.2200 g., 0.9999 Gold .2000 oz. AGW, 22 mm. **Ruler:** Elizabeth II **Series:** Year 2000 **Subject:** Birth of Christ **Obv:** Crowned bust right **Obv. Designer:** Raphael Maklouf **Rev:** Madonna and child with angels

Date	Mintage	F	VF	XF	Unc	BU
1997 Proof	Est. 2,000	Value: 165				

KM# 800 1/5 CROWN

6.2200 g., 0.9999 Gold .2000 oz. AGW, 22 mm. **Ruler:** Elizabeth II **Series:** Year 2000 **Subject:** Fall of the Roman Empire 476 **Obv:** Crowned bust right **Obv. Designer:** Raphael Maklouf **Rev:** Barbarian defeating Roman soldier

Date	Mintage	F	VF	XF	Unc	BU
1997 Proof	Est. 2,000	Value: 165				

KM# 802 1/5 CROWN

6.2200 g., 0.9999 Gold .2000 oz. AGW, 22 mm. **Ruler:** Elizabeth II **Series:** Year 2000 **Subject:** Flight of Mohammed 622 **Obv:** Crowned bust right **Obv. Designer:** Raphael Maklouf **Rev:** Arabs and camels at an oasis

Date	Mintage	F	VF	XF	Unc	BU
1997 Proof	Est. 2,000	Value: 165				

KM# 804 1/5 CROWN

6.2200 g., 0.9999 Gold .2000 oz. AGW, 22 mm. **Ruler:** Elizabeth II **Series:** Year 2000 **Subject:** Norman Conquest 1066 **Obv:** Crowned bust right **Obv. Designer:** Raphael Maklouf **Rev:** William the Conqueror rallying his troops

Date	Mintage	F	VF	XF	Unc	BU
1997 Proof	Est. 2,000	Value: 165				

KM# 807 1/5 CROWN

6.2200 g., 0.9999 Gold .2000 oz. AGW, 22 mm. **Ruler:** Elizabeth II **Series:** World Cup Soccer **Obv:** Crowned bust right **Obv. Designer:** Raphael Maklouf **Rev:** Standing figures shaking hands within circle

Date	Mintage	F	VF	XF	Unc	BU
1998 Proof	Est. 5,000	Value: 165				

KM# 814 1/5 CROWN

6.2200 g., 0.9999 Gold .2000 oz. AGW, 22 mm. **Ruler:** Elizabeth II **Series:** Year of the Tiger **Obv:** Crowned bust right **Obv. Designer:** Raphael Maklouf **Rev:** Tiger

Date	Mintage	F	VF	XF	Unc	BU
1998 Proof	Est. 12,000	Value: 165				

KM# 824 1/5 CROWN

6.2200 g., 0.9999 Gold .2000 oz. AGW, 22 mm. **Ruler:** Elizabeth II **Obv:** Crowned bust right **Obv. Designer:** Raphael Maklouf **Rev:** Portrait of Marco Polo, caravan and palace

Date	Mintage	F	VF	XF	Unc	BU
1998 Proof	Est. 5,000	Value: 165				

KM# 826 1/5 CROWN

6.2200 g., 0.9999 Gold .2000 oz. AGW, 22 mm. **Ruler:** Elizabeth II **Obv:** Crowned bust right **Obv. Designer:** Raphael Maklouf **Rev:** Bust with headdress facing, ship and African map **Note:** Similar to 1 Crown, KM#827.

Date	Mintage	F	VF	XF	Unc	BU
1998 Proof	Est. 5,000	Value: 165				

KM# 836 1/5 CROWN

6.2200 g., 0.9999 Gold .2000 oz. AGW, 22 mm. **Ruler:** Elizabeth II **Series:** Flower Fairies **Obv:** Crowned bust right **Obv. Designer:** Raphael Maklouf **Rev:** Fairy standing, lavender **Rev. Designer:** Cecily Mary Barker

Date	Mintage	F	VF	XF	Unc	BU
1998 Proof	Est. 5,000	Value: 165				

KM# 836a 1/5 CROWN

6.2200 g., 0.9999 Platinum .2000 oz. APW, 22 mm. **Ruler:** Elizabeth II **Series:** Flower Fairies **Obv:** Crowned bust right **Obv. Designer:** Raphael Maklouf **Rev:** Fairy standing, lavender **Rev. Designer:** Cecily Mary Barker

Date	Mintage	F	VF	XF	Unc	BU
1998 Proof	Est. 2,500	Value: 260				

KM# 837 1/5 CROWN

6.2200 g., 0.9999 Gold .2000 oz. AGW, 22 mm. **Ruler:** Elizabeth II **Series:** Flower Fairies **Obv:** Crowned bust right **Obv. Designer:** Raphael Maklouf **Rev:** Two fairies, sweet pea **Rev. Designer:** Cecily Mary Barker

Date	Mintage	F	VF	XF	Unc	BU
1998 Proof	Est. 5,000	Value: 165				

KM# 837a 1/5 CROWN

6.2200 g., 0.9999 Platinum .2000 oz. APW, 22 mm. **Ruler:** Elizabeth II **Series:** Flower Fairies **Obv:** Crowned bust right **Obv. Designer:** Raphael Maklouf **Rev:** Two fairies, sweet pea **Rev. Designer:** Cecily Mary Barker

Date	Mintage	F	VF	XF	Unc	BU
1998 Proof	Est. 2,500	Value: 260				

KM# 838 1/5 CROWN

6.2200 g., 0.9999 Gold .2000 oz. AGW, 22 mm. **Ruler:** Elizabeth II **Series:** Flower Fairies **Obv:** Crowned bust right **Obv. Designer:** Raphael Maklouf **Rev:** Fairy looking into flower, White Bindweed **Rev. Designer:** Cecily Mary Barker

Date	Mintage	F	VF	XF	Unc	BU
1998 Proof	Est. 5,000	Value: 165				

KM# 838a 1/5 CROWN

6.2200 g., 0.9999 Platinum .2000 oz. APW, 22 mm. **Ruler:** Elizabeth II **Series:** Flower Fairies **Obv:** Crowned bust right **Obv. Designer:** Raphael Maklouf **Rev:** Fairy looking into flower, White Bindweed **Rev. Designer:** Cecily Mary Barker

Date	Mintage	F	VF	XF	Unc	BU
1998 Proof	Est. 2,500	Value: 260				

KM# 839 1/5 CROWN

6.2200 g., 0.9999 Gold .2000 oz. AGW, 22 mm. **Ruler:** Elizabeth II **Series:** Flower Fairies **Obv:** Crowned bust right **Obv. Designer:** Raphael Maklouf **Rev:** Fairy standing, daffodil **Rev. Designer:** Cecily Mary Barker

Date	Mintage	F	VF	XF	Unc	BU
1998 Proof	Est. 5,000	Value: 165				

KM# 839a 1/5 CROWN

6.2200 g., 0.9999 Platinum .2000 oz. APW, 22 mm. **Ruler:** Elizabeth II **Series:** Flower Fairies **Obv:** Crowned bust right **Obv. Designer:** Raphael Maklouf **Rev:** Fairy standing, daffodil **Rev. Designer:** Cecily Mary Barker

Date	Mintage	F	VF	XF	Unc	BU
1998 Proof	Est. 2,500	Value: 265				

KM# 845 1/5 CROWN

6.2200 g., 0.9999 Gold .2000 oz. AGW, 22 mm. **Ruler:** Elizabeth II **Series:** Winter Olympics - Nagano **Obv:** Crowned bust right **Obv. Designer:** Raphael Maklouf **Rev:** Ski jumper

Date	Mintage	F	VF	XF	Unc	BU
1998 Proof	Est. 5,000	Value: 165				

KM# 846 1/5 CROWN

6.2200 g., 0.9999 Gold .2000 oz. AGW, 22 mm. **Ruler:** Elizabeth II **Series:** Winter Olympics - Nagano **Obv:** Crowned bust right **Obv. Designer:** Raphael Maklouf **Rev:** Slalom skier

Date	Mintage	F	VF	XF	Unc	BU
1998 Proof	Est. 5,000	Value: 165				

KM# 847 1/5 CROWN

6.2200 g., 0.9999 Gold .2000 oz. AGW, 22 mm. **Ruler:** Elizabeth II **Series:** Winter Olympics - Nagano **Obv:** Crowned bust right **Obv. Designer:** Raphael Maklouf **Rev:** Figure skaters below flames

Date	Mintage	F	VF	XF	Unc	BU
1998	Est. 5,000	Value: 165				

KM# 848 1/5 CROWN

6.2200 g., 0.9999 Gold .2000 oz. AGW, 22 mm. **Ruler:** Elizabeth II **Series:** Winter Olympics - Nagano **Obv:** Crowned bust right **Obv. Designer:** Raphael Maklouf **Rev:** Figure skater, speed skater and skier

Date	Mintage	F	VF	XF	Unc	BU
1998 Proof	Est. 5,000	Value: 165				

KM# 855 1/5 CROWN

6.2200 g., 0.9999 Gold .2000 oz. AGW, 22 mm. **Ruler:** Elizabeth II **Obv:** Crowned bust righ t **Obv. Designer:** Raphael Maklouf **Rev:** Birman cat

Date	Mintage	F	VF	XF	Unc	BU
1998 Proof	1,000	Value: 150				

KM# 855a 1/5 CROWN

6.2200 g., 0.9995 Platinum .2000 oz. APW, 22 mm. **Ruler:** Elizabeth II **Obv:** Crowned bust right **Obv. Designer:** Raphael Maklouf **Rev:** Birman cat

Date	Mintage	F	VF	XF	Unc	BU
1998 Proof	—	Value: 260				

KM# 861 1/5 CROWN

6.2200 g., 0.9999 Gold .2000 oz. AGW, 22 mm. **Ruler:** Elizabeth II **Series:** History of the Cat **Obv:** Crowned bust right **Obv. Designer:** Raphael Maklouf **Rev:** Egyptian Mau cat with earring

Date	Mintage	F	VF	XF	Unc	BU
1998 Proof	Est. 7,500	Value: 170				

KM# 871 1/5 CROWN

6.2200 g., 0.9999 Gold .2000 oz. AGW, 22 mm. **Ruler:** Elizabeth II **Subject:** 125th Anniversary of the Steam Railway **Obv:** Crowned bust right **Obv. Designer:** Raphael Maklouf **Rev:** "The General"

Date	Mintage	F	VF	XF	Unc	BU
1998 Proof	Est. 5,000	Value: 170				

KM# 873 1/5 CROWN

6.2200 g., 0.9999 Gold .2000 oz. AGW, 22 mm. **Ruler:** Elizabeth II **Subject:** 125th Anniversary of the Steam Railway **Obv:** Crowned bust right **Obv. Designer:** Raphael Maklouf **Rev:** "The Rocket" and portrait

Date	Mintage	F	VF	XF	Unc	BU
1998 Proof	Est. 5,000	Value: 170				

KM# 875 1/5 CROWN

6.2200 g., 0.9999 Gold .2000 oz. AGW, 22 mm. **Ruler:** Elizabeth II **Subject:** 125th Anniversary of the Steam Railway **Obv:** Crowned bust right **Obv. Designer:** Raphael Maklouf **Rev:** Orient Express parlor car, interior view

Date	Mintage	F	VF	XF	Unc	BU
1998 Proof	Est. 5,000	Value: 170				

KM# 877 1/5 CROWN

6.2200 g., 0.9999 Gold .2000 oz. AGW, 22 mm. **Ruler:** Elizabeth II **Subject:** 125th Anniversary of the Steam Railway **Obv:** Crowned bust right **Obv. Designer:** Raphael Maklouf **Rev:** Mount Pilatus railway

Date	Mintage	F	VF	XF	Unc	BU
1998 Proof	Est. 5,000	Value: 170				

KM# 879 1/5 CROWN

6.2200 g., 0.9999 Gold .2000 oz. AGW, 22 mm. **Ruler:** Elizabeth II **Subject:** 125th Anniversary of the Steam Railway **Obv:** Crowned bust right **Obv. Designer:** Raphael Maklouf **Rev:** No. 1 Sutherland locomotive

Date	Mintage	F	VF	XF	Unc	BU
1998 Proof	Est. 5,000	Value: 170				

KM# 881 1/5 CROWN

6.2200 g., 0.9999 Gold .2000 oz. AGW, 22 mm. **Ruler:** Elizabeth II **Subject:** 125th Anniversary of the Steam Railway **Obv:** Crowned bust right **Obv. Designer:** Raphael Maklouf **Rev:** "Flying Scotsman"

Date	Mintage	F	VF	XF	Unc	BU
1998 Proof	Est. 5,000	Value: 170				

KM# 883 1/5 CROWN

6.2200 g., 0.9999 Gold .2000 oz. AGW, 22 mm. **Ruler:** Elizabeth II **Subject:** 125th Anniversary of the Steam Railway **Obv:** Crowned bust right **Obv. Designer:** Raphael Maklouf **Rev:** Mallard locomotive

Date	Mintage	F	VF	XF	Unc	BU
1998 Proof	Est. 5,000	Value: 170				

KM# 885 1/5 CROWN

6.2200 g., 0.9999 Gold .2000 oz. AGW, 22 mm. **Ruler:** Elizabeth II **Subject:** 125th Anniversary of the Steam Railway **Obv:** Crowned bust right **Obv. Designer:** Raphael Maklouf **Rev:** The Big Boy locomotive

Date	Mintage	F	VF	XF	Unc	BU
1998 Proof	Est. 5,000	Value: 170				

KM# 887 1/5 CROWN

6.2200 g., 0.9999 Gold .2000 oz. AGW, 22 mm. **Ruler:** Elizabeth II **Series:** Year 2000 **Obv:** Crowned bust right **Obv. Designer:** Raphael Maklouf **Rev:** American Independence 1776

Date	Mintage	F	VF	XF	Unc	BU
1998 Proof	Est. 2,000	Value: 170				

KM# 889 1/5 CROWN

6.2200 g., 0.9999 Gold .2000 oz. AGW, 22 mm. **Ruler:** Elizabeth II **Series:** Year 2000 **Obv:** Crowned bust right **Obv. Designer:** Raphael Maklouf **Rev:** French Revolution 1789

Date	Mintage	F	VF	XF	Unc	BU
1998 Proof	Est. 2,000	Value: 170				

KM# 891 1/5 CROWN

6.2200 g., 0.9999 Gold .2000 oz. AGW, 22 mm. **Ruler:** Elizabeth II **Series:** Year 2000 **Obv:** Crowned bust right **Obv. Designer:** Raphael Maklouf **Rev:** Reformation of the Church 1517

Date	Mintage	F	VF	XF	Unc	BU
1998 Proof	Est. 2,000	Value: 170				

KM# 893 1/5 CROWN

6.2200 g., 0.9999 Gold .2000 oz. AGW, 22 mm. **Ruler:** Elizabeth II **Series:** Year 2000 **Obv:** Crowned bust right **Obv. Designer:** Raphael Maklouf **Rev:** 400th Anniversary of the Renaissance

Date	Mintage	F	VF	XF	Unc	BU
1998 Proof	Est. 2,000	Value: 170				

KM# 895 1/5 CROWN

6.2200 g., 0.9999 Gold .2000 oz. AGW, 22 mm. **Ruler:** Elizabeth II **Subject:** 125th Anniversary of the Steam Railway **Obv:** Crowned bust right **Obv. Designer:** Raphael Maklouf **Rev:** Ocean wave and sea gull

Date	Mintage	F	VF	XF	Unc	BU
1998 Proof	Est. 5,000	Value: 170				

KM# 913 1/5 CROWN

6.2200 g., 0.9999 Gold .2000 oz. AGW, 22 mm. **Ruler:** Elizabeth II **Subject:** Battle of Waterloo 1815 **Obv:** Crowned bust right **Obv. Designer:** Raphael Maklouf **Rev:** Wellington on horse

Date	Mintage	F	VF	XF	Unc	BU
1999 Proof	Est. 2,000	Value: 170				

KM# 915 1/5 CROWN

6.2200 g., 0.9999 Gold .2000 oz. AGW, 22 mm. **Ruler:** Elizabeth II **Subject:** U.S. Civil War **Obv:** Crowned bust right **Obv. Designer:** Raphael Maklouf **Rev:** Cameos of Lee and Grant, flags, sword and drum

Date	Mintage	F	VF	XF	Unc	BU
1999 Proof	Est. 2,000	Value: 170				

KM# 917 1/5 CROWN

6.2200 g., 0.9999 Gold .2000 oz. AGW, 22 mm. **Ruler:** Elizabeth II **Subject:** Bolshevik Revolution 1917 **Obv:** Crowned bust right **Obv. Designer:** Raphael Maklouf **Rev:** Lenin above the Aurora

Date	Mintage	F	VF	XF	Unc	BU
1999 Proof	Est. 2,000	Value: 170				

KM# 919 1/5 CROWN

6.2200 g., 0.9999 Gold .2000 oz. AGW, 22 mm. **Ruler:** Elizabeth II **Subject:** Armistice Day 1918 **Obv:** Crowned bust right **Obv. Designer:** Raphael Maklouf **Rev:** Biplane above tank

Date	Mintage	F	VF	XF	Unc	BU
1999 Proof	Est. 2,000	Value: 170				

KM# 921 1/5 CROWN

6.2200 g., 0.9999 Gold .2000 oz. AGW, 22 mm. **Ruler:** Elizabeth II **Series:** Summer Olympics - Sydney **Obv:** Crowned bust right **Obv. Designer:** Raphael Maklouf **Rev:** Three javelin throwers

Date	Mintage	F	VF	XF	Unc	BU
1999 Proof	Est. 5,000	Value: 170				

KM# 923 1/5 CROWN

6.2200 g., 0.9999 Gold .2000 oz. AGW, 22 mm. **Ruler:** Elizabeth II **Series:** Summer Olympics - Sydney **Obv:** Crowned bust right **Obv. Designer:** Raphael Maklouf **Rev:** Female diver

Date	Mintage	F	VF	XF	Unc	BU
1999 Proof	Est. 5,000	Value: 170				

KM# 925 1/5 CROWN

6.2200 g., 0.9999 Gold .2000 oz. AGW, 22 mm. **Ruler:** Elizabeth II **Series:** Summer Olympics - Sydney **Obv:** Crowned bust right **Obv. Designer:** Raphael Maklouf **Rev:** Sailboat

Date	Mintage	F	VF	XF	Unc	BU
1999 Proof	Est. 5,000	Value: 170				

KM# 927 1/5 CROWN

6.2200 g., 0.9999 Gold .2000 oz. AGW, 22 mm. **Ruler:** Elizabeth II **Series:** Summer Olympics - Sydney **Obv:** Crowned bust right **Obv. Designer:** Raphael Maklouf **Rev:** Two runners

Date	Mintage	F	VF	XF	Unc	BU
1999 Proof	Est. 5,000	Value: 170				

KM# 929 1/5 CROWN

6.2200 g., 0.9999 Gold .2000 oz. AGW, 22 mm. **Ruler:** Elizabeth II **Series:** Summer Olympics - Sydney **Obv:** Crowned bust right **Obv. Designer:** Raphael Maklouf **Rev:** Two hurdlers

Date	Mintage	F	VF	XF	Unc	BU
1999 Proof	Est. 5,000	Value: 170				

KM# 931 1/5 CROWN

6.2200 g., 0.9999 Gold .2000 oz. AGW, 22 mm. **Ruler:** Elizabeth II **Series:** World Cup Rugby 1999 **Obv:** Crowned bust right **Obv. Designer:** Raphael Maklouf **Rev:** Bust of William Webb Ellis

Date	Mintage	F	VF	XF	Unc	BU
1999 Proof	Est. 5,000	Value: 170				

KM# 933 1/5 CROWN

6.2200 g., 0.9999 Gold .2000 oz. AGW, 22 mm. **Ruler:** Elizabeth II **Series:** World Cup Rugby 1999 **Obv:** Crowned bust right **Obv. Designer:** Raphael Maklouf **Rev:** Rugby scrum

Date	Mintage	F	VF	XF	Unc	BU
1999 Proof	Est. 5,000	Value: 170				

KM# 935 1/5 CROWN

6.2200 g., 0.9999 Gold .2000 oz. AGW, 22 mm. **Ruler:** Elizabeth II **Series:** World Cup Rugby 1999 **Obv:** Crowned bust right **Obv. Designer:** Raphael Maklouf **Rev:** Player running for catch

Date	Mintage	F	VF	XF	Unc	BU
1999 Proof	Est. 5,000	Value: 170				

KM# 937 1/5 CROWN

6.2200 g., 0.9999 Gold .2000 oz. AGW, 22 mm. **Ruler:** Elizabeth II **Series:** World Cup Rugby 1999 **Obv:** Crowned bust right **Obv. Designer:** Raphael Maklouf **Rev:** Goal kick

Date	Mintage	F	VF	XF	Unc	BU
1999 Proof	Est. 5,000	Value: 170				

KM# 939 1/5 CROWN

6.2200 g., 0.9999 Gold .2000 oz. AGW, 22 mm. **Ruler:** Elizabeth II **Series:** World Cup Rugby 1999 **Obv:** Crowned bust right **Obv. Designer:** Raphael Maklouf **Rev:** Tackled ball carrier

Date	Mintage	F	VF	XF	Unc	BU
1999 Proof	Est. 5,000	Value: 170				

KM# 941 1/5 CROWN

6.2200 g., 0.9999 Gold .2000 oz. AGW, 22 mm. **Ruler:** Elizabeth II **Series:** World Cup Rugby 1999 **Obv:** Crowned bust right **Obv. Designer:** Raphael Maklouf **Rev:** Player leaping for catch

Date	Mintage	F	VF	XF	Unc	BU
1999 Proof	Est. 5,000	Value: 170				

KM# 950 1/5 CROWN
6.2200 g., 0.9999 Gold .2000 oz. AGW, 22 mm.
Ruler: Elizabeth II **Series:** Year of the Rabbit **Obv:** Crowned bust right **Obv. Designer:** Raphael Maklouf **Rev:** Two rabbits

Date	Mintage	F	VF	XF	Unc	BU
1999 Proof	Est. 12,000	Value: 170				

KM# 954 1/5 CROWN
6.2200 g., 0.9999 Gold .2000 oz. AGW, 22 mm.
Ruler: Elizabeth II **Obv:** Crowned bust right **Obv. Designer:** Raphael Maklouf **Rev:** Portrait Sir Walter Raleigh, ship and dates

Date	Mintage	F	VF	XF	Unc	BU
1999 Proof	Est. 5,000	Value: 170				

KM# 956 1/5 CROWN
6.2200 g., 0.9999 Gold .2000 oz. AGW, 22 mm.
Ruler: Elizabeth II **Obv:** Crowned bust right **Obv. Designer:** Raphael Maklouf **Rev:** Portrait Robert Falcon Scott and compass

Date	Mintage	F	VF	XF	Unc	BU
1999 Proof	Est. 5,000	Value: 170				

KM# 962 1/5 CROWN
6.2200 g., 0.9999 Gold .2000 oz. AGW, 22 mm.
Ruler: Elizabeth II **Subject:** British Blue Cat **Obv:** Crowned bust right **Obv. Designer:** Raphael Maklouf **Rev:** Cat cleaning paw

Date	Mintage	F	VF	XF	Unc	BU
1999	—	—	—	—	140	—
1999 Proof	—	Value: 145				
1999 U Y2K	Est. 5,000	—	—	—	150	—

KM# 962a 1/5 CROWN
6.2200 g., 0.9995 Platinum .2000 oz. APW, 22 mm.
Ruler: Elizabeth II **Subject:** British Blue Cat **Obv:** Crowned bust right **Obv. Designer:** Raphael Maklouf **Rev:** Cat cleaning paw

Date	Mintage	F	VF	XF	Unc	BU
1999 Proof	—	Value: 260				

KM# 975 1/5 CROWN
6.2200 g., 0.9999 Gold .2000 oz. AGW, 22 mm. **Ruler:** Elizabeth II **Series:** The Life and Times of the Queen Mother **Obv:** Crowned bust right **Obv. Designer:** Raphael Maklouf **Rev:** Child in chair

Date	Mintage	F	VF	XF	Unc	BU
1999 Proof	Est. 5,000	Value: 170				

KM# 977 1/5 CROWN
6.2200 g., 0.9999 Gold .2000 oz. AGW, 22 mm.
Ruler: Elizabeth II **Series:** The Life and Times of the Queen Mother **Obv:** Crowned bust right **Obv. Designer:** Raphael Maklouf **Rev:** Engagement portrait

Date	Mintage	F	VF	XF	Unc	BU
1999 Proof	Est. 5,000	Value: 170				

KM# 979 1/5 CROWN
6.2200 g., 0.9999 Gold .2000 oz. AGW, 22 mm.
Ruler: Elizabeth II **Series:** The Life and Times of the Queen Mother **Obv:** Crowned bust right **Obv. Designer:** Raphael Maklouf **Rev:** Honeymoon departure

Date	Mintage	F	VF	XF	Unc	BU
1999 Proof	Est. 5,000	Value: 170				

KM# 994 1/5 CROWN
6.2200 g., 0.9999 Gold .2000 oz. AGW, 22 mm.
Ruler: Elizabeth II **Subject:** The Wedding of HRH Prince Edward **Obv:** Crowned bust right **Obv. Designer:** Raphael Maklouf **R ev:** Portrait of Prince Edward

Date	Mintage	F	VF	XF	Unc	BU
1999 Proof	Est. 5,000	Value: 170				

KM# 995 1/5 CROWN
6.2200 g., 0.9999 Gold .2000 oz. AGW, 22 mm. **Ruler:** Elizabeth II **Series:** The Life and Times of the Queen Mother **Subject:** The Wedding of HRH The Prince Edward **Obv:** Crowned bust right **Obv. Designer:** Raphael Maklouf **Rev:** Head of Prince Edward

Date	Mintage	F	VF	XF	Unc	BU
1999 Proof	Est. 5,000	Value: 170				

KM# 997 1/5 CROWN
6.2200 g., 0.9999 Gold .2000 oz. AGW, 22 mm.
Ruler: Elizabeth II **Series:** The Life and Times of the Queen Mother **Subject:** The Wedding of HRH The Prince Edward **Obv:** Crowned bust right **Obv. Designer:** Raphael Maklouf **Rev:** Head of Sophie Rhys-Jones

Date	Mintage	F	VF	XF	Unc	BU
1999 Proof	Est. 5,000	Value: 170				

KM# 999 1/5 CROWN
6.2200 g., 0.9999 Gold .2000 oz. AGW, 22 mm.
Ruler: Elizabeth II **Subject:** 30th Anniversary of First Man on the Moon **Obv:** Crowned bust right **Obv. Designer:** Raphael Maklouf **Rev:** Apollo XI, two moon walkers, date

Date	Mintage	F	VF	XF	Unc	BU
1999 Proof	Est. 2,000	Value: 170				

KM# 1001 1/5 CROWN
6.2200 g., 0.9999 Gold .2000 oz. AGW, 22 mm.
Ruler: Elizabeth II **Subject:** 30th Anniversary of First Man on the Moon **Obv:** Crowned bust right **Obv. Designer:** Raphael Maklouf **Rev:** Mariner IX, 1971, space craft orbiting Mars

Date	Mintage	F	VF	XF	Unc	BU
1999 Proof	Est. 2,000	Value: 170				

KM# 1003 1/5 CROWN
6.2200 g., 0.9999 Gold .2000 oz. AGW, 22 mm.
Ruler: Elizabeth II **Subject:** 30th Anniversary of First Man on the Moon **Obv:** Crowned bust right **Obv. Designer:** Raphael Maklouf **Rev:** Apollo-Soyuz link-up

Date	Mintage	F	VF	XF	Unc	BU
1999 Proof	Est. 2,000	Value: 170				

KM# 1005 1/5 CROWN
6.2200 g., 0.9999 Gold .2000 oz. AGW, 22 mm.
Ruler: Elizabeth II **Subject:** 30th Anniversary of First Man on the Moon **Obv:** Crowned bust right **Obv. Designer:** Raphael Maklouf **Rev:** Viking Mars Lander, 1978

Date	Mintage	F	VF	XF	Unc	BU
1999 Proof	Est. 2,000	Value: 170				

KM# 1007 1/5 CROWN
6.2200 g., 0.9999 Gold .2000 oz. AGW, 22 mm.
Ruler: Elizabeth II **Subject:** 30th Anniversary of First Man on the Moon **Obv:** Crowned bust right **Obv. Designer:** Raphael Maklouf **Rev:** Shuttle Columbia, 1981

Date	Mintage	F	VF	XF	Unc	BU
1999 Proof	Est. 2,000	Value: 170				

KM# 1009 1/5 CROWN
6.2200 g., 0.9999 Gold .2000 oz. AGW, 22 mm. **Subject:** 30th Anniversary of First Man on the Moon **Obv:** Crowned bust right **Obv. Designer:** Raphael Maklouf **Rev:** Mars Pathfinder, 1997

Date	Mintage	F	VF	XF	Unc	BU
1999 Proof	Est. 2,000	Value: 170				

KM# 984 1/5 CROWN
6.2200 g., 0.9999 Gold .2000 oz. AGW, 22 mm. **Ruler:** Elizabeth II **Subject:** Founding of the UN - Millennium **Obv:** Crowned bust right **Obv. Designer:** Raphael Maklouf **Rev:** UN Building, logo

Date	Mintage	F	VF	XF	Unc	BU
2000 Proof	Est. 2,000	Value: 170				

KM# 984a 1/5 CROWN
28.2800 g., 0.9250 Silver .8410 oz. ASW **Ruler:** Elizabeth II **Subject:** Founding of the UN 1945 **Obv:** Crowned bust right **Obv. Designer:** Raphael Maklouf **Rev:** UN building and logo

Date	Mintage	F	VF	XF	Unc	BU
2000 Proof	—	Value: 50.00				

KM# 985 1/5 CROWN
6.2200 g., 0.9999 Gold .2000 oz. AGW, 22 mm.
Ruler: Elizabeth II **Subject:** First Man on the Moon - Millennium **Obv:** Crowned bust right **Obv. Designer:** Raphael Maklouf **Rev:** Landing scene, date

Date	Mintage	F	VF	XF	Unc	BU
2000 Proof	Est. 2,000	Value: 170				

KM# 987 1/5 CROWN
6.2200 g., 0.9999 Gold .2000 oz. AGW, 22 mm.
Ruler: Elizabeth II **Subject:** Fall of the Berlin Wall - Millennium **Obv:** Crowned bust right **Obv. Designer:** Raphael Maklouf **Rev:** Crowds surrounding wall

Date	Mintage	F	VF	XF	Unc	BU
2000 Proof	Est. 2,000	Value: 170				

KM# 989 1/5 CROWN
6.2200 g., 0.9999 Gold .2000 oz. AGW, 22 mm.
Ruler: Elizabeth II **Subject:** Millennium 2000 - The Future **Obv:** Crowned bust right **Obv. Designer:** Raphael Maklouf **Rev:** International space station

Date	Mintage	F	VF	XF	Unc	BU
2000 Proof	Est. 2,000	Value: 170				

KM# 1014 1/5 CROWN
6.2200 g., 0.9999 Gold .2000 oz. AGW, 22 mm. **Ruler:** Elizabeth II **Subject:** Year of the Dragon **Obv:** Crowned bust right **Obv. Designer:** Raphael Maklouf **Rev:** Dragon, Chinese characters

Date	Mintage	F	VF	XF	Unc	BU
2000 Proof	Est. 12,000	Value: 170				

KM# 1054 1/5 CROWN
6.2200 g., 0.9999 Gold .2000 oz. AGW, 22 mm.
Ruler: Elizabeth II **Obv:** Crowned bust right **Obv. Designer:** Raphael Maklouf **Rev:** Scottish kitten **Edge:** Reeded

Date	Mintage	F	VF	XF	Unc	BU
2000 Proof	—	Value: 175				
2000	—	—	—	—	145	—

KM# 1020 1/5 CROWN
6.2200 g., 0.9999 Gold .2000 oz. AGW, 22 mm. **Ruler:** Elizabeth II **Obv:** Crowned bust right **Obv. Designer:** Raphael Maklouf **Rev:** Armored portrait of Francisco Pizarro, map and ship **Edge:** Reeded

Date	Mintage	F	VF	XF	Unc	BU
2000 Proof	5,000	Value: 175				

KM# 1022 1/5 CROWN
6.2200 g., 0.9999 Gold .2000 oz. AGW, 22 mm. **Ruler:** Elizabeth II **Obv:** Crowned bust right **Obv. Designer:** Raphael Maklouf **Rev:** Portrait, ship on ice and map, Willem Barents

Date	Mintage	F	VF	XF	Unc	BU
2000 Proof	5,000	Value: 175				

KM# 1024 1/5 CROWN
6.2200 g., 0.9999 Gold .2000 oz. AGW, 22 mm. **Series:** Queen Mother **Obv:** Crowned bust right **Obv. Designer:** Raphael Maklouf **Rev:** 1931 family scene **Edge:** Reeded

Date	Mintage	F	VF	XF	Unc	BU
2000 Proof	5,000	Value: 175				

KM# 1026 1/5 CROWN
6.2200 g., 0.9999 Gold .2000 oz. AGW, 22 mm. **Ruler:** Elizabeth II **Series:** Queen Mother **Obv:** Crowned bust right **Obv. Designer:** Raphael Maklouf **Rev:** 1937 Coronation scene

Date	Mintage	F	VF	XF	Unc	BU
2000 Proof	5,000	Value: 175				

KM# 1028 1/5 CROWN
6.2200 g., 0.9999 Gold .2000 oz. AGW, 22 mm. **Ruler:** Elizabeth II **Series:** Queen Mother **Obv:** Crowned bust right **Obv. Designer:** Raphael Maklouf **Rev:** 1945 Victory Visit scene

Date	Mintage	F	VF	XF	Unc	BU
2000 Proof	5,000	Value: 175				

KM# 1030 1/5 CROWN
6.2200 g., 0.9999 Gold .2000 oz. AGW, 22 mm. **Ruler:** Elizabeth II **Series:** Queen Mother **Obv:** Crowned bust right **Obv. Designer:** Raphael Maklouf **Rev:** 1963 Royal Visit scene

Date	Mintage	F	VF	XF	Unc	BU
2000 Proof	175	Value: 175				

KM# 1032 1/5 CROWN
6.2200 g., 0.9990 Gold .2000 oz. AGW, 22 mm. **Ruler:** Elizabeth II **Subject:** Battle of Britain **Obv:** Crowned bust right **Obv. Designer:** Raphael Maklouf **Rev:** Aerial battle scene **Edge:** Reeded

Date	Mintage	F	VF	XF	Unc	BU
2000 Proof	5,000	Value: 175				

KM# 1034 1/5 CROWN
6.2200 g., 0.9990 Gold .2000 oz. AGW, 22 mm.
Ruler: Elizabeth II **Subject:** Global Challenge Yacht Race **Obv:** Crowned bust right **Obv. Designer:** Raphael Maklouf **Rev:** Partial view of ship and map

Date	Mintage	F	VF	XF	Unc	BU
2000 Proof	5,000	Value: 175				

KM# 1046 1/5 CROWN
6.2200 g., 0.9999 Gold .2000 oz. AGW, 22 mm.
Ruler: Elizabeth II **Obv:** Crowned bust right **Obv. Designer:** Raphael Maklouf **Rev:** Prince William's portrait **Edge:** Reeded

Date	Mintage	F	VF	XF	Unc	BU
2000 Proof	5,000	Value: 175				

KM# 1048 1/5 CROWN
6.2200 g., 0.9999 Gold .2000 oz. AGW, 22 mm.
Ruler: Elizabeth II **Obv:** Crowned bust right **Obv. Designer:** Raphael Maklouf **Rev:** Bust with hat facing

Date	Mintage	F	VF	XF	Unc	BU
2000 Proof	2,000	Value: 175				

KM# 1054a 1/5 CROWN
6.2200 g., 0.9995 Platinum .2000 oz. APW, 22 mm.
Ruler: Elizabeth II **Obv:** Crowned bust right **Obv. Designer:** Raphael Maklouf **Rev:** Scottish kitten

Date	Mintage	F	VF	XF	Unc	BU
2000	—	—	—	—	255	—

KM# 669 1/4 CROWN
0.9990 Bi-Metallic Gold center in Platinum ring .1249 oz.
Ruler: Elizabeth II **Series:** Legend of King Arthur **Obv:** Crowned bust right **Obv. Designer:** Raphael Maklouf **Rev:** King Arthur with sword and orb

Date	Mintage	F	VF	XF	Unc	BU
1996 Proof	Est. 5,000	Value: 250				

KM# 670 1/4 CROWN
0.9990 Bi-Metallic .1249 oz. **Ruler:** Elizabeth II **Series:** Legend of King Arthur **Obv:** Crowned bust right **Obv. Designer:** Raphael Maklouf **Rev:** Queen Guinevere

Date	Mintage	F	VF	XF	Unc	BU
1996 Proof	Est. 5,000	Value: 250				

KM# 671 1/4 CROWN
0.9990 Bi-Metallic Gold center in Platinum ring .1249 oz.
Ruler: Elizabeth II **Series:** Legend of King Arthur **Obv:** Crowned bust right **Obv. Designer:** Raphael Maklouf **Rev:** Sir Lancelot

Date	Mintage	F	VF	XF	Unc	BU
1996 Proof	Est. 5,000	Value: 250				

KM# 672 1/4 CROWN
0.9990 Bi-Metallic Gold center in Platinum ring .1249 oz.
Ruler: Elizabeth II **Series:** Legend of King Arthur **Obv:** Crowned bust right **Obv. Designer:** Raphael Maklouf **Rev:** Merlin

Date	Mintage	F	VF	XF	Unc	BU
1996 Proof	Est. 5,000	Value: 250				

KM# 673 1/4 CROWN
0.9990 Bi-Metallic Gold center in Platinum ring .1249 oz.
Ruler: Elizabeth II **Series:** Legend of King Arthur **Obv:** Crowned bust right **Obv. Designer:** Raphael Maklouf **Rev:** Camelot Castle

Date	Mintage	F	VF	XF	Unc	BU
1996 Proof	Est. 5,000	Value: 250				

KM# 674 1/4 CROWN
3.8880 g., 0.9950 Platinum .1244 oz. APW **Ruler:** Elizabeth II **Series:** Legend of King Arthur **Obv:** Crowned bust right **Obv. Designer:** Raphael Maklouf **Rev:** King Arthur with sword and orb

Date	Mintage	F	VF	XF	Unc	BU
1996 Proof	Est. 5,000	Value: 275				

KM# 675 1/4 CROWN
3.8880 g., 0.9950 Platinum .1244 oz. APW **Ruler:** Elizabeth II **Series:** Legend of King Arthur **Obv:** Crowned bust right **Obv. Designer:** Raphael Maklouf **Rev:** Queen Guinevere

Date	Mintage	F	VF	XF	Unc	BU
1996 Proof	Est. 5,000	Value: 275				

KM# 676 1/4 CROWN

3.8880 g., 0.9950 Platinum .1244 oz. APW **Ruler:** Elizabeth II **Series:** Legend of King Arthur **Obv:** Crowned bust right **Obv. Designer:** Raphael Maklouf **Rev:** Sir Lancelot

Date	Mintage	F	VF	XF	Unc	BU
1996 Proof	Est. 5,000	Value: 275				

KM# 677 1/4 CROWN

3.8880 g., 0.9950 Platinum .1244 oz. APW **Ruler:** Elizabeth II **Series:** Legend of King Arthur **Obv:** Crowned bust right **Obv. Designer:** Raphael Maklouf **Rev:** Merlin

Date	Mintage	F	VF	XF	Unc	BU
1996 Proof	Est. 5,000	Value: 275				

KM# 678 1/4 CROWN

3.8880 g., 0.9950 Platinum .1244 oz. APW **Ruler:** Elizabeth II **Series:** Legend of King Arthur **Obv:** Crowned bust right within circle **Obv. Designer:** Raphael Maklouf **Rev:** Castle within circle

Date	Mintage	F	VF	XF	Unc	BU
1996 Proof	Est. 5,000	Value: 275				

KM# 187 1/2 CROWN

15.5500 g., 0.9990 Gold .5000 oz. AGW **Ruler:** Elizabeth II **Subject:** U.S. Constitution **Obv:** Crowned bust right within circle **Obv. Designer:** Raphael Maklouf **Rev:** Statue of Liberty at center of Presidential busts within circle

Date	Mintage	F	VF	XF	Unc	BU
1987 Proof	12,000	Value: 350				

KM# 187a 1/2 CROWN

15.5500 g., 0.9990 Platinum .5000 oz. APW **Ruler:** Elizabeth II **Subject:** U.S. Constitution **Obv:** Crowned bust right **Obv. Designer:** Raphael Maklouf **Rev:** Busts of American presidents, Statue of Liberty at center

Date	Mintage	F	VF	XF	Unc	BU
1987 Proof	250	Value: 650				

KM# 238 1/2 CROWN

15.5500 g., 0.9990 Gold .5000 oz. AGW **Ruler:** Elizabeth II **Obv:** Crowned bust right **Obv. Designer:** Raphael Maklouf **Rev:** Manx cat

Date	Mintage	F	VF	XF	Unc	BU
1988	6,375	—	—	—	345	—
1988 Proof	5,000	Value: 365				

KM# 286 1/2 CROWN

16.4000 g., 0.9480 Gold .5000 oz. AGW **Ruler:** Elizabeth II **Subject:** Australian Bicentennial **Obv:** Crowned bust right within circle **Obv. Designer:** Raphael Maklouf **Rev:** Cockatoo on branch within circle

Date	Mintage	F	VF	XF	Unc	BU
1988 Proof	Est. 7,500	Value: 360				

KM# 287 1/2 CROWN

16.4000 g., 0.9480 Gold .5000 oz. AGW **Ruler:** Elizabeth II **Subject:** Australian Bicentennial **Obv:** Crowned bust right **Obv. Designer:** Raphael Maklouf **Rev:** Koala bear

Date	Mintage	F	VF	XF	Unc	BU
1988 Proof	Est. 7,500	Value: 360				

KM# 288 1/2 CROWN

16.4000 g., 0.9480 Gold .5000 oz. AGW **Ruler:** Elizabeth II **Subject:** Australian Bicentennial **Obv:** Crowned bust right **Obv. Designer:** Raphael Maklouf **Rev:** Duckbill platypus

Date	Mintage	F	VF	XF	Unc	BU
1988 Proof	Est. 7,500	Value: 360				

KM# 289 1/2 CROWN

16.4000 g., 0.9480 Gold .5000 oz. AGW **Ruler:** Elizabeth II **Subject:** Australian Bicentennial **Obv:** Crowned bust right within circle **Obv. Designer:** Raphael Maklouf **Rev:** Kangaroo within circle

Date	Mintage	F	VF	XF	Unc	BU
1988 Proof	Est. 7,500	Value: 360				

KM# 359 1/2 CROWN

15.5500 g., 0.9990 Platinum .5000 oz. APW **Ruler:** Elizabeth II **Subject:** Australian Bicentennial **Obv:** Crowned bust right **Obv. Designer:** Raphael Maklouf **Rev:** Cockatoo

Date	Mintage	F	VF	XF	Unc	BU
1988 Proof	—	Value: 650				

KM# 360 1/2 CROWN

15.5500 g., 0.9990 Platinum .5000 oz. APW **Ruler:** Elizabeth II **Subject:** Australian Bicentennial **Obv:** Crowned bust right **Obv. Designer:** Raphael Maklouf **Rev:** Koala bear

Date	Mintage	F	VF	XF	Unc	BU
1988 Proof	—	Value: 650				

KM# 361 1/2 CROWN

15.5500 g., 0.9990 Platinum .5000 oz. APW **Ruler:** Elizabeth II **Subject:** Australian Bicentennial **Obv:** Crowned bust right **Obv. Designer:** Raphael Maklouf **Rev:** Duckbill platypus

Date	Mintage	F	VF	XF	Unc	BU
1988 Proof	—	Value: 650				

KM# 362 1/2 CROWN

15.5500 g., 0.9990 Platinum .5000 oz. APW **Ruler:** Elizabeth II **Subject:** Australian Bicentennial **Obv:** Crowned bust right **Obv. Designer:** Raphael Maklouf **Rev:** Kangaroo

Date	Mintage	F	VF	XF	Unc	BU
1988 Proof	—	Value: 650				

KM# 363 1/2 CROWN

15.5500 g., 0.9990 Platinum .5000 oz. APW **Ruler:** Elizabeth II **Subject:** Australian Bicentennial **Obv:** Crowned bust right **Obv. Designer:** Raphael Maklouf **Rev:** Dingo Dog

Date	Mintage	F	VF	XF	Unc	BU
1988 Proof	—	Value: 650				

KM# 255 1/2 CROWN

16.4000 g., 0.9480 Gold .5000 oz. AGW **Ruler:** Elizabeth II **Obv:** Crowned bust right **Obv. Designer:** Raphael Maklouf **Rev:** Persian cat

Date	Mintage	F	VF	XF	Unc	BU
1989	—	—	—	—	345	—
1989 Proof	—	Value: 375				

KM# 470 1/2 CROWN

15.5500 g., 0.9990 Platinum .5000 oz. APW **Ruler:** Elizabeth II **Obv:** Crowned bust right **Obv. Designer:** Raphael Maklouf **Rev:** Persian cat

Date	Mintage	F	VF	XF	Unc	BU
1989	—	—	—	—	BV+20%	—
1989 Proof	—	BV+25%				

KM# 1265 1/2 CROWN

15.5500 g., 0.9990 Gold 0.4994 oz. AGW, 30 mm. **Ruler:** Elizabeth II **Obv:** Crowned bust right **Obv. Designer:** Raphael Maklouf **Rev:** Stamp design in black center **Edge:** Reeded

Date	Mintage	F	VF	XF	Unc	BU
1990PM	—	—	—	—	350	—

KM# 280 1/2 CROWN

16.4000 g., 0.9480 Gold .5000 oz. AGW **Ruler:** Elizabeth II **Obv:** Crowned bust right **Obv. Designer:** Raphael Maklouf **Rev:** Alley cat

Date	Mintage	F	VF	XF	Unc	BU
1990	—	—	—	—	365	—
1990 Proof	—	Value: 400				

KM# 297 1/2 CROWN

15.5500 g., 0.9990 Gold .5000 oz. AGW **Ruler:** Elizabeth II **Obv:** Crowned bust right **Obv. Designer:** Raphael Maklouf **Rev:** Norwegian cat

Date	Mintage	F	VF	XF	Unc	BU
1991	—	—	—	—	365	—
1991 Proof	—	Value: 400				

KM# 325 1/2 CROWN

15.5500 g., 0.9990 Gold .5000 oz. AGW **Ruler:** Elizabeth II **Subject:** America's Cup **Obv:** Crowned bust right **Obv. Designer:** Raphael Maklouf **Rev:** Cameo of "Star of India" above two modern sailboats

Date	Mintage	F	VF	XF	Unc	BU
1992 Prooflike	2,000	—	—	—	360	—

KM# 331 1/2 CROWN

15.5500 g., 0.9990 Gold .5000 oz. AGW **Ruler:** Elizabeth II **Obv:** Crowned bust right **Obv. Designer:** Raphael Maklouf **Rev:** Siamese cat

Date	Mintage	F	VF	XF	Unc	BU
1992	—	—	—	—	365	—
1992 Proof	—	Value: 400				

KM# 341 1/2 CROWN

15.5500 g., 0.9990 Gold .5000 oz. AGW **Ruler:** Elizabeth II **Subject:** Year of the Rooster **Obv:** Crowned bust right **Obv. Designer:** Raphael Maklouf **Rev:** Cockerel within circle **Rev. Designer:** Barry Stanton

Date	Mintage	F	VF	XF	Unc	BU
1993 Proof	Est. 5,000	Value: 375				

KM# 352 1/2 CROWN

15.5500 g., 0.9990 Gold .5000 oz. AGW **Ruler:** Elizabeth II **Obv:** Crowned bust right **Obv. Designer:** Raphael Maklouf **Rev:** Maine coon cat

Date	Mintage	F	VF	XF	Unc	BU
1993	—	—	—	—	365	—
1993 Proof	—	Value: 400				

KM# 379 1/2 CROWN

15.5500 g., 0.9990 Gold .5000 oz. AGW **Ruler:** Elizabeth II **Obv:** Crowned bust right **Obv. Designer:** Raphael Maklouf **Rev:** Japanese bobtail cat

Date	Mintage	F	VF	XF	Unc	BU
1994	—	—	—	—	365	—
1994 Proof	—	Value: 400				

KM# 405 1/2 CROWN

15.5500 g., 0.9990 Gold .5000 oz. AGW **Ruler:** Elizabeth II **Obv:** Crowned bust right **Obv. Designer:** Raphael Maklouf **Rev:** Pekingese dog

Date	Mintage	F	VF	XF	Unc	BU
1994 Proof	5,000	Value: 375				

KM# 476 1/2 CROWN
15.5500 g., 0.9990 Platinum .5000 oz. APW **Ruler:** Elizabeth II
Obv: Crowned bust right **Obv. Designer:** Raphael Maklouf
Rev: Japanese bobtail cat

Date	Mintage	F	VF	XF	Unc	BU
1994	—	—	—	—	BV+20%	—
1994 Proof	—	BV+20%				

KM# 445 1/2 CROWN
15.5500 g., 0.9990 Gold .5000 oz. AGW **Ruler:** Elizabeth II
Obv: Crowned bust right **Obv. Designer:** Raphael Maklouf
Rev: Turkish cat looking back

Date	Mintage	F	VF	XF	Unc	BU
1995 U	—	—	—	—	365	—
1995 Proof	—	Value: 400				

KM# 452 1/2 CROWN
15.5500 g., 0.9990 Gold .5000 oz. AGW **Ruler:** Elizabeth II
Subject: Year of the Pig **Obv:** Crowned bust right
Obv. Designer: Raphael Maklouf **Rev:** Sow with piglets

Date	Mintage	F	VF	XF	Unc	BU
1995 Proof	Est. 5,000	Value: 365				

KM# 481 1/2 CROWN
15.5500 g., 0.9990 Platinum .5000 oz. APW **Ruler:** Elizabeth II
Obv: Crowned bust right **Obv. Designer:** Raphael Maklouf
Rev: Turkish cat

Date	Mintage	F	VF	XF	Unc	BU
1995	—	—	—	—	BV+20%	—
1995 Proof	—	BV+20%				

KM# 731 1/2 CROWN
15.5517 g., 0.9999 Gold .5000 oz. AGW **Ruler:** Elizabeth II
Subject: Year of the Rat **Obv:** Crowned bust right
Obv. Designer: Raphael Maklouf **Rev:** Rat

Date	Mintage	F	VF	XF	Unc	BU
1996 Proof	—	Value: 365				

KM# 619 1/2 CROWN
15.5500 g., 0.9990 Gold .5000 oz. AGW **Ruler:** Elizabeth II
Obv: Crowned bust right **Obv. Designer:** Raphael Maklouf
Rev: Burmese cat

Date	Mintage	F	VF	XF	Unc	BU
1996 U	—	—	—	—	345	—
1996 Proof	—	Value: 375				

KM# 620 1/2 CROWN
15.5500 g., 0.9990 Platinum .5000 oz. APW **Ruler:** Elizabeth II
Obv: Crowned bust right **Obv. Designer:** Raphael Maklouf
Rev: Burmese cat

Date	Mintage	F	VF	XF	Unc	BU
1996 U	—	—	—	—	BV+20%	—
1996 Proof	—	Value: 650				

KM# 724 1/2 CROWN
15.5517 g., 0.9999 Gold .5000 oz. AGW **Ruler:** Elizabeth II
Subject: Year of the Ox **Obv:** Crowned bust right
Obv. Designer: Raphael Maklouf **Rev:** Ox laying down

Date	Mintage	F	VF	XF	Unc	BU
1996 Proof	Est. 6,000	Value: 350				

KM# 764a 1/2 CROWN
15.5500 g., 0.9999 Silver .5 oz. ASW **Obv:** Crowned bust right
Obv. Designer: Raphael Maklouf **Rev:** Portrait of Leif Eriksson and Viking ship with map sail

Date	Mintage	F	VF	XF	Unc	BU
1997 Proof	—	Value: 30.00				

KM# 764 1/2 CROWN
15.5517 g., 0.9999 Gold .5000 oz. AGW **Ruler:** Elizabeth II
Obv: Crowned bust right **Obv. Designer:** Raphael Maklouf
Rev: Portrait of Leif Eriksson and Viking ship with map sail

Date	Mintage	F	VF	XF	Unc	BU
1997 Proof	Est. 2,500	Value: 365				

KM# 767 1/2 CROWN
15.5517 g., 0.9999 Gold .5000 oz. AGW **Ruler:** Elizabeth II
Obv: Crowned bust right **Obv. Designer:** Raphael Maklouf
Rev: Portrait of Fridtjof Nansen, map and ship "The Fram"

Date	Mintage	F	VF	XF	Unc	BU
1997 Proof	Est. 2,500	Value: 345				

KM# 767a 1/2 CROWN
15.5500 g., 0.9990 Silver .5 oz. ASW **Ruler:** Elizabeth II
Obv: Crowned bust right **Obv. Designer:** Raphael Maklouf
Rev: Portrait of Fridtjof Nansen, map and ship "The Fram"

Date	Mintage	F	VF	XF	Unc	BU
1997 Proof	—	Value: 30.00				

KM# 773 1/2 CROWN
15.5517 g., 0.9999 Gold .5000 oz. AGW **Ruler:** Elizabeth II
Obv: Crowned bust right **Obv. Designer:** Raphael Maklouf
Rev: Long-haired Smoke cat

Date	Mintage	F	VF	XF	Unc	BU
1997	—	—	—	—	365	—
1997 Proof	—	Value: 400				

KM# 791 1/2 CROWN
15.5517 g., 0.9999 Gold .5000 oz. AGW **Ruler:** Elizabeth II
Subject: History of the Cat **Obv:** Crowned bust right
Obv. Designer: Raphael Maklouf **Rev:** Cat stalking a spider

Date	Mintage	F	VF	XF	Unc	BU
1997 Proof	Est. 2,500	Value: 375				

KM# 815 1/2 CROWN
15.5000 g., 0.9999 Gold .5000 oz. AGW **Ruler:** Elizabeth II
Subject: Year of the Tiger **Obv:** Crowned bust right
Obv. Designer: Raphael Maklouf **Rev:** Tiger

Date	Mintage	F	VF	XF	Unc	BU
1998 Proof	Est. 6,000	Value: 365				

KM# 856 1/2 CROWN
15.5517 g., 0.9999 Gold .5000 oz. AGW **Ruler:** Elizabeth II
Obv: Crowned bust right **Obv. Designer:** Raphael Maklouf
Rev: Birman cat

Date	Mintage	F	VF	XF	Unc	BU
1998	—	—	—	—	365	—
1998 Proof	1,000	Value: 400				

KM# 856a 1/2 CROWN
15.5517 g., 0.9995 Platinum .5000 oz. APW **Ruler:** Elizabeth II
Obv: Crowned bust right **Obv. Designer:** Raphael Maklouf
Rev: Birman cat

Date	Mintage	F	VF	XF	Unc	BU
1998	—	—	—	—	—	—

Note: Reported, not confirmed

KM# 862 1/2 CROWN
15.5517 g., 0.9999 Gold .5000 oz. AGW **Ruler:** Elizabeth II
Subject: History of the Cat **Obv:** Crowned bust right **Obv. Designer:** Raphael Maklouf **Rev:** Egyptain Mau cat with earring

Date	Mintage	F	VF	XF	Unc	BU
1998 Proof	Est. 250	Value: 400				

KM# 951 1/2 CROWN
15.5517 g., 0.9999 Gold .5000 oz. AGW **Ruler:** Elizabeth II
Subject: Year of the Rabbit **Obv:** Crowned bust right
Obv. Designer: Raphael Maklouf **Rev:** Two rabbits

Date	Mintage	F	VF	XF	Unc	BU
1999 Proof	Est. 6,000	Value: 365				

KM# 964 1/2 CROWN
15.5517 g., 0.9999 Gold .5000 oz. AGW **Ruler:** Elizabeth II
Subject: British Blue cat **Obv:** Crowned bust right
Obv. Designer: Raphael Maklouf **Rev:** Cat cleaning paw

Date	Mintage	F	VF	XF	Unc	BU
1999	—	—	—	—	360	—
1999 Proof	—	Value: 385				

KM# 964a 1/2 CROWN
15.5518 g., 0.9995 Platinum .5000 oz. APW **Ruler:** Elizabeth II
Subject: British Blue cat **Obv:** Crowned bust right
Obv. Designer: Raphael Maklouf **Rev:** Cat cleaning paw

Date	Mintage	F	VF	XF	Unc	BU
1999	—	—	—	—	—	—

Note: Reported, not confirmed

KM# 1084 1/2 CROWN
9.0000 g., 0.9990 Bi-Metallic Titanium center in Gold ring .2891 oz., 32.25 mm. **Ruler:** Elizabeth II **Subject:** Greenwich Meridian Time Clock **Obv:** Head with tiara right within beaded circle **Obv. Designer:** Ian Rank-Broadley **Rev:** Greenwich meridian line on map clock face **Edge:** Reeded

Date	Mintage	F	VF	XF	Unc	BU
2000 Proof	10,000	Value: 220				

KM# 1055 1/2 CROWN
15.5517 g., 0.9999 Gold .5000 oz. AGW, 30 mm.
Ruler: Elizabeth II **Subject:** Scottish Fold Kitten **Obv:** Crowned bust right **Obv. Designer:** Raphael Maklouf **Rev:** Kitten playing with world **Edge:** Reeded

Date	Mintage	F	VF	XF	Unc	BU
2000	—	—	—	—	345	—
2000 Proof	—	Value: 365				

KM# 1055a 1/2 CROWN
6.2200 g., 0.9995 Platinum .2000 oz. APW **Ruler:** Elizabeth II
Subject: Scottish Fold Kitten **Obv:** Crowned bust right
Obv. Designer: Raphael Maklouf **Rev:** Kitten playing with world

Date	Mintage	F	VF	XF	Unc	BU
2000	—	—	—	—	350	—

KM# 1263 1/2 CROWN
15.0400 g., Titanium, 38.5 mm. **Ruler:** Elizabeth II **Obv:** Crowned bust right **Rev:** Space station and shuttle **Edge:** Reeded

Date	Mintage	F	VF	XF	Unc	BU
2000PM Matte	—	—	—	—	40.00	—

KM# 1015 1/2 CROWN
15.5517 g., 0.9999 Gold .5000 oz. AGW **Ruler:** Elizabeth II
Subject: Year of the Dragon **Obv:** Head with tiara right **Obv. Designer:** Ian Rank-Broadley **Rev:** Dragon, Chinese characters

Date	Mintage	F	VF	XF	Unc	BU
2000 Proof	Est. 6,000	Value: 350				

KM# 18 CROWN
Copper-Nickel, 38.5 mm. **Ruler:** Elizabeth II **Obv:** Young bust right **Obv. Designer:** Arnold Machin **Rev:** Manx cat
Rev. Designer: Christopher Ironside **Edge:** Reeded

Date	Mintage	F	VF	XF	Unc	BU
1970	150,000	—	—	—	10.00	12.00

KM# 18a CROWN
28.2800 g., 0.9250 Silver .8411 oz. ASW, 38.5 mm.
Ruler: Elizabeth II **Obv:** Young bust right **Obv. Designer:** Arnold Machin **Rev:** Manx cat **Rev. Designer:** Christopher Ironside

Date	Mintage	F	VF	XF	Unc	BU
1970 Proof	11,000	Value: 17.50				

KM# 30 CROWN
Copper-Nickel, 38.5 mm. **Ruler:** Elizabeth II
Subject: Centenary - Birth of Winston Churchill **Obv:** Young bust right **Obv. Designer:** Arnold Machin **Rev:** Bust facing
Edge: Reeded **Note:** Most of this issue are doubled die.

Date	Mintage	F	VF	XF	Unc	BU
1974	45,000	—	—	—	5.00	6.00

KM# 30a CROWN
28.2800 g., 0.9250 Silver .8411 oz. ASW **Ruler:** Elizabeth II
Obv: Young bust right **Obv. Designer:** Arnold Machin **Rev:** Bust facing **Edge:** Reeded

Date	Mintage	F	VF	XF	Unc	BU
1974	—	—	—	—	7.50	8.50
1974 Proof	30,000	Value: 9.50				

KM# 37 CROWN
Copper-Nickel, 38.5 mm. **Ruler:** Elizabeth II
Subject: Bicentenary of American Independence **Obv:** Young bust right **Obv. Designer:** Arnold Machin **Rev:** Bust left
Edge: Reeded **Note:** Doubled die strike exists.

Date	Mintage	F	VF	XF	Unc	BU
1976	50,000	—	—	—	6.00	7.00

KM# 37a CROWN
28.2800 g., 0.9250 Silver .8411 oz. ASW, 38.5 mm. **Ruler:** Elizabeth II **Subject:** Bicentenary of American Independence
Obv: Young bust right **Obv. Designer:** Arnold Machin **Rev:** Bust left

Date	Mintage	F	VF	XF	Unc	BU
1976	—	—	—	—	7.50	8.50
1976 Proof	30,000	Value: 10.00				

KM# 38 CROWN
Copper-Nickel, 38.5 mm. **Ruler:** Elizabeth II **Obv:** Young bust right **Obv. Designer:** Arnold Machin **Rev:** Horse-drawn tram
Edge: Reeded **Note:** Doubled die strike exists.

Date	Mintage	F	VF	XF	Unc	BU
1976	50,000	—	—	—	7.50	8.50

KM# 38a CROWN
28.2800 g., 0.9250 Silver .8411 oz. ASW, 38.5 mm.
Ruler: Elizabeth II **Obv:** Young bust right **Obv. Designer:** Arnold Machin **Rev:** Horse-drawn tram

Date	Mintage	F	VF	XF	Unc	BU
1976	—	—	—	—	12.50	13.50
1976 Proof	30,000	Value: 15.00				

KM# 41 CROWN
Copper-Nickel, 38.5 mm. **Ruler:** Elizabeth II **Subject:** Silver Jubilee **Obv:** Young bust right **Obv. Designer:** Arnold Machin
Rev: Triskeles in center of crowns **Edge:** Reeded

Date	Mintage	F	VF	XF	Unc	BU
ND(1977)	—	—	—	—	4.50	6.00
ND(1977) Proof	—	Value: 15.00				

KM# 41a CROWN

28.2800 g., 0.9250 Silver .8411 oz. ASW, 38.5 mm.
Ruler: Elizabeth II **Subject:** Silver Jubilee **Obv:** Crowned bust right **Obv. Designer:** Arnold Machin **Rev:** Triskeles in center of crowns **Edge:** Reeded

Date	Mintage	F	VF	XF	Unc	BU
ND(1977)	—	—	—	—	12.00	13.00
ND(1977) Proof	30,000	Value: 13.50				

KM# 42 CROWN

Copper-Nickel, 38.5 mm. **Ruler:** Elizabeth II **Subject:** Queen's Jubilee Appeal **Obv:** Young bust right **Obv. Designer:** Arnold Machin **Rev:** Triskeles on shield and crown divide wreath with monogram at center **Edge:** Reeded

Date	Mintage	F	VF	XF	Unc	BU
1977	—	—	—	—	6.00	7.00

Note: Wide and narrow rims exist

KM# 42a CROWN

28.2800 g., 0.9250 Silver .8411 oz. ASW, 38.5 mm.
Ruler: Elizabeth II **Subject:** Queen's Jubilee Appeal **Obv:** Young bust right **Obv. Designer:** Arnold Machin **Rev:** Triskeles on shield and crown divide wreath with monogram at center

Date	Mintage	F	VF	XF	Unc	BU
1977	70,000	—	—	—	12.00	13.00
1977 Proof	30,000	Value: 13.50				

KM# 43 CROWN

Copper-Nickel, 38.5 mm. **Ruler:** Elizabeth II **Subject:** 25th Anniversary of Coronation **Obv:** Young bust right
Obv. Designer: Arnold Machin **Rev:** Falcons **Edge:** Reeded
Note: For mule of Isle of Man obverse with Ascension Island KM#1 reverse, refer to Ascension Island listings.

Date	Mintage	F	VF	XF	Unc	BU
1978	—	—	—	—	7.50	10.00
1978 Proof	—	Value: 12.00				

KM# 43a CROWN

28.2800 g., 0.9250 Silver .8411 oz. ASW, 38.5 mm.
Ruler: Elizabeth II **Subject:** 25th Anniversary of Coronation **Obv:** Young bust right **Obv. Designer:** Arnold Machin **Rev:** Falcons

Date	Mintage	F	VF	XF	Unc	BU
1978	70,000	—	—	—	12.50	13.50
1978 Proof	30,000	Value: 15.00				

KM# 45 CROWN

Copper-Nickel, 38.5 mm. **Ruler:** Elizabeth II **Subject:** 300th Anniversary of Manx Coinage **Obv:** Young bust right
Obv. Designer: Arnold Machin **Rev:** Triskeles at center of assorted coins **Edge:** Reeded

Date	Mintage	F	VF	XF	Unc	BU
1979	—	—	—	—	8.00	9.00
1979 Proof	—	Value: 10.00				

KM# 45a CROWN

28.2800 g., 0.9250 Silver .8411 oz. ASW, 38.5 mm.
Ruler: Elizabeth II **Subject:** 300th Anniversary of Manx Coinage **Obv:** Young bust right **Obv. Designer:** Arnold Machin
Rev: Triskeles at center of assorted coins

Date	Mintage	F	VF	XF	Unc	BU
1979	70,000	—	—	—	12.50	13.50
1979 Proof	30,000	Value: 15.00				

KM# 46 CROWN

Copper-Nickel, 38.5 mm. **Ruler:** Elizabeth II
Subject: Millennium of Tynwald **Obv:** Young bust right
Obv. Designer: Arnold Machin **Rev:** Viking longship, Godred Cravan **Rev. Designer:** Leslie Lindsay **Edge:** Reeded

Date	Mintage	F	VF	XF	Unc	BU
1979	100,000	—	—	—	3.50	4.50

KM# 46a CROWN

28.2800 g., 0.9250 Silver .8411 oz. ASW, 38.5 mm.
Ruler: Elizabeth II **Subject:** Millennium of Tynwald **Obv:** Young bust right **Obv. Designer:** Arnold Machin **Rev:** Viking longship, Godred Cravan **Rev. Designer:** Leslie Lindsay

Date	Mintage	F	VF	XF	Unc	BU
1979	25,000	—	—	—	12.50	13.50
1979 Proof	10,000	Value: 15.00				

KM# 46b CROWN

43.0000 g., 0.9170 Gold 1.2678 oz. AGW, 38.5 mm.
Ruler: Elizabeth II **Subject:** Millennium of Tynwald **Obv:** Young bust right **Obv. Designer:** Arnold Machin **Rev:** Viking longship
Rev. Designer: Leslie Lindsay

Date	Mintage	F	VF	XF	Unc	BU
1979 Proof	300	Value: 925				

KM# 46c CROWN

52.0000 g., 0.9500 Platinum 1.5884 oz. APW, 38.5 mm.
Ruler: Elizabeth II **Subject:** Millennium of Tynwald **Obv:** Young bust right **Obv. Designer:** Arnold Machin **Rev:** Viking longship
Rev. Designer: Leslie Lindsay

Date	Mintage	F	VF	XF	Unc	BU
1979 Proof	100	Value: 2,150				

KM# 47 CROWN

Copper-Nickel, 38.5 mm. **Ruler:** Elizabeth II
Subject: Millennium of Tynwald **Obv:** Young bust right
Obv. Designer: Arnold Machin **Rev:** English cog, Castle Rushen
Rev. Designer: Leslie Lindsay **Edge:** Reeded

Date	Mintage	F	VF	XF	Unc	BU
1979	100,000	—	—	—	6.50	7.50
1979 CB	—	—	—	—	6.50	7.50

KM# 47a CROWN

28.2800 g., 0.9250 Silver .8411 oz. ASW, 38.5 mm.
Ruler: Elizabeth II **Subject:** Millennium of Tynwald **Obv:** Young bust right **Obv. Designer:** Arnold Machin **Rev:** English cog, Castle Rushen **Rev. Designer:** Leslie Lindsay

Date	Mintage	F	VF	XF	Unc	BU
1979	25,000	—	—	—	12.50	13.50
1979 Proof	10,000	Value: 15.00				

KM# 47b CROWN

43.0000 g., 0.9170 Gold 1.2678 oz. AGW, 38.5 mm.
Ruler: Elizabeth II **Subject:** Millennium of Tynwald **Obv:** Young bust right **Obv. Designer:** Arnold Machin **Rev:** English cog, Castle Rushen **Rev. Designer:** Leslie Lindsay

Date	Mintage	F	VF	XF	Unc	BU
1979 Proof	300	Value: 925				

KM# 47c CROWN

52.0000 g., 0.9500 Platinum 1.5884 oz. APW, 38.5 mm.
Ruler: Elizabeth II **Subject:** Millennium of Tynwald **Obv:** Young bust right **Obv. Designer:** Arnold Machin **Rev:** English cog, Castle Rushen **Rev. Designer:** Leslie Lindsay

Date	Mintage	F	VF	XF	Unc	BU
1979 Proof	100	Value: 2,150				

KM# 48 CROWN

Copper-Nickel, 38.5 mm. **Ruler:** Elizabeth II
Subject: Millennium of Tynwald **Obv:** Young bust right
Obv. Designer: Arnold Machin **Rev:** Ship **Rev. Designer:** Leslie Lindsay **Edge:** Reeded

Date	Mintage	F	VF	XF	Unc	BU
1979	100,000	—	—	—	8.00	9.00

KM# 48a CROWN

28.2800 g., 0.9250 Silver .8411 oz. ASW, 38.5 mm.
Ruler: Elizabeth II **Subject:** Millennium of Tynwald **Obv:** Young bust right **Obv. Designer:** Arnold Machin **Rev:** Ship
Rev. Designer: Leslie Lindsay

Date	Mintage	F	VF	XF	Unc	BU
1979	25,000	—	—	—	12.50	13.50
1979 Proof	10,000	Value: 15.00				

KM# 48b CROWN

43.0000 g., 0.9170 Gold 1.2678 oz. AGW, 38.5 mm.
Ruler: Elizabeth II **Subject:** Millennium of Tynwald **Obv:** Young bust right **Obv. Designer:** Arnold Machin **Rev:** Ship
Rev. Designer: Leslie Lindsay

Date	Mintage	F	VF	XF	Unc	BU
1979 Proof	300	Value: 925				

KM# 48c CROWN

52.0000 g., 0.9500 Platinum 1.5884 oz. APW, 38.5 mm.
Ruler: Elizabeth II **Subject:** Millennium of Tynwald **Obv:** Young bust right **Obv. Designer:** Arnold Machin **Rev:** Ship
Rev. Designer: Leslie Lindsay

Date	Mintage	F	VF	XF	Unc	BU
1979 Proof	100	Value: 2,150				

KM# 49 CROWN

28.2800 g., Copper-Nickel, 38.5 mm. **Ruler:** Elizabeth II
Subject: Millennium of Tynwald **Obv:** Young bust right
Obv. Designer: Arnold Machin **Rev:** Standing figure and ship
Rev. Designer: Leslie Lindsay **Edge:** Reeded

Date	Mintage	F	VF	XF	Unc	BU
1979	100,000	—	—	—	8.00	9.00

KM# 49a CROWN

28.2800 g., 0.9250 Silver .8411 oz. ASW, 38.5 mm.
Ruler: Elizabeth II **Subject:** Millennium of Tynwald **Obv:** Young bust right **Obv. Designer:** Arnold Machin **Rev:** Standing figure and ship **Rev. Designer:** Leslie Lindsay

Date	Mintage	F	VF	XF	Unc	BU
1979 Proof	10,000	Value: 15.00				
1979	25,000	—	—	—	12.50	13.50

KM# 49b CROWN

43.0000 g., 0.9170 Gold 1.2678 oz. AGW, 38.5 mm.
Ruler: Elizabeth II **Subject:** Millennium of Tynwald **Obv:** Young bust right **Obv. Designer:** Arnold Machin **Rev:** Standing figure and ship **Rev. Designer:** Leslie Lindsay

Date	Mintage	F	VF	XF	Unc	BU
1979 Proof	300	Value: 925				

KM# 49c CROWN

52.0000 g., 0.9500 Platinum 1.5884 oz. APW, 38.5 mm.
Ruler: Elizabeth II **Subject:** Millennium of Tynwald **Obv:** Young bust right **Obv. Designer:** Arnold Machin **Rev:** Standing figure and ship **Rev. Designer:** Leslie Lindsay

Date	Mintage	F	VF	XF	Unc	BU
1979 Proof	100	Value: 2,150				

KM# 50 CROWN

28.2800 g., Copper-Nickel, 38.5 mm. **Ruler:** Elizabeth II
Subject: Millennium of Tynwald **Obv:** Young bust right
Obv. Designer: Arnold Machin **Rev:** Lifeboat and Sir William Hillory portrait **Rev. Designer:** Leslie Lindsay **Edge:** Reeded

Date	Mintage	F	VF	XF	Unc	BU
1979	100,000	—	—	—	8.00	9.00

KM# 50a CROWN

28.2800 g., 0.9250 Silver .8411 oz. ASW, 38.5 mm.
Ruler: Elizabeth II **Subject:** Millennium of Tynwald **Obv:** Young bust right **Obv. Designer:** Arnold Machin **Rev:** Lifeboat and Sir William Hillory portrait **Rev. Designer:** Leslie Lindsay

Date	Mintage	F	VF	XF	Unc	BU
1979	25,000	—	—	—	12.50	13.50
1979 Proof	10,000	Value: 15.00				

KM# 50b CROWN

43.0000 g., 0.9170 Gold 1.2678 oz. AGW, 38.5 mm.
Ruler: Elizabeth II **Subject:** Millennium of Tynwald **Obv:** Young bust right **Obv. Designer:** Arnold Machin **Rev:** Lifeboat and Sir William Hillory portrait **Rev. Designer:** Leslie Lindsay

Date	Mintage	F	VF	XF	Unc	BU
1979 Proof	300	Value: 925				

KM# 50c CROWN

52.0000 g., 0.9500 Platinum 1.5884 oz. APW, 38.5 mm.
Ruler: Elizabeth II **Subject:** Millennium of Tynwald **Obv:** Young bust right **Obv. Designer:** Arnold Machin **Rev:** Lifeboat and Sir William Hillory portrait **Rev. Designer:** Leslie Lindsay

Date	Mintage	F	VF	XF	Unc	BU
1979 Proof	100	Value: 2,150				

KM# 63 CROWN

Copper-Nickel, 38.5 mm. **Ruler:** Elizabeth II **Subject:** Derby Bicentennial **Obv:** Young bust right **Obv. Designer:** Arnold Machin **Rev:** Men racing horses **Edge:** Reeded

Date	Mintage	F	VF	XF	Unc	BU
1980	100,000	—	—	—	6.00	7.00

KM# 63a CROWN

28.2800 g., 0.9250 Silver .8411 oz. ASW, 38.5 mm. **Ruler:** Elizabeth II **Subject:** Derby Bicentennial **Obv:** Young bust right **Obv. Designer:** Arnold Machin **Rev:** Men racing horses

Date	Mintage	F	VF	XF	Unc	BU
1980	35,000	—	—	—	12.50	13.50
1980 Proof	20,000	Value: 15.00				

KM# 63b CROWN

52.0000 g., 0.9500 Platinum 1.5884 oz. APW, 38.5 mm. **Ruler:** Elizabeth II **Subject:** Derby Bicentennial **Obv:** Young bust right **Obv. Designer:** Arnold Machin **Rev:** Men racing horses

Date	Mintage	F	VF	XF	Unc	BU
1980 Proof	500	Value: 2,150				

KM# 63c CROWN

43.0000 g., 0.9170 Gold 1.2678 oz. AGW, 38.5 mm. **Ruler:** Elizabeth II **Subject:** Derby Bicentennial **Obv:** Young bust right **Obv. Designer:** Arnold Machin **Rev:** Men racing horses

Date	Mintage	F	VF	XF	Unc	BU
1980 Proof	—	Value: 925				

KM# 64 CROWN

Copper-Nickel, 38.5 mm. **Ruler:** Elizabeth II **Subject:** 1980 Winter Olympics - Lake Placid **Obv:** Young bust right **Obv. Designer:** Arnold Machin **Rev:** Triskeles at center of assorted olympic figures **Edge:** Reeded

Date	Mintage	F	VF	XF	Unc	BU
1980	—	—	—	—	—	—
Note: With dot between Olympics and Lake						
1980	100,000	—	—	—	3.00	4.00
Note: Without dot						
1980 Prooflike	—	—	—	—	7.50	9.00

KM# 64a CROWN

28.2800 g., 0.9250 Silver .8411 oz. ASW, 38.5 mm. **Ruler:** Elizabeth II **Subject:** 1980 Winter Olympics - Lake Placid **Obv:** Young bust right **Obv. Designer:** Arnold Machin **Rev:** Triskeles at center of assorted olympic figures

Date	Mintage	F	VF	XF	Unc	BU
1980 Matte	—	—	—	—	16.50	17.50
1980 Proof	10,000	Value: 18.50				

KM# 64b CROWN

39.8000 g., 0.9170 Gold 1.1735 oz. AGW, 38.5 mm. **Ruler:** Elizabeth II **Subject:** 1980 Winter Olympics - Lake Placid **Obv:** Young bust right **Obv. Designer:** Arnold Machin **Rev:** Triskeles at center of assorted olympic figures

Date	Mintage	F	VF	XF	Unc	BU
1980	1,500	—	—	—	850	860
Note: With dot between Olympics and Lake						
1980 Proof	500	Value: 870				

KM# 64c CROWN

52.0000 g., 0.9500 Platinum 1.5884 oz. APW, 38.5 mm. **Ruler:** Elizabeth II **Subject:** 1980 Winter Olympics - Lake Placid **Obv:** Young bust right **Obv. Designer:** Arnold Machin **Rev:** Triskeles at center of assorted olympic figures

Date	Mintage	F	VF	XF	Unc	BU
1980 Proof	100	Value: 2,150				
Note: With dot between Olympics and Lake						

KM# 65 CROWN

Copper-Nickel, 38.5 mm. **Ruler:** Elizabeth II **Subject:** 1980 Summer Olympics - Moscow **Obv:** Young bust right **Obv. Designer:** Arnold Machin **Rev:** Triskeles at center of assorted olympic figures

Date	Mintage	F	VF	XF	Unc	BU
1980	—	—	—	—	3.50	4.00
Note: Without dot between Olympiad and Moscow; without dots to right and left of One Crown						
1980	—	—	—	—	3.50	4.00
Note: Without dot between Olympiad and Moscow; with dots to right and left of One Crown						
1980	30,000	—	—	—	3.50	4.00
Note: With dot between Olympiad and Moscow; with dots to right and left of One Crown						
1980 Prooflike	—	—	—	—	7.50	9.00

KM# 65a CROWN

28.2800 g., 0.9250 Silver .8411 oz. ASW, 38.5 mm. **Ruler:** Elizabeth II **Subject:** 1980 Summer Olympics - Moscow **Obv:** Young bust right **Obv. Designer:** Arnold Machin **Rev:** Triskeles at center of assorted olympic figures

Date	Mintage	F	VF	XF	Unc	BU
1980	—	—	—	—	16.50	17.50
Note: Without dot between Olympiad and Moscow; without dots to right and left of One Crown						
1980	—	—	—	—	16.50	17.50
Note: Without dot between Olympiad and Moscow; with dots to right and left of One Crown						
1980	—	—	—	—	16.50	17.50
Note: With dot between Olympiad and Moscow; with dots to right and left of One Crown						
1980 Proof	10,000	Value: 18.50				

KM# 65b CROWN

39.8000 g., 0.9170 Gold 1.1735 oz. AGW, 38.5 mm. **Ruler:** Elizabeth II **Subject:** 1980 Summer Olympics - Moscow **Obv:** Young bust right **Obv. Designer:** Arnold Machin **Rev:** Triskeles at center of assorted olympic figures

Date	Mintage	F	VF	XF	Unc	BU
1980	1,500	—	—	—	850	860
Note: With dot between Olympiad and Moscow; with dots to right and lft of One Crown						

KM# 65c CROWN

52.0000 g., 0.9500 Platinum 1.5884 oz. APW, 38.5 mm. **Ruler:** Elizabeth II **Subject:** 1980 Summer Olympics - Moscow **Obv:** Young bust right **Obv. Designer:** Arnold Machin **Rev:** Triskeles at center of assorted olympic figures

Date	Mintage	F	VF	XF	Unc	BU
1980 Proof	100	Value: 2,150				
Note: With dot between Olympiad and Moscow; with dots to right and left of One Crown						

KM# 66 CROWN

Copper-Nickel, 38.5 mm. **Ruler:** Elizabeth II **Subject:** 1980 Summer Olympics - Moscow **Obv:** Young bust right **Obv. Designer:** Arnold Machin **Rev:** Triskeles at center of assorted olympic figures **Edge:** Reeded

Date	Mintage	F	VF	XF	Unc	BU
1980	30,000	—	—	—	6.00	7.00
1980 Prooflike	—	—	—	—	7.50	9.00

KM# 66a CROWN

28.2800 g., 0.9250 Silver .8411 oz. ASW, 38.5 mm. **Ruler:** Elizabeth II **Subject:** 1980 Summer Olympics - Moscow **Obv:** Young bust right **Obv. Designer:** Arnold Machin **Rev:** Triskeles at center of assorted olympic figures

Date	Mintage	F	VF	XF	Unc	BU
1980 Matte	—	—	—	—	16.50	17.50
1980 Proof	10,000	Value: 18.50				

KM# 66b CROWN

39.8000 g., 0.9170 Gold 1.1735 oz. AGW, 38.5 mm. **Ruler:** Elizabeth II **Subject:** 1980 Summer Olympics - Moscow **Obv:** Young bust right **Obv. Designer:** Arnold Machin **Rev:** Triskeles at center of assorted olympic figures

Date	Mintage	F	VF	XF	Unc	BU
1980	1,500	—	—	—	850	860

KM# 66c CROWN

52.0000 g., 0.9500 Platinum 1.5884 oz. APW, 38.5 mm. **Ruler:** Elizabeth II **Subject:** 1980 Summer Olympics - Moscow **Obv:** Young bust right **Obv. Designer:** Arnold Machin **Rev:** Triskeles at center of assorted olympic figures

Date	Mintage	F	VF	XF	Unc	BU
1980 Proof	100	Value: 2,150				

KM# 67 CROWN

Copper-Lead Alloy, 38.5 mm. **Ruler:** Elizabeth II **Subject:** 1980 Summer Olympics - Moscow **Obv:** Young bust right **Obv. Designer:** Arnold Machin **Rev:** Triskeles at center of assorted olympic figures **Edge:** Reeded

Date	Mintage	F	VF	XF	Unc	BU
1980	30,000	—	—	—	6.00	7.00
1980 Proof like	—	—	—	—	7.50	9.00

KM# 67a CROWN

28.2800 g., 0.9250 Silver .8411 oz. ASW, 38.5 mm. **Ruler:** Elizabeth II **Subject:** 1980 Summer Olympics - Moscow **Obv:** Young bust right **Obv. Designer:** Arnold Machin **Rev:** Triskeles at center of assorted olympic figures

Date	Mintage	F	VF	XF	Unc	BU
1980 Matte	—	—	—	—	16.50	17.50
1980 Proof	10,000	Value: 18.50				

KM# 67b CROWN

39.8000 g., 0.9170 Gold 1.1735 oz. AGW, 38.5 mm. **Ruler:** Elizabeth II **Subject:** 1980 Summer Olympics - Moscow **Obv:** Young bust right **Obv. Designer:** Arnold Machin **Rev:** Triskeles at center of assorted olympic figures

Date	Mintage	F	VF	XF	Unc	BU
1980	1,500	—	—	—	850	860

KM# 67c CROWN

52.0000 g., 0.9500 Platinum 1.5884 oz. APW, 38.5 mm. **Ruler:** Elizabeth II **Subject:** 1980 Summer Olympics - Moscow **Obv:** Young bust right **Obv. Designer:** Arnold Machin **Rev:** Triskeles at center of assorted olympic figures

Date	Mintage	F	VF	XF	Unc	BU
1980 Proof	100	Value: 2,150				

KM# 68 CROWN

Copper-Nickel, 38.5 mm. **Ruler:** Elizabeth II **Subject:** 80th Birthday of Queen Mother **Obv:** Young bust right **Obv. Designer:** Arnold Machin **Rev:** Crowned head facing divides dates **Edge:** Reeded

Date	Mintage	F	VF	XF	Unc	BU
1980	100,000	—	—	—	5.00	6.00

KM# 68a CROWN

28.2800 g., 0.5000 Silver .4546 oz. ASW, 38.5 mm. **Ruler:** Elizabeth II **Subject:** 80th Birthday of Queen Mother **Obv:** Young bust right **Obv. Designer:** Arnold Machin **Rev:** Crowned head facing divides dates

Date	Mintage	F	VF	XF	Unc	BU
1980	50,000	—	—	—	10.00	11.50

KM# 68b CROWN

28.2800 g., 0.9250 Silver .8411 oz. ASW, 38.5 mm. **Ruler:** Elizabeth II **Subject:** 80th Birthday of Queen Mother **Obv:** Young bust right **Obv. Designer:** Arnold Machin **Rev:** Crowned head facing divides dates

Date	Mintage	F	VF	XF	Unc	BU
1980 Proof	30,000	Value: 16.50				

KM# 68c CROWN

5.0000 g., 0.3740 Gold .0601 oz. AGW **Ruler:** Elizabeth II **Subject:** 80th Birthday of Queen Mother, facing **Obv:** Young bust right **Obv. Designer:** Arnold Machin **Rev:** Crowned head facing divides dates

Date	Mintage	F	VF	XF	Unc	BU
1980	50,000	—	—	—	60.00	65.00

KM# 68d CROWN

7.9600 g., 0.9170 Gold .2347 oz. AGW, 38.5 mm. **Ruler:** Elizabeth II **Subject:** 80th Birthday of Queen Mother **Obv:** Young bust right **Obv. Designer:** Arnold Machin **Rev:** Crowned head facing divides dates

Date	Mintage	F	VF	XF	Unc	BU
1980	1,000	—	—	—	165	175

KM# 73 CROWN

Copper-Nickel, 38.5 mm. **Ruler:** Elizabeth II **Subject:** Duke of Edinburgh Award Scheme **Obv:** Young bust right **Obv. Designer:** Arnold Machin **Rev:** Bust facing **Edge:** Reeded

Date	Mintage	F	VF	XF	Unc	BU
1981	50,000	—	—	—	2.50	3.50

KM# 73a CROWN

28.2800 g., 0.9250 Silver .8411 oz. ASW, 38.5 mm. **Ruler:** Elizabeth II **Subject:** Duke of Edinburgh Award Scheme **Obv:** Young bust right **Obv. Designer:** Arnold Machin **Rev:** Bust facing

Date	Mintage	F	VF	XF	Unc	BU
1981	20,000	—	—	—	12.50	13.50
1981 Proof	15,000	Value: 15.00				

KM# 73b CROWN

5.1000 g., 0.3740 Gold 0.0613 oz. AGW **Ruler:** Elizabeth II **Subject:** Duke of Edinburgh Award Scheme **Obv:** Young bust right **Obv. Designer:** Arnold Machin **Rev:** Bust facing

Date	Mintage	F	VF	XF	Unc	BU
1981 Proof	10,000	Value: 85.00				

KM# 73c CROWN

7.9600 g., 0.9170 Gold .2347 oz. AGW **Ruler:** Elizabeth II **Subject:** Duke of Edinburgh Award Scheme **Obv:** Young bust right **Obv. Designer:** Arnold Machin **Rev:** Bust facing

Date	Mintage	F	VF	XF	Unc	BU
1981 Proof	1,000	Value: 175				

KM# 73d CROWN

52.0000 g., 0.9500 Platinum 1.5884 oz. APW, 38.5 mm. **Ruler:** Elizabeth II **Subject:** Duke of Edinburgh Award Scheme **Obv:** Young bust right **Obv. Designer:** Arnold Machin **Rev:** Bust facing

Date	Mintage	F	VF	XF	Unc	BU
1981 Proof	100	Value: 2,150				

KM# 74 CROWN

Copper-Nickel, 38.5 mm. **Ruler:** Elizabeth II **Subject:** Duke of Edinburgh Award Scheme **Obv:** Young bust right **Obv. Designer:** Arnold Machin **Rev:** Monogram within crowned belt within sprigs **Edge:** Reeded

Date	Mintage	F	VF	XF	Unc	BU
1981	50,000	—	—	—	6.00	7.00

KM# 74a CROWN

28.2800 g., 0.9250 Silver .8411 oz. ASW, 38.5 mm. **Ruler:** Elizabeth II **Subject:** Duke of Edinburgh Award Scheme **Obv:** Young bust right **Obv. Designer:** Arnold Machin **Rev:** Monogram within crowned belt within sprigs

Date	Mintage	F	VF	XF	Unc	BU
1981	20,000	—	—	—	12.50	13.50
1981 Proof	15,000	Value: 15.00				

KM# 74b CROWN

5.1000 g., 0.3740 Gold .0613 oz. AGW **Ruler:** Elizabeth II **Subject:** Duke of Edinburgh Award Scheme **Obv:** Young bust right **Obv. Designer:** Arnold Machin **Rev:** Monogram within crowned belt within sprigs

Date	Mintage	F	VF	XF	Unc	BU
1981 Proof	10,000	Value: 65.00				

KM# 74c CROWN

7.9600 g., 0.9170 Gold .2347 oz. AGW **Ruler:** Elizabeth II **Subject:** Duke of Edinburgh Award Scheme **Obv:** Young bust right **Obv. Designer:** Arnold Machin **Rev:** Monogram within crowned belt within sprigs

Date	Mintage	F	VF	XF	Unc	BU
1981 Proof	1,000	Value: 175				

KM# 74d CROWN

52.0000 g., 0.9500 Platinum 1.5884 oz. APW, 38.5 mm. **Ruler:** Elizabeth II **Subject:** Duke of Edinburgh Award Scheme **Obv:** Young bust right **Obv. Designer:** Arnold Machin **Rev:** Monogram within crowned belt within sprigs

Date	Mintage	F	VF	XF	Unc	BU
1981 Proof	100	Value: 2,150				

KM# 75 CROWN

Copper-Nickel, 38.5 mm. **Ruler:** Elizabeth II **Subject:** Duke of Edinburgh Award Scheme **Obv:** Young bust right **Obv. Designer:** Arnold Machin **Rev:** Nursing, hiking, swimming **Edge:** Reeded

Date	Mintage	F	VF	XF	Unc	BU
1981	50,000	—	—	—	6.00	7.00

KM# 75a CROWN

28.2800 g., 0.9250 Silver .8411 oz. ASW, 38.5 mm. **Ruler:** Elizabeth II **Subject:** Duke of Edinburgh Award Scheme **Obv:** Young bust right **Obv. Designer:** Arnold Machin **Rev:** Nursing, hiking, swimming

Date	Mintage	F	VF	XF	Unc	BU
1981	20,000	—	—	—	12.50	13.50
1981 Proof	15,000	Value: 15.00				

KM# 75b CROWN

5.1000 g., 0.3740 Gold .0613 oz. AGW **Ruler:** Elizabeth II **Subject:** Duke of Edinburgh Award Scheme **Obv:** Young bust right **Obv. Designer:** Arnold Machin **Rev:** Nursing, hiking, swimming

Date	Mintage	F	VF	XF	Unc	BU
1981 Proof	10,000	Value: 65.00				

KM# 75c CROWN

7.9600 g., 0.9170 Gold .2347 oz. AGW **Ruler:** Elizabeth II **Subject:** Duke of Edinburgh Award Scheme **Obv:** Young bust right **Obv. Designer:** Arnold Machin **Rev:** Nursing, hiking, swimming

Date	Mintage	F	VF	XF	Unc	BU
1981 Proof	1,000	Value: 175				

KM# 75d CROWN

52.0000 g., 0.9500 Platinum 1.5884 oz. APW, 38.5 mm. **Ruler:** Elizabeth II **Subject:** Duke of Edinburgh Award Scheme **Obv:** Young bust right **Obv. Designer:** Arnold Machin **Rev:** Nursing, hiking, swimming

Date	Mintage	F	VF	XF	Unc	BU
1981 Proof	100	Value: 2,150				

KM# 76 CROWN

Copper-Nickel, 38.5 mm. **Ruler:** Elizabeth II **Subject:** Duke of Edinburgh Award Scheme **Obv:** Young bust right **Obv. Designer:** Arnold Machin **Rev:** Rock climbing, sailing, motorcycling **Edge:** Reeded

Date	Mintage	F	VF	XF	Unc	BU
1981	50,000	—	—	—	6.00	7.00

KM# 76a CROWN

28.2800 g., 0.9250 Silver .8411 oz. ASW, 38.5 mm. **Ruler:** Elizabeth II **Subject:** Duke of Edinburgh Award Scheme **Obv:** Young bust right **Obv. Designer:** Arnold Machin **Rev:** Rock climbing, sailing, motorcycling

Date	Mintage	F	VF	XF	Unc	BU
1981	20,000	—	—	—	12.50	13.50
1981 Proof	15,000	Value: 15.00				

KM# 76b CROWN

5.1000 g., 0.3740 Gold .0613 oz. AGW **Ruler:** Elizabeth II **Subject:** Duke of Edinburgh Award Scheme **Obv:** Young bust right **Obv. Designer:** Arnold Machin **Rev:** Rock climbing, sailing, motorcycling

Date	Mintage	F	VF	XF	Unc	BU
1981 Proof	10,000	Value: 65.00				

KM# 76c CROWN

7.9600 g., 0.9170 Gold .2347 oz. AGW **Ruler:** Elizabeth II **Subject:** Duke of Edinburgh Award Scheme **Obv:** Young bust right **Obv. Designer:** Arnold Machin **Rev:** Rock climbing, sailing, motorcycling

Date	Mintage	F	VF	XF	Unc	BU
1981 Proof	1,000	Value: 175				

KM# 76d CROWN

52.0000 g., 0.9500 Platinum 1.5884 oz. APW, 38.5 mm. **Ruler:** Elizabeth II **Subject:** Duke of Edinburgh Award Scheme **Obv:** Young bust right **Obv. Designer:** Arnold Machin **Rev:** Rock climbing, sailing, motorcycling

Date	Mintage	F	VF	XF	Unc	BU
1981 Proof	100	Value: 2,150				

KM# 77 CROWN

Copper-Nickel, 38.5 mm. **Ruler:** Elizabeth II **Subject:** International Year of Disabled **Obv:** Young bust right **Obv. Designer:** Arnold Machin **Rev:** Braille and bust 1/4 left **Edge:** Reeded

Date	Mintage	F	VF	XF	Unc	BU
1981	50,000	—	—	—	2.50	3.50
1981 Prooflike	—	—	—	—	5.00	6.00

KM# 77a CROWN

28.2800 g., 0.9250 Silver .8411 oz. ASW, 38.5 mm. **Ruler:** Elizabeth II **Subject:** International Year of Disabled **Obv:** Young bust right **Obv. Designer:** Arnold Machin **Rev:** Braille and bust 1/4 left

Date	Mintage	F	VF	XF	Unc	BU
1981	20,000	—	—	—	12.50	13.50
1981 Proof	15,000	Value: 15.00				

KM# 77b CROWN

5.1000 g., 0.3740 Gold .0613 oz. AGW **Ruler:** Elizabeth II **Subject:** International Year of Disabled **Obv:** Young bust right **Obv. Designer:** Arnold Machin **Rev:** Braille and bust 1/4 left

Date	Mintage	F	VF	XF	Unc	BU
1981 Proof	10,000	Value: 75.00				

KM# 77c CROWN

7.9600 g., 3917.0000 Gold .2347 oz. AGW **Ruler:** Elizabeth II **Subject:** International Year of Disabled **Obv:** Young bust right **Obv. Designer:** Arnold Machin **Rev:** Braille and bust 1/4 left

Date	Mintage	F	VF	XF	Unc	BU
1981 Proof	1,000	Value: 180				

KM# 77d CROWN

52.0000 g., 0.9500 Platinum 1.5884 oz. APW, 38.5 mm. **Ruler:** Elizabeth II **Subject:** International Year of Disabled **Obv:** Young bust right **Obv. Designer:** Arnold Machin **Rev:** Braille and bust 1/4 left

Date	Mintage	F	VF	XF	Unc	BU
1981 Proof	100	Value: 2,150				

KM# 78 CROWN

Copper-Nickel, 38.5 mm. **Ruler:** Elizabeth II **Subject:** International Year of Disabled **Obv:** Young bust right **Obv. Designer:** Arnold Machin **Rev:** Beethoven, violin and music score **Edge:** Reeded

Date	Mintage	F	VF	XF	Unc	BU
1981	50,000	—	—	—	8.00	9.00
1981 Prooflike	—	—	—	—	10.00	12.00

KM# 78a CROWN

28.2800 g., 0.9250 Silver .8411 oz. ASW, 38.5 mm. **Ruler:** Elizabeth II **Subject:** International Year of Disabled **Obv:** Young bust right **Obv. Designer:** Arnold Machin **Rev:** Beethoven, violin and music score

Date	Mintage	F	VF	XF	Unc	BU
1981	20,000	—	—	—	12.50	13.50
1981 Proof	15,000	Value: 16.50				

KM# 78b CROWN
5.1000 g., 0.3740 Gold .0613 oz. AGW **Ruler:** Elizabeth II **Subject:** International Year of Disabled **Obv:** Young bust right **Obv. Designer:** Arnold Machin **Rev:** Beethoven, violin and music score

Date	Mintage	F	VF	XF	Unc	BU
1981 Proof	10,000	Value: 75.00				

KM# 78c CROWN
7.9600 g., 0.9170 Gold .2347 oz. AGW **Ruler:** Elizabeth II **Subject:** International Year of Disabled **Obv:** Young bust right **Obv. Designer:** Arnold Machin **Rev:** Beethoven, violin and music score

Date	Mintage	F	VF	XF	Unc	BU
1981 Proof	1,000	Value: 180				

KM# 78d CROWN
52.0000 g., 0.9500 Platinum 1.5884 oz. APW, 38.5 mm. **Ruler:** Elizabeth II **Subject:** International Year of Disabled **Obv:** Young bust right **Obv. Designer:** Arnold Machin **Rev:** Beethoven, violin and music score

Date	Mintage	F	VF	XF	Unc	BU
1981 Proof	100	Value: 2,150				

KM# 79 CROWN
Copper-Nickel, 38.5 mm. **Ruler:** Elizabeth II **Subject:** International Year of Disabled **Obv:** Young bust right **Obv. Designer:** Arnold Machin **Rev:** Bust facing **Edge:** Reeded

Date	Mintage	F	VF	XF	Unc	BU
1981	50,000	—	—	—	8.00	9.00
1981 Prooflike	—	—	—	—	9.00	10.00

KM# 79a CROWN
28.2800 g., 0.9250 Silver .8411 oz. ASW, 38.5 mm. **Ruler:** Elizabeth II **Subject:** International Year of Disabled **Obv:** Young bust right **Obv. Designer:** Arnold Machin **Rev:** Bust facing

Date	Mintage	F	VF	XF	Unc	BU
1981	20,000	—	—	—	12.50	13.50
1981 Proof	15,000	Value: 15.00				

KM# 79b CROWN
5.1000 g., 0.3740 Gold 0.613 oz. AGW **Ruler:** Elizabeth II **Subject:** International Year of Disabled **Obv:** Young bust right **Obv. Designer:** Arnold Machin **Rev:** Bust facing

Date	Mintage	F	VF	XF	Unc	BU
1981 Proof	10,000	Value: 75.00				

KM# 79c CROWN
7.9600 g., 0.9170 Gold .2347 oz. AGW **Ruler:** Elizabeth II **Subject:** International Year of Disabled **Obv:** Young bust right **Obv. Designer:** Arnold Machin **Rev:** Bust facing

Date	Mintage	F	VF	XF	Unc	BU
1981 Proof	1,000	Value: 180				

KM# 79d CROWN
52.0000 g., 0.9500 Platinum 1.5884 oz. APW, 38.5 mm. **Ruler:** Elizabeth II **Subject:** International Year of Disabled **Obv:** Young bust right **Obv. Designer:** Arnold Machin **Rev:** Bust facing

Date	Mintage	F	VF	XF	Unc	BU
1981 Proof	100	Value: 2,150				

KM# 80 CROWN
Copper-Nickel, 38.5 mm. **Ruler:** Elizabeth II **Subject:** International Year of Disabled **Obv:** Young bust right **Obv. Designer:** Arnold Machin **Rev:** Uniformed bust 1/4 left and sailboat **Edge:** Reeded

Date	Mintage	F	VF	XF	Unc	BU
1981	50,000	—	—	—	8.00	9.00
1981 Prooflike	—	—	—	—	9.00	10.00

KM# 80a CROWN
28.2800 g., 0.9250 Silver .8411 oz. ASW, 38.5 mm. **Ruler:** Elizabeth II **Subject:** International Year of Disabled **Obv:** Young bust right **Obv. Designer:** Arnold Machin **Rev:** Uniformed bust 1/4 left and sailboat

Date	Mintage	F	VF	XF	Unc	BU
1981	20,000	—	—	—	14.00	16.00
1981 Proof	15,000	Value: 20.00				

KM# 80b CROWN
5.1000 g., 0.3740 Gold .0613 oz. AGW **Ruler:** Elizabeth II **Subject:** International Year of Disabled **Obv:** Young bust right **Obv. Designer:** Arnold Machin **Rev:** Uniformed bust 1/4 left and sailboat

Date	Mintage	F	VF	XF	Unc	BU
1981 Proof	10,000	Value: 75.00				

KM# 80c CROWN
7.9600 g., 0.9170 Gold .2347 oz. AGW **Ruler:** Elizabeth II **Subject:** International Year of Disabled **Obv:** Young bust right **Obv. Designer:** Arnold Machin **Rev:** Uniformed bust 1/4 left and sailboat

Date	Mintage	F	VF	XF	Unc	BU
1981 Proof	1,000	Value: 180				

KM# 80d CROWN
52.0000 g., 0.9500 Platinum 1.5884 oz. APW, 38.5 mm. **Ruler:** Elizabeth II **Subject:** International Year of Disabled **Obv:** Young bust right **Obv. Designer:** Arnold Machin **Rev:** Uniformed bust 1/4 left and sailboat

Date	Mintage	F	VF	XF	Unc	BU
1981 Proof	100	Value: 2,150				

KM# 81 CROWN
Copper-Nickel, 38.5 mm. **Ruler:** Elizabeth II **Subject:** Wedding of Prince Charles and Lady Diana **Obv:** Young bust right **Obv. Designer:** Arnold Machin **Rev:** Crown above shields

Date	Mintage	F	VF	XF	Unc	BU
1981	50,000	—	—	—	6.00	7.00

KM# 81a CROWN
28.2800 g., 0.9250 Silver .8411 oz. ASW, 38.5 mm. **Ruler:** Elizabeth II **Subject:** Wedding of Prince Charles and Lady Diana **Obv:** Young bust right **Obv. Designer:** Arnold Machin **Rev:** Crown above shields

Date	Mintage	F	VF	XF	Unc	BU
1981	20,000	—	—	—	12.50	13.50
1981 Proof	15,000	Value: 15.00				

KM# 81b CROWN
5.1000 g., 0.3740 Gold .0613 oz. AGW **Ruler:** Elizabeth II **Subject:** Wedding of Prince Charles and Lady Diana **Obv:** Young bust right **Obv. Designer:** Arnold Machin **Rev:** Crown above shields **Edge:** Reeded

Date	Mintage	F	VF	XF	Unc	BU
1981 Proof	10,000	Value: 75.00				

KM# 81c CROWN
7.9600 g., 0.9170 Gold .2347 oz. AGW **Ruler:** Elizabeth II **Subject:** Wedding of Prince Charles and Lady Diana **Obv:** Young bust right **Obv. Designer:** Arnold Machin **Rev:** Crown above shields

Date	Mintage	F	VF	XF	Unc	BU
1981 Proof	1,000	Value: 175				

KM# 81d CROWN
52.0000 g., 0.9500 Platinum 1.5884 oz. APW, 38.5 mm. **Ruler:** Elizabeth II **Subject:** Wedding of Prince Charles and Lady Diana **Obv:** Young bust right **Obv. Designer:** Arnold Machin **Rev:** Crown above shields

Date	Mintage	F	VF	XF	Unc	BU
1981 Proof	100	Value: 2,150				

KM# 82 CROWN
Copper-Nickel, 38.5 mm. **Ruler:** Elizabeth II **Subject:** Wedding of Prince Charles and Lady Diana **Obv:** Young bust right **Obv. Designer:** Arnold Machin **Rev:** Conjoined heads right **Edge:** Reeded

Date	Mintage	F	VF	XF	Unc	BU
1981	50,000	—	—	—	6.00	7.00

KM# 82a CROWN
28.2800 g., 0.9250 Silver .8411 oz. ASW, 38.5 mm. **Ruler:** Elizabeth II **Subject:** Wedding of Prince Charles and Lady Diana **Obv:** Young bust right **Obv. Designer:** Arnold Machin **Rev:** Conjoined heads right

Date	Mintage	F	VF	XF	Unc	BU
1981	20,000	—	—	—	12.50	13.50
1981	15,000	Value: 15.00				

KM# 82b CROWN
5.1000 g., 0.3740 Gold .0613 oz. AGW **Ruler:** Elizabeth II **Subject:** Wedding of Prince Charles and Lady Diana **Obv:** Young bust right **Obv. Designer:** Arnold Machin **Rev:** Conjoined heads right

Date	Mintage	F	VF	XF	Unc	BU
1981 Proof	10,000	Value: 75.00				

KM# 82c CROWN
7.9600 g., 0.9170 Gold .2347 oz. AGW **Ruler:** Elizabeth II **Subject:** Wedding of Prince Charles and Lady Diana **Obv:** Young bust right **Obv. Designer:** Arnold Machin **Rev:** Conjoined heads right

Date	Mintage	F	VF	XF	Unc	BU
1981 Proof	1,000	Value: 175				

KM# 82d CROWN
52.0000 g., 0.9500 Platinum 1.5884 oz. APW, 38.5 mm. **Ruler:** Elizabeth II **Subject:** Wedding of Prince Charles and Lady Diana **Obv:** Young bust right **Obv. Designer:** Arnold Machin **Rev:** Conjoined heads right

Date	Mintage	F	VF	XF	Unc	BU
1981 Proof	—	Value: 2,150				

KM# 91 CROWN
Copper-Nickel, 38.5 mm. **Ruler:** Elizabeth II **Series:** XII World Cup - Spain **Obv:** Young bust right **Obv. Designer:** Arnold Machin **Rev:** Half figure holding World Cup trophy within map

Date	Mintage	F	VF	XF	Unc	BU
1982	50,000	—	—	—	3.50	4.50

KM# 91a CROWN
28.2800 g., 0.9250 Silver .8411 oz. ASW, 38.5 mm. **Ruler:** Elizabeth II **Series:** XII World Cup - Spain **Obv:** Young bust right **Obv. Designer:** Arnold Machin **Rev:** Half figure holding World Cup trophy within map

Date	Mintage	F	VF	XF	Unc	BU
1982	20,000	—	—	—	16.50	18.00
1982 Proof	15,000	Value: 24.00				

KM# 91b CROWN
5.1000 g., 0.3740 Gold .0613 oz. AGW **Ruler:** Elizabeth II **Series:** XII World Cup - Spain **Obv:** Young bust right **Obv. Designer:** Arnold Machin **Rev:** Half figure holding World Cup trophy within map

Date	Mintage	F	VF	XF	Unc	BU
1982 Proof	40,000	Value: 65.00				

KM# 91c CROWN
7.9600 g., 0.9170 Gold .2347 oz. AGW **Ruler:** Elizabeth II **Series:** XII World Cup - Spain **Obv:** Young bust right **Obv. Designer:** Arnold Machin **Rev:** Half figure holding World Cup trophy within map

Date	Mintage	F	VF	XF	Unc	BU
1982 Proof	4,000	Value: 175				

KM# 91d CROWN
52.0000 g., 0.9500 Platinum 1.5884 oz. APW, 38.5 mm. **Ruler:** Elizabeth II **Series:** XII World Cup - Spain **Obv:** Young bust right **Obv. Designer:** Arnold Machin **Rev:** Half figure holding World Cup trophy within map

Date	Mintage	F	VF	XF	Unc	BU
1982 Proof	100	Value: 2,150				

KM# 92 CROWN
Copper-Nickel, 38.5 mm. **Ruler:** Elizabeth II **Series:** XII World Cup - Spain **Obv:** Young bust right **Obv. Designer:** Arnold Machin **Rev:** Triskeles at center of assorted shields

Date	Mintage	F	VF	XF	Unc	BU
1982	50,000	—	—	—	3.50	4.50

KM# 92a CROWN
28.2800 g., 0.9250 Silver .8411 oz. ASW, 38.5 mm. **Ruler:** Elizabeth II **Series:** XII World Cup - Spain **Obv:** Young bust right **Obv. Designer:** Arnold Machin **Rev:** Triskeles at center of assorted shields

Date	Mintage	F	VF	XF	Unc	BU
1982	20,000	—	—	—	14.50	16.00
1982 Proof	15,000	Value: 17.50				

KM# 92b CROWN
5.1000 g., 0.3740 Gold .0613 oz. AGW **Ruler:** Elizabeth II **Series:** XII World Cup - Spain **Obv:** Young bust right **Obv. Designer:** Arnold Machin **Rev:** Triskeles at center of assorted shields

Date	Mintage	F	VF	XF	Unc	BU
1982 Proof	40,000	Value: 65.00				

KM# 92c CROWN

7.9600 g., 0.9170 Gold .2347 oz. AGW **Ruler:** Elizabeth II **Series:** XII World Cup - Spain **Obv:** Young bust right **Rev:** Triskeles at center of assorted shields

Date	Mintage	F	VF	XF	Unc	BU
1982 Proof	4,000	Value: 175				

KM# 92d CROWN

52.0000 g., 0.9500 Platinum 1.5884 oz. APW, 38.5 mm. **Ruler:** Elizabeth II **Series:** XII World Cup - Spain **Obv:** Young bust right **Obv. Designer:** Arnold Machin **Rev:** Triskeles at center of assorted shields

Date	Mintage	F	VF	XF	Unc	BU
1982 Proof	100	Value: 2,150				

KM# 93 CROWN

Copper-Nickel, 38.5 mm. **Ruler:** Elizabeth II **Series:** XII World Cup - Spain **Obv:** Young bust right **Obv. Designer:** Arnold Machin **Rev:** Soccer scenes

Date	Mintage	F	VF	XF	Unc	BU
1982	50,000	—	—	—	8.00	9.00
1982 (sb)	—	—	—	—	9.00	10.00

KM# 93a CROWN

28.2800 g., 0.9250 Silver .8411 oz. ASW, 38.5 mm. **Ruler:** Elizabeth II **Series:** XII World Cup - Spain **Obv:** Young bust right **Obv. Designer:** Arnold Machin **Rev:** Soccer scenes

Date	Mintage	F	VF	XF	Unc	BU
1982	20,000	—	—	—	14.50	16.50
1982 Proof	15,000	Value: 20.00				

KM# 93b CROWN

5.1000 g., 0.3740 Gold .0613 oz. AGW **Ruler:** Elizabeth II **Series:** XII World Cup - Spain **Obv:** Young bust right **Obv. Designer:** Arnold Machin **Rev:** Soccer scenes

Date	Mintage	F	VF	XF	Unc	BU
1982 Proof	40,000	Value: 65.00				

KM# 93c CROWN

7.9600 g., 0.9170 Gold .2347 oz. AGW **Ruler:** Elizabeth II **Series:** XII World Cup - Spain **Obv:** Young bust right **Obv. Designer:** Arnold Machin **Rev:** Soccer scenes

Date	Mintage	F	VF	XF	Unc	BU
1982 Proof	4,000	Value: 175				

KM# 93d CROWN

52.0000 g., 0.9500 Platinum 1.5884 oz. APW, 38.5 mm. **Ruler:** Elizabeth II **Series:** XII World Cup - Spain **Obv:** Young bust right **Obv. Designer:** Arnold Machin **Rev:** Soccer scenes

Date	Mintage	F	VF	XF	Unc	BU
1982 Proof	100	Value: 2,150				

KM# 94 CROWN

Copper-Nickel, 38.5 mm. **Ruler:** Elizabeth II **Series:** XII World Cup - Spain **Obv:** Young bust right **Obv. Designer:** Arnold Machin **Rev:** Soccer scenes

Date	Mintage	F	VF	XF	Unc	BU
1982	50,000	—	—	—	8.00	9.00

KM# 94a CROWN

28.2800 g., 0.9250 Silver .8411 oz. ASW, 38.5 mm. **Ruler:** Elizabeth II **Series:** XII World Cup - Spain **Obv:** Young bust right **Obv. Designer:** Arnold Machin **Rev:** Soccer scenes

Date	Mintage	F	VF	XF	Unc	BU
1982	20,000	—	—	—	14.50	16.50
1982 Proof	15,000	Value: 20.00				

KM# 94b CROWN

5.1000 g., 0.3740 Gold .0613 oz. AGW **Ruler:** Elizabeth II **Series:** XII World Cup - Spain **Obv:** Young bust right **Obv. Designer:** Arnold Machin **Rev:** Soccer scenes

Date	Mintage	F	VF	XF	Unc	BU
1982 Proof	40,000	Value: 65.00				

KM# 94c CROWN

7.9600 g., 0.9170 Gold .2347 oz. AGW **Ruler:** Elizabeth II **Series:** XII World Cup - Spain **Obv:** Young bust right **Obv. Designer:** Arnold Machin **Rev:** Soccer scenes

Date	Mintage	F	VF	XF	Unc	BU
1982 Proof	4,000	Value: 175				

KM# 94d CROWN

52.0000 g., 0.9500 Platinum 1.5884 oz. APW, 38.5 mm. **Ruler:** Elizabeth II **Series:** XII World Cup - Spain **Obv:** Young bust right **Obv. Designer:** Arnold Machin **Rev:** Soccer scenes

Date	Mintage	F	VF	XF	Unc	BU
1982 Proof	100	Value: 2,150				

KM# 95 CROWN

Copper-Nickel, 38.5 mm. **Ruler:** Elizabeth II **Series:** XII World Cup - Spain **Obv:** Young bust right **Obv. Designer:** Arnold Machin **Rev:** Assorted shields

Date	Mintage	F	VF	XF	Unc	BU
1982	—	—	—	—	3.50	4.50

KM# 95a CROWN

28.2800 g., 0.9250 Silver .8411 oz. ASW, 38.5 mm. **Ruler:** Elizabeth II **Series:** XII World Cup - Spain **Obv:** Young bust right **Obv. Designer:** Arnold Machin **Rev:** Assorted shields

Date	Mintage	F	VF	XF	Unc	BU
1982	—	Value: 20.00				

KM# 95b CROWN

5.1000 g., 0.3740 Gold .0613 oz. AGW **Ruler:** Elizabeth II **Series:** XII World Cup - Spain **Obv:** Young bust right **Obv. Designer:** Arnold Machin **Rev:** Assorted shields

Date	Mintage	F	VF	XF	Unc	BU
1982 Proof	3,000	Value: 75.00				

KM# 95c CROWN

7.9600 g., 0.9170 Gold .2347 oz. AGW **Ruler:** Elizabeth II **Series:** XII World Cup - Spain **Obv:** Young bust right **Obv. Designer:** Arnold Machin **Rev:** Assorted shields

Date	Mintage	F	VF	XF	Unc	BU
1982 Proof	—	Value: 180				

KM# 95d CROWN

52.0000 g., 0.9500 Platinum 1.5884 oz. APW, 38.5 mm. **Ruler:** Elizabeth II **Series:** XII World Cup - Spain **Obv:** Young bust right **Obv. Designer:** Arnold Machin **Rev:** Assorted shields

Date	Mintage	F	VF	XF	Unc	BU
1982 Proof	—	Value: 2,150				

KM# 96 CROWN

Copper-Nickel, 38.5 mm. **Ruler:** Elizabeth II **Series:** Maritime Heritage **Obv:** Young bust right **Obv. Designer:** Arnold Machin **Rev:** Ship and cameo

Date	Mintage	F	VF	XF	Unc	BU
1982	Est. 50,000	—	—	—	9.00	10.00
1982 Prooflike	Inc. above	—	—	—	10.00	12.00

KM# 96a CROWN

28.2800 g., 0.9250 Silver .8411 oz. ASW, 38.5 mm. **Ruler:** Elizabeth II **Series:** Maritime Heritage **Obv:** Young bust right **Obv. Designer:** Arnold Machin **Rev:** Ship and cameo

Date	Mintage	F	VF	XF	Unc	BU
1982	15,000	—	—	—	20.00	22.50
1982 Proof	10,000	Value: 25.00				

KM# 96b CROWN

5.1000 g., 0.3740 Gold .0613 oz. AGW **Ruler:** Elizabeth II **Series:** Maritime Heritage **Obv:** Crowned bust right **Rev:** Ship and cameo

Date	Mintage	F	VF	XF	Unc	BU
1982 Proof	22,000	Value: 65.00				

KM# 96c CROWN

7.9600 g., 0.9170 Gold .2347 oz. AGW **Ruler:** Elizabeth II **Series:** Maritime Heritage **Obv:** Young bust right **Obv. Designer:** Arnold Machin **Rev:** Ship and cameo

Date	Mintage	F	VF	XF	Unc	BU
1982 Proof	2,000	Value: 175				

KM# 96d CROWN

52.0000 g., 0.9500 Platinum 1.5884 oz. APW, 38.5 mm. **Ruler:** Elizabeth II **Series:** Maritime Heritage **Obv:** Young bust right **Obv. Designer:** Arnold Machin **Rev:** Ship and cameo

Date	Mintage	F	VF	XF	Unc	BU
1982 Proof	50	Value: 2,150				

KM# 97 CROWN

Copper-Nickel, 38.5 mm. **Ruler:** Elizabeth II **Series:** Maritime Heritage **Obv:** Young bust right **Obv. Designer:** Arnold Machin **Rev:** Ship and cameo

Date	Mintage	F	VF	XF	Unc	BU
1982	Est. 50,000	—	—	—	3.00	4.00
1982 Prooflike	Inc. above	—	—	—	5.00	7.00

KM# 97a CROWN

28.2800 g., 0.9250 Silver .8411 oz. ASW, 38.5 mm. **Ruler:** Elizabeth II **Series:** Maritime Heritage **Obv:** Young bust right **Obv. Designer:** Arnold Machin **Rev:** Ship and cameo

Date	Mintage	F	VF	XF	Unc	BU
1982	15,000	—	—	—	20.00	22.50
1982 Proof	10,000	Value: 25.00				

KM# 97b CROWN

5.1000 g., 0.3740 Gold .0613 oz. AGW **Ruler:** Elizabeth II **Series:** Maritime Heritage **Obv:** Young bust right **Obv. Designer:** Arnold Machin **Rev:** Ship and cameo

Date	Mintage	F	VF	XF	Unc	BU
1982 Proof	22,000	Value: 65.00				

KM# 97c CROWN

7.9600 g., 0.9170 Gold .2347 oz. AGW **Ruler:** Elizabeth II **Series:** Maritime Heritage **Obv:** Young bust right **Obv. Designer:** Arnold Machin **Rev:** Ship and cameo

Date	Mintage	F	VF	XF	Unc	BU
1982 Proof	2,000	Value: 175				

KM# 97d CROWN

52.0000 g., 0.9500 Platinum 1.5884 oz. APW, 38.5 mm. **Ruler:** Elizabeth II **Series:** Maritime Heritage **Obv:** Young bust right **Obv. Designer:** Arnold Machin **Rev:** Ship and cameo

Date	Mintage	F	VF	XF	Unc	BU
1982 Proof	50	Value: 2,150				

KM# 98 CROWN

Copper-Nickel, 38.5 mm. **Ruler:** Elizabeth II **Series:** Maritime Heritage **Obv:** Young bust right **Obv. Designer:** Arnold Machin **Rev:** Ship and cameo

Date	Mintage	F	VF	XF	Unc	BU
1982	Est. 50,000	—	—	—	8.00	9.00
1982 Prooflike	Inc. above	—	—	—	9.00	10.00

KM# 98a CROWN

28.2800 g., 0.9250 Silver .8411 oz. ASW, 38.5 mm. **Ruler:** Elizabeth II **Series:** Maritime Heritage **Obv:** young bust right **Obv. Designer:** Arnold Machin **Rev:** Ship and cameo

Date	Mintage	F	VF	XF	Unc	BU
1982	15,000	—	—	—	20.00	22.50
1982 Proof	10,000	Value: 25.00				

KM# 98b CROWN

5.1000 g., 0.3740 Gold .0613 oz. AGW **Ruler:** Elizabeth II **Series:** Maritime Heritage **Obv:** Young bust right **Obv. Designer:** Arnold Machin **Rev:** Ship and cameo

Date	Mintage	F	VF	XF	Unc	BU
1982 Proof	22,000	Value: 65.00				

KM# 98c CROWN

7.9600 g., 0.9170 Gold .2347 oz. AGW **Ruler:** Elizabeth II **Series:** Maritime Heritage **Obv:** Young bust right **Obv. Designer:** Arnold Machin **Rev:** Ship and cameo

Date	Mintage	F	VF	XF	Unc	BU
1982 Proof	2,000	Value: 175				

KM# 98d CROWN

52.0000 g., 0.9500 Platinum 1.5884 oz. APW, 38.5 mm. **Ruler:** Elizabeth II **Series:** Maritime Heritage **Obv:** Young bust right **Obv. Designer:** Arnold Machin **Rev:** Ship and cameo

Date	Mintage	F	VF	XF	Unc	BU
1982 Proof	50	Value: 2,150				

KM# 99 CROWN

Copper-Nickel, 38.5 mm. **Ruler:** Elizabeth II **Series:** Maritime Heritage **Obv:** Young bust right **Obv. Designer:** Arnold Machin **Rev:** Ship and cameo

Date	Mintage	F	VF	XF	Unc	BU
1982	Est. 50,000	—	—	—	3.00	4.00
1982 Prooflike	Inc. above	—	—	—	5.00	7.00

KM# 99a CROWN

28.2800 g., 0.9250 Silver .8411 oz. ASW, 38.5 mm. **Ruler:** Elizabeth II **Series:** Maritime Heritage **Obv:** Young bust right **Obv. Designer:** Arnold Machin **Rev:** Ship and cameo

Date	Mintage	F	VF	XF	Unc	BU
1982	15,000	—	—	—	20.00	22.50
1982 Proof	10,000	Value: 25.00				

KM# 99b CROWN

5.1000 g., 0.3740 Gold .0613 oz. AGW **Ruler:** Elizabeth II **Series:** Maritime Heritage **Obv:** Young bust right **Obv. Designer:** Arnold Machin **Rev:** Ship and cameo

Date	Mintage	F	VF	XF	Unc	BU
1982 Proof	22,000	Value: 65.00				

KM# 99c CROWN

7.9600 g., 0.9170 Gold .2347 oz. AGW **Ruler:** Elizabeth II **Series:** Maritime Heritage **Obv:** Young bust right **Obv. Designer:** Arnold Machin **Rev:** Ship and cameo

Date	Mintage	F	VF	XF	Unc	BU
1982 Proof	2,000	Value: 175				

KM# 99d CROWN

52.0000 g., 0.9500 Platinum 1.5884 oz. APW, 38.5 mm. **Ruler:** Elizabeth II **Series:** Maritime Heritage **Obv:** Young bust right **Obv. Designer:** Arnold Machin **Rev:** Ship and cameo

Date	Mintage	F	VF	XF	Unc	BU
1982 Proof	50	Value: 2,150				

KM# 103 CROWN

Copper-Nickel, 38.5 mm. **Ruler:** Elizabeth II **Series:** Manned Flight **Obv:** Young bust right **Obv. Designer:** Arnold Machin **Rev:** Hot air balloon

Date	Mintage	F	VF	XF	Unc	BU
1983	50,000	—	—	—	8.00	10.00
1983 DMIHE	—	—	—	—	15.00	17.00

KM# 103a CROWN
28.2800 g., 0.9250 Silver .8411 oz. ASW, 38.5 mm. **Ruler:** Elizabeth II **Series:** Manned Flight **Obv:** Young bust right **Obv. Designer:** Arnold Machin **Rev:** Hot air balloon

Date	Mintage	F	VF	XF	Unc	BU
1983	15,000	—	—	—	20.00	22.50
1983	11,000	Value: 25.00				

KM# 103b CROWN
5.1000 g., 0.3740 Gold .0613 oz. AGW **Ruler:** Elizabeth II **Series:** Manned Flight **Obv:** Young bust right **Obv. Designer:** Arnold Machin **Rev:** Hot air balloon

Date	Mintage	F	VF	XF	Unc	BU
1983 Proof	5,500	Value: 80.00				

KM# 103c CROWN
7.9600 g., 0.9170 Gold .2347 oz. AGW **Ruler:** Elizabeth II **Series:** Manned Flight **Obv:** Young bust right **Obv. Designer:** Arnold Machin **Rev:** Hot air balloon

Date	Mintage	F	VF	XF	Unc	BU
1983 Proof	500	Value: 185				

KM# 103d CROWN
52.0000 g., 0.9500 Platinum 1.5884 oz. APW, 38.5 mm. **Ruler:** Elizabeth II **Series:** Manned Flight **Obv:** Young bust right **Obv. Designer:** Arnold Machin **Rev:** Hot air balloon

Date	Mintage	F	VF	XF	Unc	BU
1983 Proof	50	Value: 2,150				

KM# 104 CROWN
Copper-Nickel, 38.5 mm. **Ruler:** Elizabeth II **Series:** Manned Flight **Obv:** Young bust right **Obv. Designer:** Arnold Machin **Rev:** Biplane

Date	Mintage	F	VF	XF	Unc	BU
1983	50,000	—	—	—	8.00	10.00
1983 DMIHE	—	—	—	—	15.00	17.00

KM# 104a CROWN
28.2800 g., 0.9250 Silver .8411 oz. ASW, 38.5 mm. **Ruler:** Elizabeth II **Series:** Manned Flight **Obv:** Young bust right **Obv. Designer:** Arnold Machin **Rev:** Biplane

Date	Mintage	F	VF	XF	Unc	BU
1983	15,000	—	—	—	20.00	22.50
1983 Proof	11,000	Value: 25.00				

KM# 104b CROWN
5.1000 g., 0.3740 Gold .0613 oz. AGW **Ruler:** Elizabeth II **Series:** Manned Flight **Obv:** Young bust right **Obv. Designer:** Arnold Machin **Rev:** Biplane

Date	Mintage	F	VF	XF	Unc	BU
1983 Proof	5,500	Value: 80.00				

KM# 104c CROWN
7.9600 g., 0.9170 Gold .2347 oz. AGW **Ruler:** Elizabeth II **Series:** Manned Flight **Obv:** Young bust right **Obv. Designer:** Arnold Machin **Rev:** Biplane

Date	Mintage	F	VF	XF	Unc	BU
1983 Proof	500	Value: 185				

KM# 104d CROWN
52.0000 g., 0.9500 Platinum 1.5884 oz. APW, 38.5 mm. **Ruler:** Elizabeth II **Series:** Manned Flight **Obv:** Young bust right **Obv. Designer:** Arnold Machin **Rev:** Biplane

Date	Mintage	F	VF	XF	Unc	BU
1983 Proof	50	Value: 2,150				

KM# 105 CROWN
Copper-Nickel, 38.5 mm. **Ruler:** Elizabeth II **Series:** Manned Flight **Obv:** Young bust right **Obv. Designer:** Arnold Machin **Rev:** Jet

Date	Mintage	F	VF	XF	Unc	BU
1983	50,000	—	—	—	8.00	10.00
1983 DMIHE	—	—	—	—	15.00	17.00

KM# 105a CROWN
28.2800 g., 0.9250 Silver .8411 oz. ASW, 38.5 mm. **Ruler:** Elizabeth II **Series:** Manned Flight **Obv:** Young bust right **Obv. Designer:** Arnold Machin **Rev:** Jet

Date	Mintage	F	VF	XF	Unc	BU
1983	15,000	—	—	—	20.00	22.50
1983 Proof	11,000	Value: 25.00				

KM# 105b CROWN
5.1000 g., 0.3740 Gold .0613 oz. AGW **Ruler:** Elizabeth II **Series:** Manned Flight **Obv:** Young bust right **Obv. Designer:** Arnold Machin **Rev:** Jet

Date	Mintage	F	VF	XF	Unc	BU
1983 Proof	5,500	Value: 80.00				

KM# 105c CROWN
7.9600 g., 0.9170 Gold .2347 oz. AGW **Ruler:** Elizabeth II **Series:** Manned Flight **Obv:** Young bust right **Obv. Designer:** Arnold Machin **Rev:** Jet

Date	Mintage	F	VF	XF	Unc	BU
1983 Proof	500	Value: 185				

KM# 105d CROWN
52.0000 g., 0.9500 Platinum 1.5884 oz. APW, 38.5 mm. **Ruler:** Elizabeth II **Series:** Manned Flight **Obv:** Young bust right **Obv. Designer:** Arnold Machin **Rev:** Jet

Date	Mintage	F	VF	XF	Unc	BU
1983 Proof	50	Value: 2,150				

KM# 106 CROWN
Copper-Nickel, 38.5 mm. **Ruler:** Elizabeth II **Series:** Manned Flight **Obv:** Young bust right **Obv. Designer:** Arnold Machin **Rev:** Space Shuttle

Date	Mintage	F	VF	XF	Unc	BU
1983	50,000	—	—	—	8.00	10.00
1983 DMIHE	—	—	—	—	15.00	17.00

KM# 106a CROWN
28.2800 g., 0.9250 Silver .8411 oz. ASW, 38.5 mm. **Ruler:** Elizabeth II **Series:** Manned Flight **Obv:** Young bust right **Obv. Designer:** Arnold Machin **Rev:** Space shuttle

Date	Mintage	F	VF	XF	Unc	BU
1983	15,000	—	—	—	12.50	13.50
1983 Proof	11,000	Value: 20.00				

KM# 106b CROWN
5.1000 g., 0.3740 Gold .0613 oz. AGW **Ruler:** Elizabeth II **Series:** Manned Flight **Obv:** Young bust right **Obv. Designer:** Arnold Machin **Rev:** Space shuttle

Date	Mintage	F	VF	XF	Unc	BU
1983 Proof	5,500	Value: 80.00				

KM# 106c CROWN
7.9600 g., 0.9170 Gold .2347 oz. AGW **Ruler:** Elizabeth II **Series:** Manned Flight **Obv:** Young bust right **Obv. Designer:** Arnold Machin **Rev:** Space shuttle

Date	Mintage	F	VF	XF	Unc	BU
1983 Proof	500	Value: 185				

KM# 106d CROWN
52.0000 g., 0.9500 Platinum 1.5884 oz. APW, 38.5 mm. **Ruler:** Elizabeth II **Series:** Manned Flight **Obv:** Young bust right **Obv. Designer:** Arnold Machin **Rev:** Space Shuttle

Date	Mintage	F	VF	XF	Unc	BU
1983 Proof	50	Value: 2,150				

KM# 117 CROWN
Copper-Nickel, 38.5 mm. **Ruler:** Elizabeth II **Series:** 1984 Winter Olympics - Sarajevo **Obv:** Young bust right **Obv. Designer:** Arnold Machin **Rev:** Figure skaters **Rev. Designer:** Leslie Lindsay

Date	Mintage	F	VF	XF	Unc	BU
1984	50,000	—	—	—	8.00	9.00
1984 Proof	—	Value: 10.00				

KM# 117a CROWN
28.2800 g., 0.9250 Silver .8411 oz. ASW, 38.5 mm. **Ruler:** Elizabeth II **Series:** 1984 Winter Olympics - Sarajevo **Obv:** Young bust right **Obv. Designer:** Arnold Machin **Rev:** Figure Skaters **Rev. Designer:** Leslie Lindsay

Date	Mintage	F	VF	XF	Unc	BU
1984 Proof	15,000	Value: 30.00				

KM# 117b CROWN
5.1000 g., 0.3740 Gold .0613 oz. AGW **Ruler:** Elizabeth II **Series:** 1984 Winter Olympics - Sarajevo **Obv:** Young bust right **Obv. Designer:** Arnold Machin **Rev:** Figure skaters **Rev. Designer:** Leslie Lindsay

Date	Mintage	F	VF	XF	Unc	BU
1984 Proof	10,000	Value: 60.00				

KM# 117c CROWN
7.9600 g., 0.9170 Gold .2347 oz. AGW **Ruler:** Elizabeth II **Series:** 1984 Winter Olympics - Sarajevo **Obv:** Young bust right **Obv. Designer:** Arnold Machin **Rev:** Figure skaters **Rev. Designer:** Leslie Lindsay

Date	Mintage	F	VF	XF	Unc	BU
1984 Proof	1,000	Value: 175				

KM# 117d CROWN
52.0000 g., 0.9500 Platinum 1.5884 oz. APW, 38.5 mm. **Ruler:** Elizabeth II **Series:** 1984 Winter Olympics - Sarajevo **Obv:** Young bust right **Obv. Designer:** Arnold Machin **Rev:** Figure skaters **Rev. Designer:** Leslie Lindsay

Date	Mintage	F	VF	XF	Unc	BU
1984 Proof	100	Value: 2,150				

KM# 117e CROWN
Silver Clad Copper-Nickel, 38.5 mm. **Ruler:** Elizabeth II **Series:** 1984 Winter Olympics - Sarajevo **Obv:** Young bust right **Obv. Designer:** Arnold Machin **Rev:** Figure skaters **Rev. Designer:** Leslie Lindsay

Date	Mintage	F	VF	XF	Unc	BU
1984	20,000	—	—	—	20.00	22.50

KM# 118 CROWN
Copper-Nickel, 38.5 mm. **Ruler:** Elizabeth II **Series:** 1984 Olympics - Los Angeles **Obv:** Young bust right **Obv. Designer:** Arnold Machin **Rev:** Runners **Rev. Designer:** Leslie Lindsay

Date	Mintage	F	VF	XF	Unc	BU
1984	50,000	—	—	—	6.00	7.00
1984 Proof	—	Value: 8.50				

KM# 118a CROWN
28.2800 g., 0.9250 Silver .8411 oz. ASW, 38.5 mm. **Ruler:** Elizabeth II **Series:** 1984 Olympics - Los Angeles **Obv:** Young bust right **Obv. Designer:** Arnold Machin **Rev:** Runners **Rev. Designer:** Leslie Lindsay

Date	Mintage	F	VF	XF	Unc	BU
1984 Proof	15,000	Value: 30.00				

KM# 118b CROWN
5.1000 g., 0.3740 Gold .0613 oz. AGW **Ruler:** Elizabeth II **Series:** 1984 Olympics - Los Angeles **Obv:** Young bust right **Obv. Designer:** Arnold Machin **Rev:** Runners **Rev. Designer:** Leslie Lindsay

Date	Mintage	F	VF	XF	Unc	BU
1984 Proof	10,000	Value: 65.00				

KM# 118c CROWN
7.9600 g., 0.9170 Gold .2347 oz. AGW **Ruler:** Elizabeth II **Series:** 1984 Olympics - Los Angeles **Obv:** Young bust right **Obv. Designer:** Leslie Lindsay **Rev:** Runners

Date	Mintage	F	VF	XF	Unc	BU
1984 Proof	1,000	Value: 175				

KM# 118d CROWN
52.0000 g., 0.9500 Platinum 1.5884 oz. APW, 38.5 mm. **Ruler:** Elizabeth II **Series:** 1984 Olympics - Los Angeles **Obv:** Young bust right **Obv. Designer:** Arnold Machin **Rev:** Runners **Rev. Designer:** Leslie Lindsay

Date	Mintage	F	VF	XF	Unc	BU
1984 Proof	100	Value: 2,100				

KM# 118e CROWN
Silver Clad Copper-Nickel, 38.5 mm. **Ruler:** Elizabeth II **Series:** 1984 Olympics - Los Angeles **Obv:** Young bust right **Obv. Designer:** Arnold Machin **Rev:** Runners **Rev. Designer:** Leslie Lindsay

Date	Mintage	F	VF	XF	Unc	BU
1984	20,000	—	—	—	20.00	22.50

KM# 119 CROWN
Copper-Nickel, 38.5 mm. **Series:** 1984 Olympics - Los Angeles **Obv:** Young bust right **Obv. Designer:** Arnold Machin **Rev:** Gymnastics **Rev. Designer:** Leslie Lindsay

Date	Mintage	F	VF	XF	Unc	BU
1984	50,000	—	—	—	3.50	5.00
1984 Proof	—	Value: 8.50				

KM# 119a CROWN
28.2800 g., 0.9250 Silver .8411 oz. ASW, 38.5 mm. **Ruler:** Elizabeth II **Series:** 1984 Olympics - Los Angeles **Obv:** Young bust right **Obv. Designer:** Arnold Machin **Rev:** Gymnastics **Rev. Designer:** Leslie Lindsay

Date	Mintage	F	VF	XF	Unc	BU
1984 Proof	15,000	Value: 30.00				

KM# 119b CROWN
5.1000 g., 0.3740 Gold .0613 oz. AGW **Ruler:** Elizabeth II **Series:** 1984 Olympics - Los Angeles **Obv:** Young bust right **Obv. Designer:** Arnold Machin **Rev:** Gymnastics **Rev. Designer:** Leslie Lindsay

Date	Mintage	F	VF	XF	Unc	BU
1984 Proof	10,000	Value: 65.00				

KM# 119c CROWN
7.9600 g., 0.9170 Gold .2347 oz. AGW **Ruler:** Elizabeth II **Series:** 1984 Olympics - Los Angeles **Obv:** Young bust right **Obv. Designer:** Arnold Machin **Rev:** Gymnastics **Rev. Designer:** Leslie Lindsay

Date	Mintage	F	VF	XF	Unc	BU
1984 Proof	1,000	Value: 175				

KM# 119d CROWN
52.0000 g., 0.9500 Platinum 1.5884 oz. APW, 38.5 mm. **Ruler:** Elizabeth II **Series:** 1984 Olympics - Los Angeles **Obv:** Young bust right **Obv. Designer:** Arnold Machin **Rev:** Gymnastics **Rev. Designer:** Leslie Lindsay

Date	Mintage	F	VF	XF	Unc	BU
1984 Proof	100	Value: 2,150				

KM# 119e CROWN
Silver Clad Copper-Nickel, 38.5 mm. **Ruler:** Elizabeth II **Series:** 1984 Olympics - Los Angeles **Obv:** Young bust right **Obv. Designer:** Arnold Machin **Rev:** Gymnastics **Rev. Designer:** Leslie Lindsay

Date	Mintage	F	VF	XF	Unc	BU
1984	20,000	—	—	—	20.00	22.50

KM# 120 CROWN
Copper-Nickel, 38.5 mm. **Ruler:** Elizabeth II **Series:** 1984 Olympics - Los Angeles **Obv:** Young bust right **Obv. Designer:** Arnold Machin **Rev:** Equestrian **Rev. Designer:** Leslie Lindsay

Date	Mintage	F	VF	XF	Unc	BU
1984	50,000	—	—	—	6.00	7.00
1984 Proof	—	Value: 8.50				

KM# 120a CROWN
28.2800 g., 0.9250 Silver .8411 oz. ASW, 38.5 mm. **Ruler:** Elizabeth II **Series:** 1984 Olympics - Los Angeles **Obv:** Young bust right **Obv. Designer:** Arnold Machin **Rev:** Equestrian **Rev. Designer:** Leslie Lindsay

Date	Mintage	F	VF	XF	Unc	BU
1984 Proof	15,000	Value: 30.00				

KM# 120b CROWN
5.1000 g., 0.3740 Gold .0613 oz. AGW **Ruler:** Elizabeth II **Series:** 1984 Olympics - Los Angeles **Obv:** Young bust right **Obv. Designer:** Arnold Machin **Rev:** Equestrian **Rev. Designer:** Leslie Lindsay

Date	Mintage	F	VF	XF	Unc	BU
1984 Proof	10,000	Value: 65.00				

KM# 120c CROWN
7.9600 g., 0.9170 Gold .2347 oz. AGW **Ruler:** Elizabeth II **Series:** 1984 Olympics - Los Angeles **Obv:** Young bust right **Obv. Designer:** Arnold Machin **Rev:** Equestrian **Rev. Designer:** Leslie Lindsay

Date	Mintage	F	VF	XF	Unc	BU
1984 Proof	1,000	Value: 175				

KM# 120d CROWN
52.0000 g., 0.9500 Platinum 1.5884 oz. APW, 38.5 mm. **Ruler:** Elizabeth II **Series:** 1984 Olympics - Los Angeles **Obv:** Young bust right **Obv. Designer:** Arnold Machin **Rev:** Equestrian **Rev. Designer:** Leslie Lindsay

Date	Mintage	F	VF	XF	Unc	BU
1984 Proof	100	Value: 2,150				

KM# 120e CROWN
Silver Clad Copper-Nickel, 38.5 mm. **Ruler:** Elizabeth II **Series:** 1984 Olympics - Los Angeles **Obv:** Young bust right **Obv. Designer:** Arnold Machin **Rev:** Equestrian **Rev. Designer:** Leslie Lindsay

Date	Mintage	F	VF	XF	Unc	BU
1984	20,000	—	—	—	20.00	22.50

KM# 121 CROWN
Copper-Nickel, 38.5 mm. **Ruler:** Elizabeth II **Subject:** Quincentenary **Obv:** Young bust right **Obv. Designer:** Arnold Machin **Rev:** Arms with supporters

Date	Mintage	F	VF	XF	Unc	BU
1984	—	—	—	—	6.00	7.00
1984 Prooflike	—	—	—	—	—	8.50

KM# 121a CROWN
28.2800 g., 0.9250 Silver .8411 oz. ASW, 38.5 mm. **Ruler:** Elizabeth II **Subject:** Quincentenary **Obv:** Young bust right **Obv. Designer:** Arnold Machin **Rev:** Arms with supporters

Date	Mintage	F	VF	XF	Unc	BU
1984	—	—	—	—	12.50	13.50
1984 Proof	—	Value: 18.00				

KM# 121b CROWN
5.1000 g., 0.3740 Gold .0613 oz. AGW **Ruler:** Elizabeth II **Subject:** Quincentenary **Obv:** Young bust right **Obv. Designer:** Arnold Machin **Rev:** Arms with supporters

Date	Mintage	F	VF	XF	Unc	BU
1984 Proof	10,000	Value: 65.00				

KM# 121c CROWN
7.9600 g., 0.9170 Gold .2347 oz. AGW **Ruler:** Elizabeth II **Subject:** Quincentenary **Obv:** Young bust right **Obv. Designer:** Arnold Machin **Rev:** Arms with supporters

Date	Mintage	F	VF	XF	Unc	BU
1984 Proof	1,000	Value: 175				

KM# 121d CROWN
52.0000 g., 0.9500 Platinum 1.5884 oz. APW, 38.5 mm. **Ruler:** Elizabeth II **Subject:** Quincentenary **Obv:** Young bust right **Obv. Designer:** Arnold Machin **Rev:** Arms with supporters

Date	Mintage	F	VF	XF	Unc	BU
1984 Proof	—	Value: 2,150				

KM# 122 CROWN
Copper-Nickel, 38.5 mm. **Ruler:** Elizabeth II **Subject:** Quincentenary **Obv:** Young bust right **Obv. Designer:** Arnold Machin **Rev:** Lion above shields

Date	Mintage	F	VF	XF	Unc	BU
1984	—	—	—	—	6.00	7.00
1984 Prooflike	—	—	—	—	—	8.50

KM# 122a CROWN
28.2800 g., 0.9250 Silver .8411 oz. ASW, 38.5 mm. **Ruler:** Elizabeth II **Subject:** Quincentenary **Obv:** Young bust right **Obv. Designer:** Arnold Machin **Rev:** Lion above shields

Date	Mintage	F	VF	XF	Unc	BU
1984	—	—	—	—	12.50	13.50
1984 Proof	—	Value: 18.00				

KM# 122b CROWN
5.1000 g., 0.3740 Gold .0613 oz. AGW **Ruler:** Elizabeth II **Subject:** Quincentenary **Obv:** Young bust right **Obv. Designer:** Arnold Machin **Rev:** Lion above shields

Date	Mintage	F	VF	XF	Unc	BU
1984 Proof	10,000	Value: 65.00				

KM# 122c CROWN
7.9600 g., 0.9170 Gold .2347 oz. AGW **Ruler:** Elizabeth II **Subject:** Quincentenary **Obv:** Young bust right **Obv. Designer:** Arnold Machin **Rev:** Lion above shields

Date	Mintage	F	VF	XF	Unc	BU
1984 Proof	1,000	Value: 175				

KM# 122d CROWN
52.0000 g., 0.9500 Platinum 1.5884 oz. APW, 38.5 mm. **Ruler:** Elizabeth II **Subject:** Quincentenary **Obv:** Young bust right **Obv. Designer:** Arnold Machin **Rev:** Lion above shields

Date	Mintage	F	VF	XF	Unc	BU
1984 Proof	—	Value: 2,150				

KM# 123 CROWN
Copper-Nickel, 38.5 mm. **Ruler:** Elizabeth II **Subject:** Quincentenary **Obv:** Young bust right **Obv. Designer:** Arnold Machin **Rev:** Bird above shields

Date	Mintage	F	VF	XF	Unc	BU
1984	—	—	—	—	6.00	7.00
1984 Prooflike	—	—	—	—	—	8.50

KM# 123a CROWN
28.2800 g., 0.9250 Silver .8411 oz. ASW, 38.5 mm. **Ruler:** Elizabeth II **Subject:** Quincentenary **Obv:** Young bust right **Obv. Designer:** Arnold Machin **Rev:** Bird above shields

Date	Mintage	F	VF	XF	Unc	BU
1984	—	—	—	—	12.50	13.50
1984 Proof	—	Value: 18.00				

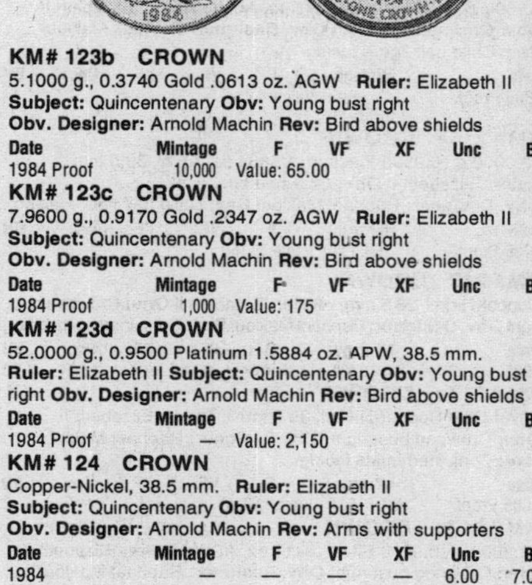

KM# 123b CROWN
5.1000 g., 0.3740 Gold .0613 oz. AGW **Ruler:** Elizabeth II **Subject:** Quincentenary **Obv:** Young bust right **Obv. Designer:** Arnold Machin **Rev:** Bird above shields

Date	Mintage	F	VF	XF	Unc	BU
1984 Proof	10,000	Value: 65.00				

KM# 123c CROWN
7.9600 g., 0.9170 Gold .2347 oz. AGW **Ruler:** Elizabeth II **Subject:** Quincentenary **Obv:** Young bust right **Obv. Designer:** Arnold Machin **Rev:** Bird above shields

Date	Mintage	F	VF	XF	Unc	BU
1984 Proof	1,000	Value: 175				

KM# 123d CROWN
52.0000 g., 0.9500 Platinum 1.5884 oz. APW, 38.5 mm. **Ruler:** Elizabeth II **Subject:** Quincentenary **Obv:** Young bust right **Obv. Designer:** Arnold Machin **Rev:** Bird above shields

Date	Mintage	F	VF	XF	Unc	BU
1984 Proof	—	Value: 2,150				

KM# 124 CROWN
Copper-Nickel, 38.5 mm. **Ruler:** Elizabeth II **Subject:** Quincentenary **Obv:** Young bust right **Obv. Designer:** Arnold Machin **Rev:** Arms with supporters

Date	Mintage	F	VF	XF	Unc	BU
1984	—	—	—	—	6.00	7.00
1984 Prooflike	—	—	—	—	—	8.50

KM# 124a CROWN
28.2800 g., 0.9250 Silver .8411 oz. ASW, 38.5 mm. **Ruler:** Elizabeth II **Subject:** Quincentenary **Obv:** Young bust right **Obv. Designer:** Arnold Machin **Rev:** Arms with supporters

Date	Mintage	F	VF	XF	Unc	BU
1984	—	—	—	—	12.50	13.50
1984 Proof	—	Value: 18.00				

KM# 124b CROWN
5.1000 g., 0.3740 Gold .0613 oz. AGW **Ruler:** Elizabeth II **Subject:** Quincentenary **Obv:** Crowned bust right **Rev:** Arms with supporters

Date	Mintage	F	VF	XF	Unc	BU
1984 Proof	10,000	Value: 65.00				

KM# 124c CROWN
7.9600 g., 0.9170 Gold .2347 oz. AGW **Ruler:** Elizabeth II **Subject:** Quincentenary **Obv:** Young bust right **Obv. Designer:** Arnold Machin **Rev:** Arms with supporters

Date	Mintage	F	VF	XF	Unc	BU
1984 Proof	1,000	Value: 175				

KM# 124d CROWN
52.0000 g., 0.9500 Platinum 1.5884 oz. APW, 38.5 mm. **Ruler:** Elizabeth II **Subject:** Quincentenary **Obv:** Young bust right **Obv. Designer:** Arnold Machin **Rev:** Arms with supporters

Date	Mintage	F	VF	XF	Unc	BU
1984 Proof	—	Value: 2,150				

KM# 130 CROWN
Copper-Nickel, 38.5 mm. **Ruler:** Elizabeth II **Subject:** 30th Commonwealth Parliamentary Conference **Obv:** Young bust right **Obv. Designer:** Arnold Machin **Rev:** Conjoined heads right within circle **Rev. Legend:** Celtic uncial script

Date	Mintage	F	VF	XF	Unc	BU
1984	—	—	—	—	3.00	4.00

KM# 130a CROWN
28.2800 g., 0.9250 Silver .8411 oz. ASW, 38.5 mm. **Ruler:** Elizabeth II **Subject:** 30th Commonwealth Parliamentary Conference **Obv:** Young bust right **Obv. Designer:** Arnold Machin **Rev:** Conjoined heads right within circle **Rev. Legend:** Celtic uncial script

Date	Mintage	F	VF	XF	Unc	BU
1984	—	—	—	—	15.00	16.50
1984 Proof	—	Value: 20.00				

KM# 130b CROWN
5.1000 g., 0.3740 Gold .0613 oz. AGW **Ruler:** Elizabeth II **Subject:** 30th Commonwealth Parliamentary Conference **Obv:** Young bust right **Obv. Designer:** Arnold Machin **Rev:** Conjoined heads right within circle **Rev. Legend:** Celtic uncial script

Date	Mintage	F	VF	XF	Unc	BU
1984 Proof	10,000	Value: 65.00				

KM# 130c CROWN
7.9600 g., 0.9170 Gold .2347 oz. AGW **Ruler:** Elizabeth II **Subject:** 30th Commonwealth Parliamentary Conference **Obv:** Young bust right **Obv. Designer:** Arnold Machin **Rev:** Conjoined heads right within circle **Rev. Legend:** Celtic uncial script

Date	Mintage	F	VF	XF	Unc	BU
1984 Proof	1,000	Value: 175				

KM# 130d CROWN
52.0000 g., 0.9500 Platinum 1.5884 oz. APW, 38.5 mm. **Ruler:** Elizabeth II **Subject:** 30th Commonwealth Parliamentary Conference **Obv:** Young bust right **Obv. Designer:** Arnold Machin **Rev:** Conjoined heads right within circle **Rev. Legend:** Celtic uncial script

Date	Mintage	F	VF	XF	Unc	BU
1984 Proof	—	Value: 2,150				

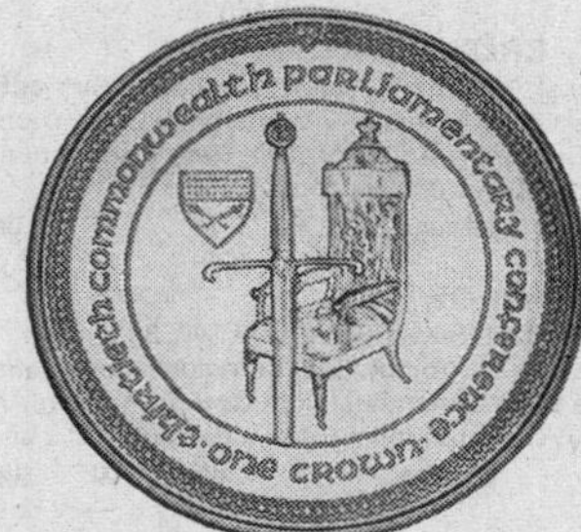

KM# 131 CROWN
Copper-Nickel, 38.5 mm. **Ruler:** Elizabeth II **Subject:** 30th Commonwealth Parliamentary Conference **Obv:** Young bust right **Obv. Designer:** Arnold Machin **Rev:** Throne, shield and sword **Rev. Legend:** Celtic uncial script

Date	Mintage	F	VF	XF	Unc	BU
1984	—	—	—	—	3.00	4.00

KM# 131a CROWN
28.2800 g., 0.9250 Silver .8411 oz. ASW, 38.5 mm. **Ruler:** Elizabeth II **Subject:** 30th Commonwealth Parliamentary Conference **Obv:** Young bust right **Obv. Designer:** Arnold Machin **Rev:** Throne, sword and shield **Rev. Legend:** Celtic uncial script

Date	Mintage	F	VF	XF	Unc	BU
1984	—	—	—	—	15.00	16.50
1984 Proof	—	Value: 20.00				

KM# 131b CROWN
5.1000 g., 0.3740 Gold .0613 oz. AGW **Ruler:** Elizabeth II **Subject:** 30th Commonwealth Parliamentary Conference **Obv:** Young bust right **Obv. Designer:** Arnold Machin **Rev:** Throne, sword and shield **Rev. Legend:** Celtic uncial script

Date	Mintage	F	VF	XF	Unc	BU
1984 Proof	10,000	Value: 65.00				

KM# 131c CROWN
7.9600 g., 0.9170 Gold .2347 oz. AGW **Ruler:** Elizabeth II **Subject:** 30th Commonwealth Parliamentary Conference **Obv:** Young bust right **Obv. Designer:** Arnold Machin **Rev:** Throne, sword and shield **Rev. Legend:** Celtic uncial script

Date	Mintage	F	VF	XF	Unc	BU
1984 Proof	1,000	Value: 175				

KM# 131d CROWN
52.0000 g., 0.9500 Platinum 1.5884 oz. APW, 38.5 mm. **Ruler:** Elizabeth II **Subject:** 30th Commonwealth Parliamentary Conference **Obv:** Young bust right **Obv. Designer:** Arnold Machin **Rev:** Throne, shield and sword **Rev. Legend:** Celtic uncial script

Date	Mintage	F	VF	XF	Unc	BU
1984 Proof	—	Value: 2,150				

KM# 132 CROWN
Copper-Nickel, 38.5 mm. **Ruler:** Elizabeth II **Subject:** 30th Commonwealth Parliamentary Conference **Obv:** Young bust right **Obv. Designer:** Arnold Machin **Rev:** Crowned head facing within circle **Rev. Legend:** Celtic uncial script

Date	Mintage	F	VF	XF	Unc	BU
1984	—	—	—	—	3.00	4.00

KM# 132a CROWN

28.2800 g., 0.9250 Silver .8411 oz. ASW, 38.5 mm.
Ruler: Elizabeth II **Subject:** 30th Commonwealth Parliamentary Conference **Obv:** Young bust right **Obv. Designer:** Arnold Machin **Rev:** Crowned head facing within circle
Rev. Legend: Celtic uncial script

Date	Mintage	F	VF	XF	Unc	BU
1984	—	—	—	—	15.00	16.50
1984 Proof	—	Value: 20.00				

KM# 132b CROWN

5.1000 g., 0.3740 Gold .0613 oz. AGW **Ruler:** Elizabeth II **Subject:** 30th Commonwealth Parliamentary Conference **Obv:** Young bust right **Obv. Designer:** Arnold Machin **Rev:** crowned head facing within circle **Rev. Legend:** Celtic uncial script

Date	Mintage	F	VF	XF	Unc	BU
1984 Proof	10,000	Value: 65.00				

KM# 132c CROWN

7.9600 g., 0.9170 Gold .2347 oz. AGW **Ruler:** Elizabeth II **Subject:** 30th Commonwealth Parliamentary Conference **Obv:** Young bust right **Obv. Designer:** Arnold Machin **Rev:** Crowned head facing within circle **Rev. Legend:** Celtic uncial script

Date	Mintage	F	VF	XF	Unc	BU
1984 Proof	1,000	Value: 175				

KM# 132d CROWN

52.0000 g., 0.9500 Platinum 1.5884 oz. APW, 38.5 mm.
Ruler: Elizabeth II **Subject:** 30th Commonwealth Parliamentary Conference **Obv:** Young bust right **Obv. Designer:** Arnold Machin **Rev:** Crowned head facing within circle
Rev. Legend: Celtic uncial script

Date	Mintage	F	VF	XF	Unc	BU
1984 Proof	—	Value: 2,150				

KM# 133 CROWN

Copper-Nickel, 38.5 mm. **Ruler:** Elizabeth II **Subject:** 30th Commonwealth Parliamentary Conference **Obv:** Young bust right **Obv. Designer:** Arnold Machin **Rev:** Conference tent
Rev. Legend: Celtic uncial script

Date	Mintage	F	VF	XF	Unc	BU
1984	—	—	—	—	3.00	4.00

KM# 133a CROWN

28.2800 g., 0.9250 Silver .8411 oz. ASW, 38.5 mm.
Ruler: Elizabeth II **Subject:** 30th Commonwealth Parliamentary Conference **Obv:** Young bust right **Obv. Designer:** Arnold Machin **Rev:** Conference tent **Rev. Legend:** Celtic uncial script

Date	Mintage	F	VF	XF	Unc	BU
1984	—	—	—	—	15.00	16.50
1984 Proof	—	Value: 20.00				

KM# 133b CROWN

5.1000 g., 0.3740 Gold .0613 oz. AGW **Ruler:** Elizabeth II
Subject: 30th Commonwealth Parliamentary Conference
Obv: Young bust right **Obv. Designer:** Arnold Machin **Rev:** Conference tent within circle **Rev. Legend:** Celtic uncial script

Date	Mintage	F	VF	XF	Unc	BU
1984 Proof	10,000	Value: 65.00				

KM# 133c CROWN

7.9600 g., 0.9170 Gold .2347 oz. AGW **Ruler:** Elizabeth II
Subject: 30th Commonwealth Parliamentary Conference
Obv: Young bust right **Obv. Designer:** Arnold Machin
Rev: Conference tent **Rev. Legend:** Celtic uncial script

Date	Mintage	F	VF	XF	Unc	BU
1984 Proof	1,000	Value: 175				

KM# 133d CROWN

52.0000 g., 0.9500 Platinum 1.5884 oz. APW, 38.5 mm.
Ruler: Elizabeth II **Subject:** 30th Commonwealth Parliamentary Conference **Obv:** Young bust right **Obv. Designer:** Arnold Machin **Rev:** Conference tent **Rev. Legend:** Celtic uncial script

Date	Mintage	F	VF	XF	Unc	BU
1984 Proof	—	Value: 2,150				

KM# 220a CROWN

Silver Clad Copper-Nickel, 38.5 mm. **Ruler:** Elizabeth II
Obv: Crowned bust right **Obv. Designer:** Raphael Maklouf
Rev: Adult and two children facing

Date	Mintage	F	VF	XF	Unc	BU
1985 Proof	Est. 20,000	Value: 15.00				
1990PM Proof	—	Value: 35.00				

KM# 216 CROWN

Copper-Nickel, 38.5 mm. **Ruler:** Elizabeth II **Obv:** Crowned bust right **Obv. Designer:** Raphael Maklouf **Rev:** Child half figure facing

Date	Mintage	F	VF	XF	Unc	BU
1985	Est. 50,000	—	—	—	2.50	3.50

KM# 216a CROWN

Silver Clad Copper-Nickel, 38.5 mm. **Ruler:** Elizabeth II
Obv: Crowned bust right **Obv. Designer:** Raphael Maklouf
Rev: Child half figure facing

Date	Mintage	F	VF	XF	Unc	BU
1985 Proof	Est. 20,000	Value: 10.00				

KM# 220 CROWN

Copper-Nickel, 38.5 mm. **Ruler:** Elizabeth II **Obv:** Crowned bust right **Obv. Designer:** Raphael Maklouf **Rev:** Adult and two children facing

Date	Mintage	F	VF	XF	Unc	BU
1985	Est. 50,000	—	—	—	2.50	3.50
1990	—	—	—	—	2.50	3.50
1990PM Proof	—	Value: 10.00				

KM# 216b CROWN

28.2800 g., 0.9250 Silver .8411 oz. ASW, 38.5 mm.
Ruler: Elizabeth II **Obv:** Crowned bust right
Obv. Designer: Raphael Maklouf **Rev:** Child half figure facing

Date	Mintage	F	VF	XF	Unc	BU
1985 Proof	Est. 15,000	Value: 25.00				

KM# 216c CROWN

5.1000 g., 0.3740 Gold .0613 oz. AGW **Ruler:** Elizabeth II
Obv: Crowned bust right **Obv. Designer:** Raphael Maklouf
Rev: Child half figure facing

Date	Mintage	F	VF	XF	Unc	BU
1985 Proof	Est. 10,000	Value: 65.00				

KM# 216d CROWN

7.9600 g., 0.9170 Gold .2347 oz. AGW **Ruler:** Elizabeth II
Obv: Crowned bust right **Obv. Designer:** Raphael Maklouf
Rev: Child half figure facing

Date	Mintage	F	VF	XF	Unc	BU
1985 Proof	Est. 1,000,000	Value: 175				

KM# 216e CROWN

52.0000 g., 0.9500 Platinum 1.5884 oz. APW, 38.5 mm.
Ruler: Elizabeth II **Obv:** Crowned bust right
Obv. Designer: Raphael Maklouf **Rev:** Child half figure facing

Date	Mintage	F	VF	XF	Unc	BU
1985 Proof	Est. 100	Value: 2,150				

KM# 217 CROWN

Copper-Nickel, 38.5 mm. **Ruler:** Elizabeth II **Obv:** Crowned bust right **Obv. Designer:** Raphael Maklouf **Rev:** Conjoined busts facing

Date	Mintage	F	VF	XF	Unc	BU
1985	Est. 50,000	—	—	—	2.50	3.50

KM# 217a CROWN

Silver Clad Copper-Nickel, 38.5 mm. **Ruler:** Elizabeth II
Obv: Crowned bust right **Obv. Designer:** Raphael Maklouf
Rev: Conjoined busts facing

Date	Mintage	F	VF	XF	Unc	BU
1985 Proof	Est. 20,000	Value: 10.00				

KM# 217b CROWN

28.2800 g., 0.9250 Silver .8411 oz. ASW **Ruler:** Elizabeth II
Obv: Crowned bust right **Obv. Designer:** Raphael Maklouf
Rev: Conjoined busts facing

Date	Mintage	F	VF	XF	Unc	BU
1985 Proof	Est. 15,000	Value: 25.00				

KM# 217c CROWN

5.1000 g., 0.3740 Gold .0613 oz. AGW **Ruler:** Elizabeth II
Obv: Crowned bust right **Obv. Designer:** Raphael Maklouf
Rev: Conjoined busts facing

Date	Mintage	F	VF	XF	Unc	BU
1985 Proof	Est. 10,000	Value: 65.00				

KM# 217d CROWN

7.9600 g., 0.9170 Gold .2347 oz. AGW **Ruler:** Elizabeth II
Obv: Crowned bust right **Obv. Designer:** Raphael Maklouf
Rev: Conjoined busts facing

Date	Mintage	F	VF	XF	Unc	BU
1985 Proof	Est. 1,000	Value: 175				

KM# 217e CROWN

52.0000 g., 0.9500 Platinum 1.5884 oz. APW, 38.5 mm.
Ruler: Elizabeth II **Obv:** Crowned bust right
Obv. Designer: Raphael Maklouf **Rev:** Conjoined busts facing

Date	Mintage	F	VF	XF	Unc	BU
1985 Proof	Est. 100	Value: 2,150				

KM# 218 CROWN

Copper-Nickel, 38.5 mm. **Ruler:** Elizabeth II **Obv:** Crowned bust right **Obv. Designer:** Raphael Maklouf **Rev:** Conjoined busts facing

Date	Mintage	F	VF	XF	Unc	BU
1985	Est. 50,000	—	—	—	2.50	3.50

KM# 218a CROWN

Silver Clad Copper-Nickel, 38.5 mm. **Ruler:** Elizabeth II
Obv: Crowned bust right **Obv. Designer:** Raphael Maklouf
Rev: Conjoined busts facing

Date	Mintage	F	VF	XF	Unc	BU
1985 Proof	Est. 20,000	Value: 10.00				

KM# 218b CROWN

28.2800 g., 0.9250 Silver .8411 oz. ASW, 38.5 mm.
Ruler: Elizabeth II **Obv:** Crowned bust right
Obv. Designer: Raphael Maklouf **Rev:** Conjoined busts facing

Date	Mintage	F	VF	XF	Unc	BU
1985 Proof	Est. 15,000	Value: 25.00				

KM# 218c CROWN

5.1000 g., 0.3740 Gold .0613 oz. AGW **Ruler:** Elizabeth II
Obv: Crowned bust right **Obv. Designer:** Raphael Maklouf
Rev: Conjoined busts facing

Date	Mintage	F	VF	XF	Unc	BU
1985 Proof	Est. 10,000	Value: 65.00				

KM# 218d CROWN

7.9600 g., 0.9170 Gold .2347 oz. AGW **Ruler:** Elizabeth II
Obv: Crowned bust right **Obv. Designer:** Raphael Maklouf
Rev: Conjoined busts facing

Date	Mintage	F	VF	XF	Unc	BU
1985 Proof	Est. 1,000	Value: 175				

KM# 218e CROWN

52.0000 g., 0.9500 Platinum 1.5884 oz. APW, 38.5 mm.
Ruler: Elizabeth II **Obv:** Crowned bust right
Obv. Designer: Raphael Maklouf **Rev:** Conjoined busts facing

Date	Mintage	F	VF	XF	Unc	BU
1985 Proof	Est. 100	Value: 2,150				

KM# 219 CROWN

Copper-Nickel, 38.5 mm. **Ruler:** Elizabeth II **Obv:** Crowned bust right **Obv. Designer:** Raphael Maklouf **Rev:** Queen Mother and Princess Elizabeth

Date	Mintage	F	VF	XF	Unc	BU
1985	Est. 50,000	—	—	—	2.50	3.50

KM# 219a CROWN

Silver Clad Copper-Nickel, 38.5 mm. **Ruler:** Elizabeth II
Obv: Crowned bust right **Obv. Designer:** Raphael Maklouf
Rev: Queen Mother and Princess Elizabeth

Date	Mintage	F	VF	XF	Unc	BU
1985 Proof	Est. 20,000	Value: 10.00				

KM# 219b CROWN

28.2800 g., 0.9250 Silver .8411 oz. ASW, 38.5 mm.
Ruler: Elizabeth II **Obv:** Crowned bust right **Obv. Designer:** Raphael Maklouf **Rev:** Queen Mother and Princess Elizabeth

Date	Mintage	F	VF	XF	Unc	BU
1985 Proof	Est. 15,000	Value: 25.00				

KM# 219c CROWN

5.1000 g., 0.3740 Gold .0613 oz. AGW **Ruler:** Elizabeth II
Obv: Crowned bust right **Obv. Designer:** Raphael Maklouf
Rev: Queen Mother and Princess Elizabeth

Date	Mintage	F	VF	XF	Unc	BU
1985 Proof	Est. 10,000	Value: 65.00				

KM# 219d CROWN

7.9600 g., 0.9170 Gold .2347 oz. AGW **Ruler:** Elizabeth II
Obv: Crowned bust right **Obv. Designer:** Raphael Maklouf
Rev: Queen Mother and Princess Elizabeth

Date	Mintage	F	VF	XF	Unc	BU
1985 Proof	Est. 1,000	Value: 175				

KM# 219e CROWN

52.0000 g., 0.9500 Platinum 1.5884 oz. APW, 38.5 mm.
Ruler: Elizabeth II **Obv:** Crowned bust right **Obv. Designer:** Raphael Maklouf **Rev:** Queen Mother and Princess Elizabeth

Date	Mintage	F	VF	XF	Unc	BU
1985 Proof	Est. 100	Value: 2,150				

KM# 220b CROWN

28.2800 g., 0.9250 Silver .8411 oz. ASW, 38.5 mm.
Ruler: Elizabeth II **Obv:** Crowned bust right **Obv. Designer:** Raphael Maklouf **Rev:** Adult and two children facing

Date	Mintage	F	VF	XF	Unc	BU
1985 Proof	Est. 15,000	Value: 25.00				
1990 Proof	—	Value: 28.00				

KM# 220c CROWN

5.1000 g., 0.3740 Gold .0613 oz. AGW **Ruler:** Elizabeth II
Obv: Crowned bust right **Obv. Designer:** Raphael Maklouf
Rev: Adult and two children facing

Date	Mintage	F	VF	XF	Unc	BU
1985 Proof	Est. 10,000	Value: 65.00				

KM# 220d CROWN

7.9600 g., 0.9170 Gold .2347 oz. AGW **Ruler:** Elizabeth II
Obv: Crowned bust right **Obv. Designer:** Raphael Maklouf
Rev: Adult and two children facing

Date	Mintage	F	VF	XF	Unc	BU
1985 Proof	Est. 1,000	Value: 175				

KM# 220e CROWN

52.0000 g., 0.9500 Platinum 1.5884 oz. APW, 38.5 mm.
Ruler: Elizabeth II **Obv:** Crowned bust right **Obv. Designer:** Raphael Maklouf **Rev:** Adult and two children facing

Date	Mintage	F	VF	XF	Unc	BU
1985 Proof	Est. 100	Value: 2,150				

KM# 221 CROWN

Copper-Nickel, 38.5 mm. **Ruler:** Elizabeth II **Subject:** 85th Birthday of Queen Mother **Obv:** Crowned bust right
Obv. Designer: Raphael Maklouf **Rev:** Queen Mother

Date	Mintage	F	VF	XF	Unc	BU
1985	Est. 50,000	—	—	—	2.50	3.50

KM# 221a CROWN

Silver Clad Copper-Nickel, 38.5 mm. **Ruler:** Elizabeth II
Subject: 85th Birthday of Queen Mother **Obv:** Crowned bust right
Obv. Designer: Raphael Maklouf **Rev:** Queen Mother

Date	Mintage	F	VF	XF	Unc	BU
1985 Proof	Est. 20,000	Value: 10.00				

KM# 221b CROWN

28.2800 g., 0.9250 Silver .8411 oz. ASW, 38.5 mm. **Ruler:** Elizabeth II **Subject:** 85th Birthday of Queen Mother **Obv:** Crowned bust right **Obv. Designer:** Raphael Maklouf **Rev:** Queen Mother

Date	Mintage	F	VF	XF	Unc	BU
1985 Proof	Est. 15,000	Value: 25.00				

KM# 221c CROWN

5.1000 g., 0.3740 Gold .0613 oz. AGW **Ruler:** Elizabeth II
Subject: 85th Birthday of Queen Mother **Obv:** Crowned bust right
Obv. Designer: Raphael Maklouf **Rev:** Queen Mother

Date	Mintage	F	VF	XF	Unc	BU
1985 Proof	Est. 10,000	Value: 65.00				

KM# 221d CROWN

7.9600 g., 0.9170 Gold .2347 oz. AGW **Ruler:** Elizabeth II **Subject:** 85th Birthday of Queen Mother **Obv:** Crowned bust right **Obv. Designer:** Raphael Maklouf **Rev:** Queen Mother

Date	Mintage	F	VF	XF	Unc	BU
1985 Proof	Est. 1,000,000	Value: 175				

KM# 221e CROWN

52.0000 g., 0.9500 Platinum 1.5884 oz. APW, 38.5 mm. **Ruler:** Elizabeth II **Subject:** 85th Birthday of Queen Mother **Obv:** Crowned bust right **Obv. Designer:** Raphael Maklouf **Rev:** Queen Mother

Date	Mintage	F	VF	XF	Unc	BU
1985 Proof	Est. 100	Value: 2,150				

KM# 160 CROWN

Copper-Nickel, 38.5 mm. **Ruler:** Elizabeth II **Series:** World Cup Soccer - Mexico **Obv:** Crowned bust right **Obv. Designer:** Raphael Maklouf **Rev:** Map and soccer players within circle **Edge:** Reeded

Date	Mintage	F	VF	XF	Unc	BU
1986	Est. 50,000	—	—	—	2.50	3.50

KM# 160a CROWN

Silver Clad Copper-Nickel, 38.5 mm. **Ruler:** Elizabeth II **Series:** World Cup Soccer - Mexico **Obv:** Crowned bust right **Obv. Designer:** Raphael Maklouf **Rev:** Map and soccer players within circle

Date	Mintage	F	VF	XF	Unc	BU
1986 Proof	Est. 20,000	Value: 10.00				

KM# 160b CROWN

28.2800 g., 0.9250 Silver .8411 oz. ASW, 38.5 mm. **Ruler:** Elizabeth II **Series:** World Cup Soccer - Mexico **Obv:** Crowned bust right **Obv. Designer:** Raphael Maklouf **Rev:** Map and soccer players within circle

Date	Mintage	F	VF	XF	Unc	BU
1986 Proof	Est. 15,000	Value: 17.50				

KM# 160c CROWN

5.1000 g., 0.3740 Gold .0613 oz. AGW **Ruler:** Elizabeth II **Series:** World Cup Soccer - Mexico **Obv:** Crowned bust right **Obv. Designer:** Raphael Maklouf **Rev:** Map and soccer players within circle

Date	Mintage	F	VF	XF	Unc	BU
1986 Proof	Est. 10,000	Value: 65.00				

KM# 160d CROWN

7.9600 g., 0.9170 Gold .2347 oz. AGW **Ruler:** Elizabeth II **Series:** World Cup Soccer - Mexico **Obv:** Crowned bust right **Obv. Designer:** Raphael Maklouf **Rev:** Map and soccer players within circle

Date	Mintage	F	VF	XF	Unc	BU
1986 Proof	Est. 1,000	Value: 175				

KM# 160e CROWN

52.0000 g., 0.9500 Platinum 1.5884 oz. APW, 38.5 mm. **Ruler:** Elizabeth II **Series:** World Cup Soccer - Mexico **Obv:** Crowned bust right **Obv. Designer:** Raphael Maklouf **Rev:** Map and soccer players within circle

Date	Mintage	F	VF	XF	Unc	BU
1986 Proof	Est. 200	Value: 2,150				

KM# 161 CROWN

Copper-Nickel, 38.5 mm. **Ruler:** Elizabeth II **Series:** World Cup Soccer - Mexico **Obv:** Crowned bust right **Obv. Designer:** Raphael Maklouf **Rev:** Soccer players within circle

Date	Mintage	F	VF	XF	Unc	BU
1986	Est. 50,000	—	—	—	2.50	3.50

KM# 161a CROWN

Silver Clad Copper-Nickel, 38.5 mm. **Ruler:** Elizabeth II **Series:** World Cup Soccer - Mexico **Obv:** Crowned bust right **Obv. Designer:** Raphael Maklouf **Rev:** Soccer players within circle

Date	Mintage	F	VF	XF	Unc	BU
1986 Proof	Est. 20,000	Value: 10.00				

KM# 161b CROWN

28.2800 g., 0.9250 Silver .8411 oz. ASW, 38.5 mm. **Ruler:** Elizabeth II **Series:** World Cup Soccer - Mexico **Obv:** Crowned bust right **Obv. Designer:** Raphael Maklouf **Rev:** Soccer players within circle

Date	Mintage	F	VF	XF	Unc	BU
1986 Proof	Est. 15,000	Value: 17.50				

KM# 161c CROWN

5.1000 g., 0.3740 Gold .0613 oz. AGW **Ruler:** Elizabeth II **Series:** World Cup Soccer - Mexico **Obv:** Raphael Maklouf **Rev:** Soccer players within circle

Date	Mintage	F	VF	XF	Unc	BU
1986 Proof	Est. 10,000	Value: 65.00				

KM# 161d CROWN

7.9600 g., 0.9170 Gold .2347 oz. AGW **Ruler:** Elizabeth II **Series:** World Cup Soccer - Mexico **Obv:** Crowned bust right **Obv. Designer:** Raphael Maklouf **Rev:** Soccer players within circle

Date	Mintage	F	VF	XF	Unc	BU
1986 Proof	Est. 1,000	Value: 175				

KM# 161e CROWN

52.0000 g., 0.9500 Platinum 1.5884 oz. APW, 38.5 mm. **Ruler:** Elizabeth II **Series:** World Cup Soccer - Mexico **Obv:** Crowned bust right **Obv. Designer:** Raphael Maklouf **Rev:** Soccer players within circle

Date	Mintage	F	VF	XF	Unc	BU
1986 Proof	Est. 200	Value: 2,150				

KM# 162 CROWN

Copper-Nickel, 38.5 mm. **Ruler:** Elizabeth II **Series:** World Cup Soccer - Mexico **Obv:** Crowned bust right **Obv. Designer:** Raphael Maklouf **Rev:** Soccer players within circle **Edge:** Reeded

Date	Mintage	F	VF	XF	Unc	BU
1986	Est. 50,000	—	—	—	2.50	3.50

KM# 162a CROWN

Silver-Clad Copper-Nickel, 38.5 mm. **Ruler:** Elizabeth II **Series:** World Cup Soccer - Mexico **Obv:** Crowned bust right **Obv. Designer:** Raphael Maklouf **Rev:** Soccer players within circle

Date	Mintage	F	VF	XF	Unc	BU
1986 Proof	Est. 20,000	Value: 10.00				

KM# 162b CROWN

28.2800 g., 0.9250 Silver .8411 oz. ASW, 38.5 mm. **Ruler:** Elizabeth II **Series:** World Cup Soccer - Mexico **Obv:** Crowned bust right **Obv. Designer:** Raphael Maklouf **Rev:** Soccer players within circle

Date	Mintage	F	VF	XF	Unc	BU
1986 Proof	Est. 15,000	Value: 17.50				

KM# 162c CROWN

5.1000 g., 0.3740 Gold .0613 oz. AGW **Ruler:** Elizabeth II **Series:** World Cup Soccer - Mexico **Obv:** Crowned bust right **Obv. Designer:** Raphael Maklouf **Rev:** Soccer players within circle

Date	Mintage	F	VF	XF	Unc	BU
1986 Proof	Est. 10,000	Value: 65.00				

KM# 162d CROWN

7.9600 g., 0.9170 Gold .2347 oz. AGW **Ruler:** Elizabeth II **Series:** World Cup Soccer - Mexico **Obv:** Crowned bust right **Obv. Designer:** Raphael Maklouf **Rev:** Soccer players within circle

Date	Mintage	F	VF	XF	Unc	BU
1986 Proof	Est. 1,000	Value: 175				

KM# 162e CROWN

52.0000 g., 0.9500 Platinum 1.5884 oz. APW, 38.5 mm. **Ruler:** Elizabeth II **Series:** World Cup Soccer - Mexico **Obv:** Crowned bust right **Obv. Designer:** Raphael Maklouf **Rev:** Soccer players within circle

Date	Mintage	F	VF	XF	Unc	BU
1986 Proof	Est. 200	Value: 2,150				

KM# 163 CROWN

Copper-Nickel, 38.5 mm. **Ruler:** Elizabeth II **Series:** World Cup Soccer - Mexico **Obv:** Crowned bust right **Obv. Designer:** Raphael Maklouf **Rev:** Net and soccer players within circle **Edge:** Reeded

Date	Mintage	F	VF	XF	Unc	BU
1986	Est. 50,000	—	—	—	2.50	3.50

KM# 163a CROWN

Silver-Clad Copper-Nickel **Ruler:** Elizabeth II **Series:** World Cup Soccer - Mexico **Obv:** Crowned bust right **Obv. Designer:** Raphael Maklouf **Rev:** Net and soccer players within circle

Date	Mintage	F	VF	XF	Unc	BU
1986 Proof	Est. 20,000	Value: 10.00				

KM# 163b CROWN

28.2800 g., 0.9250 Silver .8411 oz. ASW, 38.5 mm. **Ruler:** Elizabeth II **Series:** World Cup Soccer - Mexico **Obv:** Crowned bust right **Obv. Designer:** Raphael Maklouf **Rev:** Net and soccer players within circle

Date	Mintage	F	VF	XF	Unc	BU
1986 Proof	Est. 15,000	Value: 17.50				

KM# 163c CROWN

5.1000 g., 0.3740 Gold .0613 oz. AGW **Ruler:** Elizabeth II **Series:** World Cup Soccer - Mexico **Obv:** Crowned bust right **Obv. Designer:** Raphael Maklouf **Rev:** Net and soccer players within circle

Date	Mintage	F	VF	XF	Unc	BU
1986 Proof	Est. 10,000	Value: 65.00				

KM# 163d CROWN

7.9600 g., 0.9170 Gold .2347 oz. AGW **Ruler:** Elizabeth II **Series:** World Cup Soccer - Mexico **Obv:** Crowned bust right **Obv. Designer:** Raphael Maklouf **Rev:** Net and soccer players within circle

Date	Mintage	F	VF	XF	Unc	BU
1986 Proof	Est. 1,000	Value: 175				

KM# 163e CROWN

52.0000 g., 0.9500 Platinum 1.5884 oz. APW, 38.5 mm. **Ruler:** Elizabeth II **Series:** World Cup Soccer - Mexico **Obv:** Crowned bust right **Obv. Designer:** Raphael Maklouf **Rev:** Net and soccer players within circle

Date	Mintage	F	VF	XF	Unc	BU
1986 Proof	Est. 200	Value: 2,150				

KM# 164 CROWN

Copper-Nickel, 38.5 mm. **Ruler:** Elizabeth II **Series:** World Cup Soccer - Mexico **Obv:** Crowned bust right **Obv. Designer:** Raphael Maklouf **Rev:** Globe **Edge:** Reeded

Date	Mintage	F	VF	XF	Unc	BU
1986	Est. 50,000	—	—	—	2.50	3.50

KM# 164a CROWN

Silver-Clad Copper-Nickel, 38.5 mm. **Ruler:** Elizabeth II **Series:** World Cup Soccer - Mexico **Obv:** Crowned bust right **Obv. Designer:** Raphael Maklouf **Rev:** Globe

Date	Mintage	F	VF	XF	Unc	BU
1986	Est. 20,000	Value: 10.00				
1989	—	—	—	—	80.00	—

KM# 164b CROWN

28.2800 g., 0.9250 Silver .8411 oz. ASW, 38.5 mm. **Ruler:** Elizabeth II **Series:** World Cup Soccer - Mexico **Obv:** Crowned bust right **Obv. Designer:** Raphael Maklouf **Rev:** Globe

Date	Mintage	F	VF	XF	Unc	BU
1986 Proof	Est. 15,000	Value: 17.50				

KM# 164c CROWN

5.1000 g., 0.3740 Gold .0613 oz. AGW **Ruler:** Elizabeth II **Series:** World Cup Soccer - Mexico **Obv:** Crowned bust right **Obv. Designer:** Raphael Maklouf **Rev:** Globe

Date	Mintage	F	VF	XF	Unc	BU
1986 Proof	Est. 10,000	Value: 65.00				

KM# 164d CROWN

7.9600 g., 0.9170 Gold .2347 oz. AGW **Ruler:** Elizabeth II **Series:** World Cup Soccer - Mexico **Obv:** Crowned bust right **Obv. Designer:** Raphael Maklouf **Rev:** Globe

Date	Mintage	F	VF	XF	Unc	BU
1986 Proof	Est. 1,000	Value: 175				

KM# 164e CROWN

52.0000 g., 0.9500 Platinum 1.5884 oz. APW, 38.5 mm. **Ruler:** Elizabeth II **Series:** World Cup Soccer - Mexico **Obv:** Crowned bust right **Obv. Designer:** Raphael Maklouf **Rev:** Globe

Date	Mintage	F	VF	XF	Unc	BU
1986 Proof	Est. 200	Value: 2,150				

KM# 165 CROWN

Copper-Nickel, 38.5 mm. **Ruler:** Elizabeth II **Series:** World Cup Soccer - Mexico **Obv:** Crowned bust right **Obv. Designer:** Raphael Maklouf **Rev:** Flags within circle **Edge:** Reeded

Date	Mintage	F	VF	XF	Unc	BU
1986	Est. 50,000	—	—	—	2.50	3.50

KM# 165a CROWN

Silver-Clad Copper-Nickel, 38.5 mm. **Ruler:** Elizabeth II **Series:** World Cup Soccer - Mexico **Obv:** Crowned bust right **Obv. Designer:** Raphael Maklouf **Rev:** Flags within circle

Date	Mintage	F	VF	XF	Unc	BU
1986	Est. 20,000	Value: 10.00				
1989	—	—	—	—	80.00	—

KM# 165b CROWN

28.2800 g., 0.9250 Silver .8411 oz. ASW, 38.5 mm. **Ruler:** Elizabeth II **Series:** World Cup Soccer - Mexico **Obv:** Crowned bust right **Obv. Designer:** Raphael Maklouf **Rev:** Flags within circle

Date	Mintage	F	VF	XF	Unc	BU
1986 Proof	Est. 15,000	Value: 17.50				

KM# 165c CROWN

5.1000 g., 0.3740 Gold .0613 oz. AGW **Ruler:** Elizabeth II **Series:** World Cup Soccer - Mexico **Obv:** Crowned bust right **Obv. Designer:** Raphael Maklouf **Rev:** Flags within circle

Date	Mintage	F	VF	XF	Unc	BU
1986 Proof	Est. 10,000	Value: 65.00				

KM# 165d CROWN

7.9600 g., 0.9170 Gold .2347 oz. AGW **Ruler:** Elizabeth II **Series:** World Cup Soccer - Mexico **Obv:** Crowned bust right **Obv. Designer:** Raphael Maklouf **Rev:** Flags within circle

Date	Mintage	F	VF	XF	Unc	BU
1986 Proof	Est. 1,000	Value: 175				

KM# 165e CROWN

52.0000 g., 0.9500 Platinum 1.5884 oz. APW, 38.5 mm. **Ruler:** Elizabeth II **Series:** World Cup Soccer - Mexico **Obv:** Crowned bust right **Obv. Designer:** Raphael Maklouf **Rev:** Flags within circle

Date	Mintage	F	VF	XF	Unc	BU
1986 Proof	Est. 200	Value: 2,150				

KM# 173 CROWN

Copper-Nickel, 38.5 mm. **Ruler:** Elizabeth II **Subject:** Prince Andrew's Wedding **Obv:** Crowned bust right **Obv. Designer:** Raphael Maklouf **Rev:** Conjoined heads left **Edge:** Reeded

Date	Mintage	F	VF	XF	Unc	BU
1986	Est. 50,000	—	—	—	4.00	5.00
1986 Proof	—	Value: 8.00				

KM# 173a CROWN

Silver-Clad Copper-Nickel, 38.5 mm. **Ruler:** Elizabeth II **Subject:** Prince Andrew's Wedding **Obv:** Crowned bust right **Obv. Designer:** Raphael Maklouf **Rev:** Conjoined heads left

Date	Mintage	F	VF	XF	Unc	BU
1986 Proof	Est. 20,000	Value: 12.00				

KM# 173b CROWN

28.2800 g., 0.9250 Silver .8411 oz. ASW, 38.5 mm. **Ruler:** Elizabeth II **Subject:** Prince Andrew's Wedding **Obv:** Crowned bust right **Obv. Designer:** Raphael Maklouf **Rev:** Conjoined heads left

Date	Mintage	F	VF	XF	Unc	BU
1986	Est. 20,000	—	—	—	15.00	16.00
1986 Proof	Est. 15,000	Value: 18.00				

KM# 173c CROWN

5.1000 g., 0.3740 Gold .0613 oz. AGW **Ruler:** Elizabeth II **Subject:** Prince Andrew's Wedding **Obv:** Crowned bust right **Obv. Designer:** Raphael Maklouf **Rev:** Conjoined heads left

Date	Mintage	F	VF	XF	Unc	BU
1986 Proof	Est. 10,000	Value: 65.00				

KM# 173d CROWN

7.9600 g., 0.9170 Gold .2347 oz. AGW **Ruler:** Elizabeth II **Subject:** Prince Andrew's Wedding **Obv:** Crowned bust right **Obv. Designer:** Raphael Maklouf **Rev:** Conjoined heads left

Date	Mintage	F	VF	XF	Unc	BU
1986 Proof	Est. 1,000	Value: 175				

KM# 173e CROWN

52.0000 g., 0.9500 Platinum 1.5884 oz. APW, 38.5 mm. **Ruler:** Elizabeth II **Subject:** Prince Andrew's Wedding **Obv:** Crowned bust right **Obv. Designer:** Raphael Maklouf **Rev:** Conjoined heads left

Date	Mintage	F	VF	XF	Unc	BU
1986 Proof	Est. 100	Value: 2,150				

KM# 174 CROWN

Copper-Nickel, 38.5 mm. **Ruler:** Elizabeth II **Subject:** Prince Andrew's Wedding **Obv:** Crowned bust right **Obv. Designer:** Raphael Maklouf **Rev:** Two sets of arms **Edge:** Reeded

Date	Mintage	F	VF	XF	Unc	BU
1986	Est. 50,000	—	—	—	4.00	5.00
1986 Proof	—	Value: 8.00				

KM# 174a CROWN

Silver Clad Copper-Nickel, 38.5 mm. **Ruler:** Elizabeth II **Subject:** Prince Andrew's Wedding **Obv:** Crowned bust right **Obv. Designer:** Raphael Maklouf **Rev:** Two sets of arms

Date	Mintage	F	VF	XF	Unc	BU
1986 Proof	Est. 20,000	Value: 12.00				

KM# 174b CROWN

28.2800 g., 0.9250 Silver .8411 oz. ASW, 38.5 mm. **Ruler:** Elizabeth II **Subject:** Prince Andrew's Wedding **Obv:** Crowned bust right **Obv. Designer:** Raphael Maklouf **Rev:** Two sets of arms

Date	Mintage	F	VF	XF	Unc	BU
1986	Est. 20,000	—	—	—	15.00	16.00
1986 Proof	Est. 15,000	Value: 18.00				

KM# 174c CROWN

5.1000 g., 0.3740 Gold .0613 oz. AGW **Ruler:** Elizabeth II **Subject:** Prince Andrew's Wedding **Obv:** Crowned bust right **Obv. Designer:** Raphael Maklouf **Rev:** Two sets of arms

Date	Mintage	F	VF	XF	Unc	BU
1986 Proof	Est. 10,000	Value: 65.00				

KM# 174d CROWN

7.9600 g., 0.9170 Gold .2347 oz. AGW **Ruler:** Elizabeth II **Subject:** Prince Andrew's Wedding **Obv:** Crowned bust right **Obv. Designer:** Raphael Maklouf **Rev:** Two sets of arms

Date	Mintage	F	VF	XF	Unc	BU
1986 Proof	Est. 1,000	Value: 175				

KM# 174e CROWN

52.0000 g., 0.9500 Platinum 1.5884 oz. APW, 38.5 mm. **Ruler:** Elizabeth II **Subject:** Prince Andrew's Wedding **Obv:** Crowned bust right **Obv. Designer:** Raphael Maklouf **Rev:** Two sets of arms

Date	Mintage	F	VF	XF	Unc	BU
1986 Proof	Est. 100	Value: 2,150				

KM# 179a CROWN

28.2800 g., Silver-Clad Copper-Nickel, 38.5 mm. **Ruler:** Elizabeth II **Obv:** Crowned bust right within circle **Obv. Designer:** Raphael Maklouf **Rev:** Sailboats and map within circle **Edge:** Reeded

Date	Mintage	F	VF	XF	Unc	BU
1987PM Proof	20,000	Value: 7.00				

KM# 176 CROWN

Copper-Nickel, 38.5 mm. **Ruler:** Elizabeth II **Subject:** United States Constitution **Obv:** Crowned bust right **Obv. Designer:** Raphael Maklouf **Rev:** Statue of Liberty divides dates within circle of Presidential busts **Edge:** Reeded

Date	Mintage	F	VF	XF	Unc	BU
1987	—	—	—	—	5.00	6.00

KM# 176a CROWN

31.1000 g., 0.9990 Palladium 1.0000 oz., 38.5 mm. **Ruler:** Elizabeth II **Subject:** United States Constitution Bicentennial **Obv:** Crowned bust right **Obv. Designer:** Raphael Maklouf **Rev:** Statue of Liberty divides dates within circle of Presidential busts

Date	Mintage	F	VF	XF	Unc	BU
1987 Proof	Est. 25,000	Value: 400				

KM# 176b CROWN

31.1000 g., 0.9950 Platinum 1.0000 oz. APW, 38.5 mm. **Ruler:** Elizabeth II **Subject:** United States Constitution Bicentennial **Obv:** Crowned bust right **Obv. Designer:** Raphael Maklouf **Rev:** Statue of Liberty divides dates within circle of Presidential busts

Date	Mintage	F	VF	XF	Unc	BU
1987 Proof	Est. 1,000	Value: 1,325				

KM# 179 CROWN

Copper-Nickel, 38.5 mm. **Ruler:** Elizabeth II **Series:** Americ'a Cup **Obv:** Crowned bust right within circle **Obv. Designer:** Raphael Maklouf **Rev:** Sailboats and map within circle **Edge:** Reeded

Date	Mintage	F	VF	XF	Unc	BU
1987	50,000	—	—	—	10.00	11.50

KM# 179b CROWN

28.2800 g., 0.9250 Silver .8411 oz. ASW, 38.5 mm. **Ruler:** Elizabeth II **Series:** America's Cup **Obv:** Crowned bust right within circle **Obv. Designer:** Raphael Maklouf **Rev:** Sailboats and map within circle

Date	Mintage	F	VF	XF	Unc	BU
1987	Est. 20,000	—	—	—	26.50	28.50
1987 Proof	Est. 15,000	Value: 40.00				

KM# 179c CROWN

31.1030 g., 0.9990 Palladium 1.0000 oz. **Ruler:** Elizabeth II **Series:** America's Cup **Obv:** Crowned bust right within circle **Obv. Designer:** Raphael Maklouf **Rev:** Sailboats and map within circle

Date	Mintage	F	VF	XF	Unc	BU
1987 Proof	1,000	Value: 400				

KM# 183 CROWN

Copper-Nickel, 38.5 mm. **Ruler:** Elizabeth II **Series:** America's Cup **Obv:** Crowned bust right **Obv. Designer:** Raphael Maklouf **Rev:** Sailboats and cup **Edge:** Reeded

Date	Mintage	F	VF	XF	Unc	BU
1987	50,000	—	—	—	10.00	11.50

KM# 183b CROWN

28.2800 g., 0.9250 Silver .8411 oz. ASW, 38.5 mm. **Ruler:** Elizabeth II **Series:** America's Cup **Obv:** Crowned bust right **Obv. Designer:** Raphael Maklouf **Rev:** Sailboats and cup

Date	Mintage	F	VF	XF	Unc	BU
1987	Est. 20,000	—	—	—	26.50	28.50
1987 Proof	Est. 15,000	Value: 40.00				

KM# 183c CROWN

31.1030 g., 0.9990 Palladium 1.0000 oz. **Ruler:** Elizabeth II **Series:** America's Cup **Obv:** Crowned bust right **Obv. Designer:** Raphael Maklouf **Rev:** Sailboats and cup

Date	Mintage	F	VF	XF	Unc	BU
1987 Proof	1,000	Value: 400				

KM# 184 CROWN

Copper-Nickel, 38.5 mm. **Ruler:** Elizabeth II **Series:** America's Cup **Obv:** Crowned bust right **Obv. Designer:** Raphael Maklouf **Rev:** Statue of Liberty and sailboats **Edge:** Reeded

Date	Mintage	F	VF	XF	Unc	BU
1987	50,000	—	—	—	10.00	11.50

KM# 184b CROWN

28.2800 g., 0.9250 Silver .8411 oz. ASW, 38.5 mm. **Ruler:** Elizabeth II **Series:** Americ'a Cup **Obv:** Crowned bust right **Obv. Designer:** Raphael Maklouf **Rev:** Statue of Liberty and sailboats

Date	Mintage	F	VF	XF	Unc	BU
1987	Est. 20,000	—	—	—	26.50	28.50
1987 Proof	Est. 15,000	Value: 40.00				

KM# 184c CROWN

31.1030 g., 0.9990 Palladium 1.0000 oz. **Ruler:** Elizabeth II **Series:** America's Cup **Obv:** Crowned bust right **Obv. Designer:** Raphael Maklouf **Rev:** Statue of Liberty and sailboats

Date	Mintage	F	VF	XF	Unc	BU
1987 Proof	1,000	Value: 400				

KM# 185 CROWN

Copper-Nickel, 38.5 mm. **Ruler:** Elizabeth II **Series:** America's Cup **Obv:** Crowned bust right **Obv. Designer:** Raphael Maklouf **Rev:** Bust of George Steers and sailboat **Edge:** Reeded

Date	Mintage	F	VF	XF	Unc	BU
1987	50,000	—	—	—	10.00	11.50

KM# 185b CROWN

28.2800 g., 0.9250 Silver .8411 oz. ASW, 38.5 mm. **Ruler:** Elizabeth II **Series:** America's Cup **Obv:** Crowned bust right **Obv. Designer:** Raphael Maklouf **Rev:** Bust of George Steers and sailboat

Date	Mintage	F	VF	XF	Unc	BU
1987	Est. 20,000	—	—	—	26.50	28.50
1987 Proof	Est. 15,000	Value: 40.00				

KM# 185c CROWN

31.1030 g., 0.9990 Palladium 1.0000 oz. **Ruler:** Elizabeth II **Series:** America's Cup **Obv:** Crowned bust right **Obv. Designer:** Raphael Maklouf **Rev:** Bust of George Steers and sailboat

Date	Mintage	F	VF	XF	Unc	BU
1987 Proof	1,000	Value: 400				

KM# 186 CROWN

Copper-Nickel, 38.5 mm. **Ruler:** Elizabeth II **Series:** America's Cup **Obv:** Crowned bust right **Obv. Designer:** Raphael Maklouf **Rev:** Bust of Sir Thomas Lipton and sailboat **Edge:** Reeded

Date	Mintage	F	VF	XF	Unc	BU
1987	50,000	—	—	—	10.00	11.50

KM# 186b CROWN

28.2800 g., 0.9250 Silver .8411 oz. ASW, 38.5 mm. **Ruler:** Elizabeth II **Series:** America's Cup **Obv:** Crowned bust right **Obv. Designer:** Raphael Maklouf **Rev:** Bust of Sir Thomas Lipton and sailboat

Date	Mintage	F	VF	XF	Unc	BU
1987	Est. 20,000	—	—	—	26.50	28.50
1987 Proof	Est. 15,000	Value: 40.00				

KM# 186c CROWN

31.1030 g., 0.9990 Palladium 1.0000 oz. **Ruler:** Elizabeth II **Series:** America's Cup **Obv:** Crowned bust right **Obv. Designer:** Raphael Maklouf **Rev:** Bust of Sir Thomas LIpton and sailboat

Date	Mintage	F	VF	XF	Unc	BU
1987 Proof	1,000	Value: 400				

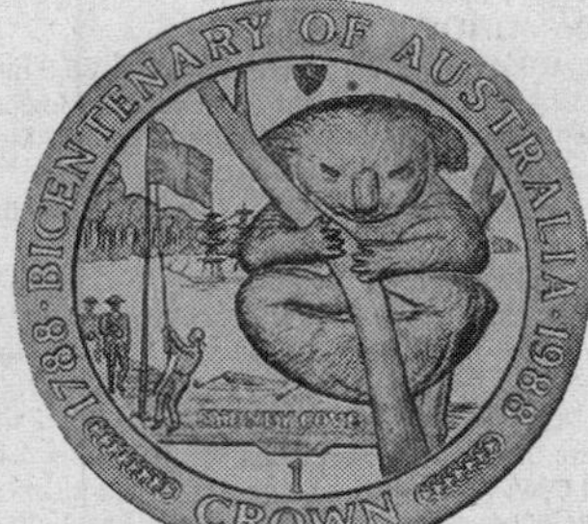

KM# 223 CROWN

Copper-Nickel, 38.5 mm. **Ruler:** Elizabeth II **Subject:** Australian Bicentennial **Obv:** Crowned bust right **Obv. Designer:** Raphael Maklouf **Rev:** Koala bear in tree within circle

Date	Mintage	F	VF	XF	Unc	BU
1988	—	—	—	—	10.00	15.00
1988 Proof	500	Value: 30.00				

KM# 222 CROWN
Copper-Nickel, 38.5 mm. **Ruler:** Elizabeth II **Subject:** Australian Bicentennial **Obv:** Crowned bust right **Obv. Designer:** Raphael Maklouf **Rev:** Cockatoo on branch within circle

Date	Mintage	F	VF	XF	Unc	BU
1988 Proof	500	Value: 30.00				
1988	—	—	—	—	10.00	15.00

KM# 222a CROWN
31.1000 g., 0.9990 Silver 1.0000 oz. ASW, 38.5 mm. **Ruler:** Elizabeth II **Subject:** Australian Bicentennial **Obv:** Crowned bust right **Obv. Designer:** Raphael Maklouf **Rev:** Cockatoo on branch within circle

Date	Mintage	F	VF	XF	Unc	BU
1988 Proof	—	Value: 175				

KM# 223a CROWN
31.1000 g., 0.9990 Silver 1.0000 oz. ASW, 38.5 mm. **Ruler:** Elizabeth II **Subject:** Australian Bicentennial **Obv:** Crowned bust right **Obv. Designer:** Raphael Maklouf **Rev:** Koala bear in tree within circle

Date	Mintage	F	VF	XF	Unc	BU
1988 Proof	—	Value: 175				

KM# 224 CROWN
Copper-Nickel, 38.5 mm. **Ruler:** Elizabeth II **Subject:** Australian Bicentennial **Obv:** Crowned bust right **Obv. Designer:** Raphael Maklouf **Rev:** Duckbill platypus below two men and tent, all within circle

Date	Mintage	F	VF	XF	Unc	BU
1988	—	—	—	—	10.00	15.00
1988 Proof	500	Value: 30.00				

KM# 224a CROWN
31.1000 g., 0.9990 Silver 1.0000 oz. ASW, 38.5 mm. **Ruler:** Elizabeth II **Subject:** Australian Bicentennial **Obv:** Crowned bust right **Obv. Designer:** Raphael Maklouf **Rev:** Duckbill platypus below two men and tent all within circle

Date	Mintage	F	VF	XF	Unc	BU
1988 Proof	—	Value: 175				

KM# 225 CROWN
Copper-Nickel, 38.5 mm. **Ruler:** Elizabeth II **Subject:** Australian Bicentennial **Obv:** Crowned bust right **Obv. Designer:** Raphael Maklouf **Rev:** Kangaroo within circle

Date	Mintage	F	VF	XF	Unc	BU
1988	—	—	—	—	10.00	15.00
1988 Proof	500	Value: 30.00				

KM# 225a CROWN
31.1000 g., 0.9999 Silver 1.0000 oz. ASW, 38.5 mm. **Ruler:** Elizabeth II **Subject:** Australian Bicentennial **Obv:** Crowned bust right **Obv. Designer:** Raphael Maklouf **Rev:** Kangaroo within circle

Date	Mintage	F	VF	XF	Unc	BU
1988 Proof	—	Value: 175				

KM# 226 CROWN
Copper-Nickel, 38.5 mm. **Ruler:** Elizabeth II **Subject:** Australian Bicentennial **Obv:** Crowned bust right **Obv. Designer:** Raphael Maklouf **Rev:** Dingo and train within circle

Date	Mintage	F	VF	XF	Unc	BU
1988	—	—	—	—	12.50	15.00

KM# 226a CROWN
31.1000 g., 0.9999 Silver 1.0000 oz. ASW, 38.5 mm. **Ruler:** Elizabeth II **Subject:** Australian Bicentennial **Obv:** Crowned bust right **Obv. Designer:** Raphael Maklouf **Rev:** Dingo and train within circle

Date	Mintage	F	VF	XF	Unc	BU
1988 Proof	—	Value: 175				

KM# 227 CROWN
Copper-Nickel, 38.5 mm. **Ruler:** Elizabeth II **Subject:** Australian Bicentennial **Obv:** Crowned bust right **Obv. Designer:** Raphael Maklouf **Rev:** Tasmanian devil and map within circle

Date	Mintage	F	VF	XF	Unc	BU
1988	—	—	—	—	10.00	15.00

KM# 227a CROWN
31.1000 g., 0.9999 Silver 1.0000 oz. ASW, 38.5 mm. **Ruler:** Elizabeth II **Subject:** Australian Bicentennial **Obv:** Crowned bust right **Obv. Designer:** Raphael Maklouf **Rev:** Tasmanian devil and map within circle

Date	Mintage	F	VF	XF	Unc	BU
1988 Proof	—	Value: 175				

KM# 228 CROWN
Copper-Nickel, 38.5 mm. **Ruler:** Elizabeth II **Series:** Steam Navigation **Obv:** Crowned bust right **Obv. Designer:** Raphael Maklouf **Rev:** Patrick Miller's Number One

Date	Mintage	F	VF	XF	Unc	BU
1988	—	—	—	—	8.00	10.00

KM# 229 CROWN
Copper-Nickel, 38.5 mm. **Ruler:** Elizabeth II **Series:** Steam Navigation **Obv:** Crowned bust right **Obv. Designer:** Raphael Maklouf **Rev:** Ship within circle

Date	Mintage	F	VF	XF	Unc	BU
1988	—	—	—	—	8.00	10.00

KM# 230 CROWN
Copper-Nickel, 38.5 mm. **Ruler:** Elizabeth II **Series:** Steam Navigation **Obv:** Crowned bust right **Obv. Designer:** Raphael Maklouf **Rev:** Steamship within circle

Date	Mintage	F	VF	XF	Unc	BU
1988	—	—	—	—	8.00	10.00

KM# 231 CROWN
Copper-Nickel, 38.5 mm. **Ruler:** Elizabeth II **Series:** Steam Navigation **Obv:** Crowned bust right **Obv. Designer:** Raphael Maklouf **Rev:** Steamship within circle

Date	Mintage	F	VF	XF	Unc	BU
1988	—	—	—	—	8.00	10.00

KM# 232 CROWN
Copper-Nickel, 38.5 mm. **Ruler:** Elizabeth II **Series:** Steam Navigation **Obv:** Crowned bust right **Obv. Designer:** Raphael Maklouf **Rev:** Steamship within circle

Date	Mintage	F	VF	XF	Unc	BU
1988	—	—	—	—	8.00	10.00

KM# 233 CROWN
Copper-Nickel, 38.5 mm. **Ruler:** Elizabeth II **Series:** Steam Navigation **Obv:** Crowned bust right **Obv. Designer:** Raphael Maklouf **Rev:** Steamship divides circle

Date	Mintage	F	VF	XF	Unc	BU
1988	—	—	—	—	8.00	10.00

KM# 234 CROWN
31.1000 g., 0.9990 Silver 1.0000 oz. ASW, 38.5 mm. **Ruler:** Elizabeth II **Obv:** Crowned bust right **Obv. Designer:** Raphael Maklouf **Rev:** Manx cat

Date	Mintage	F	VF	XF	Unc	BU
1988 Proof	15,000	Value: 16.50				

KM# 239 CROWN
31.1000 g., 0.9990 Gold 1.0000 oz. AGW **Ruler:** Elizabeth II **Obv:** Crowned bust right **Obv. Designer:** Raphael Maklouf **Rev:** Manx cat

Date	Mintage	F	VF	XF	Unc	BU
1988 U	4,300	—	—	—	675	700
1988 Proof	5,000	Value: 725				

KM# 245 CROWN
Copper-Nickel, 38.5 mm. **Ruler:** Elizabeth II **Obv:** Crowned bust right **Obv. Designer:** Raphael Maklouf **Rev:** Manx cat

Date	Mintage	F	VF	XF	Unc	BU
1988	—	—	—	—	10.00	14.00
1988 Proof	250	Value: 25.00				

KM# 240 CROWN

Copper-Nickel, 38.5 mm. **Ruler:** Elizabeth II **Series:** Bicentenary of the Mutiny on the Bounty **Obv:** Crowned bust right **Obv. Designer:** Raphael Maklouf **Rev:** Standing figures facing within circle

Date	Mintage	F	VF	XF	Unc	BU
1989	—	—	—	—	3.25	4.50
1989 Prooflike	—	—	—	—	—	15.00

KM# 240a CROWN

28.2800 g., 0.9250 Silver .8411 oz. ASW, 38.5 mm. **Ruler:** Elizabeth II **Series:** Mutiny on the Bounty **Obv:** Crowned bust right **Obv. Designer:** Raphael Maklouf **Rev:** Standing figures facing within circle

Date	Mintage	F	VF	XF	Unc	BU
1989 Proof	—	Value: 45.00				

KM# 241 CROWN

Copper-Nickel, 38.5 mm. **Ruler:** Elizabeth II **Series:** Mutiny on the Bounty **Obv:** Crowned bust right **Obv. Designer:** Raphael Maklouf **Rev:** H.M.S. Bounty

Date	Mintage	F	VF	XF	Unc	BU
1989	—	—	—	—	7.50	9.00
1989 Prooflike	—	—	—	—	—	15.00

KM# 241a CROWN

28.2800 g., 0.9250 Silver .8411 oz. ASW, 38.5 mm. **Ruler:** Elizabeth II **Series:** Mutiny on the Bounty **Obv:** Crowned bust right **Obv. Designer:** Raphael Maklouf **Rev:** H.M.S. Bounty

Date	Mintage	F	VF	XF	Unc	BU
1989 Proof	—	Value: 45.00				

KM# 242 CROWN

Copper-Nickel, 38.5 mm. **Ruler:** Elizabeth II **Series:** Mutiny on the Bounty **Obv:** Crowned bust right **Obv. Designer:** Raphael Maklouf **Rev:** Captain Bligh and crew set afloat

Date	Mintage	F	VF	XF	Unc	BU
1989	—	—	—	—	7.50	9.00
1989 Prooflike	—	—	—	—	—	15.00

KM# 242a CROWN

28.2800 g., 0.9250 Silver .8411 oz. ASW, 38.5 mm. **Ruler:** Elizabeth II **Series:** Mutiny on the Bounty **Obv:** Crowned bust right **Obv. Designer:** Raphael Maklouf **Rev:** Captain Bligh and crew set afloat

Date	Mintage	F	VF	XF	Unc	BU
1989 Proof	—	Value: 45.00				

KM# 243 CROWN

Copper-Nickel, 38.5 mm. **Ruler:** Elizabeth II **Series:** Muntiny on the Bounty **Obv:** Crowned bust right **Obv. Designer:** Raphael Maklouf **Rev:** Pitcairn Island

Date	Mintage	F	VF	XF	Unc	BU
1989	—	—	—	—	7.50	9.00
1989 Prooflike	—	—	—	—	—	15.00

KM# 243a CROWN

28.2800 g., 0.9250 Silver .8411 oz. ASW, 38.5 mm. **Ruler:** Elizabeth II **Series:** Mutiny on the Bounty **Obv:** Crowned bust right **Obv. Designer:** Raphael Maklouf **Rev:** Pitcairn Island

Date	Mintage	F	VF	XF	Unc	BU
1989 Proof	—	Value: 45.00				

KM# 246 CROWN

Copper-Nickel, 38.5 mm. **Ruler:** Elizabeth II **Obv:** Crowned bust right **Obv. Designer:** Raphael Maklouf **Rev:** Washington crossing the Delaware

Date	Mintage	F	VF	XF	Unc	BU
1989	—	—	—	—	2.75	3.50
1989 Proof	—	Value: 9.00				

KM# 246a CROWN

28.2800 g., 0.9250 Silver .8411 oz. ASW, 38.5 mm. **Ruler:** Elizabeth II **Obv:** Crowned bust right **Obv. Designer:** Raphael Maklouf **Rev:** Washington crossing the Delaware

Date	Mintage	F	VF	XF	Unc	BU
1989 Proof	—	Value: 22.50				

KM# 247 CROWN

Copper-Nickel, 38.5 mm. **Ruler:** Elizabeth II **Subject:** George Washington Inauguration **Obv:** Crowned bust right **Obv. Designer:** Raphael Maklouf **Rev:** Head of George Washington **Edge:** Reeded

Date	Mintage	F	VF	XF	Unc	BU
1989	—	—	—	—	2.75	3.50
1989 Proof	—	Value: 9.00				

KM# 247a CROWN

28.2800 g., 0.9250 Silver .8411 oz. ASW, 38.5 mm. **Ruler:** Elizabeth II **Subject:** George Washington Inauguration **Obv:** Crowned bust right **Obv. Designer:** Raphael Maklouf **Rev:** Head of George Washington

Date	Mintage	F	VF	XF	Unc	BU
1989 Proof	—	Value: 22.50				

KM# 248 CROWN

Copper-Nickel, 38.5 mm. **Ruler:** Elizabeth II **Subject:** George Washington Inauguration **Obv:** Crowned bust right **Obv. Designer:** Raphael Maklouf **Rev:** Cameo within eagle **Edge:** Reeded

Date	Mintage	F	VF	XF	Unc	BU
1989	—	—	—	—	7.00	8.00
1989 Proof	—	Value: 9.00				

KM# 248a CROWN

28.2800 g., 0.9250 Silver .8411 oz. ASW, 38.5 mm. **Ruler:** Elizabeth II **Subject:** George Washington Inauguration **Obv:** Crowned bust right **Obv. Designer:** Raphael Maklouf **Rev:** Cameo within eagle

Date	Mintage	F	VF	XF	Unc	BU
1989 Proof	—	Value: 22.50				

KM# 249 CROWN

Copper-Nickel, 38.5 mm. **Ruler:** Elizabeth II **Subject:** George Washington Inauguration **Obv:** Crowned bust right **Obv. Designer:** Raphael Maklouf **Rev:** George Washington taking oath **Edge:** Reeded

Date	Mintage	F	VF	XF	Unc	BU
1989	—	—	—	—	5.00	6.00
1989 Proof	—	Value: 9.00				

KM# 249a CROWN

28.2800 g., 0.9250 Silver .8411 oz. ASW, 38.5 mm. **Ruler:** Elizabeth II **Subject:** George Washington Inauguration **Obv:** Crowned bust right **Obv. Designer:** Raphael Maklouf **Rev:** George Washington taking oath

Date	Mintage	F	VF	XF	Unc	BU
1989 Proof	—	Value: 22.50				

KM# 250 CROWN

Copper-Nickel, 38.5 mm. **Ruler:** Elizabeth II **Obv:** Crowned bust right **Obv. Designer:** Raphael Maklouf **Rev:** Persian cat **Edge:** Reeded

Date	Mintage	F	VF	XF	Unc	BU
1989	—	—	—	—	10.00	12.00
1989 Proof	250	Value: 35.00				

KM# 251 CROWN

31.1000 g., 0.9990 Silver 1.0000 oz. ASW, 38.5 mm. **Ruler:** Elizabeth II **Obv:** Crowned bust right **Obv. Designer:** Raphael Maklouf **Rev:** Persian cat

Date	Mintage	F	VF	XF	Unc	BU
1989 Proof	—	Value: 30.00				

KM# 256 CROWN

31.1000 g., 0.9990 Gold 1.0000 oz. AGW **Ruler:** Elizabeth II **Obv:** Crowned bust right **Obv. Designer:** Raphael Maklouf **Rev:** Persian cat

Date	Mintage	F	VF	XF	Unc	BU
1989	—	—	—	—	675	700
1989 Proof	—	Value: 725				

KM# 273 CROWN

Copper-Nickel, 38.5 mm. **Ruler:** Elizabeth II **Subject:** Royal Visit **Obv:** Crowned bust right **Obv. Designer:** Raphael Maklouf **Rev:** Three scenes from ship **Edge:** Reeded

Date	Mintage	F	VF	XF	Unc	BU
1989	Est. 50,000	—	—	—	8.00	9.00

KM# 273a CROWN

31.1000 g., 0.9990 Silver 1.0000 oz. ASW, 38.5 mm. **Ruler:** Elizabeth II **Subject:** Royal Visit **Obv:** Crowned bust right **Obv. Designer:** Raphael Maklouf **Rev:** Three scenes from ship

Date	Mintage	F	VF	XF	Unc	BU
1989 Proof	Est. 20,000	Value: 35.00				

KM# 273b CROWN

31.1000 g., 0.9990 Gold 1.0000 oz. AGW **Ruler:** Elizabeth II **Subject:** Royal Visit **Obv:** Crowned bust right **Obv. Designer:** Raphael Maklouf **Rev:** Three scenes from ship

Date	Mintage	F	VF	XF	Unc	BU
1989 Proof	Est. 7,500	Value: 750				

KM# 471 CROWN

31.1035 g., 0.9995 Platinum .9995 oz. APW **Ruler:** Elizabeth II **Obv:** Crowned bust right **Obv. Designer:** Raphael Maklouf **Rev:** Persian cat

Date	Mintage	F	VF	XF	Unc	BU
1989	—	—	—	—	BV+20%	—
1989 Proof	—	BV+25%				

KM# 307a CROWN

28.2800 g., 0.9250 Silver 0.841 oz. ASW, 38.6 mm. **Ruler:** Elizabeth II **Obv:** Crowned bust right **Obv. Designer:** Raphael Maklouf **Rev:** Adult and two children facing

Date	Mintage	F	VF	XF	Unc	BU
1990PM Proof	—	Value: 50.00				

KM# 307 CROWN

28.2800 g., Copper-Nickel, 38.6 mm. **Ruler:** Elizabeth II **Obv:** Crowned bust right **Obv. Designer:** Raphael Maklouf **Rev:** Adult and two children facing **Edge:** Reeded

Date	Mintage	F	VF	XF	Unc	BU
1990PM	—	—	—	—	10.00	12.00

KM# 267 CROWN

Copper-Nickel, 38.5 mm. **Ruler:** Elizabeth II **Subject:** 150th Anniversary of "Penny Black" Stamp **Obv:** Crowned bust right **Obv. Designer:** Raphael Maklouf **Rev:** Crowned head left within stamp **Note:** Struck in "pearl black" Copper-Nickel.

Date	Mintage	F	VF	XF	Unc	BU
1990	—	—	—	—	12.50	13.50
1990 Proof	50,000	Value: 16.50				

KM# 267a CROWN

28.2800 g., 0.9250 Silver .8411 oz. ASW, 38.5 mm. **Ruler:** Elizabeth II **Subject:** 150th Anniversary of "Penny Black" Stamp **Obv:** Crowned bust right **Obv. Designer:** Raphael Maklouf **Rev:** Crowned head left within stamp

Date	Mintage	F	VF	XF	Unc	BU
1990 Proof	30,000	Value: 30.00				

KM# 267b CROWN

31.1000 g., 0.9990 Gold 1.0000 oz. AGW **Ruler:** Elizabeth II **Subject:** 150th Anniversary of "Penny Black" Stamp **Obv:** Crowned bust right **Obv. Designer:** Raphael Maklouf **Rev:** Crowned head left within stamp

Date	Mintage	F	VF	XF	Unc	BU
1990 Proof	Est. 1,000	Value: 750				

KM# 267c CROWN

52.0000 g., 0.9500 Platinum 1.5884 oz. APW, 38.5 mm. **Ruler:** Elizabeth II **Subject:** 150th Anniversary of "Penny Black" Stamp **Obv:** Crowned bust right **Obv. Designer:** Raphael Maklouf **Rev:** Crowned head left within stamp

Date	Mintage	F	VF	XF	Unc	BU
1990 Proof	Est. 50	Value: 2,150				

KM# 269 CROWN

Copper-Nickel, 38.5 mm. **Ruler:** Elizabeth II **Series:** World Cup - Italy **Obv:** Crowned bust right **Obv. Designer:** Raphael Maklouf **Rev:** Soccer players and shield **Edge:** Reeded

Date	Mintage	F	VF	XF	Unc	BU
1990	—	—	—	—	3.25	4.50

KM# 269a CROWN

28.2800 g., 0.9250 Silver .8411 oz. ASW, 38.5 mm. **Ruler:** Elizabeth II **Series:** World Cup - Italy **Obv:** Crowned bust right **Obv. Designer:** Raphael Maklouf **Rev:** Soccer players and shield

Date	Mintage	F	VF	XF	Unc	BU
1990 Proof	Est. 30,000	Value: 20.00				

KM# 269b CROWN

6.2200 g., 0.9990 Gold .2000 oz. AGW **Ruler:** Elizabeth II **Series:** World Cup - Italy **Obv:** Crowned bust right **Obv. Designer:** Raphael Maklouf **Rev:** Soccer players and shield

Date	Mintage	F	VF	XF	Unc	BU
1990 Proof	Est. 500	Value: 200				

KM# 269c CROWN

6.2230 g., 0.9990 Platinum .2000 oz. APW **Ruler:** Elizabeth II **Series:** World Cup - Italy **Obv:** Crowned bust right **Obv. Designer:** Raphael Maklouf **Rev:** Soccer players and shield

Date	Mintage	F	VF	XF	Unc	BU
1990 Proof	Est. 100	Value: 275				

KM# 270 CROWN

Copper-Nickel, 38.5 mm. **Ruler:** Elizabeth II **Series:** World Cup - Italy **Obv:** Crowned bust right **Obv. Designer:** Raphael Maklouf **Rev:** Soccer player in center of three shields

Date	Mintage	F	VF	XF	Unc	BU
1990	—	—	—	—	6.00	7.00

KM# 270a CROWN

28.2800 g., 0.9250 Silver .8411 oz. ASW, 38.5 mm. **Ruler:** Elizabeth II **Series:** World Cup - Italy **Obv:** Crowned bust right **Obv. Designer:** Raphael Maklouf **Rev:** Soccer player in center of three shields

Date	Mintage	F	VF	XF	Unc	BU
1990 Proof	Est. 30,000	Value: 20.00				

KM# 270b CROWN

6.2200 g., 0.9990 Gold .2000 oz. AGW **Ruler:** Elizabeth II **Series:** World Cup - Italy **Obv:** Crowned bust right **Obv. Designer:** Raphael Maklouf **Rev:** Soccer player in center of three shields

Date	Mintage	F	VF	XF	Unc	BU
1990 Proof	Est. 500	Value: 175				

KM# 270c CROWN

6.2230 g., 0.9990 Platinum .2000 oz. APW **Ruler:** Elizabeth II **Series:** World Cup - Italy **Obv:** Crowned bust right **Obv. Designer:** Raphael Maklouf **Rev:** Soccer player in center of three shields

Date	Mintage	F	VF	XF	Unc	BU
1990 Proof	Est. 100	Value: 285				

KM# 271 CROWN

Copper-Nickel, 38.5 mm. **Ruler:** Elizabeth II **Series:** World Cup - Italy **Obv:** Crowned bust right **Obv. Designer:** Raphael Maklouf **Rev:** Three shields flanked by emblems with soccer ball below **Edge:** Reeded

Date	Mintage	F	VF	XF	Unc	BU
1990	—	—	—	—	6.00	7.00

KM# 271a CROWN

28.2800 g., 0.9250 Silver .8411 oz. ASW, 38.5 mm. **Ruler:** Elizabeth II **Series:** World Cup - Italy **Obv:** Crowned bust right **Obv. Designer:** Raphael Maklouf **Rev:** Three shields flanked by emblems with soccer ball below

Date	Mintage	F	VF	XF	Unc	BU
1990 Proof	Est. 30,000	Value: 30.00				

KM# 271b CROWN

6.2200 g., 0.9990 Gold .2000 oz. AGW **Ruler:** Elizabeth II **Series:** World Cup - Italy **Obv:** Crowned bust right **Obv. Designer:** Raphael Maklouf **Rev:** Three shields flanked by emblems with soccer ball below

Date	Mintage	F	VF	XF	Unc	BU
1990 Proof	Est. 500	Value: 200				

KM# 271c CROWN

6.2230 g., 0.9990 Platinum .2000 oz. APW **Ruler:** Elizabeth II **Series:** World Cup - Italy **Obv:** Crowned bust right **Obv. Designer:** Raphael Maklouf **Rev:** Three shields flanked by emblems with soccer ball below

Date	Mintage	F	VF	XF	Unc	BU
1990 Proof	Est. 100	Value: 285				

KM# 272 CROWN

Copper-Nickel, 38.5 mm. **Ruler:** Elizabeth II **Series:** World Cup - Italy **Obv:** Crowned bust right **Obv. Designer:** Raphael Maklouf **Rev:** Three shields flanked by soccer players **Edge:** Reeded

Date	Mintage	F	VF	XF	Unc	BU
1990	—	—	—	—	6.00	7.00

KM# 272a CROWN

28.2800 g., 0.9250 Silver .8411 oz. ASW, 38.5 mm. **Ruler:** Elizabeth II **Series:** World Cup - Italy **Obv:** Crowned bust right **Obv. Designer:** Raphael Maklouf **Rev:** Three shields flanked by soccer players

Date	Mintage	F	VF	XF	Unc	BU
1990 Proof	Est. 30,000	Value: 20.00				

KM# 272b CROWN

6.2200 g., 0.9990 Gold .2000 oz. AGW **Ruler:** Elizabeth II **Series:** World Cup - Italy **Obv:** Crowned bust right **Obv. Designer:** Raphael Maklouf **Rev:** Three shields flanked by soccer players

Date	Mintage	F	VF	XF	Unc	BU
1990 Proof	Est. 500	Value: 200				

KM# 272c CROWN

6.2230 g., 0.9990 Platinum .2000 oz. APW **Ruler:** Elizabeth II **Series:** World Cup - Italy **Obv:** Crowned bust right **Obv. Designer:** Raphael Maklouf **Rev:** Three shields flanked by soccer players

Date	Mintage	F	VF	XF	Unc	BU
1990 Proof	Est. 100	Value: 285				

KM# 275 CROWN

Copper-Nickel, 38.5 mm. **Ruler:** Elizabeth II **Obv:** Crowned bust right **Obv. Designer:** Raphael Maklouf **Rev:** Alley cat

Date	Mintage	F	VF	XF	Unc	BU
1990	—	—	—	—	10.00	15.00
1990 Proof	250	Value: 35.00				

KM# 276 CROWN

31.1000 g., 0.9990 Silver 1.000 oz. ASW, 38.5 mm. **Ruler:** Elizabeth II **Obv:** Crowned bust right **Obv. Designer:** Raphael Maklouf **Rev:** Alley cat

Date	Mintage	F	VF	XF	Unc	BU
1990 Proof	—	Value: 30.00				

KM# 281 CROWN

31.1000 g., 0.9990 Gold 1.000 oz. AGW **Ruler:** Elizabeth II **Obv:** Crowned bust right **Obv. Designer:** Raphael Maklouf **Rev:** Alley cat

Date	Mintage	F	VF	XF	Unc	BU
1990	—	—	—	—	675	700
1990 Proof	—	Value: 725				

KM# 283 CROWN

Copper-Nickel, 38.5 mm. **Ruler:** Elizabeth II **Obv:** Crowned bust right **Obv. Designer:** Raphael Maklouf **Rev:** Bust right with hat and cigar **Edge:** Reeded

Date	Mintage	F	VF	XF	Unc	BU
1990	—	—	—	—	3.25	4.50

KM# 283a CROWN

28.2800 g., 0.9250 Silver .8411 oz. ASW, 38.5 mm. **Ruler:** Elizabeth II **Obv:** Crowned bust right **Obv. Designer:** Raphael Maklouf **Rev:** Bust right with hat and cigar

Date	Mintage	F	VF	XF	Unc	BU
1990 Proof	Est. 25,000	Value: 50.00				

KM# 283b CROWN

6.2230 g., 0.9990 Gold .2000 oz. AGW **Ruler:** Elizabeth II **Obv:** Crowned bust right **Obv. Designer:** Raphael Maklouf **Rev:** Bust right with hat and cigar

Date	Mintage	F	VF	XF	Unc	BU
1990 Proof	Est. 500	Value: 200				

KM# 283c CROWN

6.2230 g., 0.9990 Platinum .2000 oz. APW **Ruler:** Elizabeth II **Obv:** Crowned bust right **Obv. Designer:** Raphael Maklouf **Rev:** Bust right with hat and cigar

Date	Mintage	F	VF	XF	Unc	BU
1990 Proof	Est. 100	Value: 285				

KM# 284 CROWN

Copper-Nickel, 38.5 mm. **Ruler:** Elizabeth II **Obv:** Crowned bust right **Obv. Designer:** Raphael Maklouf **Rev:** Bust left **Edge:** Reeded

Date	Mintage	F	VF	XF	Unc	BU
1990	—	—	—	—	3.25	4.50

KM# 284a CROWN

28.2800 g., 0.9250 Silver .8411 oz. ASW, 38.5 mm. **Ruler:** Elizabeth II **Obv:** Crowned bust right **Obv. Designer:** Raphael Maklouf **Rev:** Bust left

Date	Mintage	F	VF	XF	Unc	BU
1990 Proof	Est. 25,000	Value: 50.00				

KM# 284b CROWN

6.2230 g., 0.9990 Gold .2000 oz. AGW **Ruler:** Elizabeth II **Obv:** Crowned bust right **Obv. Designer:** Raphael Maklouf **Rev:** Bust left

Date	Mintage	F	VF	XF	Unc	BU
1990 Proof	Est. 500	Value: 200				

KM# 284c CROWN

6.2230 g., 0.9990 Platinum .2000 oz. APW **Ruler:** Elizabeth II **Obv:** Crowned bust right **Obv. Designer:** Raphael Maklouf **Rev:** Bust left

Date	Mintage	F	VF	XF	Unc	BU
1990 Proof	Est. 100	Value: 285				

KM# 320a CROWN

28.2800 g., 0.9250 Silver .8411 oz. ASW, 38.6 mm. **Ruler:** Elizabeth II **Subject:** America's Cup - San Diego **Obv:** Crowned bust right **Obv. Designer:** Raphael Maklouf **Rev:** Cameo of sailboats **Rev. Legend:** AMERICA'S CUP CHALLENGE

Date	Mintage	F	VF	XF	Unc	BU
1991 Proof	15	Value: 485				

KM# 320 CROWN

28.2800 g., Copper-Nickel, 38.6 mm. **Ruler:** Elizabeth II **Subject:** America's Cup **Obv:** Crowned bust right **Obv. Designer:** Raphael Maklouf **Rev:** Cameo of sailboats with no roman numerals in legend **Edge:** Reeded **Note:** Officially "sales samples" about 25 pieces were sold or presented to distributors

Date	Mintage	F	VF	XF	Unc	BU
1991PM	100	—	—	—	35.00	40.00

KM# 291 CROWN

Copper-Nickel, 38.5 mm. **Ruler:** Elizabeth II **Subject:** 100th Anniversary - American Numismatic Association **Obv:** Crowned bust right **Obv. Designer:** Raphael Maklouf **Rev:** Cat within circle of assorted coins **Edge:** Reeded

Date	Mintage	F	VF	XF	Unc	BU
1991	—	—	—	—	4.50	6.50

KM# 291a CROWN

28.2800 g., 0.9250 Silver .8411 oz. ASW, 38.5 mm. **Ruler:** Elizabeth II **Subject:** 100th Anniversary - American Numismatic Association **Obv:** Crowned bust right **Obv. Designer:** Raphael Maklouf **Rev:** Cat within circle of assorted coins

Date	Mintage	F	VF	XF	Unc	BU
1991 Proof	—	Value: 22.00				

KM# 292 CROWN

Copper-Nickel, 38.5 mm. **Ruler:** Elizabeth II **Obv:** Crowned bust right **Obv. Designer:** Raphael Maklouf **Rev:** Norwegian cat **Edge:** Reeded

Date	Mintage	F	VF	XF	Unc	BU
1991	—	—	—	—	10.00	15.00
1991 Proof	25	—	—	—	—	—

KM# 293 CROWN

31.1000 g., 0.9990 Silver 1.0000 oz. ASW, 38.5 mm. **Ruler:** Elizabeth II **Obv:** Crowned bust right **Obv. Designer:** Raphael Maklouf **Rev:** Norwegian cat

Date	Mintage	F	VF	XF	Unc	BU
1991 Proof	50,000	Value: 30.00				

KM# 298 CROWN

31.1000 g., 0.9990 Gold 1.0000 oz. AGW **Ruler:** Elizabeth II **Obv:** Crowned bust right **Obv. Designer:** Raphael Maklouf **Rev:** Norwegian cat

Date	Mintage	F	VF	XF	Unc	BU
1991	—	—	—	—	675	700
1991 Proof	—	Value: 725				

KM# 304 CROWN

Copper-Nickel, 38.5 mm. **Ruler:** Elizabeth II **Subject:** 10th Wedding Anniversary **Obv:** Crowned bust right **Obv. Designer:** Raphael Maklouf **Rev:** Head of Prince Charles

Date	Mintage	F	VF	XF	Unc	BU
1991	—	—	—	—	4.00	6.00

KM# 304a CROWN

28.2800 g., 0.9250 Silver .8411 oz. ASW, 38.5 mm. **Ruler:** Elizabeth II **Subject:** 10th Wedding Anniversary **Obv:** Crowned bust right **Obv. Designer:** Raphael Maklouf **Rev:** Head of Prince Charles

Date	Mintage	F	VF	XF	Unc	BU
1991 Proof	—	Value: 40.00				

KM# 304b CROWN

6.2200 g., 0.9990 Gold .2000 oz. AGW **Ruler:** Elizabeth II **Subject:** 10th Wedding Anniversary **Obv:** Crowned bust right **Obv. Designer:** Raphael Maklouf **Rev:** Head of Prince Charles

Date	Mintage	F	VF	XF	Unc	BU
1991 Proof	—	Value: 165				

KM# 305 CROWN

Copper-Nickel, 38.5 mm. **Ruler:** Elizabeth II **Subject:** 10th Wedding Anniversary **Obv:** Crowned bust right **Obv. Designer:** Raphael Maklouf **Rev:** Head of Princess Diana

Date	Mintage	F	VF	XF	Unc	BU
1991	—	—	—	—	4.00	6.00

KM# 305a CROWN

28.2800 g., 0.9250 Silver .8411 oz. ASW, 38.5 mm. **Ruler:** Elizabeth II **Subject:** 10th Wedding Anniversary **Obv:** Crowned bust right **Obv. Designer:** Raphael Maklouf **Rev:** Head of Princess Diana

Date	Mintage	F	VF	XF	Unc	BU
1991 Proof	—	Value: 40.00				

KM# 305b CROWN

6.2200 g., 0.9990 Gold .2000 oz. AGW **Ruler:** Elizabeth II **Subject:** 10th Wedding Anniversary **Obv:** Crowned bust right **Obv. Designer:** Raphael Maklouf **Rev:** Head of Princess Diana

Date	Mintage	F	VF	XF	Unc	BU
1991 Proof	—	Value: 165				

KM# 326a CROWN

28.2800 g., 0.9250 Silver .8411 oz. ASW, 38.5 mm. **Ruler:** Elizabeth II **Subject:** America's Cup - San Diego **Obv:** Crowned bust right **Obv. Designer:** Raphael Maklouf **Rev:** Cameo above sailboats

Date	Mintage	F	VF	XF	Unc	BU
1992 Proof	25,000	—	—	—	60.00	65.00

KM# 310 CROWN

Copper-Nickel, 38.5 mm. **Ruler:** Elizabeth II **Series:** Discovery of America **Obv:** Crowned bust right **Obv. Designer:** Raphael Maklouf **Rev:** Head with hat facing and train engine within circle

Date	Mintage	F	VF	XF	Unc	BU
1992	—	—	—	—	3.75	4.50
1992 Proof	—	Value: 12.00				

KM# 311 CROWN

Copper-Nickel, 38.5 mm. **Ruler:** Elizabeth II **Series:** Discovery of America **Obv:** Crowned bust right **Obv. Designer:** Raphael Maklouf **Rev:** Head facing and train engine within circle

Date	Mintage	F	VF	XF	Unc	BU
1992	—	—	—	—	3.75	4.50
1992 Proof	—	Value: 12.00				

KM# 310a CROWN

28.2800 g., 0.9250 Silver .8411 oz. ASW, 38.5 mm. **Ruler:** Elizabeth II **Series:** Discovery of America **Obv:** Crowned bust right **Obv. Designer:** Raphael Maklouf **Rev:** Head with hat facing and train engine within circle

Date	Mintage	F	VF	XF	Unc	BU
1992 Proof	—	Value: 45.00				

KM# 311a CROWN

28.2800 g., 0.9250 Silver .8411 oz. ASW, 38.5 mm. **Ruler:** Elizabeth II **Series:** Discovery of America **Obv:** Crowned bust right **Obv. Designer:** Raphael Maklouf **Rev:** Head facing and train engine within circle

Date	Mintage	F	VF	XF	Unc	BU
1992 Proof	—	Value: 45.00				

KM# 312 CROWN

Copper-Nickel, 38.5 mm. **Ruler:** Elizabeth II **Series:** Discovery of America **Obv:** Crowned bust right **Obv. Designer:** Raphael Maklouf **Rev:** Group of standing figures within circle

Date	Mintage	F	VF	XF	Unc	BU
1992 Proof	—	Value: 10.00				
1992	—	—	—	—	3.75	4.50

KM# 312a CROWN

28.2800 g., 0.9250 Silver .8411 oz. ASW, 38.5 mm. **Ruler:** Elizabeth II **Series:** Discovery of America **Obv:** Crowned bust right **Obv. Designer:** Raphael Maklouf **Rev:** Group of standing figures within circle

Date	Mintage	F	VF	XF	Unc	BU
1992 Proof	—	Value: 45.00				

KM# 326 CROWN
Copper-Nickel, 38.5 mm. **Ruler:** Elizabeth II **Subject:** America's Cup - San Diego **Obv:** Crowned bust right **Obv. Designer:** Raphael Maklouf **Rev:** Cameo above sailboats **Rev. Legend:** AMERICA'S CUP • SAN DIEGO • 1992

Date	Mintage	F	VF	XF	Unc	BU
1992	—	—	—	—	4.75	6.00
1992 Proof	—	Value: 12.50				

KM# 313 CROWN
Copper-Nickel, 38.5 mm. **Ruler:** Elizabeth II **Series:** Discovery of America **Obv:** Crowned bust right **Obv. Designer:** Raphael Maklouf **Rev:** Triskeles on shield above crossed flags within circle

Date	Mintage	F	VF	XF	Unc	BU
1992	—	—	—	—	8.00	9.00
1992 Proof	—	Value: 10.00				

KM# 313a CROWN
28.2800 g., 0.9250 Silver .8411 oz. ASW, 38.5 mm. **Ruler:** Elizabeth II **Series:** Discovery of America **Obv:** Bust of Queen Elizabeth II right **Obv. Designer:** Raphael Maklouf **Rev:** Triskeles on shield above crossed flags within circle

Date	Mintage	F	VF	XF	Unc	BU
1992 Proof	—	Value: 25.00				

KM# 334 CROWN
31.1000 g., 0.9990 Gold 1.0000 oz. AGW **Ruler:** Elizabeth II **Obv:** Crowned bust right **Obv. Designer:** Raphael Maklouf **Rev:** Seated Siamese cat

Date	Mintage	F	VF	XF	Unc	BU
1992 Proof	—	Value: 725				
1992	—	—	—	—	675	700

KM# 326b CROWN
31.0300 g., 0.9990 Gold 1.0000 oz. AGW **Ruler:** Elizabeth II **Subject:** America's Cup - San Diego **Obv:** Crowned bust right **Obv. Designer:** Raphael Maklouf **Rev:** Cameo above sailboats

Date	Mintage	F	VF	XF	Unc	BU
1992 Proof	—*	—	—	—	800	850

KM# 332 CROWN
Copper-Nickel, 38.5 mm. **Ruler:** Elizabeth II **Obv:** Crowned bust right **Obv. Designer:** Raphael Maklouf **Rev:** Seated Siamese cat

Date	Mintage	F	VF	XF	Unc	BU
1992	—	—	—	—	10.00	15.00

KM# 333 CROWN
31.1000 g., 0.9990 Silver 1.0000 oz. ASW, 38.5 mm. **Ruler:** Elizabeth II **Obv:** Crowned bust right **Obv. Designer:** Raphael Maklouf **Rev:** Seated Siamese cat

Date	Mintage	F	VF	XF	Unc	BU
1992 Proof	50,000	Value: 30.00				

KM# 342 CROWN
31.1000 g., 0.9990 Gold 1.0000 oz. AGW **Ruler:** Elizabeth II **Subject:** Year of the Cockerel **Obv:** Crowned bust right **Obv. Designer:** Raphael Maklouf **Rev:** Cockerel within circle **Rev. Designer:** Barry Stanton

Date	Mintage	F	VF	XF	Unc	BU
1993 Proof	Est. 2,500	Value: 750				

KM# 353 CROWN
Copper-Nickel, 38.5 mm. **Ruler:** Elizabeth II **Obv:** Crowned bust right **Obv. Designer:** Raphael Maklouf **Rev:** Maine coon cat

Date	Mintage	F	VF	XF	Unc	BU
1993	—	—	—	—	10.00	15.00

KM# 354 CROWN
31.1000 g., 0.9990 Silver 1.0000 oz. ASW, 38.5 mm. **Ruler:** Elizabeth II **Obv:** Crowned bust right **Obv. Designer:** Raphael Maklouf **Rev:** Maine coon cat

Date	Mintage	F	VF	XF	Unc	BU
1993 Proof	50,000	Value: 30.00				

KM# 355 CROWN
31.1000 g., 0.9990 Gold 1.0000 oz. AGW **Ruler:** Elizabeth II **Obv:** Crowned bust right **Obv. Designer:** Raphael Maklouf **Rev:** Maine coon cat

Date	Mintage	F	VF	XF	Unc	BU
1993	—	—	—	—	675	700
1993 Proof	—	Value: 725				

KM# 357 CROWN
Copper-Nickel, 38.5 mm. **Ruler:** Elizabeth II **Series:** Preserve Planet Earth **Obv:** Crowned bust right **Obv. Designer:** Raphael Maklouf **Rev:** Dinosaur

Date	Mintage	F	VF	XF	Unc	BU
1993	—	—	—	—	10.00	12.00

KM# 358 CROWN
Copper-Nickel, 38.5 mm. **Ruler:** Elizabeth II **Series:** Preserve Planet Earth **Obv:** Crowned bust right **Obv. Designer:** Raphael Maklouf **Rev:** Diplodocus

Date	Mintage	F	VF	XF	Unc	BU
1993	—	—	—	—	9.00	12.00

KM# 364 CROWN
Copper-Nickel, 38.5 mm. **Ruler:** Elizabeth II **Series:** World Cup Soccer - U.S.A. **Obv:** Crowned bust right **Obv. Designer:** Raphael Maklouf **Rev:** Two players

Date	Mintage	F	VF	XF	Unc	BU
1994	—	—	—	—	6.00	7.00

KM# 364a CROWN
28.2800 g., 0.9250 Silver .8411 oz. ASW, 38.5 mm. **Ruler:** Elizabeth II **Series:** World Cup Soccer - U.S.A. **Obv:** Crowned bust right **Obv. Designer:** Raphael Maklouf **Rev:** Two players

Date	Mintage	F	VF	XF	Unc	BU
1994 Proof	Est. 30,000	Value: 35.00				

KM# 366 CROWN
Copper-Nickel, 38.5 mm. **Ruler:** Elizabeth II **Series:** World Cup Soccer - U.S.A. **Obv:** Crowned bust right **Obv. Designer:** Raphael Maklouf **Rev:** Three players

Date	Mintage	F	VF	XF	Unc	BU
1994	—	—	—	—	6.00	7.00

KM# 366a CROWN
28.2800 g., 0.9250 Silver .8411 oz. ASW, 38.5 mm. **Ruler:** Elizabeth II **Series:** World Cup Soccer - U.S.A. **Obv:** Crowned bust right **Obv. Designer:** Raphael Maklouf **Rev:** Three players

Date	Mintage	F	VF	XF	Unc	BU
1994 Proof	Est. 30,000	Value: 35.00				

KM# 368 CROWN
Copper-Nickel, 38.5 mm. **Ruler:** Elizabeth II **Series:** World Cup Soccer - U.S.A. **Obv:** Crowned bust right **Obv. Designer:** Raphael Maklouf **Rev:** Soccer players

Date	Mintage	F	VF	XF	Unc	BU
1994	—	—	—	—	6.00	7.00

KM# 368a CROWN
28.2800 g., 0.9250 Silver .8411 oz. ASW, 38.5 mm. **Ruler:** Elizabeth II **Series:** World Cup Soccer - U.S.A. **Obv:** Crowned bust right **Obv. Designer:** Raphael Maklouf **Rev:** Soccer players

Date	Mintage	F	VF	XF	Unc	BU
1994 Proof	Est. 30,000	Value: 35.00				

KM# 370 CROWN
Copper-Nickel, 38.5 mm. **Ruler:** Elizabeth II **Series:** World Cup Soccer - U.S.A. **Obv:** Crowned bust right **Obv. Designer:** Raphael Maklouf **Rev:** Soccer players

Date	Mintage	F	VF	XF	Unc	BU
1994	—	—	—	—	6.00	7.00

KM# 370a CROWN
28.2800 g., 0.9250 Silver .8411 oz. ASW, 38.5 mm. **Ruler:** Elizabeth II **Series:** World Cup Soccer - U.S.A. **Obv:** Crowned bust right **Obv. Designer:** Raphael Maklouf **Rev:** Soccer players

Date	Mintage	F	VF	XF	Unc	BU
1994 Proof	Est. 30,000	Value: 35.00				

KM# 372 CROWN
Copper-Nickel, 38.5 mm. **Ruler:** Elizabeth II **Series:** World Cup Soccer - U.S.A. **Obv:** Crowned bust right **Obv. Designer:** Raphael Maklouf **Rev:** Soccer players

Date	Mintage	F	VF	XF	Unc	BU
1994	—	—	—	—	8.00	9.00

KM# 372a CROWN
28.2800 g., 0.9250 Silver .8411 oz. ASW, 38.5 mm. **Ruler:** Elizabeth II **Series:** World Cup Soccer - U.S.A. **Obv:** Crowned bust right **Obv. Designer:** Raphael Maklouf **Rev:** Soccer players

Date	Mintage	F	VF	XF	Unc	BU
1994 Proof	Est. 30,000	Value: 35.00				

KM# 374 CROWN
Copper-Nickel, 38.5 mm. **Ruler:** Elizabeth II **Series:** World Cup Soccer - U.S.A. **Obv:** Crowned bust right **Obv. Designer:** Raphael Maklouf **Rev:** Soccer players

Date	Mintage	F	VF	XF	Unc	BU
1994	—	—	—	—	6.00	7.00

KM# 374a CROWN
28.2800 g., 0.9250 Silver .8411 oz. ASW, 38.5 mm. **Ruler:** Elizabeth II **Series:** World Cup Soccer - U.S.A. **Obv:** Crowned bust right **Obv. Designer:** Raphael Maklouf **Rev:** Soccer players

Date	Mintage	F	VF	XF	Unc	BU
1994 Proof	Est. 30,000	Value: 35.00				

KM# 380 CROWN
Copper-Nickel, 38.5 mm. **Ruler:** Elizabeth II **Obv:** Crowned bust right **Obv. Designer:** Raphael Maklouf **Rev:** Japanese bobtail cat

Date	Mintage	F	VF	XF	Unc	BU
1994	—	—	—	—	11.00	15.00

KM# 381 CROWN
31.1000 g., 0.9990 Silver 1.0000 oz. ASW, 38.5 mm. **Ruler:** Elizabeth II **Obv:** Crowned bust right **Obv. Designer:** Raphael Maklouf **Rev:** Japanese bobtail cat

Date	Mintage	F	VF	XF	Unc	BU
1994 Proof	—	Value: 35.00				

KM# 382 CROWN
31.1000 g., 0.9990 Gold 1.0000 oz. AGW **Ruler:** Elizabeth II **Obv:** Crowned bust right **Obv. Designer:** Raphael Maklouf **Rev:** Japanese bobtail cat

Date	Mintage	F	VF	XF	Unc	BU
1994	—	—	—	—	675	700
1994 Proof	—	Value: 725				

KM# 384 CROWN
Copper-Nickel, 38.5 mm. **Ruler:** Elizabeth II **Series:** Preserve Planet Earth **Obv:** Crowned bust right **Obv. Designer:** Raphael Maklouf **Rev:** Woolly mammoth

Date	Mintage	F	VF	XF	Unc	BU
1994	—	—	—	—	10.00	15.00

KM# 384a CROWN

28.2800 g., 0.9250 Silver .8411 oz. ASW, 38.5 mm. **Ruler:** Elizabeth II **Series:** Preserve Planet Earth **Obv:** Crowned bust right **Obv. Designer:** Raphael Maklouf **Rev:** Woolly mammoth

Date	Mintage	F	VF	XF	Unc	BU
1994 Proof	Est. 30,000	Value: 35.00				

KM# 385 CROWN

Copper-Nickel, 38.5 mm. **Ruler:** Elizabeth II **Series:** Preserve Planet Earth **Obv:** Crowned bust right **Obv. Designer:** Raphael Maklouf **Rev:** Kangaroos

Date	Mintage	F	VF	XF	Unc	BU
1994	—	—	—	—	9.00	12.00

KM# 385a CROWN

28.2800 g., 0.9250 Silver .8411 oz. ASW, 38.5 mm. **Ruler:** Elizabeth II **Series:** Preserve Planet Earth **Obv:** Crowned bust right **Obv. Designer:** Raphael Maklouf **Rev:** Kangaroos

Date	Mintage	F	VF	XF	Unc	BU
1994 Proof	Est. 30,000	Value: 35.00				

KM# 386 CROWN

Copper-Nickel, 38.5 mm. **Ruler:** Elizabeth II **Series:** Preserve Planet Earth **Obv:** Crowned bust right **Obv. Designer:** Raphael Maklouf **Rev:** Seals

Date	Mintage	F	VF	XF	Unc	BU
1994	—	—	—	—	9.00	12.00

KM# 386a CROWN

28.2800 g., 0.9250 Silver .8411 oz. ASW, 38.5 mm. **Ruler:** Elizabeth II **Series:** Preserve Planet Earth **Obv:** Crowned bust right **Obv. Designer:** Raphael Maklouf **Rev:** Seals

Date	Mintage	F	VF	XF	Unc	BU
1994 Proof	Est. 30,000	Value: 35.00				

KM# 387 CROWN

Copper-Nickel, 38.5 mm. **Ruler:** Elizabeth II **Series:** Preserve Planet Earth **Obv:** Crowned bust right **Obv. Designer:** Raphael Maklouf **Rev:** Deer

Date	Mintage	F	VF	XF	Unc	BU
1994	—	—	—	—	9.00	12.00

KM# 387a CROWN

28.2800 g., 0.9250 Silver .8411 oz. ASW, 38.5 mm. **Ruler:** Elizabeth II **Series:** Preserve Planet Earth **Obv:** Crowned bust right **Obv. Designer:** Raphael Maklouf **Rev:** Deer

Date	Mintage	F	VF	XF	Unc	BU
1994 Proof	Est. 30,000	Value: 35.00				

KM# 406 CROWN

Copper-Nickel, 38.5 mm. **Ruler:** Elizabeth II **Subject:** Year of the Dog **Obv:** Crowned bust right **Obv. Designer:** Raphael Maklouf **Rev:** Pekingese within circle

Date	Mintage	F	VF	XF	Unc	BU
1994	—	—	—	—	10.00	15.00

KM# 407 CROWN

31.1000 g., 0.9990 Silver 1.000 oz. ASW, 38.5 mm. **Ruler:** Elizabeth II **Subject:** Year of the Dog **Obv:** Crowned bust right **Obv. Designer:** Raphael Maklouf **Rev:** Pekingese within circle

Date	Mintage	F	VF	XF	Unc	BU
1994 Proof	—	Value: 40.00				

KM# 408 CROWN

31.1000 g., 0.9990 Gold 1.000 oz. AGW **Ruler:** Elizabeth II **Subject:** Year of the Dog **Obv:** Crowned bust right **Obv. Designer:** Raphael Maklouf **Rev:** Pekingese within circle

Date	Mintage	F	VF	XF	Unc	BU
1994 Proof	Est. 5,000	Value: 725				

KM# 417 CROWN

Copper-Nickel, 38.5 mm. **Ruler:** Elizabeth II **Series:** Man in Flight **Obv:** Crowned bust right **Obv. Designer:** Raphael Maklouf **Rev:** Otto Lilienthal

Date	Mintage	F	VF	XF	Unc	BU
1994	—	—	—	—	7.00	8.00

KM# 417a CROWN

28.2800 g., 0.9250 Silver .8411 oz. ASW, 38.5 mm. **Ruler:** Elizabeth II **Series:** Man in Flight **Obv:** Crowned bust right **Obv. Designer:** Raphael Maklouf **Rev:** Otto Lilienthal

Date	Mintage	F	VF	XF	Unc	BU
1994 Proof	Est. 30,000	Value: 40.00				

KM# 418 CROWN

Copper-Nickel, 38.5 mm. **Ruler:** Elizabeth II **Series:** Man in Flight **Obv:** Crowned bust right **Obv. Designer:** Raphael Maklouf **Rev:** Ferdinand von Zeppelin

Date	Mintage	F	VF	XF	Unc	BU
1994	—	—	—	—	11.00	13.50

KM# 419 CROWN

Copper-Nickel, 38.5 mm. **Ruler:** Elizabeth II **Series:** Man in Flight **Obv:** Crowned bust right **Obv. Designer:** Raphael Maklouf **Rev:** Louis Bleriot

Date	Mintage	F	VF	XF	Unc	BU
1994	—	—	—	—	8.00	9.00

KM# 419a CROWN

28.2800 g., 0.9250 Silver .8411 oz. ASW, 38.5 mm. **Ruler:** Elizabeth II **Series:** Man in Flight **Subject:** First Channel Crossing - 1909 **Obv:** Crowned bust right **Obv. Designer:** Raphael Maklouf **Rev:** Louis Bleriot

Date	Mintage	F	VF	XF	Unc	BU
1994 Proof	Est. 30,000	Value: 40.00				

KM# 420 CROWN

Copper-Nickel, 38.5 mm. **Ruler:** Elizabeth II **Series:** Man in Flight **Subject:** First Atlantic Crossing - 1919 **Obv:** Crowned bust right **Obv. Designer:** Raphael Maklouf **Rev:** Alcock and Brown

Date	Mintage	F	VF	XF	Unc	BU
1994	—	—	—	—	10.00	12.00

KM# 420a CROWN

28.2800 g., 0.9250 Silver .8411 oz. ASW, 38.5 mm. **Ruler:** Elizabeth II **Series:** Man in Flight **Subject:** First Atlantic Crossing - 1919 **Obv:** Crowned bust right **Obv. Designer:** Raphael Maklouf **Rev:** Alcock and Brown

Date	Mintage	F	VF	XF	Unc	BU
1994 Proof	Est. 30,000	Value: 40.00				

KM# 421 CROWN

Copper-Nickel, 38.5 mm. **Ruler:** Elizabeth II **Series:** Man in Flight **Subject:** First England to Australia flight **Obv:** Crowned bust right **Obv. Designer:** Raphael Maklouf **Rev:** Biplane

Date	Mintage	F	VF	XF	Unc	BU
1994	—	—	—	—	8.00	9.50

KM# 421a CROWN

28.2800 g., 0.9250 Silver .8411 oz. ASW, 38.5 mm. **Ruler:** Elizabeth II **Series:** Man in Flight **Subject:** First England to Australia flight **Obv:** Crowned bust right **Obv. Designer:** Raphael Maklouf **Rev:** Biplane

Date	Mintage	F	VF	XF	Unc	BU
1994 Proof	Est. 30,000	Value: 40.00				

KM# 422 CROWN

Copper-Nickel, 38.5 mm. **Ruler:** Elizabeth II **Series:** Man in Flight **Subject:** 60th Anniversary of Airmail **Obv:** Crowned bust right **Obv. Designer:** Raphael Maklouf **Rev:** Airplane

Date	Mintage	F	VF	XF	Unc	BU
1994	—	—	—	—	8.00	9.50

KM# 422a CROWN

28.2800 g., 0.9250 Silver .8411 oz. ASW, 38.5 mm. **Ruler:** Elizabeth II **Series:** Man in Flight **Subject:** 60th Anniversary of Airmail **Obv:** Crowned bust right **Obv. Designer:** Raphael Maklouf **Rev:** Airplane

Date	Mintage	F	VF	XF	Unc	BU
1994 Proof	Est. 30,000	Value: 40.00				

KM# 423 CROWN

Copper-Nickel, 38.5 mm. **Ruler:** Elizabeth II **Series:** Man in Flight **Subject:** 50th Anniversary of International Civil Aviation Organization **Obv:** Crowned bust right **Obv. Designer:** Raphael Maklouf **Rev:** Emblem

Date	Mintage	F	VF	XF	Unc	BU
1994	—	—	—	—	8.00	9.50

KM# 423a CROWN

28.2800 g., 0.9250 Silver .8411 oz. ASW, 38.5 mm. **Ruler:** Elizabeth II **Series:** Man in Flight **Subject:** 50th Anniversary of International Civil Aviation Organization **Obv:** Crowned bust right **Obv. Designer:** Raphael Maklouf **Rev:** Emblem

Date	Mintage	F	VF	XF	Unc	BU
1994 Proof	Est. 30,000	Value: 40.00				

KM# 424 CROWN

Copper-Nickel, 38.5 mm. **Ruler:** Elizabeth II **Series:** Man in Flight **Subject:** 25th Anniversary of First Concorde Flight **Obv:** Crowned bust right **Obv. Designer:** Raphael Maklouf **Rev:** Concorde

Date	Mintage	F	VF	XF	Unc	BU
1994	—	—	—	—	8.00	9.50

KM# 424a CROWN

28.2800 g., 0.9250 Silver .8411 oz. ASW, 38.5 mm. **Ruler:** Elizabeth II **Series:** Man in Flight **Subject:** 25th Anniversary of First Concorde Flight **Obv:** Crowned bust right **Obv. Designer:** Raphael Maklouf **Rev:** Concorde

Date	Mintage	F	VF	XF	Unc	BU
1994 Proof	Est. 30,000	Value: 40.00				

KM# 477 CROWN

31.1035 g., 0.9995 Platinum .9995 oz. APW **Ruler:** Elizabeth II **Obv:** Crowned bust right **Obv. Designer:** Raphael Maklouf **Rev:** Japanese bobtail cat

Date	Mintage	F	VF	XF	Unc	BU
1994	—	—	—	—	BV+20%	—
1994 Proof	—	BV_25%				

KM# 695 CROWN

Copper-Nickel, 38.5 mm. **Ruler:** Elizabeth II **Series:** Normandy Invasion **Obv:** Crowned bust right **Obv. Designer:** Raphael Maklouf **Rev:** Troop ship and landing craft

Date	Mintage	F	VF	XF	Unc	BU
1994	—	—	—	—	6.50	7.50

KM# 695a CROWN

28.2800 g., 0.9250 Silver .8411 oz. ASW, 38.5 mm. **Ruler:** Elizabeth II **Series:** Normandy Invasion **Obv:** Crowned bust right **Obv. Designer:** Raphael Maklouf **Rev:** Troop ship and landing craft

Date	Mintage	F	VF	XF	Unc	BU
1994 Proof	Est. 30,000	Value: 26.50				

KM# 696 CROWN

Copper-Nickel, 38.5 mm. **Ruler:** Elizabeth II **Series:** Normandy Invasion **Obv:** Crowned bust right **Obv. Designer:** Raphael Maklouf **Rev:** American troops landing

Date	Mintage	F	VF	XF	Unc	BU
1994	—	—	—	—	6.50	7.50

KM# 696a CROWN

28.2800 g., 0.9250 Silver .8411 oz. ASW, 38.5 mm. **Ruler:** Elizabeth II **Series:** Normandy Invasion **Obv:** Crowned bust right **Obv. Designer:** Raphael Maklouf **Rev:** American troops landing

Date	Mintage	F	VF	XF	Unc	BU
1994 Proof	Est. 30,000	Value: 26.50				

KM# 697 CROWN
Copper-Nickel, 38.5 mm. **Ruler:** Elizabeth II **Series:** Normandy Invasion **Obv:** Crowned bust right **Obv. Designer:** Raphael Maklouf **Rev:** American soldier behind rock

Date	Mintage	F	VF	XF	Unc	BU
1994	—	—	—	—	6.50	7.50

KM# 697a CROWN
28.2800 g., 0.9250 Silver .8411 oz. ASW, 38.5 mm. **Ruler:** Elizabeth II **Series:** Normandy Invasion **Obv:** Crowned bust right **Obv. Designer:** Raphael Maklouf **Rev:** American soldier behind rock

Date	Mintage	F	VF	XF	Unc	BU
1994 Proof	Est. 30,000	Value: 26.50				

KM# 698 CROWN
Copper-Nickel, 38.5 mm. **Ruler:** Elizabeth II **Series:** Normandy Invasion **Obv:** Crowned bust right **Obv. Designer:** Raphael Maklouf **Rev:** German machine gun nest

Date	Mintage	F	VF	XF	Unc	BU
1994	—	—	—	—	6.50	7.50

KM# 698a CROWN
28.2800 g., 0.9250 Silver .8411 oz. ASW, 38.5 mm. **Ruler:** Elizabeth II **Series:** Normandy Invasion **Obv:** Crowned bust right **Obv. Designer:** Raphael Maklouf **Rev:** German machine gun nest

Date	Mintage	F	VF	XF	Unc	BU
1994 Proof	Est. 30,000	Value: 26.50				

KM# 699 CROWN
Copper-Nickel, 38.5 mm. **Ruler:** Elizabeth II **Series:** Normandy Invasion **Obv:** Crowned bust right **Obv. Designer:** Raphael Maklouf **Rev:** British troops landing

Date	Mintage	F	VF	XF	Unc	BU
1994	—	—	—	—	6.50	7.50

KM# 699a CROWN
28.2800 g., 0.9250 Silver .8411 oz. ASW, 38.5 mm. **Ruler:** Elizabeth II **Series:** Normandy Invasion **Obv:** Crowned bust right **Obv. Designer:** Raphael Maklouf **Rev:** British troops landing

Date	Mintage	F	VF	XF	Unc	BU
1994 Proof	Est. 30,000	Value: 26.50				

KM# 700 CROWN
Copper-Nickel, 38.5 mm. **Ruler:** Elizabeth II **Series:** Normandy Invasion **Obv:** Crowned bust right **Obv. Designer:** Raphael Maklouf **Rev:** General Eisenhower left

Date	Mintage	F	VF	XF	Unc	BU
1994	—	—	—	—	6.50	7.50

KM# 700a CROWN
28.2800 g., 0.9250 Silver .8411 oz. ASW, 38.5 mm. **Ruler:** Elizabeth II **Series:** Normandy Invasion **Obv:** Crowned bust right **Obv. Designer:** Raphael Maklouf **Rev:** General Eisenhower left

Date	Mintage	F	VF	XF	Unc	BU
1994 Proof	Est. 30,000	Value: 26.50				

KM# 701 CROWN
Copper-Nickel, 38.5 mm. **Ruler:** Elizabeth II **Series:** Normandy Invasion **Obv:** Crowned bust right **Obv. Designer:** Raphael Maklouf **Rev:** General Omar Bradley looking right

Date	Mintage	F	VF	XF	Unc	BU
1994	—	—	—	—	6.50	7.50

KM# 701a CROWN
28.2800 g., 0.9250 Silver .8411 oz. ASW, 38.5 mm. **Ruler:** Elizabeth II **Series:** Normandy Invasion **Obv:** Crowned bust right **Obv. Designer:** Raphael Maklouf **Rev:** General Omar Bradley looking right

Date	Mintage	F	VF	XF	Unc	BU
1994 Proof	Est. 30,000	Value: 26.50				

KM# 702 CROWN
Copper-Nickel, 38.5 mm. **Ruler:** Elizabeth II **Series:** Normandy Invasion **Obv:** Crowned bust right **Obv. Designer:** Raphael Maklouf **Rev:** General Montgomery left

Date	Mintage	F	VF	XF	Unc	BU
1994	—	—	—	—	6.50	7.50

KM# 702a CROWN
28.2800 g., 0.9250 Silver .8411 oz. ASW, 38.5 mm. **Ruler:** Elizabeth II **Series:** Normandy Invasion **Obv:** Crowned bust right **Obv. Designer:** Raphael Maklouf **Rev:** General Montgomery left

Date	Mintage	F	VF	XF	Unc	BU
1994 Proof	Est. 30,000	Value: 26.50				

KM# 703 CROWN
6.2200 g., 0.9999 Gold .2000 oz. AGW **Ruler:** Elizabeth II **Series:** Normandy Invasion **Obv:** Crowned bust right **Obv. Designer:** Raphael Maklouf **Rev:** Troop ship and landing craft

Date	Mintage	F	VF	XF	Unc	BU
1994 Proof	Est. 5,000	Value: 165				

KM# 704 CROWN
6.2200 g., 0.9999 Gold .2000 oz. AGW **Ruler:** Elizabeth II **Series:** Normandy Invasion **Obv:** Crowned bust right **Obv. Designer:** Raphael Maklouf **Rev:** American troops landing

Date	Mintage	F	VF	XF	Unc	BU
1994 Proof	Est. 5,000	Value: 165				

KM# 705 CROWN
6.2200 g., 0.9999 Gold .2000 oz. AGW **Ruler:** Elizabeth II **Series:** Normandy Invasion **Obv:** Crowned bust right **Obv. Designer:** Raphael Maklouf **Rev:** American soldier behind rock

Date	Mintage	F	VF	XF	Unc	BU
1994 Proof	Est. 5,000	Value: 165				

KM# 706 CROWN
6.2200 g., 0.9999 Gold .2000 oz. AGW **Ruler:** Elizabeth II **Series:** Normandy Invasion **Obv:** Crowned bust right **Obv. Designer:** Raphael Maklouf **Rev:** German machine gun nest

Date	Mintage	F	VF	XF	Unc	BU
1994 Proof	Est. 5,000	Value: 165				

KM# 707 CROWN
6.2200 g., 0.9999 Gold .2000 oz. AGW **Ruler:** Elizabeth II **Series:** Normandy Invasion **Obv:** Crowned bust right **Obv. Designer:** Raphael Maklouf **Rev:** British troops landing

Date	Mintage	F	VF	XF	Unc	BU
1994 Proof	Est. 5,000	Value: 165				

KM# 708 CROWN
6.2200 g., 0.9999 Gold .2000 oz. AGW **Ruler:** Elizabeth II **Series:** Normandy Invasion **Obv:** Crowned bust right **Obv. Designer:** Raphael Maklouf **Rev:** General Eisenhower left

Date	Mintage	F	VF	XF	Unc	BU
1994 Proof	Est. 5,000	Value: 165				

KM# 709 CROWN
6.2200 g., 0.9999 Gold .2000 oz. AGW **Ruler:** Elizabeth II **Series:** Normandy Invasion **Obv:** Crowned bust right **Obv. Designer:** Raphael Maklouf **Rev:** General Omar Bradley right

Date	Mintage	F	VF	XF	Unc	BU
1994 Proof	Est. 5,000	Value: 165				

KM# 710 CROWN
6.2200 g., 0.9999 Gold .2000 oz. AGW **Ruler:** Elizabeth II **Series:** Normandy Invasion **Obv:** Crowned bust right **Obv. Designer:** Raphael Maklouf **Rev:** General Montgomery left

Date	Mintage	F	VF	XF	Unc	BU
1994 Proof	Est. 5,000	Value: 165				

KM# 434 CROWN
Copper-Nickel, 38.5 mm. **Ruler:** Elizabeth II **Series:** Man in Flight **Obv:** Crowned bust right **Obv. Designer:** Raphael Maklouf **Rev:** Icarus' wings melting

Date	Mintage	F	VF	XF	Unc	BU
1995 Proof	—	Value: 7.50				

KM# 434a CROWN
28.2800 g., 0.9250 Silver .8411 oz. ASW, 38.5 mm. **Ruler:** Elizabeth II **Series:** Man in Flight **Obv:** Crowned bust right **Obv. Designer:** Raphael Maklouf **Rev:** Icarus' wings melting

Date	Mintage	F	VF	XF	Unc	BU
1995 Proof	Est. 30,000	Value: 37.50				

KM# 435 CROWN
Copper-Nickel, 38.5 mm. **Ruler:** Elizabeth II **Series:** Man in Flight **Obv:** Crowned bust right **Obv. Designer:** Raphael Maklouf **Rev:** Leonardo Da Vinci and aircraft design

Date	Mintage	F	VF	XF	Unc	BU
1995 Proof	—	Value: 7.50				

KM# 435a CROWN
28.2800 g., 0.9250 Silver .8411 oz. ASW, 38.5 mm. **Ruler:** Elizabeth II **Series:** Man in Flight **Obv:** Crowned bust right **Obv. Designer:** Raphael Maklouf **Rev:** Leonardo da Vinci and aircraft design

Date	Mintage	F	VF	XF	Unc	BU
1995 Proof	Est. 30,000	Value: 37.50				

KM# 436 CROWN
Copper-Nickel, 38.5 mm. **Ruler:** Elizabeth II **Series:** Man in Flight **Obv:** Crowned bust right **Obv. Designer:** Raphael Maklouf **Rev:** Montgolfier Brothers' balloon

Date	Mintage	F	VF	XF	Unc	BU
1995 Proof	—	Value: 7.50				

KM# 436a CROWN
28.2800 g., 0.9250 Silver .8411 oz. ASW, 38.5 mm. **Ruler:** Elizabeth II **Series:** Man in Flight **Obv:** Crowned bust right **Obv. Designer:** Raphael Maklouf **Rev:** Montgolfier Brothers' balloon

Date	Mintage	F	VF	XF	Unc	BU
1995 Proof	Est. 30,000	Value: 35.00				

KM# 437 CROWN
Copper-Nickel, 38.5 mm. **Ruler:** Elizabeth II **Series:** Man in Flight **Obv:** Crowned bust right **Obv. Designer:** Raphael Maklouf **Rev:** Wright Brothers' airplane

Date	Mintage	F	VF	XF	Unc	BU
1995	—	—	—	—	7.00	9.00

KM# 437a CROWN
28.2800 g., 0.9250 Silver .8411 oz. ASW, 38.5 mm. **Ruler:** Elizabeth II **Series:** Man in Flight **Obv:** Crowned bust right **Obv. Designer:** Raphael Maklouf **Rev:** Wright brothers' airplane

Date	Mintage	F	VF	XF	Unc	BU
1995 Proof	Est. 30,000	Value: 38.50				

KM# 438 CROWN
Copper-Nickel, 38.5 mm. **Ruler:** Elizabeth II **Series:** Man in Flight **Subject:** First Flight Toyko to Paris **Obv:** Crowned bust right **Obv. Designer:** Raphael Maklouf **Rev:** Heads of Abe and Kawachi over airplane

Date	Mintage	F	VF	XF	Unc	BU
1995 Proof	—	Value: 6.50				

KM# 438a CROWN
28.2800 g., 0.9250 Silver .8411 oz. ASW, 38.5 mm. **Ruler:** Elizabeth II **Series:** Man in Flight **Subject:** First Flight Tokyo to Paris **Obv:** Crowned bust right **Obv. Designer:** Raphael Maklouf **Rev:** Heads of Abe and Kawachi above plane

Date	Mintage	F	VF	XF	Unc	BU
1995 Proof	Est. 30,000	Value: 40.00				

KM# 439.1 CROWN
Copper-Nickel, 38.5 mm. **Ruler:** Elizabeth II **Series:** Man in Flight **Obv:** Crowned bust right **Obv. Designer:** Raphael Maklouf **Rev:** FW190, first diesel powered aircraft

Date	Mintage	F	VF	XF	Unc	BU
1995 Proof	500	Value: 12.50				

KM# 439.1a CROWN
28.2800 g., 0.9250 Silver .8411 oz. ASW, 38.5 mm. **Ruler:** Elizabeth II **Series:** Man in Flight **Obv:** Crowned bust right **Obv. Designer:** Raphael Maklouf **Rev:** First diesel powered aircraft

Date	Mintage	F	VF	XF	Unc	BU
1995 Proof	Est. 30,000	Value: 40.00				

KM# 439.2 CROWN
Copper-Nickel, 38.5 mm. **Ruler:** Elizabeth II **Series:** Man in Flight **Obv:** Crowned bust right **Obv. Designer:** Raphael Maklouf **Rev:** FW190 BMW injection aero engine

Date	Mintage	F	VF	XF	Unc	BU
1995	—	—	—	—	6.50	7.50

KM# 440.1 CROWN
Copper-Nickel, 38.5 mm. **Ruler:** Elizabeth II **Series:** Man in Flight **Obv:** Crowned bust right **Obv. Designer:** Raphael Maklouf **Rev:** ME262, first jet aircraft 1941

Date	Mintage	F	VF	XF	Unc	BU
1995 Proof	500	Value: 12.50				

KM# 440.1a CROWN
28.2800 g., 0.9250 Silver .8411 oz. ASW, 38.5 mm. **Ruler:** Elizabeth II **Series:** Man in Flight **Obv:** Crowned bust right **Obv. Designer:** Raphael Maklouf **Rev:** ME262, first jet aircraft 1941

Date	Mintage	F	VF	XF	Unc	BU
1995 Proof	Est. 30,000	Value: 40.00				

KM# 440.2 CROWN
Copper-Nickel, 38.5 mm. **Ruler:** Elizabeth II **Series:** Man in Flight **Obv:** Crowned bust right **Obv. Designer:** Raphael Maklouf **Rev:** Jet powered aircraft 1942

Date	Mintage	F	VF	XF	Unc	BU
1995	—	—	—	—	6.50	7.50

KM# 441 CROWN
Copper-Nickel, 38.5 mm. **Ruler:** Elizabeth II **Series:** Man in Flight **Subject:** 25th Anniversary of Boeing 747 **Obv:** Crowned bust right **Obv. Designer:** Raphael Maklouf **Rev:** Boeing 747

Date	Mintage	F	VF	XF	Unc	BU
1995 Proof	—	Value: 7.50				

KM# 441a CROWN
28.2800 g., 0.9250 Silver .8411 oz. ASW, 38.5 mm. **Ruler:** Elizabeth II **Series:** Man in Flight **Subject:** 25th Anniversary of Boeing 747 **Obv:** Crowned bust right **Obv. Designer:** Raphael Maklouf **Rev:** Boeing 747

Date	Mintage	F	VF	XF	Unc	BU
1995 Proof	Est. 30,000	Value: 38.50				

KM# 446 CROWN
Copper-Nickel, 38.5 mm. **Ruler:** Elizabeth II **Obv:** Crowned bust right **Obv. Designer:** Raphael Maklouf **Rev:** Turkish cat

Date	Mintage	F	VF	XF	Unc	BU
1995	—	—	—	—	10.00	15.00

KM# 447 CROWN
31.1000 g., 0.9990 Silver 1.0000 oz. ASW, 38.5 mm. **Ruler:** Elizabeth II **Obv:** Crowned bust right **Obv. Designer:** Raphael Maklouf **Rev:** Turkish cat

Date	Mintage	F	VF	XF	Unc	BU
1995 Proof	—	Value: 30.00				

KM# 448 CROWN
31.1000 g., 0.9990 Gold 1.0000 oz. AGW **Ruler:** Elizabeth II **Obv:** Crowned bust right **Obv. Designer:** Raphael Maklouf **Rev:** Turkish cat

Date	Mintage	F	VF	XF	Unc	BU
1995 U	—	—	—	—	675	700
1995 Proof	—	Value: 725				

KM# 453 CROWN
Copper-Nickel, 38.5 mm. **Ruler:** Elizabeth II **Subject:** Year of the Pig **Obv:** Crowned bust right **Obv. Designer:** Raphael Maklouf **Rev:** Sow with piglets

Date	Mintage	F	VF	XF	Unc	BU
1995	—	—	—	—	10.00	14.00

KM# 454 CROWN
31.1035 g., 0.9990 Silver 1.0000 oz. ASW, 38.5 mm. **Ruler:** Elizabeth II **Subject:** Year of the Pig **Obv:** Crowned bust right **Obv. Designer:** Raphael Maklouf **Rev:** Sow with piglets

Date	Mintage	F	VF	XF	Unc	BU
1995 Proof	—	Value: 40.00				

KM# 455 CROWN
31.1035 g., 0.9990 Gold 1.0000 oz. AGW **Ruler:** Elizabeth II **Subject:** Year of the Pig **Obv:** Crowned bust right **Obv. Designer:** Raphael Maklouf **Rev:** Sow with piglets

Date	Mintage	F	VF	XF	Unc	BU
1995 Proof	Est. 2,500	Value: 750				

KM# 458 CROWN
Copper-Nickel, 38.5 mm. **Ruler:** Elizabeth II **Subject:** 95th Birthday of Queen Mother **Obv:** Crowned bust right **Obv. Designer:** Raphael Maklouf **Rev:** Crowned bust facing

Date	Mintage	F	VF	XF	Unc	BU
1995	—	—	—	—	6.00	7.00

KM# 458a CROWN
28.2800 g., 0.9250 Silver .8411 oz. ASW, 38.5 mm. **Ruler:** Elizabeth II **Subject:** 95th Birthday of Queen Mother **Obv:** Crowned bust right **Obv. Designer:** Raphael Maklouf **Rev:** Crowned bust facing

Date	Mintage	F	VF	XF	Unc	BU
1995 Proof	Est. 30,000	Value: 35.00				

KM# 461 CROWN
Copper-Nickel, 38.5 mm. **Ruler:** Elizabeth II **Series:** Preserve Planet Earth **Obv:** Crowned bust right **Obv. Designer:** Raphael Maklouf **Rev:** European otter

Date	Mintage	F	VF	XF	Unc	BU
1995	—	—	—	—	12.00	15.00

KM# 461a CROWN
28.2800 g., 0.9250 Silver .8411 oz. ASW, 38.5 mm. **Ruler:** Elizabeth II **Series:** Preserve Planet Earth **Obv:** Crowned bust right **Obv. Designer:** Raphael Maklouf **Rev:** European otter

Date	Mintage	F	VF	XF	Unc	BU
1995 Proof	Est. 30,000	Value: 40.00				

KM# 462 CROWN
Copper-Nickel, 38.5 mm. **Ruler:** Elizabeth II **Series:** Preserve Planet Earth **Obv:** Crowned bust right **Obv. Designer:** Raphael Maklouf **Rev:** Egrets

Date	Mintage	F	VF	XF	Unc	BU
1995	—	—	—	—	11.00	15.00

KM# 462a CROWN
28.2800 g., 0.9250 Silver .8411 oz. ASW, 38.5 mm. **Ruler:** Elizabeth II **Series:** Preserve Planet Earth **Obv:** Crowned bust right **Obv. Designer:** Raphael Maklouf **Rev:** Egrets

Date	Mintage	F	VF	XF	Unc	BU
1995 Proof	Est. 30,000	Value: 40.00				

KM# 482 CROWN
31.1035 g., 0.9995 Platinum .9995 oz. APW **Ruler:** Elizabeth II **Obv:** Crowned bust right **Obv. Designer:** Raphael Maklouf **Rev:** Turkish cat

Date	Mintage	F	VF	XF	Unc	BU
1995	—	—	—	—	BV+20%	—
1995 Proof	—	BV_25%				

KM# 502 CROWN
Copper-Nickel, 38.5 mm. **Ruler:** Elizabeth II **Series:** Aircraft of World War II **Obv:** Crowned bust right **Obv. Designer:** Raphael Maklouf **Rev:** Airplanes

Date	Mintage	F	VF	XF	Unc	BU
1995	—	—	—	—	5.50	7.50

KM# 502a CROWN
28.2800 g., 0.9250 Silver .8411 oz. ASW, 38.5 mm. **Ruler:** Elizabeth II **Series:** Aircraft of World War II **Obv:** Crowned bust right **Obv. Designer:** Raphael Maklouf **Rev:** Airplanes

Date	Mintage	F	VF	XF	Unc	BU
1995 Proof	Est. 30,000	Value: 30.00				

KM# 503 CROWN
Copper-Nickel, 38.5 mm. **Ruler:** Elizabeth II **Series:** Aircraft of World War II **Obv:** Crowned bust right **Obv. Designer:** Raphael Maklouf **Rev:** P-51 Mustang

Date	Mintage	F	VF	XF	Unc	BU
1995	—	—	—	—	5.50	7.50

KM# 503a CROWN
28.2800 g., 0.9250 Silver .8411 oz. ASW, 38.5 mm. **Ruler:** Elizabeth II **Series:** Aircraft of World War II **Obv:** Crowned bust right **Obv. Designer:** Raphael Maklouf **Rev:** P-51 Mustang

Date	Mintage	F	VF	XF	Unc	BU
1995 Proof	—	Value: 30.00				

KM# 504 CROWN
Copper-Nickel, 38.5 mm. **Ruler:** Elizabeth II **Series:** Aircraft of World War II **Obv:** Crowned bust right **Obv. Designer:** Raphael Maklouf **Rev:** Letov 5328 **Edge:** Reeded

Date	Mintage	F	VF	XF	Unc	BU
1995	—	—	—	—	5.50	7.50

KM# 504a CROWN
28.2800 g., 0.9250 Silver .8411 oz. ASW, 38.5 mm. **Ruler:** Elizabeth II **Series:** Aircraft of World War II **Obv:** Crowned bust right **Obv. Designer:** Raphael Maklouf **Rev:** Letov 5328

Date	Mintage	F	VF	XF	Unc	BU
1995 Proof	Est. 30,000	Value: 30.00				

KM# 505 CROWN
Copper-Nickel, 38.5 mm. **Ruler:** Elizabeth II **Series:** Aircraft of World War II **Obv:** Crowned bust right **Obv. Designer:** Raphael Maklouf **Rev:** Messerschmitt ME262 **Edge:** Reeded

Date	Mintage	F	VF	XF	Unc	BU
1995	—	—	—	—	5.50	7.50

KM# 505a CROWN
28.2800 g., 0.9250 Silver .8411 oz. ASW, 38.5 mm. **Ruler:** Elizabeth II **Series:** Aircraft of World War II **Obv:** Crowned bust right **Obv. Designer:** Raphael Maklouf **Rev:** Messerschmitt ME262

Date	Mintage	F	VF	XF	Unc	BU
1995 Proof	Est. 30,000	Value: 30.00				

KM# 506 CROWN
Copper-Nickel, 38.5 mm. **Ruler:** Elizabeth II **Series:** Aircraft of World War II **Obv:** Crowned bust right **Obv. Designer:** Raphael Maklouf **Rev:** JU87 Stuka **Edge:** Reeded

Date	Mintage	F	VF	XF	Unc	BU
1995	—	—	—	—	5.50	7.50

KM# 506a CROWN
28.2800 g., 0.9250 Silver .8411 oz. ASW, 38.5 mm. **Ruler:** Elizabeth II **Series:** Aircraft of World War II **Obv:** Crowned bust right **Obv. Designer:** Raphael Maklouf **Rev:** JU87 Stuka

Date	Mintage	F	VF	XF	Unc	BU
1995 Proof	Est. 30,000	Value: 30.00				

KM# 507 CROWN
Copper-Nickel, 38.5 mm. **Ruler:** Elizabeth II **Series:** Aircraft of World War II **Obv:** Crowned bust right **Obv. Designer:** Raphael Maklouf **Rev:** MIG 3 **Edge:** Reeded

Date	Mintage	F	VF	XF	Unc	BU
1995	—	—	—	—	5.50	7.50

KM# 507a CROWN
28.2800 g., 0.9250 Silver .8411 oz. ASW, 38.5 mm.
Ruler: Elizabeth II **Series:** Aircraft of World War II **Obv:** Crowned bust right **Obv. Designer:** Raphael Maklouf **Rev:** MIG 3

Date	Mintage	F	VF	XF	Unc	BU
1995 Proof	Est. 30,000	Value: 30.00				

KM# 508 CROWN
Copper-Nickel, 38.5 mm. **Ruler:** Elizabeth II **Series:** Aircraft of World War II **Obv:** Crowned bust right **Obv. Designer:** Raphael Maklouf **Rev:** Nakajima KI-49 Donryu **Edge:** Reeded

Date	Mintage	F	VF	XF	Unc	BU
1995	—	—	—	—	5.50	7.50

KM# 508a CROWN
28.2800 g., 0.9250 Silver .8411 oz. ASW, 38.5 mm. **Ruler:** Elizabeth II **Series:** Aircraft of World War II **Obv:** Crowned bust right **Obv. Designer:** Raphael Maklouf **Rev:** Nakajima KI-49 Donryu

Date	Mintage	F	VF	XF	Unc	BU
1995 Proof	Est. 30,000	Value: 30.00				

KM# 509 CROWN
Copper-Nickel, 38.5 mm. **Ruler:** Elizabeth II **Series:** Aircraft of World War II **Obv:** Crowned bust right **Obv. Designer:** Raphael Maklouf **Rev:** Vickers Wellington **Edge:** Reeded

Date	Mintage	F	VF	XF	Unc	BU
1995	—	—	—	—	5.50	7.50

KM# 509a CROWN
28.2800 g., 0.9250 Silver .8411 oz. ASW, 38.5 mm. **Ruler:** Elizabeth II **Series:** Aircraft of World War II **Obv:** Crowned bust right **Obv. Designer:** Raphael Maklouf **Rev:** Vickers Wellington

Date	Mintage	F	VF	XF	Unc	BU
1995 Proof	Est. 30,000	Value: 30.00				

KM# 510 CROWN
Copper-Nickel, 38.5 mm. **Ruler:** Elizabeth II **Series:** Aircraft of World War II **Obv:** Crowned bust right **Obv. Designer:** Raphael Maklouf **Rev:** Supermarine Spitfire **Edge:** Reeded

Date	Mintage	F	VF	XF	Unc	BU
1995 (py)	—	—	—	—	6.00	8.00
1995	—	—	—	—	6.00	8.00

KM# 510a CROWN
28.2800 g., 0.9250 Silver .8411 oz. ASW, 38.5 mm. **Ruler:** Elizabeth II **Series:** Aircraft of World War II **Obv:** Crowned bust right **Obv. Designer:** Raphael Maklouf **Rev:** Supermarine Spitfire

Date	Mintage	F	VF	XF	Unc	BU
1995 Proof	Est. 30,000	Value: 30.00				

KM# 511 CROWN
Copper-Nickel, 38.5 mm. **Ruler:** Elizabeth II **Series:** Aircraft of World War II **Obv:** Crowned bust right **Obv. Designer:** Raphael Maklouf **Rev:** Fokker G.1a **Edge:** Reeded

Date	Mintage	F	VF	XF	Unc	BU
1995	—	—	—	—	5.50	7.50

KM# 511a CROWN
28.2800 g., 0.9250 Silver .8411 oz. ASW, 38.5 mm.
Ruler: Elizabeth II **Series:** Aircraft of World War II **Obv:** Crowned bust right **Obv. Designer:** Raphael Maklouf **Rev:** Fokker G.1a

Date	Mintage	F	VF	XF	Unc	BU
1995 Proof	Est. 30,000	Value: 30.00				

KM# 512 CROWN
Copper-Nickel, 38.5 mm. **Ruler:** Elizabeth II **Series:** Aircraft of World War II **Obv:** Crowned bust right **Obv. Designer:** Raphael Maklouf **Rev:** Commonwealth Boomerang CA-13 **Edge:** Reeded

Date	Mintage	F	VF	XF	Unc	BU
1995	—	—	—	—	5.50	7.50

KM# 512a CROWN
28.2800 g., 0.9250 Silver .8411 oz. ASW, 38.5 mm. **Ruler:** Elizabeth II **Series:** Aircraft of World War II **Obv:** Crowned bust right **Obv. Designer:** Raphael Maklouf **Rev:** Boomerang CA-13

Date	Mintage	F	VF	XF	Unc	BU
1995 Proof	Est. 30,000	Value: 30.00				

KM# 513 CROWN
Copper-Nickel, 38.5 mm. **Ruler:** Elizabeth II **Series:** Aircraft of World War II **Obv:** Crowned bust right **Obv. Designer:** Raphael Maklouf **Rev:** Bristol Blenheim 142 **Edge:** Reeded

Date	Mintage	F	VF	XF	Unc	BU
1995	—	—	—	—	5.50	7.50

KM# 513a CROWN
28.2800 g., 0.9250 Silver .8411 oz. ASW, 38.5 mm. **Ruler:** Elizabeth II **Series:** Aircraft of World War II **Obv:** Crowned bust right **Obv. Designer:** Raphael Maklouf **Rev:** Bristol Blenheim 142

Date	Mintage	F	VF	XF	Unc	BU
1995 Proof	Est. 30,000	Value: 30.00				

KM# 514 CROWN
Copper-Nickel, 38.5 mm. **Ruler:** Elizabeth II **Series:** Aircraft of World War II **Obv:** Crowned bust right **Obv. Designer:** Raphael Maklouf **Rev:** Mitsubishi Zero **Edge:** Reeded

Date	Mintage	F	VF	XF	Unc	BU
1995	—	—	—	—	5.50	7.50

KM# 514a CROWN
28.2800 g., 0.9250 Silver .8411 oz. ASW, 38.5 mm. **Ruler:** Elizabeth II **Series:** Aircraft of World War II **Obv:** Crowned bust right **Obv. Designer:** Raphael Maklouf **Rev:** Mitsubishi Zero

Date	Mintage	F	VF	XF	Unc	BU
1995 Proof	Est. 30,000	Value: 30.00				

KM# 515 CROWN
Copper-Nickel, 38.5 mm. **Ruler:** Elizabeth II **Series:** Aircraft of World War II **Obv:** Crowned bust right **Obv. Designer:** Raphael Maklouf **Rev:** Heinkel HE 111 **Edge:** Reeded

Date	Mintage	F	VF	XF	Unc	BU
1995	—	—	—	—	5.50	7.50

KM# 515a CROWN
28.2800 g., 0.9250 Silver .8411 oz. ASW, 38.5 mm. **Ruler:** Elizabeth II **Series:** Aircraft of World War II **Obv:** Crowned bust right **Obv. Designer:** Raphael Maklouf **Rev:** Heinkel HE 111

Date	Mintage	F	VF	XF	Unc	BU
1995 Proof	Est. 30,000	Value: 30.00				

KM# 516 CROWN
Copper-Nickel, 38.5 mm. **Ruler:** Elizabeth II **Series:** Aircraft of World War II **Obv:** Crowned bust right **Obv. Designer:** Raphael Maklouf **Rev:** Boulton Paul P.82 Defiant **Edge:** Reeded

Date	Mintage	F	VF	XF	Unc	BU
1995	—	—	—	—	5.50	7.50

KM# 516a CROWN
28.2800 g., 0.9250 Silver .8411 oz. ASW, 38.5 mm. **Ruler:** Elizabeth II **Series:** Aircraft of World War II **Obv:** Crowned bust right **Obv. Designer:** Raphael Maklouf **Rev:** Boulton Paul P.82 Defiant

Date	Mintage	F	VF	XF	Unc	BU
1995 Proof	Est. 30,000	Value: 30.00				

KM# 517 CROWN
Copper-Nickel, 38.5 mm. **Ruler:** Elizabeth II **Series:** Aircraft of World War II **Obv:** Crowned bust right **Obv. Designer:** Raphael Maklouf **Rev:** Boeing B-29 Enola Gay **Edge:** Reeded

Date	Mintage	F	VF	XF	Unc	BU
1995	—	—	—	—	5.50	7.50

KM# 517a CROWN
28.2800 g., 0.9250 Silver .8411 oz. ASW, 38.5 mm. **Ruler:** Elizabeth II **Series:** Aircraft of World War II **Obv:** Crowned bust right **Obv. Designer:** Raphael Maklouf **Rev:** Boeing B-29 Enola Gay

Date	Mintage	F	VF	XF	Unc	BU
1995 Proof	Est. 30,000	Value: 30.00				

KM# 518 CROWN
Copper-Nickel, 38.5 mm. **Ruler:** Elizabeth II **Series:** Aircraft of World War II **Obv:** Crowned bust right **Obv. Designer:** Raphael Maklouf **Rev:** Douglas DC-3 (C-47) Dakota **Edge:** Reeded

Date	Mintage	F	VF	XF	Unc	BU
1995	—	—	—	—	5.50	7.50

KM# 518a CROWN
28.2800 g., 0.9250 Silver .8411 oz. ASW, 38.5 mm.
Ruler: Elizabeth II **Series:** Aircraft of World War II **Obv:** Crowned bust right **Obv. Designer:** Raphael Maklouf **Rev:** Douglas DC-3 (C-47) Dakota

Date	Mintage	F	VF	XF	Unc	BU
1995 Proof	Est. 30,000	Value: 30.00				

KM# 519 CROWN
Copper-Nickel, 38.5 mm. **Ruler:** Elizabeth II **Series:** Aircraft of World War II **Obv:** Crowned bust right **Obv. Designer:** Raphael Maklouf **Rev:** Fairey Swordfish **Edge:** Reeded

Date	Mintage	F	VF	XF	Unc	BU
1995	—	—	—	—	5.50	7.50

KM# 519a CROWN
28.2800 g., 0.9250 Silver .8411 oz. ASW, 38.5 mm. **Ruler:** Elizabeth II **Series:** Aircraft of World War II **Obv:** Crowned bust right **Obv. Designer:** Raphael Maklouf **Rev:** Fairey Swordfish

Date	Mintage	F	VF	XF	Unc	BU
1995 Proof	Est. 30,000	Value: 30.00				

KM# 520 CROWN
Copper-Nickel, 38.5 mm. **Ruler:** Elizabeth II **Series:** Aircraft of WWII **Obv:** Crowned bust right **Obv. Designer:** Raphael Maklouf **Rev:** Curtiss P-40 Tomahawk **Edge:** Reeded

Date	Mintage	F	VF	XF	Unc	BU
1995	—	—	—	—	5.50	7.50

KM# 520a CROWN
28.2800 g., 0.9250 Silver .8411 oz. ASW, 38.5 mm. **Ruler:** Elizabeth II **Series:** Aircraft of WWII **Obv:** Crowned bust right **Obv. Designer:** Raphael Maklouf **Rev:** Curtiss P-40 Tomahawk

Date	Mintage	F	VF	XF	Unc	BU
1995 Proof	Est. 30,000	Value: 30.00				

KM# 524 CROWN
Copper-Nickel, 38.5 mm. **Ruler:** Elizabeth II **Series:** America's Cup **Obv:** Crowned bust right **Obv. Designer:** Raphael Maklouf **Rev:** Sailboats **Edge:** Reeded

Date	Mintage	F	VF	XF	Unc	BU
1995	—	—	—	—	5.00	6.50

KM# 524a CROWN
28.2800 g., 0.9250 Silver .8411 oz. ASW, 38.5 mm.
Ruler: Elizabeth II **Series:** America's Cup **Obv:** Crowned bust right **Obv. Designer:** Raphael Maklouf **Rev:** Sailboats

Date	Mintage	F	VF	XF	Unc	BU
1995 Proof	Est. 30,000	Value: 50.00				

KM# 526 CROWN
Copper-Nickel, 38.5 mm. **Ruler:** Elizabeth II **Series:** Inventions of the Modern World **Obv:** Crowned bust right
Obv. Designer: Raphael Maklouf **Rev:** Cameo Tsai Lun, paper and tree**Edge:** Reeded

Date	Mintage	F	VF	XF	Unc	BU
1995	—	—	—	—	6.00	8.00

KM# 526a CROWN
28.2800 g., 0.9250 Silver .8411 oz. ASW, 38.5 mm.
Ruler: Elizabeth II **Series:** Inventions of the Modern World **Obv:** Crowned bust right **Obv. Designer:** Raphael Maklouf **Rev:** Cameo of Tsai Lun, paper and tree

Date	Mintage	F	VF	XF	Unc	BU
1995 Proof	Est. 30,000	Value: 40.00				

KM# 528 CROWN
Copper-Nickel, 38.5 mm. **Ruler:** Elizabeth II **Series:** Inventions of the Modern World **Obv:** Crowned bust right **Obv. Designer:** Raphael Maklouf **Rev:** Cameo of Chang Heng and seismograph **Edge:** Reeded

Date	Mintage	F	VF	XF	Unc	BU
1995	—	—	—	—	5.00	6.50

KM# 528a CROWN
28.2800 g., 0.9250 Silver .8411 oz. ASW, 38.5 mm. **Ruler:** Elizabeth II **Series:** Inventions of the Modern World **Obv:** Crowned bust right **Obv. Designer:** Raphael Maklouf **Rev:** Cameo of Chang Heng and seismograph

Date	Mintage	F	VF	XF	Unc	BU
1995 Proof	Est. 30,000	Value: 40.00				

KM# 530 CROWN
Copper-Nickel, 38.5 mm. **Ruler:** Elizabeth II **Series:** Inventions of the Modern World **Obv:** Crowned bust right **Obv. Designer:** Raphael Maklouf **Rev:** Cameo of Tsu Chung Chih and compass cart **Edge:** Reeded

Date	Mintage	F	VF	XF	Unc	BU
1995	—	—	—	—	8.00	10.00

KM# 530a CROWN
28.2800 g., 0.9250 Silver .8411 oz. ASW, 38.5 mm. **Ruler:** Elizabeth II **Series:** Inventions of the Modern World **Obv:** Crowned bust right **Obv. Designer:** Raphael Maklouf **Rev:** Cameo of Tsu Chung Chih and compass car

Date	Mintage	F	VF	XF	Unc	BU
1995 Proof	Est. 30,000	Value: 40.00				

KM# 532 CROWN
Copper-Nickel, 38.5 mm. **Ruler:** Elizabeth II **Series:** Inventions of the Modern World **Obv:** Crowned bust right **Obv. Designer:** Raphael Maklouf **Rev:** Cameo of Pi Sheng and movable type **Edge:** Reeded

Date	Mintage	F	VF	XF	Unc	BU
1995	—	—	—	—	5.00	6.50

KM# 532a CROWN
28.2800 g., 0.9250 Silver .8411 oz. ASW, 38.5 mm. **Ruler:** Elizabeth II **Series:** Inventions of the Modern World **Obv:** Crowned bust right **Obv. Designer:** Raphael Maklouf **Rev:** Cameo of Pi Sheng and movable type

Date	Mintage	F	VF	XF	Unc	BU
1995 Proof	Est. 30,000	Value: 40.00				

KM# 534 CROWN
Copper-Nickel, 38.5 mm. **Ruler:** Elizabeth II **Series:** Inventions of the Modern World **Obv:** Crowned bust right **Obv. Designer:** Raphael Maklouf **Rev:** Cameo of Charles Babbage and first computer **Edge:** Reeded

Date	Mintage	F	VF	XF	Unc	BU
1995	—	—	—	—	6.00	8.00

KM# 534a CROWN
28.2800 g., 0.9250 Silver .8411 oz. ASW, 38.5 mm. **Ruler:** Elizabeth II **Series:** Inventions of the Modern World **Obv:** Crowned bust right **Obv. Designer:** Raphael Maklouf **Rev:** Cameo of Charles Babbage and first computer

Date	Mintage	F	VF	XF	Unc	BU
1995 Proof	Est. 30,000	Value: 40.00				

KM# 536 CROWN
Copper-Nickel, 38.5 mm. **Ruler:** Elizabeth II **Series:** Inventions of the Modern World **Obv:** Crowned bust right **Obv. Designer:** Raphael Maklouf **Rev:** Cameo of Fox Talbot, photography **Edge:** Reeded

Date	Mintage	F	VF	XF	Unc	BU
1995	—	—	—	—	8.00	10.00

KM# 536a CROWN
28.2800 g., 0.9250 Silver .8411 oz. ASW, 38.5 mm. **Ruler:** Elizabeth II **Series:** Inventions of the Modern World **Obv:** Crowned bust right **Obv. Designer:** Raphael Maklouf **Rev:** Cameo of Fox Talbot, photography

Date	Mintage	F	VF	XF	Unc	BU
1995 Proof	Est. 30,000	Value: 40.00				

KM# 538 CROWN
Copper-Nickel, 38.5 mm. **Ruler:** Elizabeth II **Series:** Inventions of the Modern World **Obv:** Crowned bust right **Obv. Designer:** Raphael Maklouf **Rev:** Cameo Rudolf Diesel and engine

Date	Mintage	F	VF	XF	Unc	BU
1995	—	—	—	—	5.00	6.50

KM# 538a CROWN
28.2800 g., 0.9250 Silver .8411 oz. ASW, 38.5 mm. **Ruler:** Elizabeth II **Series:** Inventions of the Modern World **Obv:** Crowned bust right **Obv. Designer:** Raphael Maklouf **Rev:** Cameo of Rudolf Diesel and engine

Date	Mintage	F	VF	XF	Unc	BU
1995 Proof	Est. 30,000	Value: 40.00				

KM# 540 CROWN
Copper-Nickel, 38.5 mm. **Ruler:** Elizabeth II **Series:** Inventions of the Modern World **Obv:** Crowned bust right **Obv. Designer:** Raphael Maklouf **Rev:** Cameo of Wilhelm K. Roentgern, xray **Edge:** Reeded

Date	Mintage	F	VF	XF	Unc	BU
1995	—	—	—	—	5.00	6.50

KM# 540a CROWN
28.2800 g., 0.9250 Silver .8411 oz. ASW, 38.5 mm. **Ruler:** Elizabeth II **Series:** Inventions of the Modern World **Obv:** Crowned bust right **Obv. Designer:** Raphael Maklouf **Rev:** Cameo of Wilhelm K. Roentgen, xray

Date	Mintage	F	VF	XF	Unc	BU
1995 Proof	Est. 30,000	Value: 40.00				

KM# 542 CROWN
Copper-Nickel, 38.5 mm. **Ruler:** Elizabeth II **Series:** Inventions of the Modern World **Obv:** Crowned bust right **Obv. Designer:** Raphael Maklouf **Rev:** Cameo of Guglielmo Marconi, radio equipment **Edge:** Reeded

Date	Mintage	F	VF	XF	Unc	BU
1995	—	—	—	—	5.00	6.50

KM# 542a CROWN
28.2800 g., 0.9250 Silver .8411 oz. ASW, 38.5 mm. **Ruler:** Elizabeth II **Series:** Inventions of the Modern World **Obv:** Crowned bust right **Obv. Designer:** Raphael Maklouf **Rev:** Cameo of Guglielmo Marconi and radio equipment

Date	Mintage	F	VF	XF	Unc	BU
1995 Proof	Est. 30,000	Value: 40.00				

KM# 544 CROWN
Copper-Nickel, 38.5 mm. **Ruler:** Elizabeth II **Series:** Inventions of the Modern World **Obv:** Crowned bust right **Obv. Designer:** Raphael Maklouf **Rev:** Cameo L. Baird and television equipment **Edge:** Reeded

Date	Mintage	F	VF	XF	Unc	BU
1995	—	—	—	—	5.00	6.50

KM# 544a CROWN
28.2800 g., 0.9250 Silver .8411 oz. ASW, 38.5 mm. **Ruler:** Elizabeth II **Series:** Inventions of the Modern World **Obv:** Crowned bust right **Obv. Designer:** Raphael Maklouf **Rev:** Cameo of John L. Baird and television equipment

Date	Mintage	F	VF	XF	Unc	BU
1995 Proof	Est. 30,000	Value: 40.00				

KM# 546 CROWN
Copper-Nickel, 38.5 mm. **Ruler:** Elizabeth II **Series:** Inventions of the Modern World **Obv:** Crowned bust right **Obv. Designer:** Raphael Maklouf **Rev:** Cameo of Alexander Fleming and microscope **Edge:** Reeded

Date	Mintage	F	VF	XF	Unc	BU
1995	—	—	—	—	5.00	6.50

KM# 546a CROWN
28.2800 g., 0.9250 Silver .8411 oz. ASW, 38.5 mm. **Ruler:** Elizabeth II **Series:** Inventions of the Modern World **Obv:** Crowned bust right **Obv. Designer:** Raphael Maklouf **Rev:** Cameo of Alexander Fleming and microscope

Date	Mintage	F	VF	XF	Unc	BU
1995 Proof	Est. 30,000	Value: 40.00				

KM# 548 CROWN
Copper-Nickel, 38.5 mm. **Ruler:** Elizabeth II **Series:** Inventions of the Modern World **Obv:** Crowned bust right **Obv. Designer:** Raphael Maklouf **Rev:** Cameo of Lazlo Biro, ball-point pen **Edge:** Reeded

Date	Mintage	F	VF	XF	Unc	BU
1995	—	—	—	—	5.00	6.50

KM# 548a CROWN
28.2800 g., 0.9250 Silver .8411 oz. ASW, 38.5 mm. **Ruler:** Elizabeth II **Series:** Inventions of the Modern World **Obv:** Crowned bust right **Obv. Designer:** Raphael Maklouf **Rev:** Cameo of Lazlo Biro, ball-point pen

Date	Mintage	F	VF	XF	Unc	BU
1995 Proof	Est. 30,000	Value: 40.00				

KM# 555 CROWN
Copper-Nickel, 38.5 mm. **Ruler:** Elizabeth II **Series:** Inventions of the Modern World **Obv:** Crowned bust right **Obv. Designer:** Raphael Maklouf **Rev:** Cameo of Wernher von Braun and rocket **Edge:** Reeded

Date	Mintage	F	VF	XF	Unc	BU
1996	—	—	—	—	5.00	6.50

KM# 555a CROWN
28.2800 g., 0.9250 Silver .8411 oz. ASW, 38.5 mm. **Ruler:** Elizabeth II **Series:** Inventions of the Modern World **Obv:** Crowned bust right **Obv. Designer:** Raphael Maklouf **Rev:** Cameo of Wernher von Braun and rocket

Date	Mintage	F	VF	XF	Unc	BU
1996 Proof	Est. 30,000	Value: 40.00				

KM# 556 CROWN
Copper-Nickel, 38.5 mm. **Ruler:** Elizabeth II **Series:** Inventions of the Modern World **Obv:** Crowned bust right **Obv. Designer:** Raphael Maklouf **Rev:** Cameo of Thomas Edison, electricity **Edge:** Reeded

Date	Mintage	F	VF	XF	Unc	BU
1996	—	—	—	—	8.00	10.00

KM# 556a CROWN
28.2800 g., 0.9250 Silver .8411 oz. ASW, 38.5 mm. **Ruler:** Elizabeth II **Series:** Inventions of the Modern World **Obv:** Crowned bust right **Obv. Designer:** Raphael Maklouf **Rev:** Cameo of Thomas Edison, electricity

Date	Mintage	F	VF	XF	Unc	BU
1996 Proof	—	Value: 40.00				

KM# 557 CROWN
Copper-Nickel, 38.5 mm. **Ruler:** Elizabeth II **Series:** Inventions of the Modern World **Obv:** Crowned bust right **Obv. Designer:** Raphael Maklouf **Rev:** Compass

Date	Mintage	F	VF	XF	Unc	BU
1996	—	—	—	—	6.00	8.00

KM# 557a CROWN
28.2800 g., 0.9250 Silver .8411 oz. ASW, 38.5 mm. **Ruler:** Elizabeth II **Series:** Inventions of the Modern World **Obv:** Crowned bust right **Obv. Designer:** Raphael Maklouf **Rev:** Compass

Date	Mintage	F	VF	XF	Unc	BU
1996 Proof	—	Value: 40.00				

KM# 558.1 CROWN
Copper-Nickel, 38.5 mm. **Ruler:** Elizabeth II **Series:** Inventions of the Modern World **Obv:** Crowned bust right **Obv. Designer:** Raphael Maklouf **Rev:** Cameo of Michael Faraday, electricity **Edge:** Reeded

Date	Mintage	F	VF	XF	Unc	BU
1996	—	—	—	—	5.00	6.50

KM# 558.2 CROWN
Copper-Nickel, 38.5 mm. **Ruler:** Elizabeth II **Series:** Inventions of the Modern World **Obv:** Crowned bust right **Obv. Designer:** Raphael Maklouf **Rev:** Cameo of Michael Faraday, electricity; legend error **Rev. Legend:** EXRERIMENTAL **Edge:** Reeded

Date	Mintage	F	VF	XF	Unc	BU
1996	—	—	—	—	11.50	12.50

KM# 558.2a CROWN
28.2800 g., 0.9250 Silver .8411 oz. ASW, 38.5 mm. **Ruler:** Elizabeth II **Series:** Inventions of the Modern World **Obv:** Crowned bust right **Obv. Designer:** Raphael Maklouf **Rev:** Cameo of Michael Faraday, electricity; legend error **Rev. Legend:** EXRERIMENTAL

Date	Mintage	F	VF	XF	Unc	BU
1996 Proof	Est. 30,000	Value: 40.00				

KM# 559 CROWN

Copper-Nickel, 38.5 mm. **Ruler:** Elizabeth II **Series:** Inventions of the Modern World **Obv:** Crowned bust right **Obv. Designer:** Raphael Maklouf **Rev:** Emile Berliner, gramophone **Edge:** Reeded

Date	Mintage	F	VF	XF	Unc	BU
1996	—	—	—	—	5.00	6.50

KM# 559a CROWN

28.2800 g., 0.9250 Silver .8411 oz. ASW, 38.5 mm. **Ruler:** Elizabeth II **Series:** Inventions of the Modern World **Obv:** Crowned bust right **Obv. Designer:** Raphael Maklouf **Rev:** Cameo of Emile Berliner and gramophone

Date	Mintage	F	VF	XF	Unc	BU
1996 Proof	Est. 30,000	Value: 40.00				

KM# 560 CROWN

Copper-Nickel, 38.5 mm. **Ruler:** Elizabeth II **Series:** Inventions of the Modern World **Obv:** Crowned bust right **Obv. Designer:** Raphael Maklouf **Rev:** Cameo of Alexander Graham Bell, voice transmission **Edge:** Reeded

Date	Mintage	F	VF	XF	Unc	BU
1996	—	—	—	—	8.00	10.00

KM# 560a CROWN

28.2800 g., 0.9250 Silver .8411 oz. ASW, 38.5 mm. **Ruler:** Elizabeth II **Series:** Inventions of the Modern World **Obv:** Crowned bust right **Obv. Designer:** Raphael Maklouf **Rev:** Cameo of Alexander Graham Bell, voice transmission

Date	Mintage	F	VF	XF	Unc	BU
1996 Proof	30,000	Value: 40.00				

KM# 567 CROWN

Copper-Nickel, 38.5 mm. **Ruler:** Elizabeth II **Series:** 1996 Summer Olympics - Atlanta **Obv:** Crowned bust right **Obv. Designer:** Raphael Maklouf **Rev:** Hurdler within sprigs

Date	Mintage	F	VF	XF	Unc	BU
1996	—	—	—	—	6.00	8.00

KM# 567a CROWN

28.2800 g., 0.9250 Silver .8411 oz. ASW, 38.5 mm. **Ruler:** Elizabeth II **Series:** 1996 Summer Olympics - Atlanta **Obv:** Crowned bust right **Obv. Designer:** Raphael Maklouf **Rev:** Hurdler within sprigs

Date	Mintage	F	VF	XF	Unc	BU
1996 Proof	Est. 30,000	Value: 35.00				

KM# 568 CROWN

Copper-Nickel, 38.5 mm. **Ruler:** Elizabeth II **Series:** 1996 Summer Olympics - Atlanta **Obv:** Crowned bust right **Obv. Designer:** Raphael Maklouf **Rev:** Runners

Date	Mintage	F	VF	XF	Unc	BU
1996	—	—	—	—	6.00	8.00

KM# 568a CROWN

28.2800 g., 0.9250 Silver .8411 oz. ASW, 38.5 mm. **Ruler:** Elizabeth II **Series:** 1996 Summer Olympics - Atlanta **Obv:** Crowned bust right **Obv. Designer:** Raphael Maklouf **Rev:** Runners

Date	Mintage	F	VF	XF	Unc	BU
1996 Proof	Est. 30,000	Value: 35.00				

KM# 569 CROWN

Copper-Nickel, 38.5 mm. **Ruler:** Elizabeth II **Series:** 1996 Summer Olympics - Atlanta **Obv:** Crowned bust right **Obv. Designer:** Raphael Maklouf **Rev:** Sailing

Date	Mintage	F	VF	XF	Unc	BU
1996	—	—	—	—	6.00	8.00

KM# 569a CROWN

28.2800 g., 0.9250 Silver .8411 oz. ASW, 38.5 mm. **Ruler:** Elizabeth II **Series:** 1996 Summer Olympics - Atlanta **Obv:** Crowned bust right **Obv. Designer:** Raphael Maklouf **Rev:** Sailing

Date	Mintage	F	VF	XF	Unc	BU
1996 Proof	Est. 30,000	Value: 35.00				

KM# 570 CROWN

Copper-Nickel, 38.5 mm. **Ruler:** Elizabeth II **Series:** 1996 Summer Olympics - Atlanta **Obv:** Crowned bust right **Obv. Designer:** Raphael Maklouf **Rev:** Swimming

Date	Mintage	F	VF	XF	Unc	BU
1996	—	—	—	—	6.00	8.00

KM# 570a CROWN

28.2800 g., 0.9250 Silver .8411 oz. ASW, 38.5 mm. **Ruler:** Elizabeth II **Series:** 1996 Summer Olympics - Atlanta **Obv:** Crowned bust right **Obv. Designer:** Raphael Maklouf **Rev:** Swimming

Date	Mintage	F	VF	XF	Unc	BU
1996 Proof	Est. 30,000	Value: 35.00				

KM# 571 CROWN

Copper-Nickel, 38.5 mm. **Ruler:** Elizabeth II **Series:** 1996 Summer Olympics - Atlanta **Obv:** Crowned bust right **Obv. Designer:** Raphael Maklouf **Rev:** Equestrian within wreath

Date	Mintage	F	VF	XF	Unc	BU
1996	—	—	—	—	6.00	8.00

KM# 571a CROWN

28.2800 g., 0.9250 Silver .8411 oz. ASW, 38.5 mm. **Ruler:** Elizabeth II **Series:** 1996 Summer Olympics - Atlanta **Obv:** Crowned bust right **Obv. Designer:** Raphael Maklouf **Rev:** Equestrian within wreath

Date	Mintage	F	VF	XF	Unc	BU
1996 Proof	Est. 30,000	Value: 35.00				

KM# 572 CROWN

Copper-Nickel, 38.5 mm. **Ruler:** Elizabeth II **Series:** 1996 Summer Olympics - Atlanta **Obv:** Crowned bust right **Obv. Designer:** Raphael Maklouf **Rev:** Cyclists and Nike

Date	Mintage	F	VF	XF	Unc	BU
1996	—	—	—	—	6.00	8.00

KM# 572a CROWN

28.2800 g., 0.9250 Silver .8411 oz. ASW, 38.5 mm. **Ruler:** Elizabeth II **Series:** 1996 Summer Olympics - Atlanta **Obv:** Crowned bust right **Obv. Designer:** Raphael Maklouf **Rev:** Cyclists and Nike

Date	Mintage	F	VF	XF	Unc	BU
1996 Proof	Est. 30,000	Value: 35.00				

KM# 577 CROWN

Copper-Nickel, 38.5 mm. **Ruler:** Elizabeth II **Series:** Bicentenary of Robert Burns **Obv:** Crowned bust right **Obv. Designer:** Raphael Maklouf **Rev:** Seated figure facing right within circle **Edge:** Reeded

Date	Mintage	F	VF	XF	Unc	BU
1996	—	—	—	—	8.00	10.00

KM# 577a CROWN

28.2800 g., 0.9250 Silver .8411 oz. ASW, 38.5 mm. **Ruler:** Elizabeth II **Series:** Bicentenary of Robert Burns **Obv:** Crowned bust right **Obv. Designer:** Raphael Maklouf **Rev:** Seated figure facing right within circle

Date	Mintage	F	VF	XF	Unc	BU
1996 Proof	Est. 30,000	Value: 40.00				

KM# 578 CROWN

Copper-Nickel, 38.5 mm. **Ruler:** Elizabeth II **Series:** Bicentenary of Robert Burns **Obv:** Crowned bust right **Obv. Designer:** Raphael Maklouf **Rev:** Pirate ship **Edge:** Reeded

Date	Mintage	F	VF	XF	Unc	BU
1996	—	—	—	—	5.00	6.50

KM# 578a CROWN

28.2800 g., 0.9250 Silver .8411 oz. ASW, 38.5 mm. **Ruler:** Elizabeth II **Series:** Bicentenary of Robert Burns **Obv:** Crowned bust right **Obv. Designer:** Raphael Maklouf **Rev:** Pirate ship

Date	Mintage	F	VF	XF	Unc	BU
1996 Proof	Est. 30,000	Value: 40.00				

KM# 579 CROWN

Copper-Nickel, 38.5 mm. **Ruler:** Elizabeth II **Series:** Bicentenary of Robert Burns **Obv:** Crowned bust right **Obv. Designer:** Raphael Maklouf **Rev:** Auld Lang Syne

Date	Mintage	F	VF	XF	Unc	BU
1996	—	—	—	—	5.00	6.50

KM# 579a CROWN

28.2800 g., 0.9250 Silver .8411 oz. ASW, 38.5 mm. **Ruler:** Elizabeth II **Series:** Bicentenary of Robert Burns **Obv:** Crowned bust right **Obv. Designer:** Raphael Maklouf **Rev:** Auld Lang Syne

Date	Mintage	F	VF	XF	Unc	BU
1996 Proof	Est. 30,000	Value: 40.00				

KM# 580 CROWN

Copper-Nickel, 38.5 mm. **Ruler:** Elizabeth II **Series:** Bicentenary of Robert Burns **Obv:** Crowned bust right **Obv. Designer:** Raphael Maklouf **Rev:** Edinburgh Castle

Date	Mintage	F	VF	XF	Unc	BU
1996	—	—	—	—	8.00	10.00

KM# 580a CROWN

28.2800 g., 0.9250 Silver .8411 oz. ASW, 38.5 mm. **Ruler:** Elizabeth II **Series:** Bicentenary of Robert Burns **Obv:** Crowned bust right **Obv. Designer:** Raphael Maklouf **Rev:** Edinburgh Castle

Date	Mintage	F	VF	XF	Unc	BU
1996 Proof	Est. 30,000	Value: 40.00				

KM# 582 CROWN

28.2800 g., 0.9250 Silver .8411 oz. ASW, 38.5 mm. **Ruler:** Elizabeth II **Subject:** 70th Birthday of Queen Elizabeth II **Obv:** Crowned bust right **Obv. Designer:** Raphael Maklouf **Rev:** Monogram and numeral 70 flanked by flower sprigs

Date	Mintage	F	VF	XF	Unc	BU
1996	—	—	—	—	6.00	8.00

KM# 582a CROWN

28.2800 g., 0.9250 Silver .8411 oz. ASW, 38.5 mm. **Ruler:** Elizabeth II **Subject:** 70th Birthday of Queen Elizabeth II **Obv:** Crowned bust right **Obv. Designer:** Raphael Maklouf **Rev:** Monogram and numeral 70 flanked by flower sprigs

Date	Mintage	F	VF	XF	Unc	BU
1996 Proof	Est. 30,000	Value: 40.00				

KM# 585 CROWN

Copper-Nickel, 38.5 mm. **Ruler:** Elizabeth II **Series:** Preserve Planet Earth **Obv:** Crowned bust right **Obv. Designer:** Raphael Maklouf **Rev:** Killer whale

Date	Mintage	F	VF	XF	Unc	BU
1996	—	—	—	—	12.00	14.00

KM# 585a CROWN

28.2800 g., 0.9250 Silver .8411 oz. ASW, 38.5 mm. **Ruler:** Elizabeth II **Series:** Preserve Planet Earth **Obv:** Crowned bust right **Obv. Designer:** Raphael Maklouf **Rev:** Killer whale

Date	Mintage	F	VF	XF	Unc	BU
1996 Proof	Est. 30,000	Value: 40.00				

KM# 586 CROWN

Copper-Nickel, 38.5 mm. **Ruler:** Elizabeth II **Series:** Preserve Planet Earth **Obv:** Crowned bust right **Obv. Designer:** Raphael Maklouf **Rev:** Razorbill feeding chick

Date	Mintage	F	VF	XF	Unc	BU
1996	—	—	—	—	12.00	14.00

KM# 586a CROWN

28.2800 g., 0.9250 Silver .8411 oz. ASW, 38.5 mm. **Ruler:** Elizabeth II **Series:** Preserve Planet Earth **Obv:** Crowned bust right **Obv. Designer:** Raphael Maklouf **Rev:** Razorbill feeding chick

Date	Mintage	F	VF	XF	Unc	BU
1996 Proof	Est. 30,000	Value: 40.00				

KM# 609 CROWN

Copper-Nickel, 38.5 mm. **Ruler:** Elizabeth II **Series:** Flower Fairies **Obv:** Crowned bust right **Obv. Designer:** Raphael Maklouf **Rev:** Orchis **Rev. Designer:** Cecily Mary Barker

Date	Mintage	F	VF	XF	Unc	BU
1996	—	—	—	—	5.00	6.50

KM# 609a CROWN

28.2800 g., 0.9250 Silver .8411 oz. ASW, 38.5 mm. **Ruler:** Elizabeth II **Series:** Flower Fairies **Obv:** Crowned bust right **Obv. Designer:** Raphael Maklouf **Rev:** Orchis **Rev. Designer:** Cecily Mary Barker

Date	Mintage	F	VF	XF	Unc	BU
1996 Proof	Est. 30,000	Value: 40.00				

KM# 610 CROWN

Copper-Nickel, 38.5 mm. **Ruler:** Elizabeth II **Series:** Flower Fairies **Obv:** Crowned bust right **Obv. Designer:** Raphael Maklouf **Rev:** Rose **Rev. Designer:** Cecily Mary Barker

Date	Mintage	F	VF	XF	Unc	BU
1996	—	—	—	—	8.00	10.00

KM# 610a CROWN

28.2800 g., 0.9250 Silver .8411 oz. ASW, 38.5 mm. **Ruler:** Elizabeth II **Series:** Flower Fairies **Obv:** Crowned bust right **Obv. Designer:** Raphael Maklouf **Rev:** Rose **Rev. Designer:** Cecily Mary Barker

Date	Mintage	F	VF	XF	Unc	BU
1996 Proof	Est. 30,000	Value: 40.00				

KM# 611 CROWN

Copper-Nickel, 38.5 mm. **Ruler:** Elizabeth II **Series:** Flower Fairies **Obv:** Crowned bust right **Obv. Designer:** Raphael Maklouf **Rev:** Fuchsia **Rev. Designer:** Cecily Mary Barker

Date	Mintage	F	VF	XF	Unc	BU
1996	—	—	—	—	5.00	6.50

KM# 611a CROWN

28.2800 g., 0.9250 Silver .8411 oz. ASW, 38.5 mm. **Ruler:** Elizabeth II **Series:** Flower Fairies **Obv:** Crowned bust right **Obv. Designer:** Raphael Maklouf **Rev:** Fuchsia **Rev. Designer:** Cecily Mary Barker

Date	Mintage	F	VF	XF	Unc	BU
1996 Proof	Est. 30,000	Value: 40:00				

KM# 612 CROWN

Copper-Nickel, 38.5 mm. **Ruler:** Elizabeth II **Series:** Flower Fairies **Obv:** Crowned bust right **Obv. Designer:** Raphael Maklouf **Rev:** Pinks **Rev. Designer:** Cecily Mary Barker

Date	Mintage	F	VF	XF	Unc	BU
1996	—	—	—	—	5.00	6.50

KM# 612a CROWN

28.2800 g., 0.9250 Silver .8411 oz. ASW, 38.5 mm. **Ruler:** Elizabeth II **Series:** Flower Fairies **Obv:** Crowned bust right **Obv. Designer:** Raphael Maklouf **Rev:** Pinks **Rev. Designer:** Cecily Mary Barker

Date	Mintage	F	VF	XF	Unc	BU
1996 Proof	Est. 30,000	Value: 40.00				

KM# 621 CROWN

Copper-Nickel, 38.5 mm. **Ruler:** Elizabeth II **Obv:** Crowned bust right **Obv. Designer:** Raphael Maklouf **Rev:** Burmese cat

Date	Mintage	F	VF	XF	Unc	BU
1996	—	—	—	—	12.50	15.00

KM# 621a CROWN

31.1035 g., 0.9990 Silver 1.000 oz. ASW, 38.5 mm. **Ruler:** Elizabeth II **Obv:** Crowned bust right **Obv. Designer:** Raphael Maklouf **Rev:** Burmese cat

Date	Mintage	F	VF	XF	Unc	BU
1996 Proof	Est. 50,000	Value: 40.00				

KM# 621b CROWN

31.1000 g., 0.9990 Gold 1.0000 oz. AGW **Ruler:** Elizabeth II **Obv:** Crowned bust right **Obv. Designer:** Raphael Maklouf **Rev:** Burmese cat

Date	Mintage	F	VF	XF	Unc	BU
1996 U	—	—	—	—	675	700
1996 Proof	—	Value: 725				

KM# 624 CROWN

31.1035 g., 0.9995 Platinum .9995 oz. APW **Ruler:** Elizabeth II **Obv:** Crowned bust right **Obv. Designer:** Raphael Maklouf **Rev:** Burmese cat

Date	Mintage	F	VF	XF	Unc	BU
1996	—	—	—	—	BV+20%	—
1996 Proof	—	BV+25%				

KM# 626 CROWN

Copper-Nickel, 38.5 mm. **Ruler:** Elizabeth II **Obv:** Crowned bust right **Obv. Designer:** Raphael Maklouf **Rev:** Bust within map and ship

Date	Mintage	F	VF	XF	Unc	BU
1996	—	—	—	—	7.50	10.00

KM# 626a CROWN

28.2800 g., 0.9250 Silver .8411 oz. ASW, 38.5 mm. **Ruler:** Elizabeth II **Obv:** Crowned bust right **Obv. Designer:** Raphael Maklouf **Rev:** Bust within map and ship

Date	Mintage	F	VF	XF	Unc	BU
1996 Proof	Est. 30,000	Value: 40.00				

KM# 629 CROWN

Copper-Nickel, 38.5 mm. **Ruler:** Elizabeth II **Obv:** Crowned bust right **Obv. Designer:** Raphael Maklouf **Rev:** Bust, map and ship

Date	Mintage	F	VF	XF	Unc	BU
1996	—	—	—	—	7.00	9.00

KM# 629a CROWN

28.2800 g., 0.9250 Silver .8411 oz. ASW, 38.5 mm. **Ruler:** Elizabeth II **Obv:** Crowned bust right **Obv. Designer:** Raphael Maklouf **Rev:** Bust, map and ship

Date	Mintage	F	VF	XF	Unc	BU
1996 Proof	Est. 30,000	Value: 40.00				

KM# 632 CROWN

Copper-Nickel, 38.5 mm. **Ruler:** Elizabeth II **Series:** European Football Championship **Obv:** Crowned bust right **Obv. Designer:** Raphael Maklouf **Rev:** Football player flanked by emblems within broken circle

Date	Mintage	F	VF	XF	Unc	BU
1996	—	—	—	—	7.00	9.00

KM# 632a CROWN

28.2800 g., 0.9250 Silver .8411 oz. ASW, 38.5 mm. **Ruler:** Elizabeth II **Series:** European Football Championship **Obv:** Crowned bust right **Obv. Designer:** Raphael Maklouf **Rev:** Football player flanked by emblems within broken circle

Date	Mintage	F	VF	XF	Unc	BU
1996 Proof	Est. 30,000	Value: 40.00				

KM# 635 CROWN

Copper-Nickel, 38.5 mm. **Ruler:** Elizabeth II **Series:** European Football Championship **Obv:** Crowned bust right **Obv. Designer:** Raphael Maklouf **Rev:** Czech Republic vs Itay

Date	Mintage	F	VF	XF	Unc	BU
1996	—	—	—	—	7.00	9.00

KM# 635a CROWN

28.2800 g., 0.9250 Silver .8411 oz. ASW, 38.5 mm. **Ruler:** Elizabeth II **Series:** European Football Championship **Obv:** Crowned bust right **Obv. Designer:** Raphael Maklouf **Rev:** Czech Republic vs Italy

Date	Mintage	F	VF	XF	Unc	BU
1996 Proof	Est. 30,000	Value: 40.00				

KM# 638 CROWN

Copper-Nickel, 38.5 mm. **Ruler:** Elizabeth II **Series:** European Football Championship **Obv:** Crowned bust right **Obv. Designer:** Raphael Maklouf **Rev:** Germany vs Russia

Date	Mintage	F	VF	XF	Unc	BU
1996	—	—	—	—	7.00	9.00

KM# 638a CROWN

28.2800 g., 0.9250 Silver .8411 oz. ASW, 38.5 mm. **Ruler:** Elizabeth II **Series:** European Football Championship **Obv:** Crowned bust right **Obv. Designer:** Raphael Maklouf **Rev:** Germany vs Russia

Date	Mintage	F	VF	XF	Unc	BU
1996 Proof	Est. 30,000	Value: 40.00				

KM# 641 CROWN

Copper-Nickel, 38.5 mm. **Ruler:** Elizabeth II **Series:** European Football Championship **Obv:** Crowned bust right **Obv. Designer:** Raphael Maklouf **Rev:** Spain vs France

Date	Mintage	F	VF	XF	Unc	BU
1996	—	—	—	—	7.00	9.00

KM# 641a CROWN

28.2800 g., 0.9250 Silver .8411 oz. ASW, 38.5 mm. **Ruler:** Elizabeth II **Series:** European Football Championship **Obv:** Crowned bust right **Obv. Designer:** Raphael Maklouf **Rev:** Spain vs France

Date	Mintage	F	VF	XF	Unc	BU
1996 Proof	Est. 30,000	Value: 40.00				

KM# 644 CROWN

Copper-Nickel, 38.5 mm. **Ruler:** Elizabeth II **Series:** European Football Championship **Obv:** Crowned bust right **Obv. Designer:** Raphael Maklouf **Rev:** Turkey vs Croatia

Date	Mintage	F	VF	XF	Unc	BU
1996	—	—	—	—	7.00	9.00

KM# 644a CROWN

28.2800 g., 0.9250 Silver .8411 oz. ASW, 38.5 mm. **Ruler:** Elizabeth II **Series:** European Football Championship **Obv:** Crowned bust right **Obv. Designer:** Raphael Maklouf **Rev:** Turkey vs Croatia

Date	Mintage	F	VF	XF	Unc	BU
1996 Proof	Est. 30,000	Value: 40.00				

KM# 647 CROWN

Copper-Nickel, 38.5 mm. **Ruler:** Elizabeth II **Series:** European Football Championship **Obv:** Crowned bust right **Obv. Designer:** Raphael Maklouf **Rev:** Denmark vs Portugal

Date	Mintage	F	VF	XF	Unc	BU
1996	—	—	—	—	6.00	8.00

KM# 647a CROWN

28.2800 g., 0.9250 Silver .8411 oz. ASW, 38.5 mm. **Ruler:** Elizabeth II **Series:** European Football Championship **Obv:** Crowned bust right **Obv. Designer:** Raphael Maklouf **Rev:** Denmark vs Portugal

Date	Mintage	F	VF	XF	Unc	BU
1996 Proof	Est. 30,000	Value: 40.00				

KM# 650 CROWN

Copper-Nickel, 38.5 mm. **Ruler:** Elizabeth II **Series:** European Football Championship **Obv:** Crowned bust right **Obv. Designer:** Raphael Maklouf **Rev:** Scotland vs England

Date	Mintage	F	VF	XF	Unc	BU
1996	—	—	—	—	7.00	9.00

KM# 650a CROWN

28.2800 g., 0.9250 Silver .8411 oz. ASW, 38.5 mm.
Ruler: Elizabeth II **Series:** European Football Championship **Obv:** Crowned bust right **Obv. Designer:** Raphael Maklouf **Rev:** Scotland vs England

Date	Mintage	F	VF	XF	Unc	BU
1996 Proof	Est. 30,000	Value: 40.00				

KM# 653 CROWN

Copper-Nickel, 38.5 mm. **Ruler:** Elizabeth II **Series:** European Football Championship **Obv:** Crowned bust right **Obv. Designer:** Raphael Maklouf **Rev:** Holland vs Switzerland

Date	Mintage	F	VF	XF	Unc	BU
1996	—	—	—	—	7.00	9.00

KM# 653a CROWN

28.2800 g., 0.9250 Silver .8411 oz. ASW, 38.5 mm.
Ruler: Elizabeth II **Series:** European Football Championship **Obv:** Crowned bust right **Obv. Designer:** Raphael Maklouf **Rev:** Holland vs Switzerland

Date	Mintage	F	VF	XF	Unc	BU
1996 Proof	Est. 30,000	Value: 40.00				

KM# 657 CROWN

Copper-Nickel, 38.5 mm. **Ruler:** Elizabeth II **Series:** European Football Championship **Obv:** Crowned bust right **Obv. Designer:** Raphael Maklouf **Rev:** German shield, winner

Date	Mintage	F	VF	XF	Unc	BU
1996	—	—	—	—	7.00	9.00

KM# 657a CROWN

28.2800 g., 0.9250 Silver .8411 oz. ASW, 38.5 mm.
Ruler: Elizabeth II **Series:** European Football Championship **Obv:** Crowned bust right **Obv. Designer:** Raphael Maklouf **Rev:** German shield, winner

Date	Mintage	F	VF	XF	Unc	BU
1996 Proof	Est. 30,000	Value: 40.00				

KM# 679 CROWN

Copper-Nickel, 38.5 mm. **Ruler:** Elizabeth II **Series:** Legend of King Arthur **Obv:** Crowned bust right **Obv. Designer:** Raphael Maklouf **Rev:** King Arthur with sword and orb

Date	Mintage	F	VF	XF	Unc	BU
1996	Est. 30,000	—	—	—	10.00	12.50

KM# 679a CROWN

28.2800 g., 0.9250 Silver .8411 oz. ASW, 38.5 mm.
Ruler: Elizabeth II **Series:** Legend of King Arthur **Obv:** Crowned bust right **Obv. Designer:** Raphael Maklouf **Rev:** King Arthur with sword and orb

Date	Mintage	F	VF	XF	Unc	BU
1996 Proof	Est. 30,000	Value: 22.50				

KM# 680 CROWN

Copper-Nickel, 38.5 mm. **Ruler:** Elizabeth II **Series:** Legend of King Arthur **Obv:** Crowned bust right **Obv. Designer:** Raphael Maklouf **Rev:** Crowned 3/4-length figure facing walking through archway

Date	Mintage	F	VF	XF	Unc	BU
1996	—	—	—	—	10.00	12.50

KM# 680a CROWN

28.2800 g., 0.9250 Silver .8411 oz. ASW, 38.5 mm.
Ruler: Elizabeth II **Series:** Legend of King Arthur **Obv:** Crowned bust right **Obv. Designer:** Raphael Maklouf **Rev:** Crowned 3/4 length figure facing walking through archway

Date	Mintage	F	VF	XF	Unc	BU
1996 Proof	Est. 30,000	Value: 22.50				

KM# 681 CROWN

Copper-Nickel, 38.5 mm. **Ruler:** Elizabeth II **Series:** Legend of King Arthur **Obv:** Crowned bust right **Obv. Designer:** Raphael Maklouf **Rev:** Armored equestrian within circle

Date	Mintage	F	VF	XF	Unc	BU
1996	—	—	—	—	10.00	12.50

KM# 681a CROWN

28.2800 g., 0.9250 Silver .8411 oz. ASW, 38.5 mm.
Ruler: Elizabeth II **Series:** Legend of King Arthur **Obv:** Crowned bust right **Obv. Designer:** Raphael Maklouf **Rev:** Armored equestrian within circle

Date	Mintage	F	VF	XF	Unc	BU
1996 Proof	Est. 30,000	Value: 22.50				

KM# 682 CROWN

Copper-Nickel, 38.5 mm. **Ruler:** Elizabeth II **Series:** Legend of King Arthur **Obv:** Crowned bust right **Obv. Designer:** Raphael Maklouf **Rev:** Merlin

Date	Mintage	F	VF	XF	Unc	BU
1996	—	—	—	—	10.00	12.50

KM# 682a CROWN

28.2800 g., 0.9250 Silver .8411 oz. ASW, 38.5 mm.
Ruler: Elizabeth II **Series:** Legend of King Arthur **Obv:** Crowned bust right **Obv. Designer:** Raphael Maklouf **Rev:** Merlin

Date	Mintage	F	VF	XF	Unc	BU
1996 Proof	Est. 30,000	Value: 22.50				

KM# 683 CROWN

Copper-Nickel, 38.5 mm. **Ruler:** Elizabeth II **Series:** Legend of King Arthur **Obv:** Crowned bust right **Obv. Designer:** Raphael Maklouf **Rev:** Camelot Castle

Date	Mintage	F	VF	XF	Unc	BU
1996	—	—	—	—	10.00	12.50

KM# 683a CROWN

28.2800 g., 0.9250 Silver .8411 oz. ASW, 38.5 mm. **Ruler:** Elizabeth II **Series:** Legend of King Arthur **Obv:** Crowned bust right **Obv. Designer:** Raphael Maklouf **Rev:** Camelot Castle

Date	Mintage	F	VF	XF	Unc	BU
1996 Proof	Est. 30,000	Value: 25.00				

KM# 732 CROWN

Copper-Nickel, 38.5 mm. **Ruler:** Elizabeth II **Subject:** Year of the Rat **Obv:** Crowned bust right within circle **Obv. Designer:** Raphael Maklouf **Rev:** Rat within circle

Date	Mintage	F	VF	XF	Unc	BU
1996	—	—	—	—	12.00	14.00

KM# 732a CROWN

28.2800 g., 0.9250 Silver .8411 oz. ASW, 38.5 mm. **Ruler:** Elizabeth II **Subject:** Year of the Rat **Obv:** Crowned bust right within circle **Obv. Designer:** Raphael Maklouf **Rev:** Rat within circle

Date	Mintage	F	VF	XF	Unc	BU
1996 Proof	—	—	—	—	—	—

Note: Entire silver issue purchased by one buyer. Mintage, disposition and market value unknown

KM# 733 CROWN

31.1035 g., 0.9999 Gold 1.0000 oz. AGW **Ruler:** Elizabeth II **Subject:** Year of the Rat **Obv:** Crowned bust right **Obv. Designer:** Raphael Maklouf **Rev:** Rat

Date	Mintage	F	VF	XF	Unc	BU
1996 Proof	—	—	—	—	—	—

Note: Entire gold issue purchased by one buyer. Mintage, disposition and market value unknown

KM# 725 CROWN

Copper-Nickel, 38.5 mm. **Ruler:** Elizabeth II **Subject:** Year of the Ox **Obv:** Crowned bust right **Obv. Designer:** Raphael Maklouf **Rev:** Ox laying down

Date	Mintage	F	VF	XF	Unc	BU
1997	—	—	—	—	10.00	12.00

KM# 725a CROWN

28.2800 g., 0.9250 Silver .8411 oz. ASW, 38.5 mm.
Ruler: Elizabeth II **Subject:** Year of the Ox **Obv:** Crowned bust right **Obv. Designer:** Raphael Maklouf **Rev:** Ox laying down

Date	Mintage	F	VF	XF	Unc	BU
1997 Proof	Est. 30,000	Value: 40.00				

KM# 726 CROWN

31.1035 g., 0.9999 Gold 1.0000 oz. AGW **Ruler:** Elizabeth II **Subject:** Year of the Ox **Obv:** Crowned bust right **Obv. Designer:** Raphael Maklouf **Rev:** Ox laying down

Date	Mintage	F	VF	XF	Unc	BU
1997 Proof	Est. 2,000	Value: 725				

KM# 759 CROWN

Copper-Nickel, 38.5 mm. **Ruler:** Elizabeth II **Series:** Flower Fairies **Obv:** Crowned bust right **Obv. Designer:** Raphael Maklouf **Rev:** Fairy sitting on flowers **Rev. Designer:** Cecily Mary Barker

Date	Mintage	F	VF	XF	Unc	BU
1997	—	—	—	—	8.00	10.00

KM# 759a CROWN

28.2800 g., 0.9250 Silver .8411 oz. ASW, 38.5 mm.
Ruler: Elizabeth II **Series:** Flower Fairies **Obv:** Crowned bust right **Obv. Designer:** Raphael Maklouf **Rev:** Fairy sitting on flowers **Rev. Designer:** Cecily Mary Barker

Date	Mintage	F	VF	XF	Unc	BU
1997 Proof	Est. 30,000	Value: 40.00				

KM# 760 CROWN

Copper-Nickel, 38.5 mm. **Ruler:** Elizabeth II **Series:** Flower Fairies **Obv:** Crowned bust right **Obv. Designer:** Raphael Maklouf **Rev:** Snowdrop **Rev. Designer:** Cecily Mary Barker

Date	Mintage	F	VF	XF	Unc	BU
1997	—	—	—	—	8.00	10.00

KM# 760a CROWN

28.2800 g., 0.9250 Silver .8411 oz. ASW, 38.5 mm.
Ruler: Elizabeth II **Series:** Flower Fairies **Obv:** Crowned bust right **Obv. Designer:** Raphael Maklouf **Rev:** Snowdrop **Rev. Designer:** Cecily Mary Barker

Date	Mintage	F	VF	XF	Unc	BU
1997 Proof	Est. 30,000	Value: 40.00				

KM# 761 CROWN

Copper-Nickel, 38.5 mm. **Ruler:** Elizabeth II **Series:** Flower Fairies **Obv:** Crowned bust right **Obv. Designer:** Raphael Maklouf **Rev:** Tulip **Rev. Designer:** Cecily Mary Barker

Date	Mintage	F	VF	XF	Unc	BU
1997	—	—	—	—	8.00	10.00

KM# 761a CROWN

28.2800 g., 0.9250 Silver .8411 oz. ASW, 38.5 mm.
Ruler: Elizabeth II **Series:** Flower Fairies **Obv:** Crowned bust right **Obv. Designer:** Raphael Maklouf **Rev:** Tulip **Rev. Designer:** Cecily Mary Barker

Date	Mintage	F	VF	XF	Unc	BU
1997 Proof	Est. 30,000	Value: 40.00				

KM# 762 CROWN

Copper-Nickel, 38.5 mm. **Ruler:** Elizabeth II **Series:** Flower Fairies **Obv:** Crowned bust right **Obv. Designer:** Raphael Maklouf **Rev:** Jasmine **Rev. Designer:** Cecily Mary Barker

Date	Mintage	F	VF	XF	Unc	BU
1997	—	—	—	—	8.00	10.00

KM# 762a CROWN
28.2800 g., 0.9250 Silver .8411 oz. ASW, 38.5 mm.
Ruler: Elizabeth II **Series:** Flower Fairies **Obv:** Crowned bust right **Obv. Designer:** Raphael Maklouf **Rev:** Jasmine **Rev. Designer:** Cecily Mary Barker

Date	Mintage	F	VF	XF	Unc	BU
1997 Proof	Est. 30,000	Value: 40.00				

KM# 765 CROWN
Copper-Nickel, 38.5 mm. **Ruler:** Elizabeth II **Obv:** Crowned bust right **Obv. Designer:** Raphael Maklouf **Rev:** Leif Eriksson 999-1001, viking ship with map sail

Date	Mintage	F	VF	XF	Unc	BU
1997	—	—	—	—	8.00	10.00

KM# 765a CROWN
28.2800 g., 0.9250 Silver .8411 oz. ASW, 38.5 mm. **Ruler:** Elizabeth II **Obv:** Crowned bust right **Obv. Designer:** Raphael Maklouf **Rev:** Leif Eriksson 999-1001, viking ship with map sail

Date	Mintage	F	VF	XF	Unc	BU
1997 Proof	Est. 30,000	Value: 40.00				

KM# 768 CROWN
Copper-Nickel, 38.5 mm. **Ruler:** Elizabeth II **Obv:** Crowned bust right **Obv. Designer:** Raphael Maklouf **Rev:** Bust of Fridtjof Nansen, map and his ship "The Fram"

Date	Mintage	F	VF	XF	Unc	BU
1997	—	—	—	—	8.00	10.00

KM# 768a CROWN
28.2800 g., 0.9250 Silver .8411 oz. ASW, 38.5 mm. **Ruler:** Elizabeth II **Obv:** Crowned bust right **Obv. Designer:** Raphael Maklouf **Rev:** Bust of Fridtjof Nansen, map and his ship "The Fram"

Date	Mintage	F	VF	XF	Unc	BU
1997 Proof	Est. 30,000	Value: 40.00				

KM# 774 CROWN
Copper-Nickel, 38.5 mm. **Ruler:** Elizabeth II **Obv:** Crowned bust right **Obv. Designer:** Raphael Maklouf **Rev:** Long-haired Smoke cat

Date	Mintage	F	VF	XF	Unc	BU
1997	—	—	—	—	10.00	14.00
1997 Proof	—	Value: 20.00				

KM# 774a CROWN
31.1035 g., 0.9999 Silver 1.0000 oz. ASW, 38.5 mm.
Ruler: Elizabeth II **Obv:** Crowned bust right **Obv. Designer:** Raphael Maklouf **Rev:** Long-haired Smoke cat

Date	Mintage	F	VF	XF	Unc	BU
1997 Proof	Est. 50,000	Value: 40.00				

KM# 774b CROWN
31.1035 g., 0.9999 Gold 1.0000 oz. AGW **Ruler:** Elizabeth II **Obv:** Crowned bust right **Obv. Designer:** Raphael Maklouf **Rev:** Long-haired Smoke cat

Date	Mintage	F	VF	XF	Unc	BU
1997	—	—	—	—	675	700
1997 Proof	—	Value: 725				

KM# 777 CROWN
28.2800 g., 0.9250 Silver .8411 oz. ASW, 38.5 mm.
Ruler: Elizabeth II **Series:** History of the Cat **Obv:** Crowned bust right **Obv. Designer:** Raphael Maklouf **Rev:** Ancestry of Felidae, evolution of the cat

Date	Mintage	F	VF	XF	Unc	BU
1997 Proof	Est. 10,000	Value: 45.00				

KM# 778 CROWN
28.2800 g., 0.9250 Silver .8411 oz. ASW, 38.5 mm.
Ruler: Elizabeth II **Series:** History of the Cat **Obv:** Crowned bust right **Obv. Designer:** Raphael Maklouf **Rev:** Snarling cat

Date	Mintage	F	VF	XF	Unc	BU
1997 Proof	Est. 10,000	Value: 45.00				

KM# 779 CROWN
28.2800 g., 0.9250 Silver .8411 oz. ASW, 38.5 mm.
Ruler: Elizabeth II **Series:** History of the Cat **Obv:** Crowned bust right **Obv. Designer:** Raphael Maklouf **Rev:** Cat walking left

Date	Mintage	F	VF	XF	Unc	BU
1997 Proof	Est. 10,000	Value: 45.00				

KM# 780 CROWN
28.2800 g., 0.9250 Silver .8411 oz. ASW, 38.5 mm.
Ruler: Elizabeth II **Series:** History of the Cat **Obv:** Crowned bust right **Obv. Designer:** Raphael Maklouf **Rev:** Ancient Egyptian Goddess Bast and artifacts

Date	Mintage	F	VF	XF	Unc	BU
1997 Proof	Est. 10,000	Value: 45.00				

KM# 782 CROWN
Copper-Nickel, 38.5 mm. **Ruler:** Elizabeth II **Subject:** 90th Anniversary of the TT **Obv:** Crowned bust right **Obv. Designer:** Raphael Maklouf **Rev:** Motorcyclist flanked by emblems above sprigs

Date	Mintage	F	VF	XF	Unc	BU
1997	—	—	—	—	8.00	10.00

KM# 782a CROWN
28.2800 g., 0.9250 Silver .8411 oz. ASW, 38.5 mm.
Ruler: Elizabeth II **Subject:** 90th Anniversary of the TT **Obv:** Crowned bust right **Obv. Designer:** Raphael Maklouf **Rev:** Motorcyclist flanked by emblems above sprigs

Date	Mintage	F	VF	XF	Unc	BU
1997 Proof	Est. 30,000	Value: 42.50				

KM# 784 CROWN
Copper-Nickel, 38.5 mm. **Ruler:** Elizabeth II **Subject:** 90th Anniversary of the TT **Obv:** Crowned bust right **Obv. Designer:** Raphael Maklouf **Rev:** 1937 winner Omobono Tenni

Date	Mintage	F	VF	XF	Unc	BU
1997	—	—	—	—	9.50	11.50

KM# 784a CROWN
28.2800 g., 0.9250 Silver .8411 oz. ASW, 38.5 mm.
Ruler: Elizabeth II **Subject:** 90th Anniversary of the TT **Obv:** Crowned bust right **Obv. Designer:** Raphael Maklouf **Rev:** 1937 winner Omobono Tenni

Date	Mintage	F	VF	XF	Unc	BU
1997 Proof	Est. 30,000	Value: 42.50				

KM# 786 CROWN
Copper-Nickel, 38.5 mm. **Ruler:** Elizabeth II **Subject:** 90th Anniversary of the TT **Obv:** Crowned bust right **Obv. Designer:** Raphael Maklouf **Rev:** 1957 winner Bob McIntyre

Date	Mintage	F	VF	XF	Unc	BU
1997	—	—	—	—	9.50	11.50

KM# 786a CROWN
28.2800 g., 0.9250 Silver .8411 oz. ASW, 38.5 mm.
Ruler: Elizabeth II **Subject:** 90th Anniversary of the TT **Obv:** Crowned bust right **Obv. Designer:** Raphael Maklouf **Rev:** 1957 winner Bob McIntyre

Date	Mintage	F	VF	XF	Unc	BU
1997 Proof	Est. 30,000	Value: 42.50				

KM# 788 CROWN
Copper-Nickel, 38.5 mm. **Ruler:** Elizabeth II **Subject:** 90th Anniversary of the TT **Obv:** Crowned bust right **Obv. Designer:** Raphael Maklouf **Rev:** 1967 winner Mike Hailwood

Date	Mintage	F	VF	XF	Unc	BU
1997	—	—	—	—	9.50	11.50

KM# 788a CROWN
28.2800 g., 0.9250 Silver .8411 oz. ASW, 38.5 mm.
Ruler: Elizabeth II **Subject:** 90th Anniversary of the TT **Obv:** Crowned bust right **Obv. Designer:** Raphael Maklouf **Rev:** 1967 winner Mike Hailwood

Date	Mintage	F	VF	XF	Unc	BU
1997 Proof	Est. 30,000	Value: 42.50				

KM# 793 CROWN
Copper-Nickel, 38.5 mm. **Ruler:** Elizabeth II **Subject:** 50th Wedding Anniversary of Queen Elizabeth II and Prince Philip **Obv:** Crowned bust right **Obv. Designer:** Raphael Maklouf **Rev:** Conjoined 3/4 length figures facing

Date	Mintage	F	VF	XF	Unc	BU
1997	—	—	—	—	8.00	10.00

KM# 793a CROWN
28.2800 g., 0.9250 Gold Clad Silver .8411 oz., 38.5 mm. **Ruler:** Elizabeth II **Subject:** 50th Wedding Anniversary of Queen Elizabeth II and Prince Philip **Obv:** Crowned bust right **Obv. Designer:** Raphael Maklouf **Rev:** Conjoined 3/4 length figures facing

Date	Mintage	F	VF	XF	Unc	BU
1997 Proof	Est. 10,000	Value: 40.00				

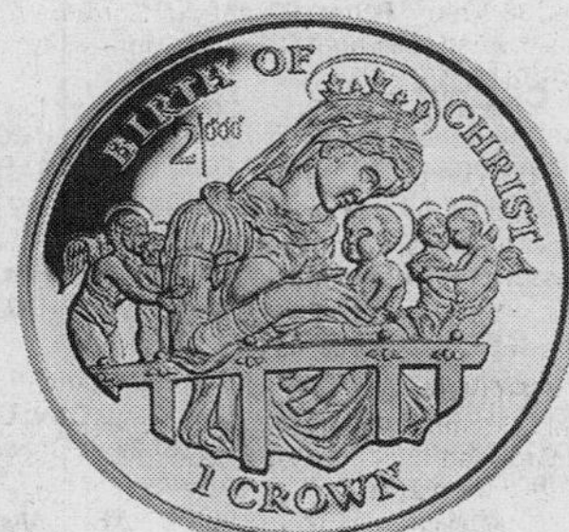

KM# 799 CROWN
Copper-Nickel, 38.5 mm. **Ruler:** Elizabeth II **Series:** Year 2000 **Subject:** Birth of Christ **Obv:** Crowned bust right **Obv. Designer:** Raphael Maklouf **Rev:** Madonna and child with angels

Date	Mintage	F	VF	XF	Unc	BU
1997	—	—	—	—	7.50	9.50

KM# 799a CROWN
28.2800 g., 0.9250 Silver .8411 oz. ASW, 38.5 mm.
Ruler: Elizabeth II **Series:** Year 2000 **Subject:** Birth of Christ **Obv:** Crowned bust right **Obv. Designer:** Raphael Maklouf **Rev:** Madonna and child with angels

Date	Mintage	F	VF	XF	Unc	BU
1997 Proof	Est. 10,000	Value: 50.00				

KM# 801 CROWN
Copper-Nickel, 38.5 mm. **Ruler:** Elizabeth II **Series:** Year 2000 **Subject:** Fall of the Roman Empire 476 **Obv:** Crowned bust right **Obv. Designer:** Raphael Maklouf **Rev:** Barbarian defeating soldier

Date	Mintage	F	VF	XF	Unc	BU
1997	—	—	—	—	7.50	9.50

KM# 801a CROWN
28.2800 g., 0.9250 Silver .8411 oz. ASW, 38.5 mm.
Ruler: Elizabeth II **Series:** Year 2000 **Subject:** Fall of the Roman Empire 476 **Obv:** Crowned bust right **Obv. Designer:** Raphael Maklouf **Rev:** Barbarian defeating soldier

Date	Mintage	F	VF	XF	Unc	BU
1997 Proof	Est. 10,000	Value: 50.00				

KM# 803 CROWN
Copper-Nickel, 38.5 mm. **Ruler:** Elizabeth II **Series:** Year 2000 **Subject:** Flight of Mohammed 622 **Obv:** Crowned bust right **Obv. Designer:** Raphael Maklouf **Rev:** Arabs and camels at oasis

Date	Mintage	F	VF	XF	Unc	BU
1997	—	—	—	—	7.50	9.50

KM# 803a CROWN
28.2800 g., 0.9250 Silver .8411 oz. ASW, 38.5 mm.
Ruler: Elizabeth II **Series:** Year 2000 **Subject:** Flight of Mohammed 622 **Obv:** Crowned bust right **Obv. Designer:** Raphael Maklouf **Rev:** Arabs and camels at oasis

Date	Mintage	F	VF	XF	Unc	BU
1997 Proof	Est. 10,000	Value: 50.00				

KM# 805 CROWN
Copper-Nickel, 38.5 mm. **Ruler:** Elizabeth II **Series:** Year 2000 **Subject:** Norman Conquest 1066 **Obv:** Crowned bust right **Obv. Designer:** Raphael Maklouf **Rev:** William the Conqueror rallying his troops

Date	Mintage	F	VF	XF	Unc	BU
1997	—	—	—	—	7.50	9.50

KM# 805a CROWN
28.2800 g., 0.9250 Silver .8411 oz. ASW, 38.5 mm. **Ruler:** Elizabeth II **Series:** Year 2000 **Subject:** Norman Conquest 1066 **Obv:** Crowned bust right **Obv. Designer:** Raphael Maklouf **Rev:** Armored equestrian rallying his troops

Date	Mintage	F	VF	XF	Unc	BU
1997 Proof	Est. 10,000	Value: 50.00				

KM# 808 CROWN
Copper-Nickel, 38.5 mm. **Ruler:** Elizabeth II **Series:** World Cup Soccer **Obv:** Crowned bust right **Obv. Designer:** Raphael Maklouf **Rev:** Soccer players within ball

Date	Mintage	F	VF	XF	Unc	BU
1998	—	—	—	—	7.50	9.50

KM# 808a CROWN
28.2800 g., 0.9250 Silver .8411 oz. ASW, 38.5 mm. **Ruler:** Elizabeth II **Series:** World Cup Soccer **Obv:** Crowned bust right **Obv. Designer:** Raphael Maklouf **Rev:** Soccer players within ball

Date	Mintage	F	VF	XF	Unc	BU
1998 Proof	Est. 30,000	Value: 45.00				

KM# 809 CROWN
Copper-Nickel, 38.5 mm. **Ruler:** Elizabeth II **Series:** World Cup Soccer **Obv:** Crowned bust right **Obv. Designer:** Raphael Maklouf **Rev:** Soccer players

Date	Mintage	F	VF	XF	Unc	BU
1998	—	—	—	—	7.50	9.50

KM# 809a CROWN
28.2800 g., 0.9250 Silver .8411 oz. ASW, 38.5 mm.
Ruler: Elizabeth II **Series:** World Cup Soccer **Obv:** Crowned bust right **Obv. Designer:** Raphael Maklouf **Rev:** Soccer players

Date	Mintage	F	VF	XF	Unc	BU
1998 Proof	Est. 30,000	Value: 45.00				

KM# 810 CROWN
Copper-Nickel, 38.5 mm. **Ruler:** Elizabeth II **Series:** World Cup Soccer **Obv:** Crowned bust right **Obv. Designer:** Raphael Maklouf **Rev:** Soccer players

Date	Mintage	F	VF	XF	Unc	BU
1998	—	—	—	—	7.50	9.50

KM# 810a CROWN
28.2800 g., 0.9250 Silver .8411 oz. ASW, 38.5 mm.
Ruler: Elizabeth II **Series:** World Cup Soccer **Obv:** Crowned bust right **Obv. Designer:** Raphael Maklouf **Rev:** Soccer players

Date	Mintage	F	VF	XF	Unc	BU
1998 Proof	Est. 30,000	Value: 45.00				

KM# 811 CROWN
Copper-Nickel, 38.5 mm. **Ruler:** Elizabeth II **Series:** World Cup Soccer **Obv:** Crowned bust right **Obv. Designer:** Raphael Maklouf **Rev:** Soccer players

Date	Mintage	F	VF	XF	Unc	BU
1998	—	—	—	—	7.50	9.50

KM# 811a CROWN
28.2800 g., 0.9250 Silver .8411 oz. ASW, 38.5 mm. **Ruler:** Elizabeth II **Series:** World Cup Soccer **Obv:** Crowned bust right **Obv. Designer:** Raphael Maklouf **Rev:** Soccer players

Date	Mintage	F	VF	XF	Unc	BU
1998 Proof	Est. 30,000	Value: 45.00				

KM# 816 CROWN
Copper-Nickel, 38.5 mm. **Ruler:** Elizabeth II **Subject:** Year of the Tiger **Obv:** Crowned bust right within circle **Obv. Designer:** Raphael Maklouf **Rev:** Tiger within circle

Date	Mintage	F	VF	XF	Unc	BU
1998	—	—	—	—	12.00	14.00

KM# 816a CROWN
28.2800 g., 0.9250 Silver .8411 oz. ASW, 38.5 mm.
Ruler: Elizabeth II **Subject:** Year of the Tiger **Obv:** Crowned bust right within circle **Obv. Designer:** Raphael Maklouf **Rev:** Tiger within circle

Date	Mintage	F	VF	XF	Unc	BU
1998 Proof	Est. 30,000	Value: 45.00				

KM# 817 CROWN
31.1035 g., 0.9999 Gold 1.0000 oz. AGW **Ruler:** Elizabeth II **Subject:** Year of the Tiger **Obv:** Crowned bust right **Obv. Designer:** Raphael Maklouf **Rev:** Tiger

Date	Mintage	F	VF	XF	Unc	BU
1998 Proof	Est. 2,000	Value: 725				

KM# 825 CROWN
Copper-Nickel, 38.5 mm. **Ruler:** Elizabeth II **Obv:** Crowned bust right **Obv. Designer:** Raphael Maklouf **Rev:** Bust right, caravan and palace

Date	Mintage	F	VF	XF	Unc	BU
1998	—	—	—	—	8.00	10.00

KM# 825a CROWN
28.2800 g., 0.9250 Silver .8411 oz. ASW, 38.5 mm.
Ruler: Elizabeth II **Obv:** Crowned bust right **Rev:** Bust right, caravan and palace

Date	Mintage	F	VF	XF	Unc	BU
1998 Proof	Est. 30,000	Value: 47.50				

KM# 827 CROWN
Copper-Nickel, 38.5 mm. **Ruler:** Elizabeth II **Obv:** Crowned bust right **Obv. Designer:** Raphael Maklouf **Rev:** Bust, ship and African map

Date	Mintage	F	VF	XF	Unc	BU
1998	—	—	—	—	8.00	10.00

KM# 827a CROWN
28.2800 g., 0.9250 Silver .8411 oz. ASW, 38.5 mm.
Ruler: Elizabeth II **Obv:** Crowned bust right **Obv. Designer:** Raphael Maklouf **Rev:** Bust, ship and African map

Date	Mintage	F	VF	XF	Unc	BU
1998 Proof	Est. 30,000	Value: 47.50				

KM# 840 CROWN
Copper-Nickel, 38.5 mm. **Ruler:** Elizabeth II **Series:** Flower Fairies **Obv:** Crowned bust right **Obv. Designer:** Raphael Maklouf **Rev:** Standing fairy **Rev. Designer:** Cecily Mary Barker

Date	Mintage	F	VF	XF	Unc	BU
1998	—	—	—	—	8.00	10.00

KM# 840a CROWN
28.2800 g., 0.9250 Silver .8411 oz. ASW, 38.5 mm.
Ruler: Elizabeth II **Series:** Flower Fairies **Obv:** Crowned bust right **Obv. Designer:** Raphael Maklouf **Rev:** Standing fairy **Rev. Designer:** Cecily Mary Barker

Date	Mintage	F	VF	XF	Unc	BU
1998 Proof	Est. 30,000	Value: 47.50				

KM# 841 CROWN
Copper-Nickel, 38.5 mm. **Ruler:** Elizabeth II **Series:** Flower Fairies **Obv:** Crowned bust right **Obv. Designer:** Raphael Maklouf **Rev:** Sweet pea, two fairies **Rev. Designer:** Cecily Mary Barker

Date	Mintage	F	VF	XF	Unc	BU
1998	—	—	—	—	7.50	9.50

KM# 841a CROWN
28.2800 g., 0.9250 Silver .8411 oz. ASW, 38.5 mm.
Ruler: Elizabeth II **Series:** Flower Fairies **Obv:** Crowned bust right **Obv. Designer:** Raphael Maklouf **Rev:** Sweet pea, two fairies **Rev. Designer:** Cecily Mary Barker

Date	Mintage	F	VF	XF	Unc	BU
1998 Proof	Est. 30,000	Value: 47.50				

KM# 842 CROWN
Copper-Nickel, 38.5 mm. **Ruler:** Elizabeth II **Series:** Flower Fairies **Obv:** Crowned bust right **Obv. Designer:** Raphael Maklouf **Rev:** Fairy looking into flower **Rev. Designer:** Cecily Mary Barker

Date	Mintage	F	VF	XF	Unc	BU
1998	—	—	—	—	7.50	9.50

KM# 842a CROWN
28.2800 g., 0.9250 Silver .8411 oz. ASW, 38.5 mm.
Ruler: Elizabeth II **Series:** Flower Fairies **Obv:** Crowned bust right **Obv. Designer:** Raphael Maklouf **Rev:** Fairy looking into flower **Rev. Designer:** Cecily Mary Barker

Date	Mintage	F	VF	XF	Unc	BU
1998 Proof	Est. 30,000	Value: 47.50				

KM# 843 CROWN
Copper-Nickel, 38.5 mm. **Ruler:** Elizabeth II **Series:** Flower Fairies **Obv:** Crowned bust right **Obv. Designer:** Raphael Maklouf **Rev:** Fairy standing with flower **Rev. Designer:** Cecily Mary Barker

Date	Mintage	F	VF	XF	Unc	BU
1998	—	—	—	—	8.00	10.00

KM# 843a CROWN
28.2800 g., 0.9250 Silver .8411 oz. ASW, 38.5 mm.
Ruler: Elizabeth II **Series:** Flower Fairies **Obv:** Crowned bust right **Obv. Designer:** Raphael Maklouf **Rev:** Fairy standing with flower **Rev. Designer:** Cecily Mary Barker

Date	Mintage	F	VF	XF	Unc	BU
1998 Proof	Est. 20,000	Value: 47.50				

KM# 849 CROWN
Copper-Nickel, 38.5 mm. **Ruler:** Elizabeth II **Series:** Winter Olympics - Nagano **Obv:** Crowned bust right **Obv. Designer:** Raphael Maklouf **Rev:** Bobsled

Date	Mintage	F	VF	XF	Unc	BU
1998	—	—	—	—	7.50	9.50

KM# 849a CROWN
28.2800 g., 0.9250 Silver .8411 oz. ASW, 38.5 mm. **Ruler:** Elizabeth II **Series:** Winter Olympics - Nagano **Obv:** Crowned bust right **Obv. Designer:** Raphael Maklouf **Rev:** Bobsled

Date	Mintage	F	VF	XF	Unc	BU
1998 Proof	Est. 30,000	Value: 47.50				

KM# 850 CROWN
Copper-Nickel, 38.5 mm. **Ruler:** Elizabeth II **Series:** Winter Olympics - Nagano **Obv:** Crowned bust right
Obv. Designer: Raphael Maklouf **Rev:** Cross-country skier

Date	Mintage	F	VF	XF	Unc	BU
1998	—	—	—	—	7.50	9.50

KM# 850a CROWN
28.2800 g., 0.9250 Silver .8411 oz. ASW, 38.5 mm. **Ruler:** Elizabeth II **Series:** Winter Olympics - Nagano **Obv:** Crowned bust right **Obv. Designer:** Raphael Maklouf **Rev:** Cross-country skier

Date	Mintage	F	VF	XF	Unc	BU
1998 Proof	Est. 30,000	Value: 47.50				

KM# 851 CROWN
Copper-Nickel, 38.5 mm. **Ruler:** Elizabeth II **Series:** Winter Olympics - Nagano **Obv:** Crowned bust right
Obv. Designer: Raphael Maklouf **Rev:** Two hockey players

Date	Mintage	F	VF	XF	Unc	BU
1998	—	—	—	—	7.50	9.50

KM# 851a CROWN
28.2800 g., 0.9250 Silver .8411 oz. ASW, 38.5 mm. **Ruler:** Elizabeth II **Series:** Winter Olympics - Nagano **Obv:** Crowned bust right **Obv. Designer:** Raphael Maklouf **Rev:** Two hockey players

Date	Mintage	F	VF	XF	Unc	BU
1998 Proof	Est. 30,000	Value: 47.50				

KM# 852 CROWN
Copper-Nickel, 38.5 mm. **Ruler:** Elizabeth II **Series:** Winter Olympics - Nagano **Obv:** Crowned bust right
Obv. Designer: Raphael Maklouf **Rev:** Two speed skaters

Date	Mintage	F	VF	XF	Unc	BU
1998	—	—	—	—	7.50	9.50

KM# 852a CROWN
28.2800 g., 0.9250 Silver .8411 oz. ASW, 38.5 mm. **Ruler:** Elizabeth II **Series:** Winter Olympics - Nagano **Obv:** Crowned bust right **Obv. Designer:** Raphael Maklouf **Rev:** Two speed skaters

Date	Mintage	F	VF	XF	Unc	BU
1998 Proof	Est. 30,000	Value: 47.50				

KM# 857 CROWN
Copper-Nickel, 38.5 mm. **Ruler:** Elizabeth II **Obv:** Crowned bust right **Obv. Designer:** Raphael Maklouf **Rev:** Birman cat

Date	Mintage	F	VF	XF	Unc	BU
1998	—	—	—	—	10.00	12.00
1998 Proof	—	Value: 15.00				

KM# 857a CROWN
31.1035 g., 0.9999 Silver 1.0000 oz. ASW, 38.5 mm.
Ruler: Elizabeth II **Obv:** Crowned bust right
Obv. Designer: Raphael Maklouf **Rev:** Birman cat

Date	Mintage	F	VF	XF	Unc	BU
1998 Proof	Est. 50,000	Value: 47.50				

KM# 857b CROWN
31.1035 g., 0.9999 Gold 1.0000 oz. AGW **Ruler:** Elizabeth II **Obv:** Crowned bust right **Obv. Designer:** Raphael Maklouf **Rev:** Birman cat

Date	Mintage	F	VF	XF	Unc	BU
1998	—	—	—	—	675	700
1998 Proof	1,000	Value: 725				

KM# 872 CROWN
Copper-Nickel, 38.5 mm. **Ruler:** Elizabeth II **Subject:** 125th Anniversary of the Steam Railway **Obv:** Crowned bust right
Obv. Designer: Raphael Maklouf **Rev:** Train

Date	Mintage	F	VF	XF	Unc	BU
1998	—	—	—	—	10.00	12.00

KM# 872a CROWN
28.2800 g., 0.9250 Silver .8410 oz. ASW, 38.5 mm. **Ruler:** Elizabeth II **Subject:** 125th Anniversary of the Steam Railway **Obv:** Crowned bust right **Obv. Designer:** Raphael Maklouf **Rev:** Train

Date	Mintage	F	VF	XF	Unc	BU
1998 Proof	Est. 30,000	Value: 47.50				

KM# 874 CROWN
Copper-Nickel, 38.5 mm. **Ruler:** Elizabeth II **Subject:** 125th Anniversary of the Steam Railway **Obv:** Crowned bust right
Obv. Designer: Raphael Maklouf **Rev:** Locomotive below bust

Date	Mintage	F	VF	XF	Unc	BU
1998	—	—	—	—	10.00	12.00

KM# 874a CROWN
28.2800 g., 0.9250 Silver .8410 oz. ASW, 38.5 mm.
Ruler: Elizabeth II **Subject:** 125th Anniversary of the Steam Railway **Obv:** Crowned bust right **Obv. Designer:** Raphael Maklouf **Rev:** Locomotive below bust

Date	Mintage	F	VF	XF	Unc	BU
1998 Proof	Est. 30,000	Value: 47.50				

KM# 876 CROWN
Copper-Nickel, 38.5 mm. **Ruler:** Elizabeth II **Subject:** 125th Anniversary of the Steam Railway **Obv:** Crowned bust right
Obv. Designer: Raphael Maklouf **Rev:** View within parlor car

Date	Mintage	F	VF	XF	Unc	BU
1998	—	—	—	—	10.00	12.00

KM# 876a CROWN
28.2800 g., 0.9250 Silver .8410 oz. ASW, 38.5 mm.
Ruler: Elizabeth II **Subject:** 125th Anniversary of the Steam Railway **Obv:** Crowned bust right **Obv. Designer:** Raphael Maklouf **Rev:** View within parlor car

Date	Mintage	F	VF	XF	Unc	BU
1998 Proof	Est. 30,000	Value: 47.50				

KM# 878 CROWN
Copper-Nickel, 38.5 mm. **Ruler:** Elizabeth II **Subject:** 125th Anniversary of the Steam Railway **Obv:** Crowned bust right
Obv. Designer: Raphael Maklouf **Rev:** Mount Pilatus Railway

Date	Mintage	F	VF	XF	Unc	BU
1998	—	—	—	—	10.00	12.00

KM# 878a CROWN
28.2800 g., 0.9250 Silver .8410 oz. ASW, 38.5 mm.
Ruler: Elizabeth II **Subject:** 125th Anniversary of the Steam Railway **Obv:** Crowned bust right **Obv. Designer:** Raphael Maklouf **Rev:** Mount Pilatus Railway

Date	Mintage	F	VF	XF	Unc	BU
1998 Proof	Est. 30,000	Value: 47.50				

KM# 880 CROWN
Copper-Nickel, 38.5 mm. **Ruler:** Elizabeth II **Subject:** 125th Anniversary of the Steam Railway **Obv:** Crowned bust right **Obv. Designer:** Raphael Maklouf **Rev:** No. 1 Sutherland locomotive

Date	Mintage	F	VF	XF	Unc	BU
1998	—	—	—	—	10.00	12.00

KM# 880a CROWN
28.2800 g., 0.9250 Silver .8410 oz. ASW, 38.5 mm.
Ruler: Elizabeth II **Subject:** 125th Anniversary of the Steam Railway **Obv:** Crowned bust right **Obv. Designer:** Raphael Maklouf **Rev:** No. 1 Sutherland locomotive

Date	Mintage	F	VF	XF	Unc	BU
1998 Proof	Est. 30,000	Value: 47.50				

KM# 882 CROWN
Copper-Nickel, 38.5 mm. **Ruler:** Elizabeth II **Subject:** 125th Anniversary of the Steam Railway **Obv:** Crowned bust right **Obv. Designer:** Raphael Maklouf **Rev:** "Flying Scotsman" locomotive

Date	Mintage	F	VF	XF	Unc	BU
1998	—	—	—	—	10.00	12.00

KM# 882a CROWN
28.2800 g., 0.9250 Silver .8410 oz. ASW, 38.5 mm.
Ruler: Elizabeth II **Subject:** 125th Anniversary of the Steam Railway **Obv:** Crowned bust right **Obv. Designer:** Raphael Maklouf **Rev:** "Flying Scotsman" locomotive

Date	Mintage	F	VF	XF	Unc	BU
1998 Proof	Est. 30,000	Value: 47.50				

KM# 884 CROWN
Copper-Nickel, 38.5 mm. **Ruler:** Elizabeth II **Subject:** 125th Anniversary of the Steam Railway **Obv:** Crowned bust right
Obv. Designer: Raphael Maklouf **Rev:** "The Mallard" locomotive

Date	Mintage	F	VF	XF	Unc	BU
1998	—	—	—	—	10.00	12.00

KM# 884a CROWN
28.2800 g., 0.9250 Silver .8410 oz. ASW, 38.5 mm.
Ruler: Elizabeth II **Subject:** 125th Anniversary of the Steam Railway **Obv:** Crowned bust right **Obv. Designer:** Raphael Maklouf **Rev:** "The Mallard" locomotive

Date	Mintage	F	VF	XF	Unc	BU
1998 Proof	Est. 30,000	Value: 47.50				

KM# 886 CROWN
Copper-Nickel, 38.5 mm. **Ruler:** Elizabeth II **Subject:** 125th Anniversary of the Steam Railway **Obv:** Crowned bust right
Obv. Designer: Raphael Maklouf **Rev:** "The Big Boy" locomotive

Date	Mintage	F	VF	XF	Unc	BU
1998	—	—	—	—	10.00	12.00

KM# 886a CROWN
28.2800 g., 0.9250 Silver .8410 oz. ASW, 38.5 mm.
Ruler: Elizabeth II **Subject:** 125th Anniversary of the Steam Railway **Obv:** Bust of Queen Elizabeth II right
Obv. Designer: Raphael Maklouf **Rev:** "The Big Boy" locomotive

Date	Mintage	F	VF	XF	Unc	BU
1998 Proof	Est. 30,000	Value: 47.50				

KM# 888 CROWN
Copper-Nickel, 38.5 mm. **Ruler:** Elizabeth II **Series:** Year 2000
Obv: Crowned bust right **Obv. Designer:** Raphael Maklouf
Rev: Group of standing figures

Date	Mintage	F	VF	XF	Unc	BU
1998	—	—	—	—	8.00	10.00

KM# 888a CROWN
28.2800 g., 0.9250 Silver .8410 oz. ASW, 38.5 mm.
Ruler: Elizabeth II **Series:** Year 2000 **Obv:** Crowned bust right
Obv. Designer: Raphael Maklouf **Rev:** Group of standing figures

Date	Mintage	F	VF	XF	Unc	BU
1998 Proof	Est. 30,000	Value: 28.50				

KM# 890 CROWN
Copper-Nickel, 38.5 mm. **Ruler:** Elizabeth II **Series:** Year 2000
Obv: Crowned bust right **Obv. Designer:** Raphael Maklouf
Rev: French Revolution 1789

Date	Mintage	F	VF	XF	Unc	BU
1998	—	—	—	—	7.50	9.50

KM# 890a CROWN
28.2800 g., 0.9250 Silver .8410 oz. ASW, 38.5 mm.
Ruler: Elizabeth II **Series:** Year 2000 **Obv:** Crowned bust right
Obv. Designer: Raphael Maklouf **Rev:** French Revolution 1789

Date	Mintage	F	VF	XF	Unc	BU
1998 Proof	Est. 30,000	Value: 28.50				

KM# 892 CROWN
Copper-Nickel, 38.5 mm. **Ruler:** Elizabeth II **Series:** Year 2000
Obv: Crowned bust right **Obv. Designer:** Raphael Maklouf
Rev: Reformation of the Church 1517

Date	Mintage	F	VF	XF	Unc	BU
1998	—	—	—	—	7.50	9.50

KM# 892a CROWN
28.2800 g., 0.9250 Silver .8410 oz. ASW, 38.5 mm. **Ruler:** Elizabeth II **Series:** Year 2000 **Obv:** Crowned bust right **Obv. Designer:** Raphael Maklouf **Rev:** Reformation of the Church 1517

Date	Mintage	F	VF	XF	Unc	BU
1998 Proof	Est. 30,000	Value: 28.50				

KM# 894 CROWN
Copper-Nickel, 38.5 mm. **Ruler:** Elizabeth II **Series:** Year 2000
Obv: Crowned bust right **Obv. Designer:** Raphael Maklouf
Rev: 400th Anniversary of the Renaissance

Date	Mintage	F	VF	XF	Unc	BU
1998	—	—	—	—	7.50	9.50

KM# 894a CROWN
28.2800 g., 0.9250 Silver .8410 oz. ASW, 38.5 mm.
Ruler: Elizabeth II **Series:** Year 2000 **Obv:** Crowned bust right **Obv. Designer:** Raphael Maklouf **Rev:** 400th Anniversary of the Renaissance

Date	Mintage	F	VF	XF	Unc	BU
1998 Proof	Est. 30,000	Value: 28.50				

KM# 896 CROWN
Copper-Nickel, 38.5 mm. **Ruler:** Elizabeth II **Series:** Year of the Ocean **Obv:** Crowned bust right **Obv. Designer:** Raphael Maklouf **Rev:** Basking shark

Date	Mintage	F	VF	XF	Unc	BU
1998	—	—	—	—	12.50	16.00

KM# 896a CROWN
28.2800 g., 0.9250 Silver .8410 oz. ASW, 38.5 mm.
Ruler: Elizabeth II **Series:** Year of the Ocean **Obv:** Crowned bust right **Obv. Designer:** Raphael Maklouf **Rev:** Basking shark

Date	Mintage	F	VF	XF	Unc	BU
1998 Proof	Est. 30,000	Value: 47.50				

KM# 897 CROWN
Copper-Nickel, 38.5 mm. **Ruler:** Elizabeth II **Series:** Year of the Ocean **Obv:** Crowned bust right **Obv. Designer:** Raphael Maklouf **Rev:** Humpback whale

Date	Mintage	F	VF	XF	Unc	BU
1998	—	—	—	—	12.50	15.00

KM# 897a CROWN
28.2800 g., 0.9250 Silver .8410 oz. ASW, 38.5 mm. **Ruler:** Elizabeth II **Series:** Year of the Ocean **Obv:** Crowned bust right **Obv. Designer:** Raphael Maklouf **Rev:** Humpback whale

Date	Mintage	F	VF	XF	Unc	BU
1998 Proof	Est. 30,000	Value: 47.50				

KM# 898 CROWN
Copper-Nickel, 38.5 mm. **Ruler:** Elizabeth II **Series:** Year of the Ocean **Obv:** Crowned bust right **Obv. Designer:** Raphael Maklouf **Rev:** Penguins and seals

Date	Mintage	F	VF	XF	Unc	BU
1998	—	—	—	—	12.00	14.00

KM# 898a CROWN
28.2800 g., 0.9250 Silver .8410 oz. ASW, 38.5 mm. **Ruler:** Elizabeth II **Series:** Year of the Ocean **Obv:** Crowned bust right **Obv. Designer:** Raphael Maklouf **Rev:** Penguins and seals

Date	Mintage	F	VF	XF	Unc	BU
1998 Proof	Est. 30,000	Value: 45.00				

KM# 899 CROWN
Copper-Nickel, 38.5 mm. **Ruler:** Elizabeth II **Series:** Year of the Ocean **Obv:** Crowned bust right **Obv. Designer:** Raphael Maklouf **Rev:** Sailboats

Date	Mintage	F	VF	XF	Unc	BU
1998	—	—	—	—	10.00	12.00

KM# 899a CROWN
28.2800 g., 0.9250 Silver .8410 oz. ASW, 38.5 mm.
Ruler: Elizabeth II **Series:** Year of the Ocean **Obv:** Crowned bust right **Obv. Designer:** Raphael Maklouf **Rev:** Sailboats

Date	Mintage	F	VF	XF	Unc	BU
1998 Proof	Est. 30,000	Value: 47.50				

KM# A984 CROWN
Copper-Nickel, 38.5 mm. **Ruler:** Elizabeth II **Subject:** Founding of the UN 1945 **Obv:** Crowned bust right **Rev:** UN Building and logo

Date	Mintage	F	VF	XF	Unc	BU
2000	—	—	—	—	8.00	10.00

KM# 914 CROWN
Copper-Nickel, 38.5 mm. **Ruler:** Elizabeth II **Subject:** Battle of Waterloo 1815 **Obv:** Crowned bust right **Obv. Designer:** Raphael Maklouf **Rev:** Equestrian

Date	Mintage	F	VF	XF	Unc	BU
1999	—	—	—	—	8.00	10.00

KM# 914a CROWN
28.2800 g., 0.9250 Silver .8410 oz. ASW, 38.5 mm. **Ruler:** Elizabeth II **Subject:** Battle of Waterloo 1815 **Obv:** Crowned bust right **Obv. Designer:** Raphael Maklouf **Rev:** Equestrian

Date	Mintage	F	VF	XF	Unc	BU
1999 Proof	Est. 10,000	Value: 50.00				

KM# 918 CROWN
Copper-Nickel, 38.5 mm. **Ruler:** Elizabeth II **Subject:** Russian Revolution 1917 **Obv:** Crowned bust right **Obv. Designer:** Raphael Maklouf **Rev:** Lenin above the Aurora

Date	Mintage	F	VF	XF	Unc	BU
1999	—	—	—	—	7.50	9.50

KM# 916 CROWN
Copper-Nickel, 38.5 mm. **Ruler:** Elizabeth II **Subject:** American Civil War 1865 **Obv:** Crowned bust right **Obv. Designer:** Raphael Maklouf **Rev:** Cameos, swords, flag and drum

Date	Mintage	F	VF	XF	Unc	BU
1999	—	—	—	—	9.50	11.50

KM# 916a CROWN
28.2800 g., 0.9250 Silver .8410 oz. ASW, 38.5 mm.
Ruler: Elizabeth II **Subject:** American Civil War 1865 **Obv:** Crowned bust right **Obv. Designer:** Raphael Maklouf **Rev:** Cameos, swords, flag and drum

Date	Mintage	F	VF	XF	Unc	BU
1999 Proof	Est. 10,000	Value: 50.00				

KM# 918a CROWN
28.2800 g., 0.9250 Silver .8410 oz. ASW, 38.5 mm. **Ruler:** Elizabeth II **Subject:** Russian Revolution 1917 **Obv:** Crowned bust right **Obv. Designer:** Raphael Maklouf **Rev:** Lenin above the Aurora

Date	Mintage	F	VF	XF	Unc	BU
1999 Proof	Est. 10,000	Value: 50.00				

KM# 988 CROWN
Copper-Nickel, 38.5 mm. **Ruler:** Elizabeth II **Subject:** Fall of Berlin Wall 1989 **Obv:** Crowned bust right **Obv. Designer:** Raphael Maklouf **Rev:** Crowds around wall **Edge:** Reeded

Date	Mintage	F	VF	XF	Unc	BU
2000	—	—	—	—	7.50	9.50

KM# 988a CROWN
28.2800 g., 0.9250 Silver .8410 oz. ASW, 38.5 mm. **Ruler:** Elizabeth II **Subject:** Fall of Berlin Wall 1989 **Obv:** Crowned bust right **Obv. Designer:** Raphael Maklouf **Rev:** Crowds around wall

Date	Mintage	F	VF	XF	Unc	BU
2000 Proof	Est. 10,000	Value: 50.00				

KM# 920 CROWN
Copper-Nickel, 38.5 mm. **Ruler:** Elizabeth II **Subject:** World War I Armistice Day 1918 **Obv:** Crowned bust right **Obv. Designer:** Raphael Maklouf **Rev:** Biplane above tank **Edge:** Reeded

Date	Mintage	F	VF	XF	Unc	BU
1999	—	—	—	—	7.50	9.50

KM# 990 CROWN
Copper-Nickel, 38.5 mm. **Ruler:** Elizabeth II **Subject:** Millennium 2000 - The Future **Obv:** Crowned bust right **Obv. Designer:** Raphael Maklouf **Rev:** International Space Station **Edge:** Reeded

Date	Mintage	F	VF	XF	Unc	BU
2000	—	—	—	—	7.50	9.50

KM# 990a CROWN
28.2800 g., 0.9250 Silver .8410 oz. ASW, 38.5 mm.
Ruler: Elizabeth II **Subject:** Millennium 2000 - The Future **Obv:** Crowned bust right **Obv. Designer:** Raphael Maklouf **Rev:** International Space Station

Date	Mintage	F	VF	XF	Unc	BU
2000 Proof	Est. 10,000	Value: 50.00				

KM# 920a CROWN
28.2800 g., 0.9250 Silver .8410 oz. ASW, 38.5 mm.
Ruler: Elizabeth II **Subject:** World War I Armistice Day 1918 **Obv:** Crowned bust right **Obv. Designer:** Raphael Maklouf **Rev:** Biplane above tank

Date	Mintage	F	VF	XF	Unc	BU
1999 Proof	Est. 10,000	Value: 50.00				

KM# 922 CROWN
Copper-Nickel, 38.5 mm. **Ruler:** Elizabeth II **Series:** Summer Olympics - Sydney **Obv:** Crowned bust right **Obv. Designer:** Raphael Maklouf **Rev:** Javelin throwers **Edge:** Reeded

Date	Mintage	F	VF	XF	Unc	BU
1999	—	—	—	—	7.50	9.50

KM# 922a CROWN
28.2800 g., 0.9250 Silver .8410 oz. ASW, 38.5 mm. **Ruler:** Elizabeth II **Series:** Summer Olympics - Sydney **Obv:** Crowned bust right **Obv. Designer:** Raphael Maklouf **Rev:** Javelin throwers

Date	Mintage	F	VF	XF	Unc	BU
1999 Proof	Est. 10,000	Value: 50.00				

KM# 924 CROWN
Copper-Nickel, 38.5 mm. **Ruler:** Elizabeth II **Series:** Summer Olympics - Sydney **Obv:** Crowned bust right **Obv. Designer:** Raphael Maklouf **Rev:** Diver divides map **Edge:** Reeded

Date	Mintage	F	VF	XF	Unc	BU
1999	—	—	—	—	7.50	9.50

KM# 924a CROWN
28.2800 g., 0.9250 Silver .8410 oz. ASW, 38.5 mm. **Ruler:** Elizabeth II **Series:** Summer Olympics - Sydney **Obv:** Crowned bust right **Obv. Designer:** Raphael Maklouf **Rev:** Diver divides map

Date	Mintage	F	VF	XF	Unc	BU
1999 Proof	Est. 10,000	Value: 50.00				

KM# 926 CROWN
Copper-Nickel, 38.5 mm. **Ruler:** Elizabeth II **Series:** Summer Olympics - Sydney **Obv:** Crowned bust right **Obv. Designer:** Raphael Maklouf **Rev:** Sailboat and Sydney Opera House **Edge:** Reeded

Date	Mintage	F	VF	XF	Unc	BU
1999	—	—	—	—	7.50	9.50

KM# 926a CROWN
28.2800 g., 0.9250 Silver .8410 oz. ASW, 38.5 mm.
Ruler: Elizabeth II **Series:** Summer Olympics - Sydney **Obv:** Crowned bust right **Obv. Designer:** Raphael Maklouf **Rev:** Sailboat and Sydney Opera House

Date	Mintage	F	VF	XF	Unc	BU
1999 Proof	Est. 10,000	Value: 50.00				

KM# 928 CROWN
Copper-Nickel, 38.5 mm. **Ruler:** Elizabeth II **Series:** Summer Olympics - Sydney **Obv:** Crowned bust right **Obv. Designer:** Raphael Maklouf **Rev:** Runners and torch **Edge:** Reeded

Date	Mintage	F	VF	XF	Unc	BU
1999	—	—	—	—	7.50	9.50

KM# 928a CROWN
28.2800 g., 0.9250 Silver .8410 oz. ASW, 38.5 mm. **Ruler:** Elizabeth II **Series:** Summer Olympics - Sydney **Obv:** Crowned bust right **Obv. Designer:** Raphael Maklouf **Rev:** Runners and torch

Date	Mintage	F	VF	XF	Unc	BU
1999 Proof	Est. 10,000	Value: 50.00				

KM# 930 CROWN
Copper-Nickel, 38.5 mm. **Ruler:** Elizabeth II **Series:** Summer Olympics - Sydney **Obv:** Crowned bust right **Obv. Designer:** Raphael Maklouf **Rev:** Hurdlers and Sydney Opera House **Edge:** Reeded

Date	Mintage	F	VF	XF	Unc	BU
1999	—	—	—	—	7.50	9.50

KM# 930a CROWN
28.2800 g., 0.9250 Silver .8410 oz. ASW, 38.5 mm.
Ruler: Elizabeth II **Series:** Summer Olympics - Sydney **Obv:** Crowned bust right **Obv. Designer:** Raphael Maklouf **Rev:** Hurdlers and Sydney Opera House

Date	Mintage	F	VF	XF	Unc	BU
1999 Proof	Est. 10,000	Value: 50.00				

KM# 932 CROWN
Copper-Nickel, 38.5 mm. **Ruler:** Elizabeth II **Series:** World Cup Rugby 1999 **Obv:** Crowned bust right **Obv. Designer:** Raphael Maklouf **Rev:** Bust 1/4 right flanked by players **Edge:** Reeded

Date	Mintage	F	VF	XF	Unc	BU
1999	—	—	—	—	8.00	10.00

KM# 932a CROWN
28.2800 g., 0.9250 Silver .8410 oz. ASW, 38.5 mm. **Ruler:** Elizabeth II **Series:** World Cup Rugby 1999 **Obv:** Crowned bust right **Obv. Designer:** Raphael Maklouf **Rev:** Bust 1/4 right flanked by players

Date	Mintage	F	VF	XF	Unc	BU
1999 Proof	Est. 10,000	Value: 50.00				

KM# 934 CROWN
Copper-Nickel, 38.5 mm. **Ruler:** Elizabeth II **Series:** World Cup Rugby 1999 **Obv:** Crowned bust right **Obv. Designer:** Raphael Maklouf **Rev:** Rugby scrum **Edge:** Reeded

Date	Mintage	F	VF	XF	Unc	BU
1999	—	—	—	—	8.00	10.00

KM# 934a CROWN
28.2800 g., 0.9250 Silver .8410 oz. ASW, 38.5 mm. **Ruler:** Elizabeth II **Series:** World Cup Rugby 1999 **Obv:** Crowned bust right **Obv. Designer:** Raphael Maklouf **Rev:** Rugby scrum

Date	Mintage	F	VF	XF	Unc	BU
1999 Proof	Est. 10,000	Value: 50.00				

KM# 936 CROWN
Copper-Nickel, 38.5 mm. **Ruler:** Elizabeth II **Series:** World Cup Rugby 1999 **Obv:** Crowned bust right **Obv. Designer:** Raphael Maklouf **Rev:** Player catching ball **Edge:** Reeded

Date	Mintage	F	VF	XF	Unc	BU
1999	—	—	—	—	8.00	10.00

KM# 936a CROWN
28.2800 g., 0.9250 Silver .8410 oz. ASW, 38.5 mm. **Ruler:** Elizabeth II **Series:** World Cup Rugby 1999 **Obv:** Crowned bust right **Obv. Designer:** Raphael Maklouf **Rev:** Player catching ball

Date	Mintage	F	VF	XF	Unc	BU
1999 Proof	Est. 10,000	Value: 50.00				

KM# 938 CROWN
Copper-Nickel, 38.5 mm. **Ruler:** Elizabeth II **Series:** World Cup Rugby 1999 **Obv:** Crowned bust right **Obv. Designer:** Raphael Maklouf **Rev:** Goal kick **Edge:** Reeded

Date	Mintage	F	VF	XF	Unc	BU
1999	—	—	—	—	8.00	10.00

KM# 938a CROWN
28.2800 g., 0.9250 Silver .8410 oz. ASW, 38.5 mm. **Ruler:** Elizabeth II **Series:** World Cup Rugby 1999 **Obv:** Crowned bust right **Obv. Designer:** Raphael Maklouf **Rev:** Goal kick

Date	Mintage	F	VF	XF	Unc	BU
1999 Proof	Est. 10,000	Value: 50.00				

KM# 940 CROWN
Copper-Nickel, 38.5 mm. **Ruler:** Elizabeth II **Series:** World Cup Rugby 1999 **Obv:** Crowned bust right **Obv. Designer:** Raphael Maklouf **Rev:** Ball runner being tackled **Edge:** Reeded

Date	Mintage	F	VF	XF	Unc	BU
1999	—	—	—	—	8.00	10.00

KM# 940a CROWN
28.2800 g., 0.9250 Silver .8410 oz. ASW, 38.5 mm. **Ruler:** Elizabeth II **Series:** World Cup Rugby 1999 **Obv:** Crowned bust right **Obv. Designer:** Raphael Maklouf **Rev:** Ball runner being tackled

Date	Mintage	F	VF	XF	Unc	BU
1999 Proof	Est. 10,000	Value: 50.00				

KM# 942 CROWN
Copper-Nickel, 38.5 mm. **Ruler:** Elizabeth II **Series:** World Cup Rugby 1999 **Obv:** Crowned bust right **Obv. Designer:** Raphael Maklouf **Rev:** Player jumping for catch **Edge:** Reeded

Date	Mintage	F	VF	XF	Unc	BU
1999	—	—	—	—	8.00	10.00

KM# 942a CROWN
28.2800 g., 0.9250 Silver .8410 oz. ASW, 38.5 mm. **Ruler:** Elizabeth II **Series:** World Cup Rugby 1999 **Obv:** Crowned bust right **Obv. Designer:** Raphael Maklouf **Rev:** Player jumping for catch

Date	Mintage	F	VF	XF	Unc	BU
1999 Proof	Est. 10,000	Value: 50.00				

KM# 952 CROWN
Copper-Nickel, 38.5 mm. **Ruler:** Elizabeth II **Subject:** Year of the Rabbit **Obv:** Crowned bust right **Obv. Designer:** Raphael Maklouf **Rev:** Rabbits **Edge:** Reeded

Date	Mintage	F	VF	XF	Unc	BU
1999	—	—	—	—	12.00	14.00

KM# 952a CROWN
28.2800 g., 0.9250 Silver .8410 oz. ASW, 38.5 mm. **Ruler:** Elizabeth II **Subject:** Year of the Rabbit **Obv:** Crowned bust right **Obv. Designer:** Raphael Maklouf **Rev:** Rabbits

Date	Mintage	F	VF	XF	Unc	BU
1999 Proof	Est. 10,000	Value: 45.00				

KM# 952b CROWN
31.1035 g., 0.9999 Gold .9999 oz. AGW **Ruler:** Elizabeth II **Subject:** Year of the Rabbit **Obv:** Crowned bust right **Obv. Designer:** Raphael Maklouf **Rev:** Rabbits

Date	Mintage	F	VF	XF	Unc	BU
1999 Proof	Est. 2,000	Value: 725				

KM# 955 CROWN
Copper-Nickel, 38.5 mm. **Ruler:** Elizabeth II **Obv:** Crowned bust right **Obv. Designer:** Raphael Maklouf **Rev:** Bust with hat, map of America and ship **Edge:** Reeded

Date	Mintage	F	VF	XF	Unc	BU
1999	—	—	—	—	8.00	10.00

KM# 955a CROWN
28.2800 g., 0.9250 Silver .8410 oz. ASW, 38.5 mm. **Ruler:** Elizabeth II **Obv:** Crowned bust right **Obv. Designer:** Raphael Maklouf **Rev:** Bust with hat, map of America and ship

Date	Mintage	F	VF	XF	Unc	BU
1999 Proof	Est. 10,000	Value: 50.00				

KM# 957 CROWN
Copper-Nickel, 38.5 mm. **Ruler:** Elizabeth II **Obv:** Crowned bust right **Obv. Designer:** Raphael Maklouf **Rev:** Compass, bust of Robert Falcon Scott and men pulling sled **Edge:** Reeded

Date	Mintage	F	VF	XF	Unc	BU
1999	—	—	—	—	8.00	10.00

KM# 957a CROWN
28.2800 g., 0.9250 Silver .8410 oz. ASW, 38.5 mm. **Ruler:** Elizabeth II **Obv:** Crowned bust right **Obv. Designer:** Raphael Maklouf **Rev:** Compass, bust of Robert Falcon Scott and men pulling sled

Date	Mintage	F	VF	XF	Unc	BU
1999 Proof	Est. 10,000	Value: 50.00				

KM# 966 CROWN
Copper-Nickel, 38.5 mm. **Ruler:** Elizabeth II **Obv:** Crowned bust right **Obv. Designer:** Raphael Maklouf **Rev:** British Blue cat cleaning its paws **Edge:** Reeded

Date	Mintage	F	VF	XF	Unc	BU
1999	—	—	—	—	9.00	12.00

KM# 967 CROWN
31.1035 g., 0.9990 Silver 1.0000 oz. ASW, 38.5 mm. **Ruler:** Elizabeth II **Obv:** Crowned bust right **Obv. Designer:** Raphael Maklouf **Rev:** British Blue cat cleaning its paws

Date	Mintage	F	VF	XF	Unc	BU
1999 Proof	Est. 50,000	Value: 40.00				

KM# 968 CROWN
31.1035 g., 0.9990 Gold 1.0000 oz. AGW **Ruler:** Elizabeth II **Obv:** Crowned bust right **Obv. Designer:** Raphael Maklouf **Rev:** British Blue cat cleaning its paws

Date	Mintage	F	VF	XF	Unc	BU
1999	—	—	—	—	675	700
1999 Proof	—	Value: 725				

KM# 976 CROWN
Copper-Nickel, 38.5 mm. **Ruler:** Elizabeth II **Series:** The Life and Times of the Queen Mother **Obv:** Crowned bust right **Obv. Designer:** Raphael Maklouf **Rev:** Seated child facing **Edge:** Reeded

Date	Mintage	F	VF	XF	Unc	BU
1999	—	—	—	—	7.50	9.50

KM# 976a CROWN
28.2800 g., 0.9250 Silver .8410 oz. ASW, 38.5 mm. **Ruler:** Elizabeth II **Series:** The Life and Times of the Queen Mother **Obv:** Crowned bust right **Obv. Designer:** Raphael Maklouf **Rev:** Seated child facing

Date	Mintage	F	VF	XF	Unc	BU
1999 Proof	Est. 10,000	Value: 50.00				

KM# 978 CROWN
Copper-Nickel, 38.5 mm. **Ruler:** Elizabeth II **Series:** The Life and Times of the Queen Mother **Obv:** Crowned bust right **Obv. Designer:** Raphael Maklouf **Rev:** Royal engagement portrait **Edge:** Reeded

Date	Mintage	F	VF	XF	Unc	BU
1999	—	—	—	—	7.50	9.50

KM# 978a CROWN
28.2800 g., 0.9250 Silver .8410 oz. ASW, 38.5 mm. **Ruler:** Elizabeth II **Series:** The Life and Times of the Queen Mother **Obv:** Crowned bust right **Obv. Designer:** Raphael Maklouf **Rev:** Royal engagement portrait

Date	Mintage	F	VF	XF	Unc	BU
1999 Proof	Est. 10,000	Value: 50.00				

KM# 980 CROWN
Copper-Nickel, 38.5 mm. **Ruler:** Elizabeth II **Series:** The Life and Times of the Queen Mother **Obv:** Crowned bust right **Obv. Designer:** Raphael Maklouf **Rev:** Wedding portrait **Edge:** Reeded

Date	Mintage	F	VF	XF	Unc	BU
1999	—	—	—	—	7.50	9.50

KM# 980a CROWN
28.2800 g., 0.9250 Silver .8410 oz. ASW **Ruler:** Elizabeth II **Series:** The Life and Times of the Queen Mother **Obv:** Crowned bust right **Obv. Designer:** Raphael Maklouf **Rev:** Wedding portrait

Date	Mintage	F	VF	XF	Unc	BU
1999 Proof	Est. 10,000	Value: 50.00				

KM# 982 CROWN
Copper-Nickel, 38.5 mm. **Ruler:** Elizabeth II **Subject:** The Life and Times of the Queen Mother **Obv:** Crowned bust right **Obv. Designer:** Raphael Maklouf **Rev:** Honeymoon departure **Edge:** Reeded

Date	Mintage	F	VF	XF	Unc	BU
1999	—	—	—	—	7.50	9.50

KM# 982a CROWN
28.2800 g., 0.9250 Silver .8410 oz. ASW, 38.5 mm. **Ruler:** Elizabeth II **Series:** The Life and Times of the Queen Mother **Obv:** Crowned bust right **Obv. Designer:** Raphael Maklouf **Rev:** Honeymoon departure

Date	Mintage	F	VF	XF	Unc	BU
1999 Proof	Est. 10,000	Value: 50.00				

KM# 996 CROWN

Copper-Nickel, 38.5 mm. **Ruler:** Elizabeth II **Subject:** The Wedding of HRH Prince Edward and Sophie Rhys-Jones **Obv:** Crowned bust right **Obv. Designer:** Raphael Maklouf **Rev:** Head right

Date	Mintage	F	VF	XF	Unc	BU
1999	—	—	—	—	7.50	9.50

KM# 996a CROWN

28.2800 g., 0.9250 Silver .8410 oz. ASW, 38.5 mm. **Ruler:** Elizabeth II **Subject:** The Wedding of HRH Prince Edward and Sophie Rhys-Jones **Obv:** Crowned bust right **Obv. Designer:** Raphael Maklouf **Rev:** Head right

Date	Mintage	F	VF	XF	Unc	BU
1999 Proof	Est. 10,000	Value: 50.00				

KM# 998 CROWN

Copper-Nickel, 38.5 mm. **Ruler:** Elizabeth II **Subject:** The Wedding of HRH Prince Edward and Sophie Rhys-Jones **Obv:** Crowned bust right **Obv. Designer:** Raphael Maklouf **Rev:** Head left

Date	Mintage	F	VF	XF	Unc	BU
1999	—	—	—	—	7.50	9.50

KM# 998a CROWN

28.2800 g., 0.9250 Silver .8410 oz. ASW, 38.5 mm. **Ruler:** Elizabeth II **Subject:** The Wedding of HRH Prince Edward and Sophie Rhys-Jones **Obv:** Crowned bust right **Obv. Designer:** Raphael Maklouf **Rev:** Head left

Date	Mintage	F	VF	XF	Unc	BU
1999 Proof	Est. 10,000	Value: 50.00				

KM# 1000 CROWN

Copper-Nickel, 38.5 mm. **Ruler:** Elizabeth II **Subject:** 30th Anniversary of First Man on the Moon **Obv:** Crowned bust right **Obv. Designer:** Raphael Maklouf **Rev:** Apollo XI and moon walkers

Date	Mintage	F	VF	XF	Unc	BU
1999	—	—	—	—	7.50	9.50

KM# 1000a CROWN

28.2800 g., 0.9250 Silver .8410 oz. ASW, 38.5 mm. **Ruler:** Elizabeth II **Subject:** 30th Anniversary of First Man on the Moon **Obv:** Crowned bust right **Obv. Designer:** Raphael Maklouf **Rev:** Apollo XI and two moon walkers

Date	Mintage	F	VF	XF	Unc	BU
1999 Proof	Est. 10,000	Value: 50.00				

KM# 1002 CROWN

Copper-Nickel, 38.5 mm. **Ruler:** Elizabeth II **Subject:** 30th Anniversary of First Man on the Moon **Obv:** Crowned bust right **Obv. Designer:** Raphael Maklouf **Rev:** Mariner IX, 1971 and orbiting Mars

Date	Mintage	F	VF	XF	Unc	BU
1999	—	—	—	—	7.50	9.50

KM# 1002a CROWN

28.2800 g., 0.9250 Silver .8410 oz. ASW, 38.5 mm. **Ruler:** Elizabeth II **Subject:** 30th Anniversary of First Man on the Moon **Obv:** Crowned bust right **Obv. Designer:** Raphael Maklouf **Rev:** Mariner IX orbiting Mars

Date	Mintage	F	VF	XF	Unc	BU
1999	Est. 10,000	Value: 50.00				

KM# 1004 CROWN

Copper-Nickel, 38.5 mm. **Ruler:** Elizabeth II **Subject:** 30th Anniversary of First Man on the Moon **Obv:** Crowned bust right **Obv. Designer:** Raphael Maklouf **Rev:** Apollo-Soyuz link-up, 1975

Date	Mintage	F	VF	XF	Unc	BU
1999	—	—	—	—	7.50	9.50

KM# 1004a CROWN

28.2800 g., 0.9250 Silver .8410 oz. ASW, 38.5 mm. **Ruler:** Elizabeth II **Subject:** 30th Anniversary of First Man on the Moon **Obv:** Crowned bust right **Obv. Designer:** Raphael Maklouf **Rev:** Apollo-Soyuz link-up, 1975

Date	Mintage	F	VF	XF	Unc	BU
1999 Proof	Est. 10,000	Value: 50.00				

KM# 1006 CROWN

Copper-Nickel, 38.5 mm. **Ruler:** Elizabeth II **Subject:** 30th Anniversary of First Man on the Moon **Obv:** Crowned bust right **Obv. Designer:** Raphael Maklouf **Rev:** Viking Mars Lander, 1978

Date	Mintage	F	VF	XF	Unc	BU
1999	—	—	—	—	7.50	9.50

KM# 1006a CROWN

28.2800 g., 0.9250 Silver .8410 oz. ASW, 38.5 mm. **Ruler:** Elizabeth II **Subject:** 30th Anniversary of First Man on the Moon **Obv:** Crowned bust right **Obv. Designer:** Raphael Maklouf **Rev:** Viking Mars lander, 1978

Date	Mintage	F	VF	XF	Unc	BU
1999 Proof	Est. 10,000	Value: 50.00				

KM# 1008 CROWN

Copper-Nickel, 38.5 mm. **Ruler:** Elizabeth II **Subject:** 30th Anniversary of First Man on the Moon **Obv:** Crowned bust right **Obv. Designer:** Raphael Maklouf **Rev:** Shuttle orbiter Columbia, 1981

Date	Mintage	F	VF	XF	Unc	BU
1999	—	—	—	—	8.00	10.00

KM# 1008a CROWN

28.2800 g., 0.9250 Silver .8410 oz. ASW, 38.5 mm. **Ruler:** Elizabeth II **Subject:** 30th Anniversary of First Man on the Moon **Obv:** Crowned bust right **Obv. Designer:** Raphael Maklouf **Rev:** Shuttle orbiter Columbia, 1981

Date	Mintage	F	VF	XF	Unc	BU
1999 Proof	Est. 10,000	Value: 50.00				

KM# 1010 CROWN

Copper-Nickel, 38.5 mm. **Ruler:** Elizabeth II **Subject:** 30th Anniversary of First Man on the Moon **Obv:** Crowned bust right **Obv. Designer:** Raphael Maklouf **Rev:** Mars Pathfinder, 1997

Date	Mintage	F	VF	XF	Unc	BU
1999	—	—	—	—	12.00	14.00

KM# 1010a CROWN

28.2800 g., 0.9250 Silver .8410 oz. ASW, 38.5 mm. **Ruler:** Elizabeth II **Subject:** 30th Anniversary of First Man on the Moon **Obv:** Crowned bust right **Obv. Designer:** Raphael Maklouf **Rev:** Mars Pathfinder, 1997

Date	Mintage	F	VF	XF	Unc	BU
1999 Proof	Est. 10,000	Value: 50.00				

KM# 1267 CROWN

28.2500 g., Silver, 38.7 mm. **Subject:** Fall of the Berlin Wall - 1989 **Obv:** Crowned bust right **Obv. Designer:** Raphael Maklouf **Rev:** Brandenburg Gate behind crowd holding pennant with slogan, Love and Peace in West & East **Edge:** Reeded

Date	Mintage	F	VF	XF	Unc	BU
2000	—	—	—	—	12.00	14.00

KM# 1264 CROWN

28.2800 g., Copper-Nickel, 38.5 mm. **Ruler:** Elizabeth II **Obv:** Crowned bust right **Obv. Designer:** Raphael Maklouf **Rev:** Space station and shuttle **Edge:** Reeded

Date	Mintage	F	VF	XF	Unc	BU
2000PM	—	—	—	—	15.00	17.00

KM# 1264a CROWN

28.2200 g., 0.9250 Silver 0.8392 oz. ASW, 38.5 mm. **Ruler:** Elizabeth II **Obv:** Crowned bust right **Obv. Designer:** Raphael Maklouf **Rev:** Space station and shuttle **Edge:** Reeded

Date	Mintage	F	VF	XF	Unc	BU
2000PM Proof	—	Value: 50.00				

KM# 1057 CROWN

31.1035 g., 0.9999 Gold 1.0000 oz. AGW, 32.7 mm. **Ruler:** Elizabeth II **Subject:** Scottish Fold Kitten **Obv:** Crowned bust right **Obv. Designer:** Raphael Maklouf **Rev:** Kitten playing with world **Edge:** Reeded

Date	Mintage	F	VF	XF	Unc	BU
2000 Proof	—	Value: 725				
2000	—	—	—	—	675	700

KM# 986 CROWN

Copper-Nickel, 38.5 mm. **Ruler:** Elizabeth II **Subject:** First Man on the Moon **Obv:** Crowned bust right **Obv. Designer:** Raphael Maklouf **Rev:** Astronauts on moon and flag

Date	Mintage	F	VF	XF	Unc	BU
2000	—	—	—	—	7.50	9.50

KM# 986a CROWN

28.2800 g., 0.9250 Silver .8410 oz. ASW, 38.5 mm. **Ruler:** Elizabeth II **Subject:** First Man on the Moon **Obv:** Crowned bust right **Obv. Designer:** Raphael Maklouf **Rev:** Astronauts on moon and flag

Date	Mintage	F	VF	XF	Unc	BU
2000 Proof	Est. 10,000	Value: 50.00				

KM# 1016 CROWN

Copper-Nickel, 38.5 mm. **Ruler:** Elizabeth II **Subject:** Year of the Dragon **Obv:** Crowned bust right **Obv. Designer:** Raphael Maklouf **Rev:** Dragon

Date	Mintage	F	VF	XF	Unc	BU
2000	—	—	—	—	12.00	15.00

KM# 1016a CROWN

28.2800 g., 0.9250 Silver .8410 oz. ASW, 38.5 mm. **Ruler:** Elizabeth II **Subject:** Year of the Dragon **Obv:** Crowned bust right **Obv. Designer:** Raphael Maklouf **Rev:** Dragon

Date	Mintage	F	VF	XF	Unc	BU
2000 Proof	Est. 30,000	Value: 50.00				

KM# 1017 CROWN

31.1035 g., 0.9999 Gold 1.0000 oz. AGW, 32.7 mm. **Ruler:** Elizabeth II **Subject:** Year of the Dragon **Obv:** Crowned bust right **Obv. Designer:** Raphael Maklouf **Rev:** Dragon

Date	Mintage	F	VF	XF	Unc	BU
2000 Proof	Est. 2,000	Value: 725				

KM# 1019 CROWN

28.2800 g., Copper-Nickel, 38.6 mm. **Ruler:** Elizabeth II **Subject:** Millennium **Obv:** Crowned bust right **Obv. Designer:** Raphael Maklouf **Rev:** Stylized monogram **Edge:** Reeded

Date	Mintage	F	VF	XF	Unc	BU
2000	—	—	—	—	8.00	10.00

KM# 1019a CROWN

28.2800 g., 0.9250 Silver .8410 oz. ASW, 38.6 mm. **Ruler:** Elizabeth II **Subject:** Millennium **Obv:** Crowned bust right **Obv. Designer:** Raphael Maklouf **Rev:** Stylized monogram **Edge:** Reeded

Date	Mintage	F	VF	XF	Unc	BU
2000 Proof	10,000	Value: 47.50				

KM# 1021 CROWN
28.2800 g., Copper-Nickel, 38.6 mm. **Ruler:** Elizabeth II **Obv:** Crowned bust right **Obv. Designer:** Raphael Maklouf **Rev:** Armored 1/2 bust, map and ship

Date	Mintage	F	VF	XF	Unc	BU
2000	—	—	—	—	8.00	10.00

KM# 1021a CROWN
28.2800 g., 0.9250 Silver .8410 oz. ASW, 38.6 mm. **Ruler:** Elizabeth II **Obv:** Crowned bust right **Obv. Designer:** Raphael Maklouf **Rev:** Armored 1/2 bust, map and ship

Date	Mintage	F	VF	XF	Unc	BU
2000 Proof	10,000	Value: 47.50				

KM# 1023 CROWN
Copper-Nickel, 38.5 mm. **Ruler:** Elizabeth II **Obv:** Crowned bust right **Obv. Designer:** Raphael Maklouf **Rev:** Portrait of Willem Barents, ship on ice, map

Date	Mintage	F	VF	XF	Unc	BU
2000	—	—	—	—	8.00	10.00

KM# 1023a CROWN
28.2800 g., 0.9250 Silver .8410 oz. ASW, 38.5 mm. **Ruler:** Elizabeth II **Obv:** Crowned bust right **Obv. Designer:** Raphael Maklouf **Rev:** Portrait of Willem Barents, ship on ice, map

Date	Mintage	F	VF	XF	Unc	BU
2000 Proof	10,000	Value: 47.50				

KM# 1025 CROWN
28.2800 g., Copper-Nickel, 38.5 mm. **Ruler:** Elizabeth II **Series:** Queen Mother **Obv:** Crowned bust right **Obv. Designer:** Raphael Maklouf **Rev:** 1931 family scene **Edge:** Reeded

Date	Mintage	F	VF	XF	Unc	BU
2000	—	—	—	—	10.00	12.00

KM# 1025a CROWN
28.2800 g., 0.9250 Silver .8410 oz. ASW, 38.5 mm. **Ruler:** Elizabeth II **Series:** Queen Mother **Obv:** Crowned bust right **Obv. Designer:** Raphael Maklouf **Rev:** 1931 family scene **Edge:** Reeded

Date	Mintage	F	VF	XF	Unc	BU
2000 Proof	10,000	Value: 47.50				

KM# 1027 CROWN
Copper-Nickel, 38.5 mm. **Ruler:** Elizabeth II **Obv:** Crowned bust right **Obv. Designer:** Raphael Maklouf **Rev:** 1937 Coronation scene

Date	Mintage	F	VF	XF	Unc	BU
2000	—	—	—	—	10.00	12.00

KM# 1027a CROWN
28.2800 g., 0.9250 Silver .8410 oz. ASW, 38.5 mm. **Ruler:** Elizabeth II **Obv:** Crowned bust right **Obv. Designer:** Raphael Maklouf **Rev:** Coronation scene

Date	Mintage	F	VF	XF	Unc	BU
2000 Proof	10,000	Value: 47.50				

KM# 1029 CROWN
Copper-Nickel, 38.5 mm. **Ruler:** Elizabeth II **Obv:** Crowned bust right **Obv. Designer:** Raphael Maklouf **Rev:** 1945 Victory Visit

Date	Mintage	F	VF	XF	Unc	BU
2000	—	—	—	—	10.00	12.00

KM# 1029a CROWN
28.2800 g., 0.9250 Silver .8410 oz. ASW, 38.5 mm. **Ruler:** Elizabeth II **Obv:** Crowned bust right **Obv. Designer:** Raphael Maklouf **Rev:** 1945 Victory Visit

Date	Mintage	F	VF	XF	Unc	BU
2000 Proof	10,000	Value: 47.50				

KM# 1029b CROWN
28.6500 g., 0.9250 Gilt Silver 0.852 oz., 38.5 mm. **Ruler:** Elizabeth II **Subject:** Queen Mother **Obv:** Crowned bust right **Obv. Designer:** Raphael Maklouf **Rev:** 1945 Royal visit to Isle of Man **Edge:** Reeded

Date	Mintage	F	VF	XF	Unc	BU
2000PM Proof	—	Value: 50.00				

KM# 1031 CROWN
Copper-Nickel, 38.5 mm. **Ruler:** Elizabeth II **Obv:** Crowned bust right **Obv. Designer:** Raphael Maklouf **Rev:** Queen Mother, coach, and man

Date	Mintage	F	VF	XF	Unc	BU
2000	—	—	—	—	10.00	12.00

KM# 1031a CROWN
28.2800 g., 0.9250 Silver .8410 oz. ASW, 38.5 mm. **Ruler:** Elizabeth II **Obv:** Crowned bust right **Obv. Designer:** Raphael Maklouf **Rev:** Queen Mother, coach, and man

Date	Mintage	F	VF	XF	Unc	BU
2000 Proof	10,000	Value: 47.50				

KM# 1031b CROWN
28.6500 g., 0.9250 Gilt Silver 0.852 oz., 38.6 mm. **Ruler:** Elizabeth II **Subject:** Queen Mother **Obv:** Crowned bust right **Obv. Designer:** Raphael Maklouf **Rev:** 1963 Visit to Isle of Man **Edge:** Reeded

Date	Mintage	F	VF	XF	Unc	BU
2000PM Proof	—	Value: 50.00				

KM# 1033 CROWN
28.2800 g., Copper-Nickel, 38.5 mm. **Ruler:** Elizabeth II **Subject:** Battle of Britain **Obv:** Crowned bust right **Obv. Designer:** Raphael Maklouf **Rev:** Aerial battle scene

Date	Mintage	F	VF	XF	Unc	BU
2000	—	—	—	—	10.00	12.00

KM# 1033a CROWN
28.2800 g., 0.9250 Silver .8410 oz. ASW, 38.5 mm. **Ruler:** Elizabeth II **Subject:** Battle of Britain **Obv:** Crowned bust right **Obv. Designer:** Raphael Maklouf **Rev:** Aerial battle scene

Date	Mintage	F	VF	XF	Unc	BU
2000 Proof	10,000	Value: 47.50				

KM# 1035 CROWN
Copper-Nickel, 38.5 mm. **Ruler:** Elizabeth II **Subject:** Global Challenge Yacht Race **Obv:** Crowned bust right **Obv. Designer:** Raphael Maklouf **Rev:** Partial ship and map

Date	Mintage	F	VF	XF	Unc	BU
2000	—	—	—	—	10.00	12.00

KM# 1035a CROWN
28.2800 g., 0.9250 Silver .8410 oz. ASW, 38.5 mm. **Ruler:** Elizabeth II **Subject:** Global Challenge Yacht Race **Obv:** Crowned bust right **Obv. Designer:** Raphael Maklouf **Rev:** Partial ship and map

Date	Mintage	F	VF	XF	Unc	BU
2000 Proof	10,000	Value: 47.50				

KM# 1047 CROWN
28.2800 g., Copper-Nickel, 38.5 mm. **Ruler:** Elizabeth II **Obv:** Crowned bust right **Obv. Designer:** Raphael Maklouf **Rev:** Head 3/4 right **Edge:** Reeded

Date	Mintage	F	VF	XF	Unc	BU
2000	—	—	—	—	7.50	9.50

KM# 1047a CROWN
28.2800 g., 0.9250 Silver .8410 oz. ASW, 38.5 mm. **Ruler:** Elizabeth II **Obv:** Crowned bust right **Obv. Designer:** Raphael Maklouf **Rev:** Head 3/4 right **Edge:** Reeded

Date	Mintage	F	VF	XF	Unc	BU
2000 Proof	10,000	Value: 47.50				

KM# 1049 CROWN
Copper-Nickel, 38.5 mm. **Ruler:** Elizabeth II **Obv:** Crowned bust right **Obv. Designer:** Raphael Maklouf **Rev:** Queen Mother's portrait

Date	Mintage	F	VF	XF	Unc	BU
2000	—	—	—	—	10.00	12.00

KM# 1049a CROWN
28.2800 g., 0.9250 Silver .8410 oz. ASW, 38.5 mm. **Ruler:** Elizabeth II **Obv:** Crowned bust right **Obv. Designer:** Raphael Maklouf **Rev:** Queen Mother's portrait

Date	Mintage	F	VF	XF	Unc	BU
2000 Proof	10,000	Value: 47.50				

KM# 1051 CROWN
28.2800 g., 0.9250 Silver .8410 oz. ASW, 38.6 mm. **Ruler:** Elizabeth II **Subject:** Millennium-Meridian **Obv:** Crowned bust right **Obv. Designer:** Raphael Maklouf **Rev:** Observatory clock face with an embedded brass strip **Edge:** Reeded

Date	Mintage	F	VF	XF	Unc	BU
2000 Proof	10,000	Value: 47.50				

KM# 1056 CROWN
Copper-Nickel, 38.6 mm. **Ruler:** Elizabeth II **Subject:** Scottish Fold Kitten **Obv:** Crowned bust right **Obv. Designer:** Raphael Maklouf **Rev:** Kitten playing with world **Edge:** Reeded

Date	Mintage	F	VF	XF	Unc	BU
2000	—	—	—	—	11.00	13.00

KM# 1056a CROWN
31.1035 g., 0.9999 Silver 1.000 oz. ASW, 38.6 mm. **Ruler:** Elizabeth II **Subject:** Scottish Fold Kitten **Obv:** Crowned bust right **Obv. Designer:** Raphael Maklouf **Rev:** Kitten playing with world **Edge:** Reeded

Date	Mintage	F	VF	XF	Unc	BU
2000 Proof	50,000	Value: 47.50				

KM# 177 5 CROWN
155.5500 g., 0.9990 Silver 5.0000 oz. ASW, 65 mm. **Ruler:** Elizabeth II **Subject:** Bicentennial of U.S. Constitution **Obv:** Crowned bust right **Obv. Designer:** Raphael Maklouf **Rev:** Statue of Liberty divides dates within circle of assorted Presidential busts **Note:** Photo reduced.

Date	Mintage	F	VF	XF	Unc	BU
1987 Proof	9,000	Value: 80.00				

KM# 180 5 CROWN
155.5500 g., 0.9990 Silver 5.0000 oz. ASW, 65 mm. **Ruler:** Elizabeth II **Series:** America's Cup **Obv:** Crowned bust right **Obv. Designer:** Raphael Maklouf **Rev:** Sailboats and trophy

Date	Mintage	F	VF	XF	Unc	BU
1987 Proof	6,000	Value: 95.00				

KM# 299 5 CROWN
155.5500 g., 0.9990 Silver 5.0000 oz. ASW, 65 mm. **Ruler:** Elizabeth II **Series:** America's Cup **Obv:** Crowned bust right **Obv. Designer:** Raphael Maklouf **Rev:** Sailboats and Statue of Liberty .

Date	Mintage	F	VF	XF	Unc	BU
1987 Proof	200	Value: 220				

KM# 308 5 CROWN
155.5500 g., 0.9990 Silver 5.0000 oz. ASW, 65 mm. **Ruler:** Elizabeth II **Series:** America's Cup **Obv:** Crowned bust

right **Obv. Designer:** Raphael Maklouf **Rev:** Sailboats and map **Note:** Photo reduced.

Date	Mintage	F	VF	XF	Unc	BU
1987 Proof	—	Value: 350				

KM# 206 5 CROWN
155.5500 g., 0.9990 Silver 5.0000 oz. ASW, 65 mm. **Ruler:** Elizabeth II **Subject:** Steam Navigation **Obv:** Crowned bust right **Obv. Designer:** Raphael Maklouf **Rev:** Ship

Date	Mintage	F	VF	XF	Unc	BU
1988	—	—	—	—	145	165

KM# 285 5 CROWN
155.5500 g., 0.9990 Silver 5.0000 oz. ASW, 65 mm. **Ruler:** Elizabeth II **Subject:** Australian Bicentennial **Obv:** Crowned bust right **Obv. Designer:** Raphael Maklouf **Rev:** Kangaroo

Date	Mintage	F	VF	XF	Unc	BU
1988 Proof	—	Value: 160				

KM# 321 5 CROWN
155.5500 g., 0.9990 Silver 5.0000 oz. ASW, 65 mm. **Ruler:** Elizabeth II **Series:** America's Cup **Obv:** Crowned bust right **Obv. Designer:** Raphael Maklouf **Rev:** Cameo above two modern sailboats **Note:** Officially a "sales sample" about 10 pieces were sold or presented to distributors

Date	Mintage	F	VF	XF	Unc	BU
1991 Proof	Est. 15	—	—	—	—	—

KM# 327 5 CROWN
155.5500 g., 0.9990 Silver 5.0000 oz. ASW, 65 mm. **Ruler:** Elizabeth II **Series:** America's Cup **Obv:** Crowned bust right **Obv. Designer:** Raphael Maklouf **Rev:** Cameo above two modern sailboats

Date	Mintage	F	VF	XF	Unc	BU
1992	—	—	—	—	145	165

KM# 348 5 CROWN
155.5500 g., 0.9990 Silver 5.0000 oz. ASW, 65 mm. **Ruler:** Elizabeth II **Obv:** Crowned bust right **Obv. Designer:** Raphael Maklouf **Rev:** Siamese cat

Date	Mintage	F	VF	XF	Unc	BU
1992 Proof	—	Value: 225				

KM# 689 5 CROWN
155.5175 g., 0.9990 Silver 5.0000 oz. ASW, 65 mm. **Ruler:** Elizabeth II **Series:** Legend of King Arthur **Obv:** Crowned bust right **Obv. Designer:** Raphael Maklouf **Rev:** King Arthur with sword and orb

Date	Mintage	F	VF	XF	Unc	BU
1996 Proof	Est. 999	Value: 85.00				

KM# 690 5 CROWN
155.5175 g., 0.9990 Silver 5.0000 oz. ASW, 65 mm. **Ruler:** Elizabeth II **Series:** Legend of King Arthur **Obv:** Crowned bust right **Obv. Designer:** Raphael Maklouf **Rev:** Queen Guinevere

Date	Mintage	F	VF	XF	Unc	BU
1996 Proof	Est. 999	Value: 85.00				

KM# 691 5 CROWN
155.5175 g., 0.9990 Silver 5.0000 oz. ASW, 65 mm. **Ruler:** Elizabeth II **Series:** Legend of King Arthur **Obv:** Crowned bust right **Obv. Designer:** Raphael Maklouf **Rev:** Sir Lancelot

Date	Mintage	F	VF	XF	Unc	BU
1996	Est. 999	Value: 85.00				

KM# 692 5 CROWN
155.5175 g., 0.9990 Silver 5.0000 oz. ASW, 65 mm. **Ruler:** Elizabeth II **Series:** Legend of King Arthur **Obv:** Crowned bust right **Obv. Designer:** Raphael Maklouf **Rev:** Merlin

Date	Mintage	F	VF	XF	Unc	BU
1996	Est. 999	Value: 95.00				

KM# 693 5 CROWN
155.5175 g., 0.9990 Silver 5.0000 oz. ASW, 65 mm. **Ruler:** Elizabeth II **Series:** Legend of King Arthur **Obv:** Crowned bust right **Obv. Designer:** Raphael Maklouf **Rev:** Camelot Castle

Date	Mintage	F	VF	XF	Unc	BU
1996	Est. 999	Value: 100				

KM# 734 5 CROWN
155.5175 g., 0.9999 Gold 5.0000 oz. AGW **Ruler:** Elizabeth II **Subject:** Year of the Rat **Obv:** Crowned bust right **Obv. Designer:** Raphael Maklouf **Rev:** Rat

Date	Mintage	F	VF	XF	Unc	BU
1996 Proof	—	—	—	—	—	—

Note: Entire series purchased by one buyer. Mintage, disposition, and market value unknown

KM# 727 5 CROWN
155.5175 g., 0.9999 Gold 5.0000 oz. AGW **Ruler:** Elizabeth II **Subject:** Year of the Ox **Obv:** Crowned bust right **Obv. Designer:** Raphael Maklouf **Rev:** Ox laying down

Date	Mintage	F	VF	XF	Unc	BU
1997 Proof	Est. 250	Value: 3,500				

KM# 818 5 CROWN
155.5175 g., 0.9999 Gold 5.0000 oz. AGW **Ruler:** Elizabeth II **Subject:** Year of the Tiger **Obv:** Crowned bust right **Obv. Designer:** Raphael Maklouf **Rev:** Tiger

Date	Mintage	F	VF	XF	Unc	BU
1998 Proof	Est. 250	Value: 3,500				

KM# 953 5 CROWN
155.5175 g., 0.9999 Gold 5.0000 oz. AGW **Ruler:** Elizabeth II **Subject:** Year of the Rabbit **Obv:** Crowned bust right **Obv. Designer:** Raphael Maklouf **Rev:** Two rabbits

Date	Mintage	F	VF	XF	Unc	BU
1999 Proof	Est. 250	Value: 3,500				

KM# 1018 5 CROWN
155.5175 g., 0.9999 Gold 5.0000 oz. AGW **Ruler:** Elizabeth II **Subject:** Year of the Dragon **Obv:** Crowned bust right **Obv. Designer:** Raphael Maklouf **Rev:** Dragon

Date	Mintage	F	VF	XF	Unc	BU
2000 Proof	Est. 250	Value: 3,500				

KM# 181 10 CROWN
311.0350 g., 0.9990 Silver 10.0000 oz. ASW, 75 mm. **Ruler:** Elizabeth II **Series:** America's Cup **Obv:** Crowned bust right **Obv. Designer:** Raphael Maklouf **Rev:** Sailboats and Statue of Liberty **Note:** Photo reduced.

Date	Mintage	F	VF	XF	Unc	BU
1987 Proof	2,000	Value: 175				

KM# 188 10 CROWN
311.0350 g., 0.9990 Silver 10.0000 oz. ASW, 75 mm. **Ruler:** Elizabeth II **Subject:** Bicentenary of America's Constitution **Obv:** Crowned bust right **Obv. Designer:** Raphael Maklouf **Rev:** Statue of Liberty within circle of assorted Presidential busts

Date	Mintage	F	VF	XF	Unc	BU
1987 Proof	6,000	Value: 155				

KM# 300 10 CROWN
311.0350 g., 0.9990 Silver 10.0000 oz. ASW, 75 mm. **Ruler:** Elizabeth II **Series:** America's Cup **Obv:** Crowned bust right **Obv. Designer:** Raphael Maklouf **Rev:** Sailboats and trophy **Note:** Photo reduced.

Date	Mintage	F	VF	XF	Unc	BU
1987 Proof	69	Value: 350				

KM# 309 10 CROWN
311.0350 g., 0.9990 Silver 10.0000 oz. ASW, 75 mm. **Ruler:** Elizabeth II **Series:** America's Cup **Obv:** Crowned bust right **Obv. Designer:** Raphael Maklouf **Rev:** Sailboats and map

Date	Mintage	F	VF	XF	Unc	BU
1987 Proof	—	Value: 525				

KM# 258 10 CROWN
311.0350 g., 0.9990 Silver 10.0000 oz. ASW, 75 mm. **Ruler:** Elizabeth II **Subject:** Australian Bicentennial **Obv:** Crowned bust right **Obv. Designer:** Raphael Maklouf **Rev:** Koala

Date	Mintage	F	VF	XF	Unc	BU
1988 Proof	Est. 13,000	Value: 200				

KM# 992 10 CROWN
311.0350 g., 0.9990 Silver 10.0000 oz. ASW, 75 mm. **Ruler:** Elizabeth II **Obv:** Crowned bust right **Obv. Designer:** Raphael Maklouf **Rev:** Siamese cat

Date	Mintage	F	VF	XF	Unc	BU
1992 Proof	—	Value: 300				

KM# 775 10 CROWN
311.0300 g., 0.9250 Silver 9.2499 oz. ASW, 75 mm. **Ruler:** Elizabeth II **Subject:** 10th Anniversary of the Manx Cat **Obv:** Crowned bust right **Obv. Designer:** Raphael Maklouf **Rev:** Cat in center of assorted cat coins **Note:** Photo reduced.

Date	Mintage	F	VF	XF	Unc	BU
1997 Proof	Est. 1,997	Value: 400				

SILVER BULLION ANGEL SERIES

KM# 522 ANGEL
31.1035 g., 0.9999 Silver 1.0000 oz. ASW, 38.5 mm.

Ruler: Elizabeth II **Obv:** Crowned bust right **Obv. Designer:** Raphael Maklouf **Rev:** Archangel Michael slaying dragon right

Date	Mintage	F	VF	XF	Unc	BU
1995 Proof	—	Value: 30.00				

GOLD BULLION COINAGE

Angel Issues

KM# 166 1/20 ANGEL

1.6970 g., 0.9170 Gold .0500 oz. AGW **Ruler:** Elizabeth II **Obv:** Crowned bust right **Obv. Designer:** Raphael Maklouf **Rev:** Archangel Michael slaying dragon

Date	Mintage	F	VF	XF	Unc	BU
1986 (pi) Proof	5,000	Value: 45.00				
1986	—	—	—	—	37.50	—
1987	—	—	—	—	37.50	—
1987 Proof	—	Value: 45.00				

KM# 193 1/20 ANGEL

1.6970 g., 0.9170 Gold .0500 oz. AGW **Obv:** Crowned bust right **Obv. Designer:** Raphael Maklouf **Rev:** Archangel Michael slaying dragon **Rev. Designer:** Leslie Lindsay

Date	Mintage	F	VF	XF	Unc	BU
1988 (pi)	—	—	—	—	50.00	—
1988	—	—	—	—	37.50	—
1989 (h) Proof	Est. 5,000	Value: 50.00				
1989 (mt) Proof	3,000	Value: 50.00				
1990 (sg) Proof	Est. 3,000	Value: 50.00				
1991 (cc) Proof	1,000	Value: 50.00				
1992 (cb) Proof	1,000	Value: 50.00				
1993 Proof	Est. 1,000	Value: 50.00				

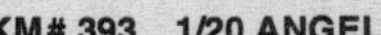

KM# 393 1/20 ANGEL

1.5551 g., 0.9999 Gold .0500 oz. AGW **Ruler:** Elizabeth II **Obv:** Crowned bust right **Obv. Designer:** Raphael Maklouf **Rev:** Archangel Michael slaying dragon right

Date	Mintage	F	VF	XF	Unc	BU
1994 (ns) Proof	—	Value: 45.00				
1995 (sc) Proof	—	Value: 50.00				
1996 (bs) Proof	Est. 1,000	Value: 50.00				
1997 (at) Proof	Est. 1,000	Value: 50.00				
1998 (x) Proof	Est. 1,000	Value: 50.00				
1999 (fw) Proof	Est. 1,000	Value: 50.00				
2000 Proof	—	Value: 45.00				
Note: Christmas candle privy mark						
2000 (ch) Proof	Est. 1,000	Value: 50.00				

KM# 138 1/10 ANGEL

3.3900 g., 0.9170 Gold .1000 oz. AGW **Ruler:** Elizabeth II **Obv:** Crowned bust right **Obv. Designer:** Raphael Maklouf **Rev:** Archangel Michael slaying dragon

Date	Mintage	F	VF	XF	Unc	BU
1984 Proof	5,000	Value: 75.00				

KM# 140 1/10 ANGEL

3.3900 g., 0.9170 Gold .1000 oz. AGW **Ruler:** Elizabeth II **Obv:** Crowned bust right **Obv. Designer:** Raphael Maklouf **Rev:** Archangel Michael slaying dragon left **Rev. Designer:** Leslie Lindsay

Date	Mintage	F	VF	XF	Unc	BU
1985 Proof	3,000	Value: 80.00				
1985	8,000	—	—	—	70.00	—
1986	—	—	—	—	70.00	—
1986 Proof	—	Value: 80.00				
1987 Proof	—	Value: 80.00				
1987	—	—	—	—	70.00	—

KM# 159 1/10 ANGEL

3.3900 g., 0.9170 Gold .1000 oz. AGW **Ruler:** Elizabeth II **Obv:** Crowned bust right **Obv. Designer:** Raphael Maklouf **Rev:** Archangel Michael slaying dragon left **Rev. Designer:** Leslie Lindsay

Date	Mintage	F	VF	XF	Unc	BU
1985 C	1,000	—	—	—	85.00	—
1985 H	1,000	—	—	—	85.00	—
1985 L	1,000	—	—	—	85.00	—
1985 A	1,000	—	—	—	85.00	—
1985	5,000	—	—	—	70.00	—
1986 T	1,000	—	—	—	85.00	—
1986 A	1,000	—	—	—	85.00	—
1986 X	1,000	—	—	—	85.00	—
1987 A	1,000	—	—	—	85.00	—
1987 L	1,000	—	—	—	85.00	—
1987 (mt) Proof	3,000	Value: 85.00				
1987 F Proof	1,000	Value: 85.00				
1988 A Proof	1,000	Value: 85.00				

KM# 194 1/10 ANGEL

3.3900 g., 0.9170 Gold .1000 oz. AGW **Ruler:** Elizabeth II **Obv:** Crowned bust right **Obv. Designer:** Raphael Maklouf **Rev:** Archangel Michael slaying dragon

Date	Mintage	F	VF	XF	Unc	BU
1988	—	—	—	—	70.00	—
1989 A Proof	250	Value: 100				
1990 A Proof	1,000	Value: 85.00				
1991 A Proof	400	Value: 95.00				
Note: 299 pieces have been melted						
1992 A	100	—	—	—	110	—

KM# 394 1/10 ANGEL

3.1103 g., 0.9999 Gold .1000 oz. AGW **Obv:** Crowned bust right **Obv. Designer:** Raphael Maklouf **Rev:** Archangel Michael

Date	Mintage	F	VF	XF	Unc	BU
1994 Proof	—	Value: 75.00				

KM# 152.1 1/4 ANGEL

8.4830 g., 0.9170 Gold .2500 oz. AGW **Ruler:** Elizabeth II **Obv:** Crowned bust right **Obv. Designer:** Raphael Maklouf **Rev:** Archangel Michael slaying dragon left **Rev. Designer:** Leslie Lindsay

Date	Mintage	F	VF	XF	Unc	BU
1985 Proof	51	Value: 200				
1985	2,117	—	—	—	175	—
1986 L	1,000	—	—	—	175	—
1986 Proof	—	Value: 185				

KM# 152.2 1/4 ANGEL

8.4830 g., 0.9170 Gold .2500 oz. AGW **Ruler:** Elizabeth II **Obv:** Crowned bust right **Obv. Designer:** Raphael Maklouf **Rev:** Archangel Michael slaying dragon **Rev. Designer:** Leslie Lindsay

Date	Mintage	F	VF	XF	Unc	BU
1987 (bb) Proof	1,000	Value: 185				
1987 (SL) Proof	568	Value: 185				
1987 Proof	—	Value: 185				
1987	—	—	—	—	175	—
1987 (s) Proof	1,000	Value: 185				

KM# 195 1/4 ANGEL

8.4830 g., 0.9170 Gold .2500 oz. AGW **Ruler:** Elizabeth II **Obv:** Crowned bust right **Obv. Designer:** Raphael Maklouf **Rev:** Archangel Michael slaying dragon left **Rev. Designer:** Leslie Lindsay

Date	Mintage	F	VF	XF	Unc	BU
1988 (f) Proof	1,000	Value: 200				
1988	—	—	—	—	175	—
1988 (p) Proof	1,000	Value: 200				
1988 (ss) Proof	1,000	Value: 200				
1989 (y)	—	—	—	—	175	—
1989 C (d) Proof	1,000	Value: 200				
1989 (p) Proof	500	Value: 200				
1989 (hk) Proof	1,000	Value: 200				
1990 (c) Proof	250	Value: 220				
1990 (ma) Proof	200	Value: 250				
Note: 40 pieces melted						
1990 (tb)	1,000	—	—	—	175	—
Note: 10 pieces melted						
1990 (ba) Proof	1,000	Value: 200				
Note: 513 pieces melted						
1990 (h) Proof	1,000	Value: 180				
1990 (fl)	1,000	—	—	—	175	—
Note: 9 pieces melted						
1991 (fr) Proof	500	Value: 200				
1991 (c) Proof	200	Value: 250				
Note: 57 pieces melted						
1993 Proof	—	Value: 175				

KM# 395 1/4 ANGEL

7.7758 g., 0.9999 Gold .2500 oz. AGW **Ruler:** Elizabeth II **Obv:** Crowned bust right **Obv. Designer:** Raphael Maklouf **Rev:** Archangel Michael slaying dragon

Date	Mintage	F	VF	XF	Unc	BU
1994 Proof	750	Value: 190				

KM# 155 1/2 ANGEL

16.9380 g., 0.9170 Gold .5000 oz. AGW **Ruler:** Elizabeth II **Obv:** Crowned bust right **Obv. Designer:** Raphael Maklouf **Rev:** Archangel Michael slaying dragon left **Rev. Designer:** Leslie Lindsay

Date	Mintage	F	VF	XF	Unc	BU
1985	1,776	—	—	—	350	—
1985 Proof	51	Value: 375				
1986 Proof	3,000	Value: 365				
1986	—	—	—	—	350	—
1987	—	—	—	—	350	—
1987 Proof	—	Value: 365				

KM# 196 1/2 ANGEL

16.9380 g., 0.9170 Gold .5000 oz. AGW **Ruler:** Elizabeth II **Obv:** Crowned bust right **Obv. Designer:** Raphael Maklouf **Rev:** Archangel Michael slaying dragon

Date	Mintage	F	VF	XF	Unc	BU
1988	—	—	—	—	350	—

KM# 396 1/2 ANGEL

15.5517 g., 0.9999 Gold .5000 oz. AGW **Ruler:** Elizabeth II **Obv:** Crowned bust right **Obv. Designer:** Raphael Maklouf **Rev:** Archangel Michael slaying dragon

Date	Mintage	F	VF	XF	Unc	BU
1994 Proof	—	Value: 350				

KM# 139 ANGEL

33.9300 g., 0.9170 Gold 1.0000 oz. AGW **Ruler:** Elizabeth II **Obv:** Young bust right **Obv. Designer:** Arnold Machin **Rev:** Archangel Michael slaying dragon left **Rev. Designer:** Leslie Lindsay

Date	Mintage	F	VF	XF	Unc	BU
1984 Proof	3,000	Value: 725				

KM# 141 ANGEL

33.9300 g., 0.9170 Gold 1.0000 oz. AGW **Ruler:** Elizabeth II **Obv:** Crowned bust right **Obv. Designer:** Raphael Maklouf **Rev:** Archangel Michael slaying dragon left **Rev. Designer:** Leslie Lindsay

Date	Mintage	F	VF	XF	Unc	BU
1985 Prooflike	—	—	—	—	—	—
1985 Proof	3,000	Value: 725				
1985	28,000	—	—	—	700	—
1986 Proof	—	Value: 725				
1986	—	—	—	—	700	—
1987	—	—	—	—	700	—
1987 Proof	—	Value: 725				

KM# 191 ANGEL

33.9300 g., 0.9170 Gold 1.0000 oz. AGW **Ruler:** Elizabeth II **Subject:** Hong Kong Coin Show **Obv:** Crowned bust right **Rev:** Archangel Michael slaying dragon left **Rev. Designer:** Leslie Lindsay

Date	Mintage	F	VF	XF	Unc	BU
1987 Proof	1,000	Value: 725				

KM# 197 ANGEL

33.9300 g., 0.9170 Gold 1.0000 oz. AGW **Ruler:** Elizabeth II **Obv:** Crowned bust right **Obv. Designer:** Raphael Maklouf **Rev:** Archangel Michael slaying dragon left **Rev. Designer:** Leslie Lindsay

Date	Mintage	F	VF	XF	Unc	BU
1988 (ss) Proof	1,000	Value: 725				
1988	—	—	—	—	700	—

KM# 397 ANGEL
31.1035 g., 0.9999 Gold 1.0000 oz. AGW **Ruler:** Elizabeth II
Obv: Crowned bust right **Obv. Designer:** Raphael Maklouf
Rev: Archangel Michael slaying dragon right

Date	Mintage	F	VF	XF	Unc	BU
1994 Proof	—	Value: 725				

KM# 156 5 ANGEL
169.6680 g., 0.9170 Gold 5.0000 oz. AGW **Ruler:** Elizabeth II
Obv: Crowned bust right **Obv. Designer:** Raphael Maklouf
Rev: Archangel Michael slaying dragon left
Rev. Designer: Leslie Lindsay

Date	Mintage	F	VF	XF	Unc	BU
1985	104	—	—	—	3,500	—
1985 Proof	90	Value: 3,500				
1986 Proof	250	Value: 3,500				
1986	89	—	—	—	3,500	—
1987 Proof	27	Value: 3,500				
1987	150	—	—	—	3,500	—

KM# 198 5 ANGEL
169.6680 g., 0.9170 Gold 5.0000 oz. AGW **Ruler:** Elizabeth II
Obv: Crowned bust right **Obv. Designer:** Raphael Maklouf
Rev: Archangel Michael slaying dragon

Date	Mintage	F	VF	XF	Unc	BU
1988	250	—	—	—	3,500	—

KM# 157 10 ANGEL
339.3350 g., 0.9170 Gold 10.0000 oz. AGW **Ruler:** Elizabeth II
Obv: Crowned bust right **Obv. Designer:** Raphael Maklouf
Rev: Archangel Michael slaying dragon left
Rev. Designer: Leslie Lindsay

Date	Mintage	F	VF	XF	Unc	BU
1985 Proof	68	Value: 7,000				
1985	79	—	—	—	7,000	—
1986	47	—	—	—	7,000	—
1986 Proof	250	Value: 7,000				
1987	150	—	—	—	7,000	—
1987 Proof	30	Value: 7,000				

KM# 199 10 ANGEL
339.3350 g., 0.9170 Gold 10.0000 oz. AGW **Ruler:** Elizabeth II
Obv: Crowned bust right **Obv. Designer:** Raphael Maklouf
Rev: Archangel Michael slaying dragon

Date	Mintage	F	VF	XF	Unc	BU
1988 Proof	250	Value: 7,000				

KM# 189 15 ANGEL
508.9575 g., 0.9170 Gold 15.0000 oz. AGW **Ruler:** Elizabeth II
Obv: Crowned bust right **Obv. Designer:** Raphael Maklouf
Rev: Archangel Michael slaying dragon

Date	Mintage	F	VF	XF	Unc	BU
1987 Proof	18	Value: 11,000				
1987	150	—	—	—	10,500	—

KM# 200 15 ANGEL
508.9575 g., 0.9170 Gold 15.0000 oz. AGW **Ruler:** Elizabeth II
Obv: Crowned bust right **Obv. Designer:** Raphael Maklouf
Rev: Archangel Michael slaying dragon left
Rev. Designer: Leslie Lindsay

Date	Mintage	F	VF	XF	Unc	BU
1988 Proof	—	Value: 10,500				

KM# 201 20 ANGEL
678.6720 g., 0.9170 Gold 20.0000 oz. AGW, 75.2 mm.
Ruler: Elizabeth II **Obv:** Crowned bust right **Obv. Designer:** Raphael Maklouf **Rev:** Archangel Michael slaying dragon left
Rev. Designer: Leslie Lindsay **Note:** Photo reduced.

Date	Mintage	F	VF	XF	Unc	BU
1988	250	—	—	—	10,500	—
1988 Proof	100	Value: 11,000				

KM# 201a 20 ANGEL
Gilt Silver **Ruler:** Elizabeth II **Obv:** Crowned bust right
Obv. Designer: Raphael Maklouf **Rev:** Archangel Michael slaying dragon left **Rev. Designer:** Leslie Lindsay

Date	Mintage	F	VF	XF	Unc	BU
1988	—	—	—	—	—	—

KM# 301 25 ANGEL
848.2750 g., 0.9170 Gold 25.0000 oz. AGW **Ruler:** Elizabeth II
Obv: Crowned bust right **Obv. Designer:** Raphael Maklouf
Rev: Archangel Michael slaying dragon

Date	Mintage	F	VF	XF	Unc	BU
1989	—	—	—	—	17,500	—

GOLD BULLION COINAGE

Sovereign Issues

KM# 969 1/5 SOVEREIGN
1.0000 g., 0.9999 Gold .0321 oz. AGW **Ruler:** Elizabeth II
Obv: Head with tiara right **Obv. Designer:** Ian Rank-Broadley
Rev: Triskeles **Shape:** Rectangular

Date	Mintage	F	VF	XF	Unc	BU
1999	—	—	—	—	BV+40%	—

KM# 970 1/2 SOVEREIGN
2.5000 g., 0.9999 Gold .0804 oz. AGW **Ruler:** Elizabeth II
Obv: Head with tiara right **Obv. Designer:** Ian Rank-Broadley
Rev: Triskeles **Shape:** Rectangular

Date	Mintage	F	VF	XF	Unc	BU
1999	—	—	—	—	BV+30%	—

KM# 971 3/4 SOVEREIGN
3.5000 g., 0.9999 Gold .1125 oz. AGW **Ruler:** Elizabeth II
Obv: Head with tiara right **Obv. Designer:** Ian Rank-Broadley
Rev: Triskeles **Shape:** Rectangular

Date	Mintage	F	VF	XF	Unc	BU
1999	—	—	—	—	BV+25%	—

KM# 972 SOVEREIGN
5.0000 g., 0.9999 Gold .1607 oz. AGW **Ruler:** Elizabeth II
Obv: Head with tiara right **Obv. Designer:** Ian Rank-Broadley
Rev: Triskeles **Shape:** Rectangular

Date	Mintage	F	VF	XF	Unc	BU
1999	—	—	—	—	BV+20%	—

KM# 973 2 SOVEREIGNS
10.0000 g., 0.9999 Gold .3215 oz. AGW **Ruler:** Elizabeth II
Obv: Head with tiara right **Obv. Designer:** Ian Rank-Broadley
Rev: Triskeles **Shape:** Rectangular

Date	Mintage	F	VF	XF	Unc	BU
1999	—	—	—	—	—	—

KM# 974 5 SOVEREIGNS
31.1035 g., 0.9999 Gold .9999 oz. AGW **Ruler:** Elizabeth II
Obv: Head with tiara right **Obv. Designer:** Ian Rank-Broadley
Rev: Triskeles **Shape:** Rectangular

Date	Mintage	F	VF	XF	Unc	BU
1999	—	—	—	—	BV+5%	—

GOLD BULLION COINAGE

Platina Issues

KM# 944 1/25 PLATINA
1.2447 g., 0.7500 White Gold .0300 oz. AGW **Ruler:** Elizabeth II
Obv: Crowned bust right **Obv. Designer:** Raphael Maklouf
Rev: Crowned arms

Date	Mintage	F	VF	XF	Unc	BU
1999 Proof	Est. 10,000	Value: 40.00				

KM# 945 1/10 PLATINA
3.1103 g., 0.7500 White Gold .0750 oz. AGW **Ruler:** Elizabeth II
Obv: Crowned bust right **Obv. Designer:** Raphael Maklouf
Rev: Crowned arms

Date	Mintage	F	VF	XF	Unc	BU
1999 Proof	Est. 7,500	Value: 75.00				

KM# 946 1/5 PLATINA
6.2200 g., 0.7500 White Gold .1500 oz. AGW **Ruler:** Elizabeth II
Obv: Crowned bust right **Obv. Designer:** Raphael Maklouf
Rev: Crowned arms flanked by falcons

Date	Mintage	F	VF	XF	Unc	BU
1999 Proof	Est. 5,000	Value: 135				

KM# 947 1/2 PLATINA
15.5517 g., 0.7500 White Gold .3750 oz. AGW
Ruler: Elizabeth II **Obv:** Crowned bust right
Obv. Designer: Raphael Maklouf **Rev:** Crowned arms

Date	Mintage	F	VF	XF	Unc	BU
1999 Proof	Est. 3,500	Value: 275				

GOLD & PLATINUM BIMETALLIC BULLION COINAGE

KM# 1065 1/4 ANGEL
Ring Weight: 3.8880 g. **Ring Composition:** 0.9995 Platinum .1244 oz. APW **Center Weight:** 3.8880 g. **Center Composition:** 0.9999 Gold .1249 oz. AGW , 22 mm. **Ruler:** Elizabeth II
Obv: Crowned bust right **Obv. Designer:** Raphael Maklouf
Rev: Archangel Michael slaying dragon **Edge:** Reeded

Date	Mintage	F	VF	XF	Unc	BU
1995 Proof	—	Value: 265				

KM# 1066 1/4 NOBLE
Bi-Metallic Platinum center in Gold ring, 22 mm.
Ruler: Elizabeth II **Obv:** Crowned bust right **Obv. Designer:** Raphael Maklouf **Rev:** Viking ship **Edge:** Reeded

Date	Mintage	F	VF	XF	Unc	BU
1995 Proof	—	Value: 265				

PLATINUM BULLION COINAGE

Noble Series

KM# 266 1/20 NOBLE
1.5551 g., 0.9995 Platinum .0500 oz. APW **Ruler:** Elizabeth II
Obv: Crowned bust right **Obv. Designer:** Raphael Maklouf
Rev: Viking ship

Date	Mintage	F	VF	XF	Unc	BU
1989	10,000	Value: 70.00				
1992	—	—	—	—	65.00	—

KM# 137 1/10 NOBLE
3.1100 g., 0.9995 Platinum .1000 oz. APW **Ruler:** Elizabeth II

Obv: Young bust right **Obv. Designer:** Arnold Machin
Rev: Viking ship

Date	Mintage	F	VF	XF	Unc	BU
1984	—	—	—	—	130	—
1984 Proof	5,000	Value: 135				

KM# 153 1/10 NOBLE
3.1100 g., 0.9995 Platinum .1000 oz. APW **Ruler:** Elizabeth II
Obv: Crowned head right **Obv. Designer:** Raphael Maklouf
Rev: Viking ship

Date	Mintage	F	VF	XF	Unc	BU
1985	99,000	—	—	—	130	—
1985 Proof	5,000	Value: 135				
1986	—	—	—	—	130	—
1986 Proof	5,000	Value: 135				
1987	—	—	—	—	130	—
1987 Proof	5,000	Value: 135				

KM# 202 1/10 NOBLE
3.1100 g., 0.9995 Platinum .1000 oz. APW **Ruler:** Elizabeth II
Obv: Crowned bust right **Obv. Designer:** Raphael Maklouf
Rev: Viking ship with hologram sail

Date	Mintage	F	VF	XF	Unc	BU
1988	5,000	—	—	—	130	—
1989	5,000	—	—	—	130	—

KM# 168 1/4 NOBLE
7.7757 g., 0.9995 Platinum .2500 oz. APW **Ruler:** Elizabeth II
Obv: Crowned bust right **Obv. Designer:** Raphael Maklouf
Rev: Viking ship

Date	Mintage	F	VF	XF	Unc	BU
1986 Proof	2,015	Value: 325				
1987 Proof	3,250	Value: 325				
1987PM Proof	750	Value: 325				

KM# 203 1/4 NOBLE
7.7757 g., 0.9995 Platinum .2500 oz. APW **Ruler:** Elizabeth II
Obv: Crowned bust right **Obv. Designer:** Raphael Maklouf
Rev: Viking ship

Date	Mintage	F	VF	XF	Unc	BU
1988	—	—	—	—	325	—
1988 (a)	100	—	—	—	325	—
1988 (p) Proof	1,000	Value: 325				
1988 (bb) Proof	1,000	Value: 325				
1989 (p) Proof	500	Value: 325				
1989 (br) Proof	250	Value: 325				
1990 (ba) Proof	1,000	Value: 325				
1990 (ti) Proof	Est. 1,000	Value: 325				

KM# 717 1/4 NOBLE
7.7757 g., 0.9995 Platinum .2500 oz. APW **Ruler:** Elizabeth II
Obv: Crowned bust right **Obv. Designer:** Raphael Maklouf
Rev: Ship with hologram sail

Date	Mintage	F	VF	XF	Unc	BU
1996 Proof	Est. 10,000	Value: 325				

KM# 169 1/2 NOBLE
15.5514 g., 0.9995 Platinum .5000 oz. APW **Ruler:** Elizabeth II
Obv: Crowned bust right **Obv. Designer:** Raphael Maklouf
Rev: Ship with hologram sail

Date	Mintage	F	VF	XF	Unc	BU
1986 Proof	15	Value: 750				
1987 Proof	3,000	Value: 650				

KM# 204 1/2 NOBLE
15.5514 g., 0.9995 Platinum .5000 oz. APW **Ruler:** Elizabeth II, The 1994 date was issued as part of a two piece set with a rhodium plated silver medal marking the 10th anniversary of the modern platinum noble coin series **Obv:** Crowned bust right **Obv. Designer:** Raphael Maklouf **Rev:** Viking ship

Date	Mintage	F	VF	XF	Unc	BU
1988	3,000	Value: 650				
1989 Proof	3,000	Value: 650				
1994PM Proof	250	Value: 750				

KM# 110 NOBLE
31.1030 g., 0.9995 Platinum .9991 oz. APW **Ruler:** Elizabeth II
Obv: Young bust right **Obv. Designer:** Arnold Machin
Rev: Viking ship

Date	Mintage	F	VF	XF	Unc	BU
1983 Proof	94	Value: 1,275				
1983	1,700	—	—	—	1,250	—
1984	—	—	—	—	1,250	—
1984 Proof	2,000	Value: 1,275				

KM# 154 NOBLE
31.1030 g., 0.9995 Platinum .9991 oz. APW **Ruler:** Elizabeth II
Obv: Crowned bust right **Obv. Designer:** Raphael Maklouf
Rev: Viking ship

Date	Mintage	F	VF	XF	Unc	BU
1985	—	—	—	—	1,250	—
1985 Proof	3,000	Value: 1,275				
1986	—	—	—	—	1,250	—
1986 Proof	3,000	Value: 1,275				
1987	—	—	—	—	1,250	—
1987 Proof	3,000	Value: 1,275				

KM# 205 NOBLE
31.1030 g., 0.9995 Platinum .9991 oz. APW **Ruler:** Elizabeth II
Obv: Crowned bust right **Obv. Designer:** Raphael Maklouf
Rev: Viking ship

Date	Mintage	F	VF	XF	Unc	BU
1988 Proof	3,000	Value: 1,250				
1989 Proof	3,000	Value: 1,250				

KM# 170 5 NOBLE
155.5140 g., 0.9995 Platinum 5.0000 oz. APW
Ruler: Elizabeth II **Obv:** Crowned bust right
Obv. Designer: Raphael Maklouf **Rev:** Viking ship

Date	Mintage	F	VF	XF	Unc	BU
1986 Proof	15	Value: 6,500				
1987 Proof	11	Value: 6,500				
1988 Proof	—	Value: 7,000				

KM# 171 10 NOBLE
311.0280 g., 0.9995 Platinum 10.0000 oz. APW, 63 mm.
Ruler: Elizabeth II **Obv:** Crowned bust right **Obv. Designer:** Raphael Maklouf **Rev:** Viking ship **Note:** Photo reduced.

Date	Mintage	F	VF	XF	Unc	BU
1986 Proof	15	Value: 12,500				
1987 Proof	11	Value: 12,500				
1988 Proof	—	Value: 13,000				

TRADE COINAGE

Ecu Series

KM# 711 15 ECUS
10.0000 g., 0.9250 Silver .2974 oz. ASW **Ruler:** Elizabeth II
Obv: Crowned bust right **Obv. Designer:** Raphael Maklouf
Rev: Manx cat within shield and wings

Date	Mintage	F	VF	XF	Unc	BU
1994	Est. 30,000	—	—	—	42.50	—

KM# 714 15 ECUS
10.0000 g., 0.9250 Silver .2974 oz. ASW **Ruler:** Elizabeth II
Subject: 50th Anniversary of United Nations **Obv:** Crowned bust right **Obv. Designer:** Raphael Maklouf **Rev:** Blacksmith

Date	Mintage	F	VF	XF	Unc	BU
1995 Proof	Est. 30,000	Value: 42.50				

KM# 712 25 ECUS
19.2000 g., 0.9250 Silver .5710 oz. ASW **Ruler:** Elizabeth II
Subject: 50th Anniversary of United Nations **Obv:** Crowned bust right **Obv. Designer:** Raphael Maklouf **Rev:** Viking boat on helmeted shield

Date	Mintage	F	VF	XF	Unc	BU
1994	Est. 15,000	—	—	—	52.50	55.00

KM# 715 25 ECUS
19.2000 g., 0.9250 Silver .5710 oz. ASW **Ruler:** Elizabeth II
Subject: 50th Anniversary of United Nations **Obv:** Crowned bust right **Obv. Designer:** Raphael Maklouf **Rev:** Ram's head within shield

Date	Mintage	F	VF	XF	Unc	BU
1995 Proof	Est. 15,000	Value: 55.00				

KM# 713 75 ECUS
6.2200 g., 0.9990 Gold .2000 oz. AGW **Ruler:** Elizabeth II
Obv: Crowned bust right **Obv. Designer:** Raphael Maklouf
Rev: Triskeles on crowned shield

Date	Mintage	F	VF	XF	Unc	BU
1994	Est. 2,000	—	—	—	190	200

KM# 716 75 ECUS
6.2200 g., 0.9990 Gold .2000 oz. AGW **Ruler:** Elizabeth II
Obv: Crowned bust right **Obv. Designer:** Raphael Maklouf
Rev: Falcons on shield

Date	Mintage	F	VF	XF	Unc	BU
1995 Proof	Est. 2,000	Value: 200				

TRADE COINAGE

Sterling Euro Series

KM# 718 10 EURO

10.0000 g., 0.9250 Silver .2974 oz. ASW **Ruler:** Elizabeth II **Subject:** Spain - 10 years Membership E.C. **Obv:** Crowned bust right **Obv. Designer:** Raphael Maklouf **Rev:** Head facing below standing figures within circle

Date	Mintage	F	VF	XF	Unc	BU
1996 Proof	Est. 30,000	Value: 40.00				

KM# 795 10 EURO

10.0000 g., 0.9250 Silver .2974 oz. ASW **Ruler:** Elizabeth II **Subject:** 200th Anniversary - Birth of Franza Schubert **Obv:** Crowned bust right **Obv. Designer:** Raphael Maklouf **Rev:** Head below piano recital scene

Date	Mintage	F	VF	XF	Unc	BU
1997 Proof	Est. 30,000	Value: 40.00				

KM# 796 10 EURO

10.0000 g., 0.9250 Silver .2974 oz. ASW **Ruler:** Elizabeth II **Obv:** Crowned bust right **Obv. Designer:** Raphael Maklouf **Rev:** Head below organ player

Date	Mintage	F	VF	XF	Unc	BU
1997 Proof	Est. 30,000	Value: 40.00				

KM# 909 10 EURO

10.0000 g., 0.9250 Silver .2974 oz. ASW **Ruler:** Elizabeth II **Subject:** 125th Anniversary of the Isle of Man Railway **Obv:** Crowned bust right **Obv. Designer:** Raphael Maklouf **Rev:** Old steam train

Date	Mintage	F	VF	XF	Unc	BU
1998 Proof	Est. 30,000	Value: 40.00				

KM# 910 10 EURO

10.0000 g., 0.9250 Silver .2974 oz. ASW **Ruler:** Elizabeth II **Subject:** Myths and Legends - Manannan **Obv:** Crowned bust right **Obv. Designer:** Raphael Maklouf **Rev:** Equestrian

Date	Mintage	F	VF	XF	Unc	BU
1998 Proof	Est. 30,000	Value: 40.00				

KM# 719 15 EURO

19.2000 g., 0.9250 Silver .5710 oz. ASW **Ruler:** Elizabeth II **Subject:** First Performance - La Boheme **Obv:** Crowned bust right **Obv. Designer:** Raphael Maklouf **Rev:** Head below standing figures

Date	Mintage	F	VF	XF	Unc	BU
1996 Proof	Est. 15,000	Value: 75.00				

KM# 720 50 EURO

6.2200 g., 0.9999 Gold .1999 oz. AGW **Ruler:** Elizabeth II **Subject:** 125th Anniversary of Aida-Verdi **Obv:** Crowned bust right **Obv. Designer:** Raphael Maklouf **Rev:** Head below standing figures

Date	Mintage	F	VF	XF	Unc	BU
1996 Proof	Est. 2,000	Value: 165				

KM# 797 50 EURO

6.2200 g., 0.9999 Gold .1999 oz. AGW **Ruler:** Elizabeth II **Obv:** Crowned bust right **Obv. Designer:** Raphael Maklouf **Rev:** Head below harp player

Date	Mintage	F	VF	XF	Unc	BU
1997 Proof	Est. 2,000	Value: 165				

KM# 911 50 EURO

6.2200 g., 0.9999 Gold .1999 oz. AGW **Ruler:** Elizabeth II **Subject:** St. George **Obv:** Crowned bust right **Obv. Designer:** Raphael Maklouf **Rev:** Rider spearing dragon as captive damsel watches

Date	Mintage	F	VF	XF	Unc	BU
1998 Proof	Est. 2,000	Value: 175				

WW II P.O.W. TOKEN COINAGE

KM# Tn23 1/2 PENNY

Brass

Date	Mintage	F	VF	XF	Unc	BU
ND	2,000	17.50	35.00	75.00	165	—

KM# Tn24 PENNY

Brass

Date	Mintage	F	VF	XF	Unc	BU
ND	20,000	6.00	15.00	35.00	80.00	—

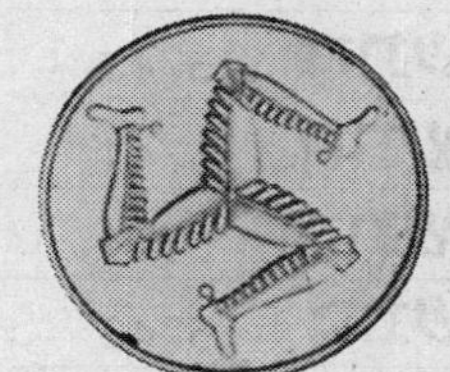

KM# Tn25 6 PENCE

Brass

Date	Mintage	F	VF	XF	Unc	BU
ND	2,500	12.00	28.00	60.00	135	—

PATTERNS

Including off metal strikes

KM#	Date	Mintage	Identification	Mkt Val
Pn20	1987	30	1/2 Crown. Silver.	325
Pn21	1989	—	Crown. Copper-Nickel. Black finish, first penny postage stamp.	—
Pn23	1992	—	5 Pounds. Virenium. Nigell Mansell, KM336.	—

PIEFORTS

KM#	Date	Mintage	Identification	Mkt Val
P4	1983	4,950	Pound. Silver. KM109.	37.50
P5	1983	4,950	Pound. Silver. KM127	37.50
P6	1983	4,950	Pound. Silver. KM130	42.50
P7	1983	4,950	Pound. Silver. KM131	42.50
P8	1984	1,000	Pound. 0.3740 Gold.	150
P9	1984	250	Pound. 0.9170 Gold.	375
P10	1985	4,950	Pound. Silver.	42.50
P11	1985	950	Pound. 0.3740 Gold.	150
P12	1985	250	Pound. 0.9170 Gold.	375
P13	1985	50	Pound. Platinum.	500

MINT SETS

KM#	Date	Mintage	Identification	Issue Price	Mkt Val
MS1	1965 (3)	1,500	KM15-17	—	1,100
MS2	1971 (6)	50,000	KM19-24	3.00	3.00
MS3	1973 (4)	2,500	KM26-29	760	820
MS4	1974 (4)	250	KM26-29	—	1,400
MS5	1975 (6)	20,000	KM19-24	—	3.00
MS6	1975 (6)	20,000	KM19a-24a	56.50	45.00
MS7	1975 (4)	200	KM26-29	—	1,400
MS8	1976 (6)	20,000	KM32-34, 35.1,36.2, 39	—	4.00
MS9	1976 (6)	20,000	KM32a-34a, 35.1a-36.1a, 39a	—	40.00
MS10	1976 (4)	—	KM26-29	—	1,400
MS11	1977 (6)	50,000	KM33-34, 35.1-36.1, 39-40	—	4.00
MS12	1977 (4)	180	KM26-29	—	1,400
MS13	1978 (6)	10,000	KM32a-34a, 35.1a-36.1a, 39a	—	50.00
MS14	1978 (6)	—	KM32-34, 35.1-36.1, 39	—	4.00
MS15	1979 (6)	—	KM32-34, 35.1-36.1, 39	—	5.00
MS16	1979 (4)	—	KM26-29	—	1,400
MS17	1980 (6)	30,000	KM58-62, 70	—	5.00
MS18	1981 (6)	—	KM58-62, 70	—	5.00
MS19	1982	—		—	6.00
MS20	1983 (9)	—	KM58-62, 70, 88, 90, 109	—	30.00
MS21	1983 (6)	—	KM58-62, 70	—	5.00
MS22	1989 (9)	—	KM207-208, 209.1, 210-215	—	28.00
MS23	1990 (9)	—	KM207-208, 209.1, 210-215	25.00	28.00
MS24	1992 (9)	—	KM207-208, 209.2, 210-215	25.00	28.00
MS25	1994 (9)	—	KM207-208, 212-213, 337, 391-392, 398-399	25.00	28.00
MS26	1995 (9)	—	KM207-208, 212-213, 337, 391-392, 465-466	—	—
MS27	1996 (9)	—	KM587-595	—	28.00
MS28	1997 (5)	5,000	KM770-773, 774b	—	1,300
MS29	1985 (9)	—	KM142-148, 150-151, plus rectangular medal	—	28.00

PROOF SETS

KM#	Date	Mintage	Identification	Issue Price	Mkt Val
PS1	1965 (3)	1,000	KM15a-17a	—	1,180
PS2	1971 (6)	10,000	KM19-24	20.00	20.00
PS3	1973 (4)	1,250	KM26-29	950	1,500
PS4	1974 (4)	2,500	KM26-29	900	1,500
PS5	1975 (6)	600	KM19b-24b	1,175	4,050
PS6	1975 (4)	—	KM26-29	—	1,500
PS7	1976 (6)	600	KM32b-34b, 35.1b-36.1b, 39b	—	4,050
PS8	1976 (4)	—	KM26-29	—	1,500
PS9	1977 (6)	10,000	KM33a-34a, 35.1a-36.1a, 39a, 40a	—	42.50
PS10	1977 (4)	1,250	KM26-29	—	1,500
PS11	1978 (7)	—	KM32-34, 35.1-36.1, 39, 44	—	15.00
PS12	1978 (7)	600	KM32b-34b, 35.1b-36.1b, 39b, 44b	—	4,425
PS13	1979 (7)	10,000	KM32a-34a, 35.1a-36.1a, 39a, 44a	110	50.00
PS14	1979 (7)	500	KM32b-34b, 35.1b, 36.1b, 39b, 44b	2,765	4,425
PS15	1979 (4)	1,000	KM26-29	—	1,500
PS16	1980 (7)	10,000	KM44d, 58a-62a, 70a	—	55.00
PSA16	1980 (7)	—	KM44, 58-62, 70	—	20.00
PS17	1980 (7)	—	KM44c, 58c-62c, 70c	—	170
PS18	1980 (7)	300	KM44b, 58d-62d, 70d	—	1,575
PS19	1982 (9)	1,000	KM44a, 58b-62b, 70a, 88a, 90a	—	130
PSA19	1981 (7)	—	KM44a, 59b-62b, 70b, 88a	—	—
PS20	1982 (9)	250	KM44c, 58b-62b, 88b, 90b	—	1,295
PS21	1982 (9)	100	KM44b, 58c-62c, 88c, 90c	—	4,000
PS22	1982 (7)	25,000	KM58-62, 70, 90	—	15.00
PSA22	1982 (8)	—	KM44a, 59b-62b, 70a, 88a, 90a	—	—
PS23	1982 (7)	9,000	KM58b-62b, 70a, 90a	—	60.00
PS24	1982 (7)	250	KM58c-62c, 70c, 90b	—	245
PS25	1982 (7)	400	KM58d-62d, 70d, 90c	—	1,720
PS26	1983 (7)	—	KM58d-62d, 90a, 109a	—	1,585
PS27	1983 (7)	—	KM58b-62b, 90b, 109b	—	290
PS28	1983 (7)	—	KM58c-62c, 90c, 109c	—	1,370
PSA29	1983 (9)	—	KM59b-62b, 70b, 88a, 90a, 109a	—	—
PS29	1985 (9)	25,000	KM142-148, 150-151	36.00	36.00
PS32	1985 (9)	100	KM135c, 142c-148c, 150c	3,600	3,850
PS31	1985 (9)	150	KM135b, 142b-148b, 150b	3,240	2,800
PS30	1985 (9)	5,000	KM135, 142a-148a, 150a	120	120
PS33	1985 (7)	25,000	KM142-148	20.00	20.00
PS34	1985 (7)	5,000	KM142a-148a	72.00	72.00
PS35	1985 (7)	150	KM142b-148b	2,160	1,875
PS37	1985 (6)	51	KM140-141, 152.1, 155-157	—	6,750
PS36	1985 (7)	100	KM142c-148c	2,400	2,450
PS38	1986 (7)	17	KM140-141, 152.1, 155-157, 166	—	6,700
PS39	1986 (6)	15	KM153-154, 168-171	—	13,350
PSA40	1983-1986 (4)	—	KM109a, 128a, 135-136	—	—
PS40	1986 (4)	2,000	KM153-154, 168-169	1,950	1,350
PS42	1987 (4)	—	KM176a, 177, 187-188	—	1,150
PS41	1986 (5)	2,500	KM140-141, 152.1, 155, 166	—	900
PS43	1987 (6)	30	KM140-141, 152.2, 155-157	—	6,950
PS44	1987 (5)	—	KM140-141, 152.2, 155, 166	—	900
PS45	1987 (4)	3,000	KM140-141, 152.2, 155	—	850
PS46	1987 (6)	11	KM153-154, 168-169, 170-171	—	12,575
PS47	1987 (4)	2,500	KM153-154, 168-169	—	1,325
PS48	1988 (5)	611	KM235-239	—	1,250
PS49	1988 (4)	500	KM222-225	—	35.00
PS50	1988 (4)	7,500	KM286-289 Medal	—	1,400
PSA51	1994 (2)	250	KM#204 plus Rhodium-plated Silver 31 g medal 10th Anniversary of the Platinum Noble Coin Series	—	1,000
PS51	1996 (5)	500	KM613, 615, 617, 619, 621b	—	845
PS52	1998 (5)	1,000	KM853-856, 857b	—	815
PS53	1999 (5)	1,000	KM958, 960, 962, 964, 968	1,300	835
PS54	2000 (5)	1,000	KM1052-1055, 1057	1,300	1,300

PROOF-LIKE SETS (PL)

KM#	Date	Mintage	Identification	Issue Price	Mkt Val
PL1	1980 (4)	—	KM64-67	—	35.00
PL2	1981 (4)	—	KM77-80	—	38.00
PL3	1982 (4)	50,000	KM96-99	—	35.00
PL4	1984 (4)	—	KM121-124 College of Arms	—	35.00
PL5	1986 (2)	—	KM173-174 Andrew and Sarah Wedding	—	16.00
PL6	1989 (6)	50,000	KM240-243	—	60.00

The state of Israel, a Middle Eastern republic at the eastern end of the Mediterranean Sea, bounded by Lebanon on the north, Syria on the northeast, Jordan on the east, and Egypt on the southwest, has an area of 9,000sq. mi. (20,770 sq. km.) and a population of 6 million. Capital: Jerusalem. Finished diamonds, chemicals, citrus, textiles, minerals, electronic and transportation equipment are exported.

HEBREW COIN DATING

Modern Israel's coins carry Hebrew dating formed from a combination of the 22 consonant letters of the Hebrew alphabet and read from right to left. The Jewish calendar dates back more than 5700 years; but five millenniums are assumed in the dating of coins (until 1981). Thus, the year 5735 (1975AD) appears as 735, with the first two characters from the right indicating the number of years in hundreds; tav (400), plus shin (300). The next is lamedh (30), followed by a separation mark which has the appearance of double quotation marks, then heh (5).

The separation mark - generally similar to a single quotation mark through 5718 (1958 AD), and like a double quotation mark thereafter - serves the purpose of indicating that the letters form a number, not a word, and on some issues can be confused with the character yodh (10), which in a stylized rendering can appear similar, although slightly larger and thicker. The separation mark does not appear in either form on a few commemorative issues.

The Jewish New Year falls in September or October by Christian calendar reckoning. Where dual dating is encountered, with but a few exceptions the Hebrew dating on the coins of modern Israel is 3760 years greater than the Christian dating; 5735 is equivalent to 1975AD, with the 5000 assumed until 1981, when full dates appear on the coins. These exceptions are most of the Hanukka coins, (Feast of Lights), the Bank of Israel gold 50 Pound commemorative of 5725 (1964AD) and others. In such special instances the differential from Christian dating is 3761 years, except in the instance of the 5720 Chanuka Pound, which is dated 1960AD, as is the issue of 5721, an arrangement reflecting the fact that the events fall early in the Jewish year and late in the Christian.

The Star of David is not a mintmark. It appears only on some coins sold by the Israel Government Coins and Medals Corporation Ltd., which is owned by the Israel government, and is a division of the Prime Minister's office and sole distributor to collectors. The Star of David was first used in 1971 on the science coin to signify that it was minted in Jerusalem, but was later used by different mint facilities.

AD Date		Jewish Era
1948	תש״ח	5708
1949	תש״ט	5709
1952	תשי״ב	5712
1954	תשי״ד	5714
1955	תשט״ו	5715
1957	תשי״ז	5717
1958	תשי״ח	5718
1959	תשי״ט	5719
1960	תש״ך	5720
1960	תשך	5720
1961	תשכ״א	5721
1962	תשכ״ב	5722
1963	תשכ״ג	5723
1964	תשכ״ד	5724
1965	תשכ״ה	5725
1966	תשכ״ו	5726
1967	תשכ״ז	5727
1968	תשכ״ח	5728
1969	תשכ״ט	5729
1970	תש״ל	5730
1971	תשל״א	5731
1972	תשל״ב	5732
1973	תשל״ג	5733
1974	תשל״ד	5734
1975	תשל״ה	5735
1976	תשל״ו	5736
1977	תשל״ז	5737
1978	תשל״ח	5738
1979	תשל״ט	5739
1980	תש״ם	5740
1981	תשמ״א	5741
1981	התשמ״א	5741
1982	התשמ״ב	5742
1983	התשמ״ג	5743
1984	התשמ״ד	5744
1985	התשמ״ה	5745
1986	התשמ״ו	5746
1987	התשמ״ז	5747
1988	התשמ״ח	5748
1989	התשמ״ט	5749
1990	התש״ן	5750
1991	התשנ״א	5751
1992	התשנ״ב	5752
1993	התשנ״ג	5753
1994	התשנ״ד	5754
1995	התשנ״ה	5755
1996	התשנ״ו	5756
1997	התשנ״ז	5757
1998	התשנ״ח	5758
1999	התשנ״ט	5759
2000	התש״ס	5760

MINT MARKS

(o) - Ottawa
(s) - San Francisco
None – Jerusalem

(M) MATTE - Normal circulation strike or a dull finish produced by sandblasting special uncirculated (polish finish) or proof quality dies.

(U) SPECIAL UNCIRCULATED - Polished or prooflike in appearance without any frosted features.

(P) PROOF - The highest quality obtainable having mirror-like fields and frosted features.

MONETARY SYSTEM

1000 Mils = 1 Pound

REPUBLIC

MIL COINAGE

KM# 8 25 MILS

Aluminum, 30 mm. **Obv:** Grape cluster **Rev:** Value within wreath **Note:** Released April 6, 1949.

Date	Mintage	F	VF	XF	Unc	BU
JE5708 (1948)	43,000	35.00	75.00	200	800	1,000
JE5709 (1949) open link	650,000	10.00	20.00	70.00	150	—
JE5709 (1949) closed link	—	5.00	10.00	15.00	35.00	—

REFORM COINAGE

1000 Pruta (Prutot) = 1 Lira

NOTE: The 1949 Pruta coins, except for the 100 and 500 Pruta values, occur with and without a small pearl under the bar connecting the wreath on the reverse. Only the 50 and 100 Pruta coins were issued in 5709. All later coins were struck with frozen dates.

KM# 9 PRUTA

Aluminum, 21 mm. **Obv:** Anchor **Rev:** Value within wreath

Date	Mintage	F	VF	XF	Unc	BU
JE5709 (1949) With pearl	2,685,000	—	0.50	1.00	2.00	—
JE5709(1949) With pearl, Prooflike	Inc. above	—	—	—	5.00	—
JE5709 (1949) Without pearl	2,500,000	—	1.00	5.00	20.00	—
JE5709 (1949) Proof	20,000	Value: 500				

KM# 12 25 PRUTA

Copper-Nickel, 19.5 mm. **Obv:** Grape cluster **Rev:** Value within wreath

Date	Mintage	F	VF	XF	Unc	BU
JE5709 (1949) With pearl	10,520,000	—	0.50	0.75	2.00	—
JE5709 (1949) Without pearl	2,500,000	—	5.00	10.00	30.00	—
JE5709 (1949) Proof	20,000	Value: 500				

KM# 12a 25 PRUTA

Nickel-Clad Steel, 19.5 mm. **Obv:** Grape cluster **Rev:** Value within wreath

Date	Mintage	F	VF	XF	Unc	BU
JE5714 (1954)	3,697,000	—	0.50	1.00	2.50	—

KM# 13.1 50 PRUTA

Copper-Nickel, 23.5 mm. **Obv:** Grape leaves **Rev:** Value within wreath **Edge:** Reeded

Date	Mintage	F	VF	XF	Unc	BU
JE5709 (1949) With pearl	12,040,000	—	5.00	10.00	25.00	—
JE5709 (1949) Proof	20,000	Value: 500				
JE5709 (1949) Without pearl	Inc. above	—	0.75	1.50	3.00	—
JE5714 (1954)	250,000	—	5.00	15.00	32.00	—

KM# 13.2 50 PRUTA

Copper-Nickel, 23.5 mm. **Obv:** Grape leaves **Rev:** Value within wreath **Edge:** Plain

Date	Mintage	F	VF	XF	Unc	BU
JE5714 (1954)	4,500,000	—	0.50	1.00	2.00	—

KM# 13.2a 50 PRUTA

Nickel-Clad Steel **Obv:** Grape leaves **Rev:** Value within wreath **Edge:** Plain

Date	Mintage	F	VF	XF	Unc	BU
JE5714 (1954)	17,774,000	—	0.50	1.00	2.00	—

KM# 14 100 PRUTA

Copper-Nickel, 28.5 mm. **Obv:** Date palm **Rev:** Value within wreath

Date	Mintage	F	VF	XF	Unc	BU
JE5709 (1949)	6,062,000	—	0.75	1.25	2.50	—
JE5709 (1949) Proof	20,000	Value: 500				
JE5715 (1955)	5,868,000	—	1.00	1.50	2.50	—

KM# 18 100 PRUTA

Nickel-Clad Steel, 25.6 mm. **Obv:** Date palm **Rev:** Value within wreath **Note:** Reduced size, Bern die.

Date	Mintage	F	VF	XF	Unc	BU
JE5714 (1954)	700,000	—	1.00	1.50	3.00	—

KM# 19 100 PRUTA

Nickel-Coated Steel, 25.6 mm. **Obv:** Date palm **Rev:** Value within wreath **Note:** Reduced size, Utrecht die.

Date	Mintage	F	VF	XF	Unc	BU
JE5714 (1954)	20,000	—	150	300	1,000	—

KM# 15 250 PRUTA

Copper-Nickel, 32.2 mm. **Obv:** Oat sprigs **Rev:** Value within wreath

Date	Mintage	F	VF	XF	Unc	BU
JE5709 (1949) With pearl	1,496,000	—	2.50	10.00	20.00	—
JE5709 (1949) Without pearl	524,000	—	1.00	2.00	5.00	—

KM# 15a 250 PRUTA

14.4000 g., 0.5000 Silver .2315 oz. ASW **Obv:** Oat sprigs **Rev:** Value within wreath

Date	Mintage	F	VF	XF	Unc	BU
JE5709 (1949) H	44,000	—	4.50	6.50	11.50	—
Note: Not placed into circulation						

KM# 16 500 PRUTA

25.5000 g., 0.5000 Silver .4099 oz. ASW, 38 mm. **Obv:** Pomegranates **Rev:** Value within wreath **Note:** Dav. #257.

Date	Mintage	F	VF	XF	Unc	BU
JE5709 (1949)	34,000	—	8.50	12.50	35.00	50.00
Note: Not placed into circulation						

KM# 10 5 PRUTOT

Bronze, 20 mm. **Obv:** 4-stringed lyre

Date	Mintage	F	VF	XF	Unc	BU
JE5709 (1949) With pearl	5,045,000	—	0.50	1.00	2.50	—
JE5709 (1949) Proof	25,000	Value: 500				
JE5709 (1949) Without pearl	5,000,000	—	0.50	5.00	20.00	—

KM# 11 10 PRUTOT

Bronze, 27 mm. **Obv:** Amphora **Rev:** Value within wreath

Date	Mintage	F	VF	XF	Unc	BU
JE5709 (1949) With pearl	7,448,000	—	0.75	5.00	20.00	—
JE5709 (1949) Without pearl	7,500,000	—	0.50	1.00	3.00	—
JE5709 (1949) Proof	20,000	Value: 500				

KM# 17 10 PRUTOT

Aluminum, 24.5 mm. **Obv:** Ceremonial pitcher flanked by sprigs **Rev:** Value within wreath **Shape:** Scalloped

Date	Mintage	F	VF	XF	Unc	BU
JE5712 (1952)	26,042,000	—	0.35	0.75	2.00	—

KM# 20 10 PRUTOT

Aluminum, 24.5 mm. **Obv:** Ceremonial pitcher flanked by sprigs **Rev:** Value within wreath

Date	Mintage	F	VF	XF	Unc	BU
JE5717 (1957)	1,000,000	—	0.35	0.75	2.50	—

KM# 20a 10 PRUTOT

Copper Electroplated Aluminum, 24.5 mm. **Obv:** Ceremonial pitcher flanked by sprigs **Rev:** Value within wreath

Date	Mintage	F	VF	XF	Unc	BU
JE5717 (1957)	1,088,000	—	0.35	0.75	2.00	—

REFORM COINAGE

100 Agorot = 1 Lira

Commencing January 1, 1960-1980

KM# 24.1 AGORA

1.0000 g., Aluminum, 20 mm. **Obv:** Text to left and below oat sprigs **Rev:** Value **Shape:** Scalloped

Date	Mintage	F	VF	XF	Unc	BU
JE5720 (1960)	12,768,000	—	4.00	8.00	20.00	—
Note: Letter "Lamed" in Israel with serif						
JE5720 (1960)	Inc. above	—	10.00	20.00	100	—
Note: Letter "Lamed" in Israel without lower serif						
JE5720 (1960)	300	—	150	300	750	—
Note: Large date						
JE5721 (1961)	19,262,000	—	0.50	2.00	5.00	—
JE5721 (1961)	Inc. above	—	5.00	15.00	100	—
Note: Thick date						
JE5721 (1961)	Inc. above	—	5.00	15.00	100	—
Note: Wide date						
JE5722 (1962)	14,500,000	—	0.10	0.40	0.75	—
Note: Large date						
JE5722 (1962)	Inc. above	—	5.00	10.00	20.00	—
Note: Small date, small serifs						
JE5723 (1963)	14,804,000	—	0.10	0.40	0.75	—
Note: Medal alignment						
JE5723 (1963)	10,000	—	3.00	5.00	15.00	30.00
Note: Coin alignment						
JE5724 (1964)	27,552,000	—	—	—	0.75	—
JE5725 (1965)	20,708,000	—	—	—	0.25	—
JE5726 (1966)	10,165,000	—	—	—	0.25	—
JE5727 (1967)	6,781,000	—	—	—	0.25	—
JE5728 (1968)	20,899,000	—	—	—	0.25	—
JE5729 (1969)	22,120,000	—	—	—	0.25	—
JE5730 (1970)	17,748,000	—	—	—	0.25	—
JE5731 (1971)	10,290,000	—	—	—	0.25	—
JE5732 (1972)	24,512,000	—	—	—	0.25	—
JE5733 (1973)	20,496,000	—	—	—	0.25	—
JE5734 (1974)	42,080,000	—	—	—	0.25	—
JE5735 (1975)	1,574,000	—	—	—	0.25	—
JE5736 (1976)	4,512,000	—	—	—	0.25	—
JE5737 (1977)	9,680,000	—	—	—	0.25	—
JE5738 (1978)	8,864,000	—	—	—	0.25	—
JE5739 (1979)	4,048,000	—	—	—	0.25	—
JE5740 (1980)	2,600,000	—	—	—	1.00	—

KM# 24.2 AGORA

1.0000 g., Aluminum, 20 mm. **Obv:** Text to left and below oat sprigs, star of David in field **Rev:** Value

Date	Mintage	F	VF	XF	Unc	BU
JE5731 (1971)(j)	125,921	—	—	—	0.75	—
JE5732 (1972)(j)	68,513	—	—	—	0.75	—
JE5734 (1974)(j)	92,868	—	—	—	0.75	—
JE5735 (1975)(j)	61,686	—	—	—	1.00	—
JE5736 (1976)(j)	64,654	—	—	—	0.75	—
JE5737 (1977)(j)	37,208	—	—	—	1.00	—
JE5738 (1978)(j)	57,072	—	—	—	0.75	—
JE5739 (1979)(j)	31,590	—	—	—	1.00	—

KM# 63 AGORA

1.0000 g., Aluminum, 20 mm. **Subject:** 25th Anniversary of Independence **Obv:** Text to left and below oat sprigs **Rev:** Value **Shape:** Scalloped **Note:** Struck for sets only.

Date	Mintage	F	VF	XF	Unc	BU
JE5733 (1973)(j)	98,107	—	—	—	0.75	—

KM# 96 AGORA

Nickel, 20 mm. **Subject:** 25th Anniversary - Bank of Israel **Obv:** Text to left and below oat sprigs **Rev:** Value **Shape:** Scalloped **Note:** Struck for sets only

Date	Mintage	F	VF	XF	Unc	BU
JE5740 (1980)(b)	35,000	—	—	—	2.00	—

Normal 1961 — 1961 I.C.I.

KM# 25 5 AGOROT

2.3000 g., Aluminum-Bronze, 17.5 mm. **Obv:** Pomegranates **Rev:** Value

Date	Mintage	F	VF	XF	Unc	BU
JE5720 (1960)	8,019,000	—	5.00	10.00	25.00	—
JE5721 (1961)	15,090,000	—	0.25	0.50	1.50	—
Note: Sharp, flat date						
JE5721 (1961)	5,000,000	—	10.00	20.00	60.00	—
Note: I.C.I. issue; high date with serifs						
JE5722 (1962) Large date	11,198,000	—	0.25	0.50	1.00	—
JE5722 (1962) Small date	Inc. above	—	5.00	10.00	25.00	—
JE5723 (1963)	1,429,000	—	0.25	0.50	1.25	—
JE5724 (1964)	21,000	—	12.00	120	400	500
JE5725 (1965)	201,000	—	—	0.10	0.25	—
JE5726 (1966)	291,000	—	—	0.10	0.25	—
JE5727 (1967)	2,195,000	—	—	0.10	0.25	—
JE5728 (1968)	4,019,999	—	—	0.10	0.25	—
JE5729 (1969)	2,200,000	—	—	0.10	0.25	—
JE5730 (1970)	4,003,999	—	—	0.10	0.25	—
JE5731 (1971)	14,010,000	—	—	0.10	0.25	—
JE5732 (1972)	9,005,000	—	—	0.10	0.25	—
JE5733 (1973)	25,720,000	—	—	0.10	0.25	—
JE5734 (1974)	10,470,000	—	—	0.10	0.25	—
JE5735 (1975)	10,232,000	—	—	0.10	0.25	—
JE5736 (1976)	—	—	—	0.10	0.25	—
JE5737 (1977)	—	—	—	0.10	0.25	—

KM# 25a 5 AGOROT

2.3000 g., Aluminum-Bronze, 17.5 mm. **Obv:** Pomegranates, Star of David in field **Rev:** Value

Date	Mintage	F	VF	XF	Unc	BU
JE5731 (1971)(j)	125,921	—	—	—	0.75	—
JE5732 (1972)(j)	68,513	—	—	—	0.75	—
JE5734 (1974)(j)	92,868	—	—	—	0.75	—
JE5735 (1975)(j)	61,686	—	—	—	1.00	—

KM# 25b 5 AGOROT

Aluminum, 17.5 mm. **Obv:** Pomegranates **Rev:** Value

Date	Mintage	F	VF	XF	Unc	BU
JE5736 (1976) (M)	13,156,000	—	—	0.10	0.50	—
JE5737 (1977) (M)	16,800,000	—	—	0.10	0.50	—
JE5737 (1977)(o)	15,000,000	—	—	0.10	0.50	—
JE5738 (1978) (M)	21,480,000	—	—	0.10	0.50	—
JE5738 (1978)(o) (U)	38,760,000	—	—	0.10	0.50	—
JE5739 (1979) (M)	12,636,000	—	—	0.10	0.50	—

KM# 25c 5 AGOROT

Copper-Nickel, 17.5 mm. **Rev:** Value

Date	Mintage	F	VF	XF	Unc	BU
JE5735 (1975)(j)	61,686	—	—	—	1.00	—
JE5736 (1976)(j)	64,654	—	—	—	0.75	—
JE5737 (1977)(j)	37,208	—	—	—	1.00	—
JE5738 (1978)(j)	57,072	—	—	—	0.75	—
JE5739 (1979)(j)	31,590	—	—	—	1.00	—

KM# 64 5 AGOROT

Copper-Nickel, 17.5 mm. **Subject:** 25th Anniversary of Independence **Obv:** Pomegranates **Rev:** Value **Note:** In sets only.

Date	Mintage	F	VF	XF	Unc	BU
JE5733 (1973)(j)	98,107	—	—	—	0.75	—

KM# 97 5 AGOROT

Nickel, 17.5 mm. **Subject:** 25th Anniversary - Bank of Israel **Obv:** Pomegranates **Rev:** Value **Note:** Struck for sets only.

Date	Mintage	F	VF	XF	Unc	BU
JE5740 (1980)(b)	35,000	—	—	—	2.00	—

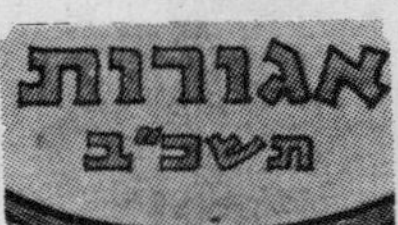
Large date, thick letters

Small date, thin letters

KM# 26 10 AGOROT

5.0000 g., Aluminum-Bronze, 21.5 mm. **Obv:** Date palm **Rev:** Value

Date	Mintage	F	VF	XF	Unc	BU
JE5720 (1960)	14,397,000	—	0.50	1.00	10.00	—
JE5721 (1961)	12,821,000	—	0.50	1.00	6.00	—
JE5721 (1961)	Inc. above	—	25.00	60.00	325	—
Note: "Fatha" in Arabic, legend: "Israel"						
JE5722 (1962) Large date, thick letters	8,845,000	—	0.25	0.50	1.00	—
JE5722 (1962) Small date, thin letters	Inc. above	—	5.00	10.00	20.00	—
JE5723 (1963)	3,931,000	—	0.25	0.50	1.00	—
JE5724 (1964) Large date	3,612,000	—	0.25	0.50	1.00	—
JE5724 (1964) Small date	Inc. above	—	8.00	15.00	50.00	—
JE5725 (1965)	201,000	—	—	0.20	0.25	—
JE5726 (1966)	7,276,000	—	—	0.10	0.25	—
JE5727 (1967)	6,426,000	—	—	0.10	0.25	—
JE5728 (1968)	4,825,000	—	—	0.10	0.25	—
JE5729 (1969)	6,810,000	—	—	0.10	0.25	—
JE5730 (1970)	6,131,000	—	—	0.10	0.25	—
JE5731 (1971)	6,810,000	—	—	0.10	0.25	—
JE5732 (1972)	19,653,000	—	—	0.10	0.25	—
JE5733 (1973)	16,205,000	—	—	0.10	0.25	—
JE5734 (1974)	22,040,000	—	—	0.10	0.25	—
JE5735 (1975)	25,135,000	—	—	0.10	0.25	—
JE5736 (1976)	54,870,000	—	—	0.10	0.25	—
JE5737 (1977)	27,886,000	—	—	0.10	0.25	—

KM# 26a 10 AGOROT

5.0000 g., Aluminum-Bronze, 21.5 mm. **Obv:** Date palm with star of David in field **Rev:** Value

Date	Mintage	F	VF	XF	Unc	BU
JE5731 (1971)(j)	125,921	—	—	—	0.75	—
JE5732 (1972)(j)	68,513	—	—	—	0.75	—

KM# 26b 10 AGOROT

Aluminum, 21.5 mm. **Obv:** Date palm **Rev:** Value

Date	Mintage	F	VF	XF	Unc	BU
JE5737 (1977)(o) (U)	30,100,000	—	—	0.10	0.25	—
JE5738 (1978) (M)	24,050,000	—	—	0.10	0.25	—
JE5738 (1978)(o) (U)	104,336,000	—	—	0.10	0.25	—
JE5739 (1979)	22,201,000	—	—	0.10	0.25	—
JE5740 (1980)	4,752,000	—	—	0.10	0.25	—
Note: Most of the 5740 dated coins were melted down before being issued.						

KM# 26c 10 AGOROT

Copper-Nickel, 21.5 mm. **Obv:** Date palm with star of David in field **Rev:** Value **Note:** In sets only.

Date	Mintage	F	VF	XF	Unc	BU
JE5734 (1974)(j)	92,868	—	—	—	0.75	—
JE5735 (1975)(j)	61,686	—	—	—	1.00	—
JE5736 (1976)(j)	64,654	—	—	—	0.75	—
JE5737 (1977)(j)	37,208	—	—	—	1.00	—
JE5738 (1978)(j)	57,072	—	—	—	0.75	—
JE5739 (1979)(j)	31,590	—	—	—	1.00	—

KM# 65 10 AGOROT

Copper-Nickel, 21.5 mm. **Subject:** 25th Anniversary of Independence **Obv:** Date palm **Rev:** Value **Note:** In sets only.

Date	Mintage	F	VF	XF	Unc	BU
JE5733 (1973)(j)	98,107	—	—	—	0.75	—

KM# 98 10 AGOROT

Nickel, 21.5 mm. **Subject:** 25th Anniversary - Bank of Israel **Obv:** Date palm **Rev:** Value **Note:** Struck for sets only.

Date	Mintage	F	VF	XF	Unc	BU
JE5740 (1980)(b)	35,000	—	—	—	2.00	—

KM# 27 25 AGOROT

6.5000 g., Aluminum-Bronze, 25.5 mm. **Obv:** Three-string lyre **Rev:** Value

Date	Mintage	F	VF	XF	Unc	BU
JE5720 (1960)	4,391,000	—	0.25	0.50	3.00	—
JE5721 (1961)	5,009,000	—	0.10	0.20	1.00	—
JE5722 (1962)	882,000	—	0.15	0.30	1.00	—
JE5723 (1963)	194,000	—	0.50	1.00	5.00	—
JE5724 (1964)	—	—	—	—	—	—
Note: Five trial pieces only						
JE5725 (1965)	187,000	—	0.10	0.20	0.50	—
JE5726 (1966)	320,000	—	—	0.10	0.40	—
JE5727 (1967)	325,000	—	—	0.10	0.40	—
JE5728 (1968)	445,000	—	—	0.10	0.40	—
JE5729 (1969)	432,000	—	—	0.10	0.40	—
JE5730 (1970)	417,000	—	—	0.10	0.40	—
JE5731 (1971)	500,000	—	—	0.10	0.40	—
JE5732 (1972)	1,883,000	—	—	0.10	0.40	—
JE5733 (1973)	3,370,000	—	—	0.10	0.40	—
JE5734 (1974)	2,320,000	—	—	0.10	0.40	—
JE5735 (1975)	3,968,000	—	—	0.10	0.40	—
JE5736 (1976)	3,901,000	—	—	0.10	0.40	—
JE5737 (1977)	1,832,000	—	—	0.10	0.40	—
JE5738 (1978)	12,200,000	—	—	0.10	0.40	—
JE5739 (1979)	10,842,000	—	—	0.10	0.40	—

KM# 27a 25 AGOROT

6.5000 g., Aluminum-Bronze, 25.5 mm. **Obv:** Three stringed lyre with star of David in field **Rev:** Value

Date	Mintage	F	VF	XF	Unc	BU
JE5731 (1971)(j)	125,921	—	—	—	0.75	—
JE5732 (1972)(j)	68,513	—	—	—	0.75	—

KM# 27b 25 AGOROT

Copper-Nickel, 25.5 mm. **Obv:** Three stringed lyre with star of David in field **Rev:** Value **Note:** Struck for sets only.

Date	Mintage	F	VF	XF	Unc	BU
JE5734 (1974)(j)	92,868	—	—	—	0.75	—
JE5735 (1975)(j)	61,686	—	—	—	1.00	—
JE5736 (1976)(j)	64,654	—	—	—	0.75	—
JE5737 (1977)(j)	37,208	—	—	—	1.00	—
JE5738 (1978)(j)	57,072	—	—	—	0.75	—
JE5739 (1979)(j)	31,590	—	—	—	1.00	—

KM# 66 25 AGOROT

Copper-Nickel, 25.5 mm. **Subject:** 25th Anniversary of Independence **Obv:** Three-string lyre **Rev:** Value **Note:** Struck for sets only.

Date	Mintage	F	VF	XF	Unc	BU
JE5733 (1973)(j)	98,107	—	—	—	0.75	—

KM# 99 25 AGOROT

Nickel, 25.5 mm. **Subject:** 25th Anniversary - Bank of Israel **Obv:** Three-string lyre **Rev:** Value **Note:** Struck for sets only.

Date	Mintage	F	VF	XF	Unc	BU
JE5740 (1980)(b)	35,000	—	—	—	2.00	—

COMMEMORATIVE COINAGE

Note: All proof commemoratives with the exception of the 1 and 5 Lirot issues of 1958 are distinguished from the uncirculated editions by the presence of the Hebrew letter 'mem'.

KM# 31 1/2 LIRA

Copper-Nickel, 30 mm. **Subject:** Feast of Purim **Obv:** Inscription **Rev:** Chalice within beaded circle

Date	Mintage	F	VF	XF	Unc	BU
JE5721 (1961)(u)	19,939	—	—	—	5.00	—
JE5721 (1961)(u) Proof	4,901	Value: 10.00				
JE5722 (1962)(u)	19,890	—	—	—	7.00	—
JE5722 (1962)(u) Proof	9,894	Value: 9.00				

KM# 36.1 1/2 LIRA

6.8000 g., Copper-Nickel, 24.5 mm. **Obv:** Menorah flanked by sprigs **Rev:** Value

Date	Mintage	F	VF	XF	Unc	BU
JE5723 (1963) Large animals	5,593,000	—	0.50	2.00	5.00	—
JE5723 (1963) Small animals	14,000	—	3.00	15.00	30.00	—
JE5724 (1964)	3,762,000	—	0.10	0.75	2.00	—
JE5725 (1965)	1,551,000	—	0.10	0.15	1.00	—
JE5726 (1966)	2,139,000	—	0.10	0.15	0.50	—
JE5727 (1967)	1,942,000	—	0.10	0.15	0.50	—
JE5728 (1968)	1,183,000	—	0.10	0.15	0.50	—
JE5729 (1969)	450,000	—	0.10	0.20	0.60	—
JE5730 (1970)	1,000,999	—	0.10	0.20	0.60	—
JE5731 (1971)	500,000	—	0.10	0.20	0.60	—
JE5732 (1972)	421,000	—	0.10	0.20	0.60	—
JE5733 (1973)	3,225,000	—	0.10	0.15	0.50	—
JE5734 (1974)	4,275,000	—	0.10	0.15	0.50	—
JE5735 (1975)	11,066,000	—	0.10	0.15	0.50	—
JE5736 (1976)	4,959,000	—	0.10	0.15	0.50	—
JE5737 (1977)	4,983,000	—	0.10	0.15	0.50	—
JE5738 (1978)	14,325,000	—	0.10	0.15	0.50	—
JE5739 (1979)	21,391,000	—	0.10	0.15	0.50	—

KM# 36.2 1/2 LIRA

6.8000 g., Copper-Nickel, 24.5 mm. **Obv:** Menorah with star of David in field flanked by sprigs **Rev:** Value **Note:** Struck for sets only.

Date	Mintage	F	VF	XF	Unc	BU
JE5731 (1971)(j)	125,921	—	—	—	1.00	—
JE5732 (1972)(j)	68,513	—	—	—	1.00	—
JE5734 (1974)(j)	92,868	—	—	—	1.00	—
JE5735(1975)(j)	61,686	—	—	—	1.00	—
JE5736 (1976)(j)	64,654	—	—	—	1.00	—
JE5737 (1977)(j)	37,208	—	—	—	1.25	—
JE5738 (1978)(j)	57,072	—	—	—	1.00	—
JE5739 (1979)(j)	31,590	—	—	—	1.25	—

KM# 67 1/2 LIRA

6.8000 g., Copper-Nickel, 24.5 mm. **Subject:** 25th Anniversary of Independence **Obv:** Menorah flanked by sprigs **Rev:** Value **Edge:** Reeded **Note:** Struck for sets only.

Date	Mintage	F	VF	XF	Unc	BU
JE5733 (1973)(j)	98,107	—	—	—	1.50	—

KM# 100 1/2 LIRA

Nickel, 24.5 mm. **Subject:** 25th Anniversary - Bank of Israel **Obv:** Menorah flanked by sprigs **Rev:** Value **Edge:** Reeded **Note:** Struck for sets only.

Date	Mintage	F	VF	XF	Unc	BU
JE5740 (1980)(b)	35,000	—	—	—	3.00	—

KM# 101 LIRA

9.0000 g., Nickel, 27.5 mm. **Subject:** 25th Anniversary - Bank of Israel **Obv:** Pomegranates with star of David in field **Rev:** Value flanked by stars above text **Edge:** Reeded, smooth alternating edge **Note:** Struck for sets only.

Date	Mintage	F	VF	XF	Unc	BU
JE5740 (1980)(b)	35,000	—	—	—	4.00	—

KM# 22 LIRA

Copper-Nickel, 32 mm. **Subject:** Hanukkah - Law Is Light **Obv:** Value to upper right of text and date **Rev:** Menorah flanked by stars with text below **Edge:** Smooth **Designer:** Zvy Narkiss

Date	Mintage	F	VF	XF	Unc	BU
JE5719-1958 Proof	5,000	Value: 28.00				
JE5719-1958(b)	149,594	—	—	—	2.00	—
JE5719-1958(b) Proof	5,000	Value: 20.00				

KM# 28 LIRA

Copper-Nickel, 32 mm. **Subject:** Hannukah - 50th Anniversary of Deganya, oldest Kibbuto founded in 1909 **Obv:** Text at upper left of desert scene **Obv. Designer:** Rothschild and Lippman **Rev:** Text at upper and lower left of value **Rev. Designer:** Miriam Karoly

Date	Mintage	F	VF	XF	Unc	BU
JE5720-1960	49,000	—	—	—	6.00	—
JE5720-1960(u)	49,455	—	—	—	5.00	—
JE5720-1960(u) Proof	4,702	Value: 25.00				

KM# 32 LIRA

Copper-Nickel, 32 mm. **Subject:** Hanukkah **Obv:** Block-like design **Obv. Designer:** Rothschild and Lippman **Rev:** Seated hooded figure holding lamb **Rev. Designer:** Jacob Zim **Edge:** Smooth

Date	Mintage	F	VF	XF	Unc	BU
JE5721-1960(u)	16,781	—	—	—	12.00	—
JE5721-1960(u) Proof	3,000	Value: 85.00				

KM# 34 LIRA

Copper-Nickel, 32 mm. **Subject:** Hanukkah **Obv:** Large torch flanked by text with small value at upper right **Rev:** Rearing elephant

Date	Mintage	F	VF	XF	Unc	BU
JE5722-1961(u)	18,801	—	—	—	6.00	12.00
JE5722-1961(u) Proof	9,324	Value: 20.00				

KM# 38 LIRA

Copper-Nickel, 32 mm. **Subject:** Hanukkah **Obv:** Italian lamp **Rev:** Value above text and date

Date	Mintage	F	VF	XF	Unc	BU
JE5723-1962(b)	9,560	—	—	—	12.50	16.50
JE5723-1962(b) Proof	5,941	Value: 25.00				

KM# 42 LIRA

Copper-Nickel, 32 mm. **Subject:** Hanukkah **Obv:** Value above text and date within rectangle **Rev:** 18th Century North African lamp

Date	Mintage	F	VF	XF	Unc	BU
JE5724-1963(u)	9,928	—	—	—	10.00	15.00
JE5724-1963(u) Proof	5,412	Value: 25.00				

KM# 37 LIRA

Copper-Nickel, 27.5 mm. **Obv:** Menorah flanked by sprigs **Rev:** Value

Date	Mintage	F	VF	XF	Unc	BU
JE5723 (1963) Large animals	4,212,000	—	0.50	1.50	3.00	—
JE5723 (1963) Large animals	4,212,000	—	0.50	1.50	3.00	—
JE5723 (1963) Small animals	Inc. above	—	1.00	10.00	20.00	—
JE5724 (1964)	—	—	—	—	—	—
Note: Only ten trial pieces struck						
JE5725 (1965)	166,000	—	0.25	0.50	1.25	—
JE5725 (1965)	166,000	—	0.25	0.50	1.25	—
JE5726 (1966)	290,000	—	0.25	0.50	1.25	—
JE5726 (1966)	290,000	—	0.25	0.50	1.25	—
JE5727 (19697)	180,000	—	0.25	0.50	1.25	—
JE5727 (1967)	180,000	—	0.25	0.50	1.25	—

KM# 47.1 LIRA

9.0000 g., Copper-Nickel, 27.5 mm. **Obv:** Pomegranates **Rev:** Value flanked by stars above text **Edge:** Reeded, smooth alternating edge

Date	Mintage	F	VF	XF	Unc	BU
JE5727 (1967)	3,830,000	—	0.10	0.25	1.00	—
JE5728 (1968)	3,932,000	—	0.10	0.25	1.00	—
JE5729 (1969)	12,484,000	—	0.10	0.25	0.75	—
JE5730 (1970)	4,794,000	—	0.10	0.25	0.75	—
JE5731 (1971)	2,993,000	—	0.10	0.25	0.75	—
JE5732 (1972)	2,489,000	—	0.10	0.25	0.75	—
JE5733 (1973)	10,265,000	—	0.10	0.25	0.75	—
JE5734 (1974)	6,287,000	—	0.10	0.25	0.75	—
JE5735 (1975)	13,225,000	—	0.10	0.25	0.75	—
JE5736 (1976)	4,268,000	—	0.10	0.25	0.75	—
JE5737 (1977)	11,129,000	—	0.10	0.25	0.75	—
JE5738 (1978)	61,752,000	—	0.10	0.25	0.75	—
JE5739 (1979)	34,815,000	—	0.10	0.25	0.75	—
JE5740 (1980)	10,840,000	—	0.10	0.25	0.75	—

Note: Most of the 5740 dated coins were melted down before being issued.

KM# 47.2 LIRA

9.0000 g., Copper-Nickel, 27.5 mm. **Obv:** Pomegranates with star of David in field **Rev:** Value flanked by stars above text **Note:** Struck for sets only.

Date	Mintage	F	VF	XF	Unc	BU
JE5731 (1971)(j)	125,921	—	—	—	1.00	—
JE5732 (1972)(j)	68,513	—	—	—	1.00	—
JE5734 (1974)(j)	92,868	—	—	—	1.00	—
JE5735 (1975)(j)	61,686	—	—	—	1.00	—
JE5736 (1976)(j)	64,654	—	—	—	1.00	—
JE5737 (1977)(j)	37,208	—	—	—	1.50	—
JE5738 (1978)(j)	57,072	—	—	—	1.00	—
JE5739 (1979)(j)	31,590	—	—	—	1.50	—

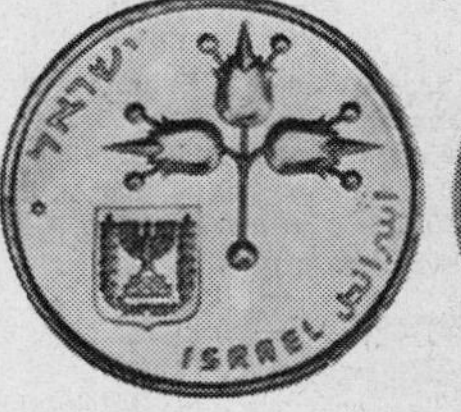

KM# 68 LIRA

9.0000 g., Copper-Nickel, 27.5 mm. **Subject:** 25th Anniversary of Independence **Obv:** Pomegranates with star of David in field **Rev:** Value flanked by stars above text **Edge:** Smooth, reeded alternating edge **Note:** Struck for sets only.

Date	Mintage	F	VF	XF	Unc	BU
JE5733 (1973)(j)	98,107	—	—	—	1.00	—

KM# 21 5 LIROT

25.0000 g., 0.9000 Silver .7234 oz. ASW, 34 mm. **Subject:** 10th Anniversary of Independence **Obv:** Large value at lower right of text **Rev:** Menorah **Designer:** Miriam Karoly **Note:** Dav. #258

Date	Mintage	F	VF	XF	Unc	BU
JE5718-1958(u)	97,860	—	—	—	12.00	17.50
JE5718-1958(u) Frosted Proof	2,000	Value: 300				

KM# 23 5 LIROT

25.0000 g., 0.9000 Silver .7234 oz. ASW, 34 mm. **Subject:** 11th Anniversary of Independence **Obv:** Value at lower right of text **Rev:** Ingathering of exiles **Designer:** Miriam Karoly **Note:** Dav. #259.

Date	Mintage	F	VF	XF	Unc	BU
JE5719-1959(b)	27,016	—	—	—	15.00	20.00
JE5719-1959(b) Proof	4,682	Value: 35.00				

KM# 29 5 LIROT

25.0000 g., 0.9000 Silver .7234 oz. ASW, 34 mm. **Subject:** 12th Anniversary of Independence **Obv:** Value at lower right of text **Obv. Designer:** Miriam Karoly **Rev:** Head left within square at upper right **Rev. Designer:** Andre Laserre **Note:** Dav. #29.

Date	Mintage	F	VF	XF	Unc	BU
JE5720-1960(b)	34,281	—	—	—	12.00	18.00
JE5720-1960(b) Proof	4,827	Value: 35.00				

KM# 33 5 LIROT

25.0000 g., 0.9000 Silver .7234 oz. ASW, 34 mm. **Subject:** 13th Anniversary of Independence **Obv:** Olive branch with 10 leaves and 3 olives **Rev:** Ark of the law with 6 torah **Note:** Dav. #261

Date	Mintage	F	VF	XF	Unc	BU
JE5721-1961(u)	19,363	—	—	—	35.00	45.00
JE5721-1961(u) Proof	4,455	Value: 60.00				

KM# 35 5 LIROT

25.0000 g., 0.9000 Silver .7234 oz. ASW, 34 mm. **Subject:** 14th Anniversary of Independence **Rev:** Negev Industrialization **Note:** Dav. #262,

Date	Mintage	F	VF	XF	Unc	BU
JE5722-1962(u)	10,380	—	—	—	25.00	35.00
JE5722-1962(u) Proof	4,960	Value: 50.00				

KM# 39 5 LIROT

25.0000 g., 0.9000 Silver .7234 oz. ASW, 34 mm. **Subject:** 15th Anniversary of Independence **Obv:** Value and star within upright design **Rev:** Longship **Note:** Dav. #263.

Date	Mintage	F	VF	XF	Unc	BU
JE5723-1963(r)	5,960	—	—	—	220	285
JE5723-1963(r) Proof	4,495	Value: 295				

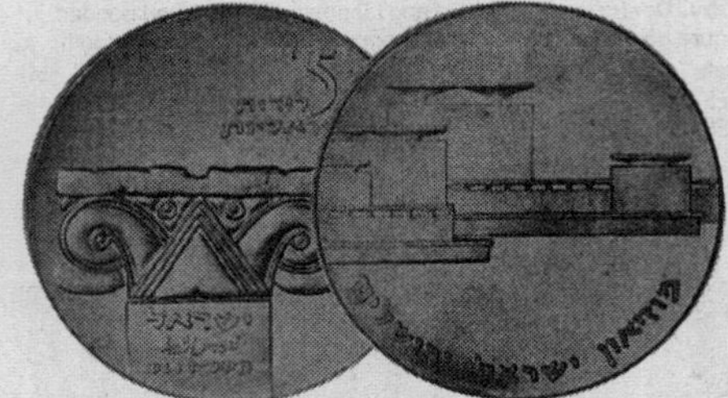

KM# 43 5 LIROT

25.0000 g., 0.9000 Silver .7234 oz. ASW, 34 mm. **Subject:** 16th Anniversary of Independence **Obv:** Israel Museum **Rev:** Ionic style column with value at upper right **Note:** Dav. #264.

Date	Mintage	F	VF	XF	Unc	BU
JE5724-1964(r)	10,967	—	—	—	30.00	40.00
JE5724-1964(r) Proof	4,421	Value: 55.00				

KM# 45 5 LIROT

25.0000 g., 0.9000 Silver .7234 oz. ASW, 34 mm. **Subject:** 17th Anniversary of Independence **Rev:** Knesset Building **Note:** Dav. #265.

Date	Mintage	F	VF	XF	Unc	BU
JE5725-1965(r)	25,147	—	—	—	11.00	14.00
JE5725-1965(r) Proof	7,537	Value: 15.00				

KM# 46 5 LIROT

25.0000 g., 0.9000 Silver .7234 oz. ASW, 34 mm. **Subject:** 18th Anniversary of Independence **Rev:** Abstract design **Note:** Dav. #266.

Date	Mintage	F	VF	XF	Unc	BU
JE5726-1966(u)	32,356	—	—	—	11.00	14.00
JE5726-1966(u) Proof	10,368	Value: 15.00				

KM# 48 5 LIROT

25.0000 g., 0.9000 Silver .7234 oz. ASW, 34 mm. **Subject:** 19th Anniversary of Independence **Obv:** Large stylized value **Rev:** Port of Eilat **Note:** Dav. #267.

Date	Mintage	F	VF	XF	Unc	BU
JE5727-1967(u)	30,158	—	—	—	12.00	14.00
JE5727-1967(u) Proof	7,680	Value: 20.00				
JE5727-1967(u) Frosted Proof	Inc. below	Value: 75.00				

KM# 69.1 5 LIROT

20.0000 g., 0.7500 Silver .4823 oz. ASW **Subject:** Hanukkah **Obv:** Menorah flanked by sprigs to left of value with text around top half **Rev:** Russian lamp

Date	Mintage	F	VF	XF	Unc	BU
JE5733-1972(j)	74,506	—	—	—	8.00	—

KM# 69.2 5 LIROT

20.0000 g., 0.7500 Silver .4823 oz. ASW **Subject:** Hanukkah **Obv:** Menorah flanked by sprigs to left of value with text arount top half **Rev:** Russian lamp **Edge:** Reeded

Date	Mintage	F	VF	XF	Unc	BU
JE5733-1972(j) Proof	22,336	Value: 8.00				

KM# 75.1 5 LIROT

20.0000 g., 0.5000 Silver .3215 oz. ASW **Subject:** Hanukkah **Rev:** Babylonian lamp **Edge:** Plain

Date	Mintage	F	VF	XF	Unc	BU
JE5734-1973(j)	94,686	—	—	—	7.00	—

KM# 75.2 5 LIROT

20.0000 g., 0.5000 Silver .3215 oz. ASW **Subject:** Hanukkah **Rev:** Babylonian lamp **Edge:** Reeded

Date	Mintage	F	VF	XF	Unc	BU
JE5734-1973(j) Proof	44,860	Value: 8.00				

KM# 90 5 LIROT

Copper-Nickel, 30 mm. **Obv:** Roaring lion left with menorah above **Rev:** Value flanked by stars **Edge:** Smooth

Date	Mintage	F	VF	XF	Unc	BU
JE5738 (1978)	8,350,000	—	0.40	1.00	3.50	6.00
JE5739 (1979)	37,646,000	—	0.40	1.00	3.00	6.00

KM# 90a 5 LIROT

Copper-Nickel, 30 mm. **Obv:** Roaring lion left with star of David in field **Rev:** Value flanked by stars **Edge:** Smooth **Note:** Struck for sets only.

Date	Mintage	F	VF	XF	Unc	BU
JE5739 (1979)(j)	31,590	—	—	—	3.50	6.00

KM# 102 5 LIROT

Nickel, 30 mm. **Subject:** 25th Anniversary - Bank of Israel **Obv:** Roaring lion left with menorah above **Rev:** Value flanked by stars **Edge:** Smooth **Note:** Struck for sets only.

Date	Mintage	F	VF	XF	Unc	BU
JE5740 (1980)(b)	35,000	—	—	3.00	5.00	—

KM# 49 10 LIROT

26.0000 g., 0.9000 Silver .7524 oz. ASW, 37 mm. **Subject:** Victory Commemorative **Obv:** Artistic star-like design with a sprig wrapped around the sword with text below **Rev:** Wailing Wall with text around bottom **Note:** Dav. #268

Date	Mintage	F	VF	XF	Unc	BU
JE5727-1967(b)	234,461	—	—	—	11.50	—

KM# 49a 10 LIROT

26.0000 g., 0.9000 Silver .7524 oz. ASW, 37 mm. **Subject:** Victory Commemorative **Obv:** Artistic star-like design with sprig wrapped around sword with text below **Rev:** Wailing Wall with text below **Note:** Dav. #268

Date	Mintage	F	VF	XF	Unc	BU
JE5727-1967 Proof	50,380	Value: 15.00				

KM# 51 10 LIROT

26.0000 g., 0.9000 Silver .7524 oz. ASW, 37 mm. **Subject:** 20th Anniversary of Independence **Obv:** Building with pillars with text and dates below **Rev:** City view to right of menorah flanked by sprigs **Edge Lettering:** Hebrew **Note:** Dav. #269.

Date	Mintage	F	VF	XF	Unc	BU
JE5728-1968(b)	49,996	—	—	—	14.00	—
JE5728-1968(b) Proof	20,494	Value: 16.00				

KM# 53 10 LIROT

26.0000 g., 0.9000 Silver .7524 oz. ASW **Subject:** 21st Anniversary of Independence **Obv:** Pyramid of block letters **Rev:** Shalom

Date	Mintage	F	VF	XF	Unc	BU
JE5729-1969(s)	39,884	—	—	—	14.00	—
JE5729-1969(s) Proof	19,838	Value: 16.00				
JE5729-1969(k)	20,185	—	—	—	14.00	—

Note: Hebrew letter KOF below helmet

KM# 55 10 LIROT

26.0000 g., 0.9000 Silver .7524 oz. ASW, 37.3 mm. **Subject:** 22nd Anniversary of Independence **Obv:** Value and text within artistic design **Rev:** Mikveh Israel Centenary **Edge Lettering:** Hebrew

Date	Mintage	F	VF	XF	Unc	BU
JE5730-1970(k)	47,509	—	—	—	12.00	—
JE5730-1970(b) Proof	22,434	Value: 15.00				

KM# 56.1 10 LIROT

26.0000 g., 0.9000 Silver .7524 oz. ASW **Subject:** Pidyon Haben **Obv:** Menorah flanked by sprigs at upper left of text **Rev:** Text among the letter M flanked by diamonds **Edge:** Plain

Date	Mintage	F	VF	XF	Unc	BU
JE5730-1970(j)	48,847	—	—	—	13.00	—

KM# 56.2 10 LIROT

26.0000 g., 0.9000 Silver .7524 oz. ASW **Subject:** Pidyon Haben **Obv:** Menorah flanked by sprigs to upper left of text **Rev:** Text within letter M flanked by diamonds **Edge:** Reeded

Date	Mintage	F	VF	XF	Unc	BU
JE5730-1970(s) Proof	14,719	Value: 15.00				

KM# 57.1 10 LIROT

26.0000 g., 0.9000 Silver .7524 oz. ASW **Subject:** Pidyon Haben **Obv:** Menorah flanked by sprigs to upper left of text **Rev:** Text within letter M flanked by diamonds **Edge:** Plain

Date	Mintage	F	VF	XF	Unc	BU
JE5731-1971(j)	30,144	—	—	—	13.00	—

KM# 57.2 10 LIROT

26.0000 g., 0.9000 Silver .7524 oz. ASW **Subject:** Pidyon Haben **Obv:** Menorah flanked by sprigs to upper left of text **Rev:** Text within letter M flanked by diamonds **Edge:** Reeded

Date	Mintage	F	VF	XF	Unc	BU
JE5731-1971(s) Proof	13,897	Value: 15.00				

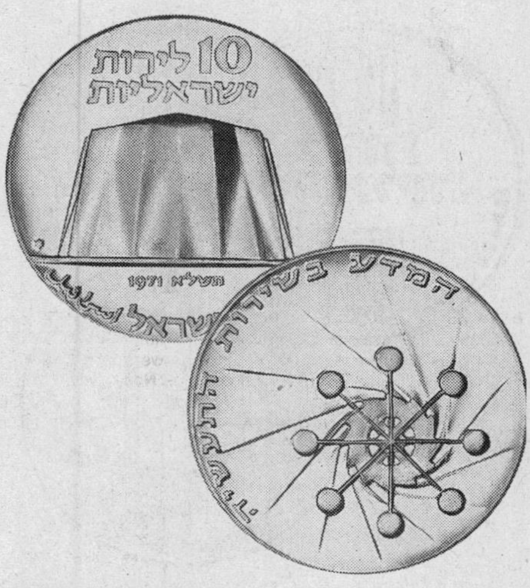

KM# 58 10 LIROT

26.0000 g., 0.9000 Silver .7524 oz. ASW **Subject:** 23rd Anniversary of Independence **Obv:** Stylized atomic reactor **Rev:** Molecule, cog wheel

Date	Mintage	F	VF	XF	Unc	BU
JE5731-1971(u)	29,943	—	—	—	12.00	—
JE5731-1971(j) Star	22,697	—	—	—	13.00	—
JE5731-1971(u) Proof	17,481	Value: 15.00				

KM# 59.1 10 LIROT

26.0000 g., 0.9000 Silver .7524 oz. ASW **Subject:** Let My People Go **Obv:** Menorah flanked by sprigs to upper left of text and date **Rev:** Text within rectangle

Date	Mintage	F	VF	XF	Unc	BU
JE5731-1971(j)	73,444	—	—	—	12.00	—
JE5731-1971(j) Proof	20,132	Value: 14.00				

KM# 59.2 10 LIROT

26.0000 g., 0.9000 Silver .7524 oz. ASW **Obv:** Menorah flanked by sprigs to upper left of text and date **Rev:** Text within rectangle **Note:** Berne die.

Date	Mintage	F	VF	XF	Unc	BU
JE5731-1971(j) Proof	80	Value: 700				

KM# 61.1 10 LIROT

26.0000 g., 0.9000 Silver .7524 oz. ASW **Subject:** Pidyon Haben **Obv:** Menorah flanked by sprigs below value and text **Rev:** Text within the letter M flanked by diamonds **Edge:** Plain

Date	Mintage	F	VF	XF	Unc	BU
JE5732-1972(j) With star	29,744	—	—	—	12.00	—
JE5732-1972(j) Without star	14,944	—	—	—	13.00	—

KM# 61.2 10 LIROT

26.0000 g., 0.9000 Silver .7524 oz. ASW **Subject:** Pidyon Haben **Obv:** Menorah flanked by sprigs below value and text **Rev:** Text within letter M flanked by diamonds **Edge:** Reeded

Date	Mintage	F	VF	XF	Unc	BU
JE5732-1972(j) Proof	12,443	Value: 15.00				

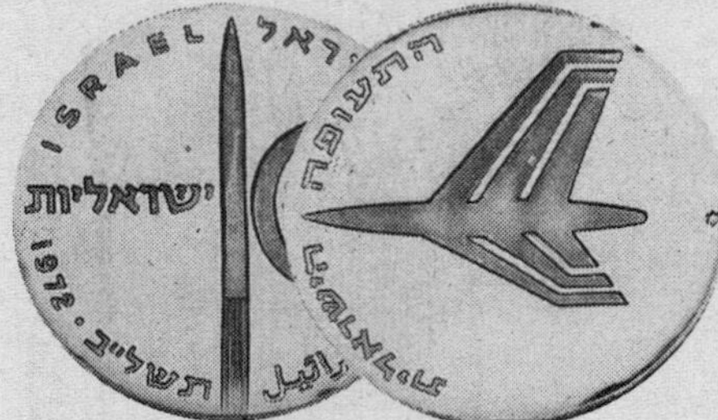

KM# 62 10 LIROT

26.0000 g., 0.9000 Silver .7524 oz. ASW, 37.3 mm. **Subject:** 24th Anniversary of Independence **Obv:** Value as the 1 being a rocket **Rev:** Flying jet **Edge:** Lettered

Date	Mintage	F	VF	XF	Unc	BU
JE5732-1972(j)	49,832	—	—	—	12.00	—
JE5732-1972(j) Proof	14,989	Value: 15.00				

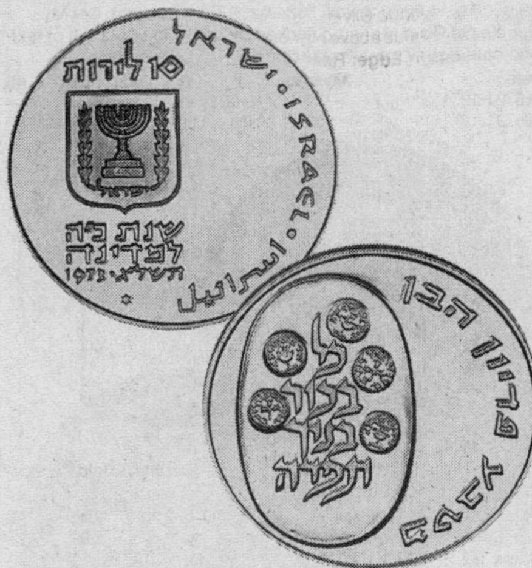

KM# 70.1 10 LIROT

26.0000 g., 0.9000 Silver .7524 oz. ASW **Subject:** Pidyon Haben **Obv:** Menorah flanked by sprigs above text **Rev:** Artistic design within oblong circle **Edge:** Plain **Designer:** Rothschild, Lippmann

Date	Mintage	F	VF	XF	Unc	BU
JE5733-1973(j)	100,676	—	—	—	12.00	—

KM# 70.2 10 LIROT

26.0000 g., 0.9000 Silver .7524 oz. ASW **Subject:** Pidyon Haben **Obv:** Menorah flanked by sprigs above text **Rev:** Artistic designs within oblong circle **Edge:** Reeded

Date	Mintage	F	VF	XF	Unc	BU
JE5733-1973(j) Proof	14,837	Value: 14.00				

KM# 71 10 LIROT

26.0000 g., 0.9000 Silver .7524 oz. ASW **Subject:** 25th Anniversary of Independence **Obv:** Menorah flanked by sprigs above text **Rev:** Text on scroll **Edge:** Lettered

Date	Mintage	F	VF	XF	Unc	BU
JE5733-1973(j)	123,953	—	—	—	11.50	—
JE5733-1973(j) Proof	41,484	Value: 13.50				

KM# 77 10 LIROT

26.0000 g., 0.9000 Silver .7524 oz. ASW **Subject:** 26th Anniversary of Independence **Obv:** Value at upper right of text **Rev:** Text to left of upright design **Edge:** Lettered

Date	Mintage	F	VF	XF	Unc	BU
JE5734-1974(j)	127,195	—	—	—	11.50	—
JE5734-1974(j) Proof	49,657	Value: 13.50				

KM# 76.1 10 LIROT

26.0000 g., 0.9000 Silver .7524 oz. ASW **Subject:** Pidyon Haben **Obv:** Value above menorah flanked by sprigs **Rev:** Artistic design within oblong circle **Edge:** Plain

Date	Mintage	F	VF	XF	Unc	BU
JE5734-1974(j)	108,547	—	—	—	11.50	—

KM# 76.2 10 LIROT

26.0000 g., 0.9000 Silver .7524 oz. ASW **Subject:** Pidyon Haben **Obv:** Value above menorah flanked by sprigs **Rev:** Artistic designs within oblong circle **Edge:** Reeded

Date	Mintage	F	VF	XF	Unc	BU
JE5734-1974(j) Proof	44,348	Value: 13.50				

KM# 78.1 10 LIROT

20.0000 g., 0.5000 Silver .3215 oz. ASW **Subject:** Hanukkah **Obv:** Value and date above text **Rev:** Damascus lamp **Edge:** Plain

Date	Mintage	F	VF	XF	Unc	BU
JE5735-1974	74,112	—	—	—	7.00	—

KM# 78.2 10 LIROT

20.0000 g., 0.5000 Silver .3215 oz. ASW **Subject:** Hanukkah **Obv:** Value and date above text **Rev:** Damascus lamp **Edge:** Reeded

Date	Mintage	F	VF	XF	Unc	BU
JE5735-1974(j) Proof	58,642	Value: 8.00				

KM# 84.1 10 LIROT

20.0000 g., 0.5000 Silver .3215 oz. ASW **Subject:** Hanukkah **Obv:** Value above text with date below **Rev:** Holland lamp **Edge:** Plain

Date	Mintage	F	VF	XF	Unc	BU
JE5736-1975(j)	44,215	—	—	—	7.50	—

KM# 84.2 10 LIROT

20.0000 g., 0.5000 Silver .3215 oz. ASW **Subject:** Hanukkah **Obv:** Value above text with date below **Rev:** Holland lamp **Edge:** Reeded

Date	Mintage	F	VF	XF	Unc	BU
JE5736-1975(j) Proof	33,537	Value: 8.50				

KM# 87.1 10 LIROT

20.0000 g., 0.5000 Silver .3215 oz. ASW **Subject:** Hanukkah **Obv:** Value within square **Rev:** U.S. lamp **Edge:** Plain

Date	Mintage	F	VF	XF	Unc	BU
JE5737-1976(j)	24,844	—	—	—	12.00	—

KM# 87.2 10 LIROT

20.0000 g., 0.5000 Silver .3215 oz. ASW **Subject:** Hanukkah **Obv:** Value within square **Rev:** U.S. lamp **Edge:** Reeded

Date	Mintage	F	VF	XF	Unc	BU
JE5737-1976(j) Proof	19,989	Value: 16.00				

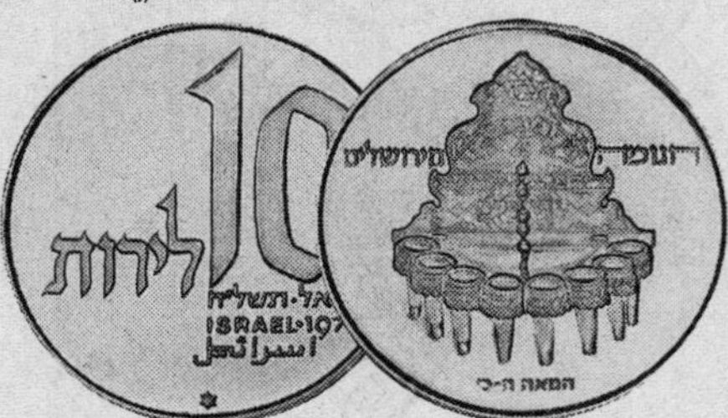

KM# 91.1 10 LIROT

Copper-Nickel, 34 mm. **Subject:** Hanukkah **Obv:** Text to left and below value **Rev:** Jerusalem lamp **Edge:** Plain

Date	Mintage	F	VF	XF	Unc	BU
JE5738-1977(j)	46,106	—	—	—	4.00	—

KM# 91.2 10 LIROT

Copper-Nickel, 34 mm. **Subject:** Hanukkah **Obv:** Text to left and below value **Rev:** Jerusalem lamp **Edge:** Reeded **Note:** Open style "mem."

Date	Mintage	F	VF	XF	Unc	BU
JE5738-1977(j) Proof	29,516	Value: 6.00				

KM# 91.3 10 LIROT

Copper-Nickel, 34 mm. **Subject:** Hanukkah **Obv:** Text to left and below value **Rev:** Jerusalem lamp **Edge:** Reeded
Note: Closed style "mem".

Date	Mintage	F	VF	XF	Unc	BU
JE5738-1977(j) Proof	Inc. above	Value: 10.00				

KM# 30 20 LIROT

7.9880 g., 0.9170 Gold .2355 oz. AGW, 22 mm. **Subject:** 100th Anniversary - Birth of Dr. Theodor Herzl **Obv:** Menorah flanked by sprigs within beaded circle **Obv. Designer:** Andre Lasserre **Rev:** Head left within rectangle **Rev. Designer:** Miriam Karoli

Date	Mintage	F	VF	XF	Unc	BU
JE5720-1960(b)	10,460	—	—	—	200	220

KM# 79.1 25 LIROT

26.0000 g., 0.9350 Silver .7816 oz. ASW **Subject:** 1st Anniversary - Death of David Ben Gurion **Obv:** Menorah flanked by sprigs **Rev:** Head left within rectangle **Edge:** Plain

Date	Mintage	F	VF	XF	Unc	BU
JE5735-1974(j)	99,291	—	—	—	14.50	—

KM# 79.2 25 LIROT

26.0000 g., 0.9350 Silver .7816 oz. ASW **Subject:** 1st Anniversary - Death of David Ben Gurion **Obv:** Menorah flanked by sprigs **Rev:** Head left within rectangle **Edge:** Reeded

Date	Mintage	F	VF	XF	Unc	BU
JE5735-1974(b) Proof	64,153	Value: 16.00				

KM# 81 25 LIROT

30.0000 g., 0.8000 Silver .7717 oz. ASW **Subject:** 25th Anniversary of Israel Bond Program **Obv:** Large value above menorah flanked by sprigs **Rev:** Artistic design **Edge:** Lettered

Date	Mintage	F	VF	XF	Unc	BU
JE5735-1975(j)	49,140	—	—	—	13.50	—
JE5735-1975(j) Proof	39,847	Value: 16.00				

KM# 80.1 25 LIROT

26.0000 g., 0.9000 Silver .7524 oz. ASW **Subject:** Pidyon Haben **Obv:** Menorah flanked by sprigs above value **Rev:** Artistic designs within oblong circle **Edge:** Plain

Date	Mintage	F	VF	XF	Unc	BU
JE5735-1975(j)	62,187	—	—	—	12.00	—

KM# 80.2 25 LIROT

26.0000 g., 0.9000 Silver .7524 oz. ASW **Subject:** Pidyon Haben **Obv:** Menorah flanked by sprigs above value **Rev:** Artistic designs within oblong circle **Edge:** Reeded

Date	Mintage	F	VF	XF	Unc	BU
JE5735-1975(j) Proof	49,192	Value: 14.00				

KM# 85 25 LIROT

26.0000 g., 0.9000 Silver .7534 oz. ASW **Subject:** 28th Anniversary of Independence **Obv:** Value menorah flanked by sprigs **Rev:** Block-like text with star to upper left **Edge:** Lettered

Date	Mintage	F	VF	XF	Unc	BU
JE5736-1976(j)	37,813	—	—	—	13.00	—
JE5736-1976(j) Proof	27,471	Value: 15.00				

KM# 86.1 25 LIROT

30.0000 g., 0.8000 Silver .7717 oz. ASW **Subject:** Pidyon Haben **Obv:** Menorah flanked by sprigs at upper left above text **Rev:** Artistic star-like design **Edge:** Plain

Date	Mintage	F	VF	XF	Unc	BU
JE5736-1976(j)	37,345	—	—	—	12.00	—

KM# 86.2 25 LIROT

30.0000 g., 0.8000 Silver .7717 oz. ASW **Subject:** Pidyon Haben **Obv:** Menorah flanked by sprigs to upper left above text **Rev:** Artistic star-like design **Edge:** Reeded

Date	Mintage	F	VF	XF	Unc	BU
JE5736-1976(j) Proof	29,430	Value: 16.00				

KM# 88 25 LIROT

20.0000 g., 0.5000 Silver .3215 oz. ASW **Subject:** 29th Anniversary of Independence **Obv:** Large value above menorah flanked by sprigs **Rev:** Stylized bird below castle **Edge:** Lettered

Date	Mintage	F	VF	XF	Unc	BU
JE5737-1977(j)	36,976	—	—	—	7.00	—
JE5737-1977(j) Proof	26,735	Value: 9.00				

KM# 89.1 25 LIROT

26.0000 g., 0.9000 Silver .7534 oz. ASW **Subject:** Pidyon Haben **Obv:** Value above menorah flanked by sprigs **Rev:** Artistic star-like design **Edge:** Plain

Date	Mintage	F	VF	XF	Unc	BU
JE5737-1977(j)	32,089	—	—	—	13.00	—

KM# 89.2 25 LIROT

26.0000 g., 0.9000 Silver .7534 oz. ASW **Subject:** Pidyon Haben **Obv:** Value above menorah flanked by sprigs **Rev:** Artistic star-like design **Edge:** Reeded

Date	Mintage	F	VF	XF	Unc	BU
JE5737-1977(j) Proof	18,541	Value: 16.50				

KM# 94.1 25 LIROT

Copper-Nickel, 34 mm. **Subject:** Hanukkah **Obv:** Value above text **Rev:** French lamp **Edge:** Plain

Date	Mintage	F	VF	XF	Unc	BU
JE5739-1978(j)	36,200	—	—	—	4.00	—

KM# 94.2 25 LIROT

26.0000 g., 0.9000 Silver .7534 oz. ASW, 34 mm. **Subject:** Hanukkah **Rev:** French lamp **Edge:** Reeded

Date	Mintage	F	VF	XF	Unc	BU
JE5739-1978(j) Proof	22,300	Value: 11.50				

KM# 40 50 LIROT
13.3400 g., 0.9170 Gold .3933 oz. AGW, 27 mm. **Subject:** 10th Anniversary - Death of Weizmann **Obv:** Menorah flanked by sprigs within circle **Rev:** Bust left within rectangle

Date	Mintage	F	VF	XF	Unc	BU
JE5723-1962(b) Proof	6,195	Value: 350				
Note: With "mem"						
JE5723-1962(b) Proof	10	Value: 1,200				
Note: Without "mem"						

KM# 44 50 LIROT
13.3400 g., 0.9170 Gold .3933 oz. AGW, 27 mm. **Subject:** 10th Anniversary - Bank of Israel **Obv:** Menorah flanked by sprigs **Rev:** Artistic design to upper right of text

Date	Mintage	F	VF	XF	Unc	BU
JE5725-1964(b)	5,975	—	—	—	300	—
JE5725-1964(b) Proof	1,502	Value: 3,250				
Note: Includes 702 used officially by the Bank of Israel						

KM# 72 50 LIROT
7.0000 g., 0.9000 Gold .2025 oz. AGW **Subject:** 25th Anniversary of Independence **Obv:** Menorah flanked by sprigs above text **Rev:** Text on scroll

Date	Mintage	F	VF	XF	Unc	BU
JE5733-1973(b) Proof	27,724	Value: 180				

KM# 92.1 50 LIROT
20.0000 g., 0.5000 Silver .3215 oz. ASW, 33 mm. **Subject:** 30th Anniversary of Independence **Obv:** Menorah flanked by sprigs above value **Rev:** Text within tree **Edge:** Lettered

Date	Mintage	F	VF	XF	Unc	BU
JE5738-1978(j)	40,402	—	—	—	8.00	—

KM# 92.2 50 LIROT
20.0000 g., 0.5000 Silver .3215 oz. ASW **Subject:** 30th Anniversary of Independence **Obv:** Menorah flanked by sprigs above value **Rev:** Text within tree **Edge:** Reeded

Date	Mintage	F	VF	XF	Unc	BU
JE5738-1978(b) Proof	21,806	Value: 9.00				

KM# 95 50 LIROT
20.0000 g., 0.5000 Silver .3215 oz. ASW **Subject:** 31st Anniversary of Independence **Obv:** Value above menorah flanked by sprigs **Rev:** Stylized mother and children **Edge:** Lettered

Date	Mintage	F	VF	XF	Unc	BU
JE5739-1979(j)	24,108	—	—	—	10.00	—
JE5739-1979(o) Proof	16,102	Value: 12.00				

KM# 41 100 LIROT
26.6800 g., 0.9170 Gold .7866 oz. AGW, 33 mm. **Subject:** 10th Anniversary - Death of Weizmann **Obv:** Menorah flanked by sprigs within circle **Rev:** Head left within rectangle

Date	Mintage	F	VF	XF	Unc	BU
JE5723-1962(b) Proof	6,196	Value: 575				
Note: With "mem"						
JE5723-1962(b) Proof	10	Value: 1,500				
Note: Without "mem"						

KM# 50 100 LIROT
26.6800 g., 0.9170 Gold .7866 oz. AGW, 33 mm. **Subject:** Victory Commemorative **Obv:** Leafy sprig around sword within artistic star-like design **Rev:** Wailing Wall

Date	Mintage	F	VF	XF	Unc	BU
JE5727-1967(b) Proof	9,004	Value: 595				

KM# 52 100 LIROT
25.0000 g., 0.8000 Gold .6430 oz. AGW, 33 mm. **Subject:** 20th Anniversary - Jerusalem Reunification **Obv:** Building pillars, text and value **Rev:** Menorah flanked by sprigs to upper left of city view

Date	Mintage	F	VF	XF	Unc	BU
JE5728-1968(b) Proof	12,490	Value: 450				

KM# 54 100 LIROT
25.0000 g., 0.8000 Gold .6430 oz. AGW, 33 mm. **Subject:** 21st Anniversary of Independence **Obv:** Block-like letters within triangular design **Rev:** Shalom

Date	Mintage	F	VF	XF	Unc	BU
JE5729-1969(u) Proof	12,500	Value: 475				

KM# 60 100 LIROT
22.0000 g., 0.9000 Gold .6366 oz. AGW, 30 mm. **Subject:** Let My People Go **Obv:** Menorah flanked by sprigs to upper left of text **Rev:** Text within rectangle to right of moon within lines

Date	Mintage	F	VF	XF	Unc	BU
JE5731-1971(b) Proof	9,956	Value: 485				

KM# 73 100 LIROT
13.5000 g., 0.9000 Gold .3906 oz. AGW **Subject:** 25th Anniversary of Independence **Obv:** Text on scroll **Rev:** Menorah flanked by sprigs above text

Date	Mintage	F	VF	XF	Unc	BU
JE5733-1973(b) Proof	27,472	Value: 325				

KM# 103.1 100 LIROT
20.0000 g., 0.5000 Silver .3215 oz. ASW **Subject:** Hanukkah **Obv:** Value **Rev:** Egyptian lamp within star design **Edge:** Plain

Date	Mintage	F	VF	XF	Unc	BU
JE5740-1979(b)	31,588	—	—	—	8.00	—

KM# 103.2 100 LIROT
20.0000 g., 0.5000 Silver .3215 oz. ASW **Subject:** Hanukkah **Obv:** Value **Rev:** Egyptian lamp **Edge:** Reeded

Date	Mintage	F	VF	XF	Unc	BU
JE5740-1979(b) Proof	19,019	Value: 10.00				

KM# 74 200 LIROT
27.0000 g., 0.9000 Gold .7813 oz. AGW **Subject:** 25th Anniversary of Independence **Obv:** Menorah flanked by sprigs above text **Rev:** Text on scroll

Date	Mintage	F	VF	XF	Unc	BU
JE5733-1973(b) Proof	17,889	Value: 650				

KM# 104 200 LIROT
26.0000 g., 0.9000 Silver .7534 oz. ASW **Subject:** 32nd Anniversary of Independence **Obv:** Menorah flanked by sprigs to upper right of text and value **Rev:** Sprig divides text **Edge:** Lettered

Date	Mintage	F	VF	XF	Unc	BU
JE5740-1980(b)	20,197	—	—	—	12.00	—
JE5740-1980(b) Proof	12,911	Value: 15.00				

KM# 82 500 LIROT
28.0000 g., 0.9000 Gold .8102 oz. AGW **Subject:** 1st Anniversary - Death of David Ben Gurion **Obv:** Menorah flanked by sprigs **Rev:** Head left within rectangle

Date	Mintage	F	VF	XF	Unc	BU
JE5735-1974(b) Proof	47,528	Value: 595				

KM# 83 500 LIROT
20.0000 g., 0.9000 Gold .5787 oz. AGW **Subject:** 25th Anniversary of Israel Bond Program **Obv:** Large value above menorah flanked by sprigs **Rev:** Artistic design

Date	Mintage	F	VF	XF	Unc	BU
JE5735-1975(u) Proof	31,693	Value: 425				

KM# 93 1000 LIROT
12.0000 g., 0.9000 Gold .3473 oz. AGW **Subject:** 30th Anniversary of Independence **Obv:** Text and value above menorah flanked by sprigs **Rev:** Text within tree

Date	Mintage	F	VF	XF	Unc	BU
JE5738-1978(b) Proof	12,043	Value: 295				

KM# 105 5000 LIROT
17.2800 g., 0.9000 Gold .50000 oz. AGW **Subject:** 32nd Anniversary of Independence **Obv:** Menorah flanked by sprigs above text and value **Rev:** Sprig divides text

Date	Mintage	F	VF	XF	Unc	BU
JE5740-1980(o) Proof	6,382	Value: 400				

REFORM COINAGE

10 (old) Agorot = 1 New Agora; 100 New Agorot = 1 Sheqel

Commencing February 24, 1980-1985

KM# 106 NEW AGORA

0.7000 g., Aluminum, 15 mm. **Obv:** Date palm **Rev:** Value

Date	Mintage	F	VF	XF	Unc	BU
JE5740 (1980)	200,000,000	—	—	—	0.10	—
Note: 110 million coins were reportedly melted down						
JE5741 (1981)	1,000,000	—	—	0.10	0.20	—
JE5742 (1982)	1,000,000	—	—	0.10	0.20	—

KM# 107 5 NEW AGOROT

1.0000 g., Aluminum, 18.5 mm. **Obv:** Menorah flanked by sprigs **Rev:** Value

Date	Mintage	F	VF	XF	Unc	BU
JE5740 (1980)	69,532,000	—	—	—	0.10	—
JE5741 (1981)	1,000,000	—	—	0.10	0.20	—
JE5742 (1982)	5,000,000	—	—	—	0.10	—

KM# 108 10 NEW AGOROT

2.1000 g., Bronze, 16 mm. **Obv:** Pomegranate **Rev:** Value

Date	Mintage	F	VF	XF	Unc	BU
JE5740 (1980)	167,932,000	—	—	—	0.10	—
Note: 70,200 million coins were reportedly melted down						
JE5741 (1981)	241,160,000	—	—	—	0.10	—
JE5742 (1982)	23,000,000	—	—	—	0.10	—
JE5743 (1983)	2,500,000	—	—	0.10	0.15	—
JE5744 (1984)	500,000	—	—	0.10	0.20	—

KM# 109 1/2 SHEQEL

3.1000 g., Copper-Nickel, 20 mm. **Obv:** Roaring lion left **Rev:** Value flanked by stars

Date	Mintage	F	VF	XF	Unc	BU
JE5740 (1980)	52,308,000	—	—	0.25	1.00	1.10
JE5741 (1981)	53,272,000	—	—	0.25	1.00	1.10
JE5742 (1982)	18,808,000	—	—	0.25	1.00	1.10
JE5743 (1983)	250,000	—	—	0.35	1.00	1.10
JE5744 (1984)	250,000	—	—	0.35	1.00	1.10

KM# 121 1/2 SHEQEL

7.2000 g., 0.8500 Silver .1967 oz. ASW **Series:** Holyland Sites **Obv:** Value **Rev:** Qumran Caves **Shape:** 12-sided

Date	Mintage	F	VF	XF	Unc	BU
JE5743-1982(p)	15,151	—	—	—	12.00	—

KM# 126 1/2 SHEQEL

7.2000 g., 0.8500 Silver .1967 oz. ASW **Series:** Holyland Sites **Obv:** Value **Obv. Designer:** Zeer Lipman **Rev:** Herodion Ruins **Rev. Designer:** Dan Gelbart **Shape:** 12-sided

Date	Mintage	F	VF	XF	Unc	BU
JE5744-1983(d)	11,044	—	—	—	10.00	—

KM# 140 1/2 SHEQEL

7.2000 g., 0.8500 Silver .1967 oz. ASW **Series:** Holyland Sites **Obv:** Value **Obv. Designer:** Zeer Lipman **Rev:** Kidron Valley **Rev. Designer:** Dan Gelbart **Shape:** 12-sided

Date	Mintage	F	VF	XF	Unc	BU
JE5745-1984(p)	7,538	—	—	—	15.00	—

KM# 152 1/2 SHEQEL

7.2000 g., 0.8500 Silver .1967 oz. ASW **Series:** Holyland Sites **Obv:** Value **Rev:** Capernaum **Shape:** 12-sided

Date	Mintage	F	VF	XF	Unc	BU
JE5746-1985(p)	6,010	—	—	—	15.00	—

KM# 110.1 SHEQEL

14.4000 g., 0.8500 Silver .3935 oz. ASW **Subject:** Hanukkah **Obv:** Value **Rev:** Corfu lamp **Edge:** Plain

Date	Mintage	F	VF	XF	Unc	BU
JE5741-1980(o)	23,753	—	—	—	9.00	10.00

KM# 110.2 SHEQEL

14.4000 g., 0.8500 Silver .3935 oz. ASW **Subject:** Hanukkah **Rev:** Corfu lamp **Edge:** Reeded

Date	Mintage	F	VF	XF	Unc	BU
JE5741-1980(o) Proof	15,428	Value: 12.00				

KM# 111 SHEQEL

5.1000 g., Copper-Nickel, 23 mm. **Obv:** Value **Rev:** Chalice

Date	Mintage	F	VF	XF	Unc	BU
JE5741 (1981)	154,540,000	—	—	0.30	0.50	—
JE5742 (1982)	15,850,000	—	—	0.30	0.50	—
JE5743 (1983)	26,360,000	—	—	0.30	0.50	—
JE5744 (1984)	32,205,000	—	—	0.30	0.50	—
JE5745 (1985)	500,000	—	—	1.00	2.00	—

KM# 116.1 SHEQEL

14.4000 g., 0.8500 Silver .3935 oz. ASW **Subject:** Hanukkah **Obv:** Value at left of menorah flanked by sprigs **Rev:** Polish lamp **Edge:** Plain

Date	Mintage	F	VF	XF	Unc	BU
JE5742 -1981(p)	16,115	—	—	—	10.00	—

KM# 116.2 SHEQEL

14.4000 g., 0.8500 Silver .3935 oz. ASW **Subject:** Hanukkah **Rev:** Polish lamp **Edge:** Reeded

Date	Mintage	F	VF	XF	Unc	BU
JE5742 -1981(f) Proof	11,186	Value: 14.00				

KM# 122 SHEQEL

14.4000 g., 0.8500 Silver .3935 oz. ASW **Series:** Holyland Sites **Obv:** Value **Rev:** Qumran caves

Date	Mintage	F	VF	XF	Unc	BU
JE5743-1982(d) Proof	9,000	Value: 25.00				

KM# 123 SHEQEL

14.4000 g., 0.8500 Silver .3935 oz. ASW **Subject:** Hanukkah **Obv:** Value below menorah flanked by sprigs **Rev:** Yemen lamp

Date	Mintage	F	VF	XF	Unc	BU
JE5743-1982(p)	14,475	—	—	—	20.00	—

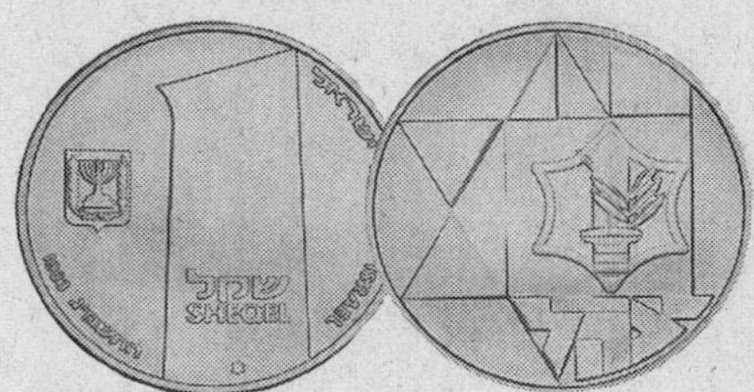

KM# 127 SHEQEL

14.4000 g., 0.8500 Silver .3935 oz. ASW **Subject:** 35th Anniversary - State of Israel **Obv:** Large value **Obv. Designer:** Gideon Keich **Rev:** Sprig wrapped around sword within star design **Rev. Designer:** Yaacov Zim

Date	Mintage	F	VF	XF	Unc	BU
JE5743-1983(f)	14,782	—	—	—	11.00	—

KM# 128 SHEQEL

14.4000 g., 0.8500 Silver .3935 oz. ASW **Series:** Holyland Sites **Obv:** Value **Obv. Designer:** Zeer Lipman **Rev:** Herodion Ruins **Rev. Designer:** Dan Gelbart **Shape:** 12-sided

Date	Mintage	F	VF	XF	Unc	BU
JE5744-1983(d) Proof	10,372	Value: 24.00				

KM# 129 SHEQEL

14.4000 g., 0.8500 Silver .3935 oz. ASW **Subject:** Hanukkah **Obv:** Value **Rev:** Prague lamp

Date	Mintage	F	VF	XF	Unc	BU
JE5744-1983(p)	12,777	—	—	—	12.00	—

KM# 144 SHEQEL
14.4000 g., 0.8500 Silver .3935 oz. ASW **Subject:** Hanukkah **Obv:** Vertical lined value **Rev:** Theresianstadt lamp

Date	Mintage	F	VF	XF	Unc	BU
JE5745-1984(p)	11,004	—	—	—	17.00	—

KM# 141 SHEQEL
14.4000 g., 0.8500 Silver .3935 oz. ASW **Series:** Holyland Sites **Obv:** Value **Rev:** Kidron Valley **Shape:** 12-sided

Date	Mintage	F	VF	XF	Unc	BU
JE5745-1984(f) Proof	6,798	Value: 30.00				

KM# 135 SHEQEL
14.4000 g., 0.8500 Silver .3935 oz. ASW **Subject:** 36th Anniversary - State of Israel **Obv:** Value below menorah flanked by sprigs **Rev:** Kinsmen

Date	Mintage	F	VF	XF	Unc	BU
JE5744-1984(p)	9,476	—	—	—	12.00	—

KM# 148 SHEQEL
14.4000 g., 0.8500 Silver .3935 oz. ASW **Subject:** 37th Anniversary of Independence **Obv:** Value **Rev:** Scientific Achievement

Date	Mintage	F	VF	XF	Unc	BU
JE5745-1985(p)	8,520	—	—	—	12.50	—

KM# 155 SHEQEL
14.4000 g., 0.8500 Silver .3935 oz. ASW **Obv:** Value **Rev:** Ancient ship

Date	Mintage	F	VF	XF	Unc	BU
JE5745-1985(f) Prooflike	12,951	—	—	—	20.00	—

KM# 153 SHEQEL
14.4000 g., 0.8500 Silver .3935 oz. ASW **Series:** Holyland Sites **Obv:** Value **Rev:** Capernaum **Shape:** 12-sided

Date	Mintage	F	VF	XF	Unc	BU
JE5746-1985(f) Proof	6,010	Value: 28.00				

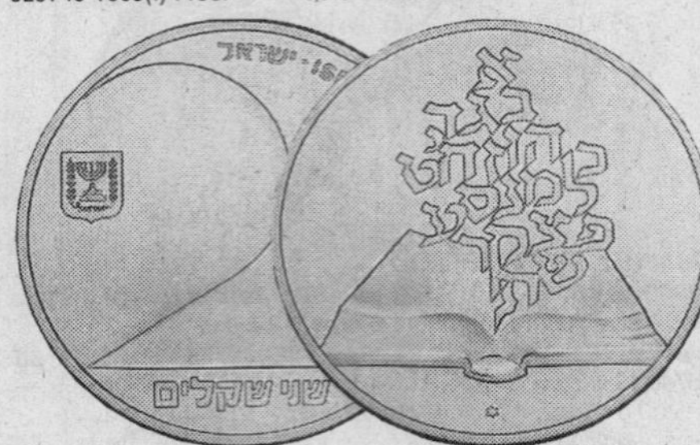

KM# 112 2 SHEQALIM
28.8000 g., 0.8250 Silver .7639 oz. ASW **Subject:** 33rd Anniversary of independence **Obv:** Large stylized value **Rev:** Stylized design within book **Edge:** Lettered

Date	Mintage	F	VF	XF	Unc	BU
JE5741-1981(o)	16,316	—	—	—	12.00	—
JE5741-1981(o) Proof	11,317	Value: 25.00				

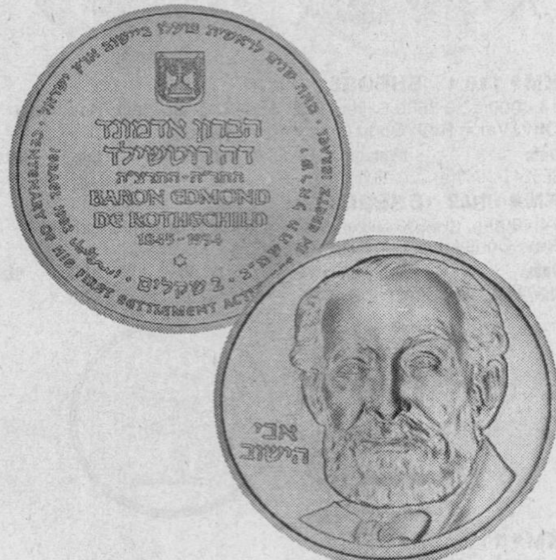

KM# 117 2 SHEQALIM
28.8000 g., 0.8500 Silver .7871 oz. ASW **Subject:** 34th Anniversary of Independence **Obv:** Menorah flanked by sprigs above text **Rev:** Head facing **Edge:** Lettered

Date	Mintage	F	VF	XF	Unc	BU
JE5742-1982(p)	13,272	—	—	—	16.00	—
JE5742-1982(f) Proof	9,506	Value: 22.00				

KM# 124 2 SHEQALIM
28.8000 g., 0.8500 Silver .7871 oz. ASW **Subject:** Hanukkah **Obv:** Menorah flanked by sprigs above text and dates **Rev:** Yemen lamp

Date	Mintage	F	VF	XF	Unc	BU
JE5743-1982(f) Proof	8,996	Value: 25.00				

KM# 130 2 SHEQALIM
28.8000 g., 0.8500 Silver .7871 oz. ASW **Subject:** 35th Anniversary of Independence **Obv. Designer:** Gideon Keich **Rev:** Sprig wrapped around sword within star design **Rev. Designer:** Yaaçov Zim

Date	Mintage	F	VF	XF	Unc	BU
JE5743-1983(f) Proof	9,999	Value: 20.00				

KM# 131 2 SHEQALIM
28.8000 g., 0.8500 Silver .7871 oz. ASW **Subject:** Hanukkah **Obv:** Value above menorah flanked by sprigs **Rev:** Prague lamp **Rev. Designer:** Nathan Karp

Date	Mintage	F	VF	XF	Unc	BU
JE5744-1983(b) Proof	10,894	Value: 22.00				

KM# 145 2 SHEQALIM
28.8000 g., 0.8500 Silver .7871 oz. ASW **Subject:** Hanukkah **Obv:** Value to right of menorah flanked by sprigs **Rev:** Theresianstadt lamp

Date	Mintage	F	VF	XF	Unc	BU
JE5745-1984(b) Proof	10,011	Value: 27.00				

KM# 136 2 SHEQALIM
28.8000 g., 0.8500 Silver .7871 oz. ASW **Subject:** 36th Anniversary of Independence **Obv:** Menorah flanked by sprigs **Rev:** Kinsmen

Date	Mintage	F	VF	XF	Unc	BU
JE5744-1984(f) Proof	8,551	Value: 22.00				

KM# 149 2 SHEQALIM
28.8000 g., 0.8500 Silver .7871 oz. ASW **Subject:** 37th Anniversary of Independence **Obv:** Menorah flanked by sprigs above text within circular designs **Rev:** Scientific achievement

Date	Mintage	F	VF	XF	Unc	BU
JE5745-1985(f) Proof	8,330	Value: 25.00				

KM# 118 5 SHEQALIM
6.2000 g., Aluminum-Bronze, 24 mm. **Series:** Cornucopiae **Obv:** Horn of Cornucopia **Rev:** Value flanked by stars

Date	Mintage	F	VF	XF	Unc	BU
JE5742 (1982)	30,000,000	—	—	0.50	0.75	—
JE5743 (1983)	994,000	—	—	1.00	2.00	—
JE5744 (1984)	17,389,000	—	—	0.50	0.75	—
JE5745 (1985)	250,000	—	—	1.00	2.50	—

KM# 125 5 SHEQALIM
8.6300 g., 0.9000 Gold .2497 oz. AGW **Series:** Holyland Sites **Rev:** Qumran Caves **Shape:** 12-sided

Date	Mintage	F	VF	XF	Unc	BU
JE5743-1982(d) Proof	4,927	Value: 200				

KM# 132 5 SHEQALIM
0.8630 g., 0.9000 Gold .2497 oz. AGW **Series:** Holyland Sites **Obv:** Value **Obv. Designer:** Zeev Lipman **Rev:** Herodion Ruins **Rev. Designer:** Dan Gelbart **Shape:** 12-sided

Date	Mintage	F	VF	XF	Unc	BU
JE5744-1983(d) Proof	4,346	Value: 200				

KM# 142 5 SHEQALIM
8.6300 g., 0.9000 Gold .2497 oz. AGW **Series:** Holyland Sites **Obv:** Value **Obv. Designer:** Zeev Lipman **Rev:** Kidron Valley **Rev. Designer:** Dan Gelbart **Shape:** 12-sided

Date	Mintage	F	VF	XF	Unc	BU
JE5745 -1984(b) Proof	2,601	Value: 350				

KM# 154 5 SHEQALIM
8.6300 g., 0.9000 Gold .2497 oz. AGW **Series:** Holyland Sites **Obv:** Value **Rev:** Capernaum **Shape:** 12-sided

Date	Mintage	F	VF	XF	Unc	BU
JE5746-1985(b) Proof	2,633	Value: 250				

KM# 113 10 SHEQALIM
17.2800 g., 0.9000 Gold .5000 oz. AGW **Subject:** 33rd Anniversary of Independence **Obv:** Large stylized value **Rev:** Stylized design within book

Date	Mintage	F	VF	XF	Unc	BU
JE5741-1981(o) Proof	5,634	Value: 400				

KM# 120 10 SHEQALIM
17.2800 g., 0.9000 Gold .5000 oz. AGW **Subject:** 34th Anniversary of Independence **Obv:** Menorah flanked by sprigs above text **Rev:** Head facing

Date	Mintage	F	VF	XF	Unc	BU
JE5742-1982(o) Proof	4,875	Value: 400				

KM# 119 10 SHEQALIM
8.0000 g., Copper-Nickel, 26 mm. **Obv:** Ancient Galley **Rev:** Value flanked by stars

Date	Mintage	F	VF	XF	Unc	BU
JE5742 (1982)	36,084,000	—	—	0.75	1.25	—
JE5743 (1983)	17,851,000	—	—	0.75	1.25	—
JE5744 (1984)	31,950,000	—	—	0.75	1.25	—
JE5745 (1985)	25,864,000	—	—	0.50	0.75	—

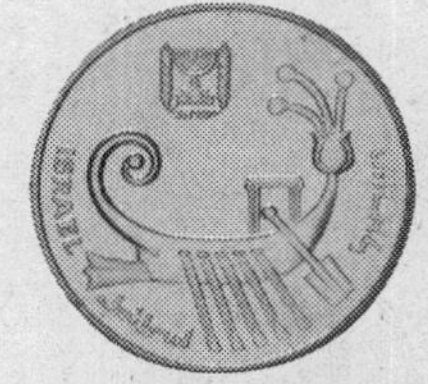

KM# 134 10 SHEQALIM
8.0000 g., Copper-Nickel, 26 mm. **Subject:** Hanukkah **Obv:** Ancient Galley **Rev:** Value flanked by stars

Date	Mintage	F	VF	XF	Unc	BU
JE5744 (1984)	2,000,000	—	—	1.00	1.50	—

KM# 133 10 SHEQALIM
17.2800 g., 0.9000 Gold .5000 oz. AGW **Subject:** 35th Anniversary of Independence **Obv:** Menorah flanked by sprigs within stylized value **Rev:** Sprig wrapped around sword within star design **Rev. Designer:** Yaacov Zim

Date	Mintage	F	VF	XF	Unc	BU
JE5743-1983(b) Proof	3,814	Value: 400				

KM# 138 10 SHEQALIM
17.2800 g., 0.9000 Gold .5000 oz. AGW **Subject:** 36th Anniversary of Independence **Obv:** Menorah flanked by sprigs **Rev:** Kinsmen

Date	Mintage	F	VF	XF	Unc	BU
JE5744-1984(o) Proof	3,798	Value: 400				

KM# 137 10 SHEQALIM
Copper-Nickel, 26 mm. **Obv:** Head left **Rev:** Value flanked by stars

Date	Mintage	F	VF	XF	Unc	BU
JE5744 (1984)	2,003,000	—	—	1.00	1.50	—

KM# 150 10 SHEQALIM
17.2800 g., 0.9000 Gold .5000 oz. AGW **Subject:** 37th Anniversary of Independence **Obv:** Menorah, text and value within circular designs **Rev:** Scientific achievement

Date	Mintage	F	VF	XF	Unc	BU
JE5745-1985(o) Proof	3,240	Value: 400				

KM# 114.1 25 SHEQEL
26.0000 g., 0.9000 Silver .7524 oz. ASW **Subject:** 100th Anniversary - Birth of Zeev Jabotinsky **Obv:** State arms above value **Rev:** Head 3/4 left **Designer:** Gabi Neuman

Date	Mintage	F	VF	XF	Unc	BU
JE5741-1980(o)	14,469	—	—	—	12.00	—

KM# 114.2 25 SHEQEL
26.0000 g., 0.9000 Silver .7524 oz. ASW **Subject:** 100th Anniversary - Birth of Zeev Jabotinsky **Obv:** State arms above value **Rev:** Head left **Edge:** Reeded

Date	Mintage	F	VF	XF	Unc	BU
JE5741-1980(o) Proof	12,236	Value: 20.00				

KM# 139 50 SHEQALIM
Aluminum-Bronze, 28 mm. **Obv:** Ancient coin **Rev:** Value flanked by stars

Date	Mintage	F	VF	XF	Unc	BU
JE5744 (1984)	13,994,000	—	—	0.50	1.00	—
JE5745 (1985)	1,000,000	—	—	1.00	2.00	—

KM# 147 50 SHEQALIM
Aluminum-Bronze, 28 mm. **Obv:** Head left **Obv. Designer:** Gabi Neuman **Rev:** Value flanked by stars

Date	Mintage	F	VF	XF	Unc	BU
JE5745 (1985)	1,000,000	—	—	1.00	2.00	—

KM# 143 100 SHEQALIM
Copper-Nickel, 29 mm. **Obv:** Menorah **Rev:** Value

Date	Mintage	F	VF	XF	Unc	BU
JE5744 (1984)	30,028,000	—	—	0.75	1.50	—
JE5745 (1985)	19,638,000	—	—	0.75	1.50	—

KM# 146 100 SHEQALIM
Copper-Nickel, 29 mm. **Subject:** Hanukkah **Obv:** Menorah **Rev:** Value

Date	Mintage	F	VF	XF	Unc	BU
JE5745 (1985)	2,000,000	—	—	1.25	2.25	—

KM# 151 100 SHEQALIM
Copper-Nickel, 29 mm. **Obv:** Head 1/4 left **Obv. Designer:** Gabi Neuman **Rev:** Value

Date	Mintage	F	VF	XF	Unc	BU
JE5745 (1985)(p)	2,000,000	—	—	1.25	2.25	—

KM# 115 500 SHEQEL
17.2800 g., 0.9000 Gold .5000 oz. AGW **Subject:** 100th Anniversary - Birth of Zeev Jabotinsky **Obv:** Menorah flanked by sprigs above value **Designer:** Gabi Neuman

Date	Mintage	F	VF	XF	Unc	BU
JE5741-1980(o) Proof	7,471	Value: 400				

REFORM COINAGE

10 Sheqalim = 1 Agora; 1000 Sheqalim = 100 Agorot = 1 New Sheqel

September 4, 1985

KM# 156 AGORA
Aluminum-Bronze **Obv:** Ancient ship **Rev:** Value within lined square

Date	Mintage	F	VF	XF	Unc	BU
JE5745 (1985)	58,144,000	—	—	—	0.50	—
JE5746 (1986)	95,272,000	—	—	—	0.50	—
JE5747 (1987)	1,080,000	—	—	—	0.50	—
JE5748 (1988)	15,768,000	—	—	—	0.50	—
JE5749 (1989)	10,801,000	—	—	—	0.50	—
JE5750 (1990)	4,968,000	—	—	—	0.50	—
JE5751 (1991)(j)	12,000	—	—	—	2.00	—
Note: In sets only						

KM# 171 AGORA
Aluminum-Bronze **Subject:** Hanukkah **Obv:** Ancient ship **Rev:** Value within lined square

Date	Mintage	F	VF	XF	Unc	BU
JE5747 (1987)	1,004,000	—	—	0.15	0.75	—
JE5748 (1988)	540,000	—	—	0.20	0.75	—
JE5749 (1989)	504,000	—	—	0.20	0.75	—
JE5750 (1990)	2,160,000	—	—	0.15	0.75	—
JE5751 (1991)(j)	432,000	—	—	0.20	0.75	—

KM# 193 AGORA
Aluminum-Bronze **Subject:** 40th Anniversary of Independence **Obv:** Ancient ship **Rev:** Value within lined square

Date	Mintage	F	VF	XF	Unc	BU
JE5748 (1988)	504,000	—	—	0.20	0.75	—

KM# 157 5 AGOROT
Aluminum-Bronze, 20.5 mm. **Obv:** Ancient coin **Rev:** Value within lined square

Date	Mintage	F	VF	XF	Unc	BU
JE5745 (1985)(p)	25,000,000	—	—	0.10	0.15	—
JE5745 (1985)(s)	9,504,000	—	—	0.10	0.15	—
JE5746 (1986)(j)	6,912,050	—	—	0.10	0.15	—
JE5746 (1986)(f)	5,472,000	—	—	0.10	0.15	—
JE5747 (1987)(j)	14,257,298	—	—	0.10	0.15	—
JE5748 (1988)(j)	9,360,000	—	—	0.10	0.15	—
JE5749 (1989)(j)	4,896,000	—	—	0.10	0.15	—
JE5750 (1990)(j)	576,000	—	—	0.15	0.25	—
JE5751 (1991)(j)	4,464,000	—	—	0.10	0.15	—
JE5752 (1992)(j)	7,664,000	—	—	0.10	0.15	—
JE5752 (1992)(so)	18,432,000	—	—	0.10	0.15	—
JE5754 (1994)(a)	5,952,000	—	—	0.10	0.15	—
JE5754 (1994)(h)	6,144,000	—	—	0.10	0.15	—
JE5755 (1995)(so)	6,144,000	—	—	0.10	0.15	—
JE5756 (1996)(sg)	6,144,000	—	—	0.10	0.15	—
JE5757 (1997)(so)	6,144,000	—	—	0.10	0.15	—
JE5758 (1998)(so)	12,288,000	—	—	0.10	0.15	—
JE5759 (1999)(so)	6,144,000	—	—	0.10	0.15	—
JE5760 (2000)(so)	12,288,000	—	—	0.10	0.15	—

KM# 172 5 AGOROT
Aluminum-Bronze, 20.5 mm. **Subject:** Hanukkah **Obv:** Ancient coin **Rev:** Value within lined square **Note:** JE5754-5760 coins contain the Star of David mint mark; the JE5747-5753 coins do not.

Date	Mintage	F	VF	XF	Unc	BU
JE5747 (1987)(p)	1,004,000	—	—	0.10	0.30	—
JE5748 (1988)(j)	536,000	—	—	0.20	0.50	—
JE5749 (1989)(j)	504,000	—	—	0.20	0.50	—
JE5750 (1990)(j)	2,016,000	—	—	0.10	0.30	—
JE5751 (1991)(j)	1,488,000	—	—	0.10	0.30	—
JE5752 (1992)(j)	960,000	—	—	0.10	0.30	—
JE5753 (1993)(j)	960,000	—	—	0.10	0.30	—
JE5754 (1994)(u)	12,000	—	—	—	2.00	—
Note: In sets only						
JE5755 (1995)(u)	10,000	—	—	—	2.00	—
Note: In sets only						
JE5756 (1996)(u)	7,500	—	—	—	2.00	—
Note: In sets only						
JE5757 (1997)(u)	7,500	—	—	—	2.00	—
Note: In sets only						
JE5758 (1998)(u)	10,000	—	—	—	2.00	—
Note: In sets only						
JE5759 (1999)(u)	6,000	—	—	—	2.50	—
Note: In sets only						
JE5760 (2000)(u)	5,000	—	—	—	2.50	—
Note: In sets only						

KM# 194 5 AGOROT
Aluminum-Bronze **Subject:** 40th Anniversary of Independence **Obv:** Ancient coin **Rev:** Value within lined square

Date	Mintage	F	VF	XF	Unc	BU
JE5748 (1988)(j)	504,000	—	—	0.20	0.50	—

KM# 158 10 AGOROT
Aluminum-Bronze **Obv:** Menorah **Rev:** Value within lined square

Date	Mintage	F	VF	XF	Unc	BU
JE5745 (1985)(f)	45,000,000	—	—	0.10	0.20	—
JE5746 (1986)(j)	20,934,048	—	—	0.10	0.20	—
JE5746 (1986)(b)	71,820,000	—	—	0.10	0.20	—
JE5747 (1987)(j)	19,351,000	—	—	0.10	0.20	—
JE5748 (1988)(j)	8,640,000	—	—	0.10	0.20	—
JE5749 (1989)(j)	420,000	—	—	0.20	0.50	—
JE5750 (1990)(j)	2,376,000	—	—	0.10	0.20	—
JE5751 (1991)(j)	11,905,000	—	—	0.10	0.20	—
Note: Exist with 6mm or 7mm long date; thick or thin letters; and 7mm or 7.5mm value 10						
JE5751 (1991)(so)	30,240,000	—	—	0.10	0.20	—
JE5751 (1991)(f)	17,280,000	—	—	0.10	0.20	—
JE5752 (1992)(j)	1,728,000	—	—	0.10	0.20	—
JE5753 (1993)(so)	25,920,000	—	—	0.10	0.20	—
JE5754 (1994)(u)	30,096,000	—	—	0.10	0.20	—
JE5754 (1994)(s)	21,600,000	—	—	0.10	0.20	—
JE5755 (1995)(h)	17,280,000	—	—	0.10	0.20	—
JE5756 (1996)(so)	43,200,000	—	—	0.10	0.20	—
JE5757 (1997)(h)	21,600,000	—	—	0.10	0.20	—
JE5757 (1997)(u)	21,600,000	—	—	0.10	0.20	—
JE5758 (1998)(so)	60,450,000	—	—	0.10	0.20	—
JE5759 (1999)(a)	21,600,000	—	—	0.10	0.20	—
JE5759 (1999)(sl)	4,601,000	—	—	0.10	0.20	—
JE5759 (1999)(w)	2,000	—	—	0.10	0.20	—
JE5760 (2000)(so)	82,944,000	—	—	0.10	0.20	—

KM# 173 10 AGOROT
Aluminum-Bronze, 22 mm. **Subject:** Hanukkah **Obv:** Menorah **Rev:** Value within lined square **Note:** JE5754-5760 have the Star of David mint mark, JE5747-5753 coins do not.

Date	Mintage	F	VF	XF	Unc	BU
JE5747 (1987)(p)	1,004,000	—	—	0.10	0.40	—
JE5748 (1988)(j)	834,000	—	—	0.10	0.40	—
JE5749 (1989)(j)	798,000	—	—	0.10	0.40	—
JE5750 (1990)(j)	2,052,000	—	—	0.10	0.40	—
JE5751 (1991)(j)	1,488,000	—	—	0.10	0.40	—
JE5752 (1992)(j)	1,404,000	—	—	0.10	0.40	—
JE5753 (1993)(j)	1,404,000	—	—	0.10	0.40	—
JE5754 (1994)(u)	12,000	—	—	—	2.00	—
Note: In sets only						
JE5755 (1995)(u)	10,000	—	—	—	2.00	—
Note: In sets only						
JE5756 (1996)(u)	7,500	—	—	—	2.00	—
Note: In sets only						
JE5757 (1997)(u)	7,500	—	—	—	2.00	—
Note: In sets only						
JE5758 (1998)(u)	10,000	—	—	—	2.00	—
Note: In sets only						
JE5759 (1999)(u)	6,000	—	—	—	2.50	—
Note: In sets only						
JE5760 (2000)(u)	5,000	—	—	—	3.00	—
Note: In sets only						

KM# 195 10 AGOROT
Aluminum-Bronze **Subject:** 40th Anniversary of Independence **Obv:** Menorah **Rev:** Value within lined square

Date	Mintage	F	VF	XF	Unc	BU
JE5748 (1988)(j)	504,000	—	—	0.20	0.50	—

KM# 161 SHEQEL

14.4000 g., 0.8500 Silver .3935 oz. ASW **Subject:** Hanukkah **Obv:** Value **Rev:** Ashkenaz lamp

Date	Mintage	F	VF	XF	Unc	BU
JE5746-1985(p)	9,460	—	—	—	15.00	—

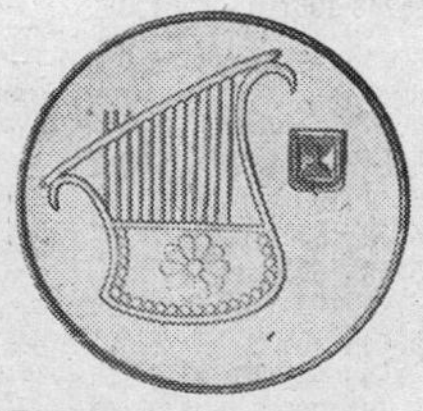

KM# 159 1/2 NEW SHEQEL

Aluminum-Bronze, 26 mm. **Obv:** Value **Rev:** Lyre

Date	Mintage	F	VF	XF	Unc	BU
JE5745 (1985)(s)	4,032,000	—	—	0.35	0.75	—
Note: Exist with thick E and trimmed thin E						
JE5745(1985)(j)	1,296,000	—	—	0.35	0.75	—
Note: Exist with thick E and trimmed thin E						
JE5745 (1985)(p)	15,000,000	—	—	0.35	0.75	—
Note: Exist with thick E and trimmed thin E						
JE5746 (1986)(j)	4,392,000	—	—	0.35	0.75	—
JE5747 (1987)(j)	144,000	—	—	1.00	2.00	—
JE5748 (1988)(j)	20,000	—	—	—	3.00	—
Note: In sets only						
JE5749 (1989)(j)	756,000	—	—	0.40	1.00	—
JE5750 (1990)(j)	648,000	—	—	0.40	1.00	—
JE5751 (1991)(j)	288,000	—	—	0.75	1.50	—
JE5752 (1992)(f)	2,688,000	—	—	0.35	0.75	—
JE5752 (1992)(j)	828,000	—	—	0.35	0.75	—
JE5752 (1992)(so)	10,752,000	—	—	0.35	0.75	—
JE5753 (1993)(c)	2,496,000	—	—	0.35	0.75	—
JE5753 (1993)(f)	2,688,000	—	—	0.35	0.75	—
JE5755 (1995)(a)	5,376,000	—	—	0.35	0.75	—
JE5755 (1995)(so)	5,376,000	—	—	0.35	0.75	—
JE5757 (1997)(so)	5,376,000	—	—	0.35	0.75	—
JE5758 (1998)(u)	5,376,000	—	—	0.35	0.75	—
JE5759 (1999)(so)	8,064,000	—	—	0.35	0.75	—
JE5760 (2000)(so)	2,880,000	—	—	—	—	—
Note: Reported in the 2000 Annual report, a correction in the 2002 Annual report, stated that it was in error.						

KM# 167 1/2 NEW SHEQEL

Aluminum-Bronze, 26 mm. **Obv:** Value **Rev:** Bust facing within names of settlements funded

Date	Mintage	F	VF	XF	Unc	BU
JE5746 (1986)(u)	2,000,000	—	—	1.00	3.00	—

KM# 168 1/2 NEW SHEQEL

7.2000 g., 0.8500 Silver .1967 oz. ASW **Series:** Holyland Sites **Obv:** Value **Rev:** Akko **Shape:** 12-sided

Date	Mintage	F	VF	XF	Unc	BU
JE5747-1986(u)	6,224	—	—	—	10.00	—

KM# 180 1/2 NEW SHEQEL

7.2000 g., 0.8500 Silver .1967 oz. ASW **Series:** Holyland Sites **Rev:** Jericho **Shape:** 12-sided

Date	Mintage	F	VF	XF	Unc	BU
JE5748-1987(p)	7,590	—	—	—	12.50	—

KM# 174 1/2 NEW SHEQEL

Aluminum-Bronze, 26 mm. **Subject:** Hanukka **Obv:** Value **Rev:** Lyre **Note:** Coins dated JE5754-5760 have the Star of David mint mark; the coins from JE5747-5753 do not.

Date	Mintage	F	VF	XF	Unc	BU
JE5747 (1987)(p)	1,004,000	—	—	0.35	0.85	—
JE5748 (1988)(j)	532,000	—	—	0.40	1.00	—
JE5749 (1989)(j)	504,000	—	—	0.40	1.00	—
JE5750 (1990)(j)	2,016,000	—	—	0.35	0.85	—
JE5751 (1991)(j)	960,000	—	—	0.35	0.85	—
JE5752 (1992)(j)	288,000	—	—	0.75	1.50	—
JE5753 (1993)(j)	304,000	—	—	0.75	1.50	—
JE5754 (1994)(u)	12,000	—	—	—	2.00	—
Note: In sets only						
JE5755 (1995)(u)	10,000	—	—	—	2.00	—
Note: In sets only						
JE5756 (1996)(u)	7,500	—	—	—	2.00	—
Note: In sets only						
JE5757 (1997)(u)	7,500	—	—	—	2.00	—
Note: In sets only						
JE5758 (1998)(u)	10,000	—	—	—	2.00	—
Note: In sets only						
JE5759 (1999)(u)	6,000	—	—	—	2.50	—
Note: In sets only						
JE5760 (2000)(u)	5,000	—	—	—	3.00	—
Note: In sets only						

KM# 188 1/2 NEW SHEQEL

7.2000 g., 0.8500 Silver .1967 oz. ASW **Series:** Holyland Sites **Obv:** Value **Rev:** Caesarea **Shape:** 12-sided

Date	Mintage	F	VF	XF	Unc	BU
JE5749-1988(p)	5,865	—	—	—	15.00	—

KM# 196 1/2 NEW SHEQEL

Aluminum-Bronze, 26 mm. **Subject:** 40th Anniversary of Independence **Obv:** Value **Rev:** Lyre

Date	Mintage	F	VF	XF	Unc	BU
JE5748 (1988)(j)	500,000	—	—	0.40	1.00	—

KM# 202 1/2 NEW SHEQEL

7.2000 g., 0.8500 Silver .1967 oz. ASW **Subject:** Holyland Sites **Obv:** Value **Rev:** Jaffa Harbor **Shape:** 12-sided

Date	Mintage	F	VF	XF	Unc	BU
JE5750-1989(f)	4,940	—	—	—	18.00	—

KM# 209 1/2 NEW SHEQEL

7.2000 g., 0.8500 Silver .1967 oz. ASW **Subject:** Holyland Sites **Obv:** Value **Rev:** Sea of Galilee sites map **Shape:** 12-sided

Date	Mintage	F	VF	XF	Unc	BU
JE5751-1990(f)	4,346	—	—	—	20.00	—

KM# 303 1/2 NEW SHEQEL

Copper-Aluminum-Nickel, 26 mm. **Series:** Hanukkah **Obv:** Value **Rev:** Theresienstadt lamp **Note:** Struck for sets only.

Date	Mintage	F	VF	XF	Unc	BU
JE5754 (1994)(u)	12,000	—	—	—	8.00	—

KM# 304 1/2 NEW SHEQEL

Copper-Aluminum-Nickel, 26 mm. **Series:** Hanukkah **Obv:** Value **Rev:** Early American lamp **Note:** Struck for sets only.

Date	Mintage	F	VF	XF	Unc	BU
JE5755 (1995)(u)	10,000	—	—	—	8.00	—

KM# 368 1/2 NEW SHEQEL

14.5000 g., Copper-Aluminum-Nickel, 26 mm. **Subject:** Environment **Obv:** Value **Rev:** Flower **Edge:** Plain **Shape:** 12-sided **Note:** Struck for sets only. Piefort only type.

Date	Mintage	F	VF	XF	Unc	BU
JE5754 (1994)(u)	8,000	—	—	—	10.00	—

KM# 392 1/2 NEW SHEQEL

Copper-Aluminum-Nickel, 26 mm. **Subject:** Medicine Anniversary **Note:** Struck for sets only. Piefort only type.

Date	Mintage	F	VF	XF	Unc	BU
JE5755 (1995)(u)	8,000	—	—	—	10.00	—

KM# 305 1/2 NEW SHEQEL

Copper-Aluminum-Nickel, 26 mm. **Series:** Hanukkah **Obv:** Value **Rev:** 14th century French lamp **Note:** Struck for sets only.

Date	Mintage	F	VF	XF	Unc	BU
JE5756 (1996)(u)	7,500	—	—	—	10.00	—

KM# 318 1/2 NEW SHEQEL

Copper-Aluminum-Nickel, 26 mm. **Series:** Hanukkah **Obv:** Value **Rev:** Russian lamp **Note:** Struck for sets only.

Date	Mintage	F	VF	XF	Unc	BU
JE5757 (1997)(u)	7,500	—	—	—	8.00	—

KM# 393 1/2 NEW SHEQEL

Copper-Aluminum-Nickel, 26 mm. **Subject:** Jerusalem 3000 **Note:** Struck for sets only. Piefort only type.

Date	Mintage	F	VF	XF	Unc	BU
JE5756 (1996)	8,000	—	—	—	10.00	—

KM# 394 1/2 NEW SHEQEL

Copper-Aluminum-Nickel, 26 mm. **Subject:** First Zionist Congress Centennial **Note:** Struck for sets only. Piefort only type.

Date	Mintage	F	VF	XF	Unc	BU
JE5757 (1997)	6,000	—	—	—	12.00	—

KM# 314 1/2 NEW SHEQEL

Copper-Aluminum-Nickel, 26 mm. **Series:** Hanukkah **Obv:** Value **Rev:** English lamp **Note:** Struck for sets only.

Date	Mintage	F	VF	XF	Unc	BU
JE5758 (1998)(u)	10,000	—	—	—	8.00	—

KM# 331 1/2 NEW SHEQEL

Copper-Aluminum-Nickel, 26 mm. **Series:** Hanukkah **Obv:** Value **Rev:** Menorah **Note:** Struck for sets only.

Date	Mintage	F	VF	XF	Unc	BU
JE5759 (1999)(u)	6,000	—	—	—	8.00	—

KM# 395 1/2 NEW SHEQEL

Copper-Aluminum-Nickel, 26 mm. **Subject:** 50th Anniversary - State of Israel **Note:** Struck for sets only. Piefort only type.

Date	Mintage	F	VF	XF	Unc	BU
JE5758 (1998)	8,000	—	—	—	10.00	—

KM# 332 1/2 NEW SHEQEL

Copper-Aluminum-Nickel, 26 mm. **Obv:** Value **Rev:** Jerusalem Hanukkah lamp **Note:** Struck for sets only.

Date	Mintage	F	VF	XF	Unc	BU
JE5760 (2000)(u)	5,000	—	—	—	8.00	—

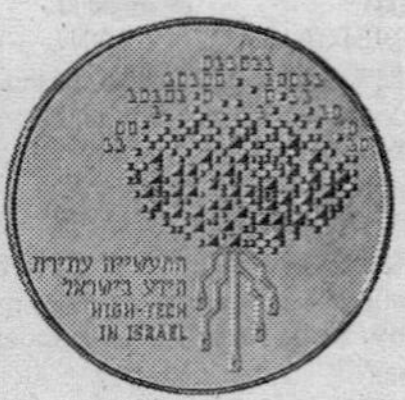

KM# 324 1/2 NEW SHEQEL
Bronze, 26 mm. **Subject:** High Tech in Israel **Obv:** Value **Rev:** Stylized mosaic bouquet **Note:** Struck for sets only. Piefort only type.

Date	Mintage	F	VF	XF	Unc	BU
JE5759 (1999)	6,000	—	—	—	12.00	—

KM# 363 1/2 NEW SHEQEL
14.3200 g., Copper-Nickel-Aluminum, 25.85 mm. **Subject:** "Love Thy Neighbor" **Obv:** Value **Rev:** Arch **Edge:** Plain **Shape:** 12-sided **Note:** Struck for sets only. Piefort only type.

Date	Mintage	F	VF	XF	Unc	BU
JE5760 (2000)	4,000	—	—	—	12.00	—

KM# 160 NEW SHEQEL
Copper-Nickel, 18 mm. **Obv:** Value

Date	Mintage	F	VF	XF	Unc	BU
JE5745 (1985)(b)	29,088,000	—	—	0.65	1.50	—
JE5746 (1986)(f)	8,000,000	—	—	0.65	1.50	—
JE5746 (1986)(j)	12,960,055	—	—	0.65	1.50	—
JE5747 (1987)(j)	216,000	—	—	1.00	3.00	—
JE5748 (1988)(j)	6,372,000	—	—	0.65	1.50	—
JE5748 (1988)(u)	14,004,000	—	—	0.65	1.50	—
JE5749 (1989)(j)	8,706,000	—	—	0.65	1.50	—
JE5750 (1990)(j)	756,000	—	—	0.75	2.00	—
JE5751 (1991)(j)	1,152,000	—	—	0.65	1.50	—
JE5752 (1992)(f)	8,640,000	—	—	0.65	1.50	—
JE5752 (1992)(j)	1,512,000	—	—	0.65	1.50	—
JE5752 (1992)(o)	17,280,000	—	—	0.65	1.50	—
JE5753 (1993)(f)	8,640,000	—	—	0.65	1.50	—

KM# 160a NEW SHEQEL
Nickel-Clad Steel, 18 mm. **Obv:** Value

Date	Mintage	F	VF	XF	Unc	BU
JE5754 (1994)(f)	8,496,000	—	—	—	1.00	—
JE5754 (1994)(u)	12,960,000	—	—	—	1.00	—
JE5755 (1995)(u)	25,920,000	—	—	—	1.00	—
JE5756 (1996)(u)	8,640,000	—	—	—	1.00	—
JE5757 (1997)(u)	30,240,000	—	—	—	1.00	—
JE5758 (1998)(sa)	4,295,500	—	—	—	1.00	—
JE5759 (1999)(u)	17,280,000	—	—	—	1.00	—
JE5760 (2000)(o)	20,738,000	—	—	—	1.00	—

KM# 163 NEW SHEQEL
Copper-Nickel, 18 mm. **Subject:** Hanukkah **Obv:** Value **Rev:** English lamp **Note:** Coins dated JE5754-5760 have the Star of David mint mark; the JE5746-5753 coins do not.

Date	Mintage	F	VF	XF	Unc	BU
JE5746 (1986)(b)	1,056,000	—	—	0.65	1.50	—
JE5747 (1987)(p)	1,004,000	—	—	0.65	1.50	—
JE5748 (1988)(j)	534,000	—	—	0.75	2.00	—
JE5749 (1989)(j)	504,000	—	—	0.75	2.00	—
JE5750 (1990)(j)	2,052,000	—	—	0.65	1.50	—
JE5751 (1991)(f)	1,080,000	—	—	0.65	1.50	—
JE5751 (1991)(j)	24,000	—	—	0.65	1.50	—
JE5752 (1992)(j)	1,044,000	—	—	0.65	1.50	—
JE5753 (1993)(j)	922,000	—	—	0.65	1.50	—
JE5754 (1994)(u)	12,000	—	—	—	2.50	—
Note: In sets only						
JE5755 (1995)(u)	10,000	—	—	—	2.50	—
Note: In sets only						
JE5756 (1996)(u)	7,500	—	—	—	2.50	—
Note: In sets only						
JE5757 (1997)(u)	7,500	—	—	—	2.50	—
Note: In sets only						
JE5758 (1998)(u)	10,000	—	—	—	2.50	—
Note: In sets only						
JE5759 (1999)(u)	6,000	—	—	—	3.00	—
Note: In sets only						
JE5760 (2000)(u)	5,000	—	—	—	3.50	—
Note: In sets only						

KM# 164 NEW SHEQEL
14.4000 g., 0.8500 Silver .3935 oz. ASW **Subject:** 38th Anniversary of Independence **Obv:** Value, half rainbow and menorah flanked by sprigs **Rev:** Artistic designs **Designer:** Asaaf Berg and Tidhar Dagan

Date	Mintage	F	VF	XF	Unc	BU
JE5746-1986(p)	8,010	—	—	—	12.50	—

KM# 169 NEW SHEQEL
14.4000 g., 0.8500 Silver .3935 oz. ASW **Series:** Holyland Sites **Obv:** Value **Rev:** Akko **Shape:** 12-sided

Date	Mintage	F	VF	XF	Unc	BU
JE5747-1986(f) Proof	6,117	Value: 20.00				

KM# 175 NEW SHEQEL
14.4000 g., 0.8500 Silver .3935 oz. ASW **Subject:** Hanukkah **Obv:** Value **Rev:** Algerian lamp **Rev. Designer:** Yaakov Enyed

Date	Mintage	F	VF	XF	Unc	BU
JE5747-1986(f)	8,227	—	—	—	20.00	—

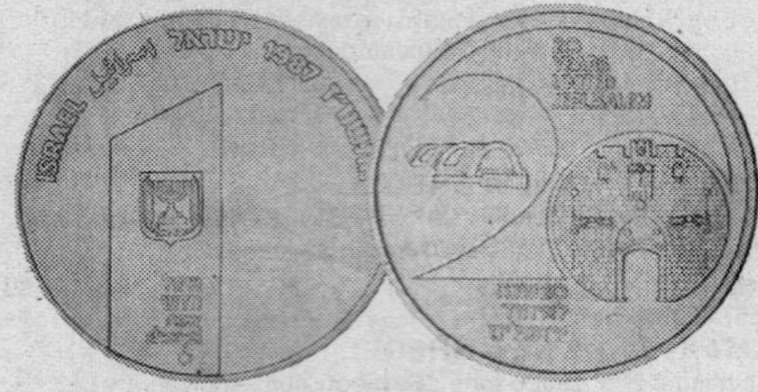

KM# 177 NEW SHEQEL
14.4000 g., 0.8500 Silver .3935 oz. ASW **Subject:** 20th Anniversary - United Jerusalem **Obv:** Menorah flanked by sprigs within rectangle **Rev:** Circular city of Jerusalem to right of numeral two

Date	Mintage	F	VF	XF	Unc	BU
JE5747-1987(p)	8,107	—	—	—	15.00	—

KM# 181 NEW SHEQEL
14.4000 g., 0.8500 Silver .3935 oz. ASW **Series:** Holyland Sites **Obv:** Value **Rev:** Jericho **Shape:** 12-sided

Date	Mintage	F	VF	XF	Unc	BU
JE5748-1987(f) Proof	8,196	Value: 20.00				

KM# 183 NEW SHEQEL
14.4000 g., 0.8500 Silver .3935 oz. ASW **Subject:** Hanukkah **Obv:** Value, text and menorah flanked by sprigs within design **Rev:** English lamp

Date	Mintage	F	VF	XF	Unc	BU
JE5748-1987(f)	7,810	—	—	—	20.00	—

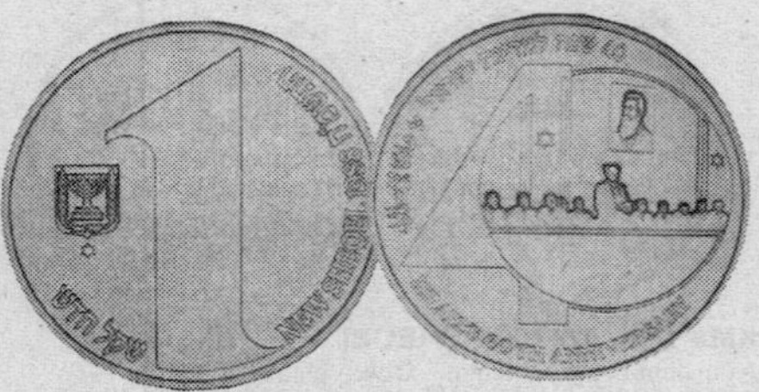

KM# 185 NEW SHEQEL
14.4000 g., 0.8500 Silver .3935 oz. ASW **Subject:** 40th Anniversary of Independence **Obv:** Large stylized value **Obv. Designer:** Asher Kalderon **Rev:** Stylized figures of government within large numeral 40 **Rev. Designer:** Ruben Nutels

Date	Mintage	F	VF	XF	Unc	BU
JE5748-1988(p)	8,990	—	—	—	12.50	—

KM# 189 NEW SHEQEL
14.4000 g., 0.8500 Silver .3935 oz. ASW **Series:** Holyland Sites **Obv:** Value **Rev:** Caesarea **Shape:** 12-sided

Date	Mintage	F	VF	XF	Unc	BU
JE5749-1988(f) Proof	6,560	Value: 30.00				

KM# 191 NEW SHEQEL
14.4000 g., 0.8500 Silver .3935 oz. ASW **Subject:** Hanukkah **Obv:** Value and text within design **Rev:** Tunisian lamp

Date	Mintage	F	VF	XF	Unc	BU
JE5749-1988(u)	6,688	—	—	—	20.00	—

KM# 197 NEW SHEQEL
Copper-Nickel, 18 mm. **Subject:** 40th Anniversary of Independence **Obv:** Value **Rev:** English lamp

Date	Mintage	F	VF	XF	Unc	BU
JE5748 (1988)(j)	504,000	—	—	—	1.75	—

KM# 198 NEW SHEQEL
Copper-Nickel, 18 mm. **Obv:** Value **Rev:** Bust facing

Date	Mintage	F	VF	XF	Unc	BU
JE5748 (1988)(d)	1,000,000	—	—	—	1.75	—

KM# 199 NEW SHEQEL
14.4000 g., 0.8500 Silver .3935 oz. ASW **Subject:** 41st Anniversary of Independence **Obv:** Value covers left side of lined area **Rev:** Roe deer standing to right in mapped area

Date	Mintage	F	VF	XF	Unc	BU
JE5749-1989(f)	6,249	—	—	—	20.00	—

KM# 203 NEW SHEQEL
14.4000 g., 0.8500 Silver .3935 oz. ASW **Subject:** Holyland Sites **Obv:** Value **Rev:** Jaffa Harbor **Shape:** 12-sided

Date	Mintage	F	VF	XF	Unc	BU
JE5750-1989(f) Proof	4,844	Value: 32.00				

KM# 205 NEW SHEQEL
14.4000 g., 0.8500 Silver .3935 oz. ASW **Subject:** Hanukkah **Obv:** Value **Rev:** Persian lamp

Date	Mintage	F	VF	XF	Unc	BU
JE5750-1989(m)	6,171	—	—	—	25.00	—

KM# 210 NEW SHEQEL
14.4000 g., 0.8500 Silver .3935 oz. ASW **Subject:** Holyland Sites **Obv:** Value **Rev:** Sea of Galilee sites map **Shape:** 12-sided

Date	Mintage	F	VF	XF	Unc	BU
JE5751-1990(f) Proof	4,735	Value: 35.00				

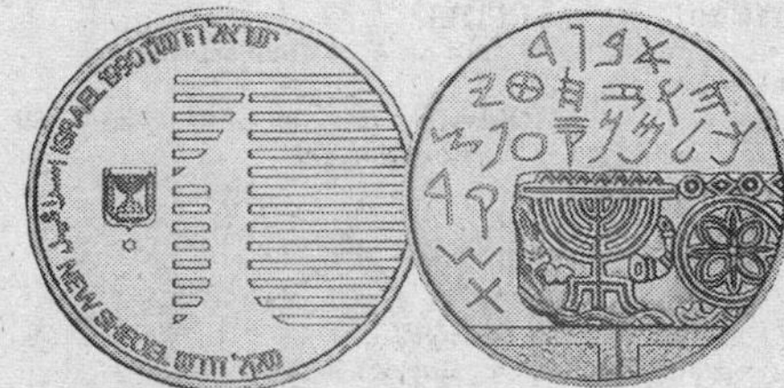

KM# 212 NEW SHEQEL
14.4000 g., 0.8500 Silver .3935 oz. ASW **Subject:** 42nd Anniversary of Independence **Obv:** Linear value **Obv. Designer:** Ruben Nutels **Rev:** Archaeology **Rev. Designer:** Ehud Shafrir

Date	Mintage	F	VF	XF	Unc	BU
JE5750-1990(f)	5,509	—	—	—	22.00	—

KM# 215 NEW SHEQEL
14.4000 g., 0.8500 Silver .3935 oz. ASW **Subject:** Hanukkah **Obv:** Value, text and menorah flanked by sprigs **Rev:** Cochin lamp

Date	Mintage	F	VF	XF	Unc	BU
JE5751-1990(f)	5,259	—	—	—	25.00	—

KM# 220 NEW SHEQEL
14.4000 g., 0.9250 Silver .4282 oz. ASW **Subject:** Wildlife **Obv:** Cedar trees and value **Rev:** Dove and tree trunk

Date	Mintage	F	VF	XF	Unc	BU
JE5752-1991(f)	4,125	—	—	—	25.00	—

KM# 218 NEW SHEQEL
14.4000 g., 0.9250 Silver .4282 oz. ASW **Subject:** 43rd Anniversary of Independence **Obv:** Value within diagonal lines **Rev:** Plane above stylized standing figures

Date	Mintage	F	VF	XF	Unc	BU
JE5751-1991(f)	5,508	—	—	—	18.00	—

KM# 223 NEW SHEQEL
14.4000 g., 0.9250 Silver .4282 oz. ASW **Series:** Judaic **Obv:** Value within diagonal lines to right of cup **Rev:** Kiddush cup flanked by dates within circular design

Date	Mintage	F	VF	XF	Unc	BU
JE5752-1991(f)	4,876	—	—	—	20.00	—

KM# 342 NEW SHEQEL
3.4600 g., 0.9000 Gold .1001 oz. AGW **Subject:** Wildlife **Obv:** Cedar trees and value **Rev:** Dove and tree trunk

Date	Mintage	F	VF	XF	Unc	BU
JE5752-1991(o) Proof	2,515	Value: 200				

KM# 225 NEW SHEQEL
14.4000 g., 0.9250 Silver .4282 oz. ASW **Subject:** 44th Anniversary of Independence **Obv:** Value **Rev:** Balance scale above arch within square

Date	Mintage	F	VF	XF	Unc	BU
JE5752-1992(p)	4,047	—	—	—	35.00	—

KM# 231 NEW SHEQEL
14.4000 g., 0.9250 Silver .4282 oz. ASW **Series:** Wildlife **Obv:** Value at upper right of lilies **Rev:** Roe and lily

Date	Mintage	F	VF	XF	Unc	BU
JE5753-1992(f)	4,105	—	—	—	25.00	—

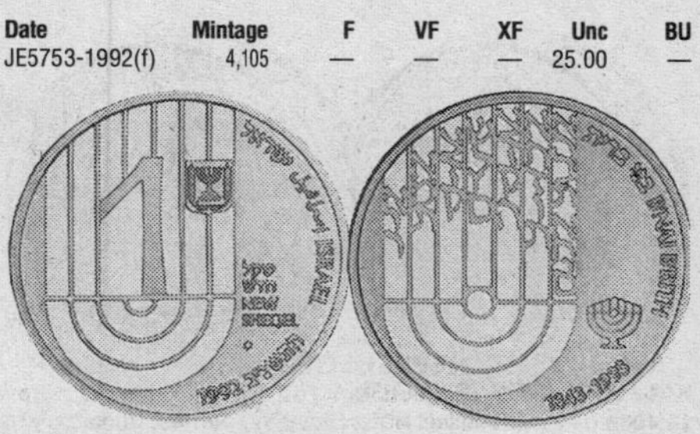

KM# 234 NEW SHEQEL
14.4000 g., 0.9250 Silver .4282 oz. ASW **Subject:** B'nai B'rith - 150th Anniversary. **Obv:** Value and menorah within stylized design **Rev:** Text within stylized design

Date	Mintage	F	VF	XF	Unc	BU
JE5752-1992	4,034	—	—	—	25.00	—

KM# 238 NEW SHEQEL
14.4000 g., 0.9250 Silver .4282 oz. ASW **Series:** Judaic **Obv:** Value within diagonal lines to right of candles on box **Rev:** Shabbat candles

Date	Mintage	F	VF	XF	Unc	BU
JE5753-1992(u)	5,564	—	—	—	25.00	—

KM# 343 NEW SHEQEL
3.4600 g., 0.9000 Gold .1001 oz. AGW **Series:** Wildlife **Rev:** Roe and lily

Date	Mintage	F	VF	XF	Unc	BU
JE5753-1992(p) Proof	2,000	Value: 200				

KM# 240 NEW SHEQEL
14.4000 g., 0.9250 Silver .4282 oz. ASW **Subject:** 45th Anniversary of Independence **Obv:** Value, text, dates and menorah flanked by sprigs **Rev:** Tourism attractions

Date	Mintage	F	VF	XF	Unc	BU
JE5753-1993(u)	6,985	—	—	—	25.00	—

KM# 243 NEW SHEQEL
14.4000 g., 0.9250 Silver .4282 oz. ASW **Series:** Wildlife **Obv:** Value at upper right of apple blossom **Rev:** Buck and young Hart deer standing in grass

Date	Mintage	F	VF	XF	Unc	BU
JE5754-1993(f)	3,761	—	—	—	25.00	—

KM# 244 NEW SHEQEL
3.4600 g., 0.9000 Gold .1001 oz. AGW **Series:** Wildlife **Obv:** Value at upper right of apple blossom **Rev:** Buck and young Hart standing in grass

Date	Mintage	F	VF	XF	Unc	BU
JE5754-1993(u) Proof	1,679	Value: 200				

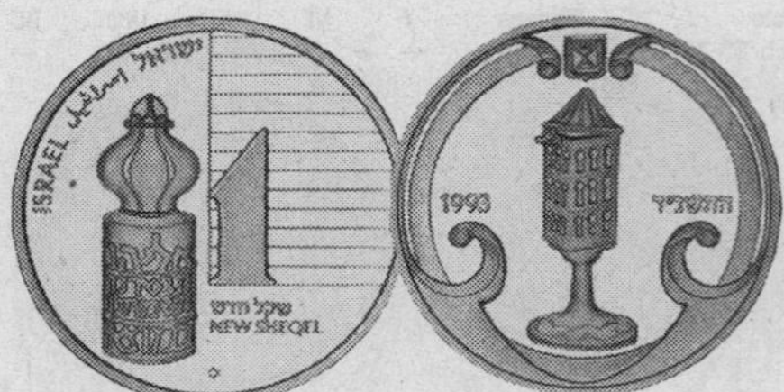

KM# 250 NEW SHEQEL
14.4000 g., 0.9250 Silver .4282 oz. ASW **Series:** Judaic **Obv:** Torah crown at left of value within lined 1/4 square **Rev:** Havdalah spicebox

Date	Mintage	F	VF	XF	Unc	BU
JE5754-1993(u)	3,288	—	—	—	20.00	—

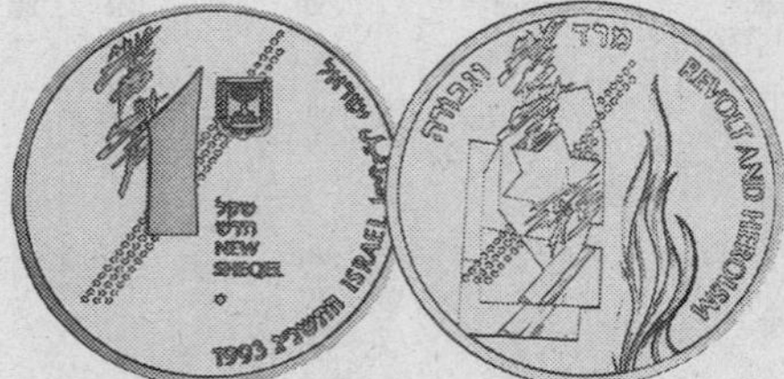

KM# 247 NEW SHEQEL
14.4000 g., 0.9250 Silver .4282 oz. ASW **Obv:** Value and menorah within beaded diagonal line **Rev:** Medal with star within beaded diagonal lines to left of flames **Note:** Revolt and Heroism.

Date	Mintage	F	VF	XF	Unc	BU
JE5753-1993(u)	4,642	—	—	—	20.00	—

KM# 252 NEW SHEQEL
14.4000 g., 0.9250 Silver .4282 oz. ASW **Subject:** Environment **Obv:** Slanted value **Rev:** Globe within flower design

Date	Mintage	F	VF	XF	Unc	BU
JE5754-1994(f)	3,490	—	—	—	25.00	—

KM# 256 NEW SHEQEL
14.4000 g., 0.9250 Silver .4282 oz. ASW **Series:** Biblical **Rev:** Abraham's willingness to sacrifice Isaac

Date	Mintage	F	VF	XF	Unc	BU
JE5755-1994(f) Prooflike	3,468	—	—	—	30.00	—

KM# 259 NEW SHEQEL
14.4000 g., 0.9250 Silver .4282 oz. ASW **Subject:** Wildlife **Obv:** Palm tree to right of value and text **Rev:** Leopard

Date	Mintage	F	VF	XF	Unc	BU
JE5755-1994(u)	3,286	—	—	—	30.00	—

KM# 260 NEW SHEQEL
3.4600 g., 0.9000 Gold .1001 oz. AGW **Subject:** Wildlife **Obv:** Palm tree to right of value and text **Rev:** Leopard

Date	Mintage	F	VF	XF	Unc	BU
JE5755-1994(o) Proof	1,355	Value: 225				

KM# 263 NEW SHEQEL
14.4000 g., 0.9250 Silver .4282 oz. ASW **Subject:** Anniversary - Medicine **Obv:** Snake on a menorrah **Rev:** Value, text and menorah flanked by sprigs **Rev. Designer:** Eleizer Weishoff

Date	Mintage	F	VF	XF	Unc	BU
JE5755-1995(f)	3,468	—	—	—	25.00	—

KM# 267 NEW SHEQEL
14.4000 g., 0.9250 Silver .4282 oz. ASW **Subject:** 50th Anniversary - Defeat of Nazi Germany **Obv:** Value above text **Rev:** V-shape design with state emblems within

Date	Mintage	F	VF	XF	Unc	BU
JE5755-1995(h) Prooflike	3,450	—	—	—	—	32.50

KM# 271 NEW SHEQEL
14.4000 g., 0.9250 Silver .4282 oz. ASW **Series:** F.A.O. **Obv:** Value within wheat sprigs and diagonal lines **Rev:** FAO logo

Date	Mintage	F	VF	XF	Unc	BU
JE5755-1995(v) Prooflike	3,564	—	—	—	—	35.00

KM# 274 NEW SHEQEL
14.4000 g., 0.9250 Silver .4327 oz. ASW **Subject:** Wildlife **Obv:** Value and cluster of grapes **Rev:** Fox

Date	Mintage	F	VF	XF	Unc	BU
JE5756-1995(v)	2,438	—	—	—	30.00	—

KM# 275 NEW SHEQEL
3.4600 g., 0.9000 Gold .1001 oz. AGW **Subject:** Wildlife **Obv:** Grapes **Rev:** Fox

Date	Mintage	F	VF	XF	Unc	BU
JE5756-1995(o) Proof	837	Value: 325				

KM# 278 NEW SHEQEL
14.4000 g., 0.9250 Silver .4282 oz. ASW **Subject:** Peace Treaty with Jordan **Obv:** Text divides value and menorah flanked by sprigs **Obv. Designer:** Shimon Keler **Rev:** Sprig divides text **Rev. Designer:** David Pesach

Date	Mintage	F	VF	XF	Unc	BU
JE5755-1995(bp)	3,301	—	—	—	—	28.00

KM# 281 NEW SHEQEL
14.4000 g., 0.9250 Silver .4282 oz. ASW **Subject:** Biblical Arts - Solomon's Judgment **Obv:** Value above text **Rev:** Medieval linear design

Date	Mintage	F	VF	XF	Unc	BU
JE5755-1995(f) Prooflike	2,826	—	—	—	30.00	—

KM# 287 NEW SHEQEL
14.4000 g., 0.9250 Silver .4282 oz. ASW **Subject:** Port of Caesarea **Obv:** Anchor to lower left of value and text **Rev:** Ancient ship

Date	Mintage	F	VF	XF	Unc	BU
JE5755-1995(f)	2,633	—	—	—	28.00	—

KM# 284 NEW SHEQEL
14.4000 g., 0.9250 Silver .4282 oz. ASW **Subject:** Jerusalem 3000 **Obv:** Value flanked by menorah and design above text **Rev:** Inscription at center

Date	Mintage	F	VF	XF	Unc	BU
JE5756-1996(f) Prooflike	4,497	—	—	—	35.00	—

KM# 290 NEW SHEQEL
14.4000 g., 0.9250 Silver .4282 oz. ASW **Subject:** Wildlife **Obv:** Fig leaves and value **Rev:** Nightingale

Date	Mintage	F	VF	XF	Unc	BU
JE5757-1996(v) Prooflike	2,451	—	—	—	—	30.00

KM# 291 NEW SHEQEL
3.4600 g., 0.9000 Gold .1001 oz. AGW **Subject:** Wildlife **Rev:** Nightingale

Date	Mintage	F	VF	XF	Unc	BU
JE5757-1996(v) Proof	912	Value: 350				

KM# 294 NEW SHEQEL
14.4000 g., 0.9250 Silver .4282 oz. ASW **Subject:** Biblical Arts **Obv:** Value above design and text **Rev:** Miriam and the women

Date	Mintage	F	VF	XF	Unc	BU
JE5757-1996(u) Prooflike	2,236	—	—	—	—	40.00

KM# 297 NEW SHEQEL
14.4000 g., 0.9250 Silver .4282 oz. ASW **Obv:** Menorah above value and text **Rev:** Head left

Date	Mintage	F	VF	XF	Unc	BU
JE5757-1996(u)	5,296	—	—	—	—	35.00

KM# 300 NEW SHEQEL
14.4000 g., 0.9250 Silver .4282 oz. ASW **Subject:** First Zionist Congress Centennial **Obv:** Value flanked by menorah, star design and text **Rev:** Half-figure left leaning on bridge **Rev. Designer:** Gideon Keich

Date	Mintage	F	VF	XF	Unc	BU
JE5757-1997(u) Prooflike	4,028	—	—	—	—	30.00

KM# 306 NEW SHEQEL
14.4000 g., 0.9250 Silver .4282 oz. ASW **Subject:** Wildlife **Obv:** Pomegranates, value and text **Rev:** Lion right

Date	Mintage	F	VF	XF	Unc	BU
JE5758-1997(u) Prooflike	2,135	—	—	—	25.00	—

KM# 307 NEW SHEQEL
3.4600 g., 0.9000 Gold .1001 oz. AGW **Subject:** Wildlife **Obv:** Pomegranates and value **Rev:** Lion **Edge:** Reeded

Date	Mintage	F	VF	XF	Unc	BU
JE5758-1997(u) Proof	770	Value: 375				

KM# 310 NEW SHEQEL
14.4300 g., 0.9250 Silver .4291 oz. ASW **Subject:** Anniversary **Obv:** Value and menorah above text **Rev:** Flag within stars

Date	Mintage	F	VF	XF	Unc	BU
JE5758-1998(u) Prooflike	9,819	—	—	—	—	25.00

KM# 316 NEW SHEQEL
14.4300 g., 0.9250 Silver .4291 oz. ASW **Subject:** Biblical - Noah's Ark **Obv:** Dove, rainbow and value **Rev:** Stylized figure releasing dove

Date	Mintage	F	VF	XF	Unc	BU
JE5758-1998(u) Prooflike	2,198	—	—	—	30.00	—

KM# 320 NEW SHEQEL
14.4300 g., 0.9250 Silver .4291 oz. ASW **Subject:** Wildlife **Obv:** Fir trees and value **Rev:** Stork

Date	Mintage	F	VF	XF	Unc	BU
JE5759-1998(u) Prooflike	2,147	—	—	—	—	30.00

KM# 321 NEW SHEQEL
3.4600 g., 0.9000 Gold .1001 oz. AGW **Subject:** Wildlife **Obv:** Fir trees and value **Rev:** Stork

Date	Mintage	F	VF	XF	Unc	BU
JE5759-1998(u) Proof	553	Value: 375				

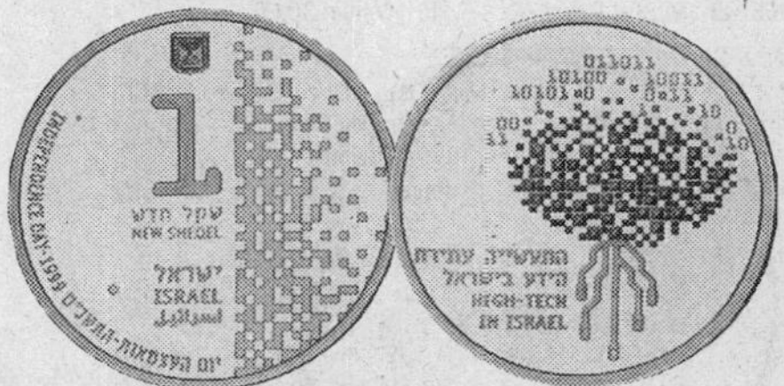

KM# 325 NEW SHEQEL
14.4000 g., 0.9250 Silver .4282 oz. ASW, 30 mm. **Subject:** High-Tech in Israel **Obv:** Value and mosaic **Obv. Designer:** Yigal Gabay **Rev:** O1 Computer code as bouquet

Date	Mintage	F	VF	XF	Unc	BU
JE5759-1999(u) Prooflike	1,713	—	—	—	—	25.00

KM# 328 NEW SHEQEL
14.4000 g., 0.9250 Silver .4282 oz. ASW **Subject:** The Millennium Coin **Obv:** Value and olive branch **Rev:** Year 2000 motif incorporating dove with olive branch

Date	Mintage	F	VF	XF	Unc	BU
JE5759-1999(u) Prooflike	4,629	—	—	—	—	25.00

KM# 333 NEW SHEQEL
14.4000 g., 0.9250 Silver .4282 oz. ASW **Subject:** Biblical **Obv:** Value, text and menorah to right of stars **Rev:** Abraham looking at the stars

Date	Mintage	F	VF	XF	Unc	BU
JE5759-1999(o) Prooflike	2,146	—	—	—	—	35.00

KM# 336 NEW SHEQEL
14.4000 g., 0.9250 Silver .4282 oz. ASW, 30 mm. **Subject:** Anniversary - Independence Day **Obv:** Value within dome design **Rev:** Arch above text **Rev. Inscription:** Love Thy Neighbor, As Thyself **Edge:** Plain

Date	Mintage	F	VF	XF	Unc	BU
JE5760-2000(u) Prooflike	2,516	—	—	—	—	25.00

KM# 339 NEW SHEQEL
14.4000 g., 0.9250 Silver .4282 oz. ASW **Subject:** Biblical - Joseph and His Brothers **Obv:** Value and text **Rev:** Joseph standing before sheaves of wheat into his brothers **Edge:** Plain

Date	Mintage	F	VF	XF	Unc	BU
JE5760-2000(u) Prooflike	2,249	—	—	—	—	25.00

KM# 347 NEW SHEQEL
14.4000 g., 0.9250 Silver .4282 oz. ASW, 30 mm. **Subject:** Wildlife **Obv:** Acacia tree and value **Rev:** Ibex **Edge:** Plain

Date	Mintage	F	VF	XF	Unc	BU
JE5761-2000(u) Prooflike	2,000	—	—	—	—	25.00

KM# 348 NEW SHEQEL
3.4600 g., 0.9000 Gold .1001 oz. AGW, 18 mm. **Subject:** Wildlife **Obv:** Acacia tree **Rev:** Ibex **Edge:** Reeded

Date	Mintage	F	VF	XF	Unc	BU
JE5761-2000(u) Proof	700	Value: 325				

KM# 162 2 SHEQALIM
28.8000 g., 0.8500 Silver .7871 oz. ASW **Subject:** Hanukkah **Obv:** Value, partial feather and menorah flanked by sprigs **Rev:** Ashkanaz lamp

Date	Mintage	F	VF	XF	Unc	BU
JE5746-1985(b) Proof	9,225	Value: 25.00				

KM# 335 10 SHEQALIM
17.2800 g., 0.9000 Gold 0.5 oz. AGW, 30 mm. **Series:** Biblical **Obv:** Arms above denomination **Rev:** Abraham gazing at the stars **Edge:** Reeded

Date	Mintage	F	VF	XF	Unc	BU
JE5759-1999(u) Proof	687	Value: 700				

KM# 165 2 NEW SHEQALIM
28.8000 g., 0.8500 Silver .7871 oz. ASW **Subject:** 38th Anniversary of Independence **Obv:** Value, partial rainbow and menorah **Rev:** Artistic designs **Designer:** Asaaf Berg and Tidbar Dagon

Date	Mintage	F	VF	XF	Unc	BU
JE5746-1986(p) Proof	7,344	Value: 25.00				

KM# 176 2 NEW SHEQALIM

28.8000 g., 0.8500 Silver .7871 oz. ASW **Subject:** Hanukkah
Obv: Value and text **Rev:** Algerian lamp

Date	Mintage	F	VF	XF	Unc	BU
JE5747-1986(f) Proof	8,343	Value: 30.00				

KM# 184 2 NEW SHEQALIM

28.8000 g., 0.8500 Silver .7871 oz. ASW **Subject:** Hanukkah
Obv: Value above text **Rev:** English lamp

Date	Mintage	F	VF	XF	Unc	BU
JE5748-1987(d) Proof	8,039	Value: 30.00				

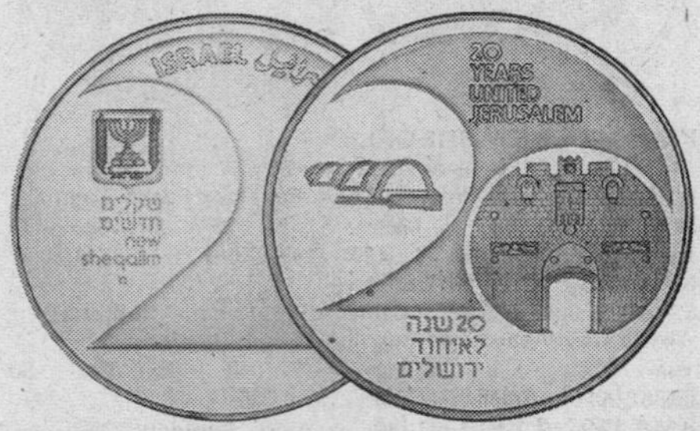

KM# 178 2 NEW SHEQALIM

28.8000 g., 0.8500 Silver .7871 oz. ASW **Subject:** 20th Anniversary - United Jerusalem **Obv:** Stylized value
Rev: Circular city within numeral value

Date	Mintage	F	VF	XF	Unc	BU
JE5747-1987(u) Proof	7,788	Value: 22.00				

KM# 186 2 NEW SHEQALIM

28.8000 g., 0.8500 Silver .7871 oz. ASW **Subject:** 40th Anniversary of Independence **Obv:** Menorah flanked by sprigs to to upper left of stylized value **Obv. Designer:** Asher Kalderon **Rev:** Stylized figures of government within large numeral 40 **Rev. Designer:** Ruben Nutels

Date	Mintage	F	VF	XF	Unc	BU
JE5748-1988(p) Proof	9,100	Value: 22.50				

KM# 192 2 NEW SHEQALIM

28.8000 g., 0.8500 Silver .7871 oz. ASW **Subject:** Hanukkah
Obv: Value above text **Rev:** Tunisian lamp

Date	Mintage	F	VF	XF	Unc	BU
JE5749-1988(u) Proof	7,110	Value: 30.00				

KM# 206 2 NEW SHEQALIM

28.8000 g., 0.8500 Silver .7871 oz. ASW **Subject:** Hanukkah
Obv: Value at upper left above text **Rev:** Persian lamp

Date	Mintage	F	VF	XF	Unc	BU
JE5750-1989(m) Proof	6,282	Value: 40.00				

KM# 200 2 NEW SHEQALIM

28.8000 g., 0.8500 Silver .7871 oz. ASW **Subject:** 41st Anniversary of Independence **Obv:** Value to left within horizontal lines **Rev:** Roe deer facing right among trees

Date	Mintage	F	VF	XF	Unc	BU
JE5749-1989(f) Proof	7,062	Value: 30.00				

KM# 213 2 NEW SHEQALIM

28.8000 g., 0.8500 Silver .7871 oz. ASW **Subject:** 42nd Anniversary of Independence **Obv:** Linear value to right of menorah flanked by sprigs **Obv. Designer:** Ruben Nutels **Rev:** Archaeology **Rev. Designer:** Ehud Shafrir

Date	Mintage	F	VF	XF	Unc	BU
JE5750-1990(f) Proof	5,457	Value: 40.00				

KM# 216 2 NEW SHEQALIM

28.8000 g., 0.8500 Silver .7871 oz. ASW **Subject:** Hanukkah
Obv: Value at lower left **Rev:** Cochin lamp

Date	Mintage	F	VF	XF	Unc	BU
JE5751-1990(f) Proof	5,383	Value: 45.00				

KM# 219 2 NEW SHEQALIM

28.8000 g., 0.9250 Silver .8565 oz. ASW **Subject:** 43rd Anniversary of Independence **Obv:** Value to left within shaded diagonal lines **Rev:** Plane above stylized standing figures

Date	Mintage	F	VF	XF	Unc	BU
JE5751-1991(u) Proof	6,695	Value: 35.00				

KM# 221 2 NEW SHEQALIM
28.8000 g., 0.9250 Silver .8565 oz. ASW **Subject:** Wildlife **Obv:** Trees and value **Rev:** Stylized dove and tree trunk

Date	Mintage	F	VF	XF	Unc	BU
JE5752-1991(f) Proof	5,005	Value: 40.00				

KM# 224 2 NEW SHEQALIM
28.8000 g., 0.9250 Silver .8565 oz. ASW **Series:** Judaic **Obv:** Value and cup **Rev:** Kiddush cup

Date	Mintage	F	VF	XF	Unc	BU
JE5752-1991(f) Proof	6,575	Value: 30.00				

KM# 226 2 NEW SHEQALIM
28.8000 g., 0.9250 Silver .8565 oz. ASW **Subject:** 44th Anniversary of Independence **Obv:** Value **Rev:** Scales above arched doorway

Date	Mintage	F	VF	XF	Unc	BU
JE5752-1992(p) Proof	4,486	Value: 50.00				

KM# 228 2 NEW SHEQALIM
28.8000 g., 0.9250 Silver .8565 oz. ASW **Subject:** IX Paralympic Games **Obv:** Value to right of menorah flanked by sprigs **Rev:** Shaded star in center of horizontal lines to right and upper left **Rev. Designer:** Abraham Patt

Date	Mintage	F	VF	XF	Unc	BU
JE5752-1992(f) Proof	3,718	Value: 45.00				

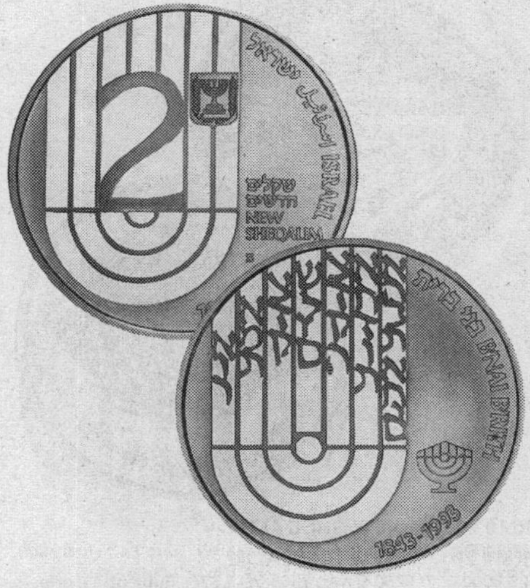

KM# 235 2 NEW SHEQALIM
28.8000 g., 0.9250 Silver .8565 oz. ASW **Obv:** Stylized design with value at center **Rev:** Stylized design with inscription

Date	Mintage	F	VF	XF	Unc	BU
JE5752-1992(f) Proof	4,622	Value: 35.00				

KM# 232 2 NEW SHEQALIM
28.8000 g., 0.9250 Silver .8565 oz. ASW **Series:** Wildlife **Obv:** Value at upper right of lillies **Rev:** Roe deer facing left

Date	Mintage	F	VF	XF	Unc	BU
JE5753-1992(p) Proof	4,724	Value: 45.00				

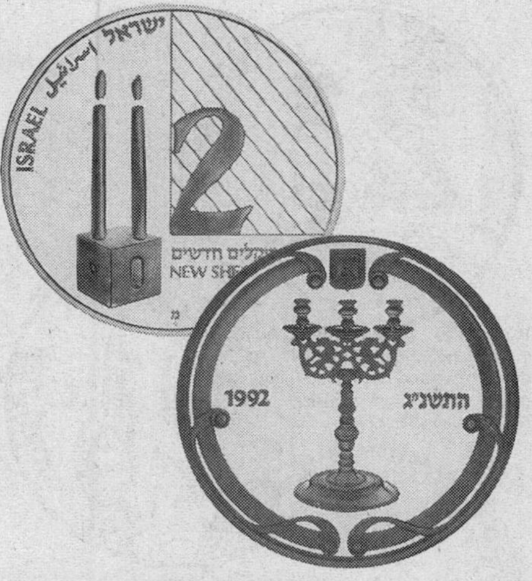

KM# 239 2 NEW SHEQALIM
28.8000 g., 0.9250 Silver .8565 oz. ASW **Series:** Judaic **Obv:** Value at center right within diagonal lines, lit candles on box at lower left **Rev:** Shabbat candles

Date	Mintage	F	VF	XF	Unc	BU
JE5753-1992(p) Proof	4,975	Value: 35.00				

KM# 241 2 NEW SHEQALIM
28.8000 g., 0.9250 Silver .8565 oz. ASW **Subject:** 45th Anniversary of Independence **Obv:** Menorah flanked by sprigs above value and date **Rev:** Tourism objects

Date	Mintage	F	VF	XF	Unc	BU
JE5753-1993(u) Proof	4,570	Value: 40.00				

KM# 245 2 NEW SHEQALIM
28.8000 g., 0.9250 Silver .8565 oz. ASW **Series:** Wildlife **Obv:** Apple tree sprig to lower left of value **Rev:** Buck and young hart deer facing left

Date	Mintage	F	VF	XF	Unc	BU
JE5754-1993(f) Proof	5,382	Value: 40.00				

KM# 248 2 NEW SHEQALIM
28.8000 g., 0.9250 Silver .8565 oz. ASW **Subject:** Revolt and Heroism **Obv:** Diagonal dotted lines with value to upper left **Rev:** Medal with diagonal dotted lines and star to left of flame

Date	Mintage	F	VF	XF	Unc	BU
JE5753-1993(u) Proof	4,994	Value: 38.00				

KM# 257 2 NEW SHEQALIM
28.8000 g., 0.9250 Silver .8565 oz. ASW **Series:** Biblical **Subject:** Abraham's willingness to sacrifice Isaac **Obv:** Value above text to right of menorah flanked by sprigs **Rev:** Stylized figures below angel

Date	Mintage	F	VF	XF	Unc	BU
JE5755-1994(u) Proof	4,439	Value: 55.00				

KM# 268 2 NEW SHEQALIM
28.8000 g., 0.9250 Silver .8565 oz. ASW **Subject:** 50th Anniversary - Defeat of Nazi Germany **Obv:** Value above text to right of menorah flanked by sprigs **Rev:** Shaded v-shape with state emblems within

Date	Mintage	F	VF	XF	Unc	BU
JE5755-1995(h) Proof	5,808	Value: 45.00				

KM# 251 2 NEW SHEQALIM
28.8000 g., 0.9250 Silver .8565 oz. ASW **Series:** Judaic **Obv:** Torah crown to left of value **Rev:** Havdalah spicebox

Date	Mintage	F	VF	XF	Unc	BU
JE5754-1993(f) Proof	4,750	Value: 40.00				

KM# 261 2 NEW SHEQALIM
28.8000 g., 0.9250 Silver .8565 oz. ASW **Subject:** Wildlife **Obv:** Palm tree **Rev:** Leopard

Date	Mintage	F	VF	XF	Unc	BU
JE5755-1994(u) Proof	4,283	Value: 45.00				

KM# 272 2 NEW SHEQALIM
28.8000 g., 0.9250 Silver .8565 oz. ASW **Series:** F.A.O. **Obv:** Barley stalks and value **Rev:** FAO logo and dates

Date	Mintage	F	VF	XF	Unc	BU
JE5755-1995(v) Proof	3,945	Value: 65.00				

KM# 279 2 NEW SHEQALIM
28.8000 g., 0.9250 Silver .8565 oz. ASW **Subject:** Peace Treaty with Jordan **Obv:** Text divides value and state arms **Rev:** Sprig divides text **Designer:** Shimon Keter and David Pesach

Date	Mintage	F	VF	XF	Unc	BU
JE5755-1995(o) Proof	3,536	Value: 45.00				

KM# 282 2 NEW SHEQALIM
28.8000 g., 0.9250 Silver .8565 oz. ASW **Series:** Biblical **Subject:** Solomon's Judgment **Obv:** Value above text **Rev:** Medieval linear design

Date	Mintage	F	VF	XF	Unc	BU
JE5755-1995(f) Proof	2,993	Value: 60.00				

KM# 253 2 NEW SHEQALIM
28.8000 g., 0.9250 Silver .8565 oz. ASW **Subject:** Environment **Rev:** World globe and flower

Date	Mintage	F	VF	XF	Unc	BU
JE5754-1994(f) Proof	4,272	—	—	—	40.00	—

KM# 264 2 NEW SHEQALIM
28.8000 g., 0.9250 Silver .8565 oz. ASW **Subject:** Anniversary - Medicine **Obv:** Snake on a menorah **Rev:** Value, text and menorah flanked by sprigs **Designer:** Eleizer Weishaff

Date	Mintage	F	VF	XF	Unc	BU
JE5755-1995(f) Proof	3,698	Value: 50.00				

KM# 288 2 NEW SHEQALIM
28.8000 g., 0.9250 Silver .8565 oz. ASW **Subject:** Port of Caesarea **Rev:** Ancient ship

Date	Mintage	F	VF	XF	Unc	BU
JE5755-1995(f) Proof	2,560	Value: 45.00				

KM# 276 2 NEW SHEQALIM
28.8000 g., 0.9250 Silver .8565 oz. ASW **Series:** Wildlife **Obv:** Value and grape cluster **Rev:** Fox

Date	Mintage	F	VF	XF	Unc	BU
JE5756-1995 Proof	Est. 4,500	Value: 50.00				
JE5756-1995(v) Proof	3,436	Value: 50.00				

KM# 301 2 NEW SHEQALIM
28.8000 g., 0.9250 Silver .8565 oz. ASW **Subject:** Anniversary - First Zionist Congress Centennial **Obv:** Value **Rev:** Half length figure leaning on rail facing left **Rev. Designer:** Gideon Keich

Date	Mintage	F	VF	XF	Unc	BU
JE5757-1997(u) Proof	4,281	Value: 38.00				

KM# 292 2 NEW SHEQALIM
28.8000 g., 0.9250 Silver .8565 oz. ASW **Subject:** Wildlife **Obv:** Value **Rev:** Nightingale

Date	Mintage	F	VF	XF	Unc	BU
JE5757-1996(v) Proof	2,500	Value: 40.00				

KM# 295 2 NEW SHEQALIM
28.8000 g., 0.9250 Silver .8565 oz. ASW **Subject:** Biblical **Obv:** Value above text, state arms and star design at left **Rev:** Miriam and the women

Date	Mintage	F	VF	XF	Unc	BU
JE5757-1996(u) Proof	2,568	Value: 60.00				

KM# 298 2 NEW SHEQALIM
28.8000 g., 0.9250 Silver .8565 oz. ASW **Obv:** National arms and denomination **Rev:** Head of Yitzhak Rabin left

Date	Mintage	F	VF	XF	Unc	BU
JE5756-1996(u) Proof	5,293	Value: 60.00				

KM# 308 2 NEW SHEQALIM
28.8000 g., 0.9250 Silver .8565 oz. ASW **Subject:** Wildlife **Obv:** Lion walking right **Rev:** Pomegranates at upper left of value

Date	Mintage	F	VF	XF	Unc	BU
JE5758-1997(u) Proof	2,277	Value: 48.00				

KM# 317 2 NEW SHEQALIM
28.8000 g., 0.9250 Silver .8565 oz. ASW **Subject:** Biblical - Noah's Ark **Obv:** Dove, rainbow and value **Rev:** Noah releasing dove

Date	Mintage	F	VF	XF	Unc	BU
JE5758-1998(u) Proof	2,164	Value: 60.00				

KM# 322 2 NEW SHEQALIM
28.8000 g., 0.9250 Silver .8565 oz. ASW **Subject:** Wildlife **Obv:** Fir tree and value **Rev:** Stork

Date	Mintage	F	VF	XF	Unc	BU
JE5759-1998(u) Proof	2,500	Value: 45.00				

KM# 311 2 NEW SHEQALIM
28.8000 g., 0.9250 Silver .8565 oz. ASW **Subject:** 50th Anniversary of Independence **Obv:** Value to right of menorah flanked by sprigs above text **Rev:** Flag within stars

Date	Mintage	F	VF	XF	Unc	BU
JE5758-1998(u) Proof	8,279	Value: 40.00				

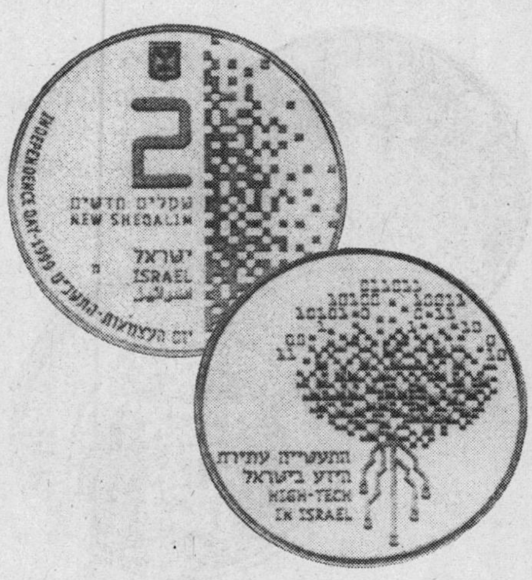

KM# 326 2 NEW SHEQALIM
28.8000 g., 0.9250 Silver .8565 oz. ASW, 38.7 mm. **Subject:** Anniversary - High Tech in Israel **Obv:** Value and 01 computer code **Obv. Designer:** Yigal Gabay **Rev:** 10 computer code as bouquet

Date	Mintage	F	VF	XF	Unc	BU
JE5759-1999 Proof	1,850	Value: 40.00				

KM# 329 2 NEW SHEQALIM
28.8000 g., 0.9250 Silver .8565 oz. ASW **Obv:** Value and olive branch **Rev:** Year 2000 motif incorporating dove with olive branch **Edge Lettering:** The Millennium

Date	Mintage	F	VF	XF	Unc	BU
JE5759-1999(u) Proof	4,092	Value: 40.00				

KM# 334 2 NEW SHEQALIM
28.8000 g., 0.9250 Silver .8565 oz. ASW **Series:** Biblical **Obv:** Menorah, value and date among stars above text **Rev:** Abraham looking at stars

Date	Mintage	F	VF	XF	Unc	BU
JE5759-1999(o) Proof	5,843	Value: 55.00				

KM# 337 2 NEW SHEQALIM
28.8000 g., 0.9250 Silver .8565 oz. ASW, 38.7 mm.
Subject: Anniversary - Independence Day **Obv:** Value **Rev:** Arch above inscription **Rev. Inscription:** Love Thy Neighbor, As Thyself **Edge:** Plain

Date	Mintage	F	VF	XF	Unc	BU
JE5760-2000(u) Proof	2,258	Value: 45.00				

KM# 340 2 NEW SHEQALIM
28.8000 g., 0.9250 Silver .8565 oz. ASW, 38.7 mm. **Subject:** Biblical - Joseph and His Brothers **Obv:** Denomination **Rev:** Joseph standing before sheaves of wheat into brothers **Edge:** Reeded

Date	Mintage	F	VF	XF	Unc	BU
JE5760-2000(u) Proof	2,100	Value: 50.00				

KM# 349 2 NEW SHEQALIM
28.8000 g., 0.9250 Silver .8564 oz. ASW, 38.7 mm.
Subject: Wildlife **Obv:** Acacia tree **Rev:** Ibex **Edge:** Reeded

Date	Mintage	F	VF	XF	Unc	BU
JE5760-2000(u) Proof	2,000	Value: 45.00				

KM# 170 5 NEW SHEQALIM
8.6300 g., 0.9000 Gold .2497 oz. AGW **Series:** Holyland Sites **Rev:** Akko **Shape:** 12-sided

Date	Mintage	F	VF	XF	Unc	BU
JE5747-1986(b) Proof	2,800	Value: 250				

KM# 182 5 NEW SHEQALIM
8.6300 g., 0.9000 Gold .2497 oz. AGW **Series:** Holyland Sites **Obv:** Value **Rev:** Jericho to left of menorah and palm trees **Shape:** 12-sided

Date	Mintage	F	VF	XF	Unc	BU
JE5748-1987(o) Proof	4,000	Value: 225				

KM# 190 5 NEW SHEQALIM
8.6300 g., 0.9000 Gold .2497 oz. AGW **Series:** Holyland Sites **Obv:** Value **Rev:** Caesarea **Shape:** 12-sided

Date	Mintage	F	VF	XF	Unc	BU
JE5749-1988(o) Proof	3,454	Value: 235				

KM# 204 5 NEW SHEQALIM
8.6300 g., 0.9000 Gold .2497 oz. AGW **Series:** Holyland Sites **Obv:** Value **Rev:** Jaffa Harbor **Shape:** 12-sided

Date	Mintage	F	VF	XF	Unc	BU
JE5750-1989(o) Proof	2,402	Value: 275				

KM# 207 5 NEW SHEQALIM
Copper-Nickel, 24 mm. **Obv:** Value **Rev:** Ancient column **Shape:** 12-sided

Date	Mintage	F	VF	XF	Unc	BU
JE5750 (1990)(f)	15,000,000	—	—	—	3.75	—
JE5751 (1991)(j)	324,000	—	—	3.00	5.00	—
JE5752 (1992)(j)	413,000	—	—	3.00	5.00	—
JE5754 (1994)(v)	2,016,000	—	—	—	3.75	—
JE5755 (1995)(v)	2,160,000	—	—	—	3.75	—
JE5757 (1997)(u)	2,160,000	—	—	—	3.75	—
JE5757 (1997)(v)	2,160,000	—	—	—	3.75	—
JE5758 (1998)(h)	2,160,000	—	—	—	3.75	—
JE5759 (1999)(h)	2,160,000	—	—	—	3.75	—
JE5759 (1999)(u)	2,160,000	—	—	—	3.75	—
JE5760 (2000)(v)	4,464,000	—	—	—	3.75	—

KM# 208 5 NEW SHEQALIM
Copper-Nickel, 24 mm. **Obv:** Value **Rev:** Bust facing

Date	Mintage	F	VF	XF	Unc	BU
JE5750 (1990)(f)	1,500,000	—	—	2.50	5.00	—

KM# 211 5 NEW SHEQALIM
8.6300 g., 0.9000 Gold .2497 oz. AGW **Series:** Holyland Sites **Obv:** Value **Rev:** Sea of Galilee map

Date	Mintage	F	VF	XF	Unc	BU
JE5751-1990(o) Proof	1,935	Value: 375				

KM# 222 5 NEW SHEQALIM
8.6300 g., 0.9000 Gold .2497 oz. AGW **Subject:** Wildlife **Obv:** Cedar trees and value **Rev:** Dove and tree trunk within legend

Date	Mintage	F	VF	XF	Unc	BU
JE5752-1991(o) Proof	2,000	Value: 300				

KM# 217 5 NEW SHEQALIM
Copper-Nickel, 24 mm. **Obv:** Value **Rev:** Ancient column
Note: Coins dated JE5754-5760 have the Star of David mint mark; the JE5751-5753 coins do not.

Date	Mintage	F	VF	XF	Unc	BU
JE5751 (1991)(j)	500,000	—	—	2.00	4.00	—
JE5751 (1991)	—	—	—	—	3.75	—
JE5752 (1992)(j)	486,000	—	—	2.00	4.00	—
JE5753 (1993)(j)	500,000	—	—	2.00	4.00	—

Date	Mintage	F	VF	XF	Unc	BU
JE5754 (1994)(u)	12,000	—	—	—	4.00	—
Note: In sets only						
JE5755 (1995)(u)	10,000	—	—	—	4.00	—
Note: In sets only						
JE5756 (1996)(u)	7,500	—	—	—	4.00	—
Note: In sets only						
JE5757 (1997)(u)	7,500	—	—	—	4.00	—
Note: In sets only						
JE5758 (1998)(u)	10,000	—	—	—	4.00	—
Note: In sets only						
JE5759 (1999)(u)	6,000	—	—	—	5.00	—
Note: In sets only						
JE5760 (2000)(u)	5,000	—	—	—	5.00	—
Note: In sets only						
JE5761 (2001)	4,000	—	—	—	3.75	—
Note: In sets only						

KM# 229 5 NEW SHEQALIM
8.6300 g., 0.9000 Gold .2497 oz. AGW **Subject:** IX Paralympic Games **Obv:** Value at center with half horizontal lines at right **Rev:** Shaded star within horizontal lines **Designer:** Abraham Patt

Date	Mintage	F	VF	XF	Unc	BU
JE5752-1992(u) Proof	1,629	Value: 425				

KM# 236 5 NEW SHEQALIM
8.6300 g., 0.9000 Gold .2497 oz. AGW **Subject:** B'nai B'rith **Obv:** Stylized design with value at upper left **Rev:** Stylized design with inscription

Date	Mintage	F	VF	XF	Unc	BU
JE5753-1992(u) Proof	2,305	Value: 325				

KM# 233 5 NEW SHEQALIM
8.6300 g., 0.9000 Gold .2497 oz. AGW **Series:** Wildlife **Obv:** Value at upper right of lily **Rev:** Roe deer facing left

Date	Mintage	F	VF	XF	Unc	BU
JE5753-1992(p) Proof	2,150	Value: 275				

KM# 246 5 NEW SHEQALIM
8.6300 g., 0.9000 Gold .2497 oz. AGW **Series:** Wildlife **Obv:** Value at upper right of apple tree sprig **Rev:** Buck and young hart

Date	Mintage	F	VF	XF	Unc	BU
JE5754-1993(u) Proof	1,782	Value: 275				

KM# 237 5 NEW SHEQALIM
Copper-Nickel **Obv:** Value **Rev:** Bust facing

Date	Mintage	F	VF	XF	Unc	BU
JE5753 (1993)(j)	1,500,000	—	—	—	5.00	—

KM# 254 5 NEW SHEQALIM
8.6300 g., 0.9000 Gold .2497 oz. AGW **Series:** Independence Day **Subject:** Environment **Obv:** Value **Rev:** World globe within flower

Date	Mintage	F	VF	XF	Unc	BU
JE5754-1994(sa) Proof	1,407	Value: 275				

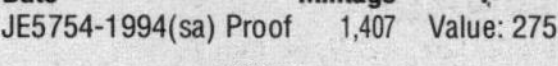

KM# 262 5 NEW SHEQALIM
8.6300 g., 0.9000 Gold .2497 oz. AGW **Subject:** Wildlife **Obv:** Palm tree and value **Rev:** Leopard

Date	Mintage	F	VF	XF	Unc	BU
JE5755-1994(o) Proof	1,355	Value: 300				

KM# 265 5 NEW SHEQALIM
8.6300 g., 0.9000 Gold .2497 oz. AGW **Series:** Independence Day **Subject:** Anniversary - Medicine **Obv:** Snake on a menorah **Rev:** Value **Designer:** Eliezer Weishoff

Date	Mintage	F	VF	XF	Unc	BU
JE5755-1995(o) Proof	1,147	Value: 325				

KM# 277 5 NEW SHEQALIM
8.6300 g., 0.9000 Gold .2497 oz. AGW **Subject:** Wildlife **Obv:** Value and grape cluster **Rev:** Fox

Date	Mintage	F	VF	XF	Unc	BU
JE5756-1995(u) Proof	872	Value: 350				

KM# 293 5 NEW SHEQALIM
8.6300 g., 0.9000 Gold .2497 oz. AGW **Subject:** Wildlife **Obv:** Fig leaves and value **Rev:** Nightingale

Date	Mintage	F	VF	XF	Unc	BU
JE5757-1996(v) Proof	805	Value: 425				

KM# 309 5 NEW SHEQALIM
8.6300 g., 0.9000 Gold .2497 oz. AGW **Subject:** Wildlife **Obv:** Pomegranates and value **Rev:** Lion walking right

Date	Mintage	F	VF	XF	Unc	BU
JE5758-1997(u) Proof	742	Value: 375				

KM# 323 5 NEW SHEQALIM
8.6300 g., 0.9000 Gold .2497 oz. AGW **Subject:** Wildlife **Obv:** Fir trees and value **Rev:** Stork

Date	Mintage	F	VF	XF	Unc	BU
JE5759-1998(u) Proof	615	Value: 400				

KM# 166 10 NEW SHEQALIM
17.2800 g., 0.9000 Gold .5000 oz. AGW **Subject:** 38th Anniversary of Independence **Obv:** Value **Rev:** Styilized designs **Designer:** Asaaf Berg and Tidhar Dagan

Date	Mintage	F	VF	XF	Unc	BU
JE5746-1986(d) Proof	2,485	Value: 425				

KM# 179 10 NEW SHEQALIM
17.2800 g., 0.9000 Gold .5000 oz. AGW **Subject:** 39th Anniversary - United Jerusalem

Date	Mintage	F	VF	XF	Unc	BU
JE5747-1987(p) Proof	3,200	Value: 375				

KM# 187 10 NEW SHEQALIM
17.2800 g., 0.9000 Gold .5000 oz. AGW **Subject:** 40th Anniversary of Independence **Obv:** Menorah within stylized value **Obv. Designer:** Asher Kalderon **Rev:** Stylized figures of government within large numeral 40 **Rev. Designer:** Ruben Nutels

Date	Mintage	F	VF	XF	Unc	BU
JE5748-1988(m) Proof	4,575	Value: 400				

KM# 201 10 NEW SHEQALIM
17.2800 g., 0.9000 Gold .5000 oz. AGW **Subject:** 41st Anniversary of Independence **Rev:** Gazelle in forest, legend at left

Date	Mintage	F	VF	XF	Unc	BU
JE5749-1989(o) Proof	2,743	Value: 400				

KM# 214 10 NEW SHEQALIM
17.2800 g., 0.9000 Gold .5000 oz. AGW **Subject:** 42nd Anniversary of Independence **Obv:** Menorah to left of large linear value **Obv. Designer:** Ruben Nutels **Rev:** Archaeology **Rev. Designer:** Ehud Shafrir

Date	Mintage	F	VF	XF	Unc	BU
JE5750-1990(p) Proof	1,815	Value: 650				

KM# 230 10 NEW SHEQALIM
17.2800 g., 0.9000 Gold .5000 oz. AGW **Subject:** 43rd Anniversary of Independence **Obv:** Value within shaded diagonal lines **Rev:** Plane above stylized standing figures

Date	Mintage	F	VF	XF	Unc	BU
JE5751-1991 Proof	2,236	Value: 475				

KM# 227 10 NEW SHEQALIM
17.2800 g., 0.9000 Gold .5000 oz. AGW **Subject:** 44th Anniversary of Independence **Obv:** Value **Rev:** Scales above arched doorway **Note:** Edge varieties exist.

Date	Mintage	F	VF	XF	Unc	BU
JE5752-1992 Proof	1,750	Value: 675				

Note: Struck at the Monnaie de Paris with narrow spaced edge reeding

Date	Mintage	F	VF	XF	Unc	BU
JE5752-1992 Proof	375	Value: 2,000				

Note: Struck at the Utrecht Mint with wide spaced edge reeding

KM# 242 10 NEW SHEQALIM
17.2800 g., 0.9000 Gold .5000 oz. AGW **Series:** Independence Day **Subject:** Tourism **Obv:** Value **Rev:** Tourism objects

Date	Mintage	F	VF	XF	Unc	BU
JE5753-1993(u) Proof	1,944	Value: 450				

KM# 249 10 NEW SHEQALIM
17.2800 g., 0.9000 Gold .5000 oz. AGW **Subject:** Revolt and Heroism **Obv:** Value within beaded diagonal lines **Rev:** Medal with star within beaded diagonal lines to left of flame

Date	Mintage	F	VF	XF	Unc	BU
JE5753-1993(u) Proof	1,583	Value: 450				

KM# 255 10 NEW SHEQALIM
17.2800 g., 0.9000 Gold .5000 oz. AGW **Series:** Independence Day **Subject:** Environment **Obv:** Slanted value **Rev:** World globe within flower

Date	Mintage	F	VF	XF	Unc	BU
JE5754-1994(sa) Proof	1,482	Value: 550				

KM# 258 10 NEW SHEQALIM
17.2800 g., 0.9000 Gold .5000 oz. AGW **Subject:** Biblical **Rev:** Abraham's willingness to sacrifice Isaac

Date	Mintage	F	VF	XF	Unc	BU
JE5755-1994(o) Proof	1,209	Value: 650				

KM# 266 10 NEW SHEQALIM
17.2800 g., 0.9000 Gold .5000 oz. AGW **Series:** Independence Day **Subject:** Anniversary - Medicine **Obv:** Value **Rev:** Snake on a menorah **Designer:** Eleizer Weishoff

Date	Mintage	F	VF	XF	Unc	BU
JE5755-1995(o) Proof	1,230	Value: 550				

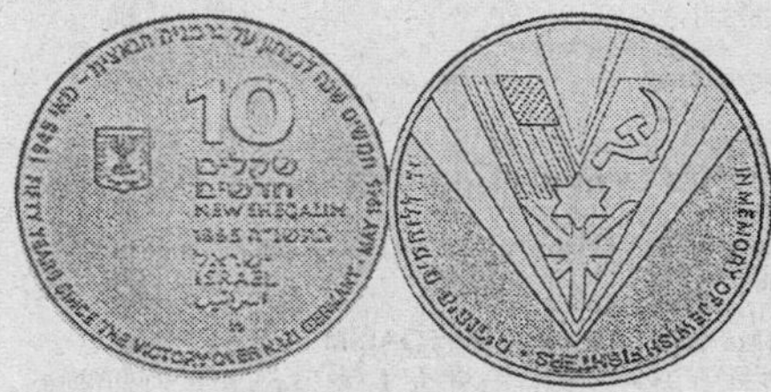

KM# 269 10 NEW SHEQALIM
16.9600 g., 0.9170 Gold .4998 oz. AGW **Subject:** 50th Anniversary - Defeat of Nazi Germany **Obv:** Value above text to right of menorah flanked by sprigs **Rev:** Flag and emblems within v-shaped design

Date	Mintage	F	VF	XF	Unc	BU
JE5755-1995(h) Proof	1,742	Value: 550				

KM# 270 10 NEW SHEQALIM
Bi-Metallic Aureate bonded Bronze center in Nickel bonded Steel ring, 22.5 mm. **Obv:** Value, vertical lines and text within circle **Rev:** Palm tree and baskets within half beaded circle

Date	Mintage	F	VF	XF	Unc	BU
JE5755 (1995)	28,224,000	—	—	—	5.00	—

KM# 273 10 NEW SHEQALIM
Bi-Metallic Aureate bonded Bronze center in Nickel bonded Steel ring, 22.5 mm. **Obv:** Value, text and vertical lines within circle **Rev:** Bust facing at right within vertical lines and circle

Date	Mintage	F	VF	XF	Unc	BU
JE5755 (1995)(u)	1,584,000	—	—	—	10.00	—

KM# 280 10 NEW SHEQALIM
16.9600 g., 0.9170 Gold .4998 oz. AGW **Subject:** Peace Treaty with Jordan **Designer:** Shimon Keter and David Pesach

Date	Mintage	F	VF	XF	Unc	BU
JE5755-1995(o) Proof	1,451	Value: 495				

KM# 283 10 NEW SHEQALIM
17.2800 g., 0.9000 Gold .5000 oz. AGW **Subject:** Biblical - Solomon's Judgment **Obv:** Value above text **Rev:** Medieval linear design

Date	Mintage	F	VF	XF	Unc	BU
JE5756-1995(o) Proof	961	Value: 650				

KM# 289 10 NEW SHEQALIM
16.9600 g., 0.9170 Gold .4998 oz. AGW **Obv:** Anchor to lower left of value and text **Rev:** Port of Caesarea, ancient ship

Date	Mintage	F	VF	XF	Unc	BU
JE5755-1995(o) Proof	927	Value: 650				

KM# 315 10 NEW SHEQALIM
Bi-Metallic Aureate bonded Bronze center in Nickel bonded Steel ring, 22.5 mm. **Subject:** Hanukkah **Obv:** Value, text and menorah within circle and vertical lines **Rev:** Palm tree and baskets within half beaded circle

Date	Mintage	F	VF	XF	Unc	BU
JE5756 (1996)(u)	7,500	—	—	—	7.00	—
Note: In sets only						
JE5757 (1997)(u)	7,500	—	—	—	7.00	—
Note: In sets only						
JE5758 (1998)(u)	10,000	—	—	—	7.00	—
Note: In sets only						
JE5759 (1999)(u)	6,000	—	—	—	8.00	—
Note: In sets only						
JE5760 (2000)(u)	5,000	—	—	—	9.00	—
Note: In sets only						

KM# 285 10 NEW SHEQALIM
16.9600 g., 0.9170 Gold .4998 oz. AGW **Subject:** Anniversary - Jerusalem's Third Millennium **Obv:** State arms left of large value **Rev:** Inscription at center

Date	Mintage	F	VF	XF	Unc	BU
JE5756-1996(sa) Proof	1,642	Value: 675				

KM# 296 10 NEW SHEQALIM
17.2800 g., 0.9000 Gold .5000 oz. AGW **Subject:** Biblical **Obv:** Value above text, state arms and star design at left **Rev:** Miriam and the women

Date	Mintage	F	VF	XF	Unc	BU
JE5757-1996(u) Proof	855	Value: 725				

KM# 302 10 NEW SHEQALIM
17.2800 g., 0.9000 Gold .5000 oz. AGW **Subject:** Anniversary - First Zionist Congress Centennial **Obv:** Denomination **Rev:** Portrait of Herzl **Rev. Designer:** Gideon Keitch

Date	Mintage	F	VF	XF	Unc	BU
JE5757-1997(u) Proof	1,326	Value: 495				

KM# 312 10 NEW SHEQALIM
15.5500 g., 0.9990 Gold .4994 oz. AGW **Subject:** 50th Anniversary of Independence **Obv:** Value **Rev:** Flag

Date	Mintage	F	VF	XF	Unc	BU
JE5758-1998(u) Proof	2,406	Value: 495				

KM# 319 10 NEW SHEQALIM
17.2800 g., 0.9000 Gold .5000 oz. AGW **Subject:** Biblical - Noah's Ark **Obv:** Rainbow, dove and value **Rev:** Noah releasing dove from ark

Date	Mintage	F	VF	XF	Unc	BU
JE5758-1998(u) Proof	744	Value: 750				

KM# 327 10 NEW SHEQALIM
16.9600 g., 0.9170 Gold .5000 oz. AGW, 30 mm. **Subject:** Anniversary - High-Tech in Israel **Obv:** Value and 01 computer code **Rev:** 01 computer code as bouquet **Designer:** Yigal Gabay

Date	Mintage	F	VF	XF	Unc	BU
JE5759-1999(u) Proof	751	Value: 750				

KM# 330 10 NEW SHEQALIM
16.9600 g., 0.9170 Gold .5000 oz. AGW **Subject:** The Millennium Coin **Obv:** Value and olive branch **Rev:** Year 2000 motif incorporating dove with olive branch

Date	Mintage	F	VF	XF	Unc	BU
JE5759-1999(u) Proof	1,859	Value: 475				

KM# 338 10 NEW SHEQALIM
16.9600 g., 0.9170 Gold .5000 oz. AGW **Subject:** Anniversary - Independence Day **Obv:** Value **Rev:** Arch above inscription **Rev. Inscription:** Love Thy Neighbor, As Thyself **Edge:** Reeded

Date	Mintage	F	VF	XF	Unc	BU
JE5760-2000(u) Proof	794	Value: 725				

KM# 341 10 NEW SHEQALIM
16.9600 g., 0.9170 Gold .5000 oz. AGW, 30 mm. **Series:** Biblical **Obv:** Value **Rev:** Joseph standing before sheaves of wheat into his brothers **Edge:** Reeded

Date	Mintage	F	VF	XF	Unc	BU
JE5760-2000(u) Proof	700	Value: 695				

KM# 299 20 NEW SHEQALIM
31.1035 g., 0.9990 Gold 1.0000 oz. AGW **Obv:** Menorah flanked by sprigs above text, value and date **Rev:** Head left

Date	Mintage	F	VF	XF	Unc	BU
JE5757-1996(va) Proof	1,949	Value: 975				

KM# 313 20 NEW SHEQALIM
31.1035 g., 0.9990 Gold 1.0000 oz. AGW **Subject:** 50th Anniversary of Independence **Obv:** Value **Rev:** Flag

Date	Mintage	F	VF	XF	Unc	BU
JE5758-1998(u) Proof	2,345	Value: 1,000				

KM# 286 30 NEW SHEQALIM
155.5175 g., 0.9990 Silver 5.0000 oz. ASW, 65 mm. **Subject:** Anniversary - Jerusalem's Third Millennium **Obv:** State arms left of value **Rev:** Inscription at center **Note:** Photo reduced.

Date	Mintage	F	VF	XF	Unc	BU
JE5756-1996(f) Proof	2,929	Value: 185				

PATTERNS

KM#	Date	Mintage	Identification	Mkt Val
Pn1	1960	2	Agora. 8 fat and wide grains. Large 9.50mm 1 and date.	7,500
Pn2	1960	4	Agora. 8 thin and narrow grains. Small 9.00mm 1 and large date.	7,500
Pn3	1960	1	Agora. 8 thin and narrow grains. Large 9.50mm 1 and date.	—
Pn4	1960	1	Agora. Aluminum. 8 fate and wide grains. Small 9 mm 1. Struck as coin turn.	6,000
Pn5	JE5722-1962	3	Lira. Copper-Nickel. As KM#38 but mis-spelling of Hanukka in Hebrew. Letter "Nun" instead of "Kof"	2,500

PIEFORTS

KM#	Date	Mintage	Identification	Mkt Val
P1	JE5741 (1981)	30,217	New Agora. Copper-Nickel. KM106.	2.00
P2	JE5741 (1981)	30,217	5 New Agorot. Copper-Nickel. KM107.	2.00
P3	JE5741 (1981)	30,217	10 New Agorot. Bronze. KM108.	2.50
P4	JE5741 (1981)	30,217	1/2 Sheqel. Copper-Nickel. KM109.	2.50
P5	JE5741 (1981)	30,217	Sheqel. Copper-Nickel. KM111.	3.50

Note: P1-5 were struck at the Bern Mint

KM#	Date	Mintage	Identification	Mkt Val
P6	JE5742 (1982)	18,735	New Agora. Copper-Nickel. KM106	2.00
P7	JE5742 (1982)	19,735	5 New Agorot. Copper-Nickel. KM107.	2.00
P8	JE5742 (1982)	18,735	10 New Agorot. Bronze. KM108.	2.50
P9	JE5742 (1982)	21,735	1/2 Sheqel. Copper-Nickel. KM109.	2.50
P10	JE5742 (1982)	19,735	Sheqel. Copper-Nickel. KM111.	3.00
P11	JE5742 (1982)	20,735	5 Sheqalim. Aluminum-Bronze. KM118.	3.50
P12	JE5743 (1983)	17,177	New Agora. Copper-Nickel. 4.2000 g. 15 mm. Plain edge. KM#106.	1.00
P13	JE5743 (1983)	17,177	5 New Agorot. Copper-Nickel. 6.3000 g. 18.5 mm. Plain edge. KM#107.	1.50
P14	JE5743 (1983)	17,177	10 New Agorot. Bronze. KM108.	1.50
P15	JE5743 (1983)	17,177	1/2 Sheqel. Copper-Nickel. KM109.	2.00
P16	JE5743 (1983)	17,177	Sheqel. Copper-Nickel. KM111.	2.00
P17	JE5743 (1983)	17,177	5 Sheqalim. Aluminum-Bronze. KM118.	2.50
P18	JE5743 (1983)	17,177	10 Sheqalim. Copper-Nickel. KM119.	3.00
P19	JE5744 (1984)	15,572	Agora. Copper-Nickel. 4.2000 g. 15 mm. Plain edge. KM#107.	1.00
P20	JE5744 (1984)	15,572	5 New Agorot. Copper-Nickel. 6.3000 g. 18.5 mm. Plain edge. KM#107.	1.50
P21	JE5744 (1984)	15,572	10 New Agorot. Bronze. KM108.	1.50
P22	JE5744 (1984)	15,572	1/2 Sheqel. Copper-Nickel. KM109.	2.00
P23	JE5744 (1984)	15,572	Sheqel. Copper-Nickel. KM111.	2.00
P24	JE5744 (1984)	15,572	5 Sheqalim. Aluminum-Bronze. KM118.	2.50
P25	JE5744 (1984)	15,572	10 Sheqalim. Copper-Nickel. KM119.	3.00

Note: P6-25 were struck at the Rome Mint

KM#	Date	Mintage	Identification	Mkt Val
P26	JE5745 (1985)	14,768	Sheqel. Copper-Nickel. KM111.	2.00
P27	JE5745 (1985)	14,768	5 Sheqalim. Aluminum-Bronze. KM118.	2.00
P28	JE5745 (1985)	14,768	10 Sheqalim. Copper-Nickel. KM119.	2.50
P29	JE5745 (1985)	14,768	50 Sheqalim. Aluminum-Bronze. KM139.	3.00
P30	JE5745 (1985)	14,768	100 Sheqalim. Copper-Nickel. KM143.	3.50

Note: P26-30 were struck at the Bern Mint

KM#	Date	Mintage	Identification	Mkt Val
P31	JE5746 (1986)	12,665	Agora. Aluminum-Bronze. KM156.	2.00
P32	JE5746 (1986)	12,665	5 Agorot. Aluminum-Bronze. KM157.	3.00
P33	JE5746 (1986)	12,665	10 Agorot. Aluminum-Bronze. KM158.	4.00
P34	JE5746 (1986)	12,665	1/2 New Sheqel. Aluminum-Bronze. KM159.	5.00
P35	JE5746 (1986)	12,665	New Sheqel. Copper-Nickel. KM160.	6.00

Note: P31-35 were struck at the Paris Mint

KM#	Date	Mintage	Identification	Mkt Val
P36	JE5747 (1987)	11,529	Agora. Aluminum-Bronze center. KM156.	2.00
P37	JE5747 (1987)	11,529	5 Agorot. Aluminum-Bronze. KM157.	3.00
P38	JE5747 (1987)	11,529	10 Agorot. Aluminum-Bronze. KM158.	4.00
P39	JE5747 (1987)	11,529	1/2 New Sheqel. Aluminum-Bronze. KM159.	5.00
P40	JE5747 (1987)	11,529	New Sheqel. Copper-Nickel. KM160.	6.00
P41	JE5748 (1988)	12,027	5 Agorot. Nickel. KM194.	3.50
PA41	JE5748 (1988)	12,027	Agora. Aluminum-Bronze center. KM193.	2.50
P42	JE5748 (1988)	12,027	10 Agorot. Nickel. KM195.	4.50
P43	JE5748 (1988)	12,027	1/2 New Sheqel. Nickel. KM196.	5.50
P44	JE5748 (1988)	12,027	New Sheqel. Nickel. KM197.	6.00

Note: P36-44 were struck at the Stuttgart Mint

KM#	Date	Mintage	Identification	Mkt Val
P45	JE5749 (1989)	9,622	Agora. Nickel. KM156.	2.00
P46	JE5749 (1989)	9,622	5 Agorot. Aluminum-Bronze. KM157.	3.00
P47	JE5749 (1989)	9,622	10 Agorot. Aluminum-Bronze. KM158.	4.00
P48	JE5749 (1989)	9,622	1/2 New Sheqel. Aluminum-Bronze. KM159.	5.00
P49	JE5749 (1989)	9,622	New Sheqel. Copper-Nickel. KM160.	6.00
P50	JE5750 (1990)	—	Agora. Bronze. KM156.	2.00
P51	JE5750 (1990)	—	5 Agorot. Bronze. KM157.	3.00
P52	JE5750 (1990)	—	10 Agorot. Bronze. KM158.	4.00
P53	JE5750 (1990)	—	1/2 New Sheqel. Bronze. KM159.	5.00
P54	JE5750 (1990)	—	New Sheqel. Copper-Nickel. KM160.	5.00
P55	JE5750 (1990)	—	5 New Sheqalim. Copper-Nickel. KM207.	6.00

Note: P45-55 were struck at the Stuttgart mint.

KM#	Date	Mintage	Identification	Mkt Val
P56	JE5751 (1991)	—	Agora. Aluminum-Bronze. KM156.	2.00
P57	JE5751 (1991)	—	5 Agorot. Aluminum-Bronze. KM157.	3.00
P58	JE5751 (1991)	—	10 Agorot. Aluminum-Bronze. KM158.	4.00
P59	JE5751 (1991)	—	1/2 New Sheqel. Aluminum-Bronze. KM159.	5.00
P60	JE5751 (1991)	—	New Sheqel. Copper-Nickel. KM160.	6.00
P61	JE5751 (1991)	—	5 New Sheqalim. Copper-Nickel. KM207.	6.00
P62	JE5752 (1992)	—	Agora. Aluminum-Bronze. KM156.	2.00
P63	JE5752 (1992)	—	5 Agorot. Aluminum-Bronze. KM157.	3.00
P64	JE5752 (1992)	—	10 Agorot. Aluminum-Bronze. KM158.	4.00
P65	JE5752 (1992)	—	1/2 New Sheqel. Aluminum-Bronze. KM159.	5.00
P66	JE5752 (1992)	—	New Sheqel. Copper-Nickel. KM160.	6.00
P67	JE5752 (1992)	—	5 New Sheqalim. Copper-Nickel. KM207.	6.00
P68	JE5753 (1993)	8,000	Agora. Aluminum-Bronze. KM156.	2.00
P69	JE5753 (1993)	8,000	5 Agorot. Aluminum-Bronze center. KM157.	3.00
P70	JE5753 (1993)	8,000	10 Agorot. Aluminum-Bronze. KM158.	4.00
P71	JE5753 (1993)	8,000	1/2 New Sheqel. Aluminum-Bronze. KM159.	5.00
P72	JE5753 (1993)	8,000	New Sheqel. Copper-Nickel. KM160.	6.00
P73	JE5753 (1993)	8,000	5 New Sheqalim. Silver. KM207.	6.00
P74	JE5754 (1994)	8,000	Agora. Aluminum-Bronze. KM156.	3.00
P75	JE5754 (1994)	8,000	5 Agorot. Aluminum-Bronze. KM157.	4.00
P76	JE5754 (1994)	8,000	10 Agorot. Aluminum-Bronze. KM158.	5.00
P77	JE5754 (1994)	8,000	1/2 New Sheqel. Aluminum-Bronze. KM159.	6.00
P78	JE5754 (1994)	8,000	1/2 New Sheqel. Copper-Aluminum-Nickel. 14.5000 g. 26 mm. Value. Flower. Plain edge. KM#368.	10.00
P79	JE5754 (1994)	8,000	New Sheqel. Copper-Nickel. KM160.	7.00
P80	JE5754 (1994)	8,000	5 New Sheqalim. Copper-Nickel. KM207.	9.00
P81	JE5755 (1995)	8,000	Agora. Aluminum-Bronze. KM156.	2.00
P82	JE5755 (1995)	8,000	5 Agorot. Aluminum-Bronze. KM157.	3.00
P83	JE5755 (1995)	8,000	10 Agorot. Aluminum-Bronze. KM158.	4.00
P84	JE5755 (1995)	8,000	1/2 New Sheqel. Aluminum-Bronze. KM159.	5.00
P85	JE5755 (1995)	8,000	1/2 New Sheqel. Copper-Aluminum-Nickel. 14.5000 g. 26 mm. Value. Medical symbols. Plain edge. KM#392.	10.00
P86	JE5755 (1995)	8,000	New Sheqel. Copper-Nickel. KM160.	6.00
P87	JE5755 (1995)	8,000	5 New Sheqalim. Copper-Nickel. KM207.	8.00
P88	JE5755 (1995)	8,000	10 New Sheqalim. Bi-Metallic. KM270.	12.00

Note: P56-88 were struck at the Utrecht mint

KM#	Date	Mintage	Identification	Mkt Val
P89	JE5756 (1996)	8,000	Agora. Aluminum-Bronze. KM#156.	2.00
P90	JE5756 (1996)	8,000	5 Agorot. Aluminum-Bronze. KM#157	3.00
P91	JE5756 (1996)	8,000	10 Agorot. Aluminum-Bronze. KM#158.	4.00
P92	JE5756 (1996)	8,000	1/2 New Sheqel. Aluminum-Bronze. KM#159.	5.00
P93	JE5756 (1996)	8,000	1/2 New Sheqel. Copper-Aluminum-Nickel. 14.5000 g. 26 mm. Value. Hebrew inscription. Plain edge. KM#393.	10.00
P94	JE5756 (1996)	8,000	New Sheqel. Copper-Nickel. KM#160.	6.00
P95	JE5756 (1996)	8,000	5 New Sheqalim. Copper-Nickel. KM#217.	8.00
P96	JE5756 (1996)	8,000	10 New Sheqalim. Bi-Metallic. KM#270.	12.00
P97	JE5757 (1997)	6,000	Agora. Aluminum-Bronze. KM#156	2.00
P98	JE5757 (1997)	6,000	5 Agorot. Aluminum-Bronze. KM#157.	3.00
P99	JE5757 (1997)	6,000	10 Agorot. Aluminum-Bronze. KM#158.	4.00
P100	JE5757 (1997)	6,000	1/2 New Sheqel. Aluminum-Bronze. KM#159.	5.00
P101	JE5757-(1997)	6,000	1/2 New Sheqel. Aluminum-Bronze. KM#394.	12.00
P102	JE5757 (1997)	6,000	New Sheqel. Aluminum-Bronze. KM#160.	6.00
P103	JE5757 (1997)	6,000	5 New Sheqalim. Copper-Nickel. KM#207.	8.00
P104	JE5757 (1997)	6,000	10 New Sheqalim. Copper-Nickel. KM#270.	12.00
P105	JE5758 (1998)	8,000	Agora. Aluminum-Bronze. KM#156.	2.00
P106	JE5758 (1998)	8,000	5 Agorot. Aluminum-Bronze. KM#157.	3.00
P107	JE5758 (1998)	8,000	10 Agorot. Aluminum-Bronze. KM#158.	4.00
P108	JE5758 (1998)	8,000	1/2 New Sheqel. Aluminum-Bronze. KM#159.	5.00
P109	JE5758 (1998)	8,000	1/2 New Sheqel. Copper-Aluminum-Nickel. 14.3300 g. 26.3 mm. Value. Flag and stars. Plain edge. KM#395.	10.00
P110	JE5758 (1998)	8,000	New Sheqel. Copper-Nickel. KM#160.	6.00
P111	JE5758 (1998)	8,000	5 New Sheqalim. Copper-Nickel. KM#207.	8.00
P112	JE5758 (1998)	8,000	10 New Sheqalim. Bi-Metallic. KM#270.	12.00
P113	JE5759 (1999)	6,000	Agora. Aluminum-Bronze. KM#156.	2.00
P114	JE5759 (1999)	6,000	5 Agorot. Aluminum-Bronze. KM#157.	3.00
P115	JE5759 (1999)	6,000	10 Agorot. Aluminum-Bronze. KM#158.	4.00
P116	JE5759 (1999)	6,000	1/2 New Sheqel. Aluminum-Bronze. KM#159.	5.00
P117	JE5759 (1999)	6,000	1/2 New Sheqel. Bronze. High Tech KM#324.	12.00
P118	JE5759 (1999)	6,000	New Sheqel. Nickel Clad Steel. KM#160a	6.00
P119	JE5759 (1999)	6,000	5 New Sheqalim. Copper-Nickel. KM#207.	8.00
P120	JE5759 (1999)	6,000	10 New Sheqalim. Bi-Metallic. KM#270.	12.00

Note: P89-120 were struck in Oslo and Utrecht mints.

KM#	Date	Mintage	Identification	Mkt Val
P121	JE5760 (2000)	4,000	Agora. Aluminum-Bronze. 4.2300 g. 16.9 mm. Plain edge. KM#156.	2.00
P122	JE5760 (2000)	4,000	5 Agorot. Aluminum-Bronze. 6.3100 g. 19.4 mm. Plain edge. KM#157.	3.00
P123	JE5760 (2000)	4,000	10 Agorot. Aluminum-Bronze. 8.6000 g. 21.9 mm. Plain edge. KM#158.	4.00
P124	JE5760 (2000)	4,000	1/2 New Sheqel. Aluminum-Bronze. 14.1000 g. 26 mm. Plain edge. KM#159.	5.00
P125	JE5760 (2000)	4,000	1/2 New Sheqel. Aluminum-Bronze. 14.3200 g. 25.85 mm. Plain edge. KM#363.	12.00
P126	JE5760 (2000)	4,000	New Sheqel. Copper-Nickel. 8.3000 g. 18 mm. Plain edge. KM#160.	6.00
P127	JE5760 (2000)	4,000	5 New Sheqalim. Copper-Nickel. 14.3300 g. 23.9 mm. Plain edge. KM#207.	8.00
P128	JE5760 (2000)	4,000	10 New Sheqalim. Bi-Metallic. 11.0500 g. 22.9 mm. Reeded edge. KM#270.	12.00

MINT SETS

KM#	Date	Mintage	Identification	Issue Price	Mkt Val
MSA1	0 (10)	—	—	—	—
MS1	JE5709 (1949) (10)	—	KM8-12 with pearl, 13.1 with pearl, 14-15 with pearl, 15 without pearl, 16 in "muffin tin" - Two-piece heavy plastic case (Light blue molded bottom and a clear swivel top.)	—	150
MS2	JE5722 (1962) (16)	4,000	KM12a, 13.2a, 17-20, 20a, 24.1, 25-27, market value is for close to perfect sets.	18.50	75.00
MS3	JE5723 (1963) (18)	7,000	As MS2 with KM#36.1, 37 in presentation holder.	22.50	50.00

KM#	Date	Mintage	Identification	Issue Price	Mkt Val
MS4	JE5723 (1963) (6)	200	KM24.1, 25-26 (1962), 27, 36.1, 37 (white folder, plastic over card), market value is for close to perfect sets.	2.50	175
MS5	JE5723 (1963) (6)	2,000	KM#24.1, 25, 26, 27, 36.1, 37 (plain white card)	2.50	125
MS6	JE5723 (1963) (6)	10,000	KM#24.1 with inverted reverse, KM#25, 26, 27, 36.1, 37 (card with map).	2.60	35.00
MS7	JE5723 (1963) (6)	10,544	KM#24.1, 25, 26, 27, 36.1, 37 (card with map) - issued in 1964.	2.60	12.00
MS8	JE5725 (1965) (6)	153,424	KM24.1, 25-27, 36.1, 37. Issued in card	3.50	3.00
MS9	JE5726 (1966) (6)	114,714	KM24.1, 25-27, 36.1, 37. Issued in card.	3.50	3.00
MS10	JE5727 (1967) (6)	128,124	KM24.1, 25-27, 36.1, 37 (card)	3.50	3.00
MS11	JE5728 (1968) (6)	184,552	KM24.1, 25-27, 36.1, 47.1 (card)	3.50	3.00
MS12	JE5729 (1969) (6)	158,052	KM24.1, 25-27, 36.1, 47.1 (card)	3.50	3.50
MS13	JE5730 (1970) (6)	60,045	KM24.1, 25-27, 36.1, 47.1, in red wallet	3.75	4.00
MS13a	JE5730 (1970) (6)	64,800	KM24.1, 25-27, 36.1, 47.1(card)	3.75	4.00
MS14	JE5731 (1971) (6)	32,543	KM24.1, 25-27, 36.1, 47.1, in blue wallet	3.50	4.00
MS14a	JE5731 (1971) (6)	125,921	KM24.1, 25-27, 36.2, 47.2, with Star of David, in pink plastic case	3.00	3.00
MS15	JE5732 (1972) (6)	21,486	KM24.1, 25-27, 36.1, 47.1, in violet wallet	3.00	5.00
MS15a	JE5782 (1972) (6)	68,513	KM24.2, 25a-27a, 36.2, 47.2, with Star of David, in violet plastic case	3.50	3.00
MS16	JE5733 (1973) (6)	98,107	KM63-68, in blue plastic case	3.50	4.00
MS17	JE5734 (1974) (6)	92,868	KM24.2, 25a-27a, 36.1, 47.1, in brown plastic case	3.50	3.00
MS18	JE 5735 (1975) (6)	61,686	KM#24.2, 25c, 26c, 27b, 36.2, 47.2 in brown plastic case.	3.50	3.00
MS19	JE5736 (1976) (6)	64,654	KM24.2, 25c, 26c, 27b, 36.2, 47.2, in green plastic case	3.50	3.00
MS20	JE5737 (1977) (6)	37,208	KM#24.2, 25c, 26c, 27b, 36.2, 47.2.	3.50	4.00
MS21	JE5738 (1978) (6)	57,072	KM#24.2, 25c, 26c, 27b, 36.2, 47.2	3.50	4.00
MS22	JE5739 (1979) (7)	31,590	KM#24.1, 25b, 26b, 27, 36.1, 47.1, 90, plastic wallet.	—	3.00
MS23	JE5739 (1979) (7)	—	KM#24.2, 25c, 26c, 27b, 36.2, 47.2, 90a, brown plastic case.	—	4.00
MS24	JE5740 (1980) (7)	—	KM#24.1, 26b, 47.1, 106-109	—	8.00
MS26	JE5740 (1980) (7)	35,000	KM96-102	13.00	12.00
MS27	JE5742 (1982) (7)	30,000	KM106-109, 111, 118-119	3.50	8.00
MS28	JE5743 (1983) (5)	17,478	KM108-109, 111, 118-119	3.50	8.00
MS29	JE5744 (1984) (9)	13,403	KM108, 109, 111, 118, 119, 134, 137, 139, 143	4.50	10.00
MS30	JE5745 (1985) (8)	15,224	KM111, 118, 119, 139, 143, 146, 147, 151	4.50	12.00
MS31	JE5745 (1985) (5)	7,760	KM156-160	10.00	15.00
MS32	JE5746-47 (1986-87) (12)	14,305	KM156-160, 163, 167, 171-174	9.00	15.00
MS33	JE5747 (1987) (5)	14,000	KM163, 171-174	—	8.00
MS34	JE5747-48 (1987-88) (10)	11,094	KM156-160, 163, 171-174	10.00	12.00
MS35	JE5748 (1988) (5)	30,000	KM163, 171-174	6.50	8.00
MS36	JE5748 (1988) (6)	15,795	KM156-60, 198, green holder	7.50	13.00
MS37	JE5748 (1988) (5)	15,000	KM193-197, blue holder	6.50	12.50
MS38	JE5749 (1989) (5)	20,000	KM163, 171-174	8.00	10.00
MS39	JE5749 (1989) (10)	9,716	KM156-160, 163, 171-174	7.00	12.00
MS40	JE5750 (1990) (5)	7,562	KM163, 171-174	5.00	10.00
MS41	JE5750 (1990) (6)	12,000	KM156-160, 207	8.00	10.00
MS42	JE5751 (1990) (6)	7,929	KM163, 171-174, 217	8.00	10.00
MS43	JE5750-51 (1990-91) (6)	6,746	KM208 (5750), 156-160, 207 (5751)	10.00	20.00
MS44	JE5752 (1992) (5)	6,886	KM163, 172-174, 217	8.00	8.00
MS45	JE5752 (1992) (7)	8,000	KM134, 147, 151, 167, 198, 208, 237, mixed dates	15.00	15.00
MS46	JE5752 (1992) (5)	8,000	KM157-160, 207	8.00	10.00
MS47	JE5753 (1993) (5)	8,000	KM163, 172-174, 217	9.50	8.00
MS48	JE5754 (1994) (6)	12,000	KM163, 172-174, 217, 303	16.00	15.00
MS49	JE5753-54 (1993-94) (7)	8,000	KM158-160 (5753), 157, 158, 160, 207 (5754)	—	15.00
MS50	JE5755 (1995) (6)	10,000	KM163, 172-174, 217, 304	17.00	25.00
MS51	JE5755 (1995) (6)	5,000	KM#157-160, 207, 270	—	15.00
MS52	JE5756 (1996) (7)	7,500	KM163, 172-174, 217, 305, 315	—	30.00
MS53	JE5757 (1997) (7)	7,500	KM163, 172-174, 217, 315, 318	—	35.00
MS54	JE5758 (1998) (7)	8,000	KM#163, 172-174, 217, 314, 315	—	35.00
MS54a	JE5758 (1998) (5)	5,000	KM#157-159, 160a, 207	—	10.00
MS55	JE5759 (1999) (7)	6,000	KM#163, 172-174, 217, 315, 331	—	35.00
MS56	JE5760 (2000) (4)	3,000	KM#157, 158, 160A, 207 Contains 2001 ANA issue	—	—
MS57	JE5760 (2000) (7)	5,000	KM163, 172-174, 217, 315, 332	—	30.00
MS58	JE5761-62 (2001-02) (9)	3,000	KM#157 (2 pcs), 158 (2 pcs), 159, 160a (2 pcs), 207, 270 mixed date set	—	—

OFFICIALLY ASSEMBLED HISTORICAL SETS

KM#	Date	Mintage	Identification	Issue Price	Mkt Val
HS1	1927-55 (7)	18,000	The Coin and the Moon Set, KM1, 10, 12-15, 17, plus medal	15.00	15.00
HS2	1948-85 (9)	26,000	KM#11, 13, 14, 27, 36, 47, 107, 108, 109 plus a medal. Historical Coin Set	15.00	15.00

PIEFORT PROOF SETS (PPS)

KM#	Date	Mintage	Identification	Issue Price	Mkt Val
PPS1	JE5741 (1981) (b) (5)	30,217	KM#P1-P5.	10.00	12.00
PPS2	JE5742 (1982) (r) (6)	18,735	KM#P6-P11.	10.00	10.00
PPS3	JE5743 (1983) (d) (7)	17,177	KM#P12-P18.	10.00	12.00
PPS4	JE5744 (1984) (b) (7)	15,572	KM#P19-P25.	10.00	10.00
PPS5	JE5745 (1985) (b) (5)	14,768	KM#P26-P30	10.00	12.00
PPS6	JE5746 (1986) (p) (5)	12,665	KM#P31-P35.	12.00	18.00
PPS7	JE5747 (1987) (f) (5)	11,529	KM#P36-P40.	15.00	18.00
PPS8	JE5748 (1988) (f) (5)	12,027	KM#PA41, P41-P44.	15.00	25.00
PPS9	JE5749 (1989) (f) (5)	9,622	KM#P45-P49.	15.00	25.00
PPS10	JE5750 (1990) (f) (6)	10,000	KM#P50-P55.	15.00	25.00
PPS11	JE5751 (1991) (u) (6)	8,000	KM#P56-P61.	15.00	25.00
PPS12	JE5752 (1992) (u) (6)	8,000	KM#P68-P73.	15.00	25.00
PPS13	JE5753 (1993) (u) (6)	8,000	KM#P68-P73.	15.00	25.00
PPS14	JE5754 (1994) (u) (7)	8,000	KM#P74-P80.	—	45.00
PPS15	JE5755 (1995) (u) (8)	8,000	KM#P81-P88.	33.00	45.00
PPS16	JE5756 (1996) (b) & (u) (8)	8,000	KM#P89-P96.	—	45.00
PPS17	JE5757 (1997) (h) & (u) (8)	6,000	KM#P97-P104.	—	48.00
PPS18	JE5758 (1998) (h) & (u) (8)	8,000	KM#P105-P112.	—	45.00
PPS19	JE5759 (1999) (h) & (u) (8)	6,000	KM#P113-P120.	—	48.00
PPS20	JE5760 (2000) (8)	4,000	KM#P121-P128.	—	48.00

PROOF SETS

KM#	Date	Mintage	Identification	Issue Price	Mkt Val
PS1	1927 (14)	34	KM1-7 two each, original case	—	7,500
PS2	1927 (7)	4	KM1-7 original case	—	5,000

SPECIAL SELECT SETS

KM#	Date	Mintage	Identification	Issue Price	Mkt Val
SS1	1949	—		—	—

ITALIAN SOMALILAND

Italian Somaliland, a former Italian Colony in East Africa, extended south from Ras Asir to Kenya. Area: 178,218 sq. miles (461,585 sq. km). Capital: Mogadisho. In 1885, Italy obtained commercial concessions in the area of the sultan of Zanzibar, and in 1905 purchased the coast from Warshek to Brava. The Italians then extended their occupation inward. Cession of the Jubaland Province by Britain in 1924, and seizure of the sultanates of Obbia and Mejertein in 1925-27 brought direct Italian administration over the whole territory. Italian dominance continued until WW II. British troops occupied Italian Somaliland in 1941. Britain administered the colony until 1950 when it became a UN trust territory administered by Italy. On July 1, 1960. Italian Somaliland united with British Somaliland to form the Independent Somali Democratic Republic.

TITLE

الصومال الايطاليانية

Al-Somal Al-Italiyaniya(t)

MONETARY SYSTEM
100 Bese = 1 Rupia

ITALIAN POSSESSION

STANDARD COINAGE

KM# 1 BESA
Bronze **Ruler:** Vittorio Emanuele III **Obv:** Uniformed bust left **Rev:** Value and date within circle

Date	Mintage	F	VF	XF	Unc	BU
1909R	2,000,000	15.00	30.00	70.00	300	—
1910R	500,000	15.00	30.00	90.00	350	—
1913R	200,000	22.50	45.00	150	700	—
1921R	500,000	18.50	35.00	100	400	—

KM# 2 2 BESE
Bronze **Ruler:** Vittorio Emanuele III **Obv:** Uniformed bust left **Rev:** Value and date within circle

Date	Mintage	F	VF	XF	Unc	BU
1909R	500,000	18.50	37.50	140	550	—
1910R	250,000	18.50	37.50	160	600	—
1913R	300,000	22.50	45.00	225	900	—
1921R	600,000	18.50	37.50	140	550	—
1923R	1,500,000	18.50	35.00	130	500	—
1924R	Inc. above	18.50	30.00	110	450	—

KM# 3 4 BESE
Bronze **Ruler:** Vittorio Emanuele III **Obv:** Uniformed bust left **Rev:** Value and date within circle

Date	Mintage	F	VF	XF	Unc	BU
1909R	250,000	27.50	55.00	180	900	—
1910R	250,000	27.50	55.00	200	1,000	—
1913R	50,000	50.00	125	500	1,500	—
1921R	200,000	30.00	60.00	200	1,000	—
1923R	1,000,000	30.00	60.00	200	1,000	—
1924R	Inc. above	30.00	75.00	225	1,100	—

KM# 4 1/4 RUPIA
2.9160 g., 0.9170 Silver .0859 oz. ASW **Ruler:** Vittorio Emanuele III **Obv:** Head right **Rev:** Crown above value and date flanked by sprigs

Date	Mintage	F	VF	XF	Unc	BU
1910R	400,000	20.00	40.00	150	400	—
1913R	100,000	50.00	100	300	600	—

KM# 5 1/2 RUPIA
5.8319 g., 0.9170 Silver .1719 oz. ASW **Ruler:** Vittorio Emanuele III **Obv:** Head right **Rev:** Crown above value and date flanked by sprigs

Date	Mintage	F	VF	XF	Unc	BU
1910R	400,000	30.00	65.00	250	650	—
1912R	100,000	35.00	70.00	225	600	—
1913R	100,000	35.00	70.00	200	550	—
1915R	50,000	55.00	120	400	1,000	—
1919R	200,000	30.00	60.00	180	450	—

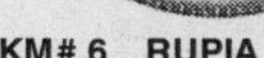

KM# 6 RUPIA
11.6638 g., 0.9170 Silver .3437 oz. ASW **Ruler:** Vittorio Emanuele III **Obv:** Head right **Rev:** Crown above value and date flanked by sprigs

Date	Mintage	F	VF	XF	Unc	BU
1910R	300,000	40.00	90.00	275	550	—
1912R	600,000	40.00	85.00	250	500	—
1913R	300,000	40.00	75.00	225	450	—
1914R	300,000	40.00	75.00	225	450	—
1915R	250,000	40.00	75.00	225	450	—
1919R	400,000	40.00	75.00	225	450	—
1920R	1,300,000	900	1,500	3,750	7,500	—
1921R	940,000	1,850	3,750	6,000	12,500	—

REFORM COINAGE

100 Centesimi = 1 Lira

KM# 7 5 LIRE
6.0000 g., 0.8350 Silver .1611 oz. ASW **Ruler:** Vittorio Emanuele III **Obv:** Crowned bust right **Rev:** Crowned shield flanked by sprigs divides value with date below **Designer:** Attilio Motti

Date	Mintage	F	VF	XF	Unc	BU
1925R	400,000	125	300	500	1,000	1,500

KM# 8 10 LIRE
12.0000 g., 0.8350 Silver .3221 oz. ASW **Ruler:** Vittorio Emanuele III **Obv:** Crowned bust right **Rev:** Crowned shield flanked by sprigs divides value with date below **Designer:** Attilio Motti

Date	Mintage	F	VF	XF	Unc	BU
1925R	100,000	200	500	700	1,200	2,000

PROVAS

KM#	Date	Mintage	Identification	Mkt Val
Pr1	1909R	—	Besa. Bronze.	—
Pr2	1909R	—	2 Bese. Bronze.	—
Pr3	1909R	—	4 Bese. Bronze.	—
Pr4	1909R	—	4 Bese. Silver.	—
Pr5	1910R	—	4 Bese. Nickel.	—
Pr6	1910R	—	1/4 Rupia. Silver. Head right. Crown above value and date flanked by sprigs.	1,500

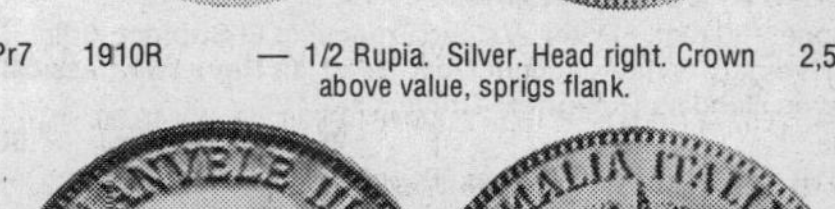

KM#	Date	Mintage	Identification	Mkt Val
Pr7	1910R	—	1/2 Rupia. Silver. Head right. Crown above value, sprigs flank.	2,500

KM#	Date	Mintage	Identification	Mkt Val
Pr8	1910R	—	Rupia. Silver. Head right. Crown above value and date flanked by sprigs.	4,000
Pr9	1915R	—	1/2 Rupia. Silver. 1 ANNO/DI GUERRA flanks crown.	—
Pr10	1915R	—	Rupia. Silver. 1 ANNO/DI GUERRA flanks crown.	—
Pr11	1925R	—	5 Lire. Silver. PROVA.	800
Pr12	1925R	—	5 Lire. Silver. PROVA DI STAMPA.	700
Pr13	1925R	—	10 Lire. Silver. PROVA.	1,000
Pr14	1925R	—	10 Lire. Silver. PROVA DI STAMPA.	850

TRIAL STRIKES

KM#	Date	Mintage	Identification	Mkt Val
TS1	1909	—	Besa. Pewter.	375
TS2	1909	—	2 Bese. Lead.	—
TS3	1910	—	4 Bese. Pewter.	750

The Italian Republic, a 700-mile-long peninsula extending into the heart of the Mediterranean Sea, has an area of 116,304 sq. mi. (301,230 sq. km.) and a population of 60 million. Capital: Rome. The economy centers around agriculture, manufacturing, forestry and fishing. Machinery, textiles, clothing and motor vehicles are exported.

From the fall of Rome until modern times, 'Italy' was little more than a geographical expression. Although nominally included in the Empire of Charlemagne and the Holy Roman Empire, it was in reality divided into a number of independent states and kingdoms presided over by wealthy families, soldiers of fortune or hereditary rulers. The 19th century unification movement fostered by Mazzini, Garibaldi and Cavour attained fruition in 1860-70 with the creation of the Kingdom of Italy and the installation of Victor Emmanuel, king of Sardinia, as king of Italy. Benito Mussolini came to power during the post-World War I period of economic and political unrest, and installed a Fascist dictatorship with a figurehead king as titular Head of State. Mussolini entered Italy into the German-Japanese anti-comitern pact (Tri-Partite Pact) and withdrew from the League of Nations. The war did not go well for Italy and Germany was forced to assist Italy in its failed invasion of Greece. The Allied invasion of Sicily on July 10, 1943 and bombings of Rome brought the Fascist council to a no vote of confidence on July 23, 1943. Mussolini was arrested but soon escaped and set up a government in Salo. Rome fell to the Allied forces in June, 1944 and the country was allowed the status of cobelligerent against Germany. The Germans held northern Italy for another year. Mussolini was eventually captured and executed by partisans.

Following the defeat of the Axis powers, the Italian monarchy was dissolved by plebiscite, and the Italian Republic proclaimed.

RULERS
Vittorio Emanuele III, 1900-1946
Umberto II, 1946
Republic, 1946-

MONETARY SYSTEM
100 Centesimi = 1 Lira

KINGDOM

DECIMAL COINAGE

KM# 35 CENTESIMO
Copper **Ruler:** Vittorio Emanuele III **Obv:** Head left **Rev:** Value and date within wreath with star above

Date	Mintage	F	VF	XF	Unc	BU
1902R	26,000	300	600	1,100	2,200	—
1903R	5,655,000	1.00	3.00	6.00	30.00	—
1904/0R	14,626,000	2.00	3.00	7.50	22.00	—
1904R	Inc. above	1.00	3.00	6.00	30.00	—
1905/0R	8,531,000	6.00	12.00	30.00	75.00	—
1905R	Inc. above	1.00	3.00	6.00	30.00	—
1908R	3,859,000	1.00	3.00	6.00	30.00	—

KM# 40 CENTESIMO
Copper **Ruler:** Vittorio Emanuele III **Obv:** Bust left **Rev:** Female standing on prow **Rev. Designer:** Pietro Canonia

Date	Mintage	F	VF	XF	Unc	BU
1908R	57,000	250	350	800	1,400	—
1909R	3,539,000	2.00	3.00	7.00	20.00	—
1910R	3,599,000	2.00	3.00	7.00	20.00	—
1911R	700,000	12.00	18.00	45.00	100	—

Date	Mintage	F	VF	XF	Unc	BU
1912R	3,995,000	2.00	3.00	7.00	20.00	—
1913R	3,200,000	2.00	4.00	8.00	25.00	—
1914R	11,585,000	2.00	3.00	7.00	20.00	—
1915R	9,757,000	2.00	3.00	7.00	20.00	—
1916R	9,845,000	2.00	3.00	7.00	20.00	—
1917R	2,400,000	2.00	3.00	7.00	20.00	—
1918R	2,710,000	10.00	20.00	50.00	100	—

KM# 38 2 CENTESIMI

Copper **Ruler:** Vittorio Emanuele III **Obv:** Head left **Rev:** Value and date within wreath

Date	Mintage	F	VF	XF	Unc	BU
1903R	5,000,000	2.00	4.00	15.00	30.00	—
1905R	1,260,000	10.00	15.00	25.00	75.00	—
1906R	3,145,000	2.00	6.00	15.00	30.00	—
1907R	230,000	50.00	95.00	220	520	—
1908R	1,518,000	2.00	5.00	15.00	30.00	—

KM# 41 2 CENTESIMI

Copper **Ruler:** Vittorio Emanuele III **Obv:** Bust left **Rev:** Female standing on prow **Rev. Designer:** Pietro Canonia

Date	Mintage	F	VF	XF	Unc	BU
1908	298,000	20.00	40.00	90.00	200	—
1909	2,419,000	1.00	3.00	7.00	30.00	—
1910	590,000	10.00	20.00	50.00	150	—
1911	2,777,000	1.00	3.00	7.00	30.00	—
1912	840,000	6.00	10.00	40.00	100	—
1914	1,648,000	1.00	3.00	7.00	30.00	—
1915	4,860,000	1.00	3.00	5.00	25.00	—
1916	1,540,000	1.00	4.00	8.00	30.00	—
1917	3,638,000	1.00	3.00	7.00	30.00	—

KM# 42 5 CENTESIMI

Copper, 25.5 mm. **Ruler:** Vittorio Emanuele III **Obv:** Bust left **Rev:** Female standing on prow **Rev. Designer:** Pietro Canonia

Date	Mintage	F	VF	XF	Unc	BU
1908R	824,000	12.00	28.00	60.00	150	—
1909R	1,734,000	2.00	5.00	20.00	60.00	—
1912R	743,000	4.00	10.00	25.00	90.00	—
1913R Dot after D	1,964,000	5.00	15.00	30.00	95.00	—
1913R Without dot after D	Inc. above	60.00	125	300	600	—
1915R	1,038,000	3.00	8.00	22.00	80.00	—
1918R	4,242,000	2.00	4.00	8.00	60.00	—

KM# 59 5 CENTESIMI

Copper, 19.8 mm. **Ruler:** Vittorio Emanuele III **Obv:** Head left **Rev:** Wheat ear divides value

Date	Mintage	F	VF	XF	Unc	BU
1919R	13,208,000	3.00	8.00	25.00	100	—
1920R	33,372,000	0.20	0.60	3.00	15.00	—
1921R	80,111,000	0.20	0.60	3.00	15.00	—
1922R	42,914,000	0.20	0.60	3.00	15.00	—
1923R	29,614,000	0.20	0.60	3.00	15.00	—
1924R	20,352,000	0.20	0.60	3.00	15.00	—
1925R	40,460,000	0.20	0.60	3.00	15.00	—
1926R	21,158,000	0.20	0.60	3.00	15.00	—
1927R	15,800,000	0.20	0.60	3.00	15.00	—
1928R	16,090,000	0.20	0.60	3.00	15.00	—
1929R	29,000,000	0.20	0.60	3.00	15.00	—
1930R	22,694,000	0.20	0.60	3.00	15.00	—
1931R	20,000,000	0.20	0.60	3.00	15.00	—
1932R	11,456,000	0.20	0.60	3.00	15.00	—
1933R	20,720,000	0.20	0.60	3.00	15.00	—
1934R	16,000,000	0.20	0.60	3.00	15.00	—
1935R	11,000,000	0.20	0.60	3.00	15.00	—

Date	Mintage	F	VF	XF	Unc	BU
1936R	9,462,000	0.30	1.00	5.00	12.00	—
1937R	972,000	7.00	15.00	30.00	100	—

KM# 73 5 CENTESIMI

Copper **Ruler:** Vittorio Emanuele III **Obv:** Head right **Rev:** Eagle with wings spread

Date	Mintage	F	VF	XF	Unc	BU
1936R Yr. XIV	4,998,000	3.00	6.00	12.00	30.00	—
1937R Yr. XV	7,207,000	1.00	2.00	6.00	15.00	—
1938R Yr. XVI	24,000,000	0.10	0.50	2.50	5.00	—
1939R Yr. XVII	22,000,000	0.10	0.50	2.50	5.00	—

KM# 73a 5 CENTESIMI

Aluminum-Bronze **Ruler:** Vittorio Emanuele III **Obv:** Head right **Rev:** Eagle with wings spread

Date	Mintage	F	VF	XF	Unc	BU
1939R Yr. XVII	10,000,000	0.20	0.50	2.00	6.00	—
1940R Yr. XVIII	16,340,000	0.20	0.50	2.00	6.00	—
1941R Yr. XIX	25,200,000	0.20	0.50	2.00	6.00	—
1942R Yr. XX	13,922,000	0.20	0.50	2.00	6.00	—
1943R Yr. XXI	372,000	3.00	6.00	15.00	30.00	—

KM# 43 10 CENTESIMI

Copper **Ruler:** Vittorio Emanuele III **Obv:** Bust left **Rev:** Female standing on prow

Date	Mintage	F	VF	XF	Unc	BU
1908R Unique	—	—	—	—	—	—

KM# 51 10 CENTESIMI

Copper, 30 mm. **Ruler:** Vittorio Emanuele III **Subject:** 50th Anniversary of the Kingdom **Obv:** Head left **Rev:** Two classical figures standing **Designer:** Trentacoste

Date	Mintage	F	VF	XF	Unc	BU
1911R	2,000,000	5.00	10.00	30.00	80.00	—

KM# 60 10 CENTESIMI

Copper, 23 mm. **Ruler:** Vittorio Emanuele III **Obv:** Head left **Rev:** Honey Bee

Date	Mintage	F	VF	XF	Unc	BU
1919R	986,000	20.00	50.00	125	300	—
1920R	37,995,000	0.30	0.75	4.00	15.00	—
1921R	66,510,000	0.30	0.75	4.00	15.00	—
1922R	45,217,000	0.30	0.75	4.00	15.00	—
1923R	31,529,000	0.30	0.75	4.00	15.00	—
1924R	35,312,000	0.30	0.75	4.00	15.00	—
1925R	22,370,000	0.30	0.75	4.00	15.00	—
1926R	25,190,000	0.30	0.75	4.00	15.00	—
1927R	22,673,000	0.30	0.75	4.00	15.00	—
1928R	15,680,000	1.00	3.00	8.00	40.00	—
1929R	15,593,000	0.30	0.75	4.00	15.00	—
1930R	17,115,000	0.30	0.75	4.00	15.00	—
1931R	10,750,000	0.30	0.75	4.00	15.00	—
1932R	5,678,000	2.00	4.00	15.00	70.00	—
1933R	10,250,000	0.30	0.75	4.00	15.00	—
1934R	18,300,000	0.30	0.75	4.00	15.00	—
1935R	10,500,000	0.30	0.75	4.00	15.00	—
1936R	8,770,000	1.00	2.50	8.00	40.00	—
1937R	5,500,000	1.00	2.50	8.00	40.00	—

KM# 74 10 CENTESIMI

Copper **Ruler:** Vittorio Emanuele III **Obv:** Head left **Rev:** Savoy arms on fasces with wheat ear and oak leaf flanking

Date	Mintage	F	VF	XF	Unc	BU
1936R Yr. XIV	8,195,000	2.50	5.00	15.00	45.00	—
1937R Yr. XV	7,212,000	1.00	2.00	5.00	20.00	—

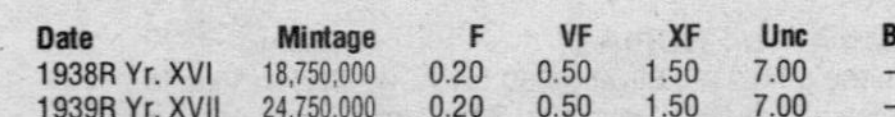

Date	Mintage	F	VF	XF	Unc	BU
1938R Yr. XVI	18,750,000	0.20	0.50	1.50	7.00	—
1939R Yr. XVII	24,750,000	0.20	0.50	1.50	7.00	—

KM# 74a 10 CENTESIMI

Aluminum-Bronze, 23 mm. **Ruler:** Vittorio Emanuele III **Obv:** Head right **Rev:** Savoy arms on fasces with wheat ear and oak leaf flanking

Date	Mintage	F	VF	XF	Unc	BU
1939R Yr. XVII	26,105,000	0.10	0.50	1.00	4.50	—
1940R Yr. XVIII	23,355,000	0.10	0.50	1.00	4.50	—
1941R Yr. XIX	27,050,000	0.10	0.50	1.00	4.50	—
1942R Yr. XX	18,100,000	0.10	0.50	1.00	4.50	—
1943R Yr. XXI	25,400,000	0.10	0.50	1.00	4.50	—

KM# 44 20 CENTESIMI

Nickel, 21.5 mm. **Ruler:** Vittorio Emanuele III **Obv:** Head left admiring wheat ear **Rev:** Victory in flight with Savoy arms below **Rev. Designer:** Leonardo Bistolfi

Date	Mintage	F	VF	XF	Unc	BU
1908R	14,315,000	0.50	2.00	6.00	40.00	—
1909R	19,280,000	0.50	2.00	6.00	40.00	—
1910R	21,887,000	0.50	2.00	6.00	60.00	—
1911R	13,671,000	0.50	2.00	6.00	60.00	—
1912R	21,040,000	0.50	2.00	6.00	40.00	—
1913R	20,729,000	0.50	2.00	6.00	40.00	—
1914R	14,308,000	0.50	2.00	6.00	60.00	—
1919R	3,475,000	2.00	2.00	30.00	120	—
1920R	27,284,000	0.50	2.00	6.00	40.00	—
1921R	50,372,000	0.50	2.00	6.00	40.00	—
1922R	17,134,000	0.50	2.00	6.00	40.00	—
1926R	500	—	—	—	500	—
1927R	100	—	—	—	600	—
1928R	50	—	—	—	700	—
1929R	50	—	—	—	700	—
1930R	50	—	—	—	700	—
1931R	50	—	—	—	700	—
1932R	50	—	—	—	700	—
1933R	50	—	—	—	700	—
1934R	50	—	—	—	700	—
1935R	50	—	—	—	700	—

KM# 58 20 CENTESIMI

Copper-Nickel, 21.5 mm. **Ruler:** Vittorio Emanuele III **Obv:** Crowned Savoy shield flanked by oak and laurel sprigs **Rev:** Value and date within hexagon box **Edge:** Plain and reeded **Note:** Overstruck on KM#28.

Date	Mintage	F	VF	XF	Unc	BU
1918R	43,097,000	0.50	1.00	6.00	60.00	—
1919R	33,432,000	0.50	1.00	6.00	60.00	—
1920R	923,000	5.00	10.00	30.00	100	—

KM# 75 20 CENTESIMI

Nickel, 21.5 mm. **Ruler:** Vittorio Emanuele III **Obv:** Head left **Rev:** Savoy shield within head right

Date	Mintage	F	VF	XF	Unc	BU
1936R Yr. XIV	117,000	40.00	80.00	210	420	—
1937R Yr. XV	50	—	—	—	700	—
1938R Yr. XVII	20	—	—	—	900	—

KM# 75a 20 CENTESIMI

Stainless Steel, 22.5 mm. **Ruler:** Vittorio Emanuele III **Obv:** Head left **Rev:** Savoy shield within head right **Edge:** Plain **Note:** Magnetic.

Date	Mintage	F	VF	XF	Unc	BU
1939R Yr. XVII	10,462,000	1.00	2.00	10.00	45.00	—
1940R Yr. XVIII	35,350,000	1.00	2.00	10.00	45.00	—
1942R Yr. XX	48,500,000	1.00	2.00	10.00	55.00	—

KM# 75b 20 CENTESIMI

Stainless Steel, 21.8 mm. **Ruler:** Vittorio Emanuele III **Obv:** Head left **Rev:** Savoy shield within head right **Edge:** Reeded **Note:** Magnetic.

Date	Mintage	F	VF	XF	Unc	BU
1939R Yr. XVIII	Inc. above	0.50	1.00	3.00	5.00	—
1939R Yr. XVII	10,462,000	0.10	0.40	1.00	3.00	—
1940R Yr. XVIII	Inc. above	0.10	0.40	1.00	3.00	—
1941R Yr. XIX	97,300,000	0.10	0.40	1.00	3.00	—
1942R Yr. XX	Inc. above	0.10	0.40	1.00	3.00	—
1943R Yr. XXI	18,453,000	0.10	0.40	1.00	3.00	—

KM# 75c 20 CENTESIMI

Stainless Steel, 22.5 mm. **Ruler:** Vittorio Emanuele III **Obv:** Head left **Rev:** Savoy shield within head right **Edge:** Plain **Note:** Non-magnetic.

Date	Mintage	F	VF	XF	Unc	BU
1939R Yr. XVII	Inc. above	2.00	6.00	14.00	38.00	—

KM# 75d 20 CENTESIMI

Stainless Steel, 21.8 mm. **Ruler:** Vittorio Emanuele III **Obv:** Head left **Rev:** Savoy shield within head right **Edge:** Reeded **Note:** Non-magnetic.

Date	Mintage	F	VF	XF	Unc	BU
1939R Yr. XVII	Inc. above	0.50	1.00	3.00	5.00	—
1939R Yr. XVIII	25,300,000	0.50	1.00	3.50	5.00	—
1940R Yr. XVIII	Inc. above	0.10	0.40	1.00	3.00	—

KM# 36 25 CENTESIMI

Nickel **Ruler:** Vittorio Emanuele III **Obv:** Crowned eagle with Savoy shield on chest **Rev:** Value above sprigs

Date	Mintage	F	VF	XF	Unc	BU
1902R	7,773,000	25.00	50.00	100	300	—
1903R	5,895,000	25.00	50.00	100	300	—

KM# 61.1 50 CENTESIMI

Nickel, 24 mm. **Ruler:** Vittorio Emanuele III **Obv:** Head left **Rev:** Four lions pulling cart with seated Aequitas **Edge:** Plain

Date	Mintage	F	VF	XF	Unc	BU
1919R	3,700,000	2.50	7.00	40.00	100	—
1920R	29,450,000	1.00	2.00	6.00	30.00	—
1921R	16,849,000	1.00	2.00	6.00	30.00	—
1924R	599,000	100	200	420	1,100	—
1925R	24,884,000	1.00	2.00	6.00	30.00	—
1926R	500	—	—	—	520	—
1927R	100	—	—	—	710	—
1928R	50	—	—	—	920	—

KM# 61.2 50 CENTESIMI

Nickel, 24 mm. **Ruler:** Vittorio Emanuele III **Obv:** Head left **Rev:** Four lions pulling cart with seated Aequitas **Edge:** Reeded

Date	Mintage	F	VF	XF	Unc	BU
1919R	Inc. above	10.00	20.00	100	600	—
1920R	Inc. above	3.50	10.00	30.00	200	—
1921R	Inc. above	3.50	10.00	30.00	200	—
1924R	Inc. above	50.00	100	250	900	—
1925R	Inc. above	4.00	10.00	30.00	150	—
1929R	50	—	—	—	700	—
1930R	50	—	—	—	700	—
1931R	50	—	—	—	700	—
1932R	50	—	—	—	700	—
1933R	50	—	—	—	700	—
1934R	50	—	—	—	700	—
1935R	50	—	—	—	700	—

KM# 76 50 CENTESIMI

Nickel, 24 mm. **Ruler:** Vittorio Emanuele III **Obv:** Head right **Obv. Designer:** Giuseppe Romagnoli **Rev:** Eagle standing right on fasces

Date	Mintage	F	VF	XF	Unc	BU
1936R Yr. XIV	118,000	20.00	50.00	120	330	—
1937R Yr. XV	50	—	—	—	1,100	—
1938R Yr. XVII	20	—	—	—	2,100	—

KM# 76a 50 CENTESIMI

Stainless Steel, 24 mm. **Ruler:** Vittorio Emanuele III **Obv:** Head right **Obv. Designer:** Giuseppe Romagnoli **Rev:** Eagle standing right on fasces **Edge:** Reeded **Note:** Non-magnetic.

Date	Mintage	F	VF	XF	Unc	BU
1939R Yr. XVII	9,373,000	0.35	0.75	2.00	12.00	—
1939R Yr. XVIII	10,005,000	0.50	1.00	3.00	16.00	—
1940R Yr. XVIII	19,005,000	0.25	0.60	1.50	5.00	—

KM# 76b 50 CENTESIMI

Stainless Steel, 24 mm. **Ruler:** Vittorio Emanuele III **Obv:** Head right **Rev:** Eagle standing right on fasces **Edge:** Reeded **Note:** Magnetic.

Date	Mintage	F	VF	XF	Unc	BU
1939R Yr. XVII	9,373,000	0.40	1.00	3.00	12.00	—
1939R Yr. XVIII	Inc. above	0.40	1.00	3.00	12.00	—
1940R Yr. XVIII	19,005,000	0.10	0.40	1.50	4.00	—
1941R Yr. XIX	58,100,000	0.10	0.40	1.50	4.00	—
1942R Yr. XX	26,450,000	0.10	0.60	1.50	4.00	—
1943R Yr. XXI	3,681,000	25.00	45.00	80.00	175	—

KM# 32 LIRA

5.0000 g., 0.8350 Silver .1342 oz. ASW **Ruler:** Vittorio Emanuele III **Obv:** Head right **Rev:** Crowned eagle with savoy shield

Date	Mintage	F	VF	XF	Unc	BU
1901R	2,590,000	7.50	18.50	90.00	450	—
1902R	4,084,000	5.00	13.50	75.00	300	—
1905R	700,000	150	300	1,000	2,500	—
1906R	4,665,000	5.00	13.50	75.00	300	—
1907R	8,472,000	4.00	10.00	60.00	250	—

KM# 45 LIRA

5.0000 g., 0.8350 Silver .1342 oz. ASW **Ruler:** Vittorio Emanuele III **Obv:** Bust right **Rev:** Quadriga with standing female figure **Rev. Designer:** Davide Calandra

Date	Mintage	F	VF	XF	Unc	BU
1908R	2,212,000	30.00	75.00	410	1,000	—
1909R	3,475,000	15.00	40.00	310	800	—
1910R	5,525,000	6.00	10.00	75.00	300	—
1912R	5,865,000	5.00	12.00	50.00	200	—
1913R	16,177,000	3.00	10.00	30.00	150	—

KM# 57 LIRA

5.0000 g., 0.8350 Silver .1342 oz. ASW **Ruler:** Vittorio Emanuele III **Obv:** Bust right **Rev:** Quadriga with standing female figure

Date	Mintage	F	VF	XF	Unc	BU
1915R	5,229,000	5.00	25.00	60.00	165	—
1916R	1,835,000	10.00	40.00	170	420	—
1917R	9,744,000	4.00	15.00	30.00	100	—

KM# 62 LIRA

Nickel, 27 mm. **Ruler:** Vittorio Emanuele III **Obv:** Female seated left **Rev:** Crowned Savoy shield and value within wreath

Date	Mintage	F	VF	XF	Unc	BU
1922R	82,267,000	0.60	2.00	15.00	50.00	—
1923R	20,175,000	1.00	5.00	40.00	120	—
1924R Closed 2	29,288,000	1.00	4.00	20.00	100	—
1926R	500	—	—	—	420	—
1927R	100	—	—	—	510	—
1928R	19,996,000	2.00	10.00	60.00	130	—
1929R	50	—	—	—	720	—
1930R	50	—	—	—	720	—
1931R	50	—	—	—	720	—
1932R	50	—	—	—	720	—
1933R	50	—	—	—	720	—
1934R	50	—	—	—	720	—
1935R	50	—	—	—	720	—

KM# 77 LIRA

Nickel, 27 mm. **Ruler:** Vittorio Emanuele III **Obv:** Head left **Rev:** Eagle with wings open

Date	Mintage	F	VF	XF	Unc	BU
1936R Yr. XIV	119,000	30.00	80.00	150	350	—
1937R Yr. XV	50	—	—	—	1,100	—
1938R XVII	20	—	—	—	1,600	—

KM# 77a LIRA

Stainless Steel, 27 mm. **Ruler:** Vittorio Emanuele III **Obv:** Head left **Rev:** Eagle with wings open **Edge:** Reeded **Note:** Non-magnetic.

Date	Mintage	F	VF	XF	Unc	BU
1939R Yr. XVII	10,034,000	0.40	1.50	4.00	8.00	—
1939R Yr. XVIII	15,977,000	0.20	0.60	3.00	7.00	—
1940R Yr. XVIII	25,997,000	0.20	0.50	2.00	6.00	—

KM# 77b LIRA

Stainless Steel, 27 mm. **Ruler:** Vittorio Emanuele III **Obv:** Head left **Rev:** Eagle with wings open **Edge:** Reeded **Note:** Magnetic.

Date	Mintage	F	VF	XF	Unc	BU
1939R Yr. XVII	Inc. above	0.40	1.50	4.00	8.00	—
1939R Yr. XVIII	Inc. above	0.20	0.60	3.00	7.00	—
1940R Yr. XVIII	Inc. above	0.20	0.50	2.00	6.00	—
1941R Yr. XIX	8,550,000	0.50	1.75	5.00	12.00	—
1942R Yr. XX	5,700,000	0.20	1.75	5.00	12.00	—
1943R Yr. XXI	11,500,000	10.00	25.00	50.00	100	—

KM# 33 2 LIRE

10.0000 g., 0.8350 Silver .2684 oz. ASW **Ruler:** Vittorio Emanuele III **Obv:** Head right **Rev:** Crowned eagle with Savoy shield on chest

Date	Mintage	F	VF	XF	Unc	BU
1901R	72,000	525	1,300	3,900	7,200	—
1902R	549,000	75.00	300	800	2,100	—
1903R	54,000	1,000	2,000	5,300	12,900	—
1904R	157,000	225	900	2,100	5,200	—
1905R	1,643,000	20.00	120	300	950	—
1906R	970,000	20.00	130	800	950	—
1907R	1,245,000	15.00	100	280	900	—

KM# 46 2 LIRE
10.0000 g., 0.8350 Silver .2684 oz. ASW **Ruler:** Vittorio Emanuele III **Obv:** Bust right **Rev:** Quadriga with standing female **Rev. Designer:** Davide Calandra

Date	Mintage	F	VF	XF	Unc	BU
1908R	2,283,000	10.00	40.00	180	700	—
1910R	719,000	50.00	140	600	1,600	—
1911R	535,000	100	350	1,000	2,500	—
1912R	2,166,000	15.00	40.00	210	810	—

KM# 52 2 LIRE
10.0000 g., 0.8350 Silver .2684 oz. ASW, 27 mm. **Ruler:** Vittorio Emanuele III **Subject:** 50th Anniversary of the Kingdom **Obv:** Head left **Rev:** Two classical figures standing **Designer:** Dominico Trentacoste

Date	Mintage	F	VF	XF	Unc	BU
1911R	1,000,000	45.00	100	210	420	—

KM# 55 2 LIRE
10.0000 g., 0.8350 Silver .2684 oz. ASW **Ruler:** Vittorio Emanuele III **Obv:** Bust right **Rev:** Quadriga with standing female

Date	Mintage	F	VF	XF	Unc	BU
1914R	10,390,000	6.00	12.00	30.00	100	—
1915R	7,948,000	6.00	12.00	30.00	120	—
1916R	10,923,000	6.00	12.00	30.00	100	—
1917R	6,123,000	15.00	30.00	80.00	200	—

KM# 63 2 LIRE
Nickel **Ruler:** Vittorio Emanuele III **Obv:** Bust right **Rev:** Axe head within fasces with value at left

Date	Mintage	F	VF	XF	Unc	BU
1923R	32,260,000	1.00	5.00	30.00	100	—
1924R	45,051,000	1.00	5.00	30.00	100	—
1925R	14,628,000	2.00	20.00	80.00	190	—
1926R	5,101,000	8.00	70.00	300	1,000	—
1927R	1,632,000	30.00	150	300	1,200	—
1928R	50	—	—	—	800	—
1929R	50	—	—	—	800	—
1930R	50	—	—	—	800	—
1931R	50	—	—	—	800	—
1932R	50	—	—	—	800	—
1933R	50	—	—	—	800	—
1934R	50	—	—	—	800	—
1935R	50	—	—	—	800	—

KM# 78 2 LIRE
Nickel **Ruler:** Vittorio Emanuele III **Obv:** Head right **Rev:** Eagle with open wings standing on fasces within wreath **Edge:** Plain

Date	Mintage	F	VF	XF	Unc	BU
1936R Yr. XIV	120,000	50.00	100	220	380	—
1937R Yr. XV	50	—	—	—	760	—
1939R Yr. XVII	20	—	—	—	1,100	—

KM# 78a 2 LIRE
Stainless Steel, 29 mm. **Ruler:** Vittorio Emanuele III **Obv:** Head right **Rev:** Eagle with open wings standing on fasces within wreath **Edge:** Reeded **Note:** Non-magnetic.

Date	Mintage	F	VF	XF	Unc	BU
1939R Yr. XVII	2,900,000	0.60	1.75	5.00	20.00	—
1939R Yr. XVIII	4,873,000	0.40	1.00	4.00	10.00	—
1940R Yr. XVIII	5,742,000	0.40	1.00	4.00	9.00	—

KM# 78b 2 LIRE
Stainless Steel, 29 mm. **Ruler:** Vittorio Emanuele III **Obv:** Head right **Rev:** Eagle with open wings standing on fasces within wreath **Edge:** Reeded **Note:** Magnetic.

Date	Mintage	F	VF	XF	Unc	BU
1939R Yr. XVII	Inc. above	1.00	2.00	6.00	24.00	—
1939R Yr. XVIII	Inc. above	0.40	0.90	2.50	6.00	—
1940R Yr. XVIII	Inc. above	0.40	0.90	2.00	5.50	—
1941R Yr. XIX	1,865,000	0.50	1.50	3.00	8.00	—
1942R Yr. XX	2,450,000	40.00	80.00	175	400	—
1943R Yr. XXI	600,000	25.00	50.00	150	300	—

KM# 34 5 LIRE
25.0000 g., 0.9000 Silver .7234 oz. ASW **Ruler:** Vittorio Emanuele III **Obv:** Head right **Obv. Designer:** Filippo Speranza **Rev:** Crowned eagle with Savoy shield on chest

Date	Mintage	F	VF	XF	Unc	BU
1901R	114	—	8,000	30,000	45,000	—

KM# 53 5 LIRE
25.0000 g., 0.9000 Silver .7234 oz. ASW, 37 mm. **Ruler:** Vittorio Emanuele III **Subject:** 50th Anniversary of the Kingdom **Obv:** Head left **Rev:** Two classical figures standing **Designer:** Dominico Trentacoste

Date	Mintage	F	VF	XF	Unc	BU
1911R	60,000	500	1,100	2,000	3,700	—

KM# 56 5 LIRE
25.0000 g., 0.9000 Silver .7234 oz. ASW **Ruler:** Vittorio Emanuele III **Obv:** Head right **Rev:** Quadriga with standing female **Rev. Designer:** Davide Calandra

Date	Mintage	F	VF	XF	Unc	BU
1914R	273,000	2,000	4,000	7,500	10,000	—

KM# 67.1 5 LIRE
5.0000 g., 0.8350 Silver .1342 oz. ASW, 23 mm. **Ruler:** Vittorio Emanuele III **Obv:** Head left **Rev:** Eagle with open wings standing on fascis **Edge Lettering:** *FERT*

Date	Mintage	F	VF	XF	Unc	BU
1926R	5,405,000	5.00	15.00	50.00	120	—
1927R	92,887,000	2.00	5.00	12.00	40.00	—
1928R	9,908,000	4.00	15.00	50.00	120	—
1929R	33,803,000	2.00	5.00	10.00	35.00	—
1930R	19,525,000	2.00	5.00	10.00	30.00	—
1931R	50	—	—	—	770	—
1932R	50	—	—	—	770	—
1933R	50	—	—	—	770	—
1934R	50	—	—	—	770	—
1935R	50	—	—	—	770	—

KM# 67.2 5 LIRE
5.0000 g., 0.8350 Silver .1342 oz. ASW, 23 mm. **Ruler:** Vittorio Emanuele III **Obv:** Head left **Rev:** Eagle with wings open standing on fascis **Edge Lettering:** ** FERT **

Date	Mintage	F	VF	XF	Unc	BU
1927R	Inc. above	2.00	5.00	12.00	35.00	—
1928R	Inc. above	8.00	20.00	80.00	120	—
1929R	Inc. above	2.00	5.00	12.00	35.00	—

KM# 79 5 LIRE
5.0000 g., 0.8350 Silver .1342 oz. ASW **Ruler:** Vittorio Emanuele III **Obv:** Head left **Rev:** Mother seated with three children

Date	Mintage	F	VF	XF	Unc	BU
1936R Yr. XIV	1,016,000	20.00	40.00	80.00	150	—
1937R Yr. XV	100,000	25.00	50.00	90.00	200	—
1938R Yr. XVIII	20	—	—	—	1,600	—
1939R Yr. XVIII	20	—	—	—	1,600	—
1940R Yr. XIX	20	—	—	—	1,600	—
1941R Yr. XX	20	—	—	—	1,600	—

KM# 47 10 LIRE
3.2258 g., 0.9000 Gold .0933 oz. AGW, 18 mm. **Ruler:** Vittorio Emanuele III **Rev. Designer:** Egidio Boninsegna

Date	Mintage	F	VF	XF	Unc	BU
1910R Rare	—	—	—	—	—	—
Note: All but one piece melted						
1912R	6,796	1,000	1,875	3,750	8,500	—
1926R	40	—	—	12,000	20,000	—
1927R	30	—	—	10,500	17,500	—

KM# 68.1 10 LIRE
10.0000 g., 0.8350 Silver .2684 oz. ASW **Ruler:** Vittorio Emanuele III **Obv:** Head left **Obv. Designer:** Giuseppe Romagnoli **Rev:** Biga with female **Edge Lettering:** *FERT*

Date	Mintage	F	VF	XF	Unc	BU
1926R	1,748,000	125	200	350	600	—
1927R	44,801,000	6.00	20.00	80.00	120	—
1928R	6,652,000	15.00	50.00	120	300	—
1929R	6,800,000	30.00	65.00	150	350	—
1930R	3,668,000	50.00	120	300	650	—
1931R	50	—	—	—	1,000	—
1932R	50	—	—	—	1,000	—
1933R	50	—	—	—	1,000	—
1934R	50	—	—	—	1,000	—

KM# 68.2 10 LIRE

10.0000 g., 0.8350 Silver .2684 oz. ASW **Ruler:** Vittorio Emanuele III **Obv:** Head left **Obv. Designer:** Giuseppe Romagnoli **Rev:** Biga with female **Edge Lettering:** **FERT**

Date	Mintage	F	VF	XF	Unc	BU
1927R	Inc. above	10.00	20.00	50.00	100	—
1928R	Inc. above	100	300	500	1,200	—
1929R	Inc. above	30.00	70.00	180	350	—

KM# 80 10 LIRE

10.0000 g., 0.8350 Silver .2684 oz. ASW **Ruler:** Vittorio Emanuele III **Obv:** Head right **Rev:** Female standing on prow **Designer:** Giuseppe Romagnoli

Date	Mintage	F	VF	XF	Unc	BU
1936R Yr. XIV	619,000	20.00	40.00	75.00	180	—
1937R Yr. XV	50	—	—	—	1,500	—
1938R Yr. XVII	20	—	—	—	2,100	—
1939R Yr. XVIII	20	—	—	—	2,100	—
1940R Yr. XIX	20	—	—	—	2,100	—
1941R Yr. XX	20	—	—	—	2,100	—

KM# 37.1 20 LIRE

6.4516 g., 0.9000 Gold .1867 oz. AGW **Ruler:** Vittorio Emanuele III **Obv:** Head left **Rev:** Crowned eagle with Savoy shield on chest

Date	Mintage	F	VF	XF	Unc	BU
1902R	181	—	15,000	25,000	35,000	—
1903R	1,800	650	1,350	2,500	4,500	—
1905R	8,715	450	800	1,350	2,500	—
1908R Rare	—	—	—	—	—	—

KM# 37.2 20 LIRE

6.4516 g., 0.9000 Gold .1867 oz. AGW **Ruler:** Vittorio Emanuele III **Obv:** Head left **Rev:** Crowned eagle with Savoy shield on chest **Note:** A small anchor below the neck indicates that the gold in the coin is from Eritrea.

Date	Mintage	F	VF	XF	Unc	BU
1902R	115	6,500	14,500	30,000	50,000	—

KM# 48 20 LIRE

6.4516 g., 0.9000 Gold .1867 oz. AGW **Ruler:** Vittorio Emanuele III **Obv:** Uniformed bust left **Rev:** Female standing on prow **Designer:** Egidio Boninsegna

Date	Mintage	F	VF	XF	Unc	BU
1910R	Est. 33,000	—	—	—	70,000	—
Note: Six pieces currently known to exist						
1912R	59,000	325	550	1,350	2,200	—
1926R	40	—	—	10,500	17,500	—
1927R	30	—	—	12,000	20,000	—

KM# 64 20 LIRE

6.4516 g., 0.9000 Gold .1867 oz. AGW, 21 mm. **Ruler:** Vittorio Emanuele III **Subject:** 1st Anniversary of Fascist Government **Obv:** Head left **Rev:** Axe head within fasces with value at left **Designer:** Attilio Motti

Date	Mintage	F	VF	XF	Unc	BU
1923R	20,000	310	620	1,300	2,100	2,500

KM# 69 20 LIRE

15.0000 g., 0.8000 Silver .3858 oz. ASW **Ruler:** Vittorio Emanuele III **Obv:** Head right **Rev:** Standing male with fasces approaching seated Italia **Designer:** Giuseppe Romagnoli

Date	Mintage	F	VF	XF	Unc	BU
1927R Yr. V	100	—	4,000	7,000	10,000	—
1927R Yr. VI	3,518,000	70.00	200	325	800	—
1928R Yr. VI	2,487,000	100	250	400	900	—
1929R Yr. VII	50	—	—	—	4,500	—
1930R Yr. VIII	50	—	—	—	4,500	—
1931R Yr. IX	50	—	—	—	4,500	—
1932R Yr. X	50	—	—	—	4,500	—
1933R Yr. XI	50	—	—	—	4,500	—
1934R Yr. XII	50	—	—	—	4,500	—

KM# 70 20 LIRE

20.0000 g., 0.6000 Silver .3858 oz. ASW, 35 mm. **Ruler:** Vittorio Emanuele III **Subject:** 10th Anniversary - End of World War I **Obv:** Helmeted head left **Rev:** Fasces, lion's head and axe head **Designer:** Giuseppe Romagnoli **Note:** Similar 20 and 100 Lire pieces were struck in gold. Silver and silvered brass items are modern fantasies.

Date	Mintage	F	VF	XF	Unc	BU
1928R	3,536,250	150	300	650	1,200	—

KM# 81 20 LIRE

20.0000 g., 0.8000 Silver .5145 oz. ASW **Ruler:** Vittorio Emanuele III **Obv:** Head left **Rev:** Quadriga and seated female **Designer:** Giuseppe Romagnoli

Date	Mintage	F	VF	XF	Unc	BU
1936R Yr. XIV	10,000	—	—	1,750	4,500	—
1937R Yr. XV	50	—	—	—	6,500	—
1938R Yr. XVII	20	—	—	—	7,500	—
1939R Yr. XVIII	20	—	—	—	7,500	—
1940R Yr. XIX	20	—	—	—	7,500	—
1941R Yr. XX	20	—	—	—	7,500	—

KM# 49 50 LIRE

16.1290 g., 0.9000 Gold .4667 oz. AGW **Ruler:** Vittorio Emanuele III **Obv:** Bust left **Rev:** Female with plow **Designer:** Egidio Boninsegna

Date	Mintage	F	VF	XF	Unc	BU
1910R Rare	2,096	—	—	—	—	—
1912R	11,000	550	1,200	2,000	3,000	4,500
1926R	40	—	—	—	30,000	—
1927R	30	—	—	—	25,000	—

KM# 54 50 LIRE

16.1290 g., 0.9000 Gold .4667 oz. AGW, 28 mm. **Ruler:** Vittorio Emanuele III **Subject:** 50th Anniversary of the Kingdom **Obv:** Head left **Rev:** Standing classical couple **Designer:** Domenico Trentacoste

Date	Mintage	F	VF	XF	Unc	BU
ND(1911)R	20,000	450	700	1,350	2,250	3,000

KM# 71 50 LIRE

4.3995 g., 0.9000 Gold .1273 oz. AGW **Ruler:** Vittorio Emanuele III **Obv:** Head left **Rev:** Man striding right

Date	Mintage	F	VF	XF	Unc	BU
1931R Yr. IX	32,000	95.00	130	325	500	—
1931R Yr. X	Inc. above	150	280	475	800	—
1932R Yr. X	12,000	200	325	500	900	—
1933R Yr. XI	6,463	300	425	775	1,500	—

KM# 82 50 LIRE

4.3995 g., 0.9000 Gold .1273 oz. AGW **Ruler:** Vittorio Emanuele III **Obv:** Head left **Rev:** Eagle with wings spread above Savoy shield

Date	Mintage	F	VF	XF	Unc	BU
1936R	790	1,250	2,200	5,000	9,000	15,000

KM# 39 100 LIRE

32.2580 g., 0.9000 Gold .9334 oz. AGW **Ruler:** Vittorio Emanuele III **Obv:** Head left **Rev:** Crowned eagle with Savoy shield on chest

Date	Mintage	F	VF	XF	Unc	BU
1903R	966	2,000	3,750	8,250	17,250	—
1905R	1,012	1,750	3,000	7,150	14,375	—

KM# 50 100 LIRE

32.2580 g., 0.9000 Gold .9334 oz. AGW **Ruler:** Vittorio Emanuele III **Obv:** Bust left **Rev:** Female with plow **Designer:** Egidio Boninsegna

Date	Mintage	F	VF	XF	Unc	BU
1910R Rare	2,013	—	—	—	—	—
1912R	4,946	—	2,500	4,000	8,000	—
1926R	40	—	13,500	19,500	38,000	—
1927R	30	—	15,750	25,000	40,000	—

KM# 65 100 LIRE
32.2580 g., 0.9000 Gold .9334 oz. AGW, 32 mm. **Ruler:** Vittorio Emanuele III **Subject:** 1st Anniversary of Fascist Government **Obv:** Head left **Rev:** Axe within fasces with value at left **Designer:** Attilio Motti

Date	Mintage	F	VF	XF	Unc	BU
1923R Matte finish	20,000	760	1,150	2,200	5,200	—
1923R Bright finish, rare	—	—	—	—	—	—

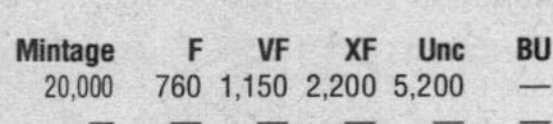

KM# 66 100 LIRE
32.2580 g., 0.9000 Gold .9334 oz. AGW, 35 mm. **Ruler:** Vittorio Emanuele III **Subject:** 25th year of reign, 10th Anniversary - World War I Entry **Obv:** Head left above oak sprigs **Rev:** Heroic male figure kneeling on large rock holding flag and small Victory **Designer:** Aurelio Mistruzzi

Date	Mintage	F	VF	XF	Unc	BU
1925R Matte finish	5,000	1,500	2,250	4,500	8,750	12,000
1925R Bright finish, rare	—	—	—	—	—	—

KM# 72 100 LIRE
8.7990 g., 0.9000 Gold .2546 oz. AGW **Ruler:** Vittorio Emanuele III **Obv:** Head left **Rev:** Female on prow **Designer:** Giuseppe Romagnoli

Date	Mintage	F	VF	XF	Unc	BU
1931R Yr. IX	34,000	BV	275	425	800	—
1931R Yr. X	Inc. above	200	300	500	1,200	—
1932R Yr. X	9,081	185	350	500	1,200	—
1933R Yr. XI	6,464	250	400	750	1,250	—

KM# 83 100 LIRE
8.7990 g., 0.9000 Gold .2546 oz. AGW, 25 mm. **Ruler:** Vittorio Emanuele III **Obv:** Head right **Rev:** Male figure striding left **Designer:** Giuseppe Romagnoli

Date	Mintage	F	VF	XF	Unc	BU
1936R	812	1,350	2,500	5,000	15,000	18,500

KM# 84 100 LIRE
5.1900 g., 0.9000 Gold .1502 oz. AGW, 20 mm. **Ruler:** Vittorio Emanuele III **Obv:** Head right **Rev:** Male figure striding left **Designer:** Giuseppe Romagnoli

Date	Mintage	F	VF	XF	Unc	BU
1937R Yr. XVI	249	—	7,500	13,500	27,000	42,500
1940R Yr. XVIII, rare	2	—	—	—	—	—

REPUBLIC

DECIMAL COINAGE

KM# 87 LIRA
Aluminum **Obv:** Wheat sprigs within head left **Rev:** Orange sprig

Date	Mintage	F	VF	XF	Unc	BU
1946R	104,000	25.00	50.00	120	200	—
1947R	12,000	100	300	600	1,100	—
1948R	9,000,000	0.40	2.00	7.00	30.00	—
1949R	13,200,000	0.40	2.00	7.00	30.00	—
1950R	1,942,000	1.00	3.00	10.00	40.00	—

KM# 91 LIRA
Aluminum, 17 mm. **Obv:** Balance scales **Rev:** Cornucopia, value and date **Designer:** Giuseppe Romagnoli **Note:** The 1968-1969 and 1982-1999 dates were issued in sets only.

Date	Mintage	F	VF	XF	Unc	BU
1951R	3,680,000	0.20	1.00	3.00	10.00	—
1952R	2,720,000	0.20	1.00	3.00	8.00	—
1953R	2,800,000	0.20	1.00	3.00	8.00	—
1954R	41,040,000	0.10	0.25	0.50	1.85	—
1955R	32,640,000	0.10	0.25	0.50	1.85	—
1956R	1,840,000	1.00	4.00	10.00	25.00	—
1957R	7,440,000	0.10	0.25	0.50	2.00	—
1958R	5,280,000	0.10	0.25	0.50	2.00	—
1959R	1,680,000	0.10	0.25	0.50	2.00	—
1968R	100,000	—	—	—	20.00	—
1969R	310,000	—	—	—	4.00	—
1970R	1,011,000	—	—	—	2.00	—
1980R	1,500,000	—	—	—	1.50	—
1981R	500,000	—	—	—	4.00	—
1982R	85,000	—	—	—	2.50	—
1983R	76,000	—	—	—	25.00	—
1984R	77,000	—	—	—	20.00	—
1985R	73,000	—	—	—	5.00	—
1985R Proof	20,000	Value: 8.00				
1986R	13,200	—	—	—	4.00	—
1986R Proof	17,500	Value: 12.00				
1987R	177,000	—	—	—	10.00	—
1987R Proof	—	Value: 25.00				
1988R	51,000	—	—	—	10.00	—
1988R Proof	9,000	Value: 12.00				
1989R	51,200	—	—	—	10.00	—
1989R Proof	9,260	Value: 12.00				
1990R	52,300	—	—	—	8.00	—
1990R Proof	9,600	Value: 12.00				
1991R	56,000	—	—	—	8.00	—
1991R Proof	11,000	Value: 12.00				
1992R	52,000	—	—	—	8.00	—
1992R Proof	9,500	Value: 12.00				
1993R	50,200	—	—	—	8.00	—
1993R Proof	8,500	Value: 12.00				
1994R	44,500	—	—	—	8.00	—
1994R Proof	8,500	Value: 12.00				
1995R Proof	7,960	Value: 20.00				
1995R	44,600	—	—	—	12.00	—
1996R Proof	8,000	Value: 12.00				
1996R	45,000	—	—	—	6.00	—
1997R Proof	8,440	Value: 15.00				
1997R	43,600	—	—	—	12.00	—
1998R Proof	9,000	Value: 12.00				
1998R	55,200	—	—	—	6.00	—
1999R Proof	8,000	Value: 10.00				
1999R	51,800	—	—	—	6.00	—
2000R	61,400	—	—	—	12.00	—
2000R Proof	9,000	Value: 20.00				

KM# 204 LIRA
14.6000 g., 0.8350 Silver .3919 oz. ASW **Series:** History of the Lira **Subject:** Lira of 1901, KM#32 **Obv:** Head right within circle **Rev:** Crowned eagle with shield on chest within beaded circle **Edge:** Reeded and plain

Date	Mintage	F	VF	XF	Unc	BU
1999R	—	—	—	—	55.00	—
1999R Proof	—	Value: 75.00				

KM# 205 LIRA
14.6000 g., 0.8350 Silver .3919 oz. ASW **Series:** History of the Lira **Subject:** Lira of 1915, KM#57 **Obv:** Head right within circle **Rev:** Quadriga with standing female within circle

Date	Mintage	F	VF	XF	Unc	BU
1999R	—	—	—	—	55.00	—
1999R Proof	—	Value: 75.00				

KM# 206 LIRA
14.6000 g., 0.8350 Silver .3919 oz. ASW, 34 mm. **Series:** History of the Lira **Subject:** Lira of 1922, KM#62 **Obv:** Seated allegorical figure within circle **Rev:** Crowned shield and value within wreath flanked by small circles **Edge:** Reeded and plain sections

Date	Mintage	F	VF	XF	Unc	BU
2000	—	—	—	—	55.00	—
2000 Proof	—	Value: 75.00				

KM# 207 LIRA
14.6000 g., 0.8350 Silver .3919 oz. ASW, 34 mm. **Series:** History of the Lire **Subject:** Lira of 1936, KM#77 **Obv:** Head left within circle **Rev:** Eagle in front of fasces within circle flanked by sprigs **Edge:** Reeded and plain sections

Date	Mintage	F	VF	XF	Unc	BU
2000	—	—	—	—	55.00	—
2000 Proof	—	Value: 75.00				

KM# 88 2 LIRE
Aluminum **Obv:** Ploughman **Rev:** Wheat ear divides value **Designer:** Giuseppe Romagnoli

Date	Mintage	F	VF	XF	Unc	BU
1946R	123,000	20.00	60.00	120	300	—
1947R	12,000	125	300	800	1,200	—
1948R	7,200,000	0.50	2.00	10.00	30.00	—
1949R	1,350,000	3.00	10.00	30.00	100	—
1950R	2,640,000	0.60	2.50	10.00	35.00	—

KM# 94 2 LIRE
Aluminum **Obv:** Honey bee **Rev:** Olive branch and value **Note:** The 1968-1969 and 1982-1999 dates were issued in sets only.

Date	Mintage	F	VF	XF	Unc	BU
1953R	4,125,000	0.20	0.50	2.00	5.00	—
1954R	22,500,000	0.20	0.50	2.00	5.00	—
1955R	2,750,000	0.20	0.50	2.00	5.00	—
1956R	1,500,000	1.50	3.00	8.00	20.00	—
1957R	6,313,000	0.20	0.50	2.00	5.00	—
1958R	125,000	25.00	60.00	100	180	—
1959R	2,000,000	0.20	0.50	2.00	5.00	—
1968R	100,000	—	—	—	20.00	—
1969R	310,000	—	—	—	4.00	—
1970R	1,140,000	—	—	—	2.50	—
1980R	500,000	—	—	—	2.00	—
1981R	500,000	—	—	—	3.00	—
1982R	85,000	—	—	—	3.00	—
1983R	76,000	6.00	15.00	20.00	40.00	—
1984R	77,000	—	—	8.00	15.00	—
1985R	91,220	—	—	—	8.00	—
1985R Proof	20,000	Value: 10.00				
1986R	73,200	—	—	—	8.00	—
1986R Proof	17,500	Value: 10.00				
1987R	57,500	—	—	—	10.00	—
1987R Proof	10,000	Value: 15.00				
1988R	51,050	—	—	—	25.00	—
1988R Proof	9,000	Value: 25.00				
1989R	51,200	—	—	—	8.00	—
1989R Proof	9,260	Value: 10.00				
1990R	53,300	—	—	—	10.00	—
1990R Proof	9,600	Value: 15.00				
1991R	54,000	—	—	—	8.00	—
1991R Proof	11,000	Value: 10.00				
1992R	52,000	—	—	—	8.00	—
1992R Proof	9,500	Value: 10.00				
1993R	50,200	—	—	—	8.00	—
1993R Proof	8,500	Value: 10.00				
1994R Proof	8,500	Value: 20.00				
1994R	44,500	—	—	—	18.00	—
1995R	44,588	—	—	—	30.00	—
1995R Proof	7,960	Value: 30.00				
1996R Proof	8,000	Value: 18.00				
1996R	65,000	—	—	—	8.00	—
1997R	43,600	—	—	—	30.00	—
1997R Proof	8,660	Value: 35.00				
1998R	55,200	—	—	—	8.00	—
1998R Proof	9,000	Value: 10.00				
1999R Proof	8,500	Value: 10.00				
1999R	51,800	—	—	—	8.00	—
2000R Proof	9,000	Value: 15.00				
2000R	61,500	—	—	—	8.00	—

KM# 89 5 LIRE

Aluminum **Obv:** Female head holding torch facing right **Rev:** Grape cluster

Date	Mintage	F	VF	XF	Unc	BU
1946R	81,000	200	350	700	1,000	—
1947R	17,000	325	425	700	1,000	—
1948R	25,125,000	0.50	2.00	8.00	50.00	—
1949R	71,100,000	0.30	2.00	5.00	25.00	—
1950R	114,790,000	0.30	2.00	5.00	25.00	—

KM# 92 5 LIRE

1.0000 g., Aluminum, 20.20 mm. **Obv:** Rudder **Rev:** Dolphin and value **Designer:** Giuseppe Romagnoli

Date	Mintage	F	VF	XF	Unc	BU
1951R	40,260,000	0.10	0.25	1.00	6.00	—
1952R	57,400,000	0.10	0.25	1.00	6.00	—
1953R	196,200,000	0.10	0.25	0.50	3.00	—
1954R	436,400,000	0.10	0.25	0.50	3.00	—
1955R	159,000,000	0.10	0.25	0.50	2.00	—
1956R	400,000	30.00	70.00	400	1,200	—
1966R	1,200,000	0.25	0.50	2.00	6.00	—
1967R	10,600,000	0.10	0.25	0.50	1.00	—
1968R	7,500,000	—	—	0.10	0.75	—
1969R	7,910,000	—	—	0.10	0.75	—
1969R Inverted 1 (die break at base of 1)	969,000	3.00	6.00	18.00	65.00	—
1970R	4,200,000	—	—	0.10	0.75	—
1971R	8,600,000	—	—	0.10	0.75	—
1972R	16,400,000	—	—	0.10	0.50	—
1973R	28,800,000	—	—	0.10	0.50	—
1974R	6,600,000	—	—	0.10	0.50	—
1975R	7,000,000	—	—	0.10	0.50	—
1976R	8,800,000	—	—	0.10	0.50	—
1977R	6,700,000	—	—	0.10	0.50	—
1978R	3,600,000	—	—	0.10	0.50	—

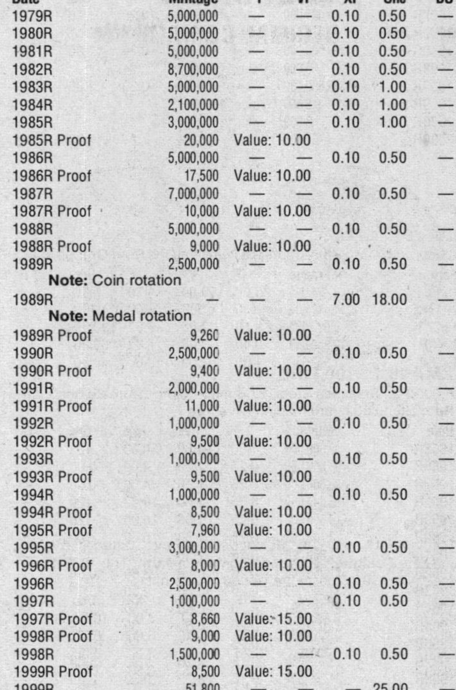

Date	Mintage	F	VF	XF	Unc	BU
1979R	5,000,000	—	—	0.10	0.50	—
1980R	5,000,000	—	—	0.10	0.50	—
1981R	5,000,000	—	—	0.10	0.50	—
1982R	8,700,000	—	—	0.10	0.50	—
1983R	5,000,000	—	—	0.10	1.00	—
1984R	2,100,000	—	—	0.10	1.00	—
1985R	3,000,000	—	—	0.10	1.00	—
1985R Proof	20,000	Value: 10.00				
1986R	5,000,000	—	—	0.10	0.50	—
1986R Proof	17,500	Value: 10.00				
1987R	7,000,000	—	—	0.10	0.50	—
1987R Proof	10,000	Value: 10.00				
1988R	5,000,000	—	—	0.10	0.50	—
1988R Proof	9,000	Value: 10.00				
1989R	2,500,000	—	—	0.10	0.50	—
Note: Coin rotation						
1989R	—	—	—	7.00	18.00	—
Note: Medal rotation						
1989R Proof	9,260	Value: 10.00				
1990R	2,500,000	—	—	0.10	0.50	—
1990R Proof	9,400	Value: 10.00				
1991R	2,000,000	—	—	0.10	0.50	—
1991R Proof	11,000	Value: 10.00				
1992R	1,000,000	—	—	0.10	0.50	—
1992R Proof	9,500	Value: 10.00				
1993R	1,000,000	—	—	0.10	0.50	—
1993R Proof	9,500	Value: 10.00				
1994R	1,000,000	—	—	0.10	0.50	—
1994R Proof	8,500	Value: 10.00				
1995R Proof	7,960	Value: 10.00				
1995R	3,000,000	—	—	0.10	0.50	—
1996R Proof	8,000	Value: 10.00				
1996R	2,500,000	—	—	0.10	0.50	—
1997R	1,000,000	—	—	0.10	0.50	—
1997R Proof	8,660	Value: 15.00				
1998R Proof	9,000	Value: 10.00				
1998R	1,500,000	—	—	0.10	0.50	—
1999R Proof	8,500	Value: 15.00				
1999R	51,800	—	—	—	25.00	—
2000R Proof	10,000	Value: 20.00				
2000R	61,400	—	—	—	20.00	—

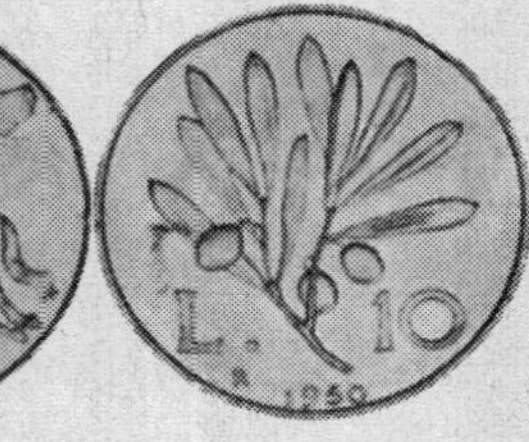

KM# 90 10 LIRE

Aluminum, 29 mm. **Obv:** Pegasus **Rev:** Olive branch divides value **Designer:** Giuseppe Romagnoli

Date	Mintage	F	VF	XF	Unc	BU
1946R	101,000	60.00	120	300	700	—
1947R	12,000	375	900	1,450	2,600	—
1948R	14,400,000	1.00	10.00	40.00	100	—
1949R	49,500,000	0.50	1.00	5.00	30.00	—
1950R	53,311,000	0.50	1.00	5.00	30.00	—

KM# 93 10 LIRE

1.6000 g., Aluminum, 23.25 mm. **Obv:** Plow **Rev:** Value within wheat ears **Designer:** Giuseppe Romagnoli

Date	Mintage	F	VF	XF	Unc	BU
1951R	96,600,000	0.10	0.50	3.00	30.00	—
1952R	105,150,000	0.10	0.50	3.00	15.00	—
1953R	151,500,000	0.10	0.50	3.00	15.00	—
1954R	95,250,000	0.50	1.00	5.00	40.00	—
1955R	274,950,000	0.10	0.15	2.00	5.00	—
1956R	76,650,000	0.10	1.00	5.00	20.00	—
1965R	1,050,000	0.25	1.00	5.00	20.00	—
1966R	16,500,000	0.10	0.25	1.00	3.00	—
1967R	29,450,000	0.10	0.25	1.00	3.00	—
1968R	32,200,000	—	—	0.10	0.75	—
1969R	23,710,000	—	—	0.10	0.75	—
1970R	14,100,000	—	—	0.10	0.75	—
1971R	23,550,000	—	—	0.10	0.75	—
1972R	61,300,000	—	—	0.10	0.50	—
1973R	145,800,000	—	—	0.10	0.50	—
1974R	85,000,000	—	—	0.10	0.50	—
1975R	76,800,000	—	—	0.10	0.50	—
1976R	82,000,000	—	—	0.10	0.50	—
1977R	80,750,000	—	—	0.10	0.50	—
1978R	43,800,000	—	—	0.10	0.50	—
1979R	98,000,000	—	—	0.10	0.50	—
1980R	89,000,000	—	—	0.10	0.50	—
1981R	91,750,000	—	—	0.10	0.50	—
1982R	44,500,000	—	—	0.10	0.50	—
1983R	15,110,000	—	—	0.50	1.00	—
1984R	11,122,000	—	—	0.50	1.00	—
1985R	15,000,000	—	—	0.10	0.50	—
1985R Proof	20,000	Value: 10.00				
1986R	16,000,000	—	—	0.10	0.50	—
1986R Proof	17,500	Value: 8.00				
1987R	13,000,000	—	—	0.10	0.50	—
1987R Proof	10,000	Value: 8.00				
1988R	13,000,000	—	—	0.10	0.50	—
1988R Proof	9,000	Value: 10.00				
1989R	16,000,000	—	—	0.10	0.50	—
1989R Proof	9,260	Value: 10.00				
1990R	14,000,000	—	—	0.10	1.00	—
1990R Proof	9,400	Value: 10.00				
1991R	5,000,000	—	—	0.10	1.00	—
1991R Proof	11,000	Value: 10.00				
1992R	1,000,000	—	—	0.10	1.00	—
1992R Proof	9,500	Value: 10.00				
1993R	1,000,000	—	—	0.10	1.00	—
1993R Proof	8,500	Value: 10.00				
1994R	1,000,000	—	—	0.10	1.00	—
1994R Proof	8,500	Value: 10.00				
1995R Proof	7,960	Value: 12.00				
1995R	2,500,000	—	—	0.10	1.00	—
1996R Proof	8,000	Value: 10.00				
1996R	3,500,000	—	—	0.10	1.00	—
1997R	2,000,000	—	—	0.10	1.00	—
1997R Proof	8,440	Value: 15.00				
1998R Proof	9,000	Value: 1.00				
1998R	1,500,000	—	—	0.10	1.00	—
1999R	1,500,000	—	—	0.10	1.00	—
1999R Proof	8,500	Value: 10.00				
2000R Proof	—	Value: 18.00				
2000R	61,400	—	—	—	20.00	—

KM# 97.1 20 LIRE

3.6000 g., Aluminum-Bronze, 21.25 mm. **Obv:** Wheat sprigs within head left **Rev:** Oak leaves divides value and date **Designer:** Pietro Giampaoli

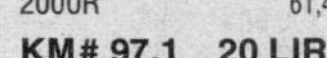

Date	Mintage	F	VF	XF	Unc	BU
1957R Serifed 7	Est. 60,075,000	0.20	0.40	2.00	10.00	—
1957R Plain 7	Inc. above	0.20	0.40	2.00	10.00	—
1958R	80,550,000	0.10	0.40	3.00	12.00	—
1959R	4,005,000	0.50	2.00	8.00	50.00	—

KM# 97.2 20 LIRE

3.6000 g., Aluminum-Bronze, 21.25 mm. **Obv:** Wheat sprigs within head left **Rev:** Oak leaves divides value and date **Edge:** Plain **Designer:** Pietro Giampaoli

Date	Mintage	F	VF	XF	Unc	BU
1968R	100,000	3.00	6.00	25.00	60.00	—
1969R	16,735,000	0.10	0.15	0.25	1.00	—
1970R	31,500,000	0.10	0.15	0.25	0.65	—
1971R	12,375,000	0.10	0.15	0.25	1.00	—
1972R	34,400,000	0.10	0.15	0.25	0.65	—
1973R	20,000,000	0.10	0.15	0.25	0.65	—
1974R	17,000,000	0.10	0.15	0.20	0.65	—
1975R	25,000,000	0.10	0.15	0.20	0.65	—
1976R	17,325,000	0.10	0.15	0.20	0.65	—
1977R	10,000,000	0.10	0.15	0.20	0.65	—
1978R	13,521,000	0.10	0.15	0.20	0.65	—
1979R	40,465,000	0.10	0.15	0.20	0.50	—
1980R	61,795,000	0.10	0.15	0.20	0.50	—
1981R	81,510,000	0.10	0.15	0.20	0.50	—
1982R	34,500,000	0.10	0.15	0.20	0.50	—
1983R	15,110,000	0.10	0.15	0.20	0.50	—
1984R	5,122,000	0.10	0.15	1.00	3.00	—
1985R	15,000,000	0.10	0.15	0.20	0.50	—
1985R Proof	20,000	Value: 10.00				
1986R	13,000,000	0.10	0.15	0.20	0.50	—
1986R Proof	17,500	Value: 10.00				
1987R	2,766,000	0.10	0.15	1.00	3.00	—
1987R Proof	10,000	Value: 5.00				
1988R	13,000,000	0.10	0.15	0.20	0.50	—
1988R Proof	9,000	Value: 5.00				
1989R	16,000,000	0.10	0.15	0.20	0.50	—
1989R Proof	9,260	Value: 5.00				
1990R	15,500,000	0.10	0.15	0.20	0.50	—
1990R Proof	9,400	Value: 5.00				
1991R	13,000,000	0.10	0.15	0.20	0.50	—
1991R Proof	11,000	Value: 5.00				
1992R	2,500,000	0.10	0.15	1.00	3.00	—
1992R Proof	9,500	Value: 5.00				
1993R	1,000,000	0.10	0.15	0.50	1.00	—
1993R Proof	8,500	Value: 5.00				
1994R	1,000,000	0.10	0.15	0.20	0.50	—
1994R Proof	8,500	Value: 5.00				
1995R Proof	7,950	Value: 5.00				
1995R	1,000,000	0.10	0.15	0.50	1.00	—
1996R	1,000,000	0.10	0.15	0.50	1.00	—
1996R Proof	8,000	Value: 5.00				
1997R Proof	8,440	Value: 5.00				
1997R	1,000,000	0.10	0.15	0.50	1.00	—
1998R	1,000,000	0.10	0.15	0.50	1.00	—

Date	Mintage	F	VF	XF	Unc	BU
1998R Proof	9,000	Value: 5.00				
1999R Proof	8,500	Value: 5.00				
1999R	500,000	0.10	0.15	1.00	3.00	—
2000R Proof	8,960	Value: 8.00				
2000R	61,400	—	—	—	20.00	—

KM# 95.1 50 LIRE

6.2500 g., Stainless Steel, 24.8 mm. **Obv:** Head right **Rev:** Vulcan standing at anvil facing left divides date and value **Designer:** Giuseppe Romagnoli

Date	Mintage	F	VF	XF	Unc	BU
1954R	17,600,000	1.00	5.00	25.00	100	—
1955R	70,500,000	0.50	1.50	10.00	40.00	—
1956R	69,400,000	0.50	1.50	10.00	40.00	—
1957R	8,925,000	2.00	8.00	30.00	120	—
1958R	825,000	5.00	15.00	60.00	200	—
1959R	8,800,000	4.00	7.00	12.00	40.00	—
1960R	2,025,000	5.00	10.00	40.00	100	—
1961R	11,100,000	0.50	1.50	10.00	40.00	—
1962R	17,700,000	0.50	1.50	5.00	30.00	—
1963R	31,600,000	0.20	0.75	2.50	20.00	—
1964R	37,900,000	0.20	0.75	2.50	18.00	—
1965R	25,300,000	0.20	0.50	1.50	12.00	—
1966R	27,400,000	0.20	0.40	0.80	8.00	—
1967R	28,000,000	0.20	0.40	0.80	6.00	—
1968R	17,800,000	0.20	0.30	0.50	1.50	—
1969R	23,010,000	0.20	0.30	0.50	1.50	—
1970R	21,411,000	0.10	0.20	0.50	1.50	—
1971R	33,410,000	0.10	0.20	0.50	1.50	—
1972R	39,000,000	0.10	0.20	0.50	1.50	—
1973R	48,700,000	0.10	0.20	0.50	1.50	—
1974R	63,000,000	0.10	0.20	0.35	1.00	—
1975R	87,000,000	0.10	0.15	0.25	0.75	—
1976R	180,600,000	0.10	0.15	0.25	0.75	—
1977R	293,800,000	0.10	0.15	0.25	0.75	—
1978R	416,808,000	0.10	0.15	0.25	0.75	—
1979R	321,086,000	0.10	0.15	0.25	0.75	—
1980R	94,819,000	0.10	0.15	0.25	0.75	—
1981R	139,080,000	0.10	0.15	0.25	0.75	—
1982R	54,500,000	0.10	0.15	0.25	0.75	—
1983R	20,000,000	0.10	0.15	0.25	0.75	—
1984R	10,000,000	0.10	0.15	0.25	0.75	—
1985R	10,000,000	0.10	0.15	0.25	0.75	—
1985R Proof	20,000	Value: 10.00				
1986R	15,000,000	0.10	0.15	0.25	0.75	—
1986R Proof	17,500	Value: 10.00				
1987R	14,682,000	0.10	0.15	0.25	0.75	—
1987R Proof	10,000	Value: 10.00				
1988R	20,000,000	0.10	0.15	0.25	0.75	—
1988R Proof	9,000	Value: 10.00				
1989R	26,500,000	0.10	0.15	0.25	0.75	—
1989R Proof	9,200	Value: 12.00				

KM# 95.2 50 LIRE

Stainless Steel, 17 mm. **Obv:** Head right **Rev:** Vulcan standing at anvil facing left divides date and value **Designer:** Giuseppe Romagnoli **Note:** Reduced size.

Date	Mintage	F	VF	XF	Unc	BU
1990R	45,500,000	—	0.10	0.20	0.50	—
1991R	60,000,000	—	0.10	0.20	0.50	—
1991R Proof	11,000	Value: 10.00				
1992R	90,000,000	—	0.10	0.20	0.50	—
1992R Proof	9,500	Value: 10.00				
1993R	160,000,000	—	0.10	0.20	0.50	—
1993R Proof	8,500	Value: 10.00				
1994R Proof	8,500	Value: 10.00				
1994R	95,255,000	—	0.10	0.20	0.50	—
1995R	82,000,000	—	0.10	0.20	0.50	—
1995R Proof	7,960	Value: 12.00				

KM# 183 50 LIRE

Copper-Nickel, 19 mm. **Obv:** Turreted head left **Rev:** Large value within wreath of produce **Designer:** L. Cretara

Date	Mintage	F	VF	XF	Unc	BU
1996R	110,000,000	—	0.10	0.20	0.50	—
1996R Proof	8,000	Value: 10.00				

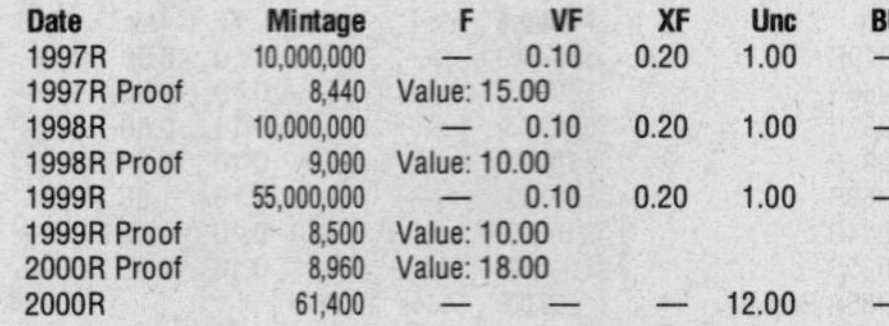

Date	Mintage	F	VF	XF	Unc	BU
1997R	10,000,000	—	0.10	0.20	1.00	—
1997R Proof	8,440	Value: 15.00				
1998R	10,000,000	—	0.10	0.20	1.00	—
1998R Proof	9,000	Value: 10.00				
1999R	55,000,000	—	0.10	0.20	1.00	—
1999R Proof	8,500	Value: 10.00				
2000R Proof	8,960	Value: 18.00				
2000R	61,400	—	—	—	12.00	—

KM# 96.1 100 LIRE

8.0000 g., Stainless Steel, 27.8 mm. **Obv:** Laureate head left **Rev:** Standing figure holding olive tree

Date	Mintage	F	VF	XF	Unc	BU
1955R	8,600,000	1.00	4.00	50.00	185	—
1956R	99,800,000	0.25	1.00	4.00	50.00	—
1957R	90,600,000	0.25	1.50	4.00	50.00	—
1958R	25,640,000	0.25	1.50	10.00	120	—
1959R	19,500,000	0.25	1.50	10.00	120	—
1960R	20,700,000	0.25	1.50	10.00	100	—
1961R	11,860,000	0.25	1.50	10.00	100	—
1962R	21,700,000	0.20	0.50	3.00	40.00	—
1963R	33,100,000	0.20	0.50	2.00	30.00	—
1964R	31,300,000	0.20	0.50	1.50	20.00	—
1965R	37,000,000	0.20	0.50	1.50	20.00	—
1966R	52,500,000	0.15	0.25	1.00	15.00	—
1967R	23,700,000	0.15	0.25	1.00	15.00	—
1968R	34,200,000	0.15	0.25	0.50	2.00	—
1969R	27,710,000	0.15	0.25	0.50	2.00	—
1970R	25,011,000	0.15	0.25	0.50	2.00	—
1971R	24,700,000	0.15	0.25	0.50	2.00	—
1972R	31,170,000	0.15	0.25	0.50	3.00	—
1973R	30,780,000	0.15	0.25	0.50	3.00	—
1974R	61,000,000	0.15	0.25	0.35	0.85	—
1975R	106,650,000	0.15	0.25	0.35	0.85	—
1976R	160,020,000	0.15	0.25	0.35	0.85	—
1977R	253,980,000	0.15	0.25	0.35	0.85	—
1978R	343,626,000	0.15	0.25	0.35	0.85	—
1979R	351,583,600	0.15	0.25	0.35	0.85	—
1980R	69,938,500	0.15	0.25	0.35	0.85	—
1981R	122,381,700	0.15	0.25	0.35	0.85	—
1982R	39,500,000	0.15	0.25	0.35	0.85	—
1983R	25,000,000	0.15	0.25	1.00	3.00	—
1984R	10,000,000	0.15	0.25	1.00	3.00	—
1985R	10,000,000	0.15	0.25	1.00	3.00	—
1985R Proof	20,000	Value: 10.00				
1986R	18,000,000	0.15	0.25	0.50	1.00	—
1986R Proof	17,500	Value: 10.00				
1987R	25,000,000	0.15	0.25	0.50	1.00	—
1987R Proof	10,000	Value: 10.00				
1988R	23,000,000	0.15	0.25	0.85	1.00	—
1988R Proof	9,000	Value: 15.00				
1989R	34,000,000	0.15	0.25	0.85	1.00	—
1989R Proof	9,260	Value: 15.00				

KM# 96.2 100 LIRE

Stainless Steel **Obv:** Laureate head left **Rev:** Standing figure holding olive tree **Note:** Reduced size. Prev. KM#96a.

Date	Mintage	F	VF	XF	Unc	BU
1990R Proof	9,600	Value: 12.00				
1990R	60,000,000	—	—	—	1.00	—
1991R	100,000,000	—	—	—	1.00	—
1991R Proof	11,000	Value: 12.00				
1992R	166,000,000	—	—	—	1.00	—
1992R Proof	9,500	Value: 12.00				

KM# 102 100 LIRE

8.0000 g., Stainless Steel, 27.8 mm. **Subject:** 100th Anniversary - Birth of Guglielmo Marconi, Physicist **Obv:** Head facing **Rev:** Early radio-wave receiver flanked by date and value **Designer:** Guerrino M. Monassi

Date	Mintage	F	VF	XF	Unc	BU
ND(1974)R	50,000,000	0.15	0.25	0.35	1.50	—

KM# 106 100 LIRE

8.0000 g., Stainless Steel, 27.8 mm. , Young head left **Series:** F.A.O. **Rev:** Cow nursing calf, value and date **Designer:** Giandomenico

Date	Mintage	F	VF	XF	Unc	BU
1979R	78,340,000	0.15	0.25	0.50	1.50	—

KM# 108 100 LIRE

8.0000 g., Stainless Steel, 27.8 mm. **Subject:** Centennial of Livorno Naval Academy **Obv:** Anchor and ship's wheel **Rev:** Building divides dates with flag and value below **Designer:** M. Vallucci

Date	Mintage	F	VF	XF	Unc	BU
ND(1981)R	39,500,000	0.15	0.25	0.35	1.50	—

KM# 127 100 LIRE

8.0000 g., 0.8350 Silver .2148 oz. ASW, 27.8 mm. **Subject:** 900th Anniversary - University of Bologna **Obv:** Medieval student in thought **Rev:** Towered building

Date	Mintage	F	VF	XF	Unc	BU
1988R	68,000	—	—	—	18.00	—
1988R Proof	13,000	Value: 28.00				

KM# 159 100 LIRE

Copper-Nickel, 22 mm. **Obv:** Turreted head left **Rev:** Large value within circle flanked by sprigs **Designer:** Laura Cretara

Date	Mintage	F	VF	XF	Unc	BU
1993R	211,501,200	0.15	0.25	0.35	0.75	—
1993R Proof	8,500	Value: 10.00				
1994R	180,000,000	0.15	0.25	0.35	0.75	—
1994R Proof	8,500	Value: 15.00				
1996R Proof	8,000	Value: 15.00				
1996R	210,000,000	0.15	0.25	0.35	0.75	—
1997R Proof	8,440	Value: 20.00				
1997R	70,000,000	0.15	0.25	0.35	0.75	—
1998R Proof	9,000	Value: 15.00				
1998R	120,000,000	0.15	0.25	0.35	0.75	—
1999R	120,000,000	0.15	0.25	0.35	0.75	—
1999R Proof	8,500	Value: 15.00				
2000R	61,400	0.15	0.25	0.35	15.00	—
2000R Proof	10,000	Value: 20.00				

KM# 171 100 LIRE

5.0000 g., 835.0000 Silver .1342 oz. ASW **Subject:** 100th Anniversary - Bank of Italy **Rev:** Printing press **Note:** Both uncirculated and proof versions were issued in sets only.

Date	Mintage	F	VF	XF	Unc	BU
ND(1993)R	52,000	—	—	—	20.00	—
ND(1993)R Proof	10,000	Value: 35.00				

KM# 180 100 LIRE
4.5300 g., Copper-Nickel, 22 mm. **Series:** F.A.O. **Obv:** Turreted head left **Rev:** Logo and value within globe design
Designer: Laura Cretara

Date	Mintage	F	VF	XF	Unc	BU
ND(1995)R	100,000,000	0.15	0.25	0.35	0.75	—
ND(1995)R Proof	7,960	Value: 25.00				

KM# 105 200 LIRE
5.0000 g., Aluminum-Bronze, 24 mm. **Obv:** Head right **Rev:** Value within gear **Designer:** M. Vallucci

Date	Mintage	F	VF	XF	Unc	BU
1977R	15,900,000	0.20	0.25	0.35	1.25	—
1978R	461,034,000	0.20	0.25	0.35	1.25	—
1979R	487,325,000	0.20	0.25	0.35	1.25	—
1980R	105,690,000	0.20	0.25	0.45	2.00	—
1981R	72,500,000	0.20	0.25	0.45	2.00	—
1982R	9,500,000	0.20	0.25	1.00	4.00	—
1983R	20,000,000	0.20	0.25	0.75	3.00	—
1984R	10,000,000	0.20	0.25	0.75	3.00	—
1985R	15,000,000	0.20	0.25	0.75	3.00	—
1985R Proof	20,000	Value: 10.00				
1986R	15,000,000	0.20	0.25	0.75	3.00	—
1986R Proof	17,500	Value: 10.00				
1987R	26,180,000	0.20	0.25	0.35	1.25	—
1987R Proof	10,000	Value: 10.00				
1988R	37,000,000	0.20	0.25	0.35	1.25	—
1988R Proof	9,000	Value: 15.00				
1991R	70,000,000	0.20	0.25	0.35	1.25	—
1991R Proof	11,000	Value: 10.00				
1995R Proof	7,960	Value: 20.00				
1995R	170,000,000	0.20	0.25	0.35	1.25	—
1998R	120,000,000	0.20	0.25	0.35	1.25	—
1998R Proof	9,000	Value: 10.00				
1999R	—	0.20	0.25	0.35	1.25	—
1999R Proof	—	Value: 10.00				
2000R	61,400	—	—	—	15.00	—
2000R Proof	8,960	Value: 12.50				

KM# 107 200 LIRE
5.0000 g., Aluminum-Bronze, 24 mm. **Series:** F.A.O. **Subject:** International Women's Year **Obv:** Bust facing **Rev:** Seated woman with knee bent and child standing at her back facing right **Designer:** Giondomenico

Date	Mintage	F	VF	XF	Unc	BU
1980R	48,500,000	0.20	0.25	0.35	2.00	—

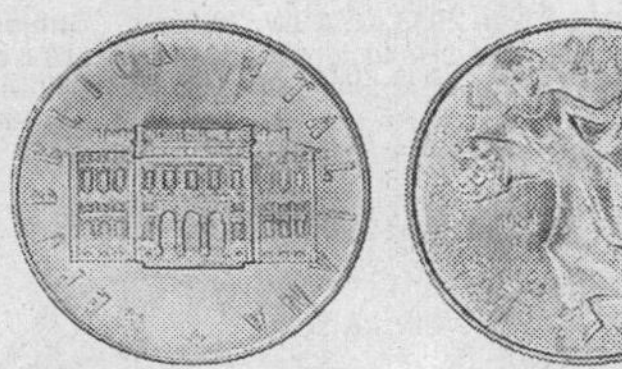

KM# 109 200 LIRE
5.0000 g., Aluminum-Bronze, 24 mm. **Subject:** World Food Day **Obv:** Villa Lubin façade **Rev:** Female advancing left holding cornucopia **Designer:** Guido Veroi

Date	Mintage	F	VF	XF	Unc	BU
1981R	45,207,600	0.20	0.25	0.35	2.00	—

KM# 128 200 LIRE
5.0000 g., 0.8350 Silver .1342 oz. ASW **Subject:** 900th Anniversary - University of Bologna **Obv:** Medieval student in thought **Rev:** Courtyard view within oval rope wreath

Date	Mintage	F	VF	XF	Unc	BU
1988R	68,000	—	—	—	20.00	—
1988R Proof	13,000	Value: 30.00				

KM# 130 200 LIRE
5.0000 g., Bronzital, 24 mm. **Subject:** Taranto Naval Yards **Obv:** Head right **Rev:** Ships and dates **Designer:** M. Vallucci

Date	Mintage	F	VF	XF	Unc	BU
ND(1989)R	48,000,000	—	—	—	2.00	—
ND(1989)R Proof	9,260	Value: 10.00				

KM# 133 200 LIRE
5.0000 g., 0.8350 Silver .1342 oz. ASW **Subject:** Soccer **Obv:** Head left **Rev:** Ball superimposed on world globe within assorted shields bordering

Date	Mintage	F	VF	XF	Unc	BU
1989R	86,000	—	—	—	15.00	—
1989R Proof	28,000	Value: 18.50				

KM# 138 200 LIRE
5.0000 g., 0.8350 Silver .1342 oz. ASW **Subject:** Christopher Columbus **Obv:** Bust 3/4 right within globe design **Rev:** Shield divides date and value above dolphin

Date	Mintage	F	VF	XF	Unc	BU
1989R	75,000	—	—	—	15.00	—
1989R Proof	25,000	Value: 22.50				

KM# 135 200 LIRE
5.0000 g., Bronzital, 24 mm. **Obv:** Head right **Obv. Designer:** M. Vallucci **Rev:** State Council building divides dates and value **Rev. Designer:** Driutti

Date	Mintage	F	VF	XF	Unc	BU
ND(1990)R	64,500,000	—	—	—	2.00	—
ND(1990)R Proof	9,600	Value: 10.00				

KM# 142 200 LIRE
9.0000 g., 0.8350 Silver .2416 oz. ASW **Subject:** Italian Flora and Fauna **Obv:** Female head left with flora and fauna in hair **Obv. Designer:** Annalisa Valentini **Rev:** Wolf divides date and value

Date	Mintage	F	VF	XF	Unc	BU
1991R	57,000	—	—	—	20.00	—
1991R Proof	10,000	Value: 27.50				

KM# 151 200 LIRE
5.0000 g., Aluminum-Bronze, 24 mm. **Subject:** Genoa Stamp Exposition **Obv:** Head right **Rev:** Stylized sailing ship **Designer:** M. Vallucci

Date	Mintage	F	VF	XF	Unc	BU
1992R	110,000,000	—	—	—	2.50	—
1992R Proof	9,500	Value: 12.00				

KM# 155 200 LIRE
5.0000 g., Aluminum-Bronze, 24 mm. **Subject:** 70th Anniversary of Military Aviation **Obv:** Head right **Obv. Designer:** M. Vallucci **Rev:** Quartered arms within circle **Rev. Designer:** Zanelli

Date	Mintage	F	VF	XF	Unc	BU
1993R Proof	8,500	Value: 10.00				
1993R	170,000,000	—	—	—	2.50	—

KM# 172 200 LIRE
5.0000 g., 0.8350 Silver .1343 oz. ASW **Subject:** 100th Anniversary - Bank of Italy **Obv:** Female head left with headdress **Rev:** Hammered minting scene **Note:** Both uncirculated and proof versions were issued in sets only.

Date	Mintage	F	VF	XF	Unc	BU
ND(1993)R	52,000	—	—	—	25.00	—
ND(1993)R Proof	10,000	Value: 40.00				

KM# 164 200 LIRE
5.0000 g., Aluminum-Bronze, 24 mm. **Subject:** 180th Anniversary - Carabinieri **Obv:** Head right **Obv. Designer:** M. Vallucci **Rev:** Flaming bomb above banner and value **Rev. Designer:** Zanelli

Date	Mintage	F	VF	XF	Unc	BU
ND(1994)R	200,000,000	—	—	—	2.00	—
ND(1994)R Proof	8,500	Value: 12.00				

KM# 184 200 LIRE
5.0000 g., Brass, 24 mm. **Subject:** Centennial - Customs Service Academy **Obv:** Old and new buildings **Rev:** Shield above value, hat and sword **Designer:** Eugnio Driutti

Date	Mintage	F	VF	XF	Unc	BU
ND(1996)R	200,000,000	—	—	—	1.50	—
ND(1996)R Proof	8,000	Value: 12.00				

KM# 186 200 LIRE
5.0000 g., Brass, 24 mm. **Subject:** Centennial - Italian Naval League **Obv:** Head right **Obv. Designer:** M. Vallucci **Rev:** Naval League seal divides dates and value **Rev. Designer:** G. C. Frapiccini

Date	Mintage	F	VF	XF	Unc	BU
ND(1997)	40,000,000	—	—	—	1.50	—
ND(1997) Proof	8,440	Value: 15.00				

KM# 218 200 LIRE
5.0000 g., Aluminum-Bronze, 24 mm. **Subject:** The Carabinieri, Protectors of Art Heritage **Obv. Designer:** M. Vallucci **Rev:** Flaming bomb and David statue **Rev. Designer:** C. Frapiccini **Edge:** Reeded

Date	Mintage	F	VF	XF	Unc	BU
ND(1999) Proof	8,500	Value: 10.00				
ND(1999)	105,000,000	—	—	—	1.50	—

KM# 98 500 LIRE
11.0000 g., 0.8350 Silver .2953 oz. ASW, 29.3 mm.
Obv: Columbus' ships **Obv. Designer:** Guido Veroi **Rev:** Bust left within wreath **Rev. Designer:** Pietro Giampaoli **Edge:** Dates in raised lettering

Date	Mintage	F	VF	XF	Unc	BU
1958R	24,240,000	—	BV	4.50	10.00	—
1958R Prooflike	Inc. above	—	—	—	30.00	—
1959R	19,360,000	—	BV	4.50	10.00	—
1959R Prooflike	Inc. above	—	—	—	30.00	—
1960R	24,080,000	—	BV	4.50	9.00	—
1960R Prooflike	Inc. above	—	—	—	30.00	—
1961R	6,560,000	—	BV	10.00	20.00	—
1961R Prooflike	Inc. above	—	—	—	50.00	—
1964R	4,880,000	—	BV	6.00	15.00	—
1964R Prooflike	Inc. above	—	—	—	30.00	—
1965R	3,120,000	—	BV	6.00	15.00	—
1965R Prooflike	Inc. above	—	—	—	30.00	—
1966R	13,120,000	—	BV	4.50	10.00	—
Note: Varieties exist						
1966R Prooflike	Inc. above	—	—	—	25.00	—
1967R	2,480,000	—	BV	4.50	10.00	—
1967R Prooflike	Inc. above	—	—	—	25.00	—
1968R	100,000	—	—	—	70.00	—
1968R Prooflike	Inc. above	—	—	—	120	—
1969R	310,000	—	—	—	30.00	—
1969R Prooflike	Inc. above	—	—	—	30.00	—
1970R	1,140,000	—	—	—	25.00	—
1970R Prooflike	Inc. above	—	—	—	25.00	—
1980R	257,270	—	—	—	15.00	—
1980R Prooflike	Inc. above	—	—	—	25.00	—
1981R	162,794	—	—	—	16.50	—
1981R Prooflike	Inc. above	—	—	—	30.00	—
1982R	115,000	—	—	—	16.50	—
1982R Prooflike	Inc. above	—	—	—	30.00	—
1983R	76,000	—	—	—	100	—
1984R	77,000	—	—	—	80.00	—
1985R	74,600	—	—	—	50.00	—
1985R Proof	15,000	Value: 60.00				
1986R	73,200	—	—	—	40.00	—
1986R Proof	Inc. above	Value: 60.00				
1987R	57,500	—	—	—	50.00	—
1987R Proof	10,000	Value: 65.00				
1988R	51,050	—	—	—	100	—
1988R Proof	10,000	Value: 85.00				
1989R	51,200	—	—	—	50.00	—
1989R Proof	10,000	Value: 75.00				
1990R	52,300	—	—	—	40.00	—
1990R Proof	10,000	Value: 60.00				
1991R	54,000	—	—	—	40.00	—
1991R Proof	11,000	Value: 70.00				
1992R	52,000	—	—	—	35.00	—
1992R Proof	9,500	Value: 70.00				
1993R	50,200	—	—	—	35.00	—
1993R Proof	8,500	Value: 80.00				
1994R	44,500	—	—	—	60.00	—
1994R Proof	8,500	Value: 80.00				
1995R	44,558	—	—	—	80.00	—
1995R Proof	7,960	Value: 120				
1996R	45,000	—	—	—	40.00	—
1996R Proof	8,000	Value: 60.00				
1997R	43,600	—	—	—	60.00	—
1997R Proof	8,440	Value: 120				
1998R	55,100	—	—	—	40.00	—
1998R Proof	9,000	Value: 60.00				
1999R	51,800	—	—	—	40.00	—
1999R Proof	8,500	Value: 55.00				
2000R	61,400	—	—	—	50.00	—
2000R Proof	8,960	Value: 55.00				

KM# 99 500 LIRE
11.0000 g., 0.8350 Silver .2953 oz. ASW, 29.3 mm.
Subject: Italian Unification Centennial **Obv:** Female seated left **Rev:** Quadriga **Designer:** Guido Veroi

Date	Mintage	F	VF	XF	Unc	BU
ND(1961)R	27,120,000	—	BV	4.50	7.00	—
ND(1961)R Prooflike	Inc. above	—	—	—	20.00	—

KM# 100 500 LIRE
11.0000 g., 0.8350 Silver .2953 oz. ASW, 29.3 mm.
Subject: 700th Anniversary - Birth of Dante Alighieri, Poet
Obv: Head left **Rev:** Radiant sun above flame, value and date

Date	Mintage	F	VF	XF	Unc	BU
1965R	4,272,000	—	BV	5.00	10.00	—
1965R Proof	Inc. above	Value: 15.00				

KM# 103 500 LIRE
11.0000 g., 0.8350 Silver .2953 oz. ASW, 29.3 mm.
Subject: 100th Anniversary - Birth of Guglielmo Marconi, Physicist **Obv:** Bust left **Rev:** Map of Italy with radio tower loops

Date	Mintage	F	VF	XF	Unc	BU
ND(1974)R	689,752	—	—	—	10.00	—
ND(1974)R Proof	Inc. above	Value: 15.00				

KM# 104 500 LIRE
11.0000 g., 0.8350 Silver .2953 oz. ASW, 29.3 mm.
Subject: 500th Anniversary - Birth of Michelangelo Buonarroti
Obv: Bust left **Rev:** Seated statue divides dates with value below

Date	Mintage	F	VF	XF	Unc	BU
1975R	269,000	—	—	—	13.00	—
1975R Proof	Inc. above	Value: 20.00				

KM# 110 500 LIRE
11.0000 g., 0.8350 Silver .2953 oz. ASW, 29.3 mm.
Subject: 200th Anniversary - Death of Virgil **Obv:** Head left
Rev: Tree divides cow, horse and dates with value below

Date	Mintage	F	VF	XF	Unc	BU
1981R (1982)	341,000	—	—	—	12.00	—
1981R (1982) Proof	Inc. above	Value: 15.00				

KM# 111 500 LIRE
6.8000 g., Bi-Metallic Bronzital center in Acmonital ring, 25.8 mm.
Obv: Head left within circle **Rev:** Plaza within circle flanked by sprigs **Designer:** Cretara

Date	Mintage	F	VF	XF	Unc	BU
1982R	162,000	—	0.40	0.60	2.00	—
Note: Obverse portrait varieties exist						
1983R	137,974,000	—	0.40	0.60	2.00	—
1984R	162,000,000	—	0.40	0.60	2.00	—
1985R	162,000,000	—	0.40	0.60	2.00	—
1985R Proof	20,000	Value: 15.00				
1986R	165,000,000	—	0.40	0.60	2.00	—
1986R Proof	17,500	Value: 15.00				
1987R	200,000,000	—	0.40	0.60	2.00	—
1987R Proof	10,000	Value: 20.00				
1988R	142,000,000	—	0.40	0.60	2.00	—
1988R Proof	9,000	Value: 25.00				
1989R	155,000,000	—	0.40	0.60	2.00	—
1989R Proof	9,250	Value: 20.00				
1990R	130,000,000	—	0.40	0.60	2.00	—
1990R Proof	9,400	Value: 18.00				
1991R	140,000,000	—	0.40	0.60	2.00	—
1991R Proof	11,400	Value: 18.00				
1992R	150,000,000	—	0.40	0.60	2.00	—
Note: Obverse portrait varieties exist						
1992R Proof	9,500	Value: 18.00				
1995R Proof	7,960	Value: 35.00				
1995R	110,000,000	—	—	0.60	2.00	—
1999R Proof	—	Value: 40.00				
1999R	—	—	—	0.60	2.00	—
2000R	61,400	—	—	—	15.00	—
2000R Proof	10,000	Value: 30.00				

KM# 112 500 LIRE
11.0000 g., 0.8350 Silver .2953 oz. ASW, 29.3 mm.
Subject: 100th Anniversary - Death of Giuseppe Garibaldi
Obv: Bust right **Rev:** Island map divides value and date

Date	Mintage	F	VF	XF	Unc	BU
1982R (1983)	193,000	—	—	—	22.00	—
1982R (1983) Proof	Inc. above	Value: 30.00				

KM# 113 500 LIRE
11.0000 g., 0.8350 Silver .2953 oz. ASW, 29.3 mm. **Obv:** Bust facing **Rev:** Dog within crowned wreath dividing dates with value below

Date	Mintage	F	VF	XF	Unc	BU
ND(1983)R	198,000	—	—	—	20.00	—
ND(1983)R Proof	Inc. above	Value: 30.00				

KM# 114 500 LIRE
11.0000 g., 0.8350 Silver .2953 oz. ASW, 29.3 mm. **Subject:** Los Angeles Olympics **Obv:** Head right between dove at left and torch at right **Obv. Designer:** Maurizio Soccorsi **Rev:** Three figures holding up Olympic flame **Rev. Designer:** Franco Pioli

Date	Mintage	F	VF	XF	Unc	BU
1984	193,000	—	—	—	20.00	—
1984 Proof	—	Value: 25.00				

KM# 115 500 LIRE
11.0000 g., 0.8350 Silver .2953 oz. ASW, 29.3 mm. **Subject:** First Italian President of Common Market **Obv:** Head left with map, stars and globe within scalp **Rev:** Flags above stylized ancient stadium **Designer:** Laura Cretara

Date	Mintage	F	VF	XF	Unc	BU
1985R	103,000	—	—	—	40.00	—

Date	Mintage	F	VF	XF	Unc	BU
1985R Proof	29,000	Value: 60.00				

KM# 116 500 LIRE

11.0000 g., 0.8350 Silver .2953 oz. ASW, 29.3 mm.
Obv: Town's architectural montage **Rev:** Hilltop castle above two hemispheres

Date	Mintage	F	VF	XF	Unc	BU
1985R	126,000	—	—	—	25.00	—
1985R Proof	Inc. above	Value: 38.00				

KM# 117 500 LIRE

11.0000 g., 0.8350 Silver .2953 oz. ASW, 29.3 mm.
Subject: European Year of Music **Obv:** Muse of music left **Rev:** Pipe organ frontal view

Date	Mintage	F	VF	XF	Unc	BU
1985R	96,000	—	—	—	20.00	—
1985R Proof	Inc. above	Value: 30.00				

KM# 118 500 LIRE

11.0000 g., 0.8350 Silver .2953 oz. ASW, 29.3 mm. **Subject:** Etruscan Culture **Obv:** Standing warrior **Rev:** Two winged horses left

Date	Mintage	F	VF	XF	Unc	BU
1985R	104,000	—	—	—	18.00	—
1985R Proof	Inc. above	Value: 30.00				

KM# 123 500 LIRE

11.0000 g., 0.8350 Silver .2953 oz. ASW, 29.3 mm.
Subject: 200th Anniversary - Birth of Alessandro Manzoni
Obv: Bust 3/4 facing **Rev:** Headdress

Date	Mintage	F	VF	XF	Unc	BU
1985R	91,218	—	—	—	45.00	—
1985R Proof	20,000	Value: 70.00				

KM# 119 500 LIRE

11.0000 g., 0.8350 Silver .2953 oz. ASW, 29.3 mm.
Subject: Soccer Championship - Mexico **Obv:** Map of Italy and soccer ball **Rev:** Aztec Calendar within soccer ball

Date	Mintage	F	VF	XF	Unc	BU
1986R	91,000	—	—	—	25.00	—
1986R Proof	21,000	Value: 40.00				

KM# 120 500 LIRE

11.0000 g., 0.8350 Silver .2953 oz. ASW, 29.3 mm.
Subject: Year of Peace **Obv:** Head right **Rev:** Ancient tree

Date	Mintage	F	VF	XF	Unc	BU
1986R	90,000	—	—	—	25.00	—
1986R Proof	19,000	Value: 35.00				

KM# 124 500 LIRE

11.0000 g., 0.8350 Silver .2953 oz. ASW, 29.3 mm. **Subject:** 600th Anniversary - Birth of Donatello **Obv:** Head with headdress 1/4 left **Rev:** Standing male statue to left of value and date

Date	Mintage	F	VF	XF	Unc	BU
1986R	73,000	—	—	—	60.00	—
1986R Proof	17,500	Value: 90.00				

KM# 121 500 LIRE

11.0000 g., 0.8350 Silver .2953 oz. ASW, 29.3 mm. **Subject:** Year of the Family **Obv:** Head left **Rev:** Family scene

Date	Mintage	F	VF	XF	Unc	BU
1987R	85,000	—	—	—	20.00	—
1987R Proof	20,000	Value: 35.00				

KM# 122 500 LIRE

11.0000 g., 0.8350 Silver .2953 oz. ASW, 29.3 mm.
Subject: World Athletic Championships **Obv:** Stylized runner left **Rev:** Ancient and modern sprinter, Coliseum in background

Date	Mintage	F	VF	XF	Unc	BU
1987R	80,000	—	—	—	20.00	—
1987R Proof	20,000	Value: 35.00				

KM# 132 500 LIRE

11.0000 g., 0.8350 Silver .2953 oz. ASW, 29.3 mm.
Subject: Giacomo Leopardi

Date	Mintage	F	VF	XF	Unc	BU
1987R	58,000	—	—	—	80.00	—
1987R Proof	10,000	Value: 135				

KM# 125 500 LIRE

11.0000 g., 0.8350 Silver .2953 oz. ASW, 29.3 mm.
Subject: Summer Olympics - Seoul **Obv:** Face left with dove and torch **Rev:** Two artistic figures within wreath above rings
Designer: Carmela Colaneri

Date	Mintage	F	VF	XF	Unc	BU
1988R	70,000	—	—	—	25.00	—
1988R Proof	13,000	Value: 45.00				

KM# 126 500 LIRE

11.0000 g., 0.8350 Silver .2953 oz. ASW, 29.3 mm.
Subject: 40th Anniversary of Constitution **Obv:** Turreted head left **Rev:** Oak and laurel sprig within partial text with dates and value below **Designer:** Laura Cretara

Date	Mintage	F	VF	XF	Unc	BU
ND(1988)R	67,000	—	—	—	25.00	—
ND(1988)R Proof	13,000	Value: 35.00				

KM# 129 500 LIRE

11.0000 g., 0.8350 Silver .2953 oz. ASW, 29.3 mm.
Subject: 900th Anniversary - University of Bologna
Obv: Medieval student in thought **Rev:** Emblem

Date	Mintage	F	VF	XF	Unc	BU
1988R	68,000	—	—	—	35.00	—
1988R Proof	13,000	Value: 60.00				

KM# 144 500 LIRE

11.0000 g., 0.8350 Silver .2953 oz. ASW, 29.3 mm.
Subject: 100th Anniversary - Death of Giovanni Bosco **Obv:** Bust facing **Rev:** Mother, father and seated child

Date	Mintage	F	VF	XF	Unc	BU
1988R	51,000	—	—	—	130	—
1988R Proof	9,000	Value: 140				

KM# 131 500 LIRE

11.0000 g., 0.8350 Silver .2953 oz. ASW, 29.3 mm.
Subject: Fight Against Cancer **Obv:** Female doctor and DNA **Rev:** Heartbeat, microscope and hand

Date	Mintage	F	VF	XF	Unc	BU
1989R	46,000	—	—	—	50.00	—
1989R Proof	7,598	Value: 100				

KM# 134 500 LIRE

11.0000 g., 0.8350 Silver .2953 oz. ASW, 29.3 mm.
Subject: Soccer **Obv:** Head left with world cup trophy within hair **Rev:** Map of Italy within world globe

Date	Mintage	F	VF	XF	Unc	BU
1989R	88,000	—	—	—	30.00	—
1989R	28,000	Value: 45.00				

KM# 139 500 LIRE
11.0000 g., 0.8350 Silver .2953 oz. ASW, 29.3 mm.
Subject: Christopher Columbus **Obv:** Bust 1/4 right within globe design **Rev:** Ships in dock

Date	Mintage	F	VF	XF	Unc	BU
1989R	75,000	—	—	—	30.00	—
1989R Proof	25,000	Value: 45.00				

KM# 145 500 LIRE
11.0000 g., 0.8350 Silver .2953 oz. ASW, 29.3 mm. **Subject:** 350th Anniversary - Death of Tommaso Campanella **Obv:** Bust 3/4 right **Rev:** Half sun face at left, half dome at right, text below

Date	Mintage	F	VF	XF	Unc	BU
1989R	51,000	—	—	—	85.00	—
1989R Proof	9,260	Value: 100				

KM# 136 500 LIRE
11.0000 g., 0.8350 Silver .2953 oz. ASW, 29.3 mm.
Subject: Soccer **Obv:** Head left with world cup trophy within hair **Rev:** Dove within globe and soccer ball

Date	Mintage	F	VF	XF	Unc	BU
1990R	67,500	—	—	—	25.00	—
1990R Proof	24,500	Value: 40.00				

KM# 137 500 LIRE
11.0000 g., 0.8350 Silver .2953 oz. ASW, 29.3 mm. **Subject:** Italian Presidency of the E.E.C. Council **Obv:** Head left **Rev:** Logo

Date	Mintage	F	VF	XF	Unc	BU
1990R	54,000	—	—	—	25.00	—
1990R Proof	10,000	Value: 50.00				

KM# 140 500 LIRE
11.0000 g., 0.8350 Silver .2953 oz. ASW, 29.3 mm.
Subject: Columbus - Discovery of America **Obv:** Head left and new world map **Rev:** Stylized ship within an instrument

Date	Mintage	F	VF	XF	Unc	BU
1990R	75,000	—	—	—	27.50	—
1990R Proof	25,000	Value: 42.50				

KM# 146 500 LIRE
11.0000 g., 0.8350 Silver .2953 oz. ASW, 29.3 mm. **Subject:** 500th Anniversary - Birth of Tizian **Obv:** Head left **Rev:** Buildings

Date	Mintage	F	VF	XF	Unc	BU
1990R	52,300	—	—	—	65.00	—
1990R Proof	9,450	Value: 100				

KM# 143 500 LIRE
15.0000 g., 0.8350 Silver .4027 oz. ASW **Subject:** Italian Flora and Fauna **Obv:** Head facing within assorted animals and flowers **Rev:** Man within center of dead and living tree

Date	Mintage	F	VF	XF	Unc	BU
1991R	50,000	—	—	—	40.00	—
1991R Proof	9,500	Value: 55.00				

KM# 147 500 LIRE
15.0000 g., 0.8350 Silver .4027 oz. ASW **Subject:** 2100th Anniversary of Ponte Milvio **Obv:** Head right with bridge and shield within hair **Rev:** Stone arch bridge

Date	Mintage	F	VF	XF	Unc	BU
1991R	59,000	—	—	—	25.00	—
1991R Proof	14,000	Value: 40.00				

KM# 141 500 LIRE
11.0000 g., 0.8350 Silver .2953 oz. ASW **Subject:** 250th Anniversary - Death of Antonio Vivaldi **Obv:** Violinist right, building in background **Rev:** Music score and mountain scene

Date	Mintage	F	VF	XF	Unc	BU
ND(1991)R	55,000	—	—	—	100	—
ND(1991)R Proof	11,000	Value: 120				

KM# 148 500 LIRE
11.0000 g., 0.8350 Silver .2953 oz. ASW **Subject:** Discovery of America **Obv:** Radiant head facing **Rev:** Mapped scroll divides compass and date

Date	Mintage	F	VF	XF	Unc	BU
1991R	75,000	—	—	—	30.00	—
1991R Proof	25,000	Value: 50.00				

KM# 149 500 LIRE
15.0000 g., 0.8350 Silver .4027 oz. ASW **Subject:** 500th Anniversary - Death of Lorenzo de' Medici **Obv:** Bust left **Rev:** Florence tower, books, dates and value

Date	Mintage	F	VF	XF	Unc	BU
ND(1992)R	50,000	—	—	—	30.00	—
ND(1992)R Proof	11,000	Value: 50.00				

KM# 150 500 LIRE
11.0000 g., 0.8350 Silver .2953 oz. ASW **Subject:** Christopher Columbus **Obv:** Bust 3/4 facing **Rev:** Landing scene

Date	Mintage	F	VF	XF	Unc	BU
1992R	67,000	—	—	—	30.00	—
1992R Proof	18,000	Value: 50.00				

KM# 152 500 LIRE
15.0000 g., 0.8350 Silver .4027 oz. ASW **Subject:** 200th Anniversary - Birth of Gioacchino Rossini **Obv:** Bust facing **Rev:** Signature on music staff sheet

Date	Mintage	F	VF	XF	Unc	BU
1992R	45,000	—	—	—	35.00	—
1992R Proof	9,000	Value: 60.00				

KM# 153 500 LIRE
15.0000 g., 0.8350 Silver .4027 oz. ASW **Subject:** Olympics **Obv:** Laureate head facing and half of oval track **Rev:** Buildings and 3/4 oval track

Date	Mintage	F	VF	XF	Unc	BU
1992R	48,040	—	—	—	30.00	—
1992R Proof	12,000	Value: 45.00				

KM# 154 500 LIRE
15.0000 g., 0.8350 Silver .4027 oz. ASW **Subject:** Flora and Fauna **Obv:** Head left with bird and flora within hair **Rev:** Square enclosing dolphin, flamingo and other animals
Designer: Carmela Colaneri

Date	Mintage	F	VF	XF	Unc	BU
1992R	43,000	—	—	—	35.00	—
1992R Proof	8,500	Value: 60.00				

KM# 161 500 LIRE

11.0000 g., 0.8350 Silver .2953 oz. ASW **Subject:** 500th Anniversary - Death of Piero Della Francesca

Date	Mintage	F	VF	XF	Unc	BU
1992R	52,000	—	—	—	70.00	—
1992R Proof	9,500	Value: 110				

KM# 156 500 LIRE

15.0000 g., 0.8350 Silver .4027 oz. ASW **Subject:** 2000th Anniversary - Death of Horace **Obv:** Column divides date and value **Rev:** Bust left

Date	Mintage	F	VF	XF	Unc	BU
1993R	50,000	—	—	—	40.00	—
1993R Proof	10,000	Value: 55.00				

KM# 157 500 LIRE

15.0000 g., 0.8350 Silver .4027 oz. ASW **Subject:** Wildlife protection **Obv:** Head facing flanked by flowers **Rev:** Storks and swordfish divide date and value **Designer:** Maria Angela Cassol

Date	Mintage	F	VF	XF	Unc	BU
1993R	36,000	—	—	—	35.00	—
1993R Proof	10,000	Value: 50.00				

KM# 158 500 LIRE

15.0000 g., 0.8350 Silver .4027 oz. ASW **Subject:** 650th Anniversary - University of Pisa **Obv:** Seated figure right with open book **Rev:** Leaning Tower of Pisa to right of building

Date	Mintage	F	VF	XF	Unc	BU
1993R	41,000	—	—	—	35.00	—
1993R Proof	9,080	Value: 50.00				

KM# 160 500 LIRE

6.8000 g., Bi-Metallic Bronzital center in Acmonital ring, 25.8 mm. **Subject:** Centennial - Bank of Italy **Obv:** Head left within circle **Obv. Designer:** Laura Cretara **Rev:** Monogram within design divides dates within circle **Rev. Designer:** G. Rossi **Note:** Large and small designer's name, G ROSSI, exist.

Date	Mintage	F	VF	XF	Unc	BU
ND(1993)R	Est. 90,000,000	—	—	—	2.50	—
ND(1993)R Proof	8,500	Value: 10.00				

KM# 163 500 LIRE

11.0000 g., 0.8350 Silver .2953 oz. ASW **Subject:** 200th Anniversary - Death of Carolo Goldoni

Date	Mintage	F	VF	XF	Unc	BU
1993R	50,000	—	—	—	50.00	—
1993R Proof	8,500	Value: 110				

KM# 173 500 LIRE

11.0000 g., 0.8350 Silver .2953 oz. ASW **Subject:** Centennial - Bank of Italy **Obv:** Head left **Rev:** Statues and building **Note:** Both uncirculated and proof versions were offered in sets only.

Date	Mintage	F	VF	XF	Unc	BU
ND(1993)R	52,000	—	—	—	40.00	—
ND(1993)R Proof	10,000	Value: 75.00				

KM# 167 500 LIRE

6.8000 g., Bi-Metallic Bronzital center in Acmonital ring, 25.8 mm. **Subject:** 500th Anniversary - Publication of Mathematical Work by Luca Pacioli **Obv:** Head left within circle **Obv. Designer:** Laura Cretara **Rev:** Bust facing within circle

Date	Mintage	F	VF	XF	Unc	BU
ND(1994)R	50,000,000	—	—	—	2.00	—
ND(1994)R Proof	8,500	Value: 15.00				

KM# 181 500 LIRE

6.8000 g., Bi-Metallic Bronzital center in Acmonital ring, 25.8 mm. **Subject:** Istituto Nazionale di Statistica **Obv:** Head left within circle **Rev:** Institute building within circle **Rev. Designer:** C. Momoni

Date	Mintage	F	VF	XF	Unc	BU
ND(1996)R	96,755,000	—	—	—	2.00	—
ND(1996)R Proof	8,000	Value: 15.00				

KM# 187 500 LIRE

6.8000 g., Bi-Metallic Bronzital center in Acmonital ring, 25.8 mm. **Subject:** 50th Anniversary - National Police Code **Obv:** Head left within circle **Obv. Designer:** Laura Cretara **Rev:** Mythological figure above crowned shield within wreath and circle **Rev. Designer:** Carmela Colaneri

Date	Mintage	F	VF	XF	Unc	BU
ND(1997)R Proof	8,440	Value: 25.00				
ND(1997)R	40,000,000	—	—	—	2.00	—

KM# 193 500 LIRE

6.8000 g., Bi-Metallic Bronzital center in Acmonital ring, 25.8 mm. **Series:** F.A.O. **Subject:** F.A.O. - 20 years **Obv:** Allegorical portrait **Obv. Designer:** Laura Cretara **Rev:** Hand and grains **Rev. Designer:** L. Desimoni

Date	Mintage	F	VF	XF	Unc	BU
ND(1998)R	100,000,000	—	—	—	2.00	—
ND(1998)R Proof	9,000	Value: 15.00				

KM# 203 500 LIRE

6.8200 g., Bi-Metallic Bronzital center in Acmonital ring, 25.9 mm. **Subject:** European Parliamentary Elections **Obv:** Allegorical portrait **Obv. Designer:** Laura Cretara **Rev:** Ballot box **Edge:** Reeded and plain sections

Date	Mintage	F	VF	XF	Unc	BU
ND(1999)R	50,000,000	—	—	—	2.00	—
ND(1999)R Proof	8,500	Value: 15.00				

KM# 101 1000 LIRE

14.6000 g., 0.8350 Silver .392 oz. ASW **Subject:** Centennial of Rome as Italian capital **Obv:** Concordia veiled bust right **Rev:** Flower-like symbol above value

Date	Mintage	F	VF	XF	Unc	BU
ND(1970)R	3,011,000	—	—	—	15.00	—
ND(1970)R Proof	—	Value: 35.00				

KM# 165 1000 LIRE

14.6000 g., 0.8350 Silver .392 oz. ASW **Subject:** 900th Anniversary - St. Mark's Basilica **Obv:** Church façade **Rev:** Figures within boat

Date	Mintage	F	VF	XF	Unc	BU
1994R	41,000	—	—	—	40.00	—
1994R Proof	8,600	Value: 70.00				

KM# 168 1000 LIRE

14.6000 g., 0.8350 Silver .392 oz. ASW **Subject:** Flora and Fauna Protection **Obv:** Female bust facing with tree as left side of hair **Rev:** Bird, tree and dolphin divides date and value

Date	Mintage	F	VF	XF	Unc	BU
1994R	40,000	—	—	—	30.00	40.00
1994R Proof	7,700	Value: 70.00				

KM# 169 1000 LIRE

14.6000 g., 0.8350 Silver .392 oz. ASW **Obv:** Tintoretto in oval **Rev:** Collage of his paintings **Designer:** Maria Angela Cassol

Date	Mintage	F	VF	XF	Unc	BU
1994R	45,000	—	—	—	80.00	—
1994R Proof	8,500	Value: 120				

KM# 185 1000 LIRE
14.6000 g., 0.8350 Silver .392 oz. ASW **Subject:** Pietro Mascagni **Obv:** Bust right **Rev:** Theater interior view

Date	Mintage	F	VF	XF	Unc	BU
1995R	45,000	—	—	—	150	—
1995R Proof	7,960	Value: 230				

KM# 182 1000 LIRE
14.6000 g., 0.8350 Silver .392 oz. ASW **Subject:** Olympics - Atlanta **Obv:** Female head right with laurel wreath and olympic rings as hair style **Rev:** Torch runner, Statue of Liberty silhouette, stadium track and value

Date	Mintage	F	VF	XF	Unc	BU
1996R	38,000	—	—	—	40.00	—
1996R Proof	7,435	Value: 70.00				

KM# 199 1000 LIRE
14.6000 g., 0.8350 Silver .392 oz. ASW **Subject:** Montale Commemorative **Note:** Both uncirculated and proof versions were offered in sets only.

Date	Mintage	F	VF	XF	Unc	BU
1996R	45,000	—	—	—	60.00	—
1996R Proof	8,000	Value: 100				

KM# 200 1000 LIRE
14.6000 g., 0.8350 Silver 0.392 oz. ASW **Subject:** Donizetti Commemorative **Note:** Both uncirculated and proof versions were offered in sets only.

Date	Mintage	F	VF	XF	Unc	BU
1997R	44,000	—	—	—	100	—
1997R Proof	8,440	Value: 150				

KM# 194 1000 LIRE
Bi-Metallic Copper-Nickel center in Aluminum-Bronze ring, 27 mm. **Subject:** European Union **Obv:** Head left within circle **Obv. Designer:** Laura Cretara **Rev:** Corrected map with United Germany within globe design **Rev. Designer:** Pernazza

Date	Mintage	F	VF	XF	Unc	BU
1997R	80,000,000	—	—	—	3.00	—
1997R Proof	8,440	Value: 25.00				
1998R	180,000,000	—	—	—	3.00	—
1998R Proof	9,000	Value: 25.00				
1999R	51,800	—	—	—	15.00	—
1999R Proof	8,500	Value: 25.00				
2000R	61,400	—	—	—	20.00	—
2000R Proof	8,960	Value: 25.00				

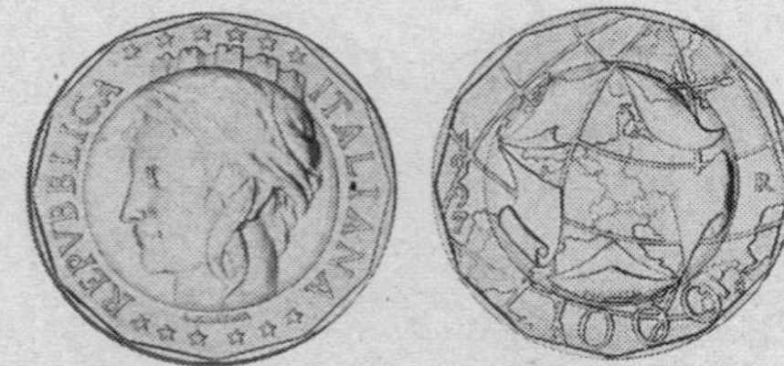

KM# 190 1000 LIRE
Bi-Metallic Copper-Nickel center in Aluminum-Bronze ring, 27 mm. **Subject:** European Union **Obv:** Allegorical portrait **Obv. Designer:** L. Cretara **Rev:** Pernazza

Date	Mintage	F	VF	XF	Unc	BU
1997R	100,000,000	—	—	—	3.50	—

KM# 201 1000 LIRE
14.6000 g., 0.8350 Silver 0.392 oz. ASW **Obv:** Bernini bust and St. Peter's Colonnade in background **Rev:** Architectural renderings and sunburst **Note:** Both uncirculated and proof versions were offered in sets only.

Date	Mintage	F	VF	XF	Unc	BU
1998R	55,200	—	—	—	45.00	—
1998R Proof	9,000	Value: 90.00				

KM# 221 1000 LIRE
14.6000 g., 0.8350 Silver 0.3919 oz. ASW, 31.4 mm. **Subject:** Vittorio Alfieri **Obv:** Bust looking right **Rev:** Rope over book **Edge:** Raised ornamentation

Date	Mintage	F	VF	XF	Unc	BU
1999R	51,800	—	—	—	80.00	—
1999R Proof	8,500	Value: 110				

KM# 235 1000 LIRE
14.6000 g., 0.8350 Silver 0.3919 oz. ASW, 31.4 mm. **Obv:** Giordano Bruno **Rev:** Three sun faces

Date	Mintage	F	VF	XF	Unc	BU
2000R	8,960	—	—	—	100	—
2000R Proof	51,400	Value: 130				

KM# 196 2000 LIRE
16.0000 g., 0.8350 Silver .4295 oz. ASW **Obv:** Stars and birds circling world globe **Rev:** Creative brain unraveling DNA above value

Date	Mintage	F	VF	XF	Unc	BU
1997R Proof	—	—	—	—	—	—
1998R	36,300	—	—	—	80.00	—
1998R Proof	7,880	Value: 100				

KM# 195 2000 LIRE
16.0000 g., 0.8350 Silver .4295 oz. ASW **Subject:** Christian Millennium **Obv:** Leaves and birds sprouting from globe top **Rev:** Jesus above value

Date	Mintage	F	VF	XF	Unc	BU
1998R	36,300	—	—	—	80.00	—
1998R Proof	7,880	Value: 100				

KM# 202 2000 LIRE
16.0000 g., 0.8350 Silver .4295 oz. ASW **Subject:** National Museum in Rome **Obv:** Head left on ancient coin **Rev:** Seated gladiator

Date	Mintage	F	VF	XF	Unc	BU
1999R	35,500	—	—	—	40.00	—
1999R Proof	6,700	Value: 80.00				

KM# 170 5000 LIRE
18.0000 g., 0.8350 Silver .4832 oz. ASW **Subject:** University of Pisa **Obv:** Wings surround head facing **Rev:** Building and design at center of circle with small towers between points

Date	Mintage	F	VF	XF	Unc	BU
1993R	42,000	—	—	—	40.00	—
1993R Proof	8,500	Value: 80.00				

KM# 175 5000 LIRE
18.0000 g., 0.8350 Silver .4832 oz. ASW **Subject:** 600th Anniversary - Birth of Pisanello **Obv:** Bust left wearing floppy hat **Rev:** Equestrian right

Date	Mintage	F	VF	XF	Unc	BU
1995R	38,000	—	—	—	45.00	—
1995R Proof	7,800	Value: 90.00				

KM# 178 5000 LIRE
18.0000 g., 0.8350 Silver .4832 oz. ASW **Subject:** Italian Presidency of the European Union **Obv:** Female head left **Rev:** Letter E, flags, stars and assorted designs

Date	Mintage	F	VF	XF	Unc	BU
1996R	38,000	—	—	—	45.00	—
1996R Proof	7,996	Value: 90.00				

KM# 189 5000 LIRE
18.0000 g., 0.8350 Silver .4832 oz. ASW **Subject:** Giovanni Antonio Canal **Obv:** Bust right and Venice city view **Rev:** Harbor full of sailboats

Date	Mintage	F	VF	XF	Unc	BU
ND(1997)R	36,000	—	—	—	35.00	—
ND(1997)R Proof	7,550	Value: 80.00				

KM# 197 5000 LIRE
18.0000 g., 0.8350 Silver .4832 oz. ASW **Subject:** 1999 **Obv:** Birds sprouting from globe **Rev:** Saint Francis selling cloth to merchant

Date	Mintage	F	VF	XF	Unc	BU
1999R	37,600	—	—	—	60.00	—
1999R Proof	8,170	Value: 70.00				

KM# 198 5000 LIRE
18.0000 g., 0.8350 Silver .4832 oz. ASW **Subject:** 1999 **Obv:** Three birds and nine stars encircle world **Rev:** Satellite dish and wheels

Date	Mintage	F	VF	XF	Unc	BU
1999R	37,600	—	—	—	60.00	—
1999R Proof	8,170	Value: 70.00				

KM# 166 10000 LIRE
22.0000 g., 0.8350 Silver .5907 oz. ASW **Subject:** World Cup Soccer **Obv:** Head right with stars in hair **Rev:** Olive branch, value and banner within globe

Date	Mintage	F	VF	XF	Unc	BU
1994R	43,000	—	—	—	80.00	—
1994R Proof	9,000	Value: 120				

KM# 174 10000 LIRE
22.0000 g., 0.8350 Silver .5907 oz. ASW **Subject:** 40th Anniversary - Conference of Messina **Obv:** Europa on bull right **Rev:** Letter E and numeral 5 within globe design and star border

Date	Mintage	F	VF	XF	Unc	BU
1995R	42,000	—	—	—	70.00	—
1995R Proof	8,050	Value: 85.00				

KM# 179 10000 LIRE
22.0000 g., 0.8350 Silver .5907 oz. ASW **Subject:** 50th Anniversary of the Republic **Obv:** Bust right with star in background **Rev:** Man leading horse right

Date	Mintage	F	VF	XF	Unc	BU
1996R	38,000	—	—	—	70.00	—
1996R Proof	7,900	Value: 120				

KM# 188 10000 LIRE
22.0000 g., 0.8350 Silver 0.5906 oz. ASW **Subject:** 200th Anniversary - Italian Flag **Obv:** Allegorical portrait **Rev:** Woman wearing flag like a cape

Date	Mintage	F	VF	XF	Unc	BU
ND(1997)	36,000	—	—	—	70.00	—
ND(1997) Proof	7,695	Value: 120				

KM# 192 10000 LIRE
22.0000 g., 0.8350 Silver .5907 oz. ASW **Subject:** Soccer **Obv:** Head left **Rev:** Stylized soccer design

Date	Mintage	F	VF	XF	Unc	BU
1998R	34,000	—	—	—	70.00	—
1998R Proof	7,000	Value: 100				

KM# 208 10000 LIRE
22.0000 g., 0.8350 Silver .5906 oz. ASW, 34 mm. **Obv:** Birds and grass sprouting **Rev:** Standing figure flanked by tall weeds **Edge:** Reeded and plain sections

Date	Mintage	F	VF	XF	Unc	BU
2000	33,700	—	—	—	50.00	—
2000 Proof	7,000	Value: 80.00				

KM# 209 10000 LIRE
22.0000 g., 0.8350 Silver .5906 oz. ASW, 34 mm. **Obv:** Doves and stars around world globe **Rev:** Da Vinci's wing and airplane design **Edge:** Reeded and plain sections

Date	Mintage	F	VF	XF	Unc	BU
2000	—	—	—	—	50.00	—
2000 Proof	—	Value: 80.00				

KM# 176 50000 LIRE
7.5000 g., 0.9000 Gold .217 oz. AGW **Subject:** Bank of Italy **Obv:** Bust left **Rev:** Building and value

Date	Mintage	F	VF	XF	Unc	BU
1993R Proof	22,560	Value: 300				

KM# 223 50000 LIRE
7.5000 g., 0.9000 Gold 0.217 oz. AGW, 20 mm. **Subject:** 800th Anniversary - Birth of Saint Anthony of Padova **Obv:** Corner view of Basilica **Rev:** Interior view - Chapel, date and value

Date	Mintage	F	VF	XF	Unc	BU
1995R Proof	9,221	Value: 300				

KM# 225 50000 LIRE
7.5000 g., 0.9000 Gold 0.217 oz. AGW, 20 mm. **Subject:** 800th Anniversary - Battistero in Parma **Obv:** Battistero **Rev:** Decorations from the Battistero, date and value

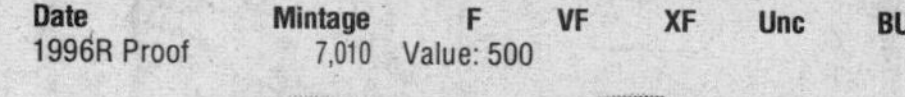

Date	Mintage	F	VF	XF	Unc	BU
1996R Proof	7,010	Value: 500				

KM# 191 50000 LIRE
7.5000 g., 0.9000 Gold .217 oz. AGW **Subject:** 1600th Anniversary - Death of St. Ambrose **Obv:** St. Ambrose Church in Milan **Rev:** Investiture of St. Ambrose

Date	Mintage	F	VF	XF	Unc	BU
ND(1997)R Proof	5,750	Value: 300				

KM# 228 50000 LIRE
7.5000 g., 0.9000 Gold 0.217 oz. AGW, 20 mm. **Subject:** 850th Anniversary - Church of San Giovanni of the Hermits in Palermo **Obv:** Church of San Giovanni **Rev:** Curved arches

Date	Mintage	F	VF	XF	Unc	BU
1998R Proof	4,900	Value: 325				

KM# 230 50000 LIRE
7.5000 g., 0.9000 Gold 0.217 oz. AGW, 20 mm. **Subject:** 900th Anniversary - Foundation of the Cathedral in Modena **Obv:** Front of Cathedral **Rev:** Arch with lion, date and denomination

Date	Mintage	F	VF	XF	Unc	BU
1999R Proof	5,500	Value: 325				

KM# 232 50000 LIRE
7.5000 g., 0.9000 Gold 0.217 oz. AGW, 20 mm. **Subject:** 500th Anniversary - Birth of Benvenuto Cellini **Obv:** Bust of Cellini **Rev:** Figure, date and denomination

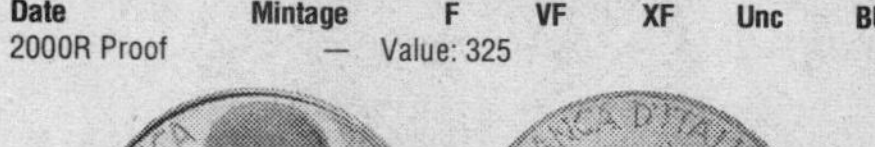

Date	Mintage	F	VF	XF	Unc	BU
2000R Proof	—	Value: 325				

KM# 177 100000 LIRE
15.0000 g., 0.9000 Gold .434 oz. AGW **Subject:** Centennial of the Bank of Italy **Obv:** Bust facing **Rev:** Value and building **Note:** 1996 strikes do not exist.

Date	Mintage	F	VF	XF	Unc	BU
1993 Proof	21,196	Value: 500				

KM# 222 100000 LIRE

15.0000 g., 0.9000 Gold 0.434 oz. AGW, 25 mm. **Subject:** 700th Anniversary - Basilica of Santa Croce in Florence **Obv:** Front of the Basilica of Santa Croce **Rev:** Interior view, date and denomination

Date	Mintage	F	VF	XF	Unc	BU
1995R Proof	8,584	Value: 650				

KM# 224 100000 LIRE

15.0000 g., 0.9000 Gold 0.434 oz. AGW, 25 mm. **Subject:** 600th Anniversary - Foundation of Certosa Di Pavia **Obv:** Exterior angled view **Rev:** Interior view

Date	Mintage	F	VF	XF	Unc	BU
1996R Proof	5,550	Value: 750				

KM# 226 100000 LIRE

15.0000 g., 0.9000 Gold 0.434 oz. AGW, 25 mm. **Subject:** 800th Anniversary - Dedication of the Basilica Superiore of San Nicola of Bari **Obv:** Exterior view of the Basilica **Rev:** Interior view

Date	Mintage	F	VF	XF	Unc	BU
1997R Proof	5,400	Value: 650				

KM# 227 100000 LIRE

15.0000 g., 0.9000 Gold 0.434 oz. AGW, 25 mm. **Subject:** 650th Anniversary - Completion of the Tower - Palace of Siena **Obv:** Tower **Rev:** Anniversary dates and denomination

Date	Mintage	F	VF	XF	Unc	BU
1998R Proof	4,800	Value: 650				

KM# 229 100000 LIRE

15.0000 g., 0.9000 Gold 0.434 oz. AGW, 25 mm. **Subject:** Repair of the Basilica of St. Francis of Assisi **Obv:** Front of Basilica **Rev:** Round seal, date and denomination

Date	Mintage	F	VF	XF	Unc	BU
1999R Proof	5,047	Value: 650				

KM# 231 100000 LIRE

15.0000 g., 0.9000 Gold 0.434 oz. AGW, 20 mm. **Subject:** 700th Anniversary - First Jubilee of 1300 **Obv:** The Quadrangle **Rev:** Detail of the fresco of Giotto

Date	Mintage	F	VF	XF	Unc	BU
2000R Proof	—	Value: 600				

TRIAL STRIKES

KM#	Date	Mintage	Identification	Mkt Val
TS1	1927R	—	20 Lire. Inscription. PROVA SENZA RITOCCO. Seated and standing figures above value. KM69.	1,200
TS2	1927R	—	20 Lire. Faceless head right. PROVA TECNICA - R. SENZA RITOCCO. KM69.	1,500
TS3	1940	—	5 Lire. Silver. Helmeted bust left. Uniface.	1,500
TS4	1940	—	5 Lire. Silver. Crowned savoy shield with fases and axe within circle. Uniface. Photo reduced.	1,500

PATTERNS

Including off metal strikes

KM#	Date	Mintage	Identification	Mkt Val
Pn2	1903R	—	10 Centesimi. Bronze.	—
Pn3	1903R	—	2 Lire. Silver Plated Bronze.	—
Pn4	1903	—	5 Lire. Silver.	1,000
PnA5	1903 (M)	—	20 Lire. Gold.	3,500
Pn5	1903R	—	20 Lire. Gilt Silver.	—
PnA6	1903 (M)	—	100 Lire. Gold.	8,500
Pn6	1903R	—	100 Lire. Gilt Bronze.	225
PnA7	1904	5	Centesimo. Bronze. KM37.	—
PnB7	1904	—	50 Lire. Brass. Head of Vittorio left.. Eagle with spread wings facing, head left, crown above.	—
Pn7	1905R	—	20 Centesimi. Bronze.	—
Pn8	1905R	—	20 Centesimi. Nickel.	—
Pn9	1906R	—	20 Lire. Gilt Bronze.	225
Pn10	1907	—	20 Centesimi. Nickel.	—
Pn11	1907	—	100 Lire.	—
PnA12	1908	—	100 Lire. Silver.	5,000
Pn12	1908	—	100 Lire. Bronze.	250
Pn13	1915R	—	10 Centesimi. Nickel. Obv: Helmeted head right. Rev: Grain ear.	—
Pn14	1915R	—	10 Centesimi. Nickel. Obv: Diademed and jeweled head right. Rev: Grain ear.	—
Pn15	1915R	—	10 Centesimi. Nickel. Obv: Diademed and jeweled head right. Rev: Grain ear.	—
Pn16	1915	—	10 Centesimi. Nickel.	—
Pn17	1918	—	5 Centesimi. Ferro-nickel.	250
Pn18	1918	—	5 Centesimi. Ferro-nickel.	250
Pn19	1918	—	5 Centesimi. Ferro-nickel.	250
Pn20	1918	—	5 Centesimi. Ferro-nickel.	250
Pn21	1918	—	5 Centesimi. Ferro-nickel.	250
Pn22	1918	—	10 Centesimi. Ferro-nickel.	—
Pn23	1918	—	20 Centesimi. Nickel.	—
Pn24	1918	—	20 Centesimi. Nickel.	—
Pn25	1918	—	20 Centesimi. Nickel.	—
Pn26	1918	—	20 Centesimi. Nickel.	—
Pn27	1918	—	20 Centesimi. Ferro-nickel.	—
PnA28	1918	—	25 Centesimi. Iron. Obv: Turreted and grain-wreathed head of Italia right. Rev: Denomination above ornament, PROVA S.J. below.	—
Pn28	1918	—	25 Centesimi. Bronze.	—
Pn29	1918	—	50 Centesimi.	—
Pn30	1918	—	50 Centesimi. Nickel.	—
Pn31	1919R	—	5 Centesimi. 17 mm. Ferro-nickel.	—
Pn32	1919	—	5 Centesimi. Bronze.	—
Pn33	ND(1919)	—	10 Centesimi. Bronze.	—
Pn34	1920R	—	Lira. Nickel.	—
Pn35	1920R	—	Lira. Nickel.	—
Pn36	1920R	—	Lira. Nickel.	—
PnA37	1922	—	2 Lire. Nickel.	—
Pn37	1922	—	2 Lire. Nickel.	—
PnA38	1922R	—	2 Lire. Nickel.	—
Pn38	1922R	—	2 Lire. Nickel.	—
Pn39	1926R	—	5 Lire. Silver.	—
Pn40	ND(1927)	—	20 Lire. Silver.	—
Pn41	ND(1927)	—	20 Lire. Silver.	—
Pn42	1950	—	50 Lire. Stainless Steel.	—
Pn43	1950	—	100 Lire. Silver. 20 mm.	—
Pn44	1950	—	100 Lire. Nickel-Silver.	—
Pn45	1950	—	100 Lire. Nickel.	—
Pn46	1951R	—	Lira. Aluminum.	—
Pn47	1951R	—	2 Lire. Aluminum.	—
Pn48	1951R	—	10 Lire. Aluminum.	—
Pn49	1955R	—	20 Lire. Aluminum-Bronze.	—
Pn50	1955R	—	20 Lire. Aluminum-Bronze.	—
Pn51	1956R	—	20 Lire. Aluminum-Bronze. Bottom of neck rounded.	—
Pn52	1956R	1,200	20 Lire. Aluminum-Bronze. Bottom of neck at angle.	—
Pn53	1957R	—	500 Lire. Silver.	—
Pn54	1957R	—	500 Lire. Silver.	—
Pn55	1957R	—	500 Lire. Silver.	—
Pn56	1957R	—	500 Lire. Silver.	—
Pn57	1957R	—	500 Lire. Silver.	—
Pn58	1957R	—	500 Lire. Silver.	—
Pn59	1957R	—	Florino. Gilt Bronze.	—
Pn60	1957R	—	Florino. Gilt Bronze.	—
Pn61	1957R	—	2 Florini. Gilt Bronze.	—
Pn62	1957R	—	2 Florini. Gilt Bronze.	—
Pn63	1970	—	1000 Lire. Silver.	—
Pn64	1970	—	1000 Lire. Silver.	—
Pn65	ND (1970)	—	10000 Lire. Gilt Bronze.	—

PROVAS

PROVA in field; Standard metals unless otherwise noted

KM#	Date	Mintage	Identification	Mkt Val
Pr1	1903	—	20 Lire. Head right. Standing figures facing.	4,000
Pr2	1903	—	100 Lire. Head right. Standing figures facing.	14,000

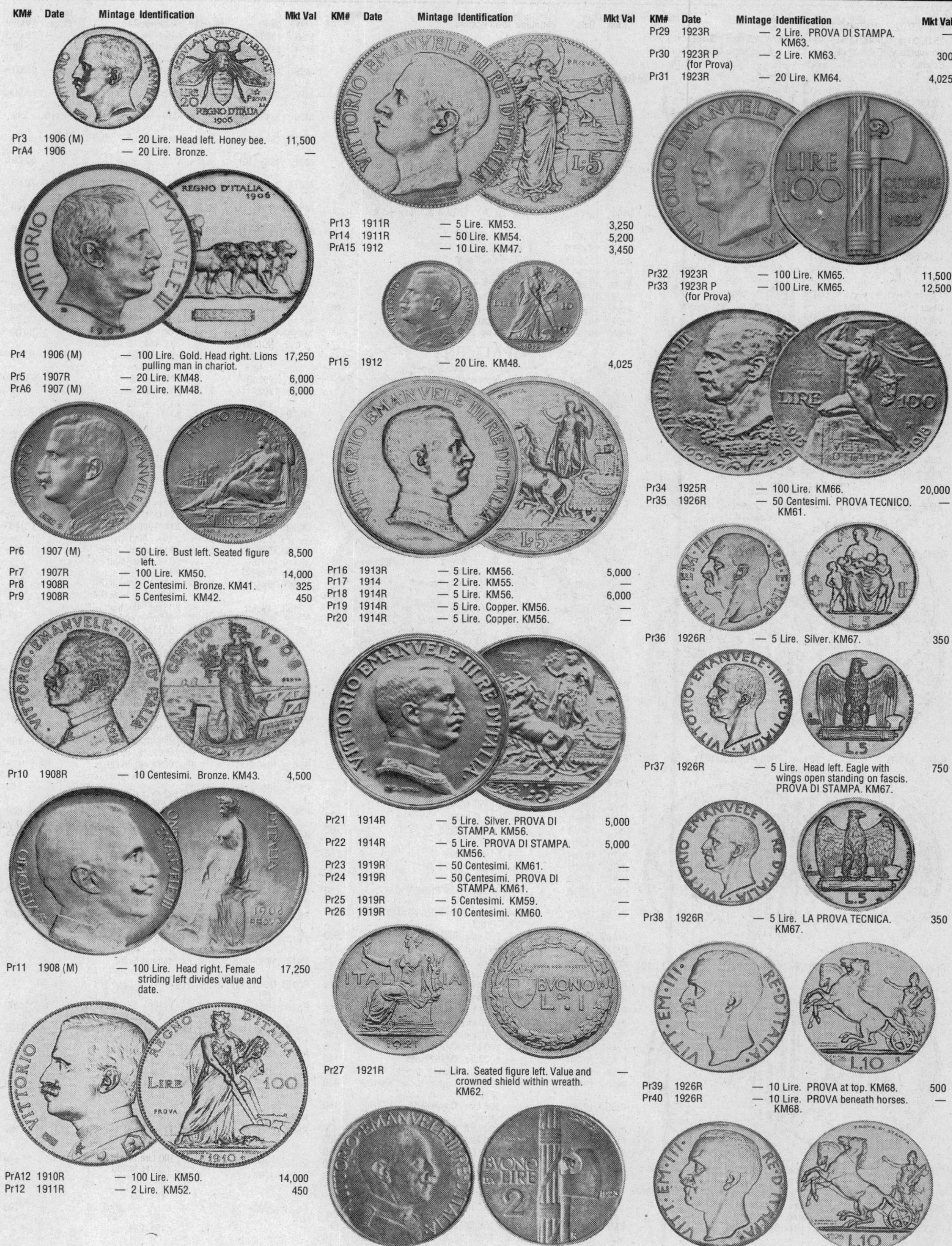

KM#	Date	Mintage	Identification	Mkt Val
Pr3	1906 (M)	—	20 Lire. Head left. Honey bee.	11,500
PrA4	1906	—	20 Lire. Bronze.	—
Pr4	1906 (M)	—	100 Lire. Gold. Head right. Lions pulling man in chariot.	17,250
Pr5	1907R	—	20 Lire. KM48.	6,000
PrA6	1907 (M)	—	20 Lire. KM48.	6,000
Pr6	1907 (M)	—	50 Lire. Bust left. Seated figure left.	8,500
Pr7	1907R	—	100 Lire. KM50.	14,000
Pr8	1908R	—	2 Centesimi. Bronze. KM41.	325
Pr9	1908R	—	5 Centesimi. KM42.	450
Pr10	1908R	—	10 Centesimi. Bronze. KM43.	4,500
Pr11	1908 (M)	—	100 Lire. Head right. Female striding left divides value and date.	17,250
PrA12	1910R	—	100 Lire. KM50.	14,000
Pr12	1911R	—	2 Lire. KM52.	450
Pr13	1911R	—	5 Lire. KM53.	3,250
Pr14	1911R	—	50 Lire. KM54.	5,200
PrA15	1912	—	10 Lire. KM47.	3,450
Pr15	1912	—	20 Lire. KM48.	4,025
Pr16	1913R	—	5 Lire. KM56.	5,000
Pr17	1914	—	2 Lire. KM55.	—
Pr18	1914R	—	5 Lire. KM56.	6,000
Pr19	1914R	—	5 Lire. Copper. KM56.	—
Pr20	1914R	—	5 Lire. Copper. KM56.	—
Pr21	1914R	—	5 Lire. Silver. PROVA DI STAMPA. KM56.	5,000
Pr22	1914R	—	5 Lire. PROVA DI STAMPA. KM56.	5,000
Pr23	1919R	—	50 Centesimi. KM61.	—
Pr24	1919R	—	50 Centesimi. PROVA DI STAMPA. KM61.	—
Pr25	1919R	—	5 Centesimi. KM59.	—
Pr26	1919R	—	10 Centesimi. KM60.	—
Pr27	1921R	—	Lira. Seated figure left. Value and crowned shield within wreath. KM62.	—
Pr28	1923R	—	2 Lire. KM63.	325
Pr29	1923R	—	2 Lire. PROVA DI STAMPA. KM63.	—
Pr30	1923R P (for Prova)	—	2 Lire. KM63.	300
Pr31	1923R	—	20 Lire. KM64.	4,025
Pr32	1923R	—	100 Lire. KM65.	11,500
Pr33	1923R P (for Prova)	—	100 Lire. KM65.	12,500
Pr34	1925R	—	100 Lire. KM66.	20,000
Pr35	1926R	—	50 Centesimi. PROVA TECNICO. KM61.	—
Pr36	1926R	—	5 Lire. Silver. KM67.	350
Pr37	1926R	—	5 Lire. Head left. Eagle with wings open standing on fascis. PROVA DI STAMPA. KM67.	750
Pr38	1926R	—	5 Lire. LA PROVA TECNICA. KM67.	350
Pr39	1926R	—	10 Lire. PROVA at top. KM68.	500
Pr40	1926R	—	10 Lire. PROVA beneath horses. KM68.	—
Pr41	1926R	—	10 Lire. PROVA DI STAMPA. KM68.	950

KM#	Date	Mintage	Identification	Mkt Val
Pr42	1926R	—	10 Lire. LA PROVA TECNICA. KM68.	500
Pr43	1927R	—	5 Lire. PROVA DI STAMPA above eagle. KM67.	—
Pr44	1927R	—	5 Lire. PROVA DI STAMPA at right side of eagle. KM67.	—
PrA45	1927R	—	10 Lire. PROVA beneath horses. KM68.	500
Pr45	1927R	—	20 Lire. KM69, Unc.	13,000
PrB45	1927R	—	10 Lire. PROVA DI STAMPA above. KM68.	400
Pr46	1927R	—	20 Lire. PROVA DI STAMPA. KM69.	1,700
Pr49	1928R	—	20 Lire. PROVA. KM70.	1,200
Pr50	1928R	—	20 Lire. PROVA DI STAMPA. KM70.	1,450
Pr51	1928R	—	20 Lire. LA PROVA. KM70.	1,200
Pr52	1928R	—	20 Lire. PROVA DI STAMPA. KM70.	—
Pr53	1928R	—	20 Lire. Gold. KM70.	—
Pr54	1928R	—	20 Lire. PROVA behind head. KM70.	1,200
Pr55	1931R	—	50 Lire. KM71.	3,000
Pr56	1931R	—	100 Lire. KM72.	3,000
Pr57	1936R	—	5 Centesimi. KM73.	—
Pr58	1936R	—	10 Centesimi. KM74.	300
Pr59	1936R	—	20 Centesimi. KM75.	300
Pr60	1936R	—	50 Centesimi. KM76.	300
Pr61	1936R	—	Lira. KM77.	350
Pr62	1936R	—	2 Lire. KM78.	350
Pr63	1936R	—	5 Lire. KM79.	800
Pr64	1936R	—	10 Lire. KM80.	700
Pr65	1936R	—	20 Lire. KM81.	2,400
Pr66	1936R	—	50 Lire. KM82.	8,600
Pr67	1936R	—	100 Lire. KM83.	12,000
Pr68	1939R	—	5 Centesimi. KM73a.	—
Pr69	1939R	—	10 Centesimi. KM74a.	—
Pr70	1939R	—	20 Centesimi. KM75a.	—
Pr71	1939R	—	50 Centesimi. KM76a.	—
Pr72	1939R	—	Lira. KM77a.	—
Pr73	1939R	—	2 Lire. KM78a.	—
Pr74	1946R	—	Lira. KM87.	950
Pr75	1946R	—	2 Lire. KM88.	1,100
Pr76	1946R	—	5 Lire. KM89.	1,750
Pr77	1946R	—	10 Lire. KM90.	2,700
Pr78	1951R	—	Lira. KM91.	1,100
Pr79	1951R	—	5 Lire. KM92.	1,250
Pr80	1951R	—	10 Lire. KM93.	1,350
Pr81	1953R	—	2 Lire. KM94.	950
Pr82	1956R	—	20 Lire. P for PROVA, KM97.1, Unc.	750
PrA82	1956R	—	20 Lire. P for PROVA, KM97.1, Proof.	1,200
PrA83	1957R	—	500 Lire. KM98, Proof.	5,500
Pr83	1957R	1,004	500 Lire. KM98, Unc.	4,500
Pr84	1965R	570	500 Lire. KM100, Unc.	1,600
PrA84	1965R	—	500 Lire.KM100, Proof.	3,000
Pr85	1968R	—	20 Lire. KM97.2, Unc.	375
PrA85	1968R	—	20 Lire. KM97.2, Proof.	—
PrA86	1970R	—	1000 Lire. KM101, Proof.	750
Pr86	1970R	2,500	1000 Lire. KM101, Unc.	350
Pr87	1974R	—	100 Lire. KM96, Unc.	150
PrA87	1974R	—	100 Lire. KM96, Proof.	300
PrA88	1974R	—	100 Lire. KM102, Unc.	140
Pr88	1974R	—	100 Lire. KM102, Proof.	300
PrA89	1974R	—	100 Lire. Copper Nickel. KM102, Proof.	300
Pr89	1974R	—	100 Lire. Copper Nickel. KM102, Unc.	150
Pr90	1974R	—	100 Lire. Silver. KM102.	400
PrA91	1974R	—	500 Lire. KM103, Unc.	300
Pr91	1974R	730	500 Lire. KM103, Proof.	450
PrA92	1977R	—	200 Lire. KM105, Proof.	550
Pr92	1977R	417	200 Lire. KM105, Unc.	300

MINT SETS

KM#	Date	Mintage	Identification	Issue Price	Mkt Val
MS1	1968 (8)	100,000	KM91-96, 97.2, 98	6.50	150
MS2	1969 (8)	310,000	KM91-96, 97.2, 98	6.50	15.00
MS3	1970 (9)	1,011,000	KM91-96, 97.2, 98, 101	—	25.00
MS4	1980 (10)	257,272	KM91-96, 97.2, 98, 105, 107	—	22.50
MS5	1981 (11)	162,794	KM91-96, 97.2, 98, 105, 108-109	—	25.00
MS7	1982 (10)	120,000	KM91-96, 97.2, 98, 105, 111	—	25.00
MS9	1983 (10)	76,000	KM91-96, 97.2, 98, 105, 111	175	240
MS11	1984 (10)	77,000	KM91-96, 97.2, 98, 105, 111	—	175
MS13	1985 (10)	5,000	KM91-96, 97.2, 105, 111, 123	—	52.00
MS14	1985 (11)	75,000	KM91-96, 97.2, 98, 105, 111, 123	—	70.00
MS17	1986 (11)	73,000	KM91-96, 97.2, 98, 105, 111, 124	—	100
MS18	1987 (11)	58,000	KM91-96, 97.2, 98, 105, 111, 132	—	100
MS19	1988 (11)	51,000	KM91-96, 97.2, 98, 105, 111, 144	46.00	250
MS21	1988 (3)	—	KM127-129	—	85.00
MS22	1989 (11)	51,000	KM91-96, 97.2, 98, 111, 130, 145	—	120
MS23	1989 (2)	—	KM133-134	—	50.00
MS24	1989 (2)	—	KM138-139	—	70.00
MS25	1990 (11)	52,800	KM91-94, 95a-96a, 97.2, 98, 111, 135, 146	—	90.00
MS26	1991 (11)	64,000	KM91-94, 95a-96a, 97.2, 98, 105, 111, 141	50.00	90.00
MS27	1991 (2)	—	KM142-143	—	70.00
MS28	1992 (11)	52,000	KM91-94, 95a-96a, 97.2, 98, 111, 151, 161	50.00	110
MS29	1993 (11)	50,000	KM91-94, 95a, 97.2, 98, 155, 159, 160, 163	—	85.00
MS31	ND (1993) (3)	—	KM171-173	31.00	90.00
MS30	1994 (11)	44,500	KM91-94, 95a, 97.2, 98, 159, 164, 167, 169	—	130
MS32	1995 (11)	44,600	KM91-94, 95a, 97.2, 98, 105, 111, 180, 185	—	210
MS33	1996 (11)	45,000	KM91-94, 97.2, 98, 159, 181, 183-184, 199	—	90.00
MS34	1997 (12)	43,500	KM91-94, 97.2, 98, 159, 183, 186-187, 196, 200	—	170
MS35	1998 (12)	55,200	KM91-94, 97.2, 98, 105, 159, 183, 193-194, 201	—	100
MS36	1998 (2)	—	KM195-196	—	70.00
MS37	1999 (12)	51,800	KM#91-94, 97.2, 98, 105, 111, 159, 183, 194, 221	—	120
MS38	2000 (12)	50,000	KM#91-94, 97.2, 98, 105, 111, 159, 183, 194, 235	—	120

PROOF SETS

KM#	Date	Mintage	Identification	Issue Price	Mkt Val
PS1	1985 (10)	5,000	KM91-96, 97.2, 105, 111, 123	—	90.00
PS2	1985 (11)	15,000	KM91-96, 97.2, 98, 105, 111, 123	—	120
PS3	1986 (10)	17,500	KM91-96, 97.2, 105, 111, 124	—	100
PS4	1986 (11)	18,000	KM91-96, 97.2, 98, 105, 111, 124	—	115
PS5	1987 (11)	10,000	KM91-96, 97.2, 98, 105, 111, 132	—	140
PS6	1988 (11)	9,000	KM91-96, 97.2, 98, 105, 111, 144	100	220
PS7	1988 (3)	—	KM127-129	—	135
PS8	1989 (11)	9,260	KM91-96, 97.2, 98, 111, 130, 145	—	120
PS9	1990 (11)	9,400	KM91-94, 95a-96a, 97.2, 98, 111, 135, 146	—	180
PS10	1989 (2)	—	KM133-134	—	60.00
PS11	1989 (2)	—	KM138-139	—	65.00
PS12	1991 (11)	11,000	KM91-94, 95a-96a, 97.2, 98, 105, 111, 141	100	160
PS13	1992 (11)	9,500	KM91-94, 95a-96a, 97.2, 98, 111, 151, 161	90.00	175
PS14	1993 (11)	8,500	KM91-94, 95a, 97.2, 98, 155, 159, 160, 163	—	180
PS15	ND (1993) (3)	—	KM171-173	60.00	150
PS16	1994 (11)	8,500	KM#91-94, 95a, 97.2, 98, 159, 164, 167, 169	—	200
PS17	1995 (11)	7,960	KM#91-94, 95a, 97.2, 98, 105, 111, 180, 185	—	280
PS18	1996 (11)	8,000	KM#91-94, 97.2, 98, 159, 181, 183, 184, 199	—	160
PS19	1997 (12)	8,450	KM#91-94, 97.2, 98, 159, 183, 186, 187, 196, 200	—	300
PS20	1998 (2)	—	KM195-196	—	120
PS21	1998 (12)	9,000	KM#91-94, 97.2, 98, 105, 159, 183, 193, 194, 201	—	150
PS22	1999 (2)	—	KM197-198	—	120
PS23	1999 (12)	8,500	KM#91-94, 97.2, 98, 105, 111, 159, 183, 194, 221	—	180
PS24	2000 (12)	—	KM#91-94, 97.2, 98, 105, 111, 159, 183, 194, 235	—	190

IVORY COAST

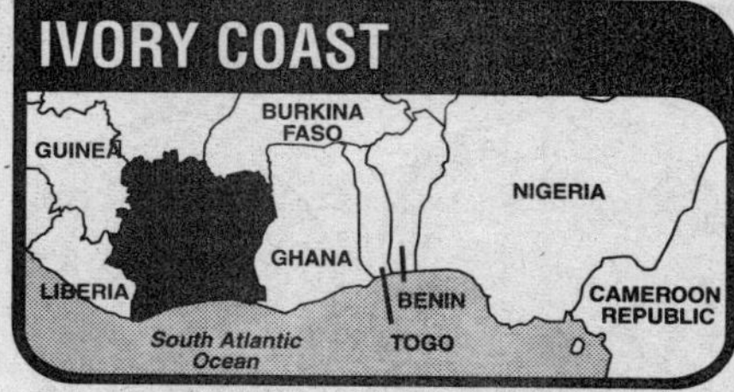

The Republic of the Ivory Coast, (Cote d'Ivoire), a former French Overseas territory located on the south side of the African bulge between Liberia and Ghana, has an area of 124,504 sq. mi. (322,463 sq. km.) and a population of 11.8 million. Capital: Yamoussoukro. The predominantly agricultural economy is one of Africa's most prosperous. Coffee, tropical woods, cocoa, and bananas are exported.

French and Portuguese navigators visited the Ivory Coast in the 15th century. French traders set up establishments in the 19th century, and gradually extended their influence along the coast and inland. The area was organized as a territory in 1893, and from 1904 to 1958 was a constituent unit of the Federation of French West Africa - as a Colony under the Third Republic and an Overseas Territory under the Fourth. In 1958 Ivory Coast became an autonomous republic within the French Community. Independence was attained on Aug. 7, 1960.

REPUBLIC

DECIMAL COINAGE

KM# 1 10 FRANCS

25.0000 g., 0.9250 Silver .7434 oz. ASW **Obv:** Head right **Rev:** Elephant and value within wreath **Note:** Varieties exist in 2.9mm and 3.5mm planchets.

Date	Mintage	F	VF	XF	Unc	BU
1966 Proof	—	Value: 45.00				

KM# 2 10 FRANCS

3.2000 g., 0.9000 Gold .0926 oz. AGW

Date	Mintage	F	VF	XF	Unc	BU
1966 Proof	2,000	Value: 85.00				

KM# 3 25 FRANCS

8.0000 g., 0.9000 Gold .2315 oz. AGW **Obv:** Head right **Rev:** Elephant and value within wreath

Date	Mintage	F	VF	XF	Unc	BU
1966 Proof	2,000	Value: 200				

KM# 4 50 FRANCS

16.0000 g., 0.9000 Gold .4630 oz. AGW **Obv:** Head right **Rev:** Elephant and value within wreath

Date	Mintage	F	VF	XF	Unc	BU
1966 Proof	2,000	Value: 345				

KM# 5 100 FRANCS

32.0000 g., 0.9000 Gold .9260 oz. AGW **Obv:** Head right **Rev:** Elephant within wreath

Date	Mintage	F	VF	XF	Unc	BU
1966 Proof	2,000	Value: 675				

ESSAIS

Standard metals unless otherwise noted

KM#	Date	Mintage	Identification	Mkt Val
E1	1966	—	100 Francs. Silver. KM5.	65.00

PIEFORTS WITH ESSAI

KM#	Date	Mintage	Identification	Mkt Val
PE1	1966	—	100 Francs. Silver. KM5.	225

PROOF SETS

KM#	Date	Mintage	Identification	Issue Price	Mkt Val
PS1	1966 (4)	2,000	KM#2-5	—	1,300

JAMAICA

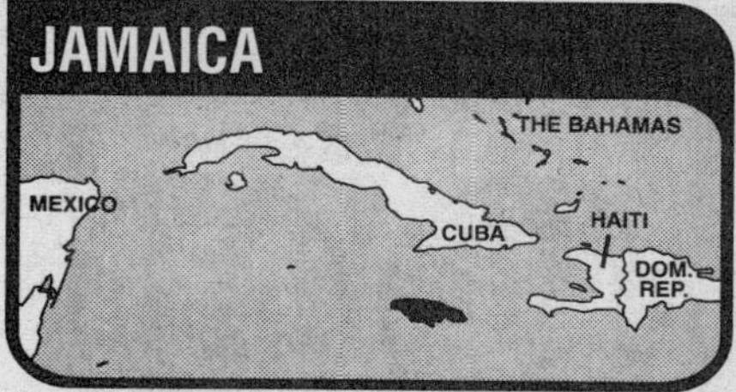

Jamaica is situated in the Caribbean Sea 90 miles south of Cuba, has an area of 4,244 sq. mi. (10,990 sq. km.) and a population of 2.1 million. Capital: Kingston. The economy is founded chiefly on mining, tourism and agriculture. Aluminum, bauxite, sugar, rum and molasses are exported.

Jamaica was discovered by Columbus on May 3, 1494, and settled by Spain in 1509. The island was captured in1655 by a British naval force under the command of Admiral William Penn, sent by Oliver Cromwell and ceded to Britain by the Treaty of Madrid, 1670. For more than 150 years, the Jamaican economy of sugar, slaves and piracy was one of the most prosperous in the new world. Dissension between the property-oriented island legislature and the home government prompted parliament to establish a crown colony government for Jamaica in 1866. From 1958 to 1961 Jamaica was a member of the West Indies Federation, withdrawing when Jamaican voters rejected the association. The colony attained independence on Aug. 6, 1962. Jamaica is a member of the Commonwealth of Nations. Elizabeth II is the Head of State, as Queen of Jamaica.

In 1758, the Jamaican Assembly authorized stamping a certain amount of Spanish milled coinage. Token coinage by merchants aided the island's monetary supply in the early19th century. Sterling coinage was introduced in Jamaica in 1825, with the additional silver three halfpence under William IV and Victoria. Certain issues of three pence of William IV and Victoria were intended for colonial use, including Jamaica, as were the last dates of three pence for George VI.

There was an extensive token and work tally coinage for Jamaica in the late 19th and early 20th centuries.

A decimal standard currency system was adopted on Sept. 8, 1969.

RULERS

British, until 1962

MINT MARKS

C - Royal Canadian Mint, Ottawa
H - Heaton
FM - Franklin Mint, U.S.A.**
(fm) - Franklin Mint, U.S.A.*
no mint mark - Royal Mint, London

***NOTE**: During 1970 the Franklin Mint produced matte and proof coins (1 cent-1 dollar) using dies similar to/or Royal Mint without the FM mint mark.

NOTE: From 1975-1985 the Franklin Mint produced coinage in up to 3 different qualities. Qualities of issue are designated in ( ) after each date and are defined as follows:

(M) MATTE - Normal circulation strike or a dull finish produced by sandblasting special uncirculated (polish finish) or proof quality dies.

(U) SPECIAL UNCIRCULATED - Polished or proof-like in appearance without any frosted features.

(P) PROOF - The highest quality obtainable having mirror-like fields and frosted features.

MONETARY SYSTEM

4 Farthings = 1 Penny
12 Pence = 1 Shilling
8 Reales = 6 Shillings, 8 Pence
(Commencing 1969)
100 Cents = 1 Dollar

BRITISH COLONY

REGULAR COINAGE

KM# 18 FARTHING

Copper-Nickel **Ruler:** Edward VII **Obv:** Crowned bust right within beaded circle **Rev:** Arms with horizontal shading within beaded circle **Designer:** G. W. DeSaulles

Date	Mintage	F	VF	XF	Unc	BU
1902	144,000	2.00	6.00	20.00	45.00	50.00
1903	144,000	2.00	6.00	20.00	45.00	50.00

KM# 21 FARTHING

Copper-Nickel **Ruler:** Edward VII **Obv:** Crowned bust right within beaded circle **Rev:** Arms with vertical shading within beaded circle **Designer:** G. W. DeSaulles

Date	Mintage	F	VF	XF	Unc	BU
1904	192,000	1.00	5.00	12.00	35.00	42.50
1904 Proof	—	Value: 250				
1905	192,000	1.00	5.00	12.00	35.00	42.50
1906	528,000	1.00	3.00	9.00	28.00	35.00
1907	192,000	1.00	5.00	12.00	35.00	42.50
1909	144,000	2.00	6.00	20.00	45.00	50.00
1910	48,000	4.00	10.00	30.00	50.00	60.00

KM# 24 FARTHING

Copper-Nickel **Ruler:** George V **Obv:** Crowned bust left within beaded circle **Obv. Designer:** E. B. MacKennal **Rev:** Arms within beaded circle **Rev. Designer:** G. W. DeSaulles

Date	Mintage	F	VF	XF	Unc	BU
1914	192,000	2.00	5.00	12.00	35.00	42.50
1916H	480,000	0.75	2.00	6.00	20.00	27.50
1916H Proof	—	Value: 250				
1918C	208,000	1.00	2.00	8.00	25.00	30.00
1918C Proof	—	Value: 225				
1919C	401,000	0.75	2.00	6.00	20.00	27.50
1926	240,000	1.00	2.00	8.00	25.00	30.00
1928	480,000	0.75	2.00	6.00	20.00	25.00
1928 Proof	—	Value: 225				
1932	480,000	0.75	2.00	6.00	20.00	27.50
1932 Proof	—	—	—	—	—	—
1934	480,000	0.75	2.00	6.00	20.00	27.50
1934 Proof	—	—	—	—	—	—

KM# 27 FARTHING

Nickel-Brass **Ruler:** George VI **Obv:** Crowned head left **Rev:** Arms divide date **Designer:** Percy Metcalfe

Date	Mintage	F	VF	XF	Unc	BU
1937	480,000	0.50	1.50	5.00	15.00	20.00
1937 Proof	—	Value: 175				

KM# 30 FARTHING

Nickel-Brass **Ruler:** George VI **Obv:** Crowned head left **Rev:** Arms divide date **Designer:** Percy Metcalfe

Date	Mintage	F	VF	XF	Unc	BU
1938	480,000	0.50	1.50	5.00	15.00	20.00
1938 Proof	—	—	—	—	—	—
1942	480,000	0.50	1.50	5.00	15.00	20.00
1945	480,000	0.50	1.50	5.00	15.00	20.00
1945 Proof	—	Value: 120				
1947	192,000	1.00	3.00	7.50	20.00	27.50
1947 Proof	—	Value: 120				

KM# 33 FARTHING

Nickel-Brass **Ruler:** George VI **Obv:** Crowned head left **Obv. Legend:** Without AND EMPEROR OF INDIA in legend **Rev:** Arms divide date **Designer:** Percy Metcalfe

Date	Mintage	F	VF	XF	Unc	BU
1950	288,000	0.10	0.25	0.80	3.25	15.00
1950 Proof	—	Value: 175				
1952	288,000	0.10	0.25	0.80	3.50	17.50
1952 Proof	—	Value: 175				

KM# 19 1/2 PENNY

Copper-Nickel **Ruler:** Edward VII **Obv:** Crowned bust right within beaded circle **Rev:** Arms with horizontal shading within beaded circle **Designer:** G. W. DeSaulles

Date	Mintage	F	VF	XF	Unc	BU
1902	48,000	2.00	5.00	20.00	50.00	60.00
1903	48,000	2.00	5.00	20.00	60.00	70.00

KM# 22 1/2 PENNY

Copper-Nickel, 25.3 mm. **Ruler:** Edward VII **Obv:** Crowned bust right within beaded circle **Rev:** Arms with vertical shading within beaded circle **Designer:** G. W. DeSaulles

Date	Mintage	F	VF	XF	Unc	BU
1904	48,000	1.50	5.00	25.00	70.00	80.00
1905	48,000	1.50	5.00	25.00	70.00	80.00
1906	432,000	0.65	1.50	7.50	25.00	32.50
1907	504,000	0.65	1.50	7.50	25.00	32.50
1909	144,000	0.75	2.00	10.00	40.00	45.00
1910	144,000	0.75	2.00	10.00	40.00	45.00

KM# 25 1/2 PENNY

Copper-Nickel **Ruler:** George V **Obv:** Crowned bust left within beaded circle **Obv. Designer:** E. B. MacKennal **Rev:** Arms within beaded circle **Rev. Designer:** G. W. DeSaulles

Date	Mintage	F	VF	XF	Unc	BU
1914	96,000	3.00	6.00	25.00	75.00	90.00
1916H	192,000	0.35	1.50	6.00	20.00	27.50
1918C	251,000	0.35	1.50	6.00	20.00	27.50
1918C Proof	—	Value: 200				
1919C	312,000	0.35	1.50	7.50	20.00	27.50
1920	480,000	0.35	1.50	7.50	20.00	27.50
1926	240,000	0.35	1.50	7.50	30.00	35.00
1928	120,000	0.35	3.00	10.00	35.00	40.00
1928 Proof	—	Value: 200				

KM# 28 1/2 PENNY

Nickel-Brass **Ruler:** George VI **Obv:** Crowned head left **Rev:** Arms divide date **Designer:** Percy Metcalfe

Date	Mintage	F	VF	XF	Unc	BU
1937	960,000	0.50	1.00	3.50	12.00	15.00
1937 Proof	—	Value: 175				

KM# 31 1/2 PENNY

Nickel-Brass **Ruler:** George VI **Obv:** Crowned head left **Rev:** Arms divide date **Designer:** Percy Metcalfe

Date	Mintage	F	VF	XF	Unc	BU
1938	960,000	0.25	0.75	3.50	12.00	15.00
1938 Proof	—	Value: 175				
1940	960,000	0.25	0.75	3.50	12.00	15.00
1940 Proof	—	Value: 175				
1942	960,000	0.25	0.75	3.50	12.00	15.00
1945	960,000	0.25	0.75	3.50	12.00	15.00
1945 Proof	—	Value: 175				
1947	960,000	0.25	0.75	3.50	12.00	15.00
1947 Proof	—	Value: 200				

KM# 34 1/2 PENNY

Nickel-Brass **Ruler:** George VI **Obv:** Crowned head left **Rev:** Arms divide date **Designer:** Percy Metcalfe

Date	Mintage	F	VF	XF	Unc	BU
1950	1,440,000	0.10	0.20	0.30	3.25	5.00
1950 Proof	—	Value: 175				
1952	1,200,000	0.10	0.20	0.30	3.25	5.00
1952 Proof	—	Value: 175				

KM# 36 1/2 PENNY

Nickel-Brass **Ruler:** Elizabeth II **Obv:** Crowned bust right **Rev:** Arms divide date **Rev. Designer:** Percy Metcalfe

Date	Mintage	F	VF	XF	Unc	BU
1955	1,440,000	0.10	0.15	0.40	2.00	3.00
1955 Proof	—	Value: 150				
1957	600,000	1.00	2.00	4.00	6.00	9.00
1957 Proof	—	—	—	—	—	—
1958	960,000	0.10	0.20	0.50	2.00	3.00
1958 Proof	—	Value: 150				
1959	960,000	0.10	0.20	0.50	2.00	3.00
1959 Proof	—	—	—	—	—	—
1961	480,000	0.20	0.40	1.00	4.00	5.00
1961 Proof	—	—	—	—	—	—
1962	960,000	0.10	0.15	0.30	1.75	2.50
1962 Proof	—	Value: 150				
1963	960,000	0.10	0.15	0.30	1.75	2.50
1963 Proof	—	Value: 150				

KM# 38 1/2 PENNY

Nickel-Brass **Ruler:** Elizabeth II **Obv:** Crowned bust right **Rev:** Arms with supporters

Date	Mintage	F	VF	XF	Unc	BU
1964	1,440,000	0.10	0.15	0.20	0.80	1.00
1965	1,200,000	0.10	0.15	0.20	0.80	1.00
1966	1,680,000	0.10	0.15	0.20	0.80	1.00

KM# 41 1/2 PENNY

Copper-Nickel-Zinc **Ruler:** Elizabeth II **Subject:** Jamaican Coinage Centennial **Obv:** Crowned bust right **Rev:** Arms with supporters

Date	Mintage	F	VF	XF	Unc	BU
1969	30,000	0.10	0.15	0.25	0.75	1.00
1969 Proof	5,000	Value: 2.50				

KM# 20 PENNY

Copper-Nickel **Ruler:** Edward VII **Obv:** Crowned bust right within beaded circle **Rev:** Arms with horizontal shading within beaded circle **Designer:** G. W. DeSaulles

Date	Mintage	F	VF	XF	Unc	BU
1902	60,000	2.25	6.00	25.00	70.00	85.00
1903	60,000	2.25	6.00	25.00	70.00	85.00

KM# 23 PENNY

Copper-Nickel **Ruler:** Edward VII **Obv:** Crowned bust right within beaded circle **Rev:** Arms with vertical shading within beaded circle **Designer:** G. W. DeSaulles

Date	Mintage	F	VF	XF	Unc	BU
1904	24,000	10.00	20.00	50.00	125	150
1904 Proof	—	Value: 250				
1905	48,000	2.00	6.50	35.00	70.00	85.00
1906	156,000	1.25	2.50	12.00	45.00	60.00
1907	108,000	1.25	2.50	12.00	45.00	60.00
1909	144,000	1.25	2.50	12.00	45.00	60.00
1910	144,000	1.25	2.50	12.00	45.00	60.00

KM# 26 PENNY

Copper-Nickel **Ruler:** George V **Obv:** Crowned bust left within beaded circle **Obv. Designer:** E. B. MacKennal **Rev:** Arms within beaded circle **Rev. Designer:** G. W. DeSaulles

Date	Mintage	F	VF	XF	Unc	BU
1914	24,000	10.00	20.00	65.00	175	200
1916H	24,000	10.00	20.00	60.00	175	200
1918C	187,000	2.00	5.00	15.00	60.00	75.00
1918C Proof	—	Value: 200				
1919C	251,000	1.25	4.75	12.00	50.00	65.00
1920	360,000	0.75	2.50	9.50	32.50	40.00
1926	240,000	0.75	2.50	9.50	35.00	40.00
1928	360,000	0.75	2.50	9.50	35.00	40.00
1928 Proof	—	Value: 200				

KM# 29 PENNY

Nickel-Brass **Ruler:** George VI **Obv:** Crowned head left **Rev:** Arms divide date **Designer:** Percy Metcalfe

Date	Mintage	F	VF	XF	Unc	BU
1937	1,200,000	1.00	1.75	3.25	12.00	15.00
1937 Proof	—	Value: 200				

KM# 32 PENNY

Nickel-Brass **Ruler:** George VI **Obv:** Crowned head left **Rev:** Arms divide date **Designer:** Percy Metcalfe

Date	Mintage	F	VF	XF	Unc	BU
1938	1,200,000	0.35	0.65	3.25	12.00	15.00
1938 Proof	—	Value: 200				
1940	1,200,000	0.35	0.65	3.25	12.00	15.00
1940 Proof	—	Value: 200				
1942	1,200,000	0.35	0.65	3.25	12.00	15.00
1942 Proof	—	Value: 200				
1945	1,200,000	0.35	0.65	3.25	12.00	15.00
1945 Proof	—	Value: 200				
1947	480,000	0.35	0.65	7.00	25.00	32.50
1947 Proof	—	Value: 200				

KM# 35 PENNY

Nickel-Brass **Ruler:** George VI **Obv:** Crowned head left **Obv. Legend:** Without AND EMPEROR OF INDIA in legend **Rev:** Arms divide date **Designer:** Percy Metcalfe

Date	Mintage	F	VF	XF	Unc	BU
1950	600,000	0.20	0.35	2.00	10.00	14.00
1950 Proof	—	Value: 200				
1952	725,000	0.20	0.35	2.00	10.00	14.00
1952 Proof	—	Value: 200				

KM# 37 PENNY

Nickel-Brass **Ruler:** Elizabeth II **Obv:** Crowned bust right **Rev:** Arms divide date **Rev. Designer:** Percy Metcalfe

Date	Mintage	F	VF	XF	Unc	BU
1953	1,200,000	0.10	0.20	0.50	1.50	2.00
1953 Proof	—	Value: 115				
1955	960,000	0.10	0.25	1.00	4.00	5.00
1955 Proof	—	Value: 115				
1957	600,000	0.10	0.25	1.00	4.00	5.00
1957 Proof	—	—	—	—	—	—
1958	1,080,000	0.10	0.20	0.30	3.00	4.50
1958 Proof	—	Value: 100				
1959	1,368,000	0.10	0.20	0.30	2.50	3.00
1959 Proof	—	—	—	—	—	—
1960	1,368,000	0.10	0.20	0.30	2.50	3.00
1960 Proof	—	—	—	—	—	—
1961	1,368,000	0.10	0.20	0.30	2.50	3.00
1961 Proof	—	—	—	—	—	—
1962	1,920,000	0.10	0.20	0.30	2.50	3.00
1962 Proof	—	Value: 100				
1963	720,000	2.00	4.00	10.00	50.00	65.00
1963 Proof	—	Value: 100				

KM# 39 PENNY

Nickel-Brass **Ruler:** Elizabeth II **Obv:** Crowned bust right **Rev:** Arms with supporters

Date	Mintage	F	VF	XF	Unc	BU
1964	480,000	0.10	0.15	0.50	1.00	1.50
1965	1,200,000	0.10	0.15	0.20	0.35	1.00
1966	1,200,000	0.10	0.15	0.20	0.35	1.00
1967	2,760,000	0.10	0.15	0.20	0.35	1.00

KM# 42 PENNY

Copper-Nickel-Zinc **Ruler:** Elizabeth II **Subject:** Jamaican Coinage Centennial **Obv:** Crowned bust right **Rev:** Arms with supporters

Date	Mintage	F	VF	XF	Unc	BU
1969	30,000	0.10	0.15	0.30	0.75	1.25
1969 Proof	5,000	Value: 2.50				

KM# 40 5 SHILLING

Copper-Nickel **Ruler:** Elizabeth II **Subject:** VIII Commonwealth Games **Obv:** Arms with supporters **Rev:** Crown divides date above inscription within chain link wreath

Date	Mintage	F	VF	XF	Unc	BU
1966	190,000	—	2.00	3.00	5.00	6.50
1966 Proof	20,000	Value: 7.00				

DECIMAL COINAGE

The Franklin Mint and Royal Mint have both been striking the 1 Cent through 1 Dollar coinage. The 1970 issues were all struck with dies similar to/or Royal Mint without the FM mint mark. The Royal Mint issues have the name JAMAICA extending beyond the native headdress feathers. Those struck after 1970 by the Franklin Mint have the name JAMAICA within the headdress feathers.

KM# 45 CENT

Bronze **Ruler:** Elizabeth II **Obv:** Arms with supporters **Rev:** Ackee fruit above value **Designer:** Christopher Ironside

Date	Mintage	F	VF	XF	Unc	BU
1969	30,200,000	—	—	0.10	0.25	0.50
1969 Proof	19,000	Value: 0.50				
1970 (RM) Small date	10,000,000	—	—	0.10	0.25	0.50
1970FM (M); Large date	5,000	—	—	0.10	0.25	0.50
1970FM (P)	12,000	Value: 0.50				
1971 (RM)	5,625,000	—	—	0.10	0.25	0.50

KM# 51 CENT

Bronze **Ruler:** Elizabeth II **Obv:** Arms with supporters **Rev:** Ackee fruit above value **Designer:** Christopher Ironside

Date	Mintage	F	VF	XF	Unc	BU
1971FM (M)	4,834	—	—	0.10	0.25	0.50
1971FM (P)	14,000	Value: 0.50				
1972FM (M)	7,982	—	—	0.10	0.25	0.50
1972FM (P)	17,000	Value: 0.50				
1973FM (M)	29,000	—	—	0.10	0.25	0.50
1973FM (P)	28,000	Value: 0.50				
1974FM (M)	28,000	—	—	0.10	0.25	0.50
1974FM (P)	22,000	Value: 0.50				
1975FM (M)	36,000	—	—	0.10	0.25	0.50
1975FM (U)	4,683	—	—	—	0.25	0.50
1975FM (P)	16,000	Value: 0.50				

KM# 52 CENT

Bronze **Ruler:** Elizabeth II **Series:** F.A.O. **Obv:** Arms with supporters **Rev:** Ackee fruit above value **Designer:** Christopher Ironside

Date	Mintage	F	VF	XF	Unc	BU
1971	20,000	—	—	0.50	1.00	1.50
1972	5,000,000	—	—	0.10	0.30	1.00
1973	5,500,000	—	—	0.10	0.30	1.00
1974	3,000,000	—	—	0.10	0.30	1.00

KM# 64 CENT

1.2000 g., Aluminum, 21.05 mm. **Ruler:** Elizabeth II **Series:** F.A.O. **Obv:** Arms with supporters **Rev:** Ackee fruit above value **Shape:** 12-sided **Designer:** Christopher Ironside

Date	Mintage	F	VF	XF	Unc	BU
1975	15,000,000	—	—	0.10	0.20	0.50
1976	16,000,000	—	—	0.10	0.20	0.50
1977	—	—	—	0.10	0.20	0.50
1978	8,400,000	—	—	0.10	0.20	0.50
1980	10,000,000	—	—	0.10	0.20	0.50
1981	8,000,000	—	—	0.10	0.20	0.50
1982	10,000,000	—	—	0.10	0.20	0.50
1983	1,342,000	—	—	—	0.15	0.50
1984	8,704,000	—	—	—	0.15	0.50
1985	5,112,000	—	—	—	0.15	0.50
1985 Proof	—	Value: 0.50				
1986	17,534,000	—	—	—	0.15	0.50
1987	9,968,000	—	—	—	0.15	0.50
1987 Proof	—	Value: 0.50				
1988 Proof	—	Value: 0.50				
1989 Proof	—	Value: 0.50				
1990	—	—	—	—	0.15	0.50
1990 Proof	—	Value: 0.50				
1991	—	—	—	—	0.15	0.50
1991 Proof	—	Value: 0.50				
1992 Proof	—	Value: 0.50				
1993 Proof	—	Value: 0.50				
2000	—	—	—	—	—	—

KM# 68 CENT

1.2000 g., Aluminum, 21.05 mm. **Ruler:** Elizabeth II **Obv:** Arms with supporters **Rev:** Ackee fruit above value **Shape:** 12-sided **Designer:** Christopher Ironside

Date	Mintage	F	VF	XF	Unc	BU
1976FM (M)	28,000	—	—	—	0.15	0.50
1976FM (U)	1,802	—	—	—	0.25	0.50
1976FM (P)	24,000	Value: 0.50				
1977FM (M)	28,000	—	—	—	0.15	0.30
1977FM (U)	597	—	—	—	1.50	2.00
1977FM (P)	10,000	Value: 0.50				
1978FM (M)	28,000	—	—	—	0.15	0.30
1978FM (U)	1,282	—	—	—	0.40	0.75
1978FM (P)	6,058	Value: 0.60				
1979FM (M)	28,000	—	—	—	0.15	0.50
1979FM (U)	2,608	—	—	—	0.40	0.75
1979FM (P)	4,049	Value: 0.60				
1980FM (M)	28,000	—	—	—	0.15	0.50
1980FM (U)	3,668	—	—	—	0.35	0.70
1980FM (P)	2,688	Value: 0.75				
1981FM (U)	482	—	—	—	1.50	2.00
1981FM (P)	1,577	Value: 0.75				
1982FM (U)	—	—	—	—	0.35	0.70
1982FM (P)	—	Value: 0.75				
1984FM (U)	—	—	—	—	0.35	0.70
1984FM (P)	—	Value: 0.75				

KM# 136 CENT

1.2000 g., Aluminum, 21.05 mm. **Note:** Mule. Two obverses of KM#64.

Date	Mintage	F	VF	XF	Unc	BU
1982FM	—	—	—	220	250	275

KM# 137 CENT

1.2000 g., Aluminum, 21.05 mm. **Note:** Mule. Two reverses of KM#64.

Date	Mintage	F	VF	XF	Unc	BU
1982FM	—	—	—	250	300	325

KM# 101 CENT

1.2000 g., Aluminum, 21.05 mm. **Subject:** 21st Anniversary of Independence **Obv:** Arms with supporters **Rev:** Ackee plant (blighia sapida) **Designer:** Christopher Ironside

Date	Mintage	F	VF	XF	Unc	BU
ND(1983)M (U)	—	—	—	—	0.35	0.75
ND(1983)FM (P)	—	Value: 0.75				

KM# 46 5 CENTS

2.8000 g., Copper-Nickel, 19.4 mm. **Ruler:** Elizabeth II **Obv:** Arms with supporters **Rev:** American crocodile above value **Designer:** Christopher Ironside

Date	Mintage	F	VF	XF	Unc	BU
1969 Proof	30,000	Value: 0.65				
1969	12,008,000	—	—	0.10	0.50	1.00
1970FM (M)	5,000	—	—	0.10	0.50	1.00
1970FM (P)	12,000	Value: 0.65				
1972	6,000,000	—	—	0.10	0.50	0.75
1975	6,010,000	—	—	0.10	0.50	0.75
1977	2,400,000	—	—	0.10	0.50	0.75
1978	2,000,000	—	—	0.10	0.50	0.75
1980	2,272,000	—	—	0.10	0.50	0.75
1981	2,001,000	—	—	0.10	0.50	0.75
1982	2,000,000	—	—	0.10	0.50	0.75
1983	992,000	—	—	0.75	1.00	1.50
1984	3,508,000	—	—	0.10	0.50	0.75
1985	4,760,000	—	—	0.10	0.50	0.75
1985 Proof	—	Value: 0.65				
1986	14,504,000	—	—	0.10	0.50	0.75
1987	13,166,000	—	—	0.10	0.50	0.75
1987 Proof	—	Value: 0.65				
1988	9,780,000	—	—	0.10	0.50	0.75
1988 Proof	—	Value: 0.65				
1989	—	—	—	0.10	0.50	0.75
1989 Proof	—	Value: 0.65				

KM# 46a 5 CENTS

Nickel Plated Steel, 19.4 mm. **Ruler:** Elizabeth II **Obv:** Arms with supporters **Rev:** American crocodile above value **Designer:** Christopher Ironside

Date	Mintage	F	VF	XF	Unc	BU
1990	—	—	—	0.10	0.50	0.75
1990 Proof	—	Value: 0.65				
1991	—	—	—	0.10	0.50	0.75
1991 Proof	—	Value: 0.65				
1992	—	—	—	0.10	0.50	0.75
1992 Proof	—	Value: 0.65				
1993	—	—	—	0.10	0.50	0.75
1993 Proof	—	Value: 0.65				

KM# 53 5 CENTS

2.8000 g., Copper-Nickel, 19.4 mm. **Ruler:** Elizabeth II **Obv:** Arms with supporters **Rev:** American crocodile above value **Designer:** Christopher Ironside

Date	Mintage	F	VF	XF	Unc	BU
1971FM (M)	4,834	—	—	0.10	0.75	1.00
1971FM (P)	14,000	Value: 0.50				
1972FM (M)	7,982	—	—	0.10	0.75	1.00
1972FM (P)	17,000	Value: 0.50				
1973FM (M)	17,000	—	—	0.10	0.75	1.00
1973FM (P)	28,000	Value: 0.50				
1974FM (M)	16,000	—	—	0.10	0.75	1.00
1974FM (P)	22,000	Value: 0.50				
1975FM (M)	6,240	—	—	0.10	0.75	1.00
1975FM (U)	4,683	—	—	—	0.75	1.00
1975FM (P)	16,000	Value: 0.50				
1976FM (M)	5,560	—	—	0.10	0.75	1.00
1976FM (U)	1,802	—	—	—	0.75	1.00
1976FM (P)	24,000	Value: 0.50				
1977FM (M)	5,560	—	—	0.10	0.75	1.00
1977FM (U)	597	—	—	—	1.50	2.00
1977FM (P)	10,000	Value: 0.50				
1978FM (M)	5,560	—	—	0.10	0.75	1.00
1978FM (U)	1,282	—	—	—	0.85	1.50
1978FM (P)	6,058	Value: 0.85				
1979FM (M)	5,560	—	—	0.10	0.75	1.50
1979FM (U)	2,608	—	—	—	0.80	1.60
1979FM (P)	4,049	Value: 0.85				
1980FM (M)	5,560	—	—	0.10	0.75	1.50
1980FM (U)	3,668	—	—	—	0.80	1.60
1980FM (P)	2,688	Value: 1.00				
1981FM (U)	482	—	—	—	1.50	2.00
1981FM (P)	1,577	Value: 1.00				
1982FM (U)	—	—	—	—	0.80	1.60
1982FM (P)	—	Value: 1.00				
1984FM (U)	—	—	—	—	0.80	1.60
1984FM (P)	—	Value: 1.00				

KM# 102 5 CENTS

2.8000 g., Copper-Nickel, 19.4 mm. **Ruler:** Elizabeth II **Subject:** 21st Anniversary of Independence **Obv:** Arms with supporters **Rev:** American crocodile above value **Designer:** Christopher Ironside

Date	Mintage	F	VF	XF	Unc	BU
ND(1983)FM (U)	—	—	—	—	1.25	1.75
ND(1983)FM (P)	—	Value: 1.75				

KM# 47 10 CENTS

5.7500 g., Copper-Nickel, 23.6 mm. **Ruler:** Elizabeth II **Obv:** Arms with supporters **Rev:** Butterfly within leafy sprigs above value **Designer:** Christopher Ironside

Date	Mintage	F	VF	XF	Unc	BU
1969	19,508,000	—	—	0.10	0.50	0.75
1969 Proof	30,000	Value: 0.75				
1970FM (M)	5,000	—	—	0.10	0.50	0.75
1970FM (P)	12,000	Value: 0.75				
1972	6,000,000	—	—	0.10	0.50	0.75
1975	10,010,000	—	—	0.10	0.40	0.65
1977	8,000,000	—	—	0.10	0.40	0.65
1981	8,000,000	—	—	0.10	0.30	0.60
1982	8,000,000	—	—	0.10	0.30	0.60
1983	2,000,000	—	—	0.10	0.30	0.60
1984	5,000,000	—	—	0.10	0.30	0.60
1985	8,310,000	—	—	0.10	0.30	0.60
1985 Proof	—	Value: 0.75				
1986	21,677,000	—	—	0.10	0.30	0.60
1987	29,089,000	—	—	0.10	0.30	0.60
1987 Proof	—	Value: 0.75				
1988	15,660,000	—	—	0.10	0.30	0.60
1988 Proof	—	Value: 0.75				
1989	—	—	—	0.10	0.30	0.60
1989 Proof	—	Value: 0.75				

KM# 47a 10 CENTS

5.7500 g., Nickel Plated Steel, 23.6 mm. **Ruler:** Elizabeth II **Obv:** Arms with supporters **Rev:** Butterfly within leafy sprigs above value **Designer:** Christopher Ironside

Date	Mintage	F	VF	XF	Unc	BU
1990	—	—	—	0.10	0.30	0.60
1990 Proof	—	Value: 0.75				

KM# 54 10 CENTS

5.7500 g., Copper-Nickel, 23.6 mm. **Ruler:** Elizabeth II **Obv:** Arms with supporters **Rev:** Butterfly within leafy sprigs above value **Designer:** Christopher Ironside

Date	Mintage	F	VF	XF	Unc	BU
1971FM (M)	4,834	—	—	0.10	0.35	0.70
1971FM (P)	14,000	Value: 0.75				
1972FM (M)	7,982	—	—	0.10	0.35	0.70
1972FM (P)	17,000	Value: 0.75				
1973FM (M)	15,000	—	—	0.10	0.35	0.70
1973FM (P)	28,000	Value: 0.75				
1974FM (M)	14,000	—	—	0.10	0.35	0.70
1974FM (P)	22,000	Value: 0.75				
1975FM (M)	3,120	—	—	0.10	0.35	0.75
1975FM (U)	4,683	—	—	—	0.35	0.75
1975FM (P)	16,000	Value: 0.75				
1976FM (M)	2,780	—	—	0.10	0.35	0.75
1976FM (U)	1,802	—	—	—	0.35	0.75
1976FM (P)	24,000	Value: 0.75				
1977FM (M)	2,780	—	—	0.10	0.50	0.80
1977FM (U)	597	—	—	—	1.50	2.50
1977FM (P)	10,000	Value: 0.75				
1978FM (M)	2,780	—	—	0.10	0.50	0.80
1978FM (U)	4,062	—	—	—	0.60	0.85
1978FM (P)	6,058	Value: 1.00				
1979FM (M)	2,780	—	—	0.10	0.50	0.80
1979FM (U)	2,608	—	—	—	0.60	0.85
1979FM (P)	4,049	Value: 1.00				
1980FM (M)	2,780	—	—	0.10	0.50	0.80
1980FM (U)	3,668	—	—	—	0.50	0.80
1980FM (P)	2,688	Value: 1.50				
1981FM (U)	482	—	—	—	1.50	2.00
1981FM (P)	1,577	Value: 1.50				
1982FM (U)	—	—	—	—	0.50	0.80
1982FM (P)	—	Value: 1.50				
1984FM (U)	—	—	—	—	0.50	0.80
1984FM (P)	—	Value: 1.50				

KM# 103 10 CENTS

5.7500 g., Copper-Nickel, 23.6 mm. **Ruler:** Elizabeth II **Subject:** 21st Anniversary of Independence **Obv:** Arms with supporters **Rev:** Butterfly within leafy sprigs above value **Designer:** Christopher Ironside

Date	Mintage	F	VF	XF	Unc	BU
ND(1983)FM (U)	—	—	—	—	0.50	0.80
ND(1983)FM (P)	—	Value: 1.50				

KM# 146.1 10 CENTS

Nickel Plated Steel **Ruler:** Elizabeth II **Subject:** Paul Bogle **Obv:** Arms with supporters **Rev:** Bust facing

Date	Mintage	F	VF	XF	Unc	BU
1991	—	—	—	—	0.50	0.80
1991 Proof	—	Value: 1.50				
1992	—	—	—	—	0.50	0.80
1992 Proof	—	Value: 1.50				
1993	—	—	—	—	0.50	0.80
1993 Proof	—	Value: 1.50				
1994	—	—	—	—	0.50	0.80
1994 Proof	—	Value: 1.50				

KM# 146.2 10 CENTS

Copper Plated Steel **Ruler:** Elizabeth II **Subject:** Paul Bogle **Obv:** Arms with supporters **Rev:** Bust facing **Note:** Reduced size.

Date	Mintage	F	VF	XF	Unc	BU
1995	—	—	—	—	0.25	0.50
1996	—	—	—	—	0.25	0.50
2000	—	—	—	—	0.25	0.50

KM# 48 20 CENTS

11.3000 g., Copper-Nickel, 28.5 mm. **Ruler:** Elizabeth II **Obv:** Arms with supporters **Rev:** Mahoe trees above value **Designer:** Christopher Ironside

Date	Mintage	F	VF	XF	Unc	BU
1969	3,758,000	—	—	0.20	0.75	1.00
1969 Proof	30,000	Value: 1.00				
1970FM (M)	5,000	—	—	0.20	0.75	1.00
1970FM (P)	12,000	Value: 1.00				
1975	10,000	—	—	0.80	2.50	3.00
1982	1,000,000	—	—	0.20	0.65	1.00
1984	2,000,000	—	—	0.20	0.65	1.00
1986	2,530,000	—	—	0.20	0.65	1.00
1987	5,545,000	—	—	0.20	0.65	1.00
1987 Proof	—	Value: 1.00				
1988	5,016,000	—	—	0.20	0.65	1.00
1988 Proof	—	Value: 1.00				
1989	—	—	—	0.20	0.65	1.00
1989 Proof	—	Value: 1.00				
1990 Proof	—	Value: 1.00				

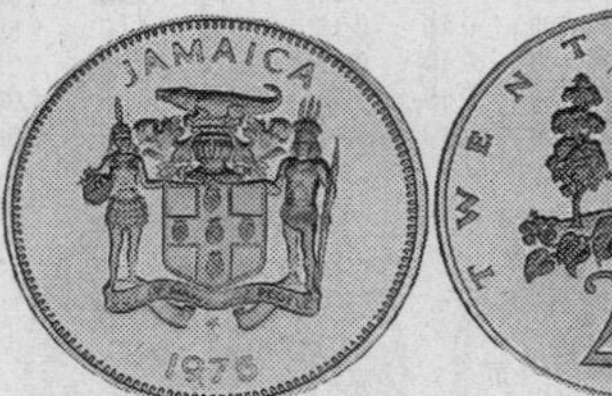

KM# 55 20 CENTS

11.3000 g., Copper-Nickel, 28.5 mm. **Ruler:** Elizabeth II **Obv:** Arms with supporters **Rev:** Mahoe trees above value **Designer:** Christopher Ironside

Date	Mintage	F	VF	XF	Unc	BU
1971FM (M)	4,834	—	—	0.20	0.50	1.00
1971FM (P)	14,000	Value: 1.00				
1972FM (M)	7,982	—	—	0.20	0.50	1.00
1972FM (P)	17,000	Value: 1.00				
1973FM (M)	13,000	—	—	0.20	0.50	1.00
1973FM (P)	28,000	Value: 1.00				
1974FM (M)	12,000	—	—	0.20	0.50	1.00
1974FM (P)	22,000	Value: 1.00				
1975FM (M)	1,560	—	—	0.20	0.50	1.00
1975FM (U)	4,683	—	—	—	0.50	1.00
1975FM (P)	16,000	Value: 1.00				
1976FM (M)	1,390	—	—	0.20	0.50	1.00
1976FM (U)	1,802	—	—	—	0.50	1.00
1976FM (P)	24,000	Value: 1.00				

KM# 69 20 CENTS
11.3000 g., Copper-Nickel, 28.5 mm. **Ruler:** Elizabeth II **Series:** F.A.O. **Obv:** Arms with supporters **Rev:** Mahoe trees above value **Designer:** Christopher Ironside

Date	Mintage	F	VF	XF	Unc	BU
1976	3,000,000	—	—	0.20	1.00	1.50
1981	—	—	—	0.20	1.00	1.50
1982	—	—	—	0.20	1.00	1.50
Note: Mintage included with KM#48						
1984	—	—	—	0.20	1.00	1.50
1987	—	—	—	0.20	1.00	1.50

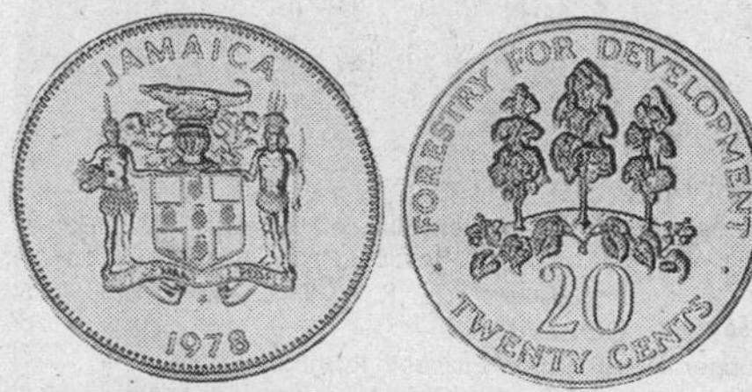

KM# 73 20 CENTS
11.3000 g., Copper-Nickel, 28.5 mm. **Ruler:** Elizabeth II **Obv:** Arms with supporters **Rev:** Mahoe trees above value **Designer:** Christopher Ironside

Date	Mintage	F	VF	XF	Unc	BU
1977FM (M)	1,390	—	—	0.20	0.75	1.25
1977FM (U)	597	—	—	—	2.00	2.50
1977FM (P)	10,000	Value: 1.00				
1978FM (M)	1,390	—	—	0.20	0.75	1.25
1978FM (U)	1,282	—	—	—	0.75	1.25
1978FM (P)	6,058	Value: 1.50				
1979FM (M)	1,390	—	—	0.20	0.75	1.25
1979FM (U)	2,608	—	—	—	0.75	1.25
1979FM (P)	4,049	Value: 1.50				
1980FM (M)	1,390	—	—	0.20	0.60	1.00
1980FM (U)	3,668	—	—	—	0.60	1.00
1980FM (P)	2,688	Value: 2.00				
1981FM (U)	482	—	—	—	2.00	2.50
1981FM (P)	1,577	Value: 2.00				
1982FM (U)	—	—	—	—	0.60	1.00
1982FM (P)	—	Value: 2.00				
1984FM (U)	—	—	—	—	0.60	1.00
1984FM (P)	—	Value: 2.00				

KM# 90 20 CENTS
11.3000 g., Copper-Nickel, 28.5 mm. **Ruler:** Elizabeth II **Subject:** World Food Day **Obv:** Arms with supporters **Rev:** Figs within leaves above value

Date	Mintage	F	VF	XF	Unc	BU
1981FM (M)	—	—	—	—	1.50	2.00

KM# 120 20 CENTS
11.3000 g., Copper-Nickel, 28.5 mm. **Ruler:** Elizabeth II **Obv:** Arms with supporters **Rev:** Figs within leaves above value

Date	Mintage	F	VF	XF	Unc	BU
1981	—	—	—	—	0.60	1.00
1984	2,000,000	—	—	—	0.60	1.00
1985	2,988,000	—	—	—	0.60	1.00
1985 Proof	—	Value: 2.00				
1986	2,530,000	—	—	—	0.60	1.00
1988	—	—	—	—	0.60	1.00

KM# 104 20 CENTS
11.3000 g., Copper-Nickel, 28.5 mm. **Ruler:** Elizabeth II **Subject:** 21st Anniversary of Independence **Obv:** Arms with supporters **Rev:** Mahoe trees above value **Designer:** Christopher Ironside

Date	Mintage	F	VF	XF	Unc	BU
ND(1983)FM (U)	—	—	—	—	0.60	1.00
ND(1983)FM (P)	—	Value: 2.00				

KM# 49 25 CENTS
14.5500 g., Copper-Nickel, 32.3 mm. **Ruler:** Elizabeth II **Obv:** Arms with supporters **Rev:** Streamer-tailed hummingbird above value **Designer:** Christopher Ironside

Date	Mintage	F	VF	XF	Unc	BU
1969	758,000	—	—	0.60	1.50	2.50
1969 Proof	30,000	Value: 3.00				
1970FM (M)	5,000	—	—	0.60	1.50	2.50
1970FM (P)	12,000	Value: 3.00				
1973	160,000	—	—	0.60	1.50	2.50
1975	3,110,000	—	—	0.60	1.50	2.50
1982	1,000,000	—	—	0.60	1.50	2.50
1984	2,002,000	—	—	0.60	1.50	2.50
1985	1,999,000	—	—	0.60	1.50	2.50
1985 Proof	—	Value: 3.00				
1986	2,635,000	—	—	0.60	1.50	2.50
1987	6,006,000	—	—	0.60	1.50	2.50
1987 Proof	—	Value: 3.00				
1988	3,034,000	—	—	0.60	1.50	2.50
1988 Proof	—	Value: 3.00				
1989	—	—	—	0.60	1.50	2.50
1989 Proof	—	Value: 3.00				
1990 Proof	—	Value: 3.00				

KM# 56 25 CENTS
14.5500 g., Copper-Nickel, 32.3 mm. **Ruler:** Elizabeth II **Obv:** Arms with supporters **Rev:** Streamer-tailed hummingbird above value **Designer:** Christopher Ironside

Date	Mintage	F	VF	XF	Unc	BU
1971FM (M)	4,834	—	—	0.75	1.50	2.50
1971FM (P)	14,000	Value: 3.00				
1972FM (M)	8,382	—	—	0.75	1.50	2.50
1972FM (P)	17,000	Value: 3.00				
1973FM (M)	13,000	—	—	0.75	1.50	2.50
1973FM (P)	28,000	Value: 3.00				
1974FM (M)	12,000	—	—	0.75	1.50	2.50
1974FM (P)	22,000	Value: 3.00				
1975FM (M)	1,503	—	—	0.75	1.50	2.50
1975FM (U)	4,683	—	—	—	1.50	2.50
1975FM (P)	16,000	Value: 3.00				
1976FM (M)	1,112	—	—	0.75	1.50	2.50
1976FM (U)	1,802	—	—	—	1.50	2.50
1976FM (P)	24,000	Value: 3.00				
1977FM (M)	1,112	—	—	0.75	1.50	2.50
1977FM (U)	597	—	—	—	3.00	4.50
1977FM (P)	10,000	Value: 3.00				
1978FM (M)	1,112	—	—	0.75	1.50	2.50
1978FM (U)	1,282	—	—	0.75	1.50	2.50
1978FM (P)	6,058	Value: 3.00				
1979FM (M)	1,112	—	—	0.75	1.50	2.50
1979FM (U)	2,608	—	—	0.75	1.50	2.50
1979FM (P)	4,049	Value: 3.00				
1980FM (M)	1,112	—	—	0.75	1.50	2.50
1980FM (U)	3,668	—	—	0.75	1.50	2.50
1980FM (P)	2,688	Value: 3.50				
1981FM (U)	482	—	—	—	3.00	4.50
1981FM (P)	1,577	Value: 3.50				
1982FM (U)	—	—	—	0.75	1.50	2.50
1982FM (P)	—	Value: 3.50				
1984FM (U)	—	—	—	0.75	1.50	2.50
1984FM (P)	—	Value: 3.50				

KM# 105 25 CENTS
14.5500 g., Copper-Nickel, 32.3 mm. **Ruler:** Elizabeth II **Subject:** 21st Anniversary of Independence **Obv:** Arms with supporters **Rev:** Streamer-tailed hummingbird above value **Designer:** Christopher Ironside

Date	Mintage	F	VF	XF	Unc	BU
ND(1983)FM (U)	—	—	—	—	1.50	3.00
ND(1983)FM (P)	—	Value: 3.00				

KM# 154 25 CENTS
14.5500 g., Copper-Nickel, 32.3 mm. **Ruler:** Elizabeth II **Subject:** 25th Anniversary - Bank of Jamaica **Obv:** Arms with supporters **Rev:** Streamer-tailed hummingbird above value **Designer:** Christopher Ironside

Date	Mintage	F	VF	XF	Unc	BU
1985	—	—	—	0.75	3.50	5.00

KM# 147 25 CENTS
Nickel Plated Steel **Ruler:** Elizabeth II **Subject:** Marcus Garvey **Obv:** Arms with supporters **Rev:** Head 1/4 right **Shape:** 7-sided

Date	Mintage	F	VF	XF	Unc	BU
1991	—	—	—	—	1.00	1.50
1991 Proof	—	Value: 3.00				
1992	—	—	—	—	1.00	1.50
1992 Proof	—	Value: 3.00				
1993	—	—	—	—	1.00	1.50
1993 Proof	—	Value: 3.00				
1994	—	—	—	—	1.00	1.50

KM# 167 25 CENTS
Copper Plated Steel **Ruler:** Elizabeth II **Subject:** Marcus Garvey **Obv:** Arms with supporters **Rev:** Head 1/4 right

Date	Mintage	F	VF	XF	Unc	BU
1995	—	—	—	—	0.50	0.75
1996	—	—	—	—	0.50	0.75
2000	—	—	—	—	0.50	0.75

KM# 65 50 CENTS

12.4500 g., Copper-Nickel, 30 mm. **Ruler:** Elizabeth II **Subject:** Marcus Garvey **Obv:** Arms with supporters **Rev:** Head 1/4 right **Shape:** 10-sided

Date	Mintage	F	VF	XF	Unc	BU
1975	12,010,000	—	0.15	0.50	1.50	2.00
1984	2,000,000	—	0.15	0.50	1.50	2.00
1985	2,119,000	—	0.15	0.50	1.50	2.00
1985 Proof	—	Value: 3.00				
1986	3,404,000	—	0.15	0.50	1.50	2.00
1987	5,545,000	—	0.15	0.50	1.50	2.00
1988	10,505,000	—	0.15	0.50	1.50	2.00
1988 Proof	—	Value: 3.00				
1989	—	—	0.15	0.50	1.50	2.00
1989 Proof	—	Value: 3.00				
1990 Proof	—	Value: 3.00				

KM# 70 50 CENTS

12.4500 g., Copper-Nickel, 30 mm. **Ruler:** Elizabeth II **S ubject:** Marcus Garvey **Obv:** Arms with supporters **Rev:** Head 1/4 right **Shape:** 10-sided

Date	Mintage	F	VF	XF	Unc	BU
1976FM (M)	1,112	—	—	0.25	1.50	2.00
1976FM (U)	1,802	—	—	—	1.50	2.00
1976FM (P)	24,000	Value: 1.50				
1977FM (M)	556	—	—	0.50	3.50	5.00
1977FM (U)	597	—	—	—	3.50	5.00
1977FM (P)	10,000	Value: 1.50				
1978FM (M)	556	—	—	0.50	3.50	5.00
1978FM (U)	1,838	—	—	—	2.00	3.00
1978FM (P)	6,058	Value: 2.50				
1979FM (M)	556	—	—	0.50	3.50	5.00
1979FM (U)	1,282	—	—	—	2.50	3.50
1979FM (P)	4,049	Value: 3.00				
1980FM (M)	556	—	—	0.50	3.50	5.00
1980FM (U)	3,668	—	—	—	2.00	3.00
1980FM (P)	2,688	Value: 3.00				
1981FM (U)	482	—	—	—	3.50	5.00
1981FM (P)	1,577	Value: 3.00				
1982FM (U)	—	—	—	—	2.00	3.00
1982FM (P)	—	Value: 3.00				
1984FM (U)	—	—	—	—	2.00	3.00
1984FM (P)	—	Value: 3.00				

KM# 106 50 CENTS

12.4500 g., Copper-Nickel, 30 mm. **Ruler:** Elizabeth II **Subject:** 21st Anniversary of Independence - Marcus Garvey **Obv:** Arms with supporters **Rev:** Head 1/4 right **Shape:** 10-sided

Date	Mintage	F	VF	XF	Unc	BU
ND(1983)FM (U)	—	—	—	—	2.00	3.00
ND(1983)FM (P)	—	Value: 4.00				

KM# 132 50 CENTS

12.4500 g., Copper-Nickel, 30 mm. **Ruler:** Elizabeth II **Subject:** 100th Anniversary - Birth of Marcus Garvey **Obv:** Arms with supporters **Rev:** Head 1/4 right

Date	Mintage	F	VF	XF	Unc	BU
1987 Proof	500	Value: 3.50				

KM# 50 DOLLAR

Copper-Nickel **Ruler:** Elizabeth II **Obv:** Arms with supporters **Rev:** Bust right

Date	Mintage	F	VF	XF	Unc	BU
1969	47,000	—	—	1.00	3.00	4.00
1969 Proof	30,000	Value: 4.50				
1970FM (M)	5,000	—	—	0.30	3.50	4.75
1970FM (P)	14,000	Value: 5.00				

KM# 57 DOLLAR

Copper-Nickel **Ruler:** Elizabeth II **Obv:** Arms with supporters **Rev:** Bust right

Date	Mintage	F	VF	XF	Unc	BU
1971FM	5,024	—	—	0.30	3.00	4.00
1971FM (P)	15,000	Value: 4.00				
1972F (M)	7,982	—	—	0.30	2.00	3.00
1972FM (P)	17,000	Value: 3.00				
1973FM	10,000	—	—	0.30	2.00	3.00
1973FM (P)	28,000	Value: 3.00				
1974FM (M)	8,961	—	—	0.30	2.00	3.00
1974FM (P)	22,000	Value: 3.00				
1975FM (M)	5,312	—	—	0.30	2.50	3.50
1975FM (U)	4,683	—	—	—	2.50	3.50
1975FM (P)	16,000	Value: 3.00				
1976FM (M)	284	—	—	—	17.50	20.00
1976FM (U)	1,802	—	—	—	4.00	5.00
1976FM (P)	24,000	Value: 2.50				
1977FM (M)	287	—	—	—	17.50	20.00
1977FM (U)	597	—	—	—	8.00	10.00
1977FM (P)	10,000	Value: 4.00				
1978FM (U)	1,566	—	—	—	4.00	5.00
1978FM (P)	6,058	Value: 5.00				
1979FM (M)	284	—	—	—	17.50	20.00
1979FM (U)	2,608	—	—	—	4.00	5.00
1979FM (P)	4,049	Value: 5.00				

KM# 84.1 DOLLAR

Copper-Nickel **Ruler:** Elizabeth II **Obv:** Arms with supporters **Rev:** Bust right

Date	Mintage	F	VF	XF	Unc	BU
1980FM (M)	284	—	—	—	20.00	22.50
1980FM (U)	3,668	—	—	—	5.00	6.00
1980FM (P)	2,688	Value: 15.00				
1981FM (U)	482	—	—	—	10.00	12.50
1981FM (P)	1,577	Value: 17.50				
1982FM (U)	—	—	—	—	7.00	10.00
1982FM (P)	—	Value: 17.50				

KM# 84.2 DOLLAR

Copper-Nickel **Ruler:** Elizabeth II **Obv:** Arms with supporters **Rev:** Bust right **Edge:** Reeded

Date	Mintage	F	VF	XF	Unc	BU
1985 Proof	—	Value: 7.50				
1985	—	—	—	—	3.00	4.00
1987 Proof	—	Value: 7.50				
1988 Proof	—	Value: 7.50				
1989 Proof	—	Value: 7.50				
1990	—	—	—	—	3.00	4.00

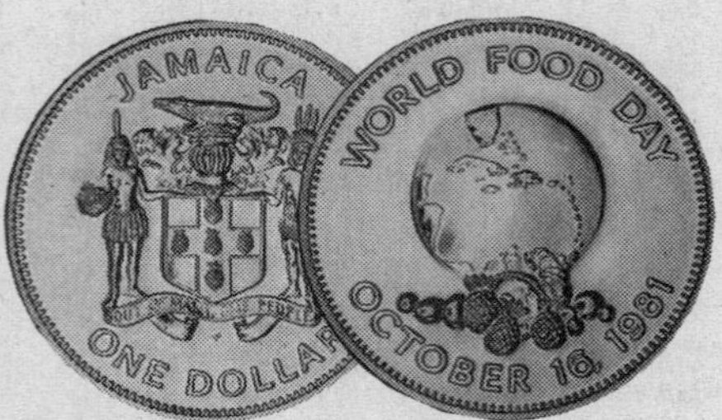

KM# 91 DOLLAR

Copper-Nickel **Ruler:** Elizabeth II **Subject:** World Food Day **Obv:** Arms with supporters **Rev:** World globe above produce

Date	Mintage	F	VF	XF	Unc	BU
ND(1981)FM (U)	—	—	—	—	7.50	8.50

KM# 96 DOLLAR

Copper-Nickel **Ruler:** Elizabeth II **Subject:** World Championship of Football **Obv:** Arms with supporters **Rev:** Goalie catching attempted score

Date	Mintage	F	VF	XF	Unc	BU
1982	—	—	—	—	4.50	5.50

KM# 107 DOLLAR

Copper-Nickel **Ruler:** Elizabeth II **Subject:** 21st Anniversary of Independence **Obv:** Arms with supporters **Rev:** Bust right

Date	Mintage	F	VF	XF	Unc	BU
ND(1983)FM (P)	609	Value: 20.00				
ND(1983)FM (U)	3,710	—	—	—	7.50	8.50

KM# 134 DOLLAR

Copper-Nickel **Ruler:** Elizabeth II **Subject:** 21st Anniversary of Independence **Obv:** Arms with supporters **Rev:** Number 21 divides heads facing above dates and braided rope

Date	Mintage	F	VF	XF	Unc	BU
ND(1983)FM (P)	—	Value: 14.00				

KM# 113 DOLLAR

Copper-Nickel **Ruler:** Elizabeth II **Subject:** 100th Anniversary - Birth of Bustamante **Obv:** Arms with supporters **Rev:** Bust 1/4 left

Date	Mintage	F	VF	XF	Unc	BU
1984FM (U)	—	—	—	—	3.00	4.00
1984FM (P)	268	Value: 25.00				

KM# 145 DOLLAR

Nickel-Brass, 23.8 mm. **Ruler:** Elizabeth II **Subject:** Sir Alexander Bustamante **Obv:** Arms with supporters **Rev:** Bust facing **Edge:** BANK OF JAMAICA

Date	Mintage	F	VF	XF	Unc	BU
1990	—	—	—	—	2.25	3.00
1990 Proof	—	Value: 5.00				
1991	—	—	—	—	2.25	3.00
1991 Proof	—	Value: 5.00				
1992	—	—	—	—	2.25	3.00
1992 Proof	—	Value: 10.00				
1993	—	—	—	—	2.25	3.00
1993 Proof	—	Value: 5.00				

KM# 145a DOLLAR

Brass Plated Steel, 23.8 mm. **Ruler:** Elizabeth II **Subject:** Sir Alexander Bustamante **Obv:** Arms with supporters **Rev:** Bust facing **Edge:** Reeded

Date	Mintage	F	VF	XF	Unc	BU
1993	—	—	—	—	2.25	3.00
1993 Proof	500	Value: 15.00				
1994	—	—	—	—	2.25	3.00

KM# 164 DOLLAR

Nickel Clad Steel **Ruler:** Elizabeth II **Obv:** Arms with supporters **Rev:** Bust facing **Shape:** 7-sided

Date	Mintage	F	VF	XF	Unc	BU
1994	—	—	—	—	1.00	1.50
1995	—	—	—	—	1.00	1.50
1996	—	—	—	—	1.00	1.50
1999	—	—	—	—	1.00	1.50
2000	—	—	—	—	1.00	1.50

KM# 58 5 DOLLARS

42.1500 g., 0.9250 Silver 1.2536 oz. ASW **Ruler:** Elizabeth II **Obv:** Arms with supporters **Rev:** Bust facing **Note:** His widow did not like this design, and the following year it was replaced by a left profile.

Date	Mintage	F	VF	XF	Unc	BU
1971FM	4,072	—	—	—	18.50	22.00
1971FM (P)	13,000	Value: 20.00				

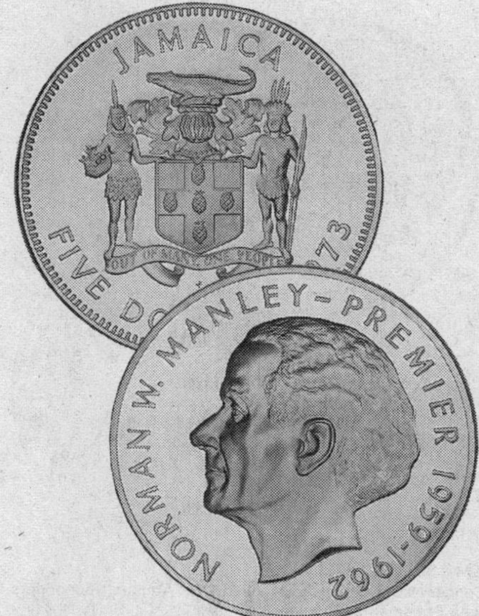

KM# 59 5 DOLLARS

41.4800 g., 0.9250 Silver 1.2336 oz. ASW **Ruler:** Elizabeth II **Obv:** Arms with supporters **Rev:** Head left

Date	Mintage	F	VF	XF	Unc	BU
1972FM	3,232	—	—	—	19.00	22.50
1972FM (P)	21,000	Value: 20.00				
1973FM	6,484	—	—	—	19.00	22.50
1973FM (P)	36,000	Value: 20.00				

KM# 62 5 DOLLARS

Copper-Nickel **Ruler:** Elizabeth II **Obv:** Arms with supporters **Rev:** Head left

Date	Mintage	F	VF	XF	Unc	BU
1974FM (M)	8,661	—	—	—	6.00	7.50
1975FM (M)	65	—	—	—	—	—
1975FM (U)	4,683	—	—	—	7.00	8.50
1976FM (M)	56	—	—	—	—	—
1976FM (U)	1,802	—	—	—	8.00	10.00
1977FM (M)	56	—	—	—	—	—
1977FM (U)	597	—	—	—	12.00	14.00
1978FM (U)	1,338	—	—	—	7.00	9.00
1979FM (M)	56	—	—	—	—	—
1979FM (U)	2,608	—	—	—	6.00	8.00

KM# 62a 5 DOLLARS

37.6000 g., 0.5000 Silver .6044 oz. ASW **Ruler:** Elizabeth II **Obv:** Arms with supporters **Rev:** Head left

Date	Mintage	F	VF	XF	Unc	BU
1974FM (P)	22,000	Value: 9.00				
1975FM (P)	16,000	Value: 10.00				
1976FM (P)	23,000	Value: 9.00				
1977FM (P)	10,000	Value: 10.00				
1978FM (P)	6,058	Value: 12.00				
1979FM (P)	4,049	Value: 15.00				

KM# 85.1 5 DOLLARS

Copper-Nickel **Ruler:** Elizabeth II **Obv:** Arms with supporters **Rev:** Head left

Date	Mintage	F	VF	XF	Unc	BU
1980FM (M)	56	—	—	—	—	—
1980FM (U)	3,668	—	—	—	15.00	17.00
1981FM (U)	482	—	—	—	20.00	22.50
1982FM (U)	—	—	—	—	10.00	12.00
1984FM (U)	—	—	—	—	10.00	12.00

KM# 85.1a 5 DOLLARS

18.5600 g., 0.5000 Silver .2983 oz. ASW **Ruler:** Elizabeth II **Obv:** Arms with supporters **Rev:** Head left

Date	Mintage	F	VF	XF	Unc	BU
1980FM (P)	2,688	Value: 15.00				
1981FM (P)	1,577	Value: 17.00				
1982FM (P)	1,040	Value: 17.00				
1984FM (P)	268	Value: 40.00				

KM# 85.2 5 DOLLARS

18.5600 g., 0.5000 Silver .2983 oz. ASW **Ruler:** Elizabeth II **Obv:** Arms with supporters **Rev:** Head left

Date	Mintage	F	VF	XF	Unc	BU
1985	—	—	—	—	30.00	—
1987 Proof	—	Value: 30.00				
1988 Proof	—	Value: 30.00				
1989 Proof	—	Value: 30.00				
1990 Proof	500	Value: 30.00				
1991 Proof	—	Value: 30.00				
1992 Proof,	—	Value: 30.00				
1993 Proof	—	Value: 30.00				

KM# 108 5 DOLLARS

Copper-Nickel **Ruler:** Elizabeth II **Subject:** 21st Anniversary of Independence **Obv:** Arms with supporters **Rev:** Head left

Date	Mintage	F	VF	XF	Unc	BU
1983FM (U)	—	—	—	—	8.00	10.00

KM# 108a 5 DOLLARS

18.5600 g., 0.5000 Silver .2983 oz. ASW **Ruler:** Elizabeth II **Obv:** Arms with supporters **Rev:** Head left

Date	Mintage	F	VF	XF	Unc	BU
1983FM (P)	—	Value: 20.00				

KM# 157 5 DOLLARS

Nickel Plated Steel **Ruler:** Elizabeth II **Subject:** Centennial - Birth of Norman Manley **Obv:** Arms with supporters **Rev:** Head left

Date	Mintage	F	VF	XF	Unc	BU
1993	—	—	—	—	3.50	5.00

KM# 157a 5 DOLLARS

18.5000 g., 0.5000 Silver .2984 oz. ASW **Ruler:** Elizabeth II **Subject:** Centennial - Birth of Norman Manley **Obv:** Arms with supporters **Rev:** Head left

Date	Mintage	F	VF	XF	Unc	BU
1993 Proof	Est. 2,000	Value: 35.00				

KM# 163 5 DOLLARS

Steel **Ruler:** Elizabeth II **Obv:** Arms with supporters **Rev:** Head left

Date	Mintage	F	VF	XF	Unc	BU
1994	—	—	—	—	2.50	3.50
1995	—	—	—	—	2.50	3.50
1996	—	—	—	—	2.50	3.50
2000	—	—	—	—	2.50	3.50

KM# 60 10 DOLLARS

49.2000 g., 0.9250 Silver 1.4632 oz. ASW **Ruler:** Elizabeth II **Subject:** 10th Anniversary of Independence **Obv:** Arms with supporters **Rev:** Conjoined heads facing each other above map

Date	Mintage	F	VF	XF	Unc	BU
ND(1972)	42,000	—	—	—	21.50	23.50
ND(1972) Proof	33,000	Value: 25.00				

KM# 63 10 DOLLARS
Copper-Nickel, 45 mm. **Ruler:** Elizabeth II **Subject:** Sir Henry Morgan **Obv:** Arms with supporters **Rev:** Bust 1/4 left

Date	Mintage	F	VF	XF	Unc	BU
1974FM (M)	15,000	—	—	—	7.50	8.50

KM# 63a 10 DOLLARS
42.8000 g., 0.9250 Silver 1.2728 oz. ASW, 45 mm. **Ruler:** Elizabeth II **Subject:** Sir Henry Morgan **Obv:** Arms with supporters **Rev:** Bust 1/4 left

Date	Mintage	F	VF	XF	Unc	BU
1974FM (P)	42,000	Value: 18.50				

KM# 66 10 DOLLARS
Copper-Nickel, 45 mm. **Ruler:** Elizabeth II **Subject:** Christopher Columbus **Obv:** Arms with supporters **Rev:** Bust looking left at right, ship at left

Date	Mintage	F	VF	XF	Unc	BU
1975FM (M)	30	—	—	—	—	—
1975FM (U)	5,758	—	—	—	12.00	13.00

KM# 66a 10 DOLLARS
42.8000 g., 0.9250 Silver 1.2728 oz. ASW, 45 mm. **Ruler:** Elizabeth II **Subject:** Christopher Columbus **Obv:** Arms with supporters **Rev:** Bust looking left at right, ship at left

Date	Mintage	F	VF	XF	Unc	BU
1975FM (P)	29,000	Value: 18.50				

KM# 71 10 DOLLARS
Copper-Nickel, 45 mm. **Ruler:** Elizabeth II **Subject:** Admiral Horatio Nelson **Obv:** Arms with supporters **Rev:** Uniformed bust 1/4 left, map and ship at far left

Date	Mintage	F	VF	XF	Unc	BU
1976FM (M)	27	—	—	—	—	—
1976FM (U)	2,302	—	—	—	15.00	17.50

KM# 71a 10 DOLLARS
42.8000 g., 0.9250 Silver 1.2728 oz. ASW, 45 mm. **Ruler:** Elizabeth II **Subject:** Admiral Horation Nelson **Obv:** Arms with supporters **Rev:** Uniformed bust 1/4 left with ship and map at far left

Date	Mintage	F	VF	XF	Unc	BU
1976FM (P)	31,000	Value: 18.50				

KM# 74 10 DOLLARS
Copper-Nickel, 45 mm. **Ruler:** Elizabeth II **Subject:** Admiral George Rodney **Obv:** Arms with supporters **Rev:** Bust right looking at ship at right

Date	Mintage	F	VF	XF	Unc	BU
1977FM (M)	27	—	—	—	—	—
1977FM (U)	847	—	—	—	30.00	35.00

KM# 74a 10 DOLLARS
42.8000 g., 0.9250 Silver 1.2728 oz. ASW, 45 mm. **Ruler:** Elizabeth II **Subject:** Admiral George Rodney **Obv:** Arms with supporters **Rev:** Bust right looking at ship at right

Date	Mintage	F	VF	XF	Unc	BU
1977FM (P)	14,000	Value: 20.00				

KM# 75 10 DOLLARS
Copper-Nickel, 45 mm. **Ruler:** Elizabeth II **Subject:** Jamaican Unity **Obv:** Arms with supporters **Rev:** Heads of many different ethnic people forming a circle

Date	Mintage	F	VF	XF	Unc	BU
1978FM (U)	1,559	—	—	—	20.00	22.50

KM# 75a 10 DOLLARS
42.8000 g., 0.9250 Silver 1.2728 oz. ASW, 45 mm. **Ruler:** Elizabeth II **Obv:** Arms with supporters **Rev:** Heads of many different ethnic people forming a circle **Edge:** Reeded **Edge Lettering:** Jamaican Unity

Date	Mintage	F	VF	XF	Unc	BU
1978FM (P)	12,000	Value: 20.00				

KM# 79 10 DOLLARS
Copper-Nickel, 45 mm. **Ruler:** Elizabeth II **Obv:** Arms with supporters **Rev:** Butterflies and flowers above date

Date	Mintage	F	VF	XF	Unc	BU
1979FM (M)	27	—	—	—	—	—
1979FM (U)	2,608	—	—	—	35.00	40.00

KM# 79a 10 DOLLARS
42.8000 g., 0.9250 Silver 1.2728 oz. ASW, 45 mm. **Ruler:** Elizabeth II **Obv:** Arms with supporters **Rev:** Butterflies and flowers above date

Date	Mintage	F	VF	XF	Unc	BU
1979FM (P)	8,308	Value: 35.00				

KM# 80 10 DOLLARS
22.4500 g., 0.9250 Silver .6677 oz. ASW **Ruler:** Elizabeth II **Subject:** International Year of the Child **Obv:** Arms with supporters **Rev:** Map back of child playing cricket

Date	Mintage	F	VF	XF	Unc	BU
1979 Proof	20,000	Value: 17.00				

KM# 87 10 DOLLARS
30.2800 g., 0.5000 Silver .4868 oz. ASW **Ruler:** Elizabeth II **Subject:** 10th Anniversary of Caribbean Development Bank **Obv:** Arms with supporters **Rev:** Legend around globe, coins below

Date	Mintage	F	VF	XF	Unc	BU
ND(1980)FM (P)	2,327	Value: 30.00				

KM# 86 10 DOLLARS
Copper-Nickel **Ruler:** Elizabeth II **Obv:** Arms with supporters **Rev:** Streamer-tailed Hummingbirds

Date	Mintage	F	VF	XF	Unc	BU
1980FM (M)	27	—	—	—	—	—
1980FM (U)	5,668	—	—	—	30.00	35.00

KM# 86a 10 DOLLARS
22.4500 g., 0.9250 Silver .6677 oz. ASW **Ruler:** Elizabeth II **Obv:** Arms with supporters **Rev:** Streamer-tailed Hummingbirds

Date	Mintage	F	VF	XF	Unc	BU
1980FM (P)	5,394	Value: 30.00				

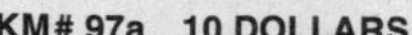

KM# 92 10 DOLLARS
28.2800 g., 0.9250 Silver .8410 oz. ASW **Ruler:** Elizabeth II **Subject:** Wedding of Prince Charles and Lady Diana **Rev:** Conjoined busts right

Date	Mintage	F	VF	XF	Unc	BU
1981 Proof	40,000	Value: 20.00				

KM# 93 10 DOLLARS
Copper-Nickel **Ruler:** Elizabeth II **Obv:** Arms with supporters **Rev:** American Crocodile above date

Date	Mintage	F	VF	XF	Unc	BU
1981FM (U)	804	—	—	—	30.00	35.00

KM# 93a 10 DOLLARS
22.4500 g., 0.9250 Silver .6677 oz. ASW **Ruler:** Elizabeth II **Obv:** Arms with supporters **Rev:** American Crocodile above date

Date	Mintage	F	VF	XF	Unc	BU
1981FM (P)	3,216	Value: 40.00				

KM# 97 10 DOLLARS
Copper-Nickel **Ruler:** Elizabeth II **Obv:** Arms with supporters **Rev:** Small Indian Mongoose

Date	Mintage	F	VF	XF	Unc	BU
1982FM (U)	—	—	—	—	30.00	35.00

KM# 97a 10 DOLLARS
22.4500 g., 0.9250 Silver .6677 oz. ASW **Ruler:** Elizabeth II **Obv:** Arms with supporters **Rev:** Small Indian Mongoose

Date	Mintage	F	VF	XF	Unc	BU
1982FM (P)	1,852	Value: 40.00				

KM# 98 10 DOLLARS
22.4500 g., 0.9250 Silver .6677 oz. ASW **Ruler:** Elizabeth II **Subject:** Soccer - World Championships **Obv:** Arms with supporters **Rev:** Standing player with ball divides circle

Date	Mintage	F	VF	XF	Unc	BU
1982 Proof	9,775	Value: 16.50				

KM# 109 10 DOLLARS
Copper-Nickel **Ruler:** Elizabeth II **Subject:** 21st Anniversary of Independence **Obv:** Arms with supporters **Rev:** Numeral 21 divides heads facing above dates and braided rope

Date	Mintage	F	VF	XF	Unc	BU
ND(1983)FM (U)	1,320	—	—	—	15.00	17.50

KM# 109a 10 DOLLARS
22.4500 g., 0.9250 Silver .6677 oz. ASW **Ruler:** Elizabeth II **Subject:** 21st Anniversary of Independence **Obv:** Arms with supporters **Rev:** Numeral 21 divides heads facing above dates and braided rope

Date	Mintage	F	VF	XF	Unc	BU
ND(1983)FM (P)	1,187	Value: 30.00				

KM# 111 10 DOLLARS
22.4500 g., 0.9250 Silver .6677 oz. ASW **Ruler:** Elizabeth II **Subject:** Royal visit **Obv:** Arms with supporters **Rev:** Conjoined busts left

Date	Mintage	F	VF	XF	Unc	BU
1983	—	Value: 25.00				

KM# 114 10 DOLLARS
Copper-Nickel **Ruler:** Elizabeth II **Obv:** Arms with supporters **Rev:** Blue Marlin breaking water

Date	Mintage	F	VF	XF	Unc	BU
1984FM (U)	—	—	—	—	30.00	35.00

KM# 114a 10 DOLLARS
22.4500 g., 0.9250 Silver .6677 oz. ASW **Ruler:** Elizabeth II **Obv:** Arms with supporters **Rev:** Blue Marlin breaking water

Date	Mintage	F	VF	XF	Unc	BU
1984FM (P)	335	Value: 75.00				

KM# 115 10 DOLLARS
22.4500 g., 0.9250 Silver .6677 oz. ASW **Ruler:** Elizabeth II **Subject:** Decade for Women **Obv:** Arms with supporters **Rev:** Woman with basket on head, map behind

Date	Mintage	F	VF	XF	Unc	BU
1984 Proof	1,100	Value: 25.00				
1985 Proof	610	Value: 35.00				

KM# 125 10 DOLLARS
22.4500 g., 0.9250 Silver .6677 oz. ASW **Ruler:** Elizabeth II **Subject:** Summer Olympics **Obv:** Arms with supporters **Rev:** Sprinter

Date	Mintage	F	VF	XF	Unc	BU
1984 Proof	10,000	Value: 20.00				

KM# 123 10 DOLLARS
22.4500 g., 0.9250 Silver .6677 oz. ASW **Ruler:** Elizabeth II **Subject:** Year of Youth **Obv:** Arms with supporters **Rev:** Collage of many youth's heads

Date	Mintage	F	VF	XF	Unc	BU
1985 Proof	1,000	Value: 30.00				

KM# 121 10 DOLLARS
22.4500 g., 0.9250 Silver .6677 oz. ASW **Ruler:** Elizabeth II **Subject:** XIII Commonwealth Games - Edinburgh **Obv:** Arms with supporters **Rev:** Relay runners

Date	Mintage	F	VF	XF	Unc	BU
1986	50,000	—	—	—	16.50	18.00

KM# 121a 10 DOLLARS
28.2800 g., 0.9250 Silver .8411 oz. ASW **Ruler:** Elizabeth II **Obv:** Arms with supporters **Rev:** Relay runners

Date	Mintage	F	VF	XF	Unc	BU
1986 Proof	20,000	Value: 22.50				

KM# 128 10 DOLLARS
22.4500 g., 0.9250 Silver .6677 oz. ASW **Ruler:** Elizabeth II **Subject:** 100th Anniversary - Birth of Marcus Garvey **Obv:** Arms with supporters **Rev:** Bust 1/4 right

Date	Mintage	F	VF	XF	Unc	BU
1987 Proof	1,000	Value: 35.00				

KM# 133 10 DOLLARS
22.4500 g., 0.9250 Silver .6677 oz. ASW **Ruler:** Elizabeth II **Subject:** 25th Anniversary of Independence **Obv:** Crowned bust right **Rev:** Arms with supporters

Date	Mintage	F	VF	XF	Unc	BU
1987 Proof	Est. 500	Value: 40.00				

KM# 138 10 DOLLARS
Copper-Nickel **Ruler:** Elizabeth II **Subject:** Year of the Worker **Obv:** Arms with supporters **Rev:** Two figures standing on board with shovel and pitch-fork above heads

Date	Mintage	F	VF	XF	Unc	BU
1988	—	—	—	—	7.00	8.00

KM# 138a 10 DOLLARS
22.4500 g., 0.9250 Silver .6677 oz. ASW **Ruler:** Elizabeth II **Subject:** Year of the Worker **Obv:** Arms with supporters **Rev:** Two standing figures on board with pitch fork and shovel raised above heads

Date	Mintage	F	VF	XF	Unc	BU
1988 Proof	Est. 1,000	Value: 40.00				

KM# 140 10 DOLLARS
Copper-Nickel **Ruler:** Elizabeth II **Subject:** Columbus' Discovery of the New World **Obv:** Arms with supporters **Rev:** Several ships at sea **Rev. Designer:** Frederick Magford

Date	Mintage	F	VF	XF	Unc	BU
1989	—	—	—	—	7.00	8.00

KM# 140a 10 DOLLARS
22.4500 g., 0.9250 Silver .6677 oz. ASW **Ruler:** Elizabeth II **Subject:** Columbus' Discovery of the New World **Obv:** Arms with supporters **Rev:** Several ships at sea **Rev. Designer:** Frederick Magford

Date	Mintage	F	VF	XF	Unc	BU
1989 Proof	Est. 5,500	Value: 35.00				

KM# 144 10 DOLLARS
Copper-Nickel **Ruler:** Elizabeth II **Subject:** Columbus' Arrival in New World **Obv:** Arms with supporters **Rev:** Bust 1/4 right and ship at far right

Date	Mintage	F	VF	XF	Unc	BU
1990	—	—	—	—	7.00	8.00

KM# 144a 10 DOLLARS
22.4500 g., 0.9250 Silver .6677 oz. ASW **Ruler:** Elizabeth II **Subject:** Columbus' Arrival in New World **Obv:** Arms with supporters **Rev:** Bust 1/4 right and ship at far right

Date	Mintage	F	VF	XF	Unc	BU
1990 Proof	Est. 11,000	Value: 32.50				

KM# 148 10 DOLLARS
Copper-Nickel **Ruler:** Elizabeth II **Subject:** Arrival in the New World **Obv:** Arms with supporters **Rev:** Columbus' ship - Pinta

Date	Mintage	F	VF	XF	Unc	BU
1991	—	—	—	—	7.00	8.00

KM# 148a 10 DOLLARS
22.4500 g., 0.9250 Silver .6677 oz. ASW **Ruler:** Elizabeth II **Subject:** Arrival in the New World **Obv:** Arms with supporters **Rev:** Columbus' ship - Pinta

Date	Mintage	F	VF	XF	Unc	BU
1991 Proof	Est. 5,500	Value: 35.00				

KM# 152 10 DOLLARS
22.4500 g., 0.9250 Silver .6677 oz. ASW **Ruler:** Elizabeth II **Subject:** 500th Anniversary of Columbus' Arrival **Obv:** Arms with supporters **Rev:** Ship

Date	Mintage	F	VF	XF	Unc	BU
1992 Proof	5,500	Value: 35.00				

KM# 155 10 DOLLARS
22.4500 g., 0.9250 Silver .6677 oz. ASW **Ruler:** Elizabeth II **Subject:** 40th Anniversary - Coronation of Queen Elizabeth II **Obv:** Arms with supporters **Rev:** Crowned bust facing holding scepters

Date	Mintage	F	VF	XF	Unc	BU
1993 Proof	Est. 5,500	Value: 35.00				

KM# 161 10 DOLLARS
28.2800 g., 0.9250 Silver .8411 oz. ASW **Ruler:** Elizabeth II **Subject:** Royal Visit **Obv:** Arms with supporters **Rev:** Standing sailor beating drum on map of Jamaica to left of ship with cameo above

Date	Mintage	F	VF	XF	Unc	BU
1994 Proof	—	Value: 35.00				

KM# 168 10 DOLLARS
20.0000 g., 0.5000 Silver .3215 oz. ASW **Ruler:** Elizabeth II **Subject:** Ernest Hemingway 1899-1961 **Obv:** Arms with supporters **Rev:** Bust at left looking right, ship at sea at right

Date	Mintage	F	VF	XF	Unc	BU
1994	Est. 10,000	—	—	—	20.00	22.50

KM# 187 10 DOLLARS
28.3000 g., 0.9250 Silver 0.8416 oz. ASW, 38.6 mm. **Ruler:** Elizabeth II **Obv:** Arms with supporters **Rev:** Two Black-billed parrots **Edge:** Reeded

Date	Mintage	F	VF	XF	Unc	BU
1995 Proof	1,000	Value: 40.00				

KM# 176 10 DOLLARS
28.2800 g., 0.9250 Silver .8411 oz. ASW **Ruler:** Elizabeth II **Subject:** Olympic Games - 1996 **Obv:** Arms with supporters **Rev:** Relay runner left

Date	Mintage	F	VF	XF	Unc	BU
1996 Proof	Est. 10,000	Value: 30.00				

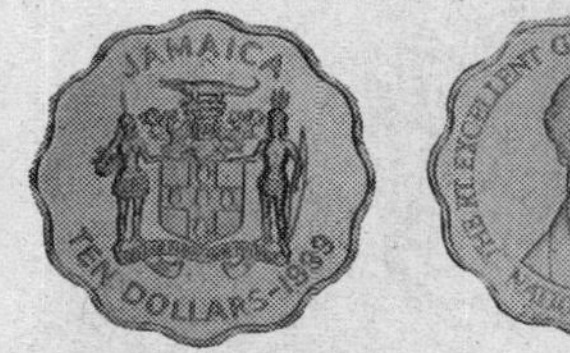

KM# 181 10 DOLLARS
Stainless Steel **Ruler:** Elizabeth II **Obv:** Arms with supporters **Rev:** Bust facing **Shape:** Scalloped

Date	Mintage	F	VF	XF	Unc	BU
1999	—	—	—	—	3.00	4.00
2000	—	—	—	—	3.00	4.00

KM# 61 20 DOLLARS
15.7484 g., 0.5000 Gold .2531 oz. AGW **Ruler:** Elizabeth II **Subject:** 10th Anniversary of Independence **Obv:** Arms with supporters and dates within rope wreath **Rev:** Map of Jamaica above ships

Date	Mintage	F	VF	XF	Unc	BU
ND(1972)	30,000	—	—	—	175	185
ND(1972) Proof	20,000	Value: 190				

KM# 182 20 DOLLARS
Ring Composition: Brass **Center Composition:** Copper-Nickel, 23 mm. **Ruler:** Elizabeth II **Obv:** Value above arms with supporters within circle **Rev:** Head 1/4 right within circle **Edge:** Reeded

Date	Mintage	F	VF	XF	Unc	BU
2000	—	—	—	—	3.00	4.00

KM# 76 25 DOLLARS
136.0800 g., 0.9250 Silver 4.0473 oz. ASW **Ruler:** Elizabeth II **Subject:** 25th Anniversary of Coronation **Obv:** Arms with supporters **Rev:** Queen left on throne with crown, sceptre and orb

Date	Mintage	F	VF	XF	Unc	BU
ND(1978)	11,000	—	—	—	60.00	62.50
ND(1978) Proof	22,000	Value: 60.00				

KM# 81 25 DOLLARS
136.0800 g., 0.9250 Silver 4.0473 oz. ASW **Ruler:** Elizabeth II **Subject:** 10th Anniversary - Investiture of Prince Charles **Obv:** Arms with supporters **Rev:** Crowned half figure left in regal dress

Date	Mintage	F	VF	XF	Unc	BU
ND(1979)	16,000	—	—	—	60.00	62.50
ND(1979) Proof	25,000	Value: 60.00				

KM# 88 25 DOLLARS
136.0800 g., 0.5000 Silver 2.1878 oz. ASW **Ruler:** Elizabeth II **Subject:** 1980 Olympics **Obv:** Arms with supporters **Rev:** Circle of heads of previous Gold Medal winners

Date	Mintage	F	VF	XF	Unc	BU
1980	—	—	—	—	50.00	52.50
1980 Proof	6,969	Value: 60.00				

KM# 94 25 DOLLARS
136.0800 g., 0.9250 Silver 4.0473 oz. ASW **Ruler:** Elizabeth II
Subject: Wedding of Prince Charles and Lady Diana **Obv:** Crowned bust right **Rev:** Conjoined busts of royal couple

Date	Mintage	F	VF	XF	Unc	BU
1981(T) Proof	6,450	Value: 100				

KM# 99 25 DOLLARS
136.0800 g., 0.9250 Silver 4.0473 oz. ASW **Ruler:** Elizabeth II
Subject: World Championship Soccer Games **Obv:** Arms with supporters **Rev:** Player kicking ball to right **Note:** Photo reduced.

Date	Mintage	F	VF	XF	Unc	BU
1982 Proof	30,000	Value: 67.50				

KM# 112 25 DOLLARS
136.0800 g., 0.9250 Silver 4.0473 oz. ASW **Ruler:** Elizabeth II
Subject: Royal Visit **Obv:** Arms with supporters **Rev:** Conjoined busts left

Date	Mintage	F	VF	XF	Unc	BU
1983 Proof	—	Value: 67.50				

KM# 116 25 DOLLARS
136.0800 g., 0.9250 Silver 4.0473 oz. ASW **Ruler:** Elizabeth II
Subject: Summer Olympics **Obv:** Arms with supporters
Rev: Sprinter

Date	Mintage	F	VF	XF	Unc	BU
1984 Proof	3,300	Value: 67.50				

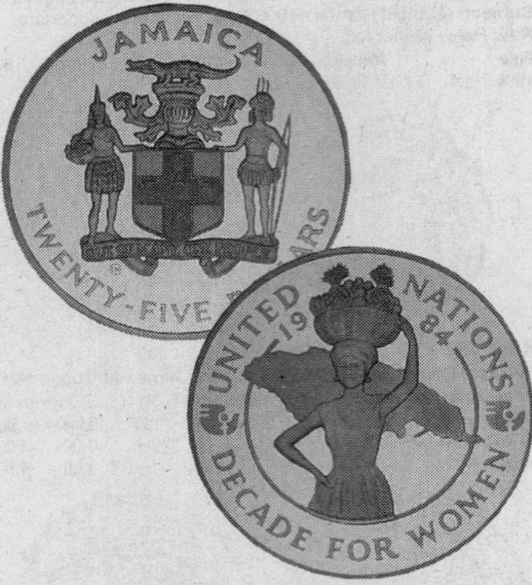

KM# 126 25 DOLLARS
23.4400 g., 0.9250 Silver .6677 oz. ASW **Ruler:** Elizabeth II
Subject: Decade For Women **Obv:** Arms with supporters
Rev: Map and female with basket of fruit on head facing
Note: Mule. Denomination error for KM#115.

Date	Mintage	F	VF	XF	Unc	BU
1984 Proof	—	Value: 160				

KM# 119 25 DOLLARS
136.0800 g., 0.9250 Silver 4.0473 oz. ASW **Ruler:** Elizabeth II
Subject: Humpback Whale Protection **Obv:** Arms with supporters **Rev:** Value and map divides humpback whales
Rev. Designer: Michael Rizzello

Date	Mintage	F	VF	XF	Unc	BU
1985 Proof	2,600	Value: 90.00				

KM# 127 25 DOLLARS
136.0800 g., 0.9250 Silver 4.0473 oz. ASW **Ruler:** Elizabeth II
Subject: World Championship Soccer - Mexico **Obv:** Arms with supporters **Rev:** Date within globe above two soccer players

Date	Mintage	F	VF	XF	Unc	BU
1986	—	—	—	—	60.00	70.00

KM# 130 25 DOLLARS
37.7800 g., 0.9250 Silver 1.1236 oz. ASW **Ruler:** Elizabeth II
Subject: 25th Anniversary of Independence **Obv:** Crowned bust right **Rev:** Arms with supporters

Date	Mintage	F	VF	XF	Unc	BU
1987 Proof	1,900	Value: 30.00				

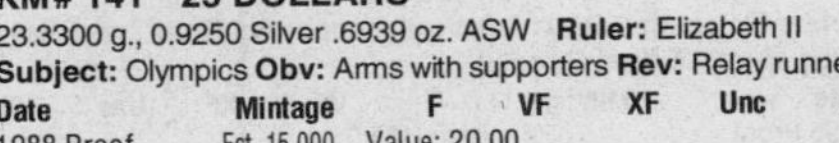

KM# 141 25 DOLLARS
23.3300 g., 0.9250 Silver .6939 oz. ASW **Ruler:** Elizabeth II
Subject: Olympics **Obv:** Arms with supporters **Rev:** Relay runners

Date	Mintage	F	VF	XF	Unc	BU
1988 Proof	Est. 15,000	Value: 20.00				

KM# 142 25 DOLLARS
23.3300 g., 0.9250 Silver .6939 oz. ASW **Ruler:** Elizabeth II
Subject: World Championship Soccer **Obv:** Arms with supporters **Rev:** Soccer player

Date	Mintage	F	VF	XF	Unc	BU
1990 Proof	—	Value: 25.00				

KM# 150 25 DOLLARS
23.3300 g., 0.9250 Silver .6939 oz. ASW **Ruler:** Elizabeth II
Subject: Columbus' Jamaican Landfall of 1494 **Obv:** Arms with supporters **Rev:** Bust of Columbus at left, Queen Isabella at right, ship between, Island of Jamaica below

Date	Mintage	F	VF	XF	Unc	BU
1991 Matte	650	—	—	—	60.00	65.00
1991 Proof	Est. 25,000	Value: 25.00				

KM# 151 25 DOLLARS
23.3300 g., 0.9250 Silver .6939 oz. ASW **Ruler:** Elizabeth II
Subject: Discovery of America - Landfall **Obv:** Arms with supporters **Rev:** Bust 1/4 right, ship within globe to right

Date	Mintage	F	VF	XF	Unc	BU
1992 Matte	550	—	—	—	60.00	65.00
1992 Proof	Est. 25,000	Value: 30.00				

KM# 159 25 DOLLARS
23.3300 g., 0.9250 Silver .6939 oz. ASW **Ruler:** Elizabeth II
Subject: Summer Olympic Games **Obv:** Arms with supporters
Rev: Bicyclists

Date	Mintage	F	VF	XF	Unc	BU
1992 Proof	15,000	Value: 35.00				

KM# 160 25 DOLLARS
23.3300 g., 0.9250 Silver .6939 oz. ASW **Ruler:** Elizabeth II
Subject: Summer Olympic Games **Obv:** Arms with supporters
Rev: Boxers

Date	Mintage	F	VF	XF	Unc	BU
1992 Proof	15,000	Value: 35.00				

KM# 165 25 DOLLARS
28.2000 g., 0.9250 Silver .8386 oz. ASW **Ruler:** Elizabeth II
Subject: World Cup Soccer **Obv:** Arms with supporters
Rev: Soccer player

Date	Mintage	F	VF	XF	Unc	BU
1994	Est. 10,000	—	—	—	40.00	45.00

KM# 169 25 DOLLARS
31.4700 g., 0.9250 Silver .9359 oz. ASW **Ruler:** Elizabeth II
Subject: Queen Elizabeth's Wedding Anniversary and Queen Mother's Birthday **Obv:** Arms with supporters **Rev:** Queen Mother's wedding portrait

Date	Mintage	F	VF	XF	Unc	BU
1994 Proof	Est. 20,000	Value: 32.00				

KM# 166 25 DOLLARS
28.2000 g., 0.9250 Silver .8386 oz. ASW **Ruler:** Elizabeth II
Subject: 25th Anniversary - Caribbean Development Bank **Obv:** Arms with supporters **Rev:** Map within grid on globe

Date	Mintage	F	VF	XF	Unc	BU
1995	Est. 2,000	—	—	—	45.00	50.00

KM# 170 25 DOLLARS
28.2800 g., 0.9250 Silver .8411 oz. ASW **Ruler:** Elizabeth II **Obv:** Arms with supporters **Rev:** Tycho Brahe at right, world globe at left

Date	Mintage	F	VF	XF	Unc	BU
1995 Proof	Est. 10,000	Value: 35.00				

KM# 173 25 DOLLARS
28.2800 g., 0.9250 Silver .8411 oz. ASW **Ruler:** Elizabeth II
Subject: U.N. 50th Anniversary **Obv:** Arms with supporters
Rev: Embracing children above logo and numeral 50

Date	Mintage	F	VF	XF	Unc	BU
ND(1995) Proof	Est. 105,000	Value: 30.00				

KM# 174 25 DOLLARS
28.2800 g., 0.9250 Silver .8411 oz. ASW **Ruler:** Elizabeth II
Subject: Endangered Wildlife **Obv:** Arms with supporters
Rev: Black-billed Amazon Parrots

Date	Mintage	F	VF	XF	Unc	BU
1995 Proof	Est. 10,000	Value: 45.00				

KM# 177 25 DOLLARS
28.2800 g., 0.9250 Silver .8411 oz. ASW **Ruler:** Elizabeth II
Subject: World Cup Soccer **Obv:** Arms with supporters
Rev: Soccer player

Date	Mintage	F	VF	XF	Unc	BU
1998 Proof	Est. 10,000	Value: 40.00				

KM# 183 25 DOLLARS
28.2800 g., 0.9250 Silver .8410 oz. ASW, 38.6 mm.
Ruler: Elizabeth II **Series:** Olympics **Obv:** Arms with supporters
Rev: Two women hurdlers **Edge:** Reeded

Date	Mintage	F	VF	XF	Unc	BU
2000 Proof	5,500	—	—	—	50.00	55.00

KM# 171 50 DOLLARS
28.2800 g., 0.9250 Silver .8411 oz. ASW **Ruler:** Elizabeth II
Subject: 50th Anniversary The Hon Robert Nesta Marley
Obv: Arms with supporters **Rev:** Head left

Date	Mintage	F	VF	XF	Unc	BU
1995 Proof	30,000	Value: 40.00				

KM# 175 50 DOLLARS
7.7760 g., 0.5833 Gold .1458 oz. AGW **Ruler:** Elizabeth II **Obv:** Arms with supporters **Rev:** Queen Mother's wedding portrait

Date	Mintage	F	VF	XF	Unc	BU
1995 Proof	Est. 5,000	Value: 115				

KM# 179 50 DOLLARS
28.2800 g., 0.9250 Silver .8410 oz. ASW **Ruler:** Elizabeth II
Subject: 50th Anniversary - University of the West Indies **Obv:** Arms with supporters **Rev:** University arms with pelican standing at top

Date	Mintage	F	VF	XF	Unc	BU
1998 Proof	20,000	Value: 40.00				

KM# 67 100 DOLLARS
7.8300 g., 0.9000 Gold .2265 oz. AGW **Ruler:** Elizabeth II
Subject: Christopher Columbus **Obv:** Arms with supporters
Rev: Bust with hat 3/4 left

Date	Mintage	F	VF	XF	Unc	BU
1975FM (M)	100	—	—	—	185	200
1975FM (U)	10,000	—	—	—	170	180
1975FM (P)	21,000	Value: 160				

KM# 72 100 DOLLARS
7.8300 g., 0.9000 Gold .2265 oz. AGW **Ruler:** Elizabeth II
Subject: Admiral Horatio Nelson **Obv:** Arms with supporters
Rev: Uniformed bust looking left, ship and map at left

Date	Mintage	F	VF	XF	Unc	BU
1976FM (M)	100	—	—	—	200	215
1976FM (P)	8,952	Value: 170				

KM# 77 100 DOLLARS
11.3400 g., 0.9000 Gold .3281 oz. AGW **Ruler:** Elizabeth II
Subject: 25th Anniversary of Coronation of Elizabeth II **Obv:** Arms with supporters **Rev:** Queen on throne with crown, sceptre and orb

Date	Mintage	F	VF	XF	Unc	BU
ND(1978)	—	—	—	—	225	235
ND(1978) Proof	5,835	Value: 230				

KM# 82 100 DOLLARS
11.3400 g., 0.9000 Gold .3281 oz. AGW **Ruler:** Elizabeth II
Subject: 10th Anniversary - Investiture of Prince Charles **Obv:** Arms with supporters **Rev:** Crowned half figure left in regal dress

Date	Mintage	F	VF	XF	Unc	BU
ND(1979) Proof	2,891	Value: 235				

KM# 110 100 DOLLARS
7.1300 g., 0.9000 Gold .2063 oz. AGW **Ruler:** Elizabeth II
Subject: 21st Anniversary of Independence **Obv:** Arms with supporters **Rev:** Number 21 divides heads facing above dates and braided rope

Date	Mintage	F	VF	XF	Unc	BU
ND(1983)FM (P)	638	Value: 220				

KM# 117 100 DOLLARS
7.1300 g., 0.9000 Gold .2063 oz. AGW **Ruler:** Elizabeth II
Subject: 100th Anniversary - Birth of Bustamante **Obv:** Arms with supporters **Rev:** Bust 1/4 left

Date	Mintage	F	VF	XF	Unc	BU
1984FM (P)	531	Value: 220				

KM# 122 100 DOLLARS
136.0800 g., 0.9250 Silver 4.0743 oz. ASW **Ruler:** Elizabeth II **Subject:** World Championship Soccer - Mexico **Obv:** Arms with supporters **Rev:** Date within globe above two soccer players

Date	Mintage	F	VF	XF	Unc	BU
1986 Proof	20,000	Value: 65.00				

KM# 129 100 DOLLARS
11.3400 g., 0.9000 Gold .3281 oz. AGW **Ruler:** Elizabeth II **Subject:** 100th Anniversary - Birth of Marcus Garvey **Obv:** Arms with supporters **Rev:** Portrait of Garvey facing

Date	Mintage	F	VF	XF	Unc	BU
1987 Proof	500	Value: 250				

KM# 139 100 DOLLARS
136.0800 g., 0.9250 Silver 4.0473 oz. ASW **Ruler:** Elizabeth II **Obv:** Arms with supporters **Rev:** Streamer-tailed Hummingbird **Note:** Photo reduced.

Date	Mintage	F	VF	XF	Unc	BU
1987 Proof	—	Value: 150				

KM# 135 100 DOLLARS
136.0800 g., 0.9250 Silver 4.0473 oz. ASW **Ruler:** Elizabeth II **Subject:** Summer Olympics - Relay Race **Obv:** Arms with supporters **Rev:** Handoff of baton during relay race

Date	Mintage	F	VF	XF	Unc	BU
1988 Proof	15,000	Value: 85.00				

KM# 143 100 DOLLARS
136.0800 g., 0.9250 Silver 4.0473 oz. ASW **Ruler:** Elizabeth II **Subject:** World Championship Soccer **Obv:** Arms with supporters **Rev:** Soccer player

Date	Mintage	F	VF	XF	Unc	BU
1990 Proof	—	Value: 140				

KM# 149 100 DOLLARS
137.8000 g., 0.9250 Silver 4.0981 oz. ASW **Ruler:** Elizabeth II **Subject:** Olympics - Boxing **Obv:** Arms with supporters **Rev:** Boxers

Date	Mintage	F	VF	XF	Unc	BU
1992 Proof	10,000	Value: 90.00				

KM# 158 100 DOLLARS
11.3400 g., 0.9000 Gold .3281 oz. AGW **Ruler:** Elizabeth II **Subject:** Centennial - Birth of Norman Manley **Obv:** Arms with supporters **Rev:** Head left

Date	Mintage	F	VF	XF	Unc	BU
1993 Proof	500	Value: 280				

KM# 172 100 DOLLARS
15.9800 g., 0.9990 Gold .5132 oz. AGW **Ruler:** Elizabeth II **Subject:** Robert Marley **Obv:** Arms with supporters **Rev:** Head left

Date	Mintage	F	VF	XF	Unc	BU
1995 Proof	2,000	Value: 375				

KM# 178 100 DOLLARS
15.9800 g., 0.9990 Gold .5132 oz. AGW **Ruler:** Elizabeth II **Subject:** World Cup Soccer **Obv:** Arms with supporters **Rev:** Soccer player

Date	Mintage	F	VF	XF	Unc	BU
1998 Proof	Est. 500	Value: 400				

KM# 180 100 DOLLARS
15.9700 g., 0.9167 Gold .4706 oz. AGW **Ruler:** Elizabeth II **Subject:** 50th Anniversary - University of the West Indies **Obv:** Arms with supporters **Rev:** University arms

Date	Mintage	F	VF	XF	Unc	BU
1998 Proof	1,000	Value: 345				

KM# 78 250 DOLLARS
43.2200 g., 0.9000 Gold 1.2507 oz. AGW **Ruler:** Elizabeth II **Subject:** 25th Anniversary of Coronation **Obv:** Arms with supporters **Rev:** Queen seated on throne with crown, sceptre and orb

Date	Mintage	F	VF	XF	Unc	BU
ND(1978) Proof	3,005	Value: 875				

KM# 83 250 DOLLARS
43.2200 g., 0.9000 Gold 1.2507 oz. AGW **Ruler:** Elizabeth II **Subject:** 10th Anniversary - Investiture of Prince Charles **Obv:** Arms with supporters **Rev:** Crowned half figure left in regal dress

Date	Mintage	F	VF	XF	Unc	BU
ND(1979) Proof	1,650	Value: 900				

KM# 89 250 DOLLARS
11.3400 g., 0.9000 Gold .3281 oz. AGW **Ruler:** Elizabeth II **Subject:** 1980 Olympics **Obv:** Arms with supporters **Rev:** Heads around outer circle of previous Gold Medal winners

Date	Mintage	F	VF	XF	Unc	BU
1980 Proof	902	Value: 255				

KM# 95 250 DOLLARS
11.3400 g., 0.9000 Gold .3281 oz. AGW **Ruler:** Elizabeth II **Subject:** Wedding of Prince Charles and Lady Diana **Obv:** Crowned bust right

Date	Mintage	F	VF	XF	Unc	BU
1981 Proof	1,491	Value: 245				

KM# 100 250 DOLLARS
11.3400 g., 0.9000 Gold .3281 oz. AGW **Ruler:** Elizabeth II
Subject: World Championship of Football **Obv:** Arms with supporters **Rev:** Goalie catching attempted score

Date	Mintage	F	VF	XF	Unc	BU
1982 Proof	694	Value: 280				

KM# 124 250 DOLLARS
11.3200 g., 0.9000 Gold .3275 oz. AGW **Ruler:** Elizabeth II
Subject: Royal Visit **Obv:** Arms with supporters **Rev:** Conjoined heads of royal couple left

Date	Mintage	F	VF	XF	Unc	BU
1983 Proof	5,000	Value: 235				

KM# 118 250 DOLLARS
11.3400 g., 0.9000 Gold .3281 oz. AGW **Ruler:** Elizabeth II
Subject: Decade for Women **Obv:** Arms with supporters
Rev: Woman with basket on head facing, map in background

Date	Mintage	F	VF	XF	Unc	BU
1984 Proof	559	Value: 275				

KM# 131 250 DOLLARS
16.0000 g., 0.9000 Gold .4630 oz. AGW **Ruler:** Elizabeth II
Subject: 25th Anniversary of Independence **Obv:** Crowned bust right **Rev:** Arms with supporters

Date	Mintage	F	VF	XF	Unc	BU
1987 Proof	250	Value: 400				

KM# 156 250 DOLLARS
11.3400 g., 0.9000 Gold .3281 oz. AGW **Ruler:** Elizabeth II
Subject: 40th Anniversary - Coronation of Queen Elizabeth
Obv: Crowned bust right **Rev:** Arms with supporters

Date	Mintage	F	VF	XF	Unc	BU
1993 Proof	Est. 500	Value: 450				

KM# 153 500 DOLLARS
11.3400 g., 0.9000 Gold .3281 oz. AGW **Ruler:** Elizabeth II
Subject: Columbus Quincentennial **Obv:** Arms with supporters
Rev: "500" on ship's sail

Date	Mintage	F	VF	XF	Unc	BU
1992 Proof	500	Value: 450				

KM# 162 500 DOLLARS
47.5400 g., 0.9170 Gold 1.4017 oz. AGW **Ruler:** Elizabeth II
Subject: Royal Visit **Obv:** Arms with supporters **Rev:** Drummer on island map with yacht at right

Date	Mintage	F	VF	XF	Unc	BU
1994 Proof	100	Value: 1,150				

PIEFORTS

KM#	Date	Mintage	Identification	Mkt Val
P1	1979	—	10 Dollars. Silver. KM#80	65.00
P2	1983	32	250 Dollars. 0.9000 Gold. Design like 10 Dollars, KM#80	1,250

MINT SETS

KM#	Date	Mintage	Identification	Issue Price	Mkt Val
MS1	1969 (2)	30,000	KM#41-42	0.90	2.00
MS2	1969 (6)	30,000	KM#45-50	—	6.50
MS3	1970 (6)	5,000	KM#45-50	16.00	6.50
MS4	1971 (7)	4,072	KM#51, 53-58	19.50	17.50
MS5	1971 (6)	4,834	KM#51, 53-57	—	10.00
MS6	1972 (7)	2,982	KM#51, 53-57, 59	19.75	25.00
MS7	1972 (6)	4,000	KM#51, 53-57	10.00	10.00
MS8	1973 (7)	6,404	KM#51, 53-57, 59	19.75	20.00
MS9	1973 (6)	3,000	KM#51, 53-57	9.95	10.00
MS10	1974 (8)	8,361	KM#51, 53-57, 59, 63	25.00	20.00
MS11	1975 (8)	4,683	KM#51, 53-57, 62, 66	27.50	20.00
MS12	1976 (9)	1,802	KM#53-57, 62, 68, 70, 71	27.50	27.50
MS13	1977 (9)	597	KM#53-54, 56-57, 62, 68, 70, 73, 74	27.50	45.00
MS14	1978 (9)	1,282	KM#53-54, 56-57, 62, 68, 70, 73, 75	27.50	40.00
MS15	1979 (9)	2,608	KM#53-54, 56-57, 62, 68, 70, 73, 79	27.50	40.00
MS16	1980 (9)	3,668	KM#53-54, 56, 68, 70, 73, 84.1-86	30.00	30.00
MS17	1981 (9)	482	KM#53-54, 56, 68, 70, 73, 84.1, 85.1, 93	31.00	45.00
MS18	1982 (9)	—	KM#53-54, 56, 68, 70, 73, 84.1-85.1, 97	31.00	40.00
MS19	1983 (9)	1,210	KM#101-109	37.00	40.00
MS20	1984 (9)	—	KM#53-54, 56, 68, 70, 73, 85.1, 113-114	37.00	35.00
MS21	2000 (7)	—	KM#64, 146.2, 163, 164, 167, 181-182	25.00	27.50

PROOF SETS

KM#	Date	Mintage	Identification	Issue Price	Mkt Val
PS1	1918C (3)	—	KM#24-26	—	600
PS2	1928 (3)	20	KM#24-26	—	600
PS3	1937 (3)	—	KM#27-29	—	550
PS4	1969 (6)	8,530	KM#45-50	15.00	10.00
PS5	1969 (2)	5,000	KM#41-42	2.70	7.00
PS6	1970 (6)	11,540	KM#45-50	15.00	10.00
PS7	1971 (7)	12,739	KM#51, 53-58	26.50	17.50
PS8	1971 (6)	1,048	KM#51, 53-57	15.00	10.00
PS9	1972 (7)	16,967	KM#51, 53-57, 59	27.50	16.00
PS10	1973 (7)	28,405	KM#51, 53-57, 59	27.50	15.00
PS11	1974 (8)	22,026	KM#51, 53-57, 62a-63a	50.00	30.00
PS12	1975 (8)	15,638	KM#51, 53-57, 62a, 66a	55.00	40.00
PS13	1976 (9)	22,900	KM#53-57, 62a, 68, 70, 71a	55.00	40.00
PS14	1976 (7)	1,503	KM#53-57, 68, 70	22.50	17.00
PS15	1977	10,054	KM#53-54, 56-57, 62a, 68, 70, 73, 74a	55.00	35.00
PS16	1978 (9)	6,058	KM#53-54, 56-57, 62a, 68, 70, 73, 75a	59.00	45.00
PS17	1979 (9)	4,049	KM#53-54, 56-57, 62a, 68, 70, 73, 79a	59.00	50.00
PS18	1980 (9)	2,688	KM#53-54, 56, 68, 70, 73, 84.1, 85.1a, 86a	90.00	60.00
PS19	1981 (9)	1,577	KM#53-54, 56, 68, 70, 73, 84.1, 85.1a, 93a	92.00	80.00
PS20	1982 (9)	—	KM#53-54, 56, 68, 70, 73, 84.1, 85.1a, 97a	92.00	75.00
PS21	1983 (9)	1,210	KM#101-107, 108a-109a	—	85.00
PS22	1984 (9)	—	KM#53-54, 56, 68, 70, 73, 85.1a, 113, 114a	92.00	75.00
PS23	1985 (9)	—	KM#46-47, 49, 64-65, 84.2-85.2, 120, 123	—	75.00
PS24	1987 (9)	500	KM#46-49, 64, 84.2, 85.2, 132, 133	90.00	75.00
PS25	1988 (9)	500	KM#46-49, 64-65, 84.2, 85.2, 138a	115	80.00
PS26	1989 (9)	500	KM#46-49, 64-65, 84.2, 85.2, 140a	120	80.00
PS27	1990 (9)	500	KM#46a-47a, 48-49, 64-65, 85.2, 144, 145	125	100
PS28	1991 (7)	500	KM#46a, 64, 85.2, 145, 146-148	—	100
PS29	1992 (7)	500	KM#46a, 64, 85.2, 145-147, 152	139	140
PS30	1993 (7)	500	KM#46a, 64, 85.2, 145a, 146-147, 155	—	140
PS31	2000 (8)	500	KM#64, 146.2, 163, 164, 167, 181-183	99.00	100

JAPAN

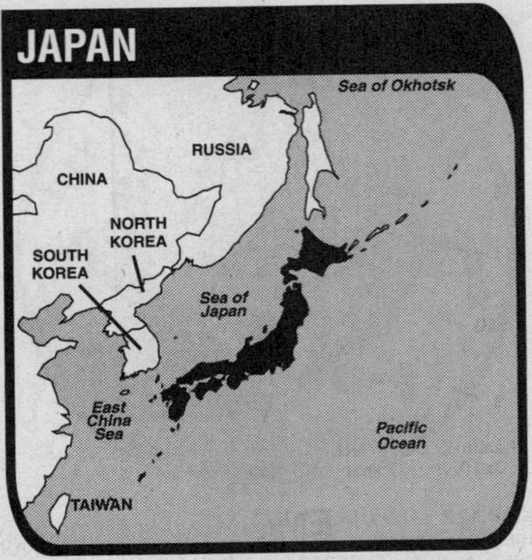

Japan, a constitutional monarchy situated off the east coast of Asia, has an area of 145,809 sq. mi. (377,835 sq. km.) and a population of 123.2 million. Capital: Tokyo. Japan, one of the major industrial nations of the world, exports machinery, motor vehicles, electronics and chemicals.

Japan, founded (so legend holds) in 660 B.C. by a direct descendant of the Sun Goddess, was first brought into contact with the west by a storm-blown Portuguese ship in 1542. European traders and missionaries proceeded to enlarge the contact until the Shogunate, sensing a military threat in the foreign presence, expelled all foreigners and restricted relations with the outside world in the 17th century. After Commodore Perry's U.S. flotilla visited in 1854, Japan rapidly industrialized, abolished the Shogunate and established a parliamentary form of government, and by the end of the 19th century achieved the status of a modern economic and military power. A series of wars with China and Russia, and participation with the allies in World War I, enlarged Japan territorially but brought its interests into conflict with the Far Eastern interests of the United States, Britain and the Netherlands, causing it to align with the Axis Powers for the pursuit of World War II. After its defeat in World War II, General Douglas MacArthur forced Japan to renounce military aggression as a political instrument, and he instituted constitutional democratic self-government. Japan quickly gained a position as an economic world power.

Japanese coinage of concern to this catalog includes those issued for the Ryukyu Islands (also called Liuchu), a chain of islands extending southwest from Japan toward Taiwan (Formosa), before the Japanese government converted the islands into a prefecture under the name Okinawa. Many of the provinces of Japan issued their own definitive coinage under the Shogunate.

RULERS

Emperors

Mutsuhito (Meiji), 1867-1912
明治 or 治明
Years 1-45

Yoshihito (Taisho), 1912-1926
大正 or 正大
Years 1-15

Hirohito (Showa), 1926-1989
昭和 or 和昭
Years 1-64

Akihito (Heisei), 1989-
平成
Years 1-

NOTE: The personal name of the emperor is followed by the name that he chose for his regnal era.

MONETARY SYSTEM

Commencing 1870

10 Rin = 1 Sen
100 Sen = 1 Yen

MONETARY UNITS

Rin 厘

Sen 銭

Yen 円 or 圓 or 圓

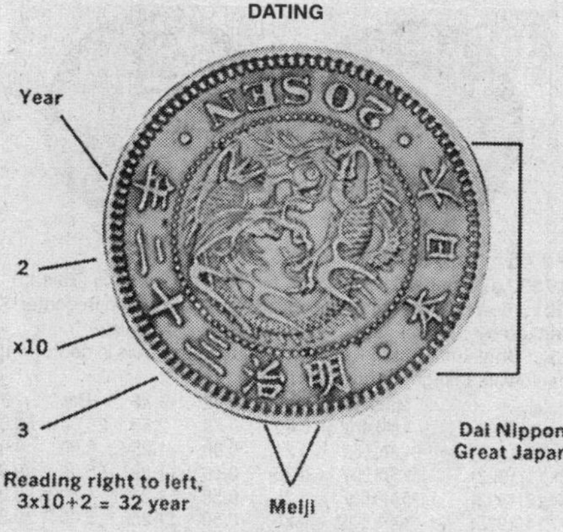

EMPIRE

DECIMAL COINAGE

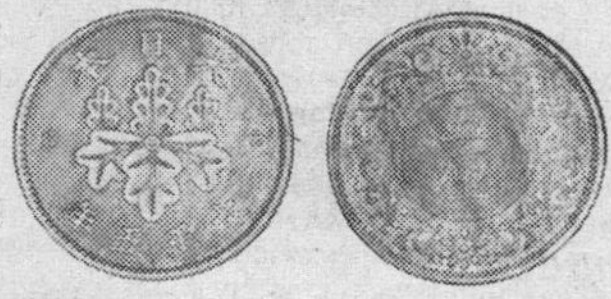

Y# 41 5 RIN

2.1000 g., Bronze, 12.8 mm. **Ruler:** Yoshihito (Taisho) **Obv:** Large paulownia crest in center flanked by cherry blossoms **Rev:** Value within circle of flowered wreath

Date	Mintage	F	VF	XF	Unc	BU
Yr.5(1916)	8,000,000	0.50	1.50	2.75	10.00	15.00
Yr.6(1917)	5,287,584	0.50	1.50	2.75	10.00	17.50
Yr.7(1918)	11,661,877	0.25	0.75	2.00	7.50	12.50
Yr.8(1919)	17,130,539	0.25	0.75	2.00	7.50	11.50

Y# 20 SEN

7.1300 g., Bronze, 27.8 mm. **Ruler:** Mutsuhito (Meiji) **Obv:** Sunburst within beaded circle with legend separated by dots around border **Rev:** Value within center of rice wreath

Date	Mintage	F	VF	XF	Unc	BU
Yr.34(1901)	5,555,155	2.00	4.50	16.00	65.00	125
Yr.35(1902)	4,444,845	5.00	10.00	25.00	145	200
Yr.39(1906)	—	—	—	—	—	—
Note: None struck for circulation						
Yr.42(1909)	—	—	—	—	—	—
Note: None struck for circulation						

Y# 35 SEN

7.1300 g., Bronze, 27.8 mm. **Ruler:** Yoshihito (Taisho) **Obv:** Sunburst within beaded circle with legend separated by dots around border **Rev:** Value within center of rice wreath

Date	Mintage	F	VF	XF	Unc	BU
Yr.2(1913)	15,000,000	1.50	2.25	4.00	32.00	65.00
Yr.3(1914)	10,000,000	1.50	2.25	4.00	32.00	50.00
Yr.4(1915)	13,000,000	1.50	2.25	4.00	32.00	50.00

Y# 42 SEN

3.7500 g., Bronze, 23 mm. **Ruler:** Yoshihito (Taisho) **Obv:** Paulownia crest flanked by cherry blossoms **Rev:** Value within circle of flowered wreath

Date	Mintage	F	VF	XF	Unc	BU
Yr.5(1916)	19,193,946	0.45	0.75	1.25	30.00	60.00
Yr.6(1917)	27,183,078	0.25	0.45	0.75	25.00	50.00
Yr.7(1918)	121,794,756	0.25	0.45	0.75	9.50	15.00
Yr.8(1919)	209,959,359	0.15	0.25	0.50	4.50	9.00
Yr.9(1920)	118,829,256	0.15	0.25	0.50	4.50	9.00
Yr.10(1921)	252,440,000	0.15	0.25	0.50	4.50	9.00
Yr.11(1922)	253,210,000	0.15	0.25	0.50	4.50	9.00
Yr.12(1923)	155,500,000	0.15	0.25	0.50	5.50	11.00
Yr.13(1924)	106,250,000	0.15	0.25	0.50	4.50	9.00

Y# 47 SEN

3.7500 g., Bronze, 23 mm. **Ruler:** Hirohito (Showa) **Obv:** Paulownia crest flanked by cherry blossoms with authority on top and date below **Rev:** Value within circle of flowered wreath

Date	Mintage	F	VF	XF	Unc	BU
Yr.2(1927)	26,500,000	1.25	2.00	2.75	32.00	50.00
Yr.4(1929)	3,000,000	2.75	5.50	12.50	45.00	75.00
Yr.5(1930)	5,000,000	2.00	3.50	6.00	70.00	150
Yr.6(1931)	25,001,222	0.25	0.45	1.25	12.50	25.00
Yr.7(1932)	35,066,715	0.25	0.45	1.25	9.00	18.00
Yr.8(1933)	38,936,907	0.15	0.25	0.50	2.50	5.00
Yr.9(1934)	100,004,950	0.15	0.25	0.50	2.50	5.00
Yr.10(1935)	200,009,912	0.15	0.25	0.50	1.50	3.00
Yr.11(1936)	109,170,428	0.15	0.25	0.50	1.50	3.00
Yr.12(1937)	133,196,568	0.15	0.25	0.50	1.50	3.00
Yr.13(1938)	87,649,338	0.15	0.25	0.50	1.50	3.00

Y# 55 SEN

3.7500 g., Bronze, 23 mm. **Ruler:** Hirohito (Showa) **Obv:** Bird within clouds flanked by cherry blossoms **Rev:** Value in center of sacred mirror within wave-like wreath

Date	Mintage	F	VF	XF	Unc	BU
Yr.13(1938)	113,600,000	0.15	0.25	0.50	1.50	2.50

Y# 56 SEN

0.9000 g., Aluminum, 17 mm. **Ruler:** Hirohito (Showa) **Obv:** Bird within clouds flanked by cherry blossoms **Rev:** Value in center of sacred mirror within wave-like wreath

Date	Mintage	F	VF	XF	Unc	BU
Yr.13(1938)	45,502,266	—	0.50	1.50	8.50	17.00
Yr.14(1939) Type A	444,602,146	—	1.25	2.25	12.00	24.00
Yr.14(1939) Type B	Inc. above	—	0.25	0.45	1.50	2.00
Yr.15(1940)	601,110,015	—	0.25	0.45	1.50	2.00

Y# 59 SEN

0.6500 g., Aluminum, 16 mm. **Ruler:** Hirohito (Showa) **Obv:** Value in center with authority above and date below **Rev:** Chrysanthemum above Mount Fuji with value below

Date	Mintage	F	VF	XF	Unc	BU
Yr.16(1941)	1,016,620,734	—	0.15	0.25	0.50	1.00
Yr.17(1942)	119,709,832	—	0.15	0.25	0.75	1.00
Yr.18(1943)	1,163,949,434	—	0.15	0.25	0.50	1.00

Y# 59a SEN

0.5500 g., Aluminum, 16 mm. **Ruler:** Hirohito (Showa) **Obv:** Value in center with authority above and date below **Rev:** Chrysanthemum above Mt. Fuji with value below **Note:** Thinner

Date	Mintage	F	VF	XF	Unc	BU
Yr.18(1943)	627,191,000	—	0.15	0.50	1.00	1.50

Y# 62 SEN

1.3000 g., Tin-Zinc, 15 mm. **Ruler:** Hirohito (Showa) **Obv:** Chrysanthemum flanked by sprigs with value above and below **Rev:** Authority inscribed vertically in center with date below

Date	Mintage	F	VF	XF	Unc	BU
Yr.19(1944)	1,629,580,000	—	0.15	0.25	0.50	1.00
Yr.20(1945)	Inc. above	—	0.25	0.50	0.75	1.50

KM# 110 SEN

0.8000 g., Reddish Brown Baked Clay, 15 mm. **Ruler:** Hirohito (Showa) **Obv:** Stylized cherry blossom in center flanked by paulownia buds below value **Rev:** Mountain with symbol at upper left

Date	Mintage	F	VF	XF	Unc	BU
ND(1945)	—	6.00	9.00	22.50	30.00	40.00

Note: Circulated unofficially for a few days before the end of WWII in Central Japan; varieties of color exist

Y# 21 5 SEN

4.6700 g., Copper-Nickel **Ruler:** Mutsuhito (Meiji) **Obv:** Sunburst within circle, 3 legends separated by dots around border **Rev:** Value within rice wreath

Date	Mintage	F	VF	XF	Unc	BU
Yr.34(1901)	7,124,824	6.00	12.00	18.50	125	150
Yr.35(1902)	2,448,544	9.00	18.50	30.00	285	350
Yr.36(1903)	372,000	120	200	300	2,500	3,000
Yr.37(1904)	1,628,000	15.00	27.50	60.00	400	600
Yr.38(1905)	6,000,000	4.00	8.00	13.50	115	150
Yr.39(1906)	—	—	—	—	—	—

Note: None struck for circulation; Spink-Taisei Hong Kong sale 9-91 BU realized $10,000

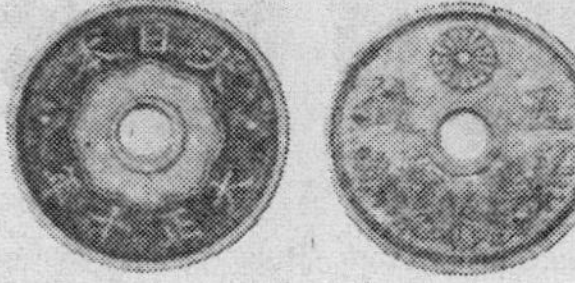

Y# 43 5 SEN

4.2800 g., Copper-Nickel, 20.6 mm. **Ruler:** Yoshihito (Taisho) **Obv:** Flower-like form of sacred mirror around hole in center flanked by dots **Rev:** Chrysanthemum flanked by value with hole in center and paulownia foliage on bottom 1/2

Date	Mintage	F	VF	XF	Unc	BU
Yr.6(1917)	6,781,830	6.00	12.00	18.50	50.00	65.00
Yr.7(1918)	9,131,201	4.00	8.00	15.00	35.00	50.00
Yr.8(1919)	44,980,633	2.50	4.50	9.00	20.00	25.00
Yr.9(1920)	21,906,326	2.50	4.50	9.00	20.00	25.00

Y# 44 5 SEN

2.6300 g., Copper-Nickel, 19.1 mm. **Ruler:** Yoshihito (Taisho) **Obv:** Flower-like form of sacred mirror around hole in center flanked by dots **Rev:** Chrysanthemum flanked by value with hole in center and paulownia foliage on bottom 1/2

Date	Mintage	F	VF	XF	Unc	BU
Yr.9(1920)	100,455,537	0.35	0.65	1.50	15.00	30.00
Yr.10(1921)	133,020,000	0.25	0.45	1.20	5.00	9.00
Yr.11(1922)	163,980,000	0.25	0.45	1.20	5.00	9.00
Yr.12(1923)	8,000,394	0.25	0.45	1.20	5.00	9.00

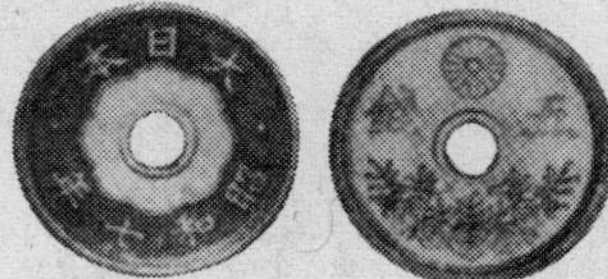

Y# 48 5 SEN

2.6300 g., Copper-Nickel, 19.1 mm. **Ruler:** Hirohito (Showa) **Obv:** Flower-like form of sacred mirror around hole in center flanked by dots **Rev:** Chrysanthemum flanked by value with hole in center and paulownia foliage on bottom 1/2

Date	Mintage	F	VF	XF	Unc	BU
Yr.7(1932)	8,000,394	0.25	0.45	1.50	7.00	14.00

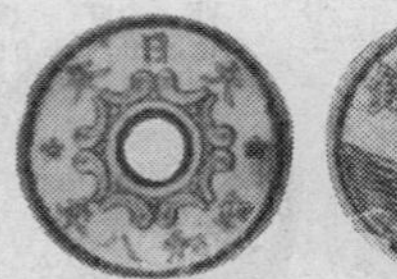

Y# 53 5 SEN

2.8000 g., Nickel, 19 mm. **Ruler:** Hirohito (Showa) **Obv:** Rings around center hole flanked by cherry blossoms with authority above and date below **Rev:** Bird with wings spread below hole in center with rays of sun on upper 1/2 of border with chrysanthemum flanked by value

Date	Mintage	F	VF	XF	Unc	BU
Yr.8(1933)	16,150,808	0.45	1.25	2.25	5.50	10.00
Yr.9(1934)	33,851,607	0.45	0.75	1.50	4.50	9.00
Yr.10(1935)	13,680,677	0.75	1.50	2.75	7.50	10.00
Yr.11(1936)	36,321,796	0.45	0.75	1.50	4.50	7.50
Yr.12(1937)	44,402,201	0.45	0.75	1.50	5.50	10.00
Yr.13(1938) 4 known	10,000,000	—	—	—	—	—

Note: Almost entire mintage remelted

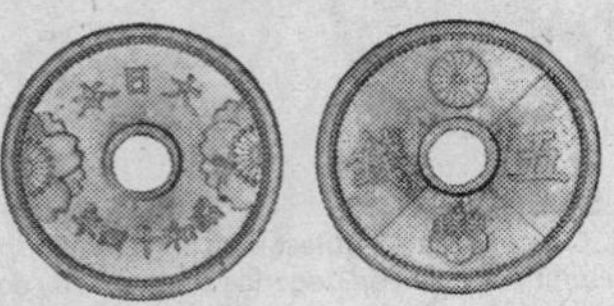

Y# 57 5 SEN

Aluminum-Bronze **Ruler:** Hirohito (Showa) **Obv:** Hole in center flanked by 1/2 cherry blossoms with authority above and date below **Rev:** Hole in center divides quarters, upper and lower quarter in relief, value at either side

Date	Mintage	F	VF	XF	Unc	BU
Yr.13(1938)	90,001,977	0.45	0.75	1.25	4.00	6.50
Yr.14(1939)	97,903,873	0.45	0.75	1.25	4.00	6.50
Yr.15(1940)	34,501,216	0.45	0.75	1.25	5.00	7.50

Y# 60 5 SEN

1.2000 g., Aluminum, 19 mm. **Ruler:** Hirohito (Showa)
Obv: Bird with wings spread with authority on top and date below
Rev: Chrysanthemum within clouds with value above and below
Note: Variety I

Date	Mintage	F	VF	XF	Unc	BU
Yr.15(1940)	167,638,000	—	0.25	0.75	3.00	6.00
Yr.16(1941)	242,361,000	—	0.25	0.50	2.25	4.50

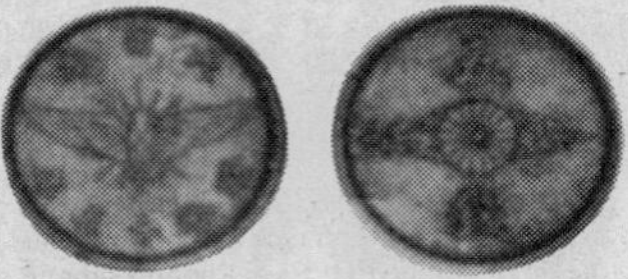

Y# 60a 5 SEN

1.0000 g., Aluminum, 19 mm. **Ruler:** Hirohito (Showa)
Obv: Bird with wings spread with authority on top and date below
Rev: Chrysanthemum among clouds with value above and below
Note: Variety 2

Date	Mintage	F	VF	XF	Unc	BU
Yr.16(1941)	478,023,877	1.25	2.75	6.00	37.50	55.00
Yr.17(1942)	Inc. above	—	0.25	0.65	1.50	2.00

Y# 60b 5 SEN

0.8000 g., Aluminum, 19 mm. **Ruler:** Hirohito (Showa)
Obv: Bird with wings spread with authority on top and date below
Rev: Chrysanthemum within clouds with value above and below
Note: Variety 3

Date	Mintage	F	VF	XF	Unc	BU
Yr.18(1943)	276,493,742	—	0.25	0.75	2.00	4.00

Y# 63 5 SEN

1.9500 g., Tin-Zinc, 17 mm. **Ruler:** Hirohito (Showa) **Obv:** Hole in center flanked by dots with authority on top and date below
Rev: Chrysanthemum on top flanked by value above hole in center with paulownia crest within cloud-like swirls below

Date	Mintage	F	VF	XF	Unc	BU
Yr.19(1944)	70,000,000	—	0.25	0.75	2.50	3.00

Y# 65 5 SEN

2.0000 g., Tin-Zinc, 17 mm. **Ruler:** Hirohito (Showa) **Obv:** Large value in center flanked by paulownia crests with authority above and date below **Rev:** Bird with wings spread flanked by value with chrysanthemum above

Date	Mintage	F	VF	XF	Unc	BU
Yr.20(1945)	180,000,000	—	0.45	1.00	3.50	6.00
Yr.21(1946)	Inc. above	—	0.45	1.00	3.50	4.50

KM# 111 5 SEN

1.3000 g., Reddish Brown Baked Clay, 18 mm. **Ruler:** Hirohito (Showa) **Obv:** Heart shapes around symbol in center with authority on top and value below **Rev:** Chrysanthemum above text

Date	Mintage	F	VF	XF	Unc	BU
Yr.20(1945)	—	250	350	450	650	750

Note: Not issued for circulation; varieties of color exist

Y# 23 10 SEN

2.6957 g., 0.8000 Silver .070 oz. ASW **Ruler:** Mutsuhito (Meiji) **Obv:** Dragon within beaded circle, 3 legends separated by dots around border **Rev:** Value within center of flowered wreath, chrysanthemum above

Date	Mintage	F	VF	XF	Unc	BU
Yr.34(1901)	797,561	95.00	135	185	800	1,150
Yr.35(1902)	1,204,439	75.00	120	150	775	1,250
Yr.37(1904)	11,106,638	3.50	5.50	7.50	35.00	70.00
Yr.38(1905)	34,182,194	3.50	5.50	7.50	35.00	70.00
Yr.39(1906)	4,710,168	3.50	5.50	7.50	35.00	70.00

Y# 29 10 SEN

2.2500 g., 0.7200 Silver .0521 oz. ASW **Ruler:** Mutsuhito (Meiji) **Obv:** Sunburst within cherry blossom circle with 3 legends separated by dots around border **Rev:** Value within center of flowered wreath with chrysanthemum above

Date	Mintage	F	VF	XF	Unc	BU
Yr.40(1907)	12,000,000	2.00	3.75	7.50	65.00	125
Yr.41(1908)	12,273,239	2.00	3.75	7.50	60.00	100
Yr.42(1909)	20,279,846	1.00	2.50	3.75	27.50	55.00
Yr.43(1910)	20,339,816	1.00	2.50	3.75	25.00	50.00
Yr.44(1911)	38,729,680	1.00	2.50	3.75	27.50	55.00
Yr.45(1912)	10,755,009	1.00	2.50	3.75	30.00	60.00

Y# 36.1 10 SEN

2.2500 g., 0.7200 Silver .0521 oz. ASW **Ruler:** Yoshihito (Taisho) **Obv:** Sunburst within cherry blossom circle with 3 legends separated by dots around border **Rev:** Value within flowered wreath with chrysanthemum on top

Date	Mintage	F	VF	XF	Unc	BU
Yr.1(1912)	10,344,307	2.00	3.75	7.50	60.00	100

Y# 36.2 10 SEN

2.2500 g., 0.7200 Silver 0.0521 oz. ASW **Ruler:** Yoshihito (Taisho) **Obv:** Sunburst within cherry blossom circle with 3 legends separated by dots around border **Rev:** Value within flowered wreath with chrysanthemum on top

Date	Mintage	F	VF	XF	Unc	BU
Yr.2(1913)	13,321,466	1.00	2.00	3.75	12.00	24.00
Yr.3(1914)	10,325,327	1.00	2.00	3.75	12.00	24.00
Yr.4(1915)	16,836,225	1.00	2.00	3.75	12.00	24.00
Yr.5(1916)	10,324,128	1.00	2.00	3.00	12.00	24.00
Yr.6(1917)	35,170,906	0.85	1.50	2.25	10.00	15.00

Y# 45 10 SEN

3.7500 g., Copper-Nickel, 22 mm. **Ruler:** Yoshihito (Taisho)
Obv: Flower-like form of sacred mirror around hole in center flanked by dots with authority on top and date below
Rev: Chrysanthemum flanked by value above hole in center with paulownia foliage on bottom 1/2

Date	Mintage	F	VF	XF	Unc	BU
Yr.9(1920)	4,894,420	0.45	0.75	2.50	25.00	50.00
Yr.10(1921)	61,870,000	0.25	0.50	1.25	5.00	9.00
Yr.11(1922)	159,770,000	0.25	0.50	1.25	5.00	9.00
Yr.12(1923)	190,010,000	0.25	0.50	1.25	4.50	9.00
Yr.14(1925)	54,475,000	0.25	0.50	1.25	5.00	9.00
Yr.15(1926)	58,675,000	0.25	0.50	1.25	5.00	9.00

Y# 49 10 SEN

3.7500 g., Copper-Nickel **Ruler:** Hirohito (Showa) **Obv:** Flower-like form of sacred mirror around hole in center flanked by dots with authority on top and date below **Rev:** Chrysanthemum flanked by value above hole in center with paulownia foliage on bottom 1/2

Date	Mintage	F	VF	XF	Unc	BU
Yr.2(1927)	36,050,000	0.25	0.45	1.25	5.00	10.00
Yr.3(1928)	41,450,000	0.25	0.45	1.25	5.00	9.00
Yr.4(1929)	10,050,000	0.45	0.75	1.50	25.00	50.00
Yr.6(1931)	1,850,087	0.60	1.25	2.00	9.00	18.00
Yr.7(1932)	23,151,177	0.25	0.45	1.25	5.00	10.00

Y# 54 10 SEN

4.0200 g., Nickel **Ruler:** Hirohito (Showa) **Obv:** Center hole within 1/3 vertical portion recessed flanked by wave-like pattern with cherry blossoms **Rev:** Hole in center flanked by value and denomination, karakusa sprays are vertical in rectangular display, chrysanthemum on top, paulownia on bottom

Date	Mintage	F	VF	XF	Unc	BU
Yr.8(1933)	14,570,714	0.45	0.75	1.50	5.50	11.00
Yr.9(1934)	37,351,832	0.25	0.50	1.25	4.75	7.50
Yr.10(1935)	35,586,755	0.30	0.75	1.50	5.25	7.50
Yr.11(1936)	77,948,804	0.25	0.50	1.25	4.75	7.50
Yr.12(1937)	40,001,969	0.30	0.75	1.50	5.50	10.00

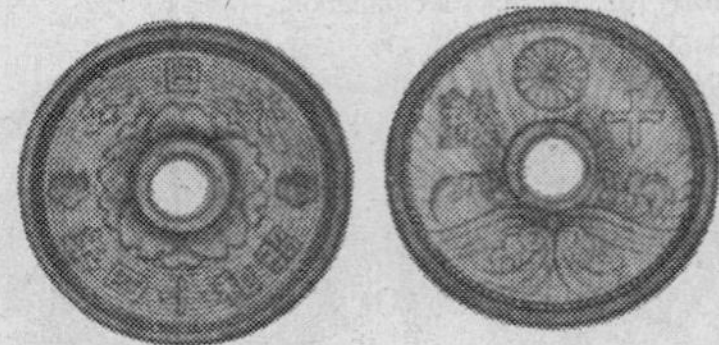

Y# 58 10 SEN

4.0000 g., Aluminum-Bronze **Ruler:** Hirohito (Showa)
Obv: Double petal cherry blossom around center hole flanked by paulownia crest with authority on top and date below
Rev: Chrysanthemum flanked by value with sun rays on upper 1/2 above hole in center with rolling waves below

Date	Mintage	F	VF	XF	Unc	BU
Yr.13(1938)	47,077,320	0.35	0.65	1.25	4.75	7.50
Yr.14(1939)	121,796,011	0.25	0.45	1.00	4.50	7.50
Yr.15(1940)	16,135,794	0.65	1.25	2.25	12.00	17.50

Y# 61 10 SEN

1.5000 g., Aluminum, 22 mm. **Ruler:** Hirohito (Showa)
Obv: Double petal cherry blossom flanked by dots with authority on top and date below **Rev:** Chrysanthemum flanked by dots with value above and paulownia foliage below

Date	Mintage	F	VF	XF	Unc	BU
Yr.15(1940)	575,600,000	—	0.20	0.35	1.50	3.00
Yr.16(1941)	Inc. above	—	0.20	0.35	1.50	3.00

Y# 61a 10 SEN

1.2000 g., Aluminum, 22 mm. **Ruler:** Hirohito (Showa) **Obv:** Double petal cherry blossom flanked by dots with authority on top and date below **Rev:** Chrysanthemum flanked by dots with value above and paulownia foliage below

Date	Mintage	F	VF	XF	Unc	BU
Yr.16(1941)	944,900,000	0.10	0.35	0.50	2.00	4.00
Yr.17(1942)	Inc. above	—	0.20	0.35	1.50	2.00
Yr.18(1943)	Inc. above	0.75	2.25	3.75	30.00	60.00

Y# 61b 10 SEN

1.0000 g., Aluminum, 22 mm. **Ruler:** Hirohito (Showa) **Obv:** Double petal cherry blossom flanked by dots with authority on top and date below **Rev:** Chrysanthemum flanked by dots with value above and paulownia foliage below

Date	Mintage	F	VF	XF	Unc	BU
Yr.18(1943)	756,000,000	—	0.20	0.35	1.25	2.50

Y# 64 10 SEN

2.4000 g., Tin-Zinc, 19 mm. **Ruler:** Hirohito (Showa) **Obv:** Hole in center flanked by dots, authority on top, date on bottom **Rev:** Chrysanthemum on top flanked by value with paulownia crest within cloud-like swirls below

Date	Mintage	F	VF	XF	Unc	BU
Yr.19(1944)	450,000,000	—	0.20	0.35	1.25	1.75

Y# 68 10 SEN

1.0000 g., Aluminum **Ruler:** Hirohito (Showa) **Obv:** Large numeral 10 overlaps double petal cherry blossom in center, authority on top, date on bottom **Rev:** Two rice stalks drooping downward, value and denomination at lower left, chrysanthemum at top

Date	Mintage	F	VF	XF	Unc	BU
Yr.20(1945)	237,590,000	—	0.20	0.35	1.00	1.50
Yr.21(1946)	Inc. above	—	0.20	0.35	1.00	1.50

KM# 112 10 SEN

2.0000 g., Reddish Brown Baked Clay, 21.9 mm. **Ruler:** Hirohito (Showa) **Obv:** Paulownia crest flanked by cherry blossoms with authority on top and date below **Rev:** Chrysandthemum in center with value above and below flanked by sprigs

Date	Mintage	F	VF	XF	Unc	BU
Yr.20(1945)	—	300	500	750	1,000	1,350

Note: Not issued for circulation; varieties of color exist

Y# 24 20 SEN

5.3900 g., 0.8000 Silver .1383 oz. ASW **Ruler:** Mutsuhito (Meiji) **Obv:** Dragon within beaded circle **Rev:** Chrysanthemum divides wreath, value within

Date	Mintage	F	VF	XF	Unc	BU
Yr.34(1901)	500,000	120	175	275	2,250	3,000
Yr.37(1904)	5,250,000	4.00	8.00	15.00	70.00	100
Yr.38(1905)	8,444,930	4.00	8.00	15.00	60.00	100

Y# 30 20 SEN

4,0500 g., 0.8000 Silver .1042 oz. ASW **Ruler:** Mutsuhito (Meiji) **Obv:** Sunburst within cherry blossom circle with 3 legends separated by dots around border **Rev:** Value and denomination within flowered wreath, chrysanthemum on top

Date	Mintage	F	VF	XF	Unc	BU
Yr.39(1906)	6,555,070	5.00	10.00	18.50	200	350
Yr.40(1907)	20,000,000	2.00	4.00	12.00	75.00	100
Yr.41(1908)	15,000,000	2.00	4.00	12.00	75.00	100
Yr.42(1909)	8,824,702	2.00	4.00	12.00	75.00	100
Yr.43(1910)	21,175,298	2.00	4.00	12.00	75.00	100
Yr.44(1911)	500,000	45.00	90.00	200	1,150	1,900

Y# 25 50 SEN

13.4800 g., 0.8000 Silver .3472 oz. ASW **Ruler:** Mutsuhito (Meiji) **Obv:** Dragon within beaded circle with 3 legends separated by dots around border **Rev:** Value within wreath, chrysanthemum above

Date	Mintage	F	VF	XF	Unc	BU
Yr.34(1901)	1,790,000	18.50	35.00	60.00	375	750
Yr.35(1902)	1,023,200	37.50	65.00	120	625	1,150
Yr.36(1903)	1,503,068	22.50	37.50	70.00	425	750
Yr.37(1904)	5,373,652	6.00	10.00	18.50	125	250
Yr.38(1905)	9,566,100	6.00	10.00	18.50	125	250

Y# 31 50 SEN

10.1000 g., 0.8000 Silver .2597 oz. ASW **Ruler:** Mutsuhito (Meiji) **Obv:** Sunburst within cherry blossom circle with 3 legends separated by dots around border **Rev:** Value and denomination within flowered wreath, chrysanthemum on top

Date	Mintage	F	VF	XF	Unc	BU
Yr.39(1906)	12,478,264	4.00	7.50	20.00	225	400
Yr.40(1907)	24,062,952	3.75	6.50	13.50	75.00	150
Yr.41(1908)	25,470,321	3.75	6.50	13.50	75.00	150
Yr.42(1909)	21,998,600	3.75	6.50	13.50	75.00	150
Yr.43(1910)	15,323,276	3.75	6.50	13.50	75.00	150
Yr.44(1911)	9,900,437	3.75	6.50	13.50	75.00	150
Yr.45(1912)	3,677,704	6.50	12.50	17.50	100	200

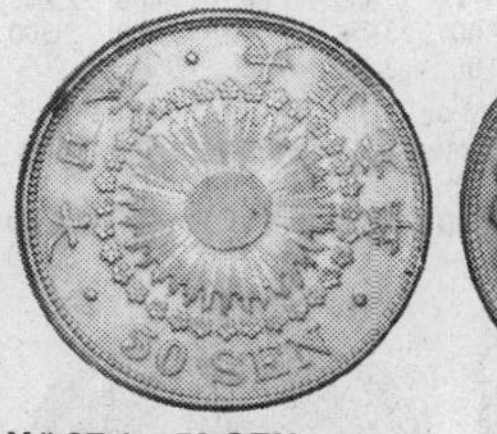

Y# 37.1 50 SEN

10.1300 g., 0.8000 Silver .2600 oz. ASW **Ruler:** Yoshihito (Taisho) **Obv:** Sunburst within cherry blossom circle, 3 legends separated by dots around border **Rev:** Value and denomination within flowered wreath, chrysanthemum on top

Date	Mintage	F	VF	XF	Unc	BU
Yr.1(1912)	1,928,649	12.50	20.00	40.00	160	300

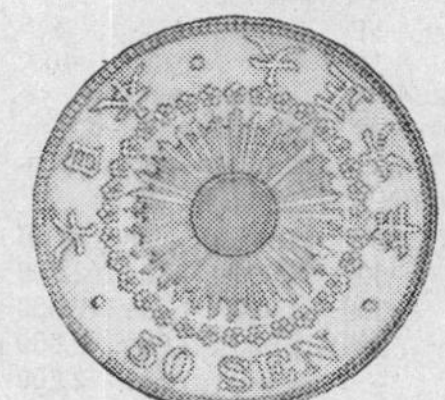

Y# 37.2 50 SEN

10.1300 g., 0.8000 Silver .2600 oz. ASW **Ruler:** Yoshihito (Taisho) **Obv:** Sunburst within cherry blossom circle, 3 legends separated by dots around border **Rev:** Value and denomination within flowered wreath, chrysanthemum on top

Date	Mintage	F	VF	XF	Unc	BU
Yr.2(1913)	5,910,063	4.50	9.00	20.00	60.00	100
Yr.3(1914)	1,872,331	20.00	35.00	55.00	200	400
Yr.4(1915)	2,011,253	17.50	30.00	50.00	160	300
Yr.5(1916)	8,736,768	4.00	7.50	15.00	35.00	70.00
Yr.6(1917)	9,963,232	4.00	7.50	15.00	35.00	70.00

Y# 46 50 SEN

4.9500 g., 0.7200 Silver .1148 oz. ASW, 23.8 mm. **Ruler:** Yoshihito (Taisho) **Obv:** Sunburst in center flanked by cherry blossoms, authority on top, date on bottom, all within sacred mirror **Rev:** Vertical value and denomination flanked by phoenix, paulownia crest flanked by karakusa sprigs, chrysanthemum on top

Date	Mintage	F	VF	XF	Unc	BU
Yr.11(1922)	76,320,000	BV	2.00	4.00	25.00	50.00
Yr.12(1923)	185,180,000	BV	1.75	2.50	18.00	25.00
Yr.13(1924)	78,520,000	BV	1.75	2.50	18.00	25.00
Yr.14(1925)	47,808,000	BV	1.75	2.50	20.00	30.00
Yr.15(1926)	32,572,000	BV	1.75	2.50	22.00	35.00

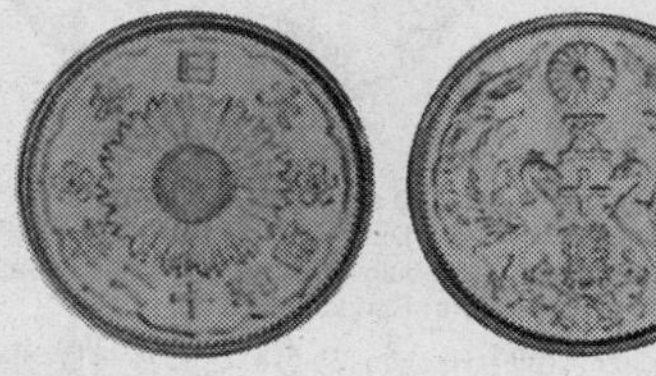

Y# 50 50 SEN

4.9500 g., 0.7200 Silver .1148 oz. ASW **Ruler:** Hirohito (Showa) **Obv:** Sunburst in center flanked by cherry blossoms, authority on top, date on bottom, all within sacred mirror **Rev:** Vertical value and denomination flanked by phoenix, paulownia crest flanked by karakusa sprigs, chrysanthemum on top

Date	Mintage	F	VF	XF	Unc	BU
Yr.3(1928)	38,592,000	—	BV	2.00	10.00	30.00
Yr.4(1929)	12,568,000	BV	2.00	5.00	30.00	60.00
Yr.5(1930)	10,200,000	BV	2.25	5.50	20.00	40.00
Yr.6(1931)	27,677,501	—	BV	2.00	9.00	12.50
Yr.7(1932)	24,132,795	—	BV	2.00	9.00	12.50
Yr.8(1933)	10,001,973	BV	2.25	7.00	22.00	40.00
Yr.9(1934)	20,003,995	—	BV	2.00	9.00	12.50
Yr.10(1935)	11,738,334	—	BV	2.00	9.00	15.00
Yr.11(1936)	44,272,796	—	BV	2.00	7.00	10.00
Yr.12(1937)	48,000,533	—	BV	2.00	7.00	10.00
Yr.13(1938)	3,600,717	50.00	75.00	125	250	350

Y# 67 50 SEN

4.5000 g., Brass **Ruler:** Hirohito (Showa) **Obv:** Stalks of wheat and rice flanked by fish, crossed pick and hoe within stalks, authority on top, date on bottom **Rev:** Phoenix among clouds, chrysanthemum on top, value and denomination on bottom **Note:** Varieties exist.

Date	Mintage	F	VF	XF	Unc	BU
Yr.21(1946)	268,161,000	0.25	0.50	1.00	2.50	3.50
Yr.22(1947)	Inc. above	—	600	900	1,700	2,250

Note: Not released to circulation

Y# 69 50 SEN

2.8000 g., Brass **Ruler:** Hirohito (Showa) **Obv:** Numeral 50 within center circle flanked by dots, authority on top, date on bottom **Rev:** Value and denomination at left of 1/2 cherry blossom wreath, chrysanthemum on top

Date	Mintage	F	VF	XF	Unc	BU
Yr.22(1947)	849,234,445	0.10	0.20	0.40	0.90	1.25
Yr.23(1948)	Inc. above	0.10	0.20	0.40	0.90	1.25

Y# A25.3 YEN

26.9600 g., 0.9000 Silver .7800 oz. ASW, 38.1 mm.
Ruler: Mutsuhito (Meiji) **Obv:** Dragon within beaded circle, legends above, written value below **Rev:** Value within wreath, chrysanthemum above **Note:** Reduced size.

Date	Mintage	F	VF	XF	Unc	BU
Yr.34(1901)	1,256,252	15.00	30.00	50.00	160	250
Yr.35(1902)	668,782	25.00	50.00	75.00	225	400
Yr.36(1903)	5,131,096	15.00	27.50	42.50	140	200
Yr.37(1904)	6,970,843	15.00	27.50	42.50	140	200
Yr.38(1905)	5,031,096	15.00	27.50	42.50	140	200
Yr.39(1906)	3,471,297	25.00	50.00	85.00	275	550
Yr.41(1908)	334,705	50.00	100	150	500	1,000
Yr.45(1912)	5,000,000	12.50	25.00	42.50	120	175

Y# 38 YEN

26.9600 g., 0.9000 Silver .7800 oz. ASW **Ruler:** Yoshihito (Taisho) **Obv:** Dragon within beaded circle, 3 legends separated by dots around border **Rev:** Value and denomination within flowered wreath, chrysanthemum on top

Date	Mintage	F	VF	XF	Unc	BU
Yr.3(1914)	11,500,000	12.50	22.50	35.00	110	150

Y# 32 5 YEN

4.1666 g., 0.9000 Gold .1205 oz. AGW **Ruler:** Mutsuhito (Meiji) **Obv:** Sunburst superimposed on sacred mirror, legends around border, value separated by paulownia crests **Rev:** Value within wreath, chrysanthemum above

Date	Mintage	F	VF	XF	Unc	BU
Yr.36(1903)	21,956	800	950	1,250	2,250	2,750
Yr.44(1911)	59,880	750	900	1,200	2,150	2,500
Yr.45(1912)	59,880	600	750	1,000	1,750	2,000

Y# 39 5 YEN

4.1666 g., 0.9000 Gold .1205 oz. AGW **Ruler:** Yoshihito (Taisho) **Obv:** Sunburst within mirror, 3 legends around border, value on bottom **Rev:** Value and denomination within flowered wreath, chrysanthemum on top

Date	Mintage	F	VF	XF	Unc	BU
Yr.2(1913)	89,820	700	900	1,150	1,850	2,250
Yr.13(1924)	76,037	600	750	950	1,650	2,000

Y# 51 5 YEN

4.1666 g., 0.9000 Gold .1205 oz. AGW **Ruler:** Hirohito (Showa)

Date	Mintage	F	VF	XF	Unc	BU
Yr.5(1930)	852,563	20,000	35,000	50,000	65,000	75,000

Y# 33 10 YEN

8.3333 g., 0.9000 Gold .2411 oz. AGW **Ruler:** Mutsuhito (Meiji) **Obv:** Sunburst superimposed on sacred mirror, legends around border, value separated by paulownia crests **Rev:** Value within wreath, chrysanthemum above

Date	Mintage	VG	F	VF	XF	BU
Yr.34(1901)	1,654,682	—	400	550	750	1,250
Yr.35(1902)	3,023,940	—	400	550	750	1,350
Yr.36(1903)	2,902,184	—	400	550	750	1,350
Yr.37(1904)	724,548	—	750	1,500	2,000	4,000
Yr.40(1907)	157,684	—	450	700	1,250	2,350
Yr.41(1908)	1,160,674	—	400	550	750	1,250
Yr.42(1909)	2,165,660	—	350	550	750	1,200
Yr.43(1910)	8,982	—	7,500	10,000	15,000	25,000

Y# 34 20 YEN

16.6666 g., 0.9000 Gold .4823 oz. AGW **Ruler:** Mutsuhito (Meiji) **Obv:** Sunburst superimposed on sacred mirror, legends around border, authority above, date below **Rev:** Value within wreath, chrysanthemum above

Date	Mintage	VG	F	VF	XF	BU
Yr.36(1903) Rare	—	—	—	—	—	—
Yr.37(1904)	2,759,470	—	550	1,250	1,750	2,400
Yr.38(1905)	1,045,904	—	550	1,250	1,750	2,400
Yr.39(1906)	1,331,332	—	550	1,250	1,750	2,400
Yr.40(1907)	817,363	—	1,000	2,000	2,500	4,500
Yr.41(1908)	458,082	—	1,250	2,500	3,500	5,500
Yr.42(1909)	557,882	—	1,500	3,000	4,000	6,500
Yr.43(1910)	2,163,644	—	500	1,000	1,600	2,200
Yr.44(1911)	1,470,057	—	500	1,000	1,600	2,200
Yr.45(1912)	1,272,450	—	525	1,100	1,700	2,300

Y40.1 20 YEN

16.6666 g., 0.9000 Gold .4823 oz. AGW **Ruler:** Yoshihito (Taisho) **Obv:** Japanese character "first" used in date **Rev:** Value and denomination within wreath, chrysanthemum on top

Date	Mintage	VG	F	VF	XF	BU
Yr.1(1912)	177,644	—	700	1,400	2,200	3,000

Y# 40.2 20 YEN

16.6666 g., 0.9000 Gold .4823 oz. AGW **Ruler:** Yoshihito (Taisho) **Obv:** Sunburst within mirror, 3 legends separated by cherry blossoms, date on bottom **Rev:** Value and denomination within wreath, chrysanthemum on top

Date	Mintage	VG	F	VF	XF	BU
Yr.2(1913)	869,248	—	500	1,000	1,700	2,300
Yr.3(1914)	1,042,890	—	500	1,000	1,700	2,300
Yr.4(1915)	1,509,960	—	500	1,000	1,700	2,300
Yr.5(1916)	2,376,641	—	450	900	1,600	2,200
Yr.6(1917)	6,208,885	—	425	850	1,550	2,150
Yr.7(1918)	3,118,647	—	450	900	1,600	2,200
Yr.8(1919)	1,531,217	—	450	900	1,600	2,200
Yr.9(1920)	370,366	—	550	1,150	1,800	2,650

Y# 52 20 YEN

16.6666 g., 0.9000 Gold .4823 oz. AGW **Ruler:** Hirohito (Showa) **Obv:** Sunburst within mirror, legends separated by cherry blossoms around border **Rev:** Value and denomination within wreath, chrysanthemum on top

Date	Mintage	VG	F	VF	XF	BU
Yr.5(1930)	11,055,500	—	15,000	25,000	35,000	45,000
Yr.6(1931)	7,526,476	—	17,500	27,500	37,500	47,500
Yr.7(1932) Rare	—	—	—	—	—	—

REFORM COINAGE

Y# 70 YEN

3.2000 g., Brass, 19.5 mm. **Ruler:** Hirohito (Showa) **Obv:** Numeral 1 within circle, flanked by dots, authority on top, date on bottom **Rev:** Value and denomination above 3/4 orange blossom wreath

Date	Mintage	F	VF	XF	Unc	BU
Yr.23(1948)	451,170,000	—	0.25	0.50	2.00	—
Yr.24(1949)	Inc. above	—	0.15	0.35	1.25	—
Yr.25(1950)	Inc. above	—	0.15	0.35	1.25	—

Y# 74 YEN

1.0000 g., Aluminum, 20 mm. **Ruler:** Hirohito (Showa) **Obv:** Sprouting branch in center, authority on top, value and denomination on bottom **Rev:** Numeral 1 within 2 inner circles, date on bottom

Date	Mintage	VG	F	VF	XF	BU
Yr.30(1955)	381,700,000	—	—	—	—	15.00
Yr.31(1956)	500,900,000	—	—	—	—	7.50
Yr.32(1957)	492,000,000	—	—	—	—	7.50
Yr.33(1958)	374,900,000	—	—	—	—	7.50
Yr.34(1959)	208,600,000	—	—	—	—	9.00
Yr.35(1960)	300,000,000	—	—	—	—	5.00
Yr.36(1961)	432,400,000	—	—	—	—	3.00
Yr.37(1962)	572,000,000	—	—	—	—	2.00
Yr.38(1963)	788,700,000	—	—	—	—	2.00
Yr.39(1964)	1,665,100,000	—	—	—	—	2.00
Yr.40(1965)	1,743,256,000	—	—	—	—	1.50
Yr.41(1966)	807,344,000	—	—	—	—	1.50
Yr.42(1967)	220,600,000	—	—	—	—	1.50
Yr.44(1969)	184,700,000	—	—	—	—	1.50
Yr.45(1970)	556,400,000	—	—	—	—	1.00
Yr.46(1971)	904,950,000	—	—	—	—	1.00
Yr.47(1972)	1,274,950,000	—	—	—	—	0.75
Yr.48(1973)	1,470,000,000	—	—	—	—	0.75
Yr.49(1974)	1,750,000,000	—	—	—	—	0.75
Yr.50(1975)	1,656,150,000	—	—	—	—	0.75
Yr.51(1976)	928,800,000	—	—	—	—	0.75
Yr.52(1977)	895,000,000	—	—	—	—	0.50
Yr.53(1978)	864,000,000	—	—	—	—	0.50
Yr.54(1979)	1,015,000,000	—	—	—	—	0.50
Yr.55(1980)	1,145,000,000	—	—	—	—	0.50
Yr.56(1981)	1,206,000,000	—	—	—	—	0.50
Yr.57(1982)	1,017,000,000	—	—	—	—	0.50
Yr.58(1983)	1,086,000,000	—	—	—	—	0.50
Yr.59(1984)	981,850,000	—	—	—	—	0.50
Yr.60(1985)	837,150,000	—	—	—	—	0.50
Yr.61(1986)	417,960,000	—	—	—	—	0.25
Yr.62(1987)	958,520,000	—	—	—	—	0.25
Yr.62(1987) Proof	230,000	Value: 1.50				
Yr.63(1988)	1,268,842,000	—	—	—	—	0.25
Yr.63(1988) Proof	200,000	Value: 1.50				
Yr.64(1989)	116,100,000	—	—	—	—	0.25

Y# 95.1 YEN

1.0000 g., Aluminum, 20 mm. **Ruler:** Akihito (Heisei) **Obv:** Sprouting branch in center, authority on top, value and denomination on bottom **Rev:** Numeral 1 within two circles, date on bottom

Date	Mintage	VG	F	VF	XF	BU
Yr.1(1989)	2,366,770,000	—	—	—	—	0.15
Yr.1(1989) Proof	200,000	Value: 1.50				

Y# 95.2 YEN

1.0000 g., Aluminum, 20 mm. **Ruler:** Akihito (Heisei) **Obv:** Sprouting branch divides authority and value **Rev:** Value within circles above date

Date	Mintage	VG	F	VF	XF	BU
Yr.2(1990)	2,768,753,000	—	—	—	—	0.15
Yr.2(1990) Proof	200,000	Value: 1.50				
Yr.3(1991)	2,300,900,000	—	—	—	—	0.15
Yr.3(1991) Proof	220,000	Value: 1.50				
Yr.4(1992)	1,298,880,000	—	—	—	—	0.15
Yr.4(1992) Proof	250,000	Value: 1.50				
Yr.5(1993)	1,260,990,000	—	—	—	—	0.15
Yr.5(1993) Proof	250,000	Value: 1.50				
Yr.6(1994)	1,040,540,000	—	—	—	—	0.15
Yr.6(1994) Proof	227,000	Value: 1.50				
Yr.7(1995)	1,041,674,000	—	—	—	—	0.15
Yr.7(1995) Proof	200,000	Value: 1.50				
Yr.8(1996)	942,024,000	—	—	—	—	0.15
Yr.8(1996) Proof	189,000	Value: 1.50				
Yr.9(1997)	782,874,000	—	—	—	—	0.15
Yr.9(1997) Proof	212,000	Value: 1.50				
Yr.10(1998)	452,412,000	—	—	—	—	0.15
Yr.10(1998) Proof	200,000	Value: 1.50				
Yr.11(1999)	66,850,000	—	—	—	—	0.15
Yr.11(1999) Proof	280,000	Value: 1.50				
Yr.12(2000)	11,800,000	—	—	—	—	0.50
Yr.12(2000) Proof	226,000	Value: 5.00				

Y# 71 5 YEN

4.0000 g., Brass **Ruler:** Hirohito (Showa) **Obv:** Pigeon within circle with authority on top, date below **Rev:** Building within circle flanked by value and denomination, all within wreath

Date	Mintage	VG	F	VF	XF	BU
Yr.23(1948)	74,520,000	—	—	0.50	0.75	12.50
Yr.24(1949)	179,692,000	—	—	0.15	0.40	8.00

Y# 72 5 YEN

3.7500 g., Brass, 22 mm. **Ruler:** Hirohito (Showa) **Obv:** Hole in center flanked by seed leaf, authority on top and date below **Rev:** Gear design around center hole with horizontal lines below, large bending stalk of rice above **Note:** Old script.

Date	Mintage	VG	F	VF	XF	BU
Yr.24(1949)	111,896,000	—	—	0.15	0.25	9.00
Yr.25(1950)	181,824,000	—	—	0.15	0.25	6.50
Yr.26(1951)	197,980,000	—	—	0.15	0.25	6.50
Yr.27(1952)	55,000,000	—	—	0.30	0.60	100
Yr.28(1953)	45,000,000	—	—	0.30	0.60	6.50
Yr.32(1957)	10,000,000	—	—	4.00	8.00	40.00
Yr.33(1958)	50,000,000	—	—	0.25	0.50	3.50

Y# 72a 5 YEN

3.7500 g., Brass, 22 mm. **Ruler:** Hirohito (Showa) **Obv:** Hole in center flanked by a seed leaf with authority on top and date below **Rev:** Gear design around center hole with horizontal lines below, large bending stalk of rice above **Note:** New script.

Date	Mintage	VG	F	VF	XF	BU
Yr.34(1959)	33,000,000	—	—	0.25	0.50	5.00
Yr.35(1960)	34,800,000	—	—	0.20	0.40	5.00
Yr.36(1961)	61,000,000	—	—	0.15	0.35	4.00
Yr.37(1962)	126,700,000	—	—	0.10	0.30	3.00
Yr.38(1963)	171,800,000	—	—	0.10	0.30	2.50
Yr.39(1964)	379,700,000	—	—	0.10	0.30	2.50
Yr.40(1965)	384,200,000	—	—	0.10	0.30	2.00
Yr.41(1966)	163,100,000	—	—	0.10	0.30	2.00
Yr.42(1967)	26,000,000	—	—	0.25	0.50	2.50
Yr.43(1968)	114,000,000	—	—	—	0.10	1.50
Yr.44(1969)	240,000,000	—	—	—	0.10	1.50
Yr.45(1970)	340,000,000	—	—	—	0.10	1.50
Yr.46(1971)	362,050,000	—	—	—	0.10	1.50
Yr.47(1972)	562,950,000	—	—	—	0.10	0.75
Yr.48(1973)	745,000,000	—	—	—	0.10	0.75
Yr.49(1974)	950,000,000	—	—	—	0.10	0.75
Yr.50(1975)	970,000,000	—	—	—	0.10	0.75
Yr.51(1976)	200,000,000	—	—	—	0.10	0.75
Yr.52(1977)	340,000,000	—	—	—	0.10	0.75
Yr.53(1978)	318,000,000	—	—	—	0.10	0.75
Yr.54(1979)	317,000,000	—	—	—	0.10	0.75
Yr.55(1980)	385,000,000	—	—	—	0.10	0.75
Yr.56(1981)	95,000,000	—	—	—	0.10	1.50
Yr.57(1982)	455,000,000	—	—	—	0.10	0.75
Yr.58(1983)	410,000,000	—	—	—	0.10	0.75
Yr.59(1984)	202,850,000	—	—	—	0.10	0.75
Yr.60(1985)	153,150,000	—	—	—	0.10	1.00
Yr.61(1986)	113,960,000	—	—	—	0.10	1.50
Yr.62(1987)	631,545,000	—	—	—	0.10	0.25
Yr.62(1987) Proof	230,000	Value: 1.75				
Yr.63(1988)	368,920,000	—	—	—	—	0.25
Yr.63(1988) Proof	200,000	Value: 1.75				
Yr.64(1989)	67,332,000	—	—	—	—	0.50

Y# 96.1 5 YEN

3.7500 g., Brass, 22 mm. **Ruler:** Akihito (Heisei) **Obv:** Hole in center flanked by a seed leaf with authority on top and date below **Rev:** Gear around center hole with bending rice stalk above value

Date	Mintage	VG	F	VF	XF	BU
Yr.1(1989)	960,460,000	—	—	—	—	0.35
Yr.1(1989) Proof	200,000	Value: 1.75				

Y# 96.2 5 YEN

3.7500 g., Brass, 22 mm. **Ruler:** Akihito (Heisei) **Obv:** Hole in center flanked by a seed leaf with authority on top and date below **Rev:** Gear design around center hole with bending rice stalk above value in horizontal lines below

Date	Mintage	VG	F	VF	XF	BU
Yr.2(1990)	520,753,000	—	—	—	—	0.35
Yr.2(1990) Proof	200,000	Value: 1.75				
Yr.3(1991)	516,900,000	—	—	—	—	0.35
Yr.3(1991) Proof	220,000	Value: 1.75				
Yr.4(1992)	300,880,000	—	—	—	—	0.35
Yr.4(1992) Proof	250,000	Value: 1.75				
Yr.5(1993)	412,990,000	—	—	—	—	0.35
Yr.5(1993) Proof	250,000	Value: 1.75				
Yr.6(1994)	197,540,000	—	—	—	—	0.35
Yr.6(1994) Proof	227,000	Value: 1.75				
Yr.7(1995)	351,674,000	—	—	—	—	0.35
Yr.7(1995) Proof	200,000	Value: 1.75				
Yr.8(1996)	207,024,000	—	—	—	—	0.35
Yr.8(1996) Proof	189,000	Value: 1.75				
Yr.9(1997)	238,874,000	—	—	—	—	0.35
Yr.9(1997) Proof	212,000	Value: 1.75				
Yr.10(1998)	172,412,000	—	—	—	—	0.35
Yr.10(1998) Proof	200,000	Value: 1.75				
Yr.11(1999)	59,850,000	—	—	—	—	0.35
Yr.11(1999) Proof	280,000	Value: 1.75				
Yr.12(2000)	8,804,000	—	—	—	—	2.50
Yr.12(2000) Proof	226,000	Value: 5.00				

Y# 73 10 YEN

4.5000 g., Bronze, 23.5 mm. **Ruler:** Hirohito (Showa) **Obv:** Temple in center with authority on top and value below **Rev:** Value and denomination within wreath **Edge:** Reeded

Date	Mintage	VG	F	VF	XF	BU
Yr.26(1951)	101,068,000	—	—	0.20	0.35	150
Yr.27(1952)	486,632,000	—	—	0.20	0.35	40.00
Yr.28(1953)	466,300,000	—	—	0.20	0.35	40.00
Yr.29(1954)	520,900,000	—	—	0.20	0.35	50.00
Yr.30(1955)	123,100,000	—	—	0.20	0.35	50.00
Yr.32(1957)	50,000,000	—	—	0.25	0.65	100
Yr.33(1958)	25,000,000	—	—	0.40	1.00	115

Y# 73a 10 YEN

4.5000 g., Bronze, 23.5 mm. **Ruler:** Hirohito (Showa) **Obv:** Temple in center with authority on top and value below **Rev:** Value and denomination within wreath **Edge:** Plain

Date	Mintage	VG	F	VF	XF	BU
Yr.34(1959)	62,400,000	—	—	—	0.20	60.00
Yr.35(1960)	225,900,000	—	—	—	0.20	45.00
Yr.36(1961)	229,900,000	—	—	—	0.20	40.00
Yr.37(1962)	284,200,000	—	—	—	0.20	5.00
Yr.38(1963)	411,300,000	—	—	—	0.20	5.00
Yr.39(1964)	479,200,000	—	—	—	0.20	3.50
Yr.40(1965)	387,600,000	—	—	—	0.20	2.50
Yr.41(1966)	395,900,000	—	—	—	0.20	2.50
Yr.42(1967)	158,900,000	—	—	—	0.20	10.00
Yr.43(1968)	363,600,000	—	—	—	0.20	2.50
Yr.44(1969)	414,800,000	—	—	—	0.20	1.50
Yr.45(1970)	382,700,000	—	—	—	0.20	2.50
Yr.46(1971)	610,050,000	—	—	—	0.20	2.00
Yr.47(1972)	634,950,000	—	—	—	0.20	1.50
Yr.48(1973)	1,345,000,000	—	—	—	0.20	1.00
Yr.49(1974)	1,780,000,000	—	—	—	0.20	1.00
Yr.50(1975)	1,280,260,000	—	—	—	0.20	1.00
Yr.51(1976)	1,369,740,000	—	—	—	0.20	1.00
Yr.52(1977)	1,467,000,000	—	—	—	0.20	1.00
Yr.53(1978)	1,435,000,000	—	—	—	0.20	1.00
Yr.54(1979)	1,207,000,000	—	—	—	0.20	1.00
Yr.55(1980)	1,127,000,000	—	—	—	0.20	0.75
Yr.56(1981)	1,369,000,000	—	—	—	0.20	0.75
Yr.57(1982)	890,000,000	—	—	—	0.20	0.75
Yr.58(1983)	870,000,000	—	—	—	0.20	0.75
Yr.59(1984)	533,850,000	—	—	—	0.20	0.75
Yr.60(1985)	335,150,000	—	—	—	0.20	0.75
Yr.61(1986)	68,960,000	—	—	—	0.25	1.50
Yr.62(1987)	165,545,000	—	—	—	0.20	0.50
Yr.62(1987) Proof	230,000	Value: 1.75				
Yr.63(1988)	617,912,000	—	—	—	—	0.50
Yr.63(1988) Proof	200,000	Value: 1.75				
Yr.64(1989)	74,692,000	—	—	—	0.25	0.75

Y# 97.1 10 YEN

4.5000 g., Bronze, 23.5 mm. **Ruler:** Akihito (Heisei) **Obv:** Temple divides authority and value **Rev:** Japanese character "first" in date

Date	Mintage	VG	F	VF	XF	BU
Yr.1(1989)	666,108,000	—	—	—	—	0.45
Yr.1(1989) Proof	200,000	Value: 1.75				

Y# 97.2 10 YEN

4.5000 g., Bronze, 23.5 mm. **Ruler:** Akihito (Heisei) **Obv:** Temple divides authority and value **Rev:** Value within wreath

Date	Mintage	VG	F	VF	XF	Unc
Yr.2(1990)	754,753,000	—	—	—	—	—
Yr.2(1990) Proof	200,000	Value: 1.75				
Yr.3(1991)	631,900,000	—	—	—	—	—
Yr.3(1991) Proof	220,000	Value: 1.75				
Yr.4(1992)	537,880,000	—	—	—	—	—
Yr.4(1992) Proof	250,000	Value: 1.75				
Yr.5(1993)	248,990,000	—	—	—	—	—
Yr.5(1993) Proof	250,000	Value: 1.75				
Yr.6(1994)	190,540,000	—	—	—	—	—
Yr.6(1994) Proof	227,000	Value: 1.75				
Yr.7(1995)	248,674,000	—	—	—	—	—
Yr.7(1995) Proof	200,000	Value: 1.75				
Yr.8(1996)	546,024,000	—	—	—	—	—
Yr.8(1996) Proof	189,000	Value: 1.75				
Yr.9(1997)	490,874,000	—	—	—	—	—
Yr.9(1997) Proof	212,000	Value: 1.75				
Yr.10(1998)	410,412,000	—	—	—	—	—
Yr.10(1998) Proof	200,000	Value: 1.75				
Yr.11(1999)	356,250,000	—	—	—	—	—
Yr.11(1999) Proof	280,000	Value: 1.75				

Date	Mintage	VG	F	VF	XF	Unc
Yr.12(2000)	314,800,000	—	—	—	—	—
Yr.12(2000) Proof	226,000	Value: 1.75				

Y# 75 50 YEN

5.5000 g., Nickel, 24 mm. **Ruler:** Hirohito (Showa) **Obv:** Chrysanthemum blossom, authority on top, value at bottom **Rev:** Numeral 50 within center design, regnal era on top, date on bottom

Date	Mintage	VG	F	VF	XF	BU
Yr.30(1955)	63,700,000	—	—	0.75	1.50	15.00
Yr.31(1956)	91,300,000	—	—	0.75	1.00	15.00
Yr.32(1957)	39,000,000	—	—	0.75	1.50	15.00
Yr.33(1958)	18,000,000	—	—	1.00	2.50	25.00

Y# 76 50 YEN

5.0000 g., Nickel, 25 mm. **Ruler:** Hirohito (Showa) **Rev:** Value above hole in center

Date	Mintage	VG	F	VF	XF	BU
Yr.34(1959)	23,900,000	—	—	1.00	2.50	12.50
Yr.35(1960)	6,000,000	—	—	12.50	22.50	50.00
Yr.36(1961)	16,000,000	—	—	2.00	4.00	15.00
Yr.37(1962)	50,300,000	—	—	0.75	1.25	5.00
Yr.38(1963)	55,000,000	—	—	0.75	1.25	5.00
Yr.39(1964)	69,200,000	—	—	0.75	1.25	5.00
Yr.40(1965)	189,300,000	—	—	0.75	1.00	2.00
Yr.41(1966)	171,500,000	—	—	0.75	1.25	2.50

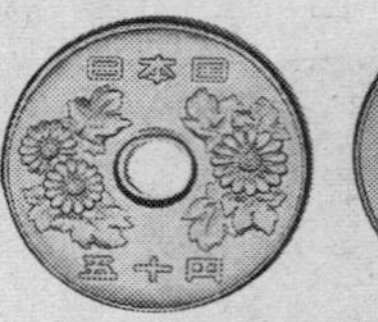

Y# 81 50 YEN

4.0000 g., Copper-Nickel, 21 mm. **Ruler:** Hirohito (Showa) **Obv:** Center hole flanked by chrysanthemums, authority on top and value below **Rev:** Numeral 50 above center hole with date below

Date	Mintage	VG	F	VF	XF	BU
Yr.42(1967)	238,400,000	—	—	—	0.75	7.50
Yr.43(1968)	200,000,000	—	—	—	0.75	5.00
Yr.44(1969)	210,000,000	—	—	—	0.75	5.00
Yr.45(1970)	269,800,000	—	—	—	0.75	5.00
Yr.46(1971)	80,950,000	—	—	—	0.75	5.00
Yr.47(1972)	138,980,000	—	—	—	0.75	4.00
Yr.48(1973)	200,970,000	—	—	—	0.75	4.00
Yr.49(1974)	470,000,000	—	—	—	0.75	2.00
Yr.50(1975)	238,120,000	—	—	—	0.75	1.50
Yr.51(1976)	241,880,000	—	—	—	0.75	1.50
Yr.52(1977)	176,000,000	—	—	—	0.75	4.00
Yr.53(1978)	234,000,000	—	—	—	0.75	1.50
Yr.54(1979)	110,000,000	—	—	—	0.75	2.00
Yr.55(1980)	51,000,000	—	—	—	0.75	2.00
Yr.56(1981)	179,000,000	—	—	—	0.75	1.00
Yr.57(1982)	30,000,000	—	—	—	0.75	2.00
Yr.58(1983)	30,000,000	—	—	—	0.75	2.00
Yr.59(1984)	29,850,000	—	—	—	0.75	2.50
Yr.60(1985)	10,150,000	—	—	—	0.75	4.00
Yr.61(1986)	9,960,000	—	—	—	0.75	2.50
Yr.62(1987)	545,000	—	—	40.00	60.00	85.00
Yr.62(1987) Proof	230,000	Value: 100				
Yr.63(1988)	108,912,000	—	—	—	—	1.50
Yr.63(1988) Proof	200,000	Value: 2.00				

Y# 101.1 50 YEN

4.0000 g., Copper-Nickel, 21 mm. **Ruler:** Akihito (Heisei) **Obv:** Center hole flanked by chrysanthemums, authority at top and value below **Rev:** Numeral 50 above center hole with date below

Date	Mintage	VG	F	VF	XF	BU
Yr.1(1989)	244,800,000	—	—	—	—	1.00
Yr.1(1989) Proof	200,000	Value: 2.00				

Y# 101.2 50 YEN

4.0000 g., Copper-Nickel, 21 mm. **Ruler:** Akihito (Heisei) **Obv:** Center hole flanked by chrysanthemums, authority at top and value below **Rev:** Value above hole in center

Date	Mintage	VG	F	VF	XF	BU
Yr.2(1990)	274,753,000	—	—	—	—	1.00
Yr.2(1990) Proof	200,000	Value: 2.00				
Yr.3(1991)	208,900,000	—	—	—	—	1.00
Yr.3(1991) Proof	220,000	Value: 2.00				
Yr.4(1992)	48,880,000	—	—	—	—	1.00
Yr.4(1992) Proof	250,000	Value: 2.00				
Yr.5(1993)	50,990,000	—	—	—	—	1.00
Yr.5(1993) Proof	250,000	Value: 2.00				
Yr.6(1994)	65,540,000	—	—	—	—	1.00
Yr.6(1994) Proof	227,000	Value: 2.00				
Yr.7(1995)	111,674,000	—	—	—	—	1.00
Yr.7(1995) Proof	200,000	Value: 2.00				
Yr.8(1996)	82,024,000	—	—	—	—	1.00
Yr.8(1996) Proof	189,000	Value: 2.00				
Yr.9(1997)	149,876,000	—	—	—	—	1.00
Yr.9(1997) Proof	212,000	Value: 2.00				
Yr.10(1998)	100,412,000	—	—	—	—	1.00
Yr.10(1998) Proof	200,000	Value: 2.00				
Yr.11(1999)	58,850,000	—	—	—	—	1.00
Yr.11(1999) Proof	280,000	Value: 2.00				
Yr.12(2000)	6,800,000	—	—	—	—	7.50
Yr.12(2000) Proof	226,000	Value: 8.00				

Y# 77 100 YEN

4.8000 g., 0.6000 Silver .0926 oz. ASW, 22.5 mm. **Ruler:** Hirohito (Showa) **Obv:** Phoenix

Date	Mintage	F	VF	XF	Unc	BU
Yr.32(1957)	30,000,000	—	1.50	2.50	7.00	9.00
Yr.33(1958)	70,000,000	—	1.50	2.50	5.00	6.00

Y# 78 100 YEN

4.8000 g., 0.6000 Silver .0926 oz. ASW, 22.5 mm. **Ruler:** Hirohito (Showa) **Obv:** Sheaf of rice in center with authority on top and value below **Rev:** Numeral 100 within circle flanked by 1/4 lined wreath with era on top and year below

Date	Mintage	VG	F	VF	XF	BU
Yr.34(1959)	110,000,000	—	—	1.50	2.50	7.00
Yr.35(1960)	50,000,000	—	—	1.50	2.50	9.00
Yr.36(1961)	15,000,000	—	—	1.50	2.50	9.00
Yr.38(1963)	45,000,000	—	—	1.50	2.50	9.00
Yr.39(1964)	10,000,000	—	—	1.75	3.50	9.00
Yr.40(1965)	62,500,000	—	—	1.50	2.50	4.00
Yr.41(1966)	97,500,000	—	—	1.50	2.50	4.00

Y# 79 100 YEN

4.8000 g., 0.6000 Silver .0926 oz. ASW, 22.5 mm. **Ruler:** Hirohito (Showa) **Subject:** 1964 Olympic Games **Obv:** Olympic circles on base of flaming torch flanked by authority above and value below **Rev:** Numeral 100 within center circle

Date	Mintage	VG	F	VF	XF	BU
Yr.39/1964	80,000,000	—	—	1.50	2.50	4.00

Y# 82 100 YEN

4.2000 g., Copper-Nickel, 22.5 mm. **Ruler:** Hirohito (Showa) **Obv:** Cherry blossoms **Rev:** Large numeral 100 in center

Date	Mintage	VG	F	VF	XF	BU
Yr.42(1967)	432,200,000	—	—	—	1.50	7.50
Note: Varieties exist						
Yr.43(1968)	471,000,000	—	—	—	1.50	5.00
Yr.44(1969)	323,700,000	—	—	—	1.50	7.50
Yr.45(1970)	237,100,000	—	—	—	1.50	5.00
Yr.46(1971)	481,050,000	—	—	—	1.50	2.50
Yr.47(1972)	468,950,000	—	—	—	1.50	2.00
Yr.48(1973)	680,000,000	—	—	—	1.50	2.00
Yr.49(1974)	660,000,000	—	—	—	1.50	2.00
Yr.50(1975)	437,160,000	—	—	—	1.50	2.00
Yr.51(1976)	322,840,000	—	—	—	1.50	2.00
Yr.52(1977)	440,000,000	—	—	—	1.50	2.00
Yr.53(1978)	292,000,000	—	—	—	1.50	2.00
Yr.54(1979)	382,000,000	—	—	—	1.50	2.00
Yr.55(1980)	588,000,000	—	—	—	1.50	2.00
Yr.56(1981)	348,000,000	—	—	—	1.50	2.00
Yr.57(1982)	110,000,000	—	—	—	1.50	3.00
Yr.58(1983)	50,000,000	—	—	—	1.50	5.00
Yr.59(1984)	41,850,000	—	—	—	1.50	5.00
Yr.60(1985)	58,150,000	—	—	—	1.50	5.00
Yr.61(1986)	99,960,000	—	—	—	1.50	2.00
Yr.62(1987)	193,545,000	—	—	—	1.50	2.00
Yr.62(1987) Proof	230,000	Value: 5.00				
Yr.63(1988)	362,912,000	—	—	—	1.50	2.00
Yr.63(1988) Proof	200,000	Value: 5.00				

Y# 83 100 YEN

9.0000 g., Copper-Nickel, 28 mm. **Ruler:** Hirohito (Showa) **Subject:** Osaka Expo '70 **Obv:** Mt. Fuji **Rev:** Circles within world globe with value above

Date	Mintage	VG	F	VF	XF	BU
Yr.45(1970)	40,000,000	—	—	2.50	3.50	6.00

Y# 84 100 YEN

12.0000 g., Copper-Nickel, 30 mm. **Ruler:** Hirohito (Showa) **Subject:** 1972 Winter Olympic Games - Sapporo **Obv:** Olympic torch with flame flanked by authority and city name **Rev:** Large numeral 100 above olympic circles flanked by flower designs

Date	Mintage	VG	F	VF	XF	BU
Yr.47/1972	30,000,000	—	—	3.00	4.50	7.50

Y# 85 100 YEN

9.8000 g., Copper-Nickel, 22.5 mm. **Ruler:** Hirohito (Showa) **Subject:** Okinawa Expo '75 **Obv:** Gate of Shurei **Rev:** Value in center flanked by dolphins with legend above and below

Date	Mintage	VG	F	VF	XF	BU
Yr.50(1975)	120,000,000	—	—	1.75	2.50	3.50

Y# 86 100 YEN

12.0000 g., Copper-Nickel, 30 mm. **Ruler:** Hirohito (Showa) **Subject:** 50th Anniversary of Reign **Obv:** Imperial Palace and Niju Bridge **Rev:** Chrysanthemum in center flanked by phoenix with inscription above and below

Date	Mintage	VG	F	VF	XF	BU
Yr.51(1976)	70,000,000	—	—	2.50	3.50	6.00

Y# 98.1 100 YEN

9.8000 g., Copper-Nickel, 22.5 mm. **Ruler:** Akihito (Heisei) **Obv:** Cherry blossoms **Rev:** Japanese character "first" in date

Date	Mintage	VG	F	VF	XF	BU
Yr.1(1989)	368,800,000	—	—	—	—	2.00
Yr.1(1989) Proof	200,000	Value: 5.00				

Y# 98.2 100 YEN

9.8000 g., Copper-Nickel, 22.5 mm. **Ruler:** Akihito (Heisei) **Obv:** Cherry blossoms **Rev:** Large numeral 100

Date	Mintage	VG	F	VF	XF	BU
Yr.2(1990)	444,753,000	—	—	—	—	2.00
Yr.2(1990) Proof	200,000	Value: 5.00				
Yr.3(1991)	374,900,000	—	—	—	—	2.00
Yr.3(1991) Proof	220,000	Value: 5.00				
Yr.4(1992)	211,050,000	—	—	—	—	2.00
Yr.4(1992) Proof	250,000	Value: 5.00				
Yr.5(1993)	81,990,000	—	—	—	—	2.00
Yr.5(1993) Proof	250,000	Value: 5.00				
Yr.6(1994)	81,540,000	—	—	—	—	2.00
Yr.6(1994) Proof	227,000	Value: 5.00				
Yr.7(1995)	92,674,000	—	—	—	—	2.00
Yr.7(1995) Proof	200,000	Value: 5.00				
Yr.8(1996)	237,024,000	—	—	—	—	2.00
Yr.8(1996) Proof	189,000	Value: 5.00				
Yr.9(1997)	271,876,000	—	—	—	—	2.00
Yr.9(1997) Proof	212,000	Value: 5.00				
Yr.10(1998)	252,412,000	—	—	—	—	2.00
Yr.10(1998) Proof	200,000	Value: 5.00				
Yr.11(1999)	178,850,000	—	—	—	—	2.00
Yr.11(1999) Proof	280,000	Value: 5.00				
Yr.12(2000)	171,800,000	—	—	—	—	2.00
Yr.12(2000) Proof	226,000	Value: 5.00				

Y# 87 500 YEN

7.2000 g., Copper-Nickel, 26.5 mm. **Ruler:** Hirohito (Showa) **Obv:** Pawlownia flower **Rev:** Numeral 500 in center flanked by cherry blossoms **Edge Lettering:** NIPPON 500

Date	Mintage	VG	F	VF	XF	BU
Yr.57(1982)	300,000,000	—	—	—	7.00	9.00
Yr.58(1983)	240,000,000	—	—	—	7.00	9.00
Yr.59(1984)	342,850,000	—	—	—	7.00	9.00
Yr.60(1985)	97,150,000	—	—	—	7.00	9.00
Yr.61(1986)	49,960,000	—	—	—	7.00	9.00
Yr.62(1987)	2,545,000	—	—	7.00	9.00	15.00
Yr.62(1987) Proof	230,000	Value: 25.00				
Yr.63(1988)	148,018,000	—	—	—	7.00	9.00
Yr.63(1988) Proof	200,000	Value: 15.00				
Yr.64(1989)	16,042,000	—	—	—	7.00	12.00

Y# 88 500 YEN

13.0000 g., Copper-Nickel, 30 mm. **Ruler:** Hirohito (Showa) **Subject:** 1985 Tsukuba Expo **Obv:** Mt. Tsukuba above cherry blossoms **Rev:** Circles within triangular design above value flanked by cherry blossom **Edge Lettering:** TSUKUBA EXPO '85

Date	Mintage	VG	F	VF	XF	BU
Yr.60(1985)	70,000,000	—	—	—	7.50	10.00

Y# 89 500 YEN

13.0000 g., Copper-Nickel, 30 mm. **Ruler:** Hirohito (Showa) **Subject:** 100th Anniversary - Governmental Cabinet System **Obv:** Prime Minister's official residence **Rev:** Large numeral 500 within center square **Edge Lettering:** NAIKAKU 100 NEN

Date	Mintage	VG	F	VF	XF	BU
Yr.60(1985)	70,000,000	—	—	—	7.50	10.00

Y# 90 500 YEN

13.0000 g., Copper-Nickel, 30 mm. **Ruler:** Hirohito (Showa) **Subject:** 60 Years of Reign of Hirohito **Obv:** Large chrysanthemum with legends around border **Rev:** Shishinden Palace **Designer:** Ikuo Hirayama

Date	Mintage	VG	F	VF	XF	BU
Yr.61(1986)	50,000,000	—	—	—	8.00	12.00

Y# 93 500 YEN

13.0000 g., Copper-Nickel, 30 mm. **Ruler:** Hirohito (Showa) **Subject:** Opening of Seikan Tunnel **Obv:** Seikan tunnel flanked by sea gulls **Rev:** Map within ribbon above value

Date	Mintage	VG	F	VF	XF	BU
Yr.63(1988)	20,000,000	—	—	—	8.50	12.50

Y# 94 500 YEN

13.0000 g., Copper-Nickel, 30 mm. **Ruler:** Hirohito (Showa) **Subject:** Opening of Seto Bridge **Obv:** Seto Bridge **Rev:** Map within ribbon above value

Date	Mintage	VG	F	VF	XF	BU
Yr.63(1988)	20,000,000	—	—	—	8.50	12.50

Y# 99.1 500 YEN

7.2000 g., Copper-Nickel, 26.5 mm. **Ruler:** Akihito (Heisei) **Obv:** Pawlownia flower **Rev:** Value flanked by cherry blossoms

Date	Mintage	VG	F	VF	XF	BU
Yr.1(1989)	192,652,000	—	—	—	7.00	9.00
Yr.1(1989) Proof	200,000	Value: 15.00				

Y# 99.2 500 YEN

7.2000 g., Copper-Nickel, 26.5 mm. **Ruler:** Akihito (Heisei) **Obv:** Pawlownia flower **Rev:** Value flanked by cherry blossoms

Date	Mintage	VG	F	VF	XF	BU
Yr.2(1990)	159,753,000	—	—	—	7.00	9.00
Yr.2(1990) Proof	200,000	Value: 15.00				
Yr.3(1991)	169,900,000	—	—	—	7.00	9.00
Yr.3(1991) Proof	220,000	Value: 15.00				
Yr.4(1992)	87,880,000	—	—	—	7.00	9.00
Yr.4(1992) Proof	250,000	Value: 15.00				
Yr.5(1993)	131,990,000	—	—	—	7.00	9.00
Yr.5(1993) Proof	250,000	Value: 15.00				
Yr.6(1994)	105,545,000	—	—	—	7.00	9.00
Yr.6(1994) Proof	227,000	Value: 15.00				
Yr.7(1995)	182,669,000	—	—	—	—	9.00
Yr.7(1995) Proof	200,000	Value: 15.00				
Yr.8(1996)	99,024,000	—	—	—	—	9.00
Yr.8(1996) Proof	189,000	Value: 15.00				
Yr.9(1997)	172,878,000	—	—	—	—	9.00
Yr.9(1997) Proof	212,000	Value: 15.00				
Yr.10(1998)	214,408,000	—	—	—	—	9.00
Yr.10(1998) Proof	200,000	Value: 15.00				
Yr.11(1999)	164,840,000	—	—	—	—	9.00
Yr.11(1999) Proof	280,000	Value: 15.00				
Yr.12(2000)	172,026,000	—	—	—	—	9.00

Y# 102 500 YEN

13.0000 g., Copper-Nickel, 30 mm. **Ruler:** Akihito (Heisei) **Subject:** Enthronement of Emperor Akihito **Obv:** Carriage **Rev:** Chrysanthemum crest among leaves above value

Date	Mintage	VG	F	VF	XF	BU
Yr.2(1990)	30,000,000	—	—	—	—	13.50

Y# 106 500 YEN

13.0000 g., Copper-Nickel, 30 mm. **Ruler:** Akihito (Heisei) **Subject:** 20th Anniversary - Reversion of Okinawa **Obv:** Building **Rev:** Value and denomination flanked by upright dragons

Date	Mintage	VG	F	VF	XF	BU
Yr.4(1992)	19,953,000	—	—	—	—	14.50
Yr.4(1992) Proof	47,000	Value: 27.50				

Y# 107 500 YEN

7.2000 g., Copper-Nickel, 26.5 mm. **Ruler:** Akihito (Heisei) **Subject:** Royal wedding of Crown Prince **Obv:** Chrysanthemum flanked by cherry blossom sprigs with legend around border **Rev:** Pair of flying herons

Date	Mintage	VG	F	VF	XF	BU
Yr.5(1993)	29,800,000	—	—	—	—	16.00
Yr.5(1993) Proof	200,000	Value: 22.50				

Y# 110 500 YEN
7.2000 g., Copper-Nickel, 26.5 mm. **Ruler:** Akihito (Heisei) **Subject:** Opening of Kansai International Airport **Obv:** Flying jet **Rev:** Design within ribbon

Date	Mintage	VG	F	VF	XF	BU
Yr.6(1994)	19,900,000	—	—	—	—	14.50
Yr.6(1994) Proof	100,000	Value: 42.50				

Y# 111 500 YEN
7.2000 g., Copper-Nickel, 26.5 mm. **Ruler:** Akihito (Heisei) **Subject:** 12th Asian Games **Obv:** Styilized runners **Rev:** Artistic design above value

Date	Mintage	VG	F	VF	XF	BU
Yr.6(1994)	9,900,000	—	—	—	—	13.50
Yr.6(1994) Proof	100,000	Value: 32.50				

Y# 112 500 YEN
7.2000 g., Copper-Nickel, 26.5 mm. **Ruler:** Akihito (Heisei) **Subject:** 12th Asian Games **Obv:** Stylized swimmers **Rev:** Artistic design above value

Date	Mintage	VG	F	VF	XF	BU
Yr.6(1994)	9,900,000	—	—	—	—	13.50
Yr.6(1994) Proof	100,000	Value: 32.50				

Y# 113 500 YEN
7.2000 g., Copper-Nickel, 26.5 mm. **Ruler:** Akihito (Heisei) **Subject:** 12th Asian Games **Obv:** Stylized jumper **Rev:** Artistic design above value

Date	Mintage	VG	F	VF	XF	BU
Yr.6(1994)	9,900,000	—	—	—	—	13.50
Yr.6(1994) Proof	100,000	Value: 32.50				

Y# 114 500 YEN
7.2000 g., Copper-Nickel, 26.5 mm. **Ruler:** Akihito (Heisei) **Series:** 1998 Nagano Winter Olympics **Obv:** Snowboarder **Rev:** Bird, value and dates

Date	Mintage	VG	F	VF	XF	BU
Yr.9(1997)	19,867,000	—	—	—	—	14.50
Yr.9(1997) Proof	133,000	Value: 35.00				

Y# 117 500 YEN
7.2000 g., Copper-Nickel, 26.5 mm. **Ruler:** Akihito (Heisei) **Series:** 1998 Nagano Winter Olympics **Obv:** Bobsledding **Rev:** Bird, value and dates

Date	Mintage	VG	F	VF	XF	BU
Yr.9(1997)	19,867,000	—	—	—	—	14.50
Yr.9(1997) Proof	133,000	Value: 35.00				

Y# 118 500 YEN
7.2000 g., Copper-Nickel, 26.5 mm. **Ruler:** Akihito (Heisei) **Series:** 1998 Nagano Winter Olympics **Obv:** Acrobat skier **Rev:** Bird, value and dates

Date	Mintage	VG	F	VF	XF	BU
Yr.10(1998)	19,867,000	—	—	—	—	14.50
Yr.10(1998) Proof	133,000	Value: 35.00				

Y# 123 500 YEN
7.2000 g., Copper-Nickel, 26.5 mm. **Ruler:** Akihito (Heisei) **Subject:** 10th Anniversary of Enthronement **Obv:** Mt. Fuji and chrysanthemums **Rev:** Chrysanthemum within wreath

Date	Mintage	VG	F	VF	XF	BU
Yr.11(1999)	14,900,000	—	—	—	—	11.50
Yr.11(1999) Proof	100,000	Value: 32.00				

Y# 125 500 YEN
7.0000 g., Nickel-Brass, 26.5 mm. **Ruler:** Akihito (Heisei) **Obv:** Pawlownia flower and highlighted legends **Rev:** Value with latent zeros **Edge:** Slanted reeding

Date	Mintage	VG	F	VF	XF	BU
Yr.12(2000)	595,746,000	—	—	—	—	9.00
Yr.12(2000) Proof	226,000	Value: 15.00				

Y# 80 1000 YEN
20.0000 g., 0.9250 Silver .5948 oz. ASW **Ruler:** Hirohito (Showa) **Series:** 1964 Olympic Games **Obv:** Mt. Fuji within sprigs of cherry blossoms **Rev:** Value and olympic circles flanked by cherry blossoms **Note:** Dav. #276

Date	Mintage	VG	F	VF	XF	BU
Yr.39(1964)	15,000,000	—	—	—	20.00	35.00

Y# 100 5000 YEN
15.0000 g., 0.9250 Silver .4461 oz. ASW **Ruler:** Akihito (Heisei) **Subject:** Osaka Exposition **Obv:** Head with flowers in hair left **Rev:** Flower design above value

Date	Mintage	F	VF	XF	Unc	BU
Yr.2 (1990)	10,000,000	—	—	—	—	65.00

Y# 103 5000 YEN
15.0000 g., 0.9250 Silver .4461 oz. ASW **Ruler:** Akihito (Heisei) **Subject:** Centennial of Parliament **Obv:** Parliament building **Rev:** Winged figures flank central figure

Date	Mintage	VG	F	VF	XF	BU
Yr.2(1990)	5,000,000	—	—	—	—	65.00

Y# 104 5000 YEN
15.0000 g., 0.9250 Silver .4461 oz. ASW **Ruler:** Akihito (Heisei) **Subject:** Centennial of Judicial System **Obv:** Court room scene **Rev:** Value within center circle and flowered wreath

Date	Mintage	VG	F	VF	XF	BU
Yr.2(1990)	5,000,000	—	—	—	—	65.00

Y# 108 5000 YEN
15.0000 g., 1.0000 Silver .4823 oz. ASW **Ruler:** Akihito (Heisei) **Subject:** Royal Wedding of Crown Prince **Obv:** Chrysanthemum flanked by sprigs **Rev:** Pair of flying herons

Date	Mintage	VG	F	VF	XF	BU
Yr.5(1993)	4,800,000	—	—	—	—	70.00
Yr.5(1993) Proof	200,000	Value: 100				

Y# 115 5000 YEN
15.0000 g., 0.9250 Silver .4461 oz. ASW **Ruler:** Akihito (Heisei) **Series:** 1998 Nagano Winter Olympics **Obv:** Hockey player **Rev:** Value, dates, and Serow

Date	Mintage	VG	F	VF	XF	BU
Yr.9(1997)	4,867,000	—	—	—	—	70.00
Yr.9(1997) Proof	133,000	Value: 120				

Y# 119 5000 YEN
15.0000 g., 0.9250 Silver .4461 oz. ASW **Ruler:** Akihito (Heisei) **Series:** 1998 Nagano Winter Olympics **Obv:** Biathlon **Rev:** Value, dates, and antelope

Date	Mintage	VG	F	VF	XF	BU
Yr.9(1997)	4,867,000	—	—	—	—	70.00
Yr.9(1997) Proof	133,000	Value: 120				

Y# 120 5000 YEN
15.0000 g., 0.9250 Silver .4461 oz. ASW **Ruler:** Akihito (Heisei) **Series:** 1998 Nagano Winter Olympics **Obv:** Paralympic skier **Rev:** Value, dates, and antelope

Date	Mintage	VG	F	VF	XF	BU
Yr.10(1998)	4,867,000	—	—	—	—	70.00
Yr.10(1998) Proof	133,000	Value: 120				

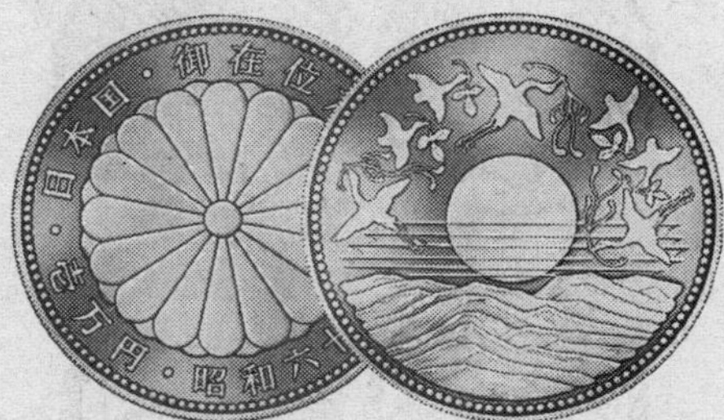

Y# 91 10000 YEN
20.0000 g., 0.9990 Silver .6430 oz. ASW **Ruler:** Hirohito (Showa) **Subject:** 60 Years - Reign of Hirohito **Obv:** Large chrysanthemum with legends around border **Rev:** Flying birds above center circle with hills and lines below **Designer:** Ikuo Hirayama

Date	Mintage	VG	F	VF	XF	BU
Yr.61(1986)	10,000,000	—	—	—	—	150

Y# 116 10000 YEN
15.6000 g., 1.0000 Gold .5022 oz. AGW **Ruler:** Akihito (Heisei) **Series:** 1998 Nagano Winter Olympics **Obv:** Ski jumper **Rev:** Value, dates, and gentian plant

Date	Mintage	F	VF	XF	Unc	BU
Yr.9(1997) Proof	55,000	Value: 675				

Y# 121 10000 YEN
15.6000 g., 1.0000 Gold .5022 oz. AGW **Ruler:** Akihito (Heisei) **Series:** 1998 Nagano Winter Olympics **Obv:** Figure skater **Rev:** Value, dates, and gentian plant

Date	Mintage	F	VF	XF	Unc	BU
Yr.9(1997) Proof	55,000	Value: 675				

Y# 122 10000 YEN
15.6000 g., 1.0000 Gold .5022 oz. AGW **Ruler:** Akihito (Heisei) **Series:** 1998 Nagano Winter Olympics **Obv:** Speed skater **Rev:** Value, dates, and gentian plant

Date	Mintage	F	VF	XF	Unc	BU
Yr.10(1998) Proof	55,000	Value: 675				

Y# 124 10000 YEN
20.0000 g., 1.0000 Gold .6430 oz. AGW **Ruler:** Akihito (Heisei) **Subject:** 15th Anniversary of Enthronement **Obv:** Chrysanthemum within wreath **Rev:** Stylized Green Phoenix

Date	Mintage	F	VF	XF	Unc	BU
Yr.11(1999) Proof	200,000	Value: 1,200				

Y# 109 50000 YEN
18.0000 g., 1.0000 Gold .5788 oz. AGW **Ruler:** Akihito (Heisei) **Subject:** Royal wedding of Crown Prince **Obv:** Chrysanthemum flanked by cherry blossom sprigs **Rev:** Pair of herons

Date	Mintage	VG	F	VF	XF	BU
Yr.5(1993)	1,900,000	—	—	—	—	650
Yr.5(1993) Proof	100,000	Value: 850				

Y# 92 100000 YEN
20.0000 g., 1.0000 Gold .6430 oz. AGW **Ruler:** Hirohito (Showa) **Subject:** 60 Years - Reign of Hirohito **Obv:** Large chrysanthemum with legends around border **Rev:** Pair of birds within artistic design **Designer:** Ikuo Hirayama

Date	Mintage	VG	F	VF	XF	BU
Yr.61(1986)	10,000,000	—	—	—	—	1,250
Yr.62(1987)	876,000	—	—	—	—	1,250
Yr.62(1987) Proof	124,000	Value: 1,350				

Y# 105 100000 YEN
30.0000 g., 1.0000 Gold .9646 oz. AGW **Ruler:** Akihito (Heisei) **Subject:** Enthronement of Emperor Akihito **Obv:** Chrysanthemum within wreath **Rev:** Stylized Green Phoenix

Date	Mintage	VG	F	VF	XF	BU
Yr.2(1990)	1,900,000	—	—	—	—	1,250
Yr.2(1990) Proof	100,000	Value: 1,350				

PLATINUM BULLION COINAGE

KM# 20 10 MOMME
Platinum 37.4 oz. APW **Ruler:** Hirohito (Showa)

Date	Mintage	VG	F	VF	XF	BU
1937	1,500	—	—	—	—	1,750

LEPROSARIUM COINAGE

KM# L11 SEN
Brass **Issuer:** Oshima-Seisho En **Obv:** Denomination with mulitple stamps **Rev:** "Ken" symbol = inspection

Date	Mintage	F	VF	XF	Unc	BU
ND(1912-25) Rare	—	—	—	—	—	—

KM# L20 SEN
Japanned (Lacquered) Brass **Issuer:** Tama-Zensei En **Note:** Uniface. Oval with central hole, denomination, rays at border.

Date	Mintage	F	VF	XF	Unc	BU
ND(1926-28) Rare	—	—	—	—	—	—

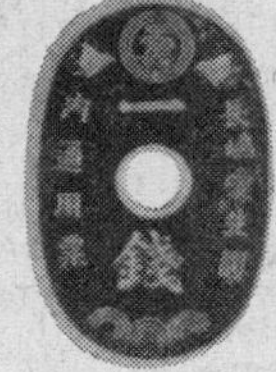

KM# L1 SEN
Japanned (Lacquered) Brass **Issuer:** Nagashima-Aisei En **Note:** Uniface. Badge of Aisei En above denomination.

Date	Mintage	F	VF	XF	Unc	BU
ND(1931-48) Rare	—	—	—	—	—	—

KM# L2 SEN
Japanned Aluminum **Issuer:** Nagashima-Aisei En

Date	Mintage	F	VF	XF	Unc	BU
ND(1931-48)	—	—	450	750	—	—

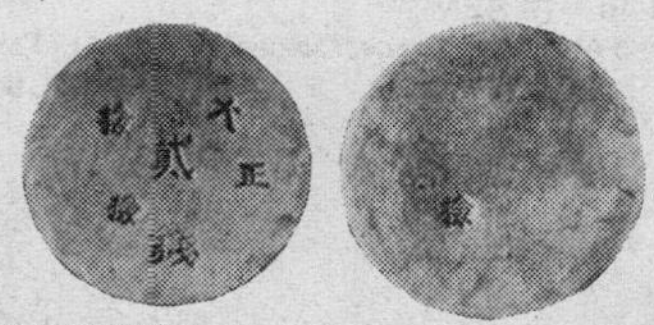

KM# L12 2 SEN
Brass **Issuer:** Oshima-Seisho En

Date	Mintage	F	VF	XF	Unc	BU
ND(1912-25) Rare	—	—	—	—	—	—

KM# L13 5 SEN
Brass **Issuer:** Oshima-Seisho En

Date	Mintage	F	VF	XF	Unc	BU
ND(1912-25) Rare	—	—	—	—	—	—

KM# L21 5 SEN
Japanned (Lacquered) Brass **Issuer:** Tama-Zensei En **Note:** Round with central hole, perpendicular rays fill border from flower.

Date	Mintage	F	VF	XF	Unc	BU
ND(1926-28) Rare	—	—	—	—	—	—

KM# L3 5 SEN
Japanned (Lacquered) Brass **Issuer:** Nagashima-Aisei En

Date	Mintage	F	VF	XF	Unc	BU
ND(1931-48) Rare	—	—	—	—	—	—

KM# L3a 5 SEN
Japanned Aluminum **Issuer:** Nagashima-Aisei En

Date	Mintage	F	VF	XF	Unc	BU
ND(1931-48)	—	—	750	1,250	—	—

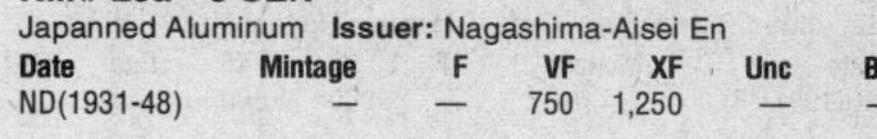

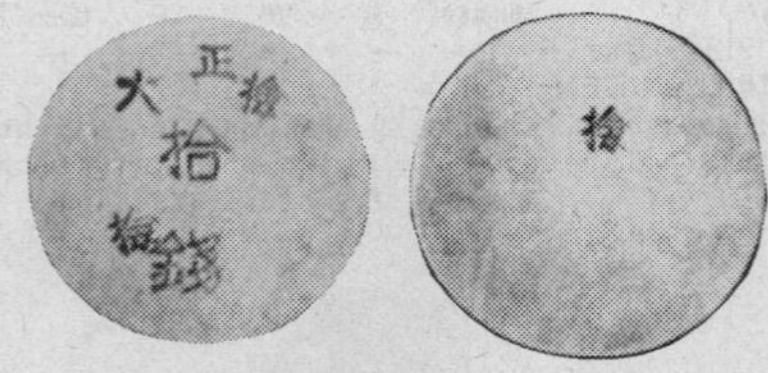

KM# L14 10 SEN

Brass **Issuer:** Oshima-Seisho En

Date	Mintage	F	VF	XF	Unc	BU
ND(1912-25) Rare	—	—	—	—	—	—

KM# L22 10 SEN

Japanned (Lacquered) Brass **Issuer:** Tama-Zensei En **Note:** Similar to 5 Sen, L21.

Date	Mintage	F	VF	XF	Unc	BU
ND(1926-28) Rare	—	—	—	—	—	—

KM# L4 10 SEN

Japanned (Lacquered) Brass **Issuer:** Nagashima-Aisei En

Date	Mintage	F	VF	XF	Unc	BU
ND(1931-48) Rare	—	—	—	—	—	—

KM# L4a 10 SEN

Japanned Aluminum **Issuer:** Nagashima-Aisei En

Date	Mintage	F	VF	XF	Unc	BU
ND(1931-48)	—	—	750	1,250	—	—

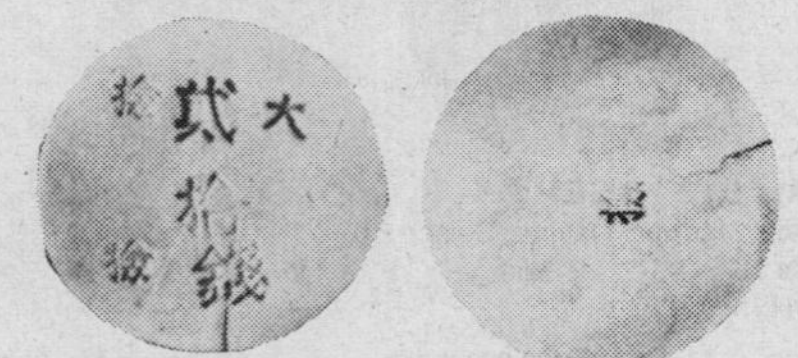

KM# L15 20 SEN

Brass **Issuer:** Oshima-Seisho En

Date	Mintage	F	VF	XF	Unc	BU
ND(1912-25) Rare	—	—	—	—	—	—

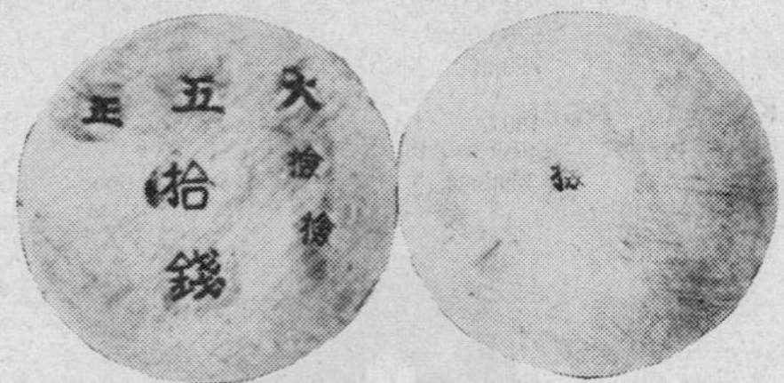

KM# L16 50 SEN

Brass **Issuer:** Oshima-Seisho En

Date	Mintage	F	VF	XF	Unc	BU
ND(1912-25) Rare	—	—	—	—	—	—

KM# L23 50 SEN

Japanned (Lacquered) Brass **Issuer:** Tama-Zensei En
Note: Rectangular with center hole. Sunset with ornate border.

Date	Mintage	F	VF	XF	Unc	BU
ND(1926-28) Rare	—	—	—	—	—	—

KM# L5 50 SEN

Japanned (Lacquered) Brass **Issuer:** Nagashima-Aisei En

Date	Mintage	F	VF	XF	Unc	BU
ND(1931-48)	—	—	900	1,500	—	—

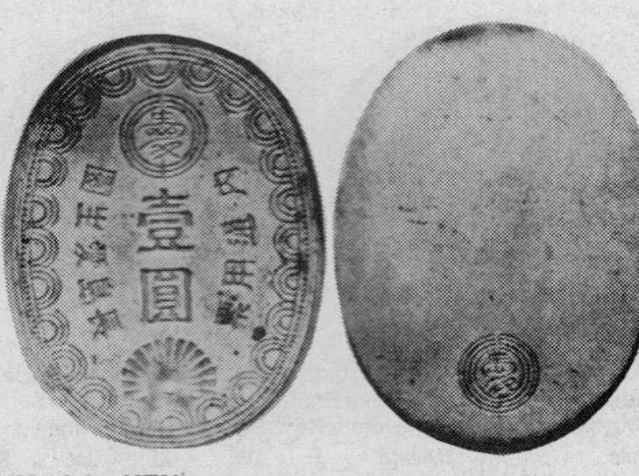

KM# L6 YEN

Brass **Issuer:** Nagashima-Aisei En **Rev:** Stylized badge of Ansei En

Date	Mintage	F	VF	XF	Unc	BU
ND(1931-48)	—	—	1,500	2,500	—	—

OCCUPATION COINAGE

The following issues were struck at the Osaka Mint for use in the Netherlands East Indies. The only inscription found on them is Dai Nippon: Great Japan. The war situation had worsened to the point that shipping the coins became virtually impossible. Consequently, none of these coins were issued in the East Indies and almost the entire issue was lost or were remelted at the mint. Y numbers are for the Netherlands Indies and dates are from the Japanese Shinto dynastic calendar.

Y# A66 SEN

Aluminum **Obv:** Stylized fish **Note:** Prev. NEI Y#22.

Date	Mintage	F	VF	XF	Unc	BU
NE2603 (1943)	233,190,000	175	200	250	400	500
NE2604 (1944)	66,810,000	125	150	200	350	450

Y# B66 5 SEN

Tin Alloy **Rev:** Stylized native figure standing **Note:** Prev. NEI Y#23.

Date	Mintage	F	VF	XF	Unc	BU
NE2603 (1943)	—	4,000	5,000	5,500	—	—

Y# 66 10 SEN

Tin Alloy **Rev:** Stylized native figure standing **Note:** Prev. NEI Y#24.

Date	Mintage	F	VF	XF	Unc	BU
NE2603 (1943)	69,490,000	90.00	125	150	225	300
NE2604 (1944)	110,510,000	60.00	75.00	100	150	250

PATTERNS

Including off metal strikes

KM#	Date	Mintage	Identification	Mkt Val
Pn31	Yr.34 (1901)	—	Yen. Copper.	3,250
Pn32	Yr.34 (1901)	—	Yen. Silver.	—
Pn33	Yr.39 (1906)	—	5 Rin. Copper.	3,250

KM#	Date	Mintage	Identification	Mkt Val
Pn34	Yr.41(1908)	—	Sen. Copper.	3,250
Pn35	Yr.42 (1909)	—	5 Rin. Copper.	3,250
Pn36	Yr.42 (1911)	—	Sen. Copper.	—

KM#	Date	Mintage	Identification	Mkt Val
Pn37	Yr.44 (1911)	—	Sen. Copper.	3,250

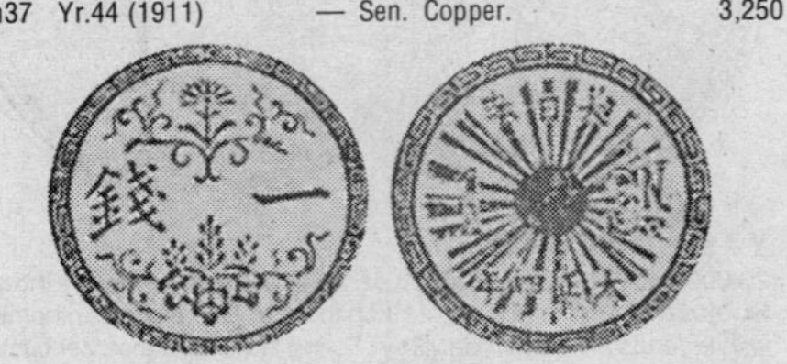

KM#	Date	Mintage	Identification	Mkt Val
Pn38	Yr.4 (1915)	—	Sen. Copper.	3,250

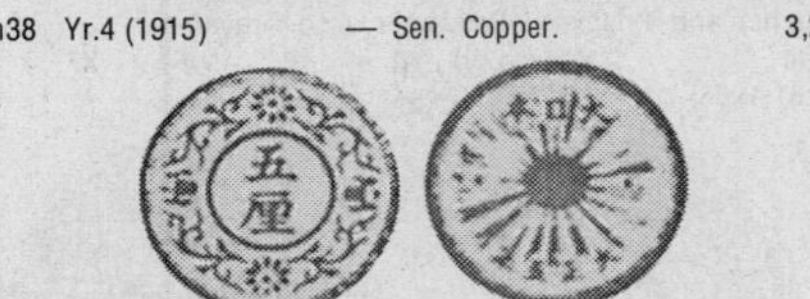

KM#	Date	Mintage	Identification	Mkt Val
Pn39	Yr.5 (1916)	—	5 Rin. Copper.	3,250

KM#	Date	Mintage	Identification	Mkt Val
Pn40	Yr.5 (1916)	—	5 Rin. Copper.	3,250
Pn42	Yr.5 (1916)	—	Sen.	—

KM#	Date	Mintage	Identification	Mkt Val
Pn43	Yr.5 (1916)	—	Sen.	—

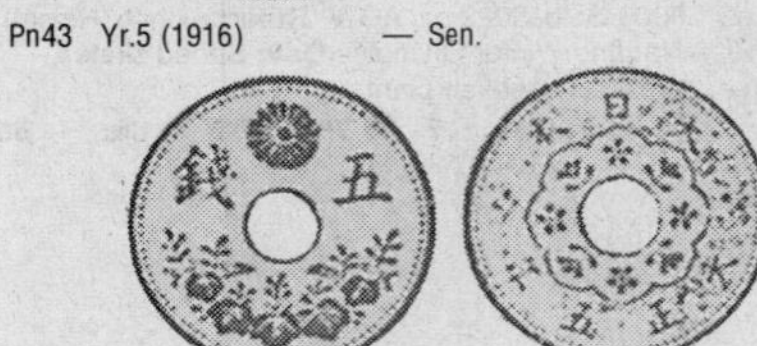

KM#	Date	Mintage	Identification	Mkt Val
Pn44	Yr.5 (1916)	—	5 Sen. Copper-Nickel.	3,250

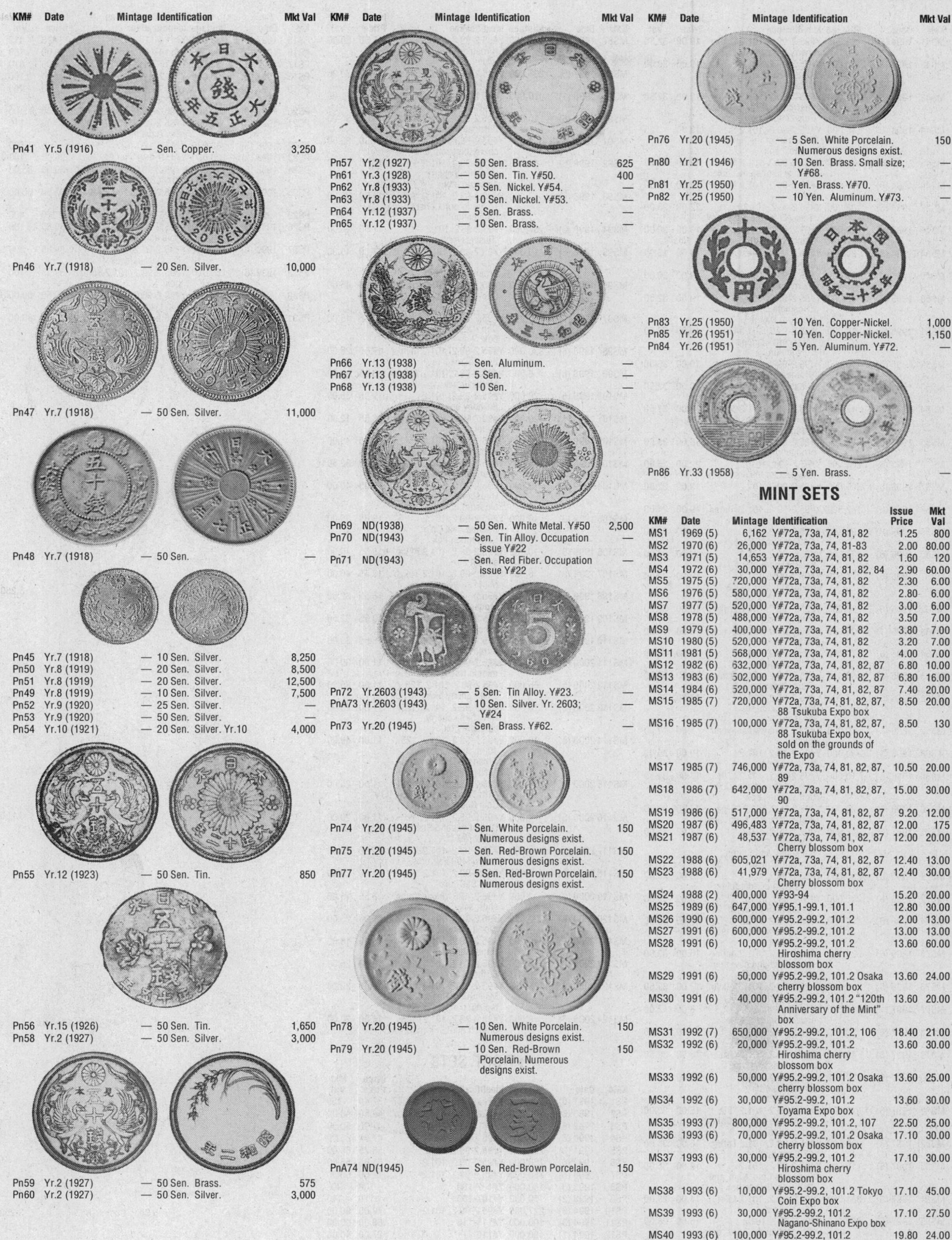

KM#	Date	Mintage	Identification	Mkt Val
Pn41	Yr.5 (1916)	—	Sen. Copper.	3,250
Pn46	Yr.7 (1918)	—	20 Sen. Silver.	10,000
Pn47	Yr.7 (1918)	—	50 Sen. Silver.	11,000
Pn48	Yr.7 (1918)	—	50 Sen.	—
Pn45	Yr.7 (1918)	—	10 Sen. Silver.	8,250
Pn50	Yr.8 (1919)	—	20 Sen. Silver.	8,500
Pn51	Yr.8 (1919)	—	20 Sen. Silver.	12,500
Pn49	Yr.8 (1919)	—	10 Sen. Silver.	7,500
Pn52	Yr.9 (1920)	—	25 Sen. Silver.	—
Pn53	Yr.9 (1920)	—	50 Sen. Silver.	—
Pn54	Yr.10 (1921)	—	20 Sen. Silver. Yr.10	4,000
Pn55	Yr.12 (1923)	—	50 Sen. Tin.	850
Pn56	Yr.15 (1926)	—	50 Sen. Tin.	1,650
Pn58	Yr.2 (1927)	—	50 Sen. Silver.	3,000
Pn59	Yr.2 (1927)	—	50 Sen. Brass.	575
Pn60	Yr.2 (1927)	—	50 Sen. Silver.	3,000

KM#	Date	Mintage	Identification	Mkt Val
Pn57	Yr.2 (1927)	—	50 Sen. Brass.	625
Pn61	Yr.3 (1928)	—	50 Sen. Tin. Y#50.	400
Pn62	Yr.8 (1933)	—	5 Sen. Nickel. Y#54.	—
Pn63	Yr.8 (1933)	—	10 Sen. Nickel. Y#53.	—
Pn64	Yr.12 (1937)	—	5 Sen. Brass.	—
Pn65	Yr.12 (1937)	—	10 Sen. Brass.	—
Pn66	Yr.13 (1938)	—	Sen. Aluminum.	—
Pn67	Yr.13 (1938)	—	5 Sen.	—
Pn68	Yr.13 (1938)	—	10 Sen.	—
Pn69	ND(1938)	—	50 Sen. White Metal. Y#50	2,500
Pn70	ND(1943)	—	Sen. Tin Alloy. Occupation issue Y#22	—
Pn71	ND(1943)	—	Sen. Red Fiber. Occupation issue Y#22	—
Pn72	Yr.2603 (1943)	—	5 Sen. Tin Alloy. Y#23.	—
PnA73	Yr.2603 (1943)	—	10 Sen. Silver. Yr. 2603; Y#24	—
Pn73	Yr.20 (1945)	—	Sen. Brass. Y#62.	—
Pn74	Yr.20 (1945)	—	Sen. White Porcelain. Numerous designs exist.	150
Pn75	Yr.20 (1945)	—	Sen. Red-Brown Porcelain. Numerous designs exist.	150
Pn77	Yr.20 (1945)	—	5 Sen. Red-Brown Porcelain. Numerous designs exist.	150
Pn78	Yr.20 (1945)	—	10 Sen. White Porcelain. Numerous designs exist.	150
Pn79	Yr.20 (1945)	—	10 Sen. Red-Brown Porcelain. Numerous designs exist.	150
PnA74	ND(1945)	—	Sen. Red-Brown Porcelain.	150

KM#	Date	Mintage	Identification	Mkt Val
Pn76	Yr.20 (1945)	—	5 Sen. White Porcelain. Numerous designs exist.	150
Pn80	Yr.21 (1946)	—	10 Sen. Brass. Small size; Y#68.	—
Pn81	Yr.25 (1950)	—	Yen. Brass. Y#70.	—
Pn82	Yr.25 (1950)	—	10 Yen. Aluminum. Y#73.	—
Pn83	Yr.25 (1950)	—	10 Yen. Copper-Nickel.	1,000
Pn85	Yr.26 (1951)	—	10 Yen. Copper-Nickel.	1,150
Pn84	Yr.26 (1951)	—	5 Yen. Aluminum. Y#72.	—
Pn86	Yr.33 (1958)	—	5 Yen. Brass.	—

MINT SETS

KM#	Date	Mintage	Identification	Issue Price	Mkt Val
MS1	1969 (5)	6,162	Y#72a, 73a, 74, 81, 82	1.25	800
MS2	1970 (6)	26,000	Y#72a, 73a, 74, 81-83	2.00	80.00
MS3	1971 (5)	14,653	Y#72a, 73a, 74, 81, 82	1.60	120
MS4	1972 (6)	30,000	Y#72a, 73a, 74, 81, 82, 84	2.90	60.00
MS5	1975 (5)	720,000	Y#72a, 73a, 74, 81, 82	2.30	6.00
MS6	1976 (5)	580,000	Y#72a, 73a, 74, 81, 82	2.80	6.00
MS7	1977 (5)	520,000	Y#72a, 73a, 74, 81, 82	3.00	6.00
MS8	1978 (5)	488,000	Y#72a, 73a, 74, 81, 82	3.50	7.00
MS9	1979 (5)	400,000	Y#72a, 73a, 74, 81, 82	3.80	7.00
MS10	1980 (5)	520,000	Y#72a, 73a, 74, 81, 82	3.20	7.00
MS11	1981 (5)	568,000	Y#72a, 73a, 74, 81, 82	4.00	7.00
MS12	1982 (6)	632,000	Y#72a, 73a, 74, 81, 82, 87	6.80	10.00
MS13	1983 (6)	502,000	Y#72a, 73a, 74, 81, 82, 87	6.80	16.00
MS14	1984 (6)	520,000	Y#72a, 73a, 74, 81, 82, 87	7.40	20.00
MS15	1985 (7)	720,000	Y#72a, 73a, 74, 81, 82, 87, 88 Tsukuba Expo box	8.50	20.00
MS16	1985 (7)	100,000	Y#72a, 73a, 74, 81, 82, 87, 88 Tsukuba Expo box, sold on the grounds of the Expo	8.50	130
MS17	1985 (7)	746,000	Y#72a, 73a, 74, 81, 82, 87, 89	10.50	20.00
MS18	1986 (7)	642,000	Y#72a, 73a, 74, 81, 82, 87, 90	15.00	30.00
MS19	1986 (6)	517,000	Y#72a, 73a, 74, 81, 82, 87	9.20	12.00
MS20	1987 (6)	496,483	Y#72a, 73a, 74, 81, 82, 87	12.00	175
MS21	1987 (6)	48,537	Y#72a, 73a, 74, 81, 82, 87 Cherry blossom box	12.00	20.00
MS22	1988 (6)	605,021	Y#72a, 73a, 74, 81, 82, 87	12.40	13.00
MS23	1988 (6)	41,979	Y#72a, 73a, 74, 81, 82, 87 Cherry blossom box	12.40	30.00
MS24	1988 (2)	400,000	Y#93-94	15.20	20.00
MS25	1989 (6)	647,000	Y#95.1-99.1, 101.1	12.80	30.00
MS26	1990 (6)	600,000	Y#95.2-99.2, 101.2	2.00	13.00
MS27	1991 (6)	600,000	Y#95.2-99.2, 101.2	13.00	13.00
MS28	1991 (6)	10,000	Y#95.2-99.2, 101.2 Hiroshima cherry blossom box	13.60	60.00
MS29	1991 (6)	50,000	Y#95.2-99.2, 101.2 Osaka cherry blossom box	13.60	24.00
MS30	1991 (6)	40,000	Y#95.2-99.2, 101.2 "120th Anniversary of the Mint" box	13.60	20.00
MS31	1992 (7)	650,000	Y#95.2-99.2, 101.2, 106	18.40	21.00
MS32	1992 (6)	20,000	Y#95.2-99.2, 101.2 Hiroshima cherry blossom box	13.60	30.00
MS33	1992 (6)	50,000	Y#95.2-99.2, 101.2 Osaka cherry blossom box	13.60	25.00
MS34	1992 (6)	30,000	Y#95.2-99.2, 101.2 Toyama Expo box	13.60	30.00
MS35	1993 (7)	800,000	Y#95.2-99.2, 101.2, 107	22.50	25.00
MS36	1993 (6)	70,000	Y#95.2-99.2, 101.2 Osaka cherry blossom box	17.10	30.00
MS37	1993 (6)	30,000	Y#95.2-99.2, 101.2 Hiroshima cherry blossom box	17.10	30.00
MS38	1993 (6)	10,000	Y#95.2-99.2, 101.2 Tokyo Coin Expo box	17.10	45.00
MS39	1993 (6)	30,000	Y#95.2-99.2, 101.2 Nagano-Shinano Expo box	17.10	27.50
MS40	1993 (6)	100,000	Y#95.2-99.2, 101.2 "Respect for the Aged" box	19.80	24.00

KM#	Date	Mintage	Identification	Issue Price	Mkt Val
MS41	1994 (6)	80,000	Y#95.2-99.2, 101.2 Osaka cherry blossom box	19.00	32.50
MS42	1994 (6)	20,000	Y#95.2-99.2, 101.2 Hiroshima cherry blossom box	19.00	30.00
MS43	1994 (6)	10,000	Y#95.2-99.2, 101.2 "5th International Tokyo Coin Convention" box	19.00	32.50
MS44	1994 (6)	10,000	Y#95.2-99.2, 101.2 "Transfer of the Heian Capitol" box	19.00	125
MS45	1994 (6)	30,000	Y#95.2-99.2, 101.2 "Mie Festival Exposition" box	19.00	30.00
MS46	1994 (6)	800,000	Y#95.2-99.2, 101.2 Mint box	18.00	23.00
MS47	1994 (6)	100,000	Y#95.2-99.2, 101.2 "Respect for the Aged" box	22.00	25.00
MS48	1994 (6)	10,000	Y#95.2-99.2, 101.2 "Tokyo Branch Mint Coin Fair" box	19.00	30.00
MSA49	1994 (1)	20,000	Y#99.2 Mint visit souvenir folder	9.00	15.00
MS49	1995 (6)	80,000	Y#95.2-99.2, 101.2 Osaka cherry blossom box	19.00	30.00
MS50	1995 (6)	10,000	Y#95.2-99.2, 101.2 Hiroshima cherry blossom box	19.00	32.50
MS51	1995 (6)	10,000	Y#95.2-99.2, 101.2 6th Tokyo International Coin Convention	19.00	32.50
MS52	1995 (6)	10,000	Y#95.2-99.2, 101.2 "Romantopia '95" box	19.00	35.00
MS53	1995 (6)	10,000	Y#95.2-99.2, 101.2 "Coin and Banknote Fair" box	19.00	32.50
MS54	1995 (6)	12,000	Y#95.2-99.2, 101.2 50th Anniversary Hiroshima Branch Mint	19.00	32.50
MS55	1995 (6)	600,000	Y#95.2-99.2, 101.2 Mint production scenes box	18.00	23.00
MS56	1995 (6)	200,000	Y#95.2-99.2, 101.2 "Respect for the Aged" box	22.00	25.00
MS57	1995 (6)	390,000	Y#95.2-99.2, 101.2 Horyuji Temple folder	19.00	22.50
MS58	1995 (6)	192,500	Y#95.2-99.2, 101.2 Himeji Castle folder	19.00	24.00
MS59	1995 (6)	191,500	Y#95.2-99.2, 101.2 Ancient Kyoto folder	19.00	24.00
MS60	1995 (6)	177,500	Y#95.2-99.2, 101.2 Yakushima folder	19.00	24.00
MS61	1995 (6)	174,500	Y#95.2-99.2, 101.2 Shirakami Mountains folder	19.00	24.00
MS62	1995 (6)	10,000	Y#95.2-99.2, 101.2 "Tokyo Mint Fair" box	18.00	30.00
MS63	1995 (1)	20,000	Y#99.2 Mint visit souvenir folder	8.50	12.00
MS64	1995 (6)	20,000	Y#95.2-99.2, 101.2 Birthday folder	20.00	30.00
MS65	1996 (6)	80,000	Y#95.2-99.2, 101.2 Osaka cherry blossom box	17.00	35.00
MS66	1996 (6)	10,000	Y#95.2-99.2, 101.2 Hiroshima cherry blossom box	17.00	35.00
MS67	1996 (1)	10,000	Y#99.2 Mint visit souvenir folder	8.00	12.00
MS68	1996 (6)	10,000	Y#95.2-99.2, 101.2 Birthday folder	19.00	35.00
MS69	1996 (6)	10,000	Y#95.2-99.2, 101.2 "7th Tokyo International Coin Convention" box	17.00	32.50
MS70	1996 (6)	20,000	Y#95.2-99.2, 101.2 "Saga World Ceramics Expo" box	17.00	30.00
MS71	1996 (6)	8,000	Y#95.2-99.2, 101.2 "Okayama Coin, Banknote, and Stamp Exhibition" box	17.00	35.00
MS72	1996 (6)	290,000	Y#95.2-99.2, 101.2 Shirakawa district folder	18.00	27.00
MS73	1996 (6)	200,000	Y#95.2-99.2, 101.2 "Respect for the Aged" box	20.00	30.00
MS74	1996 (6)	100,000	Y#95.2-99.2, 101.2 "125th Anniversary Birth of the Yen" folder	27.00	90.00
MS75	1996 (6)	321,000	Y#95.2-99.2, 101.2 Aerial view of old and new mint box	16.00	30.00
MS76	1996 (6)	6,000	Y#95.2-99.2, 101.2 Tokyo Branch Mint fair box	17.00	32.50
MS77	1997 (1)	10,000	Y#101.2 Mint visit souvenir folder	8.00	12.00
MS78	1997 (6)	10,000	Y#95.2-99.2, 101.2 Birthday folder	17.00	32.50
MS79	1997 (6)	80,000	Y#95.2-99.2, 101.2 Osaka cherry blossom box	16.00	32.50
MS80	1997 (6)	10,000	Y#95.2-99.2, 101.2 Hiroshima cherry blossom box	16.00	35.00
MS81	1997 (6)	10,000	Y#95.2-99.2, 101.2 "8th Tokyo International Coin Convention" box	16.00	30.00
MS82	1997 (6)	20,000	Y#95.2-99.2, 101.2 Tottori '97 Expo box	16.00	35.00
MS83	1997 (6)	10,000	Y#95.2-99.2, 101.2 Yamagata Coin, Note, and Stamp Exhibition box	16.00	35.00
MS84	1997 (6)	331,000	Y#95.2-99.2, 101.2 Mint Bureau box	14.00	25.00
MS85	1997 (6)	250,000	Y#95.2-99.2, 101.2 "Respect for the Aged" box	15.50	28.00
MS86	1997 (6)	8,000	Y#95.2-99.2, 101.2 Tokyo Mint Fair box	15.00	30.00
MS87	1997 (6)	195,000	Y#95.2-99.2, 101.2 Hiroshima Peace Dome folder	15.50	30.00
MS88	1997 (6)	205,000	Y#95.2-99.2, 101.2 Itsukushima Shrine folder	15.50	30.00
MS89	1998 (1)	10,000	Y#99.2 Mint visit souvenir folder	7.00	12.00
MS90	1998 (6)	10,000	Y#95.2-99.2, 101.2 Birthday folder	16.00	35.00
MS91	1998 (6)	81,000	Y#95.2-99.2, 101.2 Osaka cherry blossom box	14.50	32.50
MS92	1998 (6)	10,000	Y#95.2-99.2, 101.2 Hiroshima cherry blossom box	14.50	32.50
MS93	1998 (6)	13,000	Y#95.2-99.2, 101.2 "9th Tokyo International Coin Convention" box	14.50	30.00
MS94	1998 (6)	257,000	Y#95.2-99.2, 101.2 "Respect for the Aged" box	17.00	28.00
MS95	1998 (6)	10,000	Y#95.2-99.2, 101.2 "World Cup - Japan vs. Argentina" box	17.00	45.00
MS96	1998 (6)	10,000	Y#95.2-99.2, 101.2 "World Cup - Japan vs. Croatia" box	17.00	45.00
MS97	1998 (6)	10,000	Y#95.2-99.2, 101.2 "World Cup - Japan vs. Jamaica" box	17.00	45.00
MS98	1998 (6)	336,000	Y#95.2-99.2, 101.2 Mint Bureau box	17.50	28.00
MS99	1998 (6)	6,000	Y#95.2-99.2, 101.2 Tokyo Mint Fair box	18.05	30.00
MS100	1999 (6)	20,000	Y#95.2-99.2, 101.2 Birthday box	19.95	35.00
MS101	1999 (1)	20,000	Y#99.2 Mint visit souvenir folder	8.55	12.00
MS102	1999 (6)	6,000	Y#95.2-99.2, 101.2 Kumamoto mint box	1,805	45.00
MS103	1999 (6)	80,000	Y#95.2-99.2, 101.2 Osaka cherry blossom box	18.05	32.50
MS104	1999 (6)	10,000	Y#95.2-99.2, 101.2 Hiroshima cherry blossom box	18.05	40.00
MS105	1999 (6)	10,000	Y#95.2-99.2, 101.2 International Coin Convention box	18.05	35.00
MS106	1999 (6)	10,000	Y#95.2-99.2, 101.2 Akita exhibit box	18.55	40.00
MS107	1999 (6)	6,000	Y#95.2-99.2, 101.2 Tokyo Mint Fair box	18.55	40.00
MS108	1999 (6)	200,000	Y#95.2-99.2, 101.2 Nara Monasteries folder	18.55	32.50
MS109	1999 (6)	250,000	Y#95.2-99.2, 101.2 "Respect for the Aged" box	18.55	32.50
MS110	1999 (6)	300,000	Y#95.2-99.2, 101.2 Mint Bureau box	18.55	35.00
MS111	2000 (5)	5,000	Y#95.2-98.2, 101.2 Branch mint in Nagoya box	11.00	30.00
MS112	2000 (5)	65,000	Y#95.2-98.2, 101.2, 125 Osaka cherry blossom box	11.00	25.00
MS113	2000 (5)	10,000	Y#95.2-98.2, 101.2, 125 Hiroshima cherry blossom box	11.00	25.00
MS114	2000 (5)	10,000	Y#95.2-98.2, 101.2, 125 400th Anniversary Japanese-Dutch relation at Nagsaki box	11.00	40.00
MS115	2000 (5)	10,000	Y#95.2-98.2, 101.2, 125 11th Tokyo International Coin Convention box	11.00	25.00
MS116	2000 (5)	7,000	Y#95.2-98.2, 101.2, 125 Otaru Coin and Stamp Show box	11.00	20.00
MS117	2000 (5)	4,000	Y#95.2-98.2, 101.2, 125 Tokyo Mint Fair box	11.00	25.00
MS118	2000 (6)	5,600	Y#95.2-99.2, 101.2 "Japan Coin Set" box	17.00	20.00
MS119	2000 (2)	4,000	Y#96.2, 125 "Japan Coins" short set	8.50	15.00
MS120	2000 (6)	222,300	Y#95.2-99.2, 101.2 Nikko World Cultural Sites	17.00	25.00
MS121	2000 (6)	340,200	Y#95.2-99.2, 101.2 Mint Bureau box	15.00	18.00
MS122	2000 (2)	4,500	Y#95.2-98.2, 101.2, 125 Birthday box	18.00	25.00
MS123	2000 (6)	155,400	Y#95.2-98.2, 101.2, 125 Millennium Respect for the Aged box	19.00	22.00
MS124	2000 (6)	8,000	Y#95.2-98.2, 101.2, 125 Branch mint in Kanazawa box	16.00	20.00

PROOF SETS

KM#	Date	Mintage	Identification	Issue Price	Mkt Val
PS1	1987 (6)	230,000	Y#72a, 73a, 74, 81, 82, 87	37.40	150
PS2	1988 (6)	200,000	Y#72a, 73a, 74, 81, 82, 87	46.50	50.00
PS3	1989 (6)	200,000	Y#95.1-99.1, 101.1	47.90	50.00
PS4	1990 (6)	200,000	Y#95.2-99.2, 101.2	47.90	65.00
PS5	1991 (6)	220,000	Y#95.2-99.2, 101.2	58.75	65.00
PS6	1992 (6)	250,000	Y#95.2-99.2, 101.2	55.65	55.00
PS7	1993 (6)	250,000	Y#95.2-99.2, 101.2	72.00	60.00
PS8	1993 (3)	100,000	Y#107-109	100	900
PS9	1993 (2)	100,000	Y#107-108	110	115
PS10	1994 (6)	227,000	Y#95.2-99.2, 101.2	72.00	60.00
PS11	1994 (3)	100,000	Y#111-113	68.00	90.00
PS12	1994 (1)	100,000	Y#110	27.00	40.00
PS13	1995 (6)	200,000	Y#95.2-99.2, 101.2	72.00	65.00
PS14	1996 (6)	189,000	Y#95.2-99.2, 101.2	103	85.00
PS15	1997 (3)	33,000	Y#114-116	413	810
PS16	1997 (2)	100,000	Y#114-115	99.00	160
PS17	1997 (3)	33,000	Y#117, 119, 121	406	810
PS18	1997 (2)	100,000	Y#117, 119	97.00	160
PS19	1997 (6)	1,000	Y#95.2-99.2, 101.2 "Japan Expo Tottori '97" box	59.00	400
PS20	1997 (6)	186,000	Y#95.2-99.2, 101.2	56.00	75.00
PS21	1997 (6)	25,000	Y#95.2-99.2, 101.2 Tokyo Bay Aqualine Opening	56.00	110
PS22	1998 (3)	33,000	Y#118, 120, 122	375	800
PS23	1998 (2)	100,000	Y#118, 120	90.00	100
PS24	1998 (6)	30,000	Y#95.2-99.2, 101.2 Akashi Strait Bridge Opening	59.00	85.00
PS25	1998 (6)	170,000	Y#95.2-99.2, 101.2 Mint Bureau box	62.50	60.00
PS29	1999 (2)	100,000	Y#123, 124	370	400
PS26	1999 (6)	70,000	Y#95.2-99.2, 101.2 Type Coin series	69.85	100
PS27	1999 (6)	50,000	Y#95.2-99.2, 101.2 Coastal Highway	69.85	100
PS28	1999 (6)	150,000	Y#95.2-99.2, 101.2 Bureau box	69.85	100
PS30	2000 (6)	100,000	Y#95.2-98.2, 101.2, 125 Old Type Coin Series	62.50	80.00
PS31	2000 (6)	126,000	Y#95.2-98.2, 101.2, 125 Mint Bureau Box	62,350	80.00

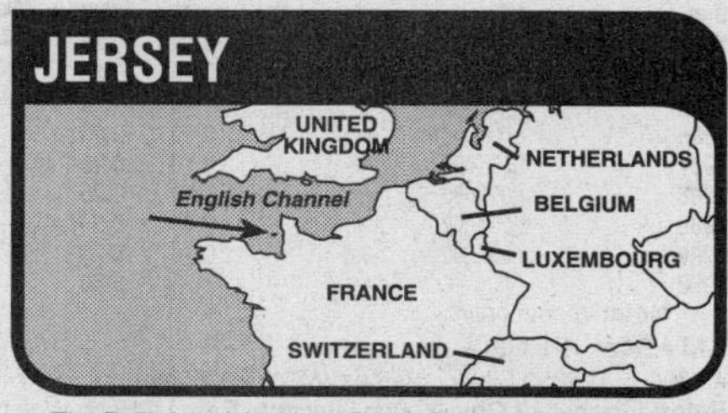

The Bailiwick of Jersey, a British Crown dependency located in the English Channel 12 miles (19 km.) west of Normandy, France, has an area of 45 sq. mi. (117 sq. km.) and a population of 74,000. Capital: St. Helier. The economy is based on agriculture and cattle breeding – the importation of cattle is prohibited to protect the purity of the island's world-famous strain of milch cows.

Jersey was occupied by Neanderthal man by 100,000 B.C., and by Iberians of 2000 B.C. who left their chamber tombs in the island's granite cliffs. Roman legions almost certainly visited the island although they left no evidence of settlement. The country folk of Jersey still speak an archaic form of Norman-French, lingering evidence of the Norman annexation of the island in 933 A.D. Jersey was annexed to England in 1206, 140 years after the Norman Conquest. The dependency is administered by its own laws and customs; laws enacted by the British Parliament do not apply to Jersey unless it is specifically mentioned. During World War II, German troops occupied the island from July1, 1940 until May 9, 1945.

Coins of pre-Roman Gaul and of Rome have been found in abundance on Jersey.

RULERS

British

MINT MARKS

H - Heaton, Birmingham

MONETARY SYSTEM

Commencing 1877

12 Pence = 1 Shilling
5 Shillings = 1 Crown
20 Shillings = 1 Pound
100 New Pence = 1 Pound

BRITISH DEPENDENCY

STANDARD COINAGE

KM# 9 1/24 SHILLING

Bronze **Obv:** Crowned bust right **Obv. Designer:** G. W. DeSaulles **Rev:** Pointed shield divides date

Date	Mintage	F	VF	XF	Unc	BU
1909	120,000	1.00	2.50	11.50	40.00	—

KM# 11 1/24 SHILLING

Bronze **Obv:** Crowned bust left **Obv. Designer:** E. B. MacKennal **Rev:** Pointed shield divides date

Date	Mintage	F	VF	XF	Unc	BU
1911	72,000	1.00	2.50	11.50	40.00	—
1913	72,000	1.00	2.50	11.50	28.00	—
1923	72,000	1.00	2.50	11.50	28.00	—

KM# 13 1/24 SHILLING

Bronze **Obv:** Crowned bust left **Obv. Designer:** E. B. MacKennal **Rev:** Shield divides date

Date	Mintage	F	VF	XF	Unc	BU
1923	72,000	0.75	3.00	5.50	22.50	—
1923 Proof	—	Value: 550				
1926	120,000	0.75	2.50	4.50	20.00	—
1926 Proof	—	Value: 550				

KM# 15 1/24 SHILLING

Bronze **Obv:** Crowned bust left **Obv. Designer:** E. B. MacKennal **Rev:** Shield divides date **Rev. Designer:** Kruger-Gray

Date	Mintage	F	VF	XF	Unc	BU
1931	72,000	0.50	1.00	3.00	15.00	—
1931 Proof	—	Value: 165				
1933	72,000	0.50	1.00	3.00	15.00	—
1933 Proof	—	Value: 165				
1935	72,000	0.50	1.00	3.00	15.00	—
1935 Proof	—	Value: 165				

KM# 17 1/24 SHILLING

Bronze **Obv:** Crowned head left **Obv. Designer:** Percy Metcalfe **Rev:** Shield divides date **Rev. Designer:** Kruger-Gray

Date	Mintage	F	VF	XF	Unc	BU
1937	72,000	0.50	1.00	3.00	15.00	—
1937 Proof	—	Value: 125				
1946	72,000	0.50	1.00	3.00	15.00	—
1946 Proof	—	Value: 125				
1947	72,000	0.50	1.00	3.00	15.00	—
1947 Proof	—	Value: 125				

KM# 10 1/12 SHILLING

Bronze **Obv:** Crowned bust right **Obv. Designer:** G. W. DeSaulles **Rev:** Pointed shield divides date

Date	Mintage	F	VF	XF	Unc	BU
1909	180,000	0.75	3.50	12.50	60.00	—

KM# 12 1/12 SHILLING

Bronze **Obv:** Crowned bust left **Obv. Designer:** E. B. MacKennal **Rev:** Pointed shield divides date

Date	Mintage	F	VF	XF	Unc	BU
1911	204,000	0.50	1.50	5.00	35.00	—
1913	204,000	0.50	1.50	5.00	35.00	—
1923	204,000	0.50	1.50	5.00	35.00	—

KM# 14 1/12 SHILLING

Bronze **Obv:** Crowned bust left **Obv. Designer:** E. B. MacKennal **Rev:** Shield divides date **Rev. Designer:** Kruger-Gray

Date	Mintage	F	VF	XF	Unc	BU
1923	301,000	0.75	2.50	8.00	30.00	—
1926	83,000	0.75	2.50	10.00	40.00	—

KM# 16 1/12 SHILLING

Bronze **Obv:** Crowned bust left **Obv. Designer:** E. B. MacKennal **Rev:** Shield divides date **Rev. Designer:** Kruger-Gray

Date	Mintage	F	VF	XF	Unc	BU
1931	204,000	0.50	1.25	3.00	19.00	—
1931 Proof	—	Value: 125				
1933	204,000	0.50	1.25	3.00	19.00	—
1933 Proof	—	Value: 125				
1935	204,000	0.50	1.25	3.00	19.00	—
1935 Proof	—	Value: 125				

KM# 18 1/12 SHILLING

Bronze **Obv:** Crowned head left **Obv. Designer:** Percy Metcalfe **Rev:** Shield divides date **Rev. Designer:** Kruger-Gray

Date	Mintage	F	VF	XF	Unc	BU
1937	204,000	0.50	1.00	2.50	10.00	—
1937 Proof	—	Value: 125				
1946	204,000	0.50	1.00	2.50	10.00	—
1946 Proof	—	Value: 125				
1947	444,000	0.25	0.50	1.50	7.50	—
1947 Proof	—	Value: 125				

KM# 19 1/12 SHILLING

Bronze **Subject:** Liberation Commemorative **Obv:** Crowned head left **Obv. Designer:** Percy Metcalfe **Rev:** Shield above written value **Rev. Designer:** Kruger-Gray

Date	Mintage	F	VF	XF	Unc	BU
1945	1,000,000	0.25	0.50	1.00	5.00	—
1945 Proof	—	Value: 100				

Note: Struck between 1949-52

KM# 20 1/12 SHILLING

Bronze **Ruler:** Elizabeth II **Obv:** Crowned head right **Rev:** Shield above written value

Date	Mintage	F	VF	XF	Unc	BU
ND (1954)	720,000	0.25	0.50	1.00	3.50	—
ND (1954) Proof	—	Value: 100				

KM# 21 1/12 SHILLING

Bronze **Ruler:** Elizabeth II **Obv:** Crowned head right **Rev:** Shield above written value

Date	Mintage	F	VF	XF	Unc	BU
1957	720,000	0.25	0.45	0.75	2.00	—
1957 Proof	2,100	Value: 7.50				
1964	1,200,000	0.25	0.45	0.75	1.50	—
1964 Proof	20,000	Value: 2.00				

KM# 24 1/12 SHILLING
Bronze **Ruler:** Elizabeth II **Obv:** Crowned head right **Rev:** Shield above dates and written value

Date	Mintage	F	VF	XF	Unc	BU
ND(1960) Proof	—	Value: 65.00				

KM# 23 1/12 SHILLING
Bronze **Ruler:** Elizabeth II **Subject:** 300th Anniversary - Accession of King Charles II **Obv:** Crowned head right **Rev:** Shield above dates and written value

Date	Mintage	F	VF	XF	Unc	BU
ND (1960)	1,200,000	0.25	0.45	0.75	1.50	—
ND (1960) Proof	4,200	Value: 4.00				

KM# 26 1/12 SHILLING
Bronze **Ruler:** Elizabeth II **Subject:** Norman Conquest **Obv:** Crowned head right **Rev:** Shield divides dates

Date	Mintage	F	VF	XF	Unc	BU
ND (1966)	1,200,000	0.25	0.45	0.75	1.50	—
ND (1966) Proof	30,000	Value: 2.00				

KM# 22 1/4 SHILLING (3 Pence)
Nickel-Brass **Ruler:** Elizabeth II **Obv:** Crowned head right

Date	Mintage	F	VF	XF	Unc	BU
1957	2,000,000	0.10	0.15	0.50	3.00	—
1957 Proof	6,300	Value: 7.50				
1960 Proof	4,200	Value: 8.50				

KM# 25 1/4 SHILLING (3 Pence)
Nickel-Brass **Ruler:** Elizabeth II **Obv:** Crowned head right **Rev:** Shield divides date **Shape:** 12-sided

Date	Mintage	F	VF	XF	Unc	BU
1964	1,200,000	0.10	0.15	0.20	0.75	—
1964 Proof	20,000	Value: 2.00				

KM# 27 1/4 SHILLING (3 Pence)
Nickel-Brass **Ruler:** Elizabeth II **Subject:** Norman Conquest **Obv:** Crowned head right **Rev:** Shield divides dates **Shape:** 12-sided

Date	Mintage	F	VF	XF	Unc	BU
ND (1966)	1,200,000	0.10	0.15	0.35	1.25	—
ND (1966) Proof	30,000	Value: 2.00				

KM# 28 5 SHILLING
Copper-Nickel **Ruler:** Elizabeth II **Subject:** Norman Conquest **Obv:** Crowned head right **Rev:** Shield divides dates

Date	Mintage	F	VF	XF	Unc	BU
ND (1966)	300,000	—	1.00	2.00	3.50	—
ND (1966) Proof	30,000	Value: 6.00				

DECIMAL COINAGE

100 New Pence = 1 Pound

Many of the following coins are also struck in silver, gold, and platinum for collectors

KM# 29 1/2 NEW PENNY
Bronze, 17.14 mm. **Ruler:** Elizabeth II **Obv:** Young bust right **Rev:** Shield above written value and date

Date	Mintage	F	VF	XF	Unc	BU
1971	3,000,000	—	—	0.10	0.20	—
1980	200,000	—	—	0.10	0.20	—
1980 Proof	10,000	Value: 1.35				

KM# 45 1/2 PENNY
Bronze, 17.14 mm. **Ruler:** Elizabeth II **Obv:** Young bust right **Rev:** Shield divides date

Date	Mintage	F	VF	XF	Unc	BU
1981	50,000	—	—	—	0.10	—
1981 Proof	15,000	Value: 0.90				

KM# 30 NEW PENNY
3.5500 g., Bronze, 20.32 mm. **Ruler:** Elizabeth II **Obv:** Young bust right **Rev:** Shield above written value

Date	Mintage	F	VF	XF	Unc	BU
1971	4,500,000	—	—	0.10	0.20	—
1980	3,000,000	—	—	0.10	0.20	—
1980 Proof	10,000	Value: 1.80				

KM# 46 PENNY
3.5500 g., Bronze, 20.32 mm. **Ruler:** Elizabeth II **Obv:** Young bust right **Rev:** Shield divides date

Date	Mintage	F	VF	XF	Unc	BU
1981	50,000	—	—	0.10	0.15	—
1981 Proof	15,000	Value: 1.10				

KM# 54 PENNY
3.5500 g., Bronze, 20.32 mm. **Ruler:** Elizabeth II **Obv:** Young bust right **Rev:** Le Hocq Watch Tower, St. Clement

Date	Mintage	F	VF	XF	Unc	BU
1983	500,000	—	—	0.10	0.25	—
1984	1,000,000	—	—	0.10	0.25	—
1985	1,000,000	—	—	0.10	0.25	—
1986	2,000,000	—	—	0.10	0.25	—
1987	1,500,000	—	—	0.10	0.25	—
1988	1,000,000	—	—	0.10	0.25	—
1989	1,500,000	—	—	0.10	0.25	—
1990	2,000,000	—	—	0.10	0.25	—
1992	—	—	—	—	0.50	—

Note: In sets only

KM# 54a PENNY
4.2000 g., 0.9250 Silver .1249 oz. ASW, 20.32 mm. **Ruler:** Elizabeth II **Obv:** Young bust right **Rev:** Le Hocq Watch Tower, St. Clement

Date	Mintage	F	VF	XF	Unc	BU
1983 Proof	5,000	Value: 7.00				

KM# 54b PENNY
Copper Plated Steel, 20.32 mm. **Ruler:** Elizabeth II **Obv:** Young bust right **Rev:** Le Hocq Watch Tower, St. Clement

Date	Mintage	F	VF	XF	Unc	BU
1994	2,000,000	—	—	0.10	0.50	—
1997	320,000	—	—	0.10	0.50	—

KM# 103 PENNY
Copper Plated Steel, 20.32 mm. **Ruler:** Elizabeth II **Obv:** Crowned head right **Obv. Designer:** Rank-Broadley

Date	Mintage	F	VF	XF	Unc	BU
1998	9,300,000	—	—	0.10	0.50	—

KM# 31 2 NEW PENCE
7.1000 g., Bronze, 25.91 mm. **Ruler:** Elizabeth II **Obv:** Young bust right **Rev:** Shield above written value

Date	Mintage	F	VF	XF	Unc	BU
1971	2,225,000	—	—	0.15	0.30	—
1975	750,000	—	—	0.15	0.40	—
1980	2,000,000	—	—	0.15	0.30	—
1980 Proof	10,000	Value: 2.25				

KM# 47 2 PENCE
7.1000 g., Bronze, 25.91 mm. **Ruler:** Elizabeth II **Obv:** Young bust right **Rev:** Shield divides date

Date	Mintage	F	VF	XF	Unc	BU
1981 Proof	15,000	Value: 1.35				
1981	50,000	—	—	0.15	0.25	—

KM# 55 2 PENCE
7.1000 g., Bronze, 25.91 mm. **Ruler:** Elizabeth II **Obv:** Young bust right **Rev:** L'Hermitage, St. Helier

Date	Mintage	F	VF	XF	Unc	BU
1983	800,000	—	—	0.15	0.25	—
1984	750,000	—	—	0.15	0.25	—
1985	250,000	—	—	0.15	0.25	—
1986	1,000,000	—	—	0.15	0.25	—
1987	2,000,000	—	—	0.15	0.25	—
1988	750,000	—	—	0.15	0.25	—
1989	1,000,000	—	—	0.15	0.25	—
1990	2,600,000	—	—	0.15	0.25	—
1997	5,500	—	—	—	0.50	—

KM# 55a 2 PENCE
8.4000 g., 0.9250 Silver .2498 oz. ASW, 25.91 mm. **Ruler:** Elizabeth II **Obv:** Young bust right **Rev:** L'Hermitage, St. Helier

Date	Mintage	F	VF	XF	Unc	BU
1983 Proof	5,000	Value: 10.00				

KM# 55b 2 PENCE
Copper Plated Steel, 25.91 mm. **Ruler:** Elizabeth II **Obv:** Young bust right **Rev:** L'Hermitage, St. Helier **Note:** Released into circulation in 1998.

Date	Mintage	F	VF	XF	Unc	BU
1992	—	—	—	0.15	0.50	—
1997	—	—	—	0.15	0.50	—

KM# 104 2 PENCE

Copper Plated Steel, 25.91 mm. **Ruler:** Elizabeth II **Obv:** Head with tiara right **Obv. Designer:** Rank-Broadley **Rev:** L'Hermitage, St. Helier

Date	Mintage	F	VF	XF	Unc	BU
1998	50,000	—	—	0.15	0.50	—

KM# 32 5 NEW PENCE

5.6500 g., Copper-Nickel, 23.59 mm. **Ruler:** Elizabeth II **Obv:** Young bust right **Rev:** Shield above written value

Date	Mintage	F	VF	XF	Unc	BU
1968	3,600,000	—	0.15	0.25	1.00	—
1980	800,000	—	0.15	0.25	1.00	—
1980 Proof	10,000	Value: 2.75				

KM# 48 5 PENCE

5.6500 g., Copper-Nickel, 23.59 mm. **Ruler:** Elizabeth II **Obv:** Young bust right **Rev:** Shield divides date

Date	Mintage	F	VF	XF	Unc	BU
1981	50,000	—	0.15	0.25	1.00	—
1981 Proof	15,000	Value: 1.80				

KM# 56.1 5 PENCE

5.6500 g., Copper-Nickel, 23.59 mm. **Ruler:** Elizabeth II **Obv:** Young bust right **Rev:** Seymour Tower, Grouville, L'Avathison

Date	Mintage	F	VF	XF	Unc	BU
1983	400,000	—	0.10	0.20	1.00	—
1984	300,000	—	0.10	0.20	1.00	—
1985	600,000	—	0.10	0.20	1.00	—
1986	200,000	—	0.10	0.20	1.00	—
1987	—	—	—	—	0.50	—
Note: In sets only						
1988	400,000	—	0.10	0.20	1.00	—

KM# 56.1a 5 PENCE

6.6000 g., 0.9250 Silver .1963 oz. ASW, 23.59 mm. **Ruler:** Elizabeth II **Obv:** Young bust right **Rev:** Seymour Tower, Grouville, L'Avathison

Date	Mintage	F	VF	XF	Unc	BU
1983 Proof	5,000	Value: 10.00				

KM# 56.2 5 PENCE

Copper-Nickel, 18 mm. **Ruler:** Elizabeth II **Obv:** Young bust right **Rev:** Seymour Tower, Grouville, L'Avathison **Note:** Reduced size.

Date	Mintage	F	VF	XF	Unc	BU
1990	4,000,000	—	—	0.15	0.35	—
1991	2,000,000	—	—	0.15	0.35	—
1992	1,000,000	—	—	0.15	0.50	—
1993	2,000,000	—	—	0.15	0.50	—
1997	5,500	—	—	—	1.00	—
Note: In sets only						

KM# 105 5 PENCE

Copper-Nickel, 18 mm. **Ruler:** Elizabeth II **Obv:** Head with tiara right **Obv. Designer:** Rank-Broadley

Date	Mintage	F	VF	XF	Unc	BU
1998	50,000	—	—	0.15	0.50	—

KM# 33 10 NEW PENCE

11.3000 g., Copper-Nickel, 28.5 mm. **Ruler:** Elizabeth II **Obv:** Young bust right **Rev:** Shield above written value

Date	Mintage	F	VF	XF	Unc	BU
1968	1,500,000	—	0.20	0.35	1.00	—
1975	1,022,000	—	0.20	0.30	0.90	—
1980	1,000,000	—	0.20	0.30	0.75	—
1980 Proof	10,000	Value: 5.50				

KM# 49 10 PENCE

11.3000 g., Copper-Nickel, 28.5 mm. **Ruler:** Elizabeth II **Obv:** Young bust right **Rev:** Shield divides date

Date	Mintage	F	VF	XF	Unc	BU
1981	50,000	—	—	0.30	1.00	—
1981 Proof	15,000	Value: 2.25				

KM# 57.1 10 PENCE

11.3000 g., Copper-Nickel, 28.5 mm. **Ruler:** Elizabeth II **Obv:** Young bust right **Rev:** La Houque Bie, Faldouet, St. Martin

Date	Mintage	F	VF	XF	Unc	BU
1983	30,000	—	—	0.30	1.00	—
1984	100,000	—	—	0.30	1.00	—
1985	100,000	—	—	0.30	1.00	—
1986	400,000	—	—	0.30	0.75	—
1987	800,000	—	—	0.30	0.75	—
1988	650,000	—	—	0.30	0.75	—
1989	700,000	—	—	0.30	0.75	—
1990	850,000	—	—	0.30	0.75	—

KM# 57.1a 10 PENCE

13.2000 g., 0.9250 Silver .3926 oz. ASW, 28.5 mm. **Ruler:** Elizabeth II **Obv:** Young bust right **Rev:** La Houque Bie, Faldouet, St. Martin

Date	Mintage	F	VF	XF	Unc	BU
1983 Proof	5,000	Value: 15.00				

KM# 57.2 10 PENCE

Copper-Nickel, 24.5 mm. **Ruler:** Elizabeth II **Obv:** Young bust right **Rev:** La Houque Bie, Faldouet, St. Martin **Note:** Reduced size.

Date	Mintage	F	VF	XF	Unc	BU
1992	7,000,000	—	—	0.30	0.50	—
1997	5,500	—	—	—	1.00	—
Note: In sets only						

KM# 106 10 PENCE

Copper-Nickel, 24.5 mm. **Ruler:** Elizabeth II **Obv:** Head with tiara right **Obv. Designer:** Rank-Broadley

Date	Mintage	F	VF	XF	Unc	BU
1998	50,000	—	—	—	1.00	—
Note: In sets only						

KM# 53 20 PENCE

5.0000 g., Copper-Nickel, 21.4 mm. **Ruler:** Elizabeth II **Subject:** 100th Anniversary of Lighthouse at Corbiere **Obv:** Young bust right **Rev:** Date below lighthouse **Rev. Designer:** Robert Lowe **Shape:** 7-sided

Date	Mintage	F	VF	XF	Unc	BU
1982	200,000	—	—	0.50	1.50	—

KM# 53a 20 PENCE

5.8300 g., 0.9250 Silver .1734 oz. ASW, 21.4 mm. **Ruler:** Elizabeth II **Subject:** 100th Anniversary of Lighthouse at Corbiere **Obv:** Young bust right **Rev:** Date below lighthouse **Rev. Designer:** Robert Lowe **Shape:** 7-sided

Date	Mintage	F	VF	XF	Unc	BU
1982 Proof	1,500	Value: 15.00				

KM# 66 20 PENCE

5.0000 g., Copper-Nickel, 21.4 mm. **Ruler:** Elizabeth II **Subject:** 100th Anniversary of Lighthouse at Corbiere **Obv:** Young bust right **Rev:** Written value below lighthouse **Rev. Designer:** Robert Lowe **Shape:** 7-sided

Date	Mintage	F	VF	XF	Unc	BU
1983	400,000	—	—	0.50	1.00	—
1984	250,000	—	—	0.50	1.00	—
1986	100,000	—	—	0.50	1.00	—
1987	100,000	—	—	0.50	1.00	—
1989	100,000	—	—	0.50	1.00	—
1990	150,000	—	—	0.50	1.00	—
1992	—	—	—	—	2.00	—
Note: In sets only						
1994	200,000	—	—	0.50	1.00	—
1996	250,000	—	—	0.50	1.00	—
1997	600,000	—	—	0.50	1.00	—
1998	—	—	—	0.50	1.00	—

KM# 66a 20 PENCE

5.8300 g., 0.9250 Silver .1734 oz. ASW, 21.4 mm. **Ruler:** Elizabeth II **Subject:** 100th Anniversary of Lighthouse at Corbiere **Obv:** Young bust right **Rev:** Written value below lighthouse **Rev. Designer:** Robert Lowe **Shape:** 7-sided

Date	Mintage	F	VF	XF	Unc	BU
1983 Proof	5,000	Value: 15.00				

KM# 107 20 PENCE

Copper-Nickel, 21.4 mm. **Ruler:** Elizabeth II **Obv:** Head with tiara right **Obv. Designer:** Rank-Broadley

Date	Mintage	F	VF	XF	Unc	BU
1998	90,000	—	—	0.50	1.00	—

KM# 44 25 PENCE

Copper-Nickel **Ruler:** Elizabeth II **Subject:** Queen's Silver Jubliee **Obv:** Young bust right **Rev:** Mont Orgueil Castle and Gorey Harbour **Rev. Designer:** Bernard Sindall

Date	Mintage	F	VF	XF	Unc	BU
ND(1977)	262,000	—	0.75	1.25	3.75	—

KM# 44a 25 PENCE

28.2800 g., 0.9250 Silver .8411 oz. ASW **Ruler:** Elizabeth II **Subject:** Queen's Silver Jubilee **Obv:** Young bust right **Rev:** Mont Orgueil and sailboats **Rev. Designer:** Bernard Sindall

Date	Mintage	F	VF	XF	Unc	BU
ND(1977) Proof	25,000	Value: 16.50				

KM# 34 50 PENCE
13.5000 g., Copper-Nickel, 30 mm. **Ruler:** Elizabeth II **Obv:** Young bust right **Rev:** Shield above written value **Shape:** 7-sided

Date	Mintage	F	VF	XF	Unc	BU
1969	480,000	—	—	0.90	1.50	—
1980	100,000	—	—	0.90	1.50	—
1980 Proof	10,000	Value: 9.00				

KM# 35 50 PENCE
5.4200 g., 0.9250 Silver .1612 oz. ASW **Ruler:** Elizabeth II **Subject:** 25th Wedding Anniversary **Obv:** Young bust right **Rev:** Mace divides map **Rev. Designer:** Norman Sillman

Date	Mintage	F	VF	XF	Unc	BU
1972	24,000	—	—	2.50	4.50	—
1972 Proof	1,500	Value: 6.50				

KM# 50 50 PENCE
13.5000 g., Copper-Nickel, 30 mm. **Ruler:** Elizabeth II **Obv:** Young bust right **Rev:** Shield divides date **Shape:** 7-sided

Date	Mintage	F	VF	XF	Unc	BU
1981 Proof	15,000	Value: 3.00				
1981	50,000	—	—	1.00	1.75	—

KM# 58.1 50 PENCE
13.5000 g., Copper-Nickel, 30 mm. **Ruler:** Elizabeth II **Obv:** Young bust right **Rev:** Grosnez Castle **Shape:** 7-sided

Date	Mintage	F	VF	XF	Unc	BU
1983	50,000	—	—	1.00	1.75	—
1984	50,000	—	—	1.00	1.75	—
1986	30,000	—	—	1.00	1.75	—
1987	150,000	—	—	1.00	1.75	—
1988	130,000	—	—	1.00	1.75	—
1989	180,000	—	—	1.00	1.75	—
1990	370,000	—	—	1.00	1.75	—
1992	—	—	—	—	2.50	—
Note: In sets only						
1994	200,000	—	—	1.00	1.75	—
1997	5,500	—	—	—	2.50	—
Note: In sets only						

KM# 58.1a 50 PENCE
15.5000 g., 0.9250 Silver .4609 oz. ASW, 30 mm. **Ruler:** Elizabeth II **Obv:** Young bust right **Rev:** Grosnez Castle **Shape:** 7-sided

Date	Mintage	F	VF	XF	Unc	BU
1983 Proof	5,000	Value: 18.00				

KM# 58.2 50 PENCE
Copper-Nickel, 27.3 mm. **Ruler:** Elizabeth II **Obv:** Young bust right **Rev:** Grosnez Castle **Shape:** 7-sided **Note:** Small size.

Date	Mintage	F	VF	XF	Unc	BU
1997	1,500,000	—	—	—	2.50	—

KM# 63 50 PENCE
13.5000 g., Copper-Nickel, 30 mm. **Ruler:** Elizabeth II **Subject:** 40th Anniversary - Liberation of 1945 **Obv:** Crowned bust right **Rev:** Crossed flags divides dates above chain links with value below **Shape:** 7-sided

Date	Mintage	F	VF	XF	Unc	BU
1985	65,000	—	—	1.25	2.00	—

KM# 108 50 PENCE
Copper-Nickel, 27.3 mm. **Ruler:** Elizabeth II **Obv:** Crowned bust right **Obv. Designer:** Rank-Broadley

Date	Mintage	F	VF	XF	Unc	BU
1998	25,000	—	—	1.00	2.50	—

KM# 36 POUND
10.8400 g., 0.9250 Silver .3224 oz. ASW **Ruler:** Elizabeth II **Subject:** 25th Wedding Anniversary **Obv:** Young bust right **Rev:** Lillies **Rev. Designer:** Norman Sillman

Date	Mintage	F	VF	XF	Unc	BU
1972	24,000	—	—	—	6.00	—
1972 Proof	1,500	Value: 12.00				

KM# 51 POUND
Copper-Nickel **Ruler:** Elizabeth II **Subject:** Bicentennial - Battle of Jersey **Obv:** Young bust right **Rev:** Badge of the Royal Jersey Militia **Shape:** 4-sided

Date	Mintage	F	VF	XF	Unc	BU
ND(1981)	200,000	—	—	2.00	3.25	—
ND(1981) Proof	15,000	Value: 8.00				

KM# 51a POUND
10.4500 g., 0.9250 Silver .3108 oz. ASW **Ruler:** Elizabeth II **Subject:** Bicentennial - Battle of Jersey **Obv:** Young bust right **Rev:** Crowned shaded pointed shield within X design divides dates **Shape:** Square

Date	Mintage	F	VF	XF	Unc	BU
ND(1981) Proof	10,000	Value: 12.50				

KM# 51b POUND
17.5500 g., 0.9170 Gold .5174 oz. AGW **Ruler:** Elizabeth II **Subject:** Bicentennial - Battle of Jersey **Obv:** Young bust right **Rev:** Crowned shaded pointed shield within X design divides dates **Shape:** Square

Date	Mintage	F	VF	XF	Unc	BU
ND(1981) Proof	5,000	Value: 380				

KM# 59 POUND
9.5000 g., Nickel-Brass, 22.5 mm. **Ruler:** Elizabeth II **Obv:** Young bust right **Rev:** Shield above written value **Edge Lettering:** CAESAREA INSULA

Date	Mintage	F	VF	XF	Unc	BU
1983	100,000	—	—	2.00	3.25	—

KM# 59a POUND
11.6800 g., 0.9250 Silver .3474 oz. ASW, 22.5 mm. **Ruler:** Elizabeth II **Obv:** Young bust right **Rev:** Shield above written value

Date	Mintage	F	VF	XF	Unc	BU
1983 Proof	2,500	Value: 20.00				

KM# 59b POUND
19.6500 g., 0.9170 Gold .5794 oz. AGW, 22.5 mm. **Ruler:** Elizabeth II **Obv:** Young bust right **Rev:** Shield above written value

Date	Mintage	F	VF	XF	Unc	BU
1983 Proof	250	Value: 425				
Note: 497 pieces were remelted						

KM# 60 POUND
9.5000 g., Nickel-Brass, 22.5 mm. **Ruler:** Elizabeth II **Obv:** Young bust right **Rev:** Shield above written value **Edge Lettering:** CAESAREA INSULA

Date	Mintage	F	VF	XF	Unc	BU
1984	20,000	—	—	2.00	3.25	—

KM# 60a POUND
11.6800 g., 0.9250 Silver .3474 oz. ASW, 22.5 mm. **Ruler:** Elizabeth II **Obv:** Young bust right **Rev:** Shield above written value

Date	Mintage	F	VF	XF	Unc	BU
1984 Proof	2,500	Value: 18.50				

KM# 60b POUND
19.6500 g., 0.9170 Gold .5794 oz. AGW, 22.5 mm. **Ruler:** Elizabeth II **Obv:** Young bust right **Rev:** Shield above written value

Date	Mintage	F	VF	XF	Unc	BU
1984 Proof	250	Value: 425				

KM# 61 POUND
9.5000 g., Nickel-Brass, 22.5 mm. **Ruler:** Elizabeth II **Obv:** Young bust right **Rev:** Shield above written value **Edge Lettering:** CAESAREA INSULA

Date	Mintage	F	VF	XF	Unc	BU
1984	20,000	—	—	2.00	3.25	—

KM# 61a POUND
11.6800 g., 0.9250 Silver .3474 oz. ASW, 22.5 mm. **Ruler:** Elizabeth II **Obv:** Young bust right **Rev:** Shield above written value

Date	Mintage	F	VF	XF	Unc	BU
1984 Proof	2,500	Value: 20.00				

KM# 61b POUND
19.6500 g., 0.9170 Gold .5794 oz. AGW, 22.5 mm. **Ruler:** Elizabeth II **Obv:** Young bust right **Rev:** Shield above written value

Date	Mintage	F	VF	XF	Unc	BU
1984 Proof	250	Value: 425				

KM# 62 POUND
9.5000 g., Nickel-Brass, 22.5 mm. **Ruler:** Elizabeth II **Obv:** Young bust right **Rev:** Shield above written value **Edge Lettering:** CAESAREA INSULA

Date	Mintage	F	VF	XF	Unc	BU
1985	25,000	—	—	2.00	3.25	—

KM# 62a POUND
11.6800 g., 0.9250 Silver .3474 oz. ASW, 22.5 mm. **Ruler:** Elizabeth II **Obv:** Young bust right **Rev:** Shield above written value

Date	Mintage	F	VF	XF	Unc	BU
1985 Proof	2,500	Value: 18.50				

KM# 62b POUND
19.6500 g., 0.9170 Gold .5794 oz. AGW, 22.5 mm. **Ruler:** Elizabeth II **Obv:** Young bust right **Rev:** Shield above written value

Date	Mintage	F	VF	XF	Unc	BU
1985 Proof	124	Value: 450				

KM# 65 POUND
9.5000 g., Nickel-Brass, 22.5 mm. **Ruler:** Elizabeth II **Obv:** Young bust right **Rev:** Shield above written value **Edge Lettering:** CAESAREA INSULA

Date	Mintage	F	VF	XF	Unc	BU
1985	10,000	—	—	2.00	3.50	—

KM# 65a POUND
11.6800 g., 0.9250 Silver .3474 oz. ASW, 22.5 mm. **Ruler:** Elizabeth II **Obv:** Young bust right **Rev:** Shield above written value

Date	Mintage	F	VF	XF	Unc	BU
1985 Proof	2,500	Value: 20.00				

KM# 65b POUND
19.6500 g., 0.9170 Gold .5794 oz. AGW, 22.5 mm. **Ruler:** Elizabeth II **Obv:** Young bust right **Rev:** Shield above written value

Date	Mintage	F	VF	XF	Unc	BU
1985 Proof	108	Value: 475				

KM# 68 POUND
9.5000 g., Nickel-Brass, 22.5 mm. **Ruler:** Elizabeth II **Obv:** Young bust right **Rev:** Shield above written value **Edge Lettering:** CAESAREA INSULA

Date	Mintage	F	VF	XF	Unc	BU
1986	10,000	—	—	2.00	3.25	—

KM# 68a POUND

11.6800 g., 0.9250 Silver .3474 oz. ASW, 22.5 mm. **Ruler:** Elizabeth II **Obv:** Young bust right **Rev:** Shield above written value

Date	Mintage	F	VF	XF	Unc	BU
1986 Proof	2,500	Value: 20.00				

KM# 68b POUND

19.6500 g., 0.9170 Gold .5794 oz. AGW, 22.5 mm. **Ruler:** Elizabeth II **Obv:** Young bust right **Rev:** Shield above written value

Date	Mintage	F	VF	XF	Unc	BU
1986 Proof	250	Value: 425				

KM# 69 POUND

9.5000 g., Nickel-Brass, 22.5 mm. **Ruler:** Elizabeth II **Obv:** Young bust right **Rev:** Shield above written value **Edge Lettering:** CAESAREA INSULA

Date	Mintage	F	VF	XF	Unc	BU
1986	10,000	—	—	2.00	3.25	—

KM# 69a POUND

11.6800 g., 0.9250 Silver .3474 oz. ASW, 22.5 mm. **Ruler:** Elizabeth II **Obv:** Young bust right **Rev:** Shield above written value

Date	Mintage	F	VF	XF	Unc	BU
1986 Proof	2,500	Value: 20.00				

KM# 69b POUND

19.6500 g., 0.9170 Gold .5794 oz. AGW, 22.5 mm. **Ruler:** Elizabeth II **Obv:** Young bust right **Rev:** Shield above written value

Date	Mintage	F	VF	XF	Unc	BU
1986 Proof	250	Value: 425				

KM# 71 POUND

9.5000 g., Nickel-Brass, 22.5 mm. **Ruler:** Elizabeth II **Obv:** Young bust right **Rev:** Shield above written value **Edge Lettering:** CAESAREA INSULA

Date	Mintage	F	VF	XF	Unc	BU
1987	10,000	—	—	2.00	3.50	—

KM# 71a POUND

11.6800 g., 0.9250 Silver .3474 oz. ASW, 22.5 mm. **Ruler:** Elizabeth II **Obv:** Young bust right **Rev:** Shield above written value

Date	Mintage	F	VF	XF	Unc	BU
1987 Proof	2,500	Value: 18.50				

KM# 71b POUND

19.6500 g., 0.9170 Gold .5794 oz. AGW, 22.5 mm. **Ruler:** Elizabeth II **Obv:** Young bust right **Rev:** Shield above written value

Date	Mintage	F	VF	XF	Unc	BU
1987 Proof	250	Value: 425				

KM# 72 POUND

9.5000 g., Nickel-Brass, 22.5 mm. **Ruler:** Elizabeth II **Obv:** Young bust right **Rev:** Shield above written value **Edge Lettering:** CAESAREA INSULA

Date	Mintage	F	VF	XF	Unc	BU
1987	10,000	—	—	2.00	3.25	—

KM# 72a POUND

11.6800 g., 0.9250 Silver .3474 oz. ASW, 22.5 mm. **Ruler:** Elizabeth II **Obv:** Young bust right **Rev:** Shield above written value

Date	Mintage	F	VF	XF	Unc	BU
1987 Proof	2,500	Value: 18.50				

KM# 72b POUND

19.6500 g., 0.9170 Gold .5794 oz. AGW, 22.5 mm. **Ruler:** Elizabeth II **Obv:** Young bust right **Rev:** Shield above written value

Date	Mintage	F	VF	XF	Unc	BU
1987 Proof	250	Value: 425				

KM# 73 POUND

9.5000 g., Nickel-Brass, 22.5 mm. **Ruler:** Elizabeth II **Obv:** Young bust right **Rev:** Shield above written value **Edge Lettering:** CAESAREA INSULA

Date	Mintage	F	VF	XF	Unc	BU
1988	10,000	—	—	2.00	4.00	—

KM# 73a POUND

11.6800 g., 0.9250 Silver .3474 oz. ASW, 22.5 mm. **Ruler:** Elizabeth II **Obv:** Young bust right **Rev:** Shield above written value

Date	Mintage	F	VF	XF	Unc	BU
1988 Proof	2,500	Value: 18.50				

KM# 73b POUND

19.6500 g., 0.9170 Gold .5794 oz. AGW, 22.5 mm. **Ruler:** Elizabeth II **Obv:** Young bust right **Rev:** Shield above written value

Date	Mintage	F	VF	XF	Unc	BU
1988 Proof	250	Value: 425				

KM# 74 POUND

9.5000 g., Nickel-Brass, 22.5 mm. **Ruler:** Elizabeth II **Obv:** Young bust right **Rev:** Shield above written value **Edge Lettering:** CAESAREA INSULA

Date	Mintage	F	VF	XF	Unc	BU
1988	10,000	—	—	2.00	3.25	—

KM# 74a POUND

11.6800 g., 0.9250 Silver .3474 oz. ASW, 22.5 mm. **Ruler:** Elizabeth II **Obv:** Young bust right **Rev:** Shield above written value

Date	Mintage	F	VF	XF	Unc	BU
1988 Proof	2,500	Value: 18.50				

KM# 74b POUND

19.6500 g., 0.9170 Gold .5794 oz. AGW, 22.5 mm. **Ruler:** Elizabeth II **Obv:** Young bust right **Rev:** Shield above written value

Date	Mintage	F	VF	XF	Unc	BU
1988 Proof	250	Value: 425				

KM# 75 POUND

9.5000 g., Nickel-Brass, 22.5 mm. **Ruler:** Elizabeth II **Obv:** Young bust right **Rev:** Shield above written value **Edge Lettering:** CAESAREA INSULA

Date	Mintage	F	VF	XF	Unc	BU
1989	25,000	—	—	2.00	3.25	—

KM# 75a POUND

11.6800 g., 0.9250 Silver .3474 oz. ASW, 22.5 mm. **Ruler:** Elizabeth II **Obv:** Young bust right **Rev:** Shield above written value

Date	Mintage	F	VF	XF	Unc	BU
1989 Proof	2,500	Value: 18.50				

KM# 75b POUND

19.6500 g., 0.9170 Gold .5794 oz. AGW, 22.5 mm. **Ruler:** Elizabeth II **Obv:** Young bust right **Rev:** Shield above written value

Date	Mintage	F	VF	XF	Unc	BU
1989 Proof	250	Value: 425				

KM# 84 POUND

9.5000 g., Nickel-Brass, 22.5 mm. **Ruler:** Elizabeth II **Obv:** Young bust right **Rev:** Schooner, The Tickler **Rev. Designer:** Robert Evans **Edge Lettering:** CAESAREA INSULA

Date	Mintage	F	VF	XF	Unc	BU
1991	15,000	—	—	—	3.25	—

KM# 84a POUND

11.6800 g., 0.9250 Silver .3474 oz. ASW, 22.5 mm. **Ruler:** Elizabeth II **Obv:** Young bust right **Rev:** Schooner, The Tickler **Rev. Designer:** Robert Evans

Date	Mintage	F	VF	XF	Unc	BU
1991 Proof	3,000	Value: 20.00				

KM# 84b POUND

19.6500 g., 0.9170 Gold .5794 oz. AGW, 22.5 mm. **Ruler:** Elizabeth II **Obv:** Young bust right **Rev:** Schooner, The Tickler **Rev. Designer:** Robert Evans

Date	Mintage	F	VF	XF	Unc	BU
1991 Proof	Est. 250	Value: 450				

KM# 85 POUND

9.5000 g., Nickel-Brass, 22.5 mm. **Ruler:** Elizabeth II **Obv:** Young bust right **Rev:** Sailing ship, Percy Douglas **Rev. Designer:** Robert Evans **Edge Lettering:** CAESAREA INSULA

Date	Mintage	F	VF	XF	Unc	BU
1991	20,000	—	—	—	3.25	—

KM# 85a POUND

11.6800 g., 0.9250 Silver .3474 oz. ASW, 22.5 mm. **Ruler:** Elizabeth II **Obv:** Young bust right **Rev:** Sailing ship, Percy Douglas **Rev. Designer:** Robert Evans

Date	Mintage	F	VF	XF	Unc	BU
1991 Proof	3,000	Value: 20.00				

KM# 85b POUND

19.6500 g., 0.9170 Gold .5794 oz. AGW, 22.5 mm. **Ruler:** Elizabeth II **Obv:** Young bust right **Rev:** Sailing ship, Percy Douglas **Rev. Designer:** Robert Evans

Date	Mintage	F	VF	XF	Unc	BU
1991 Proof	250	Value: 450				

KM# 86 POUND

9.5000 g., Nickel-Brass, 22.5 mm. **Ruler:** Elizabeth II **Obv:** Young bust right **Rev:** Brig, Hebe **Rev. Designer:** Robert Evans

Date	Mintage	F	VF	XF	Unc	BU
1992	2,000	—	—	—	3.25	—

KM# 86a POUND

11.6800 g., 0.9250 Silver .3474 oz. ASW, 22.5 mm. **Ruler:** Elizabeth II **Obv:** Young bust right **Rev:** Sailing ship, Hebe **Rev. Designer:** Robert Evans

Date	Mintage	F	VF	XF	Unc	BU
1992 Proof	Est. 3,000	Value: 20.00				

KM# 86b POUND

19.6500 g., 0.9170 Gold .5794 oz. AGW, 22.5 mm. **Ruler:** Elizabeth II **Obv:** Young bust right **Rev:** Sailing ship, Hebe **Rev. Designer:** Robert Evans

Date	Mintage	F	VF	XF	Unc	BU
1992 Proof	Est. 250	Value: 450				

KM# 87 POUND

9.5000 g., Nickel-Brass, 22.5 mm. **Ruler:** Elizabeth II **Obv:** Young bust right **Rev:** Bailiwick seal **Rev. Designer:** Robert Evans

Date	Mintage	F	VF	XF	Unc	BU
1992	20,000	—	—	—	3.50	—

KM# 87a POUND

11.6800 g., 0.9250 Silver .3474 oz. ASW, 22.5 mm. **Ruler:** Elizabeth II **Obv:** Young bust right **Rev:** Ornamented shield **Rev. Designer:** Robert Evans

Date	Mintage	F	VF	XF	Unc	BU
1992 Proof	3,000	Value: 20.00				

KM# 87b POUND

19.6500 g., 0.9170 Gold .5794 oz. AGW, 22.5 mm. **Ruler:** Elizabeth II **Obv:** Young bust right **Rev:** Ornamented shield **Rev. Designer:** Robert Evans

Date	Mintage	F	VF	XF	Unc	BU
1992 Proof	250	Value: 425				

KM# 88 POUND

9.5000 g., Nickel-Brass, 22.5 mm. **Ruler:** Elizabeth II **Obv:** Young bust right **Rev:** Barque, Gemini **Rev. Designer:** Robert Evans

Date	Mintage	F	VF	XF	Unc	BU
1993	—	—	—	—	3.25	—

KM# 88a POUND
11.6800 g., 0.9250 Silver .3474 oz. ASW, 22.5 mm.
Ruler: Elizabeth II **Obv:** Young bust right **Rev:** Sailing ship, Gemini **Rev. Designer:** Robert Evans

Date	Mintage	F	VF	XF	Unc	BU
1993 Proof	3,000	Value: 20.00				

KM# 88b POUND
19.6500 g., 0.9170 Gold .5794 oz. AGW, 22.5 mm.
Ruler: Elizabeth II **Obv:** Young bust right **Rev:** Sailing ship, Gemini **Rev. Designer:** Robert Evans

Date	Mintage	F	VF	XF	Unc	BU
1993 Proof	250	Value: 475				

KM# 90 POUND
9.5000 g., Nickel-Brass, 22.5 mm. **Ruler:** Elizabeth II **Obv:** Young bust right **Rev:** Brigantine, Century **Rev. Designer:** Robert Evans

Date	Mintage	F	VF	XF	Unc	BU
1993	—	—	—	—	3.25	—

KM# 90a POUND
11.6800 g., 0.9250 Silver .3474 oz. ASW, 22.5 mm.
Ruler: Elizabeth II **Obv:** Young bust right **Rev:** Brigantine, Century **Rev. Designer:** Robert Evans

Date	Mintage	F	VF	XF	Unc	BU
1993 Proof	Est. 3,000	Value: 20.00				

KM# 90b POUND
19.6500 g., 0.9170 Gold .5794 oz. AGW, 22.5 mm.
Ruler: Elizabeth II **Obv:** Young bust right **Rev:** Sailing ship, Century **Rev. Designer:** Robert Evans

Date	Mintage	F	VF	XF	Unc	BU
1993 Proof	Est. 250	Value: 450				

KM# 91 POUND
9.5000 g., Nickel-Brass, 22.5 mm. **Ruler:** Elizabeth II **Obv:** Young bust right **Rev:** Topsail Schooner, Resolute **Rev. Designer:** Robert Evans

Date	Mintage	F	VF	XF	Unc	BU
1994	60,000	—	—	—	3.25	—
1997	101,000	—	—	—	3.25	—

KM# 91a POUND
11.6800 g., 0.9250 Silver .3474 oz. ASW, 22.5 mm.
Ruler: Elizabeth II **Obv:** Young bust right **Rev:** Schooner, Resolute **Rev. Designer:** Robert Evans

Date	Mintage	F	VF	XF	Unc	BU
1994 Proof	3,000	Value: 20.00				

KM# 91b POUND
19.6500 g., 0.9170 Gold .5794 oz. AGW, 22.5 mm.
Ruler: Elizabeth II **Obv:** Young bust right **Rev:** Schooner, Resolute **Rev. Designer:** Robert Evans

Date	Mintage	F	VF	XF	Unc	BU
1994 Proof	250	Value: 450				

KM# 101 POUND
9.5000 g., Nickel-Brass, 22.5 mm. **Ruler:** Elizabeth II **Obv:** Head with tiara right **Obv. Designer:** Rank-Broadley **Rev:** Schooner, Resolute **Rev. Designer:** Robert Evans **Edge Lettering:** CAESAREA INSULA

Date	Mintage	F	VF	XF	Unc	BU
1998	174,000	—	—	—	3.25	—

KM# 110 SOVEREIGN
7.9800 g., 0.9167 Gold .2352 oz. AGW, 22.5 mm.
Ruler: Elizabeth II **Subject:** William I - Duke of Normandy **Obv:** Crowned bust right **Rev:** William seated on throne **Rev. Designer:** Robert Elderton

Date	Mintage	F	VF	XF	Unc	BU
2000	Est. 2,000	—	—	—	175	—
2000 Proof	Est. 2,000	Value: 225				

KM# 37 2 POUNDS
21.6800 g., 0.9250 Silver .6513 oz. ASW **Ruler:** Elizabeth II **Subject:** 25th Wedding Anniversary **Obv:** Crowned bust right **Rev:** Sailing ship "Alexandria" **Rev. Designer:** Norman Sillman

Date	Mintage	F	VF	XF	Unc	BU
1972	24,000	—	—	—	12.00	—
1972 Proof	1,500	Value: 25.00				

KM# 52 2 POUNDS
Copper-Nickel, 38.5 mm. **Ruler:** Elizabeth II **Subject:** Wedding of Prince Charles and Lady Diana **Obv:** Crowned bust right **Rev:** Conjoined busts right **Rev. Designer:** Michael Rizzello

Date	Mintage	F	VF	XF	Unc	BU
ND(1981)	150,000	—	—	—	6.00	—

KM# 52a 2 POUNDS
28.2800 g., 0.9250 Silver .8411 oz. ASW, 38.5 mm.
Ruler: Elizabeth II **Subject:** Wedding of Prince Charles and Lady Diana **Obv:** Crowned bust right **Rev:** Conjoined busts right

Date	Mintage	F	VF	XF	Unc	BU
ND(1981) Proof	35,000	Value: 15.00				

KM# 52b 2 POUNDS
15.9800 g., 0.9170 Gold .4712 oz. AGW, 38.5 mm.
Ruler: Elizabeth II **Subject:** Wedding of Prince Charles and Lady Diana **Obv:** Crowned bust right **Rev:** Conjoined busts right

Date	Mintage	F	VF	XF	Unc	BU
ND(1981) Proof	1,500	Value: 345				

KM# 64 2 POUNDS
Copper-Nickel, 38.5 mm. **Ruler:** Elizabeth II **Subject:** 40th Anniversary of Liberation of 1945 **Obv:** Crowned bust right **Rev:** H.M.S. Beagle, destroyer **Edge Lettering:** OUR DEAR CHANNEL ISLANDS WILL ALSO BE FREED TODAY

Date	Mintage	F	VF	XF	Unc	BU
1985	20,000	—	—	—	6.00	—

KM# 64a 2 POUNDS
28.2800 g., 0.9250 Silver .8411 oz. ASW, 38.5 mm.
Ruler: Elizabeth II **Subject:** 40th Anniversary of Liberation of 1945 **Obv:** Crowned bust right **Rev:** H.M.S. Beagle, destroyer

Date	Mintage	F	VF	XF	Unc	BU
1985 Proof	2,500	Value: 35.00				

KM# 64b 2 POUNDS
47.5400 g., 0.9170 Gold 1.4011 oz. AGW, 38.5 mm.
Ruler: Elizabeth II **Subject:** 40th Anniversary of Liberation of 1945 **Obv:** Crowned bust right **Rev:** H.M.S. Beagle, destroyer

Date	Mintage	F	VF	XF	Unc	BU
1985 Proof	40	Value: 2,000				

KM# 67.1 2 POUNDS
Copper-Nickel, 38.5 mm. **Ruler:** Elizabeth II **Subject:** XIII Commonwealth Games - Edinburgh **Obv:** Crowned bust right **Rev:** Two sprinters **Edge Lettering:** XIII COMMONWEALTH GAMES

Date	Mintage	F	VF	XF	Unc	BU
1986	50,000	—	—	—	6.00	—

KM# 67.1a 2 POUNDS
28.2800 g., 0.5000 Silver .4546 oz. ASW, 38.5 mm.
Ruler: Elizabeth II **Subject:** XIII Commonwealth Games - Edinburgh **Obv:** Crowned bust right **Rev:** Two sprinters

Date	Mintage	F	VF	XF	Unc	BU
1986	20,000	—	—	—	20.00	—

KM# 67.1b 2 POUNDS
28.2800 g., 0.9250 Silver .8411 oz. ASW, 38.5 mm.
Ruler: Elizabeth II **Subject:** XIII Commonwealth Games - Edinburgh **Obv:** Crowned bust right **Rev:** Two sprinters

Date	Mintage	F	VF	XF	Unc	BU
1986 Proof	20,000	Value: 40.00				

KM# 67.2 2 POUNDS
Copper-Nickel, 38.5 mm. **Ruler:** Elizabeth II **Subject:** XIII Commonwealth Games - Edinburgh **Obv:** Crowned bust right **Rev:** Two sprinters **Note:** Without edge inscription.

Date	Mintage	F	VF	XF	Unc	BU
1986	5,000	—	—	—	7.50	—

KM# 70 2 POUNDS
Copper-Nickel, 38.5 mm. **Ruler:** Elizabeth II **Subject:** World Wildlife Fund **Obv:** Crowned bust right **Rev:** Pigeons

Date	Mintage	F	VF	XF	Unc	BU
1987	23,000	—	—	—	10.00	12.00

KM# 70a 2 POUNDS
28.2800 g., 0.9250 Silver .8411 oz. ASW, 38.5 mm. **Ruler:** Elizabeth II **Subject:** World Wildlife Fund **Obv:** Crowned bust right **Rev:** Pigeons

Date	Mintage	F	VF	XF	Unc	BU
1987 Proof	25,000	Value: 25.00				

KM# 76 2 POUNDS
Copper-Nickel, 38.5 mm. **Ruler:** Elizabeth II **Subject:** Royal Visit **Obv:** Crowned bust right **Rev:** Royal Mace divides map

Date	Mintage	F	VF	XF	Unc	BU
1989	10,000	—	—	—	6.00	—

KM# 76a 2 POUNDS
28.3000 g., 0.9250 Silver .8411 oz. ASW, 38.5 mm. **Ruler:** Elizabeth II **Subject:** Royal Visit **Obv:** Crowned bust right **Rev:** Royal Mace divides map

Date	Mintage	F	VF	XF	Unc	BU
1989 Proof	3,000	Value: 30.00				

KM# 77 2 POUNDS
28.3000 g., 0.9250 Silver .8411 oz. ASW, 38.5 mm. **Ruler:** Elizabeth II **Subject:** 50th Anniversary - The Battle of Britain **Obv:** Crowned bust right **Rev:** Spitfire divides map **Rev. Designer:** Ian Rank-Broadley

Date	Mintage	F	VF	XF	Unc	BU
ND(1990) Proof	Est. 10,000	Value: 37.50				

KM# 83 2 POUNDS
Copper-Nickel, 38.5 mm. **Ruler:** Elizabeth II **Subject:** 90th Birthday of Queen Mother **Obv:** Crowned bust right **Rev:** Crowned double "E" monogram **Rev. Designer:** Robert Elderton

Date	Mintage	F	VF	XF	Unc	BU
ND(1990)	10,000	—	—	—	7.00	—

KM# 83a 2 POUNDS
28.3500 g., 0.9250 Silver .8432 oz. ASW, 38.5 mm. **Ruler:** Elizabeth II **Subject:** 90th Birthday of Queen Mother **Obv:** Crowned bust right **Rev:** Crowned double "E" monogram

Date	Mintage	F	VF	XF	Unc	BU
ND(1990) Proof	3,000	Value: 55.00				

KM# 83b 2 POUNDS
15.9800 g., 0.9170 Gold .4708 oz. AGW **Ruler:** Elizabeth II **Subject:** 90th Birthday of Queen Mother **Obv:** Crowned bust right **Rev:** Crowned double "E" monogram

Date	Mintage	F	VF	XF	Unc	BU
ND(1990) Proof	90	Value: 750				

KM# 89 2 POUNDS
Copper-Nickel, 38.5 mm. **Ruler:** Elizabeth II **Subject:** 40th Anniversary - Coronation of Queen Elizabeth II **Obv:** Crowned bust right **Rev:** Crown, royal mace and shield

Date	Mintage	F	VF	XF	Unc	BU
ND(1993)	12,000	—	—	—	6.00	—

KM# 89a 2 POUNDS
28.2800 g., 0.9250 Silver .8411 oz. ASW, 38.5 mm. **Ruler:** Elizabeth II **Subject:** 40th Anniversary - Coronation of Queen Elizabeth II **Obv:** Crowned bust right **Rev:** Crown, royal mace and shield

Date	Mintage	F	VF	XF	Unc	BU
ND(1993) Proof	Est. 10,000	Value: 55.00				

KM# 89b 2 POUNDS
15.9800 g., 0.9167 Gold .4709 oz. AGW **Ruler:** Elizabeth II **Subject:** 40th Anniversary - Coronation of Queen Elizabeth II **Obv:** Crowned bust right **Rev:** Crown, royal mace and shield

Date	Mintage	F	VF	XF	Unc	BU
ND(1993) Proof	Est. 500	Value: 500				

KM# 92 2 POUNDS
Copper-Nickel, 38.5 mm. **Ruler:** Elizabeth II **Subject:** 50th Anniversary of Liberation **Obv:** Crowned bust right **Rev:** Bird with sprig within letter V above dates within ribbon **Rev. Designer:** Robert Elderton

Date	Mintage	F	VF	XF	Unc	BU
1995	42,000	—	—	—	8.00	—

Note: Also released in special wallet with 1 Pound commemorative banknote (6,000). Market value: $20.00

KM# 92a 2 POUNDS
28.2800 g., 0.9250 Silver .8411 oz. ASW, 38.5 mm. **Ruler:** Elizabeth II **Subject:** 50th Anniversary of Liberation **Obv:** Crowned bust right **Rev:** Bird with sprig within letter V above dates within ribbon **Rev. Designer:** Robert Elderton

Date	Mintage	F	VF	XF	Unc	BU
1995 Proof	7,000	Value: 55.00				

KM# 97 2 POUNDS
Copper-Nickel, 38.5 mm. **Ruler:** Elizabeth II **Subject:** Queen Elizabeth's 70th Birthday **Obv:** Crowned bust right **Rev:** Lillies **Rev. Designer:** Norman Sillman

Date	Mintage	F	VF	XF	Unc	BU
1996	Est. 20,000	—	—	—	8.00	—

KM# 97a 2 POUNDS
28.3800 g., 0.9250 Silver .8411 oz. ASW, 38.5 mm. **Ruler:** Elizabeth II **Subject:** Queen Elizabeth's 70th Birthday **Obv:** Crowned bust right **Rev:** Lillies **Rev. Designer:** Norman Sillman

Date	Mintage	F	VF	XF	Unc	BU
1996	Est. 8,000	—	—	—	45.00	—

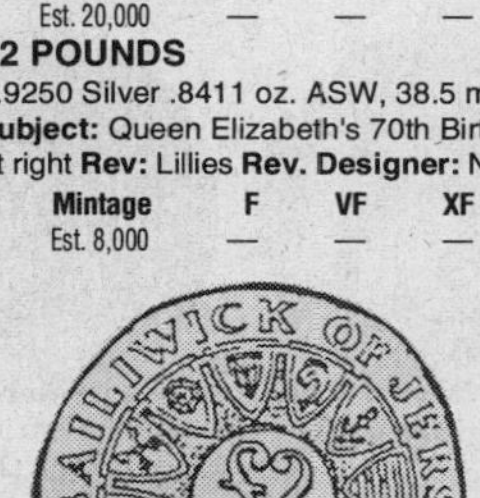

KM# 99 2 POUNDS
12.0000 g., Bi-Metallic Copper-Nickel center in Brass ring, 28.35 mm. **Ruler:** Elizabeth II **Obv:** Crowned bust right **Rev:** Value within center circle of assorted shields **Rev. Designer:** Alan Copp

Date	Mintage	F	VF	XF	Unc	BU
1997 In sets only	5,500	—	—	—	9.00	—

KM# 99a 2 POUNDS
Bi-Metallic Silver center in Gold-plated Silver ring, 28.35 mm. **Ruler:** Elizabeth II **Obv:** Crowned bust right **Rev:** Value within center circle of assorted shields **Rev. Designer:** Alan Copp

Date	Mintage	F	VF	XF	Unc	BU
1997 Proof	500	Value: 65.00				

KM# 102 2 POUNDS
12.0000 g., Bi-Metallic Copper-Nickel center in Brass ring, 28.35 mm. **Ruler:** Elizabeth II **Obv:** Head with tiara right **Obv. Designer:** Rank-Broadley **Rev:** Latent image value within circle of assorted shields **Edge Lettering:** CAESAREA INSULA

Date	Mintage	F	VF	XF	Unc	BU
1998	800,000	—	—	—	8.50	—

KM# 38 2 POUNDS 50 PENCE
27.1000 g., 0.9250 Silver .8208 oz. ASW **Ruler:** Elizabeth II **Subject:** 25th Wedding Anniversary **Obv:** Young bust right **Rev:** European Lobster **Rev. Designer:** Norman Sillman

Date	Mintage	F	VF	XF	Unc	BU
1972	24,000	—	—	—	16.00	18.00
1972 Proof	1,500	Value: 28.00				

KM# 39 5 POUNDS
2.6200 g., 0.9170 Gold .0772 oz. AGW **Ruler:** Elizabeth II **Subject:** 25th Wedding Anniversary **Obv:** Young bust right **Rev:** Garden shrew **Rev. Designer:** Norman Sillman

Date	Mintage	F	VF	XF	Unc	BU
1972	8,500	—	—	—	60.00	—
1972 Proof	1,500	Value: 75.00				

KM# 78 5 POUNDS
155.5600 g., 0.9990 Silver 5 oz. ASW, 65 mm. **Ruler:** Elizabeth II **Subject:** 50th Anniversary - The Battle of Britain **Obv:** Crowned bust right **Rev:** Spitfire divides map **Rev. Designer:** Ian Rank-Broadley **Note:** Photo reduced.

Date	Mintage	F	VF	XF	Unc	BU
ND(1990) Proof	—	Value: 145				

KM# 100 5 POUNDS
Copper-Nickel **Ruler:** Elizabeth II **Subject:** Queen's Golden Wedding Anniversary **Obv:** Crowned bust right **Rev:** Conjoined busts of royal couple and coat of arms **Rev. Designer:** Barry Stanton

Date	Mintage	F	VF	XF	Unc	BU
1997	6,000	—	—	—	15.00	—

KM# 100a 5 POUNDS
28.2800 g., 0.9250 Silver .8411 oz. ASW **Ruler:** Elizabeth II
Subject: Queen's Golden Wedding Anniversary **Obv:** Crowned bust right **Rev:** Conjoined busts of royal couple and gold-plated coat of arms **Rev. Designer:** Barry Stanton

Date	Mintage	F	VF	XF	Unc	BU
1997 Proof	Est. 30,000	Value: 65.00				

KM# 109 5 POUNDS
28.2850 g., 0.9250 Silver .8411 oz. ASW **Ruler:** Elizabeth II
Subject: Millennium **Obv:** Head with tiara right **Rev:** Gold-plated island map on globe **Rev. Designer:** Leslie Lindsay

Date	Mintage	F	VF	XF	Unc	BU
2000 Proof	32,000	Value: 47.50				

KM# 40 10 POUNDS
4.6400 g., 0.9170 Gold .1368 oz. AGW **Ruler:** Elizabeth II
Subject: 25th Wedding Anniversary **Obv:** Young bust right
Rev: Gold torque, excavated 1899 in St. Helier, Jersey.
Rev. Designer: Norman Sillman

Date	Mintage	F	VF	XF	Unc	BU
1972	8,500	—	—	—	100	—
1972 Proof	1,500	Value: 110				

KM# 79 10 POUNDS
3.1300 g., 0.9990 Gold .1005 oz. AGW **Ruler:** Elizabeth II
Subject: 50th Anniversary - The Battle of Britain **Obv:** Crowned bust right **Obv. Designer:** Ian Rank-Broadley **Rev:** Crowned air force badge divides dates

Date	Mintage	F	VF	XF	Unc	BU
ND Proof	Est. 500	Value: 125				

KM# 93 10 POUNDS
3.1300 g., 0.9990 Gold .1005 oz. AGW **Ruler:** Elizabeth II
Subject: 50th Anniversary of Liberation **Obv:** Crowned bust right **Rev:** Red Cross bringing supplies to Jersey immediately following liberation **Rev. Designer:** Robert Elderton

Date	Mintage	F	VF	XF	Unc	BU
1995 Proof sets only	500	—	—	—	85.00	—

KM# 41 20 POUNDS
9.2600 g., 0.9170 Gold .2729 oz. AGW **Ruler:** Elizabeth II
Subject: 25th Wedding Anniversary **Obv:** Young bust right
Rev: Ormer shell **Rev. Designer:** Norman Sillman

Date	Mintage	F	VF	XF	Unc	BU
1972	8,500	—	—	—	200	—
1972 Proof	1,500	Value: 220				

KM# 42 25 POUNDS
11.9000 g., 0.9170 Gold .3507 oz. AGW **Ruler:** Elizabeth II
Subject: 25th Wedding Anniversary **Obv:** Young bust right
Rev: Arms of Queen Elizabeth I

Date	Mintage	F	VF	XF	Unc	BU
1972	8,500	—	—	—	250	—
1972 Proof	1,500	Value: 270				

KM# 80 25 POUNDS
7.8100 g., 0.9990 Gold .2509 oz. AGW **Ruler:** Elizabeth II
Subject: 50th Anniversary - The Battle of Britain **Obv:** Crowned bust right **Rev:** Spitfire **Rev. Designer:** Ian Rank-Broadley

Date	Mintage	F	VF	XF	Unc	BU
1990 Proof	Est. 500	Value: 250				

KM# 94 25 POUNDS
7.8100 g., 0.9990 Gold .2509 oz. AGW **Ruler:** Elizabeth II
Subject: 50th Anniversary of Liberation **Obv:** Crowned bust right
Rev: Family encircled around flags with written value below
Rev. Designer: Robert Elderton

Date	Mintage	F	VF	XF	Unc	BU
1995 Proof sets only	500	—	—	—	215	—

KM# 43 50 POUNDS
22.6300 g., 0.9170 Gold .6670 oz. AGW **Ruler:** Elizabeth II
Subject: 25th Wedding Anniversary **Obv:** Young bust right
Rev: Shield above written value **Rev. Designer:** Norman Sillman

Date	Mintage	F	VF	XF	Unc	BU
1972	8,500	—	—	—	475	—
1972 Proof	1,500	Value: 500				

KM# 81 50 POUNDS
15.6100 g., 0.9990 Gold .5014 oz. AGW **Ruler:** Elizabeth II
Subject: 50th Anniversary - Battle of Britain **Obv:** Crowned bust right **Rev:** Crowned air force badge divides dates
Rev. Designer: Ian Rank-Broadley

Date	Mintage	F	VF	XF	Unc	BU
ND Proof	Est. 500	Value: 480				

KM# 95 50 POUNDS
15.6100 g., 0.9990 Gold .5014 oz. AGW **Ruler:** Elizabeth II
Subject: 50th Anniversary of Liberation **Obv:** Crowned bust right
Rev: Letter V divides dates above figures facing each other with flags

Date	Mintage	F	VF	XF	Unc	BU
1995 Proof sets only	500	—	—	—	435	—

KM# 82 100 POUNDS
31.2100 g., 0.9990 Gold 1.0025 oz. AGW **Ruler:** Elizabeth II
Subject: 50th Anniversary - The Battle of Britain **Obv:** Crowned bust right **Rev:** Spitfire **Rev. Designer:** Ian Rank-Broadley

Date	Mintage	F	VF	XF	Unc	BU
ND Proof	Est. 500	Value: 900				

KM# 96 100 POUNDS
31.2100 g., 0.9990 Gold 1.0025 oz. AGW **Ruler:** Elizabeth II
Subject: 50th Anniversary of Liberation **Obv:** Crowned bust right
Rev: Small shield within map with bird above within diagonal lines into map **Rev. Designer:** Robert Elderton

Date	Mintage	F	VF	XF	Unc	BU
1995 Proof sets only	500	—	—	—	865	—

PIEFORTS

KM#	Date	Mintage	Identification	Mkt Val
P1	1982	1,500	20 Pence. Silver. Date. KM53a.	25.00
P2	1995	—	2 Pounds. 0.9250 Silver. KM92a.	75.00

MINT SETS

KM#	Date	Mintage	Identification	Issue Price	Mkt Val
MS1	1972 (9)	8,500	KM35-43	348	715
MS2	1972 (4)	15,000	KM35-38	24.00	40.00
MS3	1983 (7)	25,000	KM54-59, 66	—	6.00
MS4	1987 (7)	—	KM54-55, 56.1-58.1, 66, 71	—	6.50
MSA5	1991-1994 (8)	—	Mixed dates KM#84-91	—	25.00
MS5	1992 (7)	6,000	KM54,55b, 56.2- 57.2, 58.1, 66, 86	22.50	22.50
MS6	1997 (8)	5,500	KM#54b 55b, 56.2-58.2, 66, 91, 99	—	28.00
MS7	1997 (9)	—	KM#54b, 55, 56.2, 57.2, 58.1, 58.2, 66, 91, 99	—	25.00

PROOF SETS

KM#	Date	Mintage	Identification	Issue Price	Mkt Val
PS1	1957 (4)	1,050	KM21-22 two each	—	30.00
PS2.1	1960 (4)	2,100	KM22- 23 two each	—	25.00
PS2.2	1960 (4)	I.A.	KM22, 24 two each	—	150
PS3	1964 (4)	10,000	KM21, 25 two each	—	8.00
PS4	1966 (4)	15,000	KM26-27 two each	—	8.00
PS5	1966 (2)	15,000	KM28 two pieces	—	8.00
PS6	1972 (9)	1,500	KM35-43	648	975
PS7	1980 (6)	10,000	KM29-34	—	20.00
PS8	1981 (7)	15,000	KM45-51	31.00	20.00
PS9	1983 (7)	5,000	KM54a-55a, 56.1a-57.1a, 58a-59a, 66a	—	80.00
PS10	1990 (4)	500	KM79-82	1,595	1,750
PS11	1995 (4)	500	KM93-96	1,600	1,600

JORDAN

The Hashemite Kingdom of Jordan, a constitutional monarchy in southwest Asia, has an area of 37,738 sq. mi.(91,880 sq. km.) and a population of 3.5 million. Capital: Amman. Agriculture and tourism comprise Jordan's economic base. Chief exports are phosphates, tomatoe sand oranges.

Jordan is the Edom and Moab of the time of Moses. It became part of the Roman province of Arabia in 106 A.D., was conquered by the Arabs in 633-36, and was part of the Ottoman Empire from the 16th century until World War I. At that time, the regions presently known as Jordan and Israel were mandated to Great Britain by the League of Nations as Transjordan and Palestine. In 1922 Transjordan was established as the semi-autonomous Emirate of Transjordan, ruled by the Hashemite Prince Abdullah but still nominally a part of the British mandate. The mandate over Transjordan was terminated in 1946, the country becoming the independent Hashemite Kingdom of Transjordan. The kingdom was renamed the Hashemite Kingdom of Jordan in 1950.

Several 1964 and 1965 issues were limited to respective quantities of 3,000 and 5,000 examples struck to make up sets for sale to collectors.

TITLE

المملكة الاردنية الهاسمية

el-Mamlaka(t)el-Urduniya(t)el-Hashemiya(t)

RULERS

Abdullah Ibn Al-Hussein, 1946-1951
Talal Ibn Abdullah, 1951-1952
Hussein Ibn Talal, 1952-1999
Abdullah Ibn Al-Hussein, 1999-

MONETARY SYSTEM

100 Fils = 1 Dirham
1000 Fils = 10 Dirhams = 1 Dinar
Commencing 1992
100 Piastres = 1 Dinar

KINGDOM

DECIMAL COINAGE

KM# 1 FIL

3.0000 g., Bronze, 18 mm. **Ruler:** Abdullah Ibn Al-Hussein **Obv:** Value and date within crowned circle within sprigs **Rev:** Value within circle above date **Edge:** Plain

Date	Mintage	F	VF	XF	Unc	BU
AH1368//1949	350,000	—	1.00	1.50	3.50	—
AH1368//1949 Proof	25	Value: 50.00				

Note: "FIL" is an error for "FILS," the correct Arabic singular

KM# 2 FILS

3.0000 g., Bronze, 18 mm. **Ruler:** Abdullah Ibn Al-Hussein **Obv:** Value and date within crowned circle within sprigs **Rev:** Value within circle above date **Edge:** Plain

Date	Mintage	F	VF	XF	Unc	BU
AH1368//1949	Inc. above	—	0.50	0.90	2.25	—
AH1368//1949 Proof	25	Value: 50.00				

KM# 8 FILS

3.0000 g., Bronze, 18 mm. **Ruler:** Hussein Ibn Talal **Obv:** Value and date within crowned circle within sprigs **Rev:** Value within circle above date **Edge:** Plain

Date	Mintage	F	VF	XF	Unc	BU
AH1374//1955	200,000	—	0.35	0.50	1.00	—
AH1374//1955 Proof	—	Value: 35.00				
AH1379//1960	150,000	—	0.40	0.60	1.25	—
AH1379//1960 Proof	—	Value: 35.00				
AH1382//1963	200,000	—	0.25	0.50	1.00	—
AH1382//1963 Proof	—	Value: 35.00				
AH1383//1964	3,000	—	1.50	3.00	5.00	—

Note: In sets only

Date	Mintage	F	VF	XF	Unc	BU
AH1385//1965	5,000	—	1.00	2.00	3.00	—

Note: In sets only

Date	Mintage	F	VF	XF	Unc	BU
AH1385//1965 Proof	10,000	Value: 3.00				

KM# 14 FILS

3.0000 g., Bronze, 18 mm. **Ruler:** Hussein Ibn Talal **Obv:** Head right **Rev:** Value and date within circle flanked by sprigs **Edge:** Plain

Date	Mintage	F	VF	XF	Unc	BU
AH1387-1968	60,000	—	0.15	0.25	0.75	—

KM# 35 FILS

3.0000 g., Bronze, 18 mm. **Ruler:** Hussein Ibn Talal **Obv:** Head right **Rev:** Value and date within circle flanked by sprigs **Edge:** Plain

Date	Mintage	F	VF	XF	Unc	BU
AH1398-1978 Proof	20,000	Value: 0.75				
AH1404-1984	100,000	—	0.10	0.20	0.50	—
AH1406-1985	—	—	—	1.50	2.00	—

Note: In sets only

Date	Mintage	F	VF	XF	Unc	BU
AH1406-1985 Proof	5,000	Value: 2.00				

KM# 3 5 FILS (1/2 Qirsh)

4.5000 g., Bronze, 21 mm. **Ruler:** Abdullah Ibn Al-Hussein **Obv:** Value and date within crowned circle within sprigs **Rev:** Value within circle above date **Edge:** Plain

Date	Mintage	F	VF	XF	Unc	BU
AH1368//1949	3,300,000	—	0.40	0.75	1.50	—
AH1368//1949 Proof	25	Value: 60.00				

KM# 9 5 FILS (1/2 Qirsh)

4.5000 g., Bronze, 21 mm. **Ruler:** Hussein Ibn Talal **Obv:** Value and date within crowned circle within sprigs **Rev:** Value within circle above date **Edge:** Plain

Date	Mintage	F	VF	XF	Unc	BU
AH1374-1955	3,500,000	—	0.35	0.50	0.75	—
AH1374-1955 Proof	—	Value: 35.00				
AH1379-1960	540,000	—	0.50	0.70	1.25	—
AH1379-1960 Proof	—	Value: 35.00				
AH1382-1962	250,000	—	0.45	0.70	1.25	—
AH1382-1962 Proof	—	Value: 35.00				
AH1383-1964	3,000	—	—	2.75	3.50	—

Note: In sets only

Date	Mintage	F	VF	XF	Unc	BU
AH1384-1964	2,500,000	—	0.30	0.50	1.00	—
AH1385-1965	5,000	—	1.25	2.50	3.00	—

Note: In sets only

Date	Mintage	F	VF	XF	Unc	BU
AH1385-1965 Proof	10,000	Value: 5.00				
AH1387-1967	2,000,000	—	0.10	0.20	0.40	—

KM# 15 5 FILS (1/2 Qirsh)

4.5000 g., Bronze, 21 mm. **Ruler:** Hussein Ibn Talal **Obv:** Head right **Rev:** Value and date within circle flanked by sprigs **Edge:** Plain

Date	Mintage	F	VF	XF	Unc	BU
AH1387//1968	800,000	—	0.20	0.50	0.75	—
AH1390//1970	1,400,000	—	0.10	0.25	0.50	—
AH1392//1972	400,000	—	0.10	0.25	0.65	—
AH1394//1974	2,000,000	—	0.10	0.20	0.40	—
AH1395//1975	9,000,000	—	0.10	0.15	0.30	—

KM# 36 5 FILS (1/2 Qirsh)

4.5000 g., Bronze, 21 mm. **Ruler:** Hussein Ibn Talal **Obv:** Head right **Rev:** Value and date within circle flanked by sprigs **Edge:** Plain

Date	Mintage	F	VF	XF	Unc	BU
AH1398-1978	60,200,000	—	0.10	0.15	0.30	—
AH1398-1978 Proof	20,000	Value: 1.25				
AH1406-1985	—	—	—	1.50	2.00	—

Note: In sets only

Date	Mintage	F	VF	XF	Unc	BU
AH1406-1985 Proof	5,000	Value: 2.50				

KM# 60 1/2 QIRSH (1/2 Piastre)

Copper Plated Steel **Ruler:** Hussein Ibn Talal **Obv:** Bust left **Rev:** Value at left within lines with date above and written value at lower right **Edge:** Plain

Date	Mintage	F	VF	XF	Unc	BU
AH1416-1996	—	—	—	0.35	0.65	1.00
AH1416-1996 Proof	—	Value: 5.00				

KM# 4 10 FILS (Qirsh, Piastre)

5.9000 g., Bronze, 25 mm. **Ruler:** Abdullah Ibn Al-Hussein **Obv:** Value and date within crowned circle within sprigs **Rev:** Value within circle above date and star **Edge:** Plain

Date	Mintage	F	VF	XF	Unc	BU
AH1368//1949	2,700,000	—	0.75	1.25	2.00	—
AH1368//1949 Proof	25	Value: 75.00				

KM# 10 10 FILS (Qirsh, Piastre)

5.9000 g., Bronze, 25 mm. **Ruler:** Hussein Ibn Talal **Obv:** Value and date within crowned circle within sprigs **Rev:** Value within circle above date and star **Edge:** Plain

Date	Mintage	F	VF	XF	Unc	BU
AH1374//1955	1,500,000	—	0.60	1.00	2.00	—
AH1374//1955 Proof	—	Value: 35.00				
AH1379//1960	60,000	—	1.25	2.00	3.50	—
AH1379//1960 Proof	—	Value: 35.00				
AH1382//1962	2,300,000	—	0.30	0.50	1.00	—
AH1382//1962 Proof	—	Value: 35.00				
AH1383//1964	1,253,000	—	0.30	0.50	1.00	—
AH1385//1965	1,003,000	—	0.20	0.40	1.00	—
AH1385//1965 Proof	10,000	Value: 5.00				
AH1387//1967	1,000,000	—	0.20	0.35	1.00	—

KM# 16 10 FILS (Qirsh, Piastre)

5.9000 g., Bronze, 25 mm. **Ruler:** Hussein Ibn Talal **Obv:** Head right **Rev:** Value and date within circle flanked by sprigs

Date	Mintage	F	VF	XF	Unc	BU
AH1387-1968	500,000	—	0.20	0.50	0.90	—
AH1390-1970	1,000,000	—	0.20	0.35	0.60	—
AH1392-1972	600,000	—	0.20	0.40	0.75	—
AH1394-1974	1,000,000	—	0.20	0.40	0.65	—
AH1395-1975	5,000,000	—	0.20	0.35	0.50	—

KM# 37 10 FILS (Qirsh, Piastre)

5.9000 g., Bronze, 25 mm. **Ruler:** Hussein Ibn Talal **Obv:** Head right **Rev:** Value and date within circle flanked by sprigs **Edge:** Plain

Date	Mintage	F	VF	XF	Unc	BU
AH1398-1978	30,000,000	—	0.10	0.15	0.40	—
AH1398-1978 Proof	20,000	Value: 2.00				
AH1404-1984	10,000,000	—	0.10	0.15	0.40	—
AH1406-1985	—	—	—	1.25	1.75	—
Note: In sets only						
AH1406-1985 Proof	5,000	Value: 3.00				
AH1409-1989	8,000,000	—	0.25	2.00	2.50	—

KM# 56 QIRSH (Piastre)
Bronze Plated Steel **Ruler:** Hussein Ibn Talal **Obv:** Head left **Rev:** Value to left within lines below date with written value at lower right **Edge:** Plain

Date	Mintage	F	VF	XF	Unc	BU
AH1414-1994	—	—	—	0.50	1.25	1.50
AH1416-1996	—	—	—	0.50	1.25	1.50
AH1416-1996 Proof	—	Value: 5.00				

KM# 78.1 QIRSH (Piastre)
5.4700 g., Copper Plated Steel, 24.9 mm. **Ruler:** Abdullah Ibn Al-Hussein **Obv:** King Abdullah II **Edge:** Plain

Date	Mintage	F	VF	XF	Unc	BU
AH1421-2000	—	—	—	—	1.00	1.25

KM# 78.2 QIRSH (Piastre)
5.4700 g., Chrome Plated Steel, 24.9 mm. **Ruler:** Abdullah Ibn Al-Hussein **Obv:** King Abdullah II **Edge:** Plain
Note: Gregorian and Hijra dates are flipped.

Date	Mintage	F	VF	XF	Unc	BU
AH1421-2000	—	—	—	—	7.50	10.00

KM# 5 20 FILS
Copper-Nickel **Ruler:** Abdullah Ibn Al-Hussein **Obv:** Value and date within crowned circle within sprigs **Rev:** Value within circle above date and star **Edge:** Milled

Date	Mintage	F	VF	XF	Unc	BU
AH1368//1949	1,570,000	—	0.50	1.00	1.75	—
AH1368//1949 Proof	25	Value: 90.00				

KM# 13 20 FILS
Copper-Nickel, 19.8 mm. **Ruler:** Hussein Ibn Talal **Obv:** Value and date within crowned circle within sprigs **Rev:** Value within circle above date and star **Edge:** Milled

Date	Mintage	F	VF	XF	Unc	BU
AH1383//1964	3,000	—	—	3.00	5.00	—
Note: In sets only						
AH1385//1965	5,000	—	—	3.00	5.00	—
Note: In sets only						
AH1385//1965 Proof	10,000	Value: 5.00				

KM# 17 25 FILS (1/4 Dirham)
4.7500 g., Copper-Nickel, 22 mm. **Ruler:** Hussein Ibn Talal **Obv:** Head right **Rev:** Value and date within circle flanked by sprigs **Edge:** Milled

Date	Mintage	F	VF	XF	Unc	BU
AH1387-1968	200,000	—	0.30	0.50	1.00	—
AH1390-1970	240,000	—	0.15	0.35	0.75	—
AH1394-1974	800,000	—	0.15	0.35	0.75	—
AH1395-1975	2,000,000	—	0.15	0.35	0.75	—
AH1397-1977	1,600,000	—	0.15	0.35	0.75	—

KM# 38 25 FILS (1/4 Dirham)
4.7500 g., Copper-Nickel, 22 mm. **Ruler:** Hussein Ibn Talal **Obv:** Head right **Rev:** Value and date within circle flanked by sprigs **Edge:** Milled

Date	Mintage	F	VF	XF	Unc	BU
AH1398-1978 Proof	20,000	Value: 3.00				
AH1401-1981	2,000,000	—	0.20	0.30	0.75	—
AH1404-1984	4,000,000	—	0.20	0.30	0.75	—

Date	Mintage	F	VF	XF	Unc	BU
AH1406-1985	—	—	—	2.50	3.00	—
Note: In sets only						
AH1406-1985 Proof	5,000	Value: 4.00				
AH1411-1991	5,000,000	—	0.20	0.30	0.75	—

KM# 53 2-1/2 PIASTRES
Stainless Steel **Ruler:** Hussein Ibn Talal **Obv:** Bust left **Rev:** Value at left within lines below date with written value to lower right **Edge:** Milled

Date	Mintage	F	VF	XF	Unc	BU
AH1412-1992	—	—	—	0.75	1.50	1.75
AH1416-1996	—	—	—	0.75	1.50	1.75
AH1416-1996 Proof	—	Value: 5.00				

KM# 6 50 FILS (1/2 Dirham)
7.5000 g., Copper-Nickel, 26 mm. **Ruler:** Abdullah Ibn Al-Hussein **Obv:** Value and date within crowned circle within sprigs **Rev:** Value within circle above date and star **Edge:** Milled

Date	Mintage	F	VF	XF	Unc	BU
AH1368//1949	2,500,000	—	0.75	2.00	3.50	—
AH1368//1949 Proof	25	Value: 100				

KM# 11 50 FILS (1/2 Dirham)
7.5000 g., Copper-Nickel, 26 mm. **Ruler:** Hussein Ibn Talal **Obv:** Value and date within crowned circle within sprigs **Rev:** Value within circle above date and star **Edge:** Milled

Date	Mintage	F	VF	XF	Unc	BU
AH1374//1955	2,500,000	—	0.75	1.50	3.50	—
AH1374//1955 Proof	—	Value: 35.00				
AH1382//1962	750,000	—	0.85	1.00	1.50	—
AH1382//1962 Proof	—	Value: 35.00				
AH1383//1964	1,003,000	—	0.40	0.60	1.00	—
AH1385//1965	1,505,000	—	0.40	0.60	1.00	—
AH1385//1965 Proof	10,000	Value: 4.50				

KM# 18 50 FILS (1/2 Dirham)
7.5000 g., Copper-Nickel, 26 mm. **Ruler:** Hussein Ibn Talal **Obv:** Head right **Rev:** Value and date within circle flanked by sprigs **Edge:** Milled

Date	Mintage	F	VF	XF	Unc	BU
AH1387-1968	400,000	—	0.75	1.00	2.75	—
AH1390-1970	1,000,000	—	0.40	0.60	1.25	—
AH1394-1974	1,000,000	—	0.40	0.60	1.25	—
AH1395-1975	2,000,000	—	0.40	0.60	1.25	—
AH1397-1977	6,000,000	—	0.40	0.60	1.25	—

KM# 39 50 FILS (1/2 Dirham)
7.5000 g., Copper-Nickel, 26 mm. **Ruler:** Hussein Ibn Talal **Edge:** Milled

Date	Mintage	F	VF	XF	Unc	BU
AH1398-1978	6,168,000	—	0.25	0.50	1.25	—
AH1398-1978 Proof	20,000	Value: 2.50				
AH1401-1981	5,000,000	—	0.25	0.50	1.25	—
AH1404-1984	10,000,000	—	0.25	0.50	1.25	—
AH1406-1985	—	—	—	2.75	3.25	—
Note: In sets only						
AH1406-1985 Proof	5,000	Value: 3.50				
AH1409-1989	6,000,000	—	0.25	0.50	1.25	—
AH1411-1991	10,000,000	—	0.25	0.50	1.25	—

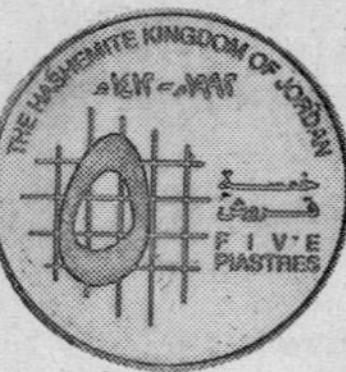

KM# 54 5 PIASTRES
Nickel Plated Steel **Ruler:** Hussein Ibn Talal **Obv:** Bust left **Rev:** Value at left within lines below date with written value at lower right **Edge:** Milled

Date	Mintage	F	VF	XF	Unc	BU
AH1412-1992	—	—	—	1.00	2.00	2.50
AH1414-1993	—	—	—	1.00	2.00	2.50
AH1416-1996	—	—	—	1.00	2.00	2.50
AH1416-1996 Proof	—	Value: 5.00				
AH1418-1998	—	—	—	1.00	2.00	2.50

KM# 73 5 PIASTRES
5.0000 g., Nickel-Clad Steel, 25.8 mm. **Ruler:** Abdullah Ibn Al-Hussein **Obv:** Bust right **Rev:** Value to left within lines below date with written value at lower right **Edge:** Milled

Date	Mintage	F	VF	XF	Unc	BU
AH1421-2000	—	—	—	—	2.00	2.50

KM# 7 100 FILS (Dirham)
12.0000 g., Copper-Nickel, 30 mm. **Ruler:** Abdullah Ibn Al-Hussein **Obv:** Value and date within crowned circle within sprigs **Rev:** Value within circle above date and star **Edge:** Milled

Date	Mintage	F	VF	XF	Unc	BU
AH1368//1949	2,000,000	—	2.00	3.00	5.00	—
AH1368//1949 Proof	25	Value: 120				

KM# 12 100 FILS (Dirham)
12.0000 g., Copper-Nickel, 30 mm. **Ruler:** Hussein Ibn Talal **Obv:** Value and date within crowned circle within sprigs **Rev:** Value within circle above date and star **Edge:** Milled

Date	Mintage	F	VF	XF	Unc	BU
AH1374//1955	500,000	—	2.00	2.50	4.00	—
AH1374//1955 Proof	—	Value: 35.00				
AH1382//1962	600,000	—	1.00	1.50	3.00	—
AH1382//1962 Proof	—	Value: 35.00				
AH1383//1964 In sets only	3,000	—	1.50	3.00	5.00	—
AH1385//1965	405,000	—	1.00	1.25	2.25	—
AH1385//1965 Proof	10,000	Value: 5.00				

KM# 19 100 FILS (Dirham)
12.0000 g., Copper-Nickel, 30 mm. **Ruler:** Hussein Ibn Talal **Obv:** Head right **Rev:** Value and date within circle flanked by sprigs **Edge:** Milled

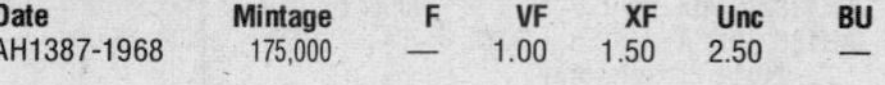

Date	Mintage	F	VF	XF	Unc	BU
AH1387-1968	175,000	—	1.00	1.50	2.50	—

Date	Mintage	F	VF	XF	Unc	BU
AH1395-1975	2,500,000	—	0.40	1.00	2.00	—
AH1397-1977	2,000,000	—	0.40	1.00	2.00	—

KM# 40 100 FILS (Dirham)

12.0000 g., Copper-Nickel, 30 mm. **Ruler:** Hussein Ibn Talal **Obv:** Head right **Rev:** Value and date within circle flanked by sprigs **Edge:** Milled

Date	Mintage	F	VF	XF	Unc	BU
AH1398-1978	3,000,000	—	0.40	1.00	2.00	—
AH1398-1978 Proof	20,000	Value: 3.50				
AH1401-1981	4,000,000	—	0.40	1.00	2.00	—
AH1404-1984	5,000,000	—	0.40	1.00	1.50	—
AH1406-1985	—	—	—	2.50	3.50	—
Note: In sets only						
AH1406-1985 Proof	5,000	Value: 4.50				
AH1409-1989	4,000,000	—	0.40	1.00	1.50	—
AH1411-1991	6,000,000	—	0.40	1.00	1.50	—

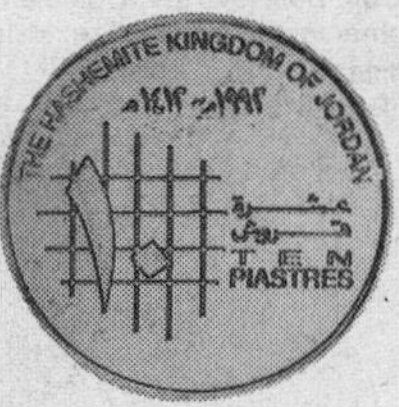

KM# 55 10 PIASTRES

Nickel Plated Steel **Ruler:** Hussein Ibn Talal **Obv:** Bust left **Rev:** Value at left within lines below date with written value at lower right **Edge:** Milled

Date	Mintage	F	VF	XF	Unc	BU
AH1412-1992	—	—	—	1.25	2.25	2.75
AH1414-1993	—	—	—	1.25	2.25	2.75
AH1416-1996	—	—	—	1.25	2.25	2.75
AH1416-1996 Proof	—	Value: 5.00				

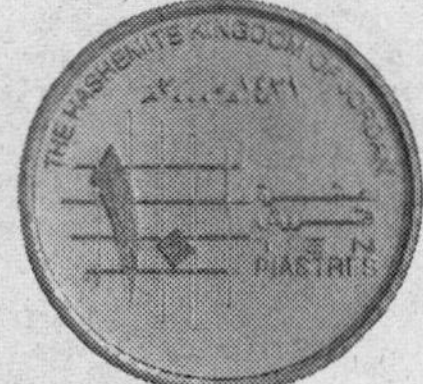

KM# 74 10 PIASTRES

8.0000 g., Nickel Clad Steel, 27.9 mm. **Ruler:** Abdullah Ibn Al-Hussein **Obv:** Bust right **Rev:** Value at left within lines below date with written value at lower right **Edge:** Milled

Date	Mintage	F	VF	XF	Unc	BU
AH1421-2000	—	—	—	—	4.00	5.00

KM# 20 1/4 DINAR

17.0000 g., Copper-Nickel, 34 mm. **Ruler:** Hussein Ibn Talal **Series:** F.A.O. **Obv:** Head right **Rev:** Date below olive tree within circled wreath with F.A.O. logo below **Edge:** Milled

Date	Mintage	F	VF	XF	Unc	BU
AH1389-1969	60,000	—	2.00	3.00	5.50	—

KM# 28 1/4 DINAR

17.0000 g., Copper-Nickel, 34 mm. **Ruler:** Hussein Ibn Talal **Obv:** Head right **Rev:** Date below olive tree within circled wreath **Edge:** Milled

Date	Mintage	F	VF	XF	Unc	BU
AH1390-1970	500,000	—	1.00	1.50	4.00	—
AH1394-1974	400,000	—	1.00	1.50	4.00	—
AH1395-1975	100,000	—	1.00	1.50	4.00	—

KM# 29 1/4 DINAR

19.0400 g., 0.9250 Silver .5663 oz. ASW, 34 mm. **Ruler:** Hussein Ibn Talal **Subject:** 10th Anniversary - Central Bank of Jordan **Obv:** Head right **Rev:** Olive tree within circled wreath with value and dates around wreath **Edge:** Milled

Date	Mintage	F	VF	XF	Unc	BU
AH1394-1974 Proof	550	Value: 100				

KM# 29a 1/4 DINAR

33.1900 g., 0.9170 Gold .9785 oz. AGW, 34 mm. **Ruler:** Hussein Ibn Talal **Subject:** 10th Anniversary - Central Bank of Jordan **Obv:** Head right **Rev:** Tree within circled wreath with dates and value around wreath **Edge:** Milled

Date	Mintage	F	VF	XF	Unc	BU
AH1394-1974 Proof	100	Value: 715				

KM# 30 1/4 DINAR

17.0000 g., Copper-Nickel, 34 mm. **Ruler:** Hussein Ibn Talal **Subject:** 25th Anniversary of Reign **Obv:** Head facing 1/4 right within small circle flanked by sprigs, all within design with crown on top and date below **Rev:** Castle above dates **Edge:** Milled

Date	Mintage	F	VF	XF	Unc	BU
AH1397-1977	200,000	—	1.00	2.00	4.50	—

KM# 41 1/4 DINAR

17.0000 g., Copper-Nickel, 34 mm. **Ruler:** Hussein Ibn Talal **Obv:** Head right **Rev:** Date below olive tree within circled wreath **Designer:** Milled

Date	Mintage	F	VF	XF	Unc	BU
AH1398-1978	200,000	—	1.00	2.00	4.50	—
AH1398-1978 Proof	20,000	Value: 5.00				
AH1401-1981	600,000	—	0.75	1.50	4.00	—
AH1406-1985	—	—	—	3.00	4.00	—
Note: In sets only						
AH1406-1985 Proof	5,000	Value: 6.50				

KM# 61 1/4 DINAR

Nickel-Brass **Ruler:** Hussein Ibn Talal **Obv:** Bust left **Rev:** Value in circle within artistic design **Edge:** Plain **Shape:** 7-sided

Date	Mintage	F	VF	XF	Unc	BU
AH1416-1996 Proof	—	Value: 7.50				
AH1416-1996	—	—	—	—	3.00	4.00
AH1417-1997	—	—	—	—	3.00	4.00

KM# 21 1/2 DINAR

20.0000 g., 0.9990 Silver .6424 oz. ASW, 35 mm. **Ruler:** Hussein Ibn Talal **Rev:** Al Harraneh Palace above value **Edge:** Milled

Date	Mintage	F	VF	XF	Unc	BU
AH1389//1969 Proof	6,100	Value: 20.00				

KM# 42 1/2 DINAR

Copper-Nickel **Ruler:** Hussein Ibn Talal **Subject:** 1400th Anniversary of Hijra (Mohammed's Pilgrimage) **Obv:** Bust facing 1/4 right **Rev:** Capitol building and sun within circle at right, sprig to left within larger circle **Edge:** Plain **Shape:** 7-sided

Date	Mintage	F	VF	XF	Unc	BU
AH1400-1980	2,006,000	—	1.50	2.50	5.00	—

KM# 58 1/2 DINAR

Brass **Ruler:** Hussein Ibn Talal **Obv:** Bust left **Rev:** Value in circle within artistic design **Edge:** Plain

Date	Mintage	F	VF	XF	Unc	BU
AH1416-1996	—	—	—	—	4.00	5.00
AH1416-1996 Proof	—	Value: 8.50				

KM# 63 1/2 DINAR

Bi-Metallic Copper-Nickel center in Aluminum-Bronze ring **Ruler:** Hussein Ibn Talal **Obv:** Bust left within circle **Rev:** Value in center of circled wreath **Edge:** Plain **Shape:** 7-sided

Date	Mintage	F	VF	XF	Unc	BU
AH1417-1997	—	—	—	—	8.00	10.00

KM# 79 1/2 DINAR
9.6700 g., Bi-Metallic Copper-Nickel center in Brass ring, 29 mm. **Ruler:** Abdullah Ibn Al-Hussein **Obv:** Bust right within circle **Rev:** Value in center of circled wreath **Edge:** Plain **Shape:** 7-sided

Date	Mintage	F	VF	XF	Unc	BU
AH1421-2000	—	—	—	—	6.00	8.00

KM# 22 3/4 DINAR
30.0000 g., 0.9990 Silver .9636 oz. ASW, 45 mm. **Ruler:** Hussein Ibn Talal **Obv:** Similar to 1/2 Dinar, KM#21 **Rev:** Shrine of the Nativity, Bethlehem **Edge:** Milled

Date	Mintage	F	VF	XF	Unc	BU
AH1389//1969 Proof	5,800	Value: 40.00				

KM# 23 DINAR
40.0000 g., 0.9990 Silver 1.2848 oz. ASW, 55 mm. **Ruler:** Hussein Ibn Talal **Obv:** Similar to 1/2 Dinar, KM#21 **Rev:** Temple Hill, Jerusalem **Edge:** Milled

Date	Mintage	F	VF	XF	Unc	BU
AH1389//1969 Proof	6,800	Value: 60.00				

KM# 47 DINAR
14.0000 g., Nickel-Bronze, 29 mm. **Ruler:** Hussein Ibn Talal **Subject:** King Hussein's 50th Birthday **Obv:** Head right within beaded circle **Rev:** Crowned sun within 3/4 wreath flanked by dates **Edge:** Milled

Date	Mintage	F	VF	XF	Unc	BU
AH1406-1985	—	—	—	—	7.50	—
AH1406-1985 Proof	5,000	Value: 10.00				

KM# 51 DINAR
15.0000 g., 0.9250 Silver .4461 oz. ASW, 30 mm. **Ruler:** Hussein Ibn Talal **Subject:** 40th Year of Reign **Obv:** Uniformed bust facing **Rev:** Tughra **Edge:** Plain

Date	Mintage	F	VF	XF	Unc	BU
AH1413-1992 Proof	4,900	Value: 22.00				

KM# 51.1 DINAR
15.0000 g., 0.9250 Silver 0.4461 oz. ASW, 30 mm. **Ruler:** Hussein Ibn Talal **Subject:** King's 40th Anniversary of Reign **Obv:** Multicolor uniformed bust facing **Rev:** Tughra **Edge:** Plain

Date	Mintage	F	VF	XF	Unc	BU
AH1413-1992 Proof	100	Value: 75.00				

KM# 52 DINAR
8.5000 g., 0.9170 Gold .2505 oz. AGW, 21 mm. **Ruler:** Hussein Ibn Talal **Subject:** 40th Year of Reign **Obv:** Uniformed bust facing **Rev:** Tughra **Edge:** Milled

Date	Mintage	F	VF	XF	Unc	BU
AH1413-1992 Proof	3,000	Value: 200				

KM# 62 DINAR
Brass **Ruler:** Hussein Ibn Talal **Subject:** 50th Anniversary - F.A.O. **Obv:** Bust left **Rev:** F.A.O. logo within artistic design **Edge:** Plain **Shape:** 7-sided

Date	Mintage	F	VF	XF	Unc	BU
AH1415-1995	—	—	—	—	10.00	12.00

KM# 59 DINAR
Brass **Ruler:** Hussein Ibn Talal **Obv:** Bust left **Rev:** Value within center of artistic design **Edge:** Plain **Shape:** 7-sided

Date	Mintage	F	VF	XF	Unc	BU
AH1416-1996	—	—	—	—	8.00	10.00
AH1416-1996 Proof	—	Value: 11.50				
AH1417-1997	—	—	—	—	7.00	9.00

KM# 68 DINAR
31.1035 g., 0.9990 Silver 1.0000 oz. ASW, 40 mm. **Ruler:** Hussein Ibn Talal **Subject:** 50 Years - Jordanian Independence **Obv:** Bust left **Rev:** Bust with headdress left with legend at upper left **Edge:** Milled

Date	Mintage	F	VF	XF	Unc	BU
ND(1996) Proof	Est. 2,000	Value: 75.00				

KM# 64 DINAR
Brass **Ruler:** Hussein Ibn Talal **Obv:** Bust left **Rev:** Value within ornamented circle **Edge:** Milled

Date	Mintage	F	VF	XF	Unc	BU
AH1419-1998	—	—	—	—	5.50	6.50

KM# 65 DINAR
Brass **Ruler:** Hussein Ibn Talal **Subject:** Human Rights **Obv:** Bust left **Rev:** Commemorative legend with value within ornamented circle **Edge:** Milled

Date	Mintage	F	VF	XF	Unc	BU
AH1419-1998	—	—	—	—	7.00	8.00

KM# 24 2 DINARS
5.5200 g., 0.9000 Gold .1597 oz. AGW, 21 mm. **Ruler:** Hussein Ibn Talal **Subject:** Forum in Jerash **Edge:** Milled

Date	Mintage	F	VF	XF	Unc	BU
AH1389 (1969) Proof	2,425	Value: 125				

KM# 31 2-1/2 DINARS
28.2800 g., 0.9250 Silver .8410 oz. ASW, 38.61 mm. **Ruler:** Hussein Ibn Talal **Subject:** Conservation **Obv:** Head right **Rev:** Rhim Gazelle **Edge:** Milled

Date	Mintage	F	VF	XF	Unc	BU
AH1397-1977	6,265	—	—	—	24.00	—
AH1397-1977 Proof	5,011	Value: 30.00				

KM# 32 3 DINARS
35.0000 g., 0.9250 Silver 1.0409 oz. ASW, 42 mm. **Ruler:** Hussein Ibn Talal **Subject:** Conservation **Obv:** Head right **Rev:** Palestine sunbird and flower **Edge:** Milled

Date	Mintage	F	VF	XF	Unc	BU
AH1397-1977	6,263	—	—	—	25.00	—
AH1397-1977 Proof	4,897	Value: 32.50				

KM# 43 3 DINARS
23.3300 g., 0.9250 Silver .6938 oz. ASW, 38.61 mm.
Ruler: Hussein Ibn Talal **Subject:** International Year of the Child **Obv:** Bust left **Rev:** Palace of culture in Amman and two children within circle **Edge:** Milled

Date	Mintage	F	VF	XF	Unc	BU
AH1401 (1981) Proof	21,000	Value: 18.50				

KM# 25 5 DINARS
13.8200 g., 0.9000 Gold .3999 oz. AGW, 31 mm. **Ruler:** Hussein Ibn Talal **Obv:** Bust left **Rev:** Treasury in Petra **Edge:** Milled

Date	Mintage	F	VF	XF	Unc	BU
AH1389-1969 Proof	1,950	Value: 285				

KM# 57 5 DINARS
Copper-Nickel, 38.61 mm. **Ruler:** Hussein Ibn Talal
Subject: UN 50 Years **Obv:** Bust left **Rev:** Black iris **Edge:** Milled

Date	Mintage	F	VF	XF	Unc	BU
ND(1995)	—	—	—	—	10.00	—

KM# 57a 5 DINARS
28.2800 g., 0.9250 Silver .8411 oz. ASW, 38.61 mm.
Ruler: Hussein Ibn Talal **Subject:** UN 50 Years **Obv:** Bust left **Rev:** Black iris **Edge:** Milled

Date	Mintage	F	VF	XF	Unc	BU
ND(1995) Proof	100,000	Value: 47.50				

KM# 66 5 DINARS
28.2800 g., 0.9250 Silver .8411 oz. ASW, 38.61 mm.
Ruler: Hussein Ibn Talal **Subject:** UNICEF: For the Children of the World **Obv:** Conjoined busts right **Rev:** Boy, girl and UNICEF logo **Edge:** Milled

Date	Mintage	F	VF	XF	Unc	BU
AH1419-1999 Proof	25,000	Value: 50.00				

KM# 71 5 DINARS
28.5000 g., Brass, 40 mm. **Ruler:** Abdullah Ibn Al-Hussein **Subject:** Millennium and Baptism of Jesus **Obv:** Bust facing **Rev:** Baptism scene **Edge:** Milled

Date	Mintage	F	VF	XF	Unc	BU
AH1420//2000 Prooflike	10,000	—	—	—	20.00	—

KM# 26 10 DINARS
27.6400 g., 0.9000 Gold .7998 oz. AGW, 40 mm.
Ruler: Hussein Ibn Talal **Subject:** Visit of Pope Paul VI
Obv: Bust left **Rev:** Pope and church within circle above value

Date	Mintage	F	VF	XF	Unc	BU
AH1389//1969 Proof	1,870	Value: 575				

KM# 44 10 DINARS
30.0000 g., 0.9250 Silver .8922 oz. ASW, 40 mm.
Ruler: Hussein Ibn Talal **Subject:** 15th century Hijrah calendar **Obv:** Bust 1/4 right **Rev:** Capitol building and sun within circle with sprig at left within larger circle **Edge:** Milled

Date	Mintage	F	VF	XF	Unc	BU
AH1400-1980 Proof	17,000	Value: 37.50				

KM# 48 10 DINARS
15.2000 g., 0.9250 Silver .4610 oz. ASW, 29 mm. **Ruler:** Hussein Ibn Talal **Subject:** King's 50th Birthday **Obv:** Head right within beaded circle **Rev:** Crowned sun within 3/4 wreath above value **Edge:** Milled

Date	Mintage	F	VF	XF	Unc	BU
AH1406-1985 Proof	—	Value: 27.50				

KM# 80 10 DINARS
31.1000 g., 0.9990 Silver 0.9989 oz. ASW, 40 mm. **Ruler:** Abdullah Ibn Al-Hussein **Subject:** Abdullah II's Accession to Throne **Obv:** Abdullah II **Rev:** Crowned and mantled arms **Edge:** Milled

Date	Mintage	F	VF	XF	Unc	BU
AH1420-1999 Proof	2,000	Value: 45.00				

KM# 72 10 DINARS
31.0000 g., 0.9990 Silver .9957 oz. ASW, 40 mm.
Ruler: Abdullah Ibn Al-Hussein **Subject:** Millennium and Baptism of Jesus **Obv:** Bust facing **Rev:** Baptism scene **Edge:** Milled **Note:** Issued in 1999.

Date	Mintage	F	VF	XF	Unc	BU
AH1420 (2000) Matte with Patina	5,000	—	—	—	45.00	—
AH1420 (2000) Proof	Inc. above	Value: 55.00				

KM# 27 25 DINARS
69.1100 g., 0.9000 Gold 1.9999 oz. AGW, 48 mm. **Ruler:** Hussein Ibn Talal **Obv:** Head right with crowned mantled arms above **Rev:** Dome of the Rock, Jerusalem, above value **Edge:** Milled

Date	Mintage	F	VF	XF	Unc	BU
AH1389-1969 Proof	1,000	Value: 1,400				

KM# 33 25 DINARS
15.0000 g., 0.9170 Gold .4422 oz. AGW, 29.01 mm. **Ruler:** Hussein Ibn Talal **Subject:** 25th Anniversary of Reign **Obv:** Bust right **Rev:** Crowned mantled arms above dates **Edge:** Milled

Date	Mintage	F	VF	XF	Unc	BU
AH1397-1977 FM Proof	4,724	Value: 325				

KM# 45 40 DINARS

14.3100 g., 0.9170 Gold .4216 oz. AGW, 27 mm.
Ruler: Hussein Ibn Talal **Subject:** 15th century Hijrah calendar **Obv:** Bust facing 1/4 right **Rev:** Sun rays, cloud, domed building and box within flower design and circle **Edge:** Milled

Date	Mintage	F	VF	XF	Unc	BU
AH1400-1980 Proof	9,500	Value: 325				

KM# 50 50 DINARS

15.9800 g., 0.9170 Gold .4710 oz. AGW, 28.40 mm. **Ruler:** Hussein Ibn Talal **Subject:** Five-Year Plan **Obv:** Head right with crowned mantled arms above **Rev:** Fruit flanked by sprigs within circled gear with writing within chain wreath **Edge:** Milled

Date	Mintage	F	VF	XF	Unc	BU
AH1396-1976	250	—	—	—	350	375
AH1396-1976 Proof	Inc. above	Value: 425				

KM# 34 50 DINARS

33.4370 g., 0.9000 Gold .9676 oz. AGW, 34 mm.
Ruler: Hussein Ibn Talal **Subject:** Conservation **Obv:** Head right **Rev:** Bird facing left **Edge:** Milled

Date	Mintage	F	VF	XF	Unc	BU
AH1397-1976	829	—	—	—	675	725
AH1397-1976 Proof	287	Value: 800				

KM# 49 50 DINARS

17.0000 g., 0.9170 Gold .5013 oz. AGW, 29 mm.
Ruler: Hussein Ibn Talal **Subject:** King Hussein's 50th Birthday **Obv:** Head right within beaded circle **Rev:** Crown above rising sun within wreath **Edge:** Milled

Date	Mintage	F	VF	XF	Unc	BU
AH1406-1985 Proof	2,029	Value: 350				
AH1406 Proof	2,000	Value: 325				

KM# 69 50 DINARS

16.9600 g., 0.9166 Gold .4998 oz. AGW, 30 mm.
Ruler: Hussein Ibn Talal **Subject:** 50 Years - Jordanian Independence **Obv:** Bust facing **Rev:** Portrait of King Abdullah

Date	Mintage	F	VF	XF	Unc	BU
ND(1996) Proof	Est. 1,000	Value: 400				

KM# 67 50 DINARS

6.2200 g., 0.9990 Gold .1998 oz. AGW, 22 mm. **Ruler:** Hussein Ibn Talal **Subject:** UNICEF: For the Children of the World **Obv:** Conjoined busts right **Rev:** Boy, girl and UNICEF logo

Date	Mintage	F	VF	XF	Unc	BU
AH1419-1999 Proof	10,000	Value: 175				

KM# 81 50 DINARS

16.9600 g., 0.9166 Gold 0.4998 oz. AGW, 30 mm.
Ruler: Abdullah Ibn Al-Hussein **Subject:** Abdullah II's Accession to the Throne **Obv:** Abdullah II **Rev:** Crowned and mantled arms **Edge:** Milled

Date	Mintage	F	VF	XF	Unc	BU
AH1420-1999 Proof	1,750	Value: 365				

KM# 82 50 DINARS

16.9600 g., 0.9166 Gold 0.4998 oz. AGW, 30 mm.
Ruler: Abdullah Ibn Al-Hussein **Subject:** Millennium and Baptism of Jesus **Obv:** Abdullah II **Rev:** River baptism scene **Edge:** Milled

Date	Mintage	F	VF	XF	Unc	BU
AH1420-2000 Proof	3,500	Value: 365				

KM# 46 60 DINARS

17.1700 g., 0.9170 Gold .5062 oz. AGW, 27 mm.
Ruler: Hussein Ibn Talal **Subject:** International Year of the Child **Obv:** Head right **Rev:** Palace of Culture in Amman and two children within circle **Edge:** Milled

Date	Mintage	F	VF	XF	Unc	BU
AH1401-1981 Proof	20,000	Value: 350				

PATTERNS

Including off metal strikes

KM#	Date	Mintage	Identification	Mkt Val
Pn1	AH1387	50	Fils. Gold. 5.6600 g. KM14.	250
Pn2	AH1387	50	5 Fils. Gold. 11.4000 g. KM15.	350
Pn3	AH1387	50	10 Fils. Gold. 18.8000 g. KM16.	400
Pn4	AH1387	50	25 Fils. Gold. 8.8100 g. KM17.	300
Pn5	AH1387	50	50 Fils. Gold. 13.7500 g. KM18.	1,000
Pn6	AH1387	50	Dirham. Gold. 22.8000 g. KM19.	1,200
Pn7	AH1395	170	Fils. Gold. 5.6600 g. As KM14.	300
Pn8	AH1395	170	5 Fils. Gold. 11.4000 g. As KM15.	500
Pn9	AH1395	170	10 Fils. Gold. 18.8000 g. As KM16.	550
Pn10	AH1395	170	25 Fils. Gold. 8.8100 g. As KM17.	350
Pn11	AH1395	170	50 Fils. Gold. 13.7500 g. As KM18.	550
Pn12	AH1395	170	Dirham. Gold. 22.8000 g. As KM19.	750
Pn13	AH1395	110	1/4 Dinar. Gold. 31.4500 g. As KM28.	950
Pn14	AH1412-1992	3	2-1/2 Piastres. Nickel-Plated Steel. as KM-53, denomination not frosted.	750
Pn15	AH1412-1992	3	5 Piastres. Nickel-Plated Steel. as KM-54, denomination not frosted	1,000
Pn16	AH1412-1992	3	10 Piastres. Nickel Plated Steel. as KM-55, denomination not frosted.	2,500
Pn17	AH1415-1995(1996)	1	1/4 Dinar. Nickel-Brass. Similar to KM-61, never released in circulation with the "1995" date.	—
Pn18	AH1415-1995(1996)	1	1/2 Dinar. Brass. Similar to KM-58, never released in circulation with the "1995" date.	—
Pn19	AH1415-1995(1996)	3	Dinar. Brass. as KM-62, lighter metal	450
Pn20	AH1417-1997	2	1/2 Dinar. Bi-Metallic. as KM-63, metal lighter in color	250

PIEFORTS

KM#	Date	Mintage	Identification	Mkt Val
P1	1981	2,050	3 Dinars. Silver. 46.6600 g. KM43.	90.00
P2	1981	61	60 Dinars. Gold. 34.3400 g. KM46.	950
P3	1985	700	50 Dinars. Gold. 34.3400 g. KM49.	700
P4	AH1413-1992	500	Dinar. 0.9167 Gold. 17.0000 g. 28.4 mm. Broad piefort of KM-52	400
P5	ND(1996)	400	50 Dinars. 0.9166 Gold. 33.9200 g. 40 mm. Milled edge. Similar to KM#69, with 40mm diameter.	800

MINT SETS

KM#	Date	Mintage	Identification	Issue Price	Mkt Val
MS1	1985 (8)	—	KM35-41, 47	10.75	15.00
MS2	1949-1964 (6)	—	KM5 (1949), 8 (1963), 9 (1962), Pn10-11 (1964), Pn12 (1962), mixed dates	—	10.00
MS3	1996 (8)	—	KM#53-56, 58-61	—	15.00

PROOF SETS

KM#	Date	Mintage	Identification	Issue Price	Mkt Val
PS1	1949 (6)	25	KM2-7	—	500
PS2	1965 (6)	10,000	KM8-13	14.40	17.50
PS3	1969 (7)	—	KM21-27	396	2,000
PS4	1969 (6)	—	KM21-26	—	925
PS5	1969 (4)	—	KM24-27	—	1,900
PS6	1969 (3)	5,800	KM21-23	36.00	125
PS7	1977 (3)	1,000	KM31-32, 34	780	825
PS8	1977 (2)	9,000	KM31-32	60.00	65.00
PS9	1978 (7)	20,000	KM35-41	27.00	15.00
PS10	1980 (2)	—	KM44-45	365	525
PS11	1985 (8)	5,000	KM35-41, 47	31.00	25.00
PS12	1996 (3)	50	KM#68, 69 & P5	—	1,000
PS13	1996 (8)	—	KM#53-56, 58-61	30.00	50.00

SPECIMEN SETS (SS)

KM#	Date	Mintage	Identification	Issue Price	Mkt Val
SS1	1964 (6)	3,000	KM8-13	—	14.00
SS2	1965 (6)	5,000	KM8-13	—	12.00
SS3	1968 (6)	50	KM14-19	—	300
SS4	1968 (6)	50	KMPn1-6	—	4,000
SS5	1975 (7)	110	KMPn7-13	—	2,000

KATANGA

Katanga, the southern province of the former Belgian Congo, had an area of 191,873 sq. mi. (496,951 sq. km.) and was noted for its mineral wealth.

MONETARY SYSTEM
100 Centimes = 1 Franc

PROVINCE

DECIMAL COINAGE

KM# 1 FRANC

Bronze **Obv:** Bananas (musax paradisiaca-Musaceae) within circle **Rev:** Cross, value and date within circle

Date	Mintage	F	VF	XF	Unc	BU
1961	—	—	1.25	2.00	4.00	—

KM# 2 5 FRANCS

Bronze, 26.3 mm. **Obv:** Bananas (musax paradisiaca-Musaceae) within circle **Rev:** Cross, value and date within circle

Date	Mintage	F	VF	XF	Unc	BU
1961	—	—	2.50	4.00	8.00	—

KM# 2a 5 FRANCS

13.3300 g., 0.9000 Gold .3857 oz. AGW **Obv:** Bananas within circle **Rev:** Cross, value and date within circle

Date	Mintage	F	VF	XF	Unc	BU
1961	20,000	—	—	—	285	500

The Republic of Kazakhstan (formerly Kazakhstan S.S.R.) is bordered to the west by the Caspian Sea and Russia, to the north by Russia, in the east by the Peoples Republic of China and in the south by Uzbekistan and Kirghizia. It has an area of 1,049,155 sq. mi. (2,717,300 sq. km.) and a population of 16.7 million. Capital: Astana. Rich in mineral resources including coal, tungsten, copper, lead, zinc and manganese with huge oil and natural gas reserves. Agriculture is very important, (it previously represented 20 percent of the total arable acreage of the combined U.S.S.R.) Non-ferrous metallurgy, heavy engineering and chemical industries are leaders in its economy.

The Kazakhs are a branch of the Turkic peoples which led the nomadic life of herdsmen until WW I. In the 13th century they came under Genghis Khan's eldest son Jujiand. Later they became a part of the Golden Horde, a western Mongol empire. Around the beginning of the 16th century they were divided into 3 confederacies, known as *zhuz* or hordes, in the steppes of Turkestan. At the end of the 17th century an incursion by the Kalmucks, a remnant of the Oirat Mongol confederacy, resulted in heavy losses on both sides which facilitated Russian penetration. Resistance to Russian settlements varied throughout the 1800's, but by 1900 over 100 million acres were declared Czarist state property and used for a planned peasant colonization. After a revolution in 1905 Kazakh deputies were elected. In 1916 the tsarist government ordered mobilization of all males, between 19 and 43, for auxiliary service. The Kazakhs rose in defiance which led the governor general of Turkestan to send troops against the rebels. Shortly after the Russian revolution, Kazakh Nationalists asked for full autonomy. The Communist *coup d'etat* of Nov. 1917 led to civil war. In 1919-20 the Red army defeated the "White" Russian forces and occupied Kazakhstan and fought against the Nationalist government formed on Nov. 17, 1917 by Ali Khan Bukey Khan. The Kazakh Autonomous Soviet Socialist Republic was proclaimed on Aug. 26, 1920 within the R.S.F.S.R. Russian and Ukrainian colonization continued while 2 purges in 1927 and 1935 quelled any Kazakh feelings of priority in the matters of their country. On Dec. 5, 1936 Kazakhstan qualified for full status as an S.S.R. and held its first congress in 1937. Independence was declared on Dec. 16, 1991 and Kazakhstan joined the C.I.S.

MONETARY SYSTEM
100 Tyin = 1 Tenge

REPUBLIC

DECIMAL COINAGE

KM# 1 2 TYIN
1.9000 g., Yellow Brass, 17.2 mm. **Obv:** National emblem **Rev:** Star design divides date with value within

Date	Mintage	F	VF	XF	Unc	BU
1993	—	—	—	—	0.45	0.75

KM# 1a 2 TYIN
1.9000 g., Copper Clad Brass, 17.2 mm. **Obv:** National emblem **Rev:** Star design divides date with value within

Date	Mintage	F	VF	XF	Unc	BU
1993	—	—	—	—	0.45	0.75

KM# 2 5 TYIN
1.9000 g., Yellow Brass, 17.2 mm. **Obv:** National emblem **Rev:** Star design divides date with value within

Date	Mintage	F	VF	XF	Unc	BU
1993	—	—	—	—	0.60	1.00

KM# 2a 5 TYIN
1.9000 g., Copper Clad Brass, 17.2 mm. **Obv:** National emblem **Rev:** Star design divides date with value within

Date	Mintage	F	VF	XF	Unc	BU
1993	—	—	—	—	0.60	1.00

KM# 3 10 TYIN
3.1000 g., Yellow Brass, 19.6 mm. **Obv:** National emblem **Rev:** Star design divides date with value within

Date	Mintage	F	VF	XF	Unc	BU
1993	—	—	—	—	0.80	1.50

KM# 3a 10 TYIN
3.1000 g., Copper Clad Brass, 19.6 mm. **Obv:** National emblem **Rev:** Star design divides date with value within

Date	Mintage	F	VF	XF	Unc	BU
1993	—	—	—	—	0.80	1.50

KM# 4 20 TYIN
4.4000 g., Brass Plated Zinc, 22 mm. **Obv:** National emblem **Rev:** Star design divides date with value within

Date	Mintage	F	VF	XF	Unc	BU
1993	—	—	—	—	1.25	2.00

KM# 5 50 TYIN
6.8000 g., Brass Plated Zinc, 25.1 mm. **Obv:** National emblem **Rev:** Star design divides date with value within

Date	Mintage	F	VF	XF	Unc	BU
1993	—	—	—	—	1.50	2.50

KM# 6 TENGE
Copper-Nickel, 17.3 mm. **Obv:** Mythical animal **Rev:** Star design with value and date within

Date	Mintage	F	VF	XF	Unc	BU
1992	—	—	—	—	1.00	1.75
1993	—	—	—	—	0.50	0.85

KM# 23 TENGE
Brass **Obv:** National emblem **Rev:** Value flanked by designs

Date	Mintage	F	VF	XF	Unc	BU
1997	—	—	—	—	0.50	0.85
2000	—	—	—	—	0.50	0.85

KM# 8 3 TENGE
Copper-Nickel **Obv:** Mythical animal within circle **Rev:** Star design with value and date within

Date	Mintage	F	VF	XF	Unc	BU
1993	—	—	—	—	0.75	1.25

KM# 9 5 TENGE
Copper-Nickel **Obv:** Mythical animal within circle **Rev:** Star design with date and value within

Date	Mintage	F	VF	XF	Unc	BU
1993	—	—	—	—	1.25	2.00

KM# 24 5 TENGE
Brass **Obv:** National emblem **Rev:** Value flanked by designs

Date	Mintage	F	VF	XF	Unc	BU
1997	—	—	—	—	0.50	0.85
2000	—	—	—	—	0.50	0.85

KM# 10 10 TENGE
Copper-Nickel **Obv:** National emblem above value **Rev:** Stylized double headed eagle within circle above date

Date	Mintage	F	VF	XF	Unc	BU
1993	—	—	—	—	2.00	3.50

KM# 25 10 TENGE
Brass **Obv:** National emblem **Rev:** Value above design

Date	Mintage	F	VF	XF	Unc	BU
1997	—	—	—	—	0.75	1.25
2000	—	—	—	—	0.75	1.25

KM# 11 20 TENGE
Copper-Nickel **Obv:** National emblem above value **Rev:** Turbaned head 1/4 right within circle

Date	Mintage	F	VF	XF	Unc	BU
1993	—	—	—	—	3.00	5.00

KM# 12 20 TENGE
Copper-Nickel **Subject:** 50th Anniversary - United Nations **Obv:** National emblem above value **Rev:** UN logo and anniversary dates within circle

Date	Mintage	F	VF	XF	Unc	BU
1995	—	—	—	—	3.50	5.50

KM# 18 20 TENGE
Copper-Nickel **Subject:** 150th Anniversary - Jambyl **Obv:** National emblem above value **Rev:** Man with stringed instrument

Date	Mintage	F	VF	XF	Unc	BU
1996	—	—	—	—	3.50	5.50

KM# 19 20 TENGE
Copper-Nickel **Subject:** 5th Anniversary - Independence **Obv:** National emblem above value **Rev:** Monument and buildings

Date	Mintage	F	VF	XF	Unc	BU
1996	—	—	—	—	3.50	5.50

KM# 20 20 TENGE
Copper-Nickel **Subject:** Centennial - Birth of Muchtar Auezov **Obv:** National emblem above value **Rev:** Head facing divides dates

Date	Mintage	F	VF	XF	Unc	BU
ND(1997)	—	—	—	—	3.50	5.50

KM# 26 20 TENGE
Copper-Nickel **Obv:** National emblem **Rev:** Value above design

Date	Mintage	F	VF	XF	Unc	BU
1997	—	—	—	—	1.00	1.75
2000	—	—	—	—	1.00	1.75

KM# 21 20 TENGE
Copper-Nickel **Subject:** Year of Peace and Harmony **Obv:** National emblem above value **Rev:** Stylized dove

Date	Mintage	F	VF	XF	Unc	BU
1997	—	—	—	—	3.50	5.50

KM# 22 20 TENGE
Copper-Nickel **Subject:** New Capital - Astana **Obv:** National emblem above value **Rev:** Flower-like design

Date	Mintage	F	VF	XF	Unc	BU
1998	—	—	—	—	3.50	5.50

KM# 28 20 TENGE
Copper-Nickel **Subject:** 100th Birthday - K.I. Satbaev **Obv:** National emblem above value **Rev:** Head facing

Date	Mintage	F	VF	XF	Unc	BU
1999	—	—	—	—	3.85	6.50

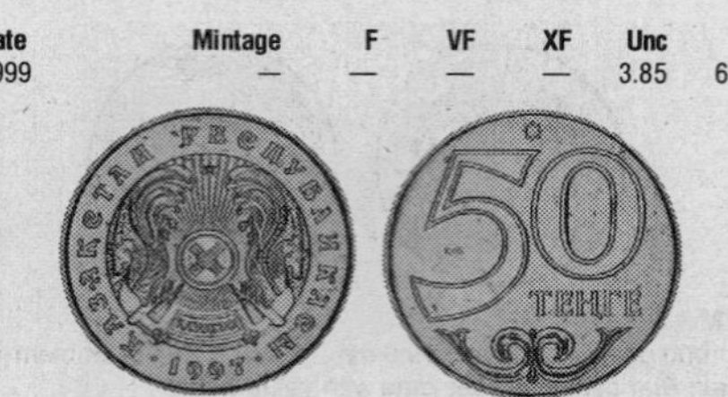

KM# 27 50 TENGE
Copper-Nickel **Obv:** National emblem **Rev:** Value above design

Date	Mintage	F	VF	XF	Unc	BU
1997	—	—	—	—	2.00	3.50
2000	—	—	—	—	2.00	3.50

KM# 30 50 TENGE
Copper-Nickel **Subject:** Millennium **Obv:** National emblem above value **Rev:** Rising sun above three blocks

Date	Mintage	F	VF	XF	Unc	BU
1999	—	—	—	—	3.50	5.50

KM# 31 50 TENGE
10.7000 g., Copper-Nickel, 31 mm. **Subject:** Victorious conclusion of World War II **Obv:** National emblem above value **Rev:** Soldiers celebrating **Edge:** Reeded and plain sections

Date	Mintage	F	VF	XF	Unc	BU
ND(2000)	—	—	—	—	4.00	6.50

KM# 48 50 TENGE
11.0600 g., Copper-Nickel, 31 mm. **Subject:** 1500th Anniversary of Akhmet Yasaui Kesenesi Mosque **Obv:** National emblem above value **Rev:** Mosque **Edge:** Reeded and plain sections

Date	Mintage	F	VF	XF	Unc	BU
2000	—	—	—	—	3.00	5.00

KM# 33 50 TENGE
11.5000 g., Copper-Nickel **Obv:** National emblem above value **Rev:** Bust 1/4 left **Edge:** Reeded and plain sections

Date	Mintage	F	VF	XF	Unc	BU
2000	—	—	—	—	4.00	6.50

KM# 13 100 TENGE
24.0000 g., 0.9250 Silver .7137 oz. ASW **Subject:** 150th Anniversary - Birth of Abaj Kunabaev **Obv:** Mother and child within circle **Rev:** Head left flanked by dates above small assorted figures **Edge:** Lettered

Date	Mintage	F	VF	XF	Unc	BU
1995 Proof	6,000	Value: 35.00				

KM# 14 100 TENGE
24.0000 g., 0.9250 Silver .7137 oz. ASW **Subject:** 150th Anniversary - Birth of Abaj Kunabaev **Obv:** Bust left **Rev:** Falconer

Date	Mintage	F	VF	XF	Unc	BU
1995 Proof	6,000	Value: 37.50				

KM# 15 100 TENGE
24.0000 g., 0.9250 Silver .7137 oz. ASW **Subject:** 150th Anniversary - Birth of Abaj Kunabaev **Obv:** Bust left **Rev:** Couple on swings

Date	Mintage	F	VF	XF	Unc	BU
1995 Proof	6,000	Value: 35.00				

KM# 16 100 TENGE
24.0000 g., 0.9250 Silver .7137 oz. ASW **Subject:** 150th Anniversary - Birth of Abaj Kunabaev **Obv:** Bust left **Rev:** Town view

Date	Mintage	F	VF	XF	Unc	BU
1995 Proof	6,000	Value: 35.00				

KM# 17 100 TENGE
24.0000 g., 0.9250 Silver .7137 oz. ASW **Subject:** 150th Anniversary - Birth of Abaj Kunabaev **Obv:** Bust left **Rev:** Elderly man

Date	Mintage	F	VF	XF	Unc	BU
1995 Proof	6,000	Value: 35.00				

KM# 32 100 TENGE
24.0000 g., 0.9250 Silver .7137 oz. ASW, 37 mm. **Subject:** Millennium **Obv:** National emblem within design **Rev:** Ancient and modern technologies **Edge:** Plain

Date	Mintage	F	VF	XF	Unc	BU
1999 Proof	2,000	Value: 45.00				

KM# 34 100 TENGE
24.0000 g., 0.9250 Silver .7137 oz. ASW, 37 mm. **Subject:** 1500th Anniversary of Turkestan **Obv:** Value **Rev:** Domed building **Edge:** Plain

Date	Mintage	F	VF	XF	Unc	BU
2000 Proof	3,000	Value: 45.00				

KM# 35 500 TENGE
24.0000 g., 0.9250 Silver .7137 oz. ASW, 37 mm. **Subject:** Snow Leopard **Obv:** Value **Rev:** Prowling leopard **Edge:** Plain

Date	Mintage	F	VF	XF	Unc	BU
2000 Proof	3,000	Value: 50.00				

KM# 36 500 TENGE
24.0000 g., 0.9250 Silver .7137 oz. ASW, 36.9 mm. **Subject:** Petroglyphs of Kazakhstan **Obv:** Value within designs **Rev:** "Sun God" petroglyph **Edge:** Plain

Date	Mintage	F	VF	XF	Unc	BU
2000 Proof	3,000	Value: 45.00				

KM# 29 1000 TENGE
3.1200 g., 0.9999 Gold .1003 oz. AGW **Subject:** Silk Road **Obv:** Value in ornamental frame **Rev:** Caravan of camels around lined cross within circle

Date	Mintage	F	VF	XF	Unc	BU
1995	—	—	—	—	85.00	100

KM# 45 2500 TENGE
7.7800 g., 0.9999 Gold 0.2501 oz. AGW, 20 mm. **Subject:** The Silk Road **Obv:** Value in ornamental frame **Rev:** Caravan of camels around lined cross within circle **Edge:** Reeded

Date	Mintage	F	VF	XF	Unc	BU
1995	—	—	—	—	220	245

KM# 46 5000 TENGE
15.5500 g., 0.9999 Gold 0.4999 oz. AGW, 25 mm. **Subject:** The Silk Road **Obv:** Value in ornamental frame **Rev:** Caravan of camels around lined cross within circle **Edge:** Reeded

Date	Mintage	F	VF	XF	Unc	BU
1995	—	—	—	—	350	375

KM# 47 10000 TENGE
31.1000 g., 0.9999 Gold 0.9998 oz. AGW, 32 mm. **Subject:** The Silk Road **Obv:** Value in ornamental frame **Rev:** Caravan of camels around lined cross within circle **Edge:** Reeded

Date	Mintage	F	VF	XF	Unc	BU
1995	—	—	—	—	700	750

PROBAS

KM#	Date	Mintage	Identification	Mkt Val
Pr1	1992	—	50 Tenge. Copper Nickel.	—
Pr2	1992	—	50 Tenge. Copper.	—
Pr3	1992	—	50 Tenge. Brass.	—
Pr4	1992	—	50 Tenge. Aluminum.	—

The Territory of Cocos (Keeling) Islands, an Australian territory, comprises a group of 27 coral islands located (see arrow on map of Australia) in the Indian Ocean 1,300 miles northwest of Australia. Only Direction and Home Islands are regularly inhabited. The group has an area of 5.4 sq. mi. and a population of about 569. Calcium, phosphate and coconut products are exported.

The islands were discovered by Capt. William Keeling of the British East India Co. in 1609. Alexander Hare, an English adventurer, established a settlement on one of the southern islands in 1823, but it lasted less than a year. A permanent settlement was established on Direction Island in 1827 by Hare and Capt. John Clunies Ross, a Scot, for the purpose of storing East Indian spices for reshipment to Europe during periods of shortage. When the experiment in spice futures did not develop satisfactorily, Hare left the islands (1829 or 1830), leaving Ross as sole owner. The coral group became a British protectorate in 1856; was attached to the colony of Ceylon in 1878; and was placed under the administration of the Straits Settlements in 1882. In 1903 the group was annexed to the Straits Settlements and incorporated into the colony of Singapore until November of 1955, when it was placed under the administration of Australia.

RULERS
British

MONETARY SYSTEM
100 Cents = 1 Rupee

AUSTRALIAN TERRITORY

TOKEN COINAGE

Plastic Ivory

Tn1-Tn7 were all issued with individual serial numbers.

KM# Tn1 5 CENTS

Date	Mintage	VG	F	VF	XF	Unc
1913	5,000	60.00	100	200	325	425

KM# Tn2 10 CENTS

Date	Mintage	VG	F	VF	XF	Unc
1913	5,000	45.00	75.00	150	275	375

KM# Tn3 25 CENTS

Date	Mintage	VG	F	VF	XF	Unc
1913	5,000	20.00	30.00	50.00	90.00	185

KM# Tn4 50 CENTS

Date	Mintage	VG	F	VF	XF	Unc
1913	2,000	75.00	125	275	475	575

KM# Tn5 RUPEE

Date	Mintage	VG	F	VF	XF	Unc
1913	2,000	25.00	40.00	75.00	125	200

KM# Tn6 2 RUPEES

Date	Mintage	VG	F	VF	XF	Unc
1913	1,000	35.00	50.00	90.00	140	225

KM# Tn7 5 RUPEES

Date	Mintage	VG	F	VF	XF	Unc
1913	1,000	35.00	50.00	100	165	250

TOKEN COINAGE

Modern Plastic

KM# Tn8 CENT
Note: Aqua-color plastic.

Date	Mintage	F	VF	XF	Unc	BU
1968	—	—	—	—	90.00	—

KM# Tn9 5 CENTS
Note: Aqua-color plastic.

Date	Mintage	F	VF	XF	Unc	BU
1968	—	—	—	—	90.00	—

KM# Tn10 10 CENTS
Note: Aqua-color plastic.

Date	Mintage	F	VF	XF	Unc	BU
1968	—	—	—	—	100	—

KM# Tn11 25 CENTS
Note: Aqua-color plastic.

Date	Mintage	F	VF	XF	Unc	BU
1968	—	—	—	—	120	—

KM# Tn12 50 CENTS
Note: Aqua-color plastic.

Date	Mintage	F	VF	XF	Unc	BU
1968	—	—	—	—	135	—

KM# Tn13 RUPEE
Note: Red-color plastic.

Date	Mintage	F	VF	XF	Unc	BU
1968	—	—	—	—	140	—

KM# Tn14 2 RUPEES
Note: Red-color plastic.

Date	Mintage	F	VF	XF	Unc	BU
1968	—	—	—	—	150	—

KM# Tn15 5 RUPEES
Note: Red-color plastic.

Date	Mintage	F	VF	XF	Unc	BU
1968	—	—	—	—	175	—

KM# Tn16 10 RUPEES
Note: Red-color plastic.

Date	Mintage	F	VF	XF	Unc	BU
1968	—	—	—	—	210	—

KM# Tn17 25 RUPEES
Note: Red-color plastic.

Date	Mintage	F	VF	XF	Unc	BU
1968	—	—	—	—	245	—

MINT SETS

KM#	Date	Mintage	Identification	Issue Price	Mkt Val
MS1	1977 (7)	—	X#1-7	—	325
MS2	1977 (2)	6,000	X#8-9	—	200

PROOF SETS

KM#	Date	Mintage	Identification	Issue Price	Mkt Val
PS1	1977 (2)	4,000	X#8-9	28.00	275

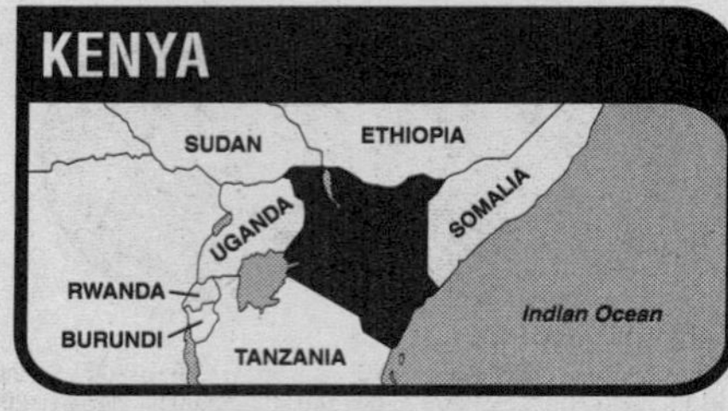

The Republic of Kenya, located on the east coast of Central Africa, has an area of 224,961 sq. mi. (582,650 sq. km.) and a population of 20.1 million. Capital: Nairobi. The predominantly agricultural country exports coffee, tea and petroleum products.

The Arabs came to the coast of Kenya in the 8th century and established posts to conduct an ivory and slave trade. The Portuguese followed in the 16th century. After a lengthy and bitter struggle with the sultans of Zanzibar who controlled much of the southeastern coast of Africa, the Portuguese were driven away (late 17th century) and for many years Kenya was simply a port of call on the route to India. German and British interests in the 19th century produced agreements defining their respective spheres of influence. The British sphere was administrated by the Imperial East Africa Co. until 1895, when the British government purchased the company's rights in the East Africa Protectorate which, in 1920, was designated as Kenya Colony and protectorate - the latter being a 10-mile-wide coastal strip together with Mombasa, Lamuand other small islands nominally retained by the Sultan of Zanzibar. Kenya achieved self-government in June of 1963 as a consequence of the 1952-60 Mau Mau terrorist campaign to secure land reforms and political rights for Africans. Independence was attained on Dec. 12, 1963. Kenya became a republic in 1964. It is a member of the Commonwealth of Nations. The president is Chief of State and Head of Government.

RULERS
British, until 1964

MONETARY SYSTEM
100 Cents = 1 Shilling

REPUBLIC

STANDARD COINAGE

KM# 1 5 CENTS
Nickel-Brass **Obv:** Arms with supporters above value **Rev:** Bust left **Rev. Designer:** Norman Sillman

Date	Mintage	F	VF	XF	Unc	BU
1966	28,000,000	—	0.25	0.50	1.00	2.00
1966 Proof	27	Value: 80.00				
1967	9,600,000	—	0.25	0.50	1.00	2.00
1968	12,000,000	—	0.25	0.50	1.00	2.00

KM# 10 5 CENTS
Nickel-Brass **Obv:** Arms with supporters divide date above value **Rev:** Bust left **Rev. Designer:** Norman Sillman

Date	Mintage	F	VF	XF	Unc	BU
1969	800,000	—	0.50	1.00	2.25	4.00
1969 Proof	15	Value: 110				
1970	10,000,000	—	0.15	0.25	1.00	—
1971	29,680,000	—	0.15	0.25	1.00	—
1973 Proof	500	Value: 25.00				
1974	5,599,000	—	0.15	0.25	1.00	—
1975	28,000,000	—	0.15	0.25	1.00	—
1978	23,168,000	—	0.15	0.25	1.00	—

KM# 17 5 CENTS
5.6000 g., Nickel-Brass, 25.5 mm. **Obv:** Arms with supporters divide date above value **Rev:** Bust right

Date	Mintage	F	VF	XF	Unc	BU
1978	—	—	—	—	1.00	—
1978 Proof	—	Value: 10.00				
1980	—	—	0.15	0.25	1.00	—
1984	—	—	0.15	0.25	1.00	—
1986	—	—	0.15	0.25	1.00	—
1987	—	—	0.15	0.25	1.00	—
1989	—	—	0.15	0.25	0.75	—
1990	—	—	0.15	0.25	0.75	—
1991	—	—	0.15	0.25	0.75	—

KM# 2 10 CENTS
Nickel-Brass, 30.8 mm. **Obv:** Arms with supporters divide date above value **Rev:** Bust left **Rev. Designer:** Norman Sillman

Date	Mintage	F	VF	XF	Unc	BU
1966	26,000,000	0.20	0.65	1.25	2.50	—
1966 Proof	27	Value: 80.00				
1967	7,300,000	0.20	0.65	1.25	2.50	—
1968	12,000,000	0.20	0.65	1.25	2.50	—

KM# 11 10 CENTS
Nickel-Brass, 30.8 mm. **Obv:** Arms with supporters divide date above value **Rev:** Bust left

Date	Mintage	F	VF	XF	Unc	BU
1969	3,900,000	—	0.15	0.25	1.00	—
1969 Proof	15	Value: 110				
1970	7,200,000	—	0.15	0.25	1.00	—
1971	32,400,000	—	0.15	0.25	0.75	—
1973	3,000,000	—	0.15	0.25	1.00	—
1973 Proof	500	Value: 25.00				
1974	3,000,000	—	0.15	0.25	1.00	—
1975	3,000,000	—	0.15	0.25	1.00	—
1977	45,600,000	—	0.15	0.25	0.75	—
1978	22,600,000	—	0.15	0.25	0.75	—

KM# 18 10 CENTS
Nickel-Brass, 30.8 mm. **Obv:** Arms with supporters divide date above value **Rev:** Bust right

Date	Mintage	F	VF	XF	Unc	BU
1978	—	—	—	—	1.00	—
1978 Proof	—	Value: 15.00				
1980	—	—	0.15	0.25	1.00	—
1984	—	—	0.15	0.25	1.25	—
1986	—	—	0.15	0.25	1.25	—
1987	—	—	0.15	0.25	1.25	—
1989	—	—	0.15	0.25	1.00	—
1990	—	—	0.15	0.25	1.00	—
1991	—	—	0.15	0.25	0.75	—

KM# 18a 10 CENTS
9.3000 g., Brass Plated Steel, 30.8 mm. **Obv:** Arms with supporters divide date above value **Rev:** Bust right

Date	Mintage	F	VF	XF	Unc	BU
1994	—	—	0.20	0.30	1.00	—

KM# 31 10 CENTS
Brass-Plated Steel **Obv:** Arms with supporters divide date below value **Rev:** Bust right

Date	Mintage	F	VF	XF	Unc	BU
1995	—	—	0.10	0.20	0.40	—

KM# 3 25 CENTS
Copper-Nickel **Obv:** Arms with supporters divide date above value **Rev:** Bust left **Rev. Designer:** Norman Sillman

Date	Mintage	F	VF	XF	Unc	BU
1966	4,000,000	0.30	1.00	2.00	3.50	—
1966 Proof	27	Value: 100				
1967	4,000,000	0.30	1.00	2.00	3.50	—

KM# 12 25 CENTS
Copper-Nickel **Obv:** Arms with supporters divide date above value **Rev:** Bust left **Rev. Designer:** Norman Sillman

Date	Mintage	F	VF	XF	Unc	BU
1969	200,000	0.50	1.00	2.50	10.00	—
1969 Proof	15	Value: 125				
1973 Proof	500	Value: 35.00				

KM# 4 50 CENTS
Copper-Nickel, 21 mm. **Obv:** Arms with supporters divide date above value **Rev:** Bust left **Rev. Designer:** Norman Sillman

Date	Mintage	F	VF	XF	Unc	BU
1966	4,000,000	0.20	0.40	1.00	2.75	—
1966 Proof	27	Value: 100				
1967	5,120,000	0.20	0.40	0.85	2.25	—
1968	6,000,000	0.20	0.40	0.85	2.00	—

KM# 13 50 CENTS
Copper-Nickel, 21 mm. **Obv:** Arms with supporters divide date above value **Rev:** Bust left **Rev. Designer:** Norman Sillman

Date	Mintage	F	VF	XF	Unc	BU
1969	400,000	0.40	0.80	1.50	3.00	—
1969 Proof	15	Value: 125				
1971	9,600,000	—	0.20	0.40	1.00	—
1973	3,360,000	0.20	0.40	0.80	1.75	—
1973 Proof	500	Value: 25.00				
1974	12,640,000	—	0.20	0.40	1.00	—
1975	8,000,000	—	0.20	0.40	1.00	—
1977	16,000,000	—	0.20	0.40	1.00	—
1978	20,480,000	—	0.20	0.40	1.00	—

KM# 19 50 CENTS
Copper-Nickel, 21 mm. **Obv:** Arms with supporters divide date above value **Rev:** Bust right

Date	Mintage	F	VF	XF	Unc	BU
1978	—	—	—	—	1.00	—
1978 Proof	—	Value: 20.00				
1980	—	—	0.15	0.25	0.75	—
1989	—	—	0.15	0.25	0.75	—

KM# 19a 50 CENTS
Nickel-Plated Steel, 21 mm. **Obv:** Arms with supporters divide date above value **Rev:** Bust right

Date	Mintage	F	VF	XF	Unc	BU
1994	—	—	0.25	0.35	1.00	—

KM# 28 50 CENTS
3.1000 g., Brass-Plated Steel, 17.9 mm. **Obv:** Arms with supporters divide date below value **Rev:** Bust right

Date	Mintage	F	VF	XF	Unc	BU
1995	—	—	0.15	0.25	0.50	—
1997	—	—	0.15	0.25	0.50	—

KM# 5 SHILLING

Copper-Nickel, 27.8 mm. **Obv:** Arms with supporters divide date above value **Rev:** Bust left **Rev. Designer:** Norman Sillman

Date	Mintage	F	VF	XF	Unc	BU
1966	20,000,000	0.25	0.50	1.00	3.00	—
1966 Proof	27	Value: 100				
1967	4,000,000	0.25	0.50	1.00	2.75	—
1968	8,000,000	0.20	0.40	0.80	2.25	—

KM# 14 SHILLING

Copper-Nickel, 27.8 mm. **Obv:** Arms with supporters divide date above value **Rev:** Bust left **Rev. Designer:** Norman Sillman

Date	Mintage	F	VF	XF	Unc	BU
1969	4,000,000	0.15	0.30	0.75	2.25	—
1969 Proof	15	Value: 125				
1971	24,000,000	0.10	0.30	0.65	2.00	—
1973	2,480,000	0.20	0.40	0.80	2.75	—
1973 Proof	500	Value: 30.00				
1974	13,520,000	0.10	0.30	0.65	2.00	—
1975	40,856,000	0.10	0.30	0.65	2.00	—
1978	20,000,000	0.10	0.30	0.65	2.00	—

KM# 20 SHILLING

Copper-Nickel, 27.8 mm. **Obv:** Arms with supporters divide date above value **Rev:** Bust right

Date	Mintage	F	VF	XF	Unc	BU
1978	—	—	—	—	1.50	—
1978 Proof	—	Value: 30.00				
1980	—	0.15	0.25	0.50	1.50	—
1989	—	0.15	0.25	0.50	1.50	—

KM# 20a SHILLING

Nickel-Plated Steel, 27.8 mm. **Obv:** Arms with supporters divide date above value **Rev:** Bust right

Date	Mintage	F	VF	XF	Unc	BU
1994	—	0.25	0.35	0.65	1.75	—

KM# 29 SHILLING

4.3500 g., Brass-Plated Steel, 22 mm. **Obv:** Arms with supporters divide date below value **Rev:** Bust right

Date	Mintage	F	VF	XF	Unc	BU
1995	—	0.10	0.20	0.40	0.75	—
1997	—	0.10	0.20	0.40	0.75	—
1998	—	0.10	0.20	0.40	0.75	—

KM# 6 2 SHILLINGS

Copper-Nickel **Obv:** Arms with supporters divide date above value **Rev:** Bust left **Rev. Designer:** Norman Sillman
Note: Similar to KM#2.

Date	Mintage	F	VF	XF	Unc	BU
1966	3,000,000	1.00	2.00	3.00	7.00	—
1966 Proof	27	Value: 120				
1968	1,100,000	1.00	2.75	4.50	10.00	—

KM# 15 2 SHILLINGS

Copper-Nickel **Obv:** Arms with supporters divide date above value **Rev:** Bust left **Rev. Designer:** Norman Sillman
Note: Similar to KM#11.

Date	Mintage	F	VF	XF	Unc	BU
1969	100,000	2.00	4.00	8.00	12.50	—
1969 Proof	15	Value: 150				
1971	1,920,000	0.60	1.25	3.50	7.50	—
1973 Proof	500	Value: 35.00				

KM# 16 5 SHILLINGS

Brass **Subject:** 10th Anniversary of Independence **Obv:** Arms with supporters divide date above value **Rev:** Bust left **Shape:** 9-sided

Date	Mintage	F	VF	XF	Unc	BU
1973	100,000	4.50	10.00	17.50	30.00	—
1973 Proof	1,500	Value: 45.00				

KM# 23 5 SHILLINGS

Copper-Nickel, 30 mm. **Obv:** Arms with supporters divide date above value **Rev:** Bust right **Shape:** 7-sided

Date	Mintage	F	VF	XF	Unc	BU
1985	—	0.35	0.75	1.50	3.00	—

KM# 23a 5 SHILLINGS

Nickel-Plated Steel **Obv:** Arms with supporters divide date above value **Rev:** Bust right **Shape:** 7-sided

Date	Mintage	F	VF	XF	Unc	BU
1994	—	0.50	1.00	2.25	4.50	—

KM# 30 5 SHILLINGS

Ring Composition: Copper-Nickel **Center Weight:** 3.4000 g. **Center Composition:** Brass, 20 mm. **Obv:** Arms with supporters below value within circle **Rev:** Bust right within circle

Date	Mintage	F	VF	XF	Unc	BU
1995	—	—	—	—	4.00	6.00
1997	—	—	—	—	4.00	6.00

KM# 27 10 SHILLINGS

Ring Composition: Brass **Center Weight:** 5.0000 g. **Center Composition:** Copper-Nickel, 22.9 mm. **Obv:** Arms with supporters below value within circle **Rev:** Bust right within circle

Date	Mintage	F	VF	XF	Unc	BU
1994	—	—	—	—	5.00	8.00
1995	—	—	—	—	5.00	8.00
1997	—	—	—	—	5.00	8.00

KM# 32 20 SHILLINGS

Ring Composition: Copper-Nickel **Center Composition:** Brass, 25.5 mm. **Obv:** Arms with supporters below value within circle **Rev:** Bust right within circle

Date	Mintage	F	VF	XF	Unc	BU
1998	—	—	—	—	8.00	10.00

KM# 7 100 SHILLINGS

7.6000 g., 0.9170 Gold .224 oz. AGW **Subject:** 75th Anniversary - Birth of President Jomo Kenyatta **Obv:** Fly whisk above value and date **Rev:** Bust left **Designer:** Norman Sillman

Date	Mintage	F	VF	XF	Unc	BU
1966	—	—	—	—	160	170
1966 Proof	7,500	Value: 185				

KM# 21 200 SHILLINGS

28.2800 g., 0.9250 Silver .841 oz. ASW **Obv:** President Moi **Rev:** Arms with supporters above value

Date	Mintage	F	VF	XF	Unc	BU
ND (1979) Proof	Est. 9,500	Value: 100				

KM# 8 250 SHILLINGS

19.0000 g., 0.9170 Gold .5602 oz. AGW **Subject:** 75th Anniversary - Birth of President Jomo Kenyatta **Obv:** Rooster with axe above value and date **Rev:** Bust left **Designer:** Norman Sillman

Date	Mintage	F	VF	XF	Unc	BU
1966	—	—	—	—	400	420
1966 Proof	1,000	Value: 445				

KM# 9 500 SHILLINGS

38.0000 g., 0.9170 Gold 1.1204 oz. AGW **Subject:** 75th Anniversary - Birth of President Jomo Kenyatta **Obv:** Mountain above value and date **Rev:** Bust left **Designer:** Norman Sillman

Date	Mintage	F	VF	XF	Unc	BU
1966	—	—	—	—	775	800
1966 Proof	500	Value: 825				

KM# 24 500 SHILLINGS
28.2800 g., 0.9250 Silver .8410 oz. ASW **Subject:** 10th Anniversary of Moi as President **Obv:** Bust right **Rev:** Arms with supporters above value **Shape:** 10-sided

Date	Mintage	F	VF	XF	Unc	BU
ND(1988) Proof	—	Value: 350				

KM# 25 500 SHILLINGS
28.3300 g., 0.9250 Silver .8425 oz. ASW **Subject:** 25th Anniversary of Independence **Obv:** Bust right **Rev:** Arms with supporters above value

Date	Mintage	F	VF	XF	Unc	BU
ND(1988) Proof	—	Value: 375				

KM# 26 1000 SHILLINGS
28.2800 g., 0.9250 Silver .8351 oz. ASW **Subject:** Silver Jubilee of Central Bank **Obv:** Bust right **Rev:** Arms with supporters above value

Date	Mintage	F	VF	XF	Unc	BU
1991 Proof	—	Value: 500				

KM# 22 3000 SHILLING
40.0000 g., 0.9170 Gold 1.1787 oz. AGW **Obv:** President Moi **Rev:** Arms with supporters above value

Date	Mintage	F	VF	XF	Unc	BU
ND (1979) Proof	2,000	Value: 875				

MINT SETS

KM#	Date	Mintage	Identification	Issue Price	Mkt Val
MS1	1966 (3)	—	KM7-9	—	1,350

PROOF SETS

KM#	Date	Mintage	Identification	Issue Price	Mkt Val
PS1	1966 (6)	27	KM1-6	—	575
PS2	1966 (3)	500	KM7-9	153	1,450
PS3	1969 (6)	15	KM10-15	—	750
PS4	1973 (7)	500	KM10-16	—	220
PS5	1978 (5)	9,500	KM#17-21	—	175

KIAU CHAU

Kiau Chau (Kiao Chau, Kiaochow, Kiautscho, now Jiaozhou), a former German trading enclave, including the port of Tsingtao (Qingdao), was located on the Shantung (Shandong) Peninsula of eastern China. Following the murder of two missionaries in Shantung in 1897, Germany occupied Kiaochow Bay, and during subsequent negotiations with the Chinese government obtained a 99 year lease on 177 sq. mi. of land. The enclave was established as a free port in 1899, and a customs house set up to collect tariffs on goods moving to and from the Chinese interior. The Japanese took siege to the port on Aug. 27, 1914, as their first action in World War I to deprive German sea marauders of their east Asian supply and refitting base. Aided by the British forces, the siege ended Nov. 7. Japan retained possession until 1922, when it was restored to China by the Washington Conference on China and naval armaments. It fell again to Japan in 1938, but not before the Chinese had destroyed its manufacturing facilities. It is presently a part of the Peoples Republic of China. The major city is Tsingtao (Qingdao) and is noted for its beer.

RULERS
Wilhelm II, 1897-1918
Japanese, 1914-1922, 1938-1945

MONETARY SYSTEM
100 Cents = 1 Dollar

GERMAN OCCUPATION

STANDARD COINAGE

Y# 1 5 CENTS
Copper-Nickel **Ruler:** Wilhelm II **Obv:** German Imperial Eagle **Obv. Legend:** DEUTSCH.KIAUTSHAU GEBIET **Rev:** Inscription within beaded circle **Rev. Inscription:** Kuang-hsü Yüan-pao

Date	Mintage	F	VF	XF	Unc	BU
1909	610,000	50.00	75.00	115	185	—
1909 Proof	—	Value: 450				

Y# 2 10 CENTS
Copper-Nickel **Ruler:** Wilhelm II **Obv:** German Imperial Eagle **Obv. Legend:** DEUTSCH.KIAUTSHAU GEBIET **Rev:** Inscription within beaded circle **Rev. Inscription:** Kuang-hsü Yüan-pao

Date	Mintage	F	VF	XF	Unc	BU
1909	670,000	30.00	50.00	90.00	160	—
1909 Proof	—	Value: 500				

KIRIBATI

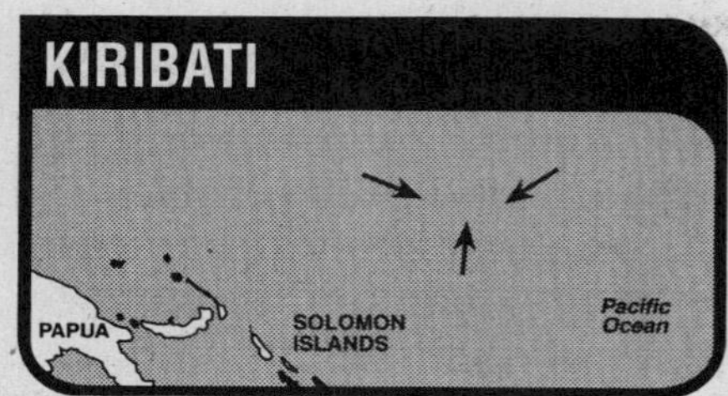

The Republic of Kiribati (formerly the Gilbert Islands), consists of 30 coral atolls and islands spread over more than one million sq. mi. (2,590,000 sq. km.) of the southwest Pacific Ocean, has an area of 332 sq. mi. (717 sq. km.) and a population of 64,200. Capital: Bairiki, on Tarawa. In addition to the Gilbert Islands proper, Kiribati includes Ocean Island, the Central and Southern Line Islands, and the Phoenix Islands, though possession of Canton and Enderbury of the Phoenix Islands is disputed with the United States. Most families engage in subsistence fishing. Copra and phosphates are exported, mostly to Australia and New Zealand.

The Gilbert Islands and the group formerly called the Ellice Islands (now Tuvalu) comprised a single British crown colony, the Gilbert and Ellice Islands.

Spanish mutineers first sighted the islands in 1537, succeeding visits were made by the English navigators John Byron (1764), James Cook (1777), and Thomas Gilbert and John Marshall (1788). An American, Edward Fanning, arrived in 1798. Britain declared a protectorate over the Gilbert and Ellice Islands, and in 1915 began the formation of a colony which was completed when the Phoenix Islands were added to the group in 1937. The Central and Southern Line Islands were administratively attached to the Gilbert and Ellice Islands colony in 1972, and remained attached to the Gilberts when Tuvalu was created in 1975. The colony became self-governing in 1971. Kiribati attained independence on July 12, 1979.

RULERS
British, until 1979

MONETARY SYSTEM
100 Cents = 1 Dollar

REPUBLIC

DECIMAL COINAGE

KM# 1 CENT
2.6000 g., Bronze, 17.5 mm. **Subject:** Christmas Island Frigate Bird **Obv:** National arms **Rev:** Frigate bird on branch **Designer:** Mike Hibbert

Date	Mintage	F	VF	XF	Unc	BU
1979	90,000	—	—	0.15	0.50	1.00
1979 Proof	10,000	Value: 1.00				
1992	—	—	—	0.15	0.50	1.00

KM# 1a CENT
2.6000 g., Bronze-Plated Steel, 17.5 mm. **Obv:** National arms **Rev:** Frigate bird on branch **Designer:** Mike Hibbert

Date	Mintage	F	VF	XF	Unc	BU
1992	—	—	—	—	0.50	1.00

KM# 2 2 CENTS
5.2000 g., Bronze, 21.6 mm. **Subject:** B'abal plant **Obv:** National arms **Rev:** B'abal plant below value **Designer:** Mike Hibbert

Date	Mintage	F	VF	XF	Unc	BU
1979	25,000	—	—	0.15	0.35	0.60
1979 Proof	10,000	Value: 1.25				
1992	—	—	—	0.15	0.35	0.60

KM# 3 5 CENTS
2.9000 g., Copper-Nickel, 19.3 mm. **Subject:** Tokai lizard **Obv:** National arms **Rev:** Lizard below value **Designer:** Mike Hibbert

Date	Mintage	F	VF	XF	Unc	BU
1979	20,000	—	0.15	0.30	1.50	2.50
1979 Proof	10,000	Value: 2.75				

KM# 3a 5 CENTS
Copper-Nickel-Plated Steel, 19.3 mm. **Obv:** National arms **Rev:** Lizard below value **Designer:** Mike Hibbert

Date	Mintage	F	VF	XF	Unc	BU
1992	—	—	—	—	1.50	2.00

KM# 4 10 CENTS
5.7000 g., Copper-Nickel, 23.6 mm. **Subject:** Bread fruit **Obv:** National arms **Rev:** Bread fruit above value **Designer:** Mike Hibbert

Date	Mintage	F	VF	XF	Unc	BU
1979	20,000	—	0.15	0.25	1.25	1.50
1979 Proof	10,000	Value: 3.00				

KM# 5 20 CENTS
11.1500 g., Copper-Nickel, 28.45 mm. **Subject:** Dolphins **Obv:** National arms **Rev:** Dolphins above value **Designer:** Mike Hibbert

Date	Mintage	F	VF	XF	Unc	BU
1979	20,000	—	0.60	1.50	6.00	8.00
1979 Proof	10,000	Value: 8.50				

KM# 6 50 CENTS
15.4000 g., Copper-Nickel, 31.65 mm. **Subject:** Panda nut **Obv:** National arms **Rev:** Panda nut above value **Designer:** Mike Hibbert

Date	Mintage	F	VF	XF	Unc	BU
1979	20,000	—	0.50	1.00	3.00	4.50
1979 Proof	10,000	Value: 6.50				

KM# 7 DOLLAR
11.7000 g., Copper-Nickel, 30 mm. **Subject:** Outrigger sailboat **Obv:** National arms **Rev:** Outrigger sailboat above written value **Shape:** 12-sided **Designer:** Mike Hibbert

Date	Mintage	F	VF	XF	Unc	BU
1979	20,000	—	0.85	1.25	4.00	5.00
1979 Proof	10,000	Value: 8.00				

KM# 41 DOLLAR
12.4000 g., Copper-Nickel, 25.8 x 38 mm. **Obv:** National arms **Rev:** Solar System **Edge:** Plain **Shape:** Irregular

Date	Mintage	F	VF	XF	Unc	BU
ND (1997) Proof	—	Value: 10.00				

KM# 14 2 DOLLARS
Nickel-Brass **Subject:** 10th Anniversary of Independence **Obv:** National arms above message within ribbon **Rev:** Meeting house with shell at lower left **Designer:** Mike Hibbert

Date	Mintage	F	VF	XF	Unc	BU
1989	—	—	—	—	5.00	6.50

KM# 21 2 DOLLARS
10.0000 g., 0.5000 Silver .1607 oz. ASW **Subject:** Titanic sinking **Obv:** National arms

Date	Mintage	F	VF	XF	Unc	BU
1998 Proof	—	Value: 15.00				

KM# 8 5 DOLLARS
28.1600 g., 0.5000 Silver .4527 oz. ASW **Subject:** Independence **Obv:** National arms **Rev:** Seated man with arms outstretched with written value below

Date	Mintage	F	VF	XF	Unc	BU
1979	1,545	—	—	—	—	22.50

KM# 8a 5 DOLLARS
28.1600 g., 0.9250 Silver .8375 oz. ASW **Subject:** Independence **Obv:** National arms **Rev:** Seated man with arms outstretched above written value

Date	Mintage	F	VF	XF	Unc	BU
1979 Proof	3,326	Value: 25.00				

KM# 12 5 DOLLARS
Copper-Nickel, 38.5 mm. **Subject:** Royal visit **Obv:** National arms **Obv. Designer:** Mike Hibbert **Rev:** Young bust right **Rev. Designer:** Arnold Machin

Date	Mintage	F	VF	XF	Unc	BU
1982	—	—	—	—	5.00	6.50

KM# 12a 5 DOLLARS
Silver, 38.5 mm. **Subject:** Royal visit **Obv:** National arms **Obv. Designer:** Mike Hibbert **Rev:** Young bust right

Date	Mintage	F	VF	XF	Unc	BU
1982 Proof	—	Value: 35.00				

KM# 19 5 DOLLARS
31.4700 g., 0.9250 Silver .9359 oz. ASW **Obv:** National arms **Rev:** Standing figure and ship

Date	Mintage	F	VF	XF	Unc	BU
1996 Proof	Est. 15,000	Value: 50.00				

KM# 20 5 DOLLARS
31.4700 g., 0.9250 Silver .9359 oz. ASW **Obv:** National arms **Rev:** High diver

Date	Mintage	F	VF	XF	Unc	BU
1996 Proof	40,000	Value: 32.50				

KM# 10 5 DOLLARS
Copper-Nickel, 38.5 mm. **Subject:** 2nd Anniversary of Independence and Wedding of Prince Charles and Lady Diana **Obv:** National arms **Rev:** Wedding crown above value

Date	Mintage	F	VF	XF	Unc	BU
1981	50,000	—	—	—	7.50	9.00

KM# 10a 5 DOLLARS
28.6000 g., 0.9250 Silver .8505 oz. ASW, 38.5 mm. **Subject:** 2nd Anniversary of Independence and Wedding of Prince Charles and Lady Diana **Obv:** National arms **Rev:** Wedding crown above value

Date	Mintage	F	VF	XF	Unc	BU
1981 Proof	25,000	Value: 22.50				

KM# 22 5 DOLLARS
15.5518 g., 0.9250 Silver .4625 oz. ASW **Subject:** Guerra & Paz **Obv:** National arms within wave-like designs **Rev:** Dove within wave-like designs **Shape:** Jagged half of coin **Note:** Half of two-part coin, combined with Western Samoa KM#115, issued in sets only. Value is determined by combining the two parts.

Date	Mintage	F	VF	XF	Unc	BU
ND(1997) Proof	Est. 10,000	Value: 35.00				

KM# 23 5 DOLLARS
15.5518 g., 0.9250 Silver .4625 oz. ASW **Subject:** Powerful empires **Obv:** National arms within wave-like designs **Rev:** Helmets and hats within wave-like designs **Shape:** Jagged half of coin **Note:** Half of two-part coin, combined with Western Samoa KM#116, issued in sets only. Value is determined by combining the two parts.

Date	Mintage	F	VF	XF	Unc	BU
ND(1997) Proof	Est. 10,000	Value: 35.00				

KM# 24 5 DOLLARS
15.5518 g., 0.9250 Silver .4625 oz. ASW **Subject:** Tempora Mutantur **Obv:** National arms within wave-like designs **Rev:** Solar system within wave-like designs **Shape:** Jagged half of coin **Note:** Half of two-part coin, combined with Western Samoa KM#117, issued in sets only. Value is determined by combining the two parts.

Date	Mintage	F	VF	XF	Unc	BU
ND(1997) Proof	Est. 10,000	Value: 35.00				

KM# 25 5 DOLLARS
15.5518 g., 0.9250 Silver .4625 oz. ASW **Subject:** People, monuments, column and compass within wave-like designs **Obv:** National arms within wave-like designs **Shape:** Jagged half of coin **Note:** Half of two-part coin, combined with Western Samoa KM#118, issued in sets only. Value is determined by combining the two parts.

Date	Mintage	F	VF	XF	Unc	BU
ND(1997) Proof	Est. 10,000	Value: 37.50				

KM# 31 5 DOLLARS
31.4000 g., 0.9250 Silver 0.9338 oz. ASW, 38.5 mm. **Subject:** British Queen Mother **Obv:** National arms **Rev:** Windsor Castle within beaded circle **Edge:** Reeded

Date	Mintage	F	VF	XF	Unc	BU
1997 Proof	—	Value: 40.00				

KM# 42 5 DOLLARS
15.8600 g., 0.9250 Silver 0.4717 oz. ASW, 25.8 mm. **Obv:** National arms **Rev:** "POWERFUL EMPIRES" Charlemagne, Spanish ship, Soviet soldier with flag **Edge:** Plain **Shape:** Irregular

Date	Mintage	F	VF	XF	Unc	BU
ND (1998) Proof	—	Value: 35.00				

KM# 30 5 DOLLARS
31.6000 g., 0.9250 Silver 0.9398 oz. ASW, 38.5 mm. **Subject:** Whaling Ship Potomac 1842 **Obv:** National arms **Rev:** Ship above sailors killing whale **Edge:** Reeded

Date	Mintage	F	VF	XF	Unc	BU
1998 Proof	—	Value: 50.00				

KM# 37 5 DOLLARS
21.6400 g., Copper-Nickel, 40 mm. **Obv:** National arms **Rev:** "Harmony" earth, moon and sun **Edge:** Reeded

Date	Mintage	F	VF	XF	Unc	BU
2000FM Proof	—	Value: 15.00				

KM# 28 5 DOLLARS
31.3000 g., 0.9990 Silver 1.0053 oz. ASW, 38.6 mm. **Subject:** 10th Anniversary of Emperor Akihito's Reign **Obv:** National arms within circle **Rev:** Conjoined busts left **Edge:** Reeded

Date	Mintage	F	VF	XF	Unc	BU
2000 Proof	2,000	Value: 75.00				

KM# 13 10 DOLLARS
28.2800 g., 0.9250 Silver .8411 oz. ASW **Subject:** 5th Anniversary of Independence **Obv:** Value above national arms **Rev:** Geographical map

Date	Mintage	F	VF	XF	Unc	BU
ND(1984)	—	—	—	—	65.00	75.00
ND(1984) Proof	2,500	Value: 45.00				

KM# 13a 10 DOLLARS
47.5200 g., 0.9170 Gold 1.4012 oz. AGW **Subject:** 5th Anniversary of Independence **Obv:** Value above national arms **Rev:** Geographical map

Date	Mintage	F	VF	XF	Unc	BU
ND(1984) Proof	50	Value: 1,250				

KM# 27 10 DOLLARS
1.2441 g., 0.9990 Gold .04 oz. AGW **Subject:** Titanic **Obv:** National arms **Rev:** Sinking ships and lifeboats

Date	Mintage	F	VF	XF	Unc	BU
1998 Proof	—	Value: 50.00				

KM# 38 10 DOLLARS
22.2200 g., 0.5000 Silver 0.3572 oz. ASW, 40 mm. **Obv:** National arms **Rev:** "Hope" earth, sun and stars **Edge:** Reeded

Date	Mintage	F	VF	XF	Unc	BU
2000FM Proof	—	Value: 40.00				

KM# 17 20 DOLLARS
31.4700 g., 0.9250 Silver .9359 oz. ASW **Subject:** Barcelona Olympics - Sailing **Obv:** National arms above message within ribbon **Rev:** Radiant sun, sailboaters and seagull flying above

Date	Mintage	F	VF	XF	Unc	BU
1992 Proof	40,000	Value: 27.50				

KM# 18 20 DOLLARS
31.4700 g., 0.9250 Silver .9359 oz. ASW **Subject:** Endangered Wildlife **Obv:** National arms above message within ribbon **Rev:** Frigate birds

Date	Mintage	F	VF	XF	Unc	BU
1992 Proof	—	Value: 40.00				

KM# 15 20 DOLLARS
31.4700 g., 0.9250 Silver .9359 oz. ASW **Subject:** Soccer - World Cup '94 **Obv:** National arms **Rev:** Soccer players

Date	Mintage	F	VF	XF	Unc	BU
1993 Proof	Est. 10,000	Value: 32.50				

KM# 16 20 DOLLARS
31.4700 g., 0.9250 Silver .9359 oz. ASW **Subject:** First Space Walk **Obv:** National arms

Date	Mintage	F	VF	XF	Unc	BU
1993 Proof	Est. 15,000	Value: 30.00				

KM# 33 20 DOLLARS
3.1103 g., 0.9990 Gold 0.0999 oz. AGW, 18 mm. **Subject:** Christmas Island Holy Year 2000 **Obv:** National arms above name and date **Rev:** Angel in flight **Edge:** Reeded

Date	Mintage	F	VF	XF	Unc	BU
1999 Proof	—	Value: 85.00				

KM# 39 20 DOLLARS
21.2200 g., 0.9990 Silver 0.6816 oz. ASW, 39.9 mm. **Obv:** National arms **Rev:** "Faith" hands below earth **Edge:** Reeded

Date	Mintage	F	VF	XF	Unc	BU
2000FM Proof	—	Value: 95.00				

KM# 26 50 DOLLARS
3.8875 g., 0.9990 Gold .25 oz. AGW **Subject:** Tempora Mutantur **Obv:** National arms **Rev:** Solar system **Shape:** Jagged half of coin **Note:** Similar to KM#24. Half of two-part coin, combined with Western Samoa KM#119, issued in sets only. Value is determined by combining the two parts.

Date	Mintage	F	VF	XF	Unc	BU
ND(1997) Proof	Est. 2,500	Value: 185				

KM# 34 50 DOLLARS
7.7759 g., 0.9990 Gold 0.2498 oz. AGW, 22 mm. **Subject:** Christmas Island Holy Year 2000 **Obv:** National arms above name and date **Rev:** The three "Wise Men" on camels **Edge:** Reeded

Date	Mintage	F	VF	XF	Unc	BU
1999 Proof	—	Value: 185				

KM# 35 100 DOLLARS
15.5518 g., 0.9990 Gold 0.4995 oz. AGW, 30 mm. **Subject:** Christmas Island Holy Year 2000 **Obv:** National arms above name and date **Rev:** Mother and child **Edge:** Reeded

Date	Mintage	F	VF	XF	Unc	BU
1999 Proof	—	Value: 375				

KM# 9 150 DOLLARS
15.9800 g., 0.9170 Gold .4711 oz. AGW **Subject:** Independence - Maneaba - a traditional meeting house **Obv:** National arms **Rev:** Maneaba - a traditional meeting house **Designer:** Mike Hibbert

Date	Mintage	F	VF	XF	Unc	BU
1979	422	—	—	—	335	—
1979 Proof	386	Value: 350				

KM# 11 150 DOLLARS
15.9800 g., 0.9170 Gold .4711 oz. AGW **Subject:** 2nd Anniversary of Independence, and wedding of Prince Charles and Lady Diana **Obv:** National arms

Date	Mintage	F	VF	XF	Unc	BU
1981	750	—	—	—	325	—
1981 Proof	1,500	Value: 340				

KM# 29 200 DOLLARS
31.3000 g., 0.9990 Gold 1.0053 oz. AGW, 35 mm. **Subject:** 10th Anniversary of Emperor Akihito's Reign **Obv:** National arms **Rev:** Conjoined busts left **Edge:** Reeded

Date	Mintage	F	VF	XF	Unc	BU
2000 Proof	500	Value: 700				

KM# 32 200 DOLLARS
16.5800 g., 0.9990 Gold 0.4003 oz. AGW, 37.8x26.2 mm. **Subject:** People and Monuments **Obv:** National arms within wave-like designs **Rev:** Eiffel Tower **Edge:** Plain **Note:** Irregular shape

Date	Mintage	F	VF	XF	Unc	BU
1999-2000 Proof	—	Value: 300				

KM# 36 500 DOLLARS
85.4700 g., 0.9990 Gold 2.7452 oz. AGW, 42.5 mm. **Obv:** National arms **Rev:** Doves, children, sword point and treaty **Edge:** Plain **Note:** Jagged coin half matching with Samoa KM-136

Date	Mintage	F	VF	XF	Unc	BU
2000 Proof	99	Value: 1,950				

COMBINED PROOF SETS (CPS)

KM#	Date	Mintage	Identification	Issue Price	Mkt Val
CPS1	1997 (8)	10,000	Kiribati KM#22-25, West Samoa KM#115-118	—	240

PROOF SETS

KM#	Date	Mintage	Identification	Issue Price	Mkt Val
PS1	1979 (7)	10,000	KM1-7	34.00	55.00
PS2	1981 (2)	—	KM10a, 11	—	360
PS3	1999 (3)	—	KM#33-35	—	645
PS4	2000 (3)	—	KM#37, 38, 39	—	150

KOREA

Korea, 'Land of the Morning Calm', occupies a mountainous peninsula in northeast Asia bounded by Manchuria, the Yellow Sea and the Sea of Japan.

According to legend, the first Korean dynasty, that of the House of Tangun, ruled from 2333 B.C. to 1122 B.C. It was followed by the dynasty of Kija, a Chinese scholar, which continued until 193 B.C. and brought a high civilization to Korea. The first recorded period in the history of Korea, the period of the Three Kingdoms, lasted from 57 B.C. to 935 A.D. and achieved the first political unification of the peninsula. The Kingdom of Koryo, from which Korea derived its name, was founded in 935 and continued until 1392, when it was superseded by the Yi Dynasty of King Yi. Sung Kye was to last until the Japanese annexation in 1910.

At the end of the 16th century Korea was invaded and occupied for 7 years by Japan, and from 1627 until the late 19th century it was a semi-independent tributary of China. Japan replaced China as the predominant foreign influence at the end of the Sino-Japanese War (1894-95), only to find her position threatened by Russian influence from 1896 to 1904. The Russian threat was eliminated by the Russo-Japanese War (1904-05) and in 1905 Japan established a direct protectorate over Korea. On Aug. 22,1910, the last Korean ruler signed the treaty that annexed Korea to Japan as a government generalcy in the Japanese Empire. Japanese suzerainty was maintained until the end of World War II.

From 1633 to 1891 the monetary system of Korea employed cast coins with a square center hole. Fifty-two agencies were authorized to procure these coins from a lesser number of coin foundries. They exist in thousands of varieties. Seed, or mother coins, were used to make the impressions in the molds in which the regular cash coins were cast. Czarist-Russian Korea experimented with Korean coins when Alexiev of Russia, Korea's Financial Advisor, founded the First Asian Branch of the Russo-Korean Bank on March 1, 1898, and authorized the issuing of a set of new Korean coins with a crowned Russian-style quasi-eagle. British-Japanese opposition and the Russo-Japanese War operated to end the Russian coinage experiment in 1904.

RULERS
Yi Hyong (Kojong), 1864-1897
as Emperor Kuang Mu, 1897-1907
Japanese Puppet
Yung Hi (Sunjong), 1907-1910

DATING

KINGDOM

MILLED COINAGE

Coinage Reform of 1892

KM# 1116 5 FUN
17.2000 g., Copper **Ruler:** Kuang Mu **Obv:** Encircled dragons within circle **Rev:** Value within wreath below flower

Date	Mintage	F	VF	XF	Unc	BU
6 (1902)	—	10.00	25.00	50.00	150	—

KM# 1117 1/4 YANG
Copper-Nickel **Ruler:** Kuang Mu **Obv:** Dragon within beaded circle **Rev:** Value within wreath below flower

Date	Mintage	F	VF	XF	Unc	BU
5 (1901)	—	200	350	600	1,350	—

RUSSIAN DOMINATION

MILLED COINAGE

Coinage Reform of 1892

KM# 1121 CHON
6.8000 g., Bronze **Ruler:** Kuang Mu **Obv:** Crowned imperial eagle within beaded circle **Rev:** Value within wreath below flower

Date	Mintage	F	VF	XF	Unc	BU
2 (1902)	3,001,000	2,000	4,000	6,750	11,000	—

KM# 1122 5 CHON
4.3000 g., Copper-Nickel **Ruler:** Kuang Mu **Obv:** Crowned imperial eagle within beaded circle **Rev:** Value within wreath below flower

Date	Mintage	F	VF	XF	Unc	BU
6 (1902)	2,800,000	1,500	2,850	4,850	7,500	—

KM# 1123 1/2 WON
13.5000 g., 0.8000 Silver .3473 oz. ASW **Ruler:** Kuang Mu **Obv:** Crowned imperial eagle within beaded circle **Rev:** Value within wreath below flower

Date	Mintage	F	VF	XF	Unc	BU
5 (1901)	1,831,000	3,000	7,000	12,500	17,500	—

Note: Ponterio & Assoc. Witte Museum sale 8-89 choice BU realized $12,500; Heritage Piedmont sale 6-2000 choice BU realized $18,400

JAPANESE PROTECTORATE

MILLED COINAGE

Coinage Reform of 1892

KM# 1124 1/2 CHON
3.5600 g., Bronze, 22 mm. **Ruler:** Kuang Mu **Obv:** Imperial eagle left within beaded circle **Rev:** Value within wreath below flower

Date	Mintage	F	VF	XF	Unc	BU
10 (1906)	24,000,000	5.00	15.00	50.00	150	—

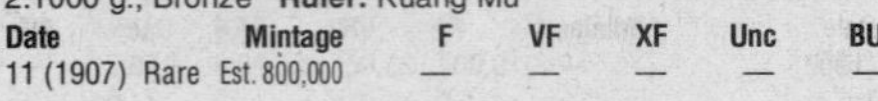

KM# 1145 1/2 CHON
2.1000 g., Bronze **Ruler:** Kuang Mu

Date	Mintage	F	VF	XF	Unc	BU
11 (1907) Rare	Est. 800,000	—	—	—	—	—

KM# 1136 1/2 CHON
2.1000 g., Bronze, 19 mm. **Ruler:** Yung Hi (Sunjong) **Obv:** Imperial eagle facing left within beaded circle **Rev:** Value within wreath below flower

Date	Mintage	F	VF	XF	Unc	BU
1 (1907)	Inc. above	125	275	550	900	—

Note: Mintage for year 1 is included in the mintage for Year 11 of KM#1124

Date	Mintage	F	VF	XF	Unc	BU
2 (1908)	21,000,000	10.00	30.00	65.00	200	—
3 (1909)	8,200,000	10.00	30.00	65.00	200	—
4 (1910)	5,070,000	85.00	200	475	900	—

KM# 1125 CHON
7.1300 g., Bronze, 28 mm. **Ruler:** Kuang Mu **Obv:** Imperial eagle facing left within beaded circle **Rev:** Value within wreath below flower

Date	Mintage	F	VF	XF	Unc	BU
9 (1905)	11,800,000	12.50	25.00	50.00	150	—
10 (1906)	Inc. above	10.00	20.00	50.00	150	—

KM# 1132 CHON
4.2000 g., Bronze, 23.5 mm. **Ruler:** Kuang Mu **Obv:** Imperial eagle facing left within beaded circle **Rev:** Value within wreath below flower

Date	Mintage	F	VF	XF	Unc	BU
11 (1907)	11,200,000	6.00	12.00	30.00	150	—

KM# 1137 CHON
4.2000 g., Bronze, 24 mm. **Ruler:** Yung Hi (Sunjong) **Obv:** Imperial eagle facing left within beaded circle **Rev:** Value within wreath below flower

Date	Mintage	F	VF	XF	Unc	BU
1 (1907)	Inc. above	8.00	20.00	50.00	150	—
2 (1908)	6,800,000	6.00	15.00	35.00	125	—
3 (1909)	9,200,000	6.00	15.00	30.00	125	—
4 (1910)	3,500,000	8.00	18.00	45.00	150	—

KM# 1126 5 CHON
4.5000 g., Copper-Nickel, 21 mm. **Ruler:** Kuang Mu **Obv:** Imperial eagle facing left within beaded circle **Rev:** Value within wreath below flower

Date	Mintage	F	VF	XF	Unc	BU
9 (1905)	20,000,000	12.50	30.00	60.00	125	—
9 (1905) Proof	—	Value: 1,500				
11 (1907)	160,000,000	15.00	35.00	75.00	150	—

KM# 1138 5 CHON
4.5000 g., Copper-Nickel, 21 mm. **Ruler:** Yung Hi (Sunjong)

Date	Mintage	F	VF	XF	Unc	BU
3 (1909)	—	900	1,750	3,500	4,750	—

KM# 1128 20 CHON
5.3900 g., 0.8000 Silver .1386 oz. ASW, 22 mm. **Ruler:** Kuang Mu **Obv:** Dragon within beaded circle **Rev:** Value within wreath below flower

Date	Mintage	F	VF	XF	Unc	BU
9 (1905)	1,000,000	50.00	100	200	400	—
9 (1905) Proof	—	Value: 2,250				
10 (1906)	2,500,000	45.00	60.00	175	350	—
10 (1906) Proof	—	Value: 1,275				

KM# 1134 20 CHON
4.0500 g., 0.8000 Silver .1042 oz. ASW, 20 mm. **Ruler:** Kuang Mu **Obv:** Dragon within beaded circle **Rev:** Value within wreath below flower

Date	Mintage	F	VF	XF	Unc	BU
11 (1907)	1,500,000	30.00	60.00	125	300	—

KM# 1140 20 CHON
4.0500 g., 0.8000 Silver .1157 oz. ASW, 20 mm. **Ruler:** Yung Hi (Sunjong) **Obv:** Dragon within beaded circle **Rev:** Value within wreath below flower

Date	Mintage	F	VF	XF	Unc	BU
2 (1908)	3,000,000	27.00	50.00	100	250	—
3 (1909)	2,000,000	27.00	50.00	100	250	—
4 (1910)	2,000,000	27.00	50.00	100	250	—

KM# 1127 10 CHON
2.7000 g., 0.8000 Silver .0695 oz. ASW, 18 mm. **Ruler:** Kuang Mu **Obv:** Dragon within beaded circle **Rev:** Value within wreath below flower **Note:** 1.5 millimeters thick

Date	Mintage	F	VF	XF	Unc	BU
10 (1906)	2,000,000	24.00	45.00	80.00	175	—

KM# 1133 10 CHON
2.0250 g., 0.8000 Silver .0695 oz. ASW, 18 mm. **Ruler:** Kuang Mu **Obv:** Dragon within beaded circle **Rev:** Value within wreath below flower **Note:** 1.0 millimeters thick

Date	Mintage	F	VF	XF	Unc	BU
11 (1907)	2,400,000	28.00	50.00	125	250	—

KM# 1139 10 CHON
2.2500 g., 0.8000 Silver .0578 oz. ASW **Ruler:** Yung Hi (Sunjong) **Obv:** Dragon within beaded circle **Rev:** Value within wreath below flower

Date	Mintage	F	VF	XF	Unc	BU
2 (1908)	6,300,000	20.00	40.00	65.00	150	—
3 (1909) Rare	—	—	—	—	—	—
4 (1910)	9,500,000	20.00	35.00	60.00	125	—

KM# 1129 1/2 WON
13.4800 g., 0.8000 Silver .3467 oz. ASW, 31 mm. **Ruler:** Kuang Mu **Obv:** Dragon within beaded circle **Rev:** Value within wreath below flower

Date	Mintage	F	VF	XF	Unc	BU
9 (1905)	600,000	80.00	150	250	500	—
9 (1905) Proof	—	Value: 1,850				
10 (1906)	1,200,000	85.00	175	300	600	—

KM# 1135 1/2 WON
10.1300 g., 0.8000 Silver .2606 oz. ASW, 26.5 mm. **Ruler:** Kuang Mu **Obv:** Dragon within beaded circle **Rev:** Value within wreath below flower

Date	Mintage	F	VF	XF	Unc	BU
11 (1907)	1,000,000	100	200	350	800	—

KM# 1141 1/2 WON
10.1300 g., 0.8000 Silver .2606 oz. ASW, 26 mm. **Ruler:** Yung Hi (Sunjong) **Obv:** Dragon within beaded circle **Rev:** Value within wreath below flower

Date	Mintage	F	VF	XF	Unc	BU
2 (1908)	1,400,000	100	200	350	650	—

KM# 1142 5 WON
4.1666 g., 0.9000 Gold .1206 oz. AGW **Ruler:** Yung Hi Sunjong) **Obv:** Dragon within beaded circle **Rev:** Value within wreath below flower

Date	Mintage	F	VF	XF	Unc	BU
2 (1908)	10,000	14,000	30,000	45,000	65,000	—
Note: Heritage Piedmont sale 6-2000 Gem BU realized $86,250						
3 (1909) 2 known	—	—	—	—	—	—

KM# 1130 10 WON
8.3333 g., 0.9000 Gold .2412 oz. AGW **Ruler:** Kuang Mu **Obv:** Dragon within beaded circle **Rev:** Value within wreath below flower

Date	Mintage	F	VF	XF	Unc	BU
10 (1906)	5,012	—	13,000	20,000	35,000	—

KM# A1130 10 WON
8.3333 g., 0.9000 Gold .2412 oz. AGW **Ruler:** Yung Hi (Sunjong) **Obv:** Dragon within beaded circle **Rev:** Value within wreath below flower

Date	Mintage	F	VF	XF	Unc	BU
3 (1909) 2 known	—	—	—	—	—	—

KM# 1131 20 WON
16.6666 g., 0.9000 Gold .4823 oz. AGW **Ruler:** Kuang Mu **Obv:** Dragon within beaded circle **Rev:** Value within wreath below flower

Date	Mintage	F	VF	XF	Unc	BU
10 (1906)	2,506	—	25,000	40,000	70,000	—

KM# 1144 20 WON
16.6666 g., 0.9000 Gold .4823 oz. AGW **Ruler:** Yung Hi (Sunjong) **Obv:** Dragon within beaded circle **Rev:** Value within wreath

Date	Mintage	F	VF	XF	Unc	BU
2 (1908) Rare	—	—	—	—	—	—
3 (1909) 2 known	—	—	—	—	—	—

Note: Reported mintages for Year 2 (1908) of 40,000 and Year 3 (1909) of 25,000 exist, but few are known today

PATTERNS

Including off metal strikes

KM#	Date	Mintage	Identification	Mkt Val
Pn33	5	—	5 Won. Copper.	—
Pn34	5	—	10 Won. Copper.	—
Pn35	6	—	20 Won. Copper.	—
Pn36	6	—	20 Won. Copper.	—
Pn37	7	—	5 Won. Copper.	—
Pn38	7	—	5 Won. Copper.	—

KOREA-NORTH

The Democratic Peoples Republic of Korea, situated in northeastern Asia on the northern half of the Korean peninsula between the Peoples Republic of China and the Republic of Korea, has an area of 46,540 sq. mi. (120,540 sq. km.) and a population of 20 million. Capital: Pyongyang. The economy is based on heavy industry and agriculture. Metals, minerals and farm produce are exported.

Japan replaced China as the predominant foreign influence in Korea in 1895 and annexed the peninsular country in 1910. Defeat in World War II brought an end to Japanese rule. U.S. troops entered Korea from the south and Soviet forces entered from the north. The Cairo conference (1943) had established that Korea should be *free and independent*. The Potsdam conference (1945) set the 38th parallel as the line dividing the occupation forces of the United States and Russia. When Russia refused to permit a U.N. commission designated to supervise reunification elections to enter North Korea, an election was held in South Korea which established the Republic of Korea on Aug. 15,1948. North Korea held an unsupervised election on Aug. 25, 1948, and on Sept. 9, 1948, proclaimed the establishment of the Democratic Peoples Republic of Korea.

NOTE: For earlier coinage see Korea.

MONETARY SYSTEM
100 Chon = 1 Won

CIRCULATION RESTRICTIONS
W/o star: KM#1-4 - General circulation
1 star: KM#5-8 - Issued to visitors from Communist countries.
2 stars: KM#9-12 - Issued to visitors from hard currency countries.

PEOPLES REPUBLIC

DECIMAL COINAGE

KM# 1 CHON
Aluminum, 16 mm. **Obv:** National arms **Rev:** Value

Date	Mintage	F	VF	XF	Unc	BU
1959	—	0.15	0.25	0.50	1.00	—
1970	—	0.20	0.35	0.75	1.50	—

KM# 5 CHON
Aluminum, 16 mm. **Obv:** National arms within circle **Rev:** Value flanked by stars

Date	Mintage	F	VF	XF	Unc	BU
1959	—	—	—	0.50	1.00	—

KM# 9 CHON
Aluminum, 16 mm. **Obv:** National arms within circle **Rev:** Star to left of value

Date	Mintage	F	VF	XF	Unc	BU
1959	—	—	—	0.50	1.00	—

KM# 2 5 CHON
Aluminum, 18 mm. **Obv:** National arms within circle **Rev:** Value

Date	Mintage	F	VF	XF	Unc	BU
1959	—	0.50	0.75	1.00	2.00	—
1974	—	0.25	0.50	1.00	2.00	—

KM# 6 5 CHON
Aluminum, 18 mm. **Obv:** National arms within circle **Rev:** Value flanked by stars

Date	Mintage	F	VF	XF	Unc	BU
1974	—	—	—	1.00	2.00	—

KM# 10 5 CHON
Aluminum, 18 mm. **Obv:** National arms within circle **Rev:** Star to left of value

Date	Mintage	F	VF	XF	Unc	BU
1974	—	—	—	1.00	2.00	—

KM# 3 10 CHON
Aluminum, 20 mm. **Obv:** National arms within circle **Rev:** Value

Date	Mintage	F	VF	XF	Unc	BU
1959	—	0.50	0.75	1.00	2.00	—

KM# 7 10 CHON
Aluminum, 20 mm. **Obv:** National arms within circle **Rev:** Value flanked by stars

Date	Mintage	F	VF	XF	Unc	BU
1959	—	—	—	1.00	2.00	—

KM# 11 10 CHON
Aluminum, 20 mm. **Obv:** National arms within circle **Rev:** Star to left of value

Date	Mintage	F	VF	XF	Unc	BU
1959	—	—	—	1.00	2.00	—

KM# 4 50 CHON
Aluminum, 25 mm. **Obv:** National arms within circle above value **Rev:** Leaping equestrian within radiant sun

Date	Mintage	F	VF	XF	Unc	BU
1978	—	0.75	1.00	1.75	3.00	—

KM# 8 50 CHON
Aluminum, 25 mm. **Obv:** National arms within circle above value **Rev:** Leaping equestrian divides stars within radiant sun

Date	Mintage	F	VF	XF	Unc	BU
1978	—	—	—	1.75	3.00	—

KM# 12 50 CHON
Aluminum, 25 mm. **Obv:** National arms within circle above value **Rev:** Star to left of leaping equestrian within radiant sun

Date	Mintage	F	VF	XF	Unc	BU
1978	—	—	—	1.75	3.00	—

KM# 13 WON
Copper-Nickel **Obv:** National arms above date **Rev:** Kim Il Sung's birthplace among radiant sun

Date	Mintage	F	VF	XF	Unc	BU
1987	—	—	—	—	4.00	—
1987 Proof	—	Value: 5.00				

KM# 18 WON
Aluminum, 27 mm. **Obv:** National arms above date **Rev:** Palace

Date	Mintage	F	VF	XF	Unc	BU
1987	—	—	—	—	3.50	—

KM# 14 WON
Copper-Nickel **Obv:** National arms above value divides date **Rev:** Kim Il Sung's Arch of Triumph within beaded circle

Date	Mintage	F	VF	XF	Unc	BU
1987	—	—	—	—	4.00	—
1987 Proof	—	Value: 5.00				

KM# 15 WON
Copper-Nickel **Obv:** National arms above value **Rev:** Kim Il Sung's Tower of Juche within beaded circle

Date	Mintage	F	VF	XF	Unc	BU
1987	—	—	—	—	4.00	—
1987 Proof	—	Value: 5.00				

KM# 179 WON
6.7000 g., Aluminum, 40 mm. **Subject:** Birds of Korea - Dryocopus Javensis **Obv:** National arms **Rev:** White-bellied woodpecker **Edge:** Plain

Date	Mintage	F	VF	XF	Unc	BU
1999 Proof	—	Value: 15.00				

KM# 180 WON
6.7000 g., Aluminum, 40 mm. **Subject:** Birds of Korea - Lyrurus Tetrix **Obv:** National arms **Rev:** Black grouse **Edge:** Plain

Date	Mintage	F	VF	XF	Unc	BU
1999 Proof	—	Value: 15.00				

KM# 181 WON
6.7000 g., Aluminum, 40 mm. **Subject:** Birds of Korea - Syrrhaptes Paradoxus **Obv:** National arms **Rev:** Pallas's sandgrouse at water's edge **Edge:** Plain

Date	Mintage	F	VF	XF	Unc	BU
1999 Proof	—	Value: 15.00				

KM# 182 WON
6.7000 g., Aluminum, 40 mm. **Subject:** Birds of Korea - Pitta Brachyura **Obv:** National arms **Rev:** Fairy pitta trilling on branch left **Edge:** Plain

Date	Mintage	F	VF	XF	Unc	BU
1999 Proof	—	Value: 15.00				

KM# 127 WON
Copper-Nickel, 35 mm. **Subject:** Blue Dragon **Obv:** National arms **Rev:** Dragon above mountains **Edge:** Reeded

Date	Mintage	F	VF	XF	Unc	BU
2000	—	—	—	—	9.00	12.00

KM# 126 WON
Copper-Nickel, 32 mm. **Obv:** National arms **Rev:** "Hyonmu" **Edge:** Reeded

Date	Mintage	F	VF	XF	Unc	BU
2000	—	—	—	—	8.00	10.00

KM# 126a WON
3.9400 g., Aluminum, 32 mm. **Obv:** National arms **Rev:** "Hyonmu" **Edge:** Plain

Date	Mintage	F	VF	XF	Unc	BU
2000 Proof	—	Value: 15.00				

KM# 127a WON
5.2000 g., Aluminum, 35 mm. **Obv:** National arms **Rev:** Dragon above mountains **Edge:** Plain

Date	Mintage	F	VF	XF	Unc	BU
2000 Proof	—	Value: 15.00				

KM# 128 WON
22.0000 g., Copper-Nickel, 35 mm. **Subject:** Tiger **Obv:** Tiger in mountains **Rev:** Tiger head **Edge:** Plain

Date	Mintage	F	VF	XF	Unc	BU
ND(1998) Proof	5,000	—	—	—	13.50	—

KM# 155 WON
16.2000 g., Brass, 35 mm. **Subject:** Seafaring Ships **Obv:** National arms **Rev:** German school ship, Prinzess Eitel Friedrich with furled sails **Edge:** Plain

Date	Mintage	F	VF	XF	Unc	BU
ND(2000) Proof	—	Value: 10.00				

KM# 155a WON
17.0000 g., Copper-Nickel, 35 mm. **Subject:** School Ships **Obv:** National arms **Rev:** German school ship, Prinzess Eitel Friedrich with furled sails **Edge:** Plain

Date	Mintage	F	VF	XF	Unc	BU
ND(2000) Proof	200	Value: 100				

KM# 156 WON
16.8600 g., Copper-Nickel, 35 mm. **Subject:** Seafaring Ships **Obv:** National arms **Rev:** German school ship, Grossherzogin Elisabeth under full sail right **Edge:** Plain

Date	Mintage	F	VF	XF	Unc	BU
ND(2000) Proof	—	Value: 10.00				

KM# 162 WON
6.7000 g., Aluminum, 40 mm. **Subject:** 3,000 Years of Korean History **Obv:** National arms **Rev:** Radiant map and landmarks **Edge:** Plain

Date	Mintage	F	VF	XF	Unc	BU
2000 Proof	—	Value: 9.00				

KM# 162a WON
26.7500 g., Brass, 40.2 mm. **Subject:** 3,000 Years of Korean History 3,000 Years of Korean History **Obv:** National arms **Rev:** Radiant Korean map and landmarks **Edge:** Plain

Date	Mintage	F	VF	XF	Unc	BU
2000 Proof	—	Value: 17.50				

KM# 198 WON
17.0000 g., Copper-Nickel, 35 mm. **Subject:** School Ships **Obv:** National arms **Rev:** SS Grossherzog Friedrich August **Edge:** Plain

Date	Mintage	F	VF	XF	Unc	BU
ND(2000) Proof	200	Value: 100				

KM# 263 WON
14.3100 g., Brass, 34.2 mm. **Obv:** National arms **Rev:** Flying squirrel **Edge:** Segmented reeding

Date	Mintage	F	VF	XF	Unc	BU
ND(2000) Proof	—	Value: 25.00				

KM# 273 WON
28.2000 g., Brass, 40.1 mm. **Obv:** National arms **Rev:** Kim Jong Il greeting diplomat, half length **Edge:** Plain

Date	Mintage	F	VF	XF	Unc	BU
2000 Proof	—	Value: 20.00				

KM# 274 WON
28.2000 g., Brass, 40.1 mm. **Obv:** National arms **Rev:** Kim Jong Il greeting diplomat, full length figures **Edge:** Plain

Date	Mintage	F	VF	XF	Unc	BU
2000 Proof	—	Value: 20.00				

KM# 275 WON
28.2000 g., Brass, 40.1 mm. **Obv:** National arms **Rev:** Kim Jong Il greeting diplomat, half length **Edge:** Plain

Date	Mintage	F	VF	XF	Unc	BU
2000 Proof	—	Value: 20.00				

KM# 277 WON
28.2000 g., Brass, 40.1 mm. **Obv:** National arms **Rev:** Treaty signing scene **Edge:** Plain

Date	Mintage	F	VF	XF	Unc	BU
2000 Proof	—	Value: 20.00				

KM# 22 5 WON
Copper-Nickel **Obv:** Value divides date below national arms **Rev:** Kim Il Sung's Arch of Triumph

Date	Mintage	F	VF	XF	Unc	BU
1987	—	—	—	—	7.00	8.00
1987 Proof	—	Value: 10.00				

KM# 23 5 WON
Copper-Nickel **Obv:** Radiant national arms above date and value **Rev:** Kim Il Sung's Tower of Juche

Date	Mintage	F	VF	XF	Unc	BU
1987	—	—	—	—	7.00	8.00
1987 Proof	—	Value: 10.00				

KM# 25 5 WON
Copper-Nickel **Obv:** National arms above date and value **Rev:** Kim Il Sung's birthplace

Date	Mintage	F	VF	XF	Unc	BU
1987	—	—	—	—	7.00	8.00
1987 Proof	—	Value: 10.00				

KM# 19 5 WON
Copper-Nickel **Subject:** World Festival of Youth and Students **Obv:** National arms with D.P.R. of Korea written below, value at lower left **Rev:** Flower-like design

Date	Mintage	F	VF	XF	Unc	BU
1989	—	—	—	—	7.00	8.00
1989 Proof	—	Value: 10.00				

KM# 92 5 WON
12.0000 g., 0.9990 Silver .3854 oz. ASW **Subject:** 50th Anniversary of Liberation **Obv:** National arms above oat sprigs and date **Rev:** Teapot in bowl

Date	Mintage	F	VF	XF	Unc	BU
1995 In proof sets only	300	Value: 50.00				

KM# 129 5 WON
13.0000 g., Copper Nickel **Subject:** 10th Singapore International Coin Show **Obv:** National arms above sprigs and date **Rev:** Multicolor logo within globe **Edge:** Plain

Date	Mintage	F	VF	XF	Unc	BU
1996	1,000	—	—	—	20.00	—

KM# 130 5 WON
27.0000 g., 0.9990 Silver .8672 oz. ASW, 35 mm. **Subject:** Kaesong - Sinuiju Railroad **Obv:** National arms **Rev:** Multicolor train **Edge:** Plain

Date	Mintage	F	VF	XF	Unc	BU
1996	2,000	—	—	—	40.00	—

KM# 131 5 WON
27.0000 g., 0.9990 Silver .8672 oz. ASW, 35 mm. **Subject:** 1st Beijing International Coin Show **Obv:** National arms **Rev:** Multicolor panda holding logo **Edge:** Plain

Date	Mintage	F	VF	XF	Unc	BU
1996	6,000	—	—	—	35.00	—

KM# 100 5 WON
26.9400 g., 0.9990 Silver .8644 oz. ASW **Subject:** Olympics **Obv:** National arms **Rev:** Two speed skaters

Date	Mintage	F	VF	XF	Unc	BU
1997 Proof	3,000	Value: 25.00				

KM# 132 5 WON
27.0000 g., 0.9990 Silver .8672 oz. ASW, 35 mm. **Subject:** 11th Singapore International Coin Show **Obv:** National arms **Rev:** Multicolor panda holding logo **Edge:** Plain

Date	Mintage	F	VF	XF	Unc	BU
1997	1,000	—	—	—	35.00	—

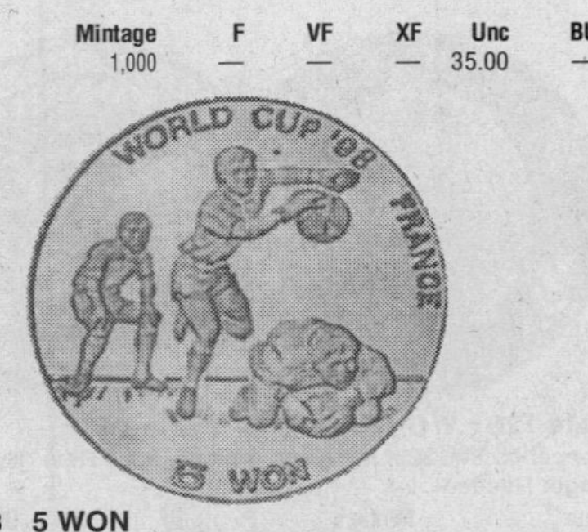

KM# 133 5 WON
27.0000 g., 0.9990 Silver .8672 oz. ASW, 35 mm. **Subject:** World Cup Soccer **Obv:** National arms **Rev:** Soccer players **Edge:** Plain

Date	Mintage	F	VF	XF	Unc	BU
1997	3,000	—	—	—	30.00	—

KM# 161 5 WON
26.8400 g., 0.9990 Silver 0.8621 oz. ASW, 40 mm. **Subject:** Korean War **Obv:** National arms **Rev:** Multicolor flags and flowers in front of monument **Edge:** Reeded

Date	Mintage	F	VF	XF	Unc	BU
1998 Proof	—	Value: 25.00				

KM# 424 5 WON
27.0000 g., 0.9990 Silver 0.8672 oz. ASW, 40 mm. **Obv:** National arms **Rev:** Rocket and satellite above Eastern Asia **Edge:** Plain

Date	Mintage	F	VF	XF	Unc	BU
1999 Proof	—	Value: 40.00				

KM# 123 5 WON
20.0000 g., 0.9990 Silver .6424 oz. ASW, 34.3 mm. **Subject:** History of Seafaring **Obv:** National arms **Rev:** Sailing Junk **Edge:** Reeded and plain sections

Date	Mintage	F	VF	XF	Unc	BU
1999 Proof	5,000	Value: 35.00				

KM# 172 5 WON
20.0000 g., 0.9990 Silver 0.6424 oz. ASW, 40 mm. **Subject:** Endangered Wildlife **Obv:** National arms **Rev:** Siberian flying squirrel **Edge:** Reeded and plain sections

Date	Mintage	F	VF	XF	Unc	BU
2000 Proof	5,000	Value: 32.50				

KM# 173 5 WON
27.0000 g., 0.9990 Silver 0.8672 oz. ASW, 40 mm.
Subject: King Tongmyong **Obv:** Mythical bird **Rev:** Crowned bust facing **Edge:** Reeded and plain sections

Date	Mintage	F	VF	XF	Unc	BU
2000 Proof	3,000	Value: 30.00				

KM# 174 5 WON
27.0000 g., 0.9990 Silver 0.8672 oz. ASW, 40 mm.
Subject: Olympics **Obv:** National arms **Rev:** Female archer drawing back her bow **Edge:** Plain

Date	Mintage	F	VF	XF	Unc	BU
2000 Proof	3,000	Value: 30.00				

KM# 175 5 WON
27.0000 g., 0.9990 Silver 0.8672 oz. ASW, 40 mm.
Subject: Olympics **Obv:** National arms **Rev:** Handball player **Edge:** Reeded and plain sections

Date	Mintage	F	VF	XF	Unc	BU
2000 Proof	3,000	Value: 30.00				

KM# 176 5 WON
27.0000 g., 0.9990 Silver 0.8672 oz. ASW, 40 mm. **Subject:** Olympics **Obv:** National arms **Rev:** Two wrestlers **Edge:** Plain

Date	Mintage	F	VF	XF	Unc	BU
2000 Proof	3,000	Value: 30.00				

KM# 177 5 WON
27.0000 g., 0.9990 Silver 0.8672 oz. ASW, 40 mm.
Subject: Mt. Kumgang **Obv:** Mythical bird **Rev:** Buddha statue facing **Edge:** Reeded and plain sections

Date	Mintage	F	VF	XF	Unc	BU
2000 Proof	3,000	Value: 30.00				

KM# 199 5 WON
15.0000 g., 0.9990 Silver 0.4818 oz. ASW, 35 mm.
Subject: School Ships **Obv:** National arms **Rev:** SS Grossherzogin Elisabeth **Edge:** Plain

Date	Mintage	F	VF	XF	Unc	BU
ND(2000) Proof	500	Value: 75.00				

KM# 200 5 WON
15.0000 g., 0.9990 Silver 0.4818 oz. ASW, 35 mm.
Subject: School Ships **Obv:** National arms **Rev:** SS Prinzess Eitel Friedrich **Edge:** Plain

Date	Mintage	F	VF	XF	Unc	BU
ND(2000) Proof	500	Value: 75.00				

KM# 201 5 WON
15.0000 g., 0.9990 Silver 0.4818 oz. ASW, 35 mm.
Subject: School Ships **Obv:** National arms **Rev:** SS Grossherzog Friedrich August **Edge:** Plain

Date	Mintage	F	VF	XF	Unc	BU
ND(2000) Proof	500	Value: 75.00				

KM# 213 5 WON
15.0000 g., 0.9990 Silver 0.4818 oz. ASW, 35 mm.
Subject: First Nobel Prize Winners Series - Sully Prudhomme **Obv:** National arms **Rev:** Writer's portrait **Edge:** Plain

Date	Mintage	F	VF	XF	Unc	BU
ND(2000) Proof	2,000	Value: 100				

KM# 214 5 WON
15.0000 g., 0.9990 Silver 0.4818 oz. ASW, 35 mm.
Subject: First Nobel Prize Winners Series - Wilhelm C. Roentgen **Obv:** National arms **Rev:** Portrait and lab scene **Edge:** Plain

Date	Mintage	F	VF	XF	Unc	BU
ND(2000) Proof	2,000	Value: 100				

KM# 215 5 WON
15.0000 g., 0.9990 Silver 0.4818 oz. ASW, 35 mm.
Subject: First Nobel Prize Winners Series - Emil A. von Behring **Obv:** National arms **Rev:** Two man lab scene **Edge:** Plain

Date	Mintage	F	VF	XF	Unc	BU
ND(2000) Proof	2,000	Value: 100				

KM# 216 5 WON
15.0000 g., 0.9990 Silver 0.4818 oz. ASW, 35 mm.
Subject: First Nobel Prize Winners Series - Henri Dunant **Obv:** National arms **Rev:** Portrait and war wounded scene **Edge:** Plain

Date	Mintage	F	VF	XF	Unc	BU
ND(2000) Proof	2,000	Value: 100				

KM# 217 5 WON
15.0000 g., 0.9990 Silver 0.4818 oz. ASW, 35 mm.
Subject: First Nobel Prize Winners Series - Jacobus Van't Hoff **Obv:** National arms **Rev:** Two chemists in lab scene **Edge:** Plain

Date	Mintage	F	VF	XF	Unc	BU
ND(2000) Proof	2,000	Value: 100				

KM# 218 5 WON
15.0000 g., 0.9990 Silver 0.4818 oz. ASW, 35 mm.
Subject: First Nobel Prize Winners Series - Frederic Passy **Obv:** National arms **Rev:** Portrait and allegorical scene **Edge:** Plain

Date	Mintage	F	VF	XF	Unc	BU
ND(2000) Proof	2,000	Value: 100				

KM# 268 5 WON
14.9600 g., 0.9990 Silver 0.4805 oz. ASW, 35 mm. **Obv:** National arms **Rev:** Mountbatten SR-N4 hovercraft **Edge:** Plain

Date	Mintage	F	VF	XF	Unc	BU
2000 Proof	—	Value: 30.00				

KM# 283 5 WON
15.0000 g., 0.9990 Silver 0.4818 oz. ASW, 35 mm.
ubject: Arirang **Obv:** National arms **Rev:** Flying female flute player **Edge:** Segmented reeding

Date	Mintage	F	VF	XF	Unc	BU
ND Proof	—	Value: 30.00				

KM# 284 5 WON
15.0000 g., 0.9990 Silver 0.4818 oz. ASW, 35 mm. **Subject:** Arirang **Obv:** National arms **Rev:** Dancers holding globe over arena **Edge:** Segmented reeding

Date	Mintage	F	VF	XF	Unc	BU
ND Proof	—	Value: 30.00				

KM# 285 5 WON
15.0000 g., 0.9990 Silver 0.4818 oz. ASW, 35 mm.
Subject: Arirang **Obv:** National arms **Rev:** Uniformed heads right and outline of dove **Edge:** Segmented reeding

Date	Mintage	F	VF	XF	Unc	BU
ND Proof	—	Value: 30.00				

KM# 286 5 WON
15.0000 g., 0.9990 Silver 0.4818 oz. ASW, 35 mm.
Subject: Arirang **Obv:** National arms **Rev:** Monument
Edge: Segmented reeding

Date	Mintage	F	VF	XF	Unc	BU
ND Proof	—	Value: 30.00				

KM# 287 5 WON
15.0000 g., 0.9990 Silver 0.4818 oz. ASW, 35 mm.
Subject: Arirang **Obv:** National arms **Rev:** Dancer in radiant sunlight **Edge:** Segmented reeding

Date	Mintage	F	VF	XF	Unc	BU
ND Proof	—	Value: 30.00				

KM# 288 5 WON
15.0000 g., 0.9990 Silver 0.4818 oz. ASW, 35 mm.
Subject: Arirang **Obv:** National arms **Rev:** Folk dancers
Edge: Segmented reeding

Date	Mintage	F	VF	XF	Unc	BU
ND Proof	—	Value: 30.00				

KM# 289 5 WON
15.0000 g., 0.9990 Silver 0.4818 oz. ASW, 35 mm. **Subject:** Arirang **Obv:** National arms **Rev:** Arena **Edge:** Segmented reeding

Date	Mintage	F	VF	XF	Unc	BU
ND Proof	—	Value: 30.00				

KM# 65 10 WON
Copper-Nickel **Subject:** 80th Birthday - Kim Il Sung
Obv: National arms **Rev:** Kim Il Sung birthplace

Date	Mintage	F	VF	XF	Unc	BU
1992	—	—	—	—	7.50	9.00

KM# 66 10 WON
Copper-Nickel **Subject:** 50th Birthday - Kim Il Jong
Obv: National arms **Rev:** Bust facing

Date	Mintage	F	VF	XF	Unc	BU
1992	—	—	—	—	7.50	9.00

KM# 73 10 WON
Copper-Nickel **Subject:** 80th Birthday - Kim Il Sung
Obv: National arms **Rev:** Bust facing

Date	Mintage	F	VF	XF	Unc	BU
1992	—	—	—	—	7.50	9.00

KM# 269 10 WON
31.0000 g., 0.9990 Silver 0.9957 oz. ASW, 40 mm.
Obv: National arms **Rev:** Olympic horse jumping **Edge:** Plain

Date	Mintage	F	VF	XF	Unc	BU
1995 Proof	—	Value: 35.00				

KM# 270 10 WON
31.0000 g., 0.9990 Silver 0.9957 oz. ASW, 40 mm.
Obv: National arms **Rev:** Olympic runners **Edge:** Plain

Date	Mintage	F	VF	XF	Unc	BU
1995 Proof	—	Value: 35.00				

KM# 87.1 10 WON
Copper-Nickel, 30 mm. **Subject:** International Sport and Culture Festival **Obv:** National arms **Rev:** Multicolor cartoon cat **Edge:** Plain

Date	Mintage	F	VF	XF	Unc	BU
1995	—	—	—	—	15.00	17.50

KM# 87.2 10 WON
12.9000 g., Copper-Nickel, 30 mm. **Subject:** International Sport and Culture Festival **Obv:** National arms **Rev:** Multicolor cartoon cat **Edge:** Plain

Date	Mintage	F	VF	XF	Unc	BU
1995	—	—	—	—	10.00	12.00

KM# 93 10 WON
28.0000 g., Silver .8993 oz. ASW **Subject:** 50th Anniversary of Liberation **Obv:** National arms above sprigs and date
Rev: Taedong gatehouse

Date	Mintage	F	VF	XF	Unc	BU
1995 In proof sets only	300	Value: 60.00				

KM# 134.1 10 WON
12.9000 g., Copper Nickel, 30 mm. **Subject:** International Sport and Culture Festival **Obv:** National arms **Rev:** Festival logo
Edge: Plain

Date	Mintage	F	VF	XF	Unc	BU
1995	—	—	—	—	10.00	12.00

KM# 134.2 10 WON
12.9000 g., Copper Nickel, 30 mm. **Subject:** International Sport and Culture Festival **Obv:** National arms **Rev:** Festival logo with pink flame **Edge:** Plain

Date	Mintage	F	VF	XF	Unc	BU
1995	—	—	—	—	10.00	12.00

KM# 230 10 WON
31.0000 g., 0.9990 Silver 0.9957 oz. ASW, 40.1 mm.
Subject: Brontosaurus **Obv:** National arms **Rev:** Two dinosaurs above value **Edge:** Plain

Date	Mintage	F	VF	XF	Unc	BU
1995 Proof	—	Value: 35.00				

KM# 105 10 WON
31.1035 g., 0.9990 Silver 1 oz. ASW **Subject:** Fauna of Asia - Ducks **Obv:** National arms **Rev:** Multicolored pair of falcated ducks

Date	Mintage	F	VF	XF	Unc	BU
1996 Proof	1,000	Value: 45.00				

KM# 115 10 WON
30.9600 g., 0.9990 Silver .9944 oz. ASW **Subject:** Fauna of Asia **Obv:** National arms **Rev:** Multicolored parrot

Date	Mintage	F	VF	XF	Unc	BU
1996 Proof	1,000	Value: 55.00				

KM# 135 10 WON
31.1035 g., 0.9990 Silver 1.0000 oz. ASW, 40 mm.
Subject: Korean Workers' Party **Obv:** National arms **Rev:** Flag and radiant setting sun **Edge:** Plain

Date	Mintage	F	VF	XF	Unc	BU
1996	1,000	—	—	—	40.00	—

KM# 271 10 WON
31.0000 g., 0.9990 Silver 0.9957 oz. ASW, 40.2 mm. **Obv:** National arms **Rev:** Two green Olympic gymnasts **Edge:** Plain

Date	Mintage	F	VF	XF	Unc	BU
1996 Proof	—	Value: 40.00				

KM# 98 10 WON
31.0000 g., 0.9990 Silver .9957 oz. ASW **Subject:** Return of Hong Kong to China **Obv:** National arms **Rev:** Temple of Heaven above Hong Kong city view

Date	Mintage	F	VF	XF	Unc	BU
1997 Proof	2,000	Value: 65.00				

KM# 222 10 WON
30.8000 g., 0.9990 Silver 0.9893 oz. ASW, 40.2 mm.
Subject: Fauna of Asia **Obv:** National arms **Rev:** Two multicolor water birds **Edge:** Reeded

Date	Mintage	F	VF	XF	Unc	BU
1997 Proof	—	Value: 50.00				

KM# 99 10 WON
31.0000 g., 0.9990 Silver .9957 oz. ASW **Subject:** Ginseng **Obv:** National arms **Rev:** Multicolored ginseng plant including root, leaves and berries

Date	Mintage	F	VF	XF	Unc	BU
1997 Proof	2,000	Value: 45.00				

KM# 101 10 WON
30.8800 g., 0.9990 Silver .9918 oz. ASW **Subject:** Shanghai Coin Show **Obv:** National arms **Rev:** Two multicolored pandas eating bamboo

Date	Mintage	F	VF	XF	Unc	BU
1997 Proof	20,000	Value: 45.00				

KM# 120 10 WON
30.9600 g., 0.9990 Silver .9944 oz. ASW, 38.6 mm. **Subject:** Korean War **Obv:** National arms **Rev:** Multicolored flags before monument **Edge:** Reeded and plain sections

Date	Mintage	F	VF	XF	Unc	BU
1997 Proof	20,000	Value: 35.00				

KM# 121 10 WON
30.9600 g., 0.9990 Silver .9944 oz. ASW, 40.3 mm. **Subject:** Korean War **Obv:** National arms **Rev:** Soldier watching bridge bombardment **Edge:** Reeded and plain sections

Date	Mintage	F	VF	XF	Unc	BU
1997 Proof	20,000	Value: 40.00				

KM# 124 10 WON
30.9500 g., 0.9990 Silver .9940 oz. ASW, 40.3 mm. **Subject:** World of Adventure **Obv:** National arms **Rev:** Multicolor sailing scene **Edge:** Segmented reeding

Date	Mintage	F	VF	XF	Unc	BU
1997 Proof	—	Value: 55.00				

KM# 136 10 WON
31.1035 g., 0.9990 Silver 1.0000 oz. ASW, 40 mm. **Subject:** Chou En Lai Centennial of Birth **Obv:** National arms above value and date **Rev:** Head facing above dates flanked by sprigs **Edge:** Plain

Date	Mintage	F	VF	XF	Unc	BU
1997	8,000	—	—	—	50.00	—

KM# 137 10 WON
31.1035 g., 0.9990 Silver 1.0000 oz. ASW, 40 mm. **Subject:** Chinese National Flower **Obv:** National arms **Rev:** Multicolor flower **Edge:** Plain

Date	Mintage	F	VF	XF	Unc	BU
1997	5,000	—	—	—	55.00	—

KM# 138.1 10 WON

31.1035 g., 0.9990 Silver 1.0000 oz. ASW, 40 mm. **Subject:** Giant Panda **Obv:** National arms **Rev:** Multicolor seated panda **Edge:** Plain **Note:** Previous KM#138.

Date	Mintage	F	VF	XF	Unc	BU
1997	10,000	—	—	—	50.00	—

KM# 349 10 WON

31.0000 g., 0.9990 Silver 0.9957 oz. ASW, 40.2 mm. **Obv:** National arms **Rev:** Multicolor parrot **Edge:** Plain

Date	Mintage	F	VF	XF	Unc	BU
1997 Proof	—	Value: 35.00				

KM# 164 10 WON

31.0000 g., 0.9990 Silver 0.9957 oz. ASW, 40 mm. **Subject:** 50th Anniversary - People's Republic **Obv:** National arms **Rev:** Flag, dates and value below mountains **Edge:** Reeded and plain sections

Date	Mintage	F	VF	XF	Unc	BU
1998 Proof	1,000	Value: 30.00				

KM# 102 10 WON

30.8800 g., 0.9990 Silver .9918 oz. ASW **Subject:** Year of the Tiger **Obv:** Tiger on mountain ledge **Rev:** Tiger head

Date	Mintage	F	VF	XF	Unc	BU
ND(1998) Proof	2,000	Value: 37.50				

KM# 110 10 WON

30.8800 g., 0.9990 Silver .9918 oz. ASW **Subject:** Korean Folk IV **Obv:** National arms **Rev:** Girl on swing

Date	Mintage	F	VF	XF	Unc	BU
1998 Proof	2,000	Value: 40.00				

KM# 111 10 WON

30.8800 g., 0.9990 Silver .9918 oz. ASW **Subject:** Korean Folk I **Obv:** National arms **Rev:** Two children flying a kite

Date	Mintage	F	VF	XF	Unc	BU
1998 Proof	2,000	Value: 40.00				

KM# 112 10 WON

30.8800 g., 0.9990 Silver .9918 oz. ASW **Subject:** Korean Folk II **Obv:** National arms **Rev:** Two girls see-sawing

Date	Mintage	F	VF	XF	Unc	BU
1998 Proof	2,000	Value: 40.00				

KM# 113 10 WON

30.8800 g., 0.9990 Silver .9918 oz. ASW **Subject:** Korean Folk III **Obv:** National arms **Rev:** Wrestling

Date	Mintage	F	VF	XF	Unc	BU
1998 Proof	2,000	Value: 40.00				

KM# 114 10 WON

30.8800 g., 0.9990 Silver .9918 oz. ASW **Subject:** Korean Folk V **Obv:** National arms **Rev:** Three girls jumping rope

Date	Mintage	F	VF	XF	Unc	BU
1998 Proof	2,000	Value: 40.00				

KM# 138.2 10 WON

31.1035 g., 0.9990 Silver 0.999 oz. ASW, 40 mm. **Subject:** Giant Panda **Obv:** National arms **Rev:** Multicolor seated Panda **Edge:** Plain

Date	Mintage	F	VF	XF	Unc	BU
1998 Proof	—	Value: 45.00				

KM# 163 10 WON

31.0000 g., 0.9990 Silver 0.9957 oz. ASW, 40 mm. **Subject:** Intrepid Symbol: Tiger **Obv:** National arms **Rev:** Snarling tiger right **Edge:** Reeded and plain sections

Date	Mintage	F	VF	XF	Unc	BU
1998 Proof	2,000	Value: 30.00				

KM# 272 10 WON

31.0000 g., 0.9990 Silver 0.9957 oz. ASW, 40 mm. **Obv:** National arms **Rev:** Olympic gymnast on high bar **Edge:** Plain

Date	Mintage	F	VF	XF	Unc	BU
1998 Proof	—	Value: 35.00				

KM# 103 10 WON

30.9600 g., 0.9990 Silver .9944 oz. ASW **Subject:** Year of the Rabbit **Obv:** National arms **Rev:** Multicolored rabbit with hearts with legend above

Date	Mintage	F	VF	XF	Unc	BU
1999 Proof	5,000	Value: 45.00				

KM# 107 10 WON
30.9600 g., 0.9990 Silver .9944 oz. ASW **Subject:** Year of the Rabbit **Obv:** National arms **Rev:** Multicolored rabbits with hearts without legend above

Date	Mintage	F	VF	XF	Unc	BU
1999 Proof	5,000	Value: 40.00				

KM# 108 10 WON
30.9600 g., 0.9990 Silver .9944 oz. ASW **Subject:** Blue dragon **Obv:** National arms **Rev:** Flying dragon above mountains

Date	Mintage	F	VF	XF	Unc	BU
1999 Proof	5,000	Value: 45.00				

KM# 109.1 10 WON
30.9600 g., 0.9990 Silver .9944 oz. ASW **Subject:** Birds of Korea **Obv:** National arms **Rev:** White-bellied woodpecker on tree limb **Edge:** Segmented reeding **Note:** Prev. KM#109

Date	Mintage	F	VF	XF	Unc	BU
1999 Proof	3,000	Value: 45.00				

KM# 109.2 10 WON
30.9600 g., 0.9990 Silver 0.9944 oz. ASW **Subject:** Birds of Korea **Obv:** National arms **Rev:** White-bellied woodpecker on tree limb **Edge:** Plain

Date	Mintage	F	VF	XF	Unc	BU
1999 Proof	Inc. above	Value: 45.00				

KM# 166 10 WON
31.0000 g., 0.9990 Silver 0.9957 oz. ASW **Subject:** Birds of Korea **Obv:** National arms **Rev:** Fairy pitta on branch **Edge:** Reeded and plain sections

Date	Mintage	F	VF	XF	Unc	BU
1999 Proof	2,000	Value: 40.00				

KM# 167 10 WON
31.0000 g., 0.9990 Silver 0.9957 oz. ASW, 40 mm. **Subject:** Olympic Games **Obv:** National arms **Rev:** Man jumping hurdles above kangaroo and value **Edge:** Reeded and plain sections

Date	Mintage	F	VF	XF	Unc	BU
1999 Proof	3,000	Value: 35.00				

KM# 168 10 WON
31.0000 g., 0.9990 Silver 0.9957 oz. ASW, 40 mm. **Subject:** Olympic Games **Obv:** National arms **Rev:** Diver **Edge:** Reeded and plain sections

Date	Mintage	F	VF	XF	Unc	BU
1999 Proof	3,000	Value: 35.00				

KM# 169 10 WON
31.0000 g., 0.9990 Silver 0.9957 oz. ASW, 40 mm. **Subject:** 7th World Track and Field Championships **Obv:** National arms **Rev:** Marathon winner Jong Song Ok **Edge:** Reeded and plain sections

Date	Mintage	F	VF	XF	Unc	BU
1999 Proof	1,000	Value: 35.00				

KM# 170 10 WON
31.0000 g., 0.9990 Silver 0.9957 oz. ASW, 40 mm. **Subject:** First North Korean Space Satellite **Obv:** National arms **Rev:** Rocket **Edge:** Reeded and plain sections

Date	Mintage	F	VF	XF	Unc	BU
1999 Proof	5,000	Value: 35.00				

KM# 171 10 WON
31.0000 g., 0.9990 Silver 0.9957 oz. ASW, 40 mm. **Subject:** Kim Il Sung and Zhou Enlai **Obv:** National arms **Rev:** Kim Il Sung and Zhou Enlai shaking hands **Edge:** Reeded and plain sections

Date	Mintage	F	VF	XF	Unc	BU
1999 Proof	5,000	Value: 35.00				

KM# 223 10 WON
30.8000 g., 0.9990 Silver, 40.2 mm. **Subject:** Birds of Korea **Obv:** National arms **Rev:** Lyrurus Tetrix, bird on ground **Edge:** Reeded

Date	Mintage	F	VF	XF	Unc	BU
1999	—	—	—	—	—	—

KM# 224 10 WON
30.8000 g., 0.9990 Silver 0.9893 oz. ASW, 40.2 mm. **Subject:** Birds of Korea **Obv:** National arms **Rev:** Syrrhaptes Paradoxus, bird on shore **Edge:** Reeded

Date	Mintage	F	VF	XF	Unc	BU
1999 Proof	—	Value: 40.00				

KM# 125 10 WON
30.9500 g., 0.9990 Silver .9940 oz. ASW, 40.3 mm. **Subject:** One Korea: 3,000 Years of History **Obv:** National arms **Rev:** Radiant map and landmarks **Edge:** Segmented reeding

Date	Mintage	F	VF	XF	Unc	BU
2000 Proof	—	Value: 45.00				

KM# 178 10 WON
31.0000 g., 0.9990 Silver 0.9957 oz. ASW, 40 mm. **Subject:** King Tangun **Obv:** National arms **Rev:** Bust facing **Edge:** Reeded and plain sections

Date	Mintage	F	VF	XF	Unc	BU
2000 Proof	5,000	Value: 35.00				

KM# 228 10 WON
31.0400 g., 0.9990 Silver 0.997 oz. ASW, 40.3 mm.
Subject: Hyonmu **Obv:** National arms and small legend
Rev: Mythical creature **Edge:** Plain

Date	Mintage	F	VF	XF	Unc	BU
2000 Proof	—	Value: 40.00				

KM# 229 10 WON
31.0400 g., 0.9990 Silver 0.997 oz. ASW, 40.3 mm.
Subject: Hyonmu **Obv:** National arms with large legend
Rev: Mythical creature **Edge:** Plain

Date	Mintage	F	VF	XF	Unc	BU
2000 Proof	—	Value: 40.00				

KM# 276 10 WON
31.0000 g., 0.9990 Silver 0.9957 oz. ASW, 40.1 mm.
Obv: National arms **Rev:** Kim greeting diplomat with Korean legend **Edge:** Plain **Note:** Similar to KM#273.

Date	Mintage	F	VF	XF	Unc	BU
2000 Proof	—	Value: 35.00				

KM# 278 10 WON
31.0000 g., 0.9990 Silver 0.9957 oz. ASW, 40.1 mm.
Obv: National arms **Rev:** Treaty signing scene **Edge:** Plain
Note: Similar to KM#277.

Date	Mintage	F	VF	XF	Unc	BU
2000 Proof	—	Value: 35.00				

KM# 279 10 WON
31.0000 g., 0.9990 Silver 0.9957 oz. ASW, 40.1 mm.
Obv: National arms **Rev:** Kim Jong Il greeting diplomat, half length **Edge:** Plain **Note:** Similar to KM#275.

Date	Mintage	F	VF	XF	Unc	BU
2000 Proof	—	Value: 35.00				

KM# 280 10 WON
31.0000 g., 0.9990 Silver, 40.1 mm. **Obv:** National arms
Rev: Kim greeting diplomat, full length view **Edge:** Plain

Date	Mintage	F	VF	XF	Unc	BU
2000 Proof	—	Value: 35.00				

KM# 281 10 WON
31.0000 g., 0.9990 Silver 0.9957 oz. ASW, 40.1 mm.
Obv: National arms **Rev:** Old couple embracing above dates and value **Edge:** Plain

Date	Mintage	F	VF	XF	Unc	BU
2000 Proof	—	Value: 35.00				

KM# 282 10 WON
31.0000 g., 0.9990 Silver 0.9957 oz. ASW, 40.1 mm.
Obv: National arms **Rev:** Two tigers **Edge:** Plain

Date	Mintage	F	VF	XF	Unc	BU
2000 Proof	—	Value: 35.00				

KM# 348 10 WON
31.0000 g., 0.9990 Silver 0.9957 oz. ASW, 40.2 mm.
Obv: National arms **Rev:** Olympic handball player **Edge:** Plain

Date	Mintage	F	VF	XF	Unc	BU
2000 Proof	—	Value: 35.00				

KM# 350 10 WON
31.0000 g., 0.9990 Silver 0.9957 oz. ASW, 40.2 mm. **Obv:** National arms **Rev:** Radiant Korean map and landmarks **Edge:** Plain

Date	Mintage	F	VF	XF	Unc	BU
2000 Proof	—	Value: 35.00				

KM# 20 20 WON
14.8000 g., 0.9990 Silver .4758 oz. ASW **Subject:** World Festival of Youth and Students **Obv:** National arms above D.P.R. of Korea, value, and date below **Rev:** Dove within circle of flower design

Date	Mintage	F	VF	XF	Unc	BU
1989 Proof	—	Value: 25.00				

KM# 97.1 20 WON
31.1035 g., 0.9990 Silver 1 oz. ASW **Subject:** Kim Il Sung's death **Obv:** National arms above value **Rev:** Bust facing
Edge: Plain **Note:** Prev. KM#97.

Date	Mintage	F	VF	XF	Unc	BU
ND(1994) Proof	5,000	Value: 85.00				

KM# 97.2 20 WON
31.1035 g., 0.9990 Silver 1 oz. ASW **Subject:** Kim Il Sung's Death **Obv:** National arms **Rev:** Bust facing **Edge:** Reeded

Date	Mintage	F	VF	XF	Unc	BU
ND(1994) Proof	—	Value: 50.00				

KM# 74 20 WON
Copper-Nickel **Subject:** 1998 World Cup Soccer **Obv:** National arms **Rev:** Soccer player in front of arch

Date	Mintage	F	VF	XF	Unc	BU
1995 Proof	10,000	Value: 30.00				

KM# 94 20 WON
50.0000 g., 0.9990 Silver 1.6059 oz. ASW, 50 mm.
Subject: 50th Anniversary of Liberation **Obv:** National arms
Rev: Fairy of Mount Kumgang

Date	Mintage	F	VF	XF	Unc	BU
1995	300	Value: 125				

Note: In proof sets only

KM# 139 20 WON
31.1035 g., 0.9990 Silver 1.0000 oz. ASW, 40 mm.
Subject: 50th Anniversary - Korean Workers' Party
Obv: National arms **Rev:** Monument **Edge:** Plain

Date	Mintage	F	VF	XF	Unc	BU
1995	—	—	—	—	40.00	—

KM# 140 20 WON
22.0000 g., Copper Nickel, 40 mm. **Subject:** 25th Basel International Coin Show **Obv:** National arms above phone fax and telex numbers **Rev:** Multicolor island and seascape **Edge:** Plain

Date	Mintage	F	VF	XF	Unc	BU
1996	1,000	—	—	—	18.00	—

KM# 26 30 WON
17.0200 g., 0.9990 Silver .5472 oz. ASW **Subject:** Friendship Art Festival **Obv:** National arms **Rev:** Head 3/4 left with hand holding microphone

Date	Mintage	F	VF	XF	Unc	BU
1989 Proof	—	Value: 40.00				

KM# 52 50 WON
17.0200 g., 0.9990 Silver .5466 oz. ASW **Subject:** 80th Birthday of Kim Il Sung **Obv:** National arms **Rev:** Kim Il Sung birthplace

Date	Mintage	F	VF	XF	Unc	BU
1992 Proof	1,000	Value: 40.00				

KM# 54 50 WON
17.0200 g., 0.9990 Silver .5466 oz. ASW **Subject:** 80th Birthday of Kim Il Sung **Obv:** National arms **Rev:** Bust facing

Date	Mintage	F	VF	XF	Unc	BU
1992 Proof	1,000	Value: 45.00				

KM# 56 50 WON
17.0200 g., 0.9990 Silver .5466 oz. ASW **Subject:** 50th Birthday of Kim Jong Il **Obv:** National arms **Rev:** Bust facing

Date	Mintage	F	VF	XF	Unc	BU
1992 Proof	5,000	Value: 50.00				

KM# 88 50 WON
Copper-Nickel **Subject:** Sportsfest **Obv:** National arms **Rev:** Wrestlers

Date	Mintage	F	VF	XF	Unc	BU
1995	—	—	—	—	22.50	25.00

KM# 141 50 WON
12.9000 g., Copper Nickel, 30 mm. **Subject:** International Friendship Exhibition **Obv:** National arms **Rev:** Building **Edge:** Plain

Date	Mintage	F	VF	XF	Unc	BU
1995	—	—	—	—	10.00	12.00

KM# 142 50 WON
12.9000 g., Copper Nickel, 30 mm. **Subject:** May Day Stadium **Obv:** National arms **Rev:** Stadium **Edge:** Plain

Date	Mintage	F	VF	XF	Unc	BU
1995	—	—	—	—	10.00	12.00

KM# 28 100 WON
3.1300 g., 0.9990 Gold .1 oz. AGW **Subject:** 40th Anniversary of People's Republic **Obv:** National arms **Rev:** Leaping equestrian

Date	Mintage	F	VF	XF	Unc	BU
1988 Proof	—	Value: 85.00				

KM# 70 100 WON
7.0000 g., 0.9990 Silver .2248 oz. ASW **Obv:** National arms **Rev:** Two multicolored Adelie penguins

Date	Mintage	F	VF	XF	Unc	BU
1995 Proof	—	Value: 45.00				

KM# 71 100 WON
7.0000 g., 0.9990 Silver .2250 oz. ASW **Subject:** 1996 Olympics **Obv:** National arms **Rev:** Sprinter

Date	Mintage	F	VF	XF	Unc	BU
1995 Proof	30,000	Value: 30.00				

KM# 72 100 WON
7.0000 g., 0.9990 Silver .2250 oz. ASW **Subject:** 1998 World Cup Soccer **Obv:** National arms **Rev:** Eiffel tower and soccer player

Date	Mintage	F	VF	XF	Unc	BU
1995 Proof	30,000	Value: 30.00				

KM# 104 100 WON
7.0000 g., 0.9990 Silver .2250 oz. ASW **Subject:** Aix Galericulata **Obv:** National arms **Rev:** Multicolor pair of mandarin ducks

Date	Mintage	F	VF	XF	Unc	BU
1995 Proof	Est. 30,000	Value: 40.00				

KM# 422 100 WON
7.0000 g., 0.9990 Silver 0.2248 oz. ASW, 30 mm. **Subject:** Return of Hong Kong **Obv:** State emblem **Rev:** Houseboat **Edge:** Plain

Date	Mintage	F	VF	XF	Unc	BU
1996 Proof	—	Value: 25.00				

KM# 122 100 WON
7.0000 g., 0.9990 Silver .2248 oz. ASW, 30 mm. **Subject:** Robinson Crusoe **Obv:** National arms **Rev:** Multicolor row boat scene **Edge:** Plain

Date	Mintage	F	VF	XF	Unc	BU
1996 Proof	—	Value: 40.00				

KM# 49 200 WON
14.9700 g., 0.9990 Silver .5 oz. ASW **Subject:** Olympics **Obv:** Silver content statement divided by national arms **Rev:** Equestrian

Date	Mintage	F	VF	XF	Unc	BU
1991 Proof	25,000	Value: 25.00				

KM# 50 200 WON
14.9700 g., 0.9990 Silver .5 oz. ASW **Subject:** Olympics **Obv:** Silver content statement below national arms **Rev:** Equestrian

Date	Mintage	F	VF	XF	Unc	BU
1991 Proof	Inc. above	Value: 22.50				

KM# 64 200 WON
15.0000 g., 0.9990 Silver .481 oz. ASW **Subject:** Summer Olympic Games - Barcelona 1992 **Obv:** National arms **Rev:** Sprinter

Date	Mintage	F	VF	XF	Unc	BU
1992 Proof	25,000	Value: 20.00				

KM# 95.1 200 WON
8.0000 g., 0.9990 Gold **Subject:** 50th Anniversary of Liberation **Obv:** National arms **Rev:** Turtle ship **Note:** Prev. KM#95.

Date	Mintage	F	VF	XF	Unc	BU
1995 In proof sets only	300	Value: 420				

KM# 95.2 200 WON
8.0000 g., 0.9990 Gold 0.2569 oz. AGW, 25 mm. **Subject:** 50th Anniversary of Liberation **Obv:** National arms with fineness closer to arms **Rev:** Turtle ship

Date	Mintage	F	VF	XF	Unc	BU
1995 Proof	—	Value: 420				

KM# 29 250 WON
7.7800 g., 0.9990 Gold .25 oz. AGW **Subject:** 40th Anniversary of People's Republic **Obv:** National arms **Rev:** Leaping equestrian

Date	Mintage	F	VF	XF	Unc	BU
1988 Proof	—	Value: 185				

KM# 21 250 WON
7.7700 g., 0.9990 Gold .25 oz. AGW **Subject:** World Festival of Youth and Students **Obv:** National arms above D.P.R. of Korea, value and date **Rev:** Flower design

Date	Mintage	F	VF	XF	Unc	BU
1989 Proof	—	Value: 285				

KM# 423 250 WON
15.0000 g., 0.9990 Silver 0.4818 oz. ASW, 35.1 mm. **Subject:** Retrun of Hong Kong **Obv:** National arms **Rev:** Multicolor Junk and city view **Edge:** Plain

Date	Mintage	F	VF	XF	Unc	BU
1996 Proof	—	Value: 35.00				

KM# 116 250 WON
20.0000 g., 0.9990 Silver .6464 oz. ASW **Subject:** Millennium **Obv:** National arms above value **Rev:** Dragon **Shape:** Rectangular

Date	Mintage	F	VF	XF	Unc	BU
1998//2000 Proof	—	Value: 40.00				

KM# 225 250 WON
14.9600 g., 0.9990 Silver 0.4805 oz. ASW, 34.9 mm. **Subject:** Beethoven **Obv:** National arms **Rev:** Bust 3/4 left writing **Edge:** Plain

Date	Mintage	F	VF	XF	Unc	BU
1999 Proof	—	Value: 35.00				

KM# 96 400 WON
16.0000 g., Gold .5138 oz. AGW **Subject:** 50th Anniversary of Liberation **Obv:** National arms **Rev:** Lake on Mount Baektu

Date	Mintage	F	VF	XF	Unc	BU
1995 In proof sets only	100	Value: 700				

KM# 39 500 WON
27.0000 g., 0.9990 Silver .8681 oz. ASW **Subject:** World Championship Soccer - Mexico '96 **Obv:** National arms **Rev:** Soccer player

Date	Mintage	F	VF	XF	Unc	BU
1987 Proof	—	Value: 35.00				

KM# 16 500 WON
27.0000 g., 0.9990 Silver .8681 oz. ASW **Series:** Winter Olympics **Subject:** Hockey **Obv:** National arms **Rev:** Hockey sticks and puck

Date	Mintage	F	VF	XF	Unc	BU
1988 Proof	20,000	Value: 20.00				

KM# 17 500 WON
27.0000 g., 0.9990 Silver .8681 oz. ASW **Subject:** 30th Anniversary of Gorch Fock **Obv:** National arms **Rev:** Ship at sea **Edge:** Plain

Date	Mintage	F	VF	XF	Unc	BU
1988 Proof	—	Value: 35.00				

KM# 24 500 WON
27.0000 g., 0.9990 Silver .8681 oz. ASW **Subject:** World Championship Soccer **Obv:** National arms above date and D.P.R. of Korea **Rev:** Soccer player

Date	Mintage	F	VF	XF	Unc	BU
1988 Proof	—	Value: 25.00				

KM# 30 500 WON
15.5700 g., 0.9990 Gold .5 oz. AGW **Subject:** 40th Anniversary of People's Republic **Obv:** National arms **Rev:** Leaping equestrian

Date	Mintage	F	VF	XF	Unc	BU
1988 Proof	—	Value: 365				

KM# 36 500 WON
27.0000 g., 0.9990 Silver .8681 oz. ASW **Series:** F.A.O. **Subject:** Food for all **Obv:** National arms

Date	Mintage	F	VF	XF	Unc	BU
1988 Proof	Est. 2,000	Value: 50.00				

KM# 27 500 WON
27.0000 g., 0.9990 Silver .8681 oz. ASW **Subject:** Amerigo Vespucci **Obv:** National arms **Rev:** Head left at right, map of 'Americas' at left

Date	Mintage	F	VF	XF	Unc	BU
1989 Proof	—	Value: 40.00				

KM# 32.1 500 WON
31.8200 g., 0.9990 Silver 1.022 oz. ASW, 40 mm. **Obv:** Number 1 in date without serifs **Rev:** Fairy of Mount Kumgang playing a flute **Edge:** Plain

Date	Mintage	F	VF	XF	Unc	BU
1989 Proof	—	Value: 50.00				

KM# 32 500 WON
31.8200 g., 0.9990 Silver 1.0231 oz. ASW, 40 mm.
Obv: National arms above date and sprigs **Rev:** Fairy of Mount Kumgang playing a flute **Edge:** Segmented reeding
Note: Sectional reeding as follows - IIIIII II IIIIII II IIIIII.

Date	Mintage	F	VF	XF	Unc	BU
1989 Proof number 1 in date without bottom serif	—	Value: 50.00				
1989 Proof	2,000	Value: 55.00				

KM# 33 500 WON
27.0000 g., 0.9990 Silver .8682 oz. ASW **Series:** Calgary Winter Olympics **Obv:** National arms **Rev:** Figure skater

Date	Mintage	F	VF	XF	Unc	BU
1989 Proof	—	Value: 35.00				

KM# 34 500 WON
27.0000 g., 0.9990 Silver .8682 oz. ASW **Series:** Barcelona Summer Olympics **Obv:** National arms **Rev:** Discus thrower

Date	Mintage	F	VF	XF	Unc	BU
1989 Proof	—	Value: 35.00				

KM# 37 500 WON
27.0000 g., 0.9990 Silver .8682 oz. ASW **Subject:** World Championship Soccer **Obv:** National arms **Rev:** Player kicking ball

Date	Mintage	F	VF	XF	Unc	BU
1989 Proof	15,000	Value: 50.00				

KM# 38 500 WON
27.0000 g., 0.9990 Silver .8682 oz. ASW **Subject:** World Championship Soccer **Obv:** National arms **Rev:** Goalie

Date	Mintage	F	VF	XF	Unc	BU
1989 Proof	—	Value: 25.00				

KM# 40 500 WON
31.8200 g., 0.9990 Silver .8682 oz. ASW **Subject:** Olympic table tennis **Obv:** National arms **Rev:** Table tennis player

Date	Mintage	F	VF	XF	Unc	BU
1990 Proof	15,000	Value: 25.00				

KM# 41 500 WON
31.8200 g., 0.9990 Silver .8682 oz. ASW **Subject:** Endangered Wildlife **Obv:** National arms **Rev:** Red-crowned crane

Date	Mintage	F	VF	XF	Unc	BU
1990 Proof	—	Value: 45.00				

KM# 44 500 WON
31.1000 g., 0.9990 Silver 1 oz. ASW **Subject:** World Championship Table Tennis **Obv:** National arms **Rev:** Two male players on doubles team

Date	Mintage	F	VF	XF	Unc	BU
1991 Proof	5,000	Value: 32.50				

KM# 45 500 WON
31.1000 g., 0.9990 Silver 1 oz. ASW **Subject:** World Championship Table Tennis **Obv:** National arms **Rev:** Male player

Date	Mintage	F	VF	XF	Unc	BU
1991 Proof	5,000	Value: 32.50				

KM# 46 500 WON
31.1000 g., 0.9990 Silver 1 oz. ASW **Subject:** 41st World Table Tennis Championships **Obv:** National arms **Rev:** Table tennis player

Date	Mintage	F	VF	XF	Unc	BU
1991 Proof	5,000	Value: 32.50				

KM# 47 500 WON
31.1000 g., 0.9990 Silver 1 oz. ASW **Subject:** 41st World Table Tennis Championships **Obv:** National arms **Rev:** Three busts facing above trophy

Date	Mintage	F	VF	XF	Unc	BU
1991 Proof	10,000	Value: 25.00				

KM# 48 500 WON
27.0000 g., 0.9990 Silver .8682 oz. ASW **Subject:** First Armoured Ship **Obv:** National arms **Rev:** First armoured ship above value

Date	Mintage	F	VF	XF	Unc	BU
1991 Proof	Est. 10,000	Value: 50.00				

KM# 63 500 WON
27.0000 g., 0.9990 Silver .8682 oz. ASW **Series:** Olympics **Obv:** National arms **Rev:** Women's volleyball

Date	Mintage	F	VF	XF	Unc	BU
1991 Proof	15,000	Value: 35.00				

KM# 59 500 WON
27.0000 g., 0.9990 Silver .8682 oz. ASW **Subject:** Environmental Protection **Obv:** National arms **Rev:** Flowers

Date	Mintage	F	VF	XF	Unc	BU
1992 Proof	1,000	Value: 55.00				

KM# 144 500 WON
27.0000 g., 0.9990 Silver .8672 oz. ASW, 35 mm. **Subject:** 1994 World Cup Soccer **Obv:** National arms **Rev:** Three soccer players **Edge:** Plain

Date	Mintage	F	VF	XF	Unc	BU
1992	—	—	—	—	35.00	—

KM# 62.1 500 WON
31.1035 g., 0.9990 Silver 1 oz. ASW, 40.3 mm.
Series: Prehistoric Animals **Obv:** National arms
Rev: Brontosaurus **Edge:** Reeded **Note:** Prev. KM#62.

Date	Mintage	F	VF	XF	Unc	BU
1993	—	—	—	—	—	—
1993 Proof	—	Value: 45.00				

KM# 60 500 WON
27.0000 g., 0.9990 Silver .8682 oz. ASW **Series:** 1994 Olympics
Obv: National arms **Rev:** Speed skating

Date	Mintage	F	VF	XF	Unc	BU
1993 Proof	1,000	Value: 30.00				

KM# 61 500 WON
27.0000 g., 0.9990 Silver .8682 oz. ASW **Series:** 1994 Olympics
Obv: National arms **Rev:** Two-man bobsled

Date	Mintage	F	VF	XF	Unc	BU
1993 Proof	1,000	Value: 40.00				

KM# 145 500 WON
31.1035 g., 0.9990 Silver 1.0000 oz. ASW, 40 mm.
Subject: 1994 World Cup Soccer **Obv:** National arms **Rev:** Two players and trophy cup **Edge:** Plain

Date	Mintage	F	VF	XF	Unc	BU
1994	—	—	—	—	40.00	—

KM# 62.2 500 WON
31.1035 g., 0.9990 Silver 0.999 oz. ASW, 40.3 mm.
Series: Prehistoric Animals **Obv:** National arms **Rev:** More vegetation by dinosaur's foot **Edge:** Reeded

Date	Mintage	F	VF	XF	Unc	BU
1995 Proof	3,000	Value: 55.00				

KM# 67 500 WON
31.1035 g., 0.9990 Silver 1 oz. ASW **Series:** 1996 Atlanta Olympics **Obv:** National arms **Rev:** Relay racers

Date	Mintage	F	VF	XF	Unc	BU
1995 Proof	3,000	Value: 40.00				

KM# 68 500 WON
31.1035 g., 0.9990 Silver 1 oz. ASW, 40 mm. **Series:** 1996 Atlanta Olympics **Obv:** National arms **Rev:** Equestrian **Edge:** Plain

Date	Mintage	F	VF	XF	Unc	BU
1995 Proof	3,000	Value: 40.00				

KM# 69 500 WON
31.1035 g., 0.9990 Silver 1 oz. ASW **Subject:** Fauna of Asia
Obv: National arms above date and sprigs **Rev:** Multicolor tiger

Date	Mintage	F	VF	XF	Unc	BU
1995 Proof	20,000	Value: 45.00				

KM# 75 500 WON
31.1035 g., 0.9990 Silver 1 oz. ASW **Subject:** 1998 World Cup Soccer **Obv:** National arms **Rev:** Soccer player in front of arch

Date	Mintage	F	VF	XF	Unc	BU
1995 Proof	10,000	Value: 45.00				

KM# 76 500 WON
31.1035 g., 0.9990 Silver 1 oz. ASW **Subject:** Fauna of Asia
Obv: National arms **Rev:** Multicolor panda

Date	Mintage	F	VF	XF	Unc	BU
1995 Proof	20,000	Value: 40.00				

KM# 77 500 WON
31.1035 g., 0.9990 Silver 1 oz. ASW **Subject:** Fauna of Asia
Obv: National arms **Rev:** Multicolor parrot

Date	Mintage	F	VF	XF	Unc	BU
1995 Proof	20,000	Value: 40.00				

KM# 78 500 WON
31.1035 g., 0.9990 Silver 1 oz. ASW **Subject:** Fauna of Asia
Obv: National arms **Rev:** Multicolor eagle

Date	Mintage	F	VF	XF	Unc	BU
1995 Proof	20,000	Value: 40.00				

KM# 79 500 WON
31.1035 g., 0.9990 Silver 1 oz. ASW **Subject:** Fauna of Asia **Obv:** National arms **Rev:** Multicolor Eurasian eagle owl

Date	Mintage	F	VF	XF	Unc	BU
1995 Proof	20,000	Value: 50.00				

KM# 80 500 WON
31.1035 g., 0.9990 Silver 1 oz. ASW **Subject:** Fauna of Asia **Obv:** National arms **Rev:** Two multicolor falcated ducks **Note:** Enameled.

Date	Mintage	F	VF	XF	Unc	BU
1995 Proof	20,000	Value: 40.00				

KM# 143 500 WON
31.1035 g., 0.9990 Silver 1.0000 oz. ASW, 40 mm. **Subject:** International Sport and Culture Festival **Obv:** National arms **Rev:** Head facing **Edge:** Plain

Date	Mintage	F	VF	XF	Unc	BU
1995	—	—	—	—	40.00	—

KM# 146 500 WON
17.0000 g., 0.9990 Silver .5460 oz. ASW **Series:** F.A.O. **Subject:** F.A.O. 50 Years **Obv:** National arms **Rev:** F.A.O. logo above dates and value within chain-like sprigs **Edge:** Plain

Date	Mintage	F	VF	XF	Unc	BU
1995	—	—	—	—	35.00	—

KM# 421 500 WON
31.1035 g., 0.9990 Silver 0.999 oz. ASW, 40 mm. **Obv:** National arms **Rev:** Multicolor lenticular hologram panda and tiger heads only one of which can be seen at a time **Edge:** Plain

Date	Mintage	F	VF	XF	Unc	BU
1996 Proof	—	Value: 35.00				

KM# 89 500 WON
31.1035 g., 0.9990 Silver .9969 oz. ASW **Series:** Olympics **Obv:** National arms **Rev:** Two eurythmic gymnasts

Date	Mintage	F	VF	XF	Unc	BU
1996	1,000	—	—	—	40.00	—

KM# 90 500 WON
31.1035 g., 0.9990 Silver .9969 oz. ASW **Series:** Olympics **Obv:** National arms **Rev:** Soccer

Date	Mintage	F	VF	XF	Unc	BU
1996	30,000	—	—	—	45.00	—

KM# 91 500 WON
31.1035 g., 0.9990 Silver .9969 oz. ASW **Subject:** Fauna of Asia **Obv:** National arms **Rev:** Multicolor holographic panda

Date	Mintage	F	VF	XF	Unc	BU
1996 Proof	5,000	Value: 60.00				

KM# 106 500 WON
31.5200 g., 0.9990 Silver 1.0124 oz. ASW **Subject:** Fauna of Asia **Obv:** National arms **Rev:** Multicolor hologram of tiger

Date	Mintage	F	VF	XF	Unc	BU
1996 Proof	—	Value: 60.00				

KM# 117 500 WON
31.1035 g., 0.9990 Silver 1 oz. ASW **Subject:** Fauna of Asia **Obv:** National arms **Rev:** Multicolor pearl gourami

Date	Mintage	F	VF	XF	Unc	BU
1996 Proof	—	Value: 50.00				

KM# 118 500 WON
31.1035 g., 0.9990 Silver 1 oz. ASW **Subject:** Fauna of Asia **Obv:** National arms **Rev:** Multicolor clown loach

Date	Mintage	F	VF	XF	Unc	BU
1996 Proof	—	Value: 50.00				

KM# 119 500 WON
31.1035 g., 0.9990 Silver 1 oz. ASW **Subject:** Fauna of Asia **Obv:** National arms **Rev:** Multicolor long-tailed angelfish

Date	Mintage	F	VF	XF	Unc	BU
1996 Proof	—	Value: 50.00				

KM# 154 500 WON
27.0000 g., 0.9990 Silver .8672 oz. ASW, 35.2 mm. **Subject:** First Asian Gymnastic Championship **Obv:** National arms **Rev:** Multicolor panda holding logo **Edge:** Coarse and finely reeded sections

Date	Mintage	F	VF	XF	Unc	BU
1996 Proof	—	Value: 60.00				

KM# 147 700 WON
31.1035 g., 0.9990 Gold 1.0000 oz. AGW, 35 mm. **Subject:** Korean Workers' Party **Obv:** National arms **Rev:** Flag and radiant setting sun **Edge:** Plain

Date	Mintage	F	VF	XF	Unc	BU
1996	100	—	—	—	775	—

KM# 165 700 WON

31.1000 g., 0.9990 Gold 0.9989 oz. AGW, 35 mm. **Subject:** 50th Anniversary of People's Republic **Obv:** National arms **Rev:** Flag **Edge:** Plain

Date	Mintage	F	VF	XF	Unc	BU
1998 Proof	500	Value: 725				

KM# 31 1000 WON

31.1300 g., 0.9990 Gold 1 oz. AGW **Subject:** 40th Anniversary of People's Republic **Obv:** National arms **Rev:** Leaping equestrian

Date	Mintage	F	VF	XF	Unc	BU
1988 Proof	—	Value: 700				

KM# 148 1000 WON

15.5500 g., 0.9990 Gold .4999 oz. AGW, 27 mm. **Subject:** Death of Kim Il Sung **Obv:** National arms **Rev:** Bust facing **Edge:** Plain

Date	Mintage	F	VF	XF	Unc	BU
ND(1994)	—	—	—	—	400	—

KM# 149 1000 WON

31.1035 g., 0.9990 Gold 1.0000 oz. AGW, 35 mm. **Subject:** 50th Anniversary - Korean Workers' Party **Obv:** National arms **Rev:** Monument **Edge:** Plain

Date	Mintage	F	VF	XF	Unc	BU
1995	—	—	—	—	725	—

KM# 58 1500 WON

8.0000 g., 0.9990 Gold .2572 oz. AGW **Series:** Olympics **Obv:** National arms **Rev:** Gymnast

Date	Mintage	F	VF	XF	Unc	BU
1990 Proof	Est. 3,000	Value: 215				

KM# 42 1500 WON

15.5500 g., 0.9990 Gold .5 oz. AGW **Subject:** Inter-parliamentary Conference **Obv:** National arms **Rev:** Buildings

Date	Mintage	F	VF	XF	Unc	BU
1991 Proof	1,000	Value: 400				

KM# 43 1500 WON

15.5500 g., 0.9990 Gold .5 oz. AGW **Subject:** Inter-parliamentary Conference **Obv:** National arms **Rev:** Building

Date	Mintage	F	VF	XF	Unc	BU
1991 Proof	800	Value: 400				

KM# 51 1500 WON

8.0000 g., 0.9990 Gold .2572 oz. AGW **Subject:** Soccer **Obv:** National arms **Rev:** Soccer player in mid-kick

Date	Mintage	F	VF	XF	Unc	BU
1991 Proof	1,000	Value: 250				

KM# 150 1500 WON

8.0000 g., 0.9990 Gold .2569 oz. AGW, 22 mm. **Series:** Olympics **Obv:** National arms **Rev:** Cyclists racing **Edge:** Plain

Date	Mintage	F	VF	XF	Unc	BU
1993	—	—	—	—	300	—

KM# 53 2000 WON

31.1000 g., 0.9990 Gold 1 oz. AGW **Subject:** 80th Birthday of Kim Il Sung **Obv:** National arms **Rev:** Kim Il Sung birthplace

Date	Mintage	F	VF	XF	Unc	BU
ND(1992) Proof	500	Value: 745				

KM# 55 2000 WON

31.1000 g., 0.9990 Gold 1 oz. AGW **Subject:** 80th Birthday of Kim Il Sung **Obv:** National arms **Rev:** Bust facing

Date	Mintage	F	VF	XF	Unc	BU
1992 Proof	500	Value: 745				

KM# 57 2000 WON

31.1000 g., 0.9990 Gold 1 oz. AGW **Subject:** 50th Birthday of Kim Jong Il **Rev:** National arms

Date	Mintage	F	VF	XF	Unc	BU
1992 Proof	500	Value: 745				

KM# 151 2000 WON

31.1035 g., 0.9990 Gold 1.0000 oz. AGW, 40 mm. **Subject:** Death of Kim Il Sung **Obv:** National arms **Rev:** Bust facing **Edge:** Plain

Date	Mintage	F	VF	XF	Unc	BU
ND(1994)	—	—	—	—	725	—

KM# 35 2500 WON

15.5500 g., 0.9990 Gold .5 oz. AGW **Subject:** 30th Anniversary of Gorch Fock **Obv:** National arms **Rev:** Sailing ship

Date	Mintage	F	VF	XF	Unc	BU
1988 Proof	Est. 500	Value: 365				

KM# 81 2500 WON

155.5175 g., 0.9990 Silver 5 oz. ASW, 65 mm. **Obv:** National arms **Rev:** Multicolor panda

Date	Mintage	F	VF	XF	Unc	BU
1995 Proof	2,500	Value: 150				

KM# 82 2500 WON

155.5175 g., 0.9990 Silver 5 oz. ASW **Obv:** National arms **Rev:** Multicolor tiger

Date	Mintage	F	VF	XF	Unc	BU
1995 Proof	2,500	Value: 160				

KM# 83 2500 WON

155.5175 g., 0.9990 Silver 5 oz. ASW **Obv:** National arms **Rev:** Multicolor parrot

Date	Mintage	F	VF	XF	Unc	BU
1995 Proof	2,500	Value: 155				

KM# 85 2500 WON

155.5175 g., 0.9990 Silver 5 oz. ASW **Obv:** National arms **Rev:** Multicolor eurasian eagle owl

Date	Mintage	F	VF	XF	Unc	BU
1995 Proof	2,500	Value: 160				

KM# 86 2500 WON

155.5175 g., 0.9990 Silver 5 oz. ASW **Obv:** National arms **Rev:** Two multicolor falcated ducks

Date	Mintage	F	VF	XF	Unc	BU
1995 Proof	2,500	Value: 160				

KM# 84 2500 WON

155.5175 g., 0.9990 Silver 5 oz. ASW **Obv:** National arms **Rev:** Multicolor eagle

Date	Mintage	F	VF	XF	Unc	BU
1995 Proof	2,500	Value: 155				

PROOF SETS

KM#	Date	Mintage	Identification	Issue Price	Mkt Val
PS1	1995 (5)	300	KM92-96	—	1,350

KOREA-SOUTH

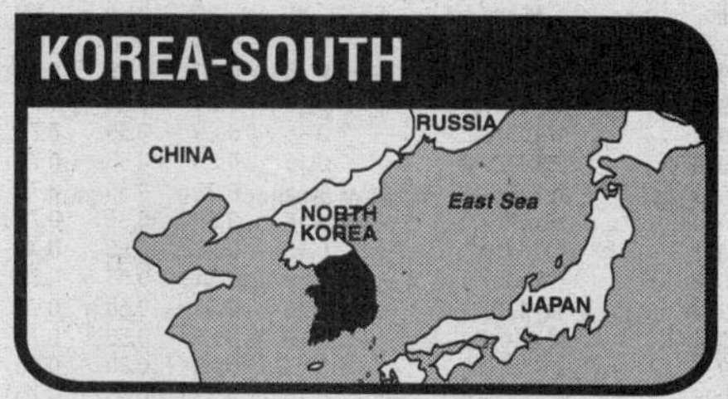

The Republic of Korea, situated in northeastern Asia on the southern half of the Korean peninsula between North Korea and the Korean Strait, has an area of 38,025 sq. mi. (98,480 sq. km.) and a population of 42.5 million. Capital: Seoul. The economy is based on agriculture and light and medium industry. Some of the world's largest oil tankers are built here. Automobiles, plywood, electronics, and textile products are exported.

Japan replaced China as the predominant foreign influence in Korea in 1895 and annexed the peninsular country in 1910. Defeat in World War II brought an end to Japanese rule. U.S. troops entered Korea from the south and Soviet forces entered from the north. The Cairo conference (1943) had established that Korea should be *free and independent*. The Potsdam conference (1945) set the 38th parallel as the line dividing the occupation forces of the United States and Russia. When Russia refused to permit a U.N. commission designated to supervise reunification elections to enter North Korea, an election was held in South Korea on May 10, 1948. By its determination, the Republic of Korea was inaugurated on Aug. 15,1948.

NOTE: For earlier coinage see Korea.

MONETARY SYSTEM
100 Chon = 1 Hwan

REPUBLIC

DECIMAL COINAGE

KM# 1 10 HWAN
2.4600 g., Bronze, 19.1 mm. **Obv:** Value **Rev:** Rose of Sharon

Date	Mintage	F	VF	XF	Unc	BU
KE4292(1959)	100,000,000	2.00	4.00	15.00	25.00	75.00
Note: Issued 10-20-59						
KE4294(1961)	100,000,000	0.30	0.70	1.00	2.50	3.00

KM# 2 50 HWAN
3.6900 g., Nickel-Brass, 22.86 mm. **Obv:** Value **Rev:** Iron-clad turtle boat

Date	Mintage	F	VF	XF	Unc	BU
KE4292(1959)	24,640,000	0.60	1.00	2.00	3.00	5.00
Note: Issued 10-20-59						
KE4294(1961)	20,000,000	0.60	1.00	2.00	3.00	5.00

KM# 3 100 HWAN
6.7400 g., Copper-Nickel, 26 mm. **Obv:** Value flanked by phoenix **Rev:** Bust left

Date	Mintage	F	VF	XF	Unc	BU
KE4292(1959)	—	2.00	3.00	4.00	10.00	15.00

Note: Issued 10-30-59. Quantities of KM#1-3 dated 4292 in uncirculated condition were countermarked "SAMPLE" in Korean for distribution to government and banking agencies. See bank samples section at end of listing. KM#3 was withdrawn from circulation June 10, 1962, and melted; KM#1 and KM#2 continued to circulate as 1 Won and 5 Won coins for 13 years, respectively, until demonetized and withdrawn from circulation March 22, 1975.

REFORM COINAGE

10 Hwan = 1 Won

KM# 4 WON
1.7000 g., Brass, 17.2 mm. **Obv:** Rose of Sharon
Rev: Inscription, value and date

Date	Mintage	F	VF	XF	Unc	BU
1966	7,000,000	0.25	0.50	1.00	9.00	20.00
Note: Issued 8-16-66						
1967	48,500,000	0.10	0.25	0.50	1.50	2.50

KM# 4a WON
0.7290 g., Aluminum, 17.2 mm. **Obv:** Rose of Sharon
Rev: Inscription, value and date

Date	Mintage	F	VF	XF	Unc	BU
1968	66,500,000	—	0.25	0.50	1.00	1.50
Note: Issued 8-26-68						
1969	85,000,000	—	0.10	0.15	0.25	0.50
1970	45,000,000	—	0.10	0.15	0.25	0.50
1974	12,000,000	—	0.25	0.50	2.00	3.00
1975	10,000,000	—	0.10	0.20	0.50	1.00
1976	20,000,000	—	—	—	0.30	0.60
1977	30,000,000	—	—	—	0.30	0.60
1978	30,000,000	—	—	—	0.15	0.25
1979	30,000,000	—	—	—	0.15	0.25
1980	20,000,000	—	—	—	0.15	0.25
1981	20,000,000	—	—	—	0.15	0.25
1982 Proof	2,000	—	—	—	—	—
1982	30,000,000	—	—	—	0.15	0.25

KM# 31 WON
0.7290 g., Aluminum, 17.2 mm. **Obv:** Rose of Sharon
Rev: Value and date

Date	Mintage	F	VF	XF	Unc	BU
1983	40,000,000	—	—	—	0.15	0.25
Note: Issued 1-15-83						
1984	20,000,000	—	—	—	0.15	0.25
1985	10,000,000	—	—	—	0.15	0.25
1987	10,000,000	—	—	—	0.15	0.25
1988	6,500,000	—	—	—	0.15	0.25
1989	10,000,000	—	—	—	0.15	0.25
1990	6,000,000	—	—	—	0.15	0.25
1991	5,000,000	—	—	—	0.15	0.25
1995	15,000	—	—	—	0.15	0.25
1996	15,000	—	—	—	0.15	0.25
1997	15,000	—	—	—	0.15	0.25
1998	—	—	—	—	0.15	0.25
1999	—	—	—	—	0.15	0.25
2000	—	—	—	—	0.15	0.25

KM# 5 5 WON
2.9500 g., Bronze, 20.4 mm. **Obv:** Iron-clad turtle boat
Rev: Value, inscription and date

Date	Mintage	F	VF	XF	Unc	BU
1966	4,500,000	0.15	0.25	1.50	22.50	50.00
Note: Issued 8-16-66						
1967	18,000,000	0.15	0.25	1.00	17.50	50.00
1968	20,000,000	0.15	0.25	1.00	17.50	50.00
1969	25,000,000	—	0.10	0.25	3.25	7.00
1970	50,000,000	—	0.10	0.25	3.00	5.00

KM# 5a 5 WON
2.9500 g., Brass, 20 mm. **Obv:** Iron-clad turtle boat **Rev:** Value, inscription and date

Date	Mintage	F	VF	XF	Unc	BU
1970	Inc. above	—	—	0.10	0.50	1.00
Note: Issued 7-16-70						
1971	64,038,000	—	—	—	0.10	0.20
1972	60,084,000	—	—	—	0.10	0.20
1977	1,000,000	—	—	0.10	0.65	1.00
1978	1,000,000	—	—	0.10	0.65	1.00
1979	1,000,000	—	—	0.10	0.65	1.00
1980	200,000	—	0.25	0.50	2.25	3.00
1981	200,000	—	0.25	0.50	1.50	2.00
1982 Proof	2,000	—	—	—	—	—
1982	200,000	—	0.25	0.50	1.50	2.00

KM# 32 5 WON
2.9500 g., Brass, 20.4 mm. **Obv:** Iron-clad turtle boat **Rev:** Value and date

Date	Mintage	F	VF	XF	Unc	BU
1983	6,000,000	—	—	0.10	0.20	0.30
Note: Issued 1-15-83						
1987	1,000,000	—	—	0.10	0.20	0.30
1988	500,000	—	—	0.10	0.20	0.30
1989	600,000	—	—	0.10	0.20	0.30
1990	600,000	—	—	0.10	0.20	0.30
1991	500,000	—	—	0.10	0.20	0.30
1995	15,000	—	—	0.10	0.20	0.30
1996	15,000	—	—	0.10	0.20	0.30
1997	15,000	—	—	0.10	0.20	0.30
1998	—	—	—	0.10	0.20	0.30
1999	—	—	—	0.10	0.20	0.30
2000	—	—	—	0.10	0.20	0.30

KM# 6 10 WON
4.0600 g., Bronze, 22.86 mm. **Obv:** Pagoda at Pul Guk Temple
Rev: Value, inscription and date

Date	Mintage	F	VF	XF	Unc	BU
1966	10,600,000	0.15	0.25	1.50	25.00	60.00
Note: Issued 8-16-66						
1967	22,500,000	0.15	0.25	1.50	25.00	60.00
1968	35,000,000	0.15	0.25	1.50	18.50	50.00
1969	46,500,000	0.15	0.25	1.50	18.50	90.00
1970	157,000,000	0.15	0.25	1.50	16.50	130

KM# 6a 10 WON
4.0600 g., Brass, 22.86 mm. **Obv:** Pagoda at Pul Guk Temple
Rev: Value, inscription and date

Date	Mintage	F	VF	XF	Unc	BU
1970	Inc. above	—	0.35	1.25	13.50	30.00
Note: Issued 7-16-70						
1971	220,000,000	—	—	0.15	1.75	3.00
1972	270,000,000	—	—	0.15	1.75	3.00
1973	30,000,000	—	0.10	0.35	6.50	15.00
1974	15,000,000	—	0.10	0.35	6.50	15.00
1975	20,000,000	—	0.10	0.50	11.50	30.00
1977	1,000,000	—	0.10	0.35	3.50	8.00
1978	80,000,000	—	0.10	0.15	1.25	2.00
1979	200,000,000	—	—	0.10	0.55	1.00
1980	150,000,000	—	—	0.10	0.55	1.00
1981	100,000	—	0.25	0.75	4.00	10.00
1982	20,000,000	—	—	0.10	0.60	1.10
1982 Proof	2,000	—	—	—	—	—

KM# 33.1 10 WON
4.0600 g., Brass, 22.86 mm. **Obv:** Pagoda at Pul Guk Temple
Rev: Value below date

Date	Mintage	F	VF	XF	Unc	BU
1983	25,000,000	—	—	0.10	0.35	0.50
Note: Issued 1-15-83						
1985	35,000,000	—	—	0.10	0.35	0.50
1986	195,000,000	—	—	0.10	0.35	0.50
1987	155,000,000	—	—	0.10	0.35	0.50
1988	189,000,000	—	—	0.10	0.35	0.50
1989	310,000,000	—	—	0.10	0.35	0.50
1990	395,000,000	—	—	0.10	0.35	0.50
1991	300,000,000	—	—	0.10	0.35	0.50
1992	150,000,000	—	—	0.10	0.35	0.50
1993	110,000,000	—	—	0.10	0.35	0.50
1994	300,000,000	—	—	0.10	0.35	0.50
1995	380,000,000	—	—	0.10	0.35	0.50
1996	290,000,000	—	—	0.10	0.35	0.50
1997	177,000,000	—	—	0.10	0.35	0.50
1999	—	—	—	0.10	0.35	0.50
2000	—	—	—	0.10	0.35	0.50

KM# 33.2 10 WON

Brass **Obv:** Pagoda at Pul Guk Temple **Rev:** Value below date

Date	Mintage	F	VF	XF	Unc	BU
1991	—	—	—	0.10	0.35	0.50
1997	—	—	—	0.10	0.35	0.50
1998	—	—	—	0.10	0.35	0.50
1999	—	—	—	0.10	0.35	0.50
2000	—	—	—	0.10	0.35	0.50

KM# 7 50 WON

2.8000 g., 0.9990 Silver .0899 oz. ASW, 16 mm. **Obv:** Arms within floral spray **Rev:** Half figure holding flag facing left

Date	Mintage	F	VF	XF	Unc	BU
KE4303-1970 Proof	4,350	Value: 100				
KE4304-1971 Rare	—	—	—	—	—	—

KM# 20 50 WON

Copper-Nickel **Series:** F.A.O. **Obv:** Text within sagging oat sprig **Rev:** Value below date

Date	Mintage	F	VF	XF	Unc	BU
1972	6,000,000	0.20	0.40	1.00	16.50	40.00
Note: Issued 12-1-72						
1973	40,000,000	—	0.15	0.25	3.50	8.00
1974	25,000,000	—	0.15	0.25	1.50	3.00
1977	1,000,000	—	0.15	0.25	2.00	3.50
1978	15,000,000	—	0.15	0.25	1.25	2.50
1979	20,000,000	—	0.10	0.20	1.25	2.00
1980	10,000,000	—	0.10	0.20	1.25	2.00
1981	25,000,000	—	0.10	0.20	1.25	2.00
1982	40,000,000	—	0.10	0.20	0.75	1.50
1982 Proof	2,000	—	—	—	—	—

KM# 34 50 WON

4.1600 g., Copper-Nickel, 21.16 mm. **Series:** F.A.O. **Obv:** Text below sagging oat sprig **Rev:** Value and date **Note:** Die varieties exist.

Date	Mintage	F	VF	XF	Unc	BU
1983	50,000,000	—	—	0.10	0.45	1.00
Note: Issued 1-15-83						
1984	40,000,000	—	—	0.10	0.45	1.00
1985	4,000,000	—	—	0.10	0.45	1.00
1987	32,000,000	—	—	0.10	0.45	1.00
1988	53,000,000	—	—	0.10	0.45	1.00
1989	70,000,000	—	—	0.10	0.45	0.60
1990	85,000,000	—	—	0.10	0.35	0.60
1991	80,000,000	—	—	0.10	0.35	0.60
1992	50,000,000	—	—	0.10	0.35	0.60
1993	5,000,000	—	—	0.10	0.35	0.50
1994	102,000,000	—	—	0.10	0.35	0.50
1995	98,000,000	—	—	0.10	0.35	0.50
1996	52,000,000	—	—	0.10	0.35	0.50
1997	129,000,000	—	—	0.10	0.35	0.50
1998	—	—	—	0.10	0.35	0.50
1999	—	—	—	0.10	0.35	0.50
2000	—	—	—	0.10	0.35	0.50

KM# 8 100 WON

5.6000 g., 0.9990 Silver .1798 oz. ASW, 21 mm. **Obv:** Arms within floral spray **Rev:** Standing figure and boat

Date	Mintage	F	VF	XF	Unc	BU
KE4303-1970 Proof	4,350	Value: 400				

KM# 9 100 WON

5.4200 g., Copper-Nickel, 24 mm. **Obv:** Bust with hat facing **Rev:** Value and date within designed wreath

Date	Mintage	F	VF	XF	Unc	BU
1970	1,500,000	0.50	0.75	1.50	18.50	50.00
Note: Issued 11-30-70						
1971	13,000,000	0.15	0.25	0.50	13.50	45.00
1972	20,000,000	—	0.20	0.40	11.50	40.00
1973	80,000,000	—	0.15	0.30	3.00	5.00
1974	50,000,000	—	0.15	0.35	4.50	10.00
Note: Die varieties exist						
1975	75,000,000	—	0.15	0.35	6.00	15.00
Note: Die varieties exist						
1977	30,000,000	—	0.15	0.35	2.25	5.00
1978	50,000,000	—	0.15	0.25	1.50	3.00
1979	130,000,000	—	0.15	0.25	1.50	3.00
1980	60,000,000	—	0.15	0.25	1.50	3.00
1981	100,000	—	0.25	0.50	4.00	6.50
1982 Proof	2,000	—	—	—	—	—
1982	70,000,000	—	0.15	0.25	1.25	2.00

KM# 21 100 WON

12.0000 g., Copper-Nickel, 30 mm. **Subject:** 30th Anniversary of Liberation **Obv:** Gate of Liberty **Rev:** Standing figures and value

Date	Mintage	F	VF	XF	Unc	BU
ND(1975)	4,998,000	0.30	0.60	0.90	2.25	—
Note: Issued 8-15-75						
ND(1975) Proof	2,000	Value: 170				

KM# 24 100 WON

12.0000 g., Copper-Nickel, 30 mm. **Subject:** 1st Anniversary of the 5th Republic **Obv:** Yin-yang symbol within rectangle above value flanked by flames **Rev:** Cluster of flowers

Date	Mintage	F	VF	XF	Unc	BU
1981	4,980,000	0.20	0.35	0.65	2.00	—
Note: Issued 8-81						
1981 Unfrosted, Proof	18,000	Value: 25.00				
1981 Proof	2,000	Value: 165				

KM# 35.1 100 WON

5.4200 g., Copper-Nickel, 24 mm. **Obv:** Bust with hat facing **Rev:** Value and date

Date	Mintage	F	VF	XF	Unc	BU
1983	8,000,000	—	0.15	0.25	0.60	1.00
Note: Issued 1-15-83						

KM# 35.2 100 WON

5.4200 g., Copper-Nickel, 24 mm. **Obv:** Bust with hat facing **Rev:** Value and date

Date	Mintage	F	VF	XF	Unc	BU
1984	40,000,000	—	0.15	0.25	0.60	1.00
1985	25,000,000	—	0.15	0.30	1.25	3.00
1986	131,000,000	—	0.15	0.25	0.60	1.00
1987	170,000,000	—	0.15	0.25	0.55	0.75
1988	298,000,000	—	0.15	0.25	0.55	0.75
1989	250,000,000	—	0.15	0.25	0.55	0.75
1990	185,000,000	—	0.15	0.25	0.55	0.75
1991	400,000,000	—	0.15	0.25	0.55	0.75
1992	425,000,000	—	0.15	0.25	0.55	0.75
1993	185,000,000	—	0.15	0.25	0.55	0.75
1994	401,000,000	—	0.15	0.25	0.55	0.75
1995	228,000,000	—	0.15	0.25	0.55	0.75
1996	447,000,000	—	0.15	0.25	0.55	0.75
1997	147,000,000	—	0.15	0.25	0.55	0.75
1999	—	—	0.15	0.25	0.55	0.75
2000	—	—	0.15	0.25	0.55	0.75

KM# 10 200 WON

11.2000 g., 0.9990 Silver .3596 oz. ASW, 28 mm. **Obv:** Arms within floral spray **Rev:** Celadon vase

Date	Mintage	F	VF	XF	Unc	BU
KE4303-1970 Proof	4,200	Value: 200				

KM# 11 250 WON

14.0000 g., 0.9990 Silver .4497 oz. ASW, 30 mm. **Obv:** Arms above flower flanked by phoenix **Rev:** Bust facing

Date	Mintage	F	VF	XF	Unc	BU
KE4303-1970 Proof	4,100	Value: 400				

KM# 12 500 WON

28.0000 g., 0.9990 Silver .8994 oz. ASW, 40 mm. **Obv:** Arms within floral spray **Rev:** Half length female figure holding tea cup within circle

Date	Mintage	F	VF	XF	Unc	BU
KE4303-1970 Proof	4,700	Value: 300				

KM# 22 500 WON

17.0000 g., Copper-Nickel, 32 mm. **Subject:** 42nd World Shooting Championships **Obv:** Symbol above value **Rev:** Marksman with text to right and below

Date	Mintage	F	VF	XF	Unc	BU
1978	980,000	0.35	0.75	1.50	4.50	—
1978 Unfrosted, proof	18,000	Value: 27.50				
1978 Proof	2,000	Value: 200				

KM# 27 500 WON
7.7000 g., Copper-Nickel, 26.5 mm. **Obv:** Manchurian crane **Rev:** Value and date

Date	Mintage	F	VF	XF	Unc	BU
1982	15,000,000	—	—	1.00	3.75	8.00
Note: Issued 6-12-82						
1982 Proof	2,000	—	—	—	—	—
1983	64,000,000	—	—	1.00	2.50	5.00
1984	70,000,000	—	—	1.00	2.50	5.00
1987	1,000,000	—	—	1.00	2.50	5.00
1988	27,000,000	—	—	1.00	2.50	5.00
1989	25,000,000	—	—	1.00	2.50	5.00
1990	60,000,000	—	—	1.00	2.50	5.00
1991	90,000,000	—	—	1.00	2.50	5.00
1992	105,000,000	—	—	1.00	2.50	5.00
1993	32,000,000	—	—	1.00	2.50	5.00
1994	50,600,000	—	—	1.00	2.50	5.00
1995	87,000,000	—	—	1.00	2.50	5.00
1996	122,000,000	—	—	1.00	2.50	5.00
1997	62,000,000	—	—	1.00	2.50	5.00
1998	—	—	—	1.00	2.50	5.00
1999	—	—	—	1.00	2.50	5.00
2000	—	—	—	1.00	2.50	5.00

KM# 13 1000 WON
56.0000 g., 0.9990 Silver 1.7988 oz. ASW **Subject:** U.N. Forces in South Korea **Obv:** Arms within floral spray **Rev:** Korean and UN flags with four uniformed heads left within circle

Date	Mintage	F	VF	XF	Unc	BU
KE4303-1970 Proof	4,050	Value: 600				

KM# 14.1 1000 WON
3.8700 g., 0.9000 Gold .1119 oz. AGW, 16 mm. **Obv:** Arms within floral spray **Rev:** Great South Gate in Seoul

Date	Mintage	F	VF	XF	Unc	BU
KE4303-1970 Proof	1,500	Value: 350				

KM# 14.2 1000 WON
3.8700 g., 0.9000 Gold .1119 oz. AGW, 16 mm. **Obv:** Arms within floral spray **Rev:** Great South Gate in Seoul

Date	Mintage	F	VF	XF	Unc	BU
KE4303-1970(a) Proof	100	Value: 1,250				

KM# 25 1000 WON
17.0000 g., Nickel, 33 mm. **Subject:** 1st Anniversary of the 5th Republic **Obv:** Yin-yang symbol within rectangle above value flanked by flames **Rev:** Imaginary bird called Bong-hwang who represents a King

Date	Mintage	F	VF	XF	Unc	BU
1981	1,880,000	1.00	1.25	1.50	6.00	—
Note: Released in 8-81						
1981 Unfrosted, proof	18,000	Value: 27.50				
1981 Proof	2,000	Value: 250				

KM# 28 1000 WON
17.0000 g., Copper-Nickel, 33 mm. **Series:** 1988 Olympics **Obv:** Dancers **Rev:** Flower design and value within sprigs

Date	Mintage	F	VF	XF	Unc	BU
1982	1,980,000	—	—	1.25	4.00	—
1982 Unfrosted, proof	10,000	Value: 20.00				
1982 Proof	10,000	Value: 35.00				

KM# 36 1000 WON
17.0000 g., Copper-Nickel, 33 mm. **Series:** 1988 Olympics **Obv:** Drummer within lined design **Rev:** Flower design and value within sprigs

Date	Mintage	F	VF	XF	Unc	BU
1983 Proof	101,000	Value: 20.00				
1983	330,000	—	—	1.25	4.00	—
1983 Unfrosted, Proof	56,000	Value: 15.00				

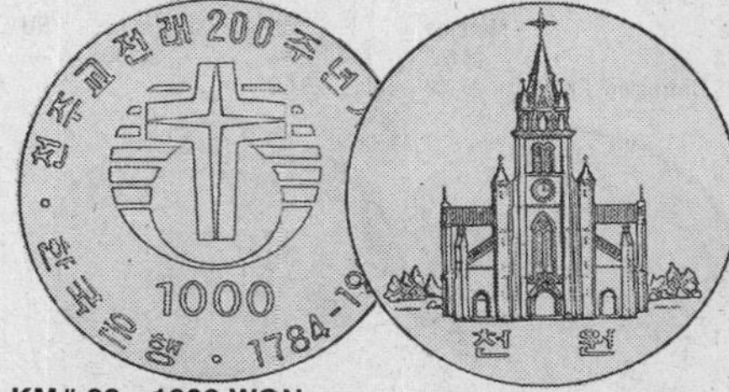

KM# 39 1000 WON
17.0000 g., Copper-Nickel, 33 mm. **Subject:** 200 Years of Catholic Church in Korea **Obv:** Cross above value **Rev:** Myung Dong Cathedral

Date	Mintage	F	VF	XF	Unc	BU
1984	572,000	—	—	1.50	5.00	—

KM# 41 1000 WON
17.0000 g., Copper-Nickel, 33 mm. **Subject:** 10th Asian Games **Obv:** Artistic design above flowers **Rev:** Lion dance

Date	Mintage	F	VF	XF	Unc	BU
1986	930,000	—	—	1.25	4.00	—
1986 Proof	70,000	Value: 10.00				

KM# 46 1000 WON
12.0000 g., Copper-Nickel, 30 mm. **Series:** 1988 Olympics **Obv:** Arms above floral spray **Rev:** Basketball players

Date	Mintage	F	VF	XF	Unc	BU
1986	560,000	—	—	—	4.00	—
1986 Proof	140,000	Value: 18.00				

KM# 47 1000 WON
Copper-Nickel, 30 mm. **Series:** 1988 Olympics **Obv:** Arms above floral spray **Rev:** Tennis player

Date	Mintage	F	VF	XF	Unc	BU
1987	560,000	—	—	—	4.00	—
1987 Proof	140,000	Value: 10.00				

KM# 48 1000 WON
12.0000 g., Copper-Nickel, 30 mm. **Series:** 1988 Olympics **Obv:** Arms above floral spray **Rev:** Handball players

Date	Mintage	F	VF	XF	Unc	BU
1987	560,000	—	—	—	4.00	—
1987 Proof	140,000	Value: 10.00				

KM# 49 1000 WON
Copper-Nickel, 30 mm. **Series:** 1988 Olympics **Obv:** Arms above floral spray **Rev:** Table tennis

Date	Mintage	F	VF	XF	Unc	BU
1988	560,000	—	—	—	4.00	—
1988 Proof	140,000	Value: 10.00				

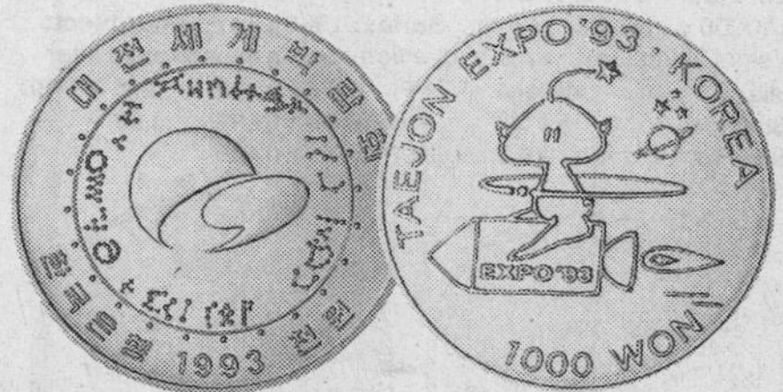

KM# 78 1000 WON
12.5600 g., Copper-Nickel, 30 mm. **Subject:** Taejon International Exposition **Obv:** Circular symbols within circle **Rev:** Mascot of the Expo, Kumdori

Date	Mintage	F	VF	XF	Unc	BU
1993	590,000	—	—	—	5.00	—

Note: Metal content is copper 94% and nickel 6% giving this coin a golden brass color

KM# 87 1000 WON

Copper-Nickel **Subject:** 50th Anniversary of U.N.

Date	Mintage	F	VF	XF	Unc	BU
1995	1,000	—	—	—	10.00	—

KM# 50 2000 WON

17.0000 g., Nickel, 33 mm. **Series:** 1988 Olympics **Obv:** Arms above floral spray **Rev:** Boxing

Date	Mintage	F	VF	XF	Unc	BU
1986	560,000	—	—	—	6.50	—
1986 Proof	140,000	Value: 22.00				

KM# 51 2000 WON

17.0000 g., Nickel, 33 mm. **Series:** 1988 Olympics **Obv:** Arms above floral spray **Rev:** Tae Kwon Do

Date	Mintage	F	VF	XF	Unc	BU
1987	560,000	—	—	—	5.50	—
1987 Proof	140,000	Value: 15.00				

KM# 52 2000 WON

17.0000 g., Nickel, 33 mm. **Series:** 1988 Olympics **Subject:** Wrestling **Obv:** Arms above floral spray **Rev:** Wrestlers

Date	Mintage	F	VF	XF	Unc	BU
1987	560,000	—	—	—	5.50	—
1987 Proof	140,000	Value: 25.00				

KM# 53 2000 WON

17.0000 g., Nickel, 33 mm. **Series:** 1988 Olympics **Subject:** Weight lifting **Obv:** Arms above floral spray **Rev:** Weight lifter

Date	Mintage	F	VF	XF	Unc	BU
1988	560,000	—	—	—	5.50	—
1988 Proof	140,000	Value: 15.00				

KM# 88 2000 WON

10.7000 g., Bi-Metallic Copper-Aluminum-Nickel center in Copper-Nickel ring, 28 mm. **Subject:** New Millennium **Obv:** Astronomical observation instrument **Rev:** Stylized design **Edge:** Reeded **Note:** Korea Minting and Security Printing Corp.

Date	Mintage	F	VF	XF	Unc	BU
2000	—	—	—	—	9.00	10.00

KM# 15.1 2500 WON

9.6800 g., 0.9000 Gold .2801 oz. AGW, 26 mm. **Obv:** Arms within floral spray **Rev:** Crowned head and temple within circle

Date	Mintage	F	VF	XF	Unc	BU
KE4303-1970 Proof	1,750	Value: 500				

KM# 15.2 2500 WON

9.6800 g., 0.9000 Gold .2801 oz. AGW **Obv:** Arms within floral spray **Rev:** Crowned head and temple within circle

Date	Mintage	F	VF	XF	Unc	BU
KE4303-1970(a) Proof	100	Value: 1,500				

KM# 16.1 5000 WON

19.3600 g., 0.9000 Gold .5602 oz. AGW, 32 mm. **Obv:** Arms within floral spray **Rev:** Iron-clad turtle boats

Date	Mintage	F	VF	XF	Unc	BU
KE4303-1970 Proof	670	Value: 1,850				

KM# 16.2 5000 WON

19.3600 g., 0.9000 Gold .5602 oz. AGW **Obv:** Arms within floral spray **Rev:** Iron-clad turtle boats

Date	Mintage	F	VF	XF	Unc	BU
KE4303-1970(a) Proof	70	Value: 2,500				

KM# 23 5000 WON

23.0000 g., 0.9000 Silver .6655 oz. ASW, 35 mm. **Subject:** 42nd World Shooting Championships **Obv:** Artistic design above value **Rev:** Shilla hunter motif

Date	Mintage	F	VF	XF	Unc	BU
1978	80,000	—	—	—	30.00	—
1978 Unfrosted, Proof	20,000	Value: 75.00				

KM# 54 5000 WON

16.8100 g., 0.9250 Silver .5000 oz. ASW, 32 mm. **Series:** 1988 Olympics **Obv:** Arms above floral spray **Rev:** Tiger mascot **Rev. Designer:** Kim Hyan Un

Date	Mintage	F	VF	XF	Unc	BU
1986	117,500	—	—	7.50	12.50	20.00
1986 Proof	227,500	Value: 22.50				

KM# 55 5000 WON

16.8100 g., 0.9250 Silver .5000 oz. ASW, 32 mm. **Series:** 1988 Olympics **Obv:** Arms above floral spray **Rev:** Tug of war

Date	Mintage	F	VF	XF	Unc	BU
1986	117,500	—	—	8.00	13.50	22.50
1986 Proof	227,500	Value: 25.00				

KM# 60 5000 WON

16.8100 g., 0.9250 Silver .5000 oz. ASW, 32 mm. **Series:** 1988 Olympics **Obv:** Arms above floral spray **Rev:** Stadium

Date	Mintage	F	VF	XF	Unc	BU
1987	117,500	—	—	7.50	12.50	20.00
1987 Proof	227,500	Value: 25.00				

KM# 61 5000 WON

16.8100 g., 0.9250 Silver .5000 oz. ASW, 32 mm. **Series:** 1988 Olympics **Obv:** Arms above floral spray **Rev:** Chegi - Kicking

Date	Mintage	F	VF	XF	Unc	BU
1987	117,500	—	—	8.00	13.50	22.50
1987 Proof	227,500	Value: 25.00				

KM# 66 5000 WON

16.8100 g., 0.9250 Silver .5000 oz. ASW, 32 mm. **Series:** 1988 Olympics **Obv:** Arms above floral spray **Rev:** Tae Kwon Do

Date	Mintage	F	VF	XF	Unc	BU
1987	117,500	—	—	7.50	12.50	20.00
1987 Proof	227,500	Value: 25.00				

KM# 67 5000 WON

16.8100 g., 0.9250 Silver .5000 oz. ASW, 32 mm. **Series:** 1988 Olympics **Obv:** Arms above floral spray **Rev:** Girls on swing

Date	Mintage	F	VF	XF	Unc	BU
1987	117,500	—	—	8.00	13.50	22.50
1987 Proof	227,500	Value: 25.00				

KM# 70 5000 WON

16.8100 g., 0.9250 Silver .5000 oz. ASW, 32 mm. **Series:** 1988 Olympics **Obv:** Arms above floral spray **Rev:** Wrestling

Date	Mintage	F	VF	XF	Unc	BU
1988	117,500	—	—	7.50	12.50	20.00
1988 Proof	227,500	Value: 25.00				

KM# 71 5000 WON

16.8100 g., 0.9250 Silver .5000 oz. ASW, 32 mm. **Series:** 1988 Olympics **Obv:** Arms above floral spray **Rev:** Boys spinning top

Date	Mintage	F	VF	XF	Unc	BU
1988	117,500	—	—	7.50	12.50	20.00
1988 Proof	227,500	Value: 25.00				

KM# 79 5000 WON

16.8100 g., 0.9250 Silver .5000 oz. ASW, 32 mm. **Subject:** Taejon International Exposition **Obv:** Circular designs within dotted circle **Rev:** Seated figure spinning yarn

Date	Mintage	F	VF	XF	Unc	BU
1993	120,000	—	—	—	18.50	—

KM# 80 5000 WON

16.8100 g., 0.9250 Silver .5000 oz. ASW, 32 mm. **Subject:** Taejon International Exposition **Obv:** Arms above floral spray **Rev:** Folk musicians

Date	Mintage	F	VF	XF	Unc	BU
1993	120,000	—	—	—	18.50	—

KM# 85 5000 WON

16.0000 g., Nickel, 32 mm. **Subject:** 50th Anniversary - Liberation from Japan **Obv:** Kim-Gu

Date	Mintage	F	VF	XF	Unc	BU
1995	25,000	—	—	—	15.00	—

KM# 96 5000 WON

22.0000 g., Bronze Enamel inlay, 38 mm. **Obv:** Head Office of the Bank of Korea old and new buildings **Rev:** 50th Anniversary of the Bank of Korea

Date	Mintage	F	VF	XF	Unc	BU
2000	—	—	—	—	—	—

KM# 17.1 10000 WON

38.7200 g., 0.9000 Gold 1.1205 oz. AGW **Obv:** Arms above floral spray flanked by phoenix **Rev:** Bust facing

Date	Mintage	F	VF	XF	Unc	BU
KE4303-1970 Proof	435	Value: 5,000				

KM# 17.2 10000 WON

38.7200 g., 0.9000 Gold 1.1205 oz. AGW **Obv:** Arms above floral spray flanked by phoenix **Rev:** Bust facing

Date	Mintage	F	VF	XF	Unc	BU
KE4303-1970(a) Proof	55	Value: 6,000				

KM# 29 10000 WON

15.0000 g., 0.9000 Silver .4340 oz. ASW, 30 mm. **Series:** 1988 Olympics **Obv:** Great South Gate, Seoul **Rev:** Stylized flower above value within wreath

Date	Mintage	F	VF	XF	Unc	BU
1982	280,000	—	—	12.00	13.50	15.00
1982 Unfrosted, proof	10,000	Value: 45.00				
1982 Proof	10,000	Value: 65.00				

KM# 37 10000 WON

15.0000 g., 0.9000 Silver .4340 oz. ASW, 30 mm. **Series:** 1988 Olympics **Obv:** Pavilion of Kyongbok Palace **Rev:** Stylized flower above value within wreath

Date	Mintage	F	VF	XF	Unc	BU
1983	137,000	—	—	12.00	13.50	15.00
1983 Unfrosted, Proof	56,000	Value: 25.00				
1983 Proof	101,000	Value: 35.00				

KM# 40 10000 WON

22.3000 g., 0.5000 Silver .3739 oz. ASW, 36 mm. **Subject:** 200 Years of Catholic Church in Korea **Obv:** Cross within sectioned circle above value **Rev:** Standing haloed figures facing

Date	Mintage	F	VF	XF	Unc	BU
1984	152,000	—	—	15.00	20.00	22.50

KM# 42 10000 WON

23.0000 g., 0.9000 Silver .6655 oz. ASW, 35 mm. **Subject:** 10th Asian Games **Obv:** Arms above floral spray **Rev:** Badminton

Date	Mintage	F	VF	XF	Unc	BU
1986	130,000	—	—	12.00	13.50	15.00
1986 Proof	70,000	Value: 24.00				

KM# 43 10000 WON

23.0000 g., 0.9000 Silver .6655 oz. ASW, 35 mm. **Subject:** 10th Asian Games **Obv:** Arms above floral spray **Rev:** Soccer players

Date	Mintage	F	VF	XF	Unc	BU
1986	130,000	—	—	12.00	13.50	15.00
1986 Proof	70,000	Value: 24.00				

KM# 56 10000 WON

33.6200 g., 0.9250 Silver 1.0000 oz. ASW, 40 mm. **Series:** 1988 Olympics **Obv:** Arms above floral spray **Rev:** Marathon runner

Date	Mintage	F	VF	XF	Unc	BU
1986	117,500	—	—	15.00	20.00	25.00
1986 Proof	227,500	Value: 30.00				

KM# 57 10000 WON

33.6200 g., 0.9250 Silver 1.0000 oz. ASW, 40 mm. **Series:** 1988 Olympics **Subject:** Diving **Obv:** Arms above floral spray **Rev:** High diver

Date	Mintage	F	VF	XF	Unc	BU
1987	117,500	—	—	15.00	20.00	25.00
1987 Proof	227,500	Value: 30.00				

Date	Mintage	F	VF	XF	Unc	BU
1988	15,000	—	—	16.00	22.50	30.00
1988 Proof	110,000	Value: 40.00				

KM# 62 10000 WON
33.6200 g., 0.9250 Silver 1.0000 oz. ASW, 40 mm. **Series:** 1988 Olympics **Subject:** Archery **Obv:** Arms above floral spray **Rev:** Archer

Date	Mintage	F	VF	XF	Unc	BU
1987	117,500	—	—	15.00	20.00	25.00
1987 Proof	227,500	Value: 30.00				
1988	Inc. above	—	—	—	200	—
1988 Proof	Inc. above	Value: 90.00				

Note: 1988 is an error date

KM# 63 10000 WON
33.6200 g., 0.9250 Silver 1.0000 oz. ASW, 40 mm. **Series:** 1988 Olympics **Subject:** Volleyball **Obv:** Arms above floral spray **Rev:** Volleyball game

Date	Mintage	F	VF	XF	Unc	BU
1987	117,500	—	—	15.00	20.00	25.00
1987 Proof	227,500	Value: 30.00				

KM# 74 10000 WON
33.6200 g., 0.9250 Silver 1.0000 oz. ASW, 40 mm. **Series:** 1988 Olympics **Subject:** Gymnastics **Obv:** Arms above floral spray **Rev:** Gymnast

Date	Mintage	F	VF	XF	Unc	BU
1988	15,000	—	—	16.00	22.50	30.00
1988 Proof	110,000	Value: 40.00				

KM# 75 10000 WON
33.6200 g., 0.9250 Silver 1.0000 oz. ASW, 40 mm. **Series:** 1988 Olympics **Subject:** Equestrian events **Obv:** Arms above floral spray **Rev:** Equestrian jumping

KM# 76 10000 WON
33.6200 g., 0.9250 Silver 1.0000 oz. ASW, 40 mm. **Series:** 1988 Olympics **Subject:** Cycling **Obv:** Arms above floral spray **Rev:** Cyclists

Date	Mintage	F	VF	XF	Unc	BU
1988	15,000	—	—	16.00	22.50	30.00
1988 Proof	110,000	Value: 40.00				

KM# 77 10000 WON
33.6200 g., 0.9250 Silver 1.0000 oz. ASW, 40 mm. **Series:** 1988 Olympics **Obv:** Arms above floral spray **Rev:** Soccer players

Date	Mintage	F	VF	XF	Unc	BU
1988	15,000	—	—	16.00	22.50	30.00
1988 Proof	110,000	Value: 40.00				

KM# 81 10000 WON
33.6200 g., 0.9250 Silver 1.0000 oz. ASW, 40 mm. **Subject:** Taejon International Exposition **Obv:** Stylized yin-yang within dotted circle **Rev:** Porcelain celadon

Date	Mintage	F	VF	XF	Unc	BU
1993	100,000	—	—	—	30.00	—

KM# 86 10000 WON
23.0000 g., 0.9000 Silver .6655 oz. ASW, 35 mm. **Subject:** 50th Anniversary of Liberation from Japan **Obv:** Ahn Jong-Kun

Date	Mintage	F	VF	XF	Unc	BU
1995	40,000	—	—	—	35.00	—

KM# 84 10000 WON
22.5000 g., 0.9250 Silver .6691 oz. ASW **Subject:** 50th Anniversary - Republic of Korea **Obv:** National yin-yang symbol within small circle above flowers **Rev:** Numeral 50 with doves on the 0 **Note:** With multicolor enamel and with gold-plated center insert.

Date	Mintage	F	VF	XF	Unc	BU
ND(1998)	100,000	—	—	—	35.00	—

KM# 18.1 20000 WON
77.4000 g., 0.9000 Gold 2.2398 oz. AGW, 55 mm. **Obv:** Arms within floral spray **Rev:** Gold crown - Silla Dynasty

Date	Mintage	F	VF	XF	Unc	BU
KE4303-1970 Proof	382	Value: 8,750				

KM# 18.2 20000 WON
77.4000 g., 0.9000 Gold 2.2398 oz. AGW **Obv:** Arms within floral spray **Rev:** Gold Crown - Silla Dynasty

Date	Mintage	F	VF	XF	Unc	BU
KE4303-1970(a) Proof	52	Value: 10,000				

KM# 26 20000 WON
22.5300 g., 0.9000 Silver .6655 oz. ASW, 35 mm. **Subject:** 1st Anniversary of the 5th Republic **Obv:** Arms above floral sprays **Rev:** Faint national yin-yang symbol above assorted uniformed busts left **Note:** Man, woman, laborer, soldier, student all symbolize the Korean will for unity.

Date	Mintage	F	VF	XF	Unc	BU
1981	80,000	—	—	25.00	30.00	—
Note: Issued 8-81						
1981 Unfrosted, proof	18,000	Value: 35.00				
1981 Proof	2,000	Value: 300				

KM# 30 20000 WON
23.0000 g., 0.9000 Silver .6655 oz. ASW, 35 mm. **Series:** 1988 Olympics **Obv:** Stylized torch and flame within globe **Rev:** Stylized flower above value within wreath

Date	Mintage	F	VF	XF	Unc	BU
1982 Unfrosted, proof	10,000	Value: 50.00				
1982 Proof	10,000	Value: 70.00				

KM# 38 20000 WON
23.0000 g., 0.9000 Silver .6655 oz. ASW, 35 mm. **Series:** 1988 Olympics **Subject:** Wrestling **Obv:** Wrestlers **Rev:** Stylized flower above value within wreath

Date	Mintage	F	VF	XF	Unc	BU
1983	123,000	—	—	25.00	30.00	—
1983 Unfrosted, proof	56,000	Value: 40.00				
1983 Proof	101,000	Value: 45.00				

KM# 44 20000 WON
28.0000 g., 0.9000 Silver, 38 mm. **Subject:** 10th Asian Games **Obv:** Artistic design above flowers **Rev:** Runner

Date	Mintage	F	VF	XF	Unc	BU
1986	130,000	—	—	25.00	30.00	—
1986 Proof	70,000	Value: 45.00				

KM# 45 20000 WON
28.0000 g., 0.9000 Silver, 38 mm. **Subject:** 10th Asian Games **Obv:** Artistic design above flowers **Rev:** Pul Guk Temple - Kyong Ju City

Date	Mintage	F	VF	XF	Unc	BU
1986	130,000	—	—	25.00	30.00	—
1986 Proof	70,000	Value: 40.00				

KM# 19.1 25000 WON
96.8000 g., 0.9000 Gold 2.8012 oz. AGW, 60 mm. **Subject:** King Sejong The Great **Obv:** Arms within floral spray **Rev:** Seated figure facing reading from a book within circle

Date	Mintage	F	VF	XF	Unc	BU
KE4303-1970 Proof	325	Value: 14,000				

KM# 19.2 25000 WON
96.8000 g., 0.9000 Gold 2.8012 oz. AGW, 60 mm. **Subject:** King Sejong The Great **Obv:** Arms within floral spray **Rev:** Seated figure facing reading from a book

Date	Mintage	F	VF	XF	Unc	BU
KE4303-1970(a) Proof	25	Value: 17,000				

KM# 58 25000 WON
16.8100 g., 0.9250 Gold .5000 oz. AGW, 27 mm. **Series:** 1988 Olympics **Obv:** Arms above floral spray **Rev:** Folk dancing

Date	Mintage	F	VF	XF	Unc	BU
1986	42,500	—	—	—	340	350
1986 Proof	117,500	Value: 360				

KM# 64 25000 WON
16.8100 g., 0.9250 Gold .5000 oz. AGW, 27 mm. **Series:** 1988 Olympics **Obv:** Arms above floral spray **Rev:** Fan dancing

Date	Mintage	F	VF	XF	Unc	BU
1987	42,500	—	—	—	340	350
1987 Proof	117,500	Value: 360				

KM# 68 25000 WON
16.8100 g., 0.9250 Gold .5000 oz. AGW, 27 mm. **Series:** 1988 Olympics **Obv:** Arms above floral spray **Rev:** Kite flying

Date	Mintage	F	VF	XF	Unc	BU
1987	47,500	—	—	—	340	350
1987 Proof	47,500	Value: 360				
1988	—	—	—	—	340	350
1988 Proof	—	Value: 360				

KM# 72 25000 WON
16.8100 g., 0.9250 Gold .5000 oz. AGW, 27 mm. **Series:** 1988 Olympics **Obv:** Arms above floral spray **Rev:** Korean Seesaw

Date	Mintage	F	VF	XF	Unc	BU
1988	42,500	—	—	—	340	350
1988 Proof	117,500	Value: 360				

KM# 82 25000 WON
16.8100 g., 0.9250 Gold .5000 oz. AGW **Subject:** Taejon International Exposition **Obv:** Stylized yin-yang within multiple circles **Rev:** Celestial globe

Date	Mintage	F	VF	XF	Unc	BU
1993	40,000	—	—	—	—	375

KM# 59 50000 WON
33.6200 g., 0.9250 Gold 1.0000 oz. AGW, 33 mm. **Series:** 1988 Olympics **Obv:** Arms above floral spray **Rev:** Turtle boat

Date	Mintage	F	VF	XF	Unc	BU
1986 Proof	30,000	Value: 725				

KM# 65 50000 WON
33.6200 g., 0.9250 Gold 1.0000 oz. AGW, 33 mm. **Series:** 1988 Olympics **Obv:** Arms above floral spray **Rev:** Great South Gate

Date	Mintage	F	VF	XF	Unc	BU
1987 Proof	30,000	Value: 725				

KM# 69 50000 WON
33.6200 g., 0.9250 Gold 1.0000 oz. AGW, 33 mm. **Series:** 1988 Olympics **Obv:** Arms above floral spray **Rev:** Stylized horse and rider

Date	Mintage	F	VF	XF	Unc	BU
1987 Proof	30,000	Value: 725				

KM# 73 50000 WON
33.6200 g., 0.9250 Gold 1.0000 oz. AGW, 33 mm. **Series:** 1988 Olympics **Obv:** Arms above floral spray **Rev:** Pul Guk Temple

Date	Mintage	F	VF	XF	Unc	BU
1988 Proof	30,000	Value: 725				

KM# 83 50000 WON
33.6200 g., 0.9250 Gold 1.0000 oz. AGW **Subject:** Taejon International Exposition **Obv:** Arms above floral spray **Rev:** Tower of Great Light

Date	Mintage	F	VF	XF	Unc	BU
1993	10,000	—	—	—	775	—

BANK SAMPLES

Korean

NOTE: Bank samples countermarked in Korean Sample have been prepared for government and banking agencies.

KM#	Date	Mintage	Identification	Issue Price	Mkt Val
S2	KE4292	—	50 Hwan. Nickel-Brass. KM2.	—	75.00
S3	KE4292	—	100 Hwan. Copper-Nickel. KM3.	—	90.00
S1	KE4292	—	10 Hwan. Bronze. KM1.	—	65.00
S4	1967	—	Won. Brass. KM4.	—	—
S5	1975	—	100 Won. Copper-Nickel. KM21.	—	—
S6	1978	—	500 Won. Copper-Nickel. KM22.	—	—
S7	1978	—	5000 Won. Silver. KM23.	—	—
S8	1984	—	20000 Won. Silver. KM26.	—	—
S9	1984	—	50000 Won. Silver. KM40.	—	—

MINT SETS

KM#	Date	Mintage	Identification	Issue Price	Mkt Val
MS1	Mixed dates (6)	75,000	KM6a(1980), 32, 34, 35.1 (1983), 27, 31 (1984) Issued as a presentation set for the World Bank Conference in Seoul, October 1985.	—	60.00
MS2	1983 (6)	—	KM27, 31-32, 33.1, 34, 35.1	—	60.00
MS3	1986 (5)	130,000	KM41-45	113	100
MSA4	1988	—	KM#46-53 Olympics	—	40.00
MS4	1991 (6)	—	KM27, 31-32, 33.1, 34, 35.2	—	12.00
MS5	1993 (6)	10,000	KM78-83	1,180	1,200
MS6	1993 (5)	30,000	KM78-82	443	450
MS7	1993 (4)	50,000	KM78-81	97.00	100
MS8	2001 (7)	—	KM#27, 31, 32, 33.2, 34, 35.2, 89	10.00	12.50

PROOF SETS

KM#	Date	Mintage	Identification	Issue Price	Mkt Val
PS1	1970 (12)	—	KM7-8, 10-13, 14.1-19.1	752	31,500
PS2	1970 (11)	—	KM7-8, 10-13, 14.2-18.2	—	22,350
PS3	1970 (6)	—	KM7-8, 10-13	53.50	1,100
PS4	1970 (6)	300	KM14.1-19.1	698	32,000
PS5	1970 (6)	25	KM14.2-19.2	—	38,250
PS6	1982 (6)	2,000	KM4a-6a, 9, 20, 27, (presentation set) Original, intact sets are worth substantially more than their individual components.	—	835
PS7	1986 (6)	350,000	KM#41, 50, 54-56, 58	275	465
PS8	1986 (5)	70,000	KM41-45	170	145
PS9	1986 (2)	—	KM46, 50	—	40.00
PSA9	1986 (6)	160,000	KM#46, 50, 54-56, 58	275	475

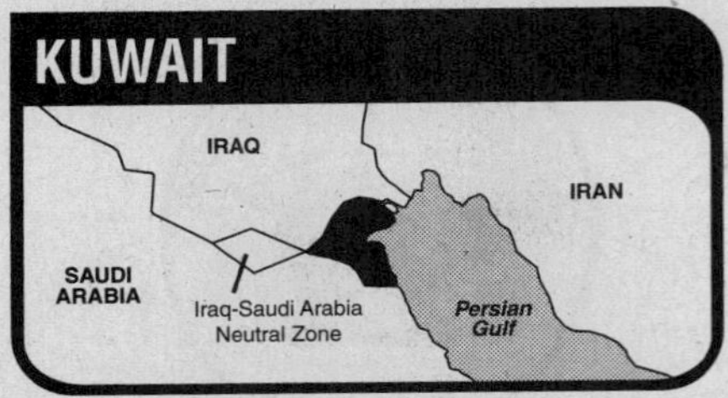

The State of Kuwait, a constitutional monarchy located on the Arabian Peninsula at the northwestern corner of the Persian Gulf, has an area of 6,880 sq. mi. (17,820 sq. km.) and a population of 1.7 million. Capital: Kuwait. Petroleum, the basis of the economy, provides 95 percent of the exports.

The modern history of Kuwait began with the founding of the city of Kuwait, 1740, by tribesmen who wandered northward from the region of the Qatar Peninsula of eastern Arabia. Fearing that the Turks would take over the sheikhdom, Sheikh Mubarak entered into an agreement with Great Britain, 1899, placing Kuwait under the protection of Britain and empowering Britain to conduct its foreign affairs. Britain terminated the protectorate on June19, 1961, giving Kuwait its independence (by a simple exchange of notes) but agreeing to furnish military aid on request.

Kuwait was invaded and occupied by an army from neighboring Iraq Aug. 2, 1990. Soon thereafter Iraq declared that the country would become a province of Iraq. An international coalition of military forces primarily based in Saudi Arabia led by the United States under terms set by the United Nations, attacked Iraqi military installations to liberate Kuwait. This occurred Jan. 17, 1991. Kuwait City was liberated Feb.27, and a cease-fire was declared Feb. 28. New paper currency was introduced March 24, 1991 to replace earlier notes.

TITLE

al-Kuwait

RULER

British Protectorate, until 1961

LOCAL

Al Sabah Dynasty

Mubarak Ibn Sabah, 1896-1915
Jabir Ibn Mubarak, 1915-1917
Salim Ibn Mubarak, 1917-1921
Ahmad Ibn Jabir, 1921-1950
Abdullah Ibn Salim, 1950-1965
Sabah Ibn Salim, 1965-1977
Jabir Ibn Ahmad, 1977-

MONETARY SYSTEM

1000 Fils = 1 Dinar

STATE OF KUWAIT

MODERN COINAGE

KM# 2 FILS

2.0000 g., Nickel-Brass, 17 mm. **Ruler:** Abdullah Ibn Salim **Obv:** Value within circle **Rev:** Ship with sails

Date	Mintage	F	VF	XF	Unc	BU
AH1380-1961	2,000,000	—	0.50	1.00	1.50	—
AH1380-1961 Proof	60	Value: 30.00				

KM# 9 FILS

2.0000 g., Nickel-Brass, 17 mm. **Ruler:** Jabir Ibn Ahmad **Obv:** Value within circle **Rev:** Ship with sails

Date	Mintage	F	VF	XF	Unc	BU
AH1382-1962 Proof	60	Value: 30.00				
AH1382-1962	500,000	—	0.10	0.15	0.35	—
AH1384-1964	600,000	—	0.25	0.75	1.50	—
AH1385-1966	500,000	—	0.25	0.75	1.50	—
AH1386-1967	1,875,000	—	0.25	0.75	1.50	—
AH1389-1970	375,000	—	0.35	1.00	2.50	—
AH1391-1971	500,000	—	0.25	0.75	1.50	—
AH1390-1971	500,000	—	0.25	0.75	1.50	—
AH1392-1972	500,000	—	0.25	0.75	1.50	—
AH1393-1973	375,000	—	0.35	1.00	2.50	—
AH1395-1975	500,000	—	0.25	0.75	1.50	—
AH1396-1976	2,500,000	—	0.15	0.25	0.50	—
AH1397-1977	2,500,000	—	0.15	0.25	0.50	—
AH1399-1979	1,500,000	—	0.15	0.25	0.50	—
AH1400-1980	—	—	0.15	0.25	0.50	—
AH1403-1983	—	—	0.15	0.25	0.50	—
AH1407-1987	—	—	0.15	0.25	0.50	—
AH1408-1988	500,000	—	0.15	0.25	0.50	—

KM# 9a FILS

2.4100 g., 0.9250 Silver .0717 oz. ASW, 17 mm. **Ruler:** Jabir Ibn Ahmad **Obv:** Value within circle **Rev:** Ship with sails

Date	Mintage	F	VF	XF	Unc	BU
AH1407-1987 Proof	—	Value: 100				

KM# 9b FILS

4.0400 g., 0.9170 Gold .1191 oz. AGW, 17 mm. **Ruler:** Jabir Ibn Ahmad **Obv:** Value within circle **Rev:** Ship with sails

Date	Mintage	F	VF	XF	Unc	BU
AH1407-1987 Proof	—	Value: 120				

KM# 3 5 FILS

2.5000 g., Nickel-Brass, 19.5 mm. **Ruler:** Abdullah Ibn Salim **Obv:** Value within circle **Rev:** Ship with sails

Date	Mintage	F	VF	XF	Unc	BU
AH1380-1961 (1961)	2,400,000	—	0.60	1.25	2.00	—
AH1380-1961 (1961) Proof	60	Value: 35.00				

KM# 10 5 FILS

2.5000 g., Nickel-Brass, 19.5 mm. **Ruler:** Jabir Ibn Ahmad **Obv:** Value within circle **Rev:** Ship with sails

Date	Mintage	F	VF	XF	Unc	BU
AH1382-1962	1,800,000	—	0.10	0.20	0.45	—
AH1382-1962 Proof	60	Value: 35.00				
AH1382-1962	1,800,000	—	0.10	0.20	0.45	—
AH1382-1962 Proof	60	Value: 35.00				
AH1384-1964	600,000	—	0.30	0.75	2.00	—
AH1386-1967	1,600,000	—	0.20	0.35	1.00	—
AH1388-1968	800,000	—	0.30	0.75	2.25	—
AH1389-1969	—	—	0.30	0.75	2.25	—
AH1389-1970	600,000	—	0.30	0.75	2.25	—
AH1390-1971	600,000	—	0.30	0.75	2.25	—
AH1391-1971	600,000	—	0.30	0.75	2.25	—
AH1392-1972	800,000	—	0.25	0.65	1.75	—
AH1393-1973	800,000	—	0.25	0.65	1.75	—
AH1394-1974	1,200,000	—	0.10	0.20	1.00	—
AH1395-1975	5,020,000	—	0.10	0.20	0.50	—
AH1396-1976	180,000	—	0.35	1.00	3.00	—
AH1397-1977	4,000,000	—	0.10	0.20	0.40	—
AH1399-1979	6,700,000	—	0.10	0.20	0.40	—
AH1400-1980	—	—	0.10	0.20	0.40	—
AH1401-1981	7,000,000	—	0.10	0.20	0.40	—
AH1403-1983	—	—	0.10	0.20	0.40	—
AH1405-1985	—	—	0.10	0.20	0.40	—
AH1407-1987	—	—	0.10	0.20	0.40	—
AH1408-1988	3,000,000	—	0.10	0.20	0.40	—
AH1410-1990	—	—	0.10	0.20	0.40	—
AH1414-1993	—	—	0.10	0.20	0.40	—
AH1415-1994	—	—	0.10	0.20	0.40	—
AH1415-1995	—	—	0.10	0.20	0.40	—
AH1415 1994	—	—	0.10	0.20	0.40	—
Note: Varieties exist						
AH1417-1997	—	—	0.10	0.20	0.40	—

KM# 10a 5 FILS

3.0100 g., 0.9250 Silver .0895 oz. ASW, 19.5 mm. **Ruler:** Jabir Ibn Ahmad **Obv:** Value within circle **Rev:** Ship with sails

Date	Mintage	F	VF	XF	Unc	BU
AH1407 Proof	—	Value: 100				

KM# 10b 5 FILS

5.0500 g., 0.9170 Gold .1488 oz. AGW, 19.5 mm. **Ruler:** Jabir Ibn Ahmad **Obv:** Value within circle **Rev:** Ship with sails

Date	Mintage	F	VF	XF	Unc	BU
AH1407-1987 Proof	—	Value: 145				

KM# 4 10 FILS

3.7500 g., Nickel-Brass, 21 mm. **Ruler:** Abdullah Ibn Salim **Obv:** Value within circle **Rev:** Ship with sails

Date	Mintage	F	VF	XF	Unc	BU
AH1380-1961	2,600,000	—	0.65	1.25	2.00	—
AH1380-1961 Proof	60	Value: 40.00				

KM# 11 10 FILS

3.7500 g., Nickel-Brass, 21 mm. **Ruler:** Jabir Ibn Ahmad **Obv:** Value within circle **Rev:** Ship with sails

Date	Mintage	F	VF	XF	Unc	BU
AH1382-1962	1,360,000	—	0.15	0.25	0.65	—
AH1382-1962 Proof	60	Value: 40.00				
AH1384-1964	800,000	—	0.35	0.85	2.50	—
AH1386-1967	1,360,000	—	0.30	0.75	1.75	—
AH1388-1968	672,000	—	0.35	0.85	2.50	—
AH1389-1969	480,000	—	0.50	1.00	2.75	—
AH1389-1970	640,000	—	0.35	0.85	2.50	—
AH1390-1971	480,000	—	0.50	1.00	2.75	—
AH1391-1971	800,000	—	0.35	0.85	2.50	—
AH1392-1972	1,120,000	—	0.15	0.40	2.00	—
AH1393-1973	1,440,000	—	0.15	0.40	2.00	—
AH1394-1974	1,280,000	—	0.15	0.40	2.00	—
AH1395-1975	5,280,000	—	0.15	0.25	0.75	—
AH1396-1976	2,400,000	—	0.15	0.25	0.75	—
AH1397-1977	—	—	0.15	0.25	0.75	—
AH1399-1979	6,160,000	—	0.15	0.25	0.75	—
AH1400-1980	—	—	0.15	0.25	0.75	—
AH1401-1981	8,320,000	—	0.15	0.25	0.75	—
AH1403-1983	—	—	0.15	0.25	0.75	—
AH1405-1985	—	—	0.15	0.25	0.75	—
AH1407-1987	—	—	0.15	0.25	0.75	—
AH1408-1988	5,000,000	—	0.15	0.25	0.75	—
AH1410-1990	—	—	0.15	0.25	0.75	—
Note: Varieties exist						
AH1415-1995	—	—	0.15	0.25	0.75	—

KM# 11a 10 FILS

4.3500 g., 0.9250 Silver .1294 oz. ASW, 21 mm. **Ruler:** Jabir Ibn Ahmad **Obv:** Value within circle **Rev:** Ship with sails

Date	Mintage	F	VF	XF	Unc	BU
AH1407-1987 Proof	—	Value: 110				

KM# 11b 10 FILS

7.6300 g., 0.9170 Gold .2250 oz. AGW, 21 mm. **Ruler:** Jabir Ibn Ahmad **Obv:** Value within circle **Rev:** Ship with sails

Date	Mintage	F	VF	XF	Unc	BU
AH1407-1987 Proof	—	Value: 225				

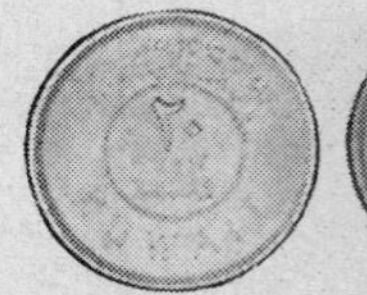

KM# 5 20 FILS

3.0000 g., Copper-Nickel, 20 mm. **Ruler:** Abdullah Ibn Salim **Obv:** Value within circle **Rev:** Ship with sails

Date	Mintage	F	VF	XF	Unc	BU
AH1380-1961	2,000,000	—	0.75	1.50	2.50	—
AH1380-1961 Proof	60	Value: 45.00				

KM# 12 20 FILS

3.0000 g., Copper-Nickel, 20 mm. **Ruler:** Jabir Ibn Ahmad **Obv:** Value within circle **Rev:** Ship with sails **Note:** Varieties exist.

Date	Mintage	F	VF	XF	Unc	BU
AH1382-1962	1,200,000	—	0.25	0.35	0.75	—
AH1382-1962 Proof	60	Value: 45.00				
AH1384-1964	480,000	—	0.50	1.00	3.00	—
AH1386-1967	1,280,000	—	0.35	0.85	2.00	—
AH1388-1968	672,000	—	0.35	0.85	2.50	—
AH1389-1969	800,000	—	0.35	0.85	2.50	—
AH1389-1970	480,000	—	0.50	1.00	3.00	—
AH1391-1971	960,000	—	0.35	0.85	2.00	—
AH1390-1971	480,000	—	0.50	1.00	3.00	—
AH1392-1972	1,440,000	—	0.20	0.45	2.00	—
AH1393-1973	1,280,000	—	0.20	0.45	2.00	—
AH1394-1974	1,600,000	—	0.20	0.45	1.50	—
AH1395-1975	2,400,000	—	0.20	0.30	1.25	—
AH1396-1976	3,200,000	—	0.20	0.30	1.25	—
AH1397-1977	3,400,000	—	0.20	0.30	1.25	—
AH1399-1979	5,520,000	—	0.20	0.30	1.25	—
AH1400-1980	—	—	0.20	0.30	1.00	—
AH1401-1981	8,960,000	—	0.20	0.30	1.00	—
AH1403-1983	—	—	0.20	0.30	1.00	—
AH1405-1985	—	—	0.20	0.30	1.00	—
AH1407-1987	—	—	0.20	0.30	1.00	—
AH1408-1988	5,000,000	—	0.20	0.30	1.00	—
AH1410-1990	—	—	0.20	0.30	1.00	—
AH1415-1995	—	—	0.20	0.30	1.00	—
AH1417-1997	—	—	0.20	0.45	2.00	—

KM# 12a 20 FILS

3.3700 g., 0.9250 Silver .1002 oz. ASW, 20 mm. **Ruler:** Jabir Ibn Ahmad **Obv:** Value within circle **Rev:** Ship with sails

Date	Mintage	F	VF	XF	Unc	BU
AH1407-1987 Proof	—	Value: 110				

KM# 12b 20 FILS

5.6700 g., 0.9170 Gold .1672 oz. AGW, 20 mm. **Ruler:** Jabir Ibn Ahmad **Obv:** Value within circle **Rev:** Ship with sails

Date	Mintage	F	VF	XF	Unc	BU
AH1407-1987 Proof	—	Value: 165				

KM# 6 50 FILS

4.5000 g., Copper-Nickel, 23 mm. **Ruler:** Sabah Ibn Salim **Obv:** Value within circle **Rev:** Ship with sails

Date	Mintage	F	VF	XF	Unc	BU
AH1380-1961	1,720,000	—	0.85	1.75	2.75	—
AH1380-1961 Proof	60	Value: 60.00				

KM# 13 50 FILS

4.5000 g., Copper-Nickel, 23 mm. **Ruler:** Jabir Ibn Ahmad **Obv:** Value within circle **Rev:** Ship with sails

Date	Mintage	F	VF	XF	Unc	BU
AH1382-1962	900,000	—	0.50	0.75	1.25	—
AH1382-1962 Proof	60	Value: 60.00				
AH1384-1964	300,000	—	0.75	1.50	4.00	—
AH1386-1966	800,000	—	0.40	0.85	2.50	—
AH1388-1968	200,000	—	1.00	2.00	6.00	—
AH1389-1969	500,000	—	0.50	1.00	3.00	—
AH1391-1971	500,000	—	0.50	1.00	3.00	—
AH1390-1970	300,000	—	0.75	1.50	4.00	—
AH1392-1972	900,000	—	0.50	0.85	2.50	—
AH1393-1973	800,000	—	0.50	0.85	2.50	—
AH1394-1974	1,000,000	—	0.35	0.50	2.00	—
AH1395-1975	1,950,000	—	0.35	0.50	2.00	—
AH1396-1976	2,250,000	—	0.25	0.35	2.00	—
AH1397-1977	6,000,000	—	0.25	0.35	1.35	—
AH1399-1979	6,050,000	—	0.25	0.35	1.35	—
AH1400-1980	—	—	0.25	0.35	1.35	—
AH1401-1981	3,000,000	—	0.25	0.35	1.35	—
AH1403-1983	—	—	0.25	0.35	1.35	—
AH1405-1985	—	—	0.25	0.35	1.35	—
AH1407-1987	2,000,000	—	0.25	0.35	1.35	—
AH1408-1988	3,000,000	—	0.25	0.35	1.35	—
AH1410-1990	—	—	0.25	0.35	1.35	—
AH1414-1993	—	—	0.25	0.35	1.35	—
AH1413-1992	—	—	0.25	0.35	1.35	—
AH1415-1995	—	—	0.20	0.35	1.35	—
AH1415-1994	—	—	0.25	0.35	1.35	—
Note: Varieties exist						
AH1417-1997	—	—	0.25	0.35	1.35	—
AH1420-1999	—	—	0.25	0.35	1.25	—

KM# 13a 50 FILS

5.0700 g., 0.9250 Silver .1511 oz. ASW, 23 mm. **Ruler:** Jabir Ibn Ahmad **Obv:** Value within circle **Rev:** Ship with sails

Date	Mintage	F	VF	XF	Unc	BU
AH1407-1987 Proof	—	Value: 120				

KM# 13b 50 FILS

8.5200 g., 0.9170 Gold .2512 oz. AGW, 23 mm. **Ruler:** Jabir Ibn Ahmad **Obv:** Value within circle **Rev:** Ship with sails

Date	Mintage	F	VF	XF	Unc	BU
AH1407-1987 Proof	—	Value: 250				

KM# 7 100 FILS

6.5000 g., Copper-Nickel, 26 mm. **Ruler:** Abdullah Ibn Salim **Obv:** Value within circle **Rev:** Ship with sails

Date	Mintage	F	VF	XF	Unc	BU
AH1380-1961	1,260,000	—	1.00	2.00	3.25	—
AH1380-1961 Proof	60	Value: 90.00				

KM# 14 100 FILS

6.5000 g., Copper-Nickel, 26 mm. **Ruler:** Jabir Ibn Ahmad **Obv:** Value within circle **Rev:** Ship with sails

Date	Mintage	F	VF	XF	Unc	BU
AH1382-1962	640,000	—	0.50	0.65	1.50	—
AH1382-1962 Proof	60	Value: 90.00				
AH1384-1964	160,000	—	1.75	3.00	6.00	—
AH1386-1967	640,000	—	1.00	1.50	3.00	—
AH1388-1968	160,000	—	1.75	3.00	6.00	—
AH1389-1969	320,000	—	1.00	2.00	4.00	—
AH1391-1971	240,000	—	1.25	2.00	4.00	—
AH1392-1972	400,000	—	1.00	1.50	3.00	—
AH1393-1973	480,000	—	1.00	1.50	3.00	—
AH1394-1974	480,000	—	1.00	1.50	3.00	—
AH1395-1975	3,040,000	—	0.50	0.75	1.75	—
AH1396-1976	—	—	0.50	0.75	1.75	—
AH1397-1977	1,600,000	—	0.50	0.75	1.75	—
AH1399-1979	3,040,000	—	0.50	0.75	1.75	—
AH1400-1980	—	—	0.50	0.75	1.75	—
AH1401-1981	2,960,000	—	0.50	0.75	1.75	—
AH1403-1983	—	—	0.50	0.75	1.75	—
AH1405-1985	—	—	0.50	0.75	1.75	—
AH1407-1987	2,000,000	—	0.50	0.75	1.75	—
AH1408-1988	2,000,000	—	0.50	0.75	1.75	—
AH1410-1990	—	—	0.50	0.75	1.75	—
AH1415-1995	—	—	0.50	0.75	1.75	—
Note: Varieties exist						
AH1418-1998	—	—	0.50	0.75	1.75	—

KM# 14a 100 FILS

7.3400 g., 0.9250 Silver .2183 oz. ASW, 26 mm. **Ruler:** Jabir Ibn Ahmad **Obv:** Value within circle **Rev:** Ship with sails

Date	Mintage	F	VF	XF	Unc	BU
AH1407 Proof	—	Value: 130				
AH1407-1987 Proof	—	Value: 130				

KM# 14b 100 FILS

12.3300 g., 0.9170 Gold .3635 oz. AGW, 26 mm. **Ruler:** Jabir Ibn Ahmad **Obv:** Value within circle **Rev:** Ship with sails

Date	Mintage	F	VF	XF	Unc	BU
AH1407-1987 Proof	—	Value: 365				

KM# 15 2 DINARS

28.2800 g., 0.5000 Silver .4546 oz. ASW **Ruler:** Sabah Ibn Salim **Subject:** 15th Anniversary of Independence **Obv:** Conjoined busts with traditional gutra headdresses on facing 3/4 left **Rev:** Castle, tower and ships

Date	Mintage	F	VF	XF	Unc	BU
ND(1976)	70,000	—	—	—	42.50	50.00

KM# 15a 2 DINARS

28.2800 g., 0.9250 Silver .8411 oz. ASW **Ruler:** Sabah Ibn Salim **Subject:** 15th Anniversary of Independence **Obv:** Castle, tower and ships **Rev:** Conjoined busts with traditional gutra headdresses on facing 3/4 left

Date	Mintage	F	VF	XF	Unc	BU
ND(1976) Proof	53,000	Value: 65.00				

KM# 24 2 DINARS

28.2800 g., 0.9250 Silver .8411 oz. ASW **Ruler:** Jabir Ibn Ahmad **Subject:** 50th Anniversary - United Nations **Obv:** Sailing ship within circle above dove with open wings within radiant circle **Rev:** United in peace written above designs, number 50, dates and emblem

Date	Mintage	F	VF	XF	Unc	BU
ND(1995) Proof	Est. 110,000	Value: 35.00				

KM# 8 5 DINARS

13.5720 g., 0.9170 Gold .4001 oz. AGW **Ruler:** Abdullah Ibn Salim **Obv:** Value in Arabic in center circle **Rev:** Dhow sailing left

Date	Mintage	F	VF	XF	Unc	BU
AH1380-1961 Rare	Est. 1,000	—	—	—	—	—

KM# 16 5 DINARS

28.2800 g., 0.9250 Silver .8411 oz. ASW **Ruler:** Jabir Ibn Ahmad **Subject:** 15th Century of the Hijira **Obv:** Capital building within circle **Rev:** Courtyard within circle

Date	Mintage	F	VF	XF	Unc	BU
AH1401-1981 Proof	10,000	Value: 55.00				

KM# 18 5 DINARS

28.2800 g., 0.9250 Silver .8411 oz. ASW **Ruler:** Jabir Ibn Ahmad **Subject:** 20th Anniversary of Independence **Obv:** Building, crescent and captains wheel within circle **Rev:** Dates, building, towers and satellite dish within chained circle

Date	Mintage	F	VF	XF	Unc	BU
ND(1981) Proof	10,000	Value: 55.00				

KM# 20 5 DINARS
33.6250 g., 0.9250 Silver 1.0000 oz. ASW **Ruler:** Jabir Ibn Ahmad **Subject:** 25th Anniversary of Kuwait Currency **Obv:** Arabic value, buildings, port scene and refinery **Rev:** English legend, falcon, dhow, building and map on globe

Date	Mintage	F	VF	XF	Unc	BU
ND (1986) Proof	—	Value: 75.00				

KM# 21 50 DINARS
16.9660 g., 0.9170 Gold .5000 oz. AGW **Ruler:** Jabir Ibn Ahmad **Subject:** 25th Anniversary of Kuwait Independence **Obv:** Arabic legend, arched design, falcon, tent, dhow and pearl in a shell **Rev:** Radiant sun, mosque and assembly building with English and Arabic legend

Date	Mintage	F	VF	XF	Unc	BU
AH1406-1986 Proof	—	Value: 400				

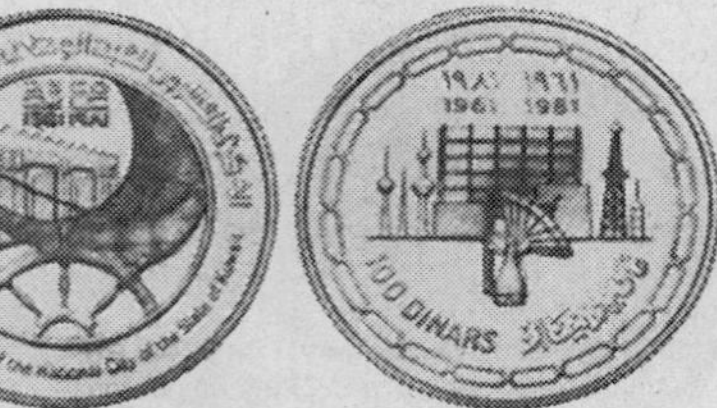

KM# 17 100 DINARS
15.9800 g., 0.9170 Gold .4711 oz. AGW **Ruler:** Jabir Ibn Ahmad **Subject:** 15th Century of the Hijira **Obv:** Building, crescent and captains wheel within circle **Rev:** Dates, building, towers and satellite dish within chained circle

Date	Mintage	F	VF	XF	Unc	BU
AH1401-1981 Proof	10,000	Value: 400				

KM# 19 100 DINARS
15.9800 g., 0.9170 Gold .4711 oz. AGW **Ruler:** Jabir Ibn Ahmad **Subject:** 20th Anniversary of Independence **Obv:** Capital building within circle **Rev:** Courtyard within circle

Date	Mintage	F	VF	XF	Unc	BU
AH1401-1981 Proof	10,000	Value: 400				

MINT SETS

KM#	Date	Mintage	Identification	Issue Price	Mkt Val
MS1	1973 (6)	—	KM9-14	1.75	30.00

PROOF SETS

KM#	Date	Mintage	Identification	Issue Price	Mkt Val
PS1	1961 (6)	60	KM2-7	—	300
PS2	1962 (6)	60	KM9-14	—	300
PS3	1987 (6)	—	KM9a-14a	—	675
PS4	1987 (6)	—	KM9b-14b	—	1,275

KYRGYZSTAN

The Republic of Kyrgyzstan, (formerly Kirghiz S.S.R., a Union Republic of the U.S.S.R.), is an independent state since Aug. 31, 1991, a member of the United Nations and of the C.I.S. It was the last state of the Union Republics to declare its sovereignty. Capital: Bishkek (formerly Frunze).

Originally part of the autonomous Turkestan S.S.R. founded on May 1, 1918, the Kyrgyz ethnic area was established on October 14, 1924, as the Kara-Kirghiz Autonomous Region within the R.S.F.S.R. Then on May 25, 1925, the name Kara (black) was dropped. It became an A.S.S.R. on Feb. 1, 1926, and a Union Republic of the U.S.S.R. in 1936. On Dec. 12, 1990, the name was then changed to the Republic of Kyrgyzstan.

REPUBLIC

STANDARD COINAGE

KM# 1 10 SOM
28.2800 g., 0.9250 Silver .8411 oz. ASW **Subject:** Millennium of Manas **Obv:** Arms within circle above date flanked by sprigs **Rev:** Armored equestrian above mountains, value and flying bird

Date	Mintage	F	VF	XF	Unc	BU
1995 Proof	Est. 20,000	Value: 55.00				

KM# 2 100 SOM
6.2200 g., 0.9990 Gold .2000 oz. AGW **Subject:** Millennium of Manas **Obv:** Arms within circle above date flanked by sprigs **Rev:** Armored equestrian above mountains, value and flying bird

Date	Mintage	F	VF	XF	Unc	BU
1995 Proof	Est. 5,000	Value: 225				

LAOS

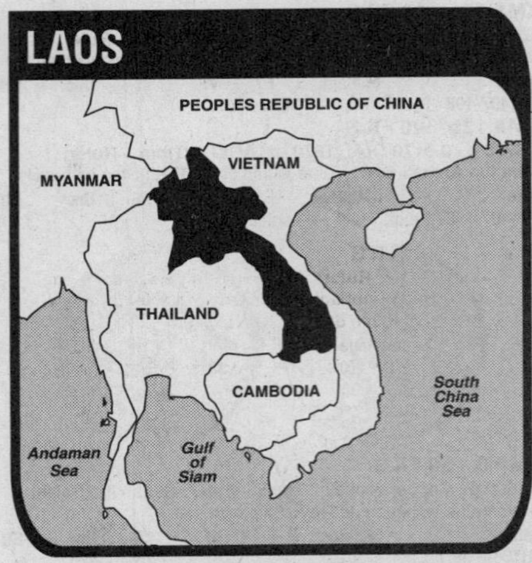

The Lao Peoples Democratic Republic, located on the Indo-Chinese Peninsula between the Socialist Republic of Vietnam and the Kingdom of Thailand, has an area of 91,428 sq. mi. (236,800 km.) and a population of 3.6 million. Capital Vientiane. Agriculture employs 95 percent of the people. Tin, lumber and coffee are exported.

The first United Kingdom of Lan Xang (Million Elephants) was established in the mid-14th century by King Fa Ngum who ruled an area including present Laos, northeastern Thailand, and the southern part of China's Yunnan province from his capital at Luang Prabang. Thailand and Vietnam obtained control over much of the present Lao territory in the 18th century and remained dominant until France established a protectorate over the area in 1893 and incorporated it into the Union of Indo-China. The Independence of Laos was proclaimed in March of 1945, during the last days of the Japanese occupation of World War-II. France reoccupied Laos in 1946, and established it as a constitutional monarchy within the French Union in 1949. In 1953 war erupted between the government and the Pathet Lao, a Communist movement supported by the Vietnamese Communist forces. Peace was declared in 1954 with Laos becoming fully independent in 1955 and the Pathet Lao being permitted to occupy two northern provinces. Civil war broke out again in 1960 with the United States supporting the government of the Kingdom of Laos and the North Vietnamese helping the Communist Pathet Lao, and continued, with intervals of truce and political compromise, until the formation of the Lao Peoples Democratic Republic on Dec. 2, 1975.

NOTE: For earlier coinage, see French Indo-China.

RULERS
Sisavang Vong, 1904-1959
Savang Vatthana, 1959-1975

MONETARY SYSTEM
100 Cents = 1 Piastre
Commencing 1955
100 Att = 1 Kip

MINT MARKS
(a) - Paris, privy marks only
Key - Havana
None - Berlin

NOTE: Private bullion issues previously listed here are now listed in *Unusual World Coins,* 4th Edition, Krause Publications, Inc., 2005.

KINGDOM

STANDARD COINAGE

KM# 4 10 CENTS
Aluminum, 23 mm. **Ruler:** Sisavang Vong **Obv:** Hole in center of head right **Rev:** Hole in center flower design above date

Date	Mintage	F	VF	XF	Unc	BU
1952(a)	2,000,000	—	0.25	0.60	1.25	2.50

KM# 5 20 CENTS
Aluminum, 27 mm. **Ruler:** Sisavang Vong **Obv:** Hole within center of conjoined elephants above date **Rev:** Hole within center of flower design above date

Date	Mintage	F	VF	XF	Unc	BU
1952(a)	3,000,000	—	0.35	0.75	2.00	4.00

KM# 6 50 CENTS
Aluminum, 31 mm. **Ruler:** Sisavang Vong **Obv:** Hole within center of table and book divides radiant sun and date **Rev:** Hole within center of flower design above date

Date	Mintage	F	VF	XF	Unc	BU
1952(a)	1,400,000	—	0.75	1.25	2.50	5.00

KM# 7 1000 KIP
10.0000 g., 0.9250 Silver .2973 oz. ASW **Ruler:** Savang Vatthana **Subject:** King Savang Vatthana Coronation **Obv:** Head right within circle **Rev:** Radiant sun above statue dividing elephant heads with lamps flanking, all within circle

Date	Mintage	F	VF	XF	Unc	BU
1971	—	—	—	—	25.00	—
1971 Proof	20,000	Value: 35.00				

KM# 8 2500 KIP
20.0000 g., 0.9250 Silver .5947 oz. ASW **Ruler:** Savang Vatthana **Subject:** King Savang Vatthana Coronation **Obv:** Head right within circle **Rev:** Radiant sun above statue dividing elephant heads with lamps flanking, all within circle

Date	Mintage	F	VF	XF	Unc	BU
1971	—	—	—	—	35.00	—
1971 Proof	20,000	Value: 45.00				

KM# 9 4000 KIP
4.0000 g., 0.9000 Gold .1157 oz. AGW **Ruler:** Savang Vatthana **Subject:** King Savang Vatthana Coronation **Obv:** Head right within circle **Rev:** Radiant sun above statue dividing elephant heads with lamps flanking, all within circle

Date	Mintage	F	VF	XF	Unc	BU
1971 Proof	10,000	Value: 125				

KM# 10 5000 KIP
40.0000 g., 0.9250 Silver 1.1895 oz. ASW **Ruler:** Savang Vatthana **Subject:** King Savang Vatthana Coronation **Obv:** Head right within circle **Rev:** Radiant sun above statue dividing elephant heads with lamps flanking, circle surrounds all

Date	Mintage	F	VF	XF	Unc	BU
1971	—	—	—	—	100	—
1971 Proof	20,000	Value: 125				

KM# 16.1 5000 KIP
11.7000 g., 0.9250 Silver .3479 oz. ASW **Ruler:** Savang Vatthana **Subject:** Laotian maiden **Obv:** Head right above conjoined elephant heads flanked by lamps **Rev:** Head right above value
Note: Hologram between denomination and "•" on reverse.

Date	Mintage	F	VF	XF	Unc	BU
1975	400	—	—	—	120	—
1975 Proof	775	Value: 125				

KM# 16.2 5000 KIP
11.7000 g., 0.9250 Silver .3479 oz. ASW **Ruler:** Savang Vatthana **Subject:** Laotian maiden **Obv:** Head right above conjoined elephant heads flanked by lamps **Rev:** Head right above value
Note: Hologram between "•" and "LAOS" on reverse.

Date	Mintage	F	VF	XF	Unc	BU
ND(1975)	—	—	—	—	100	—

KM# 17 5000 KIP
11.7000 g., 0.9250 Silver .3479 oz. ASW **Ruler:** Savang Vatthana **Subject:** Wat Phra Kio Museum, Vientiane **Obv:** Head right above conjoined elephant heads flanked by lamps **Rev:** Museum

Date	Mintage	F	VF	XF	Unc	BU
1975	400	—	—	—	120	—
1975 Proof	775	Value: 125				

KM# 11 8000 KIP
8.0000 g., 0.9000 Gold .2315 oz. AGW **Ruler:** Savang Vatthana **Subject:** King Savang Vatthana Coronation **Obv:** Head right within circle **Rev:** Radiant statue divides elephant heads with lamps flanking, all within circle

Date	Mintage	F	VF	XF	Unc	BU
1971 Proof	10,000	Value: 210				

KM# 12 10000 KIP
80.0000 g., 0.9250 Silver 2.3791 oz. ASW **Ruler:** Savang Vatthana **Subject:** King Savang Vatthana Coronation **Obv:** Head right within circle **Rev:** Radiant sun above statue dividing elephant heads with lamps flanking, circle surrounds all

Date	Mintage	F	VF	XF	Unc	BU
1971	—	—	—	—	150	—
1971 Proof	Est. 20,000	Value: 250				

KM# 18 10000 KIP
23.5000 g., 0.9250 Silver .6988 oz. ASW **Ruler:** Savang Vatthana **Subject:** Wat Xieng - Thong Temple **Obv:** Head right above elephant statue and lamps **Rev:** Temple

Date	Mintage	F	VF	XF	Unc	BU
1975	300	—	—	—	170	—
1975 Proof	650	Value: 190				

KM# 13 20000 KIP

20.0000 g., 0.9000 Gold .5787 oz. AGW **Ruler:** Savang Vatthana **Subject:** King Savang Vatthana Coronation **Obv:** Head right **Rev:** Elephant statue flanked by lamps

Date	Mintage	F	VF	XF	Unc	BU
1971 Proof	Est. 10,000	Value: 425				

KM# 14 40000 KIP

40.0000 g., 0.9000 Gold 1.1575 oz. AGW **Ruler:** Savang Vatthana **Subject:** King Savang Vatthana Coronation **Rev:** Elephant statue flanked by lamps

Date	Mintage	F	VF	XF	Unc	BU
1971 Proof	Est. 10,000	Value: 825				

KM# 19 50000 KIP

3.6000 g., 0.9000 Gold .1041 oz. AGW **Ruler:** Savang Vatthana **Obv:** Bust of King Savang Vatthana **Rev:** That Luang Temple

Date	Mintage	F	VF	XF	Unc	BU
1975	100	—	—	—	200	—
1975 Proof	175	Value: 260				

KM# 20 50000 KIP

3.6000 g., 0.9000 Gold .1041 oz. AGW **Ruler:** Savang Vatthana **Obv:** Bust of King Savana Vatthana **Rev:** Bust of Laation maiden 3/4 right

Date	Mintage	F	VF	XF	Unc	BU
1975	100	—	—	—	200	—
1975 Proof	175	Value: 260				

KM# 15 80000 KIP

80.0000 g., 0.9000 Gold 2.3151 oz. AGW **Ruler:** Savang Vatthana **Subject:** King Savang Vatthana Coronation **Obv:** Similar to 20000 Kip, KM#13, head right

Date	Mintage	F	VF	XF	Unc	BU
1971 Proof	—	Value: 1,600				

KM# 21 100000 KIP

7.3200 g., 0.9000 Gold .2118 oz. AGW **Ruler:** Savang Vatthana **Obv:** Bust of King Savang Vatthana **Rev:** Statue of Buddha

Date	Mintage	F	VF	XF	Unc	BU
1975	100	—	—	—	375	—
1975 Proof	100	Value: 450				

PEOPLES DEMOCRATIC REPUBLIC

STANDARD COINAGE

100 Att = 1 Kip

KM# 22 10 ATT

0.9000 g., Aluminum, 21 mm. **Obv:** National arms **Rev:** Half length figure facing holding wheat stalks divides sprigs with value above

Date	Mintage	F	VF	XF	Unc	BU
1980	—	—	0.20	0.40	0.85	—

KM# 23 20 ATT

1.5500 g., Aluminum, 23 mm. **Obv:** National arms **Rev:** Value flanked by designs above ox, man and plow

Date	Mintage	F	VF	XF	Unc	BU
1980	—	—	0.20	0.40	0.85	—

KM# 24 50 ATT

2.5000 g., Aluminum, 26 mm. **Obv:** National arms **Rev:** Value above fish and date flanked by palm trees

Date	Mintage	F	VF	XF	Unc	BU
1980	—	—	0.45	0.90	2.00	—

KM# 37 KIP

Copper-Nickel **Subject:** 10th Anniversary of People's Democratic Republic **Obv:** National arms **Rev:** Value flanked by designs above date

Date	Mintage	F	VF	XF	Unc	BU
1985	—	—	0.50	1.00	2.50	—

KM# 38 5 KIP

Copper-Nickel **Subject:** 10th Anniversary of People's Democratic Republic **Obv:** National arms **Rev:** Value flanked by designs above date

Date	Mintage	F	VF	XF	Unc	BU
1985	—	—	0.75	1.50	4.00	—

KM# 39 10 KIP

Copper-Nickel **Subject:** 10th Anniversary of People's Democratic Republic **Obv:** National arms **Rev:** Value flanked by designs above date

Date	Mintage	F	VF	XF	Unc	BU
1985	—	—	1.25	2.50	6.50	—

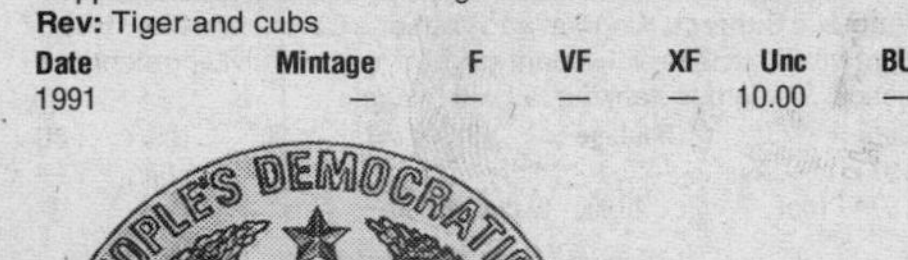

KM# 31 10 KIP

Copper-Nickel, 32.5 mm. **Obv:** National arms **Rev:** 5-masted clipper

Date	Mintage	F	VF	XF	Unc	BU
1988	30,000	—	—	—	9.00	—

KM# 31a 10 KIP

Nickel Bonded Steel, 32.5 mm. **Obv:** National arms **Rev:** 5-masted clipper

Date	Mintage	F	VF	XF	Unc	BU
1988	—	—	—	—	8.50	—

KM# 66 10 KIP

Copper **Obv:** National arms **Rev:** 5-masted clipper

Date	Mintage	F	VF	XF	Unc	BU
1988	—	—	—	—	8.50	10.00
1988 Proof	100	Value: 75.00				

KM# 30 10 KIP

Copper-Nickel **Subject:** World Soccer Championships - Italy 1990 **Obv:** National arms **Rev:** Soccer players

Date	Mintage	F	VF	XF	Unc	BU
1989	2,000	—	—	—	10.00	—

KM# 46 10 KIP

Nickel-Plated Steel **Series:** Olympics **Obv:** National arms **Rev:** Bicyclist

Date	Mintage	F	VF	XF	Unc	BU
1991	5,000	—	—	—	18.50	—

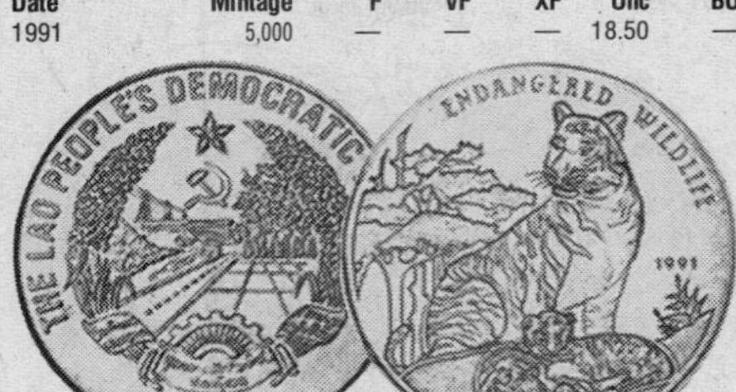

KM# 51 10 KIP

Copper-Nickel **Series:** Endangered Wildlife **Obv:** National arms **Rev:** Tiger and cubs

Date	Mintage	F	VF	XF	Unc	BU
1991	—	—	—	—	10.00	—

KM# 54 10 KIP

Copper **Series:** Endangered Wildlife **Obv:** National arms **Rev:** Tiger and cubs

Date	Mintage	F	VF	XF	Unc	BU
1991	—	—	—	—	12.00	15.00

KM# 50 10 KIP
Copper-Nickel **Series:** Prehistoric Animals **Obv:** National arms **Rev:** Tyranosaurus Rex

Date	Mintage	F	VF	XF	Unc	BU
1993	—	—	—	—	25.00	—

KM# 52 10 KIP
Copper-Nickel **Series:** Prehistoric Animals **Obv:** National arms **Rev:** Lufengosaurus

Date	Mintage	F	VF	XF	Unc	BU
1994	—	—	—	—	25.00	—

KM# 61 10 KIP
Copper-Nickel **Subject:** 1996 World Food Summit **Obv:** National arms **Rev:** Farmer plowing with ox

Date	Mintage	F	VF	XF	Unc	BU
1996	—	—	—	—	10.00	14.00

KM# 70 10 KIP
Copper-Nickel **Series:** XXVII Olympiad **Subject:** Sydney 2000 **Obv:** National arms **Rev:** Sailboats, Neptune

Date	Mintage	F	VF	XF	Unc	BU
1999	10,000	—	—	—	7.00	—

KM# 40 20 KIP
Copper-Nickel **Subject:** 10th Anniversary of People's Democratic Republic **Obv:** National arms within circle and wreath **Rev:** Value flanked by designs above date

Date	Mintage	F	VF	XF	Unc	BU
1985	—	—	1.50	2.50	7.00	—

KM# 25 50 KIP
38.2000 g., 0.9000 Silver 1.1054 oz. ASW **Subject:** 10th Anniversary of People's Democratic Republic **Obv:** National arms **Rev:** Value flanked by designs below towered building

Date	Mintage	F	VF	XF	Unc	BU
1985 Proof	2,000	Value: 42.50				

KM# 26 50 KIP
38.2000 g., 0.9000 Silver 1.1054 oz. ASW **Subject:** 10th Anniversary of People's Democratic Republic **Obv:** National arms **Rev:** Value flanked by designs below towered building

Date	Mintage	F	VF	XF	Unc	BU
1985 Proof	2,000	Value: 42.50				

KM# 27 50 KIP
38.2000 g., 0.9000 Silver 1.1054 oz. ASW **Subject:** 10th Anniversary of People's Democratic Republic **Obv:** National arms **Rev:** Value flanked by designs below building

Date	Mintage	F	VF	XF	Unc	BU
1985 Proof	2,000	Value: 42.50				

KM# 28 50 KIP
38.2000 g., 0.9000 Silver 1.1054 oz. ASW **Subject:** 10th Anniversary of People's Democratic Republic **Obv:** National arms **Rev:** Value flanked by designs below valley of jars

Date	Mintage	F	VF	XF	Unc	BU
1985 Proof	2,000	Value: 42.50				

KM# 41 50 KIP
Copper-Nickel **Subject:** 10th Anniversary of People's Democratic Republic **Obv:** National arms within circle and wreath **Rev:** Value flanked by designs above date

Date	Mintage	F	VF	XF	Unc	BU
1985	—	—	2.00	3.50	8.50	—

KM# 29 50 KIP
16.0000 g., 0.9990 Silver .5145 oz. ASW **Obv:** National arms **Rev:** 5-masted sailship "Prussia"

Date	Mintage	F	VF	XF	Unc	BU
1988 Proof	2,000	Value: 30.00				

KM# 32 50 KIP
12.0000 g., 0.9990 Silver .3855 oz. ASW **Subject:** European Soccer Championship - Germany **Obv:** National arms **Rev:** Soccer players

Date	Mintage	F	VF	XF	Unc	BU
1988	5,000	—	—	—	25.00	—

KM# 33 50 KIP
16.0000 g., 0.9990 Silver .5145 oz. ASW **Subject:** World Soccer Championship - Mexico 86 **Obv:** National arms **Rev:** Soccer players

Date	Mintage	F	VF	XF	Unc	BU
ND(1988) Proof	5,000	Value: 26.50				

KM# 34 50 KIP
16.0000 g., 0.9990 Silver .5145 oz. ASW **Subject:** World Soccer Championship - Italy 1990 **Obv:** National arms **Rev:** Soccer players

Date	Mintage	F	VF	XF	Unc	BU
1989 Proof	5,000	Value: 26.50				

KM# 35.1 50 KIP
16.0000 g., 0.9990 Silver .5145 oz. ASW **Series:** Winter Olympics **Subject:** Ice dancing **Obv:** National arms **Rev:** Ice dancers within design **Note:** Lightly frosted.

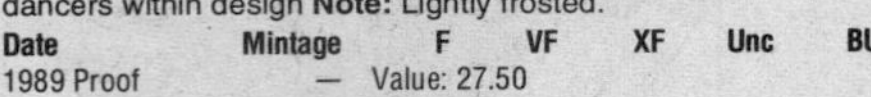

Date	Mintage	F	VF	XF	Unc	BU
1989 Proof	—	Value: 27.50				

KM# 35.2 50 KIP
16.0000 g., 0.9990 Silver .5145 oz. ASW **Series:** Winter Olympics **Subject:** Ice dancing **Obv:** National arms **Rev:** Ice dancers within design **Note:** Extensive frosting.

Date	Mintage	F	VF	XF	Unc	BU
1989 Proof	—	Value: 80.00				

KM# 36.1 50 KIP
16.0000 g., 0.9990 Silver .5145 oz. ASW **Series:** Summer Olympics **Subject:** Water polo **Obv:** National arms **Rev:** Water polo players within frosted water

Date	Mintage	F	VF	XF	Unc	BU
1989 Proof	5,000	Value: 50.00				

KM# 36.2 50 KIP
16.0000 g., 0.9990 Silver .5145 oz. ASW **Series:** Summer Olympics **Subject:** Water polo **Obv:** National arms **Rev:** Water polo players within unfrosted water

Date	Mintage	F	VF	XF	Unc	BU
1989 Proof	—	Value: 27.50				

KM# 44 50 KIP
12.0000 g., 0.9990 Silver .3858 oz. ASW **Subject:** World Cup Soccer **Obv:** National arms **Rev:** Soccer Ball

Date	Mintage	F	VF	XF	Unc	BU
1991	—	—	—	—	25.00	—

KM# 45 50 KIP
20.0000 g., 0.9990 Silver .644 oz. ASW **Subject:** Wildlife **Obv:** National arms **Rev:** Tiger and cubs

Date	Mintage	F	VF	XF	Unc	BU
1991	100	—	—	—	175	—
1991 Proof	—	Value: 35.00				

KM# 47 50 KIP
20.0000 g., 0.9990 Silver .643 oz. ASW **Subject:** Soccer **Obv:** National arms **Rev:** Goalie

Date	Mintage	F	VF	XF	Unc	BU
1991 Proof	—	Value: 32.50				

KM# 48 50 KIP
20.0000 g., 0.9990 Silver .643 oz. ASW **Subject:** Protection of Nature **Obv:** National arms **Rev:** Elephant

Date	Mintage	F	VF	XF	Unc	BU
1993 Proof	—	Value: 45.00				

KM# 49 50 KIP
15.9400 g., 0.9990 Silver .5120 oz. ASW **Series:** Prehistoric Animals **Obv:** National arms **Rev:** Sauroctonus

Date	Mintage	F	VF	XF	Unc	BU
1993 Proof	—	Value: 35.00				

KM# 53 50 KIP
16.0000 g., 0.9990 Silver .5145 oz. ASW **Series:** Prehistoric Animals **Obv:** National arms **Rev:** Elasmosaurus and tylosaurus in combat

Date	Mintage	F	VF	XF	Unc	BU
1994 Proof	—	Value: 50.00				

KM# 82 50 KIP
16.0000 g., 0.9990 Silver .5145 oz. ASW, 37.9 mm. **Subject:** Prehistoric Animals **Obv:** National arms **Rev:** Elasmosaurus fighting a Tylosaurus **Edge:** Plain

Date	Mintage	F	VF	XF	Unc	BU
1994 Proof	—	Value: 50.00				

KM# 84 50 KIP
16.1000 g., 0.9990 Silver 0.512 oz. ASW, 37.9 mm.
Obv: National arms **Rev:** Megalosaurus

Date	Mintage	F	VF	XF	Unc	BU
1994 Proof	—	Value: 30.00				

KM# 56 50 KIP
20.0000 g., 0.9990 Silver .6424 oz. ASW **Series:** Olympics
Obv: National arms **Rev:** Javelin throwers

Date	Mintage	F	VF	XF	Unc	BU
1995 Proof	Est. 15,000	Value: 25.00				

KM# 57 50 KIP
20.0000 g., 0.9990 Silver .6424 oz. ASW **Subject:** World Cup Soccer **Obv:** National arms **Rev:** Player and cathedral

Date	Mintage	F	VF	XF	Unc	BU
1996	100	—	—	—	90.00	—
1996 Proof	10,000	Value: 30.00				

KM# 97 50 KIP
Silver, 37 mm. **Subject:** World Food Summit - 1996 in Rome
Obv: National arms **Rev:** Farmer plowing with ox **Edge:** Reeded

Date	Mintage	F	VF	XF	Unc	BU
1996	—	—	—	—	—	40.00

KM# 63 50 KIP
20.0000 g., 0.9990 Silver .6424 oz. ASW **Series:** XXVII Olympiad **Obv:** National arms **Rev:** Multicolor torch and athletes
Note: Multicolor design.

Date	Mintage	F	VF	XF	Unc	BU
1996 Proof	—	Value: 42.50				

KM# 58 50 KIP
20.0000 g., 0.9990 Silver .6424 oz. ASW **Subject:** World Cup Soccer **Obv:** National arms **Rev:** Stadium within map of France
Note: Multicolor design.

Date	Mintage	F	VF	XF	Unc	BU
1996 Proof	10,000	Value: 40.00				

KM# 62 50 KIP
20.0000 g., 0.9990 Silver .6424 oz. ASW **Series:** XXVII Olympiad
Obv: National arms **Rev:** Archer - Diana, goddess of the hunt

Date	Mintage	F	VF	XF	Unc	BU
1996 Proof	—	Value: 40.00				

KM# 64 50 KIP
15.0000 g., 0.9990 Silver .6423 oz. ASW **Subject:** World of Adventure - Leif Ericson **Obv:** National arms **Rev:** Viking longship

Date	Mintage	F	VF	XF	Unc	BU
1996 Proof	—	Value: 45.00				

KM# 79 50 KIP
15.0000 g., 0.9990 Silver .4818 oz. ASW, 35 mm. **Series:** World Cup Soccer **Obv:** National arms **Rev:** Soccer player with ball and map background **Edge:** Plain

Date	Mintage	F	VF	XF	Unc	BU
1996 Proof	—	Value: 27.50				

KM# 42 100 KIP
3.1500 g., 0.9990 Gold .1012 oz. AGW **Obv:** National arms and legend above value **Rev:** 5-masted sailship "Prussia"

Date	Mintage	F	VF	XF	Unc	BU
1988	500	—	—	—	155	200

KM# 43 100 KIP
3.1500 g., 0.9990 Gold .1012 oz. AGW **Subject:** 10th Anniversary of People's Democratic Republic **Obv:** National arms
Rev: Radiant sun and temple

Date	Mintage	F	VF	XF	Unc	BU
1990	—	—	—	—	160	210

KM# 69 500 KIP
20.0000 g., 0.9250 Silver .5948 oz. ASW **Subject:** Kouprey
Obv: National arms **Rev:** Wild bull

Date	Mintage	F	VF	XF	Unc	BU
1998 Proof	10,000	Value: 50.00				

KM# 165 1000 KIP
31.6700 g., 0.9990 Silver 1.0172 oz. ASW **Series:** Endangered Wildlife **Obv:** National arms **Rev:** Gibbon

Date	Mintage	F	VF	XF	Unc	BU
1996 Proof	—	Value: 60.00				

KM# 67 1000 KIP
31.4700 g., 0.9250 Silver .9359 oz. ASW **Series:** Endangered Wildlife **Obv:** National arms **Rev:** Two long-horned saola

Date	Mintage	F	VF	XF	Unc	BU
1997 Proof	15,000	Value: 45.00				

KM# 59 1200 KIP

Nickel Bonded Steel **Subject:** Food for All **Obv:** National arms **Rev:** Three people harvesting rice below logo and dates

Date	Mintage	F	VF	XF	Unc	BU
ND(1995)	—	—	—	—	8.00	—

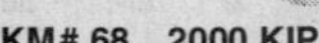

KM# 68 2000 KIP

1.2441 g., 0.9990 Gold .04 oz. AGW **Subject:** That Luang **Obv:** National arms **Rev:** Temple

Date	Mintage	F	VF	XF	Unc	BU
1998 Proof	—	Value: 60.00				

KM# 91 3000 KIP

20.0000 g., 0.9250 Silver 0.5948 oz. ASW, 38.7 mm. **Subject:** Year of the Rabbit **Obv:** National arms **Rev:** Rabbit leaping to right over latent image date **Edge:** Reeded

Date	Mintage	F	VF	XF	Unc	BU
1999 Proof	—	Value: 40.00				

KM# 72 3000 KIP

20.0000 g., 0.9250 Silver .5948 oz. ASW, 38.6 mm. **Subject:** Retrospection Rabbit **Obv:** National arms **Rev:** Multicolor rabbit looking back **Edge:** Reeded

Date	Mintage	F	VF	XF	Unc	BU
1999 Proof	—	Value: 50.00				

KM# 73 3000 KIP

20.0000 g., 0.9250 Silver .5948 oz. ASW **Subject:** Anticipation Rabbit **Obv:** National arms **Rev:** Partially gold-plated rabbit with radiant sun background

Date	Mintage	F	VF	XF	Unc	BU
1999 Proof	—	Value: 50.00				

KM# 60 5000 KIP

7.7600 g., 0.5833 Gold .1458 oz. AGW **Series:** Olympics **Obv:** National arms **Rev:** Two boxers

Date	Mintage	F	VF	XF	Unc	BU
1996	Est. 3,000	—	—	—	110	—

KM# 80 5000 KIP

15.0000 g., 0.9990 Silver .4818 oz. ASW, 35 mm. **Series:** Olympics **Obv:** National arms **Rev:** Archer with statue in background **Edge:** Plain

Date	Mintage	F	VF	XF	Unc	BU
1998 Proof	—	Value: 30.00				

KM# 81 5000 KIP

15.0000 g., 0.9990 Silver .4818 oz. ASW, 35 mm. **Obv:** National arms **Rev:** Multicolor torch and athletes **Edge:** Plain

Date	Mintage	F	VF	XF	Unc	BU
1998 Proof	—	Value: 50.00				

KM# 71 5000 KIP

20.0500 g., 0.9990 Silver .6584 oz. ASW **Series:** XXVII Olympiad **Subject:** Sydney 2000 **Obv:** National arms **Rev:** Sailboats, Neptune

Date	Mintage	F	VF	XF	Unc	BU
1999 Proof	5,000	Value: 35.00				

KM# 92 5000 KIP

15.0000 g., 0.9990 Silver 0.4818 oz. ASW, 35.1 mm. **Obv:** National arms **Rev:** St. Thomas Aquinas **Edge:** Plain

Date	Mintage	F	VF	XF	Unc	BU
1999 Proof	—	Value: 45.00				

KM# 93 5000 KIP

15.1400 g., 0.9990 Silver 0.4863 oz. ASW, 35.1 mm. **Subject:** Third Millennium **Obv:** National arms **Rev:** World map with date 2000/1999 **Edge:** Plain

Date	Mintage	F	VF	XF	Unc	BU
ND(2000) Proof	—	Value: 45.00				

KM# 74 5000 KIP

20.0000 g., 0.9250 Silver .5948 oz. ASW, 39 mm. **Subject:** Silver Dragon Fish **Obv:** National arms **Rev:** Fish **Edge:** Reeded

Date	Mintage	F	VF	XF	Unc	BU
2000-2001 Proof	10,000	Value: 40.00				

Note: Latent image date

KM# 75 5000 KIP

20.0000 g., 0.9250 Silver .5948 oz. ASW, 39 mm. **Subject:** Red Dragon Fish **Obv:** National arms **Rev:** Red colored fish **Edge:** Reeded

Date	Mintage	F	VF	XF	Unc	BU
2000-2001 Proof	10,000	Value: 40.00				

Note: Latent image date

KM# 76 5000 KIP

20.0000 g., 0.9250 Silver .5948 oz. ASW, 39 mm. **Subject:** Golden Dragon Fish **Obv:** National arms **Rev:** Jumping fish below gold cameo **Edge:** Reeded

Date	Mintage	F	VF	XF	Unc	BU
2000-2001 Proof	Est. 4,000	Value: 50.00				

Note: Latent image date

KM# 77 10000 KIP

1.2441 g., 0.9999 Gold .0400 oz. AGW, 14 mm. **Subject:** Golden Dragon Fish **Obv:** National arms **Rev:** Jumping fish **Edge:** Reeded **Note:** Date as a latent image.

Date	Mintage	F	VF	XF	Unc	BU
2000-2001	—	—	—	—	50.00	—

KM# 83 50000 KIP

7.7750 g., 0.9990 Gold 0.2497 oz. AGW, 32.2 mm. **Obv:** National arms **Rev:** Red Dragon Fish **Edge:** Reeded

Date	Mintage	F	VF	XF	Unc	BU
2000-2001 Proof	3,000	Value: 185				

KM# 78 100000 KIP

15.5518 g., 0.9999 Gold .4999 oz. AGW, 27 mm. **Subject:** Golden Dragon Fish **Obv:** National arms **Rev:** Multicolored holographic jumping fish **Edge:** Reeded

Date	Mintage	F	VF	XF	Unc	BU
2000-2001 Proof	3,000	Value: 400				

Note: Latent image date

PIEFORTS WITH ESSAI

Standard metals unless otherwise noted

Double Thickness

KM#	Date	Mintage	Identification	Issue Price	Mkt Val
PE1	1952(a)	104	10 Cents.	—	50.00
PE2	1952(a)	104	20 Cents.	—	60.00
PE3	1952(a)	104	50 Cents.	—	75.00

ESSAIS

Standard metals unless otherwise noted

KM#	Date	Mintage	Identification	Issue Price	Mkt Val
E1	1952(a)	1,200	10 Cents.	—	20.00
E2	1952(a)	1,200	20 Cents.	—	22.50
E3	1952(a)	1,200	50 Cents.	—	25.00

PIEFORTS

KM#	Date	Mintage	Identification	Issue Price	Mkt Val
P1	1988	—	50 Kip. Silver.	—	—

MINT SETS

KM#	Date	Mintage	Identification	Issue Price	Mkt Val
MS1	1971 (4)	—	KM7, 8, 10, 12	—	300
MS2	1975 (6)	100	KM16-21	—	1,300
MS3	1975 (3)	300	KM16-18	—	420

PROOF SETS

KM#	Date	Mintage	Identification	Issue Price	Mkt Val
PS1	1971 (5)	10,000	KM9, 11, 13-15	467	3,000
PS2	1971 (4)	20,000	KM7, 8, 10, 12	163	450
PS3	1975 (6)	—	KM16-21	—	1,450
PS4	1975 (3)	650	KM16-18	—	450
PS5	1975 (3)	—	KM19-21	349	960
PS6	1985 (4)	2,000	KM25-28	—	180

LATVIA

The Republic of Latvia, the central Baltic state in east Europe, has an area of 24,749 sq. mi. (43,601 sq. km.) and a population of *2.6 million. Capital: Riga. Livestock raising and manufacturing are the chief industries. Butter, bacon, fertilizers and telephone equipment are exported.

The Latvians, of Aryan descent primarily from the German Order of Livonian Knights, were nomadic tribesmen who settled along the Baltic prior to the 13th century. Ideally situated as a trade route and lacking a central government, conquered in 1561 by Poland and Sweden. Following the third partition of Poland by Austria, Prussia and Russia in 1795, Latvia came under Russian domination and did not experience autonomy until the Russian Revolution of 1917 provided an opportunity for freedom. The Latvian Republic was established on Nov. 18, 1918. The republic was occupied by Soviet troops and annexed to the Soviet Union in 1940. Following the German occupation of 1941-44, it was retaken by Russia and reestablished as a member republic of the Soviet Union. Western countries, including the United States, did not recognize Latvia's incorporation into the Soviet Union.

The coinage issued during the early 20th Century Republic is now obsolete.

Latvia declared their independence from the U.S.S.R. on August 22, 1991.

MONETARY SYSTEM
100 Santimu = 1 Lats

FIRST REPUBLIC
1918-1939

STANDARD COINAGE
100 Santimu = 1 Lats

KM# 1 SANTIMS
1.6500 g., Bronze, 17 mm. **Obv:** National arms above ribbon **Rev:** Value and date **Edge:** Plain **Note:** Struck at Huguenin Freres, Le Locle, Switzerland.

Date	Mintage	F	VF	XF	Unc	BU
1922	5,000,000	1.00	2.00	3.50	8.00	—
1923	10	—	—	—	1,500	—
1924	4,990,000	1.00	2.00	4.00	8.50	—
1926	5,000,000	1.00	2.00	4.00	8.50	—
1928	5,000,000	1.00	2.00	4.00	8.50	—
Note: Mint name below ribbon						
1928	Inc. above	3.00	6.00	12.00	32.50	—
Note: Without mint name below ribbon						
1932	5,000,000	1.00	2.00	4.00	8.50	—
1932 Proof	—	—	—	—	—	—
1935	5,000,000	1.00	2.00	4.00	8.50	—

KM# 10 SANTIMS
1.8000 g., Bronze, 17 mm. **Obv:** National arms above sprigs **Rev:** Value divides sprigs above date **Edge:** Plain

Date	Mintage	F	VF	XF	Unc	BU
1937	2,700,000	1.00	2.00	4.00	9.00	—
1938	1,900,000	2.00	3.00	6.00	10.00	—
1939	3,400,000	0.50	1.00	2.00	3.00	—
Note: Most were never placed into circulation						

KM# 2 2 SANTIMI
2.0000 g., Bronze, 19.5 mm. **Obv:** National arms above ribbon **Rev:** Value and date **Edge:** Plain

Date	Mintage	F	VF	XF	Unc	BU
1922	10,000,000	1.00	2.00	5.00	10.00	—
Note: Mint name below ribbon						
1922	Inc. above	5.00	10.00	17.50	35.00	—
Note: Without mint name below ribbon						
1923	2	—	—	—	2,000	—
1926	5,000,000	1.00	2.00	5.00	9.00	—
1928	5,000,000	1.00	2.00	5.00	9.00	—
1932	5,000,000	1.00	2.00	5.00	9.00	—
1932 Proof	—	—	—	—	—	—

KM# 11.1 2 SANTIMI
2.0000 g., Bronze, 19 mm. **Obv:** National arms above sprigs **Rev:** Value flanked by sprigs above date **Edge:** Plain

Date	Mintage	F	VF	XF	Unc	BU
1937	45,000	10.00	20.00	30.00	60.00	—

KM# 11.2 2 SANTIMI
2.0000 g., Bronze, 19.5 mm. **Obv:** National arms above sprigs **Rev:** Value flanked by sprigs above date **Edge:** Plain

Date	Mintage	F	VF	XF	Unc	BU
1939	5,000,000	2.00	3.00	4.00	9.00	—
Note: Most were never placed in circulation						

KM# 3 5 SANTIMI
3.0000 g., Bronze, 22 mm. **Obv:** National arms above ribbon **Rev:** Value and date

Date	Mintage	F	VF	XF	Unc	BU
1922	15,000,000	1.00	2.00	3.00	8.00	—
Note: Mint name below ribbon						
1922	Inc. above	3.00	6.00	10.00	20.00	—
Note: Without name below ribbon						
1923	2	—	—	—	2,250	—

KM# 4 10 SANTIMU
3.0000 g., Nickel, 19 mm. **Obv:** National arms above ribbon divides date **Rev:** Value above oat sprig **Edge:** Plain **Note:** Struck at Huguenin.

Date	Mintage	F	VF	XF	Unc	BU
1922	15,000,000	1.00	2.00	4.00	6.00	—

KM# 5 20 SANTIMU
6.0000 g., Nickel, 21 mm. **Obv:** National arms above ribbon divides date **Rev:** Value above oat sprig **Edge:** Plain **Note:** Struck at Huguenin.

Date	Mintage	F	VF	XF	Unc	BU
1922	15,000,000	1.00	2.00	5.00	9.00	—

KM# 6 50 SANTIMU
6.5000 g., Nickel, 25 mm. **Obv:** National arms above ribbon divides date **Rev:** Value to right of standing figure **Edge:** Plain **Note:** Struck at Huguenin.

Date	Mintage	F	VF	XF	Unc	BU
1922	9,000,000	2.00	4.00	6.00	10.00	—

KM# 7 LATS
5.0000 g., 0.8350 Silver .1342 oz. ASW, 23 mm. **Obv:** Arms with supporters **Rev:** Value and date within wreath **Edge:** Milled

Date	Mintage	F	VF	XF	Unc	BU
1923	—	—	—	900	—	—
1924	10,000,000	3.50	6.00	9.00	25.00	—

KM# 8 2 LATI
10.0000 g., 0.8350 Silver .2684 oz. ASW, 27 mm. **Obv:** Arms with supporters **Rev:** Value and date within wreath **Edge:** Milled

Date	Mintage	F	VF	XF	Unc	BU
1925	6,386,000	4.00	6.00	10.00	30.00	—
1926	1,114,000	4.00	6.50	12.00	32.50	—

KM# 9 5 LATI
25.0000 g., 0.8350 Silver .6712 oz. ASW, 37 mm. **Obv:** Crowned head right **Rev:** Arms with supporters above value **Edge:** Plain with DIEVS *** SVETI *** LATVOJU ***

Date	Mintage	F	VF	XF	Unc	BU
1929	1,000,000	12.00	16.00	20.00	45.00	—
1929 Proof	—	—	—	—	—	—
1931	2,000,000	11.00	15.00	18.00	40.00	—
1931 Proof	—	—	—	—	—	—
1932	600,000	15.00	20.00	25.00	50.00	—
1932 Proof	—	—	—	—	—	—

MODERN REPUBLIC
1991-present

STANDARD COINAGE
100 Santimu = 1 Lats

KM# 15 SANTIMS
Copper-Plated Iron, 15.5 mm. **Obv:** National arms **Rev:** Value flanked by diamonds below lined arch

Date	Mintage	F	VF	XF	Unc	BU
1992	—	—	—	—	0.25	0.35
1997	—	—	—	—	0.25	0.35

KM# 21 2 SANTIMI
Bronze-Plated Steel, 17 mm. **Obv:** National arms **Rev:** Lined arch above value flanked by diamonds

Date	Mintage	F	VF	XF	Unc	BU
1992	—	—	—	—	0.50	0.65
2000	—	—	—	—	0.50	0.65

KM# 16 5 SANTIMI
Brass, 18.5 mm. **Obv:** National arms **Rev:** Lined arch above value flanked by diamonds

Date	Mintage	F	VF	XF	Unc	BU
1992	—	—	—	—	0.75	1.00

KM# 17 10 SANTIMU
Brass, 20 mm. **Obv:** National arms **Rev:** Lined arch above value flanked by diamonds

Date	Mintage	F	VF	XF	Unc	BU
1992	—	—	—	—	1.25	1.50

KM# 22 20 SANTIMU
Brass **Obv:** National arms **Rev:** Lined arch above value flanked by diamonds

Date	Mintage	F	VF	XF	Unc	BU
1992	—	—	—	—	1.50	1.75

KM# 13 50 SANTIMU
Copper-Nickel **Obv:** National arms **Rev:** Triple sprig above value

Date	Mintage	F	VF	XF	Unc	BU
1992	—	—	—	—	3.00	3.50

KM# 12 LATS
Copper-Nickel **Obv:** Arms with supporters **Rev:** Fish above value

Date	Mintage	F	VF	XF	Unc	BU
1992	—	—	—	—	4.00	4.50

KM# 23 LATS
28.2800 g., 0.9250 Silver .8411 oz. ASW **Series:** UN 50th Anniversary **Obv:** National arms **Rev:** Many people holding hands

Date	Mintage	F	VF	XF	Unc	BU
1995 Proof	100,000	Value: 42.50				

KM# 39 LATS
15.2000 g., 0.9250 Silver .4520 oz. ASW **Subject:** Millennium **Obv:** Date divides holes within circle **Rev:** Vertical holes within circle, date on bottom **Note:** Button design.

Date	Mintage	F	VF	XF	Unc	BU
1999-2000 Proof	35,000	Value: 55.00				

KM# 44 LATS
20.0000 g., 0.9250 Silver .5948 oz. ASW, 34 mm. **Series:** Olympics **Obv:** National arms **Rev:** Two cyclists **Edge:** Lettered

Date	Mintage	F	VF	XF	Unc	BU
1999 Proof	—	Value: 35.00				

KM# 45 LATS
31.4700 g., 0.9250 Silver .9359 oz. ASW, 38.6 mm. **Subject:** European mink **Obv:** National arms **Rev:** Mink on rock **Edge:** Lettered

Date	Mintage	F	VF	XF	Unc	BU
1999 Proof	—	Value: 60.00				

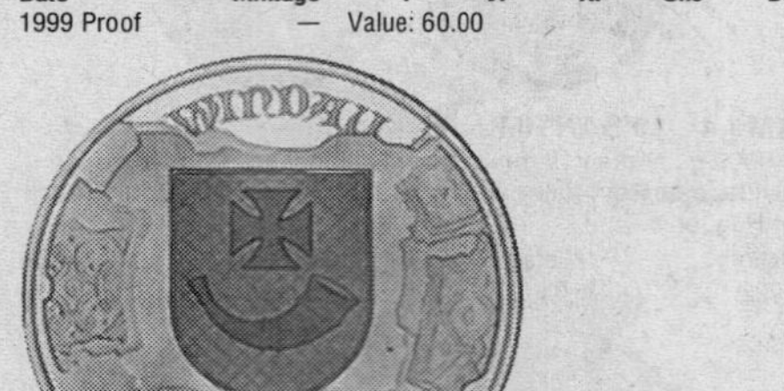

KM# 46 LATS
31.4700 g., 0.9250 Silver .9359 oz. ASW, 38.6 mm. **Subject:** Hanseatic City of Ventspils **Obv:** City arms above value **Rev:** Building and ship **Edge Lettering:** "LATVIJAS REPUBLIKA LATVIJAS BANKA"

Date	Mintage	F	VF	XF	Unc	BU
2000 Proof	—	Value: 50.00				

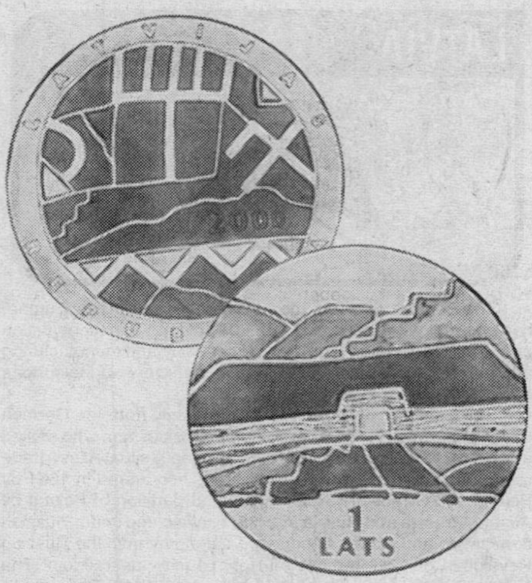

KM# 47 LATS
31.4700 g., 0.9250 Silver .9359 oz. ASW, 38.6 mm. **Subject:** Earth - Roots **Obv:** Stylized "Roots" pattern **Rev:** Landscape and value **Edge:** Plain

Date	Mintage	F	VF	XF	Unc	BU
2000 Proof	6,000	Value: 50.00				

KM# 48 LATS
31.4700 g., 0.9250 Silver .9359 oz. ASW, 38.6 mm. **Subject:** UNICEF **Obv:** National arms **Obv. Legend:** LATVIJAS REPUBLIXA above value **Rev:** Child art and logo **Edge Lettering:** "LATVIJAS BANKA" twice

Date	Mintage	F	VF	XF	Unc	BU
2000 Proof	6,000	Value: 50.00				

KM# 14 2 LATI
Copper-Nickel **Obv:** Arms with supporters **Rev:** Cow grazing above value

Date	Mintage	F	VF	XF	Unc	BU
1992	—	—	—	—	7.00	8.00

KM# 18 2 LATI
Copper-Nickel **Subject:** 75th Anniversary - Declaration of Independence **Obv:** Arms with supporters **Rev:** Artistic lined art above value and dates

Date	Mintage	F	VF	XF	Unc	BU
ND(1993)	4,000,000	—	—	—	9.00	10.00
ND(1993) Proof	200,000	Value: 15.00				

KM# 38 2 LATI
Ring Composition: Copper-Nickel **Center Composition:** Brass **Obv:** Arms with supporters within circle **Rev:** Cow above value within circle

Date	Mintage	F	VF	XF	Unc	BU
1999	—	—	—	—	10.00	12.00

KM# 19 10 LATU
25.1750 g., 0.9250 Silver .7484 oz. ASW **Subject:** 75th Anniversary - Declaration of Independence **Obv:** Arms with supporters **Rev:** Artistic lines and design above value and dates

Date	Mintage	F	VF	XF	Unc	BU
ND(1993) Proof	30,000	Value: 35.00				

KM# 24 10 LATU
31.4700 g., 0.9250 Silver .9359 oz. ASW **Series:** Olympics **Obv:** Arms with supporters **Rev:** Man paddling canoe

Date	Mintage	F	VF	XF	Unc	BU
1994 Proof	30,000	Value: 35.00				

KM# 25 10 LATU
31.4700 g., 0.9250 Silver .9359 oz. ASW **Subject:** Julia Maria **Obv:** National arms **Rev:** 3-masted schooner

Date	Mintage	F	VF	XF	Unc	BU
1995 Proof	20,000	Value: 50.00				

KM# 27 10 LATU
31.4700 g., 0.9250 Silver .9359 oz. ASW **Subject:** 800th Anniversary - Riga **Obv:** Coat of arms from 1368 **Rev:** The Great Gould's coat of arms from 1354

Date	Mintage	F	VF	XF	Unc	BU
1995 (1996) Proof	—	—	—	—	—	—
1995 (1996) Proof	—	Value: 50.00				

KM# 26 10 LATU
31.4700 g., 0.9250 Silver .9359 oz. ASW **Subject:** Riga 800 **Obv:** Standing figure in long robe with turban on head within warped circle **Rev:** First city seal within circle

Date	Mintage	F	VF	XF	Unc	BU
1995 (1996) Proof	Est. 8,000	Value: 50.00				

KM# 33 10 LATU
31.4700 g., 0.9250 Silver .9359 oz. ASW **Series:** Endangered Wildlife **Obv:** Arms with supporters **Rev:** Grieze bird **Edge:** Lettered **Edge Lettering:** LATVIJAS BANKA \ (2x)

Date	Mintage	F	VF	XF	Unc	BU
1996 Proof	15,000	Value: 50.00				

KM# 34 10 LATU
31.4700 g., 0.9250 Silver .9359 oz. ASW **Subject:** Riga - XVI Century **Obv:** Old coin design above value **Rev:** Old city view

Date	Mintage	F	VF	XF	Unc	BU
1996 Proof	—	Value: 50.00				

KM# 36 10 LATU
31.3500 g., 0.9990 Silver 1.0069 oz. ASW **Subject:** 800th Anniversary of Riga **Obv:** Old coin design with St. Christopher within warped circle **Rev:** Old coin design with city arms within partial circle **Edge:** Lettered **Edge Lettering:** LATVIJAS REPUBLIKA LATVIJAS BANKA

Date	Mintage	F	VF	XF	Unc	BU
1996 Proof	—	Value: 50.00				

KM# 28 10 LATU
31.3200 g., 0.9250 Silver .9314 oz. ASW **Obv:** Arms with supporters **Rev:** 12th-century ship above its sunken remains **Edge:** Lettered **Edge Lettering:** LATIJAS BANKAS

Date	Mintage	F	VF	XF	Unc	BU
1997 Proof	15,000	Value: 50.00				

KM# 42 10 LATU
1.2442 g., 0.9990 Gold .0400 oz. AGW, 13.92 mm. **Obv:** Arms with supporters **Rev:** Sailing ship "Julia Maria" **Edge:** Reeded

Date	Mintage	F	VF	XF	Unc	BU
1997 Proof	—	Value: 55.00				

KM# 35 10 LATU
31.4700 g., 0.9250 Silver .9359 oz. ASW **Subject:** Riga - XVII Century **Obv:** Old coin design of arms with supporters **Rev:** Aerial view of walled city

Date	Mintage	F	VF	XF	Unc	BU
1997 Proof	—	Value: 50.00				

KM# 29 10 LATU
1.2441 g., 0.9999 Gold .0400 oz. AGW **Subject:** 800th Anniversary - Riga **Obv:** City arms on old coin design **Rev:** City arms and ship on old coin design

Date	Mintage	F	VF	XF	Unc	BU
1998 Proof	—	Value: 55.00				

KM# 30 10 LATU
31.4700 g., 0.9250 Silver .9359 oz. ASW **Subject:** 800th Anniversary - Riga **Obv:** National song festival procession **Rev:** Crowned Riga city arms

Date	Mintage	F	VF	XF	Unc	BU
1998 Proof	Est. 8,000	Value: 50.00				

KM# 31 10 LATU
31.4700 g., 0.9250 Silver .9359 oz. ASW **Subject:** 800th Anniversary - Riga **Obv:** Liberty Monument **Rev:** City arms with supporters

Date	Mintage	F	VF	XF	Unc	BU
1998 Proof	Est. 8,000	Value: 55.00				

KM# 32 10 LATU
31.4700 g., 0.9250 Silver .9359 oz. ASW **Obv:** National arms **Rev:** 1925 Icebreaker "Krisjanis Valdemars"

Date	Mintage	F	VF	XF	Unc	BU
1998 Proof	10,000	Value: 50.00				

KM# 43 10 LATU
3.1100 g., 0.5830 Gold .0583 oz. AGW, 18.5 mm. **Series:** Olympics **Obv:** Arms with supporters **Rev:** Javelin thrower **Edge:** Reeded

Date	Mintage	F	VF	XF	Unc	BU
1999 Proof	—	Value: 60.00				

KM# 41 20 LATU
7.7760 g., 0.5830 Gold .1458 oz. AGW, 25 mm. **Obv:** Arms with supporters **Rev:** Sailing ship "Gekronte Ehlendt" **Edge:** Reeded

Date	Mintage	F	VF	XF	Unc	BU
1997 Proof	—	Value: 110				

KM# 37 20 LATU
31.4100 g., 0.9210 Silver .9341 oz. ASW **Obv:** City arms **Rev:** Melngalvgu **Edge:** Lettered **Edge Lettering:** LATVIJAS REPUBLIKA LATVIJAS BANKA

Date	Mintage	F	VF	XF	Unc	BU
1997 Proof	—	Value: 50.00				

KM# 20 100 LATU
13.3380 g., 0.8330 Gold .2501 oz. AGW **Subject:** 75th Anniversary - Declaration of Independence **Obv:** Arms with supporters **Rev:** Artistic lined design above value and dates

Date	Mintage	F	VF	XF	Unc	BU
ND(1993) Proof	5,000	Value: 250				

KM# 40 100 LATU
16.2000 g., 0.9990 Gold .5203 oz. AGW, 24 mm. **Subject:** Development **Obv:** Arms with supporters **Rev:** Partial circle within value **Edge:** Reeded and plain sections

Date	Mintage	F	VF	XF	Unc	BU
1998 Proof	—	Value: 500				

PATTERNS

Including off metal strikes

KM#	Date	Mintage	Identification	Mkt Val
Pn1	1922	—	10 Santimu. Silver. KM4.	225
Pn2	1922	—	10 Santimu. Aluminum-Bronze. KM4.	300
Pn3	1924	—	2 Lati. Silver.	300
Pn4	1938	—	2 Santimi. Bronze. KM11.2	600

MINT SETS

KM#	Date	Mintage	Identification	Issue Price	Mkt Val
MS1	1992 (8)	—	KM12-17, 21-22	—	25.00

PROOF SETS

KM#	Date	Mintage	Identification	Issue Price	Mkt Val
PS1	ND (1993) (3)	1,800	KM18-20	—	325

LEBANON

The Republic of Lebanon, situated on the eastern shore of the Mediterranean Sea between Syria and Israel, has an area of 4,015 sq. mi. (10,400 sq. km.) and a population of 3.5 million. Capital: Beirut. The economy is based on agriculture, trade and tourism. Fruit, other foodstuffs and textiles are exported.

Almost at the beginning of recorded history, Lebanon appeared as the well-wooded hinterland of the Phoenicians who exploited its famous forests of cedar. The mountains were a Christian refuge and a Crusader stronghold. Lebanon, the history of which is essentially the same as that of Syria, came under control of the Ottoman Turks early in the 16th century. Following the collapse of the Ottoman Empire after World War I, Lebanon, along with Syria, became a French mandate. The French drew a border around the predominantly Christian Lebanon *Sanjak* or administrative subdivision and on Sept. 1, 1920 proclaimed the area the State of Grand Lebanon (*Etat du Grand Liban*) a republic under French control. France announced the independence of Lebanon on Nov. 26, 1941, but the last British and French troops didn't leave until the end of August 1946.

TITLE

الجمهورية الليبية

al-Jomhuriya(t) al-Lubnaniya(t)

MINT MARKS
(a) - Paris, privy marks only
(u) - Utrecht, privy marks only

MONETARY SYSTEM
100 Piastres = 1 Livre (Pound)

FRENCH PROTECTORATE

STANDARD COINAGE

KM# 9 1/2 PIASTRE
Copper-Nickel, 21 mm. **Obv:** Value within sprigs above date **Rev:** Value within roped wreath flanked by oat sprigs above date

Date	Mintage	F	VF	XF	Unc	BU
1934(a)	200,000	2.00	5.00	12.50	40.00	—
1936(a)	1,200,000	1.25	3.00	7.50	25.00	—

KM# 9a 1/2 PIASTRE
Zinc **Obv:** Value within sprigs above date **Rev:** Value within roped wreath flanked by oat sprigs above date

Date	Mintage	F	VF	XF	Unc	BU
1941(a)	1,000,000	0.50	1.00	4.00	10.00	—

KM# 3 PIASTRE
Copper-Nickel **Obv:** Hole in center of wreath **Rev:** Hole in center flanked by lion heads with value and dates below

Date	Mintage	F	VF	XF	Unc	BU
1925(a)	1,500,000	0.50	2.00	7.50	25.00	—
1931(a)	300,000	1.00	4.00	12.50	45.00	—
1933(a)	500,000	1.00	4.00	10.00	45.00	—
1936(a)	2,200,000	0.50	1.00	6.50	20.00	—

KM# 3a PIASTRE

Zinc **Obv:** Hole in center of wreath **Rev:** Hole in center flanked by lion heads with value and date below

Date	Mintage	F	VF	XF	Unc	BU
1940(a)	2,000,000	0.75	1.50	4.00	10.00	—

KM# 1 2 PIASTRES

Aluminum-Bronze **Obv:** Cedar tree within circle above date **Rev:** Value flanked by stars

Date	Mintage	F	VF	XF	Unc	BU
1924(a)	1,800,000	1.25	3.00	12.50	50.00	—

KM# 4 2 PIASTRES

Aluminum-Bronze **Obv:** Cedar tree **Rev:** Ancient ship

Date	Mintage	F	VF	XF	Unc	BU
1925(a)	1,000,000	3.00	8.00	20.00	80.00	—

KM# 10 2-1/2 PIASTRES

Aluminum-Bronze **Obv:** Hole in center of wreath **Rev:** Hole in center of flowered wreath

Date	Mintage	F	VF	XF	Unc	BU
1940(a)	1,000,000	1.00	2.00	3.50	12.00	—

KM# 2 5 PIASTRES

Aluminum-Bronze **Obv:** Cedar tree within circle **Rev:** Value flanked by stars

Date	Mintage	F	VF	XF	Unc	BU
1924(a)	1,000,000	1.25	3.00	10.00	45.00	—

KM# 5.1 5 PIASTRES

Aluminum-Bronze **Obv:** Cedar tree **Rev:** Ancient ship above value and dates

Date	Mintage	F	VF	XF	Unc	BU
1925(a)	1,500,000	1.00	2.00	8.00	30.00	—

KM# 5.2 5 PIASTRES

Aluminum-Bronze **Obv:** Cedar tree **Rev:** Privy marks to left and right of "5 Piastres"

Date	Mintage	F	VF	XF	Unc	BU
1925(a)	Inc. above	1.00	2.00	7.50	30.00	—
1931(a)	400,000	1.50	4.00	12.50	40.00	—
1933(a)	500,000	1.50	4.00	12.50	40.00	—
1936(a)	900,000	1.00	2.00	7.50	25.00	—
1940(a)	1,000,000	0.75	1.50	5.00	15.00	—

KM# 6 10 PIASTRES

2.0000 g., 0.6800 Silver .0437 oz. ASW **Obv:** Cedar tree on rectangular box **Rev:** Crossed cornucopia above value

Date	Mintage	F	VF	XF	Unc	BU
1929	880,000	3.00	7.00	25.00	70.00	—

KM# 7 25 PIASTRES

5.0000 g., 0.6800 Silver .1093 oz. ASW **Obv:** Cedar tree on rectangular box **Rev:** Crossed cornucopia above value

Date	Mintage	F	VF	XF	Unc	BU
1929	600,000	3.00	7.00	25.00	75.00	—
1933(a)	200,000	4.50	15.00	40.00	125	—
1936(a)	400,000	3.50	10.00	27.50	85.00	—

KM# 8 50 PIASTRES

10.0000 g., 0.6800 Silver .2186 oz. ASW **Obv:** Cedar tree on rectangular box **Rev:** Crossed cornucopia with value above and below

Date	Mintage	F	VF	XF	Unc	BU
1929	500,000	5.00	10.00	40.00	125	—
1933(a)	100,000	7.00	20.00	65.00	190	—
1936(a)	100,000	7.00	17.50	50.00	140	—

WORLD WAR II COINAGE

KM# 11 1/2 PIASTRE

Brass **Obv:** Hole in center flanked by english value **Rev:** Hole in center flanked by value **Note:** Three varieties known. Usually crudely struck, off-center, etc. Perfectly struck, centered uncirculated specimens command a considerable premium. Finely struck coins appear with medal rotation while crude examples have coin rotation. Size of letters also vary.

Date	Mintage	F	VF	XF	Unc	BU
ND(1941)	—	1.00	2.50	5.00	12.00	—

KM# 12 PIASTRE

Brass **Obv:** English value **Rev:** Value **Note:** Two varieties known. Usually crudely struck, off-center, etc. Perfectly struck, centered unc. specimens command a considerable premium.

Date	Mintage	F	VF	XF	Unc	BU
ND(1941)	—	1.00	3.00	7.50	18.00	—

KM# 12a PIASTRE

Aluminum **Obv:** English value **Rev:** Value

Date	Mintage	F	VF	XF	Unc	BU
ND(1941)	—	—	—	—	—	—

KM# 13 2-1/2 PIASTRES

Aluminum **Obv:** English value **Rev:** Value **Designer:** Gilroy Roberts **Note:** Seven varieties known. Usually crudely struck, off-center, etc. Perfectly struck, centered unc. specimens command a considerable premium.

Date	Mintage	F	VF	XF	Unc	BU
ND(1941)	—	1.50	3.50	8.00	20.00	—

KM# 13a 2-1/2 PIASTRES

Aluminum-Bronze **Obv:** English value **Rev:** Value

Date	Mintage	F	VF	XF	Unc	BU
ND(1941)	—	—	650	850	—	—

KM# A14 5 PIASTRES

Aluminum **Obv:** English value **Rev:** Value **Note:** Did not enter circulation in significant numbers.

Date	Mintage	F	VF	XF	Unc	BU
ND(1941)	—	—	—	2,000	3,000	—

REPUBLIC

STANDARD COINAGE

KM# 19 PIASTRE

Aluminum-Bronze, 18 mm.

Date	Mintage	F	VF	XF	Unc	BU
1955(a)	4,000,000	—	0.20	0.50	1.50	3.00

KM# 20 2-1/2 PIASTRES

Aluminum-Bronze **Obv:** Hole in center of wreath flanked by value above **Rev:** Hole in center of wreath

Date	Mintage	F	VF	XF	Unc	BU
1955(a)	5,000,000	—	0.10	0.25	0.50	1.00

KM# 14 5 PIASTRES

Aluminum **Obv:** Cedar tree divides date **Rev:** Value below boat **Designer:** Gilroy Roberts

Date	Mintage	F	VF	XF	Unc	BU
1952(a)	3,600,000	0.75	1.50	3.00	6.00	10.00

KM# 18 5 PIASTRES

Aluminum **Obv:** Cedar tree **Rev:** Wreath with value above and below

Date	Mintage	F	VF	XF	Unc	BU
1954	4,440,000	0.25	0.50	1.00	2.50	5.00

KM# 21 5 PIASTRES

Aluminum-Bronze **Obv:** Cedar tree **Rev:** Lion head and value

Date	Mintage	F	VF	XF	Unc	BU
1955(a)	3,000,000	0.20	0.50	1.00	2.00	3.50
1961(a)	—	0.20	0.40	0.75	1.50	3.00

KM# 25.1 5 PIASTRES

Nickel-Brass, 18 mm. **Obv:** Cedar tree above date **Rev:** Value within wreath

Date	Mintage	F	VF	XF	Unc	BU
1968	2,000,000	—	0.10	0.15	0.20	0.45
1969	4,000,000	—	0.10	0.15	0.20	0.45
1970	—	—	0.10	0.15	0.25	0.50

KM# 25.2 5 PIASTRES
Nickel-Brass, 18 mm. **Obv:** Cedar tree above dates **Rev:** Value within wreath

Date	Mintage	F	VF	XF	Unc	BU
1972(a)	12,000,000	—	—	0.10	0.15	0.35
1975(a)	—	—	—	0.10	0.15	0.35
1980	—	—	—	0.10	0.15	0.35

KM# 15 10 PIASTRES
Aluminum, 21.8 mm. **Obv:** Cedar tree above dates **Rev:** Lion head flanked by value

Date	Mintage	F	VF	XF	Unc	BU
1952(a)	3,600,000	0.75	1.50	5.00	15.00	25.00

KM# 22 10 PIASTRES
Aluminum-Bronze, 21.8 mm. **Obv:** Boat with sail above date **Rev:** Cedar tree above value

Date	Mintage	F	VF	XF	Unc	BU
1955	2,175,000	0.50	1.00	3.50	12.50	18.50

KM# 23 10 PIASTRES
Aluminum-Bronze, 21.8 mm. **Obv:** Boat with sail above date with value at upper left **Rev:** Cedar tree above date

Date	Mintage	F	VF	XF	Unc	BU
1955(a)	6,000,000	0.20	0.40	1.00	2.00	4.00

KM# 24 10 PIASTRES
Copper-Nickel, 21.8 mm. **Obv:** Boat with sail above date with value at upper left **Rev:** Cedar tree above date

Date	Mintage	F	VF	XF	Unc	BU
1961	7,000,000	—	0.15	0.35	1.00	2.00
1961 Proof	—	—	—	—	—	—

KM# 26 10 PIASTRES
Nickel-Brass, 21.8 mm. **Obv:** Cedar tree above dates **Rev:** Value within wreath

Date	Mintage	F	VF	XF	Unc	BU
1968(a)	2,000,000	—	0.10	0.15	0.25	0.50
1969(a)	5,000,000	—	—	0.10	0.20	0.45
1970(a)	8,000,000	—	—	0.10	0.20	0.45
1972(a)	12,000,000	—	—	0.10	0.20	0.45
1975(a)	—	—	—	0.10	0.20	0.45

KM# 16.1 25 PIASTRES
Aluminum-Bronze, 23.3 mm. **Obv:** Cedar tree **Rev:** Value within rectangular box divides wreath and dates

Date	Mintage	F	VF	XF	Unc	BU
1952(u)	7,200,000	0.10	0.40	0.60	1.00	2.00

KM# 16.2 25 PIASTRES
Aluminum-Bronze, 23.3 mm. **Obv:** Cedar tree **Rev:** Value within rectangular box divides wreath and dates **Note:** Different style of inscription and larger date.

Date	Mintage	F	VF	XF	Unc	BU
1961(u)	5,000,000	0.10	0.40	0.50	0.75	1.50

KM# 27.1 25 PIASTRES
Nickel-Brass, 23.3 mm. **Obv:** Cedar tree above dates **Rev:** Value within wreath

Date	Mintage	F	VF	XF	Unc	BU
1968	1,500,000	0.10	0.15	0.25	0.50	1.00
1969	2,500,000	0.10	0.15	0.20	0.40	0.85
1970	—	0.10	0.15	0.20	0.40	0.85
1972	8,000,000	0.10	0.15	0.20	0.30	0.65
1975	—	0.10	0.15	0.20	0.30	0.65

KM# 27.2 25 PIASTRES
Nickel-Brass, 23.3 mm. **Obv:** Cedar tree above dates **Rev:** Value within wreath

Date	Mintage	F	VF	XF	Unc	BU
1980	—	0.10	0.15	0.20	0.30	0.65

KM# 17 50 PIASTRES
4.9710 g., 0.6000 Silver .0959 oz. ASW **Obv:** Cedar tree above dates **Rev:** Value within wreath

Date	Mintage	F	VF	XF	Unc	BU
1952(u)	7,200,000	—	BV	2.50	4.50	7.00

KM# 28.1 50 PIASTRES
Nickel **Obv:** Cedar tree above dates **Rev:** Value within wreath

Date	Mintage	F	VF	XF	Unc	BU
1968	2,000,000	0.20	0.40	0.60	1.00	2.00
1969	3,488,000	0.10	0.25	0.40	0.75	1.50
1970	2,000,000	0.10	0.25	0.40	0.50	1.00
1971	2,000,000	0.10	0.25	0.40	0.50	1.00
1975	—	0.10	0.25	0.40	0.50	1.00
1978	22,400,000	0.10	0.25	0.40	0.50	1.00

KM# 28.2 50 PIASTRES
Nickel **Obv:** Cedar tree above dates **Rev:** Value within wreath

Date	Mintage	F	VF	XF	Unc	BU
1980	—	0.10	0.25	0.40	0.50	1.00

KM# 29 LIVRE
Nickel **Series:** F.A.O. **Obv:** Cedar tree above dates **Rev:** Cluster of fruit above value **Rev. Designer:** Paul Koroleff

Date	Mintage	F	VF	XF	Unc	BU
1968	300,000	0.35	0.75	1.50	3.50	6.00

KM# 30 LIVRE
Nickel, 27.3 mm. **Obv:** Cedar tree above dates **Rev:** Value within wreath **Note:** Varieties exist.

Date	Mintage	F	VF	XF	Unc	BU
1975	—	0.20	0.40	0.60	1.00	2.00
1975 Proof	—	—	—	—	—	—
1977	8,000,000	0.20	0.40	0.60	1.00	2.00
1980	12,000,000	0.20	0.40	0.60	1.00	2.00
1981	—	0.20	0.40	0.60	1.00	2.00
1986	—	0.20	0.40	0.60	1.00	2.00

KM# 32 LIVRE
Copper-Nickel **Series:** 1980 Winter Olympics **Subject:** Lake Placid

Date	Mintage	F	VF	XF	Unc	BU
1980 Proof	40,000	Value: 20.00				

KM# 31 5 LIVRES
Nickel **Series:** F.A.O. **Obv:** Cedar tree above dates **Rev:** Cluster of fruit below radiant sun and value

Date	Mintage	F	VF	XF	Unc	BU
1978	1,000,000	—	—	—	3.00	5.00

KM# 33 10 LIVRES
19.0000 g., 0.5000 Silver .3054 oz. ASW **Series:** 1980 Winter Olympics **Subject:** Lake Placid **Obv:** Olympic rings on top of design **Rev:** Stylized flame

Date	Mintage	F	VF	XF	Unc	BU
1980 Proof	20,000	Value: 65.00				

KM# 35 10 LIVRES
Copper-Nickel **Series:** World Food Day **Obv:** Cedar tree above dates **Rev:** Man, oxen, radiant sun and value

Date	Mintage	F	VF	XF	Unc	BU
1981	15,000	—	—	—	8.50	11.50

KM# 37 50 LIVRES
Stainless Steel **Obv:** Arabic legend above value and cedar tree within circle **Rev:** French legend below value within circle **Shape:** 8-sided

Date	Mintage	F	VF	XF	Unc	BU
1996	—	—	—	0.45	1.00	2.00

KM# 38 100 LIVRES
Copper-Zinc **Obv:** Arabic legend above value within cedar tree **Rev:** French legend and date below value

Date	Mintage	F	VF	XF	Unc	BU
1995	—	—	—	0.65	1.50	2.00
1995 Proof	—	Value: 4.00				
1996	—	—	—	0.65	1.50	2.00
2000	—	—	—	0.65	1.50	2.00

KM# 36 250 LIVRES
Brass, 23.5 mm. **Obv:** Arabic legend above value within tree **Rev:** French legend within beaded circle and value

Date	Mintage	F	VF	XF	Unc	BU
1995	—	—	—	0.75	2.00	2.50
1995 Proof	—	Value: 5.00				
1996	—	—	—	0.75	2.00	2.50
2000	—	—	—	0.75	2.00	2.50

KM# 34 400 LIVRES
8.0000 g., 0.9000 Gold .2315 oz. AGW **Series:** 1980 Winter Olympics **Subject:** Lake Placid **Obv:** Olympic rings on top of design **Rev:** Stylized flame

Date	Mintage	F	VF	XF	Unc	BU
1980 Proof	1,000	Value: 600				

KM# 39 500 LIVRES
Stainless Steel, 24.5 mm. **Obv:** Arabic legend above value within tree **Rev:** French legend below value and dates within circle

Date	Mintage	F	VF	XF	Unc	BU
1995	—	—	—	1.00	2.50	3.00
1995 Proof	—	Value: 6.00				
1996	—	—	—	1.00	2.50	3.00
2000	—	—	—	1.00	2.50	3.00

ESSAIS

Standard metals unless otherwise noted

KM#	Date	Mintage	Identification	Mkt Val
E1	1924(a)	—	5 Piastres. Aluminum-Bronze. KM2.	100
E2	1925(a)	—	Piastre. Copper-Nickel. KM3.	80.00
E3	1925(a)	—	2 Piastres. Aluminum-Bronze. KM1.	110
E4	1925(a)	—	5 Piastres. Aluminum-Bronze. KM5.1.	90.00
E5	1929(a)	—	Piastre. Copper-Nickel. KM3.	90.00
E6	1929	—	10 Piastres. Silver. KM6.	120
E7	1929	—	25 Piastres. Silver. KM7.	125
E8	1929	—	50 Piastres. Silver. KM8.	125

KM#	Date	Mintage	Identification	Mkt Val
E9	1934 A	—	1/2 Piastre. Copper-Nickel. Value within sprigs above date. Value within roped circle flanked by sprigs above date. KM9.	100

KM#	Date	Mintage	Identification	Mkt Val
E10	1940(a)	—	2-1/2 Piastres. Aluminum-Bronze. KM10.	50.00
E11	1972	—	5 Piastres. Nickel-Brass. KM25.	15.00
E12	1972(a)	—	10 Piastres. Nickel-Brass. KM26.	15.00
E13	1980	—	25 Piastres. Nickel-Brass. KM27.	15.00
E14	1980	—	50 Piastres. Nickel. KM28.	17.50
E15	1980	—	Livre. Nickel. KM30.	20.00
E16	1981	—	10 Livres. Copper-Nickel. KM35.	40.00

PIEFORTS

KM#	Date	Mintage	Identification	Mkt Val
P1	1980	3,000	Livre. Copper-Nickel. KM32.	45.00
P2	1980	3,000	10 Livres. Silver. KM33.	120
P3	1980	750	400 Livres. Gold. KM34.	1,400

PROOF SETS

KM#	Date	Mintage	Identification	Issue Price	Mkt Val
PS1	1995 (3)	—	KM#36, 38, 39	—	15.00

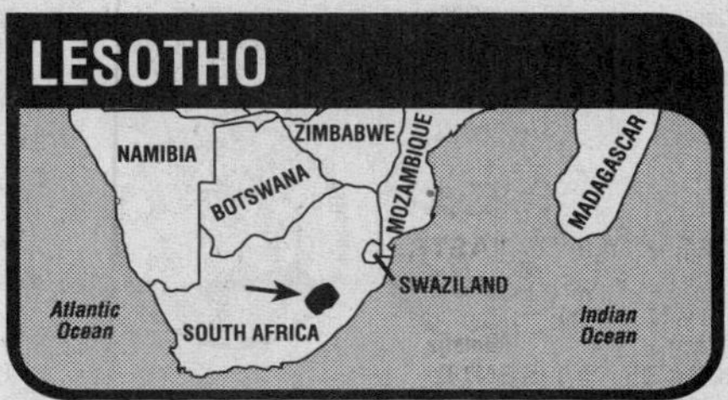

The Kingdom of Lesotho, a constitutional monarchy located within the east-central part of the Republic of South Africa, has an area of 11,720 sq. mi. (30,350 sq. km.) and a population of 1.5 million. Capital: Maseru. The economy is based on subsistence agriculture and livestock raising. Wool, mohair, and cattle are exported.

Lesotho (formerly Basutoland) was sparsely populated until the end of the 16th century. Between the 16th and 19th centuries an influx of refugees from tribal wars led to the development of a distinct Basotho group. During the reign of tribal chief Mashoeshoe I (1823-70), a series of wars with the Orange Free State resulted in the loss of large areas of territory to South Africa. Mashoeshoe appealed to the British for help, and Basutoland was constituted a native state under British protection. In 1871 it was annexed to Cape Colony, but was restored to direct control by the Crown in 1884. From 1884 to 1959 legislative and executive authority was vested in a British High Commissioner. The constitution of 1959 recognized the expressed wish of the people for independence, which was attained on Oct.4, 1966.

Lesotho is a member of the Commonwealth of Nations. The king is Head of State.

RULERS
Moshoeshoe II, 1966-1990
Letsie III, 1990-1995
Moshoeshoe II, 1995-

MONETARY SYSTEM
100 Licente/Lisente = 1 Maloti/Loti

KINGDOM

STANDARD COINAGE

100 Licente/Lisente = 1 Maloti/Loti

KM# 16 SENTE
1.5000 g., Nickel-Brass, 16.5 mm. **Ruler:** Moshoeshoe II **Obv:** Uniformed bust 1/4 left **Rev:** Basotho hat and value

Date	Mintage	F	VF	XF	Unc	BU
1979	4,500,000	—	—	0.15	0.40	0.60
1979 Proof	10,000	Value: 0.65				
1980	—	—	—	0.15	0.40	0.60
1980 Proof	10,000	Value: 0.65				
1981 Proof	2,500	Value: 0.65				
1983	—	—	—	0.15	0.40	0.60
1985	—	—	—	0.15	0.40	0.60
1989	—	—	—	0.15	0.40	0.60

KM# 54 SENTE
Brass, 16.5 mm. **Ruler:** Letsie III **Obv:** Arms with supporters **Rev:** Basotho hat and value

Date	Mintage	F	VF	XF	Unc	BU
1992	—	—	—	0.15	0.75	1.00

KM# 54a SENTE
Brass Plated Steel, 16.5 mm. **Ruler:** Letsie III **Obv:** Arms with supporters **Rev:** Traditional house and value

Date	Mintage	F	VF	XF	Unc	BU
1992	—	—	—	—	—	—

KM# 17 2 LISENTE
2.5000 g., Nickel-Brass, 19.5 mm. **Ruler:** Moshoeshoe II **Obv:** Uniformed bust 1/4 left **Rev:** Steer and value

Date	Mintage	F	VF	XF	Unc	BU
1979	3,000,000	—	—	0.20	0.50	0.75
1979 Proof	10,000	Value: 1.00				
1980	—	—	—	0.20	0.50	0.75
1980 Proof	10,000	Value: 1.00				
1981 Proof	2,500	Value: 2.00				

Date	Mintage	F	VF	XF	Unc	BU
1985	—	—	—	0.20	0.50	0.75
1989	—	—	—	0.20	0.50	0.75

KM# 55 2 LISENTE
Brass, 19.5 mm. **Ruler:** Letsie III **Obv:** Arms with supporters **Rev:** Bull and value

Date	Mintage	F	VF	XF	Unc	BU
1992	—	—	—	0.20	0.75	1.00

KM# 55a 2 LISENTE
2.2500 g., Brass-Plated Steel, 19.5 mm. **Ruler:** Letsie III **Obv:** Arms with supporters **Rev:** Bull and value **Edge:** Plain

Date	Mintage	F	VF	XF	Unc	BU
1992	—	—	—	0.20	0.75	1.00

KM# 1 5 LICENTE (Lisente)
2.8900 g., 0.9000 Silver .0836 oz. ASW **Ruler:** Moshoeshoe II **Subject:** Independence attained **Obv:** Native bust right **Rev:** Arms with supporters above value flanked by stars

Date	Mintage	F	VF	XF	Unc	BU
1966 Proof	5,000	Value: 6.00				

KM# 18 5 LICENTE (Lisente)
4.0000 g., Nickel-Brass, 23.25 mm. **Ruler:** Moshoeshoe II **Obv:** Uniformed bust 1/4 left **Rev:** Single pine tree among hills, grass and value

Date	Mintage	F	VF	XF	Unc	BU
1979	2,700,000	—	—	0.25	0.60	0.85
1979 Proof	10,000	Value: 1.25				
1980	—	—	—	0.25	0.60	0.85
1980 Proof	10,000	Value: 1.25				
1981 Proof	2,500	Value: 2.50				
1981	—	—	—	0.25	0.60	0.85
1989	—	—	—	0.25	0.60	0.85

KM# 56 5 LICENTE (Lisente)
Brass, 23.25 mm. **Ruler:** Letsie III **Obv:** Arms with supporters **Rev:** Single pine tree among grass, hills and value

Date	Mintage	F	VF	XF	Unc	BU
1994	—	—	—	0.25	0.60	0.85

KM# 62 5 LICENTE (Lisente)
Brass-Plated Steel **Ruler:** Letsie III **Obv:** Arms with supporters **Rev:** Single pine tree among grass, hills and value

Date	Mintage	F	VF	XF	Unc	BU
1998	—	—	—	0.25	0.60	0.85

KM# 2 10 LICENTE (Lisente)
5.6800 g., 0.9000 Silver .1643 oz. ASW **Ruler:** Moshoeshoe II **Subject:** Independence Attained **Obv:** Native bust right **Rev:** Arms with supporters above value flanked by stars

Date	Mintage	F	VF	XF	Unc	BU
1966 Proof	5,000	Value: 6.00				

KM# 19 10 LICENTE (Lisente)
2.0000 g., Copper-Nickel, 18.35 mm. **Ruler:** Moshoeshoe II **Obv:** Uniformed bust 1/4 left **Rev:** Angora goat

Date	Mintage	F	VF	XF	Unc	BU
1979	2,000,000	—	0.15	0.30	1.00	1.50
1979 Proof	10,000	Value: 1.75				
1980	—	—	0.15	0.30	1.00	1.50
1980 Proof	10,000	Value: 1.75				
1981 Proof	2,500	Value: 3.00				
1983	—	—	0.15	0.30	1.00	1.50
1989	—	—	0.15	0.30	1.00	1.50

KM# 61 10 LICENTE (Lisente)
2.0000 g., Copper-Nickel, 18.35 mm. **Ruler:** Letsie III **Obv:** Arms with supporters **Rev:** Angora goat

Date	Mintage	F	VF	XF	Unc	BU
1992	—	—	—	—	1.00	1.50

KM# 63 10 LICENTE (Lisente)
Brass-Plated Steel **Ruler:** Moshoeshoe II **Obv:** Arms with supporters **Rev:** Angora goat

Date	Mintage	F	VF	XF	Unc	BU
1998	—	—	—	—	1.00	1.50

KM# 3.1 20 LICENTE
11.2800 g., 0.9000 Silver .3263 oz. ASW **Ruler:** Moshoeshoe II **Subject:** Independence Attained **Obv:** Native bust right **Rev:** Small 900/1000 at right of date

Date	Mintage	F	VF	XF	Unc	BU
1966 Proof	5,000	Value: 15.00				

KM# 3.2 20 LICENTE
11.2800 g., 0.9000 Silver .3263 oz. ASW **Ruler:** Moshoeshoe II **Subject:** Independence Attained **Obv:** Native bust right **Rev:** Large 900/1000 at right of date

Date	Mintage	F	VF	XF	Unc	BU
1966 Proof	—	Value: 15.00				

KM# 64 20 LICENTE
Brass-Plated Steel **Ruler:** Moshoeshoe II **Obv:** Arms with supporters **Rev:** Flora

Date	Mintage	F	VF	XF	Unc	BU
1998	—	—	—	—	0.75	1.00

KM# 20 25 LISENTE
3.5000 g., Copper-Nickel, 21.7 mm. **Ruler:** Moshoeshoe II **Obv:** Uniformed bust 1/4 left **Rev:** Woman in native costume weaving baskets

Date	Mintage	F	VF	XF	Unc	BU
1979	1,200,000	—	0.10	0.20	1.00	1.25
1979 Proof	10,000	Value: 2.00				
1980	—	—	0.10	0.20	1.00	1.25
1980 Proof	10,000	Value: 2.00				
1981 Proof	2,500	Value: 3.50				
1985	—	—	0.10	0.20	1.00	1.25
1989	—	—	0.10	0.20	1.00	1.25

KM# 4.1 50 LICENTE (Lisente)
28.1000 g., 0.9000 Silver .8131 oz. ASW, 35 mm. **Ruler:** Moshoeshoe II **Subject:** Independence Attained **Obv:** Native bust right **Rev:** 900/1000 to right of date

Date	Mintage	F	VF	XF	Unc	BU
1966	—	—	—	—	12.00	14.00
1966 Proof	—	Value: 22.00				

KM# 4.2 50 LICENTE (Lisente)
28.1000 g., 0.9000 Silver .8131 oz. ASW **Ruler:** Moshoeshoe II **Subject:** Independence Attained **Obv:** Native bust right **Rev:** Large 900/1000 to right of date

Date	Mintage	F	VF	XF	Unc	BU
1966	—	—	—	—	12.00	14.00
1966 Proof	5,000	Value: 22.00				

KM# 4.3 50 LICENTE (Lisente)
28.1000 g., 0.9000 Silver .8131 oz. ASW **Ruler:** Moshoeshoe II **Subject:** Independence Attained **Obv:** Native bust right **Rev:** Mint mark and fineness below date

Date	Mintage	F	VF	XF	Unc	BU
1966	—	—	—	—	12.00	14.00
1966 Proof	—	Value: 22.00				

KM# 21 50 LICENTE (Lisente)
5.5000 g., Copper-Nickel, 25.5 mm. **Ruler:** Moshoeshoe II **Obv:** Uniformed bust 1/4 left **Rev:** Equestrian and value

Date	Mintage	F	VF	XF	Unc	BU
1979	480,000	—	0.35	0.50	1.25	1.50
1979 Proof	10,000	Value: 2.50				
1980	—	—	0.35	0.50	1.25	1.50
1980 Proof	10,000	Value: 2.50				
1981 Proof	2,500	Value: 4.00				

Date	Mintage	F	VF	XF	Unc	BU
1983	—	—	0.35	0.50	1.25	1.50
1989	—	—	0.35	0.50	1.25	1.50

KM# 65 50 LICENTE (Lisente)
Brass-Plated Steel **Ruler:** Moshoeshoe II

Date	Mintage	F	VF	XF	Unc	BU
1998	—	—	—	—	1.00	1.25

KM# 5 LOTI
3.9940 g., 0.9170 Gold .1177 oz. AGW **Ruler:** Moshoeshoe II
Subject: Independence Attained **Obv:** Native bust right
Rev: Arms with supporters above value flanked by stars

Date	Mintage	F	VF	XF	Unc	BU
1966 Proof	3,500	Value: 85.00				

KM# 8 LOTI
3.9940 g., 0.9170 Gold .1177 oz. AGW **Ruler:** Moshoeshoe II
Series: F.A.O. **Obv:** Native bust right **Rev:** Equestrian

Date	Mintage	F	VF	XF	Unc	BU
1969 Proof	3,000	Value: 85.00				

KM# 22 LOTI
11.3000 g., Copper-Nickel, 28.5 mm. **Ruler:** Moshoeshoe II
Obv: Uniformed bust 1/4 left **Rev:** Value at left of arms with supporters

Date	Mintage	F	VF	XF	Unc	BU
1979	1,275,000	—	0.65	1.25	3.00	3.50
1979 Proof	10,000	Value: 5.00				
1980	—	—	0.75	1.50	4.00	4.50
1980 Proof	10,000	Value: 5.00				
1981 Proof	2,500	Value: 7.00				
1989	—	—	0.75	1.50	4.00	4.50

KM# 46 LOTI
11.3100 g., 0.9250 Silver .3363 oz. ASW **Ruler:** Moshoeshoe II
Subject: Silver Jubilee of King Moshoeshoe II **Obv:** Uniformed bust 1/4 left **Rev:** Crown above arms with supporters flanked by dates

Date	Mintage	F	VF	XF	Unc	BU
1985 Proof	2,500	Value: 17.50				

KM# 46a LOTI
18.9800 g., 0.9170 Gold .5626 oz. AGW **Ruler:** Moshoeshoe II
Subject: Silver Jubilee of King Moshoeshoe II **Obv:** Uniformed bust 1/4 left **Rev:** Crown above arms with supporters flanked by dates

Date	Mintage	F	VF	XF	Unc	BU
1985 Proof	500	Value: 400				

KM# 60 LOTI
Copper-Nickel **Ruler:** Letsie III **Series:** 50th Anniversary - UN

Date	Mintage	F	VF	XF	Unc	BU
1995	—	—	—	—	8.00	9.00

KM# 66 LOTI
Nickel-Plated Steel **Ruler:** Letsie III **Obv:** Native seated right
Rev: Value at left of arms with supporters

Date	Mintage	F	VF	XF	Unc	BU
1998	—	—	—	—	1.50	2.00

KM# 6 2 MALOTI
7.9880 g., 0.9170 Gold .2355 oz. AGW **Ruler:** Moshoeshoe II
Obv: Native bust right **Rev:** Arms with supporters above value flanked by stars

Date	Mintage	F	VF	XF	Unc	BU
1966 Proof	—	Value: 175				

KM# 9 2 MALOTI
7.9880 g., 0.9170 Gold .2355 oz. AGW **Ruler:** Moshoeshoe II
Series: F.A.O. **Obv:** Native bust right **Rev:** Figure on horseback left

Date	Mintage	F	VF	XF	Unc	BU
1969 Proof	3,000	Value: 175				

KM# 58 2 MALOTI
Nickel-Clad Steel **Ruler:** Moshoeshoe II **Obv:** Arms with supporters **Rev:** Maize plants

Date	Mintage	F	VF	XF	Unc	BU
1996	—	—	—	—	2.50	3.00
1998	—	—	—	—	2.00	2.50

KM# 7 4 MALOTI
15.9760 g., 0.9170 Gold .471 oz. AGW **Ruler:** Moshoeshoe II
Obv: Native bust right **Rev:** Arms with supporters above value flanked by stars

Date	Mintage	F	VF	XF	Unc	BU
1966 Proof	3,500	Value: 345				

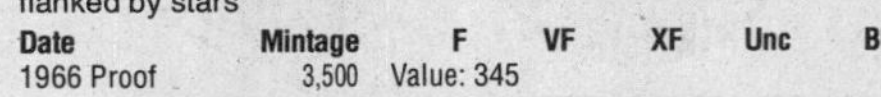

KM# 10 4 MALOTI
15.9760 g., 0.9170 Gold .471 oz. AGW **Ruler:** Moshoeshoe II
Series: F.A.O. **Obv:** Native bust right **Rev:** Figure on horseback left

Date	Mintage	F	VF	XF	Unc	BU
1969 Proof	3,000	Value: 345				

KM# 67 5 MALOTI
5.4600 g., Bi-Metallic Copper-Nickel center in Brass ring, 24 mm.
Ruler: Moshoeshoe II **Obv:** National arms **Rev:** UN logo **Note:** %0th Anniversary of UN

Date	Mintage	F	VF	XF	Unc	BU
1995	—	—	—	—	12.50	15.00

KM# 59 5 MALOTI
Nickel-Clad Steel **Ruler:** Moshoeshoe II **Obv:** Arms with supporters **Rev:** Wheat sprigs and value

Date	Mintage	F	VF	XF	Unc	BU
1996	—	—	—	—	5.50	6.00
1998	—	—	—	—	4.50	5.00

KM# 11 10 MALOTI
39.9400 g., 0.9170 Gold 1.1776 oz. AGW **Ruler:** Moshoeshoe II
Series: F.A.O. **Obv:** Arms with supporters **Rev:** Farmer leading two oxen

Date	Mintage	F	VF	XF	Unc	BU
1969 Proof	3,000	Value: 825				

KM# 13 10 MALOTI
25.0800 g., 0.9250 Silver .7459 oz. ASW **Ruler:** Moshoeshoe II
Subject: 10th Anniversary of Independence **Obv:** Uniformed bust 1/4 left divides dates **Rev:** Kneeling oriental woman with pottery within circle

Date	Mintage	F	VF	XF	Unc	BU
1976	2,300	—	—	—	20.00	25.00
1976 Proof	2,100	Value: 30.00				

KM# 23 10 MALOTI
28.2800 g., 0.9250 Silver .8411 oz. ASW **Ruler:** Moshoeshoe II
Subject: Monument of King Moshoeshoe I **Obv:** Uniformed bust 1/4 left **Rev:** Native seated right

Date	Mintage	F	VF	XF	Unc	BU
1979	10,000	—	—	—	15.00	17.50
1979 Proof	5,000	Value: 20.00				

KM# 23a 10 MALOTI
12.0000 g., 0.5000 Silver .1929 oz. ASW **Ruler:** Moshoeshoe II
Subject: Monument of King Moshoeshoe I **Obv:** Uniformed bust 1/4 left **Rev:** Native seated right

Date	Mintage	F	VF	XF	Unc	BU
1980	10,000	—	—	—	10.00	12.00
1980 Proof	5,000	Value: 15.00				

KM# 24 10 MALOTI
28.2800 g., 0.9250 Silver .8411 oz. ASW **Ruler:** Moshoeshoe II
Series: International Year of the Child **Obv:** Arms with supporters
Rev: Busts of 3 children facing, logo below **Note:** Similar to 15 Maloti, KM#25.

Date	Mintage	F	VF	XF	Unc	BU
1979 (1981)	—	—	—	—	12.00	13.50
1979 (1981) Proof	37,000	Value: 15.00				

KM# 32 10 MALOTI
23.3300 g., 0.9250 Silver .6938 oz. ASW **Ruler:** Moshoeshoe II
Subject: World Soccer Championship **Obv:** Arms with supporters **Rev:** Goalie in front of net

Date	Mintage	F	VF	XF	Unc	BU
1982 Proof	3,582	Value: 22.50				

KM# 34 10 MALOTI
23.3300 g., 0.9250 Silver .6938 oz. ASW **Ruler:** Moshoeshoe II
Subject: World Soccer Championship **Obv:** Arms with supporters **Rev:** Soccer players

Date	Mintage	F	VF	XF	Unc	BU
1982 Proof	3,000	Value: 20.00				

KM# 40 10 MALOTI
31.1000 g., 0.5000 Silver .5000 oz. ASW **Ruler:** Moshoeshoe II
Subject: George Washington **Obv:** Arms with supporters
Rev: Bust left

Date	Mintage	F	VF	XF	Unc	BU
1982 Proof	7,355	Value: 17.50				

KM# 41 10 MALOTI
31.1000 g., 0.5000 Silver .5000 oz. ASW **Ruler:** Moshoeshoe II
Subject: George Washington **Obv:** Arms with supporters
Rev: Washington on bended knee

Date	Mintage	F	VF	XF	Unc	BU
1982 Proof	4,200	Value: 17.50				

KM# 42 10 MALOTI
31.1000 g., 0.5000 Silver .5000 oz. ASW **Ruler:** Moshoeshoe II
Subject: George Washington **Obv:** Arms with supporters
Rev: Washington crossing the Delaware

Date	Mintage	F	VF	XF	Unc	BU
1982 Proof	Est. 15,000	Value: 17.50				

KM# 49 10 MALOTI
23.3300 g., 0.9250 Silver .6939 oz. ASW **Ruler:** Moshoeshoe II
Subject: Decade for Women **Obv:** Uniformed bust 1/4 left
Rev: Half-figure of woman with basket on head left

Date	Mintage	F	VF	XF	Unc	BU
1985 Proof	1,000	Value: 35.00				

KM# 50 10 MALOTI
28.2800 g., 0.9250 Silver .8411 oz. ASW **Ruler:** Moshoeshoe II
Subject: Papal visit **Obv:** Arms with supporters **Rev:** Bust left

Date	Mintage	F	VF	XF	Unc	BU
1988 Proof	Est. 15,000	Value: 45.00				

KM# 25 15 MALOTI
33.4000 g., 0.9250 Silver .9933 oz. ASW **Ruler:** Moshoeshoe II
Series: International Year of the Child **Obv:** Arms with supporters
Rev: Busts of 3 children facing, logo below

Date	Mintage	F	VF	XF	Unc	BU
1979	18,000	—	—	—	14.50	16.50
1979 Proof	7,500	Value: 22.50				

KM# 53 15 MALOTI
12.0000 g., 0.5000 Silver .1929 oz. ASW **Ruler:** Moshoeshoe II
Subject: 15th Anniversary of Independence **Obv:** Uniformed bust 1/4 left **Rev:** Eagle with ribbon in talons

Date	Mintage	F	VF	XF	Unc	BU
1981 Proof	2,500	Value: 35.00				

KM# 12 20 MALOTI
79.8810 g., 0.9170 Gold 2.3553 oz. AGW **Ruler:** Moshoeshoe II
Series: F.A.O. **Obv:** Arms with supporters **Rev:** Grazing ewe and lamb

Date	Mintage	F	VF	XF	Unc	BU
1969 Proof	3,000	Value: 1,650				

KM# 35 25 MALOTI
16.8200 g., 0.9250 Silver .5003 oz. ASW **Ruler:** Moshoeshoe II
Obv: Arms with supporters **Rev:** Bust left

Date	Mintage	F	VF	XF	Unc	BU
1981 Proof	5,000	Value: 35.00				

KM# 44 25 MALOTI
28.2800 g., 0.9250 Silver .8411 oz. ASW **Ruler:** Moshoeshoe II
Series: International Year of Disabled Persons **Obv:** Arms with supporters **Rev:** Inscription and disabled emblem divides map within circled grid

Date	Mintage	F	VF	XF	Unc	BU
1983	—	—	—	—	32.50	37.50
1983 Proof	—	Value: 55.00				

KM# 30 30 MALOTI
0.9250 Silver **Ruler:** Moshoeshoe II **Subject:** Wedding of Prince Charles and Lady Diana

Date	Mintage	F	VF	XF	Unc	BU
1981 Proof	10,000	Value: 47.50				

KM# 14 50 MALOTI
4.5000 g., 0.9000 Gold .1302 oz. AGW **Ruler:** Moshoeshoe II
Subject: 10th Anniversary of Independence **Obv:** Arms with supporters within circle **Rev:** Young bust right divides dates

Date	Mintage	F	VF	XF	Unc	BU
ND(1976)	700	—	—	—	125	130
ND(1976) Proof	1,910	Value: 130				

KM# 27 50 MALOTI
33.6200 g., 0.9250 Silver .9999 oz. ASW **Ruler:** Moshoeshoe II
Subject: 110th Anniversary - Death of King Moshoeshoe I
Obv: Arms with supporters **Rev:** Diamond with hat at center, corn ear at left, alligator at right

Date	Mintage	F	VF	XF	Unc	BU
1980	2,500	—	—	—	30.00	35.00
1980 Proof	1,400	Value: 65.00				

KM# 38 50 MALOTI
33.6200 g., 0.9250 Silver .9999 oz. ASW **Ruler:** Moshoeshoe II
Subject: 15th Anniversary of Commonwealth Membership
Obv: Arms with supporters **Rev:** Crowned bust right

Date	Mintage	F	VF	XF	Unc	BU
1981 Proof	5,000	Value: 60.00				

KM# 15 100 MALOTI
9.0000 g., 0.9000 Gold .2604 oz. AGW **Ruler:** Moshoeshoe II
Subject: 10th Anniversary of Independence **Obv:** Uniformed bust 1/4 left divides dates **Rev:** Equestrian and value within circle

Date	Mintage	F	VF	XF	Unc	BU
ND(1976)	450	—	—	—	190	200
ND(1976) Proof	1,410	Value: 180				

KM# 45 200 MALOTI
15.9800 g., 0.9000 Gold .4624 oz. AGW **Ruler:** Moshoeshoe II
Series: International Year of Disabled Persons **Obv:** Arms with supporters **Rev:** Disabled persons design within circle

Date	Mintage	F	VF	XF	Unc	BU
1983	500	—	—	—	400	420
1983 Proof	500	Value: 450				

KM# 26 250 MALOTI
33.9300 g., 0.9170 Gold 1 oz. AGW **Ruler:** Moshoeshoe II
Series: International Year of the Child **Obv:** Native bust right
Rev: Busts of 3 children facing with logo below

Date	Mintage	F	VF	XF	Unc	BU
1979	2,500	—	—	—	700	720
1979 Proof	2,000	Value: 750				

KM# 28 250 MALOTI
31.1000 g., 0.9170 Gold .917 oz. AGW **Ruler:** Moshoeshoe II
Subject: 110th Anniversary - Death of King Moshoeshoe I
Obv: Native bust right **Rev:** Diamond with hat at center, corn ear at left, alligator at right

Date	Mintage	F	VF	XF	Unc	BU
1980	1,500	—	—	—	650	660
1980 Proof	3,000	Value: 675				

KM# 31 250 MALOTI
15.9000 g., 0.9170 Gold .4688 oz. AGW **Ruler:** Moshoeshoe II
Subject: Wedding of Prince Charles and Lady Diana
Obv. Designer: Arms with supporters **Rev:** Conjoined busts left

Date	Mintage	F	VF	XF	Unc	BU
1981	1,000	—	—	—	385	400
1981 Proof	1,500	Value: 345				

KM# 31a 250 MALOTI
15.7500 g., 0.9950 Platinum .5039 oz. APW **Ruler:** Moshoeshoe II **Subject:** Wedding of Prince Charles and Lady Diana **Obv:** Arms with supporters **Rev:** Conjoined busts left

Date	Mintage	F	VF	XF	Unc	BU
1981 Proof	200	Value: 700				

KM# 36 250 MALOTI
16.9600 g., 0.9170 Gold .5001 oz. AGW **Ruler:** Moshoeshoe II
Subject: Duke of Edinburgh Youth Awards **Obv:** Arms with supporters **Rev:** Bust left

Date	Mintage	F	VF	XF	Unc	BU
1981 Proof	1,500	Value: 350				

KM# 36a 250 MALOTI
15.7500 g., 0.9950 Platinum .5039 oz. APW
Ruler: Moshoeshce II **Subject:** Duke of Edinburgh Youth Awards **Obv:** Arms with supporters **Rev:** Bust left

Date	Mintage	F	VF	XF	Unc	BU
1981 Proof	200	Value: 700				

KM# 33 250 MALOTI
7.1300 g., 0.9000 Gold .2063 oz. AGW **Ruler:** Moshoeshoe II
Subject: Soccer Games **Obv:** Arms with supporters **Rev:** Goalie

Date	Mintage	F	VF	XF	Unc	BU
1982 Proof	551	Value: 250				

KM# 51 250 MALOTI
15.9800 g., 0.9170 Gold .4708 oz. AGW **Ruler:** Moshoeshoe II
Subject: Papal Visit **Obv:** Bust left **Rev:** Arms with supporters

Date	Mintage	F	VF	XF	Unc	BU
1988 Proof	Est. 750	Value: 500				

KM# 29 500 MALOTI
33.9300 g., 0.9170 Gold 1 oz. AGW **Ruler:** Moshoeshoe II
Subject: 110th Anniversary - Death of King Moshoeshoe I
Obv: Native bust right **Rev:** Diamond with hat at center, corn ear at left, alligator at right

Date	Mintage	F	VF	XF	Unc	BU
1980	1,500	—	—	—	700	720
1980 Proof	3,000	Value: 725				

KM# 39 500 MALOTI
33.9300 g., 0.9170 Gold 1 oz. AGW **Ruler:** Moshoeshoe II
Subject: 15th Anniversary of Commonwealth Membership
Obv: Arms with supporters **Rev:** Crowned bust right

Date	Mintage	F	VF	XF	Unc	BU
1981 Proof	500	Value: 700				

KM# 39a 500 MALOTI
31.5000 g., 0.9950 Platinum 1.0078 oz. APW **Ruler:** Moshoeshoe II **Subject:** 15th Anniversary of Commonwealth Membership **Obv:** Arms with supporters **Rev:** Crowned bust right

Date	Mintage	F	VF	XF	Unc	BU
1981 Proof	200	Value: 1,350				

KM# 57 500 MALOTI
33.9300 g., 0.9166 Gold 1 oz. AGW **Ruler:** Moshoeshoe II
Subject: Royal Wedding of Prince Charles and Lady Diana
Obv: Arms with supporters **Rev:** Conjoined busts left

Date	Mintage	F	VF	XF	Unc	BU
ND(1981) Proof, rare	—	—	—	—	—	—

KM# 57a 500 MALOTI
33.4800 g., 0.9995 Platinum 1 oz. APW **Ruler:** Moshoeshoe II
Subject: Royal Wedding **Obv:** Arms with supporters
Rev: Conjoined bust left

Date	Mintage	F	VF	XF	Unc	BU
ND(1981) Proof, rare	—	—	—	—	—	—

PATTERNS

Including off metal strikes

KM#	Date	Mintage	Identification	Mkt Val
Pn1	1966	2	5 Licente. 0.9000 Silver.	—
Pn2	1966	2	10 Licente. 0.9000 Silver.	—
Pn3	1966	2	20 Licente. 0.9000 Silver.	—
Pn4	1966	2	50 Licente. 0.9000 Silver.	—
Pn6	1966	7	2 Maloti. 0.9160 Gold.	500
Pn7	1966	7	4 Maloti. 0.9160 Gold.	700

KM#	Date	Mintage	Identification	Mkt Val
Pn8	1966	7	10 Maloti. 0.9160 Gold. Head right. Arms with supporters above value and date.	950
Pn9	1966	7	20 Maloti. 0.9160 Gold.	1,250

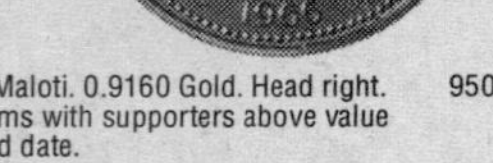

KM#	Date	Mintage	Identification	Mkt Val
Pn10	1979	5	15 Maloti. Copper-Nickel. KM25. Medallic alignment.	110
Pn10.2a	1979	—	15 Maloti. 0.9250 Silver. 33.5100 g.	—
Pn11	1979	15	15 Maloti. Copper-Nickel. KM25. Coin alignment.	80.00
Pn12	1979	15	250 Maloti. Brass. KM26.	75.00
Pn13	1979	5	250 Maloti. Copper-Nickel. KM26. Medallic alignment.	110
Pn14	1979	10	250 Maloti. Silver. 20.1500 g. KM26.	115

KM#	Date	Mintage	Identification	Mkt Val
Pn15	1980	10	50 Maloti. Copper-Nickel. KM27. Medallic alignment.	125
Pn16	1980	10	50 Maloti. Copper-Nickel. Coin alignment.	125
Pn17	1980	10	250 Maloti. Brass. KM28. Coin alignment.	110
Pn18	1980	10	250 Maloti. Copper-Nickel. KM28. Medallic alignment.	100
Pn19	1980	10	500 Maloti. Brass. KM29. Coin alignment.	110
Pn20	1980	10	500 Maloti. Copper-Nickel. KM29. Medallic alignment.	110

PIEFORTS

KM#	Date	Mintage	Identification	Mkt Val
P1	1979	50	10 Maloti. Silver. KM24.	135
P2	1981	—	250 Maloti. Gold. KM31.	550
P3	1983	—	25 Maloti. Silver. KM4.	90.00
P4	1983	100	200 Maloti. Gold. KM45.	800

MINT SETS

KM#	Date	Mintage	Identification	Issue Price	Mkt Val
MS1	1976 (3)	450	KM13-15	194	315
MS2	1989 (7)	—	KM16-22	—	11.50

PROOF SETS

KM#	Date	Mintage	Identification	Issue Price	Mkt Val
PS1	1966 (7)	1,500	KM1-7	301	525
PS2	1966 (4)	7	KMPn6-9	—	3,400
PS3	1966 (4)	2	KMPn1-4	—	—
PS4	1966 (4)	3,500	KM1, 2, 3.1, 4.1	28.00	40.00
PS5	1966 (3)	2,000	KM5-7	301	430
PSA5	1966 (4)	—	KM1, 2, 3.2, 4.2	28.00	40.00
PS6	1969 (5)	3,000	KM8-12	450	3,100
PS7	1976 (3)	1,410	KM13-15	285	300
PS8	1976 (2)	—	KM14-15	270	270
PS9	1976 (2)	—	KM13-14	—	135
PS10	1979 (7)	10,000	KM16-22	34.00	15.00
PS11	1980 (8)	10,000	KM16-22, 23a	51.00	25.00
PS12	1981 (8)	2,500	KM16-22, 53	55.00	45.00

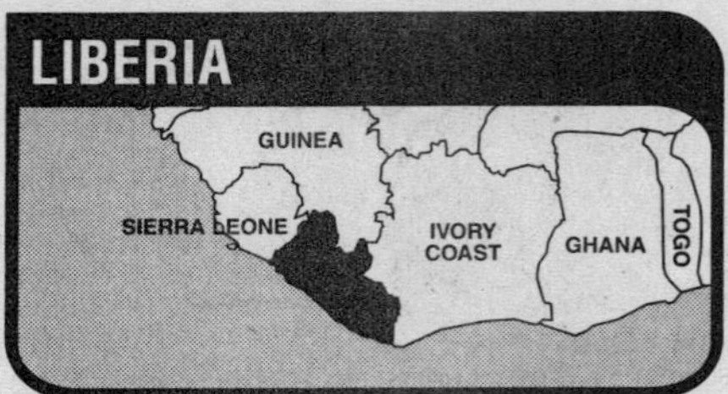

The Republic of Liberia, located on the southern side of the West African bulge between Sierra Leone and Ivory Coast, has an area of 38,250 sq. mi. (111,370 sq. km) and a population of 2.2 million. Capital: Monrovia. The major industries are agriculture, mining and lumbering. Iron ore, diamonds, rubber, coffee and coca are exported.

The Liberian coast was explored and charted by Portuguese navigator Pedro de Cintra in 1461. For the three centuries following Portuguese traders visited the area regularly to trade for gold, slaves and pepper. The modern country of Liberia, Africa's first republic, was settled in1822 by the American Colonization Society as a homeland for American freed slaves, with the U.S. government furnishing funds and assisting in negotiations for procurement of land from the native chiefs. The various settlements united in 1839 to form the Commonwealth of Liberia, and in 1847 established the country as a republic with a constitution modeled after that of the United States.

U.S. money was declared legal tender in Liberia in 1943, replacing British West African currency.

Most of the Liberian pattern series, particularly of the1888-90 period, are acknowledged to have been 'unofficial' privately sponsored issues, but they are, nonetheless, avidly collected by many collectors of Liberian coins. The 'K' number designations on these pieces refer to a listing of Liberian patterns compiled and published by Ernst Kraus.

MINT MARKS
B - Bern, Switzerland
H - Heaton, Birmingham
(l) - London
(s) - San Francisco, U.S.
FM - Franklin Mint, U.S.A.*
PM - Pobjoy Mint

***NOTE:** From 1975-1985 the Franklin Mint produced coinage in up to 3 different qualities. Qualities of issue are designated in ( ) after each date and are defined as follows:

(M) MATTE - Normal circulation strike or a dull finish produced by sandblasting special uncirculated (polish finish) or proof quality dies.

(U) SPECIAL UNCIRCULATED - Polished or prooflike in appearance without any frosted features.

(P) PROOF - The highest quality obtainable having mirror-like fields and frosted features.

MONETARY SYSTEM
100 Cents = 1 Dollar

REPUBLIC

STANDARD COINAGE

100 Cents = 1 Dollar

KM# 10 1/2 CENT
Brass **Obv:** Laureate head left with star below **Rev:** Palm tree (Elaeis guineensis-Palmae) within circle flanked by stars

Date	Mintage	F	VF	XF	Unc	BU
1937	1,000,000	0.10	0.25	0.40	1.00	2.50

KM# 10a 1/2 CENT
Copper-Nickel **Obv:** Head laureate left with star below
Rev: Palm tree within circle flanked by stars

Date	Mintage	F	VF	XF	Unc	BU
1941	250,000	0.15	0.35	0.55	1.50	2.50

KM# 5 CENT
Bronze **Obv:** Head laureate left above star **Obv. Legend:** REPUBLIC OF LIBERIA **Rev:** Palm tree divides ship and radiant sun within circle, 2 stars, date and value around border

Date	Mintage	F	VF	XF	Unc	BU
1906H	180,000	4.50	10.00	22.00	50.00	—
1906H Proof	—	Value: 130				

KM# 11 CENT

Brass **Obv:** Elephant within circle above star **Rev:** Palm tree within circle above date

Date	Mintage	F	VF	XF	Unc	BU
1937	1,000,000	0.20	0.50	1.50	6.00	12.00

KM# 11a CENT

Copper-Nickel **Obv:** Elephant within circle above star **Rev:** Palm tree within circle above date

Date	Mintage	F	VF	XF	Unc	BU
1941	250,000	0.50	2.50	7.50	40.00	—

KM# 13 CENT

2.6000 g., Bronze, 18 mm. **Obv:** Elephant within circle above star **Rev:** Ship and bird to right of palm tree within 3/4 circle above date

Date	Mintage	F	VF	XF	Unc	BU
1960	500,000	—	—	0.10	0.75	2.00
1961	7,000,000	—	—	0.10	0.75	2.00
1968(l)	3,000,000	—	—	0.10	0.75	2.00
1968(s) Proof	14,000	Value: 1.25				
1969 Proof	5,056	Value: 1.25				
1970 Proof	3,464	Value: 1.25				
1971 Proof	3,032	Value: 1.25				
1972(d)	10,000,000	—	—	0.10	0.75	2.00
1972(s) Proof	4,866	Value: 1.25				
1973 Proof	11,000	Value: 1.25				
1974 Proof	9,362	Value: 1.25				
1975	5,000,000	—	—	0.10	0.75	2.00
1975 Proof	4,056	Value: 1.25				
1976 Proof	2,131	Value: 1.25				
1977	2,500,000	—	—	0.10	0.75	2.00
1977 Proof	920	Value: 1.25				
1978FM Proof	7,311	Value: 1.25				
1983FM	2,500,000	—	—	0.10	0.75	2.00
1984	2,500,000	—	—	0.10	0.75	2.00

KM# 13a CENT

Bronze **Obv:** Elephant left **Rev:** Palm tree, bird above ship at right **Edge Lettering:** O.A.U. July 1979

Date	Mintage	F	VF	XF	Unc	BU
1979FM Proof	1,857	Value: 1.50				

KM# 6 2 CENTS

Bronze **Obv:** Laureate head left above star **Obv. Legend:** REPUBLIC OF LIBERIA **Rev:** Palm tree divides ship and radiant sun within circle, 2 stars, date and value around border

Date	Mintage	F	VF	XF	Unc	BU
1906H	108,000	5.00	12.00	30.00	75.00	—
1906H Proof	—	Value: 160				

KM# 12 2 CENTS

Brass **Obv:** Elephant within circle above star **Rev:** Palm tree divides ship and sun within circle flanked by stars above date

Date	Mintage	F	VF	XF	Unc	BU
1937	1,000,000	0.15	0.35	1.00	6.00	9.00

KM# 12a 2 CENTS

Copper-Nickel **Obv:** Elephant within circle above star **Rev:** Palm tree divides sun and ship within circle flanked by stars above date

Date	Mintage	F	VF	XF	Unc	BU
1941	810,000	0.10	0.25	0.50	2.50	3.00
1978FM Proof	7,311	Value: 2.00				

KM# 12b 2 CENTS

Copper-Nickel **Obv:** Elephant within circle above star **Rev:** Palm tree divides sun and ship within circle flanked by stars above date **Edge Lettering:** O.A.U. July 1979

Date	Mintage	F	VF	XF	Unc	BU
1979FM Proof	1,857	Value: 4.00				

KM# 14 5 CENTS

4.1000 g., Copper-Nickel, 20 mm. **Obv:** Elephant within circle above star **Rev:** Ship and bird to right of palm tree within 3/4 circle above date

Date	Mintage	F	VF	XF	Unc	BU
1960	1,000,000	—	0.10	0.15	0.50	1.50
1961	3,200,000	—	0.10	0.15	0.50	1.50
1968 Proof	15,000	Value: 1.00				
1969 Proof	5,056	Value: 1.00				
1970 Proof	3,464	Value: 1.25				
1971 Proof	3,032	Value: 1.25				
1972(d)	3,000,000	—	0.10	0.15	0.40	1.50
1972(s) Proof	4,866	Value: 1.00				
1973 Proof	11,000	Value: 1.00				
1974 Proof	9,362	Value: 1.00				
1975	3,000,000	—	0.10	0.15	0.40	1.50
1975 Proof	4,056	Value: 1.00				
1976 Proof	2,131	Value: 1.00				
1977	—	—	0.10	0.15	0.50	1.50
1977 Proof	920	Value: 1.00				
1978FM Proof	7,311	Value: 1.00				
1983FM	1,000,000	—	0.10	0.15	0.40	1.50
1984	1,000,000	—	0.10	0.15	0.40	1.50

KM# 14a 5 CENTS

Copper-Nickel **Obv:** Elephant within circle above star **Rev:** Ship and bird to right of palm tree within 3/4 circle above date **Edge Lettering:** O.A.U. July 1979

Date	Mintage	F	VF	XF	Unc	BU
1979FM Proof	1,857	Value: 2.00				

KM# 474 5 CENTS

2.2500 g., Aluminum, 26.9 mm. **Obv:** National arms **Rev:** Dragon above value **Edge:** Plain

Date	Mintage	F	VF	XF	Unc	BU
2000	—	—	—	—	1.00	1.50

KM# 7 10 CENTS

2.3200 g., 0.9250 Silver .0690 oz. ASW **Obv:** Laureate head left above star **Obv. Legend:** REPUBLIC OF LIBERIA **Rev:** Value and date within wreath

Date	Mintage	F	VF	XF	Unc	BU
1906H	35,000	5.00	15.00	40.00	150	—
1906H Proof	—	Value: 250				

KM# 15 10 CENTS

2.0700 g., 0.9000 Silver .0599 oz. ASW **Obv:** Head with headdress left above star **Rev:** Value and date within wreath

Date	Mintage	F	VF	XF	Unc	BU
1960	1,000,000	BV	1.00	1.50	3.00	5.00
1961	1,200,000	BV	1.00	1.50	3.00	5.00

KM# 15a.1 10 CENTS

2.1000 g., Copper-Nickel **Obv:** Head with headdress left above star **Rev:** Value and date within wreath

Date	Mintage	F	VF	XF	Unc	BU
1966	2,000,000	—	0.15	0.25	0.50	0.75

KM# 15a.2 10 CENTS

1.8000 g., Copper-Nickel **Obv:** Head with headdress left above star **Rev:** Value and date within wreath

Date	Mintage	F	VF	XF	Unc	BU
1968 Proof	14,000	Value: 1.25				
1969 Proof	5,056	Value: 1.25				
1970(d)	2,500,000	—	0.15	0.25	0.50	0.75
1970(s) Proof	3,464	Value: 1.50				
1971 Proof	3,032	Value: 1.50				
1972 Proof	4,866	Value: 1.25				
1973 Proof	11,000	Value: 1.00				
1974 Proof	9,362	Value: 1.00				
1975	4,500	—	0.15	0.20	0.35	0.75
1975 Proof	4,056	Value: 1.00				
1976 Proof	2,131	Value: 1.00				
1977	—	—	0.15	0.25	0.75	1.25
1977 Proof	920	Value: 1.00				
1978FM Proof	7,311	Value: 1.00				
1983FM	500,000	—	0.15	0.25	0.75	1.25
1984FM	500,000	—	0.15	0.25	0.75	1.25
1987	10,000,000	—	0.15	0.25	0.75	1.25

KM# 15b 10 CENTS

1.8000 g., Copper-Nickel **Obv:** Head with headdress left above star **Rev:** Value and date within wreath **Edge Lettering:** O.A.U. July 1979

Date	Mintage	F	VF	XF	Unc	BU
1979FM Proof	1,857	Value: 2.00				

KM# 8 25 CENTS

5.8000 g., 0.9250 Silver .1725 oz. ASW **Obv:** Head laureate left above star **Obv. Legend:** REPUBLIC OF LIBERIA **Rev:** Value and date within wreath

Date	Mintage	F	VF	XF	Unc	BU
1906H	34,000	10.00	20.00	60.00	250	—
1906H Proof	—	Value: 375				

KM# 16 25 CENTS

5.1800 g., 0.9000 Silver .1499 oz. ASW **Obv:** Head with headdress left above star **Rev:** Value and date within wreath

Date	Mintage	F	VF	XF	Unc	BU
1960	900,000	BV	2.25	2.75	5.00	7.00
1961	1,200,000	BV	2.25	2.75	5.00	7.00

KM# 16a.1 25 CENTS

5.2000 g., Copper-Nickel **Obv:** Head with headdress left above star **Rev:** Value and date within wreath

Date	Mintage	F	VF	XF	Unc	BU
1966	800,000	—	0.25	0.65	1.25	2.00

KM# 16a.2 25 CENTS

4.8000 g., Copper-Nickel, 23 mm. **Obv:** Head with headdress left above star **Rev:** Value and date within wreath **Note:** 1 and 1.15mm rim varieties exist.

Date	Mintage	F	VF	XF	Unc	BU
1968(d)	1,600,000	—	0.25	0.50	1.00	1.50
1968(s) Proof	14,000	Value: 1.50				
1969 Proof	5,056	Value: 1.50				
1970 Proof	3,464	Value: 1.75				
1971 Proof	3,032	Value: 1.75				
1972 Proof	4,866	Value: 1.50				
1973	2,000,000	—	0.25	0.50	1.00	1.50
1973 Proof	11,000	Value: 1.25				
1974 Proof	9,362	Value: 1.25				
1975	1,600,000	—	0.25	0.50	1.00	1.50
1975 Proof	4,056	Value: 1.25				

KM# 16a.3 25 CENTS

5.2000 g., Copper-Nickel **Obv:** Head with headdress left above star **Rev:** Value and date within wreath **Rev. Legend:** Large letters, higher inscription **Note:** Struck in 1988.

Date	Mintage	F	VF	XF	Unc	BU
1968 Restrike	2,400,000	—	0.25	0.50	1.00	1.50

KM# 16b 25 CENTS

4.4600 g., Nickel Clad Steel, 22.9 mm. **Obv:** Head with headdress left above star **Rev:** Value and date within wreath **Edge:** Reeded

Date	Mintage	F	VF	XF	Unc	BU
2000	—	—	—	—	1.75	—

KM# 30 25 CENTS

5.2000 g., Copper-Nickel **Series:** F.A.O. **Obv:** Head 1/4 right flanked by stars **Rev:** Woman with basket of leaves on head divides date and value within circle

Date	Mintage	F	VF	XF	Unc	BU
1976	800,000	—	0.25	0.75	1.75	3.00
1976 Proof	2,131	Value: 4.00				
1977 Proof	920	Value: 5.00				
1978FM Proof	7,311	Value: 2.50				

KM# 30a 25 CENTS

5.2000 g., Copper-Nickel **Obv:** Head 1/4 right flanked by stars **Rev:** Woman with leaves in basket on head divides date and value within circle **Edge Lettering:** O.A.U. July 1979

Date	Mintage	F	VF	XF	Unc	BU
1979FM Proof	1,857	Value: 3.50				

KM# 9 50 CENTS

11.6000 g., 0.9250 Silver .3450 oz. ASW **Obv:** Laureate head left above star **Obv. Legend:** REPUBLIC OF LIBERIA **Rev:** Value and date within wreath

Date	Mintage	F	VF	XF	Unc	BU
1906H	24,000	15.00	35.00	90.00	450	—
1906H Proof	—	Value: 600				

KM# 17 50 CENTS

10.3700 g., 0.9000 Silver .3001 oz. ASW **Obv:** Head with headdress left above star **Rev:** Value and date within wreath

Date	Mintage	F	VF	XF	Unc	BU
1960	1,100,000	BV	4.50	5.00	9.00	12.50
1961	800,000	BV	4.50	5.00	9.00	12.50

KM# 17a.1 50 CENTS

10.4000 g., Copper-Nickel **Obv:** Head with headdress left above star **Rev:** Value and date within wreath

Date	Mintage	F	VF	XF	Unc	BU
1966	200,000	—	0.75	1.00	1.50	2.50

KM# 17a.2 50 CENTS

8.9000 g., Copper-Nickel, 29 mm. **Obv:** Head with headdress left above star **Rev:** Value and date within wreath

Date	Mintage	F	VF	XF	Unc	BU
1968(l)	1,000,000	—	0.60	0.80	1.50	2.50
1968(s) Proof	14,000	Value: 1.50				
1969 Proof	5,056	Value: 1.50				
1970 Proof	3,464	Value: 2.50				
1971 Proof	3,032	Value: 2.50				
1972 Proof	4,866	Value: 1.50				
1973	1,000,000	—	0.60	0.75	1.25	2.00
1973 Proof	11,000	Value: 1.50				
1974 Proof	9,362	Value: 1.50				
1975	800,000	—	0.60	0.75	1.25	2.00
1975 Proof	4,056	Value: 1.50				

KM# 17b.2 50 CENTS

9.0000 g., Nickel-Clad Steel, 28 mm. **Obv:** Head with headdress left above star **Rev:** Value and date within wreath **Edge:** Reeded

Date	Mintage	F	VF	XF	Unc	BU
2000	—	—	—	—	3.50	—

KM# 31 50 CENTS

8.9000 g., Copper-Nickel **Obv:** Head 1/4 right flanked by stars **Rev:** National arms

Date	Mintage	F	VF	XF	Unc	BU
1976	1,000,000	—	0.60	1.00	2.50	4.00
1976 Proof	2,131	Value: 5.50				
1977 Proof	920	Value: 6.50				
1978FM Proof	7,311	Value: 4.00				
1987	1,800,000	—	0.60	1.00	2.50	4.00

KM# 31a 50 CENTS

8.9000 g., Copper-Nickel **Obv:** Head 1/4 right flanked by stars **Rev:** National arms **Edge Lettering:** O.A.U. July 1979

Date	Mintage	F	VF	XF	Unc	BU
1979FM Proof	1,857	Value: 4.50				

KM# 18 DOLLAR

20.7400 g., 0.9000 Silver .6001 oz. ASW **Obv:** Head with headdress left above star **Rev:** Value and date within wreath

Date	Mintage	F	VF	XF	Unc	BU
1961	200,000	BV	9.00	10.00	12.50	16.50
1962	1,000,000	BV	8.50	9.50	11.00	14.50

KM# 18a.1 DOLLAR

20.7000 g., Copper-Nickel, 34 mm. **Obv:** Head with headdress left above star **Rev:** Value and date within wreath

Date	Mintage	F	VF	XF	Unc	BU
1966	1,000,000	—	1.00	1.50	2.25	3.50

KM# 18a.2 DOLLAR

18.0000 g., Copper-Nickel, 34 mm. **Obv:** Head with headdress left above star **Rev:** Value and date within wreath

Date	Mintage	F	VF	XF	Unc	BU
1968(l)	1,000,000	—	1.00	1.50	2.25	3.50
1968(s) Proof	14,000	Value: 2.00				
1969 Proof	5,056	Value: 2.00				
1970(d)	2,000,000	—	1.00	1.50	3.00	4.50
1970(s) Proof	3,464	Value: 6.00				
1971 Proof	3,032	Value: 4.50				
1972 Proof	4,866	Value: 4.50				
1973 Proof	11,000	Value: 3.00				
1974 Proof	9,362	Value: 3.00				
1975	400,000	—	1.25	1.75	3.00	4.50
1975 Proof	4,056	Value: 3.00				

KM# 32 DOLLAR

18.0000 g., Copper-Nickel, 34 mm. **Obv:** Head 1/4 right flanked by stars **Rev:** Liberia, map and date within circle flanked by stars

Date	Mintage	F	VF	XF	Unc	BU
1976	2,000,000	—	2.50	4.50	8.00	12.00
1976 Proof	2,131	Value: 12.00				
1977 Proof	920	Value: 13.50				
1978FM Proof	7,311	Value: 11.00				
1987	1,500,000	—	1.50	3.00	6.00	10.00

KM# 32a DOLLAR

18.0000 g., Copper-Nickel, 34 mm. **Obv:** Head with headdress 1/4 right flanked by stars **Rev:** Liberia, map and date within circle flanked by stars **Edge Lettering:** O.A.U. July 1979

Date	Mintage	F	VF	XF	Unc	BU
1979FM Proof	1,857	Value: 10.00				

KM# 98 DOLLAR

18.0000 g., Copper-Nickel **Series:** Preserve Planet Earth **Obv:** National arms **Rev:** Protoceratops

Date	Mintage	F	VF	XF	Unc	BU
1993	—	—	—	—	10.00	12.00

KM# 101 DOLLAR

18.0000 g., Copper-Nickel **Subject:** Nolan Ryan **Obv:** National arms **Rev:** Nolan Ryan waving baseball cap **Note:** Similar to 10 Dollars, KM#102.

Date	Mintage	F	VF	XF	Unc	BU
1993	—	—	—	—	8.50	—

KM# 109 DOLLAR

28.5200 g., Copper-Nickel **Series:** Preserve Planet Earth **Obv:** National arms **Rev:** Corythosaurus

Date	Mintage	F	VF	XF	Unc	BU
1993	—	—	—	—	10.00	12.00

KM# 112 DOLLAR

28.5200 g., Copper-Nickel **Series:** Preserve Planet Earth **Obv:** National arms **Rev:** Atchaeopteryx **Note:** Incorrect spelling

Date	Mintage	F	VF	XF	Unc	BU
1993	—	—	—	—	10.00	14.00

KM# 118 DOLLAR

28.5200 g., Copper-Nickel **Series:** Preserve Planet Earth **Obv:** National arms **Rev:** Gorillas **Note:** Similar to 10 Dollars, KM#119.

Date	Mintage	F	VF	XF	Unc	BU
1994	—	—	—	—	10.00	12.00

KM# 121 DOLLAR

28.5200 g., Copper-Nickel **Series:** Preserve Planet Earth **Obv:** National arms **Rev:** Pygmy Hippopotami **Note:** Similar to 10 Dollars, KM#122.

Date	Mintage	F	VF	XF	Unc	BU
1994	—	—	—	—	10.00	12.00

KM# 124 DOLLAR

28.5200 g., Copper-Nickel **Series:** Preserve Planet Earth **Obv:** National arms **Rev:** Trionyx Turtle **Note:** Similar to 10 Dollars, KM#125.

Date	Mintage	F	VF	XF	Unc	BU
1994	—	—	—	—	10.00	12.00

KM# 115 DOLLAR
28.5200 g., Copper-Nickel **Series:** Preserve Planet Earth **Obv:** National arms **Rev:** Archaeopteryx **Note:** Correct spelling.

Date	Mintage	F	VF	XF	Unc	BU
1994	—	—	—	—	10.00	12.00

KM# 131 DOLLAR
28.5200 g., Copper-Nickel **Subject:** Babe Ruth Sultan of Swat **Obv:** National arms **Rev:** Head 1/4 right divides date within circle

Date	Mintage	F	VF	XF	Unc	BU
1994	—	—	—	—	8.00	—

KM# 131a DOLLAR
Gold Plated Copper-Nickel **Subject:** Babe Ruth Sultan of Swat **Obv:** National arms **Rev:** Head 1/4 right divides date within circle **Note:** Issued in a first day cover.

Date	Mintage	F	VF	XF	Unc	BU
1994	—	—	—	—	20.00	—

KM# 139 DOLLAR
Copper-Nickel **Subject:** Damon Hill- Fomula One Race Car **Obv:** National arms **Rev:** Bust facing flanked by helmet and flag above car and value within sprigs

Date	Mintage	F	VF	XF	Unc	BU
1994 Prooflike	—	—	—	—	7.00	—

KM# 248 DOLLAR
Copper-Nickel **Subject:** Hall of Fame - Roberto Clemente **Obv:** National arms **Rev:** Head facing

Date	Mintage	F	VF	XF	Unc	BU
1994	—	—	—	—	8.00	—

KM# 249 DOLLAR
Copper-Nickel **Subject:** Hall of Fame - Reggie Jackson **Obv:** National arms **Rev:** Baseball player divides circle above date

Date	Mintage	F	VF	XF	Unc	BU
1994	—	—	—	—	8.00	—

KM# 411 DOLLAR
Copper-Nickel **Obv:** National arms **Rev:** Head left above small gazelle and value

Date	Mintage	F	VF	XF	Unc	BU
1994	—	—	—	—	8.50	—

KM# 133 DOLLAR
Copper-Nickel **Series:** Preserve Planet Earth **Obv:** National arms **Rev:** Leopard

Date	Mintage	F	VF	XF	Unc	BU
1995	—	—	—	—	10.00	—

KM# 136 DOLLAR
Copper-Nickel **Series:** Preserve Planet Earth **Obv:** National arms **Rev:** Storks

Date	Mintage	F	VF	XF	Unc	BU
1995	—	—	—	—	9.00	—

KM# 140 DOLLAR
Copper-Nickel **Subject:** Sir Winston Churchill **Obv:** National arms **Rev:** Uniformed bust right with planes, army tanks and ship at right

Date	Mintage	F	VF	XF	Unc	BU
1995	—	—	—	—	6.00	—

KM# 141 DOLLAR
Copper-Nickel **Subject:** President Franklin D. Roosevelt **Obv:** National arms **Rev:** President Roosevelt riding in jeep

Date	Mintage	F	VF	XF	Unc	BU
1995	—	—	—	—	6.00	—

KM# 142 DOLLAR
Copper-Nickel **Subject:** General George Patton **Obv:** National arms **Rev:** General Patton in front of map

Date	Mintage	F	VF	XF	Unc	BU
1995	—	—	—	—	6.00	—

KM# 143 DOLLAR
Copper-Nickel **Subject:** President Harry S. Truman **Obv:** National arms **Rev:** President Truman facing

Date	Mintage	F	VF	XF	Unc	BU
1995	—	—	—	—	6.00	—

KM# 144 DOLLAR
Copper-Nickel **Subject:** President Charles de Gaulle **Obv:** National arms **Rev:** President on Champs Elysees

Date	Mintage	F	VF	XF	Unc	BU
1995	—	—	—	—	6.00	—

KM# 158 DOLLAR
Copper-Nickel **Subject:** Dr. Sun Yat-sen **Obv:** National arms **Rev:** Uniformed bust facing

Date	Mintage	F	VF	XF	Unc	BU
1995	—	—	—	—	6.50	—

KM# 161 DOLLAR
Copper-Nickel **Subject:** General Chiang Kai-shek **Obv:** National arms **Rev:** General Chiang kai-shek

Date	Mintage	F	VF	XF	Unc	BU
1995	—	—	—	—	6.50	—

KM# 164 DOLLAR
Copper-Nickel **Subject:** Cairo Conference **Obv:** National arms **Rev:** Chiang kai-shek, Roosevelt and Churchill

Date	Mintage	F	VF	XF	Unc	BU
1995	—	—	—	—	6.50	—

KM# 167 DOLLAR
Copper-Nickel **Subject:** 375th Anniversary - Pilgrim Fathers **Obv:** National arms **Rev:** The "Mayflower"

Date	Mintage	F	VF	XF	Unc	BU
1995	—	—	—	—	6.00	—

KM# 168 DOLLAR
Copper-Nickel **Subject:** 375th Anniversary - Pilgrim Fathers **Obv:** National arms **Rev:** First Thanksgiving scene

Date	Mintage	F	VF	XF	Unc	BU
1995	—	—	—	—	6.00	—

KM# 169 DOLLAR
Copper-Nickel **Subject:** 375th Anniversary - Pilgrim Fathers **Obv:** National arms **Rev:** Cape Cod and Pilgrims in skiff

Date	Mintage	F	VF	XF	Unc	BU
1995	—	—	—	—	6.00	—

KM# 170 DOLLAR
Copper-Nickel **Subject:** 375th Anniversary - Pilgrim Fathers **Obv:** National arms **Rev:** Pilgrim landing party

Date	Mintage	F	VF	XF	Unc	BU
1995	—	—	—	—	6.00	—

KM# 412 DOLLAR
Copper-Nickel **Subject:** Nations for Peace **Obv:** National arms **Rev:** Paper dolls, UN logo

Date	Mintage	F	VF	XF	Unc	BU
1995	—	—	—	—	8.50	—

KM# 128 DOLLAR
Copper-Nickel **Subject:** Star Trek **Obv:** National arms **Rev:** Conjoined busts facing **Note:** Similar to 10 Dollars, KM#129.

Date	Mintage	F	VF	XF	Unc	BU
1995	—	—	—	—	7.50	—

KM# 207 DOLLAR
Copper-Nickel **Subject:** Star Trek **Obv:** National arms **Rev:** Starships NCC-1701 and NCC-1701D **Note:** Similar to 10 Dollars, KM#208.

Date	Mintage	F	VF	XF	Unc	BU
1996	—	—	—	—	8.50	—

KM# 210 DOLLAR
Copper-Nickel **Subject:** Star Trek **Obv:** National arms **Rev:** Conjoined busts facing **Note:** Similar to 10 Dollars, KM#211.

Date	Mintage	F	VF	XF	Unc	BU
1996	—	—	—	—	8.50	—

KM# 213 DOLLAR
Copper-Nickel **Subject:** Star Trek **Obv:** National arms **Rev:** Conjoined busts facing **Note:** Similar to 10 Dollars, KM#214.

Date	Mintage	F	VF	XF	Unc	BU
1996	—	—	—	—	8.50	—

KM# 216 DOLLAR
Copper-Nickel **Subject:** Star Trek **Obv:** National arms **Rev:** Spock and Uhura **Note:** Similar to 10 Dollars, KM#217.

Date	Mintage	F	VF	XF	Unc	BU
1996	—	—	—	—	8.50	—

KM# 219 DOLLAR
Copper-Nickel **Subject:** Star Trek **Obv:** National arms **Rev:** Conjoined busts 1/4 left **Note:** Similar to 10 Dollars, KM#220.

Date	Mintage	F	VF	XF	Unc	BU
1996	—	—	—	—	8.50	—

KM# 222 DOLLAR
Copper-Nickel **Series:** Preserve Planet Earth **Obv:** National arms **Rev:** Grey Parrot **Note:** Similar to 10 Dollars, KM#223.

Date	Mintage	F	VF	XF	Unc	BU
1996	—	—	—	—	10.00	12.00

KM# 225 DOLLAR
Copper-Nickel **Series:** Preserve Planet Earth **Obv:** National arms **Rev:** Love Birds **Note:** Similar to 10 Dollars, KM#226.

Date	Mintage	F	VF	XF	Unc	BU
1996	—	—	—	—	10.00	12.00

KM# 254 DOLLAR
Copper-Nickel **Subject:** Chairman Mao Zedong **Obv:** National arms **Rev:** Standing figure facing **Note:** Similar to 10 Dollars, KM#256. Issued in first day cover.

Date	Mintage	F	VF	XF	Unc	BU
1996	20,000	—	—	—	7.50	—

KM# 260 DOLLAR
Copper-Nickel **Obv:** National arms **Rev:** Seated figures facing **Note:** Similar to 10 Dollars, KM#262. Issued in first day cover.

Date	Mintage	F	VF	XF	Unc	BU
1996	20,000	—	—	—	7.50	—

KM# 263 DOLLAR
Copper-Nickel **Subject:** Pioneers of the West **Obv:** National arms **Rev:** Bust facing at right of fighting indians **Note:** Similar to 10 Dollars, KM#264.

Date	Mintage	F	VF	XF	Unc	BU
1996	—	—	—	—	7.50	—

KM# 266 DOLLAR
Copper-Nickel **Subject:** Pioneers of the West **Obv:** National arms **Rev:** Davy Crockett **Note:** Similar to 10 Dollars, KM#267.

Date	Mintage	F	VF	XF	Unc	BU
1996	—	—	—	—	7.50	—

KM# 269 DOLLAR
Copper-Nickel **Subject:** Pioneers of the West **Obv:** National arms **Rev:** Jim Bowie in front of the Alamo **Note:** Similar to 10 Dollars, KM#270.

Date	Mintage	F	VF	XF	Unc	BU
1996	—	—	—	—	7.50	—

KM# 272 DOLLAR
Copper-Nickel **Subject:** Pioneers of the West **Obv:** National arms **Rev:** Kit Carson **Note:** Similar to 10 Dollars, KM#273.

Date	Mintage	F	VF	XF	Unc	BU
1996	—	—	—	—	7.50	—

KM# 275 DOLLAR
Copper-Nickel **Subject:** Pioneers of the West **Obv:** National arms **Rev:** Wild Bill Hickok **Note:** Similar to 10 Dollars, KM#276.

Date	Mintage	F	VF	XF	Unc	BU
1996	—	—	—	—	7.50	—

KM# 278 DOLLAR
Copper-Nickel **Subject:** Pioneers of the West **Obv:** National arms **Rev:** Buffalo Bill **Note:** Similar to 10 Dollars, KM#279.

Date	Mintage	F	VF	XF	Unc	BU
1996	—	—	—	—	7.50	—

KM# 560 DOLLAR
Silver **Obv:** National arms **Rev:** Multicolor fish

Date	Mintage	F	VF	XF	Unc	BU
1996B Proof	—	Value: 30.00				

KM# 569 DOLLAR
24.6100 g., Copper-Nickel, 38.6 mm. **Subject:** Marine Life Protection **Obv:** National arms **Rev:** Multicolor fish **Edge:** Reeded

Date	Mintage	F	VF	XF	Unc	BU
1996	—	—	—	—	27.50	—

KM# 570 DOLLAR
24.6100 g., Copper-Nickel, 38.6 mm. **Subject:** Marine Life Protection **Obv:** National arms **Rev:** Multicolor fish **Edge:** Reeded

Date	Mintage	F	VF	XF	Unc	BU
1997	—	—	—	—	27.50	—

KM# 426 DOLLAR
13.9400 g., Copper, 32 mm. **Subject:** AZA Species Survival Plan **Obv:** National arms **Rev:** Seated panda eating within circle **Edge:** Reeded

Date	Mintage	F	VF	XF	Unc	BU
1997	—	—	—	—	7.50	10.00

KM# 313 DOLLAR
Copper-Nickel **Subject:** Return of Hong Kong - Dragon **Obv:** National arms

Date	Mintage	F	VF	XF	Unc	BU
1997	—	—	—	—	8.50	—

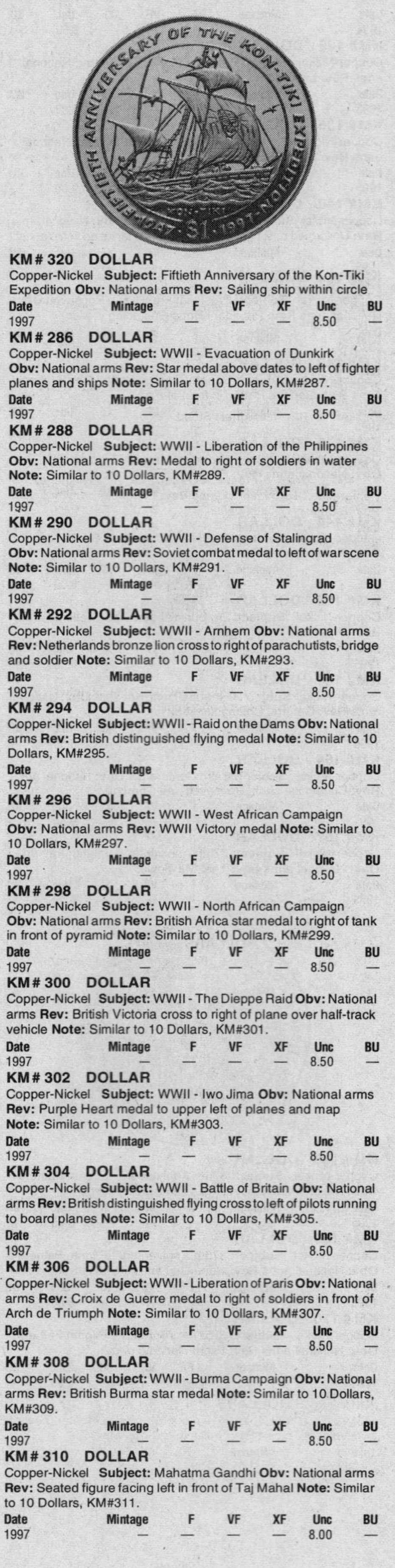

KM# 320 DOLLAR
Copper-Nickel **Subject:** Fiftieth Anniversary of the Kon-Tiki Expedition **Obv:** National arms **Rev:** Sailing ship within circle

Date	Mintage	F	VF	XF	Unc	BU
1997	—	—	—	—	8.50	—

KM# 286 DOLLAR
Copper-Nickel **Subject:** WWII - Evacuation of Dunkirk **Obv:** National arms **Rev:** Star medal above dates to left of fighter planes and ships **Note:** Similar to 10 Dollars, KM#287.

Date	Mintage	F	VF	XF	Unc	BU
1997	—	—	—	—	8.50	—

KM# 288 DOLLAR
Copper-Nickel **Subject:** WWII - Liberation of the Philippines **Obv:** National arms **Rev:** Medal to right of soldiers in water **Note:** Similar to 10 Dollars, KM#289.

Date	Mintage	F	VF	XF	Unc	BU
1997	—	—	—	—	8.50	—

KM# 290 DOLLAR
Copper-Nickel **Subject:** WWII - Defense of Stalingrad **Obv:** National arms **Rev:** Soviet combat medal to left of war scene **Note:** Similar to 10 Dollars, KM#291.

Date	Mintage	F	VF	XF	Unc	BU
1997	—	—	—	—	8.50	—

KM# 292 DOLLAR
Copper-Nickel **Subject:** WWII - Arnhem **Obv:** National arms **Rev:** Netherlands bronze lion cross to right of parachutists, bridge and soldier **Note:** Similar to 10 Dollars, KM#293.

Date	Mintage	F	VF	XF	Unc	BU
1997	—	—	—	—	8.50	—

KM# 294 DOLLAR
Copper-Nickel **Subject:** WWII - Raid on the Dams **Obv:** National arms **Rev:** British distinguished flying medal **Note:** Similar to 10 Dollars, KM#295.

Date	Mintage	F	VF	XF	Unc	BU
1997	—	—	—	—	8.50	—

KM# 296 DOLLAR
Copper-Nickel **Subject:** WWII - West African Campaign **Obv:** National arms **Rev:** WWII Victory medal **Note:** Similar to 10 Dollars, KM#297.

Date	Mintage	F	VF	XF	Unc	BU
1997	—	—	—	—	8.50	—

KM# 298 DOLLAR
Copper-Nickel **Subject:** WWII - North African Campaign **Obv:** National arms **Rev:** British Africa star medal to right of tank in front of pyramid **Note:** Similar to 10 Dollars, KM#299.

Date	Mintage	F	VF	XF	Unc	BU
1997	—	—	—	—	8.50	—

KM# 300 DOLLAR
Copper-Nickel **Subject:** WWII - The Dieppe Raid **Obv:** National arms **Rev:** British Victoria cross to right of plane over half-track vehicle **Note:** Similar to 10 Dollars, KM#301.

Date	Mintage	F	VF	XF	Unc	BU
1997	—	—	—	—	8.50	—

KM# 302 DOLLAR
Copper-Nickel **Subject:** WWII - Iwo Jima **Obv:** National arms **Rev:** Purple Heart medal to upper left of planes and map **Note:** Similar to 10 Dollars, KM#303.

Date	Mintage	F	VF	XF	Unc	BU
1997	—	—	—	—	8.50	—

KM# 304 DOLLAR
Copper-Nickel **Subject:** WWII - Battle of Britain **Obv:** National arms **Rev:** British distinguished flying cross to left of pilots running to board planes **Note:** Similar to 10 Dollars, KM#305.

Date	Mintage	F	VF	XF	Unc	BU
1997	—	—	—	—	8.50	—

KM# 306 DOLLAR
Copper-Nickel **Subject:** WWII - Liberation of Paris **Obv:** National arms **Rev:** Croix de Guerre medal to right of soldiers in front of Arch de Triumph **Note:** Similar to 10 Dollars, KM#307.

Date	Mintage	F	VF	XF	Unc	BU
1997	—	—	—	—	8.50	—

KM# 308 DOLLAR
Copper-Nickel **Subject:** WWII - Burma Campaign **Obv:** National arms **Rev:** British Burma star medal **Note:** Similar to 10 Dollars, KM#309.

Date	Mintage	F	VF	XF	Unc	BU
1997	—	—	—	—	8.50	—

KM# 310 DOLLAR
Copper-Nickel **Subject:** Mahatma Gandhi **Obv:** National arms **Rev:** Seated figure facing left in front of Taj Mahal **Note:** Similar to 10 Dollars, KM#311.

Date	Mintage	F	VF	XF	Unc	BU
1997	—	—	—	—	8.00	—

KM# 324 DOLLAR
Copper-Nickel **Subject:** Jurassic Park - Stegosaurus **Obv:** National arms **Rev:** Stegosaurus **Note:** Similar to 10 Dollars, KM#325.

Date	Mintage	F	VF	XF	Unc	BU
1997	—	—	—	—	10.00	—

KM# 327 DOLLAR
Copper-Nickel **Subject:** Golden Wedding Anniversary **Obv:** National arms **Rev:** E & P initials above two shields **Note:** Similar to 10 Dollars, KM#328.

Date	Mintage	F	VF	XF	Unc	BU
1997	—	—	—	—	7.50	—

KM# 330 DOLLAR
Copper-Nickel **Subject:** Golden Wedding Anniversary **Obv:** National arms **Rev:** Royal couple with horse **Note:** Similar to 10 Dollars, KM#331.

Date	Mintage	F	VF	XF	Unc	BU
1997	—	—	—	—	7.50	—

KM# 333 DOLLAR
Copper-Nickel **Subject:** Golden Wedding Anniversary **Obv:** National arms **Rev:** Couple with dogs **Note:** Similar to 10 Dollars, KM#334.

Date	Mintage	F	VF	XF	Unc	BU
1997	—	—	—	—	7.50	—

KM# 336 DOLLAR
Copper-Nickel **Subject:** Golden Wedding Anniversary **Obv:** National arms **Rev:** Royal couple with children **Note:** Similar to 10 Dollars, KM#337.

Date	Mintage	F	VF	XF	Unc	BU
1997	—	—	—	—	7.50	—

KM# 344 DOLLAR
Copper-Nickel **Subject:** 150th Anniversary of Independence **Obv:** National arms **Rev:** The "Ashmon" **Note:** Similar to 10 Dollars, KM#345.

Date	Mintage	F	VF	XF	Unc	BU
1997	—	—	—	—	8.50	—

KM# 368 DOLLAR
Copper-Nickel **Subject:** Star Trek - The Next Generation **Obv:** National arms **Rev:** Romulan Warbird **Note:** Similar to 10 Dollars, KM#369.

Date	Mintage	F	VF	XF	Unc	BU
1997	—	—	—	—	7.50	—

KM# 371 DOLLAR
Copper-Nickel **Subject:** Star Trek - The Next Generation **Obv:** National arms **Rev:** Klingon Attack Cruiser **Note:** Similar to 10 Dollars, KM#372.

Date	Mintage	F	VF	XF	Unc	BU
1997	—	—	—	—	7.50	—

KM# 374 DOLLAR
Copper-Nickel **Subject:** Star Trek - The Next Generation **Obv:** National arms **Rev:** U.S.S. Enterprise NCC-1701-D **Note:** Similar to 10 Dollars, KM#375.

Date	Mintage	F	VF	XF	Unc	BU
1997	—	—	—	—	7.50	—

KM# 377 DOLLAR
Copper-Nickel **Subject:** Star Trek - The Next Generation **Obv:** National arms **Rev:** Klingon Bird of Prey **Note:** Similar to 10 Dollars, KM#378.

Date	Mintage	F	VF	XF	Unc	BU
1997	—	—	—	—	7.50	—

KM# 380 DOLLAR
Copper-Nickel **Subject:** Star Trek - The Next Generation **Obv:** National arms **Rev:** Borg Cube **Note:** Similar to 10 Dollars, KM#381.

Date	Mintage	F	VF	XF	Unc	BU
1997	—	—	—	—	7.50	—

KM# 383 DOLLAR
Copper-Nickel **Subject:** Star Trek - The Next Generation **Obv:** National arms **Rev:** Ferengi Marauder **Note:** Similar to 10 Dollars, KM#384.

Date	Mintage	F	VF	XF	Unc	BU
1997	—	—	—	—	7.50	—

KM# 386 DOLLAR
Copper-Nickel **Subject:** President Ronald Reagan **Obv:** National arms **Rev:** Lincoln Memorial below head right **Note:** Similar to 10 Dollars, KM#387.

Date	Mintage	F	VF	XF	Unc	BU
1998	—	—	—	—	8.50	—

KM# 401 DOLLAR
Copper-Nickel **Subject:** Christopher Columbus **Obv:** National arms **Rev:** Bust 1/4 right above ship **Note:** Similar to 10 Dollars, KM#402.

Date	Mintage	F	VF	XF	Unc	BU
1999	—	—	—	—	8.00	—

KM# 404 DOLLAR
Copper-Nickel **Subject:** Captain Cook **Obv:** National arms **Rev:** Portrait, ship and map **Note:** Similar to 10 Dollars, KM#405.

Date	Mintage	F	VF	XF	Unc	BU
1999	—	—	—	—	8.00	—

KM# 407 DOLLAR
Copper-Nickel **Subject:** Return of Macao to China **Obv:** National arms **Rev:** Dragon and phoenix **Note:** Similar to 10 Dollars, KM#408.

Date	Mintage	F	VF	XF	Unc	BU
1999	—	—	—	—	8.50	—

KM# 413 DOLLAR
Copper-Nickel **Subject:** The Wedding of Prince Edward **Obv:** National arms **Rev:** Couple in carriage **Note:** Similar to 10 Dollars, KM#413.

Date	Mintage	F	VF	XF	Unc	BU
1999	—	—	—	—	8.00	—

KM# 571 DOLLAR

24.6100 g., Copper-Nickel, 38.6 mm. **Subject:** Marine Life Protection **Obv:** National arms **Rev:** Multicolor fish **Edge:** Reeded

Date	Mintage	F	VF	XF	Unc	BU
1999	—	—	—	—	27.50	—

KM# 612 DOLLAR

5.3500 g., Copper Nickel, 24.9 mm. **Subject:** Millennium - Year of the Dragon **Obv:** National arms within circle above date **Rev:** Chinese dragon within circle **Edge:** Reeded

Date	Mintage	F	VF	XF	Unc	BU
2000	—	—	—	—	5.00	6.00

KM# 615 DOLLAR

5.3500 g., Copper-Nickel, 24.9 mm. **Obv:** National arms within circle above date **Rev:** Dancing style dragon within circle **Edge:** Reeded

Date	Mintage	F	VF	XF	Unc	BU
2000	—	—	—	—	5.00	6.00

KM# 635 DOLLAR

0.9990 Silver, 21 mm. **Obv:** National arms **Rev:** American Quarter Horse

Date	Mintage	F	VF	XF	Unc	BU
2000 Proof	—	Value: 15.00				

KM# 696 DOLLAR

31.1000 g., 0.9990 Silver 0.9989 oz. ASW, 39 mm. **Subject:** Millennium **Obv:** American style eagle **Rev:** Morgan dollar style Liberty head **Edge:** Reeded

Date	Mintage	F	VF	XF	Unc	BU
2000 Proof	—	Value: 25.00				

KM# 442 DOLLAR

28.2800 g., Copper-Nickel, 38.6 mm. **Subject:** Greenwich Meridian **Obv:** National arms **Rev:** World landmarks and fireworks **Edge:** Reeded

Date	Mintage	F	VF	XF	Unc	BU
2000	—	—	—	—	10.00	—

KM# 47 2 DOLLARS

Copper-Nickel **Series:** F.A.O. **Subject:** World Fisheries Conference **Obv:** National arms **Rev:** Longneck croaker fish **Rev. Designer:** Stuart Devlin

Date	Mintage	F	VF	XF	Unc	BU
1983	100,000	—	—	—	15.00	20.00

KM# 47a 2 DOLLARS

28.2800 g., 0.9250 Silver .8411 oz. ASW **Subject:** World Fisheries Conference **Obv:** National arms **Rev:** Longneck croaker fish **Rev. Designer:** Stuart Devlin

Date	Mintage	F	VF	XF	Unc	BU
1983 Proof	20,000	Value: 50.00				

KM# 47b 2 DOLLARS

47.5400 g., Gold **Series:** F.A.O. **Subject:** World Fisheries Conference **Obv:** National arms **Rev:** Longneck croaker fish **Rev. Designer:** Stuart Devlin

Date	Mintage	F	VF	XF	Unc	BU
1983 Proof	600	Value: 950				

KM# 24 2-1/2 DOLLARS

4.1796 g., 0.9000 Gold .1209 oz. AGW **Subject:** Inauguration of President Tolbert **Rev:** Capitol building

Date	Mintage	F	VF	XF	Unc	BU
1972 Proof	—	Value: 95.00				

KM# 644 2-1/2 DOLLARS

11.8000 g., Copper-Nickel, 29.5 mm. **Obv:** National arms divides date **Rev:** Olympic torch runner facing right **Edge:** Plain

Date	Mintage	F	VF	XF	Unc	BU
1999 Proof	—	Value: 12.50				

KM# 62 5 DOLLARS

5.0000 g., 0.9000 Gold .1447 oz. AGW **Subject:** 25th Anniversary of Inter-Continental Hotels **Obv:** Value below hotel flanked by sprigs **Rev:** Letter I within football flanked by dates

Date	Mintage	F	VF	XF	Unc	BU
ND(1971) Proof	—	Value: 110				

KM# 25 5 DOLLARS

8.3592 g., 0.9000 Gold .2419 oz. AGW **Subject:** Inauguration of President Tolbert **Rev:** Full masted ship at sea

Date	Mintage	F	VF	XF	Unc	BU
1972 Proof	—	Value: 175				

KM# 29 5 DOLLARS

34.1000 g., 0.9000 Silver .9868 oz. ASW **Obv:** National arms, value written on top, date on bottom **Rev:** Standing elephant looking 1/4 right above star

Date	Mintage	F	VF	XF	Unc	BU
1973	500	—	—	—	25.00	—
1973 Proof	28,000	Value: 16.00				
1974 Proof	20,000	Value: 16.00				
1975 Proof	9,017	Value: 16.00				
1976 Proof	3,683	Value: 17.50				
1977 Proof	1,640	Value: 20.00				
1978FM Proof	7,311	Value: 15.00				

KM# 29a 5 DOLLARS

34.1000 g., 0.9000 Silver .9868 oz. ASW **Obv:** National arms **Rev:** Standing elephant looking 1/4 right above star **Edge Lettering:** O.A.U. July 1979

Date	Mintage	F	VF	XF	Unc	BU
1979 Proof	1,857	Value: 25.00				

KM# 44 5 DOLLARS

Copper-Nickel **Subject:** Military Memorial **Obv:** National arms above date **Rev:** Memorial statue and value flanked by shrubs **Shape:** 7-sided

Date	Mintage	F	VF	XF	Unc	BU
1982	4,000,000	—	5.00	6.50	9.00	—
1985	2,000,000	—	5.00	6.50	9.00	—

KM# 73 5 DOLLARS

15.5500 g., 0.9990 Silver .5000 oz. ASW **Subject:** Formula One - Gerhard Berger **Obv:** National arms divide date **Rev:** Head 1/4 right, racecar and flag

Date	Mintage	F	VF	XF	Unc	BU
1992 Proof	—	Value: 18.50				

KM# 76 5 DOLLARS

15.5500 g., 0.9990 Silver .5000 oz. ASW **Subject:** Formula One - Nigel Mansell **Obv:** National arms **Rev:** Head right, racecar, date and flag above sprigs

Date	Mintage	F	VF	XF	Unc	BU
1992 Proof	Est. 50,000	Value: 18.50				

KM# 78 5 DOLLARS

15.5500 g., 0.9990 Silver .5000 oz. ASW **Subject:** Formula One - Ayrton Senna **Obv:** National arms **Rev:** Bust 1/4 left above flag, racecar, dates and value

Date	Mintage	F	VF	XF	Unc	BU
1992 Proof	Est. 50,000	Value: 18.50				

KM# 79 5 DOLLARS
15.5500 g., 0.9990 Silver .5000 oz. ASW **Subject:** Formula One - Riccardo Patrese **Obv:** National arms **Rev:** Head 1/4 left to right of flag and racecar **Note:** Similar to 10 Dollars, KM#74.

Date	Mintage	F	VF	XF	Unc	BU
1992 Proof	Est. 50,000	Value: 18.50				

KM# 77 5 DOLLARS
15.5500 g., 0.9990 Silver .5000 oz. ASW **Subject:** Formula One - Aguri Suzuki **Obv:** National arms **Rev:** Racecar below bust at left **Note:** Similar to 10 Dollars, KM#84.

Date	Mintage	F	VF	XF	Unc	BU
1992 Proof	Est. 50,000	Value: 18.50				

KM# 80 5 DOLLARS
15.5500 g., 0.9990 Silver .5000 oz. ASW **Subject:** Formula One - Michael Schumacher **Obv:** National arms **Rev:** Bust at right, car at left **Note:** Similar to 10 Dollars, KM#86.

Date	Mintage	F	VF	XF	Unc	BU
1992 Proof	50,000	Value: 18.50				

KM# 81 5 DOLLARS
15.5500 g., 0.9990 Silver .5000 oz. ASW **Subject:** Formula One - Alain Prost **Obv:** National arms **Rev:** Head 3/4 left above flag, racecar, dates and value **Note:** Similar to 10 Dollars, KM#87.

Date	Mintage	F	VF	XF	Unc	BU
1992 Proof	50,000	Value: 18.50				

KM# 82 5 DOLLARS
15.5500 g., 0.9990 Silver .5000 oz. ASW **Subject:** Formula One - Ukyo Katayama **Obv:** National arms **Rev:** Racecar below bust at left **Note:** Similar to 10 Dollars, KM#88.

Date	Mintage	F	VF	XF	Unc	BU
1992 Proof	50,000	Value: 18.50				

KM# 67 5 DOLLARS
15.5500 g., 0.9990 Silver .5000 oz. ASW **Subject:** President Bill Clinton **Obv:** National arms **Rev:** Head right divides date and value above building **Note:** Similar to 10 Dollars, KM#68.

Date	Mintage	F	VF	XF	Unc	BU
1993 Proof	50,000	Value: 25.00				

KM# 97 5 DOLLARS
15.5500 g., 0.9990 Silver .5000 oz. ASW **Subject:** Chancellor Willy Brandt **Obv:** National arms **Rev:** Horses pulling casket below head right dividing dates **Note:** Similar to 10 Dollars, KM#72.

Date	Mintage	F	VF	XF	Unc	BU
1993 Proof	—	Value: 18.50				

KM# 103 5 DOLLARS
15.5500 g., 0.9990 Silver .5000 oz. ASW **Subject:** President John F. Kennedy **Obv:** National arms **Rev:** President Kennedy **Note:** Similar to 10 Dollars, KM#104.

Date	Mintage	F	VF	XF	Unc	BU
1993 Proof	50,000	Value: 20.00				

KM# 179 5 DOLLARS
15.5500 g., 0.9990 Silver .5000 oz. ASW **Subject:** Formula One - Mika Hakkinen **Obv:** National arms **Rev:** Mike Hakkinen

Date	Mintage	F	VF	XF	Unc	BU
1995 Proof	50,000	Value: 20.00				

KM# 182 5 DOLLARS
15.5500 g., 0.9990 Silver .5000 oz. ASW **Subject:** Formula One **Obv:** National arms **Rev:** Martin Brundle

Date	Mintage	F	VF	XF	Unc	BU
1995 Proof	Est. 50,000	Value: 20.00				

KM# 185 5 DOLLARS
15.5500 g., 0.9990 Silver .5000 oz. ASW **Subject:** Formula One - Rubens Barrichello **Obv:** National arms **Rev:** Rubens Barrichello

Date	Mintage	F	VF	XF	Unc	BU
1995 Proof	Est. 50,000	Value: 20.00				

KM# 188 5 DOLLARS
15.5500 g., 0.9990 Silver .5000 oz. ASW **Subject:** Formula One - David Coulthard **Obv:** National arms **Rev:** David Coulthard

Date	Mintage	F	VF	XF	Unc	BU
1995 Proof	Est. 50,000	Value: 20.00				

KM# 191 5 DOLLARS
15.5500 g., 0.9990 Silver .5000 oz. ASW **Subject:** Formula One - Jean Alesi **Obv:** National arms **Rev:** Jean Alesi

Date	Mintage	F	VF	XF	Unc	BU
1995 Proof	Est. 50,000	Value: 20.00				

KM# 562 5 DOLLARS
15.5000 g., 0.9990 Silver 0.4978 oz. ASW **Obv:** National arms **Rev:** Benz Patent motor car

Date	Mintage	F	VF	XF	Unc	BU
1995 Proof	—	Value: 24.50				

KM# 563 5 DOLLARS
15.5000 g., 0.9990 Silver, 32 mm. **Obv:** National arms **Rev:** Bughatti Royale

Date	Mintage	F	VF	XF	Unc	BU
1995	—	—	—	—	25.00	—

KM# 195 5 DOLLARS
15.5500 g., 0.9990 Silver .5000 oz. ASW **Subject:** Formula One - Mark Blundell **Obv:** National arms **Rev:** Mark Brundell **Note:** Similar to 10 Dollars, KM#199.

Date	Mintage	F	VF	XF	Unc	BU
1996 Proof	50,000	Value: 20.00				

KM# 196 5 DOLLARS
15.5500 g., 0.9990 Silver .5000 oz. ASW **Subject:** Formula One - Johnny Herbert **Obv:** National arms **Rev:** Johnny Herbert **Note:** Similar to 10 Dollars, KM#200.

Date	Mintage	F	VF	XF	Unc	BU
1996 Proof	50,000	Value: 20.00				

KM# 197 5 DOLLARS
15.5500 g., 0.9990 Silver .5000 oz. ASW **Subject:** Formula One - Eddie Irvine **Obv:** National arms **Rev:** Eddie Irvine **Note:** Similar to 10 Dollars, KM#201.

Date	Mintage	F	VF	XF	Unc	BU
1996 Proof	50,000	Value: 20.00				

KM# 198 5 DOLLARS
15.5500 g., 0.9990 Silver .5000 oz. ASW **Subject:** Formula One - Heinz Frentzen **Obv:** National arms **Rev:** Heinz Frentzen **Note:** Similar to 10 Dollars, KM#202.

Date	Mintage	F	VF	XF	Unc	BU
1996 Proof	50,000	Value: 20.00				

KM# 228 5 DOLLARS
15.5500 g., 0.9990 Silver .5000 oz. ASW **Subject:** Formula One - Ayrton Senna **Obv:** National arms **Rev:** Ayrton Senna **Note:** Similar to 10 Dollars, KM#229.

Date	Mintage	F	VF	XF	Unc	BU
1996 Proof	50,000	Value: 20.00				

KM# 255 5 DOLLARS
15.5500 g., 0.9990 Silver .5000 oz. ASW **Subject:** Chairman Mao Zedong **Obv:** National arms **Rev:** Standing figure facing above value **Note:** Similar to 10 Dollars, KM#256.

Date	Mintage	F	VF	XF	Unc	BU
1996 Proof	20,000	Value: 20.00				

KM# 261 5 DOLLARS
15.5500 g., 0.9990 Silver .5000 oz. ASW **Subject:** Chairman Mao Zedong and President Nixon **Obv:** National arms **Rev:** Seated figures facing **Note:** Similar to 10 Dollars, KM#262.

Date	Mintage	F	VF	XF	Unc	BU
1996 Proof	20,000	Value: 20.00				

KM# A452 5 DOLLARS
Copper-Nickel **Subject:** Queen of Hearts **Obv:** National arms **Rev:** Diana wearing a choker

Date	Mintage	F	VF	XF	Unc	BU
1997	—	—	—	—	15.00	—

KM# 600 5 DOLLARS
21.3000 g., Copper-Nickel, 38.5 mm. **Obv:** National arms **Rev:** Tiger at rest **Edge:** Reeded

Date	Mintage	F	VF	XF	Unc	BU
1997	—	—	—	—	10.00	—

KM# 351 5 DOLLARS
Copper-Nickel **Subject:** Chinese Astrology **Obv:** Seated Liberty **Rev:** Two rats and pumpkin

Date	Mintage	F	VF	XF	Unc	BU
1997	Est. 4,000	—	—	—	6.00	7.00

KM# 352 5 DOLLARS
Copper-Nickel **Subject:** Chinese Astrology **Obv:** Seated Liberty **Rev:** Ox

Date	Mintage	F	VF	XF	Unc	BU
1997	Est. 4,000	—	—	—	5.00	6.00

KM# 353 5 DOLLARS
Copper-Nickel **Subject:** Chinese Astrology **Obv:** Seated Liberty **Rev:** Tiger

Date	Mintage	F	VF	XF	Unc	BU
1997	Est. 4,000	—	—	—	6.00	7.00

KM# 354 5 DOLLARS
Copper-Nickel **Subject:** Chinese Astrology **Obv:** Seated Liberty **Rev:** Rabbits

Date	Mintage	F	VF	XF	Unc	BU
1997	Est. 4,000	—	—	—	5.00	6.00

KM# 355 5 DOLLARS
Copper-Nickel **Subject:** Chinese Astrology **Obv:** Seated Liberty **Rev:** Dragon

Date	Mintage	F	VF	XF	Unc	BU
1997	Est. 4,000	—	—	—	6.00	7.00

KM# 356 5 DOLLARS
Copper-Nickel **Subject:** Chinese Astrology **Obv:** Seated Liberty **Rev:** Snake

Date	Mintage	F	VF	XF	Unc	BU
1997	Est. 4,000	—	—	—	5.00	6.00

KM# 357 5 DOLLARS
Copper-Nickel **Subject:** Chinese Astrology **Obv:** Seated Liberty **Rev:** Horse

Date	Mintage	F	VF	XF	Unc	BU
1997	Est. 4,000	—	—	—	6.00	7.00

KM# 358 5 DOLLARS
Copper-Nickel **Subject:** Chinese Astrology **Obv:** Seated Liberty **Rev:** Goat

Date	Mintage	F	VF	XF	Unc	BU
1997	Est. 4,000	—	—	—	5.00	6.00

KM# 359 5 DOLLARS
Copper-Nickel **Subject:** Chinese Astrology **Obv:** Seated Liberty **Rev:** Monkey

Date	Mintage	F	VF	XF	Unc	BU
1997	Est. 4,000	—	—	—	5.00	6.00

KM# 360 5 DOLLARS
Copper-Nickel **Subject:** Chinese Astrology **Obv:** Seated Liberty **Rev:** Rooster

Date	Mintage	F	VF	XF	Unc	BU
1997	Est. 4,000	—	—	—	5.00	6.00

KM# 361 5 DOLLARS
Copper-Nickel **Subject:** Chinese Astrology **Obv:** Seated Liberty **Rev:** Wrinkled seated dog

Date	Mintage	F	VF	XF	Unc	BU
1997	Est. 4,000	—	—	—	6.00	7.00

KM# 362 5 DOLLARS
Copper-Nickel **Subject:** Chinese Astrology **Obv:** Seated Liberty **Rev:** Pig

Date	Mintage	F	VF	XF	Unc	BU
1997	Est. 4,000	—	—	—	5.00	6.00

KM# 441 5 DOLLARS
20.5600 g., Copper-Nickel, 38.5 mm. **Obv:** National arms divide date **Rev:** Polar bear **Edge:** Reeded

Date	Mintage	F	VF	XF	Unc	BU
1997	—	—	—	—	8.50	—

KM# 445 5 DOLLARS
25.1000 g., Copper-Nickel, 38.5 mm. **Subject:** Princess Diana **Obv:** National arms divides date **Rev:** Crowned bust 3/4 left **Edge:** Reeded

Date	Mintage	F	VF	XF	Unc	BU
1997 Proof	—	Value: 20.00				

KM# 446 5 DOLLARS
25.1000 g., Copper-Nickel, 38.5 mm. **Subject:** Diana Series - Lady Spencer **Obv:** National arms **Rev:** Young girl's portrait **Edge:** Reeded

Date	Mintage	F	VF	XF	Unc	BU
1997	—	—	—	—	15.00	—

KM# 447 5 DOLLARS
25.1000 g., Copper-Nickel **Subject:** First TV Interview **Obv:** National arms **Rev:** Portrait of Diana with microphone

Date	Mintage	F	VF	XF	Unc	BU
1997	—	—	—	—	15.00	—

KM# 448 5 DOLLARS
Copper-Nickel **Subject:** Diana's Official Portrait **Obv:** National arms **Rev:** Portrait

Date	Mintage	F	VF	XF	Unc	BU
1997	—	—	—	—	15.00	—

KM# 449 5 DOLLARS
Copper-Nickel **Subject:** Wedding Day **Obv:** National arms **Rev:** Diana in wedding dress

Date	Mintage	F	VF	XF	Unc	BU
1997	—	—	—	—	15.00	—

KM# 450 5 DOLLARS
Copper-Nickel **Subject:** "People's Princess" - Diana **Obv:** National arms **Rev:** Formal portrait

Date	Mintage	F	VF	XF	Unc	BU
1997	—	—	—	—	15.00	—

KM# 451 5 DOLLARS
Copper-Nickel **Subject:** England's Rose **Obv:** National arms **Rev:** Diana with bouquet of roses

Date	Mintage	F	VF	XF	Unc	BU
1997	—	—	—	—	15.00	—

KM# 452 5 DOLLARS
Copper-Nickel **Series:** Diana Princess of Wales **Obv:** National arms **Rev:** Head 3/4 left

Date	Mintage	F	VF	XF	Unc	BU
1997	—	—	—	—	—	—

KM# 453 5 DOLLARS
Copper-Nickel **Subject:** Elegance **Obv:** National arms **Rev:** Diana wearing a high collar

Date	Mintage	F	VF	XF	Unc	BU
1997	—	—	—	—	15.00	—

KM# 454 5 DOLLARS
Copper-Nickel **Subject:** Birth of William **Obv:** National arms **Rev:** Diana holding Prince William

Date	Mintage	F	VF	XF	Unc	BU
1997	—	—	—	—	15.00	—

KM# 455 5 DOLLARS
Copper-Nickel **Subject:** William's Christening **Obv:** National arms **Rev:** Diana holding Prince William

Date	Mintage	F	VF	XF	Unc	BU
1997	—	—	—	—	15.00	—

KM# 456 5 DOLLARS
Copper-Nickel **Subject:** Birth of Prince Harry **Obv:** National arms **Rev:** Diana holding Prince Harry

Date	Mintage	F	VF	XF	Unc	BU
1997	—	—	—	—	15.00	—

KM# 457 5 DOLLARS
Copper-Nickel **Subject:** Loving Mother **Obv:** National arms **Rev:** Diana with Prince William and Prince Harry

Date	Mintage	F	VF	XF	Unc	BU
1997	—	—	—	—	15.00	—

KM# 458 5 DOLLARS
Copper-Nickel **Subject:** Royal Family **Obv:** National arms **Rev:** Family portrait

Date	Mintage	F	VF	XF	Unc	BU
1997	—	—	—	—	15.00	—

KM# 459 5 DOLLARS
Copper-Nickel **Subject:** Queen Elizabeth and Lady Diana **Obv:** National arms **Rev:** Conjoined crowned busts right

Date	Mintage	F	VF	XF	Unc	BU
1997	—	—	—	—	15.00	—

KM# 460 5 DOLLARS
Copper-Nickel **Obv:** National arms **Rev:** Queen Mother and Diana

Date	Mintage	F	VF	XF	Unc	BU
1997	—	—	—	—	15.00	—

KM# 461 5 DOLLARS
Copper-Nickel **Subject:** Visit to Wales **Obv:** National arms **Rev:** Charles and Diana

Date	Mintage	F	VF	XF	Unc	BU
1997	—	—	—	—	15.00	—

KM# 462 5 DOLLARS
Copper-Nickel **Subject:** Australian Tour **Obv:** National arms **Rev:** Charles and Diana dancing

Date	Mintage	F	VF	XF	Unc	BU
1997	—	—	—	—	15.00	—

KM# 463 5 DOLLARS
Copper-Nickel **Subject:** Tour of Japan **Obv:** National arms **Rev:** Half length figures looking right

Date	Mintage	F	VF	XF	Unc	BU
1997	—	—	—	—	15.00	—

KM# 464 5 DOLLARS
Copper-Nickel, 38.5 mm. **Obv:** National arms **Rev:** Diana reading to child

Date	Mintage	F	VF	XF	Unc	BU
1997	—	—	—	—	15.00	—

KM# 465 5 DOLLARS
Copper-Nickel **Subject:** Charity **Obv:** National arms **Rev:** Diana with poor child

Date	Mintage	F	VF	XF	Unc	BU
1997	—	—	—	—	15.00	—

KM# 466 5 DOLLARS
Copper-Nickel **Obv:** National arms **Rev:** Diana with sick child

Date	Mintage	F	VF	XF	Unc	BU
1997	—	—	—	—	15.00	—

KM# 467 5 DOLLARS
Copper-Nickel **Obv:** National arms **Rev:** Diana's casket on gun carriage

Date	Mintage	F	VF	XF	Unc	BU
1997	—	—	—	—	15.00	—

KM# 496 5 DOLLARS
20.5600 g., Copper-Nickel, 38.5 mm. **Obv:** National arms **Rev:** Giraffe **Edge:** Reeded

Date	Mintage	F	VF	XF	Unc	BU
1997	—	—	—	—	7.50	—

KM# 566 5 DOLLARS
Copper-Nickel **Obv:** National arms **Rev:** Elephant

Date	Mintage	F	VF	XF	Unc	BU
1997	—	—	—	—	17.50	—

KM# 578 5 DOLLARS
23.7000 g., Copper-Nickel, 38.5 mm. **Subject:** Year of the Ox **Obv:** National arms **Rev:** Ox **Edge:** Reeded

Date	Mintage	F	VF	XF	Unc	BU
1997	—	—	—	—	7.50	—

KM# 579 5 DOLLARS
21.3000 g., Copper-Nickel, 38.4 mm. **Obv:** National arms **Rev:** Elephant **Edge:** Reeded

Date	Mintage	F	VF	XF	Unc	BU
1997	—	—	—	—	8.50	—

KM# 580 5 DOLLARS
21.3000 g., Copper-Nickel, 38.4 mm. **Obv:** National arms **Rev:** Lion **Edge:** Reeded

Date	Mintage	F	VF	XF	Unc	BU
1997	—	—	—	—	8.50	—

KM# 581 5 DOLLARS
21.3000 g., Copper-Nickel, 38.4 mm. **Obv:** National arms **Rev:** Rhinoceros **Edge:** Reeded

Date	Mintage	F	VF	XF	Unc	BU
1997	—	—	—	—	8.50	—

KM# 582 5 DOLLARS
21.3000 g., Copper-Nickel, 38.4 mm. **Obv:** National arms **Rev:** Zebra **Edge:** Reeded

Date	Mintage	F	VF	XF	Unc	BU
1997	—	—	—	—	8.50	—

KM# 583 5 DOLLARS
21.3000 g., Copper-Nickel, 38.4 mm. **Obv:** National arms **Rev:** Two kangaroos **Edge:** Reeded

Date	Mintage	F	VF	XF	Unc	BU
1997	—	—	—	—	8.50	—

KM# 339 5 DOLLARS
Copper-Nickel **Subject:** Year of the Tiger **Obv:** National arms **Rev:** Tiger with three cubs

Date	Mintage	F	VF	XF	Unc	BU
1998 (1997) Proof	—	Value: 15.00				

KM# 363 5 DOLLARS
Copper-Nickel **Subject:** RMS Titanic **Obv:** National arms **Rev:** Cameo above sinking ship **Note:** Similar to 20 Dollars, KM#364.

Date	Mintage	F	VF	XF	Unc	BU
1998	—	—	—	—	10.00	—

KM# 572 5 DOLLARS
24.9700 g., 0.9250 Silver 0.7426 oz. ASW, 38.6 mm. **Subject:** Captain Cook **Obv:** National arms **Rev:** Seated Capt. Cook at right, his ship at left **Edge:** Reeded

Date	Mintage	F	VF	XF	Unc	BU
1999 Proof	—	Value: 35.00				

KM# 593 5 DOLLARS
20.0000 g., Copper-Nickel, 38 mm. **Subject:** John F. Kennedy Jr. **Obv:** National arms **Rev:** Two portraits, flag and the White House **Edge:** Reeded

Date	Mintage	F	VF	XF	Unc	BU
1999	—	—	—	—	10.00	—

KM# 435 5 DOLLARS
11.1800 g., Copper-Nickel, 31.6 mm. **Series:** Millennium 2000 Zodiac **Obv:** National arms **Rev:** Dog **Edge:** Reeded

Date	Mintage	F	VF	XF	Unc	BU
2000	—	—	—	—	3.50	5.00

KM# 567 5 DOLLARS
11.2200 g., Copper-Nickel, 31.5 mm. **Subject:** Ulysses S. Grant **Obv:** Kennedy half dollar like design **Rev:** Bust right with two dates at lower right and below **Edge:** Reeded

Date	Mintage	F	VF	XF	Unc	BU
2000	—	—	—	—	12.00	—

KM# 584 5 DOLLARS
8.5400 g., 0.9999 Silver 0.2745 oz. ASW, 30.1 mm. **Subject:** Endangered Elephant **Obv:** National arms divide date **Rev:** Elephant and calf **Edge:** Reeded

Date	Mintage	F	VF	XF	Unc	BU
2000 Proof	—	Value: 25.00				

KM# 589 5 DOLLARS
26.9200 g., Copper-Nickel, 40.3 mm. **Subject:** First Man on Moon **Obv:** National arms **Rev:** Astronaut and American flag on moon **Edge:** Reeded

Date	Mintage	F	VF	XF	Unc	BU
2000	—	—	—	—	17.50	—

KM# 619 5 DOLLARS
11.2200 g., Copper-Nickel, 31.5 mm. **Obvz:** Heraldic eagle **Rev:** George Washington right **Edge:** Reeded

Date	Mintage	F	VF	XF	Unc	BU
2000	—	—	—	—	12.00	—

KM# 620 5 DOLLARS
11.2200 g., Copper-Nickel, 31.5 mm. **Obv:** Heraldic eagle **Rev:** Thomas Jefferson left **Edge:** Reeded

Date	Mintage	F	VF	XF	Unc	BU
2000	—	—	—	—	12.00	—

KM# 621 5 DOLLARS
11.2200 g., Copper-Nickel, 31.5 mm. **Obv:** Heraldic eagle **Rev:** George W. Bush left **Edge:** Reeded

Date	Mintage	F	VF	XF	Unc	BU
2000	—	—	—	—	12.00	—

KM# 651 5 DOLLARS
14.5600 g., Copper-Nickel, 33.1 mm. **Obv:** National arms **Rev:** Japanese "Zero" flying over Pearl Harbor **Edge:** Reeded

Date	Mintage	F	VF	XF	Unc	BU
2000	—	—	—	—	8.00	—

KM# 652 5 DOLLARS
27.3300 g., Copper-Nickel, 40.2 mm. **Obv:** National arms **Rev:** Titanic sinking **Edge:** Reeded

Date	Mintage	F	VF	XF	Unc	BU
2000	—	—	—	—	9.00	—

KM# 665 5 DOLLARS
11.2200 g., Copper-Nickel, 31.5 mm. **Obv:** Design like Kennedy half dollar **Rev:** John Adams **Edge:** Reeded

Date	Mintage	F	VF	XF	Unc	BU
2000	—	—	—	—	12.00	—

KM# 666 5 DOLLARS
11.2200 g., Copper-Nickel, 31.5 mm. **Obv:** Design like Kennedy half dollar **Rev:** James Madison **Edge:** Reeded

Date	Mintage	F	VF	XF	Unc	BU
2000	—	—	—	—	12.00	—

KM# 667 5 DOLLARS
11.2200 g., Copper-Nickel, 31.5 mm. **Obv:** Design like Kennedy half dollar **Rev:** John Q. Adams **Edge:** Reeded

Date	Mintage	F	VF	XF	Unc	BU
2000	—	—	—	—	12.00	—

KM# 668 5 DOLLARS
26.1500 g., 0.9990 Silver Clad Copper-Nickel 0.8399 oz. ASW, 38.8 mm. **Subject:** Roy Rogers, King of the Cowboys **Obv:** National arms **Rev:** Roy Rogers wearing hat flanked by stars **Edge:** Plain

Date	Mintage	F	VF	XF	Unc	BU
2000 Proof	—	Value: 35.00				

KM# 669 5 DOLLARS
11.2200 g., Copper-Nickel, 31.5 mm. **Obv:** National arms on eagle **Rev:** Andrew Jackson **Edge:** Reeded

Date	Mintage	F	VF	XF	Unc	BU
2000	—	—	—	—	8.00	—

KM# 670 5 DOLLARS
11.2200 g., Copper-Nickel, 31.5 mm. **Obv:** National arms on eagle **Rev:** Martin Van Buren **Edge:** Reeded

Date	Mintage	F	VF	XF	Unc	BU
2000	—	—	—	—	8.00	—

KM# 671 5 DOLLARS
11.2200 g., Copper-Nickel, 31.5 mm. **Obv:** National arms on eagle **Rev:** William H. Harrison **Edge:** Reeded

Date	Mintage	F	VF	XF	Unc	BU
2000	—	—	—	—	8.00	—

KM# 672 5 DOLLARS
11.2200 g., Copper-Nickel, 31.5 mm. **Obv:** National arms on eagle **Rev:** John Tyler **Edge:** Reeded

Date	Mintage	F	VF	XF	Unc	BU
2000	—	—	—	—	8.00	—

KM# 673 5 DOLLARS
11.2200 g., Copper-Nickel, 31.5 mm. **Obv:** National arms on eagle **Rev:** Bust left with two dates at lower left and below **Rev. Designer:** James K. Polk **Edge:** Reeded

Date	Mintage	F	VF	XF	Unc	BU
2000	—	—	—	—	8.00	—

KM# 674 5 DOLLARS
11.2200 g., Copper-Nickel, 31.5 mm. **Subject:** Zachary Taylor **Obv:** National arms on eagle **Rev:** Bust left with two dates at lower left and below **Edge:** Reeded

Date	Mintage	F	VF	XF	Unc	BU
2000	—	—	—	—	8.00	—

KM# 675 5 DOLLARS
11.2200 g., Copper-Nickel, 31.5 mm. **Obv:** National arms on eagle **Rev:** Millard Filmore **Edge:** Reeded

Date	Mintage	F	VF	XF	Unc	BU
2000	—	—	—	—	8.00	—

KM# 676 5 DOLLARS

11.2200 g., Copper-Nickel, 31.5 mm. **Obv:** National arms on eagle **Rev:** Franklin Pierce **Edge:** Reeded

Date	Mintage	F	VF	XF	Unc	BU
2000	—	—	—	—	8.00	—

KM# 677 5 DOLLARS

11.2200 g., Copper-Nickel, 31.5 mm. **Obv:** National arms on eagle **Rev:** Andrew Johnson **Edge:** Reeded

Date	Mintage	F	VF	XF	Unc	BU
2000	—	—	—	—	8.00	—

KM# 678 5 DOLLARS

11.2200 g., Copper-Nickel, 31.5 mm. **Obv:** National arms on eagle **Rev:** Rutherford B. Hayes **Edge:** Reeded

Date	Mintage	F	VF	XF	Unc	BU
2000	—	—	—	—	8.00	—

KM# 679 5 DOLLARS

11.2200 g., Copper-Nickel, 31.5 mm. **Obv:** National arms on eagle **Rev:** James A. Garfield **Edge:** Reeded

Date	Mintage	F	VF	XF	Unc	BU
2000	—	—	—	—	8.00	—

KM# 680 5 DOLLARS

11.2200 g., Copper-Nickel, 31.5 mm. **Obv:** National arms on eagle **Rev:** Chester A. Arthur **Edge:** Reeded

Date	Mintage	F	VF	XF	Unc	BU
2000	—	—	—	—	8.00	—

KM# 681 5 DOLLARS

11.2200 g., Copper-Nickel, 31.5 mm. **Obv:** National arms on eagle **Rev:** Grover Cleveland **Edge:** Reeded

Date	Mintage	F	VF	XF	Unc	BU
2000	—	—	—	—	8.00	—

KM# 682 5 DOLLARS

11.2200 g., Copper-Nickel, 31.5 mm. **Obv:** National arms on eagle **Rev:** Benjamin Harrison **Edge:** Reeded

Date	Mintage	F	VF	XF	Unc	BU
2000	—	—	—	—	8.00	—

KM# 683 5 DOLLARS

11.2200 g., Copper-Nickel, 31.5 mm. **Obv:** National arms on eagle **Rev:** Grover Cleveland (1893-97) **Edge:** Reeded

Date	Mintage	F	VF	XF	Unc	BU
2000	—	—	—	—	8.00	—

KM# 684 5 DOLLARS

11.2200 g., Copper-Nickel, 31.5 mm. **Obv:** National arms on eagle **Rev:** William McKinley **Edge:** Reeded

Date	Mintage	F	VF	XF	Unc	BU
2000	—	—	—	—	8.00	—

KM# 685 5 DOLLARS

11.2200 g., Copper-Nickel, 31.5 mm. **Obv:** National arms on eagle **Rev:** Theodore Roosevelt **Edge:** Reeded

Date	Mintage	F	VF	XF	Unc	BU
2000	—	—	—	—	8.00	—

KM# 686 5 DOLLARS

11.2200 g., Copper-Nickel, 31.5 mm. **Obv:** National arms on eagle **Rev:** William H. Taft **Edge:** Reeded

Date	Mintage	F	VF	XF	Unc	BU
2000	—	—	—	—	8.00	—

KM# 687 5 DOLLARS

11.2200 g., Copper-Nickel, 31.5 mm. **Obv:** National arms on eagle **Rev:** Warren G. Harding **Edge:** Reeded

Date	Mintage	F	VF	XF	Unc	BU
2000	—	—	—	—	8.00	—

KM# 688 5 DOLLARS

11.2200 g., Copper-Nickel, 31.5 mm. **Obv:** National arms on eagle **Rev:** Calvin Coolidge **Edge:** Reeded

Date	Mintage	F	VF	XF	Unc	BU
2000	—	—	—	—	8.00	—

KM# 689 5 DOLLARS

11.2200 g., Copper-Nickel, 31.5 mm. **Obv:** National arms on eagle **Rev:** Herbert Hoover **Edge:** Reeded

Date	Mintage	F	VF	XF	Unc	BU
2000	—	—	—	—	8.00	—

KM# 690 5 DOLLARS

11.2200 g., Copper-Nickel, 31.5 mm. **Obv:** National arms on eagle **Rev:** Harry S. Truman **Edge:** Reeded

Date	Mintage	F	VF	XF	Unc	BU
2000	—	—	—	—	—	8.00

KM# 691 5 DOLLARS

11.2200 g., Copper-Nickel, 31.5 mm. **Obv:** National arms on eagle **Rev:** Dwight Eisenhower **Edge:** Reeded

Date	Mintage	F	VF	XF	Unc	BU
2000	—	—	—	—	8.00	—

KM# 692 5 DOLLARS

11.2200 g., Copper-Nickel, 31.5 mm. **Obv:** National arms on eagle **Rev:** Richard M. Nixon **Edge:** Reeded

Date	Mintage	F	VF	XF	Unc	BU
2000	—	—	—	—	8.00	—

KM# 693 5 DOLLARS

11.2200 g., Copper-Nickel, 31.5 mm. **Obv:** National arms on eagle **Rev:** Gerald R. Ford **Edge:** Reeded

Date	Mintage	F	VF	XF	Unc	BU
2000	—	—	—	—	8.00	—

KM# 694 5 DOLLARS

11.2200 g., Copper-Nickel, 31.5 mm. **Obv:** National arms on eagle **Rev:** Ronald Reagan **Edge:** Reeded

Date	Mintage	F	VF	XF	Unc	BU
2000	—	—	—	—	8.00	—

KM# 695 5 DOLLARS

27.2500 g., Copper-Nickel, 40 mm. **Obv:** National arms **Rev:** The Mayflower ship **Edge:** Reeded

Date	Mintage	F	VF	XF	Unc	BU
2000 Proof	—	Value: 10.00				

KM# 723 5 DOLLARS

12.0000 g., Copper-Nickel, 31.5 mm. **Obv:** National arms **Rev:** Dragon within circle (Not KM-438) **Edge:** Reeded

Date	Mintage	F	VF	XF	Unc	BU
2000	—	—	—	—	5.00	—

KM# 427 5 DOLLARS

11.1800 g., Copper-Nickel, 31.6 mm. **Series:** Millennium 2000 Zodiac **Obv:** National arms **Rev:** Snake **Edge:** Reeded

Date	Mintage	F	VF	XF	Unc	BU
2000	—	—	—	—	4.00	5.00

KM# 429 5 DOLLARS

11.1800 g., Copper-Nickel, 31.6 mm. **Series:** Millennium 2000 Zodiac **Obv:** National arms **Rev:** Ox **Edge:** Reeded

Date	Mintage	F	VF	XF	Unc	BU
2000	—	—	—	—	4.00	5.00

KM# 428 5 DOLLARS

11.1800 g., Copper-Nickel, 31.6 mm. **Series:** Millennium 2000 Zodiac **Obv:** National arms **Rev:** Two rats and pumpkin **Edge:** Reeded

Date	Mintage	F	VF	XF	Unc	BU
2000	—	—	—	—	4.00	5.00

KM# 430 5 DOLLARS

11.1800 g., Copper-Nickel, 31.6 mm. **Series:** Millennium 2000 Zodiac **Obv:** National arms **Rev:** Tiger **Edge:** Reeded

Date	Mintage	F	VF	XF	Unc	BU
2000	—	—	—	—	4.00	5.00

KM# 431 5 DOLLARS

11.1800 g., Copper-Nickel, 31.6 mm. **Series:** Millennium 2000 Zodiac **Obv:** National arms **Rev:** Horse **Edge:** Reeded

Date	Mintage	F	VF	XF	Unc	BU
2000	—	—	—	—	4.00	5.00

KM# 432 5 DOLLARS

11.1800 g., Copper-Nickel, 31.6 mm. **Series:** Millennium 2000 Zodiac **Obv:** National arms **Rev:** Goat **Edge:** Reeded

Date	Mintage	F	VF	XF	Unc	BU
2000	—	—	—	—	4.00	5.00

KM# 433 5 DOLLARS

11.1800 g., Copper-Nickel, 31.6 mm. **Series:** Millennium 2000 Zodiac **Obv:** National arms **Rev:** Monkey **Edge:** Reeded

Date	Mintage	F	VF	XF	Unc	BU
2000	—	—	—	—	4.00	5.00

KM# 434 5 DOLLARS

11.1800 g., Copper-Nickel, 31.6 mm. **Series:** Millennium 2000 Zodiac **Obv:** National arms **Rev:** Rooster **Edge:** Reeded

Date	Mintage	F	VF	XF	Unc	BU
2000	—	—	—	—	4.00	5.00

KM# 436 5 DOLLARS

11.1800 g., Copper-Nickel, 31.6 mm. **Series:** Millennium 2000 Zodiac **Obv:** National arms **Rev:** Pig **Edge:** Reeded

Date	Mintage	F	VF	XF	Unc	BU
2000	—	—	—	—	4.00	5.00

KM# 437 5 DOLLARS

11.1800 g., Copper-Nickel, 31.6 mm. **Series:** Millennium 2000 Zodiac **Obv:** National arms **Rev:** Rabbit **Edge:** Reeded

Date	Mintage	F	VF	XF	Unc	BU
2000	—	—	—	—	4.00	5.00

KM# 438 5 DOLLARS

11.1800 g., Copper-Nickel, 31.6 mm. **Series:** Millennium 2000 Zodiac **Obv:** National arms **Rev:** Dragon **Edge:** Reeded

Date	Mintage	F	VF	XF	Unc	BU
2000	—	—	—	—	4.00	6.00

KM# 63 10 DOLLARS

11.7200 g., 0.9000 Gold .3391 oz. AGW **Subject:** 25th Anniversary of Inter-Continental Hotels **Obv:** Value below hotel building **Rev:** Letter I within football flanked by dates

Date	Mintage	F	VF	XF	Unc	BU
1971 Proof	—	Value: 245				

KM# 26 10 DOLLARS

16.7185 g., 0.9000 Gold .4838 oz. AGW **Subject:** Inauguration of President Tolbert **Rev:** Head left

Date	Mintage	F	VF	XF	Unc	BU
1972 Proof	—	Value: 350				

KM# 53 10 DOLLARS

23.3300 g., 0.9250 Silver .6939 oz. ASW **Subject:** Decade For Women **Obv:** National arms **Rev:** Coat of arms and value

Date	Mintage	F	VF	XF	Unc	BU
1985 Proof	—	Value: 30.00				

KM# 54 10 DOLLARS

31.1000 g., 0.9990 Silver 1.0000 oz. ASW **Subject:** President John F. Kennedy **Obv:** National arms **Rev:** Head left

Date	Mintage	F	VF	XF	Unc	BU
1988 Proof	25,000	Value: 37.50				

KM# 55 10 DOLLARS

31.1000 g., 0.9990 Silver 1.0000 oz. ASW **Subject:** President Samuel Kanyon Doe **Obv:** National arms **Rev:** President Samuel Kanyon Doe **Note:** Similar to 250 Dollars, KM#56.

Date	Mintage	F	VF	XF	Unc	BU
1988 Proof	25,000	Value: 37.50				

KM# 57 10 DOLLARS

31.1000 g., 0.9990 Silver 1.0000 oz. ASW **Subject:** President George Bush **Obv:** National arms **Rev:** Head left **Note:** Similar to 250 Dollars, KM#58.

Date	Mintage	F	VF	XF	Unc	BU
1989 Proof	25,000	Value: 37.50				

KM# 59 10 DOLLARS

31.1000 g., 0.9990 Silver 1.0000 oz. ASW **Subject:** Emperor Hirohito **Obv:** National arms **Rev:** Head facing divides dates **Note:** Similar to 250 Dollars, KM#60.

Date	Mintage	F	VF	XF	Unc	BU
1989 Proof	25,000	Value: 35.00				

KM# 72 10 DOLLARS
31.1000 g., 0.9990 Silver 1.0000 oz. ASW **Subject:** Chancellor Willy Brandt - In Memorium **Obv:** National arms **Rev:** Horses pulling casket below head right dividing dates

Date	Mintage	F	VF	XF	Unc	BU
1992 Proof	—	Value: 32.50				

KM# 74 10 DOLLARS
31.1000 g., 0.9990 Silver 1.0000 oz. ASW **Subject:** Formula One **Obv:** National arms **Rev:** Ricardo Patrese

Date	Mintage	F	VF	XF	Unc	BU
1992 Proof	25,000	Value: 40.00				

KM# 75 10 DOLLARS
31.1000 g., 0.9990 Silver 1.0000 oz. ASW **Subject:** Formula One **Obv:** National arms **Rev:** Nigel Mansell

Date	Mintage	F	VF	XF	Unc	BU
1992 Proof	25,000	Value: 40.00				

KM# 83 10 DOLLARS
31.1000 g., 0.9990 Silver 1.0000 oz. ASW **Subject:** Formula One **Obv:** National arms **Rev:** Gerhard Berger

Date	Mintage	F	VF	XF	Unc	BU
1992 Proof	25,000	Value: 40.00				

KM# 84 10 DOLLARS
31.1000 g., 0.9990 Silver 1.0000 oz. ASW **Subject:** Formula One **Obv:** National arms **Rev:** Aguri Suzuki

Date	Mintage	F	VF	XF	Unc	BU
1992 Proof	25,000	Value: 40.00				

KM# 85 10 DOLLARS
31.1000 g., 0.9990 Silver 1.0000 oz. ASW **Subject:** Formula One **Obv:** National arms **Rev:** Ayrton Senna

Date	Mintage	F	VF	XF	Unc	BU
1992 Proof	25,000	Value: 40.00				

KM# 86 10 DOLLARS
31.1000 g., 0.9990 Silver 1.0000 oz. ASW **Subject:** Formula One **Obv:** National arms **Rev:** Michael Schumacher

Date	Mintage	F	VF	XF	Unc	BU
1992 Proof	25,000	Value: 40.00				

KM# 87 10 DOLLARS
31.1000 g., 0.9990 Silver 1.0000 oz. ASW **Subject:** Formula One **Obv:** National arms **Rev:** Alain Prost

Date	Mintage	F	VF	XF	Unc	BU
1992 Proof	25,000	Value: 40.00				

KM# 88 10 DOLLARS
31.1000 g., 0.9990 Silver 1.0000 oz. ASW **Subject:** Formula One **Obv:** National arms **Rev:** Ukyo Katayama

Date	Mintage	F	VF	XF	Unc	BU
1992 Proof	25,000	Value: 40.00				

KM# 68 10 DOLLARS
31.1000 g., 0.9990 Silver 1.0000 oz. ASW **Subject:** President Bill Clinton **Obv:** National arms **Rev:** Head right

Date	Mintage	F	VF	XF	Unc	BU
1993 Proof	25,000	Value: 30.00				

KM# 99 10 DOLLARS
31.1000 g., 0.9990 Silver 1.0000 oz. ASW **Series:** Preserve Planet Earth **Obv:** National arms **Rev:** Protoceratops

Date	Mintage	F	VF	XF	Unc	BU
1993 Proof	25,000	Value: 35.00				

KM# 102 10 DOLLARS
31.1000 g., 0.9990 Silver 1.0000 oz. ASW **Subject:** Baseball Hall of Fame **Obv:** National arms **Rev:** Nolan Ryan waving baseball cap

Date	Mintage	F	VF	XF	Unc	BU
1993 Proof	—	Value: 30.00				

KM# 104 10 DOLLARS
31.1000 g., 0.9990 Silver 1.0000 oz. ASW **Subject:** President John F. Kennedy **Obv:** National arms **Rev:** Head left, funeral caisson below

Date	Mintage	F	VF	XF	Unc	BU
1993 Proof	25,000	Value: 40.00				

KM# 110 10 DOLLARS
31.1000 g., 0.9990 Silver 1.0000 oz. ASW **Series:** Preserve Planet Earth **Obv:** National arms **Rev:** Corythosaurus

Date	Mintage	F	VF	XF	Unc	BU
1993 Proof	25,000	Value: 35.00				

KM# 113 10 DOLLARS
31.1000 g., 0.9990 Silver 1.0000 oz. ASW **Series:** Preserve Planet Earth **Obv:** National arms **Rev:** Atchaeopteryx
Note: Incorrect spelling.

Date	Mintage	F	VF	XF	Unc	BU
1993 Proof	25,000	Value: 35.00				

KM# 116 10 DOLLARS
31.1000 g., 0.9990 Silver 1.0000 oz. ASW **Series:** Preserve Planet Earth **Obv:** National arms **Rev:** Archaeopteryx
Note: Correct spelling.

Date	Mintage	F	VF	XF	Unc	BU
1994 Proof	25,000	Value: 35.00				

KM# 561 10 DOLLARS
31.1035 g., 0.9990 Silver 1 oz. ASW **Obv:** National arms **Rev:** Mercedes Benz C-Class car

Date	Mintage	F	VF	XF	Unc	BU
1994 Proof	Est. 25,000	Value: 50.00				

KM# 119 10 DOLLARS
31.1000 g., 0.9990 Silver 1.0000 oz. ASW **Series:** Preserve Planet Earth **Obv:** National arms **Rev:** Gorillas

Date	Mintage	F	VF	XF	Unc	BU
1994 Proof	25,000	Value: 35.00				

KM# 122 10 DOLLARS
31.1000 g., 0.9990 Silver 1.0000 oz. ASW **Series:** Preserve Planet Earth **Obv:** National arms **Rev:** Pygmy Hippopotami

Date	Mintage	F	VF	XF	Unc	BU
1994 Proof	25,000	Value: 35.00				

KM# 125 10 DOLLARS
31.1000 g., 0.9990 Silver 1.0000 oz. ASW **Series:** Preserve Planet Earth **Obv:** National arms **Rev:** Nile Soft-shelled Turtle

Date	Mintage	F	VF	XF	Unc	BU
1994 Proof	25,000	Value: 40.00				

KM# 127 10 DOLLARS
31.1000 g., 0.9990 Silver 1.0000 oz. ASW **Obv:** National arms **Rev:** Head left with small gazelle below

Date	Mintage	F	VF	XF	Unc	BU
1994 Proof	25,000	Value: 30.00				

KM# 155 10 DOLLARS
31.1000 g., 0.9990 Silver 1.0000 oz. ASW **Obv:** National arms **Rev:** Uniformed bust 1/4 left

Date	Mintage	F	VF	XF	Unc	BU
1994 Proof	25,000	Value: 40.00				

KM# 156 10 DOLLARS
31.1000 g., 0.9990 Silver 1.0000 oz. ASW **Obv:** National arms **Rev:** Field Marshal Montgomery facing

Date	Mintage	F	VF	XF	Unc	BU
1994 Proof	25,000	Value: 40.00				

KM# 157 10 DOLLARS
31.1000 g., 0.9990 Silver 1.0000 oz. ASW **Obv:** National arms **Rev:** General Dwight D. Eisenhower half left

Date	Mintage	F	VF	XF	Unc	BU
1994 Proof	25,000	Value: 40.00				

KM# 281 10 DOLLARS
31.1000 g., 0.9990 Silver 1.0000 oz. ASW **Subject:** Baseball Hall of Fame, Reggie Jackson **Obv:** National arms **Rev:** Baseball player divides circle

Date	Mintage	F	VF	XF	Unc	BU
1994 Proof	—	Value: 40.00				

KM# 282 10 DOLLARS
31.1000 g., 0.9990 Silver 1.0000 oz. ASW **Subject:** Baseball Hall of Fame **Obv:** National arms **Rev:** Roberto Clemente facing

Date	Mintage	F	VF	XF	Unc	BU
1994 Proof	—	Value: 40.00				

KM# 347 10 DOLLARS
31.1000 g., 0.9990 Silver 1.0000 oz. ASW **Subject:** The History of the Motor Car **Obv:** National arms **Rev:** Mercedes-Benz C-Class car

Date	Mintage	F	VF	XF	Unc	BU
1994 Proof	—	Value: 40.00				

KM# 129 10 DOLLARS
31.1000 g., 0.9990 Silver 1.0000 oz. ASW **Subject:** Star Trek **Obv:** National arms **Rev:** Conjoined busts facing

Date	Mintage	F	VF	XF	Unc	BU
1995 Proof	—	Value: 47.50				

KM# 134 10 DOLLARS
31.1000 g., 0.9990 Silver 1.0000 oz. ASW **Series:** Preserve Planet Earth **Obv:** National arms **Rev:** Leopard

Date	Mintage	F	VF	XF	Unc	BU
1995 Proof	25,000	Value: 40.00				

KM# 137 10 DOLLARS
31.1000 g., 0.9990 Silver 1.0000 oz. ASW **Series:** Preserve Planet Earth **Obv:** National arms **Rev:** Storks

Date	Mintage	F	VF	XF	Unc	BU
1995 Proof	25,000	Value: 30.00				

KM# 145 10 DOLLARS
31.1000 g., 0.9990 Silver 1.0000 oz. ASW **Obv:** National arms **Rev:** Uniformed bust right, fighter planes, army tanks and ship

Date	Mintage	F	VF	XF	Unc	BU
1995 Proof	25,000	Value: 40.00				

KM# 146 10 DOLLARS
31.1000 g., 0.9990 Silver 1.0000 oz. ASW **Obv:** National arms **Rev:** President Franklin D. Roosevelt riding in jeep

Date	Mintage	F	VF	XF	Unc	BU
1995 Proof	25,000	Value: 40.00				

KM# 147 10 DOLLARS
31.1000 g., 0.9990 Silver 1.0000 oz. ASW **Obv:** National arms **Rev:** General George Patton in front of map

Date	Mintage	F	VF	XF	Unc	BU
1995 Proof	25,000	Value: 40.00				

KM# 148 10 DOLLARS
31.1000 g., 0.9990 Silver 1.0000 oz. ASW **Obv:** National arms **Rev:** President Harry S. Truman facing

Date	Mintage	F	VF	XF	Unc	BU
1995 Proof	25,000	Value: 40.00				

KM# 149 10 DOLLARS
31.1000 g., 0.9990 Silver 1.0000 oz. ASW **Obv:** National arms **Rev:** President Charles de Gaulle on Champs Elysees

Date	Mintage	F	VF	XF	Unc	BU
1995 Proof	25,000	Value: 40.00				

KM# 159 10 DOLLARS
31.1000 g., 0.9990 Silver 1.0000 oz. ASW **Obv:** National arms **Rev:** Bust facing

Date	Mintage	F	VF	XF	Unc	BU
1995 Proof	25,000	Value: 45.00				
1996 Proof	25,000	Value: 45.00				

KM# 162 10 DOLLARS
31.1000 g., 0.9990 Silver 1.0000 oz. ASW **Obv:** National arms **Rev:** General Chiang Kai-shek

Date	Mintage	F	VF	XF	Unc	BU
1995 Proof	25,000	Value: 45.00				
1996 Proof	25,000	Value: 45.00				

KM# 165 10 DOLLARS
31.1000 g., 0.9990 Silver 1.0000 oz. ASW **Subject:** Cairo Conference **Obv:** National arms **Rev:** Chiang Kai-shek - Roosevelt - Churchill

Date	Mintage	F	VF	XF	Unc	BU
1995 Proof	25,000	Value: 45.00				

KM# 171 10 DOLLARS
31.1000 g., 0.9990 Silver 1.0000 oz. ASW **Subject:** 375th Anniversary - Pilgrim Fathers **Obv:** National arms **Rev:** The "Mayflower"

Date	Mintage	F	VF	XF	Unc	BU
1995 Proof	25,000	Value: 40.00				

KM# 172 10 DOLLARS
31.1000 g., 0.9990 Silver 1.0000 oz. ASW **Subject:** 375th Anniversary - Pilgrim Fathers **Obv:** National arms **Rev:** Pilgrims in skiff

Date	Mintage	F	VF	XF	Unc	BU
1995 Proof	25,000	Value: 40.00				

KM# 173 10 DOLLARS
31.1000 g., 0.9990 Silver 1.0000 oz. ASW **Subject:** 375th Anniversary - Pilgrim Fathers **Obv:** National arms **Rev:** Pilgrim landing party

Date	Mintage	F	VF	XF	Unc	BU
1995 Proof	25,000	Value: 40.00				

KM# 174 10 DOLLARS
31.1000 g., 0.9990 Silver 1.0000 oz. ASW **Subject:** 375th Anniversary - Pilgrim Fathers **Obv:** National arms **Rev:** First Thanksgiving scene

Date	Mintage	F	VF	XF	Unc	BU
1995 Proof	25,000	Value: 40.00				

KM# 180 10 DOLLARS
31.1000 g., 0.9990 Silver 1.0000 oz. ASW **Subject:** Formula One **Obv:** National arms **Rev:** Mika Hakkinen

Date	Mintage	F	VF	XF	Unc	BU
1995 Proof	25,000	Value: 40.00				

KM# 183 10 DOLLARS
31.1000 g., 0.9990 Silver 1.0000 oz. ASW **Subject:** Formula One **Obv:** National arms **Rev:** Martin Brundle

Date	Mintage	F	VF	XF	Unc	BU
1995 Proof	25,000	Value: 40.00				

KM# 186 10 DOLLARS
31.1000 g., 0.9990 Silver 1.0000 oz. ASW **Subject:** Formula One **Obv:** National arms **Rev:** Rubens Barrichello

Date	Mintage	F	VF	XF	Unc	BU
1995 Proof	25,000	Value: 40.00				

KM# 189 10 DOLLARS
31.1000 g., 0.9990 Silver 1.0000 oz. ASW **Subject:** Formula One **Obv:** National arms **Rev:** David Coulthard

Date	Mintage	F	VF	XF	Unc	BU
1995 Proof	25,000	Value: 40.00				

KM# 192 10 DOLLARS
31.1000 g., 0.9990 Silver 1.0000 oz. ASW **Subject:** Formula One **Obv:** National arms **Rev:** Jean Alesi

Date	Mintage	F	VF	XF	Unc	BU
1995 Proof	25,000	Value: 40.00				

KM# 194 10 DOLLARS
31.1000 g., 0.9990 Silver 1.0000 oz. ASW **Subject:** Nations United for Peace **Obv:** National arms divides date **Rev:** Logo, paper dolls

Date	Mintage	F	VF	XF	Unc	BU
1995 Proof	25,000	Value: 37.50				

KM# 564 10 DOLLARS
31.1000 g., 0.9990 Silver 0.9989 oz. ASW, 38.6 mm.
Rev: Bugatti Royale

Date	Mintage	F	VF	XF	Unc	BU
1995	—	—	—	—	40.00	—

KM# 132 10 DOLLARS
31.1000 g., 0.9990 Silver 1.0000 oz. ASW **Subject:** Centennial - Babe Ruth - Sultan of Swat **Obv:** National arms **Rev:** Head with cap, 1/4 right divides dates within circle **Note:** Similar to 1 Dollar, KM#131.

Date	Mintage	F	VF	XF	Unc	BU
1995	—	—	—	—	42.50	—

KM# 199 10 DOLLARS
31.1000 g., 0.9990 Silver 1.0000 oz. ASW **Subject:** Formula One **Obv:** National arms **Rev:** Mark Blundell

Date	Mintage	F	VF	XF	Unc	BU
1996 Proof	25,000	Value: 40.00				

KM# 200 10 DOLLARS
31.1000 g., 0.9990 Silver 1.0000 oz. ASW **Subject:** Formula One **Obv:** National arms **Rev:** Johnny Herbert

Date	Mintage	F	VF	XF	Unc	BU
1996 Proof	25,000	Value: 40.00				

KM# 201 10 DOLLARS
31.1000 g., 0.9990 Silver 1.0000 oz. ASW **Subject:** Formula One **Obv:** National arms **Rev:** Eddie Irvine

Date	Mintage	F	VF	XF	Unc	BU
1996 Proof	25,000	Value: 40.00				

KM# 202 10 DOLLARS
31.1000 g., 0.9990 Silver 1.0000 oz. ASW **Subject:** Formula One **Obv:** National arms **Rev:** Heinz Frentzen

Date	Mintage	F	VF	XF	Unc	BU
1996 Proof	25,000	Value: 40.00				

KM# 208 10 DOLLARS
31.1000 g., 0.9990 Silver 1.0000 oz. ASW **Subject:** Star Trek **Obv:** National arms **Rev:** Starships NCC-1701 and NCC-1701D

Date	Mintage	F	VF	XF	Unc	BU
1996 Proof	25,000	Value: 45.00				

KM# 211 10 DOLLARS
31.1000 g., 0.9990 Silver 1.0000 oz. ASW **Subject:** Star Trek, Scott and McCoy **Obv:** National arms **Rev:** Conjoined busts facing

Date	Mintage	F	VF	XF	Unc	BU
1996 Proof	25,000	Value: 45.00				

KM# 214 10 DOLLARS
31.1000 g., 0.9990 Silver 1.0000 oz. ASW **Subject:** Star Trek **Obv:** National arms **Rev:** LaForge and Data

Date	Mintage	F	VF	XF	Unc	BU
1996 Proof	25,000	Value: 45.00				

KM# 217 10 DOLLARS
31.1000 g., 0.9990 Silver 1.0000 oz. ASW **Subject:** Star Trek **Obv:** National arms **Rev:** Spock and Uhura

Date	Mintage	F	VF	XF	Unc	BU
1996 Proof	25,000	Value: 45.00				

KM# 220 10 DOLLARS
31.1000 g., 0.9990 Silver 1.0000 oz. ASW **Subject:** Star Trek **Obv:** National arms **Rev:** Worf and Dr. Crusher

Date	Mintage	F	VF	XF	Unc	BU
1996 Proof	25,000	Value: 45.00				

KM# 223 10 DOLLARS
31.1000 g., 0.9990 Silver 1.0000 oz. ASW **Series:** Preserve Planet Earth **Obv:** National arms **Rev:** Grey Parrot

Date	Mintage	F	VF	XF	Unc	BU
1996 Proof	25,000	Value: 40.00				

KM# 226 10 DOLLARS
31.1000 g., 0.9990 Silver 1.0000 oz. ASW **Series:** Preserve Planet Earth **Obv:** National arms **Rev:** Love Birds

Date	Mintage	F	VF	XF	Unc	BU
1996 Proof	25,000	Value: 40.00				

KM# 229 10 DOLLARS
31.1000 g., 0.9990 Silver 1.0000 oz. ASW **Subject:** Formula One **Obv:** National arms **Rev:** Ayrton Senna

Date	Mintage	F	VF	XF	Unc	BU
1996	25,000	Value: 40.00				

KM# 242 10 DOLLARS
31.1000 g., 0.9990 Silver 1.0000 oz. ASW **Subject:** President Chiang Ching-kuo **Obv:** National arms **Rev:** Bust 1/4 right

Date	Mintage	F	VF	XF	Unc	BU
1996 Proof	25,000	Value: 42.50				

KM# 245 10 DOLLARS
31.1000 g., 0.9990 Silver 1.0000 oz. ASW **Obv:** National arms **Rev:** President Lee Ten-hui

Date	Mintage	F	VF	XF	Unc	BU
1996 Proof	25,000	Value: 42.50				

KM# 256 10 DOLLARS
31.1000 g., 0.9990 Silver 1.0000 oz. ASW **Subject:** Chairman Mao Zedong **Obv:** National arms divides date **Rev:** Standing figure facing

Date	Mintage	F	VF	XF	Unc	BU
1996 Proof	25,000	Value: 40.00				

KM# 257 10 DOLLARS
31.1000 g., 0.9990 Silver 1.0000 oz. ASW **Obv:** National arms **Rev:** Chairman Mao Zedong with gate of Heavenly Peace

Date	Mintage	F	VF	XF	Unc	BU
1996 Proof	25,000	Value: 40.00				

KM# 258 10 DOLLARS
31.1000 g., 0.9990 Silver 1.0000 oz. ASW **Obv:** National arms **Rev:** Chairman Mao Zedong proclaiming People's Republic

Date	Mintage	F	VF	XF	Unc	BU
1996 Proof	25,000	Value: 40.00				

KM# 262 10 DOLLARS
31.1000 g., 0.9990 Silver 1.0000 oz. ASW **Subject:** Chairman Mao Zedong and President Nixon **Obv:** National arms **Rev:** Seated figures facing

Date	Mintage	F	VF	XF	Unc	BU
1996 Proof	25,000	Value: 37.50				

KM# 264 10 DOLLARS
31.1000 g., 0.9990 Silver 1.0000 oz. ASW **Series:** Pioneers of the West **Obv:** National arms **Rev:** Daniel Boone

Date	Mintage	F	VF	XF	Unc	BU
1996 Proof	25,000	Value: 40.00				

KM# 267 10 DOLLARS
31.1000 g., 0.9990 Silver 1.0000 oz. ASW **Series:** Pioneers of the West **Obv:** National arms **Rev:** Davy Crockett

Date	Mintage	F	VF	XF	Unc	BU
1996 Proof	25,000	Value: 40.00				

KM# 270 10 DOLLARS
31.1000 g., 0.9990 Silver 1.0000 oz. ASW **Series:** Pioneers of the West **Obv:** National arms **Rev:** Jim Bowie in front of the Alamo

Date	Mintage	F	VF	XF	Unc	BU
1996 Proof	25,000	Value: 40.00				

KM# 273 10 DOLLARS
31.1000 g., 0.9990 Silver 1.0000 oz. ASW **Series:** Pioneers of the West **Obv:** National arms **Rev:** Kit Carson

Date	Mintage	F	VF	XF	Unc	BU
1996 Proof	25,000	Value: 40.00				

KM# 276 10 DOLLARS
31.1000 g., 0.9990 Silver 1.0000 oz. ASW **Series:** Pioneers of the West **Obv:** National arms **Rev:** Wild Bill Hickok

Date	Mintage	F	VF	XF	Unc	BU
1996 Proof	25,000	Value: 40.00				

KM# 279 10 DOLLARS
31.1000 g., 0.9990 Silver 1.0000 oz. ASW **Series:** Pioneers of the West **Obv:** National arms **Rev:** Buffalo Bill

Date	Mintage	F	VF	XF	Unc	BU
1996 Proof	25,000	Value: 40.00				

KM# 284 10 DOLLARS
31.1000 g., 0.9990 Silver 1.0000 oz. ASW **Subject:** Return of Macao to China **Obv:** National arms **Rev:** City views, old and new

Date	Mintage	F	VF	XF	Unc	BU
1996 Proof	Est. 6,000	Value: 32.50				

KM# 285 10 DOLLARS
31.1000 g., 0.9990 Silver 1.0000 oz. ASW **Subject:** Return of Hong Kong to China **Obv:** National arms divide date above value **Rev:** City views, old and new **Shape:** Rectangular

Date	Mintage	F	VF	XF	Unc	BU
1996 Proof	Est. 6,000	Value: 32.50				

KM# 287 10 DOLLARS
31.1000 g., 0.9990 Silver 1.0000 oz. ASW **Series:** WWII **Subject:** Evacuation from Dunkirk **Obv:** National arms **Rev:** British 1939-45 Star Medal to left of fighter planes and ships

Date	Mintage	F	VF	XF	Unc	BU
1997 Proof	25,000	Value: 37.50				

KM# 289 10 DOLLARS
31.1000 g., 0.9990 Silver 1.0000 oz. ASW **Series:** WWII **Subject:** Liberation of the Philippines **Obv:** National arms **Rev:** American Asian-Pacific campaign medal to right of soldiers in water

Date	Mintage	F	VF	XF	Unc	BU
1997 Proof	25,000	Value: 37.50				

KM# 291 10 DOLLARS
31.1000 g., 0.9990 Silver 1.0000 oz. ASW **Series:** WWII **Subject:** Defense of Stalingrad **Obv:** National arms **Rev:** Soviet distinguished combat medal to left of war scene

Date	Mintage	F	VF	XF	Unc	BU
1997 Proof	25,000	Value: 37.50				

KM# 293 10 DOLLARS
31.1000 g., 0.9990 Silver 1.0000 oz. ASW **Series:** WWII **Subject:** Arnhem **Obv:** National arms **Rev:** Netherlands bronze lion cross to right of parachutists, bridge and soldier

Date	Mintage	F	VF	XF	Unc	BU
1997 Proof	25,000	Value: 37.50				

KM# 295 10 DOLLARS
31.1000 g., 0.9990 Silver 1.0000 oz. ASW **Series:** WWII **Subject:** Raid on the Dams **Obv:** National arms **Rev:** British distinguished flying medal

Date	Mintage	F	VF	XF	Unc	BU
1997 Proof	25,000	Value: 37.50				

KM# 297 10 DOLLARS
31.1000 g., 0.9990 Silver 1.0000 oz. ASW **Series:** WWII **Subject:** West African Campaign **Obv:** National arms **Rev:** WWII Victory medal

Date	Mintage	F	VF	XF	Unc	BU
1997 Proof	25,000	Value: 37.50				

KM# 299 10 DOLLARS
31.1000 g., 0.9990 Silver 1.0000 oz. ASW **Series:** WWII **Subject:** North African Campaign **Obv:** National arms **Rev:** British Africa star medal to right of tank in front of pyramid

Date	Mintage	F	VF	XF	Unc	BU
1997 Proof	25,000	Value: 37.50				

KM# 301 10 DOLLARS
31.1000 g., 0.9990 Silver 1.0000 oz. ASW **Series:** WWII **Subject:** The Dieppe Raid **Obv:** National arms **Rev:** British Victoria cross to right of plane over half-track vehicle

Date	Mintage	F	VF	XF	Unc	BU
1997 Proof	25,000	Value: 37.50				

KM# 303 10 DOLLARS
31.1000 g., 0.9990 Silver 1.0000 oz. ASW **Series:** WWII **Subject:** Iwo Jima **Obv:** National arms **Rev:** Purple heart medal to upper left of planes and map

Date	Mintage	F	VF	XF	Unc	BU
1997 Proof	25,000	Value: 37.50				

KM# 305 10 DOLLARS
31.1000 g., 0.9990 Silver 1.0000 oz. ASW **Series:** WWII **Subject:** Battle of Britain **Obv:** National arms **Rev:** British distinguished flying cross to left of pilots running to board planes

Date	Mintage	F	VF	XF	Unc	BU
1997 Proof	25,000	Value: 37.50				

KM# 307 10 DOLLARS
31.1000 g., 0.9990 Silver 1.0000 oz. ASW **Series:** WWII **Subject:** Liberation of Paris **Obv:** National arms **Rev:** Croix de Guerre medal to right of soldiers in front of Arch de Triumph

Date	Mintage	F	VF	XF	Unc	BU
1997 Proof	25,000	Value: 37.50				

KM# 309 10 DOLLARS
31.1000 g., 0.9990 Silver 1.0000 oz. ASW **Series:** WWII **Subject:** Burma Campaign **Obv:** National arms **Rev:** British Burma star medal

Date	Mintage	F	VF	XF	Unc	BU
1997 Proof	25,000	Value: 37.50				

KM# 311 10 DOLLARS
31.1000 g., 0.9990 Silver 1.0000 oz. ASW **Subject:** Mahatma Gandhi **Obv:** National arms **Rev:** Seated figure facing left in front of Taj Mahal

Date	Mintage	F	VF	XF	Unc	BU
1997 Proof	25,000	Value: 40.00				

KM# 314 10 DOLLARS
31.1000 g., 0.9990 Silver 1.0000 oz. ASW **Subject:** Return of Hong Kong **Obv:** National arms **Rev:** Dragon

Date	Mintage	F	VF	XF	Unc	BU
1997 Proof	25,000	Value: 40.00				

KM# 321 10 DOLLARS
31.1000 g., 0.9990 Silver 1.0000 oz. ASW **Subject:** Fiftieth Anniversary of the Kon-Tiki Expedition **Obv:** National arms **Rev:** Mask within circle

Date	Mintage	F	VF	XF	Unc	BU
1997 Proof	25,000	Value: 40.00				

KM# 325 10 DOLLARS
31.1000 g., 0.9990 Silver 1.0000 oz. ASW **Subject:** Jurassic Park **Obv:** National arms **Rev:** Stegosaurus

Date	Mintage	F	VF	XF	Unc	BU
1997 Proof	10,000	Value: 40.00				

KM# 328 10 DOLLARS
31.1030 g., 0.9250 Gold Clad Silver .9250 oz. **Subject:** Golden Wedding Anniversary **Obv:** National arms **Rev:** E & P initials above 2 shields

Date	Mintage	F	VF	XF	Unc	BU
1997 Proof	10,000	Value: 50.00				

KM# 331 10 DOLLARS
31.1030 g., 0.9250 Gold Clad Silver .9250 oz. **Subject:** Queen Elizabeth II and Prince Philip's Golden Wedding Anniversary **Obv:** National arms **Rev:** Royal couple with horse

Date	Mintage	F	VF	XF	Unc	BU
1997 Proof	10,000	Value: 50.00				

KM# 334 10 DOLLARS
31.1030 g., 0.9250 Gold Clad Silver .9250 oz. **Subject:** Queen Elizabeth II and Prince Philip's Golden Wedding Anniversary **Obv:** National arms **Rev:** Royal couple with dogs

Date	Mintage	F	VF	XF	Unc	BU
1997 Proof	10,000	Value: 50.00				

KM# 337 10 DOLLARS
31.1030 g., 0.9250 Gold Clad Silver .9250 oz. **Subject:** Queen Elizabeth II and Prince Philip's Golden Wedding Anniversary **Obv:** National arms **Rev:** Royal couple with children

Date	Mintage	F	VF	XF	Unc	BU
1997 Proof	10,000	Value: 50.00				

KM# 345 10 DOLLARS
31.1035 g., 0.9990 Silver 1.0000 oz. ASW **Subject:** 150th Anniversary - Independence of Liberia **Obv:** National arms **Rev:** Cameo to upper left of ship above small boat

Date	Mintage	F	VF	XF	Unc	BU
1997 Proof	25,000	Value: 45.00				

KM# 346 10 DOLLARS
Copper-Nickel **Subject:** Famous Personalities of the World; Marilyn Monroe **Obv:** National arms with blank ribbons **Rev:** Head facing

Date	Mintage	F	VF	XF	Unc	BU
ND(1997) Proof	—	Value: 15.00				

KM# 348 10 DOLLARS
31.1035 g., 0.9990 Silver 1.0000 oz. ASW **Subject:** Return of Hong Kong to China **Obv:** National arms **Rev:** City view, old and new **Shape:** Rectangular

Date	Mintage	F	VF	XF	Unc	BU
1997 Proof	Est. 8,000	Value: 32.50				

KM# 349 10 DOLLARS
31.1035 g., 0.9990 Silver 1.0000 oz. ASW **Subject:** Pending Return of Macao to China **Obv:** National arms **Rev:** City view within circle

Date	Mintage	F	VF	XF	Unc	BU
1997 Proof	Est. 8,000	Value: 32.50				

KM# 350 10 DOLLARS
31.1035 g., 0.9990 Silver 1.0000 oz. ASW **Subject:** Diana - The People's Princess **Obv:** National arms **Rev:** Princess Diana in fencing attire

Date	Mintage	F	VF	XF	Unc	BU
1997 Proof	—	Value: 45.00				

KM# 369 10 DOLLARS
31.1035 g., 0.9990 Silver 1.0000 oz. ASW **Subject:** Star Trek - The Next Generation **Obv:** National arms **Rev:** Romulan Warbird

Date	Mintage	F	VF	XF	Unc	BU
1997 Proof	25,000	Value: 45.00				

KM# 372 10 DOLLARS
31.1035 g., 0.9990 Silver 1.0000 oz. ASW **Subject:** Star Trek - The Next Generation **Obv:** National arms **Rev:** Klingon Attack Cruiser

Date	Mintage	F	VF	XF	Unc	BU
1997 Proof	25,000	Value: 45.00				

KM# 375 10 DOLLARS
31.1035 g., 0.9990 Silver 1.0000 oz. ASW **Subject:** Star Trek - The Next Generation **Obv:** National arms **Rev:** U.S.S. Enterprise NCC-1701-D

Date	Mintage	F	VF	XF	Unc	BU
1997 Proof	25,000	Value: 45.00				

KM# 378 10 DOLLARS
31.1035 g., 0.9990 Silver 1.0000 oz. ASW **Subject:** Star Trek - The Next Generation **Obv:** National arms **Rev:** Klingon Bird of Prey

Date	Mintage	F	VF	XF	Unc	BU
1997 Proof	25,000	Value: 45.00				

KM# 381 10 DOLLARS
31.1035 g., 0.9990 Silver 1.0000 oz. ASW **Subject:** Star Trek - The Next Generation **Obv:** National arms **Rev:** Borg Cube

Date	Mintage	F	VF	XF	Unc	BU
1997 Proof	25,000	Value: 45.00				

KM# 384 10 DOLLARS
31.1035 g., 0.9990 Silver 1.0000 oz. ASW **Subject:** Star Trek - The Next Generation **Obv:** National arms **Rev:** Ferengi Marauder

Date	Mintage	F	VF	XF	Unc	BU
1997 Proof	25,000	Value: 45.00				

KM# 387 10 DOLLARS
31.1035 g., 0.9990 Silver 1.0000 oz. ASW **Subject:** President Ronald Reagan **Obv:** National arms **Rev:** Lincoln Memorial below head right

Date	Mintage	F	VF	XF	Unc	BU
1998 Proof	25,000	Value: 50.00				

KM# 402 10 DOLLARS
31.1035 g., 0.9990 Silver 1.0000 oz. ASW **Subject:** Christopher Columbus **Obv:** National arms **Rev:** Bust 1/4 right above ship

Date	Mintage	F	VF	XF	Unc	BU
1999 Proof	25,000	Value: 45.00				

KM# 405 10 DOLLARS
31.1035 g., 0.9990 Silver 1.0000 oz. ASW **Subject:** Captain James Cook **Obv:** National arms **Rev:** Portrait, map and ship

Date	Mintage	F	VF	XF	Unc	BU
1999 Proof	25,000	Value: 45.00				

KM# 408 10 DOLLARS
31.1035 g., 0.9990 Silver 1.0000 oz. ASW **Subject:** Return of Macao to China **Obv:** National arms **Rev:** Dragon and phoenix

Date	Mintage	F	VF	XF	Unc	BU
1999 Proof	25,000	Value: 40.00				

KM# 414 10 DOLLARS
31.1035 g., 0.9990 Silver 1.0000 oz. ASW **Subject:** The Wedding of Prince Edward and Miss Sophie Rhys-Jones **Obv:** National arms **Rev:** Couple in carriage

Date	Mintage	F	VF	XF	Unc	BU
1999 Proof	10,000	Value: 50.00				

KM# 424 10 DOLLARS
15.5517 g., 0.9990 Silver .5000 oz. ASW **Series:** Liberty **Subject:** John F. Kennedy and John Jr. **Obv:** National arms **Rev:** Conjoined heads left

Date	Mintage	F	VF	XF	Unc	BU
1999 Proof	—	Value: 22.50				

KM# 594 10 DOLLARS
31.0000 g., 0.9990 Silver 0.9957 oz. ASW, 40 mm. **Subject:** John F. Kennedy Jr. **Obv:** National arms **Rev:** Two portraits, flag and the White House **Edge:** Reeded

Date	Mintage	F	VF	XF	Unc	BU
1999 Proof	—	Value: 40.00				

KM# 471 10 DOLLARS
30.7500 g., 0.9990 Silver .9876 oz. ASW, 37.9 mm. **Subject:** Transrapid-08 Hamburg-Berlin Monorail **Obv:** National arms **Rev:** Monorail train car **Edge:** Reeded

Date	Mintage	F	VF	XF	Unc	BU
1999 Proof	—	Value: 35.00				

KM# 573 10 DOLLARS
25.1000 g., 0.9250 Silver 0.7465 oz. ASW, 38.6 mm. **Obv:** National arms **Rev:** Titanic steaming right **Edge:** Reeded

Date	Mintage	F	VF	XF	Unc	BU
1999 Proof	—	Value: 40.00				

KM# 706 10 DOLLARS
20.1000 g., 0.9250 Silver 0.5978 oz. ASW, 34 mm. **Obv:** National arms **Rev:** Sail ship "Vijia" with captains name above **Edge:** Reeded

Date	Mintage	F	VF	XF	Unc	BU
1999 Proof	—	Value: 30.00				

KM# 468 10 DOLLARS
25.0000 g., 0.9250 Silver .7435 oz. ASW, 38.7 mm. **Obv:** National arms **Rev:** Sailing ship "Mayflower" **Edge:** Reeded

Date	Mintage	F	VF	XF	Unc	BU
1999 Proof	—	Value: 25.00				

KM# 709 10 DOLLARS
0.5100 g., Gold, 11.1 mm. **Subject:** American Civil War

Obv: National arms **Rev:** Battle of Gettysburg Generals Meade and Lee **Edge:** Reeded

Date	Mintage	F	VF	XF	Unc	BU
2000 Proof	—	Value: 25.00				

KM# 423 10 DOLLARS

31.1035 g., 0.9990 Silver 1.000 oz. ASW **Subject:** Millennium **Obv:** Liberty cap, crossed flags of USA and Liberia above national arms **Rev:** Morgan dollar Liberty portrait

Date	Mintage	F	VF	XF	Unc	BU
2000 Proof	Est. 2,000	Value: 40.00				

KM# 443 10 DOLLARS

31.1035 g., 0.9990 Silver 1.0000 oz. ASW, 38.6 mm. **Subject:** Greenwich Meridian **Obv:** National arms **Rev:** World landmarks and fireworks **Edge:** Reeded

Date	Mintage	F	VF	XF	Unc	BU
2000 Proof	25,000	Value: 47.50				

KM# 444 10 DOLLARS

25.0000 g., 0.9250 Silver .7435 oz. ASW, 36.8 mm. **Subject:** Millennium - Hippocrates **Obv:** National arms **Rev:** Caduceus **Edge:** Plain **Shape:** 10-sided

Date	Mintage	F	VF	XF	Unc	BU
2000 Proof	10,000	Value: 35.00				

KM# 469 10 DOLLARS

20.5000 g., 0.9250 Silver .6097 oz. ASW, 38.6 mm. **Subject:** Millennium **Obv:** National arms **Rev:** Millennium Dome **Edge:** Reeded

Date	Mintage	F	VF	XF	Unc	BU
2000 Proof	2,000	Value: 32.50				

KM# 470 10 DOLLARS

20.5000 g., 0.9250 Silver .6097 oz. ASW **Subject:** Mutiny on the Bounty **Obv:** National arms **Rev:** Mutineers setting ship's officers adrift

Date	Mintage	F	VF	XF	Unc	BU
2000 Proof	2,000	Value: 32.50				

KM# 475 10 DOLLARS

8.4500 g., 0.9990 Silver .2714 oz. ASW, 30.1 mm. **Subject:** General Robert E. Lee **Obv:** National arms **Rev:** Equestrian left **Edge:** Reeded

Date	Mintage	F	VF	XF	Unc	BU
2000 Proof	—	Value: 15.00				

KM# 476 10 DOLLARS

8.4500 g., 0.9990 Silver .2714 oz. ASW **Obv:** National arms **Rev:** Statue of Liberty

Date	Mintage	F	VF	XF	Unc	BU
2000 Proof	—	Value: 15.00				

KM# 492 10 DOLLARS

3.3930 g., 0.9167 Gold .1000 oz. AGW, 16.5 mm. **Subject:** US Gold Indian Design Copy **Obv:** Incuse Indian design **Rev:** Incuse eagle design **Edge:** Reeded

Date	Mintage	F	VF	XF	Unc	BU
2000	—	—	—	—	125	—

KM# 499 10 DOLLARS

20.1500 g., 0.9990 Silver 0.6472 oz. ASW, 34 mm. **Obv:** National arms **Rev:** Monkeys **Edge:** Reeded

Date	Mintage	F	VF	XF	Unc	BU
2000 Proof	—	Value: 30.00				

KM# 500 10 DOLLARS

8.5500 g., 0.9990 Silver 0.2746 oz. ASW, 30 mm. **Subject:** American History **Obv:** National arms **Rev:** Washington crossing the Delaware **Edge:** Reeded **Note:** The American Mint is not an actual mint.

Date	Mintage	F	VF	XF	Unc	BU
2000 Proof	20,000	Value: 20.00				

KM# 501 10 DOLLARS

8.5500 g., 0.9990 Silver 0.2746 oz. ASW, 30 mm. **Subject:** American History - Battle of Gettysburg **Obv:** National arms **Rev:** Flags and cannon divide uniformed busts **Edge:** Reeded **Note:** The American Mint is not an actual mint.

Date	Mintage	F	VF	XF	Unc	BU
2000 Proof	20,000	Value: 20.00				

KM# 502 10 DOLLARS

8.5500 g., 0.9990 Silver 0.2746 oz. ASW, 30 mm. **Subject:** American History **Obv:** National arms **Rev:** B-17 Bomber in action **Edge:** Reeded **Note:** The American Mint is not an actual mint.

Date	Mintage	F	VF	XF	Unc	BU
2000 Proof	20,000	Value: 20.00				

KM# 503 10 DOLLARS

8.5500 g., 0.9990 Silver 0.2746 oz. ASW, 30 mm. **Subject:** American History - First Man on the Moon **Obv:** National arms **Rev:** Astronaut on the moon with American flag **Edge:** Reeded **Note:** The American Mint is not an actual mint.

Date	Mintage	F	VF	XF	Unc	BU
2000 Proof	20,000	Value: 20.00				

KM# 622 10 DOLLARS

21.0000 g., Copper-Nickel, 37 mm. **Subject:** Millennium **Obv:** National arms **Rev:** Kneeling woman with hourglass **Edge:** Reeded

Date	Mintage	F	VF	XF	Unc	BU
2000	—	—	—	—	9.00	—

KM# 645 10 DOLLARS

8.4500 g., 0.9990 Silver 0.2714 oz. ASW, 30 mm. **Obv:** National arms **Rev:** Boeing 707 **Edge:** Reeded

Date	Mintage	F	VF	XF	Unc	BU
2000 Proof	—	Value: 20.00				

KM# 653 10 DOLLARS

14.6000 g., Copper-Nickel, 33.1 mm. **Obv:** National arms **Rev:** Bust facing within U.S. flag **Edge:** Reeded

Date	Mintage	F	VF	XF	Unc	BU
2000	—	—	—	—	10.00	—

KM# 698 10 DOLLARS

29.4000 g., 0.9990 Silver 0.9443 oz. ASW, 40 mm. **Obv:** National arms **Rev:** Multicolor cougar **Edge:** Reeded

Date	Mintage	F	VF	XF	Unc	BU
2000 Proof	—	Value: 35.00				

KM# 699 10 DOLLARS

21.3200 g., 0.9990 Silver 0.6848 oz. ASW, 37.4 mm. **Obv:** National arms **Rev:** Three-dimensional multicolor timber wolf in winter **Edge:** Reeded

Date	Mintage	F	VF	XF	Unc	BU
2000	—	—	—	—	30.00	—

KM# 700 10 DOLLARS

29.0600 g., 0.9990 Silver 0.9334 oz. ASW, 40 mm. **Obv:** National arms **Rev:** Multicolor timber wolf in summer **Edge:** Reeded

Date	Mintage	F	VF	XF	Unc	BU
2000 Proof	—	Value: 35.00				

KM# 701 10 DOLLARS

31.1035 g., 0.9990 Silver 0.999 oz. ASW, 39 mm. **Obv:** Heraldic Eagle **Rev:** Type I Standing Liberty Quarter design **Edge:** Reeded

Date	Mintage	F	VF	XF	Unc	BU
2000 Proof	—	Value: 40.00				

KM# 702 10 DOLLARS
31.1035 g., 0.9990 Silver 0.999 oz. ASW, 39 mm. **Obv:** Heraldic Eagle **Rev:** Seated Liberty Dollar design **Edge:** Reeded

Date	Mintage	F	VF	XF	Unc	BU
2000 Proof	—	Value: 40.00				

KM# 703 10 DOLLARS
31.1035 g., 0.9990 Silver 0.999 oz. ASW, 39 mm. **Obv:** Heraldic Eagle **Rev:** Peace Liberty dollar design **Edge:** Reeded

Date	Mintage	F	VF	XF	Unc	BU
2000 Proof	—	Value: 40.00				

KM# 704 10 DOLLARS
Silver, 40 mm. **Subject:** Games of the XXVII Olympiad - Sydney 2000 **Obv:** National arms **Rev:** Map of Australia at upper left of man sailing **Edge:** Reeded

Date	Mintage	F	VF	XF	Unc	BU
2000 Proof	—	Value: 45.00				

KM# 20 12 DOLLARS
6.0000 g., 0.9000 Gold .1736 oz. AGW **Subject:** 70th Birthday of President Tubman **Obv:** National arms **Rev:** Bust left

Date	Mintage	F	VF	XF	Unc	BU
1965 Proof	400	Value: 130				

KM# 108 15 DOLLARS
1.0000 g., 0.9999 Gold .0321 oz. AGW **Series:** Preserve Planet Earth **Obv:** National arms **Rev:** Compsognathus

Date	Mintage	F	VF	XF	Unc	BU
1993 Proof	—	Value: 32.50				

KM# 19 20 DOLLARS
18.6500 g., 0.9000 Gold .5397 oz. AGW **Subject:** William Vacanarat Shadrach Tubman **Obv:** National arms **Rev:** Head 1/4 left above date flanked by stars

Date	Mintage	F	VF	XF	Unc	BU
1964B	10,000	—	—	—	375	—

KM# 19a 20 DOLLARS
0.9990 Gold **Obv:** National arms **Rev:** Head 1/4 left above date flanked by stars

Date	Mintage	F	VF	XF	Unc	BU
1964B L Proof	100	Value: 425				

Note: Of the total issue, 10,200 were struck of .900 fine gold and bear the "B" mint mark of the Bern Mint below the date, while 100 were struck as proofs of .999 fine gold and are designated by the presence of a small "L" above the date

KM# 64 20 DOLLARS
15.8100 g., 0.9000 Gold .8768 oz. AGW **Subject:** 25th Anniversary of Inter-Continental Hotels **Obv:** Value below hotel building **Rev:** Letter I within football flanked by dates

Date	Mintage	F	VF	XF	Unc	BU
1971 Proof	—	Value: 645				

KM# 27 20 DOLLARS
33.4370 g., 0.9000 Gold .9675 oz. AGW **Subject:** Inauguration of President Tolbert **Obv:** National arms **Rev:** Head left

Date	Mintage	F	VF	XF	Unc	BU
1972 Proof	—	Value: 700				

KM# 45 20 DOLLARS
28.2800 g., 0.9250 Silver .8411 oz. ASW **Subject:** Year of the Scout **Obv:** National arms **Rev:** Scouts at camp, three saluting, three seated

Date	Mintage	F	VF	XF	Unc	BU
1983	10,000	—	—	—	30.00	—
1983 Proof	10,000	Value: 48.50				

KM# 48 20 DOLLARS
28.2800 g., 0.9250 Silver .8411 oz. ASW **Series:** International Year of Disabled Persons **Obv:** National arms

Date	Mintage	F	VF	XF	Unc	BU
1983	—	—	—	—	32.50	—
1983 Proof	—	Value: 50.00				

KM# 283 20 DOLLARS
1.2700 g., 0.9990 Gold .0408 oz. AGW **Subject:** Formula One **Obv:** National arms divide date **Rev:** Damon Hill

Date	Mintage	F	VF	XF	Unc	BU
1994 Proof	25,000	Value: 65.00				

KM# 230 20 DOLLARS
1.2700 g., 0.9990 Gold .0408 oz. AGW **Subject:** Formula One **Obv:** National arms **Rev:** Ayrton Senna **Note:** Similar to 10 Dollars, KM#229.

Date	Mintage	F	VF	XF	Unc	BU
1996 Proof	15,000	Value: 65.00				

KM# 250 20 DOLLARS
1.2700 g., 0.9990 Gold .0408 oz. AGW **Subject:** Dalai Lama **Obv:** National arms **Rev:** Bust with praying hands facing 1/4 left **Note:** Similar to 100 Dollars, KM#252.

Date	Mintage	F	VF	XF	Unc	BU
1996 Proof	15,000	Value: 65.00				

KM# 340 20 DOLLARS
31.1035 g., 0.9990 Silver 1.0000 oz. ASW **Subject:** Year of the Ox **Obv:** National arms **Rev:** Ox above value

Date	Mintage	F	VF	XF	Unc	BU
1997 Proof	—	Value: 30.00				

KM# 416 20 DOLLARS
31.3500 g., 0.9990 Silver 1.0069 oz. ASW **Subject:** Deng Xiaoping **Obv:** National arms **Rev:** Bust 1/4 right above value

Date	Mintage	F	VF	XF	Unc	BU
1997 Proof	—	Value: 22.50				

KM# 417 20 DOLLARS
31.4000 g., 0.9990 Silver 1.0085 oz. ASW **Subject:** Princess Diana In Memoriam **Obv:** National arms **Rev:** Portrait and dates

Date	Mintage	F	VF	XF	Unc	BU
1997 Proof	—	Value: 32.50				

KM# 498 20 DOLLARS
31.2200 g., 0.9990 Silver 1.0027 oz. ASW, 38.5 mm. **Subject:** Year of the Ox - Type II **Obv:** National arms **Rev:** Ox within inner circle with legend **Edge:** Reeded

Date	Mintage	F	VF	XF	Unc	BU
1997 Proof	—	Value: 40.00				

KM# 535 20 DOLLARS
31.1300 g., 0.9990 Silver 0.9999 oz. ASW, 38.6 mm. **Subject:** Princess Diana - Compassion **Obv:** National arms **Rev:** Diana with sick child **Edge:** Reeded

Date	Mintage	F	VF	XF	Unc	BU
1997 Proof	—	Value: 40.00				

KM# 515 20 DOLLARS
31.2200 g., 0.9990 Silver 1.0027 oz. ASW, 38.5 mm. **Subject:** Princess Diana **Obv:** National arms **Rev:** Diana as a young girl **Edge:** Reeded

Date	Mintage	F	VF	XF	Unc	BU
1997 Proof	—	Value: 40.00				

KM# 518 20 DOLLARS
31.2200 g., 0.9990 Silver 1.0027 oz. ASW, 38.5 mm. **Subject:** Princess Diana **Obv:** National arms **Rev:** Diana in wedding dress **Edge:** Reeded

Date	Mintage	F	VF	XF	Unc	BU
1997 Proof	—	Value: 40.00				

KM# 520 20 DOLLARS
31.2200 g., 0.9990 Silver 1.0027 oz. ASW, 38.5 mm. **Subject:** Princess Diana "England's Rose" **Obv:** National arms **Rev:** Diana with roses **Edge:** Reeded

Date	Mintage	F	VF	XF	Unc	BU
1997 Proof	—	Value: 40.00				

KM# 523 20 DOLLARS
31.2200 g., 0.9990 Silver 1.0027 oz. ASW, 38.5 mm. **Subject:** Princess Diana **Obv:** National arms **Rev:** Diana with baby William **Edge:** Reeded

Date	Mintage	F	VF	XF	Unc	BU
1997 Proof	—	Value: 40.00				

KM# 526 20 DOLLARS
31.2200 g., 0.9990 Silver 1.0027 oz. ASW, 38.5 mm. **Subject:** Princess Diana **Obv:** National arms **Rev:** Diana with two sons **Edge:** Reeded

Date	Mintage	F	VF	XF	Unc	BU
1997 Proof	—	Value: 40.00				

KM# 527 20 DOLLARS
31.2200 g., 0.9990 Silver 1.0027 oz. ASW, 38.5 mm. **Subject:** Princess Diana **Obv:** National arms **Rev:** Royal family **Edge:** Reeded

Date	Mintage	F	VF	XF	Unc	BU
1997 Proof	—	Value: 40.00				

KM# 528 20 DOLLARS
31.2200 g., 0.9990 Silver 1.0027 oz. ASW, 38.5 mm. **Subject:** Princess Diana **Obv:** National arms **Rev:** Queen Elizabeth II and Diana **Edge:** Reeded

Date	Mintage	F	VF	XF	Unc	BU
1997 Proof	—	Value: 40.00				

KM# 533 20 DOLLARS
31.2200 g., 0.9990 Silver 1.0027 oz. ASW, 38.5 mm. **Subject:** Princess Diana **Obv:** National arms **Rev:** Diana teaching **Edge:** Reeded

Date	Mintage	F	VF	XF	Unc	BU
1997 Proof	—	Value: 40.00				

KM# 592 20 DOLLARS
31.2200 g., 0.9990 Silver 1.0027 oz. ASW, 38.5 mm. **Subject:** Princess Diana **Obv:** National arms **Rev:** Mother Teresa and Diana **Edge:** Reeded

Date	Mintage	F	VF	XF	Unc	BU
1997 Proof	—	Value: 40.00				

KM# 315 20 DOLLARS
1.2400 g., 0.9990 Gold .0400 oz. AGW **Subject:** Return of Hong Kong to China **Obv:** National arms **Rev:** Dragon **Note:** Similar to 10 Dollars, KM#314.

Date	Mintage	F	VF	XF	Unc	BU
1997 Proof	—	Value: 65.00				

KM# 341 20 DOLLARS
31.1035 g., 0.9990 Silver 1.0000 oz. ASW **Subject:** Year of the Tiger **Obv:** National arms **Rev:** Tiger in bamboo

Date	Mintage	F	VF	XF	Unc	BU
1998 (1997) Proof	—	Value: 37.50				

KM# 342 20 DOLLARS
24.9400 g., Silver **Subject:** Year of the Tiger **Obv:** National arms **Rev:** Tiger lying in bamboo

Date	Mintage	F	VF	XF	Unc	BU
1998 (1997) Proof	—	Value: 37.50				

KM# 343 20 DOLLARS
24.9400 g., Silver **Subject:** Year of the Tiger **Obv:** National arms **Rev:** Stalking tiger

Date	Mintage	F	VF	XF	Unc	BU
1998 (1997) Proof	—	Value: 37.50				

KM# 364 20 DOLLARS
31.1035 g., 0.9990 Silver 1.0000 oz. ASW **Subject:** RMS Titanic **Obv:** National arms **Rev:** Cameo above sinking ship

Date	Mintage	F	VF	XF	Unc	BU
1998 Proof	25,000	Value: 50.00				

KM# 585 20 DOLLARS
31.1035 g., 0.9990 Silver 0.999 oz. ASW, 38 mm. **Subject:** Year of the Tiger **Obv:** National arms **Rev:** Tiger above pineapple and flowers within beaded circle **Edge:** Reeded

Date	Mintage	F	VF	XF	Unc	BU
1998 Proof	—	Value: 45.00				

KM# 586 20 DOLLARS
31.1035 g., 0.9990 Silver 0.999 oz. ASW, 38 mm. **Subject:** Year of the Tiger **Obv:** National arms **Rev:** Roaring tiger **Edge:** Reeded

Date	Mintage	F	VF	XF	Unc	BU
1998 Proof	—	Value: 45.00				

KM# 587 20 DOLLARS
31.1035 g., 0.9990 Silver 0.999 oz. ASW, 38 mm. **Subject:** Year of the Tiger **Obv:** National arms **Rev:** Crouching tiger **Edge:** Reeded

Date	Mintage	F	VF	XF	Unc	BU
1998 Proof	—	Value: 45.00				

KM# 389 20 DOLLARS
31.1035 g., 0.9990 Silver 1.0000 oz. ASW **Subject:** Year of the Rabbit **Obv:** National arms **Rev:** Rabbit running left within dotted circle

Date	Mintage	F	VF	XF	Unc	BU
1999 Proof	8,000	Value: 40.00				

KM# 390 20 DOLLARS
31.1035 g., 0.9990 Silver 1.0000 oz. ASW **Subject:** Year of the Rabbit **Obv:** National arms **Rev:** Rabbit sitting

Date	Mintage	F	VF	XF	Unc	BU
1999 Proof	8,000	Value: 40.00				

KM# 391 20 DOLLARS
31.1035 g., 0.9990 Silver 1.0000 oz. ASW **Subject:** Year of the Rabbit **Obv:** National arms **Rev:** Rabbit running right

Date	Mintage	F	VF	XF	Unc	BU
1999 Proof	8,000	Value: 40.00				

KM# 418 20 DOLLARS
1.2441 g., 0.9999 Gold .0400 oz. AGW **Subject:** Return of Macao to China **Obv:** National arms **Rev:** Dragon and phoenix **Note:** Similar to 10 Dollars, KM#408.

Date	Mintage	F	VF	XF	Unc	BU
1999 Proof	25,000	Value: 55.00				

KM# 574 20 DOLLARS
20.0000 g., 0.9990 Silver 0.6424 oz. ASW, 40.1 mm. **Subject:** Captain Cook **Obv:** National arms **Rev:** Seated Capt. Cook at right, his ship at left **Edge:** Reeded

Date	Mintage	F	VF	XF	Unc	BU
2000 Proof	—	Value: 30.00				

KM# 575 20 DOLLARS
31.0000 g., 0.9990 Silver 0.9957 oz. ASW, 38.7 mm. **Obv:** National arms **Rev:** Hippopotamus **Edge:** Reeded

Date	Mintage	F	VF	XF	Unc	BU
2000 Proof	—	Value: 35.00				

KM# 576 20 DOLLARS
19.8500 g., 0.9990 Silver 0.6376 oz. ASW, 40.3 mm. **Subject:** Olympics **Obv:** National arms **Rev:** Volleyball player with city view behind **Edge:** Reeded

Date	Mintage	F	VF	XF	Unc	BU
2000 Proof	—	Value: 35.00				

KM# 577 20 DOLLARS
19.8500 g., 0.9990 Silver 0.6376 oz. ASW, 40.3 mm. **Subject:** Olympics **Obv:** National arms **Rev:** High jumper and Australian map **Edge:** Reeded

Date	Mintage	F	VF	XF	Unc	BU
2000 Proof	—	Value: 35.00				

KM# 661 20 DOLLARS
20.6000 g., 0.9990 Silver 0.6616 oz. ASW, 40.3 mm. **Obv:** National arms **Rev:** R.M.S. Queen Mary **Edge:** Reeded

Date	Mintage	F	VF	XF	Unc	BU
2000 Proof	—	Value: 25.00				

KM# 472 20 DOLLARS
20.1700 g., 0.9990 Silver .6478 oz. ASW, 40.3 mm. **Series:** American History **Obv:** National arms **Rev:** The Alamo and defenders **Edge:** Reeded

Date	Mintage	F	VF	XF	Unc	BU
2000 Proof	—	Value: 25.00				

KM# 477 20 DOLLARS
20.0400 g., 0.9990 Silver .6437 oz. ASW, 40.3 mm. **Subject:** Admiral David G. Farragut **Obv:** National arms **Rev:** Uniformed bust 1/4 left within flag **Edge:** Reeded

Date	Mintage	F	VF	XF	Unc	BU
2000 Proof	Est. 20,000	Value: 25.00				

KM# 478 20 DOLLARS
20.0400 g., 0.9990 Silver .6437 oz. ASW **Subject:** Surrender of Appomattox **Obv:** National arms **Rev:** Surrender signing scene

Date	Mintage	F	VF	XF	Unc	BU
2000 Proof	Est. 20,000	Value: 25.00				

KM# 479 20 DOLLARS
20.0400 g., 0.9990 Silver .6437 oz. ASW **Subject:** Abraham Lincoln **Obv:** National arms **Rev:** Bust 3/4 right

Date	Mintage	F	VF	XF	Unc	BU
2000 Proof	Est. 20,000	Value: 25.00				

KM# 480 20 DOLLARS
20.0400 g., 0.9990 Silver .6437 oz. ASW **Subject:** Montgolfiere Balloon **Obv:** National arms **Rev:** First hot air balloon

Date	Mintage	F	VF	XF	Unc	BU
2000 Proof	Est. 20,000	Value: 25.00				

KM# 481 20 DOLLARS
20.0400 g., 0.9990 Silver .6437 oz. ASW **Subject:** Concorde Supersonic Airliner **Obv:** National arms **Rev:** Plane in flight above runway

Date	Mintage	F	VF	XF	Unc	BU
2000 Proof	Est. 20,000	Value: 25.00				

KM# 482 20 DOLLARS
20.0400 g., 0.9990 Silver .6437 oz. ASW **Subject:** Apollo X **Obv:** National arms **Rev:** Rocket launch, space capsule, large X

Date	Mintage	F	VF	XF	Unc	BU
2000 Proof	Est. 20,000	Value: 25.00				

KM# 483 20 DOLLARS
20.0400 g., 0.9990 Silver .6437 oz. ASW **Subject:** Apollo VII **Obv:** National arms **Rev:** Space capsule above half-length busts of Schirra, Eisele, and Cunningham facing

Date	Mintage	F	VF	XF	Unc	BU
2000 Proof	Est. 20,000	Value: 25.00				

KM# 484 20 DOLLARS
20.0400 g., 0.9990 Silver .6437 oz. ASW **Subject:** STS-1 **Obv:** National arms **Rev:** 3/4-length busts of Young and Crippen facing with shuttle model

Date	Mintage	F	VF	XF	Unc	BU
2000 Proof	Est. 20,000	Value: 25.00				

KM# 485 20 DOLLARS
20.0400 g., 0.9990 Silver .6437 oz. ASW **Subject:** Skylab I **Obv:** National arms **Rev:** Half-length busts of Conrad, Kerwin, and Weitz facing below Skylab

Date	Mintage	F	VF	XF	Unc	BU
2000 Proof	Est. 20,000	Value: 25.00				

KM# 486 20 DOLLARS
20.0400 g., 0.9990 Silver .6437 oz. ASW **Series:** Olympics **Obv:** National arms **Rev:** Hurdler

Date	Mintage	F	VF	XF	Unc	BU
2000 Proof	Est. 20,000	Value: 25.00				

KM# 487 20 DOLLARS
20.0400 g., 0.9990 Silver .6437 oz. ASW **Series:** Olympics **Obv:** National arms **Rev:** Equestrian

Date	Mintage	F	VF	XF	Unc	BU
2000 Proof	Est. 20,000	Value: 25.00				

KM# 488 20 DOLLARS
20.0400 g., 0.9990 Silver .6437 oz. ASW **Series:** Olympics **Obv:** National arms **Rev:** Two basketball players in front of flags

Date	Mintage	F	VF	XF	Unc	BU
2000 Proof	Est. 20,000	Value: 25.00				

KM# 489 20 DOLLARS
20.0400 g., 0.9990 Silver .6437 oz. ASW **Series:** Olympics **Obv:** National arms **Rev:** Three cyclists

Date	Mintage	F	VF	XF	Unc	BU
2000 Proof	Est. 20,000	Value: 25.00				

KM# 490 20 DOLLARS
20.0400 g., 0.9990 Silver .6437 oz. ASW **Series:** Olympics **Obv:** National arms **Rev:** Swimmer, cyclist, and speed walker

Date	Mintage	F	VF	XF	Unc	BU
2000 Proof	Est. 20,000	Value: 25.00				

KM# 504 20 DOLLARS
20.0000 g., 0.9990 Silver 0.6424 oz. ASW, 40.4 mm. **Subject:** American History **Obv:** National arms **Rev:** Treaty of Paris signing scene **Edge:** Reeded **Note:** The American Mint is not an actual mint.

Date	Mintage	F	VF	XF	Unc	BU
2000 Proof	20,000	Value: 40.00				

KM# 505 20 DOLLARS
20.0000 g., 0.9990 Silver 0.6424 oz. ASW, 40.4 mm. **Subject:** American History - Civil War **Obv:** National arms **Rev:** Bombardment of Fort Sumter scene **Edge:** Reeded **Note:** The American Mint is not an actual mint.

Date	Mintage	F	VF	XF	Unc	BU
2000 Proof	20,000	Value: 40.00				

KM# 506 20 DOLLARS
20.0000 g., 0.9990 Silver 0.6424 oz. ASW, 40.4 mm. **Subject:** American History **Obv:** National arms **Rev:** Bust facing **Edge:** Reeded **Note:** The American Mint is not an actual mint.

Date	Mintage	F	VF	XF	Unc	BU
2000 Proof	20,000	Value: 40.00				

KM# 507 20 DOLLARS
20.0000 g., 0.9990 Silver 0.6424 oz. ASW, 40.4 mm. **Subject:** American History **Obv:** National arms **Rev:** Busts of astronauts Young and Crippen with Space Shuttle model **Edge:** Reeded **Note:** The American Mint is not an actual mint.

Date	Mintage	F	VF	XF	Unc	BU
2000 Proof	20,000	Value: 40.00				

KM# 508 20 DOLLARS
31.1035 g., 0.9990 Silver 0.999 oz. ASW, 40.7 mm. **Subject:** Millennium **Obv:** Seated Liberty **Rev:** Y2K design **Edge:** Reeded **Note:** The American Mint is not an actual mint.

Date	Mintage	F	VF	XF	Unc	BU
2000	2,000	—	—	—	30.00	—

KM# 509.1 20 DOLLARS
31.1035 g., 0.9990 Silver 0.999 oz. ASW, 39 mm. **Subject:** Millennium **Obv:** National arms **Rev:** Woman with hourglass and dove **Edge:** Reeded **Note:** The American Mint is not an actual mint.

Date	Mintage	F	VF	XF	Unc	BU
2000	—	—	—	—	30.00	—

KM# 509.2 20 DOLLARS
31.1035 g., 0.9990 Silver 0.999 oz. ASW, 39 mm. **Subject:** Millennium **Obv:** National arms **Rev:** Multicolor woman with hourglass and dove **Edge:** Reeded **Note:** The American Mint is not an actual mint.

Date	Mintage	F	VF	XF	Unc	BU
2000	—	—	—	—	30.00	—

KM# 590 20 DOLLARS
20.0000 g., 0.9990 Silver 0.6424 oz. ASW, 40 mm. **Obv:** National arms **Rev:** Titanic steaming right **Edge:** Reeded

Date	Mintage	F	VF	XF	Unc	BU
2000 Proof	—	Value: 30.00				

KM# 591 20 DOLLARS
20.0000 g., 0.9990 Silver 0.6424 oz. ASW, 40 mm. **Subject:** Apollo XVIII and Soyuz XIX **Obv:** National arms **Rev:** Two space capsules about to link up **Edge:** Reeded

Date	Mintage	F	VF	XF	Unc	BU
2000 Proof	—	Value: 30.00				

KM# 595 20 DOLLARS
20.0000 g., 0.9990 Silver 0.6424 oz. ASW, 40 mm. **Subject:** Aviation **Obv:** National arms **Rev:** Wright Brothers airplane **Edge:** Reeded

Date	Mintage	F	VF	XF	Unc	BU
2000 Proof	20,000	Value: 35.00				

KM# 596 20 DOLLARS
20.0000 g., 0.9990 Silver 0.6424 oz. ASW, 40 mm. **Subject:** Aviation **Obv:** National arms **Rev:** Russian Witiaz four-engine bi-plane **Edge:** Reeded

Date	Mintage	F	VF	XF	Unc	BU
2000 Proof	20,000	Value: 35.00				

KM# 597 20 DOLLARS
20.0000 g., 0.9990 Silver 0.6424 oz. ASW, 40 mm. **Subject:** Aviation **Obv:** National arms **Rev:** Curtiss R3C-2 floating bi-plane **Edge:** Reeded

Date	Mintage	F	VF	XF	Unc	BU
2000 Proof	20,000	Value: 35.00				

KM# 598 20 DOLLARS
20.0000 g., 0.9990 Silver 0.6424 oz. ASW, 40 mm. **Subject:** Aviation **Obv:** National arms **Rev:** Grumman F3F bi-plane fighter **Edge:** Reeded

Date	Mintage	F	VF	XF	Unc	BU
2000 Proof	20,000	Value: 35.00				

KM# 599 20 DOLLARS
20.0000 g., 0.9990 Silver 0.6424 oz. ASW, 40 mm. **Subject:** Aviation **Obv:** National arms **Rev:** Space Station **Edge:** Reeded

Date	Mintage	F	VF	XF	Unc	BU
2000 Proof	20,000	Value: 35.00				

KM# 609 20 DOLLARS
19.9000 g., 0.9990 Silver 0.6392 oz. ASW, 40.2 mm. **Obv:** National arms **Rev:** United States Bill of Rights **Edge:** Reeded

Date	Mintage	F	VF	XF	Unc	BU
2000 Proof	20,000	Value: 15.00				

KM# 610 20 DOLLARS
19.9400 g., 0.9990 Silver 0.6404 oz. ASW, 40.2 mm. **Obv:** National arms **Rev:** Louisiana Purchase map on flag behind portraits of Jefferson, Lewis and Clark **Edge:** Reeded

Date	Mintage	F	VF	XF	Unc	BU
2000 Proof	—	Value: 15.00				

KM# 613 20 DOLLARS
31.1035 g., 0.9990 Silver 0.999 oz. ASW, 39 mm. **Subject:** "King of the Cowboys" Roy Rogers **Obv:** National arms **Obv. Legend:** ROY ROGERS, King of the Cowboys below **Rev:** Bust 1/4 left **Edge:** Reeded

Date	Mintage	F	VF	XF	Unc	BU
2000 Proof	1,000	Value: 35.00				

KM# 614 20 DOLLARS
31.1035 g., 0.9990 Silver 0.999 oz. ASW, 39 mm. **Subject:** Roy Rogers **Obv:** National arms **Obv. Legend:** ROY ROGERS, Happy Trails to You! below **Rev:** Bust 1/4 left **Edge:** Reeded

Date	Mintage	F	VF	XF	Unc	BU
2000 Proof	1,000	Value: 35.00				

KM# 636 20 DOLLARS
31.1000 g., 0.9990 Silver 0.9989 oz. ASW, 38.6 mm. **Obv:** National arms **Rev:** American Quarter Horse **Edge:** Reeded

Date	Mintage	F	VF	XF	Unc	BU
2000 Proof	—	Value: 25.00				

KM# 637 20 DOLLARS
20.1000 g., 0.9990 Silver 0.6456 oz. ASW, 40.2 mm. **Obv:** National arms **Rev:** Berlin buildings **Edge:** Reeded

Date	Mintage	F	VF	XF	Unc	BU
2000 Proof	—	Value: 30.00				

KM# 638 20 DOLLARS
20.1000 g., 0.9990 Silver 0.6456 oz. ASW, 40.2 mm. **Obv:** National arms **Rev:** Brussels landmarks **Edge:** Reeded

Date	Mintage	F	VF	XF	Unc	BU
2000 Proof	—	Value: 30.00				

KM# 639 20 DOLLARS
20.1000 g., 0.9990 Silver 0.6456 oz. ASW, 20.1 mm. **Obv:** National arms **Rev:** London buildings **Edge:** Reeded

Date	Mintage	F	VF	XF	Unc	BU
2000 Proof	—	Value: 30.00				

KM# 640 20 DOLLARS
20.1000 g., 0.9990 Silver 0.6456 oz. ASW, 40.2 mm. **Obv:** National arms **Rev:** Madrid buildings **Edge:** Reeded

Date	Mintage	F	VF	XF	Unc	BU
2000 Proof	—	Value: 30.00				

KM# 641 20 DOLLARS
20.1000 g., 0.9990 Silver 0.6456 oz. ASW, 40.2 mm. **Obv:** National arms **Rev:** Rome buildings **Edge:** Reeded

Date	Mintage	F	VF	XF	Unc	BU
2000 Proof	—	Value: 30.00				

KM# 642 20 DOLLARS
20.1000 g., 0.9990 Silver 0.6456 oz. ASW, 40.2 mm. **Obv:** National arms **Rev:** Stockholm buildings **Edge:** Reeded

Date	Mintage	F	VF	XF	Unc	BU
2000 Proof	—	Value: 30.00				

KM# 646 20 DOLLARS
19.9100 g., 0.9990 Silver 0.6395 oz. ASW, 40 mm. **Obv:** National arms **Rev:** "Sovereign of the Seas" sailing ship **Edge:** Reeded

Date	Mintage	F	VF	XF	Unc	BU
2000 Proof	—	Value: 40.00				

KM# 647 20 DOLLARS
19.9100 g., 0.9990 Silver 0.6395 oz. ASW, 40 mm. **Obv:** National arms **Rev:** "Pamir" sailing ship **Edge:** Reeded

Date	Mintage	F	VF	XF	Unc	BU
2000 Proof	—	Value: 40.00				

KM# 648 20 DOLLARS
19.9100 g., 0.9990 Silver 0.6395 oz. ASW, 40 mm. **Obv:** National arms **Rev:** HMS Victory, Nelson's flag ship **Edge:** Reeded

Date	Mintage	F	VF	XF	Unc	BU
2000 Proof	—	Value: 40.00				

KM# 649 20 DOLLARS
19.9100 g., 0.9990 Silver 0.6395 oz. ASW, 40 mm. **Obv:** National arms **Rev:** LZ 127 Graf Zeppelin **Edge:** Reeded

Date	Mintage	F	VF	XF	Unc	BU
2000 Proof	—	Value: 40.00				

KM# 655 20 DOLLARS
20.6000 g., 0.9990 Silver 0.6616 oz. ASW, 40.3 mm. **Obv:** National arms **Rev:** SS Europa **Edge:** Reeded

Date	Mintage	F	VF	XF	Unc	BU
2000 Proof	—	Value: 25.00				

KM# 656 20 DOLLARS
20.6000 g., 0.9990 Silver 0.6616 oz. ASW, 40.3 mm. **Obv:** National arms **Rev:** "Royal William" ship **Edge:** Reeded

Date	Mintage	F	VF	XF	Unc	BU
2000 Proof	—	Value: 25.00				

KM# 658 20 DOLLARS
20.6000 g., 0.9990 Silver 0.6616 oz. ASW, 40.3 mm. **Obv:** National arms **Rev:** The "Great Eastern" ship **Edge:** Reeded

Date	Mintage	F	VF	XF	Unc	BU
2000 Proof	—	Value: 25.00				

KM# 659 20 DOLLARS
20.6000 g., 0.9990 Silver 0.6616 oz. ASW, 40.3 mm. **Obv:** National arms **Rev:** The German built tall ship "Pamir" **Edge:** Reeded

Date	Mintage	F	VF	XF	Unc	BU
2000 Proof	—	Value: 25.00				

KM# 660 20 DOLLARS
20.6000 g., 0.9990 Silver 0.6616 oz. ASW, 40.3 mm. **Obv:** National arms **Rev:** Signing of the Mayflower Compact **Edge:** Reeded

Date	Mintage	F	VF	XF	Unc	BU
2000 Proof	—	Value: 25.00				

KM# 663 20 DOLLARS
20.2200 g., 0.9990 Silver 0.6494 oz. ASW, 40 mm. **Obv:** National arms **Rev:** Battle of the Monitor and the Virginia **Edge:** Reeded

Date	Mintage	F	VF	XF	Unc	BU
2000 Proof	20,000	Value: 40.00				

KM# 697 20 DOLLARS
31.1035 g., 0.9990 Silver 0.999 oz. ASW, 39 mm. **Obv:** National arms **Rev:** Roy Rogers **Edge:** Reeded

Date	Mintage	F	VF	XF	Unc	BU
2000 Proof	1,000	Value: 45.00				

KM# 707 20 DOLLARS
20.1700 g., 0.9990 Silver 0.6478 oz. ASW, 40.3 mm. **Obv:** National arms **Rev:** Boston Tea Party Scene **Edge:** Reeded

Date	Mintage	F	VF	XF	Unc	BU
2000 Proof	—	Value: 35.00				

KM# 710 20 DOLLARS
20.0000 g., 0.9990 Silver 0.6424 oz. ASW, 40.3 mm. **Subject:** American History Series **Obv:** National arms **Rev:** Columbus going ashore **Edge:** Reeded

Date	Mintage	F	VF	XF	Unc	BU
2000 Proof	20,000	Value: 25.00				

KM# 711 20 DOLLARS
20.0000 g., 0.9990 Silver 0.6424 oz. ASW, 40.3 mm. **Subject:** American History Series **Obv:** National arms **Rev:** Declaration of Independence signers with document in background **Edge:** Reeded

Date	Mintage	F	VF	XF	Unc	BU
2000 Proof	20,000	Value: 25.00				

KM# 712 20 DOLLARS
20.0000 g., 0.9990 Silver 0.6424 oz. ASW, 40.3 mm. **Subject:** American History Series **Obv:** National arms **Rev:** Transcontinental Railroad Golden Spike ceremony scene **Edge:** Reeded

Date	Mintage	F	VF	XF	Unc	BU
2000 Proof	20,000	Value: 25.00				

KM# 713 20 DOLLARS
20.0000 g., 0.9990 Silver 0.6424 oz. ASW, 40.3 mm. **Subject:** American History Series **Obv:** National arms **Rev:** Great Depression, Roosevelt visiting with people in a bread line **Edge:** Reeded

Date	Mintage	F	VF	XF	Unc	BU
2000 Proof	20,000	Value: 25.00				

KM# 714 20 DOLLARS
20.0000 g., 0.9990 Silver 0.6424 oz. ASW, 40.3 mm. **Subject:** American History Series **Obv:** National arms **Rev:** Victory over Japan, surrender ceremony on the USS Missouri **Edge:** Reeded

Date	Mintage	F	VF	XF	Unc	BU
2000 Proof	20,000	Value: 25.00				

KM# 21 25 DOLLARS
23.3120 g., 0.9000 Gold .6746 oz. AGW **Subject:** 70th Birthday of President Tubman **Obv:** Head 3/4 left above date flanked by stars **Rev:** Trees and sun above value flanked by stars

Date	Mintage	F	VF	XF	Unc	BU
1965	3,000	—	—	—	475	—

KM# 21a 25 DOLLARS
23.3120 g., 0.9990 Gold 0.7487 oz. AGW **Obv:** Head 3/4 left above date flanked by stars **Rev:** Tree and sun above value flanked by stars

Date	Mintage	F	VF	XF	Unc	BU
1965B L Proof	100	Value: 525				

KM# 23 25 DOLLARS
0.9990 Gold **Subject:** 75th Birthday of President Tubman
Obv: Birthplace of President **Rev:** Head facing above dates

Date	Mintage	F	VF	XF	Unc	BU
ND(1970)B Proof	—	Value: 520				

KM# 28 25 DOLLARS
0.9990 Gold **Subject:** Sesquicentennial - Founding of Liberia **Obv:** Bust 1/4 left **Rev:** Man in canoe below tower and trees with value above

Date	Mintage	F	VF	XF	Unc	BU
ND(1972)B Proof	3,000	Value: 520				

KM# 323 25 DOLLARS
77.7587 g., 0.9990 Silver 2.5000 oz. ASW **Subject:** 25th Anniversary - Standard Catalog of World Coins **Obv:** National arms **Rev:** Children, globe and world coins

Date	Mintage	F	VF	XF	Unc	BU
1997 Proof	2,500	Value: 35.00				

KM# 623 25 DOLLARS
0.7300 g., 0.9990 Gold 0.0234 oz. AGW, 11.1 mm.
Obv: National arms **Rev:** Martin Luther **Edge:** Reeded

Date	Mintage	F	VF	XF	Unc	BU
2000 Proof	—	Value: 30.00				

KM# 624 25 DOLLARS
0.7300 g., 0.9990 Gold 0.0234 oz. AGW, 11.1 mm.
Obv: National arms **Rev:** Queen Elizabeth II **Edge:** Reeded

Date	Mintage	F	VF	XF	Unc	BU
2000 Proof	—	Value: 30.00				

KM# 625 25 DOLLARS
0.7300 g., 0.9990 Gold 0.0234 oz. AGW, 11.1 mm.
Obv: National arms **Rev:** Mozart **Edge:** Reeded

Date	Mintage	F	VF	XF	Unc	BU
2000 Proof	—	Value: 30.00				

KM# 626 25 DOLLARS
0.7300 g., 0.9990 Gold 0.0234 oz. AGW, 11.1 mm.
Obv: National arms **Rev:** Christopher Columbus **Edge:** Reeded

Date	Mintage	F	VF	XF	Unc	BU
2000 Proof	—	Value: 30.00				

KM# 627 25 DOLLARS
0.7300 g., 0.9990 Gold 0.0234 oz. AGW, 11.1 mm.
Obv: National arms **Rev:** Tutankhamen **Edge:** Reeded

Date	Mintage	F	VF	XF	Unc	BU
2000 Proof	—	Value: 30.00				

KM# 628 25 DOLLARS
0.7300 g., 0.9990 Gold 0.0234 oz. AGW, 11.1 mm.
Obv: National arms **Rev:** Charlemagne **Edge:** Reeded

Date	Mintage	F	VF	XF	Unc	BU
2000 Proof	—	Value: 30.00				

KM# 629 25 DOLLARS
0.7300 g., 0.9990 Gold 0.0234 oz. AGW, 11.1 mm.
Obv: National arms **Rev:** Peter the Great **Edge:** Reeded

Date	Mintage	F	VF	XF	Unc	BU
2000 Proof	—	Value: 30.00				

KM# 630 25 DOLLARS
0.7300 g., 0.9990 Gold 0.0234 oz. AGW, 11.1 mm.
Obv: National arms **Rev:** Mikhail Gorbachev **Edge:** Reeded

Date	Mintage	F	VF	XF	Unc	BU
2000 Proof	—	Value: 30.00				

KM# 631 25 DOLLARS
0.7300 g., 0.9990 Gold 0.0234 oz. AGW, 11.1 mm.
Obv: National arms **Rev:** Julius Caesar **Edge:** Reeded

Date	Mintage	F	VF	XF	Unc	BU
2000 Proof	—	Value: 30.00				

KM# 632 25 DOLLARS
0.7300 g., 0.9990 Gold 0.0234 oz. AGW, 11.1 mm.
Obv: National arms **Rev:** George Washington **Edge:** Reeded

Date	Mintage	F	VF	XF	Unc	BU
2000 Proof	—	Value: 30.00				

KM# 633 25 DOLLARS
0.7300 g., 0.9990 Gold 0.0234 oz. AGW, 11.1 mm.
Obv: National arms **Rev:** Mahatma Gandhi **Edge:** Reeded

Date	Mintage	F	VF	XF	Unc	BU
2000 Proof	—	Value: 30.00				

KM# 634 25 DOLLARS
0.7300 g., 0.9990 Gold 0.0234 oz. AGW, 11.1 mm.
Obv: National arms **Rev:** Joan of Arc **Edge:** Reeded

Date	Mintage	F	VF	XF	Unc	BU
2000 Proof	—	Value: 30.00				

KM# 512 25 DOLLARS
0.7300 g., 0.9990 Gold 0.0234 oz. AGW, 11.1 mm.
Obv: National arms **Rev:** Bust right **Rev. Legend:** NOFRETETE **Edge:** Reeded **Note:** The American Mint is not an actual mint.

Date	Mintage	F	VF	XF	Unc	BU
2000 Proof	—	Value: 30.00				

KM# 22 30 DOLLARS
15.0000 g., 0.9000 Gold .4340 oz. AGW **Subject:** 70th Birthday of President Tubman **Obv:** National arms **Rev:** Bust left

Date	Mintage	F	VF	XF	Unc	BU
1965 Proof	400	Value: 300				

KM# 69 50 DOLLARS
155.5150 g., 0.9990 Silver 5.0000 oz. ASW **Subject:** President Bill Clinton **Obv:** National arms **Rev:** Head right divides date and value above building **Note:** Similar to 10 Dollars, KM#68.

Date	Mintage	F	VF	XF	Unc	BU
1993 Proof	—	Value: 90.00				

KM# 410.1 50 DOLLARS
Copper-Nickel **Obv:** National arms **Rev:** Face on Mars with rough texture

Date	Mintage	F	VF	XF	Unc	BU
1996	—	—	—	—	12.00	—

KM# 410.2 50 DOLLARS
Copper-Nickel **Obv:** National arms **Rev:** Face on Mars with smooth texture

Date	Mintage	F	VF	XF	Unc	BU
1996	—	—	—	—	12.00	—

KM# 231 50 DOLLARS
3.1103 g., 0.9990 Gold .1000 oz. AGW **Subject:** Formula One **Obv:** National arms **Rev:** Ayrton Senna **Note:** Similar to 10 Dollars, KM#229.

Date	Mintage	F	VF	XF	Unc	BU
1996 Proof	10,000	Value: 110				

KM# 251 50 DOLLARS
3.1103 g., 0.9990 Gold .1000 oz. AGW **Subject:** Dalai Lama **Obv:** National arms **Rev:** Bust with praying hands 1/4 left **Note:** Similar to 100 Dollars, KM#252.

Date	Mintage	F	VF	XF	Unc	BU
1996 Proof	10,000	Value: 110				

KM# 316 50 DOLLARS
3.1103 g., 0.9990 Gold .1000 oz. AGW **Subject:** Return of Hong Kong to China **Obv:** National arms **Rev:** Dragon **Note:** Similar to 10 Dollars, KM#314.

Date	Mintage	F	VF	XF	Unc	BU
1997 Proof	—	Value: 100				

KM# 366 50 DOLLARS
3.1103 g., 0.9990 Gold .1000 oz. AGW **Subject:** RMS Titanic **Obv:** National arms **Rev:** Ship sinking **Note:** Similar to 20 Dollars, KM#364.

Date	Mintage	F	VF	XF	Unc	BU
1998 Proof	Est. 2,000	Value: 115				

KM# 419 50 DOLLARS
3.1103 g., 0.9990 Gold .1000 oz. AGW **Subject:** Return of Macao to China **Obv:** National arms **Rev:** Dragon and phoenix **Note:** Similar to 10 Dollars, KM#408.

Date	Mintage	F	VF	XF	Unc	BU
1999 Proof	10,000	Value: 100				

KM# 33 100 DOLLARS
6.0000 g., 0.9000 Gold .1736 oz. AGW **Subject:** Inauguration of President Tolbert **Obv:** Bust facing **Rev:** Joined figures form a tower

Date	Mintage	F	VF	XF	Unc	BU
1976 Proof	175	Value: 225				

KM# 36 100 DOLLARS
10.9300 g., 0.9000 Gold .3163 oz. AGW **Subject:** 130th Anniversary of the Republic **Obv:** Bust 3/4 left **Rev:** National arms

Date	Mintage	F	VF	XF	Unc	BU
1977FM (U)	787	—	—	—	235	—
1977FM (P)	4,250	Value: 220				

KM# 37 100 DOLLARS
10.9300 g., 0.9000 Gold .3163 oz. AGW **Subject:** Organization of African Unity **Obv:** National arms above value flanked by stars **Rev:** Bust facing flanked by stars

Date	Mintage	F	VF	XF	Unc	BU
1979FM (P)	1,656	Value: 220				

KM# 38 100 DOLLARS
11.2000 g., 0.9000 Gold .3241 oz. AGW **Subject:** Organization of African Unity **Obv:** National arms **Rev:** Elephant

Date	Mintage	F	VF	XF	Unc	BU
1979FM (P)	—	Value: 225				

KM# 50 100 DOLLARS
10.9300 g., 0.9000 Gold .3163 oz. AGW **Subject:** 5th Anniversary of Government **Obv:** National arms **Rev:** Leopard

Date	Mintage	F	VF	XF	Unc	BU
1985FM (P)	409	Value: 450				

KM# 61 100 DOLLARS
7.1300 g., 0.9000 Gold .2063 oz. AGW **Series:** Decade For Women **Obv:** National arms **Rev:** Woman mashing grain

Date	Mintage	F	VF	XF	Unc	BU
1985 Proof	318	Value: 200				

KM# 70 100 DOLLARS
311.0300 g., 0.9990 Silver 10.0000 oz. ASW **Subject:** President Bill Clinton **Obv:** National arms **Rev:** Head right flanked by value and date above building

Date	Mintage	F	VF	XF	Unc	BU
1993 Proof	—	Value: 165				

KM# 100 100 DOLLARS
6.2200 g., 0.9990 Gold .2000 oz. AGW **Series:** Preserve Planet Earth **Obv:** National arms **Rev:** Protoceratops

Date	Mintage	F	VF	XF	Unc	BU
1993 Proof	Est. 7,500	Value: 165				

KM# 111 100 DOLLARS
6.2200 g., 0.9990 Gold .2000 oz. AGW **Series:** Preserve Planet Earth **Obv:** National arms **Rev:** Corythosaurus

Date	Mintage	F	VF	XF	Unc	BU
1993 Proof	7,500	Value: 165				

KM# 114 100 DOLLARS
6.2200 g., 0.9990 Gold .2000 oz. AGW **Series:** Preserve Planet Earth **Obv:** National arms **Rev:** Atchaeopteryx **Note:** Incorrect spelling.

Date	Mintage	F	VF	XF	Unc	BU
1993 Proof	Est. 7,500	Value: 165				

KM# 117 100 DOLLARS
6.2200 g., 0.9990 Gold .2000 oz. AGW **Series:** Preserve Planet Earth **Obv:** National arms **Rev:** Archaeopteryx **Note:** Correct spelling.

Date	Mintage	F	VF	XF	Unc	BU
1994 Proof	7,500	Value: 165				

KM# 120 100 DOLLARS
6.2200 g., 0.9990 Gold .2000 oz. AGW **Series:** Preserve Planet Earth **Obv:** National arms **Rev:** Gorillas **Note:** Similar to 10 Dollars, KM#120.

Date	Mintage	F	VF	XF	Unc	BU
1994 Proof	Est. 7,500	Value: 165				

KM# 123 100 DOLLARS
6.2200 g., 0.9990 Gold .2000 oz. AGW **Series:** Preserve Planet Earth **Obv:** National arms **Rev:** Pygmy Hippopotami **Note:** Similar to 10 Dollars, KM#122.

Date	Mintage	F	VF	XF	Unc	BU
1994 Proof	Est. 7,500	Value: 165				

KM# 126 100 DOLLARS
6.2200 g., 0.9990 Gold .2000 oz. AGW **Series:** Preserve Planet Earth **Obv:** National arms **Rev:** Trionyx Turtle **Note:** Similar to 10 Dollars, KM#125.

Date	Mintage	F	VF	XF	Unc	BU
1994 Proof	Est. 7,500	Value: 165				

KM# 130 100 DOLLARS
6.2200 g., 0.9990 Gold .2000 oz. AGW **Subject:** Star Trek **Obv:** National arms **Rev:** Captains Kirk and Picard **Note:** Similar to 10 Dollars, KM#129.

Date	Mintage	F	VF	XF	Unc	BU
1995 Proof	—	Value: 175				

KM# 135 100 DOLLARS
6.2200 g., 0.9990 Gold .2000 oz. AGW **Series:** Preserve Planet Earth **Obv:** National arms **Rev:** Leopard

Date	Mintage	F	VF	XF	Unc	BU
1995 Proof	Est. 7,500	Value: 165				

KM# 138 100 DOLLARS
6.2200 g., 0.9990 Gold .2000 oz. AGW **Series:** Preserve Planet Earth **Obv:** National arms **Rev:** Storks

Date	Mintage	F	VF	XF	Unc	BU
1995 Proof	Est. 7,500	Value: 165				

KM# 150 100 DOLLARS
6.2200 g., 0.9990 Gold .2000 oz. AGW **Subject:** Sir Winston Churchill **Obv:** National arms **Rev:** Uniformed bust right, planes, army tanks and ship

Date	Mintage	F	VF	XF	Unc	BU
1995 Proof	Est. 7,500	Value: 145				

KM# 151 100 DOLLARS
6.2200 g., 0.9990 Gold .2000 oz. AGW **Subject:** President Franklin D. Roosevelt **Obv:** National arms **Rev:** President Roosevelt riding in jeep

Date	Mintage	F	VF	XF	Unc	BU
1995 Proof	Est. 7,500	Value: 145				

KM# 152 100 DOLLARS
6.2200 g., 0.9990 Gold .2000 oz. AGW **Subject:** General George Patton **Obv:** National arms **Rev:** General Patton in front of map

Date	Mintage	F	VF	XF	Unc	BU
1995 Proof	Est. 7,500	Value: 145				

KM# 153 100 DOLLARS
6.2200 g., 0.9990 Gold .2000 oz. AGW **Subject:** President Harry S. Truman **Obv:** National arms **Rev:** President Truman facing

Date	Mintage	F	VF	XF	Unc	BU
1995 Proof	Est. 7,500	Value: 145				

KM# 154 100 DOLLARS
6.2200 g., 0.9990 Gold .2000 oz. AGW **Subject:** President Charles de Gaulle **Obv:** National arms **Rev:** President de Gaulle on Champs Elysees

Date	Mintage	F	VF	XF	Unc	BU
1995 Proof	Est. 7,500	Value: 145				

KM# 160 100 DOLLARS
6.2200 g., 0.9990 Gold .2000 oz. AGW **Subject:** Dr. Sun Yat-Sen **Obv:** National arms **Rev:** Uniformed bust facing

Date	Mintage	F	VF	XF	Unc	BU
1995 Proof	Est. 7,500	Value: 145				

KM# 163 100 DOLLARS
6.2200 g., 0.9990 Gold .2000 oz. AGW **Subject:** General Chiang Kai-shek **Obv:** National arms **Rev:** General Chiang kai-shek

Date	Mintage	F	VF	XF	Unc	BU
1995 Proof	Est. 7,500	Value: 145				

KM# 166 100 DOLLARS
6.2200 g., 0.9990 Gold .2000 oz. AGW **Subject:** Cairo Conference **Obv:** National arms **Rev:** Chiang Kai-shek, Roosevelt and Churchill

Date	Mintage	F	VF	XF	Unc	BU
1995 Proof	Est. 7,500	Value: 145				

KM# 175 100 DOLLARS
6.2200 g., 0.9990 Gold .2000 oz. AGW **Subject:** 375th Anniversary - Pilgrim Fathers **Obv:** National arms **Rev:** Mayflower

Date	Mintage	F	VF	XF	Unc	BU
1995 Proof	7,500	Value: 145				

KM# 176 100 DOLLARS
6.2200 g., 0.9990 Gold .2000 oz. AGW **Subject:** 375th Anniversary - Pilgrim Fathers **Obv:** National arms **Rev:** Cape Cod and Pilgrims in skiff

Date	Mintage	F	VF	XF	Unc	BU
1995 Proof	7,500	Value: 145				

KM# 177 100 DOLLARS
6.2200 g., 0.9990 Gold .2000 oz. AGW **Subject:** 375th Anniversary - Pilgrim Fathers **Obv:** National arms **Rev:** Pilgrim landing party

Date	Mintage	F	VF	XF	Unc	BU
1995 Proof	7,500	Value: 145				

KM# 178 100 DOLLARS
6.2200 g., 0.9990 Gold .2000 oz. AGW **Subject:** 375th Anniversary - Pilgrim Fathers **Obv:** National arms **Rev:** First Thanksgiving scene

Date	Mintage	F	VF	XF	Unc	BU
1995 Proof	7,500	Value: 145				

KM# 209 100 DOLLARS
6.2200 g., 0.9990 Gold .2000 oz. AGW **Subject:** Star Trek **Obv:** National arms **Rev:** Star ships NCC-1701 and NCC-1701D

Date	Mintage	F	VF	XF	Unc	BU
1996 Proof	Est. 7,500	Value: 160				

KM# 252 100 DOLLARS
6.2200 g., 0.9990 Gold .2000 oz. AGW **Subject:** Dalai Lama **Obv:** National arms **Rev:** Bust with praying hands facing 1/4 left

Date	Mintage	F	VF	XF	Unc	BU
1996 Proof	Est. 7,500	Value: 140				

KM# 212 100 DOLLARS
6.2200 g., 0.9990 Gold .2000 oz. AGW **Subject:** Star Trek **Obv:** National arms **Rev:** Scott and McCoy

Date	Mintage	F	VF	XF	Unc	BU
1996 Proof	7,500	Value: 150				

KM# 215 100 DOLLARS
6.2200 g., 0.9990 Gold .2000 oz. AGW **Subject:** Star Trek **Obv:** National arms **Rev:** LaForge and Data

Date	Mintage	F	VF	XF	Unc	BU
1996 Proof	25,000	Value: 150				

KM# 218 100 DOLLARS
6.2200 g., 0.9990 Gold .2000 oz. AGW **Subject:** Star Trek **Obv:** National arms **Rev:** Spock and Uhura **Note:** Similar to 10 Dollars, KM#217.

Date	Mintage	F	VF	XF	Unc	BU
1996 Proof	25,000	Value: 150				

KM# 221 100 DOLLARS
6.2200 g., 0.9990 Gold .2000 oz. AGW **Subject:** Star Trek **Obv:** National arms **Rev:** Worf and Dr. Crusher **Note:** Similar to 10 Dollars, KM#220.

Date	Mintage	F	VF	XF	Unc	BU
1996 Proof	25,000	Value: 150				

KM# 224 100 DOLLARS
6.2200 g., 0.9990 Gold .2000 oz. AGW **Subject:** Preserve Planet Earth **Obv:** National arms **Rev:** Grey Parrot **Note:** Similar to 10 Dollars, KM#223.

Date	Mintage	F	VF	XF	Unc	BU
1996 Proof	25,000	Value: 150				

KM# 227 100 DOLLARS
6.2200 g., 0.9990 Gold .2000 oz. AGW **Subject:** Preserve Planet Earth **Obv:** National arms **Rev:** Love Birds **Note:** Similar to 10 Dollars, KM#226.

Date	Mintage	F	VF	XF	Unc	BU
1996 Proof	25,000	Value: 150				

KM# 232 100 DOLLARS
6.2200 g., 0.9990 Gold .2000 oz. AGW **Subject:** Formula One **Obv:** National arms **Rev:** Ayrton Senna **Note:** Similar to 10 Dollars, KM#229.

Date	Mintage	F	VF	XF	Unc	BU
1996 Proof	20,000	Value: 150				

KM# 237 100 DOLLARS
6.2200 g., 0.9990 Gold .2000 oz. AGW **Subject:** Dr. Sun Yat-Sen **Note:** Similar to 10 Dollars, KM#236.

Date	Mintage	F	VF	XF	Unc	BU
1996 Proof	Est. 7,500	Value: 145				

KM# 240 100 DOLLARS
6.2200 g., 0.9990 Gold .2000 oz. AGW **Subject:** General Chiang Kai-shek **Obv:** National arms **Rev:** General Chiang kai-shek **Note:** Similar to 10 Dollars, KM#162.

Date	Mintage	F	VF	XF	Unc	BU
1996 Proof	Est. 7,500	Value: 145				

KM# 243 100 DOLLARS
6.2200 g., 0.9990 Gold .2000 oz. AGW **Subject:** President Chiang Ching-kuo **Obv:** National arms **Rev:** Bust facing **Note:** Similar to 10 Dollars, KM#242.

Date	Mintage	F	VF	XF	Unc	BU
1996 Proof	Est. 7,500	Value: 145				

KM# 246 100 DOLLARS
6.2200 g., 0.9990 Gold .2000 oz. AGW **Subject:** President Lee Teng-hui **Obv:** National arms **Rev:** President Lee Ten-hui **Note:** Similar to 10 Dollars, KM#245.

Date	Mintage	F	VF	XF	Unc	BU
1996 Proof	Est. 7,500	Value: 145				

KM# 253 100 DOLLARS
6.2200 g., 0.9990 Gold .2000 oz. AGW **Subject:** Kin Rama IX of Thailand **Obv:** National arms **Rev:** King seated on radiant throne

Date	Mintage	F	VF	XF	Unc	BU
1996 Proof	Est. 7,500	Value: 145				

KM# 259 100 DOLLARS
6.2200 g., 0.9990 Gold .2000 oz. AGW **Subject:** Mao Zedong Proclaiming People's Republic **Obv:** National arms **Rev:** Chairman Mao Zedong proclaiming People's Republic **Note:** Similar to 10 Dollars, KM#258.

Date	Mintage	F	VF	XF	Unc	BU
1996 Proof	1,996	Value: 160				

KM# 312 100 DOLLARS
6.2200 g., 0.9990 Gold .2000 oz. AGW **Subject:** Mahatma Gandhi **Obv:** National arms **Rev:** Seated figure facing left in front of Taj Mahal **Note:** Similar to 10 Dollars, KM#311.

Date	Mintage	F	VF	XF	Unc	BU
1997 Proof	Est. 5,000	Value: 150				

KM# 317 100 DOLLARS
6.2200 g., 0.9990 Gold .2000 oz. AGW **Subject:** Return of Hong Kong to China **Obv:** National arms **Rev:** Dragon **Note:** Similar to 10 Dollars, KM#314.

Date	Mintage	F	VF	XF	Unc	BU
1997 Proof	Est. 5,000	Value: 150				

KM# 322 100 DOLLARS
6.2200 g., 0.9990 Gold .2000 oz. AGW **Subject:** Fiftieth Anniversary of the Kon-Tiki Expedition **Obv:** National arms **Rev:** Sailing ship within circle **Note:** Similar to 1 Dollar, KM#320.

Date	Mintage	F	VF	XF	Unc	BU
1997 Proof	Est. 7,500	Value: 150				

KM# 326 100 DOLLARS
6.2200 g., 0.9990 Gold .2000 oz. AGW **Subject:** Jurassic Park **Obv:** National arms **Rev:** Stegosaurus **Note:** Similar to 10 Dollars, KM#325.

Date	Mintage	F	VF	XF	Unc	BU
1997 Proof	Est. 2,500	Value: 160				

KM# 329 100 DOLLARS
6.2200 g., 0.9990 Gold .2000 oz. AGW **Subject:** Golden Wedding Anniversary **Obv:** National arms **Rev:** E & P initials above 2 shields **Note:** Similar to 10 Dollars, KM#328.

Date	Mintage	F	VF	XF	Unc	BU
1997 Proof	Est. 3,500	Value: 160				

KM# 332 100 DOLLARS
6.2200 g., 0.9990 Gold .2000 oz. AGW **Subject:** Golden Wedding Anniversary **Obv:** National arms **Rev:** Royal couple with horse **Note:** Similar to 10 Dollars, KM#331.

Date	Mintage	F	VF	XF	Unc	BU
1997 Proof	Est. 3,500	Value: 160				

KM# 335 100 DOLLARS
6.2200 g., 0.9990 Gold .2000 oz. AGW **Subject:** Golden Wedding Anniversary **Obv:** National arms **Rev:** Royal couple with dogs **Note:** Similar to 10 Dollars, KM#334.

Date	Mintage	F	VF	XF	Unc	BU
1997 Proof	Est. 3,500	Value: 160				

KM# 338 100 DOLLARS
6.2200 g., 0.9990 Gold .2000 oz. AGW **Subject:** Golden Wedding Anniversary **Obv:** National arms **Rev:** Royal couple with children **Note:** Similar to 10 Dollars, KM#337.

Date	Mintage	F	VF	XF	Unc	BU
1997 Proof	Est. 3,500	Value: 160				

KM# 370 100 DOLLARS
6.2200 g., 0.9990 Gold .2000 oz. AGW **Subject:** Star Trek - The Next Generation **Obv:** National arms **Rev:** Romulan Warbird **Note:** Similar to 10 Dollars, KM#369.

Date	Mintage	F	VF	XF	Unc	BU
1997 Proof	Est. 7,500	Value: 150				

KM# 373 100 DOLLARS
6.2200 g., 0.9990 Gold .2000 oz. AGW **Subject:** Star Trek - The Next Generation **Obv:** National arms **Rev:** Klingon Attack Cruiser **Note:** Similar to 10 Dollars, KM#372.

Date	Mintage	F	VF	XF	Unc	BU
1997 Proof	Est. 7,500	Value: 150				

KM# 376 100 DOLLARS
6.2200 g., 0.9990 Gold .2000 oz. AGW **Subject:** Star Trek - The Next Generation **Obv:** National arms **Rev:** U.S.S. Enterprise NCC-1701-D **Note:** Similar to 10 Dollars, KM#375.

Date	Mintage	F	VF	XF	Unc	BU
1997 Proof	Est. 7,500	Value: 150				

KM# 379 100 DOLLARS
6.2200 g., 0.9990 Gold .2000 oz. AGW **Subject:** Star Trek - The Next Generation **Obv:** National arms **Rev:** Klingon Bird of Prey **Note:** Similar to 10 Dollars, KM#378.

Date	Mintage	F	VF	XF	Unc	BU
1997 Proof	Est. 7,500	Value: 150				

KM# 382 100 DOLLARS
6.2200 g., 0.9990 Gold .2000 oz. AGW **Subject:** Star Trek - The Next Generation **Obv:** National arms **Rev:** Borg Cube **Note:** Similar to 10 Dollars, KM#381.

Date	Mintage	F	VF	XF	Unc	BU
1997 Proof	Est. 7,500	Value: 150				

KM# 385 100 DOLLARS
6.2200 g., 0.9990 Gold .2000 oz. AGW **Subject:** Star Trek - The Next Generation **Obv:** National arms **Rev:** Ferengi Marauder **Note:** Similar to 10 Dollars, KM#384.

Date	Mintage	F	VF	XF	Unc	BU
1997 Proof	Est. 7,500	Value: 150				

KM# 473 100 DOLLARS
6.2200 g., 0.9990 Gold .2000 oz. AGW **Subject:** Princess Diana in Memoriam **Obv:** National arms

Date	Mintage	F	VF	XF	Unc	BU
1997 Proof	—	Value: 165				

KM# 365 100 DOLLARS
6.2200 g., 0.9990 Gold .2000 oz. AGW **Subject:** RMS Titanic **Obv:** National arms **Rev:** Ship sinking **Note:** Similar to 20 Dollars, KM#364.

Date	Mintage	F	VF	XF	Unc	BU
1998 Proof	Est. 5,000	Value: 175				

KM# 388 100 DOLLARS
6.2200 g., 0.9990 Gold .2000 oz. AGW **Subject:** President Ronald Reagan **Obv:** National arms **Rev:** Lincoln Memorial below head right **Note:** Similar to 10 Dollars, KM#387.

Date	Mintage	F	VF	XF	Unc	BU
1998 Proof	Est. 7,500	Value: 165				

KM# 392 100 DOLLARS
6.2200 g., 0.9990 Gold .2000 oz. AGW **Subject:** Year of the Rabbit **Obv:** National arms **Rev:** Rabbit running left **Note:** Similar to 20 Dollars, KM#389.

Date	Mintage	F	VF	XF	Unc	BU
1999 Proof	5,000	Value: 165				

KM# 393 100 DOLLARS
6.2200 g., 0.9990 Gold .2000 oz. AGW **Subject:** Year of the Rabbit **Obv:** National arms **Rev:** Rabbit sitting **Note:** Similar to 20 Dollars, KM#390.

Date	Mintage	F	VF	XF	Unc	BU
1999 Proof	5,000	Value: 165				

KM# 394 100 DOLLARS
6.2200 g., 0.9990 Gold .2000 oz. AGW **Subject:** Year of the Rabbit **Obv:** National arms **Rev:** Rabbit running right **Note:** Similar to 20 Dollars, KM#391.

Date	Mintage	F	VF	XF	Unc	BU
1999 Proof	5,000	Value: 165				

KM# 403 100 DOLLARS
6.2200 g., 0.9990 Gold .2000 oz. AGW **Subject:** Christopher Columbus **Obv:** National arms **Rev:** Portrait, ship **Note:** Similar to 10 Dollars, KM#402.

Date	Mintage	F	VF	XF	Unc	BU
1999 Proof	10,000	Value: 175				

KM# 406 100 DOLLARS
6.2200 g., 0.9990 Gold .2000 oz. AGW **Subject:** Captain James Cook **Obv:** National arms **Rev:** Portrait, ship, map **Note:** Similar to 10 Dollars, KM#405.

Date	Mintage	F	VF	XF	Unc	BU
1999 Proof	10,000	Value: 175				

KM# 409 100 DOLLARS
6.2200 g., 0.9990 Gold .2000 oz. AGW **Subject:** Return of Macao to China **Obv:** National arms **Rev:** Dragon and phoenix **Note:** Similar to 10 Dollars, KM#408.

Date	Mintage	F	VF	XF	Unc	BU
1999 Proof	10,000	Value: 175				

KM# 415 100 DOLLARS
6.2200 g., 0.9990 Gold .2000 oz. AGW **Subject:** The Wedding of Prince Edward and Miss Sophie Rhys-Jones **Obv:** National arms **Rev:** Couple in carriage **Note:** Similar to 10 Dollars, KM#414.

Date	Mintage	F	VF	XF	Unc	BU
1999 Proof	Est. 5,000	Value: 175				

KM# 106 150 DOLLARS
500.0000 g., 0.9990 Silver 16.0756 oz. ASW, 85 mm. **Subject:** Preserve Planet Earth **Obv:** National arms **Rev:** Two Brachiosauros **Note:** Photo reduced.

Date	Mintage	F	VF	XF	Unc	BU
1993 Proof	121	Value: 300				

KM# 34 200 DOLLARS
12.0000 g., 0.9000 Gold .3472 oz. AGW **Subject:** Inauguration of President Tolbert **Obv:** Bust facing flanked by stars **Rev:** Man holding horn within circle

Date	Mintage	F	VF	XF	Unc	BU
1976 Proof	100	Value: 350				

KM# 46 200 DOLLARS
15.9800 g., 0.9170 Gold .4712 oz. AGW **Subject:** Year of the Scout **Obv:** National arms **Rev:** Saluting scout divides flags above dates

Date	Mintage	F	VF	XF	Unc	BU
ND(1983)	—	—	—	—	345	—
ND(1983) Proof	—	Value: 375				

KM# 49 200 DOLLARS
15.9800 g., 0.9000 Gold .4624 oz. AGW **Series:** International Year of Disabled Persons **Obv:** National arms **Rev:** Standing elderly figures above disability emblem

Date	Mintage	F	VF	XF	Unc	BU
1983	500	—	—	—	365	—
1983 Proof	500	Value: 475				

KM# 395 200 DOLLARS
12.4444 g., 0.9999 Gold .4000 oz. AGW **Subject:** Year of the Rabbit **Obv:** National arms **Rev:** Rabbit running left **Note:** Similar to 20 Dollars, KM#389.

Date	Mintage	F	VF	XF	Unc	BU
1999 Proof	1,500	Value: 285				

KM# 396 200 DOLLARS
12.4444 g., 0.9999 Gold .4000 oz. AGW **Subject:** Year of the Rabbit **Obv:** National arms **Rev:** Rabbit sitting **Note:** Similar to 20 Dollars, KM#390.

Date	Mintage	F	VF	XF	Unc	BU
1999 Proof	1,500	Value: 285				

KM# 397 200 DOLLARS
12.4444 g., 0.9999 Gold .4000 oz. AGW **Subject:** Year of the Rabbit **Obv:** National arms **Rev:** Rabbit running right **Note:** Similar to 20 Dollars, KM#391.

Date	Mintage	F	VF	XF	Unc	BU
1999 Proof	1,500	Value: 285				

KM# 601 200 DOLLARS
500.0000 g., 0.9990 Silver 16.0593 oz. ASW, 89 mm. **Obv:** National arms **Rev:** Three facing elephants **Edge:** Reeded

Date	Mintage	F	VF	XF	Unc	BU
2000 Proof	—	Value: 300				

KM# 52 250 DOLLARS
15.5000 g., 0.9990 Gold .5000 oz. AGW **Subject:** President John F. Kennedy **Obv:** National arms divides date **Rev:** Head left

Date	Mintage	F	VF	XF	Unc	BU
1988 Proof	5,000	Value: 365				

KM# 56 250 DOLLARS
15.5000 g., 0.9990 Gold .5000 oz. AGW **Subject:** President Samuel Kanyon Doe **Obv:** National arms **Rev:** Head 3/4 facing

Date	Mintage	F	VF	XF	Unc	BU
1988 Proof	Est. 5,000	Value: 375				

KM# 58 250 DOLLARS
15.5000 g., 0.9990 Gold .5000 oz. AGW **Subject:** President George Bush **Obv:** National arms **Rev:** Head left

Date	Mintage	F	VF	XF	Unc	BU
1989 Proof	600	Value: 400				

KM# 60 250 DOLLARS
15.5000 g., 0.9990 Gold .5000 oz. AGW **Subject:** Emperor Hirohito **Obv:** National arms **Rev:** Head facing divides dates

Date	Mintage	F	VF	XF	Unc	BU
1989 Proof	600	Value: 400				

KM# 89 250 DOLLARS
15.5000 g., 0.9990 Gold .5000 oz. AGW **Subject:** Formula One **Obv:** National arms **Rev:** Nigel Mansell **Note:** Similar to 10 Dollars, KM#75.

Date	Mintage	F	VF	XF	Unc	BU
1992 Proof	Est. 5,000	Value: 375				

KM# 90 250 DOLLARS
15.5000 g., 0.9990 Gold .5000 oz. AGW **Subject:** Formula One **Obv:** National arms **Rev:** Gerhard Berger **Note:** Similar to 10 Dollars, KM#83.

Date	Mintage	F	VF	XF	Unc	BU
1992 Proof	Est. 5,000	Value: 375				

KM# 91 250 DOLLARS
15.5000 g., 0.9990 Gold .5000 oz. AGW **Subject:** Formula One **Obv:** National arms **Rev:** Aguri Suzuki **Note:** Similar to 10 Dollars, KM#84.

Date	Mintage	F	VF	XF	Unc	BU
1992 Proof	Est. 5,000	Value: 375				

KM# 92 250 DOLLARS
15.5000 g., 0.9990 Gold .5000 oz. AGW **Subject:** Formula One **Obv:** National arms **Rev:** Ayrton Senna **Note:** Similar to 10 Dollars, KM#85.

Date	Mintage	F	VF	XF	Unc	BU
1992 Proof	Est. 5,000	Value: 375				

KM# 93 250 DOLLARS
15.5000 g., 0.9990 Gold .5000 oz. AGW **Subject:** Formula One **Obv:** National arms **Rev:** Ricardo Patrese **Note:** Similar to 10 Dollars, KM#74.

Date	Mintage	F	VF	XF	Unc	BU
1992 Proof	Est. 5,000	Value: 375				

KM# 94 250 DOLLARS
15.5000 g., 0.9990 Gold .5000 oz. AGW **Subject:** Formula One **Obv:** National arms **Rev:** Michael Schumacher **Note:** Similar to 10 Dollars, KM#86.

Date	Mintage	F	VF	XF	Unc	BU
1992 Proof	Est. 5,000	Value: 375				

KM# 95 250 DOLLARS
15.5000 g., 0.9990 Gold .5000 oz. AGW **Subject:** Formula One **Obv:** National arms **Rev:** Alain Prost **Note:** Similar to 10 Dollars, KM#87.

Date	Mintage	F	VF	XF	Unc	BU
1992 Proof	Est. 5,000	Value: 375				

KM# 96 250 DOLLARS
15.5000 g., 0.9990 Gold .5000 oz. AGW **Subject:** Formula One **Obv:** National arms **Rev:** Ukyo Katayama **Note:** Similar to 10 Dollars, KM#88.

Date	Mintage	F	VF	XF	Unc	BU
1992 Proof	Est. 5,000	Value: 375				

KM# 71 250 DOLLARS
15.5000 g., 0.9990 Gold .5000 oz. AGW **Subject:** President Bill Clinton **Obv:** National arms **Rev:** Head right **Note:** Similar to 10 Dollars, KM#68.

Date	Mintage	F	VF	XF	Unc	BU
1993 Proof	Est. 5,000	Value: 375				

KM# 105 250 DOLLARS
15.5000 g., 0.9990 Gold .5000 oz. AGW **Subject:** President John F. Kennedy **Obv:** National arms **Rev:** Head left, funeral caisson below **Note:** Similar to 10 Dollars, KM#104.

Date	Mintage	F	VF	XF	Unc	BU
1993 Proof	Est. 5,000	Value: 375				

KM# 181 250 DOLLARS
15.5000 g., 0.9990 Gold .5000 oz. AGW **Subject:** Formula One **Obv:** National arms **Rev:** Mika Hakkinen

Date	Mintage	F	VF	XF	Unc	BU
1995 Proof	Est. 5,000	Value: 375				

KM# 184 250 DOLLARS
15.5000 g., 0.9990 Gold .5000 oz. AGW **Subject:** Formula One **Obv:** National arms **Rev:** Martin Brundle

Date	Mintage	F	VF	XF	Unc	BU
1995 Proof	Est. 5,000	Value: 375				

KM# 187 250 DOLLARS
15.5000 g., 0.9990 Gold .5000 oz. AGW **Subject:** Formula One **Obv:** National arms **Rev:** Rubens Barricchello

Date	Mintage	F	VF	XF	Unc	BU
1995 Proof	Est. 5,000	Value: 375				

KM# 190 250 DOLLARS
15.5000 g., 0.9990 Gold .5000 oz. AGW **Subject:** Formula One **Obv:** National arms **Rev:** David Coulthard

Date	Mintage	F	VF	XF	Unc	BU
1995 Proof	Est. 5,000	Value: 375				

KM# 193 250 DOLLARS
15.5000 g., 0.9990 Gold .5000 oz. AGW **Subject:** Formula One **Obv:** National arms **Rev:** Jean Alesi

Date	Mintage	F	VF	XF	Unc	BU
1995 Proof	Est. 5,000	Value: 375				

KM# 565 250 DOLLARS
15.5000 g., 0.9990 Gold 0.4978 oz. AGW, 33 mm. **Obv:** National arms **Rev:** Bugatti Royale

Date	Mintage	F	VF	XF	Unc	BU
1995B	—	—	—	—	345	—

KM# 203 250 DOLLARS
15.5000 g., 0.9990 Gold .5000 oz. AGW **Subject:** Formula One **Obv:** National arms **Rev:** Mark Blundell

Date	Mintage	F	VF	XF	Unc	BU
1996 Proof	Est. 5,000	Value: 350				

KM# 204 250 DOLLARS
15.5000 g., 0.9990 Gold .5000 oz. AGW **Subject:** Formula One **Obv:** National arms **Rev:** Johnny Herbert **Note:** Similar to 10 Dollars, KM#200.

Date	Mintage	F	VF	XF	Unc	BU
1996 Proof	Est. 5,000	Value: 350				

KM# 205 250 DOLLARS
15.5000 g., 0.9990 Gold .5000 oz. AGW **Subject:** Formula One **Obv:** National arms **Rev:** Eddie Irvine **Note:** Similar to 10 Dollars, KM#201.

Date	Mintage	F	VF	XF	Unc	BU
1996 Proof	Est. 5,000	Value: 350				

KM# 206 250 DOLLARS
15.5000 g., 0.9990 Gold .5000 oz. AGW **Subject:** Formula One **Obv:** National arms **Rev:** Heinz Frentzen **Note:** Similar to 10 Dollars, KM#202.

Date	Mintage	F	VF	XF	Unc	BU
1996 Proof	Est. 5,000	Value: 350				

KM# 233 250 DOLLARS
15.5000 g., 0.9990 Gold .5000 oz. AGW **Subject:** Formula One **Obv:** National arms **Rev:** Ayrton Senna **Note:** Similar to 10 Dollars, KM#229.

Date	Mintage	F	VF	XF	Unc	BU
1996 Proof	Est. 5,000	Value: 350				

KM# 318 250 DOLLARS
15.5000 g., 0.9990 Gold .5000 oz. AGW **Subject:** Return of Hong Kong **Obv:** National arms **Rev:** Dragon **Note:** Similar to 10 Dollars, KM#314.

Date	Mintage	F	VF	XF	Unc	BU
1997 Proof	—	Value: 350				

KM# 420 250 DOLLARS
15.5000 g., 0.9990 Gold .5000 oz. AGW **Subject:** Return of Macao to China **Obv:** National arms **Rev:** Dragon and phoenix **Note:** Similar to 10 Dollars, KM#408.

Date	Mintage	F	VF	XF	Unc	BU
1999 Proof	Est. 5,000	Value: 350				

KM# 425 250 DOLLARS
15.5000 g., 0.9990 Gold .5000 oz. AGW **Subject:** Liberty **Obv:** National arms **Rev:** Conjoined heads left **Note:** Similar to 10 Dollars, KM#424.

Date	Mintage	F	VF	XF	Unc	BU
1999 Proof	375	Value: 400				

KM# 439 250 DOLLARS
15.5517 g., 0.9999 Gold .5000 oz. AGW, 27 mm. **Subject:** Taipai, Taiwan Rapid Transit System **Obv:** National arms above hole* and dragon **Rev:** Subway train, logo and tunnel hole* **Note:** Struck at Singapore Mint. *As first done on Albanian coins of 1988.

Date	Mintage	F	VF	XF	Unc	BU
1999 Proof	2,000	Value: 365				

KM# 107 300 DOLLARS
1000.0000 g., 0.9990 Silver 32.1512 oz. ASW, 100 mm. **Series:** Preserve Planet Earth **Obv:** National arms **Rev:** Tyrannosaurus Rex attacking Triceratops **Note:** Photo reduced.

Date	Mintage	F	VF	XF	Unc	BU
1993 Proof	151	Value: 700				

KM# 367 300 DOLLARS
1000.0000 g., 0.9990 Silver 32.1512 oz. ASW **Subject:** RMS Titanic **Obv:** National arms **Rev:** Ship sinking **Note:** Similar to 20 Dollars, KM#364.

Date	Mintage	F	VF	XF	Unc	BU
1998 Proof	Est. 500	Value: 500				

KM# 35 400 DOLLARS
24.0000 g., 0.9000 Gold .6945 oz. AGW **Subject:** Inauguration of President Tolbert **Obv:** Bust facing **Rev:** Liberia written within circle

Date	Mintage	F	VF	XF	Unc	BU
1976 Proof	25	Value: 1,250				

KM# 234 500 DOLLARS
31.1035 g., 0.9990 Gold 1.0000 oz. AGW **Subject:** Formula One **Obv:** National arms **Rev:** Ayrton Senna **Note:** Similar to 10 Dollars, KM#229.

Date	Mintage	F	VF	XF	Unc	BU
1996 Proof	Est. 2,500	Value: 725				

KM# 421 500 DOLLARS
31.1035 g., 0.9990 Gold 1.0000 oz. AGW **Subject:** Return of Macao to China **Obv:** National arms **Rev:** Dragon and phoenix **Note:** Similar to 10 Dollars, KM#408.

Date	Mintage	F	VF	XF	Unc	BU
1999 Proof	Est. 1,000	Value: 775				

KM# 247 2500 DOLLARS
155.5175 g., 0.9990 Gold 5.0000 oz. AGW **Subject:** President Lee Teng-hui **Obv:** National arms **Rev:** President Lee Teng-hui **Note:** Similar to 10 Dollars, KM#245.

Date	Mintage	F	VF	XF	Unc	BU
1996 Proof	Est. 250	Value: 3,500				

KM# 235 2500 DOLLARS
155.5175 g., 0.9990 Gold 5.0000 oz. AGW **Subject:** Formula One **Obv:** National arms **Rev:** Ayrton Senna **Note:** Similar to 10 Dollars, KM#229.

Date	Mintage	F	VF	XF	Unc	BU
1996 Proof	Est. 250	Value: 3,500				

KM# 238 2500 DOLLARS
155.5175 g., 0.9990 Gold 5.0000 oz. AGW **Subject:** Dr. Sun Yat-Sen

Date	Mintage	F	VF	XF	Unc	BU
1996 Proof	Est. 250	Value: 3,500				

KM# 241 2500 DOLLARS
155.5175 g., 0.9990 Gold 5.0000 oz. AGW **Subject:** General Chiang Kai-shek **Obv:** National arms **Rev:** General Chiang kai-shek **Note:** Similar to 10 Dollars, KM#162.

Date	Mintage	F	VF	XF	Unc	BU
1996 Proof	Est. 250	Value: 3,500				

KM# 244 2500 DOLLARS
155.5175 g., 0.9990 Gold 5.0000 oz. AGW **Subject:** President Chiang Ching-kuo **Obv:** National arms **Rev:** Bust facing **Note:** Similar to 10 Dollars, KM#242.

Date	Mintage	F	VF	XF	Unc	BU
1996 Proof	Est. 250	Value: 3,500				

KM# 319 2500 DOLLARS
155.5175 g., 0.9990 Gold 5.0000 oz. AGW **Subject:** Return of Hong Kong **Obv:** National arms **Rev:** Dragon **Note:** Similar to 10 Dollars, KM#314.

Date	Mintage	F	VF	XF	Unc	BU
1997 Proof	—	Value: 3,500				

KM# 588 2500 DOLLARS
155.5175 g., 0.9990 Gold 4.995 oz. AGW, 60 mm. **Subject:** Year of the Tiger **Obv:** National arms **Rev:** Tiger above pineapple and flowers within beaded circle **Edge:** Reeded **Note:** Photo reduced.

Date	Mintage	F	VF	XF	Unc	BU
1998 Proof	—	Value: 3,750				

KM# 398 2500 DOLLARS
155.5175 g., 0.9990 Gold 5.0000 oz. AGW **Subject:** Year of the Rabbit **Obv:** National arms **Rev:** Rabbit running left **Note:** Similar to 20 Dollars, KM#389.

Date	Mintage	F	VF	XF	Unc	BU
1999 Proof	88	Value: 4,000				

KM# 399 2500 DOLLARS
155.5175 g., 0.9990 Gold 5.0000 oz. AGW **Subject:** Year of the Rabbit **Obv:** National arms **Rev:** Rabbit sitting **Note:** Similar to 20 Dollars, KM#390.

Date	Mintage	F	VF	XF	Unc	BU
1999 Proof	88	Value: 4,000				

KM# 400 2500 DOLLARS
155.5175 g., 0.9990 Gold 5.0000 oz. AGW **Subject:** Year of the Rabbit **Obv:** National arms **Rev:** Rabbit running right **Note:** Similar to 20 Dollars, KM#391.

Date	Mintage	F	VF	XF	Unc	BU
1999 Proof	88	Value: 4,000				

KM# 422 2500 DOLLARS
155.5175 g., 0.9990 Gold 5.0000 oz. AGW **Subject:** Return of Macao to China **Obv:** National arms **Rev:** Dragon and phoenix **Note:** Similar to 10 Dollars, KM#408.

Date	Mintage	F	VF	XF	Unc	BU
1999 Proof	Est. 250	Value: 4,000				

KM# 440 2500 DOLLARS
155.5175 g., 0.9999 Gold 5.0000 oz. AGW, 55 mm.
Subject: Taipai, Taiwan Rapid Transit System **Obv:** National arms above dragon **Rev:** Dragon around subway train viewing sun with diamond inserts **Note:** Struck at Singapore Mint.

Date	Mintage	F	VF	XF	Unc	BU
ND(1999) Proof	50	Value: 3,500				

PATTERNS

Including off metal strikes

KM#	Date	Mintage	Identification	Mkt Val
Pn55	1976	—	100 Dollars. Bronze. KM#33.	150
Pn56	1976	—	200 Dollars. Bronze. KM#34.	175
Pn57	1976	—	400 Dollars. Bronze. KM#35.	200

PIEFORTS

KM#	Date	Mintage	Identification	Mkt Val
P1	1983	500	2 Dollars. Silver. KM#47a.	75.00
P2	1983	—	20 Dollars. Silver. KM#48.	100
P3	1983	100	200 Dollars. Gold. KM#49.	750

MINT SETS

KM#	Date	Mintage	Identification	Issue Price	Mkt Val
MS1	1997 (2)	4,000	KM#351-352	50.00	60.00

PROOF SETS

KM#	Date	Mintage	Identification	Issue Price	Mkt Val
PS1	1896H (5)	—	KM#5-9	—	1,625
PS2	1906H (5)	—	KM#5-9	—	1,625
PS3	1968 (6)	14,396	KM#13, 14, 15a.2-18a.2	15.25	8.00
PS4	1969 (6)	5,056	KM#13, 14, 15a.2-18a.2	15.25	8.00
PS5	1970 (6)	3,464	KM#13, 14, 15a.2-18a.2	15.25	12.50
PS6	1971 (6)	3,032	KM#13, 14, 15a.2-18a.2	15.25	10.00
PS7	1972 (6)	4,866	KM#13, 14, 15a.2-18a.2	15.50	9.00
PS8	1972 (4)	—	KM#24-27	—	1,200
PS9	1973 (7)	10,542	KM#13, 14, 15a.2-18a.2, 29	27.00	18.00
PS10	1974 (7)	9,362	KM#13, 14, 15a.2-18a.2, 29	27.00	18.00
PS11	1975 (7)	4,056	KM#13, 14, 15a.2-18a.2, 29	31.50	20.00
PS12	1976 (7)	2,131	KM#13, 14, 15a.2, 29-32	45.00	32.50
PS13	1977 (7)	920	KM#13, 14, 15a.2, 29-32	45.00	37.50
PS14	1978 (8)	7,311	KM#12a, 13, 14, 15a.2, 29-32	47.00	35.00
PS15	1979 (8)	1,857	KM#12b, 13a, 14a, 15b, 29a-32a marked O.A.U. July 1979	45.00	50.00
PS16	1997 (3)	—	KM#417, 445, 473	—	250
PS17	1999 (2)	375	KM#424-425	345	400
PS18	2000 (2)	1,000	KM#613, 614	70.00	75.00

LIBYA

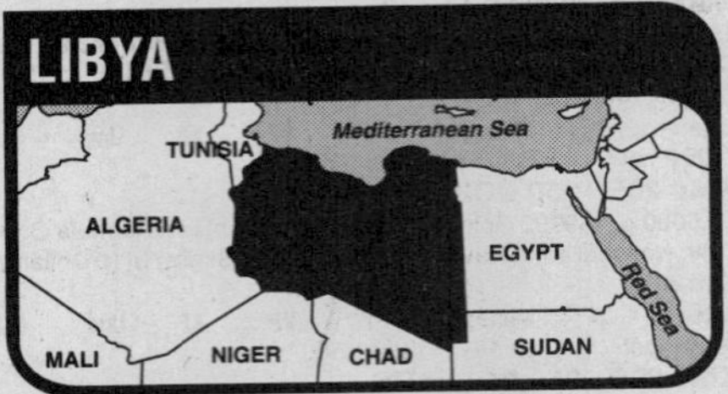

The Socialist People's Libyan Arab Jamahariya, located on the north-central coast of Africa between Tunisia and Egypt, has an area of 679,358 sq. mi. (1,759,540 sq. km.) and a population of 3.9 million. Capital: Tripoli. Crude oil, which accounts for 90 per cent of the export earnings, is the mainstay of the economy.

Libya has been subjected to foreign rule throughout most of its history, various parts of it having been ruled by the Phoenicians, Carthaginians, Vandals, Byzantines, Greeks, Romans, Egyptians, and in the following centuries the Arabs' language, culture and religion were adopted by the indigenous population. Libya was conquered by the Ottoman Turks in 1553, and remained under Turkish domination, becoming a Turkish vilayet in 1835, until it was conquered by Italy and made into a colony in 1911. The name 'Libya', the ancient Greek name for North Africa exclusive of Egypt, was given to the colony by Italy in1934. Libya came under Allied administration after the fall of Tripoli on Jan. 23, 1943, divided into zones of British and French control. On Dec. 24, 1951, in accordance with a United Nations resolution, Libya proclaimed its independence as a constitutional monarchy, thereby becoming the first country to achieve independence through the United Nations. The monarchy was overthrown by a *coup d'etat* on Sept. 1, 1969, and Libya was established as a republic.

TITLES

المملكة الليبية

al-Mamlaka(t) al-Libiya(t)

الجمهورية الليبية

al-Jomhuriya(t) al-Arabiya(t) al-Libiya(t)

RULERS
Idris I, 1951-1969

MONETARY SYSTEM
10 Milliemes = 1 Piastre
100 Piastres = 1 Pound

MONARCHY

STANDARD COINAGE

10 Milliemes = 1 Piastre; 100 Piastres = 1 Pound

KM# 1 MILLIEME
Bronze **Ruler:** Idris I **Obv:** Bust right **Rev:** Crown divides wreath with value and date within **Note:** Date in Arabic.

Date	Mintage	F	VF	XF	Unc	BU
1952	7,750,000	—	0.15	0.25	0.75	1.50
1952 Proof	32	Value: 75.00				

KM# 6 MILLIEME
Nickel-Brass **Ruler:** Idris I **Obv:** Crowned national arms above dates **Rev:** Value within wreath

Date	Mintage	F	VF	XF	Unc	BU
AH1385-1965	11,000,000	—	0.10	0.20	0.40	0.85

KM# 2 2 MILLIEMES
Bronze **Ruler:** Idris I **Obv:** Bust right **Rev:** Crown divides wreath with value and date within **Note:** Date in Arabic.

Date	Mintage	F	VF	XF	Unc	BU
1952	6,650,000	—	0.15	0.35	1.00	2.00
1952 Proof	32	Value: 75.00				

KM# 3 5 MILLIEMES
Bronze **Ruler:** Idris I **Obv:** Bust right **Rev:** Crown divides wreath with value and date within **Note:** Date in Arabic.

Date	Mintage	F	VF	XF	Unc	BU
1952	7,680,000	—	0.25	0.50	1.50	3.00
1952 Proof	32	Value: 75.00				

KM# 7 5 MILLIEMES
Nickel-Brass **Ruler:** Idris I **Obv:** Crowned national arms above dates **Rev:** Value within 3/4 wreath

Date	Mintage	F	VF	XF	Unc	BU
AH1385-1965	8,500,000	—	0.15	0.25	0.50	1.00

KM# 4 PIASTRE
Copper-Nickel **Ruler:** Idris I **Obv:** Bust right **Rev:** Crown divides wreath with value and date within **Note:** Date in Arabic.

Date	Mintage	F	VF	XF	Unc	BU
1952	10,200,000	—	0.35	0.60	1.25	2.50
1952 Proof	32	Value: 100				

KM# 5 2 PIASTRES
Copper-Nickel, 26 mm. **Ruler:** Idris I **Obv:** Bust right **Rev:** Crown divides wreath with value and dates within **Note:** Date in Arabic.

Date	Mintage	F	VF	XF	Unc	BU
1952	6,075,000	—	0.35	0.75	1.75	3.50
1952 Proof	32	Value: 125				

KM# 8 10 MILLIEMES
Copper-Nickel **Ruler:** Idris I **Obv:** Crowned national arms above dates **Rev:** Value within wreath

Date	Mintage	F	VF	XF	Unc	BU
AH1385-1965	17,000,000	—	0.15	0.25	0.50	1.00

KM# 9 20 MILLIEMES
Copper-Nickel **Ruler:** Idris I **Obv:** Crowned national arms above dates **Rev:** Value within wreath

Date	Mintage	F	VF	XF	Unc	BU
AH1385-1965	8,750,000	—	0.20	0.50	2.00	3.50

KM# 10 50 MILLIEMES
Copper-Nickel, 26 mm. **Ruler:** Idris I **Obv:** Crowned national arms above dates **Rev:** Value within wreath **Shape:** Scalloped

Date	Mintage	F	VF	XF	Unc	BU
AH1385-1965	8,000,000	—	0.35	0.75	3.00	5.00

KM# 11 100 MILLIEMES
Copper-Nickel **Ruler:** Idris I **Obv:** Crowned national arms above dates **Rev:** Value within wreath

Date	Mintage	F	VF	XF	Unc	BU
AH1385 (1965)	8,000,000	—	0.75	1.50	4.00	—

SOCIALIST PEOPLE'S REPUBLIC

STANDARD COINAGE

1000 Dirhams = 1 Dinar

KM# 12 DIRHAM
Brass Clad Steel **Obv:** Eagle flanked by dates **Rev:** Value within wreath

Date	Mintage	F	VF	XF	Unc	BU
AH1395-1975	20,000,000	—	0.25	0.50	1.50	—

KM# 18 DIRHAM
Brass Clad Steel **Obv:** Armored equestrian **Rev:** Value within wreath

Date	Mintage	F	VF	XF	Unc	BU
AH1399-1979	1,000,000	—	0.50	1.00	3.00	—

KM# 13 5 DIRHAM
Brass Clad Steel **Obv:** Eagle flanked by dates **Rev:** Value above oat sprigs within wreath

Date	Mintage	F	VF	XF	Unc	BU
AH1395-1975	23,000,000	—	0.25	0.60	2.00	—

KM# 19 5 DIRHAM
Brass Clad Steel **Obv:** Armored equestrian **Rev:** Value above oat sprigs within wreath

Date	Mintage	F	VF	XF	Unc	BU
AH1399-1979	2,000,000	—	0.75	2.00	4.00	—

KM# 14 10 DIRHAMS
Copper-Nickel Clad Steel **Obv:** Eagle flanked by dates **Rev:** Value above oat sprigs within wreath

Date	Mintage	F	VF	XF	Unc	BU
AH1395-1975	52,750,000	—	0.25	0.65	2.25	—

KM# 20 10 DIRHAMS
Copper-Nickel Clad Steel, 20 mm. **Obv:** Armored equestrian **Rev:** Value above oat sprigs within wreath

Date	Mintage	F	VF	XF	Unc	BU
AH1399-1979	4,000,000	—	0.75	2.00	4.00	—

KM# 15 20 DIRHAMS
Copper-Nickel Clad Steel **Obv:** Eagle flanked by dates **Rev:** Value above oat sprigs within wreath

Date	Mintage	F	VF	XF	Unc	BU
AH1395-1975	25,500,000	—	0.50	1.75	3.00	—

KM# 21 20 DIRHAMS
Copper-Nickel Clad Steel **Obv:** Armored equestrian **Rev:** Value above oat sprigs within wreath

Date	Mintage	F	VF	XF	Unc	BU
AH1399-1979	6,000,000	—	1.00	3.00	5.00	—

KM# 16 50 DIRHAMS
Copper-Nickel **Obv:** Eagle flanked by dates **Rev:** Value above oat sprigs within wreath

Date	Mintage	F	VF	XF	Unc	BU
AH1395-1975	25,640,000	—	1.00	2.50	6.00	—

KM# 22 50 DIRHAMS
Copper-Nickel **Obv:** Armored equestrian **Rev:** Value above oat sprigs within wreath

Date	Mintage	F	VF	XF	Unc	BU
AH1399-1979	9,120,000	—	1.50	3.50	7.00	—

KM# 17 100 DIRHAMS
Copper-Nickel **Obv:** Eagle flanked by dates
Rev. Inscription: Value above oat sprigs within wreath

Date	Mintage	F	VF	XF	Unc	BU
AH1395-1975	15,433,000	—	1.50	3.50	8.00	—

KM# 23 100 DIRHAMS
Copper-Nickel **Obv:** Armored equestrian **Rev:** Value above oat sprigs within wreath

Date	Mintage	F	VF	XF	Unc	BU
AH1399-1979	15,000,000	—	2.00	4.50	9.00	—

KM# 24 5 DINARS
28.2800 g., 0.9250 Silver .8410 oz. ASW **Subject:** International Year of Disabled Persons **Obv:** Handicap symbol within center of helping hands **Rev:** Date and emblem within globe with legend above and below

Date	Mintage	F	VF	XF	Unc	BU
1981	20,000	—	—	—	65.00	—
1981 Proof	21,000	Value: 75.00				

KM# 25 70 DINARS
15.9800 g., 0.9170 Gold .4712 oz. AGW **Subject:** International Year of Disabled Persons **Obv:** Handicap symbol within helping hands **Rev:** Date and emblem within globe with legend above and below

Date	Mintage	F	VF	XF	Unc	BU
1981	4,000	—	—	—	450	—
1981 Proof	4,000	Value: 550				

PIEFORTS

KM#	Date	Mintage	Identification	Mkt Val
P1	1981	2,150	5 Dinars. Silver. KM24.	150
P2	1981	500	70 Dinars. Gold. KM25.	1,100

MINT SETS

KM#	Date	Mintage	Identification	Issue Price	Mkt Val
MS1	1975 (6)	—	KM12-17	—	22.50

PROOF SETS

KM#	Date	Mintage	Identification	Issue Price	Mkt Val
PS1	1952 (5)	32	KM1-5	—	450

LIECHTENSTEIN

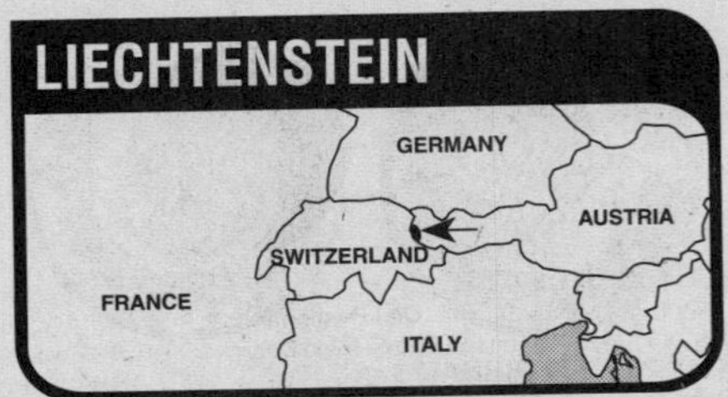

The Principality of Liechtenstein, located in central Europe on the east bank of the Rhine between Austria and Switzerland, has an area of 62 sq. mi. (160 sq. km.) and a population of 27,200. Capital: Vaduz. The economy is based on agriculture and light manufacturing. Canned goods, textiles, ceramics and precision instruments are exported.

The lordships of Schellenburg and Vaduz were merged into the principality of Liechtenstein. It was a member of the Rhine Confederation from 1806 to 1815, and of the German Confederation from 1815 to 1866 when it became independent. Liechtenstein's long and close association with Austria was terminated by World War I. In 1921 it adopted the coinage of Switzerland, and two years later entered into a customs union with the Swiss, who also operated its postal and telegraph systems and represented it in international affairs. The tiny principality abolished its army in 1868 and has avoided involvement in all European wars since that time.

RULERS

Prince John II, 1858-1929
Prince Franz I, 1929-1938
Prince Franz Josef II, 1938-1990
Prince Hans Adam II, 1990-

MINT MARKS

A - Vienna
B - Bern
M - Munich (restrikes)

MONETARY SYSTEM

100 Heller = 1 Krone

PRINCIPALITY

REFORM COINAGE

100 Heller = 1 Krone

Y# 2 KRONE

5.0000 g., 0.8350 Silver .1342 oz. ASW **Ruler:** Prince John II **Obv:** Head left **Obv. Legend:** JOHANN II.FURST... **Rev:** Crowned shield within wreath divides value, date below

Date	Mintage	F	VF	XF	Unc	BU
1904	75,000	10.00	15.00	20.00	45.00	—
1910	50,000	10.00	15.00	20.00	45.00	—
1915	75,000	10.00	15.00	20.00	45.00	—

Y# 3 2 KRONEN

10.0000 g., 0.8350 Silver .2684 oz. ASW **Ruler:** Prince John II **Obv:** Head left **Rev:** Crowned shield within wreath flanked by value and letters

Date	Mintage	F	VF	XF	Unc	BU
1912	50,000	10.00	15.00	25.00	40.00	75.00
1915	37,500	12.00	20.00	35.00	60.00	85.00

Y# 4 5 KRONEN

24.0000 g., 0.9000 Silver .6944 oz. ASW **Ruler:** Prince John II **Obv:** Head left **Obv. Legend:** JOHANN II. FURST... **Rev:** Crowned shield within wreath divides value above date

Date	Mintage	F	VF	XF	Unc	BU
1904	15,000	40.00	70.00	100	185	275
1910	10,000	50.00	85.00	140	220	335
1915	10,000	45.00	75.00	120	190	275

REFORM COINAGE

100 Rappen = 1 Frank

Y# 7 1/2 FRANK

2.5000 g., 0.8350 Silver .0751 oz. ASW **Ruler:** Prince John II **Obv:** Head left **Rev:** Crowned shield within wreath flanked by value and letters **Note:** 15,745 were melted.

Date	Mintage	F	VF	XF	Unc	BU
1924	30,000	40.00	75.00	115	200	265

Y# 8 FRANK

5.0000 g., 0.8350 Silver .1342 oz. ASW **Ruler:** Prince John II **Obv:** Head left **Rev:** Crowned shield within wreath flanked by value and letters **Note:** 45,355 were melted.

Date	Mintage	F	VF	XF	Unc	BU
1924	60,000	20.00	35.00	70.00	100	175

Y# 9 2 FRANKEN

10.0000 g., 0.8350 Silver .2684 oz. ASW **Ruler:** Prince John II **Obv:** Head left **Rev:** Crowned shield within wreath flanked by value and letters **Note:** 41,707 were melted.

Date	Mintage	F	VF	XF	Unc	BU
1924	50,000	25.00	50.00	90.00	170	250

Y# 10 5 FRANKEN

25.0000 g., 0.9000 Silver .7234 oz. ASW **Ruler:** Prince John II **Obv:** Head left **Rev:** Crowned shield within wreath flanked by value and letters **Note:** 11,260 were melted.

Date	Mintage	F	VF	XF	Unc	BU
1924	15,000	100	200	350	650	975

Y# 11 10 FRANKEN

3.2258 g., 0.9000 Gold .0933 oz. AGW **Ruler:** Prince Franz I **Obv:** Bust right **Rev:** Crowned shield within wreath flanked by value and letters

Date	Mintage	F	VF	XF	Unc	BU
1930	2,500	—	500	750	1,050	—

Y# 13 10 FRANKEN

3.2258 g., 0.9000 Gold .0933 oz. AGW **Ruler:** Prince Franz Josef II **Obv:** Head left **Rev:** Crowned shield within stars

Date	Mintage	F	VF	XF	Unc	BU
1946B	10,000	—	150	200	285	—

Y# 20 10 FRANKEN

30.0000 g., 0.9000 Silver .8682 oz. ASW **Ruler:** Prince Franz Josef II **Subject:** 50th Anniversary of Reign **Obv:** Head right **Rev:** Crowned shield

Date	Mintage	F	VF	XF	Unc	BU
1988 Proof	35,000	Value: 45.00				

Y# 22 10 FRANKEN

30.0000 g., 0.9000 Silver .8682 oz. ASW **Ruler:** Prince Hans Adam II **Subject:** Succession of Hans Adam II **Obv:** Head left divides date **Rev:** Crowned mantled shield divides value and letters

Date	Mintage	F	VF	XF	Unc	BU
1990 Proof	35,000	Value: 40.00				

Y# 12 20 FRANKEN

6.4516 g., 0.9000 Gold .1867 oz. AGW **Ruler:** Prince Franz I **Obv:** Bust right within circle **Rev:** Crowned shield within wreath divides value and letters

Date	Mintage	F	VF	XF	Unc	BU
1930	2,500	—	550	800	1,250	—

Y# 14 20 FRANKEN

6.4516 g., 0.9000 Gold .1867 oz. AGW **Ruler:** Prince Franz Josef II **Obv:** Head left **Rev:** Crowned shield within stars

Date	Mintage	F	VF	XF	Unc	BU
1946B	10,000	—	150	225	350	—

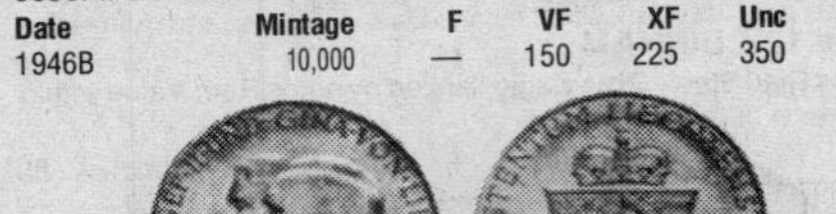

Y# 15 25 FRANKEN

5.6450 g., 0.9000 Gold .1633 oz. AGW, 22 mm. **Ruler:** Prince Franz Josef II **Subject:** Franz Josef II and Princess Gina **Obv:** Conjoined busts left **Rev:** Crowned shield **Designer:** Grienauer

Date	Mintage	F	VF	XF	Unc	BU
1956	17,000	—	—	200	275	—

Y# 18 25 FRANKEN

5.6450 g., 0.9000 Gold .1633 oz. AGW **Ruler:** Prince Franz Josef II **Subject:** 100th Anniversary - National Bank **Obv:** Head right **Rev:** Crowned mantled shield

Date	Mintage	F	VF	XF	Unc	BU
1961	20,000	—	—	—	210	—

Y# 16 50 FRANKEN
11.2900 g., 0.9000 Gold .3267 oz. AGW, 26 mm. **Ruler:** Prince Franz Josef II **Subject:** Franz Josef II and Princess Gina **Obv:** Conjoined busts left **Rev:** Crowned shield **Designer:** Grienauer

Date	Mintage	F	VF	XF	Unc	BU
1956	17,000	—	—	300	380	—

Y# 19 50 FRANKEN
11.2900 g., 0.9000 Gold .3267 oz. AGW **Ruler:** Prince Franz Josef II **Subject:** 100th Anniversary - National Bank **Obv:** Head right **Rev:** Crowned mantled shield

Date	Mintage	F	VF	XF	Unc	BU
1961	20,000	—	—	—	350	—

Y# 21 50 FRANKEN
10.0000 g., 0.9000 Gold .2894 oz. AGW **Ruler:** Prince Franz Josef II **Subject:** 50th Anniversary of Reign **Obv:** Head right **Rev:** Crowned shield divides value and letters

Date	Mintage	F	VF	XF	Unc	BU
1988 Proof	35,000	Value: 235				

Y# 23 50 FRANKEN
10.0000 g., 0.9000 Gold .2894 oz. AGW **Ruler:** Prince Hans Adam II **Subject:** Succession of Hans Adam II **Obv:** Head left divides date **Rev:** Crowned mantled shield divides value and letters

Date	Mintage	F	VF	XF	Unc	BU
1990 Proof	25,000	Value: 225				

Y# 17 100 FRANKEN
32.2580 g., 0.9000 Gold .9335 oz. AGW, 36 mm. **Ruler:** Prince Franz Josef II **Subject:** Franz Josef II and Princess Gina **Obv:** Conjoined busts left **Rev:** Crowned shield **Designer:** Grienauer

Date	Mintage	F	VF	XF	Unc	BU
1952	4,000	—	1,850	2,550	3,325	—

MINT SETS

KM#	Date	Mintage	Identification	Issue Price	Mkt Val
MS1	1930 (2)	2,500	Y11-12	—	2,250
MS2	1946 (2)	10,000	Y13-14	—	580
MS3	1956 (2)	15,000	Y15-16	—	650
MS4	1961 (2)	20,000	Y18-19	—	550

PROOF SETS

KM#	Date	Mintage	Identification	Issue Price	Mkt Val
PS1	1988 (2)	35,000	Y20-21	—	280
PS2	1990 (2)	25,000	Y22-23	—	265

The Republic of Lithuania, southernmost of the Baltic states in east Europe, has an area of 25,174 sq. mi.(65,201 sq. km.) and a population of *3.6 million. Capital: Vilnius. The economy is based on livestock raising and manufacturing. Hogs, cattle, hides and electric motors are exported.

Lithuania emerged as a grand duchy in the 14th century. In the 15th century it was a major power of central Europe, stretching from the Baltic to the Black Sea. It was joined with Poland in 1569, but lost Smolensk, Chernihiv, and the right bank of the river Dnepr Ukraina in 1667, while the left bank remained under Polish – Lithuania rule until 1793. Following the third partition of Poland by Austria, Prussia and Russia, 1795, Lithuania came under Russian domination and did not regain its independence until shortly before the end of World War I when it declared itself a sovereign republic on Feb. 16, 1918. In fall of 1920, Poland captured Vilna (Vilnius). The republic was occupied by Soviet troops and annexed to the U.S.S.R. in 1940. Following the German occupation of 1941-44, it was retaken by Russia and reestablished as a member republic of the Soviet Union. Western countries, including the United States, did not recognize Lithuania's incorporation into the Soviet Union.

Lithuania declared its independence March 11, 1990 and it was recognized by the United States on Sept. 2, 1991, followed by the Soviet government in Moscow on Sept. 6. They were seated in the UN General Assembly on Sept. 17, 1991.

REPUBLIC
1918-1940

STANDARD COINAGE
100 Centas = 1 Litas

KM# 71 CENTAS
1.6000 g., Aluminum-Bronze, 16 mm. **Obv:** National arms **Rev:** Value within circle divides stem of flowers **Edge:** Plain **Designer:** Juozas Zikaras **Note:** Struck at King's Norton.

Date	Mintage	F	VF	XF	Unc	BU
1925	5,000,000	3.00	5.00	15.00	35.00	—

KM# 79 CENTAS
Bronze, 16.6 mm. **Obv:** National arms **Rev:** Large value with oat sprig at right **Edge:** Plain **Designer:** Juozas Zikaras

Date	Mintage	F	VF	XF	Unc	BU
1936	9,995,000	2.00	3.00	5.00	28.00	—

KM# 80 2 CENTAI
2.3000 g., Bronze, 18.5 mm. **Obv:** National arms **Rev:** Large value divides date within wreath **Edge:** Plain **Designer:** Juozas Zikaras

Date	Mintage	F	VF	XF	Unc	BU
1936	4,951,000	3.00	5.00	10.00	40.00	—

KM# 72 5 CENTAI
Aluminum-Bronze **Obv:** National arms **Rev:** Value within circle divides stem of flowers **Designer:** Juozas Zikaras

Date	Mintage	F	VF	XF	Unc	BU
1925	12,000,000	2.00	4.00	8.00	30.00	—

KM# 81 5 CENTAI
2.5000 g., Bronze, 20 mm. **Obv:** National arms **Rev:** Large value within wreath, date on top **Edge:** Plain **Designer:** Juozas Zikaras

Date	Mintage	F	VF	XF	Unc	BU
1936	4,800,000	2.00	4.00	8.00	35.00	—

KM# 73 10 CENTU
3.0000 g., Aluminum-Bronze, 21 mm. **Obv:** National arms **Rev:** Value to right of sagging grain ears **Edge:** Plain **Designer:** Juozas Zikaras

Date	Mintage	F	VF	XF	Unc	BU
1925	12,000,000	3.00	5.00	8.00	30.00	—

KM# 74 20 CENTU
4.0000 g., Aluminum-Bronze, 23 mm. **Obv:** National arms **Rev:** Value to right of sagging grain ears **Edge:** Plain **Designer:** Juozas Zikaras

Date	Mintage	F	VF	XF	Unc	BU
1925	8,000,000	2.00	5.00	10.00	30.00	—

KM# 75 50 CENTU
5.0000 g., Aluminum-Bronze, 25 mm. **Obv:** National arms **Rev:** Value to right of sagging grain ears **Edge:** Plain **Designer:** Juozas Zikaras

Date	Mintage	F	VF	XF	Unc	BU
1925 Proof	2	Value: 1,000				
1925	5,000,000	4.00	8.00	15.00	35.00	—

KM# 76 LITAS
2.7000 g., 0.5000 Silver .0434 oz. ASW, 19 mm. **Obv:** National arms **Rev:** Value above oak leaves **Edge:** Milled **Designer:** Juozas Zikaras **Note:** Struck at Royal Mint, London.

Date	Mintage	F	VF	XF	Unc	BU
1925	5,985,000	2.00	3.00	8.00	30.00	—
1925 Proof	—	Value: 800				

Note: Struck as proof record specimens by the Royal Mint, less than 12 are estimated to exist

KM# 77 2 LITU
5.4000 g., 0.5000 Silver .0868 oz. ASW, 22.9 mm. **Rev:** Denomination within wreath **Edge:** Milled **Designer:** Juozas Zikaras

Date	Mintage	F	VF	XF	Unc	BU
1925	3,000,000	4.00	6.00	12.00	35.00	—
1925 Proof	—	Value: 800				

Note: Struck as proof record specimens by the Royal Mint, less than 12 are estimated to exist

KM# 78 5 LITAI
13.5000 g., 0.5000 Silver .217 oz. ASW, 29.5 mm.
Obv: National arms **Rev:** Value within flowered wreath
Edge: Milled **Designer:** Juozas Zikaras

Date	Mintage	F	VF	XF	Unc	BU
1925	1,000,000	6.00	10.00	18.00	65.00	—
1925 Proof	—	Value: 800				

Note: Struck as proof record specimens by the Royal Mint, less than 12 are estimated to exist

KM# 82 5 LITAI
9.0000 g., 0.7500 Silver .217 oz. ASW, 27 mm. **Obv:** National arms **Rev:** Head left **Edge Lettering:** TAUTOS GEROVE TAVO GEROVE **Designer:** Juozas Zikaras **Note:** Designer's initials below bust.

Date	Mintage	F	VF	XF	Unc	BU
1936	2,612,000	4.00	6.00	9.00	20.00	—

KM# 83 10 LITU
18.0000 g., 0.7500 Silver .434 oz. ASW, 32 mm. **Obv:** National arms **Rev:** Head left **Edge Lettering:** VIENYBEJE TAUTOS JEGA **Designer:** Juozas Zikaras

Date	Mintage	F	VF	XF	Unc	BU
1936	720,000	9.00	12.00	18.00	30.00	55.00

KM# 84 10 LITU
18.0000 g., 0.7500 Silver .434 oz. ASW, 32 mm. **Subject:** 20th Anniversary of Republic **Obv:** Artistic design above LIETUVA and dates **Rev:** Head left **Edge Lettering:** VIENYBEJE TAUTOS JEGA **Designer:** Juozas Zikaras

Date	Mintage	F	VF	XF	Unc	BU
ND(1938)	170,000	15.00	25.00	35.00	60.00	90.00

MODERN REPUBLIC
1991-present

REFORM COINAGE
100 Centas = 1 Litas

KM# 85 CENTAS
0.6200 g., Aluminum, 18.73 mm. **Obv:** National arms
Rev: Large value to right of design

Date	Mintage	F	VF	XF	Unc	BU
1991	—	—	—	—	0.20	—

KM# 86 2 CENTAI
0.9300 g., Aluminum, 21.75 mm. **Obv:** National arms
Rev: Large value to right of design

Date	Mintage	F	VF	XF	Unc	BU
1991	—	—	—	—	0.25	—

KM# 87 5 CENTAI
1.2400 g., Aluminum, 24.4 mm. **Obv:** National arms **Rev:** Large value to right of artistic design on pole flanked by men blowing horns

Date	Mintage	F	VF	XF	Unc	BU
1991	—	—	—	—	0.30	—

KM# 88 10 CENTU
1.2400 g., Bronze, 15.64 mm. **Obv:** National arms **Rev:** Value

Date	Mintage	F	VF	XF	Unc	BU
1991	—	—	—	—	0.50	—

KM# 106 10 CENTU
2.6000 g., Brass, 16 mm. **Obv:** National arms **Rev:** Value
Edge: Milled

Date	Mintage	F	VF	XF	Unc	BU
1997	—	—	—	—	0.40	—
1998	—	—	—	—	0.40	—
1999	—	—	—	—	0.40	—
2000	—	—	—	—	0.40	—
2000 Proof	5,000	Value: 1.00				

KM# 89 20 CENTU
1.8700 g., Bronze, 17.38 mm. **Obv:** National arms **Rev:** Value

Date	Mintage	F	VF	XF	Unc	BU
1991	—	—	—	—	1.50	—

KM# 107 20 CENTU
4.8000 g., Brass, 20 mm. **Obv:** National arms **Rev:** Value
Edge: Milled

Date	Mintage	F	VF	XF	Unc	BU
1997	—	—	—	—	0.75	—
1998	—	—	—	—	0.75	—
1999	—	—	—	—	0.75	—
2000	—	—	—	—	0.75	—
2000 Proof	5,000	Value: 1.25				

KM# 90 50 CENTU
2.7900 g., Bronze, 21.02 mm. **Obv:** National arms **Rev:** Value

Date	Mintage	F	VF	XF	Unc	BU
1991	—	—	—	—	5.00	—

KM# 108 50 CENTU
6.0000 g., Brass **Obv:** National arms **Rev:** Value within designed circle

Date	Mintage	F	VF	XF	Unc	BU
1997	—	—	—	—	1.00	—
1998	—	—	—	—	1.00	—
1999	—	—	—	—	1.00	—
2000	—	—	—	—	1.00	—
2000 Proof	5,000	Value: 2.00				

KM# 91 LITAS
Copper-Nickel, 22.3 mm. **Obv:** National arms **Rev:** Value with lines above

Date	Mintage	F	VF	XF	Unc	BU
1991	—	—	—	—	4.00	—

KM# 109 LITAS
Copper-Nickel, 22.3 mm. **Subject:** 75th Anniversary - Bank of Lithuania **Obv:** National arms above value **Rev:** Bust 1/4 right

Date	Mintage	F	VF	XF	Unc	BU
1997	200,000	—	—	—	6.00	—

KM# 109a LITAS
7.7759 g., 0.9990 Gold .25 oz. AGW, 22.3 mm. **Subject:** 75th Anniversary - Bank of Lithuania **Obv:** National arms above value **Rev:** Bust 1/4 right

Date	Mintage	F	VF	XF	Unc	BU
1997 Proof	1,500	Value: 725				

KM# 111 LITAS
Copper-Nickel, 22.3 mm. **Obv:** National arms **Rev:** Value within circle above lined designs **Edge:** Reeded

Date	Mintage	F	VF	XF	Unc	BU
1998	—	—	—	—	1.50	—
1999	—	—	—	—	1.50	—
2000	—	—	—	—	1.25	—
2000 Proof	5,000	Value: 3.00				

KM# 117 LITAS
Copper-Nickel, 22.3 mm. **Subject:** The Baltic Highway
Obv: National arms on shield within shaded circle divides date
Rev: Six clasped hands within artistic design **Edge:** Reeded and plain sections

Date	Mintage	F	VF	XF	Unc	BU
1999	1,000,000	—	—	—	3.00	—

KM# 92 2 LITAI
Copper-Nickel **Obv:** National arms **Rev:** Value within design

Date	Mintage	F	VF	XF	Unc	BU
1991	—	—	—	—	4.00	—

KM# 112 2 LITAI
Bi-Metallic Copper-Nickel ring in Brass center, 25 mm.
Obv: National arms within circle **Rev:** Value within circle
Edge: Segmented reeding

Date	Mintage	F	VF	XF	Unc	BU
1998	—	—	—	—	2.75	—
1999	—	—	—	—	2.75	—
2000 Proof	5,000	Value: 3.50				

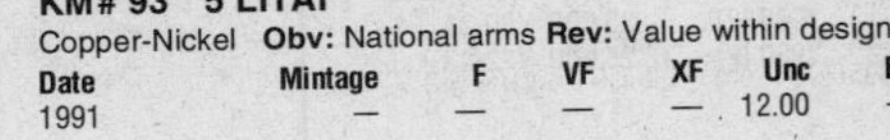

KM# 93 5 LITAI
Copper-Nickel **Obv:** National arms **Rev:** Value within design

Date	Mintage	F	VF	XF	Unc	BU
1991	—	—	—	—	12.00	—

KM# 127 5 LITAI

Outer Weight: 28.2800 g. **Outer Composition:** 0.9250 Silver .841 oz. ASW AGW, 38.61 mm. **Series:** UNICEF **Subject:** For the Children of the World **Obv:** Hill of Geoiminas Castle to right of national arms on shield above value and date **Rev:** Child with pinwheel **Edge Lettering:** LIETUVOS BANKAS

Date	Mintage	F	VF	XF	Unc	BU
1998 Proof	3,000	Value: 55.00				

KM# 113 5 LITAI

Bi-Metallic Copper-Nickel ring in Brass center, 32.5 mm. **Obv:** National arms within circle **Rev:** Value within circle **Edge Lettering:** PENKI LITAI

Date	Mintage	F	VF	XF	Unc	BU
1998	—	—	—	—	5.00	—
1999	—	—	—	—	5.00	—
2000	—	—	—	—	5.00	—
2000	5,000	Value: 6.50				

KM# 94 10 LITU

Copper-Nickel, 28.70 mm. **Subject:** 60th Anniversary - Darius and Girenas flight across the Atlantic **Obv:** National arms above value **Rev:** Conjoined pilot heads right **Edge Lettering:** SLOVE ATLANTO NUGALETOJAMS

Date	Mintage	F	VF	XF	Unc	BU
ND(1993)LMK	4,500	—	—	—	45.00	—

KM# 95 10 LITU

Copper-Nickel, 28.70 mm. **Subject:** Papal visit **Rev:** Bust right **Edge Lettering:** TIKEJIMAS MEILE VILTIS

Date	Mintage	F	VF	XF	Unc	BU
1993LMK	5,000	—	—	—	60.00	—

KM# 96 10 LITU

Copper-Nickel, 28.70 mm. **Subject:** International Song Fest **Obv:** National arms and value **Rev:** Stringed instrument below design **Edge Lettering:** SKRISKIT SKAISCIOS DAINOS

Date	Mintage	F	VF	XF	Unc	BU
1994LMK Proof	11,708	Value: 12.00				

KM# 97 10 LITU

Copper-Nickel, 28.70 mm. **Subject:** 5th World Sport Games **Obv:** National arms and value **Rev:** Runner with torch and design above divides globe **Edge Lettering:** LIETUVIAIS ESAME MES GIME

Date	Mintage	F	VF	XF	Unc	BU
1995LMK Proof	10,000	Value: 12.00				

KM# 115 10 LITU

Copper-Nickel, 28.70 mm. **Obv:** Shielded arms divide date, value below **Rev:** Vilnius building tops as seen from ground level **Edge Lettering:** VILNIUS-LIETUVOS SOSTINE

Date	Mintage	F	VF	XF	Unc	BU
1998 Proof	7,500	Value: 15.00				

KM# 116 10 LITU

Copper-Nickel, 28.70 mm. **Obv:** National arms above value **Rev:** Kaunas city arms on shield within buildings **Edge Lettering:** LAISUAS BUDAMAS, LAISVES NEISSIZADESI

Date	Mintage	F	VF	XF	Unc	BU
1999 Proof	6,028	Value: 12.00				

KM# 120 10 LITU

1.2440 g., 0.9999 Gold .04 oz. AGW, 28.70 mm. **Subject:** Lithuanian gold coinage **Obv:** National arms **Rev:** Medieval minter

Date	Mintage	F	VF	XF	Unc	BU
1999 Proof	5,500	Value: 65.00				

KM# 98 50 LITU

23.3000 g., 0.9250 Silver .6929 oz. ASW, 34 mm. **Subject:** 5th Anniversary - Independence **Obv:** National arms flanked by ribbon with value below **Rev:** Oak tree stump with leafed branch flanked by dates above **Edge Lettering:** TEGUL MEILE LIETUVOS DEGA MUSU SIRDYSE

Date	Mintage	F	VF	XF	Unc	BU
ND(1995)LMK Proof	5,000	Value: 80.00				

KM# 99 50 LITU

23.3000 g., 0.9250 Silver .6929 oz. ASW, 34 mm. **Subject:** 120th Birth Anniversary Mikalojaus K. Ciurlionis **Obv:** National arms above date at right with a pair of eagle wings at left above value **Rev:** Head right **Edge Lettering:** PASAULIS KAIP DIDELE SIMFONIJA

Date	Mintage	F	VF	XF	Unc	BU
1995LMK Proof	6,514	Value: 40.00				

KM# 100 50 LITU

23.3000 g., 0.9250 Silver .6929 oz. ASW, 34 mm. **Subject:** 5th Anniversary - 13 January 1991 Assault **Obv:** National arms flanked by ribbon with value below **Rev:** Madonna holding man **Edge Lettering:** IR KRAUJU KRIKSTYTI TAMPA VEL GYUYBE

Date	Mintage	F	VF	XF	Unc	BU
ND(1996) Proof	6,000	Value: 40.00				

KM# 103 50 LITU

23.3000 g., 0.9250 Silver .6929 oz. ASW, 34 mm. **Obv:** National arms at upper left within patterned circle, crown at lower right above lance **Rev:** Armored bust 1/4 right **Edge Lettering:** IS PRAEITIES TAVO SUNUS TE STIPRYBE SEMIA

Date	Mintage	F	VF	XF	Unc	BU
1996LMK Proof	4,421	Value: 45.00				

KM# 101 50 LITU

23.3000 g., 0.9250 Silver .6929 oz. ASW, 34 mm. **Series:** Atlanta Olympics **Obv:** National arms flanked by sprigs **Rev:** Basketball players **Edge Lettering:** CITIUS. ALTIUS. FORTIUS.

Date	Mintage	F	VF	XF	Unc	BU
1996LMK Proof	6,000	Value: 30.00				

KM# 102 50 LITU

23.3000 g., 0.9250 Silver .6929 oz. ASW, 34 mm. **Obv:** National arms at upper left within patterned circle, crown at lower right above lance **Rev:** Armored bust right **Edge Lettering:** IS PRAEITIES TAVO SUNUS TE STIPRYBE SEMIA

Date	Mintage	F	VF	XF	Unc	BU
1996LMK Proof	4,982	Value: 40.00				

KM# 104 50 LITU
23.3000 g., 0.9250 Silver .6929 oz. ASW, 34 mm. **Subject:** 450th Anniversary - First Lithuanian Book **Obv:** National arms above date **Rev:** Page from book **Edge Lettering:** MARTYNAS MAZVYDAS IMKIT MANE IR SKAITYKIT

Date	Mintage	F	VF	XF	Unc	BU
1997 Proof	3,476	Value: 47.50				

KM# 105 50 LITU
23.3000 g., 0.9250 Silver .6929 oz. ASW, 34 mm. **Subject:** 600th Anniversary - Karaims and Tartars settlement in Lithuania **Obv:** National arms above value **Rev:** Standing figures facing with weapons **Edge Lettering:** LIETUVA TEVYNE MUSU

Date	Mintage	F	VF	XF	Unc	BU
1997 Proof	2,635	Value: 47.50				

KM# 110 50 LITU
23.3000 g., 0.9250 Silver .6929 oz. ASW **Obv:** National arms within patterned circle above date **Rev:** Armored bust facing holding scepter

Date	Mintage	F	VF	XF	Unc	BU
1998 Proof	2,998	Value: 42.50				

KM# 114 50 LITU
23.3000 g., 0.9250 Silver .6929 oz. ASW **Subject:** 200th Anniversary - Birth of Adam Mickiewicz **Obv:** Feather, denomination **Rev:** Laureated profile of Adomas Mickievicius, building

Date	Mintage	F	VF	XF	Unc	BU
1998 Proof	2,860	Value: 42.50				

KM# 118 50 LITU
23.3000 g., 0.9250 Silver .6929 oz. ASW, 34 mm. **Subject:** Grand Duke Kestutis **Obv:** National arms within patterned circle **Rev:** Armored bust facing **Edge Lettering:** IS PRAEITIES TAVO SUNVS TE STIPRYBE SEMIA **Note:** Lithuanian Mint.

Date	Mintage	F	VF	XF	Unc	BU
1999 Proof	2,500	Value: 47.50				

KM# 119 50 LITU
28.2800 g., 0.9250 Silver .841 oz. ASW, 38.6 mm. **Subject:** 100th Anniversary - Death of Vincas Kudirka **Obv:** National arms within stylized bell **Rev:** Head 1/4 left **Edge Lettering:** VARDAN TOS LIETUVOS VIENYBE TEZYDI **Note:** Lithuanian Mint.

Date	Mintage	F	VF	XF	Unc	BU
1999 Proof	1,835	Value: 50.00				

KM# 123 50 LITU
28.2800 g., 0.9250 Silver .841 oz. ASW, 38.1 mm. **Subject:** 10th Anniversary - Baltic Way Highway **Obv:** National arms within circle divides date **Rev:** Three pairs of clasped hands **Edge Lettering:** VILNIUS RYGA TALINAS **Note:** Lithuanian Mint.

Date	Mintage	F	VF	XF	Unc	BU
1999 Proof	2,542	Value: 37.50				

KM# 121 50 LITU
28.2800 g., 0.9250 Silver .841 oz. ASW, 38.61 mm. **Subject:** 350th Anniversary - The Great Art of Artillery Book **Obv:** National arms within frame **Rev:** Old rocket designs **Edge Lettering:** ARS MAGNA ARTILLERIAE * MDCL

Date	Mintage	F	VF	XF	Unc	BU
2000 Proof	1,936	Value: 42.50				

KM# 125 50 LITU
23.3000 g., 0.9250 Silver .6929 oz. ASW, 34 mm. **Subject:** Grand Duke Vytautas **Obv:** National arms on shield among other shields within patterned circle below design **Rev:** Crowned armored bust holding sword facing left **Edge Lettering:** IS PRAEITIES TAVO SUNUS TESTIPRYBE SEMIA

Date	Mintage	F	VF	XF	Unc	BU
2000 Proof	2,500	Value: 40.00				

KM# 122 50 LITU
28.2800 g., 0.9250 Silver .841 oz. ASW, 38.6 mm. **Subject:** 10th Anniversary of Independence **Obv:** National arms above value **Rev:** Radiant statue of independence **Edge Lettering:** LAISVE - AMZINOJI TAUTOS VERTYBE **Note:** Struck at Lietuvos Monetu Kalykla.

Date	Mintage	F	VF	XF	Unc	BU
ND(2000) Proof	2,698	Value: 40.00				

KM# 124 50 LITU
28.2800 g., 0.9250 Silver .841 oz. ASW, 38.61 mm. **Series:** XXVII Summer Olympic Games **Obv:** National arms within lined diagonal design **Rev:** Man throwing discus, Olympic emblem and date **Edge Lettering:** NUGALI STIPRUS DVASIA IR KUNU

Date	Mintage	F	VF	XF	Unc	BU
2000 Proof	2,448	Value: 37.50				

KM# 128 50 LITU
28.2800 g., 0.9250 Silver .841 oz. ASW, 38.61 mm. **Subject:** Millennium **Obv:** National arms within lined design with stars above value **Rev:** Radiant cross within arch **Edge Lettering:** SALVE NOVUM MILLENNIUM **Designer:** Rytas Belevicius

Date	Mintage	F	VF	XF	Unc	BU
2000 Proof	2,998	Value: 38.00				

KM# 126 100 LITU
7.7800 g., 0.9999 Gold .2501 oz. AGW, 22.3 mm. **Subject:** Grand Duke Vytautas **Obv:** National arms above value **Rev:** Crowned armored bust right holding sword **Edge Lettering:** IS PRAEITIES TAVO SUNUS TE STIPRYBE SEMIA

Date	Mintage	F	VF	XF	Unc	BU
2000 Proof	2,000	Value: 600				

PATTERNS

Including off metal strikes

KM#	Date	Mintage	Identification	Mkt Val
Pn3	1936	—	5 Litai. Silver. Plain edge. Coin struck.	725
Pn4	1936	—	5 Litai. Silver. Lettered edge. Coin struck.	725
Pn5	1936	—	5 Litai. Silver. Designer's name (J. ZIKARAS) below bust. Plain edge. KM82. Medal struck.	725
Pn6	1936	—	10 Litu. Silver. Plain edge. KM83.	825
Pn7	1938	—	2 Litai. Brass. Lettered edge.	675
Pn8	1938	—	2 Litai. Silver. Reeded edge.	775
Pn9	1938	—	2 Litai. Silver. Lettered edge.	725
Pn10	1938	—	2 Litai. Silver. Plain edge.	725
Pn11	1938	—	2 Litai. Silver. Plain edge.	775
Pn12	1938	—	2 Litai. Silver. Lettered edge.	775
Pn13	1938	—	10 Litu. Silver. Coin struck.	725
Pn14	1938	2	10 Litu. Gold. Lettered edge. Medal-struck presentation pieces.	—
Pn15	1994	234	50 Litu. Silver. Lettered edge.	—

TRIAL STRIKES

KM#	Date	Mintage	Identification	Mkt Val
TS1	1925	—	Centas. Aluminum-Bronze. Uniface. Obverse.	250
TS2	1925	—	Centas. Aluminum-Bronze. Uniface. Reverse.	250
TS3	1925	—	5 Centai. Aluminum-Bronze. Uniface. Obverse.	250
TS4	1925	—	5 Centai. Aluminum-Bronze. Uniface. Reverse.	250
TS5	1925	—	10 Centu. Aluminum-Bronze. Uniface. Obverse.	275
TS6	1925	—	10 Centu. Aluminum-Bronze. Uniface. Reverse.	275
TS7	1925	—	20 Centu. Aluminum-Bronze. Uniface. Obverse.	275
TS8	1925	—	20 Centu. Aluminum-Bronze. Uniface. Reverse.	275
TS9	1925	—	50 Centu. Aluminum-Bronze. Uniface. Obverse.	285
TS10	1925	—	50 Centu. Aluminum-Bronze. Uniface. Reverse.	285

MINT SETS

KM#	Date	Mintage	Identification	Issue Price	Mkt Val
MS1	1925 (10)	—	KM71-75, 2 of each	—	1,000
MS2	1991 (9)	100,000	KM85-93	7.50	17.50
MS3	2000 (6)	5,000	KM106-108, 111-113	7.50	18.00

LUXEMBOURG

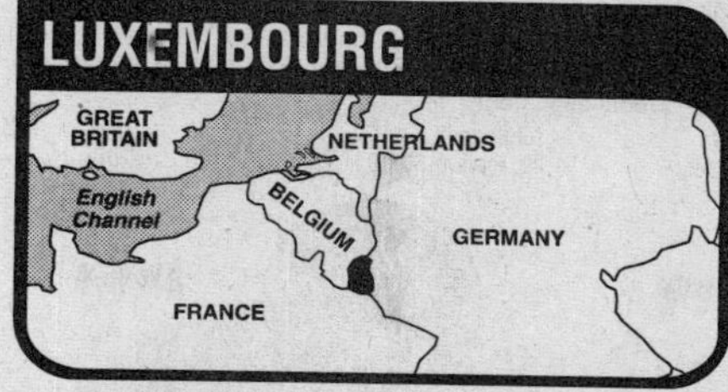

The Grand Duchy of Luxembourg is located in western Europe between Belgium, Germany and France, has an area of 1,103 sq. mi. (2,586 sq. km.) and a population of 377,100. Capital: Luxembourg. The economy is based on steel.

Founded about 963, Luxembourg was a prominent country of the Holy Roman Empire; one of its sovereigns became Holy Roman Emperor as Henry VII, 1308. After being made a duchy by Emperor Charles IV, 1354, Luxembourg passed under the domination of Burgundy, Spain, Austria and France, 1443-1815, regaining autonomy under the Treaty of Vienna, 1815, as a grand duchy in union with the Netherlands, though ostensibly a member of the German Confederation. When Belgium seceded from the Kingdom of the Netherlands, 1830, Luxembourg was forced to cede its greater western section to Belgium. The tiny duchy left the German Confederation in 1867 when the Treaty of London recognized it as an independent state and guaranteed its perpetual neutrality. Luxembourg was occupied by Germany and liberated by American troops in both World Wars.

RULERS
Adolphe, 1890-1905
William IV, 1905-1912
Marie Adelaide, 1912-1919
Charlotte, 1919-1964
Jean, 1964-2000
Henri, 2000-

MINT MARKS
A - Paris
(b) - Brussels, privy marks only
H – Gunzburg
(n) – lion - Namur
(u) - Utrecht, privy marks only

PRIVY MARKS
Angel's head, two headed eagle - Brussels
Sword, Caduceus - Utrecht (1846-74 although struck at Brussels until 1909)

NOTE: Beginning in 1994 the letters "qp" for quality proof appear on Proof coins.

MONETARY SYSTEM
100 Centimes = 1 Franc

GRAND DUCHY

STANDARD COINAGE RESUMED

100 Centimes = 1 Franc

KM# 21 2-1/2 CENTIMES
Bronze **Ruler:** William III Netherlands **Obv:** Crowned ornate shield within rope wreath **Obv. Legend:** GRAND-DUCHE DE LUXEMBOURG **Rev:** Value and date within wreath

Date	Mintage	F	VF	XF	Unc	BU
1901(u)	800,000	0.50	1.50	7.50	40.00	—
Note: BARTH on reverse						
1901(u)	Inc. above	0.50	1.50	8.50	42.00	—
Note: BAPTH on reverse						
1908(u)	400,000	0.50	1.50	9.50	45.00	—

KM# 24 5 CENTIMES
Copper-Nickel **Ruler:** Adolphe **Obv:** Head right **Rev:** Value within wreath **Designer:** A. Michaux

Date	Mintage	F	VF	XF	Unc	BU
1901	2,000,000	0.25	0.75	4.50	17.50	—

KM# 26 5 CENTIMES
Copper-Nickel **Ruler:** William IV **Obv:** Head right **Rev:** Value within wreath

Date	Mintage	F	VF	XF	Unc	BU
1908	1,500,000	0.35	1.00	6.50	20.00	—

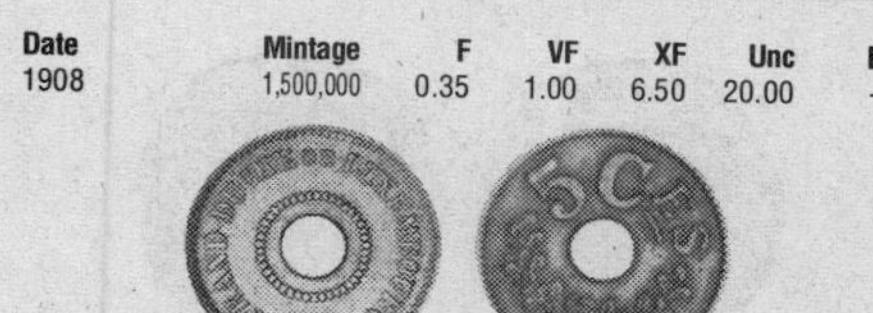

KM# 27 5 CENTIMES
Zinc **Ruler:** Marie Adelaide **Obv:** Plain and beaded circle around hole in center with date below **Rev:** Value above hole in center with 1/2 wreath below

Date	Mintage	F	VF	XF	Unc	BU
1915	1,200,000	1.00	6.00	15.00	30.00	—

KM# 30 5 CENTIMES
Iron **Ruler:** Charlotte **Obv:** National arms **Rev:** Value within wreath

Date	Mintage	F	VF	XF	Unc	BU
1918	1,200,000	1.00	4.00	8.00	30.00	—
1921	600,000	10.00	20.00	40.00	80.00	—
1922	400,000	15.00	30.00	80.00	120	—

KM# 33 5 CENTIMES
Copper-Nickel **Ruler:** Charlotte **Obv:** Crowned monogram **Rev:** Value within wreath

Date	Mintage	F	VF	XF	Unc	BU
1924	3,000,000	0.20	0.40	3.00	10.00	—

KM# 40 5 CENTIMES
Bronze **Ruler:** Charlotte **Obv:** Head left **Rev:** Value

Date	Mintage	F	VF	XF	Unc	BU
1930	5,000,000	0.10	0.25	2.00	4.00	—

KM# 25 10 CENTIMES
Copper-Nickel, 20 mm. **Ruler:** Adolphe **Obv:** Head right **Rev:** Value within wreath **Designer:** A. Michaux

Date	Mintage	F	VF	XF	Unc	BU
1901	4,000,000	0.25	0.75	6.00	14.00	—

KM# 28 10 CENTIMES
Zinc **Ruler:** Marie Adelaide **Obv:** Beaded circle around hole in center with date below **Rev:** Large value above hole in center with 1/2 wreath below

Date	Mintage	F	VF	XF	Unc	BU
1915	1,400,000	1.25	4.00	8.00	20.00	—

KM# 31 10 CENTIMES
Iron **Ruler:** Charlotte **Obv:** National arms **Rev:** Value within wreath

Date	Mintage	F	VF	XF	Unc	BU
1918	1,603,000	1.50	3.50	10.00	25.00	—
1921	626,000	2.00	10.00	20.00	40.00	—
1923	350,000	12.00	30.00	60.00	125	—

KM# 34 10 CENTIMES
Copper-Nickel **Ruler:** Charlotte **Obv:** Crowned monogram **Rev:** Value within wreath

Date	Mintage	F	VF	XF	Unc	BU
1924	3,500,000	0.25	0.50	2.00	8.00	—

KM# 41 10 CENTIMES
Bronze **Ruler:** Charlotte **Obv:** Head left **Rev:** Value flanked by sprigs with star above

Date	Mintage	F	VF	XF	Unc	BU
1930	5,000,000	0.10	0.25	2.00	4.50	—

KM# 29 25 CENTIMES
Zinc **Ruler:** Charlotte **Obv:** Beaded circle around hole in center with date below **Rev:** Large value above hole in center with wreath below

Date	Mintage	F	VF	XF	Unc	BU
1916	800,000	1.50	6.00	12.00	25.00	—
1920	—	200	400	600	1,000	—

KM# 32 25 CENTIMES
Iron **Ruler:** Charlotte **Obv:** National arms **Rev:** Value within wreath

Date	Mintage	F	VF	XF	Unc	BU
1919	804,000	2.75	6.50	12.50	35.00	—
1920	800,000	2.75	8.00	14.00	35.00	—
1922	600,000	2.75	8.50	16.00	40.00	—

KM# 37 25 CENTIMES
Copper-Nickel **Ruler:** Charlotte **Obv:** Crowned national arms flanked by stars **Rev:** Value and date to right of sprig

Date	Mintage	F	VF	XF	Unc	BU
1927	2,500,000	0.35	0.65	5.00	25.00	—

KM# 42 25 CENTIMES
Bronze **Ruler:** Charlotte **Obv:** Crowned national arms flanked by stars **Rev:** Value and date to right of sprig **Designer:** Everaerts

Date	Mintage	F	VF	XF	Unc	BU
1930	1,000,000	0.35	1.00	8.00	30.00	—

KM# 42a.1 25 CENTIMES
Copper-Nickel, 25 mm. **Ruler:** Charlotte **Obv:** Crowned national arms flanked by stars **Rev:** Value and date to right of sprig
Note: Coin alignment.

Date	Mintage	F	VF	XF	Unc	BU
1938	2,000,000	0.35	1.00	3.00	10.00	—

KM# 42a.2 25 CENTIMES
Copper-Nickel, 25 mm. **Ruler:** Charlotte **Obv:** Crowned national arms flanked by stars **Rev:** Value and date to right of sprig
Note: Medal alignment.

Date	Mintage	F	VF	XF	Unc	BU
1938	Inc. above	50.00	75.00	100	200	—

KM# 45 25 CENTIMES
Bronze, 19 mm. **Ruler:** Charlotte **Obv:** Crowned national arms flanked by diamonds **Rev:** Value and date to right of sprig

Date	Mintage	F	VF	XF	Unc	BU
1946	1,000,000	—	0.15	0.25	0.75	—
1947	1,000,000	—	0.15	0.25	0.75	—

KM# 45a.1 25 CENTIMES
Aluminum, 18.5 mm. **Ruler:** Jean **Obv:** Crowned national arms flanked by diamonds **Rev:** Value and date to right of sprig
Note: Coin alignment.

Date	Mintage	F	VF	XF	Unc	BU
1954	7,000,000	—	—	—	0.10	0.20
1957	3,020,000	—	—	—	0.10	0.20
1960	3,020,000	—	—	—	0.10	0.20
1963	4,000,000	—	—	—	0.10	0.20
1965	2,000,000	—	—	—	0.10	0.20
1967	3,000,000	—	—	—	0.10	0.20
1968	600,000	0.10	0.25	0.50	1.00	2.00
1970	4,000,000	—	—	—	0.10	0.20
1972	4,000,000	—	—	—	0.10	0.20

KM# 45a.2 25 CENTIMES
Aluminum, 18.5 mm. **Ruler:** Jean **Obv:** Crowned national arms flanked by diamonds **Rev:** Value and date to right of sprig
Note: Medal alignment.

Date	Mintage	F	VF	XF	Unc	BU
1954	Inc. above	10.00	20.00	30.00	40.00	—
1960	Inc. above	5.00	10.00	15.00	20.00	—
1963	Inc. above	5.00	10.00	15.00	20.00	—
1965	Inc. above	10.00	20.00	30.00	40.00	—
1967	Inc. above	10.00	20.00	30.00	40.00	—

KM# 45b 25 CENTIMES
2.9600 g., 0.9250 Silver .088 oz. ASW **Ruler:** Jean **Obv:** Crowned national arms flanked by diamonds **Rev:** Value and date to right of sprig

Date	Mintage	F	VF	XF	Unc	BU
1980 Proof	3,000	Value: 12.00				

KM# 43 50 CENTIMES
Nickel **Ruler:** Charlotte **Obv:** Man working field with date below **Rev:** Value divides wheat sprays

Date	Mintage	F	VF	XF	Unc	BU
1930	2,000,000	0.25	1.00	10.00	20.00	—

KM# 35 FRANC
Nickel **Ruler:** Charlotte **Obv:** Crowned monogram **Rev:** Man working field with date below

Date	Mintage	F	VF	XF	Unc	BU
1924	1,000,000	0.25	1.50	10.00	20.00	—
1928	2,000,000	0.20	1.50	10.00	20.00	—
1935	1,000,000	0.25	2.00	14.00	30.00	—

KM# 44 FRANC
Copper-Nickel, 24 mm. **Ruler:** Charlotte **Obv:** Crowned monogram flanked by flower blossoms at top **Rev:** Woman figure divides date and value

Date	Mintage	F	VF	XF	Unc	BU
1939	5,000,000	0.25	0.75	1.50	5.00	—

KM# 46.1 FRANC
Copper-Nickel, 23 mm. **Ruler:** Charlotte **Obv:** Man working field **Rev:** Crowned monogram divides value

Date	Mintage	F	VF	XF	Unc	BU
1946	4,000,000	0.15	0.35	0.50	1.50	—
1947	2,000,000	0.20	0.40	1.00	3.00	—

KM# 46.2 FRANC
Copper-Nickel, 21 mm. **Ruler:** Charlotte **Obv:** Man working field **Rev:** Crowned monogram divides value

Date	Mintage	F	VF	XF	Unc	BU
1952	5,000,000	0.10	0.25	0.50	2.00	—
1953	2,000,000	0.10	0.25	0.50	1.50	—
1955	1,000,000	0.10	0.25	0.50	1.50	—
1957	2,000,000	—	0.10	0.25	1.00	—
1960	2,000,000	—	0.10	0.25	1.00	—
1962	2,000,000	—	0.10	0.25	1.00	—
1964	2,000,000	—	0.10	0.25	1.00	—

KM# 46.2a FRANC
4.4500 g., 0.9250 Silver .1323 oz. ASW, 21 mm. **Ruler:** Jean **Obv:** Man working fields **Rev:** Crowned monogram divides value

Date	Mintage	F	VF	XF	Unc	BU
1980 Proof	3,000	Value: 20.00				

KM# 55 FRANC
Copper-Nickel, 21 mm. **Ruler:** Jean **Obv:** Head left **Rev:** Crown above value within wreath **Designer:** J. N. Lefevre

Date	Mintage	F	VF	XF	Unc	BU
1965	3,000,000	—	—	0.10	0.20	0.40
1966	1,000,000	—	—	0.10	0.20	0.40
1968	3,000,000	—	—	0.10	0.20	0.40
1970	3,000,000	—	—	0.10	0.20	0.40
1972	3,000,000	—	—	0.10	0.20	0.40
1973	3,000,000	—	—	0.10	0.20	0.40
1976	3,000,000	—	—	0.10	0.20	0.40
1977	1,000,000	—	—	0.10	0.20	0.40
1978	3,000,000	—	—	0.10	0.20	0.40
1979	2,000,000	—	—	0.10	0.20	0.40
1980	4,000,000	—	—	0.10	0.20	0.40
1981	5,000,000	—	—	0.10	0.20	0.40
1982	3,000,000	—	—	0.10	0.20	0.40
1983	3,000,000	—	—	0.10	0.20	0.40
1984	3,000,000	—	—	0.10	0.20	0.40

KM# 55a FRANC
4.4700 g., 0.9250 Silver .1329 oz. ASW, 21 mm. **Ruler:** Jean **Obv:** Head left **Rev:** Crown above value within wreath

Date	Mintage	F	VF	XF	Unc	BU
1980 Proof	3,000	Value: 20.00				

KM# 59 FRANC

Copper-Nickel, 21 mm. **Ruler:** Jean **Obv:** Head left **Rev:** IML added **Designer:** J. N. Lefevre

Date	Mintage	F	VF	XF	Unc	BU
1986	3,000,000	—	—	0.10	0.20	0.40
1987	3,000,000	—	—	0.10	0.20	0.40

KM# 63 FRANC

Nickel-Steel **Ruler:** Jean **Obv:** Head left **Rev:** Crown divides date above value **Designer:** J. N. Lefevre

Date	Mintage	F	VF	XF	Unc	BU
1988	10,000,000	—	—	—	0.40	0.60
1989	3,000,000	—	—	—	0.40	0.60
1990	25,010,000	—	—	—	0.40	0.60
1991	10,010,000	—	—	—	0.40	0.60
1992 In sets only	10,000	—	—	—	0.60	1.00
1993 In sets only	10,000	—	—	—	0.60	1.00
1994 In sets only	10,000	—	—	—	0.60	1.00
1995 In sets only	10,000	—	—	—	0.60	1.00

KM# 36 2 FRANCS

Nickel **Ruler:** Charlotte **Obv:** Crowned monogram above sprig **Rev:** Man working field

Date	Mintage	F	VF	XF	Unc	BU
1924	1,000,000	1.00	4.00	20.00	40.00	—

KM# 38 5 FRANCS

8.0000 g., 0.6250 Silver .1608 oz. ASW, 27.8 mm. **Ruler:** Charlotte **Rev:** Wing above national arms on shield divides value

Date	Mintage	F	VF	XF	Unc	BU
1929	2,000,000	BV	3.50	12.50	25.00	—

KM# 50 5 FRANCS

Copper-Nickel **Ruler:** Charlotte **Obv:** Head left **Rev:** Value flanked by flowers below crown and ribbon

Date	Mintage	F	VF	XF	Unc	BU
1949	2,000,000	0.30	0.60	1.00	3.50	—

KM# 51 5 FRANCS

Copper-Nickel **Ruler:** Charlotte **Obv:** Head right **Rev:** Crowned arms divide value

Date	Mintage	F	VF	XF	Unc	BU
1962	2,000,000	0.10	0.25	0.40	1.00	—

KM# 51a 5 FRANCS

6.7400 g., 0.9250 Silver .2004 oz. ASW **Ruler:** Jean **Obv:** Head right **Rev:** Crowned arms divide value

Date	Mintage	F	VF	XF	Unc	BU
1980 Proof	3,000	Value: 25.00				

KM# 56 5 FRANCS

Copper-Nickel **Ruler:** Jean **Obv:** Head left **Rev:** Crown above value and date within sprigs **Designer:** J. N. Lefevre

Date	Mintage	F	VF	XF	Unc	BU
1971	1,000,000	—	—	0.20	0.50	0.80
1976	1,000,000	—	—	0.20	0.50	0.80
1979	1,000,000	—	—	0.20	0.50	0.80
1981	1,000,000	—	—	0.20	0.50	0.80

KM# 56a 5 FRANCS

6.7800 g., 0.9250 Silver .2016 oz. ASW **Ruler:** Jean **Obv:** Head left **Rev:** Crown above value and date within sprigs

Date	Mintage	F	VF	XF	Unc	BU
1980 Proof	3,000	Value: 25.00				

KM# 60.1 5 FRANCS

Brass **Ruler:** Jean **Obv:** Head left **Rev:** Crown divides date above value within sprigs with IML added **Designer:** J. N. Lefevre

Date	Mintage	F	VF	XF	Unc	BU
1986	9,000,000	—	—	0.15	0.40	0.65
1987	7,000,000	—	—	0.15	0.40	0.65
1988	2,000,000	—	—	0.15	0.40	0.65

KM# 60.2 5 FRANCS

Brass **Ruler:** Jean **Obv:** Head left **Rev:** Larger crown divides date above value within sprigs **Designer:** J. N. Lefevre

Date	Mintage	F	VF	XF	Unc	BU
1987	—	—	—	0.15	0.40	0.65

KM# 65 5 FRANCS

Brass **Ruler:** Jean **Obv:** Head left **Rev:** Crown divides date above value **Designer:** J. N. Lefevre

Date	Mintage	F	VF	XF	Unc	BU
1989	2,000,000	—	—	—	0.60	1.00
1990	4,010,000	—	—	—	0.60	1.00
1991 In sets only	10,000	—	—	—	0.75	1.25
1992 In sets only	20,000	—	—	—	0.75	1.25
1993 In sets only	17,500	—	—	—	0.75	1.25
1994 In sets only	10,000	—	—	—	0.75	1.25
1995 In sets only	10,000	—	—	—	0.75	1.25

KM# 39 10 FRANCS

13.5000 g., 0.7500 Silver .3255 oz. ASW **Ruler:** Charlotte

Date	Mintage	F	VF	XF	Unc	BU
1929	1,000,000	BV	6.00	12.00	32.50	—

KM# 57 10 FRANCS

Nickel, 27 mm. **Ruler:** Jean **Obv:** Head left **Rev:** Crown above value and date flanked by leaves **Designer:** J. N. Lefevre

Date	Mintage	F	VF	XF	Unc	BU
1971	3,000,000	—	—	0.30	0.60	1.00
1972	3,000,000	—	—	0.30	0.60	1.00
1974	3,000,000	—	—	0.30	0.60	1.00
1976	3,000,000	—	—	0.30	0.60	1.00
1977	1,000,000	—	—	0.30	0.60	1.00
1978	1,000,000	—	—	0.30	0.60	1.00
1979	1,000,000	—	—	0.30	0.60	1.00
1980	1,000,000	—	—	0.30	0.60	1.00

KM# 57a 10 FRANCS

8.7900 g., 0.9250 Silver .2614 oz. ASW **Ruler:** Jean **Obv:** Head left **Rev:** Crown above value and date flanked by leaves

Date	Mintage	F	VF	XF	Unc	BU
1980 Proof	3,000	Value: 30.00				

KM# 47 20 FRANCS

8.5000 g., 0.8350 Silver .2282 oz. ASW, 27 mm. **Ruler:** Charlotte **Subject:** 600th Anniversary - John the Blind **Obv:** Head left flanked by shields **Rev:** Armored Knight on horse above dates **Designer:** Armand Bonnetain

Date	Mintage	F	VF	XF	Unc	BU
ND(1946)	100,000	BV	5.00	12.00	18.00	—
ND(1946) Proof	100	Value: 200				

KM# 58 20 FRANCS

Bronze, 25.5 mm. **Ruler:** Jean **Obv:** Head left **Rev:** Crown above value flanked by sprigs **Edge:** Dashes all around **Designer:** J. N. Lefevre

Date	Mintage	F	VF	XF	Unc	BU
1980	3,000,000	—	—	0.60	1.00	1.50
1981	3,000,000	—	—	0.60	1.00	1.50
1982	3,000,000	—	—	0.60	1.00	1.50
1983	2,000,000	—	—	0.60	1.00	1.50

KM# 58a 20 FRANCS

10.2100 g., 0.9250 Silver .3036 oz. ASW, 25.5 mm. **Ruler:** Jean **Obv:** Head left **Rev:** Crown above value flanked by sprigs

Date	Mintage	F	VF	XF	Unc	BU
1980 Proof	3,000	Value: 30.00				

KM# 64 20 FRANCS

6.2200 g., 0.9990 Gold .2 oz. AGW **Ruler:** Jean **Subject:** 150th Anniversary of the Grand Duchy **Obv:** Head left **Rev:** Crowned national arms

Date	Mintage	F	VF	XF	Unc	BU
ND(1989) Proof	50,000	Value: 145				

KM# 67 20 FRANCS

Bronze, 25.5 mm. **Ruler:** Jean **Obv:** Head left **Rev:** Crown divides date above value **Designer:** J. N. Lefevre

Date	Mintage	F	VF	XF	Unc	BU
1990	1,110,000	—	—	—	2.00	3.00
1991 In sets only	10,000	—	—	—	2.50	3.50
1992 In sets only	10,000	—	—	—	2.50	3.50
1993 In sets only	10,000	—	—	—	2.50	3.50
1994 In sets only	10,000	—	—	—	2.50	3.50
1995 In sets only	10,000	—	—	—	2.50	3.50

KM# 48 50 FRANCS

12.5000 g., 0.8350 Silver .3356 oz. ASW, 30 mm. **Ruler:** Charlotte **Subject:** 600th Anniversary - John the Blind **Designer:** Armand Bonnetain

Date	Mintage	F	VF	XF	Unc	BU
ND(1946)	100,000	—	10.00	15.00	35.00	—
ND(1946) Proof	100	Value: 225				

KM# 62 50 FRANCS

Nickel, 22.5 mm. **Ruler:** Jean **Obv:** Head left **Rev:** Crown divides date above value **Designer:** J. N. Lefevre

Date	Mintage	F	VF	XF	Unc	BU
1987	3,000,000	—	—	1.50	3.50	5.00
1988	1,000,000	—	—	1.50	3.50	5.00
1989	1,200,000	—	—	1.50	3.50	5.00

KM# 66 50 FRANCS

Nickel, 22.5 mm. **Ruler:** Jean **Designer:** J. N. Lefevre
Note: Similar to 5 Francs, KM#65.

Date	Mintage	F	VF	XF	Unc	BU
1989	2,000,000	—	—	—	3.50	5.00
1990	2,010,000	—	—	—	3.50	5.00
1991 In sets only	10,000	—	—	—	4.00	6.00
1992 In sets only	10,000	—	—	—	4.00	6.00
1993 In sets only	10,000	—	—	—	4.00	6.00
1994 In sets only	10,000	—	—	—	4.00	6.00
1995 In sets only	10,000	—	—	—	4.00	6.00

KM# 49 100 FRANCS

25.0000 g., 0.8350 Silver .6711 oz. ASW, 37 mm.
Ruler: Charlotte **Subject:** 600th Anniversary - John the Blind
Obv: Head left flanked by crowned shields **Rev:** Armored Knight on horse above dates **Designer:** Armand Bonnetain

Date	Mintage	F	VF	XF	Unc	BU
ND(1946)	98,000	—	20.00	40.00	50.00	—
ND(1946) Proof	100	Value: 250				
ND(1946) Restrike	2,000	—	—	—	100	—

Note: Without designer's name

KM# 52 100 FRANCS

18.0000 g., 0.8350 Silver .4832 oz. ASW **Ruler:** Charlotte
Obv: Head right **Rev:** Crowned arms with supporters above value

Date	Mintage	F	VF	XF	Unc	BU
1963	50,000	—	—	10.00	15.00	—

KM# 54 100 FRANCS

18.0000 g., 0.8350 Silver .4832 oz. ASW **Ruler:** Charlotte **Rev:** Crowned mantled arms with supporters **Designer:** J. N. Lefevre

Date	Mintage	F	VF	XF	Unc	BU
1964	50,000	—	—	9.00	14.00	—

KM# 70 100 FRANCS

16.1000 g., 0.9250 Silver .4788 oz. ASW **Ruler:** Jean **Subject:** 50th Anniversary - United Nations **Obv:** Head left **Rev:** Emblem and numeral 50 to lower right of building, flags and gun

Date	Mintage	F	VF	XF	Unc	BU
ND(1995) (qp) Proof	110,000	Value: 28.50				

KM# 53.1 250 FRANCS

25.0000 g., 0.8350 Silver .6772 oz. ASW **Ruler:** Charlotte
Subject: Millennium of Luxembourg City **Obv:** Head right within circular inscriptions above dates **Rev:** City view above value

Date	Mintage	F	VF	XF	Unc	BU
ND(1963)	11,500	—	—	25.00	45.00	—

KM# 53.2 250 FRANCS

25.0000 g., 0.8350 Silver .6772 oz. ASW **Ruler:** Charlotte
Subject: Millennium of Luxembourg City **Obv:** Head right within circular inscriptions above dates **Rev:** City view above value
Note: Darkly toned by the mint.

Date	Mintage	F	VF	XF	Unc	BU
ND(1963)	8,500	—	—	40.00	60.00	—

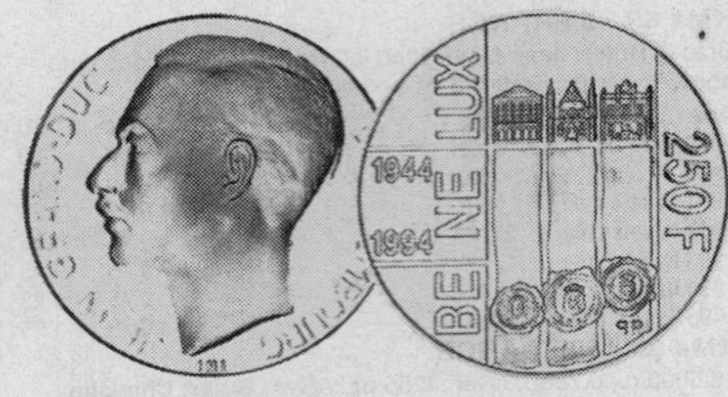

KM# 68 250 FRANCS

18.7500 g., 0.9250 Silver .5577 oz. ASW **Ruler:** Jean **Subject:** BE-NE-LUX Treaty **Obv:** Head left **Obv. Designer:** J. N. Lefevre
Rev: Houses above with flowers below dividing date and value

Date	Mintage	F	VF	XF	Unc	BU
ND(1994) (qp) Proof	30,000	Value: 30.00				

KM# 69 500 FRANCS

22.8500 g., 0.9250 Silver .6795 oz. ASW **Ruler:** Jean **Subject:** 50th Anniversary of Liberation **Obv:** Head left **Obv. Designer:** J. N. Lefevre **Rev:** Flag design below with inscription above within circle

Date	Mintage	F	VF	XF	Unc	BU
ND(1994)	25,000	—	—	—	35.00	—
ND(1994) (qp) Proof	25,000	Value: 42.50				

KM# 71 500 FRANCS

22.8500 g., 0.9250 Silver .6795 oz. ASW **Ruler:** Jean
Subject: Luxembourg - European Cultural City **Obv:** Segmented head left **Rev:** Quartered cultural pictures

Date	Mintage	F	VF	XF	Unc	BU
(19)95 (qp) Proof	10,000	Value: 45.00				

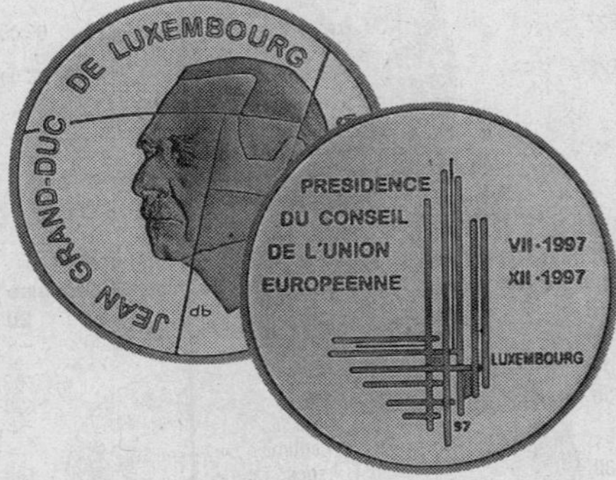

KM# 72 500 FRANCS

22.8500 g., 0.9250 Silver .6795 oz. ASW **Ruler:** Jean
Subject: Presidency of the European Community
Obv: Segmented portrait **Rev:** Symbolic design and dates

Date	Mintage	F	VF	XF	Unc	BU
(19)97 (qp) Proof	10,000	Value: 40.00				
(19)97 (qp) Proof	10,000	Value: 50.00				

KM# 73 500 FRANCS

22.8500 g., 0.9250 Silver .6795 oz. ASW **Ruler:** Jean
Subject: 1,300 years of Echternach **Obv:** Duke's segmented portrait **Rev:** City seal and anniversary dates

Date	Mintage	F	VF	XF	Unc	BU
ND(1998) (qp) Proof	10,000	Value: 40.00				

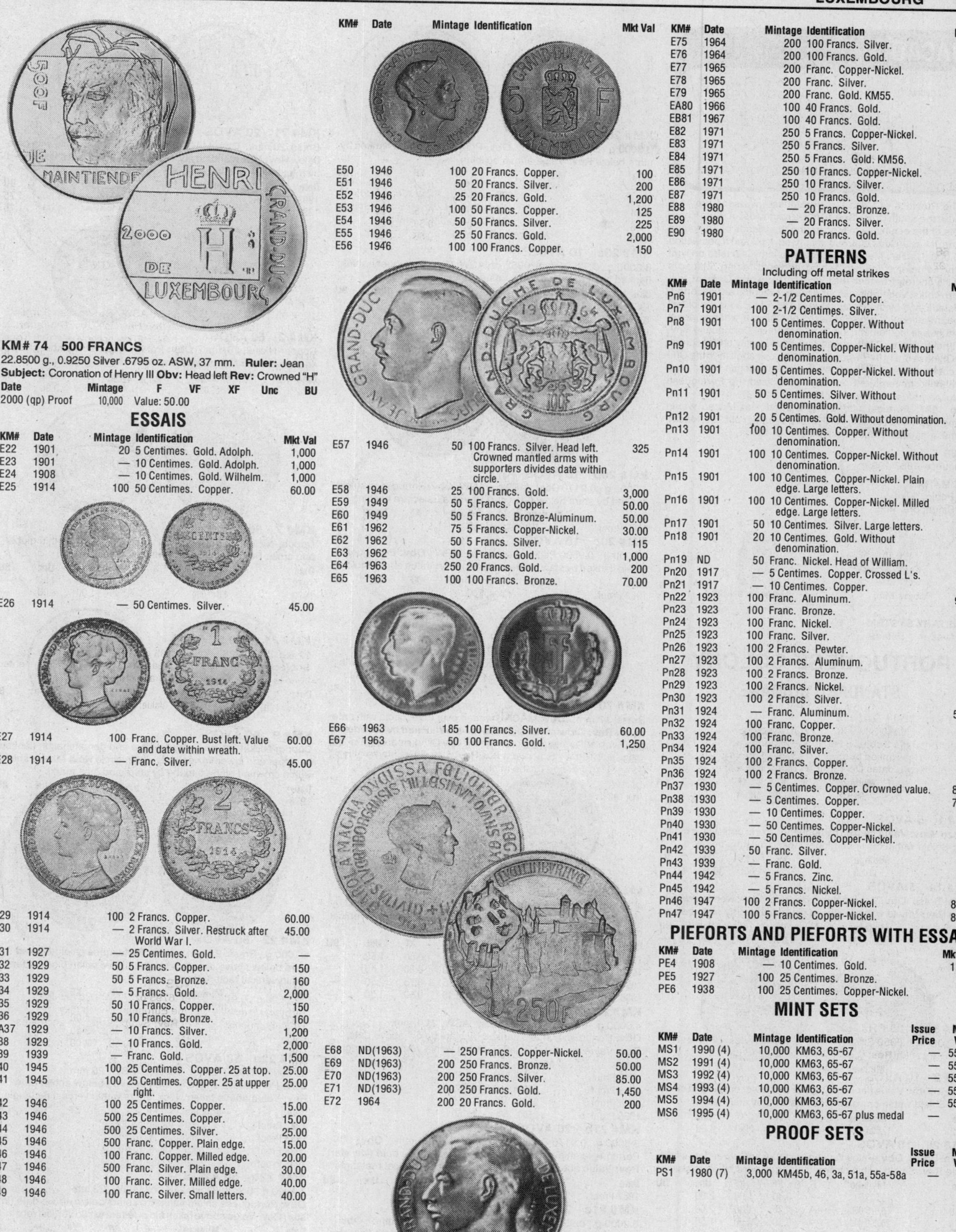

KM# 74 500 FRANCS

22.8500 g., 0.9250 Silver .6795 oz. ASW, 37 mm. **Ruler:** Jean
Subject: Coronation of Henry III **Obv:** Head left **Rev:** Crowned "H"

Date	Mintage	F	VF	XF	Unc	BU
2000 (qp) Proof	10,000	Value: 50.00				

ESSAIS

KM#	Date	Mintage	Identification	Mkt Val
E22	1901	20	5 Centimes. Gold. Adolph.	1,000
E23	1901	—	10 Centimes. Gold. Adolph.	1,000
E24	1908	—	10 Centimes. Gold. Wilhelm.	1,000
E25	1914	100	50 Centimes. Copper.	60.00
E26	1914	—	50 Centimes. Silver.	45.00
E27	1914	100	Franc. Copper. Bust left. Value and date within wreath.	60.00
E28	1914	—	Franc. Silver.	45.00
E29	1914	100	2 Francs. Copper.	60.00
E30	1914	—	2 Francs. Silver. Restruck after World War I.	45.00
E31	1927	—	25 Centimes. Gold.	—
E32	1929	50	5 Francs. Copper.	150
E33	1929	50	5 Francs. Bronze.	160
E34	1929	—	5 Francs. Gold.	2,000
E35	1929	50	10 Francs. Copper.	150
E36	1929	50	10 Francs. Bronze.	160
EA37	1929	—	10 Francs. Silver.	1,200
E38	1929	—	10 Francs. Gold.	2,000
E39	1939	—	Franc. Gold.	1,500
E40	1945	100	25 Centimes. Copper. 25 at top.	25.00
E41	1945	100	25 Centimes. Copper. 25 at upper right.	25.00
E42	1946	100	25 Centimes. Copper.	15.00
E43	1946	500	25 Centimes. Copper.	15.00
E44	1946	500	25 Centimes. Silver.	25.00
E45	1946	500	Franc. Copper. Plain edge.	15.00
E46	1946	100	Franc. Copper. Milled edge.	20.00
E47	1946	500	Franc. Silver. Plain edge.	30.00
E48	1946	100	Franc. Silver. Milled edge.	40.00
E49	1946	100	Franc. Silver. Small letters.	40.00
E50	1946	100	20 Francs. Copper.	100
E51	1946	50	20 Francs. Silver.	200
E52	1946	25	20 Francs. Gold.	1,200
E53	1946	100	50 Francs. Copper.	125
E54	1946	50	50 Francs. Silver.	225
E55	1946	25	50 Francs. Gold.	2,000
E56	1946	100	100 Francs. Copper.	150
E57	1946	50	100 Francs. Silver. Head left. Crowned mantled arms with supporters divides date within circle.	325
E58	1946	25	100 Francs. Gold.	3,000
E59	1949	50	5 Francs. Copper.	50.00
E60	1949	50	5 Francs. Bronze-Aluminum.	50.00
E61	1962	75	5 Francs. Copper-Nickel.	30.00
E62	1962	50	5 Francs. Silver.	115
E63	1962	50	5 Francs. Gold.	1,000
E64	1963	250	20 Francs. Gold.	200
E65	1963	100	100 Francs. Bronze.	70.00
E66	1963	185	100 Francs. Silver.	60.00
E67	1963	50	100 Francs. Gold.	1,250
E68	ND(1963)	—	250 Francs. Copper-Nickel.	50.00
E69	ND(1963)	200	250 Francs. Bronze.	50.00
E70	ND(1963)	200	250 Francs. Silver.	85.00
E71	ND(1963)	200	250 Francs. Gold.	1,450
E72	1964	200	20 Francs. Gold.	200
E73	1964	200	100 Francs. Copper-Nickel. Head left.	20.00
E74	1964	200	100 Francs. Bronze.	20.00
E75	1964	200	100 Francs. Silver.	20.00
E76	1964	200	100 Francs. Gold.	750
E77	1965	200	Franc. Copper-Nickel.	15.00
E78	1965	200	Franc. Silver.	15.00
E79	1965	200	Franc. Gold. KM55.	200
EA80	1966	100	40 Francs. Gold.	400
EB81	1967	100	40 Francs. Gold.	400
E82	1971	250	5 Francs. Copper-Nickel.	15.00
E83	1971	250	5 Francs. Silver.	15.00
E84	1971	250	5 Francs. Gold. KM56.	315
E85	1971	250	10 Francs. Copper-Nickel.	15.00
E86	1971	250	10 Francs. Silver.	15.00
E87	1971	250	10 Francs. Gold.	325
E88	1980	—	20 Francs. Bronze.	20.00
E89	1980	—	20 Francs. Silver.	45.00
E90	1980	500	20 Francs. Gold.	285

PATTERNS

Including off metal strikes

KM#	Date	Mintage	Identification	Mkt Val
Pn6	1901	—	2-1/2 Centimes. Copper.	125
Pn7	1901	100	2-1/2 Centimes. Silver.	165
Pn8	1901	100	5 Centimes. Copper. Without denomination.	125
Pn9	1901	100	5 Centimes. Copper-Nickel. Without denomination.	125
Pn10	1901	100	5 Centimes. Copper-Nickel. Without denomination.	—
Pn11	1901	50	5 Centimes. Silver. Without denomination.	150
Pn12	1901	20	5 Centimes. Gold. Without denomination.	1,000
Pn13	1901	100	10 Centimes. Copper. Without denomination.	90.00
Pn14	1901	100	10 Centimes. Copper-Nickel. Without denomination.	90.00
Pn15	1901	100	10 Centimes. Copper-Nickel. Plain edge. Large letters.	90.00
Pn16	1901	100	10 Centimes. Copper-Nickel. Milled edge. Large letters.	90.00
Pn17	1901	50	10 Centimes. Silver. Large letters.	150
Pn18	1901	20	10 Centimes. Gold. Without denomination.	1,000
Pn19	ND	50	Franc. Nickel. Head of William.	150
Pn20	1917	—	5 Centimes. Copper. Crossed L's.	150
Pn21	1917	—	10 Centimes. Copper.	150
Pn22	1923	100	Franc. Aluminum.	90.00
Pn23	1923	100	Franc. Bronze.	100
Pn24	1923	100	Franc. Nickel.	100
Pn25	1923	100	Franc. Silver.	135
Pn26	1923	100	2 Francs. Pewter.	125
Pn27	1923	100	2 Francs. Aluminum.	120
Pn28	1923	100	2 Francs. Bronze.	115
Pn29	1923	100	2 Francs. Nickel.	135
Pn30	1923	100	2 Francs. Silver.	150
Pn31	1924	—	Franc. Aluminum.	50.00
Pn32	1924	100	Franc. Copper.	110
Pn33	1924	100	Franc. Bronze.	110
Pn34	1924	100	Franc. Silver.	110
Pn35	1924	100	2 Francs. Copper.	100
Pn36	1924	100	2 Francs. Bronze.	110
Pn37	1930	—	5 Centimes. Copper. Crowned value.	85.00
Pn38	1930	—	5 Centimes. Copper.	75.00
Pn39	1930	—	10 Centimes. Copper.	125
Pn40	1930	—	50 Centimes. Copper-Nickel.	150
Pn41	1930	—	50 Centimes. Copper-Nickel.	160
Pn42	1939	50	Franc. Silver.	100
Pn43	1939	—	Franc. Gold.	350
Pn44	1942	—	5 Francs. Zinc.	100
Pn45	1942	—	5 Francs. Nickel.	100
Pn46	1947	100	2 Francs. Copper-Nickel.	80.00
Pn47	1947	100	5 Francs. Copper-Nickel.	85.00

PIEFORTS AND PIEFORTS WITH ESSAI

KM#	Date	Mintage	Identification	Mkt Val
PE4	1908	—	10 Centimes. Gold.	1,000
PE5	1927	100	25 Centimes. Bronze.	100
PE6	1938	100	25 Centimes. Copper-Nickel.	100

MINT SETS

KM#	Date	Mintage	Identification	Issue Price	Mkt Val
MS1	1990 (4)	10,000	KM63, 65-67	—	55.00
MS2	1991 (4)	10,000	KM63, 65-67	—	55.00
MS3	1992 (4)	10,000	KM63, 65-67	—	55.00
MS4	1993 (4)	10,000	KM63, 65-67	—	55.00
MS5	1994 (4)	10,000	KM63, 65-67	—	55.00
MS6	1995 (4)	10,000	KM63, 65-67 plus medal	—	100

PROOF SETS

KM#	Date	Mintage	Identification	Issue Price	Mkt Val
PS1	1980 (7)	3,000	KM45b, 46, 3a, 51a, 55a-58a	—	160

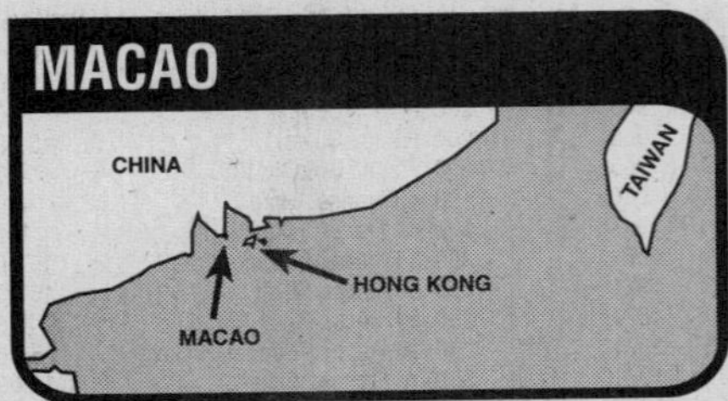

The Province of Macao, a Portuguese overseas province located in the South China Sea 40 miles southwest of Hong Kong, consists of the peninsula of Macao and the islands of Taipa and Coloane. It has an area of 6.2 sq. mi.(16 sq. km.) and a population of 500,000. Capital: Macao. Macao's economy is based on light industry, commerce, tourism, fishing, and gold trading - Macao is one of the entirely free markets for gold in the world. Cement, textiles, fireworks, vegetable oils, and metal products are exported.

Established by the Portuguese in 1557, Macao is the oldest European settlement in the Far East. The Chinese, while agreeing to Portuguese settlement, did not recognize Portuguese sovereign rights and the Portuguese remained largely under control of the Chinese until 1849, when the Portuguese abolished the Chinese customhouse and declared the independence of the port. The Manchu government formally recognized the Portuguese right to *perpetual occupation* of Macao in 1887.

In 1987, Portugal and China agreed that Macao would become a Chinese Territory in 1999. In December of 1999, Macao became a special administrative zone of China.

RULER

Portuguese 1887-1999

MINT MARKS

(p) - Pobjoy Mint

(s) - Singapore Mint

Pobjoy Mint

Singapore Mint

MONETARY SYSTEM

100 Avos = 1 Pataca

PORTUGUESE COLONY

STANDARD COINAGE

100 Avos = 1 Pataca

KM# 1 5 AVOS

Bronze **Obv:** Value flanked by upper and lower dots within circle **Rev:** Shield within crowned globe flanked by stars below

Date	Mintage	F	VF	XF	Unc	BU
1952	500,000	—	3.50	15.00	30.00	50.00

KM# 1a 5 AVOS

Nickel-Brass **Obv:** Value flanked by upper and lower dots within circle **Rev:** Shield within crowned globe flanked by stars below

Date	Mintage	F	VF	XF	Unc	BU
1967	5,000,000	—	0.50	1.00	2.50	—

KM# 2 10 AVOS

Bronze **Obv:** Value flanked by upper and lower dots within circle **Rev:** Shield within crowned globe flanked by stars below

Date	Mintage	F	VF	XF	Unc	BU
1952	12,500,000	—	0.30	0.80	6.00	—

KM# 2a 10 AVOS

Nickel-Brass **Obv:** Value flanked by upper and lower dots within circle **Rev:** Shield within crowned globe flanked by stars below

Date	Mintage	F	VF	XF	Unc	BU
1967	5,525,000	—	0.50	1.00	2.00	—
1968	6,975,000	—	0.25	1.00	2.00	—
1975	20,000,000	—	0.10	0.50	1.50	—
1976	Inc. above	—	0.10	0.50	1.50	—

KM# 20 10 AVOS

3.3000 g., Brass, 19.1 mm. **Obv:** Portuguese shield flanked by stars below **Rev:** Value above building

Date	Mintage	F	VF	XF	Unc	BU
1982	24,580,000	—	0.10	0.50	1.50	—
1983	—	—	0.10	0.50	1.50	—
1984	—	—	0.25	0.75	2.50	—
1985	—	—	0.10	0.50	1.50	—
1988	—	—	0.10	0.50	1.50	—

KM# 20a 10 AVOS

3.2000 g., 0.9250 Silver .0952 oz. ASW **Obv:** Portuguese shield flanked by stars below **Rev:** Value above building

Date	Mintage	F	VF	XF	Unc	BU
1982 Proof	2,000	Value: 7.50				
1983 Proof	2,500	Value: 7.50				
1984 Proof	2,500	Value: 7.50				
1985 Proof	2,500	Value: 7.50				

KM# 20b 10 AVOS

4.0000 g., 0.9170 Gold .1179 oz. AGW **Obv:** Portuguese shield flanked by stars below (low star) **Rev:** Value above building

Date	Mintage	F	VF	XF	Unc	BU
1982 Proof	150	Value: 125				

KM# 20c 10 AVOS

4.5000 g., 0.9500 Platinum .1374 oz. APW **Obv:** Portuguese shield flanked by stars below (low star) **Rev:** Value above building

Date	Mintage	F	VF	XF	Unc	BU
1982 Proof	375	Value: 200				

KM# 70 10 AVOS

Brass, 17 mm. **Obv:** MACAU written over inner circle with date below **Rev:** Crowned design above value flanked by mint marks

Date	Mintage	F	VF	XF	Unc	BU
1993	—	—	—	—	0.75	1.25

KM# 21 20 AVOS

4.7000 g., Brass, 21.1 mm. **Obv:** Portuguese shield flanked by stars below **Rev:** Value above block letter design within vertical rectangle

Date	Mintage	F	VF	XF	Unc	BU
1982	9,960,000	—	0.10	0.50	1.50	—
1983	—	—	0.10	0.50	1.50	—
1984	—	—	0.25	0.75	2.50	—
1985	—	—	0.10	0.50	1.50	—

KM# 21a 20 AVOS

4.6000 g., 0.9250 Silver .1368 oz. ASW, 21.1 mm. **Obv:** Portuguese shield flanked by stars below above date **Rev:** Value above block letter design within vertical rectangle

Date	Mintage	F	VF	XF	Unc	BU
1982 Proof	2,000	Value: 11.50				
1983 Proof	2,500	Value: 11.50				
1984 Proof	2,500	Value: 11.50				
1985 Proof	2,500	Value: 11.50				

KM# 21b 20 AVOS

5.5000 g., 0.9170 Gold .1621 oz. AGW, 21.1 mm. **Obv:** Portuguese shield flanked by stars below above date (low star) **Rev:** Value above block letter design within vertical rectangle

Date	Mintage	F	VF	XF	Unc	BU
1982 Proof	150	Value: 175				

KM# 21c 20 AVOS

6.2000 g., 0.9500 Platinum .1893 oz. APW, 21.1 mm. **Obv:** Portuguese shield flanked by stars below above date (low star) **Rev:** Value above block letter design within vertical rectangle

Date	Mintage	F	VF	XF	Unc	BU
1982 Proof	375	Value: 285				

KM# 71 20 AVOS

Brass, 20 mm. **Obv:** MACAU written over inner circle with date below **Rev:** Man standing above his crew on ancient ship flanked by mint marks with value above **Shape:** 12-sided

Date	Mintage	F	VF	XF	Unc	BU
1993	—	—	—	—	1.00	1.75
1998	—	—	—	—	1.00	1.75

KM# 3 50 AVOS

Copper-Nickel, 20 mm. **Obv:** Portuguese shield within globe and cross **Rev:** Macau shield within crowned globe

Date	Mintage	F	VF	XF	Unc	BU
1952	2,560,000	—	0.75	3.50	9.00	—

KM# 7 50 AVOS

Copper-Nickel, 23 mm. **Obv:** Portuguese shield within globe and cross **Rev:** Macau shield within crowned globe

Date	Mintage	F	VF	XF	Unc	BU
1972	1,600,000	—	0.50	1.50	4.00	—
1973	4,840,000	—	0.50	1.00	3.00	—

KM# 9 50 AVOS

Copper-Nickel, 23 mm. **Obv:** Value and denomination flanked by upper and lower flower buds within circle **Rev:** Macau shield within crowned globe flanked by stars and mint marks

Date	Mintage	F	VF	XF	Unc	BU
1978	3,000,000	—	0.50	1.50	4.00	—

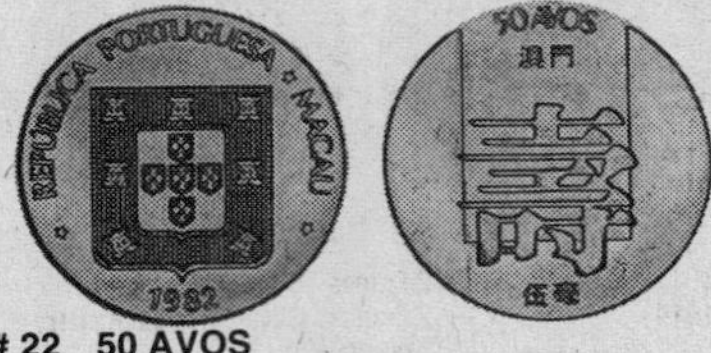

KM# 22 50 AVOS

5.1000 g., Brass, 23 mm. **Obv:** Portuguese shield flanked by stars below above date **Rev:** Value above fallen block letters within vertical rectangle

Date	Mintage	F	VF	XF	Unc	BU
1982	16,952,000	—	0.50	1.00	3.00	—
1983	—	—	0.75	4.00	9.00	—
1984	—	—	0.75	3.50	7.00	—
1985	—	—	0.50	2.00	5.00	—

KM# 22a 50 AVOS

5.7000 g., 0.9250 Silver .1695 oz. ASW, 23 mm. **Obv:** Portuguese shield flanked by stars below above date **Rev:** Value above fallen block letters within vertical rectangle

Date	Mintage	F	VF	XF	Unc	BU
1982 Proof	2,000	Value: 13.50				
1983 Proof	2,500	Value: 13.50				
1984 Proof	2,500	Value: 13.50				
1985 Proof	2,500	Value: 13.50				

KM# 22b 50 AVOS

7.4000 g., 0.9170 Gold .2181 oz. AGW, 23 mm. **Obv:** Portuguese shield flanked by stars below above date (low star) **Rev:** Value above fallen block letters within vertical rectangle

Date	Mintage	F	VF	XF	Unc	BU
1982 Proof	150	Value: 200				

KM# 22c 50 AVOS

8.4000 g., 0.9500 Platinum .2565 oz. APW, 23 mm. **Obv:** Portuguese shield flanked by stars below above date (low star) **Rev:** Value above fallen block letters within vertical rectangle

Date	Mintage	F	VF	XF	Unc	BU
1982 Proof	375	Value: 385				

KM# 72 50 AVOS

Brass, 23 mm. **Obv:** MACAU written across center of globe with date below **Rev:** Figure in ceremonial dragon costume being led by a man

Date	Mintage	F	VF	XF	Unc	BU
1993	—	—	—	—	1.50	2.50

KM# 4 PATACA

3.0000 g., 0.7200 Silver .0694 oz. ASW **Obv:** Portuguese shield within globe and long cross **Rev:** Macau shield within crowned globe

Date	Mintage	F	VF	XF	Unc	BU
1952	4,500,000	5.00	10.00	20.00	40.00	—

KM# 6 PATACA

Nickel **Obv:** Portuguese shield within globe and long cross **Rev:** Macau shield within crowned globe

Date	Mintage	F	VF	XF	Unc	BU
1968	5,000,000	—	1.00	3.00	6.50	—
1975	6,000,000	—	0.75	2.00	5.00	—

KM# 6a PATACA

Copper-Nickel **Obv:** Portuguese shield within globe and long cross **Rev:** Macau shield within crowned globe

Date	Mintage	F	VF	XF	Unc	BU
1980	—	—	3.50	12.00	25.00	—

KM# 23.1 PATACA

9.2000 g., Copper-Nickel, 26 mm. **Obv:** Portuguese shield flanked by stars below above date (high stars) **Rev:** Artistic design flanked by upright fish

Date	Mintage	F	VF	XF	Unc	BU
1982(s)	6,427,000	—	1.00	2.00	6.00	—
1983(s)	—	—	1.50	3.50	8.00	—
1984(s)	—	—	2.00	4.50	10.00	—
1985(s)	—	—	1.50	3.50	8.00	—

KM# 23.1a PATACA

9.0000 g., 0.9250 Silver .2677 oz. ASW, 26 mm. **Obv:** Portuguese shield flanked by stars below above date (high stars) **Rev:** Artistic design flanked by upright fish

Date	Mintage	F	VF	XF	Unc	BU
1982(s) Proof	2,000	Value: 17.50				
1983(s) Proof	2,500	Value: 17.50				
1984(s) Proof	2,500	Value: 17.50				
1985(s) Proof	2,500	Value: 17.50				

KM# 23.1b PATACA

11.6000 g., 0.9170 Gold .342 oz. AGW, 26 mm. **Obv:** Portuguese shield flanked by stars below above date (high stars) **Rev:** Artistic design flanked by upright fish

Date	Mintage	F	VF	XF	Unc	BU
1982(s) Proof	150	Value: 285				

KM# 23.1c PATACA

13.2000 g., 0.9500 Platinum .4032 oz. APW, 26 mm. **Obv:** Portuguese shield flanked by stars below above date (high stars) **Rev:** Artistic design flanked by upright fish

Date	Mintage	F	VF	XF	Unc	BU
1982(s) Proof	375	Value: 600				

KM# 23.2 PATACA

Copper-Nickel, 26 mm. **Obv:** Portuguese shield flanked by stars below above date (low stars) **Rev:** Artistic design flanked by upright fish

Date	Mintage	F	VF	XF	Unc	BU
1982(p)	—	—	1.00	2.00	6.00	—
1983(p)	—	—	1.50	3.50	8.00	—

KM# 23.2a PATACA

5.7000 g., 0.9250 Silver .1695 oz. ASW, 26 mm. **Obv:** Portuguese shield flanked by stars below above date (low stars) **Rev:** Artistic design flanked by upright fish

Date	Mintage	F	VF	XF	Unc	BU
1982 Proof	—	Value: 15.00				

KM# 57 PATACA

Copper-Nickel **Obv:** MACAU written across center of globe with date below **Rev:** Lighthouse above value

Date	Mintage	F	VF	XF	Unc	BU
1992	—	—	—	—	2.50	4.00
1998	—	—	—	—	2.50	4.00

KM# 97 2 PATACAS

Nickel-Brass, 27.5 mm. **Obv:** MACAU written accross center of globe above date **Rev:** Church and Chinese arch **Edge:** Plain **Shape:** Octagonal

Date	Mintage	F	VF	XF	Unc	BU
1998	—	—	—	—	3.50	5.50

KM# 5 5 PATACAS

15.0000 g., 0.7200 Silver .3472 oz. ASW **Obv:** Portuguese shield within globe and long cross **Rev:** Macau shield within crowned globe

Date	Mintage	F	VF	XF	Unc	BU
1952	900,000	6.00	8.00	12.00	25.00	—

KM# 5a 5 PATACAS

10.0000 g., 0.6500 Silver .2089 oz. ASW **Obv:** Portuguese shield within globe and long cross **Rev:** Macau shield within crowned globe

Date	Mintage	F	VF	XF	Unc	BU
1971	500,000	5.00	7.50	12.00	20.00	—

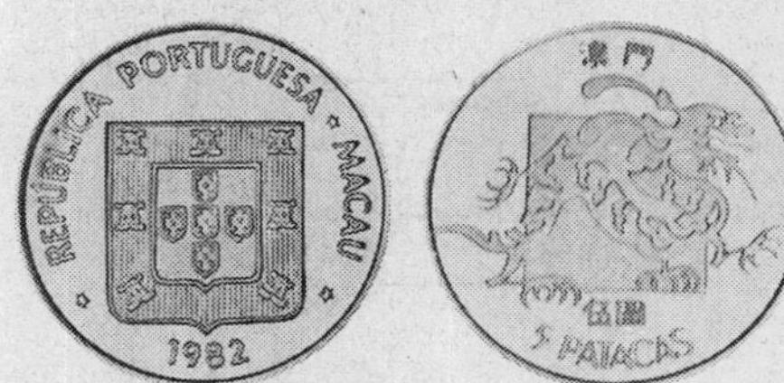

KM# 24.1 5 PATACAS

10.7000 g., Copper-Nickel, 29 mm. **Obv:** Portuguese shield flanked by stars below above date (high stars) **Rev:** Large stylized dragon above value

Date	Mintage	F	VF	XF	Unc	BU
1982(s)	1,102,000	—	1.00	2.00	6.00	—
1983(s)	—	—	3.50	7.00	20.00	—
1984(s)	—	—	5.00	10.00	60.00	—
1985(s)	—	—	3.50	7.00	45.00	—
1988(s)	—	—	1.00	2.00	6.00	—

KM# 24.1a 5 PATACAS

10.7000 g., 0.9250 Silver .3182 oz. ASW, 29 mm. **Obv:** Portuguese shield flanked by stars below above date (high stars) **Rev:** Large stylized dragon above value

Date	Mintage	F	VF	XF	Unc	BU
1982(s) Proof	2,000	Value: 32.50				
1983(s) Proof	2,500	Value: 32.50				
1984(s) Proof	2,500	Value: 32.50				
1985(s) Proof	2,500	Value: 32.50				

KM# 24.1b 5 PATACAS

16.3000 g., 0.9170 Gold .4808 oz. AGW, 29 mm. **Obv:** Portuguese shield flanked by stars below above date (high stars) **Rev:** Large stylized dragon above value

Date	Mintage	F	VF	XF	Unc	BU
1982(s) Proof	150	Value: 400				

KM# 24.1c 5 PATACAS

18.4000 g., 0.9500 Platinum .562 oz. APW, 29 mm. **Obv:** Portuguese shield flanked by stars below above date (high stars) **Rev:** Large stylized dragon above value

Date	Mintage	F	VF	XF	Unc	BU
1982(s) Proof	375	Value: 845				

KM# 24.2 5 PATACAS

10.7000 g., Copper-Nickel, 29 mm. **Obv:** Portuguese shield flanked by stars below above date (low stars) **Rev:** Small stylized dragon above value

Date	Mintage	F	VF	XF	Unc	BU
1982(p)	—	—	1.00	2.00	6.00	—
1983(p)	—	—	1.00	2.00	6.00	—

KM# 24.2a 5 PATACAS

10.7000 g., 0.9250 Silver .3182 oz. ASW, 29 mm. **Obv:** Portuguese shield flanked by stars below above date (low stars) **Rev:** Small stylized dragon above value

Date	Mintage	F	VF	XF	Unc	BU
1982(p) Proof	—	Value: 25.00				

KM# 56 5 PATACAS

Copper-Nickel **Obv:** MACAU written across center of globe with date below **Rev:** Sailing ship and building scene **Shape:** 12-sided

Date	Mintage	F	VF	XF	Unc	BU
1992	—	—	—	—	6.50	10.00

KM# 83 10 PATACAS

Bi-Metallic Copper-Nickel center in Brass ring, 28 mm. **Obv:** MACAU written across center of globe within circle above date **Rev:** Cathedral within circle above value

Date	Mintage	F	VF	XF	Unc	BU
1997	—	—	—	—	8.50	12.50

KM# 8 20 PATACAS

18.0000 g., 0.6500 Silver .3762 oz. ASW **Obv:** Macau shield within globe **Rev:** Junk (ship) passing under Taipa bridge within circle **Designer:** M. Norte

Date	Mintage	F	VF	XF	Unc	BU
1974	1,000	—	—	16.00	30.00	—

KM# 10 100 PATACAS
28.2800 g., 0.9250 Silver .8411 oz. ASW **Subject:** 25th Anniversary of Grand Prix **Obv:** Church facade flanked by stars **Rev:** Race car with advertising logos

Date	Mintage	F	VF	XF	Unc	BU
1978 Proof	610	Value: 150				

KM# 10a 100 PATACAS
Copper-Nickel **Subject:** 25th Anniversary of Grand Prix **Obv:** Church facade flanked by stars **Rev:** Race car with advertising logos

Date	Mintage	F	VF	XF	Unc	BU
1978	—	—	—	—	300	—

KM# 11 100 PATACAS
28.2800 g., 0.9250 Silver .8411 oz. ASW **Obv:** Church facade flanked by stars **Rev:** Race car without advertising **Note:** Similar to KM#10, but reissued without advertising logos on the racecar.

Date	Mintage	F	VF	XF	Unc	BU
1978 Proof	5,500	Value: 150				

KM# 14 100 PATACAS
28.2800 g., 0.9250 Silver .8411 oz. ASW **Subject:** Year of the Goat **Obv:** Crowned arms with supporters **Rev:** Goat

Date	Mintage	F	VF	XF	Unc	BU
1979(s) Proof	5,500	Value: 50.00				

KM# 16 100 PATACAS
28.2800 g., 0.9250 Silver .8411 oz. ASW **Subject:** Year of the Monkey **Obv:** Crowned arms with supporters **Rev:** Monkey swinging on a rope

Date	Mintage	F	VF	XF	Unc	BU
1980	1,000	—	—	—	65.00	—
1980 Proof	2,000	Value: 60.00				

KM# 18 100 PATACAS
28.2800 g., 0.9250 Silver .8411 oz. ASW **Subject:** Year of the Rooster **Obv:** Crowned arms with supporters **Rev:** Rooster

Date	Mintage	F	VF	XF	Unc	BU
1981(p)	1,000	—	—	—	60.00	—
1981(p) Proof	1,000	Value: 70.00				

KM# 25 100 PATACAS
28.2800 g., 0.9250 Silver .8411 oz. ASW **Subject:** Year of the Dog **Obv:** Crowned arms with supporters **Rev:** Dog

Date	Mintage	F	VF	XF	Unc	BU
1982(p)	500	—	—	—	65.00	—
1982(p) Proof	500	Value: 75.00				
1982(s)	220	—	—	—	67.50	—
1982(s) Proof	3,500	Value: 70.00				

KM# 27 100 PATACAS
28.2800 g., 0.9250 Silver .8411 oz. ASW **Subject:** Year of the Pig **Obv:** Crowned arms with supporters **Rev:** Pig

Date	Mintage	F	VF	XF	Unc	BU
1983(s)	2,500	—	—	—	50.00	—
1983(s) Proof	2,500	Value: 60.00				

KM# 29 100 PATACAS
28.2800 g., 0.9250 Silver .8411 oz. ASW **Subject:** Year of the Rat **Obv:** Crowned arms with supporters **Rev:** Rat

Date	Mintage	F	VF	XF	Unc	BU
1984(s)	2,000	—	—	—	60.00	—
1984(s) Proof	5,000	Value: 70.00				

KM# 31 100 PATACAS
28.2800 g., 0.9250 Silver .8411 oz. ASW **Subject:** Year of the Ox **Obv:** Crowned arms with supporters **Rev:** Ox

Date	Mintage	F	VF	XF	Unc	BU
1985(s)	10,000	—	—	—	50.00	—
1985(s) Proof	5,000	Value: 60.00				

KM# 33 100 PATACAS
28.2800 g., 0.9250 Silver .8411 oz. ASW **Subject:** Visit of Portugal's President Eanes **Obv:** Head left above date

Date	Mintage	F	VF	XF	Unc	BU
1985(s)	760	—	—	—	90.00	—
1985(s) Proof	2,000	Value: 65.00				

KM# 34 100 PATACAS
28.2800 g., 0.9250 Silver .8411 oz. ASW **Subject:** Year of the Tiger **Obv:** Crowned arms with supporters **Rev:** Tiger

Date	Mintage	F	VF	XF	Unc	BU
1986(p)	760	—	—	—	90.00	—
1986(p) Proof	3,000	Value: 60.00				

KM# 36 100 PATACAS
28.2800 g., 0.9250 Silver .8411 oz. ASW **Subject:** Year of the Rabbit **Obv:** Crowned arms with supporters **Rev:** Rabbit

Date	Mintage	F	VF	XF	Unc	BU
1987(p)	—	—	—	—	50.00	—
1987(p) Proof	5,000	Value: 50.00				

KM# 38 100 PATACAS
28.2800 g., 0.9250 Silver .8411 oz. ASW **Subject:** Year of the Dragon **Obv:** Crowned arms with supporters **Rev:** Dragon **Note:** Similar to 1,000 Patacas, KM#39.

Date	Mintage	F	VF	XF	Unc	BU
1988	—	—	—	—	50.00	—
1988 Proof	5,000	Value: 65.00				

KM# 40 100 PATACAS
28.2800 g., 0.9250 Silver .8411 oz. ASW **Subject:** 35th Anniversary of Grand Prix **Obv:** Sailing ship within circle **Rev:** Race car and dates within circle

Date	Mintage	F	VF	XF	Unc	BU
ND(1988) Proof	5,000	Value: 55.00				

KM# 40a 100 PATACAS
Platinum APW **Subject:** 35th Anniversary of Grand Prix **Obv:** Sailing ship within circle **Rev:** Race car within circle above dates

Date	Mintage	F	VF	XF	Unc	BU
ND(1988) Proof	10	Value: 2,750				

KM# 44 100 PATACAS
28.2800 g., 0.9250 Silver .8411 oz. ASW **Subject:** Year of the Snake **Obv:** Crowned arms with supporters **Rev:** Coiled snake **Note:** Similar to 1,000 Patacas, KM#45.

Date	Mintage	F	VF	XF	Unc	BU
1989(s)	2,000	—	—	—	50.00	—
1989(s) Proof	3,000	Value: 60.00				

KM# 46 100 PATACAS
28.2800 g., 0.9250 Silver .8411 oz. ASW **Subject:** Year of the Horse **Obv:** Crowned arms with supporters **Rev:** Horse

Date	Mintage	F	VF	XF	Unc	BU
1990(s)	1,000	—	—	—	75.00	—
1990(s) Proof	3,364	Value: 60.00				

KM# 48 100 PATACAS
28.2800 g., 0.9250 Silver .8411 oz. ASW **Subject:** Year of the Goat **Obv:** Crowned arms with supporters **Rev:** Goat **Note:** Similar to KM#51.

Date	Mintage	F	VF	XF	Unc	BU
1991(s)	1,000	—	—	—	50.00	—
1991(s) Proof	Est. 4,000	Value: 50.00				

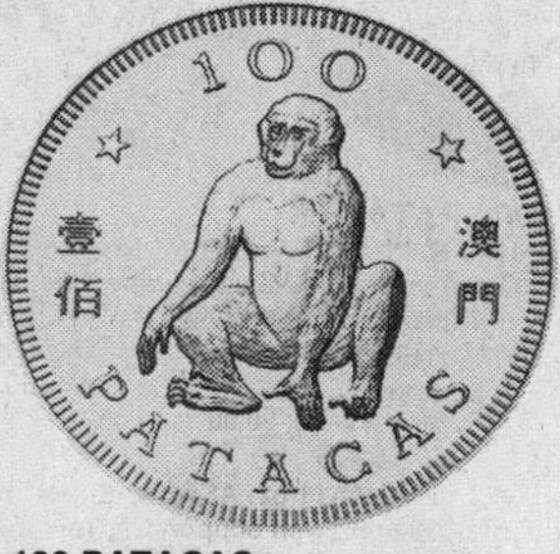

KM# 52 100 PATACAS
28.2800 g., 0.9250 Silver .8411 oz. ASW **Subject:** Year of the Monkey **Obv:** Crowned arms with supporters **Rev:** Monkey **Rev. Designer:** Robert Lowe

Date	Mintage	F	VF	XF	Unc	BU
1992(s)	1,000	—	—	—	50.00	—
1992(s) Proof	Est. 4,000	Value: 60.00				

KM# 58 100 PATACAS
28.2800 g., 0.9250 Silver .8411 oz. ASW **Subject:** Year of the Rooster **Obv:** Crowned arms with supporters **Rev:** Rooster

Date	Mintage	F	VF	XF	Unc	BU
1993	500	—	—	—	75.00	—
1993 Proof	Est. 4,000	Value: 50.00				

KM# 62 100 PATACAS
28.2800 g., 0.9250 Silver .8411 oz. ASW **Subject:** Macao Grand Prix **Obv:** Map above dates **Rev:** Checkered design divides race car and racing bike

Date	Mintage	F	VF	XF	Unc	BU
ND(1993) Proof	5,000	Value: 45.00				

KM# 66 100 PATACAS
28.2800 g., 0.9250 Silver .8411 oz. ASW **Subject:** Year of the Dog **Obv:** Crowned arms with supporters **Rev:** Dog

Date	Mintage	F	VF	XF	Unc	BU
1994	1,000	—	—	—	50.00	—
1994 Proof	Est. 4,000	Value: 50.00				

KM# 73 100 PATACAS
28.2800 g., 0.9250 Silver .8411 oz. ASW **Subject:** Year of the Pig **Obv:** Crowned arms with supporters **Rev:** Pig

Date	Mintage	F	VF	XF	Unc	BU
1995	1,000	—	—	—	60.00	—
1995 Proof	Est. 4,000	Value: 50.00				

KM# 77 100 PATACAS
28.2800 g., 0.9250 Silver .8411 oz. ASW **Subject:** Airport **Obv:** Value and date within circle **Rev:** Airport scene

Date	Mintage	F	VF	XF	Unc	BU
1995 Proof	8,000	Value: 42.50				

KM# 79 100 PATACAS
28.2800 g., 0.9250 Silver .8411 oz. ASW **Subject:** Year of the Rat **Obv:** Crowned arms with supporters **Rev:** Rat

Date	Mintage	F	VF	XF	Unc	BU
1996	1,000	—	—	—	42.50	—
1996 Proof	Est. 4,000	Value: 50.00				

KM# 84 100 PATACAS
28.2800 g., 0.9250 Silver .8411 oz. ASW **Subject:** Year of the Ox **Obv:** Church facade **Rev:** Ox

Date	Mintage	F	VF	XF	Unc	BU
1997 Proof	4,000	Value: 50.00				

KM# 88 100 PATACAS
28.2800 g., 0.9250 Silver .8411 oz. ASW **Subject:** Year of the Tiger **Obv:** Church facade **Rev:** Tiger

Date	Mintage	F	VF	XF	Unc	BU
1998 Proof	5,000	Value: 50.00				

KM# 106 100 PATACAS
28.4000 g., 0.9250 Silver .8458 oz. ASW, 38.4 mm. **Subject:** 19th East Asian Insurance Conference **Obv:** Church facade **Rev:** Two hands holding world within circle **Edge:** Reeded

Date	Mintage	F	VF	XF	Unc	BU
1998 Proof	Est. 3,000	—	—	—	50.00	—

KM# 96 100 PATACAS
31.1035 g., 0.9250 Silver .9250 oz. ASW **Subject:** Macao returns to China **Obv:** Crowned arms with supporters **Rev:** Portuguese and Chinese ships below gold-plated cameo of the Gao Temple

Date	Mintage	F	VF	XF	Unc	BU
1999	Est. 39,000	—	—	—	65.00	—

KM# 98 100 PATACAS
28.2800 g., 0.9250 Silver .8410 oz. ASW, 38.6 mm. **Subject:** Year of the Dragon **Obv:** Church facade **Rev:** Dragon **Edge:** Reeded

Date	Mintage	F	VF	XF	Unc	BU
2000	1,000	—	—	—	60.00	—
2000 Proof	4,000	Value: 55.00				

KM# 49 250 PATACAS
3.9900 g., 0.9170 Gold .1176 oz. AGW **Subject:** Year of the Goat **Obv:** Crowned arms with supporters **Rev:** Goat **Note:** Similar to 1,000 Patacas, KM#51.

Date	Mintage	F	VF	XF	Unc	BU
1991 Proof	Est. 2,500	Value: 110				

KM# 53 250 PATACAS
3.9900 g., 0.9170 Gold .1176 oz. AGW **Subject:** Year of the Monkey **Obv:** Crowned arms with supporters **Rev:** Monkey **Rev. Designer:** Robert Lowe **Note:** Similar to 1,000 Patacas, KM#51.

Date	Mintage	F	VF	XF	Unc	BU
1992 Proof	Est. 2,500	Value: 110				

KM# 59 250 PATACAS
3.9900 g., 0.9170 Gold .1176 oz. AGW **Subject:** Year of the Rooster **Obv:** Crowned arms with supporters **Rev:** Rooster **Note:** Similar to 1,000 Patacas, KM#58.

Date	Mintage	F	VF	XF	Unc	BU
1993 Proof	Est. 2,500	Value: 110				

KM# 67 250 PATACAS
3.9900 g., 0.9170 Gold .1176 oz. AGW **Subject:** Year of the Dog **Obv:** Church facade flanked by stars above date **Rev:** Dog **Note:** Similar to 1,000 Patacas, KM#69.

Date	Mintage	F	VF	XF	Unc	BU
1994 Proof	Est. 2,500	Value: 110				

KM# 74 250 PATACAS
3.9900 g., 0.9170 Gold .1176 oz. AGW **Subject:** Year of the Pig **Obv:** Church facade flanked by stars above date **Rev:** Pig

Date	Mintage	F	VF	XF	Unc	BU
1995 Proof	—	Value: 110				

KM# 80 250 PATACAS
3.9900 g., 0.9170 Gold .1176 oz. AGW **Subject:** Year of the Rat **Obv:** Church facade flanked by stars above date **Rev:** Rat

Date	Mintage	F	VF	XF	Unc	BU
1996 Proof	—	Value: 120				

KM# 85 250 PATACAS
3.9900 g., 0.9170 Gold .1176 oz. AGW **Subject:** Year of the Ox **Obv:** Church facade flanked by stars above date **Rev:** Ox **Note:** Similar to 100 Patacas, KM#84.

Date	Mintage	F	VF	XF	Unc	BU
1997 Proof	Est. 2,500	Value: 115				

KM# 89 250 PATACAS
3.9900 g., 0.9170 Gold .1176 oz. AGW **Subject:** Year of the Tiger **Obv:** Church facade flanked by stars above date **Rev:** Tiger **Note:** Similar to 100 Patacas, KM#88.

Date	Mintage	F	VF	XF	Unc	BU
1998 Proof	Est. 2,500	Value: 115				

KM# 93 250 PATACAS
3.9900 g., 0.9170 Gold .1176 oz. AGW **Subject:** Year of the Rabbit **Obv:** Church facade flanked by stars above value **Rev:** Rabbit

Date	Mintage	F	VF	XF	Unc	BU
1999 Proof	Est. 2,500	Value: 115				

KM# 99 250 PATACAS
3.9900 g., 0.9167 Gold .1176 oz. AGW, 19.3 mm. **Subject:** Year of the Dragon **Obv:** Church facade flanked by stars above date **Rev:** Dragon **Edge:** Reeded

Date	Mintage	F	VF	XF	Unc	BU
2000 Proof	2,500	Value: 125				

KM# 12 500 PATACAS
7.9600 g., 0.9170 Gold .2347 oz. AGW **Subject:** 25th Anniversary of Grand Prix **Obv:** Church facade flanked by stars above date **Rev:** Race car

Date	Mintage	F	VF	XF	Unc	BU
1978 Proof	550	Value: 300				

KM# 13 500 PATACAS
7.9600 g., 0.9170 Gold .2347 oz. AGW **Obv:** Church facade flanked by stars above date **Rev:** Race car without advertising

Date	Mintage	F	VF	XF	Unc	BU
1978 Proof	5,500	Value: 185				

KM# 15 500 PATACAS
7.9600 g., 0.9170 Gold .2347 oz. AGW **Subject:** Year of the Goat **Obv:** Crowned arms with supporters **Rev:** Goat

Date	Mintage	F	VF	XF	Unc	BU
1979 Proof	5,500	Value: 175				

KM# 41 500 PATACAS
155.5150 g., 0.9990 Silver 5 oz. ASW **Subject:** 35th Anniversary of Grand Prix **Obv:** Race car within circle **Rev:** Sailing ship within circle **Note:** Similar to KM#42.

Date	Mintage	F	VF	XF	Unc	BU
1988 Proof	2,000	Value: 145				

KM# 42 500 PATACAS
7.9881 g., 0.9170 Gold .2354 oz. AGW **Subject:** 35th Anniversary of Grand Prix **Obv:** Sailing ship within circle **Rev:** Race car within circle

Date	Mintage	F	VF	XF	Unc	BU
ND(1988) Proof	4,500	Value: 185				

KM# 50 500 PATACAS
7.9881 g., 0.9170 Gold .2354 oz. AGW **Subject:** Year of the Goat **Obv:** Crowned arms with supporters **Rev:** Goat **Note:** Similar to 1,000 Patacas, KM#51.

Date	Mintage	F	VF	XF	Unc	BU
1991 Proof	Est. 2,500	Value: 185				

KM# 54 500 PATACAS
7.9900 g., 0.9170 Gold .2352 oz. AGW **Subject:** Year of the Monkey **Obv:** Crowned arms with supporters **Rev:** Monkey **Rev. Designer:** Robert Lowe **Note:** Similar to 1,000 Patacas, KM#51.

Date	Mintage	F	VF	XF	Unc	BU
1992 Proof	Est. 2,500	Value: 200				

KM# 60 500 PATACAS
7.9900 g., 0.9170 Gold .2352 oz. AGW **Subject:** Year of the Rooster **Obv:** Church facade flanked by stars above date **Rev:** Rooster **Note:** Similar to 100 Patacas, KM#58.

Date	Mintage	F	VF	XF	Unc	BU
1993 Proof	Est. 2,500	Value: 200				

KM# 63 500 PATACAS
155.6000 g., 0.9990 Silver 5 oz. ASW **Subject:** Macao Grand Prix

Date	Mintage	F	VF	XF	Unc	BU
1993 Proof	2,000	Value: 145				

KM# 64 500 PATACAS
7.9900 g., 0.9170 Gold .2352 oz. AGW **Subject:** Macao Grand Prix **Obv:** Map above dates **Rev:** Checkered design divides race car and racing bike

Date	Mintage	F	VF	XF	Unc	BU
ND(1993) Proof	4,500	Value: 185				

KM# 68 500 PATACAS
7.9900 g., 0.9170 Gold .2352 oz. AGW **Subject:** Year of the Dog **Obv:** Church facade flanked by stars above date **Rev:** Dog **Note:** Similar to 1,000 Patacas, KM#69.

Date	Mintage	F	VF	XF	Unc	BU
1994 Proof	Est. 2,500	Value: 210				

KM# 75 500 PATACAS
7.9900 g., 0.9170 Gold .2352 oz. AGW **Subject:** Year of the Pig **Obv:** Church facade flanked by stars above date **Rev:** Pig

Date	Mintage	F	VF	XF	Unc	BU
1995 Proof	Est. 2,000	Value: 210				

KM# 81 500 PATACAS
7.9900 g., 0.9170 Gold .2352 oz. AGW **Subject:** Year of the Rat **Obv:** Church facade flanked by stars above date **Rev:** Rat

Date	Mintage	F	VF	XF	Unc	BU
1996 Proof	—	Value: 210				

KM# 86 500 PATACAS
7.9900 g., 0.9170 Gold .2352 oz. AGW **Subject:** Year of the Ox **Obv:** Church facade flanked by stars above date **Rev:** Ox **Note:** Similar to 100 Patacas, KM#84.

Date	Mintage	F	VF	XF	Unc	BU
1997 Proof	2,000	Value: 225				

KM# 90 500 PATACAS
7.9900 g., 0.9170 Gold .2352 oz. AGW **Subject:** Year of the Tiger **Obv:** Church facade flanked by stars above date **Rev:** Tiger **Note:** Similar to 100 Patacas, KM#88.

Date	Mintage	F	VF	XF	Unc	BU
1998 Proof	2,500	Value: 225				

KM# 94 500 PATACAS
7.9900 g., 0.9170 Gold .2352 oz. AGW **Subject:** Year of the Rabbit **Obv:** Church facade flanked by stars above date **Rev:** Rabbit

Date	Mintage	F	VF	XF	Unc	BU
1999 Proof	Est. 2,500	Value: 225				

KM# 100 500 PATACAS
7.9900 g., 0.9167 Gold .2355 oz. AGW, 22.05 mm. **Subject:** Year of the Dragon **Obv:** Church facade flanked by stars above date **Rev:** Dragon **Edge:** Reeded

Date	Mintage	F	VF	XF	Unc	BU
2000 Proof	2,500	Value: 250				

KM# 17 1000 PATACAS
15.9760 g., 0.9170 Gold .4711 oz. AGW **Subject:** Year of the Monkey **Obv:** Crowned arms with supporters **Rev:** Monkey

Date	Mintage	F	VF	XF	Unc	BU
1980 Proof	5,500	Value: 385				

KM# 19 1000 PATACAS
15.9760 g., 0.9170 Gold .4711 oz. AGW **Subject:** Year of the Rooster **Obv:** Crowned arms with supporters **Rev:** Rooster

Date	Mintage	F	VF	XF	Unc	BU
1981	3,500	—	—	—	345	—
1981 Proof	Inc. above	Value: 375				

KM# 26 1000 PATACAS
15.9760 g., 0.9170 Gold .4711 oz. AGW **Subject:** Year of the Dog **Obv:** Crowned arms with supporters **Rev:** Dog

Date	Mintage	F	VF	XF	Unc	BU
1982	256	—	—	—	375	—
1982 Proof	255	Value: 475				

KM# 28 1000 PATACAS
15.9760 g., 0.9170 Gold .4711 oz. AGW **Subject:** Year of the Pig **Obv:** Crowned arms with supporters **Rev:** Pig

Date	Mintage	F	VF	XF	Unc	BU
1983	400	—	—	—	375	—
1983 Proof	500	Value: 450				

KM# 30 1000 PATACAS
15.9760 g., 0.9170 Gold .4711 oz. AGW **Subject:** Year of the Rat **Obv:** Crowned arms with supporters **Rev:** Rat

Date	Mintage	F	VF	XF	Unc	BU
1984	2,000	—	—	—	345	—
1984 Proof	3,000	Value: 375				

KM# 32 1000 PATACAS
15.9760 g., 0.9170 Gold .4711 oz. AGW **Subject:** Year of the Ox **Obv:** Crowned arms with supporters **Rev:** Ox

Date	Mintage	F	VF	XF	Unc	BU
1985	10,000	—	—	—	335	—
1985 Proof	5,000	Value: 360				

KM# 35 1000 PATACAS
15.9760 g., 0.9170 Gold .4711 oz. AGW **Subject:** Year of the Tiger **Obv:** Crowned arms with supporters **Rev:** Tiger

Date	Mintage	F	VF	XF	Unc	BU
1986(p)	2,000	—	—	—	335	—
1986(p) Proof	3,000	Value: 360				

KM# 37 1000 PATACAS
15.9760 g., 0.9170 Gold .4711 oz. AGW **Subject:** Year of the Rabbit **Obv:** Crowned arms with supporters **Rev:** Rabbit

Date	Mintage	F	VF	XF	Unc	BU
1987(p)	—	—	—	—	335	—
1987(p) Proof	5,000	Value: 360				

KM# 39 1000 PATACAS
15.9760 g., 0.9170 Gold .4711 oz. AGW **Subject:** Year of the Dragon **Obv:** Crowned arms with supporters **Rev:** Dragon

Date	Mintage	F	VF	XF	Unc	BU
1988 Proof	5,000	Value: 350				

KM# 45 1000 PATACAS
15.9760 g., 0.9170 Gold .4711 oz. AGW **Subject:** Year of the Snake **Obv:** Crowned arms with supporters **Rev:** Snake

Date	Mintage	F	VF	XF	Unc	BU
1989	2,000	—	—	—	335	—
1989 Proof	3,000	Value: 360				

KM# 47 1000 PATACAS
15.9760 g., 0.9170 Gold .4711 oz. AGW **Subject:** Year of the Horse **Obv:** Crowned arms with supporters **Rev:** Horse

Date	Mintage	F	VF	XF	Unc	BU
1990	2,000	—	—	—	335	—
1990 Proof	3,000	Value: 360				

KM# 51 1000 PATACAS
15.9760 g., 0.9170 Gold .4711 oz. AGW **Subject:** Year of the Goat **Obv:** Crowned arms with supporters **Rev:** Goat

Date	Mintage	F	VF	XF	Unc	BU
1991	Est. 500	—	—	—	345	—
1991 Proof	Est. 4,500	Value: 375				

KM# 55 1000 PATACAS
15.9760 g., 0.9170 Gold .4711 oz. AGW **Subject:** Year of the Monkey **Obv:** Crowned arms with supporters **Rev:** Monkey **Rev. Designer:** Robert Lowe

Date	Mintage	F	VF	XF	Unc	BU
1992	Est. 500	—	—	—	345	—
1992 Proof	Est. 4,500	Value: 375				

KM# 61 1000 PATACAS
15.9760 g., 0.9170 Gold .4711 oz. AGW **Subject:** Year of the Rooster **Obv:** Church facade flanked by stars above date **Rev:** Rooster

Date	Mintage	F	VF	XF	Unc	BU
1993	Est. 500	—	—	—	345	—
1993 Proof	Est. 4,500	Value: 375				

KM# 69 1000 PATACAS
15.9760 g., 0.9170 Gold .4711 oz. AGW **Subject:** Year of the Dog **Obv:** Church facade flanked by stars above date **Rev:** Dog

Date	Mintage	F	VF	XF	Unc	BU
1994	Est. 500	—	—	—	345	—
1994 Proof	Est. 4,500	Value: 375				

KM# 76 1000 PATACAS
15.9760 g., 0.9170 Gold .4711 oz. AGW **Subject:** Year of the Pig **Obv:** Church facade flanked by stars above date **Rev:** Pig

Date	Mintage	F	VF	XF	Unc	BU
1995	Est. 500	—	—	—	345	—
1995 Proof	Est. 4,500	Value: 375				

KM# 78 1000 PATACAS
15.9760 g., 0.9170 Gold .4711 oz. AGW **Subject:** Airport **Obv:** Stylized form **Rev:** City aerial view

Date	Mintage	F	VF	XF	Unc	BU
1995 Proof	5,000	Value: 375				

KM# 82 1000 PATACAS
15.9760 g., 0.9170 Gold .4711 oz. AGW **Subject:** Year of the Rat **Obv:** Church facade flanked by stars above date **Rev:** Rat

Date	Mintage	F	VF	XF	Unc	BU
1996 Proof	—	Value: 375				

KM# 87 1000 PATACAS
15.9760 g., 0.9170 Gold .4711 oz. AGW **Subject:** Year of the Ox **Obv:** Church facade flanked by stars above date **Rev:** Ox

Date	Mintage	F	VF	XF	Unc	BU
1997 Proof	5,000	Value: 450				

KM# 91 1000 PATACAS
15.9760 g., 0.9170 Gold .4711 oz. AGW **Subject:** Year of the Tiger **Obv:** Church facade flanked by stars above date **Rev:** Tiger

Date	Mintage	F	VF	XF	Unc	BU
1998 Proof	5,000	Value: 450				

KM# 95 1000 PATACAS
15.9760 g., 0.9170 Gold .4711 oz. AGW **Subject:** Year of the Rabbit **Obv:** Church facade flanked by stars above date **Rev:** Rabbit

Date	Mintage	F	VF	XF	Unc	BU
1999 Proof	4,000	Value: 450				

KM# 101 1000 PATACAS
15.9760 g., 0.9167 Gold .4709 oz. AGW, 28.4 mm. **Subject:** Year of the Dragon **Obv:** Church facade flanked by stars above date **Rev:** Dragon **Edge:** Reeded

Date	Mintage	F	VF	XF	Unc	BU
2000	500	—	—	—	400	—
2000 Proof	4,000	Value: 450				

KM# 43 10000 PATACAS
155.5150 g., 0.9990 Gold 5 oz. AGW **Subject:** 35th Anniversary of Grand Prix **Obv:** Sailing ship within circle **Rev:** Race car above dates within circle **Note:** Similar to 500 Patacas, KM#42.

Date	Mintage	F	VF	XF	Unc	BU
1988 Proof	500	Value: 3,500				

KM# 65 10000 PATACAS
155.5150 g., 0.9990 Gold 5 oz. AGW **Subject:** Macao Grand Prix **Obv:** Map above dates **Rev:** Checkered design divides race car and racing bike **Note:** Similar to 500 Patacas, KM#64.

Date	Mintage	F	VF	XF	Unc	BU
1993 Proof	500	Value: 3,500				

SPECIAL ADMINISTRATIVE REGION (S.A.R.)

STANDARD COINAGE

100 Avos = 1 Pataca

KM# 111 10 AVOS
2.5000 g., Brass, 17 mm. **Subject:** Macao's Return to China **Obv:** City arms **Rev:** Sun Yat Sen Memorial above clasped hands with building in background

Date	Mintage	F	VF	XF	Unc	BU
1999	288,888	—	—	—	8.00	12.00

KM# 112 20 AVOS
3.2600 g., Brass, 19.5 mm. **Subject:** Macao's Return to China **Obv:** City arms **Rev:** Monetary and Foreign Exchange Authority Building

Date	Mintage	F	VF	XF	Unc	BU
1999	288,888	—	—	—	9.00	14.00

KM# 113 50 AVOS
4.5400 g., Brass, 23 mm. **Subject:** Macao's Return to China **Obv:** City arms **Rev:** Jet above bridge and ship

Date	Mintage	F	VF	XF	Unc	BU
1999	288,888	—	—	—	10.00	15.00

KM# 114 PATACA
6.0500 g., Copper-Nickel, 25.9 mm. **Subject:** Macao's Return to China **Obv:** City arms **Rev:** Cultural and recreational center building

Date	Mintage	F	VF	XF	Unc	BU
1999	288,888	—	—	—	12.00	17.00

KM# 115 2 PATACAS
5.5800 g., Copper-Nickel, 25 mm. **Subject:** Macao's Return to China **Obv:** City arms **Rev:** Cathedral and race car

Date	Mintage	F	VF	XF	Unc	BU
1999	288,888	—	—	—	15.00	20.00

KM# 116 5 PATACAS
6.6800 g., Copper-Nickel, 27 mm. **Subject:** Macao's Return to China **Obv:** City arms **Rev:** Racing dogs with Lisboa Hotel in background **Shape:** 12-sided

Date	Mintage	F	VF	XF	Unc	BU
1999	288,888	—	—	—	18.00	22.00

KM# 117 10 PATACAS
7.2000 g., Bi-Metallic Copper-Nickel center in Brass ring, 27.8 mm. **Subject:** Macao's Return to China **Obv:** City arms **Rev:** Government House Building **Edge:** Segmented reeding

Date	Mintage	F	VF	XF	Unc	BU
1999	288,888	—	—	—	20.00	25.00

KM# 92 100 PATACAS
28.2800 g., 0.9250 Silver 0.841 oz. ASW, 38.5 mm. **Subject:** Year of the Rabbit **Obv:** Building **Rev:** Rabbit **Edge:** Reeded

Date	Mintage	F	VF	XF	Unc	BU
1999 Proof	4,000	Value: 50.00				

PROVAS

Standard metals

Stamped PROVA in field

KM#	Date	Mintage	Identification	Issue Price	Mkt Val
Pr1	1952	—	5 Avos.	—	20.00
Pr2	1952	—	10 Avos.	—	20.00
Pr3	1952	—	50 Avos.	—	25.00
Pr4	1952	—	Pataca.	—	28.00
Pr5	1952	—	5 Patacas.	—	32.00
Pr6	1967	—	5 Avos.	—	20.00
Pr7	1967	—	10 Avos.	—	20.00
Pr8	1968	—	10 Avos.	—	20.00
Pr9	1968	—	Pataca.	—	25.00
Pr10	1969	—	10 Avos.	—	10.00
Pr11	1971	—	5 Patacas.	—	25.00
Pr12	1972	—	50 Avos.	—	20.00
Pr13	1973	—	50 Avos.	—	20.00
Pr14	1974	—	20 Patacas.	—	35.00
Pr15	1975	—	Pataca.	—	25.00

MINT SETS

KM#	Date	Mintage	Identification	Issue Price	Mkt Val
MS1	1999 (7)	288,888	KM#111-117	23.00	30.00

PROOF SETS

KM#	Date	Mintage	Identification	Issue Price	Mkt Val
PS1	1982 (5)	2,000	KM#20a-24a	—	82.50
PS1b	1982 (5)	150	KM#20b-24b	—	1,185
PS1c	1982 (5)	375	KM#20c-24c	—	2,320
PS2	1983 (5)	2,500	KM#20a-24a	55.00	82.50
PS3	1984 (5)	2,500	KM#20a-24a	55.00	82.50
PS4	1985 (5)	2,500	KM#20a-24a	55.00	82.50
PS5	1987 (2)	—	KM#36-37	—	410
PS6	1988 (2)	—	KM#38-39	—	415
PS7	1991 (3)	2,500	KM#49-51	775	670
PS8	1992 (3)	2,500	KM#53-55	825	700
PS9	1993 (3)	2,500	KM#59-61	830	700
PS10	1994 (3)	2,500	KM#67-69	825	735
PS11	1995 (3)	2,500	KM#74-76	825	735
PS12	1997 (3)	2,500	KM#85-87	849	840
PS13	1998 (3)	2,500	KM#89-91	855	840
PS14	1999 (3)	2,500	KM#93-95	850	840
PS15	2000 (3)	2,500	KM#99-101	849	825

MACEDONIA

The Republic of Macedonia is land-locked, and is bordered in the north by Yugoslavia, to the east by Bulgaria, in the south by Greece and to the west by Albania and has an area of 9,781 sq. mi. (25,713 sq. km.) and a population at the 1991 census was 2,038,847, of which the predominating ethnic groups were Macedonians. The capital is Skopje.

The Slavs settled in Macedonia since the 6th century, who had been Christianized by Byzantium, were conquered by the non-Slav Bulgars in the 7th century and in the 9th century formed a Macedo-Bulgarian empire, the western part of which survived until Byzantine conquest in 1014. In the 14th century, it fell to Serbia, and in1355 to the Ottomans. After the Balkan Wars of 1912-13 Turkey was ousted, and Serbia received the greater part of the territory, the balance going to Bulgaria and Greece. In 1918, Yugoslav Macedonia was incorporated into Serbia as 'South Serbia', becoming a republic in the S.F.R. of Yugoslavia. Claims to the historical Macedonian territory have long been a source of contention between Bulgaria and Greece.

On Nov. 20, 1991 parliament promulgated a new constitution, and declared its independence on Nov.20, 1992, but failed to secure EC and US recognition owing to Greek objections to use of the name *Macedonia.* On Dec. 11, 1992, the UN Security Council authorized the expedition of a small peacekeeping force to prevent hostilities spreading into Macedonia.

There is a 120-member single-chamber National Assembly.

REPUBLIC

STANDARD COINAGE

KM# 1 50 DENI
4.0500 g., Brass, 21.5 mm. **Obv:** Seagull flying offshore **Rev:** Radiant value

Date	Mintage	F	VF	XF	Unc	BU
1993	11,051,000	—	0.10	0.30	0.60	1.50

KM# 2 DENAR
5.1500 g., Brass, 23.7 mm. **Obv:** Sheepdog **Rev:** Radiant value

Date	Mintage	F	VF	XF	Unc	BU
1993	21,040,000	—	0.20	0.35	1.50	4.00
1997	11,200,000	—	0.20	0.35	1.50	4.00

KM# 5 DENAR
5.1500 g., Brass, 23.7 mm. **Series:** F.A.O. **Obv:** Sheep dog **Rev:** Value below F.A.O logo

Date	Mintage	F	VF	XF	Unc	BU
1995	2,314,000	—	—	—	2.00	4.00

KM# 5a DENAR
Copper-Nickel-Zinc, 23.7 mm. **Series:** F.A.O. **Obv:** Sheep dog **Rev:** F.A.O. logo above value

Date	Mintage	F	VF	XF	Unc	BU
1995	1,001,000	—	—	—	2.50	4.50

KM# 8 DENAR
15.9800 g., 0.9167 Gold .4709 oz. AGW **Subject:** 5th Anniversary - UN Membership **Obv:** National emblem within circle **Rev:** Storks within circle

Date	Mintage	F	VF	XF	Unc	BU
ND(1996) Proof	1,100	Value: 360				

KM# 10 DENAR
8.0000 g., 0.9160 Gold 0.2356 oz. AGW, 23.3 mm. **Subject:** Macedonian Orthodox Church **Obv:** Half length figure of Saint facing **Rev:** Orthodox cathedral

Date	Mintage	F	VF	XF	Unc	BU
1997	5,000	—	—	—	—	170

KM# 27 DENAR
5.1000 g., Bronze, 23.8 mm. **Obv:** Byzantine copper folis coin design **Rev:** Radiant rising sun behind value **Edge:** Plain

Date	Mintage	F	VF	XF	Unc	BU
2000	—	—	—	—	12.00	15.00

Note: Mule of KM-9 obverse and KM-2 reverse?

KM# 9 DENAR
5.1000 g., Bronze, 23.8 mm. **Subject:** 2000 Years of Christianity **Obv:** Byzantine copper folis coin **Rev:** Ornamented cross **Edge:** Plain

Date	Mintage	F	VF	XF	Unc	BU
2000	2,000	—	—	—	12.00	15.00

KM# 9a DENAR
7.0000 g., 0.9250 Silver 0.2082 oz. ASW, 23.8 mm. **Obv:** Byzantine copper folis coin **Rev:** Ornamented cross

Date	Mintage	F	VF	XF	Unc	BU
2000	2,000	—	—	—	—	190

KM# 9b DENAR
8.0000 g., 0.9160 Gold 0.2356 oz. AGW, 23.8 mm. **Obv:** Byzantine copper folis coin **Rev:** Ornamented cross

Date	Mintage	F	VF	XF	Unc	BU
2000	2,000	—	—	—	—	210

KM# 3 2 DENARI
6.2500 g., Brass, 25.5 mm. **Obv:** Trout above water **Rev:** Radiant value

Date	Mintage	F	VF	XF	Unc	BU
1993	8,998,000	—	0.25	0.50	1.25	3.00
1997	6,765,000	—	0.25	0.50	1.25	3.00

KM# 6 2 DENARI
6.2500 g., Brass, 25.5 mm. **Series:** F.A.O. **Obv:** Trout above water **Rev:** Value below F.A.O logo

Date	Mintage	F	VF	XF	Unc	BU
1995	2,637,500	—	—	—	2.00	3.50

KM# 6a 2 DENARI
Copper-Nickel-Zinc, 25.5 mm. **Series:** F.A.O. **Obv:** Trout above water **Rev:** Value below F.A.O. logo

Date	Mintage	F	VF	XF	Unc	BU
1995	1,000,000	—	—	—	2.50	4.50

KM# 12 2 DENARI
7.0000 g., 0.9160 Gold 0.2062 oz. AGW, 23 mm. **Subject:** 50th Anniversary - Faculty of Economics **Obv:** Economics building **Rev:** Economics faculty logo

Date	Mintage	F	VF	XF	Unc	BU
2000	1,000	—	—	—	—	210

KM# 4 5 DENARI
7.2500 g., Brass, 27.5 mm. **Obv:** European lynx **Rev:** Radiant value

Date	Mintage	F	VF	XF	Unc	BU
1993	12,330,000	—	0.35	0.75	1.75	3.50

KM# 7 5 DENARI
7.2500 g., Brass, 27.5 mm. **Series:** F.A.O. **Obv:** European lynx **Rev:** Value below F.A.O logo

Date	Mintage	F	VF	XF	Unc	BU
1995	3,123,000	—	—	—	2.00	3.50

KM# 7a 5 DENARI
Copper-Nickel-Zinc, 27.5 mm. **Series:** F.A.O. **Obv:** European lynx **Rev:** Value below F.A.O. logo

Date	Mintage	F	VF	XF	Unc	BU
1995	1,000,000	—	—	—	2.50	4.50

KM# 20 5 DENARI
7.9000 g., 0.9160 Gold 0.2327 oz. AGW, 23.8 mm. **Subject:** 60th Anniversary - First session of Parliament **Obv:** Logo of Association of Refugees from Aegean part of Macedonia **Rev:** Refugee mother with three children

Date	Mintage	F	VF	XF	Unc	BU
2000	1,500	—	—	—	—	200

KM# 11 10 DENARI
7.0000 g., 0.9160 Gold 0.2062 oz. AGW, 23 mm. **Subject:** Sts. Cyril and Methodus University **Obv:** Statue divides dates **Rev:** Macedonian Cyrillic alphabet

Date	Mintage	F	VF	XF	Unc	BU
1999	2,000	—	—	—	—	185

MINT SETS

KM#	Date	Mintage	Identification	Issue Price	Mkt Val
MS1	1993 (4)	—	KM1-4	—	7.50
MS2	1995 (3)	—	KM5a-7a	—	12.00

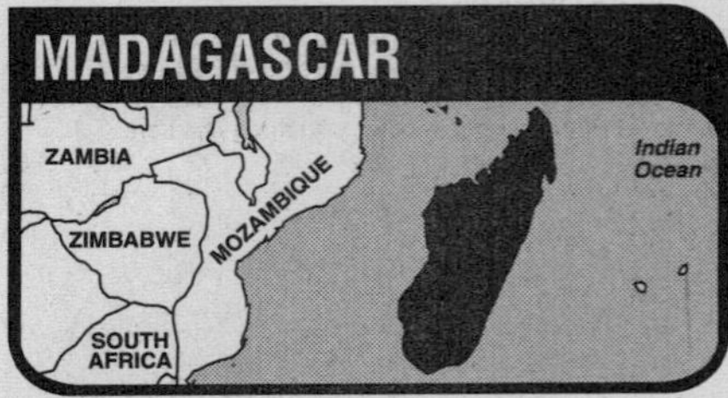

The Democratic Republic of Madagascar, an independent member of the French Community located in the Indian Ocean 250 miles (402 km.) off the southeast coast of Africa, has an area of 226,656 sq. mi. (587,040 sq. km.) and a population of 10 million. Capital: Antananarivo. The economy is primarily agricultural; large bauxite deposits are being developed. Coffee, vanilla, graphite, and rice are exported.

Successive waves of immigrants from southeast Asia, Africa, Arabia and India populated Madagascar beginning about 2,000 years ago. Diago Diaz, a Portuguese navigator, sighted the island of Madagascar on Aug. 10, 1500, when his ship became separated from an India-bound fleet. Attempts at settlement by the British during the reign of Charles I and by the French during the 17th and 18th centuries were of no avail, and the island became a refuge and supply base for Indian Ocean pirates. Despite considerable influence on the island, the British accepted the imposition of a French protectorate in 1886 in return for French recognition of Britain's sphere of influence in Zanzibar. Madagascar was made a French colony in 1896 after absolute control had been established by military force. Britain occupied the island after the fall of France, 1942, to prevent its seizure by the Japanese, returning it to the Free French in 1943. On Oct. 14, 1958, following a decade of intermittent but bitter warfare, Madagascar, as the Malagasy Republic, became an autonomous state within the French Community. On June 27, 1960, it became a sovereign, independent nation, though remaining nominally within the French Community. The Malagasy Republic was renamed the Democratic Republic of Madagascar in 1975.

MONETARY SYSTEM

100 Centimes = 1 Franc

MINT MARKS

(a) - Paris, privy marks only

SA - Pretoria

FRENCH COLONY

STANDARD COINAGE

KM# 1 50 CENTIMES

Bronze **Obv:** Rooster **Rev:** Cross of Lorraine

Date	Mintage	F	VF	XF	Unc	BU
1943SA	2,000,000	1.50	2.50	10.00	20.00	30.00

KM# 2 FRANC

Bronze **Obv:** Rooster **Rev:** Cross of Lorraine

Date	Mintage	F	VF	XF	Unc	BU
1943SA	5,000,000	3.00	6.00	22.00	65.00	95.00

KM# 3 FRANC

Aluminum **Obv:** Liberty bust left **Rev:** Conjoined ox heads flanked by sprigs, value within horns **Designer:** G.B.L. Bazor

Date	Mintage	F	VF	XF	Unc	BU
1948(a)	7,400,000	0.25	0.35	0.75	2.75	3.50
1958(a)	2,600,000	0.25	0.35	0.75	2.75	3.50

KM# 4 2 FRANCS

Aluminum **Obv:** Liberty bust left **Rev:** Conjoined ox heads flanked by sprigs, value within horns **Designer:** G.B.L. Bazor

Date	Mintage	F	VF	XF	Unc	BU
1948(a)	10,000,000	0.25	0.45	0.85	2.50	3.50

KM# 5 5 FRANCS

Aluminum **Obv:** Liberty bust left **Rev:** Conjoined ox heads flanked by sprigs, value within horns **Designer:** G.B.L. Bazor

Date	Mintage	F	VF	XF	Unc	BU
1953(a)	30,012,000	0.25	0.55	1.00	3.00	4.00

KM# 6 10 FRANCS

Aluminum-Bronze, 20 mm. **Obv:** Liberty bust left **Rev:** Value within horns flanked by cluster of sprigs with shaded area above value **Designer:** G.B.L. Bazor

Date	Mintage	F	VF	XF	Unc	BU
1953(a)	25,000,000	0.35	0.65	1.25	3.50	6.00

KM# 7 20 FRANCS

Aluminum-Bronze **Obv:** Liberty bust left **Rev:** Value within horns flanked by cluster of sprigs with shaded area above value **Designer:** G.B.L. Bazor

Date	Mintage	F	VF	XF	Unc	BU
1953(a)	15,000,000	0.75	1.50	3.00	6.50	9.00

TOKEN COINAGE

KM# Tn1 25 CENTIMES

Aluminum, 21 mm. **Issuer:** Societe des Mines d'Or de Andavakoera. **Obv:** Legend of issuer around value. **Rev:** Parakeet head left.

Date	Mintage	VG	F	VF	XF	Unc
ND(1920)	—	10.00	20.00	50.00	125	300

KM# Tn2 50 CENTIMES

Aluminum, 28 mm. **Issuer:** Societe des Mines d'Or de Andavakoera **Note:** Similar to KM#Tn1.

Date	Mintage	VG	F	VF	XF	Unc
ND(1920)	—	10.00	20.00	50.00	120	250

KM# Tn3 FRANC

Aluminum, 32 mm. **Issuer:** Societe des Mines d'Or de Andavakoera **Note:** Similar to KM#Tn1.

Date	Mintage	VG	F	VF	XF	Unc
ND(1920)	—	9.00	18.00	35.00	100	200

MALAGASY REPUBLIC

STANDARD COINAGE

KM# 8 FRANC

Stainless Steel **Obv:** Poinsettia **Rev:** Value within horns of ox head above sprigs

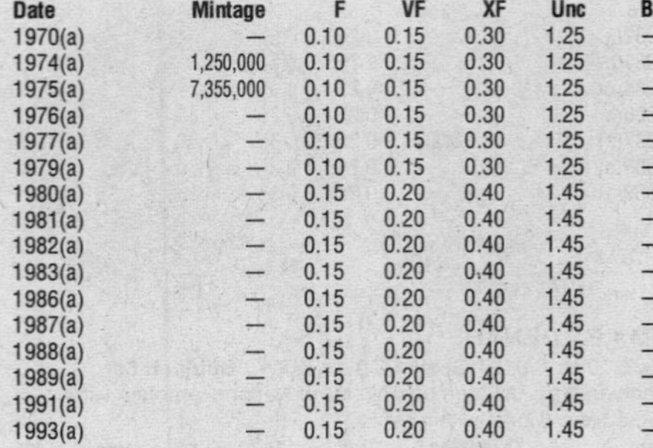

Date	Mintage	F	VF	XF	Unc	BU
1965(a)	1,170,000	0.10	0.15	0.30	1.25	—
1966(a)	—	0.10	0.15	0.30	1.25	—
1970(a)	—	0.10	0.15	0.30	1.25	—
1974(a)	1,250,000	0.10	0.15	0.30	1.25	—
1975(a)	7,355,000	0.10	0.15	0.30	1.25	—
1976(a)	—	0.10	0.15	0.30	1.25	—
1977(a)	—	0.10	0.15	0.30	1.25	—
1979(a)	—	0.10	0.15	0.30	1.25	—
1980(a)	—	0.15	0.20	0.40	1.45	—
1981(a)	—	0.15	0.20	0.40	1.45	—
1982(a)	—	0.15	0.20	0.40	1.45	—
1983(a)	—	0.15	0.20	0.40	1.45	—
1986(a)	—	0.15	0.20	0.40	1.45	—
1987(a)	—	0.15	0.20	0.40	1.45	—
1988(a)	—	0.15	0.20	0.40	1.45	—
1989(a)	—	0.15	0.20	0.40	1.45	—
1991(a)	—	0.15	0.20	0.40	1.45	—
1993(a)	—	0.15	0.20	0.40	1.45	—

KM# 9 2 FRANCS

Stainless Steel **Obv:** Poinsettia **Rev:** Value within horns of ox head above sprigs

Date	Mintage	F	VF	XF	Unc	BU
1965(a)	760,000	0.15	0.25	0.50	1.50	—
1970(a)	—	0.15	0.25	0.45	1.25	—
1974(a)	1,250,000	0.15	0.25	0.45	1.25	—
1975(a)	8,250,000	0.15	0.25	0.45	1.25	—
1976(a)	—	0.15	0.25	0.45	1.25	—
1977(a)	—	0.15	0.25	0.45	1.25	—
1979(a)	—	0.15	0.25	0.45	1.25	—
1980(a)	—	0.15	0.25	0.45	1.25	—
1981(a)	—	0.15	0.25	0.45	1.25	—
1982(a)	—	0.15	0.25	0.45	1.25	—
1983(a)	—	0.15	0.25	0.45	1.25	—
1984(a)	—	0.15	0.25	0.45	1.25	—
1986(a)	—	0.15	0.25	0.45	1.25	—
1987(a)	—	0.15	0.25	0.45	1.25	—
1988(a)	—	0.15	0.25	0.45	1.25	—
1989(a)	—	0.15	0.25	0.45	1.25	—

KM# 10 5 FRANCS (Ariary)

Stainless Steel **Obv:** Poinsettia **Rev:** Value within horns of ox head above sprigs

Date	Mintage	F	VF	XF	Unc	BU
1966(a)	—	0.15	0.25	0.60	1.75	—
1967(a)	—	0.15	0.25	0.60	1.75	—
1968(a)	7,500,000	0.15	0.25	0.60	1.75	—
1970(a)	—	0.15	0.25	0.60	1.75	—
1972(a)	19,100,000	0.15	0.25	0.60	1.75	—
1976(a)	—	0.15	0.25	0.60	1.75	—
1977(a)	—	0.15	0.25	0.60	1.75	—
1979(a)	—	0.15	0.25	0.60	1.75	—
1980(a)	—	0.20	0.30	0.65	1.85	—
1981(a)	—	0.20	0.30	0.65	1.85	—
1982(a)	—	0.20	0.30	0.65	1.85	—
1983(a)	—	0.20	0.30	0.65	1.85	—
1984(a)	—	0.20	0.30	0.65	1.85	—
1986(a)	—	0.20	0.30	0.65	1.85	—
1987(a)	—	0.20	0.30	0.65	1.85	—
1988(a)	—	0.20	0.30	0.65	1.85	—
1989(a)	—	0.20	0.30	0.65	1.85	—

KM# 11 10 FRANCS (2 Ariary)

Aluminum-Bronze **Series:** F.A.O. **Obv:** Vanilla plant **Rev:** Value within horns of ox head flanked by sprigs and marks

Date	Mintage	F	VF	XF	Unc	BU
1970(a)	7,000,000	0.20	0.30	0.70	2.00	—
1971(a)	10,000,000	0.20	0.30	0.70	2.00	—
1972(a)	5,050,000	0.20	0.30	0.70	2.00	—
1973(a)	3,000,000	0.20	0.30	0.70	2.00	—
1974(a)	—	0.20	0.30	0.70	2.00	—
1975(a)	—	0.20	0.30	0.70	2.00	—
1976(a)	9,500,000	0.20	0.30	0.70	2.00	—
1977(a)	—	0.20	0.30	0.70	2.00	—
1978(a)	—	0.20	0.30	0.70	2.00	—
1979(a)	—	0.20	0.30	0.70	2.00	—
1980(a)	—	0.25	0.35	0.80	2.25	—
1981(a)	—	0.25	0.35	0.80	2.25	—

Date	Mintage	F	VF	XF	Unc	BU
1982(a)	—	0.25	0.35	0.80	2.25	—
1983(a)	—	0.25	0.35	0.80	2.25	—
1984(a)	—	0.25	0.35	0.80	2.25	—
1986(a)	—	0.25	0.35	0.80	2.25	—
1987(a)	3,200,000	0.25	0.35	0.80	2.25	—
1988(a)	—	0.25	0.35	0.80	2.25	—
1989(a)	—	0.25	0.35	0.80	2.25	—

KM# 11a 10 FRANCS (2 Ariary)

Copper Plated Steel **Series:** F.A.O. **Obv:** Vanilla plant **Rev:** Value within horns of ox head flanked by sprigs (without other marks)

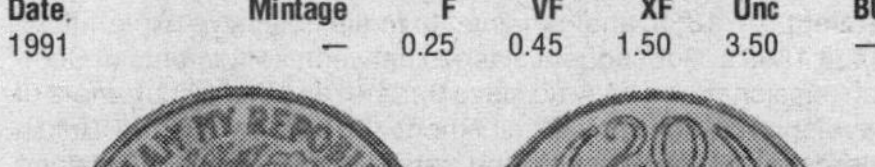

Date	Mintage	F	VF	XF	Unc	BU
1991	—	0.25	0.45	1.50	3.50	—

KM# 12 20 FRANCS (4 Ariary)

Aluminum-Bronze **Series:** F.A.O. **Obv:** Cotton plant **Rev:** Value within horns of ox head above sprigs and marks

Date	Mintage	F	VF	XF	Unc	BU
1970(a)	4,000,000	0.25	0.35	0.75	2.50	—
1971(a)	2,000,000	0.25	0.35	0.75	2.50	—
1972(a)	2,000,000	0.30	0.40	0.80	2.75	—
1973(a)	3,000,000	0.30	0.40	0.80	2.75	—
1974(a)	—	0.30	0.40	0.80	2.75	—
1975(a)	—	0.30	0.40	0.80	2.75	—
1976(a)	2,700,000	0.30	0.40	0.80	2.75	—
1977(a)	—	0.30	0.40	0.80	2.75	—
1978(a)	—	0.30	0.40	0.80	2.75	—
1979(a)	—	0.30	0.40	0.80	2.75	—
1980(a)	—	0.35	0.45	0.85	3.00	—
1981(a)	—	0.35	0.45	0.85	3.00	—
1982(a)	—	0.35	0.45	0.85	3.00	—
1983(a)	—	0.35	0.45	0.85	3.00	—
1984(a)	—	0.35	0.45	0.85	3.00	—
1986(a)	—	0.35	0.45	0.85	3.00	—
1987(a)	5,200,000	0.35	0.45	0.85	3.00	—
1988(a)	—	0.35	0.45	0.85	3.00	—
1989(a)	—	0.35	0.45	0.85	3.00	—

DEMOCRATIC REPUBLIC

NOTE: Reverse legends found on Malagasy Democratic Republic coinages.

A. - *Tanindrazana – Tolom – Piavotana – Fahafahana*; Fatherland – Revolution – Liberty

B. - *Tanindrazana – Fahafahana – Fahamarinana*; Fatherland – Liberty – Justice

C. - *Tanindrazana – Fahafahana – Fandrosoana*; Fatherland – Liberty - Progress

MONETARY SYSTEM

5 Francs = 1 Ariary
1 Ariary = 100 Iraimbilanja

STANDARD COINAGE

KM# 17 5 ARIARY

Copper Plated Steel **Obv:** Star above value within 3/4 wreath **Rev:** Rice plant within circle **Rev. Legend:** Motto A

Date	Mintage	F	VF	XF	Unc	BU
1992	—	0.65	1.25	2.25	4.00	—

KM# 13 10 ARIARY

Nickel **Series:** F.A.O. **Obv:** Star above value within 3/4 wreath **Rev:** Man cutting peat within circle **Rev. Legend:** Motto A

Date	Mintage	F	VF	XF	Unc	BU
1978	8,001,000	1.50	2.75	5.00	10.00	—

KM# 13a 10 ARIARY

9.0000 g., 0.9250 Silver .2676 oz. ASW **Obv:** Star above value within 3/4 wreath **Rev:** Man cutting peat within circle **Rev. Legend:** Motto A

Date	Mintage	F	VF	XF	Unc	BU
1978 Proof	3,800	Value: 20.00				

KM# 13b 10 ARIARY

Copper-Nickel **Obv:** Star above value within 3/4 wreath **Rev:** Man cutting peat within circle **Rev. Legend:** Motto A

Date	Mintage	F	VF	XF	Unc	BU
1983	—	2.00	4.00	8.00	15.00	—

KM# 16 10 ARIARY

10.0000 g., 0.9170 Gold .2947 oz. AGW **Subject:** World Wildlife Fund **Obv:** Star above value within 3/4 wreath **Rev:** Ibis

Date	Mintage	F	VF	XF	Unc	BU
1988 Proof	Est. 5,000	Value: 215				

KM# 18 10 ARIARY

Stainless Steel, 23.5 mm. **Obv:** Star above value within 3/4 wreath **Rev:** Man cutting peat within circle **Rev. Legend:** Motto A **Shape:** 7-sided

Date	Mintage	F	VF	XF	Unc	BU
1992	—	0.75	1.50	2.75	5.00	—

KM# 14 20 ARIARY

Nickel **Series:** F.A.O. **Obv:** Star above value within 3/4 wreath **Rev:** Farmer on tractor disking field **Rev. Legend:** Motto A

Date	Mintage	F	VF	XF	Unc	BU
1978	8,001,000	2.00	4.00	8.00	16.50	—

KM# 14a 20 ARIARY

12.0000 g., 0.9250 Silver .3569 oz. ASW **Obv:** Star above value within 3/4 wreath **Rev:** Farmer on tractor disking field **Rev. Legend:** Motto A

Date	Mintage	F	VF	XF	Unc	BU
1978 Proof	3,800	Value: 25.00				

KM# 14b 20 ARIARY

Copper-Nickel **Obv:** Star above value within 3/4 wreath **Rev:** Man on tractor disking field **Rev. Legend:** Motto A

Date	Mintage	F	VF	XF	Unc	BU
1983	—	2.50	4.50	9.00	17.50	—

KM# 15 20 ARIARY

19.4400 g., 0.9250 Silver .5782 oz. ASW **Subject:** World Wildlife Fund **Obv:** Star above value within 3/4 wreath **Rev:** Lemur

Date	Mintage	F	VF	XF	Unc	BU
1988 Proof	Est. 25,000	Value: 35.00				

KM# 19 20 ARIARY

Stainless Steel **Obv:** Star above value within 3/4 wreath **Rev:** Farmer on tractor disking field **Rev. Legend:** Motto A

Date	Mintage	F	VF	XF	Unc	BU
1992	—	1.25	2.50	4.50	10.00	—

KM# 26 20 ARIARY

19.4400 g., 0.9250 Silver .5782 oz. ASW **Series:** UNICEF **Obv:** Star above value within 3/4 wreath **Rev:** Child and ring-tailed lemur in tree

Date	Mintage	F	VF	XF	Unc	BU
1996 Proof	—	Value: 32.50				

KM# 20 50 ARIARY

Stainless Steel **Obv:** Star above value within 3/4 wreath **Rev:** Avenue of Baobabs **Rev. Legend:** Motto A

Date	Mintage	F	VF	XF	Unc	BU
1992	—	2.00	3.50	6.00	12.50	—

REPUBLIC OF MADAGASCAR

Madagasikara Republic

STANDARD COINAGE

KM# 21 5 FRANCS (Ariary)

Stainless Steel, 22 mm. **Obv:** Poinsettia **Rev:** Value within horns of ox head flanked by sprigs

Date	Mintage	F	VF	XF	Unc	BU
1996(a)	—	—	—	—	2.50	4.00

KM# 22 10 FRANCS (2 Ariary)

Copper Plated Steel, 21 mm. **Obv:** Vanilla plant **Rev:** Value within horns of ox head flanked by sprigs

Date	Mintage	F	VF	XF	Unc	BU
1996	—	—	—	—	3.00	5.00

KM# 23 5 ARIARY

Copper Plated Steel, 24 mm. **Obv:** Star above value within 3/4 wreath **Rev:** Rice plant within circle **Rev. Legend:** Motto B

Date	Mintage	F	VF	XF	Unc	BU
1994	—	—	—	—	2.50	4.00
1996	—	—	—	—	2.50	4.00

KM# 27 10 ARIARY
Stainless Steel **Issuer:** F.A.O. **Obv:** Star above value within 3/4 wreath **Rev:** Man cutting peat **Rev. Legend:** Motto C **Edge:** Plain **Shape:** 7-sided

Date	Mintage	F	VF	XF	Unc	BU
1999	—	—	—	—	4.50	6.50

KM# 24.1 20 ARIARY
Nickel Clad Steel, 28 mm. **Issuer:** F.A.O. **Obv:** Star above value within 3/4 wreath **Rev:** Farmer on tractor disking field **Rev. Legend:** Motto B

Date	Mintage	F	VF	XF	Unc	BU
1994	—	—	—	—	6.50	9.00

KM# 24.2 20 ARIARY
Nickel Clad Steel, 28 mm. **Obv:** Star above value within 3/4 wreath **Rev:** Man on tractor disking field **Rev. Legend:** Motto C

Date	Mintage	F	VF	XF	Unc	BU
1999	—	—	—	—	6.50	9.00

KM# 25 50 ARIARY
Stainless Steel, 30.5 mm. **Obv:** Star above value within 3/4 wreath **Rev:** Avenue of Baobabs **Rev. Legend:** Motto B **Shape:** 11-sided

Date	Mintage	F	VF	XF	Unc	BU
1994	—	—	—	—	8.00	12.00
1996	—	—	—	—	8.00	12.00

ESSAIS

Standard metals unless otherwise noted

KM#	Date	Mintage	Identification	Issue Price	Mkt Val
E1	1948(a)	2,000	Franc. Copper-Nickel. KM3.	—	25.00
E2	1948	2,000	2 Francs. Copper-Nickel. KM4.	—	25.00
E3	1953(a)	1,200	5 Francs. Aluminum. KM5.	—	20.00
E4	1953(a)	1,200	10 Francs. Aluminum-Bronze. KM6.	—	20.00
E5	1953(a)	1,200	20 Francs. Aluminum-Bronze. KM7.	—	20.00
E6	1965(a)	—	Franc. Stainless Steel. KM8.	—	12.00
E7	1965(a)	—	2 Francs. Stainless Steel. KM9.	—	12.00
E8	1966(a)	—	5 Francs. Stainless Steel. KM10.	—	12.00
E9	1970(a)	—	10 Francs. Aluminum-Bronze. KM11.	—	12.00
E10	1970(a)	—	20 Francs. Aluminum-Bronze. KM12.	—	12.00

PIEFORTS WITH ESSAI

Double thickness; Standard metals unless otherwise noted

KM#	Date	Mintage	Identification	Issue Price	Mkt Val
PE1	1948(a)	104	Franc. Aluminum. KM3.	—	75.00
PE2	1948(a)	104	2 Francs. Aluminum. KM4.	—	85.00
PE3	1953(a)	104	5 Francs. Aluminum. KM5.	—	60.00
PE4	1953(a)	104	10 Francs. Aluminum-Bronze. KM6.	—	65.00
PE5	1953(a)	104	20 Francs. KM7.	—	70.00

"FDC" SETS

KM#	Date	Mintage	Identification	Issue Price	Mkt Val
SS1	1970 (5)	1,500	KM8-12	2.75	11.50

PROOF SETS

KM#	Date	Mintage	Identification	Issue Price	Mkt Val
PS1	1978 (2)	3,800	KM#13a, 14a	38.00	45.00

MADEIRA ISLANDS

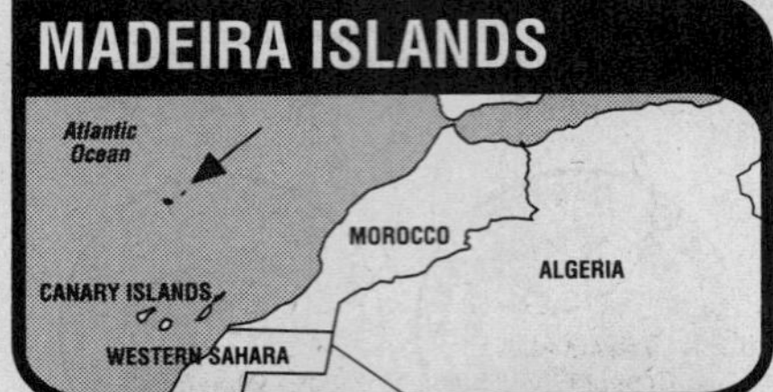

The Madeira Islands, which belong to Portugal, are located 360 miles (492 km.) off the northwest coast of Africa. They have an area of 307 sq. mi. (795 sq. km.). The group consists of two inhabited islands named Madeira and Porto Santo and two groups of uninhabited rocks named Desertas and Selvagens. Capital: Funchal. The two staple products are wine and sugar. Bananas and pineapples are also produced for export.

Although the evidence is insufficient, it is thought that the Phoenicians visited Madeira at an early period. It is also probable that the entire archipelago was explored by Genoese adventurers; an Italian map dated 1351 shows the Madeira Islands quite clearly. The Portuguese navigator Goncalvez Zarco first sighted Porto Santo in 1418, having been driven there by a storm while he was exploring the coast of West Africa. Madeira itself was discovered in 1420. The islands were uninhabited when visited by Zarco, but soon after 1418 Madeira was quickly colonized by Prince Henry the Navigator, aided by the knights of the Order of Christ. British troops occupied the islands in 1801, and again in 1807-14.

RULERS
Portuguese

PORTUGUESE COLONY

MODERN COINAGE

KM# 4 25 ESCUDOS
Copper-Nickel, 28.5 mm. **Subject:** Autonomy of Madeira **Obv:** Shields above value **Rev:** Head facing

Date	Mintage	F	VF	XF	Unc	BU
1981	750,000	—	—	—	6.00	8.00

KM# 4a 25 ESCUDOS
11.0000 g., 0.9250 Silver .3272 oz. ASW, 28.5 mm. **Subject:** Autonomy of Madeira **Obv:** Shields above value **Rev:** Head facing

Date	Mintage	F	VF	XF	Unc	BU
1981 Proof	20,000	Value: 17.50				

KM# 5 100 ESCUDOS
Copper-Nickel, 33.8 mm. **Subject:** Autonomy of Madeira **Obv:** Shields above value **Rev:** Head facing

Date	Mintage	F	VF	XF	Unc	BU
1981	250,000	—	—	—	12.00	15.00

KM# 5a 100 ESCUDOS
16.5000 g., 0.9250 Silver .4908 oz. ASW, 33.8 mm. **Subject:** Autonomy of Madeira **Obv:** Shields above value **Rev:** Head facing

Date	Mintage	F	VF	XF	Unc	BU
1981 Proof	20,000	Value: 25.00				

PROVAS

KM#	Date	Mintage	Identification	Mkt Val
Pr1	1981	—	25 Escudos. Copper-Nickel. KM4.	30.00
Pr2	1981	—	100 Escudos. Copper-Nickel. KM5.	40.00

PROOF SETS

KM#	Date	Mintage	Identification	Issue Price	Mkt Val
PS1	1981 (2)	20,000	KM4a-5a	42.00	42.50

MALAWI

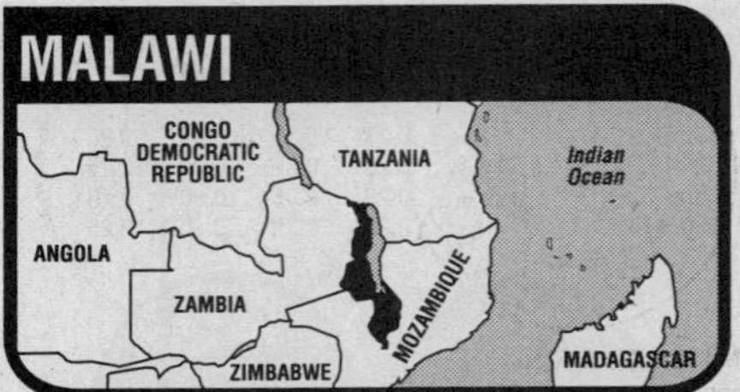

The Republic of Malawi (formerly Nyasaland), located in southeastern Africa to the west of Lake Malawi (Nyasa), has an area of 45,745 sq. mi. (118,480 sq. km.) and a population of 7 million. Capital: Lilongwe. The economy is predominantly agricultural. Tobacco, tea, peanuts and cotton are exported.

Although the Portuguese were the first Europeans to reach the Malawi area, the first meaningful contact was made by missionary-explorer Dr. David Livingstone. He arrived at Lake Malawi on Sept. 16, 1859, and remained to make extensive explorations in the 1860's. Subsequent clashes between settlements of Scottish missionaries and Arab slave traders, and the procurement of development rights by Cecil Rhodes, 1884, stimulated British interest and brought about the establishment of the Nyasaland protectorate in 1891. In 1953 Nyasaland reluctantly joined the Federation of Rhodesia and Nyasaland and, after prolonged protest, was granted self-government within the federation. Nyasaland became the independent nation of Malawi on July 6, 1964, and became a republic two years later. Malawi is a member of the Commonwealth of Nations. The president is the Chief of State and Head of Government.

NOTE: For earlier coinage see Rhodesia and Nyasaland.

MONETARY SYSTEM
12 Pence = 1 Shilling
2 Shillings = 1 Florin
5 Shillings = 1 Crown
20 Shillings = 1 Pound

REPUBLIC

STERLING COINAGE

KM# 6 PENNY
Bronze **Obv:** Malawi written above date and value **Rev:** Written and numeral value above designs

Date	Mintage	F	VF	XF	Unc	BU
1967	6,000,000	0.35	0.65	1.25	2.50	—
1968	3,600,000	3.00	6.00	12.00	25.00	—

KM# 1 6 PENCE
Copper-Nickel-Zinc **Obv:** Head right **Rev:** Rooster **Designer:** Paul Vinze

Date	Mintage	F	VF	XF	Unc	BU
1964	14,800,000	0.25	0.50	1.00	2.50	4.00
1964 Proof	10,000	Value: 1.50				
1967	6,000,000	0.50	1.00	2.50	5.00	6.50

KM# 2 SHILLING
Copper-Nickel-Zinc, 23.5 mm. **Obv:** Head right **Rev:** Bundled corncobs **Designer:** Paul Vinze

Date	Mintage	F	VF	XF	Unc	BU
1964	11,900,000	0.35	0.65	1.25	2.50	3.50
1964 Proof	10,000	Value: 1.50				
1968	3,000,000	0.75	1.50	3.00	5.50	7.00

KM# 3 FLORIN
Copper-Nickel-Zinc, 28 mm. **Obv:** Head right **Rev:** Elephants **Designer:** Paul Vinze

Date	Mintage	F	VF	XF	Unc	BU
1964	6,500,000	0.75	1.50	3.00	6.00	—
1964 Proof	10,000	Value: 4.50				

KM# 4 1/2 CROWN
Copper-Nickel-Zinc **Obv:** Head right **Rev:** Arms with supporters **Designer:** Paul Vinze

Date	Mintage	F	VF	XF	Unc	BU
1964	6,400,000	1.00	2.00	4.00	6.00	—
1964 Proof	10,000	Value: 4.50				

KM# 5 CROWN
Nickel-Brass **Subject:** Day of the Republic - July 6, 1966 **Obv:** Head right **Rev:** Arms with supporters **Designer:** Paul Vinze

Date	Mintage	F	VF	XF	Unc	BU
1966 Proof	20,000	Value: 7.50				

DECIMAL COINAGE

100 Tambala = 1 Kwacha

KM# 7.1 TAMBALA
Bronze, 17 mm. **Obv:** Head right **Rev:** Rooster **Designer:** Paul Vinze

Date	Mintage	F	VF	XF	Unc	BU
1971	15,000,000	0.15	0.20	0.40	0.75	1.50
1971 Proof	4,000	Value: 1.00				
1973	5,000,000	0.15	0.20	0.40	0.75	1.50
1974	12,500,000	0.15	0.20	0.40	0.75	1.50

KM# 7.2 TAMBALA
Bronze, 17 mm. **Obv:** Head right with accent mark above "W" in MALAWI **Rev:** Rooster

Date	Mintage	F	VF	XF	Unc	BU
1975	10,000,000	0.15	0.20	0.40	0.75	1.50
1977	10,000,000	0.15	0.20	0.40	0.75	1.50
1979	15,000,000	0.15	0.20	0.40	0.75	1.50
1982	15,000,000	0.15	0.20	0.40	0.75	1.50

KM# 7.2a TAMBALA
Copper Plated Steel **Obv:** Head right **Rev:** Rooster divides value and date

Date	Mintage	F	VF	XF	Unc	BU
1984	201,000	0.20	0.30	0.50	0.80	1.50
1985 Proof	10,000	Value: 3.00				
1987	—	0.20	0.30	0.50	0.80	1.50
1989	—	0.20	0.30	0.50	0.80	1.50
1991	—	0.20	0.30	0.50	0.80	1.50
1994	—	0.20	0.30	0.50	0.80	1.50

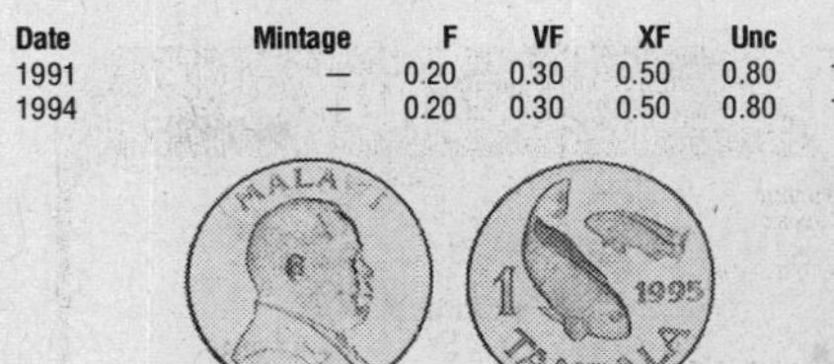

KM# 24 TAMBALA
1.8000 g., Copper Plated Steel, 17.2 mm. **Obv:** Bust right **Rev:** Two Talapia fish

Date	Mintage	F	VF	XF	Unc	BU
1995	—	—	—	—	1.00	1.50

KM# 33 TAMBALA
Bronze, 17.3 mm. **Obv:** Arms with supporters **Rev:** Two Talapia fish **Edge:** Plain

Date	Mintage	F	VF	XF	Unc	BU
1995	—	—	—	—	1.00	1.50

KM# 8.1 2 TAMBALA
Bronze **Obv:** Head right **Rev:** Paradise whydah bird divides date and value **Designer:** Paul Vinze

Date	Mintage	F	VF	XF	Unc	BU
1971	10,000,000	0.25	0.40	0.75	1.50	—
1971 Proof	4,000	Value: 1.75				
1973	5,000,000	0.25	0.40	0.75	1.50	—
1974	5,000,000	0.25	0.40	0.75	1.50	—

KM# 8.2 2 TAMBALA
Bronze **Obv:** Head right with accent mark above "W" in MALAWI **Rev:** Paradise whydah bird divides date and value

Date	Mintage	F	VF	XF	Unc	BU
1975	5,000,000	0.25	0.40	0.75	1.50	—
1977	5,000,000	0.25	0.40	0.75	1.50	—
1979	7,637,000	0.25	0.40	0.75	1.50	—
1982	15,000,000	0.25	0.40	0.75	1.50	—

KM# 8.2a 2 TAMBALA
Copper Plated Steel **Obv:** Head right **Rev:** Paradise whydah bird divides date and value

Date	Mintage	F	VF	XF	Unc	BU
1984	150,000	0.30	0.50	0.85	2.00	—
1985 Proof	10,000	Value: 4.00				
1987	—	0.30	0.50	0.85	2.00	—
1989	—	0.30	0.50	0.85	2.00	—
1991	—	0.30	0.50	0.85	1.75	—
1994	—	0.30	0.50	0.85	1.75	—

KM# 25 2 TAMBALA
3.5000 g., Copper Plated Steel, 20.3 mm. **Obv:** Bust right **Rev:** Paradise whydah bird divides date and value

Date	Mintage	F	VF	XF	Unc	BU
1995	—	—	—	—	1.00	1.50

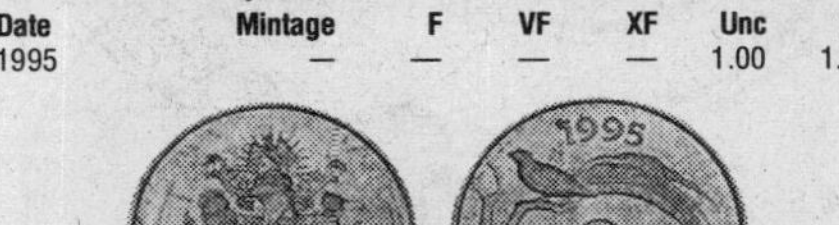

KM# 34 2 TAMBALA
3.5000 g., Bronze, 20.3 mm. **Obv:** Arms with supporters **Rev:** Paradise whydah bird divides date and value **Edge:** Plain

Date	Mintage	F	VF	XF	Unc	BU
1995	—	—	—	—	1.00	1.50

KM# 9.1 5 TAMBALA
Copper-Nickel **Obv:** Head right **Rev:** Purple heron and value **Designer:** Paul Vinze

Date	Mintage	F	VF	XF	Unc	BU
1971	7,000,000	0.25	0.45	0.85	1.75	—
1971 Proof	4,000	Value: 2.00				

KM# 9.2 5 TAMBALA
Copper-Nickel **Obv:** Head right with accent mark above "W" in MALAWI **Rev:** Purple heron and value

Date	Mintage	F	VF	XF	Unc	BU
1985 Proof	10,000	Value: 5.00				

KM# 9.2a 5 TAMBALA
2.8000 g., Nickel Clad Steel, 19.35 mm. **Obv:** Head right **Rev:** Purple heron and value

Date	Mintage	F	VF	XF	Unc	BU
1989	—	0.30	0.50	0.85	2.00	3.00
1994	—	0.30	0.50	0.85	2.00	3.00

KM# 26 5 TAMBALA
Nickel Plated Steel, 19.35 mm. **Obv:** Bust right **Rev:** Purple heron and value

Date	Mintage	F	VF	XF	Unc	BU
1995	—	—	—	—	1.50	3.00

KM# 32 5 TAMBALA
Nickel Plated Steel, 19.35 mm. **Obv:** Arms with supporters **Rev:** Purple heron and value

Date	Mintage	F	VF	XF	Unc	BU
1995	—	—	—	—	2.50	3.00

KM# 10.1 10 TAMBALA
Copper-Nickel, 23.6 mm. **Obv:** Head right **Rev:** Bundled corncob divides date and value

Date	Mintage	F	VF	XF	Unc	BU
1971	4,000,000	0.30	0.50	1.00	2.25	3.00
1971 Proof	4,000	Value: 2.50				

KM# 10.2 10 TAMBALA
Copper-Nickel, 23.6 mm. **Obv:** Head right **Rev:** Bundled corncobs divide date and value

Date	Mintage	F	VF	XF	Unc	BU
1985 Proof	10,000	Value: 6.00				
1989	—	0.40	0.80	1.50	2.75	3.50

KM# 10.2a 10 TAMBALA
Nickel Clad Steel, 23.6 mm. **Obv:** Head right **Rev:** Bundled cobs of corn divide value and date

Date	Mintage	F	VF	XF	Unc	BU
1989	—	0.40	0.80	1.50	2.75	—

KM# 27 10 TAMBALA
Nickel Plated Steel, 23.6 mm. **Obv:** Bust right **Rev:** Bundled corncobs divide date and value

Date	Mintage	F	VF	XF	Unc	BU
1995	—	—	—	—	2.25	—

KM# 11.1 20 TAMBALA
Copper-Nickel, 26.5 mm. **Obv:** Head right **Rev:** Elephants
Designer: Paul Vinze

Date	Mintage	F	VF	XF	Unc	BU
1971	3,000,000	0.75	1.50	2.50	4.00	—
1971 Proof	4,000	Value: 5.00				

KM# 11.2 20 TAMBALA
Copper-Nickel, 26.5 mm. **Obv:** Head right with accent mark above "W" in MALAWI **Rev:** Elephants

Date	Mintage	F	VF	XF	Unc	BU
1985 Proof	10,000	Value: 7.00				

KM# 11.2a 20 TAMBALA
Nickel Clad Steel, 26.5 mm. **Obv:** Head right **Rev:** Elephants

Date	Mintage	F	VF	XF	Unc	BU
1989	—	0.60	1.20	2.25	3.75	—
1994	—	0.60	1.20	2.25	3.75	—

KM# 29 20 TAMBALA
Nickel Clad Steel, 26.5 mm. **Obv:** Bust right **Rev:** Elephants

Date	Mintage	F	VF	XF	Unc	BU
1996	—	—	—	—	3.75	4.50

KM# 19 50 TAMBALA
Copper-Nickel-Zinc **Obv:** Head right **Rev:** Arms with supporters
Designer: Paul Vinze **Note:** The 1989 date for this coin does not exist.

Date	Mintage	F	VF	XF	Unc	BU
1986	—	2.00	3.00	5.00	10.00	—
1994	—	2.00	3.00	5.00	10.00	—

KM# 30 50 TAMBALA
4.4000 g., Brass Plated Steel, 22 mm. **Obv:** Bust right
Rev: Arms with supporters **Shape:** 7-sided

Date	Mintage	F	VF	XF	Unc	BU
1996	—	—	—	—	4.50	5.00

KM# 12 KWACHA
Copper-Nickel **Subject:** Decimalization of coinage **Obv:** Head right **Rev:** Arms with supporters **Edge Lettering:** DECIMAL CURRENCY INTRODUCED FEBRUARY 15TH, 1971
Designer: Paul Vinze

Date	Mintage	F	VF	XF	Unc	BU
1971	20,000	1.00	2.00	3.50	6.00	—
1971 Proof	4,000	Value: 6.50				

KM# 20 KWACHA
8.8000 g., Nickel-Brass, 26 mm. **Obv:** Head right **Rev:** Rooster

Date	Mintage	F	VF	XF	Unc	BU
1992	—	1.00	2.00	3.00	5.50	7.00

KM# 28 KWACHA
Brass Plated Steel, 26 mm. **Obv:** Bust right **Rev:** Falcon with talons out

Date	Mintage	F	VF	XF	Unc	BU
1996	—	—	—	—	7.00	10.00

KM# 15 5 KWACHA
28.2800 g., 0.9250 Silver .841 oz. ASW **Subject:** Conservation
Obv: Head right **Rev:** Zebras running right

Date	Mintage	F	VF	XF	Unc	BU
1978	4,048	—	—	—	25.00	—
1978 Proof	3,622	Value: 32.50				

KM# 23 5 KWACHA
Copper-Nickel **Subject:** United Nations 50th Anniversary
Obv: Bust right **Rev:** Child reading and UN logo

Date	Mintage	F	VF	XF	Unc	BU
ND(1995)	—	—	—	—	8.50	10.00

KM# 23a 5 KWACHA
28.2800 g., 0.9250 Silver .8410 oz. ASW **Subject:** United Nations 50th Anniversary **Obv:** Bust right **Rev:** Child reading and UN logo

Date	Mintage	F	VF	XF	Unc	BU
ND(1995) Proof	—	Value: 32.50				

KM# 40 5 KWACHA
20.3000 g., 0.9250 Silver 0.6037 oz. ASW, 34 mm. **Obv:** Arms with supporters **Rev:** Elephant **Edge:** Reeded

Date	Mintage	F	VF	XF	Unc	BU
1997 Proof	—	Value: 27.50				

KM# 41 5 KWACHA
28.5000 g., 0.9250 Silver 0.8476 oz. ASW, 38.5 mm.
Subject: Queen's Golden Wedding Anniversary **Obv:** Arms with supporters **Rev:** Child giving flowers to Queen above gold plated arms with supporters **Edge:** Reeded

Date	Mintage	F	VF	XF	Unc	BU
1997 Proof	—	Value: 45.00				

KM# 13 10 KWACHA
28.2800 g., 0.9250 Silver .8411 oz. ASW **Subject:** 10th Anniversary of Independence **Obv:** Head right **Rev:** Arms with supporters above value within chain links

Date	Mintage	F	VF	XF	Unc	BU
1974	7,556	—	—	—	13.50	15.00
1974 Proof	4,937	Value: 18.50				

KM# 14 10 KWACHA

28.2800 g., 0.9250 Silver .8411 oz. ASW **Subject:** 10th Anniversary of the Reserve Bank **Obv:** Head right **Rev:** Eagle with wings spread above lined design and value

Date	Mintage	F	VF	XF	Unc	BU
ND(1975)	6,870	—	—	—	13.50	15.00
ND(1975) Proof	Inc. above	Value: 18.50				

KM# 14a 10 KWACHA

0.9000 Gold **Subject:** 10th Anniversary of the Reserve Bank **Obv:** Head right **Rev:** Eagle with wings spread above lined design and value

Date	Mintage	F	VF	XF	Unc	BU
ND(1975)	—	—	—	—	1,250	—

KM# 16 10 KWACHA

35.0000 g., 0.9250 Silver 1.0409 oz. ASW **Series:** Conservation **Obv:** Head right **Rev:** Sable antelope

Date	Mintage	F	VF	XF	Unc	BU
1978	4,009	—	—	—	20.00	25.00
1978 Proof	3,416	Value: 35.00				

KM# 18 10 KWACHA

28.2800 g., 0.9250 Silver .8410 oz. ASW **Subject:** 20th Anniversary - Reserve Bank **Obv:** Head right **Rev:** Eagle with wings spread above lined design and value

Date	Mintage	F	VF	XF	Unc	BU
ND(1985) Proof	4,000	Value: 22.50				

KM# 18a 10 KWACHA

47.5400 g., 0.9170 Gold 1.4011 oz. AGW **Subject:** 20th Anniversary - Reserve Bank **Obv:** Head right **Rev:** Eagle with wings spread above lined design and value

Date	Mintage	F	VF	XF	Unc	BU
ND(1985) Proof	50	Value: 1,600				

KM# 21 10 KWACHA

28.2800 g., 0.9250 Silver .8411 oz. ASW **Series:** Save the Children **Subject:** Fishing **Obv:** Head right **Rev:** Children carrying fish, fishermen and sailboat in background **Rev. Designer:** Willem Vis

Date	Mintage	F	VF	XF	Unc	BU
1992 Proof	20,000	Value: 35.00				

KM# 38 10 KWACHA

20.0000 g., 0.9250 Silver 0.5948 oz. ASW, 34 mm. **Subject:** Olympics **Obv:** Arms with supporters **Rev:** Two runners **Edge:** Reeded

Date	Mintage	F	VF	XF	Unc	BU
1999 Proof	—	Value: 35.00				

KM# 22 20 KWACHA

10.0000 g., 0.9170 Gold .2948 oz. AGW **Series:** Save the Children **Subject:** Mother and children **Obv:** Head right **Rev:** Mother and child facing left, buildings and athletic players in background **Rev. Designer:** Willem Vis

Date	Mintage	F	VF	XF	Unc	BU
1992 Proof	Est. 3,000	Value: 230				

KM# 35 20 KWACHA

31.4000 g., 0.9250 Silver .9338 oz. ASW, 38.6 mm. **Series:** Endangered Wildlife **Subject:** "The Romans" **Obv:** Arms with supporters **Rev:** Female elephant with two calves in water **Edge:** Reeded

Date	Mintage	F	VF	XF	Unc	BU
1996 Proof	—	Value: 45.00				

KM# 36 20 KWACHA

31.5500 g., 0.9250 Silver 0.9383 oz. ASW, 38.6 mm. **Subject:** Queen Mother **Obv:** Arms with supporters **Rev:** Queen Mother and two girl scouts within beaded circle **Edge:** Reeded

Date	Mintage	F	VF	XF	Unc	BU
1997 Proof	—	Value: 45.00				

KM# 37 20 KWACHA

31.4300 g., 0.9250 Silver 0.9347 oz. ASW, 38.5 mm. **Subject:** British Queen Mother **Obv:** Arms with supporters **Rev:** Edward VIII making his abdication speech **Edge:** Reeded

Date	Mintage	F	VF	XF	Unc	BU
1998 Proof	—	Value: 50.00				

KM# 31 20 KWACHA

31.5300 g., 0.9250 Silver .9377 oz. ASW **Subject:** Millennium **Obv:** Head right **Rev:** Year 2000 flanked by seated figures below trees all below ears of corn within vines **Shape:** Hexagon

Date	Mintage	F	VF	XF	Unc	BU
1999 Proof	—	Value: 40.00				

KM# 17 250 KWACHA

33.4370 g., 0.9000 Gold .9676 oz. AGW **Series:** Conservation **Subject:** Nyala **Obv:** Head right **Rev:** Nyala (deer)

Date	Mintage	F	VF	XF	Unc	BU
1978	566	—	—	—	700	750
1978 Proof	208	Value: 925				

MINT SETS

KM#	Date	Mintage	Identification	Issue Price	Mkt Val
MS1	1971 (6)	10,000	KM7.1-11.1, 12	3.30	16.50
MS2	1978 (2)	—	KM15, 16	—	40.00

PROOF SETS

KM#	Date	Mintage	Identification	Issue Price	Mkt Val
PS1	1964 (4)	10,000	KM1-4	10.00	10.00
PS2	1971 (6)	4,000	KM7.1-11.1, 12	8.70	18.50
PS3	1978 (2)	—	KM15, 16	—	70.00
PS4	1985 (5)	10,000	KM7.2a-8.2a, 9.2-11.2	30.00	25.00

KELANTAN

A state in northern Malaysia, colonized by the Javanese in 1300's. It was subject to Thailand from 1780 to 1909.

TITLE

كلنتن

Khalifa(t) Al-Mu'minin

MINT

خليفة المؤمنين

Kelantan

SULTAN
Muhammed IV, 1902-1919

SULTANATE

STANDARD COINAGE

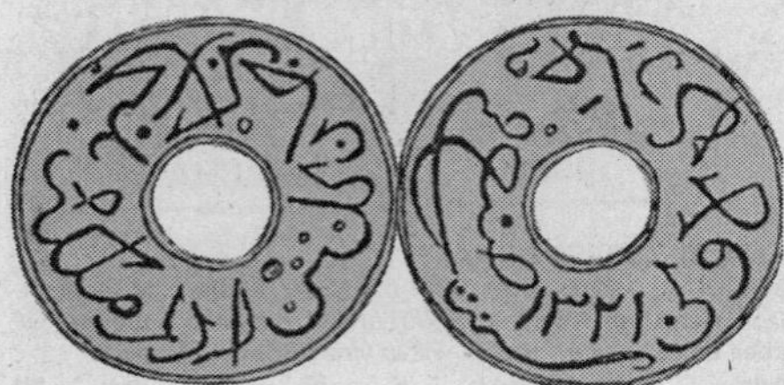

KM# 12 PITIS
Tin, 24-29 mm. **Ruler:** Muhammed IV **Obv:** Arabic legend **Obv. Legend:** Belanjaan Negri Kelantan Adama Mulkahu **Rev:** Arabic legend **Rev. Legend:** Duriba Fi Dhul Hijja Sanat 1321

Date	Mintage	VG	F	VF	XF	Unc
AH1321 (1903)	—	8.00	12.00	20.00	30.00	—

KM# 15 PITIS
Tin **Ruler:** Muhammed IV **Obv:** Arabic legend **Obv. Legend:** Belanjaan Kerajaan Kelan Tan **Rev:** Arabic legend **Rev. Legend:** Duriba Fi Dhul Hijja Sanat 1321

Date	Mintage	VG	F	VF	XF	Unc
AH1321 (1903)	—	2.00	3.00	5.00	9.00	—

KM# 18 KEPING
Tin **Ruler:** Muhammed IV **Obv:** Arabic legend **Obv. Legend:** Negri Kelantan Satu Keping **Rev:** Uninscribed, but obverse legend shows through in negative form

Date	Mintage	VG	F	VF	XF	Unc
AH1323 (1905)	—	15.00	25.00	40.00	60.00	—

KM# 20 10 KEPINGS
Tin **Ruler:** Muhammed IV **Obv:** Arabic legend **Obv. Legend:** Belanjaan Kerajaan Kelantin Sepuloh Keping **Rev:** Border of diamonds around Arabic legend **Rev. Legend:** Sunia Fi Dhul Hijja Sanat 1321

Date	Mintage	VG	F	VF	XF	Unc
AH1321 (1903)	—	6.00	12.00	25.00	40.00	—

TRENGGANU

A state in eastern Malaysia on the shore of the south China Sea. Area of dispute between Malacca and Thailand with the latter emerging with possession. Trengganu became a British dependency in 1909.

TITLE

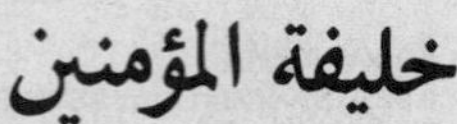

Khalifa(t) al-Mu'minin

MINT

ترغكانو

Trengganu

SULTANS
Zainal Abidin III, 1881-1918
Muhammed, 1918-1920
Sulaiman, 1920-1942

SULTANATE

STANDARD COINAGE

KM# 17 1/4 CENT
Tin **Ruler:** Zainal Abidin III **Obv:** Legend within circle **Rev:** Value within circle **Note:** Similar to 1/2 Cent, KM#16.

Date	Mintage	F	VF	XF	Unc	BU
AH1325 (1907) Rare	—	—	—	—	—	—

KM# 16 1/2 CENT
Tin, 22 mm. **Ruler:** Zainal Abidin III **Obv:** Legend within circle **Rev:** Value within circle and wreath **Note:** Recast.

Date	Mintage	VG	F	VF	XF	Unc
AH1322 (1904)	—	3.00	6.00	10.00	20.00	—

KM# 18 1/2 CENT
Tin, 22 mm. **Ruler:** Zainal Abidin III **Obv:** Legend within circle flanked by stars **Rev:** Value within circle and wreath **Note:** Recast. Originals are rare.

Date	Mintage	VG	F	VF	XF	Unc
AH1325 (1907)	—	3.00	6.00	10.00	20.00	—

KM# 19 CENT
Tin, 29 mm. **Ruler:** Zainal Abidin III **Obv:** Legend within beaded circle flanked by stars **Rev:** Value within beaded circle and wreath

Date	Mintage	VG	F	VF	XF	Unc
AH1325 (1907)	—	5.00	9.00	16.00	35.00	—

KM# 20 CENT
Tin, 29 mm. **Ruler:** Zainal Abidin III **Obv:** Legend within beaded circle flanked by stars **Rev:** Value flanked by stars within diamond shape within beaded circle and wreath **Note:** Although dated AH1325 (1907), this coin was actually struck in 1920 under Sultan Sulaiman. Authorized mintage was 1 million. Beware of thin lead counterfeits.

Date	Mintage	VG	F	VF	XF	Unc
AH1325 (1907)	—	5.00	9.00	16.00	35.00	—

BRITISH COLONY

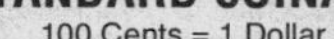

STANDARD COINAGE

100 Cents = 1 Dollar

KM# 1 1/2 CENT
Bronze **Obv:** Crowned head of King George VI left **Obv. Designer:** Percy Metcalfe **Rev:** Value within beaded circle **Shape:** 4-sided **Note:** 18 mm x 18 mm.

Date	Mintage	F	VF	XF	Unc	BU
1940	6,000,000	2.00	6.00	8.00	16.00	—
1940 Proof	—	Value: 300				

KM# 2 CENT
Bronze, 21 mm. **Obv:** Crowned head of King George VI left **Obv. Designer:** Percy Metcalfe **Rev:** Value within beaded circle **Shape:** Square

Date	Mintage	F	VF	XF	Unc	BU
1939	20,000,000	0.25	0.40	0.60	2.00	—
1939 Proof	—	Value: 300				
1940	23,600,000	0.25	0.40	0.60	2.00	—
1940 Proof	—	—	—	—	—	—
1941 I	33,620,000	0.75	1.50	10.00	28.00	—

KM# 6 CENT
Bronze, 20 mm. **Obv:** Crowned head of King George VI left **Obv. Designer:** Percy Metcalfe **Rev:** Value within beaded circle **Shape:** 4-sided **Note:** Reduced size.

Date	Mintage	F	VF	XF	Unc	BU
1943	50,000,000	0.10	0.20	0.45	1.50	—
1943 Proof	—	Value: 210				
1945	40,033,000	0.10	0.20	0.45	1.50	—

KM# 3 5 CENTS
1.3600 g., 0.7500 Silver .0327 oz. ASW **Obv:** Crowned head of King George VI left **Obv. Designer:** Percy Metcalfe **Rev:** Value within beaded circle

Date	Mintage	F	VF	XF	Unc	BU
1939	2,000,000	0.60	1.00	2.25	5.00	—
1939 Proof	—	Value: 450				
1941	4,000,000	0.50	0.65	1.20	2.50	—
1941 Proof	—	Value: 450				
1941 I	Inc. above	0.50	0.65	1.20	2.50	—

KM# 3a 5 CENTS
1.3600 g., 0.5000 Silver .0218 oz. ASW **Obv:** Crowned head of King George VI left **Obv. Designer:** Percy Metcalf **Rev:** Value within beaded circle

Date	Mintage	F	VF	XF	Unc	BU
1943	10,000,000	0.35	0.45	0.65	2.00	—
1943 Proof	—	Value: 450				
1945	8,800,000	0.35	0.45	0.65	2.00	—
1945 I	4,600,000	0.50	0.75	1.25	3.50	—

KM# 7 5 CENTS
Copper-Nickel **Obv:** Crowned head of King George VI left **Obv. Designer:** Percy Metcalfe **Rev:** Value within beaded circle

Date	Mintage	F	VF	XF	Unc	BU
1948	30,000,000	0.10	0.25	1.25	3.00	—
1948 Proof	—	Value: 450				
1950	40,000,000	0.10	0.25	1.25	3.00	—

KM# 4 10 CENTS
2.7100 g., 0.7500 Silver .0653 oz. ASW **Obv:** Crowned head of King George VI left **Obv. Designer:** Percy Metcalfe **Rev:** Value within beaded circle

Date	Mintage	F	VF	XF	Unc	BU
1939	10,000,000	1.00	1.25	1.50	3.00	—
1939 Proof	—	Value: 450				
1941	17,000,000	1.00	1.25	1.50	3.00	—
1941 Proof	—	Value: 450				
1941 I	—	—	—	2,300	2,700	—

KM# 4a 10 CENTS
2.7100 g., 0.5000 Silver .0435 oz. ASW **Obv:** Crowned head of King George VI left **Obv. Designer:** Percy Metcalf **Rev:** Value within beaded circle

Date	Mintage	F	VF	XF	Unc	BU
1943	5,000,000	0.85	1.20	1.50	3.00	—
1943 Proof	—	Value: 450				
1945	3,152,000	0.85	2.00	4.00	8.50	—
1945 I	—	—	—	2,300	2,700	—

KM# 8 10 CENTS
Copper-Nickel, 19.5 mm. **Obv:** Crowned head of George VI left **Obv. Designer:** Percy Metcalfe **Rev:** Value within beaded circle

Date	Mintage	F	VF	XF	Unc	BU
1948	23,885,000	0.15	0.30	1.40	4.50	—
1948 Proof	—	Value: 450				
1949	26,115,000	0.25	0.50	1.75	6.25	—
1950	65,000,000	0.15	0.30	1.25	4.50	—
1950 Proof	—	Value: 450				

KM# 5 20 CENTS
5.4300 g., 0.7500 Silver .1309 oz. ASW **Obv:** Crowned head of King George VI left **Obv. Designer:** Percy Metcalfe **Rev:** Value within beaded circle

Date	Mintage	F	VF	XF	Unc	BU
1939	8,000,000	2.00	2.50	3.50	6.00	—
1939 Proof	—	Value: 450				

KM# 5a 20 CENTS
5.4300 g., 0.5000 Silver .0872 oz. ASW **Obv:** Crowned head of King George VI left **Obv. Designer:** Percy Metcalf **Rev:** Value within beaded circle

Date	Mintage	F	VF	XF	Unc	BU
1943	5,000,000	1.45	1.75	2.75	5.50	—
1943 Proof	—	Value: 450				
1945	10,000,000	2.00	7.00	13.00	22.00	—
1945 I	—	—	—	2,300	2,700	—

KM# 9 20 CENTS
Copper-Nickel **Obv:** Crowned head of King George VI left **Obv. Designer:** Percy Metcalfe **Rev:** Value within beaded circle

Date	Mintage	F	VF	XF	Unc	BU
1948	40,000,000	0.35	0.75	1.75	6.00	—
1948 Proof	—	Value: 450				
1950	20,000,000	0.35	0.75	1.75	6.00	—
1950 Proof	—	Value: 450				

MALAYA & BRITISH BORNEO

South China Sea
PHILIPPINES
BRUNEI
MALAYSIA
MALAYSIA
SINGAPORE
Indian Ocean
INDONESIA

Malaya & British Borneo, a Currency Commission named the Board of Commissioners of Currency, Malaya and British Borneo, was initiated on Jan. 1, 1952, for the purpose of providing a common currency for use in Johore, Kelantan, Kedah, Perlis, Trengganu, Negri Sembilan, Pahang, Perak, Selangor, Penang, Malacca, Singapore, North Borneo, Sarawak and Brunei.

RULERS
British

MINT MARKS
KN - King's Norton, Birmingham
H - Heaton, Birmingham
No Mint mark - Royal Mint

MONETARY SYSTEM
100 Cents = 1 Dollar

BRITISH COLONY

STANDARD COINAGE

100 Cents = 1 Dollar

KM# 5 CENT
Bronze **Obv:** Crowned bust of Queen Elizabeth II right **Obv. Designer:** Cecil Thomas **Rev:** Value within beaded circle **Shape:** 4-sided

Date	Mintage	F	VF	XF	Unc	BU
1956	6,250,000	—	0.10	0.45	2.00	—
1956 Proof	—	Value: 300				
1957	12,500,000	—	0.10	0.45	2.00	—
1958	5,000,000	—	0.10	0.45	2.00	—
1958 Proof	—	Value: 300				
1961	10,000,000	—	0.10	0.45	2.00	—
1961 Proof	—	Value: 300				

KM# 6 CENT
Bronze, 18 mm. **Obv:** Value **Rev:** Crossed encased swords

Date	Mintage	F	VF	XF	Unc	BU
1962	45,000,000	—	—	0.35	1.00	—
1962 Proof	Est. 25	Value: 250				

KM# 1 5 CENTS
Copper-Nickel, 16 mm. **Obv:** Crowned bust of Queen Elizabeth II right **Obv. Designer:** Cecil Thomas **Rev:** Value within beaded circle

Date	Mintage	F	VF	XF	Unc	BU
1953	20,000,000	—	0.75	1.50	6.00	—
1953 Proof	—	Value: 300				
1957	10,000,000	—	0.75	1.75	6.00	—
1957H	10,000,000	—	0.75	1.75	6.00	—
1957KN	Inc. above	—	2.00	5.00	13.00	—
1958	10,000,000	—	1.00	2.25	6.50	—
1958 Proof	—	Value: 300				
1958H	10,000,000	—	1.25	2.00	6.50	—
1961	90,000,000	—	BV	1.35	3.00	—
1961 Proof	—	Value: 300				
1961H	5,000,000	—	2.00	7.00	19.00	—
1961KN	Inc. above	—	1.50	4.00	9.00	—

KM# 2 10 CENTS
Copper-Nickel, 19.5 mm. **Obv:** Crowned bust of Queen Elizabeth II right **Obv. Designer:** Cecil Thomas **Rev:** Value within beaded circle

Date	Mintage	F	VF	XF	Unc	BU
1953	20,000,000	—	0.75	1.50	4.50	—
1953 Proof	—	Value: 300				
1956	10,000,000	—	0.75	1.50	4.50	—
1956 Proof	—	Value: 300				
1957H	10,000,000	—	0.75	1.50	5.00	—
1957H Proof	—	Value: 300				
1957KN	10,000,000	—	1.00	2.50	5.25	—
1958	10,000,000	—	1.00	2.50	5.25	—
1960	10,000,000	—	0.75	1.50	5.00	—
1960 Proof	—	Value: 300				
1961	60,784,000	—	0.40	0.80	2.50	—
1961 Proof	—	Value: 300				
1961H	69,220,000	—	0.40	0.80	2.50	—
1961KN	Inc. above	—	1.00	2.50	5.00	—

KM# 2a 10 CENTS
Silver, 19.5 mm. **Obv:** Crowned bust right **Obv. Designer:** Cecil Thomas **Rev:** Value within beaded circle **Note:** as KM#2

Date	Mintage	F	VF	XF	Unc	BU
1953 Proof	—	Value: 860				

KM# 3 20 CENTS
Copper-Nickel **Obv:** Crowned bust of Queen Elizabeth II right **Obv. Designer:** Cecil Thomas **Rev:** Value within beaded circle

Date	Mintage	F	VF	XF	Unc	BU
1954	10,000,000	—	1.25	3.00	6.00	—
1954 Proof	—	Value: 300				
1956	5,000,000	—	1.00	3.00	6.00	—
1956 Proof	—	Value: 300				
1957H	2,500,000	—	1.50	4.00	8.00	—
1957H Proof	—	Value: 300				
1957KN	2,500,000	—	1.50	4.00	8.00	—
1961	32,000,000	—	0.75	1.50	5.00	—
1961 Proof	—	Value: 300				
1961H	23,000,000	—	0.75	1.50	5.00	—

KM# 3a 20 CENTS
Silver **Obv:** Crowned bust right **Obv. Designer:** Cecil Thomas **Rev:** Value within beaded circle **Note:** as KM#3

Date	Mintage	F	VF	XF	Unc	BU
1954 Proof	—	Value: 7,500				

KM# 4.1 50 CENTS
Copper-Nickel **Obv:** Crowned bust of Queen Elizabeth II right **Obv. Designer:** Cecil Thomas **Rev:** Value within beaded circle **Edge:** Security

Date	Mintage	F	VF	XF	Unc	BU
1954	8,000,000	—	2.00	4.00	13.00	—
1954 Proof	—	Value: 410				
1955H	4,000,000	—	2.00	4.50	14.00	—
1956	3,440,000	—	2.00	4.50	14.00	—
1956 Proof	—	Value: 410				
1957H	2,000,000	—	2.50	4.75	13.50	—
1957H Proof	—	Value: 410				
1957KN	2,000,000	—	3.00	6.00	14.00	—
1958H	4,000,000	—	1.50	3.00	12.00	—
1961	17,000,000	—	1.50	3.00	12.00	—
1961 Proof	—	Value: 410				
1961H	4,000,000	—	2.00	5.00	14.00	—
1961H Proof	—	Value: 410				

KM# 4.2 50 CENTS
Copper-Nickel **Obv:** Crowned bust of Queen Elizabeth II right **Obv. Designer:** Cecil Thomas **Rev:** Value within beaded circle **Note:** Error, without security edge.

Date	Mintage	F	VF	XF	Unc	BU
1954	Inc. above	—	155	280	550	—
1957KN	Inc. above	—	155	280	550	—
1958H	Inc. above	—	155	280	550	—
1961	Inc. above	—	155	280	550	—
1961H	Inc. above	—	155	280	550	—

MALAYSIA

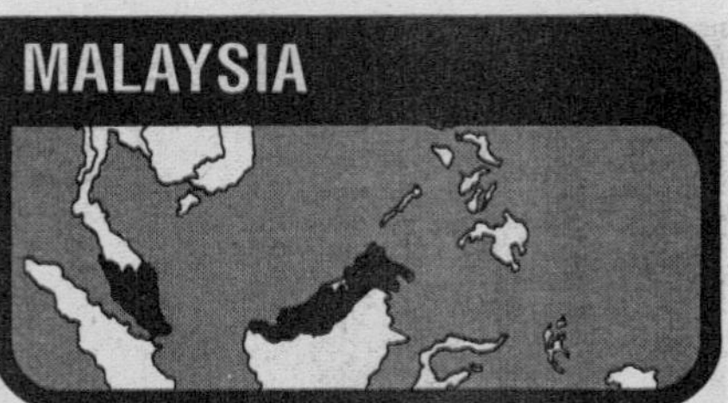

The independent limited constitutional monarchy of Malaysia, which occupies the southern part of the Malay Peninsula in Southeast Asia and the northern part of the island of Borneo, has an area of 127,316 sq. mi. (329,750 sq. km.) and a population of 15.4 million. Capital: Kuala Lumpur. The economy is based on agriculture, mining and forestry. Rubber, tin, timber and palm oil are exported.

Malaysia came into being on Sept. 16, 1963, as a federation of Malaya (Johore, Kelantan, Kedah, Perlis, Trengganu, Negri Sembilan, Pahang, Perak, Selangor, Penang, Malacca), Singapore, Sabah (British North Borneo) and Sarawak. Following two serious racial riots involving Malays and Chinese, Singapore withdrew from the federation on Aug. 9, 1965. Malaysia is a member of the Commonwealth of Nations.

MINT MARKS
FM - Franklin Mint, U.S.A.

***NOTE:** From 1975-1985 the Franklin Mint produced coinage in up to 3 different qualities. Qualities of issue are designated in ( ) after each date and are defined as follows:

(M) MATTE - Normal circulation strike or a dull finish produced by sandblasting special uncirculated (polish finish) or proof quality dies.

(U) SPECIAL UNCIRCULATED - Polished or prooflike in appearance without any frosted features.

(P) PROOF - The highest quality obtainable having mirror-like fields and frosted features.

MONETARY SYSTEM
100 Sen = 1 Ringgit (Dollar)

CONSTITUTIONAL MONARCHY

STANDARD COINAGE

100 Sen = 1 Ringgit (Dollar)

KM# 1 SEN
Bronze **Obv:** Value **Obv. Designer:** Geoffrey Colley **Rev:** Parliament house **Note:** Varieties exist.

Date	Mintage	F	VF	XF	Unc	BU
1967	45,000,000	—	—	0.50	2.00	3.00
1967 Proof	500	Value: 15.00				
1968	10,500,000	—	—	2.00	5.00	6.00
1970	2,535,000	—	—	2.00	6.00	8.00
1971	47,862,000	—	—	0.45	1.50	2.00
1973	21,400,000	—	—	0.25	0.60	1.00
1976	100	—	40.00	100	195	275
1980FM (P)	5,000	Value: 1.50				
1981FM (P)	6,628	Value: 1.50				

KM# 1a SEN
Copper-Clad Steel **Obv:** Value **Obv. Designer:** Geoffrey Colley **Rev:** Parliament house

Date	Mintage	F	VF	XF	Unc	BU
1973	Inc. above	—	—	0.65	1.50	1.80
1976	27,406,000	—	—	0.25	0.50	1.00
1977	21,751,000	—	—	0.25	0.50	0.65
1978	30,844,000	—	—	0.25	0.50	0.65
1979	15,714,000	—	—	0.25	0.50	0.65
1980	16,152,000	—	—	0.25	0.50	0.65
1981	24,633,000	—	—	0.25	0.50	0.65
1982	37,295,000	—	—	0.25	0.50	0.65
1983	19,333,000	—	—	0.45	0.75	0.90
1984	26,267,000	—	—	0.45	0.75	0.90
1985	52,402,000	—	—	0.25	0.50	0.65
1986	48,920,000	—	—	0.25	0.50	0.65
1987	35,284,000	—	—	0.25	0.50	0.65
1988	56,749,000	—	—	0.25	0.50	0.65

KM# 49 SEN
Bronze Clad Steel **Obv:** Value divides date below flower blossom **Rev:** Drum

Date	Mintage	F	VF	XF	Unc	BU
1989	28,429,000	—	—	—	0.25	0.35
1990	102,539,000	—	—	—	0.15	0.25
1991	100,315,000	—	—	—	0.15	0.25

Date	Mintage	F	VF	XF	Unc	BU
1992	122,824,000	—	—	—	0.15	0.25
1993	153,806,000	—	—	—	0.15	0.25
1994	185,085,000	—	—	—	0.15	0.25
1995	208,611,000	—	—	—	0.15	0.25
1996	183,272,598	—	—	—	0.15	0.25
1997	172,215,681	—	—	—	0.15	0.25
1998	1,917,633,834	—	—	—	0.15	0.25
1999	265,502,565	—	—	—	0.15	0.25
2000	268,762,170	—	—	—	0.15	0.25

KM# 49a SEN

0.9250 g., Silver **Obv:** Value divides date below flower blossom **Rev:** Drum

Date	Mintage	F	VF	XF	Unc	BU
1992 Proof	—	Value: 10.00				

KM# 2 5 SEN

Copper-Nickel **Obv:** Value **Obv. Designer:** Geoffrey Colley **Rev:** Parliament house **Note:** Varieties exist.

Date	Mintage	F	VF	XF	Unc	BU
1967	75,464,000	—	—	0.25	0.50	1.00
1967 Proof	500	Value: 25.00				
1968	74,536,000	—	—	0.25	0.50	1.00
1971	16,658,000	—	—	0.45	0.75	1.20
1973	102,942,000	—	—	0.25	0.50	1.00
1976	65,659,000	—	—	0.25	0.50	1.00
1977	10,609,000	—	—	0.30	0.60	1.20
1978	50,044,000	—	—	0.25	0.50	1.00
1979	38,824,000	—	—	0.25	0.50	1.00
1980	33,893,000	—	—	0.25	0.50	1.00
1980FM (P)	6,628	Value: 2.00				
1981	51,490,000	—	—	0.25	0.50	1.00
1981FM (P)	—	Value: 3.00				
1982	118,594,000	—	—	0.25	0.50	1.00
1985	15,553,000	—	—	0.25	0.50	0.65
1987	17,723,000	—	—	0.25	0.50	0.65
1988	26,788,000	—	—	0.25	0.50	0.65

KM# 50 5 SEN

Copper-Nickel, 16.3 mm. **Obv:** Value divides date below flower blossom **Rev:** Top with string

Date	Mintage	F	VF	XF	Unc	BU
1989	20,484,000	—	—	—	0.20	0.30
1990	58,909,000	—	—	—	0.20	0.30
1991	46,092,000	—	—	—	0.20	0.30
1992	67,844,000	—	—	—	0.20	0.30
1993	70,703,000	—	—	—	0.20	0.30
1994	83,026,000	—	—	—	0.20	0.30
1995	53,069,000	—	—	—	0.15	0.25
1996	51,812,529	—	—	—	0.15	0.25
1997	7,703,850	—	—	—	0.15	0.25
1998	1,293,910,233	—	—	—	0.15	0.25
1999	79,224,000	—	—	—	0.15	0.25
2000	61,198,528	—	—	—	0.15	0.25

KM# 50a 5 SEN

0.9250 g., Silver, 16.3 mm. **Obv:** Value divides date below flower blossom **Rev:** Top with string

Date	Mintage	F	VF	XF	Unc	BU
1992 Proof	—	Value: 10.00				

KM# 3 10 SEN

Copper-Nickel, 19.3 mm. **Obv:** Value **Obv. Designer:** Geoffrey Colley **Rev:** Parliament house **Note:** Varieties exist.

Date	Mintage	F	VF	XF	Unc	BU
1967	106,708,000	—	0.25	0.45	1.30	1.80
1967 Proof	500	Value: 35.00				
1968	128,292,000	—	0.25	0.45	1.10	1.50
1971	42,000	—	20.00	30.00	45.00	60.00
1973	214,832,000	—	0.10	0.30	1.00	1.30
1976	148,841,000	—	0.10	0.30	1.00	1.30
1977	52,720,000	—	0.10	0.30	1.00	1.30
1978	21,162,000	—	0.10	0.30	0.75	1.10
1979	50,633,000	—	0.10	0.25	0.60	1.10
1980	51,797,000	—	0.10	0.25	0.60	1.10
1980FM (P)	6,628	Value: 3.00				
1981	236,639,000	—	0.10	0.25	0.60	1.00
1981FM (P)	—	Value: 4.00				
1982	145,639,000	—	—	0.25	0.60	1.00
1983	30,832,000	—	—	0.25	0.60	1.00
1988	17,852,000	—	—	0.25	0.60	1.00

KM# 51 10 SEN

Copper-Nickel, 19.3 mm. **Obv:** Value divides date below flower blossom **Rev:** Ceremonial table

Date	Mintage	F	VF	XF	Unc	BU
1989	32,392,000	—	—	—	0.25	0.40
1990	132,982,000	—	—	—	0.25	0.40
1991	133,293,000	—	—	—	0.25	0.40
1992	89,919,000	—	—	—	0.25	0.40
1993	44,224,000	—	—	—	0.25	0.40
1994	7,122,000	—	—	—	0.30	0.50
1995	82,217,000	—	—	—	0.25	0.40
1996	77,347,125	—	—	—	0.25	0.40
1997	78,955,862	—	—	—	0.25	0.40
1998	1,966,056,746	—	—	—	0.25	0.40
1999	163,080,000	—	—	—	0.25	0.40
2000	162,940,000	—	—	—	0.25	0.40

KM# 51a 10 SEN

0.9250 g., Silver, 19.3 mm. **Obv:** Value divides date below flower blossom **Rev:** Ceremonial table

Date	Mintage	F	VF	XF	Unc	BU
1992 Proof	—	Value: 10.00				

KM# 4 20 SEN

Copper-Nickel, 23.4 mm. **Obv:** Value **Obv. Designer:** Geoffrey Colley **Rev:** Parliament house **Note:** Varieties exist.

Date	Mintage	F	VF	XF	Unc	BU
1967	49,560,000	—	0.25	0.50	1.50	2.20
1967 Proof	500	Value: 45.00				
1968	40,440,000	—	0.25	0.50	1.50	2.20
1969	15,000,000	—	0.25	0.50	1.50	2.20
1970	1,054,000	—	0.60	1.20	2.50	5.00
1971	9,958,000	—	0.25	0.50	1.25	2.50
1973	116,075,000	—	0.25	0.50	1.00	2.00
1976	47,396,000	—	0.25	0.50	1.00	2.00
1977	66,139,000	—	0.25	0.50	1.00	2.00
1978	6,847,000	—	0.25	0.50	1.00	2.00
1979	17,346,000	—	0.25	0.50	1.00	2.00
1980	32,837,000	—	0.15	0.30	0.65	1.20
1980FM (P)	6,628	Value: 4.00				
1981	144,128,000	—	0.15	0.30	0.65	1.20
1981FM (P)	—	Value: 5.00				
1982	97,905,000	—	—	0.25	0.60	1.20
1983	8,105,000	—	—	0.25	0.60	1.00
1987	26,225,000	—	—	0.25	0.60	1.00
1988	67,218,000	—	—	0.25	0.60	1.00

KM# 52 20 SEN

Copper-Nickel, 23.5 mm. **Obv:** Value divides date below flower blossom **Rev:** Basket with food and utensils

Date	Mintage	F	VF	XF	Unc	BU
1989	28,945,000	—	—	—	0.35	0.50
1990	56,249,000	—	—	—	0.35	0.50
1991	82,774,000	—	—	—	0.35	0.50
1992	48,975,000	—	—	—	0.35	0.50
1993	55,753,000	—	—	—	0.35	0.50
1994	2,680,000	—	—	—	0.35	0.50
1997	78,479,804	—	—	—	0.35	0.50
1998	1,161,791,361	—	—	—	0.35	0.50
2000	63,908,000	—	—	—	0.35	0.50

KM# 52a 20 SEN

0.9250 g., Silver And Enamel, 23.5 mm. **Obv:** Value divides date below flower blossom **Rev:** Basket with food and utensils

Date	Mintage	F	VF	XF	Unc	BU
1992 Proof	—	Value: 12.50				

KM# 5.1 50 SEN

Copper-Nickel, 27.8 mm. **Obv:** Value **Rev:** Parliament house

Date	Mintage	F	VF	XF	Unc	BU
1967	15,000,000	—	0.35	0.75	3.00	5.00
1967 Proof	500	Value: 55.00				
1968	12,000,000	—	0.35	0.75	3.00	5.00
1969	2,000,000	—	0.75	3.00	14.00	20.00

KM# 5.2 50 SEN

Copper-Nickel, 27.8 mm. **Obv:** Value **Rev:** Parliament house **Note:** Error, no security edge.

Date	Mintage	F	VF	XF	Unc	BU
1967	Inc. above	—	80.00	160	260	—
1968	Inc. above	—	80.00	160	260	—
1969	Inc. above	—	390	500	750	—

KM# 5.3 50 SEN

Copper-Nickel, 27.8 mm. **Obv:** Value **Rev:** Parliament house **Edge Lettering:** MALAYSIA BANK NEGARA (repeated)

Date	Mintage	F	VF	XF	Unc	BU
1971	8,404,000	—	0.30	1.00	3.00	4.00
1973	50,135,000	—	0.25	1.00	3.00	4.00
1977	17,720,000	—	0.25	0.60	2.00	3.00
1978	11,033,000	—	0.25	0.60	2.00	3.00
1979	5,361,000	—	0.25	0.60	2.00	3.00
1980	15,911,000	—	0.25	0.50	1.00	1.50
1980FM Proof	6,628	Value: 4.50				
1981	22,969,000	—	—	0.35	1.00	1.50
1982	20,585,000	—	—	0.35	1.00	1.50
1983	11,560,000	—	—	0.35	1.00	1.50
1984	10,139,000	—	—	0.35	1.00	1.50
1985	7,115,000	—	—	0.35	1.00	1.50
1986	8,193,000	—	—	0.35	1.00	1.50
1987	7,696,000	—	—	0.35	1.00	1.50
1988	26,788,000	—	—	0.35	1.00	1.50

KM# 5.4 50 SEN

Copper-Nickel, 27.8 mm. **Obv:** Value **Rev:** Parliament house **Edge:** Plain

Date	Mintage	F	VF	XF	Unc	BU
1981FM (P)	—	Value: 12.00				

KM# 53 50 SEN

Copper-Nickel, 28 mm. **Obv:** Value divides date below flower blossom **Rev:** Ceremonial kite

Date	Mintage	F	VF	XF	Unc	BU
1989	6,639,057	—	—	—	0.65	0.85
1990	26,276,464	—	—	—	0.65	0.85
1991	20,720,531	—	—	—	0.65	0.85
1992	15,134,992	—	—	—	0.65	0.85
1993	7,657,991	—	—	—	0.65	0.85
1994	6,565,914	—	—	—	0.65	0.85
1995	1,650,423	—	—	—	0.65	0.85
1996	7,475,790	—	—	—	0.65	0.85
1997	16,143,327	—	—	—	0.65	0.85
1998	401,622,135	—	—	—	0.65	0.85
1999	12,085,000	—	—	—	0.65	0.85
2000	48,206,000	—	—	—	0.65	0.85

KM# 53a 50 SEN

0.9250 g., Silver, 28 mm. **Obv:** Value divides date below flower blossom **Rev:** Ceremonial kite

Date	Mintage	F	VF	XF	Unc	BU
1992 Proof	—	Value: 15.00				

KM# 7 RINGGIT

Copper-Nickel, 33.5 mm. **Subject:** 10th Anniversary - Bank Negara **Obv:** Artistic value and dollar sign within 3/4 flower wreath **Rev:** Bust with headdress left

Date	Mintage	F	VF	XF	Unc	BU
ND(1969)	1,000,000	—	1.20	1.80	4.00	—

KM# 7a RINGGIT

19.9200 g., 0.9250 Silver .5055 oz. ASW, 33.5 mm. **Obv:** Artistic value and dollar sign within 3/4 flower wreath **Rev:** Bust with headdress left

Date	Mintage	F	VF	XF	Unc	BU
ND(1969) Proof	1,000	Value: 400				

KM# 9.1 RINGGIT

Copper-Nickel, 33.5 mm. **Obv:** Artistic value and dollar sign above date **Rev:** Parliament house within cresent
Edge Lettering: BANK NEGARA MALAYSIA

Date	Mintage	F	VF	XF	Unc	BU
1971	2,000,000	—	0.50	0.75	1.50	—
1971 Proof	500	Value: 850				
1980	472,000	—	0.60	0.85	1.65	—
1980FM (P)	6,628	Value: 8.00				
1981	765,000	—	0.60	0.85	1.65	—
1982	202,000	—	0.60	0.85	1.65	—
1984	355,000	—	0.60	0.85	1.65	—
1985	302,000	—	0.60	0.85	1.65	—
1986	253,000	—	0.60	0.85	1.65	—

KM# 9.2 RINGGIT

Copper-Nickel, 33.5 mm. **Obv:** Artistic value and dollar sign above value **Rev:** Parliament house within cresent **Edge:** Plain

Date	Mintage	F	VF	XF	Unc	BU
1981FM (P)	—	Value: 22.00				

KM# 12 RINGGIT

Copper-Nickel, 33.5 mm. **Subject:** Kuala Lumpur Anniversary **Obv:** Artistic value and dollar sign above date **Rev:** Artistic design **Edge Lettering:** MALAYSIA BANK NEGARA **Note:** Issued in 1973.

Date	Mintage	F	VF	XF	Unc	BU
1972	500,000	—	0.60	0.85	2.50	—
1972 Proof	500	Value: 410				

KM# 13 RINGGIT

Copper-Nickel, 33.5 mm. **Subject:** 25th Anniversary - Employee Provident Fund **Obv:** Value **Rev:** Two upper circles among assorted heads

Date	Mintage	F	VF	XF	Unc	BU
1976FM (U)	500,000	—	0.60	1.00	3.00	—
1976FM (P)	7,810	Value: 28.00				

KM# 16 RINGGIT

Copper-Nickel, 33 mm. **Subject:** 3rd Malaysian 5-Year Plan **Obv:** Arms with supporters **Rev:** Head with headdress facing within circle and block-like artistic design **Shape:** 14-sided

Date	Mintage	F	VF	XF	Unc	BU
ND(1976)	1,000,000	—	0.60	0.75	2.00	—
ND(1976)FM (P)	17,000	Value: 15.00				

KM# 22 RINGGIT

Copper-Nickel, 33.5 mm. **Subject:** 9th Southeast Asian Games **Obv:** Arms with supporters **Rev:** Kite flyer
Edge Lettering: MALAYSIA BANK NEGARA

Date	Mintage	F	VF	XF	Unc	BU
1977	1,000,000	—	0.60	0.75	2.00	—
1977FM (P)	11,000	Value: 25.00				

KM# 25 RINGGIT

Copper-Nickel, 33.5 mm. **Subject:** 20th Anniversary of Independence **Obv:** Head facing **Rev:** Arms with supporters

Date	Mintage	F	VF	XF	Unc	BU
ND(1977)	500,000	—	0.75	1.00	3.00	—
ND(1977)FM (P)	3,100	Value: 50.00				

KM# 26 RINGGIT

Copper-Nickel, 33.5 mm. **Subject:** 100th Anniversary of Natural Rubber Production **Obv:** Value and dollar sign above dates **Rev:** Artistic design with a pair of hands
Edge Lettering: MALAYSIA BANK NEGARA

Date	Mintage	F	VF	XF	Unc	BU
ND(1977)	500,000	—	0.60	0.75	2.00	—

KM# 27 RINGGIT

Copper-Nickel, 33.5 mm. **Subject:** 20th Anniversary of Bank Negara **Obv:** Value **Rev:** Building above dates

Date	Mintage	F	VF	XF	Unc	BU
ND(1979)	300,000	—	0.60	0.75	2.00	—

KM# 27a RINGGIT

17.0000 g., 0.9250 Silver .5055 oz. ASW, 33.5 mm. **Obv:** Value **Rev:** Building above dates

Date	Mintage	F	VF	XF	Unc	BU
ND(1979) Proof	8,000	Value: 30.00				
ND(1979)FM (P)	6,628	Value: 35.00				

KM# 28 RINGGIT

Copper-Nickel, 33.5 mm. **Subject:** 15th Century of Hejira **Obv:** Value, date **Rev:** Design within spider web
Edge Lettering: MALAYSIA BANK NEGARA

Date	Mintage	F	VF	XF	Unc	BU
AH1401(1981)	500,000	—	0.60	0.75	2.00	—

KM# 29 RINGGIT

Copper-Nickel, 33.5 mm. **Subject:** 4th Malaysian Plan **Obv:** Arms with supporters **Rev:** Bust with headdress facing 1/4 right **Edge Lettering:** MALAYSIA BANK NEGARA **Note:** Tun Hussein Onn

Date	Mintage	F	VF	XF	Unc	BU
ND(1981)	1,000,000	—	0.50	0.65	1.85	—
ND(1981) Proof	10,000	Value: 20.00				

KM# 32 RINGGIT

Copper-Nickel, 33.5 mm. **Subject:** 25th Anniversary of Independence **Obv:** Star design and bust with headdress with left arm raised facing right **Rev:** Arms with supporters

Date	Mintage	F	VF	XF	Unc	BU
ND(1982)	1,500,000	—	0.50	0.65	1.85	—
ND(1982) Proof	15,000	Value: 20.00				

KM# 36 RINGGIT

Copper-Nickel **Subject:** 5th Malaysian 5-Year Plan **Obv:** Arms with supporters with value and dollar sign below **Rev:** Tractor tire, plants, scale and sun within circle

Date	Mintage	F	VF	XF	Unc	BU
ND(1986)	1,000,000	—	0.50	0.65	1.85	—
ND(1986) Proof	8,000	Value: 12.00				

KM# 39 RINGGIT
Copper-Nickel **Subject:** 35th Annual PATA Conference
Obv: Value **Rev:** Standing turtle

Date	Mintage	F	VF	XF	Unc	BU
ND(1986)	500,000	—	0.50	1.50	5.00	12.00

KM# 39a RINGGIT
16.8500 g., 0.5000 Silver .2709 oz. ASW **Obv:** Value
Rev: Standing turtle

Date	Mintage	F	VF	XF	Unc	BU
ND(1986) Proof	11,000	Value: 20.00				

KM# 43 RINGGIT
Copper-Zinc, 24 mm. **Subject:** 30th Anniversary of Independence
Obv: Arms with supporters above value and dollar sign **Rev:** Numeral 30 divides dates below with flyin doves and sun above

Date	Mintage	F	VF	XF	Unc	BU
ND(1987) Proof	20,000	Value: 14.00				
ND(1987)	1,000,000	—	—	0.60	1.75	—

KM# 54 RINGGIT
Aluminum-Bronze, 24 mm. **Obv:** Value and dollar sign divide date with flower blossom above **Rev:** Native dagger and scabbard within designs **Note:** Varying degrees of filled die variations exist.

Date	Mintage	F	VF	XF	Unc	BU
1989	20,410,000	—	—	—	1.75	2.25
1990	80,102,000	—	—	—	1.75	2.25
1991	169,001,000	—	—	—	1.75	2.00
1992	139,042,000	—	—	—	1.75	2.00
1993	178,894,000	—	—	—	1.75	2.00

KM# 54a RINGGIT
0.9250 Silver, 24 mm. **Obv:** Value and dollar sign divide date below flower blossom **Rev:** Native dagger and scabbard within designs

Date	Mintage	F	VF	XF	Unc	BU
1992 Proof	—	Value: 15.00				

KM# 64 RINGGIT
Aluminum-Bronze, 24 mm. **Obv:** Value divides date below flower blossom **Rev:** Native dagger and scabbard within designs

Date	Mintage	F	VF	XF	Unc	BU
1993	Inc. above	—	—	—	2.00	2.25
1994	36,899,000	—	—	—	1.75	2.00
1995	132,173,000	—	—	—	1.75	2.00
1996	59,460,000	—	—	—	1.75	2.00
1997	41,842,514	—	—	—	—	—
1998	607,756,026	—	—	—	—	—

KM# 65 RINGGIT
8.1500 g., Bi-Metallic Copper-Nickel center in Nickel-Brass ring, 26.5 mm. **Subject:** Thomas-Uber Cup **Obv:** City view within circle **Rev:** Two-handled cup on radiant background **Edge:** Reeded

Date	Mintage	F	VF	XF	Unc	BU
2000	2,000,000	—	—	—	4.00	5.00

KM# 10 5 RINGGIT
Copper-Nickel **Obv:** Sultan Abdul Rahman Putra al-Haj
Rev: Government building in Kuala Lumpur

Date	Mintage	F	VF	XF	Unc	BU
1971	2,000,000	—	2.50	3.00	5.00	—
1971 Proof	500	Value: 850				

KM# 40 5 RINGGIT
29.0300 g., 0.5000 Silver .4662 oz. ASW **Subject:** PATA Conference **Obv:** Value **Rev:** Standing turtle

Date	Mintage	F	VF	XF	Unc	BU
ND(1986) Proof	11,000	Value: 50.00				

KM# 47 5 RINGGIT
Copper Plated Zinc **Subject:** 15th Southeast Asian Games
Obv: Star design within small circle above value **Rev:** Soccer players below date and design

Date	Mintage	F	VF	XF	Unc	BU
1989	500,000	—	—	—	6.00	7.00
1989 Proof	50,000	Value: 16.00				

KM# 55 5 RINGGIT
Copper Plated Zinc **Subject:** Commonwealth Heads of State Meeting **Obv:** Underlined Malaysia flanked by dots in center, arms with supporters above and value below **Rev:** City and towers with emblem at upper right

Date	Mintage	F	VF	XF	Unc	BU
1989	150,000	—	—	—	6.00	8.00
1989 Proof	8,000	Value: 18.00				

KM# 59 5 RINGGIT
Copper Plated Zinc **Subject:** 100th Anniversary of Kuala Lumpur
Obv: Artistic design within circle among horizontal lines with value below **Rev:** House and tower

Date	Mintage	F	VF	XF	Unc	BU
ND(1990)	100,000	—	—	—	6.00	8.00

KM# 61 5 RINGGIT
Copper-Zinc-Tin **Series:** World Wildlife Fund **Obv:** Value and dollar sign flanked by flowers with WWF below design
Rev: Stylized stork above dates

Date	Mintage	F	VF	XF	Unc	BU
ND(1992)	—	—	—	—	6.00	8.00
ND(1992) Proof	3,000	Value: 15.00				

KM# 44 10 RINGGIT
10.8200 g., 0.5000 Silver .1740 oz. ASW **Subject:** 30th Anniversary of Independence **Obv:** Dollar sign and value below arms with supporters **Rev:** Numeral 30 divides date below city view

Date	Mintage	F	VF	XF	Unc	BU
ND(1987)	50,000	—	—	—	10.00	12.00
ND(1987) Proof	10,000	Value: 20.00				

KM# 57 10 RINGGIT
13.6000 g., 0.9250 Silver .4045 oz. ASW **Subject:** Proclamation of Melaka as a Historical City **Obv:** Arms with supporters
Rev: Oxen pulling covered cart

Date	Mintage	F	VF	XF	Unc	BU
1989 Proof	20,000	Value: 27.00				

KM# 19 15 RINGGIT
28.2800 g., 0.9250 Silver .8411 oz. ASW **Series:** Conservation
Obv: Arms with supporters **Rev:** Malaysian Gaur

Date	Mintage	F	VF	XF	Unc	BU
1976	40,000	—	—	—	25.00	32.00
1976 Proof	8,113	Value: 75.00				

KM# 48 15 RINGGIT
16.7300 g., 0.9250 Silver .4986 oz. ASW **Subject:** 15th Southeast Asian Games **Obv:** Sun within small circle within horizontal lines above value within 3/4 circle **Rev:** Sport players below emblem and date

Date	Mintage	F	VF	XF	Unc	BU
1989 Prooflike	50,000	—	—	—	13.50	16.00
1989 Proof	20,000	Value: 25.00				

KM# 68 15 RINGGIT
17.0000 g., Copper-Nickel, 34 mm. **Subject:** First Malaysian Grand Prix **Obv:** Value **Rev:** Track route above island maps **Edge:** Reeded

Date	Mintage	F	VF	XF	Unc	BU
1999 Proof	8,000	Value: 42.50				

KM# 14 25 RINGGIT
35.0000 g., 0.9250 Silver 1.0409 oz. ASW **Subject:** 25th Anniversary - Employee Provident Fund **Obv:** Value **Rev:** Two inner circles at top divide map of Malasia within globe

Date	Mintage	F	VF	XF	Unc	BU
1976FM (U)	100,000	—	—	—	16.50	20.00
1976FM (P)	7,796	Value: 65.00				

KM# 20 25 RINGGIT
35.0000 g., 0.9250 Silver 1.0409 oz. ASW **Series:** Conservation **Obv:** Arms with supporters **Rev:** Rhinoceros Hornbill flanked by sprigs

Date	Mintage	F	VF	XF	Unc	BU
1976	40,000	—	—	—	38.00	42.00
1976 Proof	8,008	Value: 120				

KM# 23 25 RINGGIT
35.0000 g., 0.9250 Silver 1.0409 oz. ASW **Subject:** 9th Southeast Asian Games **Obv:** Arms with supporters **Rev:** Olympic circles at upper right of mapped globe

Date	Mintage	F	VF	XF	Unc	BU
1977FM (U)	100,000	—	—	—	17.50	22.00
1977FM (P)	5,877	Value: 68.00				

KM# 33 25 RINGGIT
35.0000 g., 0.9250 Silver 1.0409 oz. ASW **Subject:** 25th Anniversary of Independence **Obv:** Star design and bust with headdress with arm holding dagger facing right **Rev:** Arms with supporters **Shape:** 14-sided

Date	Mintage	F	VF	XF	Unc	BU
ND(1982)	150,000	—	—	—	17.50	20.00
ND(1982) Proof	7,000	Value: 35.00				

KM# 35 25 RINGGIT
35.0000 g., 0.5000 Silver .5627 oz. ASW **Subject:** 25th Anniversary of the National Bank **Obv:** Bust with headdress 1/4 left **Rev:** Animal figure within circle and sprigs with date and value below

Date	Mintage	F	VF	XF	Unc	BU
ND(1984)	98,000	—	—	—	20.00	22.50
ND(1984) Proof	10,000	Value: 45.00				

KM# 41 25 RINGGIT
23.3300 g., 0.9250 Silver .6939 oz. ASW **Subject:** Women's Decade **Obv:** Date to right of stylized design **Rev:** Animal figure within small circle at lower left within world globe

Date	Mintage	F	VF	XF	Unc	BU
ND(1985) Proof	2,000	Value: 70.00				

KM# 37 25 RINGGIT
35.0000 g., 0.5000 Silver .5627 oz. ASW **Subject:** 5th Malaysian 5-Year Plan **Obv:** Arms with supporters **Rev:** City scene from harbor

Date	Mintage	F	VF	XF	Unc	BU
ND(1986)	80,000	—	—	—	17.50	20.00
ND(1986) Proof	5,000	Value: 32.50				

KM# 56 25 RINGGIT
21.9000 g., 0.9250 Silver .6527 oz. ASW **Subject:** Commonwealth Heads of State Meeting **Obv:** Arms with supporters above lined Malaysia in center with value below **Rev:** Flag within 1/2 of world globe

Date	Mintage	F	VF	XF	Unc	BU
1989	30,000	—	—	—	17.50	20.00
1989 Proof	8,000	Value: 32.50				

KM# 60 25 RINGGIT
21.9000 g., 0.9250 Silver .6527 oz. ASW **Subject:** 100th Anniversary of Kuala Lumpur **Obv:** Design within circle among horizontal lines with value below **Rev:** Castle and tower

Date	Mintage	F	VF	XF	Unc	BU
ND(1990)	25,000	—	—	—	17.50	20.00
ND(1990) Proof	25,000	Value: 32.50				

KM# 62 25 RINGGIT
21.7700 g., 0.9250 Silver .6474 oz. ASW **Series:** World Wildlife Fund **Subject:** 100th Anniversary of Kuala Lumpur **Obv:** Panda above value and dollar sign **Rev:** Stylized fish

Date	Mintage	F	VF	XF	Unc	BU
ND(1992) Proof	50,000	Value: 32.50				

KM# 69 25 RINGGIT
21.7700 g., 0.9250 Silver 0.6474 oz. ASW, 36.25 mm. **Subject:** First Malaysian Grand Prix **Obv:** Value **Rev:** Trophy **Edge:** Reeded

Date	Mintage	F	VF	XF	Unc	BU
1999 Proof	3,000	Value: 60.00				

KM# 46 30 RINGGIT
22.0000 g., 0.9250 Silver .6557 oz. ASW **Subject:** 30th Anniversary of the National Bank **Obv:** Value within circle **Rev:** City view with sun and crescent

Date	Mintage	F	VF	XF	Unc	BU
1989	47,000	—	—	—	15.00	17.50
1989 Proof	10,000	Value: 30.00				

KM# 11 100 RINGGIT
18.6600 g., 0.9170 Gold .5502 oz. AGW **Subject:** Prime Minister Abdul Rahman Putra Al-haj **Obv:** Bust 3/4 facing **Rev:** Multi-storied building left of full sun

Date	Mintage	F	VF	XF	Unc	BU
1971	100,000	—	—	—	450	475
1971 Proof	500	Value: 1,400				

KM# 18 200 RINGGIT
7.3000 g., 0.9000 Gold .2212 oz. AGW **Subject:** 3rd Malaysian 5-Year Plan **Shape:** 14-sided

Date	Mintage	F	VF	XF	Unc	BU
1976FM (U)	50,000	—	—	—	150	170
1976FM (P)	887	Value: 230				

KM# 24 200 RINGGIT
7.2200 g., 0.9000 Gold .2089 oz. AGW **Subject:** 9th Southeast Asian Games **Obv:** Arms with supporters **Rev:** Man on horse right

Date	Mintage	F	VF	XF	Unc	BU
1977FM (U)	12,000	—	—	—	150	170
1977FM (P)	417	Value: 410				

KM# 15 250 RINGGIT
10.1100 g., 0.9000 Gold .2925 oz. AGW **Subject:** 25th Anniversary - Employee Provident Fund **Obv:** Value **Rev:** Inscription within circle and design

Date	Mintage	F	VF	XF	Unc	BU
1976FM (U)	30,000	—	—	—	220	235
1976FM (P)	7,706	Value: 280				

KM# 42 250 RINGGIT
8.1000 g., 0.9000 Gold .2344 oz. AGW **Series:** Womens' Decade **Obv:** Date below design **Rev:** World globe

Date	Mintage	F	VF	XF	Unc	BU
1985 Proof	1,500	Value: 260				

KM# 45 250 RINGGIT
7.4300 g., 0.9000 Gold .2144 oz. AGW **Subject:** 30th Anniversary of Independence **Obv:** Arms with supporters above value **Rev:** Numeral 30 divides dates below crossed encased swords, sun and building

Date	Mintage	F	VF	XF	Unc	BU
1987	5,000	—	—	—	160	170
1987 Proof	1,000	Value: 210				

KM# 58 250 RINGGIT
7.1300 g., 0.9000 Gold .2063 oz. AGW **Subject:** 15th Southeast Asian Games **Obv:** Value below full sun on lined background **Rev:** Games logo and stylized swimmer

Date	Mintage	F	VF	XF	Unc	BU
1989 Proof	2,500	Value: 240				

KM# 63 250 RINGGIT
8.6000 g., 0.9000 Gold .2489 oz. AGW **Series:** World Wildlife Fund **Obv:** Panda above World Wildlife Fund **Rev:** Clouded Leopard

Date	Mintage	F	VF	XF	Unc	BU
1992 Proof	3,000	Value: 210				

KM# 21 500 RINGGIT
33.4370 g., 0.9000 Gold .9676 oz. AGW **Series:** Conservation **Obv:** Arms with supporters **Rev:** Malayan Tapir

Date	Mintage	F	VF	XF	Unc	BU
1976	2,894	—	—	—	700	725
1976 Proof	508	Value: 1,700				

KM# 31 500 RINGGIT
10.2600 g., 0.9000 Gold .2969 oz. AGW **Subject:** 4th Malaysian 5-Year Plan **Obv:** Arms with supporters **Rev:** Bust 3/4 facing

Date	Mintage	F	VF	XF	Unc	BU
ND(1981)FM (U)	20,000	—	—	—	240	260
ND(1981)FM (P)	1,000	Value: 430				

KM# 34 500 RINGGIT
10.2600 g., 0.9000 Gold .2969 oz. AGW **Subject:** 25th Anniversary of Independence **Obv:** Arms with supporters **Rev:** Bust upholding dagger facing right **Note:** Similar to 1 Ringgit, KM#32.

Date	Mintage	F	VF	XF	Unc	BU
1982	20,000	—	—	—	275	290
1982 Proof	1,000	Value: 410				

KM# 38 500 RINGGIT
10.2600 g., 0.9000 Gold .2969 oz. AGW **Subject:** 5th Malaysian 5-Year Plan **Obv:** Arms with supporters **Rev:** Sun, moon and gear-like designs within circle

Date	Mintage	F	VF	XF	Unc	BU
ND(1986)	10,000	—	—	—	225	250
ND(1986) Proof	1,000	Value: 410				

KM# 70 500 RINGGIT
25.0000 g., 0.9990 Gold 0.803 oz. AGW, 35.25 mm. **Subject:** Millennium **Obv:** Arms with supporters above value **Rev:** Flags within globe **Edge:** Reeded

Date	Mintage	F	VF	XF	Unc	BU
1999 Proof	10,000	Value: 810				

PATTERNS

Including off metal strikes

KM#	Date	Mintage	Identification	Mkt Val
Pn1	SH2602 (1942)	—	20 Cents. Aluminum. Cluster of leaves within beaded circle. Value above 1/2 flower wreath. Japanese occupation.	2,500
Pn2	SH2602 (1942)	—	20 Cents. Aluminum. Japanese occupation.	2,500
Pn3	1966	—	Sen. Bronze. Cattle Egret.	—
Pn4	1966	—	Sen. Bronze. Single hibiscus flowers flank denomination. Parliament House.	—
Pn5	1966	—	5 Sen. Copper Nickel. Malayan Tapir.	—
Pn6	1966	—	5 Sen. Copper-Nickel. Single hibiscus flowers flank denomination. Parliament House.	—
Pn7	1966	—	10 Sen. Copper-Nickel. Pangolin.	—
Pn8	1966	—	10 Sen. Copper-Nickel. Proboscis Monkey.	—
Pn9	1966	—	10 Sen. Copper-Nickel. Single hibiscus flowers flank denomination. Parliament House.	—
Pn10	1966	—	20 Sen. Copper Nickel. Kijang with tall grass in background.	—
Pn11	1966	—	20 Sen. Copper Nickel. Kijang with mountains in background.	—
Pn12	1966	—	20 Sen. Copper-Nickel. Kijang on mound.	—
Pn13	1966	—	20 Sen. Copper-Nickel. Single hibiscus flowers flank denomination. Parliament House.	—

MINT SETS

KM#	Date	Mintage	Identification	Issue Price	Mkt Val
MS1	1967 (5)	10,000	KM#1-5.1	—	25.00
MS2	1973 (5)	2,000	KM#1-4, 5.3	—	6.00
MS3	1980 (6)	2,000	KM#1a, 2-4, 5.3	—	7.00
MS4	1989 (6)	2,000	KM#49-54	—	7.00
MS5	1990 (6)	2,000	KM#49-54	—	7.00

PROOF SETS

KM#	Date	Mintage	Identification	Issue Price	Mkt Val
PS1	1967 (5)	500	KM#1-5.1	—	245
PS2	1976 (3)	508	KM#19-21	808	1,800
PS3	1976 (2)	7,500	KM#19-20	—	220
PS4	1976 (3)	2,641	KM#16-18	—	245
PS5	1976 (3)	1,000	KM#13-15	—	400
PS6	1977 (3)	975	KM#22-24	164	550
PS7	1976-80 (8)	5,000	KM#1-4, 5.3, 9.1, 17, 23, 27a. Mixed date set. Minted by Franklin Mint and sold almost exclusively to employees of Bank Negara.	132	125
PS8	1981 (6)	—	KM#1-4, 5.4, 9.2 Minted and distributed by Franklin Mint.	—	65.00
PS9	1981 (3)	3,000	KM#29-31	—	440
PS10	1982 (3)	4,000	KM#32-34	—	400
PS11	1986	2,000	KM#36-38	—	400
PS12	1986 (2)	11,000	KM#39a, 40	—	55.00
PS13	1987 (3)	1,000	KM#43-45	—	220
PS14	1989 (3)	2,500	KM#47, 48, 58	—	280
PS15	1989 (2)	20,000	KM#47-48	—	42.50
PS16	1989 (2)	15,000	KM#55-56	—	45.00
PS17	1992 (6)	5,000	KM#49a-54a Minted by Bank of Negara Malaysia Mint Department and sold only to bank employees.	—	70.00
PS18	1992 (3)	3,000	KM#61-63	—	250

MALDIVE ISLANDS

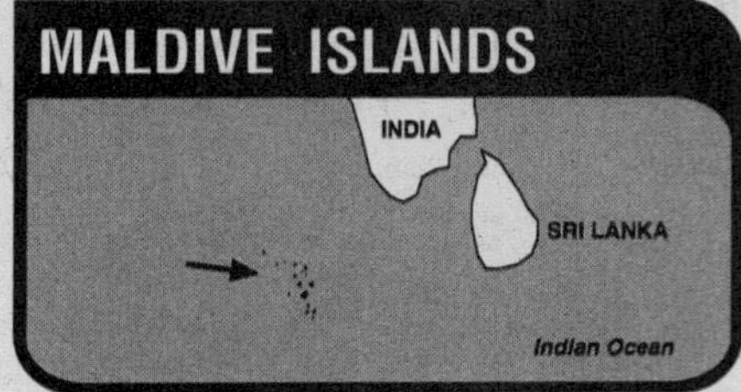

The Republic of Maldives, an archipelago of 2,000 coral islets in the northern Indian Ocean 417 miles (671 km.) west of Ceylon, has an area of 116 sq. mi. (298 sq. km.)and a population of 189,000. Capital: Male. Fishing employs 95 % of the male work force. Dried fish, copra and coir yarn are exported.

The Maldive Islands were visited by Arab traders and converted to Islam in 1153. After being harassed in the16th and 17th centuries by Mopla pirates of the Malabar coast and Portuguese raiders, the Maldivians voluntarily placed themselves under the suzerainty of Ceylon. In 1887 the islands became an internally self-governing British protectorate and a nominal dependency of Ceylon. Traditionally a sultanate, the Maldives became a republic in 1953 but restored the sultanate in 1954. The Sultanate of the Maldive Islands attained complete internal and external autonomy on July 26, 1965, and on Nov. 11,1968, again became a republic. The Maldives is a member of the Commonwealth of Nations.

RULERS

Muhammad Imad al-Din V, AH1318-1322/1900-1904AD
Muhammad Shams al-Din III, AH1322-1353/1904-1935AD
Hasan Nur al-Din II, AH1353-1364/1935-1945AD
Abdul-Majid Didi, AH1364-1371/1945-1953AD
First Republic, AH1371-1372/1953-1954AD
Muhammad Farid Didi, AH1372-1388/1954-1968AD
Second Republic, AH1388 to date/1968AD to date*

MINT NAME

Mahle (Male)

MONETARY SYSTEM

100 Lari = 1 Rupee (Rufiyaa)

SULTANATE

STANDARD COINAGE

100 Lari = 1 Rupee (Rufiyaa)

KM# 38 LARIN

Copper Or Brass **Ruler:** Muhammad Imad al-Din V AH 1318-22 / 1900-04 AD **Note:** Weight varies: 0.80-1.10 grams.

Date	Mintage	F	VF	XF	Unc	BU
AH1319 (1901)	—	1.00	1.50	2.00	4.00	—

KM# 41 LARIN

0.9000 g., Bronze, 13 mm. **Ruler:** Muhammad Shams al-Din III AH 1322-53 / 1904-35 AD **Obv:** Legend **Rev:** Legend **Note:** Struck at Birmingham, England. Rare mint proof strikes in silver and gold exist.

Date	Mintage	F	VF	XF	Unc	BU
AH1331 (1913)	—	1.00	1.25	1.75	3.00	—

KM# 39 2 LARIAT

Copper-Brass, 13 mm. **Ruler:** Muhammad Imad al-Din V AH 1318-22 / 1900-04 AD **Obv:** Legend **Rev:** Legend **Note:** 1.4-2.2 grams. Previously listed date AH1311 is merely poor die cutting of AH1319. Many die varieties exist.

Date	Mintage	F	VF	XF	Unc	BU
AH1319 (1901)	—	1.50	3.50	5.00	7.50	—

KM# 40.1 4 LARIAT

Copper-Brass **Ruler:** Muhammad Imad al-Din V AH 1318-22 / 1900-04 AD **Obv:** Legend **Rev:** Legend **Edge:** Plain or reeded **Note:** 2.5-4.5 grams. Many die varieties exist; size varies 17 - 18mm.

Date	Mintage	F	VF	XF	Unc	BU
AH1320 (1902)	—	1.50	2.50	4.50	8.00	—

KM# 40.2 4 LARIAT

Copper-Brass **Ruler:** Muhammad Imad al-Din V AH 1318-22 / 1900-04 AD **Obv:** Legend **Rev:** Legend with Arabic "Sana(t)" below date **Note:** Silver strikes are most likely presentation pieces; size varies 16.8-18mm.

Date	Mintage	F	VF	XF	Unc	BU
AH1320 (1902)	—	3.50	8.00	12.00	16.00	—

KM# 42 4 LARIAT

3.3000 g., Bronze, 19 mm. **Ruler:** Muhammad Shams al-Din III AH 1322-53 / 1904-35 AD **Obv:** Legend **Rev:** Legend **Note:** Struck at Birmingham, England. Rare mint proof strikes in silver and gold exist.

Date	Mintage	F	VF	XF	Unc	BU
AH1331 (1913)	—	1.00	1.50	2.75	6.00	—

2ND SULTANATE

STANDARD COINAGE

100 Lari = 1 Rupee (Rufiyaa)

KM# 43 LAARI

1.5000 g., Bronze, 15 mm. **Ruler:** Muhammad Farid Didi AH 1372-88 / 1954-68 AD **Obv:** National emblem divides dates above **Rev:** Value **Note:** Similar to Laari, KM#49.

Date	Mintage	F	VF	XF	Unc	BU
AH1379-1960	300,000	—	0.15	0.25	0.50	—
AH1379-1960 Proof	1,270	Value: 3.00				

KM# 44 2 LAARI

3.1500 g., Bronze, 18.2 mm. **Ruler:** Muhammad Farid Didi AH 1372-88 / 1954-68 AD **Obv:** National emblem divides dates above **Rev:** Value **Shape:** 4-sided

Date	Mintage	F	VF	XF	Unc	BU
AH1379-1960	600,000	—	0.20	0.35	0.75	—
AH1379-1960 Proof	1,270	Value: 3.50				

KM# 45 5 LAARI

2.6000 g., Nickel-Brass, 20.4 mm. **Ruler:** Muhammad Farid Didi AH 1372-88 / 1954-68 AD **Obv:** National emblem divides dates above **Rev:** Value **Shape:** Scalloped

Date	Mintage	F	VF	XF	Unc	BU
AH1379-1960	300,000	—	0.25	0.40	0.75	—
AH1379-1960 Proof	1,270	Value: 4.00				

KM# 45a 5 LAARI

Bronze **Ruler:** Muhammad Farid Didi AH 1372-88 / 1954-68 AD **Obv:** National emblem divides dates above **Rev:** Value

Date	Mintage	F	VF	XF	Unc	BU
AH1379-1960	—	—	0.25	0.40	0.75	—

KM# 45b 5 LAARI

Aluminum, 20.4 mm. **Obv:** National emblem divides dates above **Shape:** Scalloped **Note:** Similar to 5 Laari, KM#45.

Date	Mintage	F	VF	XF	Unc	BU
AH1389-1970	300,000	—	0.20	0.30	0.40	—
AH1389-1970 Proof	—	Value: 3.50				
AH1399-1979	—	—	—	0.10	0.20	—
AH1399-1979 Proof	—	Value: 2.50				

KM# 46 10 LAARI
5.2000 g., Nickel-Brass, 23 mm. **Ruler:** Muhammad Farid Didi AH 1372-88 / 1954-68 AD **Obv:** National emblem divides dates above **Rev:** Value **Shape:** Scalloped

Date	Mintage	F	VF	XF	Unc	BU
AH1379-1960	600,000	—	0.50	0.75	1.50	—
AH1379-1960 Proof	1,270	Value: 5.00				

KM# 47.1 25 LAARI
4.1000 g., Nickel-Brass, 20.4 mm. **Ruler:** Muhammad Farid Didi AH 1372-88 / 1954-68 AD **Obv:** National emblem divides dates above **Rev:** Value **Edge:** Security

Date	Mintage	F	VF	XF	Unc	BU
AH1379-1960	300,000	—	0.60	1.00	1.50	—
AH1379-1960 Proof	1,270	Value: 6.00				

KM# 47.2 25 LAARI
4.1000 g., Nickel-Brass, 20.4 mm. **Ruler:** Muhammad Farid Didi AH 1372-88 / 1954-68 AD **Obv:** National emblem divides dates above **Rev:** Value **Edge:** Reeded

Date	Mintage	F	VF	XF	Unc	BU
AH1379-1960	—	—	2.00	3.50	6.00	—

KM# 48.1 50 LAARI
5.6000 g., Nickel-Brass, 23.5 mm. **Ruler:** Muhammad Farid Didi AH 1372-88 / 1954-68 AD **Obv:** National emblem divides dates above **Rev:** Value **Edge:** Security

Date	Mintage	F	VF	XF	Unc	BU
AH1379-1960	300,000	—	1.00	1.75	2.50	—
AH1379-1960 Proof	1,270	Value: 8.00				

KM# 48.2 50 LAARI
Nickel-Brass, 23.5 mm. **Ruler:** Muhammad Farid Didi AH 1372-88 / 1954-68 AD **Obv:** National emblem divides dates above **Rev:** Value **Edge:** Reeded

Date	Mintage	F	VF	XF	Unc	BU
AH1379-1960	—	—	3.00	5.00	8.00	—

2ND REPUBLIC

STANDARD COINAGE

100 Laari = 1 Rufiyaa

KM# 49 LAARI
0.4500 g., Aluminum, 15 mm. **Obv:** National emblem divides dates above **Rev:** Value

Date	Mintage	F	VF	XF	Unc	BU
AH1389-1970	—	—	0.10	0.20	0.40	—
AH1389-1970	500,000	—	0.10	0.20	0.40	—
AH1399-1979	—	—	0.10	0.20	0.40	—
AH1399-1979 Proof	100,000	Value: 1.25				

KM# 68 LAARI
Aluminum, 18.2 mm. **Obv:** Value **Rev:** Palm tree within circle

Date	Mintage	F	VF	XF	Unc	BU
AH1404-1984	—	—	—	0.10	0.15	—
AH1404-1984 Proof	2,500	Value: 2.50				

KM# 50 2 LAARI
Aluminum, 18.2 mm.

Date	Mintage	F	VF	XF	Unc	BU
AH1389-1970 Proof	—	—	—	—	—	—
AH1389-1970	500,000	—	0.15	0.25	0.50	—
AH1399-1979	—	—	0.15	0.25	0.50	—
AH1399-1979 Proof	100,000	Value: 1.25				

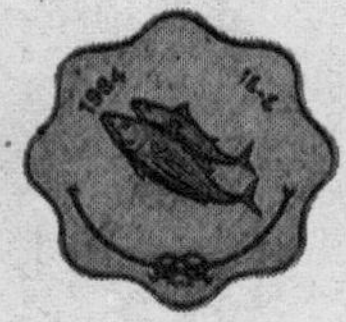

KM# 69 5 LAARI
1.0000 g., Aluminum, 20.4 mm. **Obv:** Value **Rev:** Two Bonito fish swimming upward left **Shape:** Scalloped

Date	Mintage	F	VF	XF	Unc	BU
AH1404-1984	—	—	—	0.10	0.35	0.75
AH1404-1984 Proof	2,500	Value: 3.00				
AH1411-1990	—	—	—	0.10	0.35	0.75

KM# 46a 10 LAARI
Aluminum, 23 mm. **Ruler:** Muhammad Farid Didi AH 1372-88 / 1954-68 AD **Obv:** National emblem divides dates above **Shape:** Scalloped **Note:** Similar to 10 Laari, KM#46.

Date	Mintage	F	VF	XF	Unc	BU
AH1399-1979	—	—	—	0.10	0.25	—
AH1399-1979 Proof	—	Value: 2.50				

KM# 70 10 LAARI
1.9500 g., Aluminum, 23 mm. **Obv:** Value **Rev:** Maldivian sailing ship - Odi **Shape:** Scalloped

Date	Mintage	F	VF	XF	Unc	BU
AH1404-1984	—	—	—	0.10	0.20	—
AH1404-1984 Proof	2,500	Value: 3.50				

KM# 47.3 25 LAARI
Nickel-Brass, 20.4 mm. **Obv:** National emblem divides dates above **Rev:** Palm tree **Note:** Similar to 25 Laari, KM#47.2.

Date	Mintage	F	VF	XF	Unc	BU
AH1399-1979	—	—	—	0.10	0.25	—
AH1399-1979 Proof	100,000	Value: 3.50				

KM# 71 25 LAARI
4.1500 g., Nickel-Brass, 20.4 mm. **Obv:** Value **Rev:** Mosque and minaret at Male

Date	Mintage	F	VF	XF	Unc	BU
AH1404-1984	—	—	—	0.15	0.45	—
AH1404-1984 Proof	—	Value: 4.00				
AH1411-1990	—	—	—	0.15	0.45	—
AH1416-1996	—	—	—	0.15	0.45	—

KM# 48.3 50 LAARI
Nickel-Brass, 23.5 mm. **Obv:** National emblem divides dates above **Rev:** Palm tree **Note:** Similar to 50 Laari, KM#48.2.

Date	Mintage	F	VF	XF	Unc	BU
AH1399-1979	—	—	0.10	0.20	0.40	—
AH1399-1979 Proof	100,000	Value: 6.50				

KM# 72 50 LAARI
5.6500 g., Nickel-Brass, 23.6 mm. **Obv:** Value **Rev:** Loggerhead sea turtle

Date	Mintage	F	VF	XF	Unc	BU
AH1404-1984	—	—	0.15	0.35	1.50	2.50
AH1404-1984 Proof	—	Value: 6.00				
AH1411-1990	—	—	0.15	0.35	1.50	2.50
AH1415-1994	—	—	0.15	0.35	1.50	2.50
AH1415-1995	—	—	0.15	0.35	1.50	2.50

KM# 73 RUFIYAA
Copper-Nickel Clad Steel, 25.9 mm. **Obv:** Value **Rev:** National emblem divides dates above

Date	Mintage	F	VF	XF	Unc	BU
AH1402-1982	—	—	0.20	0.50	2.00	—

KM# 73a RUFIYAA
Copper-Nickel, 25.9 mm. **Obv:** Value **Rev:** National emblem divides dates above

Date	Mintage	F	VF	XF	Unc	BU
AH1404-1984	—	—	0.20	0.50	2.00	—
AH1404-1984 Proof	—	Value: 9.00				
AH1411-1990	—	—	0.20	0.50	2.00	—
AH1416-1996	—	—	0.20	0.50	2.00	—

KM# 88 2 RUFIYAA
Brass **Obv:** Value **Rev:** Pacific triton sea shell **Edge:** Lettering over reeding **Edge Lettering:** REPUBLIC OF MALDIVES

Date	Mintage	F	VF	XF	Unc	BU
AH1415-1995	—	—	—	—	6.50	7.50

KM# 55 5 RUFIYAA
Copper-Nickel **Series:** F.A.O. **Obv:** National emblem divides dates above **Rev:** Value below Bonito fish

Date	Mintage	F	VF	XF	Unc	BU
AH1397-1977	15,000	—	—	3.50	7.50	—

KM# 57 5 RUFIYAA
Copper-Nickel, 36 mm. **Series:** F.A.O. **Obv:** National emblem divides dates above **Rev:** Spiny lobster divides circle

Date	Mintage	F	VF	XF	Unc	BU
AH1398-1978	7,000	—	—	4.00	7.50	—

KM# 57a 5 RUFIYAA
19.1500 g., 0.9250 Silver .5695 oz. ASW **Series:** F.A.O. **Obv:** National emblem divides dates above **Rev:** Spiny lobster divides circle

Date	Mintage	F	VF	XF	Unc	BU
AH1398-1978 Proof	1,887	Value: 25.00				

KM# 57b 5 RUFIYAA
18.9500 g., 0.9170 Gold .5585 oz. AGW **Series:** F.A.O. **Obv:** National emblem divides dates above **Rev:** Spiny lobster divides circle

Date	Mintage	F	VF	XF	Unc	BU
AH1398-1978 Proof	200	Value: 575				

KM# 100 5 RUFIYAA
26.0000 g., Copper-Nickel, 38.75 mm. **Subject:** International Year of the Reef **Obv:** National emblem divides dates above **Rev:** Multicolor fish scene **Edge:** Reeded

Date	Mintage	F	VF	XF	Unc	BU
AH1419-1998 Proof	—	Value: 27.50				

KM# 59 10 RUFIYAA
Copper-Nickel **Series:** F.A.O. **Obv:** National emblem divides dates above **Rev:** Woman weaving

Date	Mintage	F	VF	XF	Unc	BU
AH1399-1979	—	—	—	4.50	10.00	—

KM# 59a 10 RUFIYAA
25.0000 g., 0.9250 Silver .7435 oz. ASW **Series:** F.A.O. **Obv:** National emblem divides dates above **Rev:** Woman weaving

Date	Mintage	F	VF	XF	Unc	BU
AH1399-1979 Proof	3,000	Value: 16.50				

KM# 62 10 RUFIYAA
Copper-Nickel **Series:** F.A.O. **Obv:** National emblem divides dates above **Rev:** Girl making embroidery

Date	Mintage	F	VF	XF	Unc	BU
AH1400-1980	—	—	—	4.00	9.00	—

KM# 56 20 RUFIYAA
28.2800 g., 0.5000 Silver .4546 oz. ASW, 38.61 mm. **Series:** F.A.O. **Obv:** National emblem divides dates above **Rev:** Value flanked by fish

Date	Mintage	F	VF	XF	Unc	BU
AH1397-1977	15,000	—	—	—	12.50	—

KM# 61 20 RUFIYAA
28.2800 g., 0.9250 Silver .8411 oz. ASW, 38.61 mm. **Series:** International Year of the Child **Obv:** National emblem divides dates above **Rev:** Three children playing

Date	Mintage	F	VF	XF	Unc	BU
AH1399-1979 Proof	12,000	Value: 15.00				

KM# 65 20 RUFIYAA
Copper-Nickel, 38.61 mm. **Subject:** World Fisheries Conference **Obv:** National emblem divides dates above **Rev:** Two tuna fish **Rev. Designer:** Stuart Devlin

Date	Mintage	F	VF	XF	Unc	BU
AH1404-1984	100,000	—	—	—	12.00	15.00

KM# 65a 20 RUFIYAA
28.2800 g., 0.9250 Silver .8411 oz. ASW, 38.61 mm. **Subject:** World Fisheries Conference **Obv:** National emblem divides dates above **Rev:** Two tuna fish

Date	Mintage	F	VF	XF	Unc	BU
AH1404-1984 Proof	20,000	Value: 45.00				

KM# 74 20 RUFIYAA
19.4400 g., 0.9250 Silver .5782 oz. ASW **Series:** Decade for Women **Obv:** National emblem divides dates above **Rev:** Woman sewing lace on pillow

Date	Mintage	F	VF	XF	Unc	BU
AH1405-1985 Proof	500	Value: 40.00				

KM# 97 20 RUFIYAA
31.2200 g., 0.9990 Silver 1.0027 oz. ASW, 30.3 mm. **Subject:** Millennium **Obv:** National emblem **Rev:** Multicolor design **Edge:** Reeded **Shape:** Square

Date	Mintage	F	VF	XF	Unc	BU
AH1421-2000 Proof	—	Value: 50.00				

KM# 58 25 RUFIYAA
28.0500 g., 0.5000 Silver .4509 oz. ASW **Series:** F.A.O. **Obv:** National emblem divides dates above **Rev:** Sailing ship

Date	Mintage	F	VF	XF	Unc	BU
AH1398-1978	7,140	—	—	—	22.50	—

KM# 58a 25 RUFIYAA
28.2800 g., 0.9250 Silver .8411 oz. ASW **Series:** F.A.O. **Obv:** National emblem divides dates above **Rev:** Sailing ship

Date	Mintage	F	VF	XF	Unc	BU
AH1398-1978 (1978) Proof	2,000	Value: 32.50				

KM# 58b 25 RUFIYAA
28.2500 g., 0.9170 Gold .8326 oz. AGW **Series:** F.A.O. **Obv:** National emblem divides dates above **Rev:** Sailing ship

Date	Mintage	F	VF	XF	Unc	BU
AH1398-1978 Proof	200	Value: 825				

KM# 95 25 RUFIYAA
Copper-Nickel **Series:** 50th Anniversary - UN **Obv:** National emblem divides dates above **Rev:** UN building and logo

Date	Mintage	F	VF	XF	Unc	BU
AH1416-1996	—	—	—	—	9.50	—

KM# 89 50 RUFIYAA
1.2442 g., 0.9999 Gold .04 oz. AGW **Obv:** National emblem divides dates above **Rev:** Skylab space station

Date	Mintage	F	VF	XF	Unc	BU
AH1415-1995 (1995)	Est. 25,000	—	—	—	60.00	—

KM# 90 50 RUFIYAA
10.0000 g., 0.5000 Silver .1607 oz. ASW **Series:** 1996 Olympics **Obv:** National emblem divides dates above **Rev:** Sailboat and map

Date	Mintage	F	VF	XF	Unc	BU
AH1416-1996	Est. 10,000	—	—	—	20.00	—

KM# 99 50 RUFIYAA
31.3000 g., 0.9250 Silver 0.9308 oz. ASW, 38.5 mm.
Subject: Year of the Reef **Obv:** National emblem divides dates above **Rev:** Multicolor underwater scene **Edge:** Reeded

Date	Mintage	F	VF	XF	Unc	BU
AH1419-1998 Proof	—	Value: 50.00				

KM# 60 100 RUFIYAA
28.2800 g., 0.8000 Silver .7274 oz. ASW **Series:** F.A.O. **Obv:** National emblem divides dates above **Rev:** Woman making mats

Date	Mintage	F	VF	XF	Unc	BU
AH1399-1979	6,000	—	—	—	18.00	—

KM# 60a 100 RUFIYAA
28.2800 g., 0.9250 Silver .8411 oz. ASW **Series:** F.A.O. **Obv:** National emblem divides dates above **Rev:** Woman making mats

Date	Mintage	F	VF	XF	Unc	BU
AH1399-1979 Proof	8,000	Value: 20.00				

KM# 63 100 RUFIYAA
28.2800 g., 0.8000 Silver .7274 oz. ASW **Series:** F.A.O. **Obv:** National emblem divides dates above **Rev:** Crown of coconut and palm

Date	Mintage	F	VF	XF	Unc	BU
AH1400-1980	6,501	—	—	—	25.00	—

KM# 63a 100 RUFIYAA
28.2800 g., 0.9250 Silver .8411 oz. ASW **Series:** F.A.O. **Obv:** National emblem divides dates above **Rev:** Crown of coconut and palm

Date	Mintage	F	VF	XF	Unc	BU
AH1400-1980 Proof	3,003	Value: 45.00				

KM# 64 100 RUFIYAA
28.2800 g., 0.9250 Silver .8411 oz. ASW **Series:** World Food Day **Obv:** National emblem divides dates above **Rev:** Heads of 2 women working in a field

Date	Mintage	F	VF	XF	Unc	BU
AH1401-1981	10,000	—	—	—	27.50	—
AH1401-1981 Proof	5,000	Value: 45.00				

KM# 66 100 RUFIYAA
28.2800 g., 0.9250 Silver .8411 oz. ASW, 38.61 mm.
Series: International Year of Disabled Persons **Obv:** National emblem divides dates above **Rev:** Stylized yin and yang symbol

Date	Mintage	F	VF	XF	Unc	BU
AH1404-1984	—	—	—	—	25.00	—
AH1404-1984 Proof	—	Value: 40.00				

KM# 75 100 RUFIYAA
15.9800 g., 0.9170 Gold .4712 oz. AGW **Subject:** Opening of Grand Mosque and Islamic Centre **Obv:** National emblem divides dates above

Date	Mintage	F	VF	XF	Unc	BU
AH1405-1985 Proof	100	Value: 600				

KM# 67 100 RUFIYAA
15.9800 g., 0.9170 Gold .4712 oz. AGW **Obv:** National emblem divides dates above **Rev:** Disabled figures within lower circle under 1/2 world globe

Date	Mintage	F	VF	XF	Unc	BU
AH1404-1984	500	—	—	—	700	—
AH1404-1984 Proof	500	Value: 800				

KM# 78 100 RUFIYAA
28.2800 g., 0.9250 Silver .8411 oz. ASW **Subject:** Opening of Grand Mosque and Islamic Centre **Obv:** National emblem divides dates above **Rev:** Building and tower

Date	Mintage	F	VF	XF	Unc	BU
AH1405-1985 Proof	500	Value: 70.00				

KM# 76 100 RUFIYAA
28.2800 g., 0.9250 Silver .8411 oz. ASW
Subject: Commonwealth finance ministers meeting
Obv: National emblem divides dates above **Rev:** Grand Mosque

Date	Mintage	F	VF	XF	Unc	BU
ND(AH406) Proof	300	Value: 75.00				

KM# 87 100 RUFIYAA
10.0000 g., 0.5000 Silver .1607 oz. ASW **Obv:** National emblem divides dates above **Rev:** Sailing ship "Cutty Sark"

Date	Mintage	F	VF	XF	Unc	BU
AH1413-1993 Proof	Est. 25,000	Value: 16.50				

KM# 98 100 RUFIYAA
20.0000 g., 0.8350 Silver .5369 oz. ASW, 34 mm.
Series: Olympics **Obv:** National emblem divides dates above **Rev:** Swimmer within circle **Edge:** Reeded

Date	Mintage	F	VF	XF	Unc	BU
AH1418-1998 Proof	30,000	—	—	—	35.00	—

KM# 82 250 RUFIYAA
31.4700 g., 0.9250 Silver .9359 oz. ASW, 38.61 mm.
Series: World Football Championship **Obv:** National emblem divides dates above **Rev:** Soccer ball trailing an inscribed ribbon

Date	Mintage	F	VF	XF	Unc	BU
AH1410-1990 Proof	—	Value: 22.50				

KM# 80 250 RUFIYAA
31.4700 g., 0.9250 Silver .9359 oz. ASW **Series:** 1992 Olympics
Subject: Swimming **Obv:** National emblem divides dates above **Rev:** Swimmer and diver

Date	Mintage	F	VF	XF	Unc	BU
AH1410-1990 Proof	—	Value: 20.00				

KM# 81 250 RUFIYAA
31.4700 g., 0.9250 Silver .9359 oz. ASW, 38.61 mm. **Obv:**

National emblem divides dates above **Rev:** Maldivian Schooner - Dhivehi-Odi

Date	Mintage	F	VF	XF	Unc	BU
AH1410-1990 Proof	15,000	Value: 28.00				

KM# 83 250 RUFIYAA

31.4700 g., 0.9250 Silver .9359 oz. ASW, 38.61 mm.
Subject: World Cup '94 soccer **Obv:** National emblem divides dates above **Rev:** Two soccer players

Date	Mintage	F	VF	XF	Unc	BU
AH1413-1993 Proof	25,000	Value: 36.50				

KM# 84 250 RUFIYAA

31.4700 g., 0.9250 Silver .9359 oz. ASW, 38.61 mm. **Obv:** National emblem divides dates above **Rev:** Skylab space station

Date	Mintage	F	VF	XF	Unc	BU
AH1413-1993 Proof	1,440	Value: 32.50				

KM# 85 250 RUFIYAA

31.4700 g., 0.9250 Silver .9359 oz. ASW, 38.61 mm.
Series: 1996 Olympics **Subject:** Sailing **Obv:** National emblem divides dates above **Rev:** Sailboat divides map

Date	Mintage	F	VF	XF	Unc	BU
AH1413-1993 Proof	25,000	Value: 25.00				

KM# 86 250 RUFIYAA

31.4700 g., 0.9250 Silver .9359 oz. ASW, 38.61 mm.
Series: Endangered Wildlife **Obv:** National emblem divides dates above **Rev:** Turtle

Date	Mintage	F	VF	XF	Unc	BU
AH1414-1994 Proof	14,500	Value: 45.00				

KM# 96 250 RUFIYAA

31.2400 g., 0.9250 Silver .9291 oz. ASW, 38.61 mm.
Subject: Ibn Battuta **Obv:** National emblem divides dates above **Rev:** Bust of Ibn Battuta, dhow and map

Date	Mintage	F	VF	XF	Unc	BU
AH1416-1995 Proof	—	Value: 37.50				

KM# 101 250 RUFIYAA

28.5000 g., 0.9250 Silver 0.8476 oz. ASW, 38.6 mm.
Subject: U N 50 Years **Obv:** National emblem divides dates above **Rev:** U N building and logo **Edge:** Reeded

Date	Mintage	F	VF	XF	Unc	BU
AH1416-1996 Proof	—	Value: 100				

KM# 91 500 RUFIYAA

28.2800 g., 0.9250 Silver .8411 oz. ASW, 38.61 mm.
Subject: 25 Years of Independence

Date	Mintage	F	VF	XF	Unc	BU
AH1410-1990 Proof	1,000	Value: 60.00				

KM# 92 500 RUFIYAA

28.2800 g., 0.9250 Silver .8411 oz. ASW, 38.61 mm.
Subject: 25 Years of Republic

Date	Mintage	F	VF	XF	Unc	BU
AH1413-1993 Proof	500	Value: 65.00				

KM# 93 1000 RUFIYAA

15.9800 g., 0.9170 Gold .4712 oz. AGW, 28.4 mm. **Subject:** 25 Years of Independence

Date	Mintage	F	VF	XF	Unc	BU
AH1410-1990 Proof	1,000	Value: 500				

KM# 94 1000 RUFIYAA

15.9800 g., 0.9170 Gold .4712 oz. AGW, 28.4 mm. **Subject:** 25 Years of Republic

Date	Mintage	F	VF	XF	Unc	BU
AH1413-1993 Proof	500	Value: 550				

PATTERNS

Including off metal strikes

KM#	Date	Mintage	Identification	Mkt Val
Pn1	AH1319	—	Larin. Silver. KM38.	—
Pn2	AH1319	—	2 Lariat. Silver. KM39.	—
Pn3	AH1320	—	4 Lariat. Silver. KM40.2.	—

PIEFORTS

KM#	Date	Mintage	Identification	Mkt Val
P1	1979	100	20 Rufiyaa. Silver. National emblem - crescent moon, star and palm tree flanked by 2 flags. 3 children playing. KM61.	80.00
P2	1984	100	100 Rufiyaa. Silver. National emblem - crescent moon, star and palm tree flanked by 2 flags. Stylized Yin-Yang symbol. KM66.	100
P3	1984	100	100 Rufiyaa. Gold. National emblem - crescent moon, star and palm tree flanked by 2 flags. Disabled persons under an umbrella. KM67.	800

MINT SETS

KM#	Date	Mintage	Identification	Issue Price	Mkt Val
MS1	1984 (6)	—	KM68-73	8.75	12.50

PROOF SETS

KM#	Date	Mintage	Identification	Issue Price	Mkt Val
PS1	1960 (6)	1,270	KM43-48	—	30.00
PS2	1979 (6)	—	KM45a, 46a, 47.2, 48.2, 49-50	30.00	18.00
PS3	1979 (2)	3,000	KM59a, 60a	—	42.50
PS4	1984 (6)	2,500	KM68-72, 73a	30.00	28.00

MALI

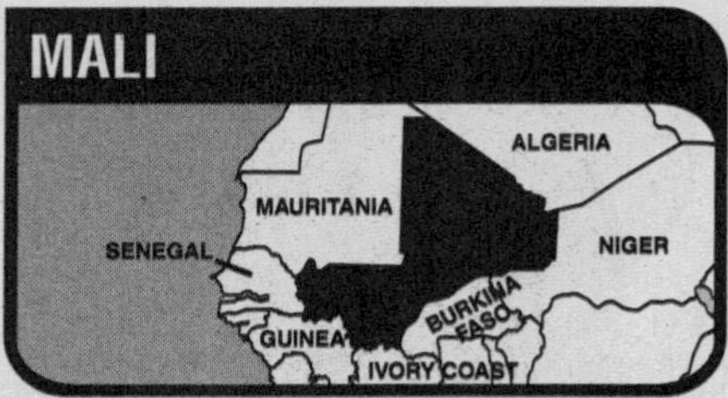

The Republic of Mali, a landlocked country in the interior of West Africa southwest of Algeria, has an area of 482,077 sq. mi. (1,240,000 sq. km.) and a population of 8.1 million. Capital: Bamako. Livestock, fish, cotton and peanuts are exported.

Malians are descendants of the ancient Malinke Kingdom of Mali that controlled the middle Niger from the 11th to the 17th centuries. The French penetrated the Sudan (now Mali) about 1880, and established their rule in 1898 after subduing fierce native resistance. In 1904 the area became the colony of Upper Senegal-Niger (changed to French Sudan in 1920), and became part of the French Union in 1946. In 1958 French Sudan became the Sudanese Republic with complete internal autonomy. Senegal joined with the Sudanese Republic in 1959 to form the Mali Federation which, in 1960, became a fully independent member of the French Community. Upon Senegal's subsequent withdrawal from the Federation, the Sudanese, on Sept. 22, 1960, proclaimed their nation the fully independent Republic of Mali and severed all ties with France.

MINT MARKS

(a) - Paris, privy marks only

REPUBLIC

STANDARD COINAGE

KM# 2 5 FRANCS

1.0000 g., Aluminum, 20 mm. **Obv:** Hippo facing **Rev:** Value above crossed leaves

Date	Mintage	F	VF	XF	Unc	BU
1961	—	0.15	0.25	0.50	2.00	5.00

KM# 1 10 FRANCS

25.0000 g., 0.9000 Silver .7234 oz. ASW
Subject: Independence **Obv:** Arms of Mali **Rev:** Bust facing

Date	Mintage	F	VF	XF	Unc	BU
ND(1960) Proof	10,000	Value: 35.00				

KM# 3 10 FRANCS

1.5500 g., Aluminum, 23.5 mm. **Obv:** Horse head left **Rev:** Value within leaf wreath

Date	Mintage	F	VF	XF	Unc	BU
1961	—	0.50	1.00	2.00	5.00	7.00

KM# 5 10 FRANCS

3.2000 g., 0.9000 Gold .0926 oz. AGW **Subject:** President Modibo Keita **Obv:** Arms of Mali **Rev:** Bust facing **Note:** Similar to 25 Francs, KM#6.

Date	Mintage	F	VF	XF	Unc	BU
1967 Proof	—	Value: 90.00				

KM# 11 10 FRANCS
1.5500 g., Aluminum, 23.5 mm. **Obv:** Value flanked by triangles with date below **Rev:** Rice plants

Date	Mintage	F	VF	XF	Unc	BU
1976(a)	10,000,000	1.25	2.50	4.50	12.50	15.00

KM# 13 10 FRANCS
3.2000 g., 0.9000 Gold .0926 oz. AGW, 23.5 mm. **Subject:** Anniversary of Independence **Obv:** Designs within circle **Rev:** Bust with hat facing **Note:** Similar to 50 Francs, KM#15.

Date	Mintage	F	VF	XF	Unc	BU
ND Proof	—	—	—	—	—	—

Note: Reported not confirmed

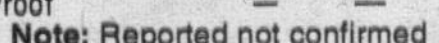

KM# 4 25 FRANCS
2.5000 g., Aluminum, 27 mm. **Obv:** Lion's head facing **Rev:** Value within leaf wreath

Date	Mintage	F	VF	XF	Unc	BU
1961	—	0.35	0.65	1.75	4.50	8.00

KM# 6 25 FRANCS
8.0000 g., 0.9000 Gold .2315 oz. AGW **Subject:** President Modibo Keita **Obv:** Arms of Mali **Rev:** Bust with hat facing

Date	Mintage	F	VF	XF	Unc	BU
1967 Proof	—	Value: 165				

KM# 12 25 FRANCS
2.5000 g., Aluminum, 27 mm. **Obv:** Value flanked by triangles with date below **Rev:** Rice plants

Date	Mintage	F	VF	XF	Unc	BU
1976(a)	10,000,000	2.50	4.00	8.00	18.00	22.00

KM# 14 25 FRANCS
8.0000 g., 0.9000 Gold .2315 oz. AGW **Subject:** Anniversary of Independence **Obv:** Arms of Mali **Rev:** Bust with hat facing

Date	Mintage	F	VF	XF	Unc	BU
ND Proof	—	Value: 325				

KM# 7 50 FRANCS
16.0000 g., 0.9000 Gold .4630 oz. AGW **Subject:** President Modibo Keita **Obv:** Arms of Mali **Rev:** Bust facing

Date	Mintage	F	VF	XF	Unc	BU
1967 Proof	—	Value: 325				

KM# 9 50 FRANCS
4.0000 g., Nickel-Brass, 23.5 mm. **Series:** F.A.O. **Obv:** Value flanked by triangles with date below **Rev:** Millet plant

Date	Mintage	F	VF	XF	Unc	BU
1975(a)	10,000,000	0.25	0.50	1.50	3.75	5.50
1977(a)	10,000,000	0.25	0.50	1.50	3.75	5.50

KM# 15 50 FRANCS
16.0000 g., 0.9000 Gold .463 oz. AGW **Subject:** Anniversary of Independence **Obv:** Arms of Mali **Rev:** Bust with hat facing

Date	Mintage	F	VF	XF	Unc	BU
ND Proof	—	Value: 575				

KM# 8 100 FRANCS
32.0000 g., 0.9000 Gold .926 oz. AGW **Subject:** President Modibo Keita **Obv:** Arms of Mali **Rev:** Bust facing

Date	Mintage	F	VF	XF	Unc	BU
1967 Proof	—	Value: 645				

KM# 10 100 FRANCS
8.0000 g., Nickel-Brass, 27.8 mm. **Series:** F.A.O. **Obv:** Value flanked by triangles with date below **Rev:** 3 Ears of corn

Date	Mintage	F	VF	XF	Unc	BU
1975(a)	23,000,000	0.65	1.25	2.50	5.00	9.00

KM# 16 100 FRANCS
32.0000 g., 0.9000 Gold .926 oz. AGW **Subject:** Anniversary of Independence **Obv:** Arms of Mali **Rev:** Bust with hat facing

Date	Mintage	F	VF	XF	Unc	BU
ND Proof	—	Value: 900				

ESSAIS

Standard metals unless otherwise noted

Some essais have surnames stamped (from die) on them. Purpose is unknown.

KM#	Date	Mintage	Identification	Issue Price	Mkt Val
E1	1975	—	50 Francs. Nickel-Brass. KM9.	—	17.50
E2	1975	—	100 Francs. Nickel-Brass. KM10.	—	20.00
E3	1976	—	10 Francs. Aluminum. KM11.	—	17.50
E4	1976	—	25 Francs. Aluminum. KM12.	—	20.00

PIEFORTS WITH ESSAIS

Standard metals unless otherwise noted

KM#	Date	Mintage	Identification	Issue Price	Mkt Val
PE1	1960	10	10 Francs. Silver. KM1.	—	250

PROOF SETS

KM#	Date	Mintage	Identification	Issue Price	Mkt Val
PS1	1967 (4)	—	KM5-8	—	1,225

The Republic of Malta, an independent parliamentary democracy, is situated in the Mediterranean Sea between Sicily and North Africa. With the islands of Gozo and Comino, Malta has an area of 124 sq. mi. (320 sq. km.) and a population of 386,000. Capital: Valletta. Malta has no proven mineral resources, an agriculture insufficient to its needs, and a small, but expanding, manufacturing facility. Clothing, textile yarns and fabrics, and knitted wear are exported.

For more than 3,500 years Malta was ruled, in succession by Phoenicians, Carthaginians, Romans, Arabs, Normans, the Knights of Malta, France and Britain. Napoleon seized Malta by treachery in 1798. The French were ousted by a Maltese insurrection assisted by Britain, and in 1814 Malta, of its own free will, became a part of the British Empire. Malta obtained full independence in Sept., 1964; electing to remain within the Commonwealth with the British monarch as the nominal head of state.

Malta became a republic on Dec. 13, 1974, but remained a member of the Commonwealth of Nations. The president is Chief of State. The prime minister is the Head of Government.

RULERS
British, until 1964

MONETARY SYSTEM
10 Mils = 1 Cent
100 Cents = 1 Pound

REPUBLIC

DECIMAL COINAGE

10 Mils = 1 Cent; 100 Cents = 1 Pound

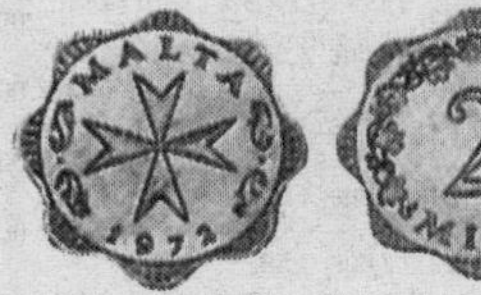

KM# 5 2 MILS
0.9500 g., Aluminum, 20.3 mm. **Obv:** Maltese cross **Rev:** Value within 3/4 wreath **Shape:** Scalloped

Date	Mintage	F	VF	XF	Unc	BU
1972	30,000	—	0.10	0.15	0.30	—
1972 Proof	13,000	Value: 0.50				
1976FM (M)	5,000	—	—	—	2.00	—
1976FM (P)	26,000	Value: 0.50				
1977FM (U)	5,252	—	—	—	1.00	—
1977FM (P)	6,884	Value: 1.00				
1978FM (U)	5,252	—	—	—	1.00	—
1978FM (P)	3,244	Value: 1.00				
1979FM (U)	537	—	—	—	3.00	—
1979FM (P)	6,577	Value: 1.00				
1980FM (U)	385	—	—	—	3.00	—
1980FM (P)	3,451	Value: 1.00				
1981FM (U)	444	—	—	—	3.00	—
1981FM (P)	1,453	Value: 1.00				

KM# 54 2 MILS
0.9500 g., Aluminum, 20.3 mm. **Subject:** 10th Anniversary of Decimalization **Obv:** Maltese cross **Rev:** Value within 3/4 wreath **Shape:** Scalloped

Date	Mintage	F	VF	XF	Unc	BU
1982FM (U)	850	—	—	—	3.00	—
1982FM (P)	1,793	Value: 1.00				

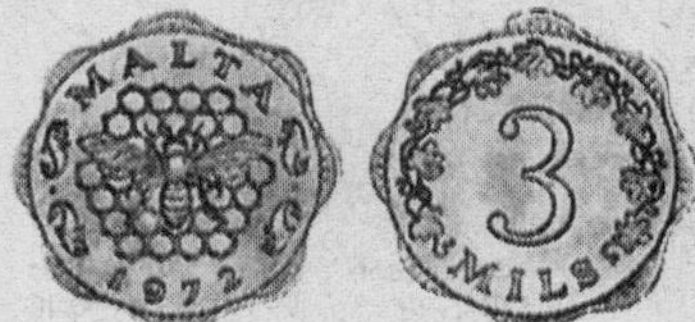

KM# 6 3 MILS
1.4500 g., Aluminum, 23.25 mm. **Obv:** Bee and honeycomb **Rev:** Value within 3/4 wreath **Shape:** Scalloped

Date	Mintage	F	VF	XF	Unc	BU
1972	—	—	0.10	0.15	1.00	—
1972 Proof	8,000	Value: 1.00				
1976FM (M)	5,000	—	—	—	2.50	—
1976FM (P)	26,000	Value: 1.00				
1977FM (U)	5,252	—	—	—	1.50	—
1977FM (P)	6,884	Value: 1.25				
1978FM (U)	5,252	—	—	—	2.50	—
1978FM (P)	3,244	Value: 1.25				
1979FM (U)	537	—	—	—	5.00	—

Date	Mintage	F	VF	XF	Unc	BU
1979FM (P)	6,577	Value: 1.25				
1980FM (U)	385	—	—	—	5.00	—
1980FM (P)	3,451	Value: 1.25				
1981FM (U)	449	—	—	—	5.00	—
1981FM (P)	1,453	Value: 1.25				

KM# 55 3 MILS

1.4500 g., Aluminum, 23.25 mm. **Subject:** 10th Anniversary of Decimalization **Obv:** Bee and honeycomb **Rev:** Value **Shape:** Scalloped

Date	Mintage	F	VF	XF	Unc	BU
1982FM (U)	850	—	—	—	4.00	—
1982FM (P)	1,793	Value: 1.25				

KM# 7 5 MILS

2.1000 g., Aluminum, 26 mm. **Obv:** Earthen lampstand **Rev:** Value within 3/4 wreath **Shape:** Scalloped

Date	Mintage	F	VF	XF	Unc	BU
1972	4,320,000	—	0.10	0.15	0.40	—
1972 Proof	13,000	Value: 1.00				
1976FM (M)	5,000	—	—	—	3.00	—
1976FM (P)	26,000	Value: 1.00				
1977FM (U)	5,252	—	—	—	2.00	—
1977FM (P)	6,884	Value: 1.50				
1978FM (U)	5,252	—	—	—	2.00	—
1978FM (P)	3,244	Value: 1.50				
1979FM (U)	537	—	—	—	7.00	—
1979FM (P)	6,577	Value: 1.50				
1980FM (U)	385	—	—	—	7.00	—
1980FM (P)	3,451	Value: 1.50				
1981FM (U)	449	—	—	—	7.00	—
1981FM (P)	1,453	Value: 1.50				

KM# 56 5 MILS

2.1000 g., Aluminum, 26 mm. **Subject:** 10th Anniversary of Decimalization **Obv:** Earthen lampstand **Rev:** Value **Shape:** Scalloped

Date	Mintage	F	VF	XF	Unc	BU
1982FM (U)	850	—	—	—	5.00	—
1982FM (P)	1,793	Value: 1.50				

KM# 8 CENT

7.1500 g., Bronze, 25.9 mm. **Obv:** The George Cross **Rev:** Value within 3/4 wreath

Date	Mintage	F	VF	XF	Unc	BU
1972	5,650,000	—	0.10	0.15	0.40	—
1972 Proof	13,000	Value: 1.25				
1975	1,500,000	—	0.10	0.20	0.50	—
1976FM (M)	5,000	—	—	—	3.50	—
1976FM (P)	26,000	Value: 1.25				
1977	2,793,000	—	0.10	0.15	0.40	—
1977FM (U)	5,252	—	—	—	2.50	—
1977FM (P)	6,884	Value: 1.75				
1978FM (U)	5,252	—	—	—	2.50	—
1978FM (P)	3,244	Value: 1.75				
1979FM (U)	537	—	—	—	9.00	—
1979FM (P)	6,577	Value: 1.75				
1980FM (U)	385	—	—	—	9.00	—
1980FM (P)	3,451	Value: 1.75				
1981FM (U)	449	—	—	—	9.00	—

Date	Mintage	F	VF	XF	Unc	BU
1981FM (P)	1,453	Value: 1.75				
1982	—	—	0.10	0.15	0.25	—

KM# 57 CENT

7.1500 g., Bronze, 25.9 mm. **Subject:** 10th Anniversary of Decimalization **Obv:** The George cross **Rev:** Value

Date	Mintage	F	VF	XF	Unc	BU
1982FM (U)	850	—	—	—	7.50	—
1982FM (P)	1,793	Value: 1.75				

KM# 9 2 CENTS

2.2500 g., Copper-Zinc, 17.75 mm. **Subject:** Penthesilea, Queen of the Amazons **Obv:** Helmeted bust right **Rev:** Value within 3/4 wreath

Date	Mintage	F	VF	XF	Unc	BU
1972	5,640,000	—	0.10	0.50	1.00	—
1972 Proof	13,000	Value: 1.50				
1976	1,000,000	—	0.15	0.20	0.60	—
1976FM (M)	2,500	—	—	—	4.50	—
1976FM (P)	26,000	Value: 1.50				
1977	6,105,000	—	0.10	0.15	0.40	—
1977FM (U)	2,752	—	—	—	4.50	—
1977FM (P)	6,884	Value: 2.50				
1978FM (U)	2,752	—	—	—	4.50	—
1978FM (P)	3,244	Value: 2.50				
1979FM (U)	537	—	—	—	12.00	—
1979FM (P)	6,577	Value: 2.50				
1980FM (U)	385	—	—	—	12.00	—
1980FM (P)	3,451	Value: 2.50				
1981FM (U)	449	—	—	—	12.00	—
1981FM (P)	1,453	Value: 2.50				
1982	—	—	0.10	0.15	0.30	—

KM# 58 2 CENTS

2.2500 g., Copper-Zinc, 17.75 mm. **Subject:** 10th Anniversary of Decimalization **Obv:** Helmeted bust right **Rev:** Value

Date	Mintage	F	VF	XF	Unc	BU
1982FM (U)	850	—	—	—	10.00	—
1982FM (P)	1,793	Value: 2.50				

KM# 10 5 CENTS

5.6500 g., Copper-Nickel, 23.6 mm. **Obv:** Ritual altar in the Temple of Hagar Qim **Rev:** Value within 3/4 wreath

Date	Mintage	F	VF	XF	Unc	BU
1972	4,180,000	—	0.20	0.30	0.50	—
1972 Proof	13,000	Value: 1.75				
1976	1,009,000	—	0.20	0.30	0.60	—
1976FM (M)	2,500	—	—	—	5.00	—
1976FM (P)	26,000	Value: 2.00				
1977	—	—	0.20	0.30	0.50	—
1977FM (U)	2,752	—	—	—	5.00	—
1977FM (P)	6,884	Value: 3.00				
1978FM (U)	2,752	—	—	—	5.00	—
1978FM (P)	3,244	Value: 3.00				
1979FM (U)	537	—	—	—	15.00	—
1979FM (P)	6,577	Value: 3.00				
1980FM (U)	385	—	—	—	15.00	—
1980FM (P)	3,451	Value: 3.00				
1981FM (U)	449	—	—	—	15.00	—
1981FM (P)	1,453	Value: 3.00				

KM# 59 5 CENTS

5.6500 g., Copper-Nickel, 23.6 mm. **Subject:** 10th Anniversary of Decimalization **Obv:** Floral altar in the Temple of Hagar Qim **Rev:** Value

Date	Mintage	F	VF	XF	Unc	BU
1982FM (U)	850	—	—	—	12.50	—
1982FM (P)	1,793	Value: 3.00				

KM# 11 10 CENTS

11.3000 g., Copper-Nickel, 28.5 mm. **Obv:** Barge of the grand master **Rev:** Value within 3/4 wreath

Date	Mintage	F	VF	XF	Unc	BU
1972	10,680,000	—	0.40	0.60	1.00	—
1972 Proof	13,000	Value: 2.25				
1976FM (M)	1,000	—	—	—	6.00	—
1976FM (P)	26,000	Value: 2.50				
1977FM (U)	1,252	—	—	—	6.00	—
1977FM (P)	6,884	Value: 3.50				
1978FM (U)	1,252	—	—	—	6.00	—
1978FM (P)	3,244	Value: 3.50				
1979FM (U)	537	—	—	—	17.50	—
1979FM (P)	6,577	Value: 3.50				
1980FM (U)	385	—	—	—	15.00	—
1980FM (P)	3,451	Value: 3.50				
1981FM (U)	449	—	—	—	15.00	—
1981FM (P)	1,453	Value: 3.50				

KM# 60 10 CENTS

11.3000 g., Copper-Nickel, 28.5 mm. **Subject:** 10th Anniversary of Decimalization **Obv:** Barge of the grand master **Rev:** Value

Date	Mintage	F	VF	XF	Unc	BU
1982FM (U)	850	—	—	—	14.00	—
1982FM (P)	1,793	Value: 3.50				

KM# 29 25 CENTS

10.5500 g., Brass, 30 mm. **Subject:** 1st Anniversary - Republic of Malta **Obv:** Republic emblem within circle **Rev:** Value within 3/4 wreath **Shape:** 8-sided

Date	Mintage	F	VF	XF	Unc	BU
1975	4,750,000	—	1.00	1.50	2.50	—
1975 Matte proof	—	—	—	—	150	—

KM# 29a 25 CENTS

Bronze, 30 mm. **Obv:** Republic emblem within circle **Rev:** Value within 3/4 wreath

Date	Mintage	F	VF	XF	Unc	BU
1975 Proof	6,000	Value: 12.50				

KM# 29b 25 CENTS

Copper-Nickel, 30 mm. **Obv:** Republic emblem within circle **Rev:** Value within 3/4 wreath

Date	Mintage	F	VF	XF	Unc	BU
1976FM (M)	300	—	—	—	40.00	—
1976FM (P)	26,000	Value: 3.00				
1977FM (U)	552	—	—	—	20.00	—
1977FM (P)	6,884	Value: 4.50				
1978FM (U)	552	—	—	—	20.00	—
1978FM (P)	3,244	Value: 4.50				
1979FM (U)	537	—	—	—	20.00	—

Date	Mintage	F	VF	XF	Unc	BU
1979FM (P)	6,577	Value: 4.50				
1980FM (U)	385	—	—	—	20.00	—
1980FM (P)	3,451	Value: 4.50				
1981FM (U)	449	—	—	—	20.00	—
1981FM (P)	1,453	Value: 4.50				

KM# 61 25 CENTS

Copper-Nickel, 30 mm. **Subject:** 10th Anniversary of Decimalization **Obv:** Republic emblem within circle **Rev:** Value **Shape:** Octagon

Date	Mintage	F	VF	XF	Unc	BU
1982FM (U)	850	—	—	—	15.00	—
1982FM (P)	1,793	Value: 4.50				

KM# 12 50 CENTS

13.6000 g., Copper-Nickel, 32.95 mm. **Obv:** Great Siege Monument **Rev:** Value within 3/4 wreath **Shape:** 10-sided

Date	Mintage	F	VF	XF	Unc	BU
1972	5,500,000	—	1.75	2.00	3.50	—
1972 Proof	13,000	Value: 4.50				
1976FM (M)	150	—	—	—	90.00	—
1976FM (P)	26,000	Value: 5.00				
1977FM (U)	402	—	—	—	25.00	—
1977FM (P)	6,884	Value: 6.00				
1978FM (U)	402	—	—	—	25.00	—
1978FM (P)	3,244	Value: 6.00				
1979FM (U)	537	—	—	—	25.00	—
1979FM (P)	6,577	Value: 6.00				
1980FM (U)	385	—	—	—	25.00	—
1980FM (P)	3,451	Value: 6.00				
1981FM (U)	449	—	—	—	25.00	—
1981FM (P)	1,453	Value: 6.00				

KM# 62 50 CENTS

13.6000 g., Copper-Nickel, 32.95 mm. **Subject:** 10th Anniversary of Decimalization **Obv:** Great Siege Monument **Rev:** Value **Shape:** 10-sided

Date	Mintage	F	VF	XF	Unc	BU
1982FM (U)	850	—	—	—	20.00	—
1982FM (P)	1,793	Value: 6.00				

KM# 13 POUND

10.0000 g., 0.9870 Silver .3173 oz. ASW **Obv:** Crowned arms with supporters **Rev:** Bust left

Date	Mintage	F	VF	XF	Unc	BU
1972	55,000	—	—	5.00	7.00	9.00

Note: Appears to be proof, but officially issued as "BU"

KM# 19 POUND

10.0000 g., 0.9870 Silver .3173 oz. ASW **Obv:** Crowned arms with supporters **Rev:** Bust left

Date	Mintage	F	VF	XF	Unc	BU
1973	30,000	—	—	5.00	7.00	9.00

KM# 45 POUND

5.6600 g., 0.9250 Silver .1683 oz. ASW **Obv:** Republic emblem within circle **Rev:** Dog

Date	Mintage	F	VF	XF	Unc	BU
1977	66,000	—	—	8.00	25.00	40.00
1977 Proof	2,500	Value: 75.00				

KM# 51 POUND

5.6600 g., 0.9250 Silver .1683 oz. ASW **Subject:** Departure of foreign forces **Obv:** Republic emblem within circle **Rev:** Flames within helping hands divide date and value

Date	Mintage	F	VF	XF	Unc	BU
1979FM (U)	50,000	—	—	4.00	7.00	—
1979FM (P)	7,871	Value: 16.50				

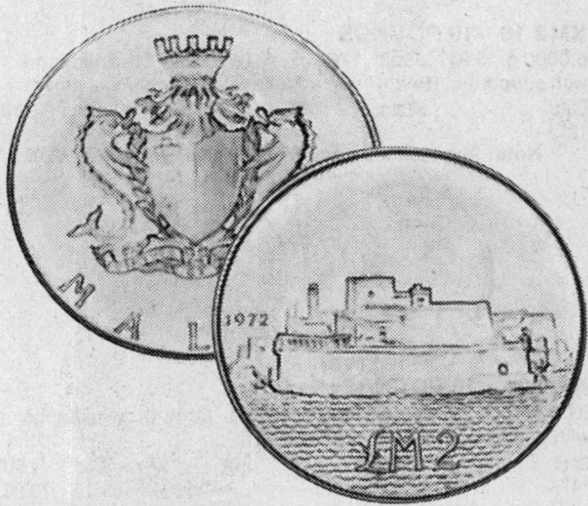

KM# 14 2 POUNDS

20.0000 g., 0.9870 Silver .6347 oz. ASW **Obv:** Crowned arms with supporters **Rev:** Fort San Angelo

Date	Mintage	F	VF	XF	Unc	BU
1972	53,000	—	—	9.50	12.50	14.50

Note: Appears to be proof, but officially issued as "BU"

KM# 20 2 POUNDS

20.0000 g., 0.9870 Silver .6347 oz. ASW **Rev:** Tal-Imdina Gate

Date	Mintage	F	VF	XF	Unc	BU
1973	30,000	—	—	10.00	15.00	17.50

KM# 24 2 POUNDS

10.0000 g., 0.9870 Silver .3173 oz. ASW **Obv:** Crowned arms with supporters **Rev:** Bust 1/4 left

Date	Mintage	F	VF	XF	Unc	BU
1974	25,000	—	—	6.50	8.50	10.00

KM# 30 2 POUNDS

10.0000 g., 0.9870 Silver .3173 oz. ASW **Obv:** Crowned arms with supporters **Rev:** Bust left

Date	Mintage	F	VF	XF	Unc	BU
1975	2,000	—	—	8.00	15.00	17.50

KM# 31 2 POUNDS

10.0000 g., 0.9870 Silver .3173 oz. ASW **Obv:** Republic emblem within circle **Rev:** Bust left

Date	Mintage	F	VF	XF	Unc	BU
1975	18,000	—	—	6.50	8.50	10.00

KM# 40 2 POUNDS

10.0000 g., 0.9870 Silver .3173 oz. ASW **Obv:** Republic emblem within circle **Rev:** Bust 1/4 right

Date	Mintage	F	VF	XF	Unc	BU
1976	11,000	—	—	8.00	10.00	12.00

KM# 46 2 POUNDS

11.3100 g., 0.9250 Silver .3363 oz. ASW **Obv:** Republic emblem within circle **Rev:** Bust left

Date	Mintage	F	VF	XF	Unc	BU
1977	15,000	—	—	—	9.00	10.00
1977 Proof	3,692	Value: 12.50				

KM# 52 2 POUNDS

11.3100 g., 0.9250 Silver .3363 oz. ASW **Series:** World Food Day **Obv:** Republic emblem within circle **Rev:** Men fishing in boat below small emblem

Date	Mintage	F	VF	XF	Unc	BU
1981	1,500	—	—	—	15.00	17.00
1981 Proof	12,000	Value: 10.00				

KM# 25 4 POUNDS
20.0000 g., 0.9870 Silver .6347 oz. ASW **Obv:** Crowned arms with supporters **Rev:** Cottonera Gate

Date	Mintage	F	VF	XF	Unc	BU
1974	24,000	—	—	10.00	15.00	17.50

KM# 32 4 POUNDS
20.0000 g., 0.9870 Silver .6347 oz. ASW **Obv:** Crowned arms with supporters **Rev:** St. Agatha's tower at Gammieh

Date	Mintage	F	VF	XF	Unc	BU
1975	2,000	—	—	15.00	27.50	32.50

KM# 33 4 POUNDS
20.0000 g., 0.9870 Silver .6347 oz. ASW **Obv:** Republic emblem within circle **Rev:** St. Agatha's Tower at Gammieh

Date	Mintage	F	VF	XF	Unc	BU
1975	18,000	—	—	13.50	17.50	20.00

KM# 41 4 POUNDS
20.0000 g., 0.9870 Silver .6347 oz. ASW **Obv:** Republic emblem **Rev:** Fort Manoel Gate

Date	Mintage	F	VF	XF	Unc	BU
1976	10,000	—	—	14.50	18.50	22.00

KM# 15 5 POUNDS
3.0000 g., 0.9160 Gold .0883 oz. AGW **Obv:** Crowned arms with supporters **Rev:** Hand holding torch within map of Malta

Date	Mintage	F	VF	XF	Unc	BU
1972	18,000	—	—	—	—	70.00

Note: Appears to be proof, but officially issued as "BU"

KM# 47 5 POUNDS
28.2800 g., 0.9250 Silver .8411 oz. ASW **Obv:** Republic emblem **Rev:** Windmill divides date and value

Date	Mintage	F	VF	XF	Unc	BU
1977	15,000	—	—	—	22.50	25.00
1977 Proof	3,938	Value: 50.00				

KM# 53 5 POUNDS
28.2800 g., 0.9250 Silver .8411 oz. ASW **Subject:** International Youth Conference - UNICEF **Obv:** Republic emblem **Rev:** Kids playing game on numeral board flanked by UNICEF emblems

Date	Mintage	F	VF	XF	Unc	BU
1981 Proof	11,000	Value: 37.50				

KM# 16 10 POUNDS
6.0000 g., 0.9170 Gold .1767 oz. AGW **Obv:** Crowned arms with supporters **Rev:** Kenur, a Maltese stone charcoal stove

Date	Mintage	F	VF	XF	Unc	BU
1972	16,000	—	—	—	—	130

Note: Appears to be proof, but officially issued as "BU"

KM# 21 10 POUNDS
3.0000 g., 0.9170 Gold .0883 oz. AGW **Obv:** Crowned arms with supporters **Rev:** Watchtower

Date	Mintage	F	VF	XF	Unc	BU
1973	9,078	—	—	—	65.00	70.00

KM# 26 10 POUNDS
3.0000 g., 0.9170 Gold .0883 oz. AGW **Obv:** Crowned arms with supporters **Rev:** Zerafa flower flanked by date and value

Date	Mintage	F	VF	XF	Unc	BU
1974	9,124	—	—	—	65.00	70.00

KM# 34 10 POUNDS
3.0000 g., 0.9170 Gold .0883 oz. AGW **Obv:** Crowned arms with supporters **Rev:** Falcon

Date	Mintage	F	VF	XF	Unc	BU
1975	2,000	—	—	—	80.00	90.00

KM# 35 10 POUNDS
3.0000 g., 0.9170 Gold .0883 oz. AGW **Obv:** Republic emblem within circle **Rev:** Maltese falcon

Date	Mintage	F	VF	XF	Unc	BU
1975	6,448	—	—	—	90.00	95.00

KM# 42 10 POUNDS
3.0000 g., 0.9170 Gold .0883 oz. AGW **Obv:** Republic emblem within circle **Rev:** Swallowtail butterfly above value

Date	Mintage	F	VF	XF	Unc	BU
1976	4,448	—	—	—	100	110

KM# 17 20 POUNDS
12.0000 g., 0.9170 Gold .3534 oz. AGW **Obv:** Crowned arms with supporters **Rev:** Merill bird

Date	Mintage	F	VF	XF	Unc	BU
1972	16,000	—	—	—	—	245

Note: Appears to be proof, but officially issued as "BU"

KM# 22 20 POUNDS
6.0000 g., 0.9170 Gold .1767 oz. AGW **Obv:** Crowned arms with supporters **Rev:** Dolphins Fountain at Floriana

Date	Mintage	F	VF	XF	Unc	BU
1973	9,075	—	—	—	125	130

KM# 27 20 POUNDS
6.0000 g., 0.9170 Gold .1767 oz. AGW **Obv:** Crowned arms with supporters **Rev:** Gozo boat with lateen sails

Date	Mintage	F	VF	XF	Unc	BU
1974	8,700	—	—	—	125	130

KM# 36 20 POUNDS
6.0000 g., 0.9170 Gold .1767 oz. AGW **Obv:** Crowned arms with supporters **Rev:** Freshwater crab

Date	Mintage	F	VF	XF	Unc	BU
1975	2,000	—	—	—	150	165

KM# 37 20 POUNDS
6.0000 g., 0.9170 Gold .1767 oz. AGW **Obv:** Republic emblem within circle **Rev:** Fresh water crab

Date	Mintage	F	VF	XF	Unc	BU
1975	5,698	—	—	—	130	135

KM# 43 20 POUNDS
6.0000 g., 0.9170 Gold .1767 oz. AGW **Obv:** Republic emblem within circle **Rev:** Storm petrel bird

Date	Mintage	F	VF	XF	Unc	BU
1976	4,098	—	—	—	135	145

KM# 48 25 POUNDS
7.9900 g., 0.9170 Gold .2353 oz. AGW **Subject:** First Gozo coin **Obv:** Republic emblem within circle **Rev:** Figure holding lance facing right within circle

Date	Mintage	F	VF	XF	Unc	BU
1977	4,000	—	—	—	165	170
1977 Proof	3,249	Value: 180				

KM# 18 50 POUNDS
30.0000 g., 0.9170 Gold .8836 oz. AGW **Obv:** Crowned arms with supporters **Rev:** Neptune divides date and value

Date	Mintage	F	VF	XF	Unc	BU
1972	16,000	—	—	—	—	615

Note: Appears to be proof, but officially issued as "BU"

KM# 23 50 POUNDS
15.0000 g., 0.9170 Gold .4418 oz. AGW **Subject:** Auberge de Castille at Valletta **Obv:** Crowned arms with supporters **Rev:** Building with small flag on top above date and value

Date	Mintage	F	VF	XF	Unc	BU
1973	9,075	—	—	—	310	320

KM# 28 50 POUNDS
15.0000 g., 0.9170 Gold .4418 oz. AGW **Subject:** First Maltese coin **Obv:** Crowned arms with supporters **Rev:** Design within wreath

Date	Mintage	F	VF	XF	Unc	BU
1974	8,667	—	—	—	310	320

KM# 38 50 POUNDS
15.0000 g., 0.9170 Gold .4418 oz. AGW **Obv:** Crowned arms with supporters **Rev:** Ornamental stone balcony

Date	Mintage	F	VF	XF	Unc	BU
1975	2,000	—	—	—	325	345

KM# 39 50 POUNDS
15.0000 g., 0.9170 Gold .4418 oz. AGW **Obv:** Republic emblem within circle **Rev:** Ornamental stone balcony

Date	Mintage	F	VF	XF	Unc	BU
1975	5,500	—	—	—	310	320

KM# 44 50 POUNDS
15.0000 g., 0.9170 Gold .4418 oz. AGW **Obv:** Republic emblem **Rev:** Ornamental door knocker

Date	Mintage	F	VF	XF	Unc	BU
1976	3,748	—	—	—	315	325

KM# 49 50 POUNDS
15.9800 g., 0.9170 Gold .4707 oz. AGW **Subject:** Mnara **Obv:** Republic emblem within circle **Rev:** Mnara design flanked by value above date

Date	Mintage	F	VF	XF	Unc	BU
1977	4,000	—	—	—	330	345
1977 Proof	846	Value: 375				

KM# 50 100 POUNDS
31.9600 g., 0.9170 Gold .9413 oz. AGW **Rev:** Father and two children sculpture above value

Date	Mintage	F	VF	XF	Unc	BU
1977	4,000	—	—	—	650	675
1977 Proof	846	Value: 725				

REFORM COINAGE

1982 - Present

100 Cents = 1 Lira

KM# 78 CENT
Copper-Zinc, 18 mm. **Obv:** Republic emblem within circle **Rev:** Common weasel

Date	Mintage	F	VF	XF	Unc	BU
1986	21,526,000	—	0.15	0.25	0.75	—
1986 Proof	10,000	Value: 75.00				

KM# 93 CENT
Copper-Zinc, 18 mm. **Obv:** Crowned shield within sprigs **Obv. Designer:** Galea Bason **Rev:** Weasel below value

Date	Mintage	F	VF	XF	Unc	BU
1991	—	—	0.15	0.25	0.75	—
1995	—	—	0.15	0.25	0.75	—
1998	—	—	0.15	0.25	0.75	—

KM# 79 2 CENTS
Copper-Zinc **Obv:** Republic emblem within circle **Rev:** Olive branch **Designer:** Noel Galea

Date	Mintage	F	VF	XF	Unc	BU
1986	280,000	—	0.15	0.25	0.45	—
1986 Proof	10,000	Value: 6.00				

KM# 94 2 CENTS
Copper-Zinc **Obv:** Crowned shield within sprigs **Obv. Designer:** Galea Bason **Rev:** Olive branch and value

Date	Mintage	F	VF	XF	Unc	BU
1991	—	—	0.30	0.60	0.90	—
1992	—	—	0.30	0.60	0.90	—
1993	—	—	0.30	0.60	0.90	—
1995	—	—	0.30	0.60	0.90	—
1998	—	—	0.30	0.60	0.90	—

KM# 77 5 CENTS
Copper-Nickel, 20 mm. **Obv:** Republic emblem within circle **Rev:** Freshwater crab **Designer:** Noel Galea

Date	Mintage	F	VF	XF	Unc	BU
1986	150,000	—	0.25	0.45	1.00	2.00
1986 Proof	10,000	Value: 7.00				

KM# 95 5 CENTS
Copper-Nickel, 20 mm. **Obv:** Crowned shield within sprigs **Obv. Designer:** Galea Bason **Rev:** Crab and value

Date	Mintage	F	VF	XF	Unc	BU
1991	—	—	0.25	0.45	1.00	2.00
1995	—	—	0.25	0.45	1.00	2.00
1998	—	—	0.25	0.45	1.00	2.00

KM# 76 10 CENTS
Copper-Nickel, 22 mm. **Obv:** Republic emblem within circle **Rev:** Dolphin fish **Designer:** Noel Galea

Date	Mintage	F	VF	XF	Unc	BU
1986	4,188,000	—	0.40	0.70	1.50	—
1986 Proof	10,000	Value: 8.00				

KM# 96 10 CENTS
Copper-Nickel, 22 mm. **Obv:** Crowned shield within sprigs **Obv. Designer:** Galea Bason **Rev:** Dolphin fish and value

Date	Mintage	F	VF	XF	Unc	BU
1991	—	—	0.40	0.70	1.50	—
1992	—	—	0.40	0.70	1.50	—
1995	—	—	0.40	0.70	6.00	—
1998	—	—	0.40	0.70	1.50	—

KM# 80 25 CENTS
Copper-Nickel, 25 mm. **Rev:** Ghirlanda flower **Designer:** Noel Galea

Date	Mintage	F	VF	XF	Unc	BU
1986	3,090,000	—	1.00	1.80	2.50	—
1986 Proof	10,000	Value: 10.00				

KM# 97 25 CENTS
Copper-Nickel, 25 mm. **Obv:** Crowned shield within sprigs **Obv. Designer:** Galea Bason **Rev:** Ghirlanda flower and value

Date	Mintage	F	VF	XF	Unc	BU
1991	—	—	1.00	1.50	2.50	—
1993	—	—	1.00	1.50	2.50	—
1995	—	—	1.00	1.50	7.00	—
1998	—	—	1.00	1.50	2.50	—

KM# 81 50 CENTS
Copper-Nickel **Obv:** Republic emblem within circle **Rev:** Tulliera plant **Designer:** Noel Galea

Date	Mintage	F	VF	XF	Unc	BU
1986	2,086,000	—	1.75	2.25	4.50	—
1986 Proof	10,000	Value: 15.00				

KM# 98 50 CENTS
Copper-Nickel **Obv:** Crowned shield within sprigs **Obv. Designer:** Galea Bason **Rev:** Tulliera plant and value

Date	Mintage	F	VF	XF	Unc	BU
1991	—	—	2.00	5.00	4.50	—
1992	—	—	2.00	5.00	4.50	—
1995	—	—	2.00	5.00	10.00	—
1998	—	—	2.00	5.00	10.00	—

KM# 116 50 CENTS
Copper-Nickel, 25 mm. **Shape:** 8-sided

Date	Mintage	F	VF	XF	Unc	BU
1995	—	—	—	—	—	—

KM# 63 LIRA
Copper-Nickel **Subject:** World Fisheries Conference **Rev:** Man in boat with fishing traps **Rev. Designer:** Stuart Devlin

Date	Mintage	F	VF	XF	Unc	BU
ND(1984)	120,000	—	—	4.00	7.50	—

KM# 82 LIRA
Nickel, 30 mm. **Obv:** Republic emblem within circle **Rev:** Merill bird **Edge Lettering:** BANK CENTRALITA MALTA **Designer:** Noel Galea

Date	Mintage	F	VF	XF	Unc	BU
1986	2,272,000	—	—	4.00	8.00	12.00
1986 Proof	10,000	Value: 20.00				

KM# 99 LIRA
Nickel **Obv:** Crowned shield within sprigs **Obv. Designer:** Galea Bason **Rev:** Merill bird and value **Rev. Designer:** Noel Galea

Date	Mintage	F	VF	XF	Unc	BU
1991	—	—	—	4.00	6.00	10.00
1992	—	—	—	4.00	6.00	10.00
1994	—	—	—	4.00	6.00	10.00
1995	—	—	—	4.00	6.00	12.00
2000	—	—	—	4.00	6.00	12.00

KM# 88 2 LIRI
17.0000 g., 0.9250 Silver .5056 oz. ASW **Subject:** 25th Anniversary of Independence **Obv:** Crowned shield within sprigs **Rev:** Bust 1/4 right flanked by dates and value

Date	Mintage	F	VF	XF	Unc	BU
1989	75,000	—	—	—	25.00	28.00
1989 Proof	7,500	Value: 45.00				

KM# 65 5 LIRI
28.2800 g., 0.9250 Silver .8411 oz. ASW **Series:** International Year of Disabled Persons **Obv:** Republic emblem **Rev:** Disabled person design, date and value within

Date	Mintage	F	VF	XF	Unc	BU
1983	—	—	—	—	45.00	50.00
1983 Proof	—	Value: 75.00				

KM# 64 5 LIRI
28.2800 g., 0.9250 Silver .8411 oz. ASW **Subject:** World Fisheries Conference **Obv:** Republic emblem **Rev:** Man in boat with fishing traps **Rev. Designer:** Stuart Devlin

Date	Mintage	F	VF	XF	Unc	BU
ND(1984) Proof	20,000	Value: 65.00				

KM# 67 5 LIRI
20.0000 g., 0.9250 Silver .5949 oz. ASW **Subject:** Maritime history "Strangier" (1813) **Obv:** Republic emblem within circle **Rev:** Saling ship among grid lines **Designer:** Noel Galea

Date	Mintage	F	VF	XF	Unc	BU
1984 Prooflike	15,000	—	—	—	42.50	45.00

KM# 68 5 LIRI
20.0000 g., 0.9250 Silver .5949 oz. ASW **Subject:** Maritime History **Obv:** Republic emblem **Rev:** "Tigre" (1839) **Designer:** Noel Galea

Date	Mintage	F	VF	XF	Unc	BU
1984 Prooflike	15,000	—	—	—	42.50	45.00

KM# 69 5 LIRI
20.0000 g., 0.9250 Silver .5949 oz. ASW **Subject:** Maritime

history **Obv:** Republic emblem **Rev:** "Wignacourt" (1844)
Designer: Noel Galea

Date	Mintage	F	VF	XF	Unc	BU
1984 Prooflike	15,000	—	—	—	42.50	45.00

KM# 70 5 LIRI
20.0000 g., 0.9250 Silver .5949 oz. ASW **Subject:** Maritime history **Obv:** Republic emblem **Rev:** "Providenza" (1848)
Designer: Noel Galea

Date	Mintage	F	VF	XF	Unc	BU
1984 Prooflike	15,000	—	—	—	42.50	45.00

KM# 71 5 LIRI
28.2800 g., 0.9250 Silver .8411 oz. ASW **Series:** Decade for Women **Obv:** Republic emblem **Rev:** Woman weaving on board within circle **Rev. Designer:** Michael Rizzello

Date	Mintage	F	VF	XF	Unc	BU
1984 Proof	17,000	Value: 90.00				

KM# 72 5 LIRI
20.0000 g., 0.9250 Silver .5949 oz. ASW **Subject:** Maritime history **Obv:** Republic emblem **Rev:** "Malta" (1862)
Designer: Noel Galea

Date	Mintage	F	VF	XF	Unc	BU
1985 Prooflike	15,000	—	—	—	42.50	45.00

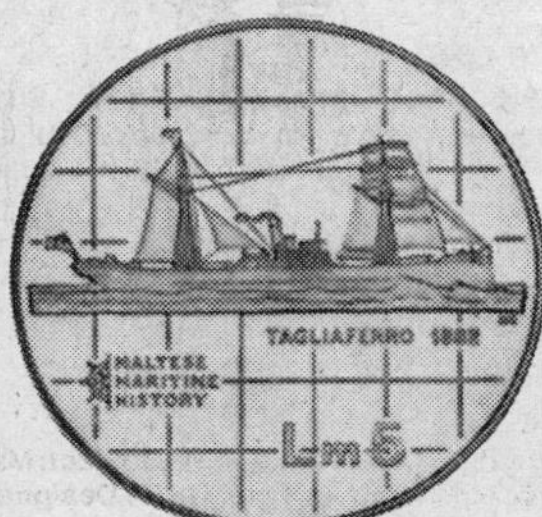

KM# 73 5 LIRI
20.0000 g., 0.9250 Silver .5949 oz. ASW **Subject:** Maritime history **Obv:** Republic emblem **Rev:** "Tagliaferro" (1882)
Designer: Noel Galea

Date	Mintage	F	VF	XF	Unc	BU
1985 Prooflike	15,000	—	—	—	42.50	45.00

KM# 74 5 LIRI
20.0000 g., 0.9250 Silver .5949 oz. ASW **Subject:** Maritime history **Obv:** Republic emblem **Rev:** "L'Isle Adam" (1883)
Designer: Noel Galea

Date	Mintage	F	VF	XF	Unc	BU
1985 Prooflike	15,000	—	—	—	42.50	45.00

KM# 75 5 LIRI
20.0000 g., 0.9250 Silver .5949 oz. ASW **Subject:** Maritime history **Obv:** Republic emblem **Rev:** "Maria Dacoutros" (1902)
Designer: Noel Galea

Date	Mintage	F	VF	XF	Unc	BU
1985 Prooflike	15,000	—	—	—	42.50	45.00

KM# 83 5 LIRI
20.0000 g., 0.9250 Silver .5949 oz. ASW **Subject:** Maritime history **Obv:** Republic emblem **Rev:** "Valetta City" (1917)
Designer: Noel Galea

Date	Mintage	F	VF	XF	Unc	BU
1986 Prooflike	15,000	—	—	—	42.50	45.00

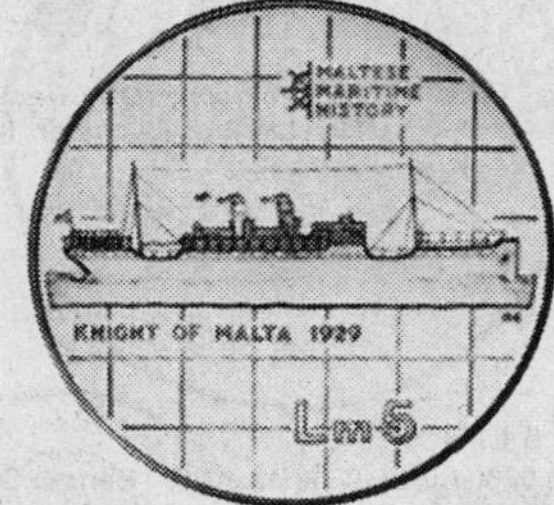

KM# 84 5 LIRI
20.0000 g., 0.9250 Silver .5949 oz. ASW **Subject:** Maritime history **Obv:** Republic emblem **Rev:** "Knight of Malta" (1929)
Designer: Noel Galea

Date	Mintage	F	VF	XF	Unc	BU
1986 Prooflike	15,000	—	—	—	42.50	45.00

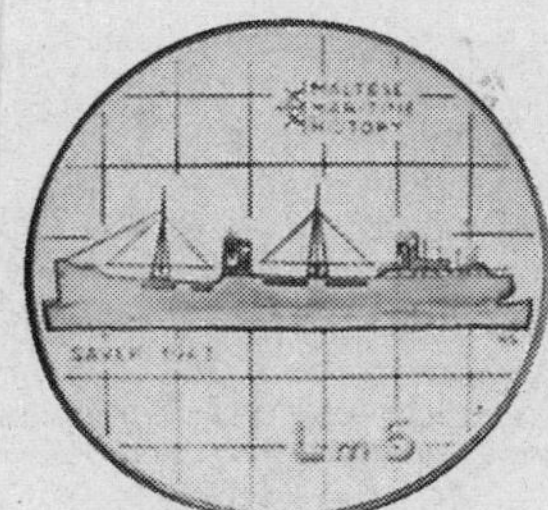

KM# 85 5 LIRI
20.0000 g., 0.9250 Silver .5949 oz. ASW **Subject:** Maritime history **Obv:** Republic emblem **Rev:** "Saver" (1943)
Designer: Noel Galea

Date	Mintage	F	VF	XF	Unc	BU
1986 Prooflike	15,000	—	—	—	42.50	45.00

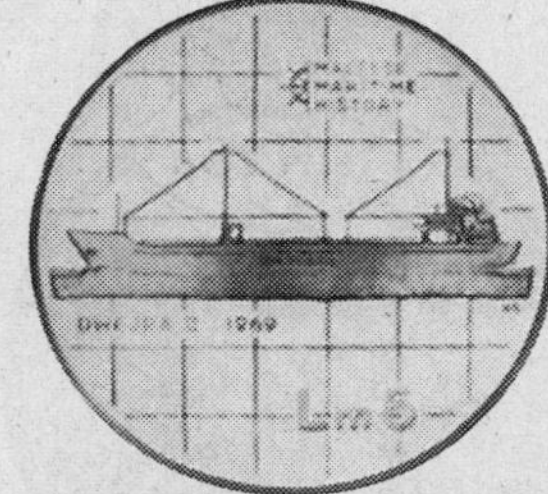

KM# 86 5 LIRI
20.0000 g., 0.9250 Silver .5949 oz. ASW **Subject:** Maritime history **Obv:** Republic emblem **Rev:** "Dwejra II" (1969) **Designer:** Noel Galea

Date	Mintage	F	VF	XF	Unc	BU
1986 Prooflike	15,000	—	—	—	42.50	45.00

KM# 87 5 LIRI
28.2800 g., 0.9250 Silver .8411 oz. ASW **Subject:** 20th Anniversary - Central Bank of Malta **Obv:** Crowned arms with supporters **Rev:** Bank of Malta

Date	Mintage	F	VF	XF	Unc	BU
1988	Est. 5,000	—	—	—	25.00	27.50
1988 Proof	Est. 2,000	Value: 40.00				

KM# 90 5 LIRI
28.6000 g., 0.9250 Silver .8506 oz. ASW **Subject:** Papal visit **Obv:** Crowned shield within sprigs **Obv. Designer:** Noel Galea **Rev:** Pope's hand with staff, city scene in background

Date	Mintage	F	VF	XF	Unc	BU
1990	5,000	—	—	—	45.00	48.00
1990 Proof	4,000	Value: 55.00				

KM# 91 5 LIRI
28.2800 g., 0.9250 Silver .8411 oz. ASW **Subject:** Entry of Malta to European Economic Community **Obv. Designer:** Galea Bason **Rev:** Two flags among the map of Malta **Rev. Designer:** John Bonnici

Date	Mintage	F	VF	XF	Unc	BU
1990	—	—	—	—	30.00	32.50
1990 Proof	4,000	Value: 50.00				

KM# 92 5 LIRI
28.2800 g., 0.9250 Silver .8411 oz. ASW **Series:** Save the Children **Obv:** Crowned shield within wreath **Rev:** Children playing

Date	Mintage	F	VF	XF	Unc	BU
1991 Proof	20,000	Value: 50.00				

KM# 100 5 LIRI
28.2800 g., 0.9250 Silver .8411 oz. ASW **Subject:** 50th Anniversary of George Cross Award **Obv:** Crowned shield within wreath **Obv. Designer:** Galea Bason **Rev:** George cross award

Date	Mintage	F	VF	XF	Unc	BU
1992	—	—	—	—	—	50.00
1992 Proof	10,000	Value: 75.00				

KM# 102 5 LIRI
28.2800 g., 0.9250 Silver .8411 oz. ASW **Subject:** 25th Anniversary of Central Bank **Obv:** Arms above Central Bank building **Rev:** Bust facing

Date	Mintage	F	VF	XF	Unc	BU
ND (1993)	—	—	—	—	—	50.00
ND(1993) Proof	1,500	Value: 65.00				

KM# 106 5 LIRI
28.2800 g., 0.9250 Silver .8411 oz. ASW **Subject:** 400th Anniversary - University of Malta **Obv:** University emblems above crowned shield within sprigs flanked by dates **Rev:** Conjoined armored busts left

Date	Mintage	F	VF	XF	Unc	BU
ND(1993) Proof	Est. 1,000	Value: 90.00				

KM# 107 5 LIRI
28.2800 g., 0.9250 Silver .8411 oz. ASW **Subject:** World Cup Soccer **Obv:** Crowned shield within wreath **Obv. Designer:** Galea Bason **Rev:** Goalie catching ball

Date	Mintage	F	VF	XF	Unc	BU
1993 Proof	Est. 20,000	Value: 50.00				

KM# 108 5 LIRI
31.4700 g., 0.9250 Silver .9359 oz. ASW **Obv:** Crowned shield within wreath **Rev:** Sailing ship "Valletta" and fortress

Date	Mintage	F	VF	XF	Unc	BU
1994 Proof	Est. 20,000	Value: 75.00				

KM# 109 5 LIRI
28.2800 g., 0.9250 Silver .8411 oz. ASW **Series:** 50th Anniversary - United Nations **Obv:** Crowned shield within wreath **Rev:** Small UN logo above two half figures shaking hands, all within circle

Date	Mintage	F	VF	XF	Unc	BU
1995 Proof	125,000	Value: 40.00				

KM# 110 5 LIRI
31.4700 g., 0.9250 Silver .9359 oz. ASW **Series:** Olympic Games **Subject:** Water polo **Obv:** Crowned shield within wreath **Rev:** Men playing water volley ball

Date	Mintage	F	VF	XF	Unc	BU
1996 Proof	Est. 35,000	Value: 35.00				

KM# 115 5 LIRI
28.2800 g., 0.9250 Silver 0.841 oz. ASW, 38.6 mm. **Subject:** UNICEF **Obv:** Crowned shield within wreath **Rev:** Boy with dog and computer **Edge:** Reeded

Date	Mintage	F	VF	XF	Unc	BU
1997 Proof	25,000	Value: 60.00				

KM# 111 5 LIRI
28.2800 g., 0.9250 Silver .841 oz. ASW **Obv:** Crowned shield within wreath **Rev:** Bank's pyramid fountain

Date	Mintage	F	VF	XF	Unc	BU
1998 Proof	1,500	Value: 60.00				

KM# 112 5 LIRI
28.2800 g., 0.9250 Silver .841 oz. ASW **Subject:** 200th Anniversary - Anti-French Revolution **Obv:** National arms **Rev:** "Blockade" medal of 1798

Date	Mintage	F	VF	XF	Unc	BU
1998 Proof	1,500	Value: 60.00				

KM# 113 5 LIRI
28.3500 g., 0.9250 Silver .8431 oz. ASW, 38.4 mm. **Subject:** Mattia Preti **Obv:** Crowned shield within wreath **Obv. Designer:** Galea Bason **Rev:** Portrait of Preti and John the Baptist **Edge:** Reeded

Date	Mintage	F	VF	XF	Unc	BU
1999 Proof	5,000	Value: 50.00				

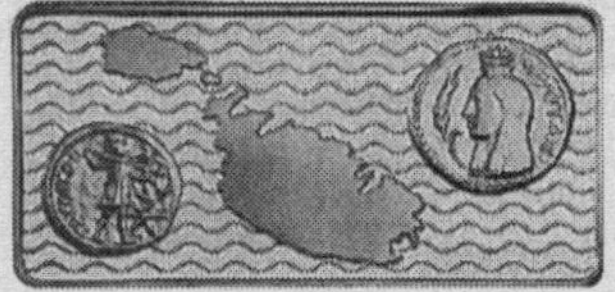

KM# 114 5 LIRI
15.0000 g., 0.9250 Silver .4461 oz. ASW **Subject:** Millennium **Obv:** Two modern gold-plated coin designs **Rev:** Two ancient coin designs, gold-plated, and Malta Island map **Edge:** Plain **Note:** 40 x 20mm.

Date	Mintage	F	VF	XF	Unc	BU
2000 Proof	32,000	Value: 125				

KM# 101 25 LIRI
7.9900 g., 0.9170 Gold .2353 oz. AGW **Subject:** 50th Anniversary of George Cross Award **Obv:** Crowned shield within wreath **Obv. Designer:** Galea Bason **Rev:** George cross award

Date	Mintage	F	VF	XF	Unc	BU
1992 Proof	Est. 500	Value: 450				

KM# 66 100 LIRI
15.9800 g., 0.9170 Gold .4709 oz. AGW **Series:** International Year of Disabled Persons **Obv:** Republic emblem within circle **Rev:** Puzzle head right with missing pieces on top

Date	Mintage	F	VF	XF	Unc	BU
1983	700	—	—	—	600	650
1983 Proof	600	Value: 1,100				

KM# 89 100 LIRI
17.0000 g., 0.9170 Gold .5007 oz. AGW **Subject:** 25th Anniversary of Independence **Obv:** Crowned shield within sprigs **Rev:** Bust 1/4 right flanked by dates and value

Date	Mintage	F	VF	XF	Unc	BU
1989	5,000	—	—	—	400	425
1989 Proof	2,500	Value: 500				

ECU / LIRA COINAGE

European Currency Unit

KM# 103 LIRA (2 Ecu)
Copper-Nickel **Subject:** Defense of Europe **Obv:** Crowned shield within sprigs **Obv. Designer:** Galea Bason **Rev:** Cluster of sailing ships within circle

Date	Mintage	F	VF	XF	Unc	BU
1993	25,000	—	—	—	30.00	32.50

KM# 104 5 LIRI (10 Ecu)
25.0000 g., 0.9250 Silver .7435 oz. ASW **Subject:** Defense of Europe **Obv:** Crowned shield within wreath **Obv. Designer:** Galea Bason **Rev:** Ships at sea

Date	Mintage	F	VF	XF	Unc	BU
1993 Proof	35,000	Value: 75.00				

KM# 105 25 LIRI (55 Ecu)
6.7200 g., 0.9000 Gold .1945 oz. AGW **Subject:** Defense of Europe

Date	Mintage	F	VF	XF	Unc	BU
1993 Proof	2,500	Value: 425				

PIEFORTS

KM#	Date	Mintage	Identification	Issue Price	Mkt Val
P1	1981	177	5 Liri. 0.9250 Silver. KM53.	—	275
P2	1983	700	5 Liri. 0.9250 Silver. KM65.	—	275
P3	1983	150	100 Pounds. 0.9170 Gold. KM66.	—	1,250
P4	1988	500	100 Pounds. 0.9250 Silver. KM87.	80.00	175

MINT SETS

KM#	Date	Mintage	Identification	Issue Price	Mkt Val
MS1	1972 (8)	8,000	KM5-12	—	50.00
MS2	1972 (4)	8,000	KM15-18	210	1,050
MS3	1972 (2)	—	KM13-14	8.50	35.00
MS4	1973 (3)	9,078	KM21-23	—	525
MS5	1973 (2)	—	KM19-20	—	35.00
MS6	1974 (3)	—	KM26-28	256	525
MS7	1974 (2)	—	KM24-25	19.60	40.00
MS8	1975 (5)	2,000	KM30, 32, 34, 36, 38	276	700
MS9	1975 (3)	—	KM34, 36, 38	256	650
MS11	1975 (3)	—	KM35, 37, 39	—	550
MSA10	1975 (2)	—	KM31, 33	—	40.00
MS10	1975 (2)	2,000	KM30, 32	20.00	75.00
MS12	1976 (3)	—	KM42-44	—	575
MS13	1976 (2)	—	KM40-41	—	30.00
MS14	1977 (9)	252	KM5-12, 29b	—	80.00
MS15	1977 (3)	4,000	KM48-50	610	1,300
MS16	1977 (3)	15,000	KM45-47	34.50	100
MS17	1978 (9)	252	KM5-12, 29b	—	60.00
MS18	1979 (9)	537	KM5-12, 29b	—	125
MS19	1980 (9)	385	KM5-12, 29b	11.00	125
MS20	1981 (9)	449	KM5-12, 29b	13.25	125
MS21	1982 (9)	850	KM54-62	13.25	175
MS22	1984 (4)	15,000	KM67-70	72.00	135
MS23	1985 (4)	15,000	KM72-75	72.00	135
MS24	1986 (4)	15,000	KM83-86	72.00	135
MS25	1995 (7)	—	KM#93-97, 99, 116	—	71.50

PROOF SETS

KM#	Date	Mintage	Identification	Issue Price	Mkt Val
PS1	1972 (8)	8,000	KM5-12; plastic case	—	75.00
PS2	1976 (9)	26,248	KM5-12, 29b	27.50	25.00
PS3	1977 (9)	6,884	KM5-12, 29b	31.50	45.00
PS4	1977 (3)	750	KM48-50	909	1,650
PS5	1977 (3)	2,500	KM45-47	72.00	250
PS6	1978 (9)	3,244	KM5-12, 29b	—	45.00
PS7	1979 (10)	6,577	KM5-12, 29b, 51	41.50	75.00
PS8	1980 (9)	3,451	KM5-12, 29b	30.00	45.00
PS9	1981 (9)	1,453	KM5-12, 29b	25.30	90.00
PS10	1982 (9)	1,793	KM54-62	32.00	195
PS11	1986 (7)	10,000	KM76-82	29.75	150

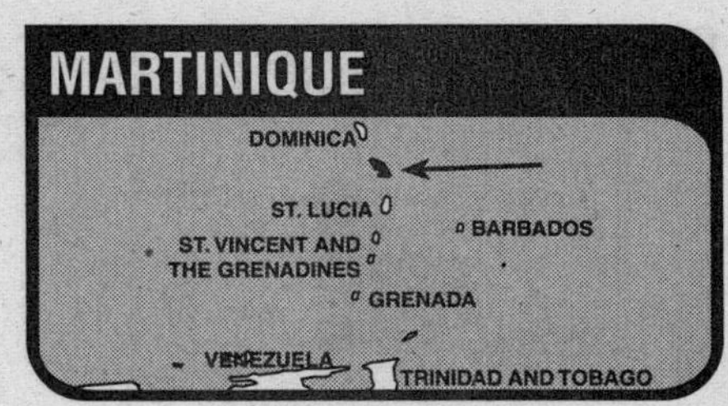

The French Overseas Department of Martinique, located in the Lesser Antilles of the West Indies between Dominica and Saint Lucia, has an area of 425 sq. mi.(1,100 sq. km.) and a population of 290,000. Capital: Fort-de-France. Agriculture and tourism are the major sources of income. Bananas, sugar, and rum are exported.

Christopher Columbus discovered Martinique, probably on June 15, 1502. France took possession on June 25, 1635, and has maintained possession since that time except for three short periods of British occupation during the Napoleonic Wars. A French department since 1946, Martinique voted a reaffirmation of that status in 1958, remaining within the new French Community. Martinique was the birthplace of Napoleon's Empress Josephine, and the site of the eruption of Mt. Pelee in 1902 that claimed 40,000 lives.

The official currency of Martinique is the French franc. The 1897-1922 coinage of the Colony of Martinique is now obsolete.

MONETARY SYSTEM
15 Sols = 1 Escalin
20 Sols = 1 Livre
66 Livres = 4 Escudos = 6400 Reis

FRENCH COLONY

DECIMAL COINAGE

KM# 40 50 CENTIMES
Copper-Nickel **Obv:** Bust left within circle with star above **Rev:** Value and date within wreath

Date	Mintage	VG	F	VF	XF	Unc
1922	500,000	12.00	22.00	40.00	150	400

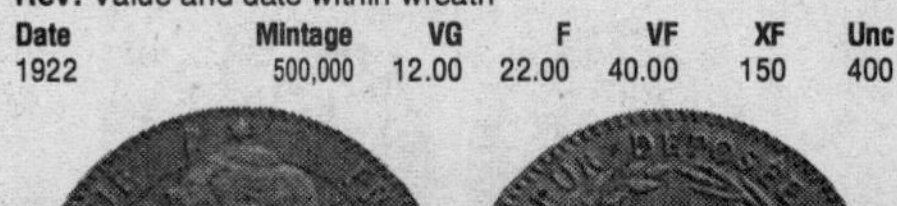

KM# 41 FRANC
Copper-Nickel **Obv:** Bust left within circle with star above **Rev:** Value and date within wreath

Date	Mintage	VG	F	VF	XF	Unc
1922	350,000	15.00	25.00	50.00	175	425

MAURITANIA

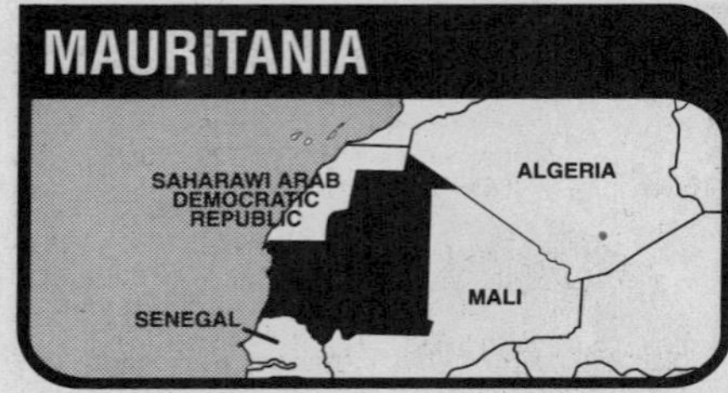

The Islamic Republic of Mauritania, located in northwest Africa bounded by Western Sahara, Mali, Algeria, Senegal and the Atlantic Ocean, has an area of 397,955 sq. mi.(1,030,700 sq. km.) and a population of 1.9 million. Capital: Nouakchott. The economy centers on herding, agriculture, fishing and mining. Iron ore, copper concentrates and fish products are exported.

The indigenous Negroid inhabitants were driven out of Mauritania by Berber invaders of the Islamic faith in the 11th century. The Berbers in turn were conquered by Arab invaders, the Beni Hassan, in the 16th century. Arab traders carried on a gainful trade in gum arabic, gold and slaves with Portuguese, Dutch, English and French traders until late in the 19th century when France took control of the area and made it a part of French West Africa, in 1920.Mauritania became a part of the French Union in 1946 and was made an autonomous republic within the new French Community in 1958, when the Islamic Republic of Mauritania was proclaimed. The republic became independent on November 28, 1960, and withdrew from the French Community in 1966.

On June 28, 1973, in a move designed to emphasize its nonalignment with France, Mauritania converted its currency from the old French-supported C.F.A. franc unit to a new unit called the Ouguiya.

MONETARY SYSTEM
5 Khoums = 1 Ouguiya

REPUBLIC

STANDARD COINAGE

KM# 1 1/5 OUGUIYA (Khoums)
Aluminum **Obv:** National emblem divides date above value **Rev:** Star and crescent divide sprigs within circle with legend around border

Date	Mintage	VG	F	VF	XF	Unc
AH1393//1973	1,000,000	—	0.35	0.75	1.50	3.00

KM# 2 OUGUIYA
Copper-Nickel-Aluminum **Obv:** National emblem divides date above value **Rev:** Star and crescent divide sprigs below value within circle, legend around border

Date	Mintage	VG	F	VF	XF	Unc
AH1393//1973	—	—	7.00	20.00	37.50	85.00

KM# 6 OUGUIYA
Copper-Nickel-Aluminum, 21 mm. **Obv:** National emblem divides date above value **Rev:** Star and crescent divide sprigs with legend below value, all within circle

Date	Mintage	VG	F	VF	XF	Unc
AH1394//1974	—	—	2.50	5.50	10.00	18.50
AH1401//1981	—	—	1.50	3.00	4.50	7.50
AH1403//1983	—	—	1.00	2.00	3.50	6.50
AH1406//1986	—	—	0.75	1.50	2.50	4.50
AH1407//1987	—	—	0.50	1.00	2.00	4.00
AH1410//1990	—	—	0.50	1.00	2.00	4.00
AH1414//1993	—	—	0.50	1.00	2.00	4.00
AH1416//1995	—	—	0.50	1.00	2.00	4.00

KM# 3 5 OUGUIYA
Copper-Nickel-Aluminum, 25 mm. **Obv:** National emblem divides date above value **Rev:** Star and crescent divide sprigs below value within circle

Date	Mintage	VG	F	VF	XF	Unc
AH1393//1973	—	—	2.50	5.50	10.00	15.00
AH1394//1974	—	—	2.50	5.50	10.00	17.50
AH1401//1981	—	—	2.00	4.00	6.00	12.50
AH1404//1984	—	—	1.50	2.50	4.50	10.00
AH1407//1987	—	—	0.75	1.50	2.50	5.00
AH1410//1990	—	—	0.50	1.00	2.00	4.00
AH1414//1993	—	—	0.50	1.00	2.00	4.00
AH1416//1995	—	—	0.50	1.00	2.00	4.00
AH1418//1997	—	—	0.50	1.00	2.00	4.00
AH1420//1999	—	—	0.50	1.00	2.00	4.00

KM# 4 10 OUGUIYA
Copper-Nickel, 25 mm. **Obv:** National emblem divides date above value **Rev:** Crescent and star divide sprigs below value within circle

Date	Mintage	VG	F	VF	XF	Unc
AH1393//1973	—	—	2.50	5.50	10.00	17.50
AH1394//1974	—	—	2.50	5.50	10.00	17.50
AH1401//1981	—	—	2.00	5.00	7.50	15.00
AH1403//1983	—	—	1.25	2.50	4.00	8.00
AH1407//1987	—	—	1.25	2.50	4.00	8.00
AH1410//1990	—	—	0.75	1.50	2.50	4.50
AH1411//1991	—	—	0.75	1.50	2.50	4.50
AH1414//1993	—	—	0.75	1.50	2.50	4.50
AH1416//1995	—	—	0.75	1.50	2.50	4.50
AH1418//1997	—	—	0.75	1.50	2.50	4.50
AH1420//1999	—	—	0.75	1.50	2.50	4.50

KM# 5 20 OUGUIYA
Copper-Nickel, 28 mm. **Obv:** National emblem divides date above value **Rev:** Star and crescent divide sprigs below value within circle

Date	Mintage	VG	F	VF	XF	Unc
AH1393//1973	—	—	2.00	5.00	10.00	18.00
AH1394//1974	—	—	2.00	5.00	10.00	18.00
AH1403//1983	—	—	1.25	2.50	4.00	8.00
AH1407//1987	—	—	1.25	2.50	4.00	8.00
AH1410//1990	—	—	1.25	2.50	4.00	8.00
AH1414//1993	—	—	1.25	2.50	4.00	8.00
AH1416//1995	—	—	1.25	2.50	4.00	8.00
AH1418//1997	—	—	1.25	2.50	4.00	8.00
AH1420//1999	—	—	1.25	2.50	4.00	8.00

KM# 7 500 OUGUIYA
26.0800 g., 0.9200 Gold .7714 oz. AGW **Subject:** 15th Anniversary of Independence **Obv:** Star and crescent flanked by palm trees below dates **Rev:** Value in square flanked by a camel head and fish with design above

Date	Mintage	F	VF	XF	Unc	BU
1975 (a)	1,800	—	—	—	575	625

MINT SETS

KM#	Date	Mintage	Identification	Issue Price	Mkt Val
MS1	1973 (10)	—	KM1-5, two each	20.00	275

MAURITIUS

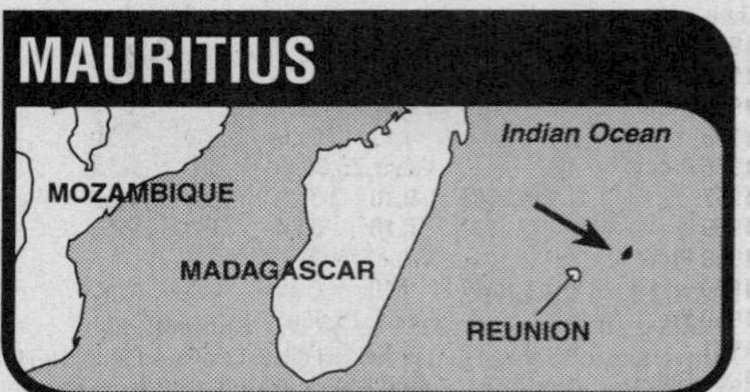

The Republic of Mauritius, is located in the Indian Ocean 500 miles (805 km.) east of Madagascar, has an area of 790 sq. mi. (1,860 sq. km.) and a population of 1 million. Capital: Port Louis. Sugar provides 90 percent of the export revenue.

Mauritius became independent on March 12, 1968. It is a member of the Commonwealth of Nations.

RULERS
British, until 1968

MINT MARKS
H - Heaton, Birmingham
SA - Pretoria Mint

MONETARY SYSTEM
100 Cents = 1 Rupee

CROWN COLONY

STANDARD COINAGE

100 Cents = 1 Rupee

KM# 12 CENT
Bronze **Obv:** Crowned bust left **Obv. Designer:** E.B. MacKennal **Rev:** Value within beaded circle

Date	Mintage	F	VF	XF	Unc	BU
1911	1,000,000	1.00	6.00	22.00	40.00	90.00
1912	500,000	1.25	6.50	28.50	55.00	100
1917	500,000	1.00	6.00	22.00	35.00	70.00
1920	500,000	1.50	8.00	32.50	60.00	120
1921	500,000	2.00	8.00	32.50	60.00	120
1922	1,800,000	0.75	1.50	9.00	25.00	50.00
1923	200,000	3.00	17.00	45.00	75.00	150
1924	200,000	3.00	17.00	45.00	75.00	150

KM# 21 CENT
Bronze **Obv:** Crowned head left **Obv. Designer:** Percy Metcalfe **Rev:** Value within beaded circle

Date	Mintage	F	VF	XF	Unc	BU
1943SA	520,000	0.50	1.25	4.00	10.00	22.00
1944SA	500,000	0.50	1.25	4.00	10.00	22.00
1945SA	500,000	0.50	1.25	4.00	10.00	22.00
1946SA	500,000	0.50	1.25	4.00	10.00	22.00
1947SA	500,000	0.50	1.25	4.00	10.00	22.00

KM# 25 CENT
Bronze **Obv:** Crowned head left **Obv. Designer:** Percy Metcalfe **Rev:** Value within beaded circle

Date	Mintage	F	VF	XF	Unc	BU
1949	500,000	0.75	1.25	2.50	7.50	15.00
1949 Proof	—	Value: 100				
1952	500,000	0.75	1.25	2.50	7.50	15.00
1952 Proof	—	Value: 100				

KM# 31 CENT
1.9500 g., Bronze, 17.8 mm. **Obv:** Crowned head of Queen Elizabeth II right **Obv. Designer:** Cecil Thomas **Rev:** Value within beaded circle

Date	Mintage	F	VF	XF	Unc	BU
1953	500,000	0.10	0.25	0.50	1.50	—

Date	Mintage	F	VF	XF	Unc	BU
1953 Proof	—	Value: 75.00				
1955	501,000	0.10	0.25	0.50	2.50	—
1955 Proof	—	Value: 75.00				
1956	500,000	0.10	0.20	0.50	2.50	—
1956 Proof	—	Value: 75.00				
1957	501,000	0.10	0.20	0.50	2.50	—
1959	501,000	0.10	0.20	0.50	2.50	—
1959 Proof	—	Value: 75.00				
1960	500,000	0.10	0.20	0.50	2.50	—
1960 Proof	—	Value: 75.00				
1961	500,000	0.10	0.20	0.50	2.50	—
1961 Proof	—	Value: 75.00				
1962	500,000	0.10	0.20	0.50	1.50	—
1962 Proof	—	Value: 50.00				
1963	500,000	0.10	0.20	0.50	1.50	—
1963 Proof	—	Value: 50.00				
1964	1,500,000	—	0.10	0.20	0.50	—
1964 Proof	—	Value: 50.00				
1965	1,500,000	—	0.10	0.20	0.50	—
1969	500,000	—	0.10	0.15	0.30	—
1970	1,500,000	—	—	0.10	0.20	—
1971	1,000,000	—	—	0.10	0.20	—
1971 Proof	750	Value: 17.50				
1975	400,000	—	—	0.10	0.20	—
1978	—	—	—	0.10	0.20	—

KM# 13 2 CENTS
Bronze **Obv:** Crowned bust left **Obv. Designer:** E.B. MacKennal **Rev:** Value within beaded circle

Date	Mintage	F	VF	XF	Unc	BU
1911	500,000	2.00	12.00	25.00	40.00	85.00
1911 Proof	—	Value: 300				
1912	250,000	3.00	15.00	40.00	70.00	140
1917	250,000	1.25	14.50	22.00	50.00	80.00
1920	250,000	1.50	14.00	28.00	55.00	90.00
1921	250,000	1.50	10.00	28.00	55.00	90.00
1922	900,000	0.50	4.00	15.00	30.00	60.00
1923	400,000	1.25	5.50	28.50	55.00	95.00
1924	400,000	1.25	5.50	28.50	50.00	90.00

KM# 22 2 CENTS
Bronze **Obv:** Crowned head left **Obv. Designer:** Percy Metcalfe **Rev:** Value within beaded circle

Date	Mintage	F	VF	XF	Unc	BU
1943SA	290,000	0.75	2.00	4.00	10.00	22.00
1944SA	500,000	0.75	2.00	4.00	10.00	22.00
1945SA	250,000	0.75	2.00	4.00	10.00	22.00
1946SA	400,000	0.75	2.00	4.00	10.00	22.00
1947SA	250,000	0.75	2.00	4.00	10.00	22.00

KM# 26 2 CENTS
3.8500 g., Bronze, 23.2 mm. **Obv:** Crowned head left **Obv. Designer:** Percy Metcalfe **Rev:** Value within beaded circle

Date	Mintage	F	VF	XF	Unc	BU
1949	250,000	0.75	1.25	2.50	6.50	12.50
1949 Proof	—	Value: 120				
1952	250,000	0.75	1.25	2.50	6.50	12.50
1952 Proof	—	Value: 120				

KM# 32 2 CENTS
3.8500 g., Bronze, 23.2 mm. **Obv:** Crowned head right **Obv. Designer:** Cecil Thomas **Rev:** Value within beaded circle

Date	Mintage	F	VF	XF	Unc	BU
1953	250,000	0.10	0.25	0.50	2.50	—
1953 Proof	—	Value: 100				
1954 Proof	—	Value: 300				
1955	501,000	0.10	0.25	0.50	2.50	—
1955 Proof	—	Value: 100				
1956	250,000	0.10	0.25	0.50	3.50	—
1956 Proof	—	Value: 100				
1957	501,000	0.10	0.25	0.50	3.50	—
1959	503,000	0.10	0.25	0.50	3.50	—
1959 Proof	—	Value: 100				
1960	250,000	0.10	0.25	0.50	3.50	—
1960 Proof	—	Value: 100				
1961	500,000	0.10	0.25	0.50	3.50	—
1961 Proof	—	Value: 100				
1962	500,000	0.10	0.25	0.50	1.50	—
1962 Proof	—	Value: 75.00				
1963	500,000	0.10	0.25	0.50	1.50	—
1963 Proof	—	Value: 75.00				
1964	1,000,000	—	0.10	0.25	0.50	—
1964 Proof	—	Value: 50.00				
1965	750,000	0.10	0.20	0.40	0.60	—
1966	500,000	0.10	0.20	0.40	0.50	—
1967	250,000	0.10	0.20	0.40	0.50	—
1969	500,000	0.10	0.20	0.40	0.50	—
1971	1,000,000	—	0.10	0.20	0.40	—
1971 Proof	750	Value: 17.50				
1975	5,200,000	—	—	0.10	0.35	—
1978	—	—	—	0.10	0.35	—
1978 Proof	9,268	Value: 1.50				

KM# 14 5 CENTS
9.7000 g., Bronze, 28.4 mm. **Obv:** Crowned bust left **Obv. Designer:** E.B. MacKennal **Rev:** Value within beaded circle

Date	Mintage	F	VF	XF	Unc	BU
1917	600,000	2.00	24.50	57.50	80.00	160
1920	200,000	2.00	24.50	60.00	100	200
1921	100,000	3.00	26.50	65.00	120	250
1922	360,000	2.00	14.50	42.50	100	200
1923	400,000	3.00	16.50	45.00	120	250
1924	400,000	2.00	14.50	42.50	100	200

KM# 20 5 CENTS
9.7000 g., Bronze, 28.4 mm. **Obv:** Crowned head left **Obv. Designer:** Percy Metcalfe **Rev:** Value within beaded circle

Date	Mintage	F	VF	XF	Unc	BU
1942SA	940,000	1.50	2.50	6.50	15.00	35.00
1944SA	1,000,000	1.25	1.75	4.00	10.00	22.00
1945SA	500,000	1.25	1.75	4.00	12.00	30.00

KM# 34 5 CENTS
9.7000 g., Bronze, 28.4 mm. **Obv:** Crowned head right **Obv. Designer:** Cecil Thomas **Rev:** Value within beaded circle

Date	Mintage	F	VF	XF	Unc	BU
1956	201,000	0.25	0.50	0.75	5.00	—
1956 Proof	—	Value: 100				
1957	203,000	0.25	0.50	2.00	8.00	—
1957 Proof	—	Value: 100				
1959	801,000	0.25	0.50	1.00	4.00	—
1959 Proof	—	Value: 75.00				
1960	400,000	0.25	0.50	1.00	4.00	—
1960 Proof	—	Value: 75.00				
1963	200,000	0.25	0.50	1.00	2.00	—
1963 Proof	—	Value: 70.00				
1964	600,000	0.25	0.50	1.00	2.00	—
1964 Proof	—	Value: 70.00				
1965	200,000	0.25	0.50	0.75	2.00	—
1966	200,000	0.25	0.50	0.75	1.50	—
1967	200,000	0.25	0.50	0.75	2.00	—
1969	500,000	0.10	0.15	0.25	0.50	—
1970	800,000	0.10	0.15	0.25	0.50	—
1971	500,000	0.10	0.15	0.25	0.50	—
1971 Proof	750	Value: 17.50				
1975	3,700,000	0.10	0.15	0.25	0.50	—
1978	8,000,000	—	0.10	0.20	0.50	—
1978 Proof	9,268	Value: 2.00				

KM# 24 10 CENTS
5.1500 g., Copper-Nickel, 23.5 mm. **Obv:** Crowned head left **Obv. Designer:** Percy Metcalfe **Rev:** Value **Shape:** Scalloped

Date	Mintage	F	VF	XF	Unc	BU
1947	500,000	1.50	4.50	18.00	45.00	—
1947 Proof	—	Value: 200				

KM# 30 10 CENTS
5.1500 g., Copper-Nickel, 23.5 mm. **Obv:** Crowned head left **Obv. Designer:** Percy Metcalfe **Rev:** Value **Shape:** Scalloped

Date	Mintage	F	VF	XF	Unc	BU
1952	250,000	0.50	1.00	3.50	9.50	17.50
1952 Proof	—	Value: 150				

KM# 33 10 CENTS
5.1500 g., Copper-Nickel, 23.5 mm. **Obv:** Crowned head right **Obv. Designer:** Cecil Thomas **Rev:** Value **Shape:** Scalloped

Date	Mintage	F	VF	XF	Unc	BU
1954	252,000	0.20	0.35	0.75	2.50	—
1954 Proof	—	Value: 150				
1957	250,000	0.20	0.35	0.75	2.50	—
1959	253,000	0.20	0.35	0.75	2.50	—
1959 Proof	—	Value: 175				
1960	50,000	0.20	0.35	0.75	2.00	—
1960 Proof	—	Value: 175				
1963	200,000	0.15	0.30	0.60	1.50	—
1963 Proof	—	Value: 175				
1964	200,000	0.15	0.30	0.60	1.00	—
1965	200,000	0.15	0.30	0.60	1.00	—
1966	200,000	0.10	0.25	0.50	0.75	—
1969	200,000	0.10	0.25	0.50	0.75	—
1970	500,000	0.10	0.25	0.50	0.75	—
1971	300,000	0.10	0.25	0.50	0.75	—
1971 Proof	750	Value: 17.50				
1975	6,675,000	0.10	0.25	0.50	0.75	—
1978	13,000,000	0.10	0.25	0.50	0.75	—
1978 Proof	9,268	Value: 2.50				

KM# 15 1/4 RUPEE
2.9200 g., 0.9160 Silver .0816 oz. ASW, 19 mm. **Obv:** Crowned bust left **Obv. Designer:** E.B. MacKennal **Rev:** Crown above 3 emblems **Rev. Designer:** G. E. Kruger-Gray

Date	Mintage	F	VF	XF	Unc	BU
1934	400,000	2.50	10.00	30.00	60.00	—
1934 Proof	—	Value: 600				
1935	400,000	2.50	10.00	30.00	60.00	—
1935 Proof	—	Value: 750				
1936	400,000	2.50	10.00	30.00	55.00	—
1936 Proof	—	Value: 650				

KM# 18 1/4 RUPEE
2.9200 g., 0.9160 Silver .0816 oz. ASW, 19 mm. **Obv:** Crowned bust left **Obv. Designer:** Percy Metcalfe **Rev. Designer:** G. E. Kruger-Gray

Date	Mintage	F	VF	XF	Unc	BU
1938	2,000,000	3.50	15.00	40.00	80.00	—
1938 Proof	—	Value: 375				

KM# 18a 1/4 RUPEE
2.9200 g., 0.5000 Silver .047 oz. ASW, 19 mm. **Obv:** Crowned bust left

Date	Mintage	F	VF	XF	Unc	BU
1946	2,000,000	7.50	30.00	60.00	100	—
1946 Proof	—	Value: 400				

KM# 27 1/4 RUPEE
2.9500 g., Copper-Nickel, 19 mm. **Obv:** Crowned head left **Obv. Designer:** Percy Metcalfe **Rev:** Crown above 3 emblems **Rev. Designer:** G. E. Kruger-Gray

Date	Mintage	F	VF	XF	Unc	BU
1950	2,000,000	0.50	1.00	2.00	9.50	18.00
1950 Proof	—	Value: 175				
1951	1,000,000	0.50	1.00	2.00	9.50	18.00
1951 Proof	—	Value: 175				

KM# 36 1/4 RUPEE
2.9500 g., Copper-Nickel, 19 mm. **Obv:** Crowned head right **Obv. Designer:** Cecil Thomas **Rev:** Crown above 3 emblems **Rev. Designer:** G. E. Kruger-Gray

Date	Mintage	F	VF	XF	Unc	BU
1960	1,000,000	0.35	0.75	1.00	2.00	—
1960 Proof	—	Value: 100				
1964	400,000	0.25	0.50	0.75	1.50	—
1964 Proof	—	Value: 100				
1965	400,000	0.25	0.50	0.75	1.25	—
1970	400,000	0.20	0.35	0.65	1.25	—
1971	540,000	0.25	0.50	0.75	1.25	—
1971 Proof	750	Value: 17.50				
1975	8,940,000	0.15	0.30	0.60	1.00	—
1978	8,800,000	0.15	0.30	0.60	1.00	—
Note: Variety exists with lower hole in 8 filled						
1978 Proof	9,268	Value: 3.50				

KM# 16 1/2 RUPEE
5.8300 g., 0.9160 Silver .1717 oz. ASW, 23.65 mm. **Obv:** Crowned bust left **Obv. Designer:** E.B. MacKennal **Rev:** Stag left **Rev. Designer:** G. E. Kruger-Gray

Date	Mintage	F	VF	XF	Unc	BU
1934	1,000,000	3.25	6.50	18.00	60.00	—
1934 Proof	—	Value: 450				

KM# 23 1/2 RUPEE
5.8300 g., 0.5000 Silver .0937 oz. ASW, 23.65 mm. **Obv:** Crowned head left **Obv. Designer:** Percy Metcalfe **Rev:** Stag left **Rev. Designer:** G. E. Kruger-Gray

Date	Mintage	F	VF	XF	Unc	BU
1946	1,000,000	10.00	25.00	125	200	—
1946 Proof	—	Value: 700				

KM# 28 1/2 RUPEE
5.8500 g., Copper-Nickel, 23.65 mm. **Obv:** Crowned head left **Obv. Designer:** Percy Metcalfe **Rev:** Stag left **Rev. Designer:** G. E. Kruger-Gray

Date	Mintage	F	VF	XF	Unc	BU
1950	1,000,000	0.50	1.00	1.75	10.00	—
1950 Proof	—	Value: 175				
1951	570,000	0.75	1.25	2.00	10.00	—
1951 Proof	—	Value: 225				

KM# 37.1 1/2 RUPEE
5.8500 g., Copper-Nickel, 23.65 mm. **Obv:** Crowned head right **Obv. Designer:** Cecil Thomas **Rev:** Stag left **Rev. Designer:** G. E. Kruger-Gray

Date	Mintage	F	VF	XF	Unc	BU
1965	200,000	0.50	1.00	2.00	8.00	—
1971	400,000	0.25	0.50	0.75	6.00	—
1971 Proof	750	Value: 22.50				
1975	4,160,000	0.25	0.50	0.75	6.00	—
1978	400,000	0.25	0.50	0.75	6.00	—
1978 Proof	9,268	Value: 6.00				

KM# 37.2 1/2 RUPEE
5.8500 g., Copper-Nickel, 23.65 mm. **Obv:** Crowned head right **Obv. Designer:** Cecil Thomas **Rev:** Stag left **Edge:** Without security feature **Note:** Error.

Date	Mintage	F	VF	XF	Unc	BU
1971	Inc. above	—	—	—	—	—

KM# 17 RUPEE
11.6600 g., 0.9160 Silver .3434 oz. ASW **Obv:** Crowned bust left **Obv. Designer:** E.B. MacKennal **Rev:** National arms divide date above value **Rev. Designer:** G. E. Kruger-Gray

Date	Mintage	F	VF	XF	Unc	BU
1934	1,500,000	6.00	10.00	25.00	65.00	85.00
1934 Proof	—	Value: 600				

KM# 19 RUPEE
11.6600 g., 0.9160 Silver .3434 oz. ASW **Obv:** Crowned head left **Obv. Designer:** Percy Metcalfe **Rev:** National arms divide date above value **Rev. Designer:** G. E. Kruger-Gray

Date	Mintage	F	VF	XF	Unc	BU
1938	200,000	10.00	20.00	60.00	175	—
1938 Proof	—	Value: 550				

KM# 29.1 RUPEE
11.7000 g., Copper-Nickel, 29.6 mm. **Obv:** Crowned head left **Obv. Designer:** Percy Metcalfe **Rev:** National arms divide date above value **Rev. Designer:** G. E. Kruger-Gray

Date	Mintage	F	VF	XF	Unc	BU
1950	1,500,000	0.75	1.50	3.00	16.00	—
1950 Proof	—	Value: 200				
1951	1,000,000	0.50	1.25	2.00	12.00	—
1951 Proof	—	Value: 300				

KM# 29.2 RUPEE
11.7000 g., Copper-Nickel, 29.6 mm. **Obv:** Crowned head left **Obv. Designer:** Percy Metcalfe **Rev:** National arms divide date above value **Rev. Designer:** G. E. Kruger-Gray **Edge:** Without security feature **Note:** Error.

Date	Mintage	F	VF	XF	Unc	BU
1951	Inc. above	—	—	—	—	—

KM# 35.1 RUPEE
11.7000 g., Copper-Nickel, 29.6 mm. **Obv:** Crowned head right **Obv. Designer:** Cecil Thomas **Rev:** National arms divide date above value **Rev. Designer:** G. E. Kruger-Gray

Date	Mintage	F	VF	XF	Unc	BU
1956	1,000,000	0.25	0.75	1.50	7.50	—
1956 Proof	—	Value: 200				
1964	200,000	0.50	1.00	3.00	5.00	—
1971	600,000	0.25	0.60	1.00	2.00	—
1971 Proof	750	Value: 45.00				
1975	4,525,000	0.25	0.60	1.00	2.00	—
1978	2,000,000	0.25	0.60	1.00	2.00	—
1978 Proof	9,268	Value: 5.00				

KM# 35.2 RUPEE
11.7000 g., Copper-Nickel, 29.6 mm. **Obv:** Crowned head right **Obv. Designer:** Cecil Thomas **Rev:** National arms divide date above value **Edge:** Without security feature **Note:** Error.

Date	Mintage	F	VF	XF	Unc	BU
1971	Inc. above	0.25	0.75	1.25	2.50	—

KM# 38 10 RUPEES
Copper-Nickel, 35 mm. **Subject:** Independence **Obv:** Crowned head right **Obv. Designer:** Cecil Thomas **Rev:** Dodo bird

Date	Mintage	F	VF	XF	Unc	BU
1971	50,000	—	1.50	4.00	8.00	12.00

COMMONWEALTH

STANDARD COINAGE

100 Cents = 1 Rupee

KM# 38a 10 RUPEES
20.0000 g., 0.9250 Silver .5948 oz. ASW, 35 mm. **Subject:** Independence **Obv:** Crowned head right **Obv. Designer:** Cecil Thomas **Rev:** Dodo bird

Date	Mintage	F	VF	XF	Unc	BU
1971 Proof	750	Value: 125				

KM# 46 10 RUPEES
Copper-Nickel **Subject:** Wedding of Prince Charles and Lady Diana **Obv:** Young bust right **Rev:** Conjoined heads left

Date	Mintage	F	VF	XF	Unc	BU
ND(1981)	—	—	1.25	2.25	6.50	—

KM# 46a 10 RUPEES
28.2800 g., 0.9250 Silver .8411 oz. ASW **Subject:** Wedding of Prince Charles and Lady Diana **Obv:** Young bust right **Rev:** Conjoined heads left

Date	Mintage	F	VF	XF	Unc	BU
ND(1981) Proof	2,090	Value: 22.50				

KM# 48 10 RUPEES

28.2800 g., 0.9250 Silver .8411 oz. ASW **Series:** World Food Day **Obv:** Young bust right **Rev:** Man harvesting sugar cane

Date	Mintage	F	VF	XF	Unc	BU
1981	10,000	—	—	—	17.50	—
1981 Proof	5,000	Value: 27.50				

KM# 40 25 RUPEES

25.5000 g., 0.5000 Silver .4099 oz. ASW **Series:** Conservation **Obv:** Young bust right **Rev:** Butterfly on flowers **Rev. Designer:** Christopher Ironside

Date	Mintage	F	VF	XF	Unc	BU
1975	—	—	—	—	24.00	—

KM# 40a 25 RUPEES

28.2800 g., 0.9250 Silver .8411 oz. ASW **Series:** Conservation **Obv:** Young bust right **Rev:** Butterfly on flowers **Rev. Designer:** Christopher Ironside

Date	Mintage	F	VF	XF	Unc	BU
1975	12	—	—	—	100	—
1975 Proof	9,869	Value: 25.00				

KM# 43 25 RUPEES

28.4000 g., 0.5000 Silver .4565 oz. ASW **Subject:** Queen's Silver Jubilee **Obv:** Young bust right **Rev:** Man harvesting sugar cane

Date	Mintage	F	VF	XF	Unc	BU
ND(1977)	—	—	—	—	9.50	11.50

KM# 43a 25 RUPEES

28.2800 g., 0.9250 Silver .8411 oz. ASW **Subject:** Queen's Silver Jubilee **Obv:** Young bust right **Rev:** Man harvesting sugar cane

Date	Mintage	F	VF	XF	Unc	BU
ND(1977) Proof	47,000	Value: 14.50				

KM# 44 25 RUPEES

28.2800 g., 0.9250 Silver .8411 oz. ASW **Subject:** 10th Anniversary of Independence **Obv:** Similar to 1,000 Rupees, KM#45: bust right **Rev:** Building

Date	Mintage	F	VF	XF	Unc	BU
1978	20,000	—	—	—	13.50	—
1978 Proof	5,100	Value: 25.00				

KM# 49 25 RUPEES

28.2800 g., 0.9250 Silver .8411 oz. ASW **Series:** International Year of Disabled Persons **Obv:** Young bust right **Rev:** Disabled persons emblem to upper left of cluster of designs

Date	Mintage	F	VF	XF	Unc	BU
1982	11,000	—	—	—	18.50	—
1982 Proof	10,000	Value: 23.50				

KM# 41 50 RUPEES

32.1500 g., 0.5000 Silver .5168 oz. ASW **Series:** Conservation **Obv:** Young bust right **Rev:** Mauritius Kestrel **Rev. Designer:** Christopher Ironside

Date	Mintage	F	VF	XF	Unc	BU
1975	—	—	—	—	24.00	—

KM# 41a 50 RUPEES

35.0000 g., 0.9250 Silver 1.0409 oz. ASW **Series:** Conservation **Obv:** Young bust right **Rev:** Mauritius Kestrel **Rev. Designer:** Christopher Ironside

Date	Mintage	F	VF	XF	Unc	BU
1975	12	—	—	—	125	—
1975 Proof	9,513	Value: 25.00				

KM# 39 200 RUPEES

15.5600 g., 0.9170 Gold .4587 oz. AGW **Subject:** Independence **Obv:** Crowned head right **Rev:** Couple in the forest

Date	Mintage	F	VF	XF	Unc	BU
1971	2,500	—	—	—	325	—
1971 Proof	750	Value: 400				

KM# 42 1000 RUPEES

33.4370 g., 0.9000 Gold .9676 oz. AGW **Series:** Conservation **Subject:** Mauritius flycatcher **Obv:** Young bust right **Rev:** Bird on nest in branch **Rev. Designer:** Christopher Ironside

Date	Mintage	F	VF	XF	Unc	BU
1975	1,966	—	—	—	675	—
1975 Proof	716	Value: 750				

KM# 45 1000 RUPEES

15.9800 g., 0.9170 Gold .4711 oz. AGW **Subject:** 10th Anniversary of Independence **Obv:** Bust right **Rev:** Building

Date	Mintage	F	VF	XF	Unc	BU
1978	1,000	—	—	—	335	—
1978 Proof	1,016	Value: 365				

KM# 47 1000 RUPEES

15.9800 g., 0.9170 Gold .4711 oz. AGW **Subject:** Wedding of Prince Charles and Lady Diana **Obv:** Young bust right **Rev:** Crowned monogram

Date	Mintage	F	VF	XF	Unc	BU
ND(1981)	28	—	—	—	600	—
ND(1981) Proof	22	Value: 950				

KM# 50 1000 RUPEES

15.9800 g., 0.9170 Gold .4711 oz. AGW **Series:** International Year of Disabled Persons **Obv:** Young bust right **Rev:** Disabled emblem within design

Date	Mintage	F	VF	XF	Unc	BU
1982	45	—	—	—	550	—
1982 Proof	48	Value: 925				

GOLD BULLION COINAGE

KM# 57 100 RUPEES
3.4120 g., 0.9170 Gold .1006 oz. AGW **Obv:** Bust 1/4 left
Rev: Dodo bird

Date	Mintage	F	VF	XF	Unc	BU
1988	—	—	—	—	85.00	—

KM# 58 250 RUPEES
8.5130 g., 0.9170 Gold .25 oz. AGW **Obv:** Bust 1/4 left
Rev: Dodo bird

Date	Mintage	F	VF	XF	Unc	BU
1988	—	—	—	—	165	—

KM# 59 500 RUPEES
17.0250 g., 0.9170 Gold .5 oz. AGW **Obv:** Bust 1/4 left
Rev: Dodo bird

Date	Mintage	F	VF	XF	Unc	BU
1988	—	—	—	—	300	—

KM# 60 1000 RUPEES
34.0500 g., 0.9170 Gold 1 oz. AGW **Obv:** Bust 1/4 left
Rev: Dodo bird

Date	Mintage	F	VF	XF	Unc	BU
1988	—	—	—	—	600	—

REPUBLIC

STANDARD COINAGE

100 Cents = 1 Rupee

KM# 51 CENT
Copper Plated Steel **Obv:** Bust 3/4 right **Rev:** Value within beaded circle

Date	Mintage	F	VF	XF	Unc	BU
1987	Est. 5,000	—	—	—	0.20	0.40
1987 Proof	Est. 2,500	Value: 1.00				

KM# 52 5 CENTS
Copper Plated Steel **Obv:** Bust 3/4 right **Rev:** Value within beaded circle

Date	Mintage	F	VF	XF	Unc	BU
1987	Est. 5,000	—	—	—	0.30	0.50
1987 Proof	Est. 2,500	Value: 2.00				
1990	—	—	—	—	0.30	0.50
1991	—	—	—	—	0.30	0.50
1993	—	—	—	—	0.30	0.50
1994	—	—	—	—	0.30	0.50
1995	—	—	—	—	0.30	0.50
1996	—	—	—	—	0.30	0.50
1999	—	—	—	—	0.30	0.50

KM# 53 20 CENTS
Nickel Plated Steel **Obv:** Bust 3/4 right **Rev:** Value within beaded circle

Date	Mintage	F	VF	XF	Unc	BU
1987	Est. 5,000	—	—	—	0.50	0.75
1987 Proof	Est. 2,500	Value: 3.00				
1990	—	—	—	—	0.50	0.75
1991	—	—	—	—	0.50	0.75
1993	—	—	—	—	0.50	0.75
1994	—	—	—	—	0.50	0.75
1995	—	—	—	—	0.50	0.75
1996	—	—	—	—	0.50	0.75
1999	—	—	—	—	0.50	0.75

KM# 54 1/2 RUPEE
Nickel Plated Steel **Obv:** Bust 3/4 right **Rev:** Stag left
Rev. Designer: G.E. Kruger-Gray

Date	Mintage	F	VF	XF	Unc	BU
1987	Est. 5,000	—	—	—	1.50	2.50
1987 Proof	Est. 2,500	Value: 5.00				
1990	—	—	—	—	1.50	2.50
1991	—	—	—	—	1.50	2.50
1997	—	—	—	—	1.50	2.50
1999	—	—	—	—	1.50	2.50

KM# 55 RUPEE
Copper-Nickel **Obv:** Bust 3/4 right **Rev:** Shield divides date above value **Rev. Designer:** G.E. Kruger-Gray

Date	Mintage	F	VF	XF	Unc	BU
1987	Est. 5,000	—	—	—	1.65	2.75
1987 Proof	Est. 2,500	Value: 10.00				
1990	—	—	—	—	1.65	2.75
1991	—	—	—	—	1.65	2.75
1993	—	—	—	—	1.65	2.75
1994	—	—	—	—	1.65	2.75
1997	—	—	—	—	1.65	2.75

KM# 56 5 RUPEES
Copper-Nickel **Obv:** Bust 3/4 right **Rev:** Value within palm trees

Date	Mintage	F	VF	XF	Unc	BU
1987	Est. 5,000	—	—	—	3.00	5.00
1987 Proof	Est. 2,500	Value: 16.00				
1991	—	—	—	—	3.00	5.00
1992	—	—	—	—	3.00	5.00

KM# 61 10 RUPEES
Copper-Nickel **Obv:** Bust 3/4 right **Rev:** Sugar cane harvesting
Shape: 7-sided

Date	Mintage	F	VF	XF	Unc	BU
1997	—	—	—	—	4.00	6.50
2000	—	—	—	—	4.00	6.50

PIEFORTS

KM#	Date	Mintage	Identification	Issue Price	Mkt Val
P2	1981	—	1000 Rupees. Gold. KM47.	—	825
P3	1982	1,100	25 Rupees. 0.9250 Silver. KM49.	—	100
P4	1982	—	1000 Rupees. Gold. KM50.	—	1,850

MINT SETS

KM#	Date	Mintage	Identification	Issue Price	Mkt Val
MS1	1987 (6)	5,000	KM51-56	16.95	17.50
MS2	1988 (4)	—	KM57-60	1,250	1,150

PROOF SETS

KM#	Date	Mintage	Identification	Issue Price	Mkt Val
PS1	1934 (3)	20	KM15-17	—	2,100
PS2	1971 (9)	750	KM31-37, 38a, 39	200	645
PS3	1975 (2)	9,268	KM40a-41a	50.00	40.00
PS4	1978 (7)	30,000	KM31-37	22.00	20.00
PS5	1981 (2)	—	KM46a, 47	—	975
PS6	1987 (6)	2,500	KM51-56	36.95	37.50

MEXICO

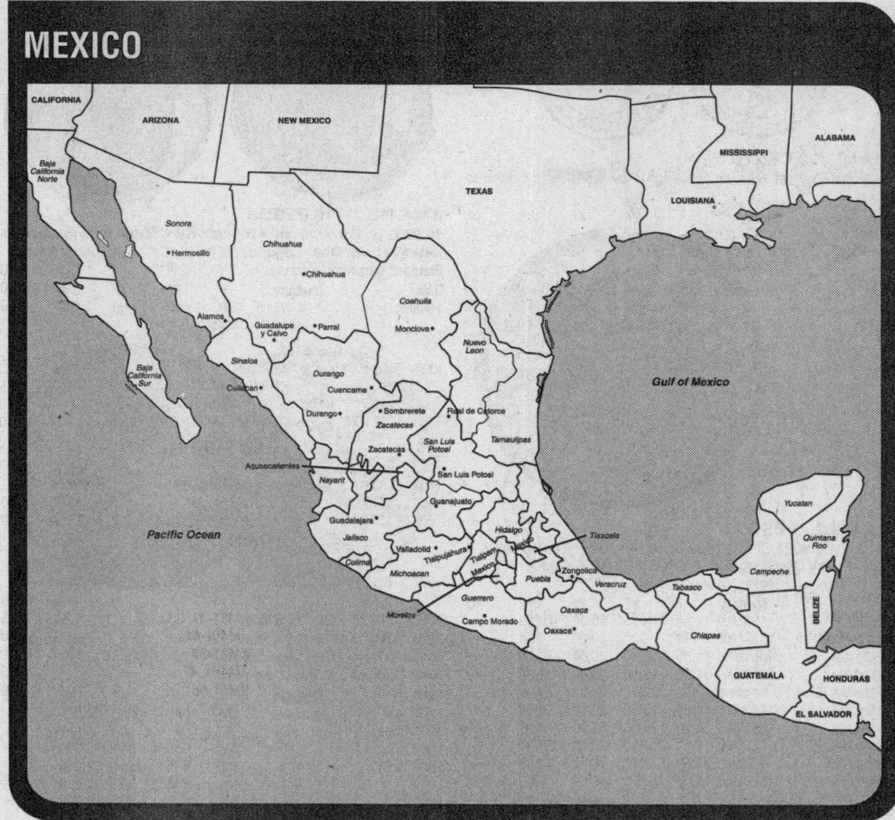

The United States of Mexico, located immediately south of the United States has an area of 759,529 sq. mi. (1,967,183 sq. km.) and an estimated population of 100 million. Capital: Mexico City. The economy is based on agriculture, manufacturing and mining. Oil, cotton, silver, coffee, and shrimp are exported.

Mexico was the site of highly advanced Indian civilizations 1,500 years before conquistador Hernando Cortes conquered the wealthy Aztec empire of Montezuma, 1519-21, and founded a Spanish colony, which lasted for nearly 300 years. During the Spanish period, Mexico, then called New Spain, stretched from Guatemala to the present states of Wyoming and California, its present northern boundary having been established by the secession of Texas during 1836 and the war of 1846-48 with the United States.

Independence from Spain was declared by Father Miguel Hidalgo on Sept. 16, 1810, (Mexican Independence Day) and was achieved by General Agustin de Iturbide in 1821. Iturbide became emperor in 1822 but was deposed when a republic was established a year later. For more than fifty years following the birth of the republic, the political scene of Mexico was characterized by turmoil, which saw two emperors (including the unfortunate Maximilian), several dictators and an average of one new government every nine months passing swiftly from obscurity to oblivion. The land, social, economic and labor reforms promulgated by the Reform Constitution of Feb. 5, 1917 established the basis for sustained economic development and participative democracy that have made Mexico one of the most politically stable countries of modern Latin America.

REPUBLIC

Second

MINT MARKS

A, AS - Alamos
CE - Real de Catorce
CA,CH - Chihuahua
C, Cn, Gn(error) - Culiacan
D, Do - Durango
EoMo - Estado de Mexico
Ga - Guadalajara
GC - Guadalupe y Calvo
G, Go - Guanajuato
H, Ho - Hermosillo
M, Mo - Mexico City
O, OA - Oaxaca
SLP, PI, P, I/P - San Luis Potosi
Z, Zs – Zacatecas

ASSAYERS INITIALS

CULIACAN MINT

Initials	Years	Mint Officials
JQ, Q	1899-1903	Jesus S. Quiroz
FV, V	1903	Francisco Valdez
MH, H	1904	Merced Hernandez
RP, P	1904-05	Ramon Ponce de Leon

MEXICO CITY MINT

Because of the great number of assayers for this mint (Mexico City is a much larger mint than any of the others) there is much confusion as to which initial stands for which assayer at any one time. Therefore we feel that it would be of no value to list the assayers.

ZACATECAS MINT

Initials	Years	Mint Officials
FZ	1886-1905	Francisco de P. Zarate
FM	1904-05	Francisco Mateos

DECIMAL COINAGE

100 Centavos = 1 Peso

KM# 394 CENTAVO

Copper **Obv:** National arms **Rev:** Value below date within wreath **Note:** Reduced size. Varieties exist.

Date	Mintage	F	VF	XF	Unc	BU
1901C	220,000	15.00	22.50	35.00	65.00	—
1902C	320,000	15.00	22.50	50.00	90.00	—
1903C	536,000	7.50	12.50	20.00	50.00	—
1904/3C	148,000	35.00	50.00	75.00	125	—
1905C	110,000	100	150	300	600	—

KM# 394.1 CENTAVO

Copper **Obv:** Facing eagle, snake in beak **Obv. Legend:** REPUBLICA MEXICANA **Rev:** Value below date within wreath **Note:** Reduced size. Varieties exist.

Date	Mintage	F	VF	XF	Unc	BU
1901M	1,494,000	3.00	8.00	17.50	50.00	—
1902/899M	2,090,000	30.00	60.00	125	225	—
1902M	Inc. above	2.25	4.00	10.00	40.00	—
1903M	8,400,000	1.50	3.00	7.00	20.00	—
1904/3M	10,250,000	1.50	10.00	20.00	55.00	—
1904M	Inc. above	1.50	3.00	8.00	25.00	—
1905M	3,643,000	2.25	4.00	10.00	40.00	—

KM# 400 5 CENTAVOS

0.9030 Silver **Obv:** Facing eagle, snake in beak **Obv. Legend:** REPUBLICA MEXICANA **Rev:** Value within 1/2 wreath **Note:** Varieties exist.

Date	Mintage	F	VF	XF	Unc	BU
1901Cn Q	148,000	1.75	2.50	4.50	15.00	—
1902Cn Q	262,000	1.75	3.00	6.00	16.50	—
Note: Narrow C, heavy serifs						
1902Cn Q	Inc. above	1.75	3.00	6.00	16.50	—
Note: Wide C, light serifs						
1903/1Cn Q	331,000	2.00	3.00	6.00	16.50	20.00
1903Cn Q	Inc. above	1.75	2.50	4.50	15.00	18.00
1903/1898Cn V	Inc. above	3.50	4.50	9.00	22.50	—
1903Cn V	Inc. above	1.75	2.50	4.50	15.00	—
1904Cn H	352,000	1.75	2.25	5.00	16.50	—
1904Cn H/C	—	1.75	2.50	5.00	16.50	—
1904Cn H 0/9	—	1.75	2.50	5.00	16.50	—

KM# 400.2 5 CENTAVOS

0.9030 Silver **Obv:** Facing eagle, snake in beak **Rev:** Value within 1/2 wreath

Date	Mintage	F	VF	XF	Unc	BU
1901Mo M	100,000	1.75	2.50	4.50	15.00	—
1902Mo M	144,000	1.25	2.00	3.75	12.00	—
1902/1Mo MoM	—	1.75	3.00	7.00	16.50	—
1903Mo M	500,000	1.25	2.00	3.75	12.00	—
1904/804Mo M	1,090,000	1.75	3.50	8.50	16.50	18.50
1904/94Mo M	Inc. above	1.75	3.75	9.00	16.50	18.50
1904Mo M	Inc. above	1.75	3.00	6.00	15.00	—
1905Mo M	344,000	1.75	3.00	7.00	16.50	—

KM# 400.3 5 CENTAVOS

0.9030 Silver **Obv:** Facing eagle, snake in beak **Rev:** Value within 1/2 wreath

Date	Mintage	F	VF	XF	Unc	BU
1901Zs Z	40,000	1.75	2.50	5.00	16.50	—
1902/1Zs Z	34,000	2.00	4.50	9.00	22.50	—
1902Zs Z	Inc. above	1.75	3.75	7.50	18.50	—
1903Zs Z	217,000	1.25	2.00	5.00	12.50	—
1904Zs Z	191,000	1.75	2.50	5.00	12.50	—
1904Zs M	Inc. above	1.75	2.50	6.00	16.50	—
1905Zs M	46,000	2.00	4.50	9.00	22.50	—
1905Zs M	Inc. above	—	—	—	—	—
Repullica - Rare						

KM# 404 10 CENTAVOS

2.7070 g., 0.9030 Silver .0785 oz. ASW **Obv:** Facing eagle, snake in beak **Obv. Legend:** REPUBLICA MEXICANA **Rev:** Value within 1/2 wreath **Note:** Varieties exist.

Date	Mintage	F	VF	XF	Unc	BU
1901Cn Q	235,000	1.50	2.50	5.00	18.00	20.00
1902Cn Q	186,000	1.50	2.50	5.00	20.00	—
1903Cn Q	256,000	1.50	2.50	6.00	20.00	—
1903Cn V	Inc. above	1.50	2.50	5.00	15.00	—
1904Cn H	307,000	1.50	2.50	5.00	15.00	—

KM# 404.2 10 CENTAVOS

2.7070 g., 0.9030 Silver .0785 oz. ASW **Obv:** Facing eagle, snake in beak **Obv. Legend:** REPUBLICA MEXICANA **Rev:** Value within 1/2 wreath

Date	Mintage	F	VF	XF	Unc	BU
1901Mo M	80,000	2.50	3.50	7.00	22.50	—
1902Mo M	181,000	1.50	2.50	6.00	20.00	—
1903Mo M	581,000	1.50	2.50	6.00	20.00	—
1904Mo M	1,266,000	1.25	2.00	4.50	18.00	—
1904Mo MM (Error)	Inc. above	2.50	5.00	10.00	25.00	—
1905Mo M	266,000	2.00	3.75	7.50	20.00	—

KM# 404.3 10 CENTAVOS

2.7070 g., 0.9020 Silver .0785 oz. ASW **Obv:** Facing eagle, snake in beak **Rev:** Value within 1/2 wreath

Date	Mintage	F	VF	XF	Unc	BU
1901Zs Z	70,000	2.50	5.00	10.00	25.00	—
1902Zs Z	120,000	2.50	5.00	10.00	25.00	—
1903Zs Z	228,000	1.50	3.00	9.00	18.00	20.00
1904Zs Z	368,000	1.50	3.00	9.00	18.00	20.00
1904Zs M	Inc. above	1.50	3.00	9.00	22.00	25.00
1905Zs M	66,000	7.50	20.00	50.00	200	—

KM# 405 20 CENTAVOS

5.4150 g., 0.9030 Silver .1572 oz. ASW **Obv:** Facing eagle, snake in beak **Rev:** Value within 1/2 wreath

Date	Mintage	F	VF	XF	Unc	BU
1901Cn Q	185,000	5.00	10.00	30.00	120	—
1902/802Cn Q	98,000	6.00	10.00	30.00	120	—
1902Cn Q	Inc. above	4.00	9.00	30.00	120	—
1903Cn Q	93,000	4.00	9.00	30.00	120	—
1904/3Cn H	258,000	—	—	—	—	—
1904Cn H	Inc. above	5.00	10.00	30.00	120	—

KM# 405.2 20 CENTAVOS
5.4150 g., 0.9030 Silver .1572 oz. ASW **Obv:** Facing eagle, snake in beak **Rev:** Value within 1/2 wreath **Note:** Varieties exist.

Date	Mintage	F	VF	XF	Unc	BU
1901Mo M	110,000	4.00	8.00	20.00	90.00	—
1902Mo M	120,000	4.00	8.00	20.00	90.00	—
1903Mo M	213,000	4.00	8.00	20.00	90.00	—
1904Mo M	276,000	4.00	8.00	20.00	90.00	—
1905Mo M	117,000	6.50	20.00	50.00	150	—

KM# 405.3 20 CENTAVOS
5.4150 g., 0.9027 Silver .1572 oz. ASW **Obv:** Facing eagle, snake in beak **Obv. Legend:** REPUBLICA MEXICANA **Rev:** Value within 1/2 wreath

Date	Mintage	F	VF	XF	Unc	BU
1901Zs Z	Inc. above	5.00	10.00	20.00	100	—
1901/0Zs Z	130,000	25.00	50.00	100	250	—
1902Zs Z	105,000	5.00	10.00	20.00	100	—
1903Zs Z	143,000	5.00	10.00	20.00	100	—
1904Zs Z	246,000	5.00	10.00	20.00	100	—
1904Zs M	Inc. above	5.00	10.00	50.00	300	—
1905Zs M	59,000	10.00	70.00	50.00	400	—

KM# 409 PESO
27.0730 g., 0.9030 Silver .7860 oz. ASW **Obv:** Facing eagle, snake in beak **Rev:** Radiant cap

Date	Mintage	F	VF	XF	Unc	BU
1901Cn JQ	1,473,000	12.00	15.00	25.00	75.00	—
1902Cn JQ	1,194,000	12.00	15.00	45.00	125	—
1903Cn JQ	1,514,000	12.00	15.00	30.00	85.00	—
1903Cn FV	Inc. above	25.00	50.00	100	225	—
1904Cn MH	1,554,000	12.00	15.00	25.00	75.00	—
1904Cn RP	Inc. above	50.00	100	150	350	—
1905Cn RP	598,000	25.00	50.00	100	250	—

KM# 410.2 PESO
1.6920 g., 0.8750 Gold .0476 oz. AGW **Obv:** Facing eagle, snake in beak **Obv. Legend:** REPUBLICA MEXICANA **Rev:** Value within 1/2 wreath

Date	Mintage	F	VF	XF	Unc	BU
1901Cn Q	Inc. above	65.00	100	150	225	—
1901/0Cn Q	2,350	65.00	100	150	225	—
1902Cn Q	2,480	65.00	100	150	225	—
1902Cn/MoQ/C	Inc. above	65.00	100	150	225	—
1904Cn H	3,614	65.00	100	150	225	—
1904Cn/Mo/ H	Inc. above	65.00	100	150	250	—
1905Cn P	1,000	—	—	—	—	—

Note: Reported, not confirmed

KM# 410.5 PESO
1.6920 g., 0.8750 Gold .0476 oz. AGW **Obv:** Facing eagle, snake in beak **Obv. Legend:** REPUBLICA MEXICANA **Rev:** Value within 1/2 wreath

Date	Mintage	F	VF	XF	Unc	BU
1901Mo M Small date	Inc. above	45.00	65.00	95.00	185	—
1901/801Mo M Large date	8,293	45.00	65.00	95.00	185	—
1902Mo M Large date	11,000	45.00	65.00	95.00	185	—
1902Mo M Small date	Inc. above	45.00	65.00	95.00	185	—
1903Mo M Large date	10,000	45.00	65.00	95.00	185	—
1903Mo M Small date	Inc. above	55.00	85.00	125	200	—
1904Mo M	9,845	45.00	65.00	95.00	185	—
1905Mo M	3,429	45.00	65.00	95.00	185	—

KM# 409.3 PESO
27.0730 g., 0.9030 Silver .7860 oz. ASW **Obv:** Facing eagle, snake in beak **Rev:** Radiant cap **Note:** Mint mark Zs. Varieties exist.

Date	Mintage	F	VF	XF	Unc	BU
1901Zs FZ	Inc. above	11.50	13.50	20.00	55.00	—
1901Zs AZ	5,706,000	4,000	6,500	10,000	—	—
1902Zs FZ	7,134,000	11.50	13.50	20.00	55.00	—
1903/2Zs FZ	3,080,000	12.50	15.00	50.00	125	—
1903Zs FZ	Inc. above	11.50	13.50	20.00	65.00	—
1904Zs FZ	2,423,000	12.00	15.00	25.00	85.00	—
1904Zs FM	Inc. above	12.00	15.00	25.00	75.00	—
1905Zs FM	995,000	20.00	40.00	60.00	150	—

KM# 409.2 PESO
27.0730 g., 0.9027 Silver .7860 oz. ASW **Obv:** Facing eagle, snake in beak **Obv. Legend:** REPUBLICA MEXICANA **Rev:** Radiant cap **Note:** Varieties exist.

Date	Mintage	F	VF	XF	Unc	BU
1901Mo AM	14,505,000	11.50	13.50	20.00	70.00	—
1902/1Mo AM	16,224,000	150	300	500	950	—
1902Mo AM	Inc. above	11.50	13.50	20.00	70.00	—
1903Mo AM	22,396,000	11.50	13.50	20.00	70.00	—
1903Mo MA (Error)	Inc. above	1,500	2,500	3,500	7,500	—
1904Mo AM	14,935,000	11.50	13.50	20.00	70.00	—
1905Mo AM	3,557,000	15.00	25.00	55.00	125	—
1908Mo AM	7,575,000	11.50	13.50	20.00	60.00	—
1908Mo GV	Inc. above	11.50	13.50	18.50	40.00	—
1909Mo GV	2,924,000	11.50	13.50	18.50	40.00	—

KM# 412.6 5 PESOS
8.4600 g., 0.8750 Gold .2380 oz. AGW **Obv:** Facing eagle, snake in beak **Obv. Legend:** REPUBLICA MEXICANA **Rev:** Radiant cap above scales

Date	Mintage	F	VF	XF	Unc	BU
1901Mo M	1,071	175	300	400	650	—
1902Mo M	1,478	175	300	400	650	—
1903Mo M	1,162	175	300	400	650	—
1904Mo M	1,415	175	300	400	650	—
1905Mo M	563	200	400	550	1,500	—

KM# 412.2 5 PESOS
8.4600 g., 0.8750 Gold .2380 oz. AGW **Obv:** Facing eagle, snake in beak **Obv. Legend:** REPUBLICA MEXICANA **Rev:** Radiant cap above scales

Date	Mintage	F	VF	XF	Unc	BU
1903Cn Q	1,000	175	300	400	750	—

KM# 413.7 10 PESOS
16.9200 g., 0.8750 Gold .4760 oz. AGW **Obv:** Facing eagle, snake in beak **Obv. Legend:** REPUBLICA MEXICANA **Rev:** Radiant cap above scales

Date	Mintage	F	VF	XF	Unc	BU
1901Mo M	562	350	500	800	1,250	—
1902Mo M	719	350	500	800	1,250	—
1903Mo M	713	350	500	800	1,250	—
1904Mo M	694	350	500	800	1,250	—
1905Mo M	401	400	600	950	1,500	—

KM# 413.2 10 PESOS
16.9200 g., 0.8750 Gold .4760 oz. AGW **Obv:** Facing eagle, snake in beak **Obv. Legend:** REPUBLICA MEXICANA **Rev:** Radiant cap above scales

Date	Mintage	F	VF	XF	Unc	BU
1903Cn Q	774	400	600	1,000	1,750	—

KM# 414.2 20 PESOS
33.8400 g., 0.8750 Gold .9520 oz. AGW **Obv:** Facing eagle, snake in beak **Obv. Legend:** REPUBLICA MEXICANA **Rev:** Radiant cap above scales

Date	Mintage	F	VF	XF	Unc	BU
1901Cn Q	Inc. above	BV	685	950	2,000	—
1901/0Cn Q	1,496	—	—	—	—	—
1902Cn Q	1,059	BV	685	950	2,000	—
1903Cn Q	1,121	BV	685	950	2,000	—
1904Cn H	4,646	BV	685	950	2,000	—
1905Cn P	1,738	BV	900	1,200	2,250	—

KM# 414.6 20 PESOS
33.8400 g., 0.8750 Gold .9520 oz. AGW **Obv:** Facing eagle, snake in beak **Obv. Legend:** REPUBLICA MEXICANA **Rev:** Radiant cap above scales

Date	Mintage	F	VF	XF	Unc	BU
1901Mo M	29,000	BV	665	850	1,500	—
1902Mo M	38,000	BV	665	850	1,500	—
1903/2Mo M	31,000	BV	665	850	1,500	—
1903Mo M	Inc. above	BV	665	850	1,500	—
1904Mo M	52,000	BV	665	850	1,500	—
1905Mo M	9,757	BV	665	850	1,500	—

UNITED STATES

DECIMAL COINAGE

100 Centavos = 1 Peso

KM# 415 CENTAVO
3.0000 g., Bronze, 20 mm. **Obv:** National arms **Rev:** Value below date within wreath **Note:** Mint mark Mo.

Date	Mintage	F	VF	XF	Unc	BU
1905 Narrow date	6,040,000	4.00	6.50	14.00	90.00	—
1905 Wide date	—	4.00	6.50	14.00	90.00	—
1906 Narrow date	Est. 67,505,000	0.50	0.75	1.25	14.00	—
Note: 50,000,000 pcs. were struck at the Birmingham Mint						
1906 Wide date	Inc. above	0.75	1.50	2.50	20.00	—
1910 Narrow date	8,700,000	2.00	3.00	6.50	85.00	—
1910 Wide date	—	2.00	3.00	6.50	85.00	—
1911 Narrow date	16,450,000	0.60	1.00	2.75	22.50	—
1911 Wide date	Inc. above	0.75	1.00	4.00	32.00	—
1912	12,650,000	1.00	1.35	3.25	32.00	—
1913	12,850,000	0.75	1.25	3.00	35.00	—

Date	Mintage	F	VF	XF	Unc	BU
1914 Narrow date	17,350,000	0.75	1.00	3.00	13.50	18.00
1914 Wide date	Inc. above	0.75	1.00	3.00	13.50	18.00
1915	2,277,000	11.00	25.00	67.50	250	—
1916	500,000	45.00	80.00	170	1,200	—
1920	1,433,000	22.00	50.00	110	400	—
1921	3,470,000	5.50	15.50	47.00	275	—
1922	1,880,000	9.00	17.00	50.00	250	—
1923	4,800,000	0.75	1.25	1.75	13.50	—
1924/3	2,000,000	65.00	170	285	525	—
1924	Inc. above	4.50	11.00	22.00	235	275
1925	1,550,000	4.50	10.00	25.00	220	—
1926	5,000,000	1.00	2.00	4.00	26.00	30.00
1927/6	6,000,000	30.00	45.00	70.00	150	—
1927	Inc. above	0.75	1.25	4.50	36.00	—
1928	5,000,000	0.75	1.00	3.25	16.50	25.00
1929	4,500,000	0.75	1.00	1.75	17.00	25.00
1930	7,000,000	0.75	1.00	2.50	19.00	—
1933	10,000,000	0.25	0.35	1.75	16.50	—
1934	7,500,000	0.25	0.95	3.25	30.00	—
1935	12,400,000	0.15	0.25	0.40	11.50	—
1936	20,100,000	0.15	0.20	0.30	8.00	—
1937	20,000,000	0.15	0.25	0.35	3.25	5.00
1938	10,000,000	0.10	0.15	0.30	2.00	2.75
1939	30,000,000	0.10	0.20	0.30	1.00	1.50
1940	10,000,000	0.20	0.30	0.60	5.50	7.50
1941	15,800,000	0.15	0.25	0.35	2.00	3.00
1942	30,400,000	0.15	0.20	0.30	1.25	2.00
1943	4,310,000	0.30	0.50	0.75	8.00	10.00
1944	5,645,000	0.15	0.25	0.50	6.00	7.50
1945	26,375,000	0.10	0.15	0.25	1.00	1.25
1946	42,135,000	—	0.15	0.20	0.60	1.00
1947	13,445,000	—	0.10	0.15	0.80	1.25
1948	20,040,000	0.10	0.15	0.30	1.10	2.00
1949	6,235,000	0.10	0.15	0.30	1.25	2.00

Note: Varieties exist.

KM# 416 CENTAVO

Bronze, 16 mm. **Obv:** National arms **Rev:** Value below date within wreath **Note:** Zapata issue. Struck at Mexico City Mint, mint mark Mo. Reduced size. Weight varies 1.39-1.5g.

Date	Mintage	F	VF	XF	Unc	BU
1915	179,000	18.00	30.00	50.00	75.00	—

KM# 417 CENTAVO

2.0000 g., Brass, 16 mm. **Obv:** National arms, eagle left **Rev:** Oat sprigs **Note:** Mint mark Mo.

Date	Mintage	F	VF	XF	Unc	BU
1950	12,815,000	—	0.15	0.35	1.65	2.00
1951	25,740,000	—	0.15	0.35	0.65	1.00
1952	24,610,000	—	0.10	0.25	0.40	0.75
1953	21,160,000	—	0.10	0.25	0.40	0.85
1954	25,675,000	—	0.10	0.15	0.85	1.20
1955	9,820,000	—	0.15	0.25	0.85	1.50
1956	11,285,000	—	0.15	0.25	0.80	1.25
1957	9,805,000	—	0.15	0.25	0.85	1.35
1958	12,155,000	—	0.10	0.25	0.45	0.75
1959	11,875,000	—	0.10	0.25	0.75	1.25
1960	10,360,000	—	0.10	0.15	0.40	0.65
1961	6,385,000	—	0.10	0.15	0.45	0.85
1962	4,850,000	—	0.10	0.15	0.55	0.90
1963	7,775,000	—	0.10	0.15	0.25	0.45
1964	4,280,000	—	0.10	0.15	0.20	0.30
1965	2,255,000	—	0.10	0.15	0.25	0.40
1966	1,760,000	—	0.10	0.25	0.60	0.75
1967	1,290,000	—	0.10	0.15	0.40	0.60
1968	1,000,000	—	0.10	0.20	0.85	1.25
1969	1,000,000	—	0.10	0.15	0.65	0.85

KM# 418 CENTAVO

1.5000 g., Brass, 13 mm. **Obv:** National arms, eagle left **Rev:** Oat sprigs **Note:** Reduced size.

Date	Mintage	F	VF	XF	Unc	BU
1970	1,000,000	—	0.20	0.40	1.45	1.75
1972	1,000,000	—	0.20	0.45	2.50	3.25
1972/2	—	—	0.50	1.25	3.50	5.00
1973	1,000,000	—	1.65	2.75	8.50	12.00

KM# 419 2 CENTAVOS

6.0000 g., Bronze, 25 mm. **Obv:** National arms **Rev:** Value below date within wreath **Note:** Mint mark Mo.

Date	Mintage	F	VF	XF	Unc	BU
1905	50,000	150	300	500	1,200	1,350
1906 Inverted 6	9,998,000	30.00	55.00	120	375	—
1906 Wide date	Inc. above	5.00	11.00	23.00	80.00	—
1906 Narrow date	Inc. above	6.50	14.00	28.00	85.00	—
Note: 5,000,000 pieces were struck at the Birmingham Mint						
1920	1,325,000	6.50	17.50	35.00	350	—
1921	4,275,000	2.50	4.75	10.00	90.00	—
1922	—	225	550	1,350	4,000	—
1924	750,000	8.50	22.50	55.00	450	—
1925	3,650,000	2.50	3.50	7.50	38.00	—
1926	4,750,000	1.00	2.25	5.50	35.00	—
1927	7,250,000	0.60	1.00	4.50	22.00	—
1928	3,250,000	0.75	1.50	4.75	30.00	—
1929	250,000	65.00	180	500	1,000	—
1935	1,250,000	4.25	9.25	22.50	200	—
1939	5,000,000	0.60	0.90	2.25	20.00	22.00
1941	3,550,000	0.45	0.60	1.25	18.00	20.00

KM# 420 2 CENTAVOS

Bronze, 20 mm. **Obv:** National arms **Rev:** Value below date within wreath **Note:** Zapata issue. Mint mark Mo. Reduced size. Weight varies 3-3.03g.

Date	Mintage	F	VF	XF	Unc	BU
1915	487,000	7.50	9.00	17.50	75.00	—

KM# 421 5 CENTAVOS

5.0000 g., Nickel, 20 mm. **Obv:** National arms **Rev:** Value and date within beaded circle **Note:** Mint mark Mo. Varieties exist.

Date	Mintage	F	VF	XF	Unc	BU
1905	1,420,000	7.00	10.00	25.00	300	375
1906/5	10,615,000	13.00	30.00	70.00	375	—
1906	Inc. above	0.75	1.35	3.25	55.00	75.00
1907	4,000,000	1.25	4.00	12.00	350	—
1909	2,052,000	3.25	10.00	48.00	360	—
1910	6,181,000	1.30	3.50	6.00	78.00	115
1911 Narrow date	4,487,000	1.00	3.00	5.00	85.00	125
1911 Wide date	Inc. above	2.50	5.00	9.00	110	160
1912 Small mint mark	420,000	90.00	100	230	725	—
1912 Large mint mark	Inc. above	70.00	95.00	175	575	—
1913	2,035,000	1.75	4.25	9.00	100	150
Note: Wide and narrow dates exist for 1913						
1914	2,000,000	1.00	2.00	3.50	70.00	95.00

Note: 5,000,000 pieces appear to have been struck at the Birmingham Mint in 1914 and all of 1909-1911. The Mexican Mint report does not mention receiving the 1914 dated coins

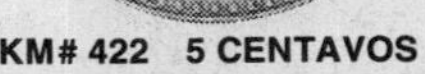

KM# 422 5 CENTAVOS

9.0000 g., Bronze, 28 mm. **Obv:** National arms **Rev:** Value below date within wreath

Date	Mintage	F	VF	XF	Unc	BU
1914Mo	2,500,000	10.00	23.00	50.00	240	—
1915Mo	11,424,000	3.00	5.00	20.00	145	—
1916Mo	2,860,000	15.00	35.00	150	645	—
1917Mo	800,000	75.00	195	375	825	—
1918Mo	1,332,000	35.00	90.00	200	625	—
1919Mo	400,000	115	225	360	925	—
1920Mo	5,920,000	3.00	8.00	40.00	265	—
1921Mo	2,080,000	10.00	24.00	75.00	275	—
1924Mo	780,000	40.00	95.00	260	625	—
1925Mo	4,040,000	5.50	11.00	47.50	200	—
1926Mo	3,160,000	5.50	11.00	48.00	300	—
1927Mo	3,600,000	4.00	7.00	30.00	215	250
1928Mo Large date	1,740,000	11.00	18.00	65.00	250	—
1928Mo Small date	Inc. above	30.00	45.00	95.00	385	—
1929Mo	2,400,000	5.50	11.00	48.00	195	—
1930Mo	2,600,000	5.00	8.00	27.50	210	—
Note: Large oval O in date						
1930Mo	Inc. above	60.00	125	250	565	—
Note: Small square O in date						
1931Mo	—	475	750	1,150	3,000	—
1933Mo	8,000,000	1.50	2.25	3.50	27.50	35.00
1934Mo	10,000,000	1.25	1.75	2.75	25.00	40.00
1935Mo	21,980,000	0.75	1.20	2.50	22.50	30.00

KM# 423 5 CENTAVOS

4.0000 g., Copper-Nickel, 20.5 mm. **Obv:** National arms, eagle left **Rev:** Value and date within circle

Date	Mintage	F	VF	XF	Unc	BU
1936M	46,700,000	—	0.65	1.25	6.50	7.50
1937M	49,060,000	—	0.50	1.00	6.00	7.00
1938M	3,340,000	—	4.00	10.00	75.00	250
1940M	22,800,000	—	0.75	1.25	8.00	10.00
1942M	7,100,000	—	1.50	3.00	35.00	45.00

KM# 424 5 CENTAVOS

6.5000 g., Bronze, 25.5 mm. **Obv:** National arms, eagle left **Rev:** Head left

Date	Mintage	F	VF	XF	Unc	BU
1942Mo	900,000	—	25.00	75.00	375	550
1943Mo	54,660,000	—	0.50	0.75	2.50	3.50
1944Mo	53,463,000	—	0.25	0.35	0.75	1.00
1945Mo	44,262,000	—	0.25	0.35	0.75	1.25
1946Mo	49,054,000	—	0.50	1.00	2.00	3.00
1951Mo	50,758,000	—	0.75	0.90	3.00	5.00
1952Mo	17,674,000	—	1.50	2.50	9.50	11.50
1953Mo	31,568,000	—	1.25	2.00	6.00	9.00
1954Mo	58,680,000	—	0.40	1.00	2.75	4.00
1955Mo	31,114,000	—	2.00	3.00	11.00	14.00

KM# 425 5 CENTAVOS

4.0000 g., Copper-Nickel, 20.5 mm. **Obv:** National arms, eagle left **Rev:** Bust right flanked by date and value

Date	Mintage	F	VF	XF	Unc	BU
1950Mo	5,700,000	—	0.75	1.50	6.00	7.00

Note: 5,600,000 pieces struck at Connecticut melted

KM# 426 5 CENTAVOS

4.0000 g., Brass, 20.5 mm. **Obv:** National arms, eagle left **Rev:** Bust right

Date	Mintage	F	VF	XF	Unc	BU
1954Mo Dot	—	—	10.00	45.00	300	375
1954Mo Without dot	—	—	15.00	30.00	250	290
1955Mo	12,136,000	—	0.75	1.50	9.00	12.50
1956Mo	60,216,000	—	0.20	0.30	0.75	1.25
1957Mo	55,288,000	—	0.15	0.20	0.90	1.50
1958Mo	104,624,000	—	0.15	0.20	0.60	1.00
1959Mo	106,000,000	—	0.15	0.25	0.75	1.25
1960Mo	99,144,000	—	0.10	0.15	0.50	0.75
1961Mo	61,136,000	—	0.10	0.15	0.50	0.75
1962Mo	47,232,000	—	0.10	0.15	0.25	0.35
1963Mo	156,680,000	—	—	0.15	0.25	0.40
1964Mo	71,168,000	—	—	0.15	0.20	0.40
1965Mo	155,720,000	—	—	0.15	0.25	0.35
1966Mo	124,944,000	—	—	0.15	0.40	0.65
1967Mo	118,816,000	—	—	0.15	0.25	0.40

Date	Mintage	F	VF	XF	Unc	BU
1968Mo	189,588,000	—	—	0.15	0.50	0.75
1969Mo	210,492,000	—	—	0.15	0.55	0.80

KM# 426a 5 CENTAVOS

Copper-Nickel, 20.5 mm. **Obv:** National arms, eagle left **Rev:** Bust right

Date	Mintage	F	VF	XF	Unc	BU
1960Mo	—	—	250	300	350	—
1962Mo	19	—	250	300	350	—
1965Mo	—	—	250	300	350	—

KM# 427 5 CENTAVOS

2.7500 g., Brass, 18 mm. **Obv:** National arms, eagle left **Rev:** Bust right **Note:** Due to some minor alloy variations this type is often encountered with a bronze-color toning. Reduced size.

Date	Mintage	F	VF	XF	Unc	BU
1970	163,368,000	—	0.10	0.15	0.35	0.45
1971	198,844,000	—	0.10	0.15	0.25	0.30
1972	225,000,000	—	0.10	0.15	0.25	0.30
1973 Flat top 3	595,070,000	—	0.10	0.15	0.25	0.40
1973 Round top 3	Inc. above	—	0.10	0.15	0.20	0.30
1974	401,584,000	—	0.10	0.15	0.30	0.40
1975	342,308,000	—	0.10	0.15	0.25	0.35
1976	367,524,000	—	0.10	0.15	0.40	0.60

KM# 428 10 CENTAVOS

2.5000 g., 0.8000 Silver .0643 oz. ASW, 18 mm. **Obv:** National arms **Rev:** Value and date within 3/4 wreath with Liberty cap above **Note:** Mint mark Mo.

Date	Mintage	F	VF	XF	Unc	BU
1905	3,920,000	—	6.00	8.00	40.00	50.00
1906	8,410,000	—	5.50	7.50	27.00	35.00
1907/6	5,950,000	—	50.00	135	275	350
1907	Inc. above	—	5.50	6.25	35.00	42.50
1909	2,620,000	—	8.50	13.00	70.00	85.00
1910/00	3,450,000	—	10.00	40.00	75.00	85.00
1910	Inc. above	—	7.00	15.00	25.00	30.00
1911 Narrow date	2,550,000	—	11.00	17.00	88.00	125
1911 Wide date	Inc. above	—	7.50	10.00	42.00	60.00
1912	1,350,000	—	10.00	18.00	130	160
1912 Low 2	Inc. above	—	10.00	18.00	115	140
1913/2	1,990,000	—	10.00	25.00	40.00	70.00
1913	Inc. above	—	7.00	10.00	33.00	40.00
1914	3,110,000	—	5.50	7.00	15.00	20.00

Note: Wide and narrow dates exist for 1914

KM# 429 10 CENTAVOS

1.8125 g., 0.8000 Silver .0466 oz. ASW, 15 mm. **Obv:** National arms **Rev:** Value and date within 3/4 wreath with Liberty cap above **Note:** Mint mark Mo. Reduced size.

Date	Mintage	F	VF	XF	Unc	BU
1919	8,360,000	—	10.00	15.00	85.00	110

KM# 430 10 CENTAVOS

12.0000 g., Bronze, 30.5 mm. **Obv:** National arms **Rev:** Value below date within wreath **Note:** Mint mark Mo.

Date	Mintage	F	VF	XF	Unc	BU
1919	1,232,000	—	25.00	70.00	450	525
1920	6,612,000	—	15.00	50.00	400	475
1921	2,255,000	—	35.00	80.00	650	800
1935	5,970,000	—	14.00	30.00	120	175

KM# 431 10 CENTAVOS

1.6600 g., 0.7200 Silver .0384 oz. ASW, 15 mm. **Obv:** National arms **Rev:** Value and date within wreath with Liberty cap above **Note:** Mint mark Mo.

Date	Mintage	F	VF	XF	Unc	BU
1925/15	5,350,000	—	30.00	75.00	125	175
1925/3	Inc. above	—	20.00	40.00	125	150
1925	Inc. above	—	2.00	5.00	40.00	45.00
1926/16	2,650,000	—	30.00	75.00	125	175
1926	Inc. above	—	3.50	7.50	65.00	85.00
1927	2,810,000	—	2.25	3.00	17.50	22.50
1928	5,270,000	—	2.00	2.75	13.50	16.50
1930	2,000,000	—	3.75	5.00	18.75	25.00
1933	5,000,000	—	1.50	3.00	10.00	11.50
1934	8,000,000	—	1.75	2.50	8.00	10.00
1935	3,500,000	—	2.75	5.00	11.00	12.50

KM# 432 10 CENTAVOS

5.5000 g., Copper-Nickel, 23.5 mm. **Obv:** National arms, eagle left **Rev:** Value and date within circle **Note:** Mint mark Mo.

Date	Mintage	F	VF	XF	Unc	BU
1936	33,030,000	—	0.75	2.50	9.00	10.00
1937	3,000,000	—	8.00	45.00	215	250
1938	3,650,000	1.25	2.00	7.00	60.00	75.00
1939	6,920,000	—	1.00	3.50	27.50	30.00
1940	12,300,000	—	0.40	1.25	5.00	6.00
1942	14,380,000	—	0.60	1.50	7.00	9.00
1945	9,558,000	—	0.40	0.70	3.50	4.00
1946	46,230,000	—	0.40	0.60	2.50	3.00

KM# 433 10 CENTAVOS

5.5000 g., Bronze, 23.5 mm. **Obv:** National arms, eagle left **Rev:** Bust left **Note:** Mint mark Mo.

Date	Mintage	F	VF	XF	Unc	BU
1955	1,818,000	—	0.75	3.25	23.00	30.00
1956	5,255,000	—	0.75	3.25	23.00	28.00
1957	11,925,000	—	0.20	0.40	5.50	8.00
1959	26,140,000	—	0.30	0.45	0.75	1.25
1966	5,873,000	—	0.15	0.25	0.60	1.75
1967	32,318,000	—	0.10	0.15	0.30	0.40

KM# 434.1 10 CENTAVOS

Copper-Nickel **Obv:** National arms, eagle left **Rev:** Upright ear of corn **Note:** Variety I- Sharp stem and wide date

Date	Mintage	F	VF	XF	Unc	BU
1974	6,000,000	—	—	0.35	0.75	1.00
1975	5,550,000	—	0.10	0.35	0.75	1.00
1976	7,680,000	—	0.10	0.20	0.30	0.40
1977	144,650,000	—	1.25	2.25	3.00	3.50
1978	271,870,000	—	—	1.00	1.50	2.25
1979	375,660,000	—	—	0.50	1.00	1.75
1980/79	21,290,000	—	2.45	3.75	6.00	7.00
1980	Inc. above	—	1.50	2.00	4.50	5.50

KM# 434.2 10 CENTAVOS

Copper-Nickel **Obv:** National arms, eagle left **Rev:** Upright ear of corn **Note:** Variety II- Blunt stem and narrow date

Date	Mintage	F	VF	XF	Unc	BU
1974	Inc. above	—	—	0.10	0.20	0.30
1977	Inc. above	—	0.15	0.50	1.25	2.25
1978	Inc. above	—	—	0.10	0.30	0.40
1979	Inc. above	—	0.15	0.35	0.85	1.50
1980	Inc. above	—	—	0.10	0.20	0.30

KM# 434.3 10 CENTAVOS

Copper-Nickel **Obv:** National arms, eagle left **Rev:** Upright ear of corn **Note:** Variety III- Blunt stem and wide date

Date	Mintage	F	VF	XF	Unc	BU
1980/79	—	—	—	—	5.00	6.00

KM# 434.4 10 CENTAVOS

Copper-Nickel **Obv:** National arms, eagle left **Rev:** Upright ear of corn **Note:** Variety IV- Sharp stem and narrow date

Date	Mintage	F	VF	XF	Unc	BU
1974	—	—	—	—	1.50	2.50
1979	—	—	—	—	1.50	2.50

KM# 435 20 CENTAVOS

5.0000 g., 0.8000 Silver .1286 oz. ASW, 22 mm. **Obv:** National arms **Rev:** Value and date within wreath with Liberty cap above **Note:** Mint mark Mo.

Date	Mintage	F	VF	XF	Unc	BU
1905	2,565,000	—	12.00	20.00	145	175
1906	6,860,000	—	9.00	16.50	60.00	80.00
1907 Straight 7	4,000,000	—	11.50	20.00	70.00	100
1907 Curved 7	5,435,000	—	7.50	13.50	65.00	90.00
1908	350,000	50.00	90.00	225	1,500	—
1910	1,135,000	—	11.00	16.00	80.00	95.00
1911	1,150,000	12.00	15.00	35.00	125	150
1912	625,000	20.00	40.00	70.00	335	375
1913	1,000,000	—	14.50	30.00	95.00	115
1914	1,500,000	—	10.00	21.50	62.50	75.00

KM# 436 20 CENTAVOS

3.6250 g., 0.8000 Silver .0932 oz. ASW, 19 mm. **Obv:** National arms **Rev:** Value and date within wreath with Liberty cap above **Note:** Mint mark Mo. Reduced size.

Date	Mintage	F	VF	XF	Unc	BU
1919	4,155,000	—	30.00	55.00	190	225

KM# 437 20 CENTAVOS

15.0000 g., Bronze, 32.5 mm. **Obv:** National arms **Rev:** Value below date within wreath **Note:** Mint mark Mo.

Date	Mintage	F	VF	XF	Unc	BU
1920	4,835,000	—	45.00	140	650	750
1935	20,000,000	—	6.00	10.00	80.00	125

KM# 438 20 CENTAVOS

3.3333 g., 0.7200 Silver .0772 oz. ASW, 19 mm. **Obv:** National arms **Rev:** Value and date within wreath with Liberty cap above **Note:** Mint mark Mo.

Date	Mintage	F	VF	XF	Unc	BU
1920	3,710,000	—	6.00	17.50	165	200
1921	6,160,000	—	6.00	14.00	100	145
1925	1,450,000	—	12.00	20.00	125	150
1926/5	1,465,000	—	20.00	65.00	325	375
1926	Inc. above	—	3.25	7.50	80.00	110
1927	1,405,000	—	3.50	8.00	85.00	115
1928	3,630,000	—	4.00	5.25	14.50	19.50
1930	1,000,000	—	5.00	8.00	25.00	35.00
1933	2,500,000	—	2.25	3.00	10.00	11.50
1934	2,500,000	—	2.25	4.00	11.00	12.50
1935	2,460,000	—	2.25	4.00	11.00	12.50
1937	10,000,000	—	1.75	2.25	4.00	5.00
1939	8,800,000	—	1.75	2.25	4.00	5.00
1940	3,000,000	—	1.75	2.25	3.50	5.00
1941	5,740,000	—	1.50	2.25	3.00	4.00
1942	12,460,000	—	1.50	2.25	3.25	3.75
1943	3,955,000	—	2.00	2.50	3.50	4.25

KM# 439 20 CENTAVOS

Bronze, 28.5 mm. **Obv:** National arms, eagle left **Rev:** Liberty cap divides value above hills, written value and date flanked by plants **Note:** Mint mark Mo.

Date	Mintage	F	VF	XF	Unc	BU
1943	46,350,000	—	1.25	3.00	18.00	25.00
1944	83,650,000	—	0.40	0.65	8.00	10.00
1945	26,801,000	—	1.25	3.50	9.50	12.00
1946	25,695,000	—	1.10	2.25	6.00	8.25
1951	11,385,000	—	3.00	8.75	90.00	110
1952	6,560,000	—	3.00	5.00	25.00	32.00
1953	26,948,000	—	0.35	0.80	8.25	12.00
1954	40,108,000	—	0.35	0.80	8.00	11.50
1955	16,950,000	—	2.75	7.00	60.00	75.00

KM# 440 20 CENTAVOS

Bronze, 28.5 mm. **Obv:** National arms, eagle left **Rev:** Liberty cap divides value above hills, written value and date flanked by plants **Note:** Mint mark Mo.

Date	Mintage	F	VF	XF	Unc	BU
1955 Inc. KM#439	Inc. above	—	0.75	1.75	17.00	22.00
1956	22,431,000	—	0.30	0.35	3.00	4.00
1957	13,455,000	—	0.45	1.25	9.00	12.00
1959	6,017,000	—	4.50	9.00	75.00	100
1960	39,756,000	—	0.15	0.25	0.75	1.00
1963	14,869,000	—	0.25	0.35	0.80	1.00
1964	28,654,000	—	0.25	0.40	0.90	1.25
1965	74,162,000	—	0.20	0.35	0.80	1.00
1966	43,745,000	—	0.15	0.25	0.75	1.00
1967	46,487,000	—	0.20	0.50	1.00	1.25
1968	15,477,000	—	0.30	0.55	1.35	1.65
1969	63,647,000	—	0.20	0.35	0.80	1.00
1970	76,287,000	—	0.15	0.20	0.90	1.30
1971	49,892,000	—	0.30	0.50	1.25	1.50

KM# 441 20 CENTAVOS

Bronze, 28.5 mm. **Obv:** National arms, eagle left **Rev:** Liberty cap divides value above hills, written value and date flanked by plants

Date	Mintage	F	VF	XF	Unc	BU
1971 Inc. KM#440	Inc. above	—	0.20	0.35	1.85	2.35
1973	78,398,000	—	0.25	0.35	0.95	1.50
1974	34,200,000	—	0.20	0.35	1.25	1.75

KM# 442 20 CENTAVOS

Copper-Nickel, 20 mm. **Obv:** National arms, eagle left **Rev:** Bust 3/4 facing flanked by value and date

Date	Mintage	F	VF	XF	Unc	BU
1974	112,000,000	—	0.10	0.15	0.25	0.30
1975	611,000,000	—	0.10	0.15	0.30	0.35
1976	394,000,000	—	0.10	0.15	0.35	0.45
1977	394,350,000	—	0.10	0.15	0.40	0.45
1978	527,950,000	—	0.10	0.15	0.25	0.30
1979	524,615,000	—	0.10	0.15	0.25	0.30
1979	—	—	1.25	2.00	4.00	8.00
Note: Doubled die obv. small letters						
1979	—	—	1.25	2.00	4.00	8.00
Note: Doubled die obv. large letters						
1980	326,500,000	—	0.15	0.20	0.30	0.40
1981 Open 8	106,205,000	—	0.30	0.50	1.00	2.00
1981 Closed 8, high date	248,500,000	—	0.30	0.50	1.00	2.00
1981 Closed 8, low date	—	—	1.00	1.50	3.50	4.25
1981/1982	—	—	40.00	75.00	175	195
Note: The 1981/1982 overdate is often mistaken as 1982/1981						
1982	286,855,000	—	0.40	0.60	0.90	1.10
1983 Round top 3	100,930,000	—	0.25	0.40	1.75	2.25
1983 Flat top 3	Inc. above	—	0.25	0.50	1.25	1.75
1983 Proof	998	Value: 15.00				

KM# 491 20 CENTAVOS

Bronze, 20 mm. **Subject:** Olmec Culture **Obv:** National arms, eagle left **Rev:** Mask 3/4 right with value below

Date	Mintage	F	VF	XF	Unc	BU
1983	260,000,000	—	0.20	0.25	1.25	1.75
1983 Proof	53	Value: 185				
1984	180,320,000	—	0.20	0.35	1.85	2.25

KM# 443 25 CENTAVOS

3.3330 g., 0.3000 Silver .0321 oz. ASW, 21.5 mm. **Obv:** National arms, eagle left **Rev:** Scale below Liberty cap **Note:** Mint mark Mo.

Date	Mintage	F	VF	XF	Unc	BU
1950	77,060,000	—	0.60	0.80	1.60	2.00
1951	41,172,000	—	0.60	0.80	1.60	2.00
1952	29,264,000	—	0.75	1.10	1.75	2.25
1953	38,144,000	—	0.65	0.85	1.60	2.00

KM# 444 25 CENTAVOS

5.5000 g., Copper-Nickel, 23 mm. **Obv:** National arms, eagle left **Rev:** Bust 3/4 facing

Date	Mintage	F	VF	XF	Unc	BU
1964	20,686,000	—	—	0.15	0.20	0.30
1966 Closed beak	180,000	—	0.65	1.00	2.25	2.50
1966 Open beak	Inc. above	—	1.75	3.50	10.00	13.50

KM# 445 50 CENTAVOS

12.5000 g., 0.8000 Silver .3215 oz. ASW, 30 mm. **Obv:** National arms **Rev:** Value and date within 3/4 wreath with Liberty cap above **Note:** Mint mark Mo.

Date	Mintage	F	VF	XF	Unc	BU
1905	2,446,000	12.50	20.00	30.00	150	225
1906 Open 9	16,966,000	—	6.00	10.00	40.00	60.00
1906 Closed 9	Inc. above	—	5.00	9.00	35.00	50.00
1907 Straight 7	18,920,000	—	5.00	9.00	25.00	28.50
1907 Curved 7	14,841,000	—	5.25	9.00	25.00	32.00
1908	488,000	—	80.00	190	545	650
1912	3,736,000	—	11.00	14.00	45.00	60.00
1913/07	10,510,000	—	40.00	90.00	240	275
1913/2	Inc. above	—	20.00	27.50	65.00	85.00
1913	Inc. above	—	5.50	8.50	27.50	35.00
1914	7,710,000	—	6.75	13.50	32.00	45.00
1916 Narrow date	480,000	—	60.00	85.00	200	290
1916 Wide date	Inc. above	—	60.00	85.00	200	290
1917	37,112,000	—	6.00	9.50	20.00	22.50
1918	1,320,000	—	70.00	135	250	335

KM# 446 50 CENTAVOS

9.0625 g., 0.8000 Silver .2331 oz. ASW, 27 mm. **Obv:** National arms **Rev:** Value and date within 3/4 wreath with Liberty cap above **Note:** Mint mark Mo. Reduced size.

Date	Mintage	F	VF	XF	Unc	BU
1918/7	2,760,000	—	525	675	1,250	—
1918	Inc. above	—	17.50	55.00	300	385
1919	29,670,000	—	9.50	22.50	95.00	125

KM# 447 50 CENTAVOS

8.3333 g., 0.7200 Silver .1929 oz. ASW, 27 mm. **Obv:** National arms **Rev:** Value and date within 3/4 wreath with Liberty cap above **Note:** Mint mark Mo.

Date	Mintage	F	VF	XF	Unc	BU
1919	10,200,000	—	10.00	20.00	90.00	110
1920	27,166,000	—	8.00	14.00	70.00	80.00
1921	21,864,000	—	8.00	14.00	85.00	100
1925	3,280,000	—	17.50	30.00	125	160
1937	20,000,000	—	4.25	5.50	7.50	8.50
1938	100,000	—	50.00	85.00	225	300
1939	10,440,000	—	6.00	8.00	15.00	18.50
1942	800,000	—	6.00	9.00	16.00	20.00
1943	41,512,000	—	3.25	4.25	5.50	6.50
1944	55,806,000	—	3.25	4.25	5.50	6.50
1945	56,766,000	—	3.25	4.25	5.50	6.50

KM# 448 50 CENTAVOS

7.9730 g., 0.4200 Silver .1076 oz. ASW, 27 mm. **Obv:** National arms **Rev:** Value and date within 3/4 wreath with Liberty cap above **Note:** Mint mark Mo.

Date	Mintage	F	VF	XF	Unc	BU
1935	70,800,000	—	2.50	3.25	5.50	7.00

KM# 449 50 CENTAVOS

6.6600 g., 0.3000 Silver .0642 oz. ASW, 26 mm. **Obv:** National arms, eagle left **Rev:** Head with head covering right **Note:** Mint mark Mo.

Date	Mintage	F	VF	XF	Unc	BU
1950	13,570,000	—	1.50	1.85	3.00	4.50
1951	3,650,000	—	2.00	2.50	3.75	5.75

KM# 450 50 CENTAVOS

14.0000 g., Bronze, 33 mm. **Obv:** National arms, eagle left **Rev:** Head with headdress left **Note:** Mint mark Mo.

Date	Mintage	F	VF	XF	Unc	BU
1955	3,502,000	—	1.50	3.00	29.00	35.00
1956	34,643,000	—	0.75	1.50	3.75	4.50
1957	9,675,000	—	1.00	2.00	6.50	7.50
1959	4,540,000	—	0.50	0.75	2.00	2.75

KM# 451 50 CENTAVOS

6.5000 g., Copper-Nickel, 25 mm. **Obv:** National arms, eagle left **Rev:** Head with headdress left

Date	Mintage	F	VF	XF	Unc	BU
1964	43,806,000	—	0.15	0.20	0.40	0.60
1965	14,326,000	—	0.20	0.25	0.45	0.65
1966	1,726,000	—	0.20	0.40	1.30	1.75
1967	55,144,000	—	0.20	0.30	0.65	1.00
1968	80,438,000	—	0.15	0.30	0.65	0.90
1969	87,640,000	—	0.20	0.35	0.80	1.00

KM# 452 50 CENTAVOS

6.5000 g., Copper-Nickel, 25 mm. **Obv:** National arms, eagle left **Rev:** Head with headdress left **Note:** Coins dated 1975 and 1976 exist with and without dots in centers of three circles on plumage on reverse. Edge varieties exist.

Date	Mintage	F	VF	XF	Unc	BU
1970	76,236,000	—	0.15	0.20	0.80	1.00
1971	125,288,000	—	0.15	0.20	0.90	1.30

Date	Mintage	F	VF	XF	Unc	BU
1972	16,000,000	—	1.25	2.00	3.00	4.75
1975 Dots	177,958,000	—	0.60	1.25	3.50	6.00
1975 No dots	Inc. above	—	0.15	0.20	0.75	1.00
1976 Dots	37,480,000	—	0.75	1.25	5.00	6.00
1976 No dots	Inc. above	—	0.15	0.20	0.50	0.75
1977	12,410,000	—	6.50	10.00	32.50	42.50
1978	85,400,000	—	0.15	0.25	0.50	0.75
1979 Round 2nd 9 in date	229,000,000	—	0.15	0.25	0.50	0.65
1979 Square 9's in date	Inc. above	—	0.20	0.40	1.60	2.00
1980 Narrow date, square 9	89,978,000	—	0.45	0.75	1.75	2.50
1980 Wide date, round 9	178,188,000	—	0.20	0.25	1.00	1.15
1981 Rectangular 9, narrow date	142,212,000	—	0.50	0.75	1.75	2.50
1981 Round 9, wide date	Inc. above	—	0.30	0.50	1.25	1.75
1982	45,474,000	—	0.20	0.40	1.00	1.25
1983	90,318,000	—	0.50	0.75	2.00	2.50
1983 Proof	998	Value: 35.00				

KM# 492 50 CENTAVOS

Stainless Steel, 22 mm. **Subject:** Palenque Culture **Obv:** National arms, eagle left **Rev:** Head with headdress 3/4 left

Date	Mintage	F	VF	XF	Unc	BU
1983	99,540,000	—	—	0.30	1.50	2.50
1983 Proof	53	Value: 195				

KM# 453 PESO

27.0700 g., 0.9030 Silver .7859 oz. ASW, 39 mm. **Subject:** Caballito **Obv:** National arms **Rev:** Horse and rider facing left among sun rays **Designer:** Charles Pillet **Note:** Mint mark Mo.

Date	Mintage	F	VF	XF	Unc	BU
1910	3,814,000	—	45.00	50.00	160	250
1911	1,227,000	—	45.00	75.00	200	275
Note: Long lower left ray on reverse						
1911	Inc. above	—	145	210	650	800
Note: Short lower left ray on reverse						
1912	322,000	—	100	210	365	500
1913/2	2,880,000	—	45.00	75.00	270	400
1913	Inc. above	—	45.00	70.00	175	250
Note: 1913 coins exist with even and unevenly spaced date						
1914	120,000	—	600	950	2,800	—

KM# 454 PESO

18.1300 g., 0.8000 Silver .4663 oz. ASW, 34 mm. **Obv:** National arms **Rev:** Value and date within 3/4 wreath with Liberty cap above **Note:** Mint mark Mo.

Date	Mintage	F	VF	XF	Unc	BU
1918	3,050,000	—	35.00	125	1,350	2,100
1919	6,151,000	—	20.00	50.00	900	1,600

KM# 455 PESO

16.6600 g., 0.7200 Silver .3856 oz. ASW, 34 mm. **Obv:** National arms **Rev:** Value and date within 3/4 wreath with Liberty cap above **Note:** Mint mark Mo.

Date	Mintage	F	VF	XF	Unc	BU
1920/10	8,830,000	—	50.00	90.00	325	—
1920	Inc. above	—	8.00	25.00	185	300
1921	5,480,000	—	8.00	25.00	155	200
1922	33,620,000	—	BV	6.00	20.00	26.00
1923	35,280,000	—	BV	6.00	20.00	28.00
1924	33,060,000	—	BV	6.00	20.00	26.00
1925	9,160,000	—	4.50	10.00	60.00	75.00
1926	28,840,000	—	BV	6.00	20.00	25.00
1927	5,060,000	—	7.00	10.00	70.00	85.00
1932 Open 9	50,770,000	—	—	BV	6.00	7.50
1932 Closed 9	Inc. above	—	—	BV	6.00	7.50
1933/2	43,920,000	—	15.00	25.00	85.00	—
1933	Inc. above	—	—	BV	6.50	8.50
1934	22,070,000	—	—	BV	8.00	10.00
1935	8,050,000	—	BV	6.00	11.50	13.50
1938	30,000,000	—	—	BV	6.00	7.50
1940	20,000,000	—	—	BV	6.50	8.00
1943	47,662,000	—	—	BV	5.75	6.50
1944	39,522,000	—	—	BV	6.00	7.00
1945	37,300,000	—	—	BV	6.00	7.00

KM# 456 PESO

14.0000 g., 0.5000 Silver .2250 oz. ASW, 32 mm. **Obv:** National arms, eagle left **Rev:** Head with headcovering right **Note:** Mint mark Mo.

Date	Mintage	F	VF	XF	Unc	BU
1947	61,460,000	—	BV	3.50	4.50	5.50
1948	22,915,000	—	3.50	4.50	5.50	6.50
1949	4,000,000	—	—	1,200	1,600	2,500
Note: Not released for circulation						
1949 Proof	—	Value: 4,000				

KM# 457 PESO

13.3300 g., 0.3000 Silver .1285 oz. ASW, 32 mm. **Obv:** National arms, eagle left **Rev:** Armored bust 3/4 left **Note:** Mint mark Mo.

Date	Mintage	F	VF	XF	Unc	BU
1950	3,287,000	—	2.50	4.00	7.00	8.50

KM# 458 PESO

16.0000 g., 0.1000 Silver .0514 oz. ASW, 34.5 mm. **Subject:** 100th Anniversary of Constitution **Obv:** National arms, eagle left within wreath **Obv. Designer:** Manuel L. Negrete **Rev:** Head left **Edge Lettering:** INDEPENDENCIA Y LIBERTAD **Note:** Mint mark Mo.

Date	Mintage	F	VF	XF	Unc	BU
1957	500,000	—	3.50	5.00	12.50	15.00

KM# 459 PESO

16.0000 g., 0.1000 Silver .0514 oz. ASW, 34.5 mm. **Obv:** National arms, eagle left within wreath **Rev:** Armored bust right within wreath **Edge Lettering:** INDEPENDENCIA Y LIBERTAD **Note:** Mint mark Mo.

Date	Mintage	F	VF	XF	Unc	BU
1957	28,273,000	—	0.75	1.00	2.50	10.00
1958	41,899,000	—	BV	0.80	1.65	2.00
1959	27,369,000	—	1.25	2.00	5.50	8.00
1960	26,259,000	—	0.75	1.10	3.25	4.50
1961	52,601,000	—	BV	0.90	2.25	3.00
1962	61,094,000	—	BV	0.80	1.75	2.25
1963	26,394,000	—	BV	0.80	1.75	2.00
1964	15,615,000	—	BV	0.80	2.00	2.40
1965	5,004,000	—	—	0.80	1.85	2.00
1966	30,998,000	—	—	0.75	1.35	1.85
1967	9,308,000	—	—	0.85	2.75	3.50

KM# 460 PESO

Copper-Nickel, 29 mm. **Obv:** National arms, eagle left **Rev:** Head left

Date	Mintage	F	VF	XF	Unc	BU
1970 Narrow date	102,715,000	—	0.25	0.35	0.65	0.80
1970 Wide date	Inc. above	—	1.25	2.50	7.50	9.00
1971	426,222,000	—	0.20	0.25	0.55	0.75
1972	120,000,000	—	0.20	0.25	0.40	0.65
1974	63,700,000	—	0.20	0.25	0.65	0.90

Date	Mintage	F	VF	XF	Unc	BU
1975 Tall narrow date	205,979,000	—	0.25	0.45	1.00	1.35

Date	Mintage	F	VF	XF	Unc	BU
1975 Short wide date	Inc. above	—	0.30	0.40	0.75	1.00
1976	94,489,000	—	0.15	0.20	0.50	0.75
1977 Thick date close to rim	94,364,000	—	0.25	0.45	1.00	1.25
1977 Thin date, space between sideburns and collar	Inc. above	—	1.00	2.00	6.50	13.50
1978 Closed 8	208,300,000	—	0.20	0.30	1.00	1.50
1978 Open 8	55,140,000	—	0.75	1.75	12.00	15.00
1979 Thin date	117,884,000	—	0.20	0.30	1.15	1.50
1979 Thick date	Inc. above	—	0.20	0.30	1.25	1.75
1980 Closed 8	318,800,000	—	0.25	0.35	1.00	1.25
1980 Open 8	23,865,000	—	0.75	1.50	8.00	12.00
1981 Closed 8	413,349,000	—	0.20	0.30	0.75	0.90
1981 Open 8	58,616,000	—	0.50	1.25	6.50	8.00
1982 Closed 8	235,000,000	—	0.25	0.75	2.25	2.50
1982 Open 8	—	—	0.75	1.50	8.00	12.00
1983 Wide date	100,000,000	—	0.30	0.45	3.00	3.50
1983 Narrow date	Inc. above	—	0.30	0.45	3.00	3.50
1983 Proof	1,051,000	Value: 38.00				

KM# 496 PESO

Stainless Steel, 24.5 mm. **Obv:** National arms, eagle left **Rev:** Armored bust right

Date	Mintage	F	VF	XF	Unc	BU
1984	722,802,000	—	0.10	0.25	0.65	1.00
1985	985,000,000	—	0.10	0.25	0.50	0.75
1986	740,000,000	—	0.10	0.25	0.50	0.75
1987	250,000,000	—	—	0.25	0.50	0.80
1987 Proof; 2 known	—	Value: 1,000				

KM# 461 2 PESOS

1.6666 g., 0.9000 Gold .0482 oz. AGW, 13 mm. **Obv:** National arms **Rev:** Date above value within wreath **Note:** Mint mark Mo.

Date	Mintage	F	VF	XF	Unc	BU
1919	1,670,000	—	BV	35.00	65.00	—
1920/10	—	BV	35.00	55.00	100	—
1920	4,282,000	—	BV	35.00	50.00	—
1944	10,000	BV	35.00	50.00	70.00	—
1945	Est. 140,000	—	—	—	BV+20%	—
1946	168,000	BV	35.00	50.00	100	—
1947	25,000	BV	35.00	50.00	75.00	—
1948 No specimens known	45,000	—	—	—	—	—

Note: During 1951-1972 a total of 4,590,493 pieces were restruck, most likely dated 1945. In 1996 matte restrikes were produced

KM# 462 2 PESOS

26.6667 g., 0.9000 Silver .7717 oz. ASW, 39 mm. **Subject:** Centennial of Independence **Obv:** National arms, eagle left within wreath **Rev:** Winged Victory **Designer:** Emilio del Moral **Note:** Mint mark Mo.

Date	Mintage	F	VF	XF	Unc	BU
1921	1,278,000	—	40.00	55.00	325	450

KM# 463 2-1/2 PESOS

2.0833 g., 0.9000 Gold .0602 oz. AGW, 15.5 mm. **Obv:** National arms **Rev:** Miguel Hidalgo y Costilla **Note:** Mint mark Mo.

Date	Mintage	F	VF	XF	Unc	BU
1918	1,704,000	—	BV	45.00	80.00	—
1919	984,000	—	BV	45.00	80.00	—
1920/10	607,000	—	BV	55.00	130	—
1920	Inc. above	—	BV	45.00	65.00	—
1944	20,000	—	BV	45.00	60.00	—
1945	Est. 180,000	—	—	—	BV+18%	—
1946	163,000	—	BV	45.00	60.00	—
1947	24,000	200	265	325	500	—
1948	63,000	—	BV	45.00	70.00	—

Note: During 1951-1972 a total of 5,025,087 pieces were restruck, most likely dated 1945. In 1996 matte restrikes were produced

KM# 464 5 PESOS

4.1666 g., 0.9000 Gold .1205 oz. AGW, 19 mm. **Obv:** National arms **Rev:** Miguel Hidalgo y Costilla **Note:** Mint mark Mo.

Date	Mintage	F	VF	XF	Unc	BU
1905	18,000	120	175	245	600	—
1906	4,638,000	—	—	BV	90.00	—
1907/6	—	—	—	—	—	—
1907	1,088,000	—	—	BV	95.00	—
1910	100,000	—	—	BV	150	—
1918/7	609,000	—	—	BV	200	—
1918	Inc. above	—	—	BV	100	—

Date	Mintage	F	VF	XF	Unc	BU
1919	506,000	—	—	BV	100	—
1920	2,385,000	—	—	BV	100	—
1955	Est. 48,000	—	—	—	BV+12%	—

Note: During 1955-1972 a total of 1,767,645 pieces were restruck, most likely dated 1955. In 1996 matte restrikes were produced

KM# 465 5 PESOS

30.0000 g., 0.9000 Silver .8681 oz. ASW, 40 mm. **Obv:** National arms, eagle left **Rev:** Head with headdress left **Note:** Mint mark Mo.

Date	Mintage	F	VF	XF	Unc	BU
1947	5,110,000	—	—	BV	12.75	14.50
1948	26,740,000	—	—	BV	12.50	13.50

KM# 466 5 PESOS

27.7800 g., 0.7200 Silver .6431 oz. ASW, 40 mm. **Subject:** Opening of Southern Railroad **Obv:** National arms, eagle left **Rev:** Radiant sun flanked by palm trees above train **Edge Lettering:** COMERCIO - AGRICULTURA - INDUSTRIA **Designer:** Manuel L. Negrete **Note:** Mint mark Mo.

Date	Mintage	F	VF	XF	Unc	BU
1950	200,000	—	22.50	40.00	50.00	55.00

Note: It is recorded that 100,000 pieces were melted to be used for the 1968 Mexican Olympic 25 Pesos

KM# 467 5 PESOS

27.7800 g., 0.7200 Silver .6431 oz. ASW, 40 mm. **Obv:** National arms, eagle left **Rev:** Head left within wreath **Edge Lettering:** COMERCIO - AGRICULTURA - INDUSTRIA **Note:** Mint mark Mo.

Date	Mintage	F	VF	XF	Unc	BU
1951	4,958,000	—	—	BV	10.00	12.00
1952	9,595,000	—	—	BV	9.50	11.00
1953	20,376,000	—	—	BV	9.50	11.00
1954	30,000	—	30.00	60.00	70.00	85.00

KM# 468 5 PESOS

27.7800 g., 0.7200 Silver .6431 oz. ASW, 40 mm. **Subject:** Bicentennial of Hidalgo's Birth **Obv:** National arms, eagle left **Rev:** Half-length figure facing to right of building and dates **Edge Lettering:** COMERCIO - AGRICULTURA - INDUSTRIA **Designer:** Manuel L. Negrete **Note:** Mint mark Mo.

Date	Mintage	F	VF	XF	Unc	BU
1953	1,000,000	—	BV	9.50	11.00	13.50

KM# 469 5 PESOS

18.0500 g., 0.7200 Silver .4179 oz. ASW, 36 mm. **Obv:** National arms, eagle left **Rev:** Head left **Note:** Mint mark Mo.

Date	Mintage	F	VF	XF	Unc	BU
1955	4,271,000	—	BV	6.25	7.00	8.50
1956	4,596,000	—	BV	6.25	7.00	8.50
1957	3,464,000	—	BV	6.25	7.00	8.50

KM# 470 5 PESOS

18.0500 g., 0.7200 Silver .4179 oz. ASW, 36 mm. **Subject:** 100th Anniversary of Constitution **Obv:** National arms, eagle left **Rev:** Head left **Edge Lettering:** INDEPENDENCIA Y LIBERTAD **Designer:** Manuel L. Negrete **Note:** Mint mark Mo.

Date	Mintage	F	VF	XF	Unc	BU
1957	200,000	—	6.50	7.50	13.50	15.50

KM# 471 5 PESOS

18.0500 g., 0.7200 Silver .4179 oz. ASW, 36 mm. **Subject:** Centennial of Carranza's Birth **Obv:** National arms, eagle left **Rev:** Head left **Edge:** Plain **Designer:** Manuel L. Negrete **Note:** Mint mark Mo.

Date	Mintage	F	VF	XF	Unc	BU
1959	1,000,000	—	—	BV	7.00	9.00

KM# 472 5 PESOS

14.0000 g., Copper-Nickel, 33 mm. **Obv:** National arms, eagle left **Rev:** Armored bust right **Edge Lettering:** INDEPENDENCIA Y LIBERTAD **Note:** Small date, large date varieties.

Date	Mintage	F	VF	XF	Unc	BU
1971	28,457,000	—	0.50	0.95	2.50	3.25
1972	75,000,000	—	0.60	1.25	2.00	2.50
1973	19,405,000	—	1.25	2.00	4.50	5.50
1974	34,500,000	—	0.50	0.80	1.75	2.25
1976 Small date	26,121,000	—	0.75	1.45	3.25	4.00
1976 Large date	121,550,000	—	0.35	0.50	1.50	1.75
1977	102,000,000	—	0.35	0.50	1.50	1.75
1978	25,700,000	—	1.00	1.50	4.50	6.25

KM# 485 5 PESOS

Copper-Nickel, 27 mm. **Subject:** Quetzalcoatl **Obv:** National arms, eagle left **Rev:** Native sculpture to lower right of value and dollar sign **Edge Lettering:** LIBERTAD Y INDEPENDENCIA **Note:** Inverted and normal edge legend varieties exist for the 1980 and 1981 dates.

Date	Mintage	F	VF	XF	Unc	BU
1980	266,899,999	—	0.25	0.50	1.75	2.25
1981	30,500,000	—	0.45	0.65	2.75	3.25
1982	20,000,000	—	1.50	2.35	4.25	5.25
1982 Proof	1,051	Value: 18.00				
1983 Proof; 7 known	—	Value: 1,200				
1984	16,300,000	—	1.25	2.00	4.75	6.00
1985	76,900,000	—	2.00	3.25	4.25	5.00

KM# 502 5 PESOS

Brass, 17 mm. **Subject:** Quetzalcoatl **Obv:** National arms, eagle left **Rev:** Date and value **Note:** Circulation coinage.

Date	Mintage	F	VF	XF	Unc	BU
1985	30,000,000	—	—	0.15	0.35	0.50
1987	81,900,000	—	8.00	9.50	12.50	15.00
1988	76,600,000	—	—	0.10	0.25	0.35
1988 Proof; 2 known	—	Value: 600				

KM# 473 10 PESOS

8.3333 g., 0.9000 Gold .2411 oz. AGW, 22.5 mm. **Obv:** National arms **Rev:** Miguel Hidalgo y Costilla **Note:** Mint mark Mo.

Date	Mintage	F	VF	XF	Unc	BU
1905	39,000	—	BV	170	225	—
1906	2,949,000	—	BV	165	185	—
1907	1,589,000	—	BV	165	185	—
1908	890,000	—	BV	165	185	—
1910	451,000	—	BV	165	185	—
1916	26,000	—	BV	175	350	—
1917	1,967,000	—	BV	165	185	—
1919	266,000	—	BV	165	200	—
1920	12,000	—	BV	425	700	—
1959	Est. 50,000	—	—	—	BV+7%	—

Note: *During 1961-1972 a total of 954,983 pieces were restruck, most likely dated 1959. In 1996 matte re-strikes were produced

KM# 474 10 PESOS

28.8800 g., 0.9000 Silver .8357 oz. ASW, 40 mm. **Obv:** National arms **Rev:** Head left **Note:** Mint mark Mo.

Date	Mintage	F	VF	XF	Unc	BU
1955	585,000	—	—	BV	12.50	14.50
1956	3,535,000	—	—	BV	12.25	13.50

KM# 475 10 PESOS

28.8800 g., 0.9000 Silver .8357 oz. ASW, 40 mm. **Subject:** 100th Anniversary of Constitution **Obv:** National arms, eagle left **Rev:** Head left **Edge Lettering:** INDEPENDENCIA Y LIBERTAD **Designer:** Manuel L. Negrete **Note:** Mint mark Mo.

Date	Mintage	F	VF	XF	Unc	BU
1957	100,000	—	13.50	27.50	45.00	50.00

KM# 476 10 PESOS

28.8800 g., 0.9000 Silver .8357 oz. ASW, 40 mm. **Subject:** 150th Anniversary - War of Independence **Obv:** National arms, eagle left **Rev:** Conjoined busts facing flanked by dates **Designer:** Manuel L. Negrete **Note:** Mint mark Mo.

Date	Mintage	F	VF	XF	Unc	BU
1960	1,000,000	—	—	BV	12.50	15.00

KM# 477.1 10 PESOS

Copper-Nickel, 30.5 mm. **Obv:** National arms, eagle left **Rev:** Miguel Hidalgo y Costilla **Shape:** 7-sided **Note:** Thin flan - 1.6mm

Date	Mintage	F	VF	XF	Unc	BU
1974	3,900,000	—	0.50	1.00	3.00	4.00
1974 Proof	—	Value: 625				
1975	1,000,000	—	2.25	3.25	7.50	8.50
1976	74,500,000	—	0.25	0.75	1.75	2.25
1977	79,620,000	—	0.50	1.00	2.00	3.00

KM# 477.2 10 PESOS

Copper-Nickel, 30.5 mm. **Obv:** National arms, eagle left **Rev:** Head left **Shape:** 7-sided **Note:** Thick flan - 2.3mm

Date	Mintage	F	VF	XF	Unc	BU
1978	124,850,000	—	0.50	0.75	2.50	2.75
1979	57,200,000	—	0.50	0.75	2.25	2.50
1980	55,200,000	—	0.50	0.75	2.50	3.75
1981	222,768,000	—	0.40	0.60	2.25	2.65
1982	151,770,000	—	0.50	0.80	2.50	3.50
1982 Proof	1,051	Value: 40.00				
1983 Proof; 3 known	—	Value: 1,800				
1985	58,000,000	—	1.25	1.75	5.75	7.50

KM# 512 10 PESOS

Stainless Steel, 19 mm. **Obv:** National arms, eagle left **Rev:** Head facing with diagonal value at left **Note:** Date varieties exist.

Date	Mintage	F	VF	XF	Unc	BU
1985	257,000,000	—	—	0.15	0.50	0.75
1986	392,000,000	—	—	0.15	0.50	1.50
1987	305,000,000	—	—	0.15	0.35	0.50
1988	500,300,000	—	—	0.15	0.25	0.35
1989	—	—	0.20	0.25	0.75	1.50
1990	—	—	—	0.25	0.75	1.25
1990 Proof; 2 known	—	Value: 550				

KM# 478 20 PESOS

16.6666 g., 0.9000 Gold .4823 oz. AGW, 27.5 mm. **Obv:** National arms, eagle left **Rev:** Gear-like design within upper circle above value **Note:** Mint mark Mo.

Date	Mintage	F	VF	XF	Unc	BU
1917	852,000	—	—	BV	345	—
1918	2,831,000	—	—	BV	345	—
1919	1,094,000	—	—	BV	345	—
1920/10	462,000	—	—	BV	345	—
1920	Inc. above	—	—	BV	345	—
1921/11	922,000	—	—	BV	345	—
1921/10	—	—	—	—	—	—
1921	Inc. above	—	—	BV	345	—
1959	Est. 13,000	—	—	—	—	—

Note: During 1960-1971 a total of 1,158,414 pieces were restruck, most likely dated 1959. In 1996 matte re-strikes were produced

KM# 486 20 PESOS

Copper-Nickel, 32 mm. **Obv:** National arms, eagle left **Rev:** Figure with headdress facing left within circle

Date	Mintage	F	VF	XF	Unc	BU
1980	84,900,000	—	0.50	0.85	2.25	3.00
1981	250,573,000	—	0.60	0.80	2.25	3.25
1982	236,892,000	—	1.00	1.75	2.50	3.50
1982 Proof	1,051	Value: 45.00				
1983 Proof; 3 known	—	Value: 575				
1984	55,000,000	—	1.00	1.50	2.50	4.75

KM# 508 20 PESOS

Brass, 21 mm. **Obv:** National arms, eagle left **Rev:** Bust facing with diagonal value at left

Date	Mintage	F	VF	XF	Unc	BU
1985 Wide date	25,000,000	—	0.10	0.20	1.00	1.25
1985 Narrow date	Inc. above	—	0.10	0.25	1.50	2.00
1986	10,000,000	—	1.00	1.75	5.00	5.50
1988	355,200,000	—	0.10	0.20	0.45	0.75
1989	—	—	0.15	0.30	1.50	2.00
1990	—	—	0.15	0.30	1.50	2.50
1990 Proof; 3 known	—	Value: 575				

KM# 479.1 25 PESOS
22.5000 g., 0.7200 Silver .5209 oz. ASW, 38 mm. **Obv:** National arms, eagle left **Rev:** Olympic rings below dancing native left, numeral design in background **Designer:** Lorenzo Rafael **Note:** Type I, Rings aligned.

Date	Mintage	F	VF	XF	Unc	BU
1968	27,182,000	—	—	BV	7.50	8.00

KM# 479.2 25 PESOS
22.5000 g., 0.7200 Silver .5209 oz. ASW, 38 mm. **Subject:** Summer Olympics - Mexico City **Obv:** National arms, eagle left **Rev:** Olympic rings below dancing native left, numeral design in background **Note:** Type II, center ring low.

Date	Mintage	F	VF	XF	Unc	BU
1968	Inc. above	—	BV	7.50	8.50	10.00

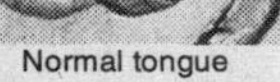
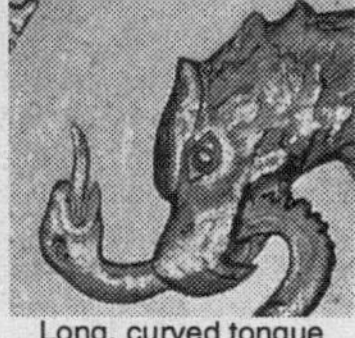
Normal tongue — Long, curved tongue

KM# 479.3 25 PESOS
22.5000 g., 0.7200 Silver .5209 oz. ASW, 38 mm. **Subject:** Summer Olympics - Mexico City **Obv:** National arms, eagle left **Rev:** Olympic rings below dancing native left, numeral design in background **Note:** Snake with long curved or normal tongue. Type III, center rings low.

Date	Mintage	F	VF	XF	Unc	BU
1968	Inc. above	—	BV	7.50	9.50	11.00

KM# 480 25 PESOS
22.5000 g., 0.7200 Silver .5209 oz. ASW, 38 mm. **Obv:** National arms, eagle left **Rev:** Bust facing

Date	Mintage	F	VF	XF	Unc	BU
1972	2,000,000	—	—	BV	7.50	8.50

KM# 514 25 PESOS
8.4060 g., 0.9250 Silver .2450 oz. ASW **Subject:** 1986 World Cup Soccer Games **Obv:** National arms, eagle left **Rev:** Value above soccer ball

Date	Mintage	F	VF	XF	Unc	BU
1985 Proof	234,000	Value: 12.00				

KM# 497 25 PESOS
7.7760 g., 0.7200 Silver .1800 oz. ASW **Subject:** 1986 World Cup Soccer Games **Obv:** National arms, eagle left **Rev:** Value above soccer ball with date below

Date	Mintage	F	VF	XF	Unc	BU
1985	354,000	—	—	—	—	7.50

KM# 497a 25 PESOS
8.4060 g., 0.9250 Silver .2450 oz. ASW **Subject:** 1986 World Cup Soccer Games **Obv:** National arms, eagle left **Rev:** Value above soccerball with date below **Note:** Without finess statement-reverse description

Date	Mintage	F	VF	XF	Unc	BU
1986 Proof	—	Value: 12.00				

KM# 503 25 PESOS
8.4060 g., 0.9250 Silver .2450 oz. ASW **Subject:** 1986 World Cup Soccer Games **Obv:** National arms, eagle left **Rev:** Pre-Columbian hieroglyphs, ojo de buey, and soccer ball

Date	Mintage	F	VF	XF	Unc	BU
1985 Proof	277,000	Value: 12.00				

KM# 519 25 PESOS
8.4060 g., 0.9250 Silver .2450 oz. ASW **Subject:** 1986 World Cup Soccer Games **Obv:** National arms, eagle left **Rev:** Soccer ball within net, date and value to left

Date	Mintage	F	VF	XF	Unc	BU
1986 Proof	—	Value: 12.00				

KM# 481 50 PESOS
41.6666 g., 0.9000 Gold 1.2057 oz. AGW, 37 mm. **Subject:** Centennial of Independence **Obv:** National arms **Rev:** Winged Victory **Edge:** Reeded **Designer:** Emilio del Moral **Note:** During 1949-1972 a total of 3,975,654 pieces were restruck, most likely dated 1947. In 1996 matte restrikes were produced. Mint mark Mo.

Date	Mintage	F	VF	XF	Unc	BU
1921	180,000	—	BV	875	950	1,000
1922	463,000	—	—	BV	825	875
1923	432,000	—	—	BV	825	875
1924	439,000	—	—	BV	825	875
1925	716,000	—	—	BV	825	875
1926	600,000	—	—	BV	825	875
1927	606,000	—	—	BV	825	875
1928	538,000	—	—	BV	825	875
1929	458,000	—	—	BV	825	875
1930	372,000	—	—	BV	825	875
1931	137,000	—	—	BV	845	900
1944	593,000	—	—	BV	820	850
1945	1,012,000	—	—	BV	820	850
1946	1,588,000	—	—	BV	820	850
1947	309,000	—	—	—	BV+3%	—
1947 Specimen	—	—	—	—	—	—

Note: Value, $6,500

KM# 482 50 PESOS
41.6666 g., 0.9000 Gold 1.2057 oz. AGW, 39 mm. **Obv:** National arms **Rev:** Winged Victory

Date	Mintage	F	VF	XF	Unc	BU
1943	89,000	—	—	—	BV	845

KM# 490 50 PESOS
Copper-Nickel, 35 mm. **Subject:** Coyolxauhqui **Obv:** National arms, eagle left **Rev:** Value to right of artistic designs **Edge:** Reeded **Note:** Doubled die examples of 1982 and 1983 dates exist.

Date	Mintage	F	VF	XF	Unc	BU
1982	222,890,000	—	1.00	2.50	5.00	6.00
1983	45,000,000	—	1.50	3.00	6.00	6.50
1983 Proof	1,051	Value: 40.00				
1984	73,537,000	—	1.00	1.35	3.50	4.00
1984 Proof; 4 known	—	Value: 750				

KM# 495 50 PESOS
Copper-Nickel, 23.5 mm. **Subject:** Benito Juarez **Obv:** National arms, eagle left **Rev:** Bust 1/4 left with diagonal value at left **Edge:** Reeded

Date	Mintage	F	VF	XF	Unc	BU
1984	94,216,000	—	0.65	1.25	2.70	3.00
1985	296,000,000	—	0.25	0.45	1.25	2.00
1986	50,000,000	—	6.00	10.00	12.00	14.00
1987	210,000,000	—	0.25	0.45	1.00	1.25
1988	80,200,000	—	6.25	9.00	13.50	15.50

KM# 495a 50 PESOS
Stainless Steel, 23.5 mm. **Subject:** Benito Juarez **Obv:** National arms, eagle left **Rev:** Bust 1/4 left with diagonal value at left **Edge:** Plain

Date	Mintage	F	VF	XF	Unc	BU
1988	353,300,000	—	—	0.20	1.25	1.75
1990	—	—	—	0.30	1.00	2.00
1992	—	—	—	0.25	1.00	2.75

KM# 498 50 PESOS
15.5520 g., 0.7200 Silver .3601 oz. ASW **Subject:** 1986 World Cup Soccer Games **Obv:** National arms, eagle left **Rev:** Pair of feet and soccer ball

Date	Mintage	F	VF	XF	Unc	BU
1985	347,000	—	—	—	—	6.50

KM# 498a 50 PESOS

16.8310 g., 0.9250 Silver .5000 oz. ASW **Subject:** 1986 World Cup Soccer Games **Obv:** National arms, eagle left **Rev:** Without fineness statement

Date	Mintage	F	VF	XF	Unc	BU
1986 Proof	10,000	Value: 20.00				

KM# 504 50 PESOS

16.8310 g., 0.9250 Silver .5000 oz. ASW **Subject:** 1986 World Cup Soccer Games **Obv:** National arms, eagle left **Rev:** Stylized athlete as soccer forerunner

Date	Mintage	F	VF	XF	Unc	BU
1985 Proof	347,000	Value: 20.00				

KM# 515 50 PESOS

16.8310 g., 0.9250 Silver .5000 oz. ASW **Subject:** 1986 World Cup Soccer Games **Obv:** National arms, eagle left **Rev:** Value to right of soccer player

Date	Mintage	F	VF	XF	Unc	BU
1985 Proof	234,000	Value: 20.00				

KM# 523 50 PESOS

16.8310 g., 0.9250 Silver .5000 oz. ASW **Subject:** 1986 World Cup Soccer Games **Obv:** National arms, eagle left **Rev:** Value to left of soccer balls

Date	Mintage	F	VF	XF	Unc	BU
1986 Proof	190,000	Value: 20.00				

KM# 532 50 PESOS

15.5500 g., 0.9990 Silver .5000 oz. ASW **Subject:** 50th Anniversary - Nationalization of Oil Industry **Obv:** National arms, eagle left **Rev:** Monument

Date	Mintage	F	VF	XF	Unc	BU
ND(1988)	30,000	—	—	—	20.00	22.00

Low 7's

High 7's

KM# 483.1 100 PESOS

27.7700 g., 0.7200 Silver .6429 oz. ASW, 39 mm. **Obv:** National arms, eagle left **Rev:** Bust facing, sloping right shoulder, round left shoulder with no clothing folds **Edge:** Reeded

Date	Mintage	F	VF	XF	Unc	BU
1977 Low 7's	5,225,000	—	—	BV	9.50	11.50
1977 High 7's	Inc. above	—	—	BV	9.50	12.00

KM# 483.2 100 PESOS

27.7700 g., 0.7200 Silver .6429 oz. ASW, 39 mm. **Obv:** National arms, eagle left **Rev:** Bust facing, higher right shoulder, left shoulder with clothing folds **Note:** Mintage inc. KM#483.1.

Date	Mintage	F	VF	XF	Unc	BU
1977 Date in line	—	—	—	BV	9.25	10.00
1978	9,879,000	—	—	BV	9.50	11.50
1979	784,000	—	—	BV	9.50	11.50
1979 Proof	—	Value: 650				

KM# 493 100 PESOS

Aluminum-Bronze, 26.5 mm. **Obv:** National arms, eagle left **Rev:** Head 1/4 right with diagonal value at right

Date	Mintage	F	VF	XF	Unc	BU
1984	227,809,000	—	0.45	0.60	2.50	4.00
1985	377,423,000	—	0.30	0.50	2.00	3.00
1986	43,000,000	—	1.00	2.50	4.75	7.50
1987	165,000,000	—	0.60	1.25	2.25	3.00
1988	433,100,000	—	0.30	0.50	2.00	2.75
1989	—	—	0.35	0.65	2.00	2.75
1990	—	—	0.15	0.40	1.50	2.50
1990 Proof; 1 known	—	Value: 650				
1991	—	—	0.15	0.25	1.00	2.50
1992	—	—	0.30	0.75	1.75	3.00

KM# 499 100 PESOS

31.1030 g., 0.7200 Silver .7201 oz. ASW **Subject:** 1986 World Cup Soccer Games **Obv:** National arms, eagle left **Rev:** Value above artistic designs and soccer ball

Date	Mintage	F	VF	XF	Unc	BU
1985	302,000	—	—	—	—	15.00

KM# 499a 100 PESOS

32.6250 g., 0.9250 Silver 1.0000 oz. ASW **Subject:** 1986 World Cup Soccer Games **Obv:** National arms, eagle left **Rev:** Without fineness statement

Date	Mintage	F	VF	XF	Unc	BU
1985 Proof	9,006	Value: 30.00				

KM# 505 100 PESOS

32.6250 g., 0.9250 Silver 1.0000 oz. ASW, 38 mm. **Subject:** 1986 World Cup Soccer Games **Obv:** National arms, eagle left **Rev:** Without fineness statement

Date	Mintage	F	VF	XF	Unc	BU
1985 Proof	9,006	Value: 30.00				

KM# 521 100 PESOS

32.6250 g., 0.9250 Silver 1.0000 oz. ASW **Subject:** 1986 World Cup Soccer Games **Obv:** National arms, eagle left **Rev:** Without fineness statement

Date	Mintage	F	VF	XF	Unc	BU
1986 Proof	208,000	Value: 30.00				

KM# 524 100 PESOS

32.6250 g., 0.9250 Silver 1.0000 oz. ASW **Subject:** 1986 World Cup Soccer Games **Obv:** National arms, eagle left **Rev:** Without fineness statement

Date	Mintage	F	VF	XF	Unc	BU
1986 Proof	190,000	Value: 30.00				

KM# 537 100 PESOS
32.6250 g., 0.9250 Silver 1.0000 oz. ASW **Subject:** World Wildlife Fund **Obv:** National arms, eagle left **Rev:** Monarch butterflies

Date	Mintage	F	VF	XF	Unc	BU
1987 Proof	Est. 30,000	Value: 50.00				

KM# 533 100 PESOS
31.1030 g., 0.9990 Silver 1.0000 oz. ASW **Subject:** 50th Anniversary - Nationalization of Oil Industry **Obv:** National arms, eagle left **Rev:** Bust facing above sprigs and dates

Date	Mintage	F	VF	XF	Unc	BU
1988	10,000	—	—	—	28.00	40.00

KM# 539 100 PESOS
33.6250 g., 0.9250 Silver 1.0000 oz. ASW **Subject:** Save the Children **Obv:** National arms, eagle left **Rev:** Child flying kite, two others sitting and playing

Date	Mintage	F	VF	XF	Unc	BU
1991 Proof	30,000	Value: 45.00				

KM# 540 100 PESOS
27.0000 g., 0.9250 Silver .8029 oz. ASW **Subject:** Ibero-American Series **Obv:** National arms, eagle left within center of assorted arms **Rev:** Maps within circles flanked by pillars above sailboats

Date	Mintage	F	VF	XF	Unc	BU
1991 Proof	50,000	Value: 55.00				
1992 Proof	75,000	Value: 45.00				

KM# 566 100 PESOS
31.1035 g., 0.9990 Silver 1.0000 oz. ASW **Subject:** Save the Vaquita Porpoise **Obv:** National arms, eagle left **Rev:** Swimming vaquita porpoise

Date	Mintage	F	VF	XF	Unc	BU
1992 Proof	—	Value: 45.00				

KM# 509 200 PESOS
Copper-Nickel, 29.5 mm. **Subject:** 175th Anniversary of Independence **Obv:** National arms, eagle left **Rev:** Conjoined busts left

Date	Mintage	F	VF	XF	Unc	BU
1985	75,000,000	—	—	0.25	3.00	4.00

KM# 510 200 PESOS
Copper-Nickel, 29.5 mm. **Subject:** 75th Anniversary of 1910 Revolution **Obv:** National arms, eagle left **Rev:** Conjoined heads left below building

Date	Mintage	F	VF	XF	Unc	BU
1985	98,590,000	—	—	0.25	3.25	4.50

KM# 525 200 PESOS
Copper-Nickel, 29.5 mm. **Subject:** 1986 World Cup Soccer Games **Obv:** National arms, eagle left **Rev:** Soccer players **Edge:** Reeded

Date	Mintage	F	VF	XF	Unc	BU
1986	50,000,000	—	—	1.00	3.50	4.50

KM# 526 200 PESOS
62.2060 g., 0.9990 Silver 2.0000 oz. ASW **Subject:** 1986 World Cup Soccer Games **Obv:** National arms, eagle left **Rev:** Value above 3 soccer balls

Date	Mintage	F	VF	XF	Unc	BU
1986	50,000	—	—	—	40.00	50.00

KM# 500.1 250 PESOS
8.6400 g., 0.9000 Gold .2500 oz. AGW **Subject:** 1986 World Cup Soccer Games **Obv:** National arms, eagle left **Rev:** Soccer ball within top 1/2 of design with value, date, and state below .

Date	Mintage	F	VF	XF	Unc	BU
1985	100,000	—	—	—	—	175
1986	—	—	—	—	—	175

KM# 500.2 250 PESOS
8.6400 g., 0.9000 Gold .2500 oz. AGW **Subject:** 1986 World Cup Soccer Games **Obv:** National arms, eagle left **Rev:** Without fineness statement

Date	Mintage	F	VF	XF	Unc	BU
1985 Proof	4,506	Value: 175				
1986 Proof	—	Value: 180				

KM# 506.1 250 PESOS
8.6400 g., 0.9000 Gold .2500 oz. AGW **Subject:** 1986 World Cup Soccer Games **Obv:** National arms, eagle left
Rev: Equestrian left within circle

Date	Mintage	F	VF	XF	Unc	BU
1985	88,000	—	—	—	—	175

KM# 506.2 250 PESOS
8.6400 g., 0.9000 Gold .2500 oz. AGW **Subject:** 1986 World Cup Soccer Games **Obv:** National arms, eagle left **Rev:** Without fineness statement

Date	Mintage	F	VF	XF	Unc	BU
1985 Proof	Est. 80,000	Value: 175				

KM# 507.1 500 PESOS
17.2800 g., 0.9000 Gold .5000 oz. AGW **Subject:** 1986 World Cup Soccer Games **Obv:** National arms, eagle left **Rev:** Soccer ball within emblem flanked by value and date

Date	Mintage	F	VF	XF	Unc	BU
1985	—	—	—	—	—	350

KM# 507.2 500 PESOS
17.2800 g., 0.9000 Gold .5000 oz. AGW **Subject:** 1986 World Cup Soccer Games **Obv:** National arms, eagle left **Rev:** Without fineness statement

Date	Mintage	F	VF	XF	Unc	BU
1985 Proof	—	Value: 350				

KM# 511 500 PESOS
33.4500 g., 0.9250 Silver 1.0000 oz. ASW **Subject:** 75th Anniversary of 1910 Revolution **Obv:** National arms, eagle left **Rev:** Conjoined heads left below building

Date	Mintage	F	VF	XF	Unc	BU
1985 Proof	40,000	Value: 35.00				

KM# 501.1 500 PESOS
17.2800 g., 0.9000 Gold .5000 oz. AGW **Subject:** 1986 World Cup Soccer Games **Obv:** National arms, eagle left **Rev:** Soccer player to right within emblem

Date	Mintage	F	VF	XF	Unc	BU
1985	102,000	—	—	—	—	350
1986	—	—	—	—	—	350

KM# 501.2 500 PESOS
17.2800 g., 0.9000 Gold .5000 oz. AGW **Subject:** 1986 World Cup Soccer Games **Obv:** National arms, eagle left **Rev:** Without fineness statement

Date	Mintage	F	VF	XF	Unc	BU
1985 Proof	5,506	Value: 350				
1986 Proof	—	Value: 350				

KM# 529 500 PESOS
Copper-Nickel, 28.5 mm. **Obv:** National arms, eagle left **Rev:** Head 1/4 right

Date	Mintage	F	VF	XF	Unc	BU
1986	20,000,000	—	—	1.00	3.25	3.50
1987	180,000,000	—	—	0.75	2.25	2.50
1988	230,000,000	—	—	0.50	2.25	2.50
1988 Proof; 2 known	—	Value: 650				
1989	—	—	—	0.75	2.25	3.00
1992	—	—	—	1.00	2.25	3.50

KM# 534 500 PESOS
17.2800 g., 0.9000 Gold .5000 oz. AGW **Subject:** 50th Anniversary - Nationalization of Oil Industry **Obv:** National arms, eagle left **Rev:** Monument **Note:** Similar to 5000 Pesos, KM#531.

Date	Mintage	F	VF	XF	Unc	BU
1988	—	—	—	—	—	350

KM# 513 1000 PESOS
17.2800 g., 0.9000 Gold .5000 oz. AGW **Subject:** 175th Anniversary of Independence **Obv:** National arms, eagle left **Rev:** Conjoined heads left below value

Date	Mintage	F	VF	XF	Unc	BU
1985 Proof	—	Value: 375				

KM# 527 1000 PESOS
31.1030 g., 0.9990 Gold 1.0000 oz. AGW **Subject:** 1986 World Cup Soccer Games **Obv:** National arms, eagle left **Rev:** Value above 3 soccer balls

Date	Mintage	F	VF	XF	Unc	BU
1986	—	—	—	—	—	700

KM# 536 1000 PESOS
Aluminum-Bronze, 30.5 mm. **Obv:** National arms, eagle left **Rev:** Bust 1/4 left with diagonal value at left **Note:** Juana de Asbaje

Date	Mintage	F	VF	XF	Unc	BU
1988	229,300,000	—	0.85	2.00	4.25	5.75
1989	—	—	0.85	2.00	4.25	5.75
1990	—	—	0.85	2.00	4.00	5.50
1990 Proof; 2 known	—	Value: 550				
1991	—	—	1.00	2.00	3.00	7.00
1992	—	—	1.00	2.00	3.00	7.00

KM# 535 1000 PESOS
34.5590 g., 0.9000 Gold 1.0000 oz. AGW **Subject:** 50th Anniversary - Nationalization of Oil Industry **Obv:** National arms, eagle left **Rev:** Portrait of Cardenas **Note:** Similar to 5000 Pesos, KM#531.

Date	Mintage	F	VF	XF	Unc	BU
1988 Proof	—	Value: 700				

KM# 643 1000 PESOS
Aluminum-Bronze, 22 mm. **Obv:** National arms, eagle left **Rev:** Stylized boat and "ATLAN" above denomination **Note:** Unissued type due to currency reform.

Date	Mintage	F	VF	XF	Unc	BU
1991Mo	—	—	—	—	15.00	—

KM# 528 2000 PESOS
62.2000 g., 0.9990 Gold 2.0000 oz. AGW **Subject:** 1986 World Cup Soccer Games **Obv:** National arms, eagle left **Rev:** Value above soccer balls

Date	Mintage	F	VF	XF	Unc	BU
1986	—	—	—	—	—	1,400

KM# 531 5000 PESOS
Copper-Nickel, 33.5 mm. **Subject:** 50th Anniversary - Nationalization of Oil Industry **Obv:** National arms, eagle left **Rev:** Monument above dates with diagonal value at left

Date	Mintage	F	VF	XF	Unc	BU
ND(1988)	50,000,000	—	—	4.75	7.75	10.00

REFORM COINAGE

1 New Peso = 1000 Old Pesos

KM# 546 5 CENTAVOS
Stainless Steel **Obv:** National arms, eagle left **Rev:** Value

Date	Mintage	F	VF	XF	Unc	BU
1992	136,800,000	—	—	0.15	0.20	0.25
1993	234,000,000	—	—	0.15	0.20	0.25
1994	125,000,000	—	—	0.15	0.20	0.25
1995	195,000,000	—	—	0.15	0.20	0.25
1995 Proof	6,981	Value: 0.50				
1996	104,831,000	—	—	0.15	0.20	0.25
1997	153,675,000	—	—	0.15	0.20	0.25
1998	64,417,000	—	—	0.15	0.20	0.25
1999	9,949,000	—	—	0.15	0.20	0.25
2000Mo	10,871,000	—	—	0.15	0.20	0.25

KM# 547 10 CENTAVOS
Stainless Steel, 17 mm. **Obv:** National arms, eagle left **Rev:** Value

Date	Mintage	F	VF	XF	Unc	BU
1992	121,250,000	—	—	0.20	0.30	0.35
1993	755,000,000	—	—	0.20	0.25	0.30
1994	557,000,000	—	—	0.20	0.25	0.30
1995	560,000,000	—	—	0.20	0.25	0.30
1995 Proof	6,981	Value: 0.50				
1996	594,216,000	—	—	0.20	0.25	0.30
1997	581,622,000	—	—	0.20	0.25	0.30
1998	602,667,000	—	—	0.20	0.25	0.30
1999	488,346,000	—	—	0.20	0.25	0.30
2000	577,546,000	—	—	0.20	0.30	0.35

KM# 548 20 CENTAVOS
Aluminum-Bronze **Obv:** National arms, eagle left **Rev:** Value and date within 3/4 wreath **Shape:** 12-sided

Date	Mintage	F	VF	XF	Unc	BU
1992	95,000,000	—	—	0.25	0.35	0.40
1993	95,000,000	—	—	0.25	0.35	0.40
1994	105,000,000	—	—	0.25	0.35	0.40
1995	180,000,000	—	—	0.25	0.35	0.40
1995 Proof	6,981	Value: 0.75				
1996	54,896,000	—	—	0.25	0.35	0.40
1997	178,807,000	—	—	0.25	0.35	0.40
1998	223,847,000	—	—	0.25	0.35	0.40
1999	233,753,000	—	—	0.25	0.35	0.40
2000	223,973,000	—	—	0.25	0.35	0.40

KM# 549 50 CENTAVOS
Aluminum-Bronze, 22 mm. **Obv:** National arms, eagle left **Rev:** Value and date within 1/2 designed wreath **Shape:** Scalloped

Date	Mintage	F	VF	XF	Unc	BU
1992	120,150,000	—	—	0.45	0.85	1.00
1993	330,000,000	—	—	0.45	0.75	1.00
1994	100,000,000	—	—	0.45	0.75	1.00
1995	60,000,000	—	—	0.45	0.75	1.00
1995 Proof	6,981	Value: 0.90				
1996	69,956,000	—	—	0.45	0.75	1.00
1997	129,029,000	—	—	0.45	0.75	1.00
1998	223,605,000	—	—	0.45	0.75	1.00
1999	89,516,000	—	—	0.45	0.75	1.00
2000	135,112,000	—	—	0.45	0.75	1.00

KM# 550 NUEVO PESO
Bi-Metallic Aluminum-Bronze center in Stainless Steel ring, 22 mm. **Obv:** National arms, eagle left **Rev:** Value

Date	Mintage	F	VF	XF	Unc	BU
1992	144,000,000	—	—	0.60	1.50	2.25
1993	329,860,000	—	—	0.60	1.50	2.25
1994	221,000,000	—	—	0.60	1.50	2.25
1995 Small date	125,000,000	—	—	0.60	1.50	2.25
1995 Large date	Inc. above	—	—	0.60	1.50	2.25
1995 Proof	6,981	Value: 2.75				

KM# 603 PESO
Bi-Metallic Stainless-steel ring in Aluminum Bronze center, 21 mm. **Obv:** National arms, eagle left within circle **Rev:** Value and date within circle **Note:** Similar to KM#550 but without N.

Date	Mintage	F	VF	XF	Unc	BU
1996Mo	169,510,000	—	—	—	1.25	2.25
1997Mo	222,870,000	—	—	—	1.25	2.25
1998Mo	261,942,000	—	—	—	1.25	2.25
1999Mo	99,168,000	—	—	—	1.25	2.25
2000Mo	158,379,000	—	—	—	1.25	2.25

KM# 551 2 NUEVOS PESOS
Bi-Metallic Aluminum-Bronze center in Stainless Steel ring, 23 mm. **Obv:** National arms, eagle left within circle **Rev:** Value and date within circle with assorted emblems around border

Date	Mintage	F	VF	XF	Unc	BU
1992	60,000,000	—	—	1.00	2.35	2.50
1993	77,000,000	—	—	1.00	2.35	2.50
1994	44,000,000	—	—	1.00	2.35	2.50
1995	20,000,000	—	—	1.00	2.35	2.50
1995 Proof	6,981	Value: 4.50				

KM# 604 2 PESOS
Bi-Metallic Aluminum-Bronze center in Stainless Steel ring, 23 mm. **Obv:** National arms, eagle left within circle **Rev:** Value and date within center circle of assorted emblems **Note:** Similar to KM#551, but denomination without N.

Date	Mintage	F	VF	XF	Unc	BU
1996Mo	24,902,000	—	—	—	2.35	2.50
1997Mo	34,560,000	—	—	—	2.35	2.50
1998Mo	104,138,000	—	—	—	2.35	2.50
1999Mo	34,713,000	—	—	—	2.35	2.50
2000Mo	69,322,000	—	—	—	2.35	2.50

KM# 552 5 NUEVOS PESOS
Bi-Metallic Aluminum-Bronze center in Stainless Steel ring, 25.5 mm. **Obv:** National arms, eagle left within circle **Rev:** Value and date within circle with bow below

Date	Mintage	F	VF	XF	Unc	BU
1992	70,000,000	—	—	2.00	4.00	4.50
1993	168,240,000	—	—	2.00	4.00	4.50
1994	58,000,000	—	—	2.00	4.00	4.50
1995 Proof	6,981	Value: 25.00				

KM# 588 5 NUEVOS PESOS
27.0000 g., 0.9250 Silver .8030 oz. ASW **Subject:** Environmental Protection **Obv:** National arms, eagle left within center of past and present arms **Rev:** Pacific Ridley Sea Turtle

Date	Mintage	F	VF	XF	Unc	BU
1994 Proof	20,000	Value: 50.00				

KM# 652 5 NUEVOS PESOS
31.1710 g., 0.9990 Silver 1.0012 oz. ASW, 40 mm. **Series:** Endangered Wildlife **Subject:** Aguila Real **Obv:** National arms, eagle left within center of past and present arms **Rev:** Golden Eagle on branch

Date	Mintage	F	VF	XF	Unc	BU
2000	50,000	—	—	—	32.50	—

KM# 655 5 NUEVOS PESOS
31.1710 g., 0.9990 Silver 1.0012 oz. ASW, 40 mm. **Series:** Endangered Wildlife **Subject:** Cocodrilo de Rio **Obv:** National arms, eagle left within center of past and present arms **Rev:** American Crocodile

Date	Mintage	F	VF	XF	Unc	BU
2000	50,000	—	—	—	32.50	—

KM# 656 5 NUEVOS PESOS
31.1710 g., 0.9990 Silver 1.0012 oz. ASW, 40 mm.
Series: Endangered Wildlife **Subject:** Nutria de Rio
Obv: National arms, eagle left within center of past and present arms **Rev:** Neotropical River Otter

Date	Mintage	F	VF	XF	Unc	BU
2000	50,000	—	—	—	32.50	—

KM# 657 5 NUEVOS PESOS
31.1710 g., 0.9990 Silver 1.0012 oz. ASW, 40 mm.
Series: Endangered Wildlife - Berrendo **Obv:** National arms, eagle left within center of past and present arms **Rev:** Peninsular Pronghorn, giant cardon cactus in back

Date	Mintage	F	VF	XF	Unc	BU
2000	50,000	—	—	—	32.50	—

KM# 605 5 PESOS
Bi-Metallic Aluminum-Bronze center in Stainless Steel ring, 25.5 mm. **Obv:** National arms, eagle left within circle **Rev:** Value within circle **Note:** Similar to KM#552 but denomination without N.

Date	Mintage	F	VF	XF	Unc	BU
1997Mo	39,468,000	—	—	3.00	4.00	5.00
1998Mo	103,729,000	—	—	3.00	4.00	5.00
1999Mo	59,427,000	—	—	3.00	4.00	5.00
2000Mo	20,869,000	—	—	3.00	4.00	5.00

KM# 629 5 PESOS
27.0000 g., 0.9250 Silver .8030 oz. ASW **Subject:** Jarabe Tapatio **Obv:** National arms, eagle left within center of assorted arms **Rev:** Mexican dancers

Date	Mintage	F	VF	XF	Unc	BU
1997 Proof	20,000	Value: 275				
1998 Proof	—	Value: 275				

KM# 627 5 PESOS
31.1035 g., 0.9990 Silver 1.0000 oz. ASW **Subject:** World Wildlife Fund **Obv:** National arms, eagle left **Rev:** Wolf with pup

Date	Mintage	F	VF	XF	Unc	BU
1998 Proof	Est. 15,000	Value: 75.00				

KM# 635 5 PESOS
19.6000 g., 0.9250 Silver .6411 oz. ASW **Subject:** Millennium Series **Obv:** National arms, eagle left **Rev:** Naval training ship Cuauhtemoc sailing into world globe

Date	Mintage	F	VF	XF	Unc	BU
1999	—	Value: 35.00				

KM# 640 5 PESOS
31.1030 g., 0.9990 Silver .9990 oz. ASW, 40 mm. **Subject:** UNICEF **Obv:** National arms, eagle left **Rev:** Two children flying kite **Edge:** Reeded

Date	Mintage	F	VF	XF	Unc	BU
1999 Proof	—	Value: 45.00				

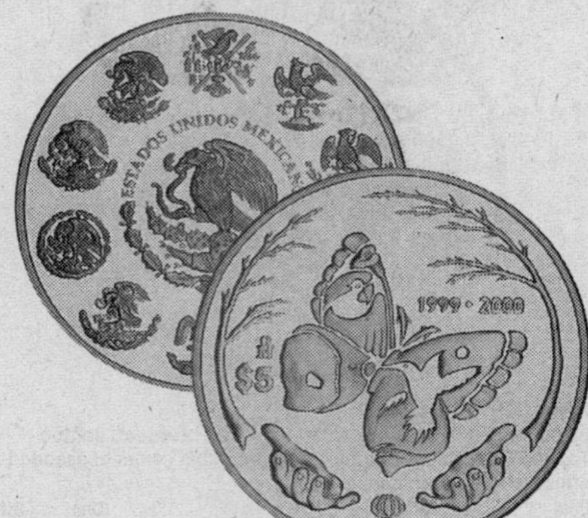

KM# 630 5 PESOS
31.1800 g., 0.9990 Silver 1.0025 oz. ASW **Subject:** Millennium Series **Obv:** National arms, eagle left within center of past and present arms **Rev:** Butterfly flanked by sprigs above hands **Rev. Designer:** Francisco Ortega Romero

Date	Mintage	F	VF	XF	Unc	BU
1999-2000 Proof	75,000	Value: 45.00				

KM# 631 5 PESOS
31.1800 g., 0.9990 Silver 1.0025 oz. ASW **Subject:** Millennium Series **Obv:** National arms, eagle left within center of past and present arms **Rev:** Stylized dove as hand of peace **Rev. Designer:** Omar Jiminez Torres

Date	Mintage	F	VF	XF	Unc	BU
1999-2000 Proof	75,000	Value: 40.00				

KM# 632 5 PESOS
31.1800 g., 0.9990 Silver 1.0025 oz. ASW **Subject:** Millennium Series **Obv:** National arms, eagle left within center of past and present arms **Rev:** Aztec bird design and value

Date	Mintage	F	VF	XF	Unc	BU
1999-2000 Proof	75,000	Value: 40.00				

KM# 670 5 PESOS
27.0000 g., 0.9250 Silver 0.803 oz. ASW, 40 mm. **Series:** Ibero-America **Obv:** National arms, eagle left within center of past and present arms **Rev:** Cowboy trick riding two horses **Edge:** Reeded

Date	Mintage	F	VF	XF	Unc	BU
2000 Proof	—	Value: 45.00				

KM# 553 10 NUEVOS PESOS
Bi-Metallic 0.925 Silver center, .1667 oz. ASW within Aluminum-Bronze ring, 27.8 mm. **Obv:** National arms, eagle left within circle **Rev:** Assorted shields within circle

Date	Mintage	F	VF	XF	Unc	BU
1992	20,000,000	—	—	—	7.50	8.50
1993	47,981,000	—	—	—	7.50	8.50
1994	15,000,000	—	—	—	7.50	8.50
1995 Proof	6,981	Value: 15.00				
1995	15,000,000	—	—	—	7.50	8.50

KM# 606 10 PESOS
Bi-Metallic 0.925 Silver .1667 ASW center within Aluminum-Bronze ring **Obv:** National arms, eagle left **Rev:** Assorted shields **Note:** Similar to KM#553, but denomination without N.

Date	Mintage	F	VF	XF	Unc	BU
1996	—	—	—	—	—	—

Note: Reported not confirmed

KM# 616 10 PESOS
Bi-Metallic Copper-Nickel-Brass center within Brass ring, 27.8 mm. **Obv:** National arms, eagle left **Rev:** Aztec design

Date	Mintage	F	VF	XF	Unc	BU
1997	44,837,000	—	—	—	5.00	6.50
1998	203,735,000	—	—	—	5.00	6.50
1998	—	—	—	—	5.00	6.50
Note: Small date, date on brass ring						
1998	—	—	—	—	5.00	6.50
Note: Large date, date partially on copper-nickel center						
1999	29,842,000	—	—	—	5.00	6.50
2000	—	—	—	—	5.00	6.50

KM# 633 10 PESOS
62.0300 g., 0.9990 Silver 1.9923 oz. ASW **Subject:** Millennium Series **Obv:** National arms, eagle left within center of past and present arms **Rev:** Ancient and modern buildings within circle

Date	Mintage	F	VF	XF	Unc	BU
1999-2000 Proof	75,000	Value: 47.50				

KM# 636 10 PESOS
Bi-Metallic Copper-Nickel center in Brass ring, 27.8 mm. **Subject:** Millennium Series **Obv:** National arms, eagle left within circle **Rev:** Aztec carving

Date	Mintage	F	VF	XF	Unc	BU
2000Mo	24,839,000	—	—	—	5.00	6.50

KM# 561 20 NUEVOS PESOS
Bi-Metallic 0.925 Silver 16.9g, (.2500 oz. ASW) center within Aluminum-Bronze ring, 32 mm. **Obv:** National arms, eagle left **Rev:** Head left within wreath

Date	Mintage	F	VF	XF	Unc	BU
1993	25,000,000	—	—	—	12.00	13.00
1994	5,000,000	—	—	—	12.00	13.00
1995	5,000,000	—	—	—	12.00	13.00

KM# 641 20 PESOS
6.2210 g., 0.9990 Gold .1998 oz. AGW, 21.9 mm. **Subject:** UNICEF **Obv:** National arms, eagle left **Rev:** Child playing with lasso **Edge:** Reeded

Date	Mintage	F	VF	XF	Unc	BU
1999 Proof	—	Value: 275				

KM# 637 20 PESOS
Bi-Metallic Copper-Nickel center within Brass ring, 32 mm. **Subject:** Xiuhtecuhtli **Obv:** National arms, eagle left within circle **Rev:** Aztec with torch within spiked circle

Date	Mintage	F	VF	XF	Unc	BU
2000	14,890,000	—	—	—	15.00	17.50

KM# 638 20 PESOS
Bi-Metallic Copper-Nickel center within Brass ring, 32 mm. **Obv:** National arms, eagle left within circle **Rev:** Head 1/4 right within circle

Date	Mintage	F	VF	XF	Unc	BU
2000	14,943,000	—	—	—	15.00	17.50

KM# 571 50 NUEVOS PESOS
Bi-Metallic 0.925 Silver .5000 ASW center within Brass ring, 38.8 mm. **Subject:** Nino Heroes **Obv:** National arms, eagle left within circle **Rev:** Six heads facing with date at upper right, all within circle and 1/2 wreath

Date	Mintage	F	VF	XF	Unc	BU
1993	2,000,000	—	—	—	25.00	28.00
1994	1,500,000	—	—	—	25.00	28.00
1995	1,500,000	—	—	—	25.00	28.00

KM# 608 50 PESOS
Bi-Metallic 0.925 Silver .5000 ASW center within Brass ring, 38.8 mm. **Obv:** National arms, eagle left **Rev:** Six heads, date at upper right, all within circle **Note:** Similar to 50 New Pesos, KM#571 without "N" before denomination.

Date	Mintage	F	VF	XF	Unc	BU
1996 Reported not confirmed	—	—	—	—	—	—

SILVER BULLION COINAGE

Libertad Series

KM# 542 1/20 ONZA (1/20 Troy Ounce of Silver)
1.5551 g., 0.9990 Silver .0500 oz. ASW **Obv:** National arms, eagle left **Rev:** Winged Victory

Date	Mintage	F	VF	XF	Unc	BU
1991	50,017	—	—	—	—	5.50
1992	295,783	—	—	—	—	4.50
1992 Proof	5,000	Value: 10.00				
1993	100,000	—	—	—	—	4.50
1993 Proof	—	Value: 10.00				
1994	90,100	—	—	—	—	4.50
1994 Proof	10,000	Value: 10.00				
1995	50,000	—	—	—	—	5.50
1995 Proof	2,000	Value: 12.00				

KM# 609 1/20 ONZA (1/20 Troy Ounce of Silver)
1.5551 g., 0.9990 Silver .0500 oz. ASW **Obv:** National arms, eagle left **Rev:** Winged Victory

Date	Mintage	F	VF	XF	Unc	BU
1996	50,000	—	—	—	—	10.00
1996 Proof	1,000	Value: 15.00				
1997	20,000	—	—	—	—	10.00
1997 Proof	800	Value: 15.00				
1998	6,400	—	—	—	—	10.00
1998 Proof	300	Value: 18.50				
1999	8,001	—	—	—	—	12.00
1999 Proof	600	Value: 16.50				
2000	57,500	—	—	—	—	12.00
2000 Proof	900	Value: 16.50				

KM# 543 1/10 ONZA (1/10 Troy Ounce of Silver)
3.1103 g., 0.9990 Silver .1000 oz. ASW **Obv:** National arms, eagle left **Rev:** Winged Victory

Date	Mintage	F	VF	XF	Unc	BU
1991	50,017	—	—	—	—	7.50
1992	299,983	—	—	—	—	6.50
1992 Proof	5,000	Value: 12.00				
1993	100,000	—	—	—	—	6.50
1993 Proof	—	Value: 12.00				
1994	90,100	—	—	—	—	6.50
1994 Proof	10,000	Value: 12.00				
1995	50,000	—	—	—	—	7.50
1995 Proof	2,000	Value: 13.50				

KM# 610 1/10 ONZA (1/10 Troy Ounce of Silver)
3.1103 g., 0.9990 Silver .1000 oz. ASW **Obv:** National arms, eagle left **Rev:** Winged Victory

Date	Mintage	F	VF	XF	Unc	BU
1996	50,000	—	—	—	—	12.00
1996 Proof	1,000	Value: 17.50				
1997	20,000	—	—	—	—	12.00
1997 Proof	800	Value: 17.50				
1998	6,400	—	—	—	—	12.00
1998 Proof	300	Value: 22.50				
1999	8,000	—	—	—	—	14.00
1999 Proof	600	Value: 20.00				
2000	27,500	—	—	—	—	14.00
2000 Proof	1,000	Value: 20.00				

KM# 544 1/4 ONZA (1/4 Troy Ounce of Silver)
7.7758 g., 0.9990 Silver .2500 oz. ASW **Obv:** National arms, eagle left **Rev:** Winged Victory

Date	Mintage	F	VF	XF	Unc	BU
1991	50,017	—	—	—	—	9.00
1992	104,000	—	—	—	—	7.50
1992 Proof	5,000	Value: 15.00				
1993	86,500	—	—	—	—	7.50
1993 Proof	—	Value: 15.00				
1994	90,100	—	—	—	—	7.50
1994 Proof	15,000	Value: 15.00				
1995	50,000	—	—	—	—	9.00
1995 Proof	2,000	Value: 16.50				

KM# 611 1/4 ONZA (1/4 Troy Ounce of Silver)
7.7758 g., 0.9990 Silver .2500 oz. ASW **Obv:** National arms, eagle left **Rev:** Winged Victory

Date	Mintage	F	VF	XF	Unc	BU
1996	50,000	—	—	—	—	15.00
1996 Proof	1,000	Value: 20.00				
1997	20,000	—	—	—	—	15.00
1997 Proof	800	Value: 20.00				
1998	6,400	—	—	—	—	15.00
1998 Proof	300	Value: 32.50				
1999	7,000	—	—	—	—	18.00
1999 Proof	600	Value: 25.00				
2000	21,000	—	—	—	—	18.00
2000 Proof	700	Value: 25.00				

KM# 545 1/2 ONZA (1/2 Troy Ounce of Silver)
15.5517 g., 0.9990 Silver .5000 oz. ASW **Obv:** National arms, eagle left **Rev:** Winged Victory

Date	Mintage	F	VF	XF	Unc	BU
1991	50,618	—	—	—	—	12.00
1992	119,000	—	—	—	—	10.00
1992 Proof	5,000	Value: 17.50				
1993	71,500	—	—	—	—	10.00
1993 Proof	—	Value: 17.50				
1994	90,100	—	—	—	—	10.00
1994 Proof	15,000	Value: 17.50				
1995	50,000	—	—	—	—	10.00
1995 Proof	2,000	Value: 18.50				

KM# 612 1/2 ONZA (1/2 Troy Ounce of Silver)
15.5517 g., 0.9990 Silver .5000 oz. ASW **Obv:** National arms, eagle left **Rev:** Winged Victory

Date	Mintage	F	VF	XF	Unc	BU
1996	50,000	—	—	—	—	20.00
1996 Proof	1,000	Value: 30.00				
1997	20,000	—	—	—	—	20.00
1997 Proof	800	Value: 30.00				
1998	6,400	—	—	—	—	22.00
1998 Proof	300	Value: 45.00				
1999	7,000	—	—	—	—	22.00
1999 Proof	600	Value: 35.00				
2000	20,000	—	—	—	—	22.00
2000 Proof	700	Value: 35.00				

KM# 494.1 ONZA (Troy Ounce of Silver)
31.1000 g., 0.9990 Silver 1.0000 oz. ASW **Subject:** Libertad **Obv:** National arms, eagle left **Rev:** Winged Victory

Date	Mintage	F	VF	XF	Unc	BU
1982	1,049,680	—	—	—	BV	17.50
1983	1,001,768	—	—	—	BV	17.50
1983 Proof	998	Value: 225				
1984	1,014,000	—	—	—	BV	17.50
1985	2,017,000	—	—	—	BV	17.50
1986	1,699,426	—	—	—	BV	17.50
1986 Proof	30,006	Value: 30.00				
1987	500,000	—	—	—	BV	50.00
1987 Proof	12,000	Value: 38.00				
1987 Proof doubled date	Inc. above	Value: 45.00				
1988	1,500,500	—	—	—	BV	47.00
1989	1,396,500	—	—	—	BV	27.00
1989 Proof	10,000	Value: 70.00				

KM# 494.2 ONZA (Troy Ounce of Silver)
31.1000 g., 0.9990 Silver 1.0000 oz. ASW **Obv:** National arms, eagle left **Rev:** Winged Victory **Edge:** Reeded

Date	Mintage	F	VF	XF	Unc	BU
1988 Proof	10,000	Value: 75.00				
1990	1,200,000	—	—	—	BV	17.50
1990 Proof	10,000	Value: 63.00				
1991	1,650,518	—	—	—	BV	30.00

KM# 494.3 ONZA (Troy Ounce of Silver)
31.1000 g., 0.9990 Silver 1.0000 oz. ASW **Subject:** Libertad **Obv:** National arms, eagle left **Rev:** Winged Victory with revised design and lettering **Edge:** Reeded edge **Note:** Mule

Date	Mintage	F	VF	XF	Unc	BU
1991	Inc. above	—	—	—	BV	45.00
1992	2,458,000	—	—	—	BV	30.00
1992 Proof	10,000	Value: 53.00				

KM# 494.4 ONZA (Troy Ounce of Silver)
31.1000 g., 0.9990 Silver 1.0000 oz. ASW **Subject:** Libertad **Obv:** National arms, eagle left **Rev:** Winged Victory with revised design and lettering **Edge:** Reeded edge **Note:** Mule

Date	Mintage	F	VF	XF	Unc	BU
1993	1,000,000	—	—	—	BV	20.00
1993 Proof	—	Value: 57.00				
1994	400,000	—	—	—	BV	25.00
1994 Proof	10,000	Value: 57.00				

Date	Mintage	F	VF	XF	Unc	BU
1995	500,000	—	—	—	BV	25.00
1995 Proof	2,000	Value: 57.00				

KM# 494.5 ONZA (Troy Ounce of Silver)
31.1000 g., 0.9990 Silver 1.0000 oz. ASW **Subject:** Libertad **Obv:** National arms, eagle left **Rev:** Winged Victory **Edge:** Reeded edge **Note:** Mule

Date	Mintage	F	VF	XF	Unc	BU
1991 Proof	10,000	Value: 57.00				

KM# 613 ONZA (Troy Ounce of Silver)
33.6250 g., 0.9250 Silver 1.0000 oz. ASW **Obv:** National arms, eagle left **Rev:** Winged Victory

Date	Mintage	F	VF	XF	Unc	BU
1996	300,000	—	—	—	—	27.00
1996 Proof	2,000	Value: 60.00				
1997	100,000	—	—	—	—	27.00
1997 Proof	1,500	Value: 60.00				
1998	67,000	—	—	—	—	42.00
1998 Proof	500	Value: 85.00				
1999	95,000	—	—	—	—	27.00
1999 Proof	600	Value: 70.00				

KM# 639 ONZA (Troy Ounce of Silver)
31.1000 g., 0.9990 Silver 1.0000 oz. ASW **Subject:** Libertad **Obv:** National arms, eagle left within center of past and present arms **Rev:** Winged Victory **Edge:** Reeded edge **Note:** Mule

Date	Mintage	F	VF	XF	Unc	BU
2000	340,000	—	—	—	—	25.00
2000 Proof	1,600	Value: 52.00				

KM# 614 2 ONZAS (2 Troy Ounces of Silver)
62.2070 g., 0.9990 Silver 2.0000 oz. ASW **Subject:** Libertad **Obv:** National arms, eagle left within center of past and present arms **Rev:** Winged Victory

Date	Mintage	F	VF	XF	Unc	BU
1996	50,000	—	—	—	—	35.00
1996 Proof	1,200	Value: 65.00				
1997	15,000	—	—	—	—	35.00
1997 Proof	1,300	Value: 70.00				
1998	7,000	—	—	—	—	45.00
1998 Proof	400	Value: 100				
1999	5,000	—	—	—	—	60.00
1999 Proof	280	Value: 175				
2000	7,500	—	—	—	—	60.00
2000 Proof	500	Value: 75.00				

KM# 615 5 ONZAS (5 Troy Ounces of Silver)
155.5175 g., 0.9990 Silver 5.0000 oz. ASW **Subject:** Libertad **Obv:** National arms, eagle left within center of past and present arms **Rev:** Winged Victory

Date	Mintage	F	VF	XF	Unc	BU
1996	20,000	—	—	—	—	110
1996 Proof	1,200	Value: 200				
1997	10,000	—	—	—	—	110
1997 Proof	1,300	Value: 200				
1998	3,500	—	—	—	—	220
1998 Proof	400	Value: 400				
1999	2,800	—	—	—	—	100
1999 Proof	100	Value: 500				
2000	4,000	—	—	—	—	100
2000 Proof	500	Value: 200				

GOLD BULLION COINAGE

KM# 530 1/20 ONZA (1/20 Ounce of Pure Gold)
1.7500 g., 0.9000 Gold .0500 oz. AGW **Obv:** Winged Victory **Rev:** Calendar stone

Date	Mintage	F	VF	XF	Unc	BU
1987	—	—	—	—	—	275
1988	—	—	—	—	—	—

KM# 589 1/20 ONZA (1/20 Ounce of Pure Gold)
1.5551 g., 0.9990 Gold .05 oz. AGW **Obv:** Winged Victory **Rev:** National arms, eagle left

Date	Mintage	F	VF	XF	Unc	BU
1991	10,000	—	—	—	—	BV+30%
1992	65,225	—	—	—	—	BV+30%
1993	10,000	—	—	—	—	BV+30%
1994	10,000	—	—	—	—	BV+30%

KM# 642 1/20 ONZA (1/20 Ounce of Pure Gold)
1.5551 g., 0.9990 Gold .05 oz. AGW **Obv:** National arms, eagle left **Rev:** Native working

Date	Mintage	F	VF	XF	Unc	BU
2000 Proof	—	Value: 50.00				

KM# 671 1/20 ONZA (1/20 Ounce of Pure Gold)
1.5551 g., 0.9990 Gold .05 oz. AGW, 16 mm. **Obv:** National arms, eagle left **Rev:** Winged Victory **Edge:** Reeded **Note:** Design similar to KM#609. Value estimates do not include the high taxes and surcharges added to the issue prices by the Mexican Government.

Date	Mintage	F	VF	XF	Unc	BU
2000	5,300	—	—	—	BV+30%	—

KM# 628 1/15 ONZA (1/15 Ounce of Pure Gold)
0.9990 Gold .0755 oz. AGW **Obv:** Winged Victory above legend **Rev:** National arms, eagle left within circle

Date	Mintage	F	VF	XF	Unc	BU
1987	—	—	—	—	—	275

KM# 541 1/10 ONZA (1/10 Ounce of Pure Gold)
3.1103 g., 0.9990 Gold .1000 oz. AGW **Obv:** National arms, eagle left **Rev:** Winged Victory

Date	Mintage	F	VF	XF	Unc	BU
1991	10,000	—	—	—	—	BV+20%
1992	50,777	—	—	—	—	BV+20%
1993	10,000	—	—	—	—	BV+20%
1994	10,000	—	—	—	—	BV+20%

KM# 672 1/10 ONZA (1/10 Ounce of Pure Gold)
3.1103 g., 0.9990 Gold 0.0999 oz. AGW, 20 mm. **Obv:** National arms, eagle left **Rev:** Winged Victory **Edge:** Reeded **Note:** Design similar to KM#610. Value estimates do not include the high taxes and surcharges added to the issue prices by the Mexican Government.

Date	Mintage	F	VF	XF	Unc	BU
2000	3,500	—	—	—	BV+20%	—

KM# 487 1/4 ONZA (1/4 Ounce of Pure Gold)
8.6396 g., 0.9000 Gold .2500 oz. AGW **Obv:** National arms, eagle left **Rev:** Winged Victory **Note:** Similar to KM#488.

Date	Mintage	F	VF	XF	Unc	BU
1981	313,000	—	—	—	—	BV+11%
1982	—	—	—	—	—	BV+11%

KM# 590 1/4 ONZA (1/4 Ounce of Pure Gold)
7.7758 g., 0.9990 Gold .2500 oz. AGW **Obv:** Winged Victory above legend **Rev:** National arms, eagle left

Date	Mintage	F	VF	XF	Unc	BU
1991	10,000	—	—	—	—	BV+11%
1992	28,106	—	—	—	—	BV+11%
1993	2,500	—	—	—	—	BV+11%
1994	2,500	—	—	—	—	BV+11%

KM# 673 1/4 ONZA (1/4 Ounce of Pure Gold)
7.7758 g., 0.9990 Gold .25 oz. AGW, 26.9 mm. **Obv:** National arms, eagle left **Rev:** Winged Victory **Edge:** Reeded **Note:** Design similar to KM#611. Value estimates do not include the high taxes and surcharges added to the issue prices by the Mexican Government.

Date	Mintage	F	VF	XF	Unc	BU
2000	2,500	—	—	—	BV+12%	—

KM# 488 1/2 ONZA (1/2 Ounce of Pure Gold)
17.2792 g., 0.9000 Gold .5000 oz. AGW **Obv:** National arms, eagle left **Rev:** Winged Victory

Date	Mintage	F	VF	XF	Unc	BU
1981	193,000	—	—	—	—	BV+8%
1982	—	—	—	—	—	BV+8%
1989 Proof	704	Value: 500				

KM# 591 1/2 ONZA (1/2 Ounce of Pure Gold)
15.5517 g., 0.9990 Gold .5000 oz. AGW **Obv:** Winged Victory above legend **Rev:** National arms, eagle left

Date	Mintage	F	VF	XF	Unc	BU
1991	10,000	—	—	—	—	BV+8%
1992	25,220	—	—	—	—	BV+8%
1993	2,500	—	—	—	—	BV+8%
1994	2,500	—	—	—	—	BV+8%

KM# 674 1/2 ONZA (1/2 Ounce of Pure Gold)
15.5517 g., 0.9990 Gold 0.4995 oz. AGW, 32.9 mm. **Obv:** National arms, eagle left **Rev:** Winged Victory **Edge:** Reeded **Note:** Design similar to KM#612. Value estimates do not include the high taxes and surcharges added to the issue prices by the Mexican Government.

Date	Mintage	F	VF	XF	Unc	BU
2000	1,500	—	—	—	BV+8%	—

KM# 489 ONZA (Ounce of Pure Gold)
34.5585 g., 0.9000 Gold 1.0000 oz. AGW **Obv:** National arms, eagle left **Rev:** Winged Victory **Note:** Similar to KM#488.

Date	Mintage	F	VF	XF	Unc	BU
1981	596,000	—	—	—	—	BV+3%
1985	—	—	—	—	—	BV+3%
1988	—	—	—	—	—	BV+3%

KM# 592 ONZA (Ounce of Pure Gold)
31.1035 g., 0.9990 Gold 1.0000 oz. AGW **Obv:** Winged Victory above legend **Rev:** National arms, eagle left

Date	Mintage	F	VF	XF	Unc	BU
1991	109,193	—	—	—	—	BV+3%
1992	46,281	—	—	—	—	BV+3%
1993	10,000	—	—	—	—	BV+3%
1994	1,000	—	—	—	—	BV+3%

KM# 675 ONZA (Ounce of Pure Gold)
31.1035 g., 0.9990 Gold 0.999 oz. AGW, 40 mm. **Obv:** National arms, eagle left **Rev:** Winged Victory **Edge:** Reeded **Note:** Design similar to KM#639. Value estimates do not include the high taxes and surcharges added to the issue prices by the Mexican Government.

Date	Mintage	F	VF	XF	Unc	BU
2000	2,730	—	—	—	BV+3%	—

PLATINUM BULLION COINAGE

KM# 538 1/4 ONZA (1/4 Ounce)
7.7775 g., 0.9990 Platinum .2500 oz. APW **Obv:** National arms, eagle left **Rev:** Winged Victory

Date	Mintage	F	VF	XF	Unc	BU
1989	704	Value: 400				

BULLION COINAGE

Pre-Columbian • Azteca Series

KM# 644 NUEVO PESO
7.7700 g., 0.9990 Silver .2496 oz. ASW, 26.8 mm. **Subject:** Eagle Warrior **Obv:** National arms, eagle left within D-shaped circle and dotted border **Rev:** Eagle warrior within D-shaped circle and dotted border **Edge:** Reeded

Date	Mintage	F	VF	XF	Unc	BU
1993Mo	1,500	—	—	—	—	15.00

Date	Mintage	F	VF	XF	Unc	BU
1993 Proof	900	Value: 22.50				

KM# 645 2 NUEVOS PESOS
15.4200 g., 0.9990 Silver .4953 oz. ASW, 32.9 mm. **Subject:** Eagle Warrior **Obv:** National arms, eagle left **Rev:** Eagle warrior **Edge:** Reeded

Date	Mintage	F	VF	XF	Unc	BU
1993Mo	1,500	—	—	—	—	15.00
1993 Proof	800	Value: 25.00				

KM# 646 5 NUEVOS PESOS
31.0500 g., 0.9990 Silver .9973 oz. ASW, 40 mm. **Subject:** Eagle Warrior **Obv:** National arms, eagle left **Rev:** Eagle warrior **Edge:** Reeded

Date	Mintage	F	VF	XF	Unc	BU
1993	2,000	—	—	—	—	22.00
1993 Proof	1,000	Value: 50.00				

KM# 647 5 NUEVOS PESOS
31.0000 g., 0.9990 Silver .9957 oz. ASW, 40 mm. **Subject:** Xochipilli **Obv:** National arms, eagle left within D-shaped circle and flower blossom border **Rev:** Seated figure sculpture within D-shaped circle and flower blossom border **Edge:** Reeded

Date	Mintage	F	VF	XF	Unc	BU
1993	2,000	—	—	—	—	25.00
1993 Proof	800	Value: 60.00				

KM# 649 5 NUEVOS PESOS
31.0000 g., 0.9990 Silver .9957 oz. ASW, 40 mm. **Subject:** Huchucteotl **Obv:** National arms, eagle left within D-shaped circle and designed border **Rev:** Aztec sculpture within D-shaped circle and designed border **Edge:** Reeded

Date	Mintage	F	VF	XF	Unc	BU
1993	5,000	—	—	—	—	20.00
1993 Proof	800	Value: 65.00				

KM# 648 5 NUEVOS PESOS
31.0000 g., 0.9990 Silver .9957 oz. ASW, 40 mm. **Subject:** Brasco Efigie **Obv:** National arms, eagle left within D-shaped circle and designed border **Rev:** Sculpture within D-shaped circle and designed border **Edge:** Reeded

Date	Mintage	F	VF	XF	Unc	BU
1993	2,000	—	—	—	—	25.00
1993 Proof	500	Value: 55.00				

KM# 650 10 NUEVOS PESOS
155.3100 g., 0.9990 Silver 4.9883 oz. ASW, 64 mm. **Subject:** Piedra de Tizoc **Obv:** National arms, eagle left **Rev:** Warrior capturing woman **Edge:** Reeded **Note:** Illustration reduced, similar to 100 Pesos, KM# 557

Date	Mintage	F	VF	XF	Unc	BU
1992 Proof	—	Value: 150				
1993 Proof	1,000	Value: 120				
1993	1,000	—	—	—	—	90.00

KM# 554 25 PESOS
7.7758 g., 0.9990 Silver .2500 oz. ASW **Obv:** National arms, eagle left within D-shaped circle and designed border **Rev:** Eagle warrior right within D-shaped circle and a designed border

Date	Mintage	F	VF	XF	Unc	BU
1992	50,000	—	—	—	14.00	—
1992 Proof	3,000	Value: 22.50				

KM# 555 50 PESOS
15.5517 g., 0.9990 Silver .5000 oz. ASW **Obv:** National arms, eagle left within D-shaped circle designed border **Rev:** Eagle warrior right within D-shaped circle and designed border

Date	Mintage	F	VF	XF	Unc	BU
1992	50,000	—	—	—	20.00	—
1992 Proof	3,000	Value: 25.00				

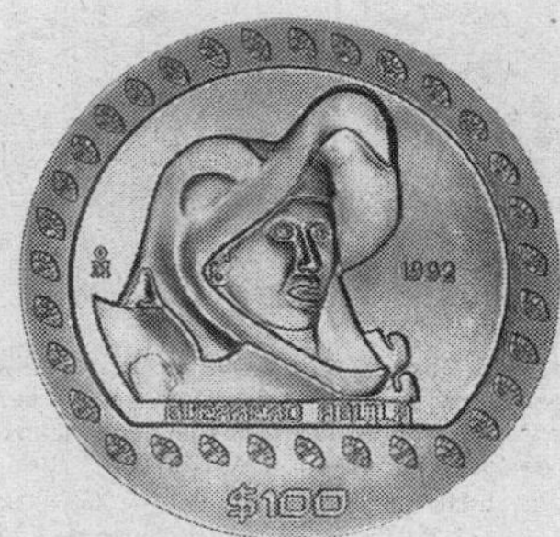

KM# 556 100 PESOS
31.1035 g., 0.9990 Silver 1.0000 oz. ASW **Obv:** National arms, eagle left **Rev:** Eagle warrior

Date	Mintage	F	VF	XF	Unc	BU
1992	205,000	—	—	—	22.00	—
1992	4,000	Value: 50.00				

KM# 562 100 PESOS
31.1035 g., 0.9990 Silver 1.0000 oz. ASW **Obv:** National arms, eagle left within D-shaped circle and designed border **Rev:** Seated figure sculpture within D-shaped circle and designed border

Date	Mintage	F	VF	XF	Unc	BU
1992 Proof	4,000	Value: 60.00				

KM# 563 100 PESOS
31.1035 g., 0.9990 Silver 1.0000 oz. ASW **Obv:** National arms, eagle left within D-shaped circle and designed border **Rev:** Brasero Efigie - The God of Rain within D-shaped circle and designed border

Date	Mintage	F	VF	XF	Unc	BU
1992 Proof	4,000	Value: 65.00				

KM# 564 100 PESOS
31.1035 g., 0.9990 Silver 1.0000 oz. ASW **Obv:** National arms, eagle left within D-shaped circle and designed border **Rev:** Huehueteotl - The God of Fire within D-shaped circle and designed border

Date	Mintage	F	VF	XF	Unc	BU
1992 Proof	4,000	Value: 50.00				

KM# 558 250 PESOS
7.7758 g., 0.9990 Gold .2500 oz. AGW **Subject:** Native Culture **Obv:** National arms, eagle left within D-shaped circle and designed border **Rev:** Sculpture of Jaguar head within D-shaped circle and designed border

Date	Mintage	F	VF	XF	Unc	BU
1992	10,000	—	—	—	185	—
1992 Proof	2,000	Value: 285				

KM# 559 500 PESOS
15.5517 g., 0.9990 Gold .5000 oz. AGW **Subject:** Native Culture **Obv:** National arms, eagle left within D-shaped circle and designed border **Rev:** Sculpture of Jaguar head within D-shaped circle and designed border

Date	Mintage	F	VF	XF	Unc	BU
1992	10,000	—	—	—	370	—
1992 Proof	2,000	Value: 485				

KM# 560 1000 PESOS
31.1035 g., 0.9990 Gold 1.0000 oz. AGW **Subject:** Native Culture **Obv:** National arms, eagle left within D-shaped circle and designed border **Rev:** Sculpture of Jaguar head within D-shaped circle and designed border

Date	Mintage	F	VF	XF	Unc	BU
1992	17,850	—	—	—	700	—
1992 Proof	2,000	Value: 750				

KM# 557 10000 PESOS
155.5175 g., 0.9990 Silver 5.0000 oz. ASW, 64 mm. **Subject:** Pieora De Tizoc **Obv:** National arms, eagle left within D-shaped circle and designed border **Rev:** Native warriors within D-shaped circle and designed border **Note:** Similar to 10 Nuevo Pesos, KM#650

Date	Mintage	F	VF	XF	Unc	BU
1992	51,900	—	—	—	—	80.00
1992 Proof	3,300	Value: 160				

BULLION COINAGE

Pre-Columbian • Central Veracruz Series

KM# 567 NUEVO PESO
7.7601 g., 0.9990 Silver .2498 oz. ASW **Subject:** Bajo relieve de el Tajin **Obv:** National arms, eagle left within D-shaped circle and designed border **Rev:** Design within D-shaped circle and designed border

Date	Mintage	F	VF	XF	Unc	BU
1993	100,000	—	—	—	—	13.50
1993 Proof	3,300	Value: 25.00				

KM# 568 2 NUEVOS PESOS
15.5516 g., 0.9990 Silver .4995 oz. ASW **Subject:** Bajo relieve de el Tajin **Obv:** National arms, eagle left within D-shaped circle and designed border **Rev:** Design within D-shaped circle and designed border

Date	Mintage	F	VF	XF	Unc	BU
1993	100,000	—	—	—	—	16.50
1993 Proof	3,000	Value: 25.00				

KM# 569 5 NUEVOS PESOS
31.1035 g., 0.9990 Silver .9991 oz. ASW **Subject:** Bajo relieve de el Tajin **Obv:** National arms, eagle left within D-shaped circle and designed border **Rev:** Design within D-shaped circle and designed border

Date	Mintage	F	VF	XF	Unc	BU
1993	100,000	—	—	—	—	20.00
1993 Proof	3,000	Value: 50.00				

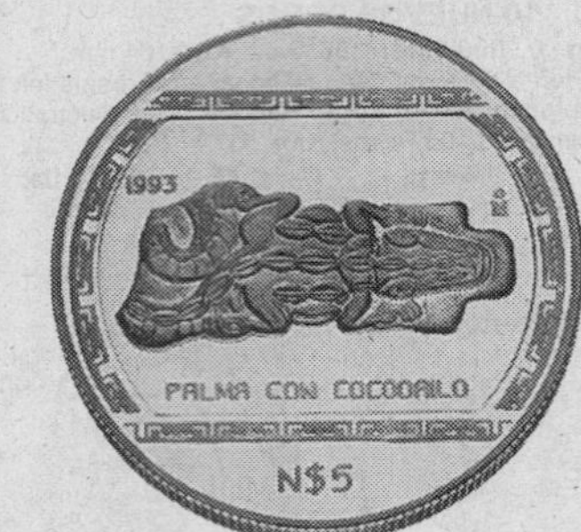

KM# 582 5 NUEVOS PESOS
31.1035 g., 0.9990 Silver .9991 oz. ASW **Subject:** Palma Con Cocodrilo **Obv:** National arms, eagle left within D-shaped circle and designed border **Rev:** Aerial view of crocodile within D-shaped circle and designed border

Date	Mintage	F	VF	XF	Unc	BU
1993	4,500	—	—	—	—	20.00
1993 Proof	2,650	Value: 50.00				

KM# 583 5 NUEVOS PESOS
31.1035 g., 0.9990 Silver .9991 oz. ASW **Subject:** Anciano Con Brasero **Obv:** National arms, eagle left within D-shaped circle and designed border **Rev:** Kneeling figure sculpture within D-shaped circle and designed border

Date	Mintage	F	VF	XF	Unc	BU
1993	2,650	—	—	—	—	25.00
1993 Proof	1,500	Value: 50.00				

KM# 584 5 NUEVOS PESOS
31.1035 g., 0.9990 Silver .9991 oz. ASW **Subject:** Carita Sonriente **Obv:** National arms, eagle left **Rev:** Sculptured head

Date	Mintage	F	VF	XF	Unc	BU
1993	4,500	—	—	—	—	20.00
1993 Proof	3,300	Value: 50.00				

KM# 570 10 NUEVOS PESOS
Center Weight: 115.5175 g. **Center Composition:** 0.9990 Silver 4.9956 oz. ASW , 64 mm. **Subject:** Piramide Del El Tajin **Obv:** National arms, eagle left within flat shaped circle and designed border **Rev:** Pyramid within flat shaped circle and designed border **Note:** Photo reduced.

Date	Mintage	F	VF	XF	Unc	BU
1993	50,000	—	—	—	—	80.00
1993 Proof	3,100	Value: 160				

KM# 585 25 NUEVOS PESOS
7.7758 g., 0.9990 Gold .2500 oz. AGW **Subject:** Hacha Ceremonial **Obv:** National arms, eagle left **Rev:** Mask left **Note:** Similar to 100 New Pesos, KM#587.

Date	Mintage	F	VF	XF	Unc	BU
1993	15,500	—	—	—	185	—
1993 Proof	800	Value: 285				

KM# 586 50 NUEVOS PESOS
15.5517 g., 0.9990 Gold .5000 oz. AGW **Subject:** Hacha Ceremonial **Obv:** National arms, eagle left **Rev:** Mask left **Note:** Similar to 100 New Pesos, KM#587.

Date	Mintage	F	VF	XF	Unc	BU
1993	15,500	—	—	—	375	—
1993 Proof	500	Value: 485				

KM# 587 100 NUEVOS PESOS
31.1035 g., 0.9990 Gold 1.0000 oz. AGW **Subject:** Hacha Ceremonial **Obv:** National arms, eagle left **Rev:** Mask left

Date	Mintage	F	VF	XF	Unc	BU
1993	7,150	—	—	—	700	—
1993 Proof	500	Value: 750				

BULLION COINAGE

Pre-Columbian • Mayan Series

KM# 572 NUEVO PESO
7.7601 g., 0.9990 Silver .2498 oz. ASW **Subject:** Chaac Mool **Obv:** National arms, eagle left within six sided shield and designed border **Rev:** Reclining figure within six sided shield and designed border

Date	Mintage	F	VF	XF	Unc	BU
1994 Matte	30,000	—	—	—	—	13.50
1994 Proof	2,500	Value: 25.00				

KM# 573 2 NUEVOS PESOS
15.5516 g., 0.9990 Silver .4995 oz. ASW **Subject:** Chaac Mool **Obv:** National arms, eagle left within six sided shield and

designed border **Rev:** Reclining figure within six sided shield and designed border

Date	Mintage	F	VF	XF	Unc	BU
1994 Matte	30,000	—	—	—	—	16.50
1994 Proof	2,500	Value: 25.00				

KM# 574 5 NUEVOS PESOS

31.1035 g., 0.9990 Silver .9991 oz. ASW **Subject:** Chaac Mool **Obv:** National arms, eagle left within six sided shield and designed border **Rev:** Reclining figure within six sided shield and designed border

Date	Mintage	F	VF	XF	Unc	BU
1994 Matte	50,000	—	—	—	—	20.00
1994 Proof	3,000	Value: 50.00				

KM# 575 5 NUEVOS PESOS

31.1035 g., 0.9990 Silver .9991 oz. ASW **Subject:** Chaac Mool **Obv:** National arms, eagle left within six sided shield and designed border **Rev:** Tomb of Palenque Memorial Stone within six sided shield and designed border

Date	Mintage	F	VF	XF	Unc	BU
1994	4,500	—	—	—	—	20.00
1994 Proof	2,800	Value: 50.00				

KM# 577 5 NUEVOS PESOS

31.1035 g., 0.9990 Silver .9991 oz. ASW **Subject:** Mascaron Del Dios Chaac **Rev:** Elaborately carved wall segment

Date	Mintage	F	VF	XF	Unc	BU
1994	4,500	—	—	—	—	20.00
1994 Proof	2,500	Value: 50.00				

KM# 578 5 NUEVOS PESOS

31.1035 g., 0.9990 Silver .9991 oz. ASW **Subject:** Dintel 26 **Obv:** National arms, eagle left within six sided shield and designed border **Rev:** Two seated figures wall carving within six sided shield and designed border

Date	Mintage	F	VF	XF	Unc	BU
1994	4,500	—	—	—	—	20.00
1994 Proof	2,600	Value: 50.00				

KM# 676 10 NUEVOS PESOS

155.5175 g., 0.9990 Silver 4.995 oz. ASW, 65 mm. **Subject:** Piramide Del Castillo **Obv:** National arms, eagle left above metal content statement **Rev:** Pyramid above two-line inscription **Rev. Inscription:** PIRAMIDE DEL CASTILLO / CHICHEN-ITZA **Edge:** Reeded

Date	Mintage	F	VF	XF	Unc	BU
1993Mo Proof	—	Value: 325				

KM# 576 10 NUEVOS PESOS

Center Weight: 115.5175 g. **Center Composition:** 0.9990 Silver 4.9956 oz. ASW , 64 mm. **Subject:** Piramide del Castillo **Obv:** National arms, eagle left **Rev:** Pyramid **Note:** Photo reduced.

Date	Mintage	F	VF	XF	Unc	BU
1994	20,000	—	—	—	—	85.00
1994 Proof	2,100	Value: 165				

KM# 579 25 NUEVOS PESOS

7.7758 g., 0.9990 Gold .2500 oz. AGW **Subject:** Personaje de Jaina **Rev:** Seated figure

Date	Mintage	F	VF	XF	Unc	BU
1994	2,000	—	—	—	185	—
1994 Proof	500	Value: 285				

KM# 580 50 NUEVOS PESOS

15.5517 g., 0.9990 Gold .5000 oz. AGW **Subject:** Personaje de Jaina **Rev:** Seated figure

Date	Mintage	F	VF	XF	Unc	BU
1994	1,000	—	—	—	375	—
1994 Proof	500	Value: 485				

KM# 581 100 NUEVOS PESOS

31.1035 g., 0.9990 Gold 1.0000 oz. AGW **Subject:** Personaje de Jaina **Obv:** National arms, eagle left within six sided shield and designed border **Rev:** Seated figure within six sided shield and designed border

Date	Mintage	F	VF	XF	Unc	BU
1994	1,000	—	—	—	700	—
1994 Proof	500	Value: 750				

BULLION COINAGE

Pre-Columbian • Olmec Series

KM# 593 PESO

7.7750 g., 0.9990 Silver .2500 oz. ASW **Subject:** Senor De Las Limas **Obv:** National arms, eagle left within square and designed border **Rev:** Sitting figure facing within square and designed border **Note:** Similar to 5 Pesos, KM#595.

Date	Mintage	F	VF	XF	Unc	BU
1996	4,000	—	—	—	—	13.50
1996 Proof	2,200	Value: 25.00				
1998 Matte	2,400	—	—	—	—	15.00

KM# 594 2 PESOS

15.5517 g., 0.9990 Silver .5000 oz. ASW **Subject:** Senor De Las Limas **Obv:** National arms, eagle left within square and designed border **Rev:** Sitting figure facing within square and designed border **Note:** Similar to 5 Pesos, KM#595.

Date	Mintage	F	VF	XF	Unc	BU
1996	4,000	—	—	—	—	16.50
1996 Proof	2,200	Value: 25.00				
1998 Matte	2,400	—	—	—	—	18.00

KM# 596 5 PESOS

31.1035 g., 0.9990 Silver 1.0000 oz. ASW **Subject:** Hombre Jaguar **Obv:** National arms, eagle left within square and designed border **Rev:** Statue facing within square and designed border

Date	Mintage	F	VF	XF	Unc	BU
1996	1,500	—	—	—	—	85.00
1996 Proof	2,800	Value: 50.00				
1998 Matte	6,000	—	—	—	—	25.00
1998 Proof	4,800	Value: 50.00				

KM# 595 5 PESOS

31.1035 g., 0.9990 Silver 1.0000 oz. ASW **Subject:** Senor De Las Limas **Obv:** National arms, eagle left within square and designed border **Rev:** Seated figure facing within square and designed border

Date	Mintage	F	VF	XF	Unc	BU
1996	4,000	—	—	—	—	20.00
1996 Proof	3,000	Value: 50.00				
1998 Matte	3,400	—	—	—	—	22.00

KM# 597 5 PESOS

31.1035 g., 0.9990 Silver 1.0000 oz. ASW **Subject:** El Luchador **Obv:** National arms, eagle left **Rev:** El Luchador

Date	Mintage	F	VF	XF	Unc	BU
1996	4,500	—	—	—	—	20.00
1996 Proof	2,700	Value: 50.00				
1998 Matte	2,000	—	—	—	—	25.00

KM# 598 5 PESOS

31.1035 g., 0.9990 Silver 1.0000 oz. ASW **Subject:** Hacha Ceremonial **Obv:** National arms, eagle left within square and designed border **Rev:** Statue within square and designed border

Date	Mintage	F	VF	XF	Unc	BU
1996	4,500	—	—	—	—	20.00
1996 Proof	2,700	Value: 50.00				
1998 Matte	2,000	—	—	—	—	25.00

KM# 599 10 PESOS
Center Weight: 1555.5175 g. **Center Composition:** 0.9990 Silver 5.0000 oz. ASW , 64 mm. **Subject:** Cabeza Olmeca **Obv:** National arms, eagle left **Rev:** Native mask **Note:** Photo reduced.

Date	Mintage	F	VF	XF	Unc	BU
1996	2,000	—	—	—	—	85.00
1996 Proof	2,750	Value: 110				
1998 Matte	2,150	—	—	—	—	85.00

KM# 600 25 PESOS
7.7758 g., 0.9990 Gold .2500 oz. AGW **Subject:** Sacerdote **Obv:** National arms, eagle left **Rev:** Sculpture **Note:** Similar to 100 Pesos, KM#602.

Date	Mintage	F	VF	XF	Unc	BU
1996	500	—	—	—	185	—
1996 Proof	750	Value: 285				

KM# 601 50 PESOS
15.5517 g., 0.9990 Gold .5000 oz. AGW **Subject:** Sacerdote **Obv:** National arms, eagle left **Rev:** Sculpture **Note:** Similar to 100 Pesos, KM#602.

Date	Mintage	F	VF	XF	Unc	BU
1996	500	—	—	—	375	—
1996 Proof	500	Value: 485				

KM# 602 100 PESOS
31.1035 g., 0.9990 Gold 1.0000 oz. AGW **Subject:** Sacerdote **Obv:** National arms, eagle left within square and designed border **Rev:** Sculpture within square and designed border

Date	Mintage	F	VF	XF	Unc	BU
1996	500	—	—	—	700	—
1996 Proof	500	Value: 750				

BULLION COINAGE

Pre-Columbian • Teotihuacan Series

KM# 617 PESO
7.7759 g., 0.9990 Silver .2500 oz. ASW **Subject:** Disco De La Muerte **Obv:** National arms, eagle left within oblong circle and designed border **Rev:** Sculpture within oblong circle and designed border

Date	Mintage	F	VF	XF	Unc	BU
1997	3,000	—	—	—	—	13.50
1997 Proof	1,600	Value: 25.00				
1998 Proof	500	Value: 30.00				
1998 Matte	2,400	—	—	—	—	15.00

KM# 618 2 PESOS
15.5517 g., 0.9990 Silver .5000 oz. ASW **Subject:** Disco De La Muerte **Obv:** National arms, eagle left within oblong circle and designed border **Rev:** Sculpture within oblong circle and designed border

Date	Mintage	F	VF	XF	Unc	BU
1997	3,000	—	—	—	—	16.50
1997 Proof	1,600	Value: 25.00				
1998	2,400	—	—	—	—	18.00
1998 Proof	500	Value: 30.00				

KM# 621 5 PESOS
31.1035 g., 0.9990 Silver 1.0000 oz. ASW **Subject:** Teotihuacan - Vasija **Obv:** National arms, eagle left within oval and designed border **Rev:** Seated woman joined to pottery vase within oval and designed border

Date	Mintage	F	VF	XF	Unc	BU
1997	4,500	—	—	—	—	20.00
1997 Proof	Est. 1,800	Value: 50.00				
1998 Proof	500	Value: 60.00				
1998 Matte	2,000	—	—	—	—	25.00

KM# 622 5 PESOS
31.1035 g., 0.9990 Silver 1.0000 oz. ASW **Subject:** Teotihuacan - Jugador de Pelota **Obv:** National arms, eagle left

Date	Mintage	F	VF	XF	Unc	BU
1997	4,500	—	—	—	—	20.00
1997 Proof	Est. 1,800	Value: 50.00				
1998 Matte	2,000	—	—	—	—	25.00
1998 Proof	500	Value: 60.00				

KM# 619 5 PESOS
31.1035 g., 0.9990 Silver 1.0000 oz. ASW **Subject:** Teotihuacan - Disco de la Muerte **Obv:** National arms, eagle left within oblong circle and designed border **Rev:** Sculpture within oblong circle and designed border

Date	Mintage	F	VF	XF	Unc	BU
1997	3,500	—	—	—	—	20.00
1997 Proof	Est. 1,800	Value: 50.00				
1998	3,400	—	—	—	—	22.00
1998 Proof	500	Value: 60.00				

KM# 620 5 PESOS
31.1035 g., 0.9990 Silver 1.0000 oz. ASW **Subject:** Teotihuacan - Mascara **Obv:** National arms, eagle left within oblong circle and designed border **Rev:** Face sculpture within oblong circle and designed border

Date	Mintage	F	VF	XF	Unc	BU
1997	4,500	—	—	—	—	20.00
1997 Proof	Est. 1,800	Value: 60.00				
1998	2,000	—	—	—	—	25.00
1998 Proof	500	Value: 65.00				

KM# 623 10 PESOS
1555.5175 g., 0.9990 Silver 5.0000 oz. ASW, 64 mm. **Subject:** Piramide Del Sol **Obv:** National arms, eagle left within oblong circle and designed border **Rev:** Pyramid within oblong circle and designed border **Note:** Photo reduced.

Date	Mintage	F	VF	XF	Unc	BU
1997	1,500	—	—	—	—	85.00
1997 Proof	2,100	Value: 165				
1998 Matte	2,150	—	—	—	—	85.00

KM# 624 25 PESOS
7.7758 g., 0.9990 Gold .2500 oz. AGW **Subject:** Serpiente Emplumada **Obv:** National arms, eagle left **Note:** Similar to 100 Pesos, KM#626.

Date	Mintage	F	VF	XF	Unc	BU
1997	500	—	—	—	185	—
1997 Proof	200	Value: 300				

KM# 625 50 PESOS
15.5517 g., 0.9990 Gold .5000 oz. AGW **Subject:** Serpiente Emplumada **Obv:** National arms, eagle left **Note:** Similar to 100 Pesos, KM#626.

Date	Mintage	F	VF	XF	Unc	BU
1997	500	—	—	—	375	—
1997 Proof	200	Value: 500				

KM# 626 100 PESOS
31.1035 g., 0.9990 Gold 1.0000 oz. AGW **Subject:** Teotihuacan - Serpiente Emplumada **Obv:** National arms, eagle left

Date	Mintage	F	VF	XF	Unc	BU
1997	500	—	—	—	700	—
1997 Proof	Est. 200	Value: 775				

BULLION COINAGE

Pre-Columbian • Tolteca Series

KM# 661 PESO
7.7759 g., 0.9990 Silver .2500 oz. ASW, 27 mm. **Subject:** Jaguar **Obv:** National arms, eagle left **Rev:** Jaguar carving **Edge:** Reeded

Date	Mintage	F	VF	XF	Unc	BU
1998	6,000	—	—	—	—	13.50
1998 Proof	4,800	Value: 25.00				

KM# 662 2 PESOS
15.5517 g., 0.9990 Silver .5000 oz. ASW, 33 mm. **Subject:** Jaguar **Obv:** National arms, eagle left **Rev:** Jaguar carving **Edge:** Reeded

Date	Mintage	F	VF	XF	Unc	BU
1998	6,000	—	—	—	—	16.50
1998 Proof	4,800	Value: 30.00				

KM# 663 5 PESOS
31.1035 g., 0.9990 Silver 1.0000 oz. ASW, 40 mm. **Subject:** Jaguar **Obv:** National arms, eagle left within shield and designed border **Rev:** Jaguar carving within shield and designed border **Edge:** Reeded

Date	Mintage	F	VF	XF	Unc	BU
1998	6,000	—	—	—	—	20.00
1998 Proof	4,800	Value: 50.00				

KM# 664 5 PESOS

31.1035 g., 0.9990 Silver 1.0000 oz. ASW, 40 mm. **Obv:** National arms, eagle left **Rev:** Sacerdote sculpture **Edge:** Reeded

Date	Mintage	F	VF	XF	Unc	BU
1998	5,000	—	—	—	—	20.00
1998 Proof	4,800	Value: 50.00				

KM# 666 5 PESOS

31.1035 g., 0.9990 Silver 1.0000 oz. ASW, 40 mm.
Subject: Serpiente con Craneo **Obv:** National arms, eagle left **Rev:** Large sculpture **Edge:** Reeded

Date	Mintage	F	VF	XF	Unc	BU
1998	5,000	—	—	—	—	20.00
1998 Proof	4,800	Value: 50.00				

KM# 665 5 PESOS

31.1035 g., 0.9990 Silver 1.0000 oz. ASW, 40 mm.
Subject: Quetzalcoatl **Obv:** National arms, eagle left **Rev:** Quetzalcoatl sculpture **Edge:** Reeded

Date	Mintage	F	VF	XF	Unc	BU
1998	5,000	—	—	—	—	20.00
1998 Proof	4,800	Value: 50.00				

KM# 634 10 PESOS

155.7300 g., 0.9990 Silver 5.0018 oz. ASW **Subject:** Atlantes **Obv:** National arms, eagle left within shield and designed border **Rev:** Three carved statues within shield and designed border

Date	Mintage	F	VF	XF	Unc	BU
1998	3,500	—	—	—	—	85.00
1998 Proof	4,200	Value: 135				

KM# 667 25 PESOS

7.7759 g., 0.9990 Gold 0.2498 oz. AGW, 23 mm. **Subject:** Aguila **Obv:** National arms, eagle left **Rev:** Eagle sculpture **Edge:** Reeded

Date	Mintage	F	VF	XF	Unc	BU
1998	300	—	—	—	200	—
1998 Proof	300	Value: 300				

KM# 668 50 PESOS

15.5517 g., 0.9990 Gold 0.4995 oz. AGW, 29 mm. **Subject:** Aguila **Obv:** National arms, eagle left **Rev:** Eagle sculpture **Edge:** Reeded

Date	Mintage	F	VF	XF	Unc	BU
1998	300	—	—	—	385	—
1998 Proof	300	Value: 500				

KM# 669 100 PESOS

31.1035 g., 0.9990 Gold 0.999 oz. AGW, 34.5 mm.
Subject: Aguila **Obv:** National arms, eagle left within designed shield **Rev:** Eagle sculpture within designed shield **Edge:** Reeded

Date	Mintage	F	VF	XF	Unc	BU
1998	300	—	—	—	725	—
1998 Proof	300	Value: 775				

PATTERNS

Including off metal strikes

KM#	Date	Mintage	Identification	Mkt Val
Pn169	1901Cn Q	—	20 Centavos. Copper.	—
Pn170	1901Cn Q	—	20 Centavos. Bronze.	425
Pn171	1904Zs FZ	—	Peso. Aluminum.	—
Pn172	1906Z	—	2 Centavos. Silver.	—
Pn173	1907Mo	—	50 Centavos. Silver. Horse and rider facing left within sun rays. National arms. Plain edge.	4,000
Pn174	1907Mo	—	50 Centavos. Silver. Incuse lettered edge, matte Proof.	3,500
Pn175	1907	—	50 Centavos. Silver. Raised lettered edge, matte Proof.	3,500
Pn176	1908Mo	—	50 Centavos. Silver. Plain edge, Proof.	3,000
Pn177	1908Mo	—	Peso. Silver. Liberty on horseback, plain edge, Proof.	—
Pn178	1909Mo	—	Peso. Silver. Plain edge, Proof.	7,000
Pn179	1909Mo	—	Peso. Silver. Incuse lettered edge, Proof.	—
Pn180	1909Mo	—	Peso. Brass. Incuse lettered edge, matte Proof.	3,250
Pn181	1909Mo	—	Peso. Brass. Raised lettered edge, matte Proof.	3,250
Pn182	1909Mo	—	Peso. Bronzed Lead. Raised lettered edge, matte Proof.	—
Pn183	1909Mo	—	Peso. Silver. Raised lettered edge, matte Proof.	—
Pn184	1910	—	2 Centavos. Bronze.	—
	1910	—	2 Centavos. Bronze.	—
Pn185	1911Mo	—	Peso. Silver. Plain edge.	2,500
Pn186	1911Mo	—	Peso. Bronze. Plain edge.	2,500
Pn187	1911Mo	—	Peso. Brass. Plain edge.	2,500
Pn188	1914Mo	—	5 Centavos. Copper.	200
Pn189	1916Mo	—	20 Pesos. Copper. Arms/Aztec calendar stone.	1,150
Pn190	1936Mo	—	Centavo. Copper-Nickel.	—
Pn191	1936Mo	—	Peso. Silver. Arms/Morelos.	3,200
Pn192	1945Mo	—	50 Centavos. Nickel. Arms/Juarez.	1,250
Pn193	1947Mo	—	Peso. Silver. Arms/Morelos.	2,500
Pn194	1947Mo	—	Peso. Silver. Arms/Juarez.	2,500
Pn195	1947Mo	—	5 Pesos. Silver. Arms/Cap, balance scale, scroll.	4,250
Pn196	1947Mo	—	Onza. 0.9250 Silver. Balance scale. Coin screw press. Coin screw press/Balance scale.	1,250
Pn197	1950Mo	—	5 Pesos. Silver. Arms/Hidalgo.	1,650
Pn198	1951Mo	2	Onza. Silver. Elephant facing right. Bust with helmet left. Miner/Elephant.	4,000
Pn199	1954Mo	—	50 Centavos. Bronze. 33mm. Arms/Cuauhtémoc.	—
Pn200	1954Mo	—	50 Centavos. Copper-Nickel. Arms/Cuauhtémoc.	—
Pn201	1955Mo	—	50 Centavos. Bronze. Arms/Cuauhtémoc.	625
Pn202	1955Mo	—	Peso. Copper-Nickel. Arms/Morelos, 32mm.	1,800
Pn203	1962Mo	—	5 Centavos. Copper-Nickel.	60.00
Pn204	1969Mo	—	Peso. Copper-Nickel. Value behind head.	2,000
Pn205	1969Mo	—	Peso. Copper-Nickel. Arms/Morelos.	1,650
Pn206	1970Mo	—	10 Centavos. Bronze. Arms/Allende.	400
Pn207	1970Mo	—	25 Centavos. Copper-Nickel. Arms/Allende.	750
Pn208	1973Mo	—	10 Pesos. Aluminum-Bronze. Arms/Hidalgo.	800
Pn209	1974Mo	—	10 Pesos. Copper-Nickel. Arms/Hidalgo.	600
Pn210	1976Mo	16	100 Pesos. 0.7200 Silver. Arms/Morelos.	—
Pn211	1978Mo	—	Onza. Silver. Coin screw press/balance scale	3,000
Pn212	1978Mo	—	Onza. 0.9250 Silver. Coin screw press / Coin belt powered press, Proof, PRUEBA	2,500
Pn213	1978Mo	—	Onza. 0.9250 Silver. Coin screw press / Coin belt powered press, Proof, PRUEBA	—
Pn214	1978Mo	—	Onza. 0.9250 Silver. Coin screw press / Native statue, Proof, PRUEBA	2,000
Pn215	1978Mo	—	Onza. 0.9250 Silver. Coin screw press / Native Statue, Proof, PRUEBA	1,750
Pn216	1979Mo	—	Onza. 0.9250 Silver.	2,000
Pn217	1979Mo	—	20 Pesos. Bronze. Arms / Mayan art	—
Pn218	1980Mo	8	20 Centavos. Copper-Nickel.	—
Pn219	1980Mo	—	Peso. Brass. Arms / Mayan art	350
Pn220	1980Mo	—	10 Pesos. 0.5000 Silver. Arms/Mayan art.	—
Pn221	1980Mo	—	10 Pesos. Bronze. Arms/Mayan art.	750
Pn222	1980Mo	—	20 Pesos. Copper-Nickel. Arms/Mayan art. Large mint mark.	300
Pn223	1980Mo	50	1/10 Onza. Silver. Arms/Radiant cap above mountain, Proof	90.00
Pn224	1981Mo	—	20 Centavos. Copper-Nickel. Small obverse design. Small arms design/Madero, Proof.	165
Pn225	1981Mo	—	20 Centavos. Copper-Nickel. Modified portrait. Small arms design/Modified portrait Madero, Proof.	135
Pn226	19xx	—	20 Centavos. Copper.	350
PnA227	1982	—	50 Pesos.	—
Pn227	1983Mo	—	50 Centavos. Proof.	650
Pn228	1983Mo	12	Peso. Stainless Steel. Arms/Morelos.	550
Pn229	1983	—	5 Pesos. Bronze. Arms/Mayan art.	350
Pn230	1983	—	Onza. Silver. Libertad.	1,350
Pn231	1984Mo	—	50 Pesos. Copper-Nickel. Arms/Juarez, Proof.	400
Pn232	ND	—	50 Pesos. Gold. Arms/Juarez, w/o JUAREZ.	—
Pn233	1985Mo	—	Peso. Copper.	325
Pn234	1985Mo	10	Peso. Silver. SUD design divided from date and denomination.	—
Pn235	1986Mo	33	Peso. Stainless Steel. SUD design w/date and denomination, no divider	65.00
Pn236	1986	—	500 Pesos. Stainless Steel. Proof.	500
Pn237	1987	3	100 Pesos. Copper. KM#537.	—
Pn238	1987	3	100 Pesos. Copper-Nickel. KM#537.	—
Pn239	1988	3	100 Pesos. Brass.	—
Pn240	1988Mo	3	500 Pesos. Aluminum-Brass. Arms/Madero, KM#529.	500
Pn241	1988Mo	—	Onza. Silver. Plain edge. Libertad.	—
Pn242	1990Mo	—	50000 Pesos. Copper-Nickel. National arms, eagle left. Bust with hat facing. Arms/Zapato.	650
Pn244	1990	—	50000 Pesos. Silver.	800
Pn245	1990	—	100000 Pesos. Bronze. Arms/Calles.	650
Pn246	1991Mo	—	100 Pesos. Aluminum. Arms/Huitzilapan.	275
Pn247	1991	—	200 Pesos. Aluminum. Arms/Xochimilco.	200
Pn248	1991	—	500 Pesos. Bronze. Arms/Atenango.	400
Pn249	1991	—	1000 Pesos. Bronze. Arms/Atlan.	35.00
Pn250	1991Mo	—	2000 Pesos. Bronze. Arms/Revolution Monument.	400
Pn251	1991Mo	—	2000 Pesos. Steel. Arms/Revolution Monument.	400
Pn252	1991Mo	34	2000 Pesos. Bi-Metallic. Arms/Revolution Monument.	250
Pn253	1996Mo	—	20 Pesos. Silver center. Aluminum-Bronze ring. W/o NUEVOS.	—
Pn254	1996Mo	—	50 Pesos. Silver. KM#571. W/o NUEVOS.	—
Pn255	1996Mo	—	5 Pesos. Silver. KM#627.	—

TRIAL STRIKES

KM#	Date	Mintage	Identification	Mkt Val
TS16	1980	—	1/10 Onza. Copper.	75.00
TS17	1980	—	1/10 Onza. Silver.	125

BANK SETS

Hard Case Sets unless otherwise noted.

KM#	Date	Mintage	Identification	Issue Price	Mkt Val
BS1	1972 (6)	—	KM#418, 427, 452, 460, 472, 480	—	30.00
BS2	1973 (5)	—	KM#418, 427 (2), 441, 472	—	20.00

KM#	Date	Mintage	Identification	Issue Price	Mkt Val
BS3	1974 (7)	—	KM#427, 434.4, 441, 442, 460, 472, 477.1	—	30.00
BS4	1975 (7)	—	KM#427, 434.1, 442, 452, 460 (2), 477.1	—	20.00
BS5	1976 (9)	—	KM#427, 434.1, 442, 452 (2), 460, 472(2), 477.1	—	15.00
BS6	1977 (9)	—	KM#434.1, 434.2, 442, 452, 460 (2), 472, 477.1, 483.1	—	35.00
BS7	1977 (9)	—	KM#434.1, 434.2, 442, 452, 460 (2), 472, 477.1, 483.2 Type II for 3-ring binder	—	—
BS8	1978 (9)	500	KM#434.1, 434.2, 442, 452, 460 (2), 472, 477.2, 483.2, Type I, flat pack	—	35.00
BS9	1978 (9)	—	KM#434.1, 434.2, 442, 452, 460 (2), 472, 477.2, 483.2 Type II for 3-ring binder,	—	15.00
BS10	1979 (9)	—	KM#434.1, 434.4, 442, 452 (2), 460 (2), 477.2, 483.2 Type I flat pack	11.00	25.00
BS11	1979 (8)	—	KM#434.1, 434.2, 442, 452 (2), 460, 477.2, 483.2 Type II for 3-ring binder	11.00	15.00
BS12	1980 (9)	—	KM#434.2, 442, 452 (2), 460 (2), 485, 486, 477.2	4.20	25.00
BS13	1981 (9)	—	KM#442 (2), 452 (2), 460 (2), 477.2, 485, 486	4.20	25.00
BS14	1982 (7)	—	KM#442, 452, 460, 477.2, 485, 486, 490	—	20.00
BS15	1983 (11)	—	KM#442 (2), 452 (2), 460 (2), 490, 491 (2), 492 (2)	—	20.00
BS16	1983 (11)	—	KM#442 (2), 452 (2), 460 (2), 490, 491 (2), 492 (2) 3-ring plastic page	—	12.50
BS17	1984 (8)	—	KM#485, 486, 490, 491, 493, 495 (2), 496,	—	25.00
BS18	1985 (12)	—	KM#477.2, 485, 493 (2), 495 (2), 496, 502, 508, 509, 510, 512	—	30.00
BS19	1985 (12)	—	KM#477.2, 485, 493 (2), 495 (2), 496, 502, 508, 509, 510, 512 3-ring plastic page	—	20.00
BS20	1986 (7)	—	KM#493, 495, 496, 508, 512, 525, 529 3-ring plastic page	—	20.00
BS21	1987 (9)	—	KM#493, 495 (2), 496, 502 (2), 512, 529 (2)	—	20.00
BS22	1988 (8)	—	KM#493, 495a, 502, 508, 512, 529, 531, 536	—	20.00
BS23	1989 (10)	—	KM#493 (3), 508 (3), 512, 529, 536 (2)	—	20.00
BS24	1990 (8)	—	KM#493 (2), 495a, 509 (2), 512, 536 (2)	—	20.00
BS25	1991 (4)	—	KM#493 (2), 536 (2)	—	15.00
BS26	1992 (5)	—	KM#493 (2), 495a, 529, 536	—	15.00
BS27	1992 (8)	—	KM#546-553	—	30.00
BS28	1993 (7)	—	KM#546-552	—	18.00
BS29	1993 (3)	—	KM#553, 561, 571	—	35.00
BS30	1994 (7)	—	KM#546-552	—	18.00
BS31	1994 (3)	—	KM#553, 561, 571	—	35.00
BS32	1995 (9)	—	KM#546-551, 553, 561, 571	—	45.00
BS33	1996 (6)	—	KM#546-549, 603, 604	12.00	30.00
BS34	1997 (8)	—	KM#546-549, 603-605, 616	—	30.00
BS35	1998 (8)	—	KM#546-549, 603-605, 616	—	30.00
BS36	1999 (8)	—	KM#546-549, 603-605, 616	—	35.00
BS37	2000 (7)	—	KM#547-549, 603-605, 636 Set in folder	—	30.00

PROOF SETS

KM#	Date	Mintage	Identification	Issue Price	Mkt Val
PS1	1982/1983 (8)	998	KM442, 452, 460, 485, 477.2, 486, 490, 494.1	495	325
PS2	1982/1983 (8)	—	KM460, 477.2, 485, 486, 490, 491, 492, PnB169 (in white box with Mo. in gold)	—	—
PS3	1982/1983 (7)	23	KM460, 477.2, 485, 486, 490, 491, 492 (in white box with Mo in gold)	—	500
PS4	1982/1983 (7)	17	KM460, 477.2, 485, 486, 490, 491, 492 (in white box)	—	500
PS5	1982/1983 (7)	8	KM460, 477.2, 485, 486, 490, 491, 492 (in white box)	—	500
PS6	1983 (7)	3	KM460, 477.2, 485, 486, 490, 491, 492	—	—
PS7	1985/1986 (12)	—	KM497a-499a, 503-505, 514-515, 519, 521, 523-524	—	250
PS8	1985 (4)	—	KM500.2-501.2, 506.2, 507.2	—	700
PS9	1985 (3)	—	KM499a, 514, 515 (in blue box)	—	60.00
PS10	1985 (3)	—	KM503-505 (in blue box)	—	60.00
PS11	1985 (2)	—	KM511, 513	—	350
PS12	1989 (3)	704	KM488, 494.1, 538, Rainbow	730	850
PS13	1992 (5)	5,000	KM494.3, 542-545	—	87.50
PS14	1993 (5)	5,000	KM494.4, 542-545	—	87.50
PS15	1994 (5)	5,000	KM494.4, 542-545	—	85.00
PS16	1995 (7)	—	KM546-550, 552, 553, 555	45.00	48.00

MEXICO-REVOLUTIONARY

Revolution, 1910-1917

The Mexican independence movement, which is of interest and concern to collectors because of the warfare induced activity of local and state mints, began with the Sept. 16, 1810 march on the capital led by Father Miguel Hidalgo, a well-intentioned man of imagination and courage who proved to be an inept organizer and leader. Hidalgo was captured and executed within 10 months. His revolution, led by such as Morelos, Guerrero and Iturbide, continued and culminated in Mexican independence in 1821. Turbulent years followed. From 1821 to 1877 there were two emperors, several dictators and enough presidents to provide a change of government on the average of once every nine months. Porfirio Diaz, who had the longest tenure of any 19th century dictator in Latin American history, seized power in 1877 and did not relinquish it until 1911.

The final phase of Mexico's lengthy revolutionary period began in 1910 and lasted through the adoption of a liberal constitution and the election of a new congress in 1917. The 1910-1917 revolution was agrarian in character and intended to destroy the regime of Diaz and make Mexico economically and diplomatically independent. The republic experienced a state of upheaval that saw most of the leading figures of the revolution (Villa, Carranza, Obregon, Zapata, Calles) fighting each other at one time or another. Carranza eventually emerged as the most powerful figure of the early revolution. As *de-facto* president in 1916, he convened a constitutional convention, which produced a constitution in which the aims of the revolution were formulized. Obregon, perhaps the ablest general and wiliest politician of the lot, became Mexico's elected president in 1920, bringing the most disastrous but significant decade in Mexico's history to an end.

AGUASCALIENTES

Aguascalientes is a state in central Mexico. Its coin issues, struck by authority of Pancho Villa, represent his deepest penetration into the Mexican heartland. Lack of silver made it necessary to make all denominations in copper.

FRANCISCO PANCHO VILLA

REVOLUTIONARY COINAGE

KM# 601 CENTAVO

Copper, 17 mm. **Obv:** Liberty cap **Rev:** Value within 3/4 wreath below date **Note:** Large date weight 3.55g.

Date	Mintage	VG	F	VF	XF	Unc
1915	—	30.00	60.00	100	200	—
Note: Large date, reeded edge						
1915	—	30.00	40.00	60.00	90.00	—
Note: Small date, reeded edge						
1915	—	250	350	450	—	—
Note: Large date, plain edge						
1915	—	30.00	50.00	75.00	115	—
Note: Small date, plain edge						

KM# 601a CENTAVO

Silver, 17 mm. **Obv:** Liberty cap **Rev:** Value within 3/4 wreath below date

Date	Mintage	F	VF	XF	Unc	BU
1915 Small date	Inc. above	—	400	650	—	—
1915 Large date	50	—	400	650	—	—

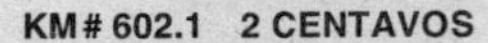

KM# 602.1 2 CENTAVOS

4.2800 g., Copper **Obv:** Liberty cap **Rev:** Value within 3/4 wreath below date

Date	Mintage	VG	F	VF	XF	Unc
1915	—	40.00	100	200	350	—
Note: Round front 2, plain edge						

KM# 602.2 2 CENTAVOS

3.3500 g., Copper, 19 mm. **Obv:** Liberty cap **Rev:** Value within 1/2 wreath below date

Date	Mintage	VG	F	VF	XF	Unc
1915	—	35.00	60.00	85.00	200	—
Note: Square front 2, reeded edge						
1915 Plain edge	—	50.00	90.00	200	300	—
Note: Square front 2						

KM# 602a 2 CENTAVOS

Silver **Obv:** Liberty cap **Rev:** Value within 1/2 wreath below date

Date	Mintage	F	VF	XF	Unc	BU
1915	50	—	700	1,200	—	—

KM# 603 5 CENTAVOS

Copper, 25 mm. **Obv:** National arms **Rev:** Liberty cap and value above sprigs

Date	Mintage	VG	F	VF	XF	Unc
1915 Plain edge; Rare	—	—	—	—	—	—
1915 Reeded edge	—	10.00	20.00	30.00	45.00	—

KM# 604.1 5 CENTAVOS

7.1300 g., Copper, 25 mm. **Obv:** National arms **Rev:** Vertically shaded 5 within sprigs

Date	Mintage	VG	F	VF	XF	Unc
1915	—	20.00	30.00	40.00	60.00	—
Note: Reeded edge						
1915	—	100	150	225	325	—
Note: Plain edge						

KM# 604.2 5 CENTAVOS

Copper, 25 mm. **Obv:** National arms **Rev:** Horizontally shaded 5 within sprigs

Date	Mintage	VG	F	VF	XF	Unc
1915	—	25.00	30.00	50.00	95.00	—
Note: Reeded edge						
1915	—	30.00	50.00	80.00	150	—
Note: Plain edge						

KM# 604a 5 CENTAVOS

Silver **Obv:** National arms **Rev:** Value within sprigs

Date	Mintage	F	VF	XF	Unc	BU
1915	50	—	2,500	3,500	—	—

KM# 606 20 CENTAVOS

Copper, 29 mm. **Obv:** National arms **Rev:** Value below Liberty cap within sprigs

Date	Mintage	VG	F	VF	XF	Unc
1915 Reeded edge	—	10.00	15.00	30.00	60.00	—

KM# 605 20 CENTAVOS

Copper, 29 mm. **Obv:** National arms **Rev:** Value below Liberty cap within sprigs

Date	Mintage	VG	F	VF	XF	Unc
1915 Reeded edge	—	10.00	15.00	30.00	60.00	—

KM# 605a 20 CENTAVOS

Silver **Obv:** National arms **Rev:** Flat-bottomed 2 **Note:** Piedfort.

Date	Mintage	F	VF	XF	Unc	BU
1915	50	—	3,000	3,800	—	—
Note: Plain edge						

KM# 600 20 CENTAVOS
Copper **Obv:** National arms **Rev:** Value below Liberty cap within sprigs **Edge:** Reeded

Date	Mintage	VG	F	VF	XF	Unc
1915	—	15.00	20.00	35.00	60.00	—

KM# 600a 20 CENTAVOS
Silver **Obv:** National arms **Rev:** Wavy-bottomed 2

Date	Mintage	VG	F	VF	XF	Unc
1915	—	1,000	1,500	2,000	3,000	—

Note: Varieties exist with both plain and milled edges and many variations in the shading of the numerals

CHIHUAHUA

Chihuahua is a northern state of Mexico bordering the U.S. It was the arena that introduced Pancho Villa to the world. Villa, an outlaw, was given a title when asked by Madero to participate in maintaining order during Madero's presidency. After Madero's death in February 1913, Villa became a persuasive leader. Chihuahua was where he made his first coins - the Parral series. The *Army of the North* pesos also came from this state. This coin helped Villa recruit soldiers because of his ability to pay in silver while others were paying in worthless paper money.

HIDALGO DEL PARRAL
Fuerzas Constitucionalistas
REVOLUTIONARY COINAGE

KM# 607 2 CENTAVOS
6.8500 g., Copper, 25 mm. **Obv:** Liberty cap within circle flanked by sprigs **Rev:** Value flanked by sprigs within circle

Date	Mintage	VG	F	VF	XF	Unc
1913	—	5.00	10.00	15.00	25.00	—

KM# 607a 2 CENTAVOS
Brass **Obv:** Liberty cap within circle flanked by sprigs **Rev:** Value flanked by sprigs within circle

Date	Mintage	VG	F	VF	XF	Unc
1913	—	95.00	150	200	350	—

KM# 608 50 CENTAVOS
12.6500 g., Silver **Obv:** Liberty cap **Rev:** Value flanked by sprigs below Liberty cap **Edge:** Reeded

Date	Mintage	VG	F	VF	XF	Unc
1913	—	15.00	30.00	50.00	75.00	—

KM# 609 50 CENTAVOS
12.1700 g., Silver, 30 mm. **Edge:** Plain

Date	Mintage	VG	F	VF	XF	Unc
1913	—	50.00	70.00	95.00	125	—

KM# 609a 50 CENTAVOS
Copper **Edge:** Plain

Date	Mintage	VG	F	VF	XF	Unc
1913 rare	—	200	300	425	600	—

KM# 610 PESO
Silver **Obv:** Inscription **Rev:** 1 through PESO and small circle above sprigs **Note:** Weight varies 29.18-30.9g.

Date	Mintage	VG	F	VF	XF	Unc
1913	—	1,200	1,800	2,500	3,000	—

KM# 611 PESO
Silver, 38 mm. **Obv:** Inscription **Rev:** Value above sprigs **Note:** Well struck counterfeits of this coin exist with the dot at the end of the word Peso even with the bottom of the O. On legitimate pieces the dot is slightly higher. Weight varies 27.3-28.85g.

Date	Mintage	VG	F	VF	XF	Unc
1913	—	35.00	40.00	75.00	165	250

CONSTITUTIONALIST ARMY
Ejercito Constitucionalista
REVOLUTIONARY COINAGE

KM# 612 5 CENTAVOS
Copper **Obv:** Liberty cap **Rev:** Value above date

Date	Mintage	VG	F	VF	XF	Unc
1914	—	25.00	35.00	60.00	95.00	—

KM# 613 5 CENTAVOS
Copper, 25 mm. **Obv:** Liberty cap **Rev:** Value above date **Note:** Numerous varieties exist. Weight varies 6.3-6.64g.

Date	Mintage	VG	F	VF	XF	Unc
1914	—	1.00	2.50	4.00	10.00	—
1915	—	1.00	2.50	4.00	10.00	—

KM# 613a 5 CENTAVOS
Brass **Obv:** Liberty cap **Rev:** Value above date **Note:** Numerous varieties exist.

Date	Mintage	VG	F	VF	XF	Unc
1914	—	2.00	3.00	8.00	10.00	—
1915	—	2.00	3.00	8.00	10.00	—

KM# 613b 5 CENTAVOS
Cast Copper **Obv:** Liberty cap **Rev:** Value above date

Date	Mintage	VG	F	VF	XF	Unc
1914	—	75.00	200	300	400	—

KM# 614 5 CENTAVOS
Copper **Obv:** National arms **Rev:** Value below date within sprigs with double-lined V

Date	Mintage	VG	F	VF	XF	Unc
1915 MS	—	150	250	325	500	—
1915 SS Unique	—	—	—	—	—	—

KM# 614a 5 CENTAVOS
Copper **Obv:** National arms **Rev:** Value below date within sprigs with solid V

Date	Mintage	VG	F	VF	XF	Unc
1915 Rare	—	—	—	—	—	—

KM# 614b 5 CENTAVOS
Copper **Obv:** National arms **Rev:** Value above date **Note:** Mule.

Date	Mintage	VG	F	VF	XF	Unc
1915	—	—	350	—	—	—

KM# 614c 5 CENTAVOS
Copper **Obv:** National arms **Rev:** Liberty cap **Note:** Mule.

Date	Mintage	VG	F	VF	XF	Unc
1915 Rare	—	—	—	—	—	—

KM# 615 10 CENTAVOS
8.7900 g., Copper, 27.5 mm. **Obv:** Liberty cap **Rev:** Value above date

Date	Mintage	VG	F	VF	XF	Unc
1915	—	1.25	2.50	3.50	5.00	—

KM# 615a 10 CENTAVOS
8.8900 g., Brass, 27.5 mm. **Obv:** Liberty cap **Rev:** Value above date

Date	Mintage	VG	F	VF	XF	Unc
1915	—	1.75	5.00	15.00	20.00	—

Note: Many varieties exist

ARMY OF THE NORTH
Ejercito Del Norte
REVOLUTIONARY COINAGE

KM# 619 PESO
29.2700 g., Silver **Obv:** National arms **Rev:** Liberty cap

Date	Mintage	VG	F	VF	XF	Unc
1915	—	20.00	30.00	40.00	100	200

KM# 619a PESO
Copper **Obv:** National arms **Rev:** Liberty cap

Date	Mintage	VG	F	VF	XF	Unc
1915	—	500	1,000	1,500	2,200	—

KM# 619b PESO
Brass **Obv:** National arms **Rev:** Liberty cap **Note:** Uniface obverse

Date	Mintage	VG	F	VF	XF	Unc
1915 Rare	—	—	—	—	—	—

PATTERNS

Constitutionalist Army

KM#	Date	Mintage	Identification	Mkt Val
Pn1	1913	—	Peso. Silver.	15,000
Pn2.1	1914	—	50 Centavos. Copper. 12.1800 g. 30 mm. Reeded edge.	3,500
Pn2.2	1914	—	50 Centavos. Copper. Plain edge.	3,000

Note: Specimens exist in silver plated copper

KM#	Date	Mintage	Identification	Mkt Val
Pn3	1914	—	Peso. Copper.	3,500
Pn4	1914	—	Peso. Silver.	3,500

Note: Silver or silver-plated copper pieces are modern fantasies

DURANGO

A state in north central Mexico. Another area of operation for Pancho Villa. The *Muera Huerta* peso originates in this state. The coins were made in Cuencame under the orders of Generals Cemceros and Contreras.

CUENCAME

Muera Huerta (Death to Huerta)

REVOLUTIONARY COINAGE

KM# 620 PESO
Silver **Obv:** National arms **Rev:** Liberty cap with written value flanked by stars

Date	Mintage	VG	F	VF	XF	Unc
1914	—	1,000	2,000	3,000	5,000	—

KM# 621 PESO
23.2000 g., Silver, 39 mm. **Obv:** National arms with continuous border **Rev:** Liberty cap with continuous border

Date	Mintage	VG	F	VF	XF	Unc
1914	—	75.00	100	150	250	550

KM# 621a PESO
Copper **Obv:** National arms with continuous border **Rev:** Liberty cap with continuous border **Note:** Varieties exist.

Date	Mintage	VG	F	VF	XF	Unc
1914	—	400	600	1,000	2,000	—

KM# 621b PESO
Brass **Obv:** National arms **Rev:** Liberty cap

Date	Mintage	VG	F	VF	XF	Unc
1914	—	—	1,000	2,000	3,500	—

KM# 622 PESO
23.4000 g., Silver, 38.5 mm. **Obv:** National arms with dot and dash border **Rev:** Liberty cap with continuous border **Note:** The so-called 20 Pesos gold Muera Huerta pieces are modern fantasies. Refer to Unusual World Coins, 4th edition, ©2005, KP Books, Inc.

Date	Mintage	VG	F	VF	XF	Unc
1914	—	60.00	100	275	350	600

ESTADO DE DURANGO

REVOLUTIONARY COINAGE

KM# 625 CENTAVO
3.2900 g., Copper, 20 mm. **Obv:** Large date in center **Rev:** Value within wreath

Date	Mintage	VG	F	VF	XF	Unc
1914	—	2.00	4.00	8.00	12.00	—

KM# 625a CENTAVO
Brass **Obv:** Large date in center **Rev:** Value within wreath

Date	Mintage	VG	F	VF	XF	Unc
1914	—	75.00	150	300	400	—

KM# 625b CENTAVO
Lead **Obv:** Large date in center **Rev:** Value within wreath

Date	Mintage	VG	F	VF	XF	Unc
1914	—	20.00	40.00	65.00	90.00	—

KM# 625c CENTAVO
Copper **Obv:** Large date in center **Rev:** Value within wreath

Date	Mintage	VG	F	VF	XF	Unc
1914	—	25.00	50.00	80.00	125	—

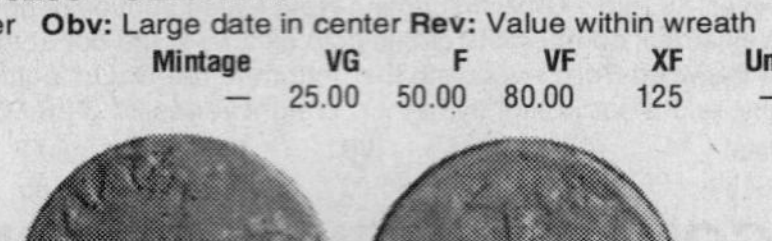

KM# 624 CENTAVO
Cast Lead **Obv:** Date **Rev:** Value within wreath

Date	Mintage	VG	F	VF	XF	Unc
1914	—	45.00	75.00	100	200	—

KM# 626a CENTAVO
Brass **Obv:** Date **Rev:** Value within wreath

Date	Mintage	VG	F	VF	XF	Unc
1914	—	75.00	100	200	350	—

KM# 626b CENTAVO
Lead **Obv:** Date **Rev:** Value within wreath

Date	Mintage	VG	F	VF	XF	Unc
1914	—	20.00	25.00	40.00	60.00	—

Note: Varieties in size exist

KM# 627 CENTAVO
Copper, 20 mm. **Obv:** Stars below date **Rev:** Value with retrograde N

Date	Mintage	VG	F	VF	XF	Unc
1914	—	6.00	10.00	15.00	20.00	—

KM# 627a CENTAVO
Lead, 20 mm. **Obv:** Stars below date **Rev:** Value with retrograde N

Date	Mintage	VG	F	VF	XF	Unc
1914	—	20.00	30.00	40.00	50.00	—

KM# 628 CENTAVO
Aluminum **Obv:** National arms within sprigs **Rev:** Value

Date	Mintage	VG	F	VF	XF	Unc
1914	—	0.65	1.00	2.00	3.00	6.00

KM# 626 CENTAVO
Copper, 20 mm. **Obv:** Date **Rev:** Value within wreath
Note: Weight varies 2.46-2.78g.

Date	Mintage	VG	F	VF	XF	Unc
1914	—	15.00	20.00	35.00	45.00	—

KM# 629 5 CENTAVOS
6.2000 g., Copper, 24 mm. **Obv:** Date above sprigs **Obv. Legend:** ESTADO DE DURANGO **Rev:** Value within designed wreath

Date	Mintage	VG	F	VF	XF	Unc
1914	—	2.00	3.00	6.00	12.00	—

KM# 630 5 CENTAVOS
Copper **Obv:** Date above sprigs **Obv. Legend:** E. DE DURANGO **Rev:** Value within designed wreath

Date	Mintage	VG	F	VF	XF	Unc
1914	—	125	275	375	600	—

KM# 631 5 CENTAVOS
5.0500 g., Copper, 23.5 mm. **Obv:** Date above sprigs **Obv. Legend:** E. DE DURANGO **Rev:** Value within designed wreath

Date	Mintage	VG	F	VF	XF	Unc
1914	—	1.25	3.00	5.00	11.00	—

KM# 631a 5 CENTAVOS
Brass **Obv:** Date above sprigs **Obv. Legend:** E. DE DURANGO **Rev:** Value within designed wreath

Date	Mintage	VG	F	VF	XF	Unc
1914	—	30.00	40.00	50.00	85.00	—

KM# 631b 5 CENTAVOS
Lead **Obv:** Date above sprigs **Obv. Legend:** E. DE DURANGO **Rev:** Value within designed wreath

Date	Mintage	VG	F	VF	XF	Unc
1914	—	45.00	70.00	100	180	—

KM# 632 5 CENTAVOS
4.6100 g., Copper, 23.5 mm. **Obv:** Date above sprigs **Obv. Legend:** E. DE DURANGO **Rev:** Roman numeral value

Date	Mintage	VG	F	VF	XF	Unc
1914	—	4.00	8.00	15.00	35.00	—

KM# 632a 5 CENTAVOS
Lead **Obv:** Date above sprigs **Obv. Legend:** E. DE DURANGO **Rev:** Roman numeral value

Date	Mintage	VG	F	VF	XF	Unc
1914	—	50.00	75.00	100	150	—

KM# 634 5 CENTAVOS
Brass **Obv:** National arms above sprigs **Rev:** Value

Date	Mintage	VG	F	VF	XF	Unc
1914	—	0.50	1.00	2.00	3.50	—

KM# 633 5 CENTAVOS
Lead **Obv:** Three stars below 1914 **Rev:** 5 CVS
Note: Counterfeits are prevalent in the market

Date	Mintage	VG	F	VF	XF	Unc
1914	—	—	600	2,000	—	—

KM# 634a 5 CENTAVOS
Copper **Obv:** National arms above sprigs **Rev:** Value
Note: There are numerous varieties of these general types of the Durango 1 and 5 Centavo pieces.

Date	Mintage	VG	F	VF	XF	Unc
1914	—	75.00	125	175	250	—

GUERRERO

Guerrero is a state on the southwestern coast of Mexico. It was one of the areas of operation of Zapata and his forces in the south of Mexico. The Zapata forces operated seven different mints in this state. The date ranges were from 1914 to 1917 and denominations from 2 Centavos to 2 Pesos. Some were cast but most were struck and the rarest coin of the group is the Suriana 1915 2 Pesos.

EMILIANO ZAPATA
(General Salgado)
REVOLUTIONARY COINAGE

KM# 638 2 CENTAVOS
Copper, 22 mm. **Obv:** National arms **Rev:** Value within wreath
Note: Weight varies 5.4-6.03g.

Date	Mintage	VG	F	VF	XF	Unc
1915	—	75.00	125	175	250	—

KM# 635 3 CENTAVOS
Copper, 25 mm. **Obv:** National arms **Rev:** Value within wreath
Note: Weight varies 4.63-6.87g.

Date	Mintage	VG	F	VF	XF	Unc
1915	—	500	1,000	1,500	2,000	—

KM# 636 5 CENTAVOS
Copper, 26 mm. **Obv:** National arms **Rev:** Value within wreath

Date	Mintage	VG	F	VF	XF	Unc
1915GRO	—	800	1,200	2,000	3,000	—

KM# 637.1 10 CENTAVOS
Copper, 27-28.5 mm. **Obv:** National arms **Rev:** Date and value within wreath **Note:** Size varies.

Date	Mintage	VG	F	VF	XF	Unc
1915GRO	—	600	800	1,000	1,500	—

KM# 637.2 10 CENTAVOS
Copper, 27-28.5 mm. **Obv:** National arms **Rev:** Value within wreath **Note:** Size varies.

Date	Mintage	VG	F	VF	XF	Unc
1915GRO	—	3.00	5.00	8.00	15.00	—

KM# 637.2a 10 CENTAVOS
8.2300 g., Brass, 26 mm. **Obv:** Snake head ends at C in REPUBLICA **Rev:** Value within wreath

Date	Mintage	VG	F	VF	XF	Unc
1915GRO	—	8.00	15.00	25.00	50.00	—

KM# 637.2b 10 CENTAVOS
Lead **Obv:** Snake head ends at C in REPUBLICA **Rev:** Value within wreath

Date	Mintage	VG	F	VF	XF	Unc
1915GRO	—	50.00	75.00	175	275	—

KM# 637.3 10 CENTAVOS
Copper **Obv:** National arms **Rev:** Date and value within wreath

Date	Mintage	VG	F	VF	XF	Unc
1915GRO	—	3.00	5.00	8.00	15.00	—

KM# 637.3a 10 CENTAVOS
Brass **Obv:** Snake head ends before A in REPUBLICA **Rev:** Value and date within wreath with dot after date

Date	Mintage	VG	F	VF	XF	Unc
1915GRO	—	12.00	20.00	50.00	100	—

KM# 639 25 CENTAVOS
Silver, 25 mm. **Obv:** Liberty cap **Rev:** Value above date
Note: Weight varies 7.41-7.5g.

Date	Mintage	VG	F	VF	XF	Unc
1915	—	125	300	500	900	—

KM# 640 50 CENTAVOS
Silver, 34 mm. **Obv:** Liberty cap **Rev:** Date and value within beaded border **Note:** Weight varies 14.5-14.8g.

Date	Mintage	VG	F	VF	XF	Unc
1915	—	900	1,500	2,100	3,000	—

KM# 641 PESO (UN)
Gold-Silver, 29-31 mm. **Obv:** National arms **Rev:** Liberty cap within sprigs **Rev. Inscription:** Oro:0,300 **Note:** Many die varieties exist. Size varies. Weight varies 10.28-14.84g. Coin is 0.30g fine Gold.

Date	Mintage	VG	F	VF	XF	Unc
1914	—	15.00	25.00	35.00	65.00	—

KM# 641a PESO (UN)
Copper **Obv:** National arms **Rev:** Liberty cap within sprigs

Date	Mintage	Good	VG	F	VF	XF
1914	—	—	100	150	225	900

KM# 642 PESO (UN)
Gold-Silver, 30.5-31 mm. **Obv:** National arms **Rev:** Liberty cap within sprigs **Rev. Inscription:** Oro:0,300 **Note:** Weight varies 12.93-14.66g. Coin is 0.300g fine Gold.

Date	Mintage	VG	F	VF	XF	Unc
1914	—	50.00	75.00	100	150	—
1915	—	600	1,000	1,500	1,800	—

KM# 643 2 PESOS (Dos)
Gold-Silver, 38.25-39.6 mm. **Obv:** National arms **Rev:** Radiant sun face above mountains **Rev. Inscription:** Oro:0,595
Note: Many varieties exist. Coin is 0.595g fine Gold.

Date	Mintage	VG	F	VF	XF	Unc
1914GRO	—	12.00	20.00	32.00	60.00	—

KM# 643a 2 PESOS (Dos)
Copper, 38-38.5 mm. **Obv:** National arms **Rev:** Radiant sun face above mountains **Note:** Size varies.

Date	Mintage	Good	VG	F	VF	XF
1914	—	—	—	1,000	1,200	1,800

KM# 644 2 PESOS (Dos)
Gold-Silver, 39-40 mm. **Obv:** National arms **Rev:** Radiant sun and mountains **Rev. Inscription:** Oro:0,595 **Note:** Weight varies 21.71-26.54g. Coin is 0.595g fine Gold.

Date	Mintage	VG	F	VF	XF	Unc
1915GRO	—	65.00	85.00	160	200	—

KM# 644a 2 PESOS (Dos)
Copper **Obv:** National arms **Rev:** Radiant sun and mountains

Date	Mintage	VG	F	VF	XF	Unc
1915GRO	—	400	800	1,000	1,500	—

ATLIXTAC

REVOLUTIONARY COINAGE

KM# 645 10 CENTAVOS
Copper, 27.5-28 mm. **Obv:** National arms **Rev:** Value within sprigs **Note:** Size varies. Weight varies 4.76-9.74g.

Date	Mintage	VG	F	VF	XF	Unc
1915	—	3.00	5.00	8.00	15.00	—

KM# 646 10 CENTAVOS
Copper, 27.55-28 mm. **Obv:** National arms **Rev:** Value within sprigs **Note:** Size varies. Weight varies 6.13-7.94g.

Date	Mintage	VG	F	VF	XF	Unc
1915	—	3.00	5.00	8.00	15.00	—

CACAHUATEPEC

REVOLUTIONARY COINAGE

KM# 648 5 CENTAVOS
12.1900 g., Copper, 28 mm. **Obv:** National arms **Rev:** Value within wreath

Date	Mintage	VG	F	VF	XF	Unc
1917	—	12.00	25.00	40.00	75.00	—

KM# 649 20 CENTAVOS
Silver, 21-23.8 mm. **Obv:** National arms **Rev:** Value within sprigs below liberty cap **Note:** Size varies. Weight varies 3.99-6.2g.

Date	Mintage	VG	F	VF	XF	Unc
1917	—	75.00	125	300	350	—

KM# 650 50 CENTAVOS
Silver, 30-30.3 mm. **Obv:** National arms **Rev:** Value and date within sprigs below Liberty cap **Note:** Size varies. Weight varies 13.45-13.78g.

Date	Mintage	VG	F	VF	XF	Unc
1917	—	10.00	30.00	45.00	90.00	—

KM# 651 PESO (UN)
Silver, 38 mm. **Obv:** National arms **Rev:** Liberty cap **Note:** Weight varies 26.81-32.05g.

Date	Mintage	VG	F	VF	XF	Unc
1917 L.V. Go	—	1,500	3,000	4,000	6,000	—

CACALOTEPEC

REVOLUTIONARY COINAGE

KM# 652 20 CENTAVOS
Silver, 22.5 mm. **Obv:** National arms **Rev:** Date and value within sprigs below Liberty cap **Note:** Weight varies 3.89-5.73g.

Date	Mintage	VG	F	VF	XF	Unc
1917	—	1,000	1,800	3,000	4,000	—

CAMPO MORADO

REVOLUTIONARY COINAGE

KM# 653 5 CENTAVOS
4.3700 g., Copper, 23.5-24 mm. **Obv:** National arms **Rev:** Value within wreath **Note:** Size varies.

Date	Mintage	VG	F	VF	XF	Unc
1915 C.M.	—	9.00	15.00	22.50	35.00	—

KM# 654 10 CENTAVOS
Copper, 25.25-26 mm. **Obv:** National arms **Rev:** Value and date within wreath **Note:** Size varies. Weight varies. 4.48-8.77g.

Date	Mintage	VG	F	VF	XF	Unc
1915 C.M. GRO	—	6.00	10.00	20.00	30.00	—

KM# 655 20 CENTAVOS
Copper, 28 mm. **Obv:** National arms **Rev:** Date above star and value within wreath **Note:** Weight varies 4.48-9g.

Date	Mintage	VG	F	VF	XF	Unc
1915 C.M. GRO	—	15.00	25.00	35.00	50.00	—

KM# 657 50 CENTAVOS
Copper, 30-31 mm. **Obv:** National arms **Rev:** Date and value within wreath **Note:** Regular obverse. Size varies. Weight varies 6.49-13.19g.

Date	Mintage	VG	F	VF	XF	Unc
1915 C.M. GRO	—	6.00	10.00	15.00	25.00	—

KM# 657a 50 CENTAVOS
Base Silver **Obv:** National arms **Rev:** Date and value within wreath **Note:** Regular obverse.

Date	Mintage	VG	F	VF	XF	Unc
1915 C.M. GRO	—	200	300	500	1,000	—

KM# 656 50 CENTAVOS
Copper, 29-31 mm. **Obv:** National arms **Rev:** Date and value within wreath **Note:** Size varies. Weight varies 9.81-16.77g.

Date	Mintage	VG	F	VF	XF	Unc
1915 C.M. GRO	—	12.00	20.00	30.00	60.00	—

KM# 659 PESO (UN)
Gold-Silver, 30-31 mm. **Obv:** National arms **Rev:** Liberty cap within sprigs **Rev. Inscription:** Oro:0,300 **Note:** Weight varies 12.26-15.81g. Coin is 0.300g fine Gold.

Date	Mintage	VG	F	VF	XF	Unc
1914 CAMPO Mo	—	15.00	30.00	45.00	60.00	—

KM# 658 PESO (UN)
Gold-Silver, 32-32.5 mm. **Obv:** National arms **Rev:** Liberty cap **Rev. Inscription:** Oro:0,300 **Note:** Weight varies 12.42-16.5g. Coin is 0.300g fine Gold.

Date	Mintage	VG	F	VF	XF	Unc
1914 Co Mo Gro	—	500	600	1,000	1,200	—

KM# 658a PESO (UN)
Brass **Obv:** National arms **Rev:** Liberty cap

Date	Mintage	VG	F	VF	XF	Unc
1914 Co Mo Gro Unique	—	—	—	—	—	—

KM# 660 2 PESOS (Dos)
Gold-Silver, 38.9-39 mm. **Obv:** National arms **Rev:** Sun over mountains **Rev. Inscription:** Oro:0,595 **Note:** Weight varies 20.6-26.02g. Coin is 0.595g fine Gold.

Date	Mintage	VG	F	VF	XF	Unc
1915 Co. Mo.	—	12.00	20.00	30.00	50.00	—

KM# 660a 2 PESOS (Dos)
Copper **Obv:** National arms **Rev:** Sun over mountains

Date	Mintage	VG	F	VF	XF	Unc
1915 Co. Mo.	—	—	800	1,000	1,200	—

KM# 662a.1 2 PESOS (Dos)
Copper **Obv:** National arms **Rev:** Liberty cap

Date	Mintage	VG	F	VF	XF	Unc
1915 C. M. GRO	—	—	—	—	1,200	—

KM# 662a.2 2 PESOS (Dos)
Copper **Obv:** National arms **Rev:** Liberty cap

Date	Mintage	VG	F	VF	XF	Unc
1915 C. M. GRO Unique	—	—	—	—	—	—

KM# 661 2 PESOS (Dos)
29.4400 g., Gold-Silver, 39 mm. **Obv:** National arms **Rev:** Sun and mountains **Rev. Inscription:** Oro:0,595 **Note:** Coin is 0.595g fine Gold.

Date	Mintage	VG	F	VF	XF	Unc
1915 Co. Mo.	—	1,600	3,000	7,000	9,000	—

KM# 662 2 PESOS (Dos)
0.5950 g., 1.0000 Gold-Silver, 34.5-35 mm. **Obv:** National arms **Rev:** Liberty cap **Note:** Size varies. Weight varies 18.27-20.08g.

Date	Mintage	VG	F	VF	XF	Unc
1915 C. M. GRO	—	20.00	30.00	45.00	85.00	—

CHILPANCINGO

REVOLUTIONARY COINAGE

KM# 663 10 CENTAVOS
2.5200 g., Cast Silver, 18 mm. **Obv:** National arms **Rev:** Sun above value and sprigs

Date	Mintage	VG	F	VF	XF	Unc
1914	—	700	1,000	1,200	1,500	—

Note: Many counterfeits exist

KM# 664 20 CENTAVOS
4.9400 g., Cast Silver, 21.5 mm. **Obv:** National arms **Rev:** Sun above value and sprigs

Date	Mintage	VG	F	VF	XF	Unc
1914	—	700	1,000	1,200	1,500	—

Note: Many counterfeits exist

SURIANA

REVOLUTIONARY COINAGE

KM# 665 2 PESOS (Dos)
22.9300 g., Gold-Silver, 39 mm. **Obv:** National arms **Rev:** Sun over mountains **Rev. Inscription:** Oro:0,595 **Note:** Coin is 0.595g fine Gold.

Date	Mintage	VG	F	VF	XF	Unc
1915 Rare	—	—	—	18,000	25,000	—

Note: Spink America Gerber sale part 2, 6-96 VF realized $16,500

TAXCO

REVOLUTIONARY COINAGE

KM# 667 2 CENTAVOS
Copper, 25.25-26 mm. **Obv:** National arms **Obv. Legend:** EDO.DE.GRO **Rev:** Value within sprigs **Note:** Size varies. Weight varies 6.81-8.55g.

Date	Mintage	VG	F	VF	XF	Unc
1915 O/T	—	25.00	40.00	60.00	90.00	—

KM# 668 5 CENTAVOS
Copper **Obv:** National arms **Rev:** Value within sprigs **Note:** Weight varies 7.13-7.39g.

Date	Mintage	VG	F	VF	XF	Unc
1915	—	9.00	15.00	25.00	35.00	—

KM# 669 10 CENTAVOS
Copper, 27-28 mm. **Obv:** National arms **Rev:** Date and value within sprigs **Note:** Size varies. Weight varies 7.51-8.67g.

Date	Mintage	VG	F	VF	XF	Unc
1915	—	9.00	20.00	35.00	50.00	—

KM# 670 50 CENTAVOS
5.4500 g., Copper, 27-28 mm. **Obv:** National arms with legend in large letters **Rev:** Value within sprigs **Note:** Size varies.

Date	Mintage	VG	F	VF	XF	Unc
1915	—	15.00	25.00	50.00	65.00	—

KM# 671 50 CENTAVOS
Silver, 27.6-28 mm. **Obv:** National arms **Rev:** Sun above value and sprigs **Note:** Size varies. Weight varies 8.95-10.85g.

Date	Mintage	VG	F	VF	XF	Unc
1915	—	25.00	40.00	60.00	100	—

KM# 672 PESO (UN)
Gold-Silver, 30-31 mm. **Obv:** National arms **Rev:** Liberty cap within sprigs **Rev. Inscription:** Oro:0,300 **Note:** Weight varies 30-31g. Coin is 0.300g fine Gold.

Date	Mintage	VG	F	VF	XF	Unc
1915	—	12.00	20.00	30.00	45.00	—

KM# 672a PESO (UN)
Brass **Obv:** National arms **Rev:** Liberty cap within sprigs

Date	Mintage	VG	F	VF	XF	Unc
1915	—	200	300	450	600	—

KM# 672b PESO (UN)
Lead **Obv:** National arms **Rev:** Liberty cap within sprigs

Date	Mintage	VG	F	VF	XF	Unc
1915	—	50.00	100	200	350	—

KM# 672c PESO (UN)
Copper **Obv:** National arms **Rev:** Liberty cap within sprigs

Date	Mintage	VG	F	VF	XF	Unc
1915	—	200	300	400	650	—

KM# 673 PESO (UN)
11.6000 g., Gold-Silver, 30 mm. **Obv:** National arms **Rev:** Liberty cap within sprigs **Rev. Inscription:** Oro:0,300 **Note:** Coin is 0.300g fine Gold.

Date	Mintage	VG	F	VF	XF	Unc
1915	—	250	400	500	800	—

KM# 674 PESO (UN)
Gold-Silver, 30 mm. **Obv:** National arms **Rev:** Liberty cap within sprigs **Rev. Inscription:** Oro:0,300 **Note:** Weight varies 10.51-12.79g. Coin is 0.300g fine Gold.

Date	Mintage	VG	F	VF	XF	Unc
1915	—	100	200	300	500	—

PATTERNS

Including off metal strikes

KM#	Date	Mintage	Identification	Mkt Val
Pn647	1914	—	2 Pesos. Gold-Silver. 0.3000 g. Atlixtac.	—
Pn674	1914	—	2 Pesos. 1.0000 Gold-Silver.	—

JALISCO

Jalisco is a state on the west coast of Mexico. The few coins made for this state show that the *Army of the North* did not restrict their operations to the northern border states. The coins were made in Guadalajara under the watchful eye of General Dieguez, commander of this segment of Villa's forces.

GUADALAJARA

REVOLUTIONARY COINAGE

KM# 675 CENTAVO
Copper **Obv:** Liberty cap **Rev:** Value

Date	Mintage	VG	F	VF	XF	Unc
1915	—	9.50	15.00	20.00	30.00	—

KM# 675a CENTAVO
Brass **Obv:** Liberty cap **Rev:** Value

Date	Mintage	VG	F	VF	XF	Unc
1915	—	—	—	300	450	—

KM# A676 CENTAVO
Copper **Obv:** Liberty cap **Rev:** Retrograde value **Note:** Varieties exist.

Date	Mintage	VG	F	VF	XF	Unc
1915	—	100	300	600	1,000	—

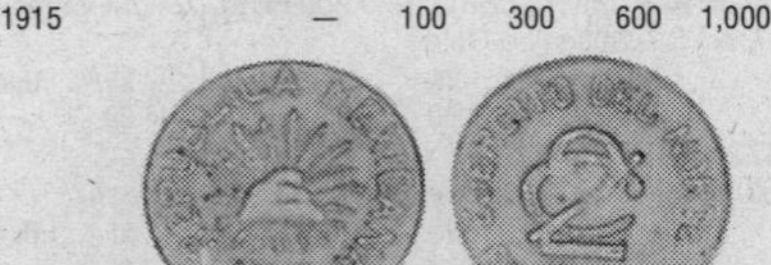

KM# 676.1 2 CENTAVOS
Copper, 20 mm. **Obv:** Liberty cap **Rev:** Value

Date	Mintage	VG	F	VF	XF	Unc
1915	—	10.00	18.00	20.00	35.00	—

Note: Varieties exist.

KM# 676.2 2 CENTAVOS
Copper **Obv:** Liberty cap **Rev:** Value

Date	Mintage	VG	F	VF	XF	Unc
1915	—	200	300	400	550	—

KM# 677 5 CENTAVOS
Copper, 24 mm. **Obv:** Liberty cap **Rev:** Value

Date	Mintage	VG	F	VF	XF	Unc
1915	—	6.50	12.00	15.00	25.00	—

KM# 677a 5 CENTAVOS
Brass **Obv:** Liberty cap **Rev:** Value

Date	Mintage	VG	F	VF	XF	Unc
1915 rare	—	—	—	—	—	—

KM# 678 10 CENTAVOS
Copper **Obv:** Liberty cap above value and date **Rev:** Crowned shield

Date	Mintage	VG	F	VF	XF	Unc
1915	—	—	—	3,000	5,000	—

KM# A678 PESO
Copper **Obv:** Liberty cap above value and date **Rev:** Crowned shield

Date	Mintage	VG	F	VF	XF	Unc
1915	—	—	—	—	15,000	—

MEXICO, ESTADO DE

Estado de Mexico is a state in central Mexico that surrounds the Federal District on three sides. The issues by the Zapata forces in this state have two distinctions – the Amecameca pieces are the crudest and the Toluca cardboard piece is the most unusual. General Tenorio authorized the crude incuse Amecameca pieces.

AMECAMECA

REVOLUTIONARY COINAGE

KM# 679 5 CENTAVOS
12.5500 g., Brass, 24.5 mm. **Obv:** Legend **Obv. Legend:** EJERCITO CONVENCIONISTA **Rev:** Value above cent sign

Date	Mintage	VG	F	VF	XF	Unc
ND unique	—	—	—	—	—	—

KM# 680 5 CENTAVOS
12.7700 g., Brass, 24.6 mm. **Obv:** National arms above RM **Rev:** Value above cent sign **Note:** Hand stamped.

Date	Mintage	VG	F	VF	XF	Unc
ND	—	300	400	600	800	—

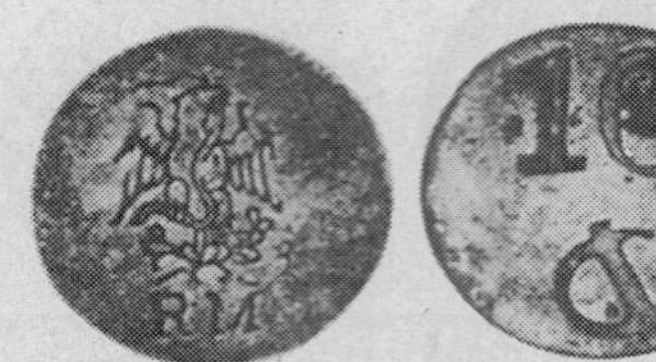

KM# 681 10 CENTAVOS
15.0000 g., Brass, 24.5-24.8 mm. **Obv:** National arms above RM **Rev:** Value above cent sign **Note:** Hand stamped. Varieties exist. Size varies.

Date	Mintage	VG	F	VF	XF	Unc
ND	—	60.00	90.00	150	200	—

KM# 681a 10 CENTAVOS
Copper **Obv:** National arms above RM **Rev:** Value above cent sign **Note:** Hand stamped.

Date	Mintage	VG	F	VF	XF	Unc
ND	—	75.00	125	225	350	—

KM# 682 20 CENTAVOS
Brass, 24-25 mm. **Obv:** National arms above RM **Rev:** Value above cent sign **Note:** Hand stamped. Varieties exist. Size varies. Weight varies 11.34-12.86g.

Date	Mintage	VG	F	VF	XF	Unc
ND	—	15.00	22.50	35.00	60.00	—

KM# 682a 20 CENTAVOS
Copper **Obv:** National arms above RM **Rev:** Value above cent sign **Note:** Hand stamped.

Date	Mintage	VG	F	VF	XF	Unc
ND	—	25.00	50.00	175	250	—

KM# 683 20 CENTAVOS
Copper, 19-20 mm. **Obv:** National arms above A. D. J. **Rev:** Value **Note:** Size varies. Weight varies 3.99-5.35g.

Date	Mintage	VG	F	VF	XF	Unc
ND	—	7.50	12.50	20.00	35.00	—

KM# 683a 20 CENTAVOS
Brass **Obv:** National arms above A. D. J. **Rev:** Value

Date	Mintage	VG	F	VF	XF	Unc
ND	—	—	—	—	300	500	—

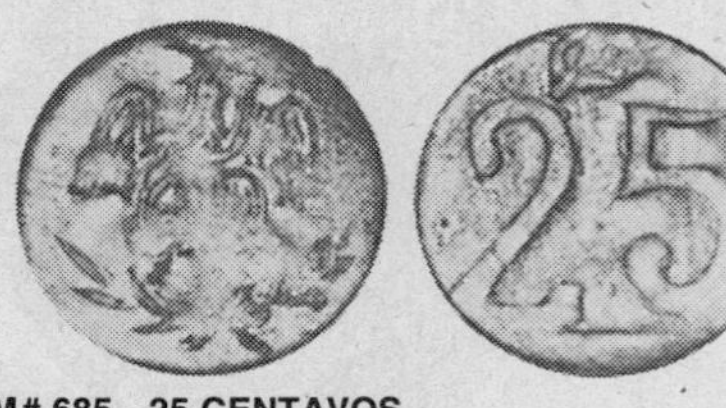

KM# 684 25 CENTAVOS
Brass **Obv:** Legend **Obv. Legend:** EJERCITO CONVENCIONISTA **Rev:** Value above cent sign

Date	Mintage	VG	F	VF	XF	Unc
ND unique	—	—	—	—	—	—

KM# 685 25 CENTAVOS
Copper, 25 mm. **Obv:** National arms above sprigs **Rev:** Large numeral value **Note:** Hand stamped. Many modern counterfeits exist in all metals. Weight varies 6.32-6.99g.

Date	Mintage	VG	F	VF	XF	Unc
ND	—	15.00	20.00	30.00	40.00	—

KM# 685a 25 CENTAVOS
7.9200 g., Brass, 25 mm. **Obv:** National arms above sprigs **Rev:** Large numeral value **Note:** Hand stamped.

Date	Mintage	VG	F	VF	XF	Unc
ND	—	—	—	100	300	—

KM# 685b 25 CENTAVOS
Silver **Obv:** National arms above sprigs **Rev:** Large numeral value **Note:** Hand stamped.

Date	Mintage	VG	F	VF	XF	Unc
ND	—	—	—	250	400	—

KM# 687 50 CENTAVOS
Copper, 23.5-29 mm. **Obv:** National arms above sprigs **Rev:** Large numeral value **Note:** Contemporary counterfeit, hand engraved. Size varies. Weight varies 8.8-10.8g.

Date	Mintage	VG	F	VF	XF	Unc
ND	—	12.00	30.00	50.00	80.00	—

Note: "¢" clears top of 5

KM# 686a 50 CENTAVOS
16.0400 g., Brass, 28.5 mm. **Obv:** National arms above sprigs **Rev:** Large numeral value **Note:** Hand stamped.

Date	Mintage	VG	F	VF	XF	Unc
ND	—	100	200	300	400	—

Note: Stem of "¢" above the 5

TENANCINGO, TOWN

(Distrito Federal Mexico)

REVOLUTIONARY COINAGE

KM# 688.1 2 CENTAVOS
Copper **Obv:** National arms **Rev:** Value within wreath without TM below value

Date	Mintage	VG	F	VF	XF	Unc
1915	—	—	—	800	2,000	—

KM# 688.2 2 CENTAVOS
Copper **Obv:** National arms **Rev:** Value within wreath with TM below value

Date	Mintage	VG	F	VF	XF	Unc
1915	—	—	400	800	2,000	—

KM# 689.1 5 CENTAVOS
Copper, 19 mm. **Obv:** National arms **Rev:** Numeral value over lined C within wreath **Note:** Weight varies 2.83-2.84g.

Date	Mintage	VG	F	VF	XF	Unc
1915	—	10.00	20.00	30.00	50.00	—

KM# 689.2 5 CENTAVOS
Copper, 19 mm. **Obv:** National arms **Rev:** Numeral value over lined C within wreath **Note:** Weight varies 2.83-2.84g.

Date	Mintage	VG	F	VF	XF	Unc
1915	—	100	300	500	800	—

KM# 690.1 10 CENTAVOS
Copper, 25.25 mm. **Obv:** National arms **Rev:** Value over lined C within wreath below date **Note:** Weight varies 4.27-5.64g.

Date	Mintage	VG	F	VF	XF	Unc
1916	—	10.00	20.00	40.00	60.00	—

KM# 690.2 10 CENTAVOS
Copper, 25.25 mm. **Obv:** National arms **Rev:** Value over lined C within wreath **Note:** Weight varies 4.27-5.64g.

Date	Mintage	VG	F	VF	XF	Unc
1916	—	100	200	400	500	—

KM# 691 20 CENTAVOS
Copper, 27.5-28 mm. **Obv:** National arms **Rev:** Value and date above sprigs **Note:** Size varies. Weight varies 8.51-11.39g.

Date	Mintage	VG	F	VF	XF	Unc
1915	—	25.00	40.00	55.00	75.00	—

TOLUCA, CITY
(Distrito Federal Mexico)

REVOLUTIONARY COINAGE

KM# 692.1 5 CENTAVOS
Grey Cardboard, 27-28 mm. **Obv:** Crowned shield within sprigs **Rev:** Banner accross large numeral value **Note:** Size varies. Weight varies 1.04-1.16g.

Date	Mintage	VG	F	VF	XF	Unc
1915	—	15.00	30.00	50.00	75.00	—

KM# 692.2 5 CENTAVOS
Grey Cardboard, 27-28 mm. **Obv:** Crowned shield within sprigs **Rev:** Banner accross large numeral value **Note:** Size varies. Weight varies 1.04-1.16g.

Date	Mintage	VG	F	VF	XF	Unc
1915	—	15.00	30.00	50.00	75.00	—

COUNTERMARKED COINAGE

KM# 693.1 20 CENTAVOS
Copper, 20 mm. **Countermark:** 20 within C **Obv:** National arms **Rev:** Numeral 20 within C and inner circle within sprigs **Note:** Countermark on 1 Centavo, KM#415. Varieties exist. Weight varies 2.65-2.95g.

CM Date	Host Date	Good	VG	F	VF	XF
ND(1915)	ND	—	20.00	30.00	45.00	60.00

KM# 693.2 20 CENTAVOS
Copper, 20 mm. **Countermark:** 20 within C **Obv:** National arms **Rev:** Numeral 20 within C and inner circle within 3/4 wreath **Note:** Countermark on 1 Centavo, KM#394.1. Weight varies 2.65-2.95g.

CM Date	Host Date	Good	VG	F	VF	XF
ND(1915)	1904	—	300	500	900	1,500

KM# 694 40 CENTAVOS
5.8600 g., Copper, 24.75-25 mm. **Countermark:** 40 within C **Obv:** National arms **Rev:** Numeral 40 within C and inner circle within wreath **Note:** Countermark on 2 Centavos, KM#419. Varieties exist. Size varies.

CM Date	Host Date	Good	VG	F	VF	XF
ND(1915)	ND	—	25.00	40.00	60.00	80.00

MORELOS

Morelos is a state in south central Mexico, adjoining the federal district on the south. It was the headquarters of Emiliano Zapata. His personal quarters were at Tlatizapan in Morelos. The Morelos coins from 2 Centavos to 1 Peso were all copper except one type of 1 Peso in silver. The two operating Zapatista mints in Morelos were Atlihuayan and Tlaltizapan.

EMILIANO ZAPATA
(Zapatista)

REVOLUTIONARY COINAGE

KM# 695 2 CENTAVOS
Copper, 23 mm. **Obv:** National arms **Obv. Legend:** E.L. DE MORELOS **Rev:** Value within wreath

Date	Mintage	VG	F	VF	XF	Unc
1915	—	1,000	1,400	1,800	2,250	—

KM# 696 5 CENTAVOS
9.0000 g., Copper, 25.9 mm. **Obv:** National arms **Rev:** Value within 3/4 wreath **Rev. Legend:** E. DE MOR. 1915

Date	Mintage	VG	F	VF	XF	Unc
1915	—	300	500	1,000	3,500	—

KM# 697 10 CENTAVOS
8.6900 g., Copper, 24 mm. **Obv:** National arms **Rev:** Value within lined C and wreath

Date	Mintage	VG	F	VF	XF	Unc
1915	—	12.00	20.00	30.00	40.00	—

KM# 698 10 CENTAVOS
Copper, 24-24.5 mm. **Obv:** National arms **Rev:** Value within lined C and wreath with date effaced from die **Note:** Size varies. Weight varies 4.83-6.8g.

Date	Mintage	VG	F	VF	XF	Unc
ND	—	12.00	20.00	35.00	55.00	—

KM# 699 10 CENTAVOS
Copper **Obv:** National arms **Rev:** Date and value within wreath **Rev. Legend:** E. DE MOR

Date	Mintage	VG	F	VF	XF	Unc
1915	—	1,000	2,000	2,500	3,000	—

KM# 700 10 CENTAVOS
Copper, 28 mm. **Obv:** National arms **Rev:** Date and value within wreath **Rev. Legend:** MOR **Note:** Weight varies 5.56-8.36g.

Date	Mintage	VG	F	VF	XF	Unc
1916	—	5.00	20.00	30.00	50.00	—

KM# 701 20 CENTAVOS
Copper, 23.75-24.75 mm. **Obv:** National arms **Rev:** Value within lined C and 3/4 wreath **Note:** Size varies. Weight varies 3.88-4.15g.

Date	Mintage	VG	F	VF	XF	Unc
1915	—	9.00	15.00	25.00	35.00	—

KM# 702 50 CENTAVOS
Copper, 28.8 mm. **Obv:** National arms with MOR beneath eagle **Rev:** 50C monogram

Date	Mintage	VG	F	VF	XF	Unc
1915	—	300	500	900	1,300	—

KM# 703 50 CENTAVOS
Copper, 28-29.5 mm. **Obv:** National arms **Rev:** Numeral value within lined C and 1/2 wreath **Note:** This coin exists with a silver and also a brass wash. Size varies. Weight varies 5.73-13.77g.

Date	Mintage	VG	F	VF	XF	Unc
1915	—	12.50	17.50	30.00	42.00	—

KM# 703a 50 CENTAVOS
Brass **Obv:** National arms above sprigs **Rev:** 50C monogram

Date	Mintage	VG	F	VF	XF	Unc
1915	—	100	200	400	600	—

KM# 706 50 CENTAVOS
Copper, 28 mm. **Obv:** National arms **Rev:** Date above large numeral value **Rev. Legend:** REFORMA LIBERTAD JUSTICIA Y LEY

Date	Mintage	VG	F	VF	XF	Unc
1915	—	350	500	800	1,000	—

KM# 704 50 CENTAVOS
Copper, 29-30 mm. **Obv:** National arms with Morelos written below **Rev:** Value within wreath **Note:** Size varies. Weight varies 8.56-11.47g.

Date	Mintage	VG	F	VF	XF	Unc
1916	—	12.50	20.00	30.00	50.00	—

KM# 708 PESO (UN)
Silver **Obv:** National arms **Rev:** Liberty cap within wreath

Date	Mintage	VG	F	VF	XF	Unc
1916	—	450	750	1,000	1,500	—

KM# 708a PESO (UN)
10.0000 g., Copper, 30 mm. **Obv:** National arms **Rev:** Liberty cap within wreath

Date	Mintage	VG	F	VF	XF	Unc
1916	—	500	1,000	1,200	2,000	—

PATTERNS

Including off metal strikes

KM#	Date	Mintage	Identification	Mkt Val
Pn1	1915	—	50 Centavos. Silver. 12.0000 g. 29.3 mm. KM#705.	1,500
Pn2	1915	—	50 Centavos. Copper. KM#705.	1,500
Pn3	191x	—	Peso. Silver. KM#707.	4,000
Pn4	191x	—	Peso. Copper. KM#707a.	4,000
Pn5	1916	—	Peso. Copper. KM#707b.	4,250

OAXACA

Oaxaca is one of the southern states in Mexico. The coins issued in this state represent the most prolific series of the Revolution. Most of the coins bear the portrait of Benito Juarez, have corded or plain edges and were issued by a provisional government in the state. The exceptions are the rectangular 1 and 3 Centavos pieces that begin the series.

PROVISIONAL GOVERNMENT

REVOLUTIONARY COINAGE

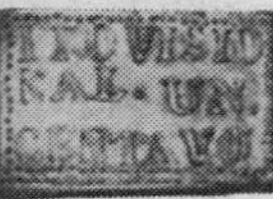

KM# 709 CENTAVO (UN)
Copper, 19 mm. **Obv:** Legend within beaded rectangle **Rev:** Legend within beaded rectangle **Note:** Rectangular flan.

Date	Mintage	VG	F	VF	XF	Unc
1915	—	60.00	90.00	300	400	—

KM# 710 CENTAVO (UN)
Copper, 18 mm. **Obv:** Bust left with date flanked by stars below **Rev:** Value within lined C and 1/2 wreath

Date	Mintage	VG	F	VF	XF	Unc
1915	—	12.00	17.50	25.00	40.00	—

KM# 710a CENTAVO (UN)
Brass **Obv:** Head left with date flanked by stars below **Rev:** Value within lined C and 1/2 wreath

Date	Mintage	VG	F	VF	XF	Unc
1915	—	50.00	100	200	300	—

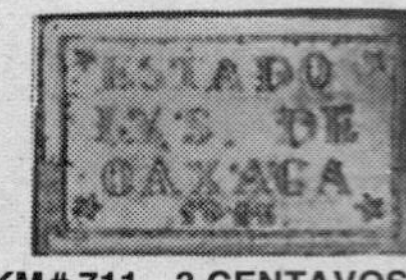

KM# 711 3 CENTAVOS (Tres)
Copper, 24 mm. **Obv:** Legend within rectangle with date below, stars in corners **Rev:** Legend within rectangle with stars in corners **Rev. Legend:** PROVISIO... **Note:** Rectangular flan.

Date	Mintage	VG	F	VF	XF	Unc
1915	—	60.00	150	300	400	—

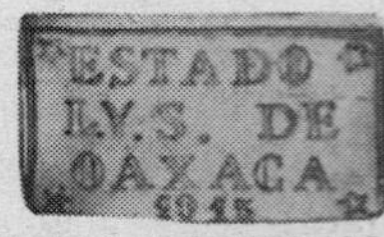
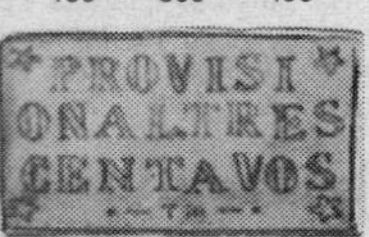

KM# 712 3 CENTAVOS (Tres)
Copper **Obv:** Legend within rectangle with date below, stars in corners **Rev:** Legend within rectangle with stars in corners **Rev. Legend:** PROVISI... **Note:** Rectangular flan.

Date	Mintage	VG	F	VF	XF	Unc
1915	—	1,000	2,000	3,000	6,000	—

KM# 713.1 3 CENTAVOS (Tres)
2.2500 g., Copper, 20 mm. **Obv:** Bust left flanked by stars below **Rev:** Value above sprigs **Note:** Without TM below value

Date	Mintage	VG	F	VF	XF	Unc
1915	—	3.00	5.00	12.00	25.00	—

KM# 713.2 3 CENTAVOS (Tres)
2.2500 g., Copper, 20 mm. **Obv:** Bust left flanked by stars below **Rev:** Value above sprigs **Edge:** Plain **Note:** Without TM below value

Date	Mintage	VG	F	VF	XF	Unc
1915	—	—	—	70.00	100	—

KM# 713.3 3 CENTAVOS (Tres)
2.2500 g., Copper, 20 mm. **Obv:** Bust left flanked by stars below **Rev:** Value above sprigs **Note:** With TM below value

Date	Mintage	VG	F	VF	XF	Unc
1915	—	100	200	400	500	—

KM# 714 3 CENTAVOS (Tres)
Copper, 20 mm. **Obv:** Bust left **Rev:** Value above sprigs **Note:** Small 3

Date	Mintage	VG	F	VF	XF	Unc
1915	—	6.00	10.00	15.00	30.00	—

KM# 715 5 CENTAVOS
Copper **Note:** JAN. 15 1915. incuse lettering

Date	Mintage	VG	F	VF	XF	Unc
1915 Rare	—	—	—	—	—	—

KM# 716 5 CENTAVOS
Copper **Obv:** Bust facing within circle **Rev:** Value above sprigs

Date	Mintage	VG	F	VF	XF	Unc
1915	—	—	—	—	8,000	—

KM# 717 5 CENTAVOS
Copper, 22 mm. **Obv:** Low relief bust left with date flanked by stars below **Rev:** Value above sprigs **Note:** Low relief with long, pointed truncation

Date	Mintage	VG	F	VF	XF	Unc
1915	—	1.50	3.00	4.50	10.00	—

KM# 718 5 CENTAVOS
Copper, 22 mm. **Obv:** Raised bust left with date flanked by stars below **Rev:** Value above sprigs **Note:** Heavy with short unfinished lapels

Date	Mintage	VG	F	VF	XF	Unc
1915	—	1.50	2.50	4.00	10.00	—

KM# 719 5 CENTAVOS
Copper, 22 mm. **Obv:** Raised bust left with date flanked by stars below **Rev:** Value above sprigs **Note:** Curved bottom

Date	Mintage	VG	F	VF	XF	Unc
1915	—	1.50	2.50	4.00	10.00	—

KM# 720 5 CENTAVOS
Copper, 22 mm. **Obv:** Bust left with date flanked by stars below **Rev:** Value above sprigs **Note:** Short truncation with closed lapels

Date	Mintage	VG	F	VF	XF	Unc
1915	—	1.50	3.00	4.50	10.00	—

KM# 721 5 CENTAVOS
Copper, 22 mm. **Obv:** Bust left with date flanked by stars below **Rev:** Value above sprigs **Note:** Short curved truncation

Date	Mintage	VG	F	VF	XF	Unc
1915	—	1.50	2.50	5.00	10.00	—

KM# 722 10 CENTAVOS
Copper **Obv:** Low relief bust left with date flanked by stars below **Rev:** Value above sprigs **Note:** Low relief with long pointed truncation

Date	Mintage	VG	F	VF	XF	Unc
1915	—	1.50	2.50	5.00	10.00	—

KM# 723 10 CENTAVOS
Copper **Obv:** Bust left with date flanked by stars below **Rev:** Value above sprigs **Note:** Obverse and reverse legend retrograde.

Date	Mintage	VG	F	VF	XF	Unc
1915 Rare	—	—	—	—	—	—

KM# 724 10 CENTAVOS
Copper, 26.5 mm. **Obv:** Raised bust left with date flanked by stars below **Rev:** Value above sprigs **Note:** Bold and unfinished truncation using 1 peso obverse die of km#740

Date	Mintage	VG	F	VF	XF	Unc
1915	—	3.00	5.00	7.00	10.00	—

KM# 725 10 CENTAVOS
Copper, 26.5 mm. **Obv:** Bust left with date flanked by stars below **Rev:** Value above sprigs **Note:** Heavy with short unfinished lapels centered high

Date	Mintage	VG	F	VF	XF	Unc
1915	—	1.50	2.50	4.00	10.00	—

KM# 726 10 CENTAVOS
Copper **Obv:** Raised bust left with date flanked by stars below **Rev:** Value above sprigs **Note:** Curved bottom

Date	Mintage	VG	F	VF	XF	Unc
1915	—	1.50	2.50	4.00	10.00	—

KM# 727.1 10 CENTAVOS
Copper **Obv:** Raised bust left with date flanked by stars below **Rev:** Value above sprigs **Note:** Short truncation with closed lapels

Date	Mintage	VG	F	VF	XF	Unc
1915	—	1.50	2.50	4.00	10.00	—

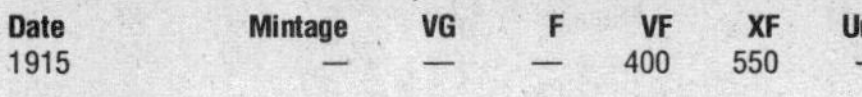

KM# 727.2 10 CENTAVOS
Copper **Obv:** Bust left with date flanked by stars below **Rev:** Value above sprigs **Note:** At present, only four pieces of this type are known. All are VF or better; T below bow with M below first leaf

Date	Mintage	VG	F	VF	XF	Unc
1915	—	—	—	400	550	—

KM# 727.3 10 CENTAVOS
Copper **Obv:** Raised bust left flanked by letters GV with date flanked by stars below **Rev:** Value above sprigs **Note:** This counterstamp appears on several different type host 10 cent coins.

Date	Mintage	VG	F	VF	XF	Unc
1915	—	100	200	300	400	—

Note: Letters GV correspond to General Garcia Vigil

KM# 730 20 CENTAVOS
Copper **Obv:** Bust left with date flanked by stars below **Rev:** Value above sprigs **Note:** 5th bust, heavy with short unfinished lapels using 20 Pesos obverse die

Date	Mintage	VG	F	VF	XF	Unc
1915	—	5.00	7.00	10.00	15.00	—

KM# 728 20 CENTAVOS
Silver, 19 mm. **Obv:** Low relief bust left with date flanked by stars below **Rev:** Value above sprigs **Note:** Low relief with long pointed truncation

Date	Mintage	VG	F	VF	XF	Unc
1915	—	800	1,000	1,500	3,000	—

KM# 728a 20 CENTAVOS
Copper, 19 mm. **Obv:** Bust left with date flanked by stars below **Rev:** Value above sprigs **Note:** Low relief with long pointed truncation

Date	Mintage	VG	F	VF	XF	Unc
1915 Rare	—	—	—	—	—	—

KM# 729.1 20 CENTAVOS
Copper **Obv:** Raised bust left with date flanked by stars below **Rev:** Value above sprigs **Note:** Unfinished truncation using 1 peso obverse die

Date	Mintage	VG	F	VF	XF	Unc
1915	—	1.50	3.00	4.50	10.00	—

KM# 729.2 20 CENTAVOS
Copper **Counterstamp:** Liberty cap **Obv:** Bust left with date flanked by stars below **Rev:** Value above sprigs **Note:** Counterstamp: Liberty cap and rays with bold unfinished truncation using 1 peso obverse die

Date	Mintage	VG	F	VF	XF	Unc
1915	—	100	150	300	350	—

KM# 731.1 20 CENTAVOS
Copper, 31 mm. **Obv:** Raised bust left with date flanked by stars below **Rev:** Value above sprigs **Note:** Curved bottom

Date	Mintage	VG	F	VF	XF	Unc
1915	—	1.50	2.50	5.00	10.00	—

KM# 731.2 20 CENTAVOS
Copper **Obv:** Raised bust left with date flanked by stars below **Rev:** Value above sprigs **Note:** Similar to KM#731.1 but with fourth bust.

Date	Mintage	VG	F	VF	XF	Unc
1915 Unique	—	—	—	—	—	—

KM# 732 20 CENTAVOS
Copper **Obv:** Raised bust left with date flanked by stars below **Rev:** Value above sprigs

Date	Mintage	VG	F	VF	XF	Unc
1915	—	1.50	2.50	4.00	10.00	—

KM# 733 20 CENTAVOS
Copper **Obv:** Bust left with date flanked by stars below **Rev:** Value above sprigs **Note:** 7th bust, short truncation with closed lapels

Date	Mintage	VG	F	VF	XF	Unc
1915	—	1.50	3.00	4.50	10.00	—

KM# 735 50 CENTAVOS
Silver, 22 mm. **Obv:** Raised bust left with date flanked by stars below **Rev:** Value above sprigs **Note:** Curved bottom

Date	Mintage	VG	F	VF	XF	Unc
1915	—	8.00	12.00	20.00	35.00	—

KM# 734 50 CENTAVOS
4.0700 g., Silver, 22 mm. **Obv:** Raised bust left with date flanked by stars below **Rev:** Value above sprigs **Note:** Heavy with short unfinished lapels

Date	Mintage	VG	F	VF	XF	Unc
1915	—	10.00	20.00	40.00	85.00	—

KM# 739 50 CENTAVOS
Billon **Obv:** Raised bust left with date flanked by stars below **Rev:** Value above sprigs **Note:** Ninth bust, high nearly straight truncation

Date	Mintage	VG	F	VF	XF	Unc
1915	—	—	—	—	4,000	—

KM# 739a 50 CENTAVOS
Copper **Obv:** Raised bust left with date flanked by stars below **Rev:** Value above sprigs **Note:** Ninth bust, high nearly straight truncation

Date	Mintage	VG	F	VF	XF	Unc
1915	—	—	—	—	—	—

KM# 736 50 CENTAVOS
Silver **Obv:** Bust left with date flanked by stars below **Rev:** Value above sprigs **Note:** Short truncation with closed lapels

Date	Mintage	VG	F	VF	XF	Unc
1915	—	6.00	9.00	15.00	25.00	—

KM# 737 50 CENTAVOS
4.5400 g., Silver, 22 mm. **Obv:** Bust left with date flanked by stars below **Rev:** Value above sprigs **Note:** Short truncation with pronounced curve

Date	Mintage	VG	F	VF	XF	Unc
1915	—	6.50	10.00	16.00	30.00	—

KM# 741 PESO (UN)
Silver **Obv:** Raised bust with date flanked by stars below **Rev:** Value above sprigs **Note:** Fifth bust, heavy with short unfinished lapels, centered high

Date	Mintage	VG	F	VF	XF	Unc
1915	—	6.00	9.00	20.00	25.00	—

KM# 740.1 PESO (UN)
Silver, 26 mm. **Obv:** Raised bust left with date flanked by stars below **Rev:** Written value above sprigs **Note:** Fourth bust with heavy unfinished truncation

Date	Mintage	VG	F	VF	XF	Unc
1915	—	3.00	5.00	10.00	20.00	—

KM# 740.2 PESO (UN)
Silver, 26 mm. **Obv:** Raised bust left with date flanked by stars below **Rev:** Written value above sprigs **Note:** Fourth bust with heavy unfinished truncation

Date	Mintage	VG	F	VF	XF	Unc
1915	—	150	300	400	600	—

KM# 742 PESO (UN)
Silver **Obv:** Low relief bust left with date flanked by stars below **Rev:** Value above sprigs **Note:** Sixth bust; Curved bottom line

Date	Mintage	VG	F	VF	XF	Unc
1915	—	6.00	9.00	20.00	25.00	—

KM# 742a PESO (UN)
Copper **Obv:** Low relief bust left with date flanked by stars below **Rev:** Value above sprigs **Note:** Sixth bust; Curved bottom line

Date	Mintage	VG	F	VF	XF	Unc
1915	—	—	—	—	500	—

KM# 743 PESO (UN)
Silver **Obv:** Low relief bust left with date flanked by stars below **Rev:** Value above sprigs **Note:** Seventh bust, short truncation with closed lapels

Date	Mintage	VG	F	VF	XF	Unc
1915	—	8.00	10.00	15.00	20.00	—

KM# 743a PESO (UN)
Silver **Obv:** Low relief bust left with date flanked by stars below **Rev:** Value above sprigs **Note:** Seventh bust, short truncation with closed lapels

Date	Mintage	VG	F	VF	XF	Unc
1915	—	35.00	75.00	150	200	—

KM# 744 2 PESOS (Dos)
Silver, 30 mm. **Obv:** Raised bust left with date flanked by stars below **Rev:** Value above sprigs **Note:** Fourth bust, using 1 peso obverse die

Date	Mintage	VG	F	VF	XF	Unc
1915	—	12.00	20.00	30.00	50.00	—

KM# 744a 2 PESOS (Dos)
Copper **Obv:** Raised bust left with date flanked by stars below **Rev:** Value above sprigs **Note:** Fourth bust, using 1 peso obverse die

Date	Mintage	VG	F	VF	XF	Unc
1915 Rare	—	—	—	—	—	—

KM# 745 2 PESOS (Dos)
Gold-Silver, 22 mm. **Obv:** Low relief bust left with date flanked by stars below **Rev:** Value above sprigs **Note:** 0.9020 Silver, 0.0100 Gold. Fifth bust, curved bottom 2 over pesos

Date	Mintage	VG	F	VF	XF	Unc
1915	—	12.00	20.00	40.00	60.00	—

KM# 745a 2 PESOS (Dos)
Copper **Obv:** Low relief bust left with date flanked by stars below **Rev:** Value above sprigs **Note:** Fifth bust, curved bottom 2 over pesos

Date	Mintage	VG	F	VF	XF	Unc
1915	—	75.00	100	150	200	—

KM# A746 2 PESOS (Dos)
Copper **Obv:** Raised bust left with date flanked by stars below **Rev:** Balance scale below liberty cap **Note:** Seventh bust, short truncation with closed lapels

Date	Mintage	VG	F	VF	XF	Unc
1915 Unique	—	—	—	—	—	—

KM# 746 2 PESOS (Dos)
Silver **Obv:** Raised bust left with date flanked by stars below **Rev:** Balance scale below liberty cap

Date	Mintage	VG	F	VF	XF	Unc
1915	—	10.00	15.00	30.00	55.00	—

KM# 746a 2 PESOS (Dos)
Copper **Obv:** Bust left with date flanked by stars below **Rev:** Balance scale below liberty cap

Date	Mintage	Good	VG	F	VF	XF
1915	—	—	150	200	600	900

KM# A747 2 PESOS (Dos)
Silver **Obv:** Bust left with date flanked by stars below **Rev:** Balance scale below liberty cap **Note:** Obverse die is free hand engraved.

Date	Mintage	VG	F	VF	XF	Unc
1915	—	—	—	185	275	—

KM# 747.1 2 PESOS (Dos)
13.4400 g., Silver, 33 mm. **Obv:** Bust left with date flanked by stars below **Rev:** Balance scale below liberty cap

Date	Mintage	VG	F	VF	XF	Unc
1915	—	10.00	15.00	30.00	60.00	—

KM# 747.2 2 PESOS (Dos)
13.4400 g., Silver, 33 mm. **Obv:** Bust left with date flanked by stars below **Rev:** Balance scale below liberty cap

Date	Mintage	VG	F	VF	XF	Unc
1915	—	10.00	20.00	30.00	60.00	—

KM# 747.3 2 PESOS (Dos)
13.4400 g., Silver, 33 mm. **Obv:** Bust left with date flanked by stars below **Rev:** Balance scale below liberty cap

Date	Mintage	VG	F	VF	XF	Unc
1915	—	10.00	20.00	30.00	60.00	—

KM# 748 2 PESOS (Dos)
0.9020 Silver, 22 mm. **Obv:** Bust left with date flanked by stars below **Rev:** Value above sprigs

Date	Mintage	VG	F	VF	XF	Unc
1915	—	12.00	20.00	40.00	60.00	—

KM# 749 2 PESOS (Dos)
Silver **Obv:** Head left with date flanked by stars below **Rev:** Value above sprigs

Date	Mintage	VG	F	VF	XF	Unc
1915 Unique	—	—	—	—	2,500	—

KM# 750 5 PESOS
0.1750 Gold, 19 mm. **Obv:** Bust left **Rev:** Value above sprigs **Note:** Third bust, heavy, with short unfinished lapels

Date	Mintage	VG	F	VF	XF	Unc
1915	—	150	200	300	450	—

KM# 750a 5 PESOS
Copper **Obv:** Bust left **Rev:** Value above sprigs **Note:** Third bust, heavy, with short unfinished lapels

Date	Mintage	VG	F	VF	XF	Unc
1915 Unique	—	—	—	—	—	—

KM# 751 5 PESOS
16.7700 g., Silver, 30 mm. **Obv:** Low relief bust left with date flanked by stars below **Rev:** Value above sprigs **Note:** Seventh bust, short truncation with closed lapels

Date	Mintage	VG	F	VF	XF	Unc
1915	—	50.00	100	200	250	—

KM# 751a 5 PESOS
Copper **Obv:** Low relief bust left with date flanked by stars below **Rev:** Value above sprigs **Note:** Seventh bust, short truncation with closed lapels

Date	Mintage	VG	F	VF	XF	Unc
1915	—	125	200	300	800	—

KM# A752 10 PESOS
0.1500 Gold **Obv:** Bust left with date flanked by stars below **Rev:** Value above sprigs

Date	Mintage	VG	F	VF	XF	Unc
1915 Rare	—	—	—	—	—	—

KM# 752 10 PESOS
0.1750 Gold, 23 mm. **Obv:** Bust left with date flanked by stars below **Rev:** Value above sprigs

Date	Mintage	VG	F	VF	XF	Unc
1915	—	200	300	400	600	—

KM# 752a 10 PESOS
Copper **Obv:** Bust left with date flanked by stars below **Rev:** Value above sprigs

Date	Mintage	VG	F	VF	XF	Unc
1915	—	500	1,000	1,500	3,000	—

KM# A753 20 PESOS
0.1500 Gold **Obv:** Bust left with date flanked by stars below **Rev:** Value above sprigs **Note:** Fourth bust

Date	Mintage	VG	F	VF	XF	Unc
1915 Unique	—	—	—	—	—	—

KM# 753 20 PESOS
0.1750 Gold **Obv:** Bust left with date flanked by stars below **Rev:** Value above sprigs

Date	Mintage	VG	F	VF	XF	Unc
1915	—	400	500	800	1,000	—

KM# 754 20 PESOS
0.1750 Gold, 27 mm. **Obv:** Bust left with date flanked by stars below **Rev:** Value above sprigs

Date	Mintage	VG	F	VF	XF	Unc
1915	—	200	300	500	800	—

KM# 755 60 PESOS
50.0000 g., 0.8590 Gold **Obv:** Head left within 3/4 wreath **Rev:** Balance scale below liberty cap **Edge:** Reeded

Date	Mintage	F	VF	XF	Unc	BU
1916 Rare	—	—	8,000	15,000	22,000	—

KM# 755a 60 PESOS
Silver **Obv:** Head left within 3/4 wreath **Rev:** Balance scales below liberty cap **Edge:** Reeded

Date	Mintage	F	VF	XF	Unc	BU
1916	—	—	—	—	1,800	—

KM# 755b 60 PESOS
Copper **Obv:** Head left within 3/4 wreath **Rev:** Balance scales below liberty cap **Edge:** Plain

Date	Mintage	F	VF	XF	Unc	BU
1916	—	—	—	1,000	1,800	—

PUEBLA

A state of central Mexico. Puebla was a state that occasionally saw Zapata forces active within its boundaries. Also active, and an issuer of coins, was the Madero brigade who issued coins with their name two years after Madero's death. The state issue of 2, 5, 10 and 20 Centavos saw limited circulation and recent hoards have been found of some values.

CHICONCUAUTLA

Madero Brigade

REVOLUTIONARY COINAGE

KM# 756 10 CENTAVOS
6.7300 g., Copper, 27 mm. **Obv:** Date below national arms **Rev:** Letters X and C entwined

Date	Mintage	VG	F	VF	XF	Unc
1915	—	7.50	12.50	17.50	25.00	—

KM# 757 20 CENTAVOS
Copper, 28 mm. **Obv:** Date below national arms **Rev:** Value **Note:** Varieties exist.

Date	Mintage	VG	F	VF	XF	Unc
1915	—	2.50	4.00	6.50	12.00	—

KM# 758 20 CENTAVOS
Copper, 28 mm. **Obv:** Date below national arms **Rev:** Value

Date	Mintage	VG	F	VF	XF	Unc
1915	—	2.50	4.00	6.50	12.00	—

TETELA DEL ORO Y OCAMPO

REVOLUTIONARY COINAGE

KM# 759 2 CENTAVOS
Copper, 16 mm. **Obv:** National arms above date **Rev:** Value

Date	Mintage	VG	F	VF	XF	Unc
1915	—	12.50	20.00	28.00	45.00	—
1915 Restrikes	—	—	1.00	1.50	2.00	—

KM# 760 2 CENTAVOS
Copper, 20 mm. **Obv:** National arms within beaded circle **Rev:** Value within beaded circle **Rev. Legend:** E. DE PU.

Date	Mintage	VG	F	VF	XF	Unc
1915	—	15.00	25.00	35.00	75.00	—

KM# 761 2 CENTAVOS
Copper, 20 mm. **Obv:** National arms within beaded circle **Rev:** Value within beaded circle **Rev. Legend:** E. DE PUE.

Date	Mintage	VG	F	VF	XF	Unc
1915	—	9.00	20.00	25.00	50.00	—

KM# 762 5 CENTAVOS
Copper, 21 mm. **Obv:** National arms within beaded circle **Rev:** Value within beaded circle

Date	Mintage	VG	F	VF	XF	Unc
1915	—	50.00	125	200	300	—

KM# 764 20 CENTAVOS
Copper, 24 mm. **Obv:** National arms **Rev:** Value above sprigs

Date	Mintage	VG	F	VF	XF	Unc
1915	—	50.00	100	150	225	—

TRIAL STRIKES

KM#	Date	Mintage	Identification	Mkt Val
TS1	1915	—	10 Centavos. Copper. Uniface, KM#763.	475
TS2	1915	—	10 Centavos. Brass. Uniface, KM#763.	750
TS3	1915	—	10 Centavos. Copper. KM#761. Eagle.	1,600

SINALOA

A state along the west coast of Mexico. The cast pieces of this state have been attributed to two people - Generals Rafael Buelna and Juan Carrasco. The cap and rays 8 Reales is usually attributed to General Buelna and the rest of the series to Carrasco. Because of their crude nature it is questionable whether separate series or mints can be determined.

BUELNA / CARRASCO

CAST COINAGE

Revolutionary

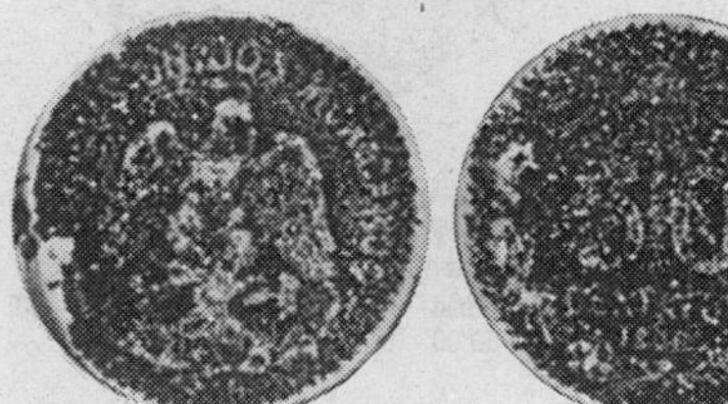

KM# 766 50 CENTAVOS
Cast Silver, 29-31 mm. **Obv:** National arms **Rev:** Numeral value within wreath **Note:** Sand molded using regular 50 Centavos, KM#445. Size varies, Weight varies 12.81-14.8g.

Date	Mintage	Good	VG	F	VF	XF
ND(1905-1918)	—	200	300	—	—	—

COUNTERMARKED COINAGE

Revolutionary

These are all crude sand cast coins using regular coins to prepare the mold. Prices below give a range for how much of the original coin from which the mold was prepared is visible.

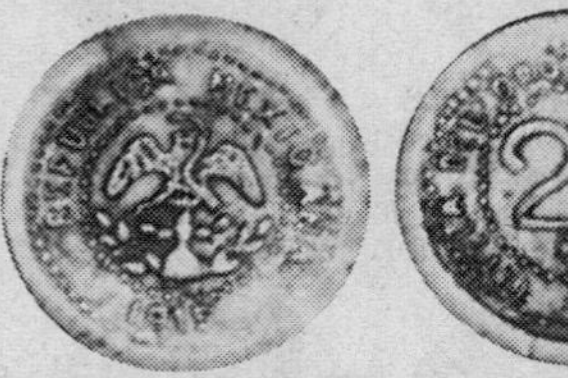

KM# 765 20 CENTAVOS

Cast Silver **Obv:** National arms within beaded circle **Rev:** Value within beaded circle **Note:** Sand molded using regular 20 Centavos.

CM Date	Host Date	Good	VG	F	VF	XF
ND(ca.1915)	ND(1898-1905)	200	300	—	—	—

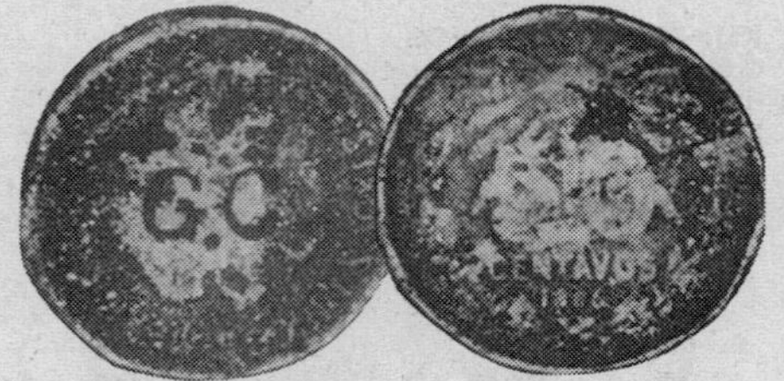

KM# 767 50 CENTAVOS

Cast Silver **Countermark:** G.C. **Obv:** National arms with additional countermark **Rev:** Value and date within wreath with liberty cap above **Note:** Sand molded using regular 50 Centavos, KM#445.

CM Date	Host Date	Good	VG	F	VF	XF
ND	ND(1905-1918)	100	150	200	300	—

KM# 768.1 PESO

Cast Silver, 38.8-39 mm. **Note:** Sand molded using regular 8 Reales, KM#377. Size varies. Weight varies 26-33.67g.

CM Date	Host Date	Good	VG	F	VF	XF
ND(ca.1915)	ND(1824-97)	17.50	35.00	45.00	55.00	—

KM# 768.2 PESO

Cast Silver, 38.5-39 mm. **Countermark:** G.C. **Obv:** With additional countermark **Note:** Sand molded using regular 8 Reales, KM#377. Size varies. Weight varies 26-33.67g.

CM Date	Host Date	Good	VG	F	VF	XF
ND(ca.1915)	ND(1824-97)	25.00	45.00	100	150	—

KM# 770 PESO

Cast Silver, 38.5 mm. **Countermark:** G.C **Obv:** National arms with additional countermark **Rev:** Liberty cap with additional countermark **Note:** Sand molded using regular Peso, KM#409.

CM Date	Host Date	Good	VG	F	VF	XF
ND(ca.1915)	ND(1898-1909)	30.00	60.00	140	175	—

MOLDOVA

The Republic of Moldova (formerly the Moldavian S.S.R.) is bordered in the north, east and south by the Ukraine and on the west by Romania. It has an area of 13,000 sq. mi. (33,700 sq. km.) and a population of 4.4 million. The capital is Chisinau. Agricultural products are mainly cereals, grapes, tobacco, sugar beets and fruits. Food processing, clothing, building materials and agricultural machinery manufacturing dominate the industry.

The historical Romanian principality of Moldova was established in the 14th century. It fell under Turkish suzerainty in the 16th century. From 1812 to 1918 Russians occupied the eastern portion of Moldova, which they named Bessarabia. In March 1918 the Bessarabian legislature voted in favor of reunification with Romania. At the Paris Peace Conference in 1920 United States, France, U.K., and Italy a.s.o officially recognized the union. The new Soviet government did not accept the union. In 1924, due to Soviet pressure against Romania a Moldavian Autonomous Soviet Socialist Republic (A.S.S.R.) was established within the USSR on the border strip that extends east of Nistru River (today it is Transdniestra or Transdniester).

Following the Molotov-Ribbentrop Pact (1939), the Soviet - German agreement, which divided Eastern Europe, the Soviet forces, reoccupied the region in June 1940 and the Moldavian S.S.R. was proclaimed. The Transdniestra region was transferred to the new republic, while Ukrainian S.S.R. obtained possession of southern part of Bessarabia. Romanian forces liberated the region in 1941. The Soviets reconquered the territory (in 1944).

A declaration of republican sovereignty was adopted in June 1990 and in Aug. 1991 the area was renamed Moldova, an independent republic. In Dec. 1991 Moldova became a member of the C.I.S. In 1992, as a result of Russian involvement, Transdniestra seceded from Moldova. In May 1992 fighting began between Moldavian separatists (Romanians) and rebels aided by contingents of Cossacks and the Russian14th Army. The Moldavian government made several futile requests for United Nations intervention. On July 3, 1992, Russian and Moldavian presidents agreed upon a neutral demarcation line with the withdrawal of Russian forces from Transdniestra. This status will remain until a more feasible constitution is proclaimed.

RULERS

Romanian, until 1940

MONETARY SYSTEM

100 Bani = 1 Leu

REPUBLIC

DECIMAL COINAGE

KM# 1 BAN

0.0700 g., Aluminum, 14.5 mm. **Obv:** National arms **Rev:** Value divides date above monogram **Edge:** Plain

Date	Mintage	F	VF	XF	Unc	BU
1993	—	—	—	—	0.20	0.40
1995	—	—	—	—	0.20	0.40
1996	—	—	—	—	0.25	0.50
2000	—	—	—	—	0.25	0.50

KM# 2 5 BANI

0.7800 g., Aluminum, 16 mm. **Obv:** National arms **Rev:** Monogram divides sprigs below value and date **Edge:** Plain

Date	Mintage	F	VF	XF	Unc	BU
1993	—	—	—	—	0.30	0.50
1995	—	—	—	—	0.30	0.50
1996	—	—	—	—	0.30	0.50
1999	—	—	—	—	0.30	0.50
2000	—	—	—	—	0.30	0.50

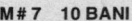

KM# 7 10 BANI

0.8400 g., Aluminum, 16.6 mm. **Obv:** National arms **Rev:** Value, date and monogram **Edge:** Plain

Date	Mintage	F	VF	XF	Unc	BU
1995	—	—	—	—	0.40	0.60
1996	—	—	—	—	0.40	0.60
1997	—	—	—	—	0.40	0.60
1998	—	—	—	—	0.40	0.60
2000	—	—	—	—	0.40	0.60

KM# 3 25 BANI

0.9200 g., Aluminum, 17.5 mm. **Obv:** National arms **Rev:** Monogram divides sprigs below value and date **Edge:** Plain

Date	Mintage	F	VF	XF	Unc	BU
1993	—	—	—	—	0.50	0.75
1995	—	—	—	—	0.50	0.75
1999	—	—	—	—	0.50	0.75
2000	—	—	—	—	0.50	0.75

KM# 4 50 BANI

Aluminum **Obv:** National arms **Rev:** Monogram divides sprigs below date and value

Date	Mintage	F	VF	XF	Unc	BU
1993	—	—	—	—	0.75	1.00

KM# 10 50 BANI

3.1000 g., Brass-Clad Steel, 19 mm. **Obv:** National arms **Rev:** Value and date within grapevine **Edge:** Reeded

Date	Mintage	F	VF	XF	Unc	BU
1997	—	—	—	—	1.50	2.00

KM# 5 LEU

Nickel Clad Steel **Obv:** National arms **Rev:** Value divides date with monogram above

Date	Mintage	F	VF	XF	Unc	BU
1992	—	—	—	—	1.50	2.00

KM# 6 5 LEI

Nickel Clad Steel **Obv:** National arms **Rev:** Value flanked by monogram and date

Date	Mintage	F	VF	XF	Unc	BU
1993	—	—	—	—	3.50	4.00

KM# 11 50 LEI

16.6300 g., 0.9850 Silver 0.5266 oz. ASW, 30 mm. **Subject:** Manastirea Rudi **Obv:** National arms **Rev:** Monastary building **Edge:** Plain

Date	Mintage	F	VF	XF	Unc	BU
2000 Proof	—	Value: 35.00				

KM# 8 100 LEI
28.2800 g., 0.9250 Silver .8411 oz. ASW **Subject:** 5th Anniversary of Independence **Obv:** National arms **Rev:** Flying stork with grapes

Date	Mintage	F	VF	XF	Unc	BU
1996	20,000	Value: 55.00				

KM# 9 100 LEI
28.2800 g., 0.9250 Silver .8411 oz. ASW **Subject:** First Olympic Games Participation **Obv:** National arms **Rev:** Two men in a canoe

Date	Mintage	F	VF	XF	Unc	BU
1996	20,000	Value: 55.00				

KM# 15 100 LEI
31.1000 g., 0.9250 Silver 0.9249 oz. ASW, 37 mm. **Obv:** National arms **Rev:** Crowned bust facing flanked by dates and shield **Edge:** Plain

Date	Mintage	F	VF	XF	Unc	BU
2000 Proof	1,000	Value: 60.00				

KM# 24 100 LEI
31.1000 g., 0.9250 Silver 0.9249 oz. ASW, 37 mm. **Subject:** Battle of Vaslui **Obv:** National arms above value **Rev:** King and soldiers **Edge:** Plain

Date	Mintage	F	VF	XF	Unc	BU
2000 Proof	1,000	Value: 60.00				

MONACO

The Principality of Monaco, located on the Mediterranean coast nine miles from Nice, has an area of 0.58 sq. mi. (1.9 sq. km.) and a population of 26,000. Capital: Monaco-Ville. The economy is based on tourism and the manufacture of cosmetics, gourmet foods and highly specialized electronics. Monaco also derives its revenue from a tobacco monopoly and the sale of postage stamps for philatelic purpose. Gambling in Monte Carlo accounts for only a small fraction of the country's revenue.

Monaco derives its name from Monoikos', the Greek surname for Hercules, the mythological strong man who, according to legend, formed the Monacan headland during one of his twelve labors. Monaco has been ruled by the Grimaldi dynasty since 1297 - Prince Albert II, the present and 32nd monarch of Monaco, is still of that line - except for a period during the French Revolution until Napoleon's downfall when the Principality was annexed to France. Since 1865, Monaco has maintained a customs union with France which guarantees its privileged position as long as the royal line remains intact. Under the new constitution proclaimed on December 17, 1962, the Prince shares his power with an 18-member unicameral National Council.

RULERS
Albert I, 1889-1922
Louis II, 1922-1949
Rainier III, 1949-2005

MINT MARKS
M - Monaco
A – Paris

MINT PRIVY MARKS
(a) - Paris (privy marks only)
(p) - Thunderbolt - Poissy

MONETARY SYSTEM
10 Centimes = 1 Decime
10 Decimes = 1 Franc

PRINCIPALITY

DECIMAL COINAGE

10 Centimes = 1 Decime; 10 Decimes = 1 Franc

KM# 110 50 CENTIMES
Aluminum-Bronze **Ruler:** Louis II **Obv:** Hercules shooting bow to right **Rev:** Shield below value within circle

Date	Mintage	F	VF	XF	Unc	BU
1924 (p)	150,000	3.50	8.00	18.00	40.00	70.00

KM# 113 50 CENTIMES
Aluminum-Bronze **Ruler:** Louis II **Obv:** Hercules shooting bow to right **Rev:** Shield below value within circle

Date	Mintage	F	VF	XF	Unc	BU
1926 (p)	100,000	4.00	9.00	20.00	45.00	75.00

KM# 111 FRANC
Aluminum-Bronze **Ruler:** Louis II **Obv:** Hercules shooting bow to right **Rev:** Shield below value within circle

Date	Mintage	F	VF	XF	Unc	BU
1924 (p)	150,000	3.00	7.00	14.00	30.00	60.00

KM# 114 FRANC
Aluminum-Bronze **Ruler:** Louis II **Obv:** Hercules shooting bow to right **Rev:** Shield below value within circle

Date	Mintage	F	VF	XF	Unc	BU
1926 (p)	100,000	4.00	9.00	16.00	35.00	65.00

KM# 120 FRANC
Aluminum, 22.9 mm. **Ruler:** Louis II **Obv:** Head left **Obv. Designer:** L. Maubert **Rev:** Crowned mantled arms flanked by value below

Date	Mintage	F	VF	XF	Unc	BU
ND(1943) (a)	2,500,000	0.50	1.00	2.00	4.50	7.00

KM# 120a FRANC
Aluminum-Bronze, 22.9 mm. **Ruler:** Louis II **Obv:** Head left **Obv. Designer:** L. Maubert **Rev:** Crowned mantled arms flanked by value below

Date	Mintage	F	VF	XF	Unc	BU
ND(1945) (a)	1,509,000	0.50	1.00	2.00	5.00	8.00

KM# 112 2 FRANCS
Aluminum-Bronze **Ruler:** Louis II **Obv:** Hercules shooting bow to right **Rev:** Shield below value within circle

Date	Mintage	F	VF	XF	Unc	BU
1924 (p)	75,000	8.00	14.00	30.00	75.00	100

KM# 115 2 FRANCS
Aluminum-Bronze **Ruler:** Louis II **Obv:** Hercules shooting bow to right **Rev:** Shield below value within circle

Date	Mintage	F	VF	XF	Unc	BU
1926 (p)	75,000	7.00	12.00	25.00	70.00	90.00

KM# 121 2 FRANCS
Aluminum **Ruler:** Louis II **Obv:** Head left **Rev:** Crowned mantled arms flanked by value below

Date	Mintage	F	VF	XF	Unc	BU
ND(1943) (a)	1,250,000	0.75	1.50	5.00	10.00	15.00

KM# 121a 2 FRANCS
Aluminum-Bronze **Ruler:** Louis II **Obv:** Head left **Rev:** Crowned mantles arms flanked by value below

Date	Mintage	F	VF	XF	Unc	BU
ND(1945) (a)	1,080,000	0.50	1.00	2.50	6.00	10.00

KM# 122 5 FRANCS
Aluminum **Ruler:** Louis II **Obv:** Head left **Rev:** Crowned mantled arms flanked by value below

Date	Mintage	F	VF	XF	Unc	BU
1945 (a)	1,000,000	1.50	3.00	7.00	15.00	20.00

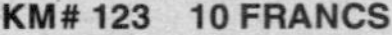

KM# 123 10 FRANCS
Copper-Nickel, 26 mm. **Ruler:** Louis II **Obv:** Bust left
Rev: Crowned mantled arms above value flanked by sprigs

Date	Mintage	F	VF	XF	Unc	BU
1946 (a)	1,000,000	1.50	3.00	6.00	12.50	20.00

KM# 130 10 FRANCS
Aluminum-Bronze **Ruler:** Rainier III **Obv:** Head left within circle
Rev: Crowned shield flanked by value

Date	Mintage	F	VF	XF	Unc	BU
1950 (a)	500,000	0.50	1.00	2.00	4.00	6.00
1951 (a)	500,000	0.50	1.00	2.00	4.00	6.00

KM# 124 20 FRANCS (Vingt)
Copper-Nickel **Ruler:** Louis II **Obv:** Bust left **Rev:** Crowned mantled arms above value flanked by sprigs

Date	Mintage	F	VF	XF	Unc	BU
1947 (a)	1,000,000	2.00	4.00	8.00	20.00	30.00

KM# 131 20 FRANCS (Vingt)
Aluminum-Bronze **Ruler:** Rainier III **Obv:** Head left divides circle
Rev: Crowned shield flanked by value

Date	Mintage	F	VF	XF	Unc	BU
1950 (a)	500,000	0.65	1.25	2.50	6.00	8.00
1951 (a)	500,000	0.65	1.25	2.50	6.00	8.00

KM# 132 50 FRANCS (Cinquante)
Aluminum-Bronze **Ruler:** Rainier III **Obv:** Head left divides circle
Rev: Armored equestrian divides circle above value

Date	Mintage	F	VF	XF	Unc	BU
1950 (a)	500,000	1.50	3.00	5.00	12.00	15.00

KM# 105 100 FRANCS (Cent)
32.2580 g., 0.9000 Gold .9335 oz. AGW **Ruler:** Albert I
Obv: Head left **Obv. Legend:** ALBERT I PRINCE.... **Rev:** Crowned oval arms within wreath with ribbon above

Date	Mintage	F	VF	XF	Unc	BU
1901A	15,000	—	BV	650	800	950
1904A	10,000	—	BV	650	800	950

KM# 133 100 FRANCS (Cent)
Copper-Nickel **Ruler:** Rainier III **Obv:** Head left divides circle
Rev: Armored equestrian divides circle above value

Date	Mintage	F	VF	XF	Unc	BU
1950 (a)	500,000	2.00	4.00	8.00	18.00	30.00

KM# 134 100 FRANCS (Cent)
Copper-Nickel **Ruler:** Rainier III **Obv:** Head left **Rev:** Value below crowned shield

Date	Mintage	F	VF	XF	Unc	BU
1956 (a)	500,000	1.50	2.50	5.50	15.00	25.00

KM# 176 100 FRANCS
15.0000 g., 0.9500 Silver 0.4581 oz. ASW, 31 mm.
Ruler: Rainier III **Subject:** 700th Anniversary - Grimaldi Dynasty
Obv: Armored equestrian **Rev:** Robed figure drawing sword at castle drawbridge **Edge:** Plain

Date	Mintage	F	VF	XF	Unc	BU
ND(1997)	30,000	—	—	—	55.00	75.00

REFORM COINAGE

100 Old Francs = 1 New Franc

KM# 155 CENTIME
Stainless Steel **Ruler:** Rainier III **Obv:** Crowned shield
Rev: Sprig divides value and date

Date	Mintage	F	VF	XF	Unc	BU
1976 (a)	25,000	—	0.15	0.30	4.00	—
1977 (a)	25,000	—	0.15	0.30	4.00	—
1978 (a)	50,000	—	0.15	0.30	4.00	—
1979 (a)	50,000	—	0.15	0.30	4.00	—
1982 (a)	10,000	—	0.15	0.30	4.00	—
1995 (a)	—	—	0.15	0.30	4.00	—

KM# 156 5 CENTIMES
Copper-Aluminum-Nickel **Ruler:** Rainier III **Obv:** Head right
Rev: Figure with hand on shield divides crown and value
Designer: G. Simon

Date	Mintage	F	VF	XF	Unc	BU
1976 (a)	25,000	—	0.20	0.40	4.50	—
1977 (a)	25,000	—	0.20	0.40	4.50	—
1978 (a)	75,000	—	0.20	0.40	4.50	—
1979 (a)	75,000	—	0.20	0.40	4.50	—
1982 (a)	10,000	—	0.20	0.40	4.50	—
1995 (a)	—	—	0.20	0.40	4.50	—

KM# 142 10 CENTIMES
Aluminum-Bronze **Ruler:** Rainier III **Obv:** Head right
Obv. Designer: G. Simon **Rev:** Figure with hand on shield divides crown and value

Date	Mintage	F	VF	XF	Unc	BU
1962 (a)	750,000	—	0.15	0.30	1.50	—
1974 (a)	172,000	—	0.15	0.30	2.25	—
1975 (a)	172,000	—	0.15	0.30	2.25	—
1976 (a)	172,000	—	0.15	0.30	2.25	—
1977 (a)	172,000	—	0.15	0.30	2.25	—
1978 (a)	300,000	—	0.15	0.30	2.50	—
1979 (a)	300,000	—	0.15	0.30	2.50	—
1982 (a)	100,000	—	0.15	0.30	2.50	—
1995 (a)	—	—	0.15	0.30	2.50	—

KM# 143 20 CENTIMES
Aluminum-Bronze, 23.5 mm. **Ruler:** Rainier III **Obv:** Head right
Obv. Designer: G. Simon **Rev:** Figure with hand on shield divides crown and value

Date	Mintage	F	VF	XF	Unc	BU
1962 (a)	750,000	—	0.25	0.50	1.75	—
1974 (a)	104,000	—	0.25	0.50	2.75	—
1975 (a)	97,000	—	0.25	0.50	2.75	—
1976 (a)	103,000	—	0.25	0.50	2.75	—
1977 (a)	97,000	—	0.25	0.50	2.75	—
1978 (a)	25,000	—	0.25	0.50	2.75	—
1979 (a)	25,000	—	0.25	0.50	2.75	—
1982 (a)	100,000	—	0.25	0.50	2.75	—
1995 (a)	30,000	—	0.25	0.50	2.75	—

KM# 144 50 CENTIMES
Aluminum-Bronze **Ruler:** Rainier III **Obv:** Head right
Obv. Designer: G. Simon **Rev:** Figure with hand on shield divides crown and value

Date	Mintage	F	VF	XF	Unc	BU
1962 (a)	375,000	—	1.25	2.50	4.50	—

KM# 145 1/2 FRANC
Nickel, 20.5 mm. **Ruler:** Rainier III **Obv:** Head right
Obv. Designer: R. Cochet **Rev:** Crown overlapping shield, value at lower left

Date	Mintage	F	VF	XF	Unc	BU
1965 (a)	375,000	0.30	0.60	1.25	2.50	—
1968 (a)	125,000	0.30	0.60	1.25	2.50	—
1974 (a)	62,500	0.35	0.70	1.50	3.50	—
1975 (a)	62,500	0.35	0.70	1.50	3.50	—
1976 (a)	62,500	0.35	0.70	1.50	3.50	—

Date	Mintage	F	VF	XF	Unc	BU
1977 (a)	62,500	0.35	0.70	1.50	3.50	—
1978 (a)	230,000	0.30	0.60	1.25	2.75	—
1979 (a)	230,000	0.30	0.60	1.25	2.75	—
1982 (a)	460,000	0.30	0.60	1.25	2.75	—
1989 (a)	10,000	0.30	0.60	1.25	2.75	—
1995 (a)	30,000	0.30	0.60	1.25	2.75	—

KM# 140 FRANC

Nickel **Ruler:** Rainier III **Obv:** Head right **Obv. Designer:** R. Cochet **Rev:** Crown overlapping shield, value at lower left

Date	Mintage	F	VF	XF	Unc	BU
1960 (a)	500,000	0.35	0.70	1.50	3.25	—
1966 (a)	175,000	0.40	0.80	1.75	4.00	—
1968 (a)	250,000	0.40	0.80	1.75	4.00	—
1974 (a)	194,000	0.40	0.80	1.75	4.00	—
1975 (a)	195,000	0.40	0.80	1.75	4.00	—
1976 (a)	193,000	0.40	0.80	1.75	4.00	—
1977 (a)	188,000	0.40	0.80	1.75	4.00	—
1978 (a)	280,000	0.40	0.80	1.75	3.50	—
1979 (a)	280,000	0.40	0.80	1.75	3.50	—
1982 (a)	525,000	0.40	0.80	1.75	3.50	—
1986 (a)	50,000	0.35	0.70	1.50	3.00	—
1989 (a)	50,000	0.35	0.70	1.50	2.75	—
1995 (a)	30,000	0.35	0.70	1.50	2.75	—

KM# 157 2 FRANCS

Nickel, 26.5 mm. **Ruler:** Rainier III **Obv:** Head right **Obv. Designer:** G. Simon **Rev:** Monogram within crowned shield

Date	Mintage	F	VF	XF	Unc	BU
1979 (a)	162,000	0.60	0.85	1.75	4.00	—
1981 (a)	275,000	0.60	0.85	1.75	4.00	—
1982 (a)	446,000	0.60	0.85	1.75	4.00	—
1995 (a)	—	0.60	0.85	1.75	4.00	—

Note: May not exist in this date

KM# 166 2 FRANCS

Nickel, 26.5 mm. **Ruler:** Rainier III **Obv:** Head left

Date	Mintage	F	VF	XF	Unc	BU
1995 (a)	—	0.60	0.85	1.75	4.00	—

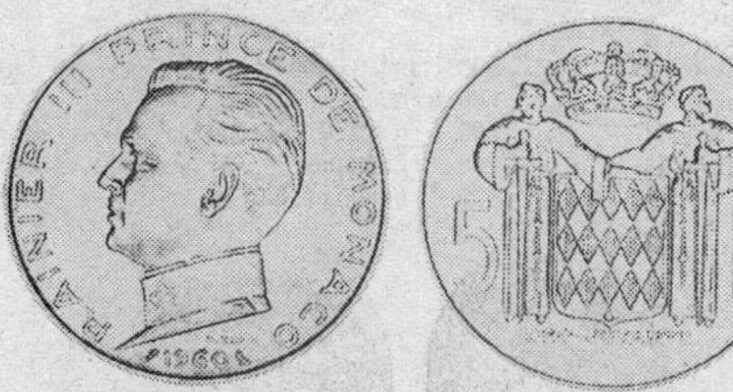

KM# 141 5 FRANCS

12.0000 g., 0.8350 Silver .3221 oz. ASW **Ruler:** Rainier III **Obv:** Head left **Rev:** Crowned arms with supporters flanked by value

Date	Mintage	F	VF	XF	Unc	BU
1960 (a)	125,000	—	—	7.50	10.00	—
1966 (a)	125,000	—	—	7.50	10.00	—

KM# 150 5 FRANCS

Nickel Clad Copper-Nickel **Ruler:** Rainier III **Obv:** Head right **Obv. Designer:** Raymond Joly **Rev:** Value below monogram and crown, all flanked by lined designs

Date	Mintage	F	VF	XF	Unc	BU
1971 (a)	250,000	—	1.50	2.50	4.50	—
1974 (a)	250,000	—	1.50	2.50	4.50	—
1975 (a)	14,000	—	2.50	6.00	12.50	—
1976 (a)	14,000	—	2.50	6.00	12.50	—
1977 (a)	14,500	—	2.00	5.00	10.00	—
1978 (a)	10,000	—	2.00	5.00	10.00	—

Date	Mintage	F	VF	XF	Unc	BU
1979 (a)	10,000	—	2.00	5.00	10.00	—
1982 (a)	152,000	—	2.00	5.00	10.00	—
1989	35,000	—	2.00	5.00	10.00	—
1995 (a)	30,000	—	2.00	5.00	10.00	—

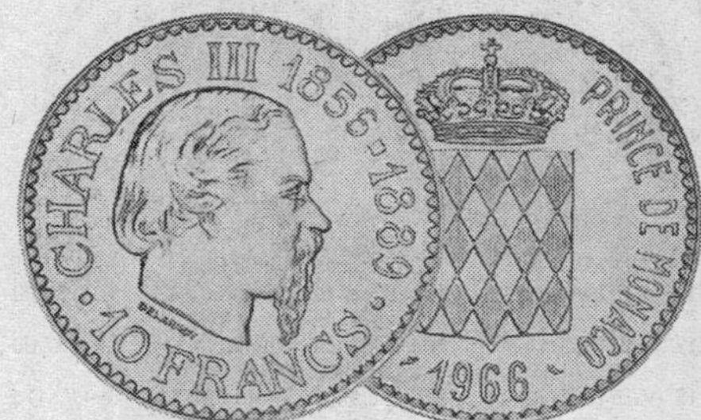

KM# 146 10 FRANCS

25.0000 g., 0.9000 Silver .7234 oz. ASW **Ruler:** Rainier III **Subject:** 100th Anniversary - Accession of Charles III **Obv:** Head right **Rev:** Crowned shield **Rev. Designer:** Delannoy

Date	Mintage	F	VF	XF	Unc	BU
1966 (a)	62,500	—	—	—	21.50	37.00

KM# 151 10 FRANCS

Copper-Nickel-Aluminum **Ruler:** Rainier III **Subject:** 25th Anniversary of Reign **Obv:** Head left **Obv. Designer:** G. Simon **Rev:** Monogram within crowned arms with supporters

Date	Mintage	F	VF	XF	Unc	BU
ND(1974) (a)	25,000	—	2.50	4.50	8.00	—

KM# 154 10 FRANCS

Copper-Nickel-Aluminum **Ruler:** Rainier III **Obv:** Head left **Rev:** Monogram within crowned arms with supporters

Date	Mintage	F	VF	XF	Unc	BU
1975 (a)	16,000	—	2.25	3.75	8.00	—
1976 (a)	16,000	—	2.50	4.00	9.00	—
1977 (a)	18,000	—	2.25	3.25	5.50	—
1978 (a)	190,000	—	2.25	3.25	5.50	—
1979 (a)	190,000	—	2.25	3.25	5.50	—
1981 (a)	230,000	—	2.25	3.25	5.50	—
1982 (a)	230,000	—	2.25	3.25	5.50	—

KM# 160 10 FRANCS

Copper-Nickel-Aluminum **Ruler:** Rainier III **Obv:** Head left **Rev:** Single rose divides value

Date	Mintage	F	VF	XF	Unc	BU
1982 (a)	30,000	—	—	—	12.50	—

KM# 163 10 FRANCS

Bi-Metallic Steel center in Aluminum-Bronze ring **Ruler:** Rainier III **Obv:** Value and monogram within circle **Rev:** Armored knight right within circle

Date	Mintage	F	VF	XF	Unc	BU
1989 (a)	100,000	—	—	—	9.00	10.00
1991 (a)	250,000	—	—	—	14.00	15.00
1992 (a)	250,000	—	—	—	12.50	13.50
1993 (a)	250,000	—	—	—	14.00	15.00
1994 (a)	250,000	—	—	—	14.00	15.00
1995 (a)	250,000	—	—	—	9.00	10.00
1996 (a)	250,000	—	—	—	9.00	10.00
1997 (a)	250,000	—	—	—	9.00	10.00
1998 (a)	250,000	—	—	—	9.00	10.00
2000 (a)	240,000	—	—	—	9.00	10.00

KM# 165 20 FRANCS

Tri-Metallic Copper-Aluminum-Nickel center; Nickel ring; Copper-Aluminum-Nickel outer ring, 26.8 mm. **Ruler:** Rainier III **Obv:** Value and monogram within circle **Rev:** Prince's palace within circle with crown above **Designer:** R. B. Baron

Date	Mintage	F	VF	XF	Unc	BU
1992 (a)	100,000	—	—	—	15.00	16.50
1995 (a)	—	—	—	—	15.00	16.50
1997 (a)	120,000	—	—	—	15.00	16.50

KM# 152.1 50 FRANCS

30.0000 g., 0.9000 Silver .8681 oz. ASW **Ruler:** Rainier III **Subject:** 25th Anniversary of Reign **Obv:** Bust right **Rev:** Crowned monograms divide diamonds **Edge:** Commemorative inscription

Date	Mintage	F	VF	XF	Unc	BU
1974 (a)	25,000	—	—	—	42.00	55.00

KM# 152.2 50 FRANCS

30.0000 g., 0.9000 Silver .8681 oz. ASW **Ruler:** Rainier III **Obv:** Bust right **Rev:** Crowned monograms divide diamonds **Edge:** Plain

Date	Mintage	F	VF	XF	Unc	BU
1975 (a)	7,500	—	—	—	60.00	65.00
1976 (a)	6,000	—	—	—	65.00	70.00

KM# 161 100 FRANCS

15.0000 g., 0.9000 Silver .4340 oz. ASW **Ruler:** Rainier III **Subject:** Heir Apparent Prince Albert **Obv:** Conjoined heads right **Rev:** Crowned arms with supporters

Date	Mintage	F	VF	XF	Unc	BU
1982 (a)	30,000	—	—	—	75.00	80.00

KM# 162 10 FRANCS

Nickel-Aluminum-Bronze **Ruler:** Rainier III **Subject:** Prince Pierre Foundation **Obv:** Bust right and single sprig on paper to left of dates **Rev:** Small doubled wreath divides date on top of shield flanked by symbols

Date	Mintage	F	VF	XF	Unc	BU
1989 (a)	100,000	—	—	—	6.50	—

KM# 164 100 FRANCS

15.0000 g., 0.9000 Silver .4340 oz. ASW **Ruler:** Rainier III
Subject: 40th Anniversary of Reign **Obv:** Head right
Rev: Crowned monogram above value

Date	Mintage	F	VF	XF	Unc	BU
1989 (a)	45,000	—	—	—	75.00	80.00

KM# 175 100 FRANCS

15.0000 g., 0.9000 Silver 0.434 oz. ASW, 31 mm. **Ruler:** Rainier III **Subject:** 50th Anniversary of Reign - Prince Ranier III **Obv:** Head right **Rev:** Crowned monogram above value **Edge:** Plain

Date	Mintage	F	VF	XF	Unc	BU
1999	20,000	—	—	—	75.00	80.00

PATTERNS

Including off metal strikes

KM#	Date	Mintage	Identification	Mkt Val
Pn15	1934A	15	500 Francs. 0.9000 Gold.	3,220

ESSAIS

Standard metals unless otherwise noted

KM#	Date	Mintage	Identification	Issue Price	Mkt Val
E1	1924	—	50 Centimes. Gold. KM#110	—	2,000
E2	1924	12	Franc. Aluminum-Bronze. KM111	—	950
E3	1924	—	Franc. Gold. KM111	—	3,000
E4	1924	12	2 Francs. Aluminum-Bronze. KM112	—	1,000
E5	1924	—	2 Francs. Gold. Hercules shooting bow to right. Shield below value within circle. KM112	—	4,000
E6	ND(1943) (a)	250	Franc. 0.9000 Gold.	—	625
E7	ND(1943) (a)	1,100	Franc. Aluminum. KM120	—	28.00
E8	ND(1943) (a)	—	Franc. Aluminum-Bronze. KM120	—	40.00
E9	ND(1943) (a)	250	Franc. Silver. KM120	—	150
E10	ND(1943) (a)	250	2 Francs. 0.9000 Gold.	—	725
E11	ND(1943) (a)	1,100	2 Francs. Aluminum. KM121	—	35.00
E12	ND(1943) (a)	1,100	2 Francs. Aluminum-Bronze. KM121	—	37.00
E13	ND(1943) (a)	250	2 Francs. Silver. KM121	—	175
E14	1945 (a)	250	5 Francs. 0.9000 Gold.	—	800
E15	1945 (a)	1,100	5 Francs. Aluminum. KM122 .	—	50.00
E16	1945 (a)	150	5 Francs. Aluminum-Bronze. KM122	—	145
E17	1945 (a)	250	5 Francs. Silver. KM122	—	225
E18	1945 (a)	1,100	10 Francs. Copper-Nickel. KM123	—	40.00
E19	1945 (a)	250	10 Francs. Silver.	—	190
E20	1945 (a)	1,100	20 Francs. Copper-Nickel. KM124	—	60.00
E21	1945 (a)	250	20 Francs. Silver.	—	180
E22	1946 (a)	250	10 Francs. 0.9000 Gold.	—	800
E23	1947 (a)	250	20 Francs. 0.9000 Gold.	—	850
E24	1950 (a)	1,100	10 Francs.	—	25.00
E25	1950 (a)	500	10 Francs. Silver.	—	50.00
E26	1950 (a)	500	10 Francs. 0.9000 Gold. 14.5100 g.	—	375
E27	1950 (a)	1,700	20 Francs.	—	32.00
E28	1950 (a)	—	20 Francs. Silver.	—	70.00
E29	1950 (a)	500	20 Francs. 0.9000 Gold.	—	450
E30	1950 (a)	1,700	50 Francs.	—	50.00
E31	1950 (a)	500	50 Francs. Silver.	—	90.00
E32	1950 (a)	500	50 Francs. 0.9000 Gold. 20.5200 g.	—	725
E33	1950 (a)	1,700	100 Francs.	—	50.00
E34	1950 (a)	500	100 Francs. Silver.	—	100
E35	1950 (a)	500	100 Francs. 0.9000 Gold. Head left divides circle. Armored knight on horse divides circle.	—	750
E36	1956 (a)	500	100 Francs. 0.9000 Gold.	—	350
E37	1956 (a)	500	100 Francs. Silver. KM134	—	150
E38	1960 (a)	—	Franc. Nickel. KM140	—	70.00
E39	1960 (a)	500	Franc. Silver.	—	70.00
E40	1960 (a)	500	Franc. 0.9200 Gold.	—	350
E41	1960 (a)	500	5 Francs. Silver.	—	100
E42	1960 (a)	500	5 Francs. 0.9200 Gold.	—	650
E43	1962 (a)	1,200	10 Centimes.	—	15.00
E44	1962 (a)	502	10 Centimes. 0.9500 Silver.	—	60.00
E45	1962 (a)	502	10 Centimes. 0.9200 Gold. Head right. Figure with hand on shield divides crown and value.	—	180
E46	1962 (a)	1,200	20 Centimes.	—	40.00
E47	1962 (a)	502	20 Centimes. 0.9500 Silver.	—	75.00
E48	1962 (a)	502	20 Centimes. 0.9200 Gold.	—	225
E49	1962 (a)	1,200	50 Centimes.	—	60.00
E50	1962 (a)	502	50 Centimes. 0.9500 Silver.	—	150
E51	1962 (a)	502	50 Centimes. 0.9200 Gold.	—	385
E52	1965 (a)	2,000	1/2 Franc. Nickel.	—	40.00
E53	1965 (a)	1,000	1/2 Franc. Silver.	—	60.00

KM#	Date	Mintage	Identification	Issue Price	Mkt Val
E54	1965 (a)	1,000	1/2 Franc. 0.9200 Gold.	—	185
E55	1966 (a)	500	5 Francs. 0.9200 Gold.	—	450
E56	1966 (a)	100	10 Francs.	—	85.00
E57	1966 (a)	1,000	10 Francs. 0.9200 Gold.	—	725
E58	1971 (a)	1,000	5 Francs.	—	40.00
E59	1971 (a)	1,000	5 Francs. Silver.	—	100
E60	1971 (a)	500	5 Francs. 0.9200 Gold.	—	375
E61	1974 (a)	1,000	5 Francs. Silver.	—	60.00
E62	1974 (a)	1,000	5 Francs. Gold.	—	325
E63	1974 (a)	1,000	10 Francs.	—	40.00
E64	1974 (a)	1,000	10 Francs. Silver.	—	110
E65	1974 (a)	1,000	10 Francs. Gold.	—	345
E66	1974 (a)	1,000	50 Francs.	—	125
E67	1974 (a)	1,000	50 Francs. Gold.	—	1,200
E68	1976	1,600	Centime. Stainless Steel. KM155	—	30.00
E69	1976	1,600	5 Centimes. Copper-Aluminum-Nickel. KM156	—	35.00
E70	1976	1,600	10 Centimes. Aluminum-Bronze. KM142	—	35.00
E71	1979	—	2 Francs. Nickel. KM157	—	70.00
E72	1982 (a)	4,000	10 Francs. Nickel-Aluminum-Bronze.	—	45.00
E73	1982 (a)	30,000	10 Francs. Silver.	—	20.00
E74	1982 (a)	1,000	10 Francs. Gold.	—	385
E75	1982 (a)	1,000	100 Francs. 0.9000 Silver. KM161	—	60.00
 E76	1982 (a)	1,000	100 Francs. Gold. Conjoined heads right. Crowned arms with supporters.	—	400

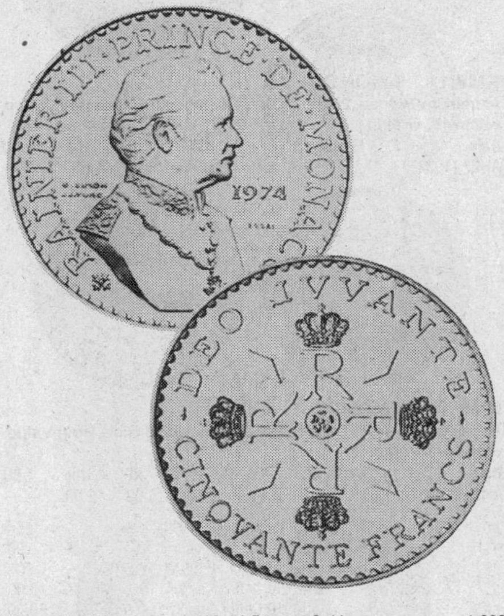

PIEFORTS

Double thickness; Standard metals unless otherwise stated

KM#	Date	Mintage	Identification	Mkt Val
P18a	1974 (a)	—	10 Francs. Gold. Without Essai	650
P19a	1974 (a)	250	50 Francs. Gold. Without Essai	1,500

PIEFORTS WITH ESSAI

Double thickness; Standard metals unless otherwise noted

KM#	Date	Mintage	Identification	Issue Price	Mkt Val
PE1	ND(1943) (a)	15	Franc. 0.9000 Gold.	—	1,200
PE2	ND(1943) (a)	15	2 Francs. 0.9000 Gold.	—	1,400
PE3	1945 (a)	15	5 Francs. 0.9000 Gold.	—	1,500
PE4	1946 (a)	16	10 Francs. 0.9000 Gold. Bust left. Crowned shield and value flanked by sprigs.	—	1,100
PE5	1947 (a)	16	20 Francs. 0.9000 Gold.	—	1,350
PE6	1950 (a)	—	10 Francs. Silver.	—	85.00
PE6a	1950 (a)	325	10 Francs. 0.9000 Gold.	—	275
PE7	1950 (a)	—	20 Francs. Silver.	—	90.00
PE7a	1950 (a)	325	20 Francs. 0.9000 Gold.	—	315
PE8	1950 (a)	—	50 Francs. Silver.	—	160
PE8a	1950 (a)	325	50 Francs. 0.9000 Gold. 40.8700 g.	—	500
PE9	1950 (a)	—	100 Francs. Silver.	—	160
PE9a	1950 (a)	325	100 Francs. 0.9000 Gold.	—	500
PE10	1956 (a)	20	100 Francs. 0.9000 Gold.	—	1,200
PE11	1960 (a)	25	Franc. 0.9200 Gold.	—	645
PE12	1960 (a)	25	5 Francs. 0.9200 Gold.	—	1,200
PE13	1962 (a)	100	10 Centimes. 0.9500 Silver.	—	140
PE13a	1962 (a)	25	10 Centimes. 0.9200 Gold.	—	725
PE14	1962 (a)	100	20 Centimes. 0.9500 Silver.	—	140
PE14a	1962 (a)	25	20 Centimes. 0.9200 Gold.	—	820
PE15	1962 (a)	100	50 Centimes. 0.9500 Silver.	—	200
PE15a	1962 (a)	25	50 Centimes. 0.9200 Gold.	—	900
PE16	1966 (a)	150	5 Francs. Nickel.	—	60.00
PE16a	1971 (a)	250	5 Francs. Silver.	—	150
PE16b	1971 (a)	250	5 Francs. 0.9200 Gold.	—	625
PE17	1974 (a)	250	5 Francs. Silver.	—	150
PE17a	1974 (a)	250	5 Francs. Gold. Head right. Crowned monogram and value flanked by lined designs.	—	625
PE18	1974 (a)	250	10 Francs. Silver.	—	200
PE18a	1974 (a)	250	10 Francs. Gold.	—	500
PE19	1974 (a)	250	50 Francs. Without Essai	—	100
PE19a	1974 (a)	250	50 Francs. Gold.	—	1,750
PE20	1982 (a)	250	10 Francs. Silver.	—	150
PE20a	1982 (a)	250	10 Francs. Gold.	—	500
PE21	1982 (a)	250	100 Francs. Silver.	—	200
PE21a	1982 (a)	250	100 Francs. Gold.	—	700

SPECIMEN SETS (SS)

KM#	Date	Mintage	Identification	Issue Price	Mkt Val
SS1	1974 (7)	7	KM140, 142, 143, 145, 150, 151, 152.1. 3,000 sets not released.	45.00	400
SS2	1975 (7)	8	KM140, 142, 143, 145, 150, 152.2, 154	—	200
SS3	1976 (9)	6,000	KM140, 142, 143, 145, 150, 152.2, 154-156	—	120
SS6	1982 (11)	10,000	KM140, 142, 143, 145, 150, 154-157, 160, 161	—	150
SS7	1995 (9)	—	KM140, 142, 143, 150, 155, 156, 163, 165, 166	—	120

The State of Mongolia, (formerly the Mongolian Peoples Republic) a landlocked country in central Asia between Russia and the People's Republic of China, has an area of 604,250 sq. mi. (1,565,000 sq. km.) and a population of 2.26 million. Capital: Ulaan Baator. Animal herds and flocks are the chief economic asset. Wool, cattle, butter, meat and hides are exported.

Mongolia (often referred to as Outer Mongolia), one of the world's oldest countries, attained its greatest power in the 13th century when Genghis Khan and his successors conquered all of China and extended their influence westward as far as Hungary and Poland. The empire dissolved in later centuries and in 1691 was brought under suzerainty of the Manchus, who had conquered China in 1644. Afterward the Chinese republican movement led by Sun Yat-sen overthrew the Manchus and set up the Chinese Republic in 1911. Mongolia, with the support of Russia, proclaimed their independence from China and, on March 13, 1921 a Provisional Peoples Government was established and later, on Nov. 26, 1924 the government proclaimed the Mongolian Peoples Republic.

Although nominally a dependency of China, Outer Mongolia voted at a plebiscite Oct. 20, 1945 to sever all ties with China and become an independent nation. Opposition to the communist party developed in late 1989 and after demonstrations and hunger strikes, the Politburo resigned on March 12, 1990 and the new State of Mongolia was organized.

On Feb. 12, 1992 it became the first to discard communism as the national political system by adopting a new constitution.

For earlier issues see Russia - Tannu Tuva.

MONETARY SYSTEM

100 Mongo = 1 Tugrik

PEOPLE'S REPUBLIC

DECIMAL COINAGE

KM# 1 MONGO

Copper, 21 mm. **Obv:** Soembo arms, text **Rev:** Value within 1/2 wreath

Date	Mintage	F	VF	XF	Unc	BU
AH15 (1925)	—	5.00	8.00	12.00	22.00	—

KM# 9 MONGO

Aluminum-Bronze **Obv:** Soembo arms, text **Rev:** Value within 1/2 wreath

Date	Mintage	F	VF	XF	Unc	BU
AH27 (1937)	—	2.50	3.50	7.50	16.50	—

KM# 15 MONGO

Aluminum-Bronze **Obv:** National arms within circle **Rev:** Value within 1/2 wreath

Date	Mintage	F	VF	XF	Unc	BU
AH35 (1945)	—	2.00	3.00	5.50	12.50	—

KM# 21 MONGO

Aluminum **Obv:** Wreath around center hole with inscription around border **Rev:** Value above hole in center and 3/4 wreath

Date	Mintage	F	VF	XF	Unc	BU
1959	9,000,000	0.25	0.60	1.00	2.00	—

KM# 27 MONGO

0.7500 g., Aluminum, 17.5 mm. **Obv:** National arms **Rev:** Value above 1/2 wreath

Date	Mintage	F	VF	XF	Unc	BU
1970	—	0.25	0.60	0.85	1.50	—
1977	—	0.25	0.60	0.85	1.50	—
1980	—	0.25	0.60	0.85	1.50	—
1981	—	0.25	0.60	0.85	1.50	—

KM# 2 2 MONGO

Copper, 24 mm. **Obv:** Soembo arms, text **Rev:** Value within 1/2 wreath

Date	Mintage	F	VF	XF	Unc	BU
AH15 (1925)	—	3.50	6.50	12.00	22.00	—

KM# 10 2 MONGO

Aluminum-Bronze, 22 mm. **Obv:** Soembo, text **Rev:** Value within 1/2 wreath

Date	Mintage	F	VF	XF	Unc	BU
AH27 (1937)	—	2.50	3.50	6.00	14.00	—

KM# 16 2 MONGO

Aluminum-Bronze **Obv:** National arms within circle **Rev:** Value within 1/2 wreath

Date	Mintage	F	VF	XF	Unc	BU
AH35 (1945)	—	1.00	2.00	4.00	9.00	—

KM# 22 2 MONGO

Aluminum **Obv:** Wreath around center hole with inscription around border **Rev:** Value above center hole and 3/4 wreath

Date	Mintage	F	VF	XF	Unc	BU
1959	4,000,000	0.25	0.65	1.50	3.50	—

KM# 28 2 MONGO

1.0500 g., Aluminum, 20 mm. **Obv:** National arms above date **Rev:** Value within 1/2 wreath

Date	Mintage	F	VF	XF	Unc	BU
1970	—	0.25	0.65	1.20	2.50	—
1977	—	0.25	0.65	1.20	2.50	—
1980	—	0.25	0.65	1.20	2.50	—
1981	—	0.25	0.65	1.20	2.50	—

KM# 3.1 5 MONGO

Copper, 32 mm. **Obv:** Soembo arms, text **Rev:** Value within 1/2 wreath

Date	Mintage	F	VF	XF	Unc	BU
AH15 (1925)	—	5.00	10.00	20.00	38.00	—

Note: Variety in obverse legend exists

KM# 3.2 5 MONGO

Copper, 32 mm. **Note:** Error: letter "m" looking like a horse's tail omitted in nayramdax (Vertically written word lower left of Soyombo)

Date	Mintage	F	VF	XF	Unc	BU
1925	—	—	—	—	40.00	—

KM# 11 5 MONGO

Aluminum-Bronze, 28 mm. **Obv:** Soembo arms, text **Rev:** Value within 1/2 wreath

Date	Mintage	F	VF	XF	Unc	BU
AH27 (1937)	—	2.75	3.50	6.00	14.00	—

KM# 17 5 MONGO

Aluminum-Bronze **Obv:** National arms within circle **Rev:** Value within 1/2 wreath

Date	Mintage	F	VF	XF	Unc	BU
AH35 (1945)	—	1.75	2.50	5.00	12.00	—

KM# 23 5 MONGO

Aluminum **Obv:** Wreath around hole in center with inscription around border **Rev:** Value above hole in center and 1/2 wreath

Date	Mintage	F	VF	XF	Unc	BU
1959	2,400,000	0.25	1.00	2.00	4.00	—

KM# 29 5 MONGO

1.6000 g., Aluminum, 23 mm. **Obv:** Date below national arms **Rev:** Value within 1/2 wreath

Date	Mintage	F	VF	XF	Unc	BU
1970	—	0.25	0.85	1.75	3.50	—
1977	—	0.25	0.85	1.75	3.50	—
1980	—	0.25	0.85	1.75	3.50	—
1981	—	0.25	0.85	1.75	3.50	—

KM# 4 10 MONGO
1.7996 g., 0.5000 Silver .0289 oz. ASW, 17 mm. **Obv:** Soembo arms, text **Rev:** Value within 1/2 wreath

Date	Mintage	VG	F	VF	XF	Unc
AH15 (1925)	1,500,000	—	3.00	5.00	9.00	20.00

KM# 12 10 MONGO
Copper-Nickel **Obv:** Soembo arms, text **Rev:** Value within 1/2 wreath

Date	Mintage	F	VF	XF	Unc	BU
AH27 (1937)	—	2.00	3.50	7.00	16.00	—

KM# 18 10 MONGO
Copper-Nickel **Obv:** National arms within circle **Rev:** Value within 1/2 wreath

Date	Mintage	F	VF	XF	Unc	BU
AH35 (1945)	—	1.50	3.00	5.00	12.00	—

KM# 24 10 MONGO
Aluminum **Obv:** National arms within circle **Rev:** Value within 3/4 wreath

Date	Mintage	F	VF	XF	Unc	BU
1959	3,000,000	0.75	1.50	3.00	6.00	—

KM# 30 10 MONGO
2.3000 g., Copper-Nickel, 18.5 mm. **Obv:** Date below national arms **Rev:** Value within 1/2 wreath

Date	Mintage	F	VF	XF	Unc	BU
1970	—	0.35	0.85	1.75	3.50	—
1977	—	0.35	0.85	1.75	3.50	—
1980	—	0.35	0.85	1.75	3.50	—
1981	—	0.35	0.85	1.75	3.50	—

KM# 5 15 MONGO
2.6994 g., 0.5000 Silver .0433 oz. ASW, 19 mm. **Obv:** Soembo arms, text **Rev:** Value within 1/2 wreath

Date	Mintage	VG	F	VF	XF	Unc
AH15 (1925)	417,000	—	3.50	6.00	12.00	22.00

KM# 13 15 MONGO
Copper-Nickel **Obv:** Soembo arms, text **Rev:** Value within 1/2 wreath

Date	Mintage	F	VF	XF	Unc	BU
AH27 (1937)	—	2.00	3.00	6.00	14.00	—

KM# 19 15 MONGO
Copper-Nickel **Obv:** National arms within circle **Rev:** Value within 3/4 wreath

Date	Mintage	F	VF	XF	Unc	BU
AH35 (1945)	—	1.50	2.25	4.00	9.00	—

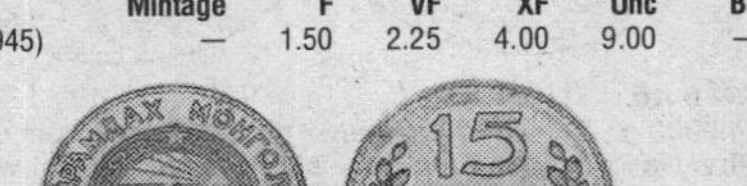

KM# 25 15 MONGO
Aluminum **Obv:** National arms within circle **Rev:** Value within 3/4 wreath

Date	Mintage	F	VF	XF	Unc	BU
1959	4,600,000	0.35	0.85	1.75	4.00	—

KM# 31 15 MONGO
4.0500 g., Copper-Nickel, 22 mm. **Obv:** Date below national arms **Rev:** Value within 1/2 wreath

Date	Mintage	F	VF	XF	Unc	BU
1970	—	0.25	0.65	1.25	2.75	—
1977	—	0.25	0.65	1.25	2.75	—
1980	—	0.25	0.65	1.25	2.75	—
1981	—	0.25	0.65	1.25	2.75	—

KM# 6 20 MONGO
3.5992 g., 0.5000 Silver .0578 oz. ASW, 22 mm. **Obv:** Soembo arms, text **Rev:** Value within 1/2 wreath

Date	Mintage	VG	F	VF	XF	Unc
AH15 (1925)	1,625,000	—	4.00	7.50	14.00	28.00

KM# 14 20 MONGO
Copper-Nickel **Obv:** Soembo arms, text **Rev:** Value within 1/2 wreath

Date	Mintage	F	VF	XF	Unc	BU
AH27 (1937)	—	2.50	4.50	10.00	20.00	—

KM# 20 20 MONGO
Copper-Nickel **Obv:** National arms within circle **Rev:** Value within 3/4 wreath

Date	Mintage	F	VF	XF	Unc	BU
AH35 (1945)	—	1.50	2.50	5.00	12.00	—

KM# 26 20 MONGO
Aluminum **Obv:** National arms within circle **Rev:** Value within 3/4 wreath

Date	Mintage	F	VF	XF	Unc	BU
1959	3,600,000	0.60	1.25	2.25	4.50	—

KM# 32 20 MONGO
5.9000 g., Copper-Nickel, 25 mm. **Obv:** Date below national arms **Rev:** Value within 1/2 wreath

Date	Mintage	F	VF	XF	Unc	BU
1970	—	0.40	0.80	1.50	3.50	—
1977	—	0.40	0.80	1.50	3.50	—
1980	—	0.40	0.80	1.50	3.50	—
1981	—	0.40	0.80	1.50	3.50	—

KM# 7 50 MONGO
9.9979 g., 0.9000 Silver .2893 oz. ASW, 27 mm. **Obv:** Soembo arms, text **Rev:** Value within 1/2 wreath

Date	Mintage	VG	F	VF	XF	Unc
AH15 (1925)	920,000	—	7.50	12.00	18.50	32.00

KM# 33 50 MONGO
8.6000 g., Copper-Nickel, 27.5 mm. **Obv:** Date below national arms **Rev:** Value within 1/2 wreath

Date	Mintage	F	VF	XF	Unc	BU
1970	—	0.50	1.00	1.75	3.75	—
1977	—	0.50	1.00	1.75	3.75	—
1980	—	0.50	1.00	1.75	3.75	—
1981	—	0.50	1.00	1.75	3.75	—

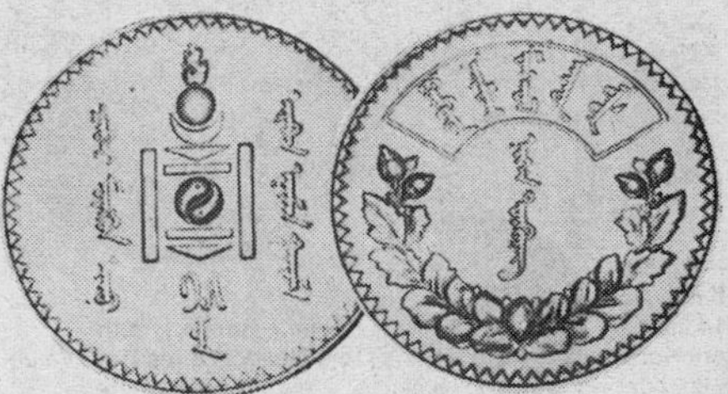

KM# 8 TUGRIK
19.9957 g., 0.9000 Silver .5786 oz. ASW, 34 mm. **Obv:** Soembo arms, text **Rev:** Value within 1/2 wreath

Date	Mintage	VG	F	VF	XF	Unc
AH15 (1925)	400,000	—	12.00	16.00	22.00	40.00

KM# 34 TUGRIK
14.9000 g., Aluminum-Bronze, 32 mm. **Subject:** 50th Anniversary of the Revolution **Obv:** National arms **Rev:** Man on horse left within beaded circle **Edge Lettering:** ONE TUGRIK 1921 - 1971 **Note:** Date on edge.

Date	Mintage	F	VF	XF	Unc	BU
ND(1971)	—	—	4.00	6.00	10.00	—

KM# 34a TUGRIK
Copper-Nickel, 32 mm. **Obv:** National arms **Rev:** Man on horse left within beaded circle

Date	Mintage	F	VF	XF	Unc	BU
ND(1971)	—	6.00	8.00	12.00	18.00	—

KM# 34b TUGRIK

18.4000 g., Silver, 32 mm. **Obv:** National arms **Rev:** Man on horse left within beaded circle

Date	Mintage	F	VF	XF	Unc	BU
(1971) Proof	—	Value: 50.00				

KM# 34c TUGRIK

30.0000 g., Gold, 32 mm. **Subject:** 50th Anniversary of the Revolution **Obv:** National arms **Rev:** Man on horse left within beaded circle **Note:** Mintage: 5-10.

Date	Mintage	F	VF	XF	Unc	BU
(1971) Proof	—	Value: 2,500				

KM# 41 TUGRIK

14.9000 g., Aluminum-Bronze, 32 mm. **Subject:** 60th Anniversary of the Revolution **Obv:** National arms **Rev:** Man on horse left within beaded circle **Edge:** Lettered

Date	Mintage	F	VF	XF	Unc	BU
1981	—	—	—	4.00	7.50	9.00

KM# 42 TUGRIK

14.9000 g., Aluminum-Bronze, 32 mm. **Subject:** Soviet - Mongolian Space Flight **Obv:** National arms **Rev:** Conjoined helmeted heads left with stars at upper left and date at lower right **Edge:** Smooth

Date	Mintage	F	VF	XF	Unc	BU
1981	—	—	—	3.00	6.00	—

KM# 43 TUGRIK

14.9000 g., Aluminum-Bronze, 32 mm. **Subject:** 60th Anniversary of the State Bank **Obv:** National arms **Rev:** Value within design with date within 1/2 wreath **Edge:** Lettered

Date	Mintage	F	VF	XF	Unc	BU
1984	—	—	—	3.00	6.00	—

Note: Edge varieties exist

KM# 44 TUGRIK

14.9000 g., Aluminum-Bronze, 32 mm. **Subject:** 60th Anniversary of the People's Republic **Obv:** National arms **Rev:** Soembo arms and value within 1/2 wreath **Edge:** Lettered

Date	Mintage	F	VF	XF	Unc	BU
1984	—	—	—	3.00	5.50	—

KM# 48 TUGRIK

14.9000 g., Aluminum-Bronze, 32 mm. **Subject:** Year of Peace **Obv:** National arms **Rev:** Dove above hands and 3/4 wreath **Edge:** Lettered

Date	Mintage	F	VF	XF	Unc	BU
1986	—	—	—	3.50	7.50	—

KM# 49 TUGRIK

14.9000 g., Aluminum-Bronze, 32 mm. **Subject:** 65th Anniversary of the Revolution **Obv:** National arms **Rev:** Bust left **Edge:** Lettered

Date	Mintage	F	VF	XF	Unc	BU
1986	—	—	—	3.00	5.50	—

KM# 52 TUGRIK

14.9000 g., Aluminum-Bronze, 32 mm. **Subject:** 170th Anniversary - Birth of Karl Marx **Obv:** National arms **Rev:** Head facing flanked by dates

Date	Mintage	F	VF	XF	Unc	BU
ND(1988)	—	—	—	4.00	12.50	—

KM# 35 10 TUGRIK

Copper-Nickel **Subject:** 50th Anniversary of State Bank **Obv:** National arms **Rev:** State bank

Date	Mintage	F	VF	XF	Unc	BU
ND(1974)	—	—	—	—	9.00	—

KM# 36 25 TUGRIK

28.2800 g., 0.9250 Silver .8411 oz. ASW **Subject:** Conservation **Obv:** National arms **Rev:** Arfali sheep

Date	Mintage	F	VF	XF	Unc	BU
1976	5,348	—	—	—	22.00	—
1976 Proof	6,096	Value: 25.00				

KM# 39.1 25 TUGRIK

19.4400 g., 0.9250 Silver .5781 oz. ASW **Series:** International Year of the Child **Obv:** National arms **Rev:** Children riding camel

Date	Mintage	F	VF	XF	Unc	BU
1980 Proof	14,000	Value: 25.00				

KM# 39.2 25 TUGRIK

19.2600 g., 0.9250 Silver 0.5728 oz. ASW, 36.1 mm. **Obv:** National arms **Rev:** Children riding camel, two countermarks at 5 o'clock **Edge:** Reeded

Date	Mintage	F	VF	XF	Unc	BU
1980 Proof	—	Value: 50.00				

KM# 47 25 TUGRIK

19.4400 g., 0.9250 Silver .5781 oz. ASW **Series:** Decade for Women **Obv:** National arms **Rev:** Figure with hat holding child

Date	Mintage	F	VF	XF	Unc	BU
1984 Proof	1,249	Value: 37.50				

KM# 50 25 TUGRIK

28.2800 g., 0.9250 Silver .8411 oz. ASW **Series:** World Wildlife Fund **Obv:** National arms **Rev:** Snow leopard

Date	Mintage	F	VF	XF	Unc	BU
1987 Matte	850	—	—	—	50.00	—
1987 Proof	25,000	Value: 27.50				

KM# 54 25 TUGRIK

28.2800 g., 0.9250 Silver .8411 oz. ASW **Series:** Save the Children Fund **Obv:** National arms **Rev:** Child playing horse head fiddle

Date	Mintage	F	VF	XF	Unc	BU
1989 Proof	20,000	Value: 28.50				

KM# 37 50 TUGRIK
35.0000 g., 0.9250 Silver 1.0409 oz. ASW **Subject:** Conservation **Obv:** National arms **Rev:** Camel running left above value flanked by bushes

Date	Mintage	F	VF	XF	Unc	BU
1976	5,328	—	—	—	24.00	—
1976 Proof	5,900	Value: 27.00				

KM# 57 50 TUGRIK
31.1000 g., 0.9990 Silver 1.0000 oz. ASW **Subject:** Discovery of America **Obv:** National arms **Rev:** Portrait of Columbus and ship within circle and legend

Date	Mintage	F	VF	XF	Unc	BU
1992 Proof	20,000	Value: 32.50				

KM# 170 50 TUGRIK
31.1000 g., 0.9990 Silver 1 oz. ASW **Subject:** Year of the Monkey **Obv:** National arms **Rev:** Monkey

Date	Mintage	F	VF	XF	Unc	BU
1992	Est. 20,000	—	—	—	80.00	—

KM# 53 100 TUGRIK
28.0000 g., 0.9000 Silver .8102 oz. ASW **Subject:** Dinosaurs **Obv:** National arms **Rev:** Nemectosaurus

Date	Mintage	F	VF	XF	Unc	BU
1989	1,000	—	—	—	80.00	—

KM# 55 100 TUGRIK
28.0000 g., 0.9000 Silver .8102 oz. ASW **Subject:** Secret history of the Mongols **Obv:** State emblem above denomination within English legend **Rev:** Portrait of Genghis Khan in light clothing

Date	Mintage	F	VF	XF	Unc	BU
1990	4,000	—	—	—	50.00	—

KM# 58 100 TUGRIK
1.5600 g., 0.9990 Gold .0500 oz. AGW **Subject:** Discovery of America - Columbus **Obv:** National arms **Rev:** Portrait of Columbus and ship within circle and legend

Date	Mintage	F	VF	XF	Unc	BU
1992 Proof	Est. 10,000	Value: 50.00				

KM# 59 200 TUGRIK
3.1100 g., 0.9990 Gold .1000 oz. AGW **Subject:** Discovery of America - Columbus **Obv:** National arms **Rev:** Portrait of Columbus and ship within circle and legend

Date	Mintage	F	VF	XF	Unc	BU
1992 Proof	Est. 10,000	Value: 75.00				

KM# 45 250 TUGRIK
7.1300 g., 0.9000 Gold .2026 oz. AGW **Series:** Decade for Women **Obv:** National arms **Rev:** Figure on horseback left, value

Date	Mintage	F	VF	XF	Unc	BU
1984 Proof	510	Value: 165				

KM# 72 300 TUGRIK
7.7700 g., 0.9990 Gold .25 oz. AGW **Subject:** Japanese royal wedding **Obv:** National arms above value **Rev:** Royal couple facing each other

Date	Mintage	F	VF	XF	Unc	BU
1993 Proof	Est. 500	Value: 235				

KM# 38 750 TUGRIK
33.4370 g., 0.9000 Gold .9676 oz. AGW **Subject:** Conservation **Rev:** Przewalski horses

Date	Mintage	F	VF	XF	Unc	BU
1976	929	—	—	—	625	—
1976 Proof	374	Value: 825				

KM# 40 750 TUGRIK
18.7900 g., 0.9000 Gold .5437 oz. AGW **Series:** International Year of the Child **Obv:** National arms **Rev:** Children dancing

Date	Mintage	F	VF	XF	Unc	BU
1980 Proof	32,000	Value: 385				

KM# 56 1000 TUGRIK
20.7000 g., 0.9000 Gold .5990 oz. AGW **Subject:** Secret history of the Mongols **Obv:** State emblem above denomination within English legend **Rev:** Portrait of Genghis Khan in heavy clothing

Date	Mintage	F	VF	XF	Unc	BU
1990	Est. 4,000	—	—	—	425	—

KM# 60 1000 TUGRIK
31.1000 g., 0.9990 Gold 1.0000 oz. AGW **Subject:** Discovery of America **Obv:** National arms divide date above value **Rev:** Portrait of Columbus and ship within circle and legend

Date	Mintage	F	VF	XF	Unc	BU
1992 Proof	2,000	Value: 700				

KM# 171 1000 TUGRIK
Gold **Subject:** Year of the Monkey **Obv:** National arms **Rev:** Monkey

Date	Mintage	F	VF	XF	Unc	BU
1992	Est. 2,000	—	—	—	750	—

STATE

DECIMAL COINAGE

KM# 122 20 TUGRIK
Aluminum **Obv:** Soembo arms, text **Rev:** Value

Date	Mintage	F	VF	XF	Unc	BU
1994	—	—	—	—	1.50	1.75

KM# 84 50 TUGRIK
15.0000 g., 0.9990 Silver .4818 oz. ASW **Obv:** State emblem above value **Rev:** Bust with hat 1/4 left

Date	Mintage	F	VF	XF	Unc	BU
1992 Proof	Est. 1,000	Value: 30.00				

KM# 86 50 TUGRIK
31.1035 g., 0.9990 Silver 1.0000 oz. ASW **Subject:** Year of the Monkey **Obv:** State emblem above value **Rev:** Sitting monkey

Date	Mintage	F	VF	XF	Unc	BU
1992 Proof	20,000	Value: 40.00				

KM# 166 50 TUGRIK
31.1035 g., 0.9990 Silver 1 oz. ASW **Subject:** Discovery of America - Columbus **Obv:** State emblem above value **Rev:** Portrait of Columbus and ship within circle and legend

Date	Mintage	F	VF	XF	Unc	BU
1992 Proof	—	Value: 42.50				

KM# 61 50 TUGRIK
31.1035 g., 0.9990 Silver 1 oz. ASW **Subject:** Year of the Rooster **Obv:** State emblem above value **Rev:** Rooster

Date	Mintage	F	VF	XF	Unc	BU
1993 Proof	20,000	Value: 40.00				

KM# 69 50 TUGRIK
31.1035 g., 0.9990 Silver 1 oz. ASW **Subject:** Japanese Royal Wedding **Obv:** State emblem above value **Rev:** Busts facing each other

Date	Mintage	F	VF	XF	Unc	BU
1993 Proof	1,962	Value: 47.50				

KM# 75 50 TUGRIK
Subject: Year of the Dog **Obv:** State emblem above value **Rev:** Two dogs

Date	Mintage	F	VF	XF	Unc	BU
1994 Proof	4,000	Value: 45.00				

KM# 123 50 TUGRIK
Aluminum **Obv:** Soembo arms, text **Rev:** Value within design

Date	Mintage	F	VF	XF	Unc	BU
1994	—	—	—	—	1.75	2.00

KM# 94 50 TUGRIK
Copper-Nickel **Subject:** Year of the Pig **Obv:** State emblem above value **Rev:** Pig

Date	Mintage	F	VF	XF	Unc	BU
1995 Proof	50,000	Value: 15.00				

KM# 104 50 TUGRIK
Copper-Nickel **Subject:** Year of the Rat **Obv:** Soembo arms within deigned circle **Rev:** Rat among flowers and plants

Date	Mintage	F	VF	XF	Unc	BU
1996 Proof	50,000	Value: 15.00				

KM# 126 50 TUGRIK
Copper-Nickel **Subject:** Year of the Ox **Obv:** National emblem **Rev:** Ox

Date	Mintage	F	VF	XF	Unc	BU
1997 Proof	25,000	Value: 15.00				

KM# 172 50 TUGRIK
Copper-Nickel **Subject:** Year of the Tiger **Obv:** National emblem **Rev:** Tiger

Date	Mintage	F	VF	XF	Unc	BU
1998	25,000	—	—	—	15.00	—

KM# 159 50 TUGRIK
20.0000 g., Copper-Nickel, 38 mm. **Subject:** Year of the Rabbit **Obv:** National emblem **Rev:** Rabbit **Edge:** Plain

Date	Mintage	F	VF	XF	Unc	BU
1999 Prooflike	25,000	—	—	—	15.00	—

KM# 87 100 TUGRIK
1.5600 g., 0.9990 Gold .0500 oz. AGW **Subject:** Year of the Monkey **Obv:** National emblem **Rev:** Monkey **Note:** Similar to 50 Tugrik, KM#86.

Date	Mintage	F	VF	XF	Unc	BU
1992 Proof	10,000	Value: 75.00				

KM# 167 100 TUGRIK
1.5600 g., 0.9990 Gold .0500 oz. AGW **Subject:** Discovery of America - Columbus **Obv:** National emblem **Rev:** Portrait of Columbus and ship within circle and legend

Date	Mintage	F	VF	XF	Unc	BU
1992 Proof	—	Value: 45.00				

KM# 62.1 100 TUGRIK
1.5600 g., 0.9990 Gold .0500 oz. AGW **Subject:** Year of the Rooster **Obv:** National emblem **Rev:** Rooster **Note:** Similar to 50 Tugrik, KM#61.

Date	Mintage	F	VF	XF	Unc	BU
1993 Proof	30,000	Value: 50.00				

KM# 62.2 100 TUGRIK
1.5600 g., 0.9990 Gold .0500 oz. AGW **Obv:** National arms above value **Rev:** Rooster left **Note:** Handstruck.

Date	Mintage	F	VF	XF	Unc	BU
1993 Proof	500	Value: 250				

Note: Strikes tend to be crude and do not have ".999" on them.

KM# 70 100 TUGRIK
1.5600 g., 0.9990 Gold .0500 oz. AGW **Subject:** Japanese Royal Wedding **Obv:** State emblem above value **Rev:** Busts facing each other **Note:** Similar to 50 Tugrik, KM#69.

Date	Mintage	F	VF	XF	Unc	BU
1993 Proof	Est. 3,000	Value: 75.00				

KM# 124 100 TUGRIK
Copper-Nickel **Obv:** Soembo arms, text **Rev:** Value below building

Date	Mintage	F	VF	XF	Unc	BU
1994	—	—	—	—	2.50	3.00

KM# 88 200 TUGRIK
3.1100 g., 0.9990 Gold .1000 oz. AGW **Subject:** Year of the Monkey **Obv:** National emblem **Rev:** Seated monkey **Note:** Similar to 50 Tugrik, KM#86.

Date	Mintage	F	VF	XF	Unc	BU
1992 Proof	—	Value: 100				

KM# 168 200 TUGRIK
3.1100 g., 0.9990 Gold .1000 oz. AGW **Subject:** Discovery of America - Columbus **Obv:** State emblem above value **Rev:** Portrait of Columbus and ship within circle and legend

Date	Mintage	F	VF	XF	Unc	BU
1992 Proof	—	Value: 75.00				

KM# 63 200 TUGRIK
3.1100 g., 0.9990 Gold .1000 oz. AGW **Subject:** Year of the Rooster **Obv:** National emblem above value at left, country name at right **Rev:** Rooster **Note:** Similar to 50 Tugrik, KM#61.

Date	Mintage	F	VF	XF	Unc	BU
1993 Proof	500	Value: 200				

KM# 71 200 TUGRIK
3.1100 g., 0.9990 Gold .1000 oz. AGW **Subject:** Japanese Royal Wedding **Obv:** National arms above value **Rev:** Busts facing each other **Note:** Similar to 50 Tugrik, KM#69.

Date	Mintage	F	VF	XF	Unc	BU
1993 Proof	100	Value: 300				

KM# 76 200 TUGRIK
3.1100 g., 0.9990 Gold .1000 oz. AGW **Subject:** Year of the Dog. **Obv:** National emblem **Rev:** Dogs

Date	Mintage	F	VF	XF	Unc	BU
1994 Proof	500	Value: 175				

KM# 125 200 TUGRIK
Copper-Nickel **Obv:** Soembo arms, text **Rev:** Value below building

Date	Mintage	F	VF	XF	Unc	BU
1994	—	—	—	—	3.00	4.00

KM# 80 250 TUGRIK
31.4700 g., 0.9250 Silver .9359 oz. ASW **Subject:** Endangered Wildlife **Obv:** Soembo arms within 3/4 wreath **Rev:** Wolves

Date	Mintage	F	VF	XF	Unc	BU
1993 Proof	Est. 15,000	Value: 40.00				

Note: KM#89 previously listed here has been reported as never released.

KM# 100 250 TUGRIK
31.4700 g., 0.9250 Silver .9359 oz. ASW **Subject:** Endangered Wildlife **Obv:** National emblem **Rev:** Przewalski's Horses

Date	Mintage	F	VF	XF	Unc	BU
1992 Proof	20,000	Value: 35.00				

KM# 110 250 TUGRIK
31.4700 g., 0.9250 Silver .9359 oz. ASW **Series:** Endangered Wildlife **Obv:** National emblem **Rev:** Saiga Antelope

Date	Mintage	F	VF	XF	Unc	BU
1993 Proof	Est. 10,000	Value: 35.00				

KM# 64 250 TUGRIK
155.5000 g., 0.9990 Silver 5.000 oz. ASW **Subject:** Year of the Rooster **Obv:** National emblem **Rev:** Rooster **Note:** Similar to 50 Tugrik, KM#61.

Date	Mintage	F	VF	XF	Unc	BU
1993	300	Value: 150				

KM# 77 250 TUGRIK
155.5000 g., 0.9990 Silver 5.0000 oz. ASW, 65 mm. **Subject:** Year of the Dog **Obv:** National emblem **Rev:** Two Pekingese **Note:** Illustration reduced.

Date	Mintage	F	VF	XF	Unc	BU
1994 Proof	200	Value: 300				

KM# 112 250 TUGRIK
31.4700 g., 0.9250 Silver .9359 oz. ASW **Series:** Olympics **Subject:** Archery **Obv:** Soembo arms within wreath **Rev:** Archer

Date	Mintage	F	VF	XF	Unc	BU
1994 Proof	—	Value: 27.50				
1995 Proof	Est. 40,000	Value: 30.00				

KM# 111 250 TUGRIK
31.4700 g., 0.9250 Silver .9359 oz. ASW **Series:** Olympics **Subject:** Boxing **Obv:** National emblem

Date	Mintage	F	VF	XF	Unc	BU
1994 Proof	Est. 5,000	Value: 50.00				

KM# 186 250 TUGRIK
31.4000 g., 0.9250 Silver .9338 oz. ASW, 38.4 mm. **Subject:** Sojus 39 and Saljut 6 **Obv:** National arms **Rev:** 2 space capsules **Edge:** Reeded

Date	Mintage	F	VF	XF	Unc	BU
1994 Proof	—	Value: 55.00				

KM# 103 250 TUGRIK
31.4700 g., 0.9250 Silver .9359 oz. ASW **Subject:** World Cup soccer **Obv:** National arms **Rev:** Soccer players

Date	Mintage	F	VF	XF	Unc	BU
1994 Proof	—	Value: 30.00				

KM# 73 500 TUGRIK
15.5500 g., 0.9990 Gold .5000 oz. AGW **Subject:** Japanese Royal Wedding **Obv:** State emblem above value **Rev:** Busts facing each other

Date	Mintage	F	VF	XF	Unc	BU
1993 Proof	160	Value: 375				

KM# 95 500 TUGRIK
31.1035 g., 0.9990 Silver 1.0000 oz. ASW **Subject:** Year of the Pig **Obv:** Soembo arms within circle **Rev:** Wild pig

Date	Mintage	F	VF	XF	Unc	BU
1995 Proof	3,000	Value: 45.00				

KM# 101.1 500 TUGRIK
31.1035 g., 0.9990 Silver 1.0000 oz. ASW **Subject:** Moscow - Beijing Railroad **Obv:** National arms **Rev:** Map without trains

Date	Mintage	F	VF	XF	Unc	BU
ND(1995) Proof	20,000	Value: 35.00				

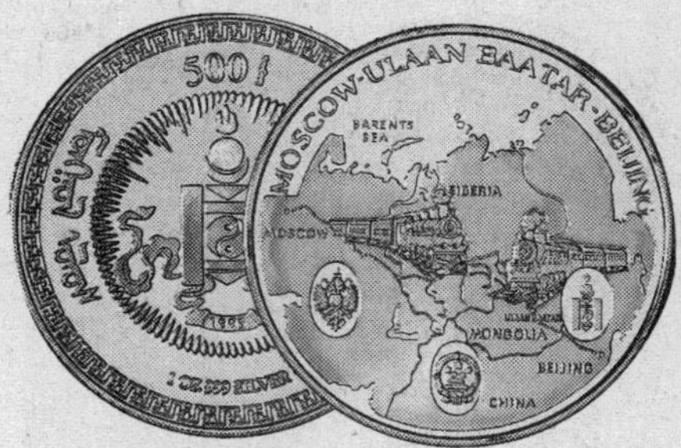

KM# 101.2 500 TUGRIK
31.1035 g., 0.9990 Silver 0.999 oz. ASW, 40.1 mm. **Obv:** Soembo arms within circle **Rev:** Map with trains **Edge:** Plain

Date	Mintage	F	VF	XF	Unc	BU
ND (1995) Proof	—	Value: 45.00				

KM# 203 500 TUGRIK
31.1500 g., 0.9990 Silver 1.0005 oz. ASW, 38 mm. **Subject:** The Straits Times 150th Anniversary **Obv:** National emblem **Rev:** Rolled newspapers and logo **Edge:** Plain

Date	Mintage	F	VF	XF	Unc	BU
ND(1995) Proof	—	Value: 40.00				

KM# 187 500 TUGRIK
31.6000 g., 0.9250 Silver .9398 oz. ASW **Series:** Endangered Wildlife **Obv:** National emblem **Rev:** Pelican

Date	Mintage	F	VF	XF	Unc	BU
1996 Proof	—	—	—	—	45.00	—

KM# 105 500 TUGRIK
31.1035 g., 0.9990 Silver 1.0000 oz. ASW **Subject:** Year of the Rat **Obv:** National emblem **Rev:** Rat **Note:** Similar to 50 Tugrik, KM#104, but with gold plated rat.

Date	Mintage	F	VF	XF	Unc	BU
1996 Proof	500	Value: 90.00				

KM# 132 500 TUGRIK
25.0000 g., 0.9250 Silver .7435 oz. ASW **Subject:** Aquila Rapax **Obv:** Soembo arms above value **Rev:** Aquila rapax sitting among rocks

Date	Mintage	F	VF	XF	Unc	BU
1996 Proof	3,500	Value: 35.00				

KM# 133 500 TUGRIK
25.0000 g., 0.9250 Silver .7435 oz. ASW **Subject:** Equus Ferus **Obv:** National emblem **Rev:** Horse running left

Date	Mintage	F	VF	XF	Unc	BU
1996 Proof	3,500	Value: 40.00				

KM# 134 500 TUGRIK
25.0000 g., 0.9250 Silver .7435 oz. ASW **Subject:** Cameleus Ferus **Obv:** National emblem **Rev:** Camel right

Date	Mintage	F	VF	XF	Unc	BU
1996 Proof	3,500	Value: 40.00				

KM# 135 500 TUGRIK
25.0000 g., 0.9250 Silver .7435 oz. ASW **Subject:** Panthera Tigris Altaica **Obv:** National emblem **Rev:** Three tigers

Date	Mintage	F	VF	XF	Unc	BU
1996 Proof	3,500	Value: 40.00				

KM# 193 500 TUGRIK
19.4400 g., 0.9250 Silver 0.5781 oz. ASW, 36 mm. **Subject:** UNICEF **Obv:** National arms **Rev:** Three costumed children **Edge:** Reeded

Date	Mintage	F	VF	XF	Unc	BU
1997 Proof	25,000	Value: 25.00				

KM# 127 500 TUGRIK
31.1035 g., 0.9990 Silver With Partial Gold Plating .1000 oz. **Subject:** Year of the Ox **Obv:** National emblem **Rev:** Ox **Note:** Similar to 50 Tugrik, KM#126.

Date	Mintage	F	VF	XF	Unc	BU
1997 Proof	3,000	Value: 50.00				

KM# 197 500 TUGRIK
Gold **Obv:** National emblem **Rev:** Sumo wrestling

Date	Mintage	F	VF	XF	Unc	BU
1998 Proof	—	Value: 50.00				

KM# 155 500 TUGRIK
15.0000 g., 0.9250 Silver .4461 oz. ASW **Series:** 1988 Olympics **Obv:** Soembo arms **Rev:** Skier

Date	Mintage	F	VF	XF	Unc	BU
1998	—	Value: 30.00				

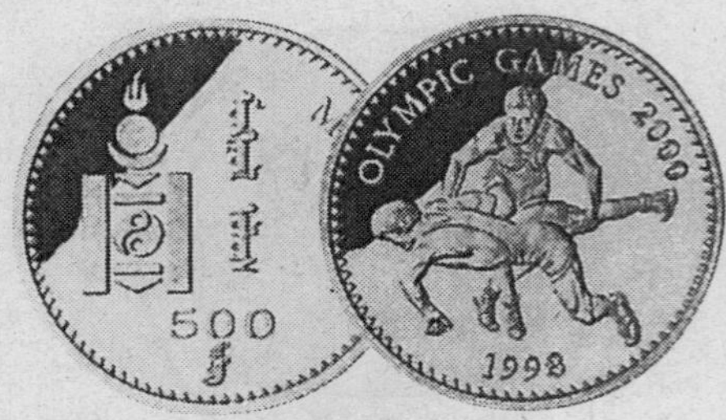

KM# 156 500 TUGRIK
20.0000 g., 0.5000 Silver .3215 oz. ASW **Series:** 2000 Olympics **Obv:** National emblem **Rev:** 2 Wrestlers

Date	Mintage	VG	F	VF	XF	Unc
1998 Proof	—	Value: 28.00				

KM# 157 500 TUGRIK
31.4700 g., 0.9990 Silver 1.0108 oz. ASW **Subject:** Endangered wildlife **Obv:** National emblem **Rev:** Tiger and cubs

Date	Mintage	F	VF	XF	Unc	BU
1998 Proof	—	Value: 50.00				

KM# 158 500 TUGRIK
1.2241 g., 0.9990 Gold .0400 oz. AGW **Subject:** Buddhist Diety Maitreya **Obv:** National emblem **Rev:** Statue

Date	Mintage	F	VF	XF	Unc	BU
1998 Proof	—	Value: 50.00				

KM# 173 500 TUGRIK
31.1045 g., 0.9990 Silver 1.0000 oz. ASW **Subject:** Year of the Tiger **Obv:** National emblem **Rev:** Tiger

Date	Mintage	F	VF	XF	Unc	BU
1998	25,000	—	—	—	25.00	—

KM# 173a 500 TUGRIK
31.1045 g., 0.9990 Silver 1.0000 oz. ASW **Subject:** Year of the Tiger **Obv:** National emblem **Rev:** Tiger **Note:** Gold-plated tiger.

Date	Mintage	F	VF	XF	Unc	BU
1998	3,000	—	—	—	50.00	—

KM# 174 500 TUGRIK
1.2441 g., 0.9990 Gold .0400 oz. AGW **Subject:** Year of the Tiger **Obv:** National emblem **Rev:** Tiger

Date	Mintage	F	VF	XF	Unc	BU
1998	—	—	—	—	45.00	—

KM# 178 500 TUGRIK
31.6100 g., 0.9250 Silver .9400 oz. ASW **Subject:** Millennium 2000 **Obv:** National emblem **Rev:** Rider and multicolor speckled hologram

Date	Mintage	F	VF	XF	Unc	BU
1998 Proof	Est. 10,000	Value: 37.50				

KM# 160 500 TUGRIK
31.1045 g., 0.9990 Silver 1.0000 oz. ASW **Subject:** Year of the Rabbit **Obv:** Soembo arms within circle **Rev:** Rabbit running left

Date	Mintage	F	VF	XF	Unc	BU
1999	3,000	—	—	—	35.00	—

KM# 202 500 TUGRIK
31.4400 g., 0.9250 Silver 0.935 oz. ASW, 38.6 mm. **Subject:** Princess Diana **Obv:** National emblem **Rev:** Diana by minefield **Edge:** Plain

Date	Mintage	F	VF	XF	Unc	BU
1999 Proof	—	Value: 45.00				

KM# 196 500 TUGRIK
19.8200 g., 0.5000 Silver 0.3186 oz. ASW, 34 mm. **Obv:** National emblem **Rev:** Two Bactrian camels **Edge:** Reeded

Date	Mintage	F	VF	XF	Unc	BU
1999 Proof	—	—	—	—	35.00	—

KM# 160a 500 TUGRIK
31.1045 g., 0.9990 Silver 1.0000 oz. ASW **Subject:** Year of the Rabbit **Obv:** Soembo arms within circle **Rev:** Rabbit running left **Note:** Gold plated rabbit.

Date	Mintage	F	VF	XF	Unc	BU
1999	3,000	—	—	—	50.00	—

KM# 161 500 TUGRIK
1.2441 g., 0.9990 Gold .0400 oz. AGW **Subject:** Year of the Rabbit **Obv:** Soembo arms within circle **Rev:** Rabbit running left

Date	Mintage	F	VF	XF	Unc	BU
1999	5,000	—	—	—	55.00	—

KM# 179 500 TUGRIK
25.2700 g., 0.9250 Silver .7515 oz. ASW **Subject:** Sita Tara **Obv:** Soembo arms above value **Rev:** Seated figure facing

Date	Mintage	F	VF	XF	Unc	BU
1999 Proof	2,500	Value: 46.50				

KM# 180 500 TUGRIK
25.0000 g., 0.9250 Bi-Metallic Goldine center in Silver ring .7435 oz. **Subject:** Genius of the Millennium - Gutenberg **Obv:** National emblem **Rev:** Open Bible, dates **Note:** Goldine center is square.

Date	Mintage	F	VF	XF	Unc	BU
1999 Proof	2,500	Value: 43.50				

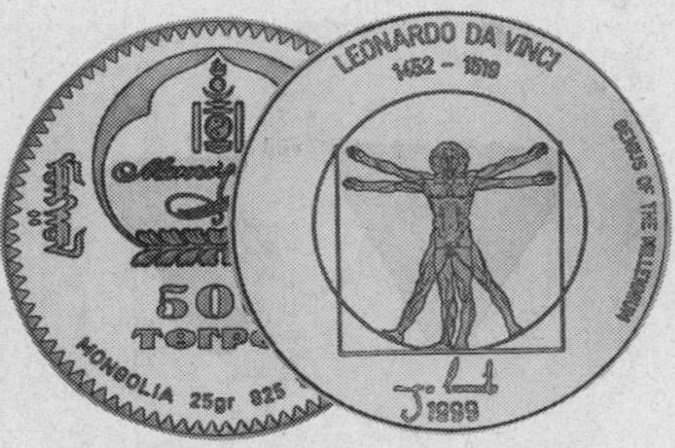

KM# 181 500 TUGRIK
25.0000 g., 0.9250 Bi-Metallic Goldine center in Silver ring .7435 oz. **Subject:** Genius of the Millennium - Da Vinci **Obv:** National emblem **Rev:** Male figure study **Note:** Goldine center is triangular.

Date	Mintage	F	VF	XF	Unc	BU
1999 Proof	2,500	Value: 46.50				

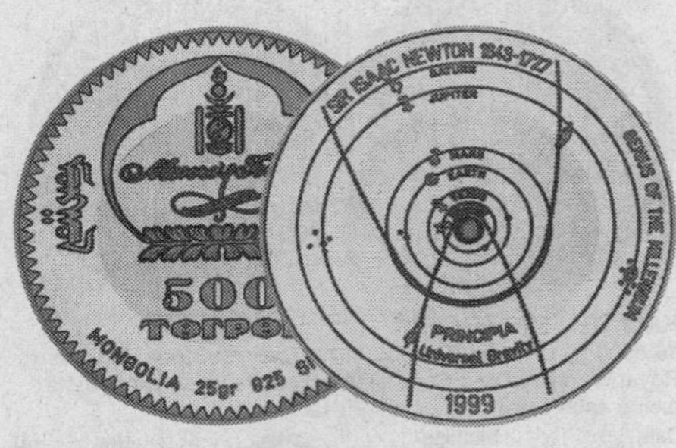

KM# 182 500 TUGRIK
25.0000 g., 0.9250 Bi-Metallic Goldine center in Silver ring .7435 oz. **Subject:** Genius of the Millennium - Newton **Obv:** National emblem **Rev:** Solar system diagram **Note:** Goldine center is round.

Date	Mintage	F	VF	XF	Unc	BU
1999 Proof	2,500	Value: 46.50				

KM# 183 500 TUGRIK
25.0000 g., 0.9250 Bi-Metallic Goldine center in Silver ring .7435 oz. **Subject:** Genius of the Millennium - von Goethe **Obv:** National emblem **Rev:** Bust facing **Note:** Goldine center is round.

Date	Mintage	F	VF	XF	Unc	BU
1999 Proof	2,500	Value: 43.50				

KM# 184 500 TUGRIK
25.0000 g., 0.9250 Bi-Metallic Goldine center in Silver ring .7435 oz. **Subject:** Genius of the Millennium - Edison **Obv:** National emblem **Rev:** Light bulb, telephone, record player **Note:** Goldine center is square.

Date	Mintage	F	VF	XF	Unc	BU
1999 Proof	2,500	Value: 43.50				

Note: KM#90, previously listed here, has been reported as never released.

KM# 65 600 TUGRIK
373.2000 g., 0.9990 Silver 12.0000 oz. ASW **Subject:** Year of the Rooster **Obv:** National emblem **Rev:** Rooster **Note:** Similar to 50 Tugrik, KM#61

Date	Mintage	F	VF	XF	Unc	BU
1993 Proof	200	Value: 500				

KM# 91 1000 TUGRIK
31.1000 g., 0.9990 Gold 1.0000 oz. AGW **Subject:** Year of the Monkey **Obv:** National emblem **Rev:** Monkey **Note:** Similar to 50 Tugrik, KM#86.

Date	Mintage	F	VF	XF	Unc	BU
1992 Proof	2,000	Value: 700				

KM# 85 1000 TUGRIK
20.0000 g., 0.9000 Gold .5788 oz. AGW **Obv:** National arms above value **Rev:** Ugedei Khan, Son of Genghis

Date	Mintage	F	VF	XF	Unc	BU
1992 Proof	500	Value: 415				

KM# 169 1000 TUGRIK
20.0000 g., 0.9000 Gold .5788 oz. AGW **Subject:** Discovery of America - Columbus **Obv:** State emblem above value **Rev:** Portrait of Columbus and ship within circle and legend

Date	Mintage	F	VF	XF	Unc	BU
1992 Proof	Est. 2,000	Value: 450				

KM# 66 1000 TUGRIK
31.1000 g., 0.9990 Gold 1.0000 oz. AGW **Subject:** Year of the Rooster **Obv:** National emblem above value at left, country name at right **Rev:** Rooster **Note:** Similar to 50 Tugrik, KM#61.

Date	Mintage	F	VF	XF	Unc	BU
1993 Proof	1,000	Value: 750				

KM# 74 1000 TUGRIK
20.0000 g., 0.9000 Gold .5788 oz. AGW **Subject:** Japanese Royal Wedding **Obv:** State emblem above value **Rev:** Busts of couple facing each other

Date	Mintage	F	VF	XF	Unc	BU
1993 Proof	145	Value: 800				

KM# 78 1000 TUGRIK
31.1035 g., 0.9990 Gold 1.0000 oz. AGW **Subject:** Year of the Dog **Obv:** National emblem **Rev:** Pekingese

Date	Mintage	F	VF	XF	Unc	BU
1994 Proof	500	Value: 725				

KM# 96 1000 TUGRIK
3.1100 g., 0.9990 Gold .1000 oz. AGW **Subject:** Year of the Pig **Obv:** National emblem **Rev:** Wild boar **Note:** Similar to 500 Tugrik, KM#95.

Date	Mintage	F	VF	XF	Unc	BU
1995 Proof	500	Value: 200				

KM# 148 1000 TUGRIK
4.4100 g., 0.9000 Gold .1276 oz. AGW **Subject:** Moscow - Ulaan Blaatar - Bejing Railroad **Obv:** Soembo arms within circle **Rev:** Steam locomotive

Date	Mintage	F	VF	XF	Unc	BU
1995 Proof	—	Value: 125				

KM# 106 1000 TUGRIK
3.1100 g., 0.9990 Gold .1000 oz. AGW **Subject:** Year of the Rat **Obv:** National emblem **Rev:** Rat **Note:** Similar to 50 Tugrik, KM#104.

Date	Mintage	F	VF	XF	Unc	BU
1996 Proof	500	Value: 150				

KM# 115 1000 TUGRIK
156.6100 g., 0.9990 Silver 5.0000 oz. ASW, 65.5 mm. **Series:** Olympics **Obv:** Soembo arms **Rev:** Ancient runners within circle **Note:** With gold inlay. Illustration reduced.

Date	Mintage	F	VF	XF	Unc	BU
1996 Matte	—	—	—	—	225	—

KM# 128 1000 TUGRIK
3.1100 g., 0.9990 Gold .1000 oz. AGW **Subject:** Year of the Ox **Obv:** National emblem **Rev:** Ox **Note:** Similar to 50 Tugrik, KM#126.

Date	Mintage	F	VF	XF	Unc	BU
1997 Proof	500	Value: 100				

KM# 201 1000 TUGRIK
7.7200 g., Gold, 24.8 mm. **Obv:** Soembo arms **Rev:** Tiger head with diamond inset eyes **Edge:** Reeded

Date	Mintage	F	VF	XF	Unc	BU
1999 Proof	—	Value: 350				

KM# 185 1000 TUGRIK
1.2441 g., 0.9999 Gold .0400 oz. AGW **Subject:** Genius of the Millennium - Da Vinci **Obv:** National arms **Rev:** Male figure study **Note:** Similar to 500 Tugrik, KM#181.

Date	Mintage	F	VF	XF	Unc	BU
1999 Proof	25,000	Value: 45.00				

KM# 116 1200 TUGRIK
7.7000 g., 0.9990 Silver .2496 oz. ASW **Subject:** Chinggis Khan **Obv:** Soemba arms **Rev:** Bust 3/4 right, dates below **Note:** Similar to 5,000 Tugrik, KM#118.

Date	Mintage	F	VF	XF	Unc	BU
1996	Est. 10,000	—	—	—	10.00	12.00
1996 Proof	Est. 10,000	Value: 15.00				

KM# 149 1200 TUGRIK
7.7000 g., 0.9990 Silver .2496 oz. ASW **Subject:** Ugedei Khan **Obv:** National emblem **Rev:** Head 3/4 facing, dates at right

Date	Mintage	F	VF	XF	Unc	BU
1997 Proof	Est. 10,000	Value: 15.00				

KM# 113 2000 TUGRIK
7.7760 g., 0.5830 Gold .1458 oz. AGW **Series:** Endangered Wildlife **Obv:** Soembo arms within wreath **Rev:** Snow leopard

Date	Mintage	F	VF	XF	Unc	BU
1994 Proof	Est. 5,000	Value: 150				

KM# 114 2000 TUGRIK
7.7760 g., 0.5830 Gold .1458 oz. AGW **Series:** Olympics **Obv:** Soembo arms within wreath **Rev:** Boxer

Date	Mintage	F	VF	XF	Unc	BU
1994 Proof	Est. 5,000	Value: 150				

KM# 175 2000 TUGRIK
7.7760 g., 0.5830 Gold .1458 oz. AGW **Subject:** Year of the Tiger **Obv:** National emblem **Rev:** Tiger

Date	Mintage	F	VF	XF	Unc	BU
1998	—	—	—	—	110	120

KM# 97 2500 TUGRIK
155.5150 g., 0.9990 Silver 5.0000 oz. ASW, 65 mm. **Subject:** Year of the Pig **Obv:** Soemba arms **Rev:** Wild pigs eating in the wild **Note:** Illustration reduced.

Date	Mintage	F	VF	XF	Unc	BU
1995 Proof	300	Value: 160				

KM# 102 2500 TUGRIK
155.5150 g., 0.9990 Silver 5.0000 oz. ASW **Subject:** Moscow - Bejing Railroad **Obv:** Soemba arms **Rev:** Locomotive on raised tracks left **Note:** Similar to 500 Tugrik, KM#101.

Date	Mintage	F	VF	XF	Unc	BU
1995 Proof	5,000	Value: 125				

KM# 107 2500 TUGRIK
155.5150 g., 0.9990 Silver 5.0000 oz. ASW, 65 mm. **Subject:** Year of the Rat **Obv:** Soemba arms **Rev:** Gold-plated rat

Date	Mintage	F	VF	XF	Unc	BU
1996 Proof	300	Value: 250				

KM# 117 2500 TUGRIK
15.5500 g., 0.9990 Silver .4994 oz. ASW **Obv:** National emblem **Rev:** Chinggis Khan **Note:** Similar to 5000 Tugrik, KM#118

Date	Mintage	F	VF	XF	Unc	BU
1996	Est. 10,000	—	—	—	20.00	22.50
1996 Proof	Est. 10,000	Value: 30.00				

KM# 129 2500 TUGRIK
155.5150 g., 0.9990 Silver With Partial Gold Plating 5.0000 oz. **Subject:** Year of the Ox **Obv:** National emblem **Rev:** Man riding ox, flowered spray around upper right

Date	Mintage	F	VF	XF	Unc	BU
1997 Proof	300	Value: 200				

KM# 150 2500 TUGRIK
15.5517 g., 0.9990 Silver .4995 oz. ASW **Obv:** Soembo arms above value **Rev:** Bust with hat 1/4 left

Date	Mintage	F	VF	XF	Unc	BU
1997 Proof	Est. 10,000	Value: 30.00				

KM# 162 2500 TUGRIK
155.1750 g., 0.9990 Silver 4.984 oz. ASW, 65 mm. **Subject:** Year of the Rabbit **Obv:** National emblem **Rev:** Rabbit **Edge:** Plain **Note:** Struck at B.H. Mayer's.

Date	Mintage	F	VF	XF	Unc	BU
1999 Proof	1,500	Value: 175				

KM# 163 2500 TUGRIK
7.7759 g., 0.9990 Gold 0.2498 oz. AGW, 22.5 mm. **Subject:** Year of the Rabbit **Obv:** National emblem **Rev:** Rabbit **Edge:** Plain **Note:** Struck at B.H. Mayer's.

Date	Mintage	F	VF	XF	Unc	BU
1999 Proof	1,500	Value: 200				

KM# 81 4000 TUGRIK
15.5940 g., 0.9999 Gold .5009 oz. AGW **Obv:** Soembo arms above value **Rev:** Horse and rider left

Date	Mintage	F	VF	XF	Unc	BU
1992 Proof	Est. 9,000	Value: 650				

KM# 67 5000 TUGRIK
155.5000 g., 0.9990 Gold 5.0000 oz. AGW **Subject:** Year of the Rooster **Obv:** National emblem above denomination at left, country name at right **Rev:** Rooster **Note:** Similar to 50 Tugrik, KM#51.

Date	Mintage	F	VF	XF	Unc	BU
1993 Proof	50	Value: 3,750				

KM# 79 5000 TUGRIK
155.5000 g., 0.9990 Gold 5.0000 oz. AGW **Subject:** Year of the Dog **Obv:** National emblem **Rev:** Dog

Date	Mintage	F	VF	XF	Unc	BU
1994 Proof	25	Value: 5,000				

KM# 118 5000 TUGRIK
3.1000 g., 0.9990 Silver .9989 oz. ASW **Obv:** Soembo arms above value **Rev:** Bust 3/4 facing, dates below

Date	Mintage	F	VF	XF	Unc	BU
1996	Est. 10,000	—	—	—	30.00	35.00
1996 Proof	Est. 10,000	Value: 50.00				

KM# 194 5000 TUGRIK
6.2200 g., 0.9990 Gold 0.1998 oz. AGW **Subject:** UNICEF **Obv:** National emblem and value **Rev:** Three costumed children **Edge:** Reeded

Date	Mintage	F	VF	XF	Unc	BU
1997 Proof	10,000	Value: 145				

KM# 136 5000 TUGRIK
155.5175 g., 0.9990 Silver 5.0000 oz. ASW **Subject:** Aquila Rapax **Obv:** National emblem and value **Rev:** Bird standing on rock **Note:** Similar to 500 Tugrik, KM#132.

Date	Mintage	F	VF	XF	Unc	BU
1997 Proof	750	Value: 225				

KM# 137 5000 TUGRIK
155.5175 g., 0.9990 Silver 5.0000 oz. ASW **Subject:** Eguus Fergus **Obv:** National emblem and value **Rev:** Horse running left **Note:** Similar to 500 Tugrik, KM#133.

Date	Mintage	F	VF	XF	Unc	BU
1997 Proof	750	Value: 225				

KM# 139 5000 TUGRIK
155.5175 g., 0.9990 Silver 5.0000 oz. ASW **Subject:** Panthera Tigris Altaica **Obv:** National emblem and value **Rev:** Tiger lying on rock **Note:** Similar to 500 Tugrik, KM#135.

Date	Mintage	F	VF	XF	Unc	BU
1997 Proof	750	Value: 225				

KM# 151 5000 TUGRIK
31.1035 g., 0.9990 Silver 1.0000 oz. ASW **Obv:** National emblem **Rev:** Ugedei Khan

Date	Mintage	F	VF	XF	Unc	BU
1997 Proof	Est. 10,000	Value: 50.00				

KM# 138 5000 TUGRIK
155.5175 g., 0.9990 Silver 5 oz. ASW **Subject:** Camelus Ferus **Obv:** National emblem and value **Rev:** Camel right **Note:** Similar to 500 Tugrik, KM#134.

Date	Mintage	F	VF	XF	Unc	BU
1997 Proof	750	Value: 225				

KM# 82 8000 TUGRIK
31.1620 g., 0.9999 Gold 1.0000 oz. AGW **Obv:** Soembo arms above value **Rev:** Chinggis Khan standing

Date	Mintage	F	VF	XF	Unc	BU
1992 Proof	Est. 3,000	Value: 1,200				

KM# 98 10000 TUGRIK
31.1035 g., 0.9990 Gold 1.0000 oz. AGW **Subject:** Year of the Pig **Obv:** National emblem **Rev:** Wild boar **Note:** Similar to 500 Tugrik, KM#95.

Date	Mintage	F	VF	XF	Unc	BU
1995 Proof	300	Value: 745				

KM# 108 10000 TUGRIK
31.1035 g., 0.9990 Gold 1.0000 oz. AGW **Subject:** Year of the Rat **Obv:** National emblem **Rev:** Rat **Note:** Similar to 50 Tugrik, KM#104.

Date	Mintage	F	VF	XF	Unc	BU
1996 Proof	300	Value: 745				

KM# 140 10000 TUGRIK
1000.1000 g., 0.9990 Silver 32.1575 oz. ASW **Subject:** Aquila Rapax **Obv:** National emblem and value **Rev:** Bird standing on rock **Note:** Similar to 500 Tugrik, KM#132.

Date	Mintage	F	VF	XF	Unc	BU
1996 Prooflike	450	—	—	—	—	600

KM# 143 10000 TUGRIK
1000.1000 g., 0.9990 Silver 32.1575 oz. ASW **Subject:** Panthera Tigris Alaica **Obv:** National emblem and value **Rev:** Tiger lying on rock **Note:** Similar to 500 Tugrik, KM#135.

Date	Mintage	F	VF	XF	Unc	BU
1996 Proof	450	—	—	—	—	600

KM# 141 10000 TUGRIK
1000.1000 g., 0.9990 Silver 32.1575 oz. ASW **Subject:** Equus Ferus **Obv:** National emblem and value **Rev:** Horse running left **Note:** Similar to 500 Tugrik, KM#133.

Date	Mintage	F	VF	XF	Unc	BU
1996 Prooflike	450	—	—	—	—	600

KM# 142 10000 TUGRIK
1000.1000 g., 0.9990 Silver 32.1575 oz. ASW **Subject:** Camelus Ferus **Obv:** National emblem and value **Rev:** Camel right **Note:** Similar to 500 Tugrik, KM#134.

Date	Mintage	F	VF	XF	Unc	BU
1996 Prooflike	450	—	—	—	—	600

KM# 130 10000 TUGRIK
31.1035 g., 0.9990 Gold 1.0000 oz. AGW **Subject:** Year of the Ox **Obv:** National emblem **Rev:** Ox **Note:** Similar to 2,500 Tugrik, KM#129.

Date	Mintage	F	VF	XF	Unc	BU
1997 Proof	300	Value: 745				

KM# 176 10000 TUGRIK
31.1035 g., 0.9990 Gold 1.0000 oz. AGW **Subject:** Year of the Tiger **Obv:** National emblem **Rev:** Tiger

Date	Mintage	F	VF	XF	Unc	BU
1998	250	—	—	—	—	745

KM# 164 10000 TUGRIK
31.1035 g., 0.9990 Gold 1 oz. AGW **Subject:** Year of the Rabbit **Obv:** National emblem **Rev:** Rabbit

Date	Mintage	F	VF	XF	Unc	BU
1999	250	—	—	—	—	745

KM# 68 12000 TUGRIK
373.2000 g., 0.9990 Gold 12.0000 oz. AGW **Subject:** Year of the Rooster **Obv:** National emblem above denomination at left, country name at right **Rev:** Rooster **Note:** Similar to 50 Tugrik, KM#61.

Date	Mintage	F	VF	XF	Unc	BU
1993 Proof	25	Value: 8,500				

KM# 119 12000 TUGRIK
7.7700 g., 0.9999 Gold .2498 oz. AGW **Subject:** Chinggis Khan **Obv:** National emblem and value **Rev:** Bust 3/4 facing **Note:** Similar to 50,000 Tugrik, KM#121.

Date	Mintage	F	VF	XF	Unc	BU
1996 Rare	10	—	—	—	—	—
1996 Proof, rare	10	—	—	—	—	—

KM# 119a 12000 TUGRIK
7.7700 g., 0.9990 Gold .2495 oz. AGW **Subject:** Chinggis Khan **Obv:** National emblem and value **Rev:** Bust 3/4 facing

Date	Mintage	F	VF	XF	Unc	BU
1996	Est. 10,000	—	—	—	175	180
1996 Proof	Est. 10,000	Value: 195				

KM# 152 12000 TUGRIK
7.7750 g., 0.9990 Gold .2500 oz. AGW **Obv:** Soembo arms above value **Rev:** Head with hat facing

Date	Mintage	F	VF	XF	Unc	BU
1997 Proof	Est. 10,000	Value: 300				

KM# 120 25000 TUGRIK
15.5500 g., 0.9999 Gold .4999 oz. AGW **Subject:** Chinggis Khan **Obv:** National emblem and value **Rev:** Bust 3/4 facing **Note:** Similar to 50,000 Tugrik, KM#121.

Date	Mintage	F	VF	XF	Unc	BU
1996 Rare	10	—	—	—	—	—
1996 Proof, Rare	10	—	—	—	—	—

KM# 120a 25000 TUGRIK
15.5500 g., 0.9990 Gold .4994 oz. AGW **Subject:** Chinggis Khan **Obv:** National emblem and value **Rev:** Bust 3/4 facing

Date	Mintage	F	VF	XF	Unc	BU
1996	Est. 10,000	—	—	—	350	360
1996 Proof	Est. 10,000	Value: 375				

KM# 144 25000 TUGRIK
15.5940 g., 0.9999 Gold .5000 oz. AGW **Subject:** Aquila Rapaz **Obv:** National emblem and value **Rev:** Bird standing on rock **Note:** Similar to 500 Tugrik, KM#132.

Date	Mintage	F	VF	XF	Unc	BU
1996 Proof	300	Value: 420				

KM# 145 25000 TUGRIK
15.5940 g., 0.9999 Gold .5000 oz. AGW **Subject:** Equus Ferus **Obv:** National emblem and value **Rev:** Horse running left **Note:** Similar to 500 Tugrik, KM#133.

Date	Mintage	F	VF	XF	Unc	BU
1996 Proof	300	Value: 420				

KM# 146 25000 TUGRIK
15.5940 g., 0.9999 Gold .5000 oz. AGW **Subject:** Cameleus Ferus **Obv:** National emblem and value **Rev:** Camel right **Note:** Similar to 500 Tugrik, KM#134.

Date	Mintage	F	VF	XF	Unc	BU
1996 Proof	300	Value: 420				

KM# 147 25000 TUGRIK
15.5940 g., 0.9999 Gold .5000 oz. AGW **Subject:** Panthera Tigris Altaica **Obv:** National emblem and value **Rev:** Tiger lying on rock **Note:** Similar to 500 Tugrik, KM#135.

Date	Mintage	F	VF	XF	Unc	BU
1996 Proof	300	Value: 420				

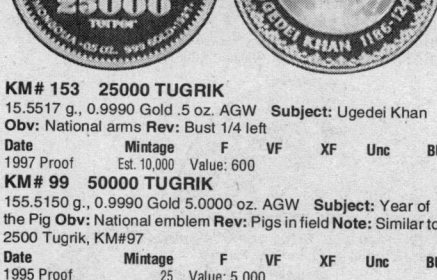

KM# 153 25000 TUGRIK
15.5517 g., 0.9990 Gold .5 oz. AGW **Subject:** Ugedei Khan **Obv:** National arms **Rev:** Bust 1/4 left

Date	Mintage	F	VF	XF	Unc	BU
1997 Proof	Est. 10,000	Value: 600				

KM# 99 50000 TUGRIK
155.5150 g., 0.9990 Gold 5.0000 oz. AGW **Subject:** Year of the Pig **Obv:** National emblem **Rev:** Pigs in field **Note:** Similar to 2500 Tugrik, KM#97

Date	Mintage	F	VF	XF	Unc	BU
1995 Proof	25	Value: 5,000				

KM# 109 50000 TUGRIK
155.5150 g., 0.9990 Gold 5.0000 oz. AGW **Subject:** Year of the Rat **Obv:** National emblem **Rev:** Rat **Note:** Similar to 50 Tugrik, KM#104.

Date	Mintage	F	VF	XF	Unc	BU
1996 Proof	25	Value: 4,250				

KM# 121 50000 TUGRIK
31.1000 g., 0.9999 Gold .9998 oz. AGW **Obv:** Soembo arms above value **Rev:** Bust 3/4 facing

Date	Mintage	F	VF	XF	Unc	BU
1996 Rare	10	—	—	—	—	—
1996 Proof, rare	10	—	—	—	—	—

KM# 121a 50000 TUGRIK
31.1000 g., 0.9990 Gold .9998 oz. AGW **Subject:** Chinggis Khan **Obv:** Soembo arms above value **Rev:** Bust 3/4 facing

Date	Mintage	F	VF	XF	Unc	BU
1996	Est. 10,000	—	—	—	700	725
1996 Proof	Est. 10,000	Value: 800				

KM# 131 50000 TUGRIK
155.5150 g., 0.9999 Gold 5.0000 oz. AGW **Subject:** Year of the Ox **Obv:** National emblem **Rev:** Ox **Note:** Similar to 2,500 Tugrik, KM#129.

Date	Mintage	F	VF	XF	Unc	BU
1997 Proof	25	Value: 4,000				

KM# 154 50000 TUGRIK
31.1035 g., 0.9990 Gold 1.0000 oz. AGW **Obv:** Soembo arms above value **Rev:** Bust 3/4 facing

Date	Mintage	F	VF	XF	Unc	BU
1997 Proof	Est. 10,000	Value: 1,200				

KM# 177 50000 TUGRIK
155.5150 g., 0.9999 Gold 5.0000 oz. AGW **Subject:** Year of the Tiger **Obv:** National emblem **Rev:** Tiger

Date	Mintage	F	VF	XF	Unc	BU
1998	99	—	—	—	3,750	—

KM# 165 50000 TUGRIK
155.5150 g., 0.9999 Gold 5.0000 oz. AGW **Subject:** Year of the Rabbit **Obv:** National emblem **Rev:** Rabbit

Date	Mintage	F	VF	XF	Unc	BU
1999	99	—	—	—	3,750	—

KM# 83 250000 TUGRIK
1000.1000 g., 0.9999 Gold 32.1575 oz. AGW, 85 mm. **Subject:** Chinggis Khan **Obv:** Soemba arms **Rev:** Head facing

Date	Mintage	F	VF	XF	Unc	BU
1992 Proof	Est. 300	Value: 25,000				

PIEFORTS

KM#	Date	Mintage	Identification	Mkt Val
P1	1980	92	25 Tugrik. Silver. KM39.	135
P2	1980	550	750 Tugrik. Gold. KM40.	775

MINT SETS

KM#	Date	Mintage	Identification	Issue Price	Mkt Val
MS1	1980 (8)	—	KM27-33, 41	—	25.00
MS2	1996 (3)	10,000	KM116-118	—	40.00
MS3	1996 (3)	10	KM119-121	—	—
MS4	1996 (3)	10,000	KM119a-121a	—	1,100

PROOF SETS

KM#	Date	Mintage	Identification	Issue Price	Mkt Val
PS1	1996 (3)	—	KM105, 106, 108	—	700
PS2	1996 (3)	10,000	KM116-118. The *10,000 mintage limit is per denomination including proof and BU single coins as well as coins included in sets.	—	70.00
PS3	1996 (3)	10	KM119-121	—	—
PS4	1996	10,000	KM119a-121a. The *10,000 mintage limit is per denomination including proof and BU single coins as well as coins included in sets.	—	1,700
PS5	1996 (4)	10	KM116-118, 121	—	—
PS6	1996 (4)	10,000	KM116-118, 121a. The *10,000 mintage limit is per denomination including proof and BU single coins as well as coins included in sets.	—	1,000
PS7	1996 (4)	10	KM118, 119-121	—	—
PS8	1996 (4)	10,000	KM118, 119a-121a. The *10,000 mintage limit is per denomination including proof and BU single coins as well as coins included in sets.	—	1,750
PS9	1997 (3)	10,000	KM149-151	—	100
PS10	1997 (3)	10,000	KM152-154	—	2,150

The former independent kingdom of Montenegro, now one of the nominally autonomous federated units of Yugoslavia, was located in southeastern Europe north of Albania. As a kingdom, it had an area of 5,333 sq. mi. (13,812 sq. km.) and a population of about 250,000. Capital: Podgorica.

Montenegro became an independent state in 1355 following the break-up of the Serb empire. During the Turkish invasion of Albania and Herzegovina in the 15th century, the Montenegrins moved their capital to the remote mountain village of Cetinje where they maintained their independence through two centuries of intermittent attack, emerging as the only one of the Balkan states not subjugated by the Turks. When World War I began, Montenegro joined with Serbia and was subsequently invaded and occupied by the Austrians. Austria withdrew upon the defeat of the Central Powers, permitting the Serbians to move in and maintain the occupation. Montenegro then joined the kingdom of the Serbs, Croats and Slovenes, which later became Yugoslavia.

The coinage, issued under the autocratic rule of Prince Nicholas, is obsolete.

RULERS
Nicholas I, as Prince, 1860-1910 as King, 1910-1918

MINT MARKS
(a) - Paris, privy marks only

MONETARY SYSTEM
100 Para, ПАРА = 1 Perper, ПЕРПЕР

KINGDOM

STANDARD COINAGE

KM# 1 PARA
Bronze **Ruler:** Nicholas I **Obv:** Crowned arms **Rev:** Value

Date	Mintage	F	VF	XF	Unc	BU
1906	200,000	10.00	20.00	40.00	90.00	—

KM# 16 PARA
Bronze **Ruler:** Nicholas I **Obv:** Crowned arms **Rev:** Value

Date	Mintage	F	VF	XF	Unc	BU
1913	100,000	13.00	30.00	70.00	140	—
1914	200,000	7.00	15.00	30.00	90.00	—

KM# 2 2 PARE
Bronze **Ruler:** Nicholas I **Obv:** Crowned arms **Rev:** Value

Date	Mintage	F	VF	XF	Unc	BU
1906	600,125	5.00	10.00	20.00	40.00	—
1908	250,000	9.00	20.00	35.00	80.00	—

KM# 17 2 PARE
Bronze **Ruler:** Nicholas I **Obv:** Crowned arms **Rev:** Value

Date	Mintage	F	VF	XF	Unc	BU
1913	500,000	5.00	8.00	17.00	32.00	—
1914	400,000	6.00	10.00	20.00	48.00	—

KM# 3 10 PARA
Nickel **Ruler:** Nicholas I **Obv:** Crowned arms **Rev:** Value

Date	Mintage	F	VF	XF	Unc	BU
1906	750,156	2.50	5.00	12.00	25.00	—
1908	250,000	3.00	6.50	16.00	36.00	—

KM# 18 10 PARA
Nickel **Ruler:** Nicholas I

Date	Mintage	F	VF	XF	Unc	BU
1913	200,000	3.50	8.00	18.00	42.00	—
1914	800,000	2.50	5.00	12.00	25.00	—

KM# 4 20 PARA
Nickel **Ruler:** Nicholas I **Obv:** Crowned arms **Rev:** Value

Date	Mintage	F	VF	XF	Unc	BU
1906	600,156	3.00	6.00	12.00	25.00	—
1908	400,000	3.00	7.00	15.00	35.00	—

KM# 19 20 PARA
Nickel **Ruler:** Nicholas I **Obv:** Crowned arms **Rev:** Value

Date	Mintage	F	VF	XF	Unc	BU
1913	200,000	4.00	8.00	18.00	45.00	—
1914	800,000	3.00	6.00	12.00	25.00	—

KM# 5 PERPER
5.0000 g., 0.8350 Silver .1342 oz. ASW **Ruler:** Nicholas I
Obv: Head right **Rev:** Crowned mantled arms within sprigs above date and value **Note:** Approximately 30 percent melted.

Date	Mintage	F	VF	XF	Unc	BU
1909(a)	500,018	12.00	22.00	42.00	95.00	—

KM# 14 PERPER
5.0000 g., 0.8350 Silver .1342 oz. ASW **Ruler:** Nicholas I
Obv: Head right **Rev:** Crowned mantled arms within sprigs above value and date

Date	Mintage	F	VF	XF	Unc	BU
1912	520,008	8.00	14.00	30.00	85.00	—
1914	500,000	9.00	18.00	35.00	90.00	—

KM# 7 2 PERPERA
10.0000 g., 0.8350 Silver .2685 oz. ASW **Ruler:** Nicholas I **Obv:** Head right **Rev:** Crowned mantled arms within sprigs above date and value

Date	Mintage	F	VF	XF	Unc	BU
1910	300,006	15.00	35.00	70.00	180	—

KM# 20 2 PERPERA
10.0000 g., 0.8350 Silver .2685 oz. ASW **Ruler:** Nicholas I
Obv: Head right **Rev:** Crowned mantled arms within sprigs above date and value

Date	Mintage	F	VF	XF	Unc	BU
1914	200,008	15.00	35.00	75.00	185	—

KM# 6 5 PERPERA
24.0000 g., 0.9000 Silver .6944 oz. ASW **Ruler:** Nicholas I
Obv: Head right **Rev:** Crowned and mantled arms **Note:** Approximately 50 percent melted.

Date	Mintage	F	VF	XF	Unc	BU
1909(a)	60,010	70.00	140	320	780	—

KM# 15 5 PERPERA
24.0000 g., 0.9000 Silver .6944 oz. ASW **Ruler:** Nicholas I
Obv: Head right **Rev:** Crowned mantled arms within sprigs above date and value

Date	Mintage	F	VF	XF	Unc	BU
1912	40,002	80.00	160	290	830	—
1914	20,002	85.00	160	320	950	1,000

KM# 8 10 PERPERA
3.3875 g., 0.9000 Gold .0980 oz. AGW **Ruler:** Nicholas I
Obv: Head right **Rev:** Crowned mantled arms within sprigs above date and value

Date	Mintage	F	VF	XF	Unc	BU
1910	40,000	120	220	310	530	—

KM# 9 10 PERPERA
3.3875 g., 0.9000 Gold .0980 oz. AGW **Ruler:** Nicholas I
Subject: 50th Year of Reign **Obv:** Head laureate left **Rev:** Crowned mantled arms within sprigs above date and value

Date	Mintage	F	VF	XF	Unc	BU
1910	35,003	130	250	330	560	—

KM# 10 20 PERPERA
6.7751 g., 0.9000 Gold .1960 oz. AGW **Ruler:** Nicholas I
Obv: Head right **Rev:** Crowned mantled arms within sprigs above date and value

Date	Mintage	F	VF	XF	Unc	BU
1910	30,000	150	275	460	720	—

KM# 11 20 PERPERA
6.7751 g., 0.9000 Gold .1960 oz. AGW **Ruler:** Nicholas I
Subject: 50th Year of Reign **Obv:** Laureate head left **Rev:** Crowned mantled arms within sprigs above date and value

Date	Mintage	F	VF	XF	Unc	BU
1910	30,003	150	275	460	720	—

KM# 12 100 PERPERA
33.8753 g., 0.9000 Gold .9802 oz. AGW **Ruler:** Nicholas I
Obv: Head right **Rev:** Crowned and mantled arms

Date	Mintage	F	VF	XF	Unc	BU
1910	301	—	4,500	7,000	12,000	—
1910 Proof	25	Value: 14,000				

KM# 13 100 PERPERA
33.8753 g., 0.9000 Gold .9802 oz. AGW **Ruler:** Nicholas I
Subject: 50th Year of Reign **Obv:** Laureate head left **Rev:** Crowned mantled arms within sprigs above date and value

Date	Mintage	F	VF	XF	Unc	BU
1910	501	—	4,500	6,500	11,000	—
1910 Proof	Inc. above	Value: 15,000				

PATTERNS

KM#	Date	Mintage	Identification	Mkt Val
Pn1	1915	—	Para. With ESSAI. Struck at Paris.	1,200
Pn2	1915	—	2 Pare. With ESSAI. Struck at Paris.	1,200
Pn3	1915	—	10 Para. With ESSAI. Struck at Paris.	—
Pn4	1915	—	20 Para. With ESSAI. Struck at Paris.	—
Pn5	1915	—	Perper. With ESSAI. Struck at Paris.	1,500
Pn6	1915	—	2 Perpera. With ESSAI. Struck at Paris.	2,000
Pn7	1915	—	5 Perpera. With ESSAI. Struck at Paris. Bears the monogram EL for Edmond Lindauer, who copied the work of S. Schwarz of the Vienna Mint, where the regular issue coinage was struck.	8,000

TRIAL STRIKES

KM#	Date	Mintage	Identification	Mkt Val
TS1	ND(1910)	—	100 Perpera. Hallmarked edge. Uniface.	6,000
TS2	ND(1910)	—	100 Perpera. TITRE ZZK ESSAI.	5,000

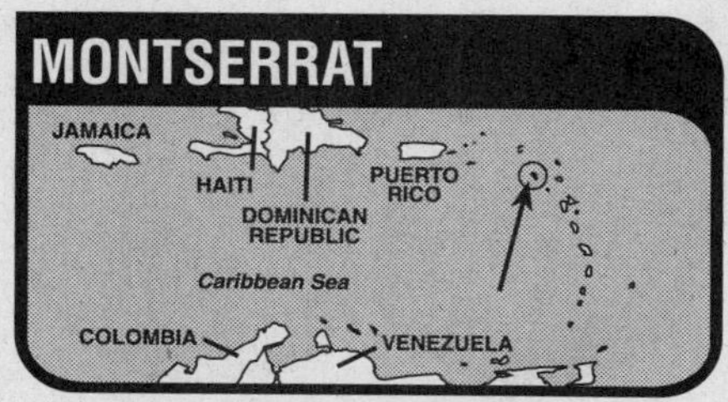

Montserrat, a British crown colony located in the Lesser Antilles of the West Indies 27 miles (43 km.) southwest of Antigua, has an area of 38 sq. mi. (100 sq. km.) and a population of 18,500. Capital: Plymouth. The island - actually a range of volcanic peaks rising from the Caribbean - exports cotton, limes and vegetables.

Columbus discovered Montserrat in 1493 and named it after Monserrado, a mountain in Spain. It was colonized by the English in 1632 and, except for brief periods of French occupancy in 1667 and 1782-83, has remained a British possession from that time. Currency of the British Caribbean Territories (Eastern Group) was used until later when the East Caribbean States coinage was introduced. Until becoming a separate colony in 1956, Montserrat was a presidency of the Leeward Islands.

The early 19th century countermarks of a crowned 3, 4, 7, 9 or 18 over M as documented by Major Pridmore have been more correctly listed under St. Bartholomew.

RULERS
British

MONETARY SYSTEM
100 Cents = 1 Dollar

BRITISH COLONY

MODERN COINAGE

KM# 30 4 DOLLARS
28.3000 g., Copper-Nickel, 38.5 mm. **Series:** F.A.O.
Obv: National shield **Rev:** Value flanked by plants

Date	Mintage	F	VF	XF	Unc	BU
1970	13,000	—	8.00	15.00	30.00	45.00
1970 Proof	2,000	Value: 50.00				

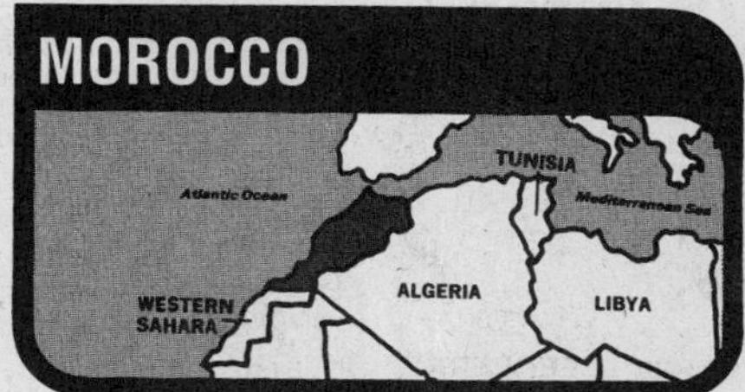

The Kingdom of Morocco, situated on the northwest corner of Africa, has an area of 275,117 sq. mi. (446,550 sq. km.) and a population of 28.5 million. Capital: Rabat. The economy is essentially agricultural. Phosphates, fresh and preserved vegetables, canned fish, and raw materials are exported.

Morocco's strategic position at the gateway to Western Europe has been the principal determinant of its violent, frequently unfortunate history. Time and again the fertile plain between the rugged Atlas Mountains and the sea has echoed the battle's trumpet as Phoenicians, Romans, Vandals, Visigoths, Byzantine Greeks and Islamic Arabs successively conquered and occupied the land. Modern Morocco is a remnant of an early empire formed by the Arabs at the close of the 7th century, which encompassed all of northwest Africa, and most of the Iberian Peninsula. During the 17th and 18th centuries, while under the control of native dynasties, it was the headquarters of the famous Sale pirates. Morocco's strategic position involved it in the competition of 19th century European powers for political influence in Africa, and resulted in the division of Morocco into French and Spanish spheres of interest, which were established as protectorates in 1912. Morocco became independent on March 2, 1956, after France agreed to end its protectorate. Spain signed similar agreements on April 7 of the same year.

TITLES

Al-Maghribiya(t)

المملكة المغربية

Al-Mamlaka(t) al-Maghribiya(t)

المحمدية الشريفة

Al-Mohammediya(t) esh-Sherifiya(t)

RULERS
Abd al-Aziz, AH1311-1326/1894-1908AD
Abd al-Hafiz, AH1326-1330/1908-1912AD

French Protectorate, AH1330/1912AD
Yusuf, AH1330-1346/1912-1927AD
Mohammed V, AH1346-1375/1927-1955AD

Kingdom
Mohammed V, AH1376-1381/1956-1962AD
Al-Hasan II, AH1381-1420/1962-1999AD
Mohammed VI, AH1420- /1999- AD

MINTS

(a) - Paris privy marks only

Silver Coins

Bronze Coins

Bi - England (Birmingham)

بانكلند

Ln = bi-England (London)

باريز

Pa = bi-Bariz (Paris)

فاس

Fs = Fes (Fas, Fez)

Py - Poissy Inscribed "Paris" but with thunderbolt privy mark.

NOTE: Some of the above forms of the mint names are shown as they appear on the coins, not in regular Arabic script.

NOTES: On the silver coins the denominations are written in words and each series has its own characteristic names:
Y#9-13 (1313-1319) Denomination in 'Preferred" Dirhams.
Y#18-22 (1320-1323) Denomination in fractions of a Rial, but on the 3 larger sizes, the equivalent is given in "Urti parts", 1 Rial 20 = Urti parts.
Y#23-25 (1329) Denomination in Dirhams and in fraction of a Rial.
Y#30-33 (1331-1336) Denomination in Yusuti or "Treasury" Dirhams.

On most of the larger denominations, the denomination is given in the form of a rhymed couplet.

NOTE: Various copper and silver coins dated AH1297-1311 are believed to be patterns. Copper coins similar to Y#14-17, but without denomination on reverse, are patterns.

NOTE: 1, 2, 5 and 10 Mazunas of AH1320 Fes exist in medal alignment and coin alignment (rare). AH1321-1323 Fes strikes are medal alignment only.

KINGDOM

Filali Sharifs - Alawi Dynasty

Abd al-Aziz

AH1311-1326 / 1894-1908AD

MILLED COINAGE

Y# 9.2 1/2 DIRHAM
1.4558 g., 0.8350 Silver .0391 oz. ASW **Obv:** Star of David within inner circle flanked by arrow heads facing inwards **Rev:** Star of David within inner circle flanked by arrow heads facing inwards

Date	Mintage	F	VF	XF	Unc
AH1319Pa	572,000	15.00	30.00	60.00	100

REFORM COINAGE

AH1320 / 1902AD

Y# 14.1 MAZUNA
1.0000 g., Bronze **Obv:** Date within circle **Rev:** Value within circle

Date	Mintage	F	VF	XF	Unc
AH1320Fs	3,000,000	4.50	9.00	20.00	40.00
AH1321Bi	900,000	6.50	13.50	32.50	60.00

Y# 14.2 MAZUNA
1.0000 g., Bronze **Obv:** Date within circle **Rev:** Value within circle **Note:** Varieties exist.

Date	Mintage	F	VF	XF	Unc
AH1320Fs	—	75.00	150	250	—

Y# 15.1 2 MAZUNAS
2.0000 g., Bronze **Obv:** Date within circle **Rev:** Value within circle

Date	Mintage	F	VF	XF	Unc
AH1320Bi	1,500,000	8.50	18.50	35.00	75.00
AH1321Bi	450,000	12.50	25.00	50.00	90.00

Y# 15.2 2 MAZUNAS
2.0000 g., Bronze **Note:** Normal rim design; varieties exist.

Date	Mintage	F	VF	XF	Unc
AH1320Fs	—	25.00	50.00	100	—
AH1322Fs	—	100	200	300	—
AH1323Fs	—	50.00	90.00	160	—

Y# 15.3 2 MAZUNAS
2.0000 g., Bronze **Obv:** Date within circle **Rev:** Value within circle, rim design reversed

Date	Mintage	F	VF	XF	Unc
AH1320Fs Rare	—	—	—	—	—

Y# 15.4 2 MAZUNAS
2.0000 g., Bronze **Note:** Normal rim design.

Date	Mintage	F	VF	XF	Unc
AH1321Pa	6,500,000	2.00	5.00	10.00	25.00

Y# 16.1 5 MAZUNAS

5.0000 g., Bronze **Obv:** Date within circle **Rev:** Value within circle

Date	Mintage	F	VF	XF	Unc
AH1320Bi	2,400,000	2.00	5.00	10.00	25.00
AH1321Bi	720,000	4.00	8.00	15.00	30.00

Y# 16.2 5 MAZUNAS

5.0000 g., Bronze **Obv:** Date within circle **Rev:** Value within circle **Note:** Varieties exist.

Date	Mintage	F	VF	XF	Unc
AH1320Fs	—	25.00	50.00	100	—
AH1322Fs	—	40.00	80.00	160	—

Y# 16.3 5 MAZUNAS

5.0000 g., Bronze **Obv:** Date within circle **Rev:** Value within circle

Date	Mintage	F	VF	XF	Unc
AH1321Pa	7,950,000	2.00	5.00	10.00	25.00

Y# 17.1 10 MAZUNAS

10.0000 g., Bronze

Date	Mintage	F	VF	XF	Unc
AH1320Be	2,400,000	2.00	5.00	10.00	25.00
AH1321Be	2,600,000	2.00	5.00	10.00	25.00

Y# 17.2 10 MAZUNAS

10.0000 g., Bronze **Obv:** Date within circle **Rev:** Value within circle

Date	Mintage	F	VF	XF	Unc
AH1320Bi	1,200,000	3.00	6.00	12.00	28.00
AH1321Bi	360,000	4.00	8.00	16.00	35.00

Y# 17.3 10 MAZUNAS

10.0000 g., Bronze **Obv:** Date within circle **Rev:** Value within circle **Note:** Varieties exist.

Date	Mintage	F	VF	XF	Unc
AH1320Fs Small letters	—	200	350	500	800
AH1320Fs Large letters	—	20.00	40.00	80.00	160
AH1321Fs	—	18.00	35.00	75.00	150
AH1323Fs Large 10	—	100	175	250	450
AH1323Fs Small 10	—	100	175	250	450

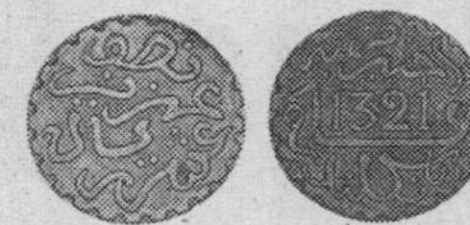

Y# 18.1 1/20 RIAL (1/2 Dirham)

1.2500 g., 0.8350 Silver .0336 oz. ASW **Obv:** Inscription **Rev:** Value and date

Date	Mintage	F	VF	XF	Unc
AH1320Ln	3,920,000	1.25	4.00	10.00	20.00
AH1321Ln	2,105,000	3.00	5.00	10.00	20.00

Y# 18.2 1/20 RIAL (1/2 Dirham)

1.2500 g., 0.8350 Silver 0.0336 oz. ASW

Date	Mintage	F	VF	XF	Unc
AH1320Pa	2,400,000	1.50	4.00	10.00	20.00

Y# 19 1/10 RIAL (Dirham)

2.5000 g., 0.8350 Silver .0671 oz. ASW

Date	Mintage	F	VF	XF	Unc
AH1320Ln	2,940,000	3.00	8.00	15.00	40.00
AH1321Ln	770,000	5.00	12.00	25.00	60.00

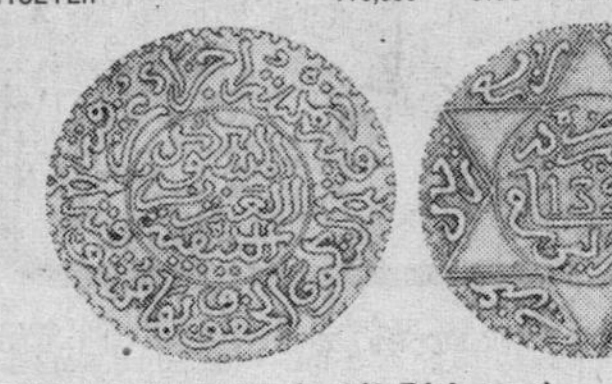

Y# 20.1 1/4 RIAL (2-1/2 Dirhams)

6.2500 g., 0.8350 Silver .1678 oz. ASW, 25 mm. **Obv:** Inscription within inner circle, legend around border **Rev:** Inscription and date within the Star of David, legend flanked by star points

Date	Mintage	F	VF	XF	Unc
AH1320	1,380,000	4.00	12.50	20.00	50.00
AH1320Be	1,380,000	4.00	12.50	20.00	50.00
AH1321Be	4,450,000	4.00	7.00	10.00	32.50
AH1321Be Proof; Rare	5	—	—	—	—

Y# 20.2 1/4 RIAL (2-1/2 Dirhams)

6.2500 g., 0.8350 Silver 0.1678 oz. ASW, 25 mm.

Date	Mintage	F	VF	XF	Unc
AH1320Ln	3,056,000	4.00	10.00	12.50	40.00
AH1321Ln	1,889,000	4.00	7.00	10.00	32.50

Y# 20.3 1/4 RIAL (2-1/2 Dirhams)

6.2500 g., 0.8350 Silver 0.1678 oz. ASW, 25 mm.

Date	Mintage	F	VF	XF	Unc
AH1320Pa	480,000	12.00	25.00	50.00	100
AH1321Pa	160,000	40.00	75.00	150	300

Y# 21.1 1/2 RIAL (5 Dirhams)

12.5000 g., 0.8350 Silver .3356 oz. ASW, 32 mm.

Date	Mintage	F	VF	XF	Unc
AH1320Be	2,510,000	7.00	15.00	30.00	75.00

Y# 21.2 1/2 RIAL (5 Dirhams)

12.5000 g., 0.8350 Silver 0.3356 oz. ASW, 32 mm.

Date	Mintage	F	VF	XF	Unc
AH1320Ln	900,000	7.00	15.00	30.00	75.00
AH1321Ln	1,041,000	7.00	15.00	30.00	75.00

Y# 21.3 1/2 RIAL (5 Dirhams)

12.5000 g., 0.8350 Silver 0.3356 oz. ASW, 32 mm.

Date	Mintage	F	VF	XF	Unc
AH1321Pa	1,800,000	7.00	17.50	35.00	85.00
AH1322Pa	540,000	15.00	30.00	75.00	150
AH1323Pa	1,090,000	12.00	25.00	50.00	110

Y# 22.1 RIAL (10 Dirhams)

25.0000 g., 0.9000 Silver .7234 oz. ASW, 37 mm.

Date	Mintage	F	VF	XF	Unc
AH1320Ln	330,000	20.00	35.00	75.00	150

Y# 22.2 RIAL (10 Dirhams)

25.0000 g., 0.9000 Silver 0.7234 oz. ASW, 37 mm. **Obv:** Inscription within circle, legend around border **Rev:** Inscription and date within the Star of David, legend flanked by star points

Date	Mintage	F	VF	XF	Unc
AH1321Pa	300,000	20.00	35.00	75.00	150

Abd al-Hafiz

AH1326-1330 / 1908-1912AD

REFORM COINAGE

AH1320 / 1902AD

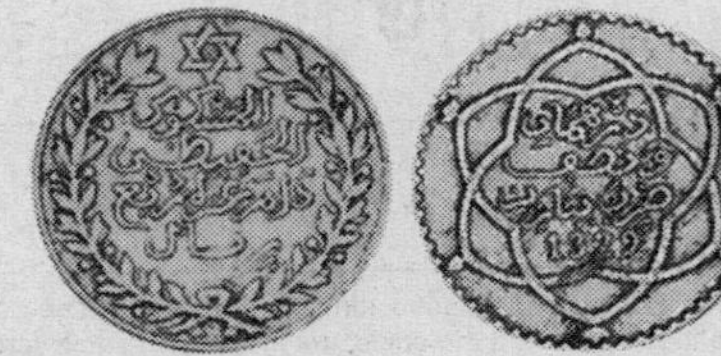

Y# 23 1/4 RIAL (2-1/2 Dirhams)

6.2500 g., 0.8350 Silver .1678 oz. ASW **Obv:** Inscription below star within sprays **Rev:** Mint, name and date within doubled tri-lobe star

Date	Mintage	F	VF	XF	Unc
AH1329Pa	3,900,000	4.00	8.50	18.00	40.00

Y# 24 1/2 RIAL (5 Dirhams)

12.5000 g., 0.8350 Silver .3356 oz. ASW **Obv:** Star above inscription within sprays **Rev:** Mint, name and date within doubled tri-lobe star

Date	Mintage	F	VF	XF	Unc
AH1329Pa	6,200,000	7.00	10.00	25.00	90.00

Y# 25 RIAL (10 Dirhams)

25.0000 g., 0.9000 Silver .7234 oz. ASW **Obv:** Star above inscription within sprays **Rev:** Mint, name and date within doubled tri-lobe star

Date	Mintage	F	VF	XF	Unc
AH1329Pa	10,100,000	12.00	20.00	40.00	100

PRIVATE TOKEN COINAGE

Enterprise Collet et Gouvernet

KM# Tn1 FRANC

Aluminum **Issuer:** Entreprise Collet et Gouvernet **Shape:** Hexagon

Date	Mintage	F	VF	XF	Unc
ND	—	20.00	50.00	75.00	125

KM# Tn2 2 FRANCS

Aluminum **Shape:** Scalloped

Date	Mintage	F	VF	XF	Unc
ND	—	20.00	35.00	60.00	100

KM# Tn3 5 FRANCS

Aluminum

Date	Mintage	F	VF	XF	Unc
ND	—	30.00	50.00	80.00	150

KM# Tn4 5 FRANCS

Aluminum

Date	Mintage	F	VF	XF	Unc
ND	—	35.00	60.00	100	175

Yusuf

AH1330-1346 / 1912-1927AD

REFORM COINAGE

AH1320 / 1902AD

Y# 26 MAZUNA

Bronze **Obv:** Value within star **Rev:** Mint name and date within doubled tri-lobe star

Date	Mintage	F	VF	XF	Unc
AH1330Pa	1,850,000	2.00	5.00	15.00	30.00

Y# 27 2 MAZUNAS

Bronze **Obv:** Value within star **Rev:** Mint name and date within doubled tri-lobe star

Date	Mintage	F	VF	XF	Unc
AH1330Pa	2,790,000	2.00	4.00	12.00	30.00

Note: Coins reportedly dated 1331Pa probably bore date AH1330

Y# 28.1 5 MAZUNAS

Bronze **Obv:** Value within star **Rev:** Mint name and date within doubled tri-lobe star

Date	Mintage	F	VF	XF	Unc
AH1330Pa	2,983,000	2.00	5.00	11.00	25.00
AH1340Pa	2,000,000	2.00	5.00	11.00	25.00

Y# 28.2 5 MAZUNAS

Bronze **Obv:** Value within star **Rev:** Mint name and date within doubled tri-lobe star

Date	Mintage	F	VF	XF	Unc
AH1340Py	2,010,000	2.00	5.00	8.00	27.50

Y# 29.1 10 MAZUNAS

Bronze **Obv:** Value within star **Rev:** Mint name and date within doubled tri-lobe star

Date	Mintage	F	VF	XF	Unc
AH1330Pa	1,500,000	0.75	2.50	10.00	30.00
AH1340Pa	1,000,000	0.75	1.50	7.50	25.00

Y# 29.2 10 MAZUNAS

Bronze **Obv:** Value within star **Rev:** Mint name and date within doubled tri-lobe star, privy marks

Date	Mintage	F	VF	XF	Unc
AH1340Py	1,000,000	1.00	3.00	12.00	30.00

Y# 30 1/10 RIAL (Dirham)

2.5000 g., 0.8350 Silver .0671 oz. ASW **Obv:** Inscription **Rev:** Mint name and date

Date	Mintage	F	VF	XF	Unc
AH1331Pa	500,000	30.00	45.00	75.00	200
AH1331Pa Proof	—	Value: 800			

Y# 31 1/4 RIAL (2-1/2 Dirhams)

6.2500 g., 0.8350 Silver .1678 oz. ASW **Obv:** Inscription and date within the Star of David, legend flanked by star points **Rev:** Mint name and date within circle

Date	Mintage	F	VF	XF	Unc
AH1331Pa	1,700,000	30.00	45.00	90.00	225

Y# 32 1/2 RIAL (5 Dirhams)

0.8350 Silver **Obv:** Inscription and date within the Star of David, legend flanked by star points **Rev:** Mint name and date within circle

Date	Mintage	F	VF	XF	Unc
AH1331Pa	4,300,000	7.00	16.00	25.00	60.00
AH1336Pa	7,200,000	6.00	11.00	20.00	50.00

Y# 33 RIAL (10 Dirhams)

25.0000 g., 0.9000 Silver .7234 oz. ASW **Obv:** Inscription and date within the Star of David, legend flanked by star points **Rev:** Mint name and date within circle

Date	Mintage	F	VF	XF	Unc
AH1331Pa	4,200,000	12.00	20.00	35.00	70.00
AH1336Pa	2,500,000	11.50	17.50	25.00	55.00

FRENCH PROTECTORATE

Yusuf

AH1330-1346 / 1912-1927AD

STANDARD COINAGE

100 Centimes = 1 Franc

Y# 34.1 25 CENTIMES

Copper-Nickel, 24 mm. **Obv:** Hole in center of the star of David within circle, without privy marks **Rev:** Hole in center flanked by value within circle, without privy marks

Date	Mintage	F	VF	XF	Unc
ND(1921)Pa	8,000,000	1.00	3.00	8.00	40.00

Y# 34.2 25 CENTIMES

Copper-Nickel, 24 mm. **Obv:** Hole in center of the star of David within circle **Rev:** Hole in center flanked by value within circle

Date	Mintage	F	VF	XF	Unc
ND(1924)Py	2,037,000	2.00	4.00	19.00	45.00

Y# 34.3 25 CENTIMES

Copper-Nickel, 24 mm. **Rev:** Thunderbolt and torch at left and right of CENTIMES

Date	Mintage	F	VF	XF	Unc
ND(1924)Py	Inc. above	3.00	8.00	15.00	60.00

Y# 35.1 50 CENTIMES

Nickel **Obv:** Star within circle ,without privy marks **Rev:** Value within artistic designed star, without privy marks

Date	Mintage	F	VF	XF	Unc
ND(1921)Pa	7,976,000	0.50	1.00	6.50	45.00

Y# 35.2 50 CENTIMES

Nickel **Obv:** Star within circle **Rev:** Value within artistic designed star, thunderbolt at bottom

Date	Mintage	F	VF	XF	Unc
ND(1924)Py	3,000,000	1.00	2.00	8.00	45.00

Y# 36.1 FRANC

Nickel, 27 mm. **Obv:** Star within circle, without privy marks **Rev:** Value within artistic designed star, without privy marks

Date	Mintage	F	VF	XF	Unc
ND(1921)Pa	8,325,000	0.50	1.00	6.50	37.50

Y# 36.2 FRANC

Nickel, 27 mm. **Obv:** Star within circle **Rev:** Value within artistic designed star, thunderbolt below 1

Date	Mintage	F	VF	XF	Unc
ND(1924)Py	4,796,000	1.25	2.50	10.00	55.00

Mohammed V
AH1346-1381 / 1927-1962AD
STANDARD COINAGE

100 Centimes = 1 Franc

Y# 40 50 CENTIMES

Aluminum-Bronze **Obv:** Star **Rev:** Value flanked by dates

Date	Mintage	F	VF	XF	Unc
AH1364-1945(a)	24,000,000	—	0.25	1.50	2.50

Y# 41 FRANC

Aluminum-Bronze **Obv:** Legend around star **Rev:** Value flanked by dates

Date	Mintage	F	VF	XF	Unc
AH1364-1945(a)	24,000,000	—	0.25	1.50	2.50

Y# 46 FRANC

Aluminum, 19.5 mm. **Obv:** Legend around star **Rev:** Value flanked by dates

Date	Mintage	F	VF	XF	Unc
AH1370-1951(a)	33,000,000	—	0.15	0.35	1.25

Note: Note: Y#46-51 were struck for more than 20 years without change of date, until a new currency was introduced in 1974

Y# 42 2 FRANCS

Aluminum-Bronze **Obv:** Legend around star **Rev:** Value flanked by dates

Date	Mintage	F	VF	XF	Unc
AH1364-1945(a)	12,000,000	—	0.75	2.50	6.00

Y# 47 2 FRANCS

Aluminum, 22 mm. **Obv:** Legend around star **Rev:** Value flanked by dates

Date	Mintage	F	VF	XF	Unc
AH1370-1951(a)	20,000,000	—	0.15	0.50	2.00

Y# 37 5 FRANCS

5.0000 g., 0.6800 Silver .1093 oz. ASW **Obv:** Date within small circle of doubled tri-lobe star, all within circle **Rev:** Value within doubled square within circle

Date	Mintage	F	VF	XF	Unc
AH1347(a)	4,000,000	—	2.50	7.00	32.00
AH1352(a)	5,000,000	—	1.75	4.00	18.00

Y# 43 5 FRANCS

Aluminum-Bronze **Obv:** Date within small circle of doubled tri-lobe star, all within circle **Rev:** Value in doubled square within circle

Date	Mintage	F	VF	XF	Unc
AH1365(a)	20,000,000	0.25	0.50	0.75	2.00

Y# 48 5 FRANCS

Aluminum, 25 mm. **Obv:** Date within small circle of doubled tri-lobe star, all within circle **Rev:** Value flanked by marks in doubled square within circle

Date	Mintage	F	VF	XF	Unc
AH1370(a)	23,000,000	0.15	0.30	0.65	1.75

Y# 38 10 FRANCS

10.0000 g., 0.6800 Silver .2186 oz. ASW **Obv:** Date in small circle of doubled tri-lobe star, all within circle **Rev:** Date in doubled square within circle

Date	Mintage	F	VF	XF	Unc
AH1347(a)	1,600,000	4.50	10.00	22.00	80.00
AH1352(a)	2,900,000	3.50	5.00	9.00	28.00

Y# 44 10 FRANCS

Copper-Nickel **Obv:** Date in small circle of doubled tri-lobe star, all within circle **Rev:** Value in doubled square within circle

Date	Mintage	F	VF	XF	Unc
AH1366(a)	20,000,000	0.50	1.00	1.50	2.50

Y# 49 10 FRANCS

Aluminum-Bronze, 20 mm. **Obv:** Star flanked by designs, date on bottom **Rev:** Value flanked by designs

Date	Mintage	F	VF	XF	Unc
AH1371(a)	40,000,000	0.15	0.40	0.85	2.00

Y# 39 20 FRANCS

20.0000 g., 0.6800 Silver .4372 oz. ASW **Obv:** Date in inner circle of doubled tri-lobe star, all within circle **Rev:** Value in doubled square within circle

Date	Mintage	F	VF	XF	Unc
AH1347(a)	177,000	7.50	12.00	32.50	80.00
AH1352(a)	2,000,000	7.00	10.00	25.00	50.00

Y# 45 20 FRANCS

Copper-Nickel **Obv:** Date in inner circle of doubled tri-lobe star, all within circle **Rev:** Value in doubled square within circle

Date	Mintage	F	VF	XF	Unc
AH1366(a)	6,000,000	0.35	0.65	1.25	2.50
AH1366(a) Proof	—	Value: 50.00			

Y# 50 20 FRANCS

Aluminum-Bronze, 23.8 mm. **Obv:** Star flanked by designs, date on bottom **Rev:** Value flanked by designs

Date	Mintage	F	VF	XF	Unc
AH1371(a)	20,000,000	0.25	0.50	1.00	2.00

Y# 51 50 FRANCS

Aluminum-Bronze, 27 mm. **Obv:** Date in inner circle of doubled tri-lobe star, all within circle **Rev:** Value in doubled square within circle

Date	Mintage	F	VF	XF	Unc
AH1371(a)	20,600,000	0.35	0.65	1.25	2.25

Y# 51a 50 FRANCS

Gold **Obv:** Date in inner circle of doubled tri-lobe star, all within circle **Rev:** Value within doubled square within circle

Date	Mintage	F	VF	XF	Unc
AH1371(a) Rare	—	—	—	—	—

Y# A54 100 FRANCS

2.5000 g., 0.7200 Silver .0579 oz. ASW **Obv:** Star flanked by designs, date on bottom **Rev:** Value flanked by designs

Date	Mintage	F	VF	XF	Unc
AH1370(a)	10,000,000	—	—	—	500

Note: Nearly all specimens were melted, only 100 known

Y# 52 100 FRANCS

4.0000 g., 0.7200 Silver .0926 oz. ASW **Obv:** Star within small circle in center of larger star with designs in points **Rev:** Value within beaded circle, legend around border

Date	Mintage	F	VF	XF	Unc
AH1372(a)	20,000,000	—	2.75	3.75	6.50

Y# 53 200 FRANCS

8.0000 g., 0.7200 Silver .1851 oz. ASW **Obv:** Star within small circle in center of larger star with designs in points **Rev:** Value and date within beaded circle

Date	Mintage	F	VF	XF	Unc
AH1372 (1953) (a)	10,176,000	—	3.00	4.50	9.00

Y# 54 500 FRANCS

22.5000 g., 0.9000 Silver .6511 oz. ASW **Obv:** Bust left within circle **Rev:** Crown in center of star flanked by dates and value

Date	Mintage	F	VF	XF	Unc
AH1376-1956(a)	2,000,000	—	10.00	12.00	20.00

KINGDOM
Resumed
Mohammed V
AH1346-1381 / 1927-1962AD
REFORM COINAGE

100 Francs = 1 Dirham

Y# 55 DIRHAM

6.0000 g., 0.6000 Silver .1157 oz. ASW **Obv:** Head left **Rev:** Crowned arms with supporters flanked by dates above and value below

Date	Mintage	F	VF	XF	Unc
AH1380-1960(a)	33,000,000	—	1.75	2.85	5.50

al-Hassan II
AH1381-1420 / 1962-1999AD
REFORM COINAGE

100 Francs = 1 Dirham

Y# 56 DIRHAM

Nickel, 23.6 mm. **Obv:** Head left **Rev:** Crowned arms with supporters

Date	Mintage	F	VF	XF	Unc
AH1384-1965(a)	30,000,000	—	0.50	0.75	1.00
AH1388-1968(a)	5,000,000	1.00	2.00	4.00	8.00
AH1389-1969(a)	17,200,000	—	0.50	0.75	1.00

Y# 57 5 DIRHAMS

11.7500 g., 0.7200 Silver .2720 oz. ASW **Obv:** Head left **Rev:** Crowned arms with supporters

Date	Mintage	F	VF	XF	Unc
AH1384-1965(a)	2,000,000	—	5.00	7.50	14.50
AH1384-1965(a) Proof	200	Value: 60.00			

REFORM COINAGE

100 Santimat = 1 Dirham

Y# 58 SANTIM

0.7000 g., Aluminum, 17 mm. **Obv:** Crowned arms with supporters **Rev:** Value flanked by designs

Date	Mintage	F	VF	XF	Unc
AH1394-1974	10,240,000	—	—	0.50	1.25
AH1395-1975	1,700,000	—	—	0.50	1.25

Y# 58a SANTIM

0.9170 Gold, 17 mm. **Obv:** Crowned arms with supporters **Rev:** Value flanked by designs

Date	Mintage	F	VF	XF	Unc
AH1394-1974 Proof	30	Value: 425			

Y# 93 SANTIM

0.7000 g., Aluminum, 17 mm. **Obv:** Crowned arms with supporters **Rev:** Fish above value

Date	Mintage	F	VF	XF	Unc
AH1407-1987	—	—	—	10.00	20.00

Note: Most were melted

Y# 59 5 SANTIMAT

2.0000 g., Brass, 17.5 mm. **Series:** F.A.O. **Obv:** Crowned arms with supporters **Rev:** Value at lower right of captains wheel

Date	Mintage	F	VF	XF	Unc
AH1394-1974	54,820,000	—	—	0.15	0.30
AH1395-1975	11,000,000	—	—	0.15	0.30
AH1398-1976	12,600,000	—	—	0.15	0.30

Y# 59a 5 SANTIMAT

0.9170 Gold, 17.5 mm. **Series:** F.A.O. **Obv:** Crowned arms with supporters **Rev:** Value at lower right of captain's wheel

Date	Mintage	F	VF	XF	Unc
AH1394-1974 Proof	30	Value: 485			

Y# 83 5 SANTIMAT

2.0000 g., Brass, 17.5 mm. **Series:** F.A.O. **Obv:** Crowned arms with supporters **Rev:** Value to upper left of center design

Date	Mintage	F	VF	XF	Unc
AH1407-1987	—	—	—	—	0.30

Y# 60 10 SANTIMAT

3.0000 g., Brass, 20 mm. **Series:** F.A.O. **Obv:** Crowned arms with supporters **Rev:** Value at lower left of designs

Date	Mintage	F	VF	XF	Unc
AH1394-1974	67,950,000	—	—	0.15	0.30
AH1395-1975	10,900,000	—	—	0.15	0.30
AH1398-1978	1,000,000	—	—	0.15	0.30

Y# 60a 10 SANTIMAT

0.9170 Gold, 20 mm. **Series:** F.A.O. **Obv:** Crowned arms with supporters **Rev:** Value at lower left of designs

Date	Mintage	F	VF	XF	Unc
AH1394-1974 Proof	30	Value: 575			

Y# 84 10 SANTIMAT

3.0000 g., Brass, 20 mm. **Series:** F.A.O. **Obv:** Crowned arms with supporters **Rev:** Single ear of corn to left of value

Date	Mintage	F	VF	XF	Unc
AH1407-1987	—	—	—	—	0.40

Y# 61 20 SANTIMAT

4.0000 g., Brass, 23 mm. **Obv:** Head left **Obv. Designer:** David Wynne **Rev:** Crowned arms with supporters

Date	Mintage	F	VF	XF	Unc
AH1394-1974	59,840,000	—	0.30	0.40	0.50
AH1395-1975	10,700,000	—	0.30	0.40	0.50
AH1397-1977	22,800,000	—	0.30	0.40	0.50
AH1398-1978	2,200,000	—	0.30	0.40	0.50

Y# 61a 20 SANTIMAT

0.9170 Gold, 23 mm. **Obv:** Head left **Rev:** Crowned arms with supporters

Date	Mintage	F	VF	XF	Unc
AH1394-1974 Proof	30	Value: 585			

Y# 85 20 SANTIMAT

4.0000 g., Brass, 23 mm. **Series:** F.A.O. **Obv:** Crowned arms with supporters **Rev:** Value to right of designs

Date	Mintage	F	VF	XF	Unc
AH1407-1987	—	—	—	—	0.50

Y# 62 50 SANTIMAT

4.0000 g., Copper-Nickel, 21 mm. **Obv:** Head left **Obv. Designer:** David Wynne **Rev:** Crowned arms with supporters

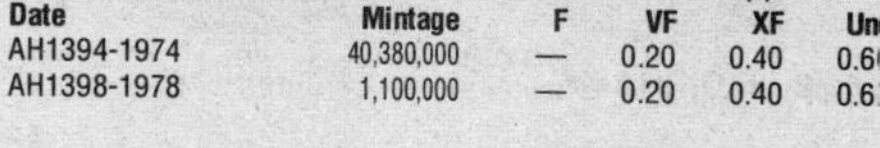

Date	Mintage	F	VF	XF	Unc
AH1394-1974	40,380,000	—	0.20	0.40	0.60
AH1398-1978	1,100,000	—	0.20	0.40	0.60

Y# 62a 50 SANTIMAT

0.9170 Gold, 21 mm. **Obv:** Head left **Rev:** Crowned arms with supporters

Date	Mintage	F	VF	XF	Unc
AH1394-1974 Proof	30	Value: 585			

Y# 87 1/2 DIRHAM

Copper-Nickel **Obv:** Head left **Obv. Designer:** David Wynne **Rev:** Crowned arms with supporters

Date	Mintage	F	VF	XF	Unc
AH1407-1987	—	—	—	—	1.25

Y# 63 DIRHAM

6.0000 g., Copper-Nickel, 24 mm. **Obv:** Head left **Obv. Designer:** David Wynne **Rev:** Crowned arms with supporters

Date	Mintage	F	VF	XF	Unc
AH1394-1974	32,850,000	—	0.30	0.50	0.75
AH1398-1978	18,100,000	—	0.30	0.50	0.75

Y# 63a DIRHAM

0.9170 Gold, 24 mm. **Obv:** Head left **Rev:** Crowned arms with supporters

Date	Mintage	F	VF	XF	Unc
AH1394-1974 Proof	30	Value: 685			

Y# 88 DIRHAM

Copper-Nickel **Obv:** Head left **Obv. Designer:** David Wynne **Rev:** Crowned arms with supporters

Date	Mintage	F	VF	XF	Unc
AH1407-1987	—	—	—	—	2.75

Y# 64 5 DIRHAMS

Copper-Nickel **Series:** World Food Conference **Obv:** Head left **Obv. Designer:** David Wynne **Rev:** Small value within center of designs

Date	Mintage	F	VF	XF	Unc
AH1395-1975	500,000	—	—	2.00	6.00
AH1395-1975 Proof	500	Value: 80.00			

Y# 64a 5 DIRHAMS

12.0000 g., 0.9250 Silver .3569 oz. ASW **Series:** World Food Conference **Obv:** Head left **Rev:** Small value within center of designs

Date	Mintage	F	VF	XF	Unc
AH1395-1975 Proof	200	Value: 150			

Y# 64b 5 DIRHAMS

23.6500 g., 0.9000 Gold .6844 oz. AGW **Series:** World Food Conference **Obv:** Head left **Rev:** Small value within center of designs

Date	Mintage	F	VF	XF	Unc
AH1395-1975 Proof	20	Value: 1,000			

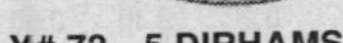

Y# 72 5 DIRHAMS

12.0000 g., Copper-Nickel, 29 mm. **Obv:** Head left **Obv. Designer:** David Wynne **Rev:** Crowned arms with supporters

Date	Mintage	F	VF	XF	Unc
AH1400-1980	10,000,000	—	1.50	4.00	6.50

Y# 82 5 DIRHAMS

6.8000 g., Bi-Metallic Aluminum-Bronze center in Stainless Steel ring Aluminum-Bronze center in Stainless Steel ring, 26.2 mm. **Obv:** Head left within circle **Obv. Designer:** David Wynne **Rev:** Crowned arms with supporters and value within circle

Date	Mintage	F	VF	XF	Unc
AH1407-1987	—	—	2.00	4.50	7.50

Y# 92 10 DIRHAMS

12.0000 g., Bi-Metallic Copper-Nickel center in Brass ring Copper-Nickel center in Brass ring, 28 mm. **Obv:** Hooded head left within circle with star below **Rev:** Crowned arms with supporters and value within circle with star above

Date	Mintage	F	VF	XF	Unc
AH1415-1995	—	—	—	—	8.00

Y# 65 50 DIRHAMS

35.0000 g., 0.9250 Silver 1.0409 oz. ASW **Subject:** 20th Anniversary of Independence **Obv:** Head left **Obv. Designer:** David Wynne **Rev:** Crowned arms with supporters

Date	Mintage	F	VF	XF	Unc
AH1395-1975	6,000	—	—	—	30.00
AH1395-1975 Proof	4,400	Value: 50.00			

Y# 65a 50 DIRHAMS

60.1400 g., 0.9000 Gold 1.7404 oz. AGW **Subject:** 20th Anniversary of Independence **Obv:** Head left **Rev:** Crowned arms with supporters

Date	Mintage	F	VF	XF	Unc
AH1395-1975 Proof	40	Value: 1,250			

Y# 67 50 DIRHAMS

35.0000 g., 0.9250 Silver 1.0409 oz. ASW **Series:** International Women's Year **Obv:** Head left **Obv. Designer:** David Wynne **Rev:** Hand within circled design

Date	Mintage	F	VF	XF	Unc
AH1395-1975	6,000	—	—	—	30.00
AH1395-1975 Proof	4,400	Value: 50.00			

Y# 67a 50 DIRHAMS

60.1400 g., 0.9000 Gold 1.7404 oz. AGW **Series:** International Women's Year **Obv:** Head left **Obv. Designer:** David Wynne **Rev:** Hand within circled design

Date	Mintage	F	VF	XF	Unc
AH1395-1975 Proof	20	Value: 1,500			

Y# 68 50 DIRHAMS

35.0000 g., 0.9250 Silver 1.0409 oz. ASW **Subject:** Anniversary - Green March **Obv:** Head left **Obv. Designer:** David Wynne **Rev:** Pointed artistic design with stars on points flanked by dates **Note:** Reverse inscriptions vary slightly for each date.

Date	Mintage	F	VF	XF	Unc
AH1396-1976	11,000	—	—	—	25.00
AH1396-1976 Proof	4,400	Value: 50.00			
AH1397-1977	3,500	—	—	—	50.00
AH1397-1977 Proof	200	Value: 150			
AH1398-1978	5,000	—	—	—	40.00
AH1398-1978 Proof	300	Value: 120			
AH1399-1979	3,000	—	—	—	50.00
AH1399-1979 Proof	300	Value: 150			
AH1400-1980	1,000	—	—	—	80.00
AH1400-1980 Proof	200	Value: 200			

Y# 68a 50 DIRHAMS

60.1400 g., 0.9000 Gold 1.7404 oz. AGW **Subject:** Anniversary - Green March **Obv:** Head left **Obv. Designer:** David Wynne **Rev:** Pointed artistic design with stars on points flanked by dates **Note:** Reverse inscriptions vary slightly for each date.

Date	Mintage	F	VF	XF	Unc
AH1396-1976 Proof	20	Value: 1,750			
AH1397-1977 Proof	20	Value: 1,700			
AH1398-1978 Proof	70	Value: 1,275			
AH1399-1979 Proof	70	Value: 1,275			
AH1400-1980 Proof	30	Value: 1,450			

Y# 70 50 DIRHAMS

35.0000 g., 0.9250 Silver 1.0409 oz. ASW **Series:** International Year of the Child **Obv:** Head left **Rev:** Design divides world globe flanked by dates

Date	Mintage	F	VF	XF	Unc
AH1399-1979	5,000	—	—	—	40.00
AH1399-1979 Proof	500	Value: 100			

Y# 70a 50 DIRHAMS

60.1400 g., 0.9000 Gold 1.7404 oz. AGW **Series:** International Year of the Child **Obv:** Head left **Rev:** Designs divide world globe flanked by dates

Date	Mintage	F	VF	XF	Unc
AH1399-1979 Proof	70	Value: 1,275			

Y# 76 50 DIRHAMS

35.0000 g., 0.9250 Silver 1.0409 oz. ASW **Subject:** 50th Birthday - King Hassan **Obv:** Head left **Rev:** Crowned arms with supporters flanked by oat sprig, curvey line and dates with value below

Date	Mintage	F	VF	XF	Unc
AH1399-1979	5,000	—	—	—	40.00
AH1399-1979 Proof	500	Value: 100			

Y# 76a 50 DIRHAMS

60.1400 g., 0.9000 Gold 1.7404 oz. AGW **Subject:** 50th Birthday - King Hassan **Obv:** Head left **Rev:** Crowned arms with supporters flanked by oat sprig, curvy line and dates with value below

Date	Mintage	F	VF	XF	Unc
AH1399-1979 Proof	70	Value: 1,400			

Y# 75 100 DIRHAMS

25.0000 g., 0.9250 Silver .7436 oz. ASW **Subject:** 9th Mediterranean Games **Obv:** Head left **Obv. Designer:** David Wynne **Rev:** Olympic circles flanked by dates

Date	Mintage	F	VF	XF	Unc
AH1403-1983	5,000	—	—	—	35.00
AH1403-1983 Proof	500	Value: 75.00			

Y# 77 100 DIRHAMS

15.0000 g., 0.9250 Silver .4461 oz. ASW **Series:** 6th Panarab Sports Games - Olympics **Obv:** Head left **Obv. Designer:** David Wynne **Rev:** Olympic rings above map

Date	Mintage	F	VF	XF	Unc
AH1405-1985	2,300	—	—	—	40.00
AH1405-1985 Proof	300	Value: 150			

Y# 78 100 DIRHAMS

15.0000 g., 0.9250 Silver .4461 oz. ASW **Subject:** 10th Anniversary of Green March **Obv:** Seated figure right **Rev:** Crowned arms with supporters

Date	Mintage	F	VF	XF	Unc
AH1406-1985	1,200	—	—	—	50.00
AH1406-1985 Proof	200	Value: 200			

Y# 78a 100 DIRHAMS

21.5000 g., 0.9000 Gold 0.6221 oz. AGW **Subject:** 10th Anniversary of the Green March **Obv:** Seated figure right **Rev:** Crowned arms with supporters

Date	Mintage	F	VF	XF	Unc
AH1406-1985 Proof	30	—	—	—	—

Y# 79 100 DIRHAMS

15.0000 g., 0.9250 Silver .4461 oz. ASW **Subject:** 25th Year - Reign of King Hassan **Obv:** Head left flanked by dates **Obv. Designer:** David Wynne **Rev:** Cheering citizens

Date	Mintage	F	VF	XF	Unc
AH1406-1986	—	—	—	—	35.00
AH1406-1986 Proof	—	Value: 100			

Y# 80 100 DIRHAMS

15.0000 g., 0.9250 Silver .4461 oz. ASW **Subject:** Visit of the Pope **Obv:** Popes shaking hands **Rev:** Crowned arms with supporters

Date	Mintage	F	VF	XF	Unc
AH1406-1986	—	—	—	—	100
AH1406-1986 Proof	2,000	Value: 200			

Y# 86 100 DIRHAMS

15.0000 g., 0.9250 Silver .4461 oz. ASW **Subject:** Opening of the Rabat Mint **Obv:** Head left **Obv. Designer:** David Wynne **Rev:** Cluster of square designs flanked by dates

Date	Mintage	F	VF	XF	Unc
AH1407-1987	—	—	—	—	25.00
AH1407-1987 Proof	—	Value: 50.00			

Y# 74 150 DIRHAMS

35.0000 g., 0.9250 Silver 1.0409 oz. ASW **Subject:** 15th Hejira Calendar Century **Obv:** Crowned arms with supporters flanked by dates **Rev:** Artistic design within circle flanked by dates

Date	Mintage	F	VF	XF	Unc
AH1401-1980	3,000	—	—	—	50.00
AH1401-1980 Proof	300	Value: 150			

Y# 74a 150 DIRHAMS

60.1400 g., 0.9000 Gold 1.7404 oz. AGW **Subject:** 15th Hejira Calendar Century **Obv:** Crowned arms with supporters flanked by dates **Rev:** Artistic design within circle flanked by dates

Date	Mintage	F	VF	XF	Unc
AH1401-1980 Proof	30	Value: 1,800			

Y# 73 150 DIRHAMS

35.0000 g., 0.9250 Silver 1.0409 oz. ASW **Subject:** 20th Anniversary - King Hassan's Coronation **Obv:** Crowned arms with supporters flanked by dates **Obv. Designer:** David Wynne **Rev:** Crowned arms with supporters

Date	Mintage	F	VF	XF	Unc
AH1401-1981	3,000	—	—	—	50.00
AH1401-1981 Proof	300	Value: 150			

Y# 73a 150 DIRHAMS

60.1400 g., 0.9000 Gold 1.7404 oz. AGW **Subject:** 20th Anniversary - King Hassan's Coronation **Obv:** Head left **Obv. Designer:** David Wynne **Rev:** Crowned arms with supporters flanked by dates

Date	Mintage	F	VF	XF	Unc
AH1401-1981 Proof	30	Value: 1,700			

Y# 81 200 DIRHAMS

15.0000 g., 0.9250 Silver .4461 oz. ASW **Subject:** Moroccan - American Friendship Treaty **Obv:** Head left **Obv. Designer:** David Wynne **Rev:** Radiant sun behind crossed flags

Date	Mintage	F	VF	XF	Unc
AH1408-1987 Proof	Est. 5,000	Value: 25.00			

Y# 81a 200 DIRHAMS

121.5000 g., 0.9000 Gold 3.5157 oz. AGW **Subject:** Moroccan - American Friendship Treaty **Obv:** Head left **Obv. Designer:** David Wynne **Rev:** Radiant sun behind crossed flags

Date	Mintage	F	VF	XF	Unc
AH1408-1987	30	—	—	—	—

Y# 97 200 DIRHAMS

15.0000 g., 0.9250 Silver 0.4461 oz. ASW, 31.3 mm. **Subject:** African Cup Soccer Games **Obv:** Head left **Obv. Designer:** David Wynne **Rev:** Games logo **Edge:** Reeded

Date	Mintage	F	VF	XF	Unc
AH1408-1988	—	—	—	—	40.00

Y# 91 200 DIRHAMS

15.0000 g., 0.9250 Silver .4461 oz. ASW **Subject:** First Francophone Games **Obv:** Head left **Obv. Designer:** David Wynne **Rev:** Games emblem

Date	Mintage	F	VF	XF	Unc
AH1409-1989	5,000	—	—	—	30.00
AH1409-1989 Proof	500	Value: 95.00			

Y# 89 200 DIRHAMS

15.0000 g., 0.9250 Silver 0.4461 oz. ASW, 31.3 mm. **Subject:** 35th Anniversary of Independence **Obv:** Head left **Rev:** Crowned arms with supporters **Edge:** Reeded

Date	Mintage	F	VF	XF	Unc
AH1411-1990	—	—	—	—	40.00
AH1411-1990 Proof	—	Value: 75.00			

Y# 90 200 DIRHAMS

15.0000 g., 0.9250 Silver 0.4461 oz. ASW, 31.3 mm. **Subject:** King's Tunisian Visit **Obv:** Head left **Obv. Designer:** David Wynne **Rev:** Inscription **Edge:** Reeded

Date	Mintage	F	VF	XF	Unc
AH1411-1990 Proof	—	Value: 95.00			
AH1411-1990	—	—	—	—	50.00

Y# 96 200 DIRHAMS

15.0000 g., 0.9250 Silver 0.4461 oz. ASW, 31.3 mm. **Subject:** 30th Anniversary of Reign **Obv:** Crowned arms with supporters **Rev:** King on horseback amidst crowd **Edge:** Reeded

Date	Mintage	F	VF	XF	Unc
AH1411-1991 Proof	—	Value: 95.00			
AH1411-1991	—	—	—	—	50.00

Y# 98 200 DIRHAMS

15.0000 g., 0.9250 Silver 0.4461 oz. ASW, 31.3 mm. **Subject:** Revolution, 40th Anniversary **Obv:** Head left **Rev:** Building within circle **Edge:** Reeded

Date	Mintage	F	VF	XF	Unc
AH1414-1993	2,000	—	—	—	40.00
AH1414-1993 Proof	300	Value: 85.00			

Y# 99 200 DIRHAMS

15.0000 g., 0.9250 Silver 0.4461 oz. ASW, 31.3 mm. **Subject:** 33rd Anniversary of Hassan's Inauguration **Obv:** Head left **Rev:** Mosque within circle **Edge:** Reeded

Date	Mintage	F	VF	XF	Unc
AH1414-1993	2,000	—	—	—	40.00
AH1414-1993 Proof	300	Value: 85.00			

Y# 100 200 DIRHAMS

15.0000 g., 0.9250 Silver 0.4461 oz. ASW, 31.3 mm. **Subject:** GATT Agreement **Obv:** Head left **Rev:** Tower within world globe **Edge:** Reeded

Date	Mintage	F	VF	XF	Unc
AH1414-1994 Proof	300	Value: 80.00			
AH1414-1994	2,000	—	—	—	40.00

Y# 100a 200 DIRHAMS

21.5000 g., 0.9000 Gold 0.6221 oz. AGW, 31.3 mm. **Subject:** GATT Agreement **Obv:** Head left **Rev:** Tower within world globe **Edge:** Reeded

Date	Mintage	F	VF	XF	Unc
AH1416-1995 Proof	—	—	—	—	—

Y# 101 200 DIRHAMS

15.0000 g., 0.9250 Silver 0.4461 oz. ASW, 31.3 mm. **Subject:** 40th Anniversary of Independence **Obv:** Head left **Rev:** Crowned arms with supporters **Edge:** Reeded

Date	Mintage	F	VF	XF	Unc
AH1416-1995	—	—	—	—	40.00
AH1416-1995 Proof	—	Value: 75.00			

Y# 102 200 DIRHAMS

15.0000 g., 0.9250 Silver 0.4461 oz. ASW, 31.3 mm. **Subject:** 50th Anniversary of United Nations **Obv:** Head left **Obv. Designer:** David Wynne **Rev:** UN logo and value within circle **Edge:** Reeded

Date	Mintage	F	VF	XF	Unc
AH1416-1995	—	—	—	—	40.00
AH1416-1995 Proof	—	Value: 75.00			

Y# 103 200 DIRHAMS

15.0000 g., 0.9250 Silver 0.4461 oz. ASW, 31.3 mm. **Subject:** Rabat 800th Anniversary **Obv:** Head left **Rev:** City view within circle **Edge:** Reeded

Date	Mintage	F	VF	XF	Unc
AH1416-1995	—	—	—	—	40.00
AH1416-1995 Proof	—	Value: 75.00			

Y# 104 200 DIRHAMS

15.0000 g., 0.9250 Silver 0.4461 oz. ASW, 31.3 mm. **Subject:** 20th Anniversary of the Green March **Obv:** Head left **Rev:** Arabic inscription **Edge:** Reeded

Date	Mintage	F	VF	XF	Unc
AH1416-1995	—	—	—	—	40.00
AH1416-1995 Proof	—	Value: 75.00			

Y# 105 200 DIRHAMS

15.0000 g., 0.9250 Silver 0.4461 oz. ASW, 31.3 mm. **Subject:** 50th Anniversary Human Rights Declaration **Obv:** Head left **Obv. Designer:** David Wynne **Rev:** Logo, legend and inscription **Edge:** Reeded

Date	Mintage	F	VF	XF	Unc
AH1419-1998	—	—	—	—	40.00

Y# 66 250 DIRHAMS

6.4500 g., 0.9000 Gold .1867 oz. AGW **Subject:** Birthday of King Hassan **Obv:** Head left **Obv. Designer:** David Wynne **Rev:** Crowned arms with supporters flanked by dates

Date	Mintage	F	VF	XF	Unc
AH1395-1975	5,000	—	—	—	130
AH1395-1975 Proof	1,270	Value: 160			
AH1396-1976	3,200	—	—	—	130
AH1396-1976 Proof	450	Value: 175			
AH1397-1977	3,000	—	—	—	130
AH1397-1977 Proof	800	Value: 150			
AH1398-1978	2,000	—	—	—	130
AH1398-1978 Proof	150	Value: 200			

Y# 71 500 DIRHAMS

12.9000 g., 0.9000 Gold .3733 oz. AGW **Subject:** Birthday of King Hassan **Obv:** Head left **Obv. Designer:** David Wynne **Rev:** Crowned arms with supporters flanked by oat sprig, curvy line and dates

Date	Mintage	F	VF	XF	Unc
AH1399-1979	3,000	—	—	—	265
AH1399-1979 Proof	300	Value: 300			
AH1400-1980	100	—	—	—	400
AH1400-1980 Proof	100	Value: 500			
AH1401-1981	100	—	—	—	400
AH1401-1981 Proof	100	Value: 500			
AH1402-1982	100	—	—	—	400
AH1402-1982 Proof	100	Value: 500			
AH1403-1983	2,500	—	—	—	265
AH1403-1983 Proof	Inc. above	Value: 285			
AH1404-1984	100	—	—	—	400
AH1404-1984 Proof	100	Value: 500			
AH1405-1985	275	—	—	—	285
AH1405-1985 Proof	125	Value: 475			
AH1406-1986 Proof	—	Value: 450			
AH1407-1987 Proof	—	Value: 450			
AH1408-1988 Proof	—	Value: 450			
AH1409-1989 Proof	—	Value: 450			
AH1410-1990 Proof	—	Value: 450			
AH1411-1991 Proof	—	Value: 450			

Date	Mintage	F	VF	XF	Unc
AH1412-1992 Proof	—	Value: 450			
AH1413-1993 Proof	—	Value: 450			

Mohammed VI
AH1420 / 1999AD
REFORM COINAGE

100 Santimat = 1 Dirham

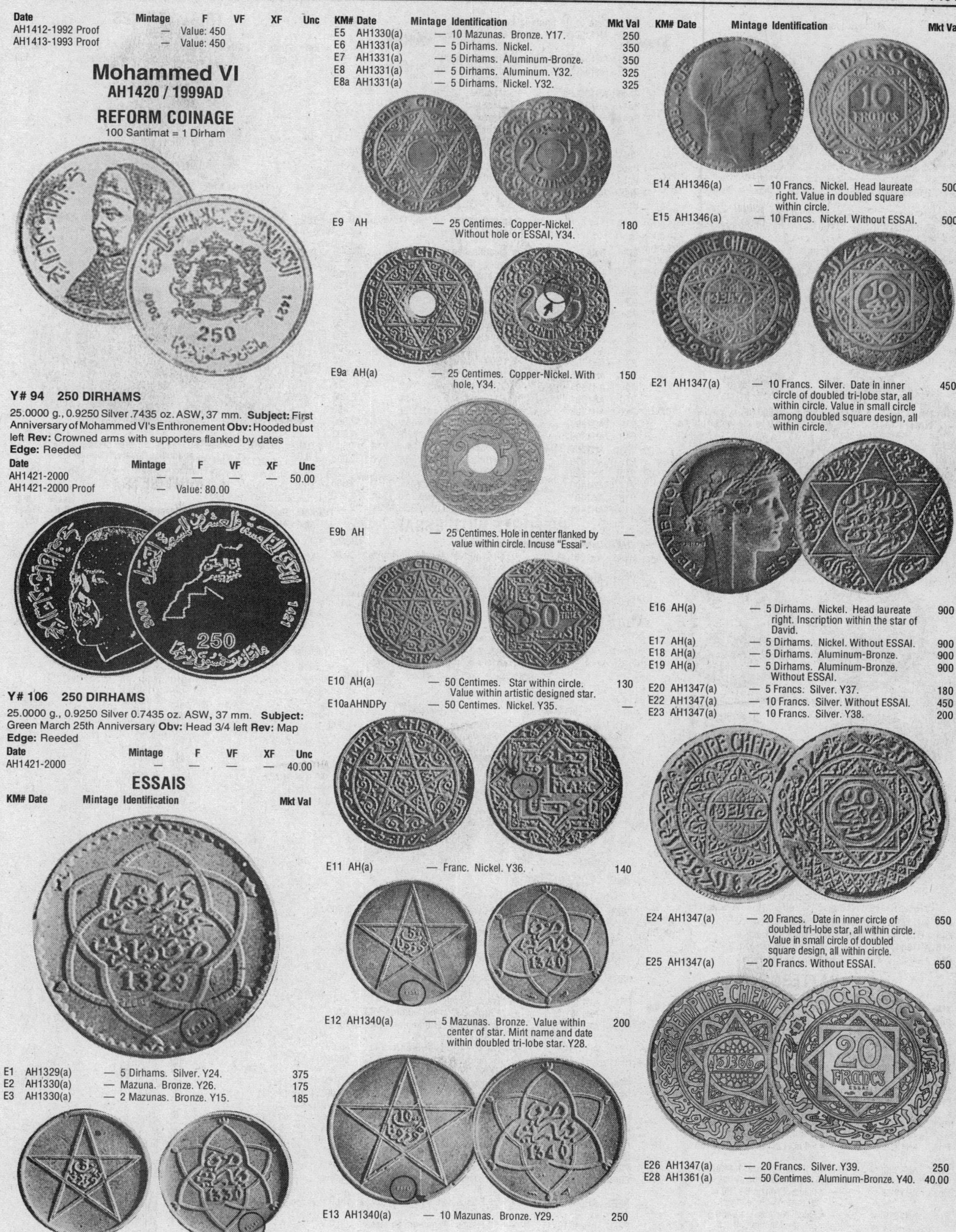

Y# 94 250 DIRHAMS

25.0000 g., 0.9250 Silver .7435 oz. ASW, 37 mm. **Subject:** First Anniversary of Mohammed VI's Enthronement **Obv:** Hooded bust left **Rev:** Crowned arms with supporters flanked by dates **Edge:** Reeded

Date	Mintage	F	VF	XF	Unc
AH1421-2000	—	—	—	—	50.00
AH1421-2000 Proof	—	Value: 80.00			

Y# 106 250 DIRHAMS

25.0000 g., 0.9250 Silver 0.7435 oz. ASW, 37 mm. **Subject:** Green March 25th Anniversary **Obv:** Head 3/4 left **Rev:** Map **Edge:** Reeded

Date	Mintage	F	VF	XF	Unc
AH1421-2000	—	—	—	—	40.00

ESSAIS

KM#	Date	Mintage	Identification	Mkt Val
E1	AH1329(a)	—	5 Dirhams. Silver. Y24.	375
E2	AH1330(a)	—	Mazuna. Bronze. Y26.	175
E3	AH1330(a)	—	2 Mazunas. Bronze. Y15.	185
E4	AH1330(a)	—	5 Mazunas. Bronze. Value within star. Mint name and date within tri-lobe star. Y16.	200
E5	AH1330(a)	—	10 Mazunas. Bronze. Y17.	250
E6	AH1331(a)	—	5 Dirhams. Nickel.	350
E7	AH1331(a)	—	5 Dirhams. Aluminum-Bronze.	350
E8	AH1331(a)	—	5 Dirhams. Aluminum. Y32.	325
E8a	AH1331(a)	—	5 Dirhams. Nickel. Y32.	325
E9	AH	—	25 Centimes. Copper-Nickel. Without hole or ESSAI, Y34.	180
E9a	AH(a)	—	25 Centimes. Copper-Nickel. With hole, Y34.	150
E9b	AH	—	25 Centimes. Hole in center flanked by value within circle. Incuse "Essai".	—
E10	AH(a)	—	50 Centimes. Star within circle. Value within artistic designed star.	130
E10a	AHNDPy	—	50 Centimes. Nickel. Y35.	—
E11	AH(a)	—	Franc. Nickel. Y36.	140
E12	AH1340(a)	—	5 Mazunas. Bronze. Value within center of star. Mint name and date within doubled tri-lobe star. Y28.	200
E13	AH1340(a)	—	10 Mazunas. Bronze. Y29.	250
E14	AH1346(a)	—	10 Francs. Nickel. Head laureate right. Value in doubled square within circle.	500
E15	AH1346(a)	—	10 Francs. Nickel. Without ESSAI.	500
E21	AH1347(a)	—	10 Francs. Silver. Date in inner circle of doubled tri-lobe star, all within circle. Value in small circle among doubled square design, all within circle.	450
E16	AH(a)	—	5 Dirhams. Nickel. Head laureate right. Inscription within the star of David.	900
E17	AH(a)	—	5 Dirhams. Nickel. Without ESSAI.	900
E18	AH(a)	—	5 Dirhams. Aluminum-Bronze.	900
E19	AH(a)	—	5 Dirhams. Aluminum-Bronze. Without ESSAI.	900
E20	AH1347(a)	—	5 Francs. Silver. Y37.	180
E22	AH1347(a)	—	10 Francs. Silver. Without ESSAI.	450
E23	AH1347(a)	—	10 Francs. Silver. Y38.	200
E24	AH1347(a)	—	20 Francs. Date in inner circle of doubled tri-lobe star, all within circle. Value in small circle of doubled square design, all within circle.	650
E25	AH1347(a)	—	20 Francs. Without ESSAI.	650
E26	AH1347(a)	—	20 Francs. Silver. Y39.	250
E28	AH1361(a)	—	50 Centimes. Aluminum-Bronze. Y40.	40.00

KM#	Date	Mintage	Identification	Mkt Val
E29	AH1361(a)	—	Franc. Aluminum-Bronze. Y41.	40.00
E30	AH1361(a)	—	2 Francs. Aluminum-Bronze. Y42.	45.00
E31	AH1365(a)	—	50 Centimes. Aluminum-Bronze center. Y40.	20.00
E32	AH1365(a)	—	Franc. Aluminum-Bronze. Y41.	22.00
E33	AH1365(a)	—	2 Francs. Aluminum-Bronze. Y42.	25.00
E34	AH1365(a)	—	5 Francs. Aluminum-Bronze. Y43.	30.00
E35	AH1366(a)	1,100	10 Francs. Copper-Nickel. Y44.	25.00
E36	AH1366(a)	1,100	20 Francs. Copper-Nickel. Y45.	30.00
E37	AH1370(a)	1,100	Franc. Aluminum center. Y46.	21.00
E38	AH1370(a)	1,100	2 Francs. Aluminum center. Y47.	24.00
E39	AH1370(a)	1,100	5 Francs. Aluminum. Y48.	30.00
E40	AH1370(a)	1,100	100 Francs. 0.7200 Silver. Y-A54.	70.00

Note: KM#E37-E40 were issued in a set with Tunisia, KM#E28-E30.

KM#	Date	Mintage	Identification	Mkt Val
E41	AH1371(a)	1,100	10 Francs. Aluminum-Bronze.Y49.	30.00
E42	AH1371(a)	1,100	20 Francs. Aluminum-Bronze. Y50.	30.00
E43	AH1371(a)	1,100	50 Francs. Aluminum-Bronze. Value in doubled square design within circle. Date in small circle within doubled tri-lobe star, all within circle. Y51.	35.00

Note: KM#E41-43 also issued in 3-piece boxed sets.

KM#	Date	Mintage	Identification	Mkt Val
E44	AH1372(a)	1,100	100 Francs. Silver. Y52.	75.00
E45	AH1372(a)	1,100	200 Francs. Silver. Y53.	90.00
E46	AH1384	—	5 Dirhams. Silver. Y#57.	—
E47	AH1384	—	Dirham. Nickel. Y#56.	—

PATTERNS

Including off metal strikes

KM#	Date	Mintage	Identification	Mkt Val
Pn29	AH1319Fs	—	1/4 Falus. Bronze. 0.7210 g. 12.5 mm. Machine struck.	—
Pn30	AH1319Fs	—	1/2 Falus. Bronze. 1.4430 g. 13 mm.	—
Pn31	AH1319Mr	—	1/2 Falus. Cast Bronze. 1.4430 g. 14 mm.	—
Pn32	AH1319Fs	—	Falus. Bronze. 2.8860 g. 16 mm.	—
Pn33	AH1319Mr	—	Falus. Cast Bronze. 2.8860 g. 17 mm.	—
Pn35	AH1319Fs	—	4 Falus. Bronze. 11.5460 g. 25 mm.	—
Pn36	AH1319Mr	—	4 Falus. Cast Bronze. 11.5460 g. 27 mm.	—
Pn37	AH1320Fs	—	1/2 Falus. Bronze. 1.4430 g. 13 mm. Machine struck.	—
Pn38	AH1320Fs	—	2 Falus. Bronze. 5.7730 g. 20 mm. Machine struck.	—
Pn39	AH1320Fs	—	4 Falus. Bronze. 11.5460 g. 25 mm. Machine struck.	—
Pn40	AH1320Be	—	Mazuna. Bronze.	—
Pn41	AH1320Pa	—	Mazuna. Bronze.	—
Pn42	AH1320Be	—	2 Mazunas. Bronze.	—
Pn43	AH1320Fs	—	2 Mazunas. Bronze. Y#15.1 without "2".	—
Pn44	AH1320Be	—	5 Mazunas. Bronze.	—
Pn45	AH1320Fs	—	5 Mazunas. Bronze. Y#16.1 without "5".	—
Pn46	AH1320Pa	—	5 Mazunas. Bronze.	—
Pn47	AH1320Be	—	10 Mazunas. Bronze. Y#17.2.	—
Pn48	AH1320Pa	—	10 Mazunas. Bronze.	—
Pn49	AH1320Be	—	1/20 Rial. Silver.	—
Pn50	AH1320Be	—	1/10 Rial. Silver.	—
Pn51	AH1320Be	—	Rial. Silver.	—
Pn53	AH1321Be	—	1/20 Rial. Silver.	—
Pn54	AH1321Be	—	1/10 Rial. Silver.	—
Pn55	AH1321Be	—	1/2 Rial. Silver.	—
Pn56	AH1321Be	—	Rial. Silver.	—

PIEFORTS

Double thickness

KM#	Date	Mintage	Identification	Mkt Val
PA1	AHPy	—	Franc. Nickel. Y#36.2.	275
P1	AH1395	10	5 Dirhams. Gold. Y64b	1,100
P1a	AH(1395)	—	Franc. Nickel. Y#36.2.	275
P2	AH1395	40	50 Dirhams. Silver. Y65	400
P3	AH1395	10	50 Dirhams. Gold. Y65a.	2,500
P4	AH1395	10	50 Dirhams. Gold. Y67a	2,500
P5	AH1395	10	250 Dirhams. Gold. Y66	400
P6	AH1395	10	50 Dirhams. Gold. Y68a.	2,100
P7	AH1396	10	250 Dirhams. Gold. Y66	400
P8	AH1396	10	50 Dirhams. Gold. Y68a.	2,500
P9	AH1397	15	250 Dirhams. Gold. Y66.	375
P10	AH1397	10	50 Dirhams. Gold. Y68a.	2,500
P11	AH1398	20	250 Dirhams. Gold. Y66.	350
P12	AH1399	20	50 Dirhams. Gold. Y68a.	2,000
P13	AH1399	20	50 Dirhams. Silver. Y70.	500
P14	AH1399	20	50 Dirhams. 0.9250 Silver. Y76	500
P15	AH1399	20	50 Dirhams. Gold. Y76a.	2,000
P16	AH1399	20	500 Dirhams. Gold. Y71.	800
P17	AH1400	10	50 Dirhams. Gold. Y68a.	2,500
P18	AH1401	10	150 Dirhams. 0.9000 Gold. Y74a.	2,500
P19	AH1401	10	150 Dirhams. 0.9000 Gold. Y73a.	2,500

PIEFORTS WITH ESSAI

KM#	Date	Mintage	Identification	Mkt Val
PEA1	AH1361(a)	—	50 Centimes. Aluminum-Bronze. Y40.	90.00
PEB1	AHPy	—	25 Centimes. Copper-Nickel. Y#34.2; Without hole.	275
PEC1	AH(a)	—	50 Centimes. Nickel. Y#35.1.	275
PED1	AHPa	—	50 Centimes. Copper-Nickel. Star within circle. Value within artistic designed star. Small module with 12 sides.	1,000
PEE1	AHPa	—	50 Centimes. Copper-Nickel. Star within circle. Value within artistic designed star. Large module with 12 sides.	1,000
PEF1	AH(AH1340) Py	—	5 Mazunas. Bronze. Y#28.2.	300
PEG1	AH(AH1340) Py	—	10 Mazunas. Bronze. Y#29.2.	400
PE1	AH1361(a)	—	Franc. Aluminum-Bronze. Y41.	110
PE2	AH1361(a)	—	2 Francs. Aluminum-Bronze. Y42.	120
PE3	AH1364(a)	104	50 Centimes. Aluminum-Bronze. Y40.	70.00
PE4	AH1364	104	Franc. Aluminum-Bronze. Y41	85.00
PE5	AH1364(a)	104	2 Francs. Aluminum-Bronze. Y42.	90.00
PE6	AH1365(a)	104	5 Francs. Aluminum-Bronze. Y43.	100
PE7	AH1366(a)	104	10 Francs. Copper-Nickel center. Y44.	95.00
PE8	AH1366(a)	104	20 Francs. Copper-Nickel. Y45.	95.00
PEA9	AH(AH1370)	—	Franc. Aluminum. . Y#46.	100
PEB9	AH(AH1370)	—	2 Francs. Aluminum. Y#47.	100
PEC9	AH(AH1370)	—	5 Francs. Aluminum. Y#48.	100
PEG9	AH(AH1370)	—	100 Francs. Silver. Y#A54.	300
PED9	AH(AH1371)	—	10 Francs. Aluminum-Bronze. Y#49.	60.00
PEE9	AH(AH1371)	—	20 Francs. Aluminum-Bronze. Y#50.	70.00
PEF9	AH(AH1371)	—	50 Francs. Aluminum-Bronze. Y#51.	80.00
PE9	AH1372(a)	104	100 Francs. Copper-Nickel. Y52.	100
PE10	AH1372(a)	104	200 Francs. Silver. Y53.	125
PE11	AH1372(a)	—	200 Francs. Gold. Y53.	1,000

TRIAL STRIKES

Uniface

KM#	Date	Mintage	Identification	Mkt Val
TS1	AH1347	—	10 Francs. Silvered Bronze.	500
TS2	AH1347	—	10 Francs. Silvered Bronze. Value in doubled square design within circle. Uniface.	500
TS3	AH1347	—	20 Francs. Silvered Bronze.	750
TS4	AH1347	—	20 Francs. Silvered Bronze. Value in doubled square design within circle. Uniface.	750

MINT SETS

KM#	Date	Mintage	Identification	Issue Price	Mkt Val
MS1	AH1370-84 (8)	—	Y#46-48(AH1370), 49-51(AH1371), 56-57 (AH1384)	—	17.50
MS2	1974-75 (7)	20,000	Y#58-63 (1974), Y#64 (1975)	20.00	30.00

PROOF SETS

KM#	Date	Mintage	Identification	Issue Price	Mkt Val
PS1	1974 (6)	30	Y#58a-63a	—	3,650

MOZAMBIQUE

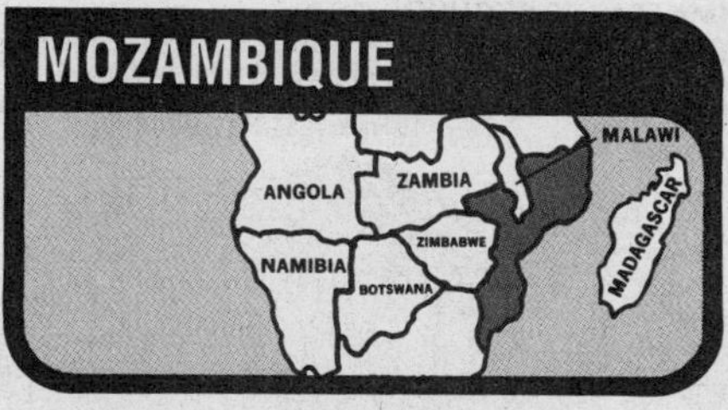

The Republic of Mozambique, a former overseas province of Portugal, stretches for 1,430 miles (2,301 km.) along the southeast coast of Africa, has an area of 302,330 sq. mi. (801,590 sq. km.) and a population of 14.1 million, 99 % of whom are native Africans of the Bantu tribes. Capital: Maputo. Agriculture is the chief industry. Cashew nuts, cotton, sugar, copra and tea are exported.

Vasco de Gama explored all the coast of Mozambique in 1498 and found Arab trading posts already established along the coast. Portuguese settlement dates from the establishment of the trading post of Mozambique in 1505. Within five years Portugal absorbed all the former Arab sultanates along the east African coast. The area was organized as a colony in 1907 and became an overseas province in 1952. In Sept. of 1974, after more than a decade of guerrilla warfare with the forces of the Mozambique Liberation Front, Portugal agreed to the independence of Mozambique, effective June 25, 1975. The Socialist party, led by President Joaquim Chissano was in power until the 2nd of November, 1990 when they became a republic.

Mozambique became a member of the Commonwealth of Nations in November 1995. The President is Head of State; the Prime Minister is Head of Government.

RULERS

Portuguese, until 1975

MONETARY SYSTEM

100 Centavos = 1 Escudo

PORTUGUESE COLONY

DECIMAL COINAGE

100 Centavos = 1 Escudo

KM# 63 10 CENTAVOS

Bronze **Obv:** Value **Rev:** Arms

Date	Mintage	F	VF	XF	Unc	BU
1936	2,000,000	2.00	10.00	35.00	50.00	—

KM# 72 10 CENTAVOS

Bronze **Obv:** Value **Rev:** Arms within crowned globe

Date	Mintage	F	VF	XF	Unc	BU
1942	2,000,000	1.00	2.50	7.50	20.00	—

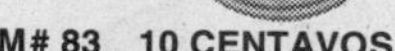

KM# 83 10 CENTAVOS

Bronze, 16 mm. **Obv:** Value **Rev:** Arms within crowned globe

Date	Mintage	F	VF	XF	Unc	BU
1960	3,750,000	—	0.50	1.25	3.00	—
1961	10,300,000	—	0.25	1.00	2.50	—

KM# 64 20 CENTAVOS

Bronze **Obv:** Value **Rev:** Arms

Date	Mintage	F	VF	XF	Unc	BU
1936	2,500,000	2.00	4.50	50.00	90.00	—

KM# 71 20 CENTAVOS

Bronze **Obv:** Value **Rev:** Arms within crowned globe

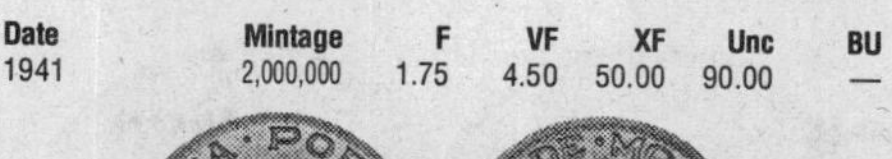

Date	Mintage	F	VF	XF	Unc	BU
1941	2,000,000	1.75	4.50	50.00	90.00	—

KM# 75 20 CENTAVOS

Bronze, 20.3 mm. **Obv:** Value **Rev:** Arms within crowned globe

Date	Mintage	F	VF	XF	Unc	BU
1949	8,000,000	0.75	1.50	4.00	10.00	—
1950	12,500,000	0.75	1.50	3.00	8.50	—

KM# 85 20 CENTAVOS

Bronze, 18 mm. **Obv:** Value **Rev:** Arms within crowned globe

Date	Mintage	F	VF	XF	Unc	BU
1961	12,500,000	—	0.25	1.00	2.50	—

KM# 88 20 CENTAVOS

Bronze, 16 mm. **Obv:** Value **Rev:** Arms within crowned globe
Note: Reduced size.

Date	Mintage	F	VF	XF	Unc	BU
1973	1,798,000	1.00	2.00	3.00	7.50	—
1974	13,044,000	1.00	2.50	3.75	9.00	—

KM# 65 50 CENTAVOS

Copper-Nickel **Obv:** Value **Rev:** Arms

Date	Mintage	F	VF	XF	Unc	BU
1936	2,500,000	5.00	45.00	125	225	—

KM# 73 50 CENTAVOS

Bronze **Obv:** Value **Rev:** Arms within crowned globe

Date	Mintage	F	VF	XF	Unc	BU
1945	2,500,000	1.50	3.50	25.00	50.00	80.00

KM# 76 50 CENTAVOS

Nickel-Bronze **Obv:** Value **Rev:** Arms within crowned globe

Date	Mintage	F	VF	XF	Unc	BU
1950	20,000,000	1.00	3.00	12.00	22.00	32.00
1951	16,000,000	1.00	3.00	10.00	20.00	30.00

KM# 81 50 CENTAVOS

Bronze **Obv:** Value **Rev:** Arms within crowned globe

Date	Mintage	F	VF	XF	Unc	BU
1953	5,010,000	0.50	1.50	4.00	10.00	—
1957	24,990,000	—	0.50	1.25	4.50	—

KM# 89 50 CENTAVOS

Bronze **Obv:** Value **Rev:** Arms within crowned globe

Date	Mintage	F	VF	XF	Unc	BU
1973	6,841,000	—	0.50	1.00	3.00	—
1974	23,810,000	—	0.50	1.00	4.00	—

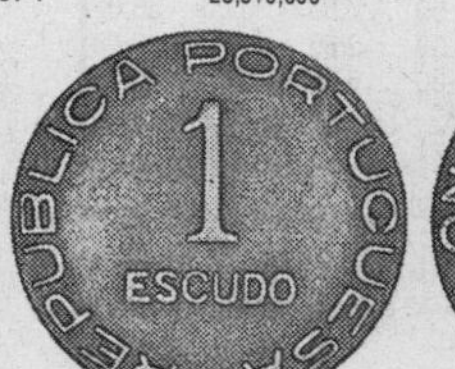

KM# 66 ESCUDO

Copper-Nickel **Obv:** Value **Rev:** Arms

Date	Mintage	F	VF	XF	Unc	BU
1936	2,000,000	4.00	25.00	150	210	—

KM# 74 ESCUDO

Bronze **Obv:** Value **Rev:** Arms within crowned globe

Date	Mintage	F	VF	XF	Unc	BU
1945	2,000,000	2.00	15.00	45.00	110	—

KM# 77 ESCUDO

Nickel-Bronze, 27 mm. **Obv:** Value **Rev:** Arms within crowned globe

Date	Mintage	F	VF	XF	Unc	BU
1950	10,000,000	2.00	15.00	45.00	90.00	—
1951	10,000,000	1.50	3.00	12.50	30.00	—

KM# 82 ESCUDO

Bronze, 26 mm. **Obv:** Value **Rev:** Arms within crowned globe

Date	Mintage	F	VF	XF	Unc	BU
1953	2,013,000	0.75	1.50	15.00	25.00	35.00
1957	2,987,000	0.75	1.50	17.50	35.00	45.00
1962	600,000	0.50	1.25	15.00	22.50	30.00
1963	3,258,000	0.50	0.75	4.00	12.50	18.00
1965	5,000,000	—	0.25	1.50	3.50	6.00
1968	4,500,000	—	0.25	1.50	3.50	6.00
1969	1,642,000	—	0.50	1.75	4.00	7.00
1973	501,000	0.20	0.50	2.00	6.50	9.00
1974	25,281,000	—	0.25	1.50	3.00	5.00

KM# 61 2-1/2 ESCUDOS

3.5000 g., 0.6500 Silver .0731 oz. ASW **Obv:** Shield within globe and maltese cross **Rev:** Arms

Date	Mintage	F	VF	XF	Unc	BU
1935	1,200,000	4.50	12.50	40.00	100	—

KM# 68 2-1/2 ESCUDOS
3.5000 g., 0.6500 Silver .0731 oz. ASW **Obv:** Shield within globe and maltese cross **Rev:** Arms within crowned globe

Date	Mintage	F	VF	XF	Unc	BU
1938	1,000,000	3.50	10.00	35.00	65.00	—
1942	1,200,000	2.50	7.50	30.00	55.00	—
1950	4,000,000	1.50	2.50	7.50	20.00	—
1951	4,000,000	2.00	6.50	25.00	50.00	—

KM# 78 2-1/2 ESCUDOS
Copper-Nickel **Obv:** Shield within globe and maltese cross **Rev:** Arms within crowned globe

Date	Mintage	F	VF	XF	Unc	BU
1952	4,000,000	0.50	8.00	50.00	80.00	—
1953	4,000,000	0.30	5.00	25.00	45.00	—
1954	4,000,000	0.25	3.00	12.00	22.00	—
1955	4,000,000	0.30	1.50	13.50	42.50	—
1965	8,000,000	0.10	0.25	1.00	4.00	—
1973	1,767,000	0.25	0.65	2.50	6.50	—

KM# 62 5 ESCUDOS
7.0000 g., 0.6500 Silver .1463 oz. ASW **Obv:** Shield within globe and maltese cross **Rev:** Arms

Date	Mintage	F	VF	XF	Unc	BU
1935	1,000,000	5.50	22.50	65.00	120	—

KM# 69 5 ESCUDOS
7.0000 g., 0.6500 Silver .1463 oz. ASW **Obv:** Shield within globe and maltese cross **Rev:** Arms within crowned globe

Date	Mintage	F	VF	XF	Unc	BU
1938	800,000	7.50	20.00	80.00	130	—
1949	8,000,000	2.75	5.50	25.00	45.00	—

KM# 84 5 ESCUDOS
4.0000 g., 0.6500 Silver .0835 oz. ASW **Obv:** Shield within globe and maltese cross **Rev:** Arms within crowned globe

Date	Mintage	F	VF	XF	Unc	BU
1960	8,000,000	1.50	2.25	3.50	7.00	10.00

KM# 86 5 ESCUDOS
Copper-Nickel **Obv:** Shield within globe and maltese cross **Rev:** Arms within crowned globe

Date	Mintage	F	VF	XF	Unc	BU
1971	8,000,000	0.20	0.50	1.00	3.00	6.00
1973	3,352,000	0.20	0.50	1.75	4.50	7.00

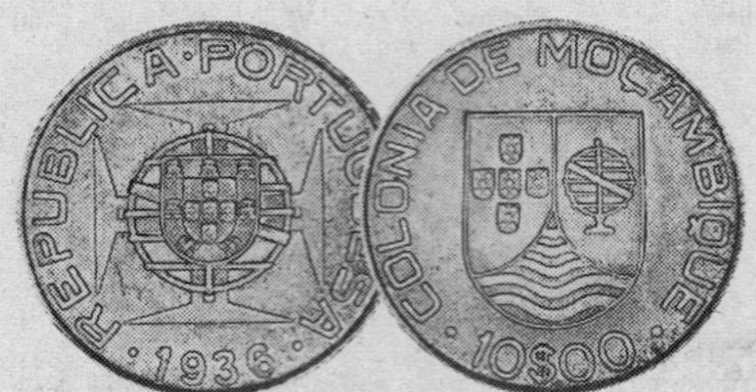

KM# 67 10 ESCUDOS
12.5000 g., 0.8350 Silver .3356 oz. ASW **Obv:** Shield within globe and maltese cross **Rev:** Arms

Date	Mintage	F	VF	XF	Unc	BU
1936	497,000	10.00	20.00	67.50	130	—

KM# 70 10 ESCUDOS
12.5000 g., 0.8350 Silver .3356 oz. ASW **Obv:** Shield within globe and maltese cross **Rev:** Arms within crowned globe

Date	Mintage	F	VF	XF	Unc	BU
1938	530,000	20.00	35.00	75.00	160	—

KM# 79 10 ESCUDOS
5.0000 g., 0.7200 Silver .1157 oz. ASW **Obv:** Shield within globe and maltese cross **Rev:** Arms within crowned globe

Date	Mintage	VG	F	VF	XF	Unc
1952	1,503,000	—	2.00	4.50	15.00	35.00
1954	1,335,000	—	2.00	4.50	20.00	50.00
1955	1,162,000	—	2.00	4.50	15.00	35.00
1960	2,000,000	—	2.00	3.00	6.00	12.00

KM# 79a 10 ESCUDOS
5.0000 g., 0.6800 Silver .1093 oz. ASW **Obv:** Shield within globe and maltese cross **Rev:** Arms within crowned globe

Date	Mintage	F	VF	XF	Unc	BU
1966	500,000	1.75	2.75	5.50	12.50	—

KM# 79b 10 ESCUDOS
Copper-Nickel **Obv:** Shield within globe and maltese cross **Rev:** Arms within crowned globe

Date	Mintage	F	VF	XF	Unc	BU
1968	5,000,000	0.30	0.70	2.50	5.00	—
1970	4,000,000	0.30	0.70	2.50	5.00	—
1974	3,366,000	0.40	1.00	3.00	6.50	—

KM# 80 20 ESCUDOS
10.0000 g., 0.7200 Silver .2315 oz. ASW **Obv:** Shield within globe and maltese cross **Rev:** Arms within crowned globe

Date	Mintage	F	VF	XF	Unc	BU
1952	1,004,000	3.75	4.50	10.00	25.00	—
1955	996,000	3.75	5.00	12.50	30.00	—
1960	2,000,000	3.75	4.25	6.50	12.50	—

KM# 80a 20 ESCUDOS
10.0000 g., 0.6800 Silver .2186 oz. ASW **Obv:** Shield within globe and maltese cross **Rev:** Arms within crowned globe

Date	Mintage	F	VF	XF	Unc	BU
1966	250,000	3.75	5.50	9.50	18.00	—

KM# 87 20 ESCUDOS
Nickel **Obv:** Shield within globe **Rev:** Arms within circle

Date	Mintage	F	VF	XF	Unc	BU
1971	2,000,000	0.35	0.75	1.75	5.00	—
1972	1,158,000	0.50	1.00	2.50	6.00	—

PEOPLE'S REPUBLIC

DECIMAL COINAGE

100 Centimos = 1 Metica

KM# 90 CENTIMO
Aluminum **Obv:** Head right **Obv. Designer:** Samora Machel **Rev:** Value and flower sprig

Date	Mintage	F	VF	XF	Unc	BU
1975	15,050,000	—	—	60.00	120	—

KM# 91 2 CENTIMOS
Copper-Zinc **Obv:** Head right **Obv. Designer:** Samora Machel **Rev:** Value and flower sprig

Date	Mintage	F	VF	XF	Unc	BU
1975	8,242,000	—	—	70.00	125	—

KM# 92 5 CENTIMOS
Copper-Zinc **Obv:** Head right **Obv. Designer:** Samora Machel **Rev:** Value and flower sprig

Date	Mintage	F	VF	XF	Unc	BU
1975	14,898,000	—	—	60.00	110	—

KM# 93 10 CENTIMOS
Copper-Zinc **Obv:** Head right **Obv. Designer:** Samora Machel **Rev:** Value and 3 flower sprigs

Date	Mintage	F	VF	XF	Unc	BU
1975	18,000,000	—	—	50.00	90.00	—

KM# 94 20 CENTIMOS
Copper-Nickel **Obv:** Head right **Obv. Designer:** Samora Machel **Rev:** Value and flower sprig

Date	Mintage	F	VF	XF	Unc	BU
1975	8,050,000	—	—	120	200	—

KM# 95 50 CENTIMOS

Copper-Nickel **Obv:** Head right **Obv. Designer:** Samora Machel **Rev:** Value and 2 1/2 seeds

Date	Mintage	F	VF	XF	Unc	BU
1975	3,050,000	—	—	145	265	—

KM# 96 METICA

Copper-Nickel **Obv:** Head right **Obv. Designer:** Samora Machel **Rev:** Plant in vase

Date	Mintage	F	VF	XF	Unc	BU
1975	2,550,000	—	—	50.00	85.00	—

KM# 97 2-1/2 METICAIS

Copper-Nickel **Obv:** Head right **Obv. Designer:** Samora Machel **Rev:** Leafy plant **Shape:** 7-sided

Date	Mintage	F	VF	XF	Unc	BU
1975	1,500,000	—	—	145	225	—

REFORM COINAGE

100 Centavos = 1 Metical; 1980

KM# 98 50 CENTAVOS

1.4000 g., Aluminum, 20 mm. **Obv:** Emblem **Rev:** Value above xylophone

Date	Mintage	F	VF	XF	Unc	BU
1980	5,160,000	0.15	0.30	0.60	1.25	2.00
1982	—	0.15	0.30	0.60	1.25	2.00

KM# 99 METICAL

8.0000 g., Brass, 26 mm. **Obv:** Emblem **Rev:** Female student and value

Date	Mintage	F	VF	XF	Unc	BU
1980	32,000	1.50	3.00	5.00	10.00	—
1982	—	1.50	3.00	5.00	10.00	—

KM# 99a METICAL

Aluminum **Obv:** Emblem **Rev:** Female student and value

Date	Mintage	F	VF	XF	Unc	BU
1986	—	0.20	0.40	0.60	1.00	—

KM# 100 2-1/2 METICAIS

Aluminum, 22.6 mm. **Obv:** Emblem **Rev:** Ship and crane in harbor **Note:** 1.80-2.00 grams.

Date	Mintage	F	VF	XF	Unc	BU
1980	1,088,000	0.25	0.50	1.00	1.75	—
1982	—	0.25	0.50	1.00	1.75	—
1986	—	0.25	0.50	1.00	1.75	—

Note: Edge varieties exist

KM# 101 5 METICAIS

2.6000 g., Aluminum, 24.5 mm. **Obv:** Emblem **Rev:** Tractor and value

Date	Mintage	F	VF	XF	Unc	BU
1980	7,736,000	0.35	0.75	1.25	2.00	—
1982	—	0.35	0.75	1.25	2.00	—
1986	—	0.35	0.75	1.25	2.00	—

KM# 102 10 METICAIS

9.1000 g., Copper-Nickel, 28 mm. **Obv:** Emblem **Rev:** Industrial skyline

Date	Mintage	F	VF	XF	Unc	BU
1980	152,000	0.75	1.50	2.50	6.00	—
1981	—	0.75	1.50	2.50	6.00	—

KM# 102a 10 METICAIS

Aluminum, 28 mm. **Obv:** Emblem **Rev:** Industrial skyline

Date	Mintage	F	VF	XF	Unc	BU
1986	—	0.25	0.45	1.00	2.00	—

KM# 103 20 METICAIS

12.0000 g., Copper-Nickel, 30 mm. **Obv:** Emblem **Rev:** Panzer tank

Date	Mintage	F	VF	XF	Unc	BU
1980	78,000	1.00	2.00	4.00	9.00	—

KM# 103a 20 METICAIS

Aluminum, 30 mm. **Obv:** Emblem **Rev:** Panzer tank

Date	Mintage	F	VF	XF	Unc	BU
1986	—	0.40	0.80	1.50	3.00	—

KM# 106 50 METICAIS

Copper-Nickel, 35 mm. **Subject:** World Fisheries Conference **Obv:** Emblem above value and date **Rev:** Traditional fishing raft **Rev. Designer:** Stuart Devlin

Date	Mintage	F	VF	XF	Unc	BU
1983	130,000	2.50	5.00	8.00	12.50	—

KM# 106a 50 METICAIS

22.0000 g., 0.9250 Silver .6543 oz. ASW, 35 mm. **Subject:** World Fisheries Conference **Obv:** Emblem above value and date **Rev:** Traditional fishing raft

Date	Mintage	F	VF	XF	Unc	BU
1983 Proof	21,000	Value: 50.00				

KM# 106b 50 METICAIS

22.0000 g., 0.9000 Gold .6366 oz. AGW **Subject:** World Fisheries Conference **Obv:** Emblem above value and date **Rev:** Traditional fishing raft

Date	Mintage	F	VF	XF	Unc	BU
1983 Proof	135	Value: 1,000				

KM# 112 50 METICAIS

Aluminum **Obv:** Emblem **Rev:** Woman and soldier with provisions

Date	Mintage	F	VF	XF	Unc	BU
1986	—	0.75	1.50	2.50	5.50	—

KM# 107 250 METICAIS

28.2800 g., 0.9250 Silver .8411 oz. ASW **Subject:** 10th Anniversary of Independence **Obv:** Emblem **Rev:** Star and map divides circle, value within 1/2 circle

Date	Mintage	F	VF	XF	Unc	BU
1985 Proof	2,000	Value: 42.50				

KM# 107a 250 METICAIS

Copper-Nickel **Obv:** Emblem **Rev:** Star and map divides circle, value within 1/2 circle

Date	Mintage	F	VF	XF	Unc	BU
1985	—	—	—	—	—	—

KM# 104 500 METICAIS

19.4000 g., 0.8000 Silver .4990 oz. ASW **Subject:** 5th Anniversary of Independence **Obv:** Emblem above value **Rev:** 1/2 Figure, corn stalks and small building

Date	Mintage	F	VF	XF	Unc	BU
1980 Proof	5,000	Value: 65.00				

KM# 110 500 METICAIS

16.0000 g., 0.9990 Silver .5145 oz. ASW **Subject:** Defense of Nature **Obv:** Emblem and value **Rev:** Lions

Date	Mintage	F	VF	XF	Unc	BU
1989 Proof	2,500	Value: 35.00				

KM# 111 500 METICAIS

16.0000 g., 0.9990 Silver .5145 oz. ASW **Subject:** Defense of Nature **Obv:** Emblem and value **Rev:** Moorish Idol Fish

Date	Mintage	F	VF	XF	Unc	BU
1989 Proof	2,000	Value: 35.00				

KM# 113 500 METICAIS

16.0000 g., 0.9990 Silver .5145 oz. ASW **Subject:** Defense of Nature **Obv:** Emblem and value **Rev:** Giraffes

Date	Mintage	F	VF	XF	Unc	BU
1990 Proof	2,000	Value: 35.00				

KM# 109 1000 METICAIS

Copper-Nickel **Subject:** Visit of Pope John Paul II **Obv:** Emblem above value **Rev:** Bust right

Date	Mintage	F	VF	XF	Unc	BU
1988	Est. 80,000	—	—	—	8.00	10.00

KM# 109a 1000 METICAIS

28.2800 g., 0.9250 Silver .8411 oz. ASW **Obv:** Emblem above value and date **Rev:** Bust right

Date	Mintage	F	VF	XF	Unc	BU
1988 Proof	Est. 3,500	Value: 42.50				

KM# 108 2000 METICAIS

17.5000 g., 0.9170 Gold .5158 oz. AGW **Subject:** 10th Anniversary of Independence **Obv:** Emblem above value **Rev:** Star and map divides circle, value at right

Date	Mintage	F	VF	XF	Unc	BU
1985 Proof	100	Value: 675				

KM# 105 5000 METICAIS

17.2790 g., 0.9000 Gold .5000 oz. AGW **Subject:** 5th Anniversary of Independence **Obv:** Emblem above value **Rev:** Figure at left, corn plants in background with tractor above

Date	Mintage	F	VF	XF	Unc	BU
1980 Proof	2,000	Value: 350				

REFORM COINAGE

100 Centavos = 1 Metical; 1994

KM# 115 METICAL

Brass Clad Steel, 17 mm. **Obv:** Emblem **Rev:** Female student

Date	Mintage	F	VF	XF	Unc	BU
1994	—	—	—	—	0.50	1.00

KM# 116 5 METICAIS

Brass Clad Steel **Obv:** Emblem **Rev:** Kingfisher

Date	Mintage	F	VF	XF	Unc	BU
1994	—	—	—	—	1.50	2.50

KM# 117 10 METICAIS

Brass Clad Steel, 23 mm. **Obv:** Emblem **Rev:** Cotton plant

Date	Mintage	F	VF	XF	Unc	BU
1994	—	—	—	—	1.25	2.00

KM# 118 20 METICAIS

Brass Clad Steel, 26 mm. **Obv:** Emblem **Rev:** Pepper plant

Date	Mintage	F	VF	XF	Unc	BU
1994	—	—	—	—	1.50	—

KM# 119 50 METICAIS

Nickel Clad Steel **Obv:** Emblem **Rev:** Leopard's head

Date	Mintage	F	VF	XF	Unc	BU
1994	—	—	—	—	3.00	5.00

KM# 120 100 METICAIS

Nickel Clad Steel, 27 mm. **Obv:** Emblem **Rev:** Lobster

Date	Mintage	F	VF	XF	Unc	BU
1994	—	—	—	—	3.50	5.50

KM# 121 500 METICAIS

Nickel Clad Steel, 30 mm. **Obv:** Emblem **Rev:** Building

Date	Mintage	F	VF	XF	Unc	BU
1994	—	—	—	—	4.50	5.50

KM# 127 500 METICAIS

Nickel Clad Steel **Series:** 2000 Summer Olympics - Sydney

Date	Mintage	F	VF	XF	Unc	BU
1998 Proof	10,000	Value: 7.50				

KM# 122 1000 METICAIS

Nickel Clad Steel, 31.5 mm. **Obv:** Emblem **Rev:** Building

Date	Mintage	F	VF	XF	Unc	BU
1994	—	—	—	—	5.00	6.00

KM# 128 1000 METICAIS

24.6200 g., 0.9250 Silver .7322 oz. ASW **Series:** 2000 Summer Olympics - Sydney

Date	Mintage	F	VF	XF	Unc	BU
1998 Proof	10,000	Value: 32.50				

KM# 125 5000 METICAIS

411.4224 g., 0.9990 Silver 13.2143 oz. ASW, 97 mm. **Obv:** National arms **Rev:** Rhinoceros right **Edge:** Reeded **Note:** Illustration reduced.

Date	Mintage	F	VF	XF	Unc	BU
1997 Proof	2,000	Value: 300				

KM# 124 5000 METICAIS

14.0000 g., Nickel Clad Steel, 28.5 mm. **Obv:** Emblem **Rev:** High power electric lines

Date	Mintage	F	VF	XF	Unc	BU
1998	—	—	—	—	5.00	6.00

KM# 114.1 10000 METICAIS

20.0000 g., 0.9990 Silver .6430 oz. ASW **Subject:** World Cup Soccer **Obv:** Emblem **Rev:** Soccer player, 999 at right

Date	Mintage	F	VF	XF	Unc	BU
1994 Proof	—	Value: 65.00				

KM# 114.2 10000 METICAIS
20.0000 g., 0.9990 Silver .6430 oz. ASW **Obv:** Emblem **Rev:** Soccer player without 999

Date	Mintage	F	VF	XF	Unc	BU
1994 Proof	—	Value: 65.00				

KM# 123 10000 METICAIS
21.0600 g., 0.9990 Silver .6764 oz. ASW **Subject:** World Cup Soccer **Obv:** Emblem **Rev:** Soccer players and net, 999 at lower left

Date	Mintage	F	VF	XF	Unc	BU
1994 Proof	—	Value: 65.00				

KM# 126 10000 METICAIS
822.8449 g., 0.9990 Silver 26.4286 oz. ASW, 100 mm. **Obv:** National arms **Rev:** Elephant charging **Edge:** Reeded **Note:** Illustration reduced.

Date	Mintage	F	VF	XF	Unc	BU
1997 Proof	2,000	Value: 500				

KM# 129 10000 METICAIS
822.8449 g., 0.9990 Silver 26.4286 oz. ASW **Series:** 2000 Summer Olympics - Sydney

Date	Mintage	F	VF	XF	Unc	BU
1998 Proof	2,000	Value: 425				

PATTERNS

Including off metal strikes

KM#	Date	Mintage	Identification	Mkt Val
Pn1	1994	—	10000 Meticais. Copper-Nickel. KM#114.1.	—
Pn2	1994	—	10000 Meticais. Copper-Nickel. KM#123.	—

PIEFORTS

KM#	Date	Mintage	Identification	Issue Price	Mkt Val
P1	1983	600	50 Meticais. 0.9250 Silver.	—	70.00

PROVAS

Standard Metals

KM#	Date	Mintage	Identification	Issue Price	Mkt Val
Pr1	1935	—	2-1/2 Escudos. Silver. KM#61	—	125
Pr2	1935	—	5 Escudos. Silver. KM62.	—	145
Pr3	1936	—	10 Centavos. Bronze. KM63.	—	60.00
Pr4	1936	—	20 Centavos. Bronze. KM64.	—	60.00
Pr5	1936	—	50 Centavos. Copper-Nickel. KM65.	—	90.00
Pr6	1936	—	Escudo. Copper-Nickel. KM66	—	90.00
Pr7	1936	—	10 Escudos. Silver. KM67.	—	180
Pr8	1938	—	2-1/2 Escudos. Silver. KM61.	—	100
Pr9	1938	—	5 Escudos. Silver. KM69.	—	120
Pr10	1938	—	10 Escudos. Silver. KM70.	—	130
Pr11	1941	—	10 Centavos. Bronze. KM71.	—	65.00
Pr12	1942	—	10 Centavos. Bronze. KM72.	—	40.00
Pr13	1942	—	2-1/2 Escudos. Silver. KM68.	—	75.00
Pr14	1945	—	50 Centavos. Bronze. KM73.	—	40.00
Pr15	1945	—	Escudo. Bronze. KM74.	—	40.00
Pr16	1948	—	2-1/2 Escudos.	—	175
Pr17	1949	—	20 Centavos. Bronze. KM75.	—	40.00
Pr18	1949	—	5 Escudos. Silver. KM69.	—	75.00
Pr19	1950	—	50 Centavos. Nickel-Bronze. KM76.	—	45.00
PrA19	1950	—	20 Centavos. Bronze. KM75.	—	85.00
Pr20	1950	—	Escudo. Nickel-Bronze. KM77.	—	45.00
Pr21	1950	—	2-1/2 Escudos. Silver. KM68.	—	80.00
Pr22	1951	—	50 Centavos. Nickel-Bronze. KM76.	—	35.00
Pr23	1951	—	Escudo. Nickel-Bronze. KM77.	—	35.00
Pr24	1951	—	2-1/2 Escudos. Silver. KM68.	—	65.00
Pr25	1951	—	5 Escudos.	—	—
Pr26	1952	—	2-1/2 Escudos. Copper-Nickel. KM78.	—	65.00
Pr27	1952	—	5 Escudos.	—	—
Pr28	1952	—	10 Escudos. Silver. KM79	—	65.00
Pr29	1952	—	20 Escudos. Silver. KM80.	—	75.00
Pr30	1953	—	50 Centavos. Bronze. KM81.	—	35.00
Pr31	1953	—	Escudo. Bronze. KM82.	—	35.00
Pr32	1953	—	2-1/2 Escudos. Copper-Nickel. KM78.	—	45.00
Pr34	1954	—	10 Escudos. Silver. KM79.	—	65.00
Pr35	1955	—	2-1/2 Escudos. Copper-Nickel. KM78.	—	45.00
Pr36	1955	—	10 Escudos. Silver. KM79.	—	65.00
Pr37	1955	—	20 Escudos. Silver. KM80.	—	65.00
Pr38	1957	—	50 Centavos. Bronze. KM81.	—	35.00
Pr39	1957	—	Escudo. Bronze. KM82.	—	35.00
Pr40	1960	—	10 Centavos. Bronze. KM83.	—	35.00
Pr41	1960	—	5 Escudos. Silver. KM84	—	65.00
Pr42	1960	—	10 Escudos. Silver. KM79.	—	65.00
Pr43	1960	—	20 Escudos. Silver. KM80.	—	65.00
Pr44	1961	—	10 Centavos. Bronze. KM83.	—	35.00
Pr45	1961	—	20 Centavos. Bronze. KM85.	—	35.00
Pr46	1962	—	Escudo. Bronze. KM82.	—	35.00
Pr47	1963	—	Escudo. Bronze. KM82.	—	35.00
Pr48	1965	—	Escudo. Bronze. KM82.	—	35.00
Pr49	1965	—	2-1/2 Escudos. Copper-Nickel. KM78.	—	45.00
Pr50	1966	—	10 Escudos. Silver. KM79a.	—	65.00
Pr51	1966	—	20 Escudos. Silver. KM80a	—	75.00
Pr52	1968	—	Escudo. Bronze. KM82.	—	35.00
Pr53	1968	—	10 Escudos. Copper-Nickel. KM79b.	—	45.00
Pr54	1968	—	20 Escudos.	—	45.00
Pr55	1969	—	Escudo. Bronze. KM82.	—	35.00
Pr56	1969	—	20 Escudos.	—	45.00
Pr57	1970	—	10 Escudos. Copper-Nickel. KM79b.	—	45.00
Pr58	1970	—	20 Escudos.	—	45.00
Pr59	1971	—	5 Escudos. Copper-Nickel. KM86.	—	45.00
Pr60	1971	—	20 Escudos. Nickel. KM87.	—	45.00
Pr61	1972	—	20 Escudos. Nickel. KM87.	—	85.00
Pr62	1973	—	20 Centavos. Bronze. KM88.	—	65.00
Pr63	1973	—	50 Centavos. Bronze. KM89.	—	85.00
Pr64	1973	—	Escudo. Bronze. KM82.	—	65.00
Pr65	1973	—	2-1/2 Escudos. Copper-Nickel. KM78.	—	85.00
Pr66	1973	—	5 Escudos. Copper-Nickel. KM86.	—	85.00
Pr68	1974	—	20 Centavos. Bronze. KM88.	—	65.00
Pr69	1974	—	50 Centavos. Bronze. KM89.	—	85.00
Pr70	1974	—	Escudo. Bronze. KM82.	—	65.00

MINT SETS

KM#	Date	Mintage	Identification	Issue Price	Mkt Val
MS1	1980 (6)	—	KM#98-103	—	30.00

SPECIMEN SETS (SS)

KM#	Date	Mintage	Identification	Issue Price	Mkt Val
SS1	1975 (8)	—	KM#90-97	—	2,250

MUSCAT & OMAN

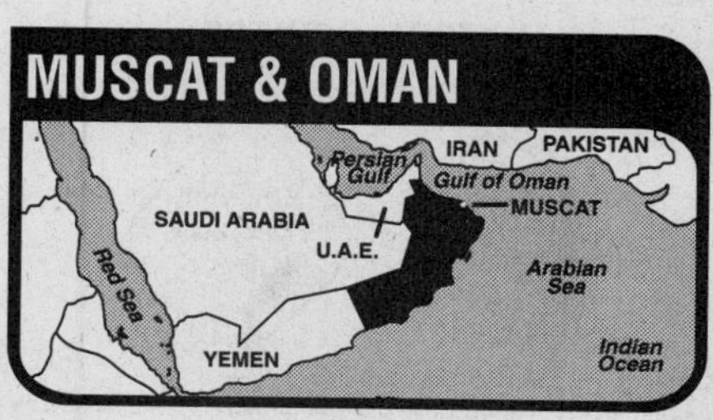

RULERS

al-Bu Sa'id Dynasty
Faisal bin Turkee, AH1306-1332/1888-1913AD
Taimur bin Faisal, AH1332-1351/1913-1932AD
Sa'id bin Taimur, AH1351-1390/1932-1970AD
Qabus bin Sa'id, AH1390-/1970-AD

MONETARY SYSTEM

Until 1970
4 Baiza = 1 Anna
64 Baiza = 1 Rupee
200 Baiza = 1 Saidi (Dasin Dog)/Dhofari Rial

1970-1972
1000 (new) Baisa = 1 Saidi Rial

Commencing 1972
1000 Baisa = 1 Omani Rial

Note: For later coin issues, please refer to Oman.

SULTANATE

COUNTERMARKED COINAGE

C# 19.1 1/4 ANNA
Copper **Ruler:** Faisal bin Turkee **Countermark:** ST
Note: Countermark in Arabic on 1/4 Anna, KM#3.

CM Date	Host Date	Good	VG	F	VF	XF
1913	AH1315	15.00	25.00	40.00	60.00	—
1913	AH1315	15.00	25.00	40.00	60.00	—

C# 19.2 1/4 ANNA
Copper **Ruler:** Faisal bin Turkee **Countermark:** ST
Note: Countermark in Arabic on 1/4 Anna, KM#8. Countermark for Sultan Taimur or Sayyid Taimur.

CM Date	Host Date	Good	VG	F	VF	XF
1913	AH1312	15.00	25.00	45.00	70.00	—

C# 20.1 1/4 ANNA
Copper **Ruler:** Faisal bin Turkee **Countermark:** SS **Note:** Large 10mm countermark in Arabic on 1/4 Anna, KM#3.

CM Date	Host Date	Good	VG	F	VF	XF
1932	AH1312	30.00	50.00	80.00	120	—
1932	AH1315	30.00	50.00	80.00	120	—

C# 20.2 1/4 ANNA
Copper **Ruler:** Faisal bin Turkee **Countermark:** SS **Note:** Large 10mm countermark in Arabic on 1/4 Anna, KM#8.

CM Date	Host Date	Good	VG	F	VF	XF
ND(1932)	AH1312	30.00	50.00	80.00	120	—

C# 21.1 1/4 ANNA
Copper **Ruler:** Faisal bin Turkee **Countermark:** SS **Note:** Small 8mm countermark in Arabic on 1/4 Anna, KM#3.

CM Date	Host Date	Good	VG	F	VF	XF
ND(1932)	AH1312	30.00	50.00	80.00	120	—

C# 21.2 1/4 ANNA
Copper **Ruler:** Faisal bin Turkee **Countermark:** SS **Note:** Small 8mm countermark in Arabic on 1/4 Anna, KM#8. Countermark for Sultan Sa'id or Sayyid Sa'id.

CM Date	Host Date	Good	VG	F	VF	XF
ND(1932)	AH1312	30.00	50.00	80.00	120	—

REFORM COINAGE

1000 (new) Baisa = 1 Saidi Rial

KM# 25 2 BAISA (Baiza)
Copper-Nickel **Ruler:** Sa'id bin Taimur **Obv:** Arms flanked by marks **Rev:** Arabic legend and inscription **Shape:** 4-sided

Date	Mintage	F	VF	XF	Unc	BU
AH1365	1,500,000	0.50	0.75	1.00	2.00	—
AH1365 Proof	—	Value: 4.00				

Note: Coins of AH1365 have the monetary unit spelled "Baiza", on all other coins it is spelled "Baisa". Most of the proof issues of the AH1359 and 1365 dated coins of Muscat and Oman now on the market are probably later restrikes produced by the Bombay Mint

KM# 36 2 BAISA (Baiza)
1.7500 g., Bronze, 16 mm. **Ruler:** Sa'id bin Taimur **Obv:** Arms **Rev:** Value flanked by marks

Date	Mintage	F	VF	XF	Unc	BU
AH1390	4,000,000	0.15	0.20	0.30	0.50	—
AH1390 Proof	—	Value: 2.50				

KM# 30 3 BAISA
Bronze, 20 mm. **Ruler:** Sa'id bin Taimur **Obv:** Arms **Rev:** Value flanked by marks

Date	Mintage	F	VF	XF	Unc	BU
AH1378	8,000,000	0.75	1.00	1.50	2.50	—
AH1378 Proof	—	—	—	—	—	—

Note: Struck for use in Dhofar Province

KM# 32 3 BAISA
Bronze, 18 mm. **Ruler:** Sa'id bin Taimur **Obv:** Arms **Rev:** Value flanked by marks

Date	Mintage	F	VF	XF	Unc	BU
AH1380	10,000,000	0.35	0.50	0.60	1.25	—
AH1380 Proof	Inc. above	—	—	—	—	—

Note: Struck for use in Muscat Province

KM# 26 5 BAISA (Baiza)
Copper-Nickel, 21 mm. **Ruler:** Sa'id bin Taimur **Obv:** Arms **Rev:** Arabic legend and inscription **Shape:** Scalloped

Date	Mintage	F	VF	XF	Unc	BU
AH1365	3,849,000	1.00	1.25	1.50	2.50	—
AH1365 Proof	—	Value: 5.00				

Note: Coins of AH1365 have the monetary unit spelled "Baiza", on all other coins it is spelled "Baisa"

KM# 33 5 BAISA (Baiza)
Copper-Nickel **Ruler:** Sa'id bin Taimur **Obv:** Arms **Rev:** Sailing ship within circle

Date	Mintage	F	VF	XF	Unc	BU
AH1381	5,000,000	0.40	0.60	1.00	2.00	—
AH1381 Proof	Inc. above	—	—	—	—	—

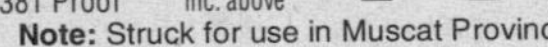

Note: Struck for use in Muscat Province

KM# 37 5 BAISA (Baiza)
3.1000 g., Bronze, 19 mm. **Ruler:** Sa'id bin Taimur **Obv:** Arms **Rev:** Value flanked by marks

Date	Mintage	F	VF	XF	Unc	BU
AH1390	3,400,000	0.15	0.20	0.30	0.50	—
AH1390 Proof	—	Value: 2.00				

KM# 22 10 BAISA
Copper-Nickel **Ruler:** Sa'id bin Taimur **Obv:** Arms **Rev:** Inscription

Date	Mintage	F	VF	XF	Unc	BU
AH1359	572,000	2.50	3.25	4.00	6.00	—
AH1359 Proof	—	Value: 8.50				

Note: Struck for use in Dhofar Province

KM# 22a 10 BAISA
Gold **Ruler:** Sa'id bin Taimur **Obv:** Arms **Rev:** Inscription

Date	Mintage	F	VF	XF	Unc	BU
AH1359 Proof	—	Value: 1,850				

KM# 38 10 BAISA
4.7000 g., Bronze, 22.5 mm. **Ruler:** Sa'id bin Taimur **Obv:** Arms **Rev:** Value flanked by marks

Date	Mintage	F	VF	XF	Unc	BU
AH1390	4,500,000	0.15	0.20	0.35	0.75	—
AH1390 Proof	—	Value: 2.50				

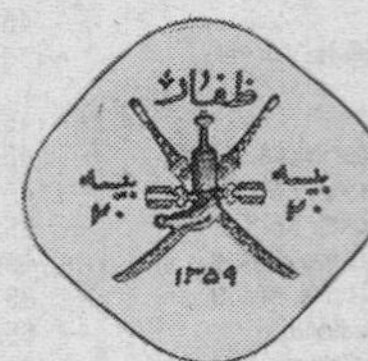

KM# 23 20 BAISA (Baiza)
Copper-Nickel **Ruler:** Sa'id bin Taimur **Obv:** Arms **Rev:** Inscription **Shape:** Square

Date	Mintage	F	VF	XF	Unc	BU
AH1359	35,000	3.00	5.00	7.50	11.50	—
AH1359 Proof	—	Value: 14.50				

Note: Struck for use in Dhofar Province

KM# 23a 20 BAISA (Baiza)
Gold **Ruler:** Sa'id bin Taimur **Obv:** Arms **Rev:** Inscription

Date	Mintage	F	VF	XF	Unc	BU
AH1359 Proof	—	Value: 1,650				

KM# 27 20 BAISA (Baiza)
Copper-Nickel **Ruler:** Sa'id bin Taimur **Obv:** Arms **Rev:** Arabic legend and inscription **Shape:** Square

Date	Mintage	F	VF	XF	Unc	BU
AH1365	1,135,000	1.00	2.00	2.75	4.50	—
AH1365 Proof	—	Value: 7.00				

KM# 28 20 BAISA (Baiza)
Copper-Nickel **Ruler:** Sa'id bin Taimur **Obv:** Arms **Rev:** Inscription **Note:** Mule.

Date	Mintage	F	VF	XF	Unc	BU
AH1359/1365 Restrike	—	—	—	—	17.50	—

KM# 39 25 BAISA
2.9000 g., Copper-Nickel, 18 mm. **Ruler:** Sa'id bin Taimur **Obv:** Arms **Rev:** Value flanked by marks

Date	Mintage	F	VF	XF	Unc	BU
AH1390	2,000,000	0.20	0.30	0.45	1.00	—
AH1390 Proof	—	Value: 2.75				

KM# 39a 25 BAISA
6.0100 g., 0.9160 Gold .1771 oz. AGW **Ruler:** Sa'id bin Taimur **Obv:** Arms **Rev:** Value flanked by marks

Date	Mintage	F	VF	XF	Unc	BU
AH1390 Proof	350	Value: 145				

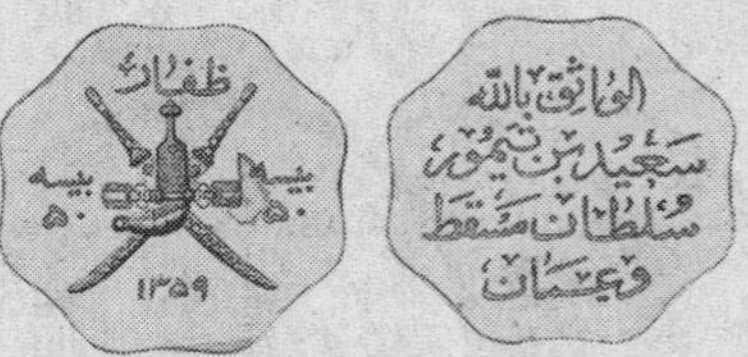

KM# 24 50 BAISA
Copper-Nickel **Ruler:** Sa'id bin Taimur **Obv:** Arms **Rev:** Inscription **Shape:** Octagon

Date	Mintage	F	VF	XF	Unc	BU
AH1359	65,000	2.00	6.50	8.50	12.50	—
AH1359 Proof	—	Value: 16.50				

Note: Struck for use in Dhofar Province

KM# 24a 50 BAISA
Gold **Ruler:** Sa'id bin Taimur **Obv:** Arms **Rev:** Inscription

Date	Mintage	F	VF	XF	Unc	BU
AH1359 Proof	—	Value: 1,750				

KM# 40 50 BAISA
6.4000 g., Copper-Nickel, 24 mm. **Ruler:** Sa'id bin Taimur **Obv:** Arms **Rev:** Value flanked by marks

Date	Mintage	F	VF	XF	Unc	BU
AH1390	1,600,000	0.25	0.45	0.75	1.50	—
AH1390 Proof	—	Value: 3.50				

KM# 40a 50 BAISA
12.8100 g., 0.9160 Gold .3775 oz. AGW **Ruler:** Sa'id bin Taimur **Obv:** Arms **Rev:** Value flanked by marks

Date	Mintage	F	VF	XF	Unc	BU
AH1390 Proof	350	Value: 300				

KM# 41 100 BAISA
Copper-Nickel **Ruler:** Sa'id bin Taimur **Obv:** Arms **Rev:** Value flanked by marks

Date	Mintage	F	VF	XF	Unc	BU
AH1390	1,000,000	0.35	0.50	0.85	1.75	—
AH1390 Proof	—	Value: 5.00				

KM# 41a 100 BAISA
22.6300 g., 0.9160 Gold .6670 oz. AGW **Ruler:** Sa'id bin Taimur **Obv:** Arms **Rev:** Value flanked by marks

Date	Mintage	F	VF	XF	Unc	BU
AH1390 Proof	350	Value: 525				

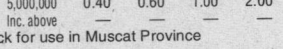

KM# 29 1/2 DHOFARI RIAL
14.0300 g., 0.5000 Silver .2256 oz. ASW
Ruler: Sa'id bin Taimur **Obv:** Arms above sprig **Rev:** Inscription within circle and wreath

Date	Mintage	F	VF	XF	Unc	BU
AH1367	200,000	12.00	14.00	18.00	28.00	—
AH1367 Proof	—	Value: 45.00				

Note: Struck for use in Dhofar Province

KM# 29a 1/2 DHOFARI RIAL

24.0300 g., 0.9170 Gold .6780 oz. AGW **Ruler:** Sa'id bin Taimur **Obv:** Arms above sprig **Rev:** Inscription within circle and wreath

Date	Mintage	F	VF	XF	Unc	BU
AH1367 Proof	2	Value: 5,500				

Note: Struck for presentation purposes

KM# 34 1/2 SAIDI RIAL

14.0300 g., 0.5000 Silver .2256 oz. ASW **Ruler:** Sa'id bin Taimur **Obv:** Arms **Rev:** Value

Date	Mintage	F	VF	XF	Unc	BU
AH1380	300,000	3.75	4.50	6.00	9.00	—
AH1380 Proof	—	Value: 75.00				
AH1381	850,000	3.75	4.50	6.00	9.00	—

KM# 34a 1/2 SAIDI RIAL

25.6000 g., 0.9160 Gold .7540 oz. AGW **Ruler:** Sa'id bin Taimur **Obv:** Arms **Rev:** Value

Date	Mintage	F	VF	XF	Unc	BU
AH1381 Proof	150	Value: 650				
AH1382 Proof	100	Value: 700				
AH1390 Proof	350	Value: 600				

Note: Struck for presentation purposes

KM# 31 SAIDI RIAL

28.0700 g., 0.8330 Silver .7518 oz. ASW **Ruler:** Sa'id bin Taimur **Obv:** Arms within circle, designs around border **Rev:** Value and date

Date	Mintage	F	VF	XF	Unc	BU
AH1378	1,000,000	—	12.50	16.00	20.00	—
AH1378 Proof	100	Value: 650				

KM# 31a SAIDI RIAL

28.0700 g., 0.5000 Silver .4512 oz. ASW **Ruler:** Sa'id bin Taimur **Obv:** Arms within circle, designs around border **Rev:** Value and date

Date	Mintage	F	VF	XF	Unc	BU
AH1378	400,000	—	10.00	12.50	15.00	—

KM# 31b SAIDI RIAL

46.6500 g., 0.9160 Gold 1.3740 oz. AGW, 33.7 mm. **Ruler:** Sa'id bin aimur **Obv:** Arms within circle, designs around border **Rev:** Value and date

Date	Mintage	F	VF	XF	Unc	BU
AH1378 Proof	100	Value: 1,250				
AH1390 Proof	350	Value: 1,000				

Note: Struck for presentation purposes

KM# 35 15 SAIDI RIALS

7.9900 g., 0.9160 Gold .2353 oz. AGW **Ruler:** Sa'id bin Taimur

Date	Mintage	F	VF	XF	Unc	BU
AH1381 Proof	100	Value: 575				
Note: Struck for presentation purposes						
AH1381	2,000	—	—	—	180	200

MINT SETS

KM#	Date	Mintage	Identification	Issue Price	Mkt Val
MS1	AH1390 (1970) (6)	5,500	KM#36-41	—	7.50

PROOF SETS

KM#	Date	Mintage	Identification	Issue Price	Mkt Val
PS1	AH1359, 65, 57 (1940, 45, 47) (6)	—	KM#22-26, 29	—	75.00
PS2	AH1359, 65, 57 (1940, 45, 47) (6)	—	KM#22, 24-27, 29	—	70.00
PS3	AH1390 (1970) (6)	2,102	KM#36-41	11.00	16.50
PS4	AH1390 (1970) (3)	350	KM#39a-41a	—	975

MYANMAR

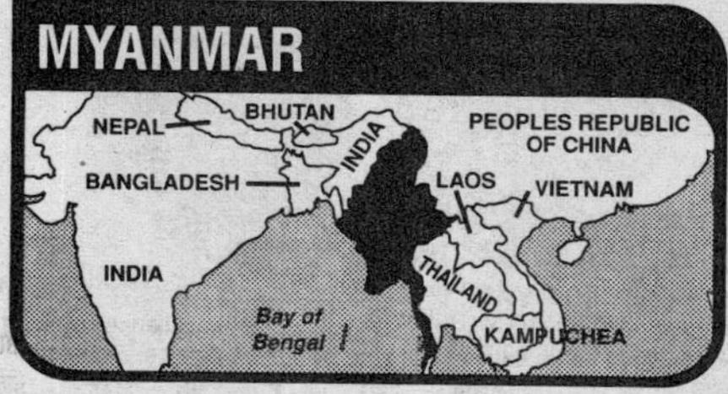

The Union of Myanmar, formerly Burma, a country of Southeast Asia fronting on the Bay of Bengal and the Andaman Sea, has an area of 261,218 sq. mi. (678,500 sq. km.) and a population of 38.8 million. Capital: Yangon (Rangoon). Myanmar is an agricultural country heavily dependent on its leading product (rice) which occupies two-thirds of the cultivated area and accounts for 40% of the value of exports. Mineral resources are extensive, but production is low. Petroleum, lead, tin, silver, zinc, nickel cobalt, and precious stones are exported.

The British East India Company, while unsuccessful in its 1612 effort to establish posts along the Bay of Bengal, was enabled by the Anglo-Burmese Wars of 1824-86 to expand to the whole of Burma and to secure its annexation to British India. In 1937, Burma was separated from India, becoming a separate British colony with limited self-government. Burma became an independent nation outside the British Commonwealth on Jan. 4, 1948, the constitution of 1948 providing for a parliamentary democracy and the nationalization of certain industries. However, political and economic problems persisted, and on March 2, 1962, Gen. Ne Win took over the government, suspended the constitution, installed himself as chief of state, and pursued a socialistic program with nationalization of nearly all industry and trade. On Jan. 4, 1974, a new constitution adopted by referendum established Burma as a socialist republic under one-party rule. The country name was changed to Myanmar in 1989.

Burmese coins are frequently known by the equivalent Indian denominations, although their values are inscribed in Burmese units. Upper Burma was annexed in 1885 and the Burmese coinage remained in circulation until 1889, when Indian coins became current throughout Burma. Coins were again issued in the old Burmese denominations after independence in 1948, but these were replaced by decimal issues in 1952. The Chula-Sakarat (CS) dating is sometimes referred to as BE-Burmese Era and began in 638AD.

RULERS

British, 1886-1948

MONETARY SYSTEM

(Until 1952)

4 Pyas = 1 Pe
2 Pe = 1 Mu
2 Mu = 1 Mat
5 Mat = 1 Kyat

NOTE: Originally 10 light Mu = 1 Kyat, eventually 8 heavy Mu = 1 Kyat.

Indian Equivalents

1 Silver Kyat = 1 Rupee = 16 Annas
1 Gold Kyat = 1 Mohur = 16 Rupees

UNION OF BURMA

STANDARD COINAGE

KM# 27 2 PYAS

Copper-Nickel **Obv:** Chinze **Rev:** Value and date flanked by sprays **Shape:** 4-sided

Date	Mintage	F	VF	XF	Unc	BU
1949	7,000,000	0.25	0.50	1.00	3.00	—
1949 Proof	100	Value: 100				

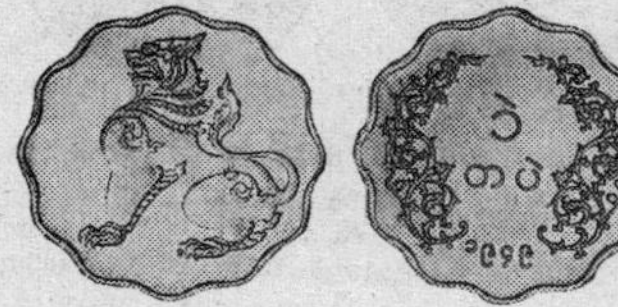

KM# 28 PE

Copper-Nickel **Obv:** Chinze **Rev:** Value and date flanked by sprays **Shape:** Scalloped

Date	Mintage	F	VF	XF	Unc	BU
1949	8,000,000	0.35	0.75	1.75	4.00	—
1949 Proof	100	Value: 100				
1950	9,500,000	0.35	0.75	1.75	4.00	—
1950 Proof	—	—	—	—	—	—
1951	6,500,000	0.50	1.00	2.00	5.00	—
1951 Proof	—	—	—	—	—	—

KM# 29 2 PE

Copper-Nickel **Obv:** Chinze **Rev:** Value and date flanked by sprays **Shape:** 4-sided

Date	Mintage	F	VF	XF	Unc	BU
1949	7,100,000	0.50	1.00	2.00	5.00	—
1949 Proof	100	Value: 100				
1950	8,500,000	0.50	1.00	2.00	5.00	—
1950 Proof	—	—	—	—	—	—
1951	7,480,000	0.50	1.00	2.00	5.00	—
1951 Proof	—	—	—	—	—	—

KM# 30 4 PE

Nickel **Obv:** Chinze **Rev:** Value and date flanked by sprays

Date	Mintage	F	VF	XF	Unc	BU
1949	6,500,000	1.25	2.50	5.00	15.00	—
1949 Proof	100	Value: 100				
1950	6,120,000	1.00	2.00	4.00	12.00	—

KM# 31 8 PE

Nickel **Obv:** Chinze **Rev:** Value and date flanked by sprays

Date	Mintage	F	VF	XF	Unc	BU
1949	3,270,000	1.50	3.00	6.00	25.00	—
1949 Proof	100	Value: 100				
1950 Proof	—	—	—	—	—	—
1950	3,900,000	1.25	2.50	5.00	20.00	—

KM# 31a 8 PE

Copper-Nickel **Obv:** Chinze flanked by stars **Rev:** Value and date flanked by sprays

Date	Mintage	VG	F	VF	XF	Unc
1952 (CS1314)	1,642,000	—	50.00	100	150	200
1952 (CS1314) Proof	—	Value: 400				

DECIMAL COINAGE

100 Pyas = 1 Kyat

KM# 32 PYA

Bronze, 18 mm. **Obv:** Chinze **Rev:** Value and date flanked by sprays

Date	Mintage	VG	F	VF	XF	Unc
1952 Proof	100	Value: 60.00				
1952	500,000	—	0.10	0.15	0.20	0.35
1953 Proof	—	—	—	—	—	—
1953	14,000,000	—	0.10	0.15	0.20	0.35
1955	30,000,000	—	0.10	0.15	0.20	0.35
1955 Proof	—	—	—	—	—	—
1956 Proof	100	Value: 60.00				
1962 Proof	100	Value: 60.00				
1965	15,000,000	—	0.10	0.15	0.20	0.35
1965 Proof	—	—	—	—	—	—

KM# 38 PYA

0.6000 g., Aluminum, 17 mm. **Subject:** Aung San **Obv:** Head 1/4 right flanked by stars below **Rev:** Value and date flanked by sprays

Date	Mintage	VG	F	VF	XF	Unc
1966	8,000,000	—	0.10	0.15	0.25	0.65

KM# 33 5 PYAS

Copper-Nickel **Obv:** Chinze **Rev:** Value and date flanked by sprays **Shape:** Scalloped

Date	Mintage	VG	F	VF	XF	Unc
1952 Proof	100	Value: 65.00				
1952	20,000,000	—	0.10	0.15	0.35	0.75
1953	59,700,000	—	0.10	0.15	0.35	0.75
1953 Proof	—	—	—	—	—	—
1955 Proof	—	—	—	—	—	—
1955	40,272,000	—	0.10	0.15	0.35	0.75
1956	20,000,000	—	0.10	0.15	0.35	0.75
1956 Proof	100	Value: 65.00				
1961 Proof	—	—	—	—	—	—
1961	12,000,000	—	0.10	0.15	0.35	0.75
1962	10,000,000	—	0.10	0.15	0.35	0.75
1962 Proof	100	Value: 65.00				
1963 Proof	—	—	—	—	—	—
1963	40,400,000	—	0.10	0.15	0.25	0.60
1965	43,600,000	—	0.10	0.15	0.20	0.40
1965 Proof	—	—	—	—	—	—
1966 Proof	—	—	—	—	—	—
1966	20,000,000	—	0.10	0.15	0.20	0.40

KM# 39 5 PYAS

0.9000 g., Aluminum, 18.4 mm. **Subject:** Aung San **Obv:** Head 1/4 right flanked by stars below **Rev:** Value and date flanked by sprays **Shape:** Scalloped

Date	Mintage	VG	F	VF	XF	Unc
1966	—	—	0.10	0.20	0.35	0.75

KM# 51 5 PYAS

Aluminum-Bronze **Series:** F.A.O. **Obv:** Rice plant **Rev:** Value and date within square

Date	Mintage	VG	F	VF	XF	Unc
1987	—	—	0.10	0.20	0.40	1.00

KM# 34 10 PYAS

Copper-Nickel **Obv:** Chinze **Rev:** Value and date flanked by sprays **Shape:** 4-sided

Date	Mintage	VG	F	VF	XF	Unc
1952 Proof	100	Value: 70.00				
1952	20,000,000	—	0.10	0.20	0.40	1.00
1953 Proof	—	—	—	—	—	—
1953	37,250,000	—	0.10	0.20	0.40	1.00
1955 Proof	—	—	—	—	—	—
1955	22,750,000	—	0.10	0.20	0.40	1.00
1956 Proof	100	Value: 70.00				
1956	35,000,000	—	0.10	0.15	0.40	1.00
1962 Proof	100	Value: 70.00				
1962	6,000,000	—	0.10	0.20	0.40	1.00
1963 Proof	10,750,000	—	—	—	—	—
1963	10,750,000	—	0.10	0.20	0.40	1.00
1965 Proof	—	—	—	—	—	—
1965	32,619,999	—	0.10	0.20	0.40	1.00

KM# 40 10 PYAS

Aluminum **Subject:** Aung San **Obv:** Head 1/4 right flanked by stars below **Rev:** Value and date flanked by sprays **Shape:** Square

Date	Mintage	VG	F	VF	XF	Unc
1966	—	—	0.15	0.30	0.60	1.25

KM# 49 10 PYAS

2.8000 g., Brass, 20.45 mm. **Series:** F.A.O. **Obv:** Rice plant **Rev:** Value within square

Date	Mintage	VG	F	VF	XF	Unc
1983	—	—	0.15	0.30	0.60	1.00

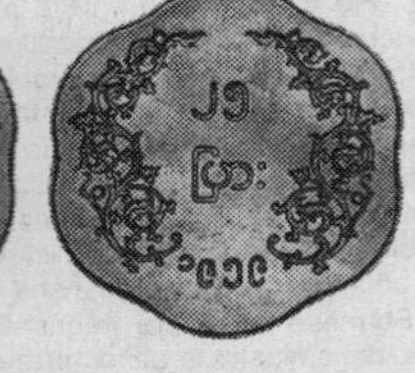

KM# 35 25 PYAS

Copper-Nickel **Obv:** Chinze flanked by stars **Rev:** Value and date flanked by sprays **Shape:** Scalloped

Date	Mintage	VG	F	VF	XF	Unc
1952	13,540,000	—	0.10	0.20	0.50	1.25
1952 Proof	100	Value: 75.00				
1954	18,000,000	—	0.10	0.20	0.50	1.25
1954 Proof	—	—	—	—	—	—
1955 Proof	—	Value: 75.00				
1956	14,000,000	—	0.10	0.20	0.50	1.25
1956 Proof	100	Value: 75.00				
1959 Proof	—	—	—	—	—	—
1959	6,000,000	—	0.10	0.20	0.50	1.25
1961	4,000,000	—	0.10	0.20	0.50	1.25
1961 Proof	—	—	—	—	—	—
1962 Proof	100	Value: 75.00				
1962	3,200,000	—	0.10	0.20	0.50	1.25
1963	16,000,000	—	0.10	0.15	0.30	0.75
1963 Proof	—	—	—	—	—	—
1965 Proof	—	—	—	—	—	—
1965	26,000,000	—	0.10	0.15	0.30	0.75

KM# 41 25 PYAS

Aluminum **Subject:** Aung San **Obv:** Head 1/4 right flanked by stars below **Rev:** Value and date flanked by sprays **Shape:** Scalloped

Date	Mintage	VG	F	VF	XF	Unc
1966	—	—	0.15	0.30	0.60	1.25

KM# 48 25 PYAS

4.3000 g., Bronze, 22.35 mm. **Series:** F.A.O. **Obv:** Rice plant **Rev:** Value and date within square

Date	Mintage	VG	F	VF	XF	Unc
1980	—	—	0.15	0.30	0.60	1.00

KM# 50 25 PYAS

Bronze **Series:** F.A.O. **Obv:** Rice plant **Rev:** Large value **Shape:** 6-sided

Date	Mintage	VG	F	VF	XF	Unc
1986	—	—	0.10	0.20	0.35	0.60

KM# 36 50 PYAS

Copper-Nickel **Obv:** Chinze flanked by stars **Rev:** Value and date flanked by vine sprigs

Date	Mintage	VG	F	VF	XF	Unc
1952	2,500,000	—	0.20	0.50	0.75	1.75
1952 Proof	100	Value: 80.00				
1954	12,000,000	—	0.20	0.50	0.75	1.75
1954 Proof	—	—	—	—	—	—
1956	8,000,000	—	0.20	0.50	0.75	1.75
1956 Proof	100	Value: 80.00				
1961	2,000,000	—	0.15	0.40	0.75	1.75
1961 Proof	—	—	—	—	—	—
1962	600,000	—	0.25	0.75	1.25	2.25
1962 Proof	100	Value: 80.00				
1963	4,800,000	—	0.15	0.25	0.65	1.25
1963 Proof	—	—	—	—	—	—
1965	2,800,000	—	0.15	0.40	0.75	1.75
1965 Proof	—	—	—	—	—	—
1966	3,400,000	—	0.10	0.30	0.75	1.75
1966 Proof	—	—	—	—	—	—

KM# 42 50 PYAS

Aluminum **Subject:** Aung San **Obv:** Head 1/4 right flanked by stars below **Rev:** Value and date flanked by sprays

Date	Mintage	VG	F	VF	XF	Unc
1966	—	—	0.15	0.40	1.00	2.25

KM# 46 50 PYAS

5.7000 g., Brass, 24.6 mm. **Series:** F.A.O. **Obv:** Rice plant **Rev:** Value within square

Date	Mintage	VG	F	VF	XF	Unc
1975	—	—	0.15	0.35	0.70	1.25
1976	—	—	0.15	0.35	0.70	1.25

KM# 37 KYAT

Copper-Nickel, 30.5 mm. **Obv:** Chinze flanked by stars **Rev:** Value and date flanked by sprays

Date	Mintage	VG	F	VF	XF	Unc
1952	2,500,000	—	0.35	0.75	1.50	3.00
1952 Proof	100	Value: 85.00				
1953	7,500,000	—	0.25	0.50	1.00	2.00
1953 Proof	—	—	—	—	—	—
1956	3,500,000	—	0.35	0.75	1.50	3.00
1956 Proof	100	Value: 85.00				

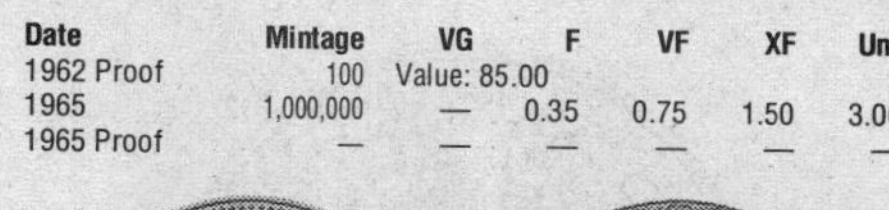

Date	Mintage	VG	F	VF	XF	Unc
1962 Proof	100	Value: 85.00				
1965	1,000,000	—	0.35	0.75	1.50	3.00
1965 Proof	—	—	—	—	—	—

KM# 47 KYAT
7.2000 g., Copper-Nickel, 26.45 mm. **Series:** F.A.O. **Obv:** Rice plant **Rev:** Value within square

Date	Mintage	VG	F	VF	XF	Unc
1975	20,000,000	—	0.25	0.50	1.00	2.00

REVOLUTIONARY COINAGE

Patriotic Liberation Army

KM# 43 MU
2.0000 g., 1.0000 Gold .0643 oz. AGW **Obv:** Peacock **Rev:** Legend within star

Date	Mintage	F	VF	XF	Unc	BU
1970-71	—	—	—	—	125	160

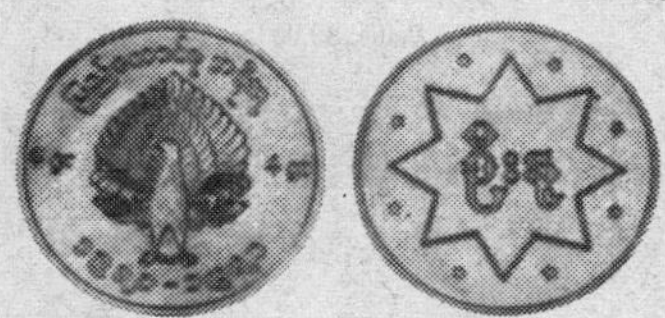

KM# 44 2 MU
4.0000 g., 1.0000 Gold .1286 oz. AGW **Obv:** Peacock **Rev:** Legend within star flanked by stars at points

Date	Mintage	F	VF	XF	Unc	BU
1970-71	—	—	—	—	245	280

KM# 45 4 MU
8.0000 g., 1.0000 Gold .2572 oz. AGW **Obv:** Peacock **Rev:** Legend within star

Date	Mintage	F	VF	XF	Unc	BU
1970-71	—	—	—	—	470	500

UNION OF MYANMAR

DECIMAL COINAGE

100 Pyas = 1 Kyat

KM# 60 KYAT
2.9500 g., Bronze **Obv:** Chinze flanked by stars **Rev:** Value **Edge:** Plain

Date	Mintage	F	VF	XF	Unc	BU
1999	—	—	—	—	0.25	0.40

KM# 57 10 PYAS
Brass **Obv:** Rice plant **Obv. Legend:** Myanmar Central Bank **Rev:** Value within square **Note:** Similar to KM#49.

Date	Mintage	VG	F	VF	XF	Unc
1991	—	—	0.15	0.30	0.60	1.00

KM# 58 25 PYAS
Copper Plated Steel **Obv:** Rice plant **Obv. Legend:** Myanmar Central Bank **Rev:** Large value **Shape:** Hexagon

Date	Mintage	VG	F	VF	XF	Unc
1991	—	—	0.15	0.30	0.60	1.00

KM# 59 50 PYAS
Brass, 24.6 mm. **Obv:** Rice plant **Obv. Legend:** Myanmar Central Bank **Rev:** Value within square **Edge:** Reeded

Date	Mintage	VG	F	VF	XF	Unc
1991	—	—	0.15	0.35	0.70	1.25

KM# 61 5 KYATS
2.7300 g., Brass, 20 mm. **Obv:** Chinze flanked by stars **Rev:** Value **Edge:** Plain

Date	Mintage	F	VF	XF	Unc	BU
1999	—	—	—	—	0.50	0.75

KM# 62 10 KYATS
Brass **Obv:** Chinze flanked by stars **Rev:** Value

Date	Mintage	F	VF	XF	Unc	BU
1999	—	—	—	—	0.75	1.00

KM# 63 50 KYATS
5.0600 g., Copper-Nickel, 23.85 mm. **Obv:** Chinze flanked by stars **Rev:** Value **Edge:** Reeded

Date	Mintage	F	VF	XF	Unc	BU
1999	—	—	—	—	1.75	2.00

KM# 64 100 KYATS
7.5200 g., Copper-Nickel, 26.8 mm. **Obv:** Chinze flanked by stars **Rev:** Value **Edge:** Reeded

Date	Mintage	F	VF	XF	Unc	BU
1999	—	—	—	—	3.00	3.50

KM# A51 300 KYAT
1.2441 g., 0.9990 Gold .04 oz. AGW **Subject:** Year of the Tiger **Obv:** Lotus flower **Rev:** Tiger

Date	Mintage	F	VF	XF	Unc	BU
1998	—	—	—	—	40.00	45.00

KM# 52 500 KYAT
20.0000 g., 0.9250 Silver .5948 oz. ASW **Subject:** Year of the Tiger **Obv:** Lotus flower **Rev:** Stalking tiger

Date	Mintage	F	VF	XF	Unc	BU
1998 Proof	Est. 15,000	Value: 50.00				

KM# 53 500 KYAT
20.0000 g., 0.9250 Silver .5948 oz. ASW **Subject:** Year of the Tiger **Obv:** Lotus flower **Rev:** Tiger drinking

Date	Mintage	F	VF	XF	Unc	BU
1998 Proof	Est. 15,000	Value: 50.00				

KM# 54 500 KYAT
20.0000 g., 0.9250 Silver .5948 oz. ASW **Subject:** Year of the Tiger **Obv:** Lotus flower **Rev:** Tiger

Date	Mintage	F	VF	XF	Unc	BU
1998 Proof	1,014,999	Value: 50.00				

KM# 55 2000 KYAT
7.7759 g., 0.9999 Gold .2500 oz. AGW **Subject:** Year of the Tiger **Obv:** Lotus flower **Rev:** Stalking tiger

Date	Mintage	F	VF	XF	Unc	BU
1998 Proof	1,998	Value: 250				

Note: In sets only

KM# 56 5000 KYAT
15.5518 g., 0.9999 Gold .5000 oz. AGW **Subject:** Year of the Tiger **Obv:** Lotus flower **Rev:** Tiger

Date	Mintage	F	VF	XF	Unc	BU
1998 Proof	5,798	Value: 425				

PROOF SETS

KM#	Date	Mintage	Identification	Issue Price	Mkt Val
PS1	1949 (5)	100	KM#27-31	—	500
PS2	1952 (6)	100	KM#32-37	—	435
PS3	1956 (6)	100	KM#32-37	—	435
PS4	1962 (6)	100	KM#32-37	—	435
PS5	1998 (3)	3,998	KM#52-54	—	145
PS6	1998 (2)	1,998	KM#55-56	—	675

NAGORNO-KARABAKH

Nagorno-Karabakh, an ethnically Armenian enclave inside Azerbaijan (pop., 1991 est.: 193,000), SW region. It occupies an area of 1,700 sq mi (4,400 square km) on the NE flank of the Karabakh Mountain Range, with the capital city of Stepanakert.

Russia annexed the area from Persia in 1813, and in 1923 it was established as an autonomous province of the Azerbaijan S.S.R. In 1988 the region's ethnic ArmenRev. Designer:an majority demonstrated against Azerbaijani rule, and in 1991, after the breakup of the U.S.S.R. brought independence to Armenia and Azerbaijan, war broke out between the two ethnic groups. On January 8, 1992 the leaders of Nagorno-Karabakh declared independence as the Republic of Mountainous Karabakh (RMK). Since 1994, following a cease-fire, ethnic Armenians have held Karabakh, though officially it remains part of Azerbaijan. Karabakh remains sovereign, but the political and military condition is volatile and tensions frequently flare into skirmishes.

Its marvelous nature and geographic situation, have all facilitated Karabakh to be a center of science, poetry and, especially, of the musical culture of Azerbaijan.

REPUBLIC

STANDARD COINAGE

KM# 13 25000 DRAMS
31.2200 g., 0.9990 Silver 1.0027 oz. ASW, 38.9 mm.
Obv: National arms **Rev:** Maps **Edge:** Plain

Date	Mintage	F	VF	XF	Unc	BU
1998 Proof	—	Value: 60.00				

KM# 14 25000 DRAMS
31.2200 g., 0.9990 Silver 1.0027 oz. ASW, 38.9 mm.
Obv: National arms **Rev:** "1700" in cross design with inscription 301AD **Edge:** Plain

Date	Mintage	F	VF	XF	Unc	BU
1998 Proof	—	Value: 60.00				

KM# 15 25000 DRAMS
31.2200 g., 0.9990 Silver 1.0027 oz. ASW, 38.9 mm.
Subject: 1700th Anniversary of Christianity in Armenia **Obv:** National arms **Rev:** Standing Saint and church **Edge:** Plain

Date	Mintage	F	VF	XF	Unc	BU
1998 Proof	—	Value: 60.00				

KM# 16 25000 DRAMS
31.2200 g., 0.9990 Silver 1.0027 oz. ASW, 38.9 mm.
Obv: National arms **Rev:** Head left **Edge:** Plain

Date	Mintage	F	VF	XF	Unc	BU
1998 Proof	—	Value: 60.00				

KM# 16a 25000 DRAMS
31.2200 g., 0.9990 Gold Plated Silver 1,0027 oz. ASW AGW, 38.9 mm. **Obv:** National arms **Rev:** Head left **Edge:** Plain

Date	Mintage	F	VF	XF	Unc	BU
1998 Proof	—	Value: 70.00				

KM# 17 25000 DRAMS
31.2200 g., 0.9990 Silver 1.0027 oz. ASW, 38.9 mm.
Obv: National arms **Rev:** Head right with laurels **Edge:** Plain

Date	Mintage	F	VF	XF	Unc	BU
1998 Proof	—	Value: 60.00				

KM# 18 25000 DRAMS
31.2200 g., 0.9990 Silver 1.0027 oz. ASW, 38.9 mm. **Obv:** National arms **Rev:** Standing figure reading book right **Edge:** Plain

Date	Mintage	F	VF	XF	Unc	BU
1998 Proof	—	Value: 60.00				

KM# 1 25000 DRAMS
31.2000 g., 0.9990 Silver 1.0021 oz. ASW, 39 mm.
Obv: National arms **Rev:** Head left above two fists **Edge:** Reeded
Note: Struck at Lialoosin Inc., Los Angeles, CA.

Date	Mintage	F	VF	XF	Unc	BU
1998 Proof	—	Value: 60.00				

KM# 1a 25000 DRAMS
Gold Plated Silver **Obv:** National arms **Rev:** Head left above two fists

Date	Mintage	F	VF	XF	Unc	BU
1998 Proof	—	Value: 65.00				

KM# 5 25000 DRAMS
30.8000 g., 0.9990 Silver .9893 oz. ASW **Obv:** National arms **Rev:** Two stone faced monuments **Edge:** Plain **Note:** Struck at Lialoosin Inc., Los Angeles, CA.

Date	Mintage	F	VF	XF	Unc	BU
1998(2000) Proof	—	Value: 60.00				

KM# 5a 25000 DRAMS
Gold Plated Silver, 38.8 mm. **Obv:** National arms **Rev:** Two stone faced monuments

Date	Mintage	F	VF	XF	Unc	BU
1998(2000) Proof	—	Value: 65.00				

KM# 2 50000 DRAMS
155.5175 g., 0.9990 Silver 5.0000 oz. ASW, 63.8 mm.
Obv: National arms **Rev:** Head left above two fists
Edge Lettering: 5 T.O. .999 A6 **Note:** Struck at Lialoosin Inc., Los Angeles, CA. Photo reduced.

Date	Mintage	F	VF	XF	Unc	BU
1998 Proof	—	Value: 235				

KM# 2a 50000 DRAMS
Gold Plated Silver . **Obv:** National arms **Rev:** Head left above two fists

Date	Mintage	F	VF	XF	Unc	BU
1998 Proof	—	Value: 250				

KM# 3 50000 DRAMS
7.8000 g., 0.9000 Gold .2257 oz. AGW, 22 mm. **Obv:** National arms **Rev:** Head left above two fists **Edge:** Plain **Note:** Struck at Lialoosin Inc., Los Angeles, CA.

Date	Mintage	F	VF	XF	Unc	BU
1998 Proof	—	Value: 300				

KM# 4 50000 DRAMS
155.5175 g., 0.9990 Silver 5.0000 oz. ASW, 63.8 mm.
Obv: National arms **Rev:** Two monumental portraits
Edge Lettering: 5 T.O. .999 AG **Note:** Struck at Lialoosin Inc., Los Angeles, CA. Photo reduced.

Date	Mintage	F	VF	XF	Unc	BU
1998 Proof	—	Value: 235				

KM# 4a 50000 DRAMS
Gold Plated Silver **Obv:** National arms **Rev:** Two monumental portraits

Date	Mintage	F	VF	XF	Unc	BU
1998 Proof	—	Value: 250				

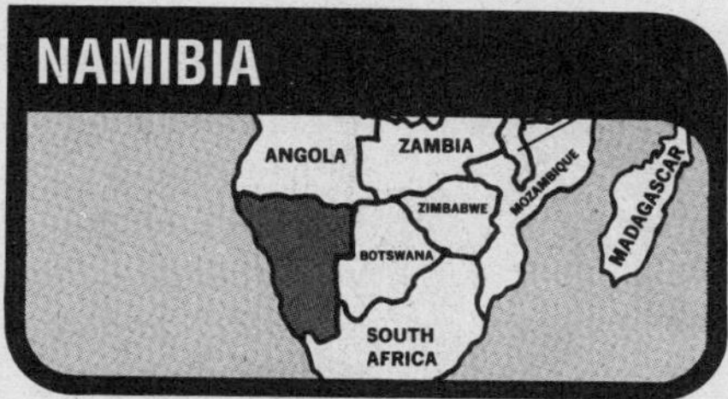

The Republic of Namibia, once the German colonial territory of German Southwest Africa, and later Southwest Africa, is situated on the Atlantic coast of southern Africa, bounded on the north by Angola, on the east by Botswana, and on the south by South Africa. It has an area of 318,261 sq. mi. (824,290 sq. km.) and a population of *1.4 million. Capital: Windhoek. Diamonds, copper, lead, zinc, and cattle are exported.

South Africa undertook the administration of Southwest Africa under the terms of a League of Nations mandate on Dec. 17, 1920. When the League of Nations was dissolved in 1946, its supervisory authority for Southwest Africa was inherited by the United Nations. In 1946 the UN denied South Africa's request to annex Southwest Africa. South Africa responded by refusing to place the territory under a UN trusteeship. In 1950 the International Court of Justice ruled that South Africa could not unilaterally modify the international status of Southwest Africa. A 1966 UN resolution declaring the mandate terminated was rejected by South Africa, and the status of the area remained in dispute. In June 1968 the UN General Assembly voted to rename the territory Namibia. In 1971 the International Court of Justice ruled that South Africa's presence in Namibia was illegal. In Dec. 1973 the UN appointed a UN Commissioner and a multi-racial Advisory Council was appointed. An interim government was formed in 1977 and independence was to be declared by Dec. 31, 1978. This resolution was rejected by major UN powers. In April 1978 South Africa accepted a plan for UN-supervised elections, which led to a political abstention by the Southwest Africa People's Organization (SWAPO) party leading to dissolving of the Minister's Council and National Assembly in Jan. 1983. A Multi-Party Conference (MPC) was formed in May 1984, which held talks with SWAPO. The MPC petitioned South Africa for self-government and on June 17, 1985 the Transitional Government of National Unity was installed. Negotiations were held in 1988 between Angola, Cuba, and South Africa reaching a peaceful settlement on Aug. 5, 1988. By April 1989 Cuban troops were to withdraw from Angola and South African troops from Namibia. The Transitional Government resigned on Feb. 28, 1988 for the upcoming elections of the constituent assembly in Nov. 1989. Independence was finally achieved on March 12, 1990 within the Commonwealth of Nations. The President is the Head of State; the Prime Minister is Head of Government.

MONETARY SYSTEM

100 Cents = 1 Namibia Dollar
1 Namibia Dollar = 1 South African Rand

REPUBLIC
1920 - present
DECIMAL COINAGE

KM# 1 5 CENTS

Nickel Plated Steel **Obv:** Arms with supporters **Rev:** Value and design within 3/4 sun design

Date	Mintage	F	VF	XF	Unc	BU
1993	—	—	—	0.20	0.50	0.75

KM# 16 5 CENTS

Stainless Steel **Series:** F.A.O **Obv:** Arms with supporters **Rev:** Fish below value

Date	Mintage	F	VF	XF	Unc	BU
2000 (1999)	—	—	—	—	1.00	1.50

KM# 2 10 CENTS

Nickel Plated Steel, 21.5 mm. **Obv:** Arms with supporters **Rev:** Tree and value

Date	Mintage	F	VF	XF	Unc	BU
1993	—	—	—	0.35	1.00	1.25
1996	—	—	—	0.35	1.00	1.25
1998	—	—	—	0.35	1.00	1.25

KM# 3 50 CENTS

Nickel Plated Steel, 24 mm. **Obv:** Arms with supporters **Rev:** Tree divides value

Date	Mintage	F	VF	XF	Unc	BU
1993	—	—	—	0.75	1.75	2.00
1996	—	—	—	0.75	1.75	2.00

KM# 4 DOLLAR

Brass **Obv:** Arms with supporters **Rev:** Bird and value

Date	Mintage	F	VF	XF	Unc	BU
1993	—	—	—	1.25	3.50	5.00
1996	—	—	—	1.25	3.50	5.00
Note: Edge varieties exist for 1996						
1998	—	—	—	1.25	3.50	5.00

KM# 6 DOLLAR

Copper-Nickel **Subject:** 5th Year of Independence **Obv:** Arms with supporters within beaded border **Rev:** Hills within beaded border

Date	Mintage	F	VF	XF	Unc	BU
1995	50,000	—	—	—	10.00	—

KM# 7 DOLLAR

Copper-Nickel **Subject:** Miss Universe **Obv:** Arms with supporters within beaded border **Rev:** Multicolor gemsbok within beaded border

Date	Mintage	F	VF	XF	Unc	BU
1995	50,000	—	—	—	12.50	—

KM# 12 DOLLAR

Copper-Nickel **Subject:** Marine Life Protection **Obv:** Arms with supporters **Rev:** Multicolor whale and calf

Date	Mintage	F	VF	XF	Unc	BU
1998 Proof	7,500	Value: 25.00				

KM# 5 5 DOLLARS

Brass **Obv:** Arms with supporters **Rev:** Eagle and value

Date	Mintage	F	VF	XF	Unc	BU
1993	—	—	—	4.00	7.50	8.00

KM# 18 5 DOLLARS

1.2700 g., 0.9999 Gold .0408 oz. AGW, 13.9 mm. **Subject:** 10 Years of Independence **Obv:** Arms with supporters **Rev:** Two lions within circle **Edge:** Reeded

Date	Mintage	F	VF	XF	Unc	BU
2000 Proof	8,000	Value: 40.00				

KM# 8 10 DOLLARS

25.0000 g., 0.9250 Silver .7435 oz. ASW **Subject:** 5th Year of Independence **Obv:** Arms with supporters **Rev:** Multicolor desert view

Date	Mintage	F	VF	XF	Unc	BU
1995 Proof	10,000	Value: 32.50				

KM# 9 10 DOLLARS

Copper-Nickel **Subject:** U.N. 50th Anniversary **Obv:** Arms with supporters **Rev:** Farm scene

Date	Mintage	F	VF	XF	Unc	BU
1995	—	—	—	—	12.50	14.50

KM# 9a 10 DOLLARS

28.2800 g., 0.9250 Silver .8410 oz. ASW **Subject:** U.N. 50th Anniversary **Obv:** Arms with supporters **Rev:** Farm scene

Date	Mintage	F	VF	XF	Unc	BU
1995 Proof	—	Value: 50.00				

KM# 10 10 DOLLARS

25.0000 g., 0.9250 Silver .7435 oz. ASW **Subject:** Miss Universe **Obv:** Arms with supporters **Rev:** Multicolor leopard

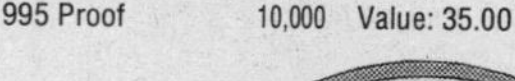

Date	Mintage	F	VF	XF	Unc	BU
1995 Proof	10,000	Value: 35.00				

KM# 11 10 DOLLARS

25.0000 g., 0.9250 Silver .7435 oz. ASW **Series:** Olympic Games 1996 **Obv:** Arms with supporters **Rev:** Runner and cheetah

Date	Mintage	F	VF	XF	Unc	BU
1996 Proof	—	Value: 35.00				

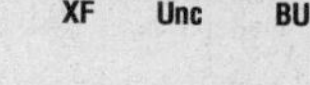

KM# 13 10 DOLLARS
25.0000 g., 0.9250 Silver .7435 oz. ASW **Subject:** Marine Life Protection **Obv:** Arms with supporters **Rev:** Multicolor whale and calf **Note:** Similar to 1 Dollar, KM#12.

Date	Mintage	F	VF	XF	Unc	BU
1998 Proof	—	Value: 60.00				

KM# 19 10 DOLLARS
25.0000 g., 0.9000 Silver .7234 oz. ASW, 37.3 mm. **Subject:** 10 Years of Independence **Obv:** Arms with supporters **Rev:** Two multicolor lions **Edge:** Reeded

Date	Mintage	F	VF	XF	Unc	BU
2000 Proof	3,000	Value: 40.00				

KM# 14 20 DOLLARS
155.5175 g., 0.9990 Silver 4.9950 oz. ASW **Obv:** Arms with supporters **Rev:** Multicolor whale and calf **Note:** Similar to 1 Dollar, KM#12.

Date	Mintage	F	VF	XF	Unc	BU
1998 Proof	—	Value: 350				

KM# 17 100 DOLLARS
31.1035 g., 0.9999 Gold 1.0000 oz. AGW **Series:** Olympic Games 1996 **Obv:** Arms with supporters **Rev:** Runner and cheetah **Note:** Similar to 10-Dollar, KM#11.

Date	Mintage	F	VF	XF	Unc	BU
1996 Proof	400	Value: 775				

KM# 15 100 DOLLARS
31.1035 g., 0.9999 Gold 1.0000 oz. AGW **Subject:** Marine Life Protection **Obv:** Arms with supporters **Rev:** Multicolor whale and calf **Note:** Similar to 1 Dollar, KM#12.

Date	Mintage	F	VF	XF	Unc	BU
1998 Proof	125	Value: 835				

ESSAIS

KM#	Date	Mintage	Identification	Mkt Val
E1	1996	30	10 Dollars. Copper-Nickel. Multi-color, KM#11.	200
E2	1996	30	100 Dollars. Copper-Nickel. Multi-color, KM#17.	220

NAURU ISLAND

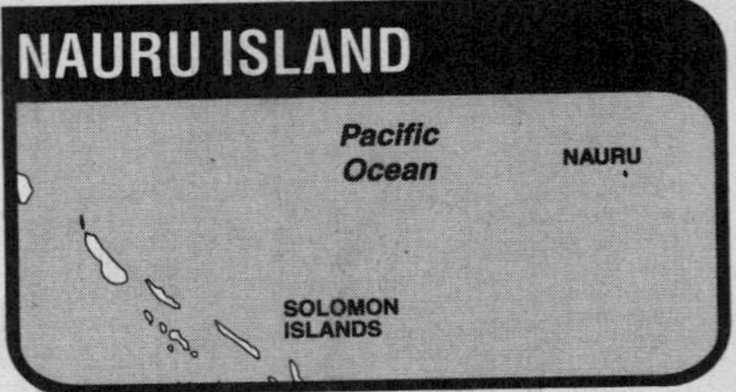

The Republic of Nauru, formerly Pleasant Island, is an island republic in the western Pacific Ocean west of the Gilbert Islands. It has an area of 8-1/2 sq. mi. and a population of 7,254. It is known for its phosphate deposits.

The island was discovered in 1798. It was annexed by Germany in 1888 and made a part of the Marshall Island protectorate. In 1914 the island was occupied by Australia and placed under mandate in 1919. During World War II it was seized by the Japanese in August, 1942. It became a joint Australian, British and New Zealand trust territory in 1947 and remained as such until it became an independent republic in 1968. Nauru has a unique relationship with the Commonwealth of Nations.

RULERS
British, until 1968

MONETARY SYSTEM
100 Cents = 1 (Australian) Dollar

REPUBLIC

DECIMAL COINAGE

KM# 12 DOLLAR
Copper-Nickel, 38.6 mm. **Subject:** British Queen Mother **Obv:** National arms **Rev:** Standing figures facing within beaded circle **Edge:** Reeded

Date	Mintage	F	VF	XF	Unc	BU
1996 Proof	—	Value: 12.00				

KM# 1 10 DOLLARS
38.7000 g., 0.9250 Silver 1.1508 oz. ASW **Subject:** Silver Jubilee of Independence **Obv:** National arms **Rev:** Value and ingot

Date	Mintage	F	VF	XF	Unc	BU
1993 Proof	1,000	Value: 85.00				

KM# 2 10 DOLLARS
31.4700 g., 0.9250 Silver .9359 oz. ASW **Subject:** Noah's Ark **Obv:** National arms **Rev:** Man, woman and animals in ark

Date	Mintage	F	VF	XF	Unc	BU
1993 Proof	Est. 15,000	Value: 65.00				

KM# 5 10 DOLLARS
31.4700 g., 0.9250 Silver .9359 oz. ASW **Series:** Endangered Wildlife **Obv:** National arms **Rev:** Songbirds

Date	Mintage	F	VF	XF	Unc	BU
1993 Proof	Est. 10,000	Value: 55.00				

KM# 3 10 DOLLARS
31.4700 g., 0.9250 Silver .9359 oz. ASW **Subject:** World Cup Soccer **Obv:** National arms **Rev:** Soccer player and soccer ball

Date	Mintage	F	VF	XF	Unc	BU
1994 Proof	30,000	Value: 45.00				

KM# 6 10 DOLLARS
31.4700 g., 0.9250 Silver .9359 oz. ASW **Subject:** Queen Mother Visits Bombed Palace **Obv:** National arms **Rev:** Figures standing in front of bombed building

Date	Mintage	F	VF	XF	Unc	BU
1994 Proof	Est. 30,000	Value: 45.00				

KM# 7 10 DOLLARS
31.4700 g., 0.9250 Silver .9359 oz. ASW **Subject:** John Fearn **Obv:** National arms **Rev:** Ship

Date	Mintage	F	VF	XF	Unc	BU
1994 Proof	Est. 15,000	Value: 50.00				

KM# 8 10 DOLLARS
31.4700 g., 0.9250 Silver .9359 oz. ASW **Obv:** National arms **Rev:** Bust with telescope facing right

Date	Mintage	F	VF	XF	Unc	BU
1994 Proof	Est. 10,000	Value: 52.50				

KM# 9 10 DOLLARS
31.4700 g., 0.9250 Silver .9359 oz. ASW **Series:** Olympics **Obv:** National arms **Rev:** Weight lifter

Date	Mintage	F	VF	XF	Unc	BU
1995 Proof	Est. 30,000	Value: 45.00				

KM# 4 50 DOLLARS
8.0500 g., 0.9000 Gold .2329 oz. AGW **Series:** 1996 Olympics **Obv:** National arms **Rev:** Javelin throwing

Date	Mintage	F	VF	XF	Unc	BU
1994 Proof	3,000	Value: 185				

KM# 10 50 DOLLARS
7.7760 g., 0.5833 Gold .1458 oz. AGW **Obv:** National arms **Rev:** Crowned emblem above steamship

Date	Mintage	F	VF	XF	Unc	BU
1994 Proof	Est. 3,000	Value: 150				

KM# 11 50 DOLLARS
7.7760 g., 0.5833 Gold .1458 oz. AGW **Subject:** Endangered Wildlife **Obv:** National arms **Rev:** Sea otter

Date	Mintage	F	VF	XF	Unc	BU
1995 Proof	Est. 2,000	Value: 165				

NEPAL

The Kingdom of Nepal, the world's only surviving Hindu kingdom, is a landlocked country occupying the southern slopes of the Himalayas. It has an area of 56,136 sq. mi. (140,800 sq. km.) and a population of 18 million. Capital: Kathmandu. Nepal has deposits of coal, copper, iron and cobalt, but they are largely unexploited. Agriculture is the principal economic activity. Rice, timber and jute are exported, with tourism being the other major foreign exchange earner.

Apart from a brief Muslim invasion in the 14th century, Nepal was able to avoid the mainstream of Northern Indian politics, due to its impregnable position in the mountains. It is therefore a unique survivor of the medieval Hindu and Buddhist culture of Northern India, which was largely destroyed by the successive waves of Muslim invasions.

Apart from agriculture, Nepal owed its prosperity to its position on one of the easiest trade routes between the great monasteries of central Tibet, and India. Nepal made full use of this, and a trading community was set up in Lhasa during the 16th century, and Nepalese coins became the accepted currency medium in Tibet.

The seeds of discord between Nepal and Tibet were sown during the first half of the 18th century, when the Nepalese debased the coinage, and the fate of the Malla kings of Nepal was sealed when Prithvi Narayan Shah, King of the small state of Gorkha, to the west of Kathmandu, was able to gain control of the trans-himalayan trade routes during the years after 1750.

Prithvi Narayan spent several years consolidating his position in hill areas before he finally succeeded in conquering the Kathmandu Valley in 1768, where he established the Shah dynasty, and moved his capital to Kathmandu.

After Prithvi Narayan's death a period of political instability ensued which lasted until the 1840's when the Rana family reduced the monarch to a figurehead and established the post of hereditary Prime Minister. A popular revolution in 1950 toppled the Rana family and reconstituted power in the throne. In 1959 King Mahendra declared Nepal a constitutional monarchy, and in 1962 a new constitution set up a system of *panchayat* (village council) democracy. In 1990, following political unrest, the king's powers were reduced. The country then adopted a system of parliamentary democracy.

On June 2, 2001 tragedy struck the royal family when Crown Prince Dipendra used an assault rifle to kill his father, mother and other members of the royal family as the result of a dispute over his current lady friend. He died 48 hours later, as King, from self inflicted gunshot wounds. Gyanendra began his second reign as King (his first was a short time as a toddler, 1950-51).

DATING

Saka Era (SE)

Up until 1888AD all coins of the Gorkha Dynasty were dated in the Saka era (SE). To convert from Saka to AD take Saka date and add 78 to arrive at the AD date. Coins dated with this era have SE before the date in the following listing.

Bikram Samvat Era (VS)

From 1888AD most copper coins were dated in the Bikram Samvat (VS) era. To convert take VS date - 57 =AD date. Coins with this era have VS before the year in the listing. With the exception of a few gold coins struck in 1890 & 1892, silver and gold coins only changed to the VS era in 1911AD, but now this era is used for all coins struck in Nepal.

RULERS

SHAH DYNASTY

पृथ्वी वीर विक्रम

Prithvi Bir Bikram
SE1803-1833/1881-1911AD, VS1938-1968/

Queen of Prithvi Bir Bikram: Lakshmi Divyeswari

त्रिभुवनवीर विक्रम

Tribhuvana Bir Bikram
VS1968-2007, 2007-2011/1911-1950, 1951-1955AD (first reign)
VS2058- / 2001- AD (second reign)

ज्ञानेन्द्रवीर विक्रम

Gyanendra Bir Bikram
VS2007/1950-1951AD

महेन्द्रवीर विक्रम

Mahendra Bir Bikram
VS2012-2028/1955-1971AD

रत्न राज लक्ष्मी

Queen of Mahendra Bir Bikram: Ratna Rajya Lakshmi

वीरेन्द्र वीर विक्रम

Birendra Bir Bikram
VS2028-2058 /1971-2001AD

ऐश्वर्य राज्य लक्ष्मी देवी

Queen of Birendra Bir Bikram: Aishvarya Rajya Lakshmi
VS2028-2058 /1971-2001AD

MONETARY SYSTEM

Many of the mohars circulated in Tibet as well as in Nepal, and on a number of occasions coins were struck from bullion supplied by the Tibetan authorities. The smaller denominations never circulated in Tibet, but some of the mohars were cut for use as small change in Tibet.

In these listings only major changes in design have been noted. There are numerous minor varieties of ornamentation or spelling.

With a few exceptions, most all coins were struck at Kathmandu.

COPPER

Initially the copper paisa was not fixed in value relative to the silver coins, and generally fluctuated in value from 1/32 mohar in 1865AD to around 1/50 mohar afterc1880AD, and was fixed at that value in 1903AD.

4 Dam = 1 Paisa
2 Paisa = 1 Dyak, Adhani

COPPER and SILVER

Decimal Series

100 Paisa = 1 Rupee

Although the value of the copper paisa was fixed at 100 paisa to the rupee in 1903, it was not until 1932 that silver coins were struck in the decimal system.

GOLD COINAGE

Nepalese gold coinage, until recently, did not carry any denominations and was traded for silver, etc. at the local bullion exchange rate. The three basic weight standards used in the following listing are distinguished for convenience, although all were known as Asarphi (gold coin) locally as follows:

GOLD MOHAR

5.60 g multiples and fractions

TOLA

12.48 g multiples and fractions

GOLD RUPEE or ASHRPHI/ASARFI

11.66 g multiples and fractions
(Reduced to 10.00 g in 1966)

NOTE: In some instances the gold and silver issues were struck from the same dies.

NUMERALS

Nepal has used more variations of numerals on their coins than any other nation. The most common are illustrated in the numeral chart in the introduction. The chart below illustrates some variations encompassing the last four centuries.

1	2	3	4	5	6	7	8	9	0
१	२	३	४	५	६	७	८	९	०

NUMERICS

Half	आधा
One	एक
Two	दुइ

Four	चार
Five	पाच
Ten	दसा
Twenty	विसा
Twenty-five	पचीसा
Fifty	पचासा
Hundred	सय

DENOMINATIONS

Paisa	पैसा
Dam	दाम
Mohar	मोरु
Rupee	रुपैयाँ
Ashrapi	असार्फी
Asarphi (Asarfi)	अश्रफी

DIE VARIETIES

Although the same dies were usually used both for silver and gold minor denominations, the gold Mohar is easily recognized being less ornate. The following illustrations are of a silver Mohar, KM#602 and a gold Mohar KM#615 issued by Surendra Bikram Saha Deva in the period SE1769-1803/1847-1881AD. Note the similar reverse legend. The obverse usually will start with the character for the word Shri either in single or multiples, the latter as Shri Shri Shri or Shri 3.

OBVERSE

SILVER SE1791

GOLD SE1793

LEGEND

श्री श्रीश्री सुरेन्द्र बिक्रम साहदेव

Shri Shri Shri Surendra Bikrama Saha Deva (date).

REVERSE

SILVER

LEGEND (in center)

GOLD

श्री ३ भवानी

Shri 3 Bhavani (around outer circle)

श्री श्री श्री गोरखनाथ

Shri Shri Shri Gorakhanatha

SHAH DYNASTY

KINGDOM

Shah Dynasty

Prithvi Bir Bikram

VS1938-1968 / 1881-1911AD

COPPER COINAGE

KM# 620.2 DAM

Copper **Rev. Inscription:** "Sarkar"

Date	Mintage	F	VF	XF	Unc
VS(19)64 (1907)	—	7.50	12.00	15.00	20.00

KM# 621 DAM

Copper

Date	Mintage	F	VF	XF	Unc
VS(19)68 (1911) Proof	—	Value: 60.00			
VS(19)68 (1911)	—	4.50	7.50	10.00	17.50

KM# 622 1/2 PAISA

Copper, 19 mm.

Date	Mintage	F	VF	XF	Unc
VS(19)64 (1907)	—	4.50	7.50	10.00	17.50
VS(19)68 (1911)	—	4.50	7.50	10.00	17.50
VS(19)68 (1911) Proof	—	Value: 60.00			

KM# 629 PAISA

Copper **Obv:** Legend within squares **Rev:** Legend within squares

Date	Mintage	Good	VG	F	VF	XF
VS1959 (1902)	—	1.00	1.50	2.50	4.00	—
VS1962 (1905)	—	1.00	1.50	2.50	4.00	—
VS1963 (1906)	—	1.00	1.50	2.50	4.00	—
VS1964 (1907)	—	1.00	1.50	2.50	4.00	—
VS1965 (1908)	—	1.00	1.50	2.50	4.00	—
VS1966 (1909)	—	1.00	1.50	2.50	4.00	—
VS1967 (1910)	—	1.00	1.50	2.50	4.00	—
VS1968 (1911)	—	1.00	1.50	2.50	4.00	—

KM# 630 PAISA

Copper-Iron Alloy **Obv:** Legend within square **Rev:** Legend within circle **Note:** Magnetic and non-magnetic alloy.

Date	Mintage	Good	VG	F	VF	XF
VS1959 (1902)	—	7.50	12.50	20.00	33.50	—

KM# 628 PAISA

Copper **Obv:** Legend within sprays **Rev:** Legend within sprays **Note:** Varieties in sprays exist. Coin and medal alignment varieties exist. Also struck between VS1343-1357.

Date	Mintage	Good	VG	F	VF	XF
VS1959 (1902)	—	1.00	1.50	3.00	5.00	—
VS1960 (1903)	—	1.00	1.50	3.00	5.00	—
VS1961 (1904)	—	1.00	1.50	3.00	5.00	—
VS1962 (1905)	—	1.00	1.50	3.00	5.00	—
VS(19)62 (1905)	—	—	—	—	—	—
VS1963 (1906)	—	1.00	1.50	3.00	5.00	—
VS1964 (1907)	—	1.00	1.50	3.00	5.00	—
VS(19)64 (1907)	—	—	—	—	—	—

KM# 631 PAISA

Copper, 23 mm. **Note:** Also Tribhuvaua Bir Bikram struck a Paisa VS1968, see KM#685.1.

Date	Mintage	F	VF	XF	Unc
VS1964 (1907)	—	5.50	9.00	15.00	22.50
VS1968 (1911)	—	8.50	13.50	20.00	30.00
VS1968 (1911) Proof	—	Value: 90.00			

KM# 633 2 PAISA (Dak)

Copper-Iron Alloy **Obv:** Legend within square **Rev:** Legend within circle **Note:** Magnetic and non-magnetic alloy. Similar to KM#630.

Date	Mintage	Good	VG	F	VF	XF
VS1959 (1902)	—	12.50	17.50	25.00	50.00	—

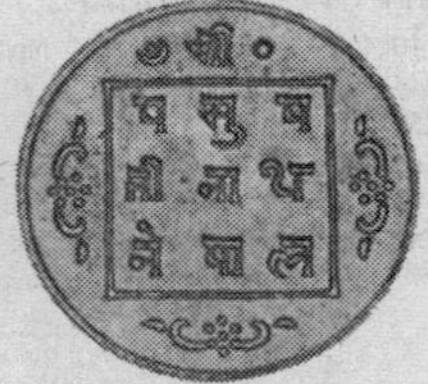

KM# 634 2 PAISA (Dak)

Copper, 26.5 mm.

Date	Mintage	F	VF	XF	Unc
VS1964 (1907)	—	8.50	13.50	20.00	30.00
VS1968 (1911)	—	9.00	15.00	22.50	35.00
VS1968 (1911) Proof	—	Value: 110			

SILVER COINAGE

KM# 635 DAM

0.0400 g., Silver **Note:** Uniface. Five characters around sword.

Date	Mintage	VG	F	VF	XF	Unc
ND(1881-1911)	—	—	8.00	10.00	15.00	25.00

KM# 636 DAM

0.0400 g., Silver **Note:** Four characters around sword.

Date	Mintage	VG	F	VF	XF	Unc
ND(1881-1911)	—	—	15.00	25.00	30.00	40.00

KM# 637 1/32 MOHAR

0.1800 g., Silver, 11 mm. **Obv:** Sun and moon

Date	Mintage	VG	F	VF	XF	Unc
ND(1881-1911)	—	5.00	8.50	12.50	16.50	—

KM# 638 1/32 MOHAR

0.1800 g., Silver, 11 mm. **Obv:** Without sun and moon

Date	Mintage	VG	F	VF	XF	Unc
ND(1881-1911)	—	5.00	8.50	12.50	16.50	—

KM# 639 1/16 MOHAR

0.3500 g., Silver, 13 mm. **Note:** Varieties exist.

Date	Mintage	VG	F	VF	XF	Unc
ND(1881-1911)	—	—	6.00	10.00	13.50	20.00

KM# 640 1/8 MOHAR

0.7000 g., Silver **Note:** Varieties exist.

Date	Mintage	VG	F	VF	XF	Unc
ND(1881-1911)	—	—	7.50	12.50	18.50	27.50

KM# 643 1/4 MOHAR

1.4000 g., Silver **Rev:** Moon and dot for sun **Note:** Machine struck. Also struck between SE1804-1817.

Date	Mintage	VG	F	VF	XF	Unc
SE1827 (1905)	—	1.75	3.00	5.00	7.00	—

KM# 644 1/4 MOHAR

1.4000 g., Silver, 15.5 mm. **Note:** Machine struck.

Date	Mintage	VG	F	VF	XF	Unc
SE1833 (1911)	—	1.75	3.00	5.00	7.00	—
SE1833 Proof	—	Value: 25.00				

KM# 647 1/2 MOHAR

2.7700 g., Silver, 21 mm. **Edge:** Plain **Note:** Machine struck. Varieties exist. Also struck between SE1803-1817.

Date	Mintage	F	VF	XF	Unc
SE1824 (1902)	—	20.00	25.00	30.00	35.00

KM# 648 1/2 MOHAR

2.7700 g., Silver, 21 mm. **Note:** Machine struck.

Date	Mintage	F	VF	XF	Unc
SE1826 (1904)	—	3.00	5.00	7.00	10.00
SE1827 (1905)	—	3.00	5.00	7.00	10.00
SE1829 (1907)	—	3.50	5.50	8.50	11.50

KM# 649 1/2 MOHAR

2.7700 g., Silver, 19 mm. **Edge:** Milled **Note:** Machine struck.

Date	Mintage	F	VF	XF	Unc
SE1832 (1910)	—	20.00	25.00	30.00	35.00

Date	Mintage	F	VF	XF	Unc
SE1833 (1911)	—	2.25	3.50	5.00	7.00
SE1833 (1911) Proof	—	Value: 35.00			

KM# 651.1 MOHAR

5.6000 g., Silver, 26 mm. **Edge:** Plain **Note:** Machine struck. Also struck between SE1807-1822.

Date	Mintage	F	VF	XF	Unc
SE1823 (1901)	—	4.50	6.50	8.00	10.00
SE1824 (1902)	—	4.50	6.50	8.00	10.00
SE1825 (1903)	—	4.50	6.50	8.00	10.00
SE1826 (1904)	—	4.50	6.50	8.00	10.00
SE1827 (1905)	—	4.50	6.50	8.00	10.00

KM# 652 MOHAR

5.6000 g., Silver, 26 mm. **Rev:** Gold die, in error

Date	Mintage	F	VF	XF	Unc
SE1825 (1903)	—	10.00	15.00	25.00	32.50

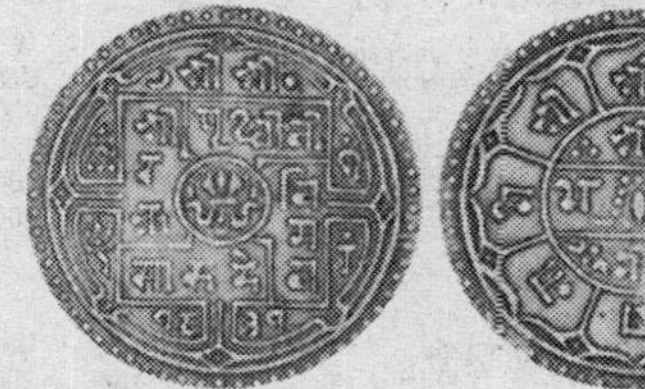

KM# 651.2 MOHAR

5.6000 g., Silver, 26 mm. **Edge:** Milled **Note:** Machine struck.

Date	Mintage	F	VF	XF	Unc
SE1826 (1904)	—	4.50	6.50	8.00	10.00
SE1827 (1905)	—	4.50	6.50	8.00	10.00
SE1828 (1906)	—	4.50	6.50	8.00	10.00
SE1829 (1907)	—	4.50	6.50	8.00	10.00
SE1830 (1908)	—	4.50	6.50	8.00	10.00
SE1831 (1909)	—	4.50	6.50	8.00	10.00
SE1832 (1910)	—	4.50	6.50	8.00	10.00
SE1833 (1911)	—	—	25.00	35.00	50.00

Note: The date SE1833 was only issued in presentation sets

KM# 655 2 MOHARS

11.2000 g., Silver, 27 mm. **Edge:** Milled **Note:** Machine struck.

Date	Mintage	F	VF	XF	Unc
SE1829 (1907)	—	15.00	27.50	40.00	60.00
SE1831 (1909)	—	6.50	9.00	12.50	20.00

KM# 656 2 MOHARS

Silver, 29 mm. **Note:** Machine struck.

Date	Mintage	F	VF	XF	Unc
SE1832 (1910)	—	7.00	9.00	11.50	18.50
SE1833 (1911) Proof	—	Value: 75.00			
SE1833 (1911)	—	6.50	8.00	10.00	16.50

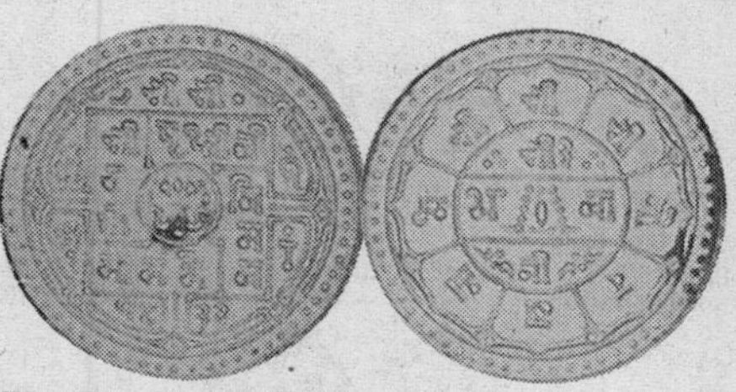

KM# 658 4 MOHARS

22.4000 g., Silver, 29 mm. **Edge:** Milled

Date	Mintage	F	VF	XF	Unc
SE1833 (1911)	—	60.00	100	140	200
SE1833 (1911) Proof	—	Value: 450			

GOLD COINAGE

KM# 659 DAM

0.0400 g., Gold **Note:** Uniface. Five characters around sword. Similar to 1/64 Mohar, KM#664.

Date	Mintage	VG	F	VF	XF	Unc
ND(1881-1911)	—	—	10.00	14.00	20.00	27.50

KM# 660 DAM

0.0400 g., Gold **Note:** Uniface. Four characters around sword. Similar to 1/64 Mohar, KM#663.

Date	Mintage	VG	F	VF	XF	Unc
ND(1881-1911)	—	—	10.00	14.00	20.00	27.50

Actual Size 2 x Actual Size

KM# 661 DAM

0.0400 g., Gold **Note:** Uniface. Circle around characters.

Date	Mintage	VG	F	VF	XF	Unc
ND(1881-1911)	—	—	10.00	14.00	20.00	27.50

Actual Size 2 x Actual Size

KM# 662 DAM

0.0400 g., Gold **Note:** Uniface. Two characters below sword. Varieties exist.

Date	Mintage	VG	F	VF	XF	Unc
ND(1881-1911)	—	—	10.00	14.00	20.00	27.50

Actual Size 2 x Actual Size

KM# 663 1/64 MOHAR

0.0900 g., Gold **Note:** Uniface. Four characters around sword.

Date	Mintage	VG	F	VF	XF	Unc
ND(1881-1911)	—	—	12.50	17.50	22.50	30.00

Actual Size 2 x Actual Size

KM# 664 1/64 MOHAR

0.0900 g., Gold **Note:** Uniface. Five characters around sword.

Date	Mintage	VG	F	VF	XF	Unc
ND(1881-1911)	—	—	12.50	17.50	22.50	30.00

KM# 665 1/32 MOHAR

0.1800 g., Gold **Note:** Uniface. Five characters around sword.

Date	Mintage	VG	F	VF	XF	Unc
ND(1881-1911)	—	—	20.00	40.00	75.00	100

KM# 666 1/32 MOHAR

0.1800 g., Gold **Note:** Uniface. Four characters around sword.

Date	Mintage	VG	F	VF	XF	Unc
ND(1881-1911)	—	—	15.00	30.00	75.00	100

KM# 667 1/16 MOHAR

0.3500 g., Gold

Date	Mintage	VG	F	VF	XF	Unc
ND(1881-1911)	—	—	15.00	40.00	75.00	100

KM# 668 1/16 MOHAR

0.3500 g., Gold

Date	Mintage	F	VF	XF	Unc
SE(18)33 (1911)	—	15.00	30.00	75.00	100
SE(18)33 (1911) Proof	—	—	—	—	—

KM# 669.1 1/8 MOHAR

0.7000 g., Gold **Obv:** Six characters

Date	Mintage	F	VF	XF	Unc
ND (1881)	—	22.50	40.00	75.00	100

KM# 669.2 1/8 MOHAR

0.7000 g., Gold **Obv:** Five characters **Note:** Varieties exist.

Date	Mintage	F	VF	XF	Unc
ND (1881)	—	22.50	40.00	75.00	100

KM# 670 1/8 MOHAR

0.7000 g., Gold

Date	Mintage	F	VF	XF	Unc
SE(18)33 (1911)	—	22.50	40.00	75.00	100

KM# 671.1 1/4 MOHAR

1.4000 g., Gold

Date	Mintage	F	VF	XF	Unc
SE1823 (1901)	—	45.00	60.00	80.00	100
SE1829 (1907)	—	40.00	50.00	60.00	80.00

KM# 671.2 1/4 MOHAR

1.4000 g., Gold

Date	Mintage	F	VF	XF	Unc
SE1833 (1911) Proof	—	—	—	—	—
SE1833 (1911)	—	40.00	50.00	60.00	80.00

KM# 672.3 1/2 MOHAR

2.8000 g., Gold

Date	Mintage	F	VF	XF	Unc
SE1823 (1901)	—	70.00	80.00	100	125

KM# 672.4 1/2 MOHAR

2.8000 g., Gold

Date	Mintage	F	VF	XF	Unc
SE1829 (1907)	—	65.00	75.00	85.00	100

KM# 672.5 1/2 MOHAR

2.8000 g., Gold

Date	Mintage	F	VF	XF	Unc
SE1833 (1911)	—	65.00	75.00	85.00	100
SE1833 (1911) Proof	—	—	—	—	—

KM# 673.1 MOHAR

5.6000 g., Gold

Date	Mintage	F	VF	XF	Unc
SE1823 (1901)	—	128	140	165	200
SE1825 (1903)	—	128	140	165	200
SE1826 (1904)	—	128	140	165	200
SE1827 (1905)	—	128	140	165	200

KM# 673.2 MOHAR

5.6000 g., Gold **Edge:** Milled

Date	Mintage	F	VF	XF	Unc
SE1828 (1906)	—	125	135	160	200
SE1829 (1907)	—	125	135	160	200
SE1831 (1909)	—	125	135	160	200
SE1833 (1911)	—	125	135	160	200
SE1833 (1911) Proof	—	—	—	—	—

KM# 674.3 TOLA

12.4800 g., Gold **Edge:** Plain

Date	Mintage	F	VF	XF	Unc
SE1823 (1901)	—	275	280	300	325
SE1824 (1902)	—	275	280	300	325
SE1825 (1903)	—	275	280	300	325
SE1826 (1904)	—	275	280	300	325

KM# 675.1 TOLA

12.4800 g., Gold **Edge:** Vertical milling

Date	Mintage	F	VF	XF	Unc
SE1828 (1906)	—	275	280	300	325
SE1829 (1907)	—	275	280	300	325
SE1831 (1909)	—	275	280	300	325
SE1832 (1910)	—	275	280	300	325
SE1833 (1911)	—	275	280	300	325
SE1833 (1911) Proof	—	—	—	—	—

KM# 678 DUITOLA ASARPHI

23.3200 g., Gold **Edge:** Plain

Date	Mintage	F	VF	XF	Unc
SE1825 (1902)	—	600	700	800	1,000

KM# 679 DUITOLA ASARPHI

23.3200 g., Gold **Edge:** Milled

Date	Mintage	F	VF	XF	Unc
SE1829 (1907)	—	550	600	700	800

KM# 680 DUITOLA ASARPHI

23.3200 g., Gold **Edge:** Milled

Date	Mintage	F	VF	XF	Unc
SE1833 (1911)	—	550	600	700	800
SE1833 (1911) Proof	—	—	—	—	—

Tribhuvana Bir Bikram

VS1968-2007 / 1911-1950AD

COPPER COINAGE

KM# 684 1/2 PAISA

Copper **Note:** Struck only for presentation sets.

Date	Mintage	F	VF	XF	Unc
VS1978 (1921)	—	—	—	50.00	75.00
VS1985 (1928)	—	—	—	50.00	75.00

KM# 685.1 PAISA

Copper **Note:** Machine struck. Also Prithvi Bir Bikram struck a Paisa VS1968, see KM#631.

Date	Mintage	Good	VG	F	VF	XF
VS1968 (1911)	—	10.00	20.00	50.00	75.00	—

KM# 685.2 PAISA

Copper **Note:** Hand struck. Many varieties exist.

Date	Mintage	Good	VG	F	VF	XF
VS1969 (1912)	—	1.00	1.50	2.25	3.50	—
VS1970 (1913)	—	1.00	1.50	2.25	3.50	—
VS1971 (1914)	—	1.00	1.50	2.25	3.50	—
VS1972 (1915)	—	1.00	1.50	2.25	3.50	—
VS1973 (1916)	—	1.00	1.50	2.25	3.50	—
VS1974 (1917)	—	1.00	1.50	2.25	3.50	—
VS1975 (1918)	—	1.00	1.50	2.25	3.50	—
VS1976 (1919)	—	1.00	1.50	2.25	3.50	—
VS1977 (1920)	—	1.00	1.50	2.25	3.50	—

KM# 686.1 PAISA

5.2000 g., Copper, 23.5 mm. **Rev:** Without "Nepal" below

Date	Mintage	F	VF	XF	Unc
VS1975 (1918)	—	—	—	37.50	50.00

KM# 686.2 PAISA

3.7000 g., Copper, 21.5 mm. **Rev:** Without "Nepal" below

Date	Mintage	Good	VG	F	VF	XF
VS1975 (1918)	—	—	—	60.00	90.00	—

Note: The above issues are believed to be patterns

KM# 687.1 PAISA

Copper, 21.5 mm. **Obv:** Outlined Khukris **Note:** Machine struck. Fine style. Weight varies: 3.50-3.80 g.

Date	Mintage	F	VF	XF	Unc
VS1977 (1920)	—	1.25	1.75	3.00	6.00
VS1977 (1920)	—	1.25	1.75	3.00	6.00
Note: Inverted date					
VS1978	—	1.25	1.75	3.00	6.00

KM# 687.2 PAISA

Copper, 22 mm. **Obv:** Outlined Khukris always right over left **Note:** Machine struck. Weight varies: 2.6-3.1 grams. Prev. KM#688.

Date	Mintage	F	VF	XF	Unc
VS1978 (1921)	—	1.25	1.75	3.00	6.00
VS1979 (1922)	—	1.25	1.75	3.00	6.00
VS1980 (1923)	—	1.50	3.00	5.00	10.00
VS1981 (1924)	—	1.50	3.00	5.00	10.00
VS1982 (1925)	—	1.25	1.75	3.00	6.00
VS1984 (1927)	—	1.25	1.75	3.00	6.00
VS1985 (1928)	—	1.25	1.75	3.00	6.00
VS1986 (1929)	—	1.25	1.75	3.00	6.00
VS1987 (1930)	—	1.25	1.75	3.00	6.00

KM# 687.3 PAISA

3.7500 g., Copper, 21 mm. **Obv:** Outlined Khukris left over right and right over left **Note:** Crude, hand struck. Varieties of the Khukris exist

Date	Mintage	Good	VG	F	VF	XF
VS1978 (1921)	—	2.00	3.00	4.50	7.50	—
VS1979 (1922)	—	2.00	3.00	4.50	7.50	—
VS1980 (1923)	—	4.00	5.00	7.50	12.50	—
VS1981 (1924)	—	4.00	5.00	7.50	12.50	—
VS1982 (1925)	—	4.00	5.00	7.50	12.50	—
VS1983 (1926)	—	4.00	5.00	7.50	12.50	—

KM# 687.4 PAISA

3.7500 g., Brass **Obv:** Fine style crossed khukris

Date	Mintage	VG	F	VF	XF	Unc
VS1975 (1918)	—	0.50	1.25	1.75	3.00	6.00
VS1976 (1919)	—	0.50	1.25	1.75	3.00	6.00

KM# 689.1 2 PAISA

Copper, 26 mm. **Obv:** Outlined Khukris **Note:** Machine struck. Varieties of the Khukris exist. Weight varies: 6.9-7.5 grams.

Date	Mintage	VG	F	VF	XF	Unc
VS1976 (1919)	—	1.00	2.00	3.00	5.00	—
VS1977 (1920)	—	1.00	2.00	3.00	5.00	—
VS1977 (1920) Inverted date	—	3.50	5.00	8.50	13.50	—

KM# 689.2 2 PAISA

Copper **Obv:** Outlined Khukris left over right and right over left **Note:** Crude struck. Varieties of the Khukris exist. Weight varies: 4.6-5.5 grams.

Date	Mintage	Good	VG	F	VF	XF
VS1978 (1921)	—	1.00	2.00	3.50	6.50	—
VS1979 (1922)	—	1.00	2.00	3.50	6.50	—
VS1980 (1923)	—	1.00	2.00	3.50	6.50	—
VS1981 (1924)	—	1.00	2.00	3.50	6.50	—
VS1982 (1925)	—	1.00	2.00	3.50	6.50	—
VS1983 (1926)	—	1.00	2.00	3.50	6.50	—
VS1984 (1927)	—	1.00	2.00	3.50	6.50	—
VS1985 (1928)	—	1.00	2.00	3.50	6.50	—
VS1986 (1929)	—	1.50	2.50	4.00	7.50	—
VS1987 (1930)	—	1.50	2.50	4.00	7.50	—
VS1988 (1931)	—	2.00	3.00	5.00	9.00	—

KM# 689.3 2 PAISA

5.0000 g., Copper **Obv:** Outlined Khukris always right over left **Note:** Machine struck. Weight varies: 5.00-5.700 grams.

Date	Mintage	VG	F	VF	XF	Unc
VS1978 (1921)	—	1.00	2.00	3.00	4.50	—
VS1979 (1922)	—	1.00	2.00	3.00	4.50	—
VS1980 (1923)	—	1.00	2.00	3.00	4.50	—
VS1981 (1924)	—	1.00	2.00	3.00	4.50	—
VS1982 (1925)	—	1.00	2.00	3.00	4.50	—
VS1983 (1926)	—	1.00	2.00	3.00	4.50	—
VS1984 (1927)	—	1.00	2.00	3.00	4.50	—
VS1991 (1934)	—	1.50	2.50	4.00	6.00	—

KM# 689.4 2 PAISA

Brass **Obv:** Fine style crossed khukris

Date	Mintage	VG	F	VF	XF	Unc
VS1976 (1919)	—	1.00	2.00	3.00	5.00	—

KM# 690.1 5 PAISA

Copper, 29.5 mm. **Obv:** Outlined Khukris **Note:** Weight varies: 18.1-18.8 g.

Date	Mintage	F	VF	XF	Unc
VS1976 (1919)	—	6.00	10.00	14.00	20.00
Note: Fine style					
VS1977 (1920)	—	1.25	2.25	3.50	6.00
VS1977 (1920) Inverted date	—	3.00	5.00	8.50	12.50

KM# 690.2 5 PAISA

Copper **Obv:** Outlined Khukris, left over right and right over left **Note:** Crude hand struck. Weight varies: 11.0-13.2 g. Size varies: 29.0-32.5mm.

Date	Mintage	F	VF	XF	Unc
VS1978 (1921)	—	1.75	3.00	5.00	8.00
VS1979 (1922)	—	1.75	3.00	5.00	8.00
VS1980 (1923)	—	1.75	3.00	5.00	8.00
VS1981 (1924)	—	1.75	3.00	5.00	8.00
VS1982 (1925)	—	1.75	3.00	5.00	8.00
VS1983 (1926)	—	1.75	3.00	5.00	8.00
VS1984 (1927)	—	1.75	3.00	5.00	8.00
VS1985 (1928)	—	1.75	3.00	5.00	8.00
VS1986 (1929)	—	1.75	3.00	5.00	8.00
VS1987 (1930)	—	1.75	3.00	5.00	8.00
VS1988 (1931)	—	6.00	10.00	14.00	20.00

KM# 690.3 5 PAISA

14.0000 g., Copper **Obv:** Outlined Khukris always right over left **Note:** Machine struck. Weight varies: 13.5-14.0 g. Varieties exist. Size varies: 29.0-30.0mm.

Date	Mintage	F	VF	XF	Unc
VS1978 (1921)	—	1.25	2.25	3.50	5.00
VS1979 (1922)	—	1.25	2.25	3.50	5.00
VS1979 (1922) Backwards date	—	1.25	2.25	3.50	5.00
VS1980 (1923)	—	1.25	2.25	3.50	5.00
VS1981 (1924)	—	1.25	2.25	3.50	5.00
VS1982 (1925)	—	1.25	2.25	3.50	5.00
VS1983 (1926)	—	1.25	2.25	3.50	5.00
VS1984 (1927)	—	1.25	2.25	3.50	5.00
VS1991 (1934)	—	15.00	20.00	25.00	30.00

KM# 690.4 5 PAISA

Brass **Obv:** Fine style crossed khukris

Date	Mintage	VG	F	VF	XF	Unc
VS1976 (1919)	—	1.25	2.25	3.50	6.00	—

SILVER COINAGE

KM# 691 DAM

0.0400 g., Silver **Note:** Uniface.

Date	Mintage	F	VF	XF	Unc
ND (1911)	—	15.00	25.00	30.00	50.00

KM# 692 1/4 MOHAR

1.4000 g., Silver, 16 mm.

Date	Mintage	VG	F	VF	XF	Unc
VS1969 (1912)	—	1.75	3.00	5.00	7.00	—
VS1970 (1913)	—	1.75	3.00	5.00	7.00	—

KM# 693 1/2 MOHAR

2.8000 g., Silver

Date	Mintage	F	VF	XF	Unc
VS1968 (1911)	—	2.25	3.50	5.00	7.00
VS1970 (1913)	—	2.25	3.50	5.00	7.00
VS1971 (1914)	—	2.25	3.50	5.00	7.00

KM# 681 1/2 MOHAR

2.7700 g., Silver **Note:** In the name of "Queen Lakshmi Divyeswari" - Regent for Tribhuvana Bir Bikram.

Date	Mintage	F	VF	XF	Unc
VS1971 (1914)	—	4.00	6.00	9.00	11.50

KM# 694 MOHAR

5.6000 g., Silver

Date	Mintage	F	VF	XF	Unc
VS1968 (1911)	—	4.50	6.50	8.00	10.00
VS1969 (1912)	—	4.50	6.50	8.00	10.00
VS1971 (1914)	—	4.50	6.50	8.00	10.00

KM# 682 MOHAR

5.6000 g., Silver **Note:** In the name of "Queen Lakshmi Divyeswari" - Regent for Tribhuvana Bir Bikram.

Date	Mintage	F	VF	XF	Unc
VS1971 (1914)	—	4.50	6.50	9.00	11.50

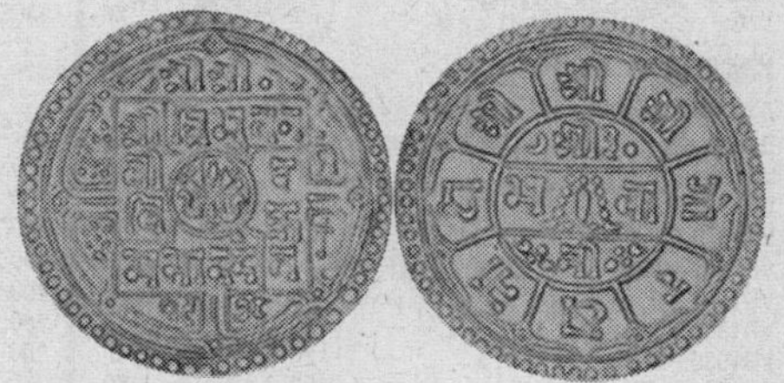

KM# 695 2 MOHARS

11.2000 g., Silver, 29 mm. **Note:** Varieties exist for this type.

Date	Mintage	F	VF	XF	Unc
VS1968 (1911)	—	BV	7.50	10.00	16.50
VS1969 (1912)	—	BV	7.50	10.00	16.50
VS1970 (1913)	—	BV	7.50	10.00	16.50
VS1971 (1914)	—	BV	7.50	10.00	16.50
VS1972 (1915)	—	BV	7.50	10.00	16.50
VS1973 (1916)	—	BV	7.50	10.00	16.50
VS1974 (1917)	—	BV	7.50	10.00	16.50
VS1975 (1918)	—	BV	7.50	10.00	16.50
VS1976 (1919)	—	BV	7.50	10.00	16.50
VS1977 (1920)	—	BV	7.50	10.00	16.50

Date	Mintage	F	VF	XF	Unc
VS1978 (1921)	—	BV	7.50	10.00	16.50
VS1979 (1922)	—	BV	7.50	10.00	16.50
VS1980 (1923)	—	BV	7.50	10.00	16.50
VS1982 (1925)	—	BV	7.50	10.00	16.50
VS1983 (1926)	—	BV	7.50	10.00	16.50
VS1984 (1927)	—	BV	7.50	10.00	16.50
VS1985 (1928)	—	BV	7.50	10.00	16.50
VS1986 (1929)	—	BV	7.50	10.00	16.50
VS1987 (1930)	—	BV	7.50	10.00	16.50
VS1988 (1931)	—	BV	7.50	10.00	16.50
VS1989 (1932)	—	BV	7.50	10.00	16.50

KM# 696 4 MOHARS

22.4000 g., Silver

Date	Mintage	F	VF	XF	Unc
VS1971 (1914)	—	40.00	75.00	125	175

GOLD COINAGE

KM# 697 DAM

0.0400 g., Gold **Note:** Uniface.

Date	Mintage	F	VF	XF	Unc
ND (1911)	—	28.00	40.00	75.00	100

KM# 697a DAM

0.0400 g., Gold **Note:** Uniface, machine struck.

Date	Mintage	F	VF	XF	Unc
ND (1911)	—	28.00	40.00	70.00	100

KM# 698 1/32 MOHAR

0.1800 g., Gold **Note:** Uniface.

Date	Mintage	F	VF	XF	Unc
ND (1911)	—	38.00	60.00	90.00	125

KM# 699 1/16 MOHAR

0.3500 g., Gold

Date	Mintage	F	VF	XF	Unc
VS(19)77 (1920)	—	50.00	90.00	120	150

KM# 700 1/8 MOHAR

0.7000 g., Gold

Date	Mintage	F	VF	XF	Unc
VS(19)76 (1919)	—	75.00	120	150	200

KM# 701 1/2 MOHAR

2.8000 g., Gold

Date	Mintage	F	VF	XF	Unc
VS1969 (1912)	—	—	—	—	—

KM# 717 1/2 MOHAR

2.8000 g., Gold

Date	Mintage	F	VF	XF	Unc
VS1995 (1938)	—	—	—	—	—

KM# 702 MOHAR

5.6000 g., Gold

Date	Mintage	F	VF	XF	Unc
VS1969 (1912)	—	120	130	150	200
VS1975 (1918)	—	120	130	150	200
VS1978 (1921)	—	120	130	150	200
VS1979 (1922)	—	120	130	150	200
VS1981 (1924)	—	120	130	150	200
VS1983 (1926)	—	120	130	150	200
VS1985 (1928)	—	120	130	150	200
VS1986 (1929)	—	120	130	150	200
VS1987 (1930)	—	120	130	150	200
VS1989 (1932)	—	120	130	150	200
VS1990 (1933)	—	120	130	150	200
VS1991 (1934)	—	120	130	150	200
VS1998 (1941)	—	120	130	150	200
VS1999 (1942)	—	120	130	150	200
VS2000 (1943)	—	120	130	150	200
VS2003 (1946)	—	120	130	150	200
VS2005 (1948)	—	120	130	150	200

KM# 683 MOHAR

5.6000 g., Gold **Note:** In the name of "Queen Lakshmi Divyeswari" - Regent for Tribhuvana Bir Bikram.

Date	Mintage	F	VF	XF	Unc
VS1971 (1914)	—	120	130	145	185

KM# 722 MOHAR

5.6000 g., Gold

Date	Mintage	F	VF	XF	Unc
VS1993 (1936)	376,000	—	—	—	—
VS1994 (1937)	283,000	—	—	—	—

KM# 703.1 ASHRAPHI (Tola)

Gold **Rev:** Moon and sun in center **Rev. Legend:** SRI 3 BHAVANI

Date	Mintage	F	VF	XF	Unc
VS1969 (1912)	—	265	270	285	315
VS1974 (1917)	—	265	270	285	315
VS1975 (1918)	—	265	270	285	315
VS1976 (1919)	—	265	270	285	315
VS1977 (1920)	—	265	270	285	315
VS1978 (1921)	—	265	270	285	315
VS1979 (1922)	—	265	270	285	315
VS1980 (1923)	—	265	270	285	315
VS1981 (1924)	—	265	270	285	315
VS1982 (1925)	—	265	270	285	315
VS1983 (1926)	—	265	270	285	315
VS1984 (1927)	—	265	270	285	315
VS1985 (1928)	—	265	270	285	315
VS1986 (1929)	—	265	270	285	315
VS1987 (1930)	—	265	270	285	315
VS1988 (1931)	—	265	270	285	315
VS1989 (1932)	—	265	270	285	315
VS1990 (1933)	—	265	270	285	315
VS1991 (1934)	—	265	270	285	315
VS1998 (1941)	—	265	270	285	315
VS1999 (1942)	—	265	270	285	315
VS2000 (1943)	—	265	270	285	315
VS2003 (1946)	—	265	270	285	315

KM# 727 ASHRAPHI (Tola)

Gold **Obv:** Trident between moon and sun above crossed Khukris in center

Date	Mintage	F	VF	XF	Unc
VS1992 (1935)	—	275	280	300	350

KM# 703.2 ASHRAPHI (Tola)

Gold

Date	Mintage	F	VF	XF	Unc
VS2005 (1948)	—	265	270	285	315

KM# 703.3 ASHRAPHI (Tola)

Gold **Rev:** 3 dots each side in center **Rev. Legend:** SRI BHAVANI

Date	Mintage	F	VF	XF	Unc
VS2033 (1976)	—	265	270	285	315

KM# 728 DUITOLA ASARPHI

Gold **Note:** Similar to 1 Tola, KM#703.

Date	Mintage	F	VF	XF	Unc
VS2005 (1948)	—	475	525	575	650

ANONYMOUS COINAGE

KM# 733 PAISA

Brass, 18 mm. **Obv:** Sun rising above three hills within grain sprigs **Rev:** Dagger in front of hills within circle

Date	Mintage	F	VF	XF	Unc
VS2010 (1953)	—	8.00	15.00	20.00	25.00
VS2011 (1954)	—	17.50	25.00	35.00	40.00
VS2012 (1955) Restrike	—	—	1.00	1.50	2.00

KM# 734 PAISA

Brass, 17.5 mm.

Date	Mintage	F	VF	XF	Unc
VS2012 (1955)	—	1.25	2.00	2.50	3.50

KM# 735 2 PAISA

Brass, 21 mm. **Obv:** Sun rising above three hills within grain sprigs **Rev:** Dagger in front of hills within circle

Date	Mintage	F	VF	XF	Unc
VS2010 (1953)	—	12.50	20.00	37.50	60.00
VS2011 (1954)	—	30.00	40.00	50.00	75.00
VS2011 (1954) Restrike	—	—	—	1.50	2.50

KM# 749 2 PAISA

Brass, 19.5 mm. **Obv:** Sun rising above three hills within grain sprigs **Rev:** Dagger in front of hills within circle

Date	Mintage	F	VF	XF	Unc
VS2012 (1955)	—	0.30	0.50	0.75	1.50
VS2013 (1956)	—	0.30	0.50	0.75	1.50
VS2014 (1957)	—	0.30	0.50	0.75	1.50

KM# 754 4 PAISA

Brass **Obv:** Legend around center circle **Rev:** Date below center circle

Date	Mintage	F	VF	XF	Unc
VS2012 (1955)	—	1.00	1.75	3.00	5.00

KM# 736 5 PAISA

3.8900 g., Bronze **Obv:** Sun rising above three hills within grain sprigs **Rev:** Hand divides date within decorative outline

Date	Mintage	F	VF	XF	Unc
VS2010 (1953)	—	2.75	4.50	7.00	10.00
VS2011 (1954)	—	0.65	1.00	2.75	5.00
VS2012 (1955)	—	0.30	0.50	0.75	1.25
VS2013 (1956)	—	0.30	0.50	0.75	1.25
VS2014 (1957)	—	0.30	0.50	0.75	1.25

KM# 736a 5 PAISA

4.0400 g., Copper-Nickel **Obv:** Sun rising above three hills within grain sprigs **Rev:** Hand divides date within decorative outline

Date	Mintage	F	VF	XF	Unc
VS2014 (1957)	—	—	—	—	—

KM# 737 10 PAISA

Bronze **Obv:** Sun rising above three hills within grain sprigs **Rev:** Dagger in front of three hills within circle

Date	Mintage	F	VF	XF	Unc
VS2010 (1953)	—	2.75	4.50	7.00	10.00
VS2011 (1954)	—	0.15	0.25	0.50	1.00
VS2011 (1954) Restrike	—	—	—	0.15	0.25
VS2012 (1955)	—	0.15	0.25	0.50	1.00

KM# 738 20 PAISA

Copper-Nickel, 18 mm. **Obv:** Sun rising above three hills within grain sprigs **Rev:** Dagger in front of three hills within circle

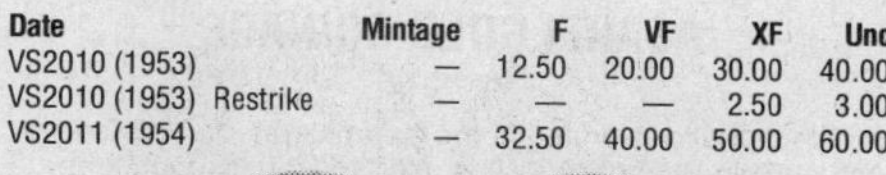

Date	Mintage	F	VF	XF	Unc
VS2010 (1953)	—	12.50	20.00	30.00	40.00
VS2010 (1953) Restrike	—	—	—	2.50	3.00
VS2011 (1954)	—	32.50	40.00	50.00	60.00

KM# 739 25 PAISA

Copper-Nickel, 19 mm. **Obv:** Sun rising above three hills within grain sprigs **Rev:** Dagger in front of three hills within circle

Date	Mintage	F	VF	XF	Unc
VS2010 (1953)	—	2.00	3.50	4.50	6.00
VS2011 (1954)	—	2.00	3.50	4.50	6.00
VS2012 (1955)	—	1.25	2.00	2.50	3.50
VS2014 (1957)	—	1.25	2.00	2.50	3.50

KM# 768 1/5 ASARPHI

2.3300 g., Gold

Date	Mintage	F	VF	XF	Unc
VS2010 (1953)	—	—	60.00	70.00	100

Note: Coins dated VS2010 are normally found as restrikes ca. 1968

Date	Mintage	F	VF	XF	Unc
VS2012 (1955)	—	—	—	—	—

KM# 774 1/4 ASARPHI

2.9000 g., Gold

Date	Mintage	F	VF	XF	Unc
VS2010 (1953)	—	70.00	80.00	90.00	120

Note: Coins dated VS2010 are normally found as restrikes ca. 1968

Date	Mintage	F	VF	XF	Unc
VS2012 (1955)	—	—	—	—	—

DECIMAL COINAGE

100 Paisa = 1 Rupee

KM# 704 1/4 PAISA

Copper, 14 mm. **Obv:** Footprints above crossed daggers within circle **Rev:** Crescent moon and star flank center dagger

Date	Mintage	F	VF	XF	Unc
VS2000 (1943)	—	15.00	25.00	30.00	40.00
VS2004 (1947)	—	15.00	25.00	30.00	40.00

KM# 705 1/2 PAISA

Copper, 16 mm. **Obv:** Footprints above crossed daggers within circle **Rev:** Crescent moon and star flank dagger at center

Date	Mintage	F	VF	XF	Unc
VS2004 (1947)	—	—	25.00	30.00	40.00

KM# 706.1 PAISA

Copper, 23 mm. **Obv:** Footprints above crossed daggers within circle **Rev:** Right wreath with sharp end **Note:** Prev. KM#706.

Date	Mintage	F	VF	XF	Unc
VS1990 (1933)	—	0.75	1.50	3.00	5.00
VS1991 (1934)	—	0.75	1.50	3.00	5.00
VS1992 (1935)	—	0.75	1.50	3.00	5.00

KM# 706.2 PAISA

Copper, 23 mm. **Obv:** Footprints above crossed daggers within circle **Rev:** Right wreath with round end

Date	Mintage	VG	F	VF	XF	Unc
VS1993	—	—	0.75	1.50	3.00	5.00
VS1994	456,000	—	0.75	1.50	3.00	5.00
VS1995	—	—	0.75	1.50	3.00	5.00
VS1996	—	—	0.75	1.50	3.00	5.00

KM# 707 PAISA

Copper, 20 mm.

Date	Mintage	F	VF	XF	Unc
VS2005 (1948)	—	0.75	1.25	1.75	2.50

KM# 707a PAISA

Brass, 20 mm. **Obv:** Footprints above crossed daggers within circle **Rev:** Crescent moon and star flank dagger at center

Date	Mintage	F	VF	XF	Unc
VS2003 (1946)	—	0.30	0.50	0.75	1.00
VS2004 (1947)	—	3.00	5.00	7.00	10.00
VS2005 (1948)	—	0.30	0.50	0.75	1.00
VS2001 (1948)	—	0.30	0.50	0.75	1.00
VS2006 (1949)	—	0.60	1.00	1.25	1.75

KM# 708 2 PAISA

Copper, 27 mm. **Obv:** Footprints above crossed daggers within circle **Rev:** Crescent moon and star flank trident at center

Date	Mintage	VG	F	VF	XF	Unc
VS1992 (1935)	—	3.00	5.00	8.50	13.50	—

KM# 709.1 2 PAISA

Copper, 27 mm. **Obv:** Footprints above crossed daggers within circle **Rev:** Crescent moon and star flank dagger ant center **Note:** 2mm wide rim.

Date	Mintage	F	VF	XF	Unc
VS1993 (1936)	473,000	1.00	2.00	3.00	5.00
VS1994 (1937)	1,133,000	1.00	2.00	3.00	5.00
VS1995 (1938)	—	1.00	2.00	3.00	5.00
VS1996 (1939)	—	1.00	2.00	3.00	5.00

KM# 709.2 2 PAISA

Copper, 25 mm. **Obv:** Footprints above crossed daggers within circle **Rev:** Crescent moon and star flank dagger at center **Note:** Rim is 1mm wide or less.

Date	Mintage	F	VF	XF	Unc
VS1993 (1936)	—	0.60	1.00	1.75	3.00
VS1994 (1937)	—	0.50	.0.75	1.50	2.50
VS1995 (1938)	—	2.00	3.50	5.00	7.50
VS1996 (1939)	—	0.30	0.50	1.00	1.50
VS1997 (1940)	—	0.50	0.75	1.50	2.50
VS1998 (1941)	—	0.50	0.75	1.50	2.50
VS1999 (1942)	—	0.50	0.75	1.50	2.50

KM# 710 2 PAISA

Copper, 23 mm. **Obv:** Footprints above crossed daggers within circle **Rev:** Crescent moon and star flank dagger at center

Date	Mintage	F	VF	XF	Unc
VS1999 (1942)	—	0.30	0.50	1.00	2.00
VS2000 (1943)	—	0.30	0.50	1.00	2.00
VS2003 (1946)	—	0.30	0.50	1.00	2.00
VS2005 (1948)	—	3.00	5.00	7.00	10.00

KM# 710a 2 PAISA

Brass **Obv:** Footprints above crossed daggers within circle **Rev:** Crescent moon and star flank dagger at center

Date	Mintage	F	VF	XF	Unc
VS1999 (1942)	—	0.30	0.50	1.00	2.00
VS2000 (1943)	—	0.30	0.50	1.00	2.00
VS2001 (1944)	—	0.30	0.50	1.00	2.00
VS2005 (1948)	—	1.75	3.00	5.00	7.50
VS2008 (1951)	—	0.30	0.50	1.00	2.00
VS2009 (1952)	—	0.30	0.50	1.00	2.00
VS2010 (1953)	—	0.30	0.50	1.00	2.00

KM# 711 5 PAISA

Copper, 30 mm. **Obv:** Footprints above crossed daggers within circle **Rev:** Crescent moon and star flank trident at center

Date	Mintage	F	VF	XF	Unc
VS1992 (1935)	—	1.50	3.00	4.50	6.50
VS1993 (1936)	878,000	1.50	3.00	4.50	6.50
VS1994 (1937)	403,000	1.50	3.00	4.50	6.50
VS1995 (1938)	—	1.00	2.00	3.00	5.00
VS1996 (1939)	—	1.50	3.00	4.50	6.50
VS1997 (1940)	—	1.50	3.00	4.50	6.50
VS1998 (1941)	—	—	—	—	—

KM# 712 5 PAISA

Copper-Nickel-Zinc **Obv:** Lamp within center circle **Rev:** Crescent moon and star flank trident above inscription

Date	Mintage	F	VF	XF	Unc
VS2000 (1943)	—	0.65	1.00	1.50	2.50
VS2009 (1952)	—	1.75	3.00	5.00	8.50
VS2010 (1953)	—	1.25	2.00	3.00	5.00

KM# 712a 5 PAISA

Copper-Nickel **Obv:** Lamp within center circle **Rev. Inscription:** Crescent moon and star flank trident above inscription

Date	Mintage	F	VF	XF	Unc
VS2010 (1953) Restrike	—	0.65	1.00	1.50	2.50

KM# 714 20 PAISA

2.2161 g., 0.3330 Silver .0237 oz. ASW **Obv:** Trident **Rev:** Dagger flanked by garlands from above

Date	Mintage	F	VF	XF	Unc
VS1989 (1932)	—	2.25	4.00	5.00	6.50
VS1991 (1934)	—	1.75	3.50	4.50	6.00
VS1992 (1935)	—	1.75	3.50	4.50	6.00
VS1993 (1936)	—	1.75	3.50	4.50	6.00
VS1994 (1937)	—	3.75	6.50	10.00	15.00
VS1995 (1938)	—	1.75	3.50	4.50	6.00
VS1996 (1939)	—	1.75	3.50	4.50	6.00
VS1997 (1940)	—	1.75	3.50	4.50	6.00
VS1998 (1941)	—	1.75	3.50	4.50	6.00
VS1999 (1942)	—	1.75	3.50	4.50	6.00
VS2000 (1943)	—	1.75	3.50	4.50	6.00
VS2001 (1944)	—	1.75	3.50	4.50	6.00
VS2003 (1946)	—	1.75	3.50	4.50	6.00
VS2004 (1947)	—	1.75	3.50	4.50	6.00

KM# 715 20 PAISA

2.2161 g., 0.3330 Silver .0237 oz. ASW

Date	Mintage	F	VF	XF	Unc
VS1989 (1932)	—	2.25	4.00	6.00	8.50

Note: The date VS1989 is given in different style characters. Refer to 50 Paisa KM#719 and 1 Rupee, KM#724 for style

KM# 716 20 PAISA

2.2161 g., 0.3330 Silver .0237 oz. ASW

Date	Mintage	F	VF	XF	Unc
VS2006 (1949)	—	0.75	1.00	1.25	1.75
VS2007 (1950)	—	—	—	—	—
VS2009 (1952)	—	0.75	1.00	1.50	2.50
VS2010 (1953)	—	0.75	1.00	1.50	2.50

KM# 718 50 PAISA

5.5403 g., 0.8000 Silver .1425 oz. ASW **Obv:** Trident within small center circle **Rev:** Dagger flanked by garlands from above

Date	Mintage	F	VF	XF	Unc
VS1989 (1932)	—	5.50	6.50	8.00	10.00
VS1991 (1934)	—	2.75	4.50	7.00	10.00
VS1992 (1935)	—	2.75	4.50	7.00	10.00
VS1993 (1936)	—	2.75	4.50	7.00	10.00
VS1994 (1937)	—	2.75	4.50	7.00	10.00
VS1995 (1938)	—	2.75	4.50	7.00	10.00
VS1996 (1939)	—	2.75	4.50	7.00	10.00
VS1997 (1940)	—	2.75	4.50	7.00	10.00
VS1998 (1941)	—	2.75	4.50	7.00	10.00
VS1999 (1942)	—	2.75	4.50	7.00	10.00
VS2000 (1943)	—	2.75	4.50	7.00	10.00
VS2001 (1944)	—	2.75	4.50	7.00	10.00
VS2003 (1946)	—	2.75	4.50	7.00	10.00
VS2004 (1947)	—	2.75	4.50	7.00	10.00
VS2005 (1948)	—	2.75	4.50	7.00	10.00

KM# 719 50 PAISA

5.5403 g., 0.8000 Silver .1425 oz. ASW **Obv:** Trident within small center circle **Rev:** Dagger flanked by garlands from above

Date	Mintage	F	VF	XF	Unc
VS1989 (1932)	—	2.50	4.50	7.00	9.00

Note: The date is given in different style characters

KM# 720 50 PAISA

5.5403 g., 0.3330 Silver .0593 oz. ASW **Obv:** Four dots around trident **Rev:** Dagger flanked by garlands from above

Date	Mintage	F	VF	XF	Unc
VS2005 (1948)	—	45.00	65.00	90.00	125

KM# 721 50 PAISA

5.5403 g., 0.3330 Silver .0593 oz. ASW **Obv:** Without dots around trident **Rev:** Dagger flanked by garlands from above

Date	Mintage	F	VF	XF	Unc
VS2006 (1949)	—	1.50	2.00	2.75	4.50
VS2007 (1950)	—	1.50	2.00	2.75	4.50
VS2009/7 (1952)	—	1.50	2.25	3.00	5.00
VS2009 (1952)	—	1.50	2.00	2.75	4.50
VS2010 (1953)	—	1.50	2.00	2.75	4.50

KM# 713 1/16 RUPEE

Silver **Obv:** Inscription **Rev:** Inscription

Date	Mintage	F	VF	XF	Unc
VS(19)96 (1939)	—	12.50	20.00	32.50	50.00

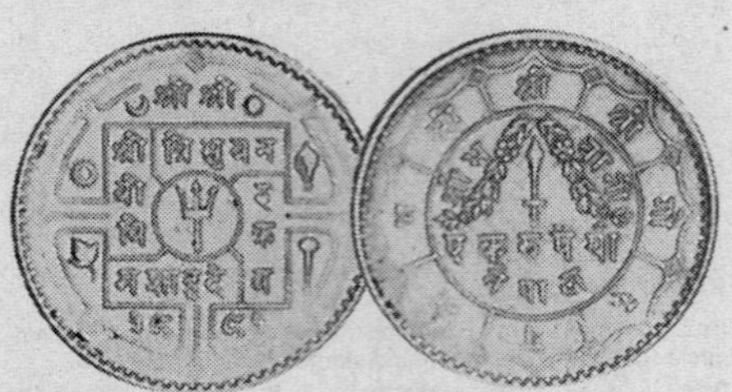

KM# 723 RUPEE

11.0806 g., 0.8000 Silver .2850 oz. ASW **Obv:** Trident within small center circle **Rev:** Dagger flanked by garlands from above

Date	Mintage	F	VF	XF	Unc
VS1989 (1932)	—	4.50	6.00	8.00	20.00
VS1991 (1934)	—	4.50	6.00	8.00	16.50
VS1992 (1935)	—	4.50	6.00	8.00	16.50
VS1993 (1936)	1,717,000	4.50	6.00	8.00	16.50
VS1994 (1937)	2,097,000	4.50	6.00	8.00	16.50
VS1995 (1938)	—	4.50	6.00	8.00	16.50
VS1996 (1939)	—	4.50	6.00	8.00	16.50
VS1997 (1940)	—	4.50	6.00	8.00	16.50
VS1998 (1941)	—	4.50	6.00	8.00	16.50
VS1999 (1942)	—	4.50	6.00	8.00	16.50
VS2000 (1943)	—	4.50	6.00	8.00	16.50
VS2001 (1944)	—	4.50	6.00	8.00	16.50
VS2003 (1946)	—	4.50	6.00	8.00	16.50
VS2005 (1948)	—	4.50	6.00	8.00	16.50

KM# 724 RUPEE

11.0806 g., 0.8000 Silver .2850 oz. ASW **Obv:** Trident within small center circle **Rev:** Dagger flanked by garlands from above

Date	Mintage	F	VF	XF	Unc
VS1989 (1932)	—	7.50	10.00	12.50	15.00

Note: The date is given in different style characters

KM# 725 RUPEE

11.0806 g., 0.3330 Silver .1186 oz. ASW **Obv:** Four dots around trident **Rev:** Dagger flanked by garlands from above

Date	Mintage	F	VF	XF	Unc
VS2005 (1948)	—	5.00	7.50	10.00	13.50

KM# 726 RUPEE

11.0806 g., 0.3330 Silver .1186 oz. ASW **Obv:** Without dots around trident **Rev:** Dagger flanked by garlands from above

Date	Mintage	F	VF	XF	Unc
VS2006 (1949)	—	2.50	3.50	5.00	7.50
VS2007 (1950)	—	2.50	3.50	5.00	7.50
VS2008 (1951)	—	2.50	3.50	5.00	7.50
VS2009 (1951)	—	2.50	3.50	5.00	7.50
VS2010 (1952)	—	2.50	3.50	5.00	7.50

ASARFI GOLD COINAGE

(Asarphi)

Fractional designations are approximate for this series. Actual Gold Weight (AGW) is used to identify each type.

Gyanendra Bir Bikram

VS2007 / 1950-51AD (first reign)

DECIMAL COINAGE

100 Paisa = 1 Rupee

KM# 729 50 PAISA

5.5403 g., 0.3330 Silver .0593 oz. ASW **Obv:** Trident within small center circle **Rev:** Dagger flanked by garlands from above

Date	Mintage	F	VF	XF	Unc
VS2007 (1950)	26	—	175	275	350

KM# 731 MOHAR

Gold

Date	Mintage	F	VF	XF	Unc
VS2007 (1950) Rare	—	—	—	—	—

KM# 730 RUPEE

11.0806 g., 0.3330 Silver .1186 oz. ASW **Obv:** Trident within small center circle **Rev:** Dagger flanked by garlands from above

Date	Mintage	F	VF	XF	Unc
VS2007 (1950)	—	4.50	6.50	9.00	12.50

KM# 732 TOLA

Gold

Date	Mintage	F	VF	XF	Unc
VS2007 (1950) Rare	—	—	—	—	—

Trivhuvan Bir Bikram

VS2007-2011 / 1951-1955AD (second reign)

DECIMAL COINAGE

100 Paisa = 1 Rupee

KM# 740 50 PAISA

Copper-Nickel, 25 mm. **Obv:** Head of Tribhuvan Bir Bikram right on 5-pointed star **Rev:** Sun rising back of hills, grain sprigs flank

Date	Mintage	F	VF	XF	Unc
VS2010 (1953)	—	0.50	1.00	2.00	4.00
VS2011 (1954)	—	0.35	0.75	1.50	3.00

KM# 742 RUPEE

Copper-Nickel **Obv:** Head of Tribhuvan Bir Bikram right on 5-pointed star **Note:** Equal denticles at rim.

Date	Mintage	F	VF	XF	Unc
VS2010 (1953)	—	0.75	1.25	2.25	4.50
VS2011 (1954)	—	0.75	1.25	2.25	4.50

KM# 743 RUPEE

Copper-Nickel **Obv:** Head of Tribhuvan Bir Bikram right on 5-pointed star **Rev:** Sun rising back of hills, grain sprigs flank **Note:** Unequal denticles at rim.

Date	Mintage	F	VF	XF	Unc
VS2011 (1954)	—	0.75	1.25	2.25	4.50

ASARFI GOLD COINAGE

(Asarphi)

Fractional designations are approximate for this series. Actual Gold Weight (AGW) is used to identify each type.

KM# 741 1/2 ASARPHI

5.8000 g., Gold **Obv:** Head of Tribhuvan Bir Bikram right on 5-pointed star **Note:** Portrait type.

Date	Mintage	F	VF	XF	Unc
VS2010 (1953)	—	—	125	145	175

Note: KM#741 is normally found as a restrike ca. 1968

KM# 744 ASARPHI

11.6600 g., Gold **Obv:** Head of Tribhuvan Bir Bikram right on 5-pointed star

Date	Mintage	F	VF	XF	Unc
VS2010 (1953)	—	—	225	245	285

Note: KM#744 normally found as a restrike ca. 1968

Mahendra Bir Bikram
VS2012-2028 / 1955-1971AD

DECIMAL COINAGE

100 Paisa = 1 Rupee

KM# 745.1 PAISA

Brass, 18 mm. **Subject:** Mahendra Coronation **Obv:** Crown **Rev:** Numeral at center, sprigs at sides **Note:** Prev. KM#745.

Date	Mintage	F	VF	XF	Unc
VS2013 (1956) Narrow rim	—	0.30	0.50	0.75	1.00

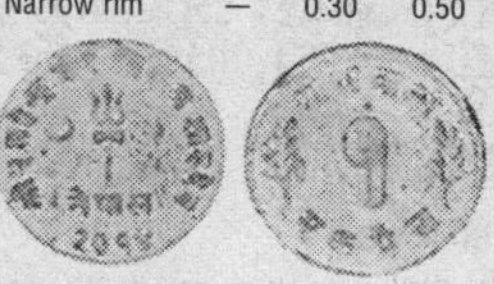

KM# 746 PAISA

Brass, 16 mm. **Obv:** Crescent and star flank trident at center **Rev:** Numerals with shading

Date	Mintage	F	VF	XF	Unc
VS2014 (1957)	—	0.10	0.15	0.25	0.40
VS2015 (1958)	—	0.10	0.15	0.25	0.40
VS2018 (1961)	—	0.10	0.15	0.25	0.40
VS2019 (1962)	—	0.10	0.15	0.25	0.40
VS2020 (1963)	—	0.10	0.15	0.25	0.40

KM# 745.2 PAISA

Brass **Subject:** Mahendra coronation

Date	Mintage	F	VF	XF	Unc
VS2013 (1958) Wide rim	—	0.30	0.50	0.75	1.00

KM# 747 PAISA

Brass **Obv:** Crescent moon and star flank trident at center **Rev:** Numerals without shading

Date	Mintage	F	VF	XF	Unc
VS2021 (1964)	—	0.10	0.15	0.20	0.30
VS2022 (1965)	—	0.10	0.15	0.25	0.40

KM# 748 PAISA

Aluminum **Obv:** Flower above hills **Rev:** National flower

Date	Mintage	F	VF	XF	Unc
VS2023 (1966)	—	—	0.10	0.15	0.25
VS2025 (1968)	—	—	0.10	0.15	0.25
VS2026 (1969)	—	—	0.10	0.15	0.25
VS2027 (1970) Proof	2,187	Value: 1.25			
VS2028 (1971)	—	—	0.10	0.15	0.25
VS2028 (1971) Proof	2,380	Value: 1.25			

KM# 750.1 2 PAISA

Brass, 20.5 mm. **Subject:** Mahendra Coronation **Obv:** Crown **Rev:** Numeral at center **Note:** Narrow rim.

Date	Mintage	F	VF	XF	Unc
VS2013 (1956)	—	0.30	0.50	0.75	1.00

KM# 750.2 2 PAISA

Brass **Subject:** Mahendra coronation **Obv:** Crown **Rev:** Numeral at center **Note:** Wide rim.

Date	Mintage	F	VF	XF	Unc
VS2013 (1956)	—	0.30	0.50	0.75	1.00

KM# 751 2 PAISA

Brass **Obv:** Crescent moon and sun flank trident **Rev:** Numerals with shading

Date	Mintage	F	VF	XF	Unc
VS2014 (1957)	—	0.10	0.15	0.25	0.40
VS2015 (1958)	—	0.10	0.15	0.25	0.40
VS2016 (1959)	—	0.10	0.15	0.25	0.40
VS2018 (1961)	—	0.10	0.15	0.25	0.40
VS2019 (1962)	—	0.10	0.15	0.25	0.40
VS2020 (1963)	—	0.10	0.15	0.25	0.40

KM# 752 2 PAISA

Brass **Obv:** Crescent moon and sun flank trident at center **Rev:** Numerals wtihout shading

Date	Mintage	F	VF	XF	Unc
VS2021 (1964)	—	0.10	0.15	0.20	0.35
VS2022 (1965)	—	0.10	0.15	0.25	0.50
VS2023 (1966)	—	0.10	0.15	0.25	0.50

KM# 753 2 PAISA

Aluminum **Obv:** Trident with sun and moon flanking above hills **Rev:** Himalayan Monal pheasant

Date	Mintage	F	VF	XF	Unc
VS2023 (1966)	—	—	0.10	0.15	0.75
VS2024 (1967)	—	—	0.10	0.15	0.75
VS2025 (1968)	—	—	0.10	0.15	0.75
VS2026 (1969)	—	—	0.10	0.15	0.75
VS2027 (1970)	—	—	0.10	0.15	0.75
VS2027 (1970) Proof	2,187	Value: 1.50			
VS2028 (1971)	—	—	0.10	0.15	0.75
VS2028 (1971) Proof	2,380	Value: 1.50			

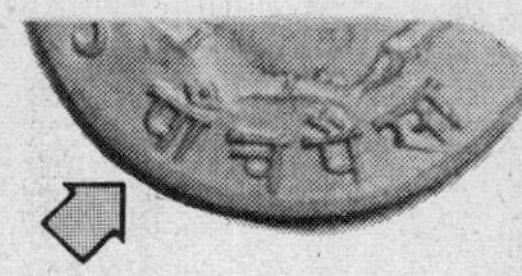

KM# 756.1 5 PAISA

Bronze, 22 mm. **Subject:** Mahendra Coronation **Obv:** Crown **Rev:** Numeral within floral outline **Note:** Wide rim with accent mark.

Date	Mintage	F	VF	XF	Unc
VS2013 (1955)	—	10.00	20.00	30.00	40.00

KM# 756.2 5 PAISA

Bronze, 22 mm. **Subject:** Mahendra coronation **Obv:** Crown **Rev:** Numeral within floral outline **Note:** Narrow rim.

Date	Mintage	F	VF	XF	Unc
VS2013 (1955) Restrike	—	0.35	0.60	1.00	1.50

KM# 756.3 5 PAISA

Bronze, 22 mm. **Subject:** Mahendra coronation **Obv:** Crown **Rev:** Numeral within floral outline **Note:** Without accent mark.

Date	Mintage	F	VF	XF	Unc
VS2013 (1955)	—	1.00	2.00	3.00	5.00

KM# 757 5 PAISA

Bronze, 22.5 mm. **Obv:** Trident at center **Rev:** Numerals with shading

Date	Mintage	F	VF	XF	Unc
VS2014 (1957)	—	0.10	0.20	0.30	0.75
VS2015 (1958)	—	0.10	0.20	0.30	0.75
VS2016 (1959)	—	0.10	0.30	0.50	1.00
VS2017 (1960)	—	0.10	0.20	0.30	0.75
VS2018 (1961)	—	0.10	0.20	0.30	0.75
VS2019 (1962)	—	0.10	0.20	0.30	0.75
VS2020 (1963)	—	0.10	0.20	0.30	0.75

KM# 758 5 PAISA

Aluminum-Bronze, 22.5 mm. **Obv:** Crescent moon and sun flank trident at center **Rev:** Numerals without shading

Date	Mintage	F	VF	XF	Unc
VS2021 (1964)	—	0.50	1.00	1.50	2.50

KM# 758a 5 PAISA

Bronze, 21 mm. **Obv:** Crescent moon and sun flank trident at center **Rev:** Numeral within shaded floral outline

Date	Mintage	F	VF	XF	Unc
VS2021 (1964)	—	0.10	0.15	0.25	0.50
VS2022 (1965)	—	0.10	0.15	0.30	0.60
VS2023 (1966)	—	0.10	0.15	0.30	0.60

KM# 759 5 PAISA

Aluminum, 21 mm. **Obv:** Trident with sun and moon flanking above hills **Rev:** Ox left

Date	Mintage	F	VF	XF	Unc
VS2023 (1966)	—	—	0.15	0.25	1.00
VS2024 (1967)	—	—	0.10	0.20	1.00
VS2025 (1968)	—	—	0.10	0.20	1.00
VS2026 (1969)	—	—	0.10	0.20	1.00
VS2027 (1970)	—	—	0.10	0.20	1.00
VS2027 (1970) Proof	2,187	Value: 1.75			

Date	Mintage	F	VF	XF	Unc
VS2028 (1971)	—	—	0.10	0.20	1.00
VS2028 (1971) Proof	2,038	Value: 1.75			

KM# 761 10 PAISA

Bronze, 24.5 mm. **Subject:** Mahendra Coronation **Obv:** Crown **Rev:** Shaded numeral

Date	Mintage	F	VF	XF	Unc
VS2013 (1956)	—	0.25	0.50	0.75	1.50

KM# 762 10 PAISA

Bronze, 25 mm. **Obv:** Crescent moon and sun flank trident **Rev:** Numerals with shading

Date	Mintage	F	VF	XF	Unc
VS2014 (1957)	—	2.75	4.50	7.00	10.00
VS2015 (1958)	—	0.15	0.25	0.50	0.75
VS2016 (1959)	—	3.00	5.00	7.00	10.00
VS2018 (1961)	—	0.15	0.25	0.50	0.75
VS2019 (1962)	—	0.15	0.25	0.50	0.75
VS2020 (1963)	—	0.15	0.25	0.50	0.75

KM# 763 10 PAISA

Aluminum-Bronze **Obv:** Crescent moon and sun flank trident at center **Rev:** Numerals without shading

Date	Mintage	F	VF	XF	Unc
VS2021 (1964)	—	0.75	1.25	2.00	3.00

KM# 764 10 PAISA

Bronze, 25 mm. **Note:** Modified design.

Date	Mintage	F	VF	XF	Unc
VS2021 (1964)	—	0.10	0.15	0.25	0.50
VS2022 (1965)	—	0.10	0.15	0.25	0.50
VS2023 (1966)	—	0.10	0.15	0.25	0.50

KM# 765 10 PAISA

Brass **Obv:** Trident with sun and moon flanking above hills **Rev:** Ox left

Date	Mintage	F	VF	XF	Unc
VS2023 (1966)	—	—	0.15	0.25	1.00
VS2024 (1967)	—	—	0.15	0.25	1.00
VS2025 (1968)	—	—	15.00	17.50	20.00
VS2026 (1969)	—	—	0.10	0.20	1.00
VS2027 (1970)	—	—	0.10	0.20	1.00
VS2027 (1970) Proof	2,187	Value: 2.00			
VS2028 (1971)	—	—	0.10	0.20	1.00
VS2028 (1971) Proof	2,380	Value: 2.00			

Note: Birendra Bir Bikram also struck a 10 Paisa VS2028, see KM#806

KM# 766 10 PAISA

Brass **Series:** F.A.O. **Obv:** Grain sprig at center **Rev:** Ox left

Date	Mintage	F	VF	XF	Unc
VS2028 (1971)	1,500,000	—	0.10	0.20	1.00

KM# 770 25 PAISA

Copper-Nickel **Subject:** Mahendra Coronation

Date	Mintage	F	VF	XF	Unc
VS2013 (1956)	—	0.30	0.50	0.70	1.00

KM# 771 25 PAISA

Copper-Nickel, 19 mm. **Obv:** Four characters in line above trident **Rev:** Small character at bottom (outer circle)

Date	Mintage	F	VF	XF	Unc
VS2015 (1958)	—	1.50	2.50	4.00	6.00
VS2018 (1961)	—	0.25	0.40	0.60	0.80
VS2020 (1963)	—	0.25	0.40	0.60	0.80
VS2021 (1964)	—	0.30	0.50	0.75	1.00
VS2022 (1965)	—	2.00	3.50	6.00	9.00

KM# 771a 25 PAISA

2.9900 g., 840.0000 Silver .0913 oz. ASW **Obv:** Trident within small center circle **Rev:** Dagger flanked by garlands from above

Date	Mintage	F	VF	XF	Unc
VS2017/6/5 (1960)	—	—	—	—	100

KM# 772 25 PAISA

Copper-Nickel, 19 mm. **Obv:** Trident within small center circle **Rev:** Large different character at bottom

Date	Mintage	F	VF	XF	Unc
VS2021 (1964)	—	0.30	0.50	0.70	1.00
VS2022 (1965)	—	0.30	0.50	0.70	1.00
VS2023 (1966)	—	0.30	0.50	0.70	1.00

KM# 773 25 PAISA

Copper-Nickel **Obv:** Five characters in line above trident **Rev:** Dagger flanked by garlands from above

Date	Mintage	F	VF	XF	Unc
VS2024 (1967)	—	—	0.35	0.50	0.75
VS2025 (1968)	—	—	15.00	20.00	25.00
VS2026 (1969)	—	—	0.35	0.50	0.75
VS2027 (1970)	—	—	0.35	0.50	0.75
VS2027 (1970) Proof	2,187	Value: 2.50			
VS2028 (1971)	—	—	0.35	0.50	0.75
VS2028 (1971) Proof	2,380	Value: 2.50			
VS2030 (1973)	—	—	0.35	0.50	0.75

KM# 777 50 PAISA

Copper-Nickel, 25 mm. **Obv:** Trident within small center circle **Rev:** Small character at bottom

Date	Mintage	F	VF	XF	Unc
VS2011 (1954)	—	0.50	1.00	1.50	3.00
VS2012 (1955)	—	0.25	0.50	0.75	1.00
VS2013 (1956)	—	0.25	0.50	1.00	2.00
VS2014 (1957)	—	0.25	0.50	1.00	2.00
VS2015 (1958)	—	0.25	0.50	1.00	2.00
VS2016 (1959)	—	0.25	0.50	1.00	2.00
VS2017 (1960)	—	0.25	0.30	0.75	1.25
VS2018 (1961)	—	0.25	0.50	1.00	2.00
VS2020 (1963)	—	0.25	0.30	0.75	1.50

KM# 795 50 PAISA

Copper-Nickel **Obv:** Trident within small center circle **Rev:** Dagger flanked by garlands from above **Note:** In the name of "Queen Ratna Rajya Lakshmi".

Date	Mintage	F	VF	XF	Unc
VS2012 (1955)	—	3,000	100	125	150

KM# 776 50 PAISA

Copper-Nickel **Subject:** Mahendra Coronation **Obv:** Crown **Rev:** Dagger flanked by garlands from above

Date	Mintage	F	VF	XF	Unc
VS2013 (1956)	—	0.35	0.75	1.00	1.50

KM# 778 50 PAISA

Copper-Nickel, 25 mm. **Obv:** Trident within small center circle **Rev:** Large different character at bottom

Date	Mintage	F	VF	XF	Unc
VS2021 (1964)	—	0.25	0.35	0.50	0.75
VS2022 (1965)	—	0.25	0.50	0.75	1.50
VS2023 (1966)	—	0.25	0.50	0.75	1.00

KM# 779 50 PAISA

Copper-Nickel **Obv:** Four characters in line above trident **Rev:** Dagger flanked by garlands from above **Note:** Reduced size, 23.5mm.

Date	Mintage	F	VF	XF	Unc
VS2023 (1966)	—	0.25	0.50	0.75	1.50

KM# 780 50 PAISA

Copper-Nickel **Obv:** Five characters in line above trident **Rev:** Dagger flanked by garlands from above

Date	Mintage	F	VF	XF	Unc
VS2025 (1968)	—	—	0.30	0.50	1.00
VS2026 (1969)	—	—	0.30	0.50	0.85
VS2027 (1970) Proof	2,187	Value: 3.00			
VS2028 (1971) Proof	2,380	Value: 3.00			
VS2030 (1973)	—	—	0.30	0.50	0.85

KM# 784 RUPEE

Copper-Nickel, 30 mm.

Date	Mintage	F	VF	XF	Unc
VS2011 (1954)	—	1.25	2.25	3.50	5.00
VS2012 (1955)	—	1.00	1.75	2.50	4.00

KM# 797 RUPEE

Copper-Nickel **Obv:** Trident within small center circle **Rev:** Dagger flanked by garlands from above **Note:** In the name of "Queen Ratna Rajya Lakshmi".

Date	Mintage	F	VF	XF	Unc
VS2012 (1955)	2,000	—	100	150	175

KM# 785 RUPEE

Copper-Nickel, 28.5 mm. **Obv:** Trident within small center circle **Rev:** Small character at bottom **Note:** Reduced size.

Date	Mintage	F	VF	XF	Unc
VS2012 (1955)	—	0.50	0.85	1.25	1.75
VS2013 (1956)	—	0.50	0.85	1.25	1.75
VS2014 (1957)	—	0.50	0.85	1.25	1.75
VS2015 (1958)	—	0.50	0.85	1.25	1.75
VS2016 (1959)	—	0.50	0.85	1.25	1.75
VS2018 (1961)	—	0.50	0.85	1.25	1.75
VS2020 (1963)	—	0.50	0.85	1.25	1.75

KM# 790 RUPEE

Copper-Nickel **Subject:** Mahendra Coronation **Obv:** Crown **Rev:** Dagger flanked by garlands from above

Date	Mintage	F	VF	XF	Unc
VS2013 (1956)	—	—	1.25	1.75	2.50

KM# 786 RUPEE

Copper-Nickel **Obv:** Trident within small center circle **Rev:** Large character at bottom **Note:** Photo reduced.

Date	Mintage	F	VF	XF	Unc
VS2021 (1964)	—	0.50	0.75	1.00	1.50
VS2022 (1965)	—	0.50	1.00	1.50	2.50
VS2023 (1966)	—	4.50	7.50	10.00	15.00

KM# 787 RUPEE

Copper-Nickel, 27 mm. **Obv:** Four characters in line above trident **Rev:** Dagger flanked by garlands from above **Note:** Reduced size, 27.5mm.

Date	Mintage	F	VF	XF	Unc
VS2023 (1966)	—	0.75	1.00	1.35	2.00

KM# 788 RUPEE

Copper-Nickel **Obv:** Five characters in line above trident **Rev:** Dagger flanked by garlands from above

Date	Mintage	F	VF	XF	Unc
VS2025 (1968)	—	—	1.00	1.50	2.00
VS2026 (1969)	—	—	1.00	1.40	2.00
VS2027 (1970) Proof	2,187	Value: 4.50			
VS2028 (1971) Proof	2,380	Value: 4.50			

KM# 794 10 RUPEE

15.6000 g., 0.6000 Silver .3009 oz. ASW **Series:** F.A.O. **Obv:** Bust of Mahendra Bir Bikram left **Rev:** Trident and 1/2 cogwheel above grain sprig

Date	Mintage	F	VF	XF	Unc
VS2025 (1968)	1,000,000	—	5.00	6.00	9.00

ASARFI GOLD COINAGE

(Asarphi)

Fractional designations are approximate for this series. Actual Gold Weight (AGW) is used to identify each type.

KM# 767 1/6 ASARPHI

1.9000 g., Gold **Subject:** Mahendra Coronation

Date	Mintage	F	VF	XF	Unc
VS2013 (1956)	—	—	50.00	60.00	100

KM# 775 1/4 ASARPHI

2.5000 g., Gold **Obv:** Trident within small circle at center **Rev:** Dagger flanked by garlands from above **Note:** Reduced weight.

Date	Mintage	F	VF	XF	Unc
VS2026 (1969)	—	—	—	75.00	110

KM# 796 1/2 ASARPHI

Gold **Note:** In the name of "Queen Ratna Rajya Lakshmi".

Date	Mintage	F	VF	XF	Unc
VS2012 (1955)	—	—	—	—	—

KM# 782 1/2 ASARPHI

5.8000 g., Gold **Obv:** Trident within small circle at center **Rev:** Dagger flanked by garlands from above

Date	Mintage	F	VF	XF	Unc
VS2012 (1955)	—	—	125	140	170
VS2019 (1962)	—	—	125	140	170

KM# 781 1/2 ASARPHI

5.8000 g., Gold **Subject:** Mahendra Coronation

Date	Mintage	F	VF	XF	Unc
VS2013 (1956)	—	—	125	140	170

KM# 783 1/2 ASARPHI

5.0000 g., Gold **Subject:** Birendra Marriage

Date	Mintage	F	VF	XF	Unc
VS2026 (1969)	—	—	—	150	180

KM# 789 ASARPHI

Gold **Obv:** Trident within small center circle **Rev:** Dagger flanked by garlands from above

Date	Mintage	F	VF	XF	Unc
VS2012 (1955)	—	—	230	250	300
VS2019 (1962)	—	—	230	250	300

KM# 798 ASARPHI

11.6600 g., Gold **Note:** In the name of "Queen Ratna Rajya Lakshmi".

Date	Mintage	F	VF	XF	Unc
VS2012 (1955)	—	—	230	250	300
VS2018 (1960)	—	—	230	250	300

KM# 791 ASARPHI

Gold **Subject:** Mahendra Coronation

Date	Mintage	F	VF	XF	Unc
VS2013 (1956)	—	—	230	250	300

KM# 792 ASARPHI

10.0000 g., Gold **Obv:** Trident within small center circle **Rev:** Dagger flanked by garlands from above

Date	Mintage	F	VF	XF	Unc
VS2026 (1969)	—	—	225	245	300

KM# 793 2 ASARFI

Gold

Date	Mintage	F	VF	XF	Unc
VS2012 (1955)	—	—	500	550	625

Birendra Bir Bikram

VS2028-2058 / 1971-2001 AD

DECIMAL COINAGE

100 Paisa = 1 Rupee

KM# 799 PAISA

Aluminum **Obv:** Trident with sun and moon flanking above hills **Rev:** National flower

Date	Mintage	F	VF	XF	Unc
VS2028 (1971)	10,000	—	0.20	0.30	0.40
VS2029 (1972)	3,036,000	—	0.10	0.15	0.25
VS2029 (1972) Proof	3,943	Value: 0.60			
VS2030 (1973)	1,279,000	—	0.10	0.15	0.25
VS2030 (1973) Proof	8,891	Value: 0.40			
VS2031 (1974)	430,000	—	0.10	0.15	0.25
VS2031 (1974) Proof	11,000	Value: 0.40			
VS2032 (1975)	324,000	—	0.10	0.15	0.25
VS2033 (1976)	217,000	—	—	0.10	0.25
VS2034 (1977)	1,040,000	—	0.10	0.15	0.25
VS2035 (1978)	394,000	—	0.10	0.15	0.25
VS2036 (1979)	—	—	0.10	0.15	0.25

KM# 800 PAISA

Aluminum **Subject:** Birendra Coronation **Obv:** Crown

Date	Mintage	F	VF	XF	Unc
VS2031 (1974)	75,000	—	0.10	0.15	0.25

KM# 800a PAISA

Copper-Nickel **Subject:** Birendra Coronation **Obv:** Crown **Rev:** Dagger flanked by garlands from above

Date	Mintage	F	VF	XF	Unc
VS2031 (1974) Proof	1,000	Value: 2.50			

KM# 1012 PAISA

Aluminum **Obv:** Crown **Rev:** Value

Date	Mintage	F	VF	XF	Unc
VS2039 (1982)	—	—	4.00	6.00	8.00
VS2040 (1983)	42,000	—	—	—	—

KM# 801 2 PAISA

Aluminum, 20 mm. **Obv:** Flower above hills with sun and moon flanking **Rev:** Himalayan Monal pheasant

Date	Mintage	F	VF	XF	Unc
VS2028 (1971)	8,319	—	0.20	0.30	0.75
VS2029 (1972)	5,206,000	—	0.10	0.15	0.75
VS2029 (1972) Proof	3,943	Value: 1.00			
VS2030 (1973)	2,563,000	—	0.10	0.15	0.75
VS2030 (1973) Proof	8,891	Value: 0.75			
VS2031 (1974) Proof	11,000	Value: 0.75			
VS2033 (1976)	72,000	—	0.10	0.15	0.75
VS2035 (1978)	26,000	—	0.10	0.15	0.75

KM# 802 5 PAISA

Aluminum, 20.5 mm. **Obv:** Trident with sun and moon flanking above hills **Rev:** Ox left

Date	Mintage	F	VF	XF	Unc
VS2028 (1971)	3,700,000	—	0.10	0.20	0.75
VS2029 (1972)	23,578,000	—	0.10	0.20	0.75
VS2029 (1972) Proof	3,943	Value: 1.00			
VS2030 (1973)	12,320,000	—	0.10	0.20	0.75
VS2030 (1973) Proof	8,891	Value: 1.00			
VS2031 (1974)	15,730,000	—	0.10	0.20	0.75
VS2031 (1974) Proof	11,000	Value: 1.00			
VS2032 (1975)	19,747,000	—	0.10	0.20	0.75
VS2033 (1976)	29,619,000	—	0.10	0.20	0.75
VS2034 (1977)	27,222,000	—	0.10	0.20	0.75
VS2035 (1978)	27,613,000	—	0.10	0.20	0.75
VS2036 (1979)	—	—	0.10	0.20	0.75
VS2037 (1980)	13,235,000	—	0.10	0.20	0.75
VS2038 (1981)	15,137,000	—	0.10	0.20	0.75
VS2039 (1982)	8,971,000	—	0.10	0.20	0.75

KM# 803 5 PAISA

Aluminum **Series:** F.A.O. **Obv:** Value Designer: Gopal Bahadur Shrestha

Date	Mintage	F	VF	XF	Unc
VS2031 (1974)	4,584,000	—	0.10	0.15	0.25

KM# 804 5 PAISA

Aluminum **Subject:** Birendra Coronation **Obv:** Crown **Rev:** Dagger flanked by garlands from above

Date	Mintage	F	VF	XF	Unc
VS2031 (1974)	2,869,000	—	0.10	0.25	0.50

KM# 804a 5 PAISA

Copper-Nickel **Subject:** Birendra Coronation **Obv:** Crown **Rev:** Dagger flanked by garlands from above

Date	Mintage	F	VF	XF	Unc
VS2031 (1974) Proof	1,000	Value: 3.00			

KM# 1013 5 PAISA

0.8500 g., Aluminum, 18 mm. **Obv:** Crown **Rev:** Value

Date	Mintage	F	VF	XF	Unc
VS2039 (1982)	8,971,000	—	7.00	10.00	15.00
VS2040 (1983)	6,430,000	—	—	0.10	0.25
VS2041 (1984)	9,634,000	—	—	0.10	0.25
VS2042 (1985)	58,000	—	—	0.10	0.25
VS2043 (1986)	2,937,000	—	—	0.10	0.25
VS2044 (1987)	3,126,000	—	—	0.10	0.25
VS2045 (1988)	1,030,000	—	—	0.10	0.25
VS2046 (1989)	—	—	—	0.10	0.25
VS2047 (1990)	—	—	—	0.10	0.25

KM# 806 10 PAISA

Brass **Obv:** Trident with sun and moon flanking above hills **Rev:** Ox left

Date	Mintage	F	VF	XF	Unc
VS2028 (1971) In sets only	5,035	—	0.25	0.40	1.50

Note: Mahendra Bir Bikram also struck a 10 Paisa VS2028, see KM#765

KM# 807 10 PAISA

Brass **Obv:** Trident with sun and moon flanking above hills **Rev:** Value with grain sprigs at sides of coin

Date	Mintage	F	VF	XF	Unc
VS2029 (1972)	3,297,000	—	0.15	0.25	0.40
VS2029 (1972) Proof	3,943	Value: 1.00			
VS2030 (1973)	5,670,000	—	0.15	0.25	0.40
VS2030 (1973) Proof	8,891	Value: 0.70			
VS2031 (1974) Proof	11,000	Value: 0.70			

KM# 808 10 PAISA

Aluminum **Subject:** Birendra Coronation **Obv:** Crown **Rev:** Dagger flanked by garlands from above

Date	Mintage	F	VF	XF	Unc
VS2031 (1974)	192,000	—	0.10	0.20	0.35

KM# 808a 10 PAISA

Copper-Nickel **Subject:** Birendra Coronation **Obv:** Crown **Rev:** Dagger flanked by garlands from above

Date	Mintage	F	VF	XF	Unc
VS2031 (1974) Proof	1,000	Value: 3.50			

KM# 809 10 PAISA

Brass **Series:** F.A.O. International Women's Year **Obv:** Busts left **Rev:** Value within grain sprigs

Date	Mintage	F	VF	XF	Unc
VS2032 (1975)	2,500,000	—	0.10	0.15	0.25

KM# 810 10 PAISA

Brass **Subject:** Agricultural Developement **Obv:** Crown **Rev:** Value

Date	Mintage	F	VF	XF	Unc
VS2033 (1976)	10,000,000	—	0.10	0.15	0.25

KM# 811 10 PAISA

Aluminum **Series:** International Year of the Child **Obv:** Trident within small circle at center **Rev:** Symbol at center, rising sun above

Date	Mintage	F	VF	XF	Unc
VS2036 (1979)	213,000	—	0.10	0.15	0.25

KM# 812 10 PAISA

Aluminum **Subject:** Education for Village Women **Obv:** Trident within small circle at center **Rev:** Open book

Date	Mintage	F	VF	XF	Unc
VS2036 (1979)	Inc. above	—	0.10	0.15	0.50

KM# 1014.1 10 PAISA

1.3000 g., Aluminum, 21.5 mm. **Obv:** Crown **Rev:** Large ears of grain

Date	Mintage	F	VF	XF	Unc
VS2039 (1982)	796	—	7.00	10.00	15.00
VS2040 (1983)	—	—	—	0.10	0.30
VS2041 (1984)	7,834,000	—	—	0.10	0.30
VS2042 (1985)	99,000	—	—	0.10	0.30

KM# 1014.2 10 PAISA

1.3000 g., Aluminum, 21.5 mm. **Obv:** Crown **Rev:** Small ears of grain

Date	Mintage	F	VF	XF	Unc
VS2041 (1984)	—	—	—	0.10	0.30
VS2042 (1985)	Inc. above	—	—	0.10	0.30
VS2043 (1986)	10,000	—	—	0.10	0.30
VS2044 (1987)	30,172,000	—	—	0.10	0.30
VS2045 (1988)	4,140,000	—	—	0.10	0.30
VS2046 (1989)	—	—	—	0.10	0.30
VS2047 (1990)	—	—	—	0.10	0.30
VS2048 (1991)	—	—	—	0.10	0.30
VS2049 (1992)	—	—	—	0.10	0.30

KM# 1014.3 10 PAISA

0.7200 g., Aluminum, 17 mm. **Obv:** Crown **Rev:** Value, grain ears flank **Edge:** Plain **Note:** Reduced size.

Date	Mintage	F	VF	XF	Unc
VS2051 (1994)	—	—	—	0.10	0.30
VS2052 (1995)	—	—	—	0.10	0.30
VS2053 (1996)	—	—	—	0.10	0.30
VS2054 (1997)	—	—	—	0.10	0.30
VS2055 (1998)	—	—	—	0.10	0.30
VS2056 (1999)	—	—	—	0.10	0.30
VS2057 (2000)	—	—	—	0.10	0.30

KM# 813 20 PAISA

Brass **Series:** F.A.O. **Obv:** Trident within small circle at center

Date	Mintage	F	VF	XF	Unc
VS2035 (1978)	234,000	—	0.35	0.75	1.00

KM# 814 20 PAISA

Brass **Series:** International Year of the Child **Obv:** Trident within small center circle **Rev:** Emblem below rising sun

Date	Mintage	F	VF	XF	Unc
VS2036 (1979)	30,000	—	0.35	0.75	1.00

KM# 815 25 PAISA

3.0000 g., Copper-Nickel **Obv:** Trident within small center circle **Rev:** Dagger flanked by garlands from above **Note:** Varieties exist.

Date	Mintage	F	VF	XF	Unc
VS2028 (1971)	5,691	—	0.40	0.60	0.80
VS2029 (1972) Proof	3,943	Value: 1.25			
VS2030 (1973)	8,676,000	—	0.30	0.40	0.50
VS2030 (1973) Proof	8,891	Value: 0.80			
VS2031 (1974)	1,172,000	—	0.35	0.50	0.75
VS2031 (1974) Proof	11,000	Value: 0.80			
VS2032 (1975)	4,584,000	—	0.30	0.40	0.50
VS2033 (1976)	1,837,000	—	0.30	0.40	0.50
VS2034 (1977)	3,808,000	—	0.30	0.40	0.50
VS2035 (1978)	5,964,000	—	0.30	0.40	0.50
VS2036 (1979)	—	—	0.30	0.40	0.50
VS2037 (1980)	2,047,000	—	0.30	0.40	0.50
VS2038 (1981)	1,580,000	—	0.30	0.40	0.50
VS2039 (1982)	7,185,000	—	0.30	0.40	0.50

KM# 816.1 25 PAISA

Copper-Nickel **Subject:** Birendra Coronation **Obv:** Crown **Rev:** Dagger flanked by garlands from above

Date	Mintage	F	VF	XF	Unc
VS2031 (1974)	431,000	—	0.35	0.50	0.75

KM# 816.2 25 PAISA

Copper-Nickel **Subject:** Birendra Coronation **Obv:** Crown **Rev:** Dagger flanked by garlands from above **Edge:** Reeded

Date	Mintage	F	VF	XF	Unc
VS2031 (1974) Proof	1,000	Value: 4.00			

KM# 817 25 PAISA

Brass **Series:** World Food Day **Obv:** Trident within small center circle **Rev:** Corn ear at left, logo at right

Date	Mintage	F	VF	XF	Unc
VS2038 (1981)	2,000,000	—	—	0.10	0.30

KM# 818 25 PAISA

Brass **Series:** International Year of Disabled Persons **Obv:** Trident within small center circle **Rev:** Emblem at center

Date	Mintage	F	VF	XF	Unc
VS2038 (1981)	Inc. above	—	0.10	0.25	0.50

KM# 1015.1 25 PAISA

1.8000 g., Aluminum, 24.5 mm. **Obv:** Crown **Rev:** Value flanked by grain ears

Date	Mintage	F	VF	XF	Unc
VS2039 (1982)	—	—	4.00	6.00	8.00
VS2040 (1983)	7,603,000	—	0.10	0.25	0.50
VS2041 (1984)	15,534,000	—	0.10	0.25	0.50
VS2042 (1985)	12,586,000	—	0.10	0.25	0.50
VS2043 (1986)	54,000	—	0.10	0.25	0.50
VS2044 (1987)	13,633,000	—	0.10	0.25	0.50
VS2045 (1988)	13,046,000	—	0.10	0.25	0.50
VS2046 (1989)	—	—	0.10	0.25	0.50
VS2047 (1990)	—	—	0.10	0.25	0.50
VS2048 (1991)	—	—	0.10	0.25	0.50
VS2049 (1992)	—	—	0.10	0.25	0.50
VS2050 (1993)	—	—	0.10	0.25	0.50

KM# 1015.2 25 PAISA

1.5000 g., Aluminum, 20 mm. **Obv:** Crown **Rev:** Value flanked by grain ears **Edge:** Plain **Note:** Reduced size.

Date	Mintage	F	VF	XF	Unc
VS2051 (1994)	—	—	0.10	0.25	0.50
VS2052 (1995)	—	—	0.10	0.25	0.50
VS2053 (1996)	—	—	0.10	0.25	0.50
VS2054 (1997)	—	—	0.10	0.25	0.50
VS2055 (1998)	—	—	0.10	0.25	0.50
VS2056 (1999)	—	—	0.10	0.25	0.50
VS2057 (2000)	—	—	0.10	0.25	0.50

KM# 821 50 PAISA

5.0000 g., Copper-Nickel, 23.5 mm. **Obv:** Trident within small center circle **Rev:** Dagger flanked by garlands from above

Date	Mintage	F	VF	XF	Unc
VS2028 (1971)	5,343	—	0.35	0.50	1.00
VS2029 (1972)	347,000	—	0.35	0.50	0.90
VS2029 (1972) Proof	3,943	Value: 1.50			
VS2030 (1973)	998,000	—	0.35	0.50	0.90
VS2030 (1973) Proof	8,891	Value: 1.00			
VS2031 (1974)	16,000	—	0.35	0.50	1.00
VS2031 (1974) Proof	11,000	Value: 1.00			
VS2032 (1975)	227,000	—	0.35	0.50	0.90
Note: Dot in moon on reverse					
VS2033 (1976)	3,446,000	—	0.35	0.50	0.75
VS2034 (1977)	6,016,000	—	0.35	0.50	0.75
VS2035 (1978)	2,355,000	—	0.35	0.50	0.75
VS2036 (1979)	—	—	0.35	0.50	0.75
VS2037 (1980)	4,861,000	—	0.35	0.50	0.75
VS2038 (1981)	929,000	—	0.35	0.50	0.75
VS2039 (1982)	2,954,000	—	0.35	0.50	0.75

KM# 821a 50 PAISA

Copper-Nickel, 20 mm. **Obv:** Trident within small center circle **Rev:** Dagger flanked by garlands from above

Date	Mintage	F	VF	XF	Unc
VS2039 (1971)	Inc. above	—	0.10	0.25	0.50
VS2040 (1983)	72,000	—	0.10	0.25	0.50
VS2041 (1984)	5,917,000	—	0.10	0.25	0.50

KM# 822.1 50 PAISA

Copper-Nickel **Subject:** Birendra Coronation **Obv:** Crown **Rev:** Dagger flanked by garlands from above **Note:** 1mm thick.

Date	Mintage	F	VF	XF	Unc
VS2031 (1974)	136,000	—	0.50	0.75	1.25

KM# 822.2 50 PAISA

Copper-Nickel **Subject:** Birendra Coronation **Edge:** Reeded **Note:** 1.5mm thick.

Date	Mintage	F	VF	XF	Unc
VS2031 (1974) Proof	1,000	Value: 5.00			

KM# 846 50 PAISA

Copper-Nickel **Obv:** Trident within small center circle **Rev:** Dagger flanked by garlands from above **Note:** In the name of Queen Aishvarya Rajya Lakshmi

Date	Mintage	F	VF	XF	Unc
VS2031 (1974)	—	—	—	—	100

KM# 823 50 PAISA

Copper-Nickel **Series:** World Food Day **Obv:** Trident within small center circle **Rev:** Corn ear at left, logo at right

Date	Mintage	F	VF	XF	Unc
VS2038 (1981)	2,000,000	—	0.10	0.30	0.60

KM# 824 50 PAISA

Copper-Nickel **Series:** International Year of Disabled Persons **Obv:** Trident within small center circle **Rev:** Emblem at center

Date	Mintage	F	VF	XF	Unc
VS2038 (1981)	Inc. above	—	0.50	0.75	1.25

KM# 1016 50 PAISA

3.0000 g., Copper-Nickel, 20 mm. **Subject:** Family Planning **Obv:** Logo above inscription **Rev:** Value

Date	Mintage	F	VF	XF	Unc
VS2041 (1984)	—	—	0.10	0.25	0.50

KM# 1018.1 50 PAISA

Stainless Steel, 23.5 mm. **Obv:** Small trident in center **Rev:** Dagger flanked by garlands from above

Date	Mintage	F	VF	XF	Unc
VS2044 (1987)	6,341,000	—	0.10	0.25	0.50
VS2045 (1988)	7,350,000	—	0.10	0.25	0.50
Note: Varieties with small and large Nepalese "5" exist					
VS2046 (1989)	—	—	0.10	0.25	0.50

KM# 1018.2 50 PAISA

Stainless Steel, 23.5 mm. **Obv:** Larger trident in center of traditional design **Rev:** Dagger flanked by garlands from above

Date	Mintage	F	VF	XF	Unc
VS2047 (1990)	—	—	0.10	0.25	0.50
VS2048 (1991)	—	—	0.10	0.25	0.50
VS2049 (1992)	—	—	0.10	0.25	0.50

KM# 1072 50 PAISA

1.4100 g., Aluminum, 22.5 mm. **Obv:** Royal crown **Rev:** Crown **Edge:** Plain **Note:** Coins dated VS2051 exist in two minor varieties being struck at Kathmandu (round edge) and Singapore (sharp edge).

Date	Mintage	F	VF	XF	Unc
VS2051 (1994)	—	—	0.10	0.20	0.40
VS2052 (1995)	—	—	0.10	0.20	0.40
VS2053 (1996)	—	—	0.10	0.20	0.40
VS2054 (1997)	—	—	0.10	0.20	0.40
VS2055 (1998)	—	—	0.10	0.20	0.40
VS2056 (1999)	—	—	0.10	0.20	0.40
VS2057 (2000)	—	—	0.10	0.20	0.40

KM# 828.1 RUPEE

10.2000 g., Copper-Nickel **Obv:** Trident within small center circle **Rev:** Dagger flanked by garlands from above

Date	Mintage	F	VF	XF	Unc
VS2028 (1971)	5,030	—	0.50	1.00	2.00
VS2029 (1972)	22,000	—	0.50	1.00	1.50
VS2029 (1972) Proof	3,943	Value: 2.50			
VS2030 (1973)	5,667	—	0.50	1.00	2.00
VS2030 (1973) Proof	8,891	Value: 2.00			
VS2031 (1974) Proof	11,000	Value: 1.50			

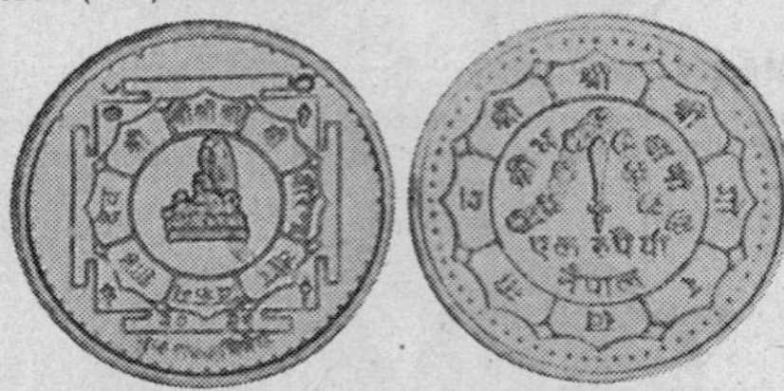

KM# 829.1 RUPEE

Copper-Nickel **Subject:** Birendra Coronation **Obv:** Crown at center of ornamental frame **Rev:** Dagger flanked by garlands from above **Note:** 2 millimeters thick.

Date	Mintage	F	VF	XF	Unc
VS2031 (1973)	—	—	0.75	1.25	1.75

KM# 829.2 RUPEE

Copper-Nickel **Subject:** Birendra Coronation **Obv:** Crown at center of ornamental frame **Rev:** Dagger flanked by garlands from above **Edge:** Reeded **Note:** 2.5 millimeters thick.

Date	Mintage	F	VF	XF	Unc
VS2031 (1973) Proof	1,000	Value: 6.00			

KM# 848 RUPEE

Copper-Nickel **Obv:** Trident within small circle at center **Rev:** Dagger flanked by garlands from above **Note:** In the name of Queen Aishvarya Rajya Lakshmi.

Date	Mintage	F	VF	XF	Unc
VS2031 (1974)	—	—	—	—	150

KM# 831 RUPEE

Copper-Nickel **Series:** F.A.O. International Women's Year **Obv:** Busts left **Rev:** Value above logo, grain ears flank

Date	Mintage	F	VF	XF	Unc
VS2032 (1975)	1,500,000	—	0.25	0.50	1.25

KM# 828a RUPEE

7.5000 g., Copper-Nickel, 27.5 mm. **Note:** Reduced weight. Coins dated VS2036 were struck at the Canberra Mint and have a very shiny surface. High quality examples of VS2034 were struck at Canberra Mint while dull surfaced examples were probably struck at Kathmandu Mint.

Date	Mintage	F	VF	XF	Unc
VS2033 (1976)	58,000	—	0.50	1.00	1.50
VS2034 (1977)	30,000,000	—	0.25	0.50	1.00
VS2035 (1978)	—	—	0.25	0.50	1.00
VS2036 (1979)	—	—	0.25	0.50	1.00
VS2036 (1979)	30,000,000	—	0.25	0.50	1.00

KM# 828.2 RUPEE

Copper-Nickel **Note:** Reduced size; 23mm. Like 821a.

Date	Mintage	F	VF	XF	Unc
VS2039 (1982)	—	—	1.50	3.00	—

KM# 1019 RUPEE

Copper-Nickel **Subject:** Family Planning **Obv:** Logo at center within design **Rev:** Value

Date	Mintage	F	VF	XF	Unc
VS2041 (1984)	21,000	—	—	—	0.75

KM# 1061 RUPEE

Stainless Steel **Obv:** Small trident in center **Rev:** Dagger flanked by garlands from above

Date	Mintage	F	VF	XF	Unc
VS2045 (1988) Prooflike	—	—	0.25	0.50	1.00
VS2048 (1991) Prooflike	—	—	0.25	0.50	1.00
Note: Varieties exist					
VS2049 (1992) Prooflike	—	—	0.25	0.50	1.25

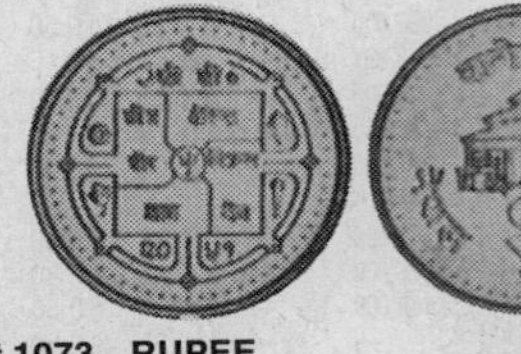

KM# 1073 RUPEE

3.5000 g., Brass Plated Steel, 22 mm. **Obv:** Small trident at center **Rev:** Large legends **Edge:** Plain **Note:** Sharp and round edge varieties.

Date	Mintage	F	VF	XF	Unc
VS2051 (1994)	—	—	0.25	0.50	1.00
VS2052 (1995)	—	—	0.25	0.50	1.00

KM# 1152 RUPEE

28.1600 g., 0.9990 Copper-Nickel 0.9045 oz., 38.5 mm. **Subject:** UN 50th Anniversary **Obv:** Traditional design **Rev:** UN 50 logo **Edge:** Reeded

Date	Mintage	F	VF	XF	Unc
VS2052 (1995)	—	—	—	—	—

KM# 1073a RUPEE

Brass, 20 mm. **Obv:** Traditional design **Rev:** Small legends

Date	Mintage	F	VF	XF	Unc
VS2052 (1995)	—	—	—	—	1.00
VS2053 (1996)	—	—	—	—	1.00
VS2054 (1997)	—	—	—	—	1.00
VS2055 (1998)	—	—	—	—	1.00
VS2056 (1999)	—	—	—	—	1.00
VS2057 (2000)	—	—	—	—	1.00

KM# 1092 RUPEE

Brass Plated Steel, 22 mm. **Series:** U.N. 50th Anniversary **Obv:** Traditional design **Rev:** UN logo and dates

Date	Mintage	F	VF	XF	Unc
VS2052 (1995)	—	—	—	—	1.75

KM# 1115 RUPEE

Brass, 20 mm. **Subject:** Visit Nepal '98 **Obv:** Traditional design **Rev:** Moon and sun flanking mountaintop

Date	Mintage	F	VF	XF	Unc
VS2054 (1997)	—	—	—	—	1.00

KM# 1139 RUPEE

Brass, 20 mm. **Subject:** Gorkhapatra Centenary **Obv:** Traditional design **Rev:** Inscription within wreath of ten people reading newspapers **Rev. Inscription:** "Gorkhapata 1958-VS2057"

Date	Mintage	F	VF	XF	Unc
VS2057 (2000)	—	—	—	—	1.00

KM# 832 2 RUPEES

Copper-Nickel **Series:** World Food Day **Obv:** Trident within small circle at center **Rev:** Corn ear at left, logo at right

Date	Mintage	F	VF	XF	Unc
VS2038 (1981)	1,000,000	—	0.50	0.75	1.50

KM# 1025 2 RUPEES

Copper-Nickel **Series:** F.A.O. **Obv:** Traditional design **Note:** Size of obverse square varies. With or without dot in reverse sun.

Date	Mintage	F	VF	XF	Unc
VS2039 (1982)	366,000	—	0.50	0.75	1.50

KM# 1020 2 RUPEES

Copper-Nickel **Subject:** Family Planning **Obv:** Emblem within decorative outlines **Rev:** Value

Date	Mintage	F	VF	XF	Unc
VS2041 (1984)	11,000	—	0.50	0.75	1.50

KM# 1074.1 2 RUPEES

4.9600 g., Brass Plated Steel, 24.4 mm. **Obv:** Small trident at center **Rev:** Building above value **Edge:** Plain **Note:** Sharp and round edge varieties exist.

Date	Mintage	F	VF	XF	Unc
VS2051 (1994)	—	—	0.35	0.60	1.25
VS2052 (1995)	—	—	0.35	0.60	1.25

KM# 1074.2 2 RUPEES

Brass, 25 mm.

Date	Mintage	F	VF	XF	Unc
VS2053 (1996)	—	—	0.35	0.60	1.25
VS2055 (1998)	—	—	0.35	0.60	1.25
VS2056 (1999)	—	—	0.35	0.60	1.25
VS2057 (2000)	—	—	0.35	0.60	1.25

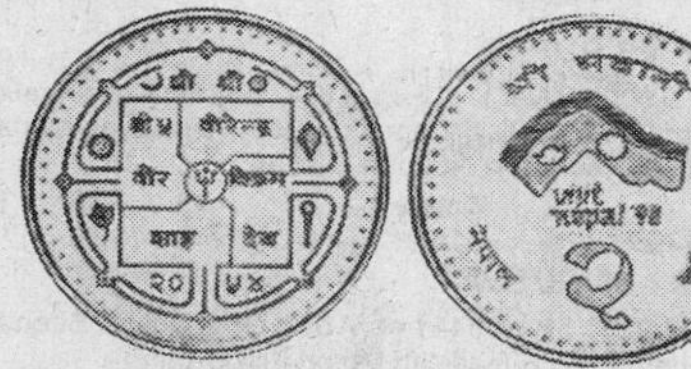

KM# 1116 2 RUPEES

Brass, 25 mm. **Subject:** Visit Nepal '98 **Obv:** Traditional design **Rev:** Moon and sun flanking mountaintop

Date	Mintage	F	VF	XF	Unc
VS2053 (1996)	—	—	—	—	1.25
VS2054 (1997)	—	—	—	—	1.25

KM# 833 5 RUPEE

Copper-Nickel **Subject:** Rural Women's Advancement **Obv:** Trident within small circle at center

Date	Mintage	F	VF	XF	Unc
VS2037 (1980)	50,000	—	0.75	1.50	3.00

KM# 834 5 RUPEE

Copper-Nickel, 28.7-30.0 mm. **Subject:** National Bank Silver Jubilee **Obv:** Trident within small circle at center **Rev:** Small figurine of native god at center **Note:** Size varies.

Date	Mintage	F	VF	XF	Unc
VS2038 (1981)	64,000	—	0.75	1.50	3.00

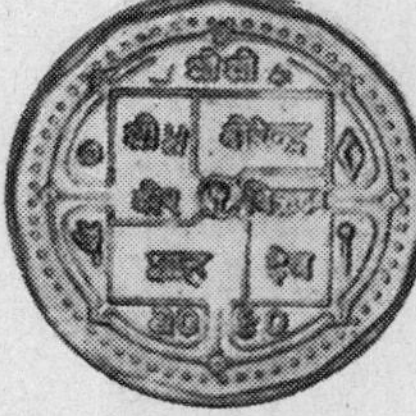

KM# 1009 5 RUPEE

Copper-Nickel **Obv:** Traditional design **Rev:** Dagger flanked by garlands from above **Note:** Circulation coinage

Date	Mintage	F	VF	XF	Unc
VS2039 (1982)	Inc. above	—	0.50	1.00	2.00
VS2040 (1983)	478,000	—	0.30	0.50	1.00

KM# 1017 5 RUPEE

Copper-Nickel **Subject:** Family Planning **Obv:** Value **Rev:** Logo above inscription

Date	Mintage	F	VF	XF	Unc
VS2041 (1984)	458,000	—	0.50	1.00	2.00

KM# 1023 5 RUPEE

Copper-Nickel **Subject:** Year of Youth **Obv:** Value **Rev:** Emblem below hills

Date	Mintage	F	VF	XF	Unc
VS2042 (1985)	1,124,000	—	—	—	2.50

KM# 1047 5 RUPEE

Copper-Nickel **Subject:** Social Services **Obv:** Value **Rev:** Ox left within small center circle

Date	Mintage	F	VF	XF	Unc
VS2042 (1985)	Inc. above	—	—	—	3.50

KM# 1028 5 RUPEE

Copper-Nickel **Series:** World Food Day **Obv:** Traditional design **Rev:** Fish left below logo

Date	Mintage	F	VF	XF	Unc
VS2043 (1986)	99,000	—	—	—	3.50

KM# 1042 5 RUPEE

Copper-Nickel **Subject:** 15th World Buddhist Conference **Obv:** Value **Rev:** Figure at center of globe within ornamented circle **Note:** Two different obverse dies exist.

Date	Mintage	F	VF	XF	Unc
VS2043//1986 (1986)	135,000	—	—	—	3.50

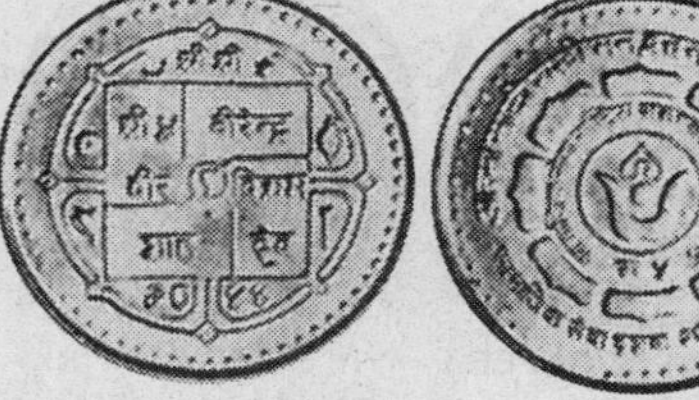

KM# 1030 5 RUPEE

Copper-Nickel **Subject:** 10th Year of National Social Security Administration **Obv:** Traditional design **Rev:** Emblem at center

Date	Mintage	F	VF	XF	Unc
VS2044 (1987)	104,000	—	—	—	3.50
VS2045 (1988)	—	—	—	—	3.50

KM# 1043 5 RUPEE

Copper **Subject:** 3rd SAARC Summit **Obv:** Traditional design **Rev:** Summit emblem

Date	Mintage	F	VF	XF	Unc
VS2044 (1987)	2,000	—	—	—	6.50

KM# 1053 5 RUPEE

Copper-Nickel **Series:** World Food Day **Obv:** Traditional design **Rev:** Emblem above symbols

Date	Mintage	F	VF	XF	Unc
VS2047 (1990)	—	—	—	—	4.00

KM# 1063 5 RUPEE

Copper-Nickel **Subject:** New Constitution **Obv:** Traditional design **Rev:** Flags above open book

Date	Mintage	F	VF	XF	Unc
VS2047 (1990)	—	—	—	—	3.25

KM# 1062 5 RUPEE

Copper-Nickel **Subject:** Parliament Session **Obv:** Traditional design **Rev:** Outlined drawings symbolizing figures of parliament

Date	Mintage	F	VF	XF	Unc
VS2048 (1991)	—	—	—	—	3.00

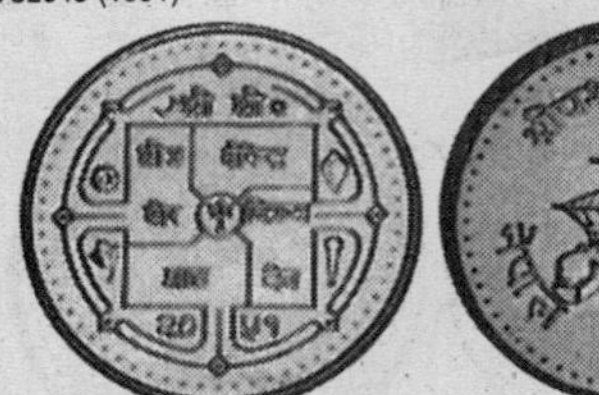

KM# 1075.1 5 RUPEE

Brass Plated Steel, 27 mm. **Obv:** Traditional design **Rev:** Temple **Edge:** Plain

Date	Mintage	F	VF	XF	Unc
VS2051 (1994)	—	—	—	—	1.50

KM# 1075.2 5 RUPEE

Brass, 25 mm. **Edge:** Reeded

Date	Mintage	F	VF	XF	Unc
VS2053 (1996)	—	—	—	—	1.50

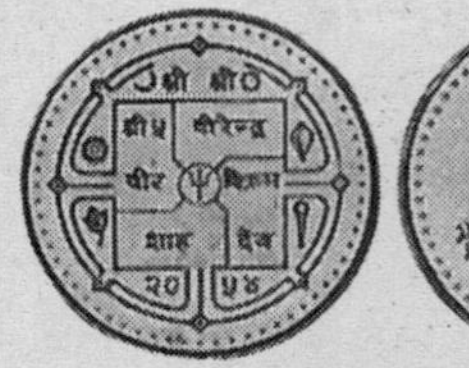

KM# 1117 5 RUPEE

Copper, 25 mm. **Subject:** Visit Nepal '98 **Obv:** Traditional design **Rev:** Sun and moon flanking mountaintop **Edge:** Reeded

Date	Mintage	F	VF	XF	Unc
VS2054 (1997)	—	—	—	—	1.50

KM# 835 10 RUPEE

8.0000 g., 0.2500 Silver .0643 oz. ASW **Series:** F.A.O. **Obv:** Value and dates **Rev:** Family scene

Date	Mintage	F	VF	XF	Unc
VS2031 (1974)	39,000	—	—	4.00	6.00

KM# 1004 10 RUPEE

Copper-Nickel, 40 mm. **Subject:** 30th Anniversary - Ascent of Mt. Everest **Obv:** Traditional design **Rev:** Mount Everest

Date	Mintage	F	VF	XF	Unc
VS2040 (1983)	2,000	—	—	—	12.50

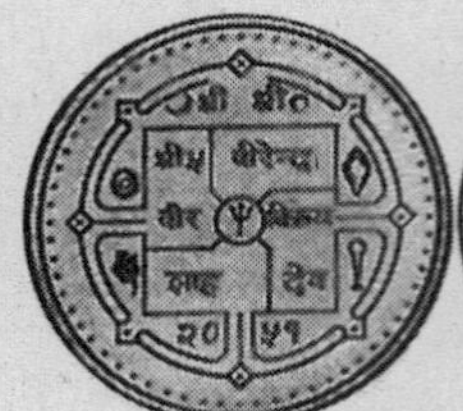

KM# 1076 10 RUPEE

Brass Plated Steel, 29 mm. **Obv:** Traditional design **Rev:** Closed book

Date	Mintage	F	VF	XF	Unc
VS2051 (1994)	—	—	—	—	2.50

KM# 1083 10 RUPEE

Copper-Nickel **Subject:** 75th Anniversary - International Labor Organization **Obv:** Traditional design **Rev:** Logo above legend

Date	Mintage	F	VF	XF	Unc
VS2051 (1994)	—	—	—	—	4.50

KM# 1089 10 RUPEE

Copper-Nickel **Subject:** 50th Anniversary - F.A.O. Logo **Obv:** Traditional design **Rev:** Logo with grain ears flanking

Date	Mintage	F	VF	XF	Unc
VS2052 (1995)	—	—	—	—	4.00

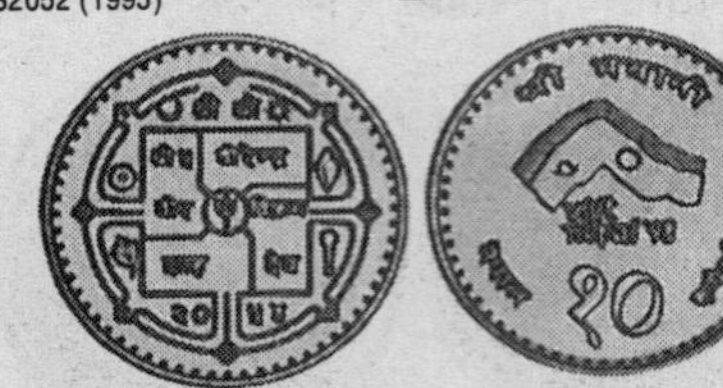

KM# 1118 10 RUPEE

Copper-Nickel, 25 mm. **Subject:** Visit Nepal '98 **Obv:** Traditional design **Rev:** Moon and sun flanking mountaintop **Edge:** Reeded

Date	Mintage	F	VF	XF	Unc
VS2054 (1997)	—	—	—	—	3.00

KM# 836 20 RUPEE

14.8500 g., 0.5000 Silver .2387 oz. ASW **Series:** F.A.O. International Women's Year **Obv:** Busts left **Rev:** Value within grain sprigs

Date	Mintage	F	VF	XF	Unc
VS2032 (1975)	50,000	—	—	4.50	7.50

KM# 837 20 RUPEE

14.8500 g., 0.5000 Silver .2387 oz. ASW **Series:** International Year of the Child **Obv:** Trident within small circle at center **Rev:** Emblem below rising sun

Date	Mintage	F	VF	XF	Unc
VS2036 (1979)	—	—	—	4.00	6.00

KM# 837a 20 RUPEE

15.0000 g., 0.9250 Silver .4461 oz. ASW **Obv:** Trident within small circle at center **Rev:** Emblem below rising sun

Date	Mintage	F	VF	XF	Unc
VS2036 (1979) Proof	1,000	Value: 27.50			

KM# 839 25 RUPEE

25.6000 g., 0.5000 Silver .4115 oz. ASW **Series:** Conservation **Obv:** Bust of Birendra Bir Bikram right **Rev:** Himalayan Monal Pheasant **Rev. Designer:** Norman Sillman

Date	Mintage	F	VF	XF	Unc
VS2031 (1974)	11,000	—	—	8.50	17.50

KM# 839a 25 RUPEE

28.2800 g., 0.9250 Silver .8411 oz. ASW **Obv:** Bust of Birendra Bir Bikram right **Rev:** Himalayan Monal Pheasant **Rev. Designer:** Norman Sillman

Date	Mintage	F	VF	XF	Unc
VS2031 (1974) Proof	11,000	Value: 20.00			

KM# 838 25 RUPEE

25.6000 g., 0.5000 Silver .4115 oz. ASW **Subject:** Birendra Coronation **Obv:** Crown **Rev:** Dagger flanked by garlands from above **Edge:** Reeded **Note:** 2mm thick.

Date	Mintage	F	VF	XF	Unc
VS2031 (1974)	75,000	—	—	7.00	10.00

KM# 838a 25 RUPEE

28.2800 g., 0.9250 Silver .8411 oz. ASW **Obv:** Crown **Rev:** Dagger flanked by garlands from above **Edge:** Reeded **Note:** 3mm thick.

Date	Mintage	F	VF	XF	Unc
VS2031 (1974) Proof	2,000	Value: 22.50			

KM# 1051 25 RUPEE

12.0000 g., 0.2500 Silver .0965 oz. ASW **Obv:** Crown **Rev:** Value

Date	Mintage	F	VF	XF	Unc
VS2041 (1984)	—	—	—	—	15.00

KM# 1048.1 25 RUPEE

12.0000 g., 0.2500 Silver .0965 oz. ASW **Subject:** 25th Anniversary of Panchayat **Obv:** Thin 25 **Rev:** Small rosette **Note:** Varieties exist with hollow or solid hand-like symbol below on obverse.

Date	Mintage	F	VF	XF	Unc
VS2042 (1985)	9,962,000	—	—	—	10.00

KM# 1048.2 25 RUPEE

12.0000 g., 0.2500 Silver 0.0965 oz. ASW **Subject:** 25th Anniversary of Panchayat **Obv:** Thick 25 **Rev:** Large rosette **Note:** Varieties exist with hollow or solid hand-like symbol below on obverse.

Date	Mintage	F	VF	XF	Unc
VS2042 (1985)	Inc. above	—	—	—	10.00

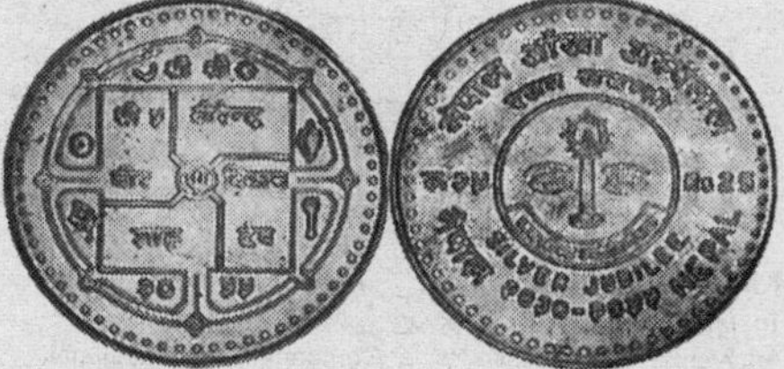

KM# 1135 25 RUPEE

8.5000 g., Copper Nickel, 29 mm. **Subject:** Silver Jubilee of King's Accession **Obv:** Traditional design **Rev:** Crown on radiant emblem **Edge:** Plain

Date	Mintage	F	VF	XF	Unc
VS2053 (1996)	—	—	—	—	3.50

KM# 1126 25 RUPEE

Copper-Nickel **Subject:** Silver Jubilee **Obv:** Traditional design **Rev:** Stylized face design

Date	Mintage	F	VF	XF	Unc
VS2055 (1998)	—	—	—	—	4.50

KM# 841 50 RUPEE

31.8000 g., 0.5000 Silver .5112 oz. ASW **Series:** Conservation **Obv:** Bust right **Rev:** Red panda **Rev. Designer:** Norman Sillman

Date	Mintage	F	VF	XF	Unc
VS2031 (1974)	11,000	—	—	10.00	17.50

KM# 841a 50 RUPEE

35.0000 g., 0.9250 Silver 1.0409 oz. ASW **Obv:** Bust right **Rev:** Red panda **Rev. Designer:** Norman Sillman

Date	Mintage	F	VF	XF	Unc
VS2031 (1974) Proof	10,000	Value: 25.00			

KM# 842 50 RUPEE

25.0000 g., 0.5000 Silver .4018 oz. ASW **Subject:** Education for Village Women **Obv:** Traditional design **Rev:** Open book

Date	Mintage	F	VF	XF	Unc
VS2036 (1979)	15,000	—	—	—	12.50

KM# 842a 50 RUPEE

25.0000 g., 0.9250 Silver .7436 oz. ASW **Obv:** Traditional design **Rev:** Open book

Date	Mintage	F	VF	XF	Unc
VS2036 (1979) Proof	1,000	Value: 40.00			

KM# 843 50 RUPEE

14.9000 g., 0.5000 Silver .2395 oz. ASW **Series:** International Year of Disabled Persons **Obv:** Traditional design **Rev:** Emblem within grain ears

Date	Mintage	F	VF	XF	Unc
VS2038 (1981)	16,000	—	—	—	8.50

KM# A851 50 RUPEE

15.0000 g., 0.4000 Silver .1929 oz. ASW **Series:** International Year of the Child **Note:** Similar to 100 Rupee, KM#851.

Date	Mintage	F	VF	XF	Unc
VS2038 (1981)	—	—	—	—	—

KM# 1046 50 RUPEE

15.0000 g., 0.5000 Silver .2406 oz. ASW **Subject:** 50th Anniversary of Kathmandu Mint **Obv:** Trident within small center circle **Rev:** Mint press

Date	Mintage	F	VF	XF	Unc
VS2039 (1982)	8,765	—	—	13.50	17.50

KM# 1119 50 RUPEE

Bronze **Obv:** Traditional square in circle design **Rev:** Buddha's portrait and Ashoka pillar **Note:** Lord Buddha; Similar to 1500 Rupee, KM#1120.

Date	Mintage	F	VF	XF	Unc
VS2055 (1998)	30,000	—	—	—	10.00

KM# 1136 50 RUPEE

Brass, 37.5 mm. **Subject:** 50th Anniversary - Radio Nepal **Obv:** Traditional design **Rev:** Stylized design **Edge:** Plain

Date	Mintage	F	VF	XF	Unc
VS2056 (1999)	—	—	—	—	10.00

KM# 1137 50 RUPEE

Brass, 37.5 mm. **Subject:** St. Xavier's Golden Jubilee **Obv:** Traditional design **Rev:** Coat of arms **Edge:** Plain

Date	Mintage	F	VF	XF	Unc
VS2057 (2000)	—	—	—	—	10.00

KM# 1127 50 RUPEE

Brass, 38.7 mm. **Subject:** Buddha **Obv:** Traditional square design **Rev:** Buddha and four figures **Edge:** Reeded

Date	Mintage	F	VF	XF	Unc
VS2057 (2000)	30,000	—	—	—	10.00

KM# 1165 100 RUPEE

25.0000 g., 0.5000 Silver 0.4019 oz. ASW, 36 mm. **Obv:** Crown in square design **Rev:** Garland draped above sword **Edge:** Reeded

Date	Mintage	F	VF	XF	Unc
VS2031 (1974) Proof	1,000	Value: 50.00			

KM# 850.2 100 RUPEE

25.4900 g., 0.9250 Silver .7580 oz. ASW **Series:** World Food Day **Obv:** Traditional design **Rev:** Figure working in field **Note:** Obverse and reverse are different.

Date	Mintage	F	VF	XF	Unc
VS2038 (1981)	—	Value: 80.00			

KM# 851 100 RUPEE

19.4400 g., 0.5000 Silver .3125 oz. ASW **Series:** International Year of the Child **Obv:** Crowned bust right **Rev:** Children filling water jug

Date	Mintage	F	VF	XF	Unc
VS2031(1974) Proof	9,270	Value: 17.50			

Note: Struck in 1981

KM# 850.1 100 RUPEE

25.4900 g., 0.5000 Silver .4050 oz. ASW **Series:** World Food Day **Obv:** Traditional design **Rev:** Figure working in field

Date	Mintage	F	VF	XF	Unc
VS2038 (1981)	18,000	—	—	—	22.50

KM# 1005 100 RUPEE

31.1000 g., 0.9250 Silver .9250 oz. ASW **Subject:** 30th Anniversary Ascent of Mt. Everest **Obv:** Trident within small circle at center **Rev:** Mount Everest

Date	Mintage	F	VF	XF	Unc
VS2040 (1983) Proof	1,500	Value: 50.00			

KM# 1024 100 RUPEE

15.0000 g., 0.5000 Silver .2411 oz. ASW **Subject:** Year of Youth **Obv:** Value **Rev:** Emblem below hills

Date	Mintage	F	VF	XF	Unc
VS2042 (1985)	8,199	—	—	—	12.00

KM# 1114 100 RUPEE

12.0400 g., 0.6000 Silver .2323 oz. ASW **Series:** 50th Anniversary - F.A.O. **Obv:** Traditional design **Rev:** Logo at center, grain ears flank

Date	Mintage	F	VF	XF	Unc
VS2052 (1995)	—	—	—	—	15.00

KM# 1102 100 RUPEE

Copper-Nickel **Series:** Nepal Wildlife **Rev:** Multicolor tiger

Date	Mintage	F	VF	XF	Unc
VS2054 (1998)	25,000	—	—	—	30.00
VS2054-1998 (1998)	25,000	—	—	—	30.00

KM# 1103 100 RUPEE

Copper-Nickel **Series:** Nepal Wildlife **Obv:** Traditional design **Rev:** Multicolor Great Indian rhino

Date	Mintage	F	VF	XF	Unc
VS2054-1998	25,000	—	—	—	35.00

KM# 1141 100 RUPEE

12.5000 g., 0.5000 Silver .200 oz. ASW **Series:** International Year of Older Persons **Obv:** Traditional design **Rev:** Emblem and inscription

Date	Mintage	F	VF	XF	Unc
VS2056 (1999)	—	—	—	—	10.00

KM# 1031 200 RUPEE

15.0000 g., 0.6000 Silver .2894 oz. ASW **Subject:** 10th Anniversary of National Social Security Administration **Obv:** Traditional design **Rev:** Emblem at center within small circle

Date	Mintage	F	VF	XF	Unc
VS2044 (1987)	4,145	—	—	—	25.00

KM# 1007 250 RUPEE

28.2800 g., 0.9250 Silver .8411 oz. ASW **Subject:** 10th Anniversary of Reign **Obv:** Conjoined busts left **Rev:** Value

Date	Mintage	F	VF	XF	Unc
VS2038 (1981) Proof	10,000	Value: 95.00			

KM# 1010 250 RUPEE

28.2800 g., 0.9250 Silver .8411 oz. ASW **Subject:** Year of the Scout **Obv:** Traditional design **Rev:** Boy and girl scouts planting seedling

Date	Mintage	F	VF	XF	Unc
VS2039 (1982)	10,000	—	—	—	45.00
VS2039 (1982) Proof	Inc. above	Value: 55.00			

KM# 1026 250 RUPEE

19.4400 g., 0.9250 Silver .5782 oz. ASW **Series:** Wildlife Preservation **Obv:** Traditional design **Rev:** Musk deer

Date	Mintage	F	VF	XF	Unc
VS2043 (1986) Proof	20,000	Value: 30.00			

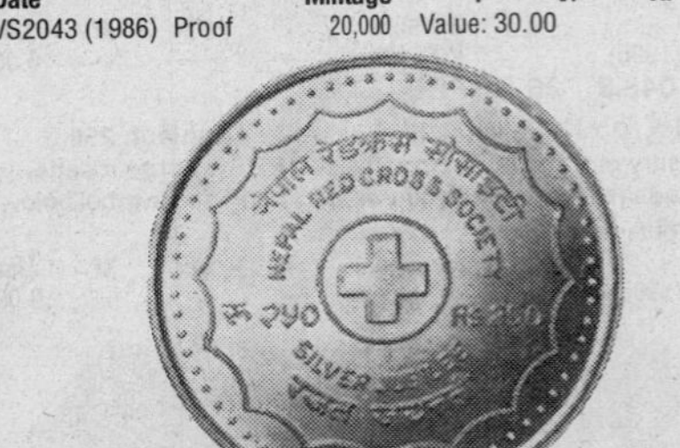

KM# 1049 250 RUPEE

19.4400 g., 0.9250 Silver .5782 oz. ASW **Subject:** Silver Jubilee of Nepal Red Cross Society **Obv:** Traditional design **Rev:** Emblem at center

Date	Mintage	F	VF	XF	Unc
VS2045 (1988)	6,360	—	—	—	23.50

KM# 1052 250 RUPEE

19.4400 g., 0.9250 Silver .5782 oz. ASW **Subject:** 25th Anniversary of Nepalese Power Company **Obv:** Traditional design **Rev:** Rising sun back of hills

Date	Mintage	F	VF	XF	Unc
VS2046 (1989)	—	—	—	—	23.50

KM# 1055 250 RUPEE

19.4400 g., 0.9250 Silver .5782 oz. ASW **Series:** Save the Children **Obv:** Traditional design **Rev:** Children dancing

Date	Mintage	F	VF	XF	Unc
VS2047 (1990) Proof	20,000	Value: 22.50			

KM# 1134.1 250 RUPEE

18.1000 g., 0.9250 Silver .5782 oz. ASW, 36 mm. **Subject:** Silver Jubilee - Nepal Disabled Association **Note:** Large figures, large inscriptions.

Date	Mintage	F	VF	XF	Unc
VS2052(1995)	—	Value: 27.50			

KM# 1134.2 250 RUPEE

17.7000 g., 0.5000 Silver 0.291 oz. ASW, 36 mm. **Subject:** Nepal Disabled Association **Obv:** Traditional square design **Rev:** Human figures Logo and value **Edge:** Reeded **Note:** Small figures, small inscriptions

Date	Mintage	F	VF	XF	Unc
VS2052(1995)	—	—	—	—	25.00

KM# 1134.3 250 RUPEE

17.7000 g., 0.5000 Silver 0.2845 oz. ASW, 36 mm. **Subject:** Nepal Disabled Association **Obv:** Traditional square design with small inscriptions **Rev:** Human figures logo and value **Edge:** Reeded

Date	Mintage	F	VF	XF	Unc
VS2052(1995)	—	—	—	—	25.00

KM# 1029 300 RUPEE

25.2900 g., 0.5000 Silver .4066 oz. ASW **Subject:** First Scout Jamboree in Nepal **Obv:** Traditional design **Rev:** Emblems within temple outline, hills in background

Date	Mintage	F	VF	XF	Unc
VS2043 (1986)	6,967	—	—	—	27.50

KM# 1044 300 RUPEE

25.0000 g., 0.9250 Silver .7436 oz. ASW **Subject:** 3rd SAARC Summit **Obv:** Traditional design **Rev:** Summit emblem

Date	Mintage	F	VF	XF	Unc
VS2044 (1987)	5,000	—	—	—	22.50

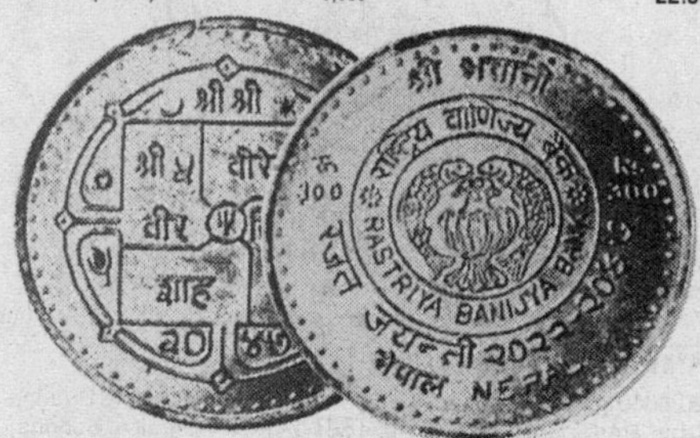

KM# 1057 300 RUPEE

18.0500 g., 0.9250 Silver .5368 oz. ASW **Obv:** Traditional design **Rev:** Rastriya Banijya Bank logo

Date	Mintage	F	VF	XF	Unc
VS2047 (1990)	—	—	—	—	22.50

KM# 1064 300 RUPEE

18.3150 g., 0.9250 Silver .5447 oz. ASW **Subject:** New Constitution **Obv:** Traditional design **Rev:** Flags above open book

Date	Mintage	F	VF	XF	Unc
VS2047 (1990)	—	—	—	—	22.50

KM# 1065 300 RUPEE

18.3150 g., 0.9250 Silver .5447 oz. ASW **Subject:** Parliament Session **Obv:** Traditional design **Rev:** Outlined figures symbolizing members of parliament

Date	Mintage	F	VF	XF	Unc
VS2048 (1991)	—	—	—	—	22.50

KM# 1068 300 RUPEE

17.8100 g., 0.9250 Silver .5297 oz. ASW **Obv:** Traditional design **Rev:** Figure between hands holding grains, hills in background

Date	Mintage	F	VF	XF	Unc
VS2049 (1992)	—	—	—	—	22.50

KM# 1094 300 RUPEE

18.1300 g., 0.9250 Silver .5392 oz. ASW **Subject:** Rastriya Beema Sansthan Silver Jubilee **Obv:** Traditional design **Rev:** Eyes below design

Date	Mintage	F	VF	XF	Unc
VS2049 (1992)	—	—	—	—	22.50

KM# 1142 300 RUPEE

18.0000 g., 0.9250 Silver .5353 oz. ASW **Subject:** 75th Anniversary of I.L.O.

Date	Mintage	F	VF	XF	Unc
VS2051 (1994)	—	—	—	—	22.50

KM# 1032 350 RUPEE

23.3000 g., 0.5000 Silver .3746 oz. ASW **Subject:** Crown Prince, Sacred Thread Ceremony **Obv:** Traditional design

Date	Mintage	F	VF	XF	Unc
VS2044 (1987)	5,217	—	—	—	30.00

KM# 1035 500 RUPEE

35.0000 g., 0.5000 Silver .5627 oz. ASW **Subject:** 50th Anniversary of National Bank **Obv:** Traditional design **Rev:** Figure at center of designed globe

Date	Mintage	F	VF	XF	Unc
VS2044 (1987)	19,000	—	—	—	45.00

KM# 1166 500 RUPEE

31.1000 g., 0.9990 Silver 0.9989 oz. ASW, 38.7 mm. **Obv:** Traditional design **Rev:** Ceremonial vase

Date	Mintage	F	VF	XF	Unc
VS2046(1989)	5,000	—	—	—	45.00

KM# 1058 500 RUPEE

31.4700 g., 0.9250 Silver .9359 oz. ASW **Series:** 1992 Olympics **Obv:** Traditional design **Rev:** Boxers

Date	Mintage	F	VF	XF	Unc
VS2049 (1992) Proof	Est. 40,000	Value: 17.50			

KM# 1069 500 RUPEE

31.4700 g., 0.9250 Silver .9359 oz. ASW **Series:** 1992 Olympics **Subject:** Soccer **Rev:** Soccer goal being scored

Date	Mintage	F	VF	XF	Unc
VS2049 (1992) Proof	20,000	Value: 28.50			

KM# 1071 500 RUPEE

31.8300 g., 0.9250 Silver .9466 oz. ASW **Series:** 1992 Olympics - Ski Jumping **Obv:** Traditional design **Rev:** Ski jumper

Date	Mintage	F	VF	XF	Unc
VS2049 (1992) Proof	Est. 40,000	Value: 16.50			

KM# 1090 500 RUPEE

31.4700 g., 0.9250 Silver .9359 oz. ASW **Series:** Endangered Wildlife **Obv:** Traditional design **Rev:** Red Panda

Date	Mintage	F	VF	XF	Unc
VS2049 (1992) Proof	Est. 15,000	Value: 30.00			

KM# 1070 500 RUPEE

31.4700 g., 0.9250 Silver .9359 oz. ASW **Series:** Endangered Wildlife **Obv:** Traditional design **Rev:** Himalayan Black Bear

Date	Mintage	F	VF	XF	Unc
VS2050 (1993) Proof	10,000	Value: 45.00			

KM# 1066 500 RUPEE

31.7500 g., 0.9250 Silver .9443 oz. ASW **Series:** 1994 Olympics **Obv:** Traditional design **Rev:** Cross-country skiing

Date	Mintage	F	VF	XF	Unc
VS2050 (1993) Proof	40,000	Value: 22.50			

KM# 1091 500 RUPEE

31.4700 g., 0.9250 Silver .9359 oz. ASW **Series:** Endangered Wildlife **Rev:** Tiger

Date	Mintage	F	VF	XF	Unc
VS2050 (1993) Proof	Est. 15,000	Value: 40.00			

KM# 1084 500 RUPEE

28.2800 g., 0.9250 Silver .8411 oz. ASW **Subject:** Conquest of Mt. Everest **Note:** Similar to 2500 Rupee, KM#1085.

Date	Mintage	F	VF	XF	Unc
VS2050 (1993) Proof	Est. 10,000	Value: 32.50			

KM# 1133 500 RUPEE

35.2000 g., 0.9000 Silver 1.0000 oz. ASW
Subject: International Monetary Fund **Obv:** Traditional design **Rev:** Conjoined globes within rectangle above banner

Date	Mintage	F	VF	XF	Unc
VS2051 (1994)	—	—	—	—	45.00

KM# 1077 500 RUPEE

31.1035 g., 0.9250 Silver .9250 oz. ASW **Obv:** Traditional design **Rev:** Buddha

Date	Mintage	F	VF	XF	Unc
VS2052 (1995) Proof	15,000	Value: 37.50			

KM# 1125 500 RUPEE

31.3500 g., 0.9990 Silver 1.0069 oz. ASW **Obv:** Traditional design **Rev:** Gold-plated lotus flowers

Date	Mintage	F	VF	XF	Unc
VS2052 (1995) Proof	Est. 7,000	Value: 45.00			

KM# 1138 500 RUPEE

19.4400 g., 0.9250 Silver 0.5781 oz. ASW, 36 mm. **Series:** UNICEF **Obv:** Traditional design **Rev:** Standing girl serving seated boy **Edge:** Reeded

Date	Mintage	F	VF	XF	Unc
1997 Proof	25,000	Value: 25.00			

KM# 1143 500 RUPEE

25.2000 g., 0.9250 Silver .7494 oz. ASW **Subject:** 50th Anniversary of Universal Declaration of Human Rights **Obv:** Traditional design **Rev:** Logo above inscription

Date	Mintage	F	VF	XF	Unc
VS2055 (1998)	—	—	—	—	22.50

KM# 1041 600 RUPEE

31.1030 g., 0.9990 Silver 1.0000 oz. ASW **Subject:** 60th Birthday - Queen Mother **Obv:** Traditional design **Rev:** Bust left

Date	Mintage	F	VF	XF	Unc
VS2045 (1988) Proof	5,000	Value: 60.00			

KM# 844 1000 RUPEE

33.4370 g., 0.9000 Gold .9676 oz. AGW **Series:** Conservation **Obv:** Crowned bust right **Rev:** Great Indian Rhinoceros **Rev. Designer:** Norman Sillman **Note:** Very small quantity restruck in 1979.

Date	Mintage	F	VF	XF	Unc
VS2031 (1974)	2,176	—	—	—	715
VS2031 (1974) Proof	671	Value: 800			

KM# 1000 1000 RUPEE

33.4370 g., 0.9000 Gold .9676 oz. AGW **Subject:** Rural Women's Advancement

Date	Mintage	F	VF	XF	Unc
VS2038 (1981) Proof	500	Value: 725			

KM# 1036 1000 RUPEE

155.5150 g., 0.9990 Silver 5.0000 oz. ASW, 65 mm. **Obv:** Traditional design **Rev:** Snow Leopard **Note:** Photo reduced.

Date	Mintage	F	VF	XF	Unc
VS2045 (1988) Proof	5,000	Value: 150			

KM# 1169 1000 RUPEE

40.0000 g., 0.5000 Silver 0.643 oz. ASW, 40 mm. **Obv:** Traditional square design **Rev:** Living Goddess Kumari **Edge:** Reeded

Date	Mintage	F	VF	XF	Unc
VS2057(2000)	—	—	—	—	50.00

KM# 1095 1500 RUPEE

31.1035 g., 0.9250 Silver .9250 oz. ASW **Subject:** Buddha's Birth **Obv:** Traditional square in circle design **Rev:** Figure standing in center, cameo at right, small figure at left

Date	Mintage	F	VF	XF	Unc
VS2054 (1997) Proof	15,000	Value: 35.00			

KM# 1120 1500 RUPEE

20.0000 g., 0.9250 Silver .5948 oz. ASW **Subject:** Lord Buddha **Obv:** Traditional square in circle design **Rev:** Portrait of Buddha, Ashoka pillar, portrait halo glows under ultraviolet light

Date	Mintage	F	VF	XF	Unc
VS2055 (1998) Proof	15,000	Value: 50.00			

KM# 1168 1500 RUPEE

0.9990 Silver, 38 mm. **Obv:** Traditional square design **Rev:** Tiger in tall grass **Edge:** Reeded

Date	Mintage	F	VF	XF	Unc
VS2054-1998	—	—	—	—	50.00

KM# 1128 1500 RUPEE

20.0000 g., 0.9250 Silver .5948 oz. ASW, 38.7 mm. **Subject:** Buddha **Obv:** Traditional square design **Rev:** Buddha with golden aura **Edge:** Reeded

Date	Mintage	F	VF	XF	Unc
VS2057 (2000)	—	—	—	—	50.00

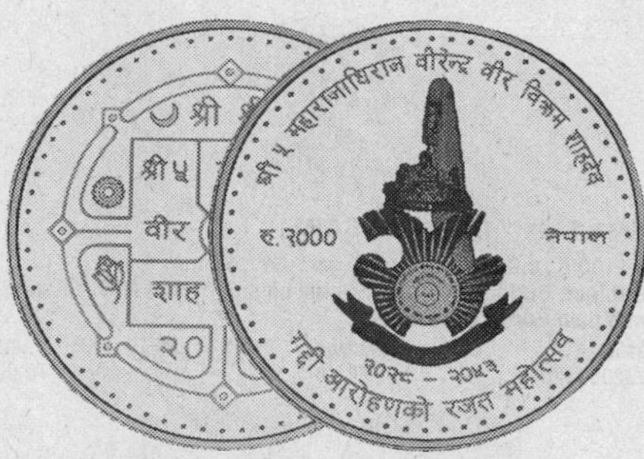

KM# 1100 2000 RUPEE

31.2400 g., 0.9990 Silver 1.0034 oz. ASW, 40 mm. **Subject:** Silver Jubilee of King's Accession **Obv:** Traditional design **Rev:** Multicolor crown

Date	Mintage	F	VF	XF	Unc
VS2053 (1996) Proof	Est. 5,000	Value: 40.00			

KM# 1121 2000 RUPEE

20.0000 g., 0.9250 Silver .5948 oz. ASW **Obv:** Traditional square in circle design **Rev:** Buddha's portrait with gold insert halo, Ashoka pillar at right **Note:** Lord Buddha; Similar to 1500 Rupee, KM#1120.

Date	Mintage	F	VF	XF	Unc
VS2055 (1998) Proof	5,000	Value: 75.00			

KM# 1104 2000 RUPEE

31.1700 g., 0.9990 Silver 1.011 oz. ASW **Series:** Nepal Wildlife **Obv:** Traditional design **Rev:** Multicolored leopard

Date	Mintage	F	VF	XF	Unc
VS2054-1998 Proof	8,000	Value: 45.00			

KM# 1105 2000 RUPEE

31.1700 g., 0.9990 Silver 1.011 oz. ASW **Series:** Nepal Wildlife **Obv:** Traditional design **Rev:** Multicolor elephants

Date	Mintage	F	VF	XF	Unc
VS2054-1998 Proof	8,000	Value: 45.00			

KM# 1085 2500 RUPEE

155.5100 g., 0.9990 Silver 5.0000 oz. ASW **Subject:** Conquest of Mt. Everest **Obv:** Traditional design **Rev:** Busts facing in front of Mount Everest **Note:** Photo reduced.Photo reduced.

Date	Mintage	F	VF	XF	Unc
VS2050 (1993) Proof	Est. 3,000	Value: 145			

KM# 1078 2500 RUPEE

155.5100 g., 0.9990 Silver 5.0000 oz. ASW **Obv:** Traditional design **Rev:** Buddha **Note:** Similar to 500 Rupee, KM#1077.

Date	Mintage	F	VF	XF	Unc
VS2052 (1995) Proof	3,000	Value: 200			

KM# 1101 5000 RUPEE

155.5000 g., 0.9990 Silver 4.9944 oz. ASW, 65 mm. **Subject:** Silver Jubilee of King's Accession **Obv:** Traditional design **Rev:** Multicolor crown

Date	Mintage	F	VF	XF	Unc
VS2053 (1996) Proof	Est. 2,500	Value: 200			

KM# 1106 5000 RUPEE

155.5518 g., 0.9990 Silver 4.9961 oz. ASW **Series:** Nepal Wildlife **Rev:** Multicolor elephants **Note:** Similar to 2000 Rupee, KM#1105.

Date	Mintage	F	VF	XF	Unc
VS2054 (1997) Proof	500	Value: 250			

ASARFI GOLD COINAGE

(Asarphi)

Fractional designations are approximate for this series. Actual Gold Weight (AGW) is used to identify each type.

KM# 1167 1/3 ASARFI

11.6500 g., 0.9000 Gold 0.3371 oz. AGW, 28.5 mm. **Obv:** Traditional design **Rev:** Ceremonial Vase **Note:** The Prince's Coming of Age

Date	Mintage	F	VF	XF	Unc
VS2046(1989)	1,000	—	—	—	275

KM# 1050a 0.3G ASARPHI

0.2500 g., 0.9990 Gold .0080 oz. AGW

Date	Mintage	F	VF	XF	Unc
VS2051 (1994)	—	—	—	—	40.00
VS2052 (1995)	—	—	—	—	40.00
VS2053 (1996)	—	—	—	—	35.00
VS2054 (1997)	—	—	—	—	35.00
VS2055 (1998)	—	—	—	—	35.00
VS2056 (1999)	—	—	—	—	35.00
VS2057 (2000)	—	—	—	—	35.00

KM# 1129 0.3G ASARPHI

0.3000 g., 0.9999 Gold .0096 oz. AGW, 7 mm. **Subject:** Buddha **Obv:** Traditional square design **Rev:** Buddha with halo **Edge:** Reeded

Date	Mintage	F	VF	XF	Unc
VS2057 (2000)	25,000	—	—	—	12.00

KM# 825 5.0G ASARPHI

5.0000 g., 0.9990 Gold .1607 oz. AGW

Date	Mintage	F	VF	XF	Unc
VS2028 (1971)	4	—	—	—	—
VS2030 (1973)	—	—	—	—	160
VS2031 (1974)	—	—	—	—	160
VS2036 (1979)	36	—	—	—	160
VS2037 (1980)	45	—	—	—	160

Note: Reports indicate a mintage of 44 pieces struck in .960 gold in 1980

Date	Mintage	F	VF	XF	Unc
VS2038 (1981)	—	—	—	—	160

KM# 822a 5.0G ASARPHI

5.0000 g., 0.9990 Gold .1607 oz. AGW **Subject:** Birendra Coronation **Obv:** Crown at center **Rev:** Dagger flanked by garlands from above

Date	Mintage	F	VF	XF	Unc
VS2031 (1974)	500	—	—	—	150

KM# 1021 5.0G ASARPHI

5.0000 g., 0.9000 Gold .1447 oz. AGW **Obv:** Traditional design **Rev:** Dagger flanked by garlands from above

Date	Mintage	F	VF	XF	Unc
VS2039 (1982)	23	—	—	—	—

KM# 1021a 5.0G ASARPHI

0.5000 g., 0.9990 Gold .1607 oz. AGW **Obv:** Traditional design **Rev:** Dagger flanked by garlands from above

Date	Mintage	F	VF	XF	Unc
VS2042 (1985)	—	—	—	—	125
VS2043 (1986)	—	—	—	—	125
VS2044 (1987)	—	—	—	—	125
VS2045 (1988)	—	—	—	—	120
VS2046 (1989)	—	—	—	—	120
VS2048 (1991)	—	—	—	—	120
VS2049 (1992)	—	—	—	—	120
VS2050 (1993)	—	—	—	—	115
VS2051 (1994)	—	—	—	—	115
VS2052 (1995)	—	—	—	—	115
VS2053 (1996)	—	—	—	—	115
VS2054 (1997)	—	—	—	—	115
VS2056 (1999)	—	—	—	—	115

KM# 1060 5.0G ASARPHI

5.0000 g., 0.9990 Gold .1600 oz. AGW **Subject:** The New Constitution **Obv:** Traditional design **Rev:** Flags above open book **Note:** Similar to 10 Asarphi, KM#1054.

Date	Mintage	F	VF	XF	Unc
VS2047 (1990)	—	—	—	—	150

KM# 1144 5.0G ASARPHI

5.0000 g., 0.9990 Gold .1606 oz. AGW **Subject:** New Parliament Session

Date	Mintage	F	VF	XF	Unc
VS2048 (1991)	—	—	—	—	120

KM# 827 10.0G ASARPHI

10.0000 g., 0.9990 Gold .3215 oz. AGW **Obv:** Traditional design **Rev:** Dagger flanked by garlands from above

Date	Mintage	F	VF	XF	Unc
VS2028 (1971)	Est. 4	—	—	—	—
VS2030 (1973)	50	—	—	—	350
VS2031 (1974)	—	—	—	—	350
VS2033 (1976)	—	—	—	—	350
VS2035 (1978)	—	—	—	—	350
VS2036 (1979)	52	—	—	—	350
VS2037 (1980)	30	—	—	—	350

Note: Reports indicate a mintage of 44 pieces struck in .960 gold in 1980

Date	Mintage	F	VF	XF	Unc
VS2038 (1981)	—	—	—	—	350

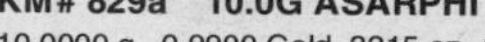

KM# 829a 10.0G ASARPHI

10.0000 g., 0.9990 Gold .3215 oz. AGW **Subject:** Birendra Coronation **Obv:** Crown **Rev:** Dagger flanked by garlands from above

Date	Mintage	F	VF	XF	Unc
VS2031 (1974) Proof	Est. 500	Value: 285			

KM# 829b 10.0G ASARPHI

10.0000 g., 0.5000 White Gold .1608 oz. AGW

Date	Mintage	F	VF	XF	Unc
VS2031 (1974) Proof	Est. 250	Value: 350			

Note: Sometimes referred to as 1000 Rupees

KM# 852 10.0G ASARPHI

11.6600 g., 0.9000 Gold .3374 oz. AGW **Series:** International Year of the Child **Obv:** Crowned bust right **Rev:** Child reading, emblems flank

Date	Mintage	F	VF	XF	Unc
VS2038 (1974) Proof	4,055	Value: 240			

Note: Struck in 1981

KM# 1022 10.0G ASARPHI

10.0000 g., 0.9000 Gold .2894 oz. AGW **Obv:** Traditional design **Rev:** Dagger flanked by garlands from above

Date	Mintage	F	VF	XF	Unc
VS2039 (1982)	25	—	—	—	—

KM# 1006 10.0G ASARPHI

10.0000 g., 0.5000 Gold .1608 oz. AGW **Subject:** 30th Anniversary Ascent of Mt. Everest **Obv:** Trident within small circle at center **Rev:** Mount Everest

Date	Mintage	F	VF	XF	Unc
VS2040 (1983) Proof	350	Value: 225			

KM# 1022a 10.0G ASARPHI

10.0000 g., 0.9990 Gold .3212 oz. AGW

Date	Mintage	F	VF	XF	Unc
VS2042 (1985)	—	—	—	—	250
VS2046 (1989)	—	—	—	—	235
VS2048 (1991)	—	—	—	—	235
VS2049 (1992)	—	—	—	—	235
VS2050 (1993)	—	—	—	—	225
VS2052 (1995)	—	—	—	—	225
VS2054 (1997)	—	—	—	—	225
VS2056 (1999)	—	—	—	—	225

KM# 1034 10.0G ASARPHI

10.0000 g., Gold **Subject:** Crown Prince, Sacred Thread Ceremony **Obv:** Traditional design

Date	Mintage	F	VF	XF	Unc
VS2044 (1987)	1,962	—	—	—	250

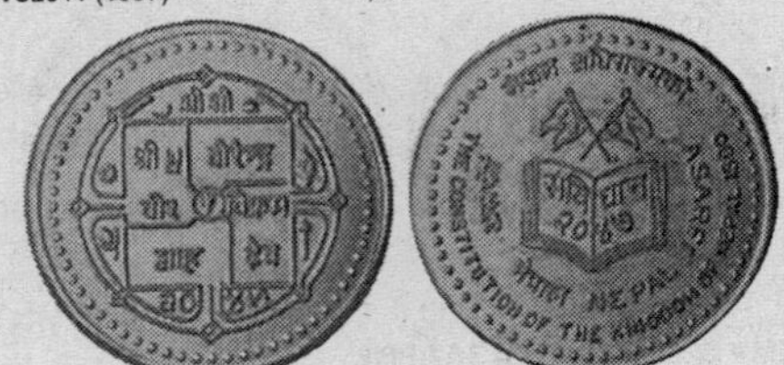

KM# 1054 10.0G ASARPHI

10.0000 g., 0.9990 Gold .3215 oz. AGW **Subject:** The New Constitution **Obv:** Traditional design **Rev:** Flags above open book

Date	Mintage	F	VF	XF	Unc
VS2047 (1990)	—	—	—	—	250

KM# 1145 10.0G ASARPHI

10.0000 g., 0.9990 Gold .3212 oz. AGW **Subject:** 50th Anniversary International Monetary Fund

Date	Mintage	F	VF	XF	Unc
VS2051 (1994)	—	—	—	—	225

KM# 1146 10.0G ASARPHI

10.0000 g., 0.9990 Gold .3212 oz. AGW **Subject:** 50th Anniversary World Bank

Date	Mintage	F	VF	XF	Unc
VS2051 (1994)	—	—	—	—	225

KM# 1147 10.0G ASARPHI

10.0000 g., 0.9990 Gold .3212 oz. AGW **Subject:** Queen Aishwariya Golden Anniversary

Date	Mintage	F	VF	XF	Unc
VS2056 (1999)	—	—	—	—	225

KM# 1122 1/25-OZ. ASARFI

1.2441 g., 0.9999 Gold .0400 oz. AGW **Obv:** Traditional square in circle design **Rev:** Buddha's portrait and Ashoka pillar **Note:** Lord Buddha; Similar to Asarfi KM#1124.

Date	Mintage	F	VF	XF	Unc
VS2055 (1998) Proof	30,000	Value: 35.00			

KM# 1130 1/25-OZ. ASARFI

1.2441 g., 0.9999 Gold .0400 oz. AGW, 18 mm. **Subject:** Buddha **Obv:** Traditional square design **Rev:** Buddha with halo **Edge:** Reeded

Date	Mintage	F	VF	XF	Unc
VS2057 (2000)	30,000	—	—	—	35.00

KM# 1033 1/20-OZ. ASARFI

5.8300 g., 0.9600 Gold .1800 oz. AGW **Subject:** Crown Prince, Sacred Thread Ceremony **Obv:** Traditional design

Date	Mintage	F	VF	XF	Unc
VS2044 (1987)	2,774	—	—	—	125

KM# 1079 1/20-OZ. ASARFI

1.5532 g., 0.9990 Gold .0500 oz. AGW **Obv:** Traditional design **Rev:** Buddha **Note:** Similar to 1-oz. Asarfi, KM#1082.

Date	Mintage	F	VF	XF	Unc
VS2052 (1995)	15,000	—	—	—	37.50

KM# 1096 1/20-OZ. ASARFI

1.5532 g., 0.9990 Gold .0500 oz. AGW **Subject:** Buddha's Birth **Obv:** Traditional design **Rev:** Standing figure at center, cameo at right, small figure at left **Note:** Similar to 1500 Rupee, KM#1095.

Date	Mintage	F	VF	XF	Unc
VS2054 (1997)	15,000	—	—	—	40.00

KM# 1107 1/20-OZ. ASARFI

1.5552 g., 0.9990 Gold .0500 oz. AGW **Series:** Nepal Wildlife **Obv:** Traditional design **Rev:** Multicolor leopard **Note:** Similar to 2000 Rupees, KM#1104.

Date	Mintage	F	VF	XF	Unc
VS2054 (1998) Proof	15,000	Value: 75.00			

KM# 1108 1/20-OZ. ASARFI

1.5552 g., 0.9990 Gold .0500 oz. AGW **Series:** Nepal Wildlife **Obv:** Traditional design **Rev:** Multicolor tiger **Note:** Similar to 100 Rupees, KM#1102.

Date	Mintage	F	VF	XF	Unc
VS2054 (1998) Proof	15,000	Value: 75.00			

KM# 1050 1/10-OZ. ASARFI

2.5000 g., 0.9000 Gold .0724 oz. AGW

Date	Mintage	F	VF	XF	Unc
VS2039 (1982)	11	—	—	—	—

KM# 1037 1/10-OZ. ASARFI

3.1100 g., 0.9990 Gold .1000 oz. AGW **Obv:** Traditional design **Rev:** Snow leopard **Note:** Similar to 1-oz. Asarphi, KM#1040.

Date	Mintage	F	VF	XF	Unc
VS2045 (1988)	Est. 10,000	—	—	—	70.00
VS2045 (1988) Proof	2,000	Value: 80.00			

KM# 1080 1/10-OZ. ASARFI

3.1100 g., 0.9990 Gold .1000 oz. AGW **Obv:** Traditional design **Rev:** Buddha **Note:** Similar to 1-oz. Asarphi, KM#1082.

Date	Mintage	F	VF	XF	Unc
VS2052 (1995)	15,000	—	—	—	70.00

KM# 1097 1/10-OZ. ASARFI

3.1100 g., 0.9990 Gold .1000 oz. AGW **Subject:** Buddha's Birth **Obv:** Traditional design **Rev:** Standing figure at center, cameo at right, small figure at left **Note:** Similar to 1500 Rupee, KM#1095.

Date	Mintage	F	VF	XF	Unc
VS2054 (1997)	15,000	—	—	—	70.00

KM# 1109 1/10-OZ. ASARFI

3.1104 g., 0.9990 Gold .1000 oz. AGW **Series:** Nepal Wildlife **Obv:** Traditional design **Rev:** Multicolor leopard **Note:** Similar to 2000 Rupees, KM#1104.

Date	Mintage	F	VF	XF	Unc
VS2054 (1998) Proof	10,000	Value: 100			

KM# 1123 1/10-OZ. ASARFI

3.1104 g., 0.9999 Gold .1000 oz. AGW **Obv:** Traditional square in circle design **Rev:** Buddha's portrait and Ashoka pillar **Note:** Lord Buddha; Similar to Asarfi KM#1124.

Date	Mintage	F	VF	XF	Unc
VS2055 (1998) Proof	15,000	Value: 70.00			

KM# 1131 1/10-OZ. ASARFI

3.1100 g., 0.9990 Gold .1000 oz. AGW, 18 mm. **Subject:** Buddha **Obv:** Traditional square design **Rev:** Buddha with halo **Edge:** Reeded

Date	Mintage	F	VF	XF	Unc
VS2057 (2000)	30,000	—	—	—	70.00

KM# 819 1/4-OZ. ASARFI

2.5000 g., 0.9990 Gold .0803 oz. AGW **Obv:** Traditional design **Rev:** Dagger flanked by garlands from above

Date	Mintage	F	VF	XF	Unc
VS2028 (1971)	4	—	—	—	—
VS2030 (1973)	—	—	—	—	110
VS2031 (1974)	—	—	—	—	110
VS2036 (1979)	—	—	—	—	110
VS2037 (1980)	48	—	—	—	110

KM# 816a 1/4-OZ. ASARFI

7.7700 g., 0.9990 Gold .250 oz. AGW **Subject:** Birendra Coronation **Obv:** Crown **Rev:** Dagger flanked by garlands from above

Date	Mintage	F	VF	XF	Unc
VS2031 (1974)	500	—	—	—	175

KM# 1038 1/4-OZ. ASARFI

7.7700 g., 0.9990 Gold .2500 oz. AGW **Obv:** Traditional design **Rev:** Snow leopard **Note:** Similar to 1-oz. Asarphi, KM#1040, Bullion Series.

Date	Mintage	F	VF	XF	Unc
VS2045 (1988)	8,000	—	—	—	175
VS2045 (1988) Proof	2,000	Value: 185			

KM# 1059 1/4-OZ. ASARFI

7.7700 g., 0.9990 Gold .25 oz. AGW **Obv:** Traditional design **Rev:** Flags above open book **Note:** Similar to 1-oz. Asarphi, KM#1054.

Date	Mintage	F	VF	XF	Unc
VS2047 (1990)	—	—	—	—	175

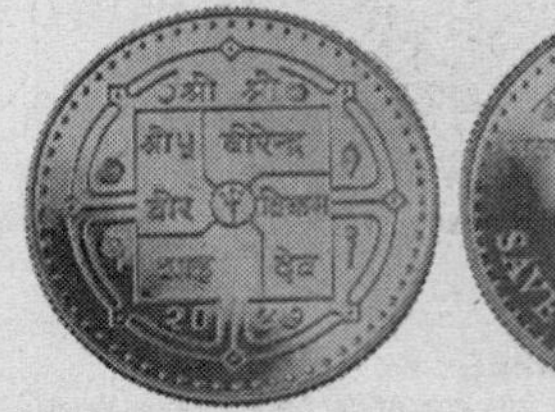

KM# 1056 1/4-OZ. ASARFI

11.6600 g., 0.9000 Gold .3374 oz. AGW **Series:** Save the Children **Obv:** Traditional design **Rev:** Older and younger children

Date	Mintage	F	VF	XF	Unc
VS2047 (1990) Proof	3,000	Value: 245			

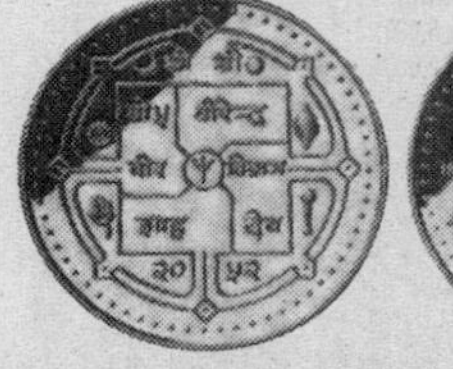

KM# 1093 1/4-OZ. ASARFI

7.7760 g., 0.9990 Gold .25 oz. AGW **Series:** Olympics **Obv:** Traditional design **Rev:** Runner and temple

Date	Mintage	F	VF	XF	Unc
VS2052 (1995)	Est. 3,000	—	—	—	175

KM# 1081 1/4-OZ. ASARFI

7.7759 g., 0.9990 Gold .2500 oz. AGW **Obv:** Traditional design **Rev:** Buddha **Note:** Similar to 1-oz. Asarphi, KM#1082.

Date	Mintage	F	VF	XF	Unc
VS2052 (1995)	15,000	—	—	—	175

KM# 1098 1/4-OZ. ASARFI

7.7759 g., 0.9990 Gold .2500 oz. AGW **Subject:** Buddha's Birth **Obv:** Traditional design **Rev:** Standing figure at center, cameo at right, small figure at left **Note:** Similar to 1500 Rupees, KM#1095.

Date	Mintage	F	VF	XF	Unc
VS2054 (1997)	15,000	—	—	—	175

KM# 1110 1/4-OZ. ASARFI

7.7759 g., 0.9990 Gold .2500 oz. AGW **Series:** Nepal Wildlife **Obv:** Traditional design **Rev:** Multicolor elephants **Note:** Similar to 2000 Rupees, KM#1105.

Date	Mintage	F	VF	XF	Unc
VS2054 (1998) Proof	2,000	Value: 185			

KM# 1111 1/4-OZ. ASARFI

7.7759 g., 0.9990 Gold .2500 oz. AGW **Series:** Nepal Wildlife **Obv:** Traditional design **Rev:** Multicolor tiger **Note:** Similar to 100 Rupees, KM#1102.

Date	Mintage	F	VF	XF	Unc
VS2054 (1998) Proof	2,000	Value: 185			

KM# 1112 1/4-OZ. ASARFI

7.7759 g., 0.9990 Gold .2500 oz. AGW **Series:** Nepal Wildlife **Obv:** Traditional design **Rev:** Multicolor rhinoceros **Note:** Similar to 100 Rupees, KM#1103.

Date	Mintage	F	VF	XF	Unc
VS2054 (1998) Proof	2,000	Value: 185			

KM# 1113 1/4-OZ. ASARFI

7.7759 g., 0.9990 Gold .2500 oz. AGW **Series:** Nepal Wildlife **Obv:** Traditional design **Rev:** Multicolor leopard **Note:** Similar to 100 Rupees, KM#1104.

Date	Mintage	F	VF	XF	Unc
VS2054 (1998) Proof	2,000	Value: 185			

KM# 1008 1/2-OZ. ASARFI

15.9800 g., 0.9000 Gold .4624 oz. AGW **Subject:** 10th Anniversary of Reign **Rev:** Dagger flanked by garlands from above

Date	Mintage	F	VF	XF	Unc
VS2038 (1981)	27	—	—	—	450
VS2038 (1981) Proof	5,092	Value: 325			

KM# 1011 1/2-OZ. ASARFI

15.9800 g., 0.9170 Gold .4712 oz. AGW **Series:** Year of the Scout **Obv:** Traditional design **Rev:** Girl scout filling water jug

Date	Mintage	F	VF	XF	Unc
VS2039 (1982)	2,000	—	—	—	400

KM# 1045 1/2-OZ. ASARFI

15.0000 g., 0.9000 Gold .4340 oz. AGW **Subject:** 3rd SAARC Summit **Obv:** Traditional design **Rev:** Summit emblem **Note:** Similar to 300 Rupees, KM#1044.

Date	Mintage	F	VF	XF	Unc
VS2044 (1987)	1,000	—	—	—	350

KM# 1039 1/2-OZ. ASARFI

15.5500 g., 0.9990 Gold .5000 oz. AGW **Obv:** Traditional design **Rev:** Snow leopard **Note:** Similar to 1-oz. Asarphi, KM#1040.

Date	Mintage	F	VF	XF	Unc
VS2045 (1988)	Est. 8,000	—	—	—	350
VS2045 (1988) Proof	2,000	Value: 375			

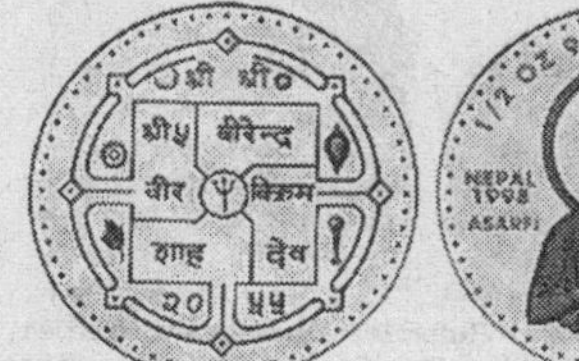

KM# 1124 1/2-OZ. ASARFI

15.5518 g., 0.9999 Gold .5000 oz. AGW **Obv:** Traditional square in circle design **Rev:** Lord Buddha, Ashoka pillar

Date	Mintage	F	VF	XF	Unc
VS2055 (1998) Proof	2,500	Value: 365			

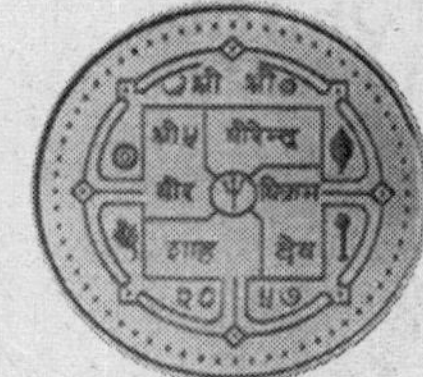

KM# 1132 1/2-OZ. ASARFI

15.5518 g., 0.9999 Gold .5000 oz. AGW, 27 mm. **Subject:** Buddha **Obv:** Traditional square design **Rev:** Buddha with halo **Edge:** Reeded

Date	Mintage	F	VF	XF	Unc
VS2057 (2000) Proof	2,500	Value: 365			

KM# 1027 1-OZ. ASARFI

31.1000 g., 0.9990 Gold 1. oz. AGW **Series:** Wildlife Protection **Obv:** Traditional design **Rev:** Ganges River Dolphins

Date	Mintage	F	VF	XF	Unc
VS2043 (1986) Proof	5,000	Value: 700			

KM# 1040 1-OZ. ASARFI

31.1000 g., 0.9999 Gold 1.0000 oz. AGW **Obv:** Traditional design **Rev:** Snow leopard

Date	Mintage	F	VF	XF	Unc
VS2045 (1988)	Est. 10,000	—	—	—	725
VS2045 (1988) Proof	2,000	Value: 750			

KM# 1082 1-OZ. ASARFI

31.1035 g., 0.9999 Gold 1.0000 oz. AGW **Obv:** Traditional design **Rev:** Buddha

Date	Mintage	F	VF	XF	Unc
VS2052 (1995) Proof	2,500	Value: 700			

KM# 1099 1-OZ. ASARFI

31.1035 g., 0.9999 Gold 1.0000 oz. AGW **Subject:** Buddha's Birth **Obv:** Traditional square in circle design **Rev:** Standing figure at center, cameo at right, small figure at left

Date	Mintage	F	VF	XF	Unc
VS2054 (1997) Proof	2,500	Value: 700			

KM# 1086 1-1/2 OZ. ASARFI

44.6400 g., 0.9167 Gold 1.5 oz. AGW **Subject:** Conquest of Mt. Everest **Obv:** Traditional design **Rev:** Mount Everest

Date	Mintage	F	VF	XF	Unc
VS2050 (1993) Proof	Est. 100	Value: 1,100			

PATTERNS

Including off metal strikes

KM#	Date	Mintage	Identification	Mkt Val
Pn3	VS1975	—	5 Paisa. Copper. KM#690.1	—

PIEFORTS

KM#	Date	Mintage	Identification	Mkt Val
P1	VS2038	88	100 Rupee. Silver. KM#851.	100
P2	VS2039	48	Asarphi.	1,250

MINT SETS

KM#	Date	Mintage	Identification	Issue Price	Mkt Val
MS1	1932 (3)	—		—	—
MS2	1949 (3)	—	KM#716, 718, 723 (restrikes)	—	8.00
MS3	1953 (8)	—	KM#733, 735-740, 742	—	160
MSA4	1953 (7)	—	KM#745.1, 750.1, 756.3, 761, 770, 776, 790	—	10.00
MS4	1955 (3)	—	KM#712 (2000); 733; 749 (2012)	0.85	5.00
MS5	1956 (7)	—	KM#745.1, 750.1, 756.2, 761, 770, 776, 790	—	50.00
MS6	1956 (7)	—	KM#745.1, 750.1, 756.3, 761, 770, 776, 790 (restrikes)	—	13.50
MS7	1957 (4)	—	KM#740 (2011), 742, 738 (2010), 769 (2014)	2.05	12.00
MS8	1957 (6)	—	KM#709.1 (1996), 755 (2014), 760 (2011); 2 pieces each	0.85	7.00
MS9	1964 (7)	—	KM#747, 752, 758, 763, 772, 778, 785	—	10.00
MS10	1964 (7)	—	KM#747, 752, 758a, 764, 772, 778, 785	—	50.00
MS11	1965 (7)	—	KM#747, 752 (2022), 758, 763, 772, 778, 786 (2021)	2.75	10.00
MS12	1966 (7)	—	KM#748, 753, 759, 765, 772, 779, 787	—	7.00
MS13	1967 (7)	—	KM#748, 753, 759, 765, 772, 779, 787	—	5.00
MS14	1971 (7)	—	KM#799, 801, 802, 806, 815, 821, 828	—	5.00
MS15	1974 (7)	—	KM#800, 804, 808, 816.1, 822.1, 829.1, 838	—	12.50
MS16	1974 (2)	—	KM#829.1, 841	32.50	30.00
MS17	1975 (5)	—	KM#808, 816.1, 822.1, 829.1, 838	—	13.00
MS18	1975 (3)	—	KM#809, 831, 836	—	9.00
MSA19	1996, 1995, 2011 (3)	—	KM#709.2 (1996); 711 (1995); 737 (2011)	—	7.00
MS19	1997 (3)	—	KM#1096-1098	—	285

PROOF SETS

KM#	Date	Mintage	Identification	Issue Price	Mkt Val
PS1	1911 (9)	—	KM621, 622, 631, 634, 644, 649, 651.2, 656, 658, Copper, Silver	—	—
PS2	1911 (6)	—	KM668, 671.2, 672.5, 673.2, 675.1, 680, Gold	—	—
PS3	1970 (7)	2,187	KM#748, 753, 759, 765, 773, 780, 788	10.00	15.00
PS4	1971 (7)	2,380	KM#748, 753, 759, 765, 773, 780, 788	10.00	15.00
PS5	1972 (7)	3,943	KM#799, 801, 802, 807, 815, 821, 828	10.00	8.50
PS6	1973 (7)	8,891	KM#799, 801, 802, 807, 815, 821, 828	10.00	6.00
PS9	1981 (7)	1,000	KM#800a, 804a, 808a, 816.2, 822.2, 829.2, 838a (dated 1974)Coins dated 2031 (1974) but this set was issued in 1981 to celebrate the 7th Anniversary of the Coronation.	62.00	50.00
PS7	1974 (7)	10,543	KM#799, 801, 802, 807, 815, 821, 828	10.00	5.50
PS8	1974 (2)	30,000	KM#839a, 841a	50.00	42.00
PS10	1988 (4)	2,000	KM#1037-1040	—	1,400
PS11	1995-97 (2)	—	KM#1077, 1099	—	740

NETHERLANDS

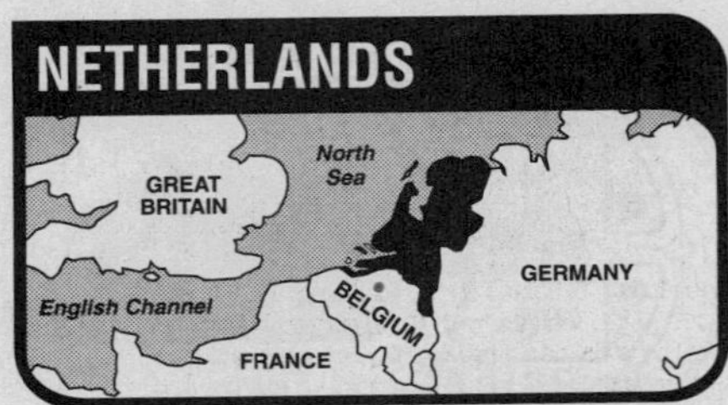

The Kingdom of the Netherlands, a country of western Europe fronting on the North Sea and bordered by Belgium and Germany, has an area of 15,770 sq. mi. (41,500 sq. km.) and a population of 16.1 million. Capital: Amsterdam, but the seat of government is at The Hague. The economy is based on dairy farming and a variety of industrial activities. Chemicals, yarns and fabrics, and meat products are exported.

After being a part of Charlemagne's empire in the 8th and 9th centuries, the Netherlands came under control of Burgundy and the Austrian Hapsburgs, and finally was subjected to Spanish dominion in the 16th century. Led by William of Orange, the Dutch revolted against Spain in 1568. The seven northern provinces formed the Union of Utrecht and declared their independence in 1581, becoming the Republic of the United Netherlands. In the following century, the *Golden Age* of Dutch history, the Netherlands became a great sea and colonial power, a patron of the arts and a refuge for the persecuted. The United Dutch Republic ended in 1795 when the French formed the Batavian Republic. Napoleon made his brother Louis, the King of Holland in 1806, however he abdicated in 1810 when Napoleon annexed Holland. The French were expelled in 1813, and all the provinces of Holland and Belgium were merged into the Kingdom of the United Netherlands under William I, in 1814. The Belgians withdrew in 1830 to form their own kingdom, the last substantial change in the configuration of European Netherlands. German forces invaded in 1940 as the royal family fled to England where a government-in-exile was formed.

WORLD WAR II COINAGE

U.S. mints in the name of the government in exile and its remaining Curacao and Suriname Colonies during the years 1941-45 minted coinage of the Netherlands Homeland Types - KM #152, 153, 163, 164, 161.1 and 161.2 -. The Curacao and Suriname strikes, distinguished by the presence of a palm tree in combination with a mint mark (P-Philadelphia; D-Denver; S-San Francisco) flanking the date, are incorporated under those titles in this volume. Pieces of this period struck in the name of the homeland bear an acorn and mint mark and are incorporated in the following tabulation.

NOTE: Excepting the World War II issues struck at U.S. mints, all of the modern coins were struck at the Utrecht Mint and bear the caduceus mint mark of that facility. They also bear the mintmasters' marks.

RULERS

KINGDOM OF THE NETHERLANDS

Wilhelmina I, 1890-1948
Juliana, 1948-1980
Beatrix, 1980—

MINT MARKS

D - Denver, 1943-1945
P - Philadelphia, 1941-1945
S - San Francisco, 1944-1945

MINT PRIVY MARKS

Utrecht

Date	Privy Mark
1806-present	Caduceus

MINTMASTERS' PRIVY MARKS

U. S. Mints

Date	Privy Mark
1941-45	Palm tree

Utrecht Mint

Date	Privy Mark
1888-1909	Halberd
1909	Halberd and star
1909-1933	Seahorse
1933-42	Grapes
1943-1945	No privy mark
1945-69	Fish
1969-79	Cock
1980	Cock and star (temporal)
1980-88	Anvil with hammer
1989-99	Bow and arrow
2000-	Bow, arrow and star

NOTE: A star adjoining the privy mark indicates that the piece was struck at the beginning of the term of office of a successor. (The star was used only if the successor had not chosen his own mark yet.)

NOTE: Since October, 1999, the Dutch Mint has taken the title of Royal Dutch Mint.

MONETARY SYSTEM

Until January 29, 2002

100 Cents = 1 Gulden

KINGDOM OF THE NETHERLANDS

DECIMAL COINAGE

KM# 109 1/2 CENT

1.2500 g., Bronze, 14 mm. **Ruler:** Wilhelmina I **Obv:** Crowned rampant lion left within beaded circle, date below **Obv. Legend:** KONINGRIJK DER NEDERLANDEN **Rev:** Value within wreath **Edge:** Reeded **Designer:** J.P.M. Menger

Date	Mintage	F	VF	XF	Unc	BU
1901	6,000,000	1.50	3.00	6.00	20.00	40.00

KM# 133 1/2 CENT

1.2500 g., Bronze, 14 mm. **Ruler:** Wilhelmina I **Obv:** Crowned arms with 17 small shields within beaded circle **Obv. Legend:** KONINGRIJK DER NEDERLANDEN **Rev:** Value within wreath **Edge:** Reeded **Designer:** J.P.M. Menger

Date	Mintage	F	VF	XF	Unc	BU
1903	10,000,000	1.00	2.00	3.00	10.00	15.00
1906	10,000,000	1.00	2.00	3.00	10.00	15.00

KM# 138 1/2 CENT

1.2500 g., Bronze, 14 mm. **Ruler:** Wilhelmina I **Obv:** Crowned arms with 15 large shields within beaded circle, date and legend **Rev:** Value within wreath **Edge:** Reeded **Designer:** J.P.M. Menger

Date	Mintage	F	VF	XF	Unc	BU
1909	5,000,000	1.00	2.00	3.00	10.00	17.50
1911	5,000,000	1.00	2.00	3.00	10.00	17.50
1912	5,000,000	1.00	2.00	3.00	10.00	17.50
1914	5,000,000	1.00	2.00	3.00	10.00	17.50
1915	2,500,000	5.00	10.00	15.00	25.00	45.00
1916	4,000,000	2.00	4.00	7.00	15.00	25.00
1917	5,000,000	1.00	2.00	4.00	10.00	15.00
1921	1,500,000	5.00	10.00	15.00	25.00	45.00
1922/1	—	100	250	400	800	1,000
1922	2,500,000	5.00	10.00	15.00	25.00	45.00
1928	4,000,000	1.00	2.00	3.00	8.00	15.00
1930	6,000,000	1.00	1.50	2.50	6.00	10.00
1934	5,000,000	0.75	1.75	2.50	5.00	8.00
1936	5,000,000	0.75	1.75	2.50	5.00	8.00
1937	1,600,000	1.00	2.50	4.00	8.00	12.50
1938	8,400,000	0.75	1.50	2.00	3.00	5.00
1940	6,000,000	0.75	1.50	2.00	3.00	5.00

KM# 130 CENT

2.5000 g., Bronze, 19 mm. **Ruler:** Wilhelmina I **Obv:** Crowned arms with 15 large shields within beaded circle **Obv. Legend:** KONINKRIJK DER NEDERLANDEN **Rev:** Value within wreath **Edge:** Reeded **Designer:** J.P.M. Menger

Date	Mintage	F	VF	XF	Unc	BU
1901	10,000,000	1.00	2.50	5.00	20.00	45.00

KM# 131 CENT

2.5000 g., Bronze, 19 mm. **Ruler:** Wilhelmina I **Obv:** Crowned arms with 10 large shields within beaded circle **Obv. Legend:** KONINGRIJK DER NEDERLANDEN **Rev:** Value within wreath **Edge:** Reeded **Designer:** J.P.M. Menger

Date	Mintage	F	VF	XF	Unc	BU
1901	10,000,000	1.00	2.50	5.00	20.00	45.00

KM# 132.1 CENT

2.5000 g., Bronze, 19 mm. **Ruler:** Wilhelmina I **Obv:** Crowned arms with 15 medium shields within beaded circle **Obv. Legend:** KONINGRIJK DER NEDERLANDEN **Rev:** Value within wreath **Edge:** Reeded **Designer:** J.P.M. Menger

Date	Mintage	F	VF	XF	Unc	BU
1902	10,000,000	1.00	2.00	3.00	15.00	25.00
1904	15,000,000	1.00	2.00	3.00	15.00	25.00
1905	10,000,000	1.00	2.00	3.00	15.00	25.00
1906	9,000,000	1.00	2.00	3.00	15.00	25.00
1907	6,000,000	6.00	12.00	30.00	60.00	100

KM# 132.2 CENT

2.5000 g., Bronze, 19 mm. **Ruler:** Wilhelmina I **Obv:** 15 medium shields in field **Obv. Legend:** KONINGRIJK DER NEDERLANDEN **Rev:** Value within wreath **Edge:** Plain **Designer:** J.P.M. Menger

Date	Mintage	F	VF	XF	Unc	BU
1906 Proof	—	Value: 875				

KM# 152 CENT

Bronze, 19 mm. **Ruler:** Wilhelmina I **Obv:** Crowned arms with 17 small shields within beaded circle **Rev:** Value within wreath

Date	Mintage	F	VF	XF	Unc	BU
1913	5,000,000	2.50	6.00	12.00	28.00	50.00
1914	9,000,000	1.00	2.00	3.00	15.00	25.00
1915	10,800,000	1.00	2.00	3.00	12.00	18.00
1916 Proof	—	Value: 110				
1916	21,700,000	0.75	1.00	2.00	10.00	15.00
1917	20,000,000	0.75	1.00	2.00	10.00	15.00
1918	10,000,000	1.00	2.00	4.00	12.00	20.00
1919	6,000,000	2.75	5.00	10.00	20.00	30.00
1920	11,400,000	0.75	1.50	2.00	10.00	15.00
1921	12,600,000	0.75	1.50	2.00	10.00	15.00
1922	20,000,000	0.75	1.50	2.00	10.00	15.00
1924	1,400,000	15.00	30.00	55.00	110	160
1925	18,600,000	0.75	1.50	2.00	10.00	15.00
1926	10,000,000	0.75	1.50	2.00	10.00	15.00
1927	10,000,000	0.75	1.50	2.00	10.00	15.00
1928	10,000,000	0.75	1.50	2.00	10.00	15.00
1929	20,000,000	0.75	1.50	2.00	8.00	12.00
1930	10,000,000	0.75	1.50	2.00	8.00	12.00
1931	3,400,000	3.50	7.50	12.50	35.00	50.00
1937	10,000,000	0.50	1.00	1.50	5.00	8.00
1938	16,600,000	0.50	1.00	1.50	5.00	8.00
1939	22,000,000	0.50	1.00	1.50	5.00	7.00
1940	24,600,000	0.50	1.00	1.50	5.00	7.00
1941	66,600,000	0.25	0.60	1.00	2.50	4.00

Note: For similar coins dated 1942P see Curacao; 1943P, 1957-1960 see Suriname

KM# 170 CENT

2.0000 g., Zinc, 17 mm. **Ruler:** Wilhelmina I **Obv:** Circled cross with banner below **Rev:** Value, waves, date and sprig **Edge:** Reeded **Designer:** N. de Haas

Date	Mintage	F	VF	XF	Unc	BU
1941	31,800,000	1.00	2.00	4.00	15.00	25.00
1942	241,000,000	0.25	0.50	1.00	3.00	8.00
1943	71,000,000	0.50	1.00	2.00	5.00	15.00
1944	29,600,000	1.00	2.00	4.00	15.00	25.00

KM# 175 CENT

2.0000 g., Bronze, 14 mm. **Ruler:** Wilhelmina I **Obv:** Head left **Rev:** Value divides date **Edge:** Plain **Designer:** L.O. Wenckebach

Date	Mintage	F	VF	XF	Unc	BU
1948	175,000,000	0.10	0.25	0.50	3.50	9.00
1948 Proof	—	Value: 80.00				

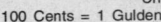

KM# 180 CENT

2.0000 g., Bronze, 14 mm. **Ruler:** Juliana **Obv:** Head right **Rev:** Value divides date **Designer:** L.O. Wenckeback

Date	Mintage	F	VF	XF	Unc	BU
1950 Proof	—	Value: 50.00				
1950	46,400,000	0.10	0.20	2.00	6.00	10.00
1951	45,800,000	0.10	0.20	2.00	6.00	10.00
1951 Proof	—	Value: 45.00				
1952	68,000,000	0.10	0.20	2.00	6.00	10.00
1952 Proof	—	Value: 45.00				
1953	54,000,000	0.10	0.20	2.00	6.00	10.00
1953 Proof	—	Value: 45.00				
1954	54,000,000	0.10	0.20	2.00	6.00	10.00
1954 Proof	—	Value: 45.00				
1955	52,000,000	0.10	0.20	2.00	6.00	10.00
1955 Proof	—	Value: 45.00				
1956	34,800,000	0.10	0.20	2.00	6.00	10.00
1956 Proof	—	Value: 45.00				
1957	48,000,000	0.10	0.20	0.25	6.00	10.00
1957 Proof	—	Value: 45.00				
1958	34,000,000	0.10	0.20	0.25	6.00	10.00
1958 Proof	—	Value: 40.00				
1959	36,000,000	0.10	0.20	1.00	6.00	10.00
1959 Proof	—	Value: 35.00				
1960	40,000,000	0.10	0.20	1.00	2.00	10.00
1960 Proof	—	Value: 35.00				
1961	52,000,000	0.10	0.20	1.00	1.50	3.00
1961 Proof	—	Value: 35.00				
1962	57,000,000	0.10	0.20	1.00	1.50	3.00
1962 Proof	—	Value: 35.00				
1963	70,000,000	0.10	0.20	1.00	1.50	3.00
1963 Proof	—	Value: 35.00				
1964	73,000,000	0.10	0.20	1.00	1.50	3.00
1964 Proof	—	Value: 35.00				
1965	91,000,000	0.10	0.20	1.00	1.50	3.00
1965 Proof	—	Value: 35.00				
1966 large date	104,000,000	0.10	0.20	1.00	1.50	3.00
1966 Proof, large date	—	Value: 35.00				
1966 small date	Inc. above	0.10	0.20	1.00	1.50	3.00
1966 Proof, small date	—	Value: 20.00				
1967	140,000,000	0.10	0.20	1.00	1.50	3.00
1967 Proof	—	Value: 25.00				
1968	28,000,000	0.10	0.20	1.00	1.50	3.00
1968 Proof	—	Value: 20.00				
1969 fish privy mark	50,000,000	0.10	0.20	0.30	0.75	1.25
1969 Proof, fish privy mark	—	Value: 20.00				
1969 cock privy mark	50,000,000	0.10	0.20	0.30	0.75	1.25
1969 Proof, cock privy mark	—	Value: 20.00				
1970	100,000,000	0.10	0.20	0.30	0.75	1.25
1970 Proof	—	Value: 20.00				
1971	70,000,000	—	—	—	0.75	1.25
1972	40,000,000	—	—	—	0.75	1.25
1973	34,000,000	—	—	—	0.75	1.25
1974	46,000,000	—	—	—	0.75	1.25
1975	25,000,000	—	—	—	0.75	1.25
1976	15,000,000	—	—	—	0.75	1.25
1977	15,000,000	—	—	—	0.75	1.25
1978	15,000,000	—	—	—	0.75	1.25
1979	15,000,000	—	—	—	0.75	1.25
1980 cock and star privy mark	15,300,000	—	—	0.10	0.20	0.50

KM# 134 2-1/2 CENT

4.0000 g., Bronze, 23.5 mm. **Ruler:** Wilhelmina I **Obv:** Crowned arms with 15 large shields within beaded circle **Obv. Legend:** KONINGRIJK DER NEDERLANDEN **Rev:** Value within wreath **Edge:** Reeded **Designer:** J.P.M. Menger

Date	Mintage	F	VF	XF	Unc	BU
1903	4,000,000	2.00	3.50	6.50	20.00	40.00
1904	4,000,000	2.00	3.50	6.50	20.00	40.00
1905	4,000,000	2.00	3.50	6.50	20.00	40.00
1906	8,000,000	2.00	3.50	6.50	20.00	35.00

KM# 150 2-1/2 CENT

Bronze **Ruler:** Wilhelmina I **Obv:** Crowned arms with 15 large shields within beaded circle **Obv. Legend:** KONINGRIJK. **Rev:** Value within wreath **Designer:** J.P.M. Menger

Date	Mintage	F	VF	XF	Unc	BU
1912	2,000,000	4.00	8.00	16.50	50.00	100
1913	4,000,000	2.50	4.50	8.00	15.00	35.00
1914	2,000,000	4.00	8.00	16.50	50.00	100
1915	3,000,000	3.00	6.00	12.00	25.00	55.00
1916	8,000,000	2.00	3.50	6.00	15.00	25.00
1918	4,000,000	2.50	4.00	8.00	22.50	45.00
1919	2,000,000	3.00	6.00	12.00	25.00	50.00
1929	8,000,000	2.00	3.50	6.00	10.00	15.00
1941	19,800,000	1.25	2.00	3.00	6.00	9.00

KM# 171 2-1/2 CENT

2.0000 g., Zinc, 20 mm. **Ruler:** Wilhelmina I **Obv:** Two swans on roof **Rev:** Value with four waves **Designer:** N. de Haas

Date	Mintage	F	VF	XF	Unc	BU
1941	27,600,000	1.00	3.00	5.00	15.00	30.00
1942	Est. 200,000	750	3,500	5,500	8,500	11,000

Note: Almost entire issue melted, about 30 pieces known

KM# 137 5 CENTS

4.5000 g., Copper-Nickel, 12 mm. **Ruler:** Wilhelmina I **Obv:** Crown flanked by sprigs **Rev:** Value within wreath **Designer:** J.C. Wienecke

Date	Mintage	F	VF	XF	Unc	BU
1907	6,000,000	3.00	6.00	10.00	20.00	35.00
1908	5,430,000	4.00	8.00	12.50	22.50	40.00
1909	2,570,000	20.00	30.00	40.00	80.00	130

KM# 153 5 CENTS

4.5000 g., Copper-Nickel, 21.3 mm. **Ruler:** Wilhelmina I **Obv:** Orange branch within circle **Rev:** Value within shells and beaded circle **Shape:** 4-sided **Designer:** J.C. Wienecke

Date	Mintage	F	VF	XF	Unc	BU
1913	6,000,000	1.50	3.00	5.00	15.00	30.00
1914	7,400,000	1.50	3.00	5.00	15.00	30.00
1923	10,000,000	1.50	3.00	5.00	15.00	30.00
1929	8,000,000	1.50	3.00	5.00	15.00	30.00
1932	2,000,000	5.50	12.00	20.00	35.00	65.00
1933	1,400,000	20.00	30.00	50.00	70.00	140
1934	2,600,000	4.00	6.00	10.00	20.00	40.00
1936	2,600,000	4.00	6.00	10.00	20.00	40.00
1938	4,200,000	2.00	3.50	4.50	10.00	20.00
1939	4,600,000	2.00	3.50	4.50	10.00	20.00
1940	7,200,000	2.00	3.00	4.00	9.00	15.00

Note: For a similar coin dated 1943, see Curacao

KM# 172 5 CENTS

2.6000 g., Zinc, 18 mm. **Ruler:** Wilhelmina I **Obv:** Two crossed horse heads and sun within square **Rev:** Value within circle flanked by nine waves and sprig **Shape:** 4-sided **Designer:** N. de Haas

Date	Mintage	F	VF	XF	Unc	BU
1941	32,200,000	1.00	2.50	6.00	18.00	35.00
1942	11,800,000	2.00	3.50	9.00	22.00	40.00
1943	7,000,000	5.00	8.00	16.50	42.50	75.00

KM# 176 5 CENTS

2.5000 g., Bronze, 21 mm. **Ruler:** Wilhelmina I **Obv:** Head left **Rev:** Value divides date and orange branch **Designer:** L.O. Wencheback

Date	Mintage	F	VF	XF	Unc	BU
1948	23,600,000	—	0.50	0.75	7.00	16.50
1948 Proof	—	Value: 100				

KM# 181 5 CENTS

3.5000 g., Bronze, 21 mm. **Ruler:** Juliana **Obv:** Head right **Rev:** Value divides date and orange branch **Designer:** L.O. Wenckeback

Date	Mintage	F	VF	XF	Unc	BU
1950	20,000,000	—	0.10	0.25	7.50	15.00
1950 Proof	—	Value: 70.00				
1951	16,200,000	—	0.10	0.25	7.50	15.00
1951 Proof	—	Value: 70.00				
1952	14,400,000	—	0.10	0.25	7.50	15.00
1952 Proof	—	Value: 70.00				
1953	12,000,000	—	0.10	0.25	7.50	15.00
1953 Proof	—	Value: 70.00				
1954	14,000,000	—	0.10	0.25	7.50	15.00
1954 Proof	—	Value: 70.00				
1955	11,400,000	—	0.10	0.25	7.50	15.00
1955 Proof	—	Value: 70.00				
1956	7,400,000	—	0.15	0.35	8.50	20.00
1956 Proof	—	Value: 70.00				
1957	16,000,000	—	0.10	0.25	6.50	15.00
1957 Proof	—	Value: 70.00				
1958	9,000,000	—	0.10	0.25	8.50	15.00
1958 Proof	—	Value: 70.00				
1960	11,000,000	—	0.10	0.25	3.50	10.00
1960 Proof	—	Value: 40.00				
1961	12,000,000	—	0.10	0.25	3.50	10.00
1961 Proof	—	Value: 40.00				
1962	15,000,000	—	0.10	0.25	2.00	6.50
1962 Proof	—	Value: 40.00				
1963	18,000,000	—	0.10	0.25	2.00	6.50
1963 Proof	—	Value: 40.00				
1964	21,000,000	—	0.10	0.25	2.00	6.50
1964 Proof	—	Value: 40.00				
1965	28,000,000	—	0.10	0.25	1.50	6.00
1965 Proof	—	Value: 40.00				
1966	22,000,000	—	0.10	0.25	2.00	6.50
1966 Proof	—	Value: 40.00				
1967 leaves far from rim	32,000,000	—	—	0.20	1.50	6.50
1967 Proof, leaves far from rim	—	Value: 50.00				
1967 leaves touching rim	Inc. above	—	0.15	0.50	1.50	6.50
1967 Proof, leaves touching rim	—	Value: 40.00				
1969 fish privy mark	5,000,000	—	0.15	0.50	3.50	15.00
1969 Proof, fish privy mark	—	Value: 40.00				
1969 cock privy mark	11,000,000	—	—	0.10	1.00	4.00
1969 Proof, cock privy mark	—	Value: 40.00				
1970	22,000,000	—	—	0.10	0.75	3.00
1970 Proof	—	Value: 40.00				
1970 date close to rim	Inc. above	—	—	0.10	0.75	3.00
1970 Proof, date close to rim	—	Value: 40.00				
1971	25,000,000	—	—	0.10	0.50	2.00
1972	25,000,000	—	—	0.10	0.50	2.00
1973	22,000,000	—	—	0.10	0.50	2.00
1974	20,000,000	—	—	—	0.50	2.00
1975	46,000,000	—	—	—	0.25	1.50
1976	50,000,000	—	—	—	0.25	1.50
1977	50,000,000	—	—	—	0.25	1.50
1978	60,000,000	—	—	—	0.25	1.50
1979	80,000,000	—	—	—	0.25	1.50
1980 cock and star privy mark	252,500,000	—	—	—	0.10	0.35

KM# 202 5 CENTS

3.5000 g., Bronze, 21 mm. **Ruler:** Beatrix **Obv:** Head left with vertical inscription **Rev:** Value within vertical lines : Bruno Ninaber von Eyben

Date	Mintage	F	VF	XF	Unc	BU
1982	47,100,000	—	—	—	0.10	0.40
1982 Proof	10,000	Value: 10.00				
1983	60,200,000	—	—	—	0.10	0.40
1983 Proof	15,000	Value: 7.50				
1984	70,700,000	—	—	—	0.10	0.40
1984 Proof	20,000	Value: 4.00				
1985	36,100,000	—	—	—	0.10	0.40
1985 Proof	17,000	Value: 4.00				
1986	7,700,000	—	—	—	0.50	1.50
1986 Proof	20,000	Value: 4.00				
1987	33,299,999	—	—	—	—	0.40
1987 Proof	18,000	Value: 4.00				
1988	22,600,000	—	—	—	—	0.40
1988 Proof	20,000	Value: 4.00				
1989	27,100,000	—	—	—	—	0.40
1989 Proof	15,000	Value: 4.00				
1990	39,300,000	—	—	—	—	0.40
1990 Proof	15,000	Value: 4.00				
1991	73,100,000	—	—	—	—	0.40
1991 Proof	14,000	Value: 4.00				
1992	52,700,000	—	—	—	—	0.40
1992 Proof	13,000	Value: 4.00				
1993	40,000,000	—	—	—	—	0.40
1993 Proof	12,000	Value: 4.00				
1994	14,000,000	—	—	—	—	1.50
1994 Proof	13,000	Value: 4.00				
1995	6,000,000	—	—	—	0.75	3.00
1995 Proof	12,000	Value: 4.00				
1996	40,000,000	—	—	—	—	0.40
1996 Proof	14,000	Value: 4.00				
1997	36,000,000	—	—	—	—	0.40
1997 Proof	12,000	Value: 4.00				
1998	65,099,999	—	—	—	—	0.40
1998 Proof	12,000	Value: 4.00				
1999	16,480,000	—	—	—	—	0.40
1999 Proof	15,000	Value: 4.00				
2000	30,076,000	—	—	—	—	0.40
2000 Proof	15,000	Value: 4.00				

KM# 119 10 CENTS

1.4000 g., 0.6400 Silver .0288 oz. ASW, 15 mm. **Ruler:** Wilhelmina I **Obv:** Small crowned head left divides legend **Obv. Legend:** WILHELMINA... **Rev:** Value and date within wreath **Edge:** Reeded **Designer:** P. Pander

Date	Mintage	F	VF	XF	Unc	BU
1901	2,000,000	10.00	25.00	70.00	150	250

KM# 135 10 CENTS

1.4000 g., 0.6400 Silver .0288 oz. ASW, 15 mm. **Ruler:** Wilhelmina I **Obv:** Head left **Rev:** Value in wreath **Designer:** P. Pander

Date	Mintage	F	VF	XF	Unc	BU
1903	6,000,000	4.00	12.00	30.00	50.00	65.00

KM# 136 10 CENTS

1.4000 g., 0.6400 Silver .0288 oz. ASW, 15 mm. **Ruler:** Wilhelmina I **Obv:** Small head left with continous legend **Rev:** Value in wreath **Designer:** P. Pander

Date	Mintage	F	VF	XF	Unc	BU
1904	3,000,000	6.00	16.50	30.00	70.00	130
1905	2,000,000	8.00	22.50	40.00	85.00	150
1906	4,000,000	4.00	14.50	25.00	55.00	110

KM# 145 10 CENTS

1.4000 g., 0.6400 Silver .0288 oz. ASW, 15 mm. **Ruler:** Wilhelmina I **Obv:** Small head left with continuous legend **Rev:** Value within wreath **Edge:** Reeded **Designer:** J.C. Wienecke

Date	Mintage	F	VF	XF	Unc	BU
1910	2,250,000	10.00	25.00	45.00	100	180
1911	4,000,000	4.00	9.00	22.00	45.00	85.00
1912	4,000,000	4.00	9.00	22.00	45.00	85.00
1913	5,000,000	3.00	7.00	15.00	40.00	75.00
1914	9,000,000	1.50	4.00	10.00	25.00	45.00
1915	5,000,000	1.75	5.00	12.00	30.00	60.00
1916	5,000,000	1.75	5.00	12.00	30.00	60.00
1917	10,000,000	1.50	3.50	8.00	16.00	30.00
1918	20,000,000	1.00	2.50	5.00	13.50	30.00
1919	10,000,000	1.50	3.50	8.00	16.00	30.00
1921	5,000,000	2.00	6.00	10.00	22.00	55.00
1925	5,000,000	2.00	6.00	10.00	22.00	55.00

KM# 163 10 CENTS

1.4000 g., 0.6400 Silver .0288 oz. ASW, 15 mm. **Ruler:** Wilhelmina I **Obv:** Small head left with continuous legend **Rev:** Value within wreath **Edge:** Reeded **Designer:** J.C. Wienecke

Date	Mintage	F	VF	XF	Unc	BU
1926	2,700,000	2.50	6.00	15.00	55.00	75.00
1927	2,300,000	2.50	6.00	15.00	60.00	85.00
1928	10,000,000	0.75	2.00	5.00	16.00	35.00
1930	5,000,000	1.00	3.50	7.50	22.00	40.00
1934	2,000,000	2.50	6.00	15.00	60.00	85.00
1935	8,000,000	0.75	1.50	3.50	10.00	15.00
1936	15,000,000	0.50	0.75	2.00	5.00	10.00
1937	18,600,000	0.50	0.75	2.00	3.50	5.00
1938	21,400,000	0.50	0.75	2.00	3.50	5.00
1939	20,000,000	0.50	0.75	2.00	3.50	5.00
1941	43,000,000	0.50	0.50	1.50	2.25	3.00
1943P Acorn privy mark	—	0.75	1.00	2.00	10.00	20.00
1944P	120,000,000	0.50	0.75	1.25	2.00	3.00
1944D	25,400,000	1,200	3,000	5,000	8,000	10,000
Note: Almost entire issue melted						
1944S	64,040,000	1.00	2.00	4.50	15.00	25.00
1945P	90,560,000	120	300	550	900	1,100

Note: For similar coins dated 1941P-1943P with palm tree privy mark, see Curacao and Suriname

KM# 173 10 CENTS

3.3000 g., Zinc, 22 mm. **Ruler:** Wilhelmina I **Obv:** Three tulips flanked by dots within circle **Rev:** Value flanked by sprigs **Edge:** Reeded **Designer:** N. de Haas

Date	Mintage	F	VF	XF	Unc	BU
1941	29,800,000	0.75	1.50	3.50	10.00	20.00
1942	95,600,000	0.25	0.50	2.00	5.00	10.00
1943	29,000,000	0.75	1.50	3.50	10.00	20.00

KM# 177 10 CENTS

1.5000 g., Nickel, 15 mm. **Ruler:** Wilhelmina I **Obv:** Head left **Rev:** Crowned value divides date **Edge:** Reeded **Designer:** L.O. Wenchaback

Date	Mintage	F	VF	XF	Unc	BU
1948 Proof	—	Value: 100				
1948	69,200,000	—	0.25	0.50	3.00	8.50

KM# 182 10 CENTS

1.5000 g., Nickel, 15 mm. **Ruler:** Juliana **Obv:** Head right **Rev:** Crowned value divides date **Edge:** Reeded **Designer:** L.O. Wenchaback

Date	Mintage	F	VF	XF	Unc	BU
1950	56,600,000	—	0.10	0.35	0.75	3.50
1950 Proof	—	Value: 80.00				
1951	54,200,000	—	0.10	0.35	0.75	3.50
1951 Proof	—	Value: 60.00				
1954	8,200,000	—	0.20	0.50	1.00	7.50
1954 Proof	—	Value: 60.00				
1955	18,200,000	—	0.10	0.35	0.75	4.00
1955 Proof	—	Value: 60.00				
1956	12,000,000	—	0.10	0.35	0.75	4.00
1956 Proof	—	Value: 60.00				
1957	18,600,000	—	0.10	0.35	0.75	4.00
1957 Proof	—	Value: 60.00				
1958	34,000,000	—	0.10	0.35	0.75	3.00
1958 Proof	—	Value: 60.00				
1959	44,000,000	—	0.10	0.35	0.75	3.00
1959 Proof	—	Value: 50.00				
1960	12,000,000	—	0.10	0.35	0.75	6.00
1960 Proof	—	Value: 50.00				
1961	25,000,000	—	—	0.10	0.25	2.50
1961 Proof	—	Value: 50.00				
1962	30,000,000	—	—	0.10	0.25	1.50
1962 Proof	—	Value: 50.00				
1963	35,000,000	—	—	0.10	0.25	1.50
1963 Proof	—	Value: 60.00				
1964	41,000,000	—	—	0.10	0.25	1.50
1964 Proof	—	Value: 60.00				
1965	59,000,000	—	—	0.10	0.25	1.50
1965 Proof	—	Value: 60.00				
1966	44,000,000	—	—	—	0.10	1.00
1966 Proof	—	Value: 50.00				
1967	39,000,000	—	—	—	0.10	1.00
1967 Proof	—	Value: 50.00				
1968	42,000,000	—	—	—	0.10	1.00
1968 Proof	—	Value: 40.00				
1969 fish privy mark	29,100,000	—	—	—	0.10	1.50
1969 Proof, fish privy mark	—	Value: 40.00				
1969 cock privy mark	24,000,000	—	—	—	0.10	1.50
1969 Proof, cock privy mark	—	Value: 40.00				
1970	50,000,000	—	—	—	0.10	1.00
1970 Proof	—	Value: 40.00				
1971	55,000,000	—	—	—	0.10	1.00
1972	60,000,000	—	—	—	0.10	1.00
1973	90,000,000	—	—	—	0.10	1.00
1974	75,000,000	—	—	—	0.10	2.00
1975	110,000,000	—	—	—	0.10	1.00
1976	85,000,000	—	—	—	0.10	1.00
1977	100,000,000	—	—	—	0.10	1.00
1978	110,000,000	—	—	—	0.10	1.00
1979	120,000,000	—	—	—	0.10	1.00
1980 cock and star privy mark	195,300,000	—	—	—	0.10	0.50

KM# 203 10 CENTS

1.5000 g., Nickel, 15 mm. **Ruler:** Beatrix **Obv:** Head left with vertical inscription **Rev:** Value and vertical lines **Edge:** Reeded **Designer:** Bruno Ninaber von Eyben

Date	Mintage	F	VF	XF	Unc	BU
1982	10,300,000	—	—	—	0.10	0.50
1982 Proof	10,000	Value: 10.00				
1983	38,200,000	—	—	—	—	0.50
1983 Proof	15,000	Value: 8.00				
1984	42,200,000	—	—	—	0.10	0.50
1984 Proof	20,000	Value: 4.00				
1985	29,100,000	—	—	—	0.10	0.50
1985 Proof	17,000	Value: 4.00				
1986	23,100,000	—	—	—	0.10	0.50
1986 Proof	20,000	Value: 4.00				
1987	21,700,000	—	—	—	0.10	0.50
1987 Proof	18,000	Value: 4.00				
1988	2,200,000	—	—	—	0.25	2.00
1988 Proof	20,000	Value: 6.00				
1989	5,300,000	—	—	—	—	1.50
1989 Proof	15,000	Value: 5.00				
1990	13,300,000	—	—	—	—	0.50
1990 Proof	15,000	Value: 4.00				
1991	41,100,000	—	—	—	—	0.50
1991 Proof	14,000	Value: 4.00				
1992	41,300,000	—	—	—	—	0.50
1992 Proof	13,000	Value: 4.00				
1993	30,100,000	—	—	—	—	0.50
1993 Proof	12,000	Value: 4.00				
1994	25,685,000	—	—	—	—	0.50
1994 Proof	13,000	Value: 4.00				
1995	35,100,000	—	—	—	—	0.50
1995 Proof	12,000	Value: 4.00				
1996	34,900,000	—	—	—	—	0.50
1996 Proof	14,000	Value: 4.00				
1997	20,100,000	—	—	—	—	0.50
1997 Proof	12,000	Value: 4.00				
1998	24,540,000	—	—	—	—	0.50
1998 Proof	12,000	Value: 4.00				
1999	50,040,000	—	—	—	—	0.50
1999 Proof	15,000	Value: 4.00				
2000	75,476,000	—	—	—	—	0.50
2000 Proof	15,000	Value: 4.00				

KM# 120.1 25 CENTS

3.5750 g., 0.6400 Silver .0736 oz. ASW, 19 mm. **Ruler:** Wilhelmina I **Obv:** Bust with wide truncation **Rev:** Value within wreath **Edge:** Reeded **Designer:** P. Pander

Date	Mintage	F	VF	XF	Unc	BU
1901	1,600,000	40.00	100	275	550	950

KM# 120.2 25 CENTS
3.5750 g., 0.6400 Silver .0736 oz. ASW, 19 mm.
Ruler: Wilhelmina I **Obv:** Head left **Rev:** Value within wreath **Edge:** Reeded **Designer:** P. Pander

Date	Mintage	F	VF	XF	Unc	BU
1901	Inc. above	8.00	22.00	45.00	110	170
1901 Proof	3	Value: 1,500				
1902	1,200,000	8.00	25.00	50.00	120	180
1903	1,200,000	8.00	25.00	50.00	120	180
1904	1,600,000	7.00	20.00	40.00	100	150
1905	1,200,000	8.00	25.00	50.00	120	180
1906	2,000,000	6.00	18.00	35.00	85.00	140

KM# 146 25 CENTS
3.5750 g., 0.6400 Silver .0736 oz. ASW, 19 mm.
Ruler: Wilhelmina I **Obv:** Bust left, legend **Rev:** Value within wreath **Edge:** Reeded **Designer:** J.C. Wienecke

Date	Mintage	F	VF	XF	Unc	BU
1910	880,000	18.00	35.00	75.00	175	300
1910 Proof	—	Value: 600				
1911	1,600,000	8.00	20.00	40.00	135	200
1912	1,600,000	8.00	20.00	40.00	135	200
1913	1,200,000	20.00	40.00	75.00	175	300
1914	5,600,000	3.50	8.00	20.00	50.00	75.00
1915	2,000,000	4.50	12.00	25.00	90.00	150
1916	2,000,000	4.50	12.00	25.00	90.00	150
1917	4,000,000	3.50	8.00	20.00	50.00	75.00
1918	6,000,000	2.00	6.00	12.00	32.00	50.00
1919	4,000,000	3.50	8.00	20.00	50.00	75.00
1925	2,000,000	4.50	12.00	20.00	55.00	100

KM# 164 25 CENTS
3.5750 g., 0.6400 Silver .0736 oz. ASW, 19 mm.
Ruler: Wilhelmina I **Obv:** Small head left **Rev:** Value within wreath **Edge:** Reeded **Designer:** J.C. Wienecke

Date	Mintage	F	VF	XF	Unc	BU
1926	2,000,000	6.00	12.00	30.00	90.00	170
1928	8,000,000	BV	1.75	5.00	18.00	30.00
1939	4,000,000	BV	1.25	2.00	5.00	8.00
1940	9,000,000	BV	1.25	2.00	5.00	8.00
1941	40,000,000	—	BV	1.50	2.50	4.50
1943P acorn privy mark	—	BV	1.50	3.50	12.50	20.00
1944P acorn privy mark	40,000,000	—	BV	1.50	2.50	5.50
1945 acorn privy mark	92,000,000	40.00	110	200	300	400

Note: For similar coins dated 1941P and 1943P with palm tree privy mark, see Curacao

KM# 174 25 CENTS
5.0000 g., Zinc, 26 mm. **Ruler:** Wilhelmina I **Obv:** Sailing boat **Rev:** Value flanked by sprigs **Designer:** N. de Haas

Date	Mintage	F	VF	XF	Unc	BU
1941	34,600,000	0.75	1.50	3.50	12.00	25.00
1942	27,800,000	0.75	1.50	3.50	12.00	25.00
1943	13,600,000	2.50	6.00	12.00	35.00	50.00

KM# 178 25 CENTS
3.0000 g., Nickel, 19 mm. **Ruler:** Wilhelmina I **Obv:** Head left **Rev:** Crowned value divides date **Edge:** Reeded **Designer:** L.O. Wencheback

Date	Mintage	F	VF	XF	Unc	BU
1948 Proof	—	Value: 150				
1948	27,400,000	—	0.25	0.50	4.00	10.00

KM# 183 25 CENTS
3.0000 g., Nickel, 19 mm. **Ruler:** Juliana **Obv:** Head right **Rev:** Crowned value divides date **Edge:** Reeded **Designer:** L.O. Wenchebach

Date	Mintage	F	VF	XF	Unc	BU
1950	43,000,000	—	0.20	0.30	1.50	6.50
1950 Proof	—	Value: 75.00				
1951	33,200,000	—	0.20	0.30	1.50	6.50
1951 Proof	—	Value: 65.00				
1954	6,400,000	—	0.50	1.50	2.00	10.00
1954 Proof	—	Value: 65.00				
1955	10,000,000	—	0.20	0.30	1.50	4.00
1955 Proof	—	Value: 65.00				
1956	8,000,000	—	0.20	0.30	1.50	4.00
1956 Proof	—	Value: 65.00				
1957	8,000,000	—	0.20	0.30	1.50	4.00
1957 Proof	—	Value: 65.00				
1958	15,000,000	—	0.20	0.30	1.00	3.00
1958 Proof	—	Value: 65.00				
1960	9,000,000	—	0.20	0.30	1.50	4.00
1960 Proof	—	Value: 60.00				
1961	6,000,000	—	0.40	1.25	1.50	5.00
1961 Proof	—	Value: 50.00				
1962	12,000,000	—	0.20	0.30	1.00	3.00
1962 Proof	—	Value: 50.00				
1963	18,000,000	—	0.20	0.30	1.00	3.00
1963 Proof	—	Value: 50.00				
1964	25,000,000	—	0.20	0.30	1.00	3.00
1964 Proof	—	Value: 50.00				
1965	18,000,000	—	0.20	0.30	1.00	1.50
1965 Proof	—	Value: 50.00				
1966	25,000,000	—	—	0.20	0.75	1.50
1966 Proof	—	Value: 50.00				
1967	18,000,000	—	—	0.20	0.75	1.50
1967 Proof	—	Value: 60.00				
1968	26,000,000	—	—	0.20	0.75	1.00
1968 Proof	—	Value: 60.00				
1969 fish privy mark	14,000,000	—	—	0.20	0.30	1.00
1969 Proof, fish privy mark	—	Value: 60.00				
1969 cock privy mark	21,000,000	—	—	0.20	0.75	1.00
1969 Proof, cock privy mark	—	Value: 60.00				
1970	39,000,000	—	—	0.20	0.30	1.00
1970 Proof	—	Value: 60.00				
1971	40,000,000	—	—	0.20	0.30	1.00
1972	50,000,000	—	—	0.20	0.30	1.00
1973	45,000,000	—	—	0.20	0.30	1.00
1974	10,000,000	—	—	0.20	0.50	1.50
1975	25,000,000	—	—	0.20	0.30	1.00
1976	64,000,000	—	—	0.20	0.30	1.00
1977	55,000,000	—	—	0.20	0.30	1.00
1978	35,000,000	—	—	0.20	0.30	1.00
1979	45,000,000	—	—	0.20	0.30	1.00
1980 cock and star privy mark	159,300,000	—	—	—	0.20	0.50

KM# 183a 25 CENTS
Aluminum **Ruler:** Juliana **Obv:** Head right **Rev:** Crowned value divides date **Note:** Thought by many sources to be a pattern.

Date	Mintage	F	VF	XF	Unc	BU
1980	15	—	—	—	—	500

KM# 204 25 CENTS
3.0000 g., Nickel, 19 mm. **Ruler:** Beatrix **Obv:** Head left with vertical inscription **Obv. Inscription:** Beatrix/Konincin Der/Nederlanden **Rev:** Value within vertical and horizontal lines **Edge:** Reeded **Designer:** Bruno Ninaber van Eyben

Date	Mintage	F	VF	XF	Unc	BU
1982	18,300,000	—	—	—	0.20	0.60
1982 Proof	10,000	Value: 15.00				
1983	18,200,000	—	—	—	0.20	0.60
1983 Proof	15,000	Value: 12.00				
1984	19,200,000	—	—	—	0.20	0.60
1984 Proof	20,000	Value: 6.00				
1985	29,100,000	—	—	—	0.20	0.60
1985 Proof	17,000	Value: 6.00				
1986	20,300,000	—	—	—	0.20	0.60
1986 Proof	20,000	Value: 6.00				
1987	30,100,000	—	—	—	0.20	0.60
1987 Proof	18,000	Value: 6.00				
1988	17,400,000	—	—	—	0.20	0.60
1988 Proof	20,000	Value: 6.00				
1989	30,500,000	—	—	—	0.20	0.60
1989 Proof	15,000	Value: 6.00				
1990	23,100,000	—	—	—	0.20	0.60
1990 Proof	15,000	Value: 6.00				
1991	25,100,000	—	—	—	0.20	0.60
1991 Proof	14,000	Value: 6.00				
1992	41,600,000	—	—	—	0.20	0.60
1992 Proof	13,000	Value: 6.00				
1993	15,100,000	—	—	—	0.25	1.00
1993 Proof	12,000	Value: 6.00				
1994	1,700,000	—	—	—	1.00	5.00
1994 Proof	13,000	Value: 10.00				
1995	30,300,000	—	—	—	0.50	1.25
1995 Proof	12,000	Value: 8.00				
1996	24,900,000	—	—	—	0.20	0.60
1996 Proof	14,000	Value: 6.00				
1997	29,900,000	—	—	—	0.20	0.60
1997 Proof	12,000	Value: 6.00				
1998	69,660,000	—	—	—	0.20	0.60
1998 Proof	12,000	Value: 6.00				
1999	10,720,074	—	—	—	0.20	0.80
1999 Proof	15,000	Value: 6.00				
2000	31,176,000	—	—	—	0.20	0.60
2000 Proof	15,000	Value: 6.00				

KM# 121.2 1/2 GULDEN
5.0000 g., 0.9450 Silver .1519 oz. ASW, 22 mm.
Ruler: Wilhelmina I **Obv:** Head left **Rev:** Crowned Arms without 50 C. below shield **Edge:** Reeded **Designer:** P. Pander

Date	Mintage	F	VF	XF	Unc	BU
1904	1,000,000	25.00	60.00	150	250	400
1905	4,000,000	7.00	15.00	35.00	90.00	135
1906	1,000,000	30.00	70.00	200	300	450
1907	3,300,000	7.00	15.00	35.00	90.00	135
1907 Proof	—	Value: 400				
1908	4,000,000	7.00	15.00	35.00	90.00	135
1909	3,000,000	7.00	15.00	35.00	90.00	135

KM# 147 1/2 GULDEN
5.0000 g., 0.9450 Silver .1519 oz. ASW, 22 mm.
Ruler: Wilhelmina I **Obv:** Head left **Rev:** Crowned Arms **Edge:** Reeded **Designer:** J.C. Wienecke

Date	Mintage	F	VF	XF	Unc	BU
1910	4,000,000	7.00	16.50	50.00	100	150
1912	4,000,000	7.00	16.50	50.00	100	150
1913	8,000,000	6.00	10.00	30.00	65.00	90.00
1919	8,000,000	6.00	10.00	30.00	65.00	90.00

KM# 160 1/2 GULDEN
5.0000 g., 0.7200 Silver .1157 oz. ASW, 22 mm.
Ruler: Wilhelmina I **Obv:** Head left **Rev:** Crowned Arms **Edge:** Reeded **Designer:** J.C. Wienecke

Date	Mintage	F	VF	XF	Unc	BU
1921	5,000,000	BV	2.75	5.00	22.00	30.00
1921 Proof	—	Value: 250				
1922	11,240,000	BV	2.50	3.50	15.00	22.00
1928	5,000,000	BV	2.75	5.00	22.00	30.00
1929	9,500,000	—	BV	3.00	12.00	18.00

Note: Varieties exist

Date	Mintage	F	VF	XF	Unc	BU
1930	18,500,000	—	BV	2.75	9.00	15.00

KM# 122.1 GULDEN

10.0000 g., 0.9450 Silver .3038 oz. ASW, 28 mm. **Ruler:** Wilhelmina I **Obv:** Crowned head left **Obv. Legend:** WILHELMINA... **Rev:** Crowned arms divide value **Rev. Legend:** DER NEDERLANDEN... **Edge Lettering:** GOD * ZIJ * MET * ONS * **Designer:** P. Pander

Date	Mintage	F	VF	XF	Unc	BU
1901	2,000,000	25.00	65.00	150	300	350
1901 Proof	—	Value: 750				

KM# 122.2 GULDEN

10.0000 g., 0.9450 Silver .3038 oz. ASW **Ruler:** Wilhelmina I **Obv:** Head left **Rev:** Crowned arms without 100 C. below shield **Edge Lettering:** GOD*ZY*MET*ONS*

Date	Mintage	F	VF	XF	Unc	BU
1904	2,000,000	12.00	35.00	75.00	150	250
1905	1,000,000	25.00	65.00	150	300	350
1905 Proof	—	Value: 800				
1906	500,000	150	300	900	1,250	1,750
1906 Proof	—	Value: 2,500				
1907	5,100,000	8.00	20.00	45.00	100	150
1908	4,700,000	8.00	20.00	45.00	100	150
1908 Proof	—	Value: 500				
1909	2,000,000	20.00	35.00	90.00	175	300

KM# 148 GULDEN

10.0000 g., 0.9450 Silver .3038 oz. ASW, 28 mm. **Ruler:** Wilhelmina I **Obv:** Head left **Obv. Legend:** Crowned arms **Edge Lettering:** GOD * ZIJ * MET * ONS * **Designer:** J.C. Wienecke

Date	Mintage	F	VF	XF	Unc	BU
1910 Proof	—	Value: 1,000				
1910	1,000,000	30.00	75.00	200	400	700
1911	2,000,000	20.00	45.00	150	300	500
1912	3,000,000	10.00	35.00	75.00	200	275
1913	8,000,000	7.00	20.00	65.00	100	150
1914	15,785,000	6.00	15.00	32.50	75.00	130
1915	14,215,000	6.00	16.50	35.00	75.00	130
1916	5,000,000	16.00	50.00	85.00	175	225
1917	2,300,000	20.00	65.00	100	200	250

KM# 161.1 GULDEN

10.0000 g., 0.7200 Silver .2315 oz. ASW, 28 mm. **Ruler:** Wilhelmina I **Obv:** Head left **Obv. Legend:** Ends below truncation **Rev:** Crowned arms **Edge Lettering:** GOD * ZIJ * MET * ONS * **Designer:** J.C. Wienecke

Date	Mintage	F	VF	XF	Unc	BU
1922	9,550,000	BV	3.75	15.00	40.00	65.00
1922 Proof	—	Value: 450				
1923	8,050,000	BV	3.75	20.00	40.00	65.00
1924	8,000,000	BV	4.50	20.00	40.00	65.00
1928	6,150,000	BV	3.75	15.00	25.00	75.00
1929	32,350,000	—	BV	4.00	10.00	18.00
1930	13,500,000	—	BV	5.00	12.00	35.00
1931	38,100,000	—	BV	4.00	10.00	15.00
1938	5,000,000	BV	4.25	7.00	18.00	25.00
1939	14,200,000	—	BV	3.75	7.00	15.00
1940	21,300,000	—	BV	3.75	7.00	15.00
1940 Proof	—	Value: 200				
1944P acorn privy mark	Inc. above	80.00	250	450	525	600

KM# 161.2 GULDEN

10.0000 g., 0.7200 Silver .2315 oz. ASW, 28 mm. **Ruler:** Wilhelmina I **Obv:** Head left **Obv. Legend:** Ends at right of truncation **Rev:** Crowned arms **Edge Lettering:** GOD * ZIJ * MET * ONS * **Note:** For similar coins dated 1943D with palm tree privy mark, see Netherlands East Indies

Date	Mintage	F	VF	XF	Unc	BU
1944P acorn privy mark	105,125,000	7.50	20.00	35.00	55.00	80.00
1945P acorn privy mark	25,375,000	225	500	1,000	1,600	2,000

Note: Only a small number placed into circulation

KM# 184 GULDEN

6.5000 g., 0.7200 Silver .1504 oz. ASW, 25 mm. **Ruler:** Juliana **Obv:** Head right **Rev:** Crowned arms divide date **Edge Lettering:** GOD * ZIJ * MET * ONS * **Designer:** L.O. Wenckebach

Date	Mintage	F	VF	XF	Unc	BU
1954	6,600,000	—	—	BV	4.00	6.00
1954 Proof	—	Value: 65.00				
1955	37,500,000	—	—	BV	3.00	5.00
1955 Proof	—	Value: 65.00				
1956	38,900,000	—	—	BV	3.00	5.00
1956 Proof	—	Value: 65.00				
1957	27,000,000	—	—	BV	3.00	5.00
1957 Proof	—	Value: 65.00				
1958	30,000,000	—	—	BV	4.50	5.00
1958 Proof	—	Value: 65.00				
1963	5,000,000	—	—	BV	4.50	7.50
1963 Proof	—	Value: 80.00				
1964	9,000,000	—	—	BV	3.00	5.00
1964 Proof	—	Value: 80.00				
1965	21,000,000	—	—	BV	3.00	4.00
1965 Proof	—	Value: 80.00				
1966	5,000,000	—	—	BV	3.00	5.00
1966 Proof	—	Value: 80.00				
1967	7,000,000	—	—	BV	4.50	6.00
1967 Proof	—	Value: 110				

KM# 184a GULDEN

6.0000 g., Nickel **Ruler:** Juliana **Obv:** Head right **Rev:** Crowned arms divide date

Date	Mintage	F	VF	XF	Unc	BU
1967	31,000,000	—	—	0.75	2.00	5.00
1967 Proof	—	Value: 55.00				
1968	61,000,000	—	—	0.75	2.00	5.00
1969 fish	27,500,000	—	—	—	2.50	6.00
1969 Proof, fish	—	Value: 50.00				
1969 cock	15,500,000	—	—	—	2.50	6.00
1969 Proof, cock	—	Value: 50.00				
1970	18,000,000	—	—	0.75	2.00	5.00
1970 Proof	—	Value: 50.00				
1971	50,000,000	—	—	—	0.75	2.00
1972	60,000,000	—	—	—	0.75	2.00
1973	27,000,000	—	—	—	0.75	3.00
1975	9,000,000	—	—	—	2.00	5.00
1976	32,000,000	—	—	—	0.75	2.00
1977	38,000,000	—	—	—	0.75	2.00
1978	30,000,000	—	—	—	0.75	2.00
1979	25,000,000	—	—	—	0.75	2.00
1980 cock and star privy mark	118,300,000	—	—	—	0.65	1.00

KM# 200 GULDEN

6.0000 g., Nickel, 25 mm. **Ruler:** Beatrix **Subject:** Investiture of New Queen **Obv:** Conjoined heads left **Rev:** Crowned arms divide date **Edge Lettering:** GOD * ZIJ * MET * ONS * **Designer:** C.E. Bruyn-van Rood

Date	Mintage	F	VF	XF	Unc	BU
1980	30,500,000	—	—	—	0.65	1.00

KM# 200b GULDEN

Gold, 25 mm. **Ruler:** Beatrix **Subject:** Investiture of New Queen **Obv:** Conjoined heads left **Rev:** Crowned arms divide date **Designer:** C. E. Bruijn-van Rood **Note:** G added (for gold).

Date	Mintage	F	VF	XF	Unc	BU
1980 Rare	7	—	—	—	—	—

KM# 200a GULDEN

6.5000 g., Silver, 25 mm. **Ruler:** Beatrix **Subject:** Investiture of New Queen **Obv:** Conjoined heads left **Rev:** Crowned arms divide date **Edge Lettering:** GOD * ZIJ * MET * ONS * **Note:** Z added (for silver).

Date	Mintage	F	VF	XF	Unc	BU
1980	157	—	—	—	—	700

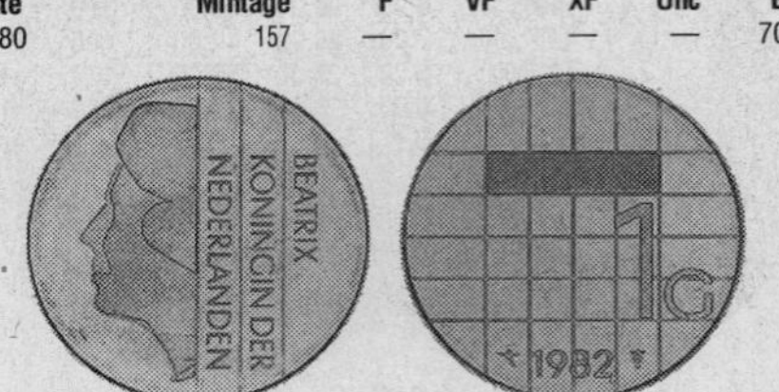

KM# 205 GULDEN

6.0000 g., Nickel, 25 mm. **Ruler:** Beatrix **Obv:** Head left with vertical inscription **Rev:** Value within vertical and horizontal lines **Edge Lettering:** GOD * ZIJ * MET * ONS * **Designer:** Bruno Ninaber von Eyben

Date	Mintage	F	VF	XF	Unc	BU
1982	31,300,000	—	—	—	—	1.25
1982 Proof	10,000	Value: 20.00				
1983	5,200,000	—	—	—	—	1.50
1983 Proof	15,000	Value: 15.00				
1984	4,200,000	—	—	—	—	1.50
1984 Proof	20,000	Value: 7.50				
1985	3,100,000	—	—	—	—	2.50
1985 Proof	17,000	Value: 7.50				
1986	12,100,000	—	—	—	—	1.75
1986 Proof	18,000	Value: 7.50				
1987	20,100,000	—	—	—	—	1.75
1987 Proof	20,000	Value: 7.50				
1988	13,600,000	—	—	—	—	1.75
1988 Proof	20,000	Value: 7.50				
1989	1,100,000	—	—	—	—	3.50
1989 Proof	15,000	Value: 7.50				
1990	1,100,000	—	—	—	—	3.50
1990 Proof	15,000	Value: 7.50				
1991	500,000	—	—	—	—	4.00
1991 Proof	14,000	Value: 7.50				
1992	10,100,000	—	—	—	—	1.50
1992 Proof	13,000	Value: 7.50				
1993	15,100,000	—	—	—	—	1.50
1993 Proof	12,000	Value: 7.50				
1994	16,600,000	—	—	—	—	1.50
1994 Proof	13,000	Value: 7.50				
1995	12,600,000	—	—	—	—	1.50
1995 Proof	12,000	Value: 7.50				
1996	6,660,000	—	—	—	—	1.50
1996 Proof	14,000	Value: 7.50				
1997	12,800,000	—	—	—	—	1.50
1997 Proof	12,000	Value: 7.50				
1998	15,100,000	—	—	—	—	1.75
1998 Proof	12,000	Value: 7.50				
1999	8,900,000	—	—	—	—	1.25
1999 Proof	15,000	Value: 7.50				
2000	37,680,000	—	—	—	—	1.25
2000 Proof	15,000	Value: 7.50				

KM# 230 GULDEN

11.0000 g., 0.7500 Gold .2652 oz. AGW **Ruler:** Beatrix **Rev:** Small tulip, "750" added **Edge Lettering:** GOD ZIJ MET ONS **Designer:** B. Ninaber van Eyben **Note:** Similar to KM#205.

Date	Mintage	F	VF	XF	Unc	BU
1999 Proof	1,000	Value: 800				

Note: Approximately 480 of the mintage were melted down

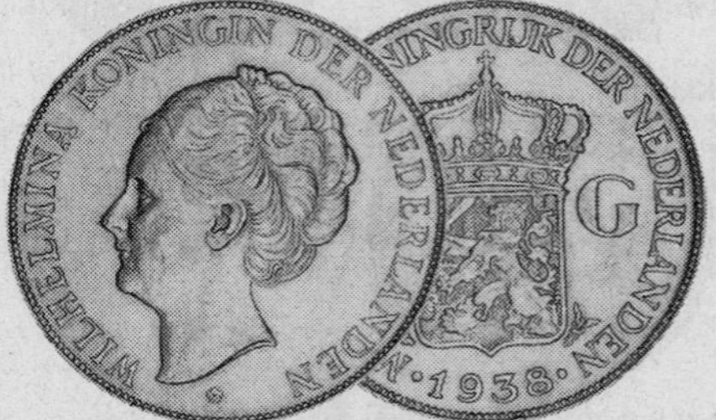

KM# 165 2-1/2 GULDEN

25.0000 g., 0.7200 Silver .5787 oz. ASW, 38 mm. **Ruler:** Wilhelmina I **Obv:** Head left **Rev:** Crowned arms divide value **Edge Lettering:** GOD * ZIJ * MET * ONS * **Designer:** J.C. Wienecke

Date	Mintage	F	VF	XF	Unc	BU
1929	4,400,000	BV	10.00	25.00	75.00	90.00
1930	11,600,000	BV	9.00	12.00	20.00	30.00

Date	Mintage	F	VF	XF	Unc	BU
1931	4,400,000	BV	9.00	12.00	20.00	30.00
1932	6,320,000	BV	9.00	12.00	20.00	30.00
1932 deep hair lines	Inc. above	70.00	125	250	350	450
1933	3,560,000	BV	9.50	15.00	25.00	50.00
1937	4,000,000	—	BV	10.00	20.00	30.00
1938	2,000,000	BV	10.00	18.00	30.00	45.00
1938 deep hair lines	Inc. above	45.00	100	235	325	425
1939	3,760,000	—	BV	10.00	20.00	30.00
1940	4,640,000	12.00	20.00	30.00	50.00	85.00

Note: For similar coins dated 1943D with palm tree privy mark, see Netherlands East Indies

KM# 185 2-1/2 GULDEN

15.0000 g., 0.7200 Silver .3472 oz. ASW, 33 mm. **Ruler:** Juliana **Obv:** Head right **Rev:** Crowned arms divide value **Edge Lettering:** GOD * ZIJ * MET * ONS * **Designer:** L.O. Wenchebach

Date	Mintage	F	VF	XF	Unc	BU
1959	7,200,000	—	—	BV	5.50	9.00
1959 Proof	—	Value: 175				
1960	12,800,000	—	—	BV	5.50	9.00
1960 Proof	—	Value: 175				
1961	10,000,000	—	—	BV	5.50	9.00
1961 Proof	—	Value: 175				
1962	5,000,000	—	—	BV	5.50	10.00
1962 Proof	—	Value: 175				
1963	4,000,000	—	BV	5.50	9.00	14.00
1963 Proof	—	Value: 175				
1964	2,800,000	—	BV	6.00	10.00	15.00
1964 Proof	—	Value: 175				
1966	5,000,000	—	—	BV	5.50	9.00
1966 Proof	—	Value: 175				

KM# 191 2-1/2 GULDEN

10.0000 g., Nickel, 29 mm. **Ruler:** Juliana **Obv:** Head right **Rev:** Crowned arms divide value **Edge Lettering:** GOD * ZIJ * MET * ONS * **Designer:** L.O. Wenckebach

Date	Mintage	F	VF	XF	Unc	BU
1969	1,200,000	—	—	1.00	4.00	10.00
Note: Fish privy mark						
1969 Proof	—	Value: 120				
Note: Fish privy mark with front hair lock						
1969 Proof; rare	—	—	—	—	—	—
Note: Fish privy mark without front hair lock						
1969	15,600,000	—	—	—	3.00	5.00
Note: Cock privy mark						
1969 Proof	—	Value: 90.00				
Note: Cock privy mark						
1970	22,000,000	—	—	—	2.50	4.00
1970 Proof	—	Value: 90.00				
1971	8,000,000	—	—	—	2.50	4.00
1972	20,000,000	—	—	—	2.50	4.00
1978	5,000,000	—	—	—	2.50	4.00
1980	37,300,000	—	—	—	2.50	4.00
Note: Cock and star privy mark						

KM# 197 2-1/2 GULDEN

10.0000 g., Nickel, 29 mm. **Ruler:** Juliana **Subject:** 400th Anniversary - The Union of Utrecht **Obv:** Head right **Obv. Designer:** L.O. Wenchkebach **Rev:** Text, value and date **Rev. Designer:** G. Noordzij **Edge Lettering:** GOD * ZIJ * MET * ONS *

Date	Mintage	F	VF	XF	Unc	BU
1979	25,000,000	—	—	—	1.50	2.00

KM# 201 2-1/2 GULDEN

10.0000 g., Nickel **Ruler:** Beatrix **Subject:** Investiture of New Queen **Obv:** Conjoined heads left **Rev:** Crowned arms divide date **Edge Lettering:** GOD * ZIJ * MET * ONS * **Designer:** L. E. Bruijn-van Rood

Date	Mintage	F	VF	XF	Unc	BU
1980	30,500,000	—	—	—	1.50	2.00

KM# 201a 2-1/2 GULDEN

Silver **Ruler:** Beatrix **Subject:** Investiture of New Queen **Obv:** Conjoined heads left **Rev:** Crowned arms divide date **Edge Lettering:** GOD * ZIJ * MET * ONS * **Designer:** C.E. Bruijn-van Rood **Note:** Z added (for silver).

Date	Mintage	F	VF	XF	Unc	BU
1980	157	—	—	—	—	800

KM# 201b 2-1/2 GULDEN

Gold **Ruler:** Beatrix **Subject:** Investiture of New Queen **Obv:** Conjoined heads left **Rev:** Crowned arms divide date **Edge Lettering:** GOD * ZIJ * MET * ONS * **Designer:** C. E. Bruijn-van Rood **Note:** G added (for gold).

Date	Mintage	F	VF	XF	Unc	BU
1980 Rare	7	—	—	—	—	—

KM# 206 2-1/2 GULDEN

10.0000 g., Nickel, 29 mm. **Ruler:** Beatrix **Obv:** Head left with vertical inscription **Rev:** Value within horizontal, vertical and diagonal lines **Edge Lettering:** GOD * ZIJ * MET * ONS * **Designer:** Bruno Ninaber van Eyben

Date	Mintage	F	VF	XF	Unc	BU
1982	14,300,000	—	—	—	—	2.00
1982 Proof	10,000	Value: 35.00				
1983	3,800,000	—	—	—	—	2.50
1983 Proof	15,000	Value: 27.50				
1984	5,200,000	—	—	—	—	2.50
1984 Proof	20,000	—	—	—	—	—
1985	3,100,000	—	—	—	—	4.50
1985 Proof	17,000	Value: 16.00				
1986	5,800,000	—	—	—	—	4.50
1986 Proof	20,000	Value: 16.00				
1987	2,500,000	—	—	—	—	8.50
1987 Proof	18,000	Value: 16.00				
1988	6,200,000	—	—	—	—	4.50
1988 Proof	20,000	Value: 16.00				
1989	4,099,999	—	—	—	—	4.00
1989 Proof	15,000	Value: 16.00				
1990	1,100,000	—	—	—	—	3.00
1990 Proof	15,000	Value: 16.00				
1991	500,000	—	—	—	—	5.00
1991 Proof	14,000	Value: 16.00				
1992	500,000	—	—	—	—	4.00
1992 Proof	13,000	Value: 16.00				
1993	500,000	—	—	—	—	6.00
1993 Proof	12,000	Value: 16.00				
1994	500,000	—	—	—	—	6.00
1994 Proof	13,000	Value: 16.00				
1995	240,000	—	—	—	—	9.00
1995 Proof	12,000	Value: 16.00				
1996	240,000	—	—	—	—	8.00
1996 Proof	14,000	Value: 16.00				
1997	300,000	—	—	—	—	8.00
1997 Proof	12,000	Value: 16.00				
1998	300,000	—	—	—	—	8.00
1998 Proof	12,000	Value: 16.00				
1999	400,000	—	—	—	—	4.00
1999 Proof	15,000	Value: 16.00				
2000	500,000	—	—	—	—	4.00
2000 Proof	15,000	Value: 16.00				

KM# 151 5 GULDEN

3.3600 g., 0.9000 Gold .0973 oz. AGW, 18 mm. **Ruler:** Wilhelmina I **Obv:** Bust right **Rev:** Crowned arms divide value **Edge:** Reeded **Designer:** J. C. Wienecke **Note:** Counterfeits are prevalent.

Date	Mintage	F	VF	XF	Unc	BU
1912	1,000,000	70.00	80.00	100	160	185
1912 Matte Proof	120	Value: 800				

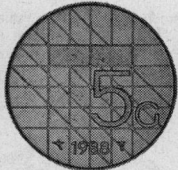

KM# 210 5 GULDEN

9.2500 g., Bronze Clad Nickel, 23.5 mm. **Ruler:** Beatrix **Obv:** Head left with vertical inscription **Rev:** Value within horizontal, vertical and diagonal lines **Edge:** GOD * ZIJ * MET * ONS * **Designer:** Bruno Ninaber van Eyben

Date	Mintage	F	VF	XF	Unc	BU
1987 Proof	2	—	—	—	—	—
1988	73,700,000	—	—	—	—	5.50
1988 Proof	20,000	Value: 12.50				
1989	69,100,000	—	—	—	—	5.50
1989 Proof	15,000	Value: 12.50				
1990	47,300,000	—	—	—	—	5.50
1990 Proof	15,000	Value: 15.00				
1991	17,100,000	—	—	—	—	5.00
1991 Proof	14,000	Value: 15.00				
1992	500,000	—	—	—	—	5.00
1992 Proof	13,000	Value: 15.00				
1993	5,500,000	—	—	—	—	5.00
1993 Proof	12,000	Value: 15.00				
1994	488,000	—	—	—	—	10.00
1994 Proof	13,000	Value: 17.50				
1995	488,000	—	—	—	—	10.00
1995 Proof	12,000	Value: 17.50				
1996	240,000	—	—	—	—	10.00
1996 Proof	14,000	Value: 17.50				
1997	278,000	—	—	—	—	10.00
1997 Proof	12,000	Value: 17.50				
1998	204,000	—	—	—	—	12.00
1998 Proof	12,000	Value: 16.00				
1999	280,000	—	—	—	—	10.00
1999 Proof	15,000	Value: 16.00				
2000	385,000	—	—	—	—	7.50
2000 Proof	15,000	Value: 16.00				

KM# 231 5 GULDEN

9.2500 g., Brass Plated Nickel **Ruler:** Beatrix **Subject:** Soccer **Obv:** Head left **Rev:** Value within soccerball **Edge:** Reeded **Edge Lettering:** GOD * ZIJ * MET * ONS * **Designer:** G. Verheus and M. Raedecker **Note:** A joint issue proof set exists containing the Netherlands KM#231, Belgium KM#213-214 plus a medal.

Date	Mintage	F	VF	XF	Unc	BU
2000	2,500,000	—	—	—	4.00	8.50
2000 Proof	Est. 1,000	Value: 200				
Note: Small mintmark						
2000 Proof	19,000	Value: 12.50				
Note: Large mintmark						

KM# 149 10 GULDEN

6.7290 g., 0.9000 Gold .1947 oz. AGW, 22.5 mm. **Ruler:** Wilhelmina I **Obv:** Head right **Rev:** Crowned arms divide value **Edge:** Reeded **Designer:** J. C. Wienecke

Date	Mintage	F	VF	XF	Unc	BU
1911	774,544	—	—	—	BV	135
1911 Proof	8	Value: 1,750				
1912	3,000,000	—	—	—	BV	135
1912 Proof	20	Value: 1,500				
1913	1,133,476	—	—	—	BV	135
1917	4,000,000	—	—	—	BV	135

KM# 162 10 GULDEN

6.7290 g., 0.9000 Gold .1947 oz. AGW, 22.5 mm.

Ruler: Wilhelmina I **Obv:** Head right **Rev:** Crowned arms divide value **Edge:** Reeded **Designer:** J. C. Wienecke

Date	Mintage	F	VF	XF	Unc	BU
1925	2,000,000	—	—	—	BV	135
1925 Proof	12	Value: 1,500				
1926	2,500,000	—	—	—	BV	135
1926 Proof	—	Value: 1,300				
1927	1,000,000	—	—	—	BV	135
1932	4,323,954	—	—	—	BV	135
1933	2,462,101	—	—	—	BV	135

KM# 195 10 GULDEN

25.0000 g., 0.7200 Silver .5787 oz. ASW, 38 mm. **Ruler:** Juliana **Subject:** 25th Anniversary of Liberation **Obv:** Head right within beaded border **Rev:** Head left within beaded border **Edge Lettering:** GOD * ZIJ * MET * ONS * **Designer:** L.O. Wenckebach

Date	Mintage	F	VF	XF	Unc	BU
ND(1970)	5,980,000	—	—	—	9.50	15.00
ND(1970) Prooflike	20,000	—	—	—	—	40.00
ND(1970) Proof	40	Value: 1,000				

KM# 196 10 GULDEN

25.0000 g., 0.7200 Silver .5787 oz. ASW, 38 mm. **Ruler:** Juliana **Subject:** 25th Anniversary of Reign **Obv:** Head right within beaded border **Rev:** Crowned arms divide date within beaded border **Edge Lettering:** GOD * ZIJ * MET * ONS * **Designer:** C.E. Bruijn van Rood

Date	Mintage	F	VF	XF	Unc	BU
1973	4,505,000	—	—	—	9.50	12.50
1973 Proof	105,570	Value: 20.00				

KM# 216 10 GULDEN

15.0000 g., 0.7200 Silver .3473 oz. ASW, 33 mm. **Ruler:** Beatrix **Subject:** BE-NE-LUX Treaty **Obv:** Head left. **Rev:** Three Parliament buildings on top, 3 designs in circles within vertical lines, all flanked by dates and value **Edge Lettering:** GOD * ZIJ * MET * ONS * **Designer:** W. Vis

Date	Mintage	F	VF	XF	Unc	BU
1994 Proof	66,500	Value: 25.00				
Note: 25,000 pieces issued in sets only						
1994	2,000,000	—	—	—	8.00	12.50
Note: 100,000 pieces melted						

KM# 220 10 GULDEN

15.0000 g., 0.8000 Silver, 33 mm. **Ruler:** Beatrix **Subject:** 300th Anniversary - Death of Hugo de Groot **Obv:** Head left **Rev:** Value and date above supine head facing upward **Edge Lettering:** GOD * ZIJ * MET * ONS * **Designer:** Jaap Drupsteen

Date	Mintage	F	VF	XF	Unc	BU
1995	1,500,000	—	—	—	8.00	12.50
Note: 110,000 pieces melted						
1995 Proof	37,500	Value: 22.50				

KM# 223 10 GULDEN

15.0000 g., 0.8000 Silver, 33 mm. **Ruler:** Beatrix **Subject:** Artist Jan Steen - Lute Player **Obv:** Head left **Rev:** Jan Steen as lute player **Edge Lettering:** GOD * ZIJ * MET * ONS * **Designer:** E. Claus

Date	Mintage	F	VF	XF	Unc	BU
1996	1,500,000	—	—	—	8.00	17.50
Note: 395,000 pieces melted						
1996 Proof	25,000	Value: 22.50				

KM# 224 10 GULDEN

15.0000 g., 0.8000 Silver .3858 oz. ASW, 33 mm. **Ruler:** Beatrix **Subject:** Marshall Plan **Obv:** Head left **Rev:** Marshall head 3/4 left divides value **Edge Lettering:** GOD * ZIJ * MET * ONS * **Designer:** B. Strik

Date	Mintage	F	VF	XF	Unc	BU
1997	1,010,000	—	—	—	8.00	20.00
Note: 55,000 pieces melted						
1997 Proof	27,000	Value: 28.00				

KM# 228 10 GULDEN

15.0000 g., 0.8000 Silver .3858 oz. ASW, 33 mm. **Ruler:** Beatrix **Subject:** Millennium **Obv:** Head above 12 concentric rings within beaded border **Rev:** Head above 12 concentric rings within beaded border **Edge:** GOD ZIJ MET ONS **Designer:** H. Jongenelis

Date	Mintage	F	VF	XF	Unc	BU
1999	1,250,000	—	—	—	8.00	20.00
1999 Proof	50,000	Value: 28.00				

KM# 207 50 GULDEN

25.0000 g., 0.9250 Silver .7435 oz. ASW, 38 mm. **Ruler:** Beatrix **Subject:** Dutch-American Friendship **Obv:** Head left **Rev:** Value within lion and eagle **Edge Lettering:** GOD * ZIJ * MET * ONS * **Designer:** E. Claus

Date	Mintage	F	VF	XF	Unc	BU
ND(1982)	189,986	—	—	—	25.00	35.00
ND(1982) Proof	49,998	Value: 55.00				

KM# 207a 50 GULDEN

Gold **Ruler:** Beatrix **Subject:** Dutch-American Friendship **Obv:** Head left **Rev:** Value within lion and eagle **Edge Lettering:** GOT ZIJ MET ONS **Designer:** E. Claus

Date	Mintage	F	VF	XF	Unc	BU
ND(1982) Rare	2	—	—	—	—	—

KM# 208 50 GULDEN

25.0000 g., 0.9250 Silver .7435 oz. ASW, 38 mm. **Ruler:** Beatrix **Subject:** 400th Anniversary - Death of William of Orange **Obv:** Head left **Rev:** Signature of William **Edge Lettering:** GOD * ZIJ * MET * ONS * **Designer:** Auke de Vries

Date	Mintage	F	VF	XF	Unc	BU
1984	1,000,000	—	—	—	25.00	30.00
Note: 145,000 pieces melted down						
1984 Prooflike	106,378	—	—	—	—	35.00
1984 Proof	56,200	Value: 40.00				

KM# 209 50 GULDEN

25.0000 g., 0.9250 Silver .7435 oz. ASW **Ruler:** Beatrix **Subject:** Golden Wedding Anniversary - Queen Mother and Prince Bernhard **Obv:** Outlined profile left, triangular points at right **Rev:** Value within conjoined outlined heads right, 1/2 star border with letters within points **Edge Lettering:** GOD * ZIJ * MET * ONS * **Designer:** Gerard Hadders

Date	Mintage	F	VF	XF	Unc	BU
1987	1,500,000	—	—	—	25.00	30.00

Date	Mintage	F	VF	XF	Unc	BU
Note: 535,000 pieces melted down						
1987 Prooflike	80,400	—	—	—	—	35.00
1987 Proof	52,872	Value: 40.00				

KM# 212 50 GULDEN
25.0000 g., 0.9250 Silver .7435 oz. ASW, 38 mm. **Ruler:** Beatrix **Subject:** 300th Anniversary of William and Mary **Obv:** Patterned head left **Rev:** Conjoined heads right **Edge Lettering:** GOD * ZIJ * MET * ONS * **Designer:** K. Martens

Date	Mintage	F	VF	XF	Unc	BU
1988	900,000	—	—	—	25.00	30.00
Note: 235,000 pieces melted						
1988 Prooflike	52,500	—	—	—	—	35.00
1988 Proof	35,500	Value: 45.00				

KM# 212a 50 GULDEN
Gold **Ruler:** Beatrix **Subject:** 300th Anniversary of William and Mary **Obv:** Patterned head left **Rev:** Conjoined heads right **Edge Lettering:** GOD ZIJ MET ONS **Designer:** K. Martens

Date	Mintage	F	VF	XF	Unc	BU
1988 Rare	4	—	—	—	—	—

KM# 214 50 GULDEN
25.0000 g., 0.9250 Silver .7435 oz. ASW, 38 mm. **Ruler:** Beatrix **Subject:** 100 Years of Queens **Obv:** Heads of Queens Emma, Wilhelmina, Juliana, and Beatrix like rocks **Edge Lettering:** GOD * ZIJ * MET * ONS * **Designer:** Peter Struycken

Date	Mintage	F	VF	XF	Unc	BU
1990	800,000	—	—	—	25.00	35.00
Note: 210,000 pieces melted						
1990 Prooflike	50,400	—	—	—	—	45.00
1990 Proof	34,500	Value: 55.00				

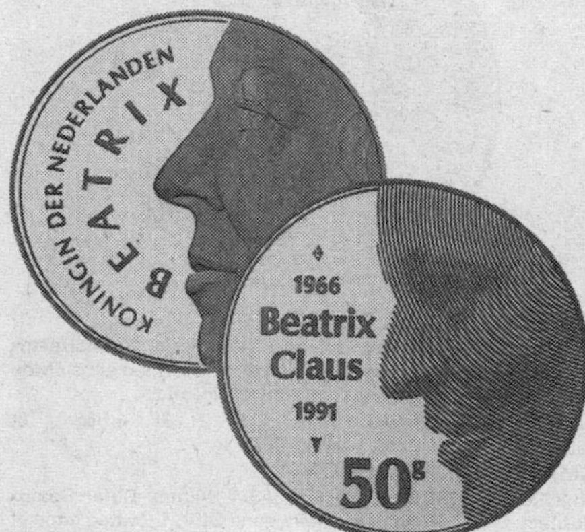

KM# 215 50 GULDEN
25.0000 g., 0.9250 Silver .7435 oz. ASW, 38 mm. **Ruler:** Beatrix **Subject:** Silver Wedding Anniversary **Obv:** Half face left **Rev:** Half face left **Edge Lettering:** GOD * ZIJ * MET * ONS * **Designer:** William van Zoetendaal

Date	Mintage	F	VF	XF	Unc	BU
1991	600,000	—	—	—	25.00	30.00
Note: 60,000 pieces melted						
1991 Prooflike	45,800	—	—	—	—	45.00
1991 Proof	34,700	Value: 50.00				

KM# 217 50 GULDEN
25.0000 g., 0.9250 Silver .7435 oz. ASW, 38 mm. **Ruler:** Beatrix **Subject:** Maastricht Treaty **Obv:** Head left with title within ribbon **Rev:** Value, date and name within rippled banner with stars **Edge Lettering:** GOD * ZIJ * MET * ONS * **Designer:** M. Roling

Date	Mintage	F	VF	XF	Unc	BU
1994	550,000	—	—	—	35.00	40.00
Note: 170,000 pieces melted						
1994 Prooflike	28,000	—	—	—	—	55.00
1994 Proof	24,500	Value: 65.00				

KM# 219 50 GULDEN
25.0000 g., 0.9250 Silver .7435 oz. ASW, 38 mm. **Ruler:** Beatrix **Subject:** 50th Anniversary of Liberation **Obv:** Head 1/4 left **Rev:** Large numeral value and legend **Edge Lettering:** GOD * ZIJ * MET * ONS * **Designer:** G. Unger

Date	Mintage	F	VF	XF	Unc	BU
ND(1995)	650,000	—	—	—	40.00	55.00
Note: 220,000 pieces melted						
ND(1995) Prooflike	27,500	—	—	—	—	60.00
ND(1995) Proof	26,000	Value: 70.00				

KM# 227 50 GULDEN
25.0000 g., 0.9250 Silver .7435 oz. ASW, 38 mm. **Ruler:** Beatrix **Subject:** 350th Anniversary - Treaty of Munster **Obv:** Head 1/4 left within circle **Rev:** Head 1/4 right within circle **Edge Lettering:** GOD*ZIJ*MET*ONS* **Designer:** H. van Houwelingen

Date	Mintage	F	VF	XF	Unc	BU
1998	450,000	—	—	—	40.00	60.00
Note: 180,000 pieces melted						
1998 Prooflike	20,000	—	—	—	—	70.00
1998 Proof	20,000	Value: 80.00				

EURO COINAGE

European Economic Community Issues

KM# 234 EURO CENT
2.3000 g., Copper Plated Steel, 16.2 mm. **Ruler:** Beatrix **Obv:** Head left among stars **Obv. Designer:** Bruno Ninaber van Eyben **Rev:** Value and globe **Rev. Designer:** Luc Luycx **Edge:** Plain

Date	Mintage	F	VF	XF	Unc	BU
1999	47,800,000	—	—	—	0.50	0.75
1999 Proof	16,500	—	—	—	—	—
2000	276,800,000	—	—	—	0.35	0.50
2000 Proof	16,500	—	—	—	—	—

KM# 235 2 EURO CENTS
3.0000 g., Copper Plated Steel, 18.7 mm. **Ruler:** Beatrix **Obv:** Head left among stars **Obv. Designer:** Bruno Ninaber van Eyben **Rev:** Value and globe **Rev. Designer:** Luc Luycx **Edge:** Grooved

Date	Mintage	F	VF	XF	Unc	BU
1999	109,000,000	—	—	—	0.50	0.75
1999 Proof	16,500	—	—	—	—	—
2000	122,000,000	—	—	—	0.50	0.75
2000 Proof	16,500	—	—	—	—	—

KM# 236 5 EURO CENTS
3.9000 g., Copper Plated Steel, 21.2 mm. **Ruler:** Beatrix **Obv:** Head left among stars **Obv. Designer:** Bruno Ninaber van Eyben **Rev:** Value and globe **Rev. Designer:** Luc Luycx **Edge:** Plain

Date	Mintage	F	VF	XF	Unc	BU
1999	213,000,000	—	—	—	0.50	0.75
2000	184,200,000	—	—	—	0.50	0.75
2000 Proof	16,500	—	—	—	—	—

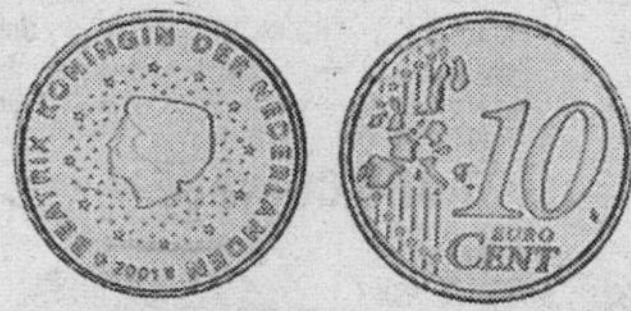

KM# 237 10 EURO CENTS
4.1000 g., Brass, 19.7 mm. **Ruler:** Beatrix **Obv:** Head left among stars **Obv. Designer:** Bruno Ninaber van Eyben **Rev:** Value and map **Rev. Designer:** Luc Luycx

Date	Mintage	F	VF	XF	Unc	BU
1999	149,700,000	—	—	—	0.75	1.00
1999 Proof	16,500	—	—	—	—	—
2000	156,700,000	—	—	—	0.75	1.00
2000 Proof	16,500	—	—	—	—	—

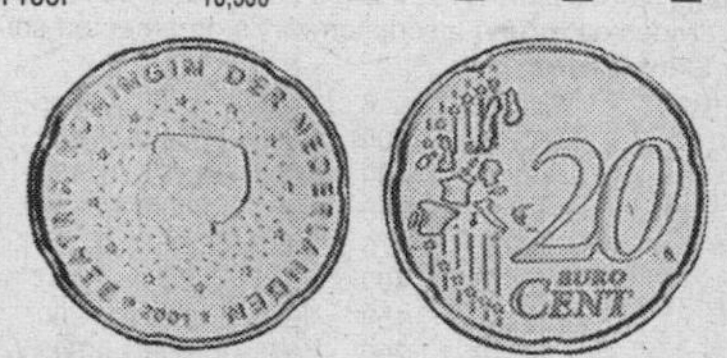

KM# 238 20 EURO CENTS
5.7000 g., Brass, 22.2 mm. **Ruler:** Beatrix **Obv:** Head left among stars **Obv. Designer:** Bruno Ninaber van Eyben **Rev:** Value and map **Rev. Designer:** Luc Luycx **Edge:** Notched

Date	Mintage	F	VF	XF	Unc	BU
1999	86,500,000	—	—	—	1.00	1.25
1999 Proof	16,500	—	—	—	—	—
2000	67,500,000	—	—	—	1.00	1.25
2000 Proof	16,500	—	—	—	—	—

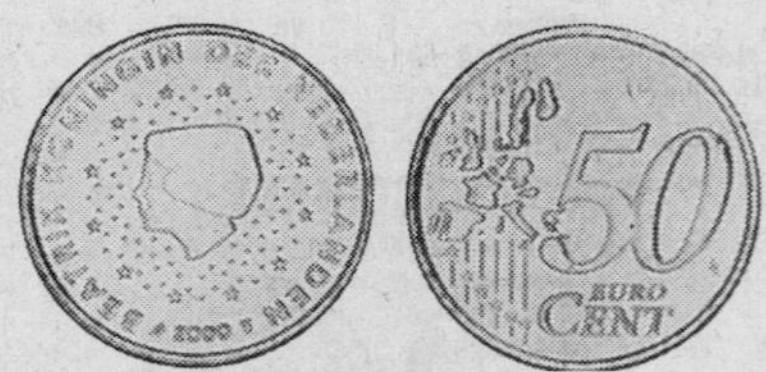

KM# 239 50 EURO CENTS

7.8000 g., Brass, 24.2 mm. **Ruler:** Beatrix **Obv:** Head left among stars **Obv. Designer:** Bruno Ninaber van Eyben **Rev:** Value and map **Rev. Designer:** Luc Luycx **Edge:** Notched

Date	Mintage	F	VF	XF	Unc	BU
1999	99,600,000	—	—	—	1.25	1.50
1999 Proof	16,500	—	—	—	—	—
2000	87,000,000	—	—	—	1.25	1.50
2000 Proof	16,500	—	—	—	—	—

KM# 240 EURO

7.5000 g., Bi-Metallic Copper-Nickel center in Brass ring, 23.2 mm. **Ruler:** Beatrix **Obv:** Half head left within 1/2 circle and star border, name within vertical lines **Obv. Designer:** Bruno Ninaber van Eyben **Rev:** Value and map within circle **Rev. Designer:** Luc Luycx **Edge:** Plain and reeded sections

Date	Mintage	F	VF	XF	Unc	BU
1999	63,500,000	—	—	—	2.50	3.00
1999 Proof	16,500	—	—	—	—	—
2000	62,800,000	—	—	—	2.50	3.00
2000 Proof	16,500	—	—	—	—	—

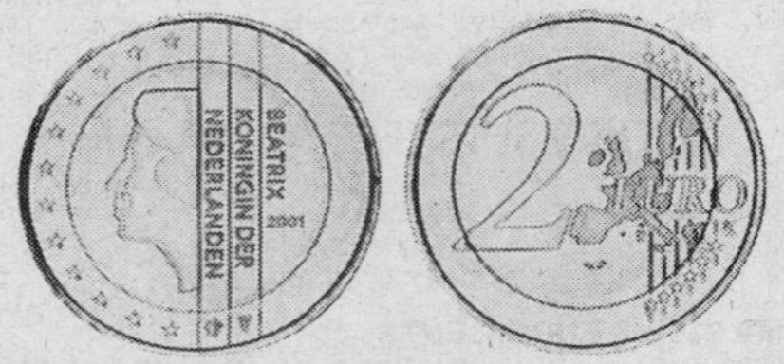

KM# 241 2 EURO

8.5000 g., Bi-Metallic Brass center in Copper-Nickel ring, 25.7 mm. **Ruler:** Beatrix **Obv:** Half head left within 1/2 circle and star border, name within vertical lines **Obv. Designer:** Bruno Ninaber van Eyben **Rev:** Value and map within circle **Rev. Designer:** Luc Luycx **Edge:** Reeded **Edge Lettering:** "GOD*ZIJ*MET*ONS*"

Date	Mintage	F	VF	XF	Unc	BU
1999	9,900,000	—	—	—	6.00	8.00
2000	24,400,000	—	—	—	5.00	6.00
2000 Proof	16,500	—	—	—	—	—

TRADE COINAGE

KM# 83.1 DUCAT

3.4940 g., 0.9830 Gold .1106 oz. AGW, 21 mm. **Obv:** Standing knight divides date **Rev:** Inscription within ornamented square **Edge:** Slant-reeded

Date	Mintage	F	VF	XF	Unc	BU
1901	29,284	400	1,000	1,500	2,400	2,700
1903/1	91,000	400	1,000	1,850	2,400	2,700
1903	Inc. above	250	700	1,000	1,600	2,000
1905	87,995	175	450	700	1,000	1,400
1906	29,379	400	1,000	1,500	2,400	2,700
1908	91,006	150	350	600	900	1,300
1909	106,021	300	600	1,000	1,600	2,000
Note: Halberd with star privy mark						
1909	30,182	400	1,000	2,000	2,700	3,600
Note: Sea horse privy mark						
1910	421,447	125	375	525	900	1,100
1910 Proof	—	Value: 1,200				
1912	147,860	125	375	525	900	1,100
1912 Proof	—	Value: 1,200				
1913	205,464	125	375	525	900	1,100
1914	246,560	125	375	525	900	1,100
1916	116,997	125	375	525	900	1,100
1916 Proof	—	Value: 1,250				
1917	216,892	—	BV	90.00	125	150
1920	293,389	—	BV	90.00	125	150
1920 Proof	—	Value: 800				
1921	409,001	—	BV	80.00	95.00	110
1922	49,837	100	350	500	900	1,100
1923	106,674	BV	80.00	250	350	450
1924	84,206	BV	80.00	250	350	450
1925	573,071	—	BV	80.00	95.00	110
1925 Proof	Inc. above	Value: 450				
1926	191,311	—	BV	85.00	110	150
1927	654,424	—	—	—	BV	60.00
1928	571,801	—	—	—	BV	60.00
1932	88,268	200	500	900	1,700	2,100
1937	116,660	BV	80.00	95.00	110	125

KM# 190.1 DUCAT

3.4940 g., 0.9830 Gold .1106 oz. AGW, 21 mm. **Ruler:** Beatrix **Obv:** Knight with right leg bent divides date **Rev:** Inscription within decorated square

Date	Mintage	F	VF	XF	Unc	BU
1960	3,605	BV	100	300	400	450
1972 Prooflike	29,205	—	—	—	—	80.00
1974 Prooflike	86,558	—	—	—	—	80.00
1974	Est. 2,000	—	—	300	600	700
Note: Medal struck						
1975 Prooflike	204,788	—	—	—	—	75.00
1976 Prooflike	37,844	—	—	85.00	150	250
Note: Of 37,844 pieces struck, 32,000 were melted						
1978 Prooflike	29,305	—	—	—	85.00	100
1985 Prooflike	103,863	—	—	—	—	80.00

KM# 190.2 DUCAT

3.4940 g., 0.9830 Gold .1106 oz. AGW **Ruler:** Beatrix **Obv:** Knight divides date with larger letters in legend **Rev:** Inscription within decorated square

Date	Mintage	F	VF	XF	Unc	BU
1986 Prooflike	95,091	—	—	—	—	85.00
1989 Proof	24,478	Value: 85.00				
1990 Proof	17,500	Value: 85.00				
1991 Proof	11,500	Value: 85.00				
1992 Proof	14,400	Value: 85.00				
1993 Proof	11,100	Value: 90.00				
1994 Proof	11,500	Value: 90.00				
1995 Proof	11,000	Value: 90.00				
1996 Proof	12,000	Value: 90.00				
1997 Proof	11,500	Value: 90.00				
1998 Proof	8,500	Value: 95.00				
1999 Proof	7,550	Value: 95.00				
2000 Proof	8,000	Value: 95.00				

KM# 211 2 DUCAT

6.9880 g., 0.9830 Gold .2209 oz. AGW, 26 mm. **Ruler:** Beatrix **Obv:** Knight divides date within beaded circle **Rev:** Inscription within decorated square

Date	Mintage	F	VF	XF	Unc	BU
1988 Prooflike	23,759	—	—	—	—	155
1989 Proof	17,862	Value: 155				
1991 Proof	10,000	Value: 160				
1992 Proof	11,800	Value: 160				
1996 Proof	10,500	Value: 160				
1999 Proof	6,250	Value: 165				
2000 Proof	7,000	Value: 160				

SILVER BULLION COINAGE

KM# 213 SILVER DUCAT

28.2500 g., 0.8730 Silver .7948 oz. ASW, 40 mm. **Ruler:** Beatrix **Obv:** Crowned arms divide date **Rev:** Knight standing with the arms of Utrecht

Date	Mintage	F	VF	XF	Unc	BU
1989 Proof	35,797	Value: 20.00				
1992 Proof	17,200	Value: 35.00				
1993 Proof	12,500	Value: 35.00				

KM# 218 SILVER DUCAT

28.2500 g., 0.8730 Silver .7948 oz. ASW, 40 mm. **Ruler:** Beatrix **Subject:** Seven Provinces - Groningen **Obv:** Crowned arms divide date **Rev:** Knight standing with arms of Groningen

Date	Mintage	F	VF	XF	Unc	BU
1994 Proof	11,000	Value: 75.00				

KM# 221 SILVER DUCAT

28.2500 g., 0.8730 Silver .7948 oz. ASW, 40 mm. **Ruler:** Beatrix **Subject:** Seven Provinces - Zeeland **Obv:** Crowned arms of the Netherlands **Rev:** Knight standing with arms of Zeeland

Date	Mintage	F	VF	XF	Unc	BU
1995 Proof	11,000	Value: 40.00				

KM# 222 SILVER DUCAT

28.2500 g., 0.8730 Silver .7948 oz. ASW, 40 mm. **Ruler:** Beatrix **Subject:** Seven Provinces - Holland **Obv:** Crowned arms divide date **Rev:** Knight standing with arms of Holland

Date	Mintage	F	VF	XF	Unc	BU
1996 Proof	12,500	Value: 40.00				

KM# 225 SILVER DUCAT

28.2500 g., 0.8730 Silver .7948 oz. ASW, 40 mm. **Ruler:** Beatrix **Subject:** Seven Provinces - Gelderland **Obv:** Crowned arms of the Netherlands **Rev:** Knight standing with arms of Gelderland

Date	Mintage	F	VF	XF	Unc	BU
1997 Proof	11,500	Value: 40.00				

KM# 226 SILVER DUCAT

28.2500 g., 0.8730 Silver .7948 oz. ASW, 40 mm. **Ruler:** Beatrix **Subject:** Seven Provinces - Friesland **Obv:** Crowned arms of the Netherlands **Rev:** Knight standing with shield of Friesland

Date	Mintage	F	VF	XF	Unc	BU
1998 Proof	11,100	Value: 40.00				

KM# 229 SILVER DUCAT

28.2500 g., 0.8730 Silver .7948 oz. ASW, 40 mm. **Ruler:** Beatrix **Subject:** Seven Provinces - Utrecht **Obv:** Crowned arms divide date **Rev:** Knight standing with arms of Utrecht

Date	Mintage	F	VF	XF	Unc	BU
1999 Proof	9,500	Value: 40.00				

KM# 232 SILVER DUCAT

28.2500 g., 0.8730 Silver .7948 oz. ASW, 40 mm. **Ruler:** Beatrix **Obv:** Crowned shield divides date **Rev:** Knight with crowned shield **Edge:** Reeded

Date	Mintage	F	VF	XF	Unc	BU
2000 Proof	10,100	Value: 45.00				

PATTERNS

Including off metal strikes

KM#	Date	Mintage	Identification	Mkt Val
Pn96	1902	—	Cent. Gold. KM132.	—
Pn97	1903	—	1/2 Cent. Gold. KM133.	—
Pn98	1903	—	2-1/2 Cent. Gold. KM134.	—
Pn99	1903	—	10 Cents. Gold. KM135.	—
Pn100	1903	—	25 Cents. Gold. KM120.2	—
Pn104	1904	—	Cent. Bronze-Nickel Plug.	—
Pn105	1904	—	5 Cents. Bronze.	—
Pn106	1904	—	5 Cents. Bronze.	—
Pn107	1904	—	5 Cents. Bronze. Holed.	—
Pn108	1904	—	5 Cents. Nickel.	—
Pn109	1904	—	5 Cents. Nickel. Holed.	—
PnA110	1904	—	5 Cents.	—
Pn110	1905	—	1/2 Gulden. Gold. KM121.2	—
Pn111	1906	—	5 Cents. Bronze.	—
PnA111	1906	—	5 Cents. Silver. Plain edge.	1,100
Pn112	1906	—	5 Cents. Nickel.	—
Pn113	1906	—	5 Cents. Nickel.	—
Pn114	1906	—	5 Cents. Nickel.	—
Pn115	1906	—	5 Cents. Silver.	—
Pn116	1906	—	10 Cents. Nickel.	—
PnA117	1906	—	10 Cents.	—
Pn117	1907	—	5 Cents. Bronze. Crown.	—
Pn118	1907	—	5 Cents. Nickel. Small crown.	—
Pn119	1908	—	Gulden. Bronze. KM122.	—
Pn120	1910	—	10 Cents. Gold. KM145.	—
PnA121	1911	—	Gulden. Bronze.	1,100
PnB121	1912	—	5 Cents. Nickel. "Proof".	—
Pn121	1913	—	2-1/2 Gulden. Silver. KM148.	—
Pn122	1928	—	Gulden. Silver. 28 mm.	350
PnA123	1928	—	Gulden. Gold. 28 mm.	700
Pn123	1928	—	Gulden. Silver. 19 mm.	250
PnA124	1928	—	Gulden. Gold. 19 mm.	550
Pn124	1929	—	Gulden. Silver.	—
PnA125	1929	—	2-1/2 Gulden. Bronze.	1,250
Pn125	1929	—	2-1/2 Gulden. Silver.	550
PnA126	1929	—	2-1/2 Gulden. Gold.	1,300
Pn126	1934	—	10 Cents. Bronze. KM163.	—
PnA127	1935	—	5 Cents. Gold.	4,000
Pn127	1941	—	Cent. Zinc. KM170 with center hole.	550
Pn128	1941	—	2-1/2 Cent. Zinc. KM171 with center hole.	550
Pn129	1941	—	10 Cents. Zinc.	180
PnA130	1969	—	Cent. Nickel.	—
Pn130	1969	—	5 Cents. Nickel. Plain edge.	—
Pn131	1969	—	5 Cents. Nickel.	—
Pn132	1969	—	5 Cents. Aluminum. 1.5000 g.	—
Pn133	1969	—	5 Cents. Aluminum. 1.2200 g.	—
PnA134	1969	—	10 Cents. Nickel-Brass.	—
PnB134	1969	—	25 Cents. Brass.	—
PnC134	1970	—	Cent. Aluminum.	—
Pn134	1973	—	10 Gulden. Silver.	—
Pn134A	1975	—	25 Cents. Aluminum. KM#183o.	—
Pn135	1979	—	10 Gulden. Nickel.	—
Pn136	1980	—	25 Cents. Aluminum. KM183a.	—
Pn137	1980	—	Gulden. Nickel. KM200b error, shield on both sides.	—
Pn138	1980	—	Gulden. Gold. KM200b.	—
Pn139	1980	—	Gulden. Silver. KM200a.	700
Pn140	1980	—	2-1/2 Gulden. Gold. KM201b.	—
Pn141	1980	—	2-1/2 Gulden. Silver. KM201a.	800
Pn142	1982	—	5 Cents. Bronze. 17 mm.	—
Pn143	1982	—	5 Cents. Tombac.	—
Pn144	1982	—	5 Cents. Brass.	—
Pn145	1982	—	5 Cents. Copper Clad Steel.	—
Pn146	1982	—	Gulden. Nickel.	—
Pn147	1982	—	50 Gulden. Gold. KM207.	—
Pn148	1984	—	5 Cents. Tombac.	200
Pn149	1984	—	10 Cents. Bronze.	200
Pn150	1985	—	5 Cents. Nickel. Plain edge.	200
Pn151	1986	—	25 Cents. Brass. KM204.	300
Pn152	1986	—	25 Cents. Aluminum. KM204.	300
Pn152A	1986	—	Gulden. Copper Nickel. KM#206.	300
Pn152B	1986	—	2-1/2 Gulden. Copper Nickel. KM#206	400
Pn153	1986	—	Ducat. Tombac. KM190.2.	500
Pn154	1987	—	5 Cents. Nickel. KM202.	—
Pn155	1988	—	5 Cents. Nickel Clad Steel.	—
Pn156	1988	—	5 Cents. Copper Clad Steel.	—
Pn157	1988	—	5 Cents. Brass Clad Steel.	—
PnA158	1988	—	50 Gulden. Tombac.	750
PnB158	1988	—	50 Gulden. Silver.	850
Pn158	1988	—	50 Gulden. Gold. KM212.	—
Pn159	1990	—	5 Cents. Aluminum.	—
Pn160	1991	—	5 Cents. Nickel. KM202.	—
Pn161	1991	—	50 Gulden. Silver. 1/4 Circle. Queen Beatrix and Prince Claus	—
Pn163	1999	—	Euro Cent. Nickel.	100
Pn164	2000	—	2 Euro Cents. Copper Nickel. KM#241	250

PIEFORTS

KM#	Date	Mintage	Identification	Mkt Val
P19	1905	—	1/2 Gulden. Silver. KM121.2	3,000
P20	1905	—	Gulden. Silver. KM122.2	4,000
P21	1910	—	25 Cents. Bronze. KM146.	—
P22	1948	—	Cent. Silver. KM175.	—
P23	1948	—	5 Cents. Silver. KM176.	—
P24	1948	—	10 Cents. Silver. KM177.	—
P25	1948	—	25 Cents. Silver. KM178.	—
PA26	1956	—	Gulden. Silver. similar to KM#184	—
P26	1958	—	Gulden. Silver. KM184.	—

MINT SETS

KM#	Date	Mintage	Identification	Issue Price	Mkt Val
MS1	1999 (8)	65,000	KM#234-241 Charity set, Clinic Clowns	15.00	17.00
MS2	2000 (6)	50,000	KM#202-206, 210	12.00	18.00
MS3	2000 (8)	68,000	KM#234-241 Charity set, Nature Monuments	15.00	17.00
MS3A	2000 (8)	13,850	KM#234-241 RABO Bank	—	35.00

PROOF SETS

KM#	Date	Mintage	Identification	Issue Price	Mkt Val
PSA1	1928-29 (3)	—	PN122-123, 125	—	1,150
PSB1	1928-29 (3)	—	PnA123-A124, A126	—	2,250
PS1	1948 (4)	50	KM175-178 with PROEF	—	1,800
PS2	1948 (4)	—	KM175-178	—	400
PS3	1949	—	KM180-183, head left, rare.	—	—
PS4	1950 (4)	—	KM180-183 with PROEF	—	1,250
PS5	1950 (4)	—	KM180-183	—	325
PS6	1951 (4)	—	KM180-183	—	275
PS7	1952 (2)	—	KM180-181	—	275
PS8	1953 (2)	—	KM180-181	—	275
PS9	1954 (5)	—	KM180-184	—	300
PS10	1955 (5)	—	KM180-184	—	250
PS11	1956 (5)	—	KM180-184	—	250
PS12	1957 (5)	—	KM18-184	—	250
PS13	1958 (5)	—	KM180-184	—	250
PS14	1959 (3)	—	KM180, 182, 185	—	450
PS15	1960 (5)	—	KM180-183, 185	—	450
PS16	1961 (5)	—	KM180-183, 185	—	450
PS17	1962 (5)	40	KM180-183, 185	—	450
PS18	1963 (6)	40	KM180-185	—	475
PS19	1964 (6)	40	KM180-185	—	475
PS20	1965 (5)	—	KM180-184	—	250
PS21	1966 (6)	—	KM180-185	—	450
PS22	1967 (5)	—	KM180-183, 184a	—	200
PS23	1968 (3)	—	KM180, 182-183	—	175
PS24	1969 (6)	—	KM180-183, 184a, 191. Cock.	—	250
PS25	1969 (6)	—	KM180-183, 184a, 191. Fish.	—	250
PS26	1970 (6)	—	KM180-183, 184a, 191	—	250
PS27	1982 (5)	10,000	KM202-206	35.00	85.00
PS28	1983 (5)	15,000	KM202-206	35.00	35.00
PS29	1984 (5)	20,406	KM202-206	35.00	22.50
PS30	1985 (5)	17,100	KM202-206	35.00	22.50
PS31	1986 (5)	19,500	KM202-206	35.00	32.50
PS32	1987 (5)	18,100	KM202-206, Utrecht medal	35.00	32.50
PS33	1988 (6)	19,550	KM202-206, 210, Groningen medal	5.50	32.50
PS34	1989 (6)	15,300	KM202-206,210, Flevoland medal	50.00	45.00
PS35	1989 (3)	6,400	LM190.2, 211, 213	260	200
PS36	1990 (6)	15,100	KM202-206, 210, N. Brabant medal. Set also includes 1974 25 Cents.	50.00	45.00
PS37	1991 (6)	14,240	KM202-206, 210,Drenthe medal	50.00	45.00
PS38	1992 (6)	12,600	KM202-206, 210, Zeeland medal	53.50	50.00
PS39	1992 (3)	6,300	KM190.2, 211, 213	270	235
PS40	1993 (6)	12,000	KM202-206, 210, Limburg medal	53.50	55.00
PS41	1994 (6)	12,500	KM202-206, 210, Friesland medal	59.50	55.00
PS42	1994 (3)	25,000	BE NE LUX, Belgium KM195, Netherlands KM216, Luxemburg KM68	65.00	55.00
PS43	1995 (6)	11,500	KM202-206, 210, Zuid-Holland medal	59.50	55.00
PS44	1996 (6)	13,500	KM202-206, 210 Booklet, 5 cents, Stuiver	60.00	75.00
PS45	1996 (2)	6,500	KM190.2, 211	248	225
PS46	1997 (6)	12,000	KM202-206, 210 Booklet, 10 Cents	60.00	70.00
PS47	1998 (6)	12,000	KM202-206, 210 Booklet, 25 Cents	60.00	70.00
PS48	1999 (6)	15,000	KM202-206, 210, Booklet, 1 Guilden	50.00	50.00
PS49	1999 (3)	2,500	KM190.2, 211, 229	—	280
PS50	1999 (2)	1,800	KM190.2, 211	—	240
PS51	2000 (6)	15,000	KM#202-206, 210 Booklet 2-1/2 Guilder	50.00	60.00
PS52	2000 (2)	500	KM#190.2, 211 Golden ducats	—	230
PS53	2000 (3)	1,000	KM#190.2, 211, 232 Golden Ducats and Silver Ducat	—	270

PROOF-LIKE SETS (PL)

KM#	Date	Mintage	Identification	Issue Price	Mkt Val
PL1	1999 (8)	16,500	KM#234-241	50.00	50.00
PL2	2000 (8)	16,500	KM#234-241	50.00	50.00

SELECT SETS (FLEUR DE COIN)

KM#	Date	Mintage	Identification	Issue Price	Mkt Val
SS1	1819 (9)	—	KM47-49, 51-56 1 set	—	60,000
SS2	1971 (6)	1,000	KM180-183, 184a, 191	—	600
SS3	1972 (1)	2,000	KM191	—	35.00
SS4	1972 (5)	2,000	KM180-183, 184a	—	200
SS5	1973 (5)	10,000	KM180-183, 184a	—	35.00
SS6	1974 (3)	10,000	KM180-182	6.50	20.00
SS7	1975 (6)	12,000	KM180-183, 184a Set also includes 1974 25 cents.	6.50	40.00
SS8	1976 (5)	15,000	KM180-183, 184a	6.50	60.00
SS9	1977 (5)	17,000	KM180-183, 184a	6.50	60.00
SS10	1978 (6)	21,500	KM180-183, 184a, 191	6.50	30.00
SS11	1979 (6)	50,000	KM180-183, 184a, 197	6.50	10.00
SS12	1980 (6)	249,732	KM180-183, 184a, 191	6.50	4.00
SS13	1980 (2)	504,000	KM200-201	12.00	4.00
SS14	1980 (2)	157	KM200-201	—	2,000
SS15	1980 (2)	7	KM200b-201b. Gold.	—	—
SS16	1982 (5)	242,701	KM202-206	12.00	4.00
SS17	1983	156,165	KM202-206	12.00	4.00
SS18	1984 (5)	131,748	KM202-206	12.00	4.00
SS19	1985 (5)	113,079	KM202-206	12.00	10.00
SS20	1986 (5)	112,190	KM202-206	12.00	10.00
SS21	1987 (5)	120,850	KM202-206, Utrecht medal	15.00	10.00
SS22	1988 (6)	132,957	KM202-206, 210, Groningen medal	15.00	12.00
SS23	1988 (6)	5,000	KM202-206, 210, ERU medal	—	150
SS24	1989 (6)	103,607	KM202-206, 210, Flevoland medal	15.00	12.00
SS25	1990 (6)	102,750	KM202-206, 210, N-Brabant medal	15.00	15.00
SS26	1991 (6)	100,000	KM202-206, 210, Drenthe medal	15.00	15.00
SS27	1991 (6)	4,000	KM202-206, 210, RABO Bank medal	—	60.00
SS28	1992 (6)	94,000	KM202-206, 210, Zeeland medal	15.00	15.00
SS29	1992 (6)	3,000	KM202-206, 210, numismatic year medal	17.50	25.00
SS30	1993 (6)	87,000	KM202-206, 210, Limburg medal	15.00	20.00
SS31	1993 (6)	2,900	KM202-206, 210, V.O.C. medal	17.50	37.50
SS32	1994 (6)	85,000	KM202-206, 210, Friesland medal	15.00	20.00
SS33	1994 (6)	3,000	KM202-206, 210, millennium of mint	17.50	30.00
SS34	1995 (6)	81,000	KM202-206, 210, Zuid-Holland medal	15.00	20.00
SS35	1995 (6)	2,500	KM202-206, 210, Rijks mint medal	17.50	40.00
SS36	1995 (6)	1,500	KM202-206, 210, Ehrbecker mint medal	—	25.00
SS37	1995 (6)	1,500	KM202-206, 210, Utrecht medal	14.50	950
SS38	1995 (6)	900	KM202-206, 210, DeCampen medal, Lion Daalder from shipwreck	200	225

KM#	Date	Mintage	Identification	Issue Price	Mkt Val
SS39	1996 (6)	1,500	KM202-206, 210, Utrecht: Town of the Mint medal	17.50	25.00
SS40	1996 (6)	80,000	KM202-206, 210, Overyssel medal	15.00	17.50
SS41	1996 (6)	3,000	KM202-206, 210, French Occupation (1795-1813) medal	17.50	30.00
SS42	1996 (6)	2,100	KM202-206, 210, Baby set	17.50	35.00
SS43	1996 (6)	350	KM202-206, 210, DeCampen medal, 1/2 Lion Daalder from shipwreck	240	375
SS44	1996 (6)	1,300	KM202-206, 210, Westpark I medal	—	25.00
SS45	1996 (6)	1,000	KM202-206, 210, Utrecht II medal	—	850
SS46	1997 (6)	85,000	KM202-206, 210, Gelderland medal	15.00	15.00
SS47	1997 (6)	3,500	KM202-206, 210, King Willem I medal	17.50	22.00
SS48	1997 (6)	—	KM202-206, 210, Baby set	17.50	32.50
SS49	1997 (6)	1,430	KM202-206, 210, Ice skating/11 cities medal	45.00	25.00
SS50	1997 (6)	700	KM202-206, 210, Westpark II medal	—	50.00
SS51	1997 (6)	1,000	KM202-206, 210, Den Besterd I medal	—	60.00
SS52	1997 (6)	500	KM202-206, 210, Den Besterd IImedal	—	140
SS53	1997 (6)	1,000	KM202-206, 210, Czar Peter medal	—	80.00
SS54	1997 (6)	500	KM202-206, 210, 't Vliegent heart medal, Ducaton from shipwreck	240	325
SS55	1997 (6)	1,150	KM202-206, 210, Royal Navy medal	—	250
SS56	1997 (6)	700	KM202-206, 210, BFBN medal	—	130
SS57	1997 (6)	1,500	KM202-206, 210, Maasdonk medal	50.00	18.00
SS58	1997 (6)	1,000	KM202-206, 210, BNN medal	75.00	75.00
SS59	1997 (6)	1,000	KM202-206, 210, Overyssel medal	—	1,100
SS60	1997 (6)	1,000	KM202-206, 210, van Rign I medal	45.00	45.00
SS61	1997 (6)	1,000	KM202-206, 210, van Gogh I medal	45.00	35.00
SS62	1997 (6)	1,000	KM202-206, 210, Stuurman medal	75.00	70.00
SS63	1998 (6)	83,500	KM202-206, 210, N. Holland medal	15.00	20.00
SS64	1998 (6)	3,500	KM202-206, 210, King Willem II medal	17.50	30.00
SS65	1998 (6)	100	KM202-206, 210, 't Vliegent heart medal, Ducaton from shipwreck	1,000	1,250
SS66	1998 (6)	8,400	KM202-206, 210, Baby set	17.50	22.50
SS67	1998 (6)	1,000	KM202-206, 210, van Rign II medal	40.00	40.00
SS68	1998 (6)	1,000	KM202-206, 210, van Gogh II medal	40.00	40.00
SS69	1998 (6)	1,000	KM202-206, 210, Frans Hals medal	50.00	50.00
SS70	1998 (6)	1,000	KM202-206, 210, Statenjacht medal	—	35.00
SS71	1998 (6)	1,000	KM202-206,210, Theo Peters medal	—	75.00
SS72	1998 (6)	1,000	KM202-206,210, Vermeer medal	—	50.00
SS73	1998 (6)	1,000	KM202-206, 210, Knippenberg medal	—	45.00
SS74	1998 (6)	2,500	KM202-206, 210, Holland medal	40.00	30.00
SS75	1998 (6)	2,500	KM202-206, 210, Zeeland medal	40.00	30.00
SS76	1999 (6)	3,500	KM202-206, 210, King Willem III medal	17.50	35.00
SS77	1999 (6)	1,000	KM202-206, 210, Statenjacht medal	30.00	30.00
SS78	1999 (6)	2,500	KM202-206, 210, Friesland medal	40.00	30.00
SS79	1999 (6)	2,500	KM202-206, 210, West Friesland medal	40.00	30.00
SS80	1999 (6)	—	KM202-206, 210, Baby set	15.50	17.50
SS80A	1999 (6)	1,000	KM#202-206, 210 P.W.S.	75.00	—
SS81	1999 (7)	74	KM#202-206, 210, VOC ship "De Akerendam" with original golden ducat dated 1724 Utrecht (KM#7)	1,250	1,200
SS83	2000 (6)	3,500	KM202-206, 210, Queen Wilhelmina medal	17.50	30.00
SS84	2000 (6)	105,000	KM#202-206, 210 Introduction of Euro coins	15.00	22.00
SS85	2000 (6)	4,000	KM#202-206, 210 400-year Nederland - Janpan	17.50	20.00
SS86	2000 (6)	18,300	KM#202-206, 210 Baby set plus bear medal	15.50	35.00
SS87	2000 (6)	1,000	KM#202-206, 210 United Seven Provinces Gelderland medal	40.00	30.00
SS88	2000 (6)	1,000	KM#202-206, 210 United Seven Provinces Overijsel Medal	40.00	30.00
SS89	2000 (6)	1,000	KM#202-206, 210 Bouwers Met Vise	45.00	145

NETHERLANDS ANTILLES

The Netherlands Antilles, comprises two groups of islands in the West Indies: Aruba (until 1986), Bonaire and Curacao and their dependencies near the Venezuelan coast and St. Eustatius, Saba, and the southern part of St. Martin (*St. Maarten*) southeast of Puerto Rico. The island group has an area of 371 sq. mi. (960 sq. km.) and a population of 225,000. Capital: Willemstad. Chief industries are the refining of crude oil and tourism. Petroleum products and phosphates are exported.

On Dec. 15, 1954, the Netherlands Antilles were given complete domestic autonomy and granted equality within the Kingdom with Surinam and the Netherlands. On Jan. I, 1986, Aruba achieved *status aparte* as the fourth part of the Dutch realm that was a step towards total independence.

RULERS

Juliana, 1948-1980
Beatrix, 1980-

MINT MARKS

Y – York Mint

Utrecht Mint
(privy marks only)

Date	Privy Mark
1945-1969	Fish
1969	Fish with star
1970-1979	Cock
1980	Cock with star
1982-1988	Anvil with hammer
1988-1999	Bow and arrow
2000	Bow and arrow with star

FM - Franklin Mint, U.S.A.

NOTE: See Kingdom of the Netherlands for more details.

NOTE: From 1975-1985 the Franklin Mint produced coinage in up to 3 different qualities. Qualities of issue are designated in ( ) after each date and are defined as follows:

(M) MATTE - Normal circulation strike or a dull finish produced by sandblasting special uncirculated (polish finish) or proof quality dies.

(U) SPECIAL UNCIRCULATED - Polished or prooflike in appearance without any frosted features.

(P) PROOF - The highest quality obtainable having mirror-like fields and frosted features.

MONETARY SYSTEM

100 Cents = 1 Gulden

KINGDOM

DECIMAL COINAGE

KM# 1 CENT

2.5000 g., Bronze, 19 mm. **Ruler:** Juliana **Obv:** Rampant lion left **Rev:** Value within wreath **Edge:** Reeded

Date	Mintage	F	VF	XF	Unc	BU
1952	1,000,000	1.50	3.00	6.00	12.50	14.00
1952 Proof	100	Value: 40.00				
1954	1,000,000	1.50	3.00	6.00	12.50	14.00
1954 Proof	200	Value: 25.00				
1957	1,000,000	0.50	1.00	2.50	5.00	14.00
1957 Proof	250	Value: 25.00				
1959	1,000,000	0.50	1.00	2.50	5.00	10.00
1959 Proof	250	Value: 20.00				
1960 Proof	300	Value: 20.00				
1961	1,000,000	0.35	0.60	1.25	2.50	4.50
1961 Proof	—	Value: 25.00				
1963	1,000,000	0.35	0.60	1.25	2.50	4.50
1963 Proof	—	Value: 20.00				
1964 Proof	—	Value: 20.00				
1965	1,200,000	0.35	0.60	1.25	2.50	4.00
1965 Proof	—	Value: 20.00				
1967	850,000	0.35	0.60	1.25	2.50	4.50
1967 Proof	—	Value: 20.00				
1968 fish	900,000	0.35	0.60	1.25	2.50	4.50
1968 star and fish	700,000	0.75	1.00	2.00	4.00	9.00
1970	200,000	0.75	1.00	2.00	4.00	9.00
1970 Proof	—	Value: 25.00				

KM# 8 CENT

2.5000 g., Bronze, 19 mm. **Ruler:** Juliana **Obv:** Crowned shield above date and ribbon **Rev:** Value flanked by stars **Edge:** Plain

Date	Mintage	F	VF	XF	Unc	BU
1970	1,200,000	0.10	0.40	0.75	1.50	2.50
1970 Proof	—	Value: 17.50				
1971	3,000,000	0.10	0.40	0.75	1.50	2.50
1971 Proof	—	Value: 17.50				
1972	1,000,000	0.10	0.40	0.75	1.50	2.50
1973	3,000,000	0.10	0.20	0.40	0.80	2.00
1973 Proof	—	Value: 17.50				
1974	3,000,000	0.10	0.20	0.40	0.80	2.00
1974 Proof	—	Value: 17.50				
1975	2,000,000	0.10	0.20	0.40	0.80	2.00
1975 Proof	—	Value: 17.50				
1976	3,000,000	—	0.20	0.40	0.80	2.00
1977	4,000,000	—	0.20	0.40	0.80	2.00
1978	2,000,000	—	0.20	0.40	0.80	2.00

Note: 1969 date is now listed in the Patterns section

KM# 8a CENT

Aluminum, 19 mm. **Ruler:** Juliana **Obv:** Crowned shield above date and ribbon **Rev:** Value flanked by stars **Edge:** Plain

Date	Mintage	F	VF	XF	Unc	BU
1979	7,512,000	—	0.10	0.25	0.50	0.75
1979 Proof	—	Value: 7.50				
1980	2,518,000	—	0.10	0.25	0.50	1.25
1981	2,423,000	—	0.10	0.25	0.50	0.75
1982	2,410,000	—	0.10	0.25	0.50	0.75
1983	2,925,000	—	0.10	0.25	0.50	0.75
1984	3,626,000	—	0.10	0.25	0.50	0.75
1985	3,024,000	—	0.10	0.25	0.50	0.75

KM# 32 CENT

0.7000 g., Aluminum, 14 mm. **Ruler:** Beatrix **Obv:** Orange blossom within circle **Rev:** Value within circle of geometric designed border **Edge:** Reeded

Date	Mintage	F	VF	XF	Unc	BU
1989	1,365,000	—	—	—	0.20	0.50
1990	2,711,000	—	—	—	0.20	0.50
1991	4,016,000	—	—	—	0.20	0.50
1992	3,049,000	—	—	—	0.20	0.50
1993	3,997,000	—	—	—	0.20	0.50
1994	1,997,000	—	—	—	0.20	0.50
1995	997,000	—	—	—	0.20	0.50
1996	3,595,000	—	—	—	0.20	0.50
1997	4,107,000	—	—	—	0.20	0.50
1998	5,757,000	—	—	—	0.20	0.50
1999	15,876,000	—	—	—	0.20	0.50
2000	6,607,500	—	—	—	0.20	0.50

KM# 5 2-1/2 CENTS

4.0000 g., Bronze, 23.5 mm. **Ruler:** Juliana **Obv:** Rampant lion left **Rev:** Value within orange wreath **Edge:** Reeded

Date	Mintage	F	VF	XF	Unc	BU
1956	400,000	0.50	1.25	2.50	5.00	8.00
1956 Proof	500	Value: 25.00				
1959	1,000,000	0.50	1.00	2.00	4.00	5.00
1959 Proof	250	Value: 25.00				
1965 fish	500,000	0.50	1.00	2.00	4.00	6.00
1965 Proof	—	Value: 25.00				
1965 fish and star	150,000	1.00	2.00	4.00	7.50	17.50

KM# 9 2-1/2 CENTS

4.0000 g., Bronze, 23.5 mm. **Ruler:** Juliana **Obv:** Crowned shield above date and ribbon **Rev:** Value flanked by stars **Edge:** Plain

Date	Mintage	F	VF	XF	Unc	BU
1970	500,000	0.40	0.75	1.50	3.00	2.75
1970 Proof	—	Value: 20.00				
1971	3,000,000	0.10	0.25	0.50	1.00	1.50
1971 Proof	—	Value: 20.00				
1973	1,000,000	0.10	0.15	0.35	0.75	1.00
1973 Proof	—	Value: 20.00				
1974	1,000,000	0.10	0.15	0.35	0.75	1.00
1974 Proof	—	Value: 20.00				
1975	1,000,000	0.10	0.15	0.35	0.75	1.00
1976	1,000,000	0.10	0.15	0.35	0.75	1.00
1977	1,000,000	0.10	0.15	0.35	0.75	1.00
1978	1,500,000	0.10	0.15	0.35	0.75	1.00

Note: 1969 date is now found in the Patterns section

KM# 9a 2-1/2 CENTS

Aluminum, 23.5 mm. **Ruler:** Juliana **Obv:** Crowned shield above date and ribbon **Rev:** Value flanked by stars **Edge:** Plain

Date	Mintage	F	VF	XF	Unc	BU
1979	2,012,000	—	0.10	0.25	0.50	0.75
1979 Proof	—	Value: 10.00				
1980	2,018,000	—	0.10	0.25	0.50	0.75
1981	1,023,000	—	0.10	0.25	0.50	0.75
1982	1,010,000	—	0.10	0.25	0.50	0.75
1983	1,025,000	—	0.10	0.25	0.50	0.75
1984	1,026,000	—	0.10	0.25	0.50	0.75
1985	1,024,000	—	0.10	0.25	0.50	0.75

KM# 6 5 CENTS

4.5000 g., Copper-Nickel, 21.3 mm. **Ruler:** Juliana **Obv:** Orange blossom within circle **Rev:** Value within circle, pearls and shells around border **Edge:** Plain **Shape:** Square

Date	Mintage	F	VF	XF	Unc	BU
1957	500,000	0.35	0.75	1.50	3.00	6.00
1957 Proof	250	Value: 40.00				
1962	250,000	1.25	2.50	5.00	10.00	12.00
1962 Proof	200	Value: 30.00				
1963	400,000	0.35	0.75	1.50	3.00	6.00
1963 Proof	—	Value: 30.00				
1965	500,000	0.35	0.75	1.50	3.00	6.00
1965 Proof	—	Value: 30.00				
1967	600,000	0.35	0.75	1.50	3.00	6.00
1967 Proof	—	Value: 30.00				
1970	450,000	0.35	0.75	1.50	3.00	6.00
1970 Proof	—	Value: 30.00				

Note: KM#A13, previously listed here, is now under Patterns

KM# 13 5 CENTS

4.5000 g., Copper-Nickel, 21.3 mm. **Ruler:** Juliana **Obv:** Crowned shield **Rev:** Value flanked by stars **Edge:** Plain **Shape:** 4-sided

Date	Mintage	F	VF	XF	Unc	BU
1971	2,000,000	0.10	0.15	0.30	0.60	0.95
1971 Proof	—	Value: 22.50				
1974	500,000	0.30	0.60	1.25	2.50	2.75
1974 Proof	—	Value: 22.50				
1975	2,000,000	0.10	0.15	0.30	0.60	0.95
1975 Proof	—	Value: 22.50				
1976	1,500,000	0.10	0.15	0.30	0.60	0.95
1977	1,000,000	0.10	0.15	0.30	0.60	0.95
1978	1,500,000	0.10	0.15	0.30	0.60	0.95
1979	1,512,000	0.10	0.15	0.30	0.60	0.95
1980	1,518,000	—	0.15	0.30	0.60	0.95
1981	1,022,999	—	0.15	0.30	0.60	0.95
1982	1,010,000	—	0.15	0.30	0.60	0.95
1983	1,024,999	—	0.15	0.30	0.60	0.95
1984	1,526,000	—	0.15	0.30	0.60	0.95
1985	1,524,000	—	0.15	0.30	0.60	0.95

KM# 33 5 CENTS

1.1600 g., Aluminum, 16 mm. **Ruler:** Beatrix **Obv:** Orange blossom within circle **Rev:** Value within circle, geometric designed border **Edge:** Reeded

Date	Mintage	F	VF	XF	Unc	BU
1989	915,000	—	—	0.25	0.60	0.75
1990	1,811,000	—	—	0.25	0.60	0.75
1991	2,513,000	—	—	—	0.60	0.75
1992	1,599,000	—	—	—	0.60	0.75
1993	2,497,000	—	—	—	0.60	0.75
1994	1,497,000	—	—	—	0.60	0.75
1995	997,000	—	—	—	0.60	0.75
1996	796,000	—	—	—	0.60	0.75
1997	2,207,000	—	—	—	0.60	0.75
1998	2,507,000	—	—	—	0.60	0.75
1999	2,501,000	—	—	—	0.60	0.75
2000	1,007,500	—	—	—	0.60	0.75

KM# 3 1/10 GULDEN

1.4000 g., 0.6400 Silver .0288 oz. ASW, 15 mm. **Ruler:** Juliana **Obv:** Head right **Rev:** Value **Edge:** Reeded

Date	Mintage	F	VF	XF	Unc	BU
1954	200,000	1.50	3.00	8.00	15.00	30.00
1954 Proof	200	Value: 40.00				
1956	250,000	1.00	2.00	4.00	8.00	12.00
1956 Proof	500	Value: 40.00				
1957	250,000	1.00	2.00	4.00	8.00	12.00
1957 Proof	250	Value: 35.00				
1959	250,000	1.00	2.00	4.00	8.00	12.00
1959 Proof	250	Value: 40.00				
1960	400,000	0.50	1.00	2.00	4.00	5.00
1960 Proof	300	Value: 40.00				
1962	400,000	0.50	1.00	2.00	4.00	5.00
1962 Proof	200	Value: 35.00				
1963	900,000	0.50	1.00	2.00	4.00	5.00
1963 Proof	—	Value: 35.00				
1966 fish	1,000,000	0.50	1.00	2.00	4.00	5.00
1966 fish and star	200,000	1.00	2.00	3.75	7.50	12.00
1970	300,000	0.50	0.75	1.50	3.00	5.00
1970 Proof	—	Value: 35.00				

KM# 10 10 CENTS

2.0000 g., Nickel, 15 mm. **Ruler:** Juliana **Obv:** Crowned shield above date and ribbon **Rev:** Value flanked by stars **Edge:** Reeded

Date	Mintage	F	VF	XF	Unc	BU
1970	1,000,000	—	0.30	0.60	1.25	1.50
1970 Proof	—	Value: 25.00				
1971	3,000,000	—	0.10	0.25	0.50	0.60
1971 Proof	—	Value: 25.00				
1974	1,000,000	—	0.30	0.60	1.25	1.50
1974 Proof	—	Value: 25.00				
1975	1,500,000	—	0.10	0.25	0.50	0.60
1975 Proof	—	Value: 25.00				
1976	2,000,000	—	0.10	0.35	0.50	0.60
1977	1,000,000	—	0.10	0.35	0.50	0.60
1978	1,500,000	—	0.10	0.35	0.50	0.60
1979	1,512,000	—	0.10	0.35	0.50	0.60
1979 Proof	—	Value: 12.50				
1980	1,518,000	—	0.10	0.35	0.50	0.60
1981	1,022,999	—	0.10	0.35	0.50	0.60
1982	1,010,000	—	0.10	0.35	0.50	0.60
1983	1,024,999	—	0.10	0.35	0.50	0.60
1984	1,026,000	—	0.10	0.35	0.50	0.60
1985	1,024,000	—	0.10	0.35	0.50	0.60

Note: 1969 date of this variety is now in the Patterns section

KM# 34 10 CENTS

3.0000 g., Nickel Bonded Steel, 18 mm. **Ruler:** Beatrix **Obv:** Orange blossom within circle **Rev:** Value within circle, geometric designed border **Edge:** Reeded

Date	Mintage	F	VF	XF	Unc	BU
1989	915,000	—	—	—	0.45	0.75
1990	1,811,000	—	—	—	0.45	0.65
1991	2,513,000	—	—	—	0.45	0.65
1992	898,000	—	—	—	0.45	0.65
1993	1,996,000	—	—	—	0.45	0.65
1994	997,000	—	—	—	0.45	0.65
1995	97,000	—	—	—	0.75	0.65
1996	895,000	—	—	—	0.45	0.65
1997	1,607,000	—	—	—	0.45	0.65
1998	2,007,000	—	—	—	0.45	0.65
1999	1,501,000	—	—	—	0.45	0.65
2000	12,500	—	—	—	2.00	2.00

KM# 4 1/4 GULDEN

3.5750 g., 0.6400 Silver .0736 oz. ASW, 19 mm. **Ruler:** Juliana **Obv:** Head right **Rev:** Value **Edge:** Reeded

Date	Mintage	F	VF	XF	Unc	BU
1954	200,000	1.75	7.75	7.50	15.00	30.00
1954 Proof	200	Value: 45.00				
1956	200,000	1.20	2.50	5.00	10.00	15.00
1956 Proof	500	Value: 45.00				
1957	200,000	1.20	2.50	5.00	10.00	15.00
1957 Proof	250	Value: 45.00				
1960	240,000	BV	1.25	2.50	5.00	8.00
1960 Proof	300	Value: 40.00				
1962	240,000	BV	1.25	2.50	5.00	8.00
1962 Proof	200	Value: 45.00				
1963	300,000	BV	1.25	2.50	5.00	8.00
1963 Proof	—	Value: 45.00				
1965	500,000	BV	1.25	2.50	5.00	8.00
1965 Proof	—	Value: 45.00				
1967 fish	310,000	BV	1.25	2.50	5.00	8.00
1967 Proof, fish	—	Value: 45.00				
1967 fish and star	200,000	BV	1.25	2.50	5.00	8.00
1970	150,000	BV	1.25	2.50	5.00	8.00
1970 Proof	—	Value: 35.00				

KM# 11 25 CENTS

3.5000 g., Nickel, 19 mm. **Ruler:** Beatrix **Obv:** Crowned shield above date and value **Rev:** Value flanked by stars **Edge:** Reeded

Date	Mintage	F	VF	XF	Unc	BU
1970	750,000	0.25	0.50	1.00	2.00	3.00
1970 Proof	—	Value: 30.00				
1971	3,000,000	—	0.15	0.30	0.60	2.00
1971 Proof	—	Value: 30.00				
1975	1,000,000	—	0.15	0.30	0.60	2.00
1975 Proof	—	Value: 30.00				
1976	1,000,000	—	0.15	0.30	0.60	1.00
1977	1,000,000	—	0.15	0.30	0.60	1.00
1978	1,000,000	—	0.15	0.30	0.60	1.00
1979	1,012,000	—	0.15	0.30	0.60	1.00
1979 Proof	—	Value: 17.50				
1980 cock and star	1,018,000	—	0.15	0.30	0.60	1.00
1981	1,022,999	—	0.15	0.30	0.60	1.00
1982	1,010,000	—	0.15	0.30	0.60	1.00
1983	1,024,999	—	0.15	0.30	0.60	1.00
1984	1,026,000	—	0.15	0.30	0.60	1.00
1985	774,000	—	0.15	0.30	0.60	1.00

KM# 35 25 CENTS

3.5000 g., Nickel Bonded Steel, 20.2 mm. **Ruler:** Beatrix **Obv:** Orange blossom within circle **Rev:** Value within circle, geometric designed border **Edge:** Reeded

Date	Mintage	F	VF	XF	Unc	BU
1989	915,000	—	—	—	0.50	1.00
1990	1,811,000	—	—	—	0.50	1.00
1991	2,013,000	—	—	—	0.50	1.00
1992	898,000	—	—	—	0.50	1.00
1993	997,000	—	—	—	0.50	1.00
1994	997,000	—	—	—	0.50	1.00
1995	297,000	—	—	—	0.50	1.00
1996	420,000	—	—	—	0.50	1.00
1997	1,297,000	—	—	—	0.50	1.00
1998	2,007,000	—	—	—	0.50	1.00
1999	1,501,000	—	—	—	0.50	1.00
2000	12,500	—	—	—	1.25	1.50

KM# 36 50 CENTS
5.0000 g., Aureate Steel, 24 mm. **Ruler:** Beatrix **Obv:** Orange blossom within circle, designed border **Rev:** Value within circle of pearls and shell border **Edge:** Plain **Shape:** 4-sided

Date	Mintage	F	VF	XF	Unc	BU
1989	315,000	—	—	—	1.00	2.00
1990	611,000	—	—	—	1.00	2.00
1991	513,000	—	—	—	1.00	2.00
1992	48,000	—	—	—	1.00	2.00
1993	8,560	—	—	—	2.00	3.00
Note: In sets only						
1994	9,000	—	—	—	1.50	2.25
Note: In sets only						
1995	9,000	—	—	—	1.50	2.25
Note: In sets only						
1996	7,500	—	—	—	1.50	2.25
Note: In sets only						
1997	9,000	—	—	—	1.00	2.00
1998	18,900	—	—	—	1.00	2.00
1999	11,000	—	—	—	1.00	2.00
2000	12,500	—	—	—	3.00	4.00

KM# 2 GULDEN
10.0000 g., 0.7200 Silver .2315 oz. ASW, 28 mm. **Ruler:** Juliana **Obv:** Head right **Rev:** Crowned arms **Edge Lettering:** GOD * ZIJ * MET * ONS *

Date	Mintage	F	VF	XF	Unc	BU
1952	1,000,000	1.00	2.00	4.00	8.00	14.00
1952 Proof	100	Value: 125				
1963	100,000	2.00	4.00	8.00	16.00	20.00
1963 Proof	—	Value: 100				
1964 fish	300,000	1.00	2.00	4.00	8.00	14.00
1964 Proof	—	Value: 100				
1964 fish and star	200,000	1.50	3.00	6.00	12.50	14.00
1970	50,000	1.50	3.00	6.00	12.50	16.00
1970 Proof	—	Value: 100				

KM# 12 GULDEN
9.0000 g., Nickel, 28 mm. **Ruler:** Juliana **Obv:** Head right **Rev:** Crowned shield above date and ribbon **Edge Lettering:** GOD * ZIJ * MET * ONS *

Date	Mintage	F	VF	XF	Unc	BU
1970	500,000	0.30	0.60	1.25	2.50	4.00
1970 Proof	—	Value: 50.00				
1971	3,000,000	0.30	0.60	1.25	2.50	3.50
1971 Proof	—	Value: 50.00				
1978	500,000	—	0.50	1.00	2.00	4.00
1979	512,000	—	0.50	1.00	2.00	4.00
1979 Proof	—	Value: 25.00				
1980 cock and star	518,000	—	0.40	0.75	1.50	2.50

Note: 1969 date is now listed in the Patterns section

KM# 24 GULDEN
9.0000 g., Nickel, 28 mm. **Ruler:** Beatrix **Obv:** Head left **Rev:** Crowned shield above date and ribbon **Edge Lettering:** GOD * ZIJ * MET * ONS *

Date	Mintage	F	VF	XF	Unc	BU
1980 anvil	223,000	—	0.50	1.00	2.00	2.50
1981	223,000	—	0.50	1.00	2.00	2.50
1982	510,000	—	0.25	0.50	1.00	2.00
1983	525,000	—	0.25	0.50	1.00	2.00
1984	526,000	—	0.25	0.50	1.00	2.00
1985	424,000	—	0.25	0.50	1.00	2.00

KM# 37 GULDEN
6.0000 g., Aureate Steel **Ruler:** Beatrix **Obv:** Head left **Rev:** Crowned shield divides value above date and ribbon **Edge Lettering:** GOD * ZIJ * MET * ONS *

Date	Mintage	F	VF	XF	Unc	BU
1989	715,000	—	—	0.50	1.00	1.00
1990	1,411,000	—	—	0.50	1.00	1.00
1991	2,013,000	—	—	0.50	1.00	1.00
1992	1,198,000	—	—	0.50	1.00	1.00
1993	1,986,000	—	—	0.50	1.00	1.00
1994	997,000	—	—	0.50	1.00	1.00
1995	9,000	—	—	—	2.00	3.00
Note: In sets only						
1996	7,500	—	—	—	2.00	3.00
Note: In sets only						
1997	9,500	—	—	0.40	3.00	1.00
1998	18,500	—	—	0.40	3.00	1.00
1999	12,000	—	—	—	3.00	4.00
2000	12,500	—	—	—	3.00	4.00

KM# 7 2-1/2 GULDEN
25.0000 g., 0.7200 Silver .5787 oz. ASW, 37 mm. **Ruler:** Juliana **Obv:** Head right **Rev:** Crowned arms **Edge Lettering:** GOD * ZIJ * MET * ONS *

Date	Mintage	F	VF	XF	Unc	BU
1964	162,400	—	—	BV	9.00	12.50
1964 Proof	—	Value: 200				

KM# 19 2-1/2 GULDEN
14.0000 g., Nickel, 32 mm. **Ruler:** Juliana **Obv:** Head right **Rev:** Crowned shield above date and ribbon **Edge Lettering:** GOD * ZIJ * MET * ONS *

Date	Mintage	F	VF	XF	Unc	BU
1978	100,000	—	—	2.50	5.00	6.00
1979	110,000	—	—	2.50	5.00	6.00
1979 Proof	—	Value: 35.00				
1980 cock and star	84,000	—	—	2.50	5.00	6.00

KM# 25 2-1/2 GULDEN
14.0000 g., Nickel, 32 mm. **Ruler:** Beatrix **Obv:** Head left **Rev:** Crowned shield above date and ribbon **Edge Lettering:** GOD * ZIJ * MET * ONS *

Date	Mintage	F	VF	XF	Unc	BU
1980 anvil	80,000	—	—	2.00	4.00	6.00
1981	30,000	—	—	2.00	4.00	6.00
1982	44,000	—	—	2.00	4.00	6.00
1984	12,500	—	—	3.00	6.00	7.00
1985	12,500	—	—	3.00	6.00	7.00

KM# 38 2-1/2 GULDEN
9.0000 g., Aureate Steel, 28 mm. **Ruler:** Beatrix **Obv:** Head left **Rev:** Crowned shield divides value above date and ribbon **Edge Lettering:** GOD * ZIJ * MET * ONS *

Date	Mintage	F	VF	XF	Unc	BU
1989	35,000	—	—	—	3.00	4.00
1990	60,000	—	—	—	3.00	4.00
1991	63,000	—	—	—	3.00	4.00
1992	23,000	—	—	—	3.00	4.00
1993	8,560	—	—	—	4.25	6.00
Note: In sets only						
1994	9,000	—	—	—	3.50	5.00
Note: In sets only						
1995	9,000	—	—	—	3.50	5.00
Note: In sets only						
1996	7,500	—	—	—	3.50	5.00
Note: In sets only						
1997	9,500	—	—	—	5.00	4.00
1998	20,000	—	—	—	3,00	4.00
1999	11,000	—	—	—	3.00	4.00
2000	12,500	—	—	—	3.00	6.00

KM# 26 5 GULDEN
3.3600 g., 0.9000 Gold .0972 oz. AGW, 18 mm. **Ruler:** Beatrix **Obv:** Head left **Rev:** Crown above joined arms of the Antilles and Netherlands **Edge:** Reeded

Date	Mintage	F	VF	XF	Unc	BU
1980 Anvil & hammer Proof	16,000	Value: 70.00				

KM# 43 5 GULDEN
11.0000 g., Brass Plated Steel, 26 mm. **Ruler:** Beatrix **Obv:** Head left **Rev:** Crowned shield divides value above date and ribbon **Edge Lettering:** GOD * ZIJ * MET * ONS *

Date	Mintage	F	VF	XF	Unc	BU
1998	607,000	—	—	—	4.50	4.00
1999	999,000	—	—	—	4.50	4.00
2000	9,000	—	—	—	7.50	5.00

KM# 20 10 GULDEN
25.0000 g., 0.7200 Silver .5787 oz. ASW, 38 mm. **Ruler:** Juliana **Subject:** 150th Anniversary of Bank **Obv:** Head right **Rev:** Crowned shield divides value **Edge Lettering:** * BANK VAN DE NEDERLANDSE ANTILLEN 1928-1978

Date	Mintage	F	VF	XF	Unc	BU
1978 Proof	14,675	Value: 15.00				
1978	35,325	—	—	—	9.00	11.00

KM# 27 10 GULDEN
6.7200 g., 0.9000 Gold .1945 oz. AGW, 22.5 mm. **Ruler:** Beatrix **Obv:** Head left **Rev:** Crown above two shields dividing value **Edge:** Reeded

Date	Mintage	F	VF	XF	Unc	BU
1980 Proof, anvil with hammer	6,000	Value: 135				

KM# 14 25 GULDEN
42.1200 g., 0.9250 Silver 1.2526 oz. ASW, 45 mm. **Ruler:** Juliana **Subject:** 25th Anniversary of Reign **Obv:** Head right **Rev:** Royal carriage on bridge **Rev. Designer:** Patrick Brindly **Edge:** DIOS KU NOS **Note:** Struck at the Ottawa Mint. Legend is in a creole version of Spanish, called Papiamento.

Date	Mintage	F	VF	XF	Unc	BU
1973	40,188	—	—	—	18.50	20.00
1973 Proof	20,207	Value: 25.00				

KM# 15 25 GULDEN
42.1200 g., 0.9250 Silver 1.2526 oz. ASW, 45 mm. **Ruler:** Juliana **Subject:** U.S. Bicentennial **Obv:** Head right **Rev:** Saling ship Andrew Doria **Edge Lettering:** IN GOD WE TRUST ST. EUSTATIUS SALUTES FIRST AMERICAN FLAG

Date	Mintage	F	VF	XF	Unc	BU
1976 FM(M)	200	—	—	—	165	185
1976 FM(U)	9,425	—	—	—	30.00	32.00
1976 FM(P)	12,788	Value: 45.00				

KM# 17 25 GULDEN
42.1200 g., 0.9250 Silver 1.2526 oz. ASW, 45 mm. **Ruler:** Juliana **Subject:** Peter Stuyvesant **Obv:** Head right **Rev:** Standing statue left **Edge:** Plain

Date	Mintage	F	VF	XF	Unc	BU
1977FM	2,000	—	—	100	200	220

KM# 22 25 GULDEN
27.2200 g., 0.9250 Silver .8095 oz. ASW, 40 mm. **Ruler:** Juliana **Series:** International Year of the Child **Obv:** Head right **Rev:** Children dancing **Edge:** Plain

Date	Mintage	F	VF	XF	Unc	BU
1979	1,000	—	—	—	75.00	80.00
1979 Prooflike	4,000	—	—	—	—	35.00
1979 Proof	17,000	Value: 17.50				

KM# 39 25 GULDEN
25.0000 g., 0.9250 Silver .7435 oz. ASW, 39 mm. **Ruler:** Beatrix **Subject:** Visit of Pope John Paul II **Obv:** Head right **Rev:** Curacao map, Juliana bridge **Edge:** Plain **Designer:** Bart Reneken

Date	Mintage	F	VF	XF	Unc	BU
1990	10,000	—	—	—	20.00	25.00
1990 Proof	8,000	Value: 40.00				

KM# 40 25 GULDEN
25.0000 g., 0.9250 Silver .7435 oz. ASW **Ruler:** Beatrix **Subject:** First Amsterdam to Curacao Flight in 1934 **Obv:** Head left **Rev:** Folker FXVIII plane over route map **Rev. Designer:** J.C. Hekman, Dutch Mint **Edge:** Plain

Date	Mintage	F	VF	XF	Unc	BU
1994	1,000	—	—	—	25.00	35.00
1994 Proof	5,300	Value: 35.00				

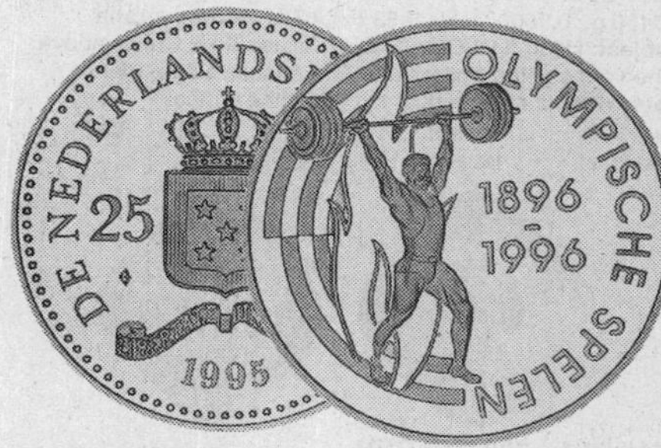

KM# 41 25 GULDEN
25.0000 g., 0.9250 Silver .7435 oz. ASW, 38 mm. **Ruler:** Beatrix **Series:** Olympics **Obv:** Crowned shield **Rev:** Weight lifter and dates **Edge:** Plain **Designer:** Dutch Mint

Date	Mintage	F	VF	XF	Unc	BU
1995	1,000	—	—	—	25.00	35.00
1995 Proof	2,500	Value: 30.00				

KM# 42 25 GULDEN
25.0000 g., 0.9250 Silver .7435 oz. ASW, 38 mm. **Ruler:** Juliana **Subject:** Fort Nassau 1797-1997 **Obv:** Head left **Rev:** Old steam sailship Curacao, dates **Edge:** Plain **Designer:** Dutch Mint

Date	Mintage	F	VF	XF	Unc	BU
ND(1997) Proof	15,000	Value: 40.00				

Date	Mintage	F	VF	XF	Unc	BU
ND(1997)	1,000	—	—	—	30.00	35.00

KM# 44 25 GULDEN
25.0000 g., 0.9250 Silver .7435 oz. ASW, 38 mm. **Ruler:** Juliana **Series:** World Wildlife Fund **Obv:** Crowned shield and value **Rev:** Whitetail buck and doe, WWF logo **Edge:** Plain **Designer:** Dutch Mint

Date	Mintage	F	VF	XF	Unc	BU
1998	500	—	—	—	35.00	45.00
1998 Proof	2,700	Value: 50.00				

KM# 45 25 GULDEN
25.0000 g., 0.9250 Silver .7435 oz. ASW, 38 mm. **Ruler:** Juliana **Subject:** 1499 Discovery of Curacao **Obv:** Crowned shield divides date within circle **Rev:** Sailing ship - Nina **Edge Lettering:** DIOS KU NOS **Designer:** Dutch Mint **Note:** Edge inscription repeats three times.

Date	Mintage	F	VF	XF	Unc	BU
1999 Proof	2,500	Value: 45.00				

KM# 48 25 GULDEN
25.0000 g., 0.9250 Silver 0.7435 oz. ASW, 38 mm. **Ruler:** Beatrix **Subject:** Olympics **Obv:** Crowned shield divides value **Rev:** Swimmer **Edge Lettering:** GOD*ZJ*MET*ONS **Designer:** Royal Dutch Mint

Date	Mintage	F	VF	XF	Unc	BU
2000 Proof	3,500	Value: 40.00				

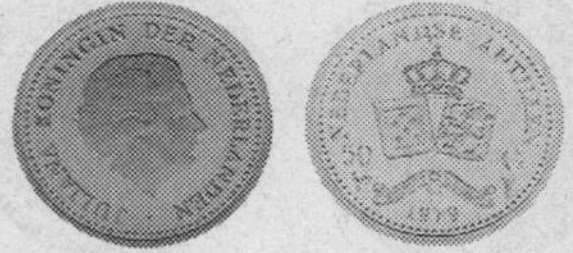

KM# 23 50 GULDEN
3.3600 g., 0.9000 Gold .0972 oz. AGW, 18 mm. **Ruler:** Juliana **Subject:** 75th Anniversary of the Royal Convenant **Obv:** Head right **Rev:** Crown above joined arms of the Antilles and Netherlands **Edge:** Reeded

Date	Mintage	F	VF	XF	Unc	BU
1979	11,000	—	—	—	65.00	70.00
1979 Proof	64,000	Value: 65.00				

KM# 28 50 GULDEN
24.0000 g., 0.5000 Silver .3859 oz. ASW, 38 mm. **Ruler:** Beatrix **Obv:** Head left **Rev:** Crown above joined arms of the Antilles and Netherlands **Edge Lettering:** GOD * XIJ * MET * ONS *

Date	Mintage	F	VF	XF	Unc	BU
1980 anvil and hammer	8,600	—	—	—	20.00	25.00
1980 Proof, anvil and hammer	16,400	Value: 25.00				

KM# 30 50 GULDEN
25.0000 g., 0.9250 Silver .7435 oz. ASW, 38 mm. **Ruler:** Beatrix **Subject:** Dutch American Friendship **Obv:** Head left **Rev:** Bust facing above three flags as banners within circle **Edge Lettering:** DIOS KU NOS

Date	Mintage	F	VF	XF	Unc	BU
1982 Y Proof	40,000	Value: 30.00				

KM# 31 50 GULDEN
25.0000 g., 0.9250 Silver .7435 oz. ASW, 38 mm. **Ruler:** Beatrix **Obv:** Head left **Rev:** Mikve Israel Emanuel Synagogue **Designer:** Plain

Date	Mintage	F	VF	XF	Unc	BU
ND(1982) Proof	10,000	Value: 40.00				

KM# 47 75 GULDEN
19.4000 g., Bi-Metallic Gold And Silver, 30 mm. **Ruler:** Beatrix **Subject:** Enkuentro Di Pueblonan **Obv:** Crowned shield divides date within circle **Rev:** World globe above five heads flanked by dates **Edge:** Plain **Designer:** Dutch Mint

Date	Mintage	F	VF	XF	Unc	BU
1999 Proof	750	Value: 250				

KM# 21 100 GULDEN
6.7200 g., 0.9000 Gold .1944 oz. AGW. **Ruler:** Juliana **Subject:** 150th Anniversary of Bank **Obv:** Head right **Rev:** Head right **Edge:** Reeded

Date	Mintage	F	VF	XF	Unc	BU
1978	26,500	—	—	—	135	140
1978 Proof	23,500	Value: 135				

KM# 46 100 GULDEN
7.7700 g., 0.9990 Gold .2500 oz. AGW, 22 mm. **Ruler:** Beatrix **Obv:** Crowned shield divides date within circle **Obv. Legend:** YEGADA DI SPAÑONAN **Rev:** The Santa Maria **Edge:** Plain **Designer:** Dutch Mint

Date	Mintage	F	VF	XF	Unc	BU
1999 Proof	850	Value: 250				

KM# 16 200 GULDEN
7.9500 g., 0.9000 Gold .2300 oz. AGW **Ruler:** Juliana **Subject:** U.S. Bicentennial **Obv:** Head right **Rev:** The Andrew Doria **Edge:** IN GOD WE TRUST ST EUSTATIUS SALUTES FIRST AMERICAN FLAG **Shape:** Octagon

Date	Mintage	F	VF	XF	Unc	BU
1976 FM(M)	100	—	—	—	350	400
1976 FM(U)	5,726	—	—	—	155	165
1976 FM(P)	15,442	Value: 165				

KM# 18 200 GULDEN
7.9500 g., 0.9000 Gold .2300 oz. AGW **Ruler:** Juliana **Obv:** Head right **Rev:** Standing statue left **Edge:** Plain **Shape:** Octagon

Date	Mintage	F	VF	XF	Unc	BU
1977 FM(M)	1,000	—	—	—	165	190
1977 FM(U)	654	—	—	—	250	265
1977 FM(P)	6,878	Value: 160				

KM# 29.2 300 GULDEN
5.0400 g., 0.9000 Gold .1458 oz. AGW **Ruler:** Juliana **Subject:** Head right **Obv:** Queen Juliana **Rev:** Crown above joined arms of the Antilles and Netherlands **Edge:** Plain **Note:** Without mint mark or mintmaster's symbol

Date	Mintage	F	VF	XF	Unc	BU
1980 Proof	Inc. above	Value: 320				

KM# 29.1 300 GULDEN
5.0400 g., 0.9000 Gold .1458 oz. AGW **Ruler:** Juliana **Subject:** Abdication of Queen Juliana **Obv:** Head right **Rev:** Crown above joined arms of the Antilles and Netherlands **Edge:** Plain **Shape:** Square

Date	Mintage	F	VF	XF	Unc	BU
1980 (u) Proof, cock and star	29,300	Value: 100				

PATTERNS

Including off metal strikes

KM#	Date	Mintage	Identification	Mkt Val
Pn1	1969	210	Cent. Nickel. KM8.	550
Pn2	1969	210	2-1/2 Cents. Nickel. KM9.	550
Pn3	1969	210	5 Cents. Nickel. KMA13.	550
Pn4	1969	210	10 Cents. Nickel. KM10.	550
Pn5	1969	210	25 Cents. Nickel. KM11.	550
Pn6	1969	210	Gulden. Nickel. (KM12).	550
Pn7	1981 Y	—	125 Gulden. Gilt Bronze.	750
Pn8	1981 Y	—	125 Gulden. Gold.	3,000
Pn9	1981 Y	—	250 Gulden. Gilt Bronze.	850
Pn10	1981 Y	—	250 Gulden. Gold.	4,000
Pn11	1981 Y	—	500 Gulden. Gilt Bronze.	950
Pn12	1981 Y	—	500 Gulden. Gold.	5,000
Pn13	1983	—	50 Guilder. 0.9250 Silver. 25.0000 g. 38 mm. Head of Beatrix left. Arms and banner above six islands of the Antilles, value 50G below. Struck at a private mint.	—

PIEFORTS

KM#	Date	Mintage	Identification	Mkt Val
P1	1998	200	5 Gulden. Brass Plated Steel. KM43.	500

MINT SETS

KM#	Date	Mintage	Identification	Issue Price	Mkt Val
MS1	1971 (7)	—	KM8-13 and Curacao KM46	—	22.00
MS2	1979 (7)	12,000	KM8a-9a, 10-13, 19	—	15.00
MS3	1980 (7)	18,000	KM8a-9a, 10-13, 19	—	10.00
MS4	1980 (2)	23,000	KM24-25	—	7.00
MS5	1981 (7)	23,000	KM8a-9a, 10-12, 24, 25	—	13.00
MS6	1982 (7)	10,000	KM8a-9a, 10-12, 24, 25	—	13.00
MS7	1983 (6)	25,000	KM8a-9a, 10-12, 24 and medallion	14.00	13.00
MS8	1984 (7)	26,000	KM8a-9a, 10-12, 24, 25	14.50	13.00
MS9	1985 (7)	24,000	KM8a-9a, 10-12, 24, 25	—	13.00
MS10	1989 (7)	15,000	KM32-38	—	13.00
MS11	1990 (7)	10,000	KM32-38	13.00	13.00
MS12	1991 (7)	12,500	KM32-38	13.50	13.00
MS13	1992 (7)	10,500	MS32-38	—	13.00
MS14	1993 (7)	8,560	KM32-38	—	13.00
MS15	1994 (7)	9,000	KM32-38	17.00	13.00
MS16	1995 (7)	9,000	KM32-38	17.50	17.50
MS17	1996 (7)	7,500	KM32-38	18.50	17.50
MS18	1997 (7)	7,000	KM32-38	15.00	17.50
MS19	1998 (8)	7,000	KM32-38, 43	15.00	17.50
MS20	1999 (8)	6,000	KM32-38, 43	15.00	17.50
MS21	2000 (8)	7,500	KM32-38, 43	15.00	17.50

PROOF SETS

KM#	Date	Mintage	Identification	Issue Price	Mkt Val
PS1	1952 (2)	100	KM1-2	—	95.00
PS2	1954 (3)	200	KM1, 3-4	—	95.00
PS3	1956 (3)	500	KM3-5	—	95.00
PS4	1957 (4)	250	KM1, 3-4, 6	—	95.00
PS5	1959 (3)	250	KM1, 3, 5	—	95.00
PS6	1960 (3)	300	KM1, 3-4	—	60.00
PS7	1962 (3)	200	KM3-4, 6	—	110
PS8	1963 (5)	—	KM1-4, 6	—	235
PS9	1964 (3)	—	KM1-2, 7	—	325
PS10	1965 (4)	—	KM1, 4-6	—	125
PS11	1967 (3)	—	KM1, 4, 6	—	100
PS12	1969 (6)	200	KM8-12, A13, Pattern set	—	700
PS13	1970 (10)	—	KM1-4, 6, 8-12	—	350
PS14	1971 (6)	—	KM8-13	—	165
PS15	1973 (3)	—	KM8-9, 14	—	87.50
PS16	1974 (4)	—	KM8-10, 13	—	85.00
PS17	1975 (4)	—	KM8, 10-11, 13	—	240
PS18	1976 (2)	13,000	KM15-16	188	325
PS19	1979 (7)	—	KM8a-9a, 10-13, 19	—	120
PS20	1999 (5)	—	KM45-47, with Aruba KM18-19	—	850

Netherlands East Indies, (Kingdom of the Netherlands) is the world's largest archipelago extending for more than 3,000 mi. along the equator from the mainland of southeast Asia to Australia. At present time, since the late 1940's, it is known as Indonesia. The Dutch were in control until 1942 when the Japanese invaded. At the end of World War II, with Japanese encouragement, Indonesia declared its independence.

World War II Coinage

Netherlands and Netherlands East Indies coins of the 1941-45 period were struck at U.S. Mints (P - Philadelphia, D – Denver, S – San Francisco) and bear the mint mark and a palm tree (acorn on Homeland issues) flanking the date. The following issues, KM#330 and KM#331, are of the usual Netherlands type, being distinguished from similar 1944-45 issues produced in the name of the Homeland by the presence of the palm tree, but were produced for release in the colony. See other related issues under Curacao and Suriname.

RULERS

Dutch, 1816-1942

MINT

Utrecht

Privy Marks

(a) – Halberd

(b) – Halberd and star

(c) – Sea horse

(d) - Grapes

KINGDOM OF NETHERLANDS

Dutch Administration 1817-1949

DECIMAL COINAGE

KM# 306 1/2 CENT

2.3000 g., Copper, 17 mm. **Ruler:** Wilhelmina I **Obv:** Crowned arms divide date within circle **Obv. Legend:** NEDERLANDSCH INDIE **Rev:** Value and inscription within circle **Edge:** Plain

Date	Mintage	F	VF	XF	Unc	BU
1902(u)	20,000,000	1.00	3.00	8.00	20.00	35.00
1902(u) Proof	—	Value: 75.00				
1908(u)	10,600,000	3.00	6.25	12.50	25.00	60.00
1908(u) Proof	—	Value: 85.00				
1909(u)	4,400,000	6.00	12.50	25.00	50.00	95.00

KM# 314.1 1/2 CENT

2.3000 g., Bronze, 17 mm. **Ruler:** Wilhelmina I **Obv:** Crowned arms divide date within circle **Obv. Legend:** NEDERLANDSCH INDIE **Rev:** Value and inscription within circle **Edge:** Plain **Note:** Mintmaster's mark: Sea horse.

Date	Mintage	F	VF	XF	Unc	BU
1914(u)	50,000,000	0.75	1.50	3.00	6.00	8.00
1916(u)	10,000,000	1.50	3.00	6.00	12.00	15.00
1921(u)	4,000,000	5.00	10.00	20.00	40.00	60.00
1932(u)	10,000,000	1.50	3.00	6.00	12.00	15.00
1933(u)	20,000,000	1.50	3.00	6.00	12.00	15.00

KM# 314.2 1/2 CENT

2.3000 g., Bronze, 17 mm. **Ruler:** Wilhelmina I **Obv:** Crowned arms divide date within circle **Obv. Legend:** NEDERLANDSCH INDIE **Rev:** Inscription and value within circle **Edge:** Plain **Note:** Mintmaster's mark: Grapes.

Date	Mintage	F	VF	XF	Unc	BU
1933(u)	Inc. above	25.00	50.00	100	200	300
1934(u)	30,000,000	0.75	1.50	3.00	6.00	8.00
1935(u)	14,000,000	1.50	2.50	5.00	10.00	12.00

Date	Mintage	F	VF	XF	Unc	BU
1936(u)	12,000,000	1.50	2.50	5.00	10.00	12.00
1936(u) Proof	—	Value: 35.00				
1937(u)	8,400,000	1.50	2.50	5.00	10.00	20.00
1937(u) Proof	—	Value: 35.00				
1938(u)	3,600,000	3.00	6.00	12.50	25.00	35.00
1939(u)	2,000,000	6.00	12.50	25.00	50.00	70.00
1945P	400,000,000	0.15	0.25	0.50	1.00	1.25

KM# 307.2 CENT

4.8000 g., Copper, 23 mm. **Ruler:** William III **Obv:** Crowned Dutch arms, legend begins and ends beside date **Obv. Legend:** NEDERLANDSCH INDIE **Rev:** Value in Javanese and Malayan text **Edge:** Plain

Date	Mintage	F	VF	XF	Unc	BU
1901(u)	15,000,000	4.00	8.00	15.00	35.00	85.00
1901(u) Proof	—	Value: 175				
1902(u)	10,000,000	4.00	8.00	15.00	30.00	60.00
1907(u)	7,500,000	4.00	8.00	15.00	30.00	60.00
1907(u) Proof	—	Value: 175				
1908(u)	12,500,000	4.00	8.00	15.00	30.00	65.00
1908(u) Proof	—	Value: 165				
1909(u)	7,500,000	4.00	8.00	15.00	30.00	80.00
1909(u) Proof	—	Value: 175				
1912(u)	25,000,000	1.50	3.00	6.00	12.00	35.00

KM# 315 CENT

Bronze **Ruler:** Wilhelmina I **Obv:** Crowned arms divide date within circle **Obv. Legend:** NEDERLANDSCH INDIE **Rev:** Inscription and value within circle

Date	Mintage	F	VF	XF	Unc	BU
1914(u)	85,000,000	1.00	2.25	4.50	9.00	15.00
1914(u) Proof	—	Value: 45.00				
1916(u)	16,440,000	2.00	4.00	8.00	16.00	30.00
1919(u)	20,000,000	2.00	4.00	8.00	16.00	30.00
1919(u) Proof	—	Value: 65.00				
1920(u)	120,000,000	1.00	2.25	4.50	9.00	8.00
1926(u)	10,000,000	2.00	4.00	8.00	16.00	30.00
1929(u)	50,000,000	1.00	2.50	5.00	10.00	15.00
1929(u) Proof	—	Value: 100				

KM# 317 CENT

4.8000 g., Bronze, 23 mm. **Ruler:** Wilhelmina I **Obv:** 3/4 spray around hole in center with value below **Obv. Legend:** NEDERLANDSCH INDIE **Rev:** Inscription and flowers around hole in center **Edge:** Plain

Date	Mintage	F	VF	XF	Unc	BU
1936(u)	52,000,000	0.50	1.00	1.75	3.50	6.00
1937(u)	120,400,000	0.50	1.00	1.75	3.50	5.00
1937(u) Proof	—	Value: 40.00				
1938(u)	150,000,000	0.50	1.00	1.75	3.50	5.00
1939(u)	81,400,000	0.50	1.00	1.75	3.50	6.00
1942P	100,000,000	0.10	0.25	0.50	1.25	2.00
1945P	335,000,000	—	0.10	0.25	0.50	1.50
1945D	133,800,000	0.10	0.25	0.50	1.25	2.00
1945S	102,568,000	0.10	0.25	0.50	1.25	2.00

KM# 308 2-1/2 CENTS

12.5000 g., Copper, 31 mm. **Ruler:** Wilhelmina I **Obv:** Crowned Dutch arms divide date **Obv. Legend:** NEDERLANDSCH INDIE **Rev:** Value in Javanese and Malayan text **Edge:** Plain

Date	Mintage	F	VF	XF	Unc	BU
1902	6,000,000	5.00	10.00	20.00	40.00	70.00
1907	3,000,000	5.00	10.00	20.00	40.00	75.00
1908	5,940,000	5.00	10.00	20.00	40.00	70.00
1908 Proof	—	Value: 160				
1909	3,060,000	8.00	15.00	30.00	60.00	95.00
1913	4,000,000	8.00	15.00	30.00	60.00	95.00
1913 Proof	—	Value: 160				

KM# 316 2-1/2 CENTS

12.5000 g., Bronze, 31 mm. **Ruler:** Wilhelmina I **Obv:** Crowned Dutch arms divide date **Obv. Legend:** NEDERLANDSCH INDIE **Rev:** Inscription and value within beaded circle **Edge:** Plain

Date	Mintage	F	VF	XF	Unc	BU
1914(u)	22,000,000	1.50	3.00	6.00	12.00	30.00
1914(u)	—	Value: 165				
1915(u)	6,000,000	5.00	10.00	20.00	40.00	70.00
1920(u)	48,000,000	1.50	3.00	6.00	12.00	25.00
1920(u)	—	Value: 165				
1945P	200,000,000	0.25	0.50	1.00	2.00	2.00

KM# 313 5 CENTS

5.0000 g., Copper-Nickel, 21 mm. **Ruler:** Wilhelmina I **Obv:** Crown above hole in center flanked by value and rice stalks **Obv. Legend:** NEDERLANDSCH INDIE **Rev:** Inscription around hole in center flanked by designs **Edge:** Plain

Date	Mintage	F	VF	XF	Unc	BU
1913(u)	60,000,000	1.00	2.00	3.75	7.50	25.00
1913(u) Proof	—	Value: 100				
1921(u)	40,000,000	1.50	3.00	6.00	12.50	35.00
1921(u) Proof	—	Value: 220				
1922(u)	20,000,000	2.50	5.00	10.00	20.00	40.00

KM# 304 1/10 GULDEN

1.2500 g., 0.7200 Silver .0289 oz. ASW, 15 mm. **Ruler:** Wilhelmina I **Obv:** Crowned Dutch arms **Obv. Legend:** NEDERL INDIE **Rev:** Inscription and value within circle **Edge:** Reeded

Date	Mintage	F	VF	XF	Unc	BU
1901(u)	5,000,000	2.50	5.00	10.00	20.00	30.00
1901(u) Proof	—	Value: 100				

KM# 309 1/10 GULDEN

1.2500 g., 0.7200 Silver .0289 oz. ASW, 15 mm. **Ruler:** Wilhelmina I **Obv:** Crowned arms divide value **Obv. Legend:** NEDERL INDIE **Rev:** Inscription within circle **Edge:** Reeded

Date	Mintage	F	VF	XF	Unc	BU
1903(u)	5,000,000	2.50	5.00	10.00	20.00	25.00
1903(u) Proof	—	Value: 110				
1904(u)	5,000,000	2.50	5.00	10.00	20.00	25.00
1904(u) Proof	—	Value: 100				
1905(u)	5,000,000	2.50	5.00	10.00	20.00	25.00
1906(u)	7,500,000	1.00	2.50	5.00	10.00	15.00
1907(u)	14,000,000	1.00	2.50	5.00	10.00	15.00
1907(u) Proof	—	Value: 60.00				
1908(u)	3,000,000	2.50	5.00	10.00	20.00	30.00
1909(u)	10,000,000	1.00	2.50	5.00	10.00	15.00
1909(u) Proof	—	Value: 110				

KM# 311 1/10 GULDEN

1.2500 g., 0.7200 Silver .0289 oz. ASW, 15 mm. **Ruler:** Wilhelmina I **Obv:** Crowned arms divide value **Obv. Legend:** NEDERL INDIE **Rev:** Inscription within circle **Edge:** Reeded **Note:** Wide rims.

Date	Mintage	F	VF	XF	Unc	BU
1910(u)	15,000,000	1.25	2.50	5.00	10.00	20.00
1910(u) Proof	—	Value: 140				
1911(u)	10,000,000	2.50	5.00	10.00	20.00	30.00
1912(u)	25,000,000	0.60	1.50	3.00	7.00	12.00
1913(u)	15,000,000	0.75	1.50	3.00	7.00	12.00
1914(u)	25,000,000	0.60	1.50	3.00	7.00	10.00
1915(u)	15,000,000	0.65	1.50	3.00	7.00	12.00
1918(u)	30,000,000	0.60	1.50	3.00	7.00	12.00
1919(u)	20,000,000	0.60	1.50	3.00	7.00	12.00
1920(u)	8,500,000	1.00	2.00	4.00	8.00	15.00
1928(u)	30,000,000	0.60	1.00	2.00	4.00	10.00
1930(u)	15,000,000	0.60	1.00	2.00	4.00	10.00

KM# 318 1/10 GULDEN
1.2500 g., 0.7200 Silver .0289 oz. ASW, 15 mm.
Ruler: Wilhelmina I **Obv:** Crowned arms divide value **Obv. Legend:** NEDERL INDIE **Rev:** Inscription within circle **Edge:** Reeded **Note:** Narrow rims.

Date	Mintage	F	VF	XF	Unc	BU
1937(u)	20,000,000	0.45	0.75	1.50	2.50	4.00
1937(u) Proof	—	Value: 130				
1938(u)	30,000,000	0.45	0.75	1.50	2.50	4.00
1939(u)	5,500,000	0.75	1.50	3.00	6.00	15.00
1939(u) Proof	—	Value: 130				
1940(u)	10,000,000	0.45	0.75	1.25	2.50	5.00
1941P	41,850,000	BV	0.50	1.00	2.00	3.00
1941S	58,150,000	BV	0.50	1.00	2.00	3.00
1942S	75,000,000	BV	0.50	1.00	2.00	3.00
1945P	100,720,000	BV	0.50	1.00	2.00	3.00
Note: Mint mark horizontal						
1945P	Inc. above	3.00	10.00	15.00	25.00	35.00
Note: Mint mark slanted with three variations						
1945S	19,280,000	BV	0.50	1.00	2.00	3.00

KM# 305 1/4 GULDEN
3.1800 g., 0.7200 Silver .0736 oz. ASW, 18.5 mm. **Ruler:** Wilhelmina I **Obv:** Crowned arms **Obv. Legend:** NEDERL INDIE **Rev:** Value in Javanese and Malayan text **Edge:** Reeded

Date	Mintage	F	VF	XF	Unc	BU
1901(u)	2,000,000	10.00	20.00	40.00	75.00	100
1901(u) Proof	—	Value: 120				

KM# 310 1/4 GULDEN
3.1800 g., 0.7200 Silver .0736 oz. ASW, 15 mm.
Ruler: Wilhelmina I **Obv:** Crowned arms divide value **Obv. Legend:** NEDERL INDIE **Rev:** Inscription within sun design flanked by small legends at points **Edge:** Reeded **Note:** Like KM#305 but with smaller privy mark and mint mark.

Date	Mintage	F	VF	XF	Unc	BU
1903(u)	2,000,000	3.75	7.50	15.00	30.00	60.00
1903(u) Proof	—	Value: 115				
1904(u)	2,000,000	2.75	7.50	15.00	30.00	50.00
1904(u) Proof	—	Value: 100				
1905(u)	2,000,000	3.75	7.50	15.00	30.00	50.00
1905(u) Proof	—	Value: 170				
1906(u)	4,000,000	2.50	5.00	10.00	20.00	35.00
1907(u)	4,400,000	2.50	5.00	10.00	20.00	35.00
1907(u) Proof	—	Value: 110				
1908(u)	2,000,000	3.75	7.50	15.00	30.00	50.00
1909(u)	4,000,000	2.50	5.00	10.00	20.00	35.00
1909(u) Proof	—	Value: 110				

KM# 312 1/4 GULDEN
3.1800 g., 0.7200 Silver .0736 oz. ASW, 15 mm.
Ruler: Wilhelmina I **Obv:** Crowned arms divide value **Obv. Legend:** NEDERL INDIE **Rev:** Inscription within sun design flanked by small legends at points **Edge:** Reeded

Date	Mintage	F	VF	XF	Unc	BU
1910(u)	6,000,000	2.50	5.00	10.00	20.00	50.00
1910(u) Proof	—	Value: 100				
1911(u)	4,000,000	2.50	5.00	10.00	20.00	50.00
1911(u) Proof	—	Value: 110				
1912(u)	10,000,000	2.50	5.00	10.00	20.00	35.00
1912 Proof	—	Value: 400				
1913(u)	6,000,000	2.50	5.00	10.00	20.00	35.00
1914(u)	10,000,000	2.50	5.00	10.00	20.00	35.00
1915(u)	6,000,000	2.50	5.00	10.00	20.00	35.00
1917(u)	12,000,000	2.00	3.75	7.50	15.00	20.00
1919(u)	6,000,000	2.50	5.00	10.00	20.00	35.00
1920(u)	20,000,000	1.20	2.00	4.00	8.00	12.00
1921(u)	24,000,000	1.20	2.00	4.00	8.00	12.00
1929(u)	5,000,000	2.00	3.75	7.50	15.00	20.00
1930(u)	7,000,000	2.00	3.75	7.50	15.00	20.00
1930(u) Proof	—	Value: 160				

KM# 319 1/4 GULDEN
3.1800 g., 0.7200 Silver .0736 oz. ASW, 18.8 mm. **Ruler:** Wilhelmina I **Obv:** Crowned arms divide value **Obv. Legend:** NEDERL INDIE **Rev:** Inscription within sun design flanked by small legends at points **Edge:** Reeded **Note:** Narrow rims.

Date	Mintage	F	VF	XF	Unc	BU
1937(u)	8,000,000	BV	1.25	2.50	5.00	8.00
1938(u)	12,000,000	BV	1.25	2.50	5.00	8.00
1939(u)	10,400,000	BV	1.25	2.50	5.00	8.00
1939 Proof	—	Value: 80.00				
1941P	34,947,000	BV	BV	1.25	2.50	3.50
1941S	5,053,000	BV	1.25	2.50	5.00	10.00
1942S	32,000,000	—	BV	1.25	2.50	3.50
1945S	56,000,000	—	BV	1.25	2.50	3.50

KM# 330 GULDEN
10.0000 g., 0.7200 Silver .2315 oz. ASW, 28 mm.
Ruler: Wilhelmina I **Obv:** Head left **Obv. Legend:** WILHELMINA KONINGIN DER NEDERLANDEN **Rev:** Crowned arms divide value **Rev. Legend:** MUNT VAN HET KONINGRIJK DER NEDERLANDEN **Edge Lettering:** GOD * ZIJ * MET * ONS *

Date	Mintage	F	VF	XF	Unc	BU
1943D	20,000,000	BV	3.75	7.50	15.00	20.00

KM# 331 2-1/2 GULDEN
25.0000 g., 0.7200 Silver .5787 oz. ASW, 38 mm. **Ruler:** Wilhelmina I **Obv:** Head left **Obv. Legend:** WILHELMINA KONINGIN DER NEDERLANDEN **Rev:** Crowned arms divide value **Rev. Legend:** MUNT VAN HET KONINGRIJK DER NEDERLANDEN **Edge Lettering:** GOD * ZIJ * MET * ONS *

Date	Mintage	F	VF	XF	Unc	BU
1943D	2,000,000	—	BV	9.00	17.50	25.00

TRADE COINAGE

These gold coins, intended primarily for circulation in the Netherlands East Indies, will be found listed as KM#83.1 in the Netherlands section.

KM# T1 DUCAT
3.4940 g., 0.9860 Gold, 21 mm. **Obv:** Standing knight with right leg bent **Rev:** Legend within square

Date	Mintage	VG	F	VF	XF	Unc
ND(1901-37)	—	—	—	—	—	—

PATTERNS

Including off metal strikes

KM#	Date	Mintage	Identification	Mkt Val
Pn11	1902(u)	—	1/2 Cent. Silver. KM#306	—
Pn12	1902(u)	—	1/2 Cent. Gold. KM#306	—
Pn13	1902(u)	—	Cent. Silver. KM#307	—
Pn14	1902(u)	—	Cent. Gold. KM#307	—
Pn15	1902(u)	—	2-1/2 Cents. Silver. 13.5000 g. KM#308	—
Pn16	1902(u)	—	2-1/2 Cents. Gold. KM#308	—
Pn17	1908(u)	—	1/10 Gulden. Gold. KM#309	—
Pn18	1903(u)	—	1/4 Gulden. Gold. KM#310	—
Pn19	1908	—	1/2 Cent. Silver.	—
Pn20	1908	—	1/2 Cent. Gold.	—
Pn21	1908	—	Cent. Iron.	—
Pn22	1908	—	Cent. Silver.	—
Pn23	1908	—	Cent. Gold.	—
Pn24	1908	—	2-1/2 Cents. Silver. KM#308	—
Pn25	1908	—	2-1/2 Cents. Gold. 22.1220 g. KM#308	—
Pn26	1934(u)	—	5 Cents. Copper-Nickel. KM#313	—
Pn27	1914	—	10 Sen. Tin.	—
Pn28	1914	—	5 Cents. Tin.	—
Pn29	1914	—	5 Cents. Gold.	—
PnA30	1934	—	1/4 Cent. Copper.	—
Pn30	1934	—	1/4 Cent. Copper. Holed	—
Pn31	1934	—	1/2 Cent. Copper. KM#314	—
Pn32	1934	—	1/4 Cent. Copper. KM#320	—
Pn33	1945	—	1/4 Gulden. Gold. KM#319	—

TRIAL STRIKES

KM#	Date	Mintage	Identification	Mkt Val
TS1	1941	1	1/10 Gulden. Silver. One side with value, Javanese and Malayan text. KM#318.	—
TS2	1941	—	1/4 Gulden. Silver. One side with value, KM#319.	—
TS3	1943	—	Gulden. Lead. One side with value, KM#330.	—
TS4	1943	—	2-1/2 Gulden. Lead. One side with value, KM#331.	—
TS5	1945	1	1/4 Cent. Lead. One side with valu5 e, KM#307.2.	—
TS6	1945	1	2-1/2 Cents. Lead. One side with value, KM#316.	—

PROOF SETS

KM#	Date	Mintage	Identification	Issue Price	Mkt Val
PS1	1854/58 (12)	—	KM303 (2 pcs.-1854), 304 (2 pcs.-1855), 305 (1855, 1858), 306 (2 pcs.-1855), 307 (2 pcs.-1856), 308 (2 pcs.-1857)	—	—

NEW CALEDONIA

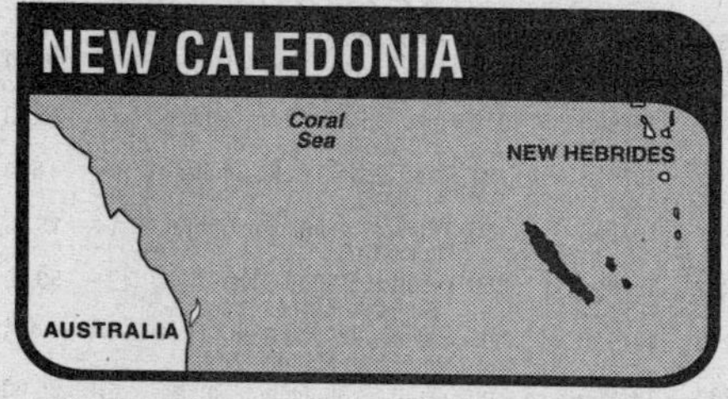

The French Overseas Territory of New Caledonia, is a group of about 25 islands in the South Pacific. They are situated about 750 miles (1,207 km.) east of Australia. The territory, which includes the dependencies of Isle des Pins, Loyalty Islands, Isle Huon, Isles Belep, Isles Chesterfield, Isle Walpole, Wallis and Futuna Islands and has a total land area of 7,358 sq. mi.(19,060 sq. km.) and a population of *156,000. Capital: Noumea. The islands are rich in minerals; New Caledonia has some of the world's largest known deposit of nickel. Nickel, nickel castings, coffee and copra are exported.

The first European to sight New Caledonia was the British navigator Capt. James Cook in 1774. The French took possession in 1853, and established a penal colony on the island in 1864. The European population of the colony remained disproportionately convict until 1897. New Caledonia became an overseas territory within the French Community in 1946, and in 1958 and 1972 chose to remain affiliated with France.

MINT MARKS
Paris, privy marks only

MONETARY SYSTEM
100 Centimes = 1 Franc

FRENCH OVERSEAS TERRITORY

DECIMAL COINAGE

KM# 1 50 CENTIMES
Aluminum, 18 mm. **Obv:** Seated figure holding torch **Rev:** Kagu bird within sprigs below value **Designer:** G.B.L. Bazor

Date	Mintage	F	VF	XF	Unc	BU
1949(a)	1,000,000	—	0.50	1.00	3.50	7.50

KM# 2 FRANC
1.3000 g., Aluminum, 23 mm. **Obv:** Seated figure holding torch **Rev:** Kagu bird within sprigs below value **Designer:** G.B.L. Bazor

Date	Mintage	F	VF	XF	Unc	BU
1949(a)	4,000,000	—	0.25	0.75	2.00	5.00

KM# 8 FRANC
1.3000 g., Aluminum, 23 mm. **Obv:** Seated figure holding torch **Rev:** Kagu bird within sprigs below value **Designer:** G.B.L. Bazor

Date	Mintage	F	VF	XF	Unc	BU
1971(a)	1,000,000	—	0.25	0.75	1.75	4.50

KM# 10 FRANC
1.3000 g., Aluminum, 23 mm. **Obv:** Seated figure holding torch, legend added **Obv. Legend:** I. E. O. M. **Rev:** Kagu bird within sprigs below value **Designer:** G.B.L. Bazor

Date	Mintage	F	VF	XF	Unc	BU
1972(a)	600,000	—	0.25	0.75	1.75	4.00
1973(a)	1,000,000	—	0.10	0.25	1.00	2.00

Date	Mintage	F	VF	XF	Unc	BU
1977(a)	1,500,000	—	0.10	0.25	1.00	2.00
1981(a)	1,000,000	—	0.10	0.20	0.75	1.50
1982(a)	1,000,000	—	0.10	0.20	0.75	1.50
1983(a)	2,000,000	—	0.10	0.20	0.75	1.50
1984(a)	—	—	0.10	0.20	0.75	1.50
1985(a)	2,000,000	—	0.10	0.20	0.75	1.50
1988(a)	2,000,000	—	0.10	0.20	0.75	1.50
1989(a)	1,000,000	—	0.10	0.20	0.75	1.50
1990(a)	1,500,000	—	0.10	0.20	0.75	1.50
1991(a)	1,600,000	—	0.10	0.20	0.75	1.50
1994(a)	2,000,000	—	0.10	0.20	0.70	1.25
1996(a)	1,900,000	—	0.10	0.20	0.70	1.25
1997(a)	1,200,000	—	0.10	0.20	0.70	1.25
1998(a)	400,000	—	0.10	0.25	0.75	1.50
1999(a)	1,200,000	—	0.10	0.20	0.70	1.25
2000(a)	1,300,000	—	—	0.15	0.50	1.00

KM# 3 2 FRANCS
Aluminum **Obv:** Seated figure holding torch **Rev:** Kagu bird within sprigs below value **Designer:** G.B.L. Bazor

Date	Mintage	F	VF	XF	Unc	BU
1949(a)	3,000,000	—	0.35	1.00	2.50	5.50

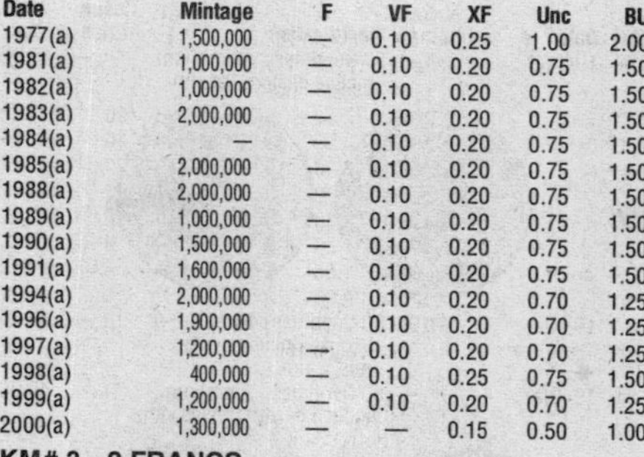

KM# 9 2 FRANCS
2.2000 g., Aluminum, 27 mm. **Obv:** Seated figure holding torch **Rev:** Kagu bird within sprigs below value **Designer:** G.B.L. Bazor

Date	Mintage	F	VF	XF	Unc	BU
1971(a)	1,000,000	—	0.35	1.25	2.25	3.50

KM# 14 2 FRANCS
2.2000 g., Aluminum, 27 mm. **Obv:** Seated figure holding torch, legend added **Obv. Legend:** I. E. O. M. **Rev:** Kagu bird and value within sprigs

Date	Mintage	F	VF	XF	Unc	BU
1973(a)	400,000	—	0.20	0.75	2.00	3.00
1977(a)	1,500,000	—	0.20	0.50	1.50	2.50
1982(a)	1,000,000	—	0.20	0.35	1.00	2.25
1983(a)	2,000,000	—	0.20	0.35	0.75	2.00
1987(a)	2,000,000	—	0.20	0.35	0.75	2.00
1989(a)	1,200,000	—	0.20	0.35	0.75	2.00
1990(a)	1,500,000	—	0.20	0.35	0.75	2.00
1991(a)	1,500,000	—	0.20	0.35	0.75	2.00
1995(a)	400,000	—	0.20	0.35	0.75	2.00
1996(a)	900,000	—	0.20	0.35	0.75	2.00
1997(a)	400,000	—	0.20	0.35	0.75	2.00
1998(a)	400,000	—	0.20	0.35	0.85	2.25
1999(a)	800,000	—	0.20	0.35	0.85	2.25
2000(a)	700,000	—	—	0.25	0.75	2.00

KM# 4 5 FRANCS
3.7500 g., Aluminum, 31 mm. **Obv:** Seated figure holding torch **Rev:** Kagu bird and value within sprigs **Designer:** G.B.L. Bazor

Date	Mintage	F	VF	XF	Unc	BU
1952(a)	4,000,000	—	0.50	1.50	3.50	6.00

KM# 16 5 FRANCS
3.7500 g., Aluminum, 31 mm. **Obv:** Seated figure holding torch, legend added **Obv. Legend:** I. E. O. M. **Rev:** Kagu bird and value within sprigs **Designer:** G.B.L. Bazor

Date	Mintage	F	VF	XF	Unc	BU
1983(a)	500,000	—	0.45	0.75	2.50	4.50
1986(a)	1,000,000	—	0.45	0.75	2.50	3.50
1989(a)	500,000	—	0.45	0.75	2.50	3.50
1990(a)	500,000	—	0.45	0.75	2.25	3.50
1991(a)	480,000	—	0.45	0.75	2.25	3.50
1992(a)	480,000	—	0.45	0.75	2.00	3.00
1994(a)	1,200,000	—	0.45	0.75	2.00	3.00
1997(a)	240,000	—	0.35	0.65	1.75	3.00
1998(a)	120,000	—	0.35	0.65	1.75	3.00
1999(a)	480,000	—	0.35	0.50	1.50	3.00
2000(a)	400,000	—	0.35	0.50	1.50	3.00

KM# 5 10 FRANCS
6.0000 g., Nickel, 24 mm. **Obv:** Liberty head left **Rev:** Sailboat above value **Designer:** R. Joly

Date	Mintage	F	VF	XF	Unc	BU
1967(a)	400,000	—	1.00	2.00	4.00	7.00
1970(a)	1,000,000	—	0.50	1.00	2.50	5.00

KM# 11 10 FRANCS
6.0000 g., Nickel, 24 mm. **Obv:** Liberty head left **Obv. Legend:** I. E. O. M. **Rev:** Sailboat above value **Designer:** R. Joly

Date	Mintage	F	VF	XF	Unc	BU
1972(a)	600,000	—	0.70	1.50	2.00	5.25
1973(a)	400,000	—	0.70	1.00	2.00	4.25
1977(a)	1,000,000	—	0.70	1.00	1.50	4.00
1983(a)	800,000	—	0.60	0.85	1.50	4.00
1986(a)	1,000,000	—	0.60	0.85	1.50	4.00
1989(a)	500,000	—	0.60	0.85	1.50	4.00
1990(a)	500,000	—	0.60	0.85	1.25	3.75
1991(a)	500,000	—	0.50	0.75	1.25	3.75
1992(a)	500,000	—	0.50	0.75	1.25	3.75
1995(a)	200,000	—	0.50	0.75	1.25	3.50
1996(a)	300,000	—	0.50	0.75	1.25	3.50
1997(a)	300,000	—	0.50	0.75	1.25	3.50
1998(a)	300,000	—	0.50	0.75	1.25	3.50
1999(a)	500,000	—	0.50	0.75	1.25	3.50
2000(a)	350,000	—	—	0.65	1.25	2.75

KM# 6 20 FRANCS
10.0000 g., Nickel, 28.5 mm. **Rev:** Three zebu heads left **Designer:** R. Joly

Date	Mintage	F	VF	XF	Unc	BU
1967(a)	300,000	—	1.25	2.50	5.00	8.50
1970(a)	1,200,000	—	0.60	1.00	3.00	5.50

KM# 12 20 FRANCS
10.0000 g., Nickel, 28.5 mm. **Obv:** Liberty head left **Obv. Legend:** I. O. E. M. **Rev:** Three ox heads above value **Designer:** R. Joly

Date	Mintage	F	VF	XF	Unc	BU
1972(a)	700,000	—	0.85	2.00	3.00	5.00
1977(a)	350,000	—	0.85	2.50	4.00	6.50

Date	Mintage	F	VF	XF	Unc	BU
1983(a)	600,000	—	0.75	1.75	3.00	5.00
1986(a)	800,000	—	0.75	1.50	2.00	4.50
1990(a)	500,000	—	0.75	1.50	2.00	4.50
1991(a)	500,000	—	0.75	1.50	2.00	4.50
1992(a)	500,000	—	0.75	1.50	2.00	4.50
1996(a)	150,000	—	0.75	1.50	2.00	4.50
1999(a)	300,000	—	0.75	15.00	2.00	4.50
2000(a)	250,000	—	0.75	1.50	200	4.50

KM# 7 50 FRANCS

15.0000 g., Nickel, 33 mm. **Obv:** Liberty head left **Rev:** Small hut within pines and palm, value at bottom **Designer:** R. Joly

Date	Mintage	F	VF	XF	Unc	BU
1967(a)	700,000	—	1.50	3.00	6.50	10.00

KM# 13 50 FRANCS

15.0000 g., Nickel, 33 mm. **Obv:** Liberty head left **Obv. Legend:** I. E. O. M. **Rev:** Hut above value in center of palm and pine trees **Designer:** R. Joly

Date	Mintage	F	VF	XF	Unc	BU
1972(a)	300,000	—	1.25	2.00	5.00	7.00
1983(a)	300,000	—	1.25	2.00	4.50	6.50
1987(a)	300,000	—	1.00	2.00	4.50	6.50
1991(a)	450,000	—	1.00	1.85	3.00	4.25
1992(a)	450,000	—	1.00	1.85	3.00	4.25
1996(a)	—	—	1.00	1.75	3.00	4.25
1997(a)	150,000	—	1.00	1.75	3.00	4.25
2000(a)	1,000,000	—	1.00	1.75	3.00	4.25

KM# 15 100 FRANCS

10.0000 g., Nickel-Bronze, 30 mm. **Obv:** Liberty head left **Rev:** Hut above value in center of palm and pine trees **Designer:** R. Joly

Date	Mintage	F	VF	XF	Unc	BU
1976(a)	2,000,000	—	1.50	2.50	6.00	9.00
1984(a)	600,000	—	1.50	2.50	6.00	8.50
1987(a)	800,000	—	1.50	2.50	5.50	7.00
1988(a)	—	—	1.50	2.50	5.50	7.00
1991(a)	500,000	—	1.35	2.25	4.00	6.00
1992(a)	500,000	—	1.35	2.25	4.00	6.00
1994	250,000	—	1.35	2.25	4.00	6.00
1995(a)	—	—	1.35	2.00	3.50	5.50
1996(a)	250,000	—	1.35	2.25	4.00	6.00
1997	190,000	—	1.35	2.00	3.50	5.50
1998(a)	310,000	—	1.25	2.00	3.50	5.50
1999(a)	400,000	—	1.25	2.00	3.50	5.50
2000(a)	300,000	—	1.25	2.00	3.50	5.50

ESSAIS

KM#	Date	Mintage	Identification	Issue Price	Mkt Val
E1	1948(a)	1,100	50 Centimes. Nickel-Bronze. Sitting figure holding sprig. Bird with wings open. Incuse design, flat rim	—	20.00
E1a	1948(a)	—	50 Centimes. Aluminum. Incuse design, flat rim	—	45.00
E2	1948(a)	1,100	50 Centimes. Nickel-Bronze. Incuse design, raised rim.	—	25.00
E2a	1948(a)	—	50 Centimes. Aluminum. Incuse design, raised rim.	—	40.00
E3	1948(a)	1,100	Franc. Nickel-Bronze. Incuse design, flat rim.	—	25.00
E3a	1948(a)	—	Franc. Aluminum. Incuse design, flat rim.	—	50.00
E4	1948(a)	1,100	Franc. Nickel-Bronze. Incuse design, raised rim.	—	30.00
E4a	1948(a)	—	Franc. Aluminum. Incuse design, raised rim.	—	45.00
E5	1948(a)	1,100	2 Francs. Nickel-Bronze. Incuse design, flat rim.	—	30.00
E5a	1948(a)	—	2 Francs. Aluminum. Incuse design, flat rim.	—	55.00
E6	1948(a)	1,100	2 Francs. Nickel-Bronze. Incuse design, raised rim.	—	20.00
E6a	1948(a)	—	2 Francs. Aluminum. Incuse design, raised rim.	—	50.00
E7	1949(a)	2,000	50 Centimes. Copper Nickel. KM1.	—	17.50
E8	1949(a)	2,000	Franc. Copper Nickel. KM2.	—	20.00
E9	1949(a)	2,000	2 Francs. Copper Nickel. KM3.	—	22.50
E10	1952(a)	1,200	5 Francs. Aluminum. KM4.	—	25.00
E11	1967(a)	1,700	10 Francs. Nickel. KM5.	—	15.00
E12	1967(a)	1,700	20 Francs. Nickel. KM6.	—	15.00
E13	1967(a)	1,700	50 Francs. Nickel. KM7.	—	15.00
E14	1976(a)	1,900	100 Francs. Nickel-Bronze. KM15.	—	27.50

PIEFORTS

An unknown quantity of gold pieforts were melted in 1983.

KM#	Date	Mintage	Identification	Issue Price	Mkt Val
P1	1967(a)	500	10 Francs. Nickel. KM5.	—	25.00
P1a	1967(a)	50	10 Francs. 0.9500 Silver. KM5.	—	150
P1b	1967(a)	20	10 Francs. 0.9200 Gold. KM5.	—	950
P2	1967(a)	500	20 Francs. Nickel. KM6.	—	30.00
P2a	1967(a)	50	20 Francs. 0.9500 Silver. KM6.	—	175
P2b	1967(a)	20	20 Francs. 0.9200 Gold. KM6.	—	1,000
P3	1967(a)	500	50 Francs. Nickel. KM7.	—	35.00
P3a	1967(a)	50	50 Francs. 0.9500 Silver. KM7.	—	200
P3b	1967(a)	20	50 Francs. 0.9200 Gold. KM7.	—	1,350
P4	1979(a)	150	Franc. Aluminum center. Similar to KM10.	—	10.00
P4a	1979(a)	250	Franc. 0.9250 Silver. Similar to KM10.	—	25.00
P4b	1979(a)	94	Franc. 0.9200 Gold. Similar to KM10.	—	550
P5	1979(a)	150	2 Francs. Aluminum. Similar to KM14.	—	15.00
P5a	1979(a)	250	2 Francs. 0.9250 Silver. Similar to KM14.	—	50.00
P5b	1979(a)	96	2 Francs. 0.9200 Gold. Similar to KM14.	—	925
P6	1979(a)	150	5 Francs. Aluminum. Similar to KM4.	—	25.00
P6a	1979(a)	250	5 Francs. 0.9250 Silver. Similar to KM4.	—	75.00
P6b	1979(a)	94	5 Francs. 0.9200 Gold. Similar to KM4.	—	1,300
P7	1979(a)	150	10 Francs. Nickel. Similar to KM11.	—	40.00
P7a	1979(a)	250	10 Francs. 0.9250 Silver. Similar to KM11.	—	100
P7b	1979(a)	93	10 Francs. 0.9200 Gold. Similar to KM11.	—	850
P8	1979(a)	150	20 Francs. Nickel center. Similar to KM12.	—	40.00
P8a	1979(a)	250	20 Francs. 0.9250 Silver. Similar to KM12.	—	100
P8b	1979(a)	95	20 Francs. 0.9200 Gold. Liberty head left. Three ox heads, value at lower left. Similar to KM12.	—	1,200
P9	1979(a)	150	50 Francs. Nickel. Similar to KM13.	—	50.00
P9a	1979(a)	250	50 Francs. 0.9250 Silver. Similar to KM13.	—	100
P10	1979(a)	150	100 Francs. Nickel-Bronze. Similar to KM15.	—	85.00
P10a	1979(a)	350	100 Francs. 0.9250 Silver. Similar to KM15.	—	125
P10b	1979(a)	96	100 Francs. 0.9200 Gold. Similar to KM15.	—	1,150

PIEFORTS WITH ESSAI

Double thickness

KM#	Date	Mintage	Identification	Issue Price	Mkt Val
PE1	1949(a)	104	50 Centimes. Aluminum. KM1.	—	60.00
PE2	1949(a)	104	Franc. Aluminum. KM2.	—	70.00
PE3	1949(a)	104	2 Francs. Aluminum. KM3.	—	80.00
PE4	1952(a)	104	5 Francs. Aluminum. KM4.	—	90.00

SPECIMEN SETS (SS)

KM#	Date	Mintage	Identification	Issue Price	Mkt Val
SS1	1967 (3)	2,200	KM5-7. This set issued with New Hebrides and French Polynesia 1967 set.	10.00	20.00

NEW GUINEA

Spanish navigator Jorge de Menezes, who landed on the northwest shore in 1527, discovered New Guinea, the world's largest island after Greenland. European interests, attracted by exaggerated estimates of the resources of the area, resulted in the island being claimed in part by Spain, the Netherlands, Great Britain and Germany.

RULERS
British, 1910-1952

MONETARY SYSTEM
12 Pence = 1 Shilling
20 Shillings = 1 Pound

AUSTRALIAN ADMINISTRATION
1914-1973

STANDARD COINAGE

12 Pence = 1 Shilling; 20 Shillings = 1 Pound

KM# 1 1/2 PENNY
Copper-Nickel **Obv:** Hole in center flanked by scepters with crown above and value below **Rev:** Hole in center flanked by designs **Designer:** G.E. Kruger-Gray **Note:** Entire mintage returned to Melbourne Mint which later sold 400 pcs. in sets with KM#2. The balance of mintage was destroyed.

Date	Mintage	F	VF	XF	Unc	BU
1929	25,000	—	—	225	375	—
1929 Proof	—	Value: 450				

KM# 1a 1/2 PENNY
Nickel **Obv:** Hole in center flanked by scepters with crown above and value below **Rev:** Hole in center flanked by designs **Designer:** G.E. Kruger-Gray

Date	Mintage	F	VF	XF	Unc	BU
1929 Proof	—	Value: 700				

KM# 2 PENNY
Copper-Nickel **Obv:** Hole in center flanked by scepters with crown above and value below **Rev:** Hole in center flanked by designs **Designer:** G.E. Kruger-Gray **Note:** Entire mintage returned to Melbourne Mint which later sold 400 pcs. in sets with KM#1. The balance of mintage was destroyed.

Date	Mintage	F	VF	XF	Unc	BU
1929	63,000	—	—	225	375	—
1929 Proof	—	Value: 450				

KM# 2a PENNY
Nickel **Obv:** Hole in center flanked by scepters with crown above and value below **Rev:** Hole in center flanked by designs **Designer:** G.E. Kruger-Gray

Date	Mintage	F	VF	XF	Unc	BU
1929 Proof	—	Value: 700				

KM# 6 PENNY
Bronze **Obv:** Hole in center flanked by swimming birds with crown above and monogram below **Rev:** Artistic design around hole in center **Designer:** G.E. Kruger-Gray

Date	Mintage	F	VF	XF	Unc	BU
1936	360,000	0.75	1.00	2.00	5.00	10.00
1936 Proof	—	Value: 275				

KM# 7 PENNY
Bronze **Obv:** Hole in center flanked by swimming birds with crown above and monogram below **Rev:** Artistic design around hole in center **Designer:** G.E. Kruger-Gray

Date	Mintage	F	VF	XF	Unc	BU
1938	360,000	1.75	3.50	7.50	12.50	18.00
1944	240,000	1.00	2.00	4.00	7.50	12.50

KM# 3 3 PENCE
Copper-Nickel **Obv:** Hole in center divides date with crown above and monogram below **Rev:** Square-star design around hole in center **Designer:** G.E. Kruger-Gray

Date	Mintage	F	VF	XF	Unc	BU
1935	1,200,000	3.00	6.00	10.00	28.00	40.00
1935 Proof	—	Value: 225				

KM# 10 3 PENCE
Copper-Nickel **Obv:** Hole in center divides date with crown above and monogram below **Rev:** Square-star design around hole in center **Designer:** G.E. Kruger-Gray

Date	Mintage	F	VF	XF	Unc	BU
1944	500,000	2.00	4.00	8.50	22.50	35.00

KM# 4 6 PENCE
Copper-Nickel **Obv:** Hole in center divides date with crown above and monogram below **Rev:** Star design around hole in center **Designer:** G.E. Kruger-Gray

Date	Mintage	F	VF	XF	Unc	BU
1935	2,000,000	2.50	4.00	8.00	28.00	40.00
1935 Proof	—	Value: 225				

KM# 9 6 PENCE
Copper-Nickel **Obv:** Hole in center divides date with crown above and monogram below **Rev:** Star design around hole in center **Designer:** G.E. Kruger-Gray

Date	Mintage	F	VF	XF	Unc	BU
1943	130,000	3.00	6.00	12.50	35.00	50.00

KM# 5 SHILLING
5.3800 g., 0.9250 Silver .16 oz. ASW, 23.5 mm. **Obv:** Hole in center flanked by crossed scepters with crown above and star below **Rev:** Hole in center flanked by artistic designs **Designer:** G.E. Kruger-Gray

Date	Mintage	F	VF	XF	Unc	BU
1935	2,100,000	BV	2.75	3.50	6.50	9.00
1936	1,360,000	BV	2.75	3.50	6.50	9.00

KM# 8 SHILLING
5.3800 g., 0.9250 Silver .16 oz. ASW, 23.5 mm. **Obv:** Hole in center flanked by crossed scepters with crown above and star below **Rev:** Hole in center flanked by artistic designs **Designer:** G.E. Kruger-Gray

Date	Mintage	F	VF	XF	Unc	BU
1938	3,400,000	BV	2.75	3.50	6.50	9.00
1945	2,000,000	BV	2.75	3.50	6.50	9.00

PROOF SETS

KM#	Date	Mintage	Identification	Issue Price	Mkt Val
PS1	1929 (2)	—	KM#1, 2	—	900
PS2	1929	20	KM#1a, 2a	—	1,400

NEW HEBRIDES

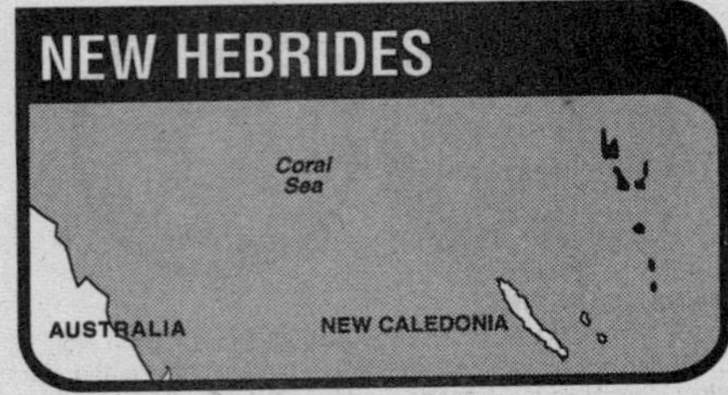

The New Hebrides were discovered by Portuguese navigator Pedro de Quiros in 1606, visited by French explorer Bougainville in 1768, and named by British navigator Capt. James Cook in 1774. Ships of all nations converged on the islands to trade for sandalwood, prompting France and Britain to relinquish their individual claims and declare the islands a neutral zone in 1878. The New Hebrides were placed under the control of a mixed Anglo-French commission of naval officers during the native uprisings of 1887, until achieving independence as Vanuatu, within the Commonwealth of nations on September 30, 1980.

MINT MARKS
(a) - Paris, privy marks only

MONETARY SYSTEM
100 Centimes = 1 Franc

FRENCH/BRITISH CONDOMINIUM
(Jointly Governed Territory)

STANDARD COINAGE

KM# 4.1 FRANC
Nickel-Brass **Obv:** Liberty head left, date below **Obv. Legend:** REPVBLIQVE FRANCAISE **Rev:** Frigate bird above value **Designer:** R. Joly

Date	Mintage	F	VF	XF	Unc	BU
1970(a)	435,000	—	0.25	0.50	0.85	1.75

KM# 4.2 FRANC
Nickel-Brass **Obv:** I.E.O.M. below head **Obv. Legend:** REPVBLIQVE FRANCAISE **Rev:** Frigate bird above value **Designer:** R. Joly

Date	Mintage	F	VF	XF	Unc	BU
1975(a)	350,000	—	0.20	0.40	0.75	—
1978(a)	200,000	—	0.20	0.40	0.75	—
1979(a)	350,000	—	0.20	0.40	0.75	—

KM# 5.1 2 FRANCS
Nickel-Brass **Obv:** Liberty head left, date below **Obv. Legend:** REPVBLIQVE FRANCAISE **Rev:** Frigate bird above value **Designer:** R. Joly

Date	Mintage	F	VF	XF	Unc	BU
1970(a)	264,000	—	0.50	0.75	1.50	2.50

KM# 5.2 2 FRANCS
Nickel-Brass **Obv:** Liberty head left, I.E.O.M. and date below head **Obv. Legend:** REPVBLIQVE FRANCAISE **Rev:** Frigate bird above value **Designer:** R. Joly

Date	Mintage	F	VF	XF	Unc	BU
1973(a)	200,000	—	0.20	0.50	1.00	—
1975(a)	300,000	—	0.20	0.50	1.00	—
1978(a)	150,000	—	0.20	0.50	1.00	—
1979(a)	250,000	—	0.20	0.50	1.00	—

KM# 6.1 5 FRANCS
Nickel-Brass **Obv:** Liberty head left, date below **Obv. Legend:** REPVBLIQVE FRANCAISE **Rev:** Frigate bird above value **Designer:** R. Joly

Date	Mintage	F	VF	XF	Unc	BU
1970(a)	375,000	—	0.50	0.75	1.65	2.75

KM# 6.2 5 FRANCS
Nickel-Brass **Obv:** Liberty head left, I.E.O.M. and date below head **Obv. Legend:** REPVBLIQVE FRANCAISE **Rev:** Frigate bird above value **Designer:** R. Joly

Date	Mintage	F	VF	XF	Unc	BU
1975(a)	350,000	—	0.30	0.75	1.25	—
1979(a)	250,000	—	0.30	0.75	1.25	—

KM# 2.1 10 FRANCS
Nickel **Obv:** Liberty head left, date below **Obv. Legend:** REPVBLIQVE FRANCAISE **Rev:** Mask left flanked by designs with value below **Designer:** R. Joly

Date	Mintage	F	VF	XF	Unc	BU
1967(a)	200,000	—	0.30	1.00	1.85	3.00
1970(a)	400,000	—	0.30	1.00	1.85	3.00

KM# 2.2 10 FRANCS
Nickel **Obv:** Liberty head left, I.E.O.M. and date below head **Obv. Legend:** REPVBLIQVE FRANCAISE **Rev:** Mask left flanked by designs with value below **Designer:** R. Joly

Date	Mintage	F	VF	XF	Unc	BU
1973(a)	200,000	—	0.30	1.15	1.85	2.75
1975(a)	300,000	—	0.30	1.15	1.85	2.75
1977(a)	200,000	—	0.30	1.15	1.85	2.75
1979(a)	400,000	—	0.30	1.15	1.85	2.75

KM# 3.1 20 FRANCS
Nickel **Obv:** Liberty head left, date below **Obv. Legend:** REPVBLEQVE FRANCAISE **Rev:** Mask left flanked by designs with value below **Designer:** R. Joly

Date	Mintage	F	VF	XF	Unc	BU
1967(a)	250,000	—	0.60	1.25	2.25	4.00
1970(a)	300,000	—	0.60	1.25	2.25	4.00

KM# 3.2 20 FRANCS
Nickel **Obv:** Liberty head left, I.E.O.M. and date below head **Obv. Legend:** REPVBLIQVE FRANCAISE **Rev:** Mask left flanked by designs, value at bottom **Designer:** R. Joly

Date	Mintage	F	VF	XF	Unc	BU
1973(a)	300,000	—	0.60	1.25	2.25	3.25
1975(a)	150,000	—	0.60	1.25	2.25	3.25
1977(a)	150,000	—	0.60	1.25	2.25	3.25
1979(a)	300,000	—	0.60	1.25	2.25	3.25

KM# 7 50 FRANCS
Nickel **Obv:** Liberty head left, I.E.O.M. and date below head **Obv. Legend:** REPVBLIQVE FRANCAISE **Rev:** Scepter above value **Designer:** R. Joly

Date	Mintage	F	VF	XF	Unc	BU
1972(a)	200,000	—	1.00	2.00	3.00	5.00

KM# 1 100 FRANCS
25.0000 g., 0.8350 Silver .6712 oz. ASW **Obv:** Liberty head left, date below **Obv. Legend:** REPVBLIQVE FRANCAISE **Rev:** Scepter above value **Designer:** R. Joly

Date	Mintage	F	VF	XF	Unc	BU
1966(a)	200,000	—	—	—	12.00	20.00

ESSAIS

KM#	Date	Mintage	Identification	Issue Price	Mkt Val
E1	1966(a)	3,000	100 Francs. Liberty head left, date below. Sword hilt above value.	—	60.00
E2	1967(a)	1,700	10 Francs.	—	20.00
E3	1967(a)	1,700	20 Francs.	—	20.00
E4	1970(a)	1,250	Franc.	—	20.00
E5	1970(a)	1,700	2 Francs.	—	20.00
E6	1970(a)	1,250	5 Francs.	—	20.00
E7	1972(a)	1,300	50 Francs.	—	22.00

PATTERNS

Including off metal strikes

KM#	Date	Mintage	Identification	Mkt Val
Pn1	1979	60	500 Francs. Copper-Nickel-Aluminum.	350
Pn2	1979	60	500 Francs. 0.9990 Silver.	500
Pn3	1979	3	500 Francs. 0.9990 Gold. 62.2000 g.	6,000
Pn4	1979	1	500 Francs. 0.9990 Platinum. 62.2000 g.	9,000

PIEFORTS WITH ESSAI

Double thickness

KM#	Date	Mintage	Identification	Issue Price	Mkt Val
PE1	1966(a)	500	100 Francs.	—	140
PE2	1966(a)	50	100 Francs. 0.9200 Gold.	—	3,750

KM#	Date	Mintage	Identification	Issue Price	Mkt Val
PE3	1967(a)	500	10 Francs. Liberty head left, date below. Mask left, flanked by designs, value on bottom.	—	15.00
PE4	1967(a)	50	10 Francs. 0.9500 Silver.	—	75.00
PE5	1967(a)	20	10 Francs. 0.9200 Gold.	—	500
PE6	1967(a)	500	20 Francs.	—	15.00

KM#	Date	Mintage	Identification	Issue Price	Mkt Val
PE7	1967(a)	50	20 Francs. 0.9500 Silver.	—	125
PE8	1967(a)	20	20 Francs. 0.9200 Gold.	—	1,000
PE10	1974(a)	500	100 Francs. 0.9250 Silver.	—	100
PE11	1974(a)	119	100 Francs. 0.9200 Gold.	—	3,500
PE12	1979(a)	150	Franc.	—	10.00
PE13	1979	250	Franc. 0.9250 Silver.	—	20.00
PE14	1979(a)	123	Franc. 0.9200 Gold.	—	200
PE15	1979(a)	150	2 Francs.	—	12.50
PE16	1979(a)	250	2 Francs. 0.9250 Silver.	—	20.00
PE17	1979(a)	115	2 Francs. 0.9200 Gold.	—	250
PE18	1979(a)	150	5 Francs.	—	15.00
PE19	1979(a)	250	5 Francs. 0.9250 Silver.	—	20.00
PE20	1979(a)	116	5 Francs. 0.9200 Gold.	—	350
PE21	1979(a)	150	10 Francs.	—	17.50
PE22	1979(a)	250	10 Francs. 0.9250 Silver.	—	20.00
PE23	1979(a)	116	10 Francs. 0.9200 Gold.	—	500
PE24	1979(a)	150	20 Francs.	—	20.00
PE25	1979(a)	250	20 Francs. 0.9250 Silver.	—	20.00
PE26	1979(a)	115	20 Francs. 0.9200 Gold.	—	625
PE27	1979(a)	150	50 Francs.	—	25.00
PE28	1979(a)	250	50 Francs. 0.9250 Silver.	—	100
PE29	1979(a)	116	50 Francs. 0.9200 Gold.	—	1,250

"FDC" SETS

This fleur-de-coin set was issued with New Caledonia and French Polynesia 1967 sets.

KM#	Date	Mintage	Identification	Issue Price	Mkt Val
SS1	1966-67 (3)	2,200	KM#1, 2.1, 3.1	10.00	10.00

NEW ZEALAND

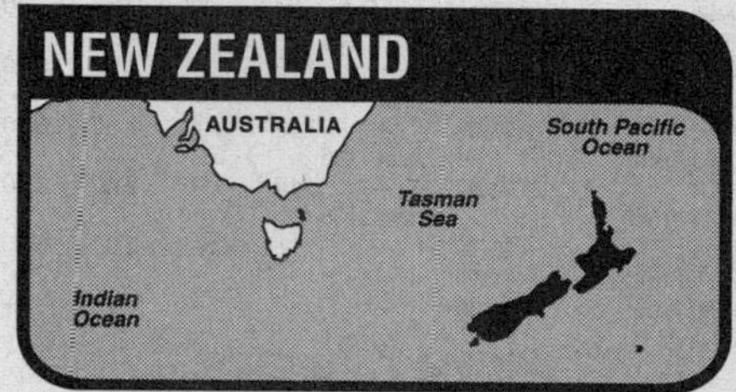

New Zealand, a parliamentary state located in the Southwest Pacific 1,250 miles (2,011 km.) east of Australia, has an area of 103,883 sq. mi. (268,680 sq. km.) and a population of *3.4 million. Capital: Wellington. Wool, meat, dairy products and some manufactured items are exported.

The first European to sight New Zealand was the Dutch navigator Abel Tasman in 1642. The islands were explored by British navigator Capt. James Cook who surveyed it in 1769 and annexed the land to Great Britain. The British government disavowed the annexation and for the next 70 years the only white settlers to arrive were adventurers attracted by the prospects of lumbering, sealing and whaling. Great Britain annexed the land in 1840 by treaty with the native chiefs and made it a dependency of New South Wales. The colony was granted self-government in1852, a ministerial form of government in 1856, and full dominion status on Sept. 26, 1907. Full internal and external autonomy, which New Zealand had in effect possessed for many years, was formally extended in 1947.New Zealand is a member of the Commonwealth of Nations. Elizabeth II is Head of State as Queen of New Zealand.

Prior to 1933 British coins were the official legal tender but Australian coins were accepted in small transactions. Currency fluctuations caused a distinctive New Zealand coinage to be introduced in 1933. The 1935 Waitangi crown and proof set were originally intended to mark the introduction but delays caused their date to be changed to 1935. The 1940 half crown marked the centennial of British rule, the 1949 and 1953 crowns commemorated Royal visits and the 1953 proof set marked the coronation of Queen Elizabeth.

Decimal Currency was introduced in 1967 with special sets commemorating the last issued of pound sterling (1965) and the first of the decimal issues. Since then dollars and set of coins have been issued nearly every year.

RULERS

British

MINTS

(L) – British Royal Mint (Llantrisant)
(C) – Royal Australian Mint (Canberra)
(O) – Royal Canadian Mint
(N) – Norwegian Mint
(P) – South African Mint (Pretoria)

MONETARY SYSTEM

4 Farthings = 1 Penny
12 Pence = 1 Shilling
20 Shillings = 1 Pound

STATE

1907 - present

POUND STERLING COINAGE

KM# 12 1/2 PENNY

Bronze, 25.3 mm. **Ruler:** George VI **Obv:** Head left **Rev:** Hei Tiki **Designer:** L.C. Mitchell

Date	Mintage	F	VF	XF	Unc	BU
1940	3,432,000	0.20	0.50	10.00	20.00	40.00
1940 Proof; 5 known	—	Value: 800				
1941	960,000	0.10	0.50	14.00	50.00	70.00
1941	—	Value: 225				
1942	1,920,000	1.00	5.00	40.00	80.00	220
1944	2,035,000	0.10	0.50	10.00	20.00	40.00
1945	1,516,000	0.10	0.50	10.00	20.00	40.00
1945 Proof	—	Value: 175				
1946	3,120,000	0.10	0.50	6.00	18.00	35.00
1946 Proof	—	Value: 175				
1947	2,726,400	0.10	0.50	6.00	12.00	22.00
1947 Proof	—	Value: 150				

KM# 20 1/2 PENNY

Bronze, 25.3 mm. **Ruler:** George VI **Obv:** Head left **Obv. Designer:** T.H. Paget **Rev:** Hei Tiki **Designer:** L.C. Mitchell

Date	Mintage	F	VF	XF	Unc	BU
1949	1,766,400	0.10	0.25	6.00	12.00	22.00
1949 Proof	—	Value: 150				
1950	1,425,600	0.10	0.25	8.00	20.00	35.00
1950 Proof	—	Value: 175				
1951	2,342,400	0.10	0.25	5.00	8.00	12.00
1951 Proof	—	Value: 150				
1952	2,400,000	0.10	0.20	4.00	7.00	10.00
1952 Proof	—	Value: 150				

KM# 23.1 1/2 PENNY

Bronze, 25.3 mm. **Ruler:** Elizabeth II **Obv:** Laureate bust right without shoulder strap **Obv. Designer:** Mary Gillick **Rev:** Hei Tiki

Date	Mintage	F	VF	XF	Unc	BU
1953	720,000	0.20	0.50	5.00	14.00	20.00
1953 Proof	7,000	Value: 5.00				
1953 Matte proof	—	Value: 100				
1954	240,000	4.00	8.00	40.00	80.00	120
1954 Proof	—	Value: 145				
1955	240,000	4.00	8.00	40.00	80.00	120
1955	—	Value: 145				

KM# 23.2 1/2 PENNY

Bronze, 25.3 mm. **Ruler:** Elizabeth II **Obv:** Laureate bust right with shoulder strap **Obv. Designer:** Mary Gillick **Rev:** Hei Tiki **Designer:** L.C. Mitchell

Date	Mintage	F	VF	XF	Unc	BU
1956	1,200,000	0.10	0.25	5.00	10.00	20.00
1956 Proof	—	Value: 135				
1957	1,440,000	0.10	0.25	5.00	10.00	20.00
1957 Proof	—	Value: 135				
1958	1,920,000	0.10	0.25	5.00	10.00	20.00
1958 Proof	—	Value: 135				
1959	1,920,000	0.10	0.20	5.00	10.00	20.00
1959 Proof	—	Value: 135				
1960	2,400,000	0.10	0.20	4.00	7.00	14.00
1960 Proof	—	Value: 135				
1961	2,880,000	0.10	0.15	3.00	5.00	10.00
1961 Proof	—	Value: 135				
1962	2,880,000	0.10	0.15	3.00	5.00	10.00
1962 Proof	—	Value: 135				
1963	1,680,000	0.10	0.15	0.30	2.00	7.00
1963 Proof	—	Value: 135				
1964	2,885,000	0.10	0.15	0.20	1.50	5.00
1964 Proof	—	Value: 135				
1965	5,200,000	0.10	0.15	0.20	0.50	3.00
1965 Prooflike	25,000	—	—	—	—	1.25
1965 Proof	10	—	—	—	—	—

KM# 13 PENNY

Bronze, 31 mm. **Ruler:** George VI **Obv:** Head left **Obv. Designer:** T.H. Paget **Rev:** Bird sitting on branch **Rev. Designer:** L.C. Mitchell

Date	Mintage	F	VF	XF	Unc	BU
1940	5,424,000	0.10	0.50	15.00	25.00	50.00
1940 Proof	—	Value: 1,000				

Date	Mintage	F	VF	XF	Unc	BU
Note: 5 known						
1941	1,200,000	0.10	0.50	45.00	100	200
1942	3,120,000	2.00	8.00	45.00	110	200
1942 Proof	—	Value: 275				
1943	8,400,000	0.10	0.50	15.00	25.00	50.00
1943 Proof	—	Value: 225				
1944	3,696,000	0.10	0.50	15.00	25.00	50.00
1944 Proof	—	Value: 225				
1945	4,764,000	0.10	0.50	15.00	25.00	50.00
1945 Proof	—	Value: 225				
1946	6,720,000	0.10	0.50	12.00	20.00	35.00
1946 Proof	—	Value: 225				
1947	5,880,000	0.10	0.50	10.00	15.00	25.00
1947 Proof	—	Value: 225				

KM# 13a PENNY

Bronze, 31 mm. **Ruler:** George VI **Obv:** Head left **Obv. Designer:** T.H. Paget **Rev:** Bird sitting on branch **Note:** Burnished

Date	Mintage	F	VF	XF	Unc	BU
1945	—	—	—	100	180	350

Note: Struck in error by the Royal Mint on Great Britain blanks

KM# 21 PENNY

Bronze, 31 mm. **Ruler:** George VI **Obv:** Head left **Obv. Designer:** T.H. Paget **Rev:** Bird sitting on branch **Rev. Designer:** L.C. Mitchell

Date	Mintage	F	VF	XF	Unc	BU
1949	2,016,000	0.10	0.50	10.00	15.00	35.00
1949 Proof	—	Value: 225				
1950	5,784,000	0.10	0.50	10.00	15.00	30.00
1950 Proof	—	Value: 175				
1951	6,888,000	0.10	0.50	10.00	15.00	25.00
1951 Proof	—	Value: 175				
1952	10,800,000	0.10	0.50	10.00	15.00	22.00
1952 Proof	—	Value: 150				

KM# 24.1 PENNY

Bronze, 31 mm. **Ruler:** Elizabeth II **Obv:** Laureate bust right without shoulder strap **Obv. Designer:** Mary Gillick **Rev:** Bird sitting on branch **Rev. Designer:** L.C. Mitchell

Date	Mintage	F	VF	XF	Unc	BU
1953	2,400,000	0.10	0.50	10.00	15.00	22.00
1953 Proof	7,000	Value: 10.00				
1953 Matte proof	—	Value: 100				
1954	1,080,000	1.00	5.00	30.00	60.00	120
1954 Proof	—	Value: 175				
1955	3,720,000	0.10	0.25	6.00	14.00	22.00
1955 Proof	—	Value: 150				
1956	Inc. below	40.00	80.00	400	800	1,200

KM# 24.2 PENNY

Bronze, 31 mm. **Ruler:** Elizabeth II **Obv:** Laureate bust right with shoulder strap **Obv. Designer:** Mary Gillick **Rev:** Bird sitting on branch **Rev. Designer:** L.C. Mitchell

Date	Mintage	F	VF	XF	Unc	BU
1956	3,600,000	0.10	0.50	5.00	10.00	20.00
1956 Proof	—	Value: 150				
1957	2,400,000	0.10	0.50	5.00	10.00	20.00
1957 Proof	—	Value: 150				
1958	10,800,000	0.10	0.20	5.00	10.00	20.00
1958 Proof	—	Value: 150				
1959	8,400,000	0.10	0.20	5.00	10.00	20.00
1959 Proof	—	Value: 150				
1960	7,200,000	0.10	0.20	4.00	8.00	15.00
1960 Proof	—	Value: 135				
1961	7,200,000	0.10	0.20	3.00	6.00	12.00

Date	Mintage	F	VF	XF	Unc	BU
1961 Proof	—	Value: 135				
1962	6,000,000	—	0.10	2.50	5.00	10.00
1962 Proof	—	Value: 135				
1963	2,400,000	—	0.10	2.00	3.50	6.00
1963 Proof	—	Value: 135				
1964	18,000,000	—	0.10	0.20	2.00	3.50
1964 Proof	—	Value: 135				
1965	200,000	—	—	—	5.00	6.00
1965 Prooflike	25,000	—	—	—	—	2.00
1965 Proof	10	—	—	—	—	—

KM# 1 3 PENCE

0.5000 Silver .0226 oz. ASW, 16.3 mm. **Ruler:** George V **Subject:** Crossed Patu **Obv:** Crowned bust left **Obv. Designer:** Percy Metcalfe **Rev:** Crossed patu flanked by value and date **Rev. Designer:** G.E. Kruger-Gray

Date	Mintage	F	VF	XF	Unc	BU
1933	6,000,000	1.00	4.00	10.00	20.00	40.00
1933 Proof	Est. 20	Value: 450				
1934	6,000,000	1.00	4.00	10.00	20.00	40.00
1934 Proof	Est. 20	Value: 1,500				
1935	40,000	100	220	500	800	1,200
1935 Proof	364	Value: 1,400				
1936	2,760,000	1.00	4.00	12.00	20.00	45.00
1936 Proof	—	Value: 450				

KM# 7 3 PENCE

0.5000 Silver .0226 oz. ASW, 16.3 mm. **Ruler:** George VI **Subject:** Crossed Patu **Obv:** Head left **Obv. Designer:** T.H. Paget **Rev:** Crossed patu flanked by value and date **Rev. Designer:** G.E. Kruger-Gray

Date	Mintage	F	VF	XF	Unc	BU
1937	2,880,000	1.00	3.00	10.00	20.00	45.00
1937 Proof	Est. 200	Value: 400				
1939	3,000,000	1.00	4.00	10.00	20.00	45.00
1939 Proof	—	Value: 400				
1940	2,000,000	1.00	4.00	10.00	25.00	50.00
1940 Proof	—	Value: 400				
1941	1,760,000	2.00	25.00	80.00	200	400
1941 Proof	—	Value: 350				
1942	3,120,000	1.00	4.00	10.00	20.00	40.00
1942 With 1 dot	Est. 250,000	4.00	80.00	200	400	800
1943	4,400,000	1.00	2.00	6.00	15.00	35.00
1944	2,840,000	1.00	3.00	8.00	15.00	35.00
1944 Proof	—	Value: 350				
1945	2,520,000	1.00	2.00	6.00	15.00	25.00
1945 Proof	—	Value: 350				
1946	6,080,000	1.00	2.00	5.00	12.00	20.00
1946 Proof	—	Value: 350				

KM# 7a 3 PENCE

Copper-Nickel, 16.3 mm. **Ruler:** George VI **Obv:** Head left **Obv. Designer:** T.H. Paget **Rev:** Crossed patu flanked by value and date **Rev. Designer:** G.E. Kruger-Gray

Date	Mintage	F	VF	XF	Unc	BU
1947	6,400,000	0.15	2.00	8.00	20.00	35.00
1947 Proof	Est. 20	Value: 300				

KM# 15 3 PENCE

Copper-Nickel, 16.3 mm. **Ruler:** George VI **Obv:** Head left **Obv. Designer:** T.H. Paget **Rev:** Crossed patu flanked by value and date **Rev. Designer:** G.E. Kruger-Gray

Date	Mintage	F	VF	XF	Unc	BU
1948	4,000,000	0.15	2.00	8.00	20.00	35.00
1948 Proof	—	Value: 175				
1950	800,000	2.00	10.00	50.00	100	220
1950 Proof	—	Value: 225				
1951	3,600,000	0.15	2.00	4.00	8.00	15.00
1951 Proof	—	Value: 175				
1952	8,000,000	0.15	2.00	3.50	6.00	10.00
1952 Proof	—	Value: 175				

KM# 25.1 3 PENCE

Copper-Nickel, 16.3 mm. **Ruler:** Elizabeth II **Obv:** Laureate bust right without shoulder strap **Obv. Designer:** Mary Gillick **Rev:** Crossed patu flanked by value and date **Rev. Designer:** G.E. Kruger-Gray

Date	Mintage	F	VF	XF	Unc	BU
1953	4,000,000	0.15	2.00	3.50	6.00	12.00
1953 Proof	7,000	Value: 7.00				
1953 Matte proof	—	Value: 125				
1954	4,000,000	0.15	2.00	4.00	8.00	15.00
1954 Proof	—	Value: 175				
1955	4,000,000	0.15	2.00	4.00	8.00	15.00
1955 Proof	—	Value: 175				
1956	Inc. below	4.00	8.00	120	220	400
1956 Proof	—	Value: 250				

KM# 25.2 3 PENCE

Copper-Nickel, 16.3 mm. **Ruler:** Elizabeth II **Obv:** Laureate bust right with shoulder strap **Obv. Designer:** Mary Gillick **Rev:** Crossed patu flanked by value and date **Rev. Designer:** G.E. Kruger-Gray

Date	Mintage	F	VF	XF	Unc	BU
1956	4,800,000	0.10	0.20	2.00	5.00	10.00
1956 Proof	—	Value: 175				
1957	8,000,000	0.10	0.20	1.00	3.00	5.00
1957 Proof	—	Value: 175				
1958	4,800,000	0.10	0.20	2.00	5.00	10.00
1958 Proof	—	Value: 175				
1959	4,000,000	0.10	0.20	2.00	5.00	10.00
1959 Proof	—	Value: 175				
1960	4,000,000	0.10	0.20	1.00	2.00	3.00
1960 Proof	—	Value: 175				
1961	4,800,000	0.10	0.15	2.00	3.00	6.00
1961 Proof	—	Value: 175				
1962	6,000,000	0.10	0.15	0.30	1.00	2.00
1962 Proof	—	Value: 175				
1963	4,000,000	0.10	0.15	0.25	1.00	2.00
1963 Proof	—	Value: 175				
1964	6,400,000	0.10	0.15	0.25	0.50	2.00
1964 Proof	—	Value: 175				
1965	4,200,000	—	0.10	0.15	0.50	1.00
1965 Prooflike	25,000	—	—	—	—	1.00
1965 Proof	10	—	—	—	—	—

KM# 2 6 PENCE

2.8300 g., 0.5000 Silver .0454 oz. ASW, 19.3 mm. **Ruler:** George V **Obv:** Crowned bust left **Obv. Designer:** Percy Metcalfe **Rev:** Bird sitting on branch **Rev. Designer:** G.E. Kruger-Gray

Date	Mintage	F	VF	XF	Unc	BU
1933	3,000,000	1.00	12.00	35.00	60.00	110
1933 Proof	20	Value: 750				
1934	3,600,000	1.00	12.00	35.00	60.00	110
1934 Proof	20	Value: 1,500				
1935 Proof	364	Value: 500				
1935	560,000	3.00	20.00	85.00	200	350
1936	1,480,000	1.00	14.00	45.00	60.00	120
1936 Proof	—	—	—	—	—	—

KM# 8 6 PENCE

2.8300 g., 0.5000 Silver .0454 oz. ASW, 19.3 mm. **Ruler:** George VI **Obv:** Head left **Obv. Designer:** T.H. Paget **Rev:** Bird sitting on branch **Rev. Designer:** G.E. Kruger-Gray

Date	Mintage	F	VF	XF	Unc	BU
1937	1,280,000	1.00	12.00	40.00	60.00	120
1937 Proof	Est. 200	Value: 350				
1939	700,000	2.00	14.00	45.00	80.00	150
1939 Proof	—	Value: 350				
1940	800,000	2.00	12.00	45.00	80.00	150
1940 Proof	—	Value: 350				
1941	440,000	3.00	50.00	120	300	500
1941 Proof	—	Value: 550				
1942	360,000	3.00	50.00	120	300	500

Date	Mintage	F	VF	XF	Unc	BU
1943	1,800,000	1.00	10.00	25.00	50.00	90.00
1944	1,160,000	2.00	10.00	25.00	50.00	90.00
1944 Proof	—	Value: 300				
1945	940,000	2.00	10.00	25.00	50.00	90.00
1945 Proof	—	Value: 300				
1946	2,120,000	1.00	5.00	12.00	25.00	45.00
1946	—	Value: 300				

KM# 8a 6 PENCE
Copper-Nickel, 19.3 mm. **Ruler:** George VI **Obv:** Head left **Obv. Designer:** T.H. Paget **Rev:** Bird sitting on branch **Rev. Designer:** G.E. Kruger-Gray

Date	Mintage	F	VF	XF	Unc	BU
1947	3,200,000	0.20	10.00	25.00	50.00	80.00
1947 Proof	Est. 20	Value: 300				

KM# 16 6 PENCE
Copper-Nickel, 19.3 mm. **Ruler:** George VI **Obv:** Head left **Obv. Designer:** T.H. Paget **Rev:** Huia bird sitting on branch **Rev. Designer:** G.E. Kruger-Gray

Date	Mintage	F	VF	XF	Unc	BU
1948	2,000,000	0.20	10.00	25.00	50.00	80.00
1948 Proof	—	Value: 275				
1950	800,000	2.00	20.00	60.00	120	200
1950 Proof	—	Value: 275				
1951	1,800,000	0.20	2.00	3.00	4.00	6.00
1951 Proof	—	Value: 275				
1952	3,200,000	0.20	8.00	20.00	35.00	50.00
1952 Proof	—	Value: 225				

KM# 26.1 6 PENCE
Copper-Nickel, 19.3 mm. **Ruler:** Elizabeth II **Obv:** Laureate bust right without shoulder strap **Obv. Designer:** Mary Gillick **Rev:** Huia bird sitting on branch **Rev. Designer:** G.E. Kruger-Gray

Date	Mintage	F	VF	XF	Unc	BU
1953	1,200,000	0.10	4.00	10.00	15.00	25.00
1953 Proof	7,000	Value: 7.00				
1953 Matte proof	—	—	—	—	125	—
1954	1,200,000	0.10	4.00	10.00	20.00	40.00
1954 Proof	—	Value: 175				
1955	1,600,000	0.10	4.00	10.00	20.00	40.00
1957	Inc. below	6.00	20.00	150	400	600
1957 Proof	—	Value: 600				

KM# 26.2 6 PENCE
Copper-Nickel, 19.3 mm. **Ruler:** Elizabeth II **Obv:** Laureate bust right with shoulder strap **Obv. Designer:** Mary Gillick **Rev:** Huia bird sitting on branch **Rev. Designer:** G.E. Kruger-Gray

Date	Mintage	F	VF	XF	Unc	BU
1955 Proof	—	Value: 200				
1956	2,000,000	0.10	3.00	8.00	12.00	25.00
1956 Proof	—	Value: 200				
1957	2,400,000	0.10	0.25	4.00	8.00	15.00
1957 Proof	—	Value: 200				
1958	3,000,000	0.10	0.25	4.00	8.00	15.00
1958 Proof	—	Value: 200				
1959	2,000,000	0.10	0.15	2.00	8.00	15.00
1959 Proof	—	Value: 200				
1960	1,600,000	0.10	0.15	2.00	2.50	5.00
1960 Proof	—	Value: 200				
1961	800,000	0.10	0.15	2.00	2.50	5.00
1961 Proof	—	Value: 200				
1962	1,200,000	0.10	0.15	2.50	4.00	10.00
1962 Proof	—	Value: 200				
1963	800,000	0.10	0.15	2.00	4.00	8.00
1963 Proof	—	Value: 200				
1964	3,800,000	—	0.10	0.15	1.00	4.00
1964 Proof	—	Value: 175				
1965	8,600,000	—	—	0.10	1.00	2.50

Date	Mintage	F	VF	XF	Unc	BU
1965 Broken wing	Inc. above	4.00	8.00	12.00	35.00	65.00
1965 Prooflike	25,000	—	—	—	—	1.00
1965 Proof	10	—	—	—	—	—

KM# 3 SHILLING
5.6500 g., 0.5000 Silver .0908 oz. ASW, 23.62 mm.
Ruler: George V **Obv:** Crowned bust left **Obv. Designer:** Percy Metcalfe **Rev:** Crouched Maori warrior left **Rev. Designer:** G.E. Kruger-Gray

Date	Mintage	F	VF	XF	Unc	BU
1933	2,000,000	2.00	20.00	45.00	110	210
1933 Proof	Est. 20	Value: 1,500				
1934	3,400,000	2.00	20.00	45.00	110	210
1934 Proof	Est. 20	Value: 2,500				
1935	1,680,000	2.00	30.00	75.00	200	400
1935 Proof	364	Value: 500				

KM# 9 SHILLING
5.6500 g., 0.5000 Silver .0908 oz. ASW, 23.62 mm. **Ruler:** George VI **Obv:** Head left **Obv. Designer:** T.H. Paget **Rev:** Crouched Maori warrior left **Rev. Designer:** G.E. Kruger-Gray

Date	Mintage	F	VF	XF	Unc	BU
1937	890,000	2.00	12.00	35.00	75.00	150
1937 Proof	Est. 200	Value: 550				
1940	500,000	3.00	15.00	40.00	100	220
1940 Proof	—	Value: 550				
1941	360,000	4.00	50.00	150	300	500
1941 Proof	—	Value: 550				
1942	240,000	4.00	50.00	150	300	500
1942 Broken back	Est. 80,000	8.00	80.00	220	400	—
1943	900,000	2.00	12.00	35.00	60.00	150
1944	480,000	3.00	15.00	40.00	75.00	180
1944 Proof	—	Value: 550				
1945	1,030,000	2.00	10.00	22.00	45.00	85.00
1945 Proof	—	Value: 550				
1946	1,060,000	2.00	10.00	20.00	40.00	80.00
1946 Proof	—	Value: 550				

KM# 9a SHILLING
Copper-Nickel, 23.62 mm. **Ruler:** George VI **Obv:** Head left **Obv. Designer:** T.H. Paget **Rev:** Crouched Maori warrior left **Rev. Designer:** G.E. Kruger-Gray

Date	Mintage	F	VF	XF	Unc	BU
1947	2,800,000	1.00	12.00	35.00	80.00	180
1947 Proof	Est. 20	Value: 350				

KM# 17 SHILLING
Copper-Nickel, 23.62 mm. **Ruler:** George VI **Obv:** Head left **Obv. Designer:** T.H. Paget **Rev:** Crouched Maori warrior left **Rev. Designer:** G.E. Kruger-Gray

Date	Mintage	F	VF	XF	Unc	BU
1948	1,000,000	1.00	12.00	35.00	80.00	180
1948 Proof	—	Value: 350				
1950	600,000	1.00	12.00	35.00	80.00	225
1950 Proof	—	Value: 350				
1951	1,200,000	1.00	12.00	35.00	75.00	150
1951 Proof	—	Value: 350				
1952	600,000	2.00	12.00	40.00	80.00	175
1952 Proof	—	Value: 350				

KM# 27.1 SHILLING
Copper-Nickel, 23.62 mm. **Ruler:** Elizabeth II **Obv:** Laureate bust right without shoulder strap **Obv. Designer:** Mary Gillick **Rev:** Crouched Maori warrior left **Rev. Designer:** G.E. Kruger-Gray

Date	Mintage	F	VF	XF	Unc	BU
1953	200,000	2.00	6.00	12.00	25.00	50.00
1953 Proof	14,000	Value: 8.00				
1953 Matte proof	—	Value: 125				
1954 Proof	—	—	—	—	—	—
1955	200,000	2.00	15.00	60.00	120	220
1955 Proof	—	Value: 350				

KM# 27.2 SHILLING
Copper-Nickel, 23.62 mm. **Ruler:** Elizabeth II **Obv:** Laureate bust right with shoulder strap **Obv. Designer:** Mary Gillick **Rev:** Crouched Maori warrior left **Rev. Designer:** G.E. Kruger-Gray

Date	Mintage	F	VF	XF	Unc	BU
1956	800,000	0.20	1.00	10.00	20.00	40.00
1956 Proof	—	Value: 350				
1957	800,000	0.20	1.00	10.00	20.00	40.00
1957 Proof	—	Value: 350				
1958	1,000,000	0.20	1.00	10.00	15.00	35.00
1958 Proof	—	Value: 350				
1958 Broken back	—	10.00	—	50.00	120	220
1959	600,000	2.00	5.00	8.00	15.00	35.00
1959 Proof	—	Value: 350				
1960	600,000	0.20	1.00	8.00	15.00	35.00
1960 Proof	—	Value: 350				
1961	400,000	0.15	0.50	8.00	12.00	25.00
1961 Proof	—	Value: 350				
1962	1,000,000	0.15	0.30	2.00	3.00	6.00
1962 Proof	—	Value: 350				
1962 No Horizon	—	10.00	—	40.00	80.00	120
1963	600,000	0.15	0.30	3.00	5.00	10.00
1963 Proof	—	Value: 350				
1964	3,400,000	0.10	0.15	2.00	2.50	4.00
1964 Proof	—	Value: 350				
1965	3,500,000	0.10	0.15	1.00	2.00	3.00
1965 Prooflike	25,000	—	—	—	—	1.25
1965 Proof	10	—	—	—	—	—

KM# 4 FLORIN
11.3100 g., 0.5000 Silver .1818 oz. ASW, 28.58 mm.
Ruler: George V **Obv:** Crowned bust left **Obv. Designer:** Percy Metcalfe **Rev:** Kiwi bird **Rev. Designer:** G.E. Kruger-Gray

Date	Mintage	F	VF	XF	Unc	BU
1933	2,100,000	2.25	20.00	50.00	150	250
1933 Proof	Est. 20	Value: 600				
1934	2,850,000	2.25	20.00	50.00	110	200
1934 Proof	Est. 20	Value: 2,000				
1935	755,000	2.25	40.00	80.00	220	500
1935 Proof	364	Value: 600				
1936	150,000	6.00	80.00	400	1,200	3,000
1936 Proof	—	Value: 1,250				

KM# 10.1 FLORIN
11.3100 g., 0.5000 Silver .1818 oz. ASW, 28.58 mm.
Ruler: George VI **Obv:** Head left **Obv. Designer:** T.H. Paget **Rev:** Kiwi bird **Rev. Designer:** G.E. Kruger-Gray

Date	Mintage	F	VF	XF	Unc	BU
1937	1,190,000	3.00	20.00	50.00	110	200
1937 Proof	Est. 200	Value: 600				
1940	500,000	4.00	45.00	200	600	1,200
1940 Proof	—	Value: 800				
1941	820,000	3.00	15.00	40.00	80.00	180
1941 Proof	—	Value: 600				
1942	150,000	3.00	22.00	45.00	110	200
1943	1,400,000	3.00	15.00	35.00	70.00	170
1944	140,000	6.00	40.00	120	250	550
1944 Proof	—	Value: 800				
1945	515,000	4.00	15.00	35.00	70.00	170
1945 Proof	—	Value: 650				

Date	Mintage	F	VF	XF	Unc	BU
1946	1,200,000	3.00	15.00	35.00	60.00	150
1946 Proof	—	Value: 650				

KM# 10.2 FLORIN
11.3100 g., 0.5000 Silver .1818 oz. ASW, 28.58 mm.
Ruler: George VI **Obv:** Head left **Obv. Designer:** T.H. Paget **Rev:** Flat back on Kiwi **Rev. Designer:** G.E. Kruger-Gray

Date	Mintage	F	VF	XF	Unc	BU
1946	Est. 300,000	4.00	50.00	200	500	800

KM# 10.2a FLORIN
Copper-Nickel, 28.58 mm. **Ruler:** George VI **Obv:** Head left **Obv. Designer:** T.H. Paget **Rev:** Kiwi bird **Rev. Designer:** G.E. Kruger-Gray

Date	Mintage	F	VF	XF	Unc	BU
1947	2,500,000	1.00	15.00	40.00	80.00	225
1947 Proof	Est. 20	Value: 450				

KM# 18 FLORIN
Copper-Nickel, 28.58 mm. **Ruler:** George VI **Obv:** Head left **Obv. Designer:** T.H. Paget **Rev:** Kiwi bird **Rev. Designer:** G.E. Kruger-Gray

Date	Mintage	F	VF	XF	Unc	BU
1948	1,750,000	1.00	15.00	40.00	80.00	225
1948 Proof	—	Value: 400				
1949	3,500,000	1.00	15.00	40.00	80.00	225
1949 Proof	—	Value: 400				
1950	3,500,000	1.00	8.00	12.00	25.00	50.00
1950 Proof	—	Value: 400				
1951	2,000,000	1.00	8.00	12.00	25.00	50.00
1951 Proof	—	Value: 400				

KM# 28.1 FLORIN
Copper-Nickel, 28.58 mm. **Ruler:** Elizabeth II **Obv:** Laureate bust right without shoulder strap **Obv. Designer:** Mary Gillick **Rev:** Kiwi bird **Rev. Designer:** G.E. Kruger-Gray

Date	Mintage	F	VF	XF	Unc	BU
1953	250,000	2.50	5.00	12.00	20.00	45.00
1953 Proof	7,000	Value: 12.50				
1953 Matte proof	—	Value: 180				
1954 Proof	—	—	—	—	—	—

KM# 28.2 FLORIN
Copper-Nickel, 28.58 mm. **Ruler:** Elizabeth II **Obv:** Laureate bust right with shoulder strap **Obv. Designer:** Mary Gillick **Rev:** Kiwi bird **Rev. Designer:** G.E. Kruger-Gray

Date	Mintage	F	VF	XF	Unc	BU
1961	1,500,000	1.00	3.00	6.00	12.00	30.00
1961 Proof	—	Value: 375				
1962	1,500,000	1.00	3.00	5.00	10.00	25.00
1962 Proof	—	Value: 375				
1963	100,000	2.50	3.50	6.00	12.00	25.00
1963 Proof	—	Value: 375				
1964	7,000,000	1.00	2.00	3.00	5.00	12.00
1964 Proof	—	Value: 375				
1965	9,450,000	0.25	0.50	1.00	2.00	3.50
1965 Prooflike	25,000	—	—	—	—	2.50
1965 Proof	10	—	—	—	—	—

KM# 5 1/2 CROWN
14.1400 g., 0.5000 Silver .2273 oz. ASW, 32 mm.
Ruler: George V **Obv:** Crowned bust left **Obv. Designer:** Percy Metcalfe **Rev:** Crowned shield within ornamental design **Rev. Designer:** G.E. Kruger-Gray

Date	Mintage	F	VF	XF	Unc	BU
1933	2,000,000	4.00	25.00	60.00	400	650
1933 Proof	Est. 20	Value: 650				
1934	2,720,000	4.00	25.00	60.00	180	300
1934 Proof	Est. 20	Value: 2,250				
1935	612,000	4.00	45.00	110	300	600
1935 Proof	364	Value: 700				

KM# 11 1/2 CROWN
14.1400 g., 0.5000 Silver .2273 oz. ASW, 32 mm.
Ruler: George VI **Obv:** Head left **Obv. Designer:** T.H. Paget **Rev:** Crowned shield within ornamental design **Rev. Designer:** G.E. Kruger-Gray

Date	Mintage	F	VF	XF	Unc	BU
1937	672,000	4.00	25.00	70.00	150	300
1937 Proof	200	Value: 700				
1941	776,000	4.00	22.00	40.00	100	220
1941 Proof	—	Value: 700				
1942	240,000	4.00	25.00	50.00	120	250
1943	1,120,000	4.00	20.00	40.00	80.00	180
1944	180,000	6.00	45.00	180	375	800
1944 Proof	—	Value: 700				
1945	420,000	4.00	20.00	50.00	120	250
1945 Proof	—	Value: 700				
1946	960,000	4.00	20.00	50.00	120	200
1946 Proof	—	Value: 700				

KM# 11a 1/2 CROWN
Copper-Nickel, 32 mm. **Ruler:** George VI **Obv:** Head left **Obv. Designer:** T.H. Paget **Rev:** Crowned shield within ornamental design **Rev. Designer:** G.E. Kruger-Gray

Date	Mintage	F	VF	XF	Unc	BU
1947	1,600,000	2.00	6.00	40.00	120	250
1947 Proof	Est. 20	Value: 550				

KM# 14 1/2 CROWN
14.1400 g., 0.5000 Silver .2273 oz. ASW, 32 mm.
Ruler: George VI **Subject:** New Zealand Centennial **Obv:** Head left **Obv. Designer:** T.H. Paget **Rev:** Radiant sun above city, standing figure in foreground **Rev. Designer:** L.C. Mitchell

Date	Mintage	F	VF	XF	Unc	BU
1940	100,800	12.00	15.00	20.00	50.00	80.00
1940 Proof	—	Value: 5,000				

KM# 19 1/2 CROWN
Copper-Nickel, 32 mm. **Ruler:** George VI **Obv:** Head left **Obv. Designer:** T.H. Paget **Rev:** Crowned shield within ornamental design **Rev. Designer:** G.E. Kruger-Gray

Date	Mintage	F	VF	XF	Unc	BU
1948	1,400,000	2.00	6.00	40.00	120	250
1948 Proof	—	Value: 500				
1949	2,800,000	2.00	6.00	40.00	120	250
1949 Proof	—	Value: 500				
1950	3,600,000	2.00	3.00	15.00	25.00	50.00
Note: K. G. close to dots						
1950 Proof	—	Value: 500				
1950	Inc. above	3.00	8.00	25.00	60.00	100
Note: K. G. close to rim						
1950 Proof	—	Value: 500				
1951	1,200,000	2.00	3.00	15.00	25.00	50.00
1951 Proof	—	Value: 500				

KM# 29.1 1/2 CROWN
Copper-Nickel, 32 mm. **Ruler:** Elizabeth II **Obv:** Laureate bust right without shoulder strap **Obv. Designer:** Mary Gillick **Rev:** Crowned shield within ornamental design **Rev. Designer:** G.E. Kruger-Gray

Date	Mintage	F	VF	XF	Unc	BU
1953	120,000	4.00	5.00	20.00	25.00	60.00
1953 Proof	7,000	Value: 20.00				
1953 Matte proof	—	Value: 245				

KM# 29.2 1/2 CROWN
Copper-Nickel, 32 mm. **Ruler:** Elizabeth II **Obv:** Laureate bust right with shoulder strap **Obv. Designer:** Mary Gillick **Rev:** Crowned shield within ornamental design **Rev. Designer:** G.E. Kruger-Gray

Date	Mintage	F	VF	XF	Unc	BU
1961	80,000	4.00	8.00	15.00	30.00	60.00
1961 Proof	—	Value: 450				
1962	600,000	2.00	2.50	3.00	4.00	10.00
1962 Proof	—	Value: 450				
1963	400,000	2.00	2.50	3.50	6.00	10.00
1963 Proof	—	Value: 450				
1965	200,000	0.50	0.70	1.00	3.50	5.00
1965 Prooflike	25,000	—	—	—	—	5.00
1965 Proof	10	—	—	—	—	—

KM# 6 CROWN

28.2800 g., 0.5000 Silver .4546 oz. ASW, 38.8 mm.
Ruler: George V **Subject:** Treaty of Waitangi in 1840. **Obv:** Crowned bust left **Obv. Designer:** E.B. MacKennal **Rev:** Crown above standing figures shaking hands **Designer:** James Berry

Date	Mintage	F	VF	XF	Unc	BU
1935	660	1,200	3,000	4,000	5,000	6,000
1935 Proof	468	Value: 6,500				

KM# 22 CROWN

28.2800 g., 0.5000 Silver .4546 oz. ASW, 38.8 mm.
Ruler: George VI **Subject:** Proposed Royal Visit **Obv:** Head left **Obv. Designer:** T.H. Paget **Rev:** Silver fern leaf flanked by stars **Rev. Designer:** James Berry

Date	Mintage	F	VF	XF	Unc	BU
1949	200,000	—	12.00	15.00	25.00	50.00
1949 Proof	Est. 3	Value: 12,000				

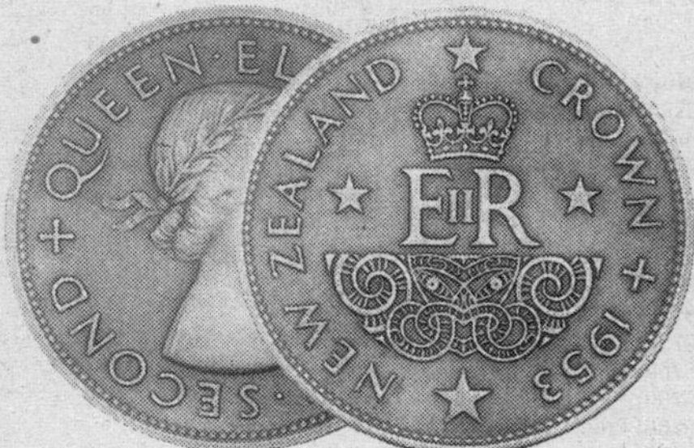

KM# 30 CROWN

Copper-Nickel, 38.8 mm. **Ruler:** Elizabeth II **Subject:** Queen Elizabeth II Coronation **Obv:** Laureate bust right **Obv. Designer:** Mary Gillick **Rev:** Crowned monogram flanked by stars above design **Rev. Designer:** R.M. Conly

Date	Mintage	F	VF	XF	Unc	BU
1953	250,000	—	6.00	8.00	12.00	15.00
1953 Proof	7,000	Value: 80.00				

DECIMAL COINAGE

100 Cents = 1 Dollar

(c) Royal Australian Mint, Canberra

(l) Royal Mint, Llantrisant

(o) Royal Canadian Mint, Ottawa

KM# 31.1 CENT

2.0500 g., Bronze, 17.5 mm. **Ruler:** Elizabeth II **Obv:** Young bust right **Obv. Designer:** Arnold Machin **Rev:** Value within silver fern leaf **Rev. Designer:** James Berry **Note:** Rounded, high relief portrait.

Date	Mintage	F	VF	XF	Unc	BU
1967(l)	120,000,000	—	—	0.10	0.15	—
1967(l) Prooflike	50,000	—	—	—	—	0.80
1967 Proof	10	—	—	—	—	—
1968	35,000	—	—	—	2.00	—
Note: In sets only						
1968 Prooflike	40,000	—	—	—	—	2.00
1969	50,000	—	—	—	2.00	—
Note: In sets only						
1969 Prooflike	50,000	—	—	—	—	2.00
1970(c)	10,060,000	—	—	0.10	1.00	—
1970 Prooflike	20,010	—	—	—	—	1.00
1971(c)	10,000,000	—	0.10	1.00	6.00	—
Note: Serifs on date numerals						
1971(l)	15,000	—	—	0.20	3.00	—
Note: Without serifs						
1971(l) Proof	5,000	Value: 12.50				
1972(c)	10,055,000	—	0.10	1.00	5.00	—
1972(c) Proof	8,045	Value: 5.00				
1973(c)	15,055,000	—	—	0.10	5.00	—
1973(c) Proof	8,000	Value: 5.00				
1974(c)	35,035,000	—	—	0.10	2.00	—
1974(c) Proof	8,000	Value: 4.00				
1975(l)	60,015,000	—	—	0.10	1.00	—
1975(l) Proof	10,000	Value: 4.00				
1976(l)	20,016,000	—	—	0.10	1.00	—
1976(l) Proof	11,000	Value: 4.00				
1977 In sets only	20,000	—	—	2.00	6.00	—
1977 Proof	12,000	Value: 6.00				
1978(o)	15,023,000	—	—	0.10	1.25	—
1978(o) Proof	15,000	Value: 2.00				
1979(o)	35,025,000	—	—	0.10	1.00	—
1979(o) Proof	16,000	Value: 2.00				
1980(l)	27,000	—	—	0.10	1.00	—
Note: Round 0 in date						
1980(l) Proof	17,000	Value: 2.00				
1980(o)	40,000,000	—	—	0.10	1.00	—
Note: Oval O in date						
1981(o)	10,000,000	—	—	0.10	1.00	—
Note: Oval hole in 8						
1981(l)	25,000	—	—	0.10	1.00	—
Note: Round hole in 8						
1981(l) Proof	18,000	Value: 2.00				
Note: Round hole in 8						
1982(o)	10,000,000	—	—	0.10	1.00	—
Note: Blunt-tipped 2						
1982(l)	25,000	—	—	0.10	1.00	—
Note: Round-tipped 2						
1982(l) Proof	18,000	Value: 2.00				
Note: Round-tipped 2						
1983(o)	40,000,000	—	—	0.10	1.00	—
Note: Round-top 3						
1983(l)	25,000	—	—	0.10	1.00	—
Note: Flat-top 3						
1983(l) Proof	18,000	Value: 2.00				
Note: Flat-top 3						
1984(l)	25,000	—	—	—	1.00	—
1984(l) Proof	15,000	Value: 2.00				
1985(c)	20,000	—	—	—	2.00	—
1985(c) Proof	12,000	Value: 2.00				

KM# 31.2 CENT

Bronze, 17.5 mm. **Obv:** Crowned bust right **Obv. Designer:** Arnold Machin **Rev:** Value within silver fern leaf **Rev. Designer:** James Berry **Note:** Die recut, low relief portrait.

Date	Mintage	F	VF	XF	Unc	BU
1984(o)	30,000,000	—	—	0.10	1.00	—
1985(o)	40,000,000	—	—	—	1.00	—

KM# 58 CENT

2.0500 g., Bronze, 17.5 mm. **Ruler:** Elizabeth II **Obv:** Crowned head right **Obv. Designer:** R.D. Maklouf **Rev:** Value within silver fern leaf **Rev. Designer:** James Berry

Date	Mintage	F	VF	XF	Unc	BU
1986(o)	25,000,000	—	—	0.10	1.00	—
1986(l)	18,000	—	—	—	1.00	—
1986(l) Proof	10,000	Value: 1.00				
1987(o)	27,500,000	—	—	0.10	0.50	—
1987(l)	18,000	—	—	—	1.00	—
1987(l) Proof	10,000	Value: 1.00				
1988(l)	15,000	—	—	—	5.00	—
Note: In sets only						
1988(l) Proof	9,000	Value: 2.00				
Note: 1988 cent was struck for sets only						

KM# 33 2 CENTS

4.1500 g., Bronze, 21.1 mm. **Ruler:** Elizabeth II **Obv:** Young bust right **Obv. Designer:** Arnold Machin **Rev:** Value within kowhai leaves **Note:** Mule.

Date	Mintage	F	VF	XF	Unc	BU
ND(1967)	Est. 50,000	—	20.00	25.00	40.00	50.00

KM# 32.1 2 CENTS

4.1500 g., Bronze, 21.1 mm. **Ruler:** Elizabeth II **Obv:** Young bust right **Obv. Designer:** Arnold Machin **Rev:** Value within kowhai leaves **Rev. Designer:** James Berry **Note:** Rounded, high relief portrait.

Date	Mintage	F	VF	XF	Unc	BU
1967(l)	75,000,000	—	—	0.10	0.25	—
1967(l) Prooflike	50,000	—	—	—	—	0.75
1967(l) Proof	10	—	—	—	—	—
1968	35,000	—	—	—	2.00	—
Note: In sets only						
1968 Prooflike	40,000	—	—	—	—	1.25
1969(c)	20,510,000	—	—	0.15	0.50	—
1969 Prooflike	50,000	—	—	—	—	1.25
1970(c)	30,000	—	—	—	2.00	—
Note: In sets only						
1970 Prooflike	20,010	—	—	—	—	1.25
1971(c)	15,050,000	—	0.10	1.00	5.00	—
Note: Serifs on date numerals						
1971(l)	15,000	—	—	2.00	4.00	—
Note: Without serifs						
1971(l) Proof	5,000	Value: 12.50				
1972(c)	17,525,000	—	0.10	1.00	5.00	—
1972(c) Proof	8,045	Value: 5.00				
1973(c)	38,565,000	—	0.10	1.00	5.00	—
1973(c) Proof	8,000	Value: 5.25				
1974(c)	50,015,000	—	0.10	0.50	2.00	—
1974(c) Proof	8,000	Value: 3.00				
1975(l)	20,015,000	—	—	0.10	1.00	—
1975(l) Proof	10,000	Value: 3.00				
1976(l)	15,016,000	—	—	0.10	1.00	—
1976(l) Proof	11,000	Value: 3.00				
1977(l)	20,000,000	—	—	0.10	1.00	—
1977(l) Proof	12,000	Value: 3.00				
1978(o)	23,000	—	—	—	6.00	—
Note: In sets only						
1978(o) Proof	15,000	Value: 3.00				
1979(o)	25,000	—	—	—	6.00	—
Note: In sets only						
1979(o) Proof	16,000	Value: 3.00				
1980(l)	27,000	—	—	0.10	1.00	—
Note: Round 0 in date						
1980(l) Proof	17,000	Value: 3.00				
1980(o)	10,000,000	—	—	0.10	1.00	—
Note: Oval 0 in date						
1981(o)	25,000,000	—	—	0.10	1.00	—
Note: Oval hole in 8						
1981(l)	25,000	—	—	0.10	1.00	—
Note: Round hole in 8						
1981(l) Proof	18,000	Value: 3.00				
1982(o)	50,000,000	—	—	0.10	1.00	—
Note: Blunt open 2						
1982(l)	25,000	—	—	0.10	1.00	—
Note: Pointed tight 2						
1982(l) Proof	18,000	Value: 3.00				
1983(o)	15,000,000	—	—	0.10	1.00	—
Note: Round-topped 3						
1983(l)	25,000	—	—	0.10	1.00	—
Note: Flat-topped 3						
1983(l) Proof	18,000	Value: 3.00				
1984(l)	25,000	—	—	0.10	1.00	—
Note: Smooth shoulder folds						
1984(l) Proof	15,000	Value: 2.00				
1985(c)	20,000	—	—	0.10	2.00	—
1985(c) Proof	12,000	Value: 2.00				

KM# 32.2 2 CENTS

Bronze, 21.1 mm. **Obv:** Crowned bust right
Obv. Designer: Arnold Machin **Rev:** Value within kowhai leaves
Rev. Designer: James Berry

Date	Mintage	F	VF	XF	Unc	BU
1984(o)	10,000,000	—	—	0.10	1.00	—
1985(o)	22,500,000	—	—	0.10	1.00	—

KM# 59 2 CENTS

4.1500 g., Bronze, 21.1 mm. **Ruler:** Elizabeth II **Obv:** Crowned head right **Obv. Designer:** R.D. Maklouf **Rev:** Kowhai **Rev. Designer:** James Berry

Date	Mintage	F	VF	XF	Unc	BU
1986(l)	18,000	—	—	—	8.00	—

Date	Mintage	F	VF	XF	Unc	BU
Note: In sets only						
1986(l) Proof	10,000	Value: 8.00				
1987(o)	36,250,000	—	—	—	1.00	—
1987(l)	18,000	—	—	—	2.00	—
1987(l) Proof	10,000	Value: 2.00				
1988(l)	15,000	—	—	—	5.00	—
Note: In sets only						
1988(l) Proof	9,000	Value: 1.25				

KM# 34.1 5 CENTS

2.8300 g., Copper-Nickel, 19.43 mm. **Ruler:** Elizabeth II **Subject:** Tuatara **Obv:** Young bust right **Obv. Designer:** Arnold Machin **Rev:** Value below tuatara **Rev. Designer:** James Berry **Note:** Rounded, high relief portrait.

Date	Mintage	F	VF	XF	Unc	BU
1967(l)	26,000,000	—	—	0.10	0.50	—
1967(l)	Inc. above	3.00	5.00	20.00	40.00	—
Note: Without sea line at right of Tuatara						
1967(l)	Inc. above	3.00	5.00	20.00	40.00	—
Note: No tail triangle under chin						
1967(l) Prooflike	50,000	—	—	—	—	1.00
1967(l) Proof	10	—	—	—	—	—
1968	35,000	—	—	0.15	1.00	—
Note: In sets only						
1968 Prooflike	40,000	—	—	—	—	2.00
1969(c)	10,260,000	—	—	0.15	0.50	—
1969 Prooflike	50,000	—	—	—	—	2.00
1970(c)	11,202,000	—	—	0.15	0.50	—
1970 Prooflike	20,010	—	—	—	—	2.00
1971(c)	11,152,000	—	0.15	0.50	5.00	—
Note: Serifs on date numerals						
1971(l)	15,000	—	—	0.50	3.00	—
Note: Without serifs						
1971(l) Proof	5,000	Value: 5.00				
1972(c)	20,015,000	—	—	0.10	2.00	—
1972(c) Proof	8,000	Value: 5.00				
1973(c)	4,038,999	—	—	0.10	2.00	—
1973(c) Proof	8,000	Value: 4.50				
1974(c)	18,015,000	—	—	0.10	3.00	—
1974(c) Proof	8,000	Value: 4.00				
1975(c)	32,015,000	—	—	0.10	2.00	—
1975(c) Proof	10,000	Value: 4.50				
1976	16,000	—	—	—	5.00	—
Note: In sets only						
1976 Proof	11,000	Value: 2.00				
1977	20,000	—	—	—	5.00	—
Note: In sets only						
1977 Proof	12,000	Value: 3.00				
1978(o)	20,023,000	—	—	0.10	0.40	—
1978(o) Proof	15,000	Value: 3.00				
1979(o)	25,000	—	—	—	6.00	—
Note: In sets only						
1979(o) Proof	16,000	Value: 3.00				
1980(l)	27,000	—	—	0.10	1.00	—
Note: Round O in date						
1980(l) Proof	17,000	Value: 2.00				
1980(o)	12,000,000	—	—	0.10	0.75	—
Note: Oval O in date						
1981(o)	20,000,000	—	—	0.10	0.75	—
Note: Oval hole in 8						
1981(l)	25,000	—	—	0.50	1.00	—
Note: Round hole in 8						
1981(l) Proof	18,000	Value: 2.00				
1982(o)	50,000,000	—	—	0.10	1.00	—
Note: Blunt 2						
1982(l)	25,000	—	—	0.50	1.00	—
Note: Pointed 2						
1982(l) Proof	18,000	Value: 2.00				
1983(l)	25,000	—	—	—	3.00	—
Note: In sets only						
1983(l) Proof	18,000	Value: 3.00				
1984(l)	25,000	—	—	—	3.00	—
Note: In sets only						
1984(l) Proof	15,000	Value: 3.00				
1985(c)	20,000	—	—	0.50	2.00	—
1985(c) Proof	12,000	Value: 2.00				

KM# 34.2 5 CENTS

2.8300 g., Copper-Nickel, 19.43 mm. **Subject:** Tuatara **Obv:** Crowned bust right **Obv. Designer:** Arnold Machin **Rev:** James Berry **Note:** Die recut, low relief.

Date	Mintage	F	VF	XF	Unc	BU
1985(o)	14,000,000	—	—	0.10	1.00	—

KM# 64 5 CENTS

Copper-Nickel **Ruler:** Elizabeth II **Obv:** Young bust right **Rev:** Small ship **Note:** Mule.

Date	Mintage	F	VF	XF	Unc	BU
1981(o) Rare; Seri on 1	—	—	—	—	—	—

KM# 60 5 CENTS

2.8300 g., Copper-Nickel, 19.43 mm. **Ruler:** Elizabeth II **Obv:** Crowned head right **Obv. Designer:** R.D. Maklouf **Rev:** Value below tuatara **Rev. Designer:** James Berry

Date	Mintage	F	VF	XF	Unc	BU
1986(o)	18,000,000	—	—	0.10	1.00	—
1986(l)	18,000	—	—	—	2.00	—
1986(l) Proof	10,000	Value: 3.00				
1987(o)	40,000,000	—	—	0.10	1.00	—
1987(l)	18,000	—	—	—	2.00	—
1987(l) Proof	10,000	Value: 3.00				
1988(c)	16,000,000	—	—	0.10	1.00	—
Note: Round-topped numerals						
1988(l)	15,000	—	—	—	2.00	—
Note: Flat-topped numerals						
1988(l) Proof	9,000	Value: 3.00				
1989(o)	36,000,000	—	—	0.10	1.00	—
1989(c)	15,000	—	—	—	1.00	—
1989(c) Proof	8,500	Value: 3.00				
1990(c)	18,000	—	—	—	3.00	—
Note: In sets only						
1990(c) Proof	10,000	Value: 3.00				
1991(c)	20,000	—	—	—	3.00	—
Note: In sets only						
1991(c) Proof	9,000	Value: 4.00				
1992(l)	15,000	—	—	—	3.00	—
Note: In sets only						
1992(l) Proof	9,000	Value: 4.00				
1993(l)	15,000	—	—	—	3.00	—
Note: In sets only						
1993(l) Proof	10,000	Value: 4.00				
1994(l)	20,026,000	—	—	0.10	1.00	—
1994(l) Proof	10,000	Value: 3.00				
1995(l)	40,010,000	—	—	0.10	1.00	—
1995(l) Proof	4,000	Value: 3.00				
1996(n)	19,008,000	—	—	0.10	1.00	—
1996(l) Proof	4,000	Value: 3.00				
1997(n)	14,000,000	—	—	0.10	1.00	—
1997(l) Proof	2,500	Value: 5.00				
1998(p)	8,000,000	—	—	0.10	1.00	—
1998(l) Proof	2,000	Value: 3.00				

KM# 72 5 CENTS

2.8300 g., Copper-Nickel, 19.43 mm. **Ruler:** Elizabeth II **Subject:** 1990 Anniversary Celebrations **Obv:** Crowned head right **Rev:** Stylized kotuku bird

Date	Mintage	F	VF	XF	Unc	BU
1990	10,000	—	—	—	10.00	—

KM# 72a 5 CENTS

3.2700 g., 0.9250 Silver .0973 oz. ASW, 19.43 mm. **Ruler:** Elizabeth II **Obv:** Crowned head right **Rev:** Stylized kotuku bird

Date	Mintage	F	VF	XF	Unc	BU
1990 Proof	7,000	Value: 15.00				

KM# 116 5 CENTS

2.8300 g., Copper-Nickel, 19.43 mm. **Ruler:** Elizabeth II **Obv:** Head with tiara right **Rev:** Value below tuatara **Rev. Designer:** James Berry **Note:** Many recalled and melted in 2006.

Date	Mintage	F	VF	XF	Unc	BU
1999(p)	25,040,000	—	—	0.10	1.00	—
1999(p) Wart on nose	—	—	—	—	6.00	—
Note: Die crack error						
1999(l)	7,000	—	—	—	5.00	—
1999(l) Proof	2,000	Value: 3.00				
2000(o)	26,000,000	—	—	0.10	1.00	—
2000(c)	3,000	—	—	—	12.00	—
2000(c) Proof	1,500	Value: 15.00				

KM# 35 10 CENTS

5.6500 g., Copper-Nickel, 23.62 mm. **Ruler:** Elizabeth II **Obv:** Young bust right **Obv. Designer:** Arnold Machin **Rev:** Value above Maori mask, koruru **Rev. Designer:** James Berry

Date	Mintage	F	VF	XF	Unc	BU
1967(l)	17,000,000	—	—	0.10	0.25	—
1967(l) Prooflike	50,000	—	—	—	—	1.00
1967(l) Proof	10	—	—	—	—	—
1968	35,000	—	—	1.00	2.00	—
Note: In sets only						
1968 Prooflike	40,000	—	—	—	—	2.00
1969	3,050,000	—	—	0.15	1.00	—
1969 Proof	50,000	Value: 2.00				

KM# 41.1 (KM41) 10 CENTS

5.6500 g., Copper-Nickel, 23.62 mm. **Ruler:** Elizabeth II **Obv:** Young bust right **Obv. Designer:** Arnold Machin **Rev:** Value above Maori mask, koruru **Rev. Designer:** James Berry **Note:** Rounded, high relief portrait.

Date	Mintage	F	VF	XF	Unc	BU
1970	2,046,000	—	—	0.15	1.00	—
1970	2,046,000	—	—	0.15	1.00	—
1970 Prooflike	20,010	—	—	—	—	1.50
1970 Prooflike	20,010	—	—	—	—	1.50
1971(c)	2,800,000	—	0.10	5.00	40.00	—
Note: Serifs on date numerals						
1971(c)	2,800,000	—	0.10	5.00	40.00	—
Note: Serifs on date numerals						
1971(l)	15,000	—	—	1.00	3.00	—
Note: Without serifs						
1971(l)	15,000	—	—	1.00	3.00	—
Note: Without serifs						
1971(l) Proof	5,000	Value: 5.00				
1971(l) Proof	5,000	Value: 5.00				
1972(c)	2,039,000	—	—	0.15	2.00	—
1972(c)	2,039,000	—	—	0.15	2.00	—
1972(c) Proof	8,000	Value: 5.00				
1972(c) Proof	8,000	Value: 5.00				
1973(c)	3,525,000	—	—	0.10	2.00	—
1973(c)	3,525,000	—	—	0.10	2.00	—
1973(c) Proof	8,000	Value: 3.00				
1973(c) Proof	8,000	Value: 3.00				
1974(c)	4,619,000	—	—	0.10	2.00	—
1974(c)	4,619,000	—	—	0.10	2.00	—
1974(c) Proof	8,000	Value: 3.00				
1974(c) Proof	8,000	Value: 3.00				
1975(l)	7,015,000	—	—	0.10	2.00	—
1975(l)	7,015,000	—	—	0.10	2.00	—
1975(l) Proof	10,000	Value: 3.00				
1975(l) Proof	10,000	Value: 3.00				
1976(l)	5,016,000	—	—	0.10	2.00	—
1976(l)	5,016,000	—	—	0.10	2.00	—
1976(l) Proof	11,000	Value: 3.00				
1976(l) Proof	11,000	Value: 3.00				
1977(l)	5,000,000	—	—	0.10	2.00	—
1977(l)	5,000,000	—	—	0.10	2.00	—
1977(o) Proof	12,000	Value: 3.00				
1977(o) Proof	12,000	Value: 3.00				
1978(o)	16,023,000	—	—	0.10	2.00	—
1978(o)	16,023,000	—	—	0.10	2.00	—
1978(o) Proof	15,000	Value: 3.00				
1978(o) Proof	15,000	Value: 3.00				
1979(o)	6,000,000	—	—	0.10	1.00	—
1979(o)	6,000,000	—	—	0.10	1.00	—
1979(o) Proof	16,000	Value: 3.00				
1979(o) Proof	16,000	Value: 3.00				
1980(l)	27,000	—	—	0.10	1.00	—
Note: Round O in date						
1980(l)	27,000	—	—	0.10	1.00	—
Note: Round O in date						
1980(l) Proof	17,000	Value: 3.00				
1980(l) Proof	17,000	Value: 3.00				
1980(o)	28,000,000	—	—	0.10	1.00	—
Note: Oval O in date						
1980(o)	28,000,000	—	—	0.10	1.00	—
Note: Oval O in date						
1981(o)	5,000,000	—	—	0.10	2.00	—
Note: Oval holes in 8						
1981(o)	5,000,000	—	—	0.10	2.00	—
Note: Oval holes in 8						
1981(l)	25,000	—	—	0.10	2.00	—
Note: Round holes in 8						

Date	Mintage	F	VF	XF	Unc	BU
1981(l)	25,000	—	—	0.10	2.00	—
Note: Round holes in 8						
1981(l) Proof	18,000	Value: 3.00				
1981(l) Proof	18,000	Value: 3.00				
1982(o)	18,000,000	—	—	0.10	1.00	—
Note: Blunt open 2						
1982(o)	18,000,000	—	—	0.10	1.00	—
Note: Blunt open 2						
1982(l)	25,000	—	—	0.10	2.00	—
Note: Point-tipped 2						
1982(l)	25,000	—	—	0.10	2.00	—
Note: Point-tipped 2						
1982(l) Proof	18,000	Value: 3.00				
1982(l) Proof	18,000	Value: 3.00				
1983(l)	25,000	—	—	—	3.00	—
Note: In sets only						
1983(l)	25,000	—	—	—	3.00	—
Note: In sets only						
1983(l) Proof	18,000	Value: 3.00				
1983(l) Proof	18,000	Value: 3.00				
1984(l)	25,000	—	—	—	3.00	—
Note: In sets only						
1984(l)	25,000	—	—	—	3.00	—
Note: In sets only						
1984(l) Proof	15,000	Value: 4.00				
1984(l) Proof	15,000	Value: 4.00				
1985(c)	20,000	—	—	1.00	3.00	—
1985(c)	20,000	—	—	1.00	3.00	—
1985(c) Proof	12,000	Value: 4.00				
1985(c) Proof	12,000	Value: 4.00				

KM# 41.2 10 CENTS

5.6500 g., Copper-Nickel, 23.62 mm. **Obv:** Crowned bust right **Rev. Designer:** James Berry **Note:** Recut due, low relief.

Date	Mintage	F	VF	XF	Unc	BU
1985(o)	8,000,000	—	—	1.00	3.00	—
Note: Wiry hair, bushy eyebrow						

KM# 61 10 CENTS

5.6500 g., Copper-Nickel, 23.62 mm. **Ruler:** Elizabeth II **Obv:** Crowned head right **Obv. Designer:** R.D. Maklouf **Rev:** Value above Maori mask, koruru **Rev. Designer:** James Berry

Date	Mintage	F	VF	XF	Unc	BU
1986(l)	18,000	—	—	—	3.00	—
Note: In sets only						
1986(l) Proof	10,000	Value: 4.00				
1987(o)	21,000,000	—	—	0.10	1.00	—
1987(l)	18,000	—	—	0.50	2.00	—
1987(l) Proof	10,000	Value: 3.00				
1988(c)	26,702,000	—	—	0.10	0.50	—
1988(l)	15,000	—	—	0.50	1.00	—
1988(l) Proof	9,000	Value: 3.00				
1989(o)	9,000,000	—	—	—	0.50	—
1989(c) Proof	8,500	Value: 3.00				
1990(c)	18,000	—	—	—	2.00	—
Note: In sets only						
1990(c) Proof	10,000	Value: 3.00				
1991(c)	20,000	—	—	—	2.00	—
Note: In sets only						
1991(c) Proof	15,000	Value: 3.00				
1992	15,000	—	—	—	2.00	—
Note: In sets only						
1992 Proof	9,000	Value: 3.00				
1993	15,000	—	—	—	2.00	—
Note: In sets only						
1993 Proof	10,000	Value: 3.00				
1994	—	—	—	—	2.00	—
Note: In sets only						
1994 Proof	10,000	Value: 3.00				
1995	—	—	—	—	1.00	—
Note: In sets only						
1995 Proof	4,000	Value: 3.00				
1996(n)	12,960,000	—	—	—	1.00	—
1996(l) Proof	4,000	Value: 3.00				
1997(n)	8,000,000	—	—	—	1.00	—
1997(l) Proof	2,500	Value: 3.00				
1998	—	—	—	—	0.80	—
Note: In sets only						
1998(l) Proof	6,000	Value: 3.00				

KM# 73 10 CENTS

5.6500 g., Copper-Nickel, 23.62 mm. **Ruler:** Elizabeth II **Subject:** 1990 Anniversary Celebrations **Obv:** Crowned head right **Rev:** Value above sailboats within rainbow design

Date	Mintage	F	VF	XF	Unc	BU
1990	10,000	—	—	—	10.00	—

KM# 73a 10 CENTS

6.5300 g., 0.9250 Silver .1942 oz. ASW, 23.62 mm. **Ruler:** Elizabeth II **Subject:** 1990 Anniversary Celebrations **Obv:** Crowned head right **Rev:** Value above sailboats within rainbow design

Date	Mintage	F	VF	XF	Unc	BU
1990 Proof	7,000	Value: 10.00				

KM# 117 10 CENTS

5.6500 g., Copper-Nickel, 23.62 mm. **Ruler:** Elizabeth II **Obv:** Head with tiara right **Rev:** Value above koruru **Rev. Designer:** James Berry **Note:** Many recalled and melted in 2006.

Date	Mintage	F	VF	XF	Unc	BU
1999(l)	7,000	—	—	—	4.00	—
Note: In sets only						
1999(l) Proof	2,000	Value: 10.00				
2000(o)	11,000,000	—	—	0.10	1.00	—
2000(l)	3,000	—	—	—	12.00	—
2000(l) Proof	1,500	Value: 15.00				

KM# 36.1 20 CENTS

11.3100 g., Copper-Nickel, 28.58 mm. **Ruler:** Elizabeth II **Obv:** Young bust right **Obv. Designer:** Arnold Machin **Rev:** Value below Kiwi bird with sprigs above **Rev. Designer:** James Berry **Note:** Rounded, high relief portrait. Prev. KM#36.

Date	Mintage	F	VF	XF	Unc	BU
1967(l)	13,000,000	—	—	0.10	1.00	—
1967(l)	13,000,000	—	—	0.10	1.00	—
1967(l) Prooflike	50,000	—	—	—	—	1.00
1967(l) Prooflike	50,000	—	—	—	—	1.00
1967(l) Proof	10	—	—	—	—	—
1967(l) Proof	10	—	—	—	—	—
1968	35,000	—	—	—	2.00	—
Note: In sets only						
1968	35,000	—	—	—	2.00	—
Note: In sets only						
1968 Prooflike	40,000	—	—	—	—	2.00
1968 Prooflike	40,000	—	—	—	—	2.00
1969	2,500,000	—	—	0.20	1.00	—
1969	2,500,000	—	—	0.20	1.00	—
1969 Prooflike	50,000	—	—	—	—	2.00
1969 Prooflike	50,000	—	—	—	—	2.00
1970	30,000	—	—	—	2.00	—
Note: In sets only						
1970	30,000	—	—	—	2.00	—
Note: In sets only						
1970 Prooflike	20,010	—	—	—	—	3.00
1970 Prooflike	20,010	—	—	—	—	3.00
1971(c)	1,600,000	—	0.20	5.00	40.00	—
Note: Serifs on date numerals						
1971(c)	1,600,000	—	0.20	5.00	40.00	—
Note: Serifs on date numerals						
1971(l)	15,000	—	—	1.00	4.00	—
Note: Without serifs						
1971(l)	15,000	—	—	1.00	4.00	—
Note: Without serifs						
1971(l) Proof	5,000	Value: 10.00				
1971(l) Proof	5,000	Value: 10.00				
1972(c)	1,531,000	—	—	0.20	2.00	—
1972(c)	1,531,000	—	—	0.20	2.00	—
1972(c) Proof	8,000	Value: 12.50				
1972(c) Proof	8,000	Value: 12.50				
1973(c)	3,043,000	—	—	0.20	2.00	—
1973(c)	3,043,000	—	—	0.20	2.00	—
1973(c) Proof	8,000	Value: 7.00				
1973(c) Proof	8,000	Value: 7.00				
1974(c)	4,527,000	—	—	0.20	5.00	—
1974(c)	4,527,000	—	—	0.20	5.00	—
1974(c) Proof	8,000	Value: 8.00				
1974(c) Proof	8,000	Value: 8.00				
1975(l)	5,015,000	—	—	0.20	2.00	—
1975(l)	5,015,000	—	—	0.20	2.00	—
1975(l) Proof	12,000	Value: 6.50				
1975(l) Proof	12,000	Value: 6.50				
1976(l)	7,516,000	—	—	0.20	2.00	—
1976(l)	7,516,000	—	—	0.20	2.00	—
1976(l) Proof	11,000	Value: 6.00				
1976(l) Proof	11,000	Value: 6.00				
1977(l)	7,500,000	—	—	0.20	2.00	—
1977(l)	7,500,000	—	—	0.20	2.00	—
1977(l) Proof	12,000	Value: 6.50				
1977(l) Proof	12,000	Value: 6.50				
1978(o)	2,523,000	—	—	0.20	2.00	—
1978(o)	2,523,000	—	—	0.20	2.00	—
1978(o) Proof	15,000	Value: 5.00				
1978(o) Proof	15,000	Value: 5.00				
1979(o)	8,025,000	—	—	0.20	2.00	—
1979(o)	8,025,000	—	—	0.20	2.00	—
1979(o) Proof	16,000	Value: 5.00				
1979(o) Proof	16,000	Value: 5.00				
1980(l)	27,000	—	—	0.15	1.00	—
Note: Round O in date						
1980(l)	27,000	—	—	0.15	1.00	—
Note: Round O in date						
1980(l) Proof	17,000	Value: 5.00				
1980(l) Proof	17,000	Value: 5.00				
1980(o)	9,000,000	—	—	0.15	2.00	—
Note: Oval O in date						
1980(o)	9,000,000	—	—	0.15	2.00	—
Note: Oval O in date						
1981(o)	7,500,000	—	—	0.15	1.00	—
Note: Oval holes in 8						
1981(o)	7,500,000	—	—	0.15	1.00	—
Note: Oval holes in 8						
1981(l)	25,000	—	—	0.15	2.00	—
Note: Round holes in 8						
1981(l)	25,000	—	—	0.15	2.00	—
Note: Round holes in 8						
1981(l) Proof	18,000	Value: 4.00				
1981(l) Proof	18,000	Value: 4.00				
1982(o)	17,500,000	—	—	0.15	2.00	—
Note: Blunt 2						
1982(o)	17,500,000	—	—	0.15	2.00	—
Note: Blunt 2						
1982(l)	25,000	—	—	0.15	1.00	—
Note: Pointed 2						
1982(l)	25,000	—	—	0.15	1.00	—
Note: Pointed 2						
1982(l) Proof	18,000	Value: 5.00				
1982(l) Proof	18,000	Value: 5.00				
1983(o)	2,500,000	—	—	0.15	3.00	—
Note: Round topped 3						
1983(o)	2,500,000	—	—	0.15	3.00	—
Note: Round topped 3						
1983(l)	25,000	—	—	0.15	1.00	—
Note: Flat topped 3						
1983(l)	25,000	—	—	0.15	1.00	—
Note: Flat topped 3						
1983(l) Proof	18,000	Value: 4.00				
1983(l) Proof	18,000	Value: 4.00				
1984(l)	25,000	—	—	0.15	1.00	—
1984(l)	25,000	—	—	0.15	1.00	—
1984(l) Proof	18,000	Value: 4.00				
1984(l) Proof	18,000	Value: 4.00				
1985(c)	20,000	—	—	0.15	1.00	—
Note: Round tip 5						
1985(c)	20,000	—	—	0.15	1.00	—
Note: Round tip 5						
1985(c) Proof	12,000	Value: 4.00				
1985(c) Proof	12,000	Value: 4.00				

KM# 36.2 20 CENTS

11.3100 g., Copper-Nickel, 28.58 mm. **Obv:** Crowned bust right **Obv. Designer:** Arnold Machin **Rev. Designer:** James Berry **Note:** Die recut, low relief.

Date	Mintage	F	VF	XF	Unc	BU
1984(o)	1,500,000	—	—	0.15	2.00	—
1985(o)	6,000,000	—	—	0.15	2.00	—

KM# 62 20 CENTS

11.3100 g., Copper-Nickel, 28.58 mm. **Ruler:** Elizabeth II **Obv:** Crowned head right **Obv. Designer:** R.D. Maklouf **Rev:** Kiwi **Rev. Designer:** James Berry

Date	Mintage	F	VF	XF	Unc	BU
1986(o)	12,500,000	—	—	0.15	1.00	—
1986(l)	18,000	—	—	0.50	2.00	—
1986(l) Proof	10,000	Value: 4.00				
1987(o)	14,000,000	—	—	0.15	1.00	—
1987(l)	18,000	—	—	0.50	2.00	—
1987(l) Proof	10,000	Value: 4.00				
1988(c)	12,500,000	—	—	0.15	1.00	—
1988(l)	15,000	—	—	0.50	2.00	—
1988(l) Proof	9,000	Value: 4.00				
1989(o)	5,000,000	—	—	0.15	1.00	—
1989(o) Proof	8,500	Value: 4.00				
1989(c)	15,000	—	—	—	2.00	—

KM# 74 20 CENTS

11.3100 g., Copper-Nickel, 28.58 mm. **Ruler:** Elizabeth II **Subject:** 1990 Anniversary Celebrations **Obv:** Crowned head right **Rev:** Ship, H.M.S. Tory

Date	Mintage	F	VF	XF	Unc	BU
1990(c)	10,000	—	—	—	10.00	—

KM# 74a 20 CENTS

13.0700 g., 0.9250 Silver .3887 oz. ASW, 28.58 mm. **Ruler:** Elizabeth II **Subject:** 1990 Anniversary Celebrations **Obv:** Crowned head right **Rev:** Ship, H.M.S. Tory

Date	Mintage	F	VF	XF	Unc	BU
1990(c) Proof	7,000	Value: 12.00				

KM# 81 20 CENTS

11.3100 g., Copper-Nickel, 28.58 mm. **Ruler:** Elizabeth II **Obv:** Crowned head right **Rev:** Value below Hei Tiki **Rev. Designer:** Pukaki

Date	Mintage	F	VF	XF	Unc	BU
1990(l)	5,000,000	—	—	0.20	1.00	—
1990(c)	18,000	—	—	0.50	2.00	—
1990(c) Proof	10,000	Value: 4.00				
1991(c)	20,000	—	—	—	3.00	—
Note: In sets only						
1991(c) Proof	15,000	Value: 4.00				
1992(l)	15,000	—	—	—	4.00	—
Note: In sets only						
1992(l) Proof	9,000	Value: 4.00				
1993(l)	15,000	—	—	—	4.00	—
Note: In sets only						
1993(l) Proof	10,000	Value: 4.00				
1994(l)	16,000	—	—	—	4.00	—
Note: In sets only						
1994(l) Proof	10,000	Value: 5.00				
1995(l)	6,000	—	—	—	4.00	—
Note: In sets only						
1995(l) Proof	6,000	Value: 10.00				
1996(l)	6,000	—	—	—	5.00	—
Note: In sets only						
1997(l)	3,500	—	—	—	5.00	—
Note: In sets only						
1997(l) Proof	2,500	Value: 10.00				
1998(l)	4,000	—	—	—	5.00	—
Note: In sets only						
1998(l) Proof	2,000	Value: 10.00				

KM# 81a 20 CENTS

13.0700 g., 0.9250 Silver .3887 oz. ASW, 28.58 mm. **Ruler:** Elizabeth II **Obv:** Crowned head right **Rev:** Value below Hei Tiki

Date	Mintage	F	VF	XF	Unc	BU
1995(l) Proof	Est. 2,500	Value: 15.00				

KM# 118 20 CENTS

11.3100 g., Copper-Nickel, 28.58 mm. **Ruler:** Elizabeth II **Obv:** Head with tiara right **Rev:** Value below Hei Tiki **Note:** Many recalled and melted in 2006.

Date	Mintage	F	VF	XF	Unc	BU
1999(l)	5,000	—	—	—	5.00	—
Note: In sets only						
1999(l) Proof	2,000	Value: 10.00				
2000(l)	3,000	—	—	—	5.00	—
Note: In sets only						
2000(l) Proof	1,500	Value: 10.00				

KM# 37.1 50 CENTS

13.6100 g., Copper-Nickel, 31.75 mm. **Ruler:** Elizabeth II **Obv:** Young bust right **Obv. Designer:** Arnold Machin **Rev:** Ship, H.M.S. Endeavour **Rev. Designer:** James Berry **Note:** Rounded, high relief portrait.

Date	Mintage	F	VF	XF	Unc	BU
1967(l)	10,000,000	—	—	0.30	1.00	—
1967(l)	Est. 750,000	—	5.00	20.00	100	—
Note: Dot above 1						
1967(l) Prooflike	50,000	—	—	—	—	2.00
1967(l)	10	—	—	—	—	—
1968	35,000	—	—	—	2.00	—
Note: In sets only						
1968 Prooflike	40,000	—	—	—	—	3.00
1970	30,000	—	—	—	2.00	—
Note: In sets only						
1970 Prooflike	20,010	—	—	—	—	3.00
1971(c)	1,123,000	0.15	1.00	5.00	40.00	—
Note: Serifs on date numerals						
1971(l)	15,000	—	—	0.50	5.00	—
Note: Without serifs						
1971(l) Proof	5,000	Value: 40.00				
1972(c)	1,423,000	—	—	0.50	5.00	—
1972(c) Proof	8,045	Value: 15.00				
1973(c)	2,523,000	—	—	0.50	5.00	—
1973(c) Proof	8,000	Value: 10.00				
1974(c)	1,215,000	—	—	0.50	5.00	—
1974(c) Proof	8,000	Value: 10.00				
1975(l)	3,815,000	—	—	0.50	4.00	—
1975(l) Proof	10,000	Value: 7.50				
1976(l)	2,016,000	—	—	0.50	3.00	—
1976(l) Proof	11,000	Value: 7.50				
1977(l)	2,000,000	—	—	0.50	3.00	—
1977(l) Proof	12,000	Value: 7.50				
1978(o)	2,023,000	—	—	0.50	3.00	—
1978(o) Proof	15,000	Value: 6.00				
1979(o)	2,425,000	—	—	0.50	3.00	—
1979(o) Proof	16,000	Value: 6.00				
1980(l)	27,000	—	—	0.50	2.00	—
Note: Thick 8 in date						
1980(l) Proof	17,000	Value: 6.00				
1980(o)	8,000,000	—	0.30	0.50	3.00	—
Note: Thin 8 in date						
1981(o)	4,000,000	—	0.30	0.50	3.00	—
Note: Blunt end on 9, oval holes in 8						
1981(l)	25,000	—	—	0.50	2.00	—
Note: Pointed end on 9, round holes in 8						
1981(l) Proof	18,000	Value: 6.00				
1982(o)	6,000,000	—	—	0.50	3.00	—
Note: Blunt end on 2						
1982(l)	25,000	—	—	0.50	3.00	—
Note: Pointed end on 2						
1982(l) Proof	18,000	Value: 6.00				
1983(l)	25,000	—	—	—	3.00	—
Note: In sets only						
1983(l) Proof	18,000	Value: 6.00				
1984(l)	25,000	—	—	0.50	3.00	—
1984(l) Proof	15,000	Value: 5.00				
1985(c)	20,000	—	—	0.50	3.00	—
1985(c) Proof	12,000	Value: 5.00				

KM# 39 50 CENTS

13.6100 g., Copper-Nickel, 31.75 mm. **Ruler:** Elizabeth II **Subject:** 200th Anniversary - Captain Cook's Voyage **Obv:** Young bust right **Obv. Designer:** Arnold Machin **Rev:** Ship, H.M.S. Endeavour **Edge Lettering:** Cook Bi-Centenary 1769-1969 **Note:** Similar to KM#37.

Date	Mintage	F	VF	XF	Unc	BU
1969	50,000	—	—	1.00	3.00	—
1969 Prooflike	50,000	—	—	—	—	3.00

KM# 37.2 50 CENTS

13.6100 g., Copper-Nickel, 31.75 mm. **Obv:** Crowned bust right **Rev:** Value in upper left **Note:** Recut die, low relief.

Date	Mintage	F	VF	XF	Unc	BU
1984(o)	2,000,000	—	—	—	3.00	—
1985(o)	2,000,000	—	—	0.50	4.00	—

KM# 95 50 CENTS

Nickel **Ruler:** Elizabeth II **Obv:** Young bust right **Obv. Designer:** Arnold Machin **Rev:** Voyageur, date and value below **Note:** Mule.

Date	Mintage	F	VF	XF	Unc	BU
1985 6 known	—	—	1,200	1,900	—	—

KM# 63 50 CENTS

13.6100 g., Copper-Nickel, 31.75 mm. **Ruler:** Elizabeth II **Obv:** Crowned head right **Obv. Designer:** R.D. Maklouf **Rev:** Ship, H.M.S. Endeavour **Rev. Designer:** James Berry

Date	Mintage	F	VF	XF	Unc	BU
1986(o)	5,200,000	—	—	0.50	2.00	—
1986(l)	18,000	—	—	1.00	2.00	—
1986(l) Proof	10,000	Value: 5.00				
1987(o)	3,600,000	—	—	0.50	2.00	—
1987(l)	18,000	—	—	1.00	2.00	—
1987(l) Proof	10,000	Value: 5.00				
1988(c)	8,800,000	—	—	0.50	2.00	—
1988(l)	15,000	—	—	1.00	2.00	—
1988(l) Proof	9,000	Value: 5.00				
1989(c)	15,000	—	—	—	3.00	—
Note: In sets only						
1989(c) Proof	8,500	Value: 5.00				
1990(c)	18,000	—	—	—	5.00	—
Note: In sets only						
1990(c) Proof	10,000	Value: 5.00				
1991(c)	20,000	—	—	—	3.00	—
Note: In sets only						
1991(c) Proof	15,000	Value: 5.00				
1992(l)	15,000	—	—	—	4.00	—
Note: In sets only						
1992(l) Proof	9,000	Value: 5.00				
1993(l)	15,000	—	—	—	4.00	—
Note: In sets only						
1993(l) Proof	10,000	Value: 5.00				
1995(l)	10,000	—	—	—	4.00	—
Note: In sets only						
1995(l) Proof	4,000	Value: 5.00				
1996(l)	6,000	—	—	—	4.00	—
Note: In sets only						
1996(l) Proof	2,500	Value: 5.00				
1997(l)	5,500	—	—	—	5.00	—
Note: In sets only						
1997(l) Proof	2,500	Value: 5.00				
1998(l)	4,000	—	—	—	4.00	—
Note: In sets only						
1998(l) Proof	2,000	Value: 5.00				

KM# 75 50 CENTS

13.6100 g., Copper-Nickel, 31.75 mm. **Ruler:** Elizabeth II **Subject:** 1990 Anniversary Celebrations **Obv:** Crowned head right **Rev:** Child with shovel sitting beside tree, value slanted at right

Date	Mintage	F	VF	XF	Unc	BU
1990(c)	10,000	—	—	—	8.00	—

KM# 75a 50 CENTS

15.7400 g., 0.9250 Silver .4682 oz. ASW, 31.75 mm. **Ruler:** Elizabeth II **Subject:** 1990 Anniversary Celebrations **Obv:** Crowned head right **Rev:** Child with shovel sitting beside tree with slanted value at right

Date	Mintage	F	VF	XF	Unc	BU
1990(c) Proof	7,000	Value: 20.00				

KM# 90 50 CENTS
Ring Composition: Copper-Nickel **Center Composition:** Aluminum-Bronze, 32 mm. **Ruler:** Elizabeth II **Subject:** H.M.S. Endeavour **Obv:** Crowned head right within circle **Rev:** Sailing ship within circle **Rev. Designer:** James Berry

Date	Mintage	F	VF	XF	Unc	BU
1994	52,500	—	—	—	15.00	—

KM# 90a 50 CENTS
Ring Composition: 0.9250 Silver **Center Composition:** Aluminum-Bronze, 32 mm. **Ruler:** Elizabeth II **Subject:** H.M.S. Endeavour **Obv:** Crowned head right within circle **Rev:** Sailing ship within circle

Date	Mintage	F	VF	XF	Unc	BU
1994 Proof	10,000	Value: 25.00				

KM# 90b 50 CENTS
Ring Composition: 0.3750 Gold **Center Composition:** 0.9160 Gold, 32 mm. **Ruler:** Elizabeth II **Subject:** H.M.S. Endeavour **Obv:** Crowned head right within circle **Rev:** Sailing ship within circle

Date	Mintage	F	VF	XF	Unc	BU
1994 Proof	500	Value: 400				

KM# 119 50 CENTS
13.6100 g., Copper-Nickel, 31.75 mm. **Ruler:** Elizabeth II **Obv:** Head with tiara right **Rev:** Ship, H.M.S. Endeavour **Rev. Designer:** James Berry **Note:** Many recalled and melted in 2006.

Date	Mintage	F	VF	XF	Unc	BU
1999	5,000	—	—	—	4.00	—
Note: In sets only						
1999 Proof	2,000	Value: 5.00				
2000	1,500	—	—	—	4.00	—
Note: In sets only						
2000 Proof	1,500	Value: 5.00				

KM# 38.1 DOLLAR
Copper-Nickel, 38.8 mm. **Ruler:** Elizabeth II **Subject:** Decimalization Commemorative **Obv:** Young bust right **Obv. Designer:** Arnold Machin **Rev:** Crowned shield within silver fern leaves **Rev. Designer:** William Gardner **Edge:** DECIMAL CURRENCY INTRODUCED JULY 10 1967

Date	Mintage	F	VF	XF	Unc	BU
1967(l)	250,000	—	—	0.75	1.00	—
1967 Prooflike	50,000	—	—	—	—	2.00
1967 Proof	10	—	—	—	—	—

KM# 38.2 DOLLAR
Copper-Nickel, 38.8 mm. **Ruler:** Elizabeth II **Obv:** Young bust right **Obv. Designer:** Arnold Machin **Rev:** Crowned shield within silver fern leaves **Rev. Designer:** William Gardner **Edge:** Reeded **Note:** Regular issue.

Date	Mintage	F	VF	XF	Unc	BU
1971(l)	45,000	—	—	2.00	3.00	—
1971 Proof	5,000	Value: 25.00				
1972(c)	42,000	—	—	2.00	3.00	—
1972 Proof	8,045	Value: 10.00				
1972 RAM case; Proof	3,000	Value: 30.00				
1973(c)	37,000	—	—	2.00	3.00	—
1973 Proof	16,000	Value: 5.00				
1975(l)	30,000	—	—	2.00	3.00	—
1975 Proof	20,000	Value: 5.00				
1976(l)	36,000	—	—	2.00	4.00	—
1976 Proof	22,000	Value: 5.00				

KM# 40.1 DOLLAR
Copper-Nickel, 38.8 mm. **Ruler:** Elizabeth II **Subject:** 200th Anniversary - Captain Cook's Voyage **Obv:** Young bust right **Obv. Designer:** Arnold Machin **Rev:** Map flanked by bust at left and ship at right **Rev. Designer:** James Berry **Edge:** COMMEMORATING COOK BI-CENTENERY 1769-1969

Date	Mintage	F	VF	XF	Unc	BU
1969(c)	450,000	—	—	1.00	2.00	—
1969 Prooflike	50,000	—	—	—	—	3.00

KM# 40.2 DOLLAR
Copper-Nickel, 38.8 mm. **Ruler:** Elizabeth II **Obv:** Young bust right **Obv. Designer:** Arnold Machin **Rev:** Map flanked by bust at left and ship at right **Rev. Designer:** James Berry **Edge:** No hyphen in edge inscription

Date	Mintage	F	VF	XF	Unc	BU
1969(c)	Inc. above	—	—	—	4.00	—

KM# 40.3 DOLLAR
Copper Nickel, 38.8 mm. **Ruler:** Elizabeth II **Obv:** Young bust right **Obv. Designer:** Arnold Machin **Rev:** Map flanked by bust at left and ship at right **Rev. Designer:** James Berry **Edge Lettering:** No I in BI-CENTENARY

Date	Mintage	F	VF	XF	Unc	BU
1969(c)	Inc. above	—	—	—	—	—

KM# 42 DOLLAR
Copper-Nickel, 38.8 mm. **Ruler:** Elizabeth II **Subject:** Royal Visit **Obv:** Young bust right **Obv. Designer:** Arnold Machin **Rev:** Mount Cook, known as Aorangi **Rev. Designer:** James Berry

Date	Mintage	F	VF	XF	Unc	BU
1970(c)	315,000	—	—	0.75	1.00	—
1970 Prooflike	20,000	—	—	—	—	2.00

KM# 43 DOLLAR
Copper-Nickel, 38.8 mm. **Ruler:** Elizabeth II **Subject:** Cook Islands **Obv:** Young bust right **Obv. Designer:** Arnold Machin **Rev:** Sailing ship to left of bust 1/4 left **Rev. Designer:** James Berry

Date	Mintage	F	VF	XF	Unc	BU
1970	25,070	—	—	4.00	9.00	—
1970 Proof	5,030	Value: 30.00				

KM# 44 DOLLAR
Copper-Nickel, 38.8 mm. **Ruler:** Elizabeth II **Subject:** Commonwealth Games **Obv:** Young bust right **Obv. Designer:** Arnold Machin **Rev:** Square emblem flanked by athletes **Rev. Designer:** Paul Beadle

Date	Mintage	F	VF	XF	Unc	BU
1974	515,000	—	—	1.00	1.75	—

KM# 44a DOLLAR
27.2160 g., 0.9250 Silver .8095 oz. ASW, 38.8 mm. **Ruler:** Elizabeth II **Subject:** Commonwealth Games **Obv:** Young bust right **Obv. Designer:** Arnold Machin **Rev:** Square emblem flanked by athletes

Date	Mintage	F	VF	XF	Unc	BU
1974 Proof	18,000	Value: 15.00				

KM# 45 DOLLAR
Copper-Nickel, 38.8 mm. **Ruler:** Elizabeth II **Subject:** New Zealand Day **Obv:** Young bust right **Obv. Designer:** Arnold Machin **Rev:** Great Egret **Rev. Designer:** James Berry

Date	Mintage	F	VF	XF	Unc	BU
1974(c)	50,000	—	—	3.00	5.00	12.00
1974 Proof	5,000	Value: 40.00				

KM# 46 DOLLAR

Copper-Nickel, 38.8 mm. **Ruler:** Elizabeth II **Subject:** Waitangi Day and Queen's 25th Anniversary **Obv:** Young bust right **Obv. Designer:** Arnold Machin **Rev:** Treaty House **Rev. Designer:** James Berry

Date	Mintage	F	VF	XF	Unc	BU
1977	90,000	—	—	2.00	3.00	—

KM# 46a DOLLAR

27.2160 g., 0.9250 Silver .8095 oz. ASW, 38.8 mm. **Ruler:** Elizabeth II **Subject:** Waitangi Day and Queen's 25th Anniversary **Obv:** Young bust right **Obv. Designer:** Arnold Machin **Rev:** Treaty House

Date	Mintage	F	VF	XF	Unc	BU
1977 Proof	27,000	Value: 12.00				

KM# 47 DOLLAR

Copper-Nickel, 38.8 mm. **Ruler:** Elizabeth II **Subject:** 25th Anniversary of Coronation and Opening of Parliament Building **Obv:** Young bust right **Obv. Designer:** Arnold Machin **Rev:** Parliament Building **Rev. Designer:** James Berry

Date	Mintage	F	VF	XF	Unc	BU
1978(l)	123,000	—	—	1.00	2.00	—

KM# 47a DOLLAR

27.2160 g., 0.9250 Silver .8095 oz. ASW, 38.8 mm. **Ruler:** Elizabeth II **Subject:** 25th Anniversary of Coronation and Opening of Parliament Building **Obv:** Young bust right **Obv. Designer:** Arnold Machin **Rev:** Parliament Building

Date	Mintage	F	VF	XF	Unc	BU
1978(o) Proof	33,000	Value: 12.00				

KM# 48 DOLLAR

Copper-Nickel, 38.8 mm. **Ruler:** Elizabeth II **Obv:** New head right **Obv. Designer:** James Berry **Rev:** Crowned shield within silver fern **Rev. Designer:** William Gardner

Date	Mintage	F	VF	XF	Unc	BU
1979(o)	25,000	—	—	1.00	2.00	—
1979(o) Proof	85,000	—	—	—	4.00	—

KM# 48a DOLLAR

27.2160 g., 0.9250 Silver .8095 oz. ASW, 38.8 mm. **Ruler:** Elizabeth II **Obv:** New head right **Obv. Designer:** John Berry **Rev:** Crowned shield within silver fern **Rev. Designer:** William Gardner

Date	Mintage	F	VF	XF	Unc	BU
1979(o) Proof	35,000	Value: 12.00				

KM# 49 DOLLAR

Copper-Nickel, 38.8 mm. **Ruler:** Elizabeth II **Obv:** New head right **Obv. Designer:** John Berry **Rev:** Fantail bird sitting on branch **Rev. Designer:** James Berry

Date	Mintage	F	VF	XF	Unc	BU
1980(l)	115,000	—	—	1.00	3.00	6.50

KM# 49a DOLLAR

27.2160 g., 0.9250 Silver .8095 oz. ASW, 38.8 mm. **Ruler:** Elizabeth II **Obv:** New head right **Obv. Designer:** John Berry **Rev:** Fantail bird sitting on branch **Rev. Designer:** James Berry

Date	Mintage	F	VF	XF	Unc	BU
1980 Proof	44,000	Value: 20.00				

KM# 50 DOLLAR

Copper-Nickel, 38.8 mm. **Ruler:** Elizabeth II **Subject:** Royal Visit **Obv:** New head right **Obv. Designer:** John Berry **Rev:** English Oak **Rev. Designer:** Paul Beadle

Date	Mintage	F	VF	XF	Unc	BU
1981(l)	100,000	—	—	1.00	2.00	—

KM# 50a DOLLAR

27.2160 g., 0.9250 Silver .8095 oz. ASW, 38.8 mm. **Ruler:** Elizabeth II **Subject:** Royal Visit **Obv:** New head right **Obv. Designer:** John Berry **Rev:** English Oak **Rev. Designer:** Paul Beadle

Date	Mintage	F	VF	XF	Unc	BU
1981 Proof	38,000	Value: 12.00				

KM# 51 DOLLAR

Copper-Nickel, 38.8 mm. **Ruler:** Elizabeth II **Obv:** New head right **Obv. Designer:** John Berry **Rev:** Takahe bird **Rev. Designer:** James Berry

Date	Mintage	F	VF	XF	Unc	BU
1982(l)	65,000	—	—	1.00	7.00	10.00

KM# 51a DOLLAR

27.2160 g., 0.9250 Silver .8095 oz. ASW, 38.8 mm. **Ruler:** Elizabeth II **Obv:** New head right **Obv. Designer:** John Berry **Rev:** Takahe bird **Rev. Designer:** James Berry

Date	Mintage	F	VF	XF	Unc	BU
1982 Proof	35,000	Value: 15.00				

KM# 52 DOLLAR

Copper-Nickel, 38.8 mm. **Ruler:** Elizabeth II **Subject:** Royal Visit **Obv:** Young bust right **Obv. Designer:** Arnold Machin **Rev:** Conjoined busts of Prince Charles and Lady Diana right **Rev. Designer:** Philip Nathan

Date	Mintage	F	VF	XF	Unc	BU
1983(l)	40,000	—	—	1.00	4.00	—

KM# 52a DOLLAR

27.2160 g., 0.9250 Silver .8095 oz. ASW, 38.8 mm. **Ruler:** Elizabeth II **Subject:** Royal Visit **Obv:** Young bust right **Obv. Designer:** Arnold Machin **Rev:** Conjoined busts of Prince Charles and Lady Diana right

Date	Mintage	F	VF	XF	Unc	BU
1983 Proof	17,000	Value: 12.00				

KM# 53 DOLLAR

Copper-Nickel, 38.8 mm. **Ruler:** Elizabeth II **Subject:** 50 Years of New Zealand Coinage **Obv:** Young bust right **Rev:** Crowned arms with supporters above various coins **Rev. Designer:** Philip Nathan

Date	Mintage	F	VF	XF	Unc	BU
1983(l)	65,000	—	—	1.00	4.00	—

KM# 53a DOLLAR

27.2160 g., 0.9250 Silver .8095 oz. ASW, 38.8 mm. **Ruler:** Elizabeth II **Subject:** 50 Years of New Zealand Coinage **Obv:** Young bust right **Obv. Designer:** Arnold Machin **Rev:** Crowned arms with supporters above various coins **Rev. Designer:** Philip Nathan

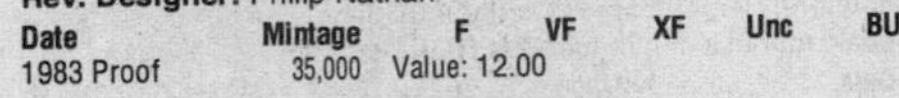

Date	Mintage	F	VF	XF	Unc	BU
1983 Proof	35,000	Value: 12.00				

KM# 54 DOLLAR

Copper-Nickel, 38.8 mm. **Ruler:** Elizabeth II **Subject:** Chatham Island Black Robin **Obv:** Young bust right **Obv. Designer:** Arnold Machin **Rev:** Black Robin on branch

Date	Mintage	F	VF	XF	Unc	BU
1984(l)	65,000	—	—	1.00	4.00	12.00

KM# 54a DOLLAR

27.2160 g., 0.9250 Silver .8095 oz. ASW, 38.8 mm. **Ruler:** Elizabeth II **Obv:** Young bust right **Obv. Designer:** Arnold Machin **Rev:** Chatham Island Black Robin

Date	Mintage	F	VF	XF	Unc	BU
1984 Proof	30,000	Value: 15.00				

KM# 55 DOLLAR

Copper-Nickel, 38.8 mm. **Ruler:** Elizabeth II **Subject:** Black Stilt **Obv:** Young bust right **Obv. Designer:** Arnold Machin

Date	Mintage	F	VF	XF	Unc	BU
1985(c)	60,000	—	—	1.00	3.00	6.50

KM# 55a DOLLAR

27.2160 g., 0.9250 Silver .8095 oz. ASW, 38.8 mm. **Ruler:** Elizabeth II **Subject:** Black Stilt **Obv:** Young bust right **Obv. Designer:** Arnold Machin **Rev:** Black stilt and chicks

Date	Mintage	F	VF	XF	Unc	BU
1985 Proof	25,000	Value: 15.00				

KM# 56 DOLLAR

Copper-Nickel, 38.8 mm. **Ruler:** Elizabeth II **Subject:** Royal Visit **Obv:** Crowned head right **Obv. Designer:** R.D. Maklouf **Rev:** Crowned E within wreath of houhere, clematis, Mt. Cook lilly, rata, pohutukawa, kowhai, kaka beak, manuka and fern fronds **Rev. Designer:** R. Maurice Conly

Date	Mintage	F	VF	XF	Unc	BU
1986(l)	40,000	—	—	1.00	3.00	—

KM# 56a DOLLAR

27.2160 g., 0.9250 Silver .8095 oz. ASW, 38.8 mm. **Ruler:** Elizabeth II **Subject:** Royal Visit **Obv:** Crowned head right **Obv. Designer:** R.D. Maklouf **Rev:** Crowned E within wreath of houhere, clematis, Mt. Cook lilly, rata, pohutukawa, kowhai, kaka beak, manuka and fern fronds **Rev. Designer:** R. Maurice Conly

Date	Mintage	F	VF	XF	Unc	BU
1986 Proof	12,500	Value: 12.00				

KM# 57 DOLLAR

Copper-Nickel, 38.8 mm. **Ruler:** Elizabeth II **Obv:** Crowned head right **Obv. Designer:** R.D. Maklouf **Rev:** Kakapo bird **Rev. Designer:** R. Maurice Conly

Date	Mintage	F	VF	XF	Unc	BU
1986(c)	53,000	—	—	1.00	3.00	6.50

KM# 57a DOLLAR

27.2160 g., 0.9250 Silver .8095 oz. ASW, 38.8 mm. **Ruler:** Elizabeth II **Obv:** Crowned head right **Obv. Designer:** R.D. Maklouf **Rev:** Kakapo bird **Rev. Designer:** R. Maurice Conly

Date	Mintage	F	VF	XF	Unc	BU
1986 Proof	20,500	Value: 20.00				

KM# 65 DOLLAR

Copper-Nickel, 38.8 mm. **Ruler:** Elizabeth II **Subject:** National Parks Centennial **Obv:** Crowned head right **Obv. Designer:** R.D. Maklouf **Rev:** Mountains within circular design

Date	Mintage	F	VF	XF	Unc	BU
1987(l)	53,000	—	—	1.00	3.00	—

KM# 65a DOLLAR

27.2160 g., 0.9250 Silver .8095 oz. ASW, 38.8 mm. **Ruler:** Elizabeth II **Subject:** National Parks Centennial **Obv:** Crowned head right **Obv. Designer:** R.D. Maklouf **Rev:** Mountains within circular design

Date	Mintage	F	VF	XF	Unc	BU
1987 Proof	20,500	Value: 12.00				

KM# 66 DOLLAR

Copper-Nickel, 38.8 mm. **Ruler:** Edward VIII **Obv:** Crowned head right **Obv. Designer:** R.D. Maklouf **Rev:** Yellow-eyed Penguin

Date	Mintage	F	VF	XF	Unc	BU
1988(l)	45,000	—	—	2.00	10.00	20.00

KM# 66a DOLLAR

27.2160 g., 0.9250 Silver .8095 oz. ASW, 38.8 mm. **Ruler:** Elizabeth II **Obv:** Crowned head right **Obv. Designer:** R.D. Maklouf **Rev:** Yellow-eyed Penguin

Date	Mintage	F	VF	XF	Unc	BU
1988 Proof	18,500	Value: 30.00				

KM# 67 DOLLAR

Copper-Nickel, 38.8 mm. **Ruler:** Elizabeth II **Subject:** XIV Commonwealth Games **Obv:** Crowned head right **Obv. Designer:** R.D. Maklouf **Rev:** Runner

Date	Mintage	F	VF	XF	Unc	BU
1989(c)	35,000	—	—	1.00	2.00	—

KM# 67a DOLLAR

27.2160 g., 0.9250 Silver .8095 oz. ASW, 38.8 mm. **Ruler:** Elizabeth II **Subject:** XIV Commonwealth Games **Obv:** Crowned head right **Obv. Designer:** R.D. Maklouf **Rev:** Runner

Date	Mintage	F	VF	XF	Unc	BU
1989 Proof	8,600	Value: 12.00				

KM# 68 DOLLAR

Copper-Nickel, 38.8 mm. **Ruler:** Elizabeth II **Subject:** XIV Commonwealth Games **Obv:** Crowned head right **Obv. Designer:** R.D. Maklouf **Rev:** Gymnast

Date	Mintage	F	VF	XF	Unc	BU
1989	35,000	—	—	1.00	2.00	—

KM# 68a DOLLAR

27.2160 g., 0.9250 Silver .8095 oz. ASW, 38.8 mm. **Ruler:** Elizabeth II **Subject:** XIV Commonwealth Games **Obv:** R.D. Maklouf **Rev:** Gymnast

Date	Mintage	F	VF	XF	Unc	BU
1989 Proof	8,600	Value: 12.00				

KM# 69 DOLLAR

Copper-Nickel, 38.8 mm. **Ruler:** Elizabeth II **Subject:** XIV Commonwealth Games **Obv:** Crowned head right **Obv. Designer:** R.D. Maklouf **Rev:** Swimmer

Date	Mintage	F	VF	XF	Unc	BU
1989	35,000	—	—	1.00	2.00	—

KM# 69a DOLLAR

27.2160 g., 0.9250 Silver .8095 oz. ASW, 38.8 mm. **Ruler:** Elizabeth II **Subject:** XIV Commonwealth Games **Obv:** Crowned head right **Obv. Designer:** R.D. Maklouf **Rev:** Swimmer

Date	Mintage	F	VF	XF	Unc	BU
1989 Proof	8,600	Value: 12.00				

KM# 70 DOLLAR

Copper-Nickel, 38.8 mm. **Ruler:** Elizabeth II **Subject:** XIV Commonwealth Games **Obv:** Crowned head right **Obv. Designer:** R.D. Maklouf **Rev:** Weight lifter

Date	Mintage	F	VF	XF	Unc	BU
1989	35,000	—	—	1.00	2.00	—

KM# 70a DOLLAR

27.2160 g., 0.9250 Silver .8095 oz. ASW, 38.8 mm. **Ruler:** Elizabeth II **Subject:** XIV Commonwealth Games **Obv:** Crowned head right **Obv. Designer:** R.D. Maklouf **Rev:** Weight lifter

Date	Mintage	F	VF	XF	Unc	BU
1989 Proof	8,600	Value: 12.00				

KM# 76 DOLLAR
Copper-Nickel, 38.8 mm. **Ruler:** Elizabeth II **Subject:** 1990 Anniversary Celebrations - Treaty of Waitangi **Obv:** Crowned head right **Obv. Designer:** R.D. Maklouf **Rev:** Treaty signing scene

Date	Mintage	F	VF	XF	Unc	BU
1990	—	—	—	1.00	3.00	—

KM# 76a DOLLAR
27.2160 g., 0.9250 Silver .8095 oz. ASW, 38.8 mm. **Ruler:** Elizabeth II **Subject:** 1990 Anniversary Celebrations - Treaty of Waitangi **Obv:** Crowned head right **Obv. Designer:** R.D. Maklouf **Rev:** Treaty signing scene

Date	Mintage	F	VF	XF	Unc	BU
1990 Proof	20,000	Value: 16.00				

KM# 78a DOLLAR
8.0000 g., 0.9250 Silver .2380 oz. ASW, 23 mm. **Ruler:** Elizabeth II **Obv:** Crowned head right **Obv. Designer:** R.D. Maklouf **Rev:** Kiwi Bird

Date	Mintage	F	VF	XF	Unc	BU
1990 Proof	10,000	Value: 30.00				

KM# 78 DOLLAR
8.0000 g., Aluminum-Bronze, 23 mm. **Ruler:** Elizabeth II **Obv:** Crowned head right **Obv. Designer:** R.D. Maklouf **Rev:** Kiwi Bird **Note:** Regular circulation issue.

Date	Mintage	F	VF	XF	Unc	BU
1990(l)	40,000,000	—	—	1.00	2.00	—
1990(c)	10,000	—	—	—	4.00	—
1991(l)	10,000,000	—	—	1.00	2.00	—
1991(c)	20,000	—	—	—	2.00	—
1991(c) Proof	15,000	Value: 20.00				
1992(l)	15,000	—	—	—	15.00	—
Note: In sets only						
1992(l) Proof	9,000	Value: 20.00				
1993(l)	15,000	—	—	—	10.00	—
Note: In sets only						
1993(l) Proof	10,000	Value: 20.00				
1994(l)	16,000	—	—	—	20.00	—
Note: In sets only						
1994(l) Proof	10,000	Value: 25.00				
1995(l)	10,000	—	—	—	20.00	—
Note: In sets only						
1995(l) Proof	4,000	Value: 25.00				
1996(l)	10,000	—	—	—	20.00	—
Note: In sets only						
1996(l) Proof	4,000	Value: 25.00				
1997(l)	2,500	—	—	—	20.00	—
Note: In sets only						
1997(l) Proof	2,500	Value: 25.00				
1998(l)	6,000	—	—	—	20.00	—
Note: In sets only						
1998(l) Proof	2,000	Value: 25.00				

KM# 120 DOLLAR
Aluminum-Bronze **Ruler:** Elizabeth II **Obv:** Head with tiara right **Obv. Designer:** Rank-Broadley **Rev:** Kiwi bird within sprigs **Rev. Designer:** R. Maurice Conly

Date	Mintage	F	VF	XF	Unc	BU
1999	5,000	—	—	—	—	20.00
Note: In sets only						
1999 Proof	2,000	Value: 20.00				
2000(o)	5,000,000	—	—	—	1.00	2.00
2000 Proof	1,500	Value: 5.00				

KM# 79 2 DOLLARS
10.0000 g., Aluminum-Bronze, 26.5 mm. **Ruler:** Elizabeth II **Obv:** Crowned head right **Obv. Designer:** R.D. Maklouf **Rev:** Kotuku, white heron **Rev. Designer:** R. Maurice Conly

Date	Mintage	F	VF	XF	Unc	BU
1990(l)	30,000,000	—	—	2.00	3.00	5.00
1990(c)	18,000	—	—	—	3.00	5.00
1990(l) Proof	10,000	Value: 6.00				
1991(l)	10,000,000	—	—	2.00	3.00	5.00
1991(c)	20,000	—	—	—	3.00	5.00
1991(c) Proof	15,000	Value: 6.00				
1992(l)	15,000	—	—	—	6.00	—
Note: In sets only						
1992(l) Proof	9,000	Value: 6.00				
1994(l)	16,000	—	—	—	6.00	—
Note: In sets only						
1994(l) Proof	10,000	Value: 6.00				
1995(l)	10,000	—	—	—	6.00	—
Note: In sets only						
1995(l) Proof	4,000	Value: 20.00				
1996(l)	10,000	—	—	—	20.00	—
Note: In sets only						
1996(l) Proof	4,000	Value: 20.00				
1997(p)	1,000,000	—	—	—	3.00	5.00
Note: Entire mintage recalled						
1998(p)	6,000,000	—	—	—	3.00	5.00
1998(p) Proof	2,000	Value: 6.00				

KM# 79a 2 DOLLARS
10.0000 g., 0.9250 Silver .2974 oz. ASW, 26.5 mm. **Ruler:** Elizabeth II **Obv:** Crowned head right **Obv. Designer:** R.D. Maklouf **Rev:** Kotuku, white heron **Rev. Designer:** R. Maurice Conly

Date	Mintage	F	VF	XF	Unc	BU
1990 Proof	10,000	Value: 25.00				

KM# 87 2 DOLLARS
Aluminum-Bronze **Ruler:** Elizabeth II **Obv:** Crowned head right **Rev:** Sacred Kingfisher

Date	Mintage	F	VF	XF	Unc	BU
1993	40,000	—	—	—	7.50	10.00

KM# 87a 2 DOLLARS
10.0000 g., 0.9250 Silver .2974 oz. ASW **Ruler:** Elizabeth II **Obv:** Crowned head right **Rev:** Sacred Kingfisher

Date	Mintage	F	VF	XF	Unc	BU
1993 Proof	10,000	Value: 20.00				

KM# 121 2 DOLLARS
10.0000 g., Aluminum-Bronze, 26.5 mm. **Ruler:** Elizabeth II **Obv:** Head with tiara right **Obv. Designer:** Rank-Broadley **Rev:** Heron above value **Rev. Designer:** R. Maurice Conley

Date	Mintage	F	VF	XF	Unc	BU
1999(p)	5,050,000	—	—	—	3.00	5.00
1999(l) Proof	2,000	Value: 25.00				
2000	3,000	—	—	—	2.50	50.00
Note: In sets only						
2000(l) Proof	1,500	Value: 25.00				

KM# 71 5 DOLLARS
Aluminum-Bronze **Ruler:** Elizabeth II **Obv:** Crowned head right **Rev:** ANZAC Memorial **Rev. Designer:** Horst Hahne

Date	Mintage	F	VF	XF	Unc	BU
1990 Proof	60,000	Value: 17.50				
Note: Set only, issued with Australian 1990 $5 as pair						

KM# 80 5 DOLLARS
Copper-Nickel **Ruler:** Elizabeth II **Subject:** Rugby World Cup **Obv:** Crowned head right **Obv. Designer:** R.D. Maklouf **Rev:** Champion cup flanked by rugby players

Date	Mintage	F	VF	XF	Unc	BU
1991	120,000	—	—	—	4.50	6.00

KM# 80a 5 DOLLARS
27.2200 g., 0.9250 Silver .8208 oz. ASW **Ruler:** Elizabeth II **Subject:** Rugby World Cup **Obv:** Crowned head right **Obv. Designer:** R.D. Maklouf **Rev:** Champion cup flanked by rugby players

Date	Mintage	F	VF	XF	Unc	BU
1991 Proof	30,000	Value: 16.00				

KM# 82 5 DOLLARS
Copper-Nickel **Ruler:** Elizabeth II **Subject:** 25th Anniversary of Decimal Currency **Obv:** Crowned head right **Obv. Designer:** R.D. Maklouf **Rev:** Silver fern leaf above various coins

Date	Mintage	F	VF	XF	Unc	BU
1992	34,000	—	—	—	5.00	6.00

KM# 82a 5 DOLLARS
27.2200 g., 0.9250 Silver .8095 oz. ASW **Ruler:** Elizabeth II **Subject:** 25th Anniversary of Decimal Currency **Obv:** Crowned head right **Obv. Designer:** R.D. Maklouf **Rev:** Silver fern leaf above various coins

Date	Mintage	F	VF	XF	Unc	BU
1992 Proof	17,000	Value: 16.00				

KM# 83 5 DOLLARS
Copper-Nickel **Ruler:** Elizabeth II **Series:** The Discoverers **Subject:** Mythological Maori Hero - Kupe **Obv:** Crowned head right **Obv. Designer:** R.D. Maklouf **Rev:** Bust right

Date	Mintage	F	VF	XF	Unc	BU
1992	40,000	—	—	—	5.00	—

KM# 84 5 DOLLARS
Copper-Nickel **Ruler:** Elizabeth II **Series:** The Discoverers **Subject:** Abel Tasman **Obv:** Crowned head right **Obv. Designer:** R.D. Maklouf **Rev. Designer:** Milena Milan

Date	Mintage	F	VF	XF	Unc	BU
1992	40,000	—	—	—	5.00	—

KM# 85 5 DOLLARS
Copper-Nickel **Ruler:** Elizabeth II **Series:** The Discoverers **Subject:** Captain James Cook **Obv:** Crowned head right **Obv. Designer:** R.D. Maklouf **Rev:** Bust 1/4 right **Rev. Designer:** Vladimir Gottwald

Date	Mintage	F	VF	XF	Unc	BU
1992	40,000	—	—	—	5.00	—

KM# 86 5 DOLLARS
Copper-Nickel **Ruler:** Elizabeth II **Series:** The Discoverers **Subject:** Christopher Columbus **Obv:** Crowned head right **Obv. Designer:** R.D. Maklouf **Rev:** Bust 1/4 right **Rev. Designer:** Vladimir Gottwald

Date	Mintage	F	VF	XF	Unc	BU
1992	40,000	—	—	—	5.00	—

KM# 88 5 DOLLARS
Copper-Nickel **Ruler:** Elizabeth II **Subject:** 40th Anniversary of Coronation **Obv:** Crowned head right **Obv. Designer:** R.D. Maklouf **Rev:** Coronation emblem within squares, all within artistic designed circle

Date	Mintage	F	VF	XF	Unc	BU
1993	15,000	—	—	—	5.00	7.00

KM# 88a 5 DOLLARS
27.2200 g., 0.9250 Silver .8095 oz. ASW **Ruler:** Elizabeth II **Subject:** 40th Anniversary of Coronation **Obv:** Crowned head right **Obv. Designer:** R.D. Maklouf **Rev:** Coronation emblem within squares, all within artistic designed circle

Date	Mintage	F	VF	XF	Unc	BU
1993 Proof	15,000	Value: 20.00				

KM# 88b 5 DOLLARS
47.5250 g., 0.9170 Gold 1.4010 oz. AGW **Ruler:** Elizabeth II **Subject:** 40th Anniversary of Coronation **Obv:** Crowned head right **Obv. Designer:** R.D. Maklouf **Rev:** Coronation emblem within squares, all within artistic designed circle

Date	Mintage	F	VF	XF	Unc	BU
1993 Proof	210	Value: 1,200				

KM# 89 5 DOLLARS
31.4700 g., 0.9250 Silver .9357 oz. ASW **Ruler:** Elizabeth II **Subject:** Endangered Wildlife **Obv:** Crowned head right **Obv. Designer:** R.D. Maklouf **Rev:** Hooker Sea Lions

Date	Mintage	F	VF	XF	Unc	BU
1993 Proof	20,000	Value: 30.00				

KM# 91 5 DOLLARS
28.2800 g., 0.9250 Silver .8410 oz. ASW **Ruler:** Elizabeth II **Obv:** Crowned head right **Obv. Designer:** R.D. Maklouf **Rev:** Queen mother and infant Elizabeth within beaded circle

Date	Mintage	F	VF	XF	Unc	BU
1994 Proof	34,600	Value: 30.00				

KM# 96 5 DOLLARS
31.4700 g., 0.9250 Silver **Ruler:** Elizabeth II **Series:** Winter Olympics - 1994 **Obv:** Crowned head right **Obv. Designer:** R.D. Maklouf **Rev:** Downhill skier

Date	Mintage	F	VF	XF	Unc	BU
1994 Proof	33,300	Value: 30.00				

KM# 92 5 DOLLARS
31.4700 g., 0.9250 Silver **Ruler:** Elizabeth II **Subject:** Antarctica **Obv:** Crowned head right **Obv. Designer:** R.D. Maklouf **Rev:** James Clark Ross

Date	Mintage	F	VF	XF	Unc	BU
1995 Proof	13,000	Value: 30.00				

KM# 93 5 DOLLARS
Copper-Nickel **Ruler:** Elizabeth II **Obv:** Crowned head right **Obv. Designer:** R.D. Maklouf **Rev:** Tui bird sitting on branch

Date	Mintage	F	VF	XF	Unc	BU
1995	11,000	—	—	—	12.50	—

KM# 93a 5 DOLLARS
28.2800 g., 0.9250 Silver .8411 oz. ASW **Ruler:** Elizabeth II **Obv:** Crowned head right **Obv. Designer:** R.D. Maklouf **Rev:** Tui bird sitting on branch

Date	Mintage	F	VF	XF	Unc	BU
1995 Proof	7,000	Value: 25.00				

KM# 97 5 DOLLARS
Copper-Nickel, 38.61 mm. **Ruler:** Elizabeth II **Obv:** Crowned head right **Obv. Designer:** R.D. Maklouf **Rev:** Kaka (Bush Parrot)

Date	Mintage	F	VF	XF	Unc	BU
1996	11,000	—	—	—	12.00	20.00

KM# 97a 5 DOLLARS
28.2800 g., 0.9250 Silver .8410 oz. ASW **Ruler:** Elizabeth II **Obv:** Crowned head right **Obv. Designer:** R.D. Maklouf **Rev:** Kaka (Bush parrot)

Date	Mintage	F	VF	XF	Unc	BU
1996 Proof	7,000	Value: 25.00				

KM# 99 5 DOLLARS
Copper-Nickel, 38.61 mm. **Ruler:** Elizabeth II
Subject: Auckland City of Sails **Obv:** Crowned head right
Obv. Designer: R.D. Maklouf **Rev:** Bridge and boats

Date	Mintage	F	VF	XF	Unc	BU
1996(l)	6,000	—	—	—	8.00	10.00

KM# 99a 5 DOLLARS
28.2800 g., 0.9250 Silver .8410 oz. ASW **Ruler:** Elizabeth II
Subject: Auckland - City of Sails **Obv:** Crowned head right
Obv. Designer: R.D. Maklouf **Rev:** Bridge and boats

Date	Mintage	F	VF	XF	Unc	BU
1996 Proof	3,000	Value: 40.00				

KM# 101 5 DOLLARS
28.4500 g., 0.9250 Silver .8461 oz. ASW **Ruler:** Elizabeth II
Obv: Crowned head right **Obv. Designer:** R.D. Maklouf
Rev: Crowned belt wreath flanked by flowers

Date	Mintage	F	VF	XF	Unc	BU
1996(l)	3,000	—	—	—	50.00	—

Note: In sets only with $20 commemorative banknote

KM# 102 5 DOLLARS
25.2200 g., 0.9250 Silver .8096 oz. ASW **Ruler:** Elizabeth II
Subject: De Heemskerck **Obv:** Crowned head right **Rev:** Sailship on globe with map

Date	Mintage	F	VF	XF	Unc	BU
1996(o) Proof	18,000	Value: 45.00				

KM# 103 5 DOLLARS
Copper-Nickel, 38.61 mm. **Ruler:** Elizabeth II **Subject:** WWF Conserving Nature **Obv:** Crowned head right
Obv. Designer: R.D. Maklouf **Rev:** Saddleback bird

Date	Mintage	F	VF	XF	Unc	BU
1997(l)	8,000	—	—	—	9.00	12.00

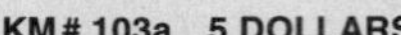

KM# 103a 5 DOLLARS
28.2800 g., 0.9250 Silver .8411 oz. ASW **Ruler:** Elizabeth II
Subject: WWF Conserving Nature **Obv:** Crowned head right
Obv. Designer: R.D. Maklouf **Rev:** Saddleback bird

Date	Mintage	F	VF	XF	Unc	BU
1997 Proof	19,000	Value: 35.00				

KM# 105 5 DOLLARS
Copper-Nickel **Ruler:** Elizabeth II **Subject:** Queen's Golden Wedding Anniversary **Obv:** Crowned head right **Obv. Designer:** R.D. Maklouf **Rev:** Coronation scene

Date	Mintage	F	VF	XF	Unc	BU
1997	9,000	—	—	—	20.00	—

KM# 105a 5 DOLLARS
28.2800 g., 0.9250 Silver 0.841 oz. ASW **Ruler:** Elizabeth II
Subject: Queen's Golden Wedding Anniversary **Obv:** Crowned head right **Obv. Designer:** R.D. Maklouf **Rev:** Coronation scene

Date	Mintage	F	VF	XF	Unc	BU
1997 Proof	32,500	Value: 25.00				

KM# 106 5 DOLLARS
Ruler: Elizabeth II **Subject:** City of Christchurch **Obv:** Crowned head right **Obv. Designer:** R.D. Maklouf **Rev:** Value above church

Date	Mintage	F	VF	XF	Unc	BU
1997	5,000	—	—	—	10.00	15.00

KM# 106a 5 DOLLARS
28.2800 g., 0.9250 Silver .8410 oz. ASW **Ruler:** Elizabeth II
Subject: City of Christchurch **Obv:** Crowned head right
Obv. Designer: R.D. Maklouf **Rev:** Value above church

Date	Mintage	F	VF	XF	Unc	BU
1997	3,000	Value: 40.00				

KM# 107 5 DOLLARS
Copper-Nickel **Ruler:** Elizabeth II **Obv:** Crowned head right
Obv. Designer: R.D. Maklouf **Rev:** Royal Albatross

Date	Mintage	F	VF	XF	Unc	BU
1998	6,500	—	—	—	10.00	15.00

KM# 107a 5 DOLLARS
29.2000 g., 0.9250 Silver .8684 oz. ASW **Ruler:** Elizabeth II
Obv: Crowned head right **Obv. Designer:** R.D. Maklouf
Rev: Royal Albatross

Date	Mintage	F	VF	XF	Unc	BU
1998 Proof	2,500	Value: 65.00				

KM# 109 5 DOLLARS
Copper-Nickel **Ruler:** Elizabeth II **Subject:** Pride in New Zealand **Obv:** Crowned head right **Rev:** Four stars

Date	Mintage	F	VF	XF	Unc	BU
1998(v) In sets only	2,000	—	—	—	10.00	—

KM# 109a 5 DOLLARS
6.0000 g., 0.9990 Silver .1927 oz. ASW **Ruler:** Elizabeth II
Subject: Pride in New Zealand **Obv:** Crowned head right
Rev: Four stars

Date	Mintage	F	VF	XF	Unc	BU
1998(v) In sets only	1,200	—	—	—	15.00	—

KM# 110 5 DOLLARS
Copper-Nickel **Ruler:** Elizabeth II **Subject:** Pride in New Zealand **Obv:** Crowned head right **Rev:** Fleece

Date	Mintage	F	VF	XF	Unc	BU
1998(v) In sets only	2,000	—	—	—	10.00	—

KM# 110a 5 DOLLARS
6.0000 g., 0.9990 Silver .1927 oz. ASW **Ruler:** Elizabeth II
Subject: Pride in New Zealand **Obv:** Crowned head right
Rev: Fleece

Date	Mintage	F	VF	XF	Unc	BU
1998(v) In sets only	1,200	—	—	—	15.00	—

KM# 111 5 DOLLARS
Copper-Nickel **Ruler:** Elizabeth II **Subject:** Pride in New Zealand **Obv:** Crowned head right **Rev:** Wheat sheaf

Date	Mintage	F	VF	XF	Unc	BU
1998(v) In sets only	2,000	—	—	—	10.00	—

KM# 111a 5 DOLLARS
6.0000 g., 0.9990 Silver .1927 oz. ASW **Ruler:** Elizabeth II
Subject: Pride in New Zealand **Obv:** Crowned head right
Rev: Wheat sheaf

Date	Mintage	F	VF	XF	Unc	BU
1998(v) In sets only	1,200	—	—	—	15.00	—

KM# 112 5 DOLLARS
Copper-Nickel **Ruler:** Elizabeth II **Subject:** Pride in New Zealand **Obv:** Crowned head right **Rev:** Crossed hammers

Date	Mintage	F	VF	XF	Unc	BU
1998(v) In sets only	2,000	—	—	—	10.00	—

KM# 112a 5 DOLLARS
6.0000 g., 0.9990 Silver .1927 oz. ASW **Ruler:** Elizabeth II
Subject: Pride in New Zealand **Obv:** Crowned head right
Rev: Crossed hammers

Date	Mintage	F	VF	XF	Unc	BU
1998(v) In sets only	1,200	—	—	—	15.00	—

KM# 113 5 DOLLARS
Copper-Nickel **Ruler:** Elizabeth II **Subject:** Dunedin
Obv: Crowned head right **Rev:** Larnach Castle

Date	Mintage	F	VF	XF	Unc	BU
1998(v)	4,000	—	—	—	10.00	—

KM# 113a 5 DOLLARS
28.2800 g., 0.9250 Silver .8684 oz. ASW **Ruler:** Elizabeth II
Subject: Dunedin **Obv:** Crowned head right **Rev:** Larnach Castle

Date	Mintage	F	VF	XF	Unc	BU
1998 Proof	2,500	Value: 30.00				

KM# 115 5 DOLLARS
Copper-Nickel **Ruler:** Elizabeth II **Obv:** Head with tiara right
Obv. Designer: Rank-Broadley **Rev:** Morepork owl on branch

Date	Mintage	F	VF	XF	Unc	BU
1999	7,500	—	—	—	12.00	25.00

KM# 115a 5 DOLLARS
28.2800 g., 0.9990 Silver .9083 oz. ASW **Ruler:** Elizabeth II
Obv: Head with tiara right **Obv. Designer:** Rank-Broadley **Rev:** Morepork owl

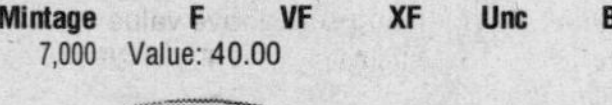

Date	Mintage	F	VF	XF	Unc	BU
1999 Proof	7,000	Value: 40.00				

KM# 123 5 DOLLARS
31.0500 g., 0.9250 Silver .9234 oz. ASW, 38.7 mm.

Ruler: Elizabeth II **Subject:** Wellington Harbour Capital **Obv:** Head with tiara right **Obv. Designer:** Rank-Broadley **Rev:** City view with ship **Edge:** Reeded

Date	Mintage	F	VF	XF	Unc	BU
1999(v) Proof	2,500	Value: 30.00				

KM# 125 5 DOLLARS
32.2000 g., Copper-Nickel, 38.6 mm. **Ruler:** Elizabeth II **Obv:** Head with tiara right **Obv. Designer:** Rank-Broadley **Rev:** Perching cormorant bird **Edge:** Reeded

Date	Mintage	F	VF	XF	Unc	BU
2000(v) Frosted finish	5,500	—	—	—	12.00	15.00

KM# 127 5 DOLLARS
32.2000 g., Copper-Nickel, 38.6 mm. **Ruler:** Elizabeth II **Obv:** Queen's portrait from dies of Solomon Islands KM67-68 **Rev:** Pied Cormorant for dies of New Zealand KM125 **Edge:** Reeded **Note:** Mule.

Date	Mintage	F	VF	XF	Unc	BU
2000(v)	Est. 50	—	—	—	—	1,000

Note: This coin is included in a New Zealand mint set dated 2000

KM# 125a 5 DOLLARS
31.1300 g., 0.9990 Silver .9998 oz. ASW **Ruler:** Elizabeth II **Obv:** Head with tiara right **Obv. Designer:** Rank-Broadley **Rev:** Perching cormorant **Note:** Heavier than the official weight of 28.28 grams.

Date	Mintage	F	VF	XF	Unc	BU
2000(v) Proof	5,000	Value: 35.00				

KM# 94 10 DOLLARS
Aluminum-Bronze **Ruler:** Elizabeth II **Obv:** Crowned head right **Obv. Designer:** R.D. Maklouf **Rev:** Gold Prospector

Date	Mintage	F	VF	XF	Unc	BU
1995(I)	7,000	—	—	—	15.00	—

KM# 94a 10 DOLLARS
0.9990 Gold .5000 oz. AGW **Ruler:** Elizabeth II **Obv:** Crowned head right **Obv. Designer:** R.D. Maklouf **Rev:** Gold Prospector

Date	Mintage	F	VF	XF	Unc	BU
1995(I) Proof	600	Value: 325				

KM# 98 10 DOLLARS
Aluminum-Bronze **Ruler:** Elizabeth II **Subject:** Sinking of General Grant **Obv:** Crowned head right **Obv. Designer:** R.D. Maklouf **Rev:** Sinking ship above value

Date	Mintage	F	VF	XF	Unc	BU
1996(I) Prooflike	6,000	—	—	—	—	15.00

KM# 98a 10 DOLLARS
0.9990 Gold .5000 oz. AGW **Ruler:** Elizabeth II **Subject:** Sinking of The General Grant **Obv:** Crowned head right **Obv. Designer:** R.D. Maklouf **Rev:** Sinking ship above value

Date	Mintage	F	VF	XF	Unc	BU
1996(I) Proof	650	Value: 350				

KM# 104 10 DOLLARS
Aluminum-Bronze **Ruler:** Elizabeth II **Subject:** Gabriel's Gully **Obv:** Crowned head right **Obv. Designer:** R.D. Maklouf **Rev:** Prospector climbing hill with shovel in hand

Date	Mintage	F	VF	XF	Unc	BU
1997(I)	3,000	—	—	—	17.50	—

KM# 104a 10 DOLLARS
0.9990 Gold .5000 oz. AGW **Ruler:** Elizabeth II **Subject:** Gabriel's Gully **Obv:** Crowned head right **Obv. Designer:** R.D. Maklouf **Rev:** Prospector climbing hill with shovel in hand

Date	Mintage	F	VF	XF	Unc	BU
1997(I) Proof	650	Value: 325				

KM# 114 10 DOLLARS
Copper-Zinc **Ruler:** Elizabeth II **Subject:** Century of Motoring **Obv:** Crowned head right **Rev:** Karl Benz driving his automobile

Date	Mintage	F	VF	XF	Unc	BU
1998(v)	2,000	—	—	—	15.00	—

KM# 114a 10 DOLLARS
Gold Plated Copper-Nickel **Ruler:** Elizabeth II **Subject:** Century of Motoring **Obv:** Crowned head right **Rev:** Karl Benz driving his automobile

Date	Mintage	F	VF	XF	Unc	BU
1998(v) Proof	1,500	Value: 45.00				

KM# 124 10 DOLLARS
15.4500 g., 0.9990 Silver .4962 oz. ASW, 29.9 mm. **Ruler:** Elizabeth II **Obv:** Crowned head right **Obv. Designer:** R.D. Maklouf **Rev:** Kiwi bird below silver fern leaf **Edge:** Reeded

Date	Mintage	F	VF	XF	Unc	BU
1998	1,500	—	—	—	110	—

KM# 122 10 DOLLARS
28.3700 g., 0.9250 Silver .8437 oz. ASW **Ruler:** Elizabeth II **Subject:** New Zealand - First to the Future **Obv:** Head with tiara right **Obv. Designer:** Rank-Broadley **Rev:** Gold-plated map of New Zealand, gold printed radiant sun **Edge:** Reeded

Date	Mintage	F	VF	XF	Unc	BU
2000(1999) Proof	33,000	Value: 40.00				

KM# 100 20 DOLLARS
31.1030 g., 0.9250 Silver .9250 oz. ASW **Ruler:** Elizabeth II **Subject:** Salute to Bravery **Obv:** Crowned head right **Rev:** Family to right of cameo

Date	Mintage	F	VF	XF	Unc	BU
1995 Proof	3,500	Value: 40.00				

KM# 108 20 DOLLARS
28.2800 g., 0.9250 Silver .8410 oz. ASW **Ruler:** Elizabeth II **Subject:** Queen's Golden Wedding Anniversary **Obv:** Crowned head right **Obv. Designer:** R.D. Maklouf **Rev:** Coronation scene **Note:** Similar to 5 Dollars, KM#105.

Date	Mintage	F	VF	XF	Unc	BU
1997 Proof	32,500	Value: 40.00				

KM# 77 150 DOLLARS
16.9500 g., 0.9170 Gold .4996 oz. AGW **Ruler:** Elizabeth II **Obv:** Crowned head right **Rev:** Kiwi

Date	Mintage	F	VF	XF	Unc	BU
1990 Proof	10,000	Value: 300				

KM# 126 150 DOLLARS
15.6000 g., 0.9950 Platinum .4990 oz. APW, 30 mm. **Ruler:** Elizabeth II **Obv:** Crowned head right **Obv. Designer:** R.D. Maklouf **Rev:** Two Kiwi and fern **Edge:** Reeded

Date	Mintage	F	VF	XF	Unc	BU
1998 Proof	350	Value: 600				

PATTERNS

Including off metal strikes

KM#	Date	Mintage	Identification	Mkt Val
Pn2	1933	—	3 Pence. Silver.	20,000

KM#	Date	Mintage	Identification	Mkt Val
Pn3	1933	—	Shilling. Silver.	50,000
Pn4	1935	—	Crown. Silver.	75,000

PIEFORTS

KM#	Date	Mintage	Identification	Mkt Val
P1	1992	5,000	Dollar. 0.9250 Silver. KM78.	100

MINT SETS

KM#	Date	Mintage	Identification	Issue Price	Mkt Val
MS1	1965 (7)	100,000	KM23.2-29.2, pink label, flat pack	2.00	3.00
MSA1	1965 (7)	75,000	KM23.2-29.2, green label, flat pack	2.50	5.00
MS2	1967 (7)	250,000	KM31-32, 34-37, 38.1	4.50	2.00
MS4	1968 (6)	35,000	KM31-32, 34-37	2.15	3.00
MS5	1969 (7)	50,000	KM31-32, 34-36, 39-40	3.25	3.00
MS7	1970 (7)	30,000	KM31-32, 34, 36-37, 41-42	3.50	5.00
MS10	1971 (7)	15,000	KM31-32, 36-37, 38.2, 41	3.50	5.00
MS12	1972 (7)	15,000	KM31-32, 34, 36-37, 38.2, 41	3.50	4.00
MS14	1973 (7)	15,000	KM31-32, 34, 36-37, 38.2, 41	3.50	5.00
MS17	1974 (7)	15,000	KM31-32, 34, 36-37, 41, 44	4.35	6.00
MS20	1975 (7)	15,000	KM31-32, 34, 36-37, 38.2, 41	4.50	4.00
MS22	1976 (7)	16,000	KM31-32, 34, 36-37, 38.2, 41	4.75	5.00
MS23	1977 (7)	20,000	KM31-32, 34, 36-37, 41, 46	4.75	5.00
MS24	1978 (7)	23,000	KM31-32, 34, 36-37, 41, 47	5.25	5.00
MS25	1979 (7)	25,000	KM31-32, 34, 36-37, 41, 48	5.50	5.00
MS26	1980 (7)	27,000	KM31-32, 34, 36-37, 41, 49	5.75	6.00
MS27	1981 (7)	25,000	KM31-32, 34, 36-37, 41, 50	5.75	5.00
MS28	1982 (7)	25,000	KM31-32, 34, 36-37, 41, 51	6.00	6.00
MS29	1983 (7)	25,000	KM31-32, 34, 36-37, 41, 53	6.25	5.00
MS30	1984 (7)	25,000	KM31-32, 34, 36-37, 41, 54	4.75	6.00
MS31	1985 (7)	20,000	KM31-32, 34, 36-37, 41, 55	4.00	6.00
MS32	1986 (7)	18,000	KM57-63	5.00	6.00
MS33	1987 (7)	18,000	KM58-63, 65	7.50	6.00
MS34	1988 (7)	15,000	KM58-63, 66	8.00	10.00
MS35	1989 (5)	14,600	KM60-63, 67	14.60	8.00
MS36	1990 (6)	18,000	KM60-61, 63, 78-79, 81	13.00	12.50
MS37	1990 (5)	10,000	KM72-76	11.00	25.00
MS38	1991 (7)	20,000	KM60-61, 63, 78-81	16.00	12.00
MS39	1992 (7)	15,000	KM60-61, 63, 78-79, 81-82	15.00	25.00
MS40	1992 (4)	40,000	KM83-86	—	20.00
MS41	1993 (6)	15,000	KM60-61, 63, 78, 81, 87	—	12.00
MS42	1994 (6)	16,000	KM60-61, 78-79,81,90	20.00	25.00
MS43	1995 (7)	6,000	KM60-61, 63, 78-79, 81, 93	17.00	25.00
MS44	1996 (7)	6,000	KM60-61, 63, 78-79, 81, 97	17.00	25.00
MS45	1997 (7)	5,500	KM60-63, 78-79, 81, 103	—	40.00
MS46	1998 (7)	4,000	KM60-61, 63, 78-79, 81, 107	15.00	25.00
MS47	1998 (4)	2,000	KM109-112	—	50.00
MS48	1999 (7)	5,000	KM115-121	20.00	30.00
MS49	2000 (7)	3,000	KM116-121, 127	18.00	50.00

PROOF SETS

KM#	Date	Mintage	Identification	Issue Price	Mkt Val
PS1	1933 (5)	20	KM1-5	—	2,850
PS2	1934 (5)	20	KM1-5	—	9,000

KM#	Date	Mintage	Identification	Issue Price	Mkt Val
PS3	1935 (6)	364	KM1-6	—	8,000
PS4	1937 (5)	200	KM7-11	—	2,700
PS5	1947 (5)	20	KM7a-11a	—	2,150
PSA6	1950 (7)	—	KM15-21	—	2,100
PS6	1953 (8)	7,000	KM23-30	—	50.00
PS7	1953 (8)	—	KM23-30, Matte Proof	—	1,350
PS8	1954 (4)	—	KM23.1-26.1	—	750
PS9	1954 (6)	—	KM23.1-28.1	—	1,350
PS10	1965 (7)	10	KM23.2-29.2	—	—
PS11	1967 (7)	10	KM31-32,34-38, V.I.P. Set	—	—
PSA12	1970 (7)	10	KM#31.1-32.1, 34.1, 36.1-37.1, 41.1-42, official card, red plush case, V.I.P. set	—	—
PS12	1971 (7)	5,000	KM31-32, 34, 36-37, 38.2, 41	15.00	70.00
PS13	1972 (7)	8,000	KM31-32, 34, 36-37, 38.2, 41	16.00	10.00
PS14	1973 (7)	8,000	KM31-32, 34, 36-37, 38.2, 41	16.00	7.00
PS15	1974 (7)	8,000	KM31-32, 34, 36-37, 41, 44a	14.00	15.00
PS16	1975 (7)	10,000	KM31-32, 34, 36-37, 38.2, 41	18.50	7.00
PS17	1976 (7)	11,000	KM31-32, 34, 36-37, 38.2, 41	19.00	7.00
PS18	1977 (7)	12,000	KM31-32, 34, 36-37, 41, 46a	19.50	12.50
PS19	1977 (7)	10	KM31-32, 34, 36-37, 41, 46a, Official card	—	—
PS20	1978 (7)	15,000	KM31-32, 34, 36-37, 41, 47a	23.50	12.50
PS21	1979 (7)	16,000	KM31-32, 34, 36-37, 41, 48a	25.50	12.50
PS22	1980 (7)	17,000	KM31-32, 34, 36-37, 41, 49a	42.00	12.50
PS23	1981 (7)	18,000	KM31-32, 34, 36-37, 41, 50a	37.00	12.50
PS24	1982 (7)	18,000	KM31-32, 34, 36-37, 41, 51a	33.00	12.50
PS25	1983 (7)	18,000	KM31-32, 34, 36-37, 41, 53a	40.00	12.50
PS26	1984 (7)	15,000	KM31-32, 34, 36-37, 41, 54a	28.00	12.50
PS27	1985 (7)	11,500	KM31-32, 34, 36-37, 41, 55a	27.00	12.50
PS28	1986 (7)	10,000	KM57a, 58-63	30.00	15.00
PS29	1987 (7)	10,000	KM58-63, 65a	38.00	15.00
PS30	1988 (7)	9,000	KM58-63, 66a	43.00	25.00
PS31	1989 (5)	8,500	KM60-63, 67a	44.50	20.00
PS32	1989 (4)	8,600	KM67a-70a	132	50.00
PS33	1990 (6)	10,000	KM60-61, 63, 78a-79a, 81	52.00	60.00
PS34	1990 (5)	7,000	KM72a-76a	110	80.00
PS35	1991 (7)	15,000	KM60-61, 63, 78-79, 80a, 81	61.00	30.00
PS36	1992 (7)	9,000	KM60-61, 63, 78-79, 81, 82a	58.00	25.00
PS37	1993 (6)	10,000	KM60-61, 63, 78, 81, 87a	75.00	25.00
PS38	1994 (6)	10,000	KM60-61, 78-79, 81, 90a	45.00	50.00
PS39	1995 (7)	4,000	KM60-61, 63, 78-79, 81, 93a	45.00	80.00
PS39A	1996 (7)	4,000	KM#60-61, 78-79, 81, 90	—	110
PS40	1997 (7)	2,500	KM60-63, 78-79, 81, 103a	—	130
PS41	1998 (7)	2,000	KM60-61, 63, 78-79, 81, 107a	55.00	180
PS42	1998 (4)	1,200	KM109a-112a	—	75.00
PS43	1999 (7)	2,000	KM115a, 116-121	59.00	180
PS44	2000 (7)	1,500	KM116-121, 128a	40.00	375

PROOF-LIKE SETS (PL)

KM#	Date	Mintage	Identification	Issue Price	Mkt Val
PLS1	1965 (7)	25,000	KM23.2-29.2 flat pack, blue label	—	7.00
PLS2	1965 (7)	400	KM23.2-29.2 red plush case	—	—
PLS3	1967 (7)	49,500	KM31-32, 34-38 flat pack, blue label	5.00	3.00
PLS4	1967	500	KM31-32, 34-38 blue plush case	—	110
PLS6	1968 (6)	40,000	KM31-32, 34-37 flat pack, blue label	5.00	2.50
PLS7	1968 (6)	I.A.	KM31-32, 34-37 blue plush case	—	7.50
PLS8	1969 (7)	50,000	KM31-32, 34-36, 39-40 flat pack, blue label	5.00	4.00
PLS9	1969 (7)	I.A.	KM31-32, 34-36, 39-40 blue plush case	—	10.00
PLS10	1970 (7)	20,000	KM31-32, 34, 36-37, 41-42, flat pack, blue label	5.00	7.00
PLS11	1970 (7)	I.A.	KM31-32, 34, 36-37, 41-42, blue plush case	—	12.50

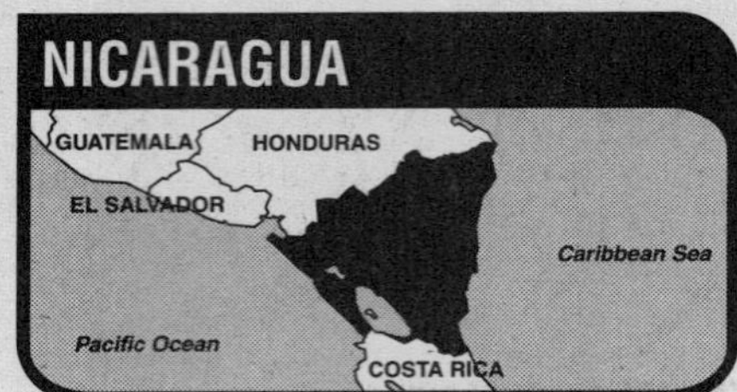

The Republic of Nicaragua, situated in Central America between Honduras and Costa Rica, has an area of 50,193 sq. mi. (129,494 sq. km.) and a population of *3.7 million. Capital: Managua. Agriculture, mining (gold and silver) and hardwood logging are the principal industries. Cotton, meat, coffee and sugar are exported.

Dissension between the Liberals and Conservatives of the contending cities kept Nicaragua in turmoil, which made it possible for William Walker to make himself President in 1855. The two major political parties finally united to drive him out and in 1857 he was expelled. A relative peace followed, but by1912, Nicaragua had requested the U.S. Marines to restore order, which began a U.S. involvement that lasted until the Good Neighbor Policy was adopted in 1933. Anastasio Somoza Garcia assumed the Presidency in 1936. This family dynasty dominated Nicaragua until its overthrow in 1979. Formal elections in 1990 renewed a democratic government in power.

MINT MARKS

H - Heaton, Birmingham
HF - Huguenin Freres, Le Locle, Switzerland
Mo - Mexico City
-Philadelphia, Pa.
-Sherritt Mint, Canada
-Waterbury, Ct.

MONETARY SYSTEM

100 Centavos = 1 Peso

REPUBLIC

DECIMAL COINAGE

KM# 10 1/2 CENTAVO

Bronze **Obv:** National emblem **Rev:** Value within sprigs

Date	Mintage	F	VF	XF	Unc	BU
1912H	900,000	1.00	2.50	15.00	40.00	—
1912H Proof	—	Value: 275				
1915H	320,000	1.50	4.00	30.00	100	—
1916H	720,000	1.50	4.00	30.00	100	—
1917	720,000	1.50	4.00	20.00	65.00	—
1922	400,000	2.00	5.00	20.00	80.00	—
1924	400,000	1.00	3.00	12.00	70.00	—
1934	500,000	1.00	3.00	10.00	45.00	—
1936	600,000	0.50	0.75	5.00	35.00	—
1937	1,000,000	0.40	0.60	4.00	20.00	—

KM# 11 CENTAVO

Bronze **Obv:** National emblem **Rev:** Value within sprigs

Date	Mintage	F	VF	XF	Unc	BU
1912H	450,000	1.00	3.00	10.00	45.00	—
1912H Proof	—	Value: 275				
1914H	300,000	5.00	10.00	30.00	85.00	—
1915H	500,000	5.00	10.00	35.00	100	—
1916H	450,000	5.00	10.00	35.00	100	—
1917	450,000	3.00	7.00	28.00	75.00	—
1919	750,000	2.00	6.00	18.00	50.00	—
1920	700,000	1.00	4.50	14.50	45.00	—
1922	500,000	1.00	4.50	14.50	45.00	—
1924	300,000	2.00	6.00	22.00	65.00	—
1927	250,000	3.50	8.50	28.00	75.00	—
1928	500,000	2.00	6.00	18.00	45.00	—
1929	500,000	2.00	5.00	13.50	35.00	—
1930	250,000	3.00	8.00	25.00	70.00	—
1934	500,000	1.50	4.00	12.00	35.00	—
1935	500,000	1.00	4.00	12.00	35.00	—
1936	500,000	1.00	3.00	8.00	25.00	—
1937	1,000,000	0.75	2.00	7.00	20.00	—
1938	2,000,000	0.75	1.50	5.00	15.00	—
1940	2,000,000	0.75	1.50	5.00	15.00	—

KM# 20 CENTAVO

Brass **Obv:** National emblem **Rev:** Value within sprigs

Date	Mintage	F	VF	XF	Unc	BU
1943	1,000,000	0.50	1.50	4.50	18.00	—

KM# 12 5 CENTAVOS

Copper-Nickel **Obv:** National emblem **Rev:** Value within sprigs

Date	Mintage	F	VF	XF	Unc	BU
1912H	460,000	4.00	10.00	25.00	75.00	—
1912H Proof	—	Value: 300				
1914H	300,000	4.00	10.00	30.00	85.00	—
1915H	160,000	8.00	20.00	50.00	225	—
1919	100,000	4.00	10.00	30.00	110	—
1920	150,000	4.00	10.00	30.00	100	—
1927	100,000	4.00	10.00	30.00	100	—
1928	100,000	4.00	10.00	30.00	100	—
1929	100,000	5.00	12.00	35.00	120	—
1930	100,000	4.00	10.00	30.00	100	—
1934	200,000	3.00	10.00	25.00	90.00	—
1935	200,000	2.00	5.00	20.00	85.00	—
1936	300,000	1.50	3.00	15.00	65.00	—
1937	300,000	1.50	3.00	10.00	40.00	—
1938	800,000	1.00	2.00	8.00	30.00	—
1940	800,000	1.00	2.00	6.00	20.00	—

KM# 21 5 CENTAVOS

Brass **Obv:** Bust facing within circle **Rev:** Radiant sun and hills within circle **Edge:** Plain

Date	Mintage	F	VF	XF	Unc	BU
1943	2,000,000	0.75	2.50	10.00	60.00	—

KM# 24.1 5 CENTAVOS

Copper-Nickel **Obv:** Bust facing within circle **Rev:** Radiant sun and hills within circle **Edge Lettering:** B. N. N **Note:** Reduced size. Medal rotation.

Date	Mintage	F	VF	XF	Unc	BU
1946	4,000,000	0.10	0.25	2.50	18.00	—
1946 Proof	—	Value: 200				
1950	—	0.10	0.25	2.50	18.00	—
1952	4,000,000	0.10	0.25	3.50	25.00	—
1952 Proof	—	Value: 250				
1954	4,000,000	0.10	0.15	0.25	5.00	—
1954 Proof	—	Value: 250				
1956	5,000,000	0.10	0.15	0.50	5.00	—
1956 Proof	—	Value: 250				

KM# 24.2 5 CENTAVOS

Copper-Nickel **Obv:** Bust facing within circle **Rev:** Radiant sun and hills within circle **Edge Lettering:** B. C. N. **Note:** Medal rotation.

Date	Mintage	F	VF	XF	Unc	BU
1962	3,000,000	—	0.10	0.15	2.00	—
1962 Proof	—	Value: 200				
1964	4,000,000	—	0.10	0.15	2.00	—
1965	10,000,000	—	0.10	0.15	2.00	—

KM# 24.2a 5 CENTAVOS

Nickel Clad Steel **Obv:** Bust facing within circle **Rev:** Radiant sun and hills within circle **Note:** Medal rotation.

Date	Mintage	F	VF	XF	Unc	BU
1972	10,020,000	—	—	0.10	0.50	—

KM# 24.3 5 CENTAVOS

Copper-Nickel **Obv:** Bust facing within circle **Rev:** Radiant sun and hills within circle **Edge:** Reeded **Note:** Coin rotation.

Date	Mintage	F	VF	XF	Unc	BU
1972 Proof	20,000	Value: 2.50				

KM# 27 5 CENTAVOS

Aluminum, 21.5 mm. **Obv:** National emblem within circle **Rev:** Value within circle **Note:** Medal rotation.

Date	Mintage	F	VF	XF	Unc	BU
1974	18,000,000	—	—	0.10	0.50	—

KM# 28 5 CENTAVOS

Aluminum, 21.5 mm. **Series:** F.A.O. **Obv:** National emblem within circle **Rev:** Value within circle **Note:** Medal rotation.

Date	Mintage	F	VF	XF	Unc	BU
1974	2,000,000	—	—	0.40	2.00	—

KM# 49 5 CENTAVOS

Aluminum **Obv:** Head with hat facing **Rev:** Value **Note:** Coin rotation.

Date	Mintage	F	VF	XF	Unc	BU
1981	5,000,000	—	—	0.40	1.50	—

KM# 55 5 CENTAVOS

0.7500 g., Aluminum, 15 mm. **Obv:** Hat above date and sprigs **Rev:** Value **Note:** Medal rotation.

Date	Mintage	F	VF	XF	Unc	BU
1987	38,000,000	—	—	0.40	1.00	—

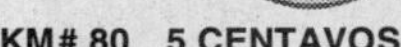

KM# 80 5 CENTAVOS

Chromium Plated Steel **Obv:** National emblem **Rev:** Bird flying over map **Note:** Coin rotation.

Date	Mintage	F	VF	XF	Unc	BU
1994	20,000,000	—	—	—	0.50	0.75

KM# 13 10 CENTAVOS

2.5000 g., 0.8000 Silver .0643 oz. ASW **Obv:** Bust facing within circle **Rev:** Radiant sun and hills within circle **Note:** All dates struck with medal rotation except 1935, which appears only in coin rotation.

Date	Mintage	F	VF	XF	Unc	BU
1912H	230,000	2.50	7.00	25.00	100	—
1912H Proof	—	Value: 300				
1914H	220,000	3.00	10.00	35.00	115	—
1914H Proof	—	Value: 375				
1927	500,000	2.00	4.00	20.00	85.00	—
1928	1,000,000	1.25	3.00	15.00	65.00	—
1930	150,000	1.50	4.00	30.00	95.00	—
1935	250,000	1.25	3.00	12.50	45.00	—
1936	250,000	1.25	3.00	10.00	30.00	—

KM# 17.1 10 CENTAVOS

Copper-Nickel **Obv:** Bust facing within circle **Rev:** Radiant sun and hills within circle **Edge Lettering:** B.N.N **Note:** Medal rotation.

Date	Mintage	F	VF	XF	Unc	BU
1939	2,500,000	1.25	3.00	10.00	30.00	—
1939 Proof	—	Value: 250				
1946	2,000,000	1.25	3.00	10.00	30.00	—
1946 Proof	—	Value: 200				
1950	2,000,000	0.25	0.50	3.00	20.00	—
1950 Proof	—	Value: 200				
1952	1,500,000	0.25	0.50	3.00	25.00	—
1952 Proof	—	Value: 200				
1954	3,000,000	0.10	0.25	1.50	10.00	—
1954 Proof	—	Value: 200				
1956	5,000,000	0.10	0.20	1.00	6.00	—
1956 Proof	—	Value: 200				

KM# 17.2 10 CENTAVOS

Copper-Nickel **Obv:** Bust facing within circle **Rev:** Radiant sun and hills within circle **Edge Lettering:** B.C.N **Note:** Medal rotation.

Date	Mintage	F	VF	XF	Unc	BU
1962	4,000,000	—	0.10	0.15	5.00	—
1962 Proof	—	Value: 225				
1964	4,000,000	—	0.10	0.15	5.00	—
1965	12,000,000	—	0.10	0.15	1.00	—

KM# 17.2a 10 CENTAVOS

Nickel Clad Steel **Obv:** Bust facing within circle **Rev:** Radiant sun and hills within circle **Note:** Medal rotation. Previous KM#17.3a.

Date	Mintage	F	VF	XF	Unc	BU
1972	10,020,000	—	0.10	0.15	0.30	—

KM# 17.3 10 CENTAVOS

Copper-Nickel **Obv:** Bust facing within circle **Rev:** Radiant sun and hills within circle **Edge:** Reeded **Note:** Coin rotation.

Date	Mintage	F	VF	XF	Unc	BU
1972 Proof	20,000	Value: 2.50				

KM# 22 10 CENTAVOS

Brass **Obv:** Bust facing within circle **Rev:** Radiant sun and hills within circle **Edge:** Reeded **Note:** Coin rotation.

Date	Mintage	F	VF	XF	Unc	BU
1943	2,000,000	0.50	1.00	5.00	50.00	—

KM# 29 10 CENTAVOS

Aluminum **Series:** F.A.O. **Obv:** Map within circle **Rev:** Value within circle **Note:** Medal rotation.

Date	Mintage	F	VF	XF	Unc	BU
1974	2,000,000	—	—	0.10	1.00	—

KM# 30 10 CENTAVOS

Aluminum **Obv:** Map within circle **Rev:** Value within circle

Date	Mintage	F	VF	XF	Unc	BU
1974	18,000,000	—	—	0.10	0.20	—

KM# 31 10 CENTAVOS

Copper-Nickel

Date	Mintage	F	VF	XF	Unc	BU
1978	20,000,000	—	—	0.40	2.00	—

KM# 50 10 CENTAVOS

Aluminum **Obv:** Head with hat facing **Rev:** Value **Note:** Coin rotation.

Date	Mintage	F	VF	XF	Unc	BU
1981	10,000,000	—	—	0.15	1.00	—

KM# 56 10 CENTAVOS

0.9000 g., Aluminum, 17 mm. **Obv:** Hat above date and sprigs **Rev:** Value **Note:** Medal rotation.

Date	Mintage	F	VF	XF	Unc	BU
1987	16,000,000	—	—	0.15	0.40	—

KM# 81 10 CENTAVOS

Chromium Plated Steel **Obv:** National emblem **Rev:** Bird flying above map **Note:** Coin rotation.

Date	Mintage	F	VF	XF	Unc	BU
1994	6,439,000	—	—	—	0.75	1.00

KM# 14 25 CENTAVOS

6.2500 g., 0.8000 Silver .1607 oz. ASW **Obv:** Bust facing within circle **Rev:** Radiant sun and hills within circle **Note:** Medal rotation.

Date	Mintage	F	VF	XF	Unc	BU
1912H	320,000	3.00	10.00	35.00	90.00	—
1912H Proof	—	Value: 350				
1914H	100,000	5.00	15.00	50.00	170	—
1928	200,000	3.00	10.00	30.00	90.00	—
1929	20,000	8.00	35.00	90.00	275	—
1930	20,000	8.00	35.00	90.00	250	—
1936	100,000	2.75	8.00	20.00	65.00	—

KM# 18.1 25 CENTAVOS

Copper-Nickel, 23 mm. **Obv:** Bust facing within circle **Rev:** Radiant sun and hills within circle **Edge Lettering:** B N N (repeated)

Date	Mintage	F	VF	XF	Unc	BU
1939	1,000,000	2.00	6.00	15.00	50.00	—
1939 Proof	—	Value: 300				
1946	1,000,000	1.50	4.00	12.00	40.00	—
1946 Proof	—	Value: 280				
1950	1,000,000	0.25	0.50	1.50	20.00	—
1950 Proof	—	Value: 300				
1952	1,000,000	0.25	0.50	1.50	15.00	—
1952 Proof	—	Value: 280				
1954	2,000,000	0.10	0.20	0.50	6.00	—
1954 Proof	—	Value: 280				
1956	3,000,000	0.10	0.20	0.50	5.00	—
1956 Proof	—	Value: 280				

KM# 18.2 25 CENTAVOS

Copper-Nickel, 23 mm. **Obv:** Bust facing within circle **Rev:** Radiant sun and hills within circle **Edge Lettering:** B. C. N. **Note:** Medal rotation.

Date	Mintage	F	VF	XF	Unc	BU
1964	3,000,000	0.10	0.20	0.40	4.00	—
1965	4,400,000	0.10	0.20	0.30	4.00	—

KM# 18.3 25 CENTAVOS

Copper-Nickel **Obv:** Bust facing within circle **Rev:** Radiant sun and hills within circle **Edge:** Reeded

Date	Mintage	F	VF	XF	Unc	BU
1972 Proof	20,000	Value: 2.50				
Note: Coin rotation						
1972	4,000,000	—	0.10	0.15	2.00	—
1974	6,000,000	—	0.10	0.15	2.00	—
Note: Medal rotation						

KM# 23 25 CENTAVOS

Brass, 26.8 mm. **Obv:** Bust facing within circle **Rev:** Radiant sun and hills within circle **Edge:** Reeded **Note:** Coin rotation.

Date	Mintage	F	VF	XF	Unc	BU
1943	1,000,000	0.50	1.50	8.50	50.00	—

KM# 51 25 CENTAVOS

Nickel Clad Steel **Obv:** Head with hat facing **Rev:** Value
Note: Coin rotation

Date	Mintage	F	VF	XF	Unc	BU
1981	10,000,000	—	—	0.25	1.50	—
1985	8,000,000	5.00	10.00	20.00	30.00	—

KM# 57 25 CENTAVOS

1.3500 g., Aluminum, 19 mm. **Obv:** Hat above date and sprigs **Rev:** Value **Note:** Medal rotation.

Date	Mintage	F	VF	XF	Unc	BU
1987	—	—	—	0.25	2.00	—

KM# 82 25 CENTAVOS

Chromium Plated Steel **Obv:** National emblem **Rev:** Bird flying above map **Note:** Coin rotation.

Date	Mintage	F	VF	XF	Unc	BU
1994	2,500,000	—	—	—	1.00	1.50

KM# 15 50 CENTAVOS

12.5000 g., 0.8000 Silver .3215 oz. ASW **Obv:** Bust facing within circle **Rev:** Radiant sun and hills within circle **Note:** Medal rotation.

Date	Mintage	F	VF	XF	Unc	BU
1912H	260,000	5.50	15.00	75.00	200	—
1912H Proof	—	Value: 500				
1929	20,000	6.50	20.00	90.00	275	—

KM# 19.1 50 CENTAVOS

Copper-Nickel **Obv:** Bust facing within circle **Rev:** Radiant sun and hills within circle **Edge Lettering:** B. N. N **Note:** Medal rotation.

Date	Mintage	F	VF	XF	Unc	BU
1939	1,000,000	3.00	8.00	20.00	65.00	—
1939 Proof	—	Value: 300				
1946	500,000	2.00	5.00	12.50	50.00	—
1946 Proof	—	Value: 300				
1950	500,000	1.00	2.00	10.00	50.00	—
1950 Proof	—	Value: 300				
1952	1,000,000	0.75	1.50	5.00	30.00	—
1952 Proof	—	Value: 300				
1954	2,000,000	0.50	1.00	4.00	15.00	—
1954 Proof	—	Value: 300				
1956	2,000,000	0.50	1.00	4.00	15.00	—
1956 Proof	—	Value: 300				

KM# 19.2 50 CENTAVOS

Copper-Nickel **Obv:** Bust facing within circle **Rev:** Radiant sun and hills within circle **Edge Lettering:** B. C. N

Date	Mintage	F	VF	XF	Unc	BU
1965	600,000	0.50	1.25	4.50	15.00	—
1965 Proof	—	Value: 150				

KM# 19.3 50 CENTAVOS

Copper-Nickel **Obv:** Bust facing within circle **Rev:** Radiant sun and hills within circle **Edge:** Reeded

Date	Mintage	F	VF	XF	Unc	BU
1972	—	—	—	—	—	—
1972 Proof	20,000	Value: 2.50				
Note: Coin rotation						
1974	2,000,000	0.10	0.25	0.50	3.50	—
Note: Medal rotation						

KM# 42 50 CENTAVOS

Copper-Nickel **Obv:** Head with hat facing **Rev:** Value
Note: Coin rotation.

Date	Mintage	F	VF	XF	Unc	BU
1980Mo	15,000,000	0.10	0.25	0.50	1.75	—

KM# 42a 50 CENTAVOS

Nickel Clad Steel **Obv:** Head with hat facing **Rev:** Value **Note:** Coin rotation.

Date	Mintage	F	VF	XF	Unc	BU
1983	10,000,000	—	—	0.40	2.50	—
1985	10,000,000	3.50	7.50	15.00	25.00	—

KM# 58 50 CENTAVOS

4.8500 g., Aluminum-Bronze, 22 mm. **Obv:** Hat above date and sprigs **Rev:** Value **Note:** Medal rotation.

Date	Mintage	F	VF	XF	Unc	BU
1987	12,000,000	—	—	0.40	2.50	—

KM# 83 50 CENTAVOS

Chromium Plated Steel, 22 mm. **Obv:** National emblem **Rev:** Bird flying above map **Note:** Coin rotation.

Date	Mintage	F	VF	XF	Unc	BU
1994	12,000,000	—	—	—	1.25	1.75

KM# 88 50 CENTAVOS

Nickel Clad Steel, 22 mm. **Obv:** National emblem **Rev:** Value above sprigs within circle, date flanked by stars

Date	Mintage	F	VF	XF	Unc	BU
1997	24,000,000	—	—	—	1.25	1.75

KM# 16 CORDOBA

25.0000 g., 0.9000 Silver .7234 oz. ASW **Obv:** Bust facing within circle **Rev:** Radiant sun and hills within circle **Note:** Medal rotation.

Date	Mintage	F	VF	XF	Unc	BU
1912H	35,000	30.00	75.00	285	1,900	—
1912H Proof	—	Value: 2,850				

KM# 26 CORDOBA

Copper-Nickel **Obv:** Bust facing within circle **Rev:** Radiant sun and hills within circle **Edge:** Reeded

Date	Mintage	F	VF	XF	Unc	BU
1972	20,000,000	0.10	0.20	2.00	4.00	—
Note: Medal rotation						
1972 Proof	40,000	Value: 10.00				
Note: Coin rotation						

KM# 43 CORDOBA

Copper-Nickel **Obv:** Head with hat facing **Rev:** Value
Note: Coin rotation.

Date	Mintage	F	VF	XF	Unc	BU
1980Mo	10,000,000	0.10	0.20	0.50	2.00	—
1983Mo	10,000,000	0.10	0.20	0.50	2.00	—

KM# 43a CORDOBA

Nickel Clad Steel **Obv:** Head with hat facing **Rev:** Value
Note: Coin rotation.

Date	Mintage	F	VF	XF	Unc	BU
1984	10,000,000	—	0.10	0.50	2.00	—
1985	10,000,000	1.00	2.00	7.00	35.00	—

KM# 59 CORDOBA

6.1500 g., Aluminum-Bronze, 24 mm. **Obv:** Hat above date and sprigs **Rev:** Value **Note:** Medal rotation.

Date	Mintage	F	VF	XF	Unc	BU
1987	23,000,000	—	0.75	1.00	3.75	—

KM# 77 CORDOBA

27.0000 g., 0.9250 Silver .8029 oz. ASW **Subject:** Ibero-American Series **Obv:** National emblem within assorted arms around border **Rev:** Map behind standing figures shaking hands within circle

Date	Mintage	F	VF	XF	Unc	BU
1991 Proof	10,000	Value: 65.00				

KM# 84 CORDOBA

13.8200 g., 0.9250 Silver .4110 oz. ASW **Subject:** National

Ruben Dario Theater **Obv:** Dancing native and map **Rev:** Theatrical masks on theatre

Date	Mintage	F	VF	XF	Unc	BU
1994 Proof	2,000	Value: 42.50				

KM# 85 CORDOBA

14.1700 g., 0.9250 Silver .4214 oz. ASW **Subject:** 100th Anniversary - City of Boaco **Obv:** National emblem **Rev:** Building

Date	Mintage	F	VF	XF	Unc	BU
1995 Proof	1,000	Value: 45.00				

KM# 87 CORDOBA

13.9600 g., 0.8250 Silver .3703 oz. ASW **Subject:** 50th Anniversary - F.A.O **Obv:** National emblem **Rev:** F.A.O. logo within circle

Date	Mintage	F	VF	XF	Unc	BU
1995 Proof	2,200	Value: 37.50				

KM# 89 CORDOBA

Nickel Clad Steel, 25 mm. **Obv:** National emblem **Rev:** Value above sprigs within circle

Date	Mintage	F	VF	XF	Unc	BU
1997	39,000,000	—	—	—	2.50	3.00
2000	35,000,000	—	—	—	2.50	3.00

KM# 44 5 CORDOBAS

Copper-Nickel, 27 mm. **Obv:** Value **Rev:** Head with hat facing **Shape:** 7-sided **Note:** Medal rotation.

Date	Mintage	F	VF	XF	Unc	BU
1980	10,000,000	0.15	0.25	1.00	3.00	—

KM# 44a 5 CORDOBAS

Nickel Clad Steel **Obv:** Value **Rev:** Head with hat facing **Shape:** 7-sided **Note:** Medal rotation.

Date	Mintage	F	VF	XF	Unc	BU
1984	8,000,000	—	0.25	1.00	3.50	—

KM# 60 5 CORDOBAS

7.5000 g., Aluminum-Bronze, 25.9 mm. **Obv:** Hat above date and sprigs **Rev:** Value

Date	Mintage	F	VF	XF	Unc	BU
1987	23,000,000	—	1.00	2.50	4.00	—

KM# 86 5 CORDOBAS

27.0000 g., 0.9250 Silver .8030 oz. ASW **Subject:** Wildlife Protection **Obv:** National emblem

Date	Mintage	F	VF	XF	Unc	BU
1994 Proof	20,000	Value: 45.00				

KM# 90 5 CORDOBAS

Nickel Clad Steel **Obv:** National emblem **Rev:** Value above sprigs within circle **Note:** Coin rotation.

Date	Mintage	F	VF	XF	Unc	BU
1997	11,000,000	—	—	—	4.00	5.00
2000	25,000,000	—	—	—	4.00	5.00

KM# 96 5 CORDOBAS

27.0000 g., 0.9250 Silver 0.803 oz. ASW, 40 mm. **Subject:** Ibero-America **Obv:** National emblem within assorted arms border **Rev:** Two folk dancers **Edge:** Reeded

Date	Mintage	F	VF	XF	Unc	BU
1997 Proof	—	Value: 60.00				

KM# 76 10 CORDOBAS

25.7000 g., 0.9990 Silver .8263 oz. ASW **Subject:** Soccer **Obv:** National emblem within circle **Rev:** Soccer champions with arms raised

Date	Mintage	F	VF	XF	Unc	BU
1991 Proof	10,000	Value: 65.00				

KM# 78 10 CORDOBAS

19.9500 g., 0.9990 Silver .6408 oz. ASW **Subject:** Spanish Royal Visit **Obv:** National emblem within circle **Rev:** Heads 1/4 left on map

Date	Mintage	F	VF	XF	Unc	BU
1991 Proof	5,000	Value: 55.00				

KM# 95 10 CORDOBAS

27.2000 g., 0.9250 Silver 0.8089 oz. ASW, 40 mm. **Subject:** Ibero-America Series **Obv:** National emblem within circle of assorted arms **Rev:** Man on horse with two milk cans **Edge:** Reeded

Date	Mintage	F	VF	XF	Unc	BU
1999 Proof	—	Value: 75.00				

KM# 32 20 CORDOBAS

5.0300 g., 0.9250 Silver .1496 oz. ASW **Subject:** Earthquake Relief Issue **Obv:** National emblem **Rev:** Bird at center of cog wheel design, plant sprigs in sections

Date	Mintage	F	VF	XF	Unc	BU
1975	2,491	—	—	—	14.50	—
1975 Proof	1,750	Value: 20.00				

Note: Medal rotation

KM# 25 50 CORDOBAS

35.6000 g., 0.9000 Gold 1.0300 oz. AGW **Subject:** 100th Anniversary - Birth of Ruben Dario **Obv:** National emblem within circle **Rev:** Bust 3/4 facing within circle

Date	Mintage	F	VF	XF	Unc	BU
1967HF Prooflike	16,000	—	—	—	—	750

Note: 500 pieces were issued in blue boxes with certificates; Boxed examples command a premium

KM# 33 50 CORDOBAS

12.5700 g., 0.9250 Silver .3738 oz. ASW **Subject:** U.S. Bicentennial **Obv:** National emblem **Rev:** Liberty bell divides dates **Note:** Mintages are included with KM#34.

Date	Mintage	F	VF	XF	Unc	BU
1975	—	—	—	—	21.50	—
1975 Proof	—	Value: 30.00				

Note: Medal rotation

KM# 34 50 CORDOBAS

12.5700 g., 0.9250 Silver .3738 oz. ASW **Subject:** Earthquake Relief Issue **Obv:** National emblem **Rev:** "The Bud" painting by Annigoni

Date	Mintage	F	VF	XF	Unc	BU
1975	4,482	—	—	—	18.00	—
1975 Proof	3,500	Value: 27.50				

KM# 61 50 CORDOBAS
16.6000 g., 0.8250 Silver .4403 oz. ASW **Series:** Winter Olympics **Obv:** National emblem within circle **Rev:** Skier

Date	Mintage	F	VF	XF	Unc	BU
1988 Proof	10,000	Value: 22.50				

KM# 62 50 CORDOBAS
16.6000 g., 0.8250 Silver .4403 oz. ASW **Series:** Olympics **Obv:** National emblem within circle **Rev:** Sailboat

Date	Mintage	F	VF	XF	Unc	BU
1988 Proof	10,000	Value: 22.50				

KM# 91 50 CORDOBAS
27.0000 g., 0.9250 Silver 0.803 oz. ASW, 40 mm.
Subject: Central Bank 40th Anniversary **Obv:** National emblem within circle and wreath **Rev:** Bust 1/4 left **Edge:** Reeded

Date	Mintage	F	VF	XF	Unc	BU
2000 Proof	1,000	Value: 75.00				

KM# 35 100 CORDOBAS
25.1400 g., 0.9250 Silver .6668 oz. ASW **Subject:** U.S. Bicentennial **Obv:** National emblem **Rev:** Betsy Ross sewing flag on left, astronaut placing flag on moon on right **Note:** Mintages included with KM#36.

Date	Mintage	F	VF	XF	Unc	BU
1975	—	—	—	—	35.00	—
1975 Proof	—	Value: 45.00				

Note: Medal rotation

KM# 36 100 CORDOBAS
25.1400 g., 0.9250 Silver .6668 oz. ASW **Subject:** Earthquake Relief Issue **Obv:** National emblem **Rev:** World globe in front of assorted flags

Date	Mintage	F	VF	XF	Unc	BU
1975	4,682	—	—	—	35.00	—
1975 Proof	3,500	Value: 45.00				

Note: Medal rotation

KM# 37 200 CORDOBAS
2.1000 g., 0.9000 Gold .0608 oz. AGW **Subject:** Pieta by Michelangelo **Obv:** National emblem **Rev:** Sitting figure holding lying figure on lap within circle

Date	Mintage	F	VF	XF	Unc	BU
1975	1,200	—	—	—	60.00	75.00
1975 Proof	1,650	Value: 85.00				

KM# 79 250 CORDOBAS
171.0700 g., 0.9990 Silver 5.4946 oz. ASW **Subject:** Spanish Royal Visit **Obv:** National emblem within circle **Rev:** Heads 1/4 left on map

Date	Mintage	F	VF	XF	Unc	BU
1992 Proof	—	Value: 135				

KM# 38 500 CORDOBAS
5.4000 g., 0.9000 Gold .1563 oz. AGW **Subject:** Colonial Church, La Merced **Obv:** National emblem **Rev:** Colonial church within circle

Date	Mintage	F	VF	XF	Unc	BU
1975	200	—	—	—	325	350
1975 Proof	100	Value: 650				

KM# 39 500 CORDOBAS
5.4000 g., 0.9000 Gold .1563 oz. AGW **Subject:** Earthquake Relief Issue **Obv:** National emblem **Rev:** "The Bud" by Annigoni

Date	Mintage	F	VF	XF	Unc	BU
1975	1,750	—	—	—	150	175
1975 Proof	1,120	Value: 220				

KM# 45 500 CORDOBAS
14.0000 g., 0.9250 Silver .4164 oz. ASW **Obv:** Map **Rev:** Head with hat facing **Note:** Medal rotation.

Date	Mintage	F	VF	XF	Unc	BU
1980Mo Proof	7,000	Value: 35.00				

KM# 46 500 CORDOBAS
14.0000 g., 0.9250 Silver .4164 oz. ASW **Obv:** Map **Rev:** Bust right **Note:** Medal rotation.

Date	Mintage	F	VF	XF	Unc	BU
1980Mo Proof	7,000	Value: 35.00				

KM# 47 500 CORDOBAS
14.0000 g., 0.9250 Silver .4164 oz. ASW **Obv:** National emblem **Rev:** Bust of Rigoberto Lopez Perez 1/4 left **Note:** Medal rotation.

Date	Mintage	F	VF	XF	Unc	BU
1980Mo Proof	7,000	Value: 35.00				

KM# 69 500 CORDOBAS
14.0000 g., 0.9990 Silver .4502 oz. ASW **Subject:** 50th Anniversary - A. C. Sandino **Obv:** National emblem
Rev: Birthplace of Augusto Cesar Sandino

Date	Mintage	F	VF	XF	Unc	BU
ND(1984) Proof	1,000	Value: 45.00				

KM# 70 500 CORDOBAS
14.0000 g., 0.9990 Silver .4502 oz. ASW **Subject:** 50th

Anniversary - Sandono's Death **Obv:** National emblem **Rev:** Facing busts of Generals Sandino, Estrada and Umanzor

Date	Mintage	F	VF	XF	Unc	BU
ND(1984) Proof	1,000	Value: 45.00				

KM# 73 500 CORDOBAS
14.0000 g., 0.9990 Silver .4502 oz. ASW **Subject:** 50th Anniversary - The Murder of General Augusto Cesar Sandino **Obv:** National emblem **Rev:** Bust with hat facing

Date	Mintage	F	VF	XF	Unc	BU
ND(1984) Proof	1,000	Value: 45.00				

KM# 63 500 CORDOBAS
Aluminum **Obv:** Hat above date and sprigs **Rev:** Value

Date	Mintage	F	VF	XF	Unc	BU
1987	—	—	—	2.50	6.50	—

KM# 40 1000 CORDOBAS
9.5000 g., 0.9000 Gold .2749 oz. AGW **Subject:** U.S. Bicentennial **Obv:** National emblem **Rev:** Liberty bell divides dates

Date	Mintage	F	VF	XF	Unc	BU
1975	3,380	—	—	—	200	225
1975 Proof	2,270	Value: 250				

KM# 48 1000 CORDOBAS
20.0000 g., 0.9000 Gold .5788 oz. AGW **Subject:** 1st Anniversary of Revolution **Obv:** Three 1/2 figures with guns raised **Rev:** Busts of Sandino and Fonseca

Date	Mintage	F	VF	XF	Unc	BU
1980Mo Proof	6,000	Value: 465				

KM# 52 1000 CORDOBAS
20.0000 g., 0.9170 Gold .5896 oz. AGW **Subject:** 50th Anniversary - The Murder of General Augusto Cesar Sandino **Obv:** National emblem **Rev:** Bust with hat facing

Date	Mintage	F	VF	XF	Unc	BU
1984 Proof	1,000	Value: 550				

KM# 53 1000 CORDOBAS
20.0000 g., 0.9170 Gold .5896 oz. AGW **Obv:** National emblem **Rev:** Birthplace of Augusto Cesar Sandino

Date	Mintage	F	VF	XF	Unc	BU
1984 Proof	1,000	Value: 550				

KM# 54 1000 CORDOBAS
20.0000 g., 0.9170 Gold .5896 oz. AGW **Obv:** National emblem **Rev:** Facing busts of Generals Sandino, Estrada and Umanzor

Date	Mintage	F	VF	XF	Unc	BU
1984 Proof	1,000	Value: 550				

KM# 41 2000 CORDOBAS
19.2000 g., 0.9000 Gold .5556 oz. AGW **Subject:** U.S. Bicentennial **Obv:** National emblem **Rev:** Betsy Ross sewing flag on left, astronaut placing flag on moon on right

Date	Mintage	F	VF	XF	Unc	BU
1975	320	—	—	—	525	550
1975 Proof	100	Value: 850				

KM# 65 2000 CORDOBAS
16.6000 g., 0.8250 Silver .4404 oz. ASW **Subject:** Soccer **Obv:** National emblem within circle **Rev:** Soccer player

Date	Mintage	F	VF	XF	Unc	BU
1988 Proof	5,000	Value: 40.00				

KM# 64 10000 CORDOBAS
20.0000 g., 0.9990 Silver .6431 oz. ASW **Subject:** Discovery of Nicaragua by Columbus **Obv:** National emblem **Rev:** Sailing ship and small boat

Date	Mintage	F	VF	XF	Unc	BU
1989 Proof	Est. 10,000	Value: 45.00				

KM# 66 10000 CORDOBAS
26.4000 g., 0.9990 Silver .8480 oz. ASW **Obv:** National emblem within circle **Rev:** Two soccer players

Date	Mintage	F	VF	XF	Unc	BU
1990 Proof	5,000	Value: 45.00				

KM# 67 10000 CORDOBAS
26.0000 g., 0.9990 Silver .8352 oz. ASW **Subject:** Discovery of America **Obv:** National emblem within circle **Rev:** Sailing ship

Date	Mintage	F	VF	XF	Unc	BU
1990 Proof	10,000	Value: 47.50				

KM# 68 10000 CORDOBAS
26.0000 g., 0.9990 Silver .8352 oz. ASW **Series:** 1992 Summer Olympics **Obv:** National emblem within circle **Rev:** Bicyclist

Date	Mintage	F	VF	XF	Unc	BU
1990 Proof	10,000	Value: 40.00				

KM# 71 10000 CORDOBAS
26.0000 g., 0.9990 Silver .8352 oz. ASW **Subject:** Wildlife Protection **Obv:** National emblem within circle **Rev:** Ocelot

Date	Mintage	F	VF	XF	Unc	BU
1990 Proof	5,000	Value: 50.00				

KM# 72.1 10000 CORDOBAS
20.4000 g., 0.9990 Silver .6553 oz. ASW **Series:** 1992 Summer Olympics **Obv:** National emblem within circle **Rev:** Horse jumping

Date	Mintage	F	VF	XF	Unc	BU
1990 Proof	10,000	Value: 60.00				

KM# 72.2 10000 CORDOBAS
20.0000 g., 0.9990 Silver .6431 oz. ASW **Series:** 1992 Summer Olympics **Obv:** National emblem within circle **Rev:** Horse jumping, 999 added at 4 o'clock

Date	Mintage	F	VF	XF	Unc	BU
1990 Proof	Inc. above	Value: 42.50				

KM# 74 10000 CORDOBAS
25.9000 g., 0.9990 Silver .8320 oz. ASW **Series:** 1992 Summer Olympics **Obv:** National emblem within circle **Rev:** Tennis player proclaiming victory

Date	Mintage	F	VF	XF	Unc	BU
1990 Proof	10,000	Value: 50.00				

KM# 75 10000 CORDOBAS
20.0000 g., 0.9990 Silver .6431 oz. ASW **Series:** 1992 Winter Olympics **Obv:** National emblem within circle **Rev:** Figure skater

Date	Mintage	F	VF	XF	Unc	BU
1990 Proof	10,000	Value: 47.50				

REVOLUTIONARY TOKEN COINAGE

KM# Tn1 10 PESOS
18.0000 g., Lead **Issuer:** General Augusto Cesar Sandino, 1925-1934

Date	Mintage	VG	F	VF	XF	Unc
ND(1927)	—	400	700	1,200	2,500	—

PATTERNS

Including off metal strikes.

KM#	Date	Mintage	Identification	Mkt Val
Pn10	1912H	2	1/2 Centavo. Silver. KM10; 2 known.	—
Pn11	1912H	1	1/2 Centavo. Gold. KM10; unique.	—
Pn12	1912H	2	Centavo. Silver. KM11; 2 known.	4,000
Pn13	1912H	1	Centavo. Gold. KM#11.	—
Pn14	1912H	2	5 Centavos. Silver. KM12.	—
Pn15	1912H	1	5 Centavos. Gold. KM12.	—
Pn16	1912H	1	10 Centavos. Gold. KM13.	—
Pn17	1912H	1	25 Centavos. Gold. KM14.	—
Pn18	1912H	1	50 Centavos. Gold. KM#15.	—
Pn19	1912H	1	Cordoba. Gold. KM16.	—
Pn20	1975	—	20 Cordobas. Silver. KM32 with 4.65 gram Plata Fino, LEY 925 below date.	—
Pn21	1975	—	50 Cordobas. Silver. KM34 with 11.63 gram. Plata Fino, LEY 925 below date.	—

KM#	Date	Mintage	Identification	Mkt Val
Pn22	1975	—	100 Cordobas. Silver. KM36 with 23.25 gram. Plata Fino, LEY 925 below date.	—

TRIAL STRIKES

KM#	Date	Mintage	Identification	Mkt Val
TS1	ND(1912)	—	10 Centavos. Aluminum. Obverse.	350

KM#	Date	Mintage	Identification	Mkt Val
TS2	ND(1912)	—	10 Centavos. Aluminum. Bust facing within circle. Radiant sun and hills within circle. Reverse.	350
TS3	ND(1912)	—	25 Centavos. Aluminum. Obverse.	360
TS4	ND(1912)	—	25 Centavos. Aluminum. Reverse.	360

KM#	Date	Mintage	Identification	Mkt Val
TS5	ND(1912)	—	50 Centavos. Aluminum. Bust facing within circle. Radiant sun and hills within circle. Obverse.	375
TS6	ND(1912)	—	50 Centavos. Aluminum.	375
TS7	ND(1912)	—	Cordoba. 18.0000 Aluminum. Obverse.	—
TS8	ND(1912)	—	Cordoba. 18.0000 Aluminum. Reverse.	—
TS9	1965	—	5 Centavos. Nickel. Raised "Trial" left of bust on obverse, above rays on reverse. KM24.2.	—
TS10	1965	—	10 Centavos. Nickel. Raised "Trial" left of bust on obverse, above rays on reverse. KM17.2.	—

MINT SETS

KM#	Date	Mintage	Identification	Issue Price	Mkt Val
MS1	1975 (5)	—	KM37-41	—	1,150
MS2	1975 (5)	2,250	KM#32-36	—	110

PROOF SETS

KM#	Date	Mintage	Identification	Issue Price	Mkt Val
PS1	1912 (7)	10	KM10-16	—	4,500
PS2	1912 (3)	2	Pn10, Pn12, Pn14	—	4,500
PS3	1912 (7)	1	Pn11, Pn13, Pn15-19	—	—
PS4	1972 (5)	20,000	KM17.3-19.3, 24.3, 26	8.00	15.00
PS5	1975 (7)	—	KM32, 33, 35, 37, 38, 40, 41	—	1,750
PS6	1975 (5)	2,000	KM32-36	—	160
PS7	1975 (3)	—	KM32, 33, 35	115	90.00
PS8	1975 (3)	—	KM34, 36, 39	—	255
PS9	1975 (2)	—	KM37, 39	—	255

NIGER

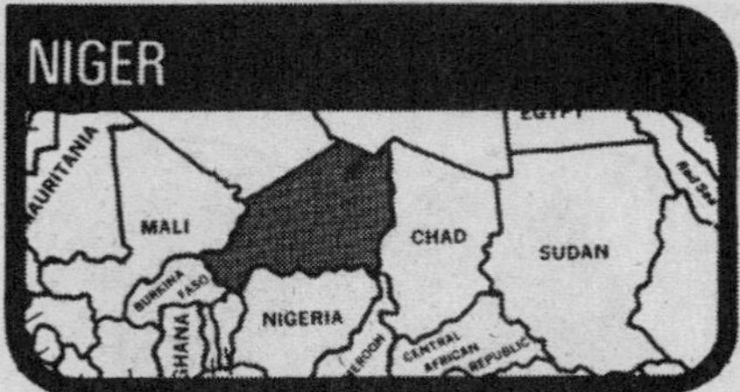

The Republic of Niger, located in West Africa's Sahara region 1,000 miles (1,609 km.) from the Mediterranean shore, has an area of 489,191 sq. mi. (1,267,000 sq. km.) and a population of *7.4 million. Capital: Niamey. The economy is based on subsistence agriculture and raising livestock. Peanuts, peanut oil, and livestock are exported.

Although four-fifths of Niger is arid desert, it was, some 6,000 years ago inhabited and an important economic crossroads. Its modern history began in the 19th century with the beginning of contacts with British and German explorers searching for the mouth of the Niger River. Niger was incorporated into French West Africa in 1896, but it was 1922 before all native resistance was quelled and Niger became a French colony. In 1958 the voters approved the new French Constitution and elected to become an autonomous republic within the French Community. On Aug. 3, 1960, Niger withdrew from the Community and proclaimed its independence.

REPUBLIC

DECIMAL COINAGE

KM# 1 10 FRANCS
4.2000 g., 0.9000 Gold .1215 oz. AGW **Subject:** Independence Commemorataive **Obv:** President Diori Hamani left **Rev:** Flagged arms

Date	Mintage	F	VF	XF	Unc	BU
ND(1960) Proof	1,000	Value: 90.00				

KM# 7 10 FRANCS
3.2000 g., 0.9000 Gold .0926 oz. AGW **Obv:** Ostriches **Rev:** Flagged arms

Date	Mintage	F	VF	XF	Unc	BU
1968 Proof	1,000	Value: 125				

KM# 8.1 10 FRANCS
20.0000 g., 0.9000 Silver .5845 oz. ASW **Obv:** Lion **Rev:** Flagged arms **Note:** Sharp details, raised rim.

Date	Mintage	F	VF	XF	Unc	BU
1968 Proof	1,000	Value: 65.00				

KM# 8.2 10 FRANCS
24.5400 g., 0.9000 Silver .7100 oz. ASW **Obv:** Exists with and without accent marks above first "E" in REPUBLIQUE **Rev:** Flagged arms **Note:** Dull details, machined-down rim

Date	Mintage	F	VF	XF	Unc	BU
1968 Proof	—	—	—	—	40.00	—

KM# 2 25 FRANCS
8.0000 g., 0.9000 Gold .2315 oz. AGW **Subject:** Independence

Commemorative **Obv:** President Diori Hamani left **Rev:** Flagged arms

Date	Mintage	F	VF	XF	Unc	BU
ND(1960) Proof	1,000	Value: 165				

KM# 9 25 FRANCS
8.0000 g., 0.9000 Gold .2315 oz. AGW **Obv:** Barbary sheep **Rev:** Flagged arms

Date	Mintage	F	VF	XF	Unc	BU
1968 Proof	1,000	Value: 185				

KM# 3 50 FRANCS
16.0000 g., 0.9000 Gold .4630 oz. AGW **Subject:** Independence Commemorative **Obv:** President Diori Hamani left **Rev:** Flagged arms

Date	Mintage	F	VF	XF	Unc	BU
ND(1960) Proof	1,000	Value: 325				

KM# 10 50 FRANCS
16.0000 g., 0.9000 Gold .4630 oz. AGW **Subject:** Independence Commemorative **Obv:** Lion **Rev:** Flagged arms

Date	Mintage	F	VF	XF	Unc	BU
1968 Proof	1,000	Value: 400				

KM# 4 100 FRANCS
32.0000 g., 0.9000 Gold .9260 oz. AGW **Subject:** Independence Commemorative **Obv:** President Diori Hamani left **Rev:** Flagged arms

Date	Mintage	F	VF	XF	Unc	BU
ND(1960) Proof	1,000	Value: 800				

KM# 11 100 FRANCS
32.0000 g., 0.9000 Gold .9260 oz. AGW **Subject:** Independence Commemorative **Obv:** President Diori Hamani left **Rev:** Flagged arms

Date	Mintage	F	VF	XF	Unc	BU
1968 Proof	1,000	Value: 800				

KM# 5 500 FRANCS
10.0000 g., 0.9000 Silver .2893 oz. ASW **Subject:** Independence Commemorative **Obv:** President Diori Hamani left **Rev:** Flagged arms

Date	Mintage	F	VF	XF	Unc	BU
ND(1960) Proof	—	Value: 35.00				

KM# 6 1000 FRANCS
20.0000 g., 0.9000 Silver .5787 oz. ASW **Subject:** Independence Commemorative **Obv:** President Diori Hamani left **Rev:** Flagged arms

Date	Mintage	F	VF	XF	Unc	BU
ND(1960) Proof	—	Value: 55.00				

ESSAIS

KM#	Date	Mintage	Identification	Issue Price	Mkt Val
E1	1960	—	10 Francs. Silver. 39.4000 g. Lion facing. Arms. Thick planchet.	—	125
E2	1960	—	25 Francs.	—	200
E3	1960	—	50 Francs.	—	325
E4	1960	—	100 Francs.	—	650
E5	ND(1960)	1,000	500 Francs. Silver. KM5.	—	40.00

KM#	Date	Mintage	Identification	Issue Price	Mkt Val
E6	ND(1960)	1,000	1000 Francs. Silver. KM6.	—	60.00

KM#	Date	Mintage	Identification	Issue Price	Mkt Val
E7	1968	—	10 Francs. Gold. 31.7800 g. KM8.	—	1,750
E8	1968	—	10 Francs. Silver.	—	35.00
E9	1968	—	25 Francs. Silver.	—	40.00
E10	1968	—	50 Francs. Silver.	—	45.00
E11	1968	—	100 Francs. Silver.	—	50.00

PATTERNS

Including off metal strikes

KM#	Date	Mintage	Identification	Mkt Val
Pn1	1968	—	10 Francs. Copper. 18.8200 g. Reeded edge. KM8.1.	200

PROOF SETS

KM#	Date	Mintage	Identification	Issue Price	Mkt Val
PS1	1960 (4)	1,000	KM1-4	—	1,380
PS2	1968 (4)	—	KM7, 9-11	—	1,500

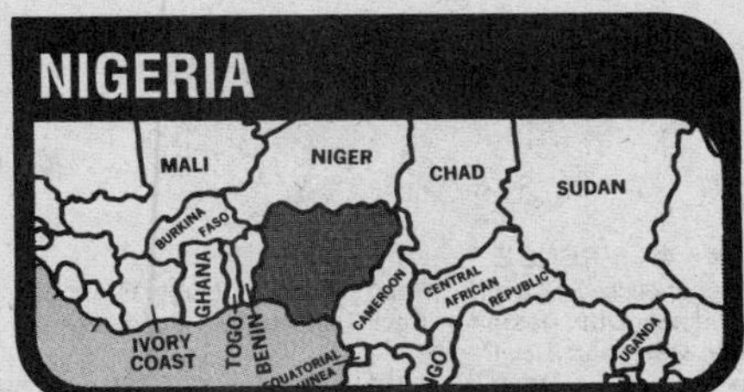

Nigeria, situated on the Atlantic coast of West Africa has an area of 356,669 sq. mi. (923,770 sq. km.).

Following the Napoleonic Wars, the British expanded their trade with the interior of Nigeria. The Berlin Conference of 1885 recognized British claims to a sphere of influence in that area, and in the following year the Royal Niger Company was chartered. Direct British control of the territory was initiated in 1900, and in 1914 the amalgamation of Northern and Southern Nigeria into the Colony and Protectorate of Nigeria was effected. In 1960, following a number of territorial and constitutional changes, Nigeria was granted independence within the British Commonwealth as a federation of the Northern, Western and Eastern regions. Nigeria altered its political relationship with Great Britain on Oct. 1, 1963, by proclaiming itself a republic. It did, however, elect to remain a member of the Commonwealth of Nations.

On May 30, 1967, the Eastern Region of the republic an area occupied principally by the proud and resourceful Ibo tribe – seceded from Nigeria and proclaimed itself the independent Republic of Biafra with Odumegwu Ojukwu as Chief of State. Civil war erupted and raged for 31 months. Casualties, including civilian, were about two million, the majority succumbing to malnutrition and disease. Biafra surrendered to the federal government on January 15, 1970.

For earlier coinage refer to British West Africa.

Arms Mottos
Short: Unity and faith
Long: Unity and Faith, Peace and Progress

BRITISH PROTECTORATE OF NIGERIA

POUND STERLING COINAGE

KM# 1 1/2 PENNY
Bronze **Ruler:** Elizabeth II **Obv:** Crown above center hole flanked by curved sprig **Rev:** Star design around center hole

Date	Mintage	F	VF	XF	Unc	BU
1959	52,800,000	—	0.15	0.25	1.00	—
1959 Proof	6,031	Value: 2.50				

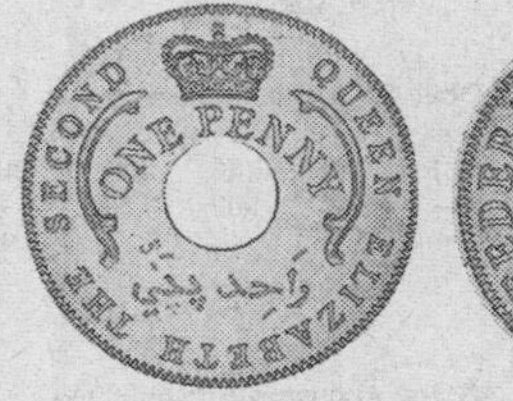

KM# 2 PENNY
Bronze, 28 mm. **Ruler:** Elizabeth II **Obv:** Crown above center hole flanked by curved sprig **Rev:** Star design around center hole

Date	Mintage	F	VF	XF	Unc	BU
1959	93,368,000	—	0.15	0.25	2.00	—
1959 Proof	6,031	Value: 2.50				

KM# 3 3 PENCE
Nickel-Brass **Ruler:** Elizabeth II **Obv:** Crowned head right **Obv. Designer:** Cecil Thomas **Rev:** Cotton plant

Date	Mintage	F	VF	XF	Unc	BU
1959	52,000,000	—	0.20	0.40	2.00	—
1959 Proof	6,031	Value: 3.50				

KM# 4 6 PENCE
Copper-Nickel, 17.8 mm. **Ruler:** Elizabeth II **Obv:** Crowned head right **Obv. Designer:** Cecil Thomas **Rev:** Cocoa beans **Rev. Designer:** T.H. Paget

Date	Mintage	F	VF	XF	Unc	BU
1959	35,000,000	—	0.40	0.80	2.50	—
1959 Proof	6,031	Value: 5.00				

KM# 5 SHILLING
Copper-Nickel, 22.8 mm. **Ruler:** Elizabeth II **Obv:** Crowned head right **Obv. Designer:** Cecil Thomas **Rev:** Palm divides date

Date	Mintage	F	VF	XF	Unc	BU
1959	18,000,000	—	0.65	1.45	3.50	—
1959 Proof	6,031	Value: 6.50				
1961	48,584,000	—	0.65	1.45	3.50	—
1962	39,416,000	—	0.65	1.45	3.50	—

KM# 6 2 SHILLING
Copper-Nickel, 27 mm. **Ruler:** Elizabeth II **Obv:** Crowned head right **Obv. Designer:** Cecil Thomas **Rev:** Flowers **Edge:** Security

Date	Mintage	F	VF	XF	Unc	BU
1959	15,000,000	—	1.25	2.50	6.00	—
1959 Proof	6,031	Value: 9.00				

BRITISH COLONY

DECIMAL COINAGE

KM# 7 1/2 KOBO
Bronze **Ruler:** Elizabeth II **Obv:** Arms with supporters **Rev:** Value flanked by flowers

Date	Mintage	F	VF	XF	Unc	BU
1973	166,618,000	—	0.45	1.00	3.50	—
1973 Proof	10,000	Value: 3.50				

KM# 8.1 KOBO
Bronze **Ruler:** Elizabeth II **Obv:** Arms with supporters and short motto **Rev:** Value flanked by oil derricks

Date	Mintage	F	VF	XF	Unc	BU
1973	586,944,000	—	0.25	0.50	2.00	—
1973 Proof	10,000	Value: 3.50				
1974	14,500,000	—	0.25	0.50	3.00	—

KM# 8.2 KOBO
Bronze **Ruler:** Elizabeth II **Obv:** Arms with supporters and long motto **Rev:** Value flanked by oil derricks

Date	Mintage	F	VF	XF	Unc	BU
1987	—	—	0.50	1.50	6.00	—
1988	—	—	0.50	1.50	6.00	—

KM# 8.2a KOBO
2.5700 g., Copper Plated Steel, 17 mm. **Ruler:** Elizabeth II **Obv:** Arms with supporters and long motto **Rev:** Value flanked by oil derricks

Date	Mintage	F	VF	XF	Unc	BU
1991	—	—	—	—	0.25	0.45

KM# 9.1 5 KOBO
Copper-Nickel **Ruler:** Elizabeth II **Obv:** Arms with supporters and short motto **Rev:** Cocoa beans

Date	Mintage	F	VF	XF	Unc	BU
1973	96,920,000	—	0.35	0.75	2.75	—
1973 Proof	10,000	Value: 4.00				
1974	—	—	0.45	0.85	3.00	—
1976	9,800,000	—	0.45	0.85	3.00	—
1986	—	—	0.45	0.85	3.00	—

KM# 9.2 5 KOBO
Copper-Nickel **Ruler:** Elizabeth II **Obv:** Arms with supporters and long motto **Rev:** Cocoa beans

Date	Mintage	F	VF	XF	Unc	BU
1987	—	—	1.00	2.50	7.00	—
1988	—	—	1.00	2.50	7.00	—
1989	—	—	1.00	2.50	7.00	—

KM# 10.1 10 KOBO
Copper-Nickel, 22.8 mm. **Ruler:** Elizabeth II **Obv:** Arms with supporters and short motto **Rev:** Value at left of oil palms

Date	Mintage	F	VF	XF	Unc	BU
1973 Proof	10,000	Value: 5.00				
1973	340,870,000	—	0.50	1.00	3.50	—
1974	—	—	0.60	1.20	3.75	—
1976	7,000,000	—	0.60	1.20	3.75	—

KM# 10.2 10 KOBO
Copper-Nickel, 22.8 mm. **Ruler:** Elizabeth II **Obv:** Arms with supporters and long motto **Rev:** Value to left of oil palms

Date	Mintage	F	VF	XF	Unc	BU
1987	—	—	1.25	3.50	9.00	—
1988	—	—	1.25	3.50	9.00	—
1989	—	—	1.25	3.50	9.00	—
1990	—	—	1.25	3.50	9.00	—

KM# 12 10 KOBO
3.4800 g., Copper Plated Steel, 19.9 mm. **Ruler:** Elizabeth II **Obv:** Arms with supporters and long motto **Rev:** Value to left of oil palms **Shape:** 12-sided

Date	Mintage	F	VF	XF	Unc	BU
1991	—	—	—	—	0.45	0.75

KM# 11 25 KOBO
Copper-Nickel **Ruler:** Elizabeth II **Obv:** Arms with supporters and short motto **Rev:** Groundnuts **Edge:** Security

Date	Mintage	F	VF	XF	Unc	BU
1973	4,616,000	—	1.00	2.50	7.50	—
1973 Proof	10,000	Value: 8.50				
1975	—	—	1.00	2.50	7.50	—

KM# 11a 25 KOBO
4.4900 g., Copper Plated Steel, 22.45 mm. **Ruler:** Elizabeth II **Obv:** Arms with supporters and long motto **Rev:** Groundnuts **Edge:** Reeded

Date	Mintage	F	VF	XF	Unc	BU
1991	—	—	—	—	0.65	1.00

KM# 13.1 50 KOBO
5.5300 g., Nickel Plated Steel, 24.72 mm. **Ruler:** Elizabeth II **Obv:** Arms with supporters with long motto **Rev:** Corn and value **Shape:** 12 rounded sides

Date	Mintage	F	VF	XF	Unc	BU
1991	—	—	—	—	1.25	1.50

KM# 13.2 50 KOBO
5.5300 g., Nickel Clad Steel, 24.72 mm. **Ruler:** Elizabeth II **Obv:** Arms with supporters with long motto **Rev:** Corn with value **Shape:** Round with a multi-sided inner rim

Date	Mintage	F	VF	XF	Unc	BU
1993	—	—	—	—	1.25	1.50

KM# 14 NAIRA
12.1500 g., Nickel Plated Steel, 27.5 mm. **Ruler:** Elizabeth II **Obv:** Arms with supporters and long motto **Rev:** Head 1/4 right

Date	Mintage	F	VF	XF	Unc	BU
1991	—	—	—	—	1.75	2.00
1993	—	—	—	—	1.75	2.00

KM# 15 100 NAIRA
28.2800 g., 0.9250 Silver .8410 oz. ASW **Ruler:** Elizabeth II **Subject:** 100 Years - Banking in Nigeria **Obv:** Arms with supporters **Rev:** Bank building **Edge:** Reeded

Date	Mintage	F	VF	XF	Unc	BU
1994 Proof	5,000	Value: 600				

Note: Issue price at Bank in Lagos approximately $1,400

KM# 16 1000 NAIRA
47.5400 g., 0.9166 Gold 1.4010 oz. AGW **Ruler:** Elizabeth II **Subject:** 100 Years - Banking in Nigeria **Obv:** Arms with supporters **Rev:** Bank building **Edge:** Reeded

Date	Mintage	F	VF	XF	Unc	BU
1994 Proof	100	Value: 2,250				

PATTERNS

Including off metal strikes

KM#	Date	Mintage	Identification	Mkt Val
Pn1	1962	—	Shilling. Bronze. KM5.	200
Pn2	1973	—	10 Kobo. Bronze. KM10.	175

TRIAL STRIKES

KM#	Date	Mintage	Identification	Mkt Val
TS1	1962	—	Shilling. Copper-Nickel. "TRIAL" in field on obverse and reverse.	120

PROOF SETS

KM#	Date	Mintage	Identification	Issue Price	Mkt Val
PS1	1959 (6)	1,031	KM1-5, 6.1, red case, originals	—	45.00
PS2	1959 (6)	5,000	KM1-5, 6.1, blue case, restrikes	—	30.00
PS3	1973 (5)	102,000	KM7, 8.1-10.1,11	14.70	25.00

NIUE

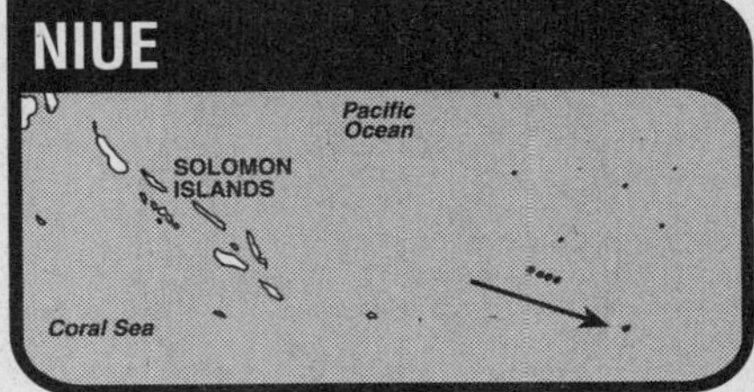

Niue, or Savage Island, a dependent state of New Zealand is located in the Pacific Ocean east of Tonga and southeast of Samoa. The size is 100 sq. mi. (260 sq. km.) with a population of *2,000. Chief village and port is Alofi. Bananas and copra are exported.

Discovered by Captain Cook in 1774, it was originally part of the Cook Islands administration but has been separate since 1922.

MINT MARKS

PM - Pobjoy Mint

NEW ZEALAND DEPENDENT STATE

DECIMAL COINAGE

KM# 85 DOLLAR

10.0200 g., 0.5000 Silver .1608 oz. ASW **Obv:** Crowned arms within sprigs **Rev:** Sailing ship, value and emblem

Date	Mintage	F	VF	XF	Unc	BU
1996 Proof	—	Value: 7.50				

KM# 113 DOLLAR

10.0200 g., 0.5000 Silver .1608 oz. ASW **Series:** Endangered Wildlife **Obv:** Crowned arms within sprigs **Rev:** Jaguar on tree limb

Date	Mintage	F	VF	XF	Unc	BU
1996 Proof	—	Value: 12.50				

KM# 122 DOLLAR

10.0000 g., 0.5000 Silver .1608 oz. ASW, 30 mm. **Series:** Protect Our World **Obv:** Crowned arms within sprigs **Rev:** Oak tree **Edge:** Reeded

Date	Mintage	F	VF	XF	Unc	BU
1996 Proof	—	Value: 8.00				

KM# 88 DOLLAR

Copper-Nickel **Obv:** Crowned arms within sprigs **Rev:** Bust facing **Rev. Legend:** . . . Princess of Wales **Note:** Similar to 10 Dollars, KM#91.

Date	Mintage	F	VF	XF	Unc	BU
1997	—	—	—	—	3.00	4.50

KM# 89 DOLLAR

Copper-Nickel **Obv:** Crowned arms within sprigs **Rev:** Head left above sprigs **Rev. Legend:** . . . Princess of Wales **Note:** Similar to 10 Dollars, KM#92.

Date	Mintage	F	VF	XF	Unc	BU
1997	—	—	—	—	3.00	4.50

KM# 87 DOLLAR

Copper-Nickel **Obv:** Crowned arms within sprigs **Rev:** Bust facing **Rev. Legend:** . . . The People's Princess

Date	Mintage	F	VF	XF	Unc	BU
1997	—	—	—	—	3.00	4.50

KM# 102 DOLLAR

Copper-Nickel **Obv:** Crowned head right **Rev:** Bust facing **Rev. Legend:** . . . In Memoriam **Note:** Similar to 10 Dollars, KM#104.

Date	Mintage	F	VF	XF	Unc	BU
1998	—	—	—	—	3.00	4.50

KM# 103 DOLLAR

Copper-Nickel **Obv:** Crowned head right **Rev:** Bust facing **Rev. Legend:** . . . Princess of Wales **Note:** Similar to 10 Dollars, KM#105.

Date	Mintage	F	VF	XF	Unc	BU
1998	—	—	—	—	3.00	4.50

KM# 115 DOLLAR

Copper-Nickel **Subject:** 50th Anniversary of Peanuts **Obv:** Crowned head right **Rev:** Snoopy and Woodstock **Note:** Similar to 10 Dollars, KM#116.

Date	Mintage	F	VF	XF	Unc	BU
2000	Est. 100,000	—	—	—	3.00	4.50

KM# 174 DOLLAR

21.0000 g., Copper-Nickel, 38.6 mm. **Subject:** Marine Life Protection **Obv:** Crowned head right **Rev:** Multicolor fish scene **Edge:** Reeded

Date	Mintage	F	VF	XF	Unc	BU
2000	—	—	—	—	12.50	20.00

KM# 1 5 DOLLARS

Copper-Nickel **Series:** Olympics **Subject:** Tennis **Obv:** Crowned arms within sprigs **Rev:** Boris Becker

Date	Mintage	F	VF	XF	Unc	BU
1987	80,000	—	—	—	6.00	8.00

KM# 5 5 DOLLARS

Copper-Nickel **Subject:** 24th Olympiad Tennis Games, Seoul 1988 **Obv:** Crowned arms within sprigs **Rev:** Steffi Graf

Date	Mintage	F	VF	XF	Unc	BU
1987	50,000	—	—	—	6.00	8.00

KM# 11 5 DOLLARS

Copper-Nickel **Subject:** 24th Olympic Games, Seoul 1988 **Obv:** Crowned arms within sprigs **Rev:** 3/4 Tennis player with cup

Date	Mintage	F	VF	XF	Unc	BU
1988	80,000	—	—	—	6.00	8.00

KM# 12 5 DOLLARS

Copper-Nickel **Series:** Olympics **Subject:** Soccer **Obv:** Crowned arms within sprigs **Rev:** Soccer player left of cameo

Date	Mintage	F	VF	XF	Unc	BU
1988	50,000	—	—	—	4.00	6.00

KM# 15 5 DOLLARS

Copper-Nickel **Subject:** 24th Olympic Games, Seoul 1988 **Obv:** Crowned arms within sprigs **Rev:** Cameos of Navratilova, Graf and Evert, tennis champions

Date	Mintage	F	VF	XF	Unc	BU
1988	80,000	—	—	—	6.00	8.00

KM# 17 5 DOLLARS

Copper-Nickel, 38.8 mm. **Obv:** Crowned arms within sprigs **Rev:** Head of John F. Kennedy left

Date	Mintage	F	VF	XF	Unc	BU
1988	80,000	—	—	—	3.50	5.00

KM# 22 5 DOLLARS

Copper-Nickel **Obv:** Crowned arms within sprigs **Rev:** Head of General Douglas MacArthur 3/4 left

Date	Mintage	F	VF	XF	Unc	BU
1989	—	—	—	—	3.50	5.00

KM# 24 5 DOLLARS

Copper-Nickel **Obv:** Crowned arms within sprigs **Rev:** Tennis player

Date	Mintage	F	VF	XF	Unc	BU
1989	Est. 50,000	—	—	—	4.00	6.00

KM# 67 5 DOLLARS

Copper-Nickel **Subject:** 24th Olympic Games, Seoul 1988 **Obv:** Crowned arms within sprigs **Rev:** Steffi Graf

Date	Mintage	F	VF	XF	Unc	BU
1989	—	—	—	—	4.00	6.00

KM# 29 5 DOLLARS

Copper-Nickel, 38.8 mm. **Obv:** Crowned arms within sprigs **Rev:** Bust of General Eisenhower facing within flags

Date	Mintage	F	VF	XF	Unc	BU
1990	—	—	—	—	3.50	5.00

KM# 31 5 DOLLARS

Copper-Nickel, 38.8 mm. **Obv:** Crowned arms within sprigs **Rev:** General George S. Patton

Date	Mintage	F	VF	XF	Unc	BU
1990	—	—	—	—	3.50	5.00

KM# 33 5 DOLLARS

Copper-Nickel, 38.8 mm. **Obv:** Crowned arms within sprigs **Rev:** Admiral William Halsey

Date	Mintage	F	VF	XF	Unc	BU
1990	—	—	—	—	3.50	5.00

KM# 35 5 DOLLARS

Copper-Nickel, 38.8 mm. **Obv:** Crowned arms within sprigs **Rev:** Bust of President Franklin D. Roosevelt facing

Date	Mintage	F	VF	XF	Unc	BU
1990	—	—	—	—	3.50	5.00

KM# 37 5 DOLLARS
Copper-Nickel, 38.8 mm. **Obv:** Crowned arms within sprigs **Rev:** Sir Winston Churchill

Date	Mintage	F	VF	XF	Unc	BU
1990	—	—	—	—	3.50	5.00

KM# 143 5 DOLLARS
28.3400 g., Copper-Nickel, 38.6 mm. **Subject:** XIV Football World Championship Italy '90 **Obv:** Crowned arms within sprigs **Rev:** Head right at lower left of map and soccer player **Edge:** Reeded

Date	Mintage	F	VF	XF	Unc	BU
1990	60,000	—	—	—	4.00	6.00

KM# 144 5 DOLLARS
28.1500 g., Copper-Nickel, 38.5 mm. **Subject:** Basketball Centennial **Obv:** Crowned arms within sprigs **Rev:** Two female basketball players **Edge:** Reeded

Date	Mintage	F	VF	XF	Unc	BU
1991	28,000	—	—	—	4.00	6.00

KM# 58 5 DOLLARS
9.9300 g., 0.5000 Silver .1596 oz. ASW **Series:** World Cup Soccer **Obv:** Crowned arms within sprigs **Rev:** Soccer player and Statue of Liberty

Date	Mintage	F	VF	XF	Unc	BU
1991 Proof	150,000	Value: 9.00				

KM# 55 5 DOLLARS
10.0000 g., 0.5000 Silver .1608 oz. ASW **Obv:** Crowned arms within sprigs **Rev:** Ship, HMS Bounty

Date	Mintage	F	VF	XF	Unc	BU
1992 Proof	Est. 150,000	Value: 9.00				

KM# 60 5 DOLLARS
10.0000 g., 0.5000 Silver .1608 oz. ASW **Series:** Endangered Wildlife **Obv:** Crowned arms within sprigs **Rev:** Jaguar

Date	Mintage	F	VF	XF	Unc	BU
1992 Proof	Est. 25,000	Value: 15.00				

KM# 61 5 DOLLARS
10.0000 g., 0.5000 Silver .1608 oz. ASW **Series:** Olympics 1996 **Obv:** Crowned arms within sprigs **Rev:** Sprinter

Date	Mintage	F	VF	XF	Unc	BU
1992 Proof	100,000	Value: 8.00				

KM# 68 5 DOLLARS
9.8500 g., 0.5000 Silver .1584 oz. ASW **Subject:** First Moon Landing **Obv:** Crowned arms within sprigs **Rev:** Man on moon

Date	Mintage	F	VF	XF	Unc	BU
1992 Proof	—	Value: 8.00				

KM# 76 5 DOLLARS
10.0000 g., 0.9250 Silver .1607 oz. ASW **Obv:** Crowned arms within sprigs **Rev:** Kennedy, Brandenburg Gate

Date	Mintage	F	VF	XF	Unc	BU
1992 Proof	Est. 50,000	Value: 10.00				

KM# 80 5 DOLLARS
9.9500 g., 0.5000 Silver .1599 oz. ASW **Series:** Endangered Wildlife **Obv:** Crowned arms within sprigs **Rev:** Dolphins

Date	Mintage	F	VF	XF	Unc	BU
1992 Proof	—	Value: 17.50				

KM# 62 5 DOLLARS
9.9500 g., 0.5000 Silver .1599 oz. ASW **Series:** Protect Our World **Obv:** Crowned arms within sprigs **Rev:** Oak tree

Date	Mintage	F	VF	XF	Unc	BU
1993 Proof	—	Value: 12.50				

KM# 114 5 DOLLARS
31.5000 g., 0.9250 Silver .9368 oz. ASW **Subject:** The Resolution **Obv:** Crowned arms within sprigs **Rev:** Sailship above value

Date	Mintage	F	VF	XF	Unc	BU
1996 Proof	—	Value: 18.00				

KM# 175 5 DOLLARS
31.8400 g., 0.9250 Silver 0.9469 oz. ASW, 38.6 mm. **Subject:** Victorian Age **Obv:** Crowned head right **Rev:** Queen Victoria and Prince Albert wedding portrait **Edge:** Reeded

Date	Mintage	F	VF	XF	Unc	BU
1996 Proof	—	Value: 25.00				

KM# 173 5 DOLLARS
31.2200 g., 0.9250 Silver 0.9285 oz. ASW, 38.6 mm. **Subject:** Queen Mother **Obv:** Crowned arms within sprigs **Rev:** Queen Mother viewing London bomb damage **Edge:** Reeded

Date	Mintage	F	VF	XF	Unc	BU
1997 Proof	—	Value: 18.00				

KM# 145 5 DOLLARS
31.3600 g., 0.9250 Silver 0.9326 oz. ASW, 38.4 mm. **Subject:** Queen Mother **Obv:** Crowned head right **Rev:** Silver Wedding scene within circle **Edge:** Reeded

Date	Mintage	F	VF	XF	Unc	BU
1998 Proof	—	Value: 18.00				

KM# 171 5 DOLLARS
31.2500 g., 0.9250 Silver 0.9294 oz. ASW, 35.5 mm. **Subject:** Pygoplites Diacantus **Obv:** Crowned head right **Rev:** Three gold-plated fish **Edge:** Plain **Shape:** 7-sided

Date	Mintage	F	VF	XF	Unc	BU
1999 Proof	—	Value: 60.00				

KM# 120 5 DOLLARS
31.4200 g., 0.9250 Silver .9344 oz. ASW **Subject:** Pterois Radiata **Obv:** Crowned head right **Rev:** Gold colored Clearfin lion fish **Edge:** Plain **Shape:** 7-sided

Date	Mintage	F	VF	XF	Unc	BU
1999 Proof	—	Value: 60.00				

KM# 121 5 DOLLARS
31.4200 g., 0.9250 Silver .9344 oz. ASW **Subject:** Fourcipiger Longirostris **Obv:** Crowned head right **Rev:** Gold colored big long nosed Butterfly fish **Edge:** Plain **Shape:** 7-sided

Date	Mintage	F	VF	XF	Unc	BU
1999 Proof	—	Value: 60.00				

KM# 172 5 DOLLARS
28.4000 g., 0.9250 Silver with gilt outer ring 0.8446 oz. ASW, 38.5 mm. **Subject:** Queen Mother **Obv:** Crowned head right **Rev:** Queen Mother's engagement portrait **Edge:** Reeded

Date	Mintage	F	VF	XF	Unc	BU
2000 Proof	—	Value: 18.00				

KM# 46 10 DOLLARS
10.0000 g., 0.9250 Silver .2974 oz. ASW **Series:** Summer Olympics **Obv:** Crowned arms within sprigs **Rev:** Runners

Date	Mintage	F	VF	XF	Unc	BU
1991 Proof	150,000	Value: 12.50				

KM# 56 10 DOLLARS
10.0000 g., 0.9250 Silver .2974 oz. ASW **Series:** Summer Olympics **Obv:** Crowned arms within sprigs **Rev:** Discus Thrower

Date	Mintage	F	VF	XF	Unc	BU
1991 Proof	50,000	Value: 11.50				

KM# 59 10 DOLLARS
31.5300 g., 0.9999 Silver 1.0128 oz. ASW **Series:** World Cup Soccer **Obv:** Crowned arms within sprigs **Rev:** Handshake above value with hands holding crowned arms below

Date	Mintage	F	VF	XF	Unc	BU
1991 Proof	20,000	Value: 16.50				

KM# 69 10 DOLLARS
31.4300 g., 0.9999 Silver 1.0106 oz. ASW **Subject:** Cook's Pacific Voyages **Obv:** Crowned arms within sprigs **Rev:** Cameo left of sailing ship

Date	Mintage	F	VF	XF	Unc	BU
1992 Proof	—	Value: 17.50				

KM# 70 10 DOLLARS
31.4300 g., 0.9999 Silver 1.0106 oz. ASW **Subject:** Moon Landing **Obv:** Crowned arms within sprigs **Rev:** Luna 9

Date	Mintage	F	VF	XF	Unc	BU
1992 Proof	Est. 15,000	Value: 18.50				

KM# 74 10 DOLLARS
31.4700 g., 0.9250 Silver .9359 oz. ASW **Series:** Endangered Wildlife **Obv:** Crowned arms within sprigs **Rev:** Whales

Date	Mintage	F	VF	XF	Unc	BU
1992 Proof	25,000	Value: 22.50				

KM# 78 10 DOLLARS
31.4700 g., 0.9250 Silver .9359 oz. ASW **Subject:** The Resolution **Obv:** Crowned arms within sprigs **Rev:** Three-masted ship

Date	Mintage	F	VF	XF	Unc	BU
1992 Proof	Est. 15,000	Value: 18.50				

KM# 86 10 DOLLARS
31.0400 g., 0.9250 Silver .9231 oz. ASW **Obv:** Crowned arms within sprigs **Rev:** Head 1/4 left and rocket launch

Date	Mintage	F	VF	XF	Unc	BU
1992 Proof	—	Value: 18.50				

KM# 81 10 DOLLARS
1.2440 g., 0.9990 Gold .0400 oz. AGW **Subject:** Liberty Gold Bullion **Obv:** Crowned head right **Rev:** Statue of Liberty

Date	Mintage	F	VF	XF	Unc	BU
1997	—	—	—	—	30.00	—

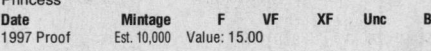

KM# 90 10 DOLLARS
28.2800 g., 0.9250 Silver .8411 oz. ASW **Obv:** Crowned arms within sprigs **Rev:** Bust facing **Rev. Legend:** . . . The People's Princess

Date	Mintage	F	VF	XF	Unc	BU
1997 Proof	Est. 10,000	Value: 15.00				

KM# 91 10 DOLLARS
28.2800 g., 0.9250 Silver .8411 oz. ASW **Obv:** Crowned arms within sprigs **Rev:** Bust facing **Rev. Legend:** . . . Princess of Wales

Date	Mintage	F	VF	XF	Unc	BU
1997 Proof	Est. 10,000	Value: 15.00				

KM# 92 10 DOLLARS
28.2800 g., 0.9250 Silver .8411 oz. ASW **Obv:** Crowned arms within sprigs **Rev:** Head left above sprigs **Rev. Legend:** . . . Princess of Wales

Date	Mintage	F	VF	XF	Unc	BU
1997 Proof	Est. 10,000	Value: 15.00				

KM# 104 10 DOLLARS
28.2800 g., 0.9250 Silver .8411 oz. ASW **Obv:** Crowned head right **Rev:** Bust facing **Rev. Legend:** . . . In Memoriam

Date	Mintage	F	VF	XF	Unc	BU
1998 Proof	Est. 10,000	Value: 15.00				

KM# 105 10 DOLLARS
28.2800 g., 0.9250 Silver .8411 oz. ASW **Obv:** Crowned head right **Rev:** Bust facing **Rev. Legend:** . . . Princess of Wales

Date	Mintage	F	VF	XF	Unc	BU
1998 Proof	Est. 10,000	Value: 15.00				

KM# 116 10 DOLLARS
28.2800 g., 0.9250 Silver .8411 oz. ASW **Subject:** 50th Anniversary of Peanuts **Obv:** Crowned head right **Rev:** Snoopy and Woodstock

Date	Mintage	F	VF	XF	Unc	BU
2000 Proof	Est. 10,000	Value: 17.50				

KM# 57 20 DOLLARS
31.4700 g., 0.9250 Silver .9359 oz. ASW **Subject:** 40th Anniversary of Coronation **Obv:** Crowned head right **Rev:** Crowned monogram within 3/4 wreath with value and dates below

Date	Mintage	F	VF	XF	Unc	BU
1993 Proof	Est. 10,000	Value: 20.00				

KM# 63 20 DOLLARS
31.4700 g., 0.9250 Silver .9359 oz. ASW **Series:** Protect Our World **Obv:** Crowned arms within sprigs **Rev:** Hand holding seedling

Date	Mintage	F	VF	XF	Unc	BU
1993 Proof	Est. 10,000	Value: 20.00				

KM# 64 20 DOLLARS
31.4700 g., 0.9250 Silver .9359 oz. ASW **Obv:** Crowned arms within sprigs **Rev:** Bust right and Statue of Liberty

Date	Mintage	F	VF	XF	Unc	BU
1993 Proof	—	Value: 20.00				

KM# 93 20 DOLLARS
1.2440 g., 0.9990 Gold .0400 oz. AGW **Obv:** Crowned arms within sprigs **Rev:** Bust facing **Rev. Legend:** ...The People's Princess

Date	Mintage	F	VF	XF	Unc	BU
1997 Proof	Est. 10,000	Value: 30.00				

KM# 94 20 DOLLARS
1.2440 g., 0.9990 Gold .0400 oz. AGW **Obv:** Crowned arms within sprigs **Rev:** Bust facing **Rev. Legend:** ...Princess of Wales

Date	Mintage	F	VF	XF	Unc	BU
1997 Proof	Est. 10,000	Value: 30.00				

KM# 95 20 DOLLARS
1.2440 g., 0.9990 Gold .0400 oz. AGW **Obv:** Crowned arms within sprigs **Rev:** Head left above sprigs **Rev. Legend:** ...Princess of Wales

Date	Mintage	F	VF	XF	Unc	BU
1997 Proof	Est. 10,000	Value: 30.00				

KM# 106 20 DOLLARS
1.2440 g., 0.9990 Gold .0400 oz. AGW **Obv:** Crowned head right **Rev:** Bust facing **Rev. Legend:** ...In Memoriam

Date	Mintage	F	VF	XF	Unc	BU
1998 Proof	Est. 10,000	Value: 30.00				

KM# 107 20 DOLLARS
1.2440 g., 0.9990 Gold .0400 oz. AGW **Obv:** Crowned head right **Rev:** Bust facing **Rev. Legend:** ...Princess of Wales

Date	Mintage	F	VF	XF	Unc	BU
1998 Proof	Est. 10,000	Value: 30.00				

KM# 117 20 DOLLARS
1.2400 g., 0.9990 Gold .0395 oz. AGW **Subject:** 50th Anniversary of Peanuts **Obv:** Crowned head right **Rev:** Snoopy and Woodstock

Date	Mintage	F	VF	XF	Unc	BU
2000 Proof	Est. 10,000	Value: 32.00				

KM# 79 25 DOLLARS
1.2441 g., 0.9990 Gold .0400 oz. AGW **Obv:** Crowned arms within sprigs **Rev:** Half length bust left

Date	Mintage	F	VF	XF	Unc	BU
1994 Proof	Est. 25,000	Value: 30.00				

KM# 82 25 DOLLARS
3.1000 g., 0.9990 Gold .1000 oz. AGW **Series:** Liberty Gold Bullion **Obv:** Crowned head right **Rev:** Statue of Liberty

Date	Mintage	F	VF	XF	Unc	BU
1997	—	—	—	—	—	70.00

KM# 96 25 DOLLARS
3.1000 g., 0.9990 Gold .1000 oz. AGW **Obv:** Crowned arms within sprigs **Rev:** Bust facing **Rev. Legend:** ...The People's Princess

Date	Mintage	F	VF	XF	Unc	BU
1997 Proof	Est. 7,500	Value: 70.00				

KM# 97 25 DOLLARS
3.1000 g., 0.9990 Gold .1000 oz. AGW **Obv:** Crowned arms within sprigs **Rev:** Bust facing **Rev. Legend:** ...Princess of Wales

Date	Mintage	F	VF	XF	Unc	BU
1997 Proof	Est. 7,500	Value: 70.00				

KM# 98 25 DOLLARS
3.1000 g., 0.9990 Gold .1000 oz. AGW **Obv:** Crowned arms within sprigs **Rev:** Head left above sprigs **Rev. Legend:** . . . Princess of Wales

Date	Mintage	F	VF	XF	Unc	BU
1997 Proof	Est. 7,500	Value: 70.00				

KM# 2 50 DOLLARS
27.1000 g., 0.6250 Silver .5446 oz. ASW **Series:** Olympics **Subject:** Tennis **Obv:** Crowned arms within sprigs **Rev:** Tennis player

Date	Mintage	F	VF	XF	Unc	BU
1987 Proof	20,000	Value: 22.50				

KM# 6 50 DOLLARS
27.1000 g., 0.6250 Silver .5446 oz. ASW **Subject:** 24th Olympiad Tennis Games, Seoul 1988 **Obv:** Crowned arms within sprigs **Rev:** Steffi Graf

Date	Mintage	F	VF	XF	Unc	BU
1987 Proof	20,000	Value: 22.50				

KM# 13 50 DOLLARS
27.1000 g., 0.6250 Silver .5446 oz. ASW **Subject:** 24th Olympic Games, Seoul 1988 **Obv:** Crowned arms within sprigs **Rev:** Steffi Graf **Note:** Similar to 5 Dollars, KM#11.

Date	Mintage	F	VF	XF	Unc	BU
1988 Proof	Est. 20,000	Value: 28.00				

KM# 14 50 DOLLARS
27.1000 g., 0.6250 Silver .5446 oz. ASW **Series:** Olympics **Subject:** Soccer **Obv:** Crowned arms within sprigs **Rev:** Soccer player to left of cameo

Date	Mintage	F	VF	XF	Unc	BU
1988 Proof	Est. 20,000	Value: 16.50				

KM# 16 50 DOLLARS
27.1000 g., 0.6250 Silver .5446 oz. ASW **Subject:** 24th Olympic Games, Seoul 1988 **Obv:** Crowned arms within sprigs **Rev:** Cameos of Navratilova, Graf and Evert, tennis champions

Date	Mintage	F	VF	XF	Unc	BU
1988 Proof	Est. 20,000	Value: 28.00				

KM# 18 50 DOLLARS
28.2800 g., 0.9250 Silver .8411 oz. ASW **Obv:** Crowned arms within sprigs **Rev:** Head left

Date	Mintage	F	VF	XF	Unc	BU
1988 Proof	20,000	Value: 18.00				

KM# 43 50 DOLLARS
28.2800 g., 0.9250 Silver .8411 oz. ASW **Subject:** Soccer **Obv:** Crowned arms within sprigs **Rev:** Soccer players divide circle

Date	Mintage	F	VF	XF	Unc	BU
1988 Proof	—	Value: 20.00				

KM# 23 50 DOLLARS
31.1030 g., 0.9990 Silver 1.0000 oz. ASW **Obv:** Crowned arms within sprigs **Rev:** General Douglas MacArthur

Date	Mintage	F	VF	XF	Unc	BU
1989 Proof	Est. 50,000	Value: 20.00				

KM# 25 50 DOLLARS
28.2800 g., 0.9250 Silver .8411 oz. ASW **Series:** Davis Cup Tennis **Obv:** Crowned arms within sprigs **Rev:** Conjoined busts of tennis players

Date	Mintage	F	VF	XF	Unc	BU
1989 Proof	Est. 20,000	Value: 22.50				

KM# 27 50 DOLLARS
28.2800 g., 0.9250 Silver .8411 oz. ASW **Series:** 1992 Olympics **Subject:** Rowing **Obv:** Crowned arms within sprigs **Rev:** Men rowing boats within circle

Date	Mintage	F	VF	XF	Unc	BU
1989 Proof	Est. 30,000	Value: 20.00				

KM# 44 50 DOLLARS
28.2800 g., 0.9250 Silver .8411 oz. ASW **Subject:** 24th Olympic Games, Seoul 1988 **Obv:** Crowned arms within sprigs **Rev:** Steffi Graf

Date	Mintage	F	VF	XF	Unc	BU
1989 Proof	20,000	Value: 20.00				

KM# 30 50 DOLLARS
31.1030 g., 0.9990 Silver 1.000 oz. ASW **Obv:** Crowned arms within sprigs **Rev:** General Eisenhower within flags

Date	Mintage	F	VF	XF	Unc	BU
1990 Proof	Est. 50,000	Value: 18.50				

KM# 32 50 DOLLARS
31.1030 g., 0.9990 Silver 1.000 oz. ASW **Obv:** Crowned arms within sprigs **Rev:** General George S. Patton

Date	Mintage	F	VF	XF	Unc	BU
1990 Proof	Est. 50,000	Value: 18.50				

KM# 34 50 DOLLARS
31.1030 g., 0.9990 Silver 1.000 oz. ASW **Obv:** Crowned arms within sprigs **Rev:** Admiral William Halsey

Date	Mintage	F	VF	XF	Unc	BU
1990 Proof	Est. 50,000	Value: 18.50				

KM# 36 50 DOLLARS
31.1030 g., 0.9990 Silver 1.000 oz. ASW **Obv:** Crowned arms within sprigs **Rev:** President Franklin D. Roosevelt

Date	Mintage	F	VF	XF	Unc	BU
1990 Proof	Est. 50,000	Value: 18.50				

KM# 38 50 DOLLARS
31.1030 g., 0.9990 Silver 1.000 oz. ASW **Obv:** Crowned arms within sprigs **Rev:** Sir Winston Churchill

Date	Mintage	F	VF	XF	Unc	BU
1990 Proof	Est. 50,000	Value: 18.50				

KM# 47 50 DOLLARS
38.2000 g., 0.9250 Silver 1.1361 oz. ASW **Subject:** Soccer **Obv:** Crowned arms within sprigs **Rev:** Player kicking soccer ball

Date	Mintage	F	VF	XF	Unc	BU
1990 Proof	20,000	Value: 22.50				

KM# 75 50 DOLLARS
28.5600 g., 0.9250 Silver .8984 oz. ASW **Subject:** Soccer **Obv:** Crowned arms within sprigs **Rev:** Soccer players

Date	Mintage	F	VF	XF	Unc	BU
1990 Proof	20,000	Value: 18.00				

KM# 71 50 DOLLARS
7.7000 g., 0.5830 Gold .1444 oz. AGW **Series:** Olympics **Obv:** Crowned arms within sprigs **Rev:** Discus thrower

Date	Mintage	F	VF	XF	Unc	BU
1992 Proof	6,000	Value: 120				

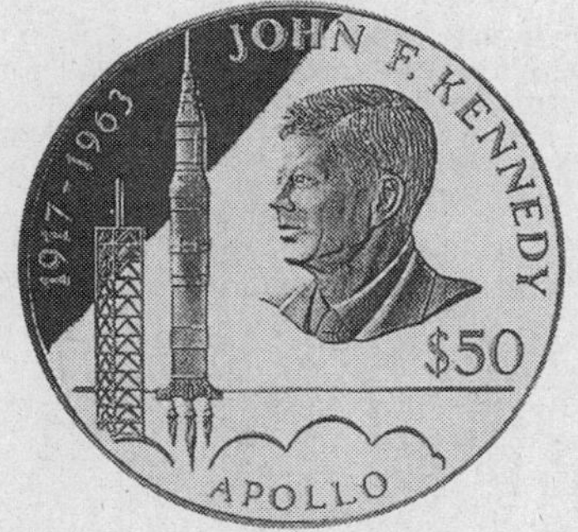

KM# 65 50 DOLLARS
155.5175 g., 0.9990 Silver 5.000 oz. ASW **Obv:** Crowned arms within sprigs **Rev:** Head left with apollo rocket

Date	Mintage	F	VF	XF	Unc	BU
1993 Proof	—	Value: 95.00				

KM# 66 50 DOLLARS
7.7760 g., 0.5830 Gold .1458 oz. AGW **Obv:** Crowned arms within sprigs **Rev:** Bust left and rocket launch

Date	Mintage	F	VF	XF	Unc	BU
1993 Proof	—	Value: 100				

KM# 72 50 DOLLARS
156.1700 g., 0.9990 Silver 5.0247 oz. ASW, 65 mm. **Series:** World Cup Soccer **Obv:** Crowned arms within sprigs **Rev:** Statue of Liberty, stars and various buildings within soccer ball design **Note:** Photo reduced.

Date	Mintage	F	VF	XF	Unc	BU
1994 Proof	Est. 3,000	Value: 135				

KM# 83 50 DOLLARS
6.2200 g., 0.9990 Gold .2000 oz. AGW **Series:** Liberty Gold Bullion **Obv:** Crowned head right **Rev:** Statue of Liberty

Date	Mintage	F	VF	XF	Unc	BU
1997	—	—	—	—	—	140

KM# 108 50 DOLLARS
3.1100 g., 0.9999 Gold .1000 oz. AGW **Obv:** Crowned head right **Rev:** Bust facing **Rev. Legend:** ...In Memoriam

Date	Mintage	F	VF	XF	Unc	BU
1998 Proof	Est. 7,500	Value: 70.00				

KM# 109 50 DOLLARS
3.1100 g., 0.9999 Gold .1000 oz. AGW **Obv:** Crowned head right **Rev:** Bust facing **Rev. Legend:** ...Princess of Wales

Date	Mintage	F	VF	XF	Unc	BU
1998 Proof	Est. 7,500	Value: 70.00				

KM# 118 50 DOLLARS
3.1103 g., 0.9990 Gold .1000 oz. AGW **Subject:** 50th Anniversary of Peanuts **Obv:** Crowned head right **Rev:** Snoopy and Woodstock

Date	Mintage	F	VF	XF	Unc	BU
2000 Proof	Est. 7,500	Value: 70.00				

KM# 7 100 DOLLARS
155.5175 g., 0.9990 Silver 5.0000 oz. ASW **Subject:** 24th Olympiad Tennis Games, Seoul 1988 **Obv:** Crowned arms within sprigs **Rev:** Steffi Graf

Date	Mintage	F	VF	XF	Unc	BU
1987	Est. 5,000	Value: 80.00				

KM# 3 100 DOLLARS
155.5175 g., 0.9990 Silver 5.0000 oz. ASW, 65 mm. **Series:** Olympics **Subject:** Tennis **Obv:** Crowned arms within sprigs **Rev:** Boris Becker **Note:** Photo reduced.

Date	Mintage	F	VF	XF	Unc	BU
1987 Proof	Est. 5,000	Value: 80.00				

KM# 77 100 DOLLARS
Silver **Obv:** Crowned arms within sprigs **Rev:** Steffi Graf with cup **Note:** Similar to $5 KM#11.

Date	Mintage	F	VF	XF	Unc	BU
1988	—	—	—	—	90.00	—

KM# 19 100 DOLLARS
155.5175 g., 0.9990 Silver 5.0000 oz. ASW **Obv:** Crowned arms within sprigs **Rev:** Head left

Date	Mintage	F	VF	XF	Unc	BU
1988 Proof	3,000	Value: 80.00				

KM# 21 100 DOLLARS
155.5175 g., 0.9990 Silver 5.0000 oz. ASW **Subject:** Soccer **Obv:** Crowned arms within sprigs **Rev:** Soccer player

Date	Mintage	F	VF	XF	Unc	BU
1988 Proof	3,000	Value: 85.00				

KM# 40 100 DOLLARS
155.5175 g., 0.9990 Silver 5.0000 oz. ASW **Subject:** 24th Olympic Games, Seoul 1988 **Obv:** Crowned arms within sprigs **Rev:** Cameos of Navratilova, Graf and Evert, tennis champions

Date	Mintage	F	VF	XF	Unc	BU
1988 Proof	Est. 3,000	Value: 90.00				

KM# 28 100 DOLLARS
155.5175 g., 0.9990 Silver 5.0000 oz. ASW, 65 mm. **Subject:** 24th Olympic Games, Seoul 1988 **Obv:** Crowned arms within sprigs **Rev:** Steffi Graf **Note:** Photo reduced.

Date	Mintage	F	VF	XF	Unc	BU
1989 Proof	3,000	Value: 90.00				

KM# 73 100 DOLLARS
154.8500 g., 0.9990 Silver 4.9791 oz. ASW, 65 mm. **Subject:** Soccer **Obv:** Crowned arms within sprigs **Rev:** 1990 World Champion Italian soccer team **Note:** Photo reduced.

Date	Mintage	F	VF	XF	Unc	BU
1990 Proof	Est. 3,000	Value: 95.00				

KM# 84 100 DOLLARS
15.5517 g., 0.9990 Gold .5000 oz. AGW **Series:** Liberty Gold Bullion **Obv:** Crowned head right **Rev:** Statue of Liberty

Date	Mintage	F	VF	XF	Unc	BU
1997 Proof	—	Value: 350				

KM# 99 100 DOLLARS
6.2200 g., 0.9990 Gold .2000 oz. AGW **Obv:** Crowned arms within sprigs **Rev:** Bust facing **Rev. Legend:** ...The People's Princess

Date	Mintage	F	VF	XF	Unc	BU
1997 Proof	Est. 5,000	Value: 140				

KM# 100 100 DOLLARS
6.2200 g., 0.9990 Gold .2000 oz. AGW **Obv:** Crowned arms within sprigs **Rev:** Bust facing **Rev. Legend:** ...Princess of Wales

Date	Mintage	F	VF	XF	Unc	BU
1997 Proof	Est. 5,000	Value: 140				

KM# 101 100 DOLLARS
6.2200 g., 0.9990 Gold .2000 oz. AGW **Obv:** Crowned arms within sprigs **Rev:** Head left above sprigs **Rev. Legend:** ...Princess of Wales

Date	Mintage	F	VF	XF	Unc	BU
1997 Proof	Est. 5,000	Value: 140				

KM# 110 100 DOLLARS
6.2200 g., 0.9990 Gold .2000 oz. AGW **Obv:** Crowned head right **Rev:** Bust facing **Rev. Legend:** ...In Memoriam

Date	Mintage	F	VF	XF	Unc	BU
1998 Proof	Est. 5,000	Value: 140				

KM# 111 100 DOLLARS
6.2200 g., 0.9990 Gold .2000 oz. AGW **Obv:** Crowned head right **Rev:** Bust facing **Rev. Legend:** ...Princess of Wales

Date	Mintage	F	VF	XF	Unc	BU
1998 Proof	Est. 5,000	Value: 140				

KM# 119 100 DOLLARS
6.2200 g., 0.9990 Gold .2000 oz. AGW **Subject:** 50th Anniversary of Peanuts **Obv:** Crowned head right **Rev:** Snoopy and Woodstock

Date	Mintage	F	VF	XF	Unc	BU
2000 Proof	Est. 5,000	Value: 140				

KM# 4 200 DOLLARS
311.0350 g., 0.9990 Silver 10.000 oz. ASW **Series:** Olympics **Subject:** Tennis **Obv:** Crowned arms within sprigs **Rev:** Tennis player

Date	Mintage	F	VF	XF	Unc	BU
1987 Proof	Est. 3,000	Value: 150				

KM# 8 200 DOLLARS
311.0350 g., 0.9990 Silver 10.000 oz. ASW **Subject:** 24th Olympiad Tennis Games, Seoul 1988 **Obv:** Crowned arms within sprigs **Rev:** Tennis player

Date	Mintage	F	VF	XF	Unc	BU
1987 Proof	Est. 3,000	Value: 150				

KM# 42 200 DOLLARS
6.9117 g., 0.9000 Gold .2000 oz. AGW **Obv:** Crowned arms within sprigs **Rev:** General Douglas MacArthur 1/4 left

Date	Mintage	F	VF	XF	Unc	BU
1989 Proof	Est. 2,500	Value: 140				

KM# 50 200 DOLLARS
6.9117 g., 0.9000 Gold .2000 oz. AGW **Obv:** Crowned arms within sprigs **Rev:** General George S. Patton

Date	Mintage	F	VF	XF	Unc	BU
1989 Proof	—	Value: 140				

KM# 45 200 DOLLARS
6.9117 g., 0.9000 Gold .2000 oz. AGW **Obv:** Crowned arms within sprigs **Rev:** General Dwight David Eisenhower in front of flags

Date	Mintage	F	VF	XF	Unc	BU
1990 Proof	2,500	Value: 140				

KM# 51 200 DOLLARS
6.9117 g., 0.9000 Gold .2000 oz. AGW **Obv:** Crowned arms within sprigs **Rev:** Admiral William Halsey

Date	Mintage	F	VF	XF	Unc	BU
1990 Proof	—	Value: 140				

KM# 52 200 DOLLARS
6.9117 g., 0.9000 Gold .2000 oz. AGW **Obv:** Crowned arms within sprigs **Rev:** President Franklin D. Roosevelt

Date	Mintage	F	VF	XF	Unc	BU
1990 Proof	—	Value: 140				

KM# 53 200 DOLLARS
6.9117 g., 0.9000 Gold .2000 oz. AGW **Obv:** Crowned arms within sprigs **Rev:** Sir Winston Churchill

Date	Mintage	F	VF	XF	Unc	BU
1990 Proof	—	Value: 140				

KM# 9 250 DOLLARS
8.4830 g., 0.9170 Gold .2500 oz. AGW **Series:** Olympics **Subject:** Tennis **Obv:** Crowned arms within sprigs **Rev:** Boris Becker

Date	Mintage	F	VF	XF	Unc	BU
1987 Proof	1,000	Value: 170				

KM# 10 250 DOLLARS
8.4830 g., 0.9170 Gold .2500 oz. AGW **Subject:** 24th Olympiad Tennis Games, Seoul 1988 **Obv:** Crowned arms within sprigs **Rev:** Steffi Graf

Date	Mintage	F	VF	XF	Unc	BU
1987 Proof	1,000	Value: 175				

KM# 20 250 DOLLARS
10.0000 g., 0.9170 Gold .2948 oz. AGW **Obv:** Crowned arms within sprigs **Rev:** John F. Kennedy left

Date	Mintage	F	VF	XF	Unc	BU
1988 Proof	5,000	Value: 200				

KM# 39 250 DOLLARS
10.0000 g., 0.9170 Gold .2948 oz. AGW **Subject:** Soccer **Obv:** Crowned arms within sprigs **Rev:** Soccer player to left of cameo

Date	Mintage	F	VF	XF	Unc	BU
1988 Proof	Est. 5,000	Value: 200				

KM# 41 250 DOLLARS
10.0000 g., 0.9170 Gold .2948 oz. AGW **Subject:** 24th Olympic Games, Seoul 1988 **Obv:** Crowned arms within sprigs **Rev:** Cameos of Navratilova, Graf and Evert, tennis champions

Date	Mintage	F	VF	XF	Unc	BU
1988 Proof	Est. 5,000	Value: 215				

KM# 48 250 DOLLARS
10.0000 g., 0.9170 Gold .2948 oz. AGW **Subject:** 24th Olympic Games, Seoul 1988 **Obv:** Crowned arms within sprigs **Rev:** Steffi Graf with cup

Date	Mintage	F	VF	XF	Unc	BU
1988 Proof	5,000	Value: 210				

KM# 26 250 DOLLARS
10.0000 g., 0.9170 Gold .2948 oz. AGW **Series:** Davis Cup Tennis **Obv:** Crowned arms within sprigs **Rev:** Davis cup

Date	Mintage	F	VF	XF	Unc	BU
1989 Proof	500	Value: 275				

KM# 49 250 DOLLARS
10.0000 g., 0.9170 Gold .2948 oz. AGW **Subject:** 24th Olympic Games, Seoul 1988 **Obv:** Crowned arms within sprigs **Rev:** Steffi Graf

Date	Mintage	F	VF	XF	Unc	BU
1989 Proof	3,000	Value: 210				

KM# 54 250 DOLLARS
10.0000 g., 0.9170 Gold .2948 oz. AGW **Subject:** Soccer - Italian **Obv:** Crowned arms within sprigs

Date	Mintage	F	VF	XF	Unc	BU
1990 Proof	Est. 2,500	Value: 210				

KM# A113 250 DOLLARS
15.5500 g., 0.9999 Gold .5 oz. AGW **Obv:** Crowned head right **Rev:** Bust facing **Rev. Legend:** ... Princess of Wales

Date	Mintage	F	VF	XF	Unc	BU
1998 Proof	3,000	Value: 345				

KM# 112 250 DOLLARS
15.5500 g., 0.9999 Gold .5000 oz. AGW **Obv:** Crowned head right **Rev:** Bust facing **Rev. Legend:** ...In Memoriam

Date	Mintage	F	VF	XF	Unc	BU
1998 Proof	Est. 3,000	Value: 345				

PATTERNS

Including off metal strikes

KM#	Date	Mintage	Identification	Mkt Val
Pn1	1990	2	5 Dollars. Silver. Silver Proof, KM33.	—
Pn2	1990	2	5 Dollars. Silver. Silver Proof, KM35.	—
Pn3	1990	2	5 Dollars. Silver. Silver Proof, KM37.	—

NORWAY

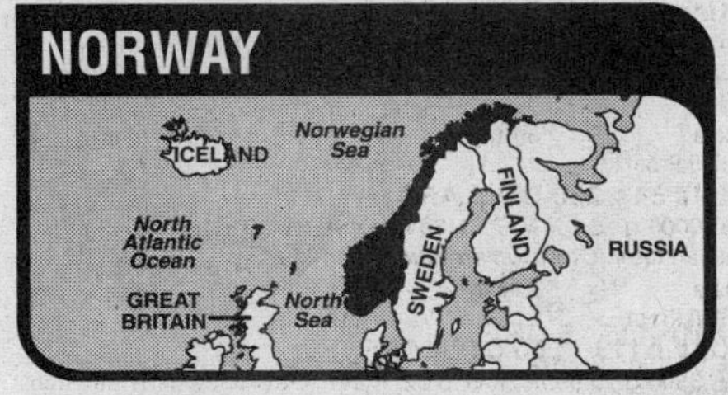

The Kingdom of Norway (*Norge, Noreg*), a constitutional monarchy located in northwestern Europe, has an area of 150,000sq. mi. (324,220 sq. km.), including the island territories of Spitzbergen (Svalbard) and Jan Mayen, and a population of *4.2 million. Capital: Oslo (Christiania). The diversified economic base of Norway includes shipping, fishing, forestry, agriculture, and manufacturing. Nonferrous metals, paper and paperboard, paper pulp, iron, steel and oil are exported.

A united Norwegian kingdom was established in the 9th century, the era of the indomitable Norse Vikings who ranged far and wide, visiting the coasts of northwestern Europe, the Mediterranean, Greenland and North America. In the 13th century the Norse kingdom was united briefly with Sweden, then passed through inheritance in 1380 to the rule of Denmark which was maintained until 1814. In 1814 Norway fell again under the rule of Sweden. The union lasted until 1905 when the Norwegian Parliament arranged a peaceful separation and invited a Danish prince (King Haakon VII) to ascend the throne of an independent Kingdom of Norway.

RULERS

Swedish, 1814-1905
Haakon VII, 1905-1957
Olav V, 1957-1991
Harald V, 1991-

MINT MARKS

(h) - Crossed hammers – Kongsberg

MINT OFFICIALS' INITIALS

Letter	Date	Name
AB, B	1961-1980	Arne Jon Bakken
AB*	1980	Ole R. Kolberg
I, IT	1880-1918	Ivar Trondsen, engraver
IAR	-	Angrid Austlid Rise, engraver
K	1981	Ole R. Kolberg
OH	1959	Oivind Hansen, engraver

MONETARY SYSTEM

100 Ore = 1 Krone (30 Skilling)

KINGDOM

DECIMAL COINAGE

KM# 352 ORE

2.0000 g., Bronze **Obv:** Crowned arms divide monograms **Rev:** Value within wreath, crossed hammers divide date below **Note:** Varieties exist.

Date	Mintage	VG	F	VF	XF	BU
1902	4,500,000	—	2.00	5.00	15.00	45.00

KM# 361 ORE

2.0000 g., Bronze **Ruler:** Haakon VII **Obv:** Crowned shield divides monogram **Rev:** Value within sprigs

Date	Mintage	VG	F	VF	XF	BU
1906	3,000,000	—	2.00	3.00	10.00	25.00
1907	2,550,000	—	2.00	3.00	12.00	27.50

KM# 367 ORE

2.0000 g., Bronze **Ruler:** Haakon VII **Obv:** Crowned monogram within circle **Rev:** Value

Date	Mintage	VG	F	VF	XF	BU
1908	1,450,000	—	10.00	20.00	45.00	165
1910	2,480,000	—	1.00	2.50	12.00	40.00
1911	3,270,000	—	1.00	2.50	15.00	65.00
1912	2,850,000	—	3.00	10.00	35.00	225
1913	2,840,000	—	1.00	2.50	7.50	35.00
1914	5,020,000	—	1.00	2.50	10.00	40.00
1915	1,540,000	—	10.00	25.00	75.00	300
1921	3,805,000	—	25.00	45.00	95.00	275
1922	Inc. above	—	0.50	2.00	15.00	55.00
1923	770,000	—	6.00	17.50	35.00	175
1925	3,000,000	—	0.50	1.50	15.00	60.00
1926	2,200,000	—	0.50	1.50	15.00	60.00
1927	800,000	—	4.00	10.00	30.00	165
1928	3,000,000	—	0.25	0.75	4.50	25.00
1929	4,990,000	—	0.25	0.75	4.50	20.00
1930 large date	2,009,999	—	0.50	1.00	6.00	27.50
1930 small date	Inc. above	—	0.50	1.00	6.00	27.50
1931	2,000,000	—	0.50	1.00	6.00	25.00
1932	2,500,000	—	0.50	1.00	6.00	25.00
1933	2,000,000	—	0.50	1.00	6.00	20.00
1934	2,000,000	—	0.50	1.00	6.00	25.00
1935	5,495,000	—	0.25	0.75	2.50	12.50
1936	6,855,000	—	0.25	0.75	2.50	12.50
1937	6,020,000	—	0.20	0.50	1.50	10.00
1938	4,920,000	—	0.20	0.50	1.50	10.00
1939	2,500,000	—	0.20	0.50	1.50	12.50
1940	5,010,000	—	0.20	0.50	1.50	10.00
1941	12,260,000	—	0.10	0.25	1.50	5.00
1946	2,200,000	—	0.10	0.25	1.50	12.00
1947	4,870,000	—	0.10	0.25	0.90	6.00
1948	9,405,000	—	0.10	0.25	0.90	5.00
1949	2,785,000	—	0.10	0.25	0.90	8.00
1950	5,730,000	—	0.10	0.25	0.90	5.00
1951	16,670,000	—	0.10	0.25	0.90	5.00
1952	Inc. above	—	0.10	0.25	0.90	4.00

KM# 367a ORE

1.7400 g., Iron **Ruler:** Haakon VII **Obv:** Crowned monogram **Rev:** Value

Date	Mintage	VG	F	VF	XF	BU
1918	6,000,000	—	5.00	10.00	20.00	65.00
1919	12,930,000	—	1.50	3.50	12.00	30.00
1920	4,445,000	—	6.00	12.50	35.00	165
1921	2,270,000	—	30.00	40.00	75.00	210

KM# 387 ORE

1.7400 g., Iron **Ruler:** Haakon VII **Subject:** World War II German Occupation **Obv:** Shield **Rev:** Value

Date	Mintage	VG	F	VF	XF	BU
1941	13,410,000	—	0.15	0.50	1.75	12.50
1942	37,710,000	—	0.15	0.50	1.75	6.00
1943	33,030,000	—	0.15	0.50	1.75	6.00
1944	8,820,000	—	0.25	0.75	2.25	6.50
1945	1,740,000	—	4.00	8.00	15.00	35.00

KM# 398 ORE

2.0000 g., Bronze, 11 mm. **Ruler:** Haakon VII **Obv:** Crowned monogram divides date **Rev:** Value

Date	Mintage	VG	F	VF	XF	BU
1952	—	—	—	0.10	1.00	6.50
Note: Mintage included with KM#367						
1953	7,440,000	—	—	0.10	0.75	4.50
1954	7,650,000	—	—	0.10	0.75	4.50
1955	8,635,000	—	—	0.10	0.75	4.50
1956	11,705,000	—	—	0.10	0.75	4.50
1957	15,750,000	—	—	0.10	0.50	3.25

KM# 403 ORE

2.0000 g., Bronze, 11 mm. **Ruler:** Olav V **Obv:** Crowned monogram **Rev:** Squirrel and value **Note:** Varieties exist.

Date	Mintage	VG	F	VF	XF	BU
1958	2,820,000	—	0.25	0.50	2.25	8.00
1959	9,120,000	—	0.10	0.20	0.85	7.00
1960	7,890,000	—	—	0.10	0.30	2.50
1961	5,670,600	—	—	0.10	0.30	2.50
1962	12,180,000	—	—	0.10	0.25	2.00
1963	8,010,000	—	—	0.10	0.30	2.50
1964	11,020,000	—	—	—	0.10	0.75
1965	8,081,000	—	—	—	0.15	2.00
1966	12,431,000	—	—	—	0.15	1.25
1967	13,026,000	—	—	—	0.10	0.75

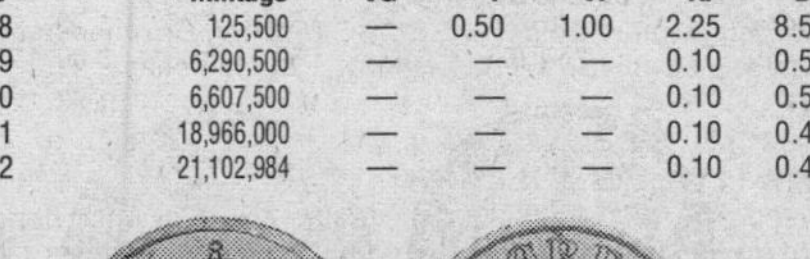

Date	Mintage	VG	F	VF	XF	BU
1968	125,500	—	0.50	1.00	2.25	8.50
1969	6,290,500	—	—	—	0.10	0.50
1970	6,607,500	—	—	—	0.10	0.50
1971	18,966,000	—	—	—	0.10	0.45
1972	21,102,984	—	—	—	0.10	0.45

KM# 353 2 ORE

4.0000 g., Bronze, 21 mm. **Obv:** Crowned arms divide monograms **Rev:** Value within wreath, crossed hammers divide date below

Date	Mintage	VG	F	VF	XF	BU
1902	1,005,000	—	1.50	4.00	15.00	150

KM# 362 2 ORE

4.0000 g., Bronze, 21 mm. **Ruler:** Haakon VII **Obv:** Crowned shield **Rev:** Value within sprigs

Date	Mintage	VG	F	VF	XF	BU
1906	500,000	—	5.00	15.00	50.00	300
1907	980,000	—	3.00	5.00	25.00	135

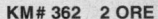

KM# 371 2 ORE

4.0000 g., Bronze, 21 mm. **Ruler:** Haakon VII **Obv:** Crowned monogram within circle **Rev:** Value

Date	Mintage	VG	F	VF	XF	BU
1909	520,000	—	6.00	17.50	60.00	250
1910	500,000	—	6.00	17.50	95.00	500
1911	195,000	—	6.00	17.50	65.00	350
1912	805,000	—	6.00	17.50	65.00	350
1913	2,010,000	—	0.75	2.00	12.00	110
1914	2,990,000	—	0.75	2.00	12.00	110
1915	Inc. above	—	5.00	20.00	85.00	450
1921	2,028,000	—	0.50	1.00	17.00	80.00
1922	2,288,000	—	0.50	1.00	17.00	70.00
1923	745,000	—	1.00	2.00	30.00	145
1928	2,250,000	—	0.50	1.00	12.50	70.00
1929	750,000	—	1.00	2.00	20.00	100
1931	1,570,000	—	0.50	1.00	15.00	75.00
1932	630,000	—	3.50	7.50	45.00	210
1933	750,000	—	0.50	1.50	10.00	75.00
1934	500,000	—	0.50	1.50	10.00	75.00
1935	2,223,000	—	0.25	1.00	7.50	45.00
1936	4,533,000	—	0.25	1.00	7.50	45.00
1937	3,790,000	—	0.20	0.50	2.75	20.00
1938	3,765,000	—	0.20	0.50	2.75	20.00
1939	4,420,000	—	0.20	0.50	2.75	20.00
1940	2,655,000	—	0.20	0.50	2.75	20.00
1946	1,575,000	—	0.20	0.50	3.50	20.00
1947	4,679,000	—	0.10	0.25	1.25	12.50
1948	1,002,999	—	1.00	3.00	5.00	12.50
1949	1,455,000	—	0.10	0.25	1.00	9.00
1950	5,790,000	—	0.10	0.25	1.00	6.00
1951	10,540,000	—	0.10	0.25	1.00	5.00
1952	Inc. above	—	0.10	0.25	1.00	5.00

KM# 371a 2 ORE

3.4800 g., Iron, 21 mm. **Ruler:** Haakon VII **Obv:** Crowned monogram **Rev:** Value

Date	Mintage	VG	F	VF	XF	BU
1917	720,000	—	80.00	145	240	475
1918	1,280,000	—	35.00	50.00	100	250
1919	3,365,000	—	10.00	15.00	55.00	265
1920	2,635,000	—	10.00	15.00	55.00	275

KM# 394 2 ORE

3.4700 g., Iron, 21 mm. **Ruler:** Haakon VII **Obv:** Shield **Rev:** Value **Note:** World War II German occupation issue.

Date	Mintage	VG	F	VF	XF	BU
1943	6,575,000	—	0.50	0.75	1.75	9.00

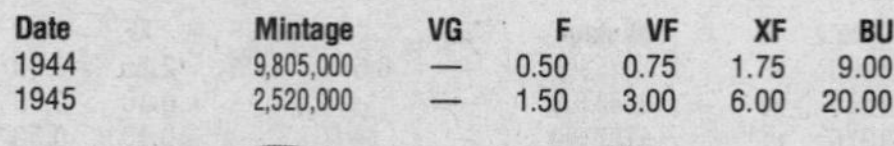

Date	Mintage	VG	F	VF	XF	BU
1944	9,805,000	—	0.50	0.75	1.75	9.00
1945	2,520,000	—	1.50	3.00	6.00	20.00

KM# 399 2 ORE

4.0000 g., Bronze, 21 mm. **Ruler:** Haakon VII **Obv:** Crowned monogram divides date **Rev:** Value

Date	Mintage	VG	F	VF	XF	BU
1952	Inc. above	—	—	0.10	0.85	8.50
1953	6,705,000	—	—	0.10	0.85	7.00
1954	2,805,000	—	—	0.10	0.85	10.00
1955	3,600,000	—	—	0.10	0.85	10.00
1956	6,780,000	—	—	0.10	0.85	7.00
1957	6,090,000	—	—	0.10	0.85	7.00

KM# 404 2 ORE

4.0000 g., Bronze, 21 mm. **Ruler:** Olav V **Obv:** Crowned monogram **Rev:** Moor hen and value, small lettering

Date	Mintage	VG	F	VF	XF	BU
1958	2,700,000	—	0.20	0.50	1.75	10.00

KM# 410 2 ORE

4.0000 g., Bronze, 21 mm. **Ruler:** Olav V **Obv:** Crowned monogram **Rev:** Moor hen and value, large lettering

Date	Mintage	VG	F	VF	XF	BU
1959	4,125,000	—	0.10	0.20	1.25	8.00
1960	3,735,000	—	—	0.10	0.85	16.50
1961	4,477,000	—	—	0.10	0.35	2.00
1962	6,205,000	—	—	0.10	0.35	2.00
1963	4,840,000	—	—	0.10	0.35	2.00
1964	7,250,000	—	—	0.10	0.20	1.50
1965	6,241,000	—	—	0.10	0.30	3.00
1966	10,485,000	—	—	—	0.15	2.50
1967	11,993,000	—	—	—	0.15	1.50
1968	3,467	—	—	—	—	900
Note: In mint sets only						
1969	315,600	—	0.50	1.00	1.75	6.00
1970	6,794,000	—	—	—	0.10	1.25
1971	15,462,000	—	—	—	0.10	1.00
1972	15,897,984	—	—	—	0.10	1.00

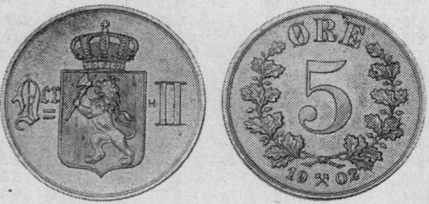

KM# 349 5 ORE

8.0000 g., Bronze, 27 mm. **Obv:** Crowned arms divide monograms **Rev:** Value within wreath, crossed hammers divide date below

Date	Mintage	VG	F	VF	XF	BU
1902	705,000	—	2.50	6.00	55.00	365

KM# 364 5 ORE

8.0000 g., Bronze, 27 mm. **Ruler:** Haakon VII **Obv:** Crowned shield divides monogram **Rev:** Value within sprigs

Date	Mintage	VG	F	VF	XF	BU
1907	200,000	—	3.50	12.50	70.00	285

KM# 368 5 ORE

Bronze, 27 mm. **Ruler:** Haakon VII **Obv:** Crowned monogram within circle **Rev:** Numeral and written value

Date	Mintage	VG	F	VF	XF	BU
1908	600,000	—	25.00	45.00	130	565
1911	480,000	—	2.00	15.00	65.00	325
1912	520,000	—	6.00	25.00	135	775
1913	1,000,000	—	1.25	5.00	30.00	190
1914	1,000,000	—	1.25	5.00	30.00	190
1915	Inc. above	—	10.00	35.00	145	850
1916	300,000	—	6.00	15.00	60.00	315
1921	683,000	—	1.50	7.50	60.00	280
1922	2,296,000	—	1.25	5.00	30.00	150
1923	456,000	—	2.50	10.00	60.00	260
1928	848,000	—	0.60	3.00	25.00	110
1929	452,000	—	3.00	10.00	60.00	300
1930	1,292,000	—	0.60	2.50	30.00	135
1931	808,000	—	0.60	2.50	30.00	120
1932	500,000	—	3.00	15.00	45.00	225
1933	300,000	—	3.00	12.00	65.00	325
1935	496,000	—	1.50	5.00	25.00	160
1936	760,000	—	1.00	2.50	20.00	115
1937	1,552,000	—	0.50	1.50	12.00	50.00
1938	1,332,000	—	0.50	1.50	12.00	50.00
1939	1,370,000	—	0.50	1.50	9.00	50.00
1940	2,554,000	—	0.30	1.00	7.00	32.50
1941	3,576,000	—	0.30	1.00	6.00	32.50
1951	8,128,000	—	0.25	0.50	2.25	20.00
1952	Inc. above	—	1.50	3.50	9.00	50.00

KM# 368a 5 ORE

6.6900 g., Iron, 27 mm. **Ruler:** Haakon VII **Obv:** Crowned monogram within circle **Rev:** Numeral and written value

Date	Mintage	VG	F	VF	XF	BU
1917	1,700,000	—	25.00	40.00	70.00	125
1918/7	432,000	—	135	225	—	850
1918	Inc. above	—	135	225	425	900
1919	3,464,000	—	12.00	30.00	70.00	250
1920	1,629,000	—	25.00	55.00	120	500

KM# 388 5 ORE

6.9400 g., Iron, 27 mm. **Ruler:** Haakon VII **Note:** World War II German occupation issue.

Date	Mintage	VG	F	VF	XF	BU
1941	6,608,000	—	0.50	1.50	5.50	40.00
1942	10,312,000	—	0.50	1.50	5.00	20.00
1943	6,184,000	—	0.75	2.00	7.00	32.50
1944	4,256,000	—	1.25	3.00	9.00	32.50
1945	408,000	—	145	165	270	575

KM# 400 5 ORE

8.0000 g., Bronze, 27 mm. **Ruler:** Haakon VII **Obv:** Crowned monogram divides date **Rev:** Value

Date	Mintage	VG	F	VF	XF	BU
1952	—	—	0.10	0.50	2.50	35.00
Note: Mintage included with KM#368						
1953	6,216,000	—	0.10	0.35	2.25	20.00
1954	4,536,000	—	0.10	0.35	2.25	20.00
1955	6,570,000	—	0.10	0.35	2.25	20.00
1956	2,959,000	—	0.10	0.35	2.25	30.00
1957	5,624,000	—	0.10	0.35	2.25	12.50

KM# 405 5 ORE

8.0000 g., Bronze, 27 mm. **Ruler:** Olav V **Obv:** Head left **Rev:** Moose

Date	Mintage	VG	F	VF	XF	BU
1958	2,205,000	—	1.00	2.00	6.00	55.00
1959	3,208,000	—	0.10	0.50	2.25	25.00
1960	5,519,000	—	0.10	0.20	1.25	17.00
1961	4,554,000	—	0.10	0.20	1.25	15.00
1962	7,764,000	—	0.10	0.15	0.75	9.00
1963	3,204,000	—	0.10	0.15	0.75	9.00
1964	6,108,000	—	—	0.10	0.50	3.00
1965	6,841,000	—	—	0.10	0.50	7.00
1966	8,415,000	—	—	0.10	0.50	3.00
1967	9,071,000	—	—	0.10	0.45	3.00
1968	4,286,000	—	—	0.10	0.85	8.00
1969	4,328,000	—	—	0.10	0.35	1.25
1970	7,350,600	—	—	0.10	0.35	1.25
1971	13,450,100	—	—	0.10	0.35	1.25
1972	19,001,784	—	—	—	0.15	1.00
1973	9,584,175	—	—	—	0.15	1.00

KM# 415 5 ORE

3.0000 g., Bronze, 19 mm. **Ruler:** Olav V **Obv:** Arms **Rev:** Value **Designer:** Oivind Hansen **Note:** Varieties exist.

Date	Mintage	VG	F	VF	XF	BU
1973	52,886,175	—	—	—	0.10	0.45
1974	37,150,223	—	—	—	0.10	0.45
1975	32,478,744	—	—	—	0.10	0.45
1976	24,232,824	—	—	—	0.10	0.25
1977	29,646,000	—	—	—	0.10	0.25
1978	13,838,000	—	—	—	0.10	0.25
1979	25,255,000	—	—	—	0.10	0.25
1980	12,315,000	—	—	—	0.10	0.25
1980 Without star	27,515,000	—	—	—	0.10	0.25
1981	24,529,000	—	—	—	0.10	0.25
1982	21,900,650	—	—	—	0.10	0.25

KM# 350 10 ORE

1.5000 g., 0.4000 Silver .0192 oz. ASW, 15 mm. **Obv:** Crowned monogram **Obv. Legend:** BRODERFOLKENES VEL **Rev:** Crowned arms divide date

Date	Mintage	VG	F	VF	XF	BU
1901	2,021,100	—	10.00	22.00	30.00	50.00
1903	1,500,700	—	12.00	24.00	40.00	50.00

KM# 372 10 ORE

1.4500 g., 0.4000 Silver, 15 mm. **Ruler:** Haakon VII **Obv:** Crowned monogram **Rev:** Value

Date	Mintage	VG	F	VF	XF	BU
1909	2,000,000	—	6.50	13.00	30.00	95.00
1911	1,650,000	—	9.00	22.00	60.00	200
1912	2,350,000	—	6.00	12.00	30.00	80.00
1913	2,000,000	—	6.00	11.00	28.00	65.00
1914	1,180,000	—	11.00	25.00	50.00	150
1915	2,820,000	—	3.00	5.00	13.00	90.00
1916	1,500,000	—	10.00	17.00	45.00	120
1917	5,950,000	—	1.50	3.00	5.00	20.00
1918/7	1,650,000	—	15.00	35.00	75.00	—
1918	Inc. above	—	3.00	5.00	13.00	45.00
1919/7	7,800,000	—	15.00	35.00	75.00	—
1919	Inc. above	—	1.50	3.00	5.00	15.00

KM# 378 10 ORE

1.5000 g., Copper-Nickel, 15 mm. **Ruler:** Haakon VII **Obv:** Crowned monogram **Rev:** Value flanked by designs

Date	Mintage	VG	F	VF	XF	BU
1920	2,535,000	—	10.00	20.00	30.00	60.00
1921	6,465,000	—	7.00	15.00	25.00	55.00
1922	3,965,000	—	7.00	15.00	20.00	50.00
1923	7,135,000	—	15.00	25.00	30.00	55.00

KM# 383 10 ORE

1.5000 g., Copper-Nickel, 15 mm. **Ruler:** Haakon VII
Obv: Crown above center hole **Rev:** Value above center hole

Date	Mintage	VG	F	VF	XF	BU
1924	12,079,100	—	0.30	0.75	9.00	40.00
1925	7,050,700	—	0.30	0.75	9.00	60.00
1926	11,764,200	—	0.30	0.75	9.00	40.00
1927	526,000	5.00	10.00	20.00	120	600
1937	5,000,000	—	0.30	0.75	5.00	35.00
1938	3,412,600	—	0.30	0.75	5.00	35.00
1939	1,538,400	—	1.00	2.50	9.50	65.00
1940	4,800,000	—	0.30	0.75	1.75	17.50
1941	10,150,000	—	0.30	0.75	1.75	10.00
1945	1,718,000	—	0.10	0.25	1.75	15.00
1946	3,723,200	—	0.10	0.25	1.75	9.00
1947	7,256,700	—	0.10	0.25	1.75	6.50
1948	3,104,500	—	0.10	0.25	2.00	7.00
1949	11,545,500	—	0.10	0.25	1.75	7.00
1951	5,150,000	—	0.10	0.25	1.75	7.00

KM# 389 10 ORE

1.2500 g., Zinc, 15 mm. **Ruler:** Haakon VII **Obv:** Crown above center hole **Rev:** Value above center hole **Note:** World War II German occupation issue.

Date	Mintage	VG	F	VF	XF	BU
1941	15,309,900	—	0.75	2.00	6.00	32.50
1942	50,387,600	—	0.35	1.00	3.50	12.50
1943	13,377,700	—	0.75	2.00	5.50	35.00
1944	3,549,400	—	7.50	12.50	30.00	135
1945	5,645,500	—	4.00	8.00	18.00	50.00

KM# 391 10 ORE

1.1500 g., Nickel-Brass, 15 mm. **Ruler:** Haakon VII **Obv:** Crown above center hole **Rev:** Value above center hole **Note:** World War II government in exile issue.

Date	Mintage	VG	F	VF	XF	BU
1942	6,000,000	—	—	—	120	225

Note: All except 9,667 were melted

KM# 396 10 ORE

1.5000 g., Copper-Nickel, 15 mm. **Ruler:** Haakon VII **Obv:** Crowned monogram divides date **Rev:** Value flanked by designs

Date	Mintage	VG	F	VF	XF	BU
1951	17,400,000	—	0.10	0.30	2.50	60.00
1952	Inc. above	—	0.10	0.20	1.50	20.00
1953	7,700,000	—	0.10	0.20	1.50	20.00
1954	10,105,000	—	0.10	0.20	1.50	20.00
1955	9,829,500	—	0.10	0.20	1.50	50.00
1956	10,066,000	—	0.10	0.20	1.50	20.00
1957	22,900,000	—	0.10	0.20	1.50	12.00

KM# 406 10 ORE

1.5000 g., Copper-Nickel, 15 mm. **Ruler:** Olav V **Obv:** Crowned monogram **Rev:** Honey bee and value, small lettering

Date	Mintage	VG	F	VF	XF	BU
1958	1,425,000	—	0.50	1.50	3.00	30.00

KM# 411 10 ORE

1.5000 g., Copper-Nickel, 15 mm. **Ruler:** Olav V **Obv:** Crowned monogram **Rev:** Honey bee and value, large lettering

Date	Mintage	VG	F	VF	XF	BU
1959	2,500,000	—	—	0.75	3.00	20.00
1960	12,490,200	—	—	0.10	0.60	7.00
1961	10,385,000	—	—	0.10	0.60	20.00
1962	16,210,000	—	—	0.10	0.60	4.00
1963	17,560,000	—	—	0.10	0.60	4.00

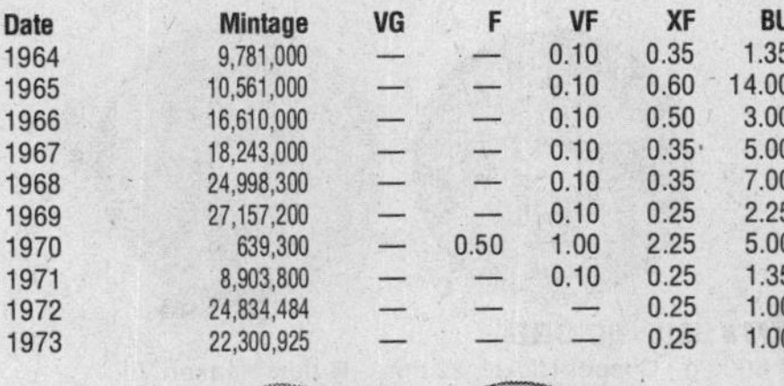

Date	Mintage	VG	F	VF	XF	BU
1964	9,781,000	—	—	0.10	0.35	1.35
1965	10,561,000	—	—	0.10	0.60	14.00
1966	16,610,000	—	—	0.10	0.50	3.00
1967	18,243,000	—	—	0.10	0.35	5.00
1968	24,998,300	—	—	0.10	0.35	7.00
1969	27,157,200	—	—	0.10	0.25	2.25
1970	639,300	—	0.50	1.00	2.25	5.00
1971	8,903,800	—	—	0.10	0.25	1.35
1972	24,834,484	—	—	—	0.25	1.00
1973	22,300,925	—	—	—	0.25	1.00

KM# 416 10 ORE

1.2500 g., Copper-Nickel, 15 mm. **Ruler:** Olav V **Obv:** Crowned monogram divides date **Rev:** Value **Designer:** Oivind Hansen
Note: Varieties exist in monogram.

Date	Mintage	VG	F	VF	XF	BU
1974	30,995,223	—	—	—	0.10	0.60
1975	21,845,496	—	—	—	0.10	0.60
1976	42,403,074	—	—	—	0.10	0.40
1977	43,304,000	—	—	—	0.10	0.40
1978	37,395,000	—	—	—	0.10	0.40
1979	25,808,000	—	—	—	0.10	0.40
1980	28,620,000	—	—	—	0.10	0.40
1980 Without star	14,050,000	—	—	—	0.10	0.40
1981	43,083,400	—	—	—	0.10	0.40
1982	40,974,256	—	—	—	0.10	0.40
1983	45,637,300	—	—	—	0.10	0.40
1984	100,066,000	—	—	—	0.10	0.35
1985	103,108,000	—	—	—	0.10	0.35
1986	146,392,000	—	—	—	0.10	0.35
1987	166,040,000	—	—	—	0.10	0.35
1988	94,677,000	—	—	—	0.10	0.35
1989	97,273,500	—	—	—	0.10	0.35
1990	150,290,000	—	—	—	0.10	0.35
1991	79,597,000	—	—	—	0.10	0.35

KM# 360 25 ORE

2.4200 g., 0.6000 Silver .0463 oz. ASW **Obv:** Crowned arms within wreath **Obv. Legend:** BRODERFOLKENES VEL **Rev:** Value within wreath, crossed hammers divide date below

Date	Mintage	VG	F	VF	XF	BU
1901	606,900	9.00	21.00	40.00	60.00	130
1902	611,700	9.00	21.00	40.00	60.00	130
1904	600,000	9.00	21.00	40.00	60.00	130

KM# 373 25 ORE

2.4200 g., 0.6000 Silver .0463 oz. ASW **Ruler:** Haakon VII **Obv:** Arms flanked by designs **Rev:** Crowned cross with monogram

Date	Mintage	VG	F	VF	XF	BU
1909	600,000	8.00	16.00	30.00	55.00	110
1911	400,000	15.00	30.00	45.00	80.00	200
1912	200,000	50.00	100	150	270	650
1913	400,000	12.00	20.00	35.00	70.00	165
1914	399,600	12.00	18.00	50.00	100	180
1915	1,032,300	4.50	10.00	15.00	40.00	110
1916	368,000	17.00	35.00	50.00	80.00	225
1917	400,000	15.00	30.00	45.00	70.00	175
1918/6	800,000	6.00	12.00	20.00	40.00	65.00
1918	Inc. above	5.00	12.00	20.00	40.00	95.00
1919	1,600,000	3.50	6.00	12.00	25.00	80.00

KM# 381 25 ORE

4.4000 g., Copper-Nickel, 17 mm. **Ruler:** Haakon VII
Obv: Crowned monogram **Rev:** Arms flanked by designs

Date	Mintage	VG	F	VF	XF	BU
1921	4,800,000	4.00	10.00	15.00	20.00	40.00
1922	14,200,000	4.00	10.00	15.00	20.00	40.00
1923	5,200,000	8.00	16.50	25.00	35.00	60.00

KM# 382 25 ORE

2.4000 g., Copper-Nickel, 17 mm. **Ruler:** Haakon VII
Obv: Crowned monogram, hole in center **Rev:** Arms flanked by designs, hole in center

Date	Mintage	VG	F	VF	XF	BU
1921	—	1.50	3.00	5.00	75.00	625
1922	—	1.50	3.00	4.00	45.00	375
1923	—	1.00	1.50	3.00	25.00	190

Note: Respective mintages included with KM#381

KM# 384 25 ORE

2.4000 g., Copper-Nickel, 17 mm. **Ruler:** Haakon VII
Obv: Crowned cross with monogram, hole in center **Rev:** Center hole flanked by designs, crown above

Date	Mintage	VG	F	VF	XF	BU
1924	4,000,000	—	0.50	2.00	7.00	65.00
1927	6,200,000	—	0.50	1.50	7.00	65.00
1929	800,000	—	1.50	6.00	42.00	250
1939	1,220,000	—	0.25	0.75	3.50	60.00
1940	1,160,000	—	0.25	0.75	3.50	50.00
1946	1,850,000	—	0.20	0.50	1.75	20.00
1947	2,592,000	—	0.20	0.50	1.75	12.00
1949	2,602,000	—	0.20	0.50	1.75	12.00
1950	2,800,000	—	0.20	0.50	1.75	12.00

KM# 392 25 ORE

2.4000 g., Nickel-Brass, 17 mm. **Ruler:** Haakon VII **Obv:** Crowned monograms form cross, hole at center **Rev:** Crown on top divides date, hole in center flanked by designs, value on bottom **Note:** World War II government in exile issue.

Date	Mintage	VG	F	VF	XF	BU
1942	2,400,000	—	—	—	120	225

Note: All but 10,300 were melted

KM# 395 25 ORE

2.0000 g., Zinc, 17 mm. **Ruler:** Haakon VII **Obv:** Shield flanked by designs **Rev:** Value flanked by designs **Note:** World War II German occupation.

Date	Mintage	VG	F	VF	XF	BU
1943	14,104,800	—	1.00	1.50	4.00	25.00
1944	3,030,500	2.00	4.00	7.50	20.00	50.00
1945	3,010,000	3.00	6.00	10.00	22.00	60.00

KM# 401 25 ORE

2.4000 g., Copper-Nickel, 17 mm. **Ruler:** Haakon VII **Obv:** Crowned monogram divides date **Rev:** Value flanked by designs
Note: Mint marks exist with mint mark on square or without square.

Date	Mintage	VG	F	VF	XF	BU
1952	4,060,000	—	0.10	0.25	1.20	30.00
1953	3,320,000	—	0.10	0.25	1.20	35.00
1954	3,140,000	—	0.10	0.25	1.20	30.00
1955	2,000,000	—	0.10	0.25	1.20	75.00
1956	3,980,000	—	0.10	0.25	1.20	30.00
1957	7,660,000	—	0.10	0.25	1.20	20.00

KM# 407 25 ORE

2.4000 g., Copper-Nickel, 17 mm. **Ruler:** Olav V **Obv:** Head left
Rev: Bird above value

Date	Mintage	VG	F	VF	XF	BU
1958	1,316,000	—	0.50	1.00	3.00	35.00
1959	1,184,000	—	0.50	1.00	3.00	30.00

Date	Mintage	VG	F	VF	XF	BU
1960	3,964,200	—	—	0.10	1.25	17.50
1961	4,656,000	—	—	0.10	1.00	7.50
1962	6,304,000	—	—	0.10	1.00	7.50
1963	3,640,000	—	—	0.10	1.00	7.50
1964	4,953,000	—	—	0.10	0.50	2.75
1965	2,798,000	—	—	0.10	0.65	30.00
1966	6,075,000	—	—	0.10	0.65	3.00
1967	6,641,000	—	—	0.10	0.65	3.00
1968	4,963,400	—	—	0.10	0.50	5.00
1969	12,426,500	—	—	0.10	0.15	2.00
1970	1,545,400	—	—	0.15	0.75	6.50
1971	5,247,200	—	—	—	0.10	1.25
1972	7,928,584	—	—	—	0.10	1.25
1973	8,516,175	—	—	—	0.10	1.25

KM# 417 25 ORE

2.0000 g., Copper-Nickel, 17 mm. **Ruler:** Olav V **Obv:** Crowned monograms in cross formation **Rev:** Value **Designer:** Oivind Hansen

Date	Mintage	VG	F	VF	XF	BU
1974	8,048,223	—	—	—	0.10	0.65
1975	15,594,696	—	—	—	0.10	0.65
1976	24,721,074	—	—	—	0.10	0.50
1977	20,150,000	—	—	—	0.10	0.50
1978	11,259,000	—	—	—	0.10	0.50
1979	16,666,000	—	—	—	0.10	0.50
1980	6,289,000	—	—	—	0.10	0.50
1980 Without star	8,176,000	—	—	—	0.10	0.50
1981	17,971,000	—	—	—	0.10	0.50
1982	16,862,650	—	—	—	0.10	0.50

KM# 356 50 ORE

5.0000 g., 0.6000 Silver .0964 oz. ASW **Obv:** Head left **Obv. Legend:** OSCAR II NORGES... **Rev:** Crowned shield within wreath, crossed hammers divide date below

Date	Mintage	VG	F	VF	XF	BU
1901	404,000	7.00	14.00	35.00	70.00	185
1902	301,200	7.00	14.00	35.00	70.00	185
1904	100,500	35.00	70.00	165	260	550

KM# 374 50 ORE

5.0000 g., 0.6000 Silver .0964 oz. ASW **Ruler:** Haakon VII **Obv:** Head right **Rev:** Crowned shield flanked by designs

Date	Mintage	VG	F	VF	XF	BU
1909	200,000	14.00	27.00	35.00	65.00	175
1911	200,000	14.00	40.00	60.00	90.00	250
1912	200,000	30.00	60.00	90.00	150	325
1913	200,000	14.00	40.00	60.00	90.00	250
1914	800,000	3.50	8.00	15.00	25.00	120
1915	300,000	12.00	23.00	40.00	60.00	150
1916	700,000	4.50	9.00	19.00	45.00	135
1918	3,090,000	2.50	5.00	8.00	12.00	90.00
1919	1,219,000	3.00	6.00	9.00	18.00	50.00

KM# 379 50 ORE

4.8000 g., Copper-Nickel, 22 mm. **Ruler:** Haakon VII **Obv:** Crowned monograms form cross **Rev:** Crowned shield flanked by designs

Date	Mintage	VG	F	VF	XF	BU
1920	1,236,000	15.00	25.00	35.00	60.00	125
1921	7,345,000	4.00	8.00	12.00	25.00	50.00
1922	3,000,000	4.00	8.00	12.00	25.00	50.00
1923	4,540,000	25.00	60.00	85.00	115	185

KM# 380 50 ORE

4.8000 g., Copper-Nickel, 22 mm. **Ruler:** Haakon VII **Obv:** Crowned monograms form cross with hole in center **Rev:** Crowned shield flanked by designs, hole in center **Note:** Respective mintages are included with KM#379.

Date	Mintage	VG	F	VF	XF	BU
1920	—	—	30.00	90.00	300	1,000
1921	—	—	3.00	15.00	135	700
1922	—	—	2.50	10.00	85.00	500
1923	—	—	2.50	6.00	70.00	350

KM# 386 50 ORE

4.8000 g., Copper-Nickel, 22 mm. **Ruler:** Haakon VII **Obv:** Crowned monograms form cross with hole in center **Rev:** Center hole flanked by designs, crown above, value below

Date	Mintage	VG	F	VF	XF	BU
1926	2,000,000	—	0.35	1.50	17.50	95.00
1927	2,502,100	—	0.35	1.50	12.00	75.00
1928/7	1,458,200	—	0.50	2.50	20.00	110
1928	Inc. above	—	0.35	1.50	20.00	110
1929	600,000	—	1.50	6.00	70.00	520
1939	900,000	—	0.25	0.60	5.00	150
1940	2,193,000	—	0.20	0.50	3.50	40.00
1941	2,373,000	—	0.20	0.50	3.50	25.00
1945	1,354,000	—	0.20	0.50	2.50	32.50
1946	1,532,500	—	0.20	0.50	3.50	20.00
1947	2,465,300	—	0.20	0.50	3.50	12.50
1948	5,911,400	—	0.20	0.40	1.75	12.50
1949	1,029,600	—	0.25	1.00	5.00	25.00

KM# 390 50 ORE

Zinc, 22 mm. **Ruler:** Haakon VII **Obv:** Shield flanked by designs **Rev:** Value flanked by designs **Note:** World War II German occupation issue.

Date	Mintage	VG	F	VF	XF	BU
1941	7,760,800	—	1.25	3.00	15.00	75.00
1942	7,605,550	—	1.00	2.50	7.00	45.00
1943	3,348,500	7.00	15.00	25.00	60.00	175
1944	1,542,400	5.00	10.00	15.00	35.00	65.00
1945	226,000	90.00	180	285	425	675

KM# 393 50 ORE

4.8000 g., Nickel-Brass, 22 mm. **Ruler:** Haakon VII **Obv:** Crowned monograms form cross with hole in center **Rev:** Center hole flanked by designs, crown above, value below **Note:** World War II government in exile issue.

Date	Mintage	VG	F	VF	XF	BU
1942	1,600,000	—	—	—	125	250

Note: All but 9,238 were melted

KM# 402 50 ORE

4.8000 g., Copper-Nickel, 22 mm. **Ruler:** Haakon VII **Obv:** Crowned monogram **Rev:** Crowned shield divides date

Date	Mintage	VG	F	VF	XF	BU
1953	2,370,000	—	0.20	0.60	1.75	35.00
1954	230,000	1.25	5.00	15.00	85.00	550

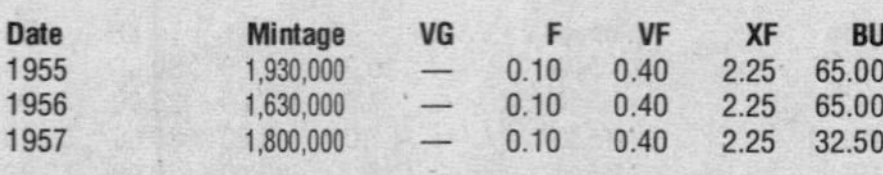

Date	Mintage	VG	F	VF	XF	BU
1955	1,930,000	—	0.10	0.40	2.25	65.00
1956	1,630,000	—	0.10	0.40	2.25	65.00
1957	1,800,000	—	0.10	0.40	2.25	32.50

KM# 408 50 ORE

4.8000 g., Copper-Nickel, 22 mm. **Ruler:** Olav V **Obv:** Head left **Rev:** Dog right divides date and value

Date	Mintage	VG	F	VF	XF	BU
1958	1,560,000	—	0.25	0.75	3.00	75.00
1959	340,000	—	1.00	2.00	12.00	75.00
1960	1,584,200	—	—	0.10	1.75	20.00
1961	2,424,600	—	—	0.10	0.85	12.50
1962	3,064,000	—	—	0.10	0.85	12.50
1963	2,168,000	—	—	0.10	0.85	12.50
1964	2,692,000	—	—	0.10	0.60	8.00
1965	1,248,000	—	0.25	0.75	3.00	55.00
1966	4,262,000	—	—	0.10	0.25	8.00
1967	4,001,000	—	—	0.10	0.25	6.50
1968	5,430,800	—	—	0.10	0.25	12.50
1969	7,591,000	—	—	0.10	0.25	3.00
1970	481,000	—	0.25	0.75	2.25	6.50
1971	2,489,300	—	—	0.10	0.25	3.00
1972	4,452,784	—	—	0.10	0.25	3.00
1973	3,317,175	—	—	0.10	0.25	3.00

KM# 418 50 ORE

4.8000 g., Copper-Nickel, 22 mm. **Ruler:** Olav V **Obv:** Crowned shield divides date **Rev:** Value **Designer:** Oivind Hansen **Note:** Varieties in shield exist.

Date	Mintage	VG	F	VF	XF	BU
1974	8,494,223	—	—	0.10	0.15	0.75
1975	10,123,496	—	—	0.10	0.15	0.75
1976	15,177,324	—	—	0.10	0.15	0.65
1977	19,411,750	—	—	0.10	0.15	0.50
1978	15,305,000	—	—	0.10	0.15	0.50
1979	10,152,000	—	—	0.10	0.15	0.50
1980	7,082,000	—	—	0.10	0.15	0.50
1980 Without star	7,066,000	—	—	0.10	0.15	0.50
1981	3,402,000	—	—	0.10	0.15	0.50
1982	11,156,650	—	—	0.10	0.15	0.40
1983	15,762,300	—	—	0.10	0.15	0.40
1984	8,615,000	—	—	0.10	0.15	0.40
1985	4,444,000	—	—	0.10	0.15	0.40
1986	4,178,000	—	—	0.10	0.15	0.40
1987	5,167,000	—	—	0.10	0.15	0.40
1988	9,610,000	—	—	0.10	0.15	0.35
1989	5,785,000	—	—	0.10	0.15	0.35
1990	1,729,000	—	—	0.10	0.15	0.50
1991	2,924,008	—	—	0.10	0.15	0.35
1992	6,802,027	—	—	0.10	0.15	0.35
1992 Proof	20,000	Value: 10.00				
1993	8,056,000	—	—	0.10	0.15	0.35
1994	7,173,000	—	—	0.10	0.15	0.35
1994 Proof	12,000	Value: 10.00				
1995	6,835,000	—	—	—	—	0.35
1995 Proof	—	Value: 10.00				
1996	4,500,000	—	—	—	—	0.40
1996 Proof	—	Value: 10.00				

KM# 460 50 ORE

3.6000 g., Bronze **Ruler:** Harald V **Obv:** Crown **Rev:** Stylized animal and value **Designer:** Grazyna Jolanta Linday

Date	Mintage	VG	F	VF	XF	BU
1996	81,956,200	—	—	—	—	0.50
1997	24,089,873	—	—	—	—	0.40
1997 Proof	—	Value: 10.00				
1998	30,913,000	—	—	—	—	0.40
1998 Proof	—	Value: 10.00				
1999	25,314,273	—	—	—	—	0.40
1999 Proof	—	Value: 10.00				
2000	18,979,552	—	—	—	—	0.40
2000 Proof	—	Value: 10.00				

KM# 357 KRONE

7.5000 g., 0.8000 Silver .1929 oz. ASW **Obv:** Head left **Obv. Legend:** OSCAR II NORGES... **Rev:** Crowned arms within wreath, crossed hammers divide date below **Note:** Without 30 SK

Date	Mintage	VG	F	VF	XF	BU
1901	151,800	17.00	30.00	60.00	175	550
1904	100,100	35.00	70.00	125	230	625

KM# 369 KRONE

7.5000 g., 0.8000 Silver .1929 oz. ASW **Ruler:** Haakon VII **Obv:** Head right **Rev:** Order of St. Olaf

Date	Mintage	VG	F	VF	XF	BU
1908	180,000	26.00	50.00	80.00	120	265
Note: Crossed hammers on shield						
1908	170,000	21.00	40.00	60.00	100	200
Note: Crossed hammers without shield						
1910	100,000	50.00	100	150	235	550
1912	200,000	30.00	45.00	100	160	325
1913	230,000	22.00	40.00	90.00	125	285
1914	602,000	11.00	19.00	35.00	50.00	125
1915	498,000	12.00	22.00	40.00	90.00	125
1916	400,000	12.00	25.00	40.00	100	265
1917	600,000	11.00	19.00	30.00	55.00	95.00

KM# 385 KRONE

7.0000 g., Copper-Nickel, 25 mm. **Ruler:** Haakon VII **Obv:** Crowned monograms form cross with hole in center **Rev:** Crowned order chain with hole in center

Date	Mintage	VG	F	VF	XF	BU
1925	8,686,000	—	0.30	3.00	25.00	140
1926	1,984,000	—	0.50	4.00	35.00	240
1927	1,000,000	—	1.00	5.00	65.00	475
1936	700,000	—	1.25	5.50	65.00	475
1937	1,000,000	—	1.00	4.00	45.00	325
1938	926,000	—	0.60	2.50	20.00	150
1939	2,253,000	—	0.60	1.50	10.00	85.00
1940	3,890,000	—	0.30	1.00	6.00	75.00
1946	5,499,000	—	0.25	0.50	3.00	20.00
1947	802,000	—	1.00	2.00	12.00	65.00
1949	7,846,000	—	0.20	0.50	3.00	15.00
1950	9,942,000	—	0.20	0.50	3.00	15.00
1951	4,761,000	—	0.20	0.50	3.00	15.00

KM# 397 KRONE

7.0000 g., Copper-Nickel, 25 mm. **Ruler:** Haakon VII **Obv:** Crowned monogram **Rev:** Crowned shield divides date

Date	Mintage	VG	F	VF	XF	BU
1951	3,819,000	—	0.20	0.50	2.50	32.50
1953	1,465,000	—	0.20	0.50	2.50	65.00
1954	3,045,000	—	0.20	0.50	2.50	65.00
1955	1,970,000	—	0.20	0.50	2.50	95.00
1956	4,300,000	—	0.20	0.50	2.50	55.00
1957	7,630,000	—	0.20	0.50	2.50	35.00

KM# 409 KRONE

7.0000 g., Copper-Nickel, 25 mm. **Ruler:** Olav V **Obv:** Head left **Rev:** Horse

Date	Mintage	VG	F	VF	XF	BU
1958	540,000	—	3.00	10.00	50.00	325
1959	4,450,000	—	—	0.20	2.50	35.00
1960	1,790,200	—	—	0.20	2.50	30.00
1961	3,933,600	—	—	0.20	0.85	15.00
1962	6,015,000	—	—	0.20	0.85	15.00
1963	4,677,000	—	—	0.20	0.85	15.00
1964	3,469,000	—	—	0.20	0.60	7.50
1965	3,222,000	—	—	0.20	1.20	65.00
1966	3,084,000	—	—	0.20	0.85	25.00
1967	6,680,000	—	—	0.20	0.85	15.00
1968	6,149,200	—	—	0.20	0.85	45.00
1969	5,185,500	—	—	0.20	0.40	5.00
1970	8,637,900	—	—	0.20	0.50	11.50
1971	10,257,800	—	—	0.20	0.40	5.00
1972	13,179,394	—	—	0.20	0.40	4.75
1973	9,140,175	—	—	0.20	0.40	4.75

KM# 419 KRONE

7.0000 g., Copper-Nickel, 25 mm. **Ruler:** Olav V **Obv:** Head left **Rev:** Value and date below crown **Designer:** Oivind Hansen **Note:** Varieties with and without star mint mark exist.

Date	Mintage	VG	F	VF	XF	BU
1974	16,537,223	—	—	0.20	0.35	1.25
1975	26,043,966	—	—	0.20	0.35	1.25
1976	35,926,574	—	—	0.20	0.35	0.85
1977	26,263,500	—	—	0.20	0.35	0.85
1978	23,360,000	—	—	0.20	0.35	0.85
1979	15,896,500	—	—	0.20	0.35	0.85
1980	5,918,000	—	—	0.20	0.35	2.50
1981	16,308,150	—	—	0.20	0.35	0.75
1982	29,187,000	—	—	0.20	0.35	0.75
1983	24,293,300	—	—	0.20	0.35	0.75
1984	3,677,000	—	—	0.20	0.35	1.50
1985	10,985,000	—	—	0.20	0.35	0.75
1986	5,612,500	—	—	0.20	0.35	0.75
1987	11,015,500	—	—	0.20	0.35	0.75
1988	14,880,000	—	—	0.20	0.35	0.75
1989	5,605,000	—	—	0.20	0.35	0.65
1990	8,804,000	—	—	0.20	0.35	0.65
1990 Proof	15,110	Value: 85.00				
1991	21,064,500	—	—	0.20	0.35	0.65

KM# 436 KRONE

7.0000 g., Copper-Nickel, 25 mm. **Ruler:** Harald V **Obv:** Head right **Rev:** Value and date below crown **Designer:** Ingrid Austlid Rase

Date	Mintage	VG	F	VF	XF	BU
1992	7,425,500	—	—	0.20	0.35	0.65
1992 Proof	20,000	Value: 10.00				
1993	12,295,000	—	—	0.20	0.35	0.65
1994	25,951,000	—	—	0.20	0.35	0.65
1994 Proof	12,000	Value: 10.00				
1995	12,883,000	—	—	0.20	0.35	0.65
1995 Proof	—	Value: 10.00				
1996	20,844,000	—	—	0.20	0.35	0.65
1996 Proof	—	Value: 10.00				

KM# 462 KRONE

4.3000 g., Copper-Nickel, 21 mm. **Ruler:** Harald V **Obv:** Crowned monograms form cross within circle with center hole **Rev:** Bird on vine above center hole date and value below

Date	Mintage	VG	F	VF	XF	BU
1997	141,099,873	—	—	—	—	0.65
1997 Proof	—	Value: 10.00				
1998	139,493,000	—	—	—	—	0.65
1998 Proof	—	Value: 10.00				
1999	74,454,273	—	—	—	—	0.65
1999 Proof	—	Value: 10.00				
2000	42,689,277	—	—	—	—	0.65
2000 Proof	—	Value: 10.00				

KM# 359 2 KRONER

15.0000 g., 0.8000 Silver .3858 oz. ASW, 31 mm. **Obv:** Head left **Obv. Legend:** OSCAR II NORGES... **Rev:** Crowned arms within wreath, crossed hammers divide date below **Note:** Restrikes are made by the Royal Mint, Norway, in gold, silver and bronze.

Date	Mintage	VG	F	VF	XF	BU
1902	153,100	50.00	85.00	125	225	500
1904	75,600	50.00	100	150	250	525

KM# 363 2 KRONER

15.0000 g., 0.8000 Silver .3858 oz. ASW, 31 mm. **Ruler:** Haakon VII **Subject:** Norway Independence **Obv:** Crowned mantled shield **Rev:** Inscription and date within tree, wreath of grasped hands surround **Designer:** Gerhard Munthe and Ivar Thorndsen

Date	Mintage	VG	F	VF	XF	BU
1906	100,000	23.00	35.00	60.00	100	175

KM# 365 2 KRONER

15.0000 g., 0.8000 Silver .3858 oz. ASW, 31 mm. **Ruler:** Haakon VII **Obv:** Crowned mantled shield **Rev:** Inscription and date within tree, wreath of grasped hands surround **Designer:** Herhard Munthe and Ivar Thorndsen

Date	Mintage	VG	F	VF	XF	BU
1907	54,600	30.00	55.00	100	175	250

KM# 366 2 KRONER

15.0000 g., 0.8000 Silver .3858 oz. ASW, 31 mm. **Ruler:** Haakon VII **Subject:** Border watch **Obv:** Crowned and mantled arms **Rev:** Inscription and date within tree, wreath of grasped hands surround **Designer:** Gerhard Munthe and Ivar Thorndsen

Date	Mintage	VG	F	VF	XF	BU
1907	27,500	100	200	350	550	850

KM# 370 2 KRONER
15.0000 g., 0.8000 Silver .3858 oz. ASW, 31 mm. **Ruler:** Haakon VII **Obv:** Head right **Rev:** Crowned shield within designed circle, various emblems around border

Date	Mintage	VG	F	VF	XF	BU
1908	200,000	—	50.00	85.00	125	250
1910	150,000	—	80.00	125	175	425
1912	150,000	—	65.00	100	150	385
1913	270,000	—	45.00	65.00	90.00	175
1914	255,000	—	45.00	70.00	95.00	215
1915	225,000	—	40.00	65.00	95.00	215
1916	250,000	—	60.00	85.00	125	265
1917	377,500	—	30.00	40.00	60.00	165

KM# 377 2 KRONER
15.0000 g., 0.8000 Silver .3858 oz. ASW, 31 mm. **Ruler:** Haakon VII **Subject:** Constitution centennial **Obv:** Crowned shield **Rev:** Standing figure facing right **Designer:** Gunner Utsand

Date	Mintage	VG	F	VF	XF	BU
1914	225,600	10.00	17.00	30.00	60.00	135

KM# 412 5 KRONER
11.5000 g., Copper-Nickel, 29.5 mm. **Ruler:** Olav V **Obv:** Head left **Rev:** Crowned shield divides value

Date	Mintage	VG	F	VF	XF	BU
1963	7,074,000	—	—	1.00	3.50	30.00
1964	7,346,000	—	—	1.00	2.25	15.00
1965	2,233,000	—	—	1.00	3.00	90.00
1966	2,502,000	—	—	1.00	3.00	65.00
1967	583,000	—	1.00	1.75	6.50	60.00
1968	1,813,400	—	—	1.00	2.25	45.00
1969	2,403,700	—	—	1.00	2.25	12.00
1970	202,300	—	1.50	2.50	6.50	22.50
1971	177,900	—	1.50	2.50	7.00	27.50
1972	2,208,704	—	—	—	1.25	3.50
1973	2,778,055	—	—	—	1.25	7.50

KM# 420 5 KRONER
11.5000 g., Copper-Nickel, 29.5 mm. **Ruler:** Olav V **Obv:** Head left **Rev:** Crowned shield divides date **Designer:** Oivind Hansen **Note:** Varieties exist with large and small shields.

Date	Mintage	VG	F	VF	XF	BU
1974	1,983,423	—	—	—	1.00	7.50
1975	2,946,442	—	—	—	1.00	4.50
1976	9,055,574	—	—	—	1.00	2.25
1977	4,629,600	—	—	—	1.00	1.50
1978	5,853,000	—	—	—	1.00	1.50
1979	6,818,000	—	—	—	1.00	1.50
1980	1,578,400	—	—	—	1.00	2.50
1981	1,104,800	—	—	—	1.00	2.25
1982	3,919,890	—	—	—	1.00	1.50
1983	2,932,260	—	—	—	1.00	1.50
1984	1,233,000	—	—	—	1.00	2.25
1985	1,399,600	—	—	—	1.00	1.50
1987	900,200	—	—	—	1.00	2.50
1988	865,200	—	—	—	1.00	2.50

KM# 421 5 KRONER
11.5000 g., Copper-Nickel, 29.5 mm. **Ruler:** Olav V **Subject:** 100th Anniversary of Krone System **Obv:** Crowned shield divides value **Rev:** Balance scale and miner **Designer:** Oivind Hansen

Date	Mintage	VG	F	VF	XF	BU
ND(1975)	1,191,813	—	—	1.00	1.50	3.50

KM# 422 5 KRONER
11.5000 g., Copper-Nickel, 29.5 mm. **Ruler:** Olav V **Subject:** 150th Anniversary - Immigration to America **Obv:** Value below arms **Rev:** Sailing ship, The "Restaurasjonen"(Restoration)

Date	Mintage	VG	F	VF	XF	BU
ND(1975)	1,222,827	—	—	1.00	1.50	3.50

KM# 423 5 KRONER
11.5000 g., Copper-Nickel, 29.5 mm. **Ruler:** Olav V **Subject:** 350th Anniversary of Norwegian Army **Obv:** Value below arms **Rev:** Sword divides crowned monograms

Date	Mintage	VG	F	VF	XF	BU
ND(1978)	2,989,768	—	—	1.00	1.50	3.00

KM# 428 5 KRONER
11.5000 g., Copper-Nickel, 29.5 mm. **Ruler:** Olav V **Subject:** 300th Anniversary of the Mint **Obv:** Crossed mining tools below crown, circle surrounds **Rev:** Conjoined heads left and right within circle **Designer:** Oivind Hansen

Date	Mintage	VG	F	VF	XF	BU
1986	2,345,500	—	—	1.00	1.50	3.00
1986 Prooflike	5,000	—	—	—	—	—

KM# 430 5 KRONER
11.5000 g., Copper-Nickel, 29.5 mm. **Ruler:** Olav V **Subject:** 175th Anniversary of the National Bank **Obv:** Arms **Rev:** Stein above date and inscription

Date	Mintage	VG	F	VF	XF	BU
1991	512,000	—	—	—	—	7.00

KM# 437 5 KRONER
11.5000 g., Copper-Nickel, 29.5 mm. **Ruler:** Harald V **Obv:** Head right **Designer:** Ingrid Austlid Rise

Date	Mintage	VG	F	VF	XF	BU
1992	549,600	—	—	—	—	2.25
Note: 100,000 are in mint sets						
1992 Proof	20,000	Value: 10.00				
1993	509,600	—	—	—	—	2.50
1994	2,111,800	—	—	—	—	2.00
1994 Proof	12,000	Value: 10.00				

KM# 456 5 KRONER
11.5000 g., Copper-Nickel, 29.5 mm. **Ruler:** Harald V **Obv:** Head right **Rev:** Old coin design divides value above legend and date **Designer:** Ingrid Austlid Rise **Note:** 1,000 years of Norwegian coinage

Date	Mintage	VG	F	VF	XF	BU
1995	500,000	—	—	—	—	3.50
1995 Proof	12,000	Value: 22.50				

KM# 458 5 KRONER
11.5000 g., Copper-Nickel, 29.5 mm. **Ruler:** Harald V **Subject:** 50th Anniversary - United Nations **Obv:** Head right **Rev:** Standing figure with arms outstretched, children holding hands by tree **Designer:** Ingrid Austlid Rise

Date	Mintage	VG	F	VF	XF	BU
ND(1995)	500,000	—	—	—	—	3.50

KM# 459 5 KRONER
11.5000 g., Copper-Nickel, 29.5 mm. **Ruler:** Harald V **Subject:** Centennial - Nansen's Return From the Arctic **Obv:** Head right **Rev:** Sailing ship facing **Designer:** Ingrid Austlid Rise

Date	Mintage	VG	F	VF	XF	BU
1996	1,381,909	—	—	—	—	3.00
1996 Proof	12,000	Value: 22.50				

KM# 461 5 KRONER
11.5000 g., Copper-Nickel, 29.5 mm. **Ruler:** Harald V

Subject: 350th Anniversary - Norwegian Postal Service
Obv: Arms **Rev:** Horse and rider left

Date	Mintage	VG	F	VF	XF	BU
ND(1997)	1,742,073	—	—	—	—	3.00
ND(1997) Proof	12,000	Value: 10.00				

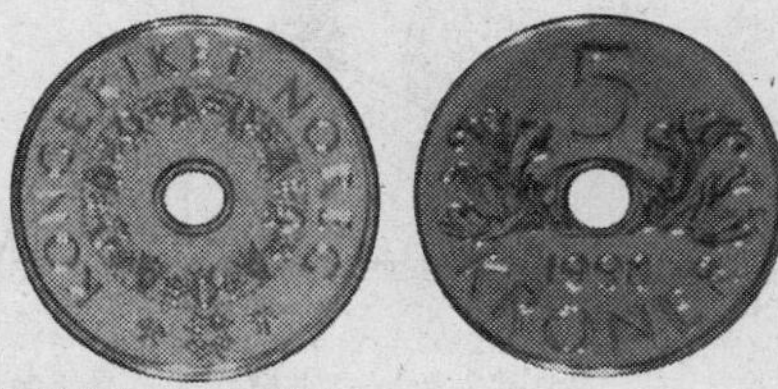

KM# 463 5 KRONER
7.8500 g., Copper-Nickel **Ruler:** Harald V **Subject:** Order of St. Olaf **Obv:** Hole at center of order chain **Rev:** Center hole flanked by sprigs, value above and date below

Date	Mintage	VG	F	VF	XF	BU
1998	47,701,000	—	—	—	—	1.50
1998 Proof	10,000	Value: 12.50				
1999	21,754,273	—	—	—	—	1.50
1999 Proof	10,000	Value: 12.50				
2000	9,691,387	—	—	—	—	1.50
2000 Proof	10,000	Value: 12.50				

KM# 358 10 KRONER
4.4803 g., 0.9000 Gold .1296 oz. AGW **Obv:** Head right **Obv. Legend:** OSCAR II NORGES... **Rev:** Crowned arms within wreath

Date	Mintage	VG	F	VF	XF	Unc
1902	24,100	BV	100	200	375	600

KM# 375 10 KRONER
4.4803 g., 0.9000 Gold .1296 oz. AGW **Ruler:** Haakon VII **Obv:** Crowned head right **Rev:** King Olaf Haraldson, the Saint

Date	Mintage	F	VF	XF	Unc	BU
1910	52,600	BV	165	275	450	—

KM# 413 10 KRONER
20.0000 g., 0.9000 Silver .5707 oz. ASW, 35 mm. **Ruler:** Haakon VII **Subject:** Constitution sesquicentennial **Obv:** Crowned shield **Rev:** Eidsval Mansion **Edge Lettering:** ENIGE OG TRO TIL DOVRE FALLER **Note:** Edge lettering varieties exist.

Date	Mintage	VG	F	VF	XF	BU
ND(1964)	1,408,000	—	—	—	9.00	11.50

KM# 427 10 KRONER
9.0000 g., Copper-Zinc-Nickel **Ruler:** Olav V **Obv:** Head left within circle **Rev:** Value within small circle at center of order chain

Date	Mintage	VG	F	VF	XF	BU
1983	20,193,060	—	—	—	2.00	5.50
1984	11,073,500	—	—	—	1.75	3.25
1985	22,457,550	—	—	—	1.75	3.00
1986	29,060,950	—	—	—	1.75	3.00
1987	8,809,750	—	—	—	1.75	3.25
1988	2,630,500	—	—	—	1.75	3.25
1989	3,259,000	—	—	—	1.75	3.25
1990	3,004,000	—	—	—	1.75	3.25
1991	20,287,150	—	—	—	1.75	2.75

KM# 457 10 KRONER
6.8000 g., Copper-Zinc-Nickel **Ruler:** Harald V **Obv:** Head right **Rev:** Stylized church rooftop, value and date **Designer:** Ingrid Austlid Rise

Date	Mintage	VG	F	VF	XF	BU
1995	60,740,000	—	—	—	—	3.50
1995 Proof	—	Value: 10.00				
1996	36,372,000	—	—	—	—	3.50
1996 Proof	—	Value: 10.00				
1997	1,229,873	—	—	—	—	3.50
1997 Proof	—	Value: 10.00				
1998	1,058,000	—	—	—	—	3.50
1998 Proof	—	Value: 10.00				
1999	1,059,273	—	—	—	—	3.50
1999 Proof	—	Value: 10.00				
2000	1,096,727	—	—	—	—	3.50
2000 Proof	—	Value: 10.00				

KM# 355 20 KRONER
8.9600 g., 0.9000 Gold .2593 oz. AGW **Obv:** Head right **Obv. Legend:** OSCAR II NORGES... **Rev:** Crowned arms within wreath

Date	Mintage	VG	F	VF	XF	Unc
1902	50,400	—	—	BV	200	350

KM# 376 20 KRONER
8.9600 g., 0.9000 Gold .2593 oz. AGW **Ruler:** Haakon VII **Obv:** Crowned head right **Rev:** King Olaf II, the Saint

Date	Mintage	F	VF	XF	Unc	BU
1910	250,000	BV	185	275	450	—

KM# 453 20 KRONER
Copper-Zinc-Nickel **Ruler:** Harald V **Obv:** Head right **Rev:** Value above 1/2 ancient boat **Designer:** Ingrid Austlid Rise

Date	Mintage	VG	F	VF	XF	BU
1994	18,598,000	—	—	—	—	6.50
1994 Proof	12,000	Value: 25.00				
1995	21,760,000	—	—	—	—	6.50
1995 Proof	—	Value: 25.00				
1996	1,519,500	—	—	—	—	6.50
1996 Proof	—	Value: 25.00				
1997	1,049,873	—	—	—	—	6.50
1997 Proof	—	Value: 25.00				
1998	5,007,000	—	—	—	—	6.50
1998 Proof	—	Value: 25.00				
1999	6,171,000	—	—	—	—	6.50
1999 Proof	—	Value: 25.00				
2000	11,113,370	—	—	—	—	6.50
2000 Proof	10,000	Value: 25.00				

KM# 464 20 KRONER
9.9000 g., Copper-Zinc-Nickel **Ruler:** Harald V **Subject:** 700th Anniversary - Akershus Fortress **Obv:** Seal of King Hadon V **Rev:** Fortress

Date	Mintage	F	VF	XF	Unc	BU
1999	5,121,986	—	—	—	7.50	—

KM# 465 20 KRONER
9.9000 g., Nickel-Bronze **Ruler:** Harald V **Subject:** Vinland **Obv:** Head right **Rev:** Viking ship hull reflected **Designer:** Ingrid Austlid Rise

Date	Mintage	F	VF	XF	Unc	BU
1999	1,048,700	—	—	—	7.50	—
1999 Proof	2,500	Value: 30.00				

Note: In sets only

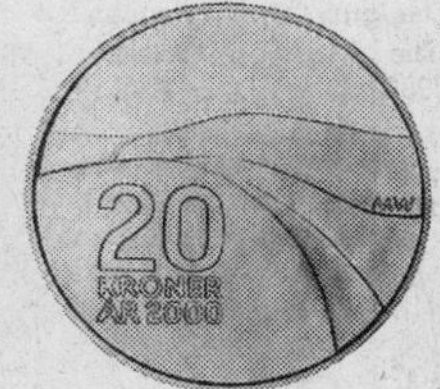

KM# 468 20 KRONER
9.9000 g., Nickel-Brass **Ruler:** Harald V **Subject:** Millennium **Obv:** Head right **Rev:** Unknown road into the future

Date	Mintage	F	VF	XF	Unc	BU
2000	1,032,307	—	—	—	12.50	—

KM# 414 25 KRONER
29.0000 g., 0.8750 Silver .8159 oz. ASW, 39 mm. **Ruler:** Olav V **Subject:** 25th Anniversary of Liberation **Obv:** Head right **Rev:** Crowned monogram **Edge:** Repeated pattern of circles and rectangles **Designer:** Oivind Hansen

Date	Mintage	VG	F	VF	XF	BU
1970	1,203,700	—	—	—	—	13.50

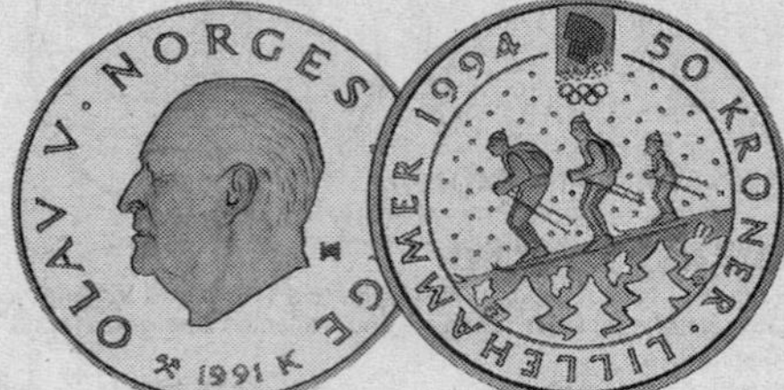

KM# 424 50 KRONER
27.0000 g., 0.9250 Silver .8030 oz. ASW **Ruler:** Olav V **Subject:** 75th Birthday of King Olav V **Obv:** Head left **Rev:** Single flowered stem divides signature and dates

Date	Mintage	VG	F	VF	XF	BU
ND(1978)	800,000	—	—	—	—	15.00

KM# 431 50 KRONER
16.8100 g., 0.9250 Silver .5000 oz. ASW **Ruler:** Olav V **Subject:** 1994 Olympics **Obv:** Head left **Rev:** Skiers within circle **Designer:** Oivind Hansen

Date	Mintage	VG	F	VF	XF	BU
1991	80,016	—	—	—	—	37.50

KM# 432 50 KRONER
16.8100 g., 0.9250 Silver .5000 oz. ASW **Ruler:** Olav V **Subject:** 1994 Olympics **Obv:** Head left **Rev:** Child skiing **Designer:** Oivind Hansen

Date	Mintage	VG	F	VF	XF	BU
1991	120,000	—	—	—	—	37.50

KM# 438 50 KRONER
16.8100 g., 0.9250 Silver .5000 oz. ASW **Ruler:** Harald V **Subject:** 1994 Olympics **Obv:** Head right **Rev:** Grandfather and child within circle **Designer:** Ingrid Austlid Rise

Date	Mintage	VG	F	VF	XF	BU
1992	74,000	—	—	—	—	37.50

KM# 439 50 KRONER
16.8100 g., 0.9250 Silver .5000 oz. ASW **Ruler:** Harald V **Subject:** 1994 Olympics **Obv:** Head right **Rev:** 2 children on sled **Designer:** Ingrid Austlid Rise

Date	Mintage	VG	F	VF	XF	BU
1992	88,000	—	—	—	—	37.50

KM# 447 50 KRONER
16.8100 g., 0.9250 Silver .5000 oz. ASW **Ruler:** Harald V **Subject:** 1994 Olympics **Obv:** Head right **Rev:** Cross-country skiers **Designer:** Ingrid Austlid Rise

Date	Mintage	VG	F	VF	XF	BU
1993	65,000	—	—	—	—	37.50

KM# 448 50 KRONER
16.8100 g., 0.9250 Silver .5000 oz. ASW **Ruler:** Harald V **Subject:** 1994 Olympics **Obv:** Head right **Rev:** Children ice skating within circle **Designer:** Ingrid Austlid Rise

Date	Mintage	VG	F	VF	XF	BU
1993	77,000	—	—	—	—	37.50

KM# 454 50 KRONER
16.8100 g., 0.9250 Silver .5000 oz. ASW **Ruler:** Harald V **Subject:** 50th Anniversary - United Nations **Obv:** Head right **Rev:** Standing figure facing, children holding hands under tree **Designer:** Ingrid Austlid Rise

Date	Mintage	VG	F	VF	XF	BU
ND(1995) Proof	200,000	Value: 42.50				

KM# 455 50 KRONER
16.8100 g., 0.9250 Silver .5000 oz. ASW **Ruler:** Harald V **Subject:** 50th Anniversary - End of World War II **Obv:** Arms **Rev:** Stylized dove above dates **Designer:** Ingrid Austlid Rise

Date	Mintage	VG	F	VF	XF	BU
ND(1995) Proof	50,000	Value: 45.00				

KM# 426 100 KRONER
24.7300 g., 0.9250 Silver .7355 oz. ASW **Ruler:** Olav V **Subject:** 25th Anniversary of King Olav's Reign **Obv:** Head left **Rev:** Tilted shield under artistic designed shield

Date	Mintage	VG	F	VF	XF	BU
1982	800,000	—	—	—	—	25.00

KM# 433 100 KRONER
33.6200 g., 0.9250 Silver 1 oz. ASW **Ruler:** Olav V **Subject:** 1994 Olympics **Obv:** Head left **Rev:** Cross-country skier within circle

Date	Mintage	VG	F	VF	XF	BU
1991	88,000	—	—	—	—	60.00

KM# 434 100 KRONER
33.6200 g., 0.9250 Silver 1 oz. ASW **Ruler:** Olav V **Subject:** 1994 Olympics **Obv:** Head left **Rev:** 2 speed skaters

Date	Mintage	VG	F	VF	XF	BU
1991	116,000	—	—	—	—	60.00

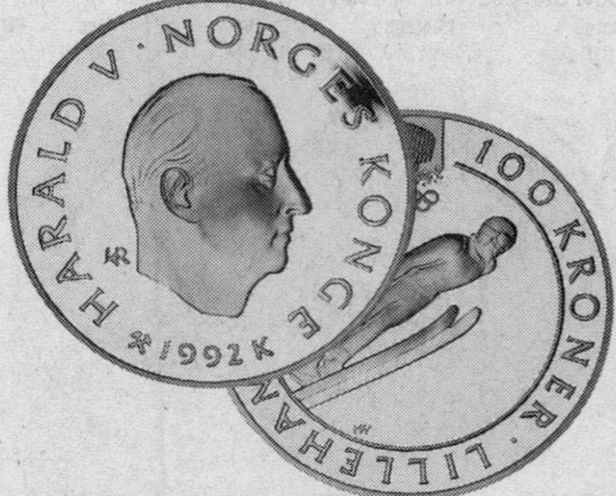

KM# 440 100 KRONER
33.6200 g., 0.9250 Silver 1 oz. ASW **Ruler:** Harald V **Subject:** 1994 Olympics **Obv:** Head right **Rev:** Ski jumper within circle **Designer:** Ingrid Austlid Rise

Date	Mintage	VG	F	VF	XF	BU
1992	85,000	—	—	—	—	60.00

KM# 441 100 KRONER
33.6200 g., 0.9250 Silver 1 oz. ASW **Ruler:** Harald V **Subject:** 1994 Olympics **Obv:** Head right **Rev:** Hockey players **Designer:** Ingrid Austlid Rise

Date	Mintage	VG	F	VF	XF	BU
1992	81,000	—	—	—	—	60.00

KM# 443 100 KRONER
33.6200 g., 0.9250 Silver 1 oz. ASW **Ruler:** Harald V
Subject: World Cycling Championships **Obv:** Arms **Rev:** Cyclist

Date	Mintage	VG	F	VF	XF	BU
1993	9,288	—	—	—	—	70.00

KM# 444 100 KRONER
33.6200 g., 0.9250 Silver 1 oz. ASW **Ruler:** Harald V **Subject:** World Cycling Championships **Obv:** Arms **Rev:** 7 cyclists

Date	Mintage	VG	F	VF	XF	BU
1993	9,288	—	—	—	—	70.00

KM# 449 100 KRONER
33.6200 g., 0.9250 Silver 1 oz. ASW **Ruler:** Harald V **Subject:** 1984 Olympics **Obv:** Head right **Rev:** Female figure skater within circle **Designer:** Ingrid Austlid Rise

Date	Mintage	VG	F	VF	XF	BU
1993	96,000	—	—	—	—	60.00

KM# 450 100 KRONER
33.6200 g., 0.9250 Silver 1 oz. ASW **Ruler:** Harald V
Subject: 1984 Olympics **Obv:** Head right **Rev:** Alpine skier
Designer: Ingrid Austlid Rise

Date	Mintage	VG	F	VF	XF	BU
1993	85,000	—	—	—	—	60.00

KM# 466 100 KRONER
33.8000 g., 0.9250 Silver 1.0052 oz. ASW **Ruler:** Harald V
Subject: Year 2000 **Obv:** National arms **Rev:** Cut tree trunk exposing rings

Date	Mintage	F	VF	XF	Unc	BU
1999 Proof	50,000	Value: 70.00				

KM# 429 175 KRONER
26.5000 g., 0.9250 Silver .7882 oz. ASW **Ruler:** Olav V
Subject: 175th Anniversary of Constitution **Obv:** Crowned arms within order chain **Rev:** Building

Date	Mintage	VG	F	VF	XF	BU
ND(1989)	85,000	—	—	—	—	75.00
ND(1989) Proof	15,000	Value: 225				

KM# 425 200 KRONER
26.8000 g., 0.6250 Silver .5385 oz. ASW **Ruler:** Olav V **Subject:** 35th Anniversary of Liberation **Obv:** Arms **Rev:** Akershus Castle

Date	Mintage	VG	F	VF	XF	BU
1980	298,399	—	—	—	—	45.00

KM# 435 1500 KRONER
17.0000 g., 0.9170 Gold .5 oz. AGW **Ruler:** Olav V **Subject:** 1994 Olympics **Obv:** Head left **Rev:** Ancient Norwegian skier

Date	Mintage	VG	F	VF	XF	BU
1991 Proof	30,000	Value: 375				

KM# 442 1500 KRONER
17.0000 g., 0.9170 Gold .5 oz. AGW **Ruler:** Harald V
Subject: 1994 Olympics **Obv:** Head right **Rev:** Birkebeiners
Designer: Ingrid Austlid Rise

Date	Mintage	VG	F	VF	XF	BU
1992 Proof	30,000	Value: 375				

KM# 445 1500 KRONER
17.0000 g., 0.9170 Gold .5 oz. AGW **Ruler:** Harald V
Subject: World Cycling Championships **Obv:** Arms **Rev:** Two 19th century cyclists

Date	Mintage	VG	F	VF	XF	BU
1993 Proof	6,390	Value: 500				

KM# 446 1500 KRONER
17.0000 g., 0.9170 Gold .5 oz. AGW **Ruler:** Harald V **Subject:** Edvard Grieg **Obv:** Crowned shield **Rev:** Figure playing piano

Date	Mintage	VG	F	VF	XF	BU
1993 Proof	5,139	Value: 550				

KM# 451 1500 KRONER
17.0000 g., 0.9170 Gold .5 oz. AGW **Ruler:** Harald V
Subject: 1994 Olympics **Obv:** Head right **Rev:** Telemark skier
Designer: Ingrid Austlid Rise

Date	Mintage	VG	F	VF	XF	BU
1993 Proof	30,000	Value: 385				

KM# 452 1500 KRONER
17.0000 g., 0.9170 Gold .5 oz. AGW **Ruler:** Harald V
Subject: Roald Amundsen **Obv:** Head right **Rev:** Bust left with skis on shoulder **Designer:** Ingrid Austlid Rise

Date	Mintage	VG	F	VF	XF	BU
1993 Proof	22,000	Value: 450				

KM# 467 1500 KRONER
16.9600 g., 0.9170 Gold .4994 oz. AGW **Ruler:** Olav V
Subject: Year 2000 **Obv:** Head right **Rev:** Tree and roots

Date	Mintage	VG	F	VF	XF	BU
2000 Proof	7,500	Value: 425				

PATTERNS

Including off metal strikes

KM#	Date	Mintage	Identification	Mkt Val
Pn40	1958	6	Ore.	—

MINT SETS

KM#	Date	Mintage	Identification	Issue Price	Mkt Val
MS1	1960 (7)	200	KM403, 405, 407-411	—	—
MS2	1961 (7)	475	KM403, 405, 407-411	—	—
MS3	1962 (7)	570	KM403, 405, 407-411	—	—
MS4	1963 (8)	430	KM403, 405, 407-412	—	—
MS6	1964 (8)	1,200	KM403, 405, 407-412	—	—
MS7	1965 (8)	1,800	KM403, 405, 407-412. Plastic.	—	400
MS8	1966 (8)	1,400	KM403, 405, 407-412. Plastic.	—	300
MS9	1967 (8)	2,490	KM403, 405, 407-412. Soft plastic.	—	250
MS11	1968 (8)	1,167	KM403, 405, 407-412. Soft plastic.	—	1,050
MS12	1968 (8)	2,300	KM403, 405, 407-412. Sandhill.	—	1,100
MS13	1969 (8)	3,140	KM403, 405, 407-412	—	55.00
MS14	1969 (8)	7,450	KM403, 405, 407-412. Sandhill.	—	125
MS15	1970 (8)	2,005	KM403, 405, 407-412. Soft plastic.	—	100
MS16	1970 (8)	7,311	KM403, 405, 407-412. Sandhill.	—	225
MS17	1971 (8)	2,010	KM403, 405, 407-412. Soft plastic.	—	100
MS18	1971 (8)	4,055	KM403, 405, 407-412. Sandhill.	—	250
MS19	1972 (8)	6,549	KM403, 405, 407-412. Soft plastic.	—	30.00
MS20	1972 (8)	6,435	KM403, 405, 407-412. Sandhill.	—	125
MS21	1973 (7)	7,085	KM405, 407-409, 411-412, 415. Soft plastic.	—	30.00
MS22	1973 (7)	13,090	KM405, 407-409, 411-412, 415. Sandhill.	6.00	100
MS23	1974 (6)	10,275	KM415-420. Soft plastic.	3.00	30.00
MS24	1974 (6)	29,695	KM415-420. Sandhill.	—	45.00
MS25	1975 (8)	30,207	KM415-422. Sandhill.	5.00	75.00
MS26	1975 (7)	5,287	KM415-421. Soft plastic.	5.00	25.00
MS27	1976 (6)	5,000	KM415-420. Soft plastic.	3.00	23.00
MS28	1976 (6)	25,000	KM415-420. Sandhill.	3.00	60.00
MS29	1977 (6)	5,000	KM415-420. Soft plastic.	3.40	25.00
MS30	1977 (6)	25,000	KM415-420. Sandhill.	3.40	60.00
MS31	1978 (6)	5,000	KM415-420. Soft plastic.	3.40	25.00
MS32	1978 (6)	30,000	KM415-420. Sandhill.	3.40	60.00
MS33	1979 (6)	8,000	KM415-420. Soft plastic.	3.40	9.00
MS34	1979 (6)	50,000	KM415-420. Sandhill.	3.40	27.00
MS35	1980 (6)	10,000	KM415-420. Soft plastic.	3.40	20.00
MS36	1980 (6)	70,000	KM415-420. Sandhill.	3.40	35.00
MS37	1981 (6)	100,000	KM415-420. Hard plastic.	4.25	19.00
MS38	1982 (6)	102,650	KM415-420	4.50	26.00
MS39	1983 (4)	102,300	KM416, 418-420	5.00	17.00
MS40	1984 (5)	101,000	KM416, 418-420, 427	5.00	21.00
MS41	1985 (5)	110,000	KM416, 418-420, 427	5.00	21.00
MS42	1986 (5)	100,000	KM416, 418-419, 427-428	7.00	30.00
MS43	1987 (5)	85,000	KM416, 418-420, 427	7.00	30.00
MS44	1988 (4)	102,000	KM416, 418, 420, 427	7.00	22.00
MS45	1989 (4)	101,000	KM416, 418-419, 427	8.00	23.00
MS46	1990 (4)	103,000	KM416, 418-419, 427, plus mint medal	8.00	23.00
MS47	1991/1992 (5)	100,000	KM416, 418, 427, 436-437	—	11.00
MS48	1991/1993 (5)	100,000	KM416, 418, 427, 436-437	—	20.00
MS49	1994 (5)	100,000	KM418, 427, 436-437, 453	—	18.00
MS50	1995 (5)	100,000	KM418, 436, 453, 456, 457	—	20.00
MS51	1996 (5)	90,000	KM418, 436, 453, 457, 459	—	25.00
MS52	1997 (5)	90,000	KM453, 457, 460, 461, 462	—	25.00
MS53	1998 (5)	90,000	KM453, 457, 460, 462, 463	—	25.00
MS54	1999 (5)	—	KM453, 457, 460, 462, 463	—	50.00
MS55	1999 (5)	50,000	KM457, 460 462-464. Souvenir folder.	13.00	15.00
MS56	1999 (5)	35,000	KM457, 460, 462-464. Baby coin set.	14.30	30.00
MS57	1999 (5)	—	KM457, 460, 462-464 plus medal.	26.00	26.00
MS58	2000 (5)	—	KM453, 457, 460, 462, 463. Hard case.	—	45.00

PROOF SETS

KM#	Date	Mintage	Identification	Issue Price	Mkt Val
PS1	1992 (3)	20,000	KM418, 436-437	—	45.00
PS2	1993 (3)	12,000	KM443-445	—	50.00
PS3	1994 (4)	15,000	KM418, 436-437, 453	—	60.00
PS4	1995 (5)	14,459	KM418, 436, 453, 456, 457	—	80.00
PS5	1996 (5)	11,551	KM418, 436, 453, 457, 459	—	80.00
PS6	1997 (5)	15,000	KM453, 457, 460, 461, 462. Norwegian Heritage Set.	—	65.00
PS7	1997 (5)	12,000	KM453, 457, 460, 461, 462	—	70.00
PS8	1998 (5)	14,097	KM453, 457, 460, 462, 463. Norwegian Heritage Set.	—	65.00
PS9	1998 (5)	12,000	KM453, 457, 460, 462, 463	—	70.00
PS10	1999 (5)	15,000	KM453, 457, 460, 462, 463	60.00	80.00
PS11	1999 (5)	2,500	KM457, 460, 462-463, 465. Heritage Set.	—	150
PS12	2000 (5)	10,000	KM453, 457, 460, 462, 463	—	65.00

OMAN

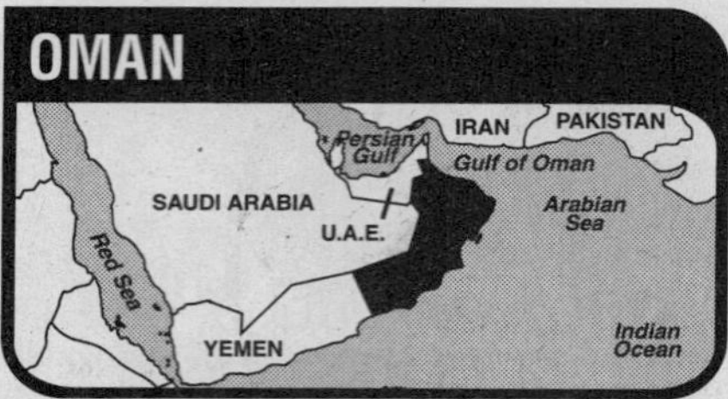

The Sultanate of Oman (formerly Muscat and Oman), an independent monarchy located in the southeastern part of the Arabian Peninsula, has an area of 82,030 sq. mi. (212,460 sq. km.) and a population of *1.3 million. Capital: Muscat. The economy is based on agriculture, herding and petroleum. Petroleum products, dates, fish and hides are exported.

The Portuguese who captured Muscat, the capital and chief port, in 1508, made the first European contact with Muscat and Oman. They occupied the city, utilizing it as a naval base and factory and holding it against land and sea attacks by Arabs and Persians until finally ejected by local Arabs in 1650. It was next occupied by the Persians who maintained control until 1741,when it was taken by Ahmed ibn Sa'id of the present ruling family. Muscat and Oman was the most powerful state in Arabia during the first half of the 19th century, until weakened by the persistent attack of interior nomadic tribes. British influence, initiated by the signing of a treaty of friendship with the Sultanate in 1798,remains a dominant fact of the civil and military phases of the government, although Britain recognizes the Sultanate as a sovereign state.

Sultan Sa'id bin Taimur was overthrown by his son, Qabus bin Sa'id, on July 23, 1970. The new sultan changed the nation's name to Sultanate of Oman.

TITLES

مسقط

Muscat

عمان

Oman

SULTANATE

DECIMAL COINAGE

1000 (new) Baisa = 1 Saidi Rial

KM# 42 1/2 SAIDI RIAL

25.6000 g., 0.9170 Gold .7548 oz. AGW **Obv:** National arms within circle **Rev:** Value and date

Date	Mintage	F	VF	XF	Unc	BU
AH1391 (1971) Proof	100	Value: 700				

Note: Struck for presentation purposes

KM# 44 SAIDI RIAL

46.6500 g., 0.9170 Gold 1.3755 oz. AGW **Obv:** National arms within circle with star and moon border **Rev:** Value and date

Date	Mintage	F	VF	XF	Unc	BU
AH1391 (1971) Proof	100	Value: 1,000				

Date	Mintage	F	VF	XF	Unc	BU
AH1394 (1974) Proof	250	Value: 1,000				

Note: Struck for presentation purposes

KM# 43 15 SAIDI RIALS

5.8100 g., 0.9170 Gold .1713 oz. AGW **Obv:** National arms **Rev:** Value

Date	Mintage	F	VF	XF	Unc	BU
AH1391 (1971) Proof	112	Value: 650				

Note: Struck for presentation purposes

KM# 53 15 SAIDI RIALS

7.9800 g., 0.9170 Gold .2353 oz. AGW **Obv:** National arms **Rev:** Value and date

Date	Mintage	F	VF	XF	Unc	BU
AH1391 (1971) Proof	224	Value: 550				

Note: Struck for presentation purposes

REFORM COINAGE

1000 Baisa = 1 Omani Rial

KM# 50 5 BAISA

3.1000 g., Bronze, 19 mm. **Obv:** National arms **Rev:** Value and date

Date	Mintage	F	VF	XF	Unc	BU
AH1395 (1975)	6,000,000	—	0.10	0.20	0.45	—
AH1400 (1979)	3,000,000	—	0.10	0.20	0.45	—
AH1406 (1985)	2,000,000	—	0.10	0.20	0.45	—
AH1410 (1989)	5,000,000	—	0.10	0.20	0.45	—

KM# 76 5 BAISA

Bronze **Subject:** 20th National Day - Sultan Qaboos **Obv:** National emblem **Rev:** Sports Complex

Date	Mintage	F	VF	XF	Unc	BU
AH1411 (1990) Proof	3,200	Value: 5.00				

KM# 150 5 BAISA

Bronze Clad Steel

Date	Mintage	F	VF	XF	Unc	BU
AH1420-1999	—	—	—	0.25	0.50	0.75

KM# 51 10 BAISA

4.7000 g., Bronze, 22.5 mm. **Series:** F.A.O. **Obv:** Date palms **Rev:** Value and date

Date	Mintage	F	VF	XF	Unc	BU
AH1395 (1975)	1,000,000	—	0.15	0.30	0.65	—

KM# 52.1 10 BAISA

4.7000 g., Bronze, 22.5 mm. **Series:** F.A.O. **Obv:** National arms **Rev:** Value and date

Date	Mintage	F	VF	XF	Unc	BU
AH1395 (1975)	6,000,000	—	0.15	0.30	0.65	—
AH1400 (1979)	5,250,000	—	0.15	0.30	0.65	—
AH1406 (1985)	3,000,000	—	0.15	0.30	0.65	—
AH1410 (1989)	6,000,000	—	0.15	0.30	0.65	—
AH1418 (1997)	—	—	0.15	0.30	0.65	—

KM# 77 10 BAISA

Bronze Clad Steel **Subject:** 20th National Day - Central Bank of Oman **Obv:** National emblem **Rev:** Central Bank building

Date	Mintage	F	VF	XF	Unc	BU
AH1411 (1990) Proof	3,200	Value: 5.00				

KM# 52.2 10 BAISA

Bronze Clad Steel, 22.5 mm. **Obv:** National arms **Rev:** Value and both AH and AD dates

Date	Mintage	F	VF	XF	Unc	BU
AH1420-1993	—	—	0.15	0.30	0.65	—
AH1425-1999	—	—	0.15	0.30	0.65	—

KM# 94 10 BAISA

Bronze Clad Steel, 22.5 mm. **Series:** F.A.O. **Subject:** 50 Years **Obv:** National arms **Rev:** FAO symbol and dates

Date	Mintage	F	VF	XF	Unc	BU
ND	—	—	—	—	1.25	—
ND(1995)	224	—	—	—	1.25	—

KM# 151 10 BAISA

Bronze Clad Steel, 22.5 mm.

Date	Mintage	F	VF	XF	Unc	BU
AH1420-1999	—	—	—	0.35	0.75	1.00

KM# 75 15 BAISA

20.0000 g., 0.9250 Silver .5949 oz. ASW **Subject:** 15th Anniversary - Reign of Sultan **Obv:** Head 1/4 left within 3/4 wreath and circular design **Rev:** Crowned Arms over country map within circle

Date	Mintage	F	VF	XF	Unc	BU
AH1406 (1985) Proof	2,000	Value: 160				

KM# 45 25 BAISA

5.9600 g., 0.9170 Gold .1757 oz. AGW, 18 mm. **Obv:** National arms **Rev:** Value and date

Date	Mintage	F	VF	XF	Unc	BU
AH1392 (1972)	100	—	—	—	150	—
AH1392 (1972) Proof	50	Value: 200				
AH1394 (1974) Proof	250	Value: 150				
AH1395 (1975) Proof	250	Value: 150				

Note: Struck for presentation purposes

KM# 45a 25 BAISA

2.9000 g., Copper-Nickel, 18 mm. **Obv:** National arms **Rev:** Value and date

Date	Mintage	F	VF	XF	Unc	BU
AH1395 (1975)	4,500,000	—	0.20	0.40	0.85	—
AH1400	5,250,000	—	0.20	0.40	0.85	—
AH1406 (1985)	4,000,000	—	0.20	0.40	0.85	—
AH1410 (1989)	7,000,000	—	0.20	0.40	0.85	—
AH1418 (1997)	—	—	0.20	0.40	0.85	—

KM# 78 25 BAISA

Copper-Nickel **Subject:** 20th National Day - Royal Hospital **Obv:** National emblem **Rev:** Royal Hospital building

Date	Mintage	F	VF	XF	Unc	BU
AH1411 (1990) Proof	3,200	Value: 7.00				

KM# 152 25 BAISA

2.9000 g., Copper-Nickel, 18 mm.

Date	Mintage	F	VF	XF	Unc	BU
AH1420-1999	—	—	—	0.50	1.00	1.25

KM# 46 50 BAISA

12.8900 g., 0.9170 Gold .3801 oz. AGW **Obv:** National arms **Rev:** Value and date

Date	Mintage	F	VF	XF	Unc	BU
AH1392 (1972)	200	—	—	—	285	—
AH1392 (1972) Proof	50	Value: 325				
AH1394 (1974) Proof	250	Value: 285				
AH1395 (1975) Proof	250	Value: 285				

Note: Struck for presentation purposes

KM# 46a 50 BAISA

6.4000 g., Copper-Nickel, 24 mm. **Obv:** National arms **Rev:** Value and date

Date	Mintage	F	VF	XF	Unc	BU
AH1395 (1975)	2,500,000	—	0.30	0.60	1.50	—
AH1400 (1979)	2,750,000	—	0.30	0.60	1.50	—
AH1406 (1985)	4,000,000	—	0.30	0.60	1.50	—
AH1410 (1989)	4,000,000	—	0.30	0.60	1.50	—
AH1418 (1997)	—	—	0.30	0.60	1.50	—

KM# 79 50 BAISA

Copper-Nickel **Subject:** 20th National Day - Irrigation Canal **Obv:** National emblem **Rev:** Canal and palm trees

Date	Mintage	F	VF	XF	Unc	BU
AH1411 (1990) Proof	3,200	Value: 8.00				

KM# 95 50 BAISA

6.4000 g., Copper-Nickel, 24 mm. **Subject:** U.N. - 50 Years **Obv:** National arms **Rev:** UN symbol and anniversary dates

Date	Mintage	F	VF	XF	Unc	BU
ND (1995)	—	—	—	—	3.00	—

KM# 153 50 BAISA

6.4000 g., Copper-Nickel, 24 mm.

Date	Mintage	F	VF	XF	Unc	BU
AH1420-1999	—	—	—	0.75	1.75	2.00

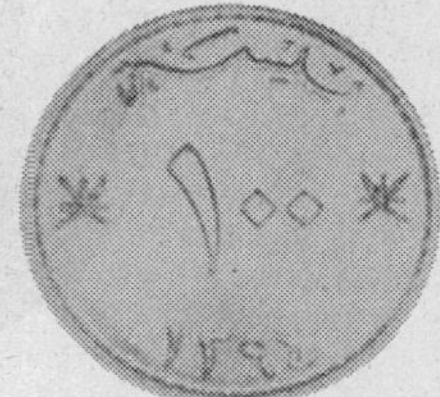

KM# 47 100 BAISA

22.7400 g., 0.9170 Gold .6705 oz. AGW **Obv:** National arms **Rev:** Value and date

Date	Mintage	F	VF	XF	Unc	BU
AH1392 (1972)	200	—	—	—	500	—
AH1392 (1972) Proof	50	Value: 550				
AH1394 (1974) Proof	250	Value: 500				
AH1395 (1975) Proof	250	Value: 500				

Note: Struck for presentation purposes

KM# 68 100 BAISA

4.2000 g., Copper-Nickel, 21.5 mm. **Obv:** National arms **Rev:** Arms and date

Date	Mintage	VG	F	VF	XF	Unc
AH1404-1983	4,000,000	—	—	0.40	0.80	2.25

KM# 80 100 BAISA

Copper-Nickel **Subject:** 20th National Day - Sultan Qaboos University **Obv:** National emblem **Rev:** University building

Date	Mintage	F	VF	XF	Unc	BU
AH1411 (1990) Proof	3,200	Value: 10.00				

KM# 82 100 BAISA

Bi-Metallic Aluminumn-Bronze center in Copper-Nickel ring, 25 mm. **Subject:** 100 Years of Coinage **Obv:** Arms within circle **Rev:** Fortress within circle

Date	Mintage	F	VF	XF	Unc	BU
AH1411-1991	—	—	—	—	5.00	7.00
AH1411-1991 Proof	1,000	Value: 20.00				

KM# 57 1/4 OMANI RIAL

12.8900 g., 0.9170 Gold .3799 oz. AGW **Subject:** Fort al Hazam **Obv:** National arms **Rev:** Fort

Date	Mintage	F	VF	XF	Unc	BU
AH1397 (1976) Proof	1,000	Value: 285				
AH1408 (1987) Proof	250	Value: 425				

KM# 66 1/4 OMANI RIAL

6.5000 g., Aluminum-Bronze, 26 mm. **Obv:** National arms and dates **Rev:** Value

Date	Mintage	VG	F	VF	XF	Unc
AH1400-1980	4,000,000	—	—	0.75	1.00	2.00

KM# 48 1/2 OMANI RIAL

25.6000 g., 0.9170 Gold .7548 oz. AGW **Obv:** National arms **Rev:** Value and date

Date	Mintage	F	VF	XF	Unc	BU
AH1392 (1972) Proof	124	Value: 675				
AH1394 (1974)	250	—	—	—	675	—
AH1395 (1975)	250	—	—	—	675	—

Note: Struck for presentation purposes

KM# 58 1/2 OMANI RIAL
19.6700 g., 0.9170 Gold .5797 oz. AGW **Subject:** Fort Mirbat **Obv:** National arms **Rev:** Fort

Date	Mintage	F	VF	XF	Unc	BU
AH1397 (1976) Proof	1,000	Value: 425				
AH1408 (1987) Proof	250	Value: 550				

KM# 64 1/2 OMANI RIAL
Copper-Nickel **Series:** F.A.O. **Obv:** National arms flanked by dates **Rev:** Fruit above value **Shape:** 7-sided

Date	Mintage	VG	F	VF	XF	Unc
AH1398-1978	15,000	—	—	2.75	3.50	5.00

KM# 69 1/2 OMANI RIAL
19.6700 g., 0.9170 Gold .5800 oz. AGW **Subject:** 10th National Day **Obv:** Crowned arms **Rev:** Value

Date	Mintage	VG	F	VF	XF	Unc
AH1400-1979 Proof	600	Value: 485				

Note: Struck for presentation purposes

KM# 67 1/2 OMANI RIAL
10.0000 g., Aluminum-Bronze, 30 mm. **Obv:** National arms and dates **Rev:** Value

Date	Mintage	VG	F	VF	XF	Unc
AH1400-1980	2,000,000	—	—	2.75	3.50	5.00

KM# 87 1/2 OMANI RIAL
10.0000 g., 0.9170 Gold .2947 oz. AGW **Subject:** Youth Year **Obv:** National arms, date and value **Rev:** Youth with banner within sprigs

Date	Mintage	VG	F	VF	XF	Unc
AH1403-1982 Proof	1,000	Value: 285				

KM# 85 1/2 OMANI RIAL
28.2800 g., 0.9250 Silver .8411 oz. ASW **Subject:** Year of Agriculture **Obv:** National arms within circle **Rev:** Dates within small circle, farm fields on top 1/2

Date	Mintage	VG	F	VF	XF	Unc
AH1409-1988 Proof	300	Value: 135				

KM# 86 1/2 OMANI RIAL
28.2800 g., 0.9250 Silver .8411 oz. ASW **Subject:** Year of Industry **Obv:** National arms **Rev:** Gears with map at center

Date	Mintage	F	VF	XF	Unc	BU
AH1411 (1990) Proof	810	Value: 110				

KM# 91 1/2 OMANI RIAL
15.0000 g., 0.9250 Silver .4461 oz. ASW **Subject:** Youth Year **Obv:** National arms within circle flanked by stars **Rev:** Radiant design

Date	Mintage	F	VF	XF	Unc	BU
AH1413 (1992) Proof	600	Value: 85.00				

KM# 134 1/2 OMANI RIAL
15.0000 g., 0.9250 Silver .4461 oz. ASW **Subject:** Youth Year **Obv:** Crowned arms **Rev:** Radiant design

Date	Mintage	F	VF	XF	Unc	BU
AH1413 (1992) Proof; Rare	310	—	—	—	—	—

KM# 92 1/2 OMANI RIAL
28.2800 g., 0.9250 Silver .8411 oz. ASW **Subject:** Heritage Year **Obv:** National arms within circle **Rev:** Radiant design

Date	Mintage	F	VF	XF	Unc	BU
AH1414 (1993) Proof	840	Value: 100				

KM# 111 1/2 OMANI RIAL
28.2800 g., 0.9250 Silver .8411 oz. ASW **Subject:** 250th Anniversary - Al Bu Sa'id Dynasty **Obv:** Bust facing flanked by dates **Rev:** National arms within artistic designed border

Date	Mintage	VG	F	VF	XF	Unc
1994 (AH1414) Proof	500	Value: 110				

KM# 54 OMANI RIAL
46.6500 g., 0.9170 Gold 1.3755 oz. AGW **Obv:** National arms **Rev:** Value and date **Note:** Similar to KM#44.

Date	Mintage	F	VF	XF	Unc	BU
AH1392 (1972) Proof	124	Value: 1,000				
AH1394 (1974) Proof	250	Value: 1,000				
AH1395 (1975) Proof	250	Value: 1,000				

Note: Struck for presentation purposes

KM# 59 OMANI RIAL
25.6000 g., 0.9170 Gold .7545 oz. AGW **Subject:** Fort Buraimi **Obv:** National arms and value **Rev:** Fort

Date	Mintage	F	VF	XF	Unc	BU
AH1397 (1976) Proof	1,000	Value: 550				
AH1408 (1987) Proof	250	Value: 675				

KM# 65 OMANI RIAL
15.0000 g., 0.5000 Silver .2412 oz. ASW **Series:** F.A.O. **Obv:** National arms flanked by dates **Rev:** Fish above value

Date	Mintage	VG	F	VF	XF	Unc
AH1398-1978	15,000	—	—	—	8.50	13.50

KM# 70 OMANI RIAL
25.6000 g., 0.9170 Gold .7548 oz. AGW **Subject:** 10th National Day

Date	Mintage	F	VF	XF	Unc	BU
AH1400 (1979) Proof	300	Value: 650				

Note: Struck for presentation purposes

KM# 84 OMANI RIAL
14.8400 g., 0.9250 Silver .4413 oz. ASW **Subject:** Youth Year **Obv:** National arms above value **Rev:** Youth with banner

Date	Mintage	VG	F	VF	XF	Unc
AH1403-1982 Proof	1,200	Value: 75.00				

KM# 84a OMANI RIAL
20.0000 g., 0.9170 Gold .5894 oz. AGW, 30 mm. **Subject:** Youth Year **Obv:** National arms above value **Rev:** Youth with banner

Date	Mintage	F	VF	XF	Unc	BU
AH1403 (1982) Proof	900	Value: 435				

KM# 135 OMANI RIAL
20.0000 g., 0.9170 Gold .5894 oz. AGW **Subject:** Youth Year **Obv:** Crowned arms **Rev:** Radiant design **Note:** Similar to 1/2 Omani Rial, KM#91.

Date	Mintage	F	VF	XF	Unc	BU
AH1413 (1992) Proof; Rare	110	—	—	—	—	—

KM# 112 OMANI RIAL
20.0000 g., 0.9170 Gold .5894 oz. AGW **Subject:** Youth Year **Obv:** National arms **Rev:** Radiant design **Note:** Similar to 1/2 Omani Rial, KM#91.

Date	Mintage	F	VF	XF	Unc	BU
AH1413 (1992) Proof	900	Value: 450				

KM# 93 OMANI RIAL
39.9400 g., 0.9167 Gold 1.1771 oz. AGW **Subject:** Heritage Year **Obv:** National arms **Rev:** Radiant design **Note:** Similar to 1/2 Omani Rial, KM#92.

Date	Mintage	F	VF	XF	Unc	BU
AH1414 (1993) Proof	1,000	Value: 900				

KM# 146 OMANI RIAL
39.9400 g., 0.9167 Gold 1.1771 oz. AGW **Subject:** 250th Anniversary - Al Bu Sa'id Dynasty **Obv:** Portrait **Rev:** National arms and value **Note:** Similar to 1/2 Omani Rial, KM#111.

Date	Mintage	F	VF	XF	Unc	BU
AH1414 (1994) Proof	500	Value: 975				

KM# 96 OMANI RIAL
10.0000 g., 0.9250 Silver .2974 oz. ASW, 30 mm. **Subject:** F.A.O. - 50 Years **Obv:** National arms within circle **Rev:** FAO symbol and anniversary dates

Date	Mintage	F	VF	XF	Unc	BU
ND (1995) Proof	—	Value: 30.00				

KM# 114 OMANI RIAL
28.2800 g., 0.9250 Silver .8410 oz. ASW **Obv:** National arms within circle **Rev:** Al-Hazm castle

Date	Mintage	VG	F	VF	XF	Unc
AH1416-1995 Proof	—	Value: 37.50				

KM# 115 OMANI RIAL
28.2800 g., 0.9250 Silver .8410 oz. ASW **Obv:** National arms **Rev:** Al-Jalali fort

Date	Mintage	VG	F	VF	XF	Unc
AH1416-1995 Proof	—	Value: 37.50				

KM# 116 OMANI RIAL
28.2800 g., 0.9250 Silver .8410 oz. ASW **Obv:** National arms **Rev:** Al-Mirani fort

Date	Mintage	VG	F	VF	XF	Unc
AH1416-1995 Proof	—	Value: 37.50				

KM# 117 OMANI RIAL
28.2800 g., 0.9250 Silver .8410 oz. ASW **Obv:** National arms **Rev:** Al-Rustaq fort

Date	Mintage	VG	F	VF	XF	Unc
AH1416-1995 Proof	—	Value: 37.50				

KM# 118 OMANI RIAL
28.2800 g., 0.9250 Silver .8410 oz. ASW **Obv:** National arms **Rev:** Al-Wafi castle

Date	Mintage	VG	F	VF	XF	Unc
AH1416-1995 Proof	—	Value: 37.50				

KM# 119 OMANI RIAL
28.2800 g., 0.9250 Silver .8410 oz. ASW **Obv:** National arms **Rev:** Bait Al-Falaj fort

Date	Mintage	VG	F	VF	XF	Unc
AH1416-1995 Proof	—	Value: 37.50				

KM# 120 OMANI RIAL
28.2800 g., 0.9250 Silver .8410 oz. ASW **Obv:** National arms **Rev:** Bait Al-Na'Aman castle

Date	Mintage	VG	F	VF	XF	Unc
AH1416-1995 Proof	—	Value: 37.50				

KM# 121 OMANI RIAL
28.2800 g., 0.9250 Silver .8410 oz. ASW **Obv:** National arms **Rev:** Bahla fort

Date	Mintage	VG	F	VF	XF	Unc
AH1416-1995 Proof	—	Value: 37.50				

KM# 122 OMANI RIAL
28.2800 g., 0.9250 Silver .8410 oz. ASW **Obv:** National arms **Rev:** Barka fort

Date	Mintage	VG	F	VF	XF	Unc
AH1416-1995 Proof	—	Value: 37.50				

KM# 123 OMANI RIAL
28.2800 g., 0.9250 Silver .8410 oz. ASW **Obv:** National arms **Rev:** Barkat-Al-Mauz castle

Date	Mintage	VG	F	VF	XF	Unc
AH1416-1995 Proof	—	Value: 37.50				

KM# 124 OMANI RIAL
28.2800 g., 0.9250 Silver .8410 oz. ASW **Obv:** National arms **Rev:** Buraimi fort

Date	Mintage	VG	F	VF	XF	Unc
AH1416-1995 Proof	—	Value: 37.50				

KM# 125 OMANI RIAL
28.2800 g., 0.9250 Silver .8410 oz. ASW **Obv:** National arms **Rev:** Ja'Alan Bani Bu Hassan castle

Date	Mintage	VG	F	VF	XF	Unc
AH1416-1995 Proof	—	Value: 37.50				

KM# 126 OMANI RIAL
28.2800 g., 0.9250 Silver .8410 oz. ASW **Obv:** National arms **Rev:** Jabrin castle

Date	Mintage	VG	F	VF	XF	Unc
AH1416-1995 Proof	—	Value: 37.50				

KM# 127 OMANI RIAL
28.2800 g., 0.9250 Silver .8410 oz. ASW **Obv:** National arms **Rev:** Khasab fort

Date	Mintage	VG	F	VF	XF	Unc
AH1416-1995 Proof	—	Value: 37.50				

KM# 128 OMANI RIAL
28.2800 g., 0.9250 Silver .8410 oz. ASW **Obv:** National arms **Rev:** Matrah fort

Date	Mintage	VG	F	VF	XF	Unc
AH1416-1995 Proof	—	Value: 37.50				

KM# 129 OMANI RIAL
28.2800 g., 0.9250 Silver .8410 oz. ASW **Obv:** National arms **Rev:** Mirbat castle

Date	Mintage	VG	F	VF	XF	Unc
AH1416-1995 Proof	—	Value: 37.50				

KM# 130 OMANI RIAL
28.2800 g., 0.9250 Silver .8410 oz. ASW **Obv:** National arms **Rev:** Nakhl fort

Date	Mintage	VG	F	VF	XF	Unc
AH1416-1995 Proof	—	Value: 37.50				

KM# 131 OMANI RIAL
28.2800 g., 0.9250 Silver .8410 oz. ASW **Obv:** National arms **Rev:** Nizwa fort

Date	Mintage	VG	F	VF	XF	Unc
AH1416-1995 Proof	—	Value: 37.50				

KM# 132 OMANI RIAL
28.2800 g., 0.9250 Silver .8410 oz. ASW **Obv:** National arms **Rev:** Sohar fort

Date	Mintage	VG	F	VF	XF	Unc
AH1416-1995 Proof	—	Value: 37.50				

KM# 133 OMANI RIAL
28.2800 g., 0.9250 Silver .8410 oz. ASW **Obv:** National arms **Rev:** Sur castle

Date	Mintage	VG	F	VF	XF	Unc
AH1416-1995 Proof	—	Value: 37.50				

KM# 140 OMANI RIAL
13.9000 g., 0.9250 Silver .4134 oz. ASW **Subject:** 25th National Day Anniversary - Burj Al Nahda **Obv:** National arms **Rev:** Burj Al Nahda

Date	Mintage	F	VF	XF	Unc	BU
1995 Proof	—	Value: 65.00				

KM# 140a OMANI RIAL
22.8000 g., 0.9160 Gold .6715 oz. AGW **Subject:** 25th National Day Anniversary - Burj Al Nahda **Obv:** National arms **Rev:** Burj Al Nahda

Date	Mintage	F	VF	XF	Unc	BU
1995 Proof	—	Value: 500				

KM# 145 OMANI RIAL
28.2800 g., 0.9250 Silver .8410 oz. ASW, 30 mm. **Subject:** U.N. - 50 Years **Obv:** National arms **Rev:** UN symbol and anniversary dates

Date	Mintage	F	VF	XF	Unc	BU
ND(1995) Proof	25,000	Value: 40.00				

KM# 101 OMANI RIAL
31.4700 g., 0.9250 Silver .9359 oz. ASW **Subject:** 26th National Day Anniversary - Sultanah **Obv:** National arms

Date	Mintage	F	VF	XF	Unc	BU
1996 Proof	—	Value: 45.00				

KM# 102 OMANI RIAL
37.8000 g., 0.9160 Gold 1.1132 oz. AGW **Subject:** 26th National Day Anniversary - Sultanah **Obv:** National arms **Rev:** Sailing ship - Sultanah within circle

Date	Mintage	F	VF	XF	Unc	BU
1996 Proof	—	Value: 825				

KM# 103 OMANI RIAL

28.2800 g., 0.9250 Silver .8411 oz. ASW **Subject:** 26th National Day Anniversary - Al Battil **Obv:** National arms **Rev:** Sailing ship - Al Battil

Date	Mintage	F	VF	XF	Unc	BU
1996 Proof	—	Value: 35.00				

KM# 104 OMANI RIAL

28.2800 g., 0.9250 Silver .8411 oz. ASW **Subject:** 26th National Day Anniversary - Al Badan **Obv:** National arms **Rev:** Sailing ship - Al Badan within circle

Date	Mintage	F	VF	XF	Unc	BU
1996 Proof	—	Value: 35.00				

KM# 105 OMANI RIAL

28.2800 g., 0.9250 Silver .8411 oz. ASW **Subject:** 26th National Day Anniversary - Al Baghlah **Obv:** National arms **Rev:** Sailing ship - Al Baghlah

Date	Mintage	F	VF	XF	Unc	BU
1996 Proof	—	Value: 35.00				

KM# 106 OMANI RIAL

28.2800 g., 0.9250 Silver .8411 oz. ASW **Subject:** 26th National Day Anniversary - Al Boum **Obv:** National arms **Rev:** Sailing ship - Al Boum within circle

Date	Mintage	F	VF	XF	Unc	BU
1996 Proof	—	Value: 35.00				

KM# 107 OMANI RIAL

28.2800 g., 0.9250 Silver .8411 oz. ASW **Subject:** 26th National Day Anniversary - Al Jalbout **Obv:** National arms **Rev:** Sailing ship - Al Jalbout

Date	Mintage	F	VF	XF	Unc	BU
1996 Proof	—	Value: 35.00				

KM# 108 OMANI RIAL

28.2800 g., 0.9250 Silver .8411 oz. ASW **Subject:** 26th National Day Anniversary - Al Sanbuq **Obv:** National arms **Rev:** Sailing ship - Al Sanbuq

Date	Mintage	F	VF	XF	Unc	BU
1996 Proof	—	Value: 35.00				

KM# 109 OMANI RIAL

28.2800 g., 0.9250 Silver .8411 oz. ASW **Subject:** 26th National Day Anniversary - Al Ghanjah **Obv:** National arms **Rev:** Sailing ship - Al Ghanjah within circle

Date	Mintage	F	VF	XF	Unc	BU
1996 Proof	—	Value: 35.00				

KM# 110 OMANI RIAL

28.2800 g., 0.9250 Silver .8411 oz. ASW **Subject:** 26th National Day Anniversary - Al Lateen **Obv:** National arms **Rev:** Sailing ship - Al Lateen

Date	Mintage	F	VF	XF	Unc	BU
1996 Proof	—	Value: 35.00				

KM# 136 OMANI RIAL

28.2800 g., 0.9250 Silver .8411 oz. ASW, 38.6 mm. **Subject:** 27th National Day Anniversary - Al Nahdha **Rev:** Al Nahdha Tower, coconut tree and Frankincense tree from the Dhofar Region

Date	Mintage	F	VF	XF	Unc	BU
AH1418-1997 Proof	—	Value: 45.00				

KM# 136a OMANI RIAL

37.8000 g., 0.9167 Gold 1.1141 oz. AGW, 38.6 mm. **Subject:** 27th National Day Anniversary - Al Nahdha **Rev:** Al Nahdha Tower, coconut tree and Frankincense tree from the Dhofar Region

Date	Mintage	F	VF	XF	Unc	BU
AH1418-1997 Proof	—	Value: 825				

KM# 138 OMANI RIAL

28.2800 g., 0.9250 Silver .8411 oz. ASW **Series:** World Wildlife Fund **Obv:** National arms and value within circle **Rev:** Leopard

Date	Mintage	F	VF	XF	Unc	BU
1997 Proof	15,000	Value: 37.50				

KM# 113 OMANI RIAL

28.2800 g., 0.9250 Silver .8411 oz. ASW, 38.6 mm. **Series:** World Wildlife Fund **Obv:** National arms **Rev:** Mountain gazelle

Date	Mintage	F	VF	XF	Unc	BU
1997 Proof	15,000	Value: 37.50				

KM# 139 OMANI RIAL

28.2800 g., 0.9250 Silver .8411 oz. ASW, 38.6 mm.
Subject: 28th National Day Anniversary - Private Sector Year
Obv: National arms within circle **Rev:** Radiant design

Date	Mintage	F	VF	XF	Unc	BU
AH1418 (1997) Proof	—	Value: 45.00				

KM# 139a OMANI RIAL

37.8000 g., 0.9167 Gold 1.1141 oz. AGW, 38.6 mm.
Subject: 28th National Day Anniversary - Private Sector Year
Obv: National arms **Rev:** Radiant design

Date	Mintage	F	VF	XF	Unc	BU
AH1418 (1997)	—	—	—	—	825	—

KM# 149 OMANI RIAL

28.2800 g., 0.9250 Silver .8410 oz. ASW, 38.61 mm.
Subject: 29th National Day Anniversary - 1420/1999
Obv: National arms **Rev:** Palm tree (Khalas) and camels caravan

Date	Mintage	F	VF	XF	Unc	BU
ND(1999)	—	—	—	—	100	—

KM# 149a OMANI RIAL

37.8000 g., 0.9167 Gold 1.1141 oz. AGW, 38.61 mm.
Subject: 29th National Day Anniversary - 1420/1999
Obv: National arms **Rev:** Palm tree (Khalas) and camels caravan

Date	Mintage	F	VF	XF	Unc	BU
ND(1999)	—	—	—	—	825	—

KM# 147a OMANI RIAL

37.8000 g., 0.9160 Gold 1.1141 oz. AGW, 38.61 mm. **Subject:** 30th National Day **Obv:** National arms **Rev:** Factory and symbols of commerce, value in center circle **Edge:** Reeded

Date	Mintage	F	VF	XF	Unc	BU
2000	—	—	—	—	825	—

KM# 147 OMANI RIAL

27.8700 g., 0.9250 Silver .8288 oz. ASW, 38.61 mm.
Subject: 30th National Day **Obv:** National arms **Rev:** Factory and symbols of commerce, value in center circle **Edge:** Reeded

Date	Mintage	F	VF	XF	Unc	BU
2000 Proof	300	—	—	—	100	—

KM# 148 OMANI RIAL
27.8700 g., 0.9250 Silver .8288 oz. ASW, 38.6 mm. **Subject:** Central Bank's 25th Anniversary **Obv:** National arms **Rev:** Central Bank of Oman

Date	Mintage	F	VF	XF	Unc	BU
ND(2000) Proof	500	—	—	—	100	—

KM# 81 2 OMANI RIALS
20.0000 g., 0.9250 Silver .5948 oz. ASW **Subject:** 20th National Day - Sultan Sa'id **Obv:** Crowned arms **Rev:** Head 1/4 left within circle

Date	Mintage	VG	F	VF	XF	Unc
AH1411-1990 Proof	3,200	Value: 50.00				

KM# 60 2-1/2 OMANI RIALS
28.2800 g., 0.9250 Silver .8411 oz. ASW **Subject:** Conservation **Obv:** National arms **Rev:** Caracal Lynx

Date	Mintage	F	VF	XF	Unc	BU
AH1397 (1976)	4,539	—	—	—	25.00	—
AH1397 (1976) Proof	4,407	Value: 30.00				

KM# 71 2-1/2 OMANI RIALS
28.2800 g., 0.9250 Silver .8411 oz. ASW **Obv:** Crowned arms **Rev:** Verreaux's eagle in flight

Date	Mintage	VG	F	VF	XF	Unc
AH1407-1986 Proof; Rare	—	—	—	—	—	—

Note: Struck for presentation purposes

KM# 73 2-1/2 OMANI RIALS
28.2800 g., 0.9250 Silver .8411 oz. ASW **Series:** World Wildlife Fund **Obv:** National arms **Rev:** Verreaux's eagle in flight

Date	Mintage	VG	F	VF	XF	Unc
AH1407-1987 Proof	25,000	Value: 30.00				

KM# 83 2-1/2 OMANI RIALS
28.2800 g., 0.9250 Silver .8411 oz. ASW **Series:** Save the Children **Obv:** Crowned arms **Rev:** Three children playing

Date	Mintage	VG	F	VF	XF	Unc
AH1411-1991 Proof	Est. 20,000	Value: 37.50				

KM# 97 2-1/2 OMANI RIALS
28.2800 g., 0.9250 Silver .8411 oz. ASW **Obv:** Crowned arms **Rev:** Three children playing

Date	Mintage	VG	F	VF	XF	Unc
AH1411-1991 Proof; Rare	—	—	—	—	—	—

Note: Struck for presentation purposes

KM# 61 5 OMANI RIALS
35.0000 g., 0.9250 Silver 1.0409 oz. ASW **Subject:** Conservation **Obv:** National arms **Rev:** Arabian White Oryx

Date	Mintage	F	VF	XF	Unc	BU
AH1397 (1976)	4,359	—	—	—	25.00	—
AH1397 (1976) Proof	4,401	Value: 30.00				

KM# 62 5 OMANI RIALS
45.6500 g., 0.9170 Gold 1.3454 oz. AGW **Subject:** 7th Anniversary - Reign of Sultan Qabus bin Sa'id **Obv:** National arms **Rev:** Bust 3/4 left

Date	Mintage	F	VF	XF	Unc	BU
AH1397 (1976) Proof	1,000	Value: 1,000				
AH1408 (1987) Proof	250	Value: 1,100				

KM# 89 5 OMANI RIALS
20.0000 g., 0.9170 Gold .5894 oz. AGW **Subject:** Agricultural Year **Obv:** National arms **Rev:** Farm fields above dates within center circle **Note:** Similar to 1/2 Omani Rial, KM#85.

Date	Mintage	F	VF	XF	Unc	BU
AH1409 (1988) Proof	200	Value: 435				

KM# 90 5 OMANI RIALS
20.0000 g., 0.9170 Gold .5894 oz. AGW **Subject:** Industry Year **Obv:** National arms **Rev:** Gears **Note:** Similar to 1/2 Omani Rial, KM#86.

Date	Mintage	F	VF	XF	Unc	BU
AH1411-1991 (1990) Proof	410	Value: 435				

KM# 141 5 OMANI RIALS
18.8000 g., 0.9250 Silver .5591 oz. ASW **Subject:** 25th National Day Anniversary - Burj Al Sahwa **Obv:** National arms and value within circle **Rev:** Monument

Date	Mintage	F	VF	XF	Unc	BU
1995 Proof	—	Value: 75.00				

KM# 141a 5 OMANI RIALS
31.0000 g., 0.9160 Gold .9130 oz. AGW **Obv:** National arms and value within circle **Rev:** Monument

Date	Mintage	F	VF	XF	Unc	BU
1995 Proof	—	Value: 675				

KM# 142 10 OMANI RIALS
23.2000 g., 0.9250 Silver .6900 oz. ASW **Subject:** 25th National Day Anniversary - Central Bank **Obv:** National arms and value **Rev:** Central Bank of Oman

Date	Mintage	F	VF	XF	Unc	BU
1995 Proof	—	Value: 85.00				

KM# 142a 10 OMANI RIALS
36.4000 g., 0.9160 Gold 1.0720 oz. AGW **Subject:** 25th National Day Anniversary - Central Bank **Obv:** National arms and value **Rev:** Central Bank of Oman

Date	Mintage	F	VF	XF	Unc	BU
1995 Proof	—	Value: 800				

KM# 49 15 OMANI RIALS
7.9900 g., 0.9170 Gold .2355 oz. AGW **Obv:** National arms **Rev:** Value

Date	Mintage	F	VF	XF	Unc	BU
AH1392 (1972) Proof	124	Value: 350				
AH1394 (1974)	300	—	—	—	250	—

Note: Struck for presentation purposes

KM# 55 15 OMANI RIALS
7.9900 g., 0.9170 Gold .2355 oz. AGW **Subject:** 10th National Day **Obv:** Crowned arms **Rev:** Value

Date	Mintage	F	VF	XF	Unc	BU
AH1400 (1979) Proof	1,000	Value: 400				

Note: Struck for presentation purposes

KM# 56 15 OMANI RIALS
20.0000 g., 0.9170 Gold .5897 oz. AGW **Subject:** 15th Anniversary - Reign of Sultan **Obv:** Head 1/4 left within 3/4 wreath and designed border **Rev:** Crowned arms over country map within circle

Date	Mintage	F	VF	XF	Unc	BU
AH1406 (1985) Proof	2,000	Value: 435				

KM# 56a 15 OMANI RIALS
31.0100 g., 0.9170 Gold .9144 oz. AGW **Subject:** 15th Anniversary - Reign of Sultan **Obv:** Head 1/4 left within 3/4 wreath and designed border **Rev:** Crowned arms over country map within circle

Date	Mintage	F	VF	XF	Unc	BU
AH1406 (1985) Proof	200	Value: 800				

KM# 98 20 OMANI RIALS
20.0000 g., 0.9170 Gold .5897 oz. AGW **Subject:** 20th National Day - Sultan Sa'id **Obv:** National arms **Rev:** Bust 1/4 left within circle and designs around border **Note:** Similar to 2 Omani Rials, KM#81.

Date	Mintage	F	VF	XF	Unc	BU
AH1411 (1990) Proof	1,200	Value: 450				

KM# 137.1 20 OMANI RIALS
48.6500 g., 0.9167 Gold 1.4338 oz. AGW **Subject:** 2oth Anniversary of Sultan's Reign **Obv:** Crowned arms within designed circle, legend above and below **Rev:** Value within designed circle with dates below flanked by leaves

Date	Mintage	F	VF	XF	Unc	BU
AH1411 (1990)	500	—	—	—	1,100	—

KM# 137.2 20 OMANI RIALS
65.3700 g., 0.9170 Gold 1.9273 oz. AGW **Subject:** 20th Anniversary of Sultan's Reign **Obv:** Crowned arms within designed circle with legend above and below **Rev:** Value within designed circle above dates flanked by leaves **Note:** Prev. KM#137.

Date	Mintage	VG	F	VF	XF	Unc
AH1411-1990 Proof	—	Value: 1,450				

KM# 143 20 OMANI RIALS
27.4000 g., 0.9250 Silver .8149 oz. ASW **Subject:** 25th National Day Anniversary **Obv:** National arms and value **Rev:** Radiant value within circle

Date	Mintage	F	VF	XF	Unc	BU
1995 Proof	—	Value: 95.00				

KM# 143a 20 OMANI RIALS
41.2000 g., 0.9160 Gold 1.2133 oz. AGW **Subject:** 25th National Day Anniversary **Obv:** National arms and value **Rev:** Radiant value within circle

Date	Mintage	F	VF	XF	Unc	BU
1995 Proof	—	Value: 900				

KM# 74 25 OMANI RIALS
10.0000 g., 0.9170 Gold .2947 oz. AGW **Series:** World Wildlife Fund **Obv:** National arms within circle **Rev:** Masked Booby

Date	Mintage	VG	F	VF	XF	Unc
AH1407-1987 Proof	5,000	Value: 225				

KM# 99 25 OMANI RIALS
10.0000 g., 0.9170 Gold .2947 oz. AGW **Series:** World Wildlife Fund **Obv:** Crown above arms with legends above and below **Rev:** Masked booby

Date	Mintage	F	VF	XF	Unc	BU
AH1407-1987 Proof; Rare	—	—	—	—	—	—

Note: Struck for presentation purposes

KM# 88 25 OMANI RIALS
10.0000 g., 0.9170 Gold .2947 oz. AGW **Series:** Save the Children **Obv:** National arms within circle **Rev:** School Master with pupils

Date	Mintage	VG	F	VF	XF	Unc
AH1411-1991 Proof	Est. 3,000	Value: 240				

KM# 100 25 OMANI RIALS
10.0000 g., 0.9170 Gold .2947 oz. AGW **Series:** Save the Children **Obv:** Crown above arms with legends above and below **Rev:** School Master with pupils

Date	Mintage	F	VF	XF	Unc	BU
AH1411-1991 Proof; Rare	—	—	—	—	—	—

Note: Struck for presentation purposes

KM# 144 25 OMANI RIALS
31.7000 g., 0.9250 Silver .9427 oz. ASW **Subject:** 25th National Day Anniversary - Sultan Qaboos bin Said **Obv:** National arms and value **Rev:** Multicolor bust facing

Date	Mintage	F	VF	XF	Unc	BU
1995 Proof	—	Value: 100				

KM# 144a 25 OMANI RIALS
50.2000 g., 0.9160 Gold 1.4784 oz. AGW **Subject:** 25th National Day Anniversary - Sultan Qaboos bin Said **Obv:** National arms and value **Rev:** Multicolor bust facing

Date	Mintage	F	VF	XF	Unc	BU
1995 Proof	—	Value: 1,100				

KM# 63 75 OMANI RIALS
33.4370 g., 0.9000 Gold .9676 oz. AGW **Subject:** Conservation **Obv:** National arms above date **Rev:** Arabian Tahr

Date	Mintage	F	VF	XF	Unc	BU
AH1397 (1976)	825	—	—	—	675	725
AH1397 (1976) Proof	325	Value: 925				

PROOF SETS

KM#	Date	Mintage	Identification	Issue Price	Mkt Val
PS1	AH1394 (3)	250	KM#45-47	—	935
PS2	AH1395 (3)	250	KM#45-47	—	935
PS3	AH1397 (3)	—	KM#60, 61, 63	780	985
PS4	AH1397 (2)	—	KM#60, 61	60.00	65.00
PS5	AH1411 (6)	3,200	KM#76-81	84.50	95.00
PS6	AH1416 (20)	—	KM#114-133	—	750
PSA6	1996 (2)	—	KM#101-102	640	875
PS7	1996 (4)	—	KM#103-106	125	140
PS8	1996 (4)	—	KM#107-110	125	140
PS9	1996 (8)	—	KM#103-110	247	280

PAKISTAN

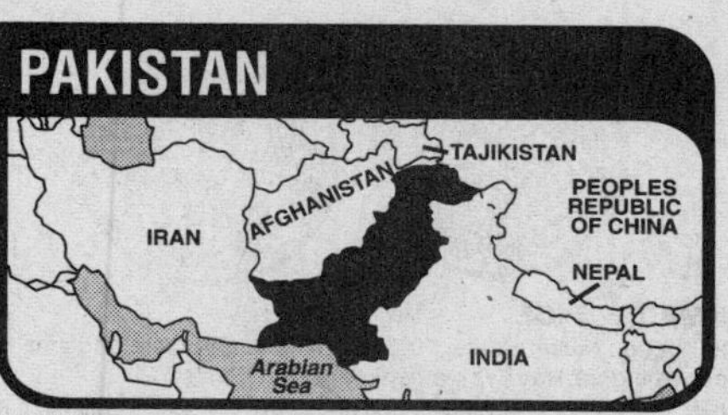

The Islamic Republic of Pakistan, located on the Indian subcontinent between India and Afghanistan, has an area of 310,404 sq. mi. (803,940 sq. km.) and a population of130 million. Capital: Islamabad. Pakistan is mainly an agricultural land although the industrial base is expanding rapidly. Yarn, textiles, cotton, rice, medical instruments, sports equipment and leather are exported.

Afghan and Turkish intrusions into northern India between the 11th and 18th centuries resulted in large numbers of Indians being converted to Islam. The idea of a separate Moslem state independent of Hindu India developed in the 1930's and was agreed to by Britain in1946. The Islamic majority areas of India, consisting of the separate geographic entities known as East and West Pakistan, achieved self-government as Pakistan, with dominion status in the British Commonwealth, when the British withdrew from India on Aug. 14, 1947. Pakistan became a republic in 1956. When a basic constitutional crisis initiated by the election of Dec. 1, 1970 - the first direct general election in Pakistani history - could not be resolved by the leaders of East and West Pakistan, the East Pakistanis seceded from the Islamic Republic of Pakistan (March 26, 1971) and formed the independent People's Republic of Bangladesh. After many years of vacillation between civilian and military regimes, the people of Pakistan held a free national election in November, 1988 and installed the first of a series of democratic governments under a parliamentary system.

TITLE

Pakistan

MONETARY SYSTEM
100 Paisa = 1 Rupee

ISLAMIC REPUBLIC

STANDARD COINAGE

3 Pies = 1 Pice; 4 Pice = 1 Anna; 16 Annas = 1 Rupee

KM# 11 PIE
1.3000 g., Bronze, 16 mm. **Obv:** Cresent and star above tughra **Rev:** Value and date flanked by stars within wreath

Date	Mintage	F	VF	XF	Unc	BU
1951	2,950,000	0.25	0.50	1.00	2.50	—
1951 Proof	—	Value: 4.00				
1953	110,000	3.00	5.00	7.00	10.00	—
1953 Proof	—	Value: 5.00				
1955	211,000	0.25	0.75	1.50	3.00	—
1955 Proof	—	Value: 15.00				
1956	3,390,000	0.25	0.50	1.00	2.50	—
1957	—	0.25	0.50	1.00	2.50	—

KM# 1 PICE
1.5500 g., Bronze, 21.3 mm. **Obv:** Legend around center hole **Rev:** Crescent and star divides value around the top, center hole divides date **Note:** Varieties exist.

Date	Mintage	F	VF	XF	Unc	BU
1948	101,070,000	0.20	0.40	0.75	1.50	—
1948 Proof	—	Value: 2.00				
1949	25,740,000	0.20	0.40	0.75	1.50	—
1949 Proof	—	Value: 2.00				
1951	14,050,000	0.20	0.45	0.85	1.75	—
1952	41,680,000	0.20	0.40	0.75	1.50	—

KM# 12 PICE

2.3000 g., Nickel-Brass, 20.6 mm. **Obv:** Crescent and star above tughra **Rev:** Value flanked by oat sprigs

Date	Mintage	F	VF	XF	Unc	BU
1953	47,540,000	0.15	0.30	0.50	1.00	—
1953 Proof	—	Value: 1.50				
1955	31,280,000	0.15	0.30	0.50	1.00	—
1956	9,710,000	0.50	0.70	1.00	1.50	—
1957	57,790,000	0.15	0.30	0.50	1.00	—
1958	52,470,000	0.15	0.30	0.50	1.00	—
1959	41,620,000	0.15	0.30	0.50	1.00	—

KM# 2 1/2 ANNA

2.9000 g., Copper-Nickel **Obv:** Tughra and date flanked by stars within sprigs, circle surrounds **Rev:** Crescent, stars and value above sprigs within circle **Shape:** 4-sided

Date	Mintage	F	VF	XF	Unc	BU
1948	73,920,000	0.15	0.30	0.50	1.00	—
1948 Proof	—	Value: 1.50				
1949 Dot after date	16,940,000	0.50	0.75	1.00	1.50	—
1951	75,360,000	0.15	0.30	0.50	1.00	—

KM# 13 1/2 ANNA

2.5000 g., Nickel-Brass **Obv:** Crescent and star above tughra **Rev:** Date divides wreath, value in center **Shape:** 4-sided

Date	Mintage	F	VF	XF	Unc	BU
1953	8,350,000	0.20	0.35	0.60	1.15	—
1953 Proof	—	Value: 1.50				
1955	17,310,000	0.15	0.30	0.50	1.00	—
1958	38,250,000	0.15	0.30	0.50	1.00	—

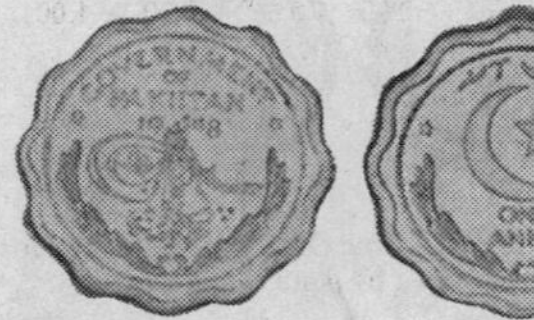

KM# 3 ANNA

3.7500 g., Copper-Nickel **Obv:** Tughra and date flanked by stars above sprigs within circle **Rev:** Crescent and star above sprigs within circle **Shape:** Scalloped

Date	Mintage	F	VF	XF	Unc	BU
1948	73,460,000	0.15	0.30	0.50	1.00	—
1948 Proof	—	Value: 1.50				
1949	11,140,000	0.20	0.35	0.60	1.15	—
1949 Dot after date	—	0.50	0.75	1.00	1.50	—
Note: Mintage included with KM#8.						
1951	40,800,000	0.15	0.30	0.50	1.00	—
1952	15,430,000	0.20	0.35	0.60	1.15	—

KM# 8 ANNA

3.7500 g., Copper-Nickel **Obv:** Tughra and date flanked by stars above sprigs within circle **Rev:** Crescent, stars and value above sprigs within circle **Shape:** Scalloped

Date	Mintage	F	VF	XF	Unc	BU
1950	94,830,000	3.00	4.50	6.50	10.00	—
1950 Proof	—	Value: 15.00				

KM# 14 ANNA

2.9000 g., Copper-Nickel **Obv:** Crescent and star above tughra **Rev:** Date divides wreath, value in center **Shape:** Scalloped

Date	Mintage	F	VF	XF	Unc	BU
1953	9,350,000	0.15	0.30	0.50	1.00	—
1953 Proof	—	Value: 1.50				
1954	35,360,000	0.15	0.30	0.50	1.00	—
1955	6,230,000	0.20	0.35	0.60	1.15	—
1956	4,580,000	0.20	0.35	0.60	1.15	—
1957	12,500,000	0.15	0.30	0.50	1.00	—
1958	44,320,000	0.15	0.30	0.50	1.00	—

KM# 4 2 ANNAS

5.8000 g., Copper-Nickel **Obv:** Tughra and date flanked by stars above sprigs within circle **Rev:** Crescent, stars and value above sprigs within circle **Shape:** 4-sided

Date	Mintage	F	VF	XF	Unc	BU
1948	55,930,000	0.15	0.30	0.50	1.00	—
1948 Proof	—	Value: 1.50				
1949	19,720,000	0.20	0.35	0.60	1.15	—
1949 Dot after date	—	0.50	0.75	1.00	1.50	—
Note: Mintage included with KM#9.						
1951	33,130,000	0.15	0.30	0.50	1.00	—

KM# 9 2 ANNAS

5.8000 g., Copper-Nickel **Obv:** Tughra and date flanked by stars above sprigs within circle **Rev:** Crescent, stars and value above sprigs within circle **Shape:** 4-sided

Date	Mintage	F	VF	XF	Unc	BU
1950	21,190,000	3.50	5.00	7.50	12.50	—
1950 Proof	—	Value: 20.00				

KM# 15 2 ANNAS

5.8000 g., Copper-Nickel **Obv:** Crescent and star above tughra **Rev:** Date divides wreath, value in center **Shape:** 4-sided

Date	Mintage	F	VF	XF	Unc	BU
1953	7,910,000	0.15	0.30	0.50	1.00	—
1953 Proof	—	Value: 1.50				
1954	5,740,000	0.15	0.30	0.50	1.00	—
1955	6,230,000	0.15	0.30	0.50	1.00	—
1956	1,370,000	0.20	0.35	0.60	1.15	—
1957	2,570,000	0.20	0.35	0.60	1.15	—
1958	6,200,000	0.15	0.30	0.50	1.00	—
1959	8,010,000	0.15	0.30	0.50	1.00	—

KM# 5 1/4 RUPEE

2.7500 g., Nickel, 19 mm. **Obv:** Tughra and date flanked by stars above sprigs **Rev:** Crescent, stars and value above sprigs **Edge:** Reeded

Date	Mintage	F	VF	XF	Unc	BU
1948	52,680,000	0.20	0.30	0.50	1.00	—
1948 Proof	—	Value: 2.25				
1949	46,000,000	0.20	0.30	0.50	1.00	—
1951	19,120,000	0.20	0.35	0.60	1.15	—

KM# 10 1/4 RUPEE

2.7500 g., Nickel, 19 mm. **Obv:** Tughra and date flanked by stars above sprigs **Rev:** Crescent, stars and value above sprigs **Edge:** Reeded

Date	Mintage	F	VF	XF	Unc	BU
1950	19,400,000	5.00	7.50	12.00	20.00	—
1950 Proof	—	Value: 25.00				

KM# 6 1/2 RUPEE

6.0000 g., Nickel, 24 mm. **Obv:** Tughra and date flanked by stars above sprigs **Rev:** Crescent, stars and value above sprigs **Edge:** Reeded

Date	Mintage	F	VF	XF	Unc	BU
1948	33,260,000	0.40	0.60	0.75	1.50	—
1948 Proof	—	Value: 2.00				
1949	20,300,000	0.40	0.60	0.75	1.50	—
1951	11,430,000	0.40	0.65	0.90	1.75	—

KM# 7 RUPEE

11.5000 g., Nickel, 28 mm. **Obv:** Tughra and date flanked by stars above sprigs **Rev:** Crescent, stars and value above sprigs **Edge:** Reeded **Note:** Varieties exist.

Date	Mintage	F	VF	XF	Unc	BU
1948	46,200,000	0.75	1.25	2.00	3.50	—
1948 Proof	—	Value: 5.00				
1949	37,100,000	0.75	1.25	2.00	3.50	—

DECIMAL COINAGE

100 Paisa = 1 Rupee

KM# 16 PICE

1.4000 g., Bronze, 16 mm. **Obv:** Crescent and star above tughra **Rev:** Date and value flanked by oat sprigs

Date	Mintage	F	VF	XF	Unc	BU
1961	74,910,000	0.15	0.30	0.50	1.00	—

KM# 17 PAISA

1.4000 g., Bronze, 16 mm. **Obv:** Crescent and star above tughra **Rev:** Value and date flanked by oat sprigs

Date	Mintage	F	VF	XF	Unc	BU
1961	134,650,000	0.15	0.25	0.40	0.80	—
1961 Proof	—	Value: 1.50				
1962	149,380,000	0.15	0.25	0.40	0.80	—
1963	127,810,000	0.15	0.25	0.40	0.80	—

KM# 24 PAISA

1.5000 g., Bronze, 17 mm. **Obv:** Crescent and star above tughra **Rev:** Value flanked by oat sprigs

Date	Mintage	F	VF	XF	Unc	BU
1964	39,890,000	0.20	0.35	0.50	1.00	—
1964 Proof	—	Value: 1.50				
1965	69,660,000	0.20	0.35	0.50	1.00	—

KM# 24a PAISA
1.5000 g., Nickel-Brass, 17 mm. **Obv:** Crescent and star above tughra **Rev:** Value flanked by oat sprigs

Date	Mintage	F	VF	XF	Unc	BU
1965	32,950,000	0.20	0.35	0.50	1.00	—
1966	179,370,000	0.15	0.25	0.40	0.80	—

KM# 29 PAISA
0.6000 g., Aluminum, 17 mm. **Obv:** Crescent and star above tughra **Rev:** Value flanked by oat sprigs

Date	Mintage	F	VF	XF	Unc	BU
1967	170,070,000	—	0.20	0.40	0.75	—
1968	—	—	0.20	0.40	0.75	—
1969	—	—	0.20	0.40	0.75	—
1970	204,606,000	—	0.20	0.40	0.75	—
1971	191,880,000	—	0.20	0.40	0.75	—
1972	108,510,000	—	0.20	0.40	0.75	—
1973	Inc. above	—	0.20	0.40	0.75	—

KM# 33 PAISA
0.6000 g., Aluminum, 17 mm. **Series:** F.A.O. **Obv:** Crescent within monument with star at upper left **Rev:** Value flanked by abstract cotton plant

Date	Mintage	F	VF	XF	Unc	BU
1974	14,230,000	—	0.20	0.40	0.75	—
1975	43,000,000	—	0.20	0.40	0.75	—
1976	49,180,000	—	0.20	0.40	0.75	—
1977	62,750,000	—	0.20	0.40	0.75	—
1978	20,380,000	—	0.20	0.40	0.75	—
1979	5,630,000	—	2.00	3.00	4.00	—

KM# 25 2 PAISA
2.2500 g., Bronze **Obv:** Crescent and star above tughra **Rev:** Value within sprigs **Shape:** Scalloped

Date	Mintage	F	VF	XF	Unc	BU
1964	67,660,000	0.15	0.35	0.50	1.00	—
1964 Proof	—	Value: 1.50				
1965	27,880,000	0.15	0.35	0.50	1.00	—
1966	50,590,000	0.15	0.35	0.50	1.00	—

KM# 28 2 PAISA
0.7500 g., Aluminum, 18 mm. **Obv:** Crescent and star above tughra **Rev:** Value within sprigs

Date	Mintage	F	VF	XF	Unc	BU
1966	11,940,000	—	0.35	0.50	1.00	—
1967	73,970,000	—	0.35	0.50	1.00	—
1968	—	—	0.35	0.50	1.00	—

KM# 25a 2 PAISA
0.7500 g., Aluminum **Obv:** Crescent and star above tughra **Rev:** Value within sprigs **Shape:** Scalloped

Date	Mintage	F	VF	XF	Unc	BU
1968	—	—	0.35	0.50	1.00	—
1969	—	—	0.35	0.50	1.00	—
1970	24,401,000	—	0.35	0.50	1.00	—
1971	10,140,000	—	0.35	0.50	1.00	—
1972	4,040,000	—	0.65	1.00	2.00	—

KM# 34 2 PAISA
1.0000 g., Aluminum, 19.5 mm. **Series:** F.A.O. **Obv:** Crescent within monument with star at upper left **Rev:** Value flanked by rice plant **Shape:** Scalloped

Date	Mintage	F	VF	XF	Unc	BU
1974	3,600,000	—	0.35	0.50	1.00	—
1975	4,020,000	—	0.35	0.50	1.00	—
1976	5,750,000	—	0.50	0.75	1.50	—

KM# 18 5 PICE
2.7500 g., Nickel-Brass **Obv:** Crescent and star above tughra **Rev:** Sailboat with value on sails **Shape:** 4-sided

Date	Mintage	F	VF	XF	Unc	BU
1961	40,050,000	0.20	0.35	0.50	1.00	—

KM# 19 5 PAISA
2.7500 g., Nickel-Brass **Obv:** Crescent and star above tughra **Rev:** Sailboat with value on sails **Shape:** 4-sided

Date	Mintage	F	VF	XF	Unc	BU
1961	40,790,000	0.20	0.35	0.50	1.00	—
1961 Proof	—	Value: 1.50				
1962	48,200,000	0.20	0.35	0.50	1.00	—
1963	45,020,000	0.20	0.35	0.50	1.00	—

KM# 26 5 PAISA
1.0000 g., Nickel-Brass, 21 mm. **Obv:** Crescent and star above tughra **Rev:** Sailboat with value on the sails **Shape:** 4-sided

Date	Mintage	F	VF	XF	Unc	BU
1964	82,730,000	0.20	0.35	0.50	1.00	—
1965	72,570,000	0.20	0.35	0.50	1.00	—
1966	32,900,000	0.20	0.35	0.50	1.00	—
1967	24,470,000	0.20	0.35	0.50	1.00	—
1968	—	0.20	0.35	0.50	1.00	—
1969	5,690,000	0.20	0.35	0.50	1.00	—
1970	24,655,000	0.20	0.35	0.50	1.00	—
1971	23,860,000	0.20	0.35	0.50	1.00	—
1972	40,345,000	0.20	0.35	0.50	1.00	—
1973	Inc. above	0.20	0.35	0.50	1.00	—
1974	7,695,000	0.65	1.00	2.00	3.00	—

KM# 35 5 PAISA
1.0000 g., Aluminum, 21 mm. **Series:** F.A.O. **Obv:** Crescent within monument with star at upper left **Rev:** Value within sugar cane **Shape:** 4-sided

Date	Mintage	F	VF	XF	Unc	BU
1974	23,395,000	—	0.35	0.50	1.00	—
1975	50,030,000	—	0.35	0.50	1.00	—
1976	58,255,000	—	0.35	0.50	1.00	—
1977	32,840,000	—	0.35	0.50	1.00	—
1978	61,940,000	—	0.35	0.50	1.00	—
1979	65,485,000	—	0.35	0.50	1.00	—
1980	55,940,000	—	0.35	0.50	1.00	—
1981	18,290,000	—	0.35	0.50	1.00	—

KM# 52 5 PAISA
1.0000 g., Aluminum, 21 mm. **Obv:** Crescent, star and date above sprigs **Rev:** Value within sugar cane flanked by stars **Shape:** 4-sided

Date	Mintage	F	VF	XF	Unc	BU
1981	16,730,000	—	0.35	0.50	1.00	—
1982	51,210,000	—	0.35	0.50	1.00	—
1983	42,915,000	—	0.35	0.50	1.00	—
1984	45,105,000	—	0.35	0.50	1.00	—
1985	46,555,000	—	0.35	0.50	1.00	—
1986	20,065,000	—	0.35	0.50	1.00	—
1987	37,710,000	—	0.35	0.50	1.00	—
1988	40,150,000	—	0.35	0.50	1.00	—
1989	—	—	0.35	0.50	1.00	—
1990	—	—	0.35	0.50	1.00	—
1991	—	—	0.35	0.50	1.00	—
1992	—	—	0.35	0.50	1.00	—

KM# 20 10 PICE
4.7500 g., Copper-Nickel **Obv:** Crescent and star above tughra **Rev:** Date divides wreath, value in center **Shape:** Scalloped

Date	Mintage	F	VF	XF	Unc	BU
1961	22,230,000	0.20	0.35	0.50	1.00	—

KM# 21 10 PAISA
4.7500 g., Copper-Nickel **Obv:** Crescent and star above tughra **Rev:** Date divides wreath, value in center **Shape:** Scalloped

Date	Mintage	F	VF	XF	Unc	BU
1961	31,090,000	0.20	0.35	0.50	1.00	—
1961 Proof	—	Value: 2.00				
1962	29,440,000	0.20	0.35	0.50	1.00	—
1963	19,760,000	0.20	0.35	0.50	1.00	—

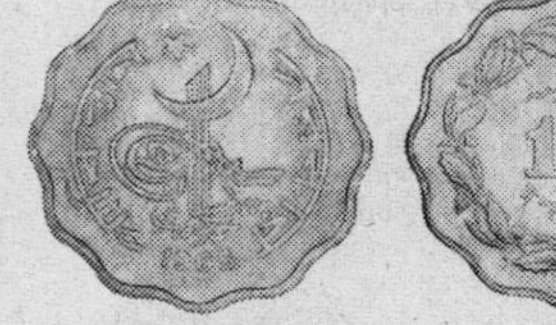

KM# 27 10 PAISA
4.7500 g., Copper-Nickel **Obv:** Crescent and star above tughra **Rev:** Value within wreath **Shape:** Scalloped

Date	Mintage	F	VF	XF	Unc	BU
1964	52,580,000	0.20	0.35	0.50	1.00	—
1965	51,540,000	0.20	0.35	0.50	1.00	—
1966	—	0.20	0.35	0.50	1.00	—
1967	16,430,000	0.20	0.35	0.50	1.00	—
1968	—	0.20	0.35	0.50	1.00	—

KM# 31 10 PAISA
4.0000 g., Copper-Nickel **Obv:** Crescent and star above tughra **Rev:** Value within wreath **Shape:** Scalloped **Note:** Reduced size.

Date	Mintage	F	VF	XF	Unc	BU
1969	—	0.20	0.35	0.50	1.00	—
1970	30,250,000	0.20	0.35	0.50	1.00	—
1971	26,270,000	0.20	0.35	0.50	1.00	—
1972	24,845,000	0.20	0.35	0.50	1.00	—
1973	Inc. above	0.20	0.35	0.50	1.00	—
1974	4,780,000	0.20	0.35	0.50	1.00	—

KM# 36 10 PAISA

1.2500 g., Aluminum **Series:** F.A.O. **Obv:** Crescent within monument with star at upper left **Rev:** Value within wheat ears **Shape:** Scalloped

Date	Mintage	F	VF	XF	Unc	BU
1974	18,640,000	—	0.35	0.50	1.00	—
1975	28,875,000	—	0.35	0.50	1.00	—
1976	43,755,000	—	0.35	0.50	1.00	—
1977	29,045,000	—	0.35	0.50	1.00	—
1978	55,185,000	—	0.35	0.50	1.00	—
1979	56,100,000	—	0.35	0.50	1.00	—
1980	40,985,000	—	0.35	0.50	1.00	—
1981	15,500,000	—	0.35	0.50	1.00	—

KM# 53 10 PAISA

1.2500 g., Aluminum **Obv:** Crescent, star and date above sprigs **Rev:** Value within square **Shape:** Scalloped

Date	Mintage	F	VF	XF	Unc	BU
1981	7,995,000	—	0.35	0.50	1.00	—
1982	39,770,000	—	0.35	0.50	1.00	—
1983	44,705,000	—	0.35	0.50	1.00	—
1984	35,255,000	—	0.35	0.50	1.00	—
1985	41,545,000	—	0.35	0.50	1.00	—
1986	43,280,000	—	0.35	0.50	1.00	—
1987	39,090,000	—	0.35	0.50	1.00	—
1988	42,510,000	—	0.35	0.50	1.00	—
1989	—	—	0.35	0.50	1.00	—
1990	—	—	0.35	0.50	1.00	—
1991	—	—	0.35	0.50	1.00	—
1992	—	—	0.35	0.50	1.00	—
1993	—	—	0.35	0.50	1.00	—
1996	—	—	0.35	0.50	1.00	—

KM# 22 25 PAISA

2.9000 g., Nickel, 19 mm. **Obv:** Crescent and star above tughra **Rev:** Value flanked by flower sprigs **Edge:** Reeded

Date	Mintage	F	VF	XF	Unc	BU
1963	16,900,000	0.20	0.35	0.50	1.00	—
1964	7,990,000	0.20	0.35	0.50	1.00	—
1965	9,290,000	0.20	0.35	0.50	1.00	—
1966	6,650,000	0.20	0.35	0.50	1.00	—
1967	3,740,000	0.20	0.35	0.50	1.00	—

KM# 30 25 PAISA

4.0000 g., Copper-Nickel, 20 mm. **Obv:** Crescent and star above tughra **Rev:** Value below flowers **Edge:** Reeded

Date	Mintage	F	VF	XF	Unc	BU
1967	5,500,000	0.20	0.35	0.50	1.00	—
Note: Mintage unconfirmed						
1968	5,500,000	0.20	0.35	0.50	1.00	—
Note: Mintage unconfirmed						
1969	—	0.20	0.35	0.50	1.00	—
1970	30,392,000	0.20	0.35	0.50	1.00	—
1971	12,664,000	0.20	0.35	0.50	1.00	—
1972	10,824,000	0.20	0.35	0.50	1.00	—
1973	—	0.20	0.35	0.50	1.00	—
1974	9,756,000	0.20	0.35	0.50	1.00	—

KM# 37 25 PAISA

4.0000 g., Copper-Nickel, 20 mm. **Obv:** Crescent within monument with star at upper left **Rev:** Value within flowers **Edge:** Reeded

Date	Mintage	F	VF	XF	Unc	BU
1975	14,264,000	0.20	0.35	0.50	1.00	—
1976	20,440,000	0.20	0.35	0.50	1.00	—
1977	22,092,000	0.20	0.35	0.50	1.00	—
1978	33,544,000	0.20	0.35	0.50	1.00	—
1979	29,648,000	0.20	0.35	0.50	1.00	—
1980	49,556,000	0.20	0.35	0.50	1.00	—
1981	33,952,000	0.20	0.35	0.50	1.00	—

KM# 58 25 PAISA

2.5000 g., Copper-Nickel, 18 mm. **Obv:** Crescent, star and date above sprigs **Rev:** Value within artistic designed wreath **Edge:** Reeded **Note:** Varieties in date and crescent size exist.

Date	Mintage	F	VF	XF	Unc	BU
1981	5,648,000	0.20	0.35	0.50	1.00	—
1982	28,940,000	0.20	0.35	0.50	1.00	—
1983	40,844,000	0.20	0.35	0.50	1.00	—
1984	50,988,000	0.20	0.35	0.50	1.00	—
1985	53,748,000	0.20	0.35	0.50	1.00	—
1986	75,764,000	0.20	0.35	0.50	1.00	—
1987	53,560,000	0.20	0.35	0.50	1.00	—
1988	58,900,000	0.20	0.35	0.50	1.00	—
1989	—	0.20	0.35	0.50	1.00	—
1990	—	0.20	0.35	0.50	1.00	—
1991	—	0.20	0.35	0.50	1.00	—
1992	—	0.20	0.35	0.50	1.00	—
1993	—	0.20	0.35	0.50	1.00	—
1994	—	0.20	0.35	0.50	1.00	—
1995	—	0.20	0.35	0.50	1.00	—

KM# 23 50 PAISA

5.8000 g., Nickel, 24 mm. **Obv:** Crescent and star above tughra **Rev:** Value flanked by flowers **Edge:** Reeded

Date	Mintage	F	VF	XF	Unc	BU
1963	8,110,000	0.20	0.35	0.50	1.00	—
1964	4,580,000	0.20	0.35	0.50	1.00	—
1965	8,980,000	0.20	0.35	0.50	1.00	—
1966	2,860,000	0.20	0.35	0.50	1.00	—
1968	—	0.20	0.35	0.50	1.00	—
1969	—	0.20	0.35	0.50	1.00	—

KM# 32 50 PAISA

5.0000 g., Copper-Nickel, 22 mm. **Obv:** Crescent and star above tughra **Rev:** Value below flowers **Edge:** Reeded

Date	Mintage	F	VF	XF	Unc	BU
1969	9,240,000	0.20	0.35	0.50	1.00	—
1970	Inc. above	0.20	0.35	0.50	1.00	—
1971	4,670,000	0.20	0.35	0.50	1.00	—
1972	4,900,000	0.20	0.35	0.50	1.00	—
1974	1,128,000	0.50	0.75	1.00	2.00	—

KM# 38 50 PAISA

5.0000 g., Copper-Nickel, 23 mm. **Obv:** Crescent within monument with star at upper left **Rev:** Value within circle and designed wreath **Edge:** Reeded **Note:** Varieties in date size exist.

Date	Mintage	F	VF	XF	Unc	BU
1975	9,180,000	0.20	0.35	0.50	1.00	—
1976	—	0.20	0.35	0.50	1.00	—
1977	5,548,000	0.20	0.35	0.50	1.00	—
1978	18,252,000	0.20	0.35	0.50	1.00	—
1979	14,596,000	0.20	0.35	0.50	1.00	—
1980	22,332,000	0.20	0.35	0.50	1.00	—
1981	13,552,000	0.20	0.35	0.50	1.00	—

KM# 39 50 PAISA

5.8300 g., Copper-Nickel, 24 mm. **Subject:** 100th Anniversary - Birth of Mohammad Ali Jinnah **Obv:** Value within circle and designed wreath **Rev:** Bust facing flanked by dates **Edge:** Reeded

Date	Mintage	F	VF	XF	Unc	BU
1976	5,600,000	0.35	0.50	1.00	1.50	2.00

KM# 54 50 PAISA

4.0000 g., Copper-Nickel, 21 mm. **Obv:** Crescent, star and date above sprigs **Rev:** Value within circle and leaf wreath **Edge:** Reeded

Date	Mintage	F	VF	XF	Unc	BU
1981	4,612,000	0.20	0.35	0.50	1.00	—
1982	15,844,000	0.20	0.35	0.50	1.00	—
1983	9,608,000	0.20	0.35	0.50	1.00	—
1984	17,520,000	0.20	0.35	0.50	1.00	—
1985	20,144,000	0.20	0.35	0.50	1.00	—
1986	14,116,000	0.20	0.35	0.50	1.00	—
1987	23,044,000	0.20	0.35	0.50	1.00	—
1988	37,140,000	0.20	0.35	0.50	1.00	—
1989	—	0.20	0.35	0.50	1.00	—
1990	—	0.20	0.35	0.50	1.00	—
1991	—	0.20	0.35	0.50	1.00	—
1992	—	0.20	0.35	0.50	1.00	—
1993	—	0.20	0.35	0.50	1.00	—
1994	—	0.20	0.35	0.50	1.00	—
1995	—	0.20	0.35	0.50	1.00	—
1996	—	0.20	0.35	0.50	1.00	—

KM# 51 50 PAISA

5.0000 g., Copper-Nickel, 23 mm. **Subject:** 1,400th Hejira Anniversary **Obv:** Crescent and star above design **Rev:** Value within wreath **Edge:** Reeded

Date	Mintage	F	VF	XF	Unc	BU
AH1401 (1981)	—	0.50	0.75	1.00	2.00	2.50

KM# 45 RUPEE

7.5000 g., Copper-Nickel **Subject:** Islamic Summit Conference **Obv:** Islamic summit minar flanked by designs **Rev:** Design within inner circle **Edge:** Reeded

Date	Mintage	F	VF	XF	Unc	BU
1977	5,074,000	0.50	0.75	1.00	2.00	2.50

KM# 46 RUPEE

7.5000 g., Copper-Nickel, 27.5 mm. **Subject:** 100th Anniversary - Birth of Allama Mohammad Iqbal **Obv:** Value and date above sprigs **Rev:** Head leaning on arm facing 1/4 left **Edge:** Reeded

Date	Mintage	F	VF	XF	Unc	BU
1977	5,000,000	0.50	0.75	1.00	2.00	2.50

KM# 57.1 RUPEE
6.5000 g., Copper-Nickel, 26.5 mm. **Obv:** Crescent, star and date above sprigs **Rev:** Value within sprigs **Edge:** Reeded

Date	Mintage	F	VF	XF	Unc	BU
1979	—	0.30	0.40	0.55	1.15	—
1980	14,522,000	0.30	0.40	0.55	1.15	—
1981	12,038,000	0.30	0.40	0.55	1.15	—

KM# 57.2 RUPEE
6.0000 g., Copper-Nickel, 25 mm. **Obv:** Crescent, star and date above sprigs **Rev:** Value within sprigs **Edge:** Reeded

Date	Mintage	F	VF	XF	Unc	BU
1981	4,084,000	0.25	0.40	0.60	1.20	—
1982	27,878,000	0.20	0.35	0.50	1.00	—
1983	18,746,000	0.20	0.35	0.50	1.00	—
1984	14,562,000	0.20	0.35	0.50	1.00	—
1985	4,934,000	0.25	0.40	0.60	1.20	—
1986	11,840,000	0.20	0.35	0.50	1.00	—
1987	50,416,000	0.20	0.35	0.50	1.00	—
1988	10,644,000	0.20	0.35	0.50	1.00	—
1990	—	0.20	0.35	0.50	1.00	—
1991	—	0.20	0.35	0.50	1.00	—

KM# 55 RUPEE
6.5000 g., Copper-Nickel, 26.5 mm. **Subject:** 1,400th Hejira Anniversary **Obv:** Crescent and star above design **Rev:** Value within wreath **Edge:** Reeded

Date	Mintage	F	VF	XF	Unc	BU
AH1401 (1981)	45,000	0.50	0.75	1.25	2.50	3.00

KM# 56 RUPEE
6.0000 g., Copper-Nickel, 25 mm. **Series:** World Food Day **Obv:** Crescent, star and date above sprigs **Rev:** F.A.O. logo within circle **Edge:** Reeded

Date	Mintage	F	VF	XF	Unc	BU
1981	45,000	0.35	0.75	1.50	3.00	3.50

KM# 62 RUPEE
4.0000 g., Bronze, 20 mm. **Obv:** Head left **Rev:** Mosque above value **Edge:** Reeded

Date	Mintage	F	VF	XF	Unc	BU
1998	—	0.20	0.25	0.35	0.65	0.75
1999	—	0.20	0.25	0.35	0.65	0.75
2000	—	0.20	0.25	0.35	0.65	0.75

KM# 63 2 RUPEES
4.0000 g., Nickel-Brass, 22.5 mm. **Obv:** Crescent, star and date above sprigs **Rev:** Mosque **Edge:** Reeded

Date	Mintage	F	VF	XF	Unc	BU
1998	—	0.20	0.30	0.45	0.85	1.00
1999	—	0.20	0.30	0.45	0.85	1.00

KM# 64 2 RUPEES
4.0000 g., Nickel-Brass, 22.5 mm. **Obv:** Crescent, star and date above sprigs **Rev:** Value below mosque and clouds **Edge:** Reeded

Date	Mintage	F	VF	XF	Unc	BU
1999	—	0.20	0.30	0.45	0.85	1.00
2000	—	0.20	0.30	0.45	0.85	1.00

KM# 59 5 RUPEES
20.0000 g., Copper, 35 mm. **Subject:** United Nations 50th Year **Obv:** Crescent and star above grain sprigs **Rev:** 50, UN logo **Edge:** Reeded **Note:** Four die varieties are reported to exist.

Date	Mintage	F	VF	XF	Unc	BU
1995	500,000	—	—	—	5.50	6.00

KM# 61 10 RUPEES
10.0000 g., Copper-Nickel, 26 mm. **Subject:** 25th Anniversary - Pakistan's Senate **Obv:** Crescent, star and date above sprigs **Rev:** Shield within sprigs above banner and dates to left of numeral 25 **Edge:** Reeded

Date	Mintage	F	VF	XF	Unc	BU
1998	100,000	—	—	4.00	6.50	7.50

KM# 60 50 RUPEES
20.0000 g., Copper-Nickel, 35 mm. **Subject:** 50th Anniversary - National Independence **Obv:** Star and crescent **Rev:** Flag and dates **Edge:** Reeded

Date	Mintage	F	VF	XF	Unc	BU
1997	500,000	—	—	4.50	7.50	8.00

KM# 40 100 RUPEES
28.2800 g., 0.9250 Silver .8411 oz. ASW, 38.6 mm.
Series: Conservation **Obv:** Crescent within monument with star at upper left **Rev:** Tropogan pheasant

Date	Mintage	F	VF	XF	Unc	BU
1976	5,120	—	—	—	30.00	40.00
1976 Proof	5,837	Value: 50.00				

KM# 41 100 RUPEES
20.4400 g., 0.9250 Silver .6079 oz. ASW, 36 mm.
Subject: 100th Anniversary - Birth of Mohammad Ali Jinnah
Obv: Crescent and star **Rev:** Bust facing flanked by dates

Date	Mintage	F	VF	XF	Unc	BU
ND(1976)	1,300	—	—	—	35.00	40.00
ND(1976) Proof	2,800	Value: 45.00				

KM# 47 100 RUPEES
20.4400 g., 0.9250 Silver .6079 oz. ASW, 36 mm.
Subject: Islamic Summit Conference **Obv:** Islamic building
Rev: Islamic summit minar

Date	Mintage	F	VF	XF	Unc	BU
1977	1,500	—	—	—	35.00	40.00
1977 Proof	2,500	Value: 45.00				

KM# 48 100 RUPEES
20.4400 g., 0.9250 Silver .6079 oz. ASW, 36 mm. **Subject:** 100th Anniversary - Birth of Allama Mohammad Iqbal **Obv:** Value and date above sprigs **Rev:** Head leaning on hand divides dates

Date	Mintage	F	VF	XF	Unc	BU
1977	3,000	—	—	—	35.00	40.00
1977 Proof	300	Value: 50.00				

KM# 42 150 RUPEES
35.0000 g., 0.9250 Silver 1.0409 oz. ASW, 42 mm.
Series: Conservation **Obv:** Crescent within monument with star at upper left **Rev:** Gavial crocodile and value

Date	Mintage	F	VF	XF	Unc	BU
1976	5,119	—	—	—	40.00	45.00
1976 Proof	5,637	Value: 50.00				

KM# 43 500 RUPEES
4.5000 g., 0.9170 Gold .1325 oz. AGW, 19 mm. **Subject:** 100th Anniversary - Birth of Mohammad Ali Jinnah **Obv:** Crescent and star **Rev:** Bust facing flanked by dates

Date	Mintage	F	VF	XF	Unc	BU
ND(1976)	500	—	—	—	125	135
ND(1976) Proof	500	Value: 150				

KM# 49 500 RUPEES
3.6400 g., 0.9170 Gold .1073 oz. AGW, 19 mm. **Subject:** 100th Anniversary - Birth of Allama Mohammad Iqbal **Obv:** Value and date above sprigs **Rev:** Head leaning on hand flanked by dates

Date	Mintage	F	VF	XF	Unc	BU
1977	500	—	—	—	120	130
1977 Proof	200	Value: 150				

KM# 50 1000 RUPEES
9.0000 g., 0.9170 Gold .2650 oz. AGW, 25 mm.
Subject: Islamic Summit Conference **Obv:** Islamic summit minar **Rev:** Design within center circle

Date	Mintage	F	VF	XF	Unc	BU
1977	400	—	—	—	220	250
1977 Proof	400	Value: 300				

KM# 44 3000 RUPEES
33.4370 g., 0.9000 Gold .9676 oz. AGW, 39 mm. **Obv:** Crescent within monument with star at upper left **Rev:** Astor Markhor and value

Date	Mintage	F	VF	XF	Unc	BU
1976	902	—	—	—	750	800
1976 Proof	273	Value: 900				

PATTERNS

Including off-metal strikes

KM#	Date	Mintage	Identification	Mkt Val
Pn1	1947	—	Rupee. Nickel Alloy. Toughra within circle. GOVERNMENT OF PAKISTAN. Crescent and star, dates flanking.	—
Pn2	1947	—	Rupee. Nickel Alloy. Toughra within circle, dates below. GOVERNMENT OF PAKISTAN. Crescent with star.	—
Pn3	1947	—	Rupee. Nickel Alloy. Crescent and star, denomination and wreath below. Toughra, date at right, wreath below. GOVERNMENT OF PAKISTAN.	—
Pn4	ND(1995)	—	Rupee. Copper Alloys. Crescent and star, wheat ears below. UN logo, large 50.	—

MINT SETS

KM#	Date	Mintage	Identification	Issue Price	Mkt Val
MS1	1948 (7)	—	KM1-7	—	10.00
MS2	1948, 1951, 1953 (8)	—	KM5-7 (1948), 11 (1951), 12-15 (1953). Restrikes have been issued.	4.00	12.50
MS3	1948, 1961 (6)	—	KM5-7 (1948), 17, 19, 21 (1961). Restrikes have been issued.	2.00	6.50
MS4	1948, 1964 (7)	—	KM7 (1948), 22-27 (1964). Restrikes have been issued.	2.00	6.50
MS5	1948, 1975 (7)	—	KM7 (1948), 33-38 (1975). Restrikes have been issued.	—	5.00
MS6	1951, 1953 (5)	—	KM11 (1951), 12-15 (1953). Restrikes have been issued.	—	8.00
MS7	1961 (3)	—	KM17, 19, 21	—	3.50
MS8	1976 (2)	—	KM41, 43	63.00	155
MS9	1976 (2)	—	KM40, 42	—	68.00
MS10	1977 (2)	—	KM47, 50	—	225

PROOF SETS

KM#	Date	Mintage	Identification	Issue Price	Mkt Val
PS1	1948 (7)	5,000	KM1-7	4.00	15.50
PS3	1950 (3)	—	KM8-10	—	60.00
PS4	1953 (5)	—	KM11-15	2.00	11.50
PS5	1961 (3)	—	KM17, 19, 21	1.00	5.00
PS6	1976 (2)	—	KM41, 43	90.50	185
PS7	1976 (2)	—	KM40, 42	—	78.00
PS8	1977 (2)	—	KM47, 50	—	300
PS9	1977 (2)	—	KM#45	—	40.00

PALAU

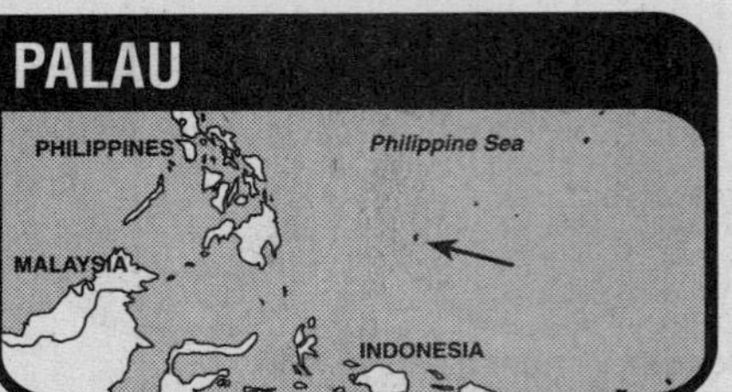

The Republic of Palau, a group of about 100 islands and islets, is generally considered a part of the Caroline Islands. It is located about 1,000 miles southeast of Manila and about the same distance southwest of Saipan and has an area of 179 sq. mi. and a population of 12,116. Capital: Koror.

The islands were administered as part of the Caroline Islands under the Spanish regime until they were sold to Germany in 1899. Seized by Japan in 1914, it was mandated to them in 1919 and Koror was made the administrative headquarters of all the Japanese mandated islands in 1921. During World War II the islands were taken by the Allies, in 1944, with the heaviest fighting taking place on Peleliu. They became part of the U.S. Trust Territory of the Pacific Islands in 1947. In 1980 they became internally self-governing and independent. Control over foreign policy, except defense, was approved in 1986. Palau became an independent nation in 1995.

REPUBLIC

COLLECTOR COINAGE

KM# 1 DOLLAR
Copper-Nickel **Subject:** Year of Marine Life Protection
Obv: Sailboat, mermaid and value within beaded circle
Rev: Multicolor design within beaded circle

Date	Mintage	F	VF	XF	Unc	BU
1992 Proof	Est. 50,000	Value: 30.00				

KM# 3 DOLLAR
Copper-Nickel **Series:** Marine Life Protection **Obv:** Mermaid sitting upright **Rev:** Multicolor ocean scene

Date	Mintage	F	VF	XF	Unc	BU
1993 Proof	50,000	Value: 27.50				

KM# 5 DOLLAR

Copper-Nickel **Series:** Marine Life Protection **Obv:** Ship, mermaid and value **Rev:** Multicolor ocean scene

Date	Mintage	F	VF	XF	Unc	BU
1994 Proof	50,000	Value: 30.00				

KM# 8 DOLLAR

Copper-Nickel **Subject:** Independence **Obv:** Neptune and mermaid **Rev:** Multicolor ocean scene

Date	Mintage	F	VF	XF	Unc	BU
1994 Proof	50,000	Value: 30.00				

KM# 11 DOLLAR

Copper-Nickel **Subject:** Marine Life Protection **Obv:** Mermaid with harp **Rev:** Multicolor sea horse and lion fish

Date	Mintage	F	VF	XF	Unc	BU
1995 Proof	30,000	Value: 35.00				

KM# 14 DOLLAR

Copper-Nickel **Subject:** United Nations 50th Anniversary **Obv:** Mermaid above seahorses, value below **Rev:** Multicolor ocean scene with emblem on bottom

Date	Mintage	F	VF	XF	Unc	BU
1995 Proof	30,000	Value: 25.00				

KM# 25 DOLLAR

Copper-Nickel **Series:** Marine Life Protection **Obv:** Two mermaids **Rev:** Multicolor high-relief dolphin

Date	Mintage	F	VF	XF	Unc	BU
1998 Proof	13,000	Value: 35.00				

KM# 26 DOLLAR

1.2441 g., 0.9999 Gold .0400 oz. AGW, 13.94 mm. **Series:** Marine Life Protection **Obv:** Two mermaids **Rev:** Jumping dolphin

Date	Mintage	F	VF	XF	Unc	BU
1998 Proof	10,000	Value: 35.00				

KM# 30 DOLLAR

Copper-Nickel **Series:** Marine Life Protection **Obv:** Mermaid with cockatoo **Rev:** Multicolor high-relief turtle

Date	Mintage	F	VF	XF	Unc	BU
1998 Proof	—	Value: 35.00				

KM# 31 DOLLAR

1.2441 g., 0.9999 Gold .0400 oz. AGW, 13.94 mm. **Series:** Marine Life Protection **Obv:** Mermaid holding cockatoo **Rev:** Sea turtle

Date	Mintage	F	VF	XF	Unc	BU
1998 Proof	—	Value: 40.00				

KM# 35 DOLLAR

Copper-Nickel **Series:** Marine Life Protection **Obv:** Mermaid and dolphin **Rev:** Multicolor high-relief manta ray

Date	Mintage	F	VF	XF	Unc	BU
1999 Proof	—	Value: 35.00				

KM# 82 DOLLAR

1.2441 g., 0.9999 Gold 0.04 oz. AGW, 13.94 mm. **Obv:** Seated Mermaid and sailboat **Rev:** Multicolor shark **Edge:** Reeded

Date	Mintage	F	VF	XF	Unc	BU
1999 Proof	—	Value: 35.00				

KM# 36 DOLLAR

1.2441 g., 0.9999 Gold .0400 oz. AGW, 13.94 mm. **Series:** Marine Life Protection **Obv:** Mermaid and dolphin **Rev:** Manta ray

Date	Mintage	F	VF	XF	Unc	BU
1999 Proof	—	Value: 37.50				

KM# 40 DOLLAR

Copper-Nickel **Series:** Marine Life Protection **Obv:** Mermaid and sailboat **Rev:** Multicolor shark

Date	Mintage	F	VF	XF	Unc	BU
1999 Proof	—	Value: 35.00				

KM# 43 DOLLAR

26.6500 g., Copper-Nickel **Series:** Marine Life Protection **Obv:** Mermaid and ship **Rev:** Multicolor fish and coral

Date	Mintage	F	VF	XF	Unc	BU
2000 Proof	—	Value: 30.00				

KM# 83 DOLLAR

1.2441 g., 0.9999 Gold 0.04 oz. AGW, 13.94 mm. **Obv:** Diving Mermaid **Rev:** Multicolor jumping Swordfish **Edge:** Reeded

Date	Mintage	F	VF	XF	Unc	BU
2000 Proof	—	Value: 35.00				

KM# 84 DOLLAR

1.2441 g., 0.9999 Gold 0.04 oz. AGW, 13.94 mm. **Obv:** Seated Mermaid **Rev:** Multicolor fish and wreck **Edge:** Reeded

Date	Mintage	F	VF	XF	Unc	BU
2000 Proof	—	Value: 35.00				

KM# 85 DOLLAR

1.2441 g., 0.9999 Gold 0.04 oz. AGW, 13.94 mm. **Obv:** Seated Mermaid and ship **Rev:** Multicolor fish and coral **Edge:** Reeded

Date	Mintage	F	VF	XF	Unc	BU
2000 Proof	—	Value: 35.00				

KM# 58 DOLLAR
26.8000 g., Copper-Nickel, 37.2 mm. **Obv:** Diving Mermaid **Rev:** Multicolor jumping swordfish **Edge:** Reeded

Date	Mintage	F	VF	XF	Unc	BU
2000 Proof	—	Value: 35.00				

KM# 59 DOLLAR
26.8000 g., Copper-Nickel, 37.2 mm. **Obv:** Seated Mermaid **Rev:** Multicolor fish and wreck **Edge:** Reeded

Date	Mintage	F	VF	XF	Unc	BU
2000 Proof	—	Value: 35.00				

KM# 2 5 DOLLARS
25.0000 g., 0.9000 Silver .7234 oz. ASW **Series:** Marine Life Protection **Obv:** Neptune and spear **Rev:** Multicolor ocean scene

Date	Mintage	F	VF	XF	Unc	BU
1992 Proof	Est. 6,000	Value: 75.00				

KM# 4 5 DOLLARS
25.0000 g., 0.9000 Silver .7234 oz. ASW **Series:** Marine Life Protection **Obv:** Neptune in shell, horses, dolphin and value **Rev:** Multicolor ocean scene

Date	Mintage	F	VF	XF	Unc	BU
1993 Proof	6,000	Value: 60.00				

KM# 6 5 DOLLARS
25.0000 g., 0.9000 Silver .7234 oz. ASW **Series:** Marine Life Protection **Obv:** Neptune and seascape **Rev:** Multicolor ocean scene

Date	Mintage	F	VF	XF	Unc	BU
1994 Proof	10,000	Value: 60.00				

KM# 9 5 DOLLARS
25.0000 g., 0.9000 Silver .7234 oz. ASW **Series:** Independence **Obv:** Mermaid and Neptune **Rev:** Nautilus and seascape

Date	Mintage	F	VF	XF	Unc	BU
1994 Proof	—	Value: 60.00				

KM# 12 5 DOLLARS
25.0000 g., 0.9000 Silver .7234 oz. ASW **Series:** Marine Life Protection **Rev:** Sea horse and lion fish

Date	Mintage	F	VF	XF	Unc	BU
1995 Proof	7,500	Value: 60.00				

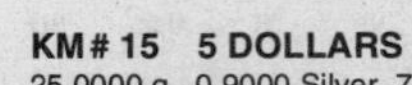

KM# 15 5 DOLLARS
25.0000 g., 0.9000 Silver .7234 oz. ASW **Subject:** United Nations 50th Anniversary **Obv:** Mermaid above seahorses **Rev:** Multicolor ocean scene

Date	Mintage	F	VF	XF	Unc	BU
1995 Proof	5,500	Value: 45.00				

KM# 46 5 DOLLARS
24.6400 g., 0.9000 Silver .7130 oz. ASW **Series:** Marine Life Protection **Obv:** Mermaid and sailboat **Rev:** Multicolor shark

Date	Mintage	F	VF	XF	Unc	BU
1998 Proof	—	Value: 60.00				
1999 Proof	—	Value: 60.00				

KM# 27 5 DOLLARS
25.0000 g., 0.9000 Silver .7234 oz. ASW **Series:** Marine Life Protection **Obv:** Two mermaids **Rev:** Multicolor high-relief dolphin **Note:** Similar to Dollar, KM#25.

Date	Mintage	F	VF	XF	Unc	BU
1998 Proof	5,000	Value: 60.00				

KM# 32 5 DOLLARS
25.0000 g., 0.9000 Silver .7234 oz. ASW **Series:** Marine Life Protection **Obv:** Mermaid holding cockatoo **Rev:** Multicolor high-relief turtle **Note:** Similar to Dollar, KM#30.

Date	Mintage	F	VF	XF	Unc	BU
1998 Proof	—	Value: 60.00				

KM# 44 5 DOLLARS
24.6400 g., 0.9000 Silver .7130 oz. ASW **Series:** Marine Life Protection **Obv:** Neptune and ship **Rev:** Multicolor dolphin jumping **Edge:** Reeded

Date	Mintage	F	VF	XF	Unc	BU
1998 Proof	5,000	Value: 60.00				

KM# 45 5 DOLLARS
24.6400 g., 0.9000 Silver .7130 oz. ASW **Series:** Marine Life Protection **Obv:** Neptune and two dolphins **Rev:** Multicolor sea turtle

Date	Mintage	F	VF	XF	Unc	BU
1998 Proof	3,000	Value: 60.00				

KM# 37 5 DOLLARS
25.0000 g., 0.9000 Silver .7234 oz. ASW, 37 mm. **Subject:** Marine Life Protection **Obv:** Mermaid and dolphin **Rev:** Multicolor high relief manta ray **Edge:** Reeded

Date	Mintage	F	VF	XF	Unc	BU
1999 Proof	—	Value: 60.00				

KM# 47 5 DOLLARS
24.6400 g., 0.9000 Silver .7130 oz. ASW **Series:** Marine Life Protection **Obv:** Mermaid in profile, sailboat **Rev:** Multicolor manta ray

Date	Mintage	F	VF	XF	Unc	BU
1999 Proof	—	Value: 60.00				

KM# 16 5 DOLLARS
25.0000 g., 0.9250 Silver .7435 oz. ASW **Series:** International Coins **Subject:** Spanish 5 Peseta - 1896-1899 **Obv:** Crowned Spanish arms **Rev:** Young head left

Date	Mintage	F	VF	XF	Unc	BU
1999 Proof	—	Value: 25.00				

KM# 17 5 DOLLARS
25.0000 g., 0.9250 Silver .7435 oz. ASW **Series:** International Coins **Subject:** Prussian 5 Mark - 1891-1908 **Obv:** Crowned arms **Rev:** Head right

Date	Mintage	F	VF	XF	Unc	BU
1999 Proof	—	Value: 25.00				

KM# 18 5 DOLLARS
25.0000 g., 0.9250 Silver .7435 oz. ASW **Series:** International Coins **Subject:** German East Africa **Obv:** Elephant above value **Rev:** Uniformed bust facing, colonial arms at lower right

Date	Mintage	F	VF	XF	Unc	BU
1999 Proof	—	Value: 35.00				

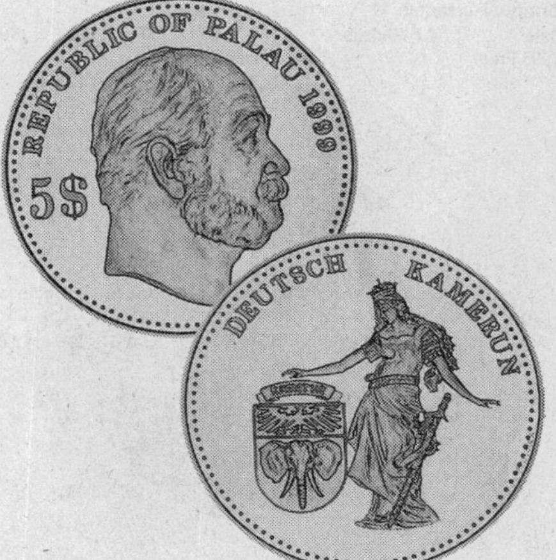

KM# 19 5 DOLLARS
25.0000 g., 0.9250 Silver .7435 oz. ASW **Series:** International Coins **Subject:** German Cameroon **Obv:** Head right **Rev:** Germania and colonial arms

Date	Mintage	F	VF	XF	Unc	BU
1999 Proof	—	Value: 27.50				

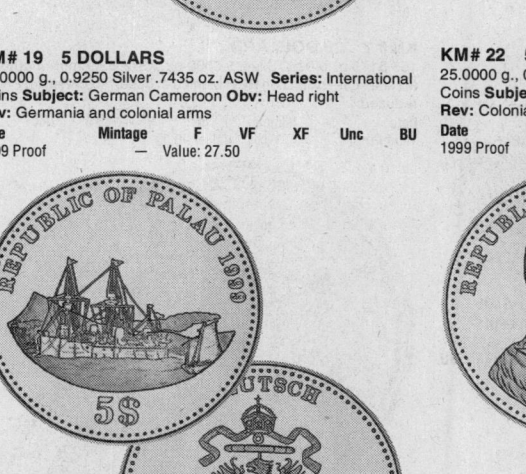

KM# 20 5 DOLLARS
25.0000 g., 0.9250 Silver .7435 oz. ASW **Series:** International Coins **Subject:** Kiau Chau **Obv:** Ships in harbor **Rev:** Emblem based on 1909 coinage

Date	Mintage	F	VF	XF	Unc	BU
1999 Proof	—	Value: 28.50				

KM# 21 5 DOLLARS
25.0000 g., 0.9250 Silver .7435 oz. ASW **Series:** International Coins **Subject:** German New Guinea **Obv:** Large ship **Rev:** Colonial arms

Date	Mintage	F	VF	XF	Unc	BU
1999 Proof	—	Value: 28.50				

KM# 22 5 DOLLARS
25.0000 g., 0.9250 Silver .7435 oz. ASW **Series:** International Coins **Subject:** German Samoa **Obv:** Armored bust left **Rev:** Colonial arms

Date	Mintage	F	VF	XF	Unc	BU
1999 Proof	—	Value: 28.50				

KM# 23 5 DOLLARS
25.0000 g., 0.9250 Silver .7435 oz. ASW **Series:** International Coins **Subject:** German South West Africa **Obv:** Whilhelm II portrait from Prussian 5 Mark coin of 1913-1914 **Rev:** Colonial arms and trooper on camel

Date	Mintage	F	VF	XF	Unc	BU
1999 Proof	—	Value: 30.00				

KM# 24 5 DOLLARS

25.0000 g., 0.9250 Silver .7435 oz. ASW **Series:** International Coins **Subject:** German Togo **Obv:** Seated Germania **Rev:** Colonial arms

Date	Mintage	F	VF	XF	Unc	BU
1999 Proof	—	Value: 25.00				

KM# 48 5 DOLLARS

24.6400 g., 0.9000 Silver .7130 oz. ASW **Series:** Marine Life Protection **Obv:** Neptune seated **Rev:** Multicolor fish and coral

Date	Mintage	F	VF	XF	Unc	BU
2000 Proof	—	Value: 55.00				

KM# 73 5 DOLLARS

25.0000 g., 0.9000 Silver, 37.2 mm. **Subject:** Marine Life Protection **Obv:** Neptune seated **Rev:** Multicolor jumping swordfish **Edge:** Reeded

Date	Mintage	F	VF	XF	Unc	BU
2000 Proof	—	Value: 60.00				

KM# 74 5 DOLLARS

25.0000 g., 0.9000 Silver, 37.2 mm. **Subject:** Marine Life Protection **Obv:** Neptune behind ancient ship **Rev:** Multicolor fish and wreck **Edge:** Reeded

Date	Mintage	F	VF	XF	Unc	BU
2000 Proof	—	Value: 60.00				

KM# 51 5 DOLLARS

24.9400 g., 0.9000 Silver .7217 oz. ASW, 38.6 mm. **Subject:** Our World - Our Future **Obv:** Half-length dancer with leis **Rev:** Multicolor world map **Edge:** Reeded

Date	Mintage	F	VF	XF	Unc	BU
2000 Proof	—	Value: 45.00				

KM# 112 10 DOLLARS

1.4900 g., 0.9990 Gold 0.0479 oz. AGW, 11 x 19 mm. **Obv:** Value, date and inscription **Rev:** Mermaid **Edge:** Plain **Shape:** Rectangle

Date	Mintage	F	VF	XF	Unc	BU
1995 Proof	—	Value: 50.00				

KM# 7 20 DOLLARS

155.5175 g., 0.9990 Silver 5.0000 oz. ASW, 63.9 mm. **Subject:** Marine - Life Protection **Rev:** Multicolor ocean scene **Note:** Photo reduced.

Date	Mintage	F	VF	XF	Unc	BU
1994 Proof	3,000	Value: 90.00				

KM# 42 20 DOLLARS

155.5175 g., 0.9990 Silver 5.0000 oz. ASW, 63.9 mm. **Subject:** Independence - October 1994 **Obv:** Mermaid and Neptune **Rev:** Multicolor seascape **Note:** Photo reduced.

Date	Mintage	F	VF	XF	Unc	BU
ND(1994) Proof	—	Value: 95.00				

KM# 13 20 DOLLARS

155.5175 g., 0.9990 Silver 5.0000 oz. ASW **Series:** Marine Life Protection **Obv:** Seated mermaid with harp **Rev:** Seahorse and lion fish **Note:** Similar to Dollar, KM#11.

Date	Mintage	F	VF	XF	Unc	BU
1995 Proof	3,000	Value: 95.00				

KM# 41 20 DOLLARS

15.6500 g., 0.9990 Silver 4.9993 oz. ASW, 64.5 mm. **Series:** 50th Anniversary - United Nations Member **Obv:** Mermaid driving quadriga **Rev:** Multicolor seascape, globe of earth below **Note:** Photo reduced.

Date	Mintage	F	VF	XF	Unc	BU
1995 Proof	—	Value: 90.00				

KM# 28 20 DOLLARS

155.5175 g., 0.9990 Silver 4.9950 oz. ASW **Series:** Marine Life Protection **Obv:** Two mermaids **Rev:** Multicolor high-relief dolphin **Note:** Similar to Dollar, KM#25.

Date	Mintage	F	VF	XF	Unc	BU
1998 Proof	700	Value: 100				

KM# 33 20 DOLLARS

155.5175 g., 0.9990 Silver 4.9950 oz. ASW **Series:** Marine Life Protection **Obv:** Mermaid with cockatoo **Rev:** Multicolor high-relief turtle **Note:** Similar to Dollar, KM#30.

Date	Mintage	F	VF	XF	Unc	BU
1998 Proof	500	Value: 110				

KM# 38 20 DOLLARS

155.5175 g., 0.9990 Silver 4.9950 oz. ASW **Series:** Marine Life Protection **Obv:** Mermaid with dolphin **Rev:** Multicolor high-relief manta ray **Note:** Similar to Dollar, KM#35.

Date	Mintage	F	VF	XF	Unc	BU
1999 Proof	500	Value: 110				

KM# 49 20 DOLLARS

153.9400 g., 0.9990 Silver 4.9443 oz. ASW **Series:** Marine Life Protection **Obv:** Seated mermaid and sailboat **Rev:** Multicolor shark **Edge:** Reeded

Date	Mintage	F	VF	XF	Unc	BU
1999 Proof	500	Value: 110				

KM# 55 20 DOLLARS

154.8400 g., 0.9990 Silver 4.9732 oz. ASW, 64.5 mm. **Subject:** Marine Life Protection **Obv:** Diving mermaid **Rev:** Multicolor jumping swordfish scene **Edge:** Reeded

Date	Mintage	F	VF	XF	Unc	BU
2000 Proof	500	Value: 110				

KM# 54 20 DOLLARS

154.8400 g., 0.9990 Silver 4.9732 oz. ASW, 64.5 mm. **Subject:** Marine Life Protection **Obv:** Seated mermaid **Rev:** Multicolor sunken ship and fish scene **Edge:** Reeded **Note:** Photo reduced.

Date	Mintage	F	VF	XF	Unc	BU
2000 Proof	500	Value: 110				

KM# 50 20 DOLLARS

153.9400 g., 0.9990 Silver 4.9443 oz. ASW **Subject:** Marine - Life Protection **Obv:** Mermaid and ship **Rev:** Multicolor fish and coral **Note:** Photo reduced.

Date	Mintage	F	VF	XF	Unc	BU
2000 Proof	500	Value: 110				

KM# 10 200 DOLLARS

31.1035 g., 0.9990 Gold 1.0000 oz. AGW **Subject:** Independence **Obv:** Mermaid and Neptune **Rev:** Nautilus and seascape

Date	Mintage	F	VF	XF	Unc	BU
1994 Proof	—	Value: 720				

KM# 29 200 DOLLARS

31.1035 g., 0.9990 Gold 1.0000 oz. AGW **Subject:** Marine - Life Protection **Obv:** Two mermaids **Rev:** Multicolor high-relief dolphin **Note:** Similar to Dollar, KM#25.

Date	Mintage	F	VF	XF	Unc	BU
1998 Proof	200	Value: 720				

KM# 34 200 DOLLARS

31.1035 g., 0.9990 Gold 1.0000 oz. AGW **Subject:** Marine - Life Protection **Obv:** Mermaid with cockatoo **Rev:** Multicolor high-relief turtle **Note:** Similar to Dollar, KM#30.

Date	Mintage	F	VF	XF	Unc	BU
1998 Proof	—	Value: 720				

KM# 39 200 DOLLARS

31.1035 g., 0.9990 Gold 1.0000 oz. AGW **Subject:** Marine - Life Protection **Obv:** Mermaid with dolphin **Rev:** Multicolor high-relief manta ray **Note:** Similar to Dollar, KM#35.

Date	Mintage	F	VF	XF	Unc	BU
1999 Proof	—	Value: 720				

ESSAIS

Standard metals unless otherwise noted

KM#	Date	Mintage	Identification	Issue Price	Mkt Val
E1	1992	—	Dollar. 0.9990 Gold. 25.9600 g. Seated mermaid and sailboat. Multicolor sea life. KM1.	—	1,500

KM#	Date	Mintage	Identification	Issue Price	Mkt Val
E2	1992	—	5 Dollars. 0.9990 Gold. 25.9700 g. Seated Neptune and ship. Multicolor sea life. Reeded edge. KM2.	—	1,500

KM#	Date	Mintage	Identification	Issue Price	Mkt Val
E3	1995	30	Dollar. Silver. KM41.	—	125

KM#	Date	Mintage	Identification	Issue Price	Mkt Val
E4	1995	30	5 Dollars. Copper-Nickel. KM41.	—	100

KM#	Date	Mintage	Identification	Issue Price	Mkt Val
E5	1995	30	200 Dollars. Copper-Nickel. KM41.	—	120
E6	1995	30	200 Dollars. Silver. KM41.	—	185

KM#	Date	Mintage	Identification	Issue Price	Mkt Val
E7	1998	20	Dollar. Silver. KM25.	—	145
E8	1998	20	5 Dollars. Copper-Nickel. KM25.	—	145
E9	1998	20	200 Dollars. Silver. KM25.	—	145

PROOF SETS

KM#	Date	Mintage	Identification	Issue Price	Mkt Val
PS1	1992	—	KME1, E2	—	3,000
PS2	1995 (4)	20	KME3, E4, E5, E6	—	600
PS3	1998 (3)	20	KME7, E8, E9	—	450

PALESTINE

Palestine, which corresponds to Canaan of the Bible, was settled by the Philistines about the 12th century B.C. and shortly thereafter was settled by the Jews who established the kingdoms of Israel and Judah. Because of its position as part of the land bridge connecting Asia and Africa, Palestine was invaded and conquered by nearly all of the historic empires of ancient Europe and Asia. In the16th century it became a part of the Ottoman Empire. After falling to the British in World War I, it, together with Transjordan, was mandated to Great Britain by the League of Nations, 1922.

For more than half a century prior to the termination of the British mandate over Palestine, 1948, Zionist leaders had sought to create a Jewish homeland for Jews who were dispersed throughout the world. For almost as long, Jews fleeing persecution had immigrated to Palestine. The Nazi persecutions of the 1930s and 1940s increased the Jewish movement to Palestine and generated international support for the creation of a Jewish state, first promulgated by the Balfour Declaration of 1917, which asserted British support for the endeavor. The state of Israel was proclaimed as the Jewish state in the territory that was Palestine. The remainder of that territory was occupied by Jordanian and Egyptian armies. Israel demonetized the coins of Palestine on Sept. 15, 1948, the Jordan government declared Palestine currency no longer legal tender on June 30, 1951, and Egypt declared it no longer legal tender in Gaza on June 9, 1951.

TITLES

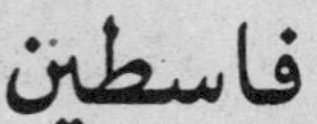

Filastin

פלשתינה (א"י).

Paleshtina (E.I.)

MONETARY SYSTEM
1000 Mils = 1 Pound
1000 Mils = 1 Pound

BRITISH ADMINISTRATION

MIL COINAGE

KM# 1 MIL
Bronze **Obv:** Inscription **Obv. Inscription:** PALESTINE 1927 (IN ENGLISH AND ARABIC) **Rev:** Value, plant

Date	Mintage	F	VF	XF	Unc	BU
1927	10,000,000	0.50	2.00	4.00	12.00	18.00
1927 Proof	66	Value: 650				
1935	704,000	2.00	3.00	5.00	25.00	40.00
1937	1,200,000	1.50	2.00	10.00	150	250
1939	3,700,000	1.00	2.00	10.00	30.00	40.00
1939 Proof	—	Value: 400				
1940	396,000	6.50	12.50	50.00	150	—
1941	1,920,000	1.00	2.00	5.00	20.00	30.00
1942	4,480,000	1.00	2.00	5.00	25.00	40.00
1943	2,800,000	0.75	2.00	5.00	35.00	45.00
1944	1,400,000	0.75	2.00	5.00	18.00	25.00
1946	1,632,000	2.00	4.00	8.00	35.00	50.00
1946 Proof	—	Value: 500				
1947	2,880,000	—	—	—	10,000	—

Note: Only 5 known; The entire issue was to be melted down

KM# 2 2 MILS
Bronze **Obv:** Inscription **Obv. Inscription:** PALESTINE, 1927 (In English and Arabic) **Rev:** Value, plant

Date	Mintage	F	VF	XF	Unc	BU
1927	5,000,000	2.00	3.00	10.00	20.00	—
1927 Proof	66	Value: 700				
1941	1,600,000	1.00	2.00	6.00	40.00	—
1941 Proof	—	Value: 400				
1942	2,400,000	1.00	2.50	10.00	25.00	40.00
1945	960,000	2.00	5.00	20.00	150	—
1946	960,000	4.00	10.00	30.00	175	—
1947	480,000	—	—	—	—	—

Note: The entire issue was melted down

KM# 3 5 MILS
Copper-Nickel, 20 mm. **Obv:** Wreath around center hole **Rev:** Value above center hole

Date	Mintage	F	VF	XF	Unc	BU
1927	10,000,000	0.75	2.00	5.00	25.00	35.00
1927 Proof	66	Value: 550				
1934	500,000	6.50	12.50	50.00	175	—
1935	2,700,000	0.75	2.00	7.00	40.00	60.00
1939	2,000,000	0.75	2.00	5.00	30.00	45.00
1939 Proof	—	Value: 425				
1941	400,000	10.00	20.00	35.00	125	175
1941 Proof	—	Value: 375				
1946	1,000,000	2.00	4.00	8.00	30.00	45.00
1946 Proof	—	Value: 450				
1947	1,000,000	—	—	—	—	25,000

Note: Almost the entire issue was melted down, with only 3 remaining pieces known to exist

KM# 3a 5 MILS
Bronze **Obv:** Wreath around center hole **Rev:** Value above center hole

Date	Mintage	F	VF	XF	Unc	BU
1942	2,700,000	1.50	2.00	8.00	45.00	60.00
1944	1,000,000	2.00	5.00	10.00	45.00	60.00

KM# 4 10 MILS
Copper-Nickel **Obv:** Date above and below center hole **Rev:** Wreath around center hole with value above and below

Date	Mintage	F	VF	XF	Unc	BU
1927	5,000,000	2.00	6.00	10.00	45.00	60.00
1927 Proof	66	Value: 575				
1933	500,000	4.00	8.00	75.00	400	—
1933 Proof	—	Value: 350				
1934	500,000	5.00	12.00	50.00	300	—
1934 Proof	—	Value: 375				
1935	1,150,000	1.00	10.00	35.00	250	—
1935 Proof	—	Value: 425				
1937	750,000	2.00	5.00	15.00	175	—
1937 Proof	—	Value: 425				
1939	1,000,000	1.00	5.00	15.00	100	—
1939 Proof	—	Value: 350				
1940	1,500,000	1.00	5.00	15.00	100	—
1940 Proof	—	Value: 100				
1941	400,000	6.00	15.00	50.00	125	200
1941 Proof	—	Value: 350				
1942	600,000	4.00	10.00	25.00	175	—
1946	1,000,000	2.00	15.00	25.00	75.00	—
1946 Proof	—	Value: 300				
1947	1,000,000	—	—	—	—	—

KM# 4a 10 MILS
Bronze **Obv:** Date above and below center hole **Rev:** Wreath around center hole with value above and below

Date	Mintage	F	VF	XF	Unc	BU
1942	1,000,000	4.00	5.00	15.00	125	—
1943	1,000,000	7.00	10.00	20.00	175	—

KM# 5 20 MILS
Copper-Nickel **Obv:** Wreath around center hole with dates below **Rev:** Value above and below center hole

Date	Mintage	F	VF	XF	Unc	BU
1927	1,500,000	7.00	12.00	35.00	100	—
1927 Proof	66	Value: 800				
1933	250,000	10.00	20.00	50.00	400	—
1934	125,000	40.00	70.00	175	750	—
1934 Proof	—	—	—	—	—	—
1935	575,000	5.00	15.00	50.00	300	—
1940	200,000	10.00	15.00	50.00	350	—
1940 Proof	—	Value: 500				
1941	100,000	50.00	75.00	150	1,000	—
1941 Proof	—	Value: 1,200				

KM# 5a 20 MILS
Bronze **Obv:** Wreath around center hole with dates below **Rev:** Value above and below center hole

Date	Mintage	F	VF	XF	Unc	BU
1942	1,100,000	10.00	12.00	30.00	175	—
1944	1,000,000	25.00	60.00	200	600	—

KM# 6 50 MILS
5.8319 g., 0.7200 Silver 0.135 oz. ASW **Obv:** Plant flanked by dates within circle **Rev:** Written and numeric value

Date	Mintage	F	VF	XF	Unc	BU
1927	8,000,000	8.00	10.00	25.00	75.00	—
1927 Proof	66	Value: 775				
1931	500,000	25.00	45.00	150	500	—
1933	1,000,000	20.00	25.00	50.00	125	—
1934	399,000	25.00	40.00	60.00	150	—
1935	5,600,000	6.00	8.00	12.00	50.00	—
1939	3,000,000	6.00	8.00	12.00	40.00	—
1939 Proof	—	Value: 275				
1940	2,000,000	8.00	20.00	30.00	75.00	—
1940 Proof	—	Value: 150				
1942	5,000,000	6.00	8.00	12.00	40.00	—

KM# 7 100 MILS
11.6638 g., 0.7200 Silver 0.27 oz. ASW **Obv:** Plant flanked by dates **Rev:** Value within circle

Date	Mintage	F	VF	XF	Unc	BU
1927	2,000,000	10.00	25.00	50.00	120	—
1927 Proof	66	Value: 850				
1931	250,000	70.00	125	250	1,000	1,500
1931 Proof	—	Value: 1,400				
1933	500,000	25.00	40.00	100	350	—
1934	200,000	90.00	125	200	450	—
1935	2,850,000	15.00	20.00	30.00	110	—
1939	1,500,000	8.00	12.00	30.00	120	—
1939 Proof	—	Value: 250				
1940	1,000,000	10.00	15.00	30.00	110	—
1942	2,500,000	10.00	15.00	25.00	90.00	—

TOKEN COINAGE

KM# Tn4 MIL
Brass **Obv:** Date 5699 on either side of shield, legend around **Obv. Legend:** 1/2 MILL...KOFER HAYISHUV...BAR TAV **Rev:** INcuse impress of the obverse with the shiled in a higher relief **Note:** Uniface. Called the "Hagana Defence Token." Struck in the Plitz factory in Holon.

Date	Mintage	F	VF	XF	Unc	BU
JE5699 (1938-39)	—	—	4.50	7.50	12.50	—

Note: The British Government did not object to the issue of these tokens which circulated until the 1950s as coins.

KM# Tn1 SOUVENIR MIL
6.8000 g., Bronze **Note:** Thin planchet, 'Y' in Holyland not fully engraved. Same beading on both sides. On top two berries, the right is higher. Hebrew Mill does not touch circle.

Date	Mintage	F	VF	XF	Unc	BU
1927	—	—	100	175	300	—

Note: This souvenir which incorporates an appropriate reproduction of a 1927 1 Mil coin of Palestine was privately created for sale to pilgrims as a souvenir of their visit to the Holy Land; The Arabic translates to Souvenir of the Holy Land. It is not known who produced them nor how many were produced

KM# Tn2 SOUVENIR MIL
8.7100 g., Bronze **Note:** Thick planchet. 'C' in Historical is re-engraved. Obverse beading is longer. Of top two berries, left one is higher. Hebrew "Mil" extends past circle.

Date	Mintage	F	VF	XF	Unc	BU
1927	—	—	100	175	300	—

KM# Tn3 SOUVENIR MIL

6.8000 g., Bronze **Note:** Similar to KM#Tn2 but struck on a thin planchet.

Date	Mintage	F	VF	XF	Unc	BU
1927	—	—	200	350	700	—

MINT SETS

KM#	Date	Mintage	Identification	Issue Price	Mkt Val
MS1	1927 (14)	—	KM1-7, two each	—	1,750

PROOF SETS

KM#	Date	Mintage	Identification	Issue Price	Mkt Val
PS1	1927 (14)	34	KM1-7, two each, original case	—	8,500
PS2	1927 (7)	4	KM1-7, original case	—	5,000

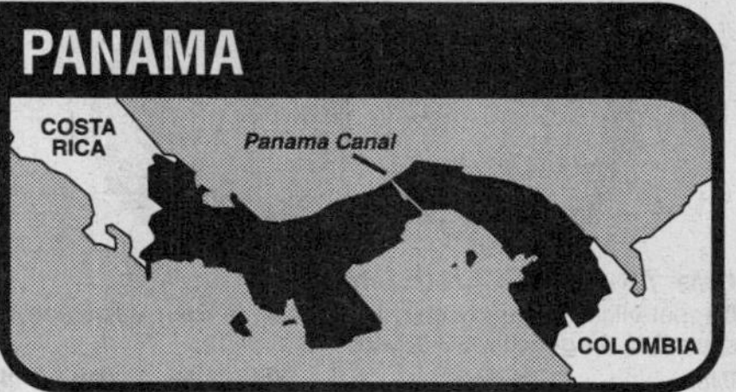

The Republic of Panama, a Central American Country situated between Costa Rica and Colombia, has an area of 29,762 sq. mi. (78,200 sq. km.) and a population of *2.4 million. Capital: Panama City. The Panama Canal is the country's biggest asset; servicing world related transit trade and international commerce. Bananas, refined petroleum, sugar and shrimp are exported.

Discovered in 1501 by the Spanish conquistador Rodrigo Galvan de Bastidas, the land of Panama was soon explored and after a few attempts at settlement was successfully colonized by the Spanish. It was in Panama in 1513 that Vasco Nunez de Balboa became the first European to see the Pacific Ocean. The first Pacific-coast settlement, founded in 1519 on the site of a village the natives called Panama, was named *Nuestra Senora de la Asuncion de Panama* (Our Lady of the Assumption of Panama). The settlement soon became a city and eventually, albeit briefly, an Audiencia (judicial tribunal).

In 1578 the city of Panama, being a primary transshipment center for treasure and supplies to and from Spain's South Pacific-coast colonies, was chosen for a new mint, and minting had begun there by 1580. By late 1582 or 1583 production was halted, possibly due to the fact that there were no nearby silver mines to sustain it. In it's brief operation, the Panama Mint must not have made many coins, as the corpus of surviving specimens known today from this colonial mint is less than 40.

The city of Panama, known today as the Old City of Panama, was sacked and burned in 1671 by the famous Henry Morgan in one of the greatest pirate victories against the Spanish Main.

Panama declared its independence in 1821 and joined the Confederation of Greater Colombia. In 1903, after Colombia rejected a treaty enabling the United States to build a canal across the Isthmus, Panama with the support of the United States proclaimed its independence from Colombia and became a sovereign republic.

The 1904 2-1/2 centesimos known as the 'Panama Pill' or 'Panama Pearl' is one of the world's smaller silver coins and a favorite with collectors.

MINT MARKS

FM - Franklin Mint, U.S.A.*
CHI in circle - Valcambi Mint, Balerna, Switzerland
RCM – Royal Canadian Mint

***NOTE:** From 1975-1985 the Franklin Mint produced coinage in up to 3 different qualities. Qualities of issue are designated in ( ) after each date and are defined as follows:

(M) MATTE - Normal circulation strike or a dull finish produced by sandblasting special uncirculated (polish finish) or proof quality dies.

(U) SPECIAL UNCIRCULATED - Polished or proof-like in appearance without any frosted features.

(P) PROOF - The highest quality obtainable having mirror-like fields and frosted features.

MONETARY SYSTEM

100 Centesimos = 1 Balboa

REPUBLIC

DECIMAL COINAGE

KM# 6 1/2 CENTESIMO

Copper-Nickel, 16 mm. **Obv:** Bust left **Rev:** Written value **Note:** Previously listed re-engraved overdates were struck from very common doubled dies. The plain date in unc. is scarcer.

Date	Mintage	F	VF	XF	Unc	BU
1907	1,000,000	1.50	2.50	3.50	10.00	15.00
1907 Proof	—	Value: 200				

KM# 14 CENTESIMO

Bronze, 19.05 mm. **Subject:** Uracca **Obv:** Written value above sprigs **Rev:** Bust with headcovering left

Date	Mintage	F	VF	XF	Unc	BU
1935	200,000	3.00	6.00	15.00	35.00	60.00
1937	200,000	2.00	4.00	10.00	25.00	50.00

KM# 17 CENTESIMO

Bronze, 19.05 mm. **Subject:** 50th Anniversary of the Republic **Obv:** Written value above sprigs **Rev:** Bust with headcovering left

Date	Mintage	F	VF	XF	Unc	BU
1953	1,500,000	0.10	0.50	1.00	4.00	7.00

KM# 22 CENTESIMO

Bronze, 19.05 mm. **Obv:** Written value above sprigs with stars above **Obv. Legend:** Bust with headcovering left **Note:** Varieties exist.

Date	Mintage	F	VF	XF	Unc	BU
1961	2,500,000	—	0.25	0.50	2.50	3.00
1962	2,000,000	—	0.25	0.50	2.00	3.00
1962 Proof	Est. 50	Value: 200				
1966	3,000,000	—	0.25	0.50	2.00	2.50
1966 Proof	13,000	Value: 1.00				
1967	7,600,000	—	0.25	0.50	2.00	2.50
1967 Proof	20,000	Value: 1.00				
1968	25,000,000	—	0.25	0.50	2.00	2.50
1968 Proof	23,000	Value: 2.00				
1969 Proof	14,000	Value: 2.00				
1970 Proof	9,528	Value: 2.00				
1971 Proof	11,000	Value: 2.00				
1972 Proof	13,000	Value: 2.00				
1973 Proof	17,000	Value: 2.00				
1974	Est. 10,000,000	—	0.10	0.25	1.00	1.50
Note: The 1974 circulation coins were stuck at West Point, NY.						
1974 Proof	Est. 18,000	Value: 2.00				
Note: The 1974 proof coins were struck at San Francisco						
1975	10,000,000	—	0.15	0.35	1.50	2.50
1977	10,000,000	—	0.15	0.35	1.50	2.00
1978	10,000,000	—	0.15	0.35	1.50	2.00
1979	10,000,000	—	0.15	0.35	1.50	2.00
1980	20,500,000	—	0.15	0.35	1.50	2.00
1982	20,000,000	—	0.25	0.50	2.00	3.50
1983FM (P)	—	Value: 2.00				
1983	5,000,000	—	0.25	0.50	2.00	3.50
1984FM (P)	—	Value: 2.00				
1985FM (P)	—	Value: 2.00				
Note: Unauthorized striking						
1986	20,000,000	—	0.25	0.50	2.00	3.50
1987	20,000,000	—	0.25	0.50	2.00	3.50

KM# 33.1 CENTESIMO

2.5000 g., Copper Coated Zinc, 19.05 mm. **Obv:** National arms **Rev:** Covered head 1/4 left **Note:** Medal rotation.

Date	Mintage	F	VF	XF	Unc	BU
1975 (RCM)	500,000	—	0.10	0.20	1.00	2.00
1975FM (M)	125,000	—	0.10	0.25	1.00	2.00
1975FM (U)	1,410	—	—	—	3.00	5.00
1975FM (P)	41,000	Value: 2.00				
1976 (RCM)	50,000	—	0.10	0.20	1.00	2.00
1976FM (M)	63,000	—	0.10	0.20	1.00	2.00
1976FM (P)	12,000	Value: 2.00				
1977FM (U)	63,000	—	0.10	0.20	1.00	2.00
1977FM (P)	9,548	Value: 2.00				
1979FM (U)	20,000	—	0.10	0.25	1.00	2.00
1979FM (P)	5,949	Value: 2.00				
1980FM (U)	40,000	—	0.10	0.25	1.00	2.00
1981FM (P)	1,973	Value: 2.00				
1982FM (U)	5,000	—	0.75	1.50	3.50	5.00
1982FM (P)	1,480	Value: 2.00				

KM# 33.2 CENTESIMO

2.5000 g., Copper Coated Zinc, 19.05 mm. **Edge Lettering:** 1830 BOLIVAR 1980

Date	Mintage	F	VF	XF	Unc	BU
1980FM (P)	2,629	Value: 2.00				

KM# 45 CENTESIMO

2.5000 g., Copper Coated Zinc, 19.05 mm. **Subject:** 75th Anniversary of Independence **Obv:** National coat of arms **Rev:** Covered head 1/4 left **Note:** Medal rotation.

Date	Mintage	F	VF	XF	Unc	BU
1978FM (U)	50,000	—	0.10	0.25	1.00	2.00
1978FM (P)	11,000	Value: 3.00				

KM# 22a CENTESIMO

2.5000 g., Copper Coated Zinc, 19.05 mm. **Obv:** Value above sprigs with stars above **Rev:** Covered head left

Date	Mintage	F	VF	XF	Unc	BU
1983	45,000,000	—	0.25	1.00	2.00	3.50

KM# 124 CENTESIMO

2.5000 g., Copper Plated Zinc, 19.05 mm. **Obv:** Written value **Rev:** Covered head 1/4 left

Date	Mintage	F	VF	XF	Unc	BU
1991	—	—	—	—	1.00	2.00
1993	30,000,000	—	—	—	1.00	2.00

KM# 125 CENTESIMO

2.5000 g., Copper Plated Zinc, 19.05 mm. **Obv:** Written value **Rev:** Covered head left

Date	Mintage	F	VF	XF	Unc	BU
1996 (RCM)	180,000,000	—	—	—	0.50	1.00

KM# 132 CENTESIMO

1.6400 g., Aluminum, 22.8 mm. **Series:** F.A.O. **Subject:** XXI Century F.A.O. Food Security **Obv:** National coat of arms **Rev:** Ship in canal **Edge:** Plain **Note:** Medal rotation.

Date	Mintage	F	VF	XF	Unc	BU
2000	—	—	—	—	3.50	5.00

KM# 15 1-1/4 CENTESIMOS

Bronze **Obv:** Written value **Rev:** Uniformed bust left

Date	Mintage	F	VF	XF	Unc	BU
1940	1,600,000	0.45	1.25	2.50	10.00	15.00

KM# 1 2-1/2 CENTESIMOS

1.2500 g., 0.9000 Silver .0362 oz. ASW **Obv:** Uniformed bust left **Rev:** National arms **Note:** This coin is popularly referred to as the "Panama Pill."

Date	Mintage	F	VF	XF	Unc	BU
1904	400,000	8.00	12.00	18.00	25.00	35.00

KM# 7.1 2-1/2 CENTESIMOS

Copper-Nickel **Obv:** National coat of arms **Rev:** Value above stars **Rev. Legend:** DOS Y MEDIOS

Date	Mintage	F	VF	XF	Unc	BU
1907	800,000	1.25	4.00	18.00	50.00	75.00

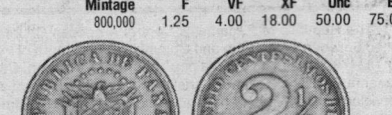

KM# 7.2 2-1/2 CENTESIMOS

Copper-Nickel **Obv:** National coat of arms **Rev:** Value above stars **Rev. Legend:** DOS Y MEDIO

Date	Mintage	F	VF	XF	Unc	BU
1916	800,000	2.50	6.00	35.00	70.00	125
1918 7 Known	—	—	1,800	3,000	—	—

Note: Unauthorized issue, 1 million pieces were struck and nearly all were melted in June 1918.

KM# 8 2-1/2 CENTESIMOS

Copper-Nickel **Obv:** Uniformed bust left **Rev:** Written value

Date	Mintage	F	VF	XF	Unc	BU
1929	1,000,000	2.00	3.50	40.00	145	200
1929 Proof	—	—	—	—	—	—

KM# 16 2-1/2 CENTESIMOS

Copper-Nickel **Obv:** Uniformed bust left **Rev:** Written value

Date	Mintage	F	VF	XF	Unc	BU
1940	1,200,000	1.00	1.25	2.50	15.00	25.00

KM# 32 2-1/2 CENTESIMOS

Copper-Nickel Clad Copper, 15 mm. **Series:** F.A.O. **Obv:** National coat of arms **Rev:** Hand holding leafy plant flanked by stars below **Designer:** Frank Gasparro

Date	Mintage	F	VF	XF	Unc	BU
1973	2,000,000	—	0.10	0.15	0.25	0.50
1975	1,000,000	—	0.25	0.50	1.00	2.00

KM# 34.1 2-1/2 CENTESIMOS

Copper-Nickel Clad Copper, 10 mm. **Subject:** Victoriano Lorenzo **Obv:** National coat of arms **Rev:** Head facing **Note:** Medal rotation.

Date	Mintage	F	VF	XF	Unc	BU
1975 (RCM)	40,000	—	0.75	1.00	2.00	2.50
1975FM (M)	50,000	—	0.75	1.00	2.00	2.50
1975FM (U)	1,410	—	1.50	2.50	3.50	4.00
1975FM (P)	41,000	Value: 2.00				
1976 (RCM)	20,000	—	0.75	1.00	2.25	3.00
1976FM (M)	25,000	—	0.75	1.00	3.00	5.00
1976FM (P)	24,000	Value: 2.00				
1977FM (U)	25,000	—	0.75	1.00	2.50	3.00
1977FM (P)	9,548	Value: 2.00				
1979FM (U)	12,000	—	0.75	1.00	2.50	3.00
1979FM (P)	5,949	Value: 2.00				
1980FM (U)	40,000	—	0.75	1.00	2.00	3.00
1981FM (P)	1,973	Value: 3.00				
1982FM (U)	2,000	—	1.50	2.50	5.00	7.00
1982FM (P)	1,480	Value: 5.00				

KM# 34.2 2-1/2 CENTESIMOS

Copper-Nickel Clad Copper, 10 mm. **Edge Lettering:** 1830 BOLIVAR 1980

Date	Mintage	F	VF	XF	Unc	BU
1980FM (P)	2,629	Value: 3.00				

KM# 46 2-1/2 CENTESIMOS

Copper-Nickel Clad Copper, 10 mm. **Subject:** 75th Anniversary of Independence **Obv:** National coat of arms **Rev:** Head facing **Note:** Medal rotation.

Date	Mintage	F	VF	XF	Unc	BU
1978FM (U)	40,000	—	0.50	1.00	2.50	3.00
1978FM (P)	11,000	Value: 2.50				

KM# 85 2-1/2 CENTESIMOS

Copper-Nickel Clad Copper, 10 mm. **Subject:** Victoriano Lorenzo **Obv:** National coat of arms **Rev:** Head facing

Date	Mintage	F	VF	XF	Unc	BU
1983FM (P)	—	Value: 5.00				
1984FM (P)	—	Value: 5.00				
1985FM (P)	—	Value: 5.00				

Note: Unauthorized striking

KM# 2 5 CENTESIMOS

2.5000 g., 0.9000 Silver .0723 oz. ASW **Obv:** Uniformed bust left **Rev:** National coat of arms

Date	Mintage	F	VF	XF	Unc	BU
1904	1,500,000	4.00	6.00	12.00	35.00	60.00
1904 Proof	12	Value: 1,500				
1916	100,000	85.00	120	185	300	400

KM# 9 5 CENTESIMOS

5.0000 g., Copper-Nickel, 21.2 mm. **Obv:** National coat of arms **Rev:** Numeric value

Date	Mintage	F	VF	XF	Unc	BU
1929	500,000	2.50	6.00	15.00	75.00	100
1932	332,000	3.00	7.00	20.00	100	120

KM# 23.1 5 CENTESIMOS

5.0000 g., Copper-Nickel, 21.2 mm. **Obv:** National coat of arms **Rev:** Numeric value

Date	Mintage	F	VF	XF	Unc	BU
1961	1,000,000	—	0.50	1.00	2.50	3.00

KM# 23.2 5 CENTESIMOS

5.0000 g., Copper-Nickel, 21.2 mm. **Obv:** National coat of arms **Rev:** Numeric value **Note:** The 1962 & 1966 Royal Mint strikes are normally sharper in detail. The stars on the reverse above the eagle are flat while previous dates are raised. Varieties exist.

Date	Mintage	F	VF	XF	Unc	BU
1962	2,600,000	—	0.25	0.50	2.00	3.00
1962 Proof	Est. 25	Value: 350				
1966	4,900,000	—	0.15	0.35	2.00	2.50
1966 Proof	13,000	Value: 1.00				
1967	2,600,000	—	0.25	0.50	2.25	3.00
1967 Proof	20,000	Value: 1.00				
1968	6,000,000	—	0.10	0.20	2.00	2.50
1968 Proof	23,000	Value: 1.00				
1969 Proof	14,000	Value: 1.00				
1970	5,000,000	—	0.10	0.20	2.00	2.50
1970 Proof	9,528	Value: 1.00				
1971 Proof	11,000	Value: 1.00				
1972 Proof	13,000	Value: 1.00				
1973	5,000,000	—	0.10	0.20	2.00	3.00
1973 Proof	17,000	Value: 1.00				
1974 Proof	19,000	Value: 1.00				

Date	Mintage	F	VF	XF	Unc	BU
1975	5,000,000	—	0.10	0.35	2.50	3.00
1982	8,000,000	—	0.10	0.35	2.50	3.00
1983	7,500,000	—	0.10	0.35	2.50	3.00
1993	6,000,000	—	0.10	0.25	2.00	2.50
1993 Proof	—	Value: 250				

Note: The 1993 proof strike was not authorized by the Panamanian government

KM# 35.1 5 CENTESIMOS

5.0000 g., Copper-Nickel Clad Copper, 21.2 mm.
Subject: Carlos J. Finlay **Obv:** National coat of arms **Rev:** Head 1/4 left **Note:** Medal rotation.

Date	Mintage	F	VF	XF	Unc	BU
1975 (RCM)	80,000	—	0.15	0.40	1.00	2.00
1975FM (M)	15,000	—	0.25	0.50	1.25	3.00
1975FM (U)	1,410	—	—	—	2.50	5.00
1975FM (P)	41,000	Value: 1.00				
1976 (RCM)	20,000	—	0.25	0.50	1.50	3.50
1976FM (M)	13,000	—	0.25	0.50	1.50	3.50
1976FM (P)	12,000	Value: 1.00				
1977FM (U)	13,000	—	0.25	0.50	1.50	3.50
1977FM (P)	9,548	Value: 1.00				
1979FM (U)	12,000	—	0.25	0.50	1.50	3.50
1979FM (P)	5,949	Value: 1.00				
1980FM (U)	43,000	—	0.25	0.50	1.50	3.00
1981FM (P)	1,973	Value: 2.50				
1982FM (U)	3,000	—	7.50	10.00	15.00	20.00
1982FM (P)	1,480	Value: 2.50				

KM# 35.2 5 CENTESIMOS

5.0000 g., Copper-Nickel Clad Copper, 21.2 mm. **Obv:** National coat of arms **Rev:** Head 1/4 left **Edge Lettering:** 1830 BOLIVAR 1980 **Note:** Medal rotation.

Date	Mintage	F	VF	XF	Unc	BU
1980FM (P)	2,629	Value: 1.50				

KM# 47 5 CENTESIMOS

5.0000 g., Copper-Nickel Clad Copper, 21.2 mm. **Subject:** 75th Anniversary of Independence **Obv:** National coat of arms **Rev:** Head 1/4 left **Note:** Medal rotation.

Date	Mintage	F	VF	XF	Unc	BU
1978FM (U)	30,000	—	0.25	0.50	1.00	3.00
1978FM (P)	11,000	Value: 1.00				

KM# 86 5 CENTESIMOS

5.0000 g., Copper-Nickel Clad Copper, 21.2 mm. **Obv:** National coat of arms **Rev:** Numeric value

Date	Mintage	F	VF	XF	Unc	BU
1983FM (P)	—	Value: 2.50				
1984FM (P)	—	Value: 2.50				
1985FM (P)	—	Value: 3.50				

Note: Unauthorized striking

KM# 126 5 CENTESIMOS

5.0000 g., Copper-Nickel, 21.2 mm. **Obv:** National coat of arms **Rev. Legend:** Numeric value

Date	Mintage	F	VF	XF	Unc	BU
1996	4,000,000	—	—	—	0.40	0.50

KM# 3 10 CENTESIMOS

5.0000 g., 0.9000 Silver .1447 oz. ASW **Obv:** Armored bust left **Rev:** National coat of arms

Date	Mintage	F	VF	XF	Unc	BU
1904	1,100,000	3.50	10.00	25.00	85.00	125
1904 Proof	12	Value: 1,500				

KM# 36.1 10 CENTESIMOS

2.2500 g., Copper-Nickel Clad Copper, 17.9 mm.
Subject: Manuel E. Amador **Obv:** National coat of arms **Rev:** Head 1/4 right **Note:** Medal rotation.

Date	Mintage	F	VF	XF	Unc	BU
1975 (RCM)	50,000	—	0.25	0.50	1.00	2.00
1975FM (M)	13,000	—	0.25	0.50	1.50	3.00
1975FM (U)	1,410	—	—	—	2.50	5.00
1975FM (P)	41,000	Value: 1.00				
1976 (RCM)	20,000	—	0.25	1.00	1.50	2.50
1976FM (M)	6,250	—	1.00	1.50	3.00	5.00
1976FM (P)	12,000	Value: 1.50				
1977FM (U)	6,250	—	1.00	1.50	5.00	7.50
1977FM (P)	9,548	Value: 1.50				
1979FM (U)	10,000	—	0.75	1.25	3.50	6.50
1979FM (P)	5,949	Value: 2.00				
1980FM (U)	40,000	—	0.50	1.00	3.50	6.50
1981FM (P)	1,973	Value: 2.50				
1982FM (U)	2,500	—	1.00	2.00	5.00	7.50
1982FM (P)	1,480	Value: 2.50				

KM# 36.2 10 CENTESIMOS

Copper-Nickel Clad Copper, 17.9 mm. **Obv:** National coat of arms **Rev:** Head 1/4 right **Edge Lettering:** 1830 BOLIVAR 1980 **Note:** Medal rotation.

Date	Mintage	F	VF	XF	Unc	BU
1980 FM (P)	2,629	Value: 2.50				

KM# 48 10 CENTESIMOS

2.2500 g., Copper-Nickel Clad Copper, 17.9 mm. **Subject:** 75th Anniversary of Independence **Obv:** National coat of arms **Rev:** Bust 1/4 right **Note:** Medal rotation.

Date	Mintage	F	VF	XF	Unc	BU
1978 FM (U)	20,000	—	0.25	0.50	1.50	3.00
1978 FM (P)	11,000	Value: 1.50				

KM# 10.1 1/10 BALBOA

2.5000 g., 0.9000 Silver .0723 oz. ASW, 17.9 mm. **Obv:** National coat of arms **Rev:** Armored bust left **Note:** High relief.

Date	Mintage	F	VF	XF	Unc	BU
1930	500,000	1.50	3.50	7.00	35.00	60.00
1930 Matte proof	20	—	—	—	1,000	—
1931	200,000	3.00	6.00	20.00	90.00	120
1932	150,000	4.00	8.00	20.00	100	150
1933	100,000	10.00	25.00	60.00	175	275
1934	75,000	12.00	30.00	60.00	200	300
1947	1,000,000	1.25	3.00	5.00	20.00	25.00

KM# 10.2 1/10 BALBOA

2.5000 g., 0.9000 Silver .0723 oz. ASW, 17.9 mm. **Obv:** National coat of arms **Rev:** Armored bust left **Note:** Low relief.

Date	Mintage	F	VF	XF	Unc	BU
1962	5,000,000	—	BV	1.25	3.00	4.50
1962 Proof	Est. 25	Value: 500				

KM# 18 1/10 BALBOA

2.5000 g., 0.9000 Silver .0723 oz. ASW, 17.9 mm.
Subject: 50th Anniversary of the Republic **Obv:** National coat of arms **Rev:** Armored bust left

Date	Mintage	F	VF	XF	Unc	BU
1953	3,300,000	—	BV	1.50	6.00	10.00

KM# 24 1/10 BALBOA

2.5000 g., 0.9000 Silver .0723 oz. ASW, 17.9 mm.
Obv: National coat of arms **Rev:** Armored bust left

Date	Mintage	F	VF	XF	Unc	BU
1961	2,500,000	—	BV	1.50	3.50	5.00

KM# 10a 1/10 BALBOA

2.2500 g., Copper-Nickel Clad Copper, 17.9 mm. **Obv:** National coat of arms **Rev:** Armored bust left

Date	Mintage	F	VF	XF	Unc	BU
1966 Type 1	6,955,000	—	0.75	1.00	3.00	3.50

Note: The Type I is similar to the 1962 strike on a thick flan (London) with diamonds on both sides of DE

Date	Mintage	F	VF	XF	Unc	BU
1966 Type 2	1,000,000	—	1.25	3.50	10.00	15.00

Note: The Type II strike similar to the 1947 strikes on a thin flan (U.S.) with elongated diamonds on both sides of DE

Date	Mintage	F	VF	XF	Unc	BU
1966	6,955,000	—	0.50	0.85	3.00	3.50

Note: The Type I variety is similar to the 1962 strike (London) on a thick flan with diamonds on both sides of DE

Date	Mintage	F	VF	XF	Unc	BU
1966	1,000,000	—	0.75	2.00	10.00	15.00

Note: The Type II variety is similar to the 1947 strike (U.S.) on a thin flan with elongated diamonds on both sides of DE

Date	Mintage	F	VF	XF	Unc	BU
1966 Proof	13,000	Value: 1.00				

Note: Thick and thin planchets

Date	Mintage	F	VF	XF	Unc	BU
1967 Proof	20,000	Value: 1.00				
1968	5,000,000	—	0.20	0.30	2.00	2.50
1968 Proof	23,000	Value: 1.00				
1969 Proof	14,000	Value: 1.00				
1970	7,500,000	—	0.15	0.25	1.00	2.00
1970 Proof	9,528	Value: 1.00				
1971 Proof	11,000	Value: 1.00				
1972 Proof	13,000	Value: 1.00				
1973	10,000,000	—	0.15	0.20	2.00	2.50
1973 Proof	17,000	Value: 1.00				
1974 Proof	18,000	Value: 1.00				
1975	500,000	—	0.25	0.50	2.50	3.50
1980	5,000,000	—	0.20	0.50	2.50	3.50
1982	7,740,000	—	0.25	0.50	2.50	3.50
1983 (RCM)	7,750,000	—	0.25	0.50	2.50	3.50
1986 (RCM)	1,000,000	—	0.25	0.50	2.50	3.50
1993	7,000,000	—	0.15	0.50	1.00	2.50
1993 Proof	—	Value: 300				

Note: Unauthorized striking

KM# 87 1/10 BALBOA

2.2500 g., Copper-Nickel Clad Copper, 17.9 mm. **Obv:** National coat of arms **Rev:** Armored bust left **Note:** Medal rotation.

Date	Mintage	F	VF	XF	Unc	BU
1983FM (P)	—	Value: 3.00				
1984FM (P)	—	Value: 3.00				
1985FM (P)	—	Value: 5.00				

Note: Unauthorized striking

KM# 127 1/10 BALBOA

2.2500 g., Copper-Nickel Clad Copper, 17.9 mm. **Obv:** National coat of arms **Rev:** Armored bust left

Date	Mintage	F	VF	XF	Unc	BU
1996	21,000,000	—	—	—	0.50	0.75

KM# 4 25 CENTESIMOS

12.5000 g., 0.9000 Silver .3617 oz. ASW **Obv:** Armored bust left **Rev:** National coat of arms

Date	Mintage	F	VF	XF	Unc	BU
1904	16,000,000	6.00	12.50	40.00	120	150
1904 Proof	12	Value: 2,500				

KM# 37.1 25 CENTESIMOS

5.6500 g., Copper-Nickel Clad Copper, 24.25 mm. **Obv:** National coat of arms **Rev:** Head 1/4 left **Note:** Medal rotation.

Date	Mintage	F	VF	XF	Unc	BU
1975 (RCM)	40,000	—	0.35	0.50	1.00	1.50
1975FM (M)	5,000	—	1.00	2.00	4.00	5.00
1975FM (U)	1,410	—	—	—	4.00	5.00
1975FM (P)	41,000	Value: 1.50				
1976 (RCM)	12,000	—	0.45	0.60	1.50	2.00
1976FM (M)	2,500	—	0.75	1.50	3.00	4.00
1976FM (P)	12,000	Value: 1.50				
1977FM (U)	2,500	—	0.75	1.50	3.50	6.50
1977FM (P)	9,548	Value: 1.50				
1979FM (U)	4,000	—	1.00	1.50	5.00	7.50
1979FM (P)	5,949	Value: 1.50				
1980FM (U)	4,000	—	1.00	2.00	4.00	6.50
1981FM (P)	1,973	Value: 2.00				
1982FM (U)	2,000	—	1.50	2.50	5.00	7.50
1982FM (P)	1,480	Value: 2.00				

KM# 37.2 25 CENTESIMOS

5.6500 g., Copper-Nickel Clad Copper, 24.25 mm. **Edge Lettering:** 1830 BOLIVAR 1980

Date	Mintage	F	VF	XF	Unc	BU
1980 FM (P)	2,629	Value: 2.00				

KM# 49 25 CENTESIMOS

5.6500 g., Copper-Nickel Clad Copper, 24.25 mm. **Subject:** 75th Anniversary of Independence **Obv:** National coat of arms **Rev:** Head 1/4 left **Note:** Medal rotation.

Date	Mintage	F	VF	XF	Unc	BU
1978 FM (U)	8,000	—	0.75	1.25	2.50	3.00
1978 FM (P)	11,000	Value: 2.00				
1978 FM (P)	11,000	Value: 2.00				

KM# 11.1 1/4 BALBOA

6.2500 g., 0.9000 Silver .1809 oz. ASW, 24.25 mm. **Obv:** National coat of arms **Rev:** Armored bust left

Date	Mintage	F	VF	XF	Unc	BU
1930	400,000	BV	3.00	25.00	50.00	85.00
1930 Matte proof	20	—	—	—	2,000	—
1931	48,000	15.00	70.00	350	1,100	2,000
1932	126,000	3.00	6.00	60.00	350	650
1933	120,000	3.00	5.00	35.00	250	350
1934	90,000	3.00	5.00	25.00	150	300
1947	700,000	BV	2.75	5.00	25.00	50.00

KM# 11.2 1/4 BALBOA

6.2500 g., 0.9000 Silver .1809 oz. ASW, 24.25 mm. **Obv:** National coat of arms **Rev:** Armored bust left **Note:** Low relief.

Date	Mintage	F	VF	XF	Unc	BU
1962	4,000,000	—	—	BV	4.00	5.00
1962 Proof	25	Value: 500				

KM# 19 1/4 BALBOA

6.2500 g., 0.9000 Silver .1809 oz. ASW, 24.25 mm. **Obv:** National coat of arms **Rev:** Armored bust left

Date	Mintage	F	VF	XF	Unc	BU
1953	1,200,000	—	BV	3.50	15.00	30.00
1953 Proof	Est. 5	Value: 1,350				

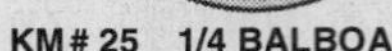

KM# 25 1/4 BALBOA

6.2500 g., 0.9000 Silver .1809 oz. ASW, 24.25 mm. **Obv:** National coat of arms **Rev:** Armored bust left

Date	Mintage	F	VF	XF	Unc	BU
1961	2,000,000	—	BV	2.75	4.00	6.00

KM# 11a 1/4 BALBOA

5.6500 g., Copper-Nickel Clad Copper, 24.25 mm. **Obv:** National coat of arms **Rev:** Armored bust left **Note:** Varieties exist.

Date	Mintage	F	VF	XF	Unc	BU
1966 (RCM)	7,400,000	—	0.35	0.50	1.50	2.50
1966 (RCM) Proof	13,000	Value: 2.00				
1967 Proof	20,000	Value: 1.50				
1968	1,200,000	—	0.35	0.60	2.00	2.50
1968 Proof	23,000	Value: 1.50				
1969 Proof	14,000	Value: 1.50				
1970	2,000,000	—	0.35	0.60	1.25	2.00
1970 Proof	9,528	Value: 2.00				
1971 Proof	11,000	Value: 2.00				
1972 Proof	13,000	Value: 2.00				
1973	800,000	—	0.40	1.00	2.00	2.50
1973 Proof	17,000	Value: 2.00				
1974 Proof	18,000	Value: 2.00				
1975	1,500,000	—	0.35	0.50	2.00	5.00
1979	2,000,000	—	0.25	0.45	3.00	5.00
1980	2,000,000	—	0.25	0.45	3.50	5.00
1982	3,000,000	—	0.25	0.45	3.50	5.00
1983 (RCM)	6,000,000	—	0.25	0.45	3.50	5.00
1986 (RCM)	3,000,000	—	0.25	0.50	3.50	5.00
1993	4,000,000	—	0.25	0.45	3.00	5.00
1993 Proof	—	Value: 350				

Note: The 1993 Proof strikes were not authorized by the Panamanian government

KM# 88 1/4 BALBOA

5.6500 g., Copper-Nickel Clad Copper, 24.25 mm. **Obv:** National coat of arms **Rev:** Armored bust left **Note:** Medal rotation

Date	Mintage	F	VF	XF	Unc	BU
1983FM (P)	—	Value: 4.00				
1984FM (P)	—	Value: 4.00				
1985FM (P)	—	Value: 7.50				

Note: Unauthorized striking

KM# 128 1/4 BALBOA

5.6500 g., Copper-Nickel Clad Copper, 24.25 mm. **Obv:** National coat of arms **Rev:** Armored bust left

Date	Mintage	F	VF	XF	Unc	BU
1996	7,200,000	—	—	—	1.00	1.50

KM# 5 50 CENTESIMOS

25.0000 g., 0.9000 Silver .7235 oz. ASW **Obv:** Armored bust left **Rev:** National coat of arms

Date	Mintage	F	VF	XF	Unc	BU
1904	1,800,000	30.00	60.00	125	250	300
1904 Proof	12	Value: 5,000				
1905	1,000,000	45.00	85.00	250	400	600

Note: 1,000,000 of both 1904 and 1905 dates were melted in 1931 for the metal to issue 1 Balboa coin at San Francisco Mint

KM# 38.1 50 CENTESIMOS

11.3000 g., Copper-Nickel Clad Copper, 30.6 mm. **Subject:** Fernando de Lesseps **Obv:** National coat of arms **Rev:** Head 1/4 right **Note:** Medal rotation.

Date	Mintage	F	VF	XF	Unc	BU
1975 (RCM)	20,000	—	1.00	1.50	2.00	3.00
1975FM (M)	2,000	—	1.50	3.00	5.00	7.00
1975FM (U)	1,410	—	—	—	6.50	8.00
1975FM (P)	41,000	Value: 2.00				
1976 (RCM)	12,000	—	1.25	2.00	4.00	6.00
1976FM (M)	1,250	—	3.00	5.00	11.50	15.00
1976FM (P)	12,000	Value: 2.50				
1977FM (U)	1,250	—	3.00	5.00	11.50	15.00
1977FM (P)	9,548	Value: 2.50				
1979FM (U)	2,000	—	3.00	5.00	11.50	15.00
1979FM (P)	5,949	Value: 3.00				
1980FM (U)	2,000	—	3.00	5.00	11.50	15.00
1981FM (P)	1,973	Value: 5.00				
1982FM (U)	1,000	—	4.00	7.50	15.00	20.00
1982FM (P)	1,480	Value: 5.00				

Note: (Error) Without edge lettering

KM# 38.2 50 CENTESIMOS

11.3000 g., Copper-Nickel Clad Copper, 30.6 mm. **Obv:** National coat of arms **Rev:** Head 1/4 right **Edge Lettering:** 1830 BOLIVAR 1980 **Note:** Medal rotation.

Date	Mintage	F	VF	XF	Unc	BU
1980 FM (P)	2,629	Value: 5.00				
1980 Proof	Inc. above	Value: 135				

Note: (error) without edge lettering

KM# 50 50 CENTESIMOS

11.3000 g., Copper-Nickel Clad Copper, 30.6 mm. **Subject:** 75th Anniversary of Independence **Obv:** National coat of arms **Rev:** Bust 1/4 right **Note:** Medal rotation.

Date	Mintage	F	VF	XF	Unc	BU
1978FM (U)	8,000	—	1.50	3.00	5.00	8.00
1978FM (P)	11,000	Value: 5.00				

KM# 12.1 1/2 BALBOA
12.5000 g., 0.9000 Silver .3617 oz. ASW, 30.6 mm.
Obv: National coat of arms **Rev:** Armored bust left
Rev. Designer: William Clark Noble **Note:** High relief.

Date	Mintage	F	VF	XF	Unc	BU
1930	300,000	BV	9.00	35.00	90.00	120
1930 Matte proof	20	Value: 2,200				
1932	63,000	6.50	15.00	120	400	850
1933	120,000	5.50	10.00	60.00	300	500
1934	90,000	5.50	10.00	60.00	300	400
1947	450,000	BV	5.50	12.00	45.00	60.00

KM# 12.2 1/2 BALBOA
12.5000 g., 0.9000 Silver .3617 oz. ASW, 30.6 mm. **Obv:** National coat of arms **Rev:** Armored bust left **Note:** Low relief.

Date	Mintage	F	VF	XF	Unc	BU
1962	700,000	—	BV	5.50	7.50	10.00
1962 Proof	25	Value: 750				

KM# 20 1/2 BALBOA
12.5000 g., 0.9000 Silver .3617 oz. ASW, 30.6 mm.
Obv: National coat of arms **Rev:** Armored bust left

Date	Mintage	F	VF	XF	Unc	BU
1953	600,000	—	BV	6.50	12.00	20.00
1953 Proof	Est. 5	Value: 1,850				

KM# 26 1/2 BALBOA
12.5000 g., 0.9000 Silver .3617 oz. ASW, 30.6 mm.
Obv: National coat of arms **Rev:** Armored bust left

Date	Mintage	F	VF	XF	Unc	BU
1961	350,000	—	BV	6.00	10.00	12.00

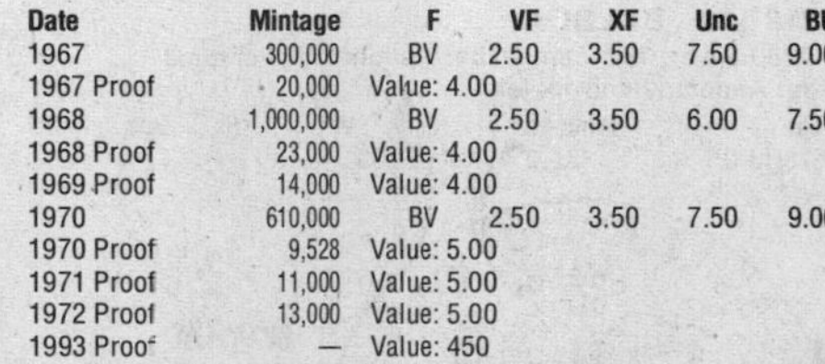

KM# 12a.1 1/2 BALBOA
12.5000 g., 0.4000 Silver Clad .1608 oz. ASW, 30.6 mm.
Obv: Normal helmet **Note:** Varieties exist.

Date	Mintage	F	VF	XF	Unc	BU
1966 (RCM)	1,000,000	BV	2.50	3.50	6.00	7.50
1966 (RCM) Proof	13,000	Value: 5.00				
1967	300,000	BV	2.50	3.50	7.50	9.00
1967 Proof	20,000	Value: 4.00				
1968	1,000,000	BV	2.50	3.50	6.00	7.50
1968 Proof	23,000	Value: 4.00				
1969 Proof	14,000	Value: 4.00				
1970	610,000	BV	2.50	3.50	7.50	9.00
1970 Proof	9,528	Value: 5.00				
1971 Proof	11,000	Value: 5.00				
1972 Proof	13,000	Value: 5.00				
1993 Proof	—	Value: 450				

Note: The 1993 Proof strike was not authorized by the Panamanian government

KM# 12a.2 1/2 BALBOA
12.5000 g., 0.4000 Silver Clad .1608 oz. ASW, 30.6 mm. **Obv:** National coat of arms **Rev:** Error: Type II helmet rim incomplete.

Date	Mintage	F	VF	XF	Unc	BU
1966	Inc. above	2.50	3.50	7.50	15.00	25.00

KM# 12b 1/2 BALBOA
11.3000 g., Copper-Nickel Clad Copper, 30.6 mm. **Obv:** National coat of arms **Rev:** Armored bust left **Note:** Varieties exist.

Date	Mintage	F	VF	XF	Unc	BU
1973	1,000,000	—	1.00	1.50	2.50	5.00
1973 Proof	17,000	Value: 2.00				
1974 Proof	18,000	Value: 2.00				
1975	1,200,000	—	0.75	1.50	2.50	5.00
1979	1,000,000	—	—	1.00	2.50	5.00
1980	400,000	—	—	1.00	2.50	5.00
1982	400,000	—	—	1.00	2.50	5.00
1983 (RCM)	1,850,000	—	—	1.00	2.50	5.00
1986 (RCM)	200,000	—	1.50	2.50	7.00	9.00
1993	600,000	—	0.75	1.25	2.00	—

KM# 89 1/2 BALBOA
11.3000 g., Copper-Nickel Clad Copper, 30.6 mm. **Obv:** National coat of arms **Rev:** Armored bust left **Note:** Medal rotation.

Date	Mintage	F	VF	XF	Unc	BU
1983FM (P)	—	Value: 6.00				
1984FM (P)	—	Value: 6.00				
1985FM (P)	—	Value: 12.50				

Note: Unauthorized striking

KM# 129 1/2 BALBOA
11.3000 g., Copper-Nickel Clad Copper, 30.6 mm.
Obv: National coat of arms **Rev:** Armored bust left

Date	Mintage	F	VF	XF	Unc	BU
1996	200,000	—	1.00	2.00	4.00	5.00

KM# 13 BALBOA
26.7300 g., 0.9000 Silver .7735 oz. ASW, 38.1 mm.
Subject: Vasco Nunez de Balboa **Obv:** Standing figure with arm on shield **Obv. Designer:** Roberto Lewis **Rev:** Armored bust left **Rev. Designer:** William Clark Noble

Date	Mintage	F	VF	XF	Unc	BU
1931	200,000	BV	12.00	20.00	75.00	100
1931 Proof	20	Value: 3,000				
1934	225,000	BV	11.50	18.50	50.00	80.00
1947	500,000	—	BV	11.50	15.00	20.00

KM# 21 BALBOA
26.7300 g., 0.9000 Silver .7735 oz. ASW, 38.1 mm.
Subject: 50th Anniversary of the Republic **Obv:** Standing figure with hand on shield **Rev:** Armored bust left

Date	Mintage	F	VF	XF	Unc	BU
1953	50,000	BV	11.50	15.00	30.00	40.00

KM# 27 BALBOA
26.7300 g., 0.9000 Silver .7735 oz. ASW, 38.1 mm.
Obv: National coat of arms **Rev:** Armored bust left **Note:** More than 200,000 of 1966 dates were melted down in 1971 for silver for the 20 Balboas. Varieties exist.

Date	Mintage	F	VF	XF	Unc	BU
1966 (RCM)	300,000	—	—	BV	12.00	13.50
1966 (RCM) Proof	13,000	Value: 16.50				
1967 Proof	20,000	Value: 14.00				
1968 Proof	23,000	Value: 14.00				
1969 Proof	14,000	Value: 14.00				
1970 Proof	13,000	Value: 16.50				
1971 Proof	18,000	Value: 15.00				
1972 Proof	10,081	Value: 18.00				
1973 Proof	30,000	Value: 14.00				
1974 Proof	30,000	Value: 14.00				

KM# 39.1 BALBOA

Copper-Nickel Clad Copper, 38.1 mm. **Obv:** National coat of arms **Rev:** Armored head 1/4 left

Date	Mintage	F	VF	XF	Unc	BU
1975FM (M)	4,035	—	—	—	15.00	20.00
1975FM (U)	1,410	—	—	—	35.00	40.00
1976FM (M)	625	—	—	—	80.00	100
1977FM (U)	625	—	—	—	80.00	100
1979FM (U)	1,000	—	—	—	60.00	75.00
1980FM (U)	1,000	—	—	—	60.00	75.00
1982FM (U)	500	—	—	—	80.00	100

KM# 39.1a BALBOA

26.7300 g., 0.9250 Silver .7950 oz. ASW, 38.1 mm. **Obv:** National coat of arms **Rev:** Armored head 1/4 left **Note:** Medal rotation.

Date	Mintage	F	VF	XF	Unc	BU
1975FM (P)	45,000	Value: 12.50				
1976FM (P)	14,000	Value: 13.50				
1977FM (P)	11,000	Value: 13.50				
1979FM (P)	7,160	Value: 20.00				

KM# 39.1b BALBOA

20.7400 g., 0.5000 Silver .3334 oz. ASW, 38.1 mm. **Obv:** National coat of arms **Rev:** Armored head 1/4 left

Date	Mintage	F	VF	XF	Unc	BU
1981FM (P)	2,633	Value: 20.00				
1982FM (P)	1,837	Value: 22.00				

KM# 39.2 BALBOA

Copper-Nickel Clad Copper, 38.1 mm. **Obv:** Erroneous silver content (LEY .925) below arms **Rev:** Armored head 1/4 left

Date	Mintage	F	VF	XF	Unc	BU
1975 (RCM)	10,000	—	—	—	8.00	10.00
1976 (RCM)	12,000	—	—	—	8.00	10.00

KM# 39.3 BALBOA

2.7400 g., 0.5000 Silver .3334 oz. ASW, 38.1 mm. **Obv:** National coat of arms **Rev:** Armored head 1/4 left **Edge Lettering:** 1830 BALBOA 1980

Date	Mintage	F	VF	XF	Unc	BU
1980FM (P)	2,629	Value: 20.00				

KM# 39.4 BALBOA

Copper-Nickel Clad Copper, 38.1 mm. **Obv:** Erroneous silver content (LEY .500) below arms **Rev:** Armored head 1/4 left

Date	Mintage	F	VF	XF	Unc	BU
1982FM (U)	11	—	—	—	500	—

KM# 51 BALBOA

Copper-Nickel Clad Copper, 38.1 mm. **Subject:** 75th Anniversary of Independence **Obv:** National coat of arms **Rev:** Armored head 1/4 left **Note:** Medal rotation.

Date	Mintage	F	VF	XF	Unc	BU
1978FM (U)	4,000	—	—	—	15.00	—

KM# 51a BALBOA

0.9250 Silver, 38.1 mm. **Obv:** National coat of arms **Rev:** Armored head 1/4 left

Date	Mintage	F	VF	XF	Unc	BU
1978FM (P)	13,000	Value: 20.00				

KM# 76 BALBOA

22.4000 g., Copper Nickel, 37.8 mm. **Subject:** Death of General Omar Torrijos **Obv:** National coat of arms **Rev:** Uniformed bust right

Date	Mintage	F	VF	XF	Unc	BU
1982	200,000	—	—	1.50	7.00	12.00
1982 Proof	200	Value: 150				
Note: Frosted obverse and reverse						
1982 Proof	50	Value: 225				
Note: Frosted obverse						
1983	200,000	—	—	1.50	7.00	15.00
1984	200,000	—	—	1.50	7.00	15.00

KM# 90 BALBOA

20.7400 g., 0.5000 Silver .3334 oz. ASW, 38.1 mm. **Obv:** National coat of arms **Rev:** Armored bust left

Date	Mintage	F	VF	XF	Unc	BU
1983FM (P)	1,602	Value: 30.00				
1984FM (P)	1,044	Value: 35.00				
1985FM (P)	954	Value: 50.00				

KM# 28 5 BALBOAS

35.7000 g., 0.9250 Silver 1.0617 oz. ASW, 39 mm. **Subject:** 11th Central American and Caribbean Games **Obv:** National coat of arms **Rev:** Discus thrower **Rev. Designer:** Gilroy Roberts **Note:** Medal rotation.

Date	Mintage	F	VF	XF	Unc	BU
1970FM	1,647,000	—	—	BV	16.00	17.50
1970FM (U)	603,000	—	—	—	16.50	18.50
1970FM (P)	59,000	Value: 20.00				

KM# 30 5 BALBOAS

35.0000 g., 0.9000 Silver 1.0128 oz. ASW, 38.8 mm. **Subject:** F.A.O. **Obv:** National coat of arms **Rev:** Hand holding leafy plant **Rev. Designer:** Frank Gasparo

Date	Mintage	F	VF	XF	Unc	BU
1972	70,000	—	—	BV	15.00	17.50
1972 Proof	10,000	Value: 30.00				

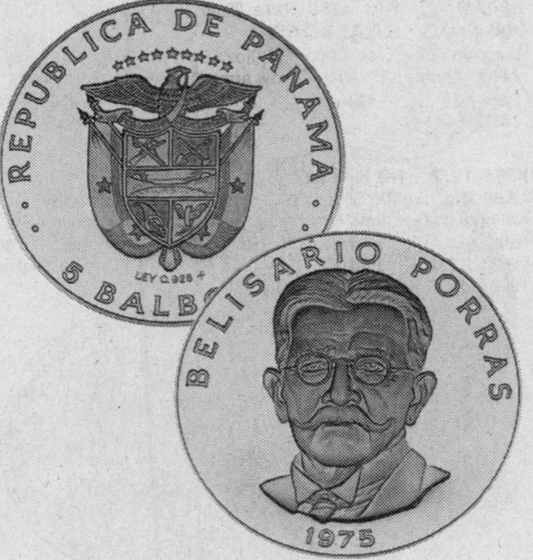

KM# 40.1 5 BALBOAS

Copper-Nickel Clad Copper, 39 mm. **Subject:** Belisario Porras **Obv:** National coat of arms **Rev:** Head facing **Note:** Medal rotation.

Date	Mintage	F	VF	XF	Unc	BU
1975FM (M)	5,125	—	—	—	12.00	15.00
1975FM (U)	1,410	—	—	—	20.00	30.00
1976FM (M)	125	—	—	—	175	200
1977FM (U)	125	—	—	—	175	200
1979FM (U)	1,000	—	—	—	25.00	30.00
1980FM (U)	1,000	—	—	—	25.00	30.00
1982FM (U)	1,200	—	—	—	20.00	30.00

KM# 40.1a 5 BALBOAS

35.1200 g., 0.9250 Silver 1.0446 oz. ASW, 39 mm. **Obv:** National coat of arms **Rev:** Head facing

Date	Mintage	F	VF	XF	Unc	BU
1975FM (P)	41,000	Value: 16.50				
1976FM (P)	12,000	Value: 16.50				
1977FM (P)	9,548	Value: 20.00				
1979FM (P)	5,949	Value: 30.00				

KM# 40.1b 5 BALBOAS

23.3300 g., 0.5000 Silver .3751 oz. ASW, 39 mm. **Obv:** National coat of arms **Rev:** Head facing **Note:** Medal rotation.

Date	Mintage	F	VF	XF	Unc	BU
1981FM (P)	1,973	Value: 30.00				
1982FM (P)	1,480	Value: 30.00				

KM# 40.2 5 BALBOAS

Copper-Nickel Clad Copper, 38.8 mm. **Obv:** Erroneous silver content (LEY .925) below arms **Rev:** Head facing

Date	Mintage	F	VF	XF	Unc	BU
1975	4,000	—	—	—	15.00	—
1976	5,000	—	—	—	15.00	—

KM# 40.3 5 BALBOAS

23.3300 g., 0.5000 Silver .3751 oz. ASW, 39 mm. **Obv:** National coat of arms **Rev:** Head facing **Edge Lettering:** 1830 BALBOA 1980

Date	Mintage	F	VF	XF	Unc	BU
1980FM (P)	2,629	Value: 20.00				

KM# 40.4 5 BALBOAS

23.3300 g., 0.5000 Silver .3751 oz. ASW, 39 mm. **Obv:** Erroneous silver content (LEY .925) below arms **Rev:** Head facing

Date	Mintage	F	VF	XF	Unc	BU
1982FM (P)	—	Value: 65.00				

KM# 58 5 BALBOAS

35.1200 g., 0.9250 Silver 1.0466 oz. ASW **Subject:** Panama Canal Treaty Implementation **Obv:** National coat of arms **Rev:** Flag

Date	Mintage	F	VF	XF	Unc	BU
1977 (P)	—	—	—	—	25.00	—
1979FM (P)	6,854	Value: 25.00				

KM# 40.5 5 BALBOAS

Copper-Nickel Clad Copper 500 oz., 39 mm. **Obv:** Erroneous silver content (LEY .500) below arms **Rev:** Head facing

Date	Mintage	F	VF	XF	Unc	BU
1982FM (U)	200	—	—	—	200	250

KM# 52 5 BALBOAS

Copper-Nickel Clad Copper **Subject:** 75th Anniversary of Independence **Obv:** National coat of arms **Rev:** Bust facing

Date	Mintage	F	VF	XF	Unc	BU
1978FM (U)	2,000	—	—	—	20.00	25.00

KM# 52a 5 BALBOAS

35.1200 g., 0.9250 Silver 1.0466 oz. ASW **Obv:** National coat of arms **Rev:** Bust facing

Date	Mintage	F	VF	XF	Unc	BU
1978FM (P)	11,000	Value: 25.00				

KM# 63 5 BALBOAS

24.1100 g., 0.5000 Silver .3875 oz. ASW **Subject:** Champions of Boxing **Obv:** National coat of arms **Rev:** Boxer and flag

Date	Mintage	F	VF	XF	Unc	BU
1980 Proof	1,261	Value: 45.00				

KM# 77 5 BALBOAS

24.1600 g., 0.9250 Silver .7186 oz. ASW **Subject:** Champions of Soccer **Obv:** National coat of arms **Rev:** Soccer ball and world globe

Date	Mintage	F	VF	XF	Unc	BU
1982 Proof	9,446	Value: 35.00				

KM# 91 5 BALBOAS

23.3300 g., 0.5000 Silver .3751 oz. ASW **Obv:** National coat of arms **Rev:** Armored bust left

Date	Mintage	F	VF	XF	Unc	BU
1983FM (P)	1,776	Value: 50.00				
1984FM (P)	889	Value: 65.00				

KM# 104 5 BALBOAS

23.3300 g., 0.5000 Silver .3751 oz. ASW **Subject:** Discovery of the Pacific Ocean

Date	Mintage	F	VF	XF	Unc	BU
1985FM (P)	765	Value: 150				

KM# 53 10 BALBOAS

42.4800 g., 0.9250 Silver 1.2635 oz. ASW, 45.6 mm. **Subject:** Panama Canal Treaty Ratification **Obv:** National coat of arms **Rev:** Map within circle

Date	Mintage	F	VF	XF	Unc	BU
1978FM (P)	12,000	Value: 32.00				
1978FM (P) FDC	Inc. above	Value: 45.00				

KM# 53a 10 BALBOAS

Nickel, 45.6 mm. **Obv:** National coat of arms **Rev:** Map within circle

Date	Mintage	F	VF	XF	Unc	BU
1978	300,000	—	—	12.00	15.00	20.00

KM# 59 10 BALBOAS

42.4800 g., 0.9250 Silver 1.2635 oz. ASW **Subject:** Panama Canal Treaty Implementation **Obv:** National coat of arms **Rev:** Ship and flag

Date	Mintage	F	VF	XF	Unc	BU
1979FM (P)	7,229	Value: 32.00				

KM# 64 10 BALBOAS

26.5000 g., 0.5000 Silver .4260 oz. ASW **Subject:** Balseria Game **Obv:** National coat of arms **Rev:** Dancing figure

Date	Mintage	F	VF	XF	Unc	BU
1980 Proof	1,267	Value: 75.00				

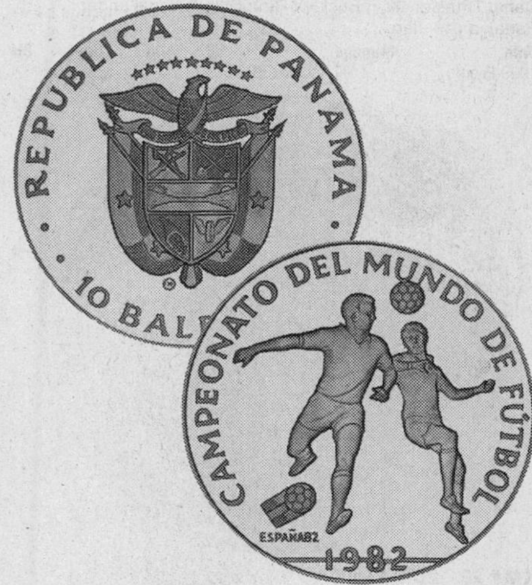

KM# 78 10 BALBOAS

26.5000 g., 0.5000 Silver .4260 oz. ASW **Subject:** Champions of Soccer **Obv:** National coat of arms **Rev:** Soccer players

Date	Mintage	F	VF	XF	Unc	BU
1982 Proof	9,076	Value: 45.00				

KM# 79 10 BALBOAS
26.5000 g., 0.5000 Silver .4260 oz. ASW **Subject:** International Year of the Child **Obv:** National coat of arms **Rev:** Three dancing figures, 2 emblems on the bottom

Date	Mintage	F	VF	XF	Unc	BU
1982 Proof	8,460	Value: 30.00				

KM# 130 10 BALBOAS
31.0000 g., 0.9250 Silver .9219 oz. ASW **Subject:** Panama Canal Transfer **Obv:** Bust left **Rev:** Ship in canal under Panamanian flag

Date	Mintage	F	VF	XF	Unc	BU
1999 Proof	4,500	Value: 30.00				

KM# 29 20 BALBOAS
129.5900 g., 0.9250 Silver 3.8544 oz. ASW, 61 mm. **Subject:** 150th Anniversary of Central American Independence **Obv:** National coat of arms **Rev:** Head right **Note:** Photo reduced.

Date	Mintage	F	VF	XF	Unc	BU
1971FM (M)	69,000	—	—	BV	60.00	65.00
1971FM (U)	—	—	BV	60.00	65.00	70.00
1971FM (P)	40,000	Value: 65.00				

KM# 31 20 BALBOAS
129.5900 g., 0.9250 Silver 3.8544 oz. ASW, 61 mm. **Subject:** Simon Bolivar **Obv:** National coat of arms **Rev:** Head right

Date	Mintage	F	VF	XF	Unc	BU
1972FM (M)	37,000	—	—	BV	60.00	65.00
1972FM (P)	48,000	Value: 50.00				
1973FM (M)	94,000	—	—	BV	60.00	65.00
1973FM (P)	74,000	Value: 50.00				
1974FM (M)	99,000	—	—	BV	60.00	65.00
1974FM (P)	161,000	Value: 50.00				
1975FM (M)	2,500	—	—	BV	65.00	70.00
1975FM (P)	62,000	Value: 50.00				
1975FM (U)	—	—	—	BV	85.00	110
1976FM (M)	2,500	60.00	65.00	85.00	115	175
Note: A substantial portion of the 1976 mintage was melted.						
1976FM (P)	22,000	Value: 65.00				

KM# 44 20 BALBOAS
129.5900 g., 0.9250 Silver 3.8544 oz. ASW, 61 mm. **Subject:** Vasco Nunez de Balboa **Obv:** National coat of arms **Rev:** 3/4-length standing armored figure facing left, raised right arm holding sword, left arm a flag **Note:** Photo reduced.

Date	Mintage	F	VF	XF	Unc	BU
1977FM (U)	2,879	BV	60.00	70.00	80.00	—
1977FM (P)	24,000	Value: 65.00				
1979FM (U)	2,500	BV	60.00	70.00	80.00	—
1979FM (P)	13,000	Value: 70.00				

KM# 54 20 BALBOAS
129.5900 g., 0.9250 Silver 3.8544 oz. ASW, 61 mm. **Subject:** 75th Anniversary of Independence **Obv:** National coat of arms **Rev:** 3/4-length Balboa standing facing left, upraised right arm holding sword, left arm a flag **Note:** Photo reduced.

Date	Mintage	F	VF	XF	Unc	BU
1978FM (U)	2,500	BV	60.00	70.00	80.00	—
1978FM (P)	23,000	Value: 60.00				

KM# 65 20 BALBOAS
119.8800 g., 0.5000 Silver 1.9273 oz. ASW, 61 mm. **Subject:** Sesquicentenarium - Death of Simon Bolivar **Obv:** National coat of arms **Rev:** Armored figure on horse **Note:** Photo reduced.

Date	Mintage	F	VF	XF	Unc	BU
1980FM (U)	1,000	—	—	—	135	—
1980FM (P)	3,714	Value: 120				

KM# 71 20 BALBOAS
118.5700 g., 0.5000 Silver 1.9060 oz. ASW, 61 mm. **Subject:** Simon Bolivar, El Libertador **Obv:** National coat of arms **Rev:** Armored figure on rearing horse in center of assorted flags **Note:** Photo reduced.

Date	Mintage	F	VF	XF	Unc	BU
1981FM (U)	500	—	—	—	180	—
1981FM (P)	3,528	Value: 120				

KM# 72 20 BALBOAS
2.1400 g., 0.5000 Gold .0344 oz. AGW **Obv:** National coat of arms **Rev:** Figure of Eight Butterfly **Rev. Designer:** Gilroy Roberts

Date	Mintage	F	VF	XF	Unc	BU
1981FM (U)	205	—	—	—	225	—
1981FM (P)	4,445	Value: 80.00				
1981FM (P) FDC	Inc. above	Value: 90.00				

KM# 81 20 BALBOAS
2.1400 g., 0.5000 Gold .0344 oz. AGW **Obv:** National coat of arms **Rev:** Hummingbird

Date	Mintage	F	VF	XF	Unc	BU
1982FM (U)	140	—	—	—	275	—
1982FM (P)	3,445	Value: 85.00				
1982FM (P) FDC	Inc. above	Value: 95.00				

KM# 80 20 BALBOAS
119.8800 g., 0.5000 Silver 1.9273 oz. ASW, 61 mm. **Subject:** Balboa - Discoverer of the Pacific **Obv:** National coat of arms **Rev:** Standing armored figures **Note:** Photo reduced.

Date	Mintage	F	VF	XF	Unc	BU
1982FM (P)	2,352	Value: 150				

KM# 92 20 BALBOAS
2.1400 g., 0.5000 Gold .0344 oz. AGW **Obv:** National coat of arms **Rev:** Banded Butterfly fish

Date	Mintage	F	VF	XF	Unc	BU
1983FM (U)	—	—	—	—	200	—
1983FM (P)	1,671	Value: 85.00				
1983FM (P) FDC	Inc. above	Value: 110				

KM# 93 20 BALBOAS
118.5700 g., 0.5000 Silver 1.9060 oz. ASW, 61 mm. **Subject:** 200th Anniversary - Birth of Bolivar **Obv:** National coat of arms **Rev:** 1/2-Length bust left holding scroll

Date	Mintage	F	VF	XF	Unc	BU
1983FM (U)	500	—	—	—	180	—
1983FM (P)	3,186	Value: 85.00				

KM# 97 20 BALBOAS
2.1400 g., 0.5000 Gold .0344 oz. AGW **Obv:** National coat of arms **Rev:** Puma

Date	Mintage	F	VF	XF	Unc	BU
1984FM (U)	100	—	—	—	600	—
1984FM (P)	357	Value: 350				
1984FM (P) FDC	Inc. above	Value: 400				

KM# 98 20 BALBOAS
119.8800 g., 0.5000 Silver 1.9273 oz. ASW, 61 mm. **Obv:** National coat of arms **Rev:** Balboa and Indian guide **Note:** Photo reduced.

Date	Mintage	F	VF	XF	Unc	BU
1984FM (P)	1,760	Value: 195				

KM# 105 20 BALBOAS
119.8800 g., 0.5000 Silver 1.9273 oz. ASW, 61 mm. **Subject:** Discovery of the Pacific Ocean **Obv:** National coat of arms **Rev:** Armored head and eagle facing left

Date	Mintage	F	VF	XF	Unc	BU
1985FM (P)	1,402	Value: 160				

KM# 102 20 BALBOAS
2.1400 g., 0.5000 Gold .0344 oz. AGW **Obv:** National coat of arms **Rev:** Harpy Eagle

Date	Mintage	F	VF	XF	Unc	BU
1985FM (P)	817	Value: 250				
1985FM (P) FDC	Inc. above	Value: 325				

KM# 73 50 BALBOAS
5.3700 g., 0.5000 Gold .0861 oz. AGW **Subject:** Christmas 1981 **Obv:** National coat of arms **Rev:** Stylized dove flanked by flowers

Date	Mintage	F	VF	XF	Unc	BU
1981FM (U)	154	—	—	—	225	—
1981FM (P)	1,940	Value: 85.00				
1981FM (P) FDC	Inc. above	Value: 100				

KM# 82 50 BALBOAS
5.3700 g., 0.5000 Gold .0861 oz. AGW **Subject:** Christmas 1982 **Obv:** National coat of arms **Rev:** Star of Bethlehem flanked by flowers

Date	Mintage	F	VF	XF	Unc	BU
1982FM (U)	60	—	—	—	450	—
1982FM (P)	1,361	Value: 95.00				
1982FM (P) FDC	Inc. above	Value: 100				

KM# 94 50 BALBOAS
5.3700 g., 0.5000 Gold .0861 oz. AGW **Subject:** Christmas 1983 **Obv:** National coat of arms **Rev:** Poinsettia

Date	Mintage	F	VF	XF	Unc	BU
1983FM (U)	—	—	—	—	225	—
1983FM (P)	1,283	Value: 110				
1983FM (P) FDC	Inc. above	Value: 130				

KM# 99 50 BALBOAS
5.3700 g., 0.5000 Gold .0861 oz. AGW **Subject:** Peace at Christmas **Obv:** National coat of arms **Rev:** Lion and lamb

Date	Mintage	F	VF	XF	Unc	BU
1984FM (P)	—	Value: 550				
1984FM (P) FDC	—	Value: 700				

KM# 55 75 BALBOAS
10.6000 g., 0.5000 Gold .1704 oz. AGW **Subject:** 75th Anniversary of Independence **Obv:** National coat of arms **Rev:** Flag flanked by dates, flowers and stars

Date	Mintage	F	VF	XF	Unc	BU
ND1978FM (U)	410	—	—	—	180	—
ND1978FM (P)	9,161	Value: 130				
1978FM (P) FDC	Inc. above	Value: 140				

KM# 41 100 BALBOAS
8.1600 g., 0.9000 Gold .2361 oz. AGW **Subject:** 500th Anniversary - Birth of Balboa **Obv:** National coat of arms **Rev:** Armored head 1/4 left

Date	Mintage	F	VF	XF	Unc	BU
1975FM (U)	44,000	—	—	—	165	—
1975FM (P)	75,000	Value: 165				
1975FM (P) FDC	Inc. above	Value: 170				
1976FM (M)	50	—	—	—	600	—
1976FM (U)	3,013	—	—	—	165	—
1976FM (P)	11,000	Value: 165				
1976FM (P) FDC	Inc. above	Value: 170				
1977FM (M)	50	—	—	—	550	—
1977FM (U)	324	—	—	—	225	—
1977FM (P)	5,092	Value: 175				
1977FM (P) FDC	Inc. above	Value: 180				

KM# 56 100 BALBOAS
8.1600 g., 0.9000 Gold .2361 oz. AGW **Subject:** Peace and Progress **Obv:** National coat of arms **Rev:** Dove orchid within circle

Date	Mintage	F	VF	XF	Unc	BU
1978FM (M)	50	—	—	—	500	—
1978FM (U)	300	—	—	—	250	—
1978FM (P)	6,086	Value: 165				
1978FM (P) FDC	Inc. above	Value: 175				

KM# 60 100 BALBOAS
8.1600 g., 0.9000 Gold .2361 oz. AGW **Subject:** Pre-Columbian Art - Golden Turtle **Obv:** National coat of arms **Rev:** Stylized turtle

Date	Mintage	F	VF	XF	Unc	BU
1979FM (M)	50	—	—	—	350	—
1979FM (U)	240	—	—	—	300	—
1979FM (P)	4,829	Value: 165				
1979FM (P) FDC	Inc. above	Value: 175				

KM# 66 100 BALBOAS
8.1600 g., 0.9000 Gold .2361 oz. AGW **Subject:** Pre-Columbian Art - Golden Condor **Obv:** National coat of arms **Rev:** Stylized condor within circle

Date	Mintage	F	VF	XF	Unc	BU
1980FM (U)	209	—	—	—	400	—
1980FM (P)	2,411	Value: 200				
1980FM (P) FDC	Inc. above	Value: 250				

KM# 67 100 BALBOAS
7.1300 g., 0.5000 Gold .1146 oz. AGW **Subject:** Panama Canal Centennial **Obv:** National coat of arms **Rev:** Bust 1/4 left

Date	Mintage	F	VF	XF	Unc	BU
ND (1980)FM (U)	77	—	—	—	700	—
ND (1980)FM (P)	2,468	Value: 135				
ND(1980)FM (P) FDC	Inc. above	Value: 150				

KM# 74 100 BALBOAS
7.1300 g., 0.5000 Gold .1146 oz. AGW **Subject:** Pre-Columbian Art **Obv:** National coat of arms **Rev:** Cocie Peoples' Ceremonial Mask

Date	Mintage	F	VF	XF	Unc	BU
1981FM (U)	174	—	—	—	325	—
1981FM (P)	1,841	Value: 150				
1981FM (P) FDC	Inc. above	Value: 160				

KM# 83 100 BALBOAS
7.1300 g., 0.5000 Gold .1146 oz. AGW **Subject:** Pre-Columbian Art **Obv:** National coat of arms **Rev:** Native design within quartered circle

Date	Mintage	F	VF	XF	Unc	BU
1982FM (U)	26	—	—	—	850	—
1982FM (P)	578	Value: 200				
FM (P) FDC	Inc. above	Value: 300				

KM# 95 100 BALBOAS
7.1300 g., 0.5000 Gold .1146 oz. AGW **Subject:** Pre-Columbian Art **Obv:** National coat of arms **Rev:** Cocie style birds

Date	Mintage	F	VF	XF	Unc	BU
1983FM (U)	—	—	—	—	350	—
1983FM (P)	1,308	Value: 150				
1983FM (P) FDC	Inc. above	Value: 160				

KM# 100 100 BALBOAS
7.1300 g., 0.5000 Gold .1146 oz. AGW **Subject:** Pre-Columbian Art **Obv:** National coat of arms **Rev:** Native art

Date	Mintage	F	VF	XF	Unc	BU
1984FM (U)	—	—	—	—	400	—
1984FM (P)	—	Value: 165				
1984FM (P) FDC	—	Value: 180				

KM# 131 100 BALBOAS
8.3000 g., 0.9000 Gold .2402 oz. AGW **Subject:** Panama Canal Transfer **Obv:** Bust left **Rev:** Ship in canal under Panamanian flag

Date	Mintage	F	VF	XF	Unc	BU
1999 Proof	1,000	Value: 300				

KM# 43 150 BALBOAS
9.3000 g., 0.9990 Platinum .2987 oz. APW **Subject:** 150th Anniversary - Panamanian Congress **Obv:** National coat of arms **Rev:** Bust left divides dates

Date	Mintage	F	VF	XF	Unc	BU
ND (1976)FM (M)	30	—	—	—	850	—
ND (1976)FM (U)	510	—	—	—	425	—
ND (1976)FM (P)	13,000	Value: 375				
ND(1976)FM (P) FDC	Inc. above	Value: 425				

KM# 68 150 BALBOAS
7.6700 g., 0.5000 Gold .1233 oz. AGW **Subject:** Sesquicentenarium - Death of Simon Bolivar **Obv:** National coat of arms **Rev:** Armored bust 1/4 left

Date	Mintage	F	VF	XF	Unc	BU
ND (1980)FM (U)	169	—	—	—	550	—
ND (1980)FM (P)	1,837	Value: 225				
ND(1980)FM (P) FDC	Inc. above	Value: 250				

KM# 61 200 BALBOAS
9.5000 g., 0.9800 Platinum .2994 oz. APW **Subject:** Panama Canal Treaty Implementation **Obv:** National coat of arms **Rev:** Flag above map

Date	Mintage	F	VF	XF	Unc	BU
1979FM (P)	2,178	Value: 340				
1979FM (P) FDC	Inc. above	Value: 375				

KM# 69 200 BALBOAS
9.9300 g., 0.9800 Platinum .2940 oz. APW **Subject:** Champions of Boxing **Obv:** National coat of arms **Rev:** Boxer and flag

Date	Mintage	F	VF	XF	Unc	BU
1980 Proof	219	Value: 600				
1980 Proof FDC	Inc. above	Value: 625				

KM# 42 500 BALBOAS
41.7000 g., 0.9000 Gold 1.2067 oz. AGW **Subject:** 500th Anniversary - Birth of Balboa **Obv:** National coat of arms **Rev:** Kneeling armored figure, sword in left hand, flag in right

Date	Mintage	F	VF	XF	Unc	BU
1975FM (M)	10	—	—	—	3,000	—
1975FM (U)	1,496	—	—	—	820	—
1975FM (P)	9,824	Value: 820				
1975FM (P) FDC	Inc. above	Value: 835				
1976FM (M)	10	—	—	—	3,000	—
1976FM (U)	160	—	—	—	875	—
1976FM (P)	2,669	Value: 825				
1976FM (P) FDC	Inc. above	Value: 845				
1977FM (M)	10	—	—	—	3,000	—
1977FM (U)	59	—	—	—	1,250	—
1977FM (P)	1,980	Value: 835				
1977FM (P) FDC	Inc. above	Value: 855				

KM# 57 500 BALBOAS
41.7000 g., 0.9000 Gold 1.2067 oz. AGW **Subject:** 30th Anniversary - Organization of American States **Obv:** National coat of arms **Rev:** Globe showing North and South America

Date	Mintage	F	VF	XF	Unc	BU
ND(1978)FM (M)	10	—	—	—	2,250	—
ND(1978)FM (U)	106	—	—	—	975	—
ND(1978)FM (P)	2,009	Value: 835				
ND(1978)FM (P) FDC	Inc. above	Value: 860				

KM# 62 500 BALBOAS
41.7000 g., 0.9000 Gold 1.2067 oz. AGW **Obv:** National coat of arms **Rev:** Jaguar

Date	Mintage	F	VF	XF	Unc	BU
1979FM (U)	130	—	—	—	965	—
1979FM (P)	1,657	Value: 835				
1979FM (P) FDC	Inc. above	Value: 900				

KM# 70 500 BALBOAS
37.1800 g., 0.5000 Gold .5977 oz. AGW **Obv:** National coat of arms **Rev:** Great egrets

Date	Mintage	F	VF	XF	Unc	BU
1980FM (U)	54	—	—	—	1,500	—
1980FM (P)	612	Value: 650				
1980FM (P) FDC	Inc. above	Value: 750				

KM# 75 500 BALBOAS
37.1800 g., 0.5000 Gold .5977 oz. AGW **Obv:** National coat of arms **Rev:** Sailfish

Date	Mintage	F	VF	XF	Unc	BU
1981FM (U)	41	—	—	—	1,850	—
1981FM (P)	487	Value: 675				
1981FM (P) FDC	Inc. above	Value: 725				

KM# 84 500 BALBOAS
37.1800 g., 0.5000 Gold .5977 oz. AGW **Subject:** Death of General Omar Torrijos **Obv:** National coat of arms **Rev:** Uniformed bust right

Date	Mintage	F	VF	XF	Unc	BU
1982FM (U)	97	—	—	—	1,200	—
1982FM (P)	398	Value: 700				
1982FM (P) FDC	Inc. above	Value: 750				

KM# 96 500 BALBOAS
37.1800 g., 0.5000 Gold .5977 oz. AGW **Obv:** National coat of arms **Rev:** Owl Butterfly **Shape:** Scalloped

Date	Mintage	F	VF	XF	Unc	BU
1983FM (U)	73	—	—	—	1,100	—
1983FM (P)	469	Value: 675				
1983FM (P) FDC	Inc. above	Value: 725				

KM# 101 500 BALBOAS
37.1200 g., 0.5000 Gold .5968 oz. AGW **Subject:** Golden Eagle **Obv:** National coat of arms **Rev:** National eagle holding a ribbon, stars above

Date	Mintage	F	VF	XF	Unc	BU
1984FM (U)	10	—	—	—	4,750	—
1984FM (P)	156	Value: 1,750				
1984FM (P) FDC	Inc. above	Value: 1,800				

KM# 103 500 BALBOAS
37.1800 g., 0.5000 Gold .5977 oz. AGW **Subject:** National Eagle **Obv:** National coat of arms **Rev:** National eagle holding an ribbon, stars above **Shape:** Scalloped

Date	Mintage	F	VF	XF	Unc	BU
1985FM (P)	184	Value: 1,600				
1985FM (P) FDC	Inc. above	Value: 1,650				

PATTERNS

Including off metal strikes.

KM#	Date	Mintage	Identification	Mkt Val
Pn1	1904	—	2-1/2 Centesimos. Silver.	1,500
Pn2	1907	—	Half Cent.	3,500
PnA3	1907	—	1/2 Centesimo. Bronze. KM6.	—
Pn3	1907	—	2-1/2 Centesimos. Silver.	—
PnA4	1953	—	Centesimo. Copper. KM17	—
PnB4	1953	—	Centesimo. Silver. 17a	—
PnC4	1953	—	Centesimo. 0.9000 Gold. 17b	—
PnD4	1953	—	1/10 Balboa. Silver.	—
PnE4	1953	—	1/10 Balboa. 0.9000 Gold. 18a	—
PnF4	1953	—	1/4 Balboa. Silver.	—
PnG4	1953	—	1/4 Balboa. 0.9000 Gold. 19a	—
PnH4	1953	—	1/2 Balboa. Silver.	—
PnI4	1953	—	1/2 Balboa. 0.9000 Gold. 20a	—
Pn4	1986	—	Balboa. Copper-Nickel. Type I.	3,500
Pn5	1986	—	Balboa. Copper Nickel. Type II.	3,500
Pn6	1987	—	1/10 Balboa. Copper-Nickel Clad Copper. Similar to KM10a.	1,000
Pn7	1987	—	1/4 Balboa. Copper-Nickel Clad Copper. Similar to KM11a.	1,500
Pn8	1987	—	1/2 Balboa. Copper-Nickel Clad Copper. Similar to KM12.	2,000
Pn9	1988	—	1/10 Balboa. Copper-Nickel. KM24.	—
Pn10	1988	—	1/4 Balboa. Copper-Nickel. KM25.	1,500
Pn11	1988	—	1/2 Balboa. Copper-Nickel. KM26.	2,000

PIEFORTS

KM#	Date	Mintage	Identification	Mkt Val
P1	1982	—	Centesimo. 0.4000 Gold. The 1982 series of 1-50 Centesimos were struck as piefort in .400 Gold outside the normal minting facility without consent from the National Bank of Panama.	550
P2	1982	—	5 Centesimos. 0.4000 Gold.	650
P3	1982	—	1/10 Balboa. 0.4000 Gold.	750
P4	1982	20	1/4 Balboa. 0.4000 Gold.	950
P5	1982	—	50 Centesimos. 0.4000 Gold.	1,000

TRIAL STRIKES

KM#	Date	Mintage	Identification	Mkt Val
TS1	1982	—	Centesimo. 0.4000 Gold. The 1982 series 1-50 Centesimos were struck as uniface trial strikes in .400 Gold outside the normal minting facility without consent from the National Bank or authorization from the Government of Panama. Reverse piefort.	250
TS2	1982	—	Centesimo. 0.4000 Gold. Obverse piefort.	250
TS3	1982	—	5 Centesimos. 0.4000 Gold. Reverse piefort	300
TS4	1982	—	5 Centesimos. 0.4000 Gold. Obverse piefort	30,000
TS5	1982	—	1/10 Balboa. 0.4000 Gold. Reverse piefort	375
TS6	1982	—	1/10 Balboa. 0.4000 Gold. Obverse piefort	375
TS7	1982	—	1/4 Balboa. 0.4000 Gold. Reverse piefort	500
TS8	1982	—	1/4 Balboa. 0.4000 Gold. Obverse piefort	500
TS9	1982	—	50 Centesimos. 0.4000 Gold. Reverse piefort	500
TS10	1982	—	50 Centesimos. 0.4000 Gold. Obverse piefort	500

MINT SETS

KM#	Date	Mintage	Identification	Issue Price	Mkt Val
MS1	1975 (8)	1,410	KM33.1-40.1	25.00	85.00

PROOF SETS

KM#	Date	Mintage	Identification	Issue Price	Mkt Val
PS1	1904 (4)	12	KM2-5	—	9,000
PS2	1930 (3)	20	KM10.1-12.1	—	4,650
PS3	1962 (5)	25	KM10.2-12.2, 22, 23.2	—	2,850
PS4	1966 (6)	12,701	KM10a-11a, 12a.1, 22, 23.2, 27	15.25	25.00
PS5	1967 (6)	19,983	KM10a-11a, 12a.1, 22, 23.2, 27	15.25	25.00
PS6	1968 (6)	23,210	KM10a-11a, 12a.1, 22, 23.2, 27	15.25	25.00
PS7	1969 (6)	14,000	KM10a-11a, 12a.1, 22, 23.2, 27	15.25	25.00
PS8	1970 (6)	9,528	KM10a-11a, 12a.1, 22, 23.2, 27	15.25	25.00
PS9	1971 (6)	10,696	KM10a-11a, 12a.1, 22, 23.2, 27	15.25	25.00
PS10	1972 (6)	13,322	KM10a-11a, 12a.1, 22, 23.2, 27	15.25	25.00
PS11	1973 (6)	16,946	KM10a-11a, 12b, 22, 23.2, 27	17.50	25.00
PS12	1974 (6)	17,521	KM10a-11a, 12b, 22, 23.2, 27	17.50	25.00
PS13	1975 (9)	37,041	KM31, 33.1-38.1, 39.1a-40.1a	130	80.00
PS14	1975 (8)	4,057	KM33.1-38.1, 39.1a-40.1a	50.00	40.00
PS15	1976 (9)	10,610	KM31, 33.1-38.1, 39.1a-40.1a	102	80.00
PS16	1976 (8)	1,792	KM33.1-38.1, 39.1a-40.1a	50.00	40.00
PS17	1976 (2)	11,479	KM31, 34.1	51.00	50.00
PS18	1977 (9)	8,093	KM33.1-38.1, 39.1a-40.1a, 44	100	100
PS19	1977 (8)	1,455	KM33.1-38.1, 39.1a-40.1a	50.00	50.00
PS20	1978 (9)	9,667	KM45-50, 51a, 52a, 54	110	120
PS21	1978 (8)	1,122	KM45-50, 51a, 52a	—	50.00
PS22	1979 (9)	4,974	KM33.1-38.1, 39.1a-40.1a, 44	132	110
PS23	1979 (8)	975	KM33.1-38.1, 39.1a-40.1a	60.00	50.00
PS24	1979 (2)	1,775	KM58-59	125	70.00
PS25	1980 (9)	1,686	KM33.2-38.2, 39.3-40.3, 65	287	150
PS26	1980 (8)	943	KM33.2-38.2, 39.3-40.3	87.00	65.00
PS27	1981 (9)	1,279	KM33.1-38.1, 39.1b-40.1b, 71	212	170
PS28	1981 (8)	694	KM33.1-38.1, 39.1b-40.1b	87.00	65.00
PS29	1982 (9)	746	KM33.1-38.1, 39.1b-40.1b, 80	212	275
PS30	1982 (9)	—	Error set; KM33.1-38.1, 39.1b, 40.4, 80	212	250
PS31	1982 (8)	734	KM33.1-38.1, 39.1b, 40.1b	87.00	100
PS32	1982 (8)	—	Error set; KM33.1-38.1, 39.1b, 40.4	—	150
PS33	1983 (9)	—	KM22, 85-91, 93	87.00	150
PS34	1983 (8)	—	KM22, 85-91	—	100
PS35	1984 (9)	—	KM22, 85-91, 98	—	225
PS36	1984 (8)	—	KM22, 85-91	72.00	100
PS37	1985 (8)	765	KM22, 85-90, 104	72.00	200
PS39	1993 (4)	—	KM10a-11a, 12a.1, 23.2	—	1,350

Palo Seco Leper Colony was established in Balboa, Canal Zone in 1907. It is known today as Palo Seco Hospital. The original issue of tokens totaled $1,800.00 of which $1,492.75 was destroyed on November 28, 1955. The issue was backed by United States Currency and was replaced by United States circulation coinage.

COLONY

LEPROSARIUM TOKEN COINAGE

KM# Tn1 CENT

Brass, 19 mm. **Obv:** Square center hole **Rev:** Square center hole divides values

Date	Mintage	F	VF	XF	Unc	BU
ND(1919)	—	125	200	—	—	—

KM# Tn2 5 CENTS

Brass, 21 mm. **Obv:** Square center hole divides legend **Rev:** Square center hole divides values

Date	Mintage	F	VF	XF	Unc	BU
ND(1919)	—	125	250	—	—	—

KM# Tn3 10 CENTS

Aluminum, 18 mm. **Obv:** Center hole divides legend **Rev:** Center hole divides values

Date	Mintage	F	VF	XF	Unc	BU
ND(1919)	—	200	350	—	—	—

KM# Tn4 25 CENTS

Aluminum, 24 mm. **Obv:** Center hole divides legend **Rev:** Center hole divides values

Date	Mintage	F	VF	XF	Unc	BU
ND(1919)	—	250	450	—	—	—

KM# Tn5 50 CENTS

Aluminum, 30.5 mm. **Obv:** Center hole divides legend **Rev:** Center hole divides values

Date	Mintage	F	VF	XF	Unc	BU
ND(1919)	—	600	1,000	—	—	—

KM# Tn6 DOLLAR

Aluminum, 38 mm. **Obv:** Center hole divides legend **Rev:** Center hole divides values

Date	Mintage	F	VF	XF	Unc	BU
ND(1919)	—	900	1,500	—	—	—

PAPUA NEW GUINEA

Papua New Guinea occupies the eastern half of the island of New Guinea. It lies north of Australia near the equator and borders on West Irian. The country, which includes nearby Bismark archipelago, Buka and Bougainville, has an area of 178,260 sq. mi. (461,690 sq. km.).and a population of 3.7 million that is divided into more than 1,000 separate tribes speaking more than 700 mutually unintelligible languages. Capital: Port Moresby. The economy is agricultural, and exports copra, rubber, cocoa, coffee, tea, gold and copper.

In 1884 Germany annexed the area known as German New Guinea (also Neu Guinea or Kaiser Wilhelmsland) comprising the northern section of eastern New Guinea, and granted its administration and development to the Neu-Guinea Compagnie. Administration reverted to Germany in 1889 following the failure of the company to exercise adequate administration. While a German protectorate, German New Guinea had an area of 92,159 sq. mi. (238,692 sq. km.) and a population of about 250,000. Capital: Herbertshohe, 1 of 4 capitals of German New Guinea. The seat of government was transferred to Rabaul in 1910. Copra was the chief crop.

Australian troops occupied German New Guinea in Aug. 1914, shortly after Great Britain declared war on Germany. It was mandated to Australia by the League of Nations in 1920, known as the Territory of New Guinea. The territory was invaded and most of it was occupied by Japan in 1942. Following the Japanese surrender, it came under U.N. trusteeship, Dec. 13, 1946, with Australia as the administering power.

The Papua and New Guinea act, 1949, provided for the government of Papua and New Guinea as one administrative unit. On Dec. 1, 1973, Papua New Guinea became self-governing with Australia retaining responsibility for defense and foreign affairs. Full independence was achieved on Sept. 16, 1975. Papua New Guinea is a member of the Commonwealth of Nations. Elizabeth II is Head of State.

MINT MARKS

FM - Franklin Mint, U.S.A.

NOTE: From 1975-1985 the Franklin Mint produced coinage in up to 3 different qualities. Qualities of issue are designated in ( ) after each date and are defined as follows:

(M) MATTE - Normal circulation strike or a dull finish produced by sandblasting special uncirculated (polish finish) or proof quality dies.

(U) SPECIAL UNCIRCULATED - Polished or prooflike in appearance without any frosted features.

(P) PROOF - The highest quality obtainable having mirror-like fields and frosted features.

MONETARY SYSTEM

100 Toea = 1 Kina

COMMONWEALTH

STANDARD COINAGE

100 Toea = 1 Kina

KM# 1 TOEA

2.0000 g., Bronze, 17.65 mm. **Obv:** National emblem **Rev:** Butterfly and value

Date	Mintage	F	VF	XF	Unc	BU
1975	14,400,000	—	—	0.15	0.35	1.00
1975FM (M)	83,000	—	—	—	0.45	1.00
1975FM (U)	4,134	—	—	—	1.00	1.50
1975FM (P)	67,000	Value: 1.00				
1976	25,175,000	—	—	—	0.35	1.00
1976FM (M)	84,000	—	—	—	0.35	1.00
1976FM (U)	976	—	—	—	1.00	1.50
1976FM (P)	16,000	Value: 1.00				
1977FM (M)	84,000	—	—	—	0.35	1.00
1977FM (U)	603	—	—	—	1.50	2.50
1977FM (P)	7,721	Value: 1.25				
1978	—	—	—	—	0.35	1.00
1978FM (M)	83,000	—	—	—	0.35	1.00
1978FM (U)	777	—	—	—	1.00	1.50
1978FM (P)	5,540	Value: 1.50				
1979FM (M)	84,000	—	—	—	0.35	1.00
1979FM (U)	1,366	—	—	—	1.00	1.50
1979FM (P)	2,728	Value: 1.50				
1980FM (U)	1,160	—	—	—	1.00	1.50
1980FM (P)	2,125	Value: 1.50				
1981	—	—	—	—	1.00	1.50
1981FM (P)	10,000	Value: 1.25				

Date	Mintage	F	VF	XF	Unc	BU
1981FM (M)	—	—	—	—	0.35	1.00
1982FM (M)	—	—	—	—	1.00	1.50
1982FM (P)	—	Value: 2.25				
1983	—	—	—	—	0.45	1.25
1983FM (U)	360	—	—	—	1.00	1.50
1983FM (P)	—	Value: 2.25				
1984	—	—	—	—	0.45	1.25
1984FM (P)	—	Value: 2.25				
1987	—	—	—	—	0.45	1.25
1990	—	—	—	—	0.45	1.25
1995	—	—	—	—	0.45	1.25

KM# 2 2 TOEA

4.0000 g., Bronze, 21.72 mm. **Obv:** National emblem **Rev:** Lion fish

Date	Mintage	F	VF	XF	Unc	BU
1975	11,400,000	—	—	0.10	0.60	1.00
1975FM (M)	42,000	—	—	—	0.65	1.00
1975FM (U)	4,134	—	—	—	1.00	1.50
1975FM (P)	67,000	Value: 1.50				
1976	15,175,000	—	—	0.10	0.50	1.00
1976FM (M)	42,000	—	—	—	0.50	1.00
1976FM (U)	976	—	—	—	1.00	1.50
1976FM (P)	16,000	Value: 1.50				
1977FM (M)	42,000	—	—	—	0.50	1.00
1977FM (U)	603	—	—	—	1.50	2.50
1977FM (P)	7,721	Value: 1.75				
1978	—	—	—	—	0.50	1.00
1978FM (M)	42,000	—	—	—	0.50	1.00
1978FM (U)	777	—	—	—	1.00	1.50
1978FM (P)	5,540	Value: 1.75				
1979FM (M)	42,000	—	—	—	0.50	1.00
1979FM (U)	1,366	—	—	—	1.00	1.50
1979FM (P)	2,728	Value: 1.75				
1980FM (U)	1,160	—	—	—	1.00	1.50
1980FM (P)	2,125	Value: 1.75				
1981	—	—	—	—	0.50	1.25
1981FM (P)	10,000	Value: 1.50				
1982FM (M)	—	—	—	—	1.00	1.50
1982FM (P)	—	Value: 2.50				
1983	—	—	—	—	0.50	1.25
1983FM (U)	360	—	—	—	1.50	2.50
1983FM (P)	—	Value: 2.50				
1984	—	—	—	—	0.50	1.25
1984 Proof	—	Value: 2.50				
1987	—	—	—	—	0.50	1.25
1990	—	—	—	—	0.50	1.25
1995	—	—	—	—	0.50	1.25
1996	—	—	—	—	0.50	1.25

KM# 3 5 TOEA

3.0000 g., Copper-Nickel, 19.53 mm. **Obv:** National emblem **Rev:** Plateless turtle

Date	Mintage	F	VF	XF	Unc	BU
1975	11,000,000	—	0.15	0.25	0.75	1.50
1975FM (M)	17,000	—	—	—	0.75	2.00
1975FM (U)	4,134	—	—	—	1.25	3.00
1975FM (P)	67,000	Value: 2.00				
1976	24,000,000	—	0.15	0.25	0.75	1.50
1976FM (M)	17,000	—	—	—	0.75	3.00
1976FM (U)	976	—	—	—	1.25	3.00
1976FM (P)	16,000	Value: 2.00				
1977FM (M)	17,000	—	—	—	0.75	2.00
1977FM (U)	603	—	—	—	1.75	3.00
1977FM (P)	7,721	Value: 2.25				
1978	2,000	—	—	—	2.50	3.00
1978FM (M)	17,000	—	—	—	0.75	2.00
1978FM (U)	777	—	—	—	1.25	3.00
1978FM (P)	5,540	Value: 2.25				
1979	—	—	—	—	0.75	1.50
1979FM (M)	17,000	—	—	—	0.75	1.50
1979FM (U)	1,366	—	—	—	1.25	2.00
1979FM (P)	2,728	Value: 2.25				
1980FM (U)	1,160	—	—	—	1.25	2.00
1980FM (P)	2,125	Value: 2.25				
1981FM (P)	10,000	Value: 2.00				
1982	—	—	—	—	0.75	2.00
1982FM (M)	—	—	—	—	1.25	2.00
1982FM (P)	—	Value: 3.00				
1983FM (U)	360	—	—	—	2.25	5.00
1983FM (P)	—	Value: 3.00				
1984	—	—	—	—	0.75	1.50
1984FM (P)	—	Value: 3.00				
1987	—	—	—	—	0.75	1.50
1990	—	—	—	—	0.75	1.50
1995	—	—	—	—	0.75	1.50

Date	Mintage	F	VF	XF	Unc	BU
1996	—	—	—	—	0.75	1.50
1998	—	—	—	—	0.75	1.50
1999	—	—	—	—	0.75	1.50

KM# 4 10 TOEA

Copper-Nickel, 23.72 mm. **Obv:** National emblem **Rev:** Cuscus and value

Date	Mintage	F	VF	XF	Unc	BU
1975	8,600,000	—	0.20	0.35	0.65	1.50
1975FM (M)	8,300	—	—	—	1.00	1.75
1975FM (U)	4,134	—	—	—	1.50	2.00
1975FM (P)	67,000	Value: 2.00				
1976	—	—	0.20	0.35	0.65	1.50
1976FM (M)	8,300	—	—	—	1.00	1.75
1976FM (U)	976	—	—	—	1.50	2.00
1976FM (P)	16,000	Value: 2.00				
1977FM (M)	8,300	—	—	—	1.00	1.75
1977FM (U)	603	—	—	—	2.25	2.75
1977FM (P)	7,721	Value: 2.50				
1978FM (M)	8,300	—	—	—	1.00	1.75
1978FM (U)	777	—	—	—	1.50	2.00
1978FM (P)	5,540	Value: 2.75				
1979FM (M)	8,300	—	—	—	1.00	1.75
1979FM (U)	1,366	—	—	—	1.50	2.00
1979FM (P)	2,728	Value: 2.75				
1980FM (U)	1,160	—	—	—	1.50	2.00
1980FM (P)	2,125	Value: 2.75				
1981FM (P)	10,000	Value: 2.75				
1982FM (M)	—	—	—	—	1.50	2.00
1982FM (P)	—	Value: 3.50				
1983FM (U)	360	—	—	—	2.50	3.00
1983FM (P)	—	Value: 3.50				
1984FM (P)	—	Value: 3.50				
1995	—	—	—	—	1.50	2.00
1996	—	—	—	—	1.50	2.00
1999	—	—	—	—	1.50	2.00

KM# 5 20 TOEA

11.3000 g., Copper-Nickel, 28.65 mm. **Obv:** National emblem **Rev:** Bennett's Cassowary and value

Date	Mintage	F	VF	XF	Unc	BU
1975	15,500,000	—	0.30	0.65	1.25	1.75
1975FM (M)	4,150	—	—	—	1.50	2.00
1975FM (U)	4,134	—	—	—	1.50	2.00
1975FM (P)	67,000	Value: 2.50				
1976FM (M)	4,150	—	—	—	1.50	2.00
1976FM (U)	976	—	—	—	1.75	2.25
1976FM (P)	16,000	Value: 2.50				
1977FM (M)	4,150	—	—	—	1.75	2.25
1977FM (U)	603	—	—	—	2.25	2.75
1977FM (P)	7,721	Value: 3.00				
1978	2,500,000	—	0.35	0.70	1.25	1.75
1978FM (M)	4,150	—	—	—	1.50	2.00
1978FM (U)	777	—	—	—	1.75	2.25
1978FM (P)	5,540	Value: 3.00				
1979FM (M)	4,150	—	—	—	1.50	2.00
1979FM (U)	1,366	—	—	—	1.75	2.25
1979FM (P)	2,728	Value: 3.00				
1980FM (U)	1,160	—	—	—	1.75	2.25
1980FM (P)	2,125	Value: 3.00				
1981	—	—	0.25	0.50	1.25	1.50
1981FM (P)	10,000	Value: 2.50				
1982FM (M)	—	—	—	—	2.00	2.25
1982FM (P)	—	Value: 4.00				
1983FM (U)	360	—	—	—	3.00	3.50
1983FM (P)	—	Value: 4.00				
1984	—	—	0.25	0.50	1.25	1.50
1984FM (P)	—	Value: 4.00				
1987	—	—	0.25	0.50	1.25	1.50
1990	—	—	0.25	0.50	1.25	1.50
1995	—	—	0.25	0.50	1.25	1.50
1998	—	—	0.25	0.50	1.25	1.50
1999	—	—	0.25	0.50	1.25	1.50

KM# 15 50 TOEA

Copper-Nickel **Subject:** South Pacific Festival of Arts **Obv:** National emblem **Rev:** Design divides circles **Shape:** 7-sided

Date	Mintage	F	VF	XF	Unc	BU
1980	—	—	0.75	1.25	2.50	—
1980FM (U)	1,160	—	—	—	10.00	—
1980FM (P)	2,125	Value: 6.50				

KM# 31 50 TOEA

Copper-Nickel **Subject:** 9th South Pacific Games **Obv:** National emblem **Rev:** Games emblem **Shape:** 7-sided

Date	Mintage	F	VF	XF	Unc	BU
1991	25,000	—	—	—	4.00	—

KM# 41 50 TOEA

13.6300 g., Copper Nickel, 30 mm. **Subject:** Silver Jubilee of Bank **Obv:** National emblem **Rev:** Symbolic design **Edge:** Reeded **Shape:** 7-sided

Date	Mintage	F	VF	XF	Unc	BU
1998	—	—	—	—	4.50	—

KM# 6 KINA

Copper-Nickel, 33 mm. **Obv:** Symbolic design around center hole **Rev:** Crocodiles flank center hole

Date	Mintage	F	VF	XF	Unc	BU
1975	2,000,000	—	1.35	2.00	3.50	7.50
1975FM (M)	829	—	—	—	8.50	9.50
1975FM (U)	4,134	—	—	—	3.50	7.50
1975FM (P)	67,000	Value: 5.00				
1976FM (M)	829	—	—	—	8.50	9.50
1976FM (U)	976	—	—	—	3.50	7.50
1976FM (P)	16,000	Value: 5.00				
1977FM (M)	829	—	—	—	8.50	9.50
1977FM (U)	603	—	—	—	12.50	13.50
1977FM (P)	7,721	Value: 6.00				
1978FM (M)	829	—	—	—	8.50	9.50
1978FM (U)	777	—	—	—	3.50	6.00
1978FM (P)	5,540	Value: 5.00				
1979FM (M)	829	—	—	—	8.50	9.50
1979FM (U)	1,366	—	—	—	3.50	6.50
1979FM (P)	2,728	Value: 6.00				
1980FM (U)	1,160	—	—	—	3.50	6.50
1980FM (P)	2,125	Value: 5.00				
1981FM (P)	10,000	Value: 5.00				
1982FM (M)	—	—	—	—	3.50	6.50
1982FM (P)	—	Value: 7.50				
1983FM (U)	360	—	—	—	14.50	15.50
1983FM (P)	—	Value: 7.00				
1984FM (P)	—	Value: 7.00				
1995	—	—	—	—	3.50	6.00
1996	—	—	—	—	3.50	6.00

Date	Mintage	F	VF	XF	Unc	BU
1998	—	—	—	—	3.50	6.00
1999	—	—	—	—	3.50	6.00

KM# 7 5 KINA
Copper-Nickel, 40 mm. **Obv:** National emblem **Rev:** New Guinea eagle

Date	Mintage	F	VF	XF	Unc	BU
1975FM (M)	166	—	—	—	32.00	—
1975FM (U)	4,134	—	—	—	6.50	—
1976FM (M)	166	—	—	—	32.00	—
1976FM (U)	976	—	—	—	8.50	—
1977FM (M)	166	—	—	—	32.00	—
1977FM (U)	603	—	—	—	18.00	—
1978FM (M)	166	—	—	—	32.00	—
1978FM (U)	777	—	—	—	10.00	—
1979FM (M)	166	—	—	—	32.00	—
1979FM (U)	1,366	—	—	—	7.50	—
1980FM (U)	1,160	—	—	—	7.50	—

KM# 7a 5 KINA
27.6000 g., 0.5000 Silver .4436 oz. ASW, 40 mm. **Obv:** National emblem **Rev:** New Guinea eagle

Date	Mintage	F	VF	XF	Unc	BU
1975FM (P)	67,000	Value: 8.50				
1976FM (P)	16,000	Value: 8.50				
1977FM (P)	7,721	Value: 8.00				
1978FM (P)	5,540	Value: 8.00				
1979FM (P)	2,728	Value: 8.50				
1980FM (P)	2,125	Value: 9.00				

KM# 18 5 KINA
28.2800 g., 0.5000 Silver .4656 oz. ASW **Series:** International Year of the Child **Obv:** National emblem **Rev:** Kneeling figure holding fish

Date	Mintage	F	VF	XF	Unc	BU
1981	8,775	—	—	—	8.50	—

KM# 20 5 KINA
Copper-Nickel, 40 mm. **Subject:** Defense of the Kokoda Trail **Obv:** National emblem **Rev:** Standing figures

Date	Mintage	F	VF	XF	Unc	BU
1982FM (M)	—	—	—	—	3.50	—

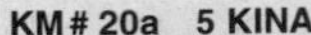

KM# 20a 5 KINA
28.2800 g., 0.9250 Silver .8411 oz. ASW, 40 mm.
Subject: Defense of the Kokoda Trail **Obv:** National emblem **Rev:** Standing figures

Date	Mintage	F	VF	XF	Unc	BU
1982FM (P)	1,795	Value: 14.50				

KM# 23 5 KINA
Copper-Nickel, 40 mm. **Subject:** 10th Anniversary - Bank of Papua New Guinea **Obv:** National emblem **Rev:** Bank divides symbolic design above and value below

Date	Mintage	F	VF	XF	Unc	BU
1983FM (U)	360	—	—	—	7.50	—

KM# 23a 5 KINA
28.2800 g., 0.9250 Silver .8411 oz. ASW, 40 mm. **Subject:** 10th Anniversary - Bank of Papua New Guinea **Obv:** National emblem **Rev:** Bank divides symbolic design above and value below

Date	Mintage	F	VF	XF	Unc	BU
1983FM (P)	673	Value: 20.00				

KM# 25 5 KINA
28.2800 g., 0.9250 Silver .8411 oz. ASW, 40 mm. **Subject:** New Parliament Building **Obv:** National emblem **Rev:** Building
Note: Prev. KM#25a.

Date	Mintage	F	VF	XF	Unc	BU
1984FM (P) Proof	—	Value: 16.50				

KM# 28 5 KINA
28.2800 g., 0.9250 Silver .8411 oz. ASW **Series:** Decade for Women **Obv:** National emblem **Rev:** Half-figure picking berries off branch **Designer:** Michael Rizzello

Date	Mintage	F	VF	XF	Unc	BU
1984FM Proof	1,050	Value: 15.00				

KM# 34 5 KINA
23.3300 g., 0.9250 Silver .6938 oz. ASW **Obv:** National emblem **Rev:** Queen Alexandra butterfly (o. alexandrae)

Date	Mintage	F	VF	XF	Unc	BU
1992FM	500	—	—	—	50.00	—
1992FM (P)	—	Value: 80.00				

KM# 37 5 KINA
27.7800 g., 0.9000 Silver .8038 oz. ASW **Subject:** Centennial of First Coinage **Obv:** National emblem within sprigs **Rev:** Raggiana Bird of Paradise

Date	Mintage	F	VF	XF	Unc	BU
ND(1994) Proof	7,500	Value: 35.00				

KM# 39 5 KINA
31.4700 g., 0.9250 Silver .9359 oz. ASW **Series:** Endangered Wildlife **Obv:** National emblem **Rev:** Two Ribbon Sweetlips fish

Date	Mintage	F	VF	XF	Unc	BU
1997 Proof	10,000	Value: 28.00				

KM# 43 5 KINA
31.5000 g., 0.9250 Silver .9368 oz. ASW, 38.6 mm.
Obv: National emblem **Rev:** Sailing ship **Edge:** Reeded

Date	Mintage	F	VF	XF	Unc	BU
1997 Proof	—	Value: 20.00				

KM# 44 5 KINA
31.4300 g., 0.9250 Silver .9347 oz. ASW, 38.6 mm.
Subject: Green Tree Python **Obv:** National emblem **Rev:** Snake in tree **Edge:** Reeded

Date	Mintage	F	VF	XF	Unc	BU
1997	—	—	—	—	—	—
1998 Proof	—	Value: 50.00				

KM# 47 5 KINA
31.3500 g., 0.9250 Silver 0.9323 oz. ASW, 38.6 mm.
Subject: British Queen Mother **Obv:** National emblem **Rev:** Cameo above Sandringham Palace **Edge:** Reeded

Date	Mintage	F	VF	XF	Unc	BU
1997 Proof	—	Value: 20.00				

KM# 40 5 KINA
20.0000 g., 0.9000 Silver .5787 oz. ASW **Series:** Olympic Games 2000 **Obv:** National emblem **Rev:** Sailboarder

Date	Mintage	F	VF	XF	Unc	BU
1997 Proof	—	Value: 14.50				

KM# 48 5 KINA
31.5300 g., 0.9250 Silver 0.9377 oz. ASW, 38.6 mm.
Subject: Princess Diana **Obv:** National emblem **Rev:** Diana and Bishop Tutu **Edge:** Reeded

Date	Mintage	F	VF	XF	Unc	BU
1998 Proof	—	Value: 25.00				

KM# 45 5 KINA
31.8500 g., 0.9250 Silver 0.9472 oz. ASW, 38.6 mm.
Subject: Queen Mother **Obv:** National emblem **Rev:** Investiture of Prince Charles **Edge:** Reeded

Date	Mintage	F	VF	XF	Unc	BU
1998 Proof	—	Value: 20.00				

KM# 8 10 KINA
Copper-Nickel, 45 mm. **Obv:** National emblem **Rev:** Raggiana Bird of Paradise

Date	Mintage	F	VF	XF	Unc	BU
1975FM (M)	82	—	—	—	60.00	—
1975FM (U)	4,134	—	—	—	9.00	—
1976FM (M)	82	—	—	—	60.00	—
1976FM (U)	976	—	—	—	12.00	—
1978FM (M)	168	—	—	—	50.00	—
1978FM (U)	777	—	—	—	15.00	—
1979FM (M)	82	—	—	—	60.00	—
1979FM (U)	1,366	—	—	—	9.00	—
1980FM (U)	776	—	—	—	12.50	—
1983FM (U)	360	—	—	—	15.00	—

KM# 8a 10 KINA
41.6000 g., 0.9250 Silver 1.2371 oz. ASW, 45 mm.
Obv: National emblem **Rev:** Raggiana Bird of Paradise

Date	Mintage	F	VF	XF	Unc	BU
1975FM (P)	79,000	Value: 20.00				
1976FM (P)	21,000	Value: 20.00				
1978FM (P)	7,352	Value: 20.00				
1979FM (P)	4,147	Value: 20.00				
1980FM (P)	2,752	Value: 22.00				
1983FM (P)	1,025	Value: 22.00				

KM# 8a.1 10 KINA
40.6000 g., 0.9250 Silver 1.2074 oz. ASW, 42 mm.
Subject: Reduced size **Obv:** National emblem **Rev:** Raggiana Bird of Paradise **Edge:** Reeded

Date	Mintage	F	VF	XF	Unc	BU
1983FM Proof	1,025	Value: 32.50				

KM# 11 10 KINA
Copper-Nickel, 45 mm. **Subject:** Silver Jubilee of Queen Elizabeth II **Obv:** National emblem **Rev:** Young bust right

Date	Mintage	F	VF	XF	Unc	BU
1977FM (M)	82	—	—	—	50.00	—
1977FM (U)	603	—	—	—	15.00	—

KM# 11a 10 KINA
40.0000 g., 0.9250 Silver 1.2046 oz. ASW, 45 mm.
Subject: Silver Jubilee of Queen Elizabeth II **Obv:** National emblem **Rev:** Young bust right

Date	Mintage	F	VF	XF	Unc	BU
1977FM (P)	14,000	Value: 18.50				

KM# 21 10 KINA
Copper-Nickel, 45 mm. **Subject:** Royal visit **Obv:** National emblem **Rev:** Conjoined heads right

Date	Mintage	F	VF	XF	Unc	BU
1982FM (M)	—	—	—	—	6.50	—

KM# 21a 10 KINA
40.5000 g., 0.9250 Silver 1.2046 oz. ASW, 45 mm. **Subject:** Royal visit **Obv:** National emblem **Rev:** Conjoined heads right

Date	Mintage	F	VF	XF	Unc	BU
1982FM (P)	1,185	Value: 20.00				

KM# 26 10 KINA
35.6000 g., 0.9250 Silver 1.0587 oz. ASW **Subject:** Papal visit **Obv:** National emblem **Rev:** Pope with arms outstretched with national arms above **Note:** Prev. KM#26a.

Date	Mintage	F	VF	XF	Unc	BU
1984FM (P)	597	Value: 22.50				

KM# 30 10 KINA

42.1200 g., 0.9250 Silver 1.2528 oz. ASW **Subject:** 9th South Pacific Games **Obv:** National emblem **Rev:** Assorted olympic athletes around emblem

Date	Mintage	F	VF	XF	Unc	BU
1991 Proof	1,971	Value: 22.50				

KM# 33 10 KINA

1.5710 g., 0.9990 Gold .0504 oz. AGW **Obv:** National emblem **Rev:** Butterfly

Date	Mintage	F	VF	XF	Unc	BU
1992 Proof	—	Value: 45.00				

KM# 33a 10 KINA

1.5710 g., 0.9950 Platinum .0502 oz. APW **Obv:** National emblem **Rev:** Butterfly

Date	Mintage	F	VF	XF	Unc	BU
1992 Proof	—	Value: 75.00				

KM# 46 10 KINA

155.5000 g., 0.9990 Silver 4.9944 oz. ASW, 64.9 mm. **Subject:** Queen Mother **Obv:** National emblem **Rev:** Queen Mary with the Duchess of York **Edge:** Reeded **Note:** Photo reduced.

Date	Mintage	F	VF	XF	Unc	BU
1998 Proof	3,000	Value: 90.00				

KM# 36 25 KINA

136.0000 g., 0.9250 Silver And Enamel 4.0445 oz., 63 mm. **Obv:** National emblem within wreath **Rev:** Raggiana Bird of Paradise **Note:** Photo reduced.

Date	Mintage	F	VF	XF	Unc	BU
ND(1994) Proof	1,000	Value: 145				

KM# 42 50 KINA

6.2200 g., 0.9000 Gold .18 oz. AGW, 21.9 mm. **Obv:** Crowned head right **Rev:** Golden butterfly and value **Edge:** Reeded

Date	Mintage	F	VF	XF	Unc	BU
1993 Proof	—	Value: 130				

KM# 38 50 KINA

7.9700 g., 0.9000 Gold .2306 oz. AGW **Subject:** Centennial of First Coinage **Obv:** National emblem within wreath **Rev:** Bird of Paradise **Note:** Similar to 5 Kina, KM#37.

Date	Mintage	F	VF	XF	Unc	BU
1994 Proof	1,500	Value: 175				

KM# 9 100 KINA

9.5700 g., 0.9000 Gold .2769 oz. AGW **Subject:** Independence **Obv:** Head 3/4 left **Rev:** Bird of paradise

Date	Mintage	F	VF	XF	Unc	BU
1975FM (M)	100	—	—	—	225	—
1975FM (U)	8,081	—	—	—	190	—
1975FM (P)	18,000	Value: 195				

KM# 10 100 KINA

9.5700 g., 0.9000 Gold .2769 oz. AGW **Subject:** 1st Anniversary of Independence **Obv:** Symbolic design around center hole **Rev:** National emblem above circular designs around center hole

Date	Mintage	F	VF	XF	Unc	BU
1976FM (M)	100	—	—	—	225	—
1976FM (U)	250	—	—	—	195	—
1976FM (P)	8,020	Value: 200				

KM# 12 100 KINA

9.5700 g., 0.9000 Gold .2769 oz. AGW **Obv:** National emblem **Rev:** Papuan hornbill

Date	Mintage	F	VF	XF	Unc	BU
1977FM (M)	100	—	—	—	225	—
1977FM (U)	362	—	—	—	200	—
1977FM (P)	3,460	Value: 210				

KM# 13 100 KINA

9.5700 g., 0.9000 Gold .2769 oz. AGW **Obv:** National emblem **Rev:** Bird-wing butterfly **Shape:** 7-sided

Date	Mintage	F	VF	XF	Unc	BU
1978FM (U)	400	—	—	—	245	—
1978FM (P)	4,751	Value: 200				

KM# 14 100 KINA

9.5700 g., 0.9000 Gold .2769 oz. AGW **Obv:** National emblem **Rev:** Four Faces of the Nation

Date	Mintage	F	VF	XF	Unc	BU
1979FM (M)	102	—	—	—	215	—
1979FM (U)	286	—	—	—	200	—
1979FM (P)	3,492	Value: 190				

KM# 16 100 KINA

7.8300 g., 0.5000 Gold .1258 oz. AGW **Subject:** South Pacific Festival of Arts **Obv:** National emblem **Rev:** Design divides circle

Date	Mintage	F	VF	XF	Unc	BU
1980 Proof	7,500	Value: 95.00				

KM# 17 100 KINA

9.5700 g., 0.9000 Gold .2769 oz. AGW **Subject:** 5th Anniversary of Independence **Obv:** National emblem **Rev:** Map and flag

Date	Mintage	F	VF	XF	Unc	BU
1980FM (M)	30	—	—	—	345	—
1980FM (P)	1,118	Value: 200				

KM# 19 100 KINA

9.5700 g., 0.9000 Gold .2769 oz. AGW **Obv:** Head 1/4 left **Rev:** Bird of paradise and stars

Date	Mintage	F	VF	XF	Unc	BU
1981FM (P)	685	Value: 210				

KM# 22 100 KINA

9.5700 g., 0.9000 Gold .2769 oz. AGW **Subject:** Royal Visit **Obv:** National emblem **Rev:** Conjoined heads right

Date	Mintage	F	VF	XF	Unc	BU
1982FM (P)	484	Value: 220				

KM# 24 100 KINA

9.5700 g., 0.9000 Gold .2769 oz. AGW **Subject:** 10th Anniversary - Bank of Papua New Guinea **Obv:** Symbol around center hole **Rev:** National emblem above center hole

Date	Mintage	F	VF	XF	Unc	BU
1983FM (P)	378	Value: 235				

KM# 27 100 KINA
9.5700 g., 0.9000 Gold .2769 oz. AGW **Subject:** 100th Anniversary - Founding of British and German Protectorates **Obv:** National emblem **Rev:** Value above flags

Date	Mintage	F	VF	XF	Unc	BU
1984FM (P)	274	Value: 250				

KM# 29 100 KINA
9.5700 g., 0.9000 Gold .2769 oz. AGW **Obv:** National emblem **Rev:** Queen Alexandra Butterfly **Shape:** 7-sided

Date	Mintage	F	VF	XF	Unc	BU
1990	500	—	—	—	225	—
1990 Proof	Est. 5,000	Value: 200				
1992 Proof	Est. 5,000	Value: 200				

KM# 29a 100 KINA
9.5700 g., 0.9950 Platinum .3061 oz. APW **Obv:** National emblem **Rev:** Queen Alexandra butterfly

Date	Mintage	F	VF	XF	Unc	BU
1992	500	—	—	—	375	—
1992 Proof	Est. 5,000	Value: 360				

KM# 35 100 KINA
9.5700 g., 0.9000 Gold .2769 oz. AGW **Subject:** 9th South Pacific Games **Obv:** National emblem **Rev:** Artistic design **Shape:** 7-sided

Date	Mintage	F	VF	XF	Unc	BU
1991 Proof	5,000	Value: 195				

PIEFORTS

KM#	Date	Mintage	Identification	Mkt Val
P1	1982	39	5 Kina. Silver. KM18.	100

MINT SETS

KM#	Date	Mintage	Identification	Issue Price	Mkt Val
MS1	1975FM (8)	4,134	KM1-8	30.00	22.50
MS2	1976FM (8)	976	KM1-8	30.00	35.00
MS3	1977FM (8)	603	KM1-7, 11	30.00	55.00
MS4	1978FM (8)	777	KM#1-8	30.00	35.00
MS5	1979FM (8)	1,366	KM1-8	31.00	30.00
MS6	1980FM (9)	—	KM1-8, 15	35.00	30.00
MS7	1982FM (8)	—	KM1-6, 20, 21	36.00	30.00
MS8	1983FM (8)	360	KM1-6, 8, 23	36.00	30.00

PROOF SETS

KM#	Date	Mintage	Identification	Issue Price	Mkt Val
PS1	1975FM (8)	42,340	KM1-6, 7a, 8a	60.00	27.50
PS2	1976FM (8)	16,323	KM1-6, 7a, 8a	60.00	27.50
PS3	1977FM (8)	7,721	KM1-6, 7a, 11a	60.00	35.00
PS4	1978FM (8)	5,540	KM1-6, 7a, 8a	70.00	40.00
PS5	1979FM (8)	2,728	KM1-6, 7a, 8a	72.00	45.00
PS6	1980FM (9)	—	KM1-6, 7a, 8a, 15	130	60.00
PS7	1981FM (6)	10,000	KM1-6	29.00	10.00
PS8	1982FM (8)	—	KM1-6, 20a, 21a	92.00	90.00
PS9	1983FM (8)	—	KM1-6, 8a.1, 23a	132	100
PS10	1984FM (8)	—	KM1-6, 25, 26	133	100
PS11	1992 (4)	250	KM29a, 33, 33a, 34	—	800

PARAGUAY

The Republic of Paraguay, a landlocked country in the heart of South America surrounded by Argentina, Bolivia and Brazil, has an area of 157,048 sq. mi. (406,750 sq. km.) and a population of *4.5 million, 95 percent of whom are of mixed Spanish and Indian descent. Capital: Asuncion. The country is predominantly agrarian, with no important mineral deposits or oil reserves. Meat, timber, hides, oilseeds, tobacco and cotton account for 70 percent of Paraguay's export revenue.

Paraguay was first visited by a ship-wrecked Spaniard named Alejo Garcia, in 1524. The interior was explored by Sebastian Cabot in 1527 and 1528, when he sailed up the Parana and Paraguay rivers. Asuncion, which would become the center of a Spanish colonial province embracing much of southern South America, was established by the Spanish explorer Juan de Salazar on Aug. 15,1537. For 150 years the history of Paraguay was largely the history of the agricultural colonies established by the Jesuits in the south and east to Christianize the Indians. In 1811, following the outbreak of the South American wars of independence, Paraguayan patriots over-threw the local Spanish authorities and proclaimed their country's independence.

During the Triple Alliance War (1864-1870) in which Paraguay faced Argentina, Brazil and Uruguay, Asuncion's ladies gathered in an Assembly on Feb. 24, 1867 and decided to give up their jewelry in order to help the national defense. The President of the Republic, Francisco Solano Lopez accepted the offering and ordered one twentieth of it be used to mint the first Paraguayan gold coins according to the Decree of the 11th of Sept.,1867.

Two dies were made, one by Bouvet, and another by an American, Leonard Charles, while only the die made by Bouvet was eventually used.

MONETARY SYSTEM
100 Centavos (Centesimos) = 1 Peso

MINT MARKS
HF – LeLocle (Swiss)

REPUBLIC

DECIMAL COINAGE

100 Centavos (Centesimos) = Peso

KM# 6 5 CENTAVOS
Copper-Nickel **Obv:** Seated lion with liberty cap on pole, date below **Obv. Legend:** REPUBLICA DEL PARAGUAY **Rev:** Value within wreath

Date	Mintage	F	VF	XF	Unc	BU
1903	600,000	2.00	8.00	25.00	75.00	—

KM# 9 5 CENTAVOS
Copper-Nickel **Obv:** Radiant star within wreath **Rev:** Value within flower chain

Date	Mintage	F	VF	XF	Unc	BU
1908	400,000	2.50	8.00	30.00	75.00	—

KM# 7 10 CENTAVOS
Copper-Nickel **Obv:** Seated lion with liberty cap on pole, date below **Obv. Legend:** REPUBLICA DEL PARAGUAY **Rev:** Value within wreath

Date	Mintage	F	VF	XF	Unc	BU
1903	1,200,000	1.50	4.00	15.00	35.00	—

KM# 10 10 CENTAVOS
Copper-Nickel **Obv:** Radiant star within wreath **Rev:** Value within flower chain

Date	Mintage	F	VF	XF	Unc	BU
1908	800,000	2.50	6.50	25.00	75.00	—

KM# 8 20 CENTAVOS
Copper-Nickel **Obv:** Seated lion with liberty cap on pole, date below **Obv. Legend:** REPUBLICA DEL PARAGUAY **Rev:** Value within wreath

Date	Mintage	F	VF	XF	Unc	BU
1903	750,000	1.50	4.00	20.00	65.00	—

KM# 11 20 CENTAVOS
Copper-Nickel **Obv:** Radiant star within wreath **Rev:** Value

Date	Mintage	F	VF	XF	Unc	BU
1908	1,000,000	2.50	7.00	35.00	80.00	—

KM# 12 50 CENTAVOS
Copper-Nickel **Obv:** Radiant star within wreath **Rev:** Value

Date	Mintage	F	VF	XF	Unc	BU
1925	4,000,000	0.50	1.50	5.00	15.00	—

KM# 15 50 CENTAVOS
Aluminum **Obv:** Radiant star within wreath **Rev:** Value

Date	Mintage	F	VF	XF	Unc	BU
1938	400,000	0.50	1.00	3.50	10.00	—

KM# 13 PESO
Copper-Nickel **Obv:** Radiant star within wreath **Rev:** Value

Date	Mintage	F	VF	XF	Unc	BU
1925	3,500,000	0.50	1.00	5.00	10.00	—

KM# 16 PESO
Aluminum **Obv:** Radiant star within wreath **Rev:** Value

Date	Mintage	F	VF	XF	Unc	BU
1938	—	0.50	1.50	3.00	8.00	—

KM# 14 2 PESOS
Copper-Nickel **Obv:** Radiant star within wreath **Rev:** Value

Date	Mintage	F	VF	XF	Unc	BU
1925	2,500,000	0.50	1.00	6.00	12.00	—

KM# 17 2 PESOS
Aluminum **Obv:** Radiant star within wreath **Rev:** Value

Date	Mintage	F	VF	XF	Unc	BU
1938	—	0.50	1.50	3.00	10.00	—

KM# 18 5 PESOS
Copper-Nickel **Obv:** Radiant star within wreath **Rev:** Value

Date	Mintage	F	VF	XF	Unc	BU
1939	4,000,000	1.00	3.50	10.00	20.00	—

KM# 19 10 PESOS
Copper-Nickel **Obv:** Radiant star within wreath **Rev:** Value

Date	Mintage	F	VF	XF	Unc	BU
1939	4,000,000	1.00	2.00	7.00	18.00	—

REFORM COINAGE

100 Centimos = 1 Guarani

KM# 20 CENTIMO
Aluminum-Bronze **Obv:** Flower within circle **Rev:** Value within wreath

Date	Mintage	F	VF	XF	Unc	BU
1944	3,500,000	0.10	0.50	1.00	5.00	—
1948HF	2,000,000	0.10	0.50	1.00	4.00	—
1950HF	1,096,000	0.10	0.25	0.75	3.00	—

KM# 21 5 CENTIMOS
Aluminum-Bronze **Obv:** Passion flower within circle **Rev:** Value within wreath

Date	Mintage	F	VF	XF	Unc	BU
1944	2,195,000	0.10	0.50	1.00	4.00	—
1947HF	13,111,000	0.10	0.20	0.50	2.00	—

KM# 22 10 CENTIMOS
Aluminum-Bronze **Obv:** Orchid within circle **Rev:** Value within wreath

Date	Mintage	F	VF	XF	Unc	BU
1944	975,000	0.25	0.75	3.00	6.00	—
1947	6,656,000	0.10	0.25	1.00	3.00	—
1947HF	—	0.20	0.50	2.00	5.00	—

KM# 25 10 CENTIMOS
Aluminum-Bronze **Obv:** Seated lion with liberty cap on pole within circle **Rev:** Value within wreath **Shape:** Scalloped

Date	Mintage	F	VF	XF	Unc	BU
1953	5,000,000	0.10	0.15	0.50	1.00	—
1953 Proof; 1 known	—	Value: 375				

Note: Medal die rotation

KM# 26 15 CENTIMOS
Aluminum-Bronze **Obv:** Seated lion with liberty cap on pole within circle **Rev:** Value within wreath **Shape:** Scalloped

Date	Mintage	F	VF	XF	Unc	BU
1953	5,000,000	0.10	0.20	0.35	1.00	—
1953 Proof; 1 known	—	Value: 375				

Note: Medal die rotation

KM# 23 25 CENTIMOS
Aluminum-Bronze **Obv:** Orchid within circle **Rev:** Value within wreath

Date	Mintage	F	VF	XF	Unc	BU
1944	700,000	0.25	1.00	3.00	12.00	—
1948HF	600,000	0.25	0.75	2.50	9.00	—
1951HF	1,000,000	0.25	0.75	1.50	5.00	—

KM# 27 25 CENTIMOS
Aluminum-Bronze **Obv:** Seated lion with liberty cap on pole within circle **Rev:** Value within wreath **Shape:** Scalloped

Date	Mintage	F	VF	XF	Unc	BU
1953	2,000,000	0.10	0.15	0.30	1.00	2.00
1953 Proof; 1 known	—	Value: 450				

Note: Medal die rotation

KM# 24 50 CENTIMOS
Aluminum-Bronze **Obv:** Seated lion with liberty cap on pole within circle **Rev:** Value within wreath

Date	Mintage	F	VF	XF	Unc	BU
1944	2,485,000	0.25	1.00	2.00	7.00	—
1951	2,893,000	0.25	0.50	1.25	3.00	4.00

KM# 28 50 CENTIMOS
Aluminum-Bronze **Obv:** Seated lion with liberty cap on pole within circle **Rev:** Value within wreath **Shape:** Scalloped

Date	Mintage	F	VF	XF	Unc	BU
1953	2,000,000	0.10	0.15	0.30	1.00	2.50
1953 Proof; 1 known	—	Value: 450				

Note: Medal die rotation

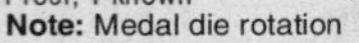

KM# 151 GUARANI
Stainless Steel **Obv:** Soldier 3/4 facing **Rev:** Tobacco plant and value

Date	Mintage	F	VF	XF	Unc	BU
1975	10,000,000	—	—	0.15	0.50	0.75
1975 Proof	1,000	Value: 6.00				
1976	12,000,000	—	—	0.10	0.40	0.65
1976 Proof	1,000	Value: 8.00				

KM# 151a GUARANI
Gold, 18 mm.

Date	Mintage	F	VF	XF	Unc	BU
1976 Proof	—	—	—	—	—	—

KM# 165a GUARANI
Gold, 18 mm.

Date	Mintage	F	VF	XF	Unc	BU
1978 Proof	—	—	—	—	—	—
1980 Proof	—	—	—	—	—	—

KM# 165 GUARANI
Stainless Steel **Series:** F.A.O. **Obv:** Standing 3/4 figure facing **Rev:** Plant and value **Note:** Varieties exist.

Date	Mintage	F	VF	XF	Unc	BU
1978	15,000,000	—	—	0.15	0.50	0.75
1980	13,000,000	—	—	0.15	0.50	0.75
1980 Proof	1,000	Value: 6.00				
1984	15,000,000	—	—	0.10	0.30	0.50
1986	15,000,000	—	—	0.10	0.30	0.50
1988	15,000,000	—	—	0.10	0.30	0.50

KM# 192 GUARANI
Brass Plated Steel **Series:** F.A.O.

Date	Mintage	F	VF	XF	Unc	BU
1992	15,000,000	—	—	0.15	0.50	0.75
1993	5,000,000	—	—	0.15	0.50	0.75

KM# 193 GUARANI
27.0000 g., 0.9250 Silver .8030 oz. ASW **Subject:** Encuentro De Dos Mundos **Obv:** National arms within circle of assorted arms **Rev:** Dancer and artistic design within circle

Date	Mintage	F	VF	XF	Unc	BU
1997 Proof	—	Value: 50.00				

KM# 196 GUARANI
27.1000 g., 0.9250 Silver 0.8059 oz. ASW, 40 mm.
Subject: Ibero-America Series **Obv:** National arms within circle of assorted arms **Rev:** Cowboy on horse **Edge:** Reeded

Date	Mintage	F	VF	XF	Unc	BU
2000 Proof	—	Value: 60.00				

KM# 152 5 GUARANIES
3.8000 g., Stainless Steel, 20 mm. **Obv:** Half-length figure with jug looking right **Rev:** Cotton plant and value

Date	Mintage	F	VF	XF	Unc	BU
1975	7,500,000	—	—	0.15	0.50	0.75
1975 Proof	1,000	Value: 6.00				

KM# 166b 5 GUARANIES
Gold, 20 mm.

Date	Mintage	F	VF	XF	Unc	BU
1978 Proof	—	—	—	—	—	—
1980 Proof	—	—	—	—	—	—

KM# 166 5 GUARANIES
3.8000 g., Stainless Steel, 20 mm. **Series:** F.A.O. **Obv:** Half-length figure with jug looking right **Rev:** Cotton plant and value **Note:** Varieties exist.

Date	Mintage	F	VF	XF	Unc	BU
1978	10,000,000	—	—	0.15	0.60	0.85
1980	12,000,000	—	—	0.15	0.60	0.85
1980 Proof	1,000	Value: 6.00				
1984	15,000,000	—	—	0.10	0.40	0.60
1986	15,000,000	—	—	0.10	0.40	0.60

KM# 166a 5 GUARANIES
Nickel-Bronze, 20 mm. **Series:** F.A.O. **Obv:** Half-length figure with jug looking right **Rev:** Cotton plant and value

Date	Mintage	F	VF	XF	Unc	BU
1992	15,000,000	—	—	0.10	0.30	0.50

KM# 153 10 GUARANIES
4.5000 g., Stainless Steel, 22 mm. **Obv:** Bust 1/4 left **Rev:** Cow head left and value

Date	Mintage	F	VF	XF	Unc	BU
1975	10,000,000	—	0.10	0.20	0.75	1.00
1975 Proof	1,000	Value: 8.00				

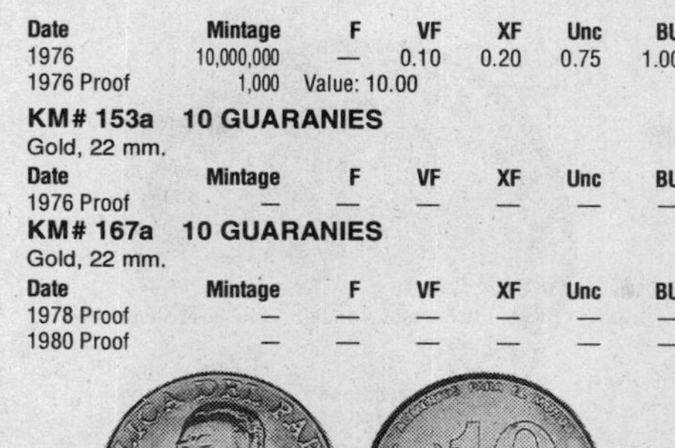

Date	Mintage	F	VF	XF	Unc	BU
1976	10,000,000	—	0.10	0.20	0.75	1.00
1976 Proof	1,000	Value: 10.00				

KM# 153a 10 GUARANIES
Gold, 22 mm.

Date	Mintage	F	VF	XF	Unc	BU
1976 Proof	—	—	—	—	—	—

KM# 167a 10 GUARANIES
Gold, 22 mm.

Date	Mintage	F	VF	XF	Unc	BU
1978 Proof	—	—	—	—	—	—
1980 Proof	—	—	—	—	—	—

KM# 167 10 GUARANIES
4.5000 g., Stainless Steel, 22 mm. **Series:** F.A.O. **Obv:** Bust 1/4 left **Rev:** Cow head left and value **Note:** Varieties exist.

Date	Mintage	F	VF	XF	Unc	BU
1978	15,000,000	—	0.10	0.20	0.75	1.00
1980	15,000,000	—	0.10	0.20	0.75	1.00
1980 Proof	1,000	Value: 8.00				
1984	20,000,000	—	0.10	0.15	0.50	0.75
1986	35,000,000	—	0.10	0.15	0.50	0.75
1988	40,000,000	—	0.10	0.15	0.50	0.75

KM# 178 10 GUARANIES
Nickel-Bronze **Series:** F.A.O. **Obv:** Bust 1/4 left **Rev:** Cow head left and value

Date	Mintage	F	VF	XF	Unc	BU
1990	40,000,000	—	—	0.10	0.40	0.60
1996	20,000,000	—	—	0.10	0.40	0.60

KM# 154 50 GUARANIES
7.4000 g., Stainless Steel, 26.1 mm. **Obv:** Uniformed bust facing **Rev:** Value above dam on the Acaray River

Date	Mintage	F	VF	XF	Unc	BU
1975	9,500,000	0.20	0.40	0.60	1.25	1.50
1975 Proof	1,000	Value: 10.00				

KM# 169a 50 GUARANIES
Gold, 25 mm.

Date	Mintage	F	VF	XF	Unc	BU
1980 Proof	—	—	—	—	—	—

KM# 169 50 GUARANIES
7.4000 g., Stainless Steel, 26.1 mm. **Obv:** Head of General Estigarribia facing **Rev:** Acaray River Dam **Note:** Varieties exist.

Date	Mintage	F	VF	XF	Unc	BU
1980	10,700,000	0.20	0.40	0.60	1.25	1.50
1980 Proof	1,000	Value: 10.00				
1986	15,000,000	0.20	0.40	0.60	1.25	1.50
1988	25,000,000	0.20	0.30	0.50	1.00	1.25

KM# 191 50 GUARANIES
Copper-Zinc-Nickel **Obv:** Uniformed bust facing **Rev:** Value above river dam

Date	Mintage	F	VF	XF	Unc	BU
1992	35,000,000	—	—	—	0.75	1.00
1995	25,000,000	—	—	—	0.75	1.00
1998	22,000,000	—	—	—	0.75	1.00

KM# 177 100 GUARANIES
10.4500 g., Copper-Zinc-Nickel **Obv:** Uniformed bust facing **Rev:** Building flanked by designs

Date	Mintage	F	VF	XF	Unc	BU
1990	35,000,000	—	—	—	2.25	2.75

KM# 177a 100 GUARANIES
5.4500 g., Brass Plated Steel **Obv:** Uniformed bust facing **Rev:** Building flanked by designs **Note:** Reduced weight and thickness.

Date	Mintage	F	VF	XF	Unc	BU
1993	35,000,000	—	—	—	1.50	2.00
1995	10,000,000	—	—	—	1.50	2.00
1996	30,000,000	—	—	—	1.50	2.00

KM# 31 150 GUARANIES
25.0000 g., 0.9990 Silver .8030 oz. ASW **Obv:** National arms **Rev:** Uniformed bust of General A. Stroessner facing

Date	Mintage	F	VF	XF	Unc	BU
1972 Proof	Est. 10,000	Value: 60.00				

KM# 32 150 GUARANIES
25.0000 g., 0.9990 Silver .8030 oz. ASW **Subject:** Munich Olympics **Obv:** National arms **Rev:** Runner flanked by design and Olympic rings

Date	Mintage	F	VF	XF	Unc	BU
1972 Proof	Est. 10,000	Value: 70.00				

KM# 33 150 GUARANIES
25.0000 g., 0.9990 Silver .8030 oz. ASW **Subject:** Munich Olympics **Obv:** National arms **Rev:** Broad jumper

Date	Mintage	F	VF	XF	Unc	BU
1972 Proof	Est. 10,000	Value: 70.00				

KM# 34 150 GUARANIES
25.0000 g., 0.9990 Silver .8030 oz. ASW **Subject:** Munich Olympics **Obv:** National arms **Rev:** Soccer player

Date	Mintage	F	VF	XF	Unc	BU
1972 Proof	Est. 10,000	Value: 70.00				

KM# 35 150 GUARANIES
25.0000 g., 0.9990 Silver .8030 oz. ASW **Subject:** Munich Olympics **Obv:** National arms **Rev:** Hurdler

Date	Mintage	F	VF	XF	Unc	BU
1972 Proof	Est. 10,000	Value: 70.00				

KM# 36 150 GUARANIES
25.0000 g., 0.9990 Silver .8030 oz. ASW **Subject:** Munich Olympics **Obv:** National arms **Rev:** High jumper

Date	Mintage	F	VF	XF	Unc	BU
1972 Proof	Est. 10,000	Value: 70.00				

KM# 37 150 GUARANIES
25.0000 g., 0.9990 Silver .8030 oz. ASW **Subject:** Munich Olympics **Obv:** National arms **Rev:** Boxer

Date	Mintage	F	VF	XF	Unc	BU
1973 Proof	Est. 10,000	Value: 70.00				

KM# 59 150 GUARANIES
25.0000 g., 0.9990 Silver .8030 oz. ASW **Obv:** National arms **Rev:** Mariscal Jose F. Estigarribia

Date	Mintage	F	VF	XF	Unc	BU
1973 Proof	Est. 10,000	Value: 55.00				

KM# 60 150 GUARANIES
25.0000 g., 0.9990 Silver .8030 oz. ASW **Obv:** National arms **Rev:** Mariscal Francisco Solano Lopez

Date	Mintage	F	VF	XF	Unc	BU
1973 Proof	Est. 10,000	Value: 55.00				

KM# 61 150 GUARANIES
25.0000 g., 0.9990 Silver .8030 oz. ASW **Obv:** National arms **Rev:** General Jose E. Diaz

Date	Mintage	F	VF	XF	Unc	BU
1973 Proof	Est. 10,000	Value: 52.50				

KM# 62 150 GUARANIES
25.0000 g., 0.9990 Silver .8030 oz. ASW **Obv:** National arms **Rev:** General Bernardino Cabaliero

Date	Mintage	F	VF	XF	Unc	BU
1973 Proof	Est. 10,000	Value: 52.50				

KM# 63 150 GUARANIES
25.0000 g., 0.9990 Silver .8030 oz. ASW **Obv:** National arms **Rev:** Teotihucana Culture sculpture

Date	Mintage	F	VF	XF	Unc	BU
1973 Proof	Est. 10,000	Value: 52.50				

KM# 64 150 GUARANIES
25.0000 g., 0.9990 Silver .8030 oz. ASW **Obv:** National arms **Rev:** Huasteca Culture sculpture

Date	Mintage	F	VF	XF	Unc	BU
1973 Proof	Est. 10,000	Value: 52.50				

KM# 65 150 GUARANIES
25.0000 g., 0.9990 Silver .8030 oz. ASW **Obv:** National arms **Rev:** Mixteca Culture animal sculpture

Date	Mintage	F	VF	XF	Unc	BU
1973 Proof	Est. 10,000	Value: 52.50				

KM# 66 150 GUARANIES
25.0000 g., 0.9990 Silver .8030 oz. ASW **Obv:** National arms **Rev:** Veracruz Ceramica Vase

Date	Mintage	F	VF	XF	Unc	BU
1973 Proof	Est. 10,000	Value: 52.50				

KM# 67 150 GUARANIES
25.0000 g., 0.9990 Silver .8030 oz. ASW **Obv:** National arms
Rev: Veracruz Culture sculpture facing

Date	Mintage	F	VF	XF	Unc	BU
1973 Proof	Est. 10,000	Value: 52.50				

KM# 68 150 GUARANIES
25.0000 g., 0.9990 Silver .8030 oz. ASW **Obv:** National arms
Rev: Albrecht Durer facing

Date	Mintage	F	VF	XF	Unc	BU
1973 Proof	Est. 10,000	Value: 65.00				

KM# 69 150 GUARANIES
25.0000 g., 0.9990 Silver .8030 oz. ASW **Obv:** National arms
Rev: Johann Wolfgang Goethe

Date	Mintage	F	VF	XF	Unc	BU
1973 Proof	Est. 10,000	Value: 65.00				

KM# 107 150 GUARANIES
25.0000 g., 0.9990 Silver .8030 oz. ASW **Obv:** National arms
Rev: Head of President Abraham Lincoln left

Date	Mintage	F	VF	XF	Unc	BU
1974 Proof	Est. 10,000	Value: 75.00				

KM# 108 150 GUARANIES
25.0000 g., 0.9990 Silver .8030 oz. ASW **Obv:** National arms
Rev: Ludwig van Beethoven

Date	Mintage	F	VF	XF	Unc	BU
1974 Proof	Est. 10,000	Value: 75.00				

KM# 109 150 GUARANIES
25.0000 g., 0.9990 Silver .8030 oz. ASW **Obv:** National arms
Rev: Head of Otto von Bismarck right

Date	Mintage	F	VF	XF	Unc	BU
1974 Proof	Est. 10,000	Value: 75.00				

KM# 110 150 GUARANIES
25.0000 g., 0.9990 Silver .8030 oz. ASW **Obv:** National arms
Rev: Head of Albert Einstein left

Date	Mintage	F	VF	XF	Unc	BU
1974 Proof	Est. 10,000	Value: 85.00				

KM# 111 150 GUARANIES
25.0000 g., 0.9990 Silver .8030 oz. ASW **Obv:** National arms
Rev: Head of Giuseppe Garibaldi facing

Date	Mintage	F	VF	XF	Unc	BU
1974 Proof	Est. 10,000	Value: 65.00				

KM# 112 150 GUARANIES
25.0000 g., 0.9990 Silver .8030 oz. ASW **Obv:** National arms
Rev: Head of Alessandro Manzoni facing

Date	Mintage	F	VF	XF	Unc	BU
1974 Proof	Est. 10,000	Value: 57.50				

KM# 113 150 GUARANIES
25.0000 g., 0.9990 Silver .8030 oz. ASW **Obv:** National arms
Rev: William Tell and son facing

Date	Mintage	F	VF	XF	Unc	BU
1974 Proof	Est. 10,000	Value: 57.50				

KM# 114 150 GUARANIES
25.0000 g., 0.9990 Silver .8030 oz. ASW **Obv:** National arms
Rev: Head of John F. Kennedy left

Date	Mintage	F	VF	XF	Unc	BU
1974 Proof	Est. 10,000	Value: 55.00				

KM# 115 150 GUARANIES
25.0000 g., 0.9990 Silver .8030 oz. ASW **Obv:** National arms
Rev: Head of Konrad Adenauer left

Date	Mintage	F	VF	XF	Unc	BU
1974 Proof	Est. 10,000	Value: 65.00				

KM# 116 150 GUARANIES
25.0000 g., 0.9990 Silver .8030 oz. ASW **Obv:** National arms
Rev: Head of Winston Churchill left

Date	Mintage	F	VF	XF	Unc	BU
1974 Proof	Est. 10,000	Value: 55.00				

KM# 117 150 GUARANIES
25.0000 g., 0.9990 Silver .8030 oz. ASW **Obv:** National arms
Rev: Head of Pope John XXIII left

Date	Mintage	F	VF	XF	Unc	BU
1974 Proof	Est. 10,000	Value: 65.00				

KM# 118 150 GUARANIES
25.0000 g., 0.9990 Silver .8030 oz. ASW **Obv:** National arms **Rev:** Head of Pope Paul VI left

Date	Mintage	F	VF	XF	Unc	BU
1974 Proof	Est. 10,000	Value: 65.00				

KM# 155 150 GUARANIES
25.0000 g., 0.9990 Silver .8030 oz. ASW **Obv:** National arms **Rev:** Parliament building

Date	Mintage	F	VF	XF	Unc	BU
1975 Proof	Est. 10,000	Value: 55.00				

KM# 156 150 GUARANIES
25.0000 g., 0.9990 Silver .8030 oz. ASW **Subject:** Apollo 11 Mission **Obv:** National arms **Rev:** Eagle landing on moon with earth at left

Date	Mintage	F	VF	XF	Unc	BU
1975 Proof	Est. 10,000	Value: 65.00				

KM# 157 150 GUARANIES
25.0000 g., 0.9990 Silver .8030 oz. ASW **Subject:** Apollo 15 Mission **Obv:** National arms **Rev:** Apollo mission design within circle

Date	Mintage	F	VF	XF	Unc	BU
1975 Proof	Est. 10,000	Value: 65.00				

KM# 158 150 GUARANIES
25.0000 g., 0.9990 Silver .8030 oz. ASW **Obv:** National arms **Rev:** Friendship Bridge

Date	Mintage	F	VF	XF	Unc	BU
1975 Proof	Est. 10,000	Value: 57.50				

KM# 159 150 GUARANIES
25.0000 g., 0.9990 Silver .8030 oz. ASW **Obv:** National arms **Rev:** Holy Trinity Church

Date	Mintage	F	VF	XF	Unc	BU
1975 Proof	Est. 10,000	Value: 57.50				

KM# 160 150 GUARANIES
25.0000 g., 0.9990 Silver .8030 oz. ASW **Obv:** National arms **Rev:** Ruins of Humaita

Date	Mintage	F	VF	XF	Unc	BU
1975 Proof	Est. 10,000	Value: 57.50				

KM# 29 300 GUARANIES
26.6000 g., 0.7200 Silver .6157 oz. ASW **Subject:** 4th Term of President Stroessner **Obv:** Seated lion with liberty cap on pole within circle **Rev:** Head left

Date	Mintage	F	VF	XF	Unc	BU
1968	250,000	—	—	7.00	10.00	14.00

KM# 194 500 GUARANIES
Brass **Obv:** Head of General Bernardino Caballero facing **Rev:** Bank of Paraguay within circle

Date	Mintage	F	VF	XF	Unc	BU
1997	20,000,000	—	—	—	2.50	3.00

KM# 195 500 GUARANIES
Brass **Obv:** Head of General Bernardino Caballero facing **Rev:** Bank above value within circle

Date	Mintage	F	VF	XF	Unc	BU
1997	—	—	—	—	35.00	50.00
1998	15,000,000	—	—	—	2.50	3.00

KM# 38 1500 GUARANIES
10.7000 g., 0.9000 Gold .3096 oz. AGW **Obv:** National arms **Rev:** Uniformed bust of General A. Stroessner facing

Date	Mintage	F	VF	XF	Unc	BU
1972 Proof	Est. 1,500	Value: 325				

KM# 39 1500 GUARANIES
10.7000 g., 0.9000 Gold .3096 oz. AGW **Subject:** Munich Olympics **Obv:** National arms **Rev:** Runner

Date	Mintage	F	VF	XF	Unc	BU
1972 Proof	Est. 1,500	Value: 750				

KM# 40 1500 GUARANIES
10.7000 g., 0.9000 Gold .3096 oz. AGW **Subject:** Munich Olympics **Obv:** National arms **Rev:** Broad jumper

Date	Mintage	F	VF	XF	Unc	BU
1972 Proof	Est. 1,500	Value: 750				

KM# 41 1500 GUARANIES
10.7000 g., 0.9000 Gold .3096 oz. AGW **Subject:** Munich Olympics **Obv:** National arms **Rev:** Soccer

Date	Mintage	F	VF	XF	Unc	BU
1972 Proof	Est. 1,500	Value: 750				

KM# 42 1500 GUARANIES
10.7000 g., 0.9000 Gold .3096 oz. AGW **Subject:** Munich Olympics **Obv:** National arms **Rev:** Hurdler

Date	Mintage	F	VF	XF	Unc	BU
1972 Proof	Est. 1,500	Value: 750				

KM# 43 1500 GUARANIES
10.7000 g., 0.9000 Gold .3096 oz. AGW **Subject:** Munich Olympics **Obv:** National arms **Rev:** High Jumper

Date	Mintage	F	VF	XF	Unc	BU
1973 Proof	1,500	Value: 750				

KM# 44 1500 GUARANIES
10.7000 g., 0.9000 Gold .3096 oz. AGW **Subject:** Munich Olympics **Obv:** National arms **Rev:** Boxer

Date	Mintage	F	VF	XF	Unc	BU
1973 Proof	Est. 1,500	Value: 750				

KM# 70 1500 GUARANIES
10.7000 g., 0.9000 Gold .3096 oz. AGW **Obv:** National arms **Rev:** Mariscal Jose F. Estigarriba

Date	Mintage	F	VF	XF	Unc	BU
1973 Proof	Est. 1,500	Value: 400				

KM# 71 1500 GUARANIES
10.7000 g., 0.9000 Gold .3096 oz. AGW **Obv:** National arms **Rev:** Head of Mariscal Francisco Solano Lopez facing

Date	Mintage	F	VF	XF	Unc	BU
1973 Proof	Est. 1,500	Value: 400				

KM# 72 1500 GUARANIES
10.7000 g., 0.9000 Gold .3096 oz. AGW **Obv:** National arms **Rev:** Bust of General Jose E. Diaz facing

Date	Mintage	F	VF	XF	Unc	BU
1973 Proof	Est. 1,500	Value: 400				

KM# 73 1500 GUARANIES
10.7000 g., 0.9000 Gold .3096 oz. AGW **Obv:** National arms **Rev:** Head of General Bernardino Caballero facing

Date	Mintage	F	VF	XF	Unc	BU
1973 Proof	Est. 1,500	Value: 400				

KM# 74 1500 GUARANIES
10.7000 g., 0.9000 Gold .3096 oz. AGW **Obv:** National arms **Rev:** Teotihucana Culture sculpture facing

Date	Mintage	F	VF	XF	Unc	BU
1973 Proof	Est. 1,500	Value: 400				

KM# 75 1500 GUARANIES
10.7000 g., 0.9000 Gold .3096 oz. AGW **Obv:** National arms **Rev:** Huasteca Culture sculpture

Date	Mintage	F	VF	XF	Unc	BU
1973 Proof	Est. 1,500	Value: 400				

KM# 76 1500 GUARANIES
10.7000 g., 0.9000 Gold .3096 oz. AGW **Obv:** National arms **Rev:** Mixteca Culture sculpture

Date	Mintage	F	VF	XF	Unc	BU
1973 Proof	Est. 1,500	Value: 400				

KM# 77 1500 GUARANIES
10.7000 g., 0.9000 Gold .3096 oz. AGW **Obv:** National arms **Rev:** Veracruz Ceramica vase

Date	Mintage	F	VF	XF	Unc	BU
1973 Proof	Est. 1,500	Value: 400				

KM# 78 1500 GUARANIES
10.7000 g., 0.9000 Gold .3096 oz. AGW **Obv:** National arms **Rev:** Veracruz Culture sculpture

Date	Mintage	F	VF	XF	Unc	BU
1973 Proof	Est. 1,500	Value: 400				

KM# 79 1500 GUARANIES
10.7000 g., 0.9000 Gold .3096 oz. AGW **Obv:** National arms **Rev:** Bust of Albrecht Durer facing

Date	Mintage	F	VF	XF	Unc	BU
1973 Proof	Est. 1,500	Value: 400				

KM# 80 1500 GUARANIES
10.7000 g., 0.9000 Gold .3096 oz. AGW **Obv:** National arms **Rev:** Bust of Johann Wolfgang Goethe facing

Date	Mintage	F	VF	XF	Unc	BU
1973 Proof	Est. 1,500	Value: 400				

KM# 119 1500 GUARANIES
10.7000 g., 0.9000 Gold .3096 oz. AGW **Obv:** National arms **Rev:** Bust of President Abraham Lincoln left

Date	Mintage	F	VF	XF	Unc	BU
1974 Proof	Est. 1,500	Value: 400				

KM# 120 1500 GUARANIES
10.7000 g., 0.9000 Gold .3096 oz. AGW **Obv:** National arms **Rev:** Bust of Ludwig van Beethoven left

Date	Mintage	F	VF	XF	Unc	BU
1974 Proof	Est. 1,500	Value: 750				

KM# 121 1500 GUARANIES
10.7000 g., 0.9000 Gold .3096 oz. AGW **Obv:** National arms **Rev:** Head of Otto von Bismarck right

Date	Mintage	F	VF	XF	Unc	BU
1974 Proof	Est. 1,500	Value: 400				

KM# 122 1500 GUARANIES
10.7000 g., 0.9000 Gold .3096 oz. AGW **Obv:** National arms **Rev:** Head of Albert Einstein left

Date	Mintage	F	VF	XF	Unc	BU
1974 Proof	Est. 1,500	Value: 400				

KM# 123 1500 GUARANIES
10.7000 g., 0.9000 Gold .3096 oz. AGW **Obv:** National arms **Rev:** Giuseppe Garibaldi facing

Date	Mintage	F	VF	XF	Unc	BU
1974 Proof	Est. 1,500	Value: 400				

KM# 124 1500 GUARANIES
10.7000 g., 0.9000 Gold .3096 oz. AGW **Obv:** National arms **Rev:** Alessandro Manzoni facing

Date	Mintage	F	VF	XF	Unc	BU
1974 Proof	Est. 1,500	Value: 400				

KM# 125 1500 GUARANIES
10.7000 g., 0.9000 Gold .3096 oz. AGW **Obv:** National arms **Rev:** William Tell and son facing

Date	Mintage	F	VF	XF	Unc	BU
1974 Proof	Est. 1,500	Value: 400				

KM# 126 1500 GUARANIES
10.7000 g., 0.9000 Gold .3096 oz. AGW **Obv:** National arms **Rev:** Head of John F. Kennedy left

Date	Mintage	F	VF	XF	Unc	BU
1974 Proof	Est. 1,500	Value: 400				

KM# 127 1500 GUARANIES
10.7000 g., 0.9000 Gold .3096 oz. AGW **Obv:** National arms **Rev:** Head of Konrad Adenauer left

Date	Mintage	F	VF	XF	Unc	BU
1974 Proof	Est. 1,500	Value: 400				

KM# 128 1500 GUARANIES
10.7000 g., 0.9000 Gold .3096 oz. AGW **Obv:** National arms **Rev:** Head of Winston Churchill left

Date	Mintage	F	VF	XF	Unc	BU
1974 Proof	Est. 1,500	Value: 400				

KM# 129 1500 GUARANIES
10.7000 g., 0.9000 Gold .3096 oz. AGW **Obv:** National arms **Rev:** Head of Pope John XXIII left

Date	Mintage	F	VF	XF	Unc	BU
1974 Proof	Est. 1,500	Value: 400				

KM# 130 1500 GUARANIES
10.7000 g., 0.9000 Gold .3096 oz. AGW **Obv:** National arms **Rev:** Head of Pope Paul VI left

Date	Mintage	F	VF	XF	Unc	BU
1974 Proof	Est. 1,500	Value: 400				

KM# 179 1500 GUARANIES
10.7000 g., 0.9000 Gold .3096 oz. AGW **Obv:** National arms **Rev:** Parliament building

Date	Mintage	F	VF	XF	Unc	BU
1975 Proof	1,500	Value: 400				

KM# 180 1500 GUARANIES
10.7000 g., 0.9000 Gold **Subject:** Apollo 11 Mission **Obv:** National arms **Rev:** Eagle landing on moon with earth at left

Date	Mintage	F	VF	XF	Unc	BU
1975 Proof	1,500	Value: 500				

KM# 181 1500 GUARANIES
10.7000 g., 0.9000 Gold **Subject:** Apollo 15 Mission **Obv:** National arms **Rev:** Apollo mission design within circle

Date	Mintage	F	VF	XF	Unc	BU
1975 Proof	1,500	Value: 500				

KM# 182 1500 GUARANIES
10.7000 g., 0.9000 Gold **Obv:** National arms **Rev:** Friendship Bridge

Date	Mintage	F	VF	XF	Unc	BU
1975 Proof	1,500	Value: 400				

KM# 183 1500 GUARANIES
10.7000 g., 0.9000 Gold **Obv:** National arms **Rev:** Holy Trinity Chruch

Date	Mintage	F	VF	XF	Unc	BU
1975 Proof	1,500	Value: 400				

KM# 184 1500 GUARANIES

10.7000 g., 0.9000 Gold **Obv:** National arms **Rev:** Ruins of Humaita

Date	Mintage	F	VF	XF	Unc	BU
1975 Proof	Est. 1,500	Value: 400				

KM# 45 3000 GUARANIES

21.3000 g., 0.9000 Gold .6164 oz. AGW **Obv:** National arms **Rev:** Uniformed bust of General A. Stroessner facing

Date	Mintage	F	VF	XF	Unc	BU
1972 Proof	Est. 1,500	Value: 500				

KM# 46 3000 GUARANIES

21.3000 g., 0.9000 Gold .6164 oz. AGW **Subject:** Munich Olympics **Obv:** National arms **Rev:** Runner

Date	Mintage	F	VF	XF	Unc	BU
1972 Proof	Est. 1,500	Value: 1,500				

KM# 47 3000 GUARANIES

21.3000 g., 0.9000 Gold .6164 oz. AGW **Subject:** Munich Olympics **Obv:** Radiant star within wreath **Rev:** Broad jumper

Date	Mintage	F	VF	XF	Unc	BU
1972 Proof	Est. 1,500	Value: 1,500				

KM# 48 3000 GUARANIES

21.3000 g., 0.9000 Gold .6164 oz. AGW **Subject:** Munich Olympics **Obv:** National arms **Rev:** Soccer

Date	Mintage	F	VF	XF	Unc	BU
1972 Proof	Est. 1,500	Value: 1,500				

KM# 49 3000 GUARANIES

21.3000 g., 0.9000 Gold .6164 oz. AGW **Subject:** Munich Olympics **Obv:** National arms **Rev:** Hurdler

Date	Mintage	F	VF	XF	Unc	BU
1972 Proof	Est. 1,500	Value: 1,500				

KM# 50 3000 GUARANIES

21.3000 g., 0.9000 Gold .6164 oz. AGW **Subject:** Munich Olympics **Obv:** National arms **Rev:** High jumper

Date	Mintage	F	VF	XF	Unc	BU
1972 Proof	Est. 1,500	Value: 1,500				

KM# 51 3000 GUARANIES

21.3000 g., 0.9000 Gold .6164 oz. AGW **Subject:** Munich Olympics **Obv:** National arms **Rev:** Boxer

Date	Mintage	F	VF	XF	Unc	BU
1973 Proof	Est. 1,500	Value: 1,500				

KM# 81 3000 GUARANIES

21.3000 g., 0.9000 Gold .6164 oz. AGW **Obv:** National arms **Rev:** Head of Mariscal Jose F. Estigarribia facing

Date	Mintage	F	VF	XF	Unc	BU
1973 Proof	Est. 1,500	Value: 750				

KM# 82 3000 GUARANIES

21.3000 g., 0.9000 Gold .6164 oz. AGW **Obv:** National arms **Rev:** Bust of Mariscal Francisco Solano Lopez facing

Date	Mintage	F	VF	XF	Unc	BU
1973 Proof	Est. 1,500	Value: 750				

KM# 83 3000 GUARANIES

21.3000 g., 0.9000 Gold .6164 oz. AGW **Obv:** National arms **Rev:** Bust of General Jose E. Diaz facing

Date	Mintage	F	VF	XF	Unc	BU
1973 Proof	Est. 1,500	Value: 750				

KM# 84 3000 GUARANIES

21.3000 g., 0.9000 Gold .6164 oz. AGW **Obv:** National arms **Rev:** Bust of General Bernardino Caballero facing

Date	Mintage	F	VF	XF	Unc	BU
1973 Proof	Est. 1,500	Value: 750				

KM# 85 3000 GUARANIES

21.3000 g., 0.9000 Gold .6164 oz. AGW **Obv:** National arms **Rev:** Teotihucana Culture sculpture facing

Date	Mintage	F	VF	XF	Unc	BU
1973 Proof	Est. 1,500	Value: 750				

KM# 86 3000 GUARANIES

21.3000 g., 0.9000 Gold .6164 oz. AGW **Obv:** National arms **Rev:** Huasteca Culture sculpture

Date	Mintage	F	VF	XF	Unc	BU
1973 Proof	Est. 1,500	Value: 750				

KM# 87 3000 GUARANIES

21.3000 g., 0.9000 Gold .6164 oz. AGW **Obv:** National arms **Rev:** Mixteca Culture sculpture

Date	Mintage	F	VF	XF	Unc	BU
1973 Proof	Est. 1,500	Value: 750				

KM# 88 3000 GUARANIES

21.3000 g., 0.9000 Gold .6164 oz. AGW **Obv:** National arms **Rev:** Veracruz Ceramica vase

Date	Mintage	F	VF	XF	Unc	BU
1973 Proof	Est. 1,500	Value: 750				

KM# 89 3000 GUARANIES
21.3000 g., 0.9000 Gold .6164 oz. AGW **Obv:** National arms **Rev:** Veracruz Culture sculpture facing

Date	Mintage	F	VF	XF	Unc	BU
1973 Proof	Est. 1,500	Value: 750				

KM# 90 3000 GUARANIES
21.3000 g., 0.9000 Gold .6164 oz. AGW **Obv:** National arms **Rev:** Bust of Albrecht Durer facing

Date	Mintage	F	VF	XF	Unc	BU
1973 Proof	Est. 1,500	Value: 750				

KM# 91 3000 GUARANIES
21.3000 g., 0.9000 Gold .6164 oz. AGW **Obv:** National arms **Rev:** Bust of Johann Wolfgang von Goethe facing

Date	Mintage	F	VF	XF	Unc	BU
1973 Proof	Est. 1,500	Value: 750				

KM# 131 3000 GUARANIES
21.3000 g., 0.9000 Gold .6164 oz. AGW **Obv:** National arms **Rev:** Bust of President Abraham Lincoln left

Date	Mintage	F	VF	XF	Unc	BU
1974 Proof	Est. 1,500	Value: 750				

KM# 132 3000 GUARANIES
21.3000 g., 0.9000 Gold .6164 oz. AGW **Obv:** National arms **Rev:** Bust of Ludwig van Beethoven left

Date	Mintage	F	VF	XF	Unc	BU
1974 Proof	Est. 1,500	Value: 1,350				

KM# 133 3000 GUARANIES
21.3000 g., 0.9000 Gold .6164 oz. AGW **Obv:** National arms **Rev:** Bust of Otto von Bismarck right

Date	Mintage	F	VF	XF	Unc	BU
1974 Proof	Est. 1,500	Value: 750				

KM# 134 3000 GUARANIES
21.3000 g., 0.9000 Gold .6164 oz. AGW **Obv:** National arms **Rev:** Head of Albert Einstein left

Date	Mintage	F	VF	XF	Unc	BU
1974 Proof	Est. 1,500	Value: 750				

KM# 135 3000 GUARANIES
21.3000 g., 0.9000 Gold .6164 oz. AGW **Obv:** National arms **Rev:** Head of Giuseppe Garibaldi facing

Date	Mintage	F	VF	XF	Unc	BU
1974 Proof	Est. 1,500	Value: 750				

KM# 136 3000 GUARANIES
21.3000 g., 0.9000 Gold .6164 oz. AGW **Obv:** National arms **Rev:** Bust of Alessandro Manzoni facing

Date	Mintage	F	VF	XF	Unc	BU
1974 Proof	Est. 1,500	Value: 750				

KM# 137 3000 GUARANIES
21.3000 g., 0.9000 Gold .6164 oz. AGW **Obv:** National arms **Rev:** William Tell and son facing

Date	Mintage	F	VF	XF	Unc	BU
1974 Proof	Est. 1,500	Value: 750				

KM# 138 3000 GUARANIES
21.3000 g., 0.9000 Gold .6164 oz. AGW **Obv:** National arms **Rev:** Head of President John F. Kennedy left

Date	Mintage	F	VF	XF	Unc	BU
1974 Proof	Est. 1,500	Value: 750				

KM# 139 3000 GUARANIES
21.3000 g., 0.9000 Gold .6164 oz. AGW **Obv:** National arms **Rev:** Head of Konrad Adenauer left

Date	Mintage	F	VF	XF	Unc	BU
1974 Proof	Est. 1,500	Value: 750				

KM# 140 3000 GUARANIES
21.3000 g., 0.9000 Gold .6164 oz. AGW **Obv:** National arms **Rev:** Head of Sir Winston Churchill left

Date	Mintage	F	VF	XF	Unc	BU
1974 Proof	Est. 1,500	Value: 750				

KM# 141 3000 GUARANIES
21.3000 g., 0.9000 Gold .6164 oz. AGW **Obv:** National arms **Rev:** Head of Pope John XXIII left

Date	Mintage	F	VF	XF	Unc	BU
1974 Proof	Est. 1,500	Value: 750				

KM# 142 3000 GUARANIES
21.3000 g., 0.9000 Gold .6164 oz. AGW **Obv:** National arms **Rev:** Head of Pope Paul VI left

Date	Mintage	F	VF	XF	Unc	BU
1974 Proof	Est. 1,500	Value: 750				

KM# 161 3000 GUARANIES
21.3000 g., 0.9000 Gold .6164 oz. AGW **Obv:** National arms **Rev:** Holy Trinity Chruch

Date	Mintage	F	VF	XF	Unc	BU
1975 Proof	—	Value: 700				

KM# 162 3000 GUARANIES
21.3000 g., 0.9000 Gold .6164 oz. AGW **Obv:** National arms **Rev:** Parliament building

Date	Mintage	F	VF	XF	Unc	BU
1975 Proof	—	Value: 700				

KM# 163 3000 GUARANIES
21.3000 g., 0.9000 Gold .6164 oz. AGW **Obv:** National arms **Rev:** Friendship bridge

Date	Mintage	F	VF	XF	Unc	BU
1975 Proof	—	Value: 700				

KM# 164 3000 GUARANIES
21.3000 g., 0.9000 Gold .6164 oz. AGW **Obv:** National arms **Rev:** Humaita ruins

Date	Mintage	F	VF	XF	Unc	BU
1975 Proof	—	Value: 700				

KM# 175 3000 GUARANIES
21.3000 g., 0.9000 Gold .6164 oz. AGW **Subject:** Apollo 11 Mission **Obv:** National arms **Rev:** Eagle landing on moon with earth at upper left

Date	Mintage	F	VF	XF	Unc	BU
1975 Proof	—	Value: 1,000				

KM# 176 3000 GUARANIES
21.3000 g., 0.9000 Gold .6164 oz. AGW **Subject:** Apollo 15 Mission within circle **Obv:** National arms **Rev:** Apollo mission design within circle

Date	Mintage	F	VF	XF	Unc	BU
1975 Proof	—	Value: 1,000				

KM# 52 4500 GUARANIES
31.9000 g., 0.9000 Gold .9231 oz. AGW **Obv:** National arms **Rev:** General A. Stroessner

Date	Mintage	F	VF	XF	Unc	BU
1972 Proof	Est. 1,500	Value: 950				

KM# 53 4500 GUARANIES
31.9000 g., 0.9000 Gold .9231 oz. AGW **Subject:** Munich Olympics **Obv:** National arms **Rev:** Runner

Date	Mintage	F	VF	XF	Unc	BU
1972 Proof	Est. 1,500	Value: 2,700				

KM# 54 4500 GUARANIES
31.9000 g., 0.9000 Gold .9231 oz. AGW **Subject:** Munich Olympics **Obv:** National arms **Rev:** Broad jumper

Date	Mintage	F	VF	XF	Unc	BU
1972 Proof	Est. 1,500	Value: 2,700				

KM# 55 4500 GUARANIES
31.9000 g., 0.9000 Gold .9231 oz. AGW **Subject:** Munich Olympics **Obv:** National arms **Rev:** Soccer

Date	Mintage	F	VF	XF	Unc	BU
1972 Proof	Est. 1,500	Value: 2,700				

KM# 56 4500 GUARANIES
31.9000 g., 0.9000 Gold .9231 oz. AGW **Subject:** Munich Olympics **Obv:** National arms **Rev:** Hurdler

Date	Mintage	F	VF	XF	Unc	BU
1972 Proof	Est. 1,500	Value: 2,700				

KM# 57 4500 GUARANIES
31.9000 g., 0.9000 Gold .9231 oz. AGW **Subject:** Munich Olympics **Obv:** National arms **Rev:** High jumper

Date	Mintage	F	VF	XF	Unc	BU
1972 Proof	Est. 1,500	Value: 2,700				

KM# 58 4500 GUARANIES
31.9000 g., 0.9000 Gold .9231 oz. AGW **Subject:** Munich Olympics **Obv:** National arms **Rev:** Boxer

Date	Mintage	F	VF	XF	Unc	BU
1972 Proof	Est. 1,500	Value: 2,700				

KM# 92 4500 GUARANIES
31.9000 g., 0.9000 Gold .9231 oz. AGW **Obv:** National arms **Rev:** Bust of Mariscal Jose F. Estigarribia facing

Date	Mintage	F	VF	XF	Unc	BU
1973 Proof	Est. 1,500	Value: 1,200				

KM# 93 4500 GUARANIES
31.9000 g., 0.9000 Gold .9231 oz. AGW **Obv:** National arms **Rev:** Bust of Mariscal Francisco Solano Lopez facing

Date	Mintage	F	VF	XF	Unc	BU
1973 Proof	Est. 1,500	Value: 1,200				

KM# 94 4500 GUARANIES
31.9000 g., 0.9000 Gold .9231 oz. AGW **Obv:** National arms **Rev:** Head of General Jose E. Diaz facing

Date	Mintage	F	VF	XF	Unc	BU
1973 Proof	Est. 1,500	Value: 1,200				

KM# 95 4500 GUARANIES
31.9000 g., 0.9000 Gold .9231 oz. AGW **Obv:** National arms **Rev:** Head of General Bernardino Caballero facing

Date	Mintage	F	VF	XF	Unc	BU
1973 Proof	Est. 1,500	Value: 1,200				

KM# 96 4500 GUARANIES
31.9000 g., 0.9000 Gold .9231 oz. AGW **Obv:** National arms **Rev:** Teotihucana Culture sculpture

Date	Mintage	F	VF	XF	Unc	BU
1973 Proof	Est. 1,500	Value: 1,200				

KM# 97 4500 GUARANIES
31.9000 g., 0.9000 Gold .9231 oz. AGW **Obv:** National arms **Rev:** Huasteca Culture sculpture

Date	Mintage	F	VF	XF	Unc	BU
1973 Proof	Est. 1,500	Value: 1,200				

KM# 98 4500 GUARANIES
31.9000 g., 0.9000 Gold .9231 oz. AGW **Obv:** National arms **Rev:** Mixteca Culture sculpture

Date	Mintage	F	VF	XF	Unc	BU
1973 Proof	Est. 1,500	Value: 1,200				

KM# 99 4500 GUARANIES
31.9000 g., 0.9000 Gold .9231 oz. AGW **Obv:** National arms **Rev:** Veracruz Ceramica sculpture

Date	Mintage	F	VF	XF	Unc	BU
1973 Proof	Est. 1,500	Value: 1,200				

KM# 100 4500 GUARANIES
31.9000 g., 0.9000 Gold .9231 oz. AGW **Obv:** National arms **Rev:** Veracruz Culture bust

Date	Mintage	F	VF	XF	Unc	BU
1973 Proof	Est. 1,500	Value: 1,200				

KM# 101 4500 GUARANIES
31.9000 g., 0.9000 Gold .9231 oz. AGW **Obv:** National arms **Rev:** Bust of Albrecht Durer facing

Date	Mintage	F	VF	XF	Unc	BU
1973 Proof	Est. 1,500	Value: 1,200				

KM# 102 4500 GUARANIES
31.9000 g., 0.9000 Gold .9231 oz. AGW **Obv:** National arms **Rev:** Johann Wolfgang Goethe facing

Date	Mintage	F	VF	XF	Unc	BU
1973 Proof	Est. 1,500	Value: 1,200				

KM# 103 4500 GUARANIES
31.9000 g., 0.9000 Gold .9231 oz. AGW **Obv:** National arms **Rev:** Ludwig van Beethoven left

Date	Mintage	F	VF	XF	Unc	BU
1974 Proof	Est. 1,500	Value: 2,100				

KM# 104 4500 GUARANIES
31.9000 g., 0.9000 Gold .9231 oz. AGW **Obv:** National arms **Rev:** Head of Otto von Biscarck right

Date	Mintage	F	VF	XF	Unc	BU
1974 Proof	Est. 1,500	Value: 1,200				

KM# 105 4500 GUARANIES
31.9000 g., 0.9000 Gold .9231 oz. AGW **Obv:** National arms **Rev:** Giuseppe Garibaldi facing

Date	Mintage	F	VF	XF	Unc	BU
1974 Proof	Est. 1,500	Value: 1,200				

KM# 106 4500 GUARANIES
31.9000 g., 0.9000 Gold .9231 oz. AGW **Obv:** National arms **Rev:** Alessandro Manzoni facing

Date	Mintage	F	VF	XF	Unc	BU
1974 Proof	Est. 1,500	Value: 1,200				

KM# 143 4500 GUARANIES
31.9000 g., 0.9000 Gold .9231 oz. AGW **Obv:** National arms **Rev:** President Abraham Lincoln left

Date	Mintage	F	VF	XF	Unc	BU
1974 Proof	Est. 1,500	Value: 1,200				

KM# 144 4500 GUARANIES
31.9000 g., 0.9000 Gold .9231 oz. AGW **Obv:** National arms **Rev:** Albert Einstein left

Date	Mintage	F	VF	XF	Unc	BU
1974 Proof	Est. 1,500	Value: 1,200				

KM# 145 4500 GUARANIES
31.9000 g., 0.9000 Gold .9231 oz. AGW **Obv:** National arms **Rev:** William Tell and son facing

Date	Mintage	F	VF	XF	Unc	BU
1974 Proof	Est. 1,500	Value: 1,200				

KM# 146 4500 GUARANIES
31.9000 g., 0.9000 Gold .9231 oz. AGW **Obv:** National arms **Rev:** President John F. Kennedy left

Date	Mintage	F	VF	XF	Unc	BU
1974 Proof	Est. 1,500	Value: 1,200				

KM# 147 4500 GUARANIES
31.9000 g., 0.9000 Gold .9231 oz. AGW **Obv:** National arms **Rev:** Konrad Adenauer left

Date	Mintage	F	VF	XF	Unc	BU
1974 Proof	Est. 1,500	Value: 1,200				

KM# 148 4500 GUARANIES
31.9000 g., 0.9000 Gold .9231 oz. AGW **Obv:** National arms **Rev:** Sir Winston Churchill left

Date	Mintage	F	VF	XF	Unc	BU
1974 Proof	Est. 1,500	Value: 1,200				

KM# 149 4500 GUARANIES
31.9000 g., 0.9000 Gold .9231 oz. AGW **Obv:** National arms **Rev:** Pope JOhn XXIII left

Date	Mintage	F	VF	XF	Unc	BU
1974 Proof	Est. 1,500	Value: 1,200				

KM# 150 4500 GUARANIES
31.9000 g., 0.9000 Gold .9231 oz. AGW **Obv:** National arms **Rev:** Pope Paul VI left

Date	Mintage	F	VF	XF	Unc	BU
1974 Proof	Est. 1,500	Value: 1,200				

KM# 185 4500 GUARANIES
31.9000 g., 0.9000 Gold .9231 oz. AGW **Obv:** National arms **Rev:** Parliament building

Date	Mintage	F	VF	XF	Unc	BU
1975 Proof	Est. 1,500	Value: 1,200				

KM# 186 4500 GUARANIES
31.9000 g., 0.9000 Gold .9231 oz. AGW **Subject:** Apollo 11 Mission **Obv:** National arms **Rev:** Eagle landing on moon with earth at upper left

Date	Mintage	F	VF	XF	Unc	BU
1975 Proof	Est. 1,500	Value: 1,200				

KM# 187 4500 GUARANIES
31.9000 g., 0.9000 Gold .9231 oz. AGW **Subject:** Apollo 15 Mission **Obv:** National arms **Rev:** Apollo mission designs within circle

Date	Mintage	F	VF	XF	Unc	BU
1975 Proof	Est. 1,500	Value: 1,200				

KM# 188 4500 GUARANIES
31.9000 g., 0.9000 Gold .9231 oz. AGW **Obv:** National arms **Rev:** Friendship bridge

Date	Mintage	F	VF	XF	Unc	BU
1975 Proof	Est. 1,500	Value: 1,200				

KM# 189 4500 GUARANIES
31.9000 g., 0.9000 Gold .9231 oz. AGW **Obv:** National arms **Rev:** Holy Trinity Church

Date	Mintage	F	VF	XF	Unc	BU
1975 Proof	Est. 1,500	Value: 1,200				

KM# 190 4500 GUARANIES
31.9000 g., 0.9000 Gold .9231 oz. AGW **Obv:** National arms **Rev:** Ruins of Humaita

Date	Mintage	F	VF	XF	Unc	BU
1975 Proof	Est. 1,500	Value: 1,200				

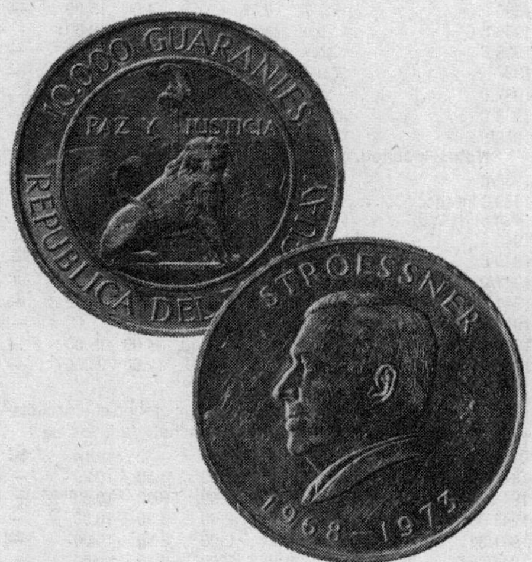

KM# 30 10000 GUARANIES
46.0100 g., 0.9000 Gold 1.3315 oz. AGW **Subject:** 4th Term of President Stroessner **Obv:** Seated lion with liberty cap on pole within circle **Rev:** Head of President Stroessner left **Note:** Similar to 300 Guaranies KM#29. KM#30 struck for presentation.

Date	Mintage	F	VF	XF	Unc	BU
ND(1968) Proof	Est. 50	Value: 4,500				

KM# 171 10000 GUARANIES
28.7000 g., 0.9990 Silver .9219 oz. ASW **Obv:** Bank building **Rev:** Conjoined busts of Caballero and Stroessner left

Date	Mintage	F	VF	XF	Unc	BU
ND(1987) Proof	1,000	Value: 42.00				

KM# 173 10000 GUARANIES
28.7000 g., 0.9990 Silver .9219 oz. ASW **Subject:** 8th Term of President A. Stroessner **Obv:** Seated lion with Liberty cap on pole within circle **Rev:** Bust of President A. Stroessner left

Date	Mintage	F	VF	XF	Unc	BU
ND(1988) Proof	1,000	Value: 42.00				

KM# 168 70000 GUARANIES
46.0000 g., 0.9000 Gold 1.3310 oz. AGW **Subject:** 6th Term of President A. Stroessner **Obv:** Seated lion with Liberty cap on pole within circle **Rev:** Bust of President A. Stroessner left

Date	Mintage	F	VF	XF	Unc	BU
ND(1978) Proof	300	Value: 1,100				

KM# 170 100000 GUARANIES
46.0000 g., 0.9000 Gold 1.3310 oz. AGW **Subject:** 7th Term of President A. Stroessner **Obv:** Seated lion with Liberty cap on pole within circle **Rev:** Bust of President A. Stroessner left

Date	Mintage	F	VF	XF	Unc	BU
ND(1983) Proof	300	Value: 1,100				

KM# 172 250000 GUARANIES
46.0000 g., 0.9170 Gold 1.3561 oz. AGW **Obv:** Bank building within circle **Rev:** Conjoined busts of Caballero and Stroessner left

Date	Mintage	F	VF	XF	Unc	BU
ND(1987) Proof	Est. 500	Value: 1,100				

Note: 250 pieces remelted

KM# 174 300000 GUARANIES
46.0000 g., 0.9170 Gold 1.3561 oz. AGW **Subject:** 8th Term of President A. Stroessner **Obv:** Seated lion with Liberty cap on pole within circle **Rev:** Bust of President A. Stroessner left

Date	Mintage	F	VF	XF	Unc	BU
ND(1988) Proof	Est. 500	Value: 1,100				

Note: 250 pieces remelted

PATTERNS

Including off metal strikes

KM#	Date	Mintage	Identification	Mkt Val
Pn40	1925	—	2 Pesos. Aluminum. Narrow flan, KM14.	100
Pn41	1925	—	2 Pesos. Aluminum. Broad flan, KM14.	125
Pn42	1939	—	5 Pesos. Brass. KM#8.	175
Pn43	1939	—	5 Pesos. Copper. KM18.	175
Pn44	1976	10	Guarani. Gold.	450
Pn45	1976	10	10 Guaranies. Gold.	750
Pn46	1978	10	Guarani. Gold.	450
Pn47	1978	10	5 Guaranies. Gold.	550
Pn48	1978	10	10 Guaranies. Gold.	750
Pn49	1980	10	Guarani. Gold.	450
Pn50	1980	10	5 Guaranies. Gold.	550
Pn51	1980	10	10 Guaranies. Gold.	750
Pn52	1980	10	50 Guaranies. Gold.	1,100

PROOF SETS

KM#	Date	Mintage	Identification	Issue Price	Mkt Val
PS1	1953 (4)	1	KM25-28	—	1,650
PS2	1972 (24)	150	KM31-36, 38-43, 45-50, 52-57	—	—
PS3	1973 (48)	150	KM37, 44, 51, 58-102	—	—
PS4	1974 (48)	150	KM103-150	—	—
PS5	1975 (24)	150	KM155-164, 175-176, 179-190	—	—
PS6	1975 (4)	1,000	KM151-154	—	30.00
PS7	1976 (2)	1,000	KM151, 153	—	20.00
PS8	1976 (2)	—	KM#151a, 153a	—	—
PS9	1978 (3)	—	KM#165, 166, 167	—	—
PS10	1978 (3)	—	KM#165a, 166b, 167a	—	—
PS11	1980 (4)	1,000	KM165-167, 169	—	30.00
PS12	1980 (4)	—	KM#165a, 166b, 167a, 169a	—	—
PS13	1988 (3)	—	KM#165, 167, 169	—	20.00

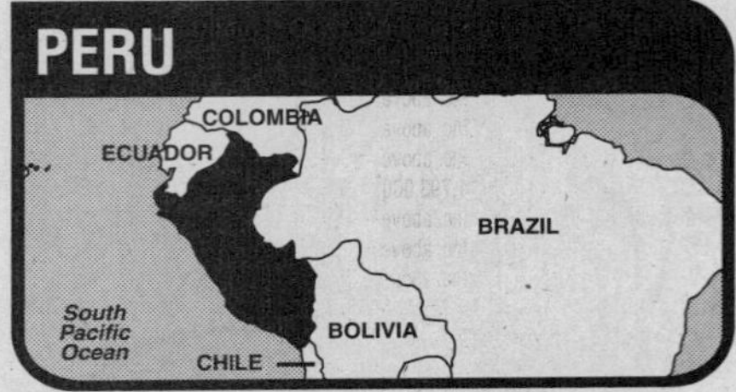

The Republic of Peru, located on the Pacific coast of South America, has an area of 496,225 sq. mi. (1,285,220sq. km.) and a population of *21.4 million. Capital: Lima. The diversified economy includes mining, fishing and agriculture. Fishmeal, copper, sugar, zinc and iron ore are exported.

Once part of the great Inca Empire that reached from northern Ecuador to central Chile, the conquest of Peru by Francisco Pizarro began in 1531. Desirable as the richest of the Spanish viceroyalties, it was torn by warfare between avaricious Spaniards until the arrival in 1569 of Francisco de Toledo, who initiated 2-1/2 centuries of efficient colonial rule, which made Lima the most aristocratic colonial capital and the stronghold of Spain's American possessions. Jose de San Martin of Argentina proclaimed Peru's independence on July 28, 1821; Simon Bolivar of Venezuela secured it in December, 1824 when he defeated the last Spanish army in South America. After several futile attempts to re-establish its South American Empire, Spain recognized Peru's independence in 1879.

Andres de Santa Cruz, whose mother was a high-ranking Inca, was the best of Bolivia's early presidents, and temporarily united Peru and Bolivia 1836-39, thus realizing his dream of a Peruvian/Bolivian confederation. This prompted the separate coinages of North and South Peru. Peruvian resistance and Chilean intervention finally broke up the confederation, sending Santa Cruz into exile. A succession of military strongman presidents ruled Peru until Marshall Castilla revitalized Peruvian politics in the mid-19th century and repulsed Spain's attempt to reclaim its one-time colony. Subsequent loss of southern territory to Chile in the War of the Pacific, 1879-81, and gradually increasing rejection of foreign economic domination, combined with recent serious inflation, affected the country numismatically.

As a result of the discovery of silver at Potosi in 1545, a mint was eventually authorized in 1565 with the first coinage taking place in 1568. The mint had an uneven life span during the Spanish Colonial period from 1568-72. It was closed from 1573-76, reopened from 1577-88. It remained closed until 1659-1660 when an unauthorized coinage in both silver and gold were struck. After being closed in 1660, it remained closed until 1684 when it struck cob style coins until 1752.

MINT MARKS

AREQUIPA, AREQ = Arequipa
AYACUCHO = Ayacucho
(B) = Brussels
CUZCO (monogram), Cuzco, Co. Cuzco
L, LIMAE (monogram), Lima
(monogram), LIMA = Lima
(L) = London
PASCO (monogram), Pasco, Paz, Po= Pasco
P, (P) = Philadelphia
S = San Francisco
(W) = Waterbury, CT, USA

NOTE: The LIMAE monogram appears in three forms. The early LM monogram form looks like a dotted L with M. The later LIMAE monogram has all the letters of LIMAE more readily distinguishable. The third form appears as an M monogram during early Republican issues.

MINT ASSAYERS' INITIALS

The letter(s) following the dates of Peruvian coins are the assayer's initials appearing on the coins. They generally appear at the 11 o'clock position on the Colonial coinage and at the 5 o'clock position along the rim on the obverse or reverse on the Republican coinage.

DATING

Peruvian 5, 10 and 20 centavos, issued from 1918-1944, bear the dates written in Spanish. The following table translates those written dates into numerals:

1918 - UN MIL NOVECIENTOS DIECIOCHO
1919 - UN MIL NOVECIENTOS DIECINUEVE
1920 - UN MIL NOVECIENTOS VEINTE
1921 - UN MIL NOVECIENTOS VEINTIUNO
1923 - UN MIL NOVECIENTOS VEINTITRES
1926 - UN MIL NOVECIENTOS VEINTISEIS
1934 - UN MIL NOVECIENTOS TREINTICUATRO
1935 - UN MIL NOVECIENTOS TREINTICINCO
1937 - UN MIL NOVECIENTOS TREINTISIETE
1939 - UN MIL NOVECIENTOS TREINTINUEVE
1940 - UN MIL NOVECIENTOS CUARENTA
1941 - UN MIL NOVECIENTOS CUARENTIUNO

U.S. Mints

1942 - MIL NOVECIENTOS CUARENTA Y DOS

Lima Mint

1942 - UN MIL NOVECIENTOS CUARENTIDOS

U.S. Mints

1943 - MIL NOVECIENTOS CUARENTA Y TRES
1944 - MIL NOVECIENTOS CUARENTA Y CUATRO

Lima Mint

1944 - MIL NOVECIENTOS CUARENTICUATRO

MONETARY SYSTEM

100 Centavos (10 Dineros) = 1 Sol
10 Soles = 1 Libra

REPUBLIC

DECIMAL COINAGE

100 Centavos (10 Dineros) = 1 Sol; 10 Soles = 1 Libra

KM# 208.1 CENTAVO

Bronze **Obv:** Radiant star design around center circle with small date below and legend above **Rev:** Value within wreath, straight centavo **Note:** Thick planchet.

Date	Mintage	F	VF	XF	Unc	BU
1901	600,000	1.00	3.00	8.00	20.00	—
1904	1,000,000	8.00	15.00	30.00	60.00	—

KM# 208.2 CENTAVO

Bronze **Obv:** Large date and legend **Rev:** Curved centavo **Note:** Thick planchet. Varieties exist.

Date	Mintage	F	VF	XF	Unc	BU
1933	275,000	1.50	3.00	8.00	20.00	—
1934	1,185,000	1.00	2.00	5.00	15.00	—
1935	1,105,000	1.00	2.00	5.00	15.00	—
1936	565,000	1.50	3.00	8.00	20.00	—
1937/6	735,000	1.00	2.00	4.00	20.00	—
1937	Inc. above	0.75	1.50	2.50	15.00	—
1938	340,000	0.75	1.50	2.50	15.00	—
1939	1,225,000	1.50	3.00	5.50	20.00	—
1940	1,250,000	1.50	3.00	5.50	20.00	—
1941	2,593,000	0.40	0.75	1.50	10.00	—

KM# 208a CENTAVO

Bronze **Obv:** Large date and legend **Rev:** Straight centavo **Note:** Thin planchet.

Date	Mintage	F	VF	XF	Unc	BU
1941 Inc. KM#208.2	—	0.40	0.75	2.00	8.00	—
1942	2,865,000	0.50	1.00	2.50	10.00	—
1944	—	10.00	20.00	35.00	70.00	—

KM# 211 CENTAVO

Bronze **Obv:** Radiant star design around center circle **Rev:** Value within wreath **Note:** Thick planchet. Engravers initial R appears below ribbon on most or all new dies, but often became weak or filled. Most coins show at least a faint trace of an R. Date varieteis also exist.

Date	Mintage	F	VF	XF	Unc	BU
1909/999 R	Inc. above	10.00	20.00	35.00	70.00	—
1909 R	Inc. above	10.00	20.00	35.00	70.00	—
1909	252,000	10.00	20.00	35.00	70.00	—
1915	250,000	3.00	6.00	10.00	30.00	—
1916	360,000	1.00	2.00	7.00	20.00	—
1916 R	Inc. above	1.00	2.00	6.00	15.00	—
1917	830,000	1.00	2.00	6.00	15.00	—
1917 R	Inc. above	1.00	2.00	6.00	15.00	—
1918	1,060,000	1.00	2.00	5.00	14.00	—
1918 R	Inc. above	1.00	2.00	5.00	14.00	—
1920	360,000	1.00	2.50	7.00	20.00	—
1920 R	Inc. above	1.00	2.50	7.00	20.00	—
1933 R Inc. KM208.2	—	1.00	2.50	7.00	20.00	—
1934 Inc. KM#208.2	—	4.50	8.00	20.00	55.00	—
1935 R Inc. KM#208.2	—	4.00	7.00	20.00	50.00	—
1936 R Inc. KM#208.2	—	1.50	3.50	7.00	20.00	—
1937	—	—	—	—	—	—
1937 R Inc. KM#208.2	—	1.50	3.50	7.00	20.00	—
1939 R Inc. KM#208.2	—	4.50	8.00	20.00	55.00	—

KM# 211a CENTAVO

Bronze **Obv:** Radiant star design around center circle, large date and legend **Rev:** Value within wreath, curved centavo **Note:** Thin planchet. Many varieties exist.

Date	Mintage	F	VF	XF	Unc	BU
1941 Inc. KM#208.2	—	1.00	2.00	5.00	15.00	—
1942 Inc. KM#208a	—	0.50	1.00	3.00	10.00	—
1943	—	2.50	5.00	15.00	35.00	—
1944	2,490,000	0.15	0.40	1.00	4.00	—
1945	2,157,000	0.15	0.40	1.00	4.00	—
1946	3,198,000	0.15	0.40	1.00	4.00	—
1947	2,976,000	0.15	0.40	1.00	4.00	—
1948	3,195,000	0.15	0.40	1.00	4.00	—
1949	1,104,000	0.25	0.65	2.00	6.00	—

KM# 227 CENTAVO

Zinc **Obv:** Radiant star design around center circle **Rev:** Value within wreath, curved centavo **Note:** Varieties exist.

Date	Mintage	F	VF	XF	Unc	BU
1950	3,196,000	0.35	0.25	1.25	5.00	—
1951	3,289,000	0.25	0.40	0.65	3.00	—
Note: Copper-plated examples of type dated 1951 are known						
1952	3,050,000	0.25	0.40	0.65	3.00	—
1953	3,260,000	0.35	0.60	1.00	4.00	—
1954	3,215,000	0.75	1.50	2.50	10.00	—
1955	3,400,000	0.25	0.40	0.65	3.00	—
1956 Pointed 6	2,500,000	0.25	0.40	0.65	3.00	—
1956 Knobbed 6	Inc. above	0.25	0.40	0.65	3.00	—
1957	4,400,000	0.40	0.85	2.00	7.00	—
1958/7	—	0.35	0.60	1.00	4.00	—
1958/8	3,200,000	0.50	1.00	2.00	7.00	—
1958	2,600,000	0.35	0.60	1.00	4.00	—
1959/8	Inc. above	0.35	0.75	1.50	5.00	—
1959	Inc. above	0.25	0.40	0.65	3.00	—
1960/50	3,060,000	0.35	0.60	1.00	4.00	—
1960	Inc. above	0.75	1.50	3.00	8.00	—
1961/51	2,600,000	0.25	0.40	1.00	3.00	—
1961	Inc. above	0.25	0.40	1.00	3.00	—
1962/52	2,600,000	0.25	0.40	1.00	3.00	—
1962	Inc. above	0.25	0.40	1.00	3.00	—
1963/53	2,400,000	0.25	0.40	1.00	3.00	—
1963	Inc. above	0.25	0.40	1.00	3.00	—
1965	360,000	0.75	1.50	3.00	10.00	—

KM# 187.2 CENTAVO

Bronze **Obv:** Radiant star design around center circle **Rev:** Value within wreath **Note:** Earlier dates 1875-1878 are listed as KM#187.1a in our 19th Century book.

Date	Mintage	F	VF	XF	Unc	BU
1919(P)	4,000,000	0.50	1.00	2.50	10.00	—

KM# 212.1 2 CENTAVOS

Copper Or Bronze **Obv:** Date at bottom **Rev:** Curved "CENTAVOS" **Note:** Thick planchet. Engraver's initial C appeared below ribbon on most or all new dies, but often became weak or filled. Most coins show at least a faint trace of C. Other varieties also exist.

Date	Mintage	F	VF	XF	Unc	BU
1917 C	73,000	4.00	6.50	15.00	40.00	—
1918/17	580,000	3.50	6.00	12.00	40.00	—
1918	Inc. above	3.50	6.00	15.00	40.00	—
1918/17 C	Inc. above	4.00	10.00	20.00	50.00	—
1918 C	Inc. above	3.50	6.00	15.00	40.00	—
1920/7 C	328,000	2.00	4.00	10.00	30.00	—
1920	Inc. above	1.00	2.00	5.00	15.00	—
1920 C	Inc. above	1.00	2.00	5.00	15.00	—
1933	285,000	1.00	2.00	5.00	15.00	—
1933 C	Inc. above	1.00	2.00	5.00	15.00	—
1934	973,000	0.75	1.50	4.00	15.00	—
1934 C	Inc. above	0.75	1.50	4.00	15.00	—
1935	950,000	0.75	1.50	4.00	15.00	—
1935 C	Inc. above	0.75	1.50	4.00	15.00	—
1936	763,000	0.75	1.50	4.00	15.00	—
1936/5 C	Inc. above	1.50	2.50	8.00	20.00	—
1936 C	Inc. above	0.75	1.25	3.00	12.00	—
1937	963,000	0.75	1.50	4.00	15.00	—
1937 C	Inc. above	0.75	1.50	4.00	15.00	—
1938 C	428,000	1.00	1.75	4.00	15.00	—
1939/8 C	—	—	—	—	—	—
Note: Reported, not confirmed						
1939/8	—	1.50	2.50	8.00	20.00	—
1939 C Inverted A for V in CENTAVOS	783,000	0.75	1.50	4.00	15.00	—
1940	—	1.00	2.00	4.00	15.00	—
1940 C	565,000	1.00	1.75	4.00	15.00	—
1941/0	Inc. above	1.00	2.00	4.00	15.00	—
1941/0 C	Inc. above	1.00	2.00	4.00	15.00	—
1941/22	Inc. above	1.00	2.00	4.00	15.00	—
1941	Inc. above	1.00	2.00	4.00	15.00	—
1941 C	Inc. above	2.00	5.00	12.00	20.00	—

KM# 212.2 2 CENTAVOS

Copper Or Bronze **Obv:** Radiant star design around center circle **Rev:** Value within wreath **Note:** Thin planchet. Varieties exist.

Date	Mintage	F	VF	XF	Unc	BU
1941/32	870,000	1.00	2.00	3.50	10.00	—
1941/33 C	Inc. above	1.00	2.00	3.50	10.00	—
1941/33	Inc. above	1.00	2.00	3.50	10.00	—
1941/38	Inc. above	1.00	2.00	3.50	10.00	—
1941/38 C	Inc. above	1.00	2.00	3.50	10.00	—
1941/39 C	Inc. above	1.00	2.00	3.50	10.00	—
1941/0	Inc. above	1.00	2.00	3.50	10.00	—
1941	Inc. above	0.50	1.00	2.00	7.00	—
1942/22	4,418,000	—	0.50	1.00	5.00	—
1942/32	4,418,000	—	0.50	1.00	5.00	—
1942	Inc. above	0.25	0.50	1.00	5.00	—
1943/2	1,829,000	0.50	1.00	3.00	10.00	—
1943	Inc. above	0.50	1.00	3.00	10.00	—
1944	2,068,000	1.00	2.00	4.00	12.00	—
1945	2,288,000	1.00	2.00	4.00	12.00	—
1946	2,121,000	0.25	0.50	0.75	4.00	—
1947	1,280,000	0.25	0.50	0.75	4.00	—
1948	1,518,000	0.25	0.50	0.75	5.00	—
1949/8	938,000	0.25	0.60	4.00	7.00	—
1949	Inc. above	0.50	1.00	4.00	7.00	—

KM# 228 2 CENTAVOS

Zinc **Obv:** Radiant star design around center circle **Rev:** Value within wreath

Date	Mintage	F	VF	XF	Unc	BU
1950	1,702,000	0.35	0.75	1.25	3.00	—
1951	3,289,000	0.35	0.75	1.25	3.00	—
Note: Copper-plated examples of type dated 1951 exist						
1952	1,155,000	0.35	0.75	1.25	3.00	—
1953	1,150,000	0.40	0.85	1.50	4.00	—
1954	—	2.00	4.00	10.00	30.00	—
1955	1,185,000	0.35	0.75	1.25	3.00	—
1956	400,000	0.50	1.00	2.00	5.00	—
1957	520,000	1.50	3.00	6.00	25.00	—
1958	200,000	1.25	2.50	4.50	15.00	—

KM# A212 2 CENTAVOS

Copper Or Bronze **Obv:** Radiant star design around center circle **Rev:** Value within wreath **Note:** Sharper diework. Earlier date 1895 listed as KM#188.2 in 19th Century book.

Date	Mintage	F	VF	XF	Unc	BU
1919(P)	3,000,000	0.35	0.75	2.00	9.00	—

KM# 213.1 5 CENTAVOS

Copper-Nickel **Obv:** Date: UN MIL NOVECIENTOS DIECIOCHO **Rev:** Value to right of sprig

Date	Mintage	F	VF	XF	Unc	BU
1918	4,000,000	0.50	1.25	2.50	10.00	—
1919	10,000,000	0.40	1.00	2.00	7.00	—
1923	2,000,000	1.00	2.00	3.50	12.50	—
1926	4,000,000	1.50	3.00	6.00	20.00	—

KM# 213.2 5 CENTAVOS

Copper-Nickel **Obv:** Head right **Rev:** Value to right of sprig

Date	Mintage	F	VF	XF	Unc	BU
1934	4,000,000	0.75	2.00	3.00	9.00	—
1934 Proof	—	Value: 200				
1935	4,000,000	0.50	1.25	2.00	6.00	—
1935 Proof	—	—	—	—	—	—
1937	2,000,000	0.75	2.00	3.00	9.00	—
1937 Proof	—	—	—	—	—	—
1939	2,000,000	0.50	1.25	2.00	6.00	—
1939 Proof	—	—	—	—	—	—
1940	2,000,000	0.50	1.25	2.00	6.00	—
1940 Proof	—	—	—	—	—	—
1941	2,000,000	0.50	1.25	2.00	6.00	—
1941 Proof	—	—	—	—	—	—

KM# 213.2a.1 5 CENTAVOS

Brass **Obv:** Date: MIL NOVECIENTOS CUARENTA Y DOS **Rev:** Value to right of sprig

Date	Mintage	F	VF	XF	Unc	BU
1942	4,000,000	1.00	3.00	5.00	20.00	—
1943	4,000,000	1.00	3.00	5.00	20.00	—
1944	4,000,000	1.00	2.75	4.50	20.00	—

KM# 213.2a.2 5 CENTAVOS

Brass **Obv:** Head right with date spelled out **Rev:** Value to right of sprig

Date	Mintage	F	VF	XF	Unc	BU
1942S	4,000,000	2.50	4.50	10.00	50.00	—
1943S	4,000,000	2.50	4.50	8.00	40.00	—

KM# 213.2a.3 5 CENTAVOS

Brass **Obv:** Date: MIL NOVECIENTOS CUARENTICUATRO **Rev:** Value to right of sprig

Date	Mintage	F	VF	XF	Unc	BU
1944	1,106,000	1.50	3.50	6.00	15.00	—

KM# 223.1 5 CENTAVOS

Brass **Obv:** Head right with short legend **Rev:** Value to right of sprig **Note:** Thick planchet.

Date	Mintage	F	VF	XF	Unc	BU
1945	2,768,000	0.35	0.75	1.50	4.00	—
1946/5	4,270,000	1.00	2.50	5.00	14.00	—
1946	Inc. above	0.25	0.50	1.00	3.50	—

KM# 223.3 5 CENTAVOS

Brass **Obv:** Head right with long legend with 3mm gap above head **Rev:** Value to right of sprig **Note:** Thick planchet.

Date	Mintage	F	VF	XF	Unc	BU
1947	7,683,000	0.25	0.50	1.00	3.00	—
1948	6,711,000	0.25	0.50	1.00	3.00	—
1949	—	0.25	0.50	1.00	3.00	—
1949/8	5,550,000	1.00	2.00	4.00	10.00	—

KM# 223.4 5 CENTAVOS

Brass **Obv:** Head right **Rev:** Value to right of sprig **Note:** Thick planchet.

Date	Mintage	F	VF	XF	Unc	BU
1949	Inc. above	1.00	2.00	4.00	10.00	—
1950	7,933,000	0.25	0.50	1.00	3.00	—
195.1	8,064,000	0.25	0.50	1.00	3.00	—
1951	Inc. above	1.00	2.00	4.00	35.00	—

KM# 223.2 5 CENTAVOS

Brass, 17 mm. **Obv:** Head right **Rev:** Value to right of sprig **Note:** Thin planchet. Varieties exist.

Date	Mintage	F	VF	XF	Unc	BU
1951	Inc. above	0.10	0.25	0.50	6.00	—
1952	7,840,000	0.10	0.25	0.50	6.00	—
1953	6,976,000	0.10	0.25	0.50	6.00	—
AFP	—	—	—	—	—	—
1954	6,244,000	0.10	0.20	0.40	1.00	—
1955	8,064,000	0.10	0.20	0.40	2.00	—
1956	16,200,000	—	0.10	0.35	1.50	—
1957 Small date	16,000,000	—	0.10	0.25	1.00	—
1957 Large date	Inc. above	—	0.10	0.25	1.00	—
1958	4,600,000	—	0.10	0.25	1.00	—
1959	8,300,000	—	0.10	0.25	1.00	—
1960/50	9,900,000	—	0.10	0.25	1.00	—
1960 Large date	Inc. above	—	0.10	0.25	1.00	—
1960 Small date	Inc. above	—	0.10	0.25	1.00	—
1961	10,200,000	—	0.10	0.20	1.00	—
1962 Curved 9	11,064,000	—	0.10	0.20	1.00	—
1962 Straight 9	Inc. above	—	0.10	0.20	1.00	—
1963	12,012,000	—	0.10	0.20	1.00	—
1964/3	12,304,000	—	0.10	0.35	1.50	—
1964	Inc. above	—	—	0.10	1.00	—
1965 Small date	12,500,000	—	—	0.10	1.00	—
1965 Large date	Inc. above	—	0.10	0.20	1.00	—
1965 Proof	—	Value: 20.00				

KM# 232 5 CENTAVOS

Brass, 17 mm. **Obv:** Head right **Rev:** Value to right of torch within chain circle **Designer:** Raymond P. Testu

Date	Mintage	F	VF	XF	Unc	BU
1954	2,080,000	1.00	2.00	4.00	8.00	—

KM# 290 5 CENTAVOS

Brass **Subject:** 400th Anniversary of Lima Mint **Obv:** National arms above value **Obv. Designer:** Armando Pareja **Rev:** Pillars of Hercules within inner circle **Rev. Designer:** Alonso de Rincon

Date	Mintage	F	VF	XF	Unc	BU
1965 Proof	—	Value: 100				
1965	712,000	—	—	0.25	1.00	—

KM# 244.1 5 CENTAVOS

Brass **Obv:** National arms within circle above date **Rev:** Value to left of flower sprig

Date	Mintage	F	VF	XF	Unc	BU
1966 Proof	1,000	Value: 15.00				
1966	14,620,000	—	—	0.10	0.20	0.35
Note: PAREJA in field at lower left of arms						
1967	14,088,000	—	—	0.10	0.20	0.35
1968	17,880,000	—	—	0.10	0.20	0.35

KM# 244.1a 5 CENTAVOS

Silver Plated Brass **Obv:** National arms within circle above date **Rev:** Value to left of flower sprig

Date	Mintage	F	VF	XF	Unc	BU
1967	—	—	—	—	—	—

KM# 244.1b 5 CENTAVOS

Silver **Obv:** National arms within circle above date **Rev:** Value to left of flower sprig

Date	Mintage	F	VF	XF	Unc	BU
1967	—	—	—	—	—	—

KM# 244.2 5 CENTAVOS

Brass **Obv:** National arms within circle **Rev:** Value to left of flower sprig **Edge:** Plain

Date	Mintage	F	VF	XF	Unc	BU
1969	17,880,000	—	—	—	0.10	0.20
1970	—	—	—	—	0.10	0.20
1971	24,320,000	—	—	—	0.10	0.20
1972	24,342,000	—	—	—	0.10	0.20
1973	25,074,000	—	—	—	0.10	0.20

KM# 244.3 5 CENTAVOS

Brass **Obv:** National arms within circle **Rev:** Value to left of flower sprig **Edge:** Plain

Date	Mintage	F	VF	XF	Unc	BU
1973	Inc. above	—	—	—	0.10	0.20
1974	—	—	—	—	0.10	0.20
1975	—	—	—	—	0.10	0.20

KM# 206.2 1/2 DINERO

1.2500 g., 0.9000 Silver .0362 oz. ASW **Obv:** National arms above date **Rev:** Seated Liberty flanked by shield and column **Note:** Most coins 1900-06 show faint to strong traces of 9/8 or 90/89 in date. Non-overdates without such traces are scarce. Most coins of 1907-17 have engraver's initial R at left of shield tip on reverse. Many other varieties exist.

Date	Mintage	F	VF	XF	Unc	BU
1901/801 JF	500,000	65.00	1.25	2.50	6.00	—
1901/801/701 JF	Inc. above	0.65	1.25	2.50	6.00	—
1901/891/791	Inc. above	0.65	1.25	2.00	5.00	—
1901/891 JF	Inc. above	0.65	1.25	2.00	5.00	—
1901 JF	Inc. above	0.75	1.50	3.50	10.00	—
1902/802 JF	616,000	0.65	1.25	2.00	5.00	—
1902/892 JF	Inc. above	0.65	1.25	2.00	5.00	—
1902/92	Inc. above	0.65	1.25	2.00	5.00	—
1902 JF	Inc. above	0.75	1.50	3.50	10.00	—
1903/803 JF	1,798,000	0.65	1.50	3.00	9.00	—
1903/893 JF	Inc. above	0.65	1.50	3.00	9.00	—
1903/897 JF	Inc. above	0.60	1.00	2.50	7.00	—
1903 JF	Inc. above	0.75	1.50	3.00	10.00	—
1904/804 JF	723,000	0.65	1.25	2.00	5.00	—
1904/804 JF FFLIZ Error	Inc. above	3.00	6.00	12.00	25.00	—
1904/884 JF	Inc. above	0.65	1.25	2.00	6.00	—
1904/891 JF	Inc. above	0.65	1.25	2.00	6.00	—
1904/893 JF	Inc. above	0.65	1.25	2.00	5.00	—
1904/894 JF	Inc. above	0.65	1.25	2.00	5.00	—
1904/894 JF FFLIZ Error	Inc. above	2.00	4.50	8.00	12.00	—
1904 JF	Inc. above	0.75	1.50	3.50	10.00	—
1904 JF FFLIZ Error	Inc. above	2.00	4.50	8.00	12.00	—
1905/805 JF	1,400,000	0.75	1.50	3.50	8.00	—
1905/891 JF	Inc. above	1.00	2.00	4.50	12.00	—
1905/893 JF	Inc. above	1.00	2.00	4.50	12.00	—
1905/894	Inc. above	1.00	2.00	4.50	12.00	—
1905/895 JF	Inc. above	0.60	1.25	2.00	5.00	—
1905/3 JF	Inc. above	1.00	2.00	4.50	12.00	—
1905 JF	Inc. above	0.75	1.50	3.50	10.00	—
1906/806 JF	900,000	0.75	1.50	3.50	8.00	—
1906/886 JF	Inc. above	0.75	1.50	3.50	8.00	—
1906/895 JF	Inc. above	0.75	1.50	3.50	8.00	—
1906/896 JF	Inc. above	0.60	1.25	2.00	5.00	—
1906 JF	Inc. above	0.75	1.50	3.00	10.00	—
1907 FG	600,000	0.75	1.50	3.00	10.00	—
1908/7 FG	200,000	1.50	3.00	6.00	15.00	—
1908 FG	Inc. above	0.75	1.50	3.50	10.00	—
1909/7 FG	—	3.00	6.00	12.50	30.00	—
1909 FG	—	0.75	1.50	3.50	8.00	—
1910 FG	640,000	0.60	1.00	2.00	5.00	—
1911 FG	460,000	0.60	1.25	2.00	5.00	—
1912 FG	120,000	0.65	1.25	2.50	6.00	—
1913 FG	480,000	0.60	1.00	2.00	5.00	—
1914/3 FG	—	0.75	1.50	3.50	10.00	—
1914/03 FG	—	1.00	2.50	5.50	15.00	—
1914/04 FG	—	1.00	2.50	5.50	15.00	—
1914 FG	—	0.60	1.00	2.00	5.00	—
1916/3 FG	860,000	0.60	1.00	2.00	5.00	—
1916/3 FG FERUANA Error	—	1.00	2.00	4.50	12.00	—
1916 FG	Inc. above	BV	0.75	1.75	4.50	—
1916/5 FG PERUANA Error	Inc. above	1.00	2.00	4.50	12.00	—
1916/5 FG FERUANA Error	Inc. above	1.00	2.00	4.50	12.00	—
1916/5 Without FERUANA	Inc. above	1.00	2.00	4.50	12.00	—
1916 FG FERUANA Error	Inc. above	1.00	2.00	4.50	15.00	—
1916 Matte	—	—	—	—	—	—
1917/87 FG	140,000	0.60	1.00	2.00	5.00	—
1917 FG	Inc. above	0.60	1.00	2.00	5.00	—

KM# 214.1 10 CENTAVOS

Copper-Nickel **Obv:** Head right **Rev:** Value to right of sprig

Date	Mintage	F	VF	XF	Unc	BU
1918	3,000,000	0.40	1.00	2.00	12.00	—
1919	2,500,000	0.40	1.00	2.00	12.00	—
1920	3,080,000	0.35	0.75	1.50	10.00	—
1921	6,920,000	0.35	0.75	1.50	10.00	—
1926	3,000,000	2.50	5.00	8.50	25.00	—

KM# 214.2 10 CENTAVOS

Copper-Nickel **Obv:** Head right **Rev:** Value to right of sprig

Date	Mintage	F	VF	XF	Unc	BU
1935	1,000,000	0.75	1.50	3.00	12.00	—
1935 Proof	—	Value: 150				
1937	1,000,000	0.40	1.00	2.00	7.00	—
1937 Proof	—	—	—	—	—	—
1939	2,000,000	0.35	0.75	1.25	5.00	—
1939 Proof	—	—	—	—	—	—
1940	2,000,000	0.35	0.75	1.25	5.00	—
1940 Proof	—	Value: 175				
1941	2,000,000	0.35	0.75	1.25	5.00	—
1941 Proof	—	—	—	—	—	—

KM# 214a.1 10 CENTAVOS

Brass **Obv:** Head right, date begins MIL..., spelled out w/a "Y" **Rev:** Value to right of sprig

Date	Mintage	F	VF	XF	Unc	BU
1942	2,000,000	1.50	3.00	6.00	20.00	—
1943	2,000,000	1.50	3.00	6.00	20.00	—
1944	2,000,000	1.50	3.50	7.00	25.00	—

KM# 214a.2 10 CENTAVOS

Brass **Obv:** Head right **Rev:** Value to right of sprig **Edge:** Plain

Date	Mintage	F	VF	XF	Unc	BU
1942S	2,000,000	6.00	12.00	20.00	50.00	—
1943S	2,000,000	1.50	3.00	6.00	20.00	—

KM# 214a.3 10 CENTAVOS

Brass **Obv:** Date behins MIL..., spelled out with an "I" **Rev:** Value to right of sprig

Date	Mintage	F	VF	XF	Unc	BU
1942	—	5.00	9.00	15.00	40.00	—

KM# 214a.4 10 CENTAVOS

Brass **Obv:** Date behins MIL..., spelled out with an "I" **Rev:** Value to right of sprig **Note:** Varieties exist.

Date	Mintage	F	VF	XF	Unc	BU
1944	—	3.50	7.00	12.00	35.00	—

KM# 226.1 10 CENTAVOS

Brass **Obv:** Long legend with 3mm gap above head **Rev:** Value to right of sprig **Note:** Thick planchet.

Date	Mintage	F	VF	XF	Unc	BU
1947	6,806,000	0.25	0.50	1.00	3.00	—
1948	5,771,000	0.25	0.50	1.25	4.00	—
1949/8	4,730,000	0.50	1.00	1.50	7.50	—

KM# 226.2 10 CENTAVOS

Brass **Obv:** Head right **Rev:** Value to right of sprig

Date	Mintage	F	VF	XF	Unc	BU
1949	Inc. above	0.25	0.50	1.00	5.00	—
1950	5,298,000	0.20	0.40	0.80	4.00	—
1950 AFP	Inc. above	0.25	0.50	1.25	8.00	—
1951	7,324,000	6.00	10.00	15.00	40.00	—
1951/0 AFP	—	0.25	0.50	1.00	4.00	—
1951 AFP	—	0.20	0.40	0.80	3.00	—

KM# 224.1 10 CENTAVOS

Brass **Obv:** Head right with short legend **Rev:** Value to right of sprig **Note:** Thick planchet.

Date	Mintage	F	VF	XF	Unc	BU
1945	2,810,000	0.25	0.50	1.50	4.00	—
1946/5	4,863,000	0.50	1.00	2.50	8.00	—
1946	Inc. above	0.35	0.75	2.00	7.00	—

KM# 224.2 10 CENTAVOS

Brass **Obv:** Head right **Rev:** Value to right of sprig **Note:** Thin planchet - 1.3mm. Date varieties exist.

Date	Mintage	F	VF	XF	Unc	BU
1951	Inc. above	0.10	0.20	0.40	2.00	—
1951 AFP	—	0.10	0.20	0.40	2.00	—
1952	6,694,000	0.10	0.20	0.40	3.00	—
1952 AFP	—	0.10	0.20	0.40	3.00	—
1953	5,668,000	0.10	0.20	0.40	2.00	—
1953 AFP	—	0.10	0.20	0.40	2.00	—
1954	7,786,000	—	0.10	0.35	1.50	—
1954 AFP	—	—	0.10	0.35	1.50	—
1955	6,690,000	—	0.10	0.35	1.50	—
1955 AFP	—	—	0.10	0.35	1.50	—
1956/5	8,410,000	0.10	0.35	0.75	3.50	—
1956	Inc. above	—	0.10	0.25	1.00	—
1956 AFP	—	—	0.20	0.40	2.00	—
1957	8,420,000	—	0.10	0.25	1.00	—
1957 AFP	—	—	0.10	0.25	1.00	—
1958	10,380,000	—	0.10	0.25	1.00	—
1958 AFP	—	—	—	—	—	—
1959	8,300,000	—	0.10	0.25	1.00	—
1959 AFP	—	—	—	—	—	—
1960	12,600,000	—	0.10	0.25	1.00	—
1961	12,700,000	—	0.10	0.15	1.00	—
1962	14,598,000	—	0.10	0.15	1.00	—
1963	16,100,000	—	0.10	0.15	1.00	—
1964	16,504,000	—	0.10	0.15	1.00	—
1965	17,808,000	—	0.10	0.15	1.00	—
1965 Proof	—	Value: 25.00				

KM# 233 10 CENTAVOS

Brass, 20 mm. **Obv:** Head right **Rev:** Value to upper right of torch, all within chain circle **Designer:** Raymond P. Testu

Date	Mintage	F	VF	XF	Unc	BU
1954	1,818,000	1.00	2.00	4.50	10.00	—

KM# 237 10 CENTAVOS

Brass **Subject:** 400th Anniversary of Lima Mint **Obv:** National arms above value **Obv. Designer:** Amando Pareja **Rev:** Pillars of Hercules within inner circle **Rev. Designer:** Alonso de Rincon

Date	Mintage	F	VF	XF	Unc	BU
1965	572,000	—	—	0.35	1.00	—
1965 Proof	—	Value: 150				

KM# 245.1 10 CENTAVOS

Brass **Obv:** National arms within circle **Rev:** Value to left of flower sprig **Edge:** Reeded **Designer:** Armando Pareja **Note:** Date varieties exist.

Date	Mintage	F	VF	XF	Unc	BU
1966	14,930,000	—	—	0.10	0.75	1.25

Note: PAREJA in field at lower left of arms

Date	Mintage	F	VF	XF	Unc	BU
1966 Proof	1,000	Value: 15.00				
1967	19,330,000	—	—	0.10	0.75	1.25
1968	24,390,000	—	—	0.10	0.75	1.25

KM# 245.1a 10 CENTAVOS

Silver Plated Brass **Obv:** National arms within circle **Rev:** Value to left of flower sprig

Date	Mintage	F	VF	XF	Unc	BU
1967	—	—	—	—	—	—

KM# 245.2 10 CENTAVOS

Brass **Obv:** National arms within circle **Rev:** Value to left of flower sprig **Edge:** Plain **Designer:** Armando Pareja **Note:** Date varieties exist.

Date	Mintage	F	VF	XF	Unc	BU
1967	—	—	—	0.10	0.25	0.40
1969	24,390,000	—	—	0.10	0.25	0.40
1970	29,110,000	—	—	0.10	0.20	0.35
1971	30,590,000	—	—	0.10	0.20	0.35
1972	34,442,000	—	—	0.10	0.20	0.35
1973	33,864,000	—	—	0.10	0.20	0.35

KM# 245.3 10 CENTAVOS

Brass **Obv:** National arms within circle **Rev:** Value to left of flower sprig **Edge:** Plain

Date	Mintage	F	VF	XF	Unc	BU
1973	Inc. above	—	—	0.10	0.15	0.25
1974	—	—	—	0.10	0.15	0.25
1975	10,430,000	—	—	0.10	0.15	0.25

KM# 263 10 CENTAVOS

Brass **Obv:** National arms within circle **Rev:** Value

Date	Mintage	F	VF	XF	Unc	BU
1975	—	—	—	0.10	0.15	0.25

KM# 204.2 DINERO

2.5000 g., 0.9000 Silver .0723 oz. ASW **Obv:** National arms above date **Rev:** Seated Liberty flanked by shield and column **Note:** Varieties exist.

Date	Mintage	F	VF	XF	Unc	BU
1902/1 JF	375,000	1.20	2.00	3.50	15.00	—
1902/891 JF	Inc. above	1.20	2.00	3.50	15.00	—
1902/892 JF	Inc. above	1.20	2.00	3.50	15.00	—
1902/897 JF	Inc. above	1.20	2.00	3.50	15.00	—
1902 JF	Inc. above	1.20	2.00	4.00	18.00	—
1903/803 JF	887,000	1.20	2.00	3.50	15.00	—
1903/807 JF	Inc. above	1.20	2.00	3.50	15.00	—
1903/892 JF	Inc. above	1.20	2.00	3.50	12.00	—
1903/893 JF	Inc. above	1.20	2.00	3.50	12.00	—
1903/92 JF	Inc. above	1.20	2.00	3.50	12.00	—
1903 JF	Inc. above	1.20	2.00	3.50	15.00	—
1904 JF	380,000	1.20	2.50	4.00	15.00	—
1905/1 JF	700,000	1.20	2.50	4.00	15.00	—
1905/3 JF	Inc. above	1.20	2.50	4.00	15.00	—
1905 JF	Inc. above	1.20	2.00	3.50	15.00	—
1906 JF	826,000	1.20	2.00	3.50	15.00	—
1907 JF Rare	500,000	—	—	—	—	—
1907 FG/JF	Inc. above	1.25	2.50	4.50	15.00	—
1907 FG	Inc. above	1.20	1.75	3.00	12.00	—
1908/6 FG/JF	Inc. above	1.20	2.25	4.00	15.00	—
1908 FG/JF	200,000	1.20	2.25	4.00	15.00	—
1908 FG/GF	Inc. above	1.20	2.25	4.00	15.00	—
1908 FG	Inc. above	1.20	1.75	3.00	15.00	—
1909 FG	—	2.00	4.00	8.00	20.00	—
1909 FG/FO	—	2.00	4.00	8.00	20.00	—
1909 FG/FF	—	2.00	4.00	8.00	20.00	—
1910 FG	210,000	BV	1.25	3.00	15.00	—
1910 FG/JF	Inc. above	1.20	2.25	4.00	18.00	—
1910 FG/JG	Inc. above	1.20	2.25	4.00	18.00	—
1911 FG	200,000	1.20	1.50	3.00	15.00	—
1911 FG/JF	Inc. above	1.20	2.25	4.00	18.00	—
1911 FG/JG	—	1.20	2.25	4.00	18.00	—
1912 FG	400,000	BV	1.25	3.00	15.00	—
1912/02 FG/JF	Inc. above	1.20	2.25	4.00	18.00	—
1912 FG/JF	Inc. above	1.20	2.25	4.00	18.00	—
1912 FG/JG	Inc. above	1.20	2.25	4.00	18.00	—
1913/1 FG/JF	Inc. above	1.20	2.25	4.00	18.00	—
1913/2 FG	360,000	1.20	2.25	4.00	18.00	—
1913/7 FG/G	Inc. above	1.20	2.25	4.00	18.00	—
1913 FG	Inc. above	BV	1.25	3.00	15.00	—
1913 FG/G	Inc. above	BV	1.25	2.50	12.00	—
1913 FG/JB	Inc. above	1.50	3.00	5.50	18.00	—
1916 FG Large date	430,000	1.25	2.50	4.50	15.00	—
1916 FG Small date	Inc. above	BV	1.25	2.00	6.00	—
1916 FG/JG	Inc. above	2.00	5.00	7.50	20.00	—
1916 FG/FF	Inc. above	2.00	5.00	7.50	20.00	—

KM# 215.1 20 CENTAVOS

Copper-Nickel, 24 mm. **Obv:** Date spelled: UN MIL NOVECIENTOS DIECIOCHO **Rev:** Value to right of sprig

Date	Mintage	F	VF	XF	Unc	BU
1918	2,500,000	0.40	1.00	5.00	20.00	—
1919	1,250,000	1.25	2.50	5.00	20.00	—
1920	1,464,000	1.25	2.25	4.00	25.00	—
1921	8,536,000	0.85	3.00	6.00	25.00	—
1926	2,500,000	2.50	5.00	9.00	30.00	—

KM# 215.2 20 CENTAVOS

Copper-Nickel, 24 mm. **Obv:** Head right **Rev:** Value to right of sprig

Date	Mintage	F	VF	XF	Unc	BU
1940	1,000,000	0.25	0.75	1.75	5.50	—
1940 Proof	—	Value: 175				
1941	1,000,000	0.35	1.00	2.50	7.50	—
1941 Proof	—	Value: 150				

KM# 215a.1 20 CENTAVOS

Brass, 24 mm. **Obv:** Date spelling: MIL NOVECIENTOS CUARENTA Y TRES **Rev:** Value to right of sprig

Date	Mintage	F	VF	XF	Unc	BU
1942	500,000	3.00	6.00	13.50	60.00	—
1943	500,000	3.00	6.00	13.50	60.00	—
1944	500,000	4.00	7.50	16.50	65.00	—

KM# 215a.2 20 CENTAVOS

Brass, 24 mm. **Obv:** Head right **Rev:** Value to right of sprig

Date	Mintage	F	VF	XF	Unc	BU
1942S	500,000	6.00	12.00	50.00	150	—
1943S	500,000	3.00	6.00	12.50	200	—

KM# 221.1 20 CENTAVOS

Brass, 24 mm. **Obv:** Head right, divided legend **Rev:** Value to right of sprig **Note:** Thick planchet.

Date	Mintage	F	VF	XF	Unc	BU
1942	300,000	1.00	2.50	5.00	12.50	—
1943	1,900,000	0.75	1.50	2.50	7.50	—
1944	2,963,000	0.60	1.25	2.00	6.00	—

KM# 221.2 20 CENTAVOS

Brass, 24 mm. **Obv:** AFP on truncation, continuous legend **Rev:** Value to right of sprig

Date	Mintage	F	VF	XF	Unc	BU
1946	3,410,000	0.25	0.50	0.85	3.00	—
1947	4,307,000	0.25	0.50	0.85	3.00	—
1948	3,578,000	0.25	0.50	0.85	3.00	—
1949/8	2,709,000	0.75	1.50	2.50	6.50	—

KM# 221.2a 20 CENTAVOS

Copper **Obv:** Head right **Rev:** Value to right of sprig

Date	Mintage	F	VF	XF	Unc	BU
1947	300	—	—	—	150	—

KM# 221.2b 20 CENTAVOS

Brass, 23 mm. **Obv:** Head right **Rev:** Value to right of sprig **Note:** Thin planchet - 1.3mm. AFP. Date varieties exist.

Date	Mintage	F	VF	XF	Unc	BU
1951	Inc. above	0.20	0.40	0.75	2.00	—
1951 Without AFP	—	—	—	—	—	—
1952	4,410,000	0.20	0.40	0.75	2.50	—
1952 Without AFP	Inc. above	—	—	—	—	—
1953	2,615,000	0.20	0.40	1.50	8.00	—
1954	1,816,000	1.50	2.50	4.00	12.00	—
1955 Large oval 9	4,050,000	0.10	0.15	0.30	1.50	—
1955 Small oval 9	Inc. above	0.20	0.40	1.50	8.00	—
1955 Round nine	Inc. above	—	—	—	—	—
1956	3,760,000	0.10	0.15	0.30	1.50	—
1957	3,680,000	0.10	0.15	0.30	1.00	—
1958	3,100,000	0.10	0.15	0.30	1.00	—
1959	5,450,000	—	0.10	0.20	1.00	—
1959 Without AFP	—	—	—	—	—	—
1960/90 With AFP	—	—	—	—	—	—
1960/90 Without AFP	—	—	—	—	—	—
1960	6,750,000	—	0.10	0.20	1.00	—
1960 Without AFP	—	0.25	0.75	1.50	4.00	—
1961	6,800,000	—	0.10	0.20	1.00	—
1961 Without AFP	—	—	—	—	—	—
1962	7,357,000	—	0.10	0.20	1.00	—
1963/2	8,843,000	0.15	0.25	0.50	2.00	—
1963	Inc. above	—	0.10	0.20	1.00	—
1964	9,550,000	—	0.10	0.20	1.00	—
1965 With inverted V for A in AFP	—	—	0.10	0.20	1.00	—
1965 Without AFP	—	0.10	0.15	0.30	1.00	—
1965 Proof	—	Value: 35.00				

KM# 221.2c 20 CENTAVOS

Copper-Nickel **Obv:** Head right **Rev:** Value to right of sprig **Edge:** Reeded **Note:** Thin planchet - 1.3mm. AFP.

Date	Mintage	F	VF	XF	Unc	BU
1958	—	—	—	—	150	—

Date	Mintage	F	VF	XF	Unc	BU
1963	—	8.00	15.00	25.00	—	—
1965 Proof	—	Value: 30.00				

KM# 221.3 20 CENTAVOS

Brass **Obv:** Head right, continuous legend **Rev:** Value to right of sprig

Date	Mintage	F	VF	XF	Unc	BU
1945	3,043,000	0.25	—	0.75	1.50	—
1946/5	Inc. above	0.25	0.65	1.00	2.00	—
1946	Inc. above	0.25	0.50	0.75	1.50	—

KM# 221.4 20 CENTAVOS

Brass **Obv:** Different style legend **Rev:** Value to right of sprig

Date	Mintage	F	VF	XF	Unc	BU
1949	Inc. above	0.50	1.00	1.75	4.50	—
1950	2,427,000	1.00	1.75	3.00	8.00	—
1951	2,941,000	3.00	7.50	15.00	40.00	—

KM# 234 20 CENTAVOS

Brass, 24 mm. **Subject:** President Castilla **Obv:** Head right **Rev:** Value to right of torch within chain circle **Edge:** Reeded **Designer:** Raymond P. Testu **Note:** Thin planchet - 1.3mm. AFP.

Date	Mintage	F	VF	XF	Unc	BU
1954	799,000	2.00	4.00	8.00	15.00	—

KM# 264 20 CENTAVOS

Brass **Obv:** National arms within circle **Rev:** Value

Date	Mintage	F	VF	XF	Unc	BU
1975	—	0.10	0.20	0.50	1.00	1.50

KM# 205.2 1/5 SOL

5.0000 g., 0.9000 Silver .1447 oz. ASW **Obv:** National arms **Rev:** Libertad incuse **Edge:** Plain **Note:** Die varieties exist. Some coins 1911-17 have engraver's initial R left of shield on reverse.

Date	Mintage	F	VF	XF	Unc	BU
1901 JF	638,000	BV	2.50	5.50	12.00	—
1903/1 JF	702,000	2.50	4.00	7.00	17.50	—
1903/13 JF	Inc. above	BV	3.50	6.00	15.00	—
1903 JF	Inc. above	BV	3.25	5.50	12.00	—
1906 JF	660,000	BV	3.25	5.50	12.00	—
1907 JF	1,370,000	BV	2.25	4.00	10.00	—
1907 FG	Inc. above	BV	3.25	5.50	12.00	—
1908/7 FG	560,000	BV	3.50	6.00	15.00	—
1908 FG	Inc. above	BV	3.25	5.50	15.00	—
1909 FG	42,000	2.50	4.00	9.00	27.50	—
1910/00 FG	165,000	3.00	7.00	15.00	35.00	—
1910 FG	Inc. above	3.00	7.00	12.00	25.00	—
1911 FG	250,000	BV	3.25	5.50	9.00	—
1911 FG-R	Inc. above	BV	3.25	5.50	9.00	—
1912 R	—	BV	2.25	4.00	—	8.00
1912 FG	300,000	BV	2.25	4.00	8.00	—
1912/1 FG-R	—	BV	2.50	5.00	—	10.00
1912 FG-R	Inc. above	BV	3.25	5.50	15.00	—
1913 FG	223,000	BV	3.50	6.00	15.00	—
1913 FG-R	Inc. above	BV	3.50	6.00	15.00	—
1914 FG	10,000	5.00	12.00	25.00	55.00	—
1915 FG	—	25.00	40.00	75.00	125	—
1916 FG	425,000	2.50	5.00	10.00	25.00	—
1916 FG-R	Inc. above	BV	3.25	5.00	9.00	—
1917 FG-R	20,000	8.00	17.00	35.00	75.00	—

KM# 238 25 CENTAVOS

Brass **Subject:** 400th Anniversary of Lima Mint **Obv:** National arms above value **Obv. Designer:** Armando Pareja **Rev:** Pillars of Hercules within inner circle **Rev. Designer:** Alonso de Rincon

Date	Mintage	F	VF	XF	Unc	BU
ND(1965)	1,113,000	—	0.25	0.35	0.75	—
1965 Proof	—	Value: 200				

KM# 246.1 25 CENTAVOS

Brass **Obv:** PAREJA in field at lower left of arms **Rev:** Value to left of flower sprig **Edge:** Reeded

Date	Mintage	F	VF	XF	Unc	BU
1966 PAREJA in field at lower left of arms	9,300,000	—	0.15	0.25	0.50	0.75
1966 Proof	1,000	Value: 15.00				
1967	8,150,000	—	0.15	0.25	0.50	0.75
1968	7,440,000	—	0.15	0.25	0.50	0.75

KM# 246.1a 25 CENTAVOS

Silver Plated Brass **Obv:** National arms within circle **Rev:** Value to left of flower sprig

Date	Mintage	F	VF	XF	Unc	BU
1967	Inc. above	—	—	—	—	—

KM# 246.2 25 CENTAVOS

Brass **Obv:** National arms within circle **Rev:** Value to left of flower sprig **Edge:** Plain **Designer:** Armando Pareja

Date	Mintage	F	VF	XF	Unc	BU
1968 AP	Inc. above	—	0.15	0.25	0.50	0.75
1969 AP on reverse	7,440,000	—	0.20	0.40	1.00	1.50
1969 With inverted V for A in AP	Inc. above	—	0.20	0.40	1.00	1.50
1969 Without AP	Inc. above	—	0.15	0.25	0.50	0.75
1970	6,341,000	—	0.20	0.40	1.00	1.50
1971	3,196,000	—	0.20	0.40	1.00	1.50
1972	5,523,000	—	0.20	0.40	1.00	1.50
1973	7,492,000	—	0.15	0.25	0.50	0.75

KM# 259 25 CENTAVOS

Brass **Obv:** National arms within circle **Rev:** Value to left of flower sprig **Designer:** Armando Pareja

Date	Mintage	F	VF	XF	Unc	BU
1973	Inc. above	—	0.10	0.15	0.25	0.40
1974	—	—	0.10	0.15	0.25	0.40
1975	—	—	0.10	0.15	0.25	0.40

KM# 203 1/2 SOL

12.5000 g., 0.9000 Silver .3617 oz. ASW **Obv:** National arms above date **Rev:** Seated Liberty flanked by shield and column **Note:** Mint mark: LIMA. Date varieties exist. Most coins have engraver's initials JR left of shield tip on reverse.

Date	Mintage	F	VF	XF	Unc	BU
1907LIMA FG-JR	1,000,000	BV	6.00	10.00	20.00	—
1908/7LIMA FG-JR	30,000	15.00	30.00	75.00	300	—
1908LIMA FG-JR	Inc. above	12.00	25.00	65.00	175	—
1914LIMA FG-JR	173,000	BV	6.50	15.00	35.00	—
1915LIMA FG-JR	570,000	BV	5.50	7.50	15.00	—
1916LIMA FG	384,000	BV	5.50	7.50	15.00	—
1916LIMA FG-JR	—	BV	5.50	7.50	15.00	—
1917LIMA FG-JR	178,000	BV	6.00	10.00	20.00	—

KM# 216 1/2 SOL

12.5000 g., 0.5000 Silver .2009 oz. ASW, 30 mm. **Obv:** National arms above date **Rev:** Seated Liberty flanked by shield and column **Note:** Date varieties exist. Engraver's initials appear on stems of obverse wreath.

Date	Mintage	F	VF	XF	Unc	BU
1922LIMA LIBERTAD incuse, J.R. on reverse	465,000	BV	7.00	25.00	80.00	—
1922LIMA LIBERTAD in relief	Inc. above	BV	7.00	25.00	80.00	—
1923LIMA GM LIBER/TAD, round-top 3	2,520,000	BV	4.00	10.00	30.00	—
1923/2LIMA Flat-top 3	Inc. above	BV	3.25	5.50	20.00	—
1923LIMA Flat-top 3	Inc. above	BV	3.50	7.00	25.00	—
1924LIMA GM	238,000	BV	6.50	20.00	50.00	—
1926LIMA GM	694,000	BV	3.50	7.50	25.00	—
1927LIMA GM	2,640,000	BV	3.25	5.50	15.00	—
1928/7LIMA GM	3,028,000	—	—	—	—	—
1928LIMA GM	Inc. above	BV	3.25	5.50	15.00	—
1929LIMA GM	3,068,000	BV	3.25	5.50	15.00	—
1935LIMA AP	2,653,000	BV	3.25	5.00	14.00	—
1935LIMA	—	—	—	—	—	—

KM# 220.1 1/2 SOL

Brass **Obv:** Five palm leaves point to llama on shield **Rev:** Value and legend

Date	Mintage	F	VF	XF	Unc	BU
1935	10,000,000	0.50	1.25	2.25	7.00	—
1935 Proof	—	Value: 200				
1941	4,000,000	0.50	1.25	2.25	7.00	—

KM# 220.2 1/2 SOL

Brass **Obv:** Arms within wreath **Rev:** Value and legend

Date	Mintage	F	VF	XF	Unc	BU
1942	4,000,000	1.50	3.00	5.00	20.00	—
1943	4,000,000	3.00	6.50	12.50	35.00	—
1944	Inc. above	1.50	3.00	5.00	20.00	—

KM# 220.3 1/2 SOL

Brass **Obv:** National arms within wreath **Rev:** Value and legend **Note:** The coins struck in Philadelphia and San Francisco have a serif on the "4" of the date; the Lima and London coins do not.

Date	Mintage	F	VF	XF	Unc	BU
1942S	1,668,000	1.50	3.00	5.00	15.00	—
1943S	6,332,000	1.50	3.00	5.00	15.00	—

KM# 220.4 1/2 SOL

Brass **Obv:** Three palm leaves point to llama on shield **Rev:** Value and legend **Note:** Dates 1941-44 have thick flat-top 4 without serifs. 1945 has narrow 4 like KM#220.5.

Date	Mintage	F	VF	XF	Unc	BU
1941	2,000,000	3.00	6.50	12.50	35.00	—
1942	Inc. above	1.50	3.00	5.00	15.00	—
1942 AP	—	—	—	—	—	—
1943	2,000,000	0.50	1.00	2.00	12.00	—
1944	Inc. above	0.40	0.85	1.75	7.00	—
1944/2	4,000,000	—	—	—	—	—
1944 AP	Inc. above	—	—	—	—	—
1945	4,000,000	0.75	1.50	3.00	10.00	—

KM# 220.5 1/2 SOL

Brass, 27 mm. **Obv:** Three palm leaves point to llama on shield **Rev:** Value and legend **Note:** 1942, 1944 AP, and all 1945-49 have narrow 4 without serif on crossbar. 1944 without AP has flat-top 4 like KM#220.4. Engraver's initials AP appear on wreath stems of some 1944-45, all 1946 and some 1947 coins. Varieties exist, including narrow and wide dates for 1956 and 1961 issues.

Date	Mintage	F	VF	XF	Unc	BU
1942 Long-top 2	Inc. above	1.50	3.00	5.00	15.00	—
1944	Inc. above	0.75	1.50	3.00	10.00	—
1944 AP	Inc. above	0.50	1.00	2.00	7.00	—
1945	Inc. above	0.75	1.50	3.00	10.00	—
1945 AP	Inc. above	0.75	1.50	3.00	10.00	—
1946/5 AP	3,744,000	2.00	3.50	6.50	17.50	—
1946 AP	Inc. above	0.40	0.75	1.25	7.00	—
1947 AP	6,066,000	0.40	0.75	1.25	7.00	—
1947	Inc. above	0.40	0.75	1.25	7.00	—
1948	3,324,000	0.40	0.75	1.25	7.00	—
1949/8	420,000	1.00	2.00	4.00	12.00	—
1949	Inc. above	1.50	3.00	6.00	18.00	—
1950	91,000	1.25	2.25	4.50	15.00	—
1951/8	930,000	0.50	1.00	2.00	7.00	—
1951	Inc. above	0.50	1.00	2.00	7.00	—
1952	935,000	0.75	1.50	3.00	10.00	—
1953	817,000	0.50	1.00	2.00	7.00	—
1954	637,000	0.75	1.50	3.00	10.00	—
1955	1,383,000	0.15	0.35	0.75	4.00	—
1956	2,309,000	0.10	0.25	0.40	1.50	—
1957	2,700,000	0.10	0.25	0.50	2.00	—
1958	2,691,000	0.10	0.25	0.40	1.50	—
1959	3,609,000	0.10	0.25	0.40	1.50	—
1960	5,600,000	0.10	0.20	0.35	0.75	—
1961 Narrow date	4,400,000	0.10	0.20	0.35	0.75	—
1961 Wide date	Inc. above	0.10	0.20	0.35	0.75	—
1962	3,540,000	0.10	0.20	0.35	1.00	—
1963	4,345,000	0.10	0.20	0.35	0.75	—
1964	5,315,000	0.10	0.20	0.35	1.50	—
1965	7,090,000	0.10	0.20	0.35	1.75	—
1965 Proof	—	Value: 75.00				

KM# 239 1/2 SOL

Brass **Subject:** 400th Anniversary of Lima Mint **Obv:** National arms above value **Obv. Designer:** Armando Pareja **Rev:** Pillars of Hercules within inner circle **Rev. Designer:** Alonso de Rincon

Date	Mintage	F	VF	XF	Unc	BU
ND(1965)	10,971,000	—	0.10	0.20	0.50	—
ND(1965) Proof	—	Value: 400				

KM# 247 1/2 SOL

Brass, 22.5 mm. **Obv:** National arms within circle **Rev:** Value to right of llama **Designer:** Armando Pareja

Date	Mintage	F	VF	XF	Unc	BU
1966	13,720,000	—	0.10	0.20	0.50	2.00
1966 Proof	1,000	Value: 20.00				
1967	15,500,000	—	0.10	0.20	0.50	2.00
1967 PAREJA on obverse and reverse	—	—	0.10	0.20	0.50	2.00
1968	13,890,000	3.00	7.00	15.00	30.00	—
1968 JAS	—	—	0.10	0.20	0.50	2.00
1969	13,890,000	—	0.10	0.20	0.50	2.00
1970	11,901,000	—	0.10	0.20	0.50	2.00
Note: Date varieties exist						
1971	7,524,000	—	0.15	0.20	0.50	2.00
1972	19,441,000	—	0.10	0.20	0.50	2.00
1973	14,951,000	—	0.10	0.20	0.50	2.00

KM# 247a 1/2 SOL

Silver Plated Brass **Obv:** National arms within circle **Rev:** Value to right of llama **Designer:** Armando Pareja

Date	Mintage	F	VF	XF	Unc	BU
1967	—	—	—	—	—	—

KM# 247b 1/2 SOL
Silver **Obv:** National arms within circle **Rev:** Value to right of llama **Designer:** Armando Pareja

Date	Mintage	F	VF	XF	Unc	BU
1967	—	—	—	—	—	—

KM# 260 1/2 SOL
Brass, 22.5 mm. **Obv:** National arms within circle **Rev:** Value to right of llama **Designer:** Armando Pareja

Date	Mintage	F	VF	XF	Unc	BU
1973	Inc. above	—	0.10	0.20	0.50	2.50
1974/1	—	—	0.10	0.20	0.50	2.50
1974	14,518,000	—	0.10	0.20	0.50	2.50
1975	14,039,000	—	0.10	0.20	0.50	2.50

KM# 265 1/2 SOL
Brass **Obv:** National arms within circle **Rev:** Value **Note:** Without mint mark.

Date	Mintage	F	VF	XF	Unc	BU
1975	62,682,000	—	0.10	0.20	0.30	0.50
1976	388,771,000	—	0.10	0.20	0.30	0.50

KM# 268 1/2 SOL
9.3500 g., 0.9000 Gold .2706 oz. AGW **Subject:** 150th Anniversary - Battle of Ayacucho **Obv:** National arms **Rev:** Monument and value

Date	Mintage	F	VF	XF	Unc	BU
1976	10,000	—	—	—	200	—

KM# 196.26 SOL
25.0000 g., 0.9000 Silver .7234 oz. ASW **Obv:** National arms above date **Rev:** Libertad incuse **Note:** Type XII. Legends have smaller lettering. Varieties exist.

Date	Mintage	F	VF	XF	Unc	BU
1914 FG	620,000	—	BV	12.50	24.00	—
1915 FG	Inc. above	—	BV	12.50	22.00	—

KM# 196.27 SOL
25.0000 g., 0.9000 Silver .7234 oz. ASW **Obv:** National arms above date **Rev:** LIBERTAD incuse

Date	Mintage	F	VF	XF	Unc	BU
1916 FG	1,927,000	—	BV	12.50	22.00	—

KM# 196.28 SOL
25.0000 g., 0.9000 Silver .7234 oz. ASW **Obv:** National arms above date **Rev:** LIBERTAD in relief **Note:** Type III.

Date	Mintage	F	VF	XF	Unc	BU
1916 FG	Inc. above	—	BV	12.50	22.00	—

KM# 217.1 SOL
25.0000 g., 0.5000 Silver .4019 oz. ASW, 37 mm. **Obv:** National arms, fineness omitted **Rev:** LEBERTAD in relief

Date	Mintage	F	VF	XF	Unc	BU
1922 Rare	—	—	—	—	—	—
1923	3,600	15.00	30.00	70.00	275	—

KM# 217.2 SOL
25.0000 g., 0.5000 Silver .4019 oz. ASW, 37 mm. **Obv:** National arms above date **Rev:** LIBERTAD incuse

Date	Mintage	F	VF	XF	Unc	BU
1923	1,400	35.00	75.00	165	475	—

KM# 218.1 SOL
25.0000 g., 0.5000 Silver .4019 oz. ASW, 37 mm. **Obv:** National arms **Rev:** Seated Liberty flanked by shield and column **Note:** Small letters. The Philadelphia and Lima strikings may be distinguished by the fact that the letters in the legends are smaller on those pieces produced at Philadelphia. All bear the name of the Lima Mint.

Date	Mintage	F	VF	XF	Unc	BU
1923	Est. 2,369,000	BV	6.50	8.50	15.00	—
1924/823	3,113,000	6.50	10.00	20.00	40.00	—
1924/824	Inc. above	6.50	10.00	20.00	40.00	—
1924	Inc. above	BV	6.50	8.50	15.00	—
1925	1,291,000	BV	6.50	10.00	20.00	—
1926	2,157,000	BV	6.50	8.50	15.00	—

KM# 218.2 SOL
25.0000 g., 0.5000 Silver .4019 oz. ASW, 37 mm. **Obv:** National arms, engraver's initials GM on stems flanking date **Rev:** Seated Liberty flanked by shield and column **Note:** Large letters.

Date	Mintage	F	VF	XF	Unc	BU
1924	96,000	6.50	9.00	20.00	65.00	—
1925	1,004,999	BV	6.50	8.50	15.00	—
1930	76,000	BV	6.50	10.00	20.00	—
1931	24,000	BV	6.50	10.00	22.00	—
1933	5,000	7.00	12.00	20.00	40.00	—
1934/3	2,855,000	BV	6.50	10.00	20.00	—
1934	Inc. above	BV	6.50	7.00	12.50	—
1935	695,000	BV	6.50	10.00	20.00	—

KM# 222 SOL
Brass, 33 mm. **Obv:** National arms **Rev:** Value within circle **Note:** Date varieties exist.

Date	Mintage	F	VF	XF	Unc	BU
1943	10,000,000	0.35	1.25	3.00	8.00	—
1944	Inc. above	0.35	1.25	3.00	7.00	—
1945	—	0.50	1.50	3.50	9.00	—
1946	1,752,000	0.50	1.50	3.00	8.00	—
1947	3,302,000	0.35	1.00	2.00	6.00	—
1948	1,992,000	0.35	1.00	2.00	6.00	—
1949/8	751,000	2.00	4.00	7.00	20.00	—
1949	Inc. above	3.50	7.50	12.00	25.00	—
1950	1,249,000	7.00	10.00	15.00	25.00	—
1951	Inc. above	0.25	0.50	1.50	6.00	—
1951/0	2,093,999	0.25	0.50	1.50	6.00	—
1952	2,037,000	0.25	0.50	1.50	6.00	—
1953	1,243,000	3.00	6.00	10.00	25.00	—
1954	1,220,000	0.35	0.75	1.75	6.00	—
1955	1,323,000	0.35	0.75	1.75	6.00	—
1956	3,450,000	0.15	0.35	0.75	3.00	—
1957	3,086,000	0.15	0.35	1.00	5.00	—
1958 Wide date	3,390,000	0.15	0.35	0.75	3.00	—
1958 Narrow date	Inc. above	0.15	0.35	0.75	3.00	—
1959	4,975,000	0.15	0.35	1.00	5.00	—
1960	5,800,000	0.15	0.35	0.75	1.50	—
1961	5,200,000	0.15	0.35	0.75	2.00	—
1962	5,102,000	0.15	0.35	0.75	1.50	—
1963	5,499,000	0.15	0.35	0.75	2.00	—
1964 Wide date	5,888,000	0.15	0.35	0.75	2.00	—
1964 Narrow date	Inc. above	0.15	0.35	0.75	2.00	—
1965	5,504,000	0.15	0.35	0.75	2.00	—
1965 Proof	—	Value: 75.00				

KM# 240 SOL
Brass, 28 mm. **Subject:** 400th Anniversary of the Lima Mint **Obv:** National arms above value **Obv. Designer:** Armando Pareja **Rev:** Pillars of Hercules within inner circle **Rev. Designer:** Alonso de Rincon

Date	Mintage	F	VF	XF	Unc	BU
ND(1965)	3,103,000	—	0.35	0.75	1.50	—
ND(1965) Proof	—	Value: 500				

KM# 248 SOL
Brass, 28 mm. **Obv:** National arms **Rev:** Llama **Designer:** Armando Pareja

Date	Mintage	F	VF	XF	Unc	BU
1966	16,410,000	—	0.10	0.25	1.00	2.50
1966 Proof	1,000	Value: 25.00				
1967	13,920,000	—	0.10	0.25	1.00	2.50
1968	12,260,000	—	0.10	0.25	1.00	2.50
1969	12,260,000	—	0.10	0.25	1.00	2.50
1970	12,336,000	—	0.10	0.25	1.00	2.50
1971	11,927,000	—	0.10	0.25	1.00	2.50
1972	3,945,000	—	0.10	0.25	1.00	2.50
1973	12,856,000	—	0.10	0.25	1.00	2.50
1974	14,966,000	—	0.10	0.25	1.00	2.50
1975	—	—	0.10	0.25	1.00	2.50

KM# 248a SOL
Silver Plated Brass **Obv:** National arms **Rev:** Llama **Designer:** Armando Pareja

Date	Mintage	F	VF	XF	Unc	BU
1967	—	—	—	—	—	—

KM# 248b SOL
Silver **Obv:** National arms **Rev:** Llama **Designer:** Armando Pareja

Date	Mintage	F	VF	XF	Unc	BU
1967	—	—	—	—	—	—

KM# 266.1 SOL
Brass, 21 mm. **Obv:** National arms within circle **Rev:** Value

Date	Mintage	F	VF	XF	Unc	BU
1975	354,485,000	—	—	0.10	0.25	0.40
1976	114,660,000	—	—	0.10	0.25	0.40

KM# 266.2 SOL
Brass **Obv:** National arms within circle **Rev:** Value **Note:** Mint mark in monogram.

Date	Mintage	F	VF	XF	Unc	BU
1978LIMA	9,000,000	—	—	0.15	0.35	0.50
1979LIMA	4,842,000	—	—	0.15	0.35	0.50
1980LIMA	28,826,000	—	—	0.15	0.35	0.50
1981LIMA	55,785,000	—	—	0.15	0.35	0.50

KM# 269 SOL

23.4000 g., 0.9000 Gold .6772 oz. AGW **Subject:** 150th Anniversary - Battle of Ayacucho **Obv:** National arms within circle **Rev:** Monument divides value within circle **Note:** Mint mark in monogram.

Date	Mintage	F	VF	XF	Unc	BU
1976LIMA	10,000	—	—	—	475	—

KM# 235 5 SOLES

2.3404 g., 0.9000 Gold .0677 oz. AGW **Obv:** National arms above date **Rev:** Seated Liberty flanked by shield and column

Date	Mintage	F	VF	XF	Unc	BU
1956	4,510	—	—	BV	55.00	—
1957	2,146	—	—	BV	55.00	—
1959	1,536	—	—	BV	65.00	—
1960	8,133	—	—	BV	55.00	—
1961	1,154	—	—	BV	65.00	—
1962	1,550	—	—	BV	65.00	—
1963	3,945	—	—	BV	55.00	—
1964	2,063	—	—	BV	60.00	—
1965	14,000	—	—	BV	55.00	—
1966	4,738	—	—	BV	55.00	—
1967	3,651	—	—	BV	55.00	—
1969	127	—	—	BV	175	—

KM# 252 5 SOLES

Copper-Nickel **Obv:** National arms within circle **Rev:** Value above designed Incan cup, written value around bottom half

Date	Mintage	F	VF	XF	Unc	BU
1969	10,000,000	0.20	0.40	0.60	1.50	2.00

KM# 254 5 SOLES

Copper-Nickel **Subject:** 150th Anniversary of Independence **Obv:** National arms **Obv. Designer:** Armando Parejo **Rev:** Bust of Tupac Amaru right **Note:** Mint mark in monogram.

Date	Mintage	F	VF	XF	Unc	BU
1971LIMA	3,480,000	0.20	0.40	0.80	2.00	—

KM# 257 5 SOLES

Copper-Nickel **Obv:** National arms within circle **Rev:** Bust of Tupac Amaru **Designer:** Armando Pareja **Note:** Regular issue. Mint mark in monogram.

Date	Mintage	F	VF	XF	Unc	BU
1972	2,068,000	—	0.10	0.35	1.00	—
1973	475,000	—	0.10	0.35	1.00	—
1974	—	—	0.10	0.35	1.50	—
1975	—	—	0.10	0.35	1.50	—

KM# 267 5 SOLES

Copper-Nickel, 22 mm. **Obv:** National arms **Rev:** Bust of Tupac Amaru **Designer:** Armando Pareja **Note:** Mint mark in monogram.

Date	Mintage	F	VF	XF	Unc	BU
1975	—	—	0.10	0.35	1.00	1.75
1976	17,016,000	—	0.10	0.35	1.00	1.75
1977	94,272,000	—	0.10	0.35	1.00	1.75

KM# 271 5 SOLES

Brass **Obv:** National arms within circle **Rev:** Value **Note:** Mint mark in monogram.

Date	Mintage	F	VF	XF	Unc	BU
1978	38,015,000	—	0.10	0.20	0.60	1.00
1979	64,524,000	—	0.10	0.20	0.60	1.00
1980	76,964,000	—	0.10	0.20	0.60	1.00
1981	31,632,000	—	0.10	0.20	0.60	1.00
1982	23,252,000	—	0.10	0.20	0.60	1.00
1983	650	20.00	30.00	40.00	60.00	—

KM# 236 10 SOLES

4.6070 g., 0.9000 Gold .1354 oz. AGW **Obv:** National arms above date **Rev:** Seated Liberty flanked by shield and column

Date	Mintage	F	VF	XF	Unc	BU
1956	5,410	—	—	BV	95.00	—
1957	1,300	—	—	BV	100	—
1959	1,103	—	—	BV	100	—
1960	7,178	—	—	BV	95.00	—
1961	1,634	—	—	BV	100	—
1962	1,676	—	—	BV	100	—
1963	3,372	—	—	BV	95.00	—
1964	1,554	—	—	BV	100	—
1965	14,000	—	—	BV	95.00	—
1966	2,601	—	—	BV	95.00	—
1967	3,002	—	—	BV	95.00	—
1968	100	—	BV	110	220	—
1969	100	—	BV	110	220	—

KM# 253 10 SOLES

Copper-Nickel **Obv:** National arms within circle **Rev:** Stylized fish below value **Designer:** Armando Parejo

Date	Mintage	F	VF	XF	Unc	BU
1969	15,000,000	0.25	0.50	0.75	1.75	2.50

KM# 255 10 SOLES

Copper-Nickel **Subject:** 150th Anniversary of Independence **Obv:** National arms **Rev:** Bust of Tupac Amaru right **Designer:** Armando Pareja **Note:** Mint mark in monogram.

Date	Mintage	F	VF	XF	Unc	BU
1971LIMA	2,460,000	0.25	0.50	1.00	2.50	—

KM# 258 10 SOLES

Copper-Nickel **Obv:** National arms within circle **Rev:** Bust of Tupac Amaru right **Designer:** Armando Pareja **Note:** Mint mark in monogram.

Date	Mintage	F	VF	XF	Unc	BU
1972	2,235	—	0.10	0.40	1.25	—
1973	1,765	—	0.10	0.40	1.25	—
1974	—	—	0.10	0.40	1.25	—
1975	—	—	0.10	0.40	1.25	—

KM# 272.1 10 SOLES

Brass **Obv:** National arms, small letters: inner circle 18.1mm **Rev:** Head with hat 3/4 right **Edge:** Plain **Designer:** Armando Pareja **Note:** Mint mark in monogram.

Date	Mintage	F	VF	XF	Unc	BU
1978	46,970,000	—	0.10	0.40	0.85	1.50

KM# 272.2 10 SOLES

Brass **Obv:** Small arms , large letters, inner circle 17.2mm **Rev:** Head with hat 3/4 right **Designer:** Armando Pareja **Note:** Mint mark in monogram.

Date	Mintage	F	VF	XF	Unc	BU
1978	—	—	0.10	0.40	0.85	1.50
1979	82,220,000	—	0.10	0.40	0.85	1.50
1980	99,595,000	—	0.10	0.40	0.85	1.50
1981	25,660,000	—	0.10	0.40	0.85	1.50
1982	61,035,000	—	0.10	0.40	0.85	1.50
1983	15,820,000	—	0.10	0.40	0.85	1.50

KM# 287 10 SOLES

Brass **Subject:** 150th Anniversary - Birth of Admiral Grau **Obv:** Value within circle **Rev:** Head 1/4 right **Note:** Mint mark in monogram.

Date	Mintage	F	VF	XF	Unc	BU
1984	30,000,000	—	—	0.20	0.50	0.75

KM# 229 20 SOLES

9.3614 g., 0.9000 Gold .2709 oz. AGW **Obv:** National arms **Rev:** Seated Liberty flanked by shield and column

Date	Mintage	F	VF	XF	Unc	BU
1950	1,800	—	—	BV	210	—
1951	9,264	—	—	BV	190	225
1952	424	—	—	BV	225	—
1953	1,435	—	—	BV	210	—
1954	1,732	—	—	BV	210	—
1955	1,971	—	—	BV	210	—
1956	1,201	—	—	BV	210	—
1957	11,000	—	—	BV	190	200
1958	11,000	—	—	BV	190	200
1959	12,000	—	—	BV	190	200
1960	7,753	—	—	BV	190	200
1961	1,825	—	—	BV	210	—
1962	2,282	—	—	BV	200	—
1963	3,892	—	—	BV	190	—
1964	1,302	—	—	BV	210	—
1965	12,000	—	—	BV	190	200
1966	4,001	—	—	BV	190	200
1967	5,003	—	—	BV	190	200
1968	640	—	—	BV	210	—
1969	640	—	—	BV	210	—

KM# 241 20 SOLES

8.0000 g., 0.9000 Silver .2315 oz. ASW **Subject:** 400th Anniversary of Lima Mint. **Obv:** National arms above value **Obv. Designer:** Armando Pareja **Rev:** Pillars of Hercules within inner circle **Rev. Designer:** Alonso de Rincon

Date	Mintage	F	VF	XF	Unc	BU
ND(1965)	150,000	—	—	—	7.00	—

KM# 249 20 SOLES

7.9700 g., 0.9000 Silver .2306 oz. ASW **Subject:** 100th Anniversary of Peru-Spain Naval Battle **Obv:** National arms above value **Rev:** Victory standing on globe flanked by dates **Designer:** Armando Pareja

Date	Mintage	F	VF	XF	Unc	BU
ND(1966)	4,001	—	—	—	16.50	—

KM# 219 50 SOLES

33.4363 g., 0.9000 Gold .9675 oz. AGW **Obv:** Head with headdress left **Rev:** Sculpture

Date	Mintage	F	VF	XF	Unc	BU
1930	5,584	BV	675	950	1,600	—
1931	5,538	BV	675	950	1,500	—
1967	10,000	—	—	—	665	—
1968	300	—	—	—	700	—
1969	403	—	—	—	700	—

KM# 230 50 SOLES

23.4056 g., 0.9000 Gold .6772 oz. AGW **Obv:** National arms **Rev:** Seated Liberty flanked by shield and column **Note:** Similar to KM#229.

Date	Mintage	F	VF	XF	Unc	BU
1950	1,927	—	—	BV	470	—
1951	5,292	—	—	BV	470	525
1952	1,201	—	—	BV	525	—
1953	1,464	—	—	BV	470	—
1954	1,839	—	—	BV	470	—
1955	1,898	—	—	BV	470	—
1956	11,000	—	—	BV	470	500
1957	11,000	—	—	BV	470	500
1958	11,000	—	—	BV	470	500
1959	5,734	—	—	BV	470	500
1960	2,139	—	—	BV	470	—
1961	1,110	—	—	BV	525	—
1962	3,319	—	—	BV	470	—
1963	3,089	—	—	BV	470	—
1964/3	2,425	—	—	BV	470	—
1964	Inc. above	—	—	BV	470	—
1965	23,000	—	—	BV	470	500
1966	3,409	—	—	BV	470	525
1967	5,805	—	—	BV	470	525
1968	443	—	—	BV	550	—
1969	443	—	—	BV	550	—
1970	553	—	—	BV	550	—

KM# 242 50 SOLES

23.4056 g., 0.9000 Gold .6772 oz. AGW **Subject:** 400th Anniversary of Lima Mint **Obv:** National arms above value **Obv. Designer:** Armando Pareja **Rev:** Pillars of Hercules within inner circle **Rev. Designer:** Alonso de Rincon

Date	Mintage	F	VF	XF	Unc	BU
ND(1965)	17,000	—	—	—	470	525

KM# 250 50 SOLES

23.4056 g., 0.9000 Gold .6772 oz. AGW **Subject:** 100th Anniversary of Peru-Spain Naval Battle **Obv:** National arms above value **Rev:** Victory standing on globe divides dates **Designer:** Armando Pareja

Date	Mintage	F	VF	XF	Unc	BU
ND(1966)	6,409	—	—	—	550	600

KM# 256 50 SOLES
21.4500 g., 0.8000 Silver .5517 oz. ASW **Subject:** 150th Anniversary of Independence **Obv:** National arms within circle **Rev:** Bust of Tupac Amaru right **Designer:** Armando Pareja **Note:** Mint mark in monogram.

Date	Mintage	F	VF	XF	Unc	BU
1971LIMA	100,000	—	—	—	9.50	—

KM# 273 50 SOLES
Aluminum-Bronze **Obv:** National arms **Rev:** Value within circle **Note:** Mint mark in monogram.

Date	Mintage	F	VF	XF	Unc	BU
1979	1,323,000	—	0.15	0.35	1.00	—
1980	452,573,000	—	0.10	0.20	0.50	—
1981	19,923,000	—	0.10	0.20	0.50	—
1982LIMA	18,471,000	—	0.10	0.20	0.50	—
1982 Without LIMA	Inc. above	—	0.15	0.35	1.00	—
1983	8,175,000	—	0.10	0.20	0.50	—

KM# 297 50 SOLES
Brass **Subject:** 150th Anniversary - Birth of Admiral Grau **Obv:** Value within circle **Rev:** Head 1/4 right **Note:** Mint mark in monogram.

Date	Mintage	F	VF	XF	Unc	BU
1984	11,475,000	—	—	0.20	0.50	—

KM# 321 50 SOLES
Brass, 17 mm. **Subject:** Admiral Grau **Obv:** Value within circle **Rev:** Head 1/4 right **Edge:** Plain

Date	Mintage	F	VF	XF	Unc	BU
1985LIMAE	8,525,000	—	—	0.20	0.50	—

KM# 231 100 SOLES
46.8071 g., 0.9000 Gold 1.3544 oz. AGW **Obv:** National arms **Rev:** Seated Liberty flanked by shield and column

Date	Mintage	F	VF	XF	Unc	BU
1950	1,176	—	—	BV	940	965
1951	8,241	—	—	BV	940	965
1952	126	—	—	2,000	3,000	3,500
1953	498	—	—	BV	940	975
1954	1,808	—	—	BV	940	965
1955	901	—	—	BV	940	965
1956	1,159	—	—	BV	940	965
1957	550	—	—	BV	940	975
1958	101	—	—	3,000	4,000	4,500
1959	4,710	—	—	BV	940	965
1960	2,207	—	—	BV	940	965
1961	6,982	—	—	BV	940	965
1962	9,678	—	—	BV	940	965
1963	7,342	—	—	BV	940	965
1964	11,000	—	—	BV	940	965
1965	23,000	—	—	BV	940	965
1966	3,409	—	—	BV	940	965
1967	6,431	—	—	BV	940	965
1968	540	—	—	BV	940	975
1969	540	—	—	BV	940	975
1970	425	—	—	BV	940	975

KM# 243 100 SOLES
46.8071 g., 0.9000 Gold 1.3544 oz. AGW **Subject:** 400th Anniversary of Lima Mint **Obv:** National arms **Obv. Designer:** Armando Pareja **Rev:** Pillars of Hercules within inner circle **Rev. Designer:** Alonso de Rincon

Date	Mintage	F	VF	XF	Unc	BU
ND(1965)	27,000	—	—	—	935	960

KM# 251 100 SOLES
46.8071 g., 0.9000 Gold 1.3544 oz. AGW **Subject:** 100th Anniversary of Peru-Spain Naval Battle **Obv:** National arms **Rev:** Victory standing on globe divides dates **Designer:** Armando Pareja

Date	Mintage	F	VF	XF	Unc	BU
ND(1966)	6,253	—	—	—	950	1,000

KM# 261 100 SOLES
22.4500 g., 0.8000 Silver .5774 oz. ASW **Subject:** Centennial Peru-Japan Trade Relations **Obv:** National arms **Rev:** Value to left of flower sprig within circle **Note:** Mint mark in monogram.

Date	Mintage	F	VF	XF	Unc	BU
1973LIMA	375,000	—	—	—	12.50	—

KM# 283 100 SOLES
Copper-Nickel **Obv:** National arms **Rev:** Value within circle **Note:** Without mint mark.

Date	Mintage	F	VF	XF	Unc	BU
1980	100,000,000	—	0.20	0.40	1.50	—
1982	—	—	0.20	0.40	1.50	—

KM# 288 100 SOLES
Brass **Subject:** 150th Anniversary - Birth of Admiral Grau **Obv:** Value within circle **Rev:** Head 1/4 right **Note:** Mint mark in monogram.

Date	Mintage	F	VF	XF	Unc	BU
1984LIMA	20,000,000	—	0.15	0.35	1.00	—

KM# 262 200 SOLES
22.0000 g., 0.8000 Silver .5659 oz. ASW **Subject:** Aviation Heroes - Chavez and Guinones **Obv:** National arms **Rev:** Conjoined heads left within circle **Note:** No mint mark.

Date	Mintage	F	VF	XF	Unc	BU
1974	25,000	—	—	—	16.00	—
1975	90,000	—	—	—	12.00	—
1976	25,000	—	—	—	20.00	—
1977	3,000	—	—	—	30.00	—
1978	3,000	—	—	—	30.00	—

KM# 270 400 SOLES
28.1000 g., 0.9000 Silver .8131 oz. ASW **Subject:** 150th Anniversary - Battle of Ayacucho **Obv:** National arms **Rev:** Monument divides value within circle **Note:** Mint mark in monogram.

Date	Mintage	F	VF	XF	Unc	BU
1976LIMA	350,000	—	—	—	16.00	—

KM# 289 500 SOLES
Brass **Subject:** 150th Anniversary - Birth of Admiral Grau **Obv:** Value within circle **Rev:** Head 1/4 right **Note:** Mint mark in monogram.

Date	Mintage	F	VF	XF	Unc	BU
1984LIMA	16,962,000	—	0.20	0.50	2.00	—

KM# 310 500 SOLES
Brass **Subject:** Admiral Grau **Obv:** National arms **Rev:** Head 1/4 right without date **Note:** Mint mark in monogram.

Date	Mintage	F	VF	XF	Unc	BU
1985LIMA	13,038,000	—	0.20	0.50	2.50	—

KM# 275 1000 SOLES
15.5500 g., 0.5000 Silver .2500 oz. ASW **Subject:** National Congress **Obv:** National arms within circle **Rev:** Building **Edge:** Smooth with incuse stars **Note:** Mint mark in monogram.

Date	Mintage	F	VF	XF	Unc	BU
1979LIMA	200,000	—	—	—	6.00	7.50

KM# 276 5000 SOLES
31.1077 g., 0.9250 Silver .9251 oz. ASW **Subject:** 100th Anniversary - Battle of Iquique **Obv:** National arms **Rev:** Ship **Note:** Mint mark in monogram.

Date	Mintage	F	VF	XF	Unc	BU
1979LIMA	100,000	—	—	15.00	20.00	22.50

KM# 284 5000 SOLES
23.3700 g., 0.9250 Silver .6951 oz. ASW **Subject:** Champions of Soccer **Obv:** National arms **Rev:** Soccer players **Note:** Mint mark in monogram.

Date	Mintage	F	VF	XF	Unc	BU
1982LIMA Proof	8,250	Value: 26.50				

KM# 285 5000 SOLES
Silver **Subject:** Champions of Soccer **Obv:** National arms **Rev:** Soccer players in front of world globe **Note:** Mint mark in monogram.

Date	Mintage	F	VF	XF	Unc	BU
1982LIMA Proof	8,300	Value: 26.50				

KM# 286 10000 SOLES
16.8000 g., 0.9250 Silver .4997 oz. ASW **Subject:** Battle of La Brena and General Caceres **Obv:** National arms **Rev:** Head left **Note:** Mint mark in monogram.

Date	Mintage	F	VF	XF	Unc	BU
1982LIMA	100,000	—	—	—	12.50	14.50

KM# 277 50000 SOLES
16.8600 g., 0.9170 Gold .5004 oz. AGW **Subject:** Alfonso Urgarte **Obv:** National arms within circle **Rev:** Head left **Note:** Mint mark in monogram.

Date	Mintage	F	VF	XF	Unc	BU
1979LIMA	10,000	—	—	—	360	385

KM# 278 50000 SOLES
16.8600 g., 0.9170 Gold .5004 oz. AGW **Subject:** Elias Aguirre **Obv:** National arms within circle **Rev:** Head left **Note:** Mint mark in monogram.

Date	Mintage	F	VF	XF	Unc	BU
1979LIMA	10,000	—	—	—	360	385

KM# 279 50000 SOLES
16.8600 g., 0.9170 Gold .5004 oz. AGW **Subject:** F. Garcia Calderon **Obv:** National arms within circle **Rev:** Bust left **Note:** Mint mark in monogram.

Date	Mintage	F	VF	XF	Unc	BU
1979LIMA	10,000	—	—	—	360	385

KM# 280 100000 SOLES
33.9000 g., 0.9170 Gold .9995 oz. AGW **Subject:** Francisco Bolognese **Obv:** National arms within circle **Rev:** Bust left **Note:** Mint mark in monogram.

Date	Mintage	F	VF	XF	Unc	BU
1979LIMA	10,000	—	—	—	700	750

KM# 281 100000 SOLES
33.9000 g., 0.9170 Gold .9995 oz. AGW **Subject:** Andres A. Caceres **Obv:** National arms within circle **Rev:** Head left **Note:** Mint mark in monogram.

Date	Mintage	F	VF	XF	Unc	BU
1979LIMA	10,000	—	—	—	700	750

KM# 282 100000 SOLES
33.9000 g., 0.9170 Gold .9995 oz. AGW **Subject:** Miguel Grau **Obv:** National arms within circle **Rev:** Bust left **Note:** Mint mark in monogram.

Date	Mintage	F	VF	XF	Unc	BU
1979LIMA	10,000	—	—	—	700	750

REFORM COINAGE

1000 Soles de Oro = 1 Inti

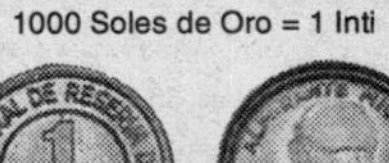

KM# 291 CENTIMO
1.5000 g., Brass, 15 mm. **Subject:** General Grau **Obv:** Value within circle **Rev:** Head 1/4 right **Note:** Mint mark: LIMA (monogram)

Date	Mintage	F	VF	XF	Unc	BU
1985LIMA	4,199,999	—	—	—	0.25	0.45

KM# 292 5 CENTIMOS
2.0000 g., Brass, 17 mm. **Subject:** General Grau **Obv:** Value within circle **Rev:** Head 1/4 right **Note:** Mint mark: LIMA (monogram)

Date	Mintage	F	VF	XF	Unc	BU
1985LIMA	20,000,000	—	—	—	0.35	0.50

KM# 293 10 CENTIMOS
2.9000 g., Brass, 19 mm. **Subject:** General Grau **Obv:** Value within circle **Rev:** Head 1/4 right **Note:** Mint mark: LIMA (monogram)

Date	Mintage	F	VF	XF	Unc	BU
1985LIMA	143,900,000	—	—	—	0.50	0.85
1986LIMA	48,730,000	—	—	—	0.65	1.00
1987LIMA	42,370,000	—	—	—	0.65	1.00

KM# 294 20 CENTIMOS
4.0000 g., Brass, 21 mm. **Subject:** General Grau **Obv:** Value within circle **Rev:** Head 1/4 right **Note:** Mint mark: LIMA (monogram)

Date	Mintage	F	VF	XF	Unc	BU
1985LIMA	4,739,000	—	—	—	1.25	1.50
1986LIMA	96,699,000	—	—	—	1.00	1.25
1987LIMA	59,668,000	—	—	—	1.00	1.25

KM# 295 50 CENTIMOS
5.2000 g., Brass, 23 mm. **Subject:** General Grau **Obv:** Value within circle **Rev:** Head 1/4 right **Note:** Mint mark: LIMA (monogram)

Date	Mintage	F	VF	XF	Unc	BU
1985LIMA	43,320,000	—	—	—	1.25	1.50
1986LIMA	72,802,000	—	—	—	1.25	1.50
1987LIMA	63,878,000	—	—	—	1.25	1.50
1988LIMA	80,000,000	—	—	—	1.25	1.50

KM# 301a 1/2 INTI
Copper-Nickel **Subject:** Pachacutec **Obv:** Map within design and styilized bow **Rev:** Native head left divides date

Date	Mintage	F	VF	XF	Unc	BU
1989	—	—	—	—	—	—

KM# 301 1/2 INTI
16.8000 g., 0.9250 Silver .4997 oz. ASW **Subject:** Pachacutec **Obv:** Map within design and stylized bow **Rev:** Native head left divides date **Note:** Mint mark: LIMA (monogram)

Date	Mintage	F	VF	XF	Unc	BU
1989LIMA	—	—	—	—	20.00	22.50

KM# 296 INTI
7.0000 g., Copper-Nickel, 25 mm. **Subject:** Admiral Grau **Obv:** National arms **Rev:** Head 1/4 right **Note:** Mint mark: LIMA (monogram)

Date	Mintage	F	VF	XF	Unc	BU
1985LIMA	15,760,000	—	—	—	1.75	2.00
1986LIMA	87,240,000	—	—	—	1.25	1.50
1987LIMA	120,000,000	—	—	—	1.00	1.25
1988LIMA	17,304,000	—	—	—	1.75	2.00

KM# 300 5 INTIS
8.2000 g., Copper-Nickel, 27 mm. **Subject:** Admiral Grau **Obv:** National arms **Rev:** Head 1/4 right **Note:** Mint mark: LIMA (monogram)

Date	Mintage	F	VF	XF	Unc	BU
1985LIMA	3,972	—	—	—	—	—
1986LIMA	28,000	—	—	—	3.50	5.00
1987LIMA	20,106,000	—	—	—	2.50	3.00
1988LIMA	34,084,000	—	—	—	2.50	3.00

KM# 298 100 INTIS
11.1100 g., 0.9250 Silver .3271 oz. ASW **Subject:** 150th Anniversary - Birth of Marshal Caceres **Obv:** National arms above value **Rev:** Head right **Note:** Mint mark: LIMA (monogram)

Date	Mintage	F	VF	XF	Unc	BU
ND(1986)LIMA	10,000	—	—	—	17.50	20.00

KM# 299 200 INTIS

22.0400 g., 0.9250 Silver .6543 oz. ASW **Subject:** 150th Anniversary - Birth of Marshal Caceres **Obv:** National arms above value **Rev:** Head right **Note:** Mint mark: LIMA (monogram)

Date	Mintage	F	VF	XF	Unc	BU
ND(1986)LIMA	—	—	—	—	32.50	35.00

REFORM COINAGE

1/M Intis = 1 Nuevo Sol; 100 (New) Centimos = 1 Nuevo Sol

KM# 303.1 CENTIMO

Brass **Obv:** National arms **Rev:** Value flanked by designs **Note:** Mint mark: LIMA (monogram)

Date	Mintage	F	VF	XF	Unc	BU
1991LIMA CHAVEZ	—	—	—	—	0.35	0.50
1992LIMA CHAVEZ	—	—	—	—	0.45	0.65
1993LIMA CHAVEZ	—	—	—	—	0.35	0.50
1994LIMA CHAVEZ	—	—	—	—	0.35	0.50

KM# 303.2 CENTIMO

Brass **Obv:** National arms **Obv. Legend:** No accent in Peru **Rev:** Large braille, no accent mark above E in centimo, no Chavez **Note:** Mint mark: LIMA (monogram)

Date	Mintage	F	VF	XF	Unc	BU
1997LIMA	—	—	—	—	0.35	—

KM# 303.3 CENTIMO

Brass **Obv:** National arms **Obv. Legend:** Accent mark in Peru **Rev:** Large braille, accent mark in centimo, no Chavez

Date	Mintage	F	VF	XF	Unc	BU
1999LIMA	—	—	—	—	2.50	—

KM# 304.1 5 CENTIMOS

Brass **Obv:** National arms **Rev:** Value flanked by designs **Note:** Mint mark: LIMA (monogram)

Date	Mintage	F	VF	XF	Unc	BU
1991LIMA CHAVEZ	—	—	—	—	0.45	0.65
1992LIMA CHAVEZ	—	—	—	—	0.50	0.75
1993LIMA	—	—	—	—	0.45	0.65
1993LIMA CHAVEZ	—	—	—	—	0.45	0.65
1994LIMA	—	—	—	—	0.45	0.65
1995	—	—	—	—	0.45	0.65
1996LIMA	—	—	—	—	0.45	0.65

KM# 304.2 5 CENTIMOS

Brass **Obv:** National arms **Rev:** Small braille with no accent mark above E in centimos, no Chavez

Date	Mintage	F	VF	XF	Unc	BU
1997LIMA	—	—	—	—	0.35	0.50
1998LIMA	—	—	—	—	0.35	0.50

KM# 304.3 5 CENTIMOS

Brass **Obv:** National arms **Rev:** Small braille with accent mark above E in centimos

Date	Mintage	F	VF	XF	Unc	BU
2000	—	—	—	—	0.35	0.50

KM# 305.1 10 CENTIMOS

Brass **Obv:** National arms within octogon **Rev:** Value flanked by designs within octogon

Date	Mintage	F	VF	XF	Unc	BU
1991LIMA	—	—	—	—	0.65	0.85
1992LIMA	—	—	—	—	0.75	1.00
1993LIMA	—	—	—	—	0.65	0.85
1993LIMA CHAVEZ	—	—	—	—	0.65	0.85
1994LIMA	—	—	—	—	0.65	0.85
1995LIMA	—	—	—	—	0.65	0.85
1996	—	—	—	—	0.65	0.85

KM# 305.2 10 CENTIMOS

Brass **Obv:** National arms within octogon **Rev:** Value flanked by designs within octogon **Note:** LIMA monogram mint mark.

Date	Mintage	F	VF	XF	Unc	BU
1997LIMA	—	—	—	—	0.65	0.85
1998LIMA	—	—	—	—	0.65	0.85

KM# 305.3 10 CENTIMOS

Brass **Obv:** National arms within octogon **Rev:** Value flanked by designs within octogon **Note:** LIMA monogram mint mark.

Date	Mintage	F	VF	XF	Unc	BU
1999	—	—	—	—	0.65	0.85
2000	—	—	—	—	0.65	0.85

KM# 306.1 20 CENTIMOS

Brass **Obv:** National arms **Rev:** Value **Note:** Mint mark in monogram. Varieties exist.

Date	Mintage	F	VF	XF	Unc	BU
1991LIMA CHAVEZ	—	—	—	—	0.85	1.20
1992LIMA CHAVEZ	—	—	—	—	0.85	1.20
1993LIMA CHAVEZ	—	—	—	—	0.85	1.20
1994LIMA	—	—	—	—	0.85	1.20
1996LIMA	—	—	—	—	0.85	1.20

KM# 306.2 20 CENTIMOS

Brass **Obv:** National arms **Rev:** Value **Note:** Mint mark in monogram

Date	Mintage	F	VF	XF	Unc	BU
2000LIMA	—	—	—	—	0.85	1.20

KM# 306.3 20 CENTIMOS

Brass **Obv:** Oval wreath above arms, accent above "u" **Rev:** Small braille dots, accent above "e"

Date	Mintage	F	VF	XF	Unc	BU
2000LM	—	—	—	—	0.85	1.20

KM# 307.1 50 CENTIMOS

Copper-Nickel, 22 mm. **Obv:** National arms within octogon **Rev:** Value flanked by sprig and monogram within octogon **Note:** Mint mark in monogram. Varieties exist.

Date	Mintage	F	VF	XF	Unc	BU
1991LIMA	—	—	—	—	1.50	1.75
1992LIMA	—	—	—	—	1.75	2.00
1993LIMA	—	—	—	—	1.50	1.75
1994LIMA	—	—	—	—	1.50	1.75
1996LIMA	—	—	—	—	1.50	1.75

KM# 307.2 50 CENTIMOS

Copper Nickel **Obv:** National arms within octogon **Rev:** Value flanked by sprig and monogram within octogon

Date	Mintage	F	VF	XF	Unc	BU
1997	—	—	—	—	1.50	1.75
1998	—	—	—	—	1.50	1.75

KM# 307.3 50 CENTIMOS

Copper Nickel **Obv:** National arms within octogon **Rev:** Value flanked by sprig and monogram within octogon **Note:** Mint mark in monogram.

Date	Mintage	F	VF	XF	Unc	BU
2000LIMA	—	—	—	—	1.50	1.75

KM# 302 NUEVO SOL

27.0000 g., 0.9250 Silver .8029 oz. ASW **Series:** Ibero - American **Obv:** National arms within assorted emblems around border **Rev:** Supine conjoined heads with hands holding a cornstalk and cross

Date	Mintage	F	VF	XF	Unc	BU
1991 Proof	60,000	Value: 50.00				

KM# 327 NUEVO SOL

27.0000 g., 0.9250 Silver 0.803 oz. ASW, 39 mm. **Series:** Ibero-American **Obv:** National arms within assorted emblems around border **Rev:** Opposite conjoined heads with hands holding cornstalk and cross

Date	Mintage	F	VF	XF	Unc	BU
ND(1991) Proof	—	Value: 55.00				

KM# 308.1 NUEVO SOL

Copper-Nickel **Obv:** National arms within octogon **Rev:** Written value flanked by sprig and monogram within octogon **Note:** Mint mark in monogram.

Date	Mintage	F	VF	XF	Unc	BU
1991LIMA	—	—	—	—	5.00	5.50
1992LIMA	—	—	—	—	5.00	5.50
1993LIMA	—	—	—	—	5.00	5.50
1994LIMA	—	—	—	—	4.00	4.50
1995LIMA	—	—	—	—	4.00	4.50
1996LIMA	—	—	—	—	4.00	4.50

KM# 308.2 NUEVO SOL

Copper-Nickel **Obv:** National arms within octogon **Rev:** Written value flanked by sprig and monogram within octogon

Date	Mintage	F	VF	XF	Unc	BU
1991	—	5.00	10.00	25.00	55.00	—

KM# 311 NUEVO SOL

33.6250 g., 0.9250 Silver 1.0000 oz. ASW **Subject:** Pre-Inca Moche Cultural Artifacts **Obv:** National arms **Rev:** Cultural artifacts within designed circle

Date	Mintage	F	VF	XF	Unc	BU
1994	3,300	—	—	—	—	—
1994 Proof	2,000	Value: 55.00				

KM# 312 NUEVO SOL

33.6250 g., 0.9170 Gold 1.0000 oz. AGW **Obv:** National arms **Rev:** Cultural artifacts within circle **Note:** Similar to KM#311.

Date	Mintage	F	VF	XF	Unc	BU
1994	899	—	—	—	—	—
1994 Proof	100	Value: 750				

KM# 314 NUEVO SOL

20.0000 g., 0.9990 Silver .6430 oz. ASW **Series:** Environmental Protection **Obv:** National arms **Rev:** Two Young Vicunas

Date	Mintage	F	VF	XF	Unc	BU
1994 Proof	30,000	Value: 47.50				

KM# 317 NUEVO SOL

20.0000 g., 0.9990 Silver .6430 oz. ASW **Series:** Environmental Protection **Obv:** National arms **Rev:** Llama, monkey and crocodile

Date	Mintage	F	VF	XF	Unc	BU
1994 Proof	20,000	Value: 47.50				

KM# 325 NUEVO SOL

33.6250 g., 0.9250 Silver 1 oz. ASW, 37.1 mm. **Obv:** National arms **Rev:** Bust half right **Edge:** Reeded

Date	Mintage	F	VF	XF	Unc	BU
1994 Proof	—	Value: 100				

KM# 318 NUEVO SOL

33.6250 g., 0.9250 Silver 1.0000 oz. ASW **Subject:** Centennial of Victor Raul Haya de la Torre **Obv:** National arms **Rev:** Head right

Date	Mintage	F	VF	XF	Unc	BU
1995	883	—	—	—	100	—

KM# 319 NUEVO SOL

33.6250 g., 0.9250 Silver 1.0000 oz. ASW **Subject:** National Mineral and Petrolium Society Centennial **Obv:** National arms **Rev:** Miner, oil derrick and cart

Date	Mintage	F	VF	XF	Unc	BU
1996	—	—	—	—	45.00	—

KM# 328 NUEVO SOL

33.5200 g., 0.9250 Silver 0.9969 oz. ASW, 37 mm. **Obv:** National arms **Rev:** Bust facing **Edge:** Reeded

Date	Mintage	F	VF	XF	Unc	BU
1997LIMAE Proof	1,000	Value: 55.00				

KM# 323 NUEVO SOL

33.4700 g., 0.9250 Silver .9954 oz. ASW, 37.1 mm. **Subject:** Centennial of Chorrillos Military School **Obv:** National arms **Rev:** Monument and building divide dates **Edge:** Reeded

Date	Mintage	F	VF	XF	Unc	BU
1998 Proof	—	Value: 47.50				

KM# 322 NUEVO SOL

33.6250 g., 0.9250 Silver 1.0000 oz. ASW **Subject:** Centennial of Japanese Immigration **Obv:** National arms **Rev:** Radiant sun above maps

Date	Mintage	F	VF	XF	Unc	BU
1999 Proof	—	Value: 47.50				

KM# 308.3 NUEVO SOL

Copper Nickel **Obv:** National arms within octogon **Rev:** Value flanked by sprig and monogram within octogon

Date	Mintage	F	VF	XF	Unc	BU
1999LIMA	—	—	—	—	4.00	4.50
2000LIMA	—	—	—	—	4.00	4.50

KM# 326 NUEVO SOL

26.9250 g., 0.9250 Silver 0.8015 oz. ASW, 40 mm. **Series:** Ibero-American **Obv:** National arms within circle of assorted arms **Rev:** Horse and rider in courtyard **Edge:** Reeded

Date	Mintage	F	VF	XF	Unc	BU
2000 Proof	—	Value: 60.00				

KM# 313.1 2 NUEVOS SOLES

5.5800 g., Bi-Metallic Brass center in Steel ring **Obv:** National arms within circle **Rev:** Stylized bird in flight to left of value within circle

Date	Mintage	F	VF	XF	Unc	BU
1994LIMA	—	—	—	—	4.50	5.00
1995LIMA	—	—	—	—	4.50	5.00

KM# 316.1 5 NUEVOS SOLES

6.5300 g., Bi-Metallic Brass center in Steel ring **Obv:** National arms within circle **Rev:** Stylized bird in flight to left of value within circle **Note:** Mint mark in monogram.

Date	Mintage	F	VF	XF	Unc	BU
1994LIMA	—	—	—	—	6.50	7.00
1995LIMA	—	—	—	—	6.50	7.00
2000LIMA	—	—	—	—	6.50	7.00

KM# 309 20 NUEVOS SOLES

33.6250 g., 0.9250 Silver 1.0000 oz. ASW **Subject:** Rio De Janeiro Protocal **Obv:** National arms **Rev:** Angel above map, dates at left

Date	Mintage	F	VF	XF	Unc	BU
1992LIMA	50,000	—	—	—	28.50	32.50

KM# 315 20 NUEVOS SOLES

33.6250 g., 0.9250 Silver 1.0000 oz. ASW **Obv:** National arms **Rev:** Head right

Date	Mintage	F	VF	XF	Unc	BU
1992LIMA Proof	—	Value: 28.50				

KM# 320 50 NUEVOS SOLES

33.6250 g., 0.9250 Silver 1.0000 oz. ASW **Subject:** Peru-Japan Commercial Exchange **Obv:** National arms **Rev:** Stylized bird design

Date	Mintage	F	VF	XF	Unc	BU
1993LIMA	—	—	—	—	42.50	47.50

TRADE COINAGE

KM# 210 1/5 LIBRA (Pound)

1.5976 g., 0.9170 Gold .0471 oz. AGW **Obv:** Shield within sprigs with small radiant sun above **Rev:** Head with headband right **Note:** Struck at Lima.

Date	Mintage	F	VF	XF	Unc	BU
1906 GOZF	106,000	—	BV	35.00	45.00	—
1907 GOZF	31,000	—	BV	35.00	45.00	—
1907 GOZG	—	—	BV	35.00	45.00	—
1909 GOZG	—	—	BV	35.00	45.00	—
1910 GOZG	—	—	BV	35.00	45.00	—
1911 GOZF	62,000	—	BV	35.00	45.00	—
1911 GOZG	—	—	BV	35.00	45.00	—
1912 GOZG	—	—	BV	35.00	45.00	—
1912 POZG	—	—	BV	35.00	45.00	—
1913 POZG	60,000	—	BV	35.00	45.00	—
1914 POZG	25,000	—	BV	35.00	45.00	—
1914 PBLG	Inc. above	—	—	—	—	—
Note: Reported, not confirmed						
1915	10,000	—	BV	30.00	45.00	—
1916	13,000	—	—	—	—	—
Note: Reported, not confirmed						
1917	3,896	—	BV	35.00	45.00	—
1918	16,000	—	BV	35.00	45.00	—
1919	10,000	—	BV	35.00	45.00	—
1920	72,000	—	BV	35.00	45.00	—
1922	8,110	—	BV	35.00	45.00	—
1923	27,000	—	BV	35.00	45.00	—
1924	—	—	BV	35.00	45.00	—
1925	20,000	—	BV	35.00	45.00	—
1926	11,000	—	BV	35.00	45.00	—
1927	14,000	—	BV	35.00	45.00	—
1928	9,322	—	BV	35.00	45.00	—
1929	8,971	—	BV	35.00	45.00	—
1930	9,991	—	BV	40.00	55.00	—
1953 BBR	9,821	—	—	BV	50.00	—
1955 ZBR	10,000	—	—	BV	50.00	—
1958 ZBR	5,098	—	—	BV	40.00	—
1959 ZBR	6,308	—	—	BV	40.00	—
1960 ZBR	6,083	—	—	BV	40.00	—
1961 ZBR	12,000	—	—	BV	40.00	—
1962 ZBR	5,431	—	—	BV	40.00	—
1963 ZBR	11,000	—	—	BV	40.00	—
1964 ZBR	25,000	—	—	BV	40.00	—
1965 ZBR	19,000	—	—	BV	40.00	—
1966 ZBR	60,000	—	—	BV	40.00	—
1967 BBR	9,914	—	—	BV	40.00	—
1968 BBR	—	—	—	BV	40.00	—
1968 BBB	4,781	—	—	BV	40.00	—
1969 BBB	15,000	—	—	BV	40.00	—

KM# 209 1/2 LIBRA (Pound)

3.9940 g., 0.9170 Gold .1177 oz. AGW **Obv:** Shield within sprigs with radiant sun above **Rev:** Head with headband right

Date	Mintage	F	VF	XF	Unc	BU
1902 ROZF	7,800	—	BV	85.00	100	—
1903 ROZF	7,245	—	BV	85.00	100	—
1904 ROZF	8,360	—	BV	85.00	100	—
1905 ROZF	8,010	—	BV	85.00	100	—
1905 GOZF	Inc. above	—	BV	85.00	100	—
1906 GOZF	9,176	—	BV	85.00	100	—
1907 GOZG	—	—	BV	85.00	100	—
1908 GOZG	8,180	—	BV	85.00	100	—
1953 BBR	9,210	—	BV	85.00	100	—
1955 ZBR	14,000	—	—	BV	90.00	—
1961 ZBR	752	—	—	BV	110	—
1962 ZBR	4,286	—	—	BV	95.00	—
1963 ZBR	908	—	—	BV	110	—
1964 ZBR	10,000	—	—	BV	90.00	—
1965 ZBR	5,490	—	—	BV	95.00	—
1966 ZBR	44,000	—	—	BV	90.00	—
1967 BBR	—	—	—	BV	90.00	—
1968 BBB	Inc. above	—	—	BV	90.00	—
1969 BBB	4,400	—	—	BV	95.00	—

KM# 207 LIBRA (Pound)

7.9881 g., 0.9170 Gold .2354 oz. AGW **Obv:** Shield within sprigs with radiant sun above **Rev:** Head with headband right

Date	Mintage	VG	F	VF	XF	Unc
1901 ROZF	81,000	—	—	—	BV	165
1902 ROZF	89,000	—	—	—	BV	165
1903 ROZF	100,000	—	—	—	BV	165
1904 ROZF	33,000	—	—	—	BV	165
1905 GOZF	—	—	—	—	BV	165
1905 ROZF	141,000	—	—	—	BV	175
1906 GOZF	201,000	—	—	—	BV	165
1907 GOZG	Inc. above	—	—	—	BV	165
1908 GOZG	36,000	—	—	—	BV	175
1909 GOZG	52,000	—	—	—	BV	175
1910 GOZG	47,000	—	—	—	BV	175
1911 GOZG	42,000	—	—	—	BV	175
1912 GOZG	54,000	—	—	—	BV	175
1912 POZG	Inc. above	—	—	—	BV	185
1913 POZG	—	—	—	—	BV	175
1914 POZG	—	—	—	—	BV	185
1914 PBLG	119,000	—	—	—	BV	175
1915 PVG	91,000	—	—	—	BV	180

Date	Mintage	VG	F	VF	XF	Unc
1915 PMGG	Inc. above	—	—	—	BV	200
1915	Inc. above	—	—	—	BV	170
1916	582,000	—	—	—	BV	165
1917	1,928,000	—	—	—	BV	165
1918	600,000	—	—	—	BV	165
1919	Inc. above	—	—	—	BV	165
1920	152,000	—	—	—	BV	175
1921	Inc. above	—	—	—	BV	180
1922	13,000	—	—	—	BV	185
1923	15,000	—	—	—	BV	185
1924	8,113	—	—	—	BV	185
1925	9,068	—	—	—	BV	180
1926	4,596	—	—	—	BV	180
1927	8,360	—	—	—	BV	180
1928	2,184	—	—	—	BV	180
1929	3,119	—	—	—	BV	180
1930	1,050	—	—	—	BV	180
1959 ZBR	605	—	—	—	BV	250
1961 ZBR	402	—	—	—	BV	250
1962 ZBR	6,203	—	—	—	BV	180
1963 ZBR	302	—	—	—	BV	260
1964 ZBR	13,000	—	—	—	BV	180
1965 ZBR	9,917	—	—	—	BV	180
1966 ZBR	39,000	—	—	—	BV	180
1967 BBR	2,002	—	—	—	BV	180
1968 BBR	7,307	—	—	—	BV	185
1969 BBR	7,307	—	—	—	BV	185

TOKEN COINAGE

KM# Tn3 50 CENTAVOS

Silver **Subject:** National Defense **Obv:** Inca warrior Cahuide attacking with war club

Date	Mintage	F	VF	XF	Unc	BU
1932	—	8.50	12.50	18.50	30.00	—

KM# Tn1 SOL

0.9000 Silver **Note:** Medal rotation.

Date	Mintage	F	VF	XF	Unc	BU
1910	—	8.50	12.50	18.50	30.00	40.00

KM# Tn4 SOL

Silver **Subject:** National Defense **Obv:** Inca warrior Cahuide attacking with war club **Note:** Medal rotation.

Date	Mintage	F	VF	XF	Unc	BU
1932	—	7.00	12.00	17.50	30.00	—

KM# Tn2 5 SOLES

2.3404 g., 0.9000 Gold .0677 oz. AGW

Date	Mintage	F	VF	XF	Unc	BU
1910	—	60.00	80.00	110	150	200

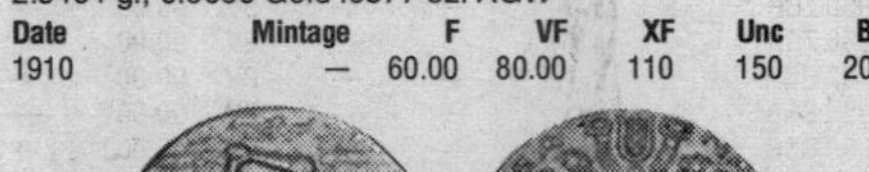

KM# Tn5 5 SOLES

Silver **Subject:** National Defense **Obv:** Inca warrior Cahuide attacking with war club

Date	Mintage	F	VF	XF	Unc	BU
1932	—	12.00	17.50	28.50	45.00	—

KM# Tn6 10 SOLES

Gold Plated Silver **Subject:** National Defense **Obv:** Inca warrior Cahuide attacking with war club

Date	Mintage	F	VF	XF	Unc	BU
1932	—	15.00	20.00	38.50	55.00	—

PATTERNS

Including off metal strikes

KM#	Date	Mintage	Identification	Mkt Val
Pn26	1932	—	Sol.	—
PnF26	1930	3	50 Soles. Native inscription.	—
PnG26	1932	—	50 Centavos.	—
Pn27	1932	—	5 Soles.	—
PnA28	1932	—	10 Soles.	—
pnB28	1946	—	1/2 Sol. Copper-Nickel.	150
Pn28	1947	—	100 Soles. Gilt Bronze.	—
Pn29	1948	—	Sol. Aluminum.	—
PnA30	1949	—	Centavo. Zinc. KM#211.	75.00
PnB30	1949	—	2 Centavos. Zinc. KM#212.2.	50.00
Pn30	1952	—	1 Sol De Oro. Brass.	—
PnA31	1958	—	20 Centavos. Copper Nickel.	50.00
Pn31	1958	—	50 Soles. Silver. With PRUEBA.	900
Pn32	1964	—	50 Soles. Silver. With PRUEBA.	900
Pn33	1965	—	50 Soles. Silver. With PRUEBA.	900

KM#	Date	Mintage	Identification	Mkt Val
PnA33	1965	—	5 Centavos. Copper-Nickel-Zinc. KM#290.	900
Pn34	1966	200	Sol. Silver. With PAREJA.	—
Pn35	1967	—	1/2 Sol. With PAREJA.	—
Pn36	1967	7	50 Soles. Silver.	—
Pn37	1988	—	Inti. Brass. KM#296.	—
Pn38	198x	—	5 Intis. Copper-Nickel-Zinc. KM#300.	—

KM#	Date	Mintage	Identification	Mkt Val
Pn39	1988	—	5 Intis. Brass.	—

TRIAL STRIKES

KM#	Date	Mintage	Identification	Mkt Val
TS4	1935	—	Sol. Silver. KM#218.1. Alloy percentage: N. 3/25, PLT/0, NKL 10 ZNC/55 CRE.	—
TS5	1935	—	Sol. Silver. KM#218.1. Alloy percentage: N. 4/20, PLT/15, NKL 10 ZNC/55 CRE.	—

PHILIPPINES

The Republic of the Philippines, an archipelago in the western Pacific 500 miles (805 km.) from the southeast coast of Asia, has an area of 115,830 sq. mi. (300,000 sq. km.) and a population of *64.9 million. Capital: Manila. The economy of the 7,000-island group is based on agriculture, forestry and fishing. Timber, coconut products, sugar and hemp are exported.

Migration to the Philippines began about 30,000 years ago when land bridges connected the islands with Borneo and Sumatra. Ferdinand Magellan claimed the islands for Spain in 1521. The first permanent settlement was established by Miguel de Legazpi at Cebu April 1565. Manila was established in 1572. A British expedition captured Manila and occupied the Spanish colony in October 1762, but returned it to Spain by the treaty of Paris, 1763. Spain held the Philippines despite growing Filipino nationalism until 1898 when they were ceded to the United States at the end of the Spanish-American War. The Philippines became a self-governing commonwealth under the United States in 1935, and attained independence as the Republic of the Philippines on July 4, 1946.

MINT MARKS

(b) Brussels, privy marks only
BSP - Bangko Sentral Pilipinas
D - Denver, 1944-1945
(Lt) - Llantrisant
M, MA - Manila
PM - Pobjoy Mint
S - San Francisco, 1903-1947
SGV - Madrid
(Sh) - Sherritt
(US) - United States
FM - Franklin Mint, U.S.A.*
(VDM) - Vereinigte Deutsche Metall Werks; Altona, Germany
Star - Manila (Spanish) = Manila

***NOTE:** From 1975-1977 the Franklin Mint produced coinage in up to 3 different qualities. Beginning in 1978only (U) and (P) were struck. Qualities of issue are designated in ( ) after each date and are defined as follows:

(M) MATTE - Normal circulation strike or a dull finish produced by sandblasting special uncirculated (polish-finish) or proof quality dies.

(U) SPECIAL UNCIRCULATED - Polished or prooflike in appearance without any frosted features.

(P) PROOF - The highest quality obtainable having mirror-like fields and frosted features.

MONETARY SYSTEM

4 Quartos = 1 Real
8 Reales = 1 Peso

UNITED STATES ADMINISTRATION

DECIMAL COINAGE

KM# 162 1/2 CENTAVO

Bronze **Obv:** Man seated beside hammer and anvil **Rev:** Eagle above stars and striped shield

Date	Mintage	F	VF	XF	Unc	BU
1903	12,084,000	0.50	1.00	2.00	12.00	20.00
1903 Proof	2,558	Value: 60.00				
1904	5,654,000	0.50	1.25	3.00	15.00	25.00
1904 Proof	1,355	Value: 75.00				
1905 Proof	471	Value: 300				
1906 Proof	500	Value: 200				
1908 Proof	500	Value: 250				

KM# 163 CENTAVO

Bronze **Obv:** Man seated beside hammer and anvil **Rev:** Eagle above stars and striped shield

Date	Mintage	F	VF	XF	Unc	BU
1903	10,790,000	0.50	1.00	2.50	15.00	30.00

Date	Mintage	F	VF	XF	Unc	BU
1903 Proof	2,558	Value: 75.00				
1904	17,040,000	0.50	1.00	2.50	17.50	32.50
1904 Proof	1,355	Value: 75.00				
1905	10,000,000	0.50	1.00	2.50	20.00	40.00
1905 Proof	471	Value: 200				
1906 Proof	500	Value: 175				
1908 Proof	500	Value: 190				
1908S	2,187,000	2.50	5.00	12.50	50.00	80.00
1909S	1,738,000	7.50	12.50	30.00	90.00	140
1910S	2,700,000	2.00	5.00	10.00	50.00	80.00
1911S	4,803,000	1.00	4.00	7.50	40.00	60.00
1912S	3,000,000	3.00	6.50	12.50	90.00	120
1913S	5,000,000	1.00	2.50	7.50	50.00	85.00
1914S	5,000,000	1.00	2.50	5.00	40.00	65.00
1915S	2,500,000	20.00	40.00	90.00	600	975
1916S	4,330,000	6.00	12.50	25.00	110	175
1917/6S	7,070,000	22.00	30.00	75.00	300	425
1917S	Inc. above	2.50	5.00	10.00	40.00	80.00
1918S	11,660,000	2.00	4.00	10.00	60.00	125
1918S Large S	Inc. above	75.00	150	325	1,300	1,800
1919S	4,540,000	0.75	2.00	6.00	35.00	65.00
1920S	2,500,000	4.00	9.00	20.00	125	265
1920	3,552,000	1.00	3.50	8.50	45.00	70.00
1921	7,283,000	0.75	3.50	7.50	40.00	70.00
1922	3,519,000	0.50	1.50	6.00	40.00	65.00
1925M	9,332,000	0.50	1.50	6.00	40.00	60.00
1926M	9,000,000	0.50	1.50	6.00	35.00	50.00
1927M	9,270,000	0.35	2.00	6.00	40.00	75.00
1928M	9,150,000	0.35	1.00	5.00	25.00	40.00
1929M	5,657,000	1.00	3.00	8.00	40.00	75.00
1930M	5,577,000	0.50	1.50	4.00	30.00	45.00
1931M	5,659,000	0.50	1.50	5.00	40.00	55.00
1932M	4,000,000	0.75	2.50	6.00	45.00	65.00
1933M	8,393,000	0.25	1.50	3.00	15.00	30.00
1934M	3,179,000	0.75	2.00	3.00	40.00	75.00
1936M	17,455,000	0.25	1.00	3.00	35.00	50.00

KM# 164 5 CENTAVOS

Copper-Nickel, 21.3 mm. **Obv:** Man seated beside hammer and anvil **Rev:** Eagle above stars and striped shield

Date	Mintage	F	VF	XF	Unc	BU
1903	8,910,000	0.50	1.25	3.00	25.00	35.00
1903 Proof	2,558	Value: 75.00				
1904	1,075,000	0.75	1.50	3.50	27.00	35.00
1904 Proof	1,355	Value: 85.00				
1905 Proof	471	Value: 200				
1906 Proof	500	Value: 175				
1908 Proof	500	Value: 175				
1916S	300,000	25.00	60.00	95.00	600	850
1917S	2,300,000	2.00	5.00	10.00	125	175
1918/7S	—	3.00	9.00	18.50	120	—
1918S	2,780,000	1.50	5.00	10.00	100	150
1919S	1,220,000	2.50	7.50	15.00	150	200
1920	1,421,000	3.00	10.00	20.00	125	150
1921	2,132,000	2.00	7.00	10.00	90.00	125
1925M	1,000,000	5.00	15.00	30.00	175	225
1926M	1,200,000	3.00	8.00	15.00	90.00	125
1927M	1,000,000	2.00	5.00	10.00	60.00	75.00
1928M	1,000,000	3.00	6.00	11.00	60.00	75.00

KM# 173 5 CENTAVOS

Copper-Nickel **Obv:** Man seated beside hammer and anvil **Rev:** Eagle above stars and striped shield **Note:** Mule.

Date	Mintage	F	VF	XF	Unc	BU
1918S	—	200	600	1,450	2,500	4,500

KM# 175 5 CENTAVOS

Copper-Nickel, 19 mm. **Obv:** Man seated beside hammer and anvil **Rev:** Eagle above stars and striped shield

Date	Mintage	F	VF	XF	Unc	BU
1930M	2,905,000	1.00	2.00	4.00	40.00	50.00
1931M	3,477,000	1.00	2.50	6.00	75.00	90.00
1932M	3,956,000	1.00	2.00	4.00	50.00	65.00
1934M	2,154,000	1.00	2.50	10.00	60.00	100
1935M	2,754,000	1.00	2.00	6.00	95.00	125

KM# 165 10 CENTAVOS

2.6924 g., 0.9000 Silver .0779 oz. ASW **Obv:** Female standing beside hammer and anvil **Rev:** Eagle above stars and striped shield

Date	Mintage	F	VF	XF	Unc	BU
1903	5,103,000	1.25	3.50	5.00	35.00	60.00
1903 Proof	2,558	Value: 80.00				
1903S	1,200,000	8.00	15.00	35.00	350	500
1904	11,000	10.00	15.00	35.00	75.00	125
1904 Proof	1,355	Value: 100				
1904S	5,040,000	1.50	2.50	6.00	40.00	75.00
1905 Proof	471	Value: 225				
1906 Proof	500	Value: 200				

KM# 169 10 CENTAVOS

2.0000 g., 0.7500 Silver .0482 oz. ASW **Obv:** Female standing beside hammer and anvil **Rev:** Eagle above stars and striped shield

Date	Mintage	F	VF	XF	Unc	BU
1907	1,501,000	1.50	3.00	5.00	50.00	75.00
1907S	4,930,000	1.00	2.00	4.00	40.00	55.00
1908 Proof	500	Value: 200				
1908S	3,364,000	1.00	2.00	4.00	60.00	90.00
1909S	312,000	15.00	35.00	60.00	350	450
1910S	—	—	—	—	—	—
Note: Unknown in any collection. Counterfeits of the 1910S are commonly encountered						
1911S	1,101,000	3.00	4.00	12.50	75.00	125
1912S	1,010,000	2.25	4.00	12.00	75.00	125
1913S	1,361,000	1.50	3.00	10.00	50.00	75.00
1914S	1,180,000	3.00	5.50	15.00	150	225
1915S	450,000	7.50	17.50	35.00	250	425
1917S	5,991,000	1.00	2.00	3.50	50.00	75.00
1918S	8,420,000	0.85	1.50	2.00	27.50	35.00
1919S	1,630,000	1.00	2.50	4.00	45.00	55.00
1920	520,000	3.50	5.00	15.00	75.00	150
1921	3,863,000	0.85	1.50	2.50	30.00	40.00
1929M	1,000,000	0.85	1.50	2.50	20.00	35.00
1935M	1,280,000	0.85	1.50	2.00	20.00	30.00

KM# 166 20 CENTAVOS

5.3849 g., 0.9000 Silver .1558 oz. ASW **Obv:** Female standing beside hammer and anvil **Rev:** Eagle above stars and striped shield

Date	Mintage	F	VF	XF	Unc	BU
1903	5,353,000	2.50	3.00	5.00	35.00	70.00
1903 Proof	2,558	Value: 125				
1903S	150,000	8.00	15.00	50.00	450	750
1904	11,000	15.00	25.00	35.00	100	150
1904 Proof	1,355	Value: 125				
1904S	2,060,000	2.75	3.50	9.00	100	150
1905 Proof	471	Value: 275				
1905S	420,000	7.50	12.00	25.00	150	200
1906 Proof	500	Value: 250				

KM# 170 20 CENTAVOS

4.0000 g., 0.7500 Silver .0965 oz. ASW **Obv:** Female standing beside hammer and anvil **Rev:** Eagle above stars and striped shield

Date	Mintage	F	VF	XF	Unc	BU
1907	1,251,000	2.00	3.00	10.00	65.00	100
1907S	3,165,000	2.00	2.50	7.50	40.00	60.00
1908 Proof	500	Value: 250				
1908S	1,535,000	2.00	3.00	12.50	50.00	75.00
1909S	450,000	6.00	22.00	45.00	300	400
1910S	500,000	6.00	20.00	45.00	350	500
1911S	505,000	5.00	15.00	35.00	225	400
1912S	750,000	4.00	7.50	25.00	200	225
1913S/S	949,000	8.00	20.00	35.00	225	325
1913S	Inc. above	3.00	7.00	15.00	150	200
1914S	795,000	3.50	6.00	20.00	140	225
1915S	655,000	10.00	15.00	30.00	250	450
1916S	1,435,000	3.00	8.00	17.50	85.00	125
1917S	3,151,000	1.65	2.50	4.00	50.00	70.00
1918S	5,560,000	1.50	2.50	4.00	40.00	50.00
1919S	850,000	1.75	4.00	7.00	75.00	125
1920	1,046,000	1.75	5.00	8.00	90.00	120
1921	1,843,000	1.50	2.50	4.00	50.00	75.00
1929M	1,970,000	1.50	2.50	4.00	40.00	50.00

KM# 174 20 CENTAVOS

4.0000 g., 0.7500 Silver .0965 oz. ASW **Obv:** Female standing beside hammer and anvil **Rev:** Eagle above stars and striped shield **Note:** Mule.

Date	Mintage	F	VF	XF	Unc	BU
1928M	100,000	5.00	13.00	35.00	550	800

KM# 167 50 CENTAVOS

13.4784 g., 0.9000 Silver .3900 oz. ASW **Obv:** Female standing beside hammer and anvil **Rev:** Eagle above stars and striped shield

Date	Mintage	F	VF	XF	Unc	BU
1903	3,102,000	6.50	8.50	12.00	75.00	110
1903 Proof	2,558	Value: 150				
1903S 2 Known	—	—	—	22,000	—	—
1904	11,000	25.00	32.00	50.00	150	200
1904 Proof	1,355	Value: 175				
1904S	2,160,000	6.50	9.50	15.00	100	140
1905 Proof	471	Value: 325				
1905S	852,000	8.00	15.00	35.00	600	1,200
1906 Proof	500	Value: 275				

KM# 171 50 CENTAVOS

10.0000 g., 0.7500 Silver .2411 oz. ASW **Obv:** Female standing beside hammer and anvil **Rev:** Eagle above stars and striped shield

Date	Mintage	F	VF	XF	Unc	BU
1907	1,201,000	5.00	10.00	30.00	175	225
1907S	2,112,000	4.00	10.00	20.00	125	150
1908 Proof	500	Value: 250				
1908S	1,601,000	4.00	9.00	25.00	250	500
1909S	528,000	5.00	15.00	45.00	275	350
1917S	674,000	5.00	10.00	25.00	125	200
1918S	2,202,000	3.75	6.00	9.00	100	125
1919S	1,200,000	3.75	5.50	10.00	150	150
1920	420,000	3.75	4.50	8.00	35.00	75.00
1921	2,317,000	BV	3.75	5.00	20.00	50.00

KM# 168 PESO

26.9568 g., 0.9000 Silver .7800 oz. ASW **Obv:** Female standing beside hammer and anvil **Rev:** Eagle above stars and striped shield

Date	Mintage	F	VF	XF	Unc	BU
1903	2,791,000	13.50	17.50	25.00	150	200
1903 Proof	2,558	Value: 300				
1903S	11,361,000	12.50	15.00	20.00	125	150
1904	11,000	65.00	85.00	110	250	325
1904 Proof	1,355	Value: 350				
1904S	6,600,000	12.50	15.00	25.00	125	165
1905 Proof	471	Value: 900				
1905S straight serif on 1	—	17.50	25.00	45.00	300	450
1905S curved serif on 1	6,056,000	14.00	20.00	30.00	200	350
1906 Proof	500	Value: 800				
1906S	201,000	750	1,200	2,500	12,000	20,000
Note: Counterfeits of the 1906S exist						

KM# 172 PESO

20.0000 g., 0.8000 Silver .5144 oz. ASW **Obv:** Female standing beside hammer and anvil **Rev:** Eagle above stars and striped shield

Date	Mintage	F	VF	XF	Unc	BU
1907 Proof, 2 known	—	—	—	—	—	—
1907S	10,276,000	8.00	9.00	12.00	60.00	100
1908 Proof	500	Value: 700				
1908S	20,955,000	8.00	9.00	12.00	60.00	90.00
1909S	7,578,000	8.00	9.00	15.00	70.00	100
1910S	3,154,000	8.00	10.00	20.00	250	400
1911S	463,000	12.00	20.00	45.00	700	1,000
1912S	680,000	12.00	25.00	75.00	750	1,200

UNITED STATES ADMINISTRATION

Commonwealth

DECIMAL COINAGE

KM# 179 CENTAVO

Bronze, 25 mm. **Obv:** Male seated beside hammer and anvil **Rev:** Eagle above shield

Date	Mintage	F	VF	XF	Unc	BU
1937M	15,790,000	0.25	1.00	4.00	12.50	25.00
1938M	10,000,000	0.25	0.75	3.00	20.00	35.00
1939M	6,500,000	0.25	2.00	4.00	15.00	30.00
1940M	4,000,000	0.25	0.75	2.00	13.00	35.00
1941M	5,000,000	0.25	2.00	5.00	20.00	35.00
1944S	58,000,000	—	0.15	0.25	2.25	5.00

KM# 180 5 CENTAVOS

Copper-Nickel **Obv:** Male seated beside hammer and anvil **Rev:** Eagle with wings open above shield

Date	Mintage	F	VF	XF	Unc	BU
1937M	2,494,000	1.00	2.50	5.50	45.00	75.00
1938M	4,000,000	0.50	1.00	2.50	15.00	30.00
1941M	2,750,000	1.00	2.50	8.00	40.00	75.00

KM# 180a 5 CENTAVOS

Copper-Nickel-Zinc, 19 mm. **Obv:** Male seated beside hammer and anvil **Rev:** Eagle with wings open above shield

Date	Mintage	F	VF	XF	Unc	BU
1944	21,198,000	—	0.20	0.50	2.00	4.00
1944S	14,040,000	—	0.20	0.25	1.00	2.00
1945S	72,796,000	—	0.20	0.25	1.00	2.00

KM# 181 10 CENTAVOS

2.0000 g., 0.7500 Silver .0482 oz. ASW, 16.7 mm. **Obv:** Female standing beside hammer and anvil **Rev:** Eagle with wings open above shield

Date	Mintage	F	VF	XF	Unc	BU
1937M	3,500,000	0.85	2.00	4.00	20.00	30.00
1938M	3,750,000	BV	0.85	2.00	10.00	15.00
1941M	2,500,000	BV	1.25	2.50	15.00	35.00
1944D	31,592,000	—	—	BV	1.25	2.50
1945D	137,208,000	—	—	BV	1.00	2.25

Note: 1937, 1938, and 1941 dated strikes have inverted W's for M's

KM# 182 20 CENTAVOS

4.0000 g., 0.7500 Silver .0965 oz. ASW, 21 mm. **Obv:** Female standing beside hammer and anvil **Rev:** Eagle with wings open above shield

Date	Mintage	F	VF	XF	Unc	BU
1937M	2,665,000	BV	1.75	3.50	15.00	30.00
1938M	3,000,000	BV	1.50	2.50	12.50	20.00
1941M	1,500,000	1.50	2.00	3.00	11.00	20.00
1944D	28,596,000	—	—	BV	1.75	2.50
1944D/S	—	12.00	16.50	20.00	50.00	75.00
1945D	82,804,000	—	—	BV	1.50	2.50

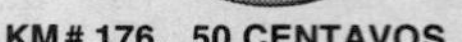

KM# 176 50 CENTAVOS

10.0000 g., 0.7500 Silver .2411 oz. ASW, 27.5 mm. **Subject:** Establishment of the Commonwealth **Obv:** Busts facing each other **Rev:** Eagle above shield **Designer:** Ambrosia Morales

Date	Mintage	F	VF	XF	Unc	BU
1936	20,000	—	30.00	45.00	75.00	110

KM# 183 50 CENTAVOS

10.0000 g., 0.7500 Silver .2411 oz. ASW, 27.5 mm. **Obv:** Female standing beside hammer and anvil **Rev:** Eagle with wings open above shield

Date	Mintage	F	VF	XF	Unc	BU
1944S	19,187,000	—	—	BV	4.50	6.50
1945S	18,120,000	—	—	BV	4.50	6.50

KM# 177 PESO

20.0000 g., 0.9000 Silver .5787 oz. ASW, 35 mm. **Subject:** Establishment of the Commonwealth **Obv:** Conjoined busts left **Rev:** Eagle with wings open above shield **Designer:** Ambrosia Morales

Date	Mintage	F	VF	XF	Unc	BU
1936	10,000	—	50.00	75.00	175	225

KM# 178 PESO

20.0000 g., 0.9000 Silver .5787 oz. ASW, 35 mm. **Subject:** Establishment of the Commonwealth **Obv:** Conjoined busts left **Rev:** Eagle with wings open above shield **Designer:** Ambrosia Morales

Date	Mintage	F	VF	XF	Unc	BU
1936	10,000	—	50.00	75.00	175	225

REPUBLIC

DECIMAL COINAGE

KM# 186 CENTAVO

Bronze, 19 mm. **Obv:** Shield of arms **Rev:** Male seated beside hammer and anvil

Date	Mintage	F	VF	XF	Unc	BU
1958	20,000,000	—	—	0.10	0.25	0.50
1960	40,000,000	—	—	0.10	0.15	0.35
1962	30,000,000	—	—	0.10	0.15	0.35
1963	130,000,000	—	—	0.10	0.15	0.25

KM# 187 5 CENTAVOS

Brass, 21 mm. **Obv:** Shield of arms **Rev:** Male seated beside hammer and anvil

Date	Mintage	F	VF	XF	Unc	BU
1958	10,000,000	—	—	0.10	0.25	0.50
1959	10,000,000	—	—	0.10	0.20	0.50
1960	40,000,000	—	—	0.10	0.15	0.40
1962	40,000,000	—	—	0.10	0.15	0.40
1963	50,000,000	—	—	0.10	0.15	0.40
1964	100,000,000	—	—	—	0.10	0.40
1966	10,000,000	—	—	0.10	0.20	0.50

KM# 188 10 CENTAVOS

Copper-Zinc-Nickel, 17.8 mm. **Obv:** Shield of arms **Rev:** Female standing beside hammer and anvil

Date	Mintage	F	VF	XF	Unc	BU
1958	10,000,000	—	—	0.15	0.25	0.50
1960	70,000,000	—	—	0.15	0.20	0.40
1962	50,000,000	—	—	0.15	0.20	0.40
1963	50,000,000	—	—	0.15	0.20	0.40
1964	100,000,000	—	—	0.10	0.20	0.40
1966	110,000,000	—	—	0.10	0.20	0.45

KM# 189.1 25 CENTAVOS

Copper-Zinc-Nickel **Obv:** Shield of arms **Rev:** Female standing beside hammer and anvil

Date	Mintage	F	VF	XF	Unc	BU
1958	10,000,000	—	—	0.25	0.50	0.75
1960	10,000,000	—	—	0.30	0.50	0.75
1962	40,000,000	—	—	0.25	0.50	0.75
1964	49,800,000	—	—	0.20	0.35	0.75
1966	50,000,000	—	0.25	0.50	1.00	1.25

KM# 189.2 25 CENTAVOS

Copper-Zinc-Nickel **Obv:** Shield of arms **Rev:** Female standing beside hammer and anvil

Date	Mintage	F	VF	XF	Unc	BU
1966	40,000,000	—	—	0.20	0.40	1.00
1966 Matte finish	Inc. above	—	—	—	—	—

KM# 184 50 CENTAVOS

10.0000 g., 0.7500 Silver .2411 oz. ASW, 27.5 mm. **Obv:** Shield of arms above date and value **Rev:** Uniformed bust right
Designer: Laura Gardin Fraser

Date	Mintage	F	VF	XF	Unc	BU
1947S	200,000	—	BV	4.00	7.50	9.00

KM# 190 50 CENTAVOS

Copper-Zinc-Nickel, 30.3 mm. **Obv:** Shield of arms **Rev:** Female standing beside hammer and anvil

Date	Mintage	F	VF	XF	Unc	BU
1958	5,000,000	—	0.30	0.45	1.00	1.50
1964	25,000,000	—	0.20	0.30	0.75	1.25

KM# 191 1/2 PESO

12.5000 g., 0.9000 Silver .3617 oz. ASW **Subject:** 100th Anniversary Birth of Dr. Jose Rizal **Obv:** Shield of arms **Rev:** Head left

Date	Mintage	F	VF	XF	Unc	BU
ND(1961)	100,000	—	—	BV	5.75	6.50
ND1961	100,000	—	—	3.00	4.00	5.00

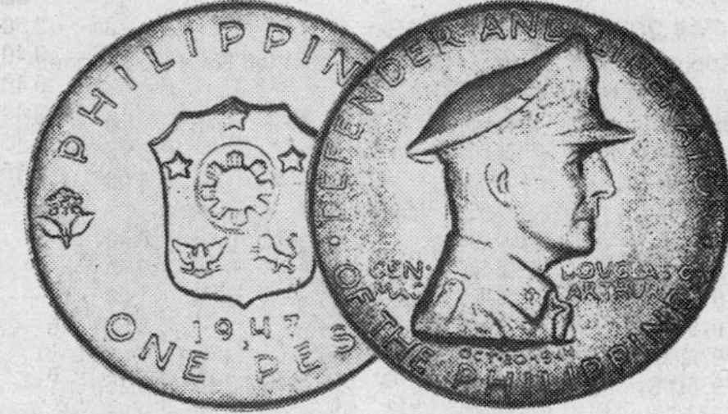

KM# 185 PESO

20.0000 g., 0.9000 Silver .5787 oz. ASW, 35.5 mm. **Obv:** Shield of arms above date and value **Rev:** Uniformed bust right
Designer: Laura Gardin Fraser

Date	Mintage	F	VF	XF	Unc	BU
1947S	100,000	—	BV	12.00	20.00	25.00

KM# 192 PESO

26.0000 g., 0.9000 Silver .7697 oz. ASW **Subject:** 100th Anniversary Birth of Dr. Jose Rizal **Obv:** Shield of arms **Rev:** Bust 1/4 right divides dates

Date	Mintage	F	VF	XF	Unc	BU
ND(1961)	100,000	—	—	BV	12.50	13.50

KM# 193 PESO

26.0000 g., 0.9000 Silver .7697 oz. ASW **Subject:** 100th Anniversary Birth of Andres Bonifacio **Obv:** Shield of arms **Rev:** Head 1/4 left divides dates

Date	Mintage	F	VF	XF	Unc	BU
ND(1963)	100,000	—	—	BV	12.50	13.50

KM# 194 PESO

26.0000 g., 0.9000 Silver .7697 oz. ASW **Subject:** 100th Anniversary Birth of Apolinario Mabini **Obv:** Shield of arms **Rev:** Head 1/4 right divides dates

Date	Mintage	F	VF	XF	Unc	BU
ND(1964)	100,000	—	—	BV	12.50	13.50

KM# 195 PESO

26.0000 g., 0.9000 Silver .7697 oz. ASW **Subject:** 25th Anniversary of Bataan Day **Obv:** Shield of arms **Rev:** Flaming broken sword flanked by sprigs, dates and stars

Date	Mintage	F	VF	XF	Unc	BU
ND(1967)	100,000	—	—	BV	12.50	13.50

Note: KM#195 is a prooflike issue

REFORM COINAGE

100 Sentimos = 1 Piso

KM# 196 SENTIMO

Aluminum **Obv:** Shield of arms **Rev:** Head left

Date	Mintage	F	VF	XF	Unc	BU
1967	10,000,000	—	—	—	0.25	—
1968	27,940,000	—	—	—	0.10	—
1969/6	12,060,000	—	—	—	0.20	—
1970	130,000,000	—	—	—	0.10	—
1974 0	165,000,000	—	—	—	0.10	—
1974 1 Proof	10,000	Value: 3.50				

KM# 205 SENTIMO

Aluminum, 19 mm. **Obv:** Head 3/4 right **Rev:** Redesigned bank seal within circle **Shape:** 4-sided

Date	Mintage	F	VF	XF	Unc	BU
1975FM (M)	108,000	—	—	—	0.50	—
1975FM (U)	5,875	—	—	—	2.00	—
1975FM (P)	37,000	Value: 1.50				
1975(Lt)	10,000,000	—	—	—	0.10	—
1975(US)	60,190,000	—	—	—	0.10	—
1976FM (M)	10,000	—	—	—	0.75	—
1976FM (U)	1,826	—	—	1.00	2.50	—
1976FM (P)	9,901	Value: 1.50				
1976(US)	60,000,000	—	—	—	0.10	—
1977	4,808,000	—	—	—	0.25	—
1977FM (M)	10,000	—	—	—	1.00	—
1977FM (U)	354	—	—	—	4.00	—
1977FM (P)	4,822	Value: 2.00				
1978	24,813,000	—	—	—	0.10	—
1978FM (U)	10,000	—	—	—	1.00	—
1978FM (P)	4,792	Value: 2.00				

KM# 224 SENTIMO

Aluminum **Obv:** Head 3/4 right **Rev:** Redesigned bank seal within circle **Shape:** Square **Note:** Varieties exist in date.

Date	Mintage	F	VF	XF	Unc	BU
1979BSP	—	—	—	—	0.25	—
1979FM (U)	10,000	—	—	—	1.00	—
1979FM (P)	3,645	Value: 2.00				
1980BSP	12,601,000	—	—	—	0.25	—
1980FM (U)	10,000	—	—	—	1.00	—
1980FM (P)	3,133	Value: 2.00				
1981BSP	33,391,000	—	—	—	0.20	—
1981FM (U)	—	—	—	—	1.00	—
1981FM (P)	1,795	Value: 2.00				
1982BSP	51,730,000	—	—	—	0.10	—
1982FM (P)	—	Value: 2.00				

KM# 238 SENTIMO

0.7000 g., Aluminum, 15.5 mm. **Obv:** Head left **Rev:** Sea shell and value within circle

Date	Mintage	F	VF	XF	Unc	BU
1983	62,090,000	—	—	—	0.50	—
1983 Proof	—	Value: 2.00				
1984	320,000	—	—	—	0.75	—
1985	16,000	—	—	—	1.00	—
1986	80,000	—	—	—	1.00	—
1987	13,570,000	—	—	—	0.75	—
1988	26,861,000	—	—	—	0.75	—
1989	—	—	—	—	0.75	—
1990	—	—	—	—	0.75	12.00
1991	—	—	—	—	—	20.00
1992	—	—	—	—	0.50	20.00
1993	—	—	0.35	1.50	9.00	16.00

KM# 273 SENTIMO

Copper Plated Steel **Obv:** Value and date **Rev:** Central bank seal within circle and gear design

Date	Mintage	F	VF	XF	Unc	BU
1995	—	—	—	—	0.25	0.45
1996	—	—	—	—	0.35	0.50
1997	—	—	—	—	0.35	0.50
1998	—	—	—	—	0.35	0.50
1999	—	—	—	—	0.35	0.50
2000	—	—	—	—	0.35	0.50

KM# 197 5 SENTIMOS

Brass, 18 mm. **Obv:** Shield above banner **Rev:** Head right

Date	Mintage	F	VF	XF	Unc	BU
1967	40,000,000	—	—	—	0.30	—
1968	50,000,000	—	—	—	0.30	—
1970	5,000,000	—	—	1.00	3.50	—
1972	71,744,000	—	—	—	0.30	—
1974	90,025,000	—	—	—	0.30	—
1974 Proof	10,000	Value: 4.00				

KM# 206 5 SENTIMOS

Brass **Obv:** Head 3/4 left **Rev:** Redesigned bank seal within circle **Shape:** Scalloped

Date	Mintage	F	VF	XF	Unc	BU
1975FM (M)	104,000	—	—	—	0.50	—
1975FM (U)	5,875	—	—	—	2.50	—
1975FM (P)	37,000	Value: 2.00				
1975(US)	98,928,000	—	—	—	0.10	—
1975(Lt)	10,000,000	—	—	—	0.10	—
1976FM (M)	10,000	—	—	—	1.50	—
1976FM (U)	1,826	—	—	—	2.50	—
1976FM (P)	9,901	Value: 1.50				
1976(US)	98,000,000	—	—	—	0.20	—
1977	19,367,000	—	—	—	0.35	—
1977FM (M)	10,000	—	—	—	1.25	—
1977FM (U)	354	—	—	—	4.00	—
1977FM (P)	4,822	Value: 2.50				
1978	61,838,000	—	—	—	0.20	—
1978FM (U)	10,000	—	—	—	1.50	—
1978FM (P)	4,792	Value: 2.50				

KM# 225 5 SENTIMOS

Brass **Obv:** Head 3/4 left **Rev:** Redesigned bank seal within circle **Shape:** Scalloped

Date	Mintage	F	VF	XF	Unc	BU
1979BSP	12,805,000	—	—	—	0.30	—
1979FM (U)	10,000	—	—	—	1.25	—
1979FM (P)	3,645	Value: 2.50				
1980BSP	111,339,000	—	—	—	0.10	—
1980FM (U)	—	—	—	—	1.00	—
1980FM (P)	3,133	Value: 2.50				
1981BSP	—	—	—	—	0.10	—
1981FM (U)	—	—	—	—	1.25	—
1981FM (P)	1,795	Value: 3.00				
1982BSP	—	—	—	—	0.10	—
1982FM (P)	—	Value: 3.00				

KM# 239 5 SENTIMOS

1.2000 g., Aluminum, 17 mm. **Obv:** Head right **Rev:** Orchid and value

Date	Mintage	F	VF	XF	Unc	BU
1983	100,016,000	—	—	—	0.50	—
1983 Proof	—	Value: 2.00				
1984	141,744,000	—	—	—	0.40	—
1985	50,416,000	—	—	—	0.25	—
1986	11,664,000	—	—	—	0.35	—
1987	79,008,000	—	—	—	0.10	—
1988	90,487,000	—	—	—	0.10	—
1989	—	—	—	—	0.25	—
1990	—	—	—	—	0.25	—
1991	—	—	—	—	0.40	—
1992	—	—	—	—	0.25	—

KM# 268 5 SENTIMOS

Copper Plated Steel **Obv:** Numeral value around center hole **Rev:** Hole in center with date, bank and name around border **Rev. Legend:** 1993 BANGKO CENTRAL NG PILIPINAS

Date	Mintage	F	VF	XF	Unc	BU
1995	—	—	—	—	0.50	0.75
1996	—	—	—	—	0.50	0.75
1997	—	—	—	—	0.50	0.75
1998	—	—	—	—	0.50	0.75
1999	—	—	—	—	0.50	0.75
2000	—	—	—	—	0.50	0.75

KM# 198 10 SENTIMOS

Copper-Zinc-Nickel, 18 mm. **Obv:** Shield of arms **Rev:** Bust left

Date	Mintage	F	VF	XF	Unc	BU
1967	50,000,000	—	—	—	0.35	—
1968	60,000,000	—	—	—	0.35	—
1969	40,000,000	—	—	—	0.35	—
1970	50,000,000	—	—	—	0.35	—
1971	80,000,000	—	—	—	0.35	—
1972	121,390,000	—	—	—	0.35	—
1974	60,208,000	—	—	—	0.35	—
1974 Proof	10,000	Value: 4.00				

KM# 207 10 SENTIMOS

Copper-Nickel **Obv:** Head 3/4 right **Rev:** Redesigned bank seal within circle

Date	Mintage	F	VF	XF	Unc	BU
1975FM (M)	104,000	—	—	—	0.50	—
1975FM (U)	5,875	—	—	—	2.50	—
1975FM (P)	37,000	Value: 2.50				
1975(VDM)	10,000,000	—	—	—	0.25	—
1975(US)	50,000,000	—	—	—	0.20	—
1976FM (M)	10,000	—	—	—	0.50	—
1976FM (U)	1,826	—	—	—	5.00	—
1976FM (P)	9,901	Value: 2.00				
1976(US)	50,000,000	—	—	—	0.20	—
1977	29,314,000	—	—	—	0.25	—
1977FM (M)	10,000	—	—	—	1.50	—
1977FM (U)	354	—	—	—	6.00	—
1977FM (P)	4,822	Value: 3.00				
1978	60,042,000	—	—	—	0.10	—
1978FM (U)	10,000	—	—	—	3.00	—
1978FM (P)	4,792	Value: 3.00				

KM# 226 10 SENTIMOS

Copper-Nickel, 18 mm. **Obv:** Head 3/4 right **Rev:** Redesigned bank seal within circle **Note:** Varieties with thick and thin legends exist for coins with BSP mint mark.

Date	Mintage	F	VF	XF	Unc	BU
1979BSP	6,446,000	—	—	—	0.50	—
1979FM (U)	10,000	—	—	—	2.00	—
1979FM (P)	3,645	Value: 3.00				
1980BSP	—	—	—	—	0.30	—
1980FM (U)	10,000	—	—	—	1.50	—
1980FM (P)	3,133	Value: 3.25				
1981BSP	—	—	—	—	0.30	—
1981FM (U)	—	—	—	—	2.00	—
1981FM (P)	1,795	Value: 3.50				
1982BSP	—	—	—	—	0.30	—
1982FM (P)	—	Value: 3.50				

KM# 240.1 10 SENTIMOS

Aluminum **Series:** F.A.O. **Subject:** World Conference on Fisheries **Obv:** Head left **Rev:** Fish and value within circle

Date	Mintage	F	VF	XF	Unc	BU
1983	95,640,000	—	—	—	8.00	—
1983 Proof	—	Value: 8.00				
1986	—	—	—	—	1.00	—
1987	Inc. below	—	—	—	1.00	—

KM# 240.2 10 SENTIMOS

1.5000 g., Aluminum, 19 mm. **Series:** F.A.O. **Subject:** World Conference on Fisheries **Obv:** Head left **Rev:** Fish and value within circle

Date	Mintage	F	VF	XF	Unc	BU
1983	—	—	—	—	0.50	1.00
1984	235,900,000	—	—	—	0.35	1.00
1985	90,169,000	—	—	—	0.35	1.00
1986	4,270,000	—	—	—	0.50	0.65
1987	99,520,000	—	—	—	0.50	0.75
1988	117,166,000	—	—	—	0.35	0.50
1989	—	—	—	—	0.35	0.50
1990	—	—	—	—	0.35	0.50
1991	—	—	—	—	0.35	0.50
1992	—	—	—	—	0.35	0.50
1993	—	—	—	—	0.50	7.00
1994	—	—	—	—	0.50	7.00

KM# 270 10 SENTIMOS

2.4600 g., Bronze Plated Steel, 16.9 mm. **Obv:** Value and date **Rev:** Central Bank seal within circle and gear design **Edge:** Reeded

Date	Mintage	F	VF	XF	Unc	BU
1995	—	—	—	—	0.25	0.40
1996	—	—	—	—	1.00	1.50
1997	—	—	—	—	0.25	0.40
1998	—	—	—	—	0.25	0.40
1999	—	—	—	—	0.25	0.40

KM# 199 25 SENTIMOS

Copper-Zinc-Nickel, 21 mm. **Obv:** Shield of arms **Rev:** Head left

Date	Mintage	F	VF	XF	Unc	BU
1967	40,000,000	—	—	0.10	0.50	—
1968	10,000,000	—	—	0.10	0.50	—
1969	10,000,000	—	—	0.10	0.50	—
1970	40,000,000	—	—	0.10	0.40	—
1971	60,000,000	—	—	0.10	0.40	—
1972	90,000,000	—	—	0.10	0.40	—
1974	10,000,000	—	—	0.10	0.50	—
1974 Proof	10,000	Value: 12.00				

KM# 208 25 SENTIMOS

Copper-Nickel, 21 mm. **Obv:** Head 3/4 left **Rev:** Redesigned bank seal within circle

Date	Mintage	F	VF	XF	Unc	BU
1975FM (M)	104,000	—	—	—	0.75	—
1975FM (U)	5,875	—	—	—	5.00	—
1975FM (P)	37,000	Value: 3.00				
1975(US)	10,000,000	—	—	0.10	0.40	—
1975(VDM)	10,000,000	—	—	0.10	0.40	—
1976FM (M)	10,000	—	—	0.10	1.00	—
1976FM (U)	1,826	—	—	—	6.50	—
1976FM (P)	9,901	Value: 3.00				
1976(US)	10,000,000	—	—	0.10	0.25	—
1977	24,654,000	—	—	0.10	0.25	—
1977FM (M)	10,000	—	—	—	1.25	—
1977FM (U)	354	—	—	—	8.00	—
1977FM (P)	4,822	Value: 4.50				
1978	40,466,000	—	—	0.10	0.25	—
1978FM (U)	10,000	—	—	—	2.50	—
1978FM (P)	4,792	Value: 4.00				

KM# 227 25 SENTIMOS

Copper-Nickel, 21 mm. **Obv:** Head 3/4 left **Rev:** Redesigned bank seal within circle

Date	Mintage	F	VF	XF	Unc	BU
1979BSP	20,725,000	—	—	0.10	0.50	—
1979FM (U)	10,000	—	—	—	2.50	—
1979FM (P)	3,645	Value: 2.00				
1980BSP	—	—	—	0.10	0.75	—
1980FM (U)	10,000	—	—	—	1.50	—
1980FM (P)	3,133	Value: 4.50				
1981BSP	—	—	—	0.10	1.00	—
1981FM (U)	—	—	—	—	3.00	—
1981FM (P)	1,795	Value: 5.00				

Date	Mintage	F	VF	XF	Unc	BU
1982BSP	—	—	—	0.10	0.50	—
1982FM (P)	—	Value: 5.00				

KM# 241.1 25 SENTIMOS

3.9000 g., Brass, 21 mm. **Obv:** Juan Luna right **Rev:** Butterfly

Date	Mintage	F	VF	XF	Unc	BU
1983	92,944,000	—	—	0.15	1.00	1.75
1983 Proof	—	Value: 2.50				
1984	254,324,000	—	—	0.15	0.75	1.50
1985	84,922,000	—	—	0.15	0.75	1.50
1986	65,284,000	—	—	0.15	0.75	1.50
1987	1,680,000	—	—	0.50	2.00	2.75
1988	51,062,000	—	—	—	0.75	1.50
1989	—	—	—	—	0.75	1.50
1990	—	—	—	—	0.75	1.50

KM# 241.2 25 SENTIMOS

Brass **Obv:** Juan Luna right **Rev:** Butterfly **Note:** Reduced size.

Date	Mintage	F	VF	XF	Unc	BU
1991	—	—	—	—	1.00	1.25
1992	—	—	—	—	1.00	1.25
1993	—	—	—	—	5.00	7.00
1994	—	—	—	—	5.00	7.00

KM# 271 25 SENTIMOS

3.8000 g., Brass, 20 mm. **Obv:** Value and date **Rev:** Central Bank seal within circle and gear design **Edge:** Plain

Date	Mintage	F	VF	XF	Unc	BU
1995	—	—	—	—	0.75	1.00
1996	—	—	—	—	1.00	1.25
1997	—	—	—	—	1.00	1.25
1998	—	—	—	—	1.00	1.25
1999	—	—	—	—	1.00	1.25
2000	—	—	—	—	1.00	1.25

KM# 200 50 SENTIMOS

Copper-Zinc-Nickel, 27.5 mm. **Obv:** Shield of arms **Rev:** Marcelo H. del Pilar right

Date	Mintage	F	VF	XF	Unc	BU
1967	20,000,000	—	0.10	0.25	0.75	1.25
1971	10,000,000	—	0.10	0.50	1.00	2.00
1972 Knob on 2	30,000,000	—	0.10	0.75	1.50	2.50
1972 Plain 2	20,517,000	—	0.10	0.50	1.25	2.25
1974	5,004,000	—	0.10	0.75	1.25	2.50
1974 Proof	10,000	Value: 20.00				
1975	5,714,000	—	0.10	0.20	1.00	2.00

KM# 242.1 50 SENTIMOS

6.0000 g., Copper-Nickel, 25 mm. **Obv:** Head of Marcelo H. del Pilar left **Rev:** Eagle with talons out **Note:** Eagle's name: PITHECOPHAGA

Date	Mintage	F	VF	XF	Unc	BU
1983	27,644,000	—	0.10	0.50	1.25	2.00
1983 Proof	—	Value: 4.25				
1984	121,408,000	—	0.10	0.20	1.00	1.50
1985	107,048,000	—	0.10	0.20	1.00	1.50
1986	120,000,000	—	0.10	0.20	0.75	1.25
1987	1,078,000	—	0.10	1.00	1.50	2.50
1988	24,008,000	—	0.10	0.20	1.00	1.50
1989	—	—	0.10	0.20	1.00	1.50
1990	—	—	0.10	0.20	1.00	1.50

KM# 242.2 50 SENTIMOS

6.0000 g., Copper-Nickel, 25 mm. **Obv:** Head of Marcelo H. del Pilar left **Rev:** Eagle attacking **Note:** Error eagle's name: PITHECOBHAGA

Date	Mintage	F	VF	XF	Unc	BU
1983	Inc. above	—	3.00	5.00	9.00	—

KM# 242.3 50 SENTIMOS

Brass **Obv:** Head of Marcelo H. Pilar left **Rev:** Eagle with talons out **Note:** Reduced size.

Date	Mintage	F	VF	XF	Unc	BU
1991	—	—	—	0.25	1.50	2.00
1992	—	—	—	0.25	1.50	2.00
1993	—	—	—	—	5.00	7.00
1994	—	—	—	—	5.00	7.00

KM# 201 PISO

26.4500 g., 0.9000 Silver .7653 oz. ASW **Subject:** Centennial - Birth of Aguinaldo **Obv:** Shield of arms **Rev:** Bust facing divides dates

Date	Mintage	F	VF	XF	Unc	BU
ND(1969) Prooflike	100,000	—	—	BV	12.00	12.50

KM# 202 PISO

Nickel, 38.3 mm. **Subject:** Pope Paul VI Visit **Obv:** Bust of Ferdinand Marcos left **Rev:** Bust of Pope Paul VI right **Designer:** Frank Gasparro

Date	Mintage	F	VF	XF	Unc	BU
1970	70,000	—	—	—	2.75	3.00

KM# 202a PISO

26.4500 g., 0.9000 Silver .7653 oz. ASW, 38.3 mm. **Obv:** Bust of Ferdinand Marcos left **Rev:** Bust of Pope Paul VI right **Designer:** Frank Gasparro

Date	Mintage	F	VF	XF	Unc	BU
1970	30,000	—	—	—	13.50	15.00

KM# 202b PISO

19.3000 g., 0.9170 Gold .5691 oz. AGW **Subject:** Pope Paul VI Visit **Obv:** Bust of Ferdinand Marcos left **Rev:** Bust of Pope Paul VI right **Designer:** Frank Gasparro

Date	Mintage	F	VF	XF	Unc	BU
1970	1,000	—	—	—	—	575

KM# 203 PISO

Copper-Zinc-Nickel, 33 mm. **Obv:** Shield of arms **Rev:** Head of Jose Rizal left

Date	Mintage	F	VF	XF	Unc	BU
1972	121,821,000	—	0.25	0.50	1.00	2.50
1974	45,631,000	—	0.25	0.50	1.00	3.00
1974 Proof	10,000	Value: 30.00				

KM# 209.1 PISO

9.5000 g., Copper-Nickel, 29 mm. **Obv:** Head of Jose Rizal 1/4 right within octogon **Rev:** Shield of arms

Date	Mintage	F	VF	XF	Unc	BU
1975FM (M)	104,000	—	—	—	2.00	—
1975FM (U)	5,877	—	—	—	5.50	—
1975FM (P)	37,000	Value: 3.00				
1975(VDM)	10,000,000	—	0.15	0.25	1.25	—
1975(US)	30,000,000	—	0.15	0.25	0.75	1.00
1976FM (M)	10,000	—	—	—	2.00	—
1976FM (U)	1,826	—	—	—	8.00	—
1976FM (P)	9,901	Value: 3.00				
1976(US)	30,000,000	—	0.15	0.25	0.75	—
1977	14,771,000	—	0.15	0.25	0.75	—
1977FM (M)	12,000	—	—	—	3.00	—
1977FM (U)	354	—	—	—	7.00	—
1977FM (P)	4,822	Value: 3.00				
1978	19,408,000	—	0.15	0.25	1.00	—
1978FM (U)	10,000	—	—	—	4.00	—
1978FM (P)	4,792	Value: 7.50				

KM# 209.2 PISO

9.5000 g., Copper-Nickel, 29 mm. **Obv:** Head of Jose Rizal 1/4 right within octogon **Rev:** Shield of arms **Rev. Inscription:** ISANG BANSA ISANG DIWA

Date	Mintage	F	VF	XF	Unc	BU
1979BSP	321,000	—	0.15	0.25	2.00	—
1979FM (U)	10,000	—	—	—	2.50	—
1979FM (P)	3,645	Value: 3.00				
1980BSP	19,693,000	—	0.15	0.25	0.75	1.00
1980FM (U)	10,000	—	—	—	7.50	—
1980FM (P)	3,133	Value: 12.50				
1981BSP	7,944,000	—	0.15	0.25	1.00	—
1981FM (U)	—	—	—	—	4.00	—
1981FM (P)	1,795	Value: 6.00				
1982FM (P)	—	Value: 7.00				
1982BSP Large date	52,110,000	—	0.15	0.25	1.00	—
1982BSP Small date	Inc. above	—	0.15	0.25	1.00	—

KM# 243.1 PISO

9.5000 g., Copper-Nickel, 28.9 mm. **Obv:** Head of Jose Rizal right **Rev:** Tamaraw bull **Edge:** Reeded **Note:** Large legends and design elements.

Date	Mintage	F	VF	XF	Unc	BU
1983	55,869,000	—	—	0.30	1.25	2.00

Date	Mintage	F	VF	XF	Unc	BU
1983 Proof	—	Value: 6.50				
1984	4,997,000	—	—	1.00	2.00	3.00
1985	182,592,000	—	—	0.30	1.00	1.75
1986	19,072,000	—	—	0.30	1.25	2.25
1987	1,391,000	—	—	3.00	5.00	6.25
1988	54,636,000	—	—	0.30	1.25	2.00

KM# 243.2 PISO

Stainless Steel, 21.6 mm. **Obv:** Head of Jose Rizal right **Rev:** Tamaraw bull **Note:** Reduced size.

Date	Mintage	F	VF	XF	Unc	BU
1991	—	—	—	0.50	1.25	2.25
1992	—	—	—	0.50	1.25	2.25
1993	—	—	—	—	5.00	6.50
1994	—	—	—	—	5.00	6.50

KM# 243.3 PISO

Copper-Nickel **Obv:** Head of Jose Rizal right **Rev:** Tamaraw bull **Note:** Smaller legends and design elements.

Date	Mintage	F	VF	XF	Unc	BU
1989	—	—	—	0.30	1.00	1.25
1990	—	—	—	0.30	1.00	1.25

KM# 251 PISO

Copper-Nickel, 28.5 mm. **Subject:** Philippine Cultures Decade **Obv:** Shield of arms divides date **Rev:** Three conjoined vertical busts right

Date	Mintage	F	VF	XF	Unc	BU
1989	—	—	—	—	2.50	—

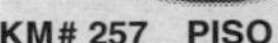

KM# 257 PISO

Copper-Nickel **Obv:** Shield of arms **Rev:** Waterfall, ship, and flower within circle

Date	Mintage	F	VF	XF	Unc	BU
ND(1991)	—	—	—	—	1.25	2.00
ND(1991) Matte	—	—	—	—	8.00	—

Note: Special striking by CB

KM# 260 PISO

Nickel Clad Steel, 21.5 mm. **Subject:** 50th Anniversary - Battle of Kagitingan **Obv:** Shield of arms **Rev:** Military head left, cross, flag and dates

Date	Mintage	F	VF	XF	Unc	BU
ND(1992)	—	—	—	—	2.50	—

KM# 269 PISO

Copper-Nickel, 24 mm. **Obv:** Head of Jose Rizal right, value and date **Rev:** Bank seal within circle and gear design

Date	Mintage	F	VF	XF	Unc	BU
1995	—	—	—	—	1.00	1.50
1996	—	—	—	—	1.25	1.75
1997	—	—	—	—	1.25	1.75
1998	—	—	—	—	1.25	1.75
1999	—	—	—	—	1.25	1.75
2000	—	—	—	—	1.25	1.75

KM# 244 2 PISO

12.0000 g., Copper-Nickel, 31 mm. **Obv:** Head of Andres Bonifacio left **Rev:** Coconut palm **Shape:** 10-sided

Date	Mintage	F	VF	XF	Unc	BU
1983	15,640,000	—	—	0.35	2.50	3.50
1983 Proof	—	Value: 8.00				
1984	121,111,000	—	—	0.35	1.00	1.50
1985	115,211,000	—	—	0.35	1.25	1.50
1986	25,260,000	—	—	0.35	1.25	1.50
1987	2,196,000	—	—	5.00	8.00	10.00
1988	16,094,000	—	—	—	7.00	10.00
1989	—	—	—	—	1.25	1.50
1990	—	—	—	—	1.25	1.50

KM# 253 2 PISO

12.0000 g., Copper-Nickel, 31 mm. **Obv:** Design within beaded circle **Rev:** Head of Elpidio Quirino right **Shape:** 10-sided

Date	Mintage	F	VF	XF	Unc	BU
ND(1991)	10,000,000	—	—	—	1.25	2.00
ND(1991) Matte	—	—	—	—	10.00	—

Note: Special striking by CB

KM# 258 2 PISO

Stainless Steel, 23.5 mm. **Obv:** Head of Andres Bonifacio left **Rev:** Coconut palm

Date	Mintage	F	VF	XF	Unc	BU
1991	—	—	—	—	2.50	3.50
1992	—	—	—	—	3.00	3.50
1993	—	—	—	—	3.00	3.50
1994	—	—	—	—	2.50	3.50

KM# 261 2 PISO

Nickel Clad Steel, 23.5 mm. **Obv:** Design within beaded circle **Rev:** Head of Manuel A. Roxas right

Date	Mintage	F	VF	XF	Unc	BU
ND(1992)	—	—	—	—	2.50	3.00
ND(1992) Matte	—	—	—	—	10.00	—

Note: Special striking by CB

KM# 256 2 PISO

Copper-Nickel **Obv:** Triangular design within circle **Rev:** Head of Jose Laurel right **Shape:** 10-sided

Date	Mintage	F	VF	XF	Unc	BU
ND(1992)	—	—	—	1.75	2.00	3.00
ND(1992) Matte	—	—	—	—	10.00	—

Note: Special striking by CB

KM# 210.1 5 PISO

Nickel, 36.5 mm. **Obv:** Shield of arms above value **Rev:** Head of Ferdinand E. Marcos left

Date	Mintage	F	VF	XF	Unc	BU
1975FM (M)	3,850	—	—	—	7.50	—
1975FM (U)	7,875	—	—	—	6.00	—
1975FM (P)	39,000	Value: 5.00				
1975(Sh)	20,000,000	—	0.50	0.75	1.00	1.50
1976FM (M)	10,000	—	—	—	4.00	—
1976FM (U)	1,826	—	—	—	15.00	—
1976FM (P)	9,901	Value: 6.00				
1977FM (M)	10,000	—	—	—	4.00	—
1977FM (U)	354	—	—	—	10.00	—
1977FM (P)	4,822	Value: 6.50				
1978FM (U)	10,000	—	—	—	2.50	—
1978FM (P)	4,792	Value: 8.00				
1982	—	—	0.50	0.75	1.50	—

KM# 210.2 5 PISO

Nickel, 36.5 mm. **Obv:** Shield of arms **Obv. Inscription:** ISANG BANSA ISANG DIWA below shield **Rev:** Head of Ferdinand E. Marcos left

Date	Mintage	F	VF	XF	Unc	BU
1979FM (U)	10,000	—	—	—	4.50	—
1979FM (P)	3,645	Value: 8.00				
1980FM (U)	10,000	—	—	—	4.50	—
1980FM (P)	3,133	Value: 10.00				
1981FM (U)	11,000	—	—	—	4.00	—
1981FM (P)	1,795	Value: 10.00				
1982FM (P)	—	Value: 10.00				
1982FM (U); Prooflike	—	—	—	—	10.00	—

KM# 259 5 PISO

Nickel-Brass, 25.5 mm. **Obv:** Head of Emilio Aguinaldo right **Rev:** Pterocarpus Indicus Flower

Date	Mintage	F	VF	XF	Unc	BU
1991	—	—	—	—	2.00	3.00
1992	—	—	—	—	3.50	4.50
1993	—	—	—	—	9.00	12.00
1994	—	—	—	—	10.00	15.00

KM# 262 5 PISO

Nickel-Brass, 25.5 mm. **Subject:** 30th Chess Olympiad **Obv:** Shield of arms **Rev:** Stylized horse head on chess board **Note:** Varieties exist.

Date	Mintage	F	VF	XF	Unc	BU
1992	—	—	—	—	11.00	12.50

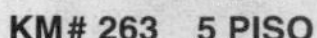

KM# 263 5 PISO

Nickel-Brass, 25.5 mm. **Subject:** Leyte Gulf Landings **Obv:** Shield of arms **Rev:** Standing figures

Date	Mintage	F	VF	XF	Unc	BU
ND(1994)	7,800	—	—	—	8.50	9.50

KM# 272 5 PISO

7.6700 g., Nickel-Brass, 25.5 mm. **Obv:** Head of Emilio Aguinaldo right, value and date within scalloped border **Rev:** Central Bank seal within circle and gear design within scalloped border **Edge:** Plain

Date	Mintage	F	VF	XF	Unc	BU
1995	—	—	—	—	2.50	3.00
1996	—	—	—	—	1.50	3.00
1997	—	—	—	—	1.50	3.00
Note: Struck at Royal Canadian Mint, without designer initials						
1997BSP	—	—	—	—	1.50	4.00
Note: With designer initials below shoulder						
1998	—	—	—	—	1.50	3.00

KM# 250 10 PISO

Nickel, 36 mm. **Subject:** People Power Revolution **Obv:** Shield of arms divides date **Rev:** Group of people

Date	Mintage	F	VF	XF	Unc	BU
1988	—	—	—	—	5.00	6.50

KM# 278 10 PISO

8.7000 g., Bi-Metallic Brass center in Copper-Nickel ring, 26.5 mm. **Obv:** Conjoined heads right within circle **Rev:** Bank seal within circle and gear design **Edge:** Plain and reeded sections

Date	Mintage	F	VF	XF	Unc	BU
2000	—	—	—	—	3.50	5.00

KM# 204 25 PISO

26.4000 g., 0.9000 Silver .7639 oz. ASW **Subject:** 25th Anniversary of Bank **Obv:** Shield of arms **Rev:** Bank in front of clouds

Date	Mintage	F	VF	XF	Unc	BU
ND(1974)	90,000	—	—	—	12.00	12.50

KM# 204a 25 PISO

26.4000 g., 0.9000 Silver .7639 oz. ASW **Obv:** Shield of arms **Rev:** Bank in front of clouds

Date	Mintage	F	VF	XF	Unc	BU
ND(1974) Proof	10,000	Value: 15.00				

KM# 211 25 PISO

25.0000 g., 0.5000 Silver .4018 oz. ASW **Obv:** Head of Emilio Aguinaldo 1/4 right **Rev:** Shield of arms

Date	Mintage	F	VF	XF	Unc	BU
1975FM (M)	10,000	—	—	—	8.00	9.00
1975FM (U)	5,875	—	—	—	15.00	16.50
1975FM (P)	37,000	Value: 11.00				

KM# 214 25 PISO

25.0000 g., 0.5000 Silver .4018 oz. ASW **Series:** F.A.O. **Obv:** Shield of arms **Rev:** Half figure with hat holding grain

Date	Mintage	F	VF	XF	Unc	BU
1976FM (M)	22,000	—	—	—	8.00	10.00
1976FM (U)	1,826	—	—	—	20.00	22.50
1976FM (P)	9,901	Value: 10.00				

KM# 217 25 PISO

25.0000 g., 0.5000 Silver .4018 oz. ASW **Subject:** Banaue Rice Terraces **Obv:** Shield of arms **Rev:** Hilly designs within circle

Date	Mintage	F	VF	XF	Unc	BU
1977FM (M)	10,000	—	—	—	13.50	15.00
1977FM (U)	354	—	—	—	30.00	35.00
1977FM (P)	4,822	Value: 15.00				

KM# 221 25 PISO

25.0000 g., 0.5000 Silver .4018 oz. ASW **Subject:** 100th Anniversary - Birth of Quezon **Obv:** Shield of arms **Rev:** Monument divides dates within beaded circle

Date	Mintage	F	VF	XF	Unc	BU
ND(1978)FM (U)	10,000	—	—	—	15.00	16.50
ND(1978)FM (P)	9,930	Value: 20.00				

KM# 228 25 PISO

25.0000 g., 0.5000 Silver .4018 oz. ASW **Subject:** UN Conference on Trade and Development **Obv:** Conference center buildings **Rev:** UN logo

Date	Mintage	F	VF	XF	Unc	BU
1979FM (U)	10,000	—	—	—	9.00	11.00
1979FM (P)	7,093	Value: 20.00				

KM# 230 25 PISO

25.0000 g., 0.5000 Silver .4018 oz. ASW **Subject:** 100th Anniversary - Birth of Gen. Douglas MacArthur **Obv:** Uniformed figures **Rev:** Uniformed bust with pipe facing 1/4 left

Date	Mintage	F	VF	XF	Unc	BU
ND(1980)FM (U)	9,800	—	—	—	20.00	22.00
ND(1980)FM (P)	6,318	Value: 40.00				

KM# 232 25 PISO

25.0000 g., 0.5000 Silver .4018 oz. ASW **Subject:** World Food Day **Obv:** Shield of arms **Rev:** Fish, corn, grain and fruit

Date	Mintage	F	VF	XF	Unc	BU
1981FM (U)	10,000	—	—	—	12.00	15.00
1981FM (P)	3,033	Value: 25.00				

KM# 235 25 PISO
25.0000 g., 0.5000 Silver .4018 oz. ASW **Obv:** Shield of arms **Rev:** Conjoined heads of Marcos and Reagan right

Date	Mintage	F	VF	XF	Unc	BU
1982	8,000	—	—	—	35.00	40.00
1982 Proof	250	Value: 450				

KM# 246 25 PISO
18.4100 g., 0.9250 Silver .5475 oz. ASW **Subject:** President Aquino's visit in Washington **Obv:** Head of President Aquino left **Rev:** Head of President Reagan right **Note:** Photo reduced.

Date	Mintage	F	VF	XF	Unc	BU
1986 Proof	Est. 1,000	Value: 350				

KM# 212 50 PISO
27.4000 g., 0.9250 Silver .8148 oz. ASW **Subject:** 3rd Anniversary of the New Society **Obv:** Shield of arms **Rev:** Head of Marcos left

Date	Mintage	F	VF	XF	Unc	BU
1975FM (M)	10,000	—	—	—	13.50	15.00
1975FM (U)	7,875	—	—	—	16.00	18.00
1975FM (P)	54,000	Value: 12.50				

KM# 215 50 PISO
27.4000 g., 0.9250 Silver .8148 oz. ASW **Subject:** I.M.F. Meeting **Obv:** Map **Rev:** Stylized star in center of world globe emblems

Date	Mintage	F	VF	XF	Unc	BU
1976 Proof	5,477	Value: 20.00				
1976FM (M)	10,000	—	—	—	15.00	17.50
1976FM (U)	1,826	—	—	—	30.00	35.00
1976FM (P)	15,000	Value: 15.00				

KM# 218 50 PISO
27.4000 g., 0.9250 Silver .8148 oz. ASW **Subject:** Inauguration of New Mint Facilities **Obv:** Shield of arms **Rev:** Two coins under star and building within circle

Date	Mintage	F	VF	XF	Unc	BU
1977FM (M)	10,000	—	—	—	16.50	18.50
1977FM (U)	354	—	—	—	35.00	40.00
1977FM (P)	6,704	Value: 16.50				

KM# 222 50 PISO
27.4000 g., 0.9250 Silver .8148 oz. ASW **Subject:** 100th Anniversary - Birth of Manuel L. Quezon **Obv:** Shield of arms **Rev:** Head right, dates and shield

Date	Mintage	F	VF	XF	Unc	BU
ND(1978)FM (U)	10,000	—	—	—	16.50	18.50
ND(1978)FM (P)	9,969	Value: 20.00				

KM# 229 50 PISO
27.4000 g., 0.9250 Silver .8148 oz. ASW **Subject:** International Year of the Child **Obv:** Shield of arms **Rev:** Child's bust facing, logo at right

Date	Mintage	F	VF	XF	Unc	BU
1979FM (U)	10,000	—	—	—	12.50	13.50
1979FM (P)	27,000	Value: 14.00				

KM# 233 50 PISO
27.4000 g., 0.9250 Silver .8148 oz. ASW **Subject:** Pope John Paul II Visit **Obv:** Standing figure praying **Rev:** Head 1/4 left

Date	Mintage	F	VF	XF	Unc	BU
1981FM (U)	10,000	—	—	—	45.00	50.00
1981FM (P)	3,353	Value: 65.00				

KM# 236 50 PISO
27.4000 g., 0.9250 Silver .8148 oz. ASW **Subject:** 40th Anniversary of Bataan-Corregidor **Obv:** Shield of arms **Rev:** Conjoined military heads left

Date	Mintage	F	VF	XF	Unc	BU
ND(1982)FM (U)	13,000	—	—	—	22.00	25.00
ND(1982)FM (P)	4,626	Value: 40.00				

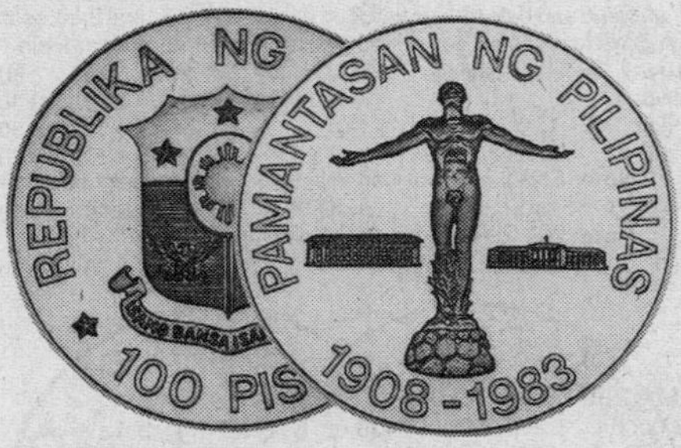

KM# 245 100 PISO
25.0000 g., 0.5000 Silver .4019 oz. ASW **Subject:** 75th Anniversary - University of the Philippines **Obv:** Shield of arms **Rev:** Nude statue divides building above dates

Date	Mintage	F	VF	XF	Unc	BU
ND(1983)	15,000	—	—	—	15.00	17.50
ND(1983) Proof	2,000	Value: 30.00				

KM# 264 100 PISO
10.0000 g., 0.9250 Silver .2974 oz. ASW **Subject:** Papal Visit 1995-Pope John Paul II **Obv:** Shield of arms **Rev:** Head left

Date	Mintage	F	VF	XF	Unc	BU
ND(1994) Proof	1,000	Value: 80.00				

KM# 279 100 PISO
16.7300 g., 0.8000 Silver .4303 oz. ASW **Subject:** Leyte Gulf Landing

Date	Mintage	F	VF	XF	Unc	BU
ND(1994) Proof	1,000	Value: 75.00				

KM# 254 150 PISO
16.8200 g., 0.9250 Silver .5002 oz. ASW **Subject:** Southeast Asian Games **Obv:** Shield of arms **Rev:** Official logo

Date	Mintage	F	VF	XF	Unc	BU
1991 Prooflike	—	—	—	—	—	60.00
1991 Proof	5,000	Value: 50.00				

KM# 248 200 PISO
25.0000 g., 0.9250 Silver .7436 oz. ASW **Subject:** World Wildlife Fund **Obv:** Shield of arms **Rev:** Mindoro Buffalo

Date	Mintage	F	VF	XF	Unc	BU
1987 Proof	25,000	Value: 50.00				

KM# 252 200 PISO
25.0000 g., 0.9250 Silver .7436 oz. ASW **Subject:** Save the Children Fund **Obv:** Shield of arms **Rev:** Children playing

Date	Mintage	F	VF	XF	Unc	BU
1990 Proof	Est. 20,000	Value: 60.00				

KM# 265 200 PISO
15.5600 g., 0.9990 Silver .4998 oz. ASW **Subject:** Papal Visit 1995 **Obv:** Shield of arms **Rev:** Bust of John Paul II left **Note:** Similar to 100 Piso, KM#264.

Date	Mintage	F	VF	XF	Unc	BU
ND(1994) Proof	1,000	Value: 100				

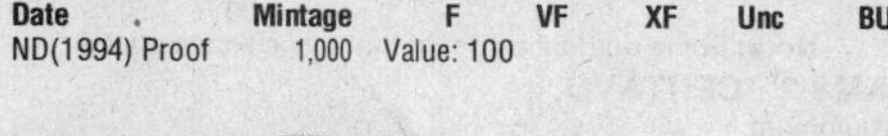

KM# 249 500 PISO
28.0000 g., 0.9250 Silver .8328 oz. ASW **Subject:** People Power Revolution **Obv:** Shield of arms divides date **Rev:** Group of people

Date	Mintage	F	VF	XF	Unc	BU
1988 Proof	Est. 7,500	Value: 50.00				

KM# 280 500 PISO
23.1000 g., 0.9250 Silver .6870 oz. ASW **Subject:** Leyte Gulf Landing

Date	Mintage	F	VF	XF	Unc	BU
ND(1994) Proof	1,000	Value: 125				

KM# 276 500 PISO
28.2800 g., 0.9250 Silver .8410 oz. ASW **Subject:** Centennial - Andres Bonifacio 1897-1997

Date	Mintage	F	VF	XF	Unc	BU
ND(1997) Proof	2,625	Value: 120				

KM# 274 500 PISO
28.2800 g., 0.9250 Silver .8410 oz. ASW **Subject:** Carlos P. Romulo Centennial **Obv:** Shield above value **Rev:** Bust left and dates

Date	Mintage	F	VF	XF	Unc	BU
ND(1998) Proof	Est. 2,100	Value: 80.00				

KM# 277 500 PISO
28.2800 g., 0.9250 Silver .8410 oz. ASW **Subject:** Centennial - Emilio F. Aguinaldo 1898-1998

Date	Mintage	F	VF	XF	Unc	BU
ND(1998) Proof	2,100	Value: 100				

KM# 275 500 PISO
28.2800 g., 0.9250 Silver .8410 oz. ASW **Subject:** 50th Anniversary - Central Bank **Obv:** Old and new bank buildings **Rev:** Old and new bank seals

Date	Mintage	F	VF	XF	Unc	BU
ND(1999) Proof	Est. 5,000	Value: 60.00				

KM# 213 1000 PISO
9.9500 g., 0.9000 Gold .2879 oz. AGW **Subject:** 3rd Anniversary of the New Society **Obv:** Shield **Rev:** Head left

Date	Mintage	F	VF	XF	Unc	BU
1975	23,000	—	—	—	200	215
1975 Proof	13,000	Value: 230				

KM# 281 1000 PISO
31.1000 g., 0.9990 Silver .9989 oz. ASW **Subject:** Leyte Gulf Landing

Date	Mintage	F	VF	XF	Unc	BU
ND(1994) Proof	1,000	Value: 175				

KM# 216 1500 PISO
20.5500 g., 0.9000 Gold .5947 oz. AGW **Subject:** I.M.F. Meeting **Obv:** Map **Rev:** Stylized star in center of world globe emblems

Date	Mintage	F	VF	XF	Unc	BU
1976	5,500	—	—	—	420	435
1976 Proof	6,500	Value: 445				

KM# 219 1500 PISO
20.5500 g., 0.9000 Gold .5947 oz. AGW **Subject:** 5th Anniversary of the New Society **Obv:** Head facing **Rev:** Redesigned bank seal within circle

Date	Mintage	F	VF	XF	Unc	BU
ND(1977)	4,000	—	—	—	420	435
ND(1977) Proof	6,000	Value: 445				

KM# 223 1500 PISO
20.5500 g., 0.9000 Gold .5947 oz. AGW **Subject:** Inauguration of New Mint Facilities **Obv:** Flowers **Rev:** Bank, gold bars, paper money and coins

Date	Mintage	F	VF	XF	Unc	BU
1978	3,000	—	—	—	420	435
1978 Proof	3,000	Value: 445				

KM# 234 1500 PISO
9.9500 g., 0.9000 Gold .2879 oz. AGW **Subject:** Pope John Paul II Visit **Obv:** Standing figure in prayer, crowd in background **Rev:** Bust 3/4 left

Date	Mintage	F	VF	XF	Unc	BU
1981 Proof	1,000	Value: 525				
1982 Proof	—	—	—	—	—	—

KM# 237 1500 PISO
9.7800 g., 0.9000 Gold .2830 oz. AGW **Subject:** 40th Anniversary of Bataan-Corregidor **Obv:** Shield of arms **Rev:** Conjoined military heads left

Date	Mintage	F	VF	XF	Unc	BU
ND(1982)FM (U)	1,000	—	—	—	300	325
ND(1982)FM (P)	445	Value: 400				

KM# 282 2000 PISO
10.0000 g., 0.5000 Gold 0.1608 oz. AGW, 27 mm. **Subject:** Asia Pacific Economic Cooperation **Obv:** Head of Fidel Ramos 3/4 right **Rev:** World globe logo and value **Edge:** Reeded

Date	Mintage	F	VF	XF	Unc	BU
1996 Proof	3,000	Value: 225				

KM# 231 2500 PISO
14.5700 g., 0.5000 Gold .2342 oz. AGW **Subject:** 100th Anniversary - Birth of General Douglas MacArthur **Obv:** Military standing figures **Rev:** Uniformed bust with pipe facing 1/4 left

Date	Mintage	F	VF	XF	Unc	BU
ND(1980)FM (P)	3,073	Value: 275				

KM# 247 2500 PISO
15.0000 g., 0.5000 Gold .2414 oz. AGW **Subject:** President Aquino's Visit in Washington **Obv:** Bust of President Aquino left **Rev:** Bust of President Reagan right

Date	Mintage	F	VF	XF	Unc	BU
1986 Proof	Est. 250	Value: 475				

KM# 266 2500 PISO
7.9800 g., 0.9167 Gold .2352 oz. AGW **Subject:** Papal Visit 1995 **Obv:** Shield of arms **Rev:** Pope John Paul II left **Note:** Similar to 100 Piso, KM#264.

Date	Mintage	F	VF	XF	Unc	BU
ND(1994) Proof	—	Value: 325				

KM# 220 5000 PISO
68.7400 g., 0.9000 Gold 1.9893 oz. AGW **Subject:** 5th Anniversary of the New Society **Obv:** Design within beaded circle **Rev:** Conjoined busts of Ferdindand and Imelda Marcos right

Date	Mintage	F	VF	XF	Unc	BU
ND(1977)FM (U)	100	—	—	—	1,650	—
ND(1977)FM (P)	3,832	Value: 1,400				

KM# 267 5000 PISO
16.8100 g., 0.9250 Gold .4999 oz. AGW **Subject:** Papal Visit 1995 **Obv:** Shield of arms **Rev:** Bust of Pope John Paul II left **Note:** Similar to 100 Piso, KM#264.

Date	Mintage	F	VF	XF	Unc	BU
ND(1994) Proof	—	Value: 500				

KM# 283 5000 PISO
Gold **Subject:** 50th Anniversary - Central Bank in the Philippines

Date	Mintage	F	VF	XF	Unc	BU
1999 Proof	2,000	Value: 475				

KM# 255 10000 PESOS
33.5500 g., 0.9250 Gold 1 oz. AGW **Subject:** People Power 1992 **Obv:** Bust of Aquino facing 3/4 right **Rev:** Map, scroll, dates and dove

Date	Mintage	F	VF	XF	Unc	BU
ND(1992) Proof	1,600	Value: 950				

PATTERNS

Including off metal strikes

KM#	Date	Mintage	Identification	Mkt Val
Pn20	1922	—	Centavo. Silver. KM#163.	—
Pn21	ND(1965-66)	—	Peso. Silver. Marcos	—
Pn22	1966	—	Centavo. Copper. Central Bank	100
Pn23	1966	—	5 Centavos. Brass.	100
Pn24	1966	—	5 Centavos. Copper.	100
Pn25	1966	—	10 Centavos. Silver.	125
Pn26	1966	—	10 Centavos. Copper.	100
Pn27	1966	—	25 Centavos. Brass.	100
PnA28	1966	—	50 Centavos. Copper. Similar to Pn28. Conjoined busts of Ferdinand and Imelda Marcos.	125
PnB28	1966	—	50 Centavos. Copper. As Pn28	125
Pn28	1966	—	50 Centavos. Silver.	200
Pn29	1966	—	Piso. Silver.	200
Pn30	1966	—	Peso. Silver. Ferd and Imelda Marcos	—
PnA31	1966	—	Piso. Copper. Similar to Pn28. As Pn38.	150
PnB31	1966	—	Piso. Brass. Similar to Pn38 wtihout eagle and lion on arms.	150
Pn31	1967	—	Sentimo. Copper.	100
Pn32	1967	—	5 Sentimos.	125
Pn33	1967	—	5 Sentimos. Copper. Similar to Pn32. Similar to Pn27.	125
PnA34	1967	—	25 Centavos. Copper. Design similar to Pn28, legend as Pn34. Similar to Pn27.	100
pnB34	1967	—	10 Centavos. Bronze. Bust of Francisco Baltazar.	125
Pn34	1967	—	25 Sentimos. Silver.	125
PnA35	1967	—	50 Centavos. Copper. As Pn36. Small conjoined busts of Ferdinand and Imelda Marcos.	125
PnB35	1967	—	50 Sentimos. Bronze. Similar to Pn28. Bust of Juan Luna.	150
Pn35	1967	—	50 Sentimos. Copper. Large conjoined busts of Ferdinand and Imelda Marcos.	150
Pn36	1967	—	50 Sentimos. Silver. Del Pilar left. Del Pilar	125
Pn37	1967	—	50 Sentimos. Copper. Del Pilar left. Del Pilar	125
PnA38	1967	—	Peso. Copper. Similar to KM#195	150
PnB38	1967	—	Peso. Brass. Similar to KM#195	150
Pn38	1968	—	Peso. Silver. Sower walking left.	225
Pn39	1968	—	Piso. Silver. Sower walking right.	225
PnA40	1969	—	Peso. Copper. Similar to KM#195. As Pn40.	150
Pn40	1969	—	Piso. Silver. Dated 1966. Aquinaldo	225
Pn41	ND(1970)	—	Peso. Copper. Similar to KM#195. Conjoined busts of Marcos and Pope Paul VI left.	150
Pn42	1970	—	Peso. Copper. Similar to KM#195. Bust of Pope Paul VI 3/4 right.	150

PIEFORTS

All standard metals unless otherwise indicated

KM#	Date	Mintage	Identification	Mkt Val
P1	1979	—	50 Piso. Silver. KM#229	150

TRIAL STRIKES

KM#	Date	Mintage	Identification	Mkt Val
TS8	1967	—	Peso. Brass. KM#195. Bataan Day	75.00

CULION ISLAND

The Culion Leper Colony was established around 1903 on the island of Culion about 150 miles southeast of Manila by the Commission of Public Health. The first issue of coins valid only in the colony was produced by a private firm, Frank & Company. Later issues were struck at the Manila Mint.

MINT MARKS
PM = Philippine Mint at Manila

MONETARY SYSTEM
100 Centavos = 1 Peso

CULION LEPER COLONY

Philippine Commission of Public Health

LEPROSARIUM COINAGE

KM# 1 1/2 CENTAVO
Aluminum **Obv:** Value **Rev:** Caduceus

Date	Mintage	F	VF	XF	Unc	BU
1913	17,000	—	—	4.00	7.50	8.50

Note: Some authorities doubt that this coin circulated

KM# 2 CENTAVO
Aluminum

Date	Mintage	Good	VG	F	VF	XF
1913	33,000	50.00	75.00	175	275	—

Note: This coin exists with thick and thin planchets

KM# 3 CENTAVO
Copper-Nickel **Obv:** Bust 1/4 right **Rev:** Eagle above shield **Note:** Similar to KM#4 but first die, better strike.

Date	Mintage	Good	VG	F	VF	XF
1927PM	30,000	10.00	15.00	20.00	50.00	140

Note: Type I - One-button coat, legible motto, "7" in date over "T" in Centavo

KM# 4 CENTAVO
Copper-Nickel **Obv:** Bust 1/4 right **Rev:** Eagle with wings open above shield **Note:** Second die, poor strike. This coin exists with thick and thin planchets.

Date	Mintage	Good	VG	F	VF	XF
1927PM	Inc. above	12.00	18.00	30.00	75.00	150

Note: Type II - One-button coat, illegible motto, end of ribbon two widths from shield edge, "7" over "N"

KM# A5 CENTAVO

Copper Nickel

Date	Mintage	Good	VG	F	VF	XF
1927PM	Inc. above	35.00	50.00	100	175	275

Note: Type III - Two-button coat, illegible motto, end of ribbon one width from shield edge

KM# 5 CENTAVO

Copper-Nickel **Obv:** Bust of Rizal in circle **Rev:** Legend **Rev. Legend:** PHILIPPINE HEALTH SERVICE/LEPER COIN ONE CENTAVO

Date	Mintage	Good	VG	F	VF	XF
1930 Rare	—	—	—	—	—	—

KM# 6 5 CENTAVOS

Aluminum **Obv:** Value, legend **Rev:** Caduceus

Date	Mintage	Good	VG	F	VF	XF
1913	6,600	35.00	65.00	100	250	—

KM# 7 5 CENTAVOS

Copper-Nickel **Obv:** Bust 1/4 right **Rev:** Eagle with wings open above shield

Date	Mintage	Good	VG	F	VF	XF
1927	16,000	3.50	7.00	12.00	20.00	35.00

KM# 8 10 CENTAVOS

Aluminum **Obv:** Value **Rev:** Caduceus **Note:** Similar to 1/2 Centavo, KM#1.

Date	Mintage	Good	VG	F	VF	XF
1913	6,600	12.50	35.00	50.00	100	—

KM# 9 10 CENTAVOS

Aluminum **Obv:** Value **Rev:** Caduceus **Note:** Similar to 1 Peso, KM#14.

Date	Mintage	Good	VG	F	VF	XF
1920	20,000	7.50	10.00	15.00	40.00	—

KM# 10 10 CENTAVOS

Copper-Nickel **Obv:** Bust 1/4 left within circle **Rev:** Value within circle

Date	Mintage	VG	F	VF	XF	Unc
1930	17,000	—	5.00	10.00	15.00	40.00

Note: One pattern in copper, has been authenticated by ANACS

KM# 11 20 CENTAVOS

Aluminum **Obv:** Value **Rev:** Caduceus **Note:** Similar to 1/2 Centavo, KM#1.

Date	Mintage	Good	VG	F	VF	XF
1913	10,000	17.50	30.00	50.00	100	—

KM# 12 20 CENTAVOS

Aluminum **Obv:** Value **Rev:** Caduceus

Date	Mintage	Good	VG	F	VF	XF
1920	10,000	7.50	12.50	20.00	40.00	—

KM# 13 20 CENTAVOS

Copper-Nickel **Obv:** Value, legend **Rev:** Caduceus

Date	Mintage	VG	F	VF	XF	Unc
1922PM	10,000	—	15.00	20.00	35.00	—

Note: This coin exists with thick and thin planchets

KM# 14 PESO

Aluminum **Obv:** Value **Rev:** Caduceus

Date	Mintage	VG	F	VF	XF	Unc
1913	8,600	12.00	15.00	25.00	40.00	—

Note: This coin exists with thick and thin planchets

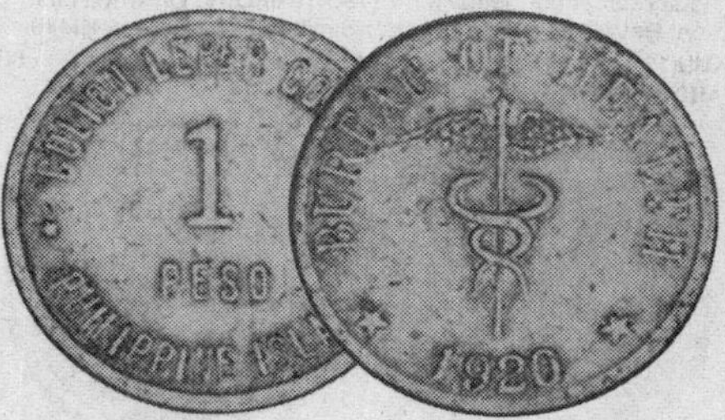

KM# 15 PESO

Aluminum **Obv:** Value **Rev:** Caduceus

Date	Mintage	VG	F	VF	XF	Unc
1920	4,000	11.00	15.00	25.00	40.00	—

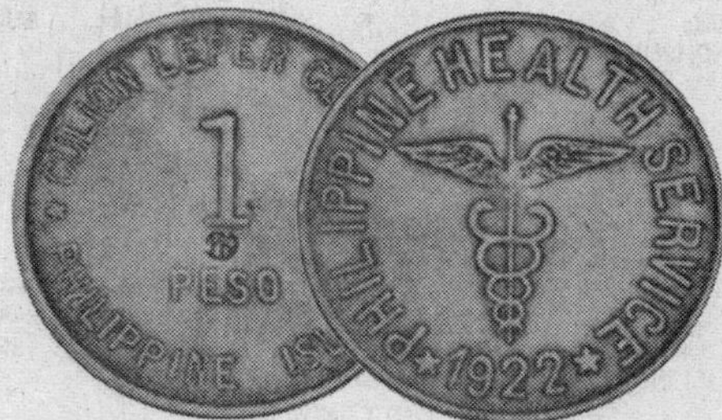

KM# 16 PESO

Copper-Nickel **Obv:** Value **Rev:** Caduceus **Note:** Varieties exist.

Date	Mintage	VG	F	VF	XF	Unc
1922	8,280	—	12.50	16.00	30.00	—

KM# 17 PESO

Copper-Nickel **Obv:** Value **Rev:** Caduceus with curved wings **Note:** Similar to KM#16, but caduceus has curved wings.

Date	Mintage	VG	F	VF	XF	Unc
1922PM	Inc. above	—	200	250	300	—

KM# 18 PESO

Copper-Nickel **Obv:** Bust 3/4 right **Rev:** Eagle with wings open above shield

Date	Mintage	VG	F	VF	XF	Unc
1925	20,000	—	7.50	12.50	15.00	75.00

PITCAIRN ISLANDS

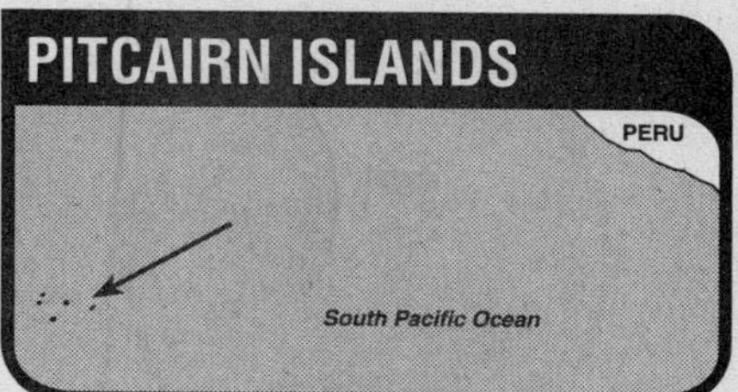

A small volcanic island, along with the uninhabited islands of Oeno, Henderson, and Ducie, constitute the British Colony of Pitcairn Islands. The main island has an area of about 2 sq. mi. (5 sq. km.) and a population of *68. It is located 1350 miles southeast of Tahiti. The islanders subsist on fishing, garden produce and crops. The sale of postage stamps and carved curios to passing ships brings cash income.

Discovered in 1767 by a British naval officer, Pitcairn was not occupied until 1790 when Fletcher Christian and nine mutineers from the British ship, *HMS Bounty*, along with some Tahitian men and women went ashore, and survived in obscurity until discovered by American whalers in 1808.

Adamstown is the chief settlement, located on the north coast, one of the few places that island-made longboats can land. The primary religion is Seventh-day Adventist and a public school provides basic education. In 1898 the settlement was placed under the jurisdiction of the Commissioner for the Western Pacific. Since 1970 this British settlement has been governed through a locally elected council under a governor.

New Zealand currency has been used since July 10, 1967.

BRITISH COLONY

REGULAR COINAGE

KM# 3 DOLLAR

Copper Nickel, 38.5 mm. **Subject:** Drafting of Constitution, 1838-1988 **Obv:** Crowned bust right **Rev:** Sailing ship

Date	Mintage	F	VF	XF	Unc	BU
ND(1988)	—	—	—	—	8.00	—

KM# 3a DOLLAR

28.2800 g., 0.9250 Silver .8411 oz. ASW, 38.5 mm. **Subject:** Drafting of constitution, 1838-1988 **Obv:** Crowned bust right **Rev:** Sailing ship

Date	Mintage	F	VF	XF	Unc	BU
ND(1988) Proof	—	Value: 40.00				

KM# 4 DOLLAR

Copper-Nickel, 38.5 mm. **Subject:** HMAV Bounty, 1789-1989 **Obv:** Crowned bust right **Rev:** Sailing ship

Date	Mintage	F	VF	XF	Unc	BU
ND(1989)	50,000	—	—	—	8.00	—

KM# 4a DOLLAR

28.2800 g., 0.9250 Silver .8411 oz. ASW, 38.5 mm. **Subject:** HMAV Bounty, 1789-1989 **Obv:** Crowned bust right **Rev:** Sailing ship

Date	Mintage	F	VF	XF	Unc	BU
ND(1989) Proof	20,000	Value: 40.00				

KM# 7 DOLLAR
Copper-Nickel, 38.5 mm. **Subject:** Establishment of Settlement, 1790-1990 **Obv:** Crowned bust right **Rev:** Ship in flames

Date	Mintage	F	VF	XF	Unc	BU
ND(1990)	—	—	—	—	8.00	—

KM# 7a DOLLAR
28.2800 g., 0.9250 Silver .8411 oz. ASW, 38.5 mm. **Subject:** Establishment of Settlement, 1790-1990 **Obv:** Crowned bust right **Rev:** Ship in flames

Date	Mintage	F	VF	XF	Unc	BU
ND(1990) Proof	10,000	Value: 45.00				

KM# 10 DOLLAR
Copper-Nickel, 38.5 mm. **Subject:** British Queen Mother **Obv:** Crowned bust right **Rev:** Bust facing 1/4 left, emblem at far left, all within beaded circle **Note:** Struck at the British Royal Mint.

Date	Mintage	F	VF	XF	Unc	BU
1997	—	—	—	—	10.00	—

KM# 11 5 DOLLARS
31.5600 g., 0.9250 Silver 0.9386 oz. ASW, 38.5 mm. **Subject:** Queen Mother **Obv:** Crowned bust right **Rev:** Queen Mother and the Order of the Garter **Edge:** Reeded

Date	Mintage	F	VF	XF	Unc	BU
1997 Proof	—	Value: 50.00				

KM# 13 10 DOLLARS
Silver **Subject:** 50th Wedding Anniversary of Queen Elizabeth II and Philip **Obv:** Bust right, legend above, date below **Rev:** Queen Elizabeth II and Philip with Prince Charles in baby buggy, legend above, value below

Date	Mintage	F	VF	XF	Unc	BU
1997 Proof	—	Value: 50.00				

KM# 1 50 DOLLARS
155.6000 g., 0.9990 Silver 5 oz. ASW, 65 mm. **Subject:** Drafting of Constitution, 1838-1988 **Obv:** Crowned bust right **Rev:** Sailing ship **Note:** Photo reduced.

Date	Mintage	F	VF	XF	Unc	BU
ND(1988) Proof	10,000	Value: 125				

KM# 5 50 DOLLARS
155.6000 g., 0.9990 Silver 5 oz. ASW, 65 mm. **Subject:** HMAV Bounty, 1789-1989 **Obv:** Crowned bust right **Rev:** Sailing ship **Note:** Similar to 250 Dollars, KM#2.

Date	Mintage	F	VF	XF	Unc	BU
ND(1989) Proof	10,000	Value: 135				

KM# 8 50 DOLLARS
155.6000 g., 0.9990 Silver 5 oz. ASW, 65 mm. **Subject:** Establishment of Settlement, 1790-1990 **Obv:** Crowned bust right **Rev:** Ship in flames **Note:** Similar to 250 Dollars, KM#9.

Date	Mintage	F	VF	XF	Unc	BU
ND(1990) Proof	2,500	Value: 165				

KM# 2 250 DOLLARS
15.9800 g., 0.9170 Gold .4708 oz. AGW **Subject:** Drafting of Constitution, 1838-1988 **Obv:** Crowned bust right **Rev:** Sailing ship

Date	Mintage	F	VF	XF	Unc	BU
ND(1988) Proof	2,500	Value: 345				

KM# 6 250 DOLLARS
15.9800 g., 0.9170 Gold .4708 oz. AGW **Subject:** HMAV Bounty, 1789-1989 **Obv:** Crowned bust right **Rev:** Ship

Date	Mintage	F	VF	XF	Unc	BU
ND(1989) Proof	2,500	Value: 345				

KM# 9 250 DOLLARS
15.9800 g., 0.9170 Gold .4708 oz. AGW **Subject:** Establishment of Settlement, 1790-1990 **Obv:** Crowned bust right **Rev:** Ship in flames within circle **Rev. Designer:** Robert Elderton

Date	Mintage	F	VF	XF	Unc	BU
ND(1990) Proof	500	Value: 365				

POLAND

The Republic of Poland, located in central Europe, has an area of 120,725 sq. mi. (312,680 sq. km.) and a population of *38.2 million. Capital: Warszawa (Warsaw). The economy is essentially agricultural, but industrial activity provides the products for foreign trade. Machinery, coal, coke, iron, steel and transport equipment are exported.

Poland, which began as a Slavic duchy in the 10th century and reached its peak of power between the 14th and 16th centuries, has had a turbulent history of invasion, occupation or partition by Mongols, Turkey, Transylvania, Sweden, Austria, Prussia and Russia.

The first partition took place in 1772. Prussia took Polish Pomerania, Russia took part of the eastern provinces, and Austria occupied Galicia and its capital city Lwów. The second partition occurred in 1793 when Russia took another slice of the eastern provinces and Prussia took what remained of western Poland. The third partition, 1795, literally removed Poland from the map. Russia took what was left of the eastern provinces. Prussia seized most of central Poland, including Warsaw. Austria took what was left of the south. Napoleon restored to Poland much of the territory lost to Prussia and Austria, but after his defeat another partition returned the Duchy of Warsaw to Prussia, made Kraków into a tiny republic, and declared what remained to be the Kingdom of Poland under the czar and in permanent union with Russia.

Poland re-emerged as an independent state recognized by the Treaty of Versailles on June 28, 1919, and maintained its independence until 1939 when it was invaded by, and partitioned between, Germany and Russia. Poland's present boundaries were determined by the U.S.-British-Russian agreement of Aug. 16, 1945. The Government of National Unity was replaced when the Polish Communist-Socialist faction claimed victory at the polls in 1947 and established a Peoples Democratic Republic' of the Soviet type in 1952. On December 29, 1989 Poland was proclaimed as the Republic of Poland.

MINT MARKS

MV, MW, MW-monogram - Warsaw Mint, 1965-
FF - Stuttgart Germany 1916-1917
(w) - Warsaw 1923-39 (opened officially in 1924) arrow mintmark
CHI - Valcambi, Switzerland

Other letters appearing with date denote the Mintmaster at the time the coin was struck.

GERMAN OCCUPATION

REGENCY COINAGE

100 Fenigow = 1 Marka

Y# 4 FENIG
Iron **Obv:** Value **Rev:** Crowned eagle with wings open

Date	Mintage	F	VF	XF	Unc	BU
1918FF	51,484,000	0.50	1.00	3.00	10.00	30.00
1918FF Proof	—	Value: 200				

Y# 5 5 FENIGOW
Iron **Obv:** Value **Rev:** Crowned eagle with wings open

Date	Mintage	F	VF	XF	Unc	BU
1917FF	18,700,000	0.25	0.75	1.50	3.50	—
1917FF Proof	—	Value: 100				
1918FF	22,690,000	0.25	0.75	1.50	3.50	—
1918FF Proof	—	Value: 200				

Y# 6a 10 FENIGOW
Zinc **Obv:** Value **Rev:** Crowned eagle with wings open **Note:** Error planchet.

Date	Mintage	F	VF	XF	Unc	BU
1917FF	—	25.00	45.00	85.00	150	—

Y# 6 10 FENIGOW

Iron **Obv:** Value **Rev:** Crowned eagle with wings open

Date	Mintage	F	VF	XF	Unc	BU
1917FF	33,000,000	7.50	15.00	20.00	28.00	—
Note: Obverse legend touches edge						
1917FF Proof	—	Value: 100				
1917FF	Inc. above	0.25	0.75	1.25	3.50	—
Note: Obverse legend away from edge						
1918FF	14,990,000	0.50	1.00	2.00	5.00	—
Note: Obverse legend away from edge						
1918FF Proof	—	Value: 200				
Note: Obverse legend away from edge						

Y# 7 20 FENIGOW

Iron **Obv:** Value **Rev:** Crowned eagle with wings open

Date	Mintage	F	VF	XF	Unc	BU
1917FF	1,900,000	2.00	4.00	6.00	11.50	—
1918FF	19,260,000	0.75	1.25	2.50	5.50	—

Y# 7a 20 FENIGOW

Zinc **Obv:** Value **Rev:** Crowned eagle with wings open **Note:** Error planchet.

Date	Mintage	F	VF	XF	Unc	BU
1917FF	—	35.00	60.00	100	200	—

REPUBLIC

STANDARD COINAGE

100 Groszy = 1 Zloty

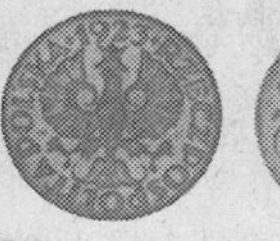

Y# 8 GROSZ

Brass **Obv:** Crowned eagle with wings open **Rev:** Stylized value **Note:** Some authorities consider this strike a pattern.

Date	Mintage	F	VF	XF	Unc	BU
1923	—	—	—	—	200	—

Y# 8a GROSZ

Bronze **Obv:** Crowned eagle with wings open **Rev:** Stylized value

Date	Mintage	F	VF	XF	Unc	BU
1923	30,000,000	0.25	0.50	1.75	10.00	—
1925(w)	40,000,000	0.25	0.50	1.75	9.00	—
1927(w)	17,000,000	0.25	0.50	1.75	10.00	—
1928(w)	13,600,000	0.25	0.50	1.75	9.00	—
1930(w)	22,500,000	4.00	10.00	25.00	40.00	—
1931(w)	9,000,000	0.50	1.00	2.00	10.00	—
1932(w)	12,000,000	0.50	1.00	2.00	10.00	—
1933(w)	7,000,000	0.50	1.00	2.00	10.00	—
1934(w)	5,900,000	0.50	1.00	2.00	12.00	—
1935(w)	7,300,000	0.50	1.00	2.00	5.00	—
1936(w)	12,600,000	0.50	1.00	2.00	5.00	—
1937(w)	17,370,000	0.25	0.50	0.75	2.50	—
1938(w)	20,530,000	0.25	0.50	0.75	2.50	—
1939(w)	12,000,000	0.25	0.50	0.75	2.50	—

Y# 9 2 GROSZE

Brass **Obv:** Crowned eagle with wings open **Rev:** Stylized value

Date	Mintage	F	VF	XF	Unc	BU
1923	20,500,000	3.50	12.50	22.50	45.00	60.00

Y# 9a 2 GROSZE

Bronze **Obv:** Crowned eagle with wings open **Rev:** Stylized value

Date	Mintage	F	VF	XF	Unc	BU
1925(w)	39,000,000	0.50	2.00	4.50	10.00	—
1927(w)	15,300,000	0.50	2.00	4.50	10.00	—
1928(w)	13,400,000	0.50	2.00	4.50	10.00	—
1930(w)	20,000,000	0.50	2.00	4.50	10.00	—
1931(w)	9,500,000	1.75	2.50	5.50	12.75	—
1932(w)	6,500,000	2.00	4.00	6.00	15.00	—
1933(w)	7,000,000	2.00	4.00	6.00	15.00	—
1934(w)	9,350,000	1.75	3.00	7.50	17.50	—
1935(w)	5,800,000	0.20	0.75	2.00	5.00	—
1936(w)	5,800,000	0.20	0.75	2.00	5.00	—
1937(w)	17,360,000	0.20	0.40	0.60	2.50	—
1938(w)	20,530,000	0.20	0.40	0.60	2.50	—
1939(w)	12,000,000	0.20	0.40	0.60	2.50	—

Y# 10 5 GROSZY

Brass, 19.5 mm. **Obv:** Crowned eagle with wings open **Rev:** Stylized value

Date	Mintage	F	VF	XF	Unc	BU
1923	32,000,000	0.50	2.00	5.00	10.00	—

Y# 10a 5 GROSZY

Bronze, 19.5 mm. **Obv:** Crowned eagle with wings open **Rev:** Stylized value

Date	Mintage	F	VF	XF	Unc	BU
1923 Proof	350	Value: 150				
1925(w)	45,500,000	0.20	0.40	4.00	8.00	—
1928(w)	8,900,000	0.20	0.40	5.00	10.00	—
1930(w)	14,200,000	0.20	0.40	5.00	12.00	—
1931(w)	1,500,000	0.50	1.00	10.00	20.00	—
1934(w)	420,000	5.00	7.50	35.00	75.00	—
1935(w)	4,660,000	0.20	0.40	0.60	5.00	—
1936(w)	4,660,000	0.20	0.40	0.60	5.00	—
1937(w)	9,050,000	0.20	0.40	0.60	2.50	—
1938(w)	17,300,000	0.20	0.40	0.60	2.50	—
1939(w)	10,000,000	0.20	0.40	0.60	2.50	—

Y# 11 10 GROSZY

Nickel, 17.5 mm. **Obv:** Crowned eagle with wings open **Rev:** Value within wreath

Date	Mintage	F	VF	XF	Unc	BU
1923	100,000,000	0.20	0.45	0.80	1.25	—

Y# 12 20 GROSZY

Nickel **Obv:** Crowned eagle with wings open **Rev:** Value within wreath

Date	Mintage	F	VF	XF	Unc	BU
1923	150,000,000	0.35	0.75	1.25	2.00	—
1923 Proof	10	Value: 300				

Y# 13 50 GROSZY

Nickel, 22.5 mm. **Obv:** Crowned eagle with wings open **Rev:** Value within wreath

Date	Mintage	F	VF	XF	Unc	BU
1923	100,000,000	0.40	0.80	1.50	3.50	—
1923 Proof	10	Value: 350				

Y# 15 ZLOTY

5.0000 g., 0.7500 Silver .1206 oz. ASW **Obv:** Crowned eagle with wings open **Rev:** Bust left **Designer:** Tadeusz Breyer

Date	Mintage	F	VF	XF	Unc	BU
1924 (Paris)	16,000,000	2.50	6.00	20.00	55.00	—
Note: Torch and cornucopia flank date						
1924 (Birmingham); Proof	8	Value: 600				
1925 (London)	24,000,000	2.50	5.00	12.00	30.00	—
Note: Dot after date						

Y# 14 ZLOTY

Nickel, 25 mm. **Obv:** Crowned eagle with wings open **Rev:** Value within stylized design

Date	Mintage	F	VF	XF	Unc	BU
1929(w)	32,000,000	0.75	1.50	2.50	7.00	—

Y# 16 2 ZLOTE

10.0000 g., 0.7500 Silver .2400 oz. ASW **Obv:** Crowned eagle with wings open **Rev:** Head left **Designer:** Tadeusz Breyer

Date	Mintage	F	VF	XF	Unc	BU
1924 (Paris)	—	5.50	10.00	20.00	85.00	—
Note: Torch and cornucopia flank date						
1924 H (Birmingham)	1,200,000	17.50	35.00	175	450	—
1924 (Birmingham); Proof	60	Value: 600				
1924 (Philadelphia)	800,000	10.00	20.00	60.00	125	—
Note: Without privy marks, coin alignment						
1925 (London)	11,000,000	5.00	9.00	17.50	47.50	—
Note: Dot after date						
1925 (Philadelphia)	5,200,000	6.50	12.00	40.00	75.00	—
Note: Without privy marks						

Y# 20 2 ZLOTE

4.4000 g., 0.7500 Silver .1061 oz. ASW **Obv:** Crowned eagle with wings open **Rev:** Veiled head left on radiant background

Date	Mintage	F	VF	XF	Unc	BU
1932(w)	15,700,000	2.25	4.00	7.00	13.50	16.50
1933(w)	9,250,000	2.25	4.00	7.00	13.50	16.50
1934(w)	250,000	4.00	7.00	12.00	27.50	—

Y# 27 2 ZLOTE

4.4000 g., 0.7500 Silver .1061 oz. ASW **Obv:** Crowned eagle with wings open **Rev:** Head left

Date	Mintage	F	VF	XF	Unc	BU
1934(w)	10,425,000	3.00	6.00	10.00	25.00	—
1936(w)	75,000	20.00	75.00	125	250	—

Y# 30 2 ZLOTE

4.4000 g., 0.7500 Silver .1061 oz. ASW **Subject:** 15th Anniversary of Gdynia Seaport **Obv:** Crowned eagle with wings open **Rev:** Sailing ship

Date	Mintage	F	VF	XF	Unc	BU
1936(w)	3,918,000	3.00	6.00	12.00	30.00	—

Y# 17.1 5 ZLOTYCH

25.0000 g., 0.9000 Silver .7234 oz. ASW **Subject:** Adoption of the Constitution **Obv:** Crowned eagle with wings open **Rev:** 100 pearls in circle **Designer:** Stanislaw Lewandowski

Date	Mintage	F	VF	XF	Unc	BU
1925(w)	100	150	300	700	1,500	—

Y# 17.1a 5 ZLOTYCH

Gold **Obv:** Crowned eagle with wings open **Rev:** Adoption of the Constitution

Date	Mintage	F	VF	XF	Unc	BU
1925(w) Rare	2	—	—	—	—	—

Y# 17.2 5 ZLOTYCH

25.0000 g., 0.9000 Silver .7234 oz. ASW **Obv:** Without monogram by date **Rev:** Adoption of the Constitution **Designer:** Stanislaw Lewandowski

Date	Mintage	F	VF	XF	Unc	BU
1925(w)	1,000	—	—	450	950	—

Y# 17.2a 5 ZLOTYCH

Bronze **Obv:** Crowned imperial eagle **Rev:** Adoption of the Constitution

Date	Mintage	F	VF	XF	Unc	BU
1925(w)	100	—	—	200	300	—

Y# 17.2c 5 ZLOTYCH

Gold **Obv:** Without monogram by date **Rev:** Adoption of the Constitution

Date	Mintage	F	VF	XF	Unc	BU
1925(w) Rare	1	—	—	—	—	—

Y# 17.3 5 ZLOTYCH

25.0000 g., 0.9000 Silver .7234 oz. ASW **Obv:** Monogram by date **Rev:** 81 pearls in circle **Designer:** Stanislaw Lewandowski

Date	Mintage	F	VF	XF	Unc	BU
1925(w)	1,000	—	—	450	950	—

Y# 17.3a 5 ZLOTYCH

43.3300 g., 0.9000 Gold 1.3407 oz. AGW **Obv:** Crowned eagle with wings open, mint mark to right of date **Rev:** Adoption of the Constitution **Edge Lettering:** SALUS REIPUBLICAE SUPREMA LEX

Date	Mintage	F	VF	XF	Unc	BU
1925(w) Rare	1	—	—	—	—	—

Y# 17.4 5 ZLOTYCH

43.3300 g., 0.9000 Gold 1.3407 oz. AGW **Obv:** Without monogram by date, with mint mark **Rev:** Adoption of the Constitution **Designer:** Stanislaw Lewandowski

Date	Mintage	F	VF	XF	Unc	BU
1925(w)	1,000	—	—	1,000	1,200	—

Y# 17.4a 5 ZLOTYCH

Tombac **Obv:** Crowned imperial eagle **Rev:** Adoption of the Constitution

Date	Mintage	F	VF	XF	Unc	BU
1925(w)	100	—	—	200	300	—

Y# 18 5 ZLOTYCH

18.0000 g., 0.7500 Silver .4340 oz. ASW **Obv:** Crowned eagle with wings open **Rev:** Winged Victory right

Date	Mintage	F	VF	XF	Unc	BU
1928(w)	7,500,000	15.00	30.00	65.00	125	—
Note: Conjoined arrow and K mint mark						
1928 Error	Inc. above	40.00	75.00	100	225	—
Note: "SUPRMA" edge inscription						
1928 Without mint mark	10,000,000	13.50	25.00	65.00	125	—
Note: 4,300,000 struck in London and 5,700,000 in Belgium						
1930(w)	5,900,000	60.00	120	275	450	—
1931(w)	2,200,000	75.00	150	200	500	—
1932(w)	3,100,000	90.00	175	350	—	—

Y# 19.1 5 ZLOTYCH

18.0000 g., 0.7500 Silver .4340 oz. ASW, 33 mm. **Subject:** Centennial of 1830 Revolution **Obv:** Crowned eagle with wings open flanked by value **Rev:** Pole with flag and banner divides dates **Edge Lettering:** SALUS REIPUBLICAE SUPREMA LEX **Designer:** Wojciech Jastrebowski

Date	Mintage	F	VF	XF	Unc	BU
1930(w)	1,000,000	8.00	16.50	35.00	100	—

Y# 19.2 5 ZLOTYCH

18.0000 g., 0.7500 Silver .4340 oz. ASW **Obv:** Crowned imperial eagle **Rev:** Pole with flag and banner divides dates **Note:** High relief.

Date	Mintage	F	VF	XF	Unc	BU
1930(w)	200	75.00	175	375	750	—

Y# 21 5 ZLOTYCH

11.0000 g., 0.7500 Silver .2652 oz. ASW **Obv:** Crowned eagle with wings open flanked by value **Rev:** Veiled head left on radiant background

Date	Mintage	F	VF	XF	Unc	BU
1932 (Warsaw : tiny arrow in space between talons of eagle's left claw)	1,000,000	15.00	50.00	200	475	—
1932 (London); without mint mark	3,000,000	—	BV	6.50	15.00	20.00
1933(w)	11,000,000	—	BV	5.00	12.50	17.50
1933(w) Proof	100	—	—	—	—	—
1934(w)	250,000	BV	4.00	8.00	20.00	—

Y# 25 5 ZLOTYCH

11.0000 g., 0.7500 Silver .2652 oz. ASW, 28 mm. **Obv:** Rifle Corps symbol below eagle with wings open **Rev:** Head left **Designer:** Stanislaw K. Ostrowski

Date	Mintage	F	VF	XF	Unc	BU
1934(w)	300,000	6.00	9.00	17.50	40.00	—

Y# 28 5 ZLOTYCH

11.0000 g., 0.7500 Silver .2652 oz. ASW, 28 mm. **Obv:** Radiant crowned eagle with wings open **Rev:** Head left **Designer:** Stanislaw K. Ostrowski

Date	Mintage	F	VF	XF	Unc	BU
1934(w)	6,510,000	BV	4.50	9.00	20.00	25.00
1935(w)	1,800,000	BV	4.75	10.00	22.00	28.00
1936(w)	1,800,000	BV	4.75	10.00	22.00	28.00
1938(w)	289,000	5.00	7.50	15.00	30.00	—

Y# 31 5 ZLOTYCH

11.0000 g., 0.7500 Silver .2652 oz. ASW **Subject:** 15th Anniversary of Gdynia Seaport **Obv:** Crowned eagle with wings open **Rev:** Sailing ship

Date	Mintage	F	VF	XF	Unc	BU
1936(w)	1,000,000	7.00	12.00	25.00	50.00	—

Y# 32 10 ZLOTYCH

3.2258 g., 0.9000 Gold .0933 oz. AGW **Obv:** Crowned eagle with wings open **Rev:** Crowned head left **Note:** Never released into circulation; similar design to Y#33.

Date	Mintage	F	VF	XF	Unc	BU
ND(1925)(w)	50,000	—	BV	85.00	165	225

Y# 22 10 ZLOTYCH

22.0000 g., 0.7500 Silver .5305 oz. ASW, 33 mm. **Obv:** Crowned eagle with wings open **Rev:** Radiant head laureate left

Date	Mintage	F	VF	XF	Unc	BU
1932(w)	3,100,000	8.50	9.50	13.50	30.00	38.00
Note: Warsaw Mint : tiny arrow in space between talons of eagle's left claw						
1932	6,000,000	8.50	9.50	13.50	30.00	38.00
Note: London Mint: without mint mark						
1932(w) Proof	100	—	—	—	—	—
1933(w)	2,800,000	8.50	9.50	13.50	30.00	38.00
1933(w) Proof	100	—	—	—	—	—

Y# 23 10 ZLOTYCH
22.0000 g., 0.7500 Silver .5305 oz. ASW, 33 mm. **Subject:** Jan III Sobieski's Victory Over the Turks **Obv:** Crowned eagle with wings open **Rev:** Uniformed bust right **Designer:** Zofia Trzcinski-Kaminska

Date	Mintage	F	VF	XF	Unc	BU
ND(1933)(w)	300,000	9.00	16.00	25.00	55.00	—
ND(1933)(w) Proof	100	—	—	—	—	—

Y# 24 10 ZLOTYCH
22.0000 g., 0.7500 Silver .5305 oz. ASW, 33 mm. **Subject:** 70th Anniversary of 1863 Insurrection **Obv:** Crowned eagle with wings open **Rev:** Head of Romuald Traugutt 3/4 facing divides dates **Designer:** Jan Wysocki

Date	Mintage	F	VF	XF	Unc	BU
ND(1933)(w)	300,000	12.00	20.00	40.00	65.00	—
ND(1933)(w)-Proof	100	—	—	—	—	—

Y# 26 10 ZLOTYCH
22.0000 g., 0.7500 Silver .5305 oz. ASW, 33 mm. **Obv:** Rifle Corps symbol below eagle with wings open **Rev:** Head of Jozef Pilsudski left **Designer:** Stanislaw K. Ostrowski

Date	Mintage	F	VF	XF	Unc	BU
1934(w)	300,000	10.00	17.50	25.00	50.00	—

Y# 29 10 ZLOTYCH
22.0000 g., 0.7500 Silver .5305 oz. ASW, 33 mm. **Obv:** Eagle with wings open with no symbols below **Rev:** Head of Jozef Pilsudski left **Designer:** Stanislaw K. Ostrowski

Date	Mintage	F	VF	XF	Unc	BU
1934(w)	200,000	12.00	18.00	25.00	55.00	—
1935(w)	1,670,000	BV	8.50	14.00	30.00	40.00
1936(w)	2,130,000	BV	8.50	14.00	30.00	40.00
1937(w)	908,000	BV	8.50	16.00	40.00	—
1938(w)	234,000	8.50	10.00	22.00	50.00	—
1939(w)	—	BV	8.50	16.00	40.00	—

Y# 33 20 ZLOTYCH
6.4516 g., 0.9000 Gold .1867 oz. AGW **Obv:** Crowned eagle with wings open **Rev:** Crowned head of Boleslaw I left **Note:** Never released into circulation.

Date	Mintage	F	VF	XF	Unc	BU
ND(1925)(w)	27,000	—	BV	145	215	325

WWII GERMAN OCCUPATION

OCCUPATION COINAGE

Y# 34 GROSZ
Zinc **Obv:** Crowned eagle with wings open **Rev:** Stylized value

Date	Mintage	F	VF	XF	Unc	BU
1939(w)	33,909,000	0.50	1.00	1.75	3.50	—

Y# 35 5 GROSZY
Zinc **Obv:** Crowned eagle with wings open, hole in center **Rev:** Stylized value, hole in center

Date	Mintage	F	VF	XF	Unc	BU
1939(w)	15,324,000	0.50	1.50	2.00	5.00	—

Y# 36 10 GROSZY
Zinc **Obv:** Crowned imperial eagle **Rev:** Value

Date	Mintage	F	VF	XF	Unc	BU
1923(w)	42,175,000	0.10	0.20	0.40	2.00	—

Note: Actually struck in 1941-44

Y# 37 20 GROSZY
Zinc **Obv:** Crowned eagle with wings open **Rev:** Value within wreath

Date	Mintage	F	VF	XF	Unc	BU
1923(w)	40,025,000	0.15	0.25	0.50	2.00	—

Note: Actually struck in 1941-44

Y# 38 50 GROSZY
Nickel Plated Iron **Obv:** Crowned eagle with wings open **Rev:** Value within wreath

Date	Mintage	F	VF	XF	Unc	BU
1938(w)	32,000,000	1.00	2.00	4.00	8.50	—

Y# 38a 50 GROSZY
Iron **Obv:** Crowned eagle with wings open **Rev:** Value within wreath

Date	Mintage	F	VF	XF	Unc	BU
1938(w)	—	1.25	2.50	5.00	10.00	—

Note: Varieties exist

TOKEN COINAGE

Lodz Ghetto, 1942-1944

A major industrial city in western Poland before World War II and site of the first wartime ghetto under German occupation (May 1940). It was also the last ghetto to close during the war (August 1944). Token coinage was struck in 1942 and 1943, in the name of the Jewish Elders of Litzmannstadt. This series has seen very little circulation, but is commonly found in conditions from slightly to badly corroded. The badly corroded specimens have the appearance of zinc.

KM# Tn1 10 PFENNIG
Aluminum-Magnesium **Rev:** Value

Date	Mintage	VG	F	VF	XF	Unc
1942	Est. 100,000	60.00	125	200	—	—

Note: Most were destroyed or remelted as the design was too similar to regular German coinage

KM# Tn5 10 PFENNIG
Aluminum-Magnesium **Obv:** Star in circle **Rev:** Value

Date	Mintage	VG	F	VF	XF	Unc
1942	100,000	35.00	50.00	65.00	125	—

KM# Tn2 5 MARK
Aluminum **Obv:** Value **Rev:** Star at upper left, GETTO and date lower right

Date	Mintage	VG	F	VF	XF	Unc
1943	600,000	5.00	10.00	25.00	45.00	—

KM# Tn2a 5 MARK
Aluminum-Magnesium **Obv:** Value **Rev:** Star at upper left, GETTO and date lower right

Date	Mintage	VG	F	VF	XF	Unc
1943	Inc. above	20.00	40.00	75.00	—	—

KM# Tn3 10 MARK
Aluminum **Obv:** Value **Rev:** Star at upper left, GETTO and date lower right **Note:** Thick and thin planchets exist.

Date	Mintage	VG	F	VF	XF	Unc
1943	100,000	5.00	10.00	25.00	45.00	—

KM# Tn3a 10 MARK
Aluminum-Magnesium **Obv:** Value **Rev:** Star at upper left, GETTO and date lower right

Date	Mintage	VG	F	VF	XF	Unc
1943	Inc. above	25.00	45.00	85.00	—	—

KM# Tn4 20 MARK
Aluminum **Obv:** Value **Rev:** Star at upper left, GETTO and date lower right **Note:** Beware of numerous counterfeits.

Date	Mintage	VG	F	VF	XF	Unc
1943	—	75.00	110	150	250	—

REPUBLIC

Post War

STANDARD COINAGE

Y# 39 GROSZ
Aluminum, 14.3 mm. **Obv:** Eagle with wings open **Rev:** Value at upper right of sprig **Note:** 116,000 were struck at Warsaw, the remainder at Budapest.

Date	Mintage	F	VF	XF	Unc	BU
1949	400,116,000	0.10	0.20	0.30	0.75	—

Y# 40 2 GROSZE
Aluminum **Obv:** Eagle with wings open **Rev:** Value at upper right of sprig **Note:** 106,000 were struck at Warsaw, the remainder at Budapest.

Date	Mintage	F	VF	XF	Unc	BU
1949	300,106,000	0.10	0.25	0.50	1.00	—

Y# 41 5 GROSZY

Bronze **Obv:** Eagle with wings open **Rev:** Value at upper right of sprig

Date	Mintage	F	VF	XF	Unc	BU
1949	300,000,000	0.10	0.25	0.50	1.00	—

Y# 41a 5 GROSZY

Aluminum **Obv:** Eagle with wings open **Rev:** Value at upper right of sprig

Date	Mintage	F	VF	XF	Unc	BU
1949	200,000,000	0.10	0.25	0.75	1.50	—

Y# 42 10 GROSZY

Copper-Nickel **Obv:** Eagle with wings open **Rev:** Value above sprig

Date	Mintage	F	VF	XF	Unc	BU
1949	200,000,000	0.20	0.40	0.60	1.50	—

Y# 42a 10 GROSZY

Aluminum **Obv:** Eagle with wings open **Rev:** Value above sprig

Date	Mintage	F	VF	XF	Unc	BU
1949	31,047,000	0.10	0.25	0.75	2.50	—

Y# 43 20 GROSZY

Copper-Nickel **Obv:** Eagle with wings open **Rev:** Value above sprig

Date	Mintage	F	VF	XF	Unc	BU
1949	133,383,000	0.25	0.45	0.75	2.00	—

Y# 43a 20 GROSZY

Aluminum **Obv:** Eagle with wings open **Rev:** Value above sprig

Date	Mintage	F	VF	XF	Unc	BU
1949	197,472,000	0.10	0.25	0.75	2.50	—

Y# 44 50 GROSZY

Copper-Nickel **Obv:** Eagle with wings open **Rev:** Value above sprig

Date	Mintage	F	VF	XF	Unc	BU
1949	109,000,000	0.35	0.65	1.00	2.50	—

Y# 44a 50 GROSZY

Aluminum **Obv:** Eagle with wings open **Rev:** Value above sprig

Date	Mintage	F	VF	XF	Unc	BU
1949	59,393,000	0.10	0.25	1.50	5.00	—

Y# 45 ZLOTY

Copper-Nickel **Obv:** Eagle with wings open **Rev:** Value within wreath

Date	Mintage	F	VF	XF	Unc	BU
1949	87,053,000	1.00	1.50	2.25	4.00	—

Y# 45a ZLOTY

Aluminum **Obv:** Eagle with wings open **Rev:** Value within wreath

Date	Mintage	F	VF	XF	Unc	BU
1949	43,000,000	0.10	0.25	2.50	6.00	—

PEOPLES REPUBLIC

STANDARD COINAGE

Y# A46 5 GROSZY

Aluminum, 16 mm. **Obv:** Eagle with wings open **Rev:** Value to upper right of sprig

Date	Mintage	F	VF	XF	Unc	BU
1958	53,521,000	—	—	0.10	0.20	—
1959	28,564,000	—	—	0.10	0.15	—
1960	12,246,000	—	0.50	1.50	2.75	—
1961	29,502,000	—	—	0.10	0.20	—
1962	90,257,000	—	—	0.10	0.15	—
1963	20,878,000	—	—	0.10	0.15	—
1965MW	5,050,000	—	0.75	2.00	4.00	—
1967MW	10,056,000	—	0.75	2.00	4.00	—
1968MW	10,196,000	—	0.75	2.00	4.00	—
1970MW	20,095,000	—	—	0.10	0.20	—
1971MW	20,000,000	—	—	0.10	0.20	—
1972MW	10,000,000	—	—	0.10	0.20	—

Y# AA47 10 GROSZY

0.7000 g., Aluminum, 17.6 mm. **Obv:** Eagle with wings open **Rev:** Value above sprig **Note:** Varieties in date size exist.

Date	Mintage	F	VF	XF	Unc	BU
1961	73,400,000	—	0.75	2.50	4.00	—
1962	25,362,000	—	1.75	5.00	20.00	—
1963	40,434,000	—	—	0.50	1.50	—
1965MW	50,521,000	—	0.25	1.00	2.00	—
1966MW	70,749,000	—	—	0.50	1.50	—
1967MW	62,059,000	—	—	0.50	1.50	—
1968MW	62,204,000	—	—	0.50	1.50	—
1969MW	71,566,000	—	—	0.50	1.00	—
1970MW	38,844,000	—	—	0.10	0.50	—
1971MW	50,000,000	—	—	0.10	0.50	—
1972MW	60,000,000	—	—	0.10	0.50	—
1973MW	80,000,000	—	—	0.10	0.25	—
1973 Rare	—	—	—	—	—	—
1974	50,000,000	—	—	0.10	0.15	—
Note: Struck at Kremnica Mint						
1975MW	50,000,000	—	—	0.10	0.15	—
1976MW	100,000,000	—	—	—	0.10	—
1977MW	100,000,000	—	—	—	0.10	—
1978MW	71,204,000	—	—	—	0.10	—
1979MW	73,191,000	—	—	—	0.10	—
1979MW Proof	5,000	Value: 1.00				
1980MW	60,623,000	—	—	—	0.10	—
1980MW Proof	5,000	Value: 1.00				
1981MW	70,000,000	—	—	—	0.10	—
1981MW Proof	5,000	Value: 1.00				
1983MW	9,600,000	—	—	—	0.10	—
1985MW	9,957,000	—	—	—	0.10	—

Y# A47 20 GROSZY

1.0000 g., Aluminum, 20 mm. **Obv:** Eagle with wings open **Rev:** Value above sprig **Note:** Date varieties exist.

Date	Mintage	F	VF	XF	Unc	BU
1957	3,940,000	—	5.00	17.00	40.00	—
1961	53,108,000	—	1.75	3.75	8.00	—
1962	19,140,000	—	2.00	5.00	12.50	—
1963	41,217,000	—	—	0.50	2.00	—
1965MW	32,022,000	—	—	0.50	2.00	—
1966MW	23,860,000	—	—	0.50	2.00	—
1967MW	29,099,000	—	—	1.00	5.00	—
1968MW	29,191,000	—	—	1.00	5.00	—
1969MW	40,227,000	—	—	0.50	1.50	—
1970MW	20,028,000	—	—	0.10	1.00	—
1971MW	20,000,000	—	—	0.10	1.00	—
1972MW	60,000,000	—	—	0.10	1.00	—
1973	50,000,000	—	—	0.10	0.50	—
Note: Struck at Kremnica Mint						
1973MW	65,000,000	—	—	0.10	0.50	—
Note: Struck at Kremnica Mint						
1975MW	50,000,000	—	—	0.10	0.50	—
1976MW Large date	100,000,000	—	—	0.10	0.50	—
1976MW Small date	Inc. above	—	—	0.10	0.50	—
1977MW	80,730,000	—	—	0.10	0.20	—
1978MW	50,730,000	—	—	0.10	0.20	—
1979MW	45,252,000	—	—	0.10	0.20	—
1979MW Proof	5,000	Value: 1.00				

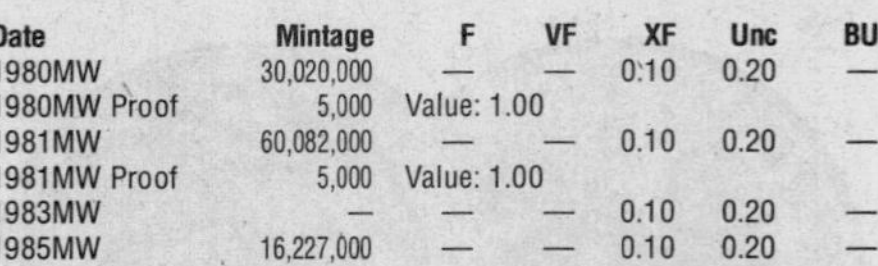

Date	Mintage	F	VF	XF	Unc	BU
1980MW	30,020,000	—	—	0.10	0.20	—
1980MW Proof	5,000	Value: 1.00				
1981MW	60,082,000	—	—	0.10	0.20	—
1981MW Proof	5,000	Value: 1.00				
1983MW	—	—	—	0.10	0.20	—
1985MW	16,227,000	—	—	0.10	0.20	—

Y# 48.1 50 GROSZY

1.6000 g., Aluminum, 23 mm. **Obv:** Eagle with wings open **Rev:** Value above sprig

Date	Mintage	F	VF	XF	Unc	BU
1957	91,316,000	—	0.75	2.00	5.00	—
1965MW	22,090,000	—	0.25	1.50	4.00	—
1967MW	2,027,000	—	1.25	4.00	15.00	—
1968MW	2,065,000	—	1.25	4.00	15.00	—
1970MW	3,273,000	—	0.15	0.30	2.00	—
1971MW	7,000,000	—	0.10	0.25	1.00	—
1972MW	10,000,000	—	0.10	0.25	0.50	—
1973MW	39,000	—	0.10	0.20	0.50	—
1974MW	33,000,000	—	0.10	0.20	0.50	—
1975	25,000,000	—	0.10	0.20	0.50	—
Note: Struck at Kremnica Mint						
1976	25,000,000	—	0.10	0.20	0.40	—
Note: Struck at Kremnica Mint						
1977MW	50,000,000	—	0.10	0.20	0.40	—
1978MW	50,020,000	—	0.10	0.20	0.40	—
1978	18,600,000	—	0.10	0.20	0.40	—
Note: Struck at Kremnica Mint						
1982MW	16,067,000	—	0.10	0.20	0.40	—
1982MW Proof	5,000	Value: 3.50				
1983MW	39,667,000	—	0.10	0.20	0.40	—
1984MW	44,217,000	—	0.10	0.20	0.40	—
1985MW	49,052,000	—	0.10	0.20	0.40	—

Y# 48.2 50 GROSZY

1.6000 g., Aluminum, 23 mm. **Obv:** Eagle with wings open **Rev:** Value above sprig

Date	Mintage	F	VF	XF	Unc	BU
1986MW	45,796,000	—	0.10	0.20	0.40	—
1986MW Proof	5,000	Value: 3.50				
1987MW	21,257,000	—	0.10	0.20	0.40	—
1987MW Proof	5,000	Value: 3.50				

Y# 49.1 ZLOTY

2.1000 g., Aluminum, 25 mm. **Obv:** Eagle with wings open **Rev:** Value within wreath

Date	Mintage	F	VF	XF	Unc	BU
1957	58,631,000	—	1.00	3.50	20.00	—
1965MW	15,015,000	—	0.50	1.00	3.00	—
1966MW	18,185,000	—	0.75	2.00	4.00	—
1967MW	1,002,000	—	2.25	6.00	15.00	—
1968MW	1,176,000	—	2.25	6.00	15.00	—
1969MW	3,024,000	—	1.25	3.00	6.00	—
1970MW	6,016,000	—	0.15	0.50	1.50	—
1971MW	6,000,000	—	0.15	0.50	1.00	—
1972MW	7,000,000	—	0.15	0.50	1.00	—
1973MW	15,000,000	—	0.10	0.50	1.00	—
1974MW	42,000,000	—	0.10	0.15	0.50	—
1975	22,000,000	—	0.10	0.15	0.50	—
Note: Struck at Kremnica Mint						
1975MW	33,000,000	—	0.10	0.15	0.50	—
1976	22,000,000	—	0.10	0.50	1.00	—
Note: Struck at Kremnica Mint						
1977MW	65,000,000	—	0.10	0.50	1.00	—
1978	16,399,999	—	0.10	0.50	1.50	—
Note: Struck at Kremnica Mint						
1978MW	80,000,000	—	0.10	0.50	1.00	—
1980MW	100,002,000	—	0.10	0.15	0.50	—
1980MW Proof	5,000	Value: 2.50				
1981MW	4,082,000	—	0.10	0.15	1.00	—
1981MW Proof	5,000	Value: 2.50				
1982MW	59,643,000	—	0.10	0.15	0.30	—

Date	Mintage	F	VF	XF	Unc	BU
1982MW Proof	5,000	Value: 3.50				
1983MW	49,636,000	—	0.10	0.15	0.25	—
1984MW	61,036,000	—	0.10	0.15	0.25	—
1985MW	167,939,000	—	0.10	0.15	0.25	—

Y# 49.2 ZLOTY

2.1000 g., Aluminum, 25 mm. **Obv:** Eagle with wings open **Rev:** Value within wreath

Date	Mintage	F	VF	XF	Unc	BU
1986MW	130,697,000	—	0.10	0.15	0.25	—
1986MW Proof	5,000	Value: 3.50				
1987MW	100,081,000	—	0.10	0.15	0.25	—
1987MW Proof	5,000	Value: 3.50				
1988MW	96,400,000	—	0.10	0.15	0.25	—
1988MW Proof	5,000	Value: 3.50				

Y# 49.3 ZLOTY

Aluminum **Obv:** Eagle with wings open **Rev:** Value within wreath

Date	Mintage	F	VF	XF	Unc	BU
1989MW	49,410,000	—	0.10	0.15	0.25	—
1989MW Proof	5,000	Value: 3.50				
1990MW	30,667,000	—	0.10	0.15	0.25	—
1990MW Proof	5,000	Value: 3.50				

Y# 46 2 ZLOTE

Aluminum, 27 mm. **Obv:** Eagle with wings open **Rev:** Value above design and fruit

Date	Mintage	F	VF	XF	Unc	BU
1958	83,640,000	—	0.20	1.50	6.00	—
1959	7,170,000	—	0.50	4.00	20.00	—
1960	36,131,000	—	0.20	0.50	3.00	—
1970MW	2,013,999	—	0.30	1.00	4.00	—
1971MW	3,000,000	—	0.20	1.00	4.00	—
1972MW	3,000,000	—	0.20	1.00	4.00	—
1973MW	10,000,000	—	0.15	0.50	1.50	—
1974MW	46,000,000	—	0.15	0.30	1.00	—

Y# 80.1 2 ZLOTE

2.9500 g., Brass, 21 mm. **Obv:** Eagle with wings open **Rev:** Value above design

Date	Mintage	F	VF	XF	Unc	BU
1975	25,000,000	—	0.15	0.25	0.50	—
Note: Struck at Leningrad Mint						
1976	60,000,000	—	0.15	0.25	0.50	—
Note: Struck at Leningrad Mint						
1977	50,000,000	—	0.15	0.25	0.50	—
Note: Struck at Leningrad Mint						
1978	2,600,000	—	0.15	0.25	1.75	—
Note: Struck at Leningrad Mint						
1978MW	2,382,000	—	0.15	0.25	1.75	—
1979MW	85,752,000	—	0.15	0.25	0.50	—
1979MW Proof	5,000	Value: 2.50				
1980MW	66,610,000	—	0.15	0.25	0.50	—
1980MW Proof	5,000	Value: 2.50				
1981MW	40,306,000	—	0.15	0.25	0.50	—
1981MW Proof	5,000	Value: 2.50				
1982MW	43,318,000	—	0.15	0.25	0.50	—
1982MW Proof	5,000	Value: 3.50				
1983MW	35,244,000	—	0.15	0.25	0.50	—
1984MW	59,999,000	—	0.15	0.25	0.50	—
1985MW	100,300,000	—	0.15	0.25	0.50	—

Y# 80.2 2 ZLOTE

Brass **Obv:** Eagle with wings open **Rev:** Value above design

Date	Mintage	F	VF	XF	Unc	BU
1986MW	60,718,000	—	0.15	0.25	0.50	—
1986MW Proof	5,000	Value: 3.50				
1987MW	44,673,000	—	0.15	0.25	0.50	—
1987MW Proof	5,000	Value: 3.50				
1988MW	94,651,000	—	0.15	0.25	0.50	—
1988MW Proof	5,000	Value: 3.50				

Y# 80.3 2 ZLOTE

Aluminum, 17.9 mm. **Obv:** Eagle with wings open **Rev:** Value above design

Date	Mintage	F	VF	XF	Unc	BU
1989MW	91,494,000	—	0.10	0.20	0.40	—
1989MW Proof	5,000	Value: 3.50				
1990MW	40,723,000	—	0.10	0.20	0.40	—
1990MW Proof	5,000	Value: 3.50				

Y# 47 5 ZLOTYCH

Aluminum **Obv:** Eagle with wings open **Rev:** Fisherman with net

Date	Mintage	F	VF	XF	Unc	BU
1958	1,328,000	—	7.50	12.50	20.00	—
Note: Two date varieties exist for strikes dated 1958						
1959	56,811,000	—	0.75	2.50	7.00	—
1960	16,300,999	—	0.25	1.50	5.00	—
1971MW	1,000,000	—	7.50	12.50	20.00	—
1973MW	5,000,000	—	0.20	1.00	4.00	—
1974MW	46,000,000	—	0.20	0.50	2.50	—

Y# 81.1 5 ZLOTYCH

4.8000 g., Brass, 24 mm. **Obv:** Eagle with wings open **Rev:** Value **Note:** Variety of size of letters exist.

Date	Mintage	F	VF	XF	Unc	BU
1975	25,000,000	—	0.20	0.40	0.85	—
Note: Struck at Leningrad Mint						
1976	60,000,000	—	0.20	0.40	0.85	—
Note: Struck at Leningrad Mint						
1977	50,000,000	—	0.20	0.40	0.85	—
Note: Struck at Leningrad Mint						
1978MW Rare	—	—	—	—	—	—
1979MW	5,098,000	—	0.20	0.40	1.50	—
1979MW	5,000	Value: 3.50				
1980MW	10,100,000	—	0.20	0.40	0.85	—
1980MW Proof	5,000	Value: 2.50				
1981MW	4,008,000	—	0.20	0.40	1.75	—
1981MW Proof	5,000	Value: 2.50				
1982MW	25,379,000	—	0.20	0.40	0.85	—
1982MW Proof	5,000	Value: 3.50				
1983MW	30,531,000	—	0.20	0.40	0.85	—
1984MW	85,598,000	—	0.20	0.40	0.85	—
1985MW	20,501,000	—	0.20	0.40	0.85	—

Y# 81.2 5 ZLOTYCH

4.8000 g., Brass, 24 mm. **Obv:** Eagle with wings open **Rev:** Value

Date	Mintage	F	VF	XF	Unc	BU
1986MW	57,108,000	—	0.20	0.40	0.85	—
1986MW Proof	5,000	Value: 3.50				
1987MW	58,843,000	—	0.20	0.40	0.85	—
1987MW Proof	5,000	Value: 3.50				
1988MW	18,668,000	—	0.20	0.40	0.85	—
1988MW Proof	5,000	Value: 3.50				

Y# 81.3 5 ZLOTYCH

Aluminum, 20 mm. **Obv:** Eagle with wings open **Rev:** Value

Date	Mintage	F	VF	XF	Unc	BU
1989MW	30,253,000	—	0.15	0.30	0.65	—
1989MW Proof	5,000	Value: 3.50				
1990MW	38,248,000	—	0.15	0.30	0.65	—
1990MW Proof	5,000	Value: 3.50				

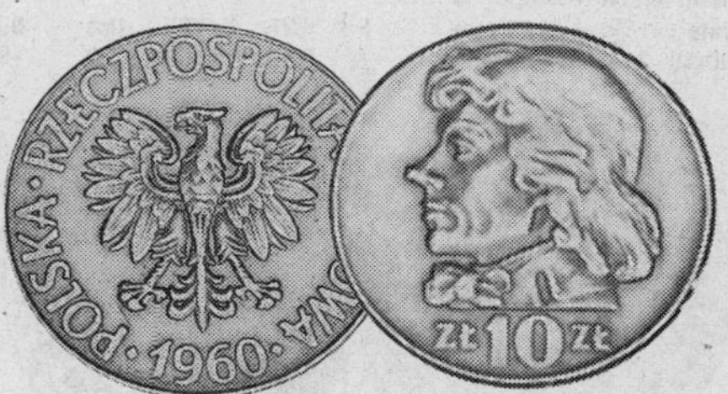

Y# 50 10 ZLOTYCH

Copper-Nickel, 31 mm. **Obv:** Eagle with wings open **Rev:** Head of Tadeusz Kosciuszko left

Date	Mintage	F	VF	XF	Unc	BU
1959	13,107,000	—	0.60	2.00	6.50	—
1960	27,551,000	—	0.60	2.00	6.50	—
1966MW	4,157,000	—	1.00	8.00	18.00	—

Y# 50a 10 ZLOTYCH

Copper-Nickel, 28 mm. **Obv:** Eagle with wings open **Rev:** Head of Tadeusz Kosciuszko left **Note:** Reduced size.

Date	Mintage	F	VF	XF	Unc	BU
1969MW	5,428,000	—	0.50	1.75	5.00	—
1970MW	13,783,000	—	0.50	1.00	2.00	—
1971MW	12,000,000	—	0.50	1.00	2.00	—
1972MW	10,000,000	—	0.50	1.00	2.00	—
1973MW	3,900,000	—	0.50	2.00	8.00	—

Y# 51 10 ZLOTYCH

Copper-Nickel, 31 mm. **Obv:** Eagle with wings open **Rev:** Bust of Mikolaj Kopernik facing **Designer:** J.G. Miedzionkiel

Date	Mintage	F	VF	XF	Unc	BU
1959	12,559,000	—	0.75	1.25	2.50	—
1965MW	3,000,000	—	1.00	5.00	15.00	—

Y# 51a 10 ZLOTYCH

Copper-Nickel, 28 mm. **Obv:** Eagle with wings open **Rev:** Bust of Mikolaj Kopernik facing **Designer:** J.G. Miedzionkiel **Note:** Reduced size.

Date	Mintage	F	VF	XF	Unc	BU
1967MW	2,128,000	—	0.75	2.00	7.50	—
1968MW	9,389,000	—	0.75	1.25	2.50	—
1969MW	8,612,000	—	0.75	1.25	2.75	—

Y# 52 10 ZLOTYCH

Copper-Nickel, 31 mm. **Subject:** 600th Anniversary of Jagiello University **Obv:** Eagle with wings open **Rev:** Stylized crowned head left **Note:** Legends raised.

Date	Mintage	F	VF	XF	Unc	BU
ND(1964)	2,610,000	—	0.50	1.50	3.50	—

Y# 52a 10 ZLOTYCH

Copper-Nickel, 31 mm. **Subject:** 600th Anniversary of Jagiello University **Obv:** Eagle with wings open **Rev:** Stylized crowned head left **Note:** Legends incuse.

Date	Mintage	F	VF	XF	Unc	BU
ND(1964)	2,612,000	—	0.50	1.50	3.50	—

Y# 54 10 ZLOTYCH

Copper-Nickel, 31 mm. **Subject:** 700th Anniversary of Warsaw **Obv:** Eagle with wings open **Rev:** Nike of Warsaw with sword **Designer:** Waclaw Kowalic

Date	Mintage	F	VF	XF	Unc	BU
1965MW	3,492,000	—	0.75	2.00	3.50	5.00

Y# 55 10 ZLOTYCH

Copper-Nickel, 31 mm. **Subject:** 700th Anniversary of Warsaw **Obv:** Stylized eagle with wings open **Rev:** Sigismund Pillar **Designer:** Jerzy Jarnuszkiewics

Date	Mintage	F	VF	XF	Unc	BU
1965MW	2,000,000	—	0.75	2.00	3.50	5.00

Y# 56 10 ZLOTYCH

Copper-Nickel, 28 mm. **Subject:** 200th Anniversary of Warsaw Mint **Obv:** Stylized eagle with wings open **Rev:** Sigismund Pillar **Edge Lettering:** W DWNSETNA ROCZNICE MENNICY WARSZAWSKIEJ **Designer:** Jerzy Jarnuszkiewicz

Date	Mintage	F	VF	XF	Unc	BU
1966MW	102,000	—	2.50	6.50	22.50	40.00

Y# 58 10 ZLOTYCH

Copper-Nickel, 28 mm. **Subject:** 20th Anniversary - Death of General Swierczewski **Obv:** Eagle with wings open **Rev:** Military head left

Date	Mintage	F	VF	XF	Unc	BU
1967MW	2,000,000	—	0.50	1.00	2.25	—

Y# 59 10 ZLOTYCH

Copper-Nickel, 28 mm. **Subject:** Centennial - Birth of Marie Sklodowska Curie **Obv:** Eagle with wings open **Rev:** Head facing

Date	Mintage	F	VF	XF	Unc	BU
1967MW	2,000,000	—	0.50	1.00	2.25	—

Y# 60 10 ZLOTYCH

Copper-Nickel, 28 mm. **Subject:** 25th Anniversary - Peoples Army **Obv:** Eagle with wings open standing on perch **Rev:** XXV and helmeted head right **Designer:** Josef Markiewicz

Date	Mintage	F	VF	XF	Unc	BU
1968MW	2,000,000	—	0.50	1.00	2.25	—

Y# 61 10 ZLOTYCH

Copper-Nickel, 28 mm. **Subject:** 25th Anniversary - Peoples Republic **Obv:** Eagle with wings open within circle **Rev:** Radiant design within circle

Date	Mintage	F	VF	XF	Unc	BU
1969MW	2,000,000	—	0.50	1.00	2.25	—

Y# 62 10 ZLOTYCH

Copper-Nickel, 28 mm. **Subject:** 25th Anniversary - Provincial Annexations **Obv:** Eagle with wings open, shield divides value **Rev:** Assorted shields **Designer:** Jerzy Jarnuszkiewicz

Date	Mintage	F	VF	XF	Unc	BU
1970MW	2,000,000	—	0.50	1.00	2.25	—

Y# 63 10 ZLOTYCH

Copper-Nickel, 28 mm. **Series:** F.A.O. **Obv:** Eagle with wings open on shield **Rev:** Atlantic turbot and ear of barley

Date	Mintage	F	VF	XF	Unc	BU
1971MW	2,000,000	—	0.75	1.50	3.50	5.00

Y# 64 10 ZLOTYCH

Copper-Nickel, 28 mm. **Subject:** 50th Anniversary - Battle of Upper Silesia **Obv:** Eagle with wings open divides date **Rev:** Design and emblem

Date	Mintage	F	VF	XF	Unc	BU
1971MW	2,000,000	—	0.50	1.00	2.25	—

Y# 65 10 ZLOTYCH

Copper-Nickel, 28 mm. **Subject:** 50th Anniversary - Gdynia Seaport **Obv:** Eagle with wings open **Rev:** Map and emblem

Date	Mintage	F	VF	XF	Unc	BU
1972MW	2,000,000	—	0.50	1.00	2.25	—

Y# 73 10 ZLOTYCH

Copper-Nickel **Obv:** Eagle with wings open divides date **Rev:** Head of Boleslaw Prus left

Date	Mintage	F	VF	XF	Unc	BU
1975MW	35,000,000	—	0.25	0.65	1.25	—
1976MW	20,000,000	—	0.25	0.65	1.25	—
1977MW	25,000,000	—	0.25	0.65	1.25	—
1978MW	4,006,999	—	0.25	0.75	2.25	—
1981MW	2,655,000	—	0.25	1.00	3.75	—
1981MW Proof	5,000	Value: 5.50				
1982MW	16,341,000	—	0.25	0.65	1.25	—
1982MW Proof	5,000	Value: 6.50				
1983MW	14,248,000	—	0.25	0.65	1.25	—
1984MW	19,064,000	—	0.25	0.65	1.25	—

Y# 74 10 ZLOTYCH

Copper-Nickel **Obv:** Eagle with wings open **Rev:** Head of Adam Micklewicz left

Date	Mintage	F	VF	XF	Unc	BU
1975MW	35,000,000	—	0.25	0.65	1.25	—
1976MW	20,000,000	—	0.25	0.65	1.25	—

Y# 152.1 10 ZLOTYCH
7.7000 g., Copper-Nickel, 25 mm. **Obv:** Eagle with wings open **Rev:** Value

Date	Mintage	F	VF	XF	Unc	BU
1984MW	15,756,000	—	0.20	0.50	1.00	—
1985MW	5,282,000	—	0.20	0.50	1.00	—
1986MW	31,043,000	—	0.20	0.50	1.00	—
1986MW Proof	5,000	Value: 4.00				
1987MW	69,636,000	—	0.20	0.50	1.00	—
1987MW Proof	5,000	Value: 4.00				
1988MW	102,493,000	—	0.20	0.50	1.00	—
1988MW Proof	5,000	Value: 4.00				

Y# 152.2 10 ZLOTYCH
Brass, 21.8 mm. **Obv:** Imperial eagle **Rev:** Value

Date	Mintage	F	VF	XF	Unc	BU
1989MW	80,800,000	—	0.20	0.40	0.80	—
1989MW Proof	5,000	Value: 4.00				
1990MW	106,892,000	—	0.20	0.40	0.80	—
1990MW Proof	5,000	Value: 4.00				

Y# 67 20 ZLOTYCH
Copper-Nickel, 28.8 mm. **Obv:** Eagle with wings open within circle **Rev:** Value within designed waterfall

Date	Mintage	F	VF	XF	Unc	BU
1973	25,000,000	—	0.25	1.00	2.50	—
Note: Struck at Kremnica Mint						
1974	12,000,000	—	0.25	0.75	1.50	—
Note: Struck at Kremnica Mint						
1976	20,000,000	—	0.25	0.75	1.50	—
Note: Struck at Warsaw Mint						

Y# 69 20 ZLOTYCH
Copper-Nickel, 28.8 mm. **Obv:** Eagle with wings open, value below **Rev:** Bust of Marceli Nowotko 1/4 left **Designer:** Stanislaw Watrobska

Date	Mintage	F	VF	XF	Unc	BU
1974MW	10,000,000	—	0.25	1.00	2.50	—
1975	10,000,000	—	0.25	1.00	2.00	—
Note: Struck at Kremnica Mint						
1976	20,000,000	—	0.25	0.75	1.50	—
Note: Struck at Kremnica Mint						
1976MW	30,000,000	—	0.25	0.75	1.50	—
1977MW	16,000,000	—	0.25	1.00	2.00	—
1983MW	152,000	—	0.25	5.00	12.50	—

Y# 70 20 ZLOTYCH
Copper-Nickel, 28.8 mm. **Subject:** 25th Anniversary of the Comcon **Obv:** Imperial eagle above value **Rev:** Half sunflower, half cog wheel

Date	Mintage	F	VF	XF	Unc	BU
1974MW	2,000,000	—	0.75	1.25	2.50	—

Y# 75 20 ZLOTYCH
Copper-Nickel, 28.8 mm. **Subject:** International Women's Year **Obv:** Imperial eagle above value **Rev:** Stylized head left

Date	Mintage	F	VF	XF	Unc	BU
1975MW	2,000,000	—	0.75	1.25	2.50	—

Y# 95 20 ZLOTYCH
Copper-Nickel, 28.8 mm. **Obv:** Imperial eagle above value **Rev:** Head of Maria Konopnicka facing

Date	Mintage	F	VF	XF	Unc	BU
1978MW	2,010,000	—	0.75	1.25	2.75	—

Y# 97 20 ZLOTYCH
Copper-Nickel, 28.8 mm. **Subject:** First Polish Cosmonaut **Obv:** Imperial eagle above value **Rev:** Cosmonaut head 1/4 left

Date	Mintage	F	VF	XF	Unc	BU
1978MW	2,009,000	—	0.75	1.25	2.75	—

Y# 99 20 ZLOTYCH
Copper-Nickel, 28.8 mm. **Series:** International Year of the Child **Obv:** Imperial eagle above value **Rev:** Children playing

Date	Mintage	F	VF	XF	Unc	BU
1979MW	2,007,000	—	1.00	1.50	3.00	—
1979MW Proof	5,000	Value: 12.00				

Y# 108 20 ZLOTYCH
Copper-Nickel, 28.8 mm. **Series:** 1980 Olympics **Obv:** Imperial eagle above value **Rev:** Runner

Date	Mintage	F	VF	XF	Unc	BU
1980MW	2,012,000	—	1.00	1.75	5.00	—
1980MW Proof	5,000	Value: 12.00				

Y# 112 20 ZLOTYCH
Copper-Nickel, 28.8 mm. **Subject:** 50th Anniversary - Training Ship Daru Pomorza **Obv:** Imperial eagle above value **Rev:** Sailing ship

Date	Mintage	F	VF	XF	Unc	BU
1980MW	2,007,000	—	1.00	1.75	3.50	—
1980MW Proof	5,000	Value: 10.00				

Y# 153.1 20 ZLOTYCH
8.7000 g., Copper-Nickel, 26.4 mm. **Obv:** Eagle with wings open **Rev:** Value **Note:** Circulation coinage.

Date	Mintage	F	VF	XF	Unc	BU
1984MW	12,703,000	—	0.25	0.60	1.25	1.50
1985MW	15,514,000	—	0.25	0.60	1.25	1.50
1986MW	37,959,000	—	0.25	0.60	1.25	1.50
1986MW Proof	5,000	Value: 4.00				
1987MW	22,213,000	—	0.25	0.60	1.25	1.50
1987MW Proof	5,000	Value: 4.00				
1988MW	14,994,000	—	0.25	0.60	1.25	1.50
1988MW Proof	5,000	Value: 4.00				

Y# 153.2 20 ZLOTYCH
Copper-Nickel, 23.9 mm. **Obv:** Eagle with wings open **Rev:** Value **Note:** Reduced size.

Date	Mintage	F	VF	XF	Unc	BU
1989MW	95,974,000	—	0.25	0.35	0.75	1.00
1989MW Proof	5,000	Value: 4.00				
1990MW	104,712,000	—	0.25	0.35	0.75	1.00
1990MW Proof	5,000	Value: 4.00				

Y# 66 50 ZLOTYCH
12.6400 g., 0.7500 Silver .3048 oz. ASW, 30 mm. **Obv:** Eagle with wings open **Rev:** Head of Fryderyk Chopin left **Designer:** Jerry Jarnuskiewicz

Date	Mintage	F	VF	XF	Unc	BU
1972MW Proof	50,000	Value: 20.00				
1974MW Proof	10,000	Value: 22.00				

Y# 100 50 ZLOTYCH

Copper-Nickel, 30 mm. **Obv:** Imperial eagle above value **Rev:** Bust of Duke Mieszko I 3/4 left

Date	Mintage	F	VF	XF	Unc	BU
1979MW	2,640,000	—	1.00	2.00	5.00	—
1979MW Proof	5,000	Value: 15.00				

Y# 114 50 ZLOTYCH

Copper-Nickel, 30 mm. **Obv:** Imperial eagle above value **Rev:** King Boleslaw I Chrobry

Date	Mintage	F	VF	XF	Unc	BU
1980MW	2,564,000	—	1.00	2.00	5.00	—
1980MW Proof	5,000	Value: 12.50				

Y# 117 50 ZLOTYCH

Copper-Nickel, 30 mm. **Obv:** Imperial eagle above value **Rev:** Crowned bust of Duke Kazimierz I Odnowiciel facing

Date	Mintage	F	VF	XF	Unc	BU
1980MW	2,504,000	—	1.00	2.00	5.00	—
1980MW Proof	5,000	Value: 12.50				

Y# 122 50 ZLOTYCH

Copper-Nickel, 30 mm. **Obv:** Imperial eagle above value **Rev:** General Broni Wladyslaw Sikorski left

Date	Mintage	F	VF	XF	Unc	BU
1981MW	2,505,000	—	1.00	2.00	5.00	—
1981MW Proof	5,000	Value: 12.50				

Y# 124 50 ZLOTYCH

Copper-Nickel, 30 mm. **Obv:** Imperial eagle above value **Rev:** Crowned bust of King Boleslaw II Smialy 1/4 right

Date	Mintage	F	VF	XF	Unc	BU
1981MW	2,538,000	—	1.00	2.00	4.50	—
1981MW Proof	5,000	Value: 12.00				

Y# 128 50 ZLOTYCH

Copper-Nickel, 30 mm. **Obv:** Imperial eagle above value **Rev:** Head of King Wladyslaw I Herman 3/4 left

Date	Mintage	F	VF	XF	Unc	BU
1981MW	2,500,000	—	1.00	2.00	4.50	—
1981MW Proof	5,000	Value: 12.00				

Y# 127 50 ZLOTYCH

Copper-Nickel, 30 mm. **Series:** F.A.O. - World Food Day **Obv:** Imperial eagle above value **Rev:** F.A.O. logo within circle

Date	Mintage	F	VF	XF	Unc	BU
1981MW	2,524,000	—	1.00	2.00	4.50	—
1981MW Proof	5,000	Value: 12.00				

Y# 133 50 ZLOTYCH

Copper-Nickel, 30 mm. **Obv:** Imperial eagle above value **Rev:** King Boleslaw III Krzywousty

Date	Mintage	F	VF	XF	Unc	BU
1982MW	2,616,000	—	1.00	2.00	4.50	—
1982MW Proof	5,000	Value: 12.50				

Y# 142 50 ZLOTYCH

Copper-Nickel, 30 mm. **Subject:** 150th Anniversary of Great Theater **Obv:** Imperial eagle above value **Rev:** Theater building

Date	Mintage	F	VF	XF	Unc	BU
1983MW	615,000	—	1.00	4.00	8.00	—

Y# 145 50 ZLOTYCH

Copper-Nickel, 30 mm. **Obv:** Imperial eagle above value **Rev:** King Jan III Sobieski facing **Designer:** Stanislawa Watrobska-Frindl

Date	Mintage	F	VF	XF	Unc	BU
1983MW	2,576,000	—	1.00	2.00	4.50	—

Y# 146 50 ZLOTYCH

Copper-Nickel, 30 mm. **Obv:** Imperial eagle above value **Rev:** Bust of Ignacy Lukasiewicz right **Designer:** Stanislawa Watrobska-Frindl

Date	Mintage	F	VF	XF	Unc	BU
1983MW	612,000	—	1.00	4.00	8.00	—

Y# 57 100 ZLOTYCH

20.0000 g., 0.9000 Silver .5787 oz. ASW **Subject:** Polish Millennium **Obv:** Eagle with wings open within assorted shields around border **Rev:** Two figures standing behind shield within circle

Date	Mintage	F	VF	XF	Unc	BU
1966MW	198,000	—	—	9.50	13.50	22.50

Y# 68 100 ZLOTYCH

16.5000 g., 0.6250 Silver .3316 oz. ASW **Subject:** 500th Anniversary - Birth of Mikolaj Kopernik, scientist **Obv:** Eagle with wings open within circle **Rev:** Head of Mikolaj Kopernik 1/4 left

Date	Mintage	F	VF	XF	Unc	BU
1973MW Proof	51,000	Value: 20.00				
1974MW Proof	50,000	Value: 20.00				

Y# 71 100 ZLOTYCH

16.5000 g., 0.6250 Silver .3316 oz. ASW **Subject:** 40th Anniversary - Death of Maria Sklodowska Curie **Obv:** Imperial eagle above value **Rev:** Profile of Curie left with radiation lines running from the symbol of the element at right

Date	Mintage	F	VF	XF	Unc	BU
1974MW Proof	50,000	Value: 15.50				

Y# 76 100 ZLOTYCH

16.5000 g., 0.6250 Silver .3316 oz. ASW **Obv:** Imperial eagle above value **Rev:** Royal castle in Warsaw

Date	Mintage	F	VF	XF	Unc	BU
1975MW Proof	50,000	Value: 15.50				

Y# 77 100 ZLOTYCH

16.5000 g., 0.6250 Silver .3316 oz. ASW **Obv:** Imperial eagle above value **Rev:** Ignacy Jan Paderewski, composer, left

Date	Mintage	F	VF	XF	Unc	BU
1975MW Proof	60,000	Value: 12.50				

Y# 78 100 ZLOTYCH

16.5000 g., 0.6250 Silver .3316 oz. ASW **Obv:** Imperial eagle above value **Rev:** Bust of Helena Modrzejewska right

Date	Mintage	F	VF	XF	Unc	BU
1975MW Proof	60,000	Value: 12.50				

Y# 82 100 ZLOTYCH

16.5000 g., 0.6250 Silver .3316 oz. ASW **Obv:** Imperial eagle above value **Rev:** Tadeusz Kosciuszko right

Date	Mintage	F	VF	XF	Unc	BU
1976MW Proof	100,000	Value: 12.50				

Y# 84 100 ZLOTYCH

16.5000 g., 0.6250 Silver .3316 oz. ASW **Obv:** Imperial eagle above value **Rev:** Head of Kazimierz Pulaski left

Date	Mintage	F	VF	XF	Unc	BU
1976MW Proof	100,000	Value: 12.50				

Y# 87 100 ZLOTYCH

16.5000 g., 0.6250 Silver .3316 oz. ASW **Series:** Environment Protection **Obv:** Imperial eagle above value **Rev:** Buffalo

Date	Mintage	F	VF	XF	Unc	BU
1977MW Proof	30,000	Value: 30.00				

Y# 88 100 ZLOTYCH

16.5000 g., 0.6250 Silver .3316 oz. ASW **Obv:** Imperial eagle above value **Rev:** Henryk Sienkiewicz, Writer, left

Date	Mintage	F	VF	XF	Unc	BU
1977MW Proof	20,000	Value: 20.00				

Y# 89 100 ZLOTYCH

16.5000 g., 0.6250 Silver .3316 oz. ASW **Obv:** Imperial eagle above value **Rev:** Head of Wladyslaw Reymont 1/4 right

Date	Mintage	F	VF	XF	Unc	BU
1977MW Proof	20,000	Value: 30.00				

Y# 91 100 ZLOTYCH

16.5000 g., 0.6250 Silver .3316 oz. ASW **Obv:** Imperial eagle above value **Rev:** Castle

Date	Mintage	F	VF	XF	Unc	BU
1977MW Proof	30,000	Value: 27.50				

Y# 92 100 ZLOTYCH

16.5000 g., 0.6250 Silver .3316 oz. ASW **Obv:** Imperial eagle above value **Rev:** Bust of Adam Mickiewicz facing

Date	Mintage	F	VF	XF	Unc	BU
1978MW Proof	30,000	Value: 16.50				

Y# 93 100 ZLOTYCH

16.5000 g., 0.6250 Silver .3316 oz. ASW **Series:** Environment Protection **Obv:** Imperial eagle above value **Rev:** Moose heading left

Date	Mintage	F	VF	XF	Unc	BU
1978MW Proof	30,000	Value: 27.50				

Y# 94 100 ZLOTYCH

16.5000 g., 0.6250 Silver .3316 oz. ASW **Subject:** 100th Anniversary - Birth of Janusz Korczak **Obv:** Imperial eagle above value **Rev:** Bust facing

Date	Mintage	F	VF	XF	Unc	BU
1978MW Proof	30,000	Value: 16.50				

Y# 96 100 ZLOTYCH

16.5000 g., 0.6250 Silver .3316 oz. ASW **Series:** Environment Protection **Obv:** Imperial eagle above value **Rev:** Beaver

Date	Mintage	F	VF	XF	Unc	BU
1978MW Proof	30,000	Value: 30.00				

Y# 98 100 ZLOTYCH

16.5000 g., 0.6250 Silver .3316 oz. ASW **Obv:** Imperial eagle above value **Rev:** Head of Henryk Wieniawski 3/4 left

Date	Mintage	F	VF	XF	Unc	BU
1979MW Proof	30,000	Value: 16.50				

Y# 103 100 ZLOTYCH

16.5000 g., 0.6250 Silver .3316 oz. ASW **Obv:** Imperial eagle above value **Rev:** Ludwik Zamenhof left

Date	Mintage	F	VF	XF	Unc	BU
1979MW Proof	30,000	Value: 16.50				

Y# 104 100 ZLOTYCH

16.5000 g., 0.6250 Silver .3316 oz. ASW **Series:** Environment Protection **Obv:** Imperial eagle above value **Rev:** Lynx

Date	Mintage	F	VF	XF	Unc	BU
1979MW Proof	20,000	Value: 27.50				

Y# 105 100 ZLOTYCH

16.5000 g., 0.6250 Silver .3316 oz. ASW **Series:** Environment Protection **Obv:** Imperial eagle above value **Rev:** Chamois

Date	Mintage	F	VF	XF	Unc	BU
1979MW Proof	20,000	Value: 27.50				

Y# 120 100 ZLOTYCH

16.5000 g., 0.6250 Silver .3316 oz. ASW **Subject:** 450th Anniversary - Birth of Jan Kochanowski, Poet **Obv:** Imperial eagle above value **Rev:** Bust of Jan Kochanowski 1/4 right

Date	Mintage	F	VF	XF	Unc	BU
1980MW Proof	10,000	Value: 45.00				

Y# 109 100 ZLOTYCH

16.5000 g., 0.6250 Silver .3316 oz. ASW **Series:** 1980 Olympics **Obv:** Imperial eagle above value **Rev:** Olympic rings and runner

Date	Mintage	F	VF	XF	Unc	BU
1980MW Proof	10,000	Value: 32.50				

Y# 121 100 ZLOTYCH

16.5000 g., 0.6250 Silver .3316 oz. ASW **Series:** Environment Protection **Obv:** Imperial eagle above value **Rev:** Cappercaillie

Date	Mintage	F	VF	XF	Unc	BU
1980MW Proof	18,000	Value: 27.50				

Y# 123 100 ZLOTYCH

16.5000 g., 0.6250 Silver .3316 oz. ASW **Obv:** Imperial eagle above value **Rev:** General Broni Wladyslaw Sikorski left

Date	Mintage	F	VF	XF	Unc	BU
1981MW Proof	12,000	Value: 20.00				

Y# 126 100 ZLOTYCH

16.5000 g., 0.6250 Silver .3316 oz. ASW **Series:** Environment Protection **Obv:** Imperial eagle above value **Rev:** Horse right

Date	Mintage	F	VF	XF	Unc	BU
1981MW Proof	12,000	Value: 27.50				

Y# 136 100 ZLOTYCH

14.1500 g., 0.7500 Silver .3412 oz. ASW **Subject:** Visit of Pope John Paul II **Obv:** Imperial eagle above value **Rev:** Bust left

Date	Mintage	F	VF	XF	Unc	BU
1982CHI	8,700	—	—	—	55.00	—
1982CHI Proof	3,750	Value: 100				
1985CHI Rare	1	—	—	—	—	—
1985CHI Proof, rare	5	—	—	—	—	—
1986CHI	80	—	—	—	450	—
1986CHI Proof	128	Value: 500				

Y# 141 100 ZLOTYCH

16.5000 g., 0.6250 Silver .3316 oz. ASW **Series:** Environment Protection **Obv:** Imperial eagle above value **Rev:** Stork walking right

Date	Mintage	F	VF	XF	Unc	BU
1982MW Proof	12,000	Value: 27.50				

Y# 147 100 ZLOTYCH

16.5000 g., 0.6250 Silver .3316 oz. ASW **Series:** Environment Protection **Obv:** Imperial eagle above value **Rev:** Bear walking right **Designer:** E. Tyc-Karpinski

Date	Mintage	F	VF	XF	Unc	BU
1983MW Proof	8,000	Value: 40.00				

Y# 148 100 ZLOTYCH
Copper-Nickel, 29 mm. **Obv:** Imperial eagle above value **Rev:** Wincenty Witos 3/4 facing

Date	Mintage	F	VF	XF	Unc	BU
1984MW	1,530,000	—	—	—	3.00	5.00

Y# 151 100 ZLOTYCH
Copper-Nickel, 29 mm. **Subject:** 40th Anniversary of Peoples Republic **Obv:** Imperial eagle above value **Rev:** 40 PRL within design

Date	Mintage	F	VF	XF	Unc	BU
1984MW	2,595,000	—	—	—	3.00	5.00

Y# 155 100 ZLOTYCH
Copper-Nickel, 29 mm. **Obv:** Imperial eagle above value **Rev:** King Przemyslaw II

Date	Mintage	F	VF	XF	Unc	BU
1985MW	2,924,000	—	—	—	3.00	5.00

Y# 157 100 ZLOTYCH
Nickel Plated Steel, 29 mm. **Subject:** Polish Women's Memorial Hospital Center **Obv:** Imperial eagle above value **Rev:** Woman breast-feeding Child

Date	Mintage	F	VF	XF	Unc	BU
1985MW	1,927,000	—	—	—	3.00	5.00

Y# 160 100 ZLOTYCH
Copper-Nickel, 29 mm. **Obv:** Imperial eagle above value **Rev:** Bust of King Wladyslaw I Lokietek 1/4 right

Date	Mintage	F	VF	XF	Unc	BU
1986MW	2,540,000	—	—	—	3.00	5.00
1986MW Proof	5,000	Value: 12.00				

Y# 167 100 ZLOTYCH
Copper-Nickel, 29 mm. **Obv:** Imperial eagle above value **Rev:** King Kazimierz III half left

Date	Mintage	F	VF	XF	Unc	BU
1987MW	2,479,000	—	—	—	3.50	5.50
1987MW Proof	5,000	Value: 12.50				

Y# 182 100 ZLOTYCH
Copper-Nickel, 29 mm. **Subject:** 70th Anniversary - Wielkopolskiego Insurrection **Obv:** Imperial eagle above value **Rev:** Uniformed conjoined busts left

Date	Mintage	F	VF	XF	Unc	BU
1988MW	2,513,000	—	—	—	3.00	5.00
1988MW Proof	5,000	Value: 12.00				

Y# 183 100 ZLOTYCH
Copper-Nickel, 29 mm. **Obv:** Imperial eagle above value **Rev:** Queen Jadwiga 1384-1399

Date	Mintage	F	VF	XF	Unc	BU
1988MW	2,469,000	—	—	—	3.00	5.00
1988MW Proof	5,000	Value: 12.00				

Y# 72 200 ZLOTYCH
14.4700 g., 0.6250 Silver .2907 oz. ASW, 31.3 mm. **Subject:** 30th Anniversary - Polish Peoples Republic **Obv:** Eagle with wings open within square with value below **Rev:** XXX LAT PRL in square within shaded design

Date	Mintage	F	VF	XF	Unc	BU
1974MW	13,062,000	—	—	—	4.50	6.50
1974MW Proof	6,000	Value: 22.50				

Y# 79 200 ZLOTYCH
14.4700 g., 0.7500 Silver .3490 oz. ASW, 31 mm. **Subject:** 30th Anniversary - Victory Over Fascism **Obv:** Eagle with wings open divides date **Rev:** Conjoined military heads left

Date	Mintage	F	VF	XF	Unc	BU
1975MW	1,826,000	—	—	—	7.00	10.00
1975MW Proof	2,600	Value: 25.00				

Y# 86 200 ZLOTYCH
14.4700 g., 0.6250 Silver .2907 oz. ASW **Series:** XXI Olympics **Obv:** Imperial eagle above value **Rev:** Rings and torch

Date	Mintage	F	VF	XF	Unc	BU
1976MW	2,072,000	—	—	—	8.50	12.00
1976MW Proof	11,000	Value: 22.50				

Y# 101 200 ZLOTYCH
17.6000 g., 0.7500 Silver .4244 oz. ASW **Obv:** Imperial eagle above value **Rev:** Uniformed bust of Duke Mieszko I 1/4 left

Date	Mintage	F	VF	XF	Unc	BU
1979MW Proof	12,000	Value: 150				

Y# 110 200 ZLOTYCH
17.6000 g., 0.7500 Silver .4244 oz. ASW **Series:** Winter Olympics **Obv:** Imperial eagle above value **Rev:** Torch below ski jumper

Date	Mintage	F	VF	XF	Unc	BU
1980MW Proof	32,000	Value: 16.50				

Y# 110a 200 ZLOTYCH
17.6000 g., 0.7500 Silver .4244 oz. ASW **Series:** Winter Olympics **Obv:** Imperial eagle above value **Rev:** Ski jumper, no torch below

Date	Mintage	F	VF	XF	Unc	BU
1980MW Proof	28,000	Value: 14.50				

Y# 115 200 ZLOTYCH
17.6000 g., 0.7500 Silver .4244 oz. ASW **Obv:** Imperial eagle above value **Rev:** King Boleslaw I Chrobry

Date	Mintage	F	VF	XF	Unc	BU
1980MW Proof	12,000	Value: 100				

Y# 118 200 ZLOTYCH
17.6000 g., 0.7500 Silver .4244 oz. ASW **Obv:** Imperial eagle above value **Rev:** Bust of Duke Kazimierz I facing

Date	Mintage	F	VF	XF	Unc	BU
1980MW Proof	12,000	Value: 45.00				

Y# 125 200 ZLOTYCH
17.6000 g., 0.7500 Silver .4244 oz. ASW **Obv:** Imperial eagle above value **Rev:** King Bolaslaw II Smialy 3/4 facing

Date	Mintage	F	VF	XF	Unc	BU
1981MW Proof	12,000	Value: 45.00				

Y# 129 200 ZLOTYCH
17.6000 g., 0.7500 Silver .4244 oz. ASW **Obv:** Imperial eagle above value **Rev:** Bust of King Wladyslaw I Herman left within circle

Date	Mintage	F	VF	XF	Unc	BU
1981MW Proof	12,000	Value: 45.00				

Y# 130 200 ZLOTYCH
17.6000 g., 0.7500 Silver .4244 oz. ASW **Subject:** World Soccer Championship Games in Spain **Obv:** Imperial eagle above value **Rev:** Stylized soccer player, date and names within grid-lined background

Date	Mintage	F	VF	XF	Unc	BU
1982MW Proof	21,000	Value: 16.50				

Y# 132 200 ZLOTYCH
17.6000 g., 0.7500 Silver .4244 oz. ASW **Obv:** Imperial eagle above value **Rev:** King Boleslaw III Krzywousty

Date	Mintage	F	VF	XF	Unc	BU
1982MW Proof	12,000	Value: 50.00				

Y# 137 200 ZLOTYCH
28.3000 g., 0.7500 Silver .6825 oz. ASW **Subject:** Visit of Pope John Paul II **Obv:** Imperial eagle above value **Rev:** Bust left

Date	Mintage	F	VF	XF	Unc	BU
1982CHI	3,000	—	—	—	475	575
1982CHI Proof	3,650	Value: 600				
1985CHI Proof, rare	5	—	—	—	—	—

Date	Mintage	F	VF	XF	Unc	BU
1985CHI Rare	1	—	—	—	—	—
1986CHI	32	—	—	—	850	—
1986CHI Proof	75	Value: 900				

Y# 143 200 ZLOTYCH

17.6000 g., 0.7500 Silver .4244 oz. ASW **Obv:** Imperial eagle above value **Rev:** King Jan III Sobieski

Date	Mintage	F	VF	XF	Unc	BU
1983MW Proof	11,000	Value: 45.00				

Y# 149 200 ZLOTYCH

17.6000 g., 0.7500 Silver .4244 oz. ASW **Series:** Winter Olympics **Obv:** Imperial eagle above value **Rev:** Ice skater

Date	Mintage	F	VF	XF	Unc	BU
1984MW Proof	15,000	Value: 22.50				

Y# 150 200 ZLOTYCH

17.6000 g., 0.7500 Silver .4244 oz. ASW **Series:** Summer Olympics **Obv:** Imperial eagle above value **Rev:** Hurdler

Date	Mintage	F	VF	XF	Unc	BU
1984MW Proof	16,000	Value: 20.00				

Y# 83 500 ZLOTYCH

30.0000 g., 0.9000 Gold .8681 oz. AGW **Obv:** Imperial eagle above value **Rev:** Head of Tadeusz Kosciuszko right

Date	Mintage	F	VF	XF	Unc	BU
1976MW	2,318	—	—	—	900	—

Y# 85 500 ZLOTYCH

30.0000 g., 0.9000 Gold .8681 oz. AGW **Obv:** Imperial eagle above value **Rev:** Kazimierz Pulaski left

Date	Mintage	F	VF	XF	Unc	BU
1976MW	2,315	—	—	—	900	—

Y# 154 500 ZLOTYCH

16.5000 g., 0.6250 Silver .3283 oz. ASW **Series:** Environment Protection **Obv:** Imperial eagle above value **Rev:** Swan and two chicks **Designer:** Ewa Olszewska-Borys

Date	Mintage	F	VF	XF	Unc	BU
1984MW Proof	10,000	Value: 35.00				

Y# 156 500 ZLOTYCH

16.5000 g., 0.7500 Silver .3979 oz. ASW **Obv:** Imperial eagle above value **Rev:** King Przemyslaw II

Date	Mintage	F	VF	XF	Unc	BU
1985MW Proof	8,000	Value: 65.00				

Y# 158 500 ZLOTYCH

16.5000 g., 0.7500 Silver .3979 oz. ASW **Subject:** 40th Anniversary of United Nations **Obv:** Imperial eagle above value **Rev:** UN logo within sprigs

Date	Mintage	F	VF	XF	Unc	BU
1985MW Proof	10,000	Value: 27.50				

Y# 159 500 ZLOTYCH

16.5000 g., 0.7500 Silver .3979 oz. ASW **Series:** Environmental Protection **Obv:** Imperial eagle above value **Rev:** Red squirrel

Date	Mintage	F	VF	XF	Unc	BU
1985MW Proof	8,000	Value: 40.00				

Y# 161 500 ZLOTYCH

16.5000 g., 0.7500 Silver .3979 oz. ASW **Obv:** Imperial eagle above value **Rev:** King Wladyslaw I Lokietek half right

Date	Mintage	F	VF	XF	Unc	BU
1986MW Proof	8,000	Value: 65.00				

Y# 162 500 ZLOTYCH

16.5000 g., 0.7500 Silver .3979 oz. ASW **Series:** Environment Protection **Obv:** Eagle with wings open divides date **Rev:** Owl with 2 chicks

Date	Mintage	F	VF	XF	Unc	BU
1986MW Proof	12,000	Value: 40.00				

Y# 225 500 ZLOTYCH

16.5000 g., 0.7500 Silver .3979 oz. ASW **Obv:** Imperial eagle above value **Rev:** Soccer ball in net

Date	Mintage	F	VF	XF	Unc	BU
1986MW Proof	16,000	Value: 30.00				

Y# 165 500 ZLOTYCH

16.5000 g., 0.7500 Silver .3979 oz. ASW **Series:** Olympics **Obv:** Imperial eagle above value **Rev:** Equestrian

Date	Mintage	F	VF	XF	Unc	BU
1987MW Proof	15,000	Value: 25.00				

Y# 166 500 ZLOTYCH

16.5000 g., 0.7500 Silver .3979 oz. ASW **Subject:** European Championship Soccer Games **Obv:** Imperial eagle above value **Rev:** Soccer player

Date	Mintage	F	VF	XF	Unc	BU
1987MW Proof	12,000	Value: 27.50				

Y# 172 500 ZLOTYCH

16.5000 g., 0.7500 Silver .3979 oz. ASW **Series:** Winter Olympics **Obv:** Imperial eagle above value **Rev:** Ice hockey goalie

Date	Mintage	F	VF	XF	Unc	BU
1987MW Proof	15,000	Value: 18.50				

Y# 173 500 ZLOTYCH

16.5000 g., 0.7500 Silver .3979 oz. ASW **Obv:** Imperial eagle above value **Rev:** Bust of King Kazimierz III 3/4 facing

Date	Mintage	F	VF	XF	Unc	BU
1987MW Proof	8,000	Value: 60.00				

Y# 181 500 ZLOTYCH

16.5000 g., 0.7500 Silver .3979 oz. ASW **Obv:** Imperial eagle above value **Rev:** Crowned bust of Queen Jadwiga facing

Date	Mintage	F	VF	XF	Unc	BU
1988MW Proof	8,000	Value: 200				

Y# 184 500 ZLOTYCH

16.5000 g., 0.7500 Silver .3979 oz. ASW **Obv:** Imperial eagle above value **Rev:** Colosseum within split soccer ball

Date	Mintage	F	VF	XF	Unc	BU
1988MW Proof	15,000	Value: 22.50				

Y# 185 500 ZLOTYCH

Copper-Nickel, 29 mm. **Subject:** 50th Anniversary - Beginning of WWII **Obv:** Imperial eagle above value **Rev:** Infantry soldiers advancing

Date	Mintage	F	VF	XF	Unc	BU
1989MW	10,135,000	—	—	—	2.50	4.00
1989MW Proof	5,000	Value: 12.00				

Y# 194 500 ZLOTYCH

Copper-Nickel, 29 mm. **Obv:** Imperial eagle above value **Rev:** Bust of King Wladyslaw II 1/4 left

Date	Mintage	F	VF	XF	Unc	BU
1989MW	2,544,000	—	—	—	3.00	5.00
1989MW Proof	5,000	Value: 12.00				

Y# 138 1000 ZLOTYCH

3.4000 g., 0.9000 Gold .0984 oz. AGW **Subject:** Visit of Pope John Paul II **Obv:** Eagle with wings open divides date **Rev:** 1/2 Figure of Pope 1/4 left

Date	Mintage	F	VF	XF	Unc	BU
1982CHI	900	—	—	—	450	—
1982CHI Proof	1,700	Value: 500				
1985CHI Rare	1	—	—	—	—	—
1985CHI Proof, rare	2	—	—	—	—	—
1986CHI	83	—	—	—	700	—
1986CHI Proof	53	Value: 850				

Y# 144 1000 ZLOTYCH

14.5000 g., 0.7500 Silver .3497 oz. ASW **Subject:** Visit of Pope John Paul II **Obv:** Imperial eagle above value **Rev:** Bust left **Designer:** Stanislawa Watrobska-Frindl

Date	Mintage	F	VF	XF	Unc	BU
1982MW	803,000	—	—	—	10.00	12.00
1983MW	1,530,000	—	—	—	9.00	10.00
1983MW Proof	10,000	Value: 27.50				

Y# 168 1000 ZLOTYCH

3.1100 g., 0.9990 Gold .1000 oz. AGW **Subject:** Papal Visit in America **Obv:** Imperial eagle above value **Rev:** Half figure of Pope 3/4 left **Note:** Similar to KM#163.

Date	Mintage	F	VF	XF	Unc	BU
1987MW Proof	201	Value: 400				

Y# 174 1000 ZLOTYCH

3.1100 g., 0.9990 Gold .1000 oz. AGW **Subject:** 10th Anniversary of Pope John Paul II **Obv:** Imperial eagle above value **Rev:** Bust left **Note:** Similar to KM#177.

Date	Mintage	F	VF	XF	Unc	BU
1988MW Proof	1,000	Value: 225				

Y# 186 1000 ZLOTYCH

3.1100 g., 0.9990 Gold .1000 oz. AGW **Subject:** Pope John Paul II **Obv:** Imperial eagle above value **Rev:** Bust left on patterned background

Date	Mintage	F	VF	XF	Unc	BU
1989MW In sets only	Est. 1,000	—	—	—	200	—

Y# 90 2000 ZLOTYCH

8.0000 g., 0.9000 Gold .2315 oz. AGW **Obv:** Eagle with wings open divides date **Rev:** Head of Fryderyk Chopin left

Date	Mintage	F	VF	XF	Unc	BU
1977MW Proof	4,000	Value: 375				

Y# 102 2000 ZLOTYCH

8.0000 g., 0.9000 Gold .2315 oz. AGW **Obv:** Eagle with wings open divides date **Rev:** Duke Mieszko I

Date	Mintage	F	VF	XF	Unc	BU
1979MW Proof	3,000	Value: 375				

Y# 106 2000 ZLOTYCH

8.0000 g., 0.9000 Gold .2315 oz. AGW **Obv:** Eagle with wings open divides date **Rev:** Head of Mikolaj Kopernik 1/4 right

Date	Mintage	F	VF	XF	Unc	BU
1979MW Proof	5,000	Value: 350				

Y# 107 2000 ZLOTYCH

8.0000 g., 0.9000 Gold .2315 oz. AGW **Obv:** Eagle with wings open divides date **Rev:** Profile of Maria Skiodowska Curie left, symbol at right

Date	Mintage	F	VF	XF	Unc	BU
1979MW Proof	5,000	Value: 350				

Y# 111 2000 ZLOTYCH

8.0000 g., 0.9000 Gold .2315 oz. AGW **Series:** Winter Olympics **Obv:** Imperial eagle above value **Rev:** Ski jumper

Date	Mintage	F	VF	XF	Unc	BU
1980MW Proof	5,250	Value: 350				

Y# 116 2000 ZLOTYCH

8.0000 g., 0.9000 Gold .2315 oz. AGW **Obv:** Imperial eagle above value **Rev:** King Boleslaw I Chrobry

Date	Mintage	F	VF	XF	Unc	BU
1980MW Proof	2,500	Value: 375				

Y# 119 2000 ZLOTYCH

8.0000 g., 0.9000 Gold .2315 oz. AGW **Obv:** Imperial eagle above value **Rev:** Kazimierz I

Date	Mintage	F	VF	XF	Unc	BU
1980MW Proof	2,500	Value: 375				

Y# 131 2000 ZLOTYCH

8.0000 g., 0.9000 Gold .2315 oz. AGW **Obv:** Imperial eagle above value **Rev:** Wladyslaw I Herman **Note:** Similar to 200 Zlotych, Y#129.

Date	Mintage	F	VF	XF	Unc	BU
1981MW Proof	3,113	Value: 375				

Y# 135 2000 ZLOTYCH

8.0000 g., 0.9000 Gold .2315 oz. AGW **Obv:** Imperial eagle above value **Rev:** Boleslaw II

Date	Mintage	F	VF	XF	Unc	BU
1981MW Proof	—	Value: 375				

Y# 139 2000 ZLOTYCH

6.8000 g., 0.9000 Gold .1968 oz. AGW **Subject:** Visit of Pope John Paul II **Obv:** Imperial eagle above value **Rev:** Half-figure of Pope 1/4 left

Date	Mintage	F	VF	XF	Unc	BU
1982CHI	500	—	—	—	800	—
1982CHI Proof	1,250	Value: 900				
1985CHI Rare	1	—	—	—	—	—
1985CHI Proof, rare	Est. 2	—	—	—	—	—
1986CHI	Est. 54	—	—	—	1,250	—
1986CHI Proof	Est. 79	Value: 1,300				

Y# 169 2000 ZLOTYCH

7.7700 g., 0.9990 Gold .2500 oz. AGW **Subject:** Papal Visit in America **Obv:** Imperial eagle above value **Rev:** Half-figure of Pope with staff left **Note:** Similar to KM#163.

Date	Mintage	F	VF	XF	Unc	BU
1987MW Proof	201	Value: 500				

Y# 175 2000 ZLOTYCH

7.7700 g., 0.9990 Gold .2500 oz. AGW **Subject:** 10th Anniversary of Pope John Paul II **Obv:** Imperial eagle above value **Rev:** Bust left **Note:** Similar to KM#177.

Date	Mintage	F	VF	XF	Unc	BU
1988 Proof	1,000	Value: 275				

Y# 187 2000 ZLOTYCH

7.7700 g., 0.9990 Gold .2500 oz. AGW **Obv:** Imperial eagle above value **Rev:** Bust left on patterned background **Note:** Pope John Paul II.

Date	Mintage	F	VF	XF	Unc	BU
1989MW In sets only	Est. 1,000	—	—	—	250	—

Y# 170 5000 ZLOTYCH

15.5500 g., 0.9990 Gold .5000 oz. AGW **Subject:** Papal Visit in America **Obv:** Imperial eagle above value **Rev:** Half-figure of Pope with staff left **Note:** Similar to KM#163.

Date	Mintage	F	VF	XF	Unc	BU
1987MW Proof	201	Value: 700				

Y# 176 5000 ZLOTYCH

15.5500 g., 0.9990 Gold .5000 oz. AGW **Subject:** 10th Anniversary of Pope John Paul II **Obv:** Imperial eagle above value **Rev:** Bust left **Note:** Similar to KM#177.

Date	Mintage	F	VF	XF	Unc	BU
1988MW Proof	1,000	Value: 500				

Y# 188 5000 ZLOTYCH

15.5500 g., 0.9990 Gold .5000 oz. AGW **Obv:** Imperial eagle above value **Rev:** Bust left on patterned background **Note:** Pope John Paul II.

Date	Mintage	F	VF	XF	Unc	BU
1989MW In sets only	Est. 1,000,000	—	—	—	475	—

Y# 191 5000 ZLOTYCH

16.5000 g., 0.7500 Silver .3978 oz. ASW **Obv:** Eagle with wings open divides date **Rev:** Circular design in front of bust facing 1/4 left, building in background

Date	Mintage	F	VF	XF	Unc	BU
1989MW Proof	20,000	Value: 45.00				

Y# 192 5000 ZLOTYCH

16.5000 g., 0.7500 Silver .3978 oz. ASW **Obv:** Imperial eagle above value **Rev:** Torunia Town Hall

Date	Mintage	F	VF	XF	Unc	BU
1989MW Proof	20,000	Value: 40.00				

Y# 193 5000 ZLOTYCH

16.5000 g., 0.7500 Silver .3978 oz. ASW **Obv:** Imperial eagle above value **Rev:** Henryk Sucharski

Date	Mintage	F	VF	XF	Unc	BU
1989MW Proof	25,000	Value: 35.00				

Y# 197 5000 ZLOTYCH

16.5000 g., 0.7500 Silver .3978 oz. ASW **Obv:** Imperial eagle above value **Rev:** Bust of King Wladyslaw II

Date	Mintage	F	VF	XF	Unc	BU
1989MW Proof	8,000	Value: 85.00				

Y# 198 5000 ZLOTYCH

16.5000 g., 0.7500 Silver .3978 oz. ASW **Obv:** Imperial eagle above value **Rev:** Half-length portrait of King Wladyslaw II

Date	Mintage	F	VF	XF	Unc	BU
1989MW Proof	2,500	Value: 300				

Y# 140 10000 ZLOTYCH

34.5000 g., 0.9000 Gold .9984 oz. AGW **Subject:** Visit of Pope John Paul II **Obv:** Imperial eagle above value **Rev:** Half-figure of Pope 1/4 left

Date	Mintage	F	VF	XF	Unc	BU
1982CHI	200	—	—	—	1,850	—
1982CHI Proof	700	Value: 1,950				
1985CHI Proof, rare	1	—	—	—	—	—
1986CHI Rare	Est. 6	—	—	—	—	—
1986CHI Proof, rare	Est. 13	—	—	—	—	—

Y# 399 10000 ZLOTYCH

28.3100 g., 0.9000 Silver .8192 oz. ASW, 40.2 mm. **Subject:** Pope John Paul II **Obv:** Imperial eagle above value **Rev:** Bust of Pope left **Edge:** Plain

Date	Mintage	F	VF	XF	Unc	BU
1986 Proof	9	Value: 2,000				

Y# 164 10000 ZLOTYCH

19.0600 g., 0.7500 Silver .4582 oz. ASW **Subject:** Papal Visit **Obv:** Imperial eagle above value **Rev:** 1/2 Figure of Pope 1/4 left

Date	Mintage	F	VF	XF	Unc	BU
1987MW	908,000	—	—	—	30.00	40.00
1987MW Proof	15,000	Value: 75.00				

Y# 171 10000 ZLOTYCH

31.1030 g., 0.9990 Gold 1.0000 oz. AGW **Subject:** Papal Visit in America **Obv:** Imperial eagle above value **Rev:** Half-figure of Pope left **Note:** Similar to KM#163.

Date	Mintage	F	VF	XF	Unc	BU
1987MW Proof	201	Value: 1,350				

Y# 177 10000 ZLOTYCH

31.1030 g., 0.9990 Gold 1.0000 oz. AGW **Subject:** 10th Anniversary of Pope John Paul II **Obv:** Imperial eagle above value **Rev:** Bust left

Date	Mintage	F	VF	XF	Unc	BU
1988MW	1,000	—	—	—	975	—
1988MW Proof	1,000	Value: 1,000				

Y# 177a 10000 ZLOTYCH

31.1030 g., 0.9990 Silver 1.0000 oz. ASW **Subject:** 10th Anniversary of Pope John Paul II **Obv:** Imperial eagle above value **Rev:** Bust left

Date	Mintage	F	VF	XF	Unc	BU
1988MW	5,000	—	—	—	—	—
1988MW Proof	—	Value: 300				

Y# 179 10000 ZLOTYCH

31.1030 g., 0.9990 Silver 1.0000 oz. ASW **Subject:** Pope John Paul - Christmas **Obv:** Imperial eagle above value **Rev:** Bust of Pope left with right hand raised

Date	Mintage	F	VF	XF	Unc	BU
1988MW Proof	5,000	Value: 250				

Y# 189 10000 ZLOTYCH

31.1030 g., 0.9990 Gold 1.0000 oz. AGW **Subject:** Pope John Paul II **Obv:** Imperial eagle above value **Rev:** Bust left on patterned background

Date	Mintage	F	VF	XF	Unc	BU
1989MW Proof	Est. 2,000	Value: 850				

Y# 189a 10000 ZLOTYCH

31.1000 g., 0.9990 Silver 1.0000 oz. ASW **Obv:** Imperial eagle above value **Rev:** Pope John Paul II

Date	Mintage	F	VF	XF	Unc	BU
1989MW	—	—	—	—	—	—
1989MW Proof	5,000	Value: 265				

Y# 237 10000 ZLOTYCH

31.1000 g., 0.9990 Silver 1.0000 oz. ASW **Obv:** Imperial eagle above value **Rev:** 3/4 Figure of Pope right

Date	Mintage	F	VF	XF	Unc	BU
1989MW Proof	—	Value: 125				

Y# 223 20000 ZLOTYCH

19.0000 g., 0.7500 Silver .4558 oz. ASW **Obv:** Imperial eagle above value **Rev:** Soccer ball, map, and globe

Date	Mintage	F	VF	XF	Unc	BU
1989 Proof	25,000	Value: 35.00				

Y# 224 20000 ZLOTYCH

19.0000 g., 0.7500 Silver .4558 oz. ASW **Obv:** Eagle with wings open divides date **Rev:** Soccer player behind vertical lines, all within circle

Date	Mintage	F	VF	XF	Unc	BU
1989 Proof	25,000	Value: 35.00				

Y# 180 50000 ZLOTYCH

19.3000 g., 0.7500 Silver .4654 oz. ASW **Subject:** 70 Years of Polish Independence **Obv:** Imperial eagle above value **Rev:** Head left

Date	Mintage	F	VF	XF	Unc	BU
1988	1,000,000	—	—	—	20.00	25.00
1988 Proof	20,000	Value: 65.00				

Y# 163 200000 ZLOTYCH

373.2420 g., 0.9990 Gold 12.0000 oz. AGW, 70 mm. **Subject:** Papal Visit in America **Obv:** Imperial eagle above value **Rev:** Half-figure with staff left **Note:** Photo reduced.

Date	Mintage	F	VF	XF	Unc	BU
1987 Proof	101	Value: 9,500				

Y# 178 200000 ZLOTYCH

373.2420 g., 0.9990 Gold 12.0000 oz. AGW, 70 mm. **Subject:** 10th Anniversary of Pope John Paul II **Obv:** Imperial eagle above value **Rev:** Bust with chin resting on thumbs left **Note:** Photo reduced.

Date	Mintage	F	VF	XF	Unc	BU
1988MW Proof	300	Value: 9,250				

Y# 190 200000 ZLOTYCH

373.2420 g., 0.9990 Gold 12.0000 oz. AGW **Obv:** Imperial eagle above value **Rev:** Pope John Paul II **Note:** Similar to KM#189.

Date	Mintage	F	VF	XF	Unc	BU
1989MW Proof	Est. 200	Value: 9,250				

REPUBLIC

Democratic

STANDARD COINAGE

Y# 216 50 ZLOTYCH
Copper-Nickel **Obv:** Crowned eagle with wings open, date below **Rev:** Value with sprig in 0

Date	Mintage	F	VF	XF	Unc	BU
1990MW	28,707,000	—	—	—	1.25	2.00
1990MW Proof	5,000	Value: 12.00				

Y# 214 100 ZLOTYCH
Copper-Nickel **Obv:** Crowned eagle with wings open **Rev:** Value with sprig in first 0

Date	Mintage	F	VF	XF	Unc	BU
1990MW	37,341,000	—	—	—	2.00	3.00
1990MW Proof	5,000	Value: 15.00				

Y# 195 10000 ZLOTYCH
Copper-Nickel, 29 mm. **Subject:** 10th Anniversary of Solidarity **Obv:** Crowned eagle with wings open divides date **Rev:** Solidarity monument with city view background **Designer:** Bohdan Chmielewski

Date	Mintage	F	VF	XF	Unc	BU
1990MW	15,164,000	—	—	—	4.50	6.00
1990MW Proof	5,000	Value: 16.50				

Y# 217 10000 ZLOTYCH
Nickel Plated Steel, 29.5 mm. **Subject:** 200th Anniversary of Polish Constitution **Obv:** Crowned eagle with wings open divides date **Rev:** Crowned eagle above inscription, crowned monogram below **Designer:** Ewa Tyc-Karpinski

Date	Mintage	F	VF	XF	Unc	BU
1991MW	2,605,000	—	—	—	6.00	8.00

Y# 246 10000 ZLOTYCH
Copper-Nickel, 29 mm. **Obv:** Crowned eagle with wings open divides date **Rev:** Wladyslaw III 3/4 left

Date	Mintage	F	VF	XF	Unc	BU
1992MW	2,500,000	—	—	—	3.50	5.00

Y# 219 20000 ZLOTYCH
3.1100 g., 0.9990 Gold .1 oz. AGW **Subject:** 10th Anniversary of Solidarity **Obv:** Crowned eagle **Rev:** Solidarity monument with city view background **Note:** Similar to 10000 Zlotych, Y#195.

Date	Mintage	F	VF	XF	Unc	BU
1990 Proof	1,004	Value: 145				

Y# 215 20000 ZLOTYCH
Bi-Metallic Copper-Nickel center in Brass ring **Subject:** 225th Anniversary of Warsaw Mint **Obv:** Crowned eagle with wings open divides date, all within circle **Rev:** Crowned monogram divides date, all within circle **Designer:** Stanislawa Watrobska-Frindl

Date	Mintage	F	VF	XF	Unc	BU
1991MW	100,000	—	—	—	18.00	22.00

Y# 243 20000 ZLOTYCH
Copper-Nickel, 29 mm. **Obv:** Imperial eagle above value **Rev:** Barn swallows

Date	Mintage	F	VF	XF	Unc	BU
1993MW	500,000	—	—	—	7.50	10.00

Y# 244 20000 ZLOTYCH
Copper-Nickel, 29 mm. **Obv:** Crowned eagle with wings open divides date, all within circle **Rev:** Lancut Castle

Date	Mintage	F	VF	XF	Unc	BU
1993MW	500,000	—	—	—	4.50	6.00

Y# 256 20000 ZLOTYCH
Copper-Nickel, 29 mm. **Obv:** Imperial eagle above value **Rev:** Kazimierz IV

Date	Mintage	F	VF	XF	Unc	BU
1993	1,500,000	—	—	—	4.50	6.00

Y# 261 20000 ZLOTYCH
Copper-Nickel, 29 mm. **Series:** Olympics **Obv:** Crowned eagle with wings open divides date **Rev:** Slalom skier

Date	Mintage	F	VF	XF	Unc	BU
1993	988,000	—	—	—	7.50	10.00

Y# 265 20000 ZLOTYCH
Copper-Nickel **Subject:** 75th Anniversary - Disabled Association **Obv:** Crowned eagle with wings open divides date **Rev:** Shield and rose within designed circle

Date	Mintage	F	VF	XF	Unc	BU
1994	75,000	—	—	—	4.50	6.00

Y# 270 20000 ZLOTYCH
Copper-Nickel **Obv:** Crowned eagle with wings open divides date **Rev:** New mint building

Date	Mintage	F	VF	XF	Unc	BU
1994	252,000	—	—	—	4.50	6.00

Y# 271 20000 ZLOTYCH
Copper-Nickel **Subject:** 200th Anniversary - Kosciuszko Insurrection **Obv:** Crowned eagle with wings open divides date **Rev:** Head left in circle within ship

Date	Mintage	F	VF	XF	Unc	BU
1994	100,000	—	—	—	5.00	7.00

Y# 272 20000 ZLOTYCH
Copper-Nickel **Obv:** Imperial eagle above value **Rev:** Zygmunt I, 1506-1548

Date	Mintage	F	VF	XF	Unc	BU
1994	1,500,000	—	—	—	4.50	6.00

Y# 220 50000 ZLOTYCH
13.1000 g., 0.9990 Gold .4212 oz. AGW **Subject:** 10th Anniversary of Solidarity **Obv:** Imperial eagle above value **Rev:** Solidarity monument with city view background **Note:** Similar to 10000 Zlotych, Y#195.

Date	Mintage	F	VF	XF	Unc	BU
1990 Proof	1,001	Value: 400				

Y# 229 50000 ZLOTYCH
Copper-Nickel **Subject:** 200th Anniversary of Order Virtuti Militari **Obv:** Crowned eagle with wings open divides date, all within beaded circle **Rev:** Military medal and crowned monogram **Shape:** Octagonal

Date	Mintage	F	VF	XF	Unc	BU
1992 Proof	100,000	Value: 12.50				

Y# 196.1 100000 ZLOTYCH
31.1000 g., 0.9990 Silver 1.0000 oz. ASW **Subject:** 10th Anniversary of Solidarity **Obv:** Imperial eagle above value **Rev:** Solidarity monument with city view background **Designer:** Bohdan Chmielewski

Date	Mintage	F	VF	XF	Unc	BU
1990	500,000	—	—	—	18.00	22.00
1990 Proof	—	Value: 85.00				

Y# 196.2 100000 ZLOTYCH
31.1000 g., 0.9990 Silver 1.0000 oz. ASW, 31.9 mm. **Subject:** 10th Anniversary of Solidarity **Obv:** Imperial eagle above value **Rev:** Solidarity monument with city view background **Designer:** Bohdan Chmielewski **Note:** Reduced size.

Date	Mintage	F	VF	XF	Unc	BU
1990 Proof	—	Value: 65.00				

Y# 199 100000 ZLOTYCH
31.1000 g., 0.9990 Silver 1.0000 oz. ASW **Obv:** Imperial eagle above value **Rev:** Fryderyk Chopin

Date	Mintage	F	VF	XF	Unc	BU
1990 Proof	10,000	Value: 35.00				

Y# 200 100000 ZLOTYCH
31.1000 g., 0.9990 Silver 1.0000 oz. ASW **Obv:** Imperial eagle above value **Rev:** Uniformed figure on horse

Date	Mintage	F	VF	XF	Unc	BU
1990 Proof	10,000	Value: 35.00				

Y# 201 100000 ZLOTYCH
31.1000 g., 0.9990 Silver 1.0000 oz. ASW **Obv:** Imperial eagle above value **Rev:** Uniformed bust of Marszalek Pilsudski 1/4 left

Date	Mintage	F	VF	XF	Unc	BU
1990 Proof	10,000	Value: 35.00				

Y# 221 100000 ZLOTYCH
15.5500 g., 0.9990 Gold .5000 oz. AGW **Subject:** 10th Anniversary of Solidarity **Obv:** Imperial eagle above value **Rev:** Buildiings, symbols **Note:** Similar to 10000 Zlotych, Y#195.

Date	Mintage	F	VF	XF	Unc	BU
1990 Proof	Est. 1,000	Value: 450				

Y# 235 100000 ZLOTYCH
16.5000 g., 0.7500 Silver .3979 oz. ASW **Series:** WWII **Obv:** Crowned eagle with wings open divides date **Rev:** Cavalry facing right, flanked by trees **Designer:** Bohdan Chmielewski

Date	Mintage	F	VF	XF	Unc	BU
1991 Proof	12,000	Value: 27.50				

Y# 236 100000 ZLOTYCH
16.5000 g., 0.7500 Silver .3979 oz. ASW **Series:** WWII **Subject:** Defense of Narvik **Obv:** Imperial eagle above value **Rev:** Polish troops

Date	Mintage	F	VF	XF	Unc	BU
1991 Proof	12,000	Value: 27.50				

Y# 238 100000 ZLOTYCH
16.5000 g., 0.7500 Silver .3979 oz. ASW **Series:** WWII **Obv:** Imperial eagle above value **Rev:** Polish troops at Battle of Tobruk

Date	Mintage	F	VF	XF	Unc	BU
1991 Proof	12,000	Value: 27.50				

Y# 239 100000 ZLOTYCH
16.5000 g., 0.7500 Silver .3979 oz. ASW **Series:** WWII **Obv:** Imperial eagle above value **Rev:** Polish pilots in Battle of Britain

Date	Mintage	F	VF	XF	Unc	BU
1991 Proof	12,000	Value: 27.50				

Y# 227 100000 ZLOTYCH
16.5000 g., 0.7500 Silver .3979 oz. ASW **Subject:** Unification of Upper Silesia and Poland **Obv:** Imperial eagle above value **Rev:** Bust 3/4 left, inscription at left

Date	Mintage	F	VF	XF	Unc	BU
1992 Proof	30,000	Value: 27.50				

Y# 268 100000 ZLOTYCH
16.5000 g., 0.9000 Silver .4775 oz. ASW **Subject:** Warsaw Uprising **Obv:** Imperial eagle above value **Rev:** Soldier with gun

Date	Mintage	F	VF	XF	Unc	BU
1994 Proof	150,000	Value: 32.50				

Y# 240 200000 ZLOTYCH
19.0600 g., 0.9990 Silver .6122 oz. ASW **Obv:** Imperial eagle above value **Rev:** Gen. Dyw. Stefan Rowecki "Grot" facing

Date	Mintage	F	VF	XF	Unc	BU
1990 Proof	25,000	Value: 45.00				
1991 Proof	—	Value: 45.00				

Y# 202 200000 ZLOTYCH
155.5000 g., 0.9990 Silver 5.0000 oz. ASW **Obv:** Imperial eagle above value **Rev:** Fryderyk Chopin **Note:** Similar to 100,000 Zlotych, Y#199.

Date	Mintage	F	VF	XF	Unc	BU
1990 Proof	10,000	Value: 175				

Y# 203 200000 ZLOTYCH
155.5000 g., 0.9990 Silver 5.0000 oz. ASW **Obv:** Imperial eagle above value **Rev:** Uniformed figure on horse **Note:** Similar to 100,000 Zlotych, Y#200.

Date	Mintage	F	VF	XF	Unc	BU
1990 Proof	10,000	Value: 175				

Y# 204 200000 ZLOTYCH
155.5000 g., 0.9990 Silver 5.0000 oz. ASW **Obv:** Imperial eagle above value **Rev:** Bust of Marszalek Pilsudski 1/4 left **Note:** Similar to 100,000 Zlotych, Y#201.

Date	Mintage	F	VF	XF	Unc	BU
1990 Proof	10,000	Value: 175				

Y# 205 200000 ZLOTYCH
31.1000 g., 0.9990 Gold 1.0000 oz. AGW **Obv:** Imperial eagle above value **Rev:** Fryderyk Chopin

Date	Mintage	F	VF	XF	Unc	BU
1990 Proof	10,000	Value: 735				

Y# 206 200000 ZLOTYCH
31.1000 g., 0.9990 Gold 1.0000 oz. AGW **Obv:** Imperial eagle above value **Rev:** Tadeusz Kosciuszko

Date	Mintage	F	VF	XF	Unc	BU
1990 Proof	10,000	Value: 735				

Y# 207 200000 ZLOTYCH
31.1000 g., 0.9990 Gold 1.0000 oz. AGW **Obv:** Imperial eagle above value **Rev:** Marszalck Pilsudski

Date	Mintage	F	VF	XF	Unc	BU
1990 Proof	10,000	Value: 735				

Y# 222 200000 ZLOTYCH
31.1000 g., 0.9990 Gold 1.0000 oz. AGW **Subject:** Solidarity **Obv:** Solidarity monument with city view background **Rev:** Solidarity monument with city view background

Date	Mintage	F	VF	XF	Unc	BU
1990 Proof	Est. 1,000	Value: 800				

Y# 250 200000 ZLOTYCH
19.2650 g., 0.9990 Silver .6188 oz. ASW **Obv:** Imperial eagle above value **Rev:** Bust of Gen. Komorowski facing

Date	Mintage	F	VF	XF	Unc	BU
1990 Proof	25,000	Value: 27.50				

Y# 218 200000 ZLOTYCH
38.9000 g., 0.9990 Silver 1.2496 oz. ASW **Subject:** 200th Anniversary of Polish Constitution **Obv:** Imperial eagle above value **Rev:** Crowned eagle perched on sprigs above engraved stone **Designer:** Ewa Tyc-Karpinski

Date	Mintage	F	VF	XF	Unc	BU
1991 Proof	100,000	Value: 22.50				

Y# 226 200000 ZLOTYCH
31.1000 g., 0.9250 Silver .9250 oz. ASW **Series:** Albertville Olympics **Obv:** Imperial eagle above value **Rev:** Slalom skier **Designer:** Ewa Tyc-Karpinski

Date	Mintage	F	VF	XF	Unc	BU
1991 Proof	20,000	Value: 28.50				

Y# 228 200000 ZLOTYCH
31.1000 g., 0.9250 Silver .9250 oz. ASW **Series:** Barcelona Olympics **Obv:** Imperial eagle above value **Rev:** Weight lifter

Date	Mintage	F	VF	XF	Unc	BU
1991 Proof	20,000	Value: 42.50				

Y# 241 200000 ZLOTYCH
31.1600 g., 0.9250 Silver .9267 oz. ASW **Series:** Barcelona Olympics **Obv:** Imperial eagle above value **Rev:** Two sailboats

Date	Mintage	F	VF	XF	Unc	BU
1991 Proof	20,000	Value: 37.50				

Y# 242 200000 ZLOTYCH
19.3300 g., 0.7500 Silver .4661 oz. ASW **Subject:** 70th Anniversary of Poznan Fair **Obv:** Imperial eagle above value **Rev:** Monument and globe design, dates above and below

Date	Mintage	F	VF	XF	Unc	BU
1991 Proof	20,000	Value: 30.00				

Y# 251 200000 ZLOTYCH
19.3300 g., 0.7500 Silver .4661 oz. ASW **Obv:** Imperial eagle above value **Rev:** Bust of Gen. Okulicki 3/4 facing

Date	Mintage	F	VF	XF	Unc	BU
1991 Proof	25,000	Value: 27.50				

Y# 252 200000 ZLOTYCH
19.3300 g., 0.7500 Silver .4661 oz. ASW **Obv:** Imperial eagle above value **Rev:** Bust of Gen. Tokarzewski - Karaszewicz

Date	Mintage	F	VF	XF	Unc	BU
1991 Proof	25,000	Value: 27.50				

Y# 230 200000 ZLOTYCH
31.1000 g., 0.9990 Silver 1.0000 oz. ASW **Subject:** Discovery of America **Obv:** Imperial eagle above value **Rev:** Portrait and ship

Date	Mintage	F	VF	XF	Unc	BU
1992 Proof	20,000	Value: 40.00				

Y# 231 200000 ZLOTYCH
31.1000 g., 0.9990 Silver 1.0000 oz. ASW **Subject:** Seville Expo '92 **Obv:** Imperial eagle above value **Rev:** Building facade and logo

Date	Mintage	F	VF	XF	Unc	BU
1992 Proof	45,000	Value: 28.00				

Y# 232 200000 ZLOTYCH
16.5000 g., 0.7500 Silver .3979 oz. ASW **Series:** WWII **Obv:** Imperial eagle above value **Rev:** Polish protection of WWII sea convoys

Date	Mintage	F	VF	XF	Unc	BU
1992 Proof	15,000	Value: 27.50				

Y# 233 200000 ZLOTYCH
16.5000 g., 0.7500 Silver .3979 oz. ASW **Obv:** Imperial eagle above value **Rev:** Bust of Stanislaw Staszic 3/4 left within sprigs

Date	Mintage	F	VF	XF	Unc	BU
1992 Proof	20,000	Value: 27.50				

Y# 253 200000 ZLOTYCH
16.5000 g., 0.7500 Silver .3979 oz. ASW **Obv:** Imperial eagle above value **Rev:** Bust of Wladyslaw II 1/4 left

Date	Mintage	F	VF	XF	Unc	BU
1992 Proof	15,000	Value: 30.00				

Y# 254 200000 ZLOTYCH
16.5000 g., 0.7500 Silver .3979 oz. ASW **Obv:** Imperial eagle above value **Rev:** Bust of Wladyslaw III 1/4 left

Date	Mintage	F	VF	XF	Unc	BU
1992 Proof	5,000	Value: 60.00				

Y# 255 200000 ZLOTYCH
16.5000 g., 0.7500 Silver .3979 oz. ASW **Subject:** 750th Anniversary - City of Stettin **Obv:** Imperial eagle above value **Rev:** Crowned phoenix head within shield flanked by dates

Date	Mintage	F	VF	XF	Unc	BU
1993 Proof	20,000	Value: 27.50				

Y# 257 200000 ZLOTYCH
16.5000 g., 0.7500 Silver .3979 oz. ASW **Obv:** Imperial eagle above value **Rev:** Bust of Kazimierz IV 3/4 right

Date	Mintage	F	VF	XF	Unc	BU
1993 Proof	15,000	Value: 32.50				

Y# 258 200000 ZLOTYCH
16.5000 g., 0.7500 Silver .3979 oz. ASW **Obv:** Crowned eagle with wings open divides date **Rev:** Kazimierz IV enthroned

Date	Mintage	F	VF	XF	Unc	BU
1993 Proof	5,000	Value: 75.00				

Y# 259 200000 ZLOTYCH
16.5000 g., 0.7500 Silver .3979 oz. ASW **Series:** WWII **Obv:** Imperial eagle above value **Rev:** Polish partisans sabotaging railways

Date	Mintage	F	VF	XF	Unc	BU
1993 Proof	10,000	Value: 55.00				

Y# 262 200000 ZLOTYCH
16.5000 g., 0.7500 Silver .3979 oz. ASW **Series:** WWII **Obv:** Imperial eagle above value **Rev:** Battle of Monte Cassino

Date	Mintage	F	VF	XF	Unc	BU
1994 Proof	15,000	Value: 37.50				

Y# 266 200000 ZLOTYCH
16.5000 g., 0.7500 Silver .3979 oz. ASW **Subject:** 75th Anniversary - Disabled Association **Obv:** Imperial eagle above value **Rev:** Shield and rose within designed circle

Date	Mintage	F	VF	XF	Unc	BU
1994 Proof	15,000	Value: 35.00				

Y# 273 200000 ZLOTYCH
16.5000 g., 0.7500 Silver .3979 oz. ASW **Obv:** Imperial eagle above value **Rev:** Half-length figure of Sigismund I 1/4 right

Date	Mintage	F	VF	XF	Unc	BU
1994 Proof	15,000	Value: 30.00				

Y# 274 200000 ZLOTYCH
16.5000 g., 0.7500 Silver .3979 oz. ASW **Obv:** Imperial eagle above value **Rev:** Bust of Sigismund facing

Date	Mintage	F	VF	XF	Unc	BU
1994 Proof	5,000	Value: 65.00				

Y# 275 200000 ZLOTYCH

16.5000 g., 0.7500 Silver .3979 oz. ASW **Subject:** 200th Anniversary - Kosciuszko Insurrection **Obv:** Imperial eagle above value **Rev:** Cameo bust left within ship

Date	Mintage	F	VF	XF	Unc	BU
1994 Proof	15,000	Value: 32.50				

Y# 245 300000 ZLOTYCH

31.1600 g., 0.9250 Silver .9267 oz. ASW **Subject:** 50th Anniversary of Warsaw Ghetto Uprising **Obv:** Imperial eagle above value **Rev:** Outreached arms above bricks

Date	Mintage	F	VF	XF	Unc	BU
1993 Proof	30,000	Value: 32.50				

Y# 247 300000 ZLOTYCH

31.1600 g., 0.9250 Silver .9267 oz. ASW **Series:** 1994 Olympics **Obv:** Eagle with wings open divides date **Rev:** Lillehammer

Date	Mintage	F	VF	XF	Unc	BU
1993 Proof	20,000	Value: 32.50				

Y# 248 300000 ZLOTYCH

31.1450 g., 0.9990 Silver 1.0004 oz. ASW **Obv:** Imperial eagle above value **Rev:** Barn swallow feeding young

Date	Mintage	F	VF	XF	Unc	BU
1993 Proof	20,000	Value: 135				

Y# 249 300000 ZLOTYCH

31.1450 g., 0.9990 Silver 1.0004 oz. ASW **Obv:** Imperial eagle above value **Rev:** Lancut Castle

Date	Mintage	F	VF	XF	Unc	BU
1993 Proof	20,000	Value: 45.00				

Y# 260 300000 ZLOTYCH

31.1000 g., 0.9990 Silver .9990 oz. ASW **Obv:** Imperial eagle above value **Rev:** Aerial view of Zamosc

Date	Mintage	F	VF	XF	Unc	BU
1993 Proof	20,000	Value: 32.50				

Y# 263 300000 ZLOTYCH

31.1600 g., 0.9250 Silver .9267 oz. ASW **Obv:** Imperial eagle above value **Rev:** St. Maksymilian Kolbe

Date	Mintage	F	VF	XF	Unc	BU
1994 Proof	15,000	Value: 40.00				

Y# 264 300000 ZLOTYCH

31.1000 g., 0.9250 Silver .9250 oz. ASW **Subject:** 70th Anniversary - Polish National Bank **Obv:** Crowned eagle with wings open divides date **Rev:** Bust facing in front of buildings **Shape:** 7-sided

Date	Mintage	F	VF	XF	Unc	BU
1994 Proof	20,000	Value: 50.00				

Y# 269 300000 ZLOTYCH

31.1035 g., 0.9990 Silver 1.0000 oz. ASW **Subject:** Warsaw Uprising **Obv:** Imperial eagle above value **Rev:** Fighting soldiers, dates, designs and cross **Designer:** Ewa Tyc-Karpinski

Date	Mintage	F	VF	XF	Unc	BU
1994 Proof	30,000	Value: 35.00				

Y# 208 500000 ZLOTYCH

62.2000 g., 0.9990 Gold 2.0000 oz. AGW **Obv:** Imperial eagle above value **Rev:** Fryderyk Chopin **Note:** Similar to 100,000 Zlotych, Y#199.

Date	Mintage	F	VF	XF	Unc	BU
1990 Proof	2,000	Value: 1,475				

Y# 209 500000 ZLOTYCH

62.2000 g., 0.9990 Gold 2.0000 oz. AGW **Obv:** Imperial eagle above value **Rev:** Uniformed figure on horse **Note:** Similar to 100,000 Zlotych, Y#200.

Date	Mintage	F	VF	XF	Unc	BU
1990 Proof	2,000	Value: 1,475				

Y# 210 500000 ZLOTYCH

62.2000 g., 0.9990 Gold 2.0000 oz. AGW **Obv:** Imperial eagle above value **Rev:** Bust of Marszalek Pilsudski 1/4 left **Note:** Similar to 100,000 Zlotych, Y#201.

Date	Mintage	F	VF	XF	Unc	BU
1990 Proof	2,000	Value: 1,475				

Y# 211 1000000 ZLOTYCH

373.2000 g., 0.9990 Gold 12.0000 oz. AGW **Obv:** Imperial eagle above value **Rev:** Fryderyk Chopin **Note:** Similar to 100,000 Zlotych, Y#199.

Date	Mintage	F	VF	XF	Unc	BU
1990 Proof	250	Value: 8,450				

Y# 212 1000000 ZLOTYCH

373.2000 g., 0.9990 Gold 12.0000 oz. AGW **Obv:** Imperial eagle above value **Rev:** Uniformed figure on horse **Note:** Similar to 100,000 Zlotych, Y#200.

Date	Mintage	F	VF	XF	Unc	BU
1990 Proof	250	Value: 8,450				

Y# 213 1000000 ZLOTYCH

373.2000 g., 0.9990 Gold 12.0000 oz. AGW **Obv:** Imperial eagle above value **Rev:** Bust of Marszalek Pilsudski 1/4 left **Note:** Similar to 100,000 Zlotych, Y#201.

Date	Mintage	F	VF	XF	Unc	BU
1990 Proof	250	Value: 8,450				

REFORM COINAGE

100 Old Zlotych = 1 Grosz; 10,000 Old Zlotych = 1 Zloty

As far back as 1990, production was initiated for the new 1 Grosz - 1 Zlotych coins for a forthcoming monetary reform. It wasn't announced until the Act of July 7, 1994 and was enacted on January 1, 1995.

Y# 276 GROSZ

Brass **Obv:** Crowned eagle with wings open **Rev:** Drooping oak leaf over value

Date	Mintage	F	VF	XF	Unc	BU
1990	29,140,000	—	—	—	0.10	0.20
1991	79,000,000	—	—	—	0.10	0.20
1992	362,000,000	—	—	—	0.10	0.20
1993	80,780,000	—	—	—	0.10	0.20
1995	102,280,109	—	—	—	0.10	0.20
1997	103,080,002	—	—	—	0.10	0.20
1998	255,830,003	—	—	—	0.10	0.20
1999	204,470,000	—	—	—	0.10	0.20
2000	211,410,000	—	—	—	0.10	0.20

Y# 277 2 GROSZE

Brass **Obv:** Crowned eagle with wings open **Rev:** Drooping oak leaves above value

Date	Mintage	F	VF	XF	Unc	BU
1990	34,400,000	—	—	—	0.15	0.25
1991	97,410,000	—	—	—	0.15	0.25
1992	157,000,003	—	—	—	0.15	0.25
1997	92,400,002	—	—	—	0.15	0.25
1998	154,840,050	—	—	—	0.15	0.25
1999	187,900,000	—	—	—	0.15	0.25
2000	92,400,000	—	—	—	0.15	0.25

Y# 278 5 GROSZY

Brass, 19.5 mm. **Obv:** Crowned eagle with wings open **Rev:** Value at upper left of oak leaves

Date	Mintage	F	VF	XF	Unc	BU
1990	70,240,000	—	—	—	0.25	0.45
1991	171,040,000	—	—	—	0.25	0.45
1992	103,784,000	—	—	—	0.25	0.45
1993	20,280,101	—	—	—	0.25	0.45
1998	93,472,002	—	—	—	0.25	0.45
1999	99,024,000	—	—	—	0.25	0.45
2000	75,600,000	—	—	—	0.25	0.45

Y# 279 10 GROSZY

Copper-Nickel, 16 mm. **Obv:** Crowned eagle with wings open **Rev:** Value within wreath

Date	Mintage	F	VF	XF	Unc	BU
1990	43,055,000	—	—	—	0.40	0.60
1991	123,164,300	—	—	—	0.40	0.60
1992	210,005,000	—	—	—	0.40	0.60
1993	80,240,008	—	—	—	0.40	0.60
1998	62,695,000	—	—	—	0.40	0.60

Date	Mintage	F	VF	XF	Unc	BU
1999	47,040,000	—	—	—	0.40	0.60
2000	104,060,000	—	—	—	0.40	0.60

Y# 280 20 GROSZY

Copper-Nickel, 18.5 mm. **Obv:** Crowned eagle with wings open **Rev:** Value within artistic design

Date	Mintage	F	VF	XF	Unc	BU
1990	25,100,000	—	—	—	0.65	0.85
1991	75,400,000	—	—	—	0.65	0.85
1992	106,100,001	—	—	—	0.65	0.85
1996	29,745,000	—	—	—	0.65	0.85
1997	59,755,000	—	—	—	0.65	0.85
1998	52,500,000	—	—	—	0.65	0.85
1999	25,985,000	—	—	—	0.65	0.85
2000	52,135,000	—	—	—	0.65	0.85

Y# 281 50 GROSZY

Copper-Nickel, 20 mm. **Obv:** Crowned eagle with wings open **Rev:** Value to right of sprig

Date	Mintage	F	VF	XF	Unc	BU
1990	29,152,000	—	—	—	1.00	1.25
1991	99,120,000	—	—	—	1.00	1.25
1992	116,000,000	—	—	—	1.00	1.25
1995	101,600,113	—	—	—	1.00	1.25

Y# 282 ZLOTY

Copper-Nickel, 23 mm. **Obv:** Crowned eagle with wings open **Rev:** Value within wreath

Date	Mintage	F	VF	XF	Unc	BU
1990	20,240,000	—	—	—	1.75	2.00
1991	60,080,000	—	—	—	1.75	2.00
1992	102,240,000	—	—	—	1.75	2.00
1993	20,904,000	—	—	—	1.75	2.00
1994	69,956,000	—	—	—	1.75	2.00
1995	99,740,122	—	—	—	1.75	2.00

Y# 283 2 ZLOTE

Bi-Metallic Copper-Nickel center in Brass ring, 21.5 mm. **Obv:** Crowned eagle with wings open within circle **Rev:** Value flanked by oak leaves

Date	Mintage	F	VF	XF	Unc	BU
1994	79,644,000	—	—	—	4.00	4.50
1995	122,880,020	—	—	—	4.00	4.50

Y# 285 2 ZLOTE

Copper-Nickel, 26.8 mm. **Subject:** 55th Anniversary - Katyn Forest Massacre **Obv:** Crowned eagle with wings open divides date **Rev:** Burned forest

Date	Mintage	F	VF	XF	Unc	BU
1995	300,000	—	—	—	3.50	5.50

Y# 289 2 ZLOTE

Copper-Nickel, 26.8 mm. **Obv:** Crowned eagle with wings open **Rev:** Catfish

Date	Mintage	F	VF	XF	Unc	BU
1995	300,000	—	—	—	14.00	16.00

Y# 297 2 ZLOTE

Copper-Nickel, 26.8 mm. **Subject:** 75th Anniversary - Battle of Warsaw **Obv:** Crowned eagle with wings open divides date **Rev:** Armored figures behind figure with cross

Date	Mintage	F	VF	XF	Unc	BU
1995	300,000	—	—	—	3.50	5.50

Y# 300 2 ZLOTE

Copper-Nickel, 26.8 mm. **Series:** 1996 Olympic Games **Obv:** Crowned eagle with wings open divides date **Rev:** Centennial

Date	Mintage	F	VF	XF	Unc	BU
1995	—	—	—	—	3.50	5.50

Y# 303 2 ZLOTE

Copper-Nickel, 26.8 mm. **Series:** 1996 Olympics - Atlanta **Obv:** Crowned eagle with wings open divides date **Rev:** Wrestling

Date	Mintage	F	VF	XF	Unc	BU
1995	—	—	—	—	3.50	5.50

Y# 310 2 ZLOTE

Copper-Nickel, 26.8 mm. **Obv:** Crowned eagle with wings open divides date, all within circle **Rev:** Lazienki Royal Palace

Date	Mintage	F	VF	XF	Unc	BU
1995	287,000	—	—	—	3.75	6.00

Y# 306 2 ZLOTE

Brass, 26.8 mm. **Obv:** Imperial eagle above value **Rev:** Bust of Zygmunt II

Date	Mintage	F	VF	XF	Unc	BU
1996	200,000	—	—	—	10.00	12.00

Y# 311 2 ZLOTE

Copper-Zinc-Tin, 26.8 mm. **Obv:** Crowned eagle with wings open **Rev:** Hedgehog with young **Designer:** Roussanka Nowakowska

Date	Mintage	F	VF	XF	Unc	BU
1996	Est. 500	—	—	—	17.50	20.00

Y# 313 2 ZLOTE

Copper-Aluminum-Zinc-Tin, 26.8 mm. **Obv:** Crowned eagle with wings open divides date, all within circle **Rev:** Castle and shield

Date	Mintage	F	VF	XF	Unc	BU
1996	Est. 500,000	—	—	—	3.00	5.00

Y# 315 2 ZLOTE

Copper-Aluminum-Zinc-Tin, 26.8 mm. **Obv:** Crowned eagle with wings open divides dates **Rev:** Heads opposite divide dates

Date	Mintage	F	VF	XF	Unc	BU
1996	Est. 500,000	—	—	—	3.00	5.00

Y# 325 2 ZLOTE

Brass, 26.8 mm. **Obv:** Crowned eagle with wings open divides date **Rev:** Head of Stefan Batory 1/4 right

Date	Mintage	F	VF	XF	Unc	BU
1997	—	—	—	—	3.50	5.50

Y# 329 2 ZLOTE

Brass, 26.8 mm. **Obv:** Crowned eagle with wings open **Rev:** Stag beetle **Note:** Jelenek Rogacz - Lucanus cervus.

Date	Mintage	F	VF	XF	Unc	BU
1997	—	—	—	—	10.00	12.00

Y# 331 2 ZLOTE

Brass, 26.8 mm. **Obv:** Crowned eagle with wings open **Rev:** Zamek W Pieskowej Skale

Date	Mintage	F	VF	XF	Unc	BU
1997	—	—	—	—	3.00	5.00

Y# 333 2 ZLOTE

Copper-Aluminum-Zinc-Tin, 26.8 mm. **Obv:** Crowned eagle with wings open divides date **Rev:** Head with headdress left, antelope and ostrich within globe design

Date	Mintage	F	VF	XF	Unc	BU
1997	Est. 500	—	—	—	5.00	7.00

Y# 335 2 ZLOTE

Brass, 26.8 mm. **Series:** Nagano Olympics **Obv:** Crowned eagle with wings open divides date **Rev:** Snow boarder

Date	Mintage	F	VF	XF	Unc	BU
1998	400,000	—	—	—	3.00	5.00

Y# 336 2 ZLOTE

Brass, 26.8 mm. **Obv:** Imperial eagle above value **Rev:** Sigismund III (1587-1632)

Date	Mintage	F	VF	XF	Unc	BU
1998	400,000	—	—	—	3.00	5.00

Y# 340 2 ZLOTE

Brass, 26.8 mm. **Obv:** Crowned eagle with wings open **Rev:** Toad right

Date	Mintage	F	VF	XF	Unc	BU
1998	400,000	—	—	—	15.00	17.00

Y# 344 2 ZLOTE

Brass, 26.8 mm. **Subject:** Discovery of Radium and Polomium **Obv:** Crowned eagle with wings open divides date **Rev:** Seated and standing figure among scientific figures of radium and polomium

Date	Mintage	F	VF	XF	Unc	BU
1998	400,000	—	—	—	3.00	5.00

Y# 347 2 ZLOTE

Brass, 26.8 mm. **Obv:** Imperial eagle above value **Rev:** Zamek W. Korniku - Palace

Date	Mintage	F	VF	XF	Unc	BU
1998	400,000	—	—	—	3.50	5.50

Y# 349 2 ZLOTE

Brass, 26.8 mm. **Subject:** 80th Anniversary - Polish Independence **Obv:** Crowned eagle with wings open divides date **Rev:** 1918 on flaming map

Date	Mintage	F	VF	XF	Unc	BU
1998	400,000	—	—	—	3.00	5.00

Y# 352 2 ZLOTE

Brass, 26.8 mm. **Subject:** 200th Birthday - Adam Mickiewicz **Obv:** Crowned eagle with wings open divides date **Rev:** Head of Adam Mickiewicz 3/4 facing

Date	Mintage	F	VF	XF	Unc	BU
1998	400,000	—	—	—	3.00	5.00

Y# 355 2 ZLOTE

Brass, 26.8 mm. **Obv:** Crowned eagle with wings open **Rev:** Gray wolves and cubs **Edge Lettering:** POLSKI NARODOWY BANK

Date	Mintage	F	VF	XF	Unc	BU
1999	420,000	—	—	—	14.00	16.00

Y# 356 2 ZLOTE

Brass, 26.8 mm. **Obv:** Crowned eagle with wings open divides date **Rev:** Bust of Juliusz Slosacki 1/4 right

Date	Mintage	F	VF	XF	Unc	BU
1999	420,000	—	—	—	3.00	5.00

Y# 357 2 ZLOTE

Brass, 26.8 mm. **Subject:** Poland's Accession to NATO **Obv:** Crowned eagle with wings open divides date **Rev:** NATO globe, soldiers rappelling from helicopter **Edge Lettering:** NARODOWY BANK POLSKI

Date	Mintage	F	VF	XF	Unc	BU
1999	450,000	—	—	—	3.00	5.00

Y# 358 2 ZLOTE

Brass, 26.8 mm. **Obv:** Crowned eagle with wings open divides date **Rev:** Head of Ernest Malinowsky facing above slanted text

Date	Mintage	F	VF	XF	Unc	BU
1999	420,000	—	—	—	3.00	5.00

Y# 363 2 ZLOTE

Brass, 26.8 mm. **Obv:** Crowned eagle with wings open divides date **Rev:** Laski and Erasmus **Edge Lettering:** NARODOWY BANK POLSKI

Date	Mintage	F	VF	XF	Unc	BU
1999	450,000	—	—	—	3.00	5.00

Y# 365 2 ZLOTE

Brass, 26.8 mm. **Obv:** Imperial eagle above value **Rev:** Fryderyk Chopin with stylized piano and music score

Date	Mintage	F	VF	XF	Unc	BU
1999	420,000	—	—	—	3.00	5.00

Y# 368 2 ZLOTE

Brass, 26.8 mm. **Obv:** Crowned eagle with wings open divides date **Rev:** Wladyslaw IV 1/4 right **Edge Lettering:** NARODOWY BANK POLSKI

Date	Mintage	F	VF	XF	Unc	BU
1999	500,000	—	—	—	3.00	5.00

Y# 372 2 ZLOTE

Brass, 26.8 mm. **Obv:** Crowned eagle with wings open divides date, all within circle **Rev:** Palace behind Potlocki family arms

Date	Mintage	F	VF	XF	Unc	BU
1999	450,000	—	—	—	3.50	5.50

Y# 404 2 ZLOTE

8.1500 g., Brass, 26.7 mm. **Subject:** Workers revolt in December 1970 **Obv:** Crowned eagle **Rev:** Fist **Edge:** "NBP" repeatedly

Date	Mintage	F	VF	XF	Unc	BU
2000	750,000	—	—	—	3.00	5.00

Y# 374 2 ZLOTE
8.3100 g., Bi-Metallic Copper-Nickel center in Brass ring, 26.8 mm. **Subject:** Millennium **Obv:** Crowned eagle in center **Rev:** Latent image dates in center **Edge Lettering:** NARODOWY BANK POLSKI

Date	Mintage	F	VF	XF	Unc	BU
2000	2,000,000	—	—	—	3.00	5.00

Y# 376 2 ZLOTE
8.1500 g., Brass, 26.8 mm. **Subject:** Holy Year **Obv:** Crowned eagle with wings open divides date **Rev:** Cross with holy symbolic animals

Date	Mintage	F	VF	XF	Unc	BU
2000	1,500,000	—	—	—	5.00	7.00

Y# 377 2 ZLOTE
8.1500 g., Brass, 26.8 mm. **Subject:** 1000th Anniversary - Gniezno Convention **Obv:** Crowned eagle with wings open divides date **Rev:** Denar coin design of Boleslaw Chrobry

Date	Mintage	F	VF	XF	Unc	BU
2000	450,000	—	—	—	5.00	7.00

Y# 388 2 ZLOTE
8.1400 g., Brass, 26.8 mm. **Subject:** "Dudek-Upupa epops" **Obv:** Crowned eagle with wings open **Rev:** Long-billed Hoopoe **Edge Lettering:** NARODOWY BANK POLSKI

Date	Mintage	F	VF	XF	Unc	BU
2000	500,000	—	—	—	4.00	6.00

Y# 389 2 ZLOTE
8.1400 g., Brass, 26.8 mm. **Subject:** 1000th Anniversary - Wroclawia (Breslau) **Obv:** Polish eagle **Rev:** Jesus with city view in background

Date	Mintage	F	VF	XF	Unc	BU
2000	500,000	—	—	—	3.00	5.00

Y# 390 2 ZLOTE
8.1400 g., Brass, 26.8 mm. **Obv:** Crowned eagle with wings open divides date, all within circle **Rev:** Wilanowie Palace

Date	Mintage	F	VF	XF	Unc	BU
2000	500,000	—	—	—	3.00	5.00

Y# 394 2 ZLOTE
8.2200 g., Brass, 26.8 mm. **Subject:** Solidarity **Obv:** Crowned eagle with wings open divides date **Rev:** Solidarity logo, map, children **Edge Lettering:** NARODOWY BANK POLSKI

Date	Mintage	F	VF	XF	Unc	BU
2000	750,000	—	—	—	3.00	5.00

Y# 398 2 ZLOTE
8.2200 g., Brass, 26.8 mm. **Obv:** Crowned eagle with wings open divides date **Rev:** Bust of Jan II Kazimierz facing 1/4 left **Edge Lettering:** POLSKA NARODOWY BANK **Note:** Jan II Kazimierz - 1648-68.

Date	Mintage	F	VF	XF	Unc	BU
2000	450,000	—	—	—	3.00	5.00

Y# 284 5 ZLOTYCH
Bi-Metallic Brass center in Copper-Nickel ring, 24 mm. **Obv:** Crowned eagle with wings open within circle **Rev:** Value within circle flanked by oak leaves

Date	Mintage	F	VF	XF	Unc	BU
1994	112,896,033	—	—	—	7.00	8.00
1996	52,940,003	—	—	—	7.00	8.00

Y# 287 10 ZLOTYCH
16.5500 g., 0.7500 Silver .3979 oz. ASW **Obv:** Crowned eagle with wings open divides date **Rev:** Capture of Berlin

Date	Mintage	F	VF	XF	Unc	BU
1995 Proof	12,000	Value: 45.00				

Y# 301 10 ZLOTYCH
16.4400 g., 0.9250 Silver .4889 oz. ASW **Series:** 1996 Olympics **Obv:** Imperial eagle above value **Rev:** Centennial - Atlanta

Date	Mintage	F	VF	XF	Unc	BU
1995 Proof	20,000	Value: 120				

Y# 305 10 ZLOTYCH
16.5000 g., 0.9250 Silver .4907 oz. ASW **Subject:** Centennial of Organized Peasant Movement **Obv:** Imperial eagle above value **Rev:** Wincenty Witos

Date	Mintage	F	VF	XF	Unc	BU
1995 Proof	20,000	Value: 45.00				

Y# 307 10 ZLOTYCH
16.5000 g., 0.9250 Silver .4907 oz. ASW **Obv:** Imperial eagle above value **Rev:** Bust of Zygmunt II August left **Designer:** Ewa Tyc-Karpinska

Date	Mintage	F	VF	XF	Unc	BU
1996 Proof	15,000	Value: 45.00				

Y# 308 10 ZLOTYCH
16.5000 g., 0.9250 Silver .4907 oz. ASW **Obv:** Imperial eagle above value **Rev:** Half-length figure facing left **Designer:** Ewa Tyc-Karpinska

Date	Mintage	F	VF	XF	Unc	BU
1996 Proof	5,000	Value: 80.00				

Y# 317 10 ZLOTYCH
16.5000 g., 0.9250 Silver .4907 oz. ASW **Obv:** Imperial eagle above value **Rev:** Stanislaw Mikolajczyk

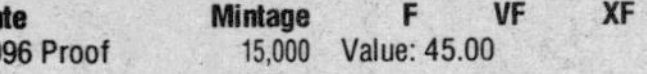

Date	Mintage	F	VF	XF	Unc	BU
1996 Proof	15,000	Value: 45.00				

Y# 318 10 ZLOTYCH
16.5000 g., 0.9250 Silver .4907 oz. ASW **Obv:** Imperial eagle above value **Rev:** Mazurka of Dabrowski

Date	Mintage	F	VF	XF	Unc	BU
1996 Proof	15,000	Value: 50.00				

Y# 324 10 ZLOTYCH
16.5000 g., 0.9250 Silver .4907 oz. ASW **Subject:** 40th Anniversary - Poznan Workers Protest **Obv:** Crowned eagle with wings open **Rev:** Figures around inscription and date

Date	Mintage	F	VF	XF	Unc	BU
1996 Proof	—	Value: 45.00				

Y# 321 10 ZLOTYCH
14.1400 g., 0.9250 Silver .4205 oz. ASW **Subject:** St. Adalbert's Martyrdom **Obv:** Crowned eagle with wings open **Rev:** Birth and funeral scenes

Date	Mintage	F	VF	XF	Unc	BU
1997 Proof	25,000	Value: 45.00				

Y# 322 10 ZLOTYCH
14.1400 g., 0.9250 Silver .4205 oz. ASW **Subject:** 46th Eucharistic Congress **Obv:** Crowned eagle with wings open within design **Rev:** Pope left with arms raised

Date	Mintage	F	VF	XF	Unc	BU
1997 Proof	Est. 50,000	Value: 40.00				

Y# 326 10 ZLOTYCH
14.1400 g., 0.9250 Silver .4205 oz. ASW **Obv:** Crowned eagle with wings open **Rev:** Stefan Batory 3/4 right

Date	Mintage	F	VF	XF	Unc	BU
1997 Proof	5,000	Value: 200				

Y# 327 10 ZLOTYCH
14.1400 g., 0.9250 Silver .4205 oz. ASW **Obv:** Crowned eagle with wings open **Rev:** Stefan Batory

Date	Mintage	F	VF	XF	Unc	BU
1997 Proof	15,000	Value: 185				

Y# 334 10 ZLOTYCH
14.1400 g., 0.9250 Silver .4205 oz. ASW **Obv:** Crowned eagle with wings open **Rev:** Pawel Edmund Strzelecki **Edge Lettering:** 200 LECIE URODZIN

Date	Mintage	F	VF	XF	Unc	BU
1997 Proof	20,000	Value: 45.00				

Y# 337 10 ZLOTYCH
14.1400 g., 0.9250 Silver .4205 oz. ASW **Obv:** Crowned eagle with wings open **Rev:** Crowned bust of Sigismund III 1/4 left

Date	Mintage	F	VF	XF	Unc	BU
1998 Proof	22,000	Value: 45.00				

Y# 338 10 ZLOTYCH
14.1400 g., 0.9250 Silver .4205 oz. ASW **Subject:** Sigismund III (1587-1632) **Obv:** Crowned eagle with wings open **Rev:** Seated King 1/4 left

Date	Mintage	F	VF	XF	Unc	BU
1998 Proof	14,000	Value: 40.00				

Y# 341 10 ZLOTYCH
14.1400 g., 0.9250 Silver .4205 oz. ASW **Series:** 1998 Winter Olympics **Obv:** Crowned eagle with wings open **Rev:** Snowboarder

Date	Mintage	F	VF	XF	Unc	BU
1998 Proof	30,000	Value: 18.50				

Y# 342 10 ZLOTYCH
14.1400 g., 0.9250 Silver .4205 oz. ASW **Obv:** Crowned eagle with wings open **Rev:** Brigadier General August Emil Fieldorf

Date	Mintage	F	VF	XF	Unc	BU
1998 Proof	17,000	Value: 45.00				

Y# 345 10 ZLOTYCH
14.1400 g., 0.9250 Silver .4205 oz. ASW **Obv:** Value and eagles in cross design **Rev:** Pope John Paul II

Date	Mintage	F	VF	XF	Unc	BU
1998 Proof	65,000	Value: 65.00				

Y# 350 10 ZLOTYCH
14.1400 g., 0.9250 Silver .4205 oz. ASW **Subject:** 80th Anniversary - Polish Independence **Obv:** Crowned eagle with wings open within stylized flames **Rev:** Anniversary dates

Date	Mintage	F	VF	XF	Unc	BU
1998 Proof	20,000	Value: 35.00				

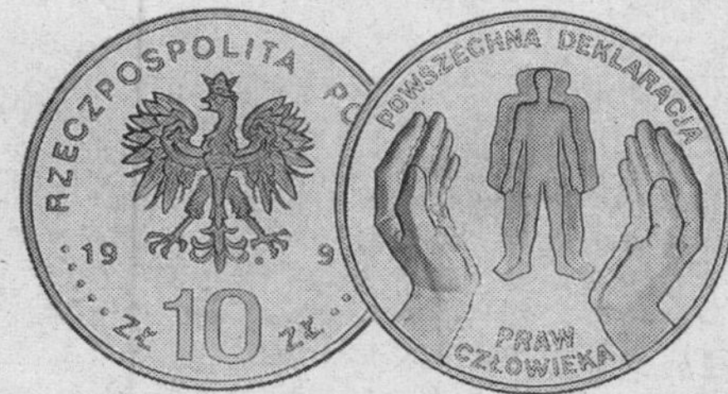

Y# 351 10 ZLOTYCH
14.1400 g., 0.9250 Silver .4205 oz. ASW **Subject:** Universal Declaration of Human Rights **Obv:** Crowned eagle with wings open divides date **Rev:** Human figure between two hands **Edge Lettering:** 50 ROCZNICA UCHWALENIA (three times)

Date	Mintage	F	VF	XF	Unc	BU
1998 Proof	14,000	Value: 35.00				

Y# 359 10 ZLOTYCH
14.1400 g., 0.9250 Silver .4205 oz. ASW **Subject:** Poland's Accession to NATO **Obv:** Crowned eagle with wings open within quartered circle **Rev:** NATO globe, soldiers rapelling from helicopter

Date	Mintage	F	VF	XF	Unc	BU
1999 Proof	25,000	Value: 30.00				

Y# 360 10 ZLOTYCH
14.1400 g., 0.9250 Silver .4205 oz. ASW **Obv:** Crucifix designs and crowned eagle **Rev:** Bust of Pope left and radiant dove

Date	Mintage	F	VF	XF	Unc	BU
1999 Proof	70,000	Value: 47.50				

Y# 362 10 ZLOTYCH
14.1400 g., 0.9250 Silver .4205 oz. ASW **Obv:** Crowned eagle with wings open **Rev:** Queen Jadwiga and coat of arms **Edge Lettering:** 1400-2000. (five times) **Note:** Cracow University.

Date	Mintage	F	VF	XF	Unc	BU
1999 Proof	20,000	Value: 32.50				

Y# 364 10 ZLOTYCH
14.1400 g., 0.9250 Silver .4205 oz. ASW **Obv:** Crowned eagle above windowed brick wall **Rev:** Laski with Erasmus in background **Note:** Jan Laski 1490-1560.

Date	Mintage	F	VF	XF	Unc	BU
1999 Proof	20,000	Value: 32.50				

Y# 366 10 ZLOTYCH

14.1400 g., 0.9250 Silver .4205 oz. ASW **Obv:** Crowned eagle over twisted chords **Rev:** Head right with stylized design

Date	Mintage	F	VF	XF	Unc	BU
1999 Proof	25,000	Value: 32.50				

Y# 369 10 ZLOTYCH

14.1400 g., 0.9250 Silver .4205 oz. ASW **Obv:** Crowned eagle with wings open **Rev:** Portrait of Wladyslaw IV, dates

Date	Mintage	F	VF	XF	Unc	BU
1999 Proof	20,000	Value: 32.50				

Y# 370 10 ZLOTYCH

14.1400 g., 0.9250 Silver .4205 oz. ASW **Obv:** Crowned eagle with wings open **Rev:** Framed half-length portrait of Wladyslaw IV

Date	Mintage	F	VF	XF	Unc	BU
1999 Proof	13,000	Value: 60.00				

Y# 378 10 ZLOTYCH

14.1400 g., 0.9250 Silver .4205 oz. ASW **Obv:** World globe and crowned eagle **Rev:** Bust of E. Malinowski facing, train in background **Edge Lettering:** 100-LECIE SMIERCI twice

Date	Mintage	F	VF	XF	Unc	BU
1999 Proof	19,000	Value: 32.50				

Y# 379 10 ZLOTYCH

14.1400 g., 0.9250 Silver .4205 oz. ASW **Obv:** Inscription and crowned eagle **Rev:** Bust of Juliusz Slowacki 1/4 right **Edge:** Plain

Date	Mintage	F	VF	XF	Unc	BU
1999 Proof	19,000	Value: 30.00				

Y# 380 10 ZLOTYCH

14.1400 g., 0.9250 Silver .4205 oz. ASW **Subject:** Holy Year **Obv:** Crowned eagle in frame **Rev:** Cross with symbols of the evangelists **Edge Lettering:** WIELKI JUBILEUSZ ROKU 2000

Date	Mintage	F	VF	XF	Unc	BU
2000 Proof	60,000	Value: 32.50				

Y# 381 10 ZLOTYCH

14.1400 g., 0.9250 Silver .4205 oz. ASW **Subject:** 1000th Anniversary - Gniezno Convention **Obv:** Old coin designs in oxidized center, crowned eagle within circle **Rev:** Seated figures of Boleslaw Chrobry and Otto III in oxidized center **Edge:** Plain

Date	Mintage	F	VF	XF	Unc	BU
2000 Proof	32,000	Value: 32.50				

Y# 392 10 ZLOTYCH

14.2000 g., 0.9250 Silver .4223 oz. ASW **Subject:** 1000 Years Wroclaw (Breslau) **Obv:** Crowned eagle in front of city view **Rev:** City arms in arch **Edge:** Plain

Date	Mintage	F	VF	XF	Unc	BU
2000 Proof	32,000	Value: 30.00				

Y# 395 10 ZLOTYCH

14.2200 g., 0.9250 Silver .4229 oz. ASW, 32 mm. **Subject:** Solidarity **Obv:** Crowned eagle with wings open divides date **Rev:** Solidarity logo and two children **Edge:** Plain

Date	Mintage	F	VF	XF	Unc	BU
2000 Proof	40,000	Value: 27.50				

Y# 400 10 ZLOTYCH

14.1400 g., 0.9250 Silver .4205 oz. ASW, 32 mm. **Subject:** Jan Kazimierz II (1648-68) **Obv:** Crowned eagle with wings open divides date **Rev:** Half-length figure facing 1/4 left **Edge:** Plain

Date	Mintage	F	VF	XF	Unc	BU
2000 Proof	14,000	Value: 30.00				

Y# 401 10 ZLOTYCH

14.1400 g., 0.9250 Silver .4205 oz. ASW **Subject:** Jan Kazimierz II (1648-68) **Obv:** Crowned eagle **Rev:** Jan II Kazimierz 1/4 left

Date	Mintage	F	VF	XF	Unc	BU
2000 Proof	20,000	Value: 30.00				

Y# 403 10 ZLOTYCH

14.1400 g., 0.9250 Silver .4205 oz. ASW **Subject:** Rapperswil Polish Museum **Obv:** Crowned eagle and value between two buildings **Rev:** Eagle-topped column **Edge:** GDANSK GDYNIA SZCZECIN ELBLAG SLUPSK

Date	Mintage	F	VF	XF	Unc	BU
2000 Proof	25,000	Value: 30.00				

Y# 405 10 ZLOTYCH

14.1400 g., 0.9250 Silver .4205 oz. ASW **Subject:** Grudnia 1970 **Obv:** Two crowned eagles **Rev:** Shadow figures on pavement

Date	Mintage	F	VF	XF	Unc	BU
2000 Proof	37,000	Value: 30.00				

Note: Antiqued finish

Y# 286 20 ZLOTYCH

31.1100 g., 0.9990 Silver .9990 oz. ASW **Subject:** Katyn Forest Massacre **Obv:** Crowned eagle with wings open divides date **Rev:** Burned forest

Date	Mintage	F	VF	XF	Unc	BU
1995 Proof	30,000	Value: 37.50				

Y# 288 20 ZLOTYCH

31.1100 g., 0.9990 Silver .9990 oz. ASW **Subject:** 500th Anniversary - Plock Province **Obv:** Imperial eagle above value **Rev:** Eagle on shield divides dates, castle in background

Date	Mintage	F	VF	XF	Unc	BU
1995 Proof	15,000	Value: 45.00				

Y# 290 20 ZLOTYCH
31.1100 g., 0.9990 Silver .9990 oz. ASW **Obv:** Crowned eagle with wings open **Rev:** Catfish

Date	Mintage	F	VF	XF	Unc	BU
1995 Proof	20,000	Value: 250				

Y# 291 20 ZLOTYCH
31.1100 g., 0.9990 Silver .9990 oz. ASW **Subject:** 50th Anniversary - United Nations **Obv:** Imperial eagle above value **Rev:** ONZ in front of half globe with designs

Date	Mintage	F	VF	XF	Unc	BU
1995 Proof	20,000	Value: 37.50				

Y# 296 20 ZLOTYCH
31.1700 g., 0.9990 Silver 1.0011 oz. ASW **Obv:** Crowned eagle with wings open divides date, all within circle **Rev:** Royal Palace and swans

Date	Mintage	F	VF	XF	Unc	BU
1995 Proof	20,000	Value: 130				

Y# 298 20 ZLOTYCH
30.9200 g., 0.9250 Silver .9195 oz. ASW **Subject:** 75th Anniversary - Battle of Warsaw **Obv:** Imperial eagle above value **Rev:** Armored figures behind figure with cross

Date	Mintage	F	VF	XF	Unc	BU
1995 Proof	20,000	Value: 40.00				

Y# 302 20 ZLOTYCH
31.0500 g., 0.9250 Silver .9234 oz. ASW **Obv:** Imperial eagle above value **Rev:** Copernicus and Ecu

Date	Mintage	F	VF	XF	Unc	BU
1995 Proof	15,000	Value: 150				

Y# 304 20 ZLOTYCH
31.1000 g., 0.9250 Silver .9240 oz. ASW **Series:** 1996 Olympics - Atlanta **Obv:** Imperial eagle above value **Rev:** Wrestlers

Date	Mintage	F	VF	XF	Unc	BU
1995 Proof	—	Value: 65.00				

Y# 309 20 ZLOTYCH
31.1000 g., 0.9250 Silver .9240 oz. ASW **Subject:** 400th Anniversary - Warsaw as Capital City **Obv:** Imperial eagle above value **Rev:** Buildings, statue and cross **Designer:** Robert Kotowicz

Date	Mintage	F	VF	XF	Unc	BU
1996 Proof	Est. 20,000	Value: 45.00				

Y# 312 20 ZLOTYCH
31.1000 g., 0.9250 Silver .9240 oz. ASW **Obv:** Crowned eagle with wings open **Rev:** Hedgehog with young **Designer:** Roussanka Nowakowska

Date	Mintage	F	VF	XF	Unc	BU
1996 Proof	Est. 20,000	Value: 400				

Y# 314 20 ZLOTYCH
31.1000 g., 0.9250 Silver .9240 oz. ASW **Obv:** Imperial eagle within circle outlined in crosses, value below **Rev:** Bishop's arms and Lidzibark Warminski castle

Date	Mintage	F	VF	XF	Unc	BU
1996 Proof	Est. 20,000	Value: 50.00				

Y# 319 20 ZLOTYCH
31.1000 g., 0.9250 Silver .9240 oz. ASW **Subject:** Millennium of Gdansk (Danzig) **Obv:** Imperial eagle above value **Rev:** Arms with supporters divide dates in front of city silhouette **Edge Lettering:** MONUMENTUM MILLENNII CIVITATIS GEDANENSIS

Date	Mintage	F	VF	XF	Unc	BU
1996 Proof	20,000	Value: 100				

Y# 330 20 ZLOTYCH
28.5200 g., 0.9250 Silver .8482 oz. ASW **Obv:** Crowned eagle with wings open **Rev:** Stag beetle **Rev. Legend:** JELOPNEK ROGACZ - Lucanus cervus

Date	Mintage	F	VF	XF	Unc	BU
1997 Proof	—	Value: 345				

Y# 332 20 ZLOTYCH
28.5200 g., 0.9250 Silver .8482 oz. ASW **Obv:** Crowned eagle with wings open divides date, all within circle **Rev:** Zamek W Pieskowej Skale

Date	Mintage	F	VF	XF	Unc	BU
1997 Proof	—	Value: 160				

Y# 343 20 ZLOTYCH
28.4700 g., 0.9250 Silver .8467 oz. ASW **Obv:** Crowned eagle with wings open **Rev:** Ropucha Paskowka - Natterjack Toad

Date	Mintage	F	VF	XF	Unc	BU
1998 Proof	22,000	Value: 175				

Y# 348 20 ZLOTYCH
28.2800 g., 0.9250 Silver .8410 oz. ASW **Subject:** Zamek W. Koniku **Obv:** Crowned eagle with wings open **Rev:** Palace among diamond design

Date	Mintage	F	VF	XF	Unc	BU
1998 Proof	20,000	Value: 70.00				

Y# 354 20 ZLOTYCH
28.1500 g., 0.9250 Silver .8372 oz. ASW **Subject:** Discovery of Radium and Polonium **Obv:** Atom design **Rev:** Madame and Monsieur Curie and formulas

Date	Mintage	F	VF	XF	Unc	BU
1998 Proof	20,000	Value: 50.00				

Y# 373 20 ZLOTYCH
28.2800 g., 0.9250 Silver .8410 oz. ASW **Subject:** Radzyn Podlaski Palace **Obv:** Crowned eagle within inner circle **Rev:** Palace behind sculptured arms

Date	Mintage	F	VF	XF	Unc	BU
1999 Proof	15,000	Value: 145				

Y# 382 20 ZLOTYCH
28.3000 g., 0.9250 Silver .8416 oz. ASW **Obv:** Imperial eagle above value **Rev:** Wolf family

Date	Mintage	F	VF	XF	Unc	BU
1999 Proof	21,000	Value: 225				

Y# 387 20 ZLOTYCH
28.3700 g., 0.9250 Silver .8437 oz. ASW **Obv:** Imperial eagle above value **Rev:** Dudek - Upupa epops - Eurasian Hoopoe

Date	Mintage	F	VF	XF	Unc	BU
2000 Proof	24,000	Value: 125				

Y# 391 20 ZLOTYCH
28.2400 g., 0.9250 Silver .8398 oz. ASW, 38.5 mm. **Obv:** Crowned eagle **Rev:** View of Palace through front gate **Edge:** Plain

Date	Mintage	F	VF	XF	Unc	BU
2000 Proof	24,000	Value: 75.00				

Y# 292 50 ZLOTYCH
3.1000 g., 0.9999 Gold .1000 oz. AGW **Obv:** Crowned eagle with wings open, all within circle **Rev:** Golden eagle

Date	Mintage	F	VF	XF	Unc	BU
1995	2,000	—	—	—	150	—

Y# 293 100 ZLOTYCH
7.7800 g., 0.9999 Gold .2500 oz. AGW **Obv:** Crowned eagle with wings open, all within circle **Rev:** Golden eagle

Date	Mintage	F	VF	XF	Unc	BU
1995	1,500	—	—	—	250	—

Y# 328 100 ZLOTYCH
8.0000 g., 0.9000 Gold .2315 oz. AGW **Obv:** Crowned eagle with wings open divides date **Rev:** Bust of Stefan Batory 1/4 right

Date	Mintage	F	VF	XF	Unc	BU
1997 Proof	2,000	Value: 275				

Y# 339 100 ZLOTYCH
8.0000 g., 0.9000 Gold .2315 oz. AGW **Obv:** Crowned eagle with wings open divides date **Rev:** Sigismund III 1/4 left

Date	Mintage	F	VF	XF	Unc	BU
1998 Proof	2,500	Value: 275				

Y# 361 100 ZLOTYCH
8.0000 g., 0.9000 Gold .2315 oz. AGW **Obv:** Crowned eagle in inner circle **Rev:** Pope John Paul II left

Date	Mintage	F	VF	XF	Unc	BU
1999 Proof	7,000	Value: 250				

Y# 371 100 ZLOTYCH
8.0000 g., 0.9000 Gold .2315 oz. AGW **Obv:** Crowned eagle with wings open divides date **Rev:** Wladyslaw IV in frame

Date	Mintage	F	VF	XF	Unc	BU
1999 Proof	2,300	Value: 275				

Y# 383 100 ZLOTYCH
8.0000 g., 0.9000 Gold .2315 oz. AGW **Obv:** Crowned eagle with wings open divides date **Rev:** Bust of Zygmunt II left

Date	Mintage	F	VF	XF	Unc	BU
1999 Proof	2,000	Value: 245				

Y# 384 100 ZLOTYCH
8.0000 g., 0.9000 Gold .2315 oz. AGW **Subject:** 100th Anniversary - Gniezno Convention **Obv:** Old coin designs **Rev:** Seated figures of Boleslaw Chrobry and Otto III

Date	Mintage	F	VF	XF	Unc	BU
2000 Proof	2,200	Value: 245				

Y# 396 100 ZLOTYCH
8.0000 g., 0.9000 Gold .2315 oz. AGW **Obv:** Crowned eagle with wings open divides date **Rev:** Queen Jadwiga facing **Edge:** Plain

Date	Mintage	F	VF	XF	Unc	BU
2000 Proof	2,000	Value: 275				

Y# 402 100 ZLOTYCH
8.0000 g., 0.9000 Gold .2315 oz. AGW, 21 mm. **Subject:** Jan Kazimierz II (1648-68) **Obv:** Crowned eagle with wings open **Rev:** Armored bust 1/4 left with names and dates on shoulder **Edge:** Plain

Date	Mintage	F	VF	XF	Unc	BU
2000 Proof	2,000	Value: 275				

Y# 294 200 ZLOTYCH
15.5000 g., 0.9000 Gold .4485 oz. AGW **Obv:** Crowned eagle with wings open within beaded circle **Rev:** Golden eagle

Date	Mintage	F	VF	XF	Unc	BU
1995	1,000	—	—	—	500	—

Y# 299 200 ZLOTYCH
15.5000 g., 0.9000 Gold .4485 oz. AGW **Subject:** XII Chopin Piano Competition **Obv:** Crowned eagle with wings open divides date **Rev:** Bust of Chopin 1/4 right below tree **Edge:** Lettered

Date	Mintage	F	VF	XF	Unc	BU
1995 Proof	500	Value: 925				

Y# 316 200 ZLOTYCH
15.5000 g., 0.9000 Gold .4485 oz. AGW **Obv:** Stylized design to right of eagle **Rev:** Henryk Sienkiewicz

Date	Mintage	F	VF	XF	Unc	BU
1996 Proof	Est. 1,000	Value: 425				

Y# 320 200 ZLOTYCH
15.5000 g., 0.9000 Gold .4485 oz. AGW **Subject:** Millennium of Gdansk (Danzig) **Obv:** Crowned eagle with wings open within shield **Rev:** City arms in old coin style

Date	Mintage	F	VF	XF	Unc	BU
1996	2,000	—	—	—	—	375

Y# 323 200 ZLOTYCH
15.5000 g., 0.9000 Gold .4485 oz. AGW **Subject:** St. Adalbert's Martyrdom **Obv:** Crowned eagle with wings open within circle **Rev:** Figure standing within center design flanked by other figures

Date	Mintage	F	VF	XF	Unc	BU
1997 Proof	2,000	Value: 375				

Y# 346 200 ZLOTYCH
15.5000 g., 0.9000 Gold .4485 oz. AGW **Obv:** Imperial eagle above value **Rev:** Standing Pope with arms wide open

Date	Mintage	F	VF	XF	Unc	BU
1998 Proof	5,000	Value: 375				

Y# 353 200 ZLOTYCH
15.5000 g., 0.9000 Gold .4485 oz. AGW **Subject:** 200th Birthday - Adam Mickiewicz **Obv:** Small crowned eagle at lower right, quote written above **Rev:** Portrait with silhouette

Date	Mintage	F	VF	XF	Unc	BU
1998 Proof	3,000	Value: 375				

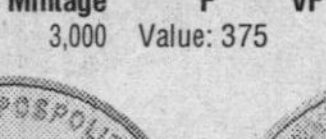

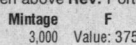

Y# 367 200 ZLOTYCH
15.5000 g., 0.9000 Gold .4485 oz. AGW **Obv:** Crowned eagle

on sash, music design **Rev:** Head of Fryderyk Chopin 1/4 left with music background

Date	Mintage	F	VF	XF	Unc	BU
1999 Proof	2,000	Value: 375				

Y# 385 200 ZLOTYCH

15.5000 g., 0.9000 Gold .4485 oz. AGW **Obv:** Crowned eagle with wings open, feather at right **Rev:** Head of Juliusz Slowacki left

Date	Mintage	F	VF	XF	Unc	BU
1999 Proof	1,900	Value: 375				

Y# 386 200 ZLOTYCH

15.5000 g., 0.9000 Gold .4485 oz. AGW **Subject:** 1000th Anniversary - Gniezno Convention **Obv:** Old coin designs **Rev:** Seated figures of Boleslaw Chrobry and Otto III

Date	Mintage	F	VF	XF	Unc	BU
2000 Proof	1,250	Value: 385				

Y# 393 200 ZLOTYCH

15.5000 g., 0.9000 Gold .4485 oz. AGW, 27 mm. **Subject:** 1000 Years - Wroclaw (Breslau) **Obv:** Crowned eagle with wings open within beaded circle **Rev:** Bust of Jesus facing, holding city arms **Edge:** Plain

Date	Mintage	F	VF	XF	Unc	BU
2000 Proof	2,000	Value: 375				

Y# 397 200 ZLOTYCH

23.3200 g., 0.9000 Gold .6748 oz. AGW **Subject:** Solidarity **Obv:** Crowned eagle with wings open **Rev:** Multicolor Soldiarity logo, map and two children **Edge:** Plain

Date	Mintage	F	VF	XF	Unc	BU
2000 Proof	2,500	Value: 550				

Y# 375 200 ZLOTYCH

13.6000 g., Gold And Silver **Subject:** Millennium **Obv:** Crowned eagle and world globe **Rev:** Various computer, DNA and atomic symbols **Note:** .900 Gold center in .925 Silver inner ring in a .900 Gold outer ring.

Date	Mintage	F	VF	XF	Unc	BU
2000 Proof	6,000	Value: 250				

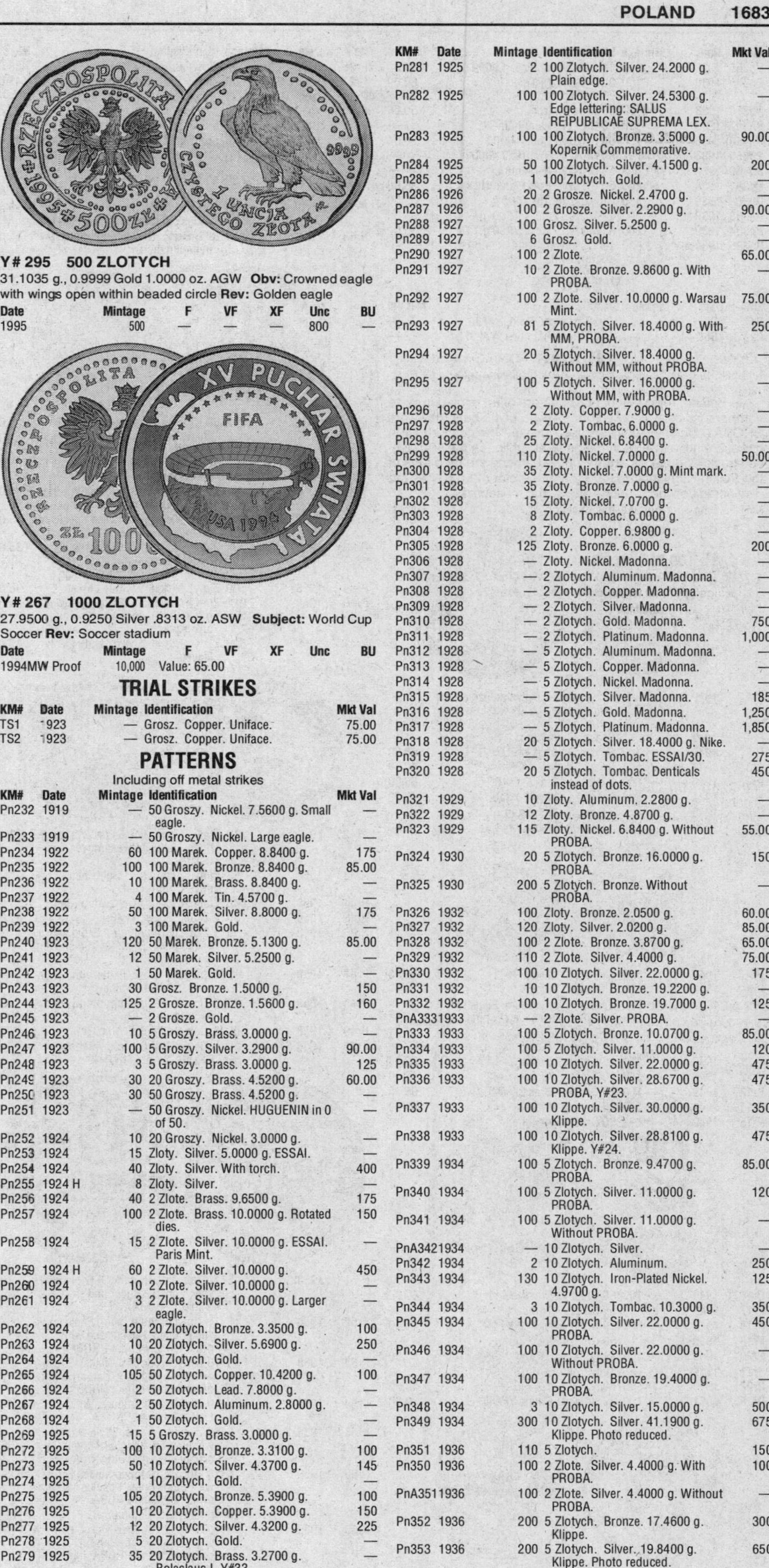

Y# 295 500 ZLOTYCH

31.1035 g., 0.9999 Gold 1.0000 oz. AGW **Obv:** Crowned eagle with wings open within beaded circle **Rev:** Golden eagle

Date	Mintage	F	VF	XF	Unc	BU
1995	500	—	—	—	800	—

Y# 267 1000 ZLOTYCH

27.9500 g., 0.9250 Silver .8313 oz. ASW **Subject:** World Cup Soccer **Rev:** Soccer stadium

Date	Mintage	F	VF	XF	Unc	BU
1994MW Proof	10,000	Value: 65.00				

TRIAL STRIKES

KM#	Date	Mintage	Identification	Mkt Val
TS1	1923	—	Grosz. Copper. Uniface.	75.00
TS2	1923	—	Grosz. Copper. Uniface.	75.00

PATTERNS

Including off metal strikes

KM#	Date	Mintage	Identification	Mkt Val
Pn232	1919	—	50 Groszy. Nickel. 7.5600 g. Small eagle.	—
Pn233	1919	—	50 Groszy. Nickel. Large eagle.	—
Pn234	1922	60	100 Marek. Copper. 8.8400 g.	175
Pn235	1922	100	100 Marek. Bronze. 8.8400 g.	85.00
Pn236	1922	10	100 Marek. Brass. 8.8400 g.	—
Pn237	1922	4	100 Marek. Tin. 4.5700 g.	—
Pn238	1922	50	100 Marek. Silver. 8.8000 g.	175
Pn239	1922	3	100 Marek. Gold.	—
Pn240	1923	120	50 Marek. Bronze. 5.1300 g.	85.00
Pn241	1923	12	50 Marek. Silver. 5.2500 g.	—
Pn242	1923	1	50 Marek. Gold.	—
Pn243	1923	30	Grosz. Bronze. 1.5000 g.	150
Pn244	1923	125	2 Grosze. Bronze. 1.5600 g.	160
Pn245	1923	—	2 Grosze. Gold.	—
Pn246	1923	10	5 Groszy. Brass. 3.0000 g.	—
Pn247	1923	100	5 Groszy. Silver. 3.2900 g.	90.00
Pn248	1923	3	5 Groszy. Brass. 3.0000 g.	125
Pn249	1923	30	20 Groszy. Brass. 4.5200 g.	60.00
Pn250	1923	30	50 Groszy. Brass. 4.5200 g.	—
Pn251	1923	—	50 Groszy. Nickel. HUGUENIN in 0 of 50.	—
Pn252	1924	10	20 Groszy. Nickel. 3.0000 g.	—
Pn253	1924	15	Zloty. Silver. 5.0000 g. ESSAI.	—
Pn254	1924	40	Zloty. Silver. With torch.	400
Pn255	1924 H	8	Zloty. Silver.	—
Pn256	1924	40	2 Zlote. Brass. 9.6500 g.	175
Pn257	1924	100	2 Zlote. Brass. 10.0000 g. Rotated dies.	150
Pn258	1924	15	2 Zlote. Silver. 10.0000 g. ESSAI. Paris Mint.	—
Pn259	1924 H	60	2 Zlote. Silver. 10.0000 g.	450
Pn260	1924	10	2 Zlote. Silver. 10.0000 g.	—
Pn261	1924	3	2 Zlote. Silver. 10.0000 g. Larger eagle.	—
Pn262	1924	120	20 Zlotych. Bronze. 3.3500 g.	100
Pn263	1924	10	20 Zlotych. Silver. 5.6900 g.	250
Pn264	1924	10	20 Zlotych. Gold.	—
Pn265	1924	105	50 Zlotych. Copper. 10.4200 g.	100
Pn266	1924	2	50 Zlotych. Lead. 7.8000 g.	—
Pn267	1924	2	50 Zlotych. Aluminum. 2.8000 g.	—
Pn268	1924	1	50 Zlotych. Gold.	—
Pn269	1925	15	5 Groszy. Brass. 3.0000 g.	—
Pn272	1925	100	10 Zlotych. Bronze. 3.3100 g.	100
Pn273	1925	50	10 Zlotych. Silver. 4.3700 g.	145
Pn274	1925	1	10 Zlotych. Gold.	—
Pn275	1925	105	20 Zlotych. Bronze. 5.3900 g.	100
Pn276	1925	10	20 Zlotych. Copper. 5.3900 g.	150
Pn277	1925	12	20 Zlotych. Silver. 4.3200 g.	225
Pn278	1925	5	20 Zlotych. Gold.	—
Pn279	1925	35	20 Zlotych. Brass. 3.2700 g. Boleslaus I, Y#33.	—
Pn280	1925	20	20 Zlotych. Nickel. 3.5000 g. Boleslaus I, Y#33.	—
Pn281	1925	2	100 Zlotych. Silver. 24.2000 g. Plain edge.	—
Pn282	1925	100	100 Zlotych. Silver. 24.5300 g. Edge lettering: SALUS REIPUBLICAE SUPREMA LEX.	—
Pn283	1925	100	100 Zlotych. Bronze. 3.5000 g. Kopernik Commemorative.	90.00
Pn284	1925	50	100 Zlotych. Silver. 4.1500 g.	200
Pn285	1925	1	100 Zlotych. Gold.	—
Pn286	1926	20	2 Grosze. Nickel. 2.4700 g.	—
Pn287	1926	100	2 Grosze. Silver. 2.2900 g.	90.00
Pn288	1927	100	Grosz. Silver. 5.2500 g.	—
Pn289	1927	6	Grosz. Gold.	—
Pn290	1927	100	2 Zlote.	65.00
Pn291	1927	10	2 Zlote. Bronze. 9.8600 g. With PROBA.	—
Pn292	1927	100	2 Zlote. Silver. 10.0000 g. Warsau Mint.	75.00
Pn293	1927	81	5 Zlotych. Silver. 18.4000 g. With MM, PROBA.	250
Pn294	1927	20	5 Zlotych. Silver. 18.4000 g. Without MM, without PROBA.	—
Pn295	1927	100	5 Zlotych. Silver. 16.0000 g. Without MM, with PROBA.	—
Pn296	1928	2	Zloty. Copper. 7.9000 g.	—
Pn297	1928	2	Zloty. Tombac. 6.0000 g.	—
Pn298	1928	25	Zloty. Nickel. 6.8400 g.	—
Pn299	1928	110	Zloty. Nickel. 7.0000 g.	50.00
Pn300	1928	35	Zloty. Nickel. 7.0000 g. Mint mark.	—
Pn301	1928	35	Zloty. Bronze. 7.0000 g.	—
Pn302	1928	15	Zloty. Nickel. 7.0700 g.	—
Pn303	1928	8	Zloty. Tombac. 6.0000 g.	—
Pn304	1928	2	Zloty. Copper. 6.9800 g.	—
Pn305	1928	125	Zloty. Bronze. 6.0000 g.	200
Pn306	1928	—	Zloty. Nickel. Madonna.	—
Pn307	1928	—	2 Zlotych. Aluminum. Madonna.	—
Pn308	1928	—	2 Zlotych. Copper. Madonna.	—
Pn309	1928	—	2 Zlotych. Silver. Madonna.	—
Pn310	1928	—	2 Zlotych. Gold. Madonna.	750
Pn311	1928	—	2 Zlotych. Platinum. Madonna.	1,000
Pn312	1928	—	5 Zlotych. Aluminum. Madonna.	—
Pn313	1928	—	5 Zlotych. Copper. Madonna.	—
Pn314	1928	—	5 Zlotych. Nickel. Madonna.	—
Pn315	1928	—	5 Zlotych. Silver. Madonna.	185
Pn316	1928	—	5 Zlotych. Gold. Madonna.	1,250
Pn317	1928	—	5 Zlotych. Platinum. Madonna.	1,850
Pn318	1928	20	5 Zlotych. Silver. 18.4000 g. Nike.	—
Pn319	1928	—	5 Zlotych. Tombac. ESSAI/30.	275
Pn320	1928	20	5 Zlotych. Tombac. Denticals instead of dots.	450
Pn321	1929	10	Zloty. Aluminum. 2.2800 g.	—
Pn322	1929	12	Zloty. Bronze. 4.8700 g.	—
Pn323	1929	115	Zloty. Nickel. 6.8400 g. Without PROBA.	55.00
Pn324	1930	20	5 Zlotych. Bronze. 16.0000 g. PROBA.	150
Pn325	1930	200	5 Zlotych. Bronze. Without PROBA.	—
Pn326	1932	100	Zloty. Bronze. 2.0500 g.	60.00
Pn327	1932	120	Zloty. Silver. 2.0200 g.	85.00
Pn328	1932	100	2 Zlote. Bronze. 3.8700 g.	65.00
Pn329	1932	110	2 Zlote. Silver. 4.4000 g.	75.00
Pn330	1932	100	10 Zlotych. Silver. 22.0000 g.	175
Pn331	1932	10	10 Zlotych. Bronze. 19.2200 g.	—
Pn332	1932	100	10 Zlotych. Bronze. 19.7000 g.	125
PnA333	1933	—	2 Zlote. Silver. PROBA.	—
Pn333	1933	100	5 Zlotych. Bronze. 10.0700 g.	85.00
Pn334	1933	100	5 Zlotych. Silver. 11.0000 g.	120
Pn335	1933	100	10 Zlotych. Silver. 22.0000 g.	475
Pn336	1933	100	10 Zlotych. Silver. 28.6700 g. PROBA, Y#23.	475
Pn337	1933	100	10 Zlotych. Silver. 30.0000 g. Klippe.	350
Pn338	1933	100	10 Zlotych. Silver. 28.8100 g. Klippe. Y#24.	475
Pn339	1934	100	5 Zlotych. Bronze. 9.4700 g. PROBA.	85.00
Pn340	1934	100	5 Zlotych. Silver. 11.0000 g. PROBA.	120
Pn341	1934	100	5 Zlotych. Silver. 11.0000 g. Without PROBA.	—
PnA342	1934	—	10 Zlotych. Silver.	—
Pn342	1934	2	10 Zlotych. Aluminum.	250
Pn343	1934	130	10 Zlotych. Iron-Plated Nickel. 4.9700 g.	125
Pn344	1934	3	10 Zlotych. Tombac. 10.3000 g.	350
Pn345	1934	100	10 Zlotych. Silver. 22.0000 g. PROBA.	450
Pn346	1934	100	10 Zlotych. Silver. 22.0000 g. Without PROBA.	—
Pn347	1934	100	10 Zlotych. Bronze. 19.4000 g. PROBA.	—
Pn348	1934	3	10 Zlotych. Silver. 15.0000 g.	500
Pn349	1934	300	10 Zlotych. Silver. 41.1900 g. Klippe. Photo reduced.	675
Pn351	1936	110	5 Zlotych.	150
Pn350	1936	100	2 Zlote. Silver. 4.4000 g. With PROBA.	100
PnA351	1936	100	2 Zlote. Silver. 4.4000 g. Without PROBA.	—
Pn352	1936	200	5 Zlotych. Bronze. 17.4600 g. Klippe.	300
Pn353	1936	200	5 Zlotych. Silver. 19.8400 g. Klippe. Photo reduced.	650
PnA356	1938	100	20 Groszy. Nickeled Iron. Without PROBA.	—

KM#	Date	Mintage	Identification	Mkt Val
Pn354	1938	100	10 Groszy. Bronze. 4.9000 g.	90.00
Pn355	1938	100	20 Groszy. Nickeled Iron. 3.4900 g. With PROBA.	60.00
Pn356	1938	120	50 Groszy. Iron.	50.00
Pn357	1938	10	50 Groszy. Aluminum.	—
Pn358	1938	100	50 Groszy. Iron. 4.5000 g.	50.00
Pn359	1938	1	50 Groszy. Bronze. 3.4000 g.	—
Pn360	1938	3	50 Groszy. Aluminum.	—
Pn361	1938	200	50 Groszy. Iron-Plated Nickel.	35.00
Pn362	1939	200	Grosz. Zinc. 14.7000 g.	35.00
Pn363	1939	200	2 Grosze. Zinc. 1.7500 g.	35.00
Pn364	1939	200	5 Groszy. Zinc. 1.7200 g. 2/hole.	35.00
Pn365	1981MW	3,000	2000 Zlotych. Gold. 8.0000 g. Boleslaw II.	—

PIEFORTS

KM#	Date	Mintage	Identification	Mkt Val
P1	1989	—	10000 Zlotych. Gold. Y#189.	—
P2	1989	—	10000 Zlotych. Silver. Y#237.	—

PROBAS

Standard metals unless otherwise stated

In Poland, rejected coin designs are often minted in large numbers for sale to collectors. These coins have the word PROBA on them, usually stamped incuse. The coins struck in nickel are not available to the general public. Of the 500 pieces struck, 250 pieces are distributed among the members of the Polish Numismatic Society and the other 250 pieces are distributed between various banks and museums.

KM#	Date	Mintage	Identification	Mkt Val
PrA1	1929	—	Zloty. Nickel. Crowned eagle with wings open. Value within fruit wreath.	—
Pr1	1949	—	Grosz. Aluminum.	—
Pr2	1949	100	Grosz. Brass. Y#39.	65.00
Pr3	1949	500	Grosz. Nickel. Y#39.	40.00
Pr4	1949	100	2 Grosze. Brass. Y#40.	65.00
Pr5	1949	500	2 Grosze. Nickel. Y#40.	45.00
Pr6	1949	—	2 Grosze. Aluminum.	—
Pr7	1949	100	5 Groszy. Brass. Y#41.	75.00
PrA7	1949	500	5 Groszy. Nickel. Y#41.	45.00
Pr8	1949	100	5 Groszy. Brass.	—
Pr9	1949	—	5 Groszy. Aluminum. Eagle with wings open. Value at upper right of spray.	—
Pr10	1949	—	10 Groszy. Aluminum.	—
Pr11	1949	100	10 Groszy. Brass. Y#42.	65.00
Pr12	1949	500	10 Groszy. Nickel. Y#42.	45.00
Pr13	1949	100	20 Groszy. Brass. Y#43.	65.00
Pr14	1949	500	20 Groszy. Nickel. Y#43.	45.00
Pr15	1949	—	20 Groszy. Aluminum.	—
Pr16	1949	100	50 Groszy. Brass. Y#44.	65.00
Pr17	1949	20	50 Groszy. Tombac. Y#44.	—
Pr18	1949	500	50 Groszy. Nickel. Y#44.	45.00
Pr19	1949	—	50 Groszy. Aluminum.	—
Pr20	1949	100	Zloty. Brass. Y#45.	80.00
Pr21	1949	—	Zloty. Aluminum.	—
Pr22	1949	500	Zloty. Nickel. Y#45.	45.00
Pr23	1957	100	20 Groszy. Brass. Y#A47.	80.00
Pr24	1957	100	50 Groszy. Brass. Y#48.1.	80.00
Pr25	1957	500	50 Groszy. Nickel. Y#48.1.	45.00
Pr26	1957	100	Zloty. Brass. Y#49.1.	80.00
Pr27	1957	500	Zloty. Nickel. Y#49.1.	45.00
Pr28	1957	5	Zloty. Copper-Nickel-Zinc. Y#49.1 without PROBA.	—
Pr29	1958	100	5 Groszy. Brass. Y#A46.	—
Pr30	1958	245	50 Groszy. Aluminum. Eagle with wings open. Value above crossed hammers.	35.00
Pr31	1958	500	50 Groszy. Nickel. Crossed hammers.	35.00
Pr32	1958	198	50 Groszy. Aluminum. Eagle with wings open. Antenna below value.	35.00
Pr33	1958	500	50 Groszy. Nickel. Antenna below denomination.	35.00
Pr34	1958	212	50 Groszy. Aluminum. Eagle with wings open. Value above spears of grain.	35.00
Pr35	1958	500	50 Groszy. Nickel. 50 above spears of grain.	35.00
Pr36	1958	234	Zloty. Aluminum. Eagle with wings open. 1 Between spears of grain.	30.00
Pr37	1958	500	Zloty. Nickel. 1 between spears of grain.	35.00
Pr38	1958	235	Zloty. Aluminum. Eagle with wings open. Value in spears of grain within diamond shape design.	35.00
Pr39	1958	500	Zloty. Nickel. 1 within circle.	35.00
Pr40	1958	211	Zloty. Aluminum. Eagle with wings open. Value among acorns and oak leaves.	30.00
Pr41	1958	500	Zloty. Nickel. Acorns and oak leaves.	35.00
Pr42	1958	210	Zloty. Aluminum. Eagle with wings open. Value between doves, low relief.	30.00
Pr43	1958	53	Zloty. Aluminum. 1 between doves, high relief.	125
Pr44	1958	500	Zloty. Nickel. 1 between birds.	35.00
Pr45	1958	100	2 Zlote. Brass. Y#46.	55.00
Pr46	1958	5	5 Zlotych. Aluminum. Eagle with wings open. Hammer and shovel without PROBA.	—
Pr47	1958	5	5 Zlotych. Brass. Eagle with wings open. Ship and value.	—
Pr48	1958	20	5 Zlotych. Aluminum. Ship, without PROBA.	150
Pr49	1958	500	5 Zlotych. Nickel. Ship.	35.00
Pr50	1958	10	5 Zlotych. Aluminum. Without PROBA, reverse of Pr49.	—
Pr51	1958	5	10 Zlotych. Aluminum. Eagle with wings open. Caliper and gear, without PROBA.	100
Pr52	1958	10	10 Zlotych. Aluminum. Eagle with wings open. Kosciuszko with ornaments, without PROBA.	—
Pr53	1958	10	10 Zlotych. Copper-Nickel. Eagle with wings open. Kosciuszko with ornaments, without PROBA.	—
Pr54	1958	5	10 Zlotych. Aluminum. With ornaments and PROBA.	100
Pr55	1958	5	10 Zlotych. Brass. Eagle with wings open. Kosciuszko with ornaments without PROBA.	—
Pr56	1958	5	10 Zlotych. Copper-Nickel. Eagle with wings open. Kosciuszko with ornaments and PROBA.	—
Pr57	1958	10	10 Zlotych. Aluminum.	—
Pr58	1958	5	10 Zlotych. Copper-Nickel. Eagle with wings open. Without ornaments and PROBA, high relief.	—
Pr59	1959	500	2 Zlote. Nickel. Y#46.	30.00
Pr60	1959	100	5 Zlotych. Brass. Y#47.	65.00
Pr61	1959	500	5 Zlotych. Nickel. Y#47.	30.00
Pr62	1959	500	5 Zlotych. Nickel. Eagle with wings open. Value within industrial collage.	30.00
Pr63	1959	500	5 Zlotych. Nickel. Eagle with wings open. Value to left of hammer and shovel.	30.00
Pr64	1959	10	10 Zlotych. Aluminum. Y#51.	—
Pr65	1959	500	10 Zlotych. Nickel. Y#51.	30.00
Pr66	1960	196	5 Zlotych. Aluminum. Ship.	—
Pr67	1960	500	5 Zlotych. Nickel. Eagle with wings open. Ship and value.	32.50
Pr68	1960	500	10 Zlotych. Nickel. Eagle with wings open. Value above caliper and gear.	30.00
Pr69	1960	500	10 Zlotych. Nickel. Eagle with wings open. Kosciuszko with ornaments and PROBA.	30.00
Pr70	1960	500	10 Zlotych. Nickel. Eagle with wings open. Kosciuszko with PROBA in front of neck.	30.00
Pr71	1960	10	100 Zlotych. Nickel. Y#57, with crosshatched field.	—
Pr72	1960	500	100 Zlotych. Nickel. Y#57, with crosshatched field.	35.00
Pr73	1960	50	100 Zlotych. 0.5000 Silver. Without PROBA, Y#57 with crosshatched field.	60.00
Pr74	1960	20	100 Zlotych. 0.7500 Silver. Y#57, with crosshatched field.	60.00
Pr75	1960	500	100 Zlotych. Nickel. Y#57.	35.00
Pr76	1960	12	100 Zlotych. 0.7500 Silver. Eagle with wings open flanked by shields. Conjoined heads right.	125
Pr77	1960	14	100 Zlotych. 0.7500 Silver.	125
Pr78	1960	4	100 Zlotych. 0.7000 Silver. High relief.	—
Pr79	1960	9	100 Zlotych. 0.7000 Silver. Flat relief.	—
Pr80	1960	20	100 Zlotych. 0.5000 Silver.	125
Pr81	1960	13	100 Zlotych. 0.7500 Silver. Eagle with wings open within circle, assorted shields around border. Conjoined heads right.	125
Pr82	1960	500	100 Zlotych. Nickel.	30.00
Pr83	1960	5	100 Zlotych. 0.7500 Silver.	150
Pr84	1960	500	100 Zlotych. Nickel.	30.00
Pr85	1960	29	100 Zlotych. 0.7000 Silver.	125
Pr86	1960	500	100 Zlotych. Nickel. Eagle with wings open within circle. Conjoined heads left within circle.	30.00
Pr87	1960	12	100 Zlotych. 0.7500 Silver.	135

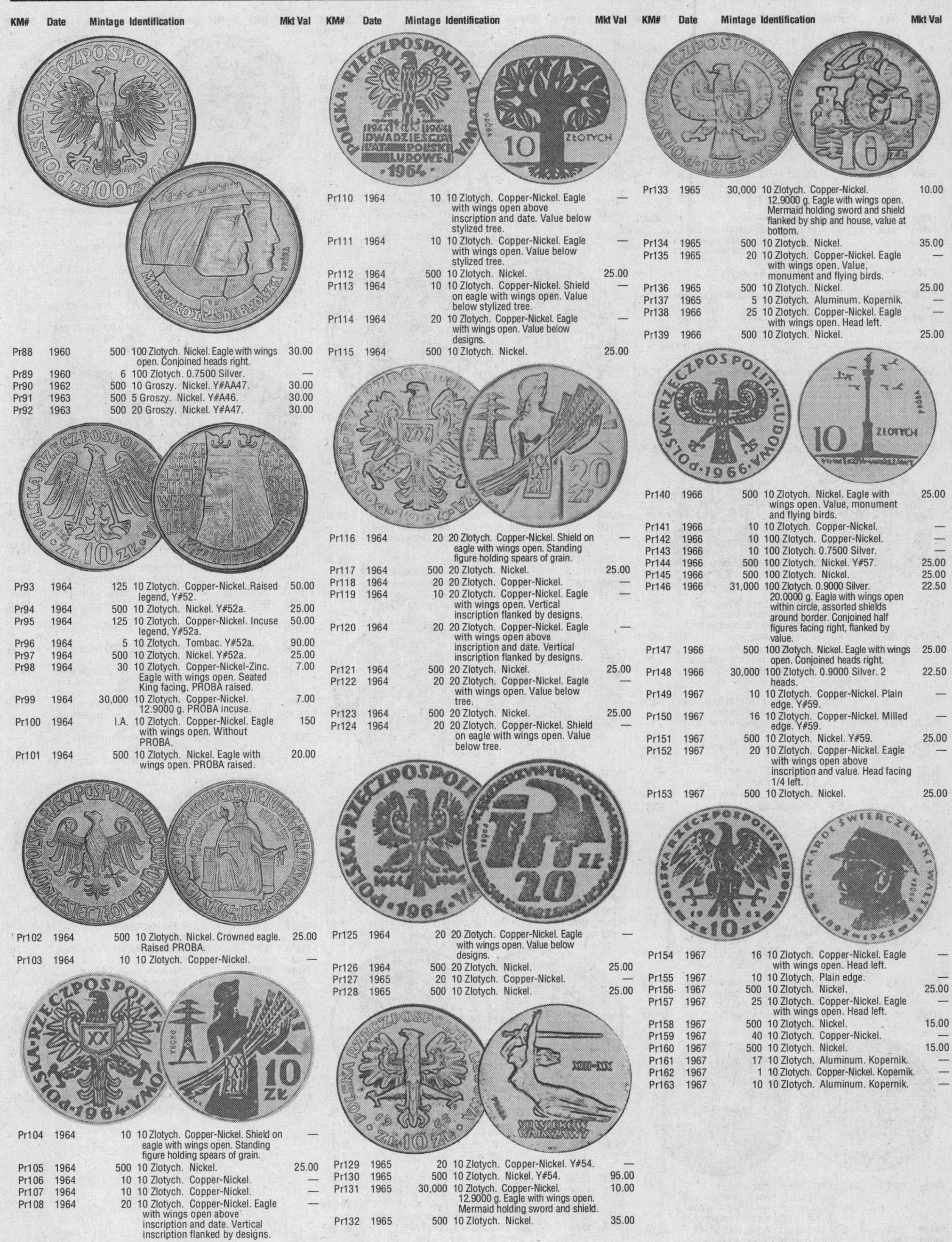

KM#	Date	Mintage	Identification	Mkt Val
Pr88	1960	500	100 Zlotych. Nickel. Eagle with wings open. Conjoined heads right.	30.00
Pr89	1960	6	100 Zlotych. 0.7500 Silver.	—
Pr90	1962	500	10 Groszy. Nickel. Y#AA47.	30.00
Pr91	1963	500	5 Groszy. Nickel. Y#A46.	30.00
Pr92	1963	500	20 Groszy. Nickel. Y#A47.	30.00
Pr93	1964	125	10 Zlotych. Copper-Nickel. Raised legend, Y#52.	50.00
Pr94	1964	500	10 Zlotych. Nickel. Y#52a.	25.00
Pr95	1964	125	10 Zlotych. Copper-Nickel. Incuse legend, Y#52a.	50.00
Pr96	1964	5	10 Zlotych. Tombac. Y#52a.	90.00
Pr97	1964	500	10 Zlotych. Nickel. Y#52a.	25.00
Pr98	1964	30	10 Zlotych. Copper-Nickel-Zinc. Eagle with wings open. Seated King facing, PROBA raised.	7.00
Pr99	1964	30,000	10 Zlotych. Copper-Nickel. 12.9000 g. PROBA incuse.	7.00
Pr100	1964	I.A.	10 Zlotych. Copper-Nickel. Eagle with wings open. Without PROBA.	150
Pr101	1964	500	10 Zlotych. Nickel. Eagle with wings open. PROBA raised.	20.00
Pr102	1964	500	10 Zlotych. Nickel. Crowned eagle. Raised PROBA.	25.00
Pr103	1964	10	10 Zlotych. Copper-Nickel.	—
Pr104	1964	10	10 Zlotych. Copper-Nickel. Shield on eagle with wings open. Standing figure holding spears of grain.	—
Pr105	1964	500	10 Zlotych. Nickel.	25.00
Pr106	1964	10	10 Zlotych. Copper-Nickel.	—
Pr107	1964	10	10 Zlotych. Copper-Nickel.	—
Pr108	1964	20	10 Zlotych. Copper-Nickel. Eagle with wings open above inscription and date. Vertical inscription flanked by designs.	—
Pr109	1964	500	10 Zlotych. Nickel.	25.00
Pr110	1964	10	10 Zlotych. Copper-Nickel. Eagle with wings open above inscription and date. Value below stylized tree.	—
Pr111	1964	10	10 Zlotych. Copper-Nickel. Eagle with wings open. Value below stylized tree.	—
Pr112	1964	500	10 Zlotych. Nickel.	25.00
Pr113	1964	10	10 Zlotych. Copper-Nickel. Shield on eagle with wings open. Value below stylized tree.	—
Pr114	1964	20	10 Zlotych. Copper-Nickel. Eagle with wings open. Value below designs.	—
Pr115	1964	500	10 Zlotych. Nickel.	25.00
Pr116	1964	20	20 Zlotych. Copper-Nickel. Shield on eagle with wings open. Standing figure holding spears of grain.	—
Pr117	1964	500	20 Zlotych. Nickel.	25.00
Pr118	1964	20	20 Zlotych. Copper-Nickel.	—
Pr119	1964	10	20 Zlotych. Copper-Nickel. Eagle with wings open. Vertical inscription flanked by designs.	—
Pr120	1964	20	20 Zlotych. Copper-Nickel. Eagle with wings open above inscription and date. Vertical inscription flanked by designs.	—
Pr121	1964	500	20 Zlotych. Nickel.	25.00
Pr122	1964	20	20 Zlotych. Copper-Nickel. Eagle with wings open. Value below tree.	—
Pr123	1964	500	20 Zlotych. Nickel.	25.00
Pr124	1964	20	20 Zlotych. Copper-Nickel. Shield on eagle with wings open. Value below tree.	—
Pr125	1964	20	20 Zlotych. Copper-Nickel. Eagle with wings open. Value below designs.	—
Pr126	1964	500	20 Zlotych. Nickel.	25.00
Pr127	1965	20	10 Zlotych. Copper-Nickel.	—
Pr128	1965	500	10 Zlotych. Nickel.	25.00
Pr129	1965	20	10 Zlotych. Copper-Nickel. Y#54.	—
Pr130	1965	500	10 Zlotych. Nickel. Y#54.	95.00
Pr131	1965	30,000	10 Zlotych. Copper-Nickel. 12.9000 g. Eagle with wings open. Mermaid holding sword and shield.	10.00
Pr132	1965	500	10 Zlotych. Nickel.	35.00
Pr133	1965	30,000	10 Zlotych. Copper-Nickel. 12.9000 g. Eagle with wings open. Mermaid holding sword and shield flanked by ship and house, value at bottom.	10.00
Pr134	1965	500	10 Zlotych. Nickel.	35.00
Pr135	1965	20	10 Zlotych. Copper-Nickel. Eagle with wings open. Value, monument and flying birds.	—
Pr136	1965	500	10 Zlotych. Nickel.	25.00
Pr137	1965	5	10 Zlotych. Aluminum. Kopernik.	—
Pr138	1966	25	10 Zlotych. Copper-Nickel. Eagle with wings open. Head left.	—
Pr139	1966	500	10 Zlotych. Nickel.	25.00
Pr140	1966	500	10 Zlotych. Nickel. Eagle with wings open. Value, monument and flying birds.	25.00
Pr141	1966	10	10 Zlotych. Copper-Nickel.	—
Pr142	1966	10	100 Zlotych. Copper-Nickel.	—
Pr143	1966	10	100 Zlotych. 0.7500 Silver.	—
Pr144	1966	500	100 Zlotych. Nickel. Y#57.	25.00
Pr145	1966	500	100 Zlotych. Nickel.	25.00
Pr146	1966	31,000	100 Zlotych. 0.9000 Silver. 20.0000 g. Eagle with wings open within circle, assorted shields around border. Conjoined half figures facing right, flanked by value.	22.50
Pr147	1966	500	100 Zlotych. Nickel. Eagle with wings open. Conjoined heads right.	25.00
Pr148	1966	30,000	100 Zlotych. 0.9000 Silver. 2 heads.	22.50
Pr149	1967	10	10 Zlotych. Copper-Nickel. Plain edge. Y#59.	—
Pr150	1967	16	10 Zlotych. Copper-Nickel. Milled edge. Y#59.	—
Pr151	1967	500	10 Zlotych. Nickel. Y#59.	25.00
Pr152	1967	20	10 Zlotych. Copper-Nickel. Eagle with wings open above inscription and value. Head facing 1/4 left.	—
Pr153	1967	500	10 Zlotych. Nickel.	25.00
Pr154	1967	16	10 Zlotych. Copper-Nickel. Eagle with wings open. Head left.	—
Pr155	1967	10	10 Zlotych. Plain edge.	—
Pr156	1967	500	10 Zlotych. Nickel.	25.00
Pr157	1967	25	10 Zlotych. Copper-Nickel. Eagle with wings open. Head left.	—
Pr158	1967	500	10 Zlotych. Nickel.	15.00
Pr159	1967	40	10 Zlotych. Copper-Nickel.	—
Pr160	1967	500	10 Zlotych. Nickel.	15.00
Pr161	1967	17	10 Zlotych. Aluminum. Kopernik.	—
Pr162	1967	1	10 Zlotych. Copper-Nickel. Kopernik.	—
Pr163	1967	10	10 Zlotych. Aluminum. Kopernik.	—

KM#	Date	Mintage	Identification	Mkt Val
Pr164	1968	20	10 Zlotych. Copper-Nickel. Eagle with wings open perched on design. 1/4 helmeted head right, XXV to left.	—
Pr165	1968	500	10 Zlotych. Nickel.	25.00
Pr166	1969	20	10 Zlotych. Copper-Nickel. Eagle with wings open within circle. Design divides date within radiant circle, PROBA at lower right.	—
Pr167	1969	500	10 Zlotych. Nickel. PROBA at lower right.	—
Pr168	1969	5	10 Zlotych. Gold. PROBA at lower right.	—
Pr169	1969	20	10 Zlotych. Copper-Nickel. Eagle with wings open within circle. PROBA at lower right.	—
Pr170	1969	500	10 Zlotych. Nickel. PROBA at right.	—
Pr171	1969	500	10 Zlotych. Nickel. Wthout PROBA.	25.00
Pr172	1969	20	10 Zlotych. Copper-Nickel. Eagle with wings open within circle, bold letters around border. 1/4 head right on mirror, bold letters around border.	—
Pr173	1969	500	10 Zlotych. Nickel.	25.00
Pr174	1969	20	10 Zlotych. Copper-Nickel. Eagle with wings open within circle. Letters and numbers within blocks.	—
Pr175	1969	500	10 Zlotych. Nickel.	25.00
Pr176	1970	20	10 Zlotych. Copper-Nickel. Eagle with wings open flanked by shields. Conjoined heads right. 25th Anniversary of Provincial Annexation	—
Pr177	1970	500	10 Zlotych. Nickel. 25th Anniversary of Provincial Annexation.	20.00
Pr178	1970	10	10 Zlotych. Copper-Nickel. Without PROBA.	—
Pr179	1970	20	10 Zlotych. Copper-Nickel. Y#62.	—
Pr180	1970	500	10 Zlotych. Nickel. Y#62.	20.00
Pr181	1970	300	10 Zlotych. Silver. Y#62.	40.00
Pr182	1970	5	10 Zlotych. Aluminum. Kopernik.	—
Pr183	1971	20	10 Zlotych. Copper-Nickel. Y#63.	—
Pr184	1971	500	10 Zlotych. Nickel. Y#63.	20.00
Pr185	1971	51,000	10 Zlotych. Copper-Nickel. Eagle with wings open. Baby nursing in front of world globe, FAO above.	12.50
Pr186	1971	500	10 Zlotych. Nickel. FAO, baby nursing.	20.00
Pr187	1971	52,000	10 Zlotych. Copper-Nickel. 9.5000 g. Eagle with wings open. Spears of grain on top of globe, F.A.O. logo between spears.	12.50
Pr188	1971	500	10 Zlotych. Nickel. FAO, wheat.	20.00
Pr189	1971	20	10 Zlotych. Copper-Nickel. Y#64.	—

KM#	Date	Mintage	Identification	Mkt Val
Pr190	1971	500	10 Zlotych. Nickel. Y#64.	20.00
Pr191	1971	20	10 Zlotych. Copper-Nickel. Eagle with wings open within eagle with wings open, all within circle. Medal in front of inscription.	—
Pr192	1971	500	10 Zlotych. Nickel. Medal.	20.00
Pr193	1972	20	10 Zlotych. Copper-Nickel. Y#65 but date inside legend.	25.00
Pr194	1972	500	10 Zlotych. Nickel. Y#65 but date inside legend.	—
Pr195	1972	20	10 Zlotych. Copper-Nickel. Y#65.	—
Pr196	1972	500	10 Zlotych. Nickel. Y#65.	20.00
Pr197	1972	—	50 Zlotych. Copper-Nickel.	—
Pr198	1972	20	50 Zlotych. 0.7500 Silver. Y#66, Chopin.	—
Pr199	1972	500	50 Zlotych. Nickel. Y#66.	18.00
Pr200	1972	—	50 Zlotych. Bronze. Chopin, without PROBA.	—
Pr201	1972	20	50 Zlotych. 0.7500 Silver. Chopin, without PROBA.	—
Pr202	1972	15,000	50 Zlotych. 0.7500 Silver. Stylized eagle with wings open within circle. Stylized head of Chopin 3/4 right. Chopin.	20.00
Pr203	1972	500	50 Zlotych. Nickel. Chopin.	20.00
Pr204	1973	20	10 Zlotych. Copper-Nickel. Eagle with wings open above inscription and date. Design above inscription and value.	—
Pr205	1973	500	10 Zlotych. Nickel.	20.00
Pr206	1973	20	10 Zlotych. Copper-Nickel. Eagle with wings open. Design within dates.	—
Pr207	1973	500	10 Zlotych. Nickel.	20.00
Pr208	1973	10	10 Zlotych. Copper-Nickel. Kopernik.	—
Pr209	1973	500	10 Zlotych. Nickel. Kopernik.	—
Pr210	1973	20	20 Zlotych. Copper-Nickel. Plain edge. Without PROBA, Y#67.	—
Pr211	1973	20	20 Zlotych. Copper-Nickel. Eagle with wings open within circle. Value within designed waterfall. Ornamented edge.	30.00
Pr212	1973	13,000	20 Zlotych. Copper-Nickel. 10.1500 g. Milled edge. Y#67.	—
Pr213	1973	500	20 Zlotych. Nickel. Y#67.	20.00
Pr214	1973	16,000	20 Zlotych. Copper-Nickel. 10.1500 g. Tree.	—
Pr215	1973	500	20 Zlotych. Nickel. Tree.	20.00
Pr216	1973	—	100 Zlotych. Copper. Kopernik.	—
Pr217	1973	20	100 Zlotych. 0.6250 Silver. Kopernik.	—
Pr218	1973	500	100 Zlotych. Nickel. Kopernik.	20.00
Pr219	1973	500	100 Zlotych. Nickel. Y#68.	15.00
Pr220	1973	5,000	100 Zlotych. 0.6250 Silver. Y#68.	15.00
Pr221	1973	1,222	100 Zlotych. 0.6250 Silver. Eagle with wings open divides date. Head of Kopernik 1/4 right.	35.00
Pr222	1973	500	100 Zlotych. Nickel. Kopernik.	20.00
Pr223	1974	40	10 Zlotych. Copper-Nickel. Sienkiewicz.	—
Pr224	1974	500	10 Zlotych. Nickel. Sienkiewicz.	20.00
Pr225	1974	40	10 Zlotych. Copper-Nickel. Y#74.	—
Pr226	1974	500	10 Zlotych. Nickel. Y#74.	20.00
Pr227	1974	10,000	20 Zlotych. Copper-Nickel. Y#69.	—
Pr228	1974	500	20 Zlotych. Nickel. Y#69.	20.00

KM#	Date	Mintage	Identification	Mkt Val
Pr229	1974	20	20 Zlotych. Copper-Nickel. 4 laborers.	—
Pr230	1974	500	20 Zlotych. Nickel. 4 laborers.	20.00
Pr231	1974	20	20 Zlotych. Copper-Nickel.	—
Pr232	1974	500	20 Zlotych. Nickel.	—
Pr233	1974	20	20 Zlotych. Copper-Nickel. XXX LAT PRL.	—
Pr234	1974	500	20 Zlotych. Nickel. XXX LAT PRL.	20.00
Pr235	1974	20	20 Zlotych. Copper-Nickel. Y#70.	—
Pr236	1974	500	20 Zlotych. Nickel. Y#70.	—
Pr237	1974	20	20 Zlotych. Copper-Nickel. Eagle with wings open above value. Letters within circle of 1/2 gear and 1/2 flower design.	—
Pr238	1974	500	20 Zlotych. Nickel.	20.00
Pr239	1974	500	100 Zlotych. Nickel. Eagle with wings open. Profile of Curie left, symbol at right.	17.50
Pr240	1974	10,000	100 Zlotych. 0.6250 Silver. Curie left.	12.50
Pr241	1974	500	100 Zlotych. Nickel. Y#71.	30.00
Pr242	1974	10	100 Zlotych. 0.6250 Silver. Y#71.	20.00
Pr243	1974	500	100 Zlotych. Nickel. Curie right.	15.00
Pr244	1974	10,000	100 Zlotych. 0.6250 Silver. Curie right.	12.50
Pr245	1974	500	100 Zlotych. Nickel. Royal Castle in Warsaw.	—
Pr246	1974	20	100 Zlotych. 0.6250 Silver. Royal Castle in Warsaw.	—
Pr247	1974	500	200 Zlotych. Nickel. Eagle with wings open within square. Triple x and letters within square.	20.00
Pr248	1974	20	200 Zlotych. 0.6250 Silver.	—
Pr249	1975	—	10 Zlotych. Aluminum. Boleslaw Prus.	—
Pr250	1975	40	10 Zlotych. Copper-Nickel. Boleslaw Prus.	—
Pr251	1975	500	10 Zlotych. Nickel. Boleslaw Prus.	20.00
Pr252	1975	20	20 Zlotych. Copper-Nickel. Year of the Woman.	—
Pr253	1975	500	20 Zlotych. Nickel. Year of the Woman.	20.00
Pr254	1975	20	20 Zlotych. Copper-Nickel. Eagle with wings open above value. Globe.	—
Pr255	1975	500	20 Zlotych. Nickel. Globe.	15.00
Pr256	1975	5,000	100 Zlotych. 0.6250 Silver. Y#76.	12.50
Pr257	1975	500	100 Zlotych. Nickel. Y#78.	17.50
Pr258	1975	20	100 Zlotych. 0.6250 Silver. Y#78.	—
Pr259	1975	500	100 Zlotych. Nickel. Modrzeiewska.	17.50
Pr260	1975	20	100 Zlotych. 0.6250 Silver. Modrzeiewska.	—
Pr261	1975	500	100 Zlotych. Nickel. Y#77.	17.50
Pr262	1975	20	100 Zlotych. 0.6250 Silver. Y#77.	—

KM#	Date	Mintage	Identification	Mkt Val
Pr263	1975	500	100 Zlotych. Nickel. Paderewski.	12.50
Pr264	1975	20	100 Zlotych. 0.6250 Silver. Paderewski.	—
Pr265	1975	500	200 Zlotych. Nickel. Eagle with wings open above value. Name written in front of swords.	20.00
Pr266	1975	10,000	200 Zlotych. 0.7500 Silver.	22.50
Pr267	1975	500	200 Zlotych. Nickel. Eagle with wings open. Hammer head flanked by dates with triple x on top.	20.00
Pr268	1975	10,000	200 Zlotych. 0.7500 Silver.	17.50
Pr269	1975	500	200 Zlotych. Nickel. Y#79.	20.00
Pr270	1975	2,600	200 Zlotych. 0.7500 Silver. Y#79.	—
Pr271	1976	20	20 Zlotych. Copper-Nickel. 30 Years of Budget Bill.	—
Pr272	1976	500	20 Zlotych. Nickel. 30 Years of Budget Bill.	—
Pr273	1976	20	20 Zlotych. Copper-Nickel. 30 Years of Budget Bill - PRL.	—
Pr274	1976	500	20 Zlotych. Nickel. PRL.	—
Pr275	1976	500	100 Zlotych. Nickel. Y#82.	20.00
Pr276	1976	20	100 Zlotych. 0.6250 Silver. Y#82.	—
Pr277	1976	3,000	100 Zlotych. 0.6250 Silver. Kosciuszko.	35.00
Pr278	1976	500	100 Zlotych. Nickel. Kosciuszko.	20.00
Pr279	1976	20	100 Zlotych.	—
Pr280	1976	500	100 Zlotych. Nickel. Pulaski.	20.00
Pr281	1976	3,000	100 Zlotych. 0.6250 Silver. Pulaski.	35.00
Pr282	1976	20	200 Zlotych. 0.6250 Silver. Olympics.	—
Pr283	1976	—	200 Zlotych. Nickel. Olympic rings and torch.	—
Pr284	1976	500	200 Zlotych. Nickel. Y#86.	30.00
Pr285	1976	6,048	200 Zlotych. 0.7500 Silver. Y#86.	20.00
Pr286	1976	500	200 Zlotych. Nickel. Eagle with wings open divides date. Stylized head with Olympic circles left.	25.00
Pr287	1976	6,050	200 Zlotych. 0.6250 Silver.	30.00
Pr288	1976	500	500 Zlotych. Nickel. Y#83.	20.00
Pr289	1976	300	500 Zlotych. 0.9000 Gold. Y#83.	700
Pr290	1976	500	500 Zlotych. Nickel. Kosciuszko.	20.00
Pr291	1976	500	500 Zlotych. Nickel. Y#85.	20.00
Pr292	1976	300	500 Zlotych. 0.9000 Gold. Y#85.	700
Pr293	1976	500	500 Zlotych. Nickel. Pulaski facing.	20.00
Pr294	1977	100	20 Zlotych. Copper-Nickel. Y#96.	—
Pr295	1977	200	20 Zlotych. Nickel. Y#96.	—
Pr296	1977	500	100 Zlotych. Nickel. Y#88.	—
Pr297	1977	3,000	100 Zlotych. 0.6250 Silver. Y#88.	42.50
Pr298	1977	500	100 Zlotych. Nickel. Sienkiewicz facing.	12.50
Pr299	1977	3,000	100 Zlotych. 0.6250 Silver. Sienkiewicz facing.	40.00
Pr300	1977	500	100 Zlotych. Nickel. Y#89.	—
Pr301	1977	3,100	100 Zlotych. 0.6250 Silver. Y#89.	25.00
Pr302	1977	500	100 Zlotych. Nickel. Reymont profile left.	—
Pr303	1977	3,100	100 Zlotych. 0.6250 Silver. Reymont profile left.	38.00
Pr304	1977	500	100 Zlotych. Nickel. Eagle with wings open divides date. Catfish.	35.00
Pr305	1977	5,100	100 Zlotych. 0.6250 Silver. Fish.	45.00
Pr306	1977	500	100 Zlotych. Nickel. Y#91.	25.00
Pr307	1977	100	100 Zlotych. 0.6250 Silver. Y#91.	—
Pr308	1977	500	100 Zlotych. Nickel. Distant Krakow castle.	—
Pr309	1977	3,100	100 Zlotych. 0.6250 Silver. Distant Krakow castle.	42.50
Pr310	1977	500	100 Zlotych. Nickel. Bison.	35.00
Pr311	1977	5,400	100 Zlotych. 0.6250 Silver. Bison.	45.00
Pr312	1977	6	2000 Zlotych. Gold. Chopin.	—
Pr313	1977	500	2000 Zlotych. Nickel. Chopin.	—
Pr314	1978	100	20 Zlotych. Copper-Nickel. Y#97.	—
Pr315	1978	500	20 Zlotych. Nickel. Y#97.	—
Pr316	1978	100	20 Zlotych. Copper-Nickel. Y#96.	—
Pr317	1978	500	20 Zlotych. Nickel. Y#96.	—
Pr318	1978	100	100 Zlotych. 0.6250 Silver. Y#92.	—
Pr319	1978	500	100 Zlotych. Nickel. Y#92.	—
Pr320	1978	100	100 Zlotych. 0.6250 Silver. Similar to KM#PrM255 but with lock of hair at left of face.	—
Pr321	1978	500	100 Zlotych. Nickel. Similar to KM#PrK255.	—
Pr322	1978	500	100 Zlotych. Nickel. Mickiewicz profile.	—
Pr323	1978	3,100	100 Zlotych. 0.6250 Silver. Eagle with wings open divides date. Head of Mickiewicz left.	40.00
Pr324	1978	100	100 Zlotych. 0.6250 Silver. Y#93.	—
Pr325	1978	500	100 Zlotych. Nickel. Y#93.	—
Pr326	1978	500	100 Zlotych. Nickel. Elk head.	—
Pr327	1978	3,100	100 Zlotych. 0.6250 Silver. Eagle with wings open divides date. Moose head.	50.00
Pr328	1978	500	100 Zlotych. Nickel. Beaver on wood.	—
Pr329	1978	3,100	100 Zlotych. 0.6250 Silver. Beaver on wood.	50.00
Pr330	1978	500	100 Zlotych. Nickel. Beaver on grass.	65.00
Pr331	1978	3,100	100 Zlotych. 0.6250 Silver. Beaver on grass.	50.00
Pr332	1978	100	100 Zlotych. 0.6250 Silver. Y#94.	—
Pr333	1978	500	100 Zlotych. Nickel. Y#94.	—
Pr334	1978	500	100 Zlotych. Nickel. Eagle with wings open divides date. Head of Korczak right.	—
Pr335	1978	3,100	100 Zlotych. 0.6250 Silver. Korczak.	22.50
Pr336	1978	500	100 Zlotych. Nickel. Eagle with wings open divides date. Globe within legend.	—
Pr337	1978	3,100	100 Zlotych. 0.6250 Silver. Globe in legend.	47.50
Pr338	1979	500	2 Zlotych. Nickel.	—
Pr339	1979	500	5 Zlotych. Nickel.	—
Pr340	1979	500	20 Zlotych. Nickel. I.Y.C., dancers.	—
Pr341	1979	4,100	20 Zlotych. 0.6250 Silver. I.Y.C.	25.00
Pr342	1979	500	20 Zlotych. Nickel. I.Y.C. Health Center.	—
Pr343	1979	30,000	20 Zlotych. Copper-Nickel. I.Y.C. Health Center.	6.00
Pr344	1979	100	50 Zlotych. Copper-Nickel. Eagle with wings open divides date. Mieszko I.	—
Pr345	1979	500	50 Zlotych. Nickel. Mieszko I.	—
Pr346	1979	100	100 Zlotych. 0.6250 Silver. Y#98.	—
Pr347	1979	500	100 Zlotych. Nickel. Y#98.	—
Pr348	1979	500	100 Zlotych. Nickel. Wieniawski profile.	—
Pr349	1979	3,100	100 Zlotych. 0.6250 Silver. Wieniawski profile.	25.00
Pr350	1979	100	100 Zlotych. 0.6250 Silver. Y#104.	—
Pr351	1979	500	100 Zlotych. Nickel. Y#104.	—
Pr352	1979	500	100 Zlotych. Nickel. Eagle with wings open divides date. Lynx.	65.00
Pr353	1979	4,100	100 Zlotych. 0.6250 Silver. Lynx.	45.00
Pr354	1979	100	100 Zlotych. 0.6250 Silver. Y#105.	—
Pr355	1979	500	100 Zlotych. Nickel. Y#105.	—

KM#	Date	Mintage	Identification	Mkt Val
Pr356	1979	500	100 Zlotych. Nickel. Mountain goat on rock.	55.00
Pr357	1979	4,100	100 Zlotych. 0.6250 Silver. Mountain goat on rock.	45.00
Pr358	1979	100	100 Zlotych. 0.6250 Silver. Y#103.	—
Pr359	1979	500	100 Zlotych. Nickel. Y#103.	—
Pr360	1979	500	100 Zlotych. Nickel. Eagle with wings open divides date. Head of Zamenhof facing.	—
Pr361	1979	3,100	100 Zlotych. 0.6250 Silver. Zamenhof facing.	30.00
Pr362	1979	100	200 Zlotych. 0.7500 Silver. Y#101.	—
Pr363	1979	500	200 Zlotych. Nickel. Y#101.	—
Pr364	1979	500	200 Zlotych. Nickel. Mieszko.	—
Pr365	1979	4,100	200 Zlotych. 0.7500 Silver. Mieszko I.	25.00
Pr366	1979	5	2000 Zlotych. 0.9000 Gold. Y#106.	—
Pr367	1979	500	2000 Zlotych. Nickel. Y#106.	—
Pr368	1979	6	2000 Zlotych. 0.9000 Gold. Y#107.	—
Pr369	1979	500	2000 Zlotych. Nickel. Y#107.	—
Pr370	1979	4	2000 Zlotych. 0.9000 Gold. Y#102.	—
Pr371	1979	—	2000 Zlotych. Bronze. Y#102.	—
Pr372	1979	500	2000 Zlotych. Nickel. Y#102.	—
Pr373	1979	4	2000 Zlotych. 0.9000 Gold. Mieszko I, PrG266.	—
Pr374	1979	—	2000 Zlotych. Bronze. PrG266.	—
Pr375	1979	500	2000 Zlotych. Nickel. PrG266.	—
Pr376	1980	100	20 Zlotych. 0.6250 Silver. Y#108.	—
Pr377	1980	500	20 Zlotych. Nickel. Y#108.	75.00
PrA378	1980	100	20 Zlotych. Nickel. Eagle with wings open divides date. Stylized runner with torch, Olympic rings at right.	90.00
Pr378	1980	100	20 Zlotych. Copper-Nickel. Y#112.	—
Pr379	1980	500	20 Zlotych. Nickel. Y#112.	—
Pr380	1980	20	20 Zlotych. Copper-Nickel. Ship.	—
Pr381	1980	500	20 Zlotych. Nickel. Ship.	—
Pr382	1980	500	20 Zlotych. Nickel. 1905-Lodz.	—
Pr383	1980	10,000	20 Zlotych. Copper-Nickel. 1905-Lodz.	—
Pr384	1980	20	20 Zlotych. Copper-Nickel. 75th Anniversary of Lodz riots.	—
Pr385	1980	500	20 Zlotych. Nickel. 75th Anniversary of Lodz riots.	—
Pr386	1980	20	50 Zlotych. Copper-Nickel. Y#114.	—
Pr387	1980	500	50 Zlotych. Nickel. Y#114.	—
Pr388	1980	20	50 Zlotych. Copper-Nickel. Boleslaw I inscription below.	—
Pr389	1980	500	50 Zlotych. Nickel. Boleslaw I, inscription below.	—
Pr390	1980	20	50 Zlotych. Copper-Nickel. Y#117.	—
Pr391	1980	500	100 Zlotych. Nickel. Eagle with wings open divides date. Ship.	—
Pr392	1980	4,000	100 Zlotych. 0.6250 Silver. Ship.	38.50
Pr393	1980	100	100 Zlotych. Copper-Nickel. Olympic flame and rings.	—
Pr394	1980	500	100 Zlotych. Nickel. Eagle with wings open divides date. Stylized runner holding torch, Olympic rings at right.	90.00
Pr395	1980	4,100	100 Zlotych. 0.6250 Silver. Olympic flame and rings.	35.00
PrA396	1980	500	100 Zlotych. Nickel. Y#109.	90.00
Pr396	1980	20	100 Zlotych. 0.6250 Silver. Y#121.	—
Pr397	1980	500	100 Zlotych. Nickel. Y#121.	—
Pr398	1980	500	100 Zlotych. Nickel. Eagle with wings open divides date. Birds.	65.00
Pr399	1980	4,018	100 Zlotych. 0.6250 Silver. Birds.	45.00
Pr400	1980	100	100 Zlotych. 0.6250 Silver. Y#120.	—
Pr401	1980	500	100 Zlotych. Nickel.	—
Pr402	1980	500	100 Zlotych. Nickel. Larger head of Kochanowski.	—
Pr403	1980	4,100	100 Zlotych. 0.6250 Silver. Larger head of Kochanowski.	20.00
Pr404	1980	100	200 Zlotych. 0.7500 Silver. Y#110.	—
Pr405	1980	500	200 Zlotych. Nickel. Y#110.	90.00
Pr406	1980	100	200 Zlotych. 0.7500 Silver. Y#110a.	—
Pr407	1980	500	200 Zlotych. Nickel. Y#110a.	90.00
Pr408	1980	500	200 Zlotych. Nickel. Eagle with wings open divides date. Olympic skier with torch mm.	100
Pr409	1980	3,620	200 Zlotych. 0.7500 Silver. Olympic skier with torch mm.	45.00
Pr410	1980	500	200 Zlotych. Nickel. Olympic skier without mm.	100
Pr411	1980	3,620	200 Zlotych. 0.7500 Silver. Olympic skier without mm.	45.00
Pr412	1980	20	200 Zlotych. 0.7500 Silver. Y#115.	—
Pr413	1980	500	200 Zlotych. Nickel. Y#115.	—
Pr414	1980	500	200 Zlotych. Nickel. Boleslaw I torso.	—
Pr415	1980	4,020	200 Zlotych. 0.7500 Silver. Boleslaw I torso.	25.00
Pr416	1980	20	200 Zlotych. 0.7500 Silver. Y#118.	—
Pr417	1980	500	200 Zlotych. Nickel. Y#118.	—
Pr418	1980	500	200 Zlotych. Nickel. Kazimierz I torso.	—
Pr419	1980	4,020	200 Zlotych. 0.7500 Silver. Kazimierz I torso.	25.00
Pr420	1980	3	2000 Zlotych. 0.9000 Gold. Y#111.	—
Pr421	1980	—	2000 Zlotych. Bronze. Y#111.	—
Pr422	1980	500	2000 Zlotych. Nickel. Y#111.	—
Pr423	1980	6	2000 Zlotych. 0.9000 Gold. Y#116.	—
Pr424	1980	500	2000 Zlotych. Nickel. Y#116.	—
Pr425	1980	6	2000 Zlotych. 0.9000 Gold. Odnowiciel.	—
Pr426	1980	500	2000 Zlotych. Nickel. Odnowiciel.	—
Pr427	1980	500	2000 Zlotych. Nickel. Olympic skier without torch mm.	—
Pr428	1980	1,500	2000 Zlotych. 0.9000 Gold. Eagle with wings open divides date. Olympic skier without torch mm.	350
Pr429	1981	500	20 Zlotych. Nickel. Restoration of Krakow.	—
Pr430	1981	30,000	20 Zlotych. Copper-Nickel. Restoration of Krakow.	8.50
Pr431	1981	20	50 Zlotych. Copper-Nickel. Y#122.	—
Pr432	1981	500	50 Zlotych. Nickel. Y#122.	—
Pr433	1981	20	50 Zlotych. Copper-Nickel. Y#124.	—
Pr434	1981	500	50 Zlotych. Nickel. Y#124.	—
Pr435	1981	20	50 Zlotych. Copper-Nickel. Y#128.	—
Pr436	1981	500	50 Zlotych. Nickel. Y#128.	—
Pr437	1981	20	50 Zlotych. Copper-Nickel. Y#127.	—
Pr438	1981	500	50 Zlotych. Nickel. Y#127.	—
Pr439	1981	120	100 Zlotych. 0.6250 Silver. Y#123.	—
Pr440	1981	500	100 Zlotych. Nickel. Y#123.	—
Pr441	1981	500	100 Zlotych. Nickel. Sikorski.	—
Pr442	1981	5,020	100 Zlotych. 0.6250 Silver. Sikorski.	27.50
Pr443	1981	500	100 Zlotych. Nickel. St. Mary's Church.	—
Pr444	1981	4,020	100 Zlotych. 0.6250 Silver. St. Mary's Church.	26.50
Pr445	1981	20	100 Zlotych. 0.6250 Silver. Y#126.	—
Pr446	1981	500	100 Zlotych. Nickel. Y#126.	—
Pr447	1981	500	100 Zlotych. Nickel.	40.00
Pr448	1981	4,020	100 Zlotych. 0.6250 Silver. Horses.	40.00
Pr449	1981	20	100 Zlotych. 0.7500 Silver. Y#125.	—
Pr450	1981	500	200 Zlotych. Nickel. Y#125.	—
Pr451	1981	500	200 Zlotych. Nickel. Boleslaw II.	—
Pr452	1981	4,020	200 Zlotych. 0.7500 Silver. Boleslaw II.	25.00
Pr453	1981	20	200 Zlotych. 0.7500 Silver. Y#129.	—
Pr454	1981	500	200 Zlotych. Nickel. Y#129.	—
Pr455	1981	500	200 Zlotych. Nickel. Wladyslaw I Herman.	—
Pr456	1981	4,020	200 Zlotych. 0.7500 Silver.	—
Pr457	1981	—	200 Zlotych. 0.7500 Silver. Wladyslaw I.	—
Pr458	1981	4	2000 Zlotych. 0.9000 Gold. Y#126.	—
Pr459	1981	500	2000 Zlotych. Nickel. Y#126.	—
Pr460	1981	4	2000 Zlotych. 0.9000 Gold. Y#131.	—
Pr461	1981	500	2000 Zlotych. 0.9000 Gold. Y#131.	—
Pr462	1982	20	50 Zlotych. Copper-Nickel. Y#133.	—
Pr463	1982	500	50 Zlotych. Nickel. Y#133.	—
Pr464	1982	500	100 Zlotych. Nickel. Y#141.	—
Pr465	1982	500	100 Zlotych. Nickel. Eagle with wings open divides date. Storks.	65.00
Pr466	1982	4,000	100 Zlotych. 0.6250 Silver. Storks.	45.00
Pr467	1982	20	200 Zlotych. 0.7500 Silver. Y#132.	—
Pr468	1982	500	200 Zlotych. Nickel. Y#132.	—
Pr469	1982	500	200 Zlotych. Nickel.	—
Pr470	1982	3,000	200 Zlotych. 0.7500 Silver.	60.00
Pr471	1982	6,000	200 Zlotych. 0.7500 Silver. Soccer player leaning right.	30.00
Pr472	1982	6,002	200 Zlotych. 0.7500 Silver. Soccer player leaning left.	60.00
Pr473	1982	500	200 Zlotych. Nickel. Soccer player leaning right.	—
Pr474	1982	500	200 Zlotych. Nickel. Without Espana 82, Y#130.	—
Pr475	1982	500	200 Zlotych. Nickel. Eagle with wings open divides date. Stylized soccer player leaning left.	—
Pr476	1982	500	500 Zlotych. Nickel. Eagle with wings open divides date. Ship.	—
Pr477	1982	25,000	500 Zlotych. 0.6250 Silver. Ship.	25.00
Pr478	1982	10,000	1000 Zlotych. 0.7500 Silver. Pope John Paul II.	35.00
Pr479	1982	500	1000 Zlotych. Nickel. Y#144.	—
Pr480	1982	500	1000 Zlotych. Nickel.	—
Pr481	1983	20	50 Zlotych. Copper-Nickel. Y#142.	—
Pr482	1983	500	50 Zlotych. Nickel. Y#142.	—
Pr483	1983	20	50 Zlotych. Copper-Nickel. Y#145.	—
Pr484	1983	500	50 Zlotych. Nickel. Y#145.	—
Pr485	1983	20	50 Zlotych. Copper-Nickel. Y#146.	—
Pr486	1983	500	50 Zlotych. Nickel. Y#146.	—
Pr487	1983	500	100 Zlotych. Nickel. Y#147.	—
Pr488	1983	500	100 Zlotych. Nickel.	—
Pr489	1983	3,000	100 Zlotych. 0.6250 Silver. Bears.	45.00
Pr490	1983	500	200 Zlotych. Nickel. Y#143.	—

KM#	Date	Mintage	Identification	Mkt Val
Pr491	1983	500	200 Zlotych. Nickel. Eagle with wings open divides date. Horse and rider rearing above fallen indian.	—
Pr492	1983	4,000	200 Zlotych. 0.7500 Silver. Jan III Sobieski.	60.00
Pr493	1983	500	500 Zlotych. Nickel. Eagle with wings open divides date. Gymnast.	—
Pr494	1983	7,000	500 Zlotych. 0.7500 Silver. Gymnast.	35.00
Pr495	1983	500	500 Zlotych. Nickel. Eagle with wings open divides date. Speed skater within horizontal lines.	—
Pr496	1983	6,000	500 Zlotych. 0.7500 Silver. Speed skater.	35.00
Pr497	1984	500	10 Zlotych. Nickel. Y#152.1.	—
Pr498	1984	500	20 Zlotych. Nickel. Y#153.1.	—
Pr499	1984	500	100 Zlotych. Nickel. Y#148.	—
Pr500	1984	500	100 Zlotych. Nickel. Y#151.	—
Pr501	1984	500	200 Zlotych. Nickel. Y#149.	—
Pr502	1984	500	200 Zlotych. Nickel. Y#150.	—
Pr503	1984	500	500 Zlotych. Nickel. Y#154.	—
Pr504	1984	500	1000 Zlotych. Nickel. Wincenty Witos.	—
Pr505	1984	3,000	1000 Zlotych. 0.6250 Silver. Wincenty Witos.	35.00
Pr506	1984	500	1000 Zlotych. Nickel. PRL.	—
Pr507	1984	2,004	1000 Zlotych. 0.6250 Silver. 40th Anniversary of Peoples Republic.	35.00
Pr508	1984	500	1000 Zlotych. Nickel. Eagle with wings open divides date. Swan.	—
Pr509	1984	5,700	1000 Zlotych. 0.6250 Silver. Environment.	45.00
Pr510	1985	500	100 Zlotych. Nickel. Y#155.	—
Pr511	1985	500	100 Zlotych. Nickel. Y#157.	—
Pr512	1985	500	200 Zlotych. Nickel. Eagle with wings open divides date. Fallen soccer player within net design.	—
Pr513	1985	15,000	200 Zlotych. Copper-Nickel.	8.50
Pr514	1985	500	200 Zlotych. Nickel. Hospital Center.	—
Pr515	1985	37,300	200 Zlotych. Nickel Plated Iron. Hospital Center	16.50
Pr516	1985	500	500 Zlotych. Nickel. Y#156.	—
Pr517	1985	500	500 Zlotych. Nickel. Y#158.	—
Pr518	1985	500	500 Zlotych. Nickel. Y#159.	—
Pr519	1985	500	1000 Zlotych. Nickel. Przemyslaw II.	—
Pr520	1985	2,500	1000 Zlotych. 0.7500 Silver. Przemyslaw II.	15.00
Pr521	1985	500	1000 Zlotych. Nickel. Eagle with wings open divides date. Heart design. Hospital Center.	—
Pr522	1985	2,500	1000 Zlotych. 0.7500 Silver. Hospital Center.	25.00
Pr523	1985	500	1000 Zlotych. Nickel. U.N.	—
Pr524	1985	2,500	1000 Zlotych. 0.7500 Silver. U.N.	40.00
Pr525	1985	500	1000 Zlotych. Nickel. Eagle with wings open divides date. Squirrel.	—
Pr526	1985	2,500	1000 Zlotych. 0.7500 Silver. Squirrel.	85.00
Pr527	1986	500	50 Groszy. Nickel. Y#48.2.	—
Pr528	1986	500	Zloty. Nickel. Y#49.2.	—
Pr529	1986	500	2 Zlote. Nickel. Y#80.2.	—
Pr530	1986	500	5 Zlotych. Nickel. Y#81.2.	—
Pr531	1986	500	100 Zlotych. Nickel. Y#160.	—
Pr532	1986	500	200 Zlotych. Nickel. Y#162.	60.00
Pr533	1986	6,000	200 Zlotych. Copper-Nickel. Y#162.	45.00
Pr534	1986	500	200 Zlotych. Nickel. Wladyslaw.	—
Pr535	1986	10,000	200 Zlotych. Copper-Nickel. Wladyslaw.	15.00
Pr536	1986	500	500 Zlotych. Nickel. Y#161.	—
Pr537	1986	500	500 Zlotych. Nickel. Y#162.	—
Pr538	1986	500	500 Zlotych. Nickel. Y#166.	—
Pr539	1986	—	500 Zlotych. Nickel. Y#225.	—
Pr540	1986	500	1000 Zlotych. Nickel. Soccer.	—
Pr541	1986	9,000	1000 Zlotych. 0.7500 Silver. Eagle with wings open divides date. Soccer ball and globe.	—
Pr542	1986	500	1000 Zlotych. Nickel. Education.	—
Pr543	1986	25,400	1000 Zlotych. 0.6250 Silver. Education.	—
Pr544	1986	22,000	1000 Zlotych. 0.7500 Silver. Hospital Center.	—
Pr545	1986	500	1000 Zlotych. Nickel. Wladyslaw I.	—
Pr546	1986	2,500	1000 Zlotych. 0.7500 Silver. Wladyslaw I.	30.00
Pr547	1986	500	1000 Zlotych. Nickel. Eagle with wings open divides date. Owl.	75.00
Pr548	1986	6,000	1000 Zlotych. 0.7500 Silver. Owl.	50.00
Pr549	1986	—	1000 Zlotych. Nickel. Eagle with wings open divides date. School design.	—
Pr550	1986	—	1000 Zlotych. 0.6250 Silver. School aid.	—
Pr551	1987	500	100 Zlotych. Nickel. Y#167.	—
Pr552	1987	500	200 Zlotych. Nickel. Eagle with wings open divides date. Europe soccer.	—
Pr553	1987	15,000	200 Zlotych. Copper-Nickel. Europe soccer.	12.00
Pr554	1987	500	200 Zlotych. Nickel. Olympics - Tennis.	—
Pr555	1987	10,000	200 Zlotych. Copper-Nickel. Olympics - Tennis.	13.50
Pr556	1987	500	500 Zlotych. Nickel. Y#165.	—
Pr557	1987	500	500 Zlotych. Nickel. Y#166.	—
Pr558	1987	500	500 Zlotych. Nickel. Y#172.	—
Pr559	1987	500	500 Zlotych. Nickel. Y#173.	—
Pr560	1987	500	1000 Zlotych. Nickel. Wratislavia.	—
Pr561	1987	24,000	1000 Zlotych. 0.7500 Silver. Wratislavia.	15.00
Pr562	1987	500	1000 Zlotych. Nickel. Slaskie Museum.	—
Pr563	1987	11,500	1000 Zlotych. 0.7500 Silver. Slaskie Museum.	20.00
Pr564	1987	500	1000 Zlotych. Nickel. Olympic cross country skier.	—
Pr565	1987	10,000	1000 Zlotych. 0.7500 Silver. Olympic cross country skier.	15.00
Pr566	1987	500	1000 Zlotych. Nickel. Eagle with wings open divides date. Olympic archery.	—
Pr567	1987	10,000	1000 Zlotych. 0.7500 Silver. Olympic archery.	37.50
Pr568	1987	500	1000 Zlotych. Nickel. Eagle with wings open divides date. Kazimierz III.	—
Pr569	1987	2,500	1000 Zlotych. 0.7500 Silver. Kazimierz III.	75.00
Pr570	1987	9	1000 Zlotych. Gold. Y#168.	—
Pr571	1987	9	2000 Zlotych. Gold. Y#169; Similar design to Pr570.	—
Pr572	1987	9	5000 Zlotych. Gold. Y#170; Similar design to Pr570.	—
Pr573	1987	9	10000 Zlotych. Gold. Y#171; Similar design to Pr570.	—
Pr574	1987	5	200000 Zlotych. Gold. Y#163; Similar design to Pr570. Photo reduced.	—
Pr575	1988	500	200 Zlotych. Nickel. Eagle with wings open divides date. Soccer 1990.	—
Pr576	1988	10,000	200 Zlotych. Copper-Nickel. Soccer 1990.	12.50
Pr577	1988	7,000	500 Zlotych. Silver. Soccer 1990, Y#184.	—

KM#	Date	Mintage	Identification	Mkt Val

KM#	Date	Mintage	Identification	Mkt Val
Pr578	1988	500	1000 Zlotych. Nickel. Queen Jadwiga.	—
Pr579	1988	2,500	1000 Zlotych. 0.7500 Silver. Queen Jadwiga.	250
Pr580	1988	500	1000 Zlotych. Nickel. Eagle with wings open divides date. Soccer 1990.	—
Pr581	1988	7,000	1000 Zlotych. 0.7500 Silver. Soccer 1990.	27.50
Pr582	1991	300	20000 Zlotych. 0.9990 Gold. Pope John Paul II right. Similar design to Pr583.	375
Pr583	1991	—	50000 Zlotych. 0.9990 Gold. Pope John Paul II right.	500

KM#	Date	Mintage	Identification	Mkt Val
Pr584	1991	—	100000 Zlotych. 0.9990 Gold. Eagle with wings open divides date. Bust of Pope 1/4 right. Similar design to Pr583.	600
Pr585	1991	—	200000 Zlotych. 0.9990 Gold. Pope John Paul II right. Similar design to Pr583.	750
Pr586	1994	—	1000 Zlotych. Copper-Nickel. Y#267.	—

MINT SETS

KM#	Date	Mintage	Identification	Issue Price	Mkt Val
MS1	1964 (2)	—	Y#52, 52a	—	15.00
MS2	1983 (11)	—	Y#AA47, A47, 48.1, 49.1, 69, 80.1, 81.1, 73, 142, 145, 146	—	37.50
MS3	1984 (9)	—	Y#48.1, 49.1, 80.1, 81.1, 73, 152.1, 153.1(Part 1), 148, 151 (Part 2)	—	18.50
MS4	1985 (10)	—	Y#AA47, A47, 48.1, 49.1, 73, 80.1, 81.1, 152.1, 153.1 (Part 1), 155, 157 (Part 2)	—	17.50

PROOF SETS

KM#	Date	Mintage	Identification	Issue Price	Mkt Val
PS1	1979 (6)	5,000	Y#AA47, A47, 80.1, 81.1, 99, 100	—	35.00
PS2	1980 (9)	5,000	Y#AA47, A47, 49.1, 80.1, 81.1, 108, 112, 114, 117	—	55.00
PS3	1981 (10)	5,000	Y#AA47, A47, 49.1, 80.1, 81.1, 73, 122, 124, 127, 128	—	60.00
PS4	1982 (6)	5,000	Y#48.1, 49.1, 80.1, 81.1, 73, 133	—	35.00
PS5	1986 (7)	5,000	Y#48.2, 49.2, 80.2, 81.2, 152.1, 153.1, 160	—	35.00
PS6	1987 (7)	5,000	Y#48.2, 49.2, 80.2, 81.2, 152.1, 153.1, 167	—	35.00
PS7	1988 (7)	5,000	Y#49.2, 80.2, 81.2, 152.1, 153.1, 182, 183 plus medal	—	42.50
PS8	1989 (7)	5,000	Y#49.3, 80.3, 81.3, 152.2, 153.2, 185, 194	—	42.50
PS9	1990 (8)	5,000	Y#49.3, 80.3, 81.3, 152.2, 153.2, 216, 214, 195	—	62.50

PORTUGAL

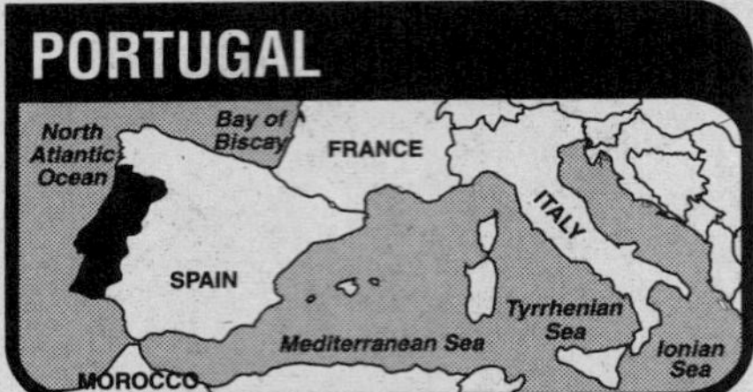

The Portuguese Republic, located in the western part of the Iberian Peninsula in southwestern Europe, has an area of 35,553 sq. mi. (92,080 sq. km.) and a population of *10.5 million. Capital: Lisbon. Portugal's economy is based on agriculture, tourism, minerals, fisheries and a rapidly expanding industrial sector. Textiles account for 33% of the exports and Portuguese wine is world famous. Portugal has become Europe's number one producer of copper and the world's largest producer of cork.

After centuries of domination by Romans, Visigoths and Moors, Portugal emerged in the 12th century as an independent kingdom financially and philosophically prepared for the great period of exploration that would soon follow. Attuned to the inspiration of Prince Henry the Navigator (1394-1460), Portugal's daring explorers of the15th and 16th centuries roamed the world's oceans from Brazil to Japan in an unprecedented burst of energy and endeavor that culminated in 1494 with Portugal laying claim to half the transoceanic world. Unfortunately for the fortunes of the tiny kingdom, the Portuguese population was too small to colonize this vast territory. Less than a century after Portugal laid claim to half the world, English, French and Dutch trading companies had seized the lion's share of the world's colonies and commerce, and Portugal's place as an imperial power was lost forever. The monarchy was overthrown in 1910 and a republic was established.

On April 25, 1974, the government of Portugal was seized by a military junta which reached agreements providing for independence for the Portuguese overseas provinces of Portuguese Guinea (*Guinea-Bissau*), Mozambique, Cape Verde Islands, Angola, and St. Thomas and Prince Islands (*Sao Tome and Principe*).

On January 1, 1986, Portugal became the eleventh member of the European Economic Community and in the first half of 1992 held its first EEC Presidency.

RULERS

Carlos I, 1889-1908
Manuel II, 1908-1910
Republic, 1910 to date

MONETARY SYSTEM

Beginning in 1836 all coins were expressed in terms of Reis and arranged in a decimal sequence (until 1910).

Commencing 1910

100 Centavos = 1 Escudo

KINGDOM

DECIMAL COINAGE

KM# 530 5 REIS

Bronze **Ruler:** Carlos I **Obv:** Head right **Obv. Legend:** CARLOS I REI... **Rev:** Value within wreath

Date	Mintage	F	VF	XF	Unc	BU
1901	1,070,000	2.50	12.50	40.00	90.00	—
1904	720,000	0.75	1.75	12.50	28.00	—
1905	1,340,000	0.75	1.50	6.00	15.00	—
1906/0	1,260	0.30	1.00	2.50	8.00	—
1906/9	Inc. above	0.25	0.75	2.00	7.00	—
1906	Inc. above	0.75	2.00	4.00	10.00	—

KM# 555 5 REIS

Bronze **Ruler:** Manuel II **Obv:** Head left **Rev:** Value within wreath

Date	Mintage	F	VF	XF	Unc	BU
1910	1,000,000	0.30	1.00	2.50	7.00	—

KM# 548 100 REIS

2.5000 g., 0.8350 Silver .0671 oz. ASW **Ruler:** Manuel II **Obv:** Bust left

Date	Mintage	F	VF	XF	Unc	BU
1909	6,363,000	1.50	3.50	6.50	22.00	—
1910	Inc. above	1.25	2.50	4.00	10.00	—

KM# 534 200 REIS

5.0000 g., 0.9170 Silver .1474 oz. ASW **Ruler:** Carlos I **Obv:** Head right **Obv. Legend:** CARLOS I... **Rev:** Value within wreath

Date	Mintage	VG	F	VF	XF	Unc
1901	205,000	30.00	75.00	125	300	—
1903	200,000	12.50	35.00	65.00	115	—

KM# 549 200 REIS

5.0000 g., 0.8350 Silver .1342 oz. ASW **Ruler:** Manuel II **Obv:** Head left **Obv. Legend:** EMANVEL II... **Rev:** Crown above value within wreath

Date	Mintage	VG	F	VF	XF	Unc
1909	7,656,000	2.25	3.50	6.50	12.00	25.00

KM# 535 500 REIS

12.5000 g., 0.9170 Silver .3684 oz. ASW, 30 mm. **Ruler:** Carlos I **Obv:** Head right **Obv. Legend:** CARLOS I... **Rev:** Crowned arms within wreath

Date	Mintage	VG	F	VF	XF	Unc
1901	1,050,000	7.50	22.50	40.00	75.00	150
1903	680,000	6.50	9.00	15.00	30.00	60.00
1906/3	240,000	15.00	35.00	70.00	100	250
1906	Inc. above	12.00	30.00	60.00	90.00	200
1907	384,000	6.00	8.00	12.00	18.00	35.00
1908	1,840,000	5.50	7.50	11.50	16.00	25.00

KM# 547 500 REIS

12.5000 g., 0.9170 Silver .3684 oz. ASW, 30 mm. **Ruler:** Manuel II **Obv:** Head left **Obv. Legend:** EMANVEL II.. **Rev:** Crowned shield within sprigs

Date	Mintage	VG	F	VF	XF	Unc
1908	2,500,000	BV	6.00	10.00	18.00	30.00
1909	Inc. above	8.00	25.00	45.00	85.00	190
1909/8	1,513,000	8.00	25.00	45.00	85.00	195

KM# 556 500 REIS

12.5000 g., 0.9170 Silver .3684 oz. ASW, 30 mm. **Ruler:** Manuel II **Subject:** Peninsular War Centennial **Obv:** Head left **Obv. Legend:** EMANVEL II... **Rev:** Crowned shield **Designer:** Valancio Alves

Date	Mintage	VG	F	VF	XF	Unc
1910	200,000	12.50	35.00	55.00	90.00	175

KM# 557 500 REIS

12.5000 g., 0.9170 Silver ,3684 oz. ASW, 30 mm. **Ruler:** Manuel II **Subject:** Marquis De Pombal **Obv:** Head left **Obv. Legend:** EMANVEL II... **Rev:** Seated Victory flanked by crowned shield and bust statue **Designer:** Venancio Alves

Date	Mintage	VG	F	VF	XF	Unc
1910	400,000	10.00	15.00	25.00	45.00	85.00
1910 Proof	—	Value: 600				

KM# 558 1000 REIS
25.0000 g., 0.9170 Silver .7368 oz. ASW, 37 mm. **Ruler:** Manuel II **Subject:** Peninsular War Centennial **Obv:** Head left **Obv. Legend:** EMANVEL II... **Rev:** Crowned shield **Designer:** Valancio Alves

Date	Mintage	VG	F	VF	XF	Unc
1910	200,000	20.00	45.00	75.00	125	250
1910 Proof	—	Value: 900				

REPUBLIC

DECIMAL COINAGE

KM# 565 CENTAVO
Bronze **Obv:** Value **Rev:** Shield within designed circle

Date	Mintage	F	VF	XF	Unc	BU
1917	2,250,000	0.50	1.00	2.00	4.00	6.00
1918	22,996,000	0.50	1.00	2.00	4.00	6.00
1920	12,535,000	0.50	1.00	2.50	5.00	7.00
1921	4,492,000	10.00	30.00	40.00	70.00	—
1922 Rare	Inc. above	—	—	—	—	—

KM# 567 2 CENTAVOS
Iron **Obv:** Value **Rev:** Shield within designed circle

Date	Mintage	F	VF	XF	Unc	BU
1918	170,000	65.00	150	300	700	—

KM# 568 2 CENTAVOS
Bronze

Date	Mintage	F	VF	XF	Unc	BU
1918	4,295,000	0.50	0.75	2.00	4.00	6.00
1920	10,109,000	0.50	1.50	2.50	5.00	7.00
1921	679,000	25.00	50.00	100	150	—

KM# 566 4 CENTAVOS
Copper-Nickel **Obv:** Value **Rev:** Liberty head left

Date	Mintage	F	VF	XF	Unc	BU
1917	4,961,000	0.35	0.65	1.50	4.00	7.00
1919	10,067,000	0.35	0.65	1.75	4.50	8.00

KM# 569 5 CENTAVOS
Bronze **Obv:** Value **Rev:** Shield within designed circle

Date	Mintage	F	VF	XF	Unc	BU
1920	114,000	35.00	70.00	120	200	—
1921	5,916,000	0.75	2.00	4.00	7.00	9.00
1922	Inc. above	125	250	500	750	—

KM# 572 5 CENTAVOS
Bronze **Obv:** Value **Rev:** Liberty head left

Date	Mintage	F	VF	XF	Unc	BU
1924	6,480,000	0.50	1.50	4.50	10.00	—
1925	7,260,000	3.50	7.50	22.00	40.00	—
1927	26,320,000	0.25	0.75	1.50	5.00	10.00

KM# 563 10 CENTAVOS
2.5000 g., 0.8350 Silver .0671 oz. ASW **Obv:** Liberty head left **Rev:** Shield within designed circle within wreath

Date	Mintage	F	VF	XF	Unc	BU
1915	3,418,000	1.25	2.50	3.50	8.00	12.00

KM# 570 10 CENTAVOS
Copper-Nickel **Obv:** Value **Rev:** Liberty head left

Date	Mintage	F	VF	XF	Unc	BU
1920	1,120,000	3.00	6.00	12.00	20.00	—
1921	1,285,000	3.00	6.00	15.00	25.00	—

KM# 573 10 CENTAVOS
Bronze **Obv:** Value **Rev:** Liberty head left

Date	Mintage	F	VF	XF	Unc	BU
1924	1,210,000	3.00	12.50	45.00	100	—
1925	9,090,000	0.75	1.50	11.00	35.00	—
1926	26,250,000	0.75	2.75	14.50	40.00	—
1930	1,730,000	55.00	125	250	550	—
1938	2,000,000	5.00	20.00	40.00	100	—
1940	3,384,000	1.50	4.00	10.00	25.00	—

KM# 583 10 CENTAVOS
Bronze, 17 mm. **Obv:** Circles within cross **Rev:** Value above sprig **Designer:** M. Norte

Date	Mintage	F	VF	XF	Unc	BU
1942	1,035,000	2.00	4.00	22.50	45.00	—
1943	18,765,000	2.00	5.00	10.00	40.00	—
1944	5,090,000	2.00	5.00	15.00	40.00	—
1945	6,090,000	2.00	4.50	15.00	35.00	—
1946	7,740,000	1.00	2.50	8.00	30.00	—
1947	9,283,000	1.00	2.00	7.50	15.00	—
1948	5,900,000	10.00	30.00	100	150	—
1949	15,240,000	0.25	1.00	5.00	15.00	20.00
1950	8,860,000	1.50	5.00	20.00	60.00	—
1951	5,040,000	1.50	5.00	35.00	75.00	—
1952	4,960,000	2.50	12.00	50.00	125	—
1953	7,548,000	1.50	3.00	5.00	10.00	15.00
1954	2,452,000	1.50	5.00	15.00	60.00	—
1955	10,000,000	0.10	0.50	2.50	6.00	—
1956	3,336,000	0.10	0.50	2.00	5.00	7.50
1957	6,654,000	0.10	0.25	2.00	5.00	—
1958	7,320,000	0.10	0.25	2.00	5.00	—
1959	7,140,000	0.10	0.25	2.00	4.00	5.00
1960	15,055,000	0.10	0.25	2.00	2.00	—
1961	5,020,000	—	0.10	1.50	4.00	—
1962	14,980,000	—	0.10	0.50	1.00	1.50
1963	5,393,000	—	0.10	1.25	2.50	—
1964	10,257,000	—	0.10	0.75	1.50	2.00
1965	15,550,000	—	0.10	1.00	1.75	—
1966	10,200,000	—	0.10	0.50	1.00	—
1967	18,592,000	—	0.10	0.50	1.00	1.50
1968	22,515,000	—	0.10	0.50	1.00	2.00
1969	3,871,000	0.10	0.25	1.25	2.50	—

KM# 594 10 CENTAVOS
Aluminum **Obv:** Circles within cross **Rev:** Value above sprig **Designer:** M. Norte

Date	Mintage	F	VF	XF	Unc	BU
1969	—	—	500	750	1,000	—
1970 Rare	—	—	—	—	—	—
1971	25,673,000	—	—	0.50	1.00	—
1972	10,558,000	—	—	0.50	1.00	—
1973	3,149,000	—	—	1.25	3.50	—
1974	17,043,000	—	—	0.50	1.00	—
1975	22,410,000	—	—	0.50	1.00	—
1976	19,907,000	—	—	0.50	1.00	—
1977	8,431,000	—	—	0.50	1.00	—
1978	2,205,000	—	—	0.50	1.00	—
1979	9,083,000	—	—	1.00	2.50	—

KM# 562 20 CENTAVOS
5.0000 g., 0.8350 Silver .1342 oz. ASW **Obv:** Liberty head left **Rev:** Shield within designed circle and wreath

Date	Mintage	F	VF	XF	Unc	BU
1913	540,000	5.00	35.00	75.00	175	—
1916	706,000	3.00	30.00	40.00	100	—

KM# 571 20 CENTAVOS
Copper-Nickel **Obv:** Value and date within circle **Rev:** Liberty head left within circle

Date	Mintage	F	VF	XF	Unc	BU
1920	1,568,000	3.50	7.00	15.00	20.00	—
1921	3,030,000	4.00	8.00	14.00	22.50	—
1922	580,000	500	900	1,500	3,000	—

KM# 574 20 CENTAVOS
Bronze, 24 mm. **Obv:** Value **Rev:** Liberty head left

Date	Mintage	F	VF	XF	Unc	BU
1924	6,220,000	1.00	4.00	20.00	50.00	—
1925	10,580,000	1.00	4.00	20.00	50.00	—

KM# 584 20 CENTAVOS
Bronze **Obv:** Circles within cross **Rev:** Value above sprig **Designer:** M. Norte

Date	Mintage	F	VF	XF	Unc	BU
1942	10,170,000	1.50	3.50	25.00	60.00	—
1943	Inc. above	1.50	3.00	20.00	60.00	—
1944	7,290,000	1.50	3.00	20.00	60.00	—
1945	7,552,000	1.00	2.00	25.00	60.00	—
1948	2,750,000	2.50	12.00	35.00	135	—
1949	12,250,000	0.10	0.50	6.00	15.00	20.00
1951	3,185,000	0.50	2.00	20.00	150	—
1952	1,815,000	2.00	12.00	35.00	200	—
1953	9,426,000	—	0.75	4.00	8.00	—
1955	5,574,000	—	0.75	4.00	8.00	—
1956	6,450,000	—	0.50	2.75	5.50	7.50
1958	7,470,000	—	0.50	2.75	5.50	7.50
1959	4,780,000	—	0.50	2.75	5.50	7.50
1960	4,790,000	—	0.50	3.50	8.00	—
1961	5,180,000	—	0.50	3.50	8.00	—
1962	2,500,000	0.25	1.50	10.00	18.00	25.00
1963	7,990,000	—	0.25	2.00	3.50	4.50

Date	Mintage	F	VF	XF	Unc	BU
1964	7,010,000	—	0.25	1.50	3.00	4.00
1965	7,365,000	—	0.25	1.00	2.50	—
1966	8,074,999	—	0.25	0.50	2.00	—
1967	9,220,000	—	0.25	0.50	2.00	—
1968	10,372,000	—	0.25	0.50	1.50	2.00
1969	8,657,000	—	0.25	1.00	3.00	—

KM# 595 20 CENTAVOS

Bronze, 16 mm. **Obv:** Circles within cross **Rev:** Value above sprig **Designer:** M. Norte

Date	Mintage	F	VF	XF	Unc	BU
1969	10,891,000	—	0.25	0.75	2.50	—
1970	16,120,000	—	0.25	1.00	3.00	—
1971	1,933,000	—	1.00	2.50	7.50	—
1972	16,354,000	—	—	0.25	1.00	—
1973	4,900,000	—	—	0.25	1.00	—
1974	26,975,000	—	—	0.25	1.00	—

KM# 561 50 CENTAVOS

12.5000 g., 0.8350 Silver .3356 oz. ASW **Obv:** Liberty head left **Rev:** Shield within designed circle and wreath

Date	Mintage	F	VF	XF	Unc	BU
1912	1,695,000	5.50	8.00	15.00	30.00	—
1913	4,443,000	BV	6.00	10.00	20.00	—
1914	4,992,000	5.50	8.00	15.00	30.00	—
1916	5,080,000	BV	6.00	10.00	20.00	—

KM# 575 50 CENTAVOS

Aluminum-Bronze **Obv:** Seated figure **Rev:** Shield within designed circle and wreath

Date	Mintage	F	VF	XF	Unc	BU
1924	810,000	65.00	125	250	400	—
1925	—	1,000	1,500	3,500	7,000	—
1926	4,340,000	2.00	6.00	18.00	40.00	55.00

KM# 577 50 CENTAVOS

Copper-Nickel, 23 mm. **Obv:** Liberty head right **Rev:** Shield within designed circle and wreath above value

Date	Mintage	F	VF	XF	Unc	BU
1927	2,330,000	2.50	12.50	30.00	125	150
1928	6,823,000	2.50	12.50	35.00	220	—
1929	9,779,000	2.50	12.50	30.00	125	150
1930	1,116,000	2.50	20.00	200	550	—
1931	7,127,000	8.00	22.00	225	550	—
1935	902,000	25.00	55.00	400	900	—
Note: For exclusive use in Azores						
1938	923,000	25.00	55.00	325	950	—
1940	2,000,000	1.00	5.00	30.00	125	—
1944	2,974,000	0.25	1.00	7.00	15.00	25.00
1945	5,700,000	0.25	1.00	5.50	20.00	30.00
1946	4,334,000	—	2.00	10.00	35.00	45.00
1947	6,998,000	0.10	1.00	9.00	20.00	30.00
1951	4,610,000	—	0.50	2.75	10.00	15.00
1952	2,421,000	0.10	1.00	4.00	20.00	30.00
1953	2,369,000	0.10	1.00	12.50	50.00	65.00
1955	3,057,000	0.10	0.50	3.00	9.00	12.00
1956	3,003,000	—	0.50	3.00	6.00	8.00
1957	3,940,000	—	0.50	3.00	6.50	9.00
1958	2,687,000	—	0.50	4.00	9.00	12.00
1959	4,027,000	—	0.50	2.00	6.00	8.00
1960	2,592,000	—	0.50	2.00	5.50	7.50
1961	3,324,000	—	0.50	2.00	4.00	6.00
1962	6,678,000	—	0.25	1.00	2.50	3.50

Date	Mintage	F	VF	XF	Unc	BU
1963	2,346,000	—	0.25	3.00	9.00	12.00
1964	7,654,000	—	0.25	1.00	1.75	2.75
1965	3,366,000	—	0.25	1.00	2.50	3.50
1966	6,085,000	—	0.25	1.00	2.50	3.50
1967	19,391,000	—	0.25	1.00	2.50	3.50
1968	11,448,000	—	0.25	1.00	2.00	3.00

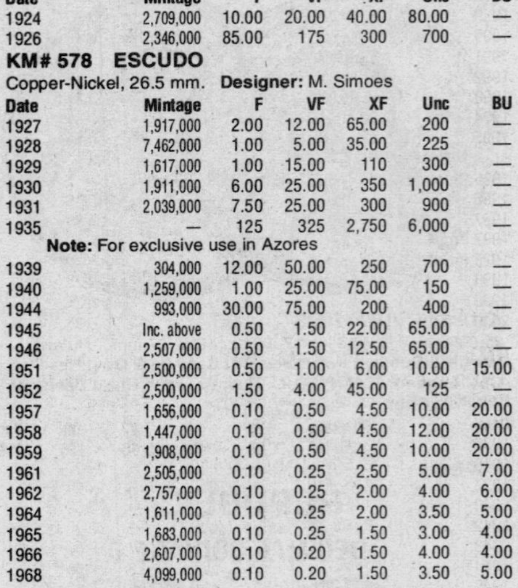

KM# 596 50 CENTAVOS

Bronze **Obv:** Circles within cross **Rev:** Value above spears of grain

Date	Mintage	F	VF	XF	Unc	BU
1969	3,481,000	—	—	1.00	3.50	—
1970	17,280,000	—	—	1.00	3.00	—
1971	9,139,000	—	—	1.00	3.00	—
1972	24,729,000	—	—	1.00	3.00	—
1973	35,588,000	—	—	0.75	2.50	—
1974	28,719,000	—	—	0.75	2.50	—
1975	17,793,000	—	—	0.75	2.50	—
1976	23,734,000	—	—	0.75	2.50	—
1977	16,340,000	—	—	0.75	2.50	—
1978	48,348,000	—	—	0.75	2.25	—
1979	61,652,000	—	—	0.75	2.00	—

KM# 560 ESCUDO

25.0000 g., 0.8350 Silver .6711 oz. ASW, 37 mm. **Subject:** October 5, 1910, Birth of the Republic **Obv:** Bust holding torch facing left **Rev:** Shield within designed circle and wreath **Designer:** Domingos Rego

Date	Mintage	F	VF	XF	Unc	BU
1910	Est. 1,000	40.00	80.00	125	200	—
Note: Struck in 1914						

KM# 564 ESCUDO

25.0000 g., 0.8350 Silver .6711 oz. ASW, 37 mm. **Obv:** Liberty head left

Date	Mintage	F	VF	XF	Unc	BU
1915	1,818,000	15.00	35.00	50.00	80.00	—
1916	1,405,000	15.00	40.00	60.00	90.00	—

KM# 576 ESCUDO

Aluminum-Bronze **Obv:** Sitting figure **Rev:** Shield within designed circle, value divides wreath

Date	Mintage	F	VF	XF	Unc	BU
1924	2,709,000	10.00	20.00	40.00	80.00	—
1926	2,346,000	85.00	175	300	700	—

KM# 578 ESCUDO

Copper-Nickel, 26.5 mm. **Designer:** M. Simoes

Date	Mintage	F	VF	XF	Unc	BU
1927	1,917,000	2.00	12.00	65.00	200	—
1928	7,462,000	1.00	5.00	35.00	225	—
1929	1,617,000	1.00	15.00	110	300	—
1930	1,911,000	6.00	25.00	350	1,000	—
1931	2,039,000	7.50	25.00	300	900	—
1935	—	125	325	2,750	6,000	—
Note: For exclusive use in Azores						
1939	304,000	12.00	50.00	250	700	—
1940	1,259,000	1.00	25.00	75.00	150	—
1944	993,000	30.00	75.00	200	400	—
1945	Inc. above	0.50	1.50	22.00	65.00	—
1946	2,507,000	0.50	1.50	12.50	65.00	—
1951	2,500,000	0.50	1.00	6.00	10.00	15.00
1952	2,500,000	1.50	4.00	45.00	125	—
1957	1,656,000	0.10	0.50	4.50	10.00	20.00
1958	1,447,000	0.10	0.50	4.50	12.00	20.00
1959	1,908,000	0.10	0.50	4.50	10.00	20.00
1961	2,505,000	0.10	0.25	2.50	5.00	7.00
1962	2,757,000	0.10	0.25	2.00	4.00	6.00
1964	1,611,000	0.10	0.25	2.00	3.50	5.00
1965	1,683,000	0.10	0.25	1.50	3.00	4.00
1966	2,607,000	0.10	0.20	1.50	4.00	4.00
1968	4,099,000	0.10	0.20	1.50	3.50	5.00

KM# 597 ESCUDO

Bronze, 26 mm. **Obv:** Circles within cross **Rev:** Value above spears of grain **Designer:** M. Norte

Date	Mintage	F	VF	XF	Unc	BU
1969	3,020,000	—	0.10	1.50	5.00	—
1970	6,009,000	—	0.10	1.50	4.00	—
1971	7,860,000	—	0.10	1.50	4.00	—
1972	3,815,000	—	0.10	1.50	4.50	—
1973	20,467,000	—	0.10	1.00	3.00	—
1974	11,444,000	—	0.10	1.00	3.00	—
1975	8,473,000	—	0.10	1.00	3.00	—
1976	7,353,000	—	0.10	0.50	2.00	—
1977	6,218,000	—	0.10	0.50	2.00	—
1978	7,061,000	—	0.10	0.50	2.00	—
1979	14,241,000	—	0.10	0.25	1.50	—

KM# 614 ESCUDO

3.0000 g., Nickel-Brass, 18 mm. **Obv:** Shield **Rev:** Value **Note:** Prev. KM#611.

Date	Mintage	F	VF	XF	Unc	BU
1981	30,165,000	—	—	0.10	1.00	—
1982	53,018,000	—	—	0.10	1.00	—
1983	53,165,000	—	—	0.10	0.50	—
1984	59,463,000	—	—	0.10	0.50	—
1985	46,832,000	—	—	0.10	0.50	—
1986	8,029,999	—	—	0.10	4.00	—

KM# 612 ESCUDO

Nickel-Brass, 18 mm. **Subject:** World Roller Hockey Championship Games **Obv:** Shield **Rev:** Hockey player

Date	Mintage	F	VF	XF	Unc	BU
ND(1983)	1,990,000	—	0.10	0.25	0.75	—

KM# 631 ESCUDO

Nickel-Brass, 16 mm. **Obv:** Design above shield **Rev:** Flower design above value **Designer:** Helder Batista

Date	Mintage	F	VF	XF	Unc	BU
1986	14,882,000	—	—	0.10	0.35	—
1987	21,922,000	—	—	0.10	0.35	—
1988	17,168,000	—	—	0.10	0.35	—

Date	Mintage	F	VF	XF	Unc	BU
1989	17,194,000	—	—	0.10	0.35	—
1990	19,008,000	—	—	0.10	0.35	—
1991	21,500,000	—	—	—	0.35	—
1992	22,000,000	—	—	—	0.35	—
1993	10,505,000	—	—	—	0.35	—
1994	—	—	—	—	0.35	—
1995	—	—	—	—	0.50	—
Note: In Mint sets only						
1996 Proof	7,000	Value: 0.50				
1996	—	—	—	—	0.35	—
1997	—	—	—	—	0.35	—
1997 Proof	—	Value: 0.50				
1998 Proof	—	Value: 2.00				
1998	—	—	—	—	0.35	—
1999	—	—	—	—	0.35	—
2000	—	—	—	—	0.35	—

KM# 580 2-1/2 ESCUDOS

3.5000 g., 0.6500 Silver .0731 oz. ASW, 20.5 mm. **Obv:** Ship **Rev:** Shield in front of circular design

Date	Mintage	F	VF	XF	Unc	BU
1932	2,592,000	5.00	20.00	50.00	120	—
1933	2,457,000	15.00	40.00	100	200	—
1937	1,000,000	150	350	700	1,500	—
1940	2,763,000	3.00	10.00	25.00	70.00	—
1942	3,847,000	BV	3.00	6.50	20.00	—
1943	8,302,000	BV	1.75	2.50	10.00	15.00
1944	9,134,000	BV	1.50	2.25	7.00	10.00
1945	6,316,000	BV	3.50	10.00	20.00	30.00
1946	3,208,000	BV	3.00	7.50	15.00	25.00
1947	2,610,000	BV	3.00	7.50	15.00	25.00
1948	1,814,000	10.00	20.00	40.00	110	—
1951	4,000,000	BV	1.25	2.00	5.00	7.00

KM# 590 2-1/2 ESCUDOS

3.5000 g., Copper-Nickel, 20 mm. **Obv:** Ship **Obv. Designer:** Martins Barata **Rev:** Shield flanked by stars **Rev. Designer:** M. Norte

Date	Mintage	F	VF	XF	Unc	BU
1963	12,711,000	—	0.50	20.00	32.00	45.00
1964	17,948,000	—	0.50	20.00	32.00	45.00
1965	19,512,000	—	0.25	5.00	11.00	15.00
1966	3,828,000	—	2.00	35.00	55.00	80.00
1967	5,545,000	—	0.25	7.00	18.00	—
1968	6,087,000	—	0.25	2.00	3.50	5.00
1969	9,969,000	—	0.25	1.75	3.00	4.00
1970	2,400,000	—	0.25	2.25	4.00	5.00
1971	6,791,000	—	0.25	1.50	3.00	4.00
1972	6,713,000	—	0.25	1.75	3.00	4.00
1973	9,104,000	—	0.25	1.00	2.00	3.00
1974	22,743,000	—	0.10	0.75	2.50	3.50
1975	16,623,999	—	0.10	0.50	1.50	2.00
1976	21,516,000	—	0.10	0.50	1.50	2.00
1977	45,726,000	—	0.10	0.50	1.50	2.00
1978	27,375,000	—	0.10	0.25	0.75	1.00
1979	44,804,000	—	0.10	0.25	0.75	1.00
1980	22,319,000	—	0.10	0.25	1.00	1.25
1981	25,420,000	—	0.10	0.20	1.00	1.25
1982	45,910,000	—	0.10	0.20	0.75	1.00
1983	62,946,000	—	0.10	0.20	0.75	1.00
1984	58,210,000	—	0.10	0.20	0.75	1.00
1985	60,142,000	—	0.10	0.20	0.75	1.00

KM# 605 2-1/2 ESCUDOS

3.5000 g., Copper-Nickel, 20 mm. **Subject:** 100th Anniversary - Death of Alexandre Herculano, Poet **Obv:** Shield **Rev:** Bust facing flanked by dates

Date	Mintage	F	VF	XF	Unc	BU
ND(1977)	5,990,000	—	0.20	0.75	2.00	—
ND(1977) Proof	13,000	Value: 3.50				

KM# 613 2-1/2 ESCUDOS

3.5000 g., Copper-Nickel, 20 mm. **Subject:** World Rolller Hockey Championship Games **Obv:** Shield **Rev:** Hockey player

Date	Mintage	F	VF	XF	Unc	BU
ND(1983)	1,990,000	—	0.10	0.25	1.00	—

KM# 617 2-1/2 ESCUDOS

3.5000 g., Copper-Nickel, 20 mm. **Series:** F.A.O. **Obv:** Shield **Rev:** Ear of corn, FAO and date

Date	Mintage	F	VF	XF	Unc	BU
1983	995,000	—	0.10	0.35	1.25	—

KM# 581 5 ESCUDOS

7.0000 g., 0.6500 Silver .1463 oz. ASW, 25 mm. **Obv:** Ship **Rev:** Shield in front of circular design

Date	Mintage	F	VF	XF	Unc	BU
1932	800,000	10.00	35.00	200	600	—
1933	6,717,000	2.50	5.50	20.00	60.00	—
1934	1,012,000	4.00	15.00	30.00	120	—
1937	1,500,000	30.00	80.00	200	600	—
1940	1,500,000	4.00	15.00	50.00	120	—
1942	2,051,000	2.50	4.50	9.00	20.00	25.00
1943	1,354,000	6.00	20.00	60.00	140	—
1946	404,000	4.00	12.50	25.00	55.00	—
1947	2,420,000	BV	3.00	5.00	12.00	—
1948	2,017,999	BV	3.00	5.00	11.00	15.00
1951	966,000	BV	3.00	5.00	11.00	15.00

KM# 587 5 ESCUDOS

7.0000 g., 0.6500 Silver .1463 oz. ASW, 25 mm. **Subject:** 500th Anniversary - Death of Prince Henry the Navigator **Obv:** Shield **Rev:** Head with sombrero facing 1/4 left **Designer:** M. Norte

Date	Mintage	F	VF	XF	Unc	BU
1960	800,000	—	2.50	3.50	6.50	10.00
1960 Matte	—	—	—	—	20.00	—

Note: A small quantity of these coins were given a matte finish by the Lisbon Mint on private contract

KM# 591 5 ESCUDOS

7.0000 g., Copper-Nickel, 24.5 mm. **Obv:** Ship **Rev:** Shield flanked by stars **Designer:** M. Norte

Date	Mintage	F	VF	XF	Unc	BU
1963	2,200,000	—	0.50	15.00	30.00	—
1964	4,268,000	—	0.50	12.50	25.00	35.00
1965	7,294,000	—	0.35	12.50	25.00	35.00
1966	8,119,999	—	0.35	10.00	25.00	35.00
1967	8,128,000	—	0.25	7.00	20.00	25.00
1968	5,023,000	—	0.25	3.00	5.00	10.00
1969	3,571,000	—	0.10	2.00	5.00	6.00
1970	1,200,000	—	0.10	2.50	5.50	7.00
1971	2,721,000	—	0.10	2.00	5.00	6.00
1972	1,880,000	—	0.10	2.00	6.00	—
1973	2,836,000	—	0.10	1.25	4.00	—
1974	3,984,000	—	0.10	1.00	3.50	—
1975	7,496,000	—	0.10	1.00	2.50	3.50
1976	11,379,000	—	0.10	1.00	2.50	3.50
1977	29,058,000	—	0.10	0.50	1.50	2.00
1978	672,000	—	2.00	5.00	10.00	—
1979	19,546,000	—	0.10	0.50	1.50	—
1980	46,244,000	—	0.10	0.50	1.50	2.00
1981	15,267,000	—	0.10	0.50	1.50	2.00
1982	31,318,000	—	0.10	0.50	1.50	2.00
1983	51,056,000	—	0.10	0.50	1.50	2.00
1984	46,794,000	—	0.10	0.50	1.50	2.00
1985	45,441,000	—	0.10	0.50	1.25	1.75
1986	18,753,000	—	0.10	0.50	1.50	—

KM# 606 5 ESCUDOS

7.0000 g., Copper-Nickel, 24.5 mm. **Subject:** 100th Anniversary - Death of Alexandre Herculano, Poet **Obv:** Shield **Rev:** Bust 1/4 right flanked by dates **Designer:** M. Norte

Date	Mintage	F	VF	XF	Unc	BU
ND(1977)	9,176,000	—	0.35	1.00	2.00	2.50
ND(1977) Proof	10,000	Value: 4.00				

KM# 615 5 ESCUDOS

7.0000 g., Copper-Nickel, 24.5 mm. **Subject:** World Roller Hockey Championship Games **Obv:** Shield **Rev:** Hockey player

Date	Mintage	F	VF	XF	Unc	BU
ND(1983)	1,990,000	—	0.25	0.50	1.00	1.50

KM# 618 5 ESCUDOS

7.0000 g., Copper-Nickel, 24.5 mm. **Series:** F.A.O. **Obv:** Shield **Rev:** Bull

Date	Mintage	F	VF	XF	Unc	BU
ND(1983)	995,000	—	0.30	0.75	1.50	2.50

KM# 632 5 ESCUDOS

Nickel-Brass **Obv:** Design above shield **Rev:** Star design above value **Designer:** Helder Batista

Date	Mintage	F	VF	XF	Unc	BU
1986	21,426,000	—	0.10	0.25	0.50	—
1987	40,548,000	—	0.10	0.25	0.50	—
1988	19,382,000	—	0.10	0.25	0.50	—
1989	27,641,000	—	0.10	0.25	0.50	—
1990	77,977,000	—	0.10	0.25	0.50	—
1991	32,000,000	—	—	—	0.50	—
1992	16,000,000	—	—	—	0.50	—
1993	8,300,000	—	—	—	0.50	—
1994	—	—	—	—	0.50	—
1995	—	—	—	—	0.50	—
1996	—	—	—	—	0.50	—
1996 Proof	7,000	Value: 0.75				
1997	—	—	—	—	0.50	—
1997 Proof	—	Value: 0.75				
1998	—	—	—	—	0.50	—
1998 Proof	—	Value: 0.75				
1999	—	—	—	—	0.50	—
2000	—	—	—	—	0.50	—

KM# 579 10 ESCUDOS

12.5000 g., 0.8350 Silver .3356 oz. ASW, 30 mm. **Subject:** Battle of Ourique **Obv:** Crowned shield flanked by value **Rev:** Armored figure on horse holding sword **Designer:** Domingos Rega

Date	Mintage	F	VF	XF	Unc	BU
1928	200,000	7.00	15.00	25.00	40.00	50.00

KM# 582 10 ESCUDOS

12.5000 g., 0.8350 Silver .3356 oz. ASW, 30 mm. **Obv:** Ship **Rev:** Shield in front of circular design

Date	Mintage	F	VF	XF	Unc	BU
1932	3,220,000	5.50	10.00	20.00	60.00	—
1933	1,780,000	30.00	70.00	200	500	—

Date	Mintage	F	VF	XF	Unc	BU
1934	400,000	15.00	30.00	50.00	150	—
1937	500,000	60.00	150	400	650	—
1940	1,200,000	10.00	20.00	40.00	60.00	—
1942	186,000	200	400	700	1,200	—
1948	507,000	30.00	75.00	150	220	—

KM# 586 10 ESCUDOS
12.5000 g., 0.8350 Silver .3356 oz. ASW, 30 mm. **Obv:** Ship **Rev:** Shield above circular design flanked by value

Date	Mintage	F	VF	XF	Unc	BU
1954	5,764,000	—	BV	5.50	8.00	10.00
1955	4,056,000	—	BV	5.50	8.00	10.00

KM# 588 10 ESCUDOS
12.5000 g., 0.6800 Silver .2732 oz. ASW, 30 mm. **Subject:** 500th Anniversary - Death of Prince Henry the Navigator **Obv:** Shield flanked by designs **Rev:** Head with sombrero facing 1/4 left **Designer:** M. Norte

Date	Mintage	F	VF	XF	Unc	BU
1960	200,000	—	9.00	20.00	30.00	35.00
1960 Matte	—	—	—	—	50.00	—

Note: A small quantity of these coins were given a matte finish by the Lisbon Mint on private contract

KM# 600 10 ESCUDOS
Copper-Nickel Clad Nickel **Obv:** Ship **Rev:** Shield flanked by stars **Designer:** M. Norte

Date	Mintage	F	VF	XF	Unc	BU
1971	3,876,000	—	0.25	0.75	2.00	2.50
1972	2,694,000	—	0.25	1.00	2.50	3.50
1973	5,418,000	—	0.25	0.75	2.00	2.50
1974	4,043,000	—	0.25	0.75	2.00	2.50

KM# 633 10 ESCUDOS
Nickel-Brass **Obv:** Design above shield **Rev:** Artistic design above value **Designer:** Helder Batista

Date	Mintage	F	VF	XF	Unc	BU
1986	12,818,000	—	0.20	0.40	1.00	1.50
1987	32,814,999	—	0.20	0.40	1.00	1.50
1988	32,579,000	—	0.20	0.40	1.00	1.50
1989	12,788,000	—	0.20	0.40	1.00	1.50
1990	26,500,000	—	0.20	0.40	1.00	1.50
1991	9,500,000	—	—	—	1.00	1.75
1992	5,600,000	—	—	—	1.00	1.75
1993	20,000	—	—	—	10.00	—
Note: In Mint sets only						
1994	20,000	—	—	—	10.00	—
Note: In Mint sets only						
1995	—	—	—	—	10.00	—
Note: In Mint sets only						
1996	—	—	—	—	1.00	—
1996 Proof	7,000	Value: 2.50				
1997	—	—	—	—	1.00	—
1997 Proof	—	Value: 2.50				
1998	—	—	—	—	1.00	—

Date	Mintage	F	VF	XF	Unc	BU
1998 Proof	—	Value: 3.00				
1999	—	—	—	—	1.00	—
2000	—	—	—	—	1.00	—

KM# 638 10 ESCUDOS
Nickel-Brass **Subject:** Rural World **Obv:** Design above shield **Rev:** Hand holding sprig flanked by stars all around **Designer:** Helder Batista

Date	Mintage	F	VF	XF	Unc	BU
1987	2,000,000	—	0.40	0.60	1.50	—

KM# 585 20 ESCUDOS
21.0000 g., 0.8000 Silver .5401 oz. ASW, 34 mm. **Subject:** 25th Anniversary of Financial Reform **Obv:** Shield above globe, value at left, all within circle **Rev:** Seated figure facing left reading a book **Designer:** Joao daSilva

Date	Mintage	F	VF	XF	Unc	BU
1953	1,000,000	—	BV	8.50	9.50	11.50
1953 Matte	—	—	—	—	—	—

Note: A small quantity of these coins were given a matte finish by the Lisbon Mint on private contract

KM# 589 20 ESCUDOS
21.0000 g., 0.8000 Silver .5401 oz. ASW, 34 mm. **Subject:** 500th Anniversary - Death of Prince Henry the Navigator **Obv:** Shield flanked by designs **Rev:** Head with sombrero facing 1/4 left **Designer:** M. Norte

Date	Mintage	F	VF	XF	Unc	BU
1960	200,000	—	12.00	20.00	30.00	40.00
1960 Matte	—	—	—	—	55.00	—

Note: A small quantity of these coins were given a matte finish by the Lisbon Mint on private contract

KM# 592 20 ESCUDOS
10.0000 g., 0.6500 Silver .2090 oz. ASW **Subject:** Opening of Salazar Bridge **Obv:** Shield and value within artistic design **Rev:** Salazar bridge

Date	Mintage	F	VF	XF	Unc	BU
1966	2,000,000	—	BV	3.50	4.50	6.00
1966 Matte	200	—	—	—	35.00	—

Note: A small quantity of these coins were given a matte finish by the Lisbon Mint on private contract

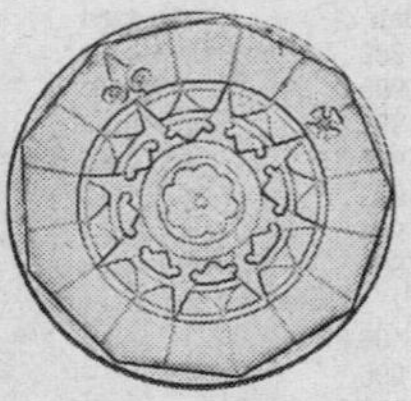

KM# 634 20 ESCUDOS
Copper-Nickel, 26.5 mm. **Obv:** Shield divides date with value below **Rev:** Nautical windrose **Designer:** Euclides Vaz

Date	Mintage	F	VF	XF	Unc	BU
1986	45,361,000	—	0.15	0.25	1.00	1.50
1987	68,216,000	—	0.15	0.25	1.00	1.50
1988	57,482,000	—	0.15	0.25	1.00	1.50
1989	25,060,000	—	0.15	0.25	1.00	1.50
1990	50,000	—	—	—	10.00	—
Note: In Mint sets only						
1991	50,000	—	—	—	10.00	—
Note: In Mint sets only						
1992	20,000	—	—	—	10.00	—
Note: In Mint sets only						
1993	20,000	—	—	—	10.00	—
Note: In Mint sets only						
1994	20,000	—	—	—	10.00	—
Note: In Mint sets only						
1995	—	—	—	—	10.00	—
Note: In Mint sets only						
1996	—	—	—	—	10.00	—
Note: In Mint sets only						
1996 Proof	7,000	Value: 2.50				
1997	—	—	—	—	10.00	—
Note: In Mint sets only						
1997 Proof	—	Value: 2.50				
1998	—	—	—	—	1.00	—
1998 Proof	—	Value: 4.00				
1999	—	—	—	—	1.00	—
2000	—	—	—	—	1.00	—

KM# 607 25 ESCUDOS
Copper-Nickel **Obv:** Value to right of shield **Rev:** Head laureate left **Designer:** Norte d'Almeida

Date	Mintage	F	VF	XF	Unc	BU
1977	7,657,000	—	0.40	1.00	2.00	4.50
1978	12,277,000	—	0.40	1.50	3.00	5.00

KM# 608 25 ESCUDOS
Copper-Nickel, 26.5 mm. **Subject:** 100th Anniversary - Death of Alexandre Herculano, Poet **Obv:** Shield **Rev:** Bust flanked by dates facing 1/4 right **Designer:** M. Norte

Date	Mintage	F	VF	XF	Unc	BU
ND(1977)	5,990,000	—	0.50	1.00	2.50	4.75
ND(1977) Proof	13,000	Value: 7.00				

KM# 609 25 ESCUDOS
Copper-Nickel **Subject:** International Year of the Child **Obv:** Shield **Rev:** Two faces, one facing left, the other 3/4 right

Date	Mintage	F	VF	XF	Unc	BU
1979	990,000	—	0.50	1.00	2.50	—
1979 Prooflike	10,000	—	—	—	8.00	—

KM# 607a 25 ESCUDOS

10.8000 g., Copper-Nickel, 28.5 mm. **Obv:** Value to right of shield **Rev:** Head laureate left **Designer:** Norte d'Almeida **Note:** Increased size; prev. KM#610.

Date	Mintage	F	VF	XF	Unc	BU
1980	750,000	—	0.40	0.80	1.50	—
1981	19,924,000	—	0.40	0.80	1.50	3.50
1982	12,158,000	—	0.40	0.80	1.50	3.50
1983	5,622,000	—	0.40	0.80	1.50	—
1984	3,453,000	—	0.40	1.00	3.00	—
1985	25,027,000	—	0.40	0.80	1.50	2.50
1986	—	—	0.50	1.00	4.00	—

KM# 616 25 ESCUDOS

Copper-Nickel, 28.5 mm. **Subject:** World Roller Hockey Championship Games **Obv:** Shield **Rev:** Suited hockey player

Date	Mintage	F	VF	XF	Unc	BU
ND(1983)	1,990,000	—	0.50	1.00	2.00	2.50

KM# 619 25 ESCUDOS

Copper-Nickel, 28.5 mm. **Series:** F.A.O. **Obv:** Shield **Rev:** Fish, F.A.O. and date

Date	Mintage	F	VF	XF	Unc	BU
1983	995,000	—	0.60	1.25	2.25	3.00

KM# 623 25 ESCUDOS

Copper-Nickel, 28.5 mm. **Subject:** 10th Anniversary of Revolution **Obv:** Waves breaking over shield **Rev:** Stylized 25 **Designer:** Helder Batista

Date	Mintage	F	VF	XF	Unc	BU
ND(1984)	1,980,000	—	0.40	1.00	1.50	2.00

KM# 624 25 ESCUDOS

Copper-Nickel, 28.5 mm. **Subject:** International Year of Disabled Persons **Obv:** Shield **Rev:** Head 1/4 left with legend above **Designer:** M. Simoes

Date	Mintage	F	VF	XF	Unc	BU
ND(1984)	1,990,000	—	0.40	1.00	2.00	2.50

KM# 627 25 ESCUDOS

Copper-Nickel, 28.5 mm. **Subject:** 600th Anniversary - Battle of Aljubarrota **Obv:** Shield within circle **Rev:** Seated crowned figure flanked by shields **Designer:** C. Meneres

Date	Mintage	F	VF	XF	Unc	BU
ND(1985)	500,000	—	0.50	1.00	2.75	—

KM# 627a 25 ESCUDOS

10.8300 g., 0.9250 Silver .3270 oz. ASW, 28.5 mm. **Obv:** Shield within circle **Rev:** Seated crowned figure flanked by shields

Date	Mintage	F	VF	XF	Unc	BU
ND(1985)	20,000	—	—	—	15.00	—

Note: In Mint sets only

Date	Mintage	F	VF	XF	Unc	BU
ND(1985)	5,000	Value: 40.00				

Note: In Proof sets only

KM# 635 25 ESCUDOS

Copper-Nickel, 28.5 mm. **Subject:** Admission to European Common Market **Obv:** Shield **Rev:** Small square and lined design **Designer:** Armando Matos Simoes

Date	Mintage	F	VF	XF	Unc	BU
1986	4,990,000	—	0.40	1.00	2.00	—

KM# 635a 25 ESCUDOS

11.0000 g., 0.9250 Silver .3272 oz. ASW, 28.5 mm. **Obv:** Shield **Rev:** Small square and lined design

Date	Mintage	F	VF	XF	Unc	BU
1986 Proof	5,000	Value: 200				

KM# 593 50 ESCUDOS

18.0000 g., 0.6500 Silver .3761 oz. ASW **Subject:** 500th Anniversary - Birth of Pedro Alvares Cabral, Navigator, Discoverer of Brazil **Obv:** Crowned shield **Rev:** Bust with headdress right within circle **Designer:** M. Norte

Date	Mintage	F	VF	XF	Unc	BU
1968	1,000,000	—	—	—	6.50	7.50
1968 Matte	400	—	—	—	32.50	—

Note: A small quantity of these coins were given a matte finish by the Lisbon Mint on private contract

KM# 598 50 ESCUDOS

18.0000 g., 0.6500 Silver .3761 oz. ASW **Subject:** 500th Anniversary - Birth of Vasco daGama, Discoverer of the sea route to India **Obv:** Shield within maltese cross **Rev:** Head with headdress left **Designer:** A. Lucas

Date	Mintage	F	VF	XF	Unc	BU
ND(1969)	1,000,000	—	—	—	6.50	7.50
ND(1969) Matte	400	—	—	—	32.50	—

Note: A small quantity of these coins were given a matte finish by the Lisbon Mint on private contract

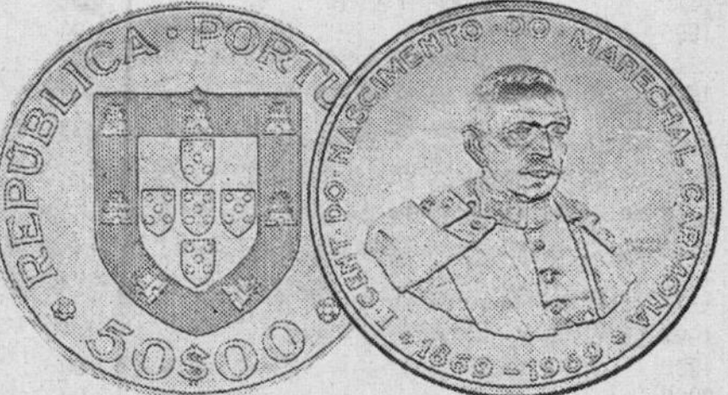

KM# 599 50 ESCUDOS

18.0000 g., 0.6500 Silver .3761 oz. ASW **Subject:** 100th Anniversary - Birth of Marechal Carmona, President **Obv:** Shield **Rev:** Uniformed bust 3/4 right

Date	Mintage	F	VF	XF	Unc	BU
ND(1969)	500,000	—	—	—	7.50	10.00
ND(1969) Matte	400	—	—	—	32.50	—

Note: A small quantity of these coins were given a matte finish by the Lisbon Mint on private contract

KM# 601 50 ESCUDOS

18.0000 g., 0.6500 Silver .3761 oz. ASW **Subject:** 125th Anniversary - Bank of Portugal **Obv:** Circles within circled cross design **Rev:** Stylized tree

Date	Mintage	F	VF	XF	Unc	BU
ND(1971)	500,000	—	—	—	8.50	11.50
ND(1971) Matte	—	—	—	—	32.50	—

Note: A small quantity of these coins were given a matte finish by the Lisbon Mint on private contract

KM# 602 50 ESCUDOS

18.0000 g., 0.6500 Silver .3761 oz. ASW, 34.5 mm. **Subject:** 400th Anniversary of Heroic Epic 'Os Lusiadas' **Obv:** Book appears as part of Quinas Cross, all within circle **Rev:** Victory within design flanked by dates, all within circle **Designer:** M. Norte

Date	Mintage	F	VF	XF	Unc	BU
ND(1972)	1,000,000	—	—	—	7.00	9.00
ND(1972) Matte	—	—	—	—	32.50	—

Note: A small quantity of these coins were given a matte finish by the Lisbon Mint on private contract

KM# 636 50 ESCUDOS

Copper-Nickel, 31 mm. **Obv:** Shield divides date with value below **Rev:** Sailboat, water and fish **Designer:** Euclides Vaz

Date	Mintage	F	VF	XF	Unc	BU
1986	51,110,000	—	—	—	2.25	2.75
1987	28,248,000	—	—	—	2.25	2.75
1988	41,905,000	—	—	—	2.25	2.75
1989	18,327,000	—	—	—	2.25	2.75
1990	50,000	—	—	—	15.00	—
Note: In Mint sets only						
1991	2,000,000	—	—	—	3.00	—
1992	20,000	—	—	—	15.00	—
Note: In Mint sets only						
1993	20,000	—	—	—	15.00	—
Note: In Mint sets only						
1994	20,000	—	—	—	15.00	—
Note: In Mint sets only						

Date	Mintage	F	VF	XF	Unc	BU
1995	20,000	—	—	—	15.00	—
Note: In Mint sets only						
1996	—	—	—	—	8.00	—
Note: In Mint sets only						
1996 Proof	7,000	Value: 5.00				
1997	—	—	—	—	8.00	—
Note: In Mint sets only						
1997 Proof	—	Value: 5.00				
1998	—	—	—	—	8.00	—
Note: In Mint sets only						
1998 Proof	—	Value: 6.00				
1999	—	—	—	—	3.00	—
2000	—	—	—	—	3.00	—

KM# 603 100 ESCUDOS

18.0000 g., 0.6500 Silver .3762 oz. ASW **Subject:** 1974 Revolution **Obv:** Small cross design within circle with numeral and written value above **Rev:** Inscription and date flanked by vertical block designs

Date	Mintage	F	VF	XF	Unc	BU
ND(1976)	950,000	—	BV	6.00	7.50	8.50
ND(1976) Proof	10,000	Value: 15.00				

KM# 625 100 ESCUDOS

Copper-Nickel, 33.5 mm. **Subject:** International Year of Disabled Persons **Obv:** Shield **Rev:** Stylized head facing 1/4 right **Designer:** M. Simoes

Date	Mintage	F	VF	XF	Unc	BU
ND(1984)	990,000	—	0.75	1.50	2.50	3.50

KM# 628 100 ESCUDOS

Copper-Nickel, 33.5 mm. **Subject:** 50th Anniversary - Death of Fernando Pessoa - Poet **Obv:** Shield above value **Rev:** Four conjoined faces facing right and flying birds within circle **Designer:** Jose Aurelio

Date	Mintage	F	VF	XF	Unc	BU
1985	480,000	—	0.75	2.00	3.50	4.50

KM# 628a 100 ESCUDOS

16.5000 g., 0.9250 Silver .4907 oz. ASW, 33.5 mm. **Obv:** Shield above value **Rev:** Four conjoined faces facing right and flying birds within circle

Date	Mintage	F	VF	XF	Unc	BU
1985 Proof	5,000	Value: 200				

KM# 629 100 ESCUDOS

Copper-Nickel, 33.5 mm. **Subject:** 800th Anniversary - Death of King Alfonso Henriques **Obv:** Cross design within oblong circle flanked by designs, date and value **Rev:** Armored head left

Date	Mintage	F	VF	XF	Unc	BU
1985	500,000	—	0.75	2.00	4.00	—

KM# 629a 100 ESCUDOS

16.5000 g., 0.9250 Silver .4907 oz. ASW, 33.5 mm. **Subject:** 800th Anniversary - Death of King Alfonso Henriques **Obv:** Cross design within oblong circle flanked by designs, date and value **Rev:** Armored head left

Date	Mintage	F	VF	XF	Unc	BU
1985 Proof	5,000	Value: 110				
1985	20,000	—	—	—	27.00	—

KM# 630 100 ESCUDOS

Copper-Nickel, 33.5 mm. **Subject:** 600th Anniversary - Battle of Aljubarrota **Obv:** Shield within circle **Rev:** Standing figure facing within pillar arch **Designer:** C. Meneres

Date	Mintage	F	VF	XF	Unc	BU
ND(1985)	500,000	—	0.75	2.00	3.50	4.50

KM# 630a 100 ESCUDOS

16.5000 g., 0.9250 Silver .4907 oz. ASW, 33.5 mm. **Subject:** 600th Anniversary - Battle of Aljubarrota **Obv:** Shield within circle **Rev:** Standing figure facing within pillar arch

Date	Mintage	F	VF	XF	Unc	BU
ND(1985)	20,000	—	—	—	22.00	—
ND(1985) Proof	5,000	Value: 80.00				

KM# 637 100 ESCUDOS

Copper-Nickel, 33.5 mm. **Subject:** World Cup Soccer - Mexico

Date	Mintage	F	VF	XF	Unc	BU
1986	500,000	—	0.75	2.00	3.50	4.50

KM# 637a 100 ESCUDOS

16.5000 g., 0.9250 Silver .4907 oz. ASW, 33.5 mm. **Subject:** World Cup Soccer - Mexico

Date	Mintage	F	VF	XF	Unc	BU
1986	50,000	—	—	—	12.50	—
1986 Proof	20,000	Value: 27.50				

KM# 639 100 ESCUDOS

Copper Nickel, 34 mm. **Subject:** Golden Age of Portuguese Discoveries - Gil Eanes **Obv:** Shield within circle **Rev:** Ship with flag on top of sails **Designer:** S. Machado

Date	Mintage	F	VF	XF	Unc	BU
1987	1,000,000	—	0.75	1.00	2.50	3.50

KM# 639a 100 ESCUDOS

16.5000 g., 0.9250 Silver .4907 oz. ASW, 34 mm. **Subject:** Golden Age of Portuguese Discoveries - Gil Eanes **Obv:** Shield within circle **Rev:** Ship with flag on top of sails

Date	Mintage	F	VF	XF	Unc	BU
1987	50,000	—	—	—	10.00	12.50
1987 Proof	22,000	Value: 20.00				

KM# 639b 100 ESCUDOS

24.0000 g., 0.9170 Gold .7075 oz. AGW, 34 mm. **Subject:** Golden Age of Portuguese Discoveries - Gil Eanes **Obv:** Shield within circle **Rev:** Ship with flag on top of sails

Date	Mintage	F	VF	XF	Unc	BU
1987	5,772	—	—	—	540	—

KM# 640 100 ESCUDOS

Copper-Nickel, 34 mm. **Subject:** Golden Age of Portuguese Discoveries - Nuno Tristao **Obv:** Shield flanked by crowns within circle **Rev:** Ship **Designer:** Isabel C. Branco and F. Branco

Date	Mintage	F	VF	XF	Unc	BU
1987	1,000,000	—	0.75	1.00	2.50	3.50

KM# 640a 100 ESCUDOS

16.5000 g., 0.9250 Silver .4907 oz. ASW, 34 mm. **Subject:** Golden Age of Portuguese Discoveries - Nuno Tristao **Obv:** Shield flanked by crowns within circle **Rev:** Ship

Date	Mintage	F	VF	XF	Unc	BU
1987	50,000	—	—	—	12.50	—
1987 Proof	20,000	Value: 20.00				

KM# 640b 100 ESCUDOS

24.0000 g., 0.9170 Gold .7075 oz. AGW, 34 mm. **Subject:** Golden Age of Portuguese Discoveries - Nuno Tristao **Obv:** Shield flanked by crowns within circle **Rev:** Ship

Date	Mintage	F	VF	XF	Unc	BU
1987	5,497	—	—	—	540	—

KM# 640c 100 ESCUDOS

31.1190 g., 0.9990 Palladium 1.0000 oz. **Subject:** Golden Age of Portuguese Discoveries - Nuno Tristao **Obv:** Shield flanked by crowns within circle **Rev:** Ship

Date	Mintage	F	VF	XF	Unc	BU
1987 Proof	2,000	Value: 450				
1987	323	—	—	—	475	—

KM# 641 100 ESCUDOS

Copper-Nickel, 34 mm. **Subject:** Golden Age of Portuguese Discoveries - Diogo Cao **Obv:** Shield to upper right of design with value below **Rev:** Compass within center of sailboat and map **Designer:** Dega

Date	Mintage	F	VF	XF	Unc	BU
1987	1,000,000	—	0.75	1.00	2.50	3.50

KM# 641a 100 ESCUDOS

16.5000 g., 0.9250 Silver .4907 oz. ASW, 34 mm. **Subject:** Golden Age of Portuguese Discoveries - Diogo Cao **Obv:** Shield to upper right of center design with value below **Rev:** Compass within center of sailboat and map

Date	Mintage	F	VF	XF	Unc	BU
1987 Proof	20,000	Value: 20.00				
1987	50,000	—	—	—	12.50	—

KM# 641b 100 ESCUDOS

24.0000 g., 0.9170 Gold .7075 oz. AGW, 34 mm. **Subject:** Golden Age of Portuguese Discoveries - Diogo Cao **Obv:** Shield to upper right of center design with value below **Rev:** Compass within center of sailboat and map

Date	Mintage	F	VF	XF	Unc	BU
1987 Proof	5,387	Value: 540				
1987	5,256	—	—	—	520	—

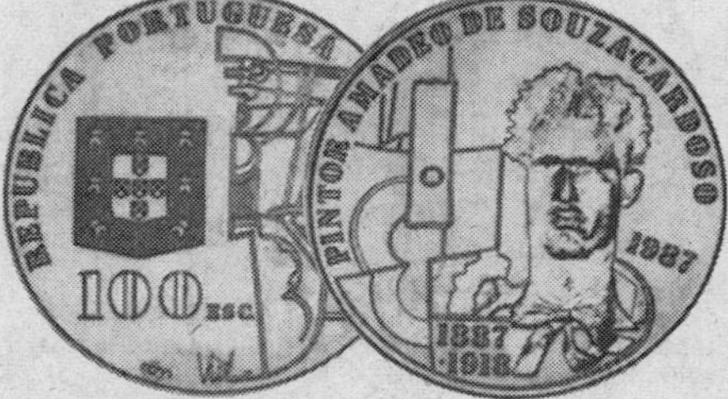

KM# 644 100 ESCUDOS

Copper-Nickel, 34 mm. **Subject:** Amadeo de Souza Cardoso **Obv:** Shield and value to left of design **Rev:** Head facing flanked by dates with design at left **Designer:** Vilar

Date	Mintage	F	VF	XF	Unc	BU
1987	800,000	—	0.75	1.25	2.50	3.50

KM# 644a 100 ESCUDOS
21.0000 g., 0.9250 Silver .6246 oz. ASW, 34 mm. **Subject:** Amadeo De Souza Cardoso **Obv:** Shield and value to left of design **Rev:** Head facing flanked by dates to right of design

Date	Mintage	F	VF	XF	Unc	BU
1987	30,000	—	—	—	18.50	—
1987 Proof	15,000	Value: 28.50				

KM# 642 100 ESCUDOS
Copper-Nickel, 34 mm. **Subject:** Golden Age of Portuguese Discoveries - Bartolomeu Dias **Obv:** Shield within circle **Rev:** Stylized boat and map **Designer:** Jorge Vieira

Date	Mintage	F	VF	XF	Unc	BU
ND(1988)	1,000,000	—	0.75	1.00	2.50	3.50

KM# 642a 100 ESCUDOS
16.5000 g., 0.9250 Silver .4907 oz. ASW, 34 mm. **Subject:** Golden Age of Portuguese Discoveries - Bartolomeu Dias **Obv:** Shield within circle **Rev:** Styilized boat and map

Date	Mintage	F	VF	XF	Unc	BU
ND(1988) Proof	20,000	Value: 20.00				
ND(1988)	50,000	—	—	—	10.00	12.50

KM# 642b 100 ESCUDOS
24.0000 g., 0.9170 Gold .7077 oz. AGW, 34 mm. **Subject:** Golden Age of Portuguese Discoveries - Bartolomeu Dias **Obv:** Shield within circle **Rev:** Stylized boat and map

Date	Mintage	F	VF	XF	Unc	BU
ND(1988)	5,503	—	—	—	520	—

KM# 642c 100 ESCUDOS
31.1190 g., 0.9990 Platinum 1.0000 oz. APW **Subject:** Golden Age of Portuguese Discoveries - Bartolomeu Dias **Obv:** Shield within circle **Rev:** Stylized boat and map

Date	Mintage	F	VF	XF	Unc	BU
ND(1988)	907	—	—	—	1,350	—
ND(1988) Proof	2,000	Value: 1,450				

KM# 646 100 ESCUDOS
Copper-Nickel, 34 mm. **Subject:** Discovery of the Canary Islands **Obv:** Shield with supporters above value **Rev:** Ship

Date	Mintage	F	VF	XF	Unc	BU
1989	2,000,000	—	—	1.00	2.50	4.00

KM# 646a 100 ESCUDOS
21.0000 g., 0.9250 Silver .6246 oz. ASW, 34 mm. **Subject:** Discovery of the Canary Islands **Obv:** Shield with supporters above value **Rev:** Ship

Date	Mintage	F	VF	XF	Unc	BU
1989	50,000	—	—	—	12.50	—
1989 Proof	23,000	Value: 20.00				

KM# 646b 100 ESCUDOS
24.0000 g., 0.9170 Gold .7077 oz. AGW **Subject:** Discovery of the Canary Islands **Obv:** Shield with supporters above value **Rev:** Ship

Date	Mintage	F	VF	XF	Unc	BU
1989 Proof	2,981	Value: 560				

KM# 647 100 ESCUDOS
Copper-Nickel, 34 mm. **Subject:** Discovery of Madeira **Obv:** Cross and shield **Rev:** Ship **Designer:** Isabel C. Branco and F. Branco

Date	Mintage	F	VF	XF	Unc	BU
1989	2,000,000	—	—	1.00	2.50	4.00

KM# 647a 100 ESCUDOS
21.0000 g., 0.9250 Silver .6246 oz. ASW, 34 mm. **Subject:** Discovery of Madeira **Obv:** Cross and shield **Rev:** Ship

Date	Mintage	F	VF	XF	Unc	BU
1989	50,000	—	—	—	12.50	—
1989 Proof	20,000	Value: 20.00				

KM# 647b 100 ESCUDOS
24.0000 g., 0.9170 Gold .7077 oz. AGW, 34 mm. **Subject:** Discovery of Madeira **Obv:** Cross and shield **Rev:** Ship

Date	Mintage	F	VF	XF	Unc	BU
1989 Proof	2,996	Value: 560				

KM# 647c 100 ESCUDOS
31.1190 g., 0.9990 Palladium 1.0000 oz. **Subject:** Discovery of Madeira **Obv:** Cross and shield **Rev:** Ship

Date	Mintage	F	VF	XF	Unc	BU
1989 Proof	2,500	Value: 450				

KM# 648 100 ESCUDOS
Copper-Nickel, 34 mm. **Subject:** Discovery of the Azores **Obv:** Shield at right within design **Rev:** Ship and stars within design

Date	Mintage	F	VF	XF	Unc	BU
ND(1989)	2,000,000	—	—	1.00	2.50	—

KM# 648a 100 ESCUDOS
21.0000 g., 0.9250 Silver .6246 oz. ASW, 34 mm. **Subject:** Discovery of the Azores **Obv:** Shield at right within design **Rev:** Ship and stars within design

Date	Mintage	F	VF	XF	Unc	BU
ND(1989)	50,000	—	—	—	12.50	—
ND(1989) Proof	20,000	Value: 20.00				

KM# 648b 100 ESCUDOS
24.0000 g., 0.9170 Gold .7077 oz. AGW **Subject:** Discovery of the Avores **Obv:** Shield to right within design **Rev:** Ship and stars within design

Date	Mintage	F	VF	XF	Unc	BU
ND(1989) Proof	5,495	Value: 540				

KM# 645.1 100 ESCUDOS
Bi-Metallic, Aluminum-Bronze center in Copper-Nickel ring, 25.5 mm. **Obv:** Shield within globe above value within circle **Rev:** Armored 1/2 length figure holding globe facing left within circle **Edge:** Five reeded and five plain sections **Designer:** Jose Candido **Note:** Varieties exist with fine and bold letters.

Date	Mintage	F	VF	XF	Unc	BU
1989	20,000,000	—	—	1.00	2.50	3.00
1990	52,000,000	—	—	1.00	2.50	3.00
1991	45,500,000	—	—	1.00	2.50	3.00
1992	14,500,000	—	—	1.00	2.50	3.00
1993	20,000	—	—	—	15.00	—
Note: In Mint sets only						
1994	20,000	—	—	—	15.00	—
Note: In Mint sets only						
1996	—	—	—	—	15.00	—
Note: In Mint sets only						
1996 Proof	7,000	Value: 10.00				
1997	—	—	—	—	2.50	—
1997 Proof	—	Value: 2.50				
1998	—	—	—	—	2.50	—
1998 Proof	—	Value: 10.00				
1999	—	—	—	—	2.50	—
2000	—	—	—	—	2.50	—

KM# 645.2 100 ESCUDOS
Ring Composition: Copper-Nickel **Center Composition:** Aluminum-Bronze, 25.5 mm. **Rev:** Pedro Nunes **Edge:** Six reeded and six plain sections

Date	Mintage	F	VF	XF	Unc	BU
1989	Inc. above	—	1.00	1.50	3.00	5.00
1990	Inc. above	—	1.25	2.00	3.50	5.50
1991	Inc. above	—	1.00	1.50	3.00	5.00

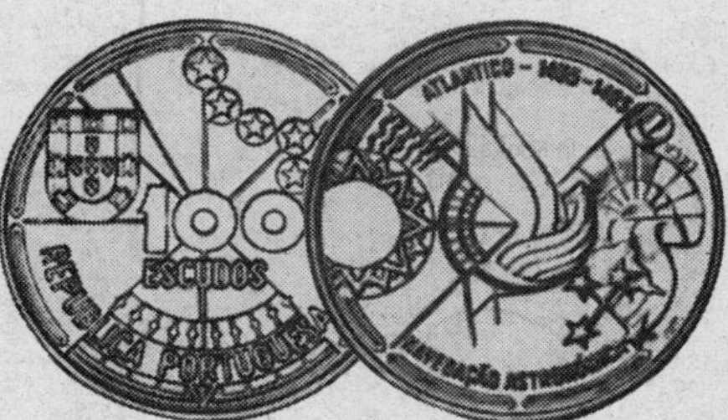

KM# 649 100 ESCUDOS
Copper-Nickel, 34 mm. **Subject:** Celestial Navigation **Obv:** Value in center flanked by shield and circled star designs **Rev:** Artistic designs

Date	Mintage	F	VF	XF	Unc	BU
1990	2,000,000	—	—	1.00	2.50	—

KM# 649a 100 ESCUDOS
21.0000 g., 0.9250 Silver .6246 oz. ASW, 34 mm. **Subject:** Celestial Navigation **Obv:** Value in center flanked by shield and circled star designs **Rev:** Artistic designs

Date	Mintage	F	VF	XF	Unc	BU
1990	50,000	—	—	—	12.50	—
1990 Proof	20,000	Value: 20.00				

KM# 649b 100 ESCUDOS
24.0000 g., 0.9170 Gold .7077 oz. AGW, 34 mm. **Subject:** Celestial Navigation **Obv:** Value in center flanked by shield and circled star designs **Rev:** Artistic designs

Date	Mintage	F	VF	XF	Unc	BU
1990 Proof	2,958	Value: 560				

KM# 649c 100 ESCUDOS
31.1190 g., 0.9990 Platinum 1.0000 oz. APW **Subject:** Celestial Navigation **Obv:** Value in center flanked by shield and circled star designs **Rev:** Artistic designs

Date	Mintage	F	VF	XF	Unc	BU
1990 Proof	2,500	Value: 1,500				

KM# 651 100 ESCUDOS
Copper-Nickel, 33 mm. **Subject:** 350th Anniversary - Restoration of Portuguese Independence **Obv:** Shield within beaded circle **Rev:** Half length figure facing left holding sword under design **Designer:** A. Marinho

Date	Mintage	F	VF	XF	Unc	BU
ND(1990)	1,000,000	—	—	1.00	2.50	4.00

KM# 651a 100 ESCUDOS
18.5000 g., 0.9250 Silver .5502 oz. ASW, 33 mm. **Subject:** 350th Anniversary - Restoration of Portuguese **Obv:** Shield within beaded circle **Rev:** Half length figure facing left holding sword under design

Date	Mintage	F	VF	XF	Unc	BU
ND(1990)	25,000	—	—	—	20.00	—
ND(1990) Proof	10,000	Value: 40.00				

KM# 656 100 ESCUDOS
Copper-Nickel, 33 mm. **Rev:** Camilo Castelo Branco **Designer:** Vilar

Date	Mintage	F	VF	XF	Unc	BU
1990	1,000,000	—	—	1.00	2.50	3.50

KM# 656a 100 ESCUDOS
18.5000 g., 0.9250 Silver .5502 oz. ASW, 33 mm. **Rev:** Camilo Castelo Branco

Date	Mintage	F	VF	XF	Unc	BU
1990 Proof	10,000	Value: 42.00				
1990	25,000	—	—	—	18.50	—

KM# 664 100 ESCUDOS
26.0000 g., Copper-Nickel, 36 mm. **Subject:** Antero DeQuental **Obv:** Hand above national arms and value **Rev:** Portrait, signature, life dates and name **Edge:** Reeded

Date	Mintage	F	VF	XF	Unc	BU
1991INCM	—	—	—	—	3.00	—

KM# 664a 100 ESCUDOS
26.5000 g., 0.9250 Silver 0.7881 oz. ASW, 36 mm. **Subject:** Antero DeQuental **Obv:** Hand above national arms and value **Rev:** Portrait, signature, name and life dates **Edge:** Reeded

Date	Mintage	F	VF	XF	Unc	BU
1991INCM	20,000	—	—	—	18.50	—
1991INCM Proof	—	Value: 42.00				

KM# 678 100 ESCUDOS
Bi-Metallic Aluminum-Bronze center in Copper-Nickel ring, 25.5 mm. **Subject:** 50th Anniversary - F.A.O. **Obv:** Shield within globe above value within circle **Obv. Designer:** Jose Candido **Rev:** F.A.O. logo within oat wreath **Rev. Designer:** J. Duarte

Date	Mintage	F	VF	XF	Unc	BU
1995 Proof	17,000	Value: 15.00				
1995	500,000	—	—	1.50	4.00	—

KM# 680 100 ESCUDOS
Copper-Nickel, 33 mm. **Subject:** 400th Anniversary - Antonio Prior de Crato **Obv:** Bird, shield, cross and designs within circle **Rev:** Bust 1/4 right within circle

Date	Mintage	F	VF	XF	Unc	BU
ND(1995)	—	—	—	1.00	2.50	4.00

KM# 680a 100 ESCUDOS
18.5000 g., 0.9250 Silver .5502 oz. ASW, 33 mm. **Subject:** 400th Anniversary - Antonio Prior de Crato **Obv:** Bird, shield, cross and designs within circle **Rev:** Bust 1/4 right within circle

Date	Mintage	F	VF	XF	Unc	BU
ND(1995)	5,000	—	—	—	30.00	—
ND(1995) Proof	10,000	Value: 32.50				

KM# 693 100 ESCUDOS
Bi-Metallic Aluminum-Bronze center in Copper-Nickel ring, 25.5 mm. **Subject:** Lisbon World Expo '98 **Obv:** Shield and flying bird above value **Rev:** Sea Lion

Date	Mintage	F	VF	XF	Unc	BU
1997	—	—	—	1.50	3.00	6.00
1997 Proof	7,000	Value: 15.00				

KM# 722.1 100 ESCUDOS
Bi-Metallic Brass center in Copper-Nickel ring, 25 mm. **Obv:** National arms, value and country name **Rev:** UNICEF logo **Edge:** Reeded and plain sections

Date	Mintage	F	VF	XF	Unc	BU
1999INCM	—	—	—	—	5.00	6.50

KM# 722.2 100 ESCUDOS
Bi-Metallic Brass center in Copper-Nickel ring, 25 mm. **Obv:** Shield within globe in center circle, numeral and written value in outer circle **Rev:** Silhouette heads of mother and baby and partial globe in center circle flanked by sprigs **Edge:** Reeded and plain sections

Date	Mintage	F	VF	XF	Unc	BU
1999INCM	—	—	—	—	6.00	7.50

KM# 655 200 ESCUDOS
Bi-Metallic Copper-Nickel center in Aluminum-Bronze ring, 28 mm. **Obv:** Shield within globe above value **Rev:** Armored 1/2 length bust right holding flower within circle **Designer:** S. Candido

Date	Mintage	F	VF	XF	Unc	BU
1991	33,000,000	—	—	1.25	3.00	4.00
1992	11,000,000	—	—	1.50	3.50	5.00
1993	20,000	—	—	—	18.00	—
Note: In Mint sets only						
1996	—	—	—	—	18.00	—
Note: In Mint sets only						
1996 Proof	7,000	Value: 20.00				
1997	—	—	—	1.50	4.00	—
1997 Proof	—	Value: 20.00				
1998	—	—	—	1.50	4.00	—
1998 Proof	—	Value: 20.00				
1999	—	—	—	1.50	4.00	—
2000	—	—	—	1.50	4.00	—

KM# 658 200 ESCUDOS
Copper-Nickel, 36 mm. **Subject:** Columbus and Portugal **Obv:** Shield and value to left of design **Rev:** Head left, map, cross, dates and 1/2 star design **Designer:** A. Marinho

Date	Mintage	F	VF	XF	Unc	BU
1991	1,500,000	—	—	1.50	3.50	5.00

KM# 658a 200 ESCUDOS
26.5000 g., 0.9250 Silver .788 oz. ASW, 36 mm. **Subject:** Columbus and Portugal **Obv:** Shield and value to left of design **Rev:** Head left, map, cross, dates and 1/2 star design

Date	Mintage	F	VF	XF	Unc	BU
1991	10,000	—	—	—	16.50	—
1991 Proof	15,000	Value: 30.00				

KM# 658b 200 ESCUDOS
27.2000 g., 0.9170 Gold .8000 oz. AGW **Subject:** Columbus and Portugal **Obv:** Shield, value and date to left of design **Rev:** Head left, map, cross, dates and 1/2 star design

Date	Mintage	F	VF	XF	Unc	BU
1991 Proof	3,500	Value: 585				

KM# 658c 200 ESCUDOS
31.1190 g., 0.9990 Platinum 1.000 oz. APW **Subject:** Columbus and Portugal **Obv:** Shield, value and date to left of design **Rev:** Head left, map, cross, dates and 1/2 star design

Date	Mintage	F	VF	XF	Unc	BU
1991 Proof	2,500	Value: 1,350				

KM# 658d 200 ESCUDOS
31.1190 g., 0.9990 Palladium 1.0000 oz. **Subject:** Columbus and Portugal **Obv:** Shield, value and date to left of design **Rev:** Head left, map, cross, dates and 1/2 star design

Date	Mintage	F	VF	XF	Unc	BU
1991 Proof	2,500	Value: 450				

KM# 659 200 ESCUDOS
Copper-Nickel, 36 mm. **Subject:** Westward Navigation **Obv:** Shield and value within design **Rev:** Stylized ship **Designer:** Paulo d'Eca Leal

Date	Mintage	F	VF	XF	Unc	BU
1991	1,500,000	—	—	1.50	4.50	—

KM# 659a 200 ESCUDOS
26.5000 g., 0.9250 Silver .7880 oz. ASW, 36 mm. **Subject:** Westward Navigation **Obv:** Shield and value within design **Rev:** Stylized ship

Date	Mintage	F	VF	XF	Unc	BU
1991	10,000	—	—	—	15.00	16.50
1991 Proof	15,000	Value: 25.00				

KM# 659b 200 ESCUDOS
27.2000 g., 0.9170 Gold .8000 oz. AGW **Subject:** Westward Navigation **Obv:** Shield and value within design **Rev:** Stylized ship

Date	Mintage	F	VF	XF	Unc	BU
1991 Proof	3,500	Value: 585				

KM# 659c 200 ESCUDOS
31.1190 g., 0.9990 Platinum 1.0000 oz. APW **Subject:** Westward Navigation **Obv:** Shield and value within design **Rev:** Stylized ship

Date	Mintage	F	VF	XF	Unc	BU
1991 Proof	2,500	Value: 1,350				

KM# 659d 200 ESCUDOS
31.1190 g., 0.9990 Palladium 1.0000 oz. **Subject:** Westward Navigation **Obv:** Shield and value within design **Rev:** Stylized ship

Date	Mintage	F	VF	XF	Unc	BU
1991 Proof	2,500	Value: 450				

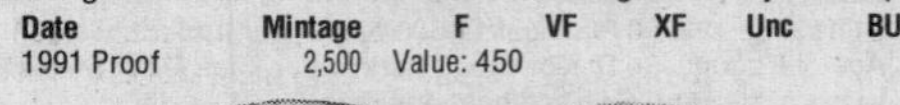

KM# 660 200 ESCUDOS
Copper-Nickel, 36 mm. **Subject:** New World - America **Obv:** Shield within design **Rev:** Head 1/4 left and ships

Date	Mintage	F	VF	XF	Unc	BU
ND(1992)	1,300,000	—	—	1.50	4.50	—

KM# 660a 200 ESCUDOS
26.5000 g., 0.9250 Silver .7880 oz. ASW, 36 mm. **Subject:** New World - America **Obv:** Shield within design **Rev:** Head 1/4 left and ships

Date	Mintage	F	VF	XF	Unc	BU
ND(1992)	10,000	—	—	—	16.50	—
ND(1992) Proof	15,000	Value: 25.00				

KM# 660b 200 ESCUDOS
27.2000 g., 0.9170 Gold .8000 oz. AGW **Subject:** New World - America **Obv:** Shield within design **Rev:** Head 1/4 left and ships

Date	Mintage	F	VF	XF	Unc	BU
ND(1992) Proof	6,000	Value: 585				

KM# 660c 200 ESCUDOS
31.1190 g., 0.9990 Platinum 1.0000 oz. APW **Subject:** New World - America **Obv:** Shield within design **Rev:** Head 1/4 left and ships

Date	Mintage	F	VF	XF	Unc	BU
ND(1992) Proof	2,500	Value: 1,350				

KM# 660d 200 ESCUDOS
31.1190 g., 0.9990 Palladium 1.0000 oz. **Subject:** New World - America **Obv:** Shield within design **Rev:** Head 1/4 left and ships

Date	Mintage	F	VF	XF	Unc	BU
ND(1992) Proof	2,500	Value: 450				

KM# 661 200 ESCUDOS
Copper-Nickel, 36 mm. **Obv:** Shield and value within thin lined cross **Rev:** Standing figure and map **Designer:** Isabel C.-F. Branco

Date	Mintage	F	VF	XF	Unc	BU
ND(1992)	1,300,000	—	—	1.50	4.50	—

KM# 661a 200 ESCUDOS
26.5000 g., 0.9250 Silver .7880 oz. ASW, 36 mm. **Obv:** Shield and value within thin lined cross **Rev:** Standing figure and map

Date	Mintage	F	VF	XF	Unc	BU
ND(1992)	10,000	—	—	—	16.50	—
ND(1992) Proof	15,000	Value: 25.00				

KM# 661b 200 ESCUDOS
27.2000 g., 0.9170 Gold .8000 oz. AGW **Obv:** Shield and value within thin lined cross **Rev:** Standing figure and map

Date	Mintage	F	VF	XF	Unc	BU
ND(1992) Proof	3,500	Value: 585				

KM# 661c 200 ESCUDOS
31.1190 g., 0.9990 Platinum 1.0000 oz. APW **Obv:** Shield and value within thin lined cross **Rev:** Standing figure and map

Date	Mintage	F	VF	XF	Unc	BU
ND(1992) Proof	2,500	Value: 1,350				

KM# 661d 200 ESCUDOS
31.1190 g., 0.9990 Palladium 1.0000 oz. **Obv:** Shield and value within thin lined cross **Rev:** Standing figure and map

Date	Mintage	F	VF	XF	Unc	BU
ND(1992) Proof	2,500	Value: 450				

KM# 662 200 ESCUDOS
Copper-Nickel, 36 mm. **Series:** Olympics **Rev:** Stylized runner **Designer:** A. Marinho

Date	Mintage	F	VF	XF	Unc	BU
1992	1,000,000	—	—	1.50	4.50	—

KM# 662a 200 ESCUDOS
26.5000 g., 0.9250 Silver .7881 oz. ASW, 36 mm. **Series:** Olympics **Rev:** Stylized runner

Date	Mintage	F	VF	XF	Unc	BU
1992	20,000	—	—	—	17.50	—
1992 Proof	30,000	Value: 32.50				

KM# 663 200 ESCUDOS
Copper-Nickel, 36 mm. **Subject:** Portugal's Presidency of the European Community **Obv:** Shield within wave-like design **Rev:** Circle of stars within wave-like design **Designer:** Isabel F. Branco

Date	Mintage	F	VF	XF	Unc	BU
1992	1,000,000	—	—	1.50	4.50	—

KM# 663a 200 ESCUDOS
26.5000 g., 0.9250 Silver .7881 oz. ASW, 36 mm. **Subject:** Portugal's Presidency of the European Community **Obv:** Shield within wave-like design **Rev:** Circle of stars within wave-like design

Date	Mintage	F	VF	XF	Unc	BU
1992	20,000	—	—	—	20.00	—
1992 Proof	30,000	Value: 35.00				

KM# 665 200 ESCUDOS
Copper-Nickel, 36 mm. **Subject:** Tanegashima - Site 1st Portuguese Landing in Japan **Obv:** Shield **Rev:** Ship **Designer:** E. Byrne

Date	Mintage	F	VF	XF	Unc	BU
ND(1993)	1,000,000	—	—	1.50	4.50	—

KM# 665a 200 ESCUDOS
26.5000 g., 0.9250 Silver .7881 oz. ASW, 36 mm. **Subject:** Tanegashima - Site 1st Portuguese Landing in Japan **Obv:** Shield **Rev:** Ship

Date	Mintage	F	VF	XF	Unc	BU
ND(1993)	30,000	—	—	—	18.50	—
ND(1993) Proof	22,000	Value: 30.00				

KM# 665b 200 ESCUDOS
27.2000 g., 0.9170 Gold .8020 oz. AGW **Subject:** Tanegashima - 1st Portuguese Ship to Japan **Obv:** Shield **Rev:** Ship

Date	Mintage	F	VF	XF	Unc	BU
ND(1993) Proof	7,000	Value: 600				

KM# 666 200 ESCUDOS
Copper-Nickel, 36 mm. **Subject:** Espingarda **Obv:** Inscription divides globe and shield **Rev:** Mounted cavalryman shooting rifle **Designer:** A. Marinho

Date	Mintage	F	VF	XF	Unc	BU
1993	1,000,000	—	—	1.50	4.50	—

KM# 666a 200 ESCUDOS
26.5000 g., 0.9250 Silver .7881 oz. ASW, 36 mm. **Subject:** Espingarda **Obv:** Inscription divides globe and shield **Rev:** Mounted cavalryman shooting rifle

Date	Mintage	F	VF	XF	Unc	BU
1993	30,000	—	—	—	18.50	—
1993 Proof	20,000	Value: 35.00				

KM# 666b 200 ESCUDOS
27.2000 g., 0.9170 Gold .8020 oz. AGW **Subject:** Espingarda **Obv:** Inscription divides globe and shield **Rev:** Mounted cavalryman shooting rifle

Date	Mintage	F	VF	XF	Unc	BU
1993 Proof	7,000	Value: 600				

KM# 666c 200 ESCUDOS
31.1190 g., 0.9990 Palladium 1.0000 oz. **Subject:** Espingarda **Obv:** Inscription divides globe and shield **Rev:** Mounted cavalryman shooting rifle

Date	Mintage	F	VF	XF	Unc	BU
1993 Proof	2,000	Value: 450				

KM# 667 200 ESCUDOS
Copper-Nickel, 36 mm. **Obv:** Ship at right of shield **Rev:** Armored busts and date to right of column

Date	Mintage	F	VF	XF	Unc	BU
1993	1,000,000	—	—	1.50	4.50	—

KM# 667a 200 ESCUDOS
26.5000 g., 0.9250 Silver .7881 oz. ASW, 36 mm. **Obv:** Ship at right of shield **Rev:** Armored busts and date to right of column

Date	Mintage	F	VF	XF	Unc	BU
1993 Proof	20,000	Value: 35.00				
1993	30,000	—	—	—	18.50	—

KM# 667b 200 ESCUDOS
27.2000 g., 0.9170 Gold .8020 oz. AGW **Obv:** Ship at right of shield **Rev:** Armored busts and date to right of column

Date	Mintage	F	VF	XF	Unc	BU
1993 Proof	7,000	Value: 600				

KM# 668 200 ESCUDOS
Copper-Nickel, 36 mm. **Rev:** Arte Namban

Date	Mintage	F	VF	XF	Unc	BU
1993	1,000,000	—	—	1.50	4.50	—

KM# 668a 200 ESCUDOS
26.5000 g., 0.9250 Silver .7881 oz. ASW, 36 mm. **Rev:** Arte Namban

Date	Mintage	F	VF	XF	Unc	BU
1993	30,000	—	—	—	18.50	—
1993 Proof	22,000	Value: 35.00				

KM# 668b 200 ESCUDOS
27.2000 g., 0.9170 Gold .8020 oz. AGW **Rev:** Arte Namban

Date	Mintage	F	VF	XF	Unc	BU
1993 Proof	7,000	Value: 600				

KM# 668c 200 ESCUDOS
31.1190 g., 0.9990 Platinum 1.0000 oz. APW **Rev:** Arte Namban

Date	Mintage	F	VF	XF	Unc	BU
1993 Proof	2,000	Value: 1,350				

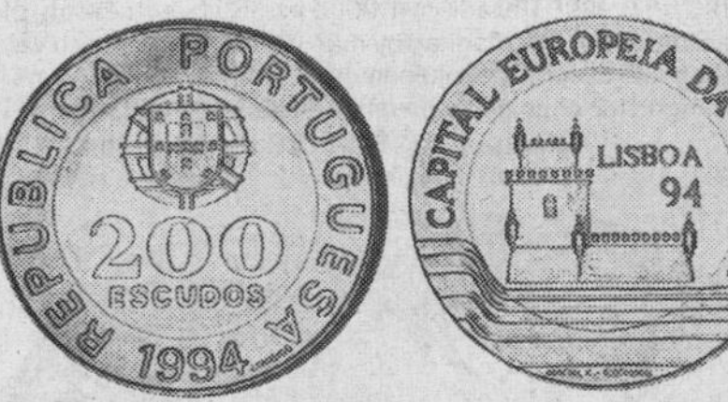

KM# 669 200 ESCUDOS
Bi-Metallic Copper-Nickel center in Aluminum-Bronze ring, 28 mm. **Subject:** Lisbon - European Cultural Capital **Obv:** Shield within globe above value within circle **Rev:** Cultural building within circle

Date	Mintage	F	VF	XF	Unc	BU
1994	1,000,000	—	—	—	4.50	—
1994 Proof	7,000	Value: 20.00				

KM# 670 200 ESCUDOS
Copper-Nickel, 36 mm. **Obv:** Shield to left of ships **Rev:** Bust 1/4 right flanked by dates and symbol **Designer:** S. Machado

Date	Mintage	F	VF	XF	Unc	BU
ND(1994)	750,000	—	—	—	5.50	—

KM# 670a 200 ESCUDOS
26.5000 g., 0.9250 Silver .7881 oz. ASW, 36 mm. **Obv:** Shield to upper left of ships **Rev:** Bust 1/4 right flanked by dates and symbol

Date	Mintage	F	VF	XF	Unc	BU
ND(1994)	20,000	—	—	—	17.50	—
ND(1994) Proof	13,000	Value: 27.50				

KM# 670b 200 ESCUDOS
27.2000 g., 0.9170 Gold .8020 oz. AGW **Obv:** Shield to upper left of ships **Rev:** Bust 1/4 right flanked by dates and symbol

Date	Mintage	F	VF	XF	Unc	BU
ND(1994) Proof	2,000	Value: 600				

KM# 671 200 ESCUDOS
Copper-Nickel, 36 mm. **Subject:** Treaty of Tordesilhas **Obv:** Ship flanked by map, shield, designs and value **Rev:** Left 1/2 of coin is conjoined crowned heads right, arms above, right 1/2 of coin is crown head left, arms on bottom **Designer:** Isabel C.-F. Branco

Date	Mintage	F	VF	XF	Unc	BU
ND(1994)	750,000	—	—	—	5.50	—

KM# 671a 200 ESCUDOS
26.5000 g., 0.9250 Silver .7881 oz. ASW, 36 mm. **Subject:** Treaty of Tordesilhas **Obv:** Ship flanked by map, shield, designs and value **Rev:** Left 1/2 of coin is conjoined crowned heads right, arms above, right 1/2 of coin is crown head left, arms on bottom

Date	Mintage	F	VF	XF	Unc	BU
ND(1994)	20,000	—	—	—	17.50	—
ND(1994) Proof	13,000	Value: 27.50				

KM# 671b 200 ESCUDOS
27.2000 g., 0.9170 Gold .8020 oz. AGW **Subject:** Treaty of Tordesilhas **Obv:** Ship flanked by map, shield, designs and value **Rev:** Left 1/2 of coin is conjoined crowned heads right, arms above, right 1/2 of coin is crown head left, arms on bottom

Date	Mintage	F	VF	XF	Unc	BU
ND(1994) Proof	2,000	Value: 600				

KM# 671c 200 ESCUDOS
31.1190 g., 0.9990 Palladium 1.0000 oz. **Subject:** Treaty of Tordesilhas **Obv:** Ship flanked by map, shield, designs and value **Rev:** Left 1/2 of coin is conjoined crowned heads right, arms above, right 1/2 of coin is crown head left, arms on bottom

Date	Mintage	F	VF	XF	Unc	BU
ND(1994) Proof	1,000	Value: 450				

KM# 672 200 ESCUDOS
Copper-Nickel, 36 mm. **Subject:** Dividing Up The World **Obv:** Shield, map, value and date **Rev:** Ship, map and divided arms

Date	Mintage	F	VF	XF	Unc	BU
1994	750,000	—	—	—	5.50	—

KM# 672a 200 ESCUDOS
26.5000 g., 0.9250 Silver .7881 oz. ASW, 36 mm. **Subject:** Dividing up the World **Obv:** Shield, value, date and map **Rev:** Ship, map and divided arms

Date	Mintage	F	VF	XF	Unc	BU
1994	20,000	—	—	—	17.50	—
1994 Proof	12,000	Value: 27.50				

KM# 672b 200 ESCUDOS
27.2000 g., 0.9170 Gold .8020 oz. AGW **Subject:** Dividing Up The World **Obv:** Shield, map, value and date **Rev:** Ship, map and divided arms

Date	Mintage	F	VF	XF	Unc	BU
1994 Proof	3,000	Value: 600				

KM# 673 200 ESCUDOS
Copper-Nickel, 36 mm. **Obv:** Water divides shield and design **Rev:** Crowned 1/2 length figure facing

Date	Mintage	F	VF	XF	Unc	BU
ND(1994)	750,000	—	—	—	5.50	—

KM# 673a 200 ESCUDOS
26.5000 g., 0.9250 Silver .7881 oz. ASW, 36 mm. **Obv:** Water divides shield and design **Rev:** Crowned 1/2 length figure facing

Date	Mintage	F	VF	XF	Unc	BU
ND(1994)	20,000	—	—	—	18.50	—
ND(1994) Proof	13,000	Value: 37.50				

KM# 673b 200 ESCUDOS
27.2000 g., 0.9170 Gold .8020 oz. AGW **Obv:** Water divides shield and design **Rev:** Crowned 1/2 length figure facing

Date	Mintage	F	VF	XF	Unc	BU
ND(1994) Proof	2,000	Value: 600				

KM# 673c 200 ESCUDOS
31.1190 g., 0.9990 Platinum 1.0000 oz. APW **Obv:** Water divides shield and design **Rev:** Crowned 1/2 length figure facing

Date	Mintage	F	VF	XF	Unc	BU
ND(1994) Proof	1,000	Value: 1,350				

KM# 679 200 ESCUDOS
Bi-Metallic Copper-Nickel center in Aluminum-Bronze ring, 28 mm. **Subject:** 50th Anniversary - United Nations **Obv:** Shield within globe above value **Obv. Designer:** J. Candido **Rev:** Numeral 50 and emblem in center of puzzle pieces **Rev. Designer:** J. Duarte

Date	Mintage	F	VF	XF	Unc	BU
1995	500,000	—	—	—	5.50	—
1995 Proof	17,000	Value: 20.00				

KM# 681 200 ESCUDOS
Copper-Nickel, 36 mm. **Obv:** Shield and globe above date and value **Rev:** Armored standing figure **Designer:** S. Machado

Date	Mintage	F	VF	XF	Unc	BU
1995	750,000	—	—	—	5.00	—

KM# 681a 200 ESCUDOS
26.5000 g., 0.9250 Silver .7881 oz. ASW, 36 mm. **Obv:** Shield and globe above date and value **Rev:** Armored standing figure

Date	Mintage	F	VF	XF	Unc	BU
1995	20,000	—	—	—	18.50	—
1995 Proof	13,000	Value: 32.50				

KM# 681b 200 ESCUDOS
27.2000 g., 0.9170 Gold .8016 oz. AGW **Obv:** Shield and globe above date and value **Rev:** Armored standing figure

Date	Mintage	F	VF	XF	Unc	BU
1995 Proof	4,000	Value: 565				

KM# 682 200 ESCUDOS
Copper-Nickel, 36 mm. **Obv:** Shield, value, fruit sprig and flower sprig **Rev:** Moluca Islands and ship **Designer:** A. Marinho

Date	Mintage	F	VF	XF	Unc	BU
1995	750,000	—	—	—	5.00	—

KM# 682a 200 ESCUDOS
26.5000 g., 0.9250 Silver .7881 oz. ASW, 36 mm. **Obv:** Shield, value, fruit sprig and flower sprig **Rev:** Moluca Islands and ship

Date	Mintage	F	VF	XF	Unc	BU
1995	20,000	—	—	—	18.50	—
1995 Proof	13,000	Value: 35.00				

KM# 682b 200 ESCUDOS
27.2000 g., 0.9170 Gold .8016 oz. AGW **Obv:** Shield, value, fruit sprig and flower sprig **Rev:** Moluca Islands and ship

Date	Mintage	F	VF	XF	Unc	BU
1995 Proof	4,000	Value: 565				

KM# 682c 200 ESCUDOS
31.1190 g., 0.9995 Palladium 1.0000 oz. **Obv:** Shield, value, fruit sprig and flower sprig **Rev:** Moluca Islands and ship

Date	Mintage	F	VF	XF	Unc	BU
1995	1,000	Value: 450				

Note: In proof sets only

KM# 683 200 ESCUDOS
Copper-Nickel, 36 mm. **Obv:** Tree, ship and shield **Rev:** Solor and Timor Islands **Designer:** E. Byrne

Date	Mintage	F	VF	XF	Unc	BU
1995	750,000	—	—	—	5.00	—

KM# 683a 200 ESCUDOS
26.5000 g., 0.9250 Silver .7881 oz. ASW, 36 mm. **Obv:** Shield, tree and ship **Rev:** Solor and Timor Islands

Date	Mintage	F	VF	XF	Unc	BU
1995	20,000	—	—	—	18.50	—
1995 Proof	13,000	Value: 35.00				

KM# 683b 200 ESCUDOS
27.2000 g., 0.9170 Gold .8016 oz. AGW **Obv:** Ship, tree and shield **Rev:** Solar and Timor Islands

Date	Mintage	F	VF	XF	Unc	BU
1995 Proof	4,000	Value: 565				

KM# 684 200 ESCUDOS
Copper-Nickel, 36 mm. **Obv:** Shield, dates, globe and value **Rev:** Map and ships **Designer:** Isabel C. F. Branco

Date	Mintage	F	VF	XF	Unc	BU
1995	750,000	—	—	—	5.00	—

KM# 684a 200 ESCUDOS
26.5000 g., 0.9250 Silver .7881 oz. ASW, 36 mm. **Obv:** Shield, dates, globe and value **Rev:** Map and ships

Date	Mintage	F	VF	XF	Unc	BU
1995	20,000	—	—	—	18.50	—
1995 Proof	13,000	Value: 35.00				

KM# 684b 200 ESCUDOS
27.2000 g., 0.9170 Gold .8016 oz. AGW **Obv:** Shield, dates, globe and value **Rev:** Map and ships

Date	Mintage	F	VF	XF	Unc	BU
1995 Proof	4,000	Value: 565				

KM# 684c 200 ESCUDOS
31.1190 g., 0.9995 Platinum 1.0000 oz. APW **Obv:** Shield, dates, globe and value **Rev:** Map and ships

Date	Mintage	F	VF	XF	Unc	BU
1995	1,000	Value: 1,350				

Note: In proof sets only

KM# 687 200 ESCUDOS
Bi-Metallic Copper-Nickel center in Brass ring, 28 mm. **Series:** Olympics **Obv:** Shield, value and olympic circles **Rev:** High jumper **Designer:** Vitor Santos

Date	Mintage	F	VF	XF	Unc	BU
1996	—	—	—	—	5.00	—
1996 Proof	7,000	Value: 20.00				

KM# 687a 200 ESCUDOS
26.4500 g., 0.9250 Silver .7866 oz. ASW **Series:** Olympics **Obv:** Shield, value and olympic circles **Rev:** High jumper

Date	Mintage	F	VF	XF	Unc	BU
1996 Proof	20,000	Value: 50.00				

KM# 689 200 ESCUDOS
Copper-Nickel, 36 mm. **Subject:** 1512 Portugal - Siam Alliance **Obv:** Ship, shield, dates and value **Rev:** Portuguese and Siamese arms

Date	Mintage	F	VF	XF	Unc	BU
1996	—	—	—	—	5.00	—

KM# 689a 200 ESCUDOS
26.5000 g., 0.9250 Silver .7881 oz. ASW, 36 mm. **Subject:** 1512 Portugal - Siam Alliance **Obv:** Ship, shield, dates and value **Rev:** Portuguese and Siamese arms

Date	Mintage	F	VF	XF	Unc	BU
1996	20,000	—	—	—	17.50	—
1996 Proof	11,000	Value: 32.50				

KM# 689b 200 ESCUDOS
27.0000 g., 0.9166 Gold .8015 oz. AGW **Subject:** 1512 Portugal - Siam Alliance **Obv:** Ship, shield, dates and value **Rev:** Portuguese and Siamese arms

Date	Mintage	F	VF	XF	Unc	BU
1996 Proof	3,000	Value: 565				

KM# 690 200 ESCUDOS
Copper-Nickel, 36 mm. **Subject:** 1513 Portuguese Arrival in China **Obv:** Shield within globe flanked by leafy sprigs **Rev:** Ship, map and building

Date	Mintage	F	VF	XF	Unc	BU
1996	—	—	—	—	6.00	—

KM# 690a 200 ESCUDOS
26.5000 g., 0.9250 Silver .7881 oz. ASW, 36 mm. **Subject:** 1513 Portuguese Arrival in China **Obv:** Shield within globe flanked by leafy sprigs **Rev:** Ship, map and building

Date	Mintage	F	VF	XF	Unc	BU
1996	20,000	—	—	—	22.50	—
1996 Proof	10,000	Value: 40.00				

KM# 690b 200 ESCUDOS
27.2000 g., 0.9166 Gold .8015 oz. AGW **Subject:** 1513 Portuguese Arrival in China **Obv:** Shield within globe flanked by leafy sprigs **Rev:** Ship, map and building

Date	Mintage	F	VF	XF	Unc	BU
1996 Proof	3,000	Value: 565				

KM# 690c 200 ESCUDOS
31.1190 g., 0.9995 Palladium 1.0000 oz. **Subject:** 1513 Portuguese Arrival in China **Obv:** Shield within globe flanked by leafy sprigs **Rev:** Ship, map and building

Date	Mintage	F	VF	XF	Unc	BU
1996 Proof	1,000	Value: 450				

KM# 691 200 ESCUDOS
Copper-Nickel, 36 mm. **Subject:** 1557 Portuguese Establishment in Macau **Obv:** Shield at upper left above building **Rev:** Building at upper left of ship

Date	Mintage	F	VF	XF	Unc	BU
1996	—	—	—	—	5.00	—

KM# 691a 200 ESCUDOS
26.5000 g., 0.9250 Silver .7881 oz. ASW, 36 mm. **Subject:** 1557 Portuguese Establishment in Macau **Obv:** Shield at upper left above building **Rev:** Building at upper left of ship

Date	Mintage	F	VF	XF	Unc	BU
1996 Proof	10,000	Value: 32.50				
1996	20,000	—	—	—	17.50	—

KM# 691b 200 ESCUDOS
27.2000 g., 0.9166 Gold .8015 oz. AGW **Subject:** 1557 Portuguese Establishment in Macau **Obv:** Shield at upper left above building **Rev:** Building at upper left of ship

Date	Mintage	F	VF	XF	Unc	BU
1996 Proof	4,000	Value: 565				

KM# 692 200 ESCUDOS
Copper-Nickel, 36 mm. **Subject:** 1582 Portuguese Discovery of Taiwan **Obv:** Flower sprig to left of shield **Rev:** Ship

Date	Mintage	F	VF	XF	Unc	BU
1996	—	—	—	—	5.00	—

KM# 692a 200 ESCUDOS
26.5000 g., 0.9250 Silver .7881 oz. ASW, 36 mm. **Subject:** 1582 Portuguese Discovery of Taiwan **Obv:** Flower sprig to left of shield **Rev:** Ship

Date	Mintage	F	VF	XF	Unc	BU
1996	20,000	—	—	—	17.50	—
1996 Proof	10,000	Value: 32.50				

KM# 692b 200 ESCUDOS
27.2000 g., 0.9166 Gold .8015 oz. AGW **Subject:** 1582 Portuguese Discovery of Taiwan **Obv:** Flower sprig to left of shield **Rev:** Ship

Date	Mintage	F	VF	XF	Unc	BU
1996 Proof	3,000	Value: 585				

KM# 692c 200 ESCUDOS
31.1190 g., 0.9995 Platinum 1.0000 oz. APW **Subject:** 1582 Portuguese Discovery of Taiwan **Obv:** Flower sprig to left of shield **Rev:** Ship

Date	Mintage	F	VF	XF	Unc	BU
1996 Proof	1,000	Value: 1,350				

KM# 694 200 ESCUDOS
Bi-Metallic Copper-Nickel center in Copper-Aluminum ring, 28 mm. **Subject:** Lisbon World Expo '98 **Obv:** Shield and value within circle **Rev:** Dolphins **Rev. Designer:** Jose Simão

Date	Mintage	F	VF	XF	Unc	BU
1997	—	—	—	—	6.00	—
1997 Proof	7,000	Value: 20.00				

KM# 697 200 ESCUDOS
Copper-Nickel, 36 mm. **Obv:** National arms **Rev:** S. Francisco Xavier

Date	Mintage	F	VF	XF	Unc	BU
1997	—	—	—	—	5.00	—

KM# 697a 200 ESCUDOS
26.5000 g., 0.9250 Silver .7881 oz. ASW, 36 mm. **Obv:** National arms **Rev:** S. Francisco Xavier

Date	Mintage	F	VF	XF	Unc	BU
1997	25,000	—	—	—	17.50	—
1997 Proof	25,000	Value: 30.00				

KM# 697b 200 ESCUDOS
27.2000 g., 0.9167 Gold .8017 oz. AGW **Obv:** National arms **Rev:** S. Francisco Xavier

Date	Mintage	F	VF	XF	Unc	BU
1997 Proof	4,000	Value: 565				

KM# 698 200 ESCUDOS
Copper-Nickel, 36 mm. **Obv:** Shield to left of designs and value **Rev:** Two seated figures talking

Date	Mintage	F	VF	XF	Unc	BU
1997	—	—	—	—	5.00	—

KM# 698a 200 ESCUDOS
26.5000 g., 0.9250 Silver .7881 oz. ASW, 36 mm. **Obv:** Shield to left of designs and value **Rev:** Two seated figures talking

Date	Mintage	F	VF	XF	Unc	BU
1997	25,000	—	—	—	17.50	—
1997 Proof	24,000	Value: 32.50				

KM# 698b 200 ESCUDOS
27.2000 g., 0.9167 Gold .8017 oz. AGW **Obv:** Shield to left of designs and value **Rev:** Two seated figures talking

Date	Mintage	F	VF	XF	Unc	BU
1997 Proof	5,000	Value: 565				

KM# 699 200 ESCUDOS
Copper-Nickel, 36 mm. **Obv:** Shield and map of South America **Rev:** Bto. Jose de Anchieta

Date	Mintage	F	VF	XF	Unc	BU
1997	—	—	—	—	5.00	—

KM# 699a 200 ESCUDOS
26.5000 g., 0.9250 Silver .7881 oz. ASW, 36 mm. **Obv:** Shield and map of South America **Rev:** Bto. Jose de Anchieta

Date	Mintage	F	VF	XF	Unc	BU
1997	25,000	—	—	—	17.50	—
1997 Proof	24,000	Value: 32.50				

KM# 699b 200 ESCUDOS
27.2000 g., 0.9167 Gold .8017 oz. AGW **Obv:** Shield and map of South America **Rev:** Bto. Jose de Anchieta

Date	Mintage	F	VF	XF	Unc	BU
1997 Proof	4,000	Value: 565				

KM# 699c 200 ESCUDOS
31.1190 g., 0.9995 Palladium 1.0000 oz. **Obv:** Shield and map of South America **Rev:** Bto. Jose de Anchieta

Date	Mintage	F	VF	XF	Unc	BU
1997 Proof	1,000	Value: 450				

KM# 700 200 ESCUDOS
Copper-Nickel, 36 mm. **Obv:** National cross and shield **Rev:** Irmao Bento de Gois, map of China's coast

Date	Mintage	F	VF	XF	Unc	BU
1997	—	—	—	—	5.00	—

KM# 700a 200 ESCUDOS
26.5000 g., 0.9250 Silver .7881 oz. ASW, 36 mm. **Obv:** National cross and shield **Rev:** Irmao Bento de Gois, map of China's coast

Date	Mintage	F	VF	XF	Unc	BU
1997	25,000	—	—	—	17.50	—
1997 Proof	24,000	Value: 32.50				

KM# 700b 200 ESCUDOS

27.2000 g., 0.9160 Gold .8017 oz. AGW **Obv:** National cross and shield **Rev:** Irmao Bento de Gois, map of China's coast

Date	Mintage	F	VF	XF	Unc	BU
1997 Proof	4,000	Value: 565				

KM# 700c 200 ESCUDOS

31.1190 g., 0.9995 Platinum 1.0000 oz. APW **Obv:** National cross and shield **Rev:** Irmao Bento de Gois, map of China's coast

Date	Mintage	F	VF	XF	Unc	BU
1997 Proof	1,000	Value: 1,350				

KM# 706 200 ESCUDOS

Bi-Metallic Copper-Nickel center in Aluminum-Bronze ring, 28 mm. **Subject:** International Year of the Oceans Expo **Obv:** Small shield within sprigs above value **Rev:** Expo 98 and fish within sprigs

Date	Mintage	F	VF	XF	Unc	BU
1998	Est. 50,000	—	—	—	4.50	—
1998 Proof	Est. 20,000	Value: 12.00				

KM# 709 200 ESCUDOS

Copper-Nickel, 36 mm. **Obv:** Three ships, shield, and value **Rev:** Portrait of Vasco Da Gama, dates

Date	Mintage	F	VF	XF	Unc	BU
1998	—	—	—	—	5.00	—

KM# 709a 200 ESCUDOS

26.5000 g., 0.9250 Silver .7881 oz. ASW, 36 mm. **Obv:** Three ships, shield, and value **Rev:** Bust of Vasco da Gama left, dates

Date	Mintage	F	VF	XF	Unc	BU
1998 Proof	25,000	Value: 32.50				

KM# 709b 200 ESCUDOS

27.2000 g., 0.9167 Gold .8017 oz. AGW **Obv:** Three ships, shield, and value **Rev:** Bust of Vasco Da Gama left, dates

Date	Mintage	F	VF	XF	Unc	BU
1998 Proof	5,000	Value: 565				

KM# 709c 200 ESCUDOS

31.1190 g., 0.9995 Platinum 1.0000 oz. APW **Obv:** Three ships, shield, and value **Rev:** Bust of Vasco da Gama, dates

Date	Mintage	F	VF	XF	Unc	BU
1998 Proof	1,000	Value: 1,350				

KM# 710 200 ESCUDOS

Copper-Nickel, 36 mm. **Subject:** Discovery of Africa **Obv:** Shield, ship, and palm tree **Rev:** Ship, map, and hunter

Date	Mintage	F	VF	XF	Unc	BU
1998	—	—	—	—	5.00	—

KM# 710a 200 ESCUDOS

26.5000 g., 0.9250 Silver .7881 oz. ASW, 36 mm. **Subject:** Discovery of Africa **Obv:** Shield, ship, and palm tree **Rev:** Ship, map, and hunter

Date	Mintage	F	VF	XF	Unc	BU
1998	25,000	—	—	—	17.50	—
1998 Proof	26,000	Value: 30.00				

KM# 710b 200 ESCUDOS

27.2000 g., 0.9167 Gold .8017 oz. AGW **Subject:** Discovery of Africa **Obv:** Shield, ship, and palm tree **Rev:** Ship, map, and hunter

Date	Mintage	F	VF	XF	Unc	BU
1998 Proof	5,000	Value: 565				

KM# 711 200 ESCUDOS

Copper-Nickel, 36 mm. **Subject:** Mozambique **Obv:** Shield above mermaid **Rev:** Two ships and island map

Date	Mintage	F	VF	XF	Unc	BU
1998	—	—	—	—	5.00	—

KM# 711a 200 ESCUDOS

26.5000 g., 0.9250 Silver .7881 oz. ASW, 36 mm. **Subject:** Mozambique **Obv:** Shield above mermaid **Rev:** Two ships and island map

Date	Mintage	F	VF	XF	Unc	BU
1998 Proof	25,000	Value: 30.00				
1998	25,000	—	—	—	17.50	—

KM# 711b 200 ESCUDOS

27.2000 g., 0.9167 Gold .8017 oz. AGW **Subject:** Mozambique **Obv:** Shield above mermaid **Rev:** Two ships and island map

Date	Mintage	F	VF	XF	Unc	BU
1998 Proof	6,000	Value: 565				

KM# 712 200 ESCUDOS

Copper-Nickel, 36 mm. **Subject:** India 1498 **Obv:** Shield and sailing ship **Rev:** Ship and coastal map of India

Date	Mintage	F	VF	XF	Unc	BU
1998	—	—	—	—	5.00	—

KM# 712a 200 ESCUDOS

26.5000 g., 0.9250 Silver .7881 oz. ASW, 36 mm. **Subject:** India 1498 **Obv:** Shield and sailing ship **Rev:** Ship and coastal map of India

Date	Mintage	F	VF	XF	Unc	BU
1998	25,000	—	—	—	17.50	—
1998 Proof	25,000	Value: 32.50				

KM# 712b 200 ESCUDOS

27.2000 g., 0.9167 Gold .8017 oz. AGW **Subject:** India 1498 **Obv:** Shield and sailing ship **Rev:** Ship and coastal map of India

Date	Mintage	F	VF	XF	Unc	BU
1998 Proof	5,000	Value: 565				

KM# 712c 200 ESCUDOS

31.1190 g., 0.9995 Palladium 1.0000 oz. **Subject:** India 1498 **Obv:** Shield and sailing ship **Rev:** Ship and coastal map of India

Date	Mintage	F	VF	XF	Unc	BU
1998 Proof	1,000	Value: 450				

KM# 716 200 ESCUDOS

Copper-Nickel 1.0000 oz., 36 mm. **Subject:** Death on the Sea **Obv:** Shield, globe and ropes **Rev:** Stylized sinking ship **Edge:** Reeded **Designer:** A. Marinho

Date	Mintage	F	VF	XF	Unc	BU
1999INCM	—	—	—	—	4.00	—

KM# 716a 200 ESCUDOS

26.5000 g., 0.9250 Silver .7881 oz. ASW, 36 mm. **Subject:** Death on the Sea **Obv:** Shield, globe and ropes **Rev:** Stylized sinking ship **Edge:** Reeded

Date	Mintage	F	VF	XF	Unc	BU
1999INCM	10,000	—	—	—	20.00	—
1999INCM Proof	10,000	Value: 35.00				

KM# 716b 200 ESCUDOS

27.2000 g., 0.9167 Gold .8017 oz. AGW, 36 mm. **Subject:** Death on the Sea **Obv:** Shield, globe and ropes **Rev:** Stylized sinking ship **Edge:** Reeded

Date	Mintage	F	VF	XF	Unc	BU
1999INCM Proof	1,000	Value: 600				

KM# 717 200 ESCUDOS

Copper-Nickel, 36 mm. **Subject:** Brasil 1500 **Obv:** Fleet of sailing ships **Rev:** Head right **Designer:** S. Machado

Date	Mintage	F	VF	XF	Unc	BU
1999INCM	—	—	—	—	4.00	—

KM# 717a 200 ESCUDOS

26.5000 g., 0.9250 Silver .7881 oz. ASW, 36 mm. **Subject:** Brasil 1500 **Obv:** Fleet of sailing ships **Rev:** Head right

Date	Mintage	F	VF	XF	Unc	BU
1999INCM	1,000	—	—	—	20.00	—
1999 Proof	1,000	Value: 35.00				

KM# 717b 200 ESCUDOS

27.2000 g., 0.9167 Gold .8017 oz. AGW **Subject:** Brasil 1500 **Obv:** Fleet of sailing ships **Rev:** Head right

Date	Mintage	F	VF	XF	Unc	BU
1999INCM Proof	1,000	Value: 600				

KM# 718 200 ESCUDOS

Copper-Nickel, 36 mm. **Subject:** Brasil **Obv:** Natives, palm trees **Rev:** Ship, native, and map **Designer:** Isabel C.F. Branco

Date	Mintage	F	VF	XF	Unc	BU
1999	—	—	—	—	4.00	—

KM# 718a 200 ESCUDOS

26.5000 g., 0.9250 Silver .7881 oz. ASW, 36 mm. **Subject:** Brasil **Obv:** Natives, palm trees **Rev:** Ship, native, and map

Date	Mintage	F	VF	XF	Unc	BU
1999	Est. 10,000	—	—	—	20.00	—
1999 Proof	Est. 10,000	Value: 35.00				

KM# 718b 200 ESCUDOS

27.2000 g., 0.9167 Gold .8017 oz. AGW **Subject:** Brasil **Obv:** Natives and palm trees **Rev:** Ship, native, and map

Date	Mintage	F	VF	XF	Unc	BU
1999 Proof	1,000	Value: 600				

KM# 719 200 ESCUDOS

Copper-Nickel, 36 mm. **Subject:** Duarte Pacheco Pereira **Rev:** Armored half-length bust facing **Designer:** E. Byrne

Date	Mintage	F	VF	XF	Unc	BU
1999	—	—	—	—	4.00	—

KM# 719a 200 ESCUDOS

26.5000 g., 0.9250 Silver .7881 oz. ASW, 36 mm. **Subject:** Duarte Pacheco Pereira **Rev:** Armored half-length bust facing

Date	Mintage	F	VF	XF	Unc	BU
1999	1,000	—	—	—	20.00	—
1999 Proof	1,000	Value: 35.00				

KM# 719b 200 ESCUDOS
27.2000 g., 0.9167 Gold .8017 oz. AGW **Subject:** Duarte Pacheco Pereira **Rev:** Armored half-length bust facing

Date	Mintage	F	VF	XF	Unc	BU
1999INCM Proof	1,000	Value: 600				

KM# 720 200 ESCUDOS
Bi-Metallic Copper-Nickel center in Brass ring, 28 mm. **Obv:** Shield within globe above value **Rev:** Stylized dove on wheels and logo **Edge:** Reeded and plain sections **Designer:** Meneres

Date	Mintage	F	VF	XF	Unc	BU
1999INCM	—	—	—	—	6.50	7.50

KM# 726 200 ESCUDOS
Bi-Metallic Copper-Nickel center in Nickel-Brass ring, 28 mm. **Obv:** Torch, cross design and value **Rev:** Olympic logo **Edge:** Reeded and plain sections **Designer:** Nogueira DaSilva

Date	Mintage	F	VF	XF	Unc	BU
2000INCM	10,000	—	—	—	4.00	—
2000INCM Proof	5,000	Value: 7.50				

KM# 728 200 ESCUDOS
21.1000 g., Copper-Nickel, 36 mm. **Subject:** Terra Do Lavrado **Obv:** Compass and shield **Rev:** Labrador coast and ship **Edge:** Reeded

Date	Mintage	F	VF	XF	Unc	BU
2000INCM	—	—	—	—	4.00	—

KM# 728a 200 ESCUDOS
26.5000 g., 0.9250 Silver .7881 oz. ASW, 36 mm. **Subject:** Terra do Lavrado **Obv:** Shield and compass **Rev:** Labrador coast and ship **Edge:** Reeded

Date	Mintage	F	VF	XF	Unc	BU
2000 Proof	Est. 10,000	Value: 37.50				
2000	Est. 10,000	—	—	—	25.00	—

KM# 728b 200 ESCUDOS
27.2000 g., 0.9166 Gold .8016 oz. AGW, 36 mm. **Subject:** Terra Do Lavrado **Obv:** Shield and compass **Rev:** Labrador coast and ship **Edge:** Reeded

Date	Mintage	F	VF	XF	Unc	BU
2000 Proof	Est. 1,375	Value: 585				

KM# 729 200 ESCUDOS
21.1400 g., Copper-Nickel, 36 mm. **Subject:** Terra Dos Corte-Real **Obv:** Cross above shield **Rev:** Ship above 1501-1502 **Edge:** Reeded

Date	Mintage	F	VF	XF	Unc	BU
2000INCM	—	—	—	—	4.00	—

KM# 729a 200 ESCUDOS
26.5000 g., 0.9250 Silver .7881 oz. ASW, 36 mm. **Subject:** Terra Dos Corte-Real **Obv:** Cross above shield **Rev:** Ship above 1501-1502 **Edge:** Reeded

Date	Mintage	F	VF	XF	Unc	BU
2000 Proof	Est. 10,000	Value: 37.50				
2000	Est. 10,000	—	—	—	25.00	—

KM# 729b 200 ESCUDOS
27.2000 g., 0.9166 Gold .8016 oz. AGW **Subject:** Terra Dos Corte-Real **Obv:** Cross above shield **Rev:** Ship above 1501-1502 **Designer:** Reeded

Date	Mintage	F	VF	XF	Unc	BU
2000 Proof	Est. 1,375	Value: 585				

KM# 729c 200 ESCUDOS
31.1190 g., 0.9995 Palladium 1.0000 oz. **Subject:** Terra Dos Corte-Real **Obv:** Cross above shield **Rev:** Ship above 1501-1502 **Edge:** Reeded

Date	Mintage	F	VF	XF	Unc	BU
2000 Proof	Est. 250	Value: 600				

KM# 730 200 ESCUDOS
21.1400 g., Copper-Nickel, 36 mm. **Subject:** Terra Florida **Obv:** Maltese crosses above compass **Rev:** Ship below maltese cross within map **Edge:** Reeded

Date	Mintage	F	VF	XF	Unc	BU
2000INCM	—	—	—	—	4.00	—

KM# 730a 200 ESCUDOS
26.5000 g., 0.9250 Silver .7881 oz. ASW **Subject:** Terra Florida **Obv:** Maltese crosses above compass **Rev:** Ship below maltese cross within map **Edge:** Reeded

Date	Mintage	F	VF	XF	Unc	BU
2000 Proof	Est. 10,000	Value: 37.50				
2000	Est. 10,000	—	—	—	25.00	—

M# 730b 200 ESCUDOS
27.2000 g., 0.9166 Gold .8016 oz. AGW **Obv:** Maltese crosses above compass **Rev:** Ship below maltese cross within map **Edge:** Reeded **Edge Lettering:** Terra Florida

Date	Mintage	F	VF	XF	Unc	BU
2000 Proof	Est. 1,375	Value: 585				

KM# 731 200 ESCUDOS
21.1400 g., Copper-Nickel, 36 mm. **Subject:** Fernao De Magalhaes **Obv:** Shield, ship, and value **Rev:** Bearded portrait **Edge:** Reeded

Date	Mintage	F	VF	XF	Unc	BU
2000INCM	—	—	—	—	4.00	—

KM# 731a 200 ESCUDOS
26.5000 g., 0.9250 Silver .7881 oz. ASW **Subject:** Fernao de Magalhaes **Obv:** Shield, ship, and value **Rev:** Bearded portrait **Edge:** Reeded

Date	Mintage	F	VF	XF	Unc	BU
2000	Est. 10,000	—	—	—	25.00	—
2000 Proof	Est. 10,000	Value: 37.50				

KM# 731b 200 ESCUDOS
27.2000 g., 0.9166 Gold .8016 oz. AGW **Subject:** Fernao de Magalhaes **Obv:** Shield, ship, and value **Rev:** Bearded portrait **Edge:** Reeded

Date	Mintage	F	VF	XF	Unc	BU
2000 Proof	Est. 1,375	Value: 585				

KM# 731c 200 ESCUDOS
31.1190 g., 0.9995 Platinum 1.0000 oz. APW **Subject:** Fernao de Magalhaes **Obv:** Shield, ship, and value **Rev:** Bearded portrait **Edge:** Reeded

Date	Mintage	F	VF	XF	Unc	BU
2000 Proof	Est. 250	Value: 1,350				

KM# 604 250 ESCUDOS
25.0000 g., 0.6800 Silver .5466 oz. ASW **Subject:** 1974 Revolution **Obv:** Value above cross design within circle **Rev:** Design flanked by dates with value above

Date	Mintage	F	VF	XF	Unc	BU
ND(1976)	950,000	—	—	6.00	10.00	—
ND(1976) Proof	10,000	Value: 18.50				

KM# 626 250 ESCUDOS
Copper-Nickel, 37 mm. **Subject:** World Fisheries Conference **Obv:** Shield within horizontal lines **Rev:** Cluster of fish within triangular design facing right **Rev. Designer:** Jose Aurelio

Date	Mintage	F	VF	XF	Unc	BU
ND(1984)	24,000	—	—	30.00	65.00	—

KM# 626a 250 ESCUDOS
23.0000 g., 0.9250 Silver .6841 oz. ASW, 37 mm. **Obv:** Shield within horizontal lines **Rev:** Cluster of fish within triangular design facing right **Edge Lettering:** World Fisheries Conference

Date	Mintage	F	VF	XF	Unc	BU
ND(1984) Proof	8,000	Value: 120				

KM# 643 250 ESCUDOS
Copper-Nickel, 37 mm. **Subject:** Seoul Olympics **Obv:** Shield in front of lined flower-like design **Rev:** Runners **Designer:** Helder Batista

Date	Mintage	F	VF	XF	Unc	BU
1988	850,000	—	—	2.50	5.00	—

KM# 643a 250 ESCUDOS
28.0000 g., 0.9250 Silver .8327 oz. ASW, 37 mm. **Subject:** Seoul Olympics **Obv:** Shield in front of lined flower-like design **Rev:** Runners

Date	Mintage	F	VF	XF	Unc	BU
1988 Proof	30,000	Value: 27.50				
1988	70,000	—	—	—	17.50	—

KM# 650 250 ESCUDOS
Copper-Nickel, 37 mm. **Subject:** 850th Anniversary - Founding of Portugal **Obv:** Small churches in cross formation at left of

design **Rev:** Sword divides cresent flanked by dates below design within circle

Date	Mintage	F	VF	XF	Unc	BU
1989	750,000	—	—	2.50	5.00	—

KM# 650a 250 ESCUDOS

28.0000 g., 0.9250 Silver .8327 oz. ASW, 37 mm. **Subject:** 850th Anniversary - Founding of Portugal **Obv:** Small churches in cross formation to left of design **Rev:** Sword divides cresent flanked by dates below design within circle

Date	Mintage	F	VF	XF	Unc	BU
1989 Proof	30,000	Value: 40.00				
1989	15,000	—	—	—	22.50	—

KM# 620 500 ESCUDOS

7.0000 g., 0.8350 Silver .1879 oz. ASW **Subject:** XVII European Art Exhibition **Obv:** Cross and globe divides date **Rev:** Styilized castle within 1/2 beaded circle

Date	Mintage	F	VF	XF	Unc	BU
1983	200,000	—	—	6.00	12.00	—
1983 Proof	8,500	Value: 30.00				

KM# 686 500 ESCUDOS

14.0000 g., 0.5000 Silver .2250 oz. ASW **Subject:** 800th Anniversary - Birth of Saint Anthony **Obv:** Castle to left of shield, date and value **Rev:** Seated figure holding cross and book within arch **Note:** Prev. KM686a

Date	Mintage	F	VF	XF	Unc	BU
1995	—	—	—	—	8.50	10.00

KM# 686b 500 ESCUDOS

14.0000 g., 0.9250 Silver .4163 oz. ASW **Subject:** 800th Anniversary - Birth of Saint Anthony **Obv:** Church to left of shield, date and value **Rev:** Seated figure holding cross and book within arch

Date	Mintage	F	VF	XF	Unc	BU
1995 Proof	10,000	Value: 45.00				

KM# 686c 500 ESCUDOS

17.5000 g., 0.9177 Gold .5159 oz. AGW **Subject:** 800th Anniversary - Birth of Saint Anthony **Obv:** Church to left of shield, date and value **Rev:** Seated figure holding cross and book within arch

Date	Mintage	F	VF	XF	Unc	BU
1995 Proof	5,000	Value: 380				

KM# 702 500 ESCUDOS

13.8700 g., 0.5000 Silver .2230 oz. ASW **Obv:** Shield **Rev:** Bank seal - Banco de Portugal

Date	Mintage	F	VF	XF	Unc	BU
ND(1996)	—	—	—	—	8.50	10.00

KM# 701 500 ESCUDOS

14.0000 g., 0.5000 Silver 0.2250 oz. ASW **Obv:** Shield superimposed on radiant sun **Rev:** Head facing

Date	Mintage	F	VF	XF	Unc	BU
ND(1997)	—	—	—	—	7.50	9.50

KM# 701a 500 ESCUDOS

14.0000 g., 0.9250 Silver .4051 oz. ASW **Obv:** Shield superimposed on radiant sun **Rev:** Head facing

Date	Mintage	F	VF	XF	Unc	BU
ND(1997) Proof	—	Value: 37.50				

KM# 701b 500 ESCUDOS

Silver And Gold **Obv:** Shield superimposed on radiant sun **Rev:** Head facing **Note:** 14.0000 gram, .925 Silver, .4051 ounce with 3.1000 gram .9167 gold, .0914 ounce lamination on reverse.

Date	Mintage	F	VF	XF	Unc	BU
ND(1997) Proof	15,000	Value: 125				

KM# 705 500 ESCUDOS

14.0000 g., 0.5000 Silver .2250 oz. ASW **Obv:** Shield, design within circle and value **Rev:** Bridge

Date	Mintage	F	VF	XF	Unc	BU
1998	—	—	—	—	7.50	9.50
1998 Proof	30,000	Value: 42.50				

KM# 705a 500 ESCUDOS

Bi-Metallic Gold center in Silver ring **Obv:** Shield, design within circle and value **Rev:** Bridge **Note:** 14.000 gram, .925 Silver, .4164 ounce with 3.1000 gram .9167 gold, .0914 ounce lamination on reverse.

Date	Mintage	F	VF	XF	Unc	BU
1998 Proof	15,000	Value: 135				

KM# 723 500 ESCUDOS

14.0000 g., 0.5000 Silver .2236 oz. ASW **Subject:** Macao's Return to China **Obv:** Partial bridge above shield and value **Rev:** Bridge above monument **Edge:** Reeded

Date	Mintage	F	VF	XF	Unc	BU
1999INCM	—	—	—	—	6.00	7.50

KM# 725 500 ESCUDOS

14.0000 g., 0.5000 Silver .2250 oz. ASW **Subject:** Eca de Queiroz **Obv:** Shield in center flanked by sprigs **Rev:** Stylized portrait left **Edge:** Reeded

Date	Mintage	F	VF	XF	Unc	BU
ND(2000)	450,000	—	—	—	8.50	10.00
ND(2000) Proof	10,000	Value: 45.00				

KM# 725a 500 ESCUDOS

14.0000 g., 0.9250 Silver .4164 oz. ASW **Subject:** Eca de Queiroz **Obv:** Shield flanked by sprigs above value **Rev:** Stylized portrait left **Edge:** Reeded **Note:** 14.000 gram, .925 Silver, .4164 ounce with 3.1000 gram .9167 gold, .1000 ounce lamination on reverse.

Date	Mintage	F	VF	XF	Unc	BU
ND(2000) Proof	10,000	Value: 125				

KM# 621 750 ESCUDOS

12.5000 g., 0.8350 Silver .3356 oz. ASW **Subject:** XVII European Art Exhibition **Obv:** Cross and globe divides date **Rev:** Crowned shield within circle

Date	Mintage	F	VF	XF	Unc	BU
1983	200,000	—	—	7.50	15.00	—
1983 Proof	8,500	Value: 35.00				

KM# 611 1000 ESCUDOS

17.0000 g., 0.9250 Silver .5056 oz. ASW **Subject:** 400th Anniversary - Death of Louis de Camoes **Obv:** Shield within globe above sprig **Rev:** Armored bust 1/4 right flanked by dates

Date	Mintage	F	VF	XF	Unc	BU
ND(1983)	150,000	—	—	—	18.50	—
ND(1983) Proof	10,000	Value: 42.50				

KM# 622 1000 ESCUDOS

21.0000 g., 0.8350 Silver .5638 oz. ASW **Subject:** XVII European Art Exhibition **Obv:** Cross and globe divides date **Rev:** Crowned shield within center circle

Date	Mintage	F	VF	XF	Unc	BU
1983	200,000	—	—	9.50	17.50	—
1983 Proof	8,500	Value: 40.00				

KM# 657 1000 ESCUDOS

27.0000 g., 0.5000 Silver .4340 oz. ASW **Series:** Ibero - American **Obv:** Shield within globe in center of assorted emblems around border **Rev:** Ship and assorted emblems within map and circle

Date	Mintage	F	VF	XF	Unc	BU
ND(1992)	326,000	—	—	—	17.50	—

KM# 657a 1000 ESCUDOS

27.0000 g., 0.9250 Silver .8029 oz. ASW **Series:** Ibero - American **Obv:** Shield within globe in center of assorted emblems around border **Rev:** Ship and assorted emblems within circle

Date	Mintage	F	VF	XF	Unc	BU
ND(1992) Proof	30,000	Value: 65.00				

KM# 675 1000 ESCUDOS

28.0000 g., 0.5000 Silver .4501 oz. ASW **Subject:** Treaty of Tordesilhas **Obv:** Upright design above value **Rev:** Cross on top of shield within mapped scroll

Date	Mintage	F	VF	XF	Unc	BU
ND(1994)	—	—	—	—	14.50	16.50

KM# 675a 1000 ESCUDOS

28.0000 g., 0.9250 Silver .8327 oz. ASW **Subject:** Treaty of Tordesilhas **Obv:** Upright design above value **Rev:** Cross on top of shield within mapped scroll

Date	Mintage	F	VF	XF	Unc	BU
ND(1994) Proof	10,000	Value: 45.00				

KM# 676 1000 ESCUDOS

28.0000 g., 0.5000 Silver .4501 oz. ASW **Subject:** Endangered Wildlife **Obv:** Shield within globe in center of assorted emblems **Rev:** Gray wolves within circle

Date	Mintage	F	VF	XF	Unc	BU
1994	70,000	—	—	—	100	—

KM# 676a 1000 ESCUDOS

28.0000 g., 0.9250 Silver .8327 oz. ASW **Subject:** Endangered Wildlife **Obv:** Shield within globe in center of assorted emblems **Rev:** Grey wolves within circle

Date	Mintage	F	VF	XF	Unc	BU
1994 Proof	30,000	Value: 150				

KM# 685 1000 ESCUDOS

28.0000 g., 0.5000 Silver .4501 oz. ASW **Subject:** 500th Anniversary - Death of John II **Obv:** Design within circle **Rev:** Head right and 1/2 of ship

Date	Mintage	F	VF	XF	Unc	BU
ND(1995)	650,000	—	—	—	13.50	15.00

KM# 685a 1000 ESCUDOS

28.0000 g., 0.9250 Silver .8327 oz. ASW **Subject:** 500th Anniversary - Death of John II **Obv:** Design within circle **Rev:** Head right and 1/2 of ship

Date	Mintage	F	VF	XF	Unc	BU
ND(1995) Proof	15,000	Value: 40.00				

KM# 688 1000 ESCUDOS

28.0000 g., 0.5000 Silver .4501 oz. ASW **Subject:** Restoration of the Frigate Ferdinand II and Gloria **Obv:** Shield, figure head, ship's hull **Rev:** Ship below two facing busts

Date	Mintage	F	VF	XF	Unc	BU
ND(1996)	—	—	—	—	14.50	16.50

KM# 688a 1000 ESCUDOS

28.0000 g., 0.9250 Silver .8327 oz. ASW **Subject:** Restoration of the Frigate Ferdinand II and Gloria **Obv:** Shield, figure head, ship's hull **Rev:** Two facing busts above ship

Date	Mintage	F	VF	XF	Unc	BU
ND(1996) Proof	15,000	Value: 45.00				

KM# 696 1000 ESCUDOS

28.0000 g., 0.5000 Silver .4501 oz. ASW **Subject:** N. S. Da Conceicao Padroeira de Portugal **Obv:** Shield **Rev:** Madonna and child

Date	Mintage	F	VF	XF	Unc	BU
ND(1996)	—	—	—	—	13.50	15.00

KM# 696a 1000 ESCUDOS

28.0000 g., 0.9250 Silver .8327 oz. ASW **Subject:** N. S. Da Conceicao Padroeira de Portugal **Obv:** Shield **Rev:** Madonna and child

Date	Mintage	F	VF	XF	Unc	BU
ND(1996) Proof	—	Value: 45.00				

KM# 695 1000 ESCUDOS

28.0000 g., 0.5000 Silver .4501 oz. ASW **Subject:** 100th Anniversary - Portuguese Oceanic Expedition **Obv:** Shield and fish **Rev:** Ship below two facing busts

Date	Mintage	F	VF	XF	Unc	BU
1997	—	—	—	—	14.50	16.50

KM# 695a 1000 ESCUDOS

28.0000 g., 0.9250 Silver .8327 oz. ASW **Subject:** 100th Anniversary - Portuguese Oceanic Expedition **Obv:** Shield and fish **Rev:** Two busts above ship

Date	Mintage	F	VF	XF	Unc	BU
1997 Proof	Est. 15,000	Value: 45.00				

KM# 703 1000 ESCUDOS

28.0000 g., 0.5000 Silver .4501 oz. ASW **Subject:** Credito Publico **Obv:** Shield within hexagonal design **Rev:** Hexagonal design

Date	Mintage	F	VF	XF	Unc	BU
1997	Est. 335,000	—	—	—	13.50	15.00

KM# 703a 1000 ESCUDOS

28.0000 g., 0.9250 Silver .8327 oz. ASW **Subject:** Credito Publico **Obv:** Shield within hexagonal design **Rev:** Hexagonal design

Date	Mintage	F	VF	XF	Unc	BU
1997 Proof	Est. 15,000	Value: 50.00				

KM# 704 1000 ESCUDOS

27.0000 g., 0.5000 Silver .4340 oz. ASW **Obv:** Shield within circle of assorted shields **Rev:** Pauliteiros dancers

Date	Mintage	F	VF	XF	Unc	BU
1997	—	—	—	—	13.50	15.00

KM# 704a 1000 ESCUDOS

27.0000 g., 0.9250 Silver .8327 oz. ASW **Obv:** Shield within circle of assorted shields **Rev:** Pauliteiros dancers

Date	Mintage	F	VF	XF	Unc	BU
1997 Proof	—	Value: 45.00				

KM# 707 1000 ESCUDOS

27.0000 g., 0.5000 Silver .4340 oz. ASW **Subject:** International Year of the Oceans Expo **Obv:** Shield and logo **Rev:** Stylized expo designs

Date	Mintage	F	VF	XF	Unc	BU
1998	—	—	—	—	13.50	15.00

KM# 707a 1000 ESCUDOS

27.0000 g., 0.9250 Silver .8030 oz. ASW **Subject:** International Year of the Oceans Expo **Obv:** Shield and logo **Rev:** Stylized expo designs

Date	Mintage	F	VF	XF	Unc	BU
1998 Proof	Est. 20,000	Value: 45.00				

KM# 708 1000 ESCUDOS
27.0000 g., 0.5000 Silver .4340 oz. ASW **Subject:** 500th Anniversary - Misericordia Church **Obv:** Basket and rope design **Rev:** Crowned praying figure flanked by cherubs and other figures below

Date	Mintage	F	VF	XF	Unc	BU
ND(1998)	—	—	—	—	13.50	15.00

KM# 708a 1000 ESCUDOS
27.0000 g., 0.9250 Silver .8030 oz. ASW **Subject:** 500th Anniversary - Misericordia Church **Obv:** Basket and rope design **Rev:** Crowned praying figure flanked by cherubs and other figures below

Date	Mintage	F	VF	XF	Unc	BU
ND(1998) Proof	—	Value: 45.00				

KM# 713 1000 ESCUDOS
27.0000 g., 0.5000 Silver .4340 oz. ASW **Obv:** Two ships, crowned shield, armillary sphere **Rev:** King Dom Manuel I seated on throne with sword

Date	Mintage	F	VF	XF	Unc	BU
1998	—	—	—	—	13.50	15.00

KM# 713a 1000 ESCUDOS
27.0000 g., 0.9250 Silver .8030 oz. ASW **Obv:** Two ships, crowned shield, armillary sphere **Rev:** King Dom Manuel I seated on throne with sword

Date	Mintage	F	VF	XF	Unc	BU
1998 Proof	Est. 15,000	Value: 45.00				

KM# 714 1000 ESCUDOS
27.0000 g., 0.5000 Silver .4340 oz. ASW **Subject:** 75th Anniversary - League of Combatants **Obv:** Stylized shield **Rev:** Sword and laurel branch

Date	Mintage	F	VF	XF	Unc	BU
1998	—	—	—	—	13.50	15.00

KM# 714a 1000 ESCUDOS
27.0000 g., 0.9250 Silver .8030 oz. ASW **Subject:** 75th Anniversary - League of Combatants **Obv:** Stylized shield **Rev:** Sword and laurel branch

Date	Mintage	F	VF	XF	Unc	BU
1998 Proof	—	Value: 45.00				

KM# 715 1000 ESCUDOS
27.0000 g., 0.5000 Silver .4340 oz. ASW **Subject:** 25th Anniversary - Revolution of April 25 **Obv:** Circles within cross design above value and date **Rev:** Date and mirrored anniversary number **Designer:** Jose Aurelio

Date	Mintage	F	VF	XF	Unc	BU
1999	—	—	—	—	13.50	15.00

KM# 715a 1000 ESCUDOS
27.0000 g., 0.9250 Silver .8030 oz. ASW **Subject:** 25th Anniversary - Revolution of April 25 **Obv:** Circles within cross design above value and date **Rev:** Date and mirrored anniversary number

Date	Mintage	F	VF	XF	Unc	BU
1999 Proof	Est. 15,000	Value: 45.00				

KM# 721 1000 ESCUDOS
27.2000 g., 0.5000 Silver .4372 oz. ASW **Subject:** Millennium of Atlantic Sailing **Obv:** Shield above logo **Rev:** Stylized face looking down on ship **Edge:** Reeded

Date	Mintage	F	VF	XF	Unc	BU
1999INCM	—	—	—	—	18.50	20.00

KM# 721a 1000 ESCUDOS
27.0000 g., 0.9250 Silver .8030 oz. ASW **Subject:** Millennium of Atlantic Sailing **Obv:** Shield above logo **Rev:** Stylized face looking down on ship **Edge:** Reeded

Date	Mintage	F	VF	XF	Unc	BU
1999INCM Proof	15,000	Value: 45.00				

KM# 724 1000 ESCUDOS
27.0000 g., 0.5000 Silver .4340 oz. ASW, 40.2 mm. **Subject:** Presidency of the European Union **Obv:** Shield and cave drawings **Rev:** Stylized design **Edge:** Reeded

Date	Mintage	F	VF	XF	Unc	BU
2000	450,000	—	—	—	13.50	15.00

KM# 724a 1000 ESCUDOS
27.0500 g., 0.9250 Silver 0.8045 oz. ASW **Obv:** Shield and cave drawings **Rev:** Stylized design

Date	Mintage	F	VF	XF	Unc	BU
2000 Proof	10,000	Value: 75.00				

KM# 727 1000 ESCUDOS
27.0000 g., 0.5000 Silver .4340 oz. ASW, 40 mm. **Series:** Ibero-America **Obv:** Shield within center of assorted shields **Rev:** Lusitano horses and rider **Edge:** Reeded

Date	Mintage	F	VF	XF	Unc	BU
2000INCM	Est. 450,000	—	—	—	22.50	25.00

KM# 727a 1000 ESCUDOS
27.0000 g., 0.9250 Silver .8030 oz. ASW, 40 mm. **Series:** Ibero-America **Obv:** Shield within center of assorted shields **Rev:** Lusitano horses and rider **Edge:** Reeded

Date	Mintage	F	VF	XF	Unc	BU
2000 Proof	Est. 20,000	—	—	—	100	120

KM# 732 1000 ESCUDOS
27.0000 g., 0.5000 Silver .4340 oz. ASW **Subject:** D. Joso De Castro **Obv:** Shield within globe above value **Rev:** Bearded stylized bust

Date	Mintage	F	VF	XF	Unc	BU
2000	—	—	—	—	20.00	22.50

ESSAIS

KM#	Date	Mintage	Identification	Mkt Val
E1	1986	30	100 Escudos. Copper Nickel. KM637	—
E2	1998	—	100 Escudos. Silver. "ENSAIO" on obverse and reverse.	—
E3	1998	—	100 Escudos. Silver. "ENSAIO" on reverse only.	—

PATTERNS

Including off metal strikes

KM#	Date	Mintage	Identification	Mkt Val
Pn200	1903	—	2 Reis. Nickel. Plain royal arms.	—
Pn201	1903	—	20 Reis. Nickel. Royal arms with wreath.	350
Pn202	1903	—	20 Reis. Nickel. Plain edge. Without wreath.	350
Pn203	1903	—	20 Reis. Nickel. Reeded edge. Value on reeded edge.	275
Pn204	1903	—	20 Reis. Nickel. Plain edge. Value on plain edge.	275
Pn205	1903	—	100 Reis. Silver. Crowned value.	1,500
Pn206	1903	—	200 Reis. Silver. Crowned value.	2,200
Pn207	ND	—	20 Centavos. Silver. Two reverses.	600
Pn208	1912	—	50 Centavos. Copper. Plain edge. Type as adopted.	750
Pn209	1912	—	50 Centavos. Silver. Reeded edge. Type as adopted.	1,000
Pn210	1912	—	Escudo. Gold. 'October 5, 1910'.	600
Pn211	1912	—	Escudo. Gold. Obverse variety.	600
Pn212	1912	—	Escudo. Gold.	600
Pn213	1919	—	4 Centavos. Copper Nickel. Plain edge. Wide border.	—
Pn214	1919	—	4 Centavos. Copper Nickel. Reeded edge. Wide border.	—
Pn215	1919	—	4 Centavos. Copper Nickel. Plain edge. Semi-wide border.	—
Pn216	1919	—	4 Centavos. Copper Nickel. Alternate edge. Narrow border.	—
Pn217	1920	—	10 Centavos. Copper Nickel. Plain edge. Larger type.	1,500
Pn218	1920	—	10 Centavos. Brass. Plain edge. Larger type.	—
Pn219	1920	—	5 Escudos. Copper. 'Abundance Through Labor'	1,000
Pn220	1920	—	5 Escudos. Copper Nickel. 'Abundance Through Labor'	1,000
Pn221	1920	—	5 Escudos. Gold. 'Abundance Through Labor'	—
Pn222	1921	—	10 Centavos. Bronze. Reeded edge. 19mm	500
Pn223	1927	—	50 Centavos. Silver. Reeded edge. Large type.	500
Pn224	1927	—	50 Centavos. Silver. Obverse 1924 type.	500
Pn225	1927	—	Escudo. Silver. Reverse 1924 type.	—
Pn226	1928	—	Escudo. Brass.	650
Pn227	1928	—	10 Escudos. Copper. 'Battle of Orique'.	750
Pn228	1929	—	10 Escudos. Brass. 'Battle of Orique'.	—
Pn229	1932	—	5 Escudos. Copper Nickel. Type adopted.	—
Pn230	1932	—	10 Escudos. Copper.	225
Pn231	1932	—	10 Escudos. Copper Nickel. Type adopted.	225
Pn232	1940	—	10 Escudos. Copper Nickel. Large type.	225

KM#	Date	Mintage	Identification	Mkt Val
Pn233	1953	—	20 Escudos. Copper. 'National Revival'.	650
Pn234	1953	—	20 Escudos. Gold. 'National Revival'.	—
Pn235	1953	—	20 Escudos. Silver. Variety of type adopted.	1,250
Pn236	1961	—	2-1/2 Escudos. Nickel. Reeded edge.	—
Pn237	1961	—	2-1/2 Escudos. Nickel. Reeded edge.	—
Pn238	1961	—	2-1/2 Escudos. Copper Nickel.	—
Pn239	1961	—	10 Escudos. Silver. Legend incuse.	600
Pn240	1961	—	10 Escudos. Copper Nickel.	350
Pn241	1961	—	10 Escudos. Silver.	—
Pn242	1961	—	10 Escudos. Copper Nickel. Legend in relief.	—
Pn243	ND	—	10 Centavos. Aluminum.	—
Pn244	ND	—	20 Centavos. Brass.	225
Pn246	ND	—	10 Escudos. Nickel. Reeded edge. Type adopted.	—
Pn247	ND	—	10 Escudos. Nickel. Plain edge. Type adopted.	—
Pn248	ND	—	10 Centavos. Bronze-Aluminum. Plain edge.	—
Pn249	1966	—	Escudo. Bronze-Aluminum.	200
Pn250	1966	—	Escudo. Bronze-Aluminum. Reeded edge.	200
Pn251	1966	—	20 Escudos. Nickel. Reeded edge.	350
Pn252	1968	—	10 Centavos. Aluminum. Similar to 1942 type.	225
Pn253	1969	—	10 Centavos. Aluminum. Large type as adopted.	—
Pn254	1970	—	Escudo. Nickel. Type adopted.	100
Pn255	1970	—	20 Escudos. Nickel. Reeded edge.	200
Pn256	1970	—	20 Escudos. Nickel. Plain edge.	200
Pn257	1970	—	20 Escudos. Nickel. Reeded edge.	200
Pn258	1970	—	20 Escudos. Nickel. Plain edge.	200
Pn259	1979	—	50 Centavos. Reeded edge.	125
Pn260	1979	—	Escudo. Reeded edge.	125
Pn261	1979	—	5 Escudos. Aluminum.	150
Pn262	ND	—	250 Escudos. Copper Nickel. Decade of Women, United Nations.	—
Pn263	1989	—	100 Escudos.	1,650

PROVAS

Stamped

KM#	Date	Mintage	Identification	Mkt Val
PrA7	1942	—	10 Centavos. Bronze. KM583.	—
PrB7	1942	—	20 Centavos. Bronze. KM584.	55.00
Pr7	1943	—	5 Escudos. Silver. KM581.	35.00
Pr8	1943	—	10 Centavos. Bronze. KM583.	20.00
Pr9	1943	—	20 Centavos. Bronze. KM584.	20.00
Pr10	1960	—	5 Escudos. Silver. KM587.	15.00
Pr11	1960	—	10 Escudos. Silver. KM588.	20.00
Pr12	1960	—	20 Escudos.	30.00
PrA13	1962	—	10 Centavos. Bronze. KM583.	—
PrB13	1962	—	20 Centavos. Bronze. KM584.	—
PrC13	1962	—	50 Centavos. Copper Nickel. KM577.	—
PrD13	1962	—	Escudo. Copper Nickel. KM578.	—
Pr13	1964	—	Escudo. Copper-Nickel. KM578.	—
Pr14	1964	—	2-1/2 Escudos. Copper-Nickel. KM590.	—
Pr15	1966	—	20 Centavos. Bronze. KM584.	—
Pr16	1966	—	Escudo. Copper-Nickel. KM578.	—
Pr17	1966	—	2-1/2 Escudos. Copper-Nickel. KM590.	17.50
Pr18	1966	—	5 Escudos. Copper-Nickel. KM591.	15.00
Pr19	1966	—	20 Escudos. Silver. Salazar Bridge, KM592.	25.00
Pr20	1966	—	20 Escudos. Gold. Salazar Bridge, KM592.	2,500
Pr21	1968	—	50 Escudos. Silver. KM593.	30.00
Pr22	1969	—	50 Escudos. Silver. KM598, 'Prova' incuse.	30.00
Pr23	1969	—	50 Escudos. Silver. KM598, 'Prova' in relief.	35.00
Pr24	1969	—	50 Escudos. Silver. KM599.	30.00
Pr25	1971	—	50 Escudos. Silver. KM601.	30.00
Pr26	1972	—	50 Escudos. Silver. KM602.	30.00
Pr27	ND(1984)	100	25 Escudos. Copper-Nickel. Shield below wave-like design. Stylized value. KM623, Revolution.	15.00
Pr28	1985	5,000	100 Escudos. Copper-Nickel. KM629, Henrique.	—

TRIAL STRIKES

KM#	Date	Mintage	Identification	Mkt Val
TS33	1910	—	1000 Reis. Nickel Alloy. KM558; ALP	400
TS34	1915	—	Escudo. Nickel Alloy. KM564; ALP.	400
TS35	1927	—	5 Centavos. Bronze. Reverse.	—
TS36	ND	—	20 Centavos. Brass. Reverse, Roman numeral.	—
TS37	ND(1927)	—	50 Centavos. Brass. Reverse.	—
TS38	ND(1927)	—	2 Escudos. Brass. Uniface, KM#591.	25.00

MINT SETS

KM#	Date	Mintage	Identification	Issue Price	Mkt Val
MS1	1960 (3)	—	KM587-589	—	45.00
MS2	1982 (4)	10,000	KM612-613, 615-616	3.00	7.00
MS3	1983 (3)	50,000	KM620-622	30.00	30.00
MS4	1983 (3)	5,000	KM617-619	4.00	25.00
MS5	1984 (2)	10,000	KM624-625	3.00	25.00
MS6	1985 (2)	20,000	KM627a, 630a	20.00	37.50
MSA6	1985 (2)	—	KM627, 630	—	10.00
MS7	1986 (5)	50,000	KM631-634, 636	6.00	30.00
MS8	1987/8 (4)	40,000	KM639a-642a	78.00	70.00
MS9	1987/8 (4)	5,000	KM639b-642b	2,080	2,200
MS10	1987 (6)	5,000	KM631-634, 636, 638	10.00	30.00
MS11	1988 (5)	30,000	KM631-634, 636	10.00	20.00
MS12	1989 (6)	50,000	KM631-634, 636, 645.1	12.00	20.00
MS13	1990 (6)	50,000	KM631-634, 636, 645.1	15.00	17.50
MS14	1989/90 (4)	30,000	KM646a-649a	79.50	80.00
MSA14	1989/90 (4)	—	KM646-649	—	15.00
MS15	1991 (7)	—	KM631-634, 636, 645.1, 655	17.50	17.50
MS16	1992 (7)	—	KM631-634, 636, 645.1, 655	—	32.50
MS17	1993 (7)	—	KM631-634, 636, 645.1, 655	—	25.00
MS18	1993 (4)	30,000	KM665a-668a	79.50	75.00
MS19	1994 (7)	—	KM631-634, 636, 645.1, 669	—	32.50
MS20	1994 (4)	—	KM670a-673a	—	90.00
MS21	1995 (7)	—	KM631-634, 636, 678-679	—	20.00
MS22	1995 (4)	20,000	KM681a-684a	77.50	70.00
MS23	1995 (2)	5,000	KM678-679	—	60.00
MS24	1996 (8)	—	KM631-634, 636, 645.1, 655, 687	—	35.00
MS25	1996 (4)	10,000	KM689a, 690a, 691a, 692a	105	70.00
MS26	1997 (9)	20,000	KM631-634, 636, 645.1, 655, 693-694	32.50	30.00
MS27	1998 (8)	50,000	KM631-634, 636, 645.1, 655, 706	32.50	30.00
MS28	1998 (4)	25,000	KM709a-712a	95.00	95.00
MS29	1999 (9)	—	KM631-634, 636, 645.1, 655, 720, 722	—	30.00
MS30	1999 (4)	10,000	KM716a-719a	95.00	95.00
MS31	2000 (4)	10,000	KM#728a-731a	65.00	95.00

PROOF SETS

KM#	Date	Mintage	Identification	Issue Price	Mkt Val
PS1	1960 (3)	—	KM587-589; matte finish	—	115
PS2	1974 (2)	10,000	KM603-604	6.00	35.00
PS3	1977 (3)	10,000	KM605-606, 608	2.50	25.00
PS4	1983 (3)	8,500	KM620-622	60.00	100
PS5	1985 (2)	5,000	KM627a, 630a	40.00	150
PS6	1985 (2)	5,000	KM628, 628a	35.00	300
PS7	1987 (4)	20,000	KM639a-642a	128	150
PS8	1987/88 (4)	2,000	KM639a, 640c, 641b, 642c; Prestige	2,200	2,750
PS9	1989/90 (4)	20,000	KM646a-649a	138	150
PS10	1989/90 (4)	5,000	KM646b-649b	2,425	2,450
PS11	1989/90 (4)	2,500	KM646a, 647c, 648b, 649c; Prestige	2,650	2,800
PS12	1991/92 (4)	15,000	KM658a-661a	150	150
PS13	1991/92 (4)	3,500	KM658b-661b	2,350	2,350
PS14	1991/92 (4)	2,500	KM658c-661c; Prestige	2,400	3,000
PS15	1993 (7)	—	KM631-634, 636, 645.1, 655	—	100
PS16	1993 (4)	22,000	KM665a-668a	150	150
PS17	1993 (4)	5,000	KM665b-668b	1,980	2,500
PS18	1993 (4)	2,000	KM665a, 666c, 667b, 668c; Prestige	2,300	2,150
PS19	1994 (7)	—	KM631-634, 636, 645.1, 669	—	50.00
PS20	1994 (4)	10,000	KM670a-673a	—	150
PS21	1994 (4)	—	KM670b-673b	—	2,400
PS22	1994 (4)	1,000	KM670a, 671c, 672b, 673c; Prestige	—	2,175
PS23	1995 (7)	7,000	KM631-634, 636, 678, 679	47.50	50.00
PS24	1995 (4)	13,000	KM681a-684a	150	150
PS25	1995 (4)	2,000	KM681b-684b	1,980	2,000
PS26	1995 (4)	1,000	KM681a, 682c, 683b, 684c	1,800	2,100
PS27	1995 (2)	10,000	KM678, 679	—	35.00
PS28	1996 (8)	7,000	KM631-634, 636, 645.1, 655, 687	—	50.00
PS29	1996 (4)	10,000	KM689a, 690a, 691a, 692a	160	150
PS30	1996 (4)	2,000	KM689b, 690b, 691b, 692b	—	2,000
PS31	1996 (4)	1,000	KM689a, 690c, 691b, 692c	—	2,100
PS32	1997 (9)	7,000	KM631-634, 636, 645.1, 655, 693-694	55.00	50.00
PS33	1997 (4)	24,000	KM697a-700a	145	150
PS34	1997 (4)	4,000	KM697b-700b	1,980	2,000
PS35	1997 (4)	1,000	KM697a, 698b, 699c, 700c	2,000	2,250
PS36	1998 (8)	20,000	KM631-634, 636, 645.1, 655, 706	52.50	50.00
PS37	1998 (4)	25,000	KM709a-712a	150	150
PS38	1998 (4)	5,000	KM709b-712b	1,980	1,980
PS39	1998 (4)	1,000	KM709c, 710a, 711b, 712c	2,000	2,250
PS40	1999 (4)	10,000	KM716a-719a	150	150
PS41	1999 (4)	1,000	KM716b-719b	1,800	1,800
PS42	2000 (4)	10,000	KM#728a-731a	125	150
PS43	2000 (4)	1,000	KM#728b-731b	1,405	1,850
PS44	2000 (4)	250	KM#728a, 729c, 730b, 731c	2,988	3,000

QATAR

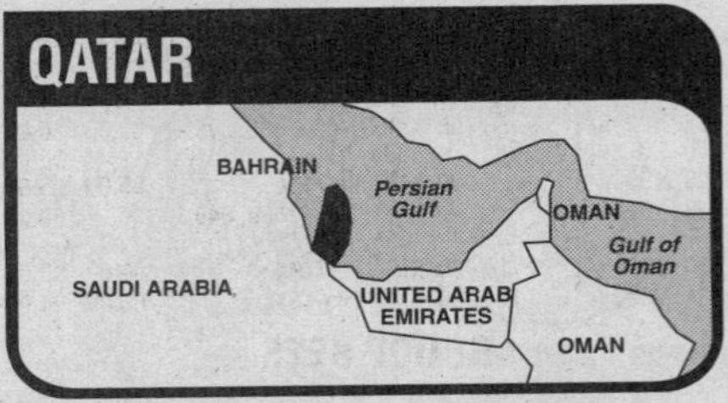

The State of Qatar, an emirate in the Persian Gulf between Bahrain and Trucial Oman, has an area of 4,247sq. mi. (11,000 sq. km.) and a population of *469,000. Capital: Doha. Oil is the chief industry and export.

Qatar was under Turkish control from 1872 until the beginning of World War I when the Ottoman Turks evacuated the Qatar Peninsula. In 1916 Sheikh Abdullah placed Qatar under the protection of Great Britain and gave Britain responsibility for its defense and foreign relations. Qatar joined with Dubai in a Monetary Union and issued coins and paper money in 1966 and 1969. When Britain announced in 1968 that it would end treaty relationships with the Persian Gulf sheikhdoms in 1971, this union was dissolved; Qatar joined Bahrain and the seven trucial sheikhdoms (called the United Arab Emirates) in an effort to form a union of Arab Emirates. However the nine sheikhdoms were unable to agree on terms of union, and Qatar declared its independence as the State of Qatar on Sept. 3, 1971.

TITLE

Daulat Qatar

RULERS

Al-Thani Dynasty

Qasim Bin Muhammad, 1876-1913
Abdullah Bin Qasim, 1913-1948
Ali Bin Abdullah, 1948-1960
Ahmad Bin Ali, 1960-1972
Khalifah bin Hamad, 1972-1995
Hamad bin Khalifah, 1995-

MONETARY SYSTEM

100 Dirhem = 1 Riyal

EMIRATE

STANDARD COINAGE

KM# 2 DIRHAM

1.5000 g., Bronze, 15 mm. **Ruler:** Khalifah Bin Hamad **Obv:** Value **Rev:** Sail boat and palm trees flanked by beads

Date	Mintage	F	VF	XF	Unc	BU
AH1393 - 1973	500,000	—	0.25	0.50	1.00	2.00

KM# 3 5 DIRHAMS

3.7500 g., Bronze, 22 mm. **Ruler:** Khalifah Bin Hamad **Obv:** Value **Rev:** Sail boat and palm trees flanked by beads

Date	Mintage	F	VF	XF	Unc	BU
AH1393 - 1973	1,000,000	—	0.15	0.30	0.75	1.50
AH1398 - 1978	1,000,000	—	0.15	0.30	0.75	1.50

KM# 1 10 DIRHAMS

7.5000 g., Bronze, 27 mm. **Ruler:** Khalifah Bin Hamad **Obv:** Value **Rev:** Sail boat and palm trees flanked by beads

Date	Mintage	F	VF	XF	Unc	BU
AH1392 - 1972	1,500,000	—	0.50	1.00	2.50	4.00
AH1393 - 1973	1,500,000	—	0.25	0.50	1.50	3.00

KM# 4 25 DIRHAMS

3.5000 g., Copper-Nickel, 20 mm. **Ruler:** Hamad bin Khalifah **Obv:** Value **Rev:** Sail boat and palm trees flanked by beads

Date	Mintage	F	VF	XF	Unc	BU
AH1393 - 1973	1,500,000	—	0.30	0.65	1.50	2.25
AH1396 - 1976	2,000,000	—	0.30	0.65	1.75	2.50
AH1398 - 1978	—	—	0.30	0.65	1.75	2.50
AH1401 - 1981	—	—	0.30	0.65	1.75	2.50
AH1407 - 1987	—	—	0.30	0.65	1.75	2.50
AH1410 - 1990	—	—	0.30	0.65	1.75	2.50
AH1414 - 1993	—	—	0.30	0.65	1.75	2.50
AH1419 - 1998	—	—	0.30	0.65	1.75	2.50
AH1421 - 2000	—	—	0.30	0.65	1.75	2.50

KM# 8 25 DIRHAMS

3.5000 g., Copper-Nickel, 19 mm. **Ruler:** Hamad bin Khalifah **Obv:** Value **Rev:** Sail boat and palm trees flanked by beads **Edge:** Reeded

Date	Mintage	F	VF	XF	Unc	BU
AH1421 - 2000	—	—	—	—	1.50	2.50

KM# 5 50 DIRHAMS

6.5000 g., Copper-Nickel, 25 mm. **Ruler:** Khalifah Bin Hamad **Obv:** Value **Rev:** Sail boat and palm trees flanked by beads

Date	Mintage	F	VF	XF	Unc	BU
AH1393 - 1973	1,500,000	—	0.40	0.85	2.00	3.00
AH1398 - 1978	2,000,000	—	0.40	0.85	2.25	3.25
AH1401 - 1981	—	—	0.40	0.85	2.25	3.25
AH1407 - 1987	—	—	0.40	0.85	2.25	3.25
AH1410 - 1990	—	—	0.40	0.85	2.25	3.25
AH1414 - 1993	—	—	0.40	0.85	2.25	3.25
AH1419 - 1998	—	—	0.40	0.85	2.25	3.25

KM# 9 50 DIRHAMS

6.5000 g., Copper-Nickel, 24 mm. **Ruler:** Hamad bin Khalifah **Obv:** Value **Rev:** Sail boat and palm trees flanked by beads **Edge:** Reeded

Date	Mintage	F	VF	XF	Unc	BU
AH1421-2000	—	—	—	—	2.00	3.00

KM# 6 100 RIYALS

22.2000 g., 0.9250 Silver .6602 oz. ASW, 37 mm. **Ruler:** Hamad bin Khalifah **Subject:** Central Bank **Obv:** National arms **Rev:** Bank building **Edge:** Plain

Date	Mintage	F	VF	XF	Unc	BU
ND(1998) Proof	400	Value: 250				

KM# 10 200 RIYALS

22.2000 g., 0.9250 Silver 0.6602 oz. ASW, 37 mm. **Ruler:** Hamad bin Khalifah **Subject:** Qatar University 25th Anniversary **Obv:** National arms **Rev:** University logo, value and dates **Edge:** Plain

Date	Mintage	F	VF	XF	Unc	BU
ND(1998) Proof	1,000	Value: 275				

KM# 7 500 RIYALS

17.0000 g., 0.9170 Gold .5012 oz. AGW, 31 mm. **Ruler:** Hamad bin Khalifah **Subject:** Central Bank **Obv:** National arms **Rev:** Bank building **Edge:** Plain

Date	Mintage	F	VF	XF	Unc	BU
ND(1998) Proof	100	Value: 700				

QATAR & DUBAI

The State of Qatar, which occupies the Qatar Peninsula jutting into the Persian Gulf from eastern Saudi Arabia, has an area of 4,247 sq. mi. (11,000 sq. km.) and a population of *469,000. Capital: Doha. The traditional occupations of pearling, fishing, and herding have been replaced in economics by petroleum-related industries. Crude oil, petroleum products, and tomatoes are exported.

Dubai is one of the seven sheikhdoms comprising the United Arab Emirates (formerly Trucial States) located along the southern shore of the Persian Gulf. It has a population of about 60,000. Capital (of the United Arab Emirates): Abu Dhabi.

Qatar, which initiated protective treaty relations with Great Britain in 1916, achieved independence on Sept. 3,1971, upon withdrawal of the British military presence from the Persian Gulf, and replaced its special treaty arrangement with Britain with a treaty of general friendship. Dubai attained independence on Dec. 1, 1971, upon termination of Britain's protective treaty with the trucial Sheikhdoms, and on Dec. 2, 1971, entered into the union of the United Arab Emirates.

Despite the fact that the Emirate of Qatar and the Sheikhdom of Dubai were merged under a monetary union, the two territories were governed independently from each other. Qatar now uses its own currency while Dubai uses the United Arab Emirates currency and coins.

TITLE

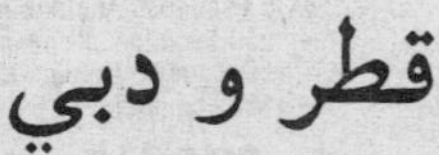

Qatar Wa Dubai

RULER

Ahmad II, 1960-1972

MONETARY SYSTEM

100 Dirhem = 1 Riyal

BRITISH PROTECTORATE

STANDARD COINAGE

KM# 1 DIRHEM

1.5000 g., Bronze, 15 mm. **Ruler:** Ahmad II **Obv:** Value **Rev:** Goitered gazelle

Date	Mintage	F	VF	XF	Unc	BU
AH1386 - 1966	1,000,000	Value: 2.00				

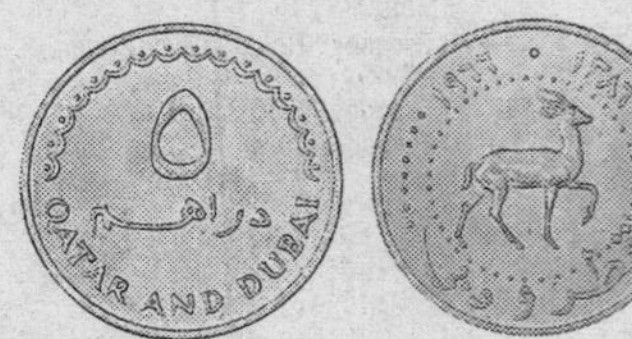

KM# 2 5 DIRHEMS

3.7500 g., Bronze, 22 mm. **Ruler:** Ahmad II **Obv:** Value **Rev:** Goitered gazelle

Date	Mintage	F	VF	XF	Unc	BU
AH1386 - 1966	2,000,000	—	2.50	4.50	8.00	15.00
AH1389 - 1969	2,000,000	—	2.50	4.50	8.00	15.00

KM# 3 10 DIRHEMS

7.5000 g., Bronze, 27 mm. **Ruler:** Ahmad II **Obv:** Value **Rev:** Goitered gazelle

Date	Mintage	F	VF	XF	Unc	BU
AH1386 - 1966	2,000,000	—	3.50	6.00	10.00	18.00
AH1391 - 1971	1,500	—	—	—	—	—

Note: Official mintage figure reported for Qatar by British Royal Mint.

KM# 4 25 DIRHEMS
3.5000 g., Copper-Nickel, 20 mm. **Ruler:** Ahmad II **Obv:** Value **Rev:** Goitered gazelle

Date	Mintage	F	VF	XF	Unc	BU
AH1386 - 1966	2,000,000	—	4.50	7.50	12.50	20.00
AH1389 - 1969	2,000,000	—	4.50	7.50	12.50	20.00

KM# 5 50 DIRHEMS
6.5000 g., Copper-Nickel, 25 mm. **Ruler:** Ahmad II **Obv:** Value **Rev:** Goitered gazelle

Date	Mintage	F	VF	XF	Unc	BU
AH1386 - 1966	2,000,000	—	6.00	9.00	15.00	22.00

RAS AL-KHAIMAH

Ras Al Khaimah
Umm Al-Qalwain
Ajman
Sharjah
Dubai
Abu-Dhabi
Fujairah
OMAN
QATAR
Persian Gulf
Gulf of Oman
SAUDI ARABIA
OMAN

Ras al-Khaimah is only one of the coin issuing emirates that was not one of the original members of the United Arab Emirates. It was a part of Sharjah. It has an estimated area of 650 sq. mi. (1700 sq. km.) and a population of 30,000. Ras al Khaimah is the only member of the United Arab Emirates that has agriculture as its principal industry.

TITLE

Ras al-Khaimah(t)

RULERS
Sultan bin Salim al-Qasimi,/1921-1948
Saqr Bin Muhammad al-Qasimi,/1948—

MONETARY SYSTEM
100 Dirhams = 1 Rial

UNITED ARAB EMIRATE

NON-CIRCULATING LEGAL TENDER COINAGE

KM# 28 50 DIRHAMS
Copper-Nickel **Ruler:** Saqr bin Muhammad al Qasimi **Obv:** Value within circle **Rev:** Falcon within circle flanked by stars

Date	Mintage	F	VF	XF	Unc	BU
AH1390 - 1970	—	—	—	—	45.00	—

KM# 1 RIAL
3.9500 g., 0.6400 Silver .0812 oz. ASW **Ruler:** Saqr bin Muhammad al Qasimi **Obv:** Value within circle **Rev:** Crossed flags within wreath

Date	Mintage	F	VF	XF	Unc	BU
AH1389 - 1969	—	—	—	—	12.50	—
AH1389 - 1969 Proof	1,500	Value: 25.00				

KM# 2 2 RIALS
6.4500 g., 0.8350 Silver .1731 oz. ASW **Ruler:** Saqr bin Muhammad al Qasimi **Obv:** Value within circle **Rev:** Crossed flags within wreath

Date	Mintage	F	VF	XF	Unc	BU
AH1389 - 1969	—	—	—	—	17.50	—
AH1389 - 1969 Proof	1,500	Value: 35.00				

KM# 29 2-1/2 RIALS
7.5000 g., 0.9250 Silver .2231 oz. ASW **Ruler:** Saqr bin Muhammad al Qasimi **Obv:** Head with headdress 1/4 right within circle flanked by stars **Rev:** Falcon within circle

Date	Mintage	F	VF	XF	Unc	BU
AH1390 - 1970	—	—	—	—	75.00	—

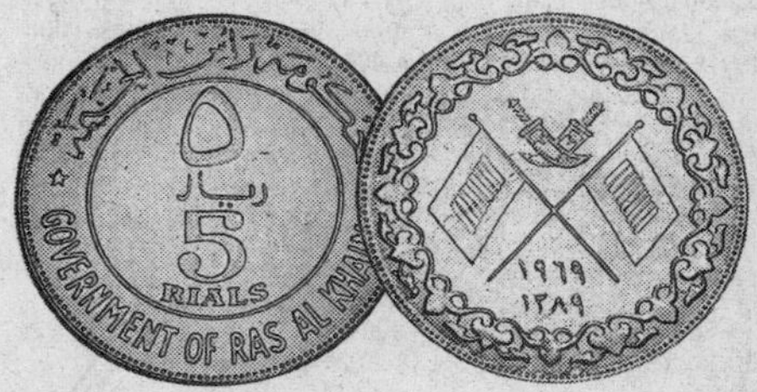

KM# 3 5 RIALS
15.0000 g., 0.8350 Silver .4027 oz. ASW **Ruler:** Saqr bin Muhammad al Qasimi **Obv:** Value within circle **Rev:** Crossed flags within wreath

Date	Mintage	F	VF	XF	Unc	BU
AH1389 - 1969	—	—	—	—	25.00	—
AH1389 - 1969 Proof	1,500	Value: 45.00				

KM# 17 7-1/2 RIYALS
22.5000 g., 0.9250 Silver .6692 oz. ASW **Ruler:** Saqr bin Muhammad al Qasimi **Subject:** Centennial of Rome **Obv:** Value within circle **Rev:** Man plowing

Date	Mintage	F	VF	XF	Unc	BU
1970 Proof	Est. 2,000	Value: 120				

KM# 32 7-1/2 RIYALS
22.5000 g., 0.9250 Silver .6692 oz. ASW **Ruler:** Saqr bin Muhammad al Qasimi **Subject:** World Championship Football **Obv:** Value within circle **Rev:** Jules Rimet Cup flanked by shields

Date	Mintage	F	VF	XF	Unc	BU
1970 Proof	Est. 2,000	Value: 235				

KM# 30 7-1/2 RIYALS
22.5000 g., 0.9250 Silver .6692 oz. ASW **Ruler:** Saqr bin Muhammad al Qasimi **Obv:** Head with headdress 1/4 right within circle flanked by stars **Rev:** Falcon within circle

Date	Mintage	F	VF	XF	Unc	BU
AH1390 (1970)	—	—	—	—	90.00	—

KM# 5 7-1/2 RIYALS
22.5000 g., 0.9250 Silver .6692 oz. ASW **Ruler:** Saqr bin Muhammad al Qasimi **Obv:** Value within circle **Rev:** Head of Giacomo Agostini left

Date	Mintage	F	VF	XF	Unc	BU
ND (1970) Proof	Est. 2,000	Value: 400				

KM# 31 10 RIYALS
30.0000 g., 0.9250 Silver .8921 oz. ASW **Ruler:** Saqr bin Muhammad al Qasimi **Subject:** 1st Anniversary - Death of Dwight Eisenhower **Obv:** Value within circle **Rev:** Head left

Date	Mintage	F	VF	XF	Unc	BU
1970	4,500	—	—	—	18.50	—
1970 Proof	1,400	Value: 37.50				

KM# 6 10 RIYALS
30.0000 g., 0.9250 Silver .8921 oz. ASW **Ruler:** Saqr bin Muhammad al Qasimi **Subject:** World Championship Football **Obv:** Value within circle **Rev:** Jules Rimet Cup in front of soccer ball

Date	Mintage	F	VF	XF	Unc	BU
1970 Proof	Est. 2,000	Value: 350				

KM# 18 10 RIYALS
30.0000 g., 0.9250 Silver .8921 oz. ASW **Ruler:** Saqr bin Muhammad al Qasimi **Subject:** Centennial of Rome **Obv:** Value within circle **Rev:** Emperor standing with charging horses

Date	Mintage	F	VF	XF	Unc	BU
1970 Proof	Est. 2,000	Value: 175				

KM# 7 10 RIYALS
30.0000 g., 0.9250 Silver .8921 oz. ASW **Ruler:** Saqr bin Muhammad al Qasimi **Subject:** Felice Gimondi **Obv:** Value within circle **Rev:** Head left

Date	Mintage	F	VF	XF	Unc	BU
ND (1970) Proof	Est. 2,000	Value: 450				

KM# 8 15 RIYALS
45.0000 g., 0.9250 Silver 1.3384 oz. ASW **Ruler:** Saqr bin Muhammad al Qasimi **Subject:** Champions of Sport **Obv:** Value within circle **Rev:** Cluster of heads all facing left

Date	Mintage	F	VF	XF	Unc	BU
ND(1970) Proof	Est. 2,000	Value: 625				

KM# 19 15 RIYALS
45.0000 g., 0.9250 Silver 1.3384 oz. ASW **Ruler:** Saqr bin Muhammad al Qasimi **Subject:** Centennial of Rome **Obv:** Value within circle **Rev:** Three heads facing right

Date	Mintage	F	VF	XF	Unc	BU
1970 Proof	Est. 2,000	Value: 220				

KM# 33 15 RIYALS
45.0000 g., 0.9250 Silver 1.3384 oz. ASW **Ruler:** Saqr bin Muhammad al Qasimi **Subject:** World Championship Football - Jules Rimet Cup **Obv:** Value within circle **Rev:** Jules Rimet Cup flanked by shields

Date	Mintage	F	VF	XF	Unc	BU
1970 Proof	—	Value: 525				

KM# 21 50 RIYALS
10.3500 g., 0.9000 Gold .2995 oz. AGW **Ruler:** Saqr bin Muhammad al Qasimi **Subject:** Centennial of Italian Unification **Obv:** Value within circle **Rev:** Head left

Date	Mintage	F	VF	XF	Unc	BU
1970 Proof	Est. 2,000	Value: 375				

KM# 10 50 RIYALS
10.3500 g., 0.9000 Gold .2995 oz. AGW **Ruler:** Saqr bin Muhammad al Qasimi **Subject:** Gigi Riva **Obv:** Value within circle **Rev:** Head left

Date	Mintage	F	VF	XF	Unc	BU
ND (1970) Proof	Est. 2,000	Value: 400				

KM# 22 75 RIYALS
15.5300 g., 0.9000 Gold .4494 oz. AGW **Ruler:** Saqr bin Muhammad al Qasimi **Subject:** Centennial of Italian Unification, Rome as the Capital **Obv:** Value within circle **Rev:** Figure with gun walking left

Date	Mintage	F	VF	XF	Unc	BU
1970 Proof	Est. 2,000	Value: 500				

KM# 11 75 RIYALS
15.5300 g., 0.9000 Gold .4494 oz. AGW **Ruler:** Saqr bin Muhammad al Qasimi **Subject:** Gianni Rivera **Obv:** Value within circle **Rev:** Head left

Date	Mintage	F	VF	XF	Unc	BU
ND (1970) Proof	Est. 2,000	Value: 475				

KM# 12 100 RIYALS

20.7000 g., 0.9000 Gold .5990 oz. AGW **Ruler:** Saqr bin Muhammad al Qasimi **Subject:** World Chmapionship Football - Jules Rimet Cup **Obv:** Value within circle **Rev:** Jules Rimet Cup in front of soccer ball

Date	Mintage	F	VF	XF	Unc	BU
1970 Proof	Est. 2,000	Value: 675				

KM# 23 100 RIYALS

20.7000 g., 0.9000 Gold .5990 oz. AGW **Ruler:** Saqr bin Muhammad al Qasimi **Subject:** Centennial of Italian Unification - WWI Victory

Date	Mintage	F	VF	XF	Unc	BU
1970 Proof	Est. 2,000	Value: 600				

KM# 24 100 RIYALS

31.0500 g., 0.9000 Gold .8985 oz. AGW **Ruler:** Saqr bin Muhammad al Qasimi **Subject:** Centennial of Italian Unification **Rev:** Standing Italia

Date	Mintage	F	VF	XF	Unc	BU
1970 Proof	Est. 2,000	Value: 1,000				

KM# 13 150 RIYALS

31.0500 g., 0.9000 Gold .8985 oz. AGW **Ruler:** Saqr bin Muhammad al Qasimi **Series:** 1972 Munich Olympics **Obv:** Value within circle **Rev:** Figures within olympic circles and flaming torch

Date	Mintage	F	VF	XF	Unc	BU
ND (1970) Proof	3,060	Value: 1,850				

KM# 25 200 RIYALS

41.4000 g., 0.9000 Gold 1.1980 oz. AGW **Ruler:** Saqr bin Muhammad al Qasimi **Subject:** Centennial of Italian Unification - Romulus and Remus **Obv:** Value within circle **Rev:** Wolf within designed circle

Date	Mintage	F	VF	XF	Unc	BU
1970 Proof	Est. 2,000	Value: 1,250				

KM# 14 200 RIYALS

41.4000 g., 0.9000 Gold 1.1980 oz. AGW **Ruler:** Saqr bin Muhammad al Qasimi **Subject:** Champions of Sport **Note:** Similar to KM#8.

Date	Mintage	F	VF	XF	Unc	BU
ND (1970) Proof	Est. 2,000	Value: 1,450				

ESSAIS

KM#	Date	Mintage	Identification	Issue Price	Mkt Val
E2	1969	—	2 Riyals. Value within circle. Crossed flags within wreath. With ASSAY.	—	22.50

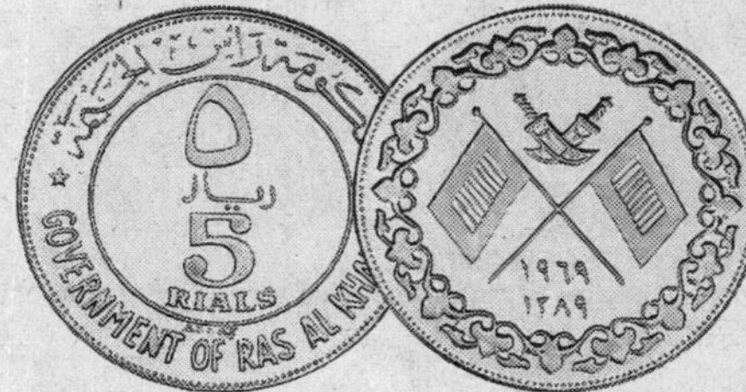

KM#	Date	Mintage	Identification	Issue Price	Mkt Val
E3	1969	—	5 Riyals. Value within circle. Crossed flags within wreath. With ASSAY.	—	37.50

KM#	Date	Mintage	Identification	Issue Price	Mkt Val
E1	1969	—	Riyal. Value within circle. Crossed flags within wreath. With ASSAY.	—	15.00
E4	1970	—	10 Riyals. With ASSAY.	—	45.00

MINT SETS

KM#	Date	Mintage	Identification	Issue Price	Mkt Val
MS1	1969 (3)	—	KM#1-3	—	55.00

PROOF SETS

KM#	Date	Mintage	Identification	Issue Price	Mkt Val
PS1	1969 (3)	1,500	KM#1-3	10.80	100
PS2	(1970) (9)	—	KM#5-8, 10-14	—	6,700
PS3	1970 (8)	—	KM#17-19, 21-25	—	4,250
PS4	(1970) (5)	—	KM#10-14	—	4,850
PS5	1970 (5)	—	KM#21-25	—	3,750
PS6	(1970) (4)	—	KM#5-8	41.50	1,850
PS7	1970 (3)	—	KM#17-19	—	500
PS8	1970 (4)	—	KM#6, 10-12	—	1,900

REUNION

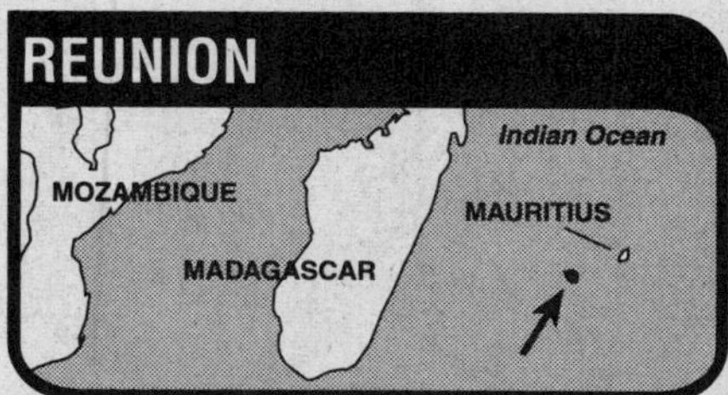

The Department of Reunion, an overseas department of France located in the Indian Ocean 400 miles (640 km.) east of Madagascar, has an area of 969 sq. mi. (2,510 sq. km.) and a population of *566,000. Capital: Saint-Denis. The island's volcanic soil is extremely fertile. Sugar, vanilla, coffee and rum are exported.

Although first visited by Portuguese navigators in the 16th century, Reunion was uninhabited when claimed for France by Capt. Goubert in 1638. The French first colonized the Isle de Bourbon in 1662 as a layover station for ships rounding the Cape of Good Hope to India. It was renamed Reunion in 1793. The island remained in French possession except for the period of 1810-15, when the British occupied it. Reunion became an overseas department of France in 1946, and in 1958 voted to continue that status within the new French Union.

During the first half of the 19th century, Reunion was officially known as Isle de Bonaparte (1801-14) and Isle de Bourbon (1814-48). Reunion coinage of those periods is so designated.

The world debut of the Euro was here on January 1, 2002.

Mint Marks

(a) – Paris, privy marks only

MONETARY SYSTEM

100 Centimes = 1 Franc

FRENCH DEPARTMENT

STANDARD COINAGE

KM# 6.1 FRANC

Aluminum, 23 mm. **Obv:** Winged liberty head left **Rev:** Sugar cane plants divide value **Edge:** Plain **Designer:** G.B.L. Bazor

Date	Mintage	F	VF	XF	Unc	BU
1948(a)	3,000,000	—	0.35	0.60	2.50	3.00
1964(a)	1,000,000	—	0.35	0.60	3.00	3.50
1968(a)	450,000	—	0.60	1.25	4.50	5.50
1969(a)	500,000	—	0.60	0.85	3.50	4.00
1971(a)	800,000	—	0.60	0.85	3.00	3.50
1973(a)	500,000	—	0.60	0.85	3.50	4.00

KM# 6.2 FRANC

Aluminum **Designer:** G.B.L. Bazor **Note:** Thinner planchet.

Date	Mintage	F	VF	XF	Unc	BU
1969(a)	Inc. above	—	0.75	1.50	5.00	6.00

KM# 7 FRANC

Aluminum **Obv:** Winged liberty head left **Rev:** Sugar cane plants divide value **Designer:** G.B.L. Bazor **Note:** Mule.

Date	Mintage	F	VF	XF	Unc	BU
1948(a)	Inc. above	—	650	1,300	2,600	—

KM# 8 2 FRANCS

Aluminum **Obv:** Winged liberty head left **Rev:** Sugar cane plants divide value **Designer:** G.B.L. Bazor

Date	Mintage	F	VF	XF	Unc	BU
1948(a)	2,000,000	—	0.35	0.85	3.50	4.00
1968(a)	100,000	—	3.00	5.00	10.00	12.50
1969(a)	150,000	—	1.75	3.50	6.50	9.00
1970(a)	300,000	—	0.85	1.75	4.00	4.50
1971(a)	300,000	—	0.85	1.75	4.00	4.50
1973(a)	500,000	—	0.85	1.75	4.00	4.50

KM# 9 5 FRANCS

Aluminum **Obv:** Winged liberty head left **Rev:** Sugar cane plants divides value **Designer:** G.B.L. Bazor

Date	Mintage	F	VF	XF	Unc	BU
1955(a)	3,000,000	—	0.60	1.00	3.00	3.50
1969(a)	100,000	—	2.50	5.00	9.00	11.50
1970(a)	200,000	—	1.75	3.50	6.50	9.00
1971(a)	100,000	—	1.75	3.50	6.50	9.00
1972(a)	300,000	—	0.85	1.75	3.50	4.00
1973(a)	250,000	—	0.85	1.75	3.50	4.00

KM# 10 10 FRANCS

Aluminum-Bronze **Obv:** Winged liberty head left **Rev:** Crowned shield divides value **Designer:** G.B.L. Bazor

Date	Mintage	F	VF	XF	Unc	BU
1955(a)	1,500,000	—	0.45	0.75	3.00	3.50
1962(a)	700,000	—	1.75	3.50	6.50	9.00
1964(a)	1,000,000	—	0.45	0.75	3.00	3.50

KM# 10a 10 FRANCS

Aluminum-Nickel-Bronze **Obv:** Winged Liberty head left **Rev:** Crowned shield divides value **Designer:** G.B.L. Bazor

Date	Mintage	F	VF	XF	Unc	BU
1964(a)	Inc. above	—	0.45	0.75	3.00	3.50
1969(a)	300,000	—	1.25	2.50	6.00	7.00
1970(a)	300,000	—	1.25	2.50	5.00	6.00
1971(a)	200,000	—	1.75	3.75	7.50	10.00
1972(a)	400,000	—	1.25	2.50	6.00	7.00
1973(a)	700,000	—	0.85	1.75	3.50	4.00

KM# 11 20 FRANCS

Aluminum-Bronze **Obv:** Winged liberty head left **Rev:** Crowned shield divides value **Designer:** G.B.L. Bazor

Date	Mintage	F	VF	XF	Unc	BU
1955(a)	1,250,000	—	0.75	1.50	4.00	4.50
1960(a)	100,000	—	3.00	6.00	12.00	15.00
1961(a)	300,000	—	2.50	4.75	8.00	10.00
1962(a)	190,000	—	2.75	5.50	9.00	12.00
1964(a)	750,000	—	0.75	1.50	3.50	4.00

KM# 11a 20 FRANCS

Aluminum-Nickel-Bronze **Obv:** Winged Liberty head left **Rev:** Crowned shield divides value **Designer:** G.B.L. Bazor

Date	Mintage	F	VF	XF	Unc	BU
1969(a)	200,000	—	2.75	5.50	9.00	12.00
1970(a)	200,000	—	2.75	5.50	9.00	12.00
1971(a)	200,000	—	2.75	5.50	9.00	12.00
1972(a)	300,000	—	2.00	3.50	6.50	8.50
1973(a)	550,000	—	0.75	1.50	3.50	4.50

KM# 12 50 FRANCS

Nickel **Obv:** Winged liberty head left **Rev:** Crowned shield divides value **Designer:** G.B.L. Bazor

Date	Mintage	F	VF	XF	Unc	BU
1962(a)	1,000,000	—	1.50	2.50	5.00	6.00
1964(a)	500,000	—	2.00	3.00	6.00	7.50
1969(a)	100,000	—	2.75	5.00	9.00	12.00
1970(a)	100,000	—	2.75	5.00	9.00	12.00
1973(a)	350,000	—	2.00	3.50	6.50	8.00

KM# 13 100 FRANCS

Nickel, 26.5 mm. **Obv:** Winged liberty head left **Rev:** Crowned shield divides value **Designer:** G.B.L. Bazor

Date	Mintage	F	VF	XF	Unc	BU
1964(a)	2,000,000	—	1.00	2.00	4.00	5.00
1969(a)	200,000	—	2.25	4.50	7.50	9.50
1970(a)	150,000	—	2.25	5.00	9.00	12.00
1971(a)	200,000	—	2.75	6.00	12.50	15.00
1972(a)	300,000	—	2.00	3.50	6.00	7.50
1973(a)	550,000	—	2.25	4.50	7.50	9.50

TOKEN COINAGE

KM# Tn1 5 CENTIMES

Aluminum **Shape:** Hexagon **Note:** Bank token. Demonetized 1941.

Date	Mintage	F	VF	XF	Unc	BU
1920	500,000	30.00	65.00	200	500	900

KM# Tn2 10 CENTIMES

Aluminum **Shape:** Hexagon **Note:** Bank token. Demonetized 1941.

Date	Mintage	F	VF	XF	Unc	BU
1920	250,000	35.00	75.00	200	500	900

KM# Tn3 25 CENTIMES

Aluminum **Shape:** Hexagon **Note:** Bank token. Demonetized 1941.

Date	Mintage	F	VF	XF	Unc	BU
1920	120,000	50.00	100	275	800	1,250

ESSAIS

Standard metals unless otherwise noted

KM#	Date	Mintage	Identification	Mkt Val
E3	1948(a)	2,000	Franc. Copper-Nickel. KM6.1.	35.00
E4	1948(a)	2,000	2 Francs. Copper-Nickel. KM8.	40.00
E5	1955(a)	1,200	5 Francs. Aluminum. KM9.	20.00
E6	1955(a)	2,000	10 Francs. Aluminum-Bronze. KM10.	22.00
E7	1955(a)	1,200	20 Francs. Aluminum-Bronze. KM11.	25.00
E8	1962(a)	1,200	50 Francs. Nickel. KM12.	25.00
E9	1964(a)	2,000	50 Francs. Nickel. KM12.	30.00
E10	1964(a)	2,000	100 Francs. Nickel. KM13.	40.00

PIEFORTS WITH ESSAI

Double thickness; standard metals unless otherwise noted

KM#	Date	Mintage	Identification	Mkt Val
PE3	1948(a)	104	Franc. Aluminum. KM6.1.	85.00
PE4	1948(a)	104	2 Francs. Aluminum. KM8.	95.00

"FDC" SETS

KM#	Date	Mintage	Identification	Issue Price	Mkt Val
SS1	1964 (5)	—	KM6.1, 10-13. Issued with Comoros set.	—	25.00

RHODESIA

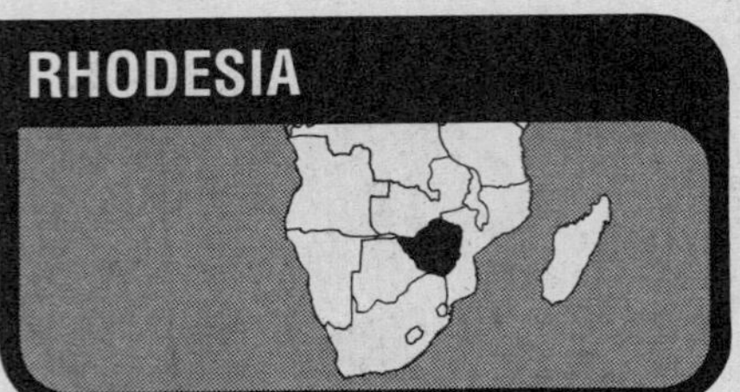

The Republic of Rhodesia or Southern Rhodesia (now known as the Republic of Zimbabwe), located in the east-central part of southern Africa, has an area of 150,804 sq. mi. (390,580sq. km.) and a population of *10.1 million. Capital: Harare (formerly Salisbury). The economy is based on agriculture and mining. Tobacco, sugar, asbestos, copper, chrome, ore and coal are exported.

The Rhodesian area contains extensive evidence of the habitat of paleolithic man and earlier civilizations, notably the world-famous ruins of Zimbabwe, a gold-trading center that flourished about the 14th or 15th century A.D. The Portuguese of the 16th century were the first Europeans to attempt to develop south-central Africa, but it remained for Cecil Rhodes and the British South Africa Co. to open the hinterlands. Rhodes obtained a concession for mineral rights from local chiefs in 1888 and administered his African empire (named Southern Rhodesia in 1895) through the British South Africa Co. until 1923, when the British government annexed the area after the white settlers voted for existence as a separate entity, rather than for incorporation into the Union of South Africa. From Sept. of 1953 through 1963 Southern Rhodesia was joined with the British Protectorates of Northern Rhodesia and Nyasaland into a multiracial federation, known as the Federation of Rhodesia and Nyasaland. When the federation was dissolved at the end of 1963, Northern Rhodesia and Nyasaland became the independent states of Zambia and Malawi.

Britain was prepared to grant independence to Southern Rhodesia but declined to do so when the politically dominant white Rhodesians refused to give assurances of representative government. On Nov. 11, 1965, following two years of unsuccessful negotiation with the British government, Prime Minister Ian Smith issued an unilateral declaration of independence. Britain responded with economic sanctions supported by the United Nations. After further futile attempts to effect an accommodation, the Rhodesian Parliament severed all ties with Britain and on March 2, 1970, established the Republic of Rhodesia.

On March 3, 1978, Prime Minister Ian Smith and three moderate black nationalist leaders signed an agreement providing for black majority rule. The name of the country was changed to Zimbabwe Rhodesia. Following a conference in London in December 1979, the opposition government conceded and it was agreed that the British Government should resume control. A British Governor soon returned to Southern Rhodesia. One of his first acts was to affirm the nullification of the purported declaration of independence. On April 18, 1980 pursuant to an act of the British Parliament, the colony of Southern Rhodesia became independent as the Republic of Zimbabwe, which remains a member of the British Commonwealth of Nations.

RULERS
British, until 1966

MONETARY SYSTEM
12 Pence = 1 Shilling = 10 Cents
10 Shillings = 1 Dollar
20 Shillings = 1 Pound

BRITISH COLONY
Self-Governing

POUND COINAGE

KM# 8 3 PENCE = 2-1/2 CENTS

Copper-Nickel **Obv:** Crowned bust of Queen Elizabeth II right **Obv. Designer:** Arnold Machin **Rev:** Three spear points divides date

Date	Mintage	F	VF	XF	Unc	BU
1968	2,400,000	0.25	0.50	0.75	2.00	—
1968 Doubleshaft error	—	—	10.00	20.00	35.00	—
1968 Proof	10	Value: 1,200				

KM# 1 6 PENCE = 5 CENTS

Copper-Nickel, 19.5 mm. **Obv:** Crowned bust of Queen Elizabeth II right **Obv. Designer:** Arnold Machin **Rev:** Flame lily **Rev. Designer:** Thomas Sasseen

Date	Mintage	F	VF	XF	Unc	BU
1964	13,500,000	0.15	0.25	0.40	1.25	—
1964 Proof	2,060	Value: 10.00				

KM# 2 SHILLING = 10 CENTS

Copper-Nickel, 23.5 mm. **Obv:** Crowned bust of Queen Elizabeth II right **Obv. Designer:** Arnold Machin **Rev:** Shield **Rev. Designer:** Thomas Sasseen

Date	Mintage	F	VF	XF	Unc	BU
1964	15,500,000	0.15	0.25	0.65	1.50	—
1964 Proof	2,060	Value: 10.00				

KM# 3 2 SHILLINGS = 20 CENTS

Copper-Nickel **Obv:** Crowned bust of Queen Elizabeth II right **Obv. Designer:** Arnold Machin **Rev:** Native headdress **Rev. Designer:** Thomas Sasseen

Date	Mintage	F	VF	XF	Unc	BU
1964	10,500,000	0.25	0.50	1.25	3.00	—
1964 Proof	2,060	Value: 12.50				

KM# 4 2-1/2 SHILLINGS = 25 CENTS

Copper-Nickel, 32.5 mm. **Obv:** Crowned bust of Queen Elizabeth II right **Obv. Designer:** Arnold Machin **Rev:** Sable antelope **Rev. Designer:** Thomas Sasseen

Date	Mintage	F	VF	XF	Unc	BU
1964	11,500,000	0.50	1.00	2.00	4.50	6.00
1964 Proof	2,060	Value: 17.50				

KM# 5 10 SHILLINGS

3.9940 g., 0.9160 Gold .1177 oz. AGW **Obv:** Crowned bust right **Rev:** Sable antelope **Rev. Designer:** Thomas Sasseen

Date	Mintage	F	VF	XF	Unc	BU
1966 Proof	6,000	Value: 100				

KM# 6 POUND

7.9881 g., 0.9160 Gold .2354 oz. AGW **Obv:** Crowned bust right **Rev:** Lion **Rev. Designer:** Thomas Sasseen

Date	Mintage	F	VF	XF	Unc	BU
1966 Proof	5,000	Value: 200				

KM# 7 5 POUNDS

39.9403 g., 0.9160 Gold 1.1772 oz. AGW **Obv:** Crowned bust of Queen Elizabeth II right **Obv. Designer:** Arnold Machin **Rev:** Arms with supporters divides date **Rev. Designer:** Thomas Sasseen

Date	Mintage	F	VF	XF	Unc	BU
1966 Proof	3,000	Value: 875				

REPUBLIC

DECIMAL COINAGE

KM# 9 1/2 CENT

Bronze, 20 mm. **Obv:** Value and date to upper left of sprig **Rev:** Arms with supporters **Designer:** Thomas Sasseen

Date	Mintage	F	VF	XF	Unc	BU
1970	10,000,000	—	0.10	0.50	1.00	—
1970 Proof	12	Value: 750				
1971	2,000,000	—	0.10	0.50	1.25	—
1972	2,000,000	—	0.10	0.50	1.25	—
1972 Proof	12	Value: 750				
1975	10,001,000	—	0.10	0.20	0.50	—
1975 Proof	10	Value: 750				
1977	—	—	—	800	1,500	—

Note: Circulation mintage melted, less than 10 surviving specimens known

Date	Mintage	F	VF	XF	Unc	BU
1977 Proof	10	Value: 1,250				

KM# 10 CENT

Bronze, 22.5 mm. **Obv:** Value and date to upper left of sprig **Rev:** Arms with supporters **Designer:** Thomas Sasseen

Date	Mintage	F	VF	XF	Unc	BU
1970	25,000,000	—	0.10	0.50	1.00	—
1970 Proof	12	Value: 750				
1971	15,000,000	—	0.10	0.50	1.00	—
1972	10,000,000	—	0.10	0.50	1.00	—
1972 Proof	12	Value: 800				
1973	5,000,000	—	0.10	0.50	1.50	—
1973 Proof	10	Value: 750				
1974	—	—	0.10	0.50	1.00	—
1975	10,000,000	—	0.10	0.50	1.00	—
1975 Proof	10	Value: 800				
1976	20,000,000	—	0.10	0.20	0.50	—
1976 Proof	10	Value: 750				
1977	10,000,000	—	0.10	0.20	0.50	—

KM# 11 2-1/2 CENTS

Copper-Nickel **Obv:** Three spear points divides date below value **Rev:** Arms with supporters **Designer:** Thomas Sasseen

Date	Mintage	F	VF	XF	Unc	BU
1970	4,000,000	0.15	0.25	0.70	1.50	—
1970 Proof	12	Value: 800				

KM# 12 5 CENTS

Copper-Nickel **Obv:** Flame lily divides date **Rev:** Arms with supporters **Designer:** Thomas Sasseen

Date	Mintage	F	VF	XF	Unc	BU
1973	—	0.25	0.75	1.50	3.00	—
1973 Proof	10	Value: 800				

KM# 13 5 CENTS

Copper-Nickel **Obv:** Flame lily **Rev:** Arms with supporters **Designer:** Thomas Sasseen

Date	Mintage	F	VF	XF	Unc	BU
1975	3,500,000	0.15	0.25	0.50	1.00	—
1975 Proof	10	Value: 750				

Date	Mintage	F	VF	XF	Unc	BU
1976	8,038,000	0.15	0.25	0.50	1.00	—
1977	3,015,000	0.25	0.75	1.50	3.00	—

KM# 14 10 CENTS

Copper-Nickel **Obv:** Arms with supporters **Rev:** Shield, value and date **Designer:** Thomas Sasseen

Date	Mintage	F	VF	XF	Unc	BU
1975	2,003,000	0.15	0.30	0.60	1.50	—
1975 Proof	10	Value: 800				

KM# 15 20 CENTS

Copper-Nickel **Obv:** Arms with supporters **Rev:** Native headdress, value and date **Designer:** Thomas Sasseen

Date	Mintage	F	VF	XF	Unc	BU
1975	1,937,000	0.50	0.75	1.00	3.00	—
1975 Proof	10	Value: 800				
1977	—	0.50	0.75	1.50	3.50	—

KM# 16 25 CENTS

Copper-Nickel **Obv:** Arms with supporters **Rev:** Sable antelope, value and date **Designer:** Thomas Sasseen

Date	Mintage	F	VF	XF	Unc	BU
1975	1,011,000	0.50	1.00	2.00	5.00	7.50
1975 Proof	10	Value: 800				

PROOF SETS

KM#	Date	Mintage	Identification	Issue Price	Mkt Val
PS1	1964 (8)	10	KM#1-4 Double set	—	250
PS2	1964 (4)	2,060	KM#1-4	—	50.00
PS3	1966 (3)	2,000	KM#5-7	280	1,000
PS4	1968 (2)	3	KM#8 Double set	—	2,250
PS5	1970 (6)	3	KM#9-11 Double set	—	5,000
PS6	19[illegible] (2)	2	KM#12 Double set	—	1,500
PS7	1975 (8)	1	KM#13-16 Double set	—	7,000
PS8	1975 (6)	4	KM#9, 10, 13-16	—	5,000
PS9	1975 (4)	4	KM#13-16	—	3,500

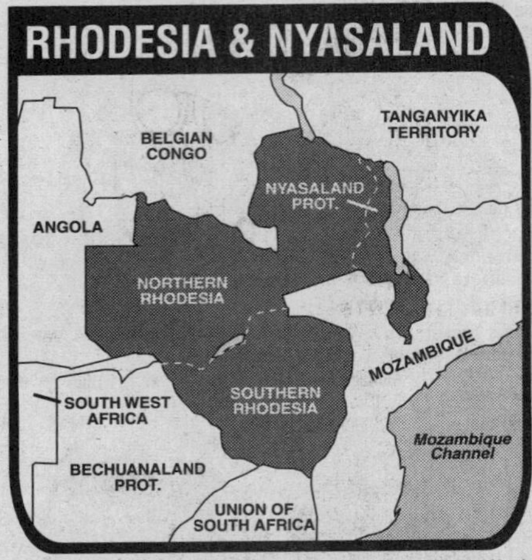

The Federation of Rhodesia and Nyasaland was located in the east-central part of southern Africa. The multiracial federation has an area of about 487,000 sq. mi. (1,261,330 sq. km.) and a population of 6.8 million. Capital: Salisbury, in Southern Rhodesia.

The geographical unity of the three British possessions suggested the desirability of political and economic union as early as 1924. Despite objections by the African constituency of Northern Rhodesia and Nyasaland, who feared that African self-determination would be retarded by the dominant influence of prosperous and self-governing Southern Rhodesia. The Central African Federation was established in Sept. of 1953. As feared by the European constituency, Southern Rhodesia despite the fact that the three component countries largely retained their pre-federation political structure effectively and profitably dominated the Federation. It was dissolved at the end of 1963, largely because of the effective opposition of the Nyasaland African Congress. Northern Rhodesia and Nyasaland became the independent states of Zambia and Malawi in 1964. Southern Rhodesia unilaterally declared its independence the following year, which was not recognized by the British Government.

For earlier coinage refer to Southern Rhodesia. For later coinage refer to Malawi, Zambia, Rhodesia and Zimbabwe.

RULERS
Elizabeth II, 1952-1964

MONETARY SYSTEM
12 Pence = 1 Shilling
5 Shillings = 1 Crown
20 Shillings = 1 Pound

FEDERATION

STANDARD COINAGE

KM# 1 1/2 PENNY

Bronze, 21 mm. **Ruler:** Elizabeth II **Obv:** Hole in center flanked by giraffes with crown above **Rev:** Value around hole in center flanked by sprigs

Date	Mintage	F	VF	XF	Unc	BU
1955	720,000	0.15	0.25	0.50	3.00	5.00
1955 Proof	2,010	Value: 5.00				
1956	480,000	0.20	0.50	1.00	3.50	5.50
1956 Proof	—	Value: 400				
1957	1,920,000	0.10	0.15	0.25	3.00	5.00
1957 Proof	—	Value: 400				
1958	2,400,000	0.10	0.15	0.25	3.00	5.00
1958 Proof	—	Value: 400				
1964	1,440,000	0.10	0.15	0.25	3.00	5.00

KM# 2 PENNY

Bronze **Ruler:** Elizabeth II **Obv:** Hole in center and crown flanked by elephants **Rev:** Value around hole in center flanked by sprigs

Date	Mintage	F	VF	XF	Unc	BU
1955	2,040,000	0.15	0.25	0.75	3.75	6.75
1955 Proof	2,010	Value: 5.50				
1956	4,800,000	0.15	0.25	0.50	3.50	6.50
1956 Proof	—	Value: 400				
1957	7,200,000	0.10	0.15	0.25	3.00	6.00
1957 Proof	—	—	—	—	—	—
1958	2,880,000	0.10	0.15	0.25	3.00	6.00
1958 Proof	—	Value: 400				
1961	4,800,000	0.10	0.15	0.25	3.00	6.00
1961 Proof	—	—	—	—	—	—
1962	6,000,000	0.10	0.15	0.25	3.00	6.00
1963	6,000,000	0.10	0.15	0.25	3.00	6.00
1963 Proof	—	Value: 400				

KM# 3 3 PENCE

Copper-Nickel, 16.3 mm. **Ruler:** Elizabeth II **Obv:** Bust right **Obv. Designer:** Mary Gillick **Rev:** Flame lily divides date

Date	Mintage	F	VF	XF	Unc	BU
1955	1,200,000	0.20	0.50	1.00	4.00	—
1955 Proof	10	Value: 400				
1956	3,200,000	0.50	1.00	2.50	20.00	—
1956 Proof	—	Value: 600				
1957	6,000,000	0.20	0.50	0.75	3.00	—
1957 Proof	—	Value: 600				
1962	4,000,000	0.20	0.50	0.75	3.00	—
1962 Proof	—	—	—	—	—	—
1963	2,000,000	0.20	0.50	0.75	3.00	—
1963 Proof	—	—	—	—	—	—
1964	3,600,000	0.15	0.25	0.50	1.50	—

KM# 3a 3 PENCE

1.4100 g., 0.5000 Silver .0226 oz. ASW, 16.3 mm. **Ruler:** Elizabeth II **Obv:** Bust laureate right **Rev:** Flame lily divides date

Date	Mintage	F	VF	XF	Unc	BU
1955 Proof	2,000	Value: 7.50				

KM# 4 6 PENCE

Copper-Nickel **Ruler:** Elizabeth II **Obv:** Bust right **Obv. Designer:** Mary Gillick **Rev:** Lion standing on rock

Date	Mintage	F	VF	XF	Unc	BU
1955	400,000	0.50	1.00	2.50	7.50	10.00
1955 Proof	10	Value: 400				
1956	800,000	0.75	2.00	7.00	40.00	—
1956 Proof	—	—	—	—	—	—
1957	4,000,000	0.20	0.50	1.00	4.00	7.50
1957 Proof	—	—	—	—	—	—
1962	2,800,000	0.20	0.50	1.00	4.00	8.00
1962 Proof	—	—	—	—	—	—
1963	800,000	5.00	10.00	20.00	45.00	—
1963 Proof	—	—	—	—	—	—

KM# 4a 6 PENCE

2.8300 g., 0.5000 Silver .0454 oz. ASW **Ruler:** Elizabeth II **Obv:** Bust laureate right **Rev:** Lion staning on rock

Date	Mintage	F	VF	XF	Unc	BU
1955 Proof	2,000	Value: 10.00				

KM# 5 SHILLING

Copper-Nickel **Ruler:** Elizabeth II **Obv:** Bust right **Obv. Designer:** Mary Gillick **Rev:** Sable antelope

Date	Mintage	F	VF	XF	Unc	BU
1955	200,000	1.50	2.50	7.00	18.00	—
1955 Proof	10	Value: 400				
1956	1,700,000	0.75	1.50	3.50	30.00	—
1956 Proof	—	—	—	—	—	—
1957	3,500,000	0.50	1.00	2.50	8.00	10.00
1957 Proof	—	—	—	—	—	—

KM# 5a SHILLING

5.6600 g., 0.5000 Silver .0909 oz. ASW **Ruler:** Elizabeth II **Obv:** Bust laureate right **Rev:** Antelope

Date	Mintage	F	VF	XF	Unc	BU
1955 Proof	2,000	Value: 25.00				

KM# 6 2 SHILLINGS

Copper-Nickel **Ruler:** Elizabeth II **Obv:** Bust right **Obv. Designer:** Mary Gillick **Rev:** Eagle with talons in fish flanked by initials

Date	Mintage	F	VF	XF	Unc	BU
1955	1,750,000	1.25	2.50	5.00	12.50	—
1955 Proof	10	Value: 400				
1956	1,850,000	1.25	2.50	4.50	12.00	—
1956 Proof	—	—	—	—	—	—
1957	1,500,000	1.25	2.50	4.50	12.00	—
1957 Proof	—	—	—	—	—	—

KM# 6a 2 SHILLINGS

11.3100 g., 0.5000 Silver .1818 oz. ASW **Ruler:** Elizabeth II **Obv:** Bust laureate right **Rev:** Eagle with talons in fish

Date	Mintage	F	VF	XF	Unc	BU
1955 Proof	2,000	Value: 30.00				

KM# 7 1/2 CROWN

Copper-Nickel **Ruler:** Elizabeth II **Obv:** Bust right **Obv. Designer:** Mary Gillick **Rev:** Arms with supporters **Rev. Designer:** T.H. Paget

Date	Mintage	F	VF	XF	Unc	BU
1955	1,600,000	1.50	3.00	6.00	15.00	—
1955 Proof	10	Value: 550				
1956	160,000	7.50	15.00	35.00	250	—
1956 Proof	—	—	—	—	—	—
1957	2,400,000	7.50	15.00	35.00	75.00	—
1957 Proof	—	—	—	—	—	—

KM# 7a 1/2 CROWN

14.1400 g., 0.5000 Silver .2273 oz. ASW **Ruler:** Elizabeth II **Obv:** Bust laureate right **Rev:** Arms with supporters

Date	Mintage	F	VF	XF	Unc	BU
1955 Proof	2,000	Value: 35.00				

PROOF SETS

KM#	Date	Mintage	Identification	Issue Price	Mkt Val
PS1	1955 (7)	10	KM1-7	—	2,200
PS2	1955 (7)	2,000	KM1-2, 3a-7a	—	110

Romania (formerly the Socialist Republic of Romania), a country in southeast Europe, has an area of 91,699 sq. mi. (237,500 sq. km.) and a population of 23.2 million. Capital: Bucharest. Machinery, foodstuffs, raw minerals and petroleum products are exported. Heavy industry and oil have become increasingly important to the economy since 1959.

A new constitution was adopted in 1923. During this period in history, the Romanian government struggled with domestic problems, agrarian reform and economic reconstruction.

On August 23, 1944, King Mihai I proclaimed an armistice with the Allied Forces. The Romanian army drove out the Germans and Hungarians in northern Transylvania, but the country was subsequently occupied by the Soviet army. That monarchy was abolished on December 30, 1947, and Romania became a "People's Republic" based on the Soviet regime. The process of sovietization included Soviet regime. The anti-Communist combative resistance movement developed frequent purges of dissidents: mainly political but also clerical, cultural and peasants. Romanian elite disappeared into the concentration camps. The anti-Communist combative resistance movement developed in spite of the Soviet army presence until 1956. The partisans remained in the mountains until 1964. With the accession of N. Ceausescu to power, Romania began to exercise a considerable degree of independence, refusing to participate in the invasion of Czechoslovakia (August 1968). In 1965, it was proclaimed a "Socialist Republic". After 1977, an oppressed and impoverished domestic scene worsened.

On December 17, 1989, an anti-Communist revolt in Timisoara. On December 22, 1989 the Communist government was overthrown. Ceausescu and his wife were arrested and later executed. The new government established a republic, the constitutional name being Romania.

RULERS

Carol I (as Prince), 1866-81 (as King), 1881-1914
Ferdinand I, 1914-1927
Mihai I, 1927-1930
Carol II, 1930-1940
Mihai I, 1940-1947

MINT MARKS

(a) - Paris, privy marks only
(b) - Brussels, privy marks only
angel head (1872-1876),
no marks (1894-1924)
B - Bucharest (1870-1900)
B - Hamburg, Germany
C - Candescu, chief engineer of the Bucharest Mint (1870-)
FM - Franklin Mint, USA
H - Heaton, Birmingham, England
HF - Huguenin Freres & Co., Le Locle, Switzerland
J - Hamburg
KN - Kings Norton, Birmingham, England
(p) - Thunderbolt - Poissy, France
zig zag (1924)
V - Vienna, Austria
W - Watt (James Watt & Co.)
Huguenin - Le Locle, Switzerland
( ) - no marks, 1930 (10, 20 Lei),
1932 (100 Lei), Royal Mint – London

MINT OFFICIALS' INITIALS

Initials	Date	Name
BASSARAB		Costache Bassarab
IOANA BASSARAB	1941-45	Ioana Bassarab Starostescu
E.W. BECKER	1939-40	E.W. Becker
(wing)		Lucien Bazor
P.M. DAMMANN	1922	P.M. Dammann
C.D.	1990	C. Dumitrescu
V.G.	1990	Vasile Gabor
H.I.; H.IONESCU	1939-52	Haralamb Ionescu
I. Jalea	1935-41	Ion Jalea
LAVRILLIER	1930-32	A. Larrillier
A.M.; A. MICHAUX	1906	Alfons Michaux
A. MURNU	1940	A. Murnu
(torch)		Henry Auguste Jules Patey
A. ROMANESCU	1946	A.Rromanescu
A. SCHARFF	1894-1901	Anton Scharff
TASSET	1910-14	Ernst Paulini Tasset

MONETARY SYSTEM

100 Bani = 1 Leu

KINGDOM

STANDARD COINAGE

KM# 31 5 BANI

2.5000 g., Copper-Nickel, 19 mm. **Ruler:** Carol I **Obv:** Crown above banner and hole in center **Rev:** Hole in center flanked by designs with value above and date below **Designer:** A. Scharff

Date	Mintage	F	VF	XF	Unc	BU
1905	2,000,000	0.50	1.50	6.00	16.00	—
1905 Proof	—	Value: 42.00				
1906	48,000,000	0.25	0.50	2.00	7.50	—
1906J	24,000,000	0.25	0.50	2.50	9.00	—

KM# 32 10 BANI

4.0000 g., Copper-Nickel, 22 mm. **Ruler:** Carol I **Obv:** Crown above banner and hole in center **Rev:** Hole in center flanked by designs with value above and date below **Designer:** A. Scharff

Date	Mintage	F	VF	XF	Unc	BU
1905	10,820,000	0.50	1.50	5.00	16.00	—
1906	24,180,000	0.25	0.75	2.00	8.50	—
1906J	17,000,000	0.25	0.75	3.00	10.00	—

KM# 33 20 BANI

6.0000 g., Copper-Nickel, 25 mm. **Ruler:** Carol I **Obv:** Crown above banner and hole in center **Rev:** Hole in center flanked by designs with value above and date below **Designer:** A. Scharff

Date	Mintage	F	VF	XF	Unc	BU
1905	2,500,000	2.00	6.00	18.00	62.00	—
1906	3,000,000	2.00	4.50	15.00	42.00	—
1906J	2,500,000	2.00	4.50	14.00	38.00	—

KM# 44 25 BANI

0.8960 g., Aluminum, 19 mm. **Ruler:** Ferdinand I **Obv:** Eagle above hole in center **Rev:** Hole in center of value with crown at right **Note:** Center hole sizes vary from 4 to 4.5mm. No engraver's name.

Date	Mintage	F	VF	XF	Unc	BU
1921	20,000,000	0.50	1.50	3.00	8.00	—

KM# 23 50 BANI

2.5000 g., 0.8350 Silver .0671 oz. ASW **Ruler:** Carol I **Obv:** Head left **Rev:** Value, date within wreath **Designer:** Tasset

Date	Mintage	F	VF	XF	Unc	BU
1901	194,205	10.00	25.00	65.00	210	—

KM# 41 50 BANI

2.5000 g., 0.8350 Silver .0671 oz. ASW, 18 mm. **Ruler:** Carol I **Obv:** Head left **Rev:** Crown above design **Designer:** Tasset

Date	Mintage	F	VF	XF	Unc	BU
1910	3,600,000	1.50	3.00	8.00	18.00	—
Note: Edge varieties (round or flat) exist						
1910 Proof	—	Value: 150				
1911	3,000,000	2.00	4.00	12.00	25.00	—
1912	1,800,000	1.50	3.50	12.50	28.00	—
1914	1,600,000	1.25	2.00	5.00	14.00	—
Note: Edge varieties (round or flat) exist						
1914 Proof	—	Value: 110				

KM# 45 50 BANI

1.2030 g., Aluminum, 21 mm. **Ruler:** Ferdinand I **Obv:** Eagle above hole in center **Rev:** Hole in center of value with crown at right **Note:** Center hole size varies from 4 to 4.5mm.

Date	Mintage	F	VF	XF	Unc	BU
1921	30,000,000	0.50	1.50	4.00	9.00	—

KM# 24 LEU

5.0000 g., 0.8350 Silver .1342 oz. ASW, 23 mm. **Ruler:** Carol I **Designer:** A. Scharff

Date	Mintage	F	VF	XF	Unc	BU
1901	369,614	5.00	18.00	50.00	180	—
1901 Proof	—	Value: 260				

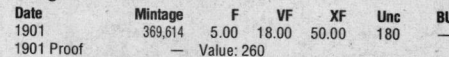

KM# 34 LEU

5.0000 g., 0.8350 Silver .1342 oz. ASW, 14 mm. **Ruler:** Carol I **Subject:** 40th Anniversary - Reign of Carol I **Obv:** Bearded head left **Rev:** Head left **Edge:** Reeded **Designer:** A. Michaux **Note:** Designer's name below truncation on reverse.

Date	Mintage	F	VF	XF	Unc	BU
ND(1906)	2,500,000	5.00	13.00	28.00	68.00	—
ND(1906) Proof	—	Value: 200				

KM# 42 LEU

5.0000 g., 0.8350 Silver .1342 oz. ASW **Ruler:** Carol I **Obv:** Bearded head left **Obv. Designer:** Tasset **Rev:** Standing figure walking right **Rev. Designer:** Bassarab

Date	Mintage	F	VF	XF	Unc	BU
1910	4,600,000	3.00	6.00	12.00	30.00	—
Note: Edge varieties (round or flat) exist						
1910 Proof	—	Value: 350				
1911	2,573,000	4.00	8.00	15.00	38.00	—
1912	3,540,000	3.00	5.00	9.50	26.00	—
1914	4,282,935	2.50	3.50	8.00	20.00	—
Note: Edge varieties (round or flat) exist						
1914 Proof	—	Value: 120				

KM# 46 LEU

3.5000 g., Copper-Nickel, 21 mm. **Ruler:** Ferdinand I **Obv:** Crowned arms with supporters flanked by stars **Rev:** Value above sprig **Edge:** Reeded

Date	Mintage	F	VF	XF	Unc	BU
1924(b) Thin	100,000,000	0.50	1.50	4.00	12.00	—
1924(p) Thick	100,006,000	0.50	1.50	4.50	14.00	—

KM# 56 LEU

2.7500 g., Nickel-Brass **Ruler:** Carol II **Obv:** Crown and date above sprig **Rev:** Ear of corn divides value **Edge:** Plain **Designer:** I. Jalea **Note:** Without mint mark.

Date	Mintage	F	VF	XF	Unc	BU
1938	27,900,000	0.20	0.60	1.60	4.50	—
1939	72,200,000	0.20	0.50	1.50	3.00	—
1940	Inc. above	0.20	0.50	1.00	3.00	—
1941	Inc. above	0.20	0.50	1.50	3.50	—

KM# 25 2 LEI
10.0000 g., 0.8350 Silver .2684 oz. ASW **Ruler:** Carol I **Obv:** Head left **Obv. Inscription:** CAROL I.... **Obv. Designer:** Tasset **Rev:** Crowned arms with supporters within crowned mantle, divided value **Rev. Designer:** A. Scharff **Edge:** Reeded

Date	Mintage	F	VF	XF	Unc	BU
1901	12,476	400	650	1,200	2,600	—

KM# 43 2 LEI
10.0000 g., 0.8350 Silver .2684 oz. ASW **Ruler:** Carol I **Obv:** Bearded head left **Obv. Designer:** Tasset **Rev:** Standing figure walking right **Rev. Designer:** Bassarab

Date	Mintage	F	VF	XF	Unc	BU
1910	1,800,000	5.00	8.00	16.00	40.00	—
Note: Edge varieties (round and flat) exist						
1910 Proof	—	Value: 220				
1911	1,000,000	6.00	12.00	25.00	55.00	—
1912	1,500,000	5.00	7.50	13.50	35.00	—
1914	2,452,000	4.50	6.00	11.00	25.00	—
Note: Edge varieties (round and flat) exist						
1914 Proof	—	Value: 130				

KM# 47 2 LEI
7.0000 g., Copper-Nickel, 25 mm. **Ruler:** Ferdinand I **Obv:** Crowned arms with supporters flanked by stars **Rev:** Value above sprig **Edge:** Reeded

Date	Mintage	F	VF	XF	Unc	BU
1924(b)	50,000,000	1.00	1.75	4.50	12.00	—
1924(p)	50,008,000	1.00	1.75	5.00	15.00	—

KM# 58 2 LEI
3.2000 g., Zinc, 20 mm. **Ruler:** Mihai I **Obv:** Crown above date **Rev:** Value within wreath **Designer:** H. Ionescu

Date	Mintage	F	VF	XF	Unc	BU
1941	101,778,000	0.50	1.50	4.50	10.00	—

KM# 17.2 5 LEI
25.0000 g., 0.9000 Silver .7234 oz. ASW, 38 mm. **Ruler:** Carol I **Edge:** Reeded **Designer:** Kullrich

Date	Mintage	F	VF	XF	Unc	BU
1901B	82,460	45.00	90.00	200	400	—
1901B Proof	—	Value: 950				

KM# 35 5 LEI
25.0000 g., 0.9000 Silver .7234 oz. ASW, 38 mm. **Ruler:** Carol I **Subject:** 40th Anniversary - Reign of Carol I **Obv:** Bearded head left **Rev:** Head left **Edge:** Reeded **Designer:** A. Michaux

Date	Mintage	F	VF	XF	Unc	BU
ND(1906)	200,000	50.00	100	200	400	—
ND(1906) Proof	—	Value: 950				

KM# 48 5 LEI
3.5000 g., Nickel-Brass, 21 mm. **Ruler:** Mihai I **Obv:** Head left **Rev:** Crowned shield divides value flanked by stars **Edge:** Reeded **Designer:** A. J. Patey

Date	Mintage	F	VF	XF	Unc	BU
1930H	15,000,000	1.50	2.50	8.00	25.00	—
1930KN	15,000,000	1.50	3.50	9.00	28.00	—
1930(a)	30,000,000	1.00	2.50	6.00	20.00	—

KM# 61 5 LEI
4.5000 g., Zinc, 23 mm. **Ruler:** Mihai I **Obv:** Crown above date **Rev:** Oat sprigs to right of value **Designer:** H. Ionescu

Date	Mintage	F	VF	XF	Unc	BU
1942	140,000,000	0.50	1.25	3.00	8.00	—

KM# 49 10 LEI
5.0000 g., Nickel-Brass, 23 mm. **Ruler:** Carol II **Obv:** Head left **Rev:** Crowned eagle with crowned shield on chest divides value **Edge:** Reeded **Designer:** A. Lavrillier

Date	Mintage	F	VF	XF	Unc	BU
1930	15,000,000	1.00	3.50	8.50	25.00	—
1930 Proof	—	—	—	—	—	—
1930(a)	30,000,000	1.00	3.00	8.00	24.00	—
1930H	7,500,000	2.50	4.50	11.00	32.00	—
1930KN	7,500,000	3.00	7.00	15.00	38.00	—
1930(a) Proof	—	Value: 175				

KM# 36 12-1/2 LEI
4.0325 g., 0.9000 Gold .1167 oz. AGW, 19 mm. **Ruler:** Carol I **Subject:** 40th Anniversary - Reign of Carol I **Obv:** Bearded bust left **Rev:** Crowned eagle and banner **Designer:** A. Michaux

Date	Mintage	F	VF	XF	Unc	BU
1906	32,000	110	180	320	450	—

KM# 37 20 LEI
6.4516 g., 0.9000 Gold .1867 oz. AGW, 20 mm. **Ruler:** Carol I **Subject:** 40th Anniversary - Reign of Carol I **Obv:** Bearded head left **Rev:** Head left **Edge:** Reeded **Designer:** A. Michaux

Date	Mintage	F	VF	XF	Unc	BU
ND(1906)(b)	15,000	135	185	260	425	—

KM# 50 20 LEI
7.5000 g., Nickel-Brass, 27 mm. **Ruler:** Mihai I **Obv:** Young head left **Rev:** Figures holding hands divides value **Rev. Designer:** Bassarab **Edge:** Reeded

Date	Mintage	F	VF	XF	Unc	BU
1930 London	40,000,000	2.00	6.50	18.00	38.00	—
1930 Proof	—	—	—	—	—	—
1930H	5,000,000	3.00	8.00	25.00	52.00	—
1930KN	5,000,000	3.00	10.00	30.00	70.00	—

KM# 51 20 LEI
7.5000 g., Nickel-Brass, 27 mm. **Ruler:** Carol II **Obv:** Head left **Rev:** Crowned eagle with crowned shield on chest divides value **Edge:** Reeded **Designer:** A. Lavrillier

Date	Mintage	F	VF	XF	Unc	BU
1930	6,750,000	1.50	3.00	12.00	24.00	—
1930 Proof	—	—	—	—	—	—
1930(a)	17,500,000	1.00	2.00	10.00	22.00	—
1930(a) Proof	—	Value: 165				
1930KN	7,750,000	2.50	6.00	25.00	56.00	—
1930KN Proof	—	Value: 150				
1930H	7,750,000	2.00	4.00	16.00	40.00	—
1930H Proof	—	Value: 200				

KM# 62 20 LEI
6.0000 g., Zinc, 26 mm. **Ruler:** Mihai I **Obv:** Crown above date **Rev:** Value within wreath **Edge:** Reeded **Designer:** H. Ionescu

Date	Mintage	F	VF	XF	Unc	BU
1942	44,000,000	0.75	1.50	3.00	8.50	—
1943	25,783,000	1.00	2.25	4.00	9.00	—
1944	5,034,000	1.50	3.00	5.00	13.00	—

KM# 38 25 LEI
8.0650 g., 0.9000 Gold .2333 oz. AGW, 30 mm. **Ruler:** Carol I **Subject:** 40th Anniversary - Reign of Carol I **Obv:** Uniformed bust left **Rev:** Crowned eagle and banner **Designer:** A. Michaux

Date	Mintage	F	VF	XF	Unc	BU
ND(1906)(b)	24,000	210	320	540	800	—

KM# 39 50 LEI
16.1300 g., 0.9000 Gold .4667 oz. AGW, 35 mm. **Ruler:** Carol I **Subject:** 40th Anniversary - Reign of Carol I **Obv:** Uniformed bust left **Rev:** Equestrian **Designer:** A. Michaux

Date	Mintage	F	VF	XF	Unc	BU
ND(1906)(b)	28,000	325	500	800	1,500	—

KM# 55 50 LEI
5.8300 g., Nickel, 24 mm. **Ruler:** Carol II **Obv:** Helmeted head left **Rev:** Crowned shield within sprigs divides value **Edge:** Reeded **Designer:** I. Jalea **Note:** 16,731 pieces melted.

Date	Mintage	F	VF	XF	Unc	BU
1937	12,000,000	1.25	2.50	6.00	14.00	—
1938	8,000,000	3.00	6.00	15.00	42.00	—

KM# 40 100 LEI
32.2600 g., 0.9000 Gold .9335 oz. AGW, 36 mm. **Ruler:** Carol I **Subject:** 40th Anniversary - Reign of Carol I **Designer:** Alfons Michaux **Note:** Similar to KM#35.

Date	Mintage	F	VF	XF	Unc	BU
ND(1906)(b)	3,000	650	900	1,900	3,200	—

KM# 52 100 LEI
14.0000 g., 0.5000 Silver .1929 oz. ASW, 31 mm. **Ruler:** Carol II **Obv:** Head right **Rev:** Crowned eagle divides wreath with value within **Edge:** Reeded **Designer:** A. Lavrillier

Date	Mintage	F	VF	XF	Unc	BU
1932(a)	2,000,000	10.00	20.00	50.00	250	—
1932	16,400,000	5.00	10.00	30.00	175	—
1932 Proof	—	Value: 750				

KM# 54 100 LEI
8.2000 g., Nickel, 27 mm. **Ruler:** Carol II **Obv:** Head left **Rev:** Crowned shield within sprigs flanked by value **Edge:** Reeded **Designer:** I. Jalea **Note:** 17,030 pieces melted.

Date	Mintage	F	VF	XF	Unc	BU
1936	20,230,000	2.00	4.00	12.00	35.00	—
1938	3,250,000	3.00	7.00	15.00	45.00	—

KM# 64 100 LEI
8.5000 g., Nickel Clad Steel, 28 mm. **Ruler:** Mihai I **Obv:** Head right **Rev:** Crown divides wreath with date and value within **Edge:** Incuse lettering **Edge Lettering:** NIHIL SINE DEO **Designer:** H. Ionescu

Date	Mintage	F	VF	XF	Unc	BU
1943	40,590,000	0.25	0.50	1.50	5.00	—
Note: Portrait varieties exist						
1944	21,289,000	0.25	0.50	2.00	8.00	—

KM# 63 200 LEI
6.0000 g., 0.8350 Silver .1611 oz. ASW, 24 mm. **Ruler:** Mihai I **Obv:** Head right **Rev:** Crowned arms with supporters **Edge:** Incuse lettering **Edge Lettering:** NIHIL SINE DEO **Designer:** H. Ionescu

Date	Mintage	F	VF	XF	Unc	BU
1942	30,025,000	2.75	3.50	6.50	15.00	—

KM# 66 200 LEI
7.5000 g., Brass, 27 mm. **Ruler:** Mihai I **Obv:** Head right **Rev:** Crown divides wreath with date and value within **Designer:** H. Ionescu **Note:** Many were silver-plated privately.

Date	Mintage	F	VF	XF	Unc	BU
1945	1,399,000	1.00	2.00	5.50	14.00	—

KM# 53 250 LEI
13.5000 g., 0.7500 Silver .3255 oz. ASW, 29 mm. **Ruler:** Carol II **Obv:** Head left **Rev:** Crowned eagle with shield on chest **Designer:** I. Jalea

Date	Mintage	F	VF	XF	Unc	BU
1935	4,500,000	16.00	50.00	120	220	—

Note: Bank reports show that between 1937-39 4,490,670 pieces were withdrawn and remelted

KM# 57 250 LEI
12.0000 g., 0.8350 Silver .3222 oz. ASW, 30 mm. **Ruler:** Carol II **Obv:** Head right **Rev:** Crowned shield divides wreath with date and value within **Edge:** Incuse lettering, line interrupted by two rhombs **Edge Lettering:** MUNCA CREDINTA REGE NATIUNE **Designer:** H. Ionescu

Date	Mintage	F	VF	XF	Unc	BU
1939	10,000,000	6.00	12.00	30.00	75.00	—
1940	8,000,000	12.00	20.00	45.00	140	—

KM# 59.1 250 LEI
12.0000 g., 0.8350 Silver .3222 oz. ASW **Ruler:** Carol II **Obv:** Head left **Rev:** Date divided by portcullis **Edge:** Incuse lettering **Edge Lettering:** TOTUL PENTRU TARA **Designer:** H. Ionescu **Note:** Mintage unissued and reportedly melted.

Date	Mintage	F	VF	XF	Unc	BU
1940	—	—	—	3,000	4,000	—

KM# 59.2 250 LEI
12.0000 g., 0.8350 Silver .3222 oz. ASW **Ruler:** Mihai I **Obv:** Head left **Rev:** Crowned shield divides date with value and date within **Edge:** Incuse lettering **Edge Lettering:** TOTUL PENTRU TARA **Designer:** H. Ionescu

Date	Mintage	F	VF	XF	Unc	BU
1941	2,250,000	9.00	15.00	35.00	90.00	—

KM# 59.3 250 LEI
12.0000 g., 0.8350 Silver .3222 oz. ASW **Ruler:** Mihai I **Obv:** Head left **Edge:** Lettered **Edge Lettering:** NIHIL SINE DEO **Designer:** H. Ionescu

Date	Mintage	F	VF	XF	Unc	BU
1941B	13,750,000	6.50	9.50	16.00	30.00	—

KM# 60 500 LEI
25.0000 g., 0.8350 Silver .6711 oz. ASW, 37 mm. **Ruler:** Mihai I **Subject:** Basarabia Reunion **Obv:** Young head left **Rev:** Crowned kneeling figure presenting putna monastery to Lord **Edge:** Incuse lettering **Edge Lettering:** PRIN STATORNICIE LA IZBANADA + **Designer:** Ioana Bassarab

Date	Mintage	F	VF	XF	Unc	BU
1941	775,000	BV	11.50	16.50	36.00	—

KM# 65 500 LEI
12.0000 g., 0.7000 Silver .2701 oz. ASW, 32 mm. **Ruler:** Mihai I **Obv:** Head left **Rev:** Crowned arms with supporters within crowned mantle divides date **Edge:** Incuse lettering **Edge Lettering:** NIHIL SINE DEO **Designer:** H. Ionescu

Date	Mintage	F	VF	XF	Unc	BU
1944	9,731,000	BV	4.50	6.50	12.50	—

KM# 67 500 LEI
10.0000 g., Brass, 30 mm. **Ruler:** Mihai I **Obv:** Head left **Rev:** Crowned arms with supporters within crowned mantle divides date **Edge:** Reeded **Designer:** H. Ionescu **Note:** Many were silver-plated privately.

Date	Mintage	F	VF	XF	Unc	BU
1945	3,422,000	1.00	2.00	4.00	8.00	—

KM# 68 500 LEI
1.5000 g., Aluminum, 24 mm. **Ruler:** Mihai I **Obv:** Head right **Rev:** Value above sprig **Edge:** Reeded **Designer:** H. Ionescu **Note:** Without designer's name, the result of a filled die.

Date	Mintage	F	VF	XF	Unc	BU
1946	5,823,000	0.50	1.00	3.00	8.00	—

KM# 69 2000 LEI
5.1000 g., Brass, 24 mm. **Ruler:** Mihai I **Obv:** Head right **Rev:** Crowned arms with supporters **Edge:** Incuse lettering **Edge Lettering:** NIHIL SINE DEO **Designer:** H. Ionescu **Note:** Many were silver-plated privately.

Date	Mintage	F	VF	XF	Unc	BU
1946	24,619,000	0.50	1.00	3.00	8.00	—

KM# 76 10000 LEI
10.0000 g., Brass, 27 mm. **Ruler:** Mihai I **Obv:** Head right **Rev:** Crowned shield to left of value and sprigs **Edge:** Incuse lettering **Edge Lettering:** NIHIL SINE DEO **Designer:** H. Ionescu **Note:** Many were silver-plated privately.

Date	Mintage	F	VF	XF	Unc	BU
1947	11,850,000	1.00	2.00	4.00	9.00	—

KM# 70 25000 LEI
12.5000 g., 0.7000 Silver .2813 oz. ASW, 32 mm. **Ruler:** Mihai I **Obv:** Head right **Rev:** Crowned shield to left of value and sprigs **Edge:** Incuse lettering **Edge Lettering:** NIHIL SINE DEO **Designer:** H. Ionescu

Date	Mintage	F	VF	XF	Unc	BU
1946	2,372,000	BV	4.50	7.50	18.00	—

KM# 71 100000 LEI
25.0000 g., 0.7000 Silver .5626 oz. ASW, 37 mm. **Ruler:** Mihai I **Obv:** Head right **Obv. Designer:** H. Ionescu **Rev:** Standing figure releasing dove with crowned shield at lower right, value at lower left **Rev. Designer:** A. Romanescu **Edge:** Incuse lettering **Edge Lettering:** NIHIL SINE DEO

Date	Mintage	F	VF	XF	Unc	BU
1946	2,002,000	BV	9.00	12.50	20.00	—

REFORM COINAGE

Aug. 15, 1947; 100 Bani = 1 Leu

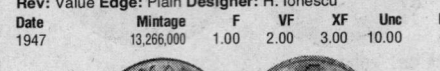

KM# 72 50 BANI
1.7000 g., Brass, 16 mm. **Ruler:** Mihai I **Obv:** Crown above date **Rev:** Value **Edge:** Plain **Designer:** H. Ionescu

Date	Mintage	F	VF	XF	Unc	BU
1947	13,266,000	1.00	2.00	3.00	10.00	—

KM# 73 LEU
2.5000 g., Brass, 18 mm. **Ruler:** Mihai I **Obv:** Crowned shield **Rev:** Value within oat sprig **Edge:** Plain **Designer:** H. Ionesw

Date	Mintage	F	VF	XF	Unc	BU
1947	88,341,000	1.00	2.25	4.00	11.00	—

KM# 74 2 LEI
3.5000 g., Bronze, 21 mm. **Ruler:** Mihai I **Obv:** Crowned shield and date **Rev:** Value within oat sprigs **Edge:** Plain **Designer:** H. Ionesw

Date	Mintage	F	VF	XF	Unc	BU
1947	40,000,000	1.00	2.50	5.00	16.00	—

KM# 75 5 LEI
1.5000 g., Aluminum, 23 mm. **Ruler:** Mihai I **Obv:** Head right **Rev:** Value to left of oat sprig **Designer:** H. Ionescu

Date	Mintage	F	VF	XF	Unc	BU
1947	56,026,000	1.50	2.50	8.00	24.00	—

PEOPLE'S REPUBLIC

STANDARD COINAGE

KM# 78 LEU
1.8300 g., Copper-Nickel-Zinc, 16 mm. **Obv:** Radiant sun and lighthouse **Rev:** Value and date **Edge:** Plain **Designer:** H. Ionescu

Date	Mintage	F	VF	XF	Unc	BU
1949	—	0.75	1.50	3.00	9.00	—
1950	—	0.75	1.50	4.00	12.00	—
1951	—	1.00	2.00	9.00	20.00	—

KM# 78a LEU
0.6100 g., Aluminum, 16 mm. **Obv:** Radiant sun and lighthouse **Rev:** Value and date **Designer:** H. Ionescu

Date	Mintage	F	VF	XF	Unc	BU
1951	—	1.00	2.00	5.00	12.00	—
1952	—	8.00	14.00	26.00	75.00	—

KM# 79 2 LEI
2.4400 g., Copper-Nickel-Zinc, 18 mm. **Obv:** Ear of corn flanked by oat and flower sprig **Rev:** Value and date **Edge:** Plain **Designer:** H. Ionescu

Date	Mintage	F	VF	XF	Unc	BU
1950	—	1.00	2.50	5.00	11.50	—
1951	—	2.00	5.00	10.00	22.00	—

KM# 79a 2 LEI
0.8400 g., Aluminum, 18 mm. **Obv:** Ear of corn flanked by oat and flower sprig **Rev:** Value and date **Designer:** H. Ionescu

Date	Mintage	F	VF	XF	Unc	BU
1951	—	0.75	2.00	5.00	12.00	—
1952	—	8.00	14.00	28.00	80.00	—

KM# 77 5 LEI
1.5000 g., Aluminum, 23 mm. **Obv:** National emblem **Rev:** Value within wreath **Edge:** Plain **Designer:** H. Ionescu

Date	Mintage	F	VF	XF	Unc	BU
1948	—	1.50	2.50	5.00	18.00	—
1949	—	1.25	2.00	4.00	12.00	—
1950	—	1.25	2.00	3.50	11.00	—
1951	—	1.25	2.00	5.00	16.00	—

KM# 80 20 LEI
2.1200 g., Aluminum, 26 mm. **Obv:** National emblem **Rev:** Blacksmith at anvil, factory in background **Edge:** Plain **Designer:** H. Ionescu

Date	Mintage	F	VF	XF	Unc	BU
1951	—	3.00	7.00	18.00	48.00	—

REFORM COINAGE

Jan. 26, 1952; 20 "old" Lei + 1 "new" Lei; 100 Bani = 1 Leu

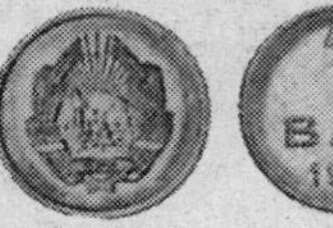

KM# 81.1 BAN
1.0000 g., Copper-Nickel-Zinc, 16 mm. **Obv:** National emblem **Rev:** Value and date **Edge:** Reeded **Designer:** H. Ionescu

Date	Mintage	F	VF	XF	Unc	BU
1952	—	0.20	0.50	1.20	3.00	—

KM# 81.2 BAN
1.0000 g., Copper-Nickel-Zinc **Obv:** National emblem **Rev:** Value and date **Designer:** H. Ionescu

Date	Mintage	F	VF	XF	Unc	BU
1953	—	1.00	2.00	8.00	18.00	—
1954	—	3.00	6.00	15.00	48.00	—

KM# 82.1 3 BANI
2.0000 g., Copper-Nickel-Zinc, 18 mm. **Obv:** National emblem **Rev:** Value and date **Edge:** Reeded **Designer:** H. Ionescu

Date	Mintage	F	VF	XF	Unc	BU
1952	—	1.00	2.00	4.00	10.00	—

KM# 82.2 3 BANI
2.0000 g., Copper-Nickel-Zinc **Obv:** National emblem **Rev:** Value and date

Date	Mintage	F	VF	XF	Unc	BU
1953	—	0.50	1.00	2.50	9.00	—
1954	—	20.00	50.00	75.00	180	—

KM# 83.1 5 BANI
2.4000 g., Copper-Nickel-Zinc, 20 mm. **Obv:** National emblem **Rev:** Value and date **Edge:** Reeded **Designer:** H. Ionescu

Date	Mintage	F	VF	XF	Unc	BU
1952	—	0.50	1.00	3.00	8.00	—

KM# 83.2 5 BANI
2.4000 g., Copper-Nickel-Zinc, 20 mm. **Obv:** National emblem **Rev:** Value and date **Designer:** H. Ionescu

Date	Mintage	F	VF	XF	Unc	BU
1953	—	0.25	0.50	2.00	8.00	—
1954	—	0.25	0.50	1.50	6.00	—
1955	—	0.25	0.50	1.50	5.00	—
1956	—	0.25	0.50	1.25	4.50	—
1957	—	0.25	0.50	1.75	5.00	—

KM# 89 5 BANI
1.7000 g., Nickel Clad Steel, 16 mm. **Obv:** National emblem, RPR on ribbon **Rev:** Value and date **Edge:** Plain **Designer:** H. Ionescu

Date	Mintage	F	VF	XF	Unc	BU
1963	—	0.20	0.50	1.00	2.00	—

KM# 84.1 10 BANI
1.8000 g., Copper-Nickel, 17 mm. **Obv:** National emblem **Rev:** Value and date within wreath **Edge:** Reeded **Designer:** H. Ionescu

Date	Mintage	F	VF	XF	Unc	BU
1952	—	2.00	3.00	9.00	24.00	—

KM# 84.2 10 BANI
1.8000 g., Copper-Nickel **Obv:** National emblem **Obv. Legend:** ROMANA **Rev:** Value and date within wreath **Designer:** H. Ionescu

Date	Mintage	F	VF	XF	Unc	BU
1954	—	0.30	1.50	3.50	9.00	—

KM# 84.3 10 BANI
1.8000 g., Copper-Nickel **Obv:** National emblem **Obv. Legend:** ROMINA **Rev:** Value and date within wreath **Designer:** H. Ionescu

Date	Mintage	F	VF	XF	Unc	BU
1955	—	0.10	0.20	0.75	4.00	—
1956	—	0.10	0.20	0.75	3.50	—

KM# 87 15 BANI
2.8700 g., Nickel Clad Steel, 19.5 mm. **Obv:** National emblem **Rev:** Value within wreath **Edge:** Plain **Designer:** H. Ionescu

Date	Mintage	F	VF	XF	Unc	BU
1960	—	0.10	0.25	0.60	2.50	—

KM# 85.1 25 BANI
3.6000 g., Copper-Nickel, 22 mm. **Obv:** National emblem **Rev:** Value and date within wreath **Edge:** Reeded **Designer:** H. Ionescu

Date	Mintage	F	VF	XF	Unc	BU
1952	—	2.00	4.00	14.00	30.00	—

KM# 85.2 25 BANI
3.6000 g., Copper-Nickel **Obv:** National emblem **Obv. Legend:** ROMANA **Rev:** Value and date within wreath **Designer:** H. Ionescu

Date	Mintage	F	VF	XF	Unc	BU
1953	—	0.20	0.75	2.50	7.00	—
1954	—	0.20	0.60	2.00	6.00	—

KM# 85.3 25 BANI
3.6000 g., Copper-Nickel **Obv:** National emblem **Obv. Legend:** ROMINA **Rev:** Value and date within wreath **Designer:** H. Ionescu

Date	Mintage	F	VF	XF	Unc	BU
1955	—	0.15	0.35	1.00	4.00	—

KM# 88 25 BANI
3.3800 g., Nickel Clad Steel **Obv:** National emblem **Rev:** Value above tractor **Edge:** Plain **Designer:** H. Ionescu

Date	Mintage	F	VF	XF	Unc	BU
1960	—	0.15	0.30	1.00	4.00	—

KM# 86 50 BANI
4.5500 g., Copper-Nickel, 25 mm. **Obv:** National emblem **Rev:** Blacksmith at anvil, factory in background **Edge:** Reeded **Designer:** H. Ionescu

Date	Mintage	F	VF	XF	Unc	BU
1955	—	0.50	1.00	3.00	14.00	—
1956	—	0.50	1.00	4.00	15.00	—

KM# 90 LEU
5.0600 g., Nickel Clad Steel, 24 mm. **Obv:** National emblem **Rev:** Tractor **Edge:** Plain **Designer:** H. Ionescu

Date	Mintage	F	VF	XF	Unc	BU
1963	—	0.25	0.50	1.00	2.50	—

KM# 91 3 LEI
5.8600 g., Nickel Clad Steel, 27 mm. **Obv:** National emblem **Rev:** Oil refinery **Edge:** Plain **Designer:** H. Ionescu

Date	Mintage	F	VF	XF	Unc	BU
1963	—	0.25	0.50	1.50	4.00	—

SOCIALIST REPUBLIC

STANDARD COINAGE

KM# 92 5 BANI
1.7000 g., Nickel Clad Steel, 16 mm. **Obv:** National emblem, ROMANIA on ribbon **Rev:** Value and date **Edge:** Plain

Date	Mintage	F	VF	XF	Unc	BU
1966	—	0.10	0.50	1.00	2.00	—

KM# 92a 5 BANI
0.6000 g., Aluminum, 16 mm. **Obv:** National emblem, ROMANIA on ribbon **Rev:** Value and date **Edge:** Plain

Date	Mintage	F	VF	XF	Unc	BU
1975	—	—	0.10	0.50	1.00	—

KM# 93 15 BANI
2.8800 g., Nickel Clad Steel, 19.5 mm. **Obv:** National emblem **Rev:** Value within wreath **Edge:** Plain

Date	Mintage	F	VF	XF	Unc	BU
1966	—	—	0.50	1.00	2.00	—

KM# 93a 15 BANI
1.0000 g., Aluminum, 19.5 mm. **Obv:** National emblem **Rev:** Value within wreath **Edge:** Plain

Date	Mintage	F	VF	XF	Unc	BU
1975	—	—	0.10	0.50	1.20	—

KM# 94 25 BANI
3.3800 g., Nickel Clad Steel, 22 mm. **Obv:** National emblem **Rev:** Value above tractor **Edge:** Plain

Date	Mintage	F	VF	XF	Unc	BU
1966	—	—	0.20	1.00	2.50	—

KM# 94a 25 BANI
1.3000 g., Aluminum, 22 mm. **Obv:** National emblem **Rev:** Value above tractor **Edge:** Plain

Date	Mintage	F	VF	XF	Unc	BU
1982	—	0.20	0.50	1.00	3.00	—

KM# 95 LEU
5.0600 g., Nickel Clad Steel, 24.6 mm. **Obv:** National emblem **Rev:** Tractor

Date	Mintage	F	VF	XF	Unc	BU
1966	—	0.10	0.25	0.75	2.00	—

KM# 96 3 LEI
5.8600 g., Nickel Clad Steel, 27 mm. **Obv:** National emblem **Rev:** Oil refinery **Edge:** Plain

Date	Mintage	F	VF	XF	Unc	BU
1966	—	0.25	0.50	1.20	4.00	—

KM# 97 5 LEI
2.8000 g., Aluminum, 29 mm. **Obv:** National emblem **Rev:** Value within design **Edge:** Security

Date	Mintage	F	VF	XF	Unc	BU
1978	—	0.25	0.50	1.50	4.50	—

KM# 100 50 LEI
15.0000 g., 0.9250 Silver .4128 oz. ASW **Subject:** 2,050th Anniversary of First Independent State **Obv:** National emblem **Rev:** Fighting figures within circle

Date	Mintage	F	VF	XF	Unc	BU
1983FM	591	—	—	—	400	—

Note: Serially numbered on edges

KM# 98 100 LEI
30.0000 g., 0.9250 Silver .8253 oz. ASW **Subject:** 2,050th Anniversary of First Independent State **Obv:** National emblem divides date **Rev:** Head with headdress left flanked by diamonds

Date	Mintage	F	VF	XF	Unc	BU
1982FM	928	—	—	—	600	—
1983FM	595	—	—	—	650	—

Note: Serially numbered on edge

KM# 99 500 LEI
8.0000 g., 0.9000 Gold .2038 oz. AGW **Subject:** 2,050th Anniversary of First Independent State **Obv:** National emblem divides date **Rev:** Fighting figures within circle

Date	Mintage	F	VF	XF	Unc	BU
1982FM	508	—	—	—	900	—
1983FM	346	—	—	—	1,000	—

Note: Edge numbered

KM# 101 1000 LEI
16.0000 g., 0.9000 Gold .4167 oz. AGW **Subject:** 2,050th Anniversary of First Independent State **Obv:** National emblem divides date **Rev:** Head with headdress left flanked by diamonds

Date	Mintage	F	VF	XF	Unc	BU
1983FM	342	—	—	—	2,250	—

Note: Edge numbered

REPUBLIC

STANDARD COINAGE

KM# 113 LEU
2.5000 g., Copper Clad Steel, 19 mm. **Subject:** National Bank of Romania **Obv:** Monogram above date and sprigs **Rev:** Value above oat sprigs **Edge:** Plain

Date	Mintage	F	VF	XF	Unc	BU
1992	Est. 60,000,000	0.20	0.50	1.25	3.50	—

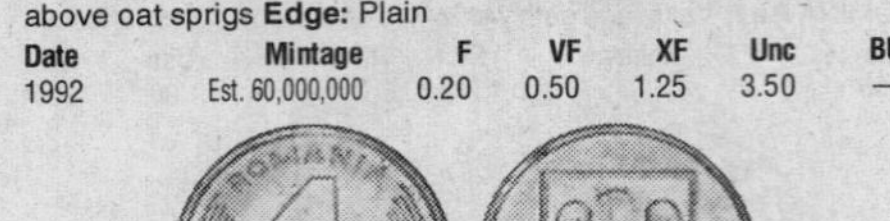

KM# 115 LEU
Copper Clad Steel **Obv:** Value flanked by sprigs **Rev:** Shield divides date

Date	Mintage	F	VF	XF	Unc	BU
1993	Est. 61,000,000	—	0.10	0.25	1.50	—
1994	Est. 10,000,000	—	—	0.20	1.00	—
1995	2,000,000	—	—	0.10	1.00	—

Date	Mintage	F	VF	XF	Unc	BU
1996	272,000	—	0.50	1.00	4.00	—
2000 Proof	4,500	Value: 4.50				

KM# 112 5 LEI
3.3500 g., Aluminum, 21 mm. **Subject:** Prince Mihai Viteazul **Designer:** Vasile Gabor **Note:** Similar to 100 Lei, KM#111. Not released for circulation; majority were melted.

Date	Mintage	F	VF	XF	Unc	BU
1991	—	—	—	—	95.00	—

KM# 114 5 LEI
Nickel Plated Steel **Obv:** Value flanked by oak leaves **Rev:** Shield divides date **Edge:** Plain

Date	Mintage	F	VF	XF	Unc	BU
1992 CD VG	Est. 30,000,000	—	0.25	0.60	3.00	—
1993 CD	Est. 70,000,000	—	—	0.30	2.00	—
1994	Est. 10,000,000	—	—	0.30	1.50	—
1995	25,000,000	—	—	0.20	1.00	—
1996	—	—	—	0.20	1.00	—
2000 Proof	4,500	Value: 4.50				

KM# 108 10 LEI
4.6500 g., Nickel-Clad Steel, 23 mm. **Subject:** Revolution Anniversary **Obv:** Flag and sprig **Rev:** Value within wreath **Edge:** Security scroll **Designer:** Vasile Gabor **Note:** Rotated die varieties exist.

Date	Mintage	F	VF	XF	Unc	BU
1990	30,000,000	—	0.50	1.00	3.00	—
1991	31,303,000	—	0.25	0.60	2.20	—
1992	60,000,000	—	0.25	0.50	1.50	—

KM# 116 10 LEI
Nickel-Clad Steel **Obv:** Value within sprigs **Rev:** Shield divides date

Date	Mintage	F	VF	XF	Unc	BU
1993	Est. 6,000,000	—	0.75	1.50	3.50	—
1994	Est. 7,000,000	—	0.50	1.00	3.00	—
1995	30,000,000	—	—	0.30	1.50	—
1996	5,000	—	—	—	—	—
2000 Proof	4,500	Value: 4.50				

KM# 117.1 10 LEI
Nickel Plated Steel **Series:** F.A.O. **Subject:** 50 Years - F.A.O. **Obv:** Shield flanked by sprigs and diamonds above value **Rev:** F.A.O logo and dates **Edge:** Plain

Date	Mintage	F	VF	XF	Unc	BU
1995	200,000	—	—	3.50	7.00	—

KM# 117.2 10 LEI
Nickel Plated Steel **Series:** F.A.O. **Subject:** 50 Years - F.A.O. **Obv:** Shield flanked by sprigs and diamonds **Rev:** F.A.O logo and dates **Note:** Obverse description: N in diamond at right for Numismatists

Date	Mintage	F	VF	XF	Unc	BU
1995	30,000	—	—	4.00	10.00	—

KM# 120 10 LEI

Nickel Plated Steel **Series:** 1996 Olympic Games - U.S.A. **Obv:** Shield above sprigs flanked by value **Rev:** Swimmer

Date	Mintage	F	VF	XF	Unc	BU
1996	10,000	—	—	5.00	12.00	—

KM# 121 10 LEI

Nickel Plated Steel **Series:** 1996 Olympic Games - U.S.A. **Obv:** Shield above sprig flanked by value **Rev:** Four Olympic scenes

Date	Mintage	F	VF	XF	Unc	BU
1996	10,000	—	—	5.00	12.00	—

KM# 122 10 LEI

Nickel Plated Steel **Series:** 1996 Olympic Games - U.S.A. **Obv:** Shield above sprig flanked by value **Rev:** Windsurfer

Date	Mintage	F	VF	XF	Unc	BU
1996	10,000	—	—	5.00	12.00	—

KM# 123 10 LEI

Nickel Plated Steel **Series:** 1996 Olympic Games - U.S.A. **Obv:** Shield above sprig flanked by value **Rev:** Sailboat with two racers

Date	Mintage	F	VF	XF	Unc	BU
1996	10,000	—	—	5.00	12.00	—

KM# 124 10 LEI

Nickel Plated Steel **Series:** 1996 Olympic Games - U.S.A. **Obv:** Shield above sprigs divide value **Rev:** Canoe with two racers

Date	Mintage	F	VF	XF	Unc	BU
1996	10,000	—	—	5.00	12.00	—

KM# 125 10 LEI

Nickel Plated Steel **Series:** 1996 Olympic Games - U.S.A. **Obv:** Shield above sprigs divide value **Rev:** Scullcraft with racers

Date	Mintage	F	VF	XF	Unc	BU
1996	10,000	—	—	5.00	12.00	—

KM# 126 10 LEI

Nickel Plated Steel **Subject:** World Food Summit - Rome **Obv:** Shield above value **Rev:** Logo above inscription

Date	Mintage	F	VF	XF	Unc	BU
1996	50,000	—	—	4.00	12.00	—

KM# 134 10 LEI

Nickel Plated Steel **Subject:** Euro Soccer **Obv:** Shield divides value **Rev:** Stylized soccer players

Date	Mintage	F	VF	XF	Unc	BU
1996	50,000	—	—	4.00	12.00	—

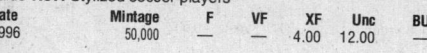

KM# 109 20 LEI

5.0000 g., Brass Clad Steel, 24 mm. **Obv:** Crowned bust facing flanked by dots **Rev:** Value and date within half sprigs and dots **Edge:** Plain **Designer:** Constantin Dumitrescu **Note:** Date varieties exist.

Date	Mintage	F	VF	XF	Unc	BU
1991	Est. 43,200,000	—	—	1.00	3.00	—
1992	Est. 48,000,000	—	—	0.80	3.00	—
1993	Est. 33,800,000	—	—	0.80	3.00	—
1994	Est. 5,000,000	—	—	1.25	3.00	—
1995	8,000,000	—	—	0.75	3.00	—
1996	500,000	—	0.75	2.00	7.00	—
2000 Proof	4,500	Value: 6.00				

KM# 110 50 LEI

5.9000 g., Brass Clad Steel, 26 mm. **Obv:** Bust left flanked by dots **Rev:** Sprig divides date and value **Edge:** Plain **Designer:** Vasile Gabor

Date	Mintage	F	VF	XF	Unc	BU
1991	Est. 29,600,000	—	—	1.50	3.00	—
1992	Est. 70,800,000	—	—	1.00	2.00	—
Note: 1992 date varieties exist						
1993	Est. 34,600,000	—	—	1.00	2.00	—
1994	Est. 30,000,000	—	—	1.00	2.00	—
1995	20,000,000	—	—	1.00	2.20	—
1996	4,900,000	—	—	2.00	4.00	—
2000 Proof	4,500	Value: 7.00				

KM# 111 100 LEI

8.7500 g., Nickel Plated Steel, 29 mm. **Obv:** Bust with headdress 1/4 right **Rev:** Value within sprigs **Edge Lettering:** ROMANIA **Designer:** Vasile Gabor

Date	Mintage	F	VF	XF	Unc	BU
1991	Est. 12,600,000	—	—	2.50	6.00	—
1992	Est. 70,500,000	—	—	1.50	3.50	—
Note: Reported edge varieties for 1992 with TOTUL PENTRU TARA; without ROMANIA are presumed essais						
1993	Est. 78,000,000	—	—	1.50	3.00	—
1994	Est. 125,000,000	—	—	1.50	2.50	—
1995	30,000,000	—	—	1.50	3.50	—
1996	11,000,000	—	—	2.50	9.00	—
2000 Proof	4,500	Value: 7.50				

KM# 118 100 LEI

27.5000 g., 0.9250 Silver .8178 oz. ASW, 37 mm. **Series:** F.A.O. **Subject:** 50 Years - F.A.O. **Obv:** Shield flanked by sprigs and diamonds above value **Rev:** F.A.O logo and dates **Edge:** Plain

Date	Mintage	F	VF	XF	Unc	BU
1995	30,000	—	—	—	24.00	—

KM# 119 100 LEI

27.0000 g., 0.9250 Silver .8030 oz. ASW, 37 mm. **Subject:** Euro Soccer **Obv:** Shield **Rev:** Players **Edge:** Plain

Date	Mintage	F	VF	XF	Unc	BU
1996 Proof	12,000	Value: 28.00				

KM# 127 100 LEI

27.0000 g., 0.9250 Silver .8030 oz. ASW **Series:** 1996 Olympic Games - U.S.A. **Obv:** Shield divides value above sprig **Rev:** Swimmer **Edge:** Plain

Date	Mintage	F	VF	XF	Unc	BU
1996 Proof	10,000	Value: 28.00				

KM# 128 100 LEI

27.0000 g., 0.9250 Silver .8030 oz. ASW **Series:** 1996 Olympic Games - U.S.A. **Obv:** Shield divides value above sprig **Rev:** Four olympic scenes **Edge:** Plain

Date	Mintage	F	VF	XF	Unc	BU
1996 Proof	10,000	Value: 28.00				

KM# 129 100 LEI

27.0000 g., 0.9250 Silver .8030 oz. ASW **Series:** 1996 Olympic Games - U.S.A. **Obv:** Shield divides value above sprig **Rev:** Windsurfer

Date	Mintage	F	VF	XF	Unc	BU
1996 Proof	10,000	Value: 28.00				

KM# 130 100 LEI

27.0000 g., 0.9250 Silver .8030 oz. ASW **Series:** 1996 Olympic Games - U.S.A. **Obv:** Shield divides value above sprig **Rev:** Sailboat with three crewmen

Date	Mintage	F	VF	XF	Unc	BU
1996 Proof	10,000	Value: 28.00				

KM# 131 100 LEI

27.0000 g., 0.9250 Silver .8030 oz. ASW **Series:** 1996 Olympic Games - U.S.A. **Obv:** Shield divides value above sprig **Rev:** Canoe with two canoeists

Date	Mintage	F	VF	XF	Unc	BU
1996 Proof	10,000	Value: 28.00				

KM# 132 100 LEI

27.0000 g., 0.9250 Silver .8030 oz. ASW **Series:** 1996 Olympic Games - U.S.A. **Obv:** Shield divides value above sprig **Rev:** Scullcraft with rowers

Date	Mintage	F	VF	XF	Unc	BU
1996 Proof	10,000	Value: 28.00				

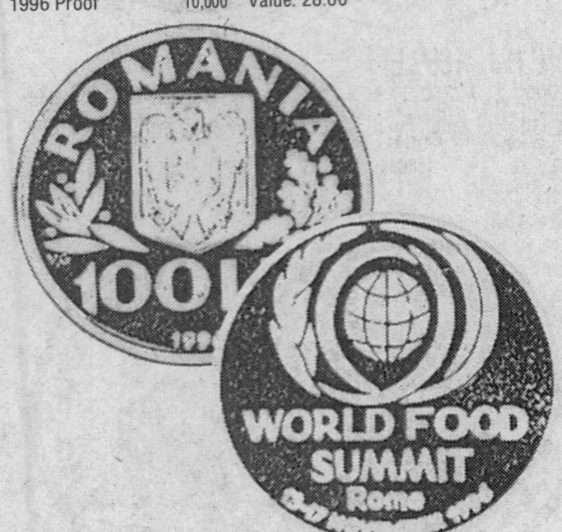

KM# 133 100 LEI

27.5000 g., 0.9250 Silver .8178 oz. ASW **Subject:** World Food Summit - Rome **Edge:** Plain

Date	Mintage	F	VF	XF	Unc	BU
1996 Proof	5,000	Value: 35.00				

KM# 135 100 LEI

27.0000 g., 0.9250 Silver .8030 oz. ASW **Subject:** 50th Anniversary - UNICEF **Obv:** Shield above value **Rev:** UNICEF logo on world globe **Edge:** Plain

Date	Mintage	F	VF	XF	Unc	BU
1996 Proof	5,000	Value: 35.00				

KM# 138 100 LEI

27.0000 g., 0.9250 Silver .8030 oz. ASW **Subject:** 120th Anniversary of Independence **Obv:** Shield above value **Rev:** Three soldiers with flag behind cannon **Edge:** Plain

Date	Mintage	F	VF	XF	Unc	BU
1998 Proof	Est. 5,000	Value: 37.50				

KM# 139 100 LEI

27.0000 g., 0.9250 Silver .8030 oz. ASW **Subject:** Andrei Saguna **Obv:** Shield divides value **Rev:** Bust facing 1/4 right with dates and church towers **Edge:** Plain

Date	Mintage	F	VF	XF	Unc	BU
1998 Proof	2,000	Value: 48.00				

KM# 140 100 LEI

27.0000 g., 0.9250 Silver .8030 oz. ASW **Series:** Olympic Games - Nagano 1998 **Obv:** Value above shield to right of stylized flame and snow flakes **Rev:** Bobsled **Edge:** Plain

Date	Mintage	F	VF	XF	Unc	BU
1998 Proof	2,000	Value: 45.00				

KM# 141 100 LEI

27.0000 g., 0.9250 Silver .8030 oz. ASW **Series:** Olympic Games - Nagano 1998 **Rev:** Figure skaters

Date	Mintage	F	VF	XF	Unc	BU
1998 Proof	2,000	Value: 45.00				

KM# 142 100 LEI

27.0000 g., 0.9250 Silver .8030 oz. ASW **Series:** Olympic Games - Nagano 1998 **Rev:** Slalom skier

Date	Mintage	F	VF	XF	Unc	BU
1998 Proof	2,000	Value: 45.00				

KM# 143 100 LEI

27.0000 g., 0.9250 Silver .8030 oz. ASW **Subject:** World Cup Soccer - France 1998 **Obv:** Value within goal net with shield at right **Rev:** Eiffel Tower in front of soccer ball **Edge:** Plain

Date	Mintage	F	VF	XF	Unc	BU
1998 Proof	5,000	Value: 40.00				

KM# 149 100 LEI
27.0000 g., 0.9250 Silver .8030 oz. ASW **Subject:** Visit of Pope John Paul II **Obv:** Shield on quatrefoil **Rev:** Portraits of Pope and Patriarch Theoctist **Edge:** Plain

Date	Mintage	F	VF	XF	Unc	BU
1999 Proof	2,000	Value: 55.00				

KM# 152 100 LEI
1.2240 g., 0.9990 Gold 0.0393 oz. AGW **Subject:** History of Gold **Obv:** Shield within ornamental circle above value **Rev:** Gold Dacian helmet found at Poiana Cotofeneti

Date	Mintage	F	VF	XF	Unc	BU
1999 Proof	25,000	Value: 300				

KM# 148 100 LEI
27.0000 g., 0.9250 Silver .8030 oz. ASW **Subject:** 100th Anniversary - Belgica Expedition **Obv:** Shield, birds and compas face **Rev:** The sailing ship Belgica and bust of scientist Emil Racovita **Edge:** Plain

Date	Mintage	F	VF	XF	Unc	BU
1999 Proof	20,000	Value: 45.00				

KM# 136 500 LEI
8.6400 g., 0.9000 Gold .25 oz. AGW, 24 mm. **Subject:** Revolution of 1848 **Obv:** Upper and lower shield divides value **Rev:** Half length figure with head facing right flanked by dates

Date	Mintage	F	VF	XF	Unc	BU
1998 Proof	Est. 2,000	Value: 300				

KM# 145 500 LEI
3.7000 g., Aluminum, 25 mm. **Obv:** Shield within sprigs **Rev:** Value within 3/4 wreath **Edge:** Lettered **Edge Lettering:** ROMANIA (three times)

Date	Mintage	F	VF	XF	Unc	BU
1998	—	—	—	0.75	2.00	—
1999	—	—	—	0.75	2.00	—
2000	—	—	—	0.75	2.00	—
2000 Proof	4,500	Value: 6.00				

KM# 146 500 LEI
Aluminum, 25 mm. **Obv:** Shield, value and date within design **Rev:** Solar eclipse **Edge:** Lettered **Edge Lettering:** ROMANIA (three times)

Date	Mintage	VG	F	VF	XF	Unc
1999	4,000,000	—	—	—	1.00	4.00

KM# 147 500 LEI
Aluminum, 25 mm. **Subject:** Solar eclipse **Obv:** Shield, eclipse and observatory **Rev:** Solar eclipse **Edge:** Lettered **Edge Lettering:** ROMANIA (3x)

Date	Mintage	VG	F	VF	XF	Unc
1999	—	—	—	—	—	—

Note: This design never gained broad release and is considered to be a pattern by several authorities

KM# 154 500 LEI
27.0000 g., 0.9990 Silver .8030 oz. ASW, 37 mm. **Subject:** Alexander the Good of Moldavia **Obv:** Old seal design and value **Rev:** Crowned bust 1/4 left, church at left **Edge:** Plain

Date	Mintage	F	VF	XF	Unc	BU
2000 Proof	Est. 1,000	Value: 65.00				

KM# 137 1000 LEI
31.1035 g., 0.9990 Gold 1 oz. AGW, 35 mm. **Subject:** Revolution of 1848 **Obv:** Crossed flags and shield flanked by value **Rev:** Victory flanked by dates **Edge:** Plain

Date	Mintage	F	VF	XF	Unc	BU
1998 Proof	Est. 1,000	Value: 775				

KM# 144 1000 LEI
31.1035 g., 0.9990 Gold 1 oz. AGW, 35 mm. **Subject:** 80th Anniversary - Union of Transylvania **Obv:** Shield to right of value **Rev:** Large building and the arms of Wallachia, Moldova and Transylvania **Edge:** Plain

Date	Mintage	F	VF	XF	Unc	BU
1998 Proof	2,000	Value: 750				

KM# 151 1000 LEI
31.1035 g., 0.9990 Gold 1 oz. AGW, 35 mm. **Subject:** Visit of Pope John Paul II **Obv:** Shield **Rev:** Portraits of Pope and Patriarch Theoctist **Edge:** Plain

Date	Mintage	F	VF	XF	Unc	BU
1999 Proof	1,000	Value: 800				

KM# 153 1000 LEI
2.0000 g., Aluminum, 22.2 mm. **Subject:** Constantin Brancoveanu **Obv:** Value above shield within lined circle **Rev:** Bust with headdress facing **Edge:** Reeded and plain sections

Date	Mintage	VG	F	VF	XF	Unc
2000	—	—	—	—	0.50	3.00
2000 Proof	4,500	Value: 10.00				

Note: In proof sets only

KM# 157 2000 LEI
31.1030 g., 0.9990 Gold .9990 oz. AGW, 35 mm. **Obv:** Shield and quill within circle **Rev:** Bust 3/4 left **Edge:** Plain

Date	Mintage	VG	F	VF	XF	Unc
2000 Proof	1,500	Value: 775				

KM# 155 5000 LEI
31.1030 g., 0.9990 Gold .9990 oz. AGW, 35 mm. **Subject:** Michael the Brave's Unification of Romania in 1600 **Obv:** Shield and old seal within circle **Rev:** Bust with headdress and church **Edge:** Plain

Date	Mintage	F	VF	XF	Unc	BU
2000 Proof	Est. 1,500	Value: 825				

KM# 182 5000 LEI
31.1030 g., 0.9990 Gold 0.999 oz. AGW, 35 mm. **Subject:** 2000 Years of Christianity **Rev:** Jesus Christ

Date	Mintage	F	VF	XF	Unc	BU
2000 Proof	—	Value: 775				

ESSAIS

KM#	Date	Mintage	Identification	Mkt Val
E1	1905	—	10 Bani. Copper-Nickel. KM29. With center hole.	200

KM#	Date	Mintage	Identification	Mkt Val
E2	1910	—	50 Bani. Silver. Head left. Crown above sprigs.	300
E3	1910	—	Leu. Silver.	300
E4	1910	—	2 Lei. Silver.	300
E5	1914	—	50 Bani. Silver.	200
E6	1914	—	50 Bani. Silver. KM41	150

KM#	Date	Mintage	Identification	Mkt Val
E7	1914	—	Leu. Silver.	250
E8	1914	—	Leu. Silver. KM42.	—
E9	1914	—	2 Lei. Silver. Head left. Crowned arms with supporters within crowned mantle flanked by value.	275
E10	1914	—	2 Lei. Silver. KM43.	—
E11	1924	—	2 Lei. Silver.	125

PATTERNS

Including off metal strikes

KM#	Date	Mintage	Identification	Mkt Val
Pn49	1905	—	5 Bani. White Metal. KM28.	100
Pn50	1905	—	5 Bani. Pewter. KM28.	—
Pn51	1905	—	5 Bani. Aluminum. KM28.	—
Pn52	1905	—	5 Bani. Zinc. KM28.	—
Pn53	1905	—	5 Bani. Bronze. KM28.	—
Pn54	1905	—	5 Bani. Brass. KM28.	125
Pn55	1905	—	5 Bani. Copper. KM28. With center hole.	125
Pn56	1905	—	5 Bani. Copper. KM28.	500
Pn57	1905	—	5 Bani. Gilt Copper. KM28.	—
Pn58	1905	—	5 Bani. Silver. KM31. Without center hole.	250
Pn59	1905	—	5 Bani. Bronze. KM31. Without center hole.	—
Pn60	1905	—	5 Bani. Pewter. KM31. Without center hole.	100
Pn61	1905	—	5 Bani. Aluminum. KM31. Without center hole.	—
Pn62	1905	—	5 Bani. Zinc. KM31. Without center hole.	—
Pn63	1905	—	5 Bani. Copper-Nickel. KM31. Without center hole.	—
Pn64	1905	—	5 Bani. Gold. Without center hole.	1,500
Pn65	1905	—	5 Bani. Gold. Without center hole.	1,200
PnA66	1905	—	10 Bani. White Metal. With center hole.	—
PnB66	1905	—	10 Bani. White Metal. Without center hole.	—
Pn66	1905	—	10 Bani. Pewter. KM29. With center hole.	125
Pn67	1905	—	10 Bani. Brass. KM29. With center hole.	125
Pn68	1905	—	10 Bani. Aluminum. KM29. With center hole.	75.00
PnA69	1905	—	10 Bani. Bronze. KM29. Red. With center hole.	—
Pn69	1905	—	10 Bani. Bronze. KM29. Red. Without center hole.	100
Pn70	1905	—	10 Bani. Bronze. KM29. Green. Without center hole.	100
Pn71	1905	—	10 Bani. Zinc. KM29.	160
PnA72	1905	—	10 Bani. Gilt Bronze. KM29. With center hole.	—
Pn72	1905	—	10 Bani. Gilt Bronze. KM29. Without center hole.	100
Pn73	1905	—	10 Bani. Copper-Nickel-Zinc. With center hole.	150
Pn74	1905	—	10 Bani. Nickel. KM29. With center hole.	—
Pn75	1905	—	10 Bani. Silver. KM29. Without center hole.	350
Pn76	1905	—	10 Bani. Silver. KM29. With center hole.	250
PnA77	1905	—	10 Bani. Gilt Copper. With branches and small date. Without center hole.	—
Pn77	1905	—	10 Bani. Copper. KM29. Without center hole.	100
Pn78	1905	—	10 Bani. Gold. Without branches. KM29. Without center hole.	1,650
Pn79	1905	—	10 Bani. Gold. KM29. With center hole.	1,400
Pn80	1905	—	10 Bani. Pewter. KM32. Without center hole.	150
Pn81	1905	—	10 Bani. Brass. KM32. Without center hole.	150
Pn82	1905	—	10 Bani. Aluminum. KM32. Without center hole.	100
Pn83	1905	—	10 Bani. Bronze. KM32. Without center hole.	125
Pn84	1905	—	10 Bani. Gold. KM32. Without center hole.	1,250
Pn85	1905	—	20 Bani. Lead. KM30.	100
Pn86	1905	—	20 Bani. Brass. KM30.	150
Pn87	1905	—	20 Bani. Copper. KM30.	125
Pn88	1905	—	20 Bani. Aluminum. KM30.	100
Pn89	1905	—	20 Bani. White Metal. KM30.	100
Pn90	1905	—	20 Bani. Zinc. KM30.	—
Pn91	1905	—	20 Bani. Pewter. KM30.	—
Pn92	1905	—	20 Bani. Gilt Bronze. KM30.	125
PnA93	1905	—	20 Bani. Bronze. KM30.	—

KM#	Date	Mintage	Identification	Mkt Val
Pn93	1905	—	20 Bani. Silver. KM30.	250
Pn94	1905	—	20 Bani. Gold. Without center hole.	1,750
Pn95	1905	—	20 Bani. Gold. With center hole.	1,500
Pn96	1905	—	20 Bani. Brass. KM33. Without center hole.	—
Pn97	1905	—	20 Bani. Copper. KM33. Without center hole.	200
Pn98	1905	—	20 Bani. Aluminum. KM33. Without center hole.	—
Pn99	1905	—	20 Bani. Pewter. KM33. Without center hole.	200
Pn100	1905	—	20 Bani. Silver. KM33. Without center hole.	400
Pn101	1906	—	Leu. White Metal.	125
Pn102	1906	—	Leu. Brass.	150
Pn103	1906	—	Leu. Aluminum.	100
Pn104	1906	—	Leu. Copper.	125
Pn105	1906	—	Leu. Gilt Bronze.	125
Pn106	1906	—	Leu. Copper-Nickel.	—
Pn107	1906	—	Leu. Gilt Bronze.	125
Pn108	1906	—	Leu. Silver.	250
Pn109	1906	—	Leu. Gold.	—
Pn110	1906	—	5 Lei. Silver.	4,500
Pn111	1906	—	12-1/2 Lei. Lead.	250
Pn112	1906	—	12-1/2 Lei. White Metal.	250
Pn113	1906	—	12-1/2 Lei. Brass.	250
Pn114	1906	—	12-1/2 Lei. Pewter.	—
Pn115	1906	—	12-1/2 Lei. Gilt Bronze.	250
PnA116	1906	—	12-1/2 Lei. Bronze. Plain edge.	250
Pn116	1906	—	12-1/2 Lei. Aluminum.	250
Pn117	1906	—	12-1/2 Lei. Aluminum. Gilt.	250
Pn118	1906	—	12-1/2 Lei. Copper.	350
Pn119	1906	—	12-1/2 Lei. Copper-Nickel.	—
Pn120	1906	—	12-1/2 Lei. Silver.	550
Pn121	1906	—	12-1/2 Lei. Gold.	1,200
Pn122	1906	—	12-1/2 Lei. Gold. Pale.	2,150
Pn123	1906	—	20 Lei. Copper.	350
Pn124	1906	—	20 Lei. Bronze.	200
Pn125	1906	—	20 Lei. White Metal.	—
Pn126	1906	—	20 Lei. White Metal. Gilt.	—
Pn127	1906	—	20 Lei. Gold.	1,200
Pn128	1906	—	20 Lei. Gold. Pale.	2,150
Pn129	1906	—	25 Lei. Pewter.	250
Pn130	1906	—	25 Lei. Zinc.	400
Pn131	1906	—	25 Lei. Lead.	200
Pn132	1906	—	25 Lei. Copper.	175
Pn133	1906	—	25 Lei. Gilt Copper.	—
Pn134	1906	—	25 Lei. Aluminum.	175
Pn135	1906	—	25 Lei. Brass.	175
Pn136	1906	—	25 Lei. Bronze. Antique.	175
Pn137	1906	—	25 Lei. Gilt Bronze.	175
Pn138	1906	—	25 Lei. Silver.	800
Pn139	1906	—	25 Lei. Gold.	2,400
Pn140	1906	—	25 Lei. Gold. Pale.	4,000
Pn141	1906	—	50 Lei. Aluminum.	350
Pn142	1906	—	50 Lei. Bronze.	400
Pn143	1906	—	50 Lei. White Metal.	—
Pn144	1906	—	50 Lei. Pewter.	425
Pn145	1906	—	50 Lei. Brass.	400
Pn146	1906	—	50 Lei. Silver.	850
Pn147	1906	12	50 Lei. Gold.	12,500
Pn148	1906	—	100 Lei. Copper.	650
Pn149	1906	—	100 Lei. Bronze.	650
Pn150	1906	—	100 Lei. Silver.	—
Pn151	1906	—	100 Lei. Gold.	5,000
PnA152	1910	—	10 Bani. Zinc.	—
Pn152	1910	—	10 Bani. Copper.	—
Pn153	1910	—	50 Bani. Lead.	—
Pn154	1910	—	50 Bani. Tin.	—
PnA155	1910	—	50 Bani. Pewter. Plain edge.	—
Pn155	1910	—	50 Bani. Pewter. Milled edge.	100
Pn156	1910	—	50 Bani. White Metal.	75.00
Pn157	1910	—	50 Bani. Aluminum.	60.00
Pn158	1910	—	50 Bani. Zinc.	—
Pn159	1910	—	50 Bani. Copper.	—
Pn160	1910	—	50 Bani. Copper-Nickel.	—
Pn161	1910	—	50 Bani. Brass.	75.00
PnA162	1910	—	50 Bani. Bronze. Plain edge. Thin planchet.	—
PnB162	1910	—	50 Bani. Bronze. Plain edge. Thick planchet.	—
PnC162	1910	—	50 Bani. Bronze. Milled edge. Thin planchet.	—
PnD162	1910	—	50 Bani. Bronze. Milled edge. Thick planchet.	—
Pn162	1910	—	50 Bani. Nickel.	100
Pn163	1910	—	Leu. Lead.	100
Pn164	1910	—	Leu. Aluminum.	100
Pn165	1910	—	Leu. Bronze.	85.00
Pn166	1910	—	Leu. Gilt Bronze.	85.00
Pn167	1910	—	Leu. Pewter.	125
Pn168	1910	—	Leu. Zinc.	—
PnA169	1910	—	Leu. Gilt Copper.	—
Pn169	1910	—	Leu. Copper.	—
Pn170	1910	—	Leu. Copper-Nickel.	—
Pn171	1910	—	2 Lei. Lead.	100
Pn172	1910	—	2 Lei. Tin.	150
Pn173	1910	—	2 Lei. Pewter.	150
Pn174	1910	—	2 Lei. Aluminum.	100
Pn175	1910	—	2 Lei. Brass.	100
PnA176	1910	—	2 Lei. Gilt Copper.	—
Pn176	1910	—	2 Lei. Copper.	—

KM#	Date	Mintage	Identification	Mkt Val
Pn177	1910	—	2 Lei. Gilt Bronze.	100
PnA178	1910	—	2 Lei. Bronze.	—
Pn178	1910	—	2 Lei. Nickel.	—
PnA179	1910	—	2 Lei. Silver.	—
Pn179	1921	—	25 Bani. Aluminum. HF at left of date.	125
PnA180	1921	—	25 Bani. Bronze. HF at left of date.	200
PnB180	1921	—	25 Bani. Copper-Nickel.	185
PnC180	1921	—	25 Bani. Bronze. Without hole.	185
PnD180	1921	—	25 Bani. Nickel.	200
PnE180	1921	—	25 Bani. Copper. Without hole.	300
PnF180	1921	—	25 Bani. Bronze. With hole.	200
Pn180	1921	—	50 Bani. Nickel. With hole.	200
PnA181	1921	—	50 Bani. Bronze. Without hole.	300
PnB181	1921	—	50 Bani. Bronze. With hole.	200
PnD181	1921	—	1.25 Leu. Nickel. Without hole.	700
PnC181	1921	—	50 Bani. Bronze. With hole.	200
Pn181	1921	—	1.25 Leu. Nickel. With hole.	500
PnA182	1921	—	5 Lei. Billon. Arms, cornucopia. Hand numbered 1-15. Struck at Paris.	—
Pn182	1921	—	5 Lei. Copper-Nickel.	450
Pn183	1921	—	5 Lei. Nickel.	—
Pn184	1922	—	25 Bani. Aluminum.	—
Pn185	1922	—	50 Bani. Aluminum.	175
Pn186	1922	—	Leu. Bronze.	220
Pn187	1922	—	Leu. Nickel.	250
Pn188	1922	—	Leu. Copper-Nickel.	210
Pn189	1922	—	2 Lei. Bronze.	250
Pn190	1922	—	2 Lei. Nickel.	250
Pn191	1922	—	2 Lei. Brass.	150
Pn192	1922	—	5 Lei. Bronze.	300
Pn193	1922	—	5 Lei. Copper-Nickel.	300
Pn194	1922	—	5 Lei. Nickel.	300
PnA195	1922	—	5 Bani. Copper.	300
Pn195	1922	—	5 Lei. Brass.	300
Pn196	1922	—	5 Lei. Copper-Nickel.	300
Pn197	1922	—	20 Lei. Gold.	2,000
Pn198	1922	—	25 Lei. Gold.	2,500
Pn199	1922	—	50 Lei. Gold.	4,000
Pn200	1922	—	100 Lei. Gold.	5,500
PnA201	1923	—	Leu. Nickel.	275
PnB201	1923	—	2 Lei. Copper.	600
Pn201	1924	—	Leu. Nickel.	65.00
Pn202	1924	—	Leu. Aluminum.	45.00
Pn203	1924	—	Leu. Tin.	45.00
Pn204	1924	—	Leu. Zinc.	—
Pn205	1924	—	Leu. Copper.	—
Pn206	1924	—	Leu. Brass.	110
Pn207	1924	—	Leu. Bronze.	60.00
Pn208	1924	—	Leu. Gilt Bronze.	50.00
Pn209	1924	—	Leu. Silver. Plain edge.	125
Pn210	1924	—	Leu. Silver. Reeded edge.	125
Pn211	1924	—	2 Lei. Zinc.	75.00
Pn212	1924	—	2 Lei. Aluminum.	50.00
Pn213	1924	—	2 Lei. Tin.	—
Pn214	1924	—	2 Lei. Bronze.	240
Pn215	1924	—	2 Lei. Brass.	100
Pn216	1924	—	2 Lei. Copper.	65.00
PnA217	1924	—	2 Lei. Copper-Nickel.	—
Pn217	1924	—	2 Lei. Nickel.	75.00
Pn218	1924	—	2 Lei. Silver. Plain edge. Thick planchet.	200
PnA219	1930	—	10 Lei. Copper-Nickel. KM49.	100
Pn219	1930	—	20 Lei. Gold. Plain.	—
Pn220	1930	—	20 Lei. Gold. Ornamented.	—
Pn221	1930	—	100 Lei. Gold. Plain.	—
Pn222	1930	—	100 Lei. Gold. Ornamented.	—
Pn223	1931	—	20 Lei. Gold. Plain.	—
Pn224	1931	—	20 Lei. Gold. Ornamented.	—
Pn225	1931	—	100 Lei. Gold. Plain.	—
Pn226	1931	—	100 Lei. Gold. Ornamented.	—
Pn227	1932	—	20 Lei. Gold. Plain.	—
Pn228	1932	—	20 Lei. Gold. Ornamented.	—
Pn229	1932	—	100 Lei. Silver. Y62.	75.00
Pn230	1932	—	100 Lei. Gold. Plain.	—
Pn231	1932	—	100 Lei. Gold. Ornamented.	—
Pn232	1933	—	20 Lei. Gold. Plain.	—
Pn233	1933	—	20 Lei. Gold. Ornamented.	—
Pn234	1933	—	100 Lei. Gold. Plain.	—
Pn235	1933	—	100 Lei. Gold. Ornamented.	—
Pn236	1934	—	20 Lei. Gold. Plain.	—
Pn237	1934	—	20 Lei. Gold. Ornamented.	—
	1934	—	20 Lei. Gold. Ornamented.	—
Pn238	1934	—	100 Lei. Gold. Plain.	—
Pn239	1934	—	100 Lei. Gold. Ornamented.	—
Pn240	1935	—	20 Lei. Gold. Plain.	—
Pn241	1935	—	20 Lei. Gold. Ornamented.	—
Pn242	1935	—	50 Lei. Silver.	—
Pn243	1935	—	100 Lei. Gold. Plain.	—
Pn244	1935	—	100 Lei. Gold. Ornamented.	—
Pn245	1935	—	200 Lei. Silver.	450
PnA245	1935	—	250 Lei. Nickel.	—
PnB245	1935	—	250 Lei. Brass.	—
Pn246	1936	—	20 Lei. Gold. Plain.	—
Pn247	1936	—	20 Lei. Gold. Ornamented.	—
Pn248	1936	—	50 Lei. Nickel.	—
Pn249	1936	—	100 Lei. Gold. Plain.	—
PnA250	1936	—	100 Lei. Copper.	500
Pn250	1936	—	100 Lei. Gold. Ornamented.	—
PnA251	1937	—	50 Lei. Nickel. KM55.	120
Pn251	1937	—	Leu. Copper-Nickel-Zinc.	—

KM#	Date	Mintage	Identification	Mkt Val
Pn252	ND 1937	—	Leu. Copper-Nickel-Zinc.	—
Pn253	1937	—	2 Lei. Copper-Nickel-Zinc.	—
Pn254	1937	—	20 Lei. Gold. Plain.	—
Pn255	1937	—	20 Lei. Gold. Ornamented.	—
Pn256	1937	—	50 Lei. Copper-Nickel-Zinc.	240
Pn257	1937	—	100 Lei. Gold. Plain.	—
Pn258	1937	—	100 Lei. Gold. Ornamented.	—
Pn259	1938	—	Leu. Copper-Nickel-Zinc.	400
Pn260	1938	—	20 Lei. Gold. Plain.	—
Pn261	1938	—	20 Lei. Gold. Ornamented.	—
Pn262	1938	—	100 Lei. Gold. Plain.	—
Pn263	1938	—	100 Lei. Gold. Ornamented.	—
Pn264	1939	—	20 Lei. Gold. Plain.	—
Pn265	1939	—	20 Lei. Gold. Ornamented.	—
Pn266	1939	—	20 Lei. Gold. Arms.	—
Pn267	1939	—	20 Lei. Gold. Eagle.	—
Pn268	1939	—	100 Lei. Gold. Plain.	—
Pn269	1939	—	100 Lei. Gold. Ornamented.	—
Pn270	1939	—	100 Lei. Gold. Bust.	—
Pn271	1940	—	20 Lei. Gold. Plain.	3,000
Pn272	1940	—	20 Lei. Gold. Ornamented.	3,000
Pn273	1940	—	100 Lei. Gold. Plain.	—
Pn274	1940	—	100 Lei. Gold. Ornamented.	—
Pn275	1940	—	250 Lei. 0.7500 Silver. Iron guard emblem.	9,000
Pn276	1941	—	Leu. Zinc.	—
Pn277	1941	—	Leu. Copper-Nickel-Zinc.	—
PnA278	1944	—	20 Lei. Gilt Copper.	200
Pn278	1944	—	20 Lei. Copper-Nickel-Zinc.	—
PnA279	1944	—	500 Lei. Silver. Plain edge.	180
Pn279	1944	—	500 Lei. Aluminum.	115
Pn280	1945	—	100 Lei. Nickel Clad Steel.	125
PnA280	1945	—	200 Lei. Aluminum.	—
Pn281	1945	—	500 Lei. Brass. Nickel plated.	125
Pn282	1945	—	2000 Lei. Brass. Nickel plated.	—
PnA283	1946	—	1000 Lei. Aluminum.	—
PnB283	1946	—	500 Lei. Aluminum.	—
Pn283	1946	—	25000 Lei. Silver.	800
PnA284	1952	—	10 Bani. Copper-Nickel. With cogged wheel instead of wreath.	—
PnB284	1956	—	10 Bani. Aluminum.	100
PnC284	1956	—	50 Bani. Aluminum.	150
PnD284	ND 1958	—	5 Bani. Aluminum-Bronze.	—
Pn284	1958	—	5 Bani. Copper-Nickel-Zinc.	100
PnA285	1960	—	10 Bani. Nickel. 12 teeth to wheel.	190
PnB285	1966	—	5 Bani. Aluminum.	—
PnC285	1966	—	15 Bani. Aluminum.	—
PnD285	1966	—	15 Bani. Brass.	—
PnE285	1966	—	15 Bani. Copper.	—
PnF285	1966	—	3 Lei. Silver.	—
PnG285	1966	—	5 Lei. Copper. Factory.	—
PnH285	1966	—	5 Lei. Copper.	—
PnI285	1966	—	5 Lei. Brass.	—
PnJ285	1984	—	100 Lei. Silver.	—
PnK285	ND (1984)	—	100 Lei.	—
PnL285	1987	—	2 Lei. Nickel Plated Steel.	180
Pn285	1960	—	10 Bani. Nickel. 20 teeth to wheel.	100
Pn286	1987	—	10 Lei. Nickel. Steel plated.	75.00
Pn287	1987	—	10 Lei. Aluminum.	70.00
Pn288	1987	—	10 Lei. Aluminum.	70.00
Pn289	1987	—	10 Lei. Bronze.	80.00
PnA290	1987	—	10 Lei. Nickel Plated Steel.	—
PnB290	1987	—	10 Lei. Aluminum.	—
PnC290	1987	—	10 Lei. Brass.	—
Pn290	1987	—	10 Lei. Nickel. Steel plated.	75.00
Pn291	1988	—	10 Lei. Aluminum.	75.00
Pn292	1988	—	10 Lei. Aluminum.	75.00
PnA293	1990	—	10 Lei. Aluminum.	100
PnB293	1991	—	Leu. Copper-Nickel. 3 oak leaves.	60.00
Pn293	1991	—	5 Lei. Iron. Nickel clad. Similar to 100 Lei, KM#111.	70.00
Pn294	1991	—	5 Lei. Brass. Similar to 100 Lei, KM#111.	70.00
PnA296	1991	—	20 Lei. Aluminum.	70.00
PnB296	1991	—	20 Lei. Nickel Plated Steel. Similar to 100 Lei, KM#111.	95.00
PnC296	1991	—	50 Lei. Aluminum.	60.00
PnD296	1991	—	50 Lei. Copper-Nickel.	60.00
Pn296	1991	—	50 Lei. Silver. KM110.	150
PnA297	1991	—	100 Lei. Brass. King Stephen.	300
PnB297	1991	—	100 Lei. Brass. Prince M. Viteazul.	200
PnC297	1991	—	100 Lei. Aluminum. Prince M. Viteazul.	150
PnD297	1991	—	100 Lei. Nickel Plated Steel. Lettered edge.	180
PnE297	1991	—	100 Lei. Nickel Plated Steel. Sinus line edge.	90.00
PnF297	1991	—	100 Lei. Nickel Plated Steel. Lettered edge.	90.00
PnG297	1991	—	100 Lei. Nickel Plated Steel. Lettered edge.	90.00
PnH297	ND (1992)	—	Leu. Nickel.	—
Pn297	1992	—	Leu. Silver.	100
Pn298	ND (1992)	—	Leu. Nickel.	80.00
PnA299	1992	—	Leu. Silver.	—
PnB299	1992	—	5 Lei. Brass.	70.00
PnC299	1992	—	5 Lei. Copper-Nickel.	70.00
PnD299	1992	—	5 Lei. Nickel Plated Steel.	70.00
Pn299	1992	—	5 Lei. Aluminum.	50.00
PnA300	1993	—	Leu. Copper. Like KM#113.	80.00
PnB300	1995	—	100 Lei. Aluminum. KM#118.	40.00
Pn300	1996	—	10 Lei. Nickel Plated Steel. Similar to KM#117. KM#134.	35.00
Pn301	1996	—	100 Lei. Aluminum. KM#119.	45.00
Pn302	1996	—	100 Lei. Brass. KM#119.	50.00
Pn303	1996	—	100 Lei. Copper-Nickel. KM#127. Brass plated.	45.00
Pn304	1996	—	100 Lei. Aluminum. KM#127.	40.00
Pn305	1996	—	100 Lei. Copper-Nickel. KM#128. Brass plated.	45.00
Pn306	1996	—	100 Lei. Aluminum. KM#128.	40.00
Pn307	1996	—	100 Lei. Copper-Nickel. KM#129. Brass plated.	45.00
Pn308	1996	—	100 Lei. Aluminum. KM#129.	40.00
Pn309	1996	—	100 Lei. Copper-Nickel. KM#130. Brass plated.	45.00
Pn310	1996	—	100 Lei. Aluminum. KM#130.	40.00
Pn311	1996	—	100 Lei. Copper-Nickel. KM#131. Brass plated.	45.00
Pn312	1996	—	100 Lei. Aluminum. KM#131.	40.00
Pn313	1996	—	100 Lei. Copper-Nickel. KM#132. Brass plated.	45.00
Pn314	1996	—	100 Lei. Aluminum. KM#132.	40.00
PnA315C1	1996	125	100 Lei. Brass center. Copper-Nickel ring. 37 mm. Nationl arms. Gymnast on balance beam. Plain with denomination edge. Piefort version.	—
Pn316	1996	—	100 Lei. Aluminum. KM#133.	45.00
Pn317	1996	—	100 Lei. Brass. KM#135.	50.00
Pn318	1996	—	500 Lei. Brass. KM#147. Arms without outline.	—
Pn319	1996	—	500 Lei. Aluminum. KM#147. Arms without outline.	—
Pn320	1996	—	500 Lei. Nickel. KM#147. Arms without outline.	—
Pn321	1996	—	500 Lei. Aluminum. KM#147. Arms without outline. Bimetal.	—
Pn322	1996	—	3000 Lei. Copper. 1 ECU. Dracula.	—
Pn323	1996	—	3000 Lei. 1 ECU. Dracula. Golden brass.	—
Pn324	1996	—	3000 Lei. Silver. 1 ECU. Dracula.	—
Pn325	1996	—	3000 Lei. Aluminum. 1 ECU. Dracula.	—
Pn326	1998	—	100 Lei. Silver. KM#119. Eiffel Tower. Golden brass.	—
PnB326	1996	125	100 Lei. Bronze.	30.00
Pn327	1998	—	100 Lei. Aluminum. KM#119. Eiffel Tower.	—
Pn328	1998	—	100 Lei. Brass. One player.	—
Pn329	1998	—	100 Lei. One player. Bimetal.	—
Pn330	1998	—	100 Lei. Brass. Two players.	—
Pn331	1998	—	100 Lei. Bi-Metallic. Two players.	—
Pn332	1998	—	100 Lei. Bi-Metallic. Gaelic cock.	—
Pn333	1998	—	500 Lei. Silver.	—
Pn334	1998	—	500 Lei. Golden brass.	—
Pn335	1998	—	500 Lei. Brass. KM#136.	25.00
Pn336	1998	—	1000 Lei. Silver. Arms at 6.	—
Pn337	1998	—	1000 Lei. Brass. Arms at 6.	45.00
Pn338	1998	—	1000 Lei. Arms at 9. Golden brass.	50.00
Pn339	1998	—	500 Lei. Brass. KM#147. Arms without outline.	35.00
Pn340	1998	—	500 Lei. Nickel. KM#147. Arms without outline.	40.00
Pn341	1998	—	500 Lei. Aluminum. KM#147. Arms without outline.	30.00
Pn342	1998	—	500 Lei. Aluminum. KM#147. Arms without outline. Bimetal.	45.00
Pn343	1998	—	100 Lei. Brass.	—
Pn344	1998	—	100 Lei. Bi-Metallic. KM#138.	—
Pn345	1998	—	100 Lei. Aluminum. KM#138.	—
Pn346	1998	—	100 Lei. Brass.	—
Pn347	1998	—	100 Lei. Silver.	—
Pn348	1998	—	100 Lei. Bi-Metallic.	—
Pn349	1998	—	100 Lei. Aluminum.	—
Pn350	1998	125	100 Lei. Aluminum. 37 mm. National arms. Two hockey players. Plain with denomination edge.	30.00
Pn350a	1998	—	100 Lei. Brass. Hockey.	35.00
Pn351A	1996	—	100 Lei. Brass. 37 mm. National arms. Skier. Plain with denomination edge.	30.00
Pn352	1998	—	100 Lei. Brass. Women single.	35.00
Pn353A	1998	—	100 Lei. Brass. Ice dancing.	35.00
Pn353	1998	125	100 Lei. Aluminum. 37 mm. National arms. Two ice dancers. Plain with denomination edge.	30.00
Pn354	1998	—	100 Lei. Brass. Ice dancing, without inscription.	35.00
Pn355	1998	—	100 Lei. Brass. Bobsled, without inscription.	40.00
Pn356	1998	—	100 Lei. Brass. Slalom, without inscription.	40.00
Pn357	1998	—	1000 Lei. Brass. Large.	—
Pn358	1998	—	1000 Lei. Brass. Thin.	—
Pn359	1998	—	1000 Lei. Golden brass.	—
Pn360	1999	—	100 Lei. Brass. Young.	—
Pn361	1999	—	100 Lei. Brass. Old.	—
Pn362	1999	—	100 Lei. Brass.	—
Pn363	1999	—	100 Lei. Brass.	—
Pn364	1999	—	100 Lei. Aluminum. Plain edge. KM146.	100
Pn365	1999	—	100 Lei. Aluminum. Plain edge. KM147.	100

PIEFORTS

KM#	Date	Mintage	Identification	Mkt Val
P3	1905	—	20 Bani. Aluminum-Bronze.	200
P4	1905	—	20 Bani. Bronze.	200
P5	1906	—	12-1/2 Lei. Gold.	—
P6	1906	—	25 Lei. Gold.	—
P7	1906	—	50 Lei. Lead.	325
P8	1906	—	50 Lei. Copper.	325
P9	1906	—	50 Lei. Silver.	1,200
P10	1906	—	50 Lei. Gold.	—

TRIAL STRIKES

KM#	Date	Mintage	Identification	Mkt Val
TS1	1906	—	5 Lei. Silver.	4,500
TS2	1906	—	100 Lei. Silver.	400
TS3	1910	—	Leu. Pewter. Milled edge. Thin planchet.	—
TS4	1910	—	Leu. Pewter. Milled edge. Thick planchet.	—
TS5	1996	—	10 Lei. Nickel Plated Steel. KM#134.	100

MINT SETS

KM#	Date	Mintage	Identification	Issue Price	Mkt Val
MS1	1982FM	—	KM#98-99	429	1,600
MS2	1983FM (4)	—	KM#98-101	850	4,300

PROOF SETS

KM#	Date	Mintage	Identification	Issue Price	Mkt Val
PS3	2000 (8)	—	KM109-111, 114-116, 145, 153	—	45.00

RUSSIA (U.S.S.R.)

Russia, formerly the central power of the Union of Soviet Socialist Republics and now of the Commonwealth of Independent States occupies the northern part of Asia and the eastern part of Europe, has an area of 17,075,400 sq. km. and a population of *146.2 million. Capital: Moscow. Exports include iron and steel, crude oil, timber, and nonferrous metals.

The first Russian dynasty was founded in Novgorod by the Viking Rurik in 862 A.D. under Yaroslav the Wise (1019-54). The subsequent Kievan state became one of the great commercial and cultural centers of Europe before falling to the Mongols of the Batu Khan, 13th century, who were suzerains of Russia until late in the 15th century when Ivan III threw off the Mongol yoke. The Russian Empire was enlarged, solidified and Westernized during the reigns of Ivan the Terrible, Peter the Great and Catherine the Great, and by 1881 extended to the Pacific and into Central Asia. Contemporary Russian history began in March of 1917 when Tsar Nicholas II abdicated under pressure and was replaced by a provisional government composed of both radical and conservative elements. This government rapidly lost ground to the Bolshevik wing of the Socialist Democratic Labor Party which attained power following the Bolshevik Revolution which began on Nov. 7, 1917. After the Russian Civil War, the regional governments, national states and armies became federal republics of the Russian Socialist Federal Soviet Republic. These autonomous republics united to form the Union of Soviet Socialist Republics that was established as a federation under the premiership of Lenin on Dec. 30, 1922.

In the fall of 1991, events moved swiftly in the Soviet Union. Estonia, Latvia and Lithuania won their independence and were recognized by Moscow, Sept. 6. The Commonwealth of Independent States was formed Dec. 8, 1991 in Mensk by Belarus, Russia and Ukraine. It was expanded at a summit Dec. 21, 1991 to include 11 of the 12 remaining republics (excluding Georgia) of the old U.S.S.R.

EMPIRE

RULER
Nicholas II, 1894-1917

MINT MARKS
Л – Leningrad, 1991
М – Moscow, 1990
СП – St. Petersburg, 1999
СПБ – St. Petersburg, 1724-1914
СПМД – St. Petersburg, 1999

(sp) (l) – LMD (ЛМД) monogram in oval, (Leningrad), (St. Petersburg) 1977-1997

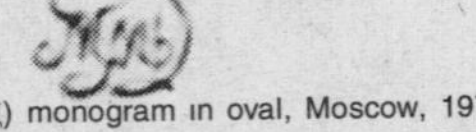

(m) – MMD (ММД) monogram in oval, Moscow, 1977-

MINT OFFICIALS' INITIALS

Leningrad Mint

Initials	Years	Mint Official
АГ	1921-22	A.F. Hartman
ПЛ	1922-27	P.V. Latishev

London Mint

Initials	Years	Mint Official
Т.Р.	1924	Thomas Ross
ФР	1924	Thomas Ross

St. Petersburg Mint

Initials	Years	Mint Official
ФЗ	1899-1901	Felix Zaleman
АР	1901-05	Alexander Redko
ЭБ	1906-13	Elikum Babayantz
ВС	1913-17	Victor Smirnov

NOTE: St. Petersburg Mint became Petrograd in 1914 and Leningrad in 1924. It was renamed St. Petersburg in 1991.

MONETARY SYSTEM
1/4 Kopek = Polushka ПОЛУШКА
1/2 Kopek = Denga, Denezhka ДЕНГА, ДЕНЕЖКА
Kopek = КОП_ИКА
(2, 3 & 4) Kopeks КОП_ИКИ
(5 and up) Kopeks КОП_ЕКЪ
(1924 – 5 and up) Kopeks КОПЕЕК
50 Kopeks = Poltina, Poltinnik ПОЛТИНА,...ПОЛРУБЛЪ
100 Kopeks = Rouble, Ruble РУБЛЪ
10 Roubles = Imperial ИМПЕРІАЛЪ
10 Roubles = Chervonetz ЧЕРВОНЕЦ

NOTE: Mintage figures for years after 1885 are for fiscal years and may or may not reflect actual rarity, the commemorative and 1917 silver figures being exceptions.

STANDARD COINAGE

Y# 47.1 1/4 KOPEK

3.0000 g., Copper **Ruler:** Nicholas II **Obv:** Crowned monogram above sprays **Rev:** Value, date

Date	Mintage	F	VF	XF	Unc	BU
1909	2,000,000	1.50	3.00	7.00	15.00	—
1910	8,000,000	4.00	8.00	15.00	30.00	—
1909-1910 Common date Proof	—	Value: 125				

Y# 47.2 POLUSHKA (1/4 KOPEK)

3.0000 g., Copper **Ruler:** Nicholas II **Obv:** Crowned monogram above sprays **Rev:** Value, date

Date	Mintage	F	VF	XF	Unc	BU
1915	500,000	2.00	5.00	10.00	20.00	—
1916	1,200,000	40.00	80.00	150	300	—

Y# 48.1 1/2 KOPEK

4.0000 g., Copper, 16 mm. **Ruler:** Nicholas II **Obv:** Crowned monogram above sprays **Rev:** Value and date

Date	Mintage	F	VF	XF	Unc	BU
1908СПБ	8,000,000	1.00	2.00	5.00	10.00	—
1909СПБ	49,500,000	1.00	2.00	5.00	15.00	—
1910СПБ	24,000,000	1.00	2.00	5.00	10.00	15.00
1911СПБ	35,800,000	1.00	2.00	5.00	10.00	15.00
1912СПБ	28,000,000	1.00	2.00	5.00	10.00	15.00
1913СПБ	50,000,000	0.75	1.50	3.00	6.00	10.00
1914СПБ	14,000,000	1.50	3.00	7.00	15.00	20.00
1908-14 Common date Proof	—	Value: 200				

Y# 48.2 1/2 KOPEK

4.0000 g., Copper **Ruler:** Nicholas II **Obv:** Crowned monogram above sprays **Rev:** Value and date **Note:** Struck at Petrograd without mint mark.

Date	Mintage	F	VF	XF	Unc	BU
1915	12,000,000	1.50	3.00	7.00	15.00	20.00
1916	9,400,000	1.50	3.00	7.00	15.00	20.00

Y# 9.2 KOPEK

4.0000 g., Copper, 21.5 mm. **Ruler:** Nicholas II **Obv:** Crowned double-headed imperial eagle within circle **Rev:** Value flanked by stars within beaded circle

Date	Mintage	F	VF	XF	Unc	BU
1901СПБ	30,000,000	0.50	1.00	2.00	8.00	—
1902СПБ	20,000,000	0.50	5.00	10.00	20.00	—
1903СПБ	74,400,000	0.50	1.00	2.00	8.00	—
1904СПБ	30,600,000	0.50	1.00	2.00	8.00	—
1905СПБ	23,000,000	0.50	1.00	2.00	8.00	—
1906СПБ	20,000,000	0.50	1.00	2.00	8.00	—
1907СПБ	20,000,000	0.50	1.00	2.00	8.00	—
1908СПБ	40,000,000	0.50	1.00	2.00	8.00	—
1909СПБ	27,500,000	0.50	1.00	2.00	8.00	—
1910СПБ	36,500,000	0.50	1.00	2.00	8.00	—
1911СПБ	38,150,000	0.50	1.00	2.00	8.00	—
1912СПБ	31,850,000	0.50	1.00	2.00	8.00	—
1913СПБ	61,500,000	0.50	1.00	2.00	8.00	—
1914СПБ	32,500,000	0.50	1.00	2.00	8.00	—
1901-14 Common date Proof	—	Value: 150				

Y# 9.3 KOPEK

4.0000 g., Copper **Ruler:** Nicholas II **Obv:** Crowned double-headed imperial eagle within circle **Rev:** Value flanked by stars within beaded circle **Note:** Struck at Petrograd without mint mark.

Date	Mintage	F	VF	XF	Unc	BU
1915	58,000,000	0.50	1.00	2.00	8.00	—
1916	46,500,000	1.00	2.00	3.00	8.00	—
1917 Unique	—	—	—	—	—	—

Y# 10.2 2 KOPEKS

Copper **Ruler:** Nicholas II **Obv:** Crowned double-headed imperial eagle within circle **Rev:** Value flanked by stars within circle

Date	Mintage	F	VF	XF	Unc	BU
1901СПБ	20,000,000	1.50	2.50	5.00	10.00	—
1902СПБ	10,000,000	1.50	2.50	5.00	10.00	—
1903СПБ	29,200,000	1.50	2.50	5.00	10.00	—
1904СПБ	13,300,000	1.50	2.50	5.00	10.00	—
1905СПБ	15,000,000	1.50	2.50	5.00	10.00	—
1906СПБ	6,250,000	1.50	2.50	5.00	10.00	—
1907СПБ	7,500,000	1.50	2.50	5.00	10.00	—
1908СПБ	19,000,000	1.50	2.50	5.00	10.00	—
1909СПБ	16,250,000	1.50	2.50	5.00	10.00	—
1910СПБ	12,000,000	1.50	2.50	5.00	10.00	—
1911СПБ	17,200,000	1.50	2.50	5.00	10.00	—
1912СПБ	17,050,000	1.50	2.50	5.00	10.00	—
1913СПБ	26,000,000	1.50	2.50	5.00	10.00	—
1914СПБ	20,000,000	1.50	2.50	5.00	10.00	—
1901-14 Common date proof	—	Value: 175				

Y# 10.3 2 KOPEKS

Copper **Ruler:** Nicholas II **Obv:** Crowned double-headed imperial eagle **Rev:** Value within circle **Note:** Struck at Petrograd without mint mark.

Date	Mintage	F	VF	XF	Unc	BU
1915	33,750,000	1.00	2.00	3.00	5.00	—
1916	31,500,000	1.00	2.00	3.00	5.00	—
Rare	—	—	—	—	—	—

Y# 11.2 3 KOPEKS

Copper **Ruler:** Nicholas II **Obv:** Crowned double imperial eagle within circle **Rev:** Value flanked by stars within beaded circle

Date	Mintage	F	VF	XF	Unc	BU
1901СПБ	10,000,000	1.50	3.00	6.00	15.00	—
1902СПБ	3,333,000	2.00	4.00	8.00	20.00	—
1903СПБ	11,400,000	1.50	3.00	6.00	15.00	—
1904СПБ	6,934,000	2.00	4.00	8.00	20.00	—
1905СПБ	3,333,000	2.00	4.00	8.00	20.00	—
1906СПБ	5,667,000	2.00	4.00	8.00	20.00	—
1907СПБ	2,500,000	2.00	4.00	8.00	20.00	—
1908СПБ	12,667,000	1.50	3.00	6.00	15.00	—
1909СПБ	6,733,000	1.50	3.00	6.00	15.00	—
1910СПБ	6,667,000	1.50	3.00	6.00	15.00	—
1911СПБ	9,467,000	1.50	3.00	6.00	15.00	—
1912СПБ	8,533,000	2.00	4.00	8.00	20.00	—
1913СПБ	15,333,000	1.50	3.00	6.00	15.00	—
1914СПБ	8,167,000	1.50	3.00	6.00	15.00	—
1901-14СПБ Common date proof	—	Value: 200				

Y# 11.3 3 KOPEKS

Copper **Ruler:** Nicholas II **Obv:** Crowned double-headed imperial eagle **Rev:** Value flanked by stars within beaded circle **Note:** Struck at Petrograd without mint mark.

Date	Mintage	F	VF	XF	Unc	BU
1915	19,833,000	1.00	2.00	6.00	20.00	—
1916	25,667,000	1.00	2.00	6.00	20.00	—
1917 Rare	—	—	—	—	—	—

Y# 19a.1 5 KOPEKS

0.8998 g., 0.5000 Silver .0144 oz. ASW **Ruler:** Nicholas II **Obv:** Crowned double-headed imperial eagle **Rev:** Crown above date and value within wreath **Edge:** Reeded

Date	Mintage	F	VF	XF	Unc	BU
1901СПБ ФЗ	5,790,000	1.50	3.00	7.00	15.00	30.00
1901СПБ АР	Inc. above	1.50	3.00	7.00	15.00	30.00
1902СПБ АР	6,000,000	1.50	3.00	7.00	15.00	30.00
1903СПБ АР	9,000,000	1.50	3.00	7.00	15.00	30.00
1904СПБ АР Rare	9	—	—	—	—	—
1905СПБ АР	10,000,000	1.50	3.00	7.00	15.00	30.00
1906СПБ ЭБ	4,000,000	1.50	3.00	7.00	15.00	30.00
1908СПБ ЭБ	400,000	1.50	3.00	7.00	15.00	30.00
1909СПБ ЭБ	3,100,000	1.50	3.00	7.00	15.00	30.00
1910СПБ ЭБ	2,500,000	1.50	3.00	7.00	15.00	30.00
1911СПБ ЭБ	2,700,000	1.50	3.00	7.00	15.00	30.00
1912СПБ ЭБ	3,000,000	1.50	3.00	7.00	15.00	30.00
1913СПБ ЭБ Proof	Inc. below	Value: 150				
1913СПБ ВС	1,300,000	1.50	3.00	7.00	15.00	30.00
1914СПБ ВС	4,200,000	1.50	3.00	7.00	15.00	30.00
1901-14 Common date proof	—	Value: 150				

Y# 19a.2 5 KOPEKS

0.8998 g., 0.5000 Silver .0144 oz. ASW **Ruler:** Nicholas II **Obv:** Crowned double-headed imperial eagle **Rev:** Crown above value and date within wreath **Note:** Struck at Petrograd without mint mark.

Date	Mintage	F	VF	XF	Unc	BU
1915 ВС	3,000,000	1.50	3.00	7.00	15.00	30.00

Y# 12.2 5 KOPEKS

Copper, 32.6 mm. **Ruler:** Nicholas II **Obv:** Crowned double-headed imperial eagle within circle **Rev:** Value flanked by stars within beaded circle

Date	Mintage	F	VF	XF	Unc	BU
1911СПБ	3,800,000	6.00	12.50	25.00	50.00	—
1912СПБ	2,700,000	10.00	17.50	35.00	70.00	—

Y# 12.3 5 KOPEKS

Copper **Ruler:** Nicholas II **Obv:** Crowned double-headed imperial eagle **Rev:** Value flanked by stars within beaded circle **Note:** Struck at Petrograd without mint mark.

Date	Mintage	F	VF	XF	Unc	BU
1916	8,000,000	40.00	80.00	150	250	—
1917 Rare	—	—	—	—	—	—

Y# 20a.1 10 KOPEKS

1.7996 g., 0.5000 Silver .0289 oz. ASW **Ruler:** Nicholas II **Obv:** Crowned double-headed imperial eagle, ribbons on crown **Rev:** Crown above value and date within wreath **Note:** Struck at Osaka, Japan without mintmaster initials.

Date	Mintage	F	VF	XF	Unc	BU
1916	70,001,000	BV	1.00	2.00	10.00	—

Y# 20a.2 10 KOPEKS

1.7996 g., 0.5000 Silver .0289 oz. ASW **Ruler:** Nicholas II **Obv:** Crowned double-headed imperial eagle, ribbons on crown **Rev:** Crown above value and date within wreath **Edge:** Reeded

Date	Mintage	F	VF	XF	Unc	BU
1901СПБ ФЗ	15,000,000	1.00	2.00	3.50	15.00	—
1901СПБ АР	Inc. above	1.00	2.00	3.50	15.00	—
1902СПБ АР	17,000,000	1.00	2.00	3.50	15.00	—
1903СПБ АР	28,500,000	1.00	2.00	3.50	15.00	—
1904СПБ АР	20,000,000	1.00	2.00	3.50	15.00	—
1905СПБ АР	25,000,000	1.00	2.00	3.50	15.00	—
1906СПБ ЭБ	17,500,000	1.00	2.00	3.50	15.00	—
1907СПБ ЭБ	—	1.00	2.00	3.50	15.00	—
1908СПБ ЭБ	8,210,000	1.00	2.00	3.50	15.00	—
1909СПБ ЭБ	25,290,000	1.00	2.00	4.00	15.00	—
1910СПБ ЭБ	20,000,000	1.00	2.00	4.00	15.00	—
1911СПБ ЭБ	19,180,000	1.00	2.00	4.00	15.00	—
1912СПБ ЭБ	20,000,000	1.00	2.00	4.00	15.00	—
1913СПБ ЭБ Proof	Inc. below	Value: 250				
1913СПБ ВС	7,250,000	1.00	2.00	4.00	15.00	—
1914СПБ ВС	51,250,000	1.00	2.00	4.00	15.00	—
1901-14 Common date proof	—	Value: 250				

Y# 20a.3 10 KOPEKS

1.7996 g., 0.5000 Silver .0289 oz. ASW **Ruler:** Nicholas II **Obv:** Crowned double-headed imperial eagle, ribbons on crown **Rev:** Crown above value and date within wreath **Note:** Struck at Petrograd without mintmaster initials.

Date	Mintage	F	VF	XF	Unc	BU
1915 ВС	82,500,000	1.00	2.00	3.00	6.00	—
1916 ВС	121,500,000	1.00	2.00	3.00	6.00	—
1917 ВС	17,600,000	—	20.00	30.00	80.00	—

Y# 21a.2 15 KOPEKS

2.6994 g., 0.5000 Silver .0434 oz. ASW **Ruler:** Nicholas II **Obv:** Crowned double-headed imperial eagle, ribbons on crown **Rev:** Crown above date and value within wreath **Edge:** Reeded

Date	Mintage	F	VF	XF	Unc	BU
1901СПБ ФЗ	6,670,000	3.00	6.00	12.00	25.00	—
1901СПБ АР	Inc. above	3.00	6.00	12.00	25.00	—
1902СПБ АР	28,667,000	1.50	3.00	7.00	15.00	—
1903СПБ АР	16,667,000	1.50	3.00	7.00	15.00	—
1904СПБ АР	15,600,000	1.50	3.00	7.00	15.00	—
1905СПБ АР	24,000,000	1.50	3.00	7.00	15.00	—
1906СПБ ЭБ	23,333,000	1.50	3.00	7.00	15.00	—
1907СПБ ЭБ	30,000,000	1.50	3.00	7.00	15.00	—
1908СПБ ЭБ	29,000,000	1.50	3.00	7.00	15.00	—
1909СПБ ЭБ	21,667,000	1.50	3.00	7.00	15.00	—
1911СПБ ЭБ	6,313,000	3.00	6.00	12.00	25.00	—
1912СПБ ВС	Inc. above	4.00	8.00	16.00	40.00	—
1912СПБ ЭБ Rare	13,333,000	—	—	—	—	—
1913СПБ ЭБ Proof	Inc. below	Value: 250				
1913СПБ ВС	5,300,000	3.00	6.00	12.00	25.00	—
1914СПБ ВС	43,367,000	1.50	3.00	7.00	15.00	—
1901-14 Common date proof	—	Value: 250				

Y# 21a.3 15 KOPEKS

2.6994 g., 0.5000 Silver .0434 oz. ASW **Ruler:** Nicholas II **Obv:** Crowned double-headed imperial eagle, ribbons on crown **Rev:** Crown above value and date within wreath **Note:** Struck at Petrograd without mintmaster initials.

Date	Mintage	F	VF	XF	Unc	BU
1915 ВС	59,333,000	1.00	2.00	3.00	10.00	—
1916 ВС	96,773,000	1.00	2.00	3.00	10.00	—
1917 ВС	14,320,000	—	20.00	30.00	80.00	—

Y# 21a.1 15 KOPEKS

2.6994 g., 0.5000 Silver .0434 oz. ASW **Ruler:** Nicholas II **Obv:** Crowned double-headed imperial eagle, ribbons on crown **Rev:** Crown above value and date within wreath **Edge:** Reeded **Note:** Struck at Osaka, Japan without mintmaster initials.

Date	Mintage	F	VF	XF	Unc	BU
1916	96,666,000	BV	1.50	3.00	10.00	—

Y# 22a.1 20 KOPEKS

3.5992 g., 0.5000 Silver .0579 oz. ASW **Ruler:** Nicholas II **Obv:** Crowned double-headed imperial eagle, ribbons on crown **Rev:** Crown above value and date within wreath

Date	Mintage	F	VF	XF	Unc	BU
1901СПБ ФЗ	7,750,000	2.00	4.00	8.00	15.00	—
1901СПБ АР Proof	Inc. above	Value: 300				
1902СПБ АР	10,000,000	2.00	4.00	8.00	15.00	—
1903СПБ АР	Inc. above	2.00	4.00	8.00	15.00	—
1904СПБ АР	13,000,000	2.00	4.00	8.00	15.00	—
1905СПБ АР	11,000,000	2.00	4.00	8.00	15.00	—
1906СПБ ЭБ	15,000,000	2.00	4.00	8.00	15.00	—
1907СПБ ЭБ	20,000,000	2.00	4.00	8.00	15.00	—
1908СПБ ЭБ	5,000,000	2.00	4.00	8.00	15.00	—
1909СПБ ЭБ	18,875,000	2.00	4.00	8.00	15.00	—
1910СПБ ЭБ	11,000,000	2.00	4.00	8.00	15.00	—
1911СПБ ЭБ	7,100,000	2.00	4.00	8.00	15.00	—
1912СПБ ЭБ	15,000,000	2.00	4.00	8.00	15.00	—
1912СПБ ВС Rare	Inc. above	—	—	—	—	—
1913СПБ ЭБ Proof	Inc. below	Value: 250				
1913СПБ ВС	4,250,000	2.00	4.00	8.00	15.00	—
1914СПБ ВС	52,750,000	BV	2.00	5.00	10.00	15.00
1901-14 Common date proof	—	Value: 250				

Y# 22a.2 20 KOPEKS

3.5992 g., 0.5000 Silver .0579 oz. ASW **Ruler:** Nicholas II **Obv:** Crowned double-headed imperial eagle, ribbons on crown **Rev:** Crown above value and date within wreath **Note:** Struck at Petrograd without mint mark.

Date	Mintage	F	VF	XF	Unc	BU
1915 ВС	105,500,000	BV	2.00	4.00	10.00	15.00
1916 ВС	131,670,000	BV	2.00	4.00	10.00	15.00
1917 ВС	3,500,000	—	25.00	35.00	100	—
1915-17 Common date proof	—	Value: 250				

Y# 57 25 KOPEKS

4.9990 g., 0.9000 Silver .1446 oz. ASW **Ruler:** Nicholas II **Obv:** Head left **Rev:** Crowned double-headed imperial eagle, ribbons on crown **Note:** Struck at St. Petersburg without mint mark.

Date	Mintage	F	VF	XF	Unc	BU
1901 Proof	Est. 200	Value: 1,250				

Y# 58.2 50 KOPEKS

9.9980 g., 0.9000 Silver .2893 oz. ASW **Ruler:** Nicholas II **Obv:** Head left **Rev:** Crowned double-headed imperial eagle, ribbons on crown **Note:** Without mint mark, moneyer's initials on edge.

Date	Mintage	F	VF	XF	Unc	BU
1901 АР	412,000	7.50	15.00	35.00	175	—
1901 ФЗ	Inc. above	7.50	15.00	35.00	175	—
1902 АР	36,000	10.00	20.00	50.00	200	—
1903 АР Proof	—	Value: 2,000				
1904 АР	4,010,000	100	200	400	1,200	—
1906 ЭБ	10,000	25.00	50.00	100	350	—
1907 ЭБ	200,000	10.00	20.00	50.00	200	—
1908 ЭБ	40,000	10.00	20.00	50.00	200	—
1909 ЭБ	50,000	10.00	20.00	50.00	200	—
1910 ЭБ	150,000	10.00	20.00	50.00	200	—
1911 ЭБ	800,000	10.00	20.00	40.00	150	—
1912 ЭБ	7,085,000	5.00	8.00	15.00	45.00	—
1913 ЭБ	6,420,000	7.50	15.00	35.00	125	—
1913 ВС	Inc. above	5.00	10.00	20.00	50.00	—

Date	Mintage	F	VF	XF	Unc	BU
1914 ВС	1,200,000	5.00	10.00	20.00	50.00	—
1901-14 Common date proof	—	Value: 500				

Y# 59.3 ROUBLE

19.9960 g., 0.9000 Silver .5786 oz. ASW **Ruler:** Nicholas II **Obv:** Head left **Rev:** Crowned double-headed imperial eagle, ribbons on crown **Note:** Without mint mark, moneyer's initials on edge.

Date	Mintage	F	VF	XF	Unc	BU
1901 ФЗ	2,608,000	12.00	25.00	45.00	275	600
1901 АР	Inc. above	40.00	80.00	150	575	4,000
1902 АР	140,000	25.00	45.00	75.00	425	1,200
1903 АР	56,000	45.00	90.00	185	750	—
1904 АР	12,000	85.00	165	350	950	—
1905 АР	21,000	45.00	90.00	185	750	—
1906 ЭБ	46,000	45.00	90.00	185	750	—
1907 ЭБ	400,000	25.00	45.00	75.00	425	2,000
1908 ЭБ	130,000	85.00	165	350	950	—
1909 ЭБ	51,000	40.00	80.00	180	600	—
1910 ЭБ	75,000	30.00	50.00	100	500	3,750
1911 ЭБ	129,000	28.00	48.00	85.00	450	2,750
1912 ЭБ	2,111,000	12.00	25.00	45.00	250	375
1913 ЭБ	22,000	60.00	120	250	750	—
1913 ВС	Inc. above	60.00	120	250	750	—
1914 ВС	536,000	25.00	45.00	90.00	425	2,000
1915 ВС	5,000	35.00	65.00	145	475	3,600

Note: Varieties exist with plain edge, these are mint errors and rare

Date	Mintage	F	VF	XF	Unc	BU
1901-15 Common date proof	—	Value: 4,000				

Y# 68 ROUBLE

19.9960 g., 0.9000 Silver .5786 oz. ASW, 34 mm. **Ruler:** Nicholas II **Subject:** Centennial - Napolean's Defeat **Obv:** Crowned double-headed imperial eagle with various crowned shields **Rev:** Inscription and date within beaded circle **Designer:** Alexander Vasulinskil

Date	Mintage	F	VF	XF	Unc	BU
1912 ЭБ	46,000	175	350	650	950	2,750
1912 ЭБ Proof	—	Value: 4,500				

Y# 69 ROUBLE

19.9960 g., 0.9000 Silver .5786 oz. ASW, 34 mm. **Ruler:** Nicholas II **Subject:** Alexander III Memorial **Obv:** Head left **Rev:** Monument **Designer:** Abraham Grilikez

Date	Mintage	F	VF	XF	Unc	BU
1912 ЭБ	2,100	750	1,600	2,750	5,000	9,500
1912 ЭБ Proof	—	Value: 10,000				

Y# 70 ROUBLE

19.9960 g., 0.9000 Silver .5786 oz. ASW, 34 mm. **Ruler:** Nicholas II **Subject:** 300th Anniversary - Romanov Dynasty **Obv:** Conjoined heads facing 1/4 right **Rev:** Crowned double-headed imperial eagle **Designer:** M.A. Kerzin **Note:** Struck at St. Petersburg without mint mark.

Date	Mintage	F	VF	XF	Unc	BU
1913 ВС	1,472,000	15.00	25.00	65.00	125	185

Y# 71 ROUBLE

19.9960 g., 0.9000 Silver .5786 oz. ASW, 34 mm. **Ruler:** Nicholas II **Subject:** 200th Anniversary - Battle of Gangut **Obv:** Armored bust right **Rev:** Crowned double-headed imperial eagle **Designer:** Alexander Vasulinskil

Date	Mintage	F	VF	XF	Unc	BU
1914 ВС	Est. 30,000	1,250	3,500	6,000	8,000	9,500

Note: Only 317 pieces were issued through 1917, but an unknown number of restrikes were made in the 1920's

Date	Mintage	F	VF	XF	Unc	BU
1914 ВС Proof	—	Value: 12,500				

Y# 62 5 ROUBLES

4.3013 g., 0.9000 Gold .1244 oz. AGW **Ruler:** Nicholas II **Obv:** Head left **Rev:** Crowned double-headed imperial eagle, ribbons on crown **Note:** Struck at St. Petersburg without mint mark.

Date	Mintage	F	VF	XF	Unc	BU
1901 ФЗ	7,500,000	—	—	BV	95.00	200
1901 АР	Inc. above	—	BV	90.00	110	220
1902 АР	6,240,000	—	—	BV	95.00	200
1903 АР	5,148,000	—	—	BV	95.00	200
1904 АР	2,016,000	—	—	BV	95.00	200
1906 ЭБ	10	—	—	7,000	10,000	—
1907 ЭБ	109	—	—	4,000	7,500	—
1909 ЭБ	—	—	BV	90.00	110	220
1910 ЭБ	200,000	—	BV	90.00	110	220
1911 ЭБ	100,000	BV	100	200	400	650
1901-11 Common date proof	—	Value: 2,500				

Y# 64 10 ROUBLES

8.6026 g., 0.9000 Gold .2489 oz. AGW **Ruler:** Nicholas II **Obv:** Head left **Rev:** Crowned double-headed imperial eagle, ribbons on crown **Note:** Without mint mark. Moneyer's initials on edge.

Date	Mintage	F	VF	XF	Unc	BU
1901 ФЗ	2,377,000	—	—	BV	190	360
1901 АР	Inc. above	—	—	BV	200	365
1902 АР	2,019,000	—	—	BV	190	360
1903 АР	2,817,000	—	—	BV	190	360
1904 АР	1,025,000	—	—	BV	190	360
1906 ЭБ Proof	10	Value: 15,000				
1909 ЭБ	50,000	—	BV	175	250	450
1910 ЭБ	100,000	—	BV	175	250	450
1911 ЭБ	50,000	—	BV	175	250	450
1901-11 Common date proof	—	Value: 4,500				

Y# A65 25 ROUBLES

32.2500 g., 0.9000 Gold .9332 oz. AGW **Ruler:** Nicholas II **Obv:** Head left **Rev:** Crowned double imperial eagle, ribbons on crown, within circle flanked by rosettes **Rev. Legend:** 2-1/2 ИМПЕРIАЛЪА (IMPERIALS) **Note:** Struck at St. Petersburg without mint mark.

Date	Mintage	F	VF	XF	Unc	BU
1908	150	—	—	70,000	90,000	—
1908 Proof	25	Value: 95,000				

Y# B65 37 ROUBLES 50 KOPEKS

32.2500 g., 0.9000 Gold .9335 oz. AGW **Ruler:** Nicholas II **Obv:** Head left **Rev:** Crowned double-headed imperial eagle within beaded circle **Rev. Legend:** 100 ФРАНКОВЪ **Note:** Without mint mark.

Date	Mintage	F	VF	XF	Unc	BU
1902	225	—	—	—	75,000	—

Note: UBS sale #67 9-06, near Unc realized $68,750.

Date	Mintage	F	VF	XF	Unc	BU
1902 Proof	—	Value: 75,000				

Note: Impaired Proofs are valued at approximately $60,000.

Y# B65a 37 ROUBLES 50 KOPEKS

Copper-Nickel **Ruler:** Nicholas II **Obv:** Head left **Rev:** Crowned double headed imperial eagle within beaded circle **Rev. Inscription:** Letter "P" after "1902 G" **Edge:** Plain **Note:** Gold plated specimens were done outside the mint.

Date	Mintage	F	VF	XF	Unc	BU
1902 (1991) P Restrike	—	—	—	—	15.00	—

GOLD MINE INGOTS

During the late 19th and early 20th century, Russian law provided that gold mine owners who supplied gold to the mints should receive back whatever silver was recovered during refining of the gold. The silver was returned in the form of circular ingots of various weights which resembled coins. These pieces have often been erroneously described as Russian trade coins for use in Mongolia, China, and Turkestan.

Note: Both the Doyla and the Zolotnik are weights, not denominations.

KM# 1 24 DOLYA

1.0664 g., 0.9900 Silver .0343 oz. ASW **Ruler:** Nicholas II **Obv:** Crowned double headed eagle within circle **Rev:** Value

Date	Mintage	F	VF	XF	Unc	BU
ND(1901)	—	—	350	450	650	—

KM# 2 ZOLOTNIK

4.2656 g., 0.9900 Silver .1371 oz. ASW **Ruler:** Nicholas II **Obv:** Crowned double headed eagle within small circle **Rev:** Value

Date	Mintage	F	VF	XF	Unc	BU
ND(1901)	—	—	300	400	600	—

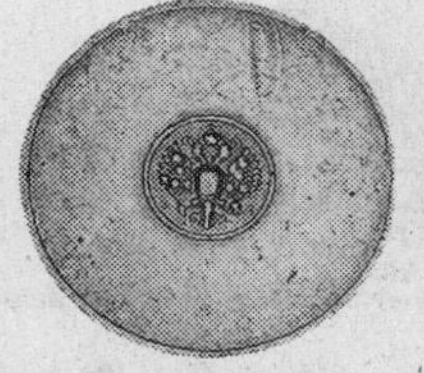

KM# 3 3 ZOLOTNIKS
12.7969 g., 0.9900 Silver .4114 oz. ASW **Ruler:** Nicholas II **Obv:** Crowned double headed eagle within small circle **Rev:** Value

Date	Mintage	F	VF	XF	Unc	BU
ND(1901)	—	—	1,000	1,500	2,000	—

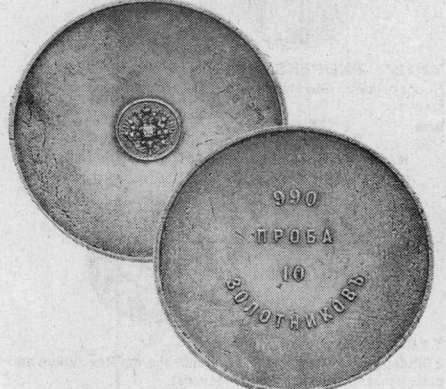

KM# 4 10 ZOLOTNIKS
42.6563 g., 0.9900 Silver 1.3714 oz. ASW **Ruler:** Nicholas II **Obv:** Crowned double headed eagle within small circle **Rev:** Value

Date	Mintage	F	VF	XF	Unc	BU
ND(1901)	—	—	350	550	850	—

РСФСР (R.S.F.S.R.)
(Russian Soviet Federated Socialist Republic)
STANDARD COINAGE

Y# 80 10 KOPEKS
1.8000 g., 0.5000 Silver .0289 oz. ASW **Obv:** National arms **Rev:** Value and date within beaded circle, star on top divides wreath

Date	Mintage	F	VF	XF	Unc	BU
1921	950,000	5.00	10.00	25.00	50.00	—
1921 Proof	—	Value: 375				
1922	18,640,000	1.00	2.00	4.50	12.00	—
1922 Proof	—	Value: 275				
1923	33,424,000	1.00	2.00	4.00	10.00	—
1923 Proof	—	Value: 225				

Y# 81 15 KOPEKS
2.7000 g., 0.5000 Silver .0434 oz. ASW **Obv:** National arms within circle **Rev:** Value and date within beaded circle, star on top divides wreath

Date	Mintage	F	VF	XF	Unc	BU
1921	933,000	6.00	12.00	30.00	60.00	—
1921 Proof	—	Value: 400				
1922	13,633,000	2.00	3.00	6.00	16.00	—
1922 Proof	—	Value: 250				
1923	28,504,000	1.50	2.50	4.50	12.00	—
1923 Proof	—	Value: 200				

Y# 82 20 KOPEKS
3.6000 g., 0.5000 Silver .0578 oz. ASW **Obv:** National arms within circle **Rev:** Value and date within beaded circle, star on top divides wreath **Note:** Varieties exist.

Date	Mintage	F	VF	XF	Unc	BU
1921	825,000	6.00	12.00	30.00	60.00	—
1921 Proof	—	Value: 500				
1922	14,220,000	2.00	4.00	8.00	20.00	—
1922 Proof	—	Value: 275				
1923	27,580,000	2.00	3.50	7.00	15.00	—
1923 Proof	—	Value: 225				

Y# 83 50 KOPEKS
9.9980 g., 0.9000 Silver .2893 oz. ASW **Obv:** National arms within beaded circle **Rev:** Value in center of star within beaded circle **Edge Lettering:** Mintmaster's initials

Date	Mintage	F	VF	XF	Unc	BU
1921 АГ	1,400,000	5.50	7.50	12.00	28.00	—
1921 АГ Proof	—	Value: 750				
1922 АГ	8,224,000	5.50	7.50	12.00	28.00	—
1922 АГ Proof	—	Value: 950				
1922 ПЛ	Inc. above	5.50	7.50	12.00	28.00	—
1922 ПЛ Proof	—	Value: 650				

Y# 84 ROUBLE
19.9960 g., 0.9000 Silver .5786 oz. ASW **Obv:** National arms within beaded circle **Rev:** Value in center of star within beaded circle **Edge Lettering:** Mintmaster's initials **Note:** Varieties exist.

Date	Mintage	F	VF	XF	Unc	BU
1921 АГ	1,000,000	9.50	13.50	25.00	70.00	95.00
1921 АГ Proof	—	Value: 2,250				
1922 АГ	2,050,000	11.00	18.50	35.00	90.00	115
1922 АГ Proof	—	Value: 3,000				
1922 ПЛ	Inc. above	11.00	18.50	35.00	90.00	115
1922 ПЛ Proof	—	Value: 2,750				

TRADE COINAGE

Y# 85 CHERVONETZ (10 Roubles)
8.6026 g., 0.9000 Gold .2489 oz. AGW **Obv:** National arms, PCØCP below arms **Rev:** Standing figure with head right **Edge Lettering:** Mintmaster's initials

Date	Mintage	F	VF	XF	Unc	BU
1923 ПЛ	2,751,000	275	400	600	750	1,250
1923 ПЛ Proof	—	Value: 8,000				
1975	250,000	—	—	—	BV+10%	—
1976 ЛМД	1,000,000	—	—	—	BV+10%	—
1976 Rare	—	—	—	—	—	—
1977 ММД	1,000,000	—	—	—	BV+10%	—
1977 ЛМД	1,000,000	—	—	—	BV+10%	—
1978 ММД	350,000	—	—	—	BV+10%	—
1979 ММД	1,000,000	—	—	—	BV+10%	—
1980 ЛМД	900,000	—	—	—	BV+10%	—
1980 ММД	—	—	—	—	—	—
1980 ММД Proof	100,000	Value: 195				
1981 ММД	1,000,000	—	—	—	BV+10%	—
1981 ЛМД Rare	—	—	—	—	—	—
1982 ММД	65,000	—	—	—	BV+10%	—
1982 ЛМД Rare	—	—	—	—	—	—

Y# A86 CHERVONETZ (10 Roubles)
8.6026 g., 0.9000 Gold .2489 oz. AGW **Obv:** National arms with CCCP below **Rev:** Standing figure with head right

Date	Mintage	F	VF	XF	Unc	BU
1925 Unique	600,000	—	—	—	—	—

Note: Chervonetz were first struck in 1923 under the R.S.F.S.R. government; in 1925 the U.S.S.R. government attempted a new issue of these coins, of which only one remaining coin is known; from 1975 to 1982 the U.S.S.R. government continued striking the original type with new dates

СССР (U.S.S.R.)
(Union of Soviet Socialist Republics)
STANDARD COINAGE

Y# 75 1/2 KOPEK
Copper **Obv:** CCCP within circle **Rev:** Value and date

Date	Mintage	F	VF	XF	Unc	BU
1925	45,380,000	4.00	8.00	16.00	30.00	—
1927	45,380,000	4.00	8.00	16.00	30.00	—
1927 Proof	—	Value: 350				
1928	—	6.00	11.00	21.00	45.00	—

Y# 76 KOPEK
Bronze **Obv:** National arms within circle **Rev:** Value and date within oat sprigs

Date	Mintage	F	VF	XF	Unc	BU
1924	34,705,000	5.00	10.00	20.00	45.00	—
Note: Reeded edge						
1924 Proof	—	Value: 400				
Note: Reeded edge						
1924	Inc. above	30.00	60.00	120	250	—
Note: Plain edge						
1925	141,806,000	45.00	90.00	160	275	—

Y# 91 KOPEK
Aluminum-Bronze **Obv:** National arms within circle **Rev:** Value and date within oat sprigs **Note:** Varieties exist.

Date	Mintage	F	VF	XF	Unc	BU
1926	87,915,000	1.00	2.00	4.00	8.00	—
1926 Proof	—	Value: 200				
1927	—	1.00	2.00	4.00	8.00	—
1928	—	0.50	1.00	2.00	5.00	—
1929	95,950,000	0.50	1.00	2.00	5.00	—
1930	85,351,000	1.50	4.00	6.00	10.00	—
1931	106,100,000	0.50	1.00	2.00	5.00	—
1932	56,900,000	0.50	1.00	2.00	5.00	—
1933	111,257,000	0.50	1.00	2.00	5.00	—
1934	100,245	1.00	3.00	5.00	10.00	—
1935	66,405,000	0.50	1.00	2.00	6.00	—

Y# 98 KOPEK
Aluminum-Bronze **Obv:** National arms **Rev:** Value and date within oat sprigs

Date	Mintage	F	VF	XF	Unc	BU
1935	—	4.00	8.00	10.00	15.00	—
Note: Mintage inc.Y91						
1936	132,204,000	1.00	2.00	4.00	8.00	—

Y# 105 KOPEK
Aluminum-Bronze **Obv:** National arms **Rev:** Value and date within oat sprigs **Note:** Varieties exist.

Date	Mintage	F	VF	XF	Unc	BU
1937	—	0.50	1.00	2.00	4.00	—
1938	—	0.50	1.00	2.00	4.00	—
1939	—	0.50	1.00	2.00	4.00	—
1940	—	0.50	1.00	2.00	4.00	—
1941	—	1.00	2.00	3.00	6.00	—
1945	—	1.00	2.00	3.00	6.00	—
1946	—	1.00	2.00	3.00	6.00	—

Y# 112 KOPEK

Aluminum-Bronze **Obv:** National arms **Rev:** Value and date within oat sprigs **Note:** Varieties exist.

Date	Mintage	F	VF	XF	Unc	BU
1948	—	1.00	2.00	3.00	5.00	—
1949	—	1.00	2.00	3.00	5.00	—
1950	—	1.00	2.00	3.00	8.00	—
1951	—	1.00	2.00	3.00	8.00	—
1952	—	0.70	1.00	2.00	3.00	—
1953	—	0.70	1.00	2.00	3.00	—
1954	—	0.70	1.00	2.00	3.00	—
1955	—	0.70	1.00	2.00	3.00	—
1956	—	0.70	1.00	2.00	3.00	—
1957 Rare	—	—	—	—	—	—

Y# 119 KOPEK

Aluminum-Bronze **Obv:** National arms **Rev:** Value and date within oat sprigs

Date	Mintage	F	VF	XF	Unc	BU
1957	—	1.00	2.00	4.00	12.00	—

Y# 126 KOPEK

Copper-Nickel **Obv:** National arms **Rev:** Value and date within oat sprigs

Date	Mintage	F	VF	XF	Unc	BU
1958	30,265,000	—	—	—	300	—

Note: Never officially released for circulation; majority of mintage remelted

Y# 126a KOPEK

1.0000 g., Brass, 15.05 mm. **Obv:** National arms **Rev:** Value and date above spray **Note:** Varieties exist.

Date	Mintage	F	VF	XF	Unc	BU
1961	—	0.10	0.15	0.25	1.00	—
1962	—	0.10	0.15	0.25	0.50	—
1963	—	0.10	0.15	0.25	0.50	—
1964	—	0.20	0.30	0.50	2.00	—
1965	—	0.10	0.15	0.25	0.50	—
1966	—	0.10	0.15	0.25	0.50	—
1967	—	0.10	0.15	0.25	0.50	—
1968	—	0.10	0.15	0.25	0.50	—
1969	—	0.10	0.15	0.25	0.50	—
1970	—	0.10	0.15	0.25	0.50	—
1971	—	0.10	0.15	0.25	0.50	—
1972	—	0.10	0.15	0.25	0.50	—
1973	—	0.10	0.15	0.25	0.50	—
1974	—	0.10	0.15	0.25	0.50	—
1975	—	0.10	0.15	0.25	0.50	—
1976	—	0.10	0.15	0.25	0.50	—
1977	—	0.10	0.15	0.25	0.50	—
1978	—	0.10	0.15	0.25	0.50	—
1979	—	0.10	0.15	0.25	0.50	—
1980	—	0.10	0.15	0.25	0.50	—
1981	—	0.10	0.15	0.25	0.50	—
1982	—	0.10	0.15	0.25	0.50	—
1983	—	0.10	0.15	0.25	0.50	—
1984	—	0.10	0.15	0.25	0.50	—
1985	—	0.10	0.15	0.25	0.50	—
1986	—	0.10	0.15	0.25	0.50	—
1987	—	0.10	0.15	0.25	0.50	—
1988	—	0.10	0.15	0.25	0.50	—
1989	—	0.10	0.15	0.20	0.30	—
1990	—	0.10	0.15	0.20	0.30	—
1991 М	—	0.10	0.15	0.20	0.30	—
1991 Л	—	0.10	0.15	0.20	0.30	—

Y# 77 2 KOPEKS

Bronze **Obv:** National arms **Rev:** Value and date within oat sprigs **Note:** Varieties exist.

Date	Mintage	F	VF	XF	Unc	BU
1924	119,996,000	5.00	12.00	22.00	50.00	—
Note: Reeded edge						
1924	Inc. above	30.00	60.00	120	250	—
Note: Plain edge						
1925 Rare	Inc. above	—	—	—	800	—

Y# 92 2 KOPEKS

Aluminum-Bronze **Obv:** National arms within circle **Rev:** Value and date within oat sprigs **Note:** Varieties exist.

Date	Mintage	F	VF	XF	Unc	BU
1926	105,053,000	0.50	1.00	2.00	4.00	—
1926 Proof	—	Value: 200				
1927 Rare	—	—	—	—	800	—
1928	—	0.50	1.00	2.00	4.00	—
1929	80,000,000	0.65	1.25	2.50	5.00	—
1930	134,186,000	0.50	1.00	2.00	4.00	—
1931	99,523,000	0.50	1.00	2.00	4.00	—
1932	39,573,000	0.65	1.25	2.50	4.50	—
1933	54,874,000	2.00	4.00	6.00	10.00	—
1934	61,574,000	0.65	1.25	2.50	4.50	—
1935	81,121,000	0.65	1.25	2.50	5.00	—

Y# 99 2 KOPEKS

Aluminum-Bronze **Obv:** National arms **Rev:** Value and date within oat sprigs **Note:** Varieties exist.

Date	Mintage	F	VF	XF	Unc	BU
1935	—	1.00	2.00	3.50	9.00	—
1936	94,354,000	1.00	2.00	3.00	7.00	—

Y# 106 2 KOPEKS

Aluminum-Bronze **Obv:** National arms **Rev:** Value and date within oat sprigs

Date	Mintage	F	VF	XF	Unc	BU
1937	—	0.50	1.00	2.00	3.00	—
1938	—	0.50	1.00	2.00	3.00	—
1939	—	0.50	1.00	2.00	3.00	—
1940	—	0.50	1.00	2.00	3.00	—
1941	—	0.50	1.00	2.00	3.00	—
1945	—	0.65	1.25	2.50	5.00	—
1946	—	0.50	1.00	2.00	4.00	—
1948	—	40.00	70.00	130	225	—
Note: Five ribbons on each wreath						

Y# 113 2 KOPEKS

Aluminum-Bronze **Obv:** National arms **Rev:** Value and date within oat sprigs **Note:** Varieties exist.

Date	Mintage	F	VF	XF	Unc	BU
1948	—	0.50	1.00	1.50	2.50	—
1949	—	0.50	1.00	1.50	2.50	—
1950	—	0.25	0.50	1.00	2.50	—
1951	—	0.50	1.00	2.00	6.00	—
1952	—	0.50	1.00	1.50	3.00	—
1953	—	0.50	1.00	1.50	2.50	—
1954	—	0.50	1.00	1.50	2.50	—
1955	—	0.50	1.00	1.50	2.50	—
1956	—	0.50	1.00	1.50	2.50	—

Y# 120 2 KOPEKS

Aluminum-Bronze **Obv:** National arms **Rev:** Value and date within oat sprigs

Date	Mintage	F	VF	XF	Unc	BU
1957	—	1.00	2.00	4.00	9.00	—

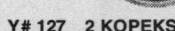

Y# 127 2 KOPEKS

Copper-Nickel **Obv:** National arms **Rev:** Value and date within sprays

Date	Mintage	F	VF	XF	Unc	BU
1958	39,591,000	—	—	—	300	—

Note: Never officially released for circulation; majority of mintage remelted

Y# 127a 2 KOPEKS

2.0000 g., Brass, 18 mm. **Obv:** National arms **Rev:** Value and date within sprays **Note:** Varieties exist.

Date	Mintage	F	VF	XF	Unc	BU
1961	—	0.10	0.15	0.25	0.50	—
1962	—	0.10	0.15	0.25	0.50	—
1963	—	0.10	0.15	0.25	0.50	—
1964	—	0.15	0.25	0.50	1.00	—
1965	—	0.10	0.15	0.25	0.50	—
1966	—	0.10	0.15	0.25	0.50	—
1967	—	0.10	0.15	0.25	0.50	—
1968	—	0.10	0.15	0.25	0.50	—
1969	—	0.10	0.15	0.25	0.50	—
1970	—	0.10	0.15	0.25	0.50	—
1971	—	0.10	0.15	0.25	0.50	—
1972	—	0.10	0.15	0.25	0.50	—
1973	—	0.10	0.15	0.25	0.50	—
1974	—	0.10	0.15	0.25	0.50	—
1975	—	0.10	0.15	0.25	0.50	—
1976	—	0.10	0.15	0.25	0.50	—
1977	—	0.10	0.15	0.25	0.50	—
1978	—	0.10	0.15	0.25	0.50	—
1979	—	0.10	0.15	0.25	0.50	—
1980	—	0.10	0.15	0.25	0.50	—
1981	—	0.10	0.15	0.25	0.50	—
1982	—	0.10	0.15	0.25	0.50	—
1983	—	0.10	0.15	0.25	0.50	—
1984	—	0.10	0.15	0.25	0.50	—
1985	—	0.10	0.15	0.25	0.50	—
1986	—	0.10	0.15	0.25	0.50	—
1987	—	0.10	0.15	0.25	0.50	—
1988	—	0.10	0.15	0.25	0.50	—
1989	—	0.10	0.15	0.20	0.35	—
1990	—	0.10	0.15	0.20	0.35	—
1991 М	—	0.10	0.15	0.20	0.35	—
1991 Л	—	0.10	0.15	0.20	0.35	—

Y# 78 3 KOPEKS

Bronze **Obv:** National arms within circle **Rev:** Value and date within oat sprigs **Note:** Varieties exist.

Date	Mintage	F	VF	XF	Unc	BU
1924	101,283,000	50.00	100	175	275	—
Note: Reeded edge						
1924	Inc. above	6.00	12.50	25.00	65.00	—
Note: Plain edge						

Y# 93 3 KOPEKS

Aluminum-Bronze **Obv:** National arms within circle **Rev:** Value and date within oat sprigs **Note:** Varieties exist.

Date	Mintage	F	VF	XF	Unc	BU
1926	19,940,000	1.25	2.00	4.00	7.00	—
1926 Proof	—	Value: 225				
1926 Rare	—	—	—	—	—	—
Note: Obverse of Y#100						
1927	—	5.00	10.00	20.00	40.00	—
1928	—	1.00	2.00	4.00	7.00	—
1929	50,150,000	1.00	2.00	4.00	8.00	—
1930	74,159,000	0.75	1.50	3.00	5.00	—
1931	121,168,000	1.00	2.00	3.00	5.00	—
1931 Rare	—	—	—	—	—	—
Note: Without CCCP obverse						
1932	37,718,000	1.00	2.00	3.00	5.00	—
1933	44,764,000	1.00	2.00	3.50	6.00	—
1934	44,529,000	1.00	2.00	3.50	6.00	—
1935	58,303,000	1.00	2.00	4.00	7.00	—
1937 Rare	—	—	—	—	—	—

Y# 100 3 KOPEKS

Aluminum-Bronze **Obv:** National arms **Rev:** Value and date within oat sprigs **Note:** Varieties exist.

Date	Mintage	F	VF	XF	Unc	BU
1935	—	1.00	3.00	7.00	14.00	—
1936	62,757,000	1.00	2.00	5.00	10.00	—

Y# 107 3 KOPEKS

Aluminum-Bronze **Obv:** National arms **Rev:** Value and date within oat sprigs **Note:** Varieties exist.

Date	Mintage	F	VF	XF	Unc	BU
1937	—	0.50	1.00	2.00	4.00	—
1938	—	0.50	1.00	2.00	4.00	—
1939	—	0.50	1.00	2.00	4.00	—
1940	—	0.50	1.00	2.00	3.00	—
1941	—	0.50	1.00	2.00	4.00	—
1943	—	0.50	1.00	2.50	5.00	—
1945	—	3.00	5.00	10.00	12.50	—
1946	—	0.50	1.00	2.50	5.00	—
1948 Five ribbons on each wreath	—	40.00	70.00	130	225	—

Y# 114 3 KOPEKS

Aluminum-Bronze **Obv:** National arms **Rev:** Value and date within oat sprigs **Note:** Varieties exist.

Date	Mintage	F	VF	XF	Unc	BU
1946 Rare	—	—	—	—	—	—
1948	—	0.50	1.00	2.50	5.00	—
1949	—	0.50	1.00	2.00	4.00	—
1950	—	0.50	1.00	2.00	4.00	—
1951	—	0.75	1.50	3.00	7.00	—
1952	—	0.50	1.00	2.00	4.00	—
1953	—	0.50	1.00	2.00	3.50	—
1954	—	0.50	1.00	2.00	3.50	—
1955	—	0.50	1.00	2.00	3.50	—
1956	—	0.50	1.00	2.00	3.50	—
1957	—	5.00	10.00	30.00	50.00	—

Y# 121 3 KOPEKS

Aluminum-Bronze **Obv:** National arms **Rev:** Value and date within oat sprigs

Date	Mintage	F	VF	XF	Unc	BU
1957	—	1.00	2.00	4.00	9.00	—

Y# 128 3 KOPEKS

Copper-Zinc **Obv:** National arms **Rev:** Value and date within sprigs

Date	Mintage	F	VF	XF	Unc	BU
1958	26,676,000	—	—	—	300	—

Note: Never officially released for circulation; majority of mintage remelted

Y# 128a 3 KOPEKS

3.0000 g., Aluminum-Bronze, 22.05 mm. **Obv:** National arms **Rev:** Value and date within sprigs **Note:** Varieties exist.

Date	Mintage	F	VF	XF	Unc	BU
1961	—	0.10	0.15	0.25	0.60	—
1962	—	0.25	0.50	1.00	2.00	—
1965	—	0.25	0.50	1.00	2.00	—
1966	—	0.10	0.15	0.25	0.60	—
1967	—	0.10	0.15	0.25	0.60	—
1968	—	0.10	0.15	0.25	0.60	—
1969	—	0.10	0.15	0.25	0.60	—
1970	—	0.10	0.15	0.25	0.60	—
1971	—	0.10	0.15	0.25	0.60	—
1972	—	0.10	0.15	0.25	0.60	—
1973	—	0.10	0.15	0.25	0.60	—
1974	—	0.10	0.15	0.25	0.60	—
1975	—	0.10	0.15	0.25	0.60	—
1976	—	0.10	0.15	0.25	0.60	—
1977	—	0.10	0.15	0.25	0.60	—
1978	—	0.10	0.15	0.25	0.60	—
1979	—	0.10	0.15	0.25	0.60	—
1980	—	0.10	0.15	0.25	0.60	—
1981	—	0.10	0.15	0.25	0.60	—
1982	—	0.10	0.15	0.25	0.60	—
1983	—	0.10	0.15	0.25	0.60	—
1984	—	0.10	0.15	0.25	0.60	—
1985	—	0.10	0.15	0.25	0.60	—
1986	—	0.10	0.15	0.25	0.60	—
1987	—	0.10	0.15	0.25	0.60	—
1988	—	0.10	0.15	0.25	0.60	—
1989	—	0.10	0.15	0.20	0.40	—
1990	—	0.10	0.15	0.20	0.40	—
1991 М	—	0.10	0.15	0.20	0.40	—
1991 Л	—	0.10	0.15	0.20	0.40	—

Y# 79 5 KOPEKS

Bronze **Obv:** National arms within circle **Rev:** Value and date within oat sprigs **Note:** Várieties exist.

Date	Mintage	F	VF	XF	Unc	BU
1924	88,510,000	50.00	100	175	275	—
Note: Reeded edge						
1924	Inc. above	7.00	15.00	30.00	75.00	—
Note: Plain edge						

Y# 94 5 KOPEKS

Aluminum-Bronze **Obv:** National arms **Rev:** Value and date **Note:** Varieties exist.

Date	Mintage	F	VF	XF	Unc	BU
1926	14,697,000	2.00	4.00	8.00	15.00	—
1926 Proof	—	Value: 250				
1927	—	20.00	60.00	100	150	—
1928	—	2.00	4.00	8.00	12.00	—
1929	20,220,000	5.00	10.00	12.00	15.00	—
1930	44,490,000	1.00	2.00	3.00	6.00	—
1931	89,540,000	1.00	2.00	3.00	6.00	—
1932	65,100,000	1.00	2.00	3.00	6.00	—
1933	18,135,000	25.00	50.00	100	300	—
1934	5,354,000	25.00	50.00	90.00	120	—
1935	11,735,000	3.00	6.00	15.00	50.00	—

Y# 101 5 KOPEKS

Aluminum-Bronze **Obv:** National arms **Rev:** Value and date within oat sprigs **Note:** Varieties exist.

Date	Mintage	F	VF	XF	Unc	BU
1935	—	2.00	4.00	9.00	26.00	—
1936	5,242,000	2.00	4.00	9.00	28.00	—

Y# 108 5 KOPEKS

Aluminum-Bronze **Obv:** National arms **Rev:** Value and date within oat sprigs **Note:** Varieties exist.

Date	Mintage	F	VF	XF	Unc	BU
1937	—	2.00	4.00	9.00	28.00	—
1938	—	1.00	2.00	3.00	5.00	—
1939	—	1.00	2.00	3.00	5.00	—
1940	—	1.00	2.00	3.00	5.00	—
1941	—	1.00	2.00	3.00	5.00	—
1943	—	1.00	2.00	3.00	5.00	—
1945	—	5.00	8.00	15.00	20.00	—
1946	—	2.00	3.00	4.00	8.00	—

Y# 115 5 KOPEKS

Aluminum-Bronze **Obv:** National arms **Rev:** Value and date withing oat sprigs **Note:** Varieties exist.

Date	Mintage	F	VF	XF	Unc	BU
1948	—	1.00	2.00	3.00	5.00	—
1949	—	1.00	2.00	3.00	4.00	—
1950	—	1.00	2.00	3.00	4.00	—
1951	—	4.00	6.00	8.00	12.00	—
1952	—	1.00	2.00	3.00	5.00	—
1953	—	1.00	2.00	3.00	5.00	—
1954	—	1.00	2.00	3.00	5.00	—
1955	—	1.00	2.00	3.00	5.00	—
1956	—	1.00	2.00	3.00	5.00	—

Y# 122 5 KOPEKS

Aluminum-Bronze **Obv:** National arms **Rev:** Value and date within oat sprigs **Note:** Varieties exist.

Date	Mintage	F	VF	XF	Unc	BU
1957	—	2.00	4.00	6.00	9.00	—

Y# 129 5 KOPEKS

Copper-Zinc **Obv:** National arms **Rev:** Value and date within sprigs

Date	Mintage	F	VF	XF	Unc	BU
1958	61,119,000	—	—	—	600	—

Note: Never officially released for circulation; majority of mintage remelted

Y# 129a 5 KOPEKS

5.0000 g., Aluminum-Bronze, 25.1 mm. **Obv:** National arms **Rev:** Value and date within sprigs **Note:** Varieties exist.

Date	Mintage	F	VF	XF	Unc	BU
1961	—	0.20	0.30	0.50	1.00	—
1962	—	0.20	0.30	0.50	1.00	—
1965	—	3.00	5.00	8.00	12.00	—
1966	—	2.00	4.00	7.00	12.00	—
1967	—	0.50	1.00	1.50	3.00	—
1968	—	0.50	1.00	1.50	3.00	—
1969	—	2.00	4.00	6.00	10.00	—
1970	—	10.00	15.00	35.00	60.00	—
1971	—	2.00	4.00	6.00	10.00	—
1972	—	2.00	4.00	6.00	10.00	—
1973	—	1.00	1.50	2.00	3.00	—
1974	—	0.10	0.20	0.50	1.00	—
1975	—	0.10	0.20	0.50	1.00	—
1976	—	0.10	0.15	0.30	0.75	—
1977	—	0.10	0.15	0.30	0.75	—
1978	—	0.10	0.15	0.30	0.75	—
1979	—	0.10	0.15	0.30	0.75	—
1980	—	0.10	0.15	0.30	0.75	—
1981	—	0.10	0.15	0.30	0.75	—
1982	—	0.10	0.15	0.30	0.70	—
1983	—	0.10	0.15	0.30	0.75	—
1984	—	0.10	0.15	0.30	0.75	—
1985	—	0.10	0.15	0.30	0.75	—
1986	—	0.10	0.15	0.30	0.75	—
1987	—	0.10	0.15	0.30	0.75	—
1988	—	0.10	0.15	0.30	0.75	—
1989	—	0.10	0.15	0.25	0.50	—
1990	—	0.15	0.25	0.45	1.25	—
1990M	—	7.00	10.00	20.00	30.00	—
1991M	—	0.10	0.15	0.25	0.50	—
1991	—	0.10	0.15	0.25	0.50	—

Y# 86 10 KOPEKS

1.8000 g., 0.5000 Silver .0289 oz. ASW **Obv:** National arms within circle **Rev:** Value and date within oat sprigs **Note:** Varieties exist.

Date	Mintage	F	VF	XF	Unc	BU
1924	67,351,000	1.00	2.00	5.00	9.00	—
1924 Proof	—	Value: 450				
1925	101,013,000	1.00	2.00	5.00	8.00	—
1925 Proof	—	Value: 225				
1927	—	1.00	2.00	5.00	9.00	—
1927 Proof	—	Value: 225				
1928	—	1.00	2.00	5.00	8.00	—
1929	64,900,000	1.00	2.00	5.00	9.00	—
1930	163,424,000	1.00	2.00	5.00	8.00	—
1931 Rare	8,791,000	—	—	—	—	—

Y# 95 10 KOPEKS

Copper-Nickel **Obv:** National arms within circle **Rev:** Value on shield held by figure at left looking right **Note:** Varieties exist.

Date	Mintage	F	VF	XF	Unc	BU
1931	122,511,000	3.00	5.00	8.00	14.00	—
1932	171,641,000	1.00	2.00	3.00	4.00	—
1933	163,125,000	1.00	2.00	3.00	4.00	—
1934	104,059,000	1.00	2.00	3.00	5.00	—

Y# 102 10 KOPEKS

Copper-Nickel **Obv:** National arms **Rev:** Value within octagon flanked by sprigs with date below

Date	Mintage	F	VF	XF	Unc	BU
1935	79,628,000	1.00	2.00	3.00	6.00	—
1936	122,260,000	1.00	2.00	3.00	5.00	—

Y# 109 10 KOPEKS

Copper-Nickel **Obv:** National arms **Rev:** Value within octagon flanked by sprigs with date below **Note:** Varieties exist.

Date	Mintage	F	VF	XF	Unc	BU
1937	—	1.00	2.00	3.00	6.00	—
1938	—	0.50	1.00	2.00	3.00	—
1939	—	0.50	1.00	2.00	3.00	—
1940	—	0.50	1.00	2.00	3.00	—
1941	—	0.50	1.00	2.00	3.00	—
1942	—	15.00	40.00	75.00	100	—
1943	—	0.50	1.00	2.00	3.00	—
1944	—	4.00	10.00	20.00	40.00	—
1945	—	0.50	1.00	2.00	5.00	—
1946	—	0.50	1.00	2.00	5.00	—

Y# A110 10 KOPEKS

Copper-Nickel **Obv:** National arms **Rev:** Value within octagon flanked by sprigs **Note:** Mule.

Date	Mintage	F	VF	XF	Unc	BU
1946 Rare	—	—	—	—	—	—

Y# 116 10 KOPEKS

Copper-Nickel **Obv:** National arms, 8 and 7 ribbons on wreath **Rev:** Value within octagon flanked by sprigs with date below **Note:** Varieties exist.

Date	Mintage	F	VF	XF	Unc	BU
1948	—	1.00	2.00	3.00	5.00	—
1949	—	0.50	1.00	2.00	3.00	—
1950	—	0.50	1.00	1.50	2.50	—
1951	—	0.50	1.00	2.00	5.00	—
1952	—	0.50	1.00	2.00	4.00	—
1953	—	0.50	1.00	1.50	2.50	—
1954	—	0.50	1.00	1.50	2.50	—
1955	—	0.50	1.00	1.50	2.50	—
1956	—	0.50	1.00	1.50	2.50	—
1956	—	20.00	35.00	60.00	100	—

Note: Reverse of Y#123

Y# 123 10 KOPEKS

Copper-Nickel **Obv:** National arms, 7 and 7 ribbons on wreath **Rev:** Value within octagon flanked by sprigs with date below

Date	Mintage	F	VF	XF	Unc	BU
1957	—	20.00	30.00	60.00	100	—

Note: Reverse of Y#116

Date	Mintage	F	VF	XF	Unc	BU
1957	—	0.50	1.00	3.00	6.00	—

Y# A130 10 KOPEKS

Copper-Nickel **Obv:** National arms **Rev:** Value and date within sprigs

Date	Mintage	F	VF	XF	Unc	BU
1958	108,023,000	—	—	—	300	—

Note: Never officially released for circulation; majority of mintage remelted

Y# 130 10 KOPEKS

1.6000 g., Copper-Nickel-Zinc, 17.35 mm. **Obv:** National arms **Rev:** Value and date flanked by sprigs

Date	Mintage	F	VF	XF	Unc	BU
1961	—	0.10	0.20	0.35	0.75	—
1962	—	0.10	0.20	0.35	0.75	—
1965	—	3.00	5.00	10.00	15.00	—
1966	—	1.00	2.50	5.00	10.00	—
1967	—	0.50	0.80	1.50	3.00	—
1968	—	0.10	0.20	0.35	0.75	—
1969	—	0.10	0.20	0.35	0.75	—
1970	—	0.10	0.20	0.35	0.75	—
1971	—	0.10	0.20	0.35	0.75	—
1972	—	0.10	0.20	0.35	0.75	—
1973	—	0.10	0.20	0.35	0.75	—
1974	—	0.10	0.20	0.35	0.75	—
1975	—	0.10	0.20	0.35	0.75	—
1976	—	0.10	0.20	0.35	0.75	—
1977	—	0.10	0.20	0.35	0.75	—
1978	—	0.10	0.20	0.35	0.75	—
1979	—	0.10	0.20	0.35	0.75	—
1980	—	0.10	0.20	0.35	0.75	—
1981	—	0.10	0.20	0.35	0.75	—
1982	—	0.10	0.20	0.35	0.75	—
1983	—	0.10	0.20	0.35	0.75	—
1984	—	0.10	0.20	0.35	0.75	—
1985	—	0.10	0.20	0.35	0.75	—
1986	—	0.10	0.20	0.35	0.75	—
1987	—	0.10	0.20	0.35	0.75	—
1988	—	0.10	0.20	0.35	0.75	—
1989	—	0.10	0.20	0.30	0.50	—
1990	—	0.25	0.50	1.00	2.50	—
1990 Л	—	0.10	0.20	0.30	0.50	—
1990 M	—	4.00	7.50	12.50	20.00	—
1991	—	0.15	0.25	0.50	1.25	—
1991 Л	—	0.10	0.20	0.30	0.50	—
1991 M	—	0.10	0.20	0.30	0.50	—

Y# 136 10 KOPEKS

Copper-Nickel-Zinc, 17 mm. **Subject:** 50th Anniversary of Revolution **Obv:** National arms within radiant circle with dates at right **Rev:** Value above radiant sun and design

Date	Mintage	F	VF	XF	Unc	BU
1967	49,789,000	—	0.20	0.30	1.00	—
1967 Prooflike	211,000	—	—	—	—	—

Y# 87 15 KOPEKS

2.7000 g., 0.5000 Silver .0434 oz. ASW **Obv:** National arms within circle **Rev:** Value and date within oat sprigs **Note:** Varieties exist.

Date	Mintage	F	VF	XF	Unc	BU
1924	72,426,000	1.25	2.50	5.00	10.00	—
1924 Proof	—	Value: 450				
1925	112,709,000	1.25	2.50	5.00	8.00	—
1925 Proof	—	Value: 225				
1927	—	1.25	2.50	5.00	8.00	—
1927 Proof	—	Value: 225				
1928	—	1.25	2.50	5.00	8.00	—
1929	46,400,000	1.25	2.50	5.00	8.00	—
1930	79,868,000	1.25	2.50	5.00	8.00	—
1931 Rare	5,099,000	—	—	—	—	—

Y# 96 15 KOPEKS
Copper-Nickel, 20 mm. **Obv:** National arms within circle **Rev:** Value on shield held by figure at left looking right **Note:** Varieties exist.

Date	Mintage	F	VF	XF	Unc	BU
1931	75,859,000	1.00	2.00	3.00	7.00	—
1932	136,046,000	1.00	2.00	3.00	5.00	—
1933	127,591,000	1.00	2.00	3.00	5.00	—
1934	58,367,000	1.00	2.00	3.00	5.50	—

Y# 103 15 KOPEKS
Copper-Nickel, 20 mm. **Obv:** National arms **Rev:** Value within octagon flanked by sprigs with date below

Date	Mintage	F	VF	XF	Unc	BU
1935	51,308,000	1.00	2.00	3.00	5.00	—
1936	52,183,000	1.00	2.00	3.00	5.00	—

Y# 110 15 KOPEKS
Copper-Nickel, 20 mm. **Obv:** National arms **Rev:** Value within octagon flanked by sprigs with date below **Note:** Varieties exist.

Date	Mintage	F	VF	XF	Unc	BU
1937	—	1.00	2.00	3.00	5.00	—
1938	—	0.50	1.00	2.00	3.00	—
1939	—	0.50	1.00	2.00	3.00	—
1940	—	0.50	1.00	2.00	3.00	—
1941	—	0.50	1.00	2.00	3.00	—
1942	—	18.00	50.00	80.00	100	—
1943	—	0.50	1.00	2.00	4.00	—
1944	—	1.00	2.00	5.00	10.00	—
1945	—	1.00	2.00	3.00	5.00	—
1946	—	0.50	1.00	2.50	4.00	—

Y# 117 15 KOPEKS
Copper-Nickel, 20 mm. **Obv:** National arms, 8 and 7 ribbons on wreath **Rev:** Value within octagon flanked by sprigs with date below **Note:** Varieties exist.

Date	Mintage	F	VF	XF	Unc	BU
1948	—	0.50	1.00	2.50	4.50	—
1949	—	0.50	1.00	2.00	4.00	—
1950	—	0.50	1.00	2.00	3.00	—
1951	—	1.00	2.00	4.00	8.00	—
1952	—	0.50	1.00	2.00	3.00	—
1953	—	0.50	1.00	2.00	3.00	—
1954	—	0.50	1.00	2.00	3.00	—
1955	—	0.50	1.00	2.00	3.00	—
1956	—	0.50	1.00	2.00	3.00	—

Y# 124 15 KOPEKS
Copper-Nickel, 20 mm. **Obv:** National arms **Rev:** Value within octagon flanked by sprigs with date below

Date	Mintage	F	VF	XF	Unc	BU
1957	—	1.00	2.00	3.00	5.00	—

Y# A131 15 KOPEKS
Copper-Nickel, 20 mm. **Obv:** National arms **Rev:** Value and date within sprigs

Date	Mintage	F	VF	XF	Unc	BU
1958	80,052,000	—	—	—	1,000	—

Note: Never officially released for circulation; majority of mintage remelted

Y# 131 15 KOPEKS
2.5000 g., Copper-Nickel-Zinc, 19.5 mm. **Obv:** National arms **Rev:** Value and date flanked by sprigs

Date	Mintage	F	VF	XF	Unc	BU
1961	—	0.10	0.20	0.40	0.75	—
1962	—	0.10	0.20	0.40	1.00	—
1965	—	1.00	2.00	4.00	7.50	—
1966	—	1.00	2.00	4.00	7.50	—
1967	—	0.50	1.00	2.00	4.00	—
1968	—	0.25	0.50	1.00	2.00	—
1969	—	0.10	0.20	0.40	0.75	—
1970	—	15.00	25.00	40.00	75.00	—
1971	—	1.00	3.00	5.00	10.00	—
1972	—	1.00	3.00	5.00	10.00	—
1973	—	1.00	3.00	5.00	10.00	—
1974	—	0.10	0.20	0.40	0.75	—
1975	—	0.10	0.20	0.40	0.75	—
1976	—	0.10	0.20	0.40	0.75	—
1977	—	0.10	0.20	0.40	0.75	—
1978	—	0.10	0.20	0.40	0.75	—
1979	—	0.10	0.20	0.40	0.75	—
1980	—	0.10	0.20	0.40	0.75	—
1981	—	0.10	0.20	0.40	0.75	—
1982	—	0.10	0.20	0.40	0.75	—
1983	—	0.10	0.20	0.40	0.75	—
1984	—	0.10	0.20	0.40	0.75	—
1985	—	0.10	0.20	0.40	0.75	—
1986	—	0.10	0.20	0.40	0.75	—
1987	—	0.10	0.20	0.40	0.75	—
1988	—	0.10	0.20	0.40	0.75	—
1989	—	0.10	0.20	0.30	0.50	—
1990	—	0.10	0.20	0.30	0.50	—
1991 М	—	0.10	0.20	0.30	0.50	—
1991 Л	—	0.10	0.20	0.30	0.50	—

Y# 137 15 KOPEKS
Copper-Nickel-Zinc, 20 mm. **Subject:** 50th Anniversary of Revolution **Obv:** National arms above value **Rev:** Statue of Laborers and dates **Rev. Designer:** Vera Muchina

Date	Mintage	F	VF	XF	Unc	BU
1967	49,789,000	0.30	0.50	1.00	2.00	—
1967 Prooflike	211,000	—	—	—	—	3.00

Y# 88 20 KOPEKS
3.6000 g., 0.5000 Silver .0578 oz. ASW **Obv:** National arms within circle **Rev:** Value and date within oat sprigs

Date	Mintage	F	VF	XF	Unc	BU
1924	93,810,000	2.00	4.00	8.00	15.00	—
1924 Proof	—	Value: 500				
1925	135,188,000	2.00	4.00	7.00	12.00	—
1925 Proof	—	Value: 225				
1927	—	2.00	3.00	5.00	12.00	—
1928	—	2.00	3.00	5.00	9.00	—
1929	67,250,000	2.00	3.00	5.00	9.00	—
1930	125,658,000	2.00	3.00	5.00	9.00	—
1931	9,530,000	—	—	—	800	—

Y# 97 20 KOPEKS
Copper-Nickel, 22 mm. **Obv:** National arms within circle **Rev:** Value on shield held by figure at left looking right **Note:** Varieties exist.

Date	Mintage	F	VF	XF	Unc	BU
1931	82,200,000	1.00	2.00	3.00	5.00	—
1932	175,350,000	1.00	2.00	3.00	5.00	—
1933	143,927,000	1.00	2.00	3.00	5.00	—
1934	70,425,000	—	—	—	—	—

Y# 104 20 KOPEKS
Copper-Nickel **Obv:** National arms **Rev:** Value within octagon flanked by sprigs with date below **Note:** Varieties exist.

Date	Mintage	F	VF	XF	Unc	BU
1935	125,165,000	1.00	1.50	2.50	5.00	—
1936	52,968,000	1.00	1.50	2.50	6.00	—
1941 Rare	—	—	—	—	—	—

Y# 111 20 KOPEKS
Copper-Nickel **Obv:** National arms **Rev:** Value within octagon flanked by sprigs with date below **Note:** Varieties exist.

Date	Mintage	F	VF	XF	Unc	BU
1937	—	0.40	0.60	1.00	3.00	—
1938	—	0.40	0.60	1.00	3.00	—
1939	—	0.40	0.60	1.00	3.00	—
1940	—	0.40	0.60	1.00	3.00	—
1941	—	0.40	0.60	1.00	3.00	—
1942	—	0.50	0.75	1.50	4.00	—
1943	—	0.40	0.60	1.00	3.00	—
1944	—	0.60	1.25	2.50	6.00	—
1945	—	0.50	0.75	1.50	4.00	—
1946	—	0.60	1.25	2.50	5.00	—

Y# 118 20 KOPEKS
Copper-Nickel **Obv:** National arms, 8 and 7 ribbons on wreath **Rev:** Value within octagon flanked by sprigs with date below **Note:** Varieties exist.

Date	Mintage	F	VF	XF	Unc	BU
1948	—	0.50	1.00	2.00	4.00	—
1949	—	0.50	1.00	2.00	4.00	—
1950	—	1.00	2.00	5.00	10.00	—
1951	—	1.00	2.00	3.00	7.00	—
1952	—	0.50	0.75	1.25	2.00	—
1953	—	0.50	0.75	1.25	2.00	—
1954	—	0.50	0.75	1.25	2.00	—
1955	—	0.50	0.75	1.25	2.00	—
1956	—	0.50	0.75	1.25	2.00	—

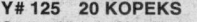

Y# 125 20 KOPEKS
Copper-Nickel **Obv:** National arms **Rev:** Value within octagon flanked by sprigs with date below

Date	Mintage	F	VF	XF	Unc	BU
1957	—	1.00	2.00	3.00	5.00	—

Y# A132 20 KOPEKS

Copper-Nickel **Obv:** National arms **Rev:** Value and date within sprigs

Date	Mintage	F	VF	XF	Unc	BU
1958	175,355,000	—	—	—	450	—

Note: Never officially released for circulation; majority of mintage remelted

Y# 132 20 KOPEKS

3.3000 g., Copper-Nickel-Zinc, 22 mm. **Obv:** National arms **Rev:** Value and date flanked by sprigs **Note:** Varieties exist.

Date	Mintage	F	VF	XF	Unc	BU
1961	—	0.15	0.30	0.50	1.00	—
1962	—	0.15	0.35	0.75	1.50	—
1965	—	1.00	3.00	5.00	10.00	—
1966	—	1.00	3.00	5.00	10.00	—
1967	—	0.50	1.00	2.00	3.00	—
1968	—	0.15	0.30	0.50	1.00	—
1969	—	0.50	1.00	2.00	4.00	—
1970	—	10.00	22.50	30.00	40.00	—
1971	—	0.50	1.00	2.00	3.00	—
1972	—	1.00	2.00	4.00	7.50	—
1973	—	10.00	15.00	25.00	40.00	—
1974	—	1.50	3.00	5.00	9.00	—
1975	—	1.00	3.00	4.00	7.50	—
1976	—	15.00	25.00	40.00	60.00	—
1977	—	0.15	0.30	0.50	1.00	—
1978	—	0.15	0.30	0.50	1.00	—
1979	—	0.15	0.30	0.50	1.00	—
1980	—	0.15	0.30	0.50	1.00	—
1981	—	0.15	0.30	0.50	1.00	—
1982	—	0.15	0.30	0.50	1.00	—
1983	—	0.15	0.30	0.50	1.00	—
1984	—	0.15	0.30	0.50	1.00	—
1985	—	0.15	0.30	0.50	1.00	—
1986	—	0.15	0.30	0.50	1.00	—
1987	—	0.15	0.30	0.50	1.00	—
1988	—	0.15	0.30	0.50	1.00	—
1989	—	0.10	0.20	0.30	0.75	—
1990	—	0.10	0.20	0.30	0.75	—
1991	—	30.00	70.00	100	300	—
1991 М	—	0.10	0.20	0.30	0.75	—
1991 Л	—	0.10	0.20	0.30	0.50	—

Y# 138 20 KOPEKS

Copper-Nickel-Zinc **Subject:** 50th Anniversary of Revolution **Obv:** National arms flanked by dates with inscription below **Rev:** Cruiser ship below value

Date	Mintage	F	VF	XF	Unc	BU
1967	49,789,000	0.40	0.60	1.00	2.00	—
1967 Prooflike	211,000	—	—	—	—	—

Y# 89.1 50 KOPEKS

9.9980 g., 0.9000 Silver .2893 oz. ASW **Obv:** National arms divide CCCP above inscription, circle surrounds all **Rev:** Blacksmith at anvil **Rev. Designer:** Thomas Ross **Edge Lettering:** Weight shown in old Russian units

Date	Mintage	F	VF	XF	Unc	BU
1924 ПЛ	26,559,000	6.50	8.50	13.50	30.00	—
1924 ПЛ Proof	—	Value: 550				
1924 ТР	40,000,000	6.50	8.50	13.50	30.00	—

Y# 89.2 50 KOPEKS

9.9980 g., 0.9000 Silver .2893 oz. ASW **Obv:** National arms divide CCCP above inscription, circle surrounds all **Rev:** Blacksmith at anvil **Rev. Designer:** Thomas Ross **Edge Lettering:** Weight shown in Грамм (grams) only **Note:** Varieties exist.

Date	Mintage	F	VF	XF	Unc	BU
1925 ПЛ	43,558,000	6.50	8.50	13.50	30.00	—
1925 ПЛ Proof	—	Value: 400				
1926 ПЛ	24,374,000	6.50	8.50	13.50	30.00	—
1926 ПЛ Proof	—	Value: 400				
1927 ПЛ	—	6.50	9.50	17.50	40.00	—
1927 ПЛ Proof	—	Value: 500				

Y# 133 50 KOPEKS

Copper-Nickel **Obv:** National arms **Rev:** Value and date within sprigs

Date	Mintage	F	VF	XF	Unc	BU
1958	40,600,000	—	—	—	1,000	—

Note: Never officially released for circulation; majority of mintage remelted

Y# 133a.1 50 KOPEKS

Copper-Nickel-Zinc **Obv:** National arms **Rev:** Value and date within sprigs **Edge:** Plain **Note:** Varieties exist.

Date	Mintage	F	VF	XF	Unc	BU
1961	—	1.00	2.00	5.00	12.00	—

Y# 133a.2 50 KOPEKS

4.4000 g., Copper-Nickel-Zinc, 24.05 mm. **Obv:** National arms **Rev:** Value and date within sprigs **Edge:** Lettered with date **Note:** Varieties exist for 1970, 1971, and 1975.

Date	Mintage	F	VF	XF	Unc	BU
1964	—	0.20	0.40	0.75	1.50	—
1965	—	0.20	0.40	0.75	1.50	—
1966	—	0.20	0.40	0.75	1.50	—
1967	—	1.00	1.50	3.00	5.00	—
1968	—	0.20	0.40	0.75	1.50	—
1969	—	0.20	0.40	0.75	1.50	—
1970	—	2.00	5.00	10.00	20.00	—
1971	—	2.00	5.00	10.00	10.00	—
1972	—	0.20	0.40	0.75	1.50	—
1973	—	0.20	0.40	0.75	1.50	—
1974	—	0.20	0.40	0.75	1.50	—
1975	—	1.00	2.50	5.00	10.00	—
1976	—	0.50	1.00	3.00	6.00	—
1977	—	0.20	0.40	0.75	1.50	—
1978	—	0.20	0.40	0.75	1.50	—
1979	—	0.20	0.40	0.75	1.50	—
1980	—	0.20	0.40	0.75	1.50	—
1981	—	0.20	0.40	0.75	1.50	—
1982	—	0.20	0.40	0.75	1.50	—
1983	—	0.20	0.40	0.75	1.50	—
1984	—	0.20	0.40	0.75	1.50	—
1985	—	0.20	0.40	0.75	1.50	—
1986	—	6.00	12.50	25.00	50.00	—
Note: With 1985 on edge						
1986	—	0.20	0.40	0.75	1.50	—
1987	—	0.20	0.40	0.75	1.50	—
1988	—	1.00	2.00	4.00	10.00	—
Note: With 1987 on edge						
1988	—	0.20	0.40	0.75	1.50	—
1989	—	6.00	12.50	25.00	50.00	—
Note: With 1988 on edge						
1989	—	0.15	0.25	0.50	1.00	—
1990	—	0.15	0.25	0.50	1.00	—
1990 Rare	—	—	—	—	—	—
Note: With 1989 on edge						
1991 М	—	0.15	0.25	0.50	1.00	—
1991 Л	—	0.15	0.25	0.50	1.00	—

Y# 139 50 KOPEKS

Copper-Nickel-Zinc, 25 mm. **Subject:** 50th Anniversary of Revolution **Obv:** National arms **Rev:** Lenin with right arm raised facing left, star at upper left

Date	Mintage	F	VF	XF	Unc	BU
ND(1967)	49,789,000	—	1.00	1.50	2.50	—
ND(1967) Prooflike	—	—	—	—	3.00	—

Y# 90.1 ROUBLE

19.9960 g., 0.9000 Silver .5786 oz. ASW **Obv:** National arms divides circle with inscription within **Rev:** Two figures walking right, radiant sun rising at right **Edge Lettering:** 18 Грамм (grams) (43.21d) **Note:** Varieties exist.

Date	Mintage	F	VF	XF	Unc	BU
1924 ПЛ	12,998,000	10.00	15.00	28.00	75.00	150
1924 ПЛ Proof	—	Value: 2,500				

Y# 90.2 ROUBLE

19.9960 g., 0.9000 Silver .5786 oz. ASW **Obv:** National arms divides circle holding inscription **Rev:** Two figures walking right, sun rising at right **Edge:** 4 Zolotniks 21 Dolyas

Date	Mintage	F	VF	XF	Unc	BU
1924 Rare	—	—	—	—	—	—

Y# 134 ROUBLE

Copper-Nickel **Obv:** National arms **Rev:** Value and date within sprigs

Date	Mintage	F	VF	XF	Unc	BU
1958	30,700,000	—	—	—	900	—

Note: Never officially released for circulation; majority of mintage remelted

Y# 134a.1 ROUBLE

Copper-Nickel-Zinc **Obv:** National arms within circle **Rev:** Value and date within sprigs **Edge:** Plain

Date	Mintage	F	VF	XF	Unc	BU
1961	—	2.00	3.50	6.00	15.00	—

Y# 134a.2 ROUBLE

7.4000 g., Copper-Nickel-Zinc, 27 mm. **Obv:** National arms within circle **Rev:** Value and date within sprigs **Edge:** Lettered with date

Date	Mintage	F	VF	XF	Unc	BU
1964	—	0.40	0.75	1.50	2.50	—
1965	—	1.00	1.50	2.50	4.00	—
1966	—	0.40	0.75	1.50	2.50	—
1967 Rare	—	—	—	—	—	—
Note: With 1966 on edge						
1967	—	0.40	0.75	1.50	2.50	—
1968	—	0.40	0.75	1.50	2.50	—
1969	—	0.40	0.75	1.50	2.50	—
1970	—	0.40	0.75	1.50	2.50	—
1971	—	0.40	0.75	1.50	2.50	—
1972	—	0.40	0.75	1.50	2.50	—
1973	—	0.40	0.75	1.50	2.50	—
1974	—	0.40	0.75	1.50	2.50	—

Date	Mintage	F	VF	XF	Unc	BU
1975	—	0.40	0.75	1.50	2.50	—
1976	—	0.40	0.75	1.50	2.50	—
1977	—	0.40	0.75	1.50	2.50	—
1978	—	0.40	0.75	1.50	2.50	—
1979	—	0.40	0.75	1.50	2.50	—
1980	—	0.40	0.75	1.50	2.50	—
1981	—	0.40	0.75	1.50	2.50	—
1982	—	0.40	0.75	1.50	2.50	—
1983	—	0.40	0.75	1.50	2.50	—
1984	—	0.40	0.75	1.50	2.50	—
1985	—	0.40	0.75	1.50	2.50	—
1986	—	0.40	0.75	1.50	2.50	—
1987	—	0.40	0.75	1.50	2.50	—
1988	—	0.40	0.75	1.50	2.50	—
1988	—	1.50	3.00	6.00	15.00	—
Note: With 1989 on edge						
1989	—	0.25	0.50	1.00	2.50	—
1990	—	1.50	3.00	6.00	15.00	—
Note: With 1989 on edge						
1990	—	0.25	0.50	1.00	2.50	—
1991 М	—	0.25	0.50	1.00	2.50	—
1991 Л	—	0.25	0.50	1.00	2.50	—

Y# 135.1 ROUBLE

Copper-Nickel-Zinc, 31 mm. **Subject:** 20th Anniversary of World War II Victory **Obv:** National arms divide CCCP with inscription below **Rev:** Statue by Vouchetic

Date	Mintage	F	VF	XF	Unc	BU
1965	59,989,000	—	0.50	1.00	2.50	—
1965 Prooflike	—	—	—	—	3.00	—
1965 Proof	—	Value: 30.00				

Y# 135.2 ROUBLE

Copper-Nickel-Zinc, 31 mm. **Obv:** National arms divide CCCP with inscription below **Rev:** Victory monument **Edge Lettering:** 1988.N.

Date	Mintage	F	VF	XF	Unc	BU
1965 Proof, restrike	55,000	Value: 3.50				

Y# 140.1 ROUBLE

Copper-Nickel-Zinc, 31 mm. **Subject:** 50th Anniversary of Revolution **Obv:** National arms **Rev:** Lenin with right arm raised facing left, star at upper left **Edge:** Lettered, with date

Date	Mintage	F	VF	XF	Unc	BU
1967	52,289,000	—	0.50	1.00	2.50	—
1967 Prooflike	—	—	—	—	3.00	—
1967 Proof	—	Value: 30.00				

Y# 140.2 ROUBLE

Copper-Nickel-Zinc, 31 mm. **Obv:** National arms **Rev:** Lenin with right arm raised facing left, star at upper left **Edge Lettering:** 1988.N.

Date	Mintage	F	VF	XF	Unc	BU
1967 Proof, restrike	55,000	Value: 4.00				

Y# 141 ROUBLE

Copper-Nickel-Zinc, 31 mm. **Subject:** Centennial of Lenin's Birth **Obv:** National arms divide CCCP **Rev:** Head right

Date	Mintage	F	VF	XF	Unc	BU
ND(1970)	99,889,000	—	0.50	1.00	2.50	—

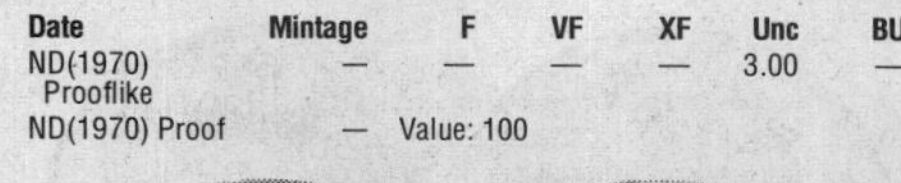

Date	Mintage	F	VF	XF	Unc	BU
ND(1970) Prooflike	—	—	—	—	3.00	—
ND(1970) Proof	—	Value: 100				

Y# 142.1 ROUBLE

Copper-Nickel-Zinc, 31 mm. **Subject:** 30th Anniversary of World War II Victory **Obv:** National arms divide CCCP **Obv. Designer:** V. Ermokov **Rev:** Volgograd monument **Rev. Designer:** J. Komschicov **Edge:** Date **Note:** Date appears on the edge in English and Russian as "9 March 1975". Varieties exist.

Date	Mintage	F	VF	XF	Unc	BU
1975	14,989,000	—	0.50	1.00	2.50	—
1975 Prooflike	—	—	—	—	3.00	—
1975 Proof	—	Value: 30.00				

Y# 142.2 ROUBLE

Copper-Nickel-Zinc, 31 mm. **Obv:** National arms divide CCCP, value below **Obv. Designer:** V. Ermokov **Rev:** Volgograd monument **Rev. Designer:** J. Komschicov **Edge Lettering:** 1988.N.

Date	Mintage	F	VF	XF	Unc	BU
ND(1975) Proof, restrike	55,000	Value: 3.50				

Y# 143.1 ROUBLE

Copper-Nickel-Zinc, 31 mm. **Subject:** 60th Anniversary of Bolshevik Revolution **Obv:** National arms divide CCCP **Rev:** Head left above ship, dates below

Date	Mintage	F	VF	XF	Unc	BU
ND(1977)	4,987,000	—	0.50	1.00	2.50	—
ND(1977) Prooflike	—	—	—	—	3.00	—
ND(1977) Proof	—	Value: 30.00				

Y# 143.2 ROUBLE

Copper-Nickel-Zinc, 31 mm. **Obv:** National arms divide CCCP, value below **Rev:** Head left above ship, dates below **Edge Lettering:** 1988.N.

Date	Mintage	F	VF	XF	Unc	BU
ND(1977) Proof, restrike	55,000	Value: 3.50				

Y# A144 ROUBLE

Copper-Nickel-Zinc, 31 mm. **Obv:** National arms divide CCCP above value **Rev:** Design with star on top with Olympic rings below **Note:** Mule

Date	Mintage	F	VF	XF	Unc	BU
1977 Rare	Inc. below	—	—	—	—	—

Y# 144 ROUBLE

Copper-Nickel-Zinc, 31 mm. **Series:** 1980 Olympics **Obv:** National arms divide CCCP above value **Rev:** Design with star on top with Olympic rings below **Rev. Designer:** V. Arsentiev

Date	Mintage	F	VF	XF	Unc	BU
1977	8,665,000	—	0.50	1.00	2.50	—
1977 Prooflike	—	—	—	—	3.00	—
1977 Proof	—	Value: 25.00				

Y# 153.1 ROUBLE

Copper-Nickel-Zinc, 31 mm. **Series:** 1980 Olympics **Obv:** National arms divide CCCP with value below **Rev:** Moscow Kremlin with stars on top of steeples **Rev. Designer:** Nikolay Nosov

Date	Mintage	F	VF	XF	Unc	BU
1978	6,490,000	—	0.50	1.00	2.50	—
1978 Prooflike	—	—	—	—	3.00	—
1978 Proof	—	Value: 60.00				

Y# 153.2 ROUBLE

Copper-Nickel-Zinc, 31 mm. **Obv:** National arms divide CCCP, value below **Rev:** Clock on tower shows Roman numeral 6 (VI) instead of 4 (IV)

Date	Mintage	F	VF	XF	Unc	BU
1978	Inc. above	—	8.00	16.00	25.00	—

Y# 165 ROUBLE

Copper-Nickel-Zinc, 31 mm. **Series:** 1980 Olympics **Obv:** National arms divide CCCP, value below **Rev:** Monument, Sputnik and Sojuz **Rev. Designer:** Nikolay Nosov

Date	Mintage	F	VF	XF	Unc	BU
1979	4,665,000	—	0.50	1.00	2.50	—
1979 Prooflike	—	—	—	—	3.00	—
1979 Proof	—	Value: 25.00				

Y# 164 ROUBLE

Copper-Nickel-Zinc, 31 mm. **Series:** 1980 Olympics **Obv:** National arms divide CCCP, value below **Rev:** Moscow University **Note:** Varieties in window arrangements exist.

Date	Mintage	F	VF	XF	Unc	BU
1979	4,665,000	—	0.50	1.00	2.50	—
1979 Prooflike	—	—	—	—	3.00	—
1979 Proof	—	Value: 25.00				

Y# 177 ROUBLE

Copper-Nickel, 31 mm. **Series:** 1980 Olympics **Obv:** National arms divide CCCP with value below **Rev:** Dolgorukij Monument **Rev. Designer:** Nikolay Nosov

Date	Mintage	F	VF	XF	Unc	BU
1980	4,490,000	—	0.50	1.00	2.50	—
1980 Prooflike	—	—	—	—	3.00	—
1980 Proof	—	Value: 25.00				

Y# 178 ROUBLE

Copper-Nickel, 31 mm. **Series:** 1980 Olympics **Obv:** National arms divide CCCP, value below **Rev:** Torch **Rev. Designer:** Nikolay Nosov

Date	Mintage	F	VF	XF	Unc	BU
1980	4,490,000	—	0.50	1.00	2.50	—
1980 Prooflike	—	—	—	—	3.00	—
1980 Proof	—	Value: 25.00				

Y# 188.1 ROUBLE

Copper-Nickel, 31 mm. **Subject:** 20th Anniversary of Manned Space Flights **Obv:** National arms divide CCCP with value below **Rev:** Cosmonaut facing flanked by rockets, hammer and sickle above

Date	Mintage	F	VF	XF	Unc	BU
ND(1981)	3,962,000	—	0.50	1.00	3.00	—
ND(1981) Proof	—	Value: 12.50				

Y# 188.2 ROUBLE

Copper-Nickel, 31 mm. **Subject:** 20th Anniversary of Manned Space Flights **Obv:** National arms divide CCCP, value below **Rev:** Cosmonaut facing flanked by rockets, hammer and sickle above **Edge Lettering:** 1988.N.

Date	Mintage	F	VF	XF	Unc	BU
ND(1981) Proof; restrike	55,000	Value: 9.00				

Y# 189.1 ROUBLE
Copper-Nickel, 31 mm. **Subject:** Russian-Bulgarian Friendship **Obv:** National arms divide CCCP with value below **Rev:** Grasped hands divide flags above and sprigs below within beaded circle **Edge Lettering:** Cyrillic lettering

Date	Mintage	F	VF	XF	Unc	BU
1981	1,984,000	—	0.50	1.00	4.00	—
1981 Proof	16,000	Value: 22.50				

Note: The same reverse die was used for both Russia 1 Rouble KM #189 and Bulgaria 1 Lev KM#119

Y# 189.2 ROUBLE
Copper-Nickel, 31 mm. **Subject:** Russian-Bulgarian Friendship **Obv:** National arms divide CCCP, value below **Rev:** Grasped hands divide flags above and sprigs below within beaded circle **Edge Lettering:** 1988.N.

Date	Mintage	F	VF	XF	Unc	BU
1981 Proof; restrike	55,000	Value: 3.50				

Note: The same reverse die was used for both Russia 1 Rouble KM#189 and Bulgaria 1 Lev KM#119

Y# 190.1 ROUBLE
Copper-Nickel, 31 mm. **Subject:** 60th Anniversary of the Soviet Union **Obv:** National arms divide CCCP with value below **Rev:** Radiant sun and standing statue facing left **Edge Lettering:** Cyrillic lettering

Date	Mintage	F	VF	XF	Unc	BU
ND(1982)	1,921,000	—	0.50	1.50	4.50	—
ND(1982) Proof	79,000	Value: 6.00				

Y# 190.2 ROUBLE
Copper-Nickel, 31 mm. **Subject:** 60th Anniversary of the Soviet Union **Obv:** National arms divide CCCP, value below **Rev:** Radiant sun back of statue **Edge Lettering:** 1988.N.

Date	Mintage	F	VF	XF	Unc	BU
ND(1982) Proof; restrike	55,000	Value: 4.50				

Y# 191.1 ROUBLE
Copper-Nickel, 31 mm. **Subject:** Death of Karl Marx Centennial **Obv:** National arms divide CCCP with value below **Rev:** Bust 3/4 left and dates **Edge:** Cyrillic lettering

Date	Mintage	F	VF	XF	Unc	BU
1983	1,921,000	—	0.50	1.50	3.50	—
1983 Proof	79,000	Value: 6.00				

Y# 191.2 ROUBLE
Copper-Nickel, 31 mm. **Subject:** Death of Karl Marx Centennial **Obv:** National arms divide CCCP, value below **Rev:** Bust 3/4 left with dates **Edge Lettering:** 1988.N.

Date	Mintage	F	VF	XF	Unc	BU
1983 Proof; restrike	55,000	Value: 4.50				

Y# 192.1 ROUBLE
Copper-Nickel, 31 mm. **Subject:** 20th Anniversary of First Woman in Space **Obv:** National arms divide CCCP with value below **Rev:** Cosmonaut head facing flanked by stars

Date	Mintage	F	VF	XF	Unc	BU
1983	1,945,000	—	0.50	1.00	4.00	—
1983 Proof	55,000	Value: 6.00				

Y# 192.2 ROUBLE
Copper-Nickel, 31 mm. **Subject:** 20th Anniversary of First Woman in Space **Obv:** National arms divide CCCP, value below **Rev:** Cosmonaut head facing flanked by stars **Edge Lettering:** 1988.N.

Date	Mintage	F	VF	XF	Unc	BU
1983 Proof; restrike	55,000	Value: 3.50				

Y# 193.1 ROUBLE
Copper-Nickel, 31 mm. **Subject:** First Russian Printer **Obv:** National arms divide CCCP with value below **Rev:** Ivan Fedorov **Edge:** Cyrillic lettering

Date	Mintage	F	VF	XF	Unc	BU
1983	1,965,000	—	0.50	1.00	3.00	—
1983 Proof	35,000	Value: 7.50				

Y# 193.2 ROUBLE
Copper-Nickel, 31 mm. **Subject:** First Russian Printer **Obv:** National arms divide CCCP, value below **Rev:** Ivan Fedorov **Edge Lettering:** 1988.N.

Date	Mintage	F	VF	XF	Unc	BU
1983 Proof; restrike	55,000	Value: 3.50				

Y# 194.1 ROUBLE
Copper-Nickel, 31 mm. **Subject:** 150th Anniversary - Birth of Dmitri Ivanovich Mendeleyev **Obv:** National arms divide CCCP with value below **Rev:** Head facing and dates **Edge:** Cyrillic lettering

Date	Mintage	F	VF	XF	Unc	BU
1984	1,965,000	—	0.50	1.00	3.00	—
1984 Proof	35,000	Value: 7.50				

Y# 194.2 ROUBLE
Copper-Nickel, 31 mm. **Subject:** 150th Anniversary - birth of Dmitri Ivanovich Mendeleyev **Obv:** National arms divide CCCP, value below **Rev:** Head facing with dates at right **Edge Lettering:** 1988.N.

Date	Mintage	F	VF	XF	Unc	BU
1984 Proof; restrike	55,000	Value: 3.50				

Y# 195.1 ROUBLE
Copper-Nickel, 31 mm. **Subject:** 125th Anniversary - Birth of Alexander Popov **Obv:** National arms divide CCCP with value below **Rev:** Head facing and dates **Edge:** Cyrillic lettering

Date	Mintage	F	VF	XF	Unc	BU
1984	1,965,000	—	0.50	1.00	3.00	—
1984 Proof	35,000	Value: 6.00				

Y# 195.2 ROUBLE
Copper-Nickel, 31 mm. **Subject:** 125th Anniversary - Birth of Alexander Popov **Obv:** National arms divide CCCP, value below **Rev:** Head facing with dates at right **Edge Lettering:** 1988.N.

Date	Mintage	F	VF	XF	Unc	BU
1984 Proof; restrike	55,000	Value: 3.50				

Y# 196.1 ROUBLE
Copper-Nickel, 31 mm. **Subject:** 185th Anniversary - Birth of Alexander Sergeyevich Pushkin **Obv:** National arms divide CCCP with value below **Rev. Designer:** Head left **Edge:** Cyrillic lettering

Date	Mintage	F	VF	XF	Unc	BU
1984	1,965,000	—	0.50	1.00	3.00	—
1984 Proof	35,000	Value: 7.50				

Y# 196.2 ROUBLE
Copper-Nickel, 31 mm. **Subject:** 185th Anniversary - Birth of Alexander Sergeyevich Pushkin **Obv:** National arms divide CCCP, value below **Rev:** Head left with dates at right **Edge Lettering:** 1988.N.

Date	Mintage	F	VF	XF	Unc	BU
1984 Proof; restrike	55,000	Value: 3.50				
1985 Proof; Restrike/ Error	—	Value: 50.00				

Y# 197.1 ROUBLE
Copper-Nickel, 31 mm. **Subject:** 115th Anniversary - Birth of Vladimir Lenin **Obv:** National arms divide CCCP with value below **Rev:** Bust left with dates **Edge:** Cyrillic lettering

Date	Mintage	F	VF	XF	Unc	BU
1985	1,960,000	—	0.50	1.50	5.00	—
1985 Proof	40,000	Value: 7.50				

Y# 197.2 ROUBLE
Copper-Nickel, 31 mm. **Subject:** 115th Anniversary of Vladimir Lenin **Obv:** National arms divide CCCP, value below **Rev:** Bust left with dates **Edge Lettering:** 1988.N.

Date	Mintage	F	VF	XF	Unc	BU
1985 Proof; Restrike/Error	55,000	Value: 4.50				
1988 Error	—	—	—	—	—	—

Y# 198.1 ROUBLE
Copper-Nickel, 31 mm. **Subject:** 40th Anniversary - World War II Victory **Obv:** National arms divide CCCP with value below **Rev:** Hammer and sickle within radiant star, sprig and dates below **Edge:** Cyrillic lettering

Date	Mintage	F	VF	XF	Unc	BU
1985	5,960,000	—	0.50	1.00	3.00	—
1985 Proof	40,000	Value: 6.00				

Y# 198.2 ROUBLE
Copper-Nickel, 33 mm. **Subject:** 40th Anniversary - World War II Victory **Obv:** National arms divide CCCP, value below **Rev:** Hammer and sickle within radiant star, sprig and dates below **Edge Lettering:** 1988.N.

Date	Mintage	F	VF	XF	Unc	BU
1985 Proof; restrike	55,000	Value: 3.50				

Y# 199.1 ROUBLE
Copper-Nickel, 31 mm. **Subject:** 12th World Youth Festival in Moscow **Obv:** National arms divide CCCP with value below **Rev:** Festival emblem **Edge:** Cyrillic lettering

Date	Mintage	F	VF	XF	Unc	BU
1985	5,960,000	—	0.50	1.00	3.00	—
1985 Proof	40,000	Value: 6.00				

Y# 199.2 ROUBLE
Copper-Nickel, 31 mm. **Subject:** 12th World Youth Festival in Moscow **Obv:** National arms divide CCCP, value below **Rev:** Festival emblem **Edge Lettering:** 1988.N.

Date	Mintage	F	VF	XF	Unc	BU
1985 Proof; restrike	55,000	Value: 3.50				

Y# 200.1 ROUBLE
Copper-Nickel, 31 mm. **Subject:** 165th Anniversary - Birth of Friedrich Engels **Obv:** National arms divide CCCP with value below **Rev:** Bust 3/4 left with dates **Rev. Designer:** Nikolay Nosov

Date	Mintage	F	VF	XF	Unc	BU
1985	1,960,000	—	0.50	1.50	4.50	—
1985 Proof	—	Value: 6.00				

Y# 200.2 ROUBLE
Copper-Nickel, 31 mm. **Subject:** 165th Anniversary - Birth of Friedrich Engels **Obv:** National arms divide CCCP, value below **Rev:** Bust 3/4 left with dates **Edge Lettering:** 1988.N.

Date	Mintage	F	VF	XF	Unc	BU
1983 Proof; restrike	—	Value: 55.00				
Note: Error date						
1985 Proof; restrike	55,000	Value: 4.50				

Y# 201.1 ROUBLE
Copper-Nickel, 31 mm. **Subject:** International Year of Peace **Obv:** National arms divide CCCP with value below **Rev:** Hands within wreath releasing dove **Edge:** Cyrillic lettering **Note:** Rouble written with inverted "V" for Л.

Date	Mintage	F	VF	XF	Unc	BU
1986	—	—	—	—	10.00	—

Y# 201.3 ROUBLE
Copper-Nickel, 31 mm. **Subject:** International Year of Peace **Obv:** National arms divide CCCP with value below **Rev:** Hands within wreath releasing dove **Note:** Rouble written **РУБЛЬ**.

Date	Mintage	F	VF	XF	Unc	BU
1986	3,955,000	—	0.50	1.50	5.00	—
1986 Proof	45,000	Value: 6.00				

Y# 201.4 ROUBLE
Copper-Nickel, 31 mm. **Subject:** International Year of Peace **Obv:** National arms divide CCCP, value below **Rev:** Hands within wreath releasing dove **Edge Lettering:** 1988.N.

Date	Mintage	F	VF	XF	Unc	BU
1986	—	—	0.50	1.50	5.00	—
1986 Proof, rare	—	—	—	—	—	—

Y# 202.1 ROUBLE
Copper-Nickel, 31 mm. **Subject:** 275th Anniversary - Birth of Mikhail Lomonosov **Obv:** National arms divide CCCP with value below **Rev:** Bust 1/4 left **Edge:** Cyrillic lettering

Date	Mintage	F	VF	XF	Unc	BU
1986	1,965,000	—	0.50	1.00	3.00	—
1986 Proof	35,000	Value: 5.00				

Y# 202.2 ROUBLE
Copper-Nickel, 31 mm. **Subject:** 275th Anniversary - Birth of Mikhail Lomonosov **Obv:** National arms divide CCCP, value below **Rev:** Bust looking left with dates at right **Edge Lettering:** 1988.N.

Date	Mintage	F	VF	XF	Unc	BU
1984 Error	—	—	—	—	—	—
1986 Proof; restrike	55,000	Value: 3.50				

Y# 205 ROUBLE
Copper-Nickel, 31 mm. **Subject:** 130th Anniversary - Birth of Constantin Tsiolkovsky **Obv:** National arms with CCCP and value below **Rev:** Seated figure facing left with stars and dates **Edge:** Cyrillic lettering

Date	Mintage	F	VF	XF	Unc	BU
1987	3,830,000	—	0.50	1.00	3.00	—
1987 Proof	170,000	Value: 5.00				

Y# 203 ROUBLE
Copper-Nickel, 31 mm. **Subject:** 175th Anniversary - Battle of Borodino **Obv:** National arms with CCCP and value below **Rev:** Group of soldiers **Edge:** Cyrillic lettering **Note:** Varieties with wheat in coat of arms.

Date	Mintage	F	VF	XF	Unc	BU
1987	3,780,000	—	0.50	1.00	3.00	—
1987 Proof	220,000	Value: 5.00				

Y# 204 ROUBLE
Copper-Nickel, 31 mm. **Subject:** 175th Anniversary - Battle of Borodino **Obv:** National arms with CCCP and value below **Rev:** Kutuzov Monument **Edge:** Cyrillic lettering **Note:** Varieties with wheat in coat of arms.

Date	Mintage	F	VF	XF	Unc	BU
1987	3,780,000	—	0.50	1.00	3.00	—
1987 Proof	220,000	Value: 5.00				

Y# 206 ROUBLE
Copper-Nickel, 31 mm. **Subject:** 70th Anniversary of Bolshevik Revolution **Obv:** National arms with CCCP and value below **Rev:** Hammer and sickle with ship on globe background at center of ribbon design, date and sprig below **Edge:** Cyrillic lettering **Note:** Varieties with wheat in coat of arms.

Date	Mintage	F	VF	XF	Unc	BU
1987	3,800,000	—	0.50	1.00	3.00	—
1987 Proof	200,000	Value: 6.00				

Y# 216 ROUBLE
Copper-Nickel, 31 mm. **Subject:** 160th Anniversary - Birth of Leo Tolstoi **Obv:** National arms with CCCP and value below **Rev:** Head facing **Edge:** Cyrillic lettering

Date	Mintage	F	VF	XF	Unc	BU
1987 Error	—	—	—	—	—	—
1988	3,775,000	—	0.50	1.00	3.00	—
1988 Proof	225,000	Value: 5.00				

Y# 209 ROUBLE
Copper-Nickel, 31 mm. **Subject:** 120th Anniversary - Birth of Maxin Gorky **Obv:** National arms with CCCP and value below **Rev:** Bust 1/4 right, designs and flying bird in background **Rev. Designer:** Albert Miroshnichenko **Edge:** Cyrillic lettering

Date	Mintage	F	VF	XF	Unc	BU
1988	3,775,000	—	0.50	1.00	3.00	—
1988 Proof	225,000	Value: 6.00				

Y# 220 ROUBLE
Copper-Nickel, 31 mm. **Subject:** 150th Anniversary - Birth of Musorgsky **Obv:** National arms with CCCP and value below **Rev:** Head 3/4 left divides dates **Edge:** Cyrillic lettering

Date	Mintage	F	VF	XF	Unc	BU
1989	2,700,000	—	0.50	1.00	3.00	—
1989 Proof	300,000	Value: 5.50				

Y# 228 ROUBLE

Copper-Nickel, 31 mm. **Subject:** 175th Anniversary - Birth of M.Y. Lermontov **Obv:** National arms with CCCP and value below **Rev:** Head 1/4 left, quill below, dates at right **Rev. Designer:** Nikolay Nosov **Edge:** Cyrillic lettering

Date	Mintage	F	VF	XF	Unc	BU
1989	2,700,000	—	0.50	1.00	3.00	—
1989 Proof	300,000	Value: 6.00				

Y# 232 ROUBLE

Copper-Nickel, 31 mm. **Subject:** 100th Anniversary - Birth of Hamza Hakim-zade Niyazi **Obv:** National arms with CCCP and value below **Rev:** Bust facing, dates at right **Edge:** Cyrillic lettering

Date	Mintage	F	VF	XF	Unc	BU
1989	1,800,000	—	0.50	1.00	3.00	—
1989 Proof	200,000	Value: 6.00				

Y# 233 ROUBLE

Copper-Nickel, 31 mm. **Subject:** 100th Anniversary - Death of Mihai Eminescu **Obv:** National arms with CCCP and value below **Rev:** Head 3/4 left flanked by dates **Edge:** Cyrillic lettering

Date	Mintage	F	VF	XF	Unc	BU
1989	1,800,000	—	0.50	1.00	3.00	—
1989 Proof	200,000	Value: 6.00				

Y# 235 ROUBLE

Copper-Nickel, 31 mm. **Subject:** 175th Anniversary - Birth of T.G. Shevchenko **Obv:** National arms with CCCP and value below **Rev:** Head looking down facing 3/4 left **Edge:** Cyrillic lettering

Date	Mintage	F	VF	XF	Unc	BU
1989	2,700,000	—	0.50	1.00	3.00	—
1989 Proof	300,000	Value: 5.50				

Y# 236 ROUBLE

Copper-Nickel, 31 mm. **Subject:** 100th Anniversary - Birth of Tschaikovsky - Composer **Obv:** National arms with CCCP and value below **Rev:** Seated figure left, musical notes in background **Edge:** Cyrillic lettering

Date	Mintage	F	VF	XF	Unc	BU
1990	2,600,000	—	—	—	3.00	—
1990 Proof	400,000	Value: 6.50				

Y# 237 ROUBLE

Copper-Nickel, 31 mm. **Subject:** Anniversary - Marshal Zhukov **Obv:** National arms with CCCP and value below **Rev:** Uniformed bust left **Edge:** Cyrillic lettering

Date	Mintage	F	VF	XF	Unc	BU
1990	1,600,000	—	—	—	5.00	—
1990 Proof	400,000	Value: 7.00				

Y# 240 ROUBLE

Copper-Nickel, 31 mm. **Subject:** 130th Anniversary - Birth of Anton Chekhov **Obv:** National arms with CCCP and value below **Rev:** Head 1/4 left divides design and dates **Edge:** Cyrillic lettering

Date	Mintage	F	VF	XF	Unc	BU
1990	2,600,000	—	—	—	3.00	—
1990 Proof	400,000	Value: 6.50				

Y# 257 ROUBLE

Copper-Nickel, 31 mm. **Subject:** 125th Anniversary - Birth of Janis Rainis **Obv:** National arms with CCCP and value below **Rev:** Head facing with dates at right **Edge:** Cyrillic lettering

Date	Mintage	F	VF	XF	Unc	BU
1990	2,600,000	—	—	—	3.00	—
1990 Proof	400,000	Value: 6.50				

Y# 258 ROUBLE

Copper-Nickel, 31 mm. **Subject:** 500th Anniversary - Birth of Francisk Scorina **Obv:** National arms with CCCP and value below **Rev:** Half figure facing **Edge:** Cyrillic lettering

Date	Mintage	F	VF	XF	Unc	BU
1990	2,600,000	—	—	—	3.00	—
1990 Proof	400,000	Value: 6.50				

Y# 260 ROUBLE

Copper-Nickel, 31 mm. **Subject:** 550th Anniversary - Birth of Alisher Navoi **Obv:** National arms with CCCP and value below **Rev:** Bust with hand on chin left **Edge:** Cyrillic lettering

Date	Mintage	F	VF	XF	Unc	BU
1990 Error	—	—	—	—	—	10.00
1991 Л	2,150,000	—	—	—	3.00	—
1991 Л Proof	350,000	Value: 3.50				
1991 M	—	—	—	—	3.00	—
1991 M Proof	—	Value: 3.50				

Y# 261 ROUBLE

Copper-Nickel, 31 mm. **Subject:** 125th Anniversary - Birth of P. N. Lebedev **Obv:** National arms with CCCP and value below **Rev:** Half figure right with hand on book, designs on bottom, dates and fomulas at right **Edge:** Cyrillic lettering

Date	Mintage	F	VF	XF	Unc	BU
1990 Error, rare	—	—	—	—	—	—
1991	2,150,000	—	—	—	3.00	—
1991 Proof	350,000	Value: 5.50				

Y# 282 ROUBLE

Copper-Nickel, 31 mm. **Subject:** K.B. Ivanov **Obv:** National arms with CCCP and value below **Rev:** Head left **Edge:** Cyrillic lettering

Date	Mintage	F	VF	XF	Unc	BU
1991	3,150,000	—	—	—	3.00	—
1991 Proof	350,000	Value: 5.50				

Y# 283 ROUBLE

Copper-Nickel, 31 mm. **Subject:** Turkman Poet Makhtumkuli **Obv:** National arms with CCCP and value below **Rev:** Bust left **Edge:** Cyrillic lettering

Date	Mintage	F	VF	XF	Unc	BU
1991	2,150,000	—	—	—	5.00	—
1991 Proof	350,000	Value: 5.50				

Y# 284 ROUBLE

Copper-Nickel, 31 mm. **Subject:** 850th Anniversary - Birth of Nizami Gyanzhevi - Poet **Obv:** National arms with CCCP and value below **Rev:** Bust right writing with quill **Edge:** Cyrillic lettering

Date	Mintage	F	VF	XF	Unc	BU
1991	2,200,000	—	—	—	5.00	—
1991 Proof	300,000	Value: 5.50				

Y# 289 ROUBLE

Copper-Nickel, 31 mm. **Series:** 1992 Olympics **Obv:** National arms with CCCP and value below **Rev:** Wrestlers

Date	Mintage	F	VF	XF	Unc	BU
1991 Proof	250,000	Value: 7.50				

Y# 290 ROUBLE

Copper-Nickel, 31 mm. **Series:** 1992 Olympics **Obv:** National arms with CCCP and value below **Rev:** Javelin throwers

Date	Mintage	F	VF	XF	Unc	BU
1991 Proof	250,000	Value: 7.50				

Y# 291 ROUBLE

Copper-Nickel, 31 mm. **Series:** 1992 Olympics **Obv:** National arms with CCCP and value below **Rev:** Cyclist and charioteer

Date	Mintage	F	VF	XF	Unc	BU
1991 Proof	250,000	Value: 7.50				

Y# 299 ROUBLE

Copper-Nickel, 31 mm. **Series:** 1992 Olympics **Obv:** National arms with CCCP and value below **Rev:** Weight lifters

Date	Mintage	F	VF	XF	Unc	BU
1991 Proof	250,000	Value: 7.50				

Y# 300 ROUBLE

Copper-Nickel, 31 mm. **Series:** 1992 Olympics **Obv:** National arms with CCCP and value below **Rev:** Broad jumpers

Date	Mintage	F	VF	XF	Unc	BU
1991 Proof	250,000	Value: 7.50				

Y# 302 ROUBLE

Copper-Nickel, 31 mm. **Series:** 1992 Olympics **Obv:** National arms with CCCP and value below **Rev:** Runners

Date	Mintage	F	VF	XF	Unc	BU
1991 Proof	250,000	Value: 7.50				

Y# 263.1 ROUBLE

Copper-Nickel, 31 mm. **Subject:** 100th Birthday of Sergey Prokofiev **Obv:** National arms with CCCP and value below **Rev:** Head right **Edge:** Cyrillic lettering

Date	Mintage	F	VF	XF	Unc	BU
1991	2,150,000	—	—	—	3.00	—
1991 Proof	350,000	Value: 5.50				

Y# 263.2 ROUBLE

Copper-Nickel, 31 mm. **Subject:** 100th Birthday of Sergey Prokofiev **Obv:** National arms with CCCP and value below **Rev:** Head right, dates below **Note:** Error death date: 1952.

Date	Mintage	F	VF	XF	Unc	BU
1991 Rare	—	—	—	—	—	—

Y# A134 2 ROUBLES

Copper-Nickel **Obv:** National arms **Rev:** Value above date within wreath

Date	Mintage	F	VF	XF	Unc	BU
1958	20,976,000	—	—	—	350	—

Note: Never officially released for circulation; majority of mintage remelted

Y# B134 3 ROUBLES

Copper-Nickel **Obv:** National arms **Rev:** Value above date within wreath

Date	Mintage	F	VF	XF	Unc	BU
1958	4,050,000	—	—	—	2,300	—

Note: Never officially released for circulation; majority of mintage remelted

Y# 207 3 ROUBLES

Copper-Nickel **Subject:** 70th Anniversary - Bolshevik Revolution **Obv:** National arms with CCCP and value below **Rev:** Date above three unifomed standing figures with weapons

Date	Mintage	F	VF	XF	Unc	BU
1987	2,300,000	—	—	—	5.00	—
1987 Proof	200,000	Value: 7.50				

Y# 210 3 ROUBLES

34.5600 g., 0.9000 Silver 1.0000 oz. ASW **Subject:** 1000th Anniversary of Russian Architecture **Obv:** National arms with CCCP and value below **Rev:** Cathedral of St. Sophia in Kiev

Date	Mintage	F	VF	XF	Unc	BU
1988 (m) Proof	Est. 35,000	Value: 110				

Y# 211 3 ROUBLES

34.5600 g., 0.9000 Silver 1.0000 oz. ASW **Subject:** 1000th Anniversary of Minting in Russian **Obv:** National arms with CCCP and value below **Rev:** Coin design of St. Vladimir, 977-1015

Date	Mintage	F	VF	XF	Unc	BU
1988 (l) Proof	Est. 35,000	Value: 110				

Y# 222 3 ROUBLES

34.5600 g., 0.9000 Silver 1.0000 oz. ASW **Subject:** 500th Anniversary United Russia **Obv:** National arms with CCCP and value below **Rev:** Kremlin

Date	Mintage	F	VF	XF	Unc	BU
1989 (l) Proof	Est. 40,000	Value: 75.00				

Y# 223 3 ROUBLES

34.5600 g., 0.9000 Silver 1.0000 oz. ASW **Subject:** 500th Anniversary of the First All-Russian Coinage **Obv:** National arms with CCCP and value below **Rev:** Three ancient coins

Date	Mintage	F	VF	XF	Unc	BU
1989 (l) Proof	Est. 40,000	Value: 75.00				

Y# 234 3 ROUBLES

Copper-Nickel **Subject:** Armenian Earthquake Relief **Obv:** National arms with CCCP and value below **Rev:** Stylized hand with flame in palm, wings form mountains in background **Rev. Designer:** Nikolay Nisov **Edge:** Cyrillic lettering

Date	Mintage	F	VF	XF	Unc	BU
1989	2,700,000	—	—	—	5.00	—
1989 Proof	300,000	Value: 6.50				

Y# 242 3 ROUBLES

34.5600 g., 0.9000 Silver 1.0000 oz. ASW **Obv:** National arms with CCCP and value below **Rev:** Captain Cook on Unalaska Island

Date	Mintage	F	VF	XF	Unc	BU
1990 (l) Proof	25,000	Value: 60.00				

Y# 247 3 ROUBLES

34.5600 g., 0.9000 Silver 1.0000 oz. ASW **Subject:** World Summit for Children **Obv:** National arms with CCCP and value below **Rev:** Baby and flower within wreath above seated figures around v-shaped design **Rev. Designer:** Nikolay Nosov

Date	Mintage	F	VF	XF	Unc	BU
1990 (l) Proof	20,000	Value: 65.00				

Y# 248 3 ROUBLES

34.5600 g., 0.9000 Silver 1.0000 oz. ASW **Obv:** National arms with CCCP and value below **Rev:** Peter the Great's Fleet

Date	Mintage	F	VF	XF	Unc	BU
1990 (m) Proof	40,000	Value: 40.00				

Y# 249 3 ROUBLES

34.5600 g., 0.9000 Silver 1.0000 oz. ASW **Obv:** National arms with CCCP and value below **Rev:** St. Peter and Paul Fortress in Leningrad

Date	Mintage	F	VF	XF	Unc	BU
1990 (l) Proof	40,000	Value: 40.00				

Y# 262 3 ROUBLES

34.5600 g., 0.9000 Silver 1.0000 oz. ASW **Obv:** National arms with CCCP and value below **Rev:** Yuri Gagarin Monument **Rev. Designer:** Nikolay Nosov

Date	Mintage	F	VF	XF	Unc	BU
1991 (l) Proof	35,000	Value: 45.00				

Y# 264 3 ROUBLES

34.5600 g., 0.9000 Silver 1.0000 oz. ASW **Obv:** National arms with CCCP and value below **Rev:** Fort Ross in California

Date	Mintage	F	VF	XF	Unc	BU
1991 (l) Proof	Est. 25,000	Value: 50.00				

Y# 274 3 ROUBLES

34.5600 g., 0.9000 Silver 1.0000 oz. ASW **Obv:** National arms with CCCP and value below **Rev:** Bolshoi Theater

Date	Mintage	F	VF	XF	Unc	BU
1991 (l) Proof	40,000	Value: 35.00				

Y# 275 3 ROUBLES

34.5600 g., 0.9000 Silver 1.0000 oz. ASW **Obv:** National arms with CCCP and value below **Rev:** Moscow's Arch of Triumph

Date	Mintage	F	VF	XF	Unc	BU
1991 (m) Proof	40,000	Value: 35.00				

Y# 301 3 ROUBLES

Copper-Nickel **Subject:** 50th Anniversary - Defense of Moscow **Obv:** National arms with CCCP and value below **Rev:** Marching soldiers **Edge:** Cyrillic lettering

Date	Mintage	F	VF	XF	Unc	BU
1991	2,150,000	—	—	—	5.00	—
1991 Proof	—	Value: 6.50				

Y# C134 5 ROUBLES

Copper-Nickel **Obv:** National arms **Rev:** Value and date within sprigs

Date	Mintage	F	VF	XF	Unc	BU
1958	5,150,000	—	—	—	300	—

Note: Never officially released for circulation; majority of mintage remelted

Y# 145 5 ROUBLES

16.6700 g., 0.9000 Silver .4824 oz. ASW **Series:** 1980 Olympics **Obv:** National arms flanked by CCCP with value below **Rev:** Scenes of Kiev **Rev. Designer:** Nikolay Nosov

Date	Mintage	F	VF	XF	Unc	BU
1977 (l)	250,000	—	—	—	8.50	—
1977 (l) Frosted unc.	Inc. above	—	—	—	—	—
1977 (l) Proof	121,000	Value: 10.00				
1977 (m) Proof	—	Value: 10.00				

Y# 146 5 ROUBLES

16.6700 g., 0.9000 Silver .4824 oz. ASW **Series:** 1980 Olympics **Obv:** National arms divide CCCP with value below **Rev:** Scenes of Leningrad

Date	Mintage	F	VF	XF	Unc	BU
1977 (l)	250,000	—	—	—	8.50	—
1977 (l) Frosted unc.	Inc. above	—	—	—	—	—
1977 (l) Proof	121,000	Value: 10.00				
1977 (m)	Inc. above	—	—	—	8.50	—
1977 (m) Proof	Inc. above	Value: 10.00				

Y# 147 5 ROUBLES

16.6700 g., 0.9000 Silver .4824 oz. ASW **Series:** 1980 Olympics **Obv:** National arms divide CCCP with value below **Rev:** Scenes of Minsk

Date	Mintage	F	VF	XF	Unc	BU
1977(l)	250,000	—	—	—	8.50	—
1977(l) Proof	121,000	Value: 10.00				
1977(m) Proof	Inc. above	Value: 10.00				

Y# 148 5 ROUBLES

16.6700 g., 0.9000 Silver .4824 oz. ASW **Series:** 1980 Olympics **Obv:** National arms divide CCCP with value below **Rev:** Scenes of Tallinn

Date	Mintage	F	VF	XF	Unc	BU
1977(l)	252,000	—	—	—	8.50	—
1977(l) Frosted	Inc. above	—	—	—	—	—
1977(l) Proof	122,000	Value: 10.00				
1977(m)	Inc. above	—	—	—	8.50	—
1977(m) Proof	Inc. above	Value: 10.00				

Y# 154 5 ROUBLES

16.6700 g., 0.9000 Silver .4824 oz. ASW **Series:** 1980 Olympics **Obv:** National arms divide CCCP with value below **Rev:** Runner in front of stadium

Date	Mintage	F	VF	XF	Unc	BU
1978(l)	227,000	—	—	—	8.50	—
1978(m) Proof	118,000	Value: 10.00				
1978(l) Matte proof	—	Value: 30.00				

Y# 155 5 ROUBLES

16.6700 g., 0.9000 Silver .4824 oz. ASW **Series:** 1980 Olympics **Obv:** National arms divide CCCP with value below **Rev:** Swimming

Date	Mintage	F	VF	XF	Unc	BU
1978(l)	227,000	—	—	—	8.50	—
1978(l) Frosted	Inc. above	—	—	—	—	—
1978(l) Proof	118,000	Value: 10.00				
1978(l) Matte proof	—	Value: 30.00				

Y# 156 5 ROUBLES

16.6700 g., 0.9000 Silver .4824 oz. ASW **Series:** 1980 Olympics **Obv:** National arms divide CCCP with value below **Rev:** High jumping **Rev. Designer:** Nikolay Nosov

Date	Mintage	F	VF	XF	Unc	BU
1978(l)	221,000	—	—	—	8.50	—
1978(l) Proof	119,000	Value: 10.00				
1978(m)	Inc. above	—	—	—	8.50	—
1978(m) Proof	Inc. above	Value: 10.00				

Y# 157 5 ROUBLES

16.6700 g., 0.9000 Silver .4824 oz. ASW **Series:** 1980 Olympics **Obv:** National arms divide CCCP with value below **Rev:** Equestrian show jumping **Rev. Designer:** Nicolay Nosov

Date	Mintage	F	VF	XF	Unc	BU
1978(l)	221,000	—	—	—	8.50	—
1978(l) Proof	119,000	Value: 10.00				
1978(m)	Inc. above	—	—	—	8.50	—
1978(m) Proof	Inc. above	Value: 10.00				

Y# 166 5 ROUBLES

16.6700 g., 0.9000 Silver 0.4824 oz. ASW **Series:** 1980 Olympics **Obv:** National arms divide CCCP with value below **Rev:** Weight lifting **Rev. Designer:** Nikolay Nosov

Date	Mintage	F	VF	XF	Unc	BU
1979(l)	207,000	—	—	—	8.50	—
1979(l) Proof	108,000	Value: 10.00				
1979(m)	Inc. above	—	—	—	8.50	—
1979(m) Proof	Inc. above	Value: 10.00				

Y# 167 5 ROUBLES

16.6700 g., 0.9000 Silver .4824 oz. ASW **Series:** 1980 Olympics **Obv:** National arms divide CCCP with value below **Rev:** Hammer throw

Date	Mintage	F	VF	XF	Unc	BU
1979(l)	207,000	—	—	—	8.50	—
1979(l) Proof	119,000	Value: 10.00				
1979(m)	Inc. above	—	—	—	8.50	—
1979(m) Proof	Inc. above	Value: 10.00				

Y# 179 5 ROUBLES

16.6700 g., 0.9000 Silver **Series:** 1980 Olympics **Obv:** National arms divide CCCP with value below **Rev:** Archery

Date	Mintage	F	VF	XF	Unc	BU
1980(l)	126,000	—	—	—	8.50	—
1980(l) Proof	95,000	Value: 11.00				
1980(m)	Inc. above	—	—	—	8.50	—
1980(m) Proof	Inc. above	Value: 11.00				

Y# 180 5 ROUBLES

16.6700 g., 0.9000 Silver **Series:** 1980 Olympics **Obv:** National arms divide CCCP with value below **Rev:** Gymnastics **Rev. Designer:** Nikolay Nosov

Date	Mintage	F	VF	XF	Unc	BU
1980(l)	126,000	—	—	—	8.50	—
1980(l) Proof	95,000	Value: 11.00				
1980(m)	Inc. above	—	—	—	8.50	—
1980(m) Proof	Inc. above	Value: 11.00				

Y# 181 5 ROUBLES

16.6700 g., 0.9000 Silver **Series:** 1980 Olympics **Subject:** Equestrian - Isindi **Obv:** National arms divide CCCP with value below **Rev:** Polo players

Date	Mintage	F	VF	XF	Unc	BU
1980(l)	126,000	—	—	—	8.50	—
1980(l) Proof	96,000	Value: 11.00				

Y# 182 5 ROUBLES

16.6700 g., 0.9000 Silver **Series:** 1980 Olympics **Obv:** National arms divide CCCP with value below **Rev:** Gorodki - stick throwing

Date	Mintage	F	VF	XF	Unc	BU
1980(l)	126,000	—	—	—	8.50	—
1980(l) Proof	96,000	Value: 11.00				

Y# 208 5 ROUBLES

Copper-Nickel **Subject:** 70th Anniversary - Bolshevik Revolution **Obv:** National arms with CCCP and value below **Rev:** Head left and date within banner **Rev. Designer:** Nikolay Nosov

Date	Mintage	F	VF	XF	Unc	BU
1987	1,300,000	—	—	—	5.00	—
1987 Proof	200,000	Value: 7.00				

Y# 217 5 ROUBLES

Copper-Nickel, 35 mm. **Obv:** National arms with CCCP and value below **Rev:** Leningrad - Peter the Great

Date	Mintage	F	VF	XF	Unc	BU
1988	1,675,000	—	—	—	5.00	—
1988 Proof	325,000	Value: 7.00				

Y# 218 5 ROUBLES

Copper-Nickel, 35 mm. **Obv:** National arms with CCCP and value below **Rev:** Novgorood Monument to the Russian Millennium **Rev. Designer:** Nikolay Nosov

Date	Mintage	F	VF	XF	Unc	BU
1988	1,675,000	—	—	—	5.00	—
1988 Proof	325,000	Value: 7.00				

Y# 219 5 ROUBLES

Copper-Nickel, 35 mm. **Obv:** National arms with CCCP and value below **Rev:** St. Sophia Cathedral in Kiev

Date	Mintage	F	VF	XF	Unc	BU
1988	1,675,000	—	—	—	5.00	—
1988 Proof	325,000	Value: 7.00				

Y# 221 5 ROUBLES

Copper-Nickel, 35 mm. **Obv:** National arms with CCCP and value below **Rev:** Pokrowsky Cathedral in Moscow

Date	Mintage	F	VF	XF	Unc	BU
1989	1,700,000	—	—	—	5.00	—
1989 Proof	300,000	Value: 7.00				

Y# 229 5 ROUBLES

Copper-Nickel, 35 mm. **Obv:** National arms with CCCP and value below **Rev:** Samarkand

Date	Mintage	F	VF	XF	Unc	BU
1989	1,700,000	—	—	—	5.00	—
1989 Proof	300,000	Value: 7.00				

Y# 230 5 ROUBLES

Copper-Nickel, 35 mm. **Obv:** National arms with CCCP and value below **Rev:** Cathedral of the Annunciation in Moscow

Date	Mintage	F	VF	XF	Unc	BU
1989	1,700,000	—	—	—	5.00	—
1989 Proof	300,000	Value: 7.00				

Y# 241 5 ROUBLES

Copper-Nickel, 35 mm. **Obv:** National arms with CCCP and value below **Rev:** St. Petersburg Palace

Date	Mintage	F	VF	XF	Unc	BU
1990	2,600,000	—	—	—	5.00	—
1990 Proof	400,000	Value: 7.00				

Y# 246 5 ROUBLES

Copper-Nickel, 35 mm. **Obv:** National arms with CCCP and value below **Rev:** Uspenski Cathedral **Edge:** Cyrillic lettering

Date	Mintage	F	VF	XF	Unc	BU
1990	2,600,000	—	—	—	5.00	—
1990 Proof	400,000	Value: 7.00				

Y# 259 5 ROUBLES

Copper-Nickel, 35 mm. **Obv:** National arms with CCCP and value below **Rev:** Matenadarin Depository of Ancient Armenian Manuscripts **Rev. Designer:** Nikolay Nosov

Date	Mintage	F	VF	XF	Unc	BU
1990	2,600,000	—	—	—	5.00	—
1990 Proof	350,000	Value: 7.00				

Y# 271 5 ROUBLES

Copper-Nickel, 35 mm. **Obv:** National arms with CCCP and value below **Rev:** Cathedral of the Archangel Michael in Moscow **Edge:** Cyrillic lettering

Date	Mintage	F	VF	XF	Unc	BU
1991	2,150,000	—	—	—	5.00	—
1991 Proof	350,000	Value: 7.00				

Y# 272 5 ROUBLES

Copper-Nickel, 35 mm. **Obv:** National arms with CCCP and value below **Rev:** State bank building in Moscow

Date	Mintage	F	VF	XF	Unc	BU
1991	2,600,000	—	—	—	5.00	—
1991 Proof	400,000	Value: 7.00				

Y# 273 5 ROUBLES

Copper-Nickel, 35 mm. **Obv:** National arms with CCCP and value below **Rev:** Monument **Rev. Designer:** Nikolay Nosov **Edge:** Cyrillic lettering

Date	Mintage	F	VF	XF	Unc	BU
1991	2,150,000	—	—	—	5.00	—
1991 Proof	350,000	Value: 7.00				

Y# 268 5 ROUBLES

7.7758 g., 0.9990 Palladium .2500 oz. **Series:** Ballet **Obv:** National arms with CCCP and value below **Rev:** Ballerina

Date	Mintage	F	VF	XF	Unc	BU
1991(l)	9,000	—	—	—	150	—

Y# 149 10 ROUBLES

33.3000 g., 0.9000 Silver .9636 oz. ASW **Series:** 1980 Olympics **Obv:** National arms divide CCCP with value below **Rev:** Scenes of Moscow

Date	Mintage	F	VF	XF	Unc	BU
1977(l)	250,000	—	—	—	17.50	—
1977(l) Proof	121,000	Value: 20.00				
1977(m)	Inc. above	—	—	—	17.50	—
1977(m) Proof	Inc. above	Value: 20.00				

Y# 150 10 ROUBLES

33.3000 g., 0.9000 Silver .9636 oz. ASW **Series:** 1980 Olympics **Obv:** National arms divide CCCP with value below **Rev:** Map of USSR back of design above rings

Date	Mintage	F	VF	XF	Unc	BU
1977(l)	250,000	—	—	—	17.50	—
1977(l) Proof	121,000	Value: 20.00				

Y# 158.1 10 ROUBLES

33.3000 g., 0.9000 Silver .9636 oz. ASW **Series:** 1980 Olympics **Obv:** National arms divide CCCP with value below **Rev:** Cycling

Date	Mintage	F	VF	XF	Unc	BU
1978(l)	227,000	—	—	—	17.50	—
1978(l) Proof	118,000	Value: 20.00				

Y# 158.2 10 ROUBLES

33.3000 g., 0.9000 Silver .9636 oz. ASW **Series:** 1980 Olympics **Obv:** National arms divide CCCP with value below **Rev:** Without mint mark

Date	Mintage	F	VF	XF	Unc	BU
1978 Rare	—	—	—	—	—	—
1978 Proof, rare	100	—	—	—	—	—

Y# 159 10 ROUBLES

33.3000 g., 0.9000 Silver .9636 oz. ASW **Series:** 1980 Olympics **Obv:** National arms divide CCCP with value below **Rev:** Canoeing

Date	Mintage	F	VF	XF	Unc	BU
1978(l) Rare	34,000	—	—	—	—	—
1978(m)	192,000	—	—	—	17.50	—
1978(m) Proof	118,000	Value: 20.00				

Y# 160 10 ROUBLES

33.3000 g., 0.9000 Silver .9636 oz. ASW **Series:** 1980 Olympics **Obv:** National arms divide CCCP with value below **Rev:** Equestrian sports

Date	Mintage	F	VF	XF	Unc	BU
1978(l) Rare	34,000	—	—	—	—	—
1978(m)	192,000	—	—	—	17.50	—
1978(m) Proof	118,000	Value: 20.00				

Y# 161 10 ROUBLES

33.3000 g., 0.9000 Silver .9636 oz. ASW **Series:** 1980 Olympics **Obv:** National arms divide CCCP with value below **Rev:** Pole vaulting

Date	Mintage	F	VF	XF	Unc	BU
1978(l)	221,000	—	—	—	17.50	—
1978(l) Proof	119,000	Value: 20.00				
1978(m)	Inc. above	—	—	—	17.50	—
1978(m) Proof	Inc. above	Value: 20.00				

Y# 168 10 ROUBLES

33.3000 g., 0.9000 Silver .9636 oz. ASW **Series:** 1980 Olympics **Obv:** National arms divide CCCP with value below **Rev:** Basketball

Date	Mintage	F	VF	XF	Unc	BU
1979(l)	221,000	—	—	—	17.50	—
1979(l) Proof	119,000	Value: 20.00				
1979 Rare	—	—	—	—	—	—

Y# 169 10 ROUBLES

33.3000 g., 0.9000 Silver .9636 oz. ASW **Series:** 1980 Olympics **Obv:** National arms divide CCCP with value below **Rev:** Volleyball

Date	Mintage	F	VF	XF	Unc	BU
1979(l)	221,000	—	—	—	17.50	—
1979(l) Proof	119,000	Value: 20.00				

Y# 170 10 ROUBLES

33.3000 g., 0.9000 Silver .9636 oz. ASW **Series:** 1980 Olympics **Obv:** National arms divide CCCP with value below **Rev:** Boxing **Rev. Designer:** Nikolay Nosov

Date	Mintage	F	VF	XF	Unc	BU
1979(l)	207,000	—	—	—	17.50	—
1979(l) Proof	108,000	Value: 20.00				

Y# 171 10 ROUBLES

33.3000 g., 0.9000 Silver .9636 oz. ASW **Series:** 1980 Olympics **Obv:** National arms divide CCCP with value below **Rev:** Judo

Date	Mintage	F	VF	XF	Unc	BU
1979(l)	207,000	—	—	—	17.50	—
1979(l) Proof	108,000	Value: 20.00				
1979(m)	Inc. above	—	—	—	17.50	—
1979(m) Proof	Inc. above	Value: 20.00				

Y# 172 10 ROUBLES

33.3000 g., 0.9000 Silver .9636 oz. ASW **Series:** 1980 Olympics **Obv:** National arms divide CCCP with value below **Rev:** Weight lifting

Date	Mintage	F	VF	XF	Unc	BU
1979(l)	207,000	—	—	—	17.50	—
1979(l) Proof	108,000	Value: 20.00				

Y# 183 10 ROUBLES

33.3000 g., 0.9000 Silver .9636 oz. ASW **Series:** 1980 Olympics **Obv:** National arms divide CCCP with value below **Rev:** Wrestlers

Date	Mintage	F	VF	XF	Unc	BU
1980(l)	126,000	—	—	—	17.50	60.00
1980(l) Proof	95,000	Value: 20.00				
1980(m)	Inc. above	—	—	—	17.50	—
1980(m) Proof	Inc. above	Value: 20.00				

Y# 184 10 ROUBLES

33.3000 g., 0.9000 Silver .9636 oz. ASW **Series:** 1980 Olympics **Obv:** National arms divide CCCP with value below **Rev:** Tug of war

Date	Mintage	F	VF	XF	Unc	BU
1980(l)	126,000	—	—	—	17.50	—
1980(l) Proof	95,000	Value: 20.00				

Y# 185 10 ROUBLES

33.3000 g., 0.9000 Silver .9636 oz. ASW **Series:** 1980 Olympics **Obv:** National arms divide CCCP with value below **Rev:** Reindeer racing

Date	Mintage	F	VF	XF	Unc	BU
1980(l)	126,000	—	—	—	17.50	—
1980(l) Proof	95,000	Value: 20.00				

Y# 238 10 ROUBLES

15.5500 g., 0.9990 Palladium .5000 oz. **Series:** Ballet **Obv:** National arms with CCCP and value below **Rev:** Ballerina

Date	Mintage	F	VF	XF	Unc	BU
1990(l)	Est. 15,000	—	—	—	265	—

Y# 269 10 ROUBLES

15.5500 g., 0.9990 Palladium .5000 oz. **Series:** Ballet **Obv:** National arms with CCCP and value below **Rev:** Ballerina

Date	Mintage	F	VF	XF	Unc	BU
1991(l)	15,000	—	—	—	265	—

Y# 285 10 ROUBLES

2.6600 g., 0.5850 Gold .0500 oz. AGW **Series:** Ballet **Obv:** National arms with CCCP and value below **Rev:** Ballerina

Date	Mintage	F	VF	XF	Unc	BU
1991(l)	6,000	—	—	—	55.00	—

Y# 212 25 ROUBLES

31.1000 g., 0.9990 Palladium 1.0000 oz. **Subject:** Monument to

Vladimir, Grand Duke of Kiev and Millennium of Christianity in Russia **Obv:** National arms with CCCP and value below **Rev:** Monument

Date	Mintage	F	VF	XF	Unc	BU
1988(l)	7,000	—	—	—	500	—

Y# 231 25 ROUBLES

31.1000 g., 0.9990 Palladium 1.0000 oz. **Series:** Ballet **Obv:** National arms with CCCP and value below **Rev:** Ballerina

Date	Mintage	F	VF	XF	Unc	BU
1989(l) Matte proof	—	Value: 525				
1989(l) Proof	3,000	Value: 525				
1989(l)	27,000	—	—	—	500	—

Y# 224 25 ROUBLES

31.1000 g., 0.9990 Palladium 1.0000 oz. **Subject:** 500th Anniversary of Russian State **Obv:** National arms with CCCP and value below **Rev:** Ivan III on throne

Date	Mintage	F	VF	XF	Unc	BU
1989(l) Proof	Est. 12,000	Value: 500				

Y# 239 25 ROUBLES

31.1000 g., 0.9990 Palladium 1.0000 oz. **Series:** Ballet **Obv:** National arms with CCCP and value below **Rev:** Ballerina

Date	Mintage	F	VF	XF	Unc	BU
1990(l) Proof	3,000	Value: 525				
1990(l)	27,000	—	—	—	500	—

Y# 243 25 ROUBLES

31.1000 g., 0.9990 Palladium 1.0000 oz. **Subject:** 250th Anniversary - Discovery of Russian America **Obv:** National arms with CCCP and value below **Rev:** Ship, St. Peter

Date	Mintage	F	VF	XF	Unc	BU
1990(l) Proof	6,500	Value: 500				

Y# 244 25 ROUBLES

31.1000 g., 0.9990 Palladium 1.0000 oz. **Subject:** 250th Anniversary - Discovery of Russian America **Obv:** National arms with CCCP and value below **Rev:** Ship, St. Paul

Date	Mintage	F	VF	XF	Unc	BU
1990(l) Proof	6,500	Value: 500				

Y# 250 25 ROUBLES

31.1000 g., 0.9990 Palladium 1.0000 oz. **Subject:** 500th Anniversary of Russian State **Obv:** National arms with CCCP and value below **Rev:** Peter the Great

Date	Mintage	F	VF	XF	Unc	BU
1990(l) Proof	12,000	Value: 500				

Y# 270 25 ROUBLES

31.1000 g., 0.9990 Palladium 1.0000 oz. **Series:** Ballet **Obv:** National arms with CCCP and value below **Rev:** Ballerina

Date	Mintage	F	VF	XF	Unc	BU
1991(l) Proof	30,000	Value: 500				
1991(l)	30,000	—	—	—	500	—

Y# 265 25 ROUBLES

31.1000 g., 0.9990 Palladium 1.0000 oz. **Note:** Three Saints Harbor - Russian settlement in America.

Date	Mintage	F	VF	XF	Unc	BU
1991 Proof	Est. 6,500	Value: 500				

Y# 266 25 ROUBLES

31.1000 g., 0.9990 Palladium 1.0000 oz. **Note:** Novo Archangelsk 1799 - three-masted ship

Date	Mintage	F	VF	XF	Unc	BU
1991(l) Proof	Est. 6,500	Value: 500				

Y# 276 25 ROUBLES

31.1000 g., 0.9990 Palladium 1.0000 oz. **Subject:** 500th Anniversary of Russian State **Obv:** National arms with CCCP and value below **Rev:** Abolition of Serfdom in Russia **Rev. Designer:** Nikolay Nosov

Date	Mintage	F	VF	XF	Unc	BU
1991(l) Proof	Est. 12,000	Value: 500				

Y# 286 25 ROUBLES

5.3200 g., 0.5850 Gold .1 oz. AGW **Series:** Ballet **Obv:** National arms with CCCP and value below **Rev:** Ballerina

Date	Mintage	F	VF	XF	Unc	BU
1991(l)	5,000	—	—	—	110	—

Y# 286a 25 ROUBLES

3.1100 g., 0.9990 Gold .1 oz. AGW **Series:** Ballet **Obv:** National arms with CCCP and value below **Rev:** Ballerina

Date	Mintage	F	VF	XF	Unc	BU
1991(l) Proof	1,500	Value: 250				

Y# 213 50 ROUBLES

8.6397 g., 0.9000 Gold .2500 oz. AGW **Subject:** 1000th Anniversary of Russian Architecture **Obv:** National arms divide CCCP with value below **Rev:** Cathedral of st. Sophia in Novgorod

Date	Mintage	F	VF	XF	Unc	BU
1988(m)	25,000	—	—	—	185	—

Y# 225 50 ROUBLES

8.6397 g., 0.9000 Gold .2500 oz. AGW **Subject:** 500th Anniversary of Russian State **Obv:** National arms with CCCP and value below **Rev:** Cathedral of the Ascension

Date	Mintage	F	VF	XF	Unc	BU
1989(m) Proof	Est. 25,000	Value: 185				

Y# 251 50 ROUBLES

8.6397 g., 0.9000 Gold .2500 oz. AGW **Subject:** 500th Anniversary of Russian State **Obv:** National arms with CCCP and value below **Rev:** Moscow Church of the Archangel

Date	Mintage	F	VF	XF	Unc	BU
1990(m) Proof	25,000	Value: 185				

Y# 277 50 ROUBLES

8.6440 g., 0.9000 Gold .2500 oz. AGW **Subject:** 500th Anniversary of Russian State **Obv:** National arms with CCCP and value below **Rev:** St. Isaac Cathedral in St. Petersburg

Date	Mintage	F	VF	XF	Unc	BU
1991(m) Proof	25,000	Value: 185				

Y# 287 50 ROUBLES

13.3000 g., 0.5850 Gold .2500 oz. AGW **Subject:** Bolshoi Ballet **Obv:** National arms with CCCP and value below **Rev:** Ballerina

Date	Mintage	F	VF	XF	Unc	BU
1991(l)	2,400	—	—	—	250	—

Y# 287a 50 ROUBLES

7.7800 g., 0.9990 Gold .2500 oz. AGW **Subject:** Bolshoi Ballet **Obv:** National arms with CCCP and value below **Rev:** Ballerina

Date	Mintage	F	VF	XF	Unc	BU
1991(l) Proof	1,500	Value: 450				

Y# A163 100 ROUBLES

17.2800 g., 0.9000 Gold .5000 oz. AGW **Series:** 1980 Olympics **Obv:** National arms divide CCCP with value below **Rev:** Upright design with star on top and sprig within world globe, olympic rings below

Date	Mintage	F	VF	XF	Unc	BU
1977(l) Proof	38,000	Value: 375				
1977(m)	Inc. above	—	—	—	350	—
1977(m) Proof	Inc. above	Value: 375				
1977(l)	44,000	—	—	—	350	—

Y# 151 100 ROUBLES

17.2800 g., 0.9000 Gold .5000 oz. AGW **Series:** 1980 Olympics **Obv:** National arms divide CCCP with value below **Rev:** Lenin Stadium

Date	Mintage	F	VF	XF	Unc	BU
1978(l)	62,000	—	—	—	350	—
1978(l) Proof	45,000	Value: 375				
1978(m)	Inc. above	—	—	—	350	—
1978(m) Proof	Inc. above	Value: 375				

Y# 162 100 ROUBLES

17.2800 g., 0.9000 Gold .5000 oz. AGW **Series:** 1980 Olympics **Obv:** National arms divide CCCP with value below **Rev:** Waterside Grandstand **Rev. Designer:** Nikolay Nosov

Date	Mintage	F	VF	XF	Unc	BU
1978 Rare	—	—	—	—	—	—
1978 Proof, rare	—	—	—	—	—	—
1978(l)	57,000	—	—	—	350	—
1978(l) Proof	43,000	Value: 375				
1978(m) Rare	Inc. above	—	—	—	—	—
1978(m) Proof, rare	Inc. above	—	—	—	—	—

Y# 173 100 ROUBLES

17.2800 g., 0.9000 Gold .5000 oz. AGW **Series:** 1980 Olympics **Obv:** National arms divide CCCP with value below **Rev:** Velodrome Building

Date	Mintage	F	VF	XF	Unc	BU
1979(l)	55,000	—	—	—	350	—
1979(l) Proof	42,000	Value: 375				
1979(m) Rare	Inc. above	—	—	—	—	—
1979(m) Proof	Inc. above	Value: 375				

Y# 174 100 ROUBLES

17.2800 g., 0.9000 Gold .5000 oz. AGW **Series:** 1980 Olympics **Obv:** National arms divide CCCP with value below **Rev:** Druzhba Sports Hall

Date	Mintage	F	VF	XF	Unc	BU
1979(m)	54,000	—	—	—	350	—
1979(l) Proof	38,000	Value: 375				

Y# 186 100 ROUBLES

17.2800 g., 0.9000 Gold .5000 oz. AGW **Series:** 1980 Olympics **Obv:** National arms divide CCCP with value below **Rev:** Torch

Date	Mintage	F	VF	XF	Unc	BU
1980(m)	25,000	—	—	—	350	—
1980(l) Proof	28,000	Value: 375				

Y# 214 100 ROUBLES

17.2800 g., 0.9000 Gold .5000 oz. AGW **Series:** 1980 Olympics **Subject:** 1000th Anniversary of Minting in Russia - Coin design of St. Vladimir (977-1015) **Obv:** National arms divide CCCP with value below **Rev:** Ancient coin design

Date	Mintage	F	VF	XF	Unc	BU
1988(m)	14,000	—	—	—	385	—

Y# 226 100 ROUBLES

17.2800 g., 0.9000 Gold .5000 oz. AGW **Series:** 1980 Olympics **Subject:** 500th Anniversary of Russian State **Obv:** National arms with CCCP and value below **Rev:** Seal of Ivan III

Date	Mintage	F	VF	XF	Unc	BU
1989(m) Proof	Est. 14,000	Value: 450				

Y# 252 100 ROUBLES

17.2800 g., 0.9000 Gold .5000 oz. AGW **Series:** 1980 Olympics **Subject:** 500th Anniversary of Russian State **Obv:** National arms divide CCCP with value below **Rev:** Peter the Great Monument

Date	Mintage	F	VF	XF	Unc	BU
1990(m) Proof	14,000	Value: 450				

Y# 288a 100 ROUBLES

15.5500 g., 0.9990 Gold .5000 oz. AGW **Subject:** Bolshoi Ballet **Obv:** National arms with CCCP and value below **Rev:** Ballerina

Date	Mintage	F	VF	XF	Unc	BU
1991(l) Proof	1,500	Value: 750				

Y# 278 100 ROUBLES

17.2800 g., 0.9000 Gold .5000 oz. AGW **Series:** 1980 Olympics **Subject:** 500th Anniversary of Russian State **Obv:** National arms with CCCP and value below **Rev:** Tolstoi Monument

Date	Mintage	F	VF	XF	Unc	BU
1991(m) Proof	14,000	Value: 385				

Y# 288 100 ROUBLES

26.5900 g., 0.5850 Gold .5000 oz. AGW **Subject:** Bolshoi Ballet **Obv:** CCCP and value below building **Rev:** Ballerina

Date	Mintage	F	VF	XF	Unc	BU
1991(l)	1,200	—	—	—	500	—

Y# 152 150 ROUBLES

15.5400 g., 0.9990 Platinum .4991 oz. APW **Series:** 1980 Olympics **Obv:** National arms divide CCCP with value below **Rev:** Upright design with star on top within wreath, Olympic rings below

Date	Mintage	F	VF	XF	Unc	BU
1977(l)	9,910	—	—	—	650	—
1977(m) Proof	24,000	Value: 675				

Y# 163 150 ROUBLES

15.5400 g., 0.9990 Platinum .4991 oz. APW **Series:** 1980 Olympics **Obv:** National arms divide CCCP with value below **Rev:** Throwing discus

Date	Mintage	F	VF	XF	Unc	BU
1978(l)	13,000	—	—	—	650	—
1978(l) Proof	20,000	Value: 675				

Y# 175 150 ROUBLES

15.5400 g., 0.9990 Platinum .4991 oz. APW **Series:** 1980 Olympics **Obv:** National arms divide CCCP with value below **Rev:** Greek wrestlers **Rev. Designer:** Nikolay Nosov

Date	Mintage	F	VF	XF	Unc	BU
1979(l)	14,000	—	—	—	650	—
1979(l)	19,000	—	—	—	650	—

Y# 176 150 ROUBLES

15.5400 g., 0.9990 Platinum .4991 oz. APW **Series:** 1980 Olympics **Obv:** National arms divide CCCP with value below **Rev:** Roman chariot racers

Date	Mintage	F	VF	XF	Unc	BU
1979(l)	9,728	—	—	—	650	—
1979(l) Proof	17,000	Value: 675				

Y# 187 150 ROUBLES

15.5400 g., 0.9990 Platinum .4991 oz. APW **Series:** 1980 Olympics **Obv:** National arms divide CCCP with value below **Rev:** Ancient Greek runners

Date	Mintage	F	VF	XF	Unc	BU
1980(l)	7,820	—	—	—	650	—
1980(l) Proof	13,000	Value: 675				

Y# 215 150 ROUBLES

15.5500 g., 0.9990 Platinum .5000 oz. APW **Subject:** 1000th Anniversary of Russian Literature **Obv:** National arms with CCCP and value below **Rev:** Chronicler writing epic about Grand Duke Igor

Date	Mintage	F	VF	XF	Unc	BU
1988(l)	16,000	—	—	—	650	—

Y# 227 150 ROUBLES

15.5500 g., 0.9990 Platinum .5000 oz. APW **Subject:** 500th Anniversary of Russian State **Obv:** National arms with CCCP and value below **Rev:** Ugra River Encounter

Date	Mintage	F	VF	XF	Unc	BU
1989(l) Proof	Est. 16,000	Value: 650				

Y# 245 150 ROUBLES
15.5500 g., 0.9990 Platinum .5000 oz. APW **Subject:** 250th Anniversary - Discovery of Russian America **Obv:** National arms with CCCP and value below **Rev:** Ship - St. Gavriil **Rev. Designer:** Nikolay Nosov

Date	Mintage	F	VF	XF	Unc	BU
1990(l) Proof	6,500	Value: 675				

Y# 253 150 ROUBLES
15.5500 g., 0.9990 Platinum .5000 oz. APW **Subject:** 500th Anniversary of Russian State **Obv:** National arms with CCCP and value below **Rev:** Battle of Poltava River **Rev. Designer:** Nikolay Nosov

Date	Mintage	F	VF	XF	Unc	BU
1990(l) Proof	16,000	Value: 650				

Y# 267 150 ROUBLES
15.5500 g., 0.9990 Platinum .5000 oz. APW **Subject:** 250th Anniversary - Discovery of Russian America **Obv:** National arms with CCCP and value below **Rev:** Bishop Veniaminov with ship in background

Date	Mintage	F	VF	XF	Unc	BU
1991(l) Proof	Est. 6,500	Value: 675				

Y# 279 150 ROUBLES
17.5000 g., 0.9990 Platinum .5000 oz. APW **Subject:** 500th Anniversary of Russian State - War of Liberation Against Napoleon **Obv:** National arms with CCCP and value below **Rev:** Monument divides heads

Date	Mintage	F	VF	XF	Unc	BU
1991(l) Proof	16,000	Value: 650				

GOVERNMENT BANK ISSUES

1991-1992

Y# 296 10 KOPEKS
Copper Clad Steel **Obv:** Kremlin Tower and Dome **Rev:** Value flanked by sprigs above date

Date	Mintage	F	VF	XF	Unc	BU
1991М	—	0.10	0.15	0.25	0.50	—

Y# 292 50 KOPEKS
Copper-Nickel **Obv:** Kremlin Tower and Dome **Rev:** Value flanked by sprigs above date

Date	Mintage	F	VF	XF	Unc	BU
1991Л	—	0.15	0.25	0.35	1.00	—

Y# 293 ROUBLE
Copper-Nickel **Obv:** Kremlin Tower and Dome **Rev:** Value flanked by sprigs above date

Date	Mintage	F	VF	XF	Unc	BU
1991Л	—	—	—	—	1.00	—
1991М	—	—	—	—	1.50	—

Y# 280 5 ROUBLES
Bi-Metallic Brass center in Copper-Nickel ring, 25 mm. **Series:** Wildlife **Obv:** Value flanked by sprigs within circle **Rev:** Owl flanked by grassy sprigs within circle **Edge:** Alternating reeded and smooth

Date	Mintage	F	VF	XF	Unc	BU
1991Л	500,000	—	—	—	3.00	6.00

Y# 281 5 ROUBLES
Bi-Metallic Brass center in Copper-Nickel ring, 25 mm. **Series:** Wildlife **Obv:** Value flanked by sprigs within circle **Rev:** Mountain Goat within circle **Edge:** Alternating reeded and smooth

Date	Mintage	F	VF	XF	Unc	BU
1991Л	500,000	—	—	—	2.00	5.00

Y# 294 5 ROUBLES
Copper-Nickel, 24 mm. **Obv:** Kremlin Tower and Dome **Rev:** Value flanked by sprigs above date **Edge:** Alternating reeded and smooth

Date	Mintage	F	VF	XF	Unc	BU
1991Л	—	—	—	—	3.00	—
1991М	—	—	—	—	5.00	—

Y# 295 10 ROUBLES
5.9700 g., Bi-Metallic Copper-Nickel ring, Aluminum-Bronze center, 25 mm. **Obv:** Kremlin Tower and Dome **Rev:** Value flanked by sprigs above date **Edge:** Alternating reeded and smooth

Date	Mintage	F	VF	XF	Unc	BU
1991(l)	—	0.50	1.00	2.00	3.00	—
1991(m)	—	1.50	3.00	5.00	10.00	—
1992(l) Error	—	—	30.00	50.00	80.00	—

RUSSIAN FEDERATION

Issued by БАНК РОССИИ (Bank Russia)

STANDARD COINAGE

Y# 303 ROUBLE
Copper-Nickel, 31 mm. **Subject:** Rebirth of Russian Sovereignty and Democracy **Obv:** Tower and steeples, value below **Rev:** Winged Victory and small building with flag on top

Date	Mintage	F	VF	XF	Unc	BU
1992Л	700,000	—	—	—	2.50	—
1992Л Proof	300,000	Value: 5.00				

Y# 305 ROUBLE
Copper-Nickel, 31 mm. **Subject:** 110th Anniversary - Birth of Jacob Kolas **Obv:** Tower and steeples, value below **Rev:** Head 1/4 right **Edge:** Cyrillic lettering

Date	Mintage	F	VF	XF	Unc	BU
1992Л	700,000	—	—	—	2.50	—
1992Л Proof	300,000	Value: 5.00				

Y# 306 ROUBLE
Copper-Nickel, 31 mm. **Subject:** 190th Anniversary - Birth of Admiral Nakhimov **Obv:** Tower and steeples, value below **Rev:** Uniformed bust with back facing, ship at right **Edge:** Cyrillic lettering

Date	Mintage	F	VF	XF	Unc	BU
1992Л	700,000	—	—	—	2.50	—
1992Л Proof	300,000	Value: 5.00				

Y# 311 ROUBLE
3.2500 g., Brass Clad Steel, 19.5 mm. **Obv:** Double headed eagle **Rev:** Value flanked by sprigs above date

Date	Mintage	F	VF	XF	Unc	BU
1992	—	2.00	5.00	10.00	20.00	—
1992Л	—	—	—	—	1.25	—
1992М	—	—	—	—	1.00	—
1992Л	—	—	—	—	2.50	—
1992М	—	—	—	—	2.00	—

Y# 320 ROUBLE
Copper-Nickel, 31 mm. **Obv:** Tower and steeples, value below **Rev:** Head of Yanka Kupala left **Edge:** Cyrillic lettering

Date	Mintage	F	VF	XF	Unc	BU
1992Л	1,000,000	—	—	—	2.50	—
1992Л Prooflike	200,000	—	—	—	—	—
1992Л Proof	350,000	Value: 5.00				

Y# 321 ROUBLE

Copper-Nickel, 31 mm. **Obv:** Double-headed eagle within beaded circle **Rev:** N.I. Lobachevsky 1/4 right

Date	Mintage	F	VF	XF	Unc	BU
1992М	1,000,000	—	—	—	2.50	—
1992М Prooflike	500,000	—	—	—	—	—
1992М Proof	—	Value: 5.00				

Y# 319.1 ROUBLE

Copper-Nickel, 31 mm. **Subject:** Vladimir Ivanovich Vernadsky **Obv:** Double-headed eagle within beaded circle **Rev:** Head looking down with hand on head 1/4 right

Date	Mintage	F	VF	XF	Unc	BU
1993Л	450,000	—	—	—	2.50	—
1993 Proof	15,000	Value: 3.50				
1993Л Proof	35,000	Value: 5.50				

Y# 319.2 ROUBLE

Copper-Nickel, 31 mm. **Subject:** Vladimir Ivanovich Vernadsky **Obv:** Without mint mark below eagle's claw **Rev:** Head looking down with hand on head 1/4 right

Date	Mintage	F	VF	XF	Unc	BU
1993	—	—	—	—	2.50	—
1993 Proof	—	Value: 15.00				

Y# 325 ROUBLE

Copper-Nickel, 31 mm. **Subject:** Gavrila Romanovich Derzhavin **Obv:** Double-headed eagle within beaded circle **Rev:** Bust 1/4 left above date and objects

Date	Mintage	F	VF	XF	Unc	BU
1993М	500,000	—	—	—	2.50	—
1993М Proof	—	Value: 5.00				

Y# 326 ROUBLE

Copper-Nickel, 31 mm. **Subject:** K.A. Timiryazev **Obv:** Double-headed eagle within beaded circle **Rev:** Bust facing, plant in vase at upper left

Date	Mintage	F	VF	XF	Unc	BU
1993М	500,000	—	—	—	2.50	—
1993М Proof	—	Value: 5.00				

Y# 327 ROUBLE

Copper-Nickel, 31 mm. **Subject:** V. Maikovski **Obv:** Kremlin Tower and Dome within beaded circle **Rev:** Head 1/4 left

Date	Mintage	F	VF	XF	Unc	BU
1993Л	500,000	—	—	—	2.50	—
1993М Proof	—	Value: 5.00				

Y# 335 ROUBLE

15.5500 g., 0.9000 Silver .4500 oz. ASW **Series:** Red Book Wildlife **Obv:** Double-headed eagle **Rev:** Tiger

Date	Mintage	F	VF	XF	Unc	BU
1993 Proof	50,000	Value: 27.50				

Y# 336 ROUBLE

15.5500 g., 0.9000 Silver .4500 oz. ASW **Series:** Red Book Wildlife **Obv:** Double-headed eagle **Rev:** Owl flanked by grassy designs

Date	Mintage	F	VF	XF	Unc	BU
1993 Proof	50,000	Value: 30.00				

Y# 337 ROUBLE

15.5500 g., 0.9000 Silver .4500 oz. ASW **Series:** Red Book Wildlife **Obv:** Double-headed eagle **Rev:** Mountain goat

Date	Mintage	F	VF	XF	Unc	BU
1993 Proof	50,000	Value: 27.50				

Y# 347 ROUBLE

Copper-Nickel, 31 mm. **Subject:** A.P. Borodin **Obv:** Double-headed eagle **Rev:** Bust facing 1/4 left, music notes and design in background

Date	Mintage	F	VF	XF	Unc	BU
1993М	500,000	—	—	—	2.50	—
1993М Proof	—	Value: 5.00				

Y# 348 ROUBLE

Copper-Nickel, 31 mm. **Subject:** I.S. Turgenev **Obv:** Double-headed eagle **Rev:** Head left

Date	Mintage	F	VF	XF	Unc	BU
1993Л	500,000	—	—	—	2.50	—
1993Л Proof	—	Value: 5.00				

Y# 372 ROUBLE

15.5500 g., 0.9000 Silver .4500 oz. ASW **Series:** Wildlife **Obv:** Double-headed eagle **Rev:** Red-breasted Kazarka

Date	Mintage	F	VF	XF	Unc	BU
1994 Proof	50,000	Value: 25.00				

Y# 373 ROUBLE

15.5500 g., 0.9000 Silver .4500 oz. ASW **Series:** Wildlife **Obv:** Double-headed eagle **Rev:** Asiatic Cobra

Date	Mintage	F	VF	XF	Unc	BU
1994 Proof	50,000	Value: 27.50				

Y# 374 ROUBLE

15.5500 g., 0.9000 Silver .4500 oz. ASW **Series:** Wildlife **Obv:** Double-headed eagle **Rev:** Asiatic black bear

Date	Mintage	F	VF	XF	Unc	BU
1994 Proof	50,000	Value: 27.50				

Y# 399 ROUBLE

Aluminum-Bronze, 19.5 mm. **Subject:** WWII Victory **Obv:** Double-headed eagle **Rev:** Mother Russia calling for volunteers

Date	Mintage	F	VF	XF	Unc	BU
1995	200,000	—	—	—	1.50	—

Note: In mint sets only

Y# 446 ROUBLE

17.4600 g., 0.9000 Silver .5052 oz. ASW **Series:** Wildlife **Obv:** Double-headed eagle **Rev:** White Stork

Date	Mintage	F	VF	XF	Unc	BU
1995 Proof	50,000	Value: 50.00				

Y# 447 ROUBLE

17.4600 g., 0.9000 Silver .5052 oz. ASW **Series:** Wildlife **Obv:** Double-headed eagle **Rev:** Caucasian Black Grouse

Date	Mintage	F	VF	XF	Unc	BU
1995 Proof	50,000	Value: 50.00				

Y# 448 ROUBLE

17.4600 g., 0.9000 Silver .5052 oz. ASW **Series:** Wildlife **Obv:** Double-headed eagle **Rev:** Black Sea Dolphin

Date	Mintage	F	VF	XF	Unc	BU
1995 Proof	50,000	Value: 50.00				

Y# 492 ROUBLE

17.4600 g., 0.9000 Silver .5052 oz. ASW **Series:** Wildlife **Obv:** Double-headed eagle **Rev:** Falcon

Date	Mintage	F	VF	XF	Unc	BU
1996 Proof	50,000	Value: 50.00				

Y# 493 ROUBLE

17.4600 g., 0.9000 Silver .5052 oz. ASW **Series:** Wildlife **Obv:** Double-headed eagle **Rev:** Gecko

Date	Mintage	F	VF	XF	Unc	BU
1996 Proof	50,000	Value: 50.00				

Y# 494 ROUBLE

17.4600 g., 0.9000 Silver .5052 oz. ASW **Series:** Wildlife **Obv:** Double-headed eagle **Rev:** Blind Mole Rat

Date	Mintage	F	VF	XF	Unc	BU
1996 Proof	50,000	Value: 50.00				

Y# 504 ROUBLE

Brass, 19.5 mm. **Subject:** 300th Anniversary - Russian Fleet **Obv:** Double-headed eagle **Rev:** Ship

Date	Mintage	F	VF	XF	Unc	BU
1996	100,000	—	—	—	1.50	—

Note: In sets only

Y# 611 ROUBLE

17.5500 g., 0.9000 Silver .5078 oz. ASW **Series:** Wildlife **Obv:** Double-headed eagle **Rev:** Two flamingos

Date	Mintage	F	VF	XF	Unc	BU
1996(l) Proof	—	—	—	—	—	—
1997(l) Proof	15,000	Value: 50.00				

Y# 612 ROUBLE

17.5500 g., 0.9000 Silver .5078 oz. ASW **Series:** Wildlife **Obv:** Double-headed eagle within beaded circle **Rev:** Gazelle

Date	Mintage	F	VF	XF	Unc	BU
1996(l) Proof, rare	—	—	—	—	—	—
1997(l) Proof	15,000	Value: 45.00				

Y# 613 ROUBLE

17.5500 g., 0.9000 Silver .5078 oz. ASW **Series:** Wildlife **Obv:** Double-headed eagle **Rev:** European Bison

Date	Mintage	F	VF	XF	Unc	BU
1997 Proof	15,000	Value: 45.00				

Y# 561 ROUBLE

8.4150 g., 0.9250 Silver .2502 oz. ASW **Subject:** 850th Anniversary - Moscow **Obv:** Double-headed eagle within beaded circle **Rev:** Shield flanked by buildings

Date	Mintage	F	VF	XF	Unc	BU
1997 (l)	20,000	—	—	—	—	10.00
1997 (m) Proof	5,000	Value: 25.00				

Y# 562 ROUBLE

8.4150 g., 0.9250 Silver .2502 oz. ASW **Subject:** 850th Anniversary - Moscow **Obv:** Double-headed eagle within beaded circle **Rev:** Cathedral of the Kazan Icon of the Holy Virgin

Date	Mintage	F	VF	XF	Unc	BU
1997	20,000	—	—	—	—	10.00
1997 (m) Proof	5,000	Value: 25.00				

Y# 563 ROUBLE

8.4150 g., 0.9250 Silver .2502 oz. ASW **Subject:** 850th Anniversary - Moscow **Obv:** Double-headed eagle within beaded circle **Rev:** University and shield

Date	Mintage	F	VF	XF	Unc	BU
1997 (l)	20,000	—	—	—	—	10.00
1997 (m) Proof	5,000	Value: 25.00				

Y# 564 ROUBLE

8.4150 g., 0.9250 Silver .2502 oz. ASW **Subject:** 850th Anniversary - Moscow **Obv:** Double-headed eagle within beaded circle **Rev:** Bolshoi Theatre and shield

Date	Mintage	F	VF	XF	Unc	BU
1997 Proof	25,000	Value: 15.00				

Y# 565 ROUBLE

8.4150 g., 0.9250 Silver .2502 oz. ASW **Subject:** 850th Anniversary - Moscow **Obv:** Double-headed eagle within beaded circle **Rev:** Resurrection Gate on Red Square

Date	Mintage	F	VF	XF	Unc	BU
1997 Proof	25,000	Value: 15.00				

Y# 566 ROUBLE

8.4150 g., 0.9250 Silver .2502 oz. ASW **Subject:** 850th Anniversary - Moscow **Obv:** Double-headed eagle within beaded circle **Rev:** Temple of Christ the Savior

Date	Mintage	F	VF	XF	Unc	BU
1997 Proof	25,000	Value: 15.00				

Y# 576 ROUBLE

8.4150 g., 0.9250 Silver .2502 oz. ASW **Subject:** World Soccer Championship - Paris 1998 **Obv:** Double-headed eagle **Rev:** Soccer players, Eiffel Tower and 1/2 globe

Date	Mintage	F	VF	XF	Unc	BU
1997(l) Proof	20,000	Value: 15.00				

Y# 577 ROUBLE

8.4150 g., 0.9250 Silver .2502 oz. ASW **Subject:** 1998 Winter Olympics **Obv:** Double-headed eagle within beaded circle **Rev:** Ice Hockey

Date	Mintage	F	VF	XF	Unc	BU
1997(m) Proof	20,000	Value: 17.50				

Y# 578 ROUBLE

8.4150 g., 0.9250 Silver .2502 oz. ASW **Subject:** 1998 Winter Olympics - Biathalon **Obv:** Double-headed eagle within beaded circle **Rev:** Skier within snow-flake design, marksman at left

Date	Mintage	F	VF	XF	Unc	BU
1997(m) Proof	20,000	Value: 17.50				

Y# 579 ROUBLE

8.4150 g., 0.9250 Silver .2502 oz. ASW **Subject:** 1897 Soccer **Obv:** Double-headed eagle within beaded circle **Rev:** Three soccer players

Date	Mintage	F	VF	XF	Unc	BU
1997(l) Proof	25,000	Value: 17.50				

Y# 580 ROUBLE
8.4150 g., 0.9250 Silver .2502 oz. ASW **Subject:** 1945 Soccer **Obv:** Double-headed eagle within beaded circle **Rev:** Goalie

Date	Mintage	F	VF	XF	Unc	BU
1997(l) Proof	25,000	Value: 17.50				

Y# 581 ROUBLE
8.4150 g., 0.9250 Silver .2502 oz. ASW **Subject:** 1956 Soccer **Obv:** Double-headed eagle within beaded circle **Rev:** Soccer players and kangaroo

Date	Mintage	F	VF	XF	Unc	BU
1997(l) Proof	25,000	Value: 17.50				

Y# 582 ROUBLE
8.4150 g., 0.9250 Silver .2502 oz. ASW **Subject:** 1960 Soccer **Obv:** Double-headed eagle within beaded circle **Rev:** Soccer players

Date	Mintage	F	VF	XF	Unc	BU
1997(l) Proof	25,000	Value: 17.50				

Y# 583 ROUBLE
8.4150 g., 0.9250 Silver .2502 oz. ASW **Subject:** 1988 Soccer **Obv:** Double-headed eagle **Rev:** Three players

Date	Mintage	F	VF	XF	Unc	BU
1997(l) Proof	25,000	Value: 17.50				

Y# 342 2 ROUBLES
15.8700 g., 0.5000 Silver .2552 oz. ASW **Subject:** Pavel Bazhov - Author of Ural Tales **Obv:** Double-headed eagle **Rev:** Head right

Date	Mintage	F	VF	XF	Unc	BU
1994(l) Proof	250,000	Value: 12.50				

Y# 343 2 ROUBLES
15.8700 g., 0.5000 Silver .2552 oz. ASW **Subject:** Ivan Krylov - Author of Fables **Obv:** Double-headed eagle **Rev:** Head 1/4 left with assorted animals below

Date	Mintage	F	VF	XF	Unc	BU
1994(l) Proof	250,000	Value: 12.50				

Y# 344 2 ROUBLES
15.8700 g., 0.5000 Silver .2552 oz. ASW **Subject:** Nikolai Gogol - Writer **Obv:** Double-headed eagle **Rev:** Head right

Date	Mintage	F	VF	XF	Unc	BU
1994(m) Proof	250,000	Value: 12.50				

Y# 363 2 ROUBLES
15.8700 g., 0.5000 Silver .2552 oz. ASW **Obv:** Double-headed eagle within beaded circle **Rev:** Admiral Ushakov

Date	Mintage	F	VF	XF	Unc	BU
1994(m) Proof	250,000	Value: 12.50				

Y# 364 2 ROUBLES
15.8700 g., 0.5000 Silver .2552 oz. ASW **Obv:** Double-headed eagle **Rev:** Ilya Repin, painter

Date	Mintage	F	VF	XF	Unc	BU
1994(m) Proof	250,000	Value: 12.50				

Y# 377 2 ROUBLES
15.8700 g., 0.5000 Silver .2552 oz. ASW **Subject:** A.S. Griboyedov **Obv:** Double-headed eagle **Rev:** Bust 1/4 left divides dates

Date	Mintage	F	VF	XF	Unc	BU
1995(m) Proof	200,000	Value: 14.50				

Y# 391 2 ROUBLES
15.8700 g., 0.5000 Silver .2552 oz. ASW **Subject:** WWII Victory Parade **Obv:** Kremlin Tower and Dome within beaded circle **Rev:** Victory Parade

Date	Mintage	F	VF	XF	Unc	BU
1995(l) Proof	200,000	Value: 30.00				

Y# 392 2 ROUBLES
15.8700 g., 0.5000 Silver .2552 oz. ASW **Series:** WWII **Obv:** Kremlin Tower and Dome within beaded circle **Rev:** Marshal Zhukov on horseback

Date	Mintage	F	VF	XF	Unc	BU
1995(m) Proof	200,000	Value: 30.00				

Y# 393 2 ROUBLES
15.8700 g., 0.5000 Silver .2552 oz. ASW **Series:** WWII **Obv:** Kremlin Tower and Dome within beaded circle **Rev:** Nuremberg trial

Date	Mintage	F	VF	XF	Unc	BU
1995(l) Proof	200,000	Value: 30.00				

Y# 414 2 ROUBLES
15.8700 g., 0.5000 Silver .2552 oz. ASW **Subject:** Sergei Esenin **Obv:** Double-headed eagle **Rev:** Head 1/4 right flanked by designs

Date	Mintage	F	VF	XF	Unc	BU
1995(l) Proof	200,000	Value: 14.50				

Y# 415 2 ROUBLES
15.8700 g., 0.5000 Silver .2552 oz. ASW **Subject:** Field Marshal Kutuzov **Obv:** Double-headed eagle **Rev:** Bust 3/4 left

Date	Mintage	F	VF	XF	Unc	BU
1995(m) Proof	200,000	Value: 13.50				

Y# 449 2 ROUBLES
15.8700 g., 0.5000 Silver .2552 oz. ASW **Subject:** Ivan Bunin **Obv:** Double-headed eagle **Rev:** Bust 1/4 right divides buildings and dates

Date	Mintage	F	VF	XF	Unc	BU
1995(m) Proof	200,000	Value: 14.50				

Y# A391 2 ROUBLES
15.8700 g., 0.5000 Silver 0.2551 oz. ASW **Obv:** Double-headed eagle **Rev:** Victory Parade **Note:** Mule of 1994 eagle obverse with Y#391 Victory Parade reverse.

Date	Mintage	F	VF	XF	Unc	BU
1995 Proof	—	Value: 250				

Y# 514 2 ROUBLES
15.8700 g., 0.5000 Silver .2552 oz. ASW **Subject:** Nikolai Nekrasov **Obv:** Double-headed eagle **Rev:** Bust 1/4 right with building, horse in harness, book and quill

Date	Mintage	F	VF	XF	Unc	BU
1996(m) Proof	50,000	Value: 25.00				

Y# 515 2 ROUBLES
15.8700 g., 0.5000 Silver .2552 oz. ASW **Subject:** Fyodor Dostoevsky **Obv:** Double-headed eagle **Rev:** Bust facing with standing figure holding child, building and dates

Date	Mintage	F	VF	XF	Unc	BU
1996(l) Proof	50,000	Value: 25.00				

Y# 549 2 ROUBLES
15.8700 g., 0.5000 Silver .2552 oz. ASW **Subject:** N.E. Zhukovsky **Obv:** Double-headed eagle **Rev:** Head 1/4 left

Date	Mintage	F	VF	XF	Unc	BU
1997(l) Proof	50,000	Value: 25.00				

Y# 550 2 ROUBLES
15.8700 g., 0.5000 Silver .2552 oz. ASW **Subject:** A.N. Skryabin - Musician **Obv:** Double-headed eagle **Rev:** Bust 3/4 right divides music notes and design

Date	Mintage	F	VF	XF	Unc	BU
1997(m) Proof	50,000	Value: 25.00				

Y# 551 2 ROUBLES
15.8700 g., 0.5000 Silver .2552 oz. ASW **Subject:** A.L. Chizhevsky **Obv:** Double-headed eagle **Rev:** Bust with chin on hand 1/4 right, trees, sun and kneeling figure at right

Date	Mintage	F	VF	XF	Unc	BU
1997(m) Proof	10,000	Value: 80.00				

Y# 558 2 ROUBLES
15.8700 g., 0.5000 Silver .2552 oz. ASW **Obv:** Double-headed eagle **Rev:** Sailing ship and Afanasi Nikitin

Date	Mintage	F	VF	XF	Unc	BU
1997(m) Proof	7,500	Value: 150				

Y# 559 2 ROUBLES
15.8700 g., 0.5000 Silver .2552 oz. ASW **Subject:** Afanasi Nikitin - Indian Scene **Obv:** Double-headed eagle **Rev:** Head facing in center of assorted animal and ship designs

Date	Mintage	F	VF	XF	Unc	BU
1997(l) Proof	7,500	Value: 155				

Y# 584 2 ROUBLES
15.8700 g., 0.5000 Silver .2552 oz. ASW **Subject:** A.K. Savrasov **Obv:** Double-headed eagle **Rev:** Head facing within square at upper left of church and trees

Date	Mintage	F	VF	XF	Unc	BU
1997(m) Proof	15,000	Value: 40.00				

Y# 297 3 ROUBLES
Copper-Nickel, 33 mm. **Subject:** International Space Year **Obv:** Tower and steeples, value below **Rev:** Floating nude figure with planet at right **Edge:** Cyrillic lettering

Date	Mintage	F	VF	XF	Unc	BU
1992(m)	600,000	—	—	—	3.50	5.00
1992(m) Proof	400,000	Value: 6.50				

Y# 298 3 ROUBLES
Copper-Nickel, 33 mm. **Subject:** Battle of Chudskoye Lake **Obv:** Tower and steeples, value below **Rev:** Armored figures in battle **Edge:** Cyrillic lettering

Date	Mintage	F	VF	XF	Unc	BU
1992(l)	600,000	—	—	—	3.50	—
1992(l) Proof	400,000	Value: 5.50				

Y# 304 3 ROUBLES
Copper-Nickel, 33 mm. **Series:** WWII **Obv:** Tower and steeples, value below **Rev:** Allied supply convoys to Murmansk

Date	Mintage	F	VF	XF	Unc	BU
1992(l) Proof	400,000	Value: 5.50				

Y# 317 3 ROUBLES
Copper-Nickel, 33 mm. **Subject:** 1st Anniversary - Defeat of Communist Attempted Coup **Obv:** Tower and steeples, value below **Rev:** Winged Victory holding harp-shaped shield above sprigs, building at right

Date	Mintage	F	VF	XF	Unc	BU
1992(m)	1,000,000	—	—	—	3.50	5.00
1992(m) Prooflike	—	—	—	—	4.00	6.00
1992(m) Proof	—	Value: 6.50				

Y# 349 3 ROUBLES
34.5600 g., 0.9000 Silver 1.0000 oz. ASW **Obv:** Double-headed eagle **Rev:** St. Petersburg Trinity Cathedral

Date	Mintage	F	VF	XF	Unc	BU
1992 Proof	40,000	Value: 35.00				

Y# 350 3 ROUBLES
34.5600 g., 0.9000 Silver 1.0000 oz. ASW **Obv:** Double-headed eagle **Rev:** St. Petersburg Academy of Science and ship

Date	Mintage	F	VF	XF	Unc	BU
1992 Proof	40,000	Value: 35.00				

Y# 318 3 ROUBLES
Copper-Nickel, 33 mm. **Subject:** Battle of Stalingrad **Obv:** Kremlin Tower and Dome within beaded circle **Rev:** Half length figure looking right, monument at right

Date	Mintage	F	VF	XF	Unc	BU
1993(m)	150,000	—	—	—	3.50	—
1993(m) Prooflike	—	—	—	—	4.00	—
1993(m) Proof	350,000	Value: 5.50				

Y# 323 3 ROUBLES
34.5600 g., 0.9000 Silver 1.0000 oz. ASW **Subject:** Bolshoi Ballet **Obv:** Double-headed eagle **Rev:** Ballet couple **Note:** Struck at Moscow without mint mark.

Date	Mintage	F	VF	XF	Unc	BU
1993 Proof	40,000	Value: 30.00				
1993	125,000	—	—	—	25.00	—

Y# 328 3 ROUBLES
Copper-Nickel, 33 mm. **Subject:** 50th Anniversary - Battle of Kursk **Obv:** Kremlin Tower and Dome **Rev:** Armored tank and map **Edge:** Cyrillic lettering

Date	Mintage	F	VF	XF	Unc	BU
1993(l)	500,000	—	—	—	3.50	—
1993(l) Proof	—	Value: 5.50				

Y# 340 3 ROUBLES
Copper-Nickel, 33 mm. **Subject:** 50th Anniversary - Kiev's Liberation from German Fascists **Obv:** Kremlin Tower and Dome within beaded circle **Rev:** Variety of monuments

Date	Mintage	F	VF	XF	Unc	BU
1993(m)	500,000	—	—	—	3.50	—
1993(m) Proof	—	Value: 5.50				

Y# 351 3 ROUBLES
34.5600 g., 0.9000 Silver 1.0000 oz. ASW **Series:** Olympics **Obv:** Double-headed eagle **Rev:** Soccer

Date	Mintage	F	VF	XF	Unc	BU
1993 Proof	40,000	Value: 32.50				

Y# 409 3 ROUBLES
34.5600 g., 0.9000 Silver 1.0000 oz. ASW **Series:** Wildlife **Obv:** Double-headed eagle **Rev:** Bear

Date	Mintage	F	VF	XF	Unc	BU
1993 Proof	5,000	Value: 203				

Y# 450 3 ROUBLES
34.5600 g., 0.9000 Silver 1.0000 oz. ASW **Subject:** Ballet **Obv:** Double-headed eagle **Rev:** Ballerina and building

Date	Mintage	F	VF	XF	Unc	BU
1993 Proof	45,000	Value: 50.00				

Y# 451 3 ROUBLES
34.5600 g., 0.9000 Silver 1.0000 oz. ASW **Subject:** Fedor Schalyapin **Obv:** Double-headed eagle **Rev:** Half-length bust left and building

Date	Mintage	F	VF	XF	Unc	BU
1993 Proof	45,000	Value: 50.00				

Y# 456 3 ROUBLES
34.5600 g., 0.9000 Silver 1.0000 oz. ASW **Obv:** Double-headed eagle **Rev:** Vasilyblazheny Cathedral in Moscow

Date	Mintage	F	VF	XF	Unc	BU
1993 Proof	30,000	Value: 30.00				

Y# 457 3 ROUBLES
34.5600 g., 0.9000 Silver 1.0000 oz. ASW **Obv:** Double-headed eagle **Rev:** Ivan the Great Cathedral, Moscow

Date	Mintage	F	VF	XF	Unc	BU
1993 Proof	30,000	Value: 30.00				

Y# 464 3 ROUBLES
34.5600 g., 0.9000 Silver 1.0000 oz. ASW **Obv:** Double-headed eagle **Rev:** Ships Nadezhda and Neva on world voyage

Date	Mintage	F	VF	XF	Unc	BU
1993 Proof	25,000	Value: 32.50				

Y# 465 3 ROUBLES
34.5600 g., 0.9000 Silver 1.0000 oz. ASW **Subject:** Russo-French Space Flight **Rev:** Cosmonauts holding flags above 1/4 globe

Date	Mintage	F	VF	XF	Unc	BU
1993 Proof	40,000	Value: 32.50				

Y# 341 3 ROUBLES
Copper-Nickel, 33 mm. **Subject:** 50th Anniversary - Battle of Leningrad **Obv:** Kremlin Tower and Dome within beaded circle **Rev:** Soldiers, monument and tower

Date	Mintage	F	VF	XF	Unc	BU
1994(l) Proof	500,000	Value: 5.50				

Y# 345 3 ROUBLES
34.5600 g., 0.9000 Silver 1.0000 oz. ASW **Obv:** Double-headed eagle **Rev:** Cathedral of the Nativity of the Mother of God

Date	Mintage	F	VF	XF	Unc	BU
1994 Proof	30,000	Value: 30.00				

Y# 346 3 ROUBLES
Copper-Nickel **Subject:** 50th Anniversary - Liberation of Sevastopol from German Fascists **Obv:** Kremlin Tower and Dome within beaded circle **Rev:** Sevastopol scene, stylized soldier above

Date	Mintage	F	VF	XF	Unc	BU
1994(l) Proof	250,000	Value: 5.50				

Y# 362 3 ROUBLES
Copper-Nickel, 33 mm. **Subject:** Normandy Invasion **Obv:** Kremlin Tower and Dome **Rev:** World globe with date in center divides designs

Date	Mintage	F	VF	XF	Unc	BU
1994(m) Proof	250,000	Value: 5.50				

Y# 365 3 ROUBLES
Copper-Nickel, 33 mm. **Series:** WWII **Subject:** Partisans Activities **Obv:** Kremlin Tower and Dome within beaded circle **Rev:** Figures with weapons in bushes **Edge:** Cyrillic lettering

Date	Mintage	F	VF	XF	Unc	BU
1994(m) Proof	250,000	Value: 5.50				

Y# 366 3 ROUBLES
Copper-Nickel, 33 mm. **Series:** WWII **Subject:** Liberation of Belgrade **Obv:** Kremlin Tower and Dome within beaded circle **Rev:** Armored figures marching, building in background

Date	Mintage	F	VF	XF	Unc	BU
1994(m) Proof	250,000	Value: 5.50				

Y# 405 3 ROUBLES
34.5600 g., 0.9000 Silver 1.0000 oz. ASW **Subject:** Ballet **Obv:** Double-headed eagle **Rev:** Ballet couple

Date	Mintage	F	VF	XF	Unc	BU
1994 Proof	40,000	Value: 35.00				

Y# 458 3 ROUBLES
34.5600 g., 0.9000 Silver 1.0000 oz. ASW **Obv:** Double-headed eagle **Rev:** Pocrov Church on the Neri

Date	Mintage	F	VF	XF	Unc	BU
1994 Proof	30,000	Value: 35.00				

Y# 460 3 ROUBLES
34.5600 g., 0.9000 Silver 1.0000 oz. ASW **Series:** Wildlife **Obv:** Double-headed eagle **Rev:** Sable on tree limb

Date	Mintage	F	VF	XF	Unc	BU
1994 Proof	10,000	Value: 60.00				

Y# 466 3 ROUBLES
34.5600 g., 0.9000 Silver 1.0000 oz. ASW **Subject:** Discovery of Antarctica **Rev:** Sailing ships Vostok and Mirny

Date	Mintage	F	VF	XF	Unc	BU
1994 Proof	25,000	Value: 55.00				

Y# 513 3 ROUBLES
34.6800 g., 0.9000 Silver 1.0034 oz. ASW **Obv:** Double-headed eagle **Rev:** Smolny Institute & Monastery - St. Petersburg

Date	Mintage	F	VF	XF	Unc	BU
1994 Proof	30,000	Value: 35.00				

Y# 520 3 ROUBLES
34.6800 g., 0.9000 Silver 1.0034 oz. ASW **Obv:** Double-headed eagle **Rev:** Ryazin Kremlin, city view

Date	Mintage	F	VF	XF	Unc	BU
1994 Proof	30,000	Value: 35.00				

Y# 528 3 ROUBLES
34.6800 g., 0.9000 Silver 1.0034 oz. ASW **Subject:** Vassili Ivanovich Surikov **Obv:** Double-headed eagle **Rev:** Head facing above Siberian sled scene

Date	Mintage	F	VF	XF	Unc	BU
1994 Proof	40,000	Value: 70.00				

Y# 529 3 ROUBLES
34.6800 g., 0.9000 Silver 1.0034 oz. ASW **Subject:** Alexander Andreyevich Ivannov **Obv:** Double-headed eagle **Rev:** Head facing 1/4 right above assorted figures

Date	Mintage	F	VF	XF	Unc	BU
1994 Proof	40,000	Value: 70.00				

Y# 380 3 ROUBLES
Copper-Nickel, 33 mm. **Series:** WWII **Subject:** Capture of Konigsberg **Obv:** Kremlin Tower and Dome within beaded circle **Rev:** Crouched soldiers in front of building

Date	Mintage	F	VF	XF	Unc	BU
1994 (m) Proof, error	—	Value: 50.00				
1995 (m) Proof	200,000	Value: 6.00				

Y# 389 3 ROUBLES
34.8800 g., 0.9000 Silver 1.0093 oz. ASW **Subject:** Trans-Siberian railway **Obv:** Double-headed eagle **Rev:** Bridge, train and map

Date	Mintage	F	VF	XF	Unc	BU
1994 Proof	25,000	Value: 35.00				

Y# 382 3 ROUBLES
Copper-Nickel, 33 mm. **Series:** WWII **Obv:** Kremlin Tower and Dome within beaded circle **Rev:** American and Russian soldiers **Note:** 50-star U.S.A. flag.

Date	Mintage	F	VF	XF	Unc	BU
1994 (m)	—	—	—	—	—	—
1995 (m) Proof	200,000	Value: 6.00				

Y# 381 3 ROUBLES
Copper-Nickel, 33 mm. **Series:** WWII **Subject:** Capture of Vienna **Obv:** Kremlin Tower and Dome within beaded circle **Rev:** Two uniformed figures with weapons, one holding flag, building in background

Date	Mintage	F	VF	XF	Unc	BU
1995(l) Proof	200,000	Value: 6.00				

Y# 383 3 ROUBLES
Copper-Nickel, 33 mm. **Series:** WWII **Subject:** Capture of Berlin **Obv:** Kremlin Tower and Dome within beaded circle **Rev:** Soldiers in front of building

Date	Mintage	F	VF	XF	Unc	BU
1995(l) Proof	200,000	Value: 6.00				

Y# 384 3 ROUBLES
Copper-Nickel, 33 mm. **Series:** WWII **Subject:** German Surrender **Obv:** Kremlin Tower and Dome within beaded circle **Rev:** Seated figures at table below flags

Date	Mintage	F	VF	XF	Unc	BU
1995(l) Proof	200,000	Value: 6.00				

Y# 385 3 ROUBLES
Copper-Nickel, 33 mm. **Series:** WWII **Subject:** Liberation of Prague **Obv:** Kremlin Tower and Dome within beaded circle **Rev:** Armored tank divides building and standing figures

Date	Mintage	F	VF	XF	Unc	BU
1995(m) Proof	200,000	Value: 6.00				

Y# 386 3 ROUBLES
Copper-Nickel, 33 mm. **Series:** WWII **Subject:** Surrender of Japanese Army in Kwantung **Obv:** Kremlin Tower and Dome within beaded circle **Rev:** Surrender scene

Date	Mintage	F	VF	XF	Unc	BU
1995(m) Proof	200,000	Value: 6.00				

Y# 387 3 ROUBLES
Copper-Nickel, 33 mm. **Series:** WWII **Obv:** Kremlin Tower and Dome within beaded circle **Rev:** Japanese formal surrender on Battleship U.S.S. Missouri

Date	Mintage	F	VF	XF	Unc	BU
1995(l) Proof	200,000	Value: 6.00				

Y# 388 3 ROUBLES
34.5600 g., 0.9000 Silver 1.0000 oz. ASW **Obv:** Double-headed eagle **Rev:** Vladimir's Golden Gate

Date	Mintage	F	VF	XF	Unc	BU
1995 Proof	30,000	Value: 37.50				

Y# 394 3 ROUBLES
34.5600 g., 0.9000 Silver 1.0000 oz. ASW **Subject:** Ballet **Obv:** Double-headed eagle **Rev:** Scene from Sleeping Beauty

Date	Mintage	F	VF	XF	Unc	BU
1995 Proof	40,000	Value: 40.00				

Y# 407 3 ROUBLES
34.5600 g., 0.9000 Silver 1.0000 oz. ASW **Subject:** 50th Anniversary - United Nations **Obv:** Double-headed eagle **Rev:** Blacksmith, UN logo at top, building at left

Date	Mintage	F	VF	XF	Unc	BU
1995 Proof	20,000	Value: 45.00				

Y# 445 3 ROUBLES

34.5600 g., 0.9000 Silver 1.0000 oz. ASW **Obv:** Double-headed eagle **Rev:** Smolensk Kremlin

Date	Mintage	F	VF	XF	Unc	BU
1995 Proof	30,000	Value: 37.50				

Y# 459 3 ROUBLES

34.5600 g., 0.9000 Silver 1.0000 oz. ASW **Obv:** Double-headed eagle **Rev:** Kizhi Church on Onega Lake

Date	Mintage	F	VF	XF	Unc	BU
1995 Proof	30,000	Value: 37.50				

Y# 461 3 ROUBLES

34.5600 g., 0.9000 Silver 1.0000 oz. ASW **Subject:** Arctic Explorers 1733-43 **Obv:** Double-headed eagle **Rev:** Busts of arctic explorers, ship, map and sled dogs

Date	Mintage	F	VF	XF	Unc	BU
1995 Proof	25,000	Value: 45.00				

Y# 462 3 ROUBLES

34.5600 g., 0.9000 Silver 1.0000 oz. ASW **Subject:** Roald Amundsen - Arctic Explorer **Obv:** Double-headed eagle **Rev:** Head left, ship and designs

Date	Mintage	F	VF	XF	Unc	BU
1995 Proof	25,000	Value: 45.00				

Y# 463 3 ROUBLES

34.5600 g., 0.9000 Silver 1.0000 oz. ASW **Subject:** 200th Anniversary - Russian National Library **Obv:** Double-headed eagle **Rev:** Book, scroll and quill in front of building

Date	Mintage	F	VF	XF	Unc	BU
1995 Proof	15,000	Value: 50.00				

Y# 467 3 ROUBLES

34.5600 g., 0.9000 Silver 1.0000 oz. ASW **Subject:** Millennium of Belgorod **Obv:** Double-headed eagle **Rev:** Scroll and building below crowned shield

Date	Mintage	F	VF	XF	Unc	BU
1995 Proof	30,000	Value: 35.00				

Y# 468 3 ROUBLES

34.5600 g., 0.9000 Silver 1.0000 oz. ASW **Subject:** Russian Millennium **Obv:** Double-headed eagle within beaded circle **Rev:** Novgorod Kremlin

Date	Mintage	F	VF	XF	Unc	BU
1995 Proof	40,000	Value: 35.00				

Y# 469 3 ROUBLES

34.5600 g., 0.9000 Silver 1.0000 oz. ASW **Subject:** Russian Millennium **Obv:** Double-headed eagle **Rev:** Spaso-Preobrazhensky Cathedral

Date	Mintage	F	VF	XF	Unc	BU
1995 Proof	40,000	Value: 30.00				

Y# 473 3 ROUBLES

34.5600 g., 0.9000 Silver 1.0000 oz. ASW **Series:** Wildlife **Obv:** Double-headed eagle **Rev:** Sable on branch

Date	Mintage	F	VF	XF	Unc	BU
1995(l) Matte	500,000	—	—	—	27.50	—
1995(m) Matte	500,000	—	—	—	27.50	—

Y# 474 3 ROUBLES

34.5600 g., 0.9000 Silver 1.0000 oz. ASW **Series:** Wildlife **Obv:** Double-headed eagle **Rev:** Lynx

Date	Mintage	F	VF	XF	Unc	BU
1995(l)	25,000	—	—	—	40.00	60.00

Y# 378 3 ROUBLES

Copper-Nickel, 33 mm. **Subject:** Liberation of Warsaw **Obv:** Kremlin Tower and Dome within beaded circle **Rev:** Standing figures holding flag

Date	Mintage	F	VF	XF	Unc	BU
1995(l) Proof	200,000	Value: 6.00				

Y# 379 3 ROUBLES

Copper-Nickel, 33 mm. **Subject:** Liberation of Budapest **Obv:** Kremlin Tower and Dome within beaded circle **Rev:** Soldiers and building

Date	Mintage	F	VF	XF	Unc	BU
1995(m) Proof	200,000	Value: 6.00				

Y# 470 3 ROUBLES

34.5600 g., 0.9000 Silver 1.0000 oz. ASW **Obv:** Double-headed eagle **Rev:** Ilya the Prophet's Church in Yaroslavl

Date	Mintage	F	VF	XF	Unc	BU
1996 Proof	30,000	Value: 40.00				

Y# 477 3 ROUBLES

34.5600 g., 0.9000 Silver 1.0000 oz. ASW **Subject:** Combat between Peresvet and Chelubey **Obv:** Double-headed eagle **Rev:** Two armored figures on rearing horses with swords

Date	Mintage	F	VF	XF	Unc	BU
1996 Proof	40,000	Value: 30.00				

Y# 478 3 ROUBLES

34.5600 g., 0.9000 Silver 1.0000 oz. ASW **Obv:** Double-headed eagle **Rev:** Old Testament Trinity icon

Date	Mintage	F	VF	XF	Unc	BU
1996 Proof	40,000	Value: 30.00				

Y# 482 3 ROUBLES

34.5600 g., 0.9000 Silver 1.0000 oz. ASW **Subject:** Ballet **Obv:** Double-headed eagle **Rev:** Nutcracker Ballet

Date	Mintage	F	VF	XF	Unc	BU
1996 Proof	25,000	Value: 35.00				

Y# 483 3 ROUBLES

34.5600 g., 0.9000 Silver 1.0000 oz. ASW **Subject:** Ballet - Nutcracker **Obv:** Double-headed eagle **Rev:** Duel with the Mouse King

Date	Mintage	F	VF	XF	Unc	BU
1996 Proof	25,000	Value: 35.00				

Y# 490 3 ROUBLES

34.5600 g., 0.9000 Silver 1.0000 oz. ASW **Obv:** Double-headed eagle **Rev:** Kremlin of Kazan

Date	Mintage	F	VF	XF	Unc	BU
1996 Proof	25,000	Value: 40.00				

Y# 491 3 ROUBLES

34.5600 g., 0.9000 Silver 1.0000 oz. ASW **Obv:** Double-headed eagle **Rev:** Kremlin of Tobolsk - city view

Date	Mintage	F	VF	XF	Unc	BU
1996 Proof	25,000	Value: 37.50				

Y# 510 3 ROUBLES

34.5600 g., 0.9000 Silver 1.0000 oz. ASW **Obv:** Double-headed eagle **Rev:** Alexander Column and Hermitage

Date	Mintage	F	VF	XF	Unc	BU
1996 Proof	15,000	Value: 45.00				

Y# 511 3 ROUBLES

34.5600 g., 0.9000 Silver 1.0000 oz. ASW **Subject:** 300th Anniversary - Russian Navy **Obv:** Double-headed eagle **Rev:** Icebreaker ship and bust left

Date	Mintage	F	VF	XF	Unc	BU
1996 Proof	10,000	Value: 50.00				

Y# 512 3 ROUBLES

34.5600 g., 0.9000 Silver 1.0000 oz. ASW **Subject:** 300th Anniversary - Russian Navy **Obv:** Double-headed eagle **Rev:** Carrier ship below bust facing

Date	Mintage	F	VF	XF	Unc	BU
1996 Proof	10,000	Value: 50.00				

Y# 535 3 ROUBLES

34.5600 g., 0.9000 Silver 1.0000 oz. ASW **Series:** Wildlife **Obv:** Double-headed eagle **Rev:** Tiger

Date	Mintage	F	VF	XF	Unc	BU
1996 Proof	10,000	Value: 70.00				

Y# 552 3 ROUBLES

34.5600 g., 0.9000 Silver 1.0000 oz. ASW **Subject:** 850th Anniversary - Moscow **Obv:** Double-headed eagle **Rev:** Workers building original Moscow, modern skyline behind

Date	Mintage	F	VF	XF	Unc	BU
1997 Proof	40,000	Value: 35.00				

Y# 553 3 ROUBLES

34.5600 g., 0.9000 Silver 1.0000 oz. ASW **Subject:** 850th Anniversary - Moscow **Obv:** Double-headed eagle **Rev:** Riverside city view

Date	Mintage	F	VF	XF	Unc	BU
1997 Proof	40,000	Value: 35.00				

Y# 560 3 ROUBLES

34.5600 g., 0.9000 Silver 1.0000 oz. ASW **Obv:** Double-headed eagle within beaded circle **Rev:** Monastery of the Saint Virgin in Yaroslavl

Date	Mintage	F	VF	XF	Unc	BU
1997 Proof	15,000	Value: 45.00				

Y# 567 3 ROUBLES

34.5600 g., 0.9000 Silver 1.0000 oz. ASW **Subject:** Ballet - Swan Lake **Obv:** Double-headed eagle **Rev:** Four ballerinas below crowned swan

Date	Mintage	F	VF	XF	Unc	BU
1997 Proof	10,000	Value: 50.00				

Y# 568 3 ROUBLES

34.5600 g., 0.9000 Silver 1.0000 oz. ASW **Subject:** Ballet - Swan Lake **Obv:** Double-headed eagle **Rev:** Rothbart and Prince Siegfried

Date	Mintage	F	VF	XF	Unc	BU
1997 Proof	10,000	Value: 50.00				

Y# 575 3 ROUBLES

34.5600 g., 0.9000 Silver 1.0000 oz. ASW **Subject:** First Anniversary - Russian-Belarus Treaty **Obv:** Double-headed eagle **Rev:** Two city views

Date	Mintage	F	VF	XF	Unc	BU
1997 Proof	10,000	Value: 50.00				

Y# 585 3 ROUBLES

34.5600 g., 0.9000 Silver 1.0000 oz. ASW **Subject:** Underroot Nativity of the Virgin Hermitage Monastery of Kursk **Obv:** Double-headed eagle **Rev:** Painting above monastery

Date	Mintage	F	VF	XF	Unc	BU
1997 Proof	15,000	Value: 45.00				

Y# 586 3 ROUBLES

34.5600 g., 0.9000 Silver 1.0000 oz. ASW **Subject:** Serge Julievich Witte **Obv:** Double-headed eagle **Rev:** Bust facing

Date	Mintage	F	VF	XF	Unc	BU
1997 Proof	10,000	Value: 50.00				

Y# 587 3 ROUBLES

34.5600 g., 0.9000 Silver 1.0000 oz. ASW **Subject:** Year of Reconciliation **Obv:** Double-headed eagle **Rev:** Standing figure facing holding quill and shield

Date	Mintage	F	VF	XF	Unc	BU
1997 Proof	10,000	Value: 60.00				

Y# 591 3 ROUBLES

34.5600 g., 0.9000 Silver 1.0000 oz. ASW **Obv:** Double-headed eagle **Rev:** Solovetski Monastery

Date	Mintage	F	VF	XF	Unc	BU
1997 Proof	15,000	Value: 45.00				

Y# 593 3 ROUBLES

34.5600 g., 0.9000 Silver 1.0000 oz. ASW **Series:** Wildlife **Obv:** Double-headed eagle **Rev:** Polar bear watching walrus

Date	Mintage	F	VF	XF	Unc	BU
1997 Proof	10,000	Value: 100				

Y# 312 5 ROUBLES

4.0500 g., Brass Clad Steel, 21.9 mm. **Obv:** Double-headed eagle **Rev:** Value flanked by sprigs above date

Date	Mintage	F	VF	XF	Unc	BU
1992Л	—	—	—	—	1.75	—
1992M	—	—	—	—	1.50	—
1992Л	—	—	—	—	2.00	—
1992M	—	—	—	—	2.50	—

Y# 322 5 ROUBLES

Copper-Nickel, 35 mm. **Obv:** Value flanked by sprigs above date **Rev:** Kazakhstan

Date	Mintage	F	VF	XF	Unc	BU
1992(I)	300,000	—	—	—	4.00	5.00
1992(I) Proof	200,000	Value: 10.00				

Y# 324 5 ROUBLES

Copper-Nickel **Subject:** Troitsk - Sergievsk Monastery **Obv:** Double-headed eagle **Rev:** Monastery

Date	Mintage	F	VF	XF	Unc	BU
1993(I)	500,000	—	—	—	6.00	7.00
1993(I) Proof	—	Value: 9.00				

Y# 339 5 ROUBLES

Copper-Nickel **Subject:** 2500 Years of Merv Minaret, Turkmenistan **Obv:** Value flanked by sprigs above date **Rev:** Building

Date	Mintage	F	VF	XF	Unc	BU
1993(I)	500,000	—	—	—	4.00	5.00
1993(I) Proof	—	Value: 10.00				

Y# 420 5 ROUBLES

7.7758 g., 0.9990 Palladium .2500 oz. **Subject:** Ballet **Obv:** Double-headed eagle **Rev:** Ballerina

Date	Mintage	F	VF	XF	Unc	BU
1993	6,000	—	—	—	150	—
1993 Proof	2,000	Value: 160				

Y# 431 5 ROUBLES

7.7758 g., 0.9990 Palladium .2500 oz. **Subject:** Ballet - Sleeping Beauty **Obv:** Double-headed eagle **Rev:** Ballerina

Date	Mintage	F	VF	XF	Unc	BU
1994	4,000	—	—	—	150	—
1994 Proof	5,000	Value: 160				

Y# 400 5 ROUBLES

4.0500 g., Aluminum-Bronze, 21.9 mm. **Series:** WWII **Obv:** Double-headed eagle **Rev:** Infantry officer leading attack

Date	Mintage	F	VF	XF	Unc	BU
1995	200,000	—	—	—	1.50	—

Note: In mint sets only

Y# 435 5 ROUBLES

7.7758 g., 0.9990 Palladium .2500 oz. **Obv:** Double-headed eagle **Rev:** Ballerina

Date	Mintage	F	VF	XF	Unc	BU
1995 Proof	4,000	Value: 160				

Y# 505 5 ROUBLES

4.0500 g., Brass, 21.9 mm. **Subject:** 300th Anniversary - Russian Fleet **Obv:** Double-headed eagle **Rev:** Sailing ship

Date	Mintage	F	VF	XF	Unc	BU
1996	100,000	—	—	—	2.50	—

Note: In mint sets only

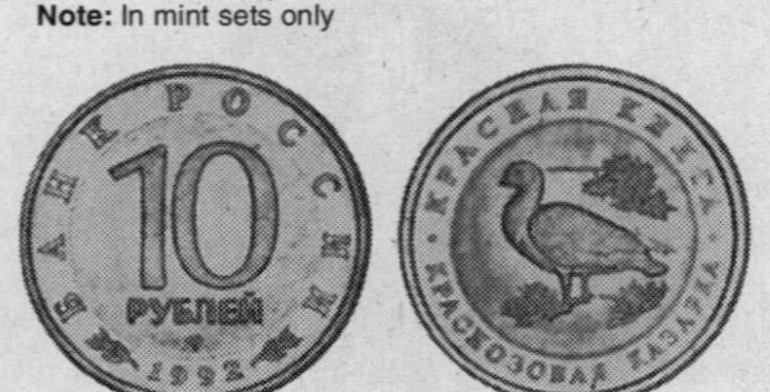

Y# 307 10 ROUBLES

5.9500 g., Bi-Metallic Aluminum-Bronze center in Copper-Nickel ring, 25 mm. **Series:** Wildlife **Obv:** Value **Rev:** Red-breasted Kazarka left **Edge:** Alternating reeded and smooth

Date	Mintage	F	VF	XF	Unc	BU
1992Л	300,000	—	—	—	2.50	6.50

Y# 308 10 ROUBLES

5.9500 g., Bi-Metallic Aluminum-Bronze center in Copper-Nickel ring, 25 mm. **Series:** Wildlife **Obv:** Value **Rev:** Tiger **Edge:** Alternating reeded and smooth

Date	Mintage	F	VF	XF	Unc	BU
1992Л	300,000	—	—	—	3.00	6.50

Y# 309 10 ROUBLES

5.9500 g., Bi-Metallic Aluminum-Bronze center in Copper-Nickel ring, 25 mm. **Series:** Wildlife **Obv:** Value **Rev:** Cobra **Edge:** Alternating reeded and smooth

Date	Mintage	F	VF	XF	Unc	BU
1992Л	300,000	—	—	—	3.00	6.50

Y# 313 10 ROUBLES

3.6500 g., Copper-Nickel, 21.1 mm. **Obv:** Double-headed eagle **Rev:** Value flanked by sprigs **Edge:** Reeded **Note:** St. Petersburg minted coins have a round-top 3 in date. Moscow minted coins have a flat-top 3 in date.

Date	Mintage	F	VF	XF	Unc	BU
1992Л	—	—	—	—	1.50	—
1992M	—	—	—	—	2.00	—
1993Л	—	—	—	—	1.50	—
1993M	—	—	—	—	10.00	—

Y# 313a 10 ROUBLES

Copper-Nickel Clad Steel, 21.1 mm. **Obv:** Double-headed eagle **Rev:** Value flanked by sprigs **Edge:** Plain **Note:** St. Petersburg minted coins have a round-top 3 in date. Moscow minted coins have a flat-top 3 in date.

Date	Mintage	F	VF	XF	Unc	BU
1992M	—	—	—	—	10.00	—
1992(sp) (I)	—	—	—	—	1.50	—
1993Л	—	—	—	—	1.50	—
1993Л	—	—	—	—	1.50	—

Y# 352 10 ROUBLES

15.5517 g., 0.9990 Palladium .5000 oz. **Series:** Olympics **Obv:** Double-headed eagle **Rev:** Cubertin and Butovsky and torch

Date	Mintage	F	VF	XF	Unc	BU
1993 Proof	7,500	Value: 250				

Y# 416 10 ROUBLES
1.5552 g., 0.9990 Gold .0500 oz. AGW **Subject:** Ballet **Obv:** Double-headed eagle **Rev:** Ballerina

Date	Mintage	F	VF	XF	Unc	BU
1993	57,000	—	—	—	50.00	—
1993 Proof	11,500	Value: 60.00				

Y# 421 10 ROUBLES
15.5500 g., 0.9990 Palladium .5000 oz. **Subject:** Russian Ballet **Obv:** Double-headed eagle **Rev:** Ballerina **Designer:** A. Baklanov

Date	Mintage	F	VF	XF	Unc	BU
1993(l)	4,000	—	—	—	250	—
1993(l) Proof	2,000	Value: 265				

Y# 424 10 ROUBLES
1.5552 g., 0.9990 Gold .0500 oz. AGW **Subject:** Russian Ballet **Obv:** Double-headed eagle **Rev:** Ballerina **Designer:** A. Baklanov

Date	Mintage	F	VF	XF	Unc	BU
1994(m) Proof	7,000	Value: 60.00				

Y# 432 10 ROUBLES
15.5500 g., 0.9990 Palladium .5000 oz. **Subject:** Russian Ballet **Obv:** Double-headed eagle **Rev:** Ballerina **Designer:** A. Baklanov

Date	Mintage	F	VF	XF	Unc	BU
1994(l)	3,000	—	—	—	250	—
1994(l) Proof	1,500	Value: 275				

Y# 401 10 ROUBLES
3.6500 g., Copper-Nickel, 21.1 mm. **Series:** WWII **Obv:** Double-headed eagle **Rev:** Munitions workers **Designer:** A. Baklanov

Date	Mintage	F	VF	XF	Unc	BU
1995(l)	200,000	—	—	—	2.00	—

Note: In mint sets only

Y# 436 10 ROUBLES
15.5500 g., 0.9990 Palladium .5000 oz. **Subject:** Ballet - Sleeping Beauty **Obv:** Double-headed eagle **Rev:** Ballerina **Designer:** A. Baklanov

Date	Mintage	F	VF	XF	Unc	BU
1995(sp) Proof	1,500	Value: 275				

Y# 438 10 ROUBLES
1.5552 g., 0.9990 Gold .0500 oz. AGW **Subject:** Ballet - Sleeping Beauty **Obv:** Double-headed eagle **Rev:** Ballerina **Designer:** A. Baklanov

Date	Mintage	F	VF	XF	Unc	BU
1995(m) Proof	7,000	Value: 60.00				

Y# 506 10 ROUBLES
3.6500 g., Copper-Nickel, 21.1 mm. **Subject:** 300th Anniversary - Russian Fleet **Obv:** Double-headed eagle **Rev:** Cargo ship **Designer:** A. Baklanov

Date	Mintage	F	VF	XF	Unc	BU
1996(sp)	100,000	—	—	—	3.00	—

Note: In mint sets only

Y# 484 10 ROUBLES
1.5552 g., 0.9990 Gold .0500 oz. AGW **Subject:** Ballet - Nutcracker **Obv:** Double-headed eagle **Rev:** Nutcracker doll **Designer:** A. Baklanov

Date	Mintage	F	VF	XF	Unc	BU
1996(m) Proof	7,500	Value: 60.00				

Y# 569 10 ROUBLES
1.5500 g., 0.9990 Gold .0498 oz. AGW **Subject:** Ballet - Swan Lake **Obv:** Double-headed eagle **Rev:** Ballerina **Designer:** A. Baklanov

Date	Mintage	F	VF	XF	Unc	BU
1997(sp) Proof	2,500	Value: 65.00				

Y# 314 20 ROUBLES
5.6000 g., Copper-Nickel, 24.1 mm. **Obv:** Double-headed eagle **Rev:** Value flanked by sprigs **Edge:** Reeded and plain sections

Date	Mintage	F	VF	XF	Unc	BU
1992Л	—	—	—	—	2.00	—
1992М	—	—	—	—	2.50	—
1992Л Rare	—	—	—	—	—	—
Note: Plain edge error						
1992М	—	—	—	—	20.00	—
Note: Plain edge error						

Y# 314a 20 ROUBLES
Copper-Nickel Clad Steel, 24.1 mm. **Obv:** Double-headed eagle **Rev:** Value flanked by sprigs **Edge:** Plain

Date	Mintage	F	VF	XF	Unc	BU
1993М	—	—	—	—	2.50	—

Y# 402 20 ROUBLES
5.6000 g., Copper-Nickel, 24.1 mm. **Series:** WWII **Obv:** Double-headed eagle **Rev:** Soldiers and tanks

Date	Mintage	F	VF	XF	Unc	BU
1995	200,000	—	—	—	3.00	—

Note: In mint sets only

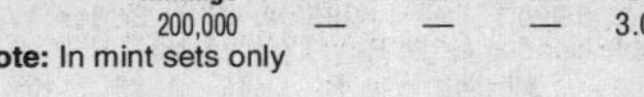

Y# 507 20 ROUBLES
5.6500 g., Copper-Nickel, 24.1 mm. **Subject:** 300th Anniversary - Russian Fleet **Obv:** Double-headed eagle **Rev:** Scientific research ship

Date	Mintage	F	VF	XF	Unc	BU
1996	100,000	—	—	—	4.50	—

Note: In mint sets only

Y# 353 25 ROUBLES
31.1035 g., 0.9990 Palladium 1.0000 oz. **Subject:** Age of enlightenment 17th century. **Obv:** Double-headed eagle **Rev:** Catherine the Great **Designer:** A. Baklanov

Date	Mintage	F	VF	XF	Unc	BU
1992(l) Proof	5,500	Value: 500				

Y# 406 25 ROUBLES
156.0400 g., 0.9990 Silver 5.0118 oz. ASW **Subject:** Russian Ballet **Obv:** Theatre within beaded circle **Rev:** Ballet couple **Designer:** A. Baklanov

Date	Mintage	F	VF	XF	Unc	BU
1993(m) Proof	10,000	Value: 95.00				
1993(l) Proof	Inc. above	Value: 95.00				

Y# 395 25 ROUBLES
3.1104 g., 0.9990 Platinum .1000 oz. APW **Subject:** Russian Ballet **Obv:** Double-headed eagle **Rev:** Ballerina **Designer:** A. Baklanov

Date	Mintage	F	VF	XF	Unc	BU
1993(l) Proof	750	—	—	—	185	—

Y# 410 25 ROUBLES
3.1100 g., 0.9990 Gold .1000 oz. AGW **Series:** Wildlife **Obv:** Double-headed eagle **Rev:** Bear **Designer:** A. Baklanov

Date	Mintage	F	VF	XF	Unc	BU
1993(m) Proof	2,000	Value: 125				

Y# 417 25 ROUBLES
3.1100 g., 0.9990 Gold .1000 oz. AGW **Subject:** Russian Ballet **Obv:** Double-headed eagle **Rev:** Ballerina **Designer:** A. Baklanov

Date	Mintage	F	VF	XF	Unc	BU
1993(m)	12,500	—	—	—	110	—
1993(m) Proof	6,000	Value: 125				

Y# 422 25 ROUBLES
31.1035 g., 0.9990 Palladium 1.0000 oz. **Subject:** Russian Ballet **Obv:** Double-headed eagle **Rev:** Ballerina **Designer:** A. Baklanov

Date	Mintage	F	VF	XF	Unc	BU
1993(l)	3,000	—	—	—	500	—
1993(l) Proof	2,000	Value: 525				

Y# 452 25 ROUBLES
31.1035 g., 0.9990 Palladium 1.0000 oz. **Subject:** Russian and World Culture **Obv:** Double-headed eagle **Rev:** M.P. Musorgsky **Designer:** A. Baklanov

Date	Mintage	F	VF	XF	Unc	BU
1993(m) Proof	5,500	Value: 500				

Y# 517 25 ROUBLES
31.1035 g., 0.9990 Palladium 1.0000 oz., 37 mm. **Subject:** First Russian Global Circumnavigation **Obv:** Double-headed eagle **Rev:** Sloop Nadyezhda **Designer:** A. Baklanov

Date	Mintage	F	VF	XF	Unc	BU
1993(l) Proof	2,500	Value: 500				

Y# 518 25 ROUBLES
31.1035 g., 0.9990 Palladium 1.0000 oz., 37 mm. **Series:** First Russian Global Circumnavigation **Obv:** Double-headed eagle **Rev:** Sloop Neva **Designer:** A. Baklanov

Date	Mintage	F	VF	XF	Unc	BU
1993(l) Proof	25,000	Value: 500				

Y# 390 25 ROUBLES
172.8300 g., 0.9000 Silver 5.0009 oz. ASW **Subject:** 100th Anniversary - Trans-Siberian Railroad **Rev:** Steam train, workers laying ties on track **Designer:** A. Baklanov

Date	Mintage	F	VF	XF	Unc	BU
1994(l) Proof	3,000	Value: 400				

Y# 423 25 ROUBLES
172.8300 g., 0.9000 Silver 5.0009 oz. ASW **Subject:** Russian Ballet **Designer:** A. Baklanov

Date	Mintage	F	VF	XF	Unc	BU
1994(m) Proof	7,500	Value: 160				

Y# 425 25 ROUBLES
3.1100 g., 0.9990 Gold .1000 oz. AGW **Subject:** Russian Ballet **Obv:** Double-headed eagle **Rev:** Ballerina **Designer:** A. Baklanov

Date	Mintage	F	VF	XF	Unc	BU
1994(m) Proof	5,000	Value: 115				

Y# 428 25 ROUBLES
3.1104 g., 0.9990 Platinum .1000 oz. APW **Subject:** Russian Ballet **Obv:** Double-headed eagle **Rev:** Ballerina **Designer:** A. Baklanov

Date	Mintage	F	VF	XF	Unc	BU
1994(l) Proof	900	Value: 185				

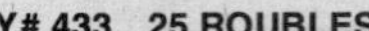

Y# 433 25 ROUBLES
31.1035 g., 0.9990 Palladium 1.0000 oz. **Subject:** Russian Ballet **Obv:** Double-headed eagle **Rev:** Ballerina **Designer:** A. Baklanov

Date	Mintage	F	VF	XF	Unc	BU
1994(l)	2,000	—	—	—	525	—
1994(l) Proof	1,500	Value: 525				

Y# 521 25 ROUBLES
31.1035 g., 0.9990 Palladium 1.0000 oz. **Subject:** First Russian Antartic Expedition, 1819-21 **Obv:** Double-headed eagle **Rev:** Sloop Mirny **Designer:** A. Baklanov

Date	Mintage	F	VF	XF	Unc	BU
1994 Proof	4,000	Value: 500				

Y# 522 25 ROUBLES
31.1035 g., 0.9990 Palladium 1.0000 oz. **Obv:** Double-headed eagle **Rev:** Sloop Vostok

Date	Mintage	F	VF	XF	Unc	BU
1994 Proof	4,000	Value: 500				

Y# 524 25 ROUBLES
3.1103 g., 0.9990 Gold .1000 oz. AGW **Series:** Wildlife **Obv:** Double-headed eagle **Rev:** Sable's head

Date	Mintage	F	VF	XF	Unc	BU
1994 Proof	4,000	Value: 110				

Y# 530 25 ROUBLES
31.1035 g., 0.9990 Palladium 1.0000 oz. **Obv:** Double-headed eagle **Rev:** Andre Ruble

Date	Mintage	F	VF	XF	Unc	BU
1994 Proof	6,000	Value: 500				

Y# 534 25 ROUBLES
4.3198 g., 0.9000 Gold .1245 oz. AGW **Obv:** Double-headed eagle **Rev:** Baikal railroad tunnel

Date	Mintage	F	VF	XF	Unc	BU
1994 Proof	3,000	Value: 140				

Y# 471 25 ROUBLES
155.5000 g., 0.9000 Silver 4.4995 oz. ASW **Series:** Wildlife **Obv:** Double-headed eagle **Rev:** Lynx on log

Date	Mintage	F	VF	XF	Unc	BU
1995 Proof	5,000	Value: 250				

Y# 472 25 ROUBLES
155.5000 g., 0.9000 Silver 4.4995 oz. ASW **Subject:** First Station at North Pole **Obv:** Double-headed eagle **Rev:** Men, ship, and airplane **Note:** Photo reduced.

Date	Mintage	F	VF	XF	Unc	BU
1995 Proof	5,000	Value: 175				

Y# 437 25 ROUBLES
31.1035 g., 0.9990 Palladium 1.0000 oz. **Obv:** Double-headed eagle **Rev:** Ballerina

Date	Mintage	F	VF	XF	Unc	BU
1995 Proof	1,500	Value: 525				

Y# 439 25 ROUBLES
3.1100 g., 0.9990 Gold .1000 oz. AGW **Obv:** Double-headed eagle **Rev:** Ballerina

Date	Mintage	F	VF	XF	Unc	BU
1995 Proof	5,000	Value: 120				

Y# 442 25 ROUBLES
3.1104 g., 0.9990 Platinum .1000 oz. APW **Obv:** Double-headed eagle **Rev:** Ballerina

Date	Mintage	F	VF	XF	Unc	BU
1995 Proof	900	Value: 185				

Y# 475 25 ROUBLES
31.1035 g., 0.9990 Palladium 1.0000 oz. **Obv:** Double-headed eagle **Rev:** Alexander Nevski

Date	Mintage	F	VF	XF	Unc	BU
1995 Proof	6,000	Value: 500				

Y# 485 25 ROUBLES
155.5175 g., 0.9990 Silver 5.0000 oz. ASW **Subject:** Ballet - Nutcracker **Obv:** Double-headed eagle **Rev:** Children dancing around tree

Date	Mintage	F	VF	XF	Unc	BU
1996 Proof	5,000	Value: 250				

Y# 479 25 ROUBLES
155.5000 g., 0.9000 Silver 4.4995 oz. ASW **Obv:** Double-headed eagle **Rev:** Battle of Kulikova Plains **Note:** Photo reduced.

Date	Mintage	F	VF	XF	Unc	BU
1996 Proof	5,000	Value: 250				

Y# 536 25 ROUBLES
172.7972 g., 0.9000 Silver 5.0000 oz. ASW **Series:** Wildlife **Obv:** Double-headed eagle **Rev:** Amur Tiger

Date	Mintage	F	VF	XF	Unc	BU
1996 Proof	3,000	Value: 250				

Y# 542 25 ROUBLES
172.7972 g., 0.9000 Silver 5.0000 oz. ASW **Obv:** Double-headed eagle **Rev:** Battle of Gangut, 1714 **Note:** Photo reduced.

Date	Mintage	F	VF	XF	Unc	BU
1996 Proof	3,000	Value: 300				

Y# 543 25 ROUBLES
172.7972 g., 0.9000 Silver 5.0000 oz. ASW **Subject:** Battle of Chesme, 1770 **Obv:** Double-headed eagle **Rev:** Battle of Chesme, 1770 **Note:** Photo reduced.

Date	Mintage	F	VF	XF	Unc	BU
1996 Proof	3,000	Value: 300				

Y# 544 25 ROUBLES
172.7972 g., 0.9000 Silver 5.0000 oz. ASW **Obv:** Double-headed eagle **Rev:** Battle of Corfu, 1799 **Note:** Photo reduced.

Date	Mintage	F	VF	XF	Unc	BU
1996 Proof	3,000	Value: 300				

Y# 545 25 ROUBLES
172.7972 g., 0.9000 Silver 5.0000 oz. ASW **Obv:** Double-headed eagle **Rev:** Battle of Sinop, 1853 **Note:** Photo reduced.

Date	Mintage	F	VF	XF	Unc	BU
1996 Proof	3,000	Value: 300				

Y# 486 25 ROUBLES
3.1103 g., 0.9990 Gold .1000 oz. AGW **Subject:** Ballet - Nutcracker **Obv:** Double headed eagle **Rev:** Figure with nutcracker doll

Date	Mintage	F	VF	XF	Unc	BU
1996 Proof	7,500	Value: 125				

Y# 554 25 ROUBLES
172.7972 g., 0.9000 Silver 5.0000 oz. ASW **Subject:** 850th Anniversary - Moscow **Obv:** Double-headed eagle **Rev:** Monument flanked by trees

Date	Mintage	F	VF	XF	Unc	BU
1997 Proof	5,000	Value: 220				

Y# 570 25 ROUBLES
172.7972 g., 0.9000 Silver 5.0000 oz. ASW **Subject:** Ballet - Swan Lake **Obv:** Double-headed eagle **Rev:** Prince Siegfried dancing with Odile

Date	Mintage	F	VF	XF	Unc	BU
1997 Proof	3,000	Value: 250				

Y# 592 25 ROUBLES
172.7972 g., 0.9000 Silver 5.0000 oz. ASW **Series:** Wildlife **Obv:** Double-headed eagle **Rev:** Bear with cub

Date	Mintage	F	VF	XF	Unc	BU
1997 Proof	1,000	Value: 350				

Y# 594 25 ROUBLES
172.7972 g., 0.9000 Silver 5.0000 oz. ASW **Series:** Wildlife **Obv:** Double-headed eagle **Rev:** Polar bear, caribou, seal

Date	Mintage	F	VF	XF	Unc	BU
1997 Proof	3,000	Value: 300				

Y# 622 25 ROUBLES
173.2900 g., 0.9000 Silver 5.0143 oz. ASW **Series:** Wildlife **Obv:** Double-headed eagle **Rev:** Sable in tree

Date	Mintage	F	VF	XF	Unc	BU
1997 Proof	1,000	Value: 350				

Y# 571 25 ROUBLES
3.1103 g., 0.9990 Gold .1000 oz. AGW **Subject:** Ballet - Swan Lake **Obv:** Double-headed eagle **Rev:** Winged figure of Rothbart and Swan

Date	Mintage	F	VF	XF	Unc	BU
1997 Proof	2,000	Value: 175				

Y# 315 50 ROUBLES
5.9500 g., Bi-Metallic Aluminum-Bronze center in Copper-Nickel ring, 25 mm. **Obv:** Double-headed eagle **Rev:** Value flanked by sprigs **Note:** Off-metal strikes exist from both mints. The strike is on the planchet reserved for Y#316, 100 Roubles.

Date	Mintage	F	VF	XF	Unc	BU
1992Л	—	0.50	0.75	1.00	2.50	—
1992М	—	0.75	1.00	1.50	3.50	—

Y# 354 50 ROUBLES
8.6397 g., 0.9000 Gold .2500 oz. AGW **Obv:** Double-headed eagle **Rev:** Moscow's Pashkov Palace

Date	Mintage	F	VF	XF	Unc	BU
1992 Proof	7,500	Value: 215				

Y# 516 50 ROUBLES
8.6397 g., 0.9000 Gold .2500 oz. AGW **Obv:** Double-headed eagle **Rev:** Chubuku (snow) ram on map **Note:** Yakutia.

Date	Mintage	F	VF	XF	Unc	BU
1992 Proof	25,000	Value: 225				

Y# 329.1 50 ROUBLES
Aluminum-Bronze, 25 mm. **Obv:** Double-headed eagle **Rev:** Value flanked by sprigs **Edge:** Alternating reeded and plain

Date	Mintage	F	VF	XF	Unc	BU
1993Л	—	—	—	—	2.50	—
1993М	—	—	—	—	2.50	—

Y# 329.2 50 ROUBLES
Brass Clad Steel, 25 mm. **Obv:** Double-headed eagle **Rev:** Value **Edge:** Plain

Date	Mintage	F	VF	XF	Unc	BU
1993(l)	—	—	—	—	3.50	—
1993(m)	—	—	—	—	2.50	—

Y# 330 50 ROUBLES
5.9500 g., Bi-Metallic Aluminum-Bronze center in Copper-Nickel ring, 25 mm. **Series:** Wildlife **Obv:** Double-headed eagle **Rev:** Black bear **Edge:** Alternating reeded and smooth

Date	Mintage	F	VF	XF	Unc	BU
1993Л	300,000	—	—	—	4.00	6.00

Y# 331 50 ROUBLES
5.9500 g., Bi-Metallic Aluminum-Bronze center in Copper-Nickel ring, 25 mm. **Series:** Wildlife **Obv:** Double-headed eagle **Rev:** Gecko **Edge:** Alternating reeded and smooth

Date	Mintage	F	VF	XF	Unc	BU
1993Л	300,000	—	—	—	5.00	7.50

Y# 332 50 ROUBLES
5.9500 g., Bi-Metallic Aluminum-Bronze center in Copper-Nickel ring, 25 mm. **Series:** Wildlife **Obv:** Double-headed eagle **Rev:** Grouse **Edge:** Alternating reeded and smooth

Date	Mintage	F	VF	XF	Unc	BU
1993Л	300,000	—	—	—	4.00	6.00

Y# 333 50 ROUBLES
5.9500 g., Bi-Metallic Aluminum-Bronze center in Copper-Nickel ring, 25 mm. **Series:** Wildlife **Obv:** Double-headed eagle **Rev:** Far Eastern Stork **Edge:** Alternating reeded and smooth

Date	Mintage	F	VF	XF	Unc	BU
1993Л	300,000	—	—	—	4.00	6.00

Y# 334 50 ROUBLES
5.9500 g., Bi-Metallic Aluminum-Bronze center in Copper-Nickel ring, 25 mm. **Series:** Wildlife **Obv:** Double-headed eagle **Rev:** Black Sea Porpoise **Edge:** Alternating reeded and smooth

Date	Mintage	F	VF	XF	Unc	BU
1993Л	300,000	—	—	—	4.00	7.50

Y# 355 50 ROUBLES
8.6397 g., 0.9000 Gold .2500 oz. AGW **Series:** Olympics **Obv:** Double-headed eagle **Rev:** Figure skater

Date	Mintage	F	VF	XF	Unc	BU
1993 Proof	7,500	Value: 215				

Y# 356 50 ROUBLES
7.7758 g., 0.9990 Platinum .2498 oz. APW **Series:** Olympics **Obv:** Double-headed eagle **Rev:** Formal riding

Date	Mintage	F	VF	XF	Unc	BU
1993 Proof	7,500	Value: 375				

Y# 396 50 ROUBLES
7.7758 g., 0.9990 Platinum .2498 oz. APW **Subject:** Bolshoi Ballet **Obv:** Double-headed eagle **Rev:** Ballerina

Date	Mintage	F	VF	XF	Unc	BU
1993 Proof	750	—	—	—	400	—

Y# 411 50 ROUBLES
7.7800 g., 0.9990 Gold .2500 oz. AGW **Series:** Wildlife **Obv:** Double-headed eagle **Rev:** Bear between trees and sprigs

Date	Mintage	F	VF	XF	Unc	BU
1993 Proof	1,480	Value: 245				

Y# 418 50 ROUBLES
7.7800 g., 0.9990 Gold .2500 oz. AGW **Subject:** Bolshoi Ballet **Obv:** Double-headed eagle **Rev:** Ballerina

Date	Mintage	F	VF	XF	Unc	BU
1993	4,700	—	—	—	300	—
1993 Proof	1,500	Value: 350				

Y# 453 50 ROUBLES
7.7800 g., 0.9990 Gold .2500 oz. AGW **Subject:** Sergei Rachmaninov **Obv:** Double-headed eagle **Rev:** Head right

Date	Mintage	F	VF	XF	Unc	BU
1993 Proof	7,500	Value: 215				

Y# 367 50 ROUBLES
5.9500 g., Bi-Metallic Aluminum-Bronze center in Copper-Nickel ring, 25 mm. **Series:** Wildlife **Obv:** Double-headed eagle **Rev:** Blind mole rat **Edge:** Alternating reeded and smooth

Date	Mintage	F	VF	XF	Unc	BU
1994Л	300,000	—	—	—	4.00	6.00

Y# 368 50 ROUBLES
5.9500 g., Bi-Metallic Aluminum-Bronze center in Copper-Nickel ring, 25 mm. **Series:** Wildlife **Obv:** Double-headed eagle **Rev:** Bison **Edge:** Alternating reeded and smooth

Date	Mintage	F	VF	XF	Unc	BU
1994Л	300,000	—	—	—	4.00	6.00

Y# 369 50 ROUBLES
5.9500 g., Bi-Metallic Alunimum-Bronze center in Copper-Nickel ring, 25 mm. **Series:** Wildlife **Obv:** Double-headed eagle **Rev:** Goitered Gazelle **Edge:** Alternating reeded and smooth

Date	Mintage	F	VF	XF	Unc	BU
1994Л	300,000	—	—	—	4.00	6.00

Y# 370 50 ROUBLES
5.9500 g., Bi-Metallic Aluminum-Bronze center in Copper-Nickel ring, 25 mm. **Series:** Wildlife **Obv:** Double-headed eagle **Rev:** Peregrine Falcon **Edge:** Alternating reeded and smooth

Date	Mintage	F	VF	XF	Unc	BU
1994Л	300,000	—	—	—	4.00	6.00

Y# 371 50 ROUBLES
5.9500 g., Bi-Metallic Aluminum-Bronze center in Copper-Nickel ring, 25 mm. **Series:** Wildlife **Obv:** Double-headed eagle **Rev:** Two flamingos **Edge:** Alternating reeded and smooth

Date	Mintage	F	VF	XF	Unc	BU
1994Л	300,000	—	—	—	4.00	6.00

Y# 426 50 ROUBLES
7.7759 g., 0.9990 Gold .2500 oz. AGW **Subject:** Bolshoi Ballet **Obv:** Double-headed eagle **Rev:** Ballerina

Date	Mintage	F	VF	XF	Unc	BU
1994 Proof	2,500	Value: 250				

Y# 429 50 ROUBLES
7.7759 g., 0.9990 Platinum .2500 oz. APW **Subject:** Bolshoi Ballet **Obv:** Double-headed eagle **Rev:** Ballerina

Date	Mintage	F	VF	XF	Unc	BU
1994 Proof	900	Value: 475				

Y# 525 50 ROUBLES
7.7759 g., 0.9990 Gold .2500 oz. AGW **Series:** Wildlife **Obv:** Double-headed eagle **Rev:** Sable in tree

Date	Mintage	F	VF	XF	Unc	BU
1994 Proof	2,500	Value: 220				

Y# 531 50 ROUBLES
7.7759 g., 0.9990 Gold .2500 oz. AGW **Rev:** Dmitri Grigorievich Levitsky

Date	Mintage	F	VF	XF	Unc	BU
1994 Proof	8,000	Value: 240				

Y# 403 50 ROUBLES
Aluminum-Bronze **Series:** WWII **Obv:** Double-headed eagle **Rev:** Two sailors, ship, and plane

Date	Mintage	F	VF	XF	Unc	BU
1995	200,000	—	—	—	4.00	—

Note: In mint sets only

Y# A475 50 ROUBLES
7.7800 g., 0.9990 Gold .2499 oz. AGW **Series:** Wildlife **Obv:** Double-headed eagle **Rev:** Lynx

Date	Mintage	F	VF	XF	Unc	BU
1995 Proof	10,000	Value: 215				

Y# 408 50 ROUBLES
7.7800 g., 0.9990 Gold .2499 oz. AGW **Subject:** 50th Anniversary - United Nations **Obv:** Double-headed eagle **Rev:** Blacksmith with anvil at feet, UN logo at top, building at left **Note:** Similar to 3 Roubles, Y#407.

Date	Mintage	F	VF	XF	Unc	BU
1995 Proof	5,000	Value: 220				

Y# 440 50 ROUBLES
7.7800 g., 0.9990 Gold .2499 oz. AGW **Subject:** Bolshoi Ballet - Sleeping Beauty **Obv:** Double-headed eagle **Rev:** Ballerina

Date	Mintage	F	VF	XF	Unc	BU
1995 Proof	2,500	Value: 350				

Y# 443 50 ROUBLES
7.7759 g., 0.9990 Platinum .2500 oz. APW **Subject:** Bolshoi Ballet - Sleeping Beauty **Obv:** Double-headed eagle **Rev:** Male dancer

Date	Mintage	F	VF	XF	Unc	BU
1995 Proof	900	Value: 475				

Y# 496 50 ROUBLES
8.6397 g., 0.9000 Gold .2500 oz. AGW **Subject:** F. Nansen and the "Fram" **Obv:** Double-headed eagle **Rev:** F. Nansen and the "Fram"

Date	Mintage	F	VF	XF	Unc	BU
1995 Proof	5,000	Value: 210				

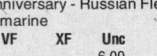

Y# 508 50 ROUBLES
Aluminum-Bronze **Subject:** 300th Anniversary - Russian Fleet **Obv:** Double-headed eagle **Rev:** Submarine

Date	Mintage	F	VF	XF	Unc	BU
1996	100,000	—	—	—	6.00	—

Note: In mint sets only

Y# 480 50 ROUBLES
7.7800 g., 0.9990 Gold .2499 oz. AGW **Obv:** Double-headed eagle **Rev:** Dmitri Donskoy Monument

Date	Mintage	F	VF	XF	Unc	BU
1996 Proof	10,000	Value: 210				

Y# 487 50 ROUBLES
7.7800 g., 0.9990 Gold .2499 oz. AGW **Subject:** Ballet - Nutcracker **Obv:** Double-headed eagle **Rev:** Marsha and Drosselmeyer with broken doll

Date	Mintage	F	VF	XF	Unc	BU
1996 Proof	2,500	Value: 250				

Y# 501 50 ROUBLES
8.6397 g., 0.9000 Gold .2500 oz. AGW **Obv:** Double-headed eagle **Rev:** Church of the Savior on the Nereditza River

Date	Mintage	F	VF	XF	Unc	BU
1996 Proof	10,000	Value: 200				

Y# 537 50 ROUBLES
7.7759 g., 0.9990 Gold .2500 oz. AGW **Series:** Wildlife **Obv:** Double-headed eagle **Rev:** Tiger head

Date	Mintage	F	VF	XF	Unc	BU
1996 Proof	1,500	Value: 225				

Y# 546 50 ROUBLES
8.6397 g., 0.9000 Gold .2500 oz. AGW **Obv:** Double-headed eagle **Rev:** Cruiser Varyag 1904

Date	Mintage	F	VF	XF	Unc	BU
1996 Proof	1,500	Value: 250				

Y# 555 50 ROUBLES
8.6397 g., 0.9000 Gold .2500 oz. AGW **Subject:** 850th Anniversary - Moscow **Obv:** Double-headed eagle **Rev:** Shield flanked by designs

Date	Mintage	F	VF	XF	Unc	BU
1997 Proof	10,000	Value: 210				

Y# 572 50 ROUBLES
7.7759 g., 0.9990 Gold .2500 oz. AGW **Subject:** Ballet - Swan Lake **Obv:** Double-headed eagle **Rev:** Prince Siegfried with crossbow and swan

Date	Mintage	F	VF	XF	Unc	BU
1997 Proof	1,500	Value: 225				

Y# 595 50 ROUBLES
7.7759 g., 0.9990 Gold .2500 oz. AGW **Series:** Wildlife **Obv:** Double-headed eagle **Rev:** Polar bear

Date	Mintage	F	VF	XF	Unc	BU
1997 Proof	1,500	Value: 220				

Y# 712 50 ROUBLES
8.7500 g., 0.9000 Gold .2532 oz. AGW **Series:** Three Millenniums **Subject:** Scientific and Technical Progress **Obv:** Double-headed eagle **Rev:** Icarus and space travel

Date	Mintage	F	VF	XF	Unc	BU
2000(m) Proof	1,000	Value: 250				

Y# 316 100 ROUBLES
6.0000 g., Bi-Metallic Copper-Nickel center in Aluminum-Bronze ring, 25.3 mm. **Obv:** Double-headed eagle **Rev:** Value flanked by sprigs **Note:** Off-metal strikes exist from the Moscow mint. The strike is on the planchet reserved for Y#315, 50 Roubles.

Date	Mintage	F	VF	XF	Unc	BU
1992Л	—	0.50	0.75	1.00	3.00	—
1992M	—	0.75	1.00	1.50	4.50	—

Y# 357 100 ROUBLES
17.5000 g., 0.9000 Gold .5000 oz. AGW **Obv:** Double-headed eagle **Rev:** Michael Lomonossov

Date	Mintage	F	VF	XF	Unc	BU
1992 Proof	5,700	Value: 375				

Y# 375 100 ROUBLES
17.5000 g., 0.9000 Gold .5000 oz. AGW **Obv:** Double-headed eagle **Rev:** Wooly Mammoth within radiant map **Note:** Yakutia

Date	Mintage	F	VF	XF	Unc	BU
1992	14,000	—	—	—	385	—

Y# 338 100 ROUBLES
Copper-Nickel-Zinc **Obv:** Double-headed eagle **Rev:** Value flanked by sprigs

Date	Mintage	F	VF	XF	Unc	BU
1993Л	—	0.25	0.50	1.00	3.00	—
1993М	—	0.25	0.50	1.00	3.00	—

Y# 412 100 ROUBLES
15.5500 g., 0.9990 Gold .5000 oz. AGW **Series:** Wildlife **Obv:** Double-headed eagle **Rev:** Black bear

Date	Mintage	F	VF	XF	Unc	BU
1993 Proof	1,400	Value: 365				

Y# 419 100 ROUBLES
15.5500 g., 0.9990 Gold .5000 oz. AGW **Subject:** Bolshoi Ballet **Obv:** Double-headed eagle **Rev:** Ballerina

Date	Mintage	F	VF	XF	Unc	BU
1993	2,700	—	—	—	500	—
1993 Proof	1,500	Value: 575				

Y# 454 100 ROUBLES
17.5000 g., 0.9000 Gold .5000 oz. AGW **Obv:** Double-headed eagle **Rev:** Peter Tchaikovsky

Date	Mintage	F	VF	XF	Unc	BU
1993 Proof	5,700	Value: 500				

Y# 427 100 ROUBLES
15.5500 g., 0.9990 Gold .5000 oz. AGW **Subject:** Bolshoi Ballet **Obv:** Double-headed eagle **Rev:** Ballerina

Date	Mintage	F	VF	XF	Unc	BU
1994 Proof	2,500	Value: 550				

Y# 526 100 ROUBLES
15.5500 g., 0.9990 Gold .5000 oz. AGW **Series:** Wildlife **Obv:** Double-headed eagle **Rev:** Sable in tree

Date	Mintage	F	VF	XF	Unc	BU
1994 Proof	2,500	Value: 400				

Y# 532 100 ROUBLES
15.5500 g., 0.9990 Gold .5000 oz. AGW **Obv:** Double-headed eagle **Rev:** Vassili Vassilievich Kandinsky - The Blue Horse

Date	Mintage	F	VF	XF	Unc	BU
1994 Proof	6,000	Value: 400				

Y# 404 100 ROUBLES
Copper-Nickel **Series:** WWII **Obv:** Double-headed eagle **Rev:** Berlin Soldier Monument

Date	Mintage	F	VF	XF	Unc	BU
1995	200,000	—	—	—	5.00	—

Note: In mint sets only

Y# 498 100 ROUBLES
912.3693 g., 0.9000 Silver 26.4000 oz. ASW **Series:** Wildlife **Obv:** Double-headed eagle **Rev:** Lynx with two kits

Date	Mintage	F	VF	XF	Unc	BU
1995 Proof	500	Value: 1,350				

Y# 502 100 ROUBLES
17.5000 g., 0.9000 Gold .5000 oz. AGW **Obv:** Double-headed eagle **Rev:** Order of Alexander Nevsky

Date	Mintage	F	VF	XF	Unc	BU
1995 Proof	5,000	Value: 500				

Y# 376 100 ROUBLES
1111.0861 g., 0.9000 Silver 32.1500 oz. ASW, 100 mm. **Series:** Wildlife **Obv:** Double-headed eagle **Rev:** Mother bear with cubs

Date	Mintage	F	VF	XF	Unc	BU
1995 Proof	500	Value: 2,500				

Y# A387 100 ROUBLES
1000.2108 g., 0.9000 Silver 28.9417 oz. ASW, 103 mm. **Series:** WWII **Subject:** WWII Victory **Rev:** Allied Commanders **Note:** Photo reduced.

Date	Mintage	F	VF	XF	Unc	BU
1995 Proof	1,500	Value: 1,600				

Y# 434 100 ROUBLES
912.3693 g., 0.9000 Silver 26.4000 oz. ASW, 100 mm. **Subject:** Ballet - Sleeping Beauty **Obv:** Building in back of double-headed eagle **Rev:** Theater above dancers

Date	Mintage	F	VF	XF	Unc	BU
1995 Proof	1,000	Value: 1,600				

Y# 441 100 ROUBLES
15.5500 g., 0.9990 Gold .5000 oz. AGW **Subject:** Ballet - Sleeping Beauty **Obv:** Double-headed eagle **Rev:** Ballerina

Date	Mintage	F	VF	XF	Unc	BU
1995 Proof	2,500	Value: 695				

Y# 497 100 ROUBLES
17.5000 g., 0.9000 Gold .5000 oz. AGW **Obv:** Double-headed eagle **Rev:** Icebreaker "Krassin"

Date	Mintage	F	VF	XF	Unc	BU
1995 Proof	2,500	Value: 500				

Y# 499 100 ROUBLES
17.5000 g., 0.9000 Gold .5000 oz. AGW **Series:** Wildlife **Obv:** Double-headed eagle **Rev:** Lynx

Date	Mintage	F	VF	XF	Unc	BU
1995 Proof	3,500	Value: 500				

Y# 495 100 ROUBLES
912.3693 g., 0.9000 Silver 26.4000 oz. ASW **Obv:** Double-headed eagle **Rev:** Sables around city **Note:** Photo reduced

Date	Mintage	F	VF	XF	Unc	BU
1996 Proof	500	Value: 1,600				

Y# 509 100 ROUBLES
Copper-Nickel **Subject:** 300th Anniversary - Russian Fleet **Obv:** Double-headed eagle **Rev:** Atlantic Icebreader "Arctic"

Date	Mintage	F	VF	XF	Unc	BU
1996	100,000	—	—	—	7.00	—

Note: In mint sets only

Y# 488 100 ROUBLES
1111.0861 g., 0.9990 Silver 32.1500 oz. ASW **Subject:** Ballet - Nutcracker **Obv:** Double-headed eagle **Rev:** Marsha cradling nutcracker doll

Date	Mintage	F	VF	XF	Unc	BU
1996 Proof	1,000	Value: 1,500				

Y# 538 100 ROUBLES
1111.0861 g., 0.9000 Silver 32.1500 oz. ASW **Series:** Wildlife **Obv:** Double-headed eagle **Rev:** Tiger

Date	Mintage	F	VF	XF	Unc	BU
1996 Proof	1,000	Value: 1,500				

Y# 547 100 ROUBLES
912.3693 g., 0.9000 Silver 26.4000 oz. ASW **Obv:** Double-headed eagle **Rev:** Warship Poltava, 1712 **Note:** Photo reduced.

Date	Mintage	F	VF	XF	Unc	BU
1996 Proof	3,000	Value: 1,000				

Y# 481 100 ROUBLES
17.5000 g., 0.9000 Gold .5000 oz. AGW **Obv:** Double-headed eagle **Rev:** All Saints Church in Kulishki

Date	Mintage	F	VF	XF	Unc	BU
1996 Proof	5,000	Value: 365				

Y# 489 100 ROUBLES
15.5517 g., 0.9990 Gold .5000 oz. AGW **Subject:** Ballet - Nutcracker **Obv:** Double-headed eagle **Rev:** Dancing Prince

Date	Mintage	F	VF	XF	Unc	BU
1996 Proof	2,500	Value: 400				

Y# 539 100 ROUBLES
15.5517 g., 0.9990 Gold .5000 oz. AGW **Series:** Wildlife **Obv:** Double-headed eagle **Rev:** Amur tiger

Date	Mintage	F	VF	XF	Unc	BU
1996 Proof	1,000	Value: 420				

Y# 548 100 ROUBLES
17.5000 g., 0.9000 Gold .5000 oz. AGW **Subject:** Battleships of WWII **Obv:** Double-headed eagle **Rev:** Destroyers, "Gremysiy and Soobrazitelny"

Date	Mintage	F	VF	XF	Unc	BU
1996 Proof	1,000	Value: 500				

Y# 597 100 ROUBLES
1111.0861 g., 0.9000 Silver 32.1500 oz. ASW **Series:** Wildlife **Obv:** Double-headed eagle **Rev:** Two polar bears

Date	Mintage	F	VF	XF	Unc	BU
1997 Proof	1,000	Value: 1,300				

Y# 556 100 ROUBLES
1111.0861 g., 0.9000 Silver 32.1500 oz. ASW **Subject:** 850th Anniversary - Moscow **Obv:** Double-headed eagle **Rev:** Kuzma Minin and Dmitri Pozharsky Monument **Note:** Photo reduced.

Date	Mintage	F	VF	XF	Unc	BU
1997 Proof	1,000	Value: 1,000				

Y# 573 100 ROUBLES
1111.0861 g., 0.9000 Silver 32.1500 oz. ASW **Subject:** Ballet - Swan Lake **Obv:** Double-headed eagle **Rev:** Prince Siegfried dancing with Odette **Note:** Photo reduced.

Date	Mintage	F	VF	XF	Unc	BU
1997 Proof	1,000	Value: 1,000				

Y# 588 100 ROUBLES
1111.0861 g., 0.9000 Silver 32.1500 oz. ASW **Obv:** Double-headed eagle **Rev:** 4-Masted Ship - "The Bark Krusenstern" **Note:** Photo reduced.

Date	Mintage	F	VF	XF	Unc	BU
1997 Proof	500	Value: 1,400				

Y# 557 100 ROUBLES
17.2890 g., 0.9000 Gold .5000 oz. AGW **Subject:** 850th Anniversary - Moscow **Obv:** Double-headed eagle **Rev:** Yuri Dolgoruky Monument

Date	Mintage	F	VF	XF	Unc	BU
1997 Proof	5,000	Value: 500				

Y# 574 100 ROUBLES
15.5517 g., 0.9990 Gold .5000 oz. AGW **Subject:** Ballet - Swan Lake **Obv:** Double-headed eagle **Rev:** Prince Siegfried and Odette'd Duet

Date	Mintage	F	VF	XF	Unc	BU
1997 Proof	1,500	Value: 400				

Y# 596 100 ROUBLES
15.5517 g., 0.9990 Gold .5000 oz. AGW **Series:** Wildlife **Obv:** Double-headed eagle **Rev:** Polar bear on ice floe

Date	Mintage	F	VF	XF	Unc	BU
1997 Proof	1,000	Value: 425				

Note: Notice the face on the bear's hind quarter

Y# 623 100 ROUBLES
15.7200 g., 0.9990 Gold .5049 oz. AGW **Obv:** Double-headed eagle **Rev:** Serge Julievech Witte

Date	Mintage	F	VF	XF	Unc	BU
1997 Proof	1,000	Value: 400				

Y# 699 100 ROUBLES
1111.1200 g., 0.9000 Silver 32.1510 oz. ASW, 100 mm. **Subject:** Russian Ballet **Obv:** Double-headed eagle **Rev:** Raymonda wedding scene **Edge:** Reeded **Note:** Photo reduced.

Date	Mintage	F	VF	XF	Unc	BU
1999(sp) Proof	1,000	Value: 1,200				

Y# 358 150 ROUBLES
15.5517 g., 0.9990 Platinum .5000 oz. APW **Subject:** Naval Battle of Chesme **Obv:** Double-headed eagle **Rev:** Two battle ships

Date	Mintage	F	VF	XF	Unc	BU
1992 Proof	3,000	Value: 675				

Y# 397 150 ROUBLES
15.5517 g., 0.9990 Platinum .5000 oz. APW **Subject:** Ballet **Obv:** Double-headed eagle **Rev:** Ballerina

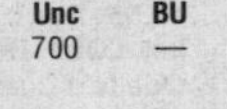

Date	Mintage	F	VF	XF	Unc	BU
1993 Proof	750	—	—	—	700	—

Y# 455 150 ROUBLES
15.5517 g., 0.9990 Platinum .5000 oz. APW **Obv:** Double-headed eagle **Rev:** Igor Stravinsky

Date	Mintage	F	VF	XF	Unc	BU
1993 Proof	3,000	Value: 675				

Y# 519 150 ROUBLES
15.5517 g., 0.9990 Platinum .5000 oz. APW **Subject:** First Global Circumnavigation **Obv:** Double-headed eagle **Rev:** Sloops - Nadyezdha and Neva

Date	Mintage	F	VF	XF	Unc	BU
1993 Proof	2,500	Value: 675				

Y# 430 150 ROUBLES
15.5517 g., 0.9990 Platinum .5000 oz. APW **Subject:** Bolshoi Ballet **Obv:** Double-headed eagle **Rev:** Ballerina

Date	Mintage	F	VF	XF	Unc	BU
1994 Proof	900	Value: 950				

Y# 523 150 ROUBLES
15.5517 g., 0.9990 Platinum .5000 oz. APW **Subject:** First Global Circumnavigation **Obv:** Double-headed eagle **Rev:** Sloops - "Mirny" and "Vostok"

Date	Mintage	F	VF	XF	Unc	BU
1994 Proof	4,000	Value: 675				

Y# 533 150 ROUBLES
15.5517 g., 0.9990 Platinum .5000 oz. APW **Subject:** Michail Alexandrowich Vrubel - The Demon **Obv:** Double-headed eagle **Rev:** Michail Alexandrowich Vrubel - The Demon

Date	Mintage	F	VF	XF	Unc	BU
1994 Proof	3,000	Value: 675				

Y# 444 150 ROUBLES
15.5517 g., 0.9990 Platinum .5000 oz. APW **Subject:** Ballet - Sleeping Beauty **Obv:** Double-headed eagle **Rev:** Male dancer

Date	Mintage	F	VF	XF	Unc	BU
1995 Proof	900	Value: 900				

Y# 503 150 ROUBLES
15.5517 g., 0.9990 Platinum .5000 oz. APW **Subject:** Battle of the Neva River in 1240 **Obv:** Double-headed eagle **Rev:** Armored equestrians fighting

Date	Mintage	F	VF	XF	Unc	BU
1995 Proof	3,000	Value: 675				

Y# 413 200 ROUBLES
31.1035 g., 0.9990 Gold 1.0000 oz. AGW **Series:** Wildlife **Obv:** Double-headed eagle **Rev:** Bear with cub

Date	Mintage	F	VF	XF	Unc	BU
1993 Proof	1,000	Value: 1,200				

Y# 527 200 ROUBLES
31.1035 g., 0.9990 Gold 1.0000 oz. AGW **Series:** Wildlife **Obv:** Double-headed eagle **Rev:** Two sables

Date	Mintage	F	VF	XF	Unc	BU
1994 Proof	2,000	Value: 1,200				

Y# 500 200 ROUBLES
31.1035 g., 0.9990 Gold 1.0000 oz. AGW **Series:** Wildlife **Obv:** Double-headed eagle **Rev:** Seated lynx

Date	Mintage	F	VF	XF	Unc	BU
1995 Proof	1,750	Value: 1,250				

Y# 540 200 ROUBLES
31.1035 g., 0.9990 Gold 1.0000 oz. AGW **Series:** Wildlife **Obv:** Double-headed eagle **Rev:** Amur tiger

Date	Mintage	F	VF	XF	Unc	BU
1996 Proof	1,000	Value: 1,200				

Y# 598 200 ROUBLES
31.1035 g., 0.9990 Gold 1.0000 oz. AGW **Series:** Wildlife **Obv:** Double-headed eagle **Rev:** Seated polar bear

Date	Mintage	F	VF	XF	Unc	BU
1997 Proof	1,000	Value: 1,100				

Y# 589 1000 ROUBLES
155.5000 g., 0.9990 Gold 4.9944 oz. AGW **Obv:** Double-headed eagle **Rev:** The Bark "Krusenstern" - 4-masted ship **Note:** Photo reduced

Date	Mintage	F	VF	XF	Unc	BU
1997 Proof	250	Value: 5,000				

Y# 541 10000 ROUBLES
1111.0861 g., 0.9990 Gold 35.6865 oz. AGW, 100 mm. **Series:** Wildlife **Obv:** Double-headed eagle **Rev:** Amur tiger with two cubs

Date	Mintage	F	VF	XF	Unc	BU
1996 Prooflike	100	—	—	—	—	25,000

Y# 599 10000 ROUBLES
1111.0861 g., 0.9990 Gold 35.6865 oz. AGW, 100 mm. **Series:** Wildlife **Obv:** Double-headed eagle **Rev:** Seated polar bear with two cubs

Date	Mintage	F	VF	XF	Unc	BU
1997 Proof	100	Value: 25,000				

REFORM COINAGE

January 1, 1998

1,000 Old Roubles = 1 New Rouble

Y# 600 KOPEK
Nickel **Obv:** St. George **Rev:** Value above vine sprig

Date	Mintage	F	VF	XF	Unc	BU
1997 M	—	—	—	—	0.30	0.40
1997 SP	—	—	—	—	0.30	0.40
1998 M	—	—	—	—	0.30	0.40
1998 SP	—	—	—	—	0.30	0.40
1999 M	—	—	—	—	0.30	0.40
1999 SP	—	—	—	—	0.30	0.40
2000 M	—	—	—	—	0.30	0.40
2000 SP	—	—	—	—	0.30	0.40

Y# 601 5 KOPEKS
Nickel, 19 mm. **Obv:** St. George **Rev:** Value above vine sprig **Edge:** Plain

Date	Mintage	F	VF	XF	Unc	BU
1997 M	—	—	—	—	0.35	0.50
1997 SP	—	—	—	—	0.35	0.50
1998 M	—	—	—	—	0.45	0.65
1998 SP	—	—	—	—	0.45	0.65
1999 M	—	—	—	—	0.35	0.50
1999 SP	—	—	—	—	0.35	0.50
2000 M	—	—	—	—	0.35	0.50
2000 SP	—	—	—	—	0.35	0.50

Y# 602 10 KOPEKS
Brass **Obv:** St. George **Rev:** Value above vine sprig

Date	Mintage	F	VF	XF	Unc	BU
1997 M	—	—	—	—	0.50	0.75
1997 SP	—	—	—	—	0.50	0.75
1998 M	—	—	—	—	0.65	1.00
1998 SP	—	—	—	—	0.65	1.00
1999 M	—	—	—	—	0.50	0.75
1999 SP	—	—	—	—	0.50	0.75
2000 M	—	—	—	—	0.50	0.75
2000 SP	—	—	—	—	0.50	0.75

Y# 603 50 KOPEKS
Brass, 19.5 mm. **Obv:** St. George **Rev:** Value above vine sprig **Edge:** Reeded

Date	Mintage	F	VF	XF	Unc	BU
1997 M	—	—	—	—	0.75	1.00
1997 SP	—	—	—	—	0.75	1.00
1998 M	—	—	—	—	1.00	1.50
1998 SP	—	—	—	—	1.00	1.50
1999 M	—	—	—	—	0.75	1.00
1999 SP	—	—	—	—	0.75	1.00

Y# 604 ROUBLE
3.2500 g., Copper-Nickel-Zinc, 20.6 mm. **Obv:** Double headed eagle **Rev:** Value **Edge:** Reeded

Date	Mintage	F	VF	XF	Unc	BU
1997 M	—	—	—	—	1.00	1.50
1997 SP	—	—	—	—	1.00	1.50
1998 M	—	—	—	—	1.00	1.50
1998 SP	—	—	—	—	1.00	1.50
1999 M	—	—	—	—	1.00	1.50
1999 SP	—	—	—	—	1.00	1.50

Y# 614 ROUBLE
8.5300 g., 0.9250 Silver .2357 oz. ASW **Series:** World Youth Games **Obv:** Double-headed eagle **Rev:** Female tennis player

Date	Mintage	F	VF	XF	Unc	BU
1998 Proof	25,000	Value: 30.00				

Y# 615 ROUBLE
8.5300 g., 0.9250 Silver .2357 oz. ASW **Series:** World Youth Games **Obv:** Double headed eagle **Rev:** Female-gymnast

Date	Mintage	F	VF	XF	Unc	BU
1998 Proof	25,000	Value: 30.00				

Y# 616 ROUBLE
8.5300 g., 0.9250 Silver .2357 oz. ASW **Series:** World Youth Games **Obv:** Double-headed eagle **Rev:** Fencer

Date	Mintage	F	VF	XF	Unc	BU
1998 Proof	25,000	Value: 30.00				

Y# 617 ROUBLE
8.5300 g., 0.9250 Silver .2357 oz. ASW **Series:** World Youth Games **Obv:** Double-headed eagle **Rev:** Hammer thrower

Date	Mintage	F	VF	XF	Unc	BU
1998 Proof	25,000	Value: 30.00				

Y# 618 ROUBLE
8.5300 g., 0.9250 Silver .2357 oz. ASW **Series:** World Youth Games **Obv:** Double-headed eagle **Rev:** Female gymnast

Date	Mintage	F	VF	XF	Unc	BU
1998 Proof	25,000	Value: 30.00				

Y# 619 ROUBLE
8.5300 g., 0.9250 Silver .2357 oz. ASW **Series:** World Youth Games **Obv:** Double-headed eagle **Rev:** Volleyball player

Date	Mintage	F	VF	XF	Unc	BU
1998 Proof	25,000	Value: 30.00				

Y# 628 ROUBLE

17.5500 g., 0.9000 Silver .5078 oz. ASW **Series:** Wildlife **Obv:** Double-headed eagle **Rev:** Far Eastern Skink

Date	Mintage	F	VF	XF	Unc	BU
1998 Proof	15,000	Value: 50.00				

Y# 629 ROUBLE

17.5500 g., 0.9000 Silver .5078 oz. ASW **Series:** Wildlife **Obv:** Double-headed eagle **Rev:** Lavtev Walrus

Date	Mintage	F	VF	XF	Unc	BU
1998 Proof	15,000	Value: 50.00				

Y# 630 ROUBLE

17.5500 g., 0.9000 Silver .5078 oz. ASW **Series:** Wildlife **Obv:** Double-headed eagle **Rev:** Emperor Goose

Date	Mintage	F	VF	XF	Unc	BU
1998 Proof	15,000	Value: 45.00				

Y# 640 ROUBLE

Copper-Nickel-Zinc, 20.5 mm. **Obv:** Double-headed eagle **Rev:** Stylized head of Pushkin left **Edge:** Reeded

Date	Mintage	F	VF	XF	Unc	BU
1999(m)	5,000,000	—	—	—	0.75	1.25
1999(SP)	5,000,000	—	—	—	0.75	1.25

Y# 641 ROUBLE

17.4400 g., 0.9000 Silver .5046 oz. ASW **Series:** Wildlife **Obv:** Double-headed eagle **Rev:** Daurian Hedgehog

Date	Mintage	F	VF	XF	Unc	BU
1999 Proof	15,000	Value: 50.00				

Y# 642 ROUBLE

17.4400 g., 0.9000 Silver .5046 oz. ASW **Series:** Wildlife **Obv:** Double-headed eagle **Rev:** Caucasian viper

Date	Mintage	F	VF	XF	Unc	BU
1999 Proof	15,000	Value: 50.00				

Y# 643 ROUBLE

17.4400 g., 0.9000 Silver .5046 oz. ASW **Series:** Wildlife **Obv:** Double-headed eagle **Rev:** Ross's Gull standing on shore

Date	Mintage	F	VF	XF	Unc	BU
1999 Proof	15,000	Value: 45.00				

Y# 719 ROUBLE

17.4400 g., 0.9000 Silver .5046 oz. ASW, 33 mm. **Subject:** Wildlife **Obv:** Double-headed eagle **Rev:** Two Black-hooded cranes **Edge:** Reeded

Date	Mintage	F	VF	XF	Unc	BU
2000(SP) Proof	3,000	Value: 200				

Y# 720 ROUBLE

17.4400 g., 0.9000 Silver .5046 oz. ASW **Obv:** Double-headed eagle **Rev:** Leopard Runner snake

Date	Mintage	F	VF	XF	Unc	BU
2000(SP) Proof	3,000	Value: 200				

Y# 721 ROUBLE

17.4400 g., 0.9000 Silver .5046 oz. ASW **Obv:** Double-headed eagle **Rev:** Russian Desman

Date	Mintage	F	VF	XF	Unc	BU
2000(SP) Proof	3,000	Value: 200				

Y# 605 2 ROUBLES

Copper-Nickel-Zinc, 23 mm. **Obv:** Double-headed eagle **Rev:** Value and vine sprig **Edge:** Alternating reeded and smooth

Date	Mintage	F	VF	XF	Unc	BU
1997(m)	—	—	—	—	1.65	2.25
1997(sp)	—	—	—	—	1.65	2.25
1998(m)	—	—	—	—	1.65	2.25
1998(sp)	—	—	—	—	1.65	2.25
1999(m)	—	—	—	—	2.00	3.00
1999(sp)	—	—	—	—	2.00	3.00

Y# 607 2 ROUBLES

16.8108 g., 0.9250 Silver .4999 oz. ASW **Subject:** 100th Anniversary - Sergei Eisenstein **Obv:** Double-headed eagle **Rev:** Head facing on movie screen with camera on stand at left

Date	Mintage	F	VF	XF	Unc	BU
1998	15,000	—	—	—	27.50	30.00

Y# 608 2 ROUBLES

16.8108 g., 0.9250 Silver .4999 oz. ASW **Subject:** 50th Anniversary - Sergei Eisenstein **Obv:** Double-headed eagle **Rev:** Figure looking at film strip, ship in background

Date	Mintage	F	VF	XF	Unc	BU
1998	15,000	—	—	—	27.50	30.00

Y# 609 2 ROUBLES

16.8108 g., 0.9250 Silver .4999 oz. ASW **Obv:** Double-headed eagle **Rev:** K.S. Stanslavski

Date	Mintage	F	VF	XF	Unc	BU
1998	15,000	—	—	—	27.50	30.00

Y# 610 2 ROUBLES

16.8108 g., 0.9250 Silver .4999 oz. ASW **Obv:** Double-headed eagle **Rev:** Maxim Gorky play - Stanislavsky method

Date	Mintage	F	VF	XF	Unc	BU
1998	15,000	—	—	—	27.50	30.00

Y# 620 2 ROUBLES
17.0000 g., 0.9250 Silver .5056 oz. ASW **Obv:** Double-headed eagle **Rev:** Victor Mikhailovich Vasnetsov - 3 ancient warriors

Date	Mintage	F	VF	XF	Unc	BU
1998	15,000	—	—	—	27.50	30.00

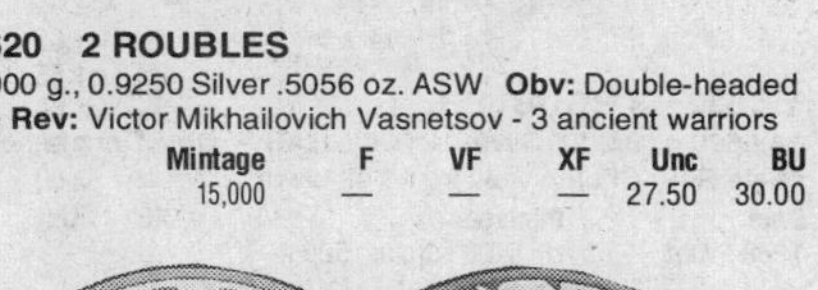

Y# 621 2 ROUBLES
17.0000 g., 0.9250 Silver .5056 oz. ASW **Obv:** Double-headed eagle **Rev:** Victor Mikhailovich Vasnetsov - 3 seated figures

Date	Mintage	F	VF	XF	Unc	BU
1998	15,000	—	—	—	27.50	30.00

Y# 649 2 ROUBLES
17.0000 g., 0.9250 Silver .5056 oz. ASW **Subject:** K. L. Khetagurov 1859-1906 **Obv:** Double-headed eagle **Rev:** Portrait with mountain tops and buildings

Date	Mintage	F	VF	XF	Unc	BU
1999 Proof	3,000	Value: 400				

Y# 650 2 ROUBLES
17.0000 g., 0.9250 Silver .5056 oz. ASW **Subject:** N. K. Rerikh 1874-1947 **Obv:** Double-headed eagle **Rev:** Painter with mountains in the background

Date	Mintage	F	VF	XF	Unc	BU
1999 Proof	15,000	Value: 25.00				

Y# 651 2 ROUBLES
17.0000 g., 0.9250 Silver .5056 oz. ASW **Subject:** The Human Acts by Rerikh. **Obv:** Double-headed eagle **Rev:** Detail from painting, artist's portrait above

Date	Mintage	F	VF	XF	Unc	BU
1999 Proof	15,000	Value: 25.00				

Y# 652 2 ROUBLES
17.0000 g., 0.9250 Silver .5056 oz. ASW **Subject:** K. P. Bryulov 1799-1852 **Obv:** Double-headed eagle **Rev:** Half length bust facing

Date	Mintage	F	VF	XF	Unc	BU
1999 Proof	15,000	Value: 20.00				

Y# 653 2 ROUBLES
17.0000 g., 0.9250 Silver .5056 oz. ASW **Subject:** The Last Day of Pompei **Obv:** Double-headed eagle **Rev:** Detail from painting, portrait in exergue

Date	Mintage	F	VF	XF	Unc	BU
1999 Proof	15,000	Value: 20.00				

Y# 654 2 ROUBLES
17.0000 g., 0.9250 Silver .5056 oz. ASW **Subject:** I.P. Pavlov **Obv:** Double-headed eagle **Rev:** Half bust 1/4 left, dog, books, cap, and gown

Date	Mintage	F	VF	XF	Unc	BU
1999 Proof	15,000	Value: 18.50				

Y# 655 2 ROUBLES
17.0000 g., 0.9250 Silver .5056 oz. ASW **Subject:** I.P. Pavlov **Obv:** Double-headed eagle **Rev:** Seated figure left and silence tower

Date	Mintage	F	VF	XF	Unc	BU
1999 Proof	15,000	Value: 18.50				

Y# 659 2 ROUBLES
17.0000 g., 0.9250 Silver .5056 oz. ASW **Subject:** Eugeny Abramovich Baratynsky **Obv:** Double-headed eagle **Rev:** Cameo to right of scenery **Edge:** Reeded

Date	Mintage	F	VF	XF	Unc	BU
2000 Proof	5,000	Value: 75.00				

Y# 660 2 ROUBLES
17.0000 g., 0.9250 Silver .5056 oz. ASW **Subject:** F. A. Vassiliyev **Obv:** Double-headed eagle **Rev:** Cameo to right of scenery

Date	Mintage	F	VF	XF	Unc	BU
2000 Proof	5,000	Value: 50.00				

Y# 662 2 ROUBLES
17.0000 g., 0.9250 Silver .5056 oz. ASW **Subject:** S. V. Kovaleuskaya **Obv:** Double-headed eagle **Rev:** Cameo to left of academic items

Date	Mintage	F	VF	XF	Unc	BU
2000 Proof	5,000	Value: 45.00				

Y# 663 2 ROUBLES
5.1000 g., Copper-Nickel-Zinc, 23 mm. **Series:** World War II **Obv:** Value **Rev:** Infantry assault at Stalingrad **Edge:** Reeded and plain sections

Date	Mintage	F	VF	XF	Unc	BU
2000(SP)	10,000,000	—	—	—	1.25	1.50

Y# 664 2 ROUBLES
Copper-Nickel-Zinc, 23 mm. **Obv:** Value at left of vine sprig **Rev:** Cannon manufacturing scene in Tula **Edge:** Alternating reeded and smooth

Date	Mintage	F	VF	XF	Unc	BU
2000(M)	10,000,000	—	—	—	1.25	1.50

Y# 665 2 ROUBLES
Copper-Nickel-Zinc, 23 mm. **Obv:** Value at left of vine sprig **Rev:** Truck-mounted rocket launchers in Smolensk **Edge:** Alternating reeded and smooth

Date	Mintage	F	VF	XF	Unc	BU
2000(M)	10,000,000	—	—	—	1.25	1.50

Y# 666 2 ROUBLES
Copper-Nickel-Zinc, 23 mm. **Obv:** Value at left of vine sprig **Rev:** Murmansk ship convoy **Edge:** Alternating reeded and smooth

Date	Mintage	F	VF	XF	Unc	BU
2000(M)	10,000,000	—	—	—	1.25	1.50

Y# 667 2 ROUBLES
Copper-Nickel-Zinc, 23 mm. **Obv:** Value at left of vine sprig **Rev:** Defense of Moscow scene **Edge:** Alternating reeded and smooth

Date	Mintage	F	VF	XF	Unc	BU
2000(M)	10,000,000	—	—	—	1.25	1.50

Y# 668 2 ROUBLES
Copper-Nickel-Zinc, 23 mm. **Obv:** Value at left of vine sprig **Rev:** Marine landing scene in Novorusiisk **Edge:** Alternating reeded and smooth

Date	Mintage	F	VF	XF	Unc	BU
2000(SP)	10,000,000	—	—	—	1.25	1.50

Y# 669 2 ROUBLES
Copper-Nickel-Zinc, 23 mm. **Obv:** Value at left of vine sprig **Rev:** Siege of Leningrad truck convoy scene **Edge:** Alternating reeded and smooth

Date	Mintage	F	VF	XF	Unc	BU
2000(SP)	10,000,000	—	—	—	1.25	1.50

Y# 704 2 ROUBLES
17.4400 g., 0.9250 Silver .5056 oz. ASW, 33 mm. **Subject:** M.I. Chigorin **Obv:** Double-headed eagle **Rev:** Cameo to left of chess pieces **Edge:** Reeded

Date	Mintage	F	VF	XF	Unc	BU
2000(SP) Proof	5,000	Value: 45.00				

Y# 624 3 ROUBLES
34.5600 g., 0.9000 Silver 1.0000 oz. ASW **Obv:** Double-headed eagle **Rev:** Soldier Devydov

Date	Mintage	F	VF	XF	Unc	BU
1998 Proof	15,000	Value: 50.00				

Y# 625 3 ROUBLES
34.5600 g., 0.9000 Silver 1.0000 oz. ASW **Obv:** Double-headed eagle **Rev:** "Russian Sosaveta" sculpture

Date	Mintage	F	VF	XF	Unc	BU
1998 Proof	15,000	Value: 50.00				

Y# 626 3 ROUBLES
34.5600 g., 0.9000 Silver 1.0000 oz. ASW **Obv:** Double-headed eagle **Rev:** Archangel's head within square

Date	Mintage	F	VF	XF	Unc	BU
1998 Proof	15,000	Value: 50.00				

Y# 627 3 ROUBLES
34.5600 g., 0.9000 Silver 1.0000 oz. ASW **Obv:** Double-headed eagle **Rev:** Merchant woman drinking tea within square

Date	Mintage	F	VF	XF	Unc	BU
1998 Proof	15,000	Value: 50.00				

Y# 631 3 ROUBLES
34.5600 g., 0.9000 Silver 1.0000 oz. ASW **Subject:** Nilo Stolobenskaya Hermitage **Obv:** Double-headed eagle **Rev:** Monastery, ships, boats and kneeling Saint at upper left

Date	Mintage	F	VF	XF	Unc	BU
1998 Proof	15,000	Value: 75.00				

Y# 632 3 ROUBLES
34.5600 g., 0.9000 Silver 1.0000 oz. ASW **Obv:** Double-headed eagle **Rev:** Church view from bell tower

Date	Mintage	F	VF	XF	Unc	BU
1998 Proof	5,000	Value: 500				

Y# 633 3 ROUBLES
34.8800 g., 0.9000 Silver 1.0093 oz. ASW **Subject:** Russian Human Rights Year **Obv:** Double-headed eagle **Rev:** Document, people, and map **Edge:** Reeded

Date	Mintage	F	VF	XF	Unc	BU
1998 Proof	15,000	Value: 47.50				

Y# 634 3 ROUBLES
34.7700 g., 0.9000 Silver 1.0061 oz. ASW **Subject:** 275th Anniversary - St. Petersburg University **Obv:** Double-headed eagle **Rev:** Four heads facing in front of building

Date	Mintage	F	VF	XF	Unc	BU
1999 Proof	15,000	Value: 50.00				

Y# 635 3 ROUBLES
34.7300 g., 0.9000 Silver 1.0049 oz. ASW **Obv:** Double-headed eagle **Rev:** Mardjany Mosque in Kazan

Date	Mintage	F	VF	XF	Unc	BU
1999 Proof	15,000	Value: 57.50				

Y# 636 3 ROUBLES
34.7300 g., 0.9000 Silver 1.0049 oz. ASW **Subject:** 200th Birthday - A. S. Pushkin **Obv:** Double headed eagle **Rev:** Seated figure at desk facing 1/4 left

Date	Mintage	F	VF	XF	Unc	BU
1999 Proof	15,000	Value: 45.00				

Y# 637 3 ROUBLES
34.7300 g., 0.9000 Silver 1.0049 oz. ASW **Subject:** 200th Birthday - A. S. Pushkin **Obv:** Double-headed eagle **Rev:** Standing 1/2 length figure right

Date	Mintage	F	VF	XF	Unc	BU
1999 Proof	15,000	Value: 45.00				

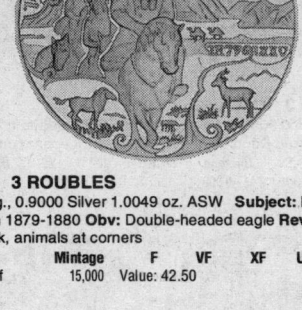

Y# 638 3 ROUBLES
34.7300 g., 0.9000 Silver 1.0049 oz. ASW **Subject:** First Tibet Exhibition 1879-1880 **Obv:** Double-headed eagle **Rev:** Men on horseback, animals at corners

Date	Mintage	F	VF	XF	Unc	BU
1999 Proof	15,000	Value: 42.50				

Y# 639 3 ROUBLES
34.7300 g., 0.9000 Silver 1.0049 oz. ASW **Subject:** Second Tibet Exhibition 1883-1885 **Obv:** Double-headed eagle **Rev:** Camp scene

Date	Mintage	F	VF	XF	Unc	BU
1999 Proof	15,000	Value: 42.50				

Y# 644 3 ROUBLES
34.7100 g., 0.9000 Silver 1.0044 oz. ASW **Subject:** Science Academy. **Obv:** Double-headed eagle **Rev:** Allegorical figure, building, portraits, crowned double headed eagle

Date	Mintage	F	VF	XF	Unc	BU
1999 Proof	5,000	Value: 300				

Y# 645 3 ROUBLES
34.7100 g., 0.9000 Silver 1.0044 oz. ASW **Subject:** Estada Kuskovo Palace **Obv:** Double-headed eagle **Rev:** Palace from three perspectives

Date	Mintage	F	VF	XF	Unc	BU
1999 Proof	15,000	Value: 60.00				

Y# 646 3 ROUBLES
34.7100 g., 0.9000 Silver 1.0044 oz. ASW **Subject:** Juryev Monastery, Novgorod **Obv:** Double-headed eagle **Rev:** Building view and detail from interior

Date	Mintage	F	VF	XF	Unc	BU
1999 Proof	15,000	Value: 75.00				

Y# 647 3 ROUBLES
34.8800 g., 0.9000 Silver 1.0093 oz. ASW **Subject:** 50th Anniversary - Diplomacy with China **Obv:** Double-headed eagle **Rev:** Moscow Kremlin and Tiananmen Gate

Date	Mintage	F	VF	XF	Unc	BU
1999 Proof	3,000	Value: 350				

Y# 657 3 ROUBLES
34.7300 g., 0.9000 Silver 1.0049 oz. ASW **Subject:** Ballet **Obv:** Double-headed eagle **Rev:** Sword fight

Date	Mintage	F	VF	XF	Unc	BU
1999 Proof	10,000	Value: 45.00				

Y# 658 3 ROUBLES
34.7300 g., 0.9000 Silver 1.0049 oz. ASW **Subject:** Ballet **Obv:** Double-headed eagle **Rev:** Couple dancing, Arabic soldiers in background

Date	Mintage	F	VF	XF	Unc	BU
1999 Proof	10,000	Value: 45.00				

Y# 690 3 ROUBLES
34.7300 g., 0.9000 Silver 1.0049 oz. ASW, 38.8 mm. **Subject:** Ufa Friendship Monument **Obv:** Double-headed eagle **Rev:** Five figures and monument **Edge:** Reeded

Date	Mintage	F	VF	XF	Unc	BU
1999 Proof	3,000	Value: 65.00				

Y# 661 3 ROUBLES
34.8800 g., 0.9000 Silver 1.0093 oz. ASW **Subject:** World Ice Hockey Championship **Obv:** Double-headed eagle **Rev:** Two hockey players **Edge:** Reeded

Date	Mintage	F	VF	XF	Unc	EU
2000 Proof	3,000	Value: 275				

Y# 671 3 ROUBLES
34.7600 g., 0.9000 Silver 1.0058 oz. ASW **Series:** Olympics **Obv:** Double-headed eagle **Rev:** 2000 Olympic design in front of map **Edge:** Reeded

Date	Mintage	F	VF	XF	Unc	BU
2000 Proof	5,000	Value: 70.00				

Y# 673 3 ROUBLES
34.6700 g., 0.9990 Silver 1.1135 oz. ASW **Subject:** Soccer **Obv:** Double-headed eagle **Rev:** Two soccer players, map, and net **Edge:** Reeded

Date	Mintage	F	VF	XF	Unc	BU
2000 Proof	3,000	Value: 65.00				

Y# 674 3 ROUBLES
34.9400 g., 0.9000 Silver 1.0110 oz. ASW **Series:** WWII **Subject:** 55th Anniversary - WWII **Obv:** Seated soldier **Rev:** Soviet Order of Glory **Edge:** Lettered **Edge Lettering:** BANK of RUSSIA THREE ROUBLES 2000

Date	Mintage	F	VF	XF	Unc	BU
2000 Proof	5,000	Value: 70.00				

Y# 705 3 ROUBLES
34.8800 g., 0.9000 Silver 1.0093 oz. ASW, 39 mm. **Subject:** St. Nicholas Monastery **Obv:** Double-headed eagle **Rev:** Saint and buildings **Edge:** Reeded

Date	Mintage	F	VF	XF	Unc	BU
2000(m) Proof	5,000	Value: 65.00				

Y# 706 3 ROUBLES
34.8800 g., 0.9000 Silver 1.0093 oz. ASW **Subject:** Novgorod Kremlin **Obv:** Double-headed eagle **Rev:** Buildings

Date	Mintage	F	VF	XF	Unc	BU
2000(m) Proof	5,000	Value: 60.00				

Y# 707 3 ROUBLES
34.8800 g., 0.9000 Silver 1.0093 oz. ASW **Subject:** City of Pushkin **Obv:** Double-headed eagle **Rev:** Park and city view

Date	Mintage	F	VF	XF	Unc	BU
2000(m) Proof	5,000	Value: 75.00				

Y# 708 3 ROUBLES
34.8800 g., 0.9000 Silver 1.0093 oz. ASW, 39 mm. **Series:** Third Millennium **Subject:** Science **Obv:** Double-headed eagle **Rev:** Astronaut, atomic elements chart, etc. **Edge:** Reeded

Date	Mintage	F	VF	XF	Unc	BU
2000(m) Proof	5,000	Value: 45.00				

Y# 709 3 ROUBLES
34.8800 g., 0.9000 Silver 1.0093 oz. ASW **Series:** Third Millennium **Subject:** Human Role **Obv:** Double-headed eagle **Rev:** People between cog wheel and computer

Date	Mintage	F	VF	XF	Unc	BU
2000(m) Proof	5,000	Value: 45.00				

Y# 714 3 ROUBLES
34.8800 g., 0.9000 Silver 1.0093 oz. ASW **Subject:** 140th Anniversary - State Bank of Russia **Obv:** Double-headed eagle **Rev:** Seated allegorical woman

Date	Mintage	F	VF	XF	Unc	BU
2000(m) Proof	3,000	Value: 400				

Y# 716 3 ROUBLES
34.8800 g., 1.0093 Silver **Subject:** Field Marshal Suvorov in Switzerland **Obv:** Double-headed eagle **Rev:** Battle scene

Date	Mintage	F	VF	XF	Unc	BU
2000(sp) Proof	5,000	Value: 70.00				

Y# 722 3 ROUBLES
34.8800 g., 0.9000 Silver 1.0093 oz. ASW **Subject:** Snow Leopard **Obv:** Double-headed eagle **Rev:** Leopard on log

Date	Mintage	F	VF	XF	Unc	BU
2000(m) Proof	5,000	Value: 70.00				

Y# 606 5 ROUBLES
Copper-Nickel Clad Copper, 25 mm. **Obv:** Double-headed eagle **Rev:** Value at left of vine sprig **Edge:** Reeded and plain sections

Date	Mintage	F	VF	XF	Unc	BU
1997(m)	—	—	—	—	2.00	3.00
1997(sp)	—	—	—	—	2.00	3.00
1998(m)	—	—	—	—	2.00	3.00
1998(sp)	—	—	—	—	2.00	3.00

Y# 695 10 ROUBLES
1.5500 g., 0.9990 Gold .0499 oz. AGW, 12 mm. **Subject:** Russian Ballet **Obv:** Double-headed eagle **Rev:** Standing knight within flower wreath **Edge:** Reeded

Date	Mintage	F	VF	XF	Unc	BU
1999(m) Proof	2,500	Value: 70.00				

Y# 670 10 ROUBLES
8.2600 g., Bi-Metallic Copper-Nickel center in Brass ring, 27 mm. **Series:** WWII **Subject:** 55th Anniversary - Victorious Conclusion of WWII **Obv:** Value **Rev:** Infantry officer within star design **Edge:** Reeded and lettered

Date	Mintage	F	VF	XF	Unc	BU
2000(sp)	10,000,000	—	—	—	3.50	5.00
2000(m)	10,000,000	—	—	—	3.50	5.00

Y# 691 25 ROUBLES
173.2900 g., 0.9000 Silver 5.0143 oz. ASW, 60 mm. **Subject:** Alexander Pushkin **Obv:** Double-headed eagle **Rev:** Walking figure with hat and cane **Edge:** Reeded **Note:** Photo reduced

Date	Mintage	F	VF	XF	Unc	BU
1999(m) Proof	3,000	Value: 215				

Y# 696 25 ROUBLES
173.2900 g., 0.9000 Silver 5.0143 oz. ASW, 60 mm. **Subject:** Russian Ballet **Obv:** Double-headed eagle **Rev:** Raymonda and the Knight dance scene **Edge:** Reeded **Note:** Photo reduced.

Date	Mintage	F	VF	XF	Unc	BU
1999(m) Proof	3,000	Value: 215				

Y# 701 25 ROUBLES
173.2900 g., 0.9000 Silver 5.0143 oz. ASW, 60 mm. **Subject:** Russian Explorers: N.M. Przhevalsky **Obv:** Double-headed eagle **Rev:** Caravan in center of other designs **Edge:** Reeded **Note:** Photo reduced.

Date	Mintage	F	VF	XF	Unc	BU
1999(sp) Proof	3,000	Value: 215				

Y# 697 25 ROUBLES
3.2000 g., 0.9990 Gold .1028 oz. AGW, 16 mm. **Subject:** Russian Ballet **Obv:** Double-headed eagle **Rev:** Dancing Saracen **Edge:** Reeded

Date	Mintage	F	VF	XF	Unc	BU
1999(sp) Proof	2,000	Value: 175				

Y# 710 25 ROUBLES
173.2900 g., 0.9000 Silver 5.0143 oz. ASW, 60 mm. **Series:** Third Millennium **Subject:** Education **Obv:** Double-headed eagle **Rev:** Ancient monk and modern student **Edge:** Reeded **Note:** Photo reduced.

Date	Mintage	F	VF	XF	Unc	BU
2000(m) Proof	1,000	Value: 650				

Y# 715 25 ROUBLES
173.2900 g., 0.9000 Silver 5.0143 oz. ASW, 60 mm. **Subject:** State Bank of Russia 140th Anniversary **Obv:** Double-headed eagle **Rev:** Document, portrait and building **Edge:** Reeded **Note:** Photo reduced.

Date	Mintage	F	VF	XF	Unc	BU
2000(m) Proof	1,000	Value: 1,000				

Y# 717 25 ROUBLES
173.2900 g., 0.9000 Silver 5.0143 oz. ASW, 60 mm. **Obv:** Double-headed eagle **Rev:** Field Marshal Suvorov **Edge:** Reeded **Note:** Photo reduced.

Date	Mintage	F	VF	XF	Unc	BU
2000(m) Proof	1,000	Value: 700				

Y# 723 25 ROUBLES
173.2900 g., 0.9000 Silver 5.0143 oz. ASW, 60 mm. **Obv:** Double-headed eagle **Rev:** Leopard on branch **Edge:** Reeded **Note:** Photo reduced.

Date	Mintage	F	VF	XF	Unc	BU
2000(m) Proof	1,000	Value: 550				

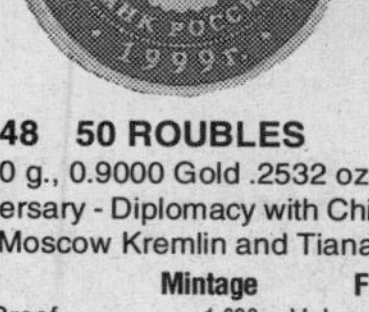

Y# 648 50 ROUBLES
8.7500 g., 0.9000 Gold .2532 oz. AGW **Subject:** 50th Anniversary - Diplomacy with China **Obv:** Double-headed eagle **Rev:** Moscow Kremlin and Tiananmen Gate

Date	Mintage	F	VF	XF	Unc	BU
1999 Proof	1,000	Value: 400				

Y# 692 50 ROUBLES
8.7500 g., 0.9000 Gold .2532 oz. AGW, 22.6 mm. **Obv:** Double-headed eagle **Rev:** Alexander Pushkin **Edge:** Reeded

Date	Mintage	F	VF	XF	Unc	BU
1999(m) Proof	1,500	Value: 245				

Y# 698 50 ROUBLES
8.7500 g., 0.9990 Gold .2534 oz. AGW, 22.6 mm. **Subject:** Russian Ballet **Obv:** Double-headed eagle **Rev:** Dancing figures **Edge:** Reeded

Date	Mintage	F	VF	XF	Unc	BU
1999(m) Proof	1,500	Value: 245				

Y# 702 50 ROUBLES
8.7500 g., 0.9000 Gold .2532 oz. AGW, 22.6 mm. **Subject:** Russian Explorer N.M. Przhevalsky **Obv:** Double-headed eagle **Rev:** Armored bust 1/4 right **Edge:** Reeded

Date	Mintage	F	VF	XF	Unc	BU
1999(sp) Proof	1,500	Value: 245				

Y# 672 50 ROUBLES
8.7100 g., 0.9000 Gold .2520 oz. AGW **Series:** Olympics **Obv:** Double-headed eagle **Rev:** Torch runner on map

Date	Mintage	F	VF	XF	Unc	BU
2000 Proof	1,000	Value: 275				

Y# 718 50 ROUBLES
8.7500 g., 0.9000 Gold .2532 oz. AGW, 22.6 mm. **Subject:** Field Marshal Suvorov **Obv:** Double-headed eagle **Rev:** Cameo above cannons **Edge:** Reeded

Date	Mintage	F	VF	XF	Unc	BU
2000(sp) Proof	500	Value: 285				

Y# 725 50 ROUBLES
7.8900 g., 0.9990 Gold .2534 oz. AGW, 22.6 mm. **Obv:** Double-headed eagle **Rev:** Snow leopard head **Edge:** Reeded

Date	Mintage	F	VF	XF	Unc	BU
2000(sp) Proof	1,000	Value: 250				

Y# 693 100 ROUBLES
1111.1200 g., 0.9000 Silver 32.1510 oz. ASW, 100 mm. **Subject:** Alexander Pushkin **Obv:** Double-headed eagle **Rev:** Statue, monuments and buildings **Edge:** Reeded **Note:** Photo reduced.

Date	Mintage	F	VF	XF	Unc	BU
1999(m) Proof	1,000	Value: 1,250				

Y# 694 100 ROUBLES
17.4500 g., 0.9000 Gold .5049 oz. AGW, 30 mm. **Subject:** Alexander Pushkin **Obv:** Double-headed eagle **Rev:** Head 1/4 right, tree and scenes **Edge:** Reeded

Date	Mintage	F	VF	XF	Unc	BU
1999 Proof	1,000	Value: 425				

Y# 700 100 ROUBLES
15.7200 g., 0.9990 Gold .5049 oz. AGW, 30 mm. **Subject:** Russian Ballet **Obv:** Double-headed eagle **Rev:** Ballerina **Edge:** Reeded

Date	Mintage	F	VF	XF	Unc	BU
1999(sp) Proof	1,500	Value: 425				

Y# 703 100 ROUBLES
17.4500 g., 0.9000 Gold .5049 oz. AGW, 30 mm. **Subject:** Russian Explorer N.M. Przhevalsky **Obv:** Double-headed eagle **Rev:** Two men viewing lake **Edge:** Reeded

Date	Mintage	F	VF	XF	Unc	BU
1999(sp) Proof	1,000	Value: 425				

Y# 724 100 ROUBLES
1111.1200 g., 0.9000 Silver 32.1510 oz. ASW, 100 mm. **Obv:** Double-headed eagle **Rev:** Two snow leopards **Edge:** Reeded

Date	Mintage	F	VF	XF	Unc	BU
2000(sp) Proof	500	Value: 1,300				

Y# 711 100 ROUBLES
1111.1200 g., 0.9000 Silver 32.1510 oz. ASW, 100 mm. **Subject:** Russian State **Obv:** Double-headed eagle **Rev:** Mother Russia, mythological bird and map **Edge:** Reeded **Note:** Photo reduced.

Date	Mintage	F	VF	XF	Unc	BU
2000(m) Proof	500	Value: 1,500				

Y# 729 100 ROUBLES
1111.1200 g., 0.9000 Silver 32.1510 oz. ASW, 100 mm. **Subject:** WWII Victory 55th Anniversary **Obv:** Russian soldier writing on Reichstag building pillar **Rev:** Conference scene **Edge:** Reeded **Note:** Photo reduced.

Date	Mintage	F	VF	XF	Unc	BU
2000(sp) Proof	500	Value: 1,400				

Y# 713 100 ROUBLES
17.4500 g., 0.9000 Gold .5049 oz. AGW, 30 mm. **Subject:** Department of Mining 300 Years **Obv:** Double-headed eagle **Rev:** Miner and equipment **Edge:** Reeded

Date	Mintage	F	VF	XF	Unc	BU
2000(m) Proof	1,000	Value: 425				

Y# 726 100 ROUBLES
15.7200 g., 0.9990 Gold .5049 oz. AGW, 30 mm. **Obv:** Double-headed eagle **Rev:** Snow leopard on branch **Edge:** Reeded

Date	Mintage	F	VF	XF	Unc	BU
2000(sp) Proof	1,000	Value: 425				

Y# 656 200 ROUBLES
3342.3899 g., 0.9000 Silver 96.7142 oz. ASW **Subject:** 275th Anniversary - St. Petersburg Mint **Obv:** Double-headed eagle **Rev:** Peter the Great, mint view, coin designs, and medal of the Imperial Order **Note:** Photo reduced.

Date	Mintage	F	VF	XF	Unc	BU
1999 Proof	150	Value: 2,000				

Y# 727 200 ROUBLES
31.3700 g., 0.9990 Gold 1.0076 oz. AGW, 33 mm. **Obv:** Double-headed eagle **Rev:** Snow leopard on branch **Edge:** Reeded

Date	Mintage	F	VF	XF	Unc	BU
2000(sp) Proof	500	Value: 1,000				

PATTERNS

Including off metal strikes

KM#	Date	Mintage	Identification	Mkt Val
Pn160	1911	—	5 Kopeks. Nickel.	—
Pn161	1911	—	10 Kopeks. Nickel.	—
Pn162	1911	—	20 Kopeks. Nickel.	—
Pn163	1911	—	20 Kopeks. Nickel.	—
Pn164	1911	—	25 Kopeks. Nickel. Eagle, date below. 25 in circle.	—
Pn165	1916	—	Kopek. Copper. Dotted background in circle, date.	—
Pn166	1916	—	Kopek. Copper. Plain background.	—
Pn167	1916	—	Kopek. Copper. Value, date below.	—
Pn168	1916	—	2 Kopeks. Copper. Eagle in circle. 2 in circle, value, date below.	—
Pn169	1916	—	3 Kopeks. Copper. Eagle in circle. 3 in circle, value, date below.	—
Pn170	1916	—	5 Kopeks. Copper.	—
Pn171	1916	—	5 Roubles. Unknown Metal.	2,250
Pn172	1917	—	3 Kopeks. Copper. 8.2500 g. Plain edge. 1/2mm larger than 1916.	2,250
Pn173	1922	—	20 Kopeks. Bronze. Y#82	—
Pn174	1922	—	50 Kopeks. Silver. Plain edge. Y#89	—
Pn175	1923	—	20 Kopeks. Bronze. Y#82	250
Pn176	1923	—	20 Kopeks. Copper. Y#82	250
Pn177	1924	—	Kopek. Copper-Aluminum. Y#76	—
Pn178	1924	—	Kopek. Bronze. Y#76	—
Pn179	1924	—	Kopek. Aluminum. Y#76	—
Pn180	1924	—	Kopek. Copper-Nickel. Y#76	—
Pn181	1924	—	Kopek. Copper-Zinc. Y#76	—
Note: Additional metals exist				
Pn182	1924	—	2 Kopeks. Copper-Aluminum. Y#77	—
Pn183	1924	—	2 Kopeks. Bronze. Y#77	—
Pn184	1924	—	2 Kopeks. Aluminum. Y#77	—
Pn185	1924	—	2 Kopeks. Copper-Nickel. Y#77	—
Pn186	1924	—	2 Kopeks. Copper-Zinc. Y#77	—
Note: Additional metals exist				
Pn187	1924	—	3 Kopeks. Copper-Aluminum. Y#78	—
Pn188	1924	—	3 Kopeks. Bronze. Y#78	—
Pn189	1924	—	3 Kopeks. Aluminum. Y#78	—
Pn190	1924	—	3 Kopeks. Copper-Nickel. Y#78	—
Pn191	1924	—	3 Kopeks. Copper-Zinc. Y#78	—
Note: Additional metals exist				
Pn192	1924	—	5 Kopeks. Unknown Metal.	—
Pn193	1924	—	5 Kopeks. Copper-Zinc. 12.0000 g. Y#79	—
Pn194	1924	—	5 Kopeks. Copper-Zinc. 18.0000 g. Y#79	—
Pn195	1924	—	5 Kopeks. Copper-Zinc. 20.0000 g. Y#79	—
Pn196	1924	—	10 Kopeks. Bronze. Y#86	—
Pn197	1924	—	15 Kopeks. Bronze. Y#87	—
Pn198	1924	—	15 Kopeks. Copper. Y#87	—
Pn199	1924	—	20 Kopeks. Bronze. Y#88	—
Pn200	1924	—	50 Kopeks. Bronze. Y#89	—
Pn201	1924	—	50 Kopeks. Unknown Metal. Y#89	—

KM#	Date	Mintage	Identification	Mkt Val
Pn202	1924	—	50 Kopeks. Copper-Nickel. Plain edge. Y#89; London Mint.	750
Pn203	1924	—	50 Kopeks. Copper-Nickel. Plain edge. Y#89	1,150
Pn204	1924	—	Rouble. Aluminum. Y#90	—

Note: There are additional 1924 patterns but information is sketchy at present

KM#	Date	Mintage	Identification	Mkt Val
Pn205	1925	—	1/2 Kopek. Copper-Aluminum. Y#75	—
Pn206	1925	—	1/2 Kopek. Aluminum. Y#75	—
Pn207	1925	—	1/2 Kopek. Copper-Nickel. Y#75	—
Pn208	1925	—	1/2 Kopek. Bronze. Y#75	—
Pn209	1925	—	1/2 Kopek. Copper-Zinc. Y#75	—

Note: Additional metals exist

KM#	Date	Mintage	Identification	Mkt Val
Pn210	1925	—	10 Kopeks. Nickel. Y#86	—
Pn211	1925	—	10 Kopeks. Aluminum-Bronze. Y#86	—
Pn212	1925	—	15 Kopeks. Nickel. Y#87	—
Pn213	1925	—	15 Kopeks. Copper. Y#87	—
Pn214	1925	—	15 Kopeks. Aluminum-Bronze. Y#87	—
Pn215	1925	—	20 Kopeks. Nickel. Y#88	—
Pn216	1925	—	20 Kopeks. Copper. Y#88	—
Pn217	1925	—	20 Kopeks. Aluminum-Bronze. Y#88	—
Pn218	1925	—	50 Kopeks. Silver. Plain edge. Y#89.2	—
Pn219	1925	—	50 Kopeks. Bronze. Y#89.2	—
Pn220	1925	—	50 Kopeks. Lead. Y#89.2	275
Pn221	1925	—	Chervonetz. Copper. Y#85	—
Pn222	1926	—	3 Kopeks. Aluminum.	—
Pn223	1926	—	3 Kopeks. Aluminum.	—
Pn224	1926	—	3 Kopeks. Unknown Metal. Y#100	—
Pn225	1929	—	10 Kopeks. Nickel.	—
Pn226	1929	—	15 Kopeks. Silver. 35% Silver; Y#87	—
Pn227	1929	—	50 Kopeks. Unknown Metal.	—
Pn228	1931	—	2 Kopeks. Copper. Y#92	—
Pn229	1931	—	3 Kopeks. Copper. Y#93	—
Pn230	1931	—	10 Kopeks. Unknown Metal. Y#93	—
Pn231	1931	—	20 Kopeks. Bronze. Y#97	—
Pn232	1932	—	3 Kopeks. Copper. KM#93	—

Note: Additional metals exist

KM#	Date	Mintage	Identification	Mkt Val
Pn233	1932	—	15 Kopeks. Unknown Metal. Y#96	—
Pn234	1933	—	10 Kopeks. Unknown Metal. Similar to Y#95	—
Pn235	1934	—	2 Kopeks. Copper. Y#92	—
Pn236	1934	—	3 Kopeks. Copper. Y#93	—
Pn237	1936	—	20 Kopeks. Aluminum. Y#104	—
Pn238	1937	—	20 Kopeks. Aluminum. Y#111	—
Pn239	1938	—	5 Kopeks. Unknown Metal. Y#101	—
Pn240	1938	—	15 Kopeks. Aluminum. Plain edge. Y#110	—
Pn241	1941	—	3 Kopeks. Unknown Metal. Y#107	—
Pn242	1941	—	50 Kopeks. Unknown Metal. Similar to Y#109	—
Pn243	1943	—	Rouble. Unknown Metal. Portrait Stalin.	—
Pn244	1946	—	10 Kopeks. Unknown Metal. Y#102	—
Pn245	1946	—	20 Kopeks. Unknown Metal. Y#111	—
Pn246	1947	—	Kopek. Aluminum-Bronze. Similar to Y#112; 16 bands on wreath.	—
Pn247	1947	—	2 Kopeks. Aluminum-Bronze. Similar to Y#113; 16 bands on wreath.	—
Pn248	1947	—	3 Kopeks. Unknown Metal. Similar to Y#114; 16 bands on wreath.	—
Pn249	1947	—	5 Kopeks. Aluminum-Bronze. Similar to Y#115; 16 bands on wreath.	—
Pn250	1947	—	10 Kopeks. Nickel. Similar to Y#116; 16 bands on wreath.	—
Pn251	1947	—	15 Kopeks. Unknown Metal. Similar to Y#117; 16 bands on wreath.	—
Pn252	1947	—	20 Kopeks. Nickel. Similar to Y#118; 16 bands on wreath.	—
Pn253	1949	—	Chervonetz. Copper.	—
Pn254	1953	—	Kopek. Copper-Nickel. With legend. Hammer and sickle, value above, date below.	500
Pn255	1953	—	Kopek. Aluminum.	—
Pn256	1953	—	Kopek. Nickel.	—

Note: Additional metals exist

KM#	Date	Mintage	Identification	Mkt Val
Pn257	1953	—	Kopek. Copper-Nickel. With legend. Hammer and sickle, value above, date below.	—
Pn258	1953	—	Kopek. Aluminum.	—
Pn259	1953	—	Kopek. Nickel.	—

Note: Additonal metals exist

KM#	Date	Mintage	Identification	Mkt Val
Pn260	1953	—	2 Kopeks. Copper-Nickel. With legend.	500
Pn261	1953	—	2 Kopeks. Aluminum.	—
Pn262	1953	—	2 Kopeks. Nickel.	—

Note: Additional metals exist

KM#	Date	Mintage	Identification	Mkt Val
Pn263	1953	—	2 Kopeks. Copper-Nickel. Without legend.	500
Pn264	1953	—	2 Kopeks. Aluminum.	—
Pn265	1953	—	2 Kopeks. Nickel.	—

Note: Additional metals exist

KM#	Date	Mintage	Identification	Mkt Val
Pn266	1953	—	3 Kopeks. Copper-Nickel. With legend.	500
Pn267	1953	—	3 Kopeks. Aluminum.	—
Pn268	1953	—	3 Kopeks. Nickel.	—

Note: Additional metals exist

KM#	Date	Mintage	Identification	Mkt Val
Pn269	1953	—	3 Kopeks. Copper-Nickel. Without legend.	500
Pn270	1953	—	3 Kopeks. Aluminum.	—
Pn271	1953	—	3 Kopeks. Nickel.	—

Note: Additional metals exist

KM#	Date	Mintage	Identification	Mkt Val
Pn272	1953	—	5 Kopeks. Aluminum. With legend.	—
Pn273	1953	—	5 Kopeks. Nickel.	—

Note: Additional metals exist

KM#	Date	Mintage	Identification	Mkt Val
Pn274	1953	—	5 Kopeks. Aluminum. Without legend.	—
Pn275	1953	—	5 Kopeks. Nickel.	—

Note: Additional metals exist

KM#	Date	Mintage	Identification	Mkt Val
Pn276	1953	—	10 Kopeks. Aluminum. With legend. Value and date within wreath.	—
Pn277	1953	—	10 Kopeks. Aluminum. Value, star above, date below.	—
Pn278	1953	—	10 Kopeks. Aluminum. Value, date below.	—
Pn279	1953	—	10 Kopeks. Aluminum. Value in wreath, star above date.	—
Pn280	1953	—	10 Kopeks. Aluminum. Value in wreath, date incircle at bottom.	—
Pn281	1953	—	10 Kopeks. Aluminum. Value in wreath in pellet border, date in circle at bottom.	—
Pn282	1953	—	10 Kopeks. Aluminum. Oak leaves behind value.	—
Pn283	1953	—	10 Kopeks. Aluminum. Without legend. Similar to KM#Pn276.	—
Pn284	1953	—	10 Kopeks. Aluminum. Similar to KM#Pn277.	—
Pn285	1953	—	10 Kopeks. Aluminum. Similar to KM#Pn278.	—
Pn286	1953	—	10 Kopeks. Aluminum. Similar to KM#Pn279.	—
Pn287	1953	—	10 Kopeks. Aluminum. Similar to KM#Pn280.	—
Pn288	1953	—	10 Kopeks. Aluminum. Similar to KM#Pn281.	—
Pn289	1953	—	10 Kopeks. Aluminum. Similar to KM#Pn282.	—

Note: For Pn276-Pn289 at least four other base metal strikings exist of each

KM#	Date	Mintage	Identification	Mkt Val
Pn290	1953	—	15 Kopeks. Aluminum. With legend. Value and date within wreath.	—
Pn291	1953	—	15 Kopeks. Aluminum. Value, star above, date below.	—
Pn292	1953	—	15 Kopeks. Aluminum. Value, date below.	—
Pn293	1953	—	15 Kopeks. Aluminum. Value in wreath, star above date in circle at bottom.	—
Pn294	1953	—	15 Kopeks. Aluminum. Value in wreath, date in circle at bottom.	—
Pn295	1953	—	15 Kopeks. Aluminum. Value in wreath, pellet border, date in circle at bottom.	—
Pn296	1953	—	15 Kopeks. Aluminum. Oak leaves behind value, date below.	—
Pn297	1953	—	15 Kopeks. Aluminum. Legend. Similar to KM#Pn290.	—
Pn298	1953	—	15 Kopeks. Aluminum. Similar to KM#Pn291.	—
Pn299	1953	—	15 Kopeks. Aluminum. Similar to KM#Pn292.	—
Pn300	1953	—	15 Kopeks. Aluminum. Similar to KM#Pn293.	—
Pn301	1953	—	15 Kopeks. Aluminum. Similar to KM#Pn294.	—
Pn302	1953	—	15 Kopeks. Aluminum. Similar to KM#Pn295.	—
Pn303	1953	—	15 Kopeks. Aluminum. Similar to KM#Pn296.	—

Note: For Pn290-Pn303 at least four other base metal strikings exist of each

KM#	Date	Mintage	Identification	Mkt Val
Pn304	1953	—	20 Kopeks. Aluminum. With legend. Value and date within wreath.	—
Pn305	1953	—	20 Kopeks. Aluminum. Value, star above, date below.	—
Pn306	1953	—	20 Kopeks. Aluminum. Value, date below.	—
Pn307	1953	—	20 Kopeks. Aluminum. Value in wreath, star above date in circle at bottom.	—
Pn308	1953	—	20 Kopeks. Aluminum. Value in wreath, date in circle at bottom.	—
Pn309	1953	—	20 Kopeks. Aluminum. Value in wreath, pellet border, date in circle at bottom.	—
Pn310	1953	—	20 Kopeks. Aluminum. Oak leaves behind value, date below.	—
Pn311	1953	—	20 Kopeks. Aluminum. Without legend. Similar to KM#Pn304.	—
Pn312	1953	—	20 Kopeks. Aluminum. Similar to KM#Pn305.	—
Pn313	1953	—	20 Kopeks. Aluminum. Similar to KM#Pn306.	—
Pn314	1953	—	20 Kopeks. Aluminum. Similar to KM#Pn307.	—
Pn315	1953	—	20 Kopeks. Aluminum. Similar to KM#Pn308.	—
Pn316	1953	—	20 Kopeks. Aluminum. Similar to KM#Pn309.	—
Pn317	1953	—	20 Kopeks. Aluminum. Similar to KM#Pn310.	—

Note: Pn304-Pn317 exist in at least four additional metals

KM#	Date	Mintage	Identification	Mkt Val
Pn318	1953	—	50 Kopeks. Bronze.	—
Pn319	1953	—	50 Kopeks. Aluminum.	—
Pn320	1953	—	50 Kopeks. Bronze.	—
Pn321	1953	—	50 Kopeks. Aluminum.	—
Pn322	1953	—	50 Kopeks. Bronze.	—
Pn323	1953	—	50 Kopeks. Aluminum.	—
Pn324	1953	—	50 Kopeks. Bronze.	—
Pn325	1953	—	50 Kopeks. Aluminum.	—

Note: Pn318-Pn325 exist in at least one other metal

KM#	Date	Mintage	Identification	Mkt Val
Pn326	1955	—	25 Kopeks. Probably copper-nickel	—
Pn327	1956	—	10 Kopeks. Nickel.	—
Pn328	1956	—	10 Kopeks. Brass.	—
Pn329	1956	—	10 Kopeks. Copper.	—
Pn330	1956	—	10 Kopeks. Aluminum.	—
Pn331	1956	—	15 Kopeks. Nickel.	—
Pn332	1956	—	15 Kopeks. Brass.	—
Pn333	1956	—	15 Kopeks. Copper.	—
Pn334	1956	—	15 Kopeks. Aluminum.	—
Pn335	1956	—	20 Kopeks. Nickel.	—
Pn336	1956	—	20 Kopeks. Brass.	—
Pn337	1956	—	20 Kopeks. Copper.	—
Pn338	1956	—	20 Kopeks. Aluminum.	—
Pn339	1956	—	50 Kopeks. Nickel.	—
Pn340	1956	—	50 Kopeks. Brass.	—
Pn341	1956	—	50 Kopeks. Copper.	—
Pn342	1956	—	50 Kopeks. Aluminum.	—
Pn343	1956	—	Rouble. Nickel.	—
Pn344	1956	—	Rouble. Brass.	—
Pn345	1956	—	Rouble. Copper.	—
Pn346	1956	—	Rouble. Aluminum.	—
Pn347	1956	—	2 Roubles. Nickel.	—
Pn348	1956	—	2 Roubles. Brass.	—
Pn349	1956	—	2 Roubles. Copper.	—
Pn350	1956	—	2 Roubles. Aluminum.	—
Pn351	1956	—	3 Roubles. Nickel.	—
Pn352	1956	—	3 Roubles. Brass.	—
Pn353	1956	—	3 Roubles. Copper.	—
Pn354	1956	—	3 Roubles. Aluminum.	—
Pn355	1956	—	5 Roubles. Nickel.	—
Pn356	1956	—	5 Roubles. Brass.	—
Pn357	1956	—	5 Roubles. Copper.	—
Pn358	1956	—	5 Roubles. Aluminum.	—
Pn359	1957	—	10 Kopeks. Copper-Nickel. Y#123	—
Pn360	1957	—	10 Kopeks. Aluminum. Y#123	—
Pn361	1957	—	20 Kopeks. Copper-Nickel. Y#125	—
Pn362	1958	—	Kopek. Aluminum. Y#126	—
Pn363	1958	—	2 Kopeks. Aluminum. Y#127	—
Pn364	1958	—	3 Kopeks. Aluminum. Y#128	—
Pn365	1958	—	5 Kopeks. Aluminum. Y#129	—
Pn366	1958	—	10 Kopeks. Aluminum. Y#A130	—
Pn367	1958	—	15 Kopeks. Aluminum. Y#A131	—
Pn368	1958	—	20 Kopeks. Aluminum. Y#A132	—
Pn369	1958	—	50 Kopeks. Aluminum. Y#133	—
Pn370	1958	—	Rouble. Aluminum. Y#134	—
Pn371	1958	—	2 Roubles. Aluminum. Y#A134	—
Pn372	1958	—	3 Roubles. Aluminum. Y#B134	—
Pn373	1958	—	5 Roubles. Aluminum. Y#C134	—
Pn374	1959	—	10 Kopeks. Copper-Nickel.	—
Pn375	1959	—	15 Kopeks. Copper-Nickel.	—
Pn376	1959	—	20 Kopeks. Copper-Nickel.	—
Pn377	1961	—	1/2 Kopek. Copper.	—
Pn378	1961	—	Kopek. Copper. Y#126	—
Pn379	1961	—	2 Kopeks. Copper. Y#127	—
Pn380	1961	—	3 Kopeks. Copper. Y#128	—
Pn381	1961	—	5 Kopeks. Copper. Y#129	—
Pn382	1961	—	10 Kopeks. Copper. Y#130	—
Pn383	1961	—	15 Kopeks. Copper. Y#131	—
Pn384	1961	—	20 Kopeks. Copper. Y#132	—
Pn385	1962	—	50 Kopeks. Copper-Nickel. Y#133.1	—
Pn386	1962	—	50 Kopeks. Copper-Nickel.	—
Pn387	1962	—	Rouble. Copper-Nickel. Y#134.1	—
Pn388	1962	—	Rouble. Copper-Nickel.	—
Pn389	1963	—	50 Kopeks. Copper-Nickel.	—
Pn390	1963	—	Rouble. Copper-Nickel.	—
Pn391	1967	—	10 Kopeks. Copper-Nickel-Zinc. Arms. Ship.	250
Pn392	1967	—	10 Kopeks. Copper-Nickel-Zinc. Arms. Worker and soldier.	250
Pn393	1967	—	15 Kopeks. Unknown Metal. Uncertain 1917-67 commemorative design	—
Pn394	1967	—	20 Kopeks. Unknown Metal. Uncertain 1917-67 commemorative design	—
Pn395	1967	—	50 Kopeks. Unknown Metal. Uncertain 1917-67 commemorative design	—
Pn396	ND	—	100 Roubles. 0.9000 Gold. Y#162	—

Note: Pn390-Pn396 minor varieties exist

KM#	Date	Mintage	Identification	Mkt Val
PN397	1993	—	3 Roubles. Copper-Nickel. 34.0000 g. 38.8 mm. Same as Y-323 including silver content statement. Same as Y-323 including silver content statement. Reeded edge.	—

TRIAL STRIKES

KM#	Date	Mintage	Identification	Mkt Val
TS1	1924	—	5 Kopeks. Copper. Y#79.	350
TS2	1924	—	5 Kopeks. Copper. Y#79.	350

MINT SETS

KM#	Date	Mintage	Identification	Issue Price	Mkt Val
MS1	1957 (4)	—	Y#122-125	2.25	35.00
MS2	1961 (9)	—	Y#126-132, 133a.1, 134a.1	4.50	32.00
MS3	1962 (7)	—	Y#126-132	2.25	4.50
MS4	1964 (4)	—	Y#126, 127, 133a.2, 134a.2	2.55	4.00
MS5	1965 (9)	—	Y#126-132, 133a.2, 134a.2	4.50	8.00
MS6	1966 (9)	—	Y#126-132, 133a.2, 134a.2	4.50	14.00
MS7	1967 (9)	—	Y#126-132, 133a.2, 134a.2	4.50	8.00
MS8	1967 (5)	211,250	Y#136-140	6.00	8.00
MS9	1968 (9)	—	Y#126-132, 133a.2, 134a.2 and mint token	6.00	10.00
MS10	1969 (9)	—	Y#126-132, 133a.2, 134a.2	7.00	8.00
MS11	1970 (9)	—	Y#126-132, 133a.2, 134a.2	11.00	15.00
MS12	1971 (9)	—	Y#126-132, 133a.2, 134a.2	6.00	10.00
MS13	1972 (9)	10,000	Y#126-132, 133a.2, 134a.2	7.00	8.00
MS14	1973 (9)	8,000	Y#126-132, 133a.2, 134a.2	11.00	8.00
MS15	1974 (9)	27,500	Y#126-132, 133a.2, 134a.2, square mint token	11.00	8.00
MS16	1975 (9)	27,000	Y#126-132, 133a.2, 134a.2	11.00	8.00
MS17	1976 (9)	55,000	Y#126-132, 133a.2, 134a.2	11.00	10.00
MS18	1977 (9)	58,750	Y#126-132, 133a.2, 134a.2	11.00	8.00
MS19	1978 (9)	62,500	Y#126-132, 133a.2, 134a.2	11.00	8.00
MS20	1979 (9)	75,000	Y#126-132, 133a.2, 134a.2	19.00	8.00
MS21	1980 (9)	—	Y#126-132, 133a.2, 134a.2	19.00	8.00
MS22	1981 (9)	—	Y#126-132, 133a.2, 134a.2	—	8.00
MS23	1982 (9)	—	Y#126-132, 133a.2, 134a.2	—	8.00
MS24	1983 (9)	—	Y#126-132, 133a.2, 134a.2	—	8.00
MS25	1984 (9)	—	Y#126-132, 133a.2, 134a.2	—	8.00
MS26	1985 (9)	—	Y#126-132, 133a.2, 134a.2	—	8.00
MSA27	1986 (9)	—	Y#126a-129a, 130-132, 133a.2, 134a.2	—	14.00
MS27	Mixed dates (9)	—	Y#135, 140-143, 188-189	—	25.00
MS28	Mixed dates (8)	—	Y#135, 140-143, 188-189	—	25.00
MS29	1987 (9)	—	Y#126-132, 133a.2-134a.2	—	10.00
MS30	1988 (9)	—	Y#126-133, 134a.2	—	8.00
MS31	1989 (9)	—	Y#126-133, 134a.2	—	8.00
MS32	1990 (9)	—	Y#126a-129a, 130-132, 133a.2, 134a.2	—	12.00
MSA32	1990 (9)	—	Y#126a-129a, 130-132, 133a.2, 134a.2	—	12.00
MSA33	1991 (9)	—	Y#126a-129a, 130-132, 133a.2, 134a.2	—	10.00
MS33	1991 (3)	—	Y#268-270	245	1,950
MS34	1992 (6)	—	Y#311-316	15.00	10.00
MS35	1993 (4)	2,700	Y#416-419	—	960
MS36	1993 (3)	3,000	Y#420-422	—	1,950
MS37	1994 (3)	2,000	Y#431-433	—	1,950
MS38	1995 (6)	200,000	Y#399-404 and medal	—	17.00
MS39	1996 (6)	100,000	Y#504-509 and medal	—	25.00
MS40	1997(SP) (7)	—	Y#600-606	—	12.50

PROOF SETS

KM#	Date	Mintage	Identification	Issue Price	Mkt Val
PS1	Mixed dates (5)	—	Y#152, 163, 175-176, 187	—	1,500
PS2	1987 (3)	—	Y#206-208	—	37.50
PS3	1990 (9)	—	Y#126a-129a, 130-132, 133a.2, 134a.2	—	15.00
PS4	1991(L) (9)	—	Y#126a-129a, 130-132, 133a.2, 134a.2	—	15.00
PS5	1991 (3)	1,500	Y#286a-288a	—	1,450
PS6	1993 (4)	1,500	Y#416-419	—	1,230
PS7	1993 (3)	750	Y#395-397	—	725
PS8	1993 (3)	2,000	Y#420-422	—	2,050
PS9	1993 (2)	10,000	Y#323, 406	—	150
PS10	1994 (4)	2,500	Y#424-427	—	1,255
PS11	1994 (3)	900	Y#428-430	—	1,360
PS12	1994 (3)	1,500	Y#431-433	—	2,050
PS13	1994 (2)	7,500	Y#405, 423	—	180
PS14	1995 (4)	2,500	Y#438-441	1,250	1,250
PS15	1995 (3)	1,500	Y#435-437	875	875
PS16	1995 (3)	900	Y#442-444	1,350	1,350

RUSSIAN CAUCASIA

Russian Caucasia, a natural area in Russia located between the Black and Caspian Seas, was a region of mystery and myth to the Ancient Greeks. It was there that Prometheus was bound for the eagle's torment and the Argonauts sought the Golden Fleece. For more than a thousand years Caucasia was the refuge for wave after wave of migrating peoples. Greeks, Romans, Persians, Turks, Huns, Mongols and finally the Russians invaded the treeless steppes and wooded highlands of this range-flanked granite bridge between Europe and Asia. Russian aggression, heroically resisted by the independent mountain races, began early in the 18th century and continued until the last opposition was stifled. The several states of Caucasia made a futile attempt to establish an independent federated republic during the Russian February Revolution of 1917, but were quickly reconquered after the triumph of Bolshevism over the Kerensky administration.

The following areas of Russian Caucasia were coin-issuing entities of interest to numismatists.

ARMAVIR

Armavir is a city located in Krasnodar Territory, Southern Russia north of the Caucasus.

LOCAL CURRENCY UNDER THE WHITE RUSSIANS

CITY

LOCAL COINAGE

KM# 1 ROUBLE

Copper **Obv:** Double-headed eagle with monogram below tail **Rev:** Value and date flanked by sprigs **Edge:** Reeded **Note:** Thin planchet.

Date	Mintage	VG	F	VF	XF	Unc
1918	—	100	150	250	450	—

KM# 2.1 3 ROUBLES

Copper, 28 mm. **Obv:** Double-headed eagle with monogram below tail **Rev:** Value and date flanked by sprigs **Edge:** Reeded **Note:** Varieties exist.

Date	Mintage	VG	F	VF	XF	Unc
1918	—	60.00	80.00	150	250	—

KM# 2.2 3 ROUBLES

Copper, 28 mm. **Obv:** Monogram below claw **Rev:** Value flanked by sprigs

Date	Mintage	VG	F	VF	XF	Unc
1918	—	75.00	100	175	275	—

KM# 3 5 ROUBLES

Copper, 31 mm. **Obv:** Double-headed eagle with monogram below tail **Rev:** Value and date flanked by sprigs

Date	Mintage	VG	F	VF	XF	Unc
1918	—	150	225	400	600	—

PATTERNS

Including off metal strikes

KM#	Date	Mintage	Identification	Mkt Val
Pn1	1918	—	Rouble. Copper. 28 mm. Reeded edge. Thin planchet. Y1.	—
Pn2	1918	—	Rouble. Copper. 28 mm. Plain edge. Thin planchet. Y1.	—
Pn3	1918	—	Rouble. Copper. 28 mm. Plain edge. Thick planchet. Y1.	—
Pn3a	1918	—	Rouble. Brass.	—
Pn4	1918	—	3 Roubles. Copper. 31 mm. Monogram under tail. Y2.1.	375
Pn5	1918	—	3 Roubles. Silver. Y2.1.	700
Pn6	1918	—	5 Roubles. Aluminum. Y3.	850

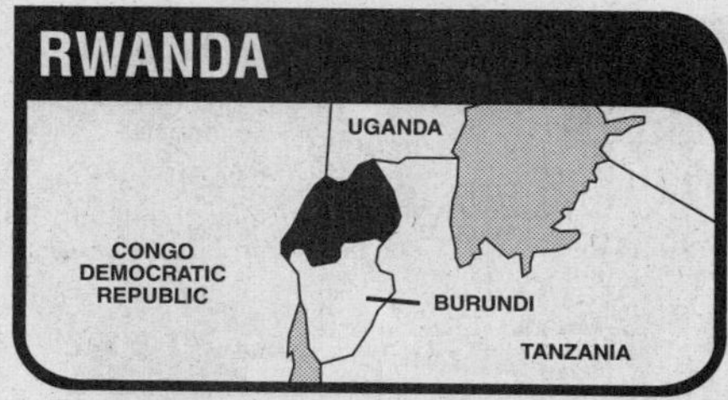

The Republic of Rwanda, located in central Africa between the Republic of the Congo and Tanzania, has an area of 10,169 sq. mi. (26,340 sq. km.) and a population of 7.3 million. Capital: Kigali. The economy is based on agriculture and mining. Coffee and tin are exported.

German Lieutenant Count von Goetzen was the first European to visit Rwanda, 1894. Four years later the court of the Mwami (the Tutsi king of Rwanda) willingly permitted the kingdom to become a protectorate of Germany. In 1916, during the African campaigns of World War I, Belgian troops from Congo occupied Rwanda. After the war it, together with Burundi, became a Belgian League of Nations mandate under the name of the Territory of Ruanda-Urundi. Following World War II, Ruanda-Urundi became a Belgian administered U.N. trust territory. The Tutsi monarchy was deposed by the U.N. supervised election of 1961, after which Belgium granted Rwanda internal autonomy. On July 1, 1962, the U.N. terminated the Belgian trusteeship and granted full independence to both Rwanda and Burundi.

For earlier coinage see Belgian Congo, and Rwanda and Burundi.

MINT MARKS

(a) - Paris, privy marks only
(b) - Brussels, privy marks only

MONETARY SYSTEM

100 Centimes = 1 Franc

REPUBLIC

STANDARD COINAGE

KM# 9 1/2 FRANC

Aluminum **Obv:** Value divides design within circle **Rev:** Inscription within circle

Date	Mintage	F	VF	XF	Unc	BU
1970	5,000,000	—	0.50	0.85	1.75	—

KM# 5 FRANC

Copper-Nickel, 21 mm. **Obv:** Head 1/4 right **Rev:** Value above flag draped arms **Edge:** Plain

Date	Mintage	F	VF	XF	Unc	BU
1964(b)	3,000,000	—	5.00	10.00	20.00	—
1965(b)	4,500,000	—	0.50	0.85	1.75	—

KM# 8 FRANC

Aluminum **Obv:** Head right **Rev:** Value above flag draped arms

Date	Mintage	F	VF	XF	Unc	BU
1969	5,000,000	—	0.50	1.50	3.50	—

KM# 12 FRANC

Aluminum **Obv:** Millet flower **Rev:** Value above flag draped arms

Date	Mintage	F	VF	XF	Unc	BU
1974	13,000,000	—	0.20	0.50	1.00	—
1977	15,000,000	—	0.15	0.25	0.75	—
1985	—	—	0.10	0.15	0.65	—

KM# 10 2 FRANCS

Aluminum **Series:** F.A.O. **Obv:** Seated figure facing above monogramed banner **Rev:** Value above flag draped arms **Shape:** Scalloped

Date	Mintage	F	VF	XF	Unc	BU
1970	5,000,000	—	0.10	0.20	0.50	—

KM# 6 5 FRANCS

Bronze **Obv:** Head 3/4 right **Rev:** Value above flag draped arms

Date	Mintage	F	VF	XF	Unc	BU
1964(b)	4,000,000	—	0.25	0.50	1.75	—
1965(b)	3,000,000	—	5.00	10.00	20.00	—

KM# 13 5 FRANCS

Bronze **Obv:** Coffee tree branch **Rev:** Value above flag draped arms

Date	Mintage	F	VF	XF	Unc	BU
1974	7,000,000	—	1.00	3.00	6.00	—
1977	7,002,000	—	1.00	2.00	4.00	—
1987	—	—	0.25	0.50	1.85	—

KM# 7 10 FRANCS

Copper-Nickel **Obv:** Head 1/4 right **Rev:** Value above flag draped arms

Date	Mintage	F	VF	XF	Unc	BU
1964(b)	6,000,000	—	1.00	2.00	4.50	—

KM# 1 10 FRANCS

3.0000 g., 0.9000 Gold .1085 oz. AGW **Obv:** Value above flag draped arms **Rev:** Head 3/4 right

Date	Mintage	VG	F	VF	XF	Unc
1965	10,000	—	—	—	—	85.00
1965 Proof	—	Value: 90.00				

KM# 14.1 10 FRANCS

Copper-Nickel **Obv:** Coffee tree branch **Rev:** Value above flag draped arms

Date	Mintage	F	VF	XF	Unc	BU
1974	6,000,000	—	3.00	5.00	10.00	15.00

KM# 14.2 10 FRANCS

Copper-Nickel **Obv:** Coffee tree branch **Rev:** Value above flag draped arms **Note:** Reduced size.

Date	Mintage	F	VF	XF	Unc	BU
1985	—	—	0.50	0.85	1.85	—

KM# 15 20 FRANCS

Brass, 27 mm. **Obv:** Millet flower bud **Rev:** Value above flag draped arms

Date	Mintage	F	VF	XF	Unc	BU
1977(a)	22,000,000	—	1.00	2.00	4.00	—

KM# 2 25 FRANCS

7.5000 g., 0.9000 Gold .2170 oz. AGW **Obv:** Value above flag draped arms **Rev:** Head 3/4 right **Note:** Similar to 10 Francs, KM#1.

Date	Mintage	F	VF	XF	Unc	BU
1965 Proof	4,000	Value: 180				

KM# 3 50 FRANCS

15.0000 g., 0.9000 Gold .4340 oz. AGW **Obv:** Value above flag draped arms **Rev:** Head 3/4 right **Note:** Similar to 10 Francs, KM#1.

Date	Mintage	F	VF	XF	Unc	BU
1965 Proof	3,000	Value: 325				

KM# 16 50 FRANCS

Brass **Obv:** Leafy branch **Rev:** Value above flag draped arms

Date	Mintage	F	VF	XF	Unc	BU
1977(a)	9,000,000	—	2.50	3.50	7.00	—

KM# 4 100 FRANCS

30.0000 g., 0.9000 Gold .8681 oz. AGW **Obv:** Value above flag draped arms **Rev:** Head 3/4 right

Date	Mintage	F	VF	XF	Unc	BU
1965 Proof	3,000	Value: 625				

KM# 18 100 FRANCS
31.2300 g., 0.9990 Silver 1.0041 oz. ASW **Subject:** Nelson Mandela **Obv:** Flag draped arms **Rev:** Head facing

Date	Mintage	F	VF	XF	Unc	BU
1990	—	—	—	—	32.00	35.00
1990 Proof	Est. 50,000	Value: 45.00				

KM# 21 100 FRANCS
31.1035 g., 0.9990 Silver 1 oz. ASW **Subject:** Environmental Protection **Obv:** Flag draped arms **Rev:** Gorilla

Date	Mintage	F	VF	XF	Unc	BU
1993 Proof	Est. 20,000	Value: 65.00				

KM# 11 200 FRANCS
18.0000 g., 0.8000 Silver .4630 oz. ASW **Series:** F.A.O. **Subject:** 10th Anniversary of Independence **Obv:** Flag divides figures shaking hands **Rev:** Figure picking coffee beans, F.A.O logo within plants

Date	Mintage	F	VF	XF	Unc	BU
1972	30,000	—	—	8.50	12.50	15.00

KM# 17 1000 FRANCS
31.6400 g., 0.9990 Silver 1.0173 oz. ASW **Subject:** 25th Anniversary of National Bank **Obv:** Bust facing **Rev:** National bank within circle

Date	Mintage	F	VF	XF	Unc	BU
ND(1989)	—	—	—	—	42.50	47.50

KM# 19 2000 FRANCS
7.8000 g., 0.9990 Gold .25 oz. AGW **Subject:** Nelson Mandela **Obv:** Flag draped arms above value **Rev:** Head facing **Note:** Similar to 5,000 Francs, KM#20.

Date	Mintage	F	VF	XF	Unc	BU
1990 Proof	Est. 50,000	Value: 225				

KM# 20 5000 FRANCS
15.5300 g., 0.9990 Gold .5 oz. AGW **Subject:** Nelson Mandela **Obv:** Value below flag draped arms **Rev:** Head facing

Date	Mintage	F	VF	XF	Unc	BU
1990 Proof	3,000	Value: 450				

ESSAIS

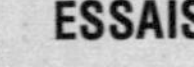

KM#	Date	Mintage	Identification	Issue Price	Mkt Val
E1	1964(b)	—	Franc. Aluminum.	—	35.00

KM#	Date	Mintage	Identification	Issue Price	Mkt Val
E2	1964(b)	—	5 Francs. Bronze. Head 1/4 right. Value above flag draped arms.	—	50.00
E3	1964(b)	—	10 Francs. Copper-Nickel.	—	65.00
E4	1977(a)	—	Franc. Aluminum.	—	20.00
E5	1977(a)	—	5 Francs. Bronze.	—	25.00
E6	1977(a)	—	20 Francs. Brass.	—	30.00
E7	1977(a)	—	50 Francs. Brass.	—	35.00

RWANDA-BURUNDI

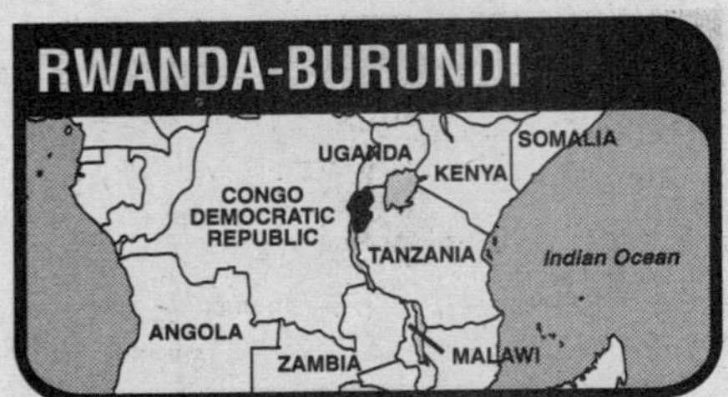

Rwanda-Burundi, a Belgian League of Nations mandate and United Nations trust territory comprising the provinces of Ruanda-Urundi of the former colony of German East Africa, was located in central Africa between the present Democratic Republic of the Congo, Uganda and mainland Tanzania. The mandate-trust territory had an area of 20,916 sq. mi. (54,272 sq. km.) and a population of 4.3 million.

For specific statistics and history of Ruanda and of Urundi see individual entries.

When Rwanda and Burundi were formed into a mandate for administration by Belgium, their names were combined as Ruanda-Urundi and they were organized as an integral part of the Belgian Congo. During the mandate-trust territory period, they utilized the coinage of the Belgian Congo, which from 1954 through 1960carried the appropriate dual identification. After the Belgian Congo acquired independence as the Democratic Republic of the Congo, the provinces of Ruanda and Urundi reverted to their former names of Rwanda and Burundi and utilized a common currency issued by a Central Bank (B.E.R.B.) established for that purpose until the time when, as independent republics, each issued its own national coinage.

For earlier coinage see Belgian Congo.

MONETARY SYSTEM
100 Centimes = 1 Franc

PROVINCES

STANDARD COINAGE

KM# 1 FRANC
Brass **Obv:** Value **Rev:** Lion

Date	Mintage	F	VF	XF	Unc	BU
1960	2,000,000	—	3.50	7.50	17.50	20.00
1961	16,000,000	—	0.50	1.00	3.50	6.00
1964	3,000,000	—	3.00	6.50	15.00	18.00

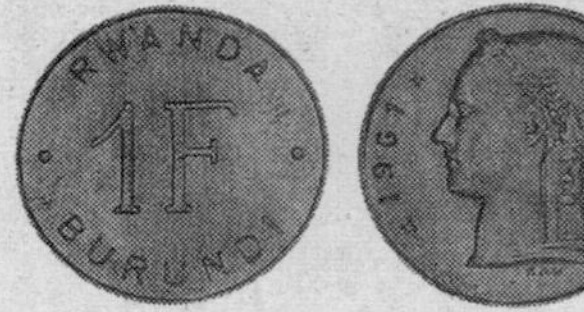

KM# 2 FRANC
Copper-Nickel **Obv:** Value **Rev:** Head left **Note:** Mule.

Date	Mintage	F	VF	XF	Unc	BU
1961	50	—	—	—	500	—

ESSAIS

KM#	Date	Mintage	Identification	Issue Price	Mkt Val
E1	1960	—	Franc. Bronze. Crowned shield divides date. Palm tree divides value.	—	160

KM#	Date	Mintage	Identification	Issue Price	Mkt Val
E2	1960	—	Franc. Brass. KM1.	—	70.00
E3	1960	—	Franc. Silver. KM1.	—	220

SAARLAND

The Saar, the 10th state of the German Federal Republic, is located in the coal-rich Saar basin on the Franco-German frontier, and has an area of 991 sq. mi. and a population of 1.2 million. Capital: Saarbrucken. It is an important center of mining and heavy industry.

From the late 14th century until the fall of Napoleon, the city of Saarbrucken was ruled by the counts of Nassau-Saarbrucken, but the surrounding territory was subject to the political and cultural domination of France. At the close of the Napoleonic era, the Saarland came under the control of Prussia. France was awarded the Saar coal mines following World War I, and the Saarland was made an autonomous territory of the League of Nations, its future political affiliation to be determined by referendum. The plebiscite, 1935, chose re-incorporation into Germany. France reoccupied the Saarland, 1945, establishing strong economic ties and assuming the obligation of defense and foreign affairs. After sustained agitation by West Germany, France agreed, 1955, to there turn of the Saar to Germany by Jan. 1957.

MINT MARKS

(a) - Paris - privy marks only

GERMAN REPUBLIC STATE

STANDARD COINAGE

KM# 1 10 FRANKEN

Aluminum-Bronze **Obv:** Industrial scene, arms at center **Rev:** Value and date **Designer:** Theo Siegal

Date	Mintage	F	VF	XF	Unc	BU
1954(a)	11,000,000	1.00	2.00	4.00	7.00	9.00

KM# 2 20 FRANKEN

Aluminum-Bronze, 23.5 mm. **Obv:** Industrial scene, arms at center **Rev:** Value and date **Edge:** Plain **Designer:** Theo Siegal

Date	Mintage	F	VF	XF	Unc	BU
1954(a)	12,950,000	1.00	2.00	4.00	7.00	9.00

KM# 3 50 FRANKEN

Aluminum-Bronze **Obv:** Industrial scene, arms in center **Rev:** Value and date **Designer:** Theo Siegal

Date	Mintage	F	VF	XF	Unc	BU
1954(a)	5,300,000	4.00	7.00	15.00	30.00	35.00

KM# 4 100 FRANKEN

Copper-Nickel **Obv:** Arms within circular design **Rev:** Value and date **Designer:** Theo Siegal

Date	Mintage	F	VF	XF	Unc	BU
1955(a)	11,000,000	2.00	4.00	7.00	17.50	22.50

ESSAIS

Standard metals unless otherwise noted

KM#	Date	Mintage	Identification	Issue Price	Mkt Val
E1	1954(a)	1,100	10 Franken. Aluminum-Bronze. KM1.	—	60.00
E2	1954(a)	—	10 Franken. Gold. KM1. Reported, not confirmed.	—	—
E3	1954(a)	1,100	20 Franken. Aluminum-Bronze. KM2.	—	60.00
E4	1954(a)	50	20 Franken. Gold. KM2.	—	2,000
E5	1954(a)	1,100	50 Franken. Aluminum-Bronze center. KM3.	—	60.00
E6	1954(a)	—	50 Franken. Gold. KM3. Reported, not confirmed.	—	—

KM#	Date	Mintage	Identification	Issue Price	Mkt Val
E7	1955(a)	50	100 Franken. Gold. Arms within circular design. Value. KM4.	—	2,500

SAHARAWI ARAB D.R.

The Saharawi Arab Democratic Republic, located in northwest Africa has an area of 102,703 sq. mi. and a population (census taken 1974) of 76,425. Formerly known as Spanish Sahara, the area is bounded on the north by Morocco, on the east and southeast by Mauritania, on the northeast by Algeria, and on the west by the Atlantic Ocean. Capital: El Aaium. Agriculture, fishing and mining are the two main industries. Exports are barley, livestock and phosphates.

A Spanish trading post was established in 1476 but was abandoned in 1524. A Spanish protectorate for the region was proclaimed in 1884. The status of the Spanish Sahara changed from a colony to an overseas province in 1958. Spain relinquished its holdings in 1975 and it was divided between Mauritania, which gave up its claim in August 1979 and Morocco, which subsequently occupied the entire territory. The official languages are Spanish and an Arab dialect: The Hassaniya.

DEMOCRATIC REPUBLIC

NON-CIRCULATING COLLECTOR COINAGE

KM# 14 PESETA

Copper-Nickel **Obv:** National arms and value **Rev:** Arab and camel

Date	Mintage	F	VF	XF	Unc	BU
1992	—	—	—	—	1.25	2.00

KM# 15 2 PESETAS

Copper-Nickel **Obv:** National arms and value **Rev:** Arab and camel

Date	Mintage	F	VF	XF	Unc	BU
1992	—	—	—	—	1.50	2.50

KM# 16 5 PESETAS

Copper-Nickel, 21.5 mm. **Obv:** National arms and value **Rev:** Arab and camel **Edge:** Plain

Date	Mintage	F	VF	XF	Unc	BU
1992	—	—	—	—	2.50	3.00

KM# 1 50 PESETAS

Copper-Nickel **Obv:** National arms and value **Rev:** Arab and camel

Date	Mintage	F	VF	XF	Unc	BU
1990	—	—	—	—	5.00	6.00

KM# 18 100 PESETAS
Copper-Nickel **Obv:** National arms and value **Rev:** Arab and sailing ship

Date	Mintage	F	VF	XF	Unc	BU
1990	—	—	—	—	10.00	11.50

KM# 20 100 PESETAS
Copper, 38 mm. **Obv:** National arms and value **Rev:** Arab and camel

Date	Mintage	F	VF	XF	Unc	BU
1990	—	—	—	—	15.00	20.00

KM# 25 100 PESETAS
Copper, 38 mm. **Obv:** National arms and value **Rev:** Arab and sailboat

Date	Mintage	F	VF	XF	Unc	BU
1990	—	—	—	—	8.00	9.00
1990 Proof	—	Value: 60.00				

KM# 7 100 PESETAS
Nickel Plated Steel **Series:** Olympics **Obv:** National arms and value **Rev:** Equestrian event

Date	Mintage	F	VF	XF	Unc	BU
1991	5,000	—	—	—	12.00	13.50

KM# 26 100 PESETAS
Nickel Plated Steel **Obv:** National arms and value **Rev:** Ship above Canary Islands map

Date	Mintage	F	VF	XF	Unc	BU
1992	—	—	—	—	12.00	13.50

KM# 40 100 PESETAS
Copper **Subject:** Columbus' ship - Santa Maria **Obv:** National arms and value

Date	Mintage	F	VF	XF	Unc	BU
1992 Proof	78	Value: 65.00				

KM# 13 100 PESETAS
Copper-Nickel **Series:** Prehistoric Animals **Obv:** National arms and value **Rev:** Brontosaurus

Date	Mintage	F	VF	XF	Unc	BU
1992	—	—	—	—	25.00	27.50

KM# 19 100 PESETAS
Copper, 38 mm. **Series:** Prehistoric Animals **Obv:** National arms and value **Rev:** Tarbosaurus Bataar

Date	Mintage	F	VF	XF	Unc	BU
1993	—	—	—	—	25.00	27.50

KM# 17 100 PESETAS
Nickel Clad Steel **Series:** Prehistoric Animals **Obv:** National arms and value **Rev:** Triceratops

Date	Mintage	F	VF	XF	Unc	BU
1994	—	—	—	—	25.00	27.50

KM# 41 100 PESETAS
Nickel Clad Steel **Series:** Prehistoric Animals **Obv:** National arms and value **Rev:** Camarasaurus

Date	Mintage	F	VF	XF	Unc	BU
1994 Proof	100	Value: 80.00				

KM# 23 100 PESETAS
Nickel Clad Steel And Enamel **Obv:** National arms and value **Rev:** WWII British Spitfire MK II

Date	Mintage	F	VF	XF	Unc	BU
1995	—	—	—	—	20.00	22.50

KM# 22 100 PESETAS
Copper, 38 mm. **Series:** Olympics **Obv:** National arms and value **Rev:** Wrestlers

Date	Mintage	F	VF	XF	Unc	BU
1996	—	—	—	—	8.50	10.00

KM# 31 200 PESETAS
Copper **Subject:** 20th Anniversary - Proclamation of Republic **Obv:** National arms and value **Rev:** Armored standing figure facing

Date	Mintage	F	VF	XF	Unc	BU
1996 Proof	—	Value: 9.50				

KM# 2 500 PESETAS
16.0000 g., 0.9990 Silver .5145 oz. ASW **Series:** Transportation **Obv:** National arms **Rev:** Arab walking camel

Date	Mintage	F	VF	XF	Unc	BU
1990	—	—	—	—	27.50	40.00

KM# 3 500 PESETAS
16.0000 g., 0.9990 Silver .5145 oz. ASW **Obv:** National arms **Rev:** Arab and sailing ship

Date	Mintage	F	VF	XF	Unc	BU
1990	—	—	—	—	30.00	45.00
1990 Proof	—	Value: 50.00				

KM# 42 500 PESETAS
Copper **Obv:** National arms **Rev:** Antique sailing ship

Date	Mintage	F	VF	XF	Unc	BU
1990 Proof	13	Value: 1,450				

KM# 4 500 PESETAS
6.0000 g., 0.9990 Silver .1929 oz. ASW **Series:** 1992 Olympics **Obv:** National arms **Rev:** Tennis player, skier

Date	Mintage	F	VF	XF	Unc	BU
1991	—	—	—	—	20.00	22.50

KM# 5 500 PESETAS
12.0000 g., 0.9990 Silver .3858 oz. ASW **Subject:** 1994 American States Games - Soccer **Obv:** National arms **Rev:** Player kicking ball

Date	Mintage	F	VF	XF	Unc	BU
1991	—	—	—	—	30.00	32.50

KM# 8 500 PESETAS
15.8400 g., 0.9990 Silver .5093 oz. ASW **Subject:** Soccer **Obv:** National arms **Rev:** Ball divided by inscription

Date	Mintage	F	VF	XF	Unc	BU
1991	15,000	—	—	—	25.00	27.50

KM# 9.1 500 PESETAS
20.0000 g., 0.9990 Silver .6430 oz. ASW **Subject:** Meeting of Two Worlds **Obv:** National arms **Rev:** Sailing ship above Canary Islands map **Note:** Thick letters.

Date	Mintage	F	VF	XF	Unc	BU
1992	—	—	—	—	27.50	30.00

KM# 9.1a 500 PESETAS
Copper **Subject:** Meeting of Two Worlds **Obv:** National arms **Rev:** Sailing ship above Canary Islands map

Date	Mintage	F	VF	XF	Unc	BU
1992 Proof	22	Value: 1,250				
1992 Proof	—	Value: 32.50				

KM# 9.2 500 PESETAS
Copper **Subject:** Meeting of Two Worlds **Obv:** National arms **Rev:** Sailing ship above Canary Islands map **Note:** Thin letters.

Date	Mintage	F	VF	XF	Unc	BU
1992 Proof	—	Value: 35.00				

KM# 11 500 PESETAS
Copper **Subject:** Defense of Nature **Obv:** National arms **Rev:** Elephant

Date	Mintage	F	VF	XF	Unc	BU
1993	—	—	—	—	40.00	45.00

KM# 12 500 PESETAS
16.0000 g., 0.9990 Silver .5140 oz. ASW **Series:** Prehistoric Animals **Obv:** National arms **Rev:** Tarbosaurus Bataar

Date	Mintage	F	VF	XF	Unc	BU
1993	—	—	—	—	35.00	45.00

KM# 27 500 PESETAS
16.0000 g., 0.9990 Silver .5140 oz. ASW **Series:** Prehistoric Animals **Obv:** National arms **Rev:** Camarasaurus

Date	Mintage	F	VF	XF	Unc	BU
1994	—	—	—	—	35.00	45.00

KM# 21 500 PESETAS
20.0000 g., 0.9990 Silver .6430 oz. ASW **Series:** 1996 Olympics **Obv:** National arms **Rev:** Wrestlers

Date	Mintage	F	VF	XF	Unc	BU
1995 Proof	15,000	—	—	—	22.50	27.50

KM# 24 500 PESETAS
20.0000 g., 0.9990 Silver .6430 oz. ASW **Obv:** National arms **Rev:** WWII British Spitfire MK II

Date	Mintage	F	VF	XF	Unc	BU
1995 Proof	15,000	Value: 32.50				

KM# 28 500 PESETAS
16.0000 g., 0.9990 Silver .5140 oz. ASW **Series:** Prehistoric Animals **Obv:** National arms **Rev:** Plateosaurus

Date	Mintage	F	VF	XF	Unc	BU
1995 Proof	—	Value: 45.00				

KM# 29 500 PESETAS
20.0000 g., 0.9990 Silver .6424 oz. ASW **Obv:** National arms **Rev:** Multicolor leopard

Date	Mintage	F	VF	XF	Unc	BU
1996 Proof	—	Value: 47.50				

KM# 32 500 PESETAS
20.0000 g., 0.9990 Silver .6430 oz. ASW **Subject:** XVI Copa Mundial - Francia 1998 - Soccer **Obv:** National arms **Rev:** Player kicking ball

Date	Mintage	F	VF	XF	Unc	BU
1996 Proof	—	Value: 50.00				

KM# 33 500 PESETAS
20.0000 g., 0.9990 Silver .6430 oz. ASW **Subject:** XVI Copa Mundial - Francia 1998 - Soccer **Obv:** National arms **Rev:** Multicolor player kicking ball

Date	Mintage	F	VF	XF	Unc	BU
1996 Proof	—	Value: 32.50				

KM# 34 500 PESETAS
20.0000 g., 0.9990 Silver .6430 oz. ASW **Series:** XXVII Olympiada - Sydney 2000 **Obv:** National arms **Rev:** Multicolor kayaker

Date	Mintage	F	VF	XF	Unc	BU
1997 Proof	—	Value: 32.50				

KM# 30 500 PESETAS
16.0000 g., 0.9990 Silver .6424 oz. ASW **Series:** Sydney Olympics **Obv:** National arms **Rev:** Weight lifter

Date	Mintage	F	VF	XF	Unc	BU
1997 Proof	—	Value: 37.50				

KM# 6 1000 PESETAS
3.1000 g., 0.9990 Gold .1000 oz. AGW **Series:** Transportation **Obv:** National arms **Rev:** Arab walking with camel **Note:** Similar to 500 Pesetas, KM#2.

Date	Mintage	F	VF	XF	Unc	BU
1991	508	—	—	—	145	165

KM# 44 1000 PESETAS
30.5000 g., 0.9990 Silver .9796 oz. ASW **Subject:** Thor Heyerdahl **Obv:** National arms **Rev:** Multicolor reed boats **Edge:** Plain

Date	Mintage	F	VF	XF	Unc	BU
1996	—	Value: 37.50				

KM# 45 1000 PESETAS
30.5000 g., 0.9990 Silver .9796 oz. ASW **Subject:** Horudsch Chaireddin **Obv:** National arms **Rev:** Multicolor pirates sailing vessels in background

Date	Mintage	F	VF	XF	Unc	BU
1996 Proof	—	Value: 50.00				

KM# 37 1000 PESETAS
31.5000 g., 0.9990 Silver 1.0117 oz. ASW **Subject:** 15th Anniversary - Diplomacy between Venezuela and Arabic Sahara **Obv:** Pillar between national emblems **Rev:** Head facing and equestrian

Date	Mintage	F	VF	XF	Unc	BU
1997	200	—	—	—	65.00	70.00
1997 Proof	800	Value: 55.00				

KM# 46 1000 PESETAS
14.9400 g., 0.9990 Silver 0.4799 oz. ASW, 35 mm. **Subject:** World Cup Soccer **Obv:** National arms **Rev:** Soccer ball and trophy **Edge:** Plain

Date	Mintage	F	VF	XF	Unc	BU
1997 Proof	—	Value: 30.00				

KM# 47 1000 PESETAS
15.0000 g., 0.9990 Silver 0.4818 oz. ASW, 35 mm. **Obv:** National arms **Rev:** Multicolor Thompsons Gazelle **Edge:** Plain

Date	Mintage	F	VF	XF	Unc	BU
1997 Proof	50	Value: 50.00				

KM# 53 1000 PESETAS
29.0000 g., Copper-Nickel, 38.1 mm. **Obv:** National arms **Rev:** Multicolor Graf Ferdinand von Zeppelin and two Zeppelins in flight **Edge:** Reeded

Date	Mintage	F	VF	XF	Unc	BU
ND (1997) Proof	—	Value: 50.00				

KM# 55 1000 PESETAS
15.4800 g., 0.9990 Silver 0.4972 oz. ASW, 35 mm. **Obv:** National arms **Rev:** Weight lifter **Edge:** Plain **Note:** Sydney Olympics

Date	Mintage	F	VF	XF	Unc	BU
1998 Proof	—	Value: 45.00				

KM# 43 1000 PESETAS
Silver **Obv:** National emblem **Rev:** Viking ship

Date	Mintage	F	VF	XF	Unc	BU
1998 Proof	100	Value: 110				

KM# 49 1000 PESETAS
15.0000 g., 0.9990 Silver 0.4818 oz. ASW, 35 mm. **Obv:** National arms **Rev:** Leonardo Da Vinci **Edge:** Plain

Date	Mintage	F	VF	XF	Unc	BU
1999 Proof	—	Value: 22.50				

KM# 50 1000 PESETAS
15.0000 g., 0.9990 Silver 0.4818 oz. ASW, 35.1 mm. **Obv:** National arms **Rev:** Pedro Cabral, two sail ships and Brazilian map **Edge:** Plain

Date	Mintage	F	VF	XF	Unc	BU
ND(2000) Proof	—	Value: 25.00				

KM# 10 1000 PESETAS - 10 ECU
31.0000 g., 0.9990 Silver .9957 oz. ASW **Subject:** European Community **Obv:** National arms **Rev:** Knight on horse and King

Date	Mintage	F	VF	XF	Unc	BU
ND(1992) Proof	15,000	Value: 40.00				

KM# 35 5000 PESETAS
33.5400 g., 0.9200 Silver .9975 oz. ASW **Subject:** 20th Anniversary - Proclamation of Republic **Obv:** National arms **Rev:** Female guerilla with rifle

Date	Mintage	F	VF	XF	Unc	BU
1996 Proof	—	Value: 65.00				

KM# 36 5000 PESETAS
33.5400 g., 0.9200 Silver .9975 oz. ASW **Subject:** 20th Anniversary - Proclamation of Republic **Obv:** National arms **Rev:** Land Rover with armed guerillas

Date	Mintage	F	VF	XF	Unc	BU
1996 Proof	—	Value: 65.00				

KM# 38 40000 PESETAS
15.5200 g., 0.9000 Gold .4491 oz. AGW **Subject:** 20th Anniversary - Diplomacy between Venezuela and Saharawi Arab Democratic Republic **Obv:** Arms of Venezuela and Saharawi Arab Democratic Republic **Rev:** Bolivar and El Uali

Date	Mintage	F	VF	XF	Unc	BU
1997 Proof	90	Value: 1,000				

KM# 38a 40000 PESETAS
15.5000 g., 0.9990 Gold .4978 oz. AGW **Subject:** 20th Anniversary - Diplomacy between Venezuela and Saharawi Arab Democratic Republic **Obv:** Arms of Venezuela and Saharawi Arab Democratic Republic **Rev:** Bolivar and El Uali

Date	Mintage	F	VF	XF	Unc	BU
1997 Proof, Rare	10	—	—	—	—	—

ESSAIS

KM#	Date	Mintage	Identification	Mkt Val
E1	1997	8	1000 Pesetas. Copper. KM#37.	3,000

PATTERNS

KM#	Date	Mintage	Identification	Mkt Val
Pn2	1997	8	40000 Pesetas. Copper. KM#38.	3,000
Pn3	1997	8	40000 Pesetas. Silver. KM#38.	3,000

PIEFORTS

KM#	Date	Mintage	Identification	Mkt Val
P2	1997	8	40000 Pesetas. Gold. KM#38.	6,000
P3	1998	—	1000 Pesetas. 0.9990 Silver. 31.2000 g. 35 mm. National arms. Viking ship. Plain edge.	—

SAINT HELENA

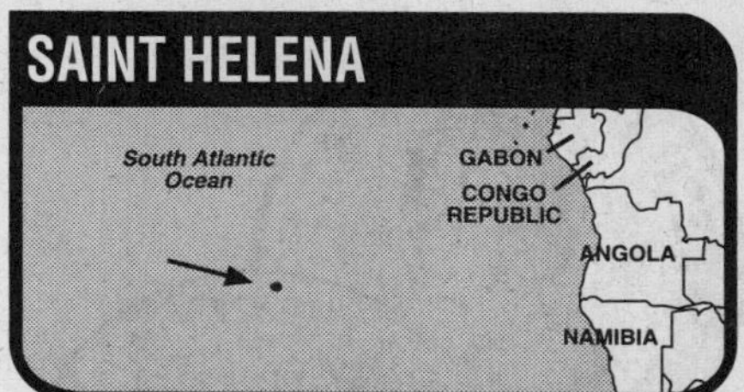

Saint Helena, a British colony located about 1,150 miles (1,850 km.) from the west coast of Africa, has an area of 47 sq. mi. (410 sq. km.) and a population of *7,000. Capital: Jamestown. Flax, lace, and rope are produced for export. Ascension and Tristan da Cunha are dependencies of Saint Helena.

The island was discovered and named by the Portuguese navigator Joao de Nova Castella in 1502. The Portuguese imported livestock, fruit trees, and vegetables but established no permanent settlement. The Dutch occupied the island temporarily, 1645-51. The original European settlement was founded by representatives of the British East India Company sent to annex the island after the departure of the Dutch. The Dutch returned and captured Saint Helena from the British on New Year's Day, 1673, but were in turn ejected by a British force under Sir Richard Munden. Thereafter Saint Helena was the undisputed possession of Great Britain. The island served as the place of exile for Napoleon, several Zulu chiefs, and an ex-sultan of Zanzibar.

RULERS
British

MINT MARKS
PM - Pobjoy Mint

MONETARY SYSTEM
12 Pence = 1 Shilling
100 Pence = 1 Pound

BRITISH COLONY

STANDARD COINAGE

KM# 5 25 PENCE (Crown)
Copper-Nickel, 38.5 mm. **Ruler:** Elizabeth II **Subject:** St. Helena Tercentenary **Obv:** Young bust right **Rev:** Sailing ship **Rev. Designer:** Leslie Durbin

Date	Mintage	VG	F	VF	XF	Unc
ND(1973)	100,000	—	—	—	—	4.00

KM# 5a 25 PENCE (Crown)
28.2800 g., 0.9250 Silver .8411 oz. ASW, 38.5 mm. **Ruler:** Elizabeth II **Subject:** St. Helena Tercentenary **Obv:** Young bust right **Rev:** Sailing ship

Date	Mintage	VG	F	VF	XF	Unc
ND(1973) Proof	10,000	Value: 22.00				

KM# 6 25 PENCE (Crown)
Copper-Nickel, 38.5 mm. **Ruler:** Elizabeth II **Subject:** Queen Elizabeth II Silver Jubilee **Obv:** Young bust right **Rev:** Aldabra giant tortoise

Date	Mintage	VG	F	VF	XF	Unc
ND(1977)	50,000	—	—	—	—	9.00

KM# 6a 25 PENCE (Crown)
28.2800 g., 0.9250 Silver .8411 oz. ASW, 38.5 mm. **Ruler:** Elizabeth II **Subject:** Queen Elizabeth II Silver Jubilee **Obv:** Young bust right **Rev:** Aldabra giant tortoise

Date	Mintage	VG	F	VF	XF	Unc
ND(1977) Proof	25,000	Value: 18.50				

KM# 7 25 PENCE (Crown)
Copper-Nickel, 38.5 mm. **Ruler:** Elizabeth II **Subject:** 25th Anniversary of Coronation **Obv:** Young bust right **Rev:** Crowned portrait with supporters

Date	Mintage	VG	F	VF	XF	Unc
1978PM	—	—	—	—	—	4.00

KM# 7a 25 PENCE (Crown)
28.2800 g., 0.9250 Silver .8411 oz. ASW, 38.5 mm. **Ruler:** Elizabeth II **Subject:** 25th Anniversary of Coronation **Obv:** Young bust right **Rev:** Crowned portrait with supporters

Date	Mintage	VG	F	VF	XF	Unc
1978PM	70,000	—	—	—	—	14.50
1978PM Proof	25,000	Value: 17.50				

KM# 8 25 PENCE (Crown)
Copper-Nickel, 38.5 mm. **Ruler:** Elizabeth II **Subject:** Queen Mother's 80th Birthday **Obv:** Young bust right **Rev:** Cameo portrait above ship and hills

Date	Mintage	VG	F	VF	XF	Unc
1980	100,000	—	—	—	—	3.50

KM# 8a 25 PENCE (Crown)
28.2800 g., 0.9250 Silver, 38.5 mm. **Ruler:** Elizabeth II **Subject:** Queen Mother's 80th Birthday **Obv:** Young bust right **Rev:** Cameo portrait above hills

Date	Mintage	VG	F	VF	XF	Unc
1980 Proof	25,000	Value: 16.50				

KM# 9 25 PENCE (Crown)
Copper-Nickel, 38.5 mm. **Ruler:** Elizabeth II **Subject:** Wedding of Prince Charles and Lady Diana **Obv:** Young bust right **Rev:** Nosegay separates facing heads of couple, ship above

Date	Mintage	VG	F	VF	XF	Unc
ND(1981)	50,000	—	—	—	—	3.50

KM# 9a 25 PENCE (Crown)
28.2800 g., 0.9250 Silver .8411 oz. ASW, 38.5 mm. **Ruler:** Elizabeth II **Subject:** Wedding of Prince Charles and Lady Diana **Obv:** Young bust right **Rev:** Nosegay separates facing heads of couple, ship above

Date	Mintage	VG	F	VF	XF	Unc
ND(1981) Proof	30,000	Value: 20.00				

KM# 10 25 PENCE (Crown)
28.2800 g., 0.9250 Silver .8411 oz. ASW, 38.5 mm. **Ruler:** Elizabeth II **Series:** International Year of the Scout **Obv:** Young bust right **Rev:** Stylized value above dates

Date	Mintage	VG	F	VF	XF	Unc
ND(1983)	10,000	—	—	—	—	30.00
ND(1983) Proof	10,000	Value: 42.50				

KM# 12 50 PENCE
Copper-Nickel, 38.5 mm. **Ruler:** Elizabeth II **Subject:** 150th Anniversary - Saint Helena Colony **Obv:** Young bust right **Rev:** Half figure above crowned shield flanked by designs

Date	Mintage	VG	F	VF	XF	Unc
ND(1984)	10,000	—	—	—	—	4.50

KM# 12a 50 PENCE
28.2800 g., 0.9250 Silver .8411 oz. ASW, 38.5 mm. **Ruler:** Elizabeth II **Subject:** 150th Anniversary - Saint Helena Colony **Obv:** Young bust right **Rev:** Half figure above crowned shield flanked by designs

Date	Mintage	VG	F	VF	XF	Unc
ND(1984) Proof	5,000	Value: 28.00				

KM# 12b 50 PENCE
47.5400 g., 0.9170 Gold 1.4017 oz. AGW, 38.5 mm. **Ruler:** Elizabeth II **Subject:** 150th Anniversary - Saint Helena Colony **Obv:** Young bust right **Rev:** Half figure above crowned shield flanked by designs

Date	Mintage	VG	F	VF	XF	Unc
ND(1984) Proof	150	Value: 985				

KM# 13 50 PENCE
Copper-Nickel, 38.5 mm. **Ruler:** Elizabeth II **Subject:** Royal Visit of Prince Andrew **Obv:** Young bust right **Rev:** Bust left

Date	Mintage	VG	F	VF	XF	Unc
1984	125,000	—	—	—	—	3.00

KM# 13a 50 PENCE
28.2800 g., 0.9250 Silver .8411 oz. ASW, 38.5 mm. **Ruler:** Elizabeth II **Subject:** Royal Visit of Prince Andrew **Obv:** Young bust right **Rev:** Bust left

Date	Mintage	VG	F	VF	XF	Unc
1984 Proof	5,000	Value: 30.00				

KM# 14 50 PENCE
Copper-Nickel, 38.5 mm. **Ruler:** Elizabeth II **Subject:** Queen Mother **Obv:** Crowned bust right **Rev:** Queen Mother and equestrian within circle

Date	Mintage	VG	F	VF	XF	Unc
1995	—	—	—	—	—	7.50

KM# 14a 50 PENCE
28.2800 g., 0.9250 Silver .8411 oz. ASW, 38.5 mm. **Ruler:** Elizabeth II **Subject:** Queen Mother **Obv:** Crowned bust right **Rev:** Queen Mother and equestrian within circle

Date	Mintage	VG	F	VF	XF	Unc
1995 Proof	10,000	Value: 35.00				

KM# 14b 50 PENCE
47.5400 g., 0.9160 Gold 1.4011 oz. AGW, 38.5 mm. **Ruler:** Elizabeth II **Subject:** Queen Mother **Obv:** Crowned bust right **Rev:** Queen Mother and equestrian within circle

Date	Mintage	VG	F	VF	XF	Unc
1995 Proof	150	Value: 1,000				

KM# 15 50 PENCE
Copper-Nickel, 38.5 mm. **Ruler:** Elizabeth II **Subject:** Queen Elizabeth II's 70th Birthday **Obv:** Crowned bust right **Rev:** Mounted guardsman **Rev. Designer:** Willem Vis

Date	Mintage	VG	F	VF	XF	Unc
1996	—	—	—	—	—	6.00

KM# 15a 50 PENCE
28.2800 g., 0.9250 Silver .8411 oz. ASW, 38.5 mm. **Ruler:** Elizabeth II **Subject:** Queen Elizabeth II's 70th Birthday **Obv:** Crowned bust right **Rev:** Mounted guardsman

Date	Mintage	VG	F	VF	XF	Unc
1996 Proof	5,000	Value: 50.00				

KM# 18 50 PENCE
Copper-Nickel, 38.5 mm. **Ruler:** Elizabeth II **Subject:** Elizabeth and Philip **Obv:** Crowned bust right **Rev:** Royal couple reviewing troops **Rev. Designer:** Willem Vis

Date	Mintage	VG	F	VF	XF	Unc
ND(1997)	—	—	—	—	—	6.50

KM# 16a 50 PENCE
28.2800 g., 0.9250 Silver .8411 oz. ASW, 38.5 mm. **Ruler:** Elizabeth II **Series:** World Wildlife Fund **Subject:** Conserving Nature **Obv:** Crowned bust right **Rev:** Three Blue Whales

Date	Mintage	VG	F	VF	XF	Unc
1998 Proof	—	Value: 45.00				

KM# 16 50 PENCE
Copper-Nickel, 38.5 mm. **Ruler:** Elizabeth II **Series:** World Wildlife Fund **Subject:** Conserving Nature **Obv:** Crowned bust right **Rev:** Three blue whales

Date	Mintage	VG	F	VF	XF	Unc
1998	—	—	—	—	—	13.00

KM# 17 50 PENCE
Copper-Nickel, 38.5 mm. **Ruler:** Elizabeth II **Series:** World Wildlife Fund **Subject:** Conserving Nature **Obv:** Crowned bust right **Rev:** Rainpiper bird, shoreline, lily **Rev. Designer:** Willem Vis

Date	Mintage	VG	F	VF	XF	Unc
1998	—	—	—	—	—	12.00

KM# 22 50 PENCE
28.2800 g., Copper-Nickel, 38.6 mm. **Ruler:** Elizabeth II **Obv:** Crowned bust right **Rev:** Crowned bust of the Queen Mother right **Edge:** Reeded

Date	Mintage	F	VF	XF	Unc	BU
ND(2000)	—	—	—	—	10.00	12.00

KM# 22a 50 PENCE
28.2800 g., 0.9250 Silver 0.841 oz. ASW, 38.6 mm. **Ruler:** Elizabeth II **Obv:** Crowned bust right **Rev:** Crowned bust of the Queen Mother right **Edge:** Reeded

Date	Mintage	F	VF	XF	Unc	BU
ND(2000) Proof	10,000	Value: 50.00				

KM# 22b 50 PENCE
47.5400 g., 0.9166 Gold 1.401 oz. AGW, 38.6 mm. **Ruler:** Elizabeth II **Obv:** Crowned bust right **Rev:** Crowned bust of the Queen Mother right **Edge:** Reeded

Date	Mintage	F	VF	XF	Unc	BU
ND(2000) Proof	100	Value: 1,050				

KM# 21 POUND
4.2000 g., Brass Plated Steel, 22 mm. **Ruler:** Elizabeth II **Obv:** Young bust right **Rev:** Coat of arms and value **Edge:** Reeded and plain sections

Date	Mintage	F	VF	XF	Unc	BU
1980PM	—	—	—	—	—	—

KM# 11 2 POUNDS
15.9800 g., 0.9170 Gold .4712 oz. AGW **Ruler:** Elizabeth II **Series:** International Year of the Scout **Obv:** Young bust right **Rev:** Scouts and tent

Date	Mintage	VG	F	VF	XF	Unc
ND(1983)	2,000	—	—	—	—	450
ND(1983) Proof	2,000	Value: 500				

PIEFORTS

KM#	Date	Mintage	Identification	Mkt Val
P1	1984	500	50 Pence. Silver. KM13a.	50.00
P2	1995	500	50 Pence. Silver. KM14a.	90.00

SAINT HELENA & ASCENSION

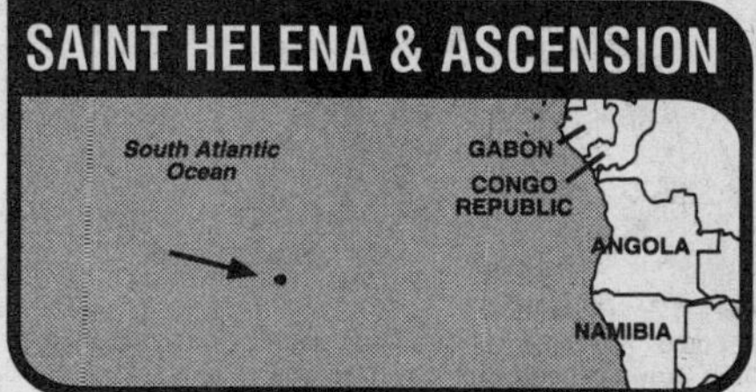

BRITISH COLONY

STANDARD COINAGE

100 Pence = 1 Pound

KM# 1 PENNY
3.6000 g., Bronze, 20.32 mm. **Ruler:** Queen Elizabeth II **Obv:** Young bust right **Rev:** Tuna fish and value

Date	Mintage	F	VF	XF	Unc	BU
1984	—	—	—	0.20	0.50	1.25
1984 Proof	10,000	Value: 1.50				

KM# 13 PENNY
3.6000 g., Bronze, 20.32 mm. **Ruler:** Queen Elizabeth II **Obv:** Crowned head right **Obv. Designer:** Raphael David Maklouf **Rev:** Tuna fish and value

Date	Mintage	F	VF	XF	Unc	BU
1991	—	—	—	0.15	0.35	1.00

KM# 13a PENNY
Copper Plated Steel, 20.32 mm. **Ruler:** Queen Elizabeth II **Obv:** Crowned head right **Obv. Designer:** Raphael David Maklouf **Rev:** Tuna above value

Date	Mintage	F	VF	XF	Unc	BU
1997	—	—	—	0.15	0.35	1.00

KM# 2 2 PENCE
7.1000 g., Bronze, 25.91 mm. **Ruler:** Queen Elizabeth II **Obv:** Young bust right **Rev:** Donkey with firewood

Date	Mintage	F	VF	XF	Unc	BU
1984	—	—	—	0.25	0.65	1.25
1984 Proof	10,000	Value: 2.00				

KM# 12 2 PENCE
7.1000 g., Bronze, 25.91 mm. **Ruler:** Queen Elizabeth II **Obv:** Crowned head right **Obv. Designer:** Raphael David Maklouf **Rev:** Value below donkey

Date	Mintage	F	VF	XF	Unc	BU
1991	—	—	—	0.20	0.60	1.25

KM# 3 5 PENCE
5.7000 g., Copper-Nickel, 23.59 mm. **Ruler:** Queen Elizabeth II **Obv:** Young bust right **Rev:** Rainpiper

Date	Mintage	F	VF	XF	Unc	BU
1984	—	—	—	0.25	0.65	1.25
1984 Proof	—	Value: 2.00				

KM# 14 5 PENCE
Copper-Nickel, 18 mm. **Ruler:** Queen Elizabeth II **Obv:** Crowned head right **Obv. Designer:** Raphael David Maklouf **Rev:** Value below rainpiper

Date	Mintage	F	VF	XF	Unc	BU
1991	—	—	—	0.20	0.50	1.00

KM# 22 5 PENCE
Copper-Nickel, 18 mm. **Ruler:** Queen Elizabeth II **Obv:** Crowned head right **Rev:** Giant tortoise

Date	Mintage	F	VF	XF	Unc	BU
1998	—	—	—	1.00	2.50	4.50

KM# 4 10 PENCE
11.3000 g., Copper-Nickel, 28.5 mm. **Ruler:** Queen Elizabeth II **Obv:** Young bust right **Rev:** Value below arum lily

Date	Mintage	F	VF	XF	Unc	BU
1984	—	—	—	0.50	1.25	2.00
1984 Proof	—	Value: 3.00				

KM# 15 10 PENCE
11.3000 g., Copper-Nickel, 28.5 mm. **Ruler:** Queen Elizabeth II **Obv:** Crowned head right **Obv. Designer:** Raphael David Maklouf

Date	Mintage	F	VF	XF	Unc	BU
1991	—	—	—	0.30	1.00	1.50

KM# 23 10 PENCE
Copper-Nickel, 24.5 mm. **Ruler:** Queen Elizabeth II **Obv:** Crowned head right **Obv. Designer:** Raphael David Maklouf **Rev:** Dolphins

Date	Mintage	F	VF	XF	Unc	BU
1998	—	—	—	1.00	3.00	5.00

KM# 21 20 PENCE
Copper-Nickel, 21.4 mm. **Ruler:** Queen Elizabeth II **Obv:** Crowned head right **Rev:** Flower **Shape:** 7-sided

Date	Mintage	F	VF	XF	Unc	BU
1998	—	—	—	0.75	1.50	2.50

KM# 5 50 PENCE
13.5000 g., Copper-Nickel, 30 mm. **Ruler:** Queen Elizabeth II **Obv:** Young bust right **Rev:** Green sea turtle **Shape:** 7-sided

Date	Mintage	F	VF	XF	Unc	BU
1984	—	—	—	1.75	3.75	6.00
1984 Proof	—	Value: 7.50				

KM# 7 50 PENCE
Copper-Nickel, 38.5 mm. **Ruler:** Queen Elizabeth II **Subject:** Wedding of Prince Andrew and Sarah Ferguson **Obv:** Crowned bust right **Rev:** Conjoined busts of couple right within circle

Date	Mintage	F	VF	XF	Unc	BU
ND(1986)	13,000	—	—	—	4.00	6.00

KM# 7a 50 PENCE
28.2800 g., 0.9250 Silver .8411 oz. ASW, 38.5 mm. **Ruler:** Queen Elizabeth II **Subject:** Wedding of Prince Andrew and Sarah Ferguson **Obv:** Crowned bust right **Rev:** Conjoined busts of couple right within circle

Date	Mintage	F	VF	XF	Unc	BU
ND(1986) Proof	2,500	Value: 27.50				

KM# 7b 50 PENCE
47.5400 g., 0.9170 Gold 1.4017 oz. AGW, 38.5 mm. **Ruler:** Queen Elizabeth II **Subject:** Wedding of Prince Andrew and Sarah Ferguson **Obv:** Crowned bust right **Rev:** Conjoined busts of couple right within circle

Date	Mintage	F	VF	XF	Unc	BU
ND(1986) Proof	50	Value: 1,150				

KM# 8 50 PENCE
Copper-Nickel, 38.5 mm. **Ruler:** Queen Elizabeth II **Subject:** 165th Anniversary of Napoleon's Death **Obv:** Crowned bust right **Rev:** Sailing ship and 1/2 figure facing right

Date	Mintage	F	VF	XF	Unc	BU
1986	50,000	—	—	—	5.00	7.00

KM# 16 50 PENCE
13.5000 g., Copper-Nickel, 30 mm. **Ruler:** Queen Elizabeth II **Obv:** Crowned head right **Obv. Designer:** Raphael David Maklouf **Rev:** Green sea turtle **Shape:** 7-sided

Date	Mintage	F	VF	XF	Unc	BU
1991	—	—	—	1.50	3.50	5.00

KM# 19 50 PENCE
Copper-Nickel, 38.5 mm. **Ruler:** Queen Elizabeth II **Subject:** Normandy Invasion **Obv:** Crowned bust right **Rev:** Barbed wire above fence, artistic arrows pointing downward

Date	Mintage	F	VF	XF	Unc	BU
ND(1994)	—	—	—	—	6.00	8.00

KM# 19a 50 PENCE
28.2800 g., 0.9250 Silver .8411 oz. ASW, 38.5 mm. **Ruler:** Queen Elizabeth II **Subject:** Normandy Invasion **Obv:** Crowned bust right **Rev:** Barbed wire above fence, artistic arrows pointing downward

Date	Mintage	F	VF	XF	Unc	BU
ND(1994) Proof	5,000	Value: 40.00				

KM# 6 POUND
9.5000 g., Nickel-Brass, 22.5 mm. **Ruler:** Queen Elizabeth II **Obv:** Young bust right **Rev:** Flying birds

Date	Mintage	F	VF	XF	Unc	BU
1984	—	—	—	2.50	5.50	8.00
1984 Proof	—	Value: 9.00				

KM# 6a POUND
9.5000 g., 0.9250 Silver .2826 oz. ASW, 22.5 mm. **Ruler:** Queen Elizabeth II **Obv:** Young bust right **Rev:** Flying birds

Date	Mintage	F	VF	XF	Unc	BU
1984 Proof	10,000	Value: 18.00				

KM# 17 POUND
9.5000 g., Nickel-Brass, 22.5 mm. **Ruler:** Queen Elizabeth II **Obv:** Crowned head right **Obv. Designer:** Raphael David Maklouf **Rev:** Two birds in flight left

Date	Mintage	F	VF	XF	Unc	BU
1991	—	—	—	2.25	5.00	7.50

KM# 11 2 POUNDS
Copper-Nickel, 38.5 mm. **Ruler:** Queen Elizabeth II **Subject:** Queen Mother **Obv:** Crowned bust right **Rev:** Crowned monogram flanked by flowers **Rev. Designer:** Robert Elderton

Date	Mintage	F	VF	XF	Unc	BU
ND(1990)	—	—	—	—	12.00	13.50

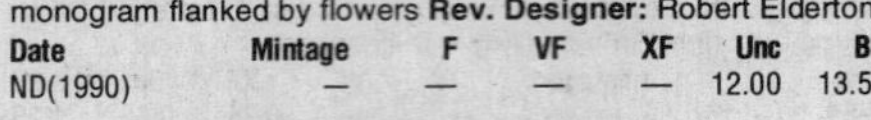

KM# 18 2 POUNDS
28.2800 g., 0.9250 Silver .8411 oz. ASW, 38.5 mm. **Ruler:** Queen Elizabeth II **Subject:** 40th Anniversary - Coronation of Elizabeth II **Obv:** Crowned bust right **Rev:** Church figures

Date	Mintage	F	VF	XF	Unc	BU
ND(1993) Proof	10,000	Value: 55.00				

KM# 24 5 POUNDS
28.2800 g., 0.9250 Silver .8411 oz. ASW, 38.5 mm. **Ruler:** Queen Elizabeth II **Subject:** Queen Mother **Obv:** Crowned bust right **Rev:** Queen Mother's monogram **Note:** Prev. KM#11a.

Date	Mintage	F	VF	XF	Unc	BU
ND(1990) Proof	10,000	Value: 50.00				

KM# 9 25 POUNDS
155.0000 g., 0.9990 Silver 4.9839 oz. ASW, 65 mm. **Ruler:** Queen Elizabeth II **Subject:** 165th Anniversary of Napoleon's Death **Obv:** Crowned bust right **Rev:** Sailing ship at right and 1/2 figure facing right **Note:** Photo reduced.

Date	Mintage	F	VF	XF	Unc	BU
1986 Proof	15,000	Value: 115				

KM# 20 25 POUNDS
155.5175 g., 0.9990 Silver 4.9950 oz. ASW, 65 mm. **Ruler:** Queen Elizabeth II **Subject:** 70th Birthday - Queen Elizabeth II **Obv:** Crowned bust right **Rev:** Mounted drummer and cameo head right **Rev. Designer:** Willem Vis **Note:** Photo reduced.

Date	Mintage	F	VF	XF	Unc	BU
1996 Proof	1,000	Value: 200				

KM# 10 50 POUNDS
32.2600 g., 0.9990 Platinum 1.0051 oz. APW **Ruler:** Queen Elizabeth II **Subject:** 165th Anniversary of Napoleon's Death **Obv:** Crowned bust right **Rev:** Sailing ship at right and 1/2 figure at left looking right **Note:** Similar to KM#9.

Date	Mintage	F	VF	XF	Unc	BU
1986 Proof	5,000	Value: 1,350				

PIEFORTS

KM#	Date	Mintage	Identification	Issue Price	Mkt Val
P1	1984	2,500	Pound. Silver. KM#6a.	49.75	30.00
P2	1986	250	50 Pence. Silver. KM#7a.	74.00	75.00
P3	1994	500	50 Pence. Copper-Nickel center. KM#19.	—	60.00

MINT SETS

KM#	Date	Mintage	Identification	Issue Price	Mkt Val
MS1	1984 (6)	—	KM#1-6	—	12.50

PROOF SETS

KM#	Date	Mintage	Identification	Issue Price	Mkt Val
PS1	1984 (6)	—	KM#1-6	—	22.50

SAINT KITTS & NEVIS

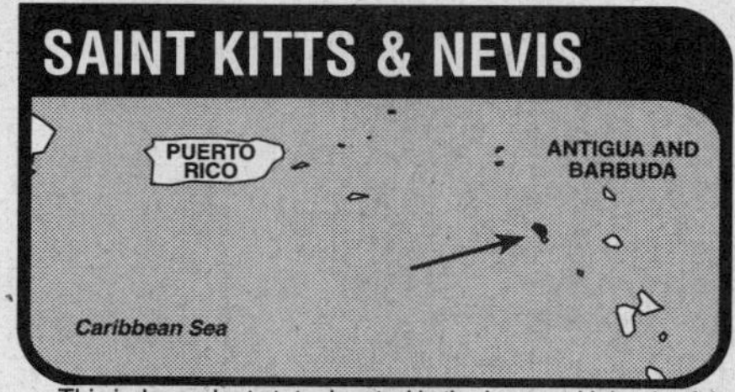

This independent state, located in the Leeward Islands of the West Indies, south of Puerto Rico, comprises the islands of St. Kitts, Nevis and Anguilla. The country has an area of 101 sq. mi. (261 sq. km.) and a population of 41,000. Capital: Basseterre, on St. Kitts (as it may be called in abbreviated form). The islands export sugar, cotton, lobsters, beverages and electrical equipment.

St. Kitts was discovered by Columbus in 1493 and was settled by Thomas Warner, an Englishman, in 1623. The Treaty of Utrecht, 1713, ceded the island to the British. France protested British occupancy, and on three occasions between 1616 and 1782 seized the island and held it for short periods. St. Kitts used the coins and currency of the British Caribbean Territories (Eastern Group).

In early 1967 the Colony was, together with the islands of Nevis and Anguilla, united politically as a self-governing British Associated State. However, in June 1967 Anguilla declared its independence, severing ties with Britain and established a so-called 'Republic of Anguilla". Britain refused to accept this and established a Commissioner to govern Anguilla; this arrangement continues to the present time.

St. Kitts and Nevis became a member of the Commonwealth of Nations on Sept. 19, 1983. Queen Elizabeth II is Head of State.

From approximately 1750-1830, billon 2 sous of the French colony of Cayenne were countermarked SK' and used on St. Kitts. They were valued at 1-1/2 Pence Sterling. (St. Kitts and Nevis now use East Caribbean Currency.)

RULERS
British

MONETARY SYSTEM
100 Cents = 1 East Caribbean Dollar

BRITISH ASSOCIATED STATE

STANDARD COINAGE

100 Cents = 1 Dollar

KM# 1 4 DOLLARS
Copper-Nickel, 38.5 mm. **Series:** F.A.O. **Obv:** Crowned arms with supporters **Rev:** Sugar cane and banana tree branch divided by value below

Date	Mintage	F	VF	XF	Unc	BU
1970	13,000	—	6.00	10.00	20.00	30.00
1970 Proof	2,000	Value: 35.00				

KM# 3 10 DOLLARS
Copper-Nickel, 38.8 mm. **Subject:** Royal Visit **Obv:** Crowned bust right **Obv. Designer:** Raphael Maklouf **Rev:** Crowned arms with supporters

Date	Mintage	F	VF	XF	Unc	BU
1985	100,000	—	—	—	10.00	12.50

KM# 3a 10 DOLLARS
28.2800 g., 0.9250 Silver .8411 oz. ASW, 38.8 mm. **Subject:** Royal Visit **Obv:** Crowned bust right **Obv. Designer:** Raphael Maklouf **Rev:** Crowned arms with supporters

Date	Mintage	F	VF	XF	Unc	BU
1985 Proof	5,000	Value: 40.00				

KM# 3b 10 DOLLARS
47.5400 g., 0.9170 Gold 1.4013 oz. AGW, 38.8 mm. **Subject:** Royal Visit **Obv:** Crowned bust right **Obv. Designer:** Raphael Maklouf **Rev:** Crowned arms with supporters

Date	Mintage	F	VF	XF	Unc	BU
1985 Proof	250	Value: 1,150				

KM# 4 20 DOLLARS
Copper-Nickel, 38.8 mm. **Subject:** 200th Anniversary - Battle of the Saints **Obv:** Crowned arms with supporters **Rev:** Dates above ship

Date	Mintage	F	VF	XF	Unc	BU
ND(1982)	—	—	—	—	12.50	15.00

KM# 4a 20 DOLLARS
28.2800 g., 0.9250 Silver .8411 oz. ASW, 38.8 mm. **Subject:** 200th Anniversary - Battle of the Saints **Obv:** Crowned arms with supporters **Rev:** Dates above ship

Date	Mintage	F	VF	XF	Unc	BU
ND(1982) Proof	2,500	Value: 42.50				

KM# 2 20 DOLLARS
28.2800 g., Copper-Nickel, 38.61 mm. **Subject:** Attainment of Independence, September 19 **Obv:** Young bust right **Rev:** Ship, map and compass

Date	Mintage	F	VF	XF	Unc	BU
1983	—	—	—	—	15.00	17.50

KM# 2a 20 DOLLARS
28.2800 g., 0.9250 Silver .8411 oz. ASW **Subject:** Attainment of Independence, September 19 **Obv:** Young bust right **Rev:** Compass, ship and map

Date	Mintage	F	VF	XF	Unc	BU
1983 Proof	5,000	Value: 40.00				

KM# 5 100 DOLLARS
7.9900 g., 0.9170 Gold .2356 oz. AGW **Subject:** 200th Anniversary - Siege of Brimstone Hill **Rev:** Brimstone hill

Date	Mintage	F	VF	XF	Unc	BU
ND(1982)	250	—	—	—	200	220
ND(1982) Proof	15	Value: 675				

KM# 6 100 DOLLARS
129.5900 g., 0.9250 Silver 3.8543 oz. ASW, 63 mm. **Subject:** Tropical birds **Rev:** Green-throated Carib Hummingbird **Note:** Photo reduced.

Date	Mintage	F	VF	XF	Unc	BU
1988 Proof	Est. 10,000	Value: 125				

SAINT LUCIA

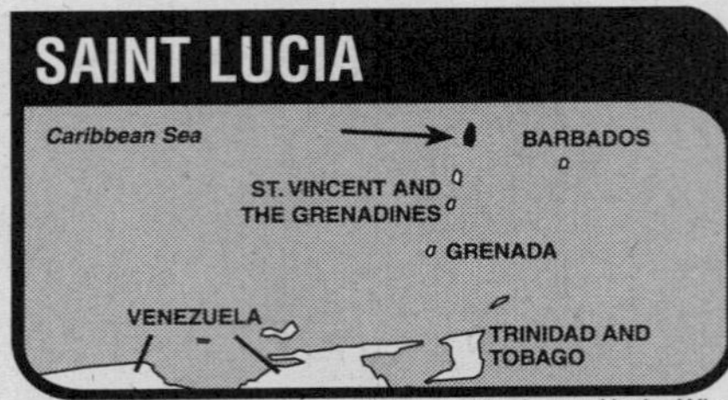

Saint Lucia, an independent island nation located in the Windward Islands of the West Indies between Saint Vincent and Martinique, has an area of 238 sq. mi. (620 sq. km.) and a population of *150,000. Capital: Castries. The economy is agricultural. Bananas, copra, cocoa, sugar and logwood are exported.

Columbus discovered Saint Lucia in 1502. The first attempts at settlement undertaken by the British in 1605 and 1638 were frustrated by sickness and the determined hostility of the fierce Carib inhabitants. The French settled it in 1650 and made a treaty with the natives. Until 1814, when the island became a definite British possession, it was the scene of a continuous conflict between the British and French, which saw the island change, hands on at least 14 occasions. In 1967, under the West Indies Act, Saint Lucia was established as a British associated state, self-governing in internal affairs. Complete independence was attained on February 22, 1979. Saint Lucia is a member of the Commonwealth of Nations. Elizabeth II is Head of State as Queen of Saint Lucia.

Prior to 1950, the island used sterling, which was superseded by the currency of the British Caribbean Territories (Eastern Group) and the East Caribbean State.

RULERS
British

MONETARY SYSTEM
100 Cents = 1 Dollar

BRITISH ASSOCIATED STATE

MODERN COINAGE

100 Cents = 1 Dollar

KM# 11 4 DOLLARS
Copper-Nickel, 38.5 mm. **Series:** F.A.O. **Obv:** Crowned arms with supporters **Rev:** Sugar cane and banana tree branch divided by value below

Date	Mintage	F	VF	XF	Unc	BU
1970	13,000	—	6.00	10.00	20.00	30.00
1970 Proof	2,000	Value: 35.00				

KM# 14 5 DOLLARS
Copper-Nickel **Subject:** Papal Visit - John Paul II **Obv:** Crowned arms with supporters **Obv. Legend:** • SAINT LUCIA • FIVE DOLLARS below **Rev:** Bust left **Rev. Legend:** • PAPAL VISIT JULY 1986 •JOHN PAUL II on shoulder **Designer:** Michael Rizzello

Date	Mintage	F	VF	XF	Unc	BU
1986	—	—	—	—	8.50	11.50

KM# 14a 5 DOLLARS
28.2800 g., 0.9250 Silver .8411 oz. ASW **Subject:** Papal Visit - John Paul II **Obv:** Crowned arms with supporters **Obv. Legend:** • SAINT LUCIA • FIVE DOLLARS below **Rev:** Bust left **Rev. Legend:** • PAPAL VISIT JULY 1986 • JOHN PAUL II on shoulder

Date	Mintage	F	VF	XF	Unc	BU
1986 Proof	2,120	Value: 42.50				

KM# 12 10 DOLLARS
Copper-Nickel, 38.8 mm. **Subject:** 200th Anniversary - Battle of the Saints **Obv:** Crowned arms with supporters **Rev:** Dates above battleships

Date	Mintage	F	VF	XF	Unc	BU
1982	—	—	—	—	12.50	14.50

KM# 12a 10 DOLLARS
28.2800 g., 0.9250 Silver .8411 oz. ASW, 38.8 mm. **Subject:** 200th Anniversary - Battle of the Saints **Obv:** Crowned arms with supporters **Rev:** Dates above battleships

Date	Mintage	F	VF	XF	Unc	BU
1982 Proof	2,500	Value: 42.50				

KM# 13 10 DOLLARS
Copper-Nickel, 38.8 mm. **Subject:** Royal Visit - Queen Elizabeth II **Obv:** Crowned bust right **Rev:** Crowned arms with supporters **Rev. Legend:** • ROYAL VISIT 1985 • TEN DOLLARS below **Designer:** Raphael Maklouf

Date	Mintage	F	VF	XF	Unc	BU
1985	100,000	—	—	—	9.50	12.50

KM# 13a 10 DOLLARS
28.2800 g., 0.9250 Silver .8411 oz. ASW, 38.8 mm. **Subject:** Royal Visit - Queen Elizabeth II **Obv:** Crowned bust right **Obv. Designer:** Raphael Maklouf **Rev:** Crowned arms with supporters **Rev. Legend:** • ROYAL VISIT 1985 • TEN DOLLARS below

Date	Mintage	F	VF	XF	Unc	BU
1985 Proof	5,000	Value: 40.00				

KM# 13b 10 DOLLARS
47.5400 g., 0.9170 Gold 1.4013 oz. AGW, 38.8 mm. **Subject:** Royal Visit - Queen Elizabeth II **Obv:** Crowned bust right **Obv. Designer:** Raphael Maklouf **Rev:** Crowned arms with supporters **Rev. Legend:** • ROYAL VISIT 1985 • TEN DOLLARS below

Date	Mintage	F	VF	XF	Unc	BU
1985 Proof	250	Value: 1,150				

KM# 16 10 DOLLARS
28.2800 g., 0.9250 Silver .8411 oz. ASW **Subject:** Commonwealth Finance Ministers' Meeting **Obv:** Monogram flanked by sprigs within circle **Rev:** Crowned arms with supporters above lake and mountains

Date	Mintage	F	VF	XF	Unc	BU
1986 Proof	1,000	Value: 65.00				

KM# 17 100 DOLLARS
129.5900 g., 0.9250 Silver 3.8543 oz. ASW, 63 mm. **Subject:** Tropical Birds **Rev:** Two amazon parrots **Note:** Photo reduced.

Date	Mintage	F	VF	XF	Unc	BU
1988 Proof	Est. 10,000	Value: 125				

KM# 15 500 DOLLARS
15.9800 g., 0.9170 Gold .4709 oz. AGW **Subject:** Papal Visit - John Paul II **Obv:** Crowned arms with supporters within circle **Rev:** Bust left **Rev. Legend:** • PAPAL VISIT JULY 1986 •

Date	Mintage	F	VF	XF	Unc	BU
1986 Proof	100	Value: 850				

SAINT PIERRE & MIQUELON

CANADA (Quebec)
Newfoundland
Atlantic Ocean

The Territorial Collectivity of Saint Pierre and Miquelon, a French overseas territory located 10 miles (16 km.) off the south coast of Newfoundland, has an area of 93 sq. mi. (242 sq. km.) and a population of *6,000. Capital: Saint Pierre. The economy of the barren archipelago is based on cod fishing and fur farming. Fish and fish products, and mink and silver fox pelts are exported.

The islands were occupied by the French in 1604, then were captured by the British in 1702 and held until 1763, at which time they were returned to the possession of France and employed as a fishing station. They passed between France and England on six more occasions between 1778 and 1814 when the Treaty of Paris awarded them permanently to France. The rugged, soil-poor granite islands, which will support only evergreen shrubs, are all that remain of France's extensive North American colonies. In 1958 Saint Pierre and Miquelon voted in favor of the new constitution of the Fifth Republic of France, thereby choosing to remain within the new French Community.

RULERS
French

MINT MARKS
(a) - Paris, privy marks only

MONETARY SYSTEM
100 Centimes = 1 Franc

FRENCH TERRITORY

STANDARD COINAGE

KM# 1 FRANC
Aluminum, 23 mm. **Obv:** Winged Liberty head left **Rev:** Ship above value **Designer:** G.B.L. Bazor

Date	Mintage	F	VF	XF	Unc	BU
1948(a)	600,000	0.50	0.75	1.50	5.50	10.00

KM# 2 2 FRANCS
Aluminum **Obv:** Winged Liberty head left **Rev:** Ship above value **Designer:** G.B.L. Bazor

Date	Mintage	F	VF	XF	Unc	BU
1948(a)	300,000	0.75	1.00	2.00	6.50	12.00

ESSAIS

Standard metals unless otherwise noted

KM#	Date	Mintage	Identification	Issue Price	Mkt Val
E1a	1948(a)	2,000	Franc. Copper-Nickel.	—	40.00
E2a	1948(a)	2,000	2 Francs. Copper-Nickel.	—	45.00

PIEFORTS WITH ESSAIS

Double thickness, standard metals unless otherwise noted

KM#	Date	Mintage	Identification	Issue Price	Mkt Val
PE1	1948(a)	104	Franc.	—	120
PE2	1948(a)	104	2 Francs.	—	150

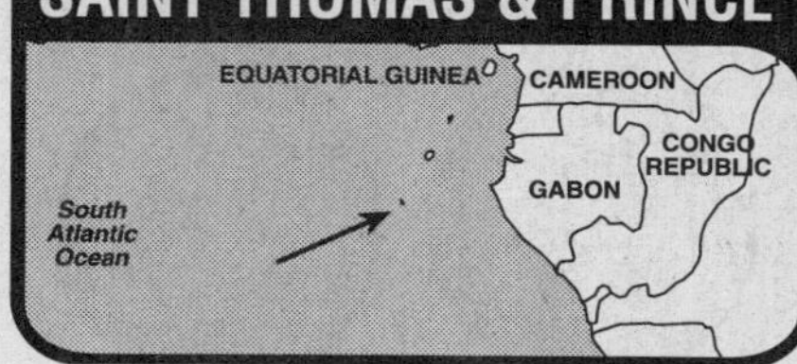

The Democratic Republic of St. Thomas & Prince (São Tomé e Príncipe) is located in the Gulf of Guinea 150 miles (241 km.) off the western coast of Africa. It has an area of 372 sq. mi. (960 sq. km.) and a population of *121,000. Capital: São Tomé. The economy of the islands is based on cocoa, copra and coffee.

Saint Thomas and Saint Prince were uninhabited when discovered by Portuguese navigators Joao de Santarem and Pedro de Escobar in 1470. After the failure of their initial settlement of 1485, the Portuguese successfully colonized St. Thomas with a colony of prisoners and exiled Jews in 1493. An initial prosperity based on the sugar trade gave way to a time of misfortune, 1567-1709, that saw the colony attacked and occupied or plundered by the French and Dutch, ravaged by the slave revolt of 1595; and finally rendered destitute by the transfer of the world sugar trade to Brazil. In the late 1800s, the colony turned from the production of sugar to cocoa, the basis of its present economy

The islands were designated a Portuguese overseas province in 1951. On April 25, 1974, the government of Portugal was seized by a military junta, which reached agreements providing for independence for the Portuguese overseas provinces of Portuguese Guinea (Guinea-Bissau), Mozambique, Cape Verde Islands, Angola, and Saint Thomas and Prince Islands. The Democratic Republic of São Tomé and Principe was declared on July 12, 1975.

RULERS
Portuguese, until 1975

MINT MARKS
R – Rio

MONETARY SYSTEM
100 Centavos = 1 Escudo

PORTUGUESE COLONY

REFORM COINAGE

100 Centavos = 1 Escudo

KM# 2 10 CENTAVOS
Nickel-Bronze **Obv:** Liberty head left **Rev:** Shield within globe above value

Date	Mintage	F	VF	XF	Unc	BU
1929	500,000	2.00	6.00	20.00	50.00	—

KM# 15 10 CENTAVOS
Bronze **Obv:** Value **Rev:** Shield within crowned globe

Date	Mintage	F	VF	XF	Unc	BU
1962	500,000	0.50	1.25	4.50	12.00	—

KM# 15a 10 CENTAVOS
Aluminum **Obv:** Value **Rev:** Shield within crowned globe

Date	Mintage	F	VF	XF	Unc	BU
1971	1,000,000	0.35	0.65	1.25	3.50	—

KM# 3 20 CENTAVOS
Nickel-Bronze **Obv:** Liberty head left **Rev:** Shield within globe above value

Date	Mintage	F	VF	XF	Unc	BU
1929	250,000	2.50	6.50	22.50	55.00	—

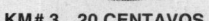

KM# 16.1 20 CENTAVOS
Bronze, 18 mm. **Obv:** Value **Rev:** Shield within crowned globe

Date	Mintage	F	VF	XF	Unc	BU
1962	250,000	0.50	1.25	5.50	15.00	—

KM# 16.2 20 CENTAVOS
Bronze, 16 mm. **Obv:** Value **Rev:** Shield within crowned globe

Date	Mintage	F	VF	XF	Unc	BU
1971	750,000	0.35	0.75	1.50	4.00	—

KM# 1 50 CENTAVOS
Nickel-Bronze **Obv:** Liberty head left **Rev:** Shield within globe above value

Date	Mintage	F	VF	XF	Unc	BU
1928	—	30.00	90.00	350	900	—
1929	400,000	4.00	12.00	50.00	150	—

KM# 8 50 CENTAVOS
Nickel-Bronze **Obv:** Value **Rev:** Shield within crowned globe

Date	Mintage	F	VF	XF	Unc	BU
1948	80,000	10.00	30.00	100	265	—

KM# 10 50 CENTAVOS
Copper-Nickel **Obv:** Value **Rev:** Shield within crowned globe

Date	Mintage	F	VF	XF	Unc	BU
1951	48,000	1.75	3.50	25.00	70.00	—

KM# 17.1 50 CENTAVOS
Bronze, 20 mm. **Obv:** Value **Rev:** Shield within crowned globe

Date	Mintage	F	VF	XF	Unc	BU
1962	480,000	0.25	0.50	2.50	5.00	—

KM# 17.2 50 CENTAVOS
Bronze, 22 mm. **Obv:** Value **Rev:** Shield within crowned globe

Date	Mintage	F	VF	XF	Unc	BU
1971	600,000	0.20	0.35	1.50	3.00	—

KM# 4 ESCUDO
Copper-Nickel **Obv:** Value **Rev:** Shield within crowned globe

Date	Mintage	F	VF	XF	Unc	BU
1939	100,000	9.00	25.00	100	285	—

KM# 9 ESCUDO
Nickel-Bronze **Obv:** Value **Rev:** Shield within crowned globe

Date	Mintage	F	VF	XF	Unc	BU
1948	60,000	12.50	40.00	120	300	—

KM# 11 ESCUDO
Copper-Nickel **Obv:** Value **Rev:** Shield within crowned globe

Date	Mintage	F	VF	XF	Unc	BU
1951	18,000	3.50	12.00	60.00	175	—

KM# 18 ESCUDO
Bronze **Obv:** Value **Rev:** Shield within crowned globe

Date	Mintage	F	VF	XF	Unc	BU
1962	160,000	0.75	2.50	15.00	35.00	—
1971	350,000	0.35	0.75	1.50	3.50	—

KM# 5 2-1/2 ESCUDOS
3.5000 g., 0.6500 Silver .0732 oz. ASW **Obv:** Shield within globe on cross **Rev:** Shield within crowned globe

Date	Mintage	F	VF	XF	Unc	BU
1939	80,000	10.00	30.00	100	300	—
1948	120,000	15.00	35.00	100	300	—

KM# 12 2-1/2 ESCUDOS
3.5000 g., 0.6500 Silver .0732 oz. ASW **Obv:** Shield within globe on cross **Rev:** Shield within crowned globe

Date	Mintage	F	VF	XF	Unc	BU
1951	64,000	2.50	6.00	30.00	100	—

KM# 19 2-1/2 ESCUDOS
Copper-Nickel **Obv:** Shield within globe on cross **Rev:** Shield within crowned globe

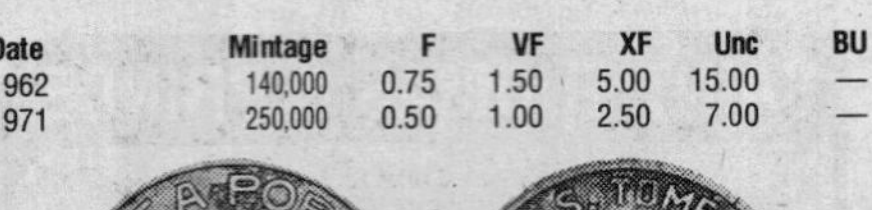

Date	Mintage	F	VF	XF	Unc	BU
1962	140,000	0.75	1.50	5.00	15.00	—
1971	250,000	0.50	1.00	2.50	7.00	—

KM# 6 5 ESCUDOS
7.0000 g., 0.6500 Silver .1462 oz. ASW **Obv:** Shield within globe on cross **Rev:** Shield within crowned globe

Date	Mintage	F	VF	XF	Unc	BU
1939	60,000	12.50	35.00	100	300	—
1948	100,000	18.00	45.00	110	300	—

KM# 13 5 ESCUDOS
7.0000 g., 0.6500 Silver .1462 oz. ASW, 25 mm. **Obv:** Shield within globe on cross **Rev:** Shield within crowned globe

Date	Mintage	F	VF	XF	Unc	BU
1951	72,000	3.50	7.00	20.00	45.00	—

KM# 20 5 ESCUDOS
4.0000 g., 0.6000 Silver .0771 oz. ASW, 22 mm. **Obv:** Shield within globe **Rev:** Shield within crowned globe

Date	Mintage	F	VF	XF	Unc	BU
1962	88,000	1.50	2.50	6.00	12.50	—

KM# 22 5 ESCUDOS
Copper-Nickel **Obv:** Shield within globe on cross **Rev:** Shield within crowned globe

Date	Mintage	F	VF	XF	Unc	BU
1971	100,000	0.75	1.50	3.50	8.00	—

KM# 7 10 ESCUDOS
12.5000 g., 0.8350 Silver .3356 oz. ASW **Obv:** Shield within globe on cross **Rev:** Shield within crowned globe

Date	Mintage	F	VF	XF	Unc	BU
1939	40,000	12.00	25.00	65.00	250	—

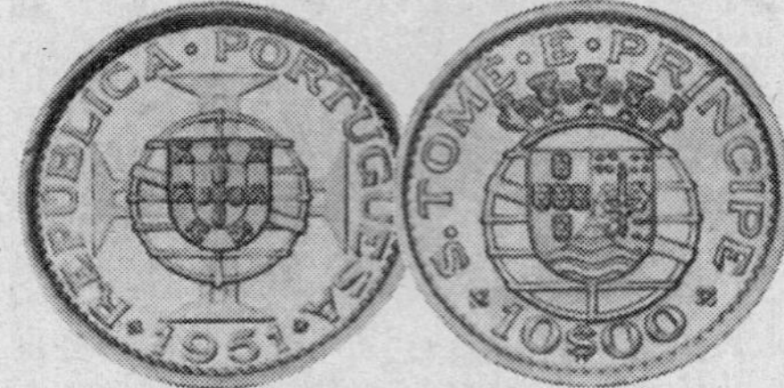

KM# 14 10 ESCUDOS
12.5000 g., 0.7200 Silver .2894 oz. ASW **Obv:** Shield within globe on cross **Rev:** Shield within crowned globe

Date	Mintage	F	VF	XF	Unc	BU
1951	40,000	5.00	9.00	16.50	35.00	—

KM# 23 10 ESCUDOS
Copper-Nickel **Obv:** Shield within globe on cross **Rev:** Shield within crowned globe

Date	Mintage	F	VF	XF	Unc	BU
1971	100,000	1.25	2.50	5.50	12.50	—

KM# 24 20 ESCUDOS
Nickel **Obv:** Shield within globe **Rev:** Shield within circle

Date	Mintage	F	VF	XF	Unc	BU
1971	75,000	1.50	3.00	6.00	13.50	—

KM# 21 50 ESCUDOS
18.0000 g., 0.6500 Silver .3762 oz. ASW **Subject:** 500th Anniversary of Discovery **Obv:** Cross within designed circle **Rev:** Double shields flanked by dates, star design at top

Date	Mintage	F	VF	XF	Unc	BU
1970	150,000	—	—	—	8.00	10.00
1970 Matte proof	Est. 200	—	—	—	—	—

Note: Produced at the Lisbon Mint on private contract.

DEMOCRATIC REPUBLIC

STANDARD COINAGE

100 Centimos = 1 Dobra

KM# 25 50 CENTIMOS
Brass, 17 mm. **Series:** F.A.O. **Obv:** Arms with supporters **Rev:** Fish above value

Date	Mintage	F	VF	XF	Unc	BU
1977	2,000,000	—	0.10	0.20	0.75	1.00
1977 Proof	2,500	Value: 3.00				

KM# 26 DOBRA
Brass, 20 mm. **Series:** F.A.O. **Obv:** Arms with supporters **Rev:** Cocoa beans on stem and value

Date	Mintage	F	VF	XF	Unc	BU
1977	1,500,000	—	0.15	0.25	1.00	1.25
1977 Proof	2,500	Value: 3.00				

KM# 27 2 DOBRAS
Copper-Nickel, 18.5 mm. **Series:** F.A.O. **Obv:** Arms with supporters **Rev:** Goats

Date	Mintage	F	VF	XF	Unc	BU
1977	1,000,000	—	0.25	0.40	1.50	1.75
1977 Proof	2,500	Value: 3.50				

KM# 28 5 DOBRAS
Copper-Nickel, 24 mm. **Series:** F.A.O. **Obv:** Arms with supporters **Rev:** Corn and value

Date	Mintage	F	VF	XF	Unc	BU
1977	750,000	—	0.35	0.65	2.00	2.50
1977 Proof	2,500	Value: 5.00				

KM# 29 10 DOBRAS
Copper-Nickel, 26 mm. **Series:** F.A.O. **Obv:** Arms with supporters **Rev:** Chickens with eggs in cartons

Date	Mintage	F	VF	XF	Unc	BU
1977	300,000	—	0.60	1.25	4.00	5.00
1977 Proof	2,500	Value: 7.00				

KM# 29a 10 DOBRAS
Copper-Nickel Clad Steel, 26 mm. **Series:** F.A.O. **Obv:** Arms with supporters **Rev:** Chickens with eggs in cartons

Date	Mintage	F	VF	XF	Unc	BU
1990	—	—	0.60	1.25	4.00	5.00

KM# 30 20 DOBRAS
Copper-Nickel Clad Steel, 29 mm. **Series:** F.A.O. **Obv:** Arms with supporters **Rev:** Logo and value to right of various plants and produce

Date	Mintage	F	VF	XF	Unc	BU
1977	500,000	—	1.00	2.00	6.00	7.00
1977 Proof	2,500	Value: 10.00				

KM# 52 50 DOBRAS
Copper-Nickel Clad Steel **Series:** F.A.O. **Obv:** Arms with supporters **Rev:** Value within octogon design with bird above and snake below

Date	Mintage	F	VF	XF	Unc	BU
1990	—	—	—	—	6.00	8.00

KM# 41 100 DOBRAS
Copper-Nickel **Subject:** World Fisheries Conference **Obv:** Arms with supporters **Rev:** Figure standing in boat with fish net **Rev. Designer:** Stuart Devlin

Date	Mintage	F	VF	XF	Unc	BU
ND(1984)	1,000,000	—	—	—	9.00	10.00

KM# 41a 100 DOBRAS
28.2800 g., 0.9250 Silver .8411 oz. ASW **Subject:** World Fisheries Conference **Obv:** Arms with supporters **Rev:** Figure standing in boat with fish net

Date	Mintage	F	VF	XF	Unc	BU
ND(1984) Proof	20,000	Value: 40.00				

KM# 41b 100 DOBRAS
47.5400 g., 0.9170 Gold 1.4017 oz. AGW **Subject:** World Fisheries Conference **Obv:** Arms with supporters **Rev:** Figure standing in boat with fish net

Date	Mintage	F	VF	XF	Unc	BU
ND(1984) Proof	100	Value: 1,250				

KM# 42 100 DOBRAS
Copper-Nickel **Subject:** 10th Anniversary of Independence **Obv:** Arms with supporters **Rev:** Value, stars and map

Date	Mintage	F	VF	XF	Unc	BU
ND(1985)	—	—	—	—	6.50	7.50

KM# 42a 100 DOBRAS
28.2800 g., 0.9250 Silver .8411 oz. ASW **Subject:** 10th Anniversary of Independence **Obv:** Arms with supporters **Rev:** Value, stars and map

Date	Mintage	F	VF	XF	Unc	BU
ND(1985) Proof	1,000	Value: 42.50				

KM# 42b 100 DOBRAS
47.5400 g., 0.9170 Gold 1.4017 oz. AGW **Subject:** 10th Anniversary of Independence **Obv:** Arms with supporters **Rev:** Value, stars and map

Date	Mintage	F	VF	XF	Unc	BU
ND(1985) Proof	50	Value: 1,400				

KM# 87 100 DOBRAS
Chrome Clad Steel, 17.5 mm. **Obv:** Arms with supporters **Rev:** Value below bird

Date	Mintage	F	VF	XF	Unc	BU
1997	—	—	—	—	1.25	1.75

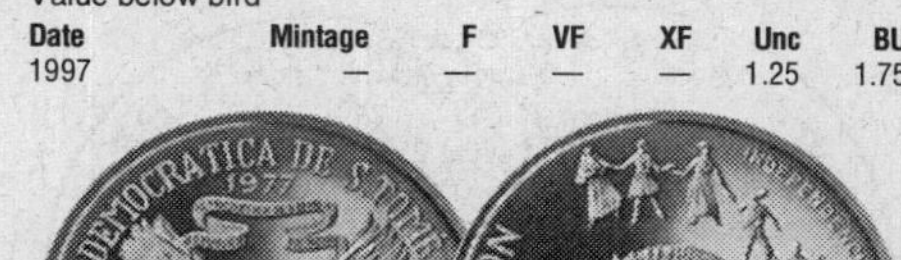

KM# 31 250 DOBRAS
17.4000 g., 0.9250 Silver .5175 oz. ASW **Subject:** Independence **Obv:** Arms with supporters **Rev:** World population

Date	Mintage	F	VF	XF	Unc	BU
1977	450	—	—	—	42.50	47.50
1977 Proof	750	Value: 40.00				

KM# 32 250 DOBRAS
17.4000 g., 0.9250 Silver .5175 oz. ASW **Subject:** Independence **Obv:** Arms with supporters **Rev:** World friendship

Date	Mintage	F	VF	XF	Unc	BU
1977	450	—	—	—	42.50	47.50
1977 Proof	800	Value: 40.00				

KM# 33 250 DOBRAS
17.4000 g., 0.9250 Silver .5175 oz. ASW **Subject:** Independence **Obv:** Arms with supporters **Rev:** Folklore statue

Date	Mintage	F	VF	XF	Unc	BU
1977	300	—	—	—	42.50	47.50
1977 Proof	600	Value: 40.00				

KM# 34 250 DOBRAS
17.4000 g., 0.9250 Silver .5175 oz. ASW **Subject:** Independence **Obv:** Arms with supporters **Rev:** World unity emblems

Date	Mintage	F	VF	XF	Unc	BU
1977	400	—	—	—	42.50	47.50
1977 Proof	700	Value: 40.00				

KM# 35 250 DOBRAS
17.4000 g., 0.9250 Silver .5175 oz. ASW **Subject:** Independence **Obv:** Arms with supporters **Rev:** Mother and child

Date	Mintage	F	VF	XF	Unc	BU
1977	350	—	—	—	42.50	47.50
1977 Proof	700	Value: 40.00				

KM# 88 250 DOBRAS
Chrome Clad Steel **Obv:** Arms with supporters **Rev:** Value above bird

Date	Mintage	F	VF	XF	Unc	BU
1997	—	—	—	—	1.50	2.00

KM# 70 500 DOBRAS
Copper-Nickel **Obv:** Arms with supporters **Rev:** Elvis Presley

Date	Mintage	F	VF	XF	Unc	BU
1993	—	—	—	—	12.50	14.50

KM# 89 500 DOBRAS
Chrome Clad Steel **Obv:** Arms with supporters **Rev:** Monkey in trees **Shape:** 7-sided

Date	Mintage	F	VF	XF	Unc	BU
1997	—	—	—	—	2.00	3.00

KM# 44 1000 DOBRAS
23.3300 g., 0.9250 Silver .6938 oz. ASW **Subject:** Soccer **Obv:** Arms with supporters **Rev:** 2 players

Date	Mintage	F	VF	XF	Unc	BU
1990 Proof	15,000	Value: 30.00				

KM# 45 1000 DOBRAS
23.3300 g., 0.9250 Silver .6938 oz. ASW **Subject:** Soccer **Obv:** Arms with supporters **Rev:** 2 players running

Date	Mintage	F	VF	XF	Unc	BU
1990 Proof	15,000	Value: 30.00				

KM# 47 1000 DOBRAS
25.9600 g., 0.9990 Silver .8347 oz. ASW **Subject:** Soccer **Obv:** Arms with supporters **Rev:** Soccer player

Date	Mintage	F	VF	XF	Unc	BU
1990 Proof	—	Value: 45.00				

KM# 48 1000 DOBRAS
25.9600 g., 0.9990 Silver .8347 oz. ASW **Subject:** Soccer **Obv:** Arms with supporters **Rev:** Soccer players

Date	Mintage	F	VF	XF	Unc	BU
1990 Proof	—	Value: 45.00				

KM# 49 1000 DOBRAS
20.0000 g., 0.9990 Silver .6431 oz. ASW **Subject:** National independence **Obv:** Arms with supporters **Rev:** Cheering figures

Date	Mintage	F	VF	XF	Unc	BU
1990 Proof	—	Value: 40.00				

KM# 50 1000 DOBRAS
20.0000 g., 0.9990 Silver .6431 oz. ASW **Subject:** Vasco de Gama **Obv:** Arms with supporters **Rev:** Cameo to right of ship

Date	Mintage	F	VF	XF	Unc	BU
1990 Proof	—	Value: 37.50				

KM# 53 1000 DOBRAS
20.0000 g., 0.9990 Silver .6431 oz. ASW **Subject:** Olympics and Discovery of America **Obv:** Arms with supporters **Rev:** Seated figure, partial map and ship, book with olympic circles on cover

Date	Mintage	F	VF	XF	Unc	BU
1990 Proof	—	Value: 35.00				

KM# 73 1000 DOBRAS
23.7400 g., 0.9250 Silver .7060 oz. ASW **Series:** 1992 Olympics **Obv:** Arms with supporters **Rev:** Date below flames and mountains

Date	Mintage	F	VF	XF	Unc	BU
1990 Proof	10,000	Value: 32.50				

KM# 74 1000 DOBRAS
23.7400 g., 0.9250 Silver .7060 oz. ASW **Series:** 1992 Olympics **Obv:** Arms with supporters **Rev:** Diver

Date	Mintage	F	VF	XF	Unc	BU
1990 Proof	10,000	Value: 27.50				

KM# 54 1000 DOBRAS
Copper-Nickel **Series:** Atlanta Olympics **Obv:** Arms with supporters **Rev:** Wrestling

Date	Mintage	F	VF	XF	Unc	BU
ND(1993) Proof	—	Value: 28.50				

KM# 63 1000 DOBRAS
Copper-Nickel **Series:** Atlanta Olympics **Obv:** Arms with supporters **Rev:** Swimmers

Date	Mintage	F	VF	XF	Unc	BU
ND(1993) Proof	—	Value: 28.50				

KM# 55 1000 DOBRAS
Copper-Nickel **Series:** Atlanta Olympics **Obv:** Arms with supporters **Rev:** Soccer players

Date	Mintage	F	VF	XF	Unc	BU
ND(1993) Proof	—	Value: 28.50				

KM# 56 1000 DOBRAS
Copper-Nickel **Series:** Atlanta Olympics **Obv:** Arms with supporters **Rev:** Boxer

Date	Mintage	F	VF	XF	Unc	BU
ND(1993) Proof	—	Value: 28.50				

KM# 57 1000 DOBRAS
Copper-Nickel **Series:** Atlanta Olympics **Obv:** Arms with supporters **Rev:** Bicyclist

Date	Mintage	F	VF	XF	Unc	BU
ND(1993) Proof	—	Value: 28.50				

KM# 58 1000 DOBRAS
Copper-Nickel **Series:** Atlanta Olympics **Obv:** Arms with supporters **Rev:** Karate competition

Date	Mintage	F	VF	XF	Unc	BU
ND(1993) Proof	—	Value: 28.50				

KM# 59 1000 DOBRAS
Copper-Nickel **Series:** Atlanta Olympics **Obv:** Arms with supporters **Rev:** Runner

Date	Mintage	F	VF	XF	Unc	BU
ND(1993) Proof	—	Value: 28.50				

KM# 60 1000 DOBRAS
Copper-Nickel **Series:** Atlanta Olympics **Obv:** Arms with supporters **Rev:** Field hockey players

Date	Mintage	F	VF	XF	Unc	BU
ND(1993) Proof	—	Value: 28.50				

KM# 61 1000 DOBRAS
Copper-Nickel **Series:** Atlanta Olympics **Obv:** Arms with supporters **Rev:** Four track and field events

Date	Mintage	F	VF	XF	Unc	BU
ND(1993) Proof	—	Value: 28.50				

KM# 62 1000 DOBRAS
Copper-Nickel **Series:** Atlanta Olympics **Obv:** Arms with supporters **Rev:** Surfer

Date	Mintage	F	VF	XF	Unc	BU
ND(1993) Proof	—	Value: 28.50				

KM# 64 1000 DOBRAS
Copper-Nickel **Series:** Atlanta Olympics **Obv:** Arms with supporters **Rev:** Three gymnastic events

Date	Mintage	F	VF	XF	Unc	BU
ND(1993) Proof	—	Value: 28.50				

KM# 65 1000 DOBRAS
Copper-Nickel **Series:** Atlanta Olympics **Obv:** Arms with supporters **Rev:** Tennis players

Date	Mintage	F	VF	XF	Unc	BU
ND(1993) Proof	—	Value: 28.50				

KM# 71 1000 DOBRAS
25.0000 g., 0.9250 Silver .7242 oz. ASW **Obv:** Arms with supporters **Rev:** Elvis Presley

Date	Mintage	F	VF	XF	Unc	BU
1993 Proof	—	Value: 32.50				

KM# 76 1000 DOBRAS
25.0000 g., 0.9250 Silver .7242 oz. ASW **Obv:** Arms with supporters **Rev:** Falcon **Note:** Enamel.

Date	Mintage	F	VF	XF	Unc	BU
1995 Proof	15,000	Value: 35.00				

KM# 77 1000 DOBRAS
25.0000 g., 0.9250 Silver .7242 oz. ASW **Obv:** Arms with supporters **Rev:** Porcelain rose **Note:** Enamel.

Date	Mintage	F	VF	XF	Unc	BU
1995 Proof	15,000	Value: 35.00				

KM# 78 1000 DOBRAS
25.0000 g., 0.9250 Silver .7242 oz. ASW **Obv:** Arms with supporters **Rev:** Seahorse and crab **Note:** Enamel.

Date	Mintage	F	VF	XF	Unc	BU
1995 Proof	15,000	Value: 40.00				

KM# 85a 1000 DOBRAS
31.1035 g., 0.9990 Silver 1 oz. ASW **Subject:** Diana - Queen of the Hearts **Obv:** Arms with supporters **Rev:** Bust with hat left **Note:** Prev. KM#85.1.

Date	Mintage	F	VF	XF	Unc	BU
1997 Proof	5,000	Value: 32.50				

KM# 102 1000 DOBRAS
1.2500 g., 0.9990 Gold .0402 oz. AGW **Subject:** Diana - Queen of the Hearts **Obv:** Arms with supporters **Rev:** Bust with hat left **Note:** Prev. KM#85.2.

Date	Mintage	F	VF	XF	Unc	BU
1997 Proof	3,000	Value: 60.00				

KM# 90 1000 DOBRAS
Chrome Clad Steel **Obv:** Arms with supporters **Rev:** Flowers and value **Shape:** 7-sided

Date	Mintage	F	VF	XF	Unc	BU
1997	—	—	—	—	2.75	3.75

KM# 92 1000 DOBRAS
Copper-Nickel **Subject:** Heidiland **Obv:** Arms with supporters **Rev:** Girl with goats

Date	Mintage	F	VF	XF	Unc	BU
1998	15,000	—	—	—	10.00	12.00

KM# 114 1000 DOBRAS
15.1000 g., 0.9990 Silver 0.485 oz. ASW, 30 mm. **Obv:** Arms with supporters **Rev:** Empress Elizabeth of Austria (1837-1898) **Edge:** Reeded

Date	Mintage	F	VF	XF	Unc	BU
1998 Proof	—	Value: 30.00				

KM# 93 1000 DOBRAS
25.0000 g., 0.9250 Silver .7435 oz. ASW **Subject:** Heidiland **Obv:** Arms with supporters **Rev:** Girl holding hat and flowers, bird, trees and mountains

Date	Mintage	F	VF	XF	Unc	BU
1998 Proof	10,000	Value: 32.50				

KM# 79 1000 DOBRAS
31.1035 g., 0.9990 Silver 1 oz. ASW **Obv:** Arms with supporters **Rev:** Peacock hologram

Date	Mintage	F	VF	XF	Unc	BU
1998(1997) Prooflike	10,000	—	—	—	—	60.00

KM# 80 1000 DOBRAS
31.1035 g., 0.9990 Silver 1 oz. ASW **Obv:** Arms with supporters **Rev:** Hummingbird hologram

Date	Mintage	F	VF	XF	Unc	BU
1998(1997) Prooflike	10,000	—	—	—	—	60.00

KM# 94 1000 DOBRAS
25.1400 g., 0.9250 Silver .7476 oz. ASW **Subject:** World Cup Soccer - France 1998 **Obv:** Arms with supporters **Rev:** Soccer players and goalie net **Shape:** 10-sided

Date	Mintage	F	VF	XF	Unc	BU
1998 Proof	10,000	Value: 35.00				

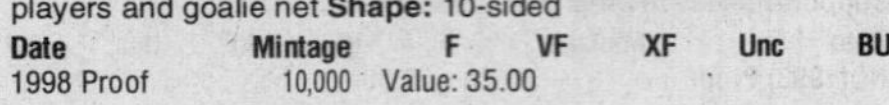

KM# 82 1000 DOBRAS
31.1035 g., 0.9990 Silver 1 oz. ASW **Obv:** Arms with supporters **Rev:** Butterfly hologram

Date	Mintage	F	VF	XF	Unc	BU
1998(1997) Prooflike	10,000	—	—	—	—	60.00

KM# 81 1000 DOBRAS
31.1035 g., 0.9990 Silver 1 oz. ASW **Obv:** Arms with supporters **Rev:** Fish hologram

Date	Mintage	F	VF	XF	Unc	BU
1998(1997) Prooflike	10,000	—	—	—	—	60.00

KM# 99 1000 DOBRAS
36.5500 g., , 34.9 mm. **Subject:** Millennium **Obv:** Arms with supporters **Rev:** Perforated gold insert exposing digital clock **Edge:** Reeded **Note:** Silver shell with gold insert encased digital clock. 8.1mm thick.

Date	Mintage	F	VF	XF	Unc	BU
1999 Proof	—	Value: 32.50				

KM# 91 2000 DOBRAS
Chrome Clad Steel **Obv:** Arms with supporters **Rev:** Tropical food plants within circle **Shape:** 7-sided

Date	Mintage	F	VF	XF	Unc	BU
1997	—	—	—	—	3.75	5.00

KM# 86 2000 DOBRAS
25.0000 g., 0.9250 Silver .7435 oz. ASW **Subject:** Third Christian millennium **Obv:** Arms with supporters **Rev:** Year 2000 CE calendar

Date	Mintage	F	VF	XF	Unc	BU
1998 Proof	5,000	Value: 28.00				

KM# 86a 2000 DOBRAS
Copper-Nickel **Subject:** Third Christian millennium **Obv:** Arms with supporters **Rev:** Year 2000 CE calendar **Note:** Calendar detailing is acid etched, not struck.

Date	Mintage	F	VF	XF	Unc	BU
1998 Prooflike	—	—	—	—	10.00	12.00

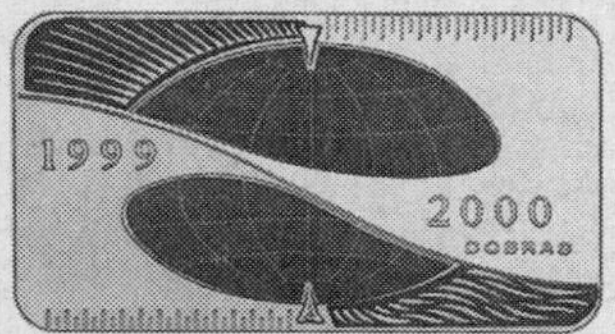

KM# 98 2000 DOBRAS
31.1600 g., 0.9990 Silver 1 oz. ASW, 27.1x47.2 mm. **Subject:** Pseudo - Millennium **Obv:** Arms with supporters **Rev:** Multicolor world and year split **Edge:** Plain **Shape:** Rectangle

Date	Mintage	VG	F	VF	XF	Unc
1998 Proof	—	Value: 47.50				

KM# 36 2500 DOBRAS
6.4800 g., 0.9000 Gold .1875 oz. AGW **Subject:** Independence **Obv:** Arms with supporters **Rev:** World friendship

Date	Mintage	F	VF	XF	Unc	BU
1977	100	—	—	—	225	250
1977 Proof	170	Value: 200				

KM# 37 2500 DOBRAS
6.4800 g., 0.9000 Gold .1875 oz. AGW **Subject:** Independence - World Population **Obv:** Arms with supporters **Rev:** World population

Date	Mintage	F	VF	XF	Unc	BU
1977	100	—	—	—	225	250
1977 Proof	170	Value: 200				

KM# 38 2500 DOBRAS
6.4800 g., 0.9000 Gold .1875 oz. AGW **Subject:** Independence **Obv:** Arms with supporters **Rev:** Folklore monument

Date	Mintage	F	VF	XF	Unc	BU
1977	100	—	—	—	225	250
1977 Proof	170	Value: 200				

KM# 39 2500 DOBRAS
6.4800 g., 0.9000 Gold .1875 oz. AGW **Subject:** Independence **Obv:** Arms with supporters **Rev:** World unity

Date	Mintage	F	VF	XF	Unc	BU
1977	100	—	—	—	225	250
1977 Proof	170	Value: 200				

KM# 40 2500 DOBRAS
6.4800 g., 0.9000 Gold .1875 oz. AGW **Subject:** Independence **Obv:** Arms with supporters **Rev:** Mother and child

Date	Mintage	F	VF	XF	Unc	BU
1977	100	—	—	—	225	250
1977 Proof	170	Value: 200				

KM# 83 2500 DOBRAS
6.2207 g., 0.9999 Gold .2000 oz. AGW **Obv:** Arms with supporters **Rev:** Hummingbird hologram **Note:** Similar to 1,000 Dobras, KM#80.

Date	Mintage	F	VF	XF	Unc	BU
1998(1997) Proof	2,500	Value: 250				

KM# 84 2500 DOBRAS
6.2207 g., 0.9999 Gold .2000 oz. AGW **Obv:** Arms with supporters **Rev:** Butterfly hologram **Note:** Similar to 1,000 Dobras, KM#82.

Date	Mintage	F	VF	XF	Unc	BU
1998(1997) Proof	2,500	Value: 250				

KM# 46 3500 DOBRAS
136.0800 g., 0.9250 Silver 4.3755 oz. ASW, 63 mm. **Subject:** Wildlife Protection **Obv:** Arms with supporters **Rev:** Sea turtle **Note:** Photo reduced.

Date	Mintage	F	VF	XF	Unc	BU
1990 Proof	750	Value: 150				

KM# 100 5000 DOBRAS
168.5600 g., **Subject:** Millennium **Obv:** Arms with supporters **Rev:** Perforated silver insert exposing digital clock **Edge:** Reeded **Note:** Silver shell with encased digital clock. 9mm thick.

Date	Mintage	F	VF	XF	Unc	BU
1999 Proof	—	Value: 100				

KM# 51 10000 DOBRAS
7.7750 g., 0.9000 Gold .2250 oz. AGW **Obv:** Arms with supporters **Rev:** Sea turtle

Date	Mintage	F	VF	XF	Unc	BU
1992 Proof	500	Value: 325				

KM# 72 25000 DOBRAS
15.5500 g., 0.9990 Gold .5 oz. AGW **Obv:** Arms with supporters **Rev:** Elvis Presley

Date	Mintage	F	VF	XF	Unc	BU
1993 Proof	—	Value: 550				

DUAL DENOMINATED COINAGE

KM# 67 500 DOBRAS - 1 ECU
Copper-Nickel **Subject:** 15th Anniversary of Association With European Common Market **Obv:** Arms with supporters **Rev:** Circular star design above ships and city view

Date	Mintage	F	VF	XF	Unc	BU
1993	20,000	—	—	—	11.50	13.50

KM# 68 2500 DOBRAS - 5 ECU
25.0000 g., 0.9250 Silver .7434 oz. ASW **Subject:** 15th Anniversary of Association With European Common Market **Obv:** Arms with supporters **Rev:** Circular star design above ships and city view

Date	Mintage	F	VF	XF	Unc	BU
1993 Proof	12,000	Value: 32.50				

KM# 69 25000 DOBRAS - 50 ECU
6.7200 g., 0.9000 Gold .1944 oz. AGW **Subject:** 15th Anniversary of Association With European Common Market **Obv:** Arms with supporters **Rev:** Old harbor scene **Note:** Similar to 2500 Dobras, 5 Ecu, KM#68.

Date	Mintage	F	VF	XF	Unc	BU
1993 Proof	1,000	Value: 220				

KM# 95 2000 DOBRAS - 1 EURO
Copper-Nickel **Obv:** Arms with supporters **Rev:** Head left and multicolor Swiss flag in circle of stars, value at lower left

Date	Mintage	F	VF	XF	Unc	BU
1997 Proof	5,000	Value: 12.50				

KM# 103 2000 DOBRAS - 1 EURO
31.1000 g., 0.9250 Silver The Belgian one franc coin adds 2.74g for a total weight of 33.85g 0.9249 oz. ASW, 38.6 mm. **Subject:** Year of the Euro **Obv:** Arms with supporters **Rev:** Map with inset Belgian 1 franc coin **Edge:** Reeded

Date	Mintage	F	VF	XF	Unc	BU
1999 Proof	—	Value: 45.00				

KM# 104 2000 DOBRAS - 1 EURO
31.2100 g., 0.9250 Silver The Italian 50 lire adds 4.46g for a total weight of 35.67 0.9282 oz. ASW, 38.6 mm. **Subject:** Year of the Euro **Obv:** Arms with supporters **Rev:** Map with inset Italian 50 lire coin **Edge:** Reeded

Date	Mintage	F	VF	XF	Unc	BU
1999 Proof	—	Value: 45.00				

KM# 105 2000 DOBRAS - 1 EURO

30.9500 g., 0.9250 Silver The French 1/2 franc adds 4.5g for a total weight of 35.45g 0.9204 oz. ASW, 38.6 mm. **Subject:** Year of the Euro **Obv:** Arms with supporters **Rev:** Map with inset French 1/2 franc coin **Edge:** Reeded

Date	Mintage	F	VF	XF	Unc	BU
1999 Proof	—	Value: 45.00				

KM# 110 2000 DOBRAS - 1 EURO

31.1000 g., 0.9250 Silver 0.9249 oz. ASW, 38.5 mm. **Subject:** Year of the Euro **Obv:** Arms with supporters **Rev:** Luxembourg 25 centimes KM-45a.1 glued to map design **Edge:** Reeded **Note:** Total weight 31.83g with Luxembourg coin

Date	Mintage	F	VF	XF	Unc	BU
1999 Proof	—	Value: 45.00				

KM# 112 2000 DOBRAS - 1 EURO

31.1000 g., 0.9250 Silver 0.9249 oz. ASW, 38.5 mm. **Subject:** Year of the Euro **Obv:** Arms with supporters **Rev:** Portuguese 1 escudo KM-631 glued to map design **Edge:** Reeded **Note:** Total weight 32.82g with Portuguese coin

Date	Mintage	F	VF	XF	Unc	BU
1999 Proof	—	Value: 45.00				

KM# 107 2000 DOBRAS - 1 EURO

31.1000 g., 0.9250 Silver 0.9249 oz. ASW, 38.5 mm. **Subject:** Year of the Euro **Obv:** Arms with supporters **Rev:** Finnland 10 penni KM-65 glued to map design **Edge:** Reeded **Note:** Total weight 32.84g with Finnish coin

Date	Mintage	F	VF	XF	Unc	BU
1999 Proof	—	Value: 45.00				

KM# 113 2000 DOBRAS - 1 EURO

31.1000 g., 0.9250 Silver 0.9249 oz. ASW, 38.5 mm. **Subject:** Year of the Euro **Obv:** Arms with supporters **Rev:** Spanish 5 pesetas KM-833 glued to map design **Edge:** Reeded **Note:** Total weight 34.14g with Spanish coin

Date	Mintage	F	VF	XF	Unc	BU
1999 Proof	—	Value: 45.00				

KM# 108 2000 DOBRAS - 1 EURO

31.1000 g., 0.9250 Silver 0.9249 oz. ASW, 38.5 mm. **Subject:** Year of the Euro **Obv:** Arms with supporters **Rev:** German 5 pfennig KM-107 glued to map design **Edge:** Reeded **Note:** Total weight 34.1g with German coin

Date	Mintage	F	VF	XF	Unc	BU
1999 Proof	—	Value: 45.00				

KM# 111 2000 DOBRAS - 1 EURO

31.1000 g., 0.9250 Silver 0.9249 oz. ASW, 38.5 mm. **Subject:** Year of the Euro **Obv:** Arms with supporters **Rev:** Netherlands 25 cents KM-183 glued to map design **Edge:** Reeded **Note:** Total weight 34.2g with Dutch coin

Date	Mintage	F	VF	XF	Unc	BU
1999 Proof	—	Value: 45.00				

KM# 109 2000 DOBRAS - 1 EURO

31.1000 g., 0.9250 Silver 0.9249 oz. ASW, 38.5 mm. **Subject:** Year of the Euro **Obv:** Arms with supporters **Rev:** Irish 5 pence KM-28.1 glued to map design **Edge:** Reeded **Note:** Total weight 34.33g with Irish coin

Date	Mintage	F	VF	XF	Unc	BU
1999 Proof	—	Value: 45.00				

KM# 106 2000 DOBRAS - 1 EURO

31.1000 g., 0.9250 Silver 0.9249 oz. ASW, 38.5 mm. **Subject:** Year of the Euro **Obv:** Arms with supporters **Rev:** Austrian 50 groschen KM-2885 glued to map design **Edge:** Reeded **Note:** Total weight with Austrian coin 34.1g

Date	Mintage	F	VF	XF	Unc	BU
1999	—	Value: 45.00				

KM# 96 10000 DOBRAS - 5 EURO

25.0000 g., 0.9250 Silver .7435 oz. ASW **Obv:** Arms with supporters **Rev:** Head left and Swiss flag in star circle, date at lower left

Date	Mintage	F	VF	XF	Unc	BU
1998 Proof	5,000	Value: 35.00				

KM# 101 15000 DOBRAS - 7.5 EUROS

25.0000 g., Silver, 38.55 mm. **Subject:** Switzerland and the European **Obv:** Arms with supporters **Rev:** Helvetia viewing a Swiss flag within a circle of stars **Edge:** Reeded

Date	Mintage	F	VF	XF	Unc	BU
1997 Proof	—	Value: 40.00				

PATTERNS

KM#	Date	Mintage	Identification	Mkt Val
Pn1	ND(1994)	—	1000 Dobras. Copper-Nickel. 1 player.	55.00
Pn2	ND(1994)	—	1000 Dobras. Copper-Nickel. With denticles.	55.00
Pn3	ND(1994)	—	1000 Dobras. 0.9990 Silver. 19.7100 g. With 999 CuNi in error.	65.00
Pn4	ND(1994)	—	1000 Dobras. Copper-Nickel. 2 soccer players and E.P. 999.	55.00
Pn5	ND(1994)	—	1000 Dobras. 0.9990 Silver. 21.0000 g. E.P. 999.	65.00

PIEFORTS

KM#	Date	Mintage	Identification	Mkt Val
P1	1984	500	100 Dobras. Silver.	65.00

PROVAS

Standard metals; stamped 'PROVA' in field

KM#	Date	Mintage	Identification	Mkt Val
Pr1	1928	—	50 Centavos. Nickel-Bronze. KM1.	200
Pr2	1929	—	10 Centavos. Nickel-Bronze center. KM2.	50.00
Pr3	1929	—	20 Centavos. Nickel-Bronze. KM3.	50.00
Pr4	1929	—	50 Centavos. Nickel-Bronze. KM1.	125
Pr5	1939	—	Escudo. Silver. KM5.	225
Pr6	1939	—	2-1/2 Escudos. Silver. KM5.	165
Pr7	1939	—	5 Escudos. Silver. KM6.	175
Pr8	1939	—	10 Escudos. Silver. KM7.	300
Pr9	1948	—	50 Centavos. Nickel-Bronze. KM8.	65.00
Pr10	1948	—	Escudo. Nickel-Bronze. KM9.	65.00
Pr11	1948	—	2-1/2 Escudos. Silver. KM5.	75.00
Pr12	1948	—	5 Escudos. Silver. KM6.	80.00
Pr13	1951	—	50 Centavos. Copper-Nickel. KM10.	85.00
Pr14	1951	—	Escudo. Copper-Nickel. KM11.	125
Pr15	1951	—	2-1/2 Escudos. Silver. KM12.	45.00
Pr16	1951	—	5 Escudos. Silver center. KM13.	65.00
Pr17	1951	—	10 Escudos. Silver. KM14.	125
Pr18	1962	—	10 Centavos. Bronze. KM15.	20.00
Pr19	1962	—	20 Centavos. Bronze. KM16.	22.50
Pr20	1962	—	50 Centavos. Bronze. KM17.	22.50
Pr21	1962	—	Escudo. Bronze. KM18.	25.00
Pr22	1962	—	2-1/2 Escudos. Copper-Nickel. KM19.	27.50
Pr23	1962	—	5 Escudos. Silver. KM20.	45.00
Pr24	1970	—	50 Escudos. Silver. KM21.	75.00
Pr25	1971	—	10 Centavos. Aluminum. KM15a.	20.00
Pr26	1971	—	20 Centavos. Bronze. KM16.2.	20.00
Pr27	1971	—	50 Centavos. Bronze. KM17.2.	20.00
Pr28	1971	—	Escudo. Bronze. KM18.	20.00
Pr29	1971	—	2-1/2 Escudos. Copper-Nickel. KM19.	22.50
Pr30	1971	—	5 Escudos. Copper-Nickel. KM22.	25.00
Pr31	1971	—	10 Escudos. Copper-Nickel. KM23.	27.50
Pr32	1971	—	20 Escudos. Nickel. KM24.	30.00

MINT SETS

KM#	Date	Mintage	Identification	Issue Price	Mkt Val
MS1	1977 (5)	—	KM31-35	71.00	215
MS2	1977 (5)	100	KM36-40	655	1,200

PROOF SETS

KM#	Date	Mintage	Identification	Issue Price	Mkt Val
PS1	1977 (5)	—	KM31-35	93.50	200
PS2	1977 (5)	170	KM36-40	805	950

SAINT VINCENT

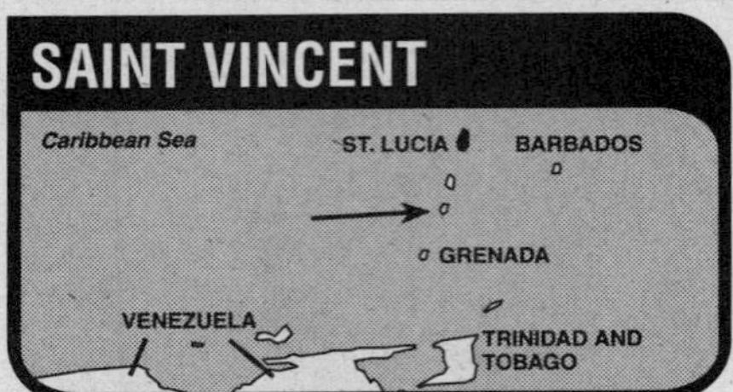

Saint Vincent and the Grenadines, consisting of the island of Saint Vincent and the northern Grenadines (a string of islets stretching southward from Saint Vincent), is located in the Windward Islands of the West Indies, West of Barbados and south of Saint Lucia. The tiny nation has an area of 150sq. mi. (340 sq. km.) and a population of *105,000.Capital: Kingstown. Arrowroot, cotton, sugar, molasses, rum and cocoa are exported. Tourism is a principal industry.

Saint Vincent was discovered by Columbus on Jan. 22,1498, but was left undisturbed for more than a century. The British began colonization early in the 18th century against bitter and prolonged Carib resistance. The island was taken by the French in 1779, but was restored to the British in 1783, at the end of the American Revolution. Saint Vincent and the northern Grenadines became a British associated state in Oct. 1969. Independence under the name of Saint Vincent and the Grenadines was attained at midnight of Oct. 26, 1979. The new nation chose to become a member of the Commonwealth of Nations with Elizabeth II as Head of State and Queen of Saint Vincent.

A local coinage was introduced in 1797, with the gold withdrawn in 1818 and the silver in 1823. This was replaced by sterling. From the mid-1950's, Saint Vincent used the currency of the British Caribbean Territories (Eastern Group), then that of the East Caribbean States.

RULERS

British

MONETARY SYSTEM

Commencing 1979

100 Cents = 1 Dollar

BRITISH COLONY

MODERN COINAGE

KM# 13 4 DOLLARS

Copper-Nickel, 38.5 mm. **Series:** F.A.O. **Obv:** Flower above shield with banner and date below **Rev:** Value below divides sugar cane plant and banana tree branch

Date	Mintage	F	VF	XF	Unc	BU
1970	13,000	—	6.00	10.00	20.00	30.00
1970 Proof	2,000	Value: 35.00				

KM# 14 10 DOLLARS

Copper-Nickel **Subject:** Royal Visit **Obv:** Crowned bust right **Obv. Designer:** Raphael Maklouf **Rev:** Flower above shield within circle

Date	Mintage	F	VF	XF	Unc	BU
1985	100,000	—	—	10.00	20.00	32.50

KM# 14a 10 DOLLARS

28.2800 g., 0.9250 Silver .8411 oz. ASW **Subject:** Royal Visit **Obv:** Crowned bust right **Rev:** Flower above shield within circle

Date	Mintage	F	VF	XF	Unc	BU
1985 Proof	5,000	Value: 60.00				

KM# 14b 10 DOLLARS

47.5400 g., 0.9170 Gold 1.4013 oz. AGW **Subject:** Royal Visit **Obv:** Crowned bust right **Rev:** Flower above shield within circle

Date	Mintage	F	VF	XF	Unc	BU
1985 Proof	250	Value: 1,050				

KM# 15 100 DOLLARS

129.5900 g., 0.9250 Silver 3.8543 oz. ASW, 63 mm. **Subject:** Tropical Birds - Pelican **Obv:** Coat of arms **Rev:** Pelican **Note:** Photo reduced.

Date	Mintage	F	VF	XF	Unc	BU
1988 Proof	Est. 10,000	Value: 135				

SAMOA

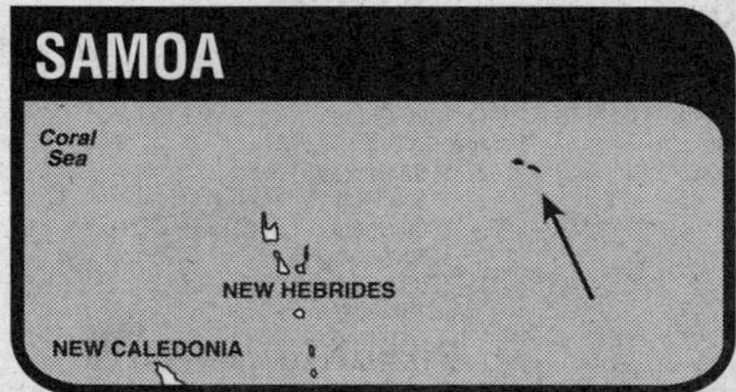

The Independent State of Samoa (formerly Western Samoa), located in the Pacific Ocean 1,600 miles (2,574 km.) northeast of New Zealand, has an area of 1,097 sq. mi. (2,860 sq. km.) and a population of *182,000. Capital: Apia. The economy is based on agriculture, fishing and tourism. Copra, cocoa and bananas are exported.

The first European to sight the Samoan group of islands was the Dutch navigator Jacob Roggeveen in 1722. Great Britain, the United States and Germany established consular representation at Apia in 1847, 1853 and 1861 respectively. The conflicting interests of the three powers produced the Berlin agreement of 1889, which declared Samoa neutral and had the effect of establishing a tripartite protectorate over the islands. A further agreement, 1899, recognized the rights of the United States in those islands east of 171 deg. west longitude (American Samoa) and of Germany in the other islands (Western Samoa).New Zealand occupied Western Samoa at the start of World War I and administered it as a League of Nations mandate and U. N. trusteeship until Jan. 1, 1962, when it became an independent state.

Samoa is a member of the Commonwealth of Nations. The Chief Executive is Chief of State. The prime minister is the Head of Government. The present Head of State, Malietoa Tanumafili II, holds his position for life. The Legislative Assembly will elect future Heads of State for 5-year terms.

Samoa, which had used New Zealand coinage, converted to a decimal coinage in 1967.

RULERS

British, until 1962
Malietoa Tanumafili II, 1962—

MONETARY SYSTEM

100 Sene = 1 Tala

INDEPENDENT STATE

STANDARD COINAGE

KM# 1 SENE

1.7500 g., Bronze, 17.5 mm. **Obv:** Head left **Obv. Designer:** T.H. Paget **Rev:** Stars and value within wreath

Date	Mintage	F	VF	XF	Unc	BU
1967	915,000	—	0.10	0.15	0.30	—
1967 Proof	15,000	Value: 0.50				

KM# 12 SENE

1.7500 g., Bronze, 17.5 mm. **Obv:** Head left **Obv. Designer:** T.H. Paget **Rev:** Stars and value within wreath **Rev. Designer:** James Berry

Date	Mintage	F	VF	XF	Unc	BU
1974	3,380,000	—	—	0.10	0.25	—
1987	—	—	—	0.10	0.25	—
1988	—	—	—	0.10	0.25	—
1993	—	—	—	0.10	0.25	—
1996	—	—	—	0.10	0.25	—

KM# 12a SENE

1.9500 g., 0.9250 Silver .0579 oz. ASW, 17.5 mm. **Obv:** Head left **Obv. Designer:** T.H. Paget **Rev:** Stars and value within wreath **Rev. Designer:** James Berry

Date	Mintage	F	VF	XF	Unc	BU
1974 Proof	5,578	Value: 1.25				

KM# 2 2 SENE

3.2500 g., Bronze, 21.1 mm. **Obv:** Head left **Obv. Designer:** T.H. Paget **Rev:** Stars and value within wreath

Date	Mintage	F	VF	XF	Unc	BU
1967	465,000	—	0.10	0.20	0.40	—
1967 Proof	15,000	Value: 0.50				

KM# 13 2 SENE

3.2500 g., Bronze, 21.1 mm. **Obv:** Head left **Obv. Designer:** T.H. Paget **Rev:** Value below nut sprig **Rev. Designer:** James Berry

Date	Mintage	F	VF	XF	Unc	BU
1974	1,640,000	—	0.10	0.15	0.30	—
1988	—	—	0.10	0.15	0.30	—
1996	—	—	0.10	0.15	0.30	—

KM# 13a 2 SENE

3.8000 g., 0.9250 Silver .1130 oz. ASW, 21.1 mm. **Obv:** Head left **Obv. Designer:** T.H. Paget **Rev:** Value below nut sprig **Rev. Designer:** James Berry

Date	Mintage	F	VF	XF	Unc	BU
1974 Proof	5,578	Value: 2.25				

KM# 122 2 SENE

3.2500 g., Bronze, 21.1 mm. **Series:** F.A.O. **Obv:** Head left **Rev:** Stars and value within wreath

Date	Mintage	F	VF	XF	Unc	BU
2000(1999)	—	—	—	—	0.35	—

KM# 3 5 SENE

2.8000 g., Copper-Nickel, 19.4 mm. **Obv:** Head left **Rev:** Value and stars

Date	Mintage	F	VF	XF	Unc	BU
1967	495,000	—	0.15	0.25	0.50	—
1967 Proof	15,000	Value: 1.00				

KM# 14 5 SENE

2.8000 g., Copper-Nickel, 19.4 mm. **Obv:** Head left **Obv. Designer:** T.H. Paget **Rev:** Pineapple and value

Date	Mintage	F	VF	XF	Unc	BU
1974	1,736,000	—	0.10	0.20	0.40	—
1987	—	—	0.10	0.20	0.40	—
1988	—	—	0.10	0.20	0.40	—
1993	—	—	0.10	0.20	0.40	—
1996	—	—	0.10	0.20	0.40	—

KM# 14a 5 SENE

3.2500 g., 0.9250 Silver .0966 oz. ASW, 19.4 mm. **Obv:** Head left **Obv. Designer:** T.H. Paget **Rev:** Pineapple and value

Date	Mintage	F	VF	XF	Unc	BU
1974 Proof	5,578	Value: 2.50				

KM# 4 10 SENE

5.6500 g., Copper-Nickel, 23.6 mm. **Obv:** Head left **Obv. Designer:** T.H. Paget **Rev:** National arms

Date	Mintage	F	VF	XF	Unc	BU
1967	400,000	—	0.20	0.35	0.70	—
1967 Proof	15,000	Value: 1.00				

KM# 15 10 SENE

5.6500 g., Copper-Nickel, 23.6 mm. **Obv:** Head left **Obv. Designer:** T.H. Paget **Rev:** Value to lower left of leafy plants **Rev. Designer:** James Berry

Date	Mintage	F	VF	XF	Unc	BU
1974	1,580,000	—	0.15	0.30	0.60	—
1987	—	—	0.15	0.30	0.60	—

Date	Mintage	F	VF	XF	Unc	BU
1988	—	—	0.15	0.30	0.60	—
1993	—	—	0.15	0.30	0.60	—
1996	—	—	0.15	0.30	0.60	—

KM# 15a 10 SENE

6.3700 g., 0.9250 Silver .1894 oz. ASW, 23.6 mm. **Obv:** Head left **Obv. Designer:** T.H. Paget **Rev:** Value to lower left of leafy plants **Rev. Designer:** James Berry

Date	Mintage	F	VF	XF	Unc	BU
1974 Proof	5,578	Value: 3.25				

KM# 5 20 SENE

11.3000 g., Copper-Nickel, 28.5 mm. **Obv:** Head left **Obv. Designer:** T.H. Paget **Rev:** National arms

Date	Mintage	F	VF	XF	Unc	BU
1967	400,000	—	0.25	0.50	1.00	—
1967 Proof	15,000	Value: 1.50				

KM# 16 20 SENE

11.3000 g., Copper-Nickel, 28.5 mm. **Obv:** Head left **Obv. Designer:** T.H. Paget **Rev:** Breadfruit and value **Rev. Designer:** James Berry

Date	Mintage	F	VF	XF	Unc	BU
1974	1,380,000	—	0.20	0.40	0.80	—
1987	—	—	0.20	0.40	0.80	—
1988	—	—	0.20	0.40	0.80	—
1993	—	—	0.20	0.40	0.80	—
1996	—	—	0.20	0.40	0.80	—

KM# 16a 20 SENE

12.7000 g., 0.9250 Silver .3776 oz. ASW, 28.5 mm. **Obv:** Head left **Obv. Designer:** T.H. Paget **Rev:** Breadfruit and value **Rev. Designer:** James Berry

Date	Mintage	F	VF	XF	Unc	BU
1974 Proof	5,578	Value: 6.00				

KM# 6 50 SENE

14.0000 g., Copper-Nickel, 32.4 mm. **Obv:** Head left **Obv. Designer:** T.H. Paget **Rev:** National arms

Date	Mintage	F	VF	XF	Unc	BU
1967	80,000	—	0.75	1.25	2.00	—
1967 Proof	15,000	Value: 2.50				

KM# 17 50 SENE

14.0000 g., Copper-Nickel, 32.4 mm. **Obv:** Head left **Obv. Designer:** T.H. Paget **Rev:** Banana tree and value **Rev. Designer:** James Berry

Date	Mintage	F	VF	XF	Unc	BU
1974	50,000	—	0.75	1.25	2.00	—
1988	—	—	0.75	1.25	2.00	—
1996	—	—	0.75	1.25	2.00	—
2000	—	—	0.75	1.25	2.00	—

KM# 17a 50 SENE

15.4000 g., 0.9250 Silver .4579 oz. ASW, 32.4 mm. **Obv:** Head left **Obv. Designer:** T.H. Paget **Rev:** Banana tree and value **Rev. Designer:** James Berry

Date	Mintage	F	VF	XF	Unc	BU
1974 Proof	5,578	Value: 7.00				

KM# 80 50 SENE

14.0000 g., Copper-Nickel, 32.4 mm. **Subject:** 25th Anniversary of Independence **Obv:** Head left **Rev:** National arms

Date	Mintage	F	VF	XF	Unc	BU
1987	—	—	—	—	2.25	—

KM# 7 TALA

Copper-Nickel, 38.8 mm. **Obv:** Head left **Rev:** National arms **Edge Lettering:** DECIMAL CURRENCY INTRODUCED 10 JULY 1967

Date	Mintage	F	VF	XF	Unc	BU
1967	20,000	—	—	—	2.50	—
1967 Proof	15,000	Value: 5.00				

KM# 8 TALA

Copper-Nickel, 38.8 mm. **Subject:** 75th Anniversary - Death of Robert Louis Stevenson **Obv:** National arms **Rev:** Reclining figure holding pen and paper left **Rev. Designer:** After Augustus Saint-Gaudens

Date	Mintage	F	VF	XF	Unc	BU
1969	25,000	—	—	—	2.50	—
1969 Proof	1,500	Value: 5.00				

KM# 9 TALA

Copper-Nickel, 38.8 mm. **Subject:** 200th Anniversary - Capt. Cook voyages **Obv:** National arms **Rev:** Head right **Rev. Designer:** James Berry

Date	Mintage	F	VF	XF	Unc	BU
1970	32,000	—	—	—	2.50	—
1970 Proof	3,000	Value: 5.00				

KM# 10 TALA

Copper-Nickel, 38.8 mm. **Subject:** Visit of Pope Paul VI **Obv:** National arms **Rev:** Bust right

Date	Mintage	F	VF	XF	Unc	BU
1970	35,000	—	—	—	3.00	—
1970 Proof	3,000	Value: 6.00				

KM# 11 TALA

Copper-Nickel, 38.8 mm. **Subject:** Roggeveen's Pacific voyage **Obv:** National arms **Rev:** Sailing ship **Rev. Designer:** James Berry

Date	Mintage	F	VF	XF	Unc	BU
1972	35,000	—	—	—	3.00	—
1972 Proof	3,000	Value: 6.50				

KM# 18 TALA

Copper-Nickel, 38.8 mm. **Subject:** 10th British Commonwealth Games **Obv:** National arms **Rev:** Boxing match

Date	Mintage	F	VF	XF	Unc	BU
1974	40,000	—	—	—	3.50	—

KM# 18a TALA

27.7000 g., 0.9250 Silver .8239 oz. ASW, 38.8 mm. **Subject:** 10th British Commonwealth Games **Obv:** National arms **Rev:** Boxing match

Date	Mintage	F	VF	XF	Unc	BU
1974 Proof	1,500	Value: 14.50				

KM# 19 TALA

Copper-Nickel, 38.8 mm. **Obv:** Head of Malietoa Tanumafili II left **Obv. Designer:** T.H. Paget **Rev:** Coconut palm and value

Date	Mintage	F	VF	XF	Unc	BU
1974	24,000	—	—	—	2.50	—

KM# 19a TALA

31.1500 g., 0.9250 Silver .9263 oz. ASW, 38.8 mm. **Obv:** Head of Malietoa Tanumafili II left **Obv. Designer:** T.H. Paget **Rev:** Coconut palm and value

Date	Mintage	F	VF	XF	Unc	BU
1974 Proof	11,000	Value: 14.00				

KM# 20 TALA

Copper-Nickel, 38.8 mm. **Subject:** U.S. Bicentennial **Obv:** Head of Malietoa Tanumafili II left **Obv. Designer:** T.H. Paget **Rev:** Equestrian and USA map **Rev. Designer:** James Berry

Date	Mintage	F	VF	XF	Unc	BU
ND(1976)	40,000	—	—	—	2.50	—

KM# 20a TALA

30.4000 g., 0.9250 Silver .9040 oz. ASW, 38.8 mm. **Subject:** U.S. Bicentennial **Obv:** Head of Malietoa Tanumafili II left **Obv. Designer:** T.H. Paget **Rev:** Equestrian and USA map **Rev. Designer:** James Berry

Date	Mintage	F	VF	XF	Unc	BU
ND(1976) Proof	4,127	Value: 13.50				

KM# 22 TALA

Copper-Nickel, 38.8 mm. **Series:** Montreal Olympics **Obv:** National arms **Rev:** Weight lifter **Rev. Designer:** James Berry

Date	Mintage	F	VF	XF	Unc	BU
1976	40,000	—	—	—	3.00	—

KM# 22a TALA

30.4000 g., 0.9250 Silver .9040 oz. ASW, 38.8 mm. **Series:** Montreal Olympics **Obv:** National arms **Rev:** Weight lifter **Rev. Designer:** James Berry

Date	Mintage	F	VF	XF	Unc	BU
1976 Proof	6,000	Value: 13.50				

KM# 24 TALA

Copper-Nickel, 38.8 mm. **Subject:** Queen's Silver Jubilee **Obv:** National arms **Rev:** Cameo flanked by palm trees **Rev. Designer:** James Berry

Date	Mintage	F	VF	XF	Unc	BU
1977	27,000	—	—	—	2.50	—

KM# 24a TALA

30.4000 g., 0.9250 Silver .9040 oz. ASW, 38.8 mm. **Subject:** Queen's Silver Jubilee **Obv:** National arms **Rev:** Cameo flanked by palm trees **Rev. Designer:** James Berry

Date	Mintage	F	VF	XF	Unc	BU
1977 Proof	6,171	Value: 13.50				

KM# 26 TALA

Copper-Nickel, 38.8 mm. **Subject:** Lindbergh's New York to Paris flight **Obv:** National arms **Rev:** Bust of Lindbergh at left, plane above, Eiffel tower at right, Statue of Liberty at left, ocean in background **Rev. Designer:** James Berry

Date	Mintage	F	VF	XF	Unc	BU
1977	17,000	—	—	—	3.00	—

KM# 26a TALA

30.4000 g., 0.9250 Silver .9040 oz. ASW, 38.8 mm. **Subject:** Lindbergh's New York to Paris flight **Obv:** National arms **Rev:** Bust of Lindbergh at left, plane above, Eiffel tower at right, Statue of Liberty at left, ocean in background **Rev. Designer:** James Berry

Date	Mintage	F	VF	XF	Unc	BU
1977 Proof	4,522	Value: 14.00				

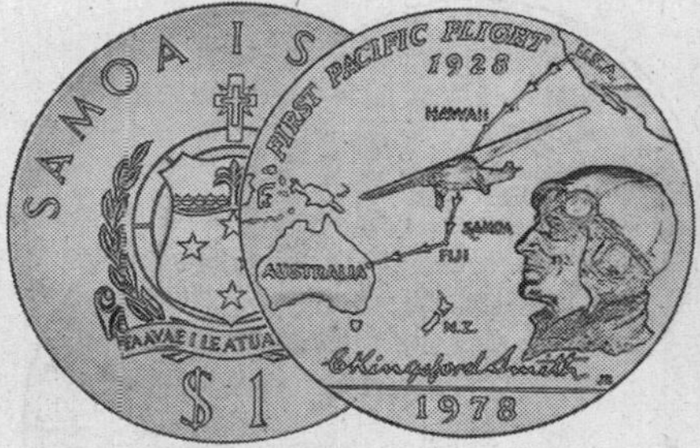

KM# 28 TALA

Copper-Nickel, 38.8 mm. **Subject:** 50th Anniversary - First Transpacific Flight **Obv:** National arms **Rev:** Head left, map, plane and date **Rev. Designer:** James Berry

Date	Mintage	F	VF	XF	Unc	BU
1978	20,000	—	—	—	3.00	—

KM# 28a TALA

30.4000 g., 0.9250 Silver .9040 oz. ASW, 38.8 mm. **Subject:** 50th Anniversary - First Transpacific Flight **Obv:** National arms **Rev:** Head left, map, plane and date

Date	Mintage	F	VF	XF	Unc	BU
1978 Proof	5,000	Value: 13.50				

KM# 30 TALA

Copper-Nickel, 38.8 mm. **Subject:** XI Commonwealth Games **Obv:** National arms **Rev:** Runners **Rev. Designer:** James Berry

Date	Mintage	F	VF	XF	Unc	BU
1978	7,710	—	—	—	3.00	—

KM# 30a TALA

30.4000 g., 0.9250 Silver .9040 oz. ASW, 38.8 mm. **Subject:** XI Commonwealth Games **Obv:** National arms **Rev:** Runners **Rev. Designer:** James Berry

Date	Mintage	F	VF	XF	Unc	BU
1978 Proof	5,000	Value: 13.50				

KM# 32 TALA

Copper-Nickel, 38.8 mm. **Subject:** Bicentenary - Death of Capt. James Cook **Obv:** National arms **Rev:** Head right and sailing ship **Rev. Designer:** James Berry

Date	Mintage	F	VF	XF	Unc	BU
1979	5,000	—	—	—	2.50	—

KM# 35 TALA

Copper-Nickel, 38.8 mm. **Series:** 1980 Olympics **Obv:** National arms **Rev:** Hurdles event **Rev. Designer:** E.W. Roberts

Date	Mintage	F	VF	XF	Unc	BU
1980	5,000	—	—	—	3.00	5.00

KM# 38 TALA

Copper-Nickel, 38.8 mm. **Series:** F.A.O. **Obv:** National arms **Rev:** Coconut palm and value **Rev. Designer:** James Berry

Date	Mintage	F	VF	XF	Unc	BU
1980	10,000	—	—	—	2.50	4.00

KM# 40 TALA

Copper-Nickel, 38.8 mm. **Subject:** Gov. Wilhelm Solf **Obv:** National arms **Rev:** Armored bust left flanked by palm trees **Rev. Designer:** E.W. Roberts

Date	Mintage	F	VF	XF	Unc	BU
1980	5,000	—	—	—	3.00	5.00

KM# 43 TALA

Copper-Nickel, 38.8 mm. **Subject:** Wedding of Prince Charles and Lady Diana **Obv:** National arms **Rev:** Conjoined heads left

Date	Mintage	F	VF	XF	Unc	BU
1981	12,000	—	—	—	2.50	3.00

KM# 47 TALA

Copper-Nickel, 38.8 mm. **Subject:** IYDP - President Franklin Roosevelt **Obv:** National arms **Rev:** Seated figure in wheelchair facing

Date	Mintage	F	VF	XF	Unc	BU
1981	8,000	—	—	—	2.50	3.00

KM# 50 TALA

Copper-Nickel, 38.8 mm. **Subject:** Commonwealth Games **Obv:** National arms **Rev:** Javelin thrower **Rev. Designer:** E.W. Roberts

Date	Mintage	F	VF	XF	Unc	BU
1982	6,000	—	—	—	3.00	4.00

KM# 53 TALA

Copper-Nickel, 38.8 mm. **Subject:** South Pacific Games **Obv:** National arms **Rev:** Runner **Rev. Designer:** E.W. Roberts

Date	Mintage	F	VF	XF	Unc	BU
1983	8,000	—	—	—	3.00	4.00

KM# 57 TALA

9.5000 g., Aluminum-Bronze, 30.6 mm. **Subject:** Circulation coinage **Obv:** Head left **Rev:** National arms **Shape:** 7-sided

Date	Mintage	F	VF	XF	Unc	BU
1984	1,000,000	—	0.50	0.75	1.00	1.50

KM# 57a TALA

27.2200 g., Copper-Nickel, 30 mm. **Obv:** Head left **Rev:** National arms **Edge:** Plain **Shape:** 7-sided

Date	Mintage	F	VF	XF	Unc	BU
1984	5,000	—	—	—	5.00	6.50

KM# 58 TALA

Copper-Nickel, 38.8 mm. **Series:** Summer Olympics **Obv:** National arms **Rev:** Boxing match **Rev. Designer:** E.W. Roberts

Date	Mintage	F	VF	XF	Unc	BU
1984	8,000	—	—	—	3.50	5.00

KM# 63 TALA

Copper-Nickel, 38.8 mm. **Subject:** Prince Andrew and Sarah Ferguson's Marriage **Obv:** National arms **Rev:** Conjoined busts **Rev. Designer:** Philip Nathan

Date	Mintage	F	VF	XF	Unc	BU
1986	10,000	—	—	—	2.50	4.00

KM# 74 TALA

Copper-Nickel, 38.8 mm. **Subject:** 25th Anniversary of World Wildlife Fund **Obv:** National arms **Rev:** Samoan Fantail bird

Date	Mintage	F	VF	XF	Unc	BU
1986	—	—	—	—	7.00	9.00

KM# 88 TALA

Copper-Nickel, 38.8 mm. **Subject:** 40th Anniversary - Reign of Queen Elizabeth II **Obv:** National arms **Rev:** Cross in center circle, equestrians and chariot around border **Rev. Designer:** Willem Vis

Date	Mintage	F	VF	XF	Unc	BU
ND(1992)	—	—	—	—	3.00	4.50

KM# 111 TALA

Copper-Nickel, 38.8 mm. **Subject:** Queen Mother **Obv:** National arms **Rev:** Glamis Castle within beaded circle

Date	Mintage	F	VF	XF	Unc	BU
1995	Est. 30,000	—	—	—	3.00	4.50

KM# 112 TALA

10.0000 g., 0.5000 Silver .1607 oz. ASW **Series:** Olympics **Obv:** National arms **Rev:** Gymnast and pommel horse

Date	Mintage	F	VF	XF	Unc	BU
1996	Est. 10,000	—	—	—	7.50	10.00

KM# 120 2 TALA

42.4139 g., 0.9250 Silver 1.3636 oz. ASW **Obv:** National arms **Rev:** Value and three scenes **Note:** Part of a tri-national, three-coin matching set with Cook Islands and Fiji.

Date	Mintage	F	VF	XF	Unc	BU
1998 Proof	Est. 20,000	Value: 35.00				

KM# 125 5 TALA

19.8300 g., Copper Nickel, 38.7 mm. **Subject:** Robert Louis Stevenson **Obv:** National arms **Rev:** Ship, portrait and pirate scene **Edge:** Reeded

Date	Mintage	F	VF	XF	Unc	BU
ND(1994)	100,000	—	—	—	5.00	6.50

KM# 115 5 TALA

15.5518 g., 0.9250 Silver .4625 oz. ASW **Subject:** War and peace **Obv:** National arms **Rev:** Arrows and sword **Note:** 1/2 of 2-part coin, combined with Kiribati KM#22, issued in sets only. Value is determined by combining the 2 parts.

Date	Mintage	F	VF	XF	Unc	BU
ND(1997) Proof	Est. 10,000	Value: 22.50				

KM# 116 5 TALA

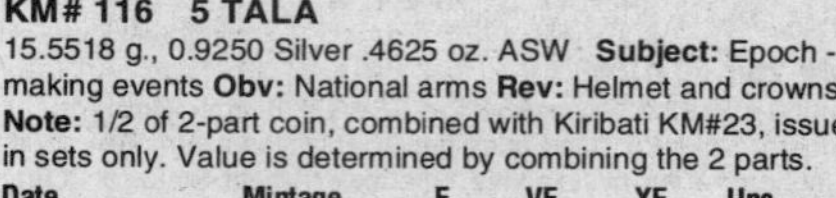

15.5518 g., 0.9250 Silver .4625 oz. ASW **Subject:** Epoch - making events **Obv:** National arms **Rev:** Helmet and crowns **Note:** 1/2 of 2-part coin, combined with Kiribati KM#23, issued in sets only. Value is determined by combining the 2 parts.

Date	Mintage	F	VF	XF	Unc	BU
ND(1997) Proof	Est. 10,000	Value: 22.50				

KM# 117 5 TALA
15.5518 g., 0.9250 Silver .4625 oz. ASW **Subject:** Tempora mutantur **Obv:** National arms **Rev:** Man with torch **Note:** 1/2 of 2-part coin, combined with Kiribati KM#24, issued in sets only. Value is determined by combining the 2 parts.

Date	Mintage	F	VF	XF	Unc	BU
ND(1997) Proof	Est. 10,000	Value: 22.50				

KM# 118 5 TALA
15.5518 g., 0.9250 Silver .4625 oz. ASW **Subject:** People and buildings **Obv:** National arms **Rev:** Working hands **Note:** 1/2 of 2-part coin, combined with Kiribati KM#25, issued in sets only. Value is determined by combining the 2 parts.

Date	Mintage	F	VF	XF	Unc	BU
ND(1997) Proof	Est. 10,000	Value: 22.50				

KM# 138 5 TALA
14.8000 g., 0.9250 Silver 0.4401 oz. ASW, 24.5 mm. **Subject:** Epoch Making Events **Obv:** National arms **Rev:** Topless Marianne and Guru **Edge:** Pain **Shape:** Irregular

Date	Mintage	F	VF	XF	Unc	BU
ND (1998) Proof	—	Value: 22.50				

KM# 33 10 TALA
31.3300 g., 0.5000 Silver .5036 oz. ASW **Subject:** Bicentenary - Death of Capt. James Cook **Obv:** National arms **Rev:** Head right and ship **Rev. Designer:** James Berry

Date	Mintage	F	VF	XF	Unc	BU
1979	3,000	—	—	—	8.50	10.00

KM# 33a 10 TALA
31.4700 g., 0.9250 Silver .9359 oz. ASW **Subject:** Bicentenary - Death of Capt. James Cook **Obv:** National arms **Rev:** Head right and ship **Rev. Designer:** James Berry

Date	Mintage	F	VF	XF	Unc	BU
1979 Proof	5,000	Value: 14.50				

KM# 36 10 TALA
31.3300 g., 0.5000 Silver .5036 oz. ASW **Series:** 1980 Olympics **Obv:** National arms **Rev:** Hurdles event **Rev. Designer:** E.W. Roberts

Date	Mintage	F	VF	XF	Unc	BU
1980	3,000	—	—	—	8.50	10.00

KM# 36a 10 TALA
31.4700 g., 0.9250 Silver .9359 oz. ASW **Series:** 1980 Olympics **Obv:** National arms **Rev:** Hurdles event **Rev. Designer:** E.W. Roberts

Date	Mintage	F	VF	XF	Unc	BU
1980 Proof	4,000	Value: 14.50				

KM# 39 10 TALA
31.3300 g., 0.5000 Silver .5036 oz. ASW, 38.8 mm. **Series:** F.A.O. **Obv:** National arms **Rev:** Palm tree with coconuts **Rev. Designer:** James Berry

Date	Mintage	F	VF	XF	Unc	BU
1980 Proof	3,000	Value: 14.50				

KM# 41 10 TALA
31.3300 g., 0.5000 Silver .5036 oz. ASW **Subject:** Gov. Wilhelm Solf **Obv:** National arms **Rev:** Uniformed bust left flanked by palm trees

Date	Mintage	F	VF	XF	Unc	BU
1980	3,000	—	—	—	8.50	10.00

KM# 41a 10 TALA
31.4700 g., 0.9250 Silver .9359 oz. ASW **Subject:** Gov. Wilhelm Solf **Obv:** National arms **Rev:** Uniformed bust left flanked by palm trees

Date	Mintage	F	VF	XF	Unc	BU
1980 Proof	4,000	Value: 14.50				

KM# 44 10 TALA
31.4700 g., 0.9250 Silver .9359 oz. ASW **Subject:** Wedding of Prince Charles and Lady Diana **Obv:** National arms **Rev:** Conjoined busts left **Rev. Designer:** E.W. Roberts

Date	Mintage	F	VF	XF	Unc	BU
1981 Proof	5,000	Value: 14.50				

KM# 48 10 TALA
31.4700 g., 0.9250 Silver .9359 oz. ASW **Subject:** IYDP - President Franklin Roosevelt **Obv:** National arms **Rev:** Seated figure in wheelchair facing

Date	Mintage	F	VF	XF	Unc	BU
1981 Proof	5,000	Value: 14.50				

KM# 51 10 TALA
31.4700 g., 0.9250 Silver .9359 oz. ASW **Subject:** Commonwealth Games **Obv:** National arms **Rev:** Javelin thrower **Rev. Designer:** E.W. Roberts

Date	Mintage	F	VF	XF	Unc	BU
1982 Proof	4,000	Value: 14.50				

KM# 54 10 TALA
31.4700 g., 0.9250 Silver .9359 oz. ASW **Subject:** South Pacific Games **Obv:** National arms **Rev:** Runner **Rev. Designer:** E.W. Roberts

Date	Mintage	F	VF	XF	Unc	BU
1983 Proof	3,000	Value: 14.50				

KM# 59 10 TALA
31.4700 g., 0.9250 Silver .9359 oz. ASW **Series:** Summer Olympics **Obv:** National arms **Rev:** Boxing match **Rev. Designer:** E.W. Roberts

Date	Mintage	F	VF	XF	Unc	BU
1984 Proof	3,000	Value: 22.50				

KM# 64 10 TALA
31.4700 g., 0.9250 Silver .9359 oz. ASW **Subject:** Prince Andrew and Sara Ferguson's Marriage **Obv:** National arms **Rev:** Conjoined busts left **Note:** Similar to Tala, KM#63.

Date	Mintage	F	VF	XF	Unc	BU
1986 Proof	2,500	Value: 14.50				

KM# 72 10 TALA
31.4700 g., 0.9250 Silver .9360 oz. ASW **Subject:** 25th Anniversary of World Wildlife Fund **Obv:** National arms **Rev:** Samoan Fantail bird

Date	Mintage	F	VF	XF	Unc	BU
1986 Proof	25,000	Value: 20.00				

KM# 66 10 TALA
31.1000 g., 0.9990 Silver 1 oz. ASW **Subject:** America's Cup Race - 1987 Perth **Obv:** The Cup **Rev:** Sailing scene

Date	Mintage	F	VF	XF	Unc	BU
1987 Proof	50,000	Value: 16.50				

KM# 70 10 TALA
31.1000 g., 0.9990 Silver 1 oz. ASW **Series:** 1988 Olympics **Obv:** National arms **Rev:** Three torches and athletes

Date	Mintage	F	VF	XF	Unc	BU
1988	20,000	—	—	—	16.50	18.50

KM# 75 10 TALA
31.1030 g., 0.9990 Silver 1 oz. ASW **Obv:** National arms **Rev:** Kon-Tiki raft and map

Date	Mintage	F	VF	XF	Unc	BU
1988 Proof	Est. 16,500	Value: 16.50				

KM# 79 10 TALA
31.4700 g., 0.9250 Silver .9360 oz. ASW **Series:** Save the Children Fund **Obv:** National arms **Rev:** Two children flanked by palms leaves

Date	Mintage	F	VF	XF	Unc	BU
1990 Proof	Est. 20,000	Value: 15.00				

KM# 82 10 TALA
31.4700 g., 0.9250 Silver .9360 oz. ASW **Series:** Summer Olympics **Obv:** National arms **Rev:** Shot putter

Date	Mintage	F	VF	XF	Unc	BU
1991 Proof	Est. 70,000	Value: 14.50				

KM# 83 10 TALA
31.1030 g., 0.9250 Silver .9250 oz. ASW **Subject:** RA expeditions **Obv:** National arms **Rev:** Map within circle to right of ship

Date	Mintage	F	VF	XF	Unc	BU
1991 Proof	15,000	Value: 17.50				

KM# 85 10 TALA
31.4700 g., 0.9250 Silver .9360 oz. ASW **Series:** Olympics **Obv:** National arms **Rev:** Javelin thrower

Date	Mintage	F	VF	XF	Unc	BU
1991 Proof	Est. 70,000	Value: 14.50				

KM# 86 10 TALA
31.4700 g., 0.9250 Silver .9360 oz. ASW **Series:** Olympics **Obv:** National arms **Rev:** Hammer thrower

Date	Mintage	F	VF	XF	Unc	BU
1992 Proof	Est. 70,000	Value: 14.50				

KM# 89 10 TALA
31.8600 g., 0.9250 Silver .9476 oz. ASW **Subject:** World Cup Soccer **Obv:** National arms **Rev:** Arena behind player's legs kicking ball

Date	Mintage	F	VF	XF	Unc	BU
1992 Proof	Est. 20,000	Value: 16.00				

KM# 93 10 TALA
31.4700 g., 0.9250 Silver .9359 oz. ASW **Subject:** Jakob Roggeveen **Obv:** National arms

Date	Mintage	F	VF	XF	Unc	BU
1992 Proof	15,000	Value: 14.50				

KM# 98 10 TALA
31.3500 g., 0.9250 Silver .9323 oz. ASW **Series:** Endangered Wildlife **Obv:** National arms **Rev:** Pair of birds

Date	Mintage	F	VF	XF	Unc	BU
1992 Proof	Est. 20,000	Value: 27.50				

KM# 99 10 TALA
31.7700 g., 0.9250 Silver .9448 oz. ASW **Obv:** National arms **Rev:** Roggeveen's fleet

Date	Mintage	F	VF	XF	Unc	BU
1992 Proof	Est. 15,000	Value: 15.00				

KM# 109 10 TALA
31.4700 g., 0.9250 Silver .9359 oz. ASW **Subject:** 40th Anniversary - Reign of Queen Elizabeth II **Obv:** National arms **Rev:** Royal carriage and guard around Order of the Garter

Date	Mintage	F	VF	XF	Unc	BU
1992 Proof	Est. 5,000	Value: 22.50				

KM# 97 10 TALA
31.8100 g., 0.9250 Silver .9461 oz. ASW **Series:** 1996 Olympics **Obv:** National arms **Rev:** Gymnast on pommel horse

Date	Mintage	F	VF	XF	Unc	BU
1993 Proof	50,000	Value: 14.50				

KM# 91 10 TALA
31.8100 g., 0.9250 Silver .9461 oz. ASW **Series:** Olympics **Obv:** National arms **Rev:** Diver

Date	Mintage	F	VF	XF	Unc	BU
1994 Proof	Est. 50,000	Value: 14.50				

KM# 121 10 TALA
31.2300 g., 0.9250 Silver 0.9288 oz. ASW, 38.6 mm. **Obv:** National arms **Rev:** Seated Robert Louis Stephenson **Edge:** Reeded

Date	Mintage	F	VF	XF	Unc	BU
1994 Proof	10,000	Value: 30.00				

KM# 94 10 TALA
31.1035 g., 0.9250 Silver 1 oz. ASW **Subject:** Tigris Expedition **Obv:** National arms **Rev:** Pyramid behind boat

Date	Mintage	F	VF	XF	Unc	BU
1994 Proof	10,000	Value: 25.00				

KM# 95 10 TALA
31.1035 g., 0.9250 Silver 1 oz. ASW **Subject:** Tigris Expedition **Obv:** National arms **Rev:** Burning Tigris

Date	Mintage	F	VF	XF	Unc	BU
1994 Proof	10,000	Value: 25.00				

KM# 100 10 TALA
31.7700 g., 0.9250 Silver .9448 oz. ASW **Obv:** National arms **Rev:** Two figures sighting land

Date	Mintage	F	VF	XF	Unc	BU
1994 Proof	10,000	Value: 16.50				

KM# 101 10 TALA
31.2300 g., 0.9250 Silver .9288 oz. ASW **Series:** Endangered Wildlife **Obv:** National arms **Rev:** Flying bat

Date	Mintage	F	VF	XF	Unc	BU
1994 Proof	Est. 20,000	Value: 27.50				

KM# 102 10 TALA
31.4700 g., 0.9250 Silver .9359 oz. ASW **Subject:** Comte de la Perouse **Obv:** National arms **Rev:** World globe on stand flanked by figures, ship and date above

Date	Mintage	F	VF	XF	Unc	BU
1994 Proof	Est. 20,000	Value: 16.50				

KM# 103 10 TALA
31.4700 g., 0.9250 Silver .9359 oz. ASW **Subject:** Protect Our World **Obv:** National arms **Rev:** Flowers

Date	Mintage	F	VF	XF	Unc	BU
1994 Proof	Est. 10,000	Value: 18.50				

KM# 104 10 TALA
31.4700 g., 0.9250 Silver .9359 oz. ASW **Subject:** Queen Mother **Obv:** National arms **Rev:** Glamis Castle within beaded circle

Date	Mintage	F	VF	XF	Unc	BU
1994 Proof	Est. 30,000	Value: 17.50				

KM# 105 10 TALA
31.4700 g., 0.9250 Silver .9359 oz. ASW **Subject:** Edmond Halley **Obv:** National arms **Rev:** Bust 1/4 right

Date	Mintage	F	VF	XF	Unc	BU
1995 Proof	10,000	Value: 18.50				

KM# 124 10 TALA
31.6200 g., 0.9250 Silver 0.9404 oz. ASW, 38.5 mm. **Subject:** Queen Elizabeth - Queen Mother **Obv:** National arms **Rev:** Young Lady sitting on horse **Edge:** Reeded

Date	Mintage	F	VF	XF	Unc	BU
1995 Proof	—	Value: 25.00				

KM# 113 10 TALA
1.2442 g., 0.9999 Gold .04 oz. AGW **Series:** Olympics **Obv:** National arms **Rev:** Discus thrower

Date	Mintage	F	VF	XF	Unc	BU
1995	Est. 25,000	—	—	—	45.00	—

KM# 114 10 TALA
31.7000 g., 0.9250 Silver .9427 oz. ASW **Subject:** Jakob le Maire **Obv:** National arms **Rev:** Sailing ship

Date	Mintage	F	VF	XF	Unc	BU
1996 Proof	—	Value: 20.00				

KM# 127 10 TALA
31.8000 g., 0.9250 Silver 0.9457 oz. ASW, 38.6 mm. **Subject:** Victorian Age **Obv:** National arms **Rev:** Queen Victoria and family within circle **Edge:** Reeded

Date	Mintage	F	VF	XF	Unc	BU
1996 Proof	—	Value: 30.00				

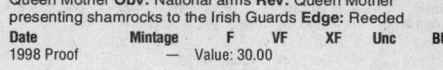

KM# 128 10 TALA
31.8000 g., 0.9250 Silver 0.9457 oz. ASW, 38.6 mm. **Subject:** Queen Mother **Obv:** National arms **Rev:** Queen Mother presenting shamrocks to the Irish Guards **Edge:** Reeded

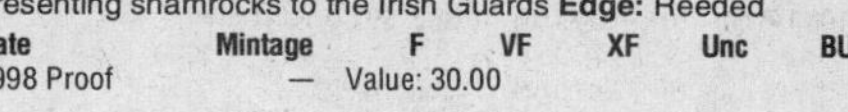

Date	Mintage	F	VF	XF	Unc	BU
1998 Proof	—	Value: 30.00				

KM# 123 10 TALA
31.5000 g., 0.9250 Silver .9368 oz. ASW, 38.6 mm. **Subject:** Princess Diana **Obv:** National arms **Rev:** Diana holding child **Edge:** Reeded

Date	Mintage	F	VF	XF	Unc	BU
1998 Proof	—	Value: 17.50				

KM# 129 10 TALA
31.4200 g., 0.9250 Silver 0.9344 oz. ASW, 38.6 mm. **Subject:** Olympics **Obv:** National arms **Rev:** Two volleyball players **Edge:** Reeded

Date	Mintage	F	VF	XF	Unc	BU
2000 Proof	—	Value: 35.00				

KM# 62 25 TALA
155.5000 g., 0.9990 Silver 5 oz. ASW, 65 mm. **Subject:** Kon-Tiki **Obv:** National arms **Rev:** Sailing ship **Note:** Photo reduced.

Date	Mintage	F	VF	XF	Unc	BU
1986 Proof	25,000	Value: 85.00				

KM# 67 25 TALA
155.5000 g., 0.9990 Silver 5 oz. ASW, 65 mm. **Subject:** America's Cup Race **Obv:** National arms **Rev:** Sailing ship **Note:** Photo reduced.

Date	Mintage	F	VF	XF	Unc	BU
1987 Proof	35,000	Value: 85.00				

KM# 76 50 TALA
31.1030 g., 0.9990 Palladium 1 oz. **Subject:** Kon-Tiki **Obv:** National arms **Rev:** Raft and bamboo poles

Date	Mintage	F	VF	XF	Unc	BU
1988 Proof	6,500	Value: 450				

KM# 78 50 TALA
7.7700 g., 0.9990 Gold .25 oz. AGW **Subject:** Trans-Antarctica Expedition **Obv:** Sled dogs and musher and single dog head facing left **Rev:** Six doves above snake on rock, value at upper left

Date	Mintage	F	VF	XF	Unc	BU
1988 Proof	30,000	Value: 175				

KM# 90 50 TALA
7.7760 g., 0.5833 Gold .1458 oz. AGW **Series:** 1996 Olympics **Obv:** National arms **Rev:** Discus thrower

Date	Mintage	F	VF	XF	Unc	BU
1993 Proof	7,500	Value: 115				

KM# 92 50 TALA
7.7760 g., 0.5833 Gold .1458 oz. AGW **Subject:** World Cup Soccer **Obv:** National arms **Rev:** Soccer players

Date	Mintage	F	VF	XF	Unc	BU
1993 Proof	Est. 3,000	Value: 115				

KM# 106 50 TALA
7.7760 g., 0.5833 Gold .1458 oz. AGW **Obv:** National arms **Rev:** Portrait

Date	Mintage	F	VF	XF	Unc	BU
1993 Proof	Est. 3,000	Value: 115				

KM# 107 50 TALA
7.7760 g., 0.5833 Gold .1458 oz. AGW **Subject:** The Endeavor **Obv:** National arms **Rev:** Sailing ship within radiant sun

Date	Mintage	F	VF	XF	Unc	BU
1994 Proof	Est. 2,500	Value: 115				

KM# 108 50 TALA
7.7760 g., 0.5833 Gold .1458 oz. AGW **Series:** Endangered Wildlife **Obv:** National arms **Rev:** Dolphins

Date	Mintage	F	VF	XF	Unc	BU
1995 Proof	Est. 2,500	Value: 125				

KM# 119 50 TALA
3.8875 g., 0.9990 Gold .25 oz. AGW **Subject:** Tempora Mutantur **Obv:** National arms **Rev:** Man with torch **Note:** 1/2 of 2-part coin, combined with Kiribati KM#26, issued in sets only; Value is determined by combining the 2 parts.

Date	Mintage	F	VF	XF	Unc	BU
ND(1997) Proof	Est. 2,500	Value: 175				

KM# 21 100 TALA
15.5500 g., 0.9170 Gold .4583 oz. AGW **Subject:** U.S. Bicentennial **Obv:** National arms **Rev:** Equestrian and USA map **Rev. Designer:** James Berry

Date	Mintage	F	VF	XF	Unc	BU
1976 Proof	2,000	Value: 320				

KM# 23 100 TALA
15.5500 g., 0.9170 Gold .4583 oz. AGW **Series:** Montreal Olympics **Obv:** National arms **Rev:** Weight lifter

Date	Mintage	F	VF	XF	Unc	BU
1976 Proof	2,500	Value: 320				

KM# 25 100 TALA
15.5500 g., 0.9170 Gold .4583 oz. AGW **Subject:** Queen's Silver Jubilee **Rev. Designer:** James Berry

Date	Mintage	F	VF	XF	Unc	BU
1977 Proof	2,500	Value: 320				

KM# 27 100 TALA
15.5500 g., 0.9170 Gold .4583 oz. AGW **Subject:** Lindbergh's New York to Paris flight **Obv:** National arms **Rev:** Bust 1/4 right, plane, statue of Liberty, Eiffel tower and dates

Date	Mintage	F	VF	XF	Unc	BU
1977 Proof	660	Value: 335				

KM# 29 100 TALA
15.5500 g., 0.9170 Gold .4583 oz. AGW **Subject:** 50th Anniversary - Transpacific Flight **Obv:** National arms **Rev:** Globe with plane flying across Pacific Ocean, portrait of Lindbergh facing left

Date	Mintage	F	VF	XF	Unc	BU
1978 Proof	1,500	Value: 325				

KM# 31 100 TALA
15.5500 g., 0.9170 Gold .4583 oz. AGW **Subject:** XI Commonwealth Games **Obv:** National arms **Rev:** Runners

Date	Mintage	F	VF	XF	Unc	BU
1978 Proof	1,000	Value: 325				

KM# 34 100 TALA
12.5000 g., 0.9170 Gold .3686 oz. AGW **Subject:** Bicentenary - death of Capt. James Cook **Obv:** National arms **Rev:** Portrait of Cook at left of sailing ship

Date	Mintage	F	VF	XF	Unc	BU
1979 Proof	1,000	Value: 255				

KM# 37 100 TALA
7.5000 g., 0.9170 Gold .2211 oz. AGW **Series:** 1980 Olympics **Obv:** National arms **Rev:** Hurdles event **Rev. Designer:** E.W. Roberts

Date	Mintage	F	VF	XF	Unc	BU
1980	250	—	—	—	175	—
1980 Proof	1,000	Value: 155				

KM# 42 100 TALA
7.5000 g., 0.9170 Gold .2211 oz. AGW **Subject:** Gov. Wilhelm Solf **Obv:** National arms **Rev:** Uniformed bust left flanked by huts and palm trees

Date	Mintage	F	VF	XF	Unc	BU
1980	250	—	—	—	165	—
1980 Proof	1,000	Value: 155				

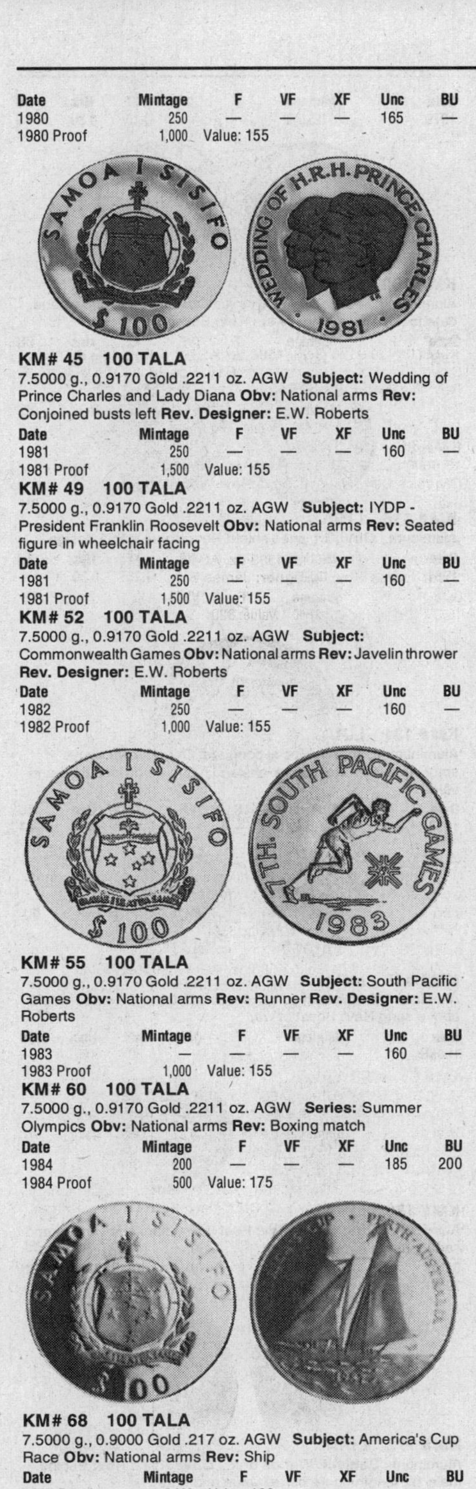

KM# 45 100 TALA
7.5000 g., 0.9170 Gold .2211 oz. AGW **Subject:** Wedding of Prince Charles and Lady Diana **Obv:** National arms **Rev:** Conjoined busts left **Rev. Designer:** E.W. Roberts

Date	Mintage	F	VF	XF	Unc	BU
1981	250	—	—	—	160	—
1981 Proof	1,500	Value: 155				

KM# 49 100 TALA
7.5000 g., 0.9170 Gold .2211 oz. AGW **Subject:** IYDP - President Franklin Roosevelt **Obv:** National arms **Rev:** Seated figure in wheelchair facing

Date	Mintage	F	VF	XF	Unc	BU
1981	250	—	—	—	160	—
1981 Proof	1,500	Value: 155				

KM# 52 100 TALA
7.5000 g., 0.9170 Gold .2211 oz. AGW **Subject:** Commonwealth Games **Obv:** National arms **Rev:** Javelin thrower **Rev. Designer:** E.W. Roberts

Date	Mintage	F	VF	XF	Unc	BU
1982	250	—	—	—	160	—
1982 Proof	1,000	Value: 155				

KM# 55 100 TALA
7.5000 g., 0.9170 Gold .2211 oz. AGW **Subject:** South Pacific Games **Obv:** National arms **Rev:** Runner **Rev. Designer:** E.W. Roberts

Date	Mintage	F	VF	XF	Unc	BU
1983	—	—	—	—	160	—
1983 Proof	1,000	Value: 155				

KM# 60 100 TALA
7.5000 g., 0.9170 Gold .2211 oz. AGW **Series:** Summer Olympics **Obv:** National arms **Rev:** Boxing match

Date	Mintage	F	VF	XF	Unc	BU
1984	200	—	—	—	185	200
1984 Proof	500	Value: 175				

KM# 68 100 TALA
7.5000 g., 0.9000 Gold .217 oz. AGW **Subject:** America's Cup Race **Obv:** National arms **Rev:** Ship

Date	Mintage	F	VF	XF	Unc	BU
1987 Proof	5,000	Value: 160				

KM# 77 100 TALA
7.5000 g., 0.9000 Gold .217 oz. AGW **Subject:** Kon-Tiki **Obv:** National arms **Rev:** Boat and inscription

Date	Mintage	F	VF	XF	Unc	BU
1988 Proof	1,500	Value: 165				

KM# 81 100 TALA
7.5000 g., 0.9170 Gold .2211 oz. AGW **Series:** Save the Children **Obv:** National arms **Rev:** Children playing

Date	Mintage	F	VF	XF	Unc	BU
1990 Proof	3,000	Value: 155				

KM# 84 100 TALA
7.5000 g., 0.9170 Gold .2211 oz. AGW **Subject:** RA expeditions **Obv:** National arms **Rev:** Ship (RA II)

Date	Mintage	F	VF	XF	Unc	BU
1991 Proof	5,000	Value: 155				

KM# 87 100 TALA
7.5000 g., 0.9000 Gold .217 oz. AGW **Series:** Olympics **Obv:** National arms **Rev:** Torch runner

Date	Mintage	F	VF	XF	Unc	BU
1991 Proof	6,000	Value: 150				

KM# 96 100 TALA
7.5000 g., 0.9170 Gold .2211 oz. AGW **Subject:** Tigris Expedition **Obv:** National arms **Rev:** Tigris sailing

Date	Mintage	F	VF	XF	Unc	BU
1994 Proof	2,000	Value: 185				

KM# 126 100 TALA
7.5000 g., 0.9160 Gold 0.2209 oz. AGW, 28.5 mm. **Subject:** Robert Louis Stevenson **Obv:** National arms **Rev:** Ship and portrait **Edge:** Reeded

Date	Mintage	F	VF	XF	Unc	BU
ND(1994) Proof	2,000	Value: 165				

KM# 130 200 TALA
14.7000 g., 0.9990 Gold 0.3561 oz. AGW, 38.7x22.85 mm. **Subject:** People and Buildings **Obv:** National arms, value and dates **Rev:** Statue of Liberty **Edge:** Plain **Shape:** Coin halved, with jagged inside edge

Date	Mintage	F	VF	XF	Unc	BU
1999-2000 Proof	—	Value: 250				

KM# 136 500 TALA
69.8200 g., 0.9990 Gold 2.2425 oz. AGW, 36.4 mm. **Obv:** National arms **Rev:** Dove and sword handle above two soldiers **Edge:** Plain **Note:** Jagged coin half matching with Kiribati KM-36

Date	Mintage	F	VF	XF	Unc	BU
2000 Proof	99	Value: 1,600				

KM# 46 1000 TALA
33.9500 g., 0.9170 Gold 1.001 oz. AGW **Subject:** Wedding of Prince Charles and Lady Diana **Obv:** National arms **Rev:** Conjoined busts left

Date	Mintage	F	VF	XF	Unc	BU
1981 Proof	100	Value: 700				

KM# 56 1000 TALA
31.1000 g., 0.9170 Gold .917 oz. AGW **Subject:** South Pacific Games **Obv:** National arms **Rev:** Runner

Date	Mintage	F	VF	XF	Unc	BU
1983 Proof	100	Value: 645				

KM# 61 1000 TALA
31.1000 g., 0.9170 Gold .917 oz. AGW **Series:** 1984 Olympics **Obv:** National arms **Rev:** Boxing match **Rev. Designer:** E.W. Roberts

Date	Mintage	F	VF	XF	Unc	BU
1984 Proof	100	Value: 635				

KM# 65 1000 TALA
33.9500 g., 0.9170 Gold 1.001 oz. AGW **Subject:** Prince Andrew and Sarah Fereguson's Marriage **Obv:** National arms **Rev:** Conjoined busts left

Date	Mintage	F	VF	XF	Unc	BU
1986 Proof	50	Value: 750				

KM# 110 1000 TALA
33.9500 g., 0.9170 Gold 1.001 oz. AGW **Subject:** 40th Anniversary - Reign of Queen Elizabeth II **Obv:** National arms **Rev:** Royal carriage and guard around Order of the Garter

Date	Mintage	F	VF	XF	Unc	BU
1992 Proof	Est. 150	Value: 685				

PIEFORTS

KM#	Date	Mintage	Identification	Mkt Val
P1	1984	3,000	Tala. 0.9250 Silver. KM57.	22.00
P2	1992	—	Tala. 0.9250 Silver. KM109.	50.00

COMBINED PROOF SETS (CPS)

KM#	Date	Mintage	Identification	Issue Price	Mkt Val
CPS1	1997 (8)	10,000	West Samoa KM#115-118, Kiribati KM#22-25	—	240

MINT SETS

KM#	Date	Mintage	Identification	Issue Price	Mkt Val
MS1	1967 (6)	—	KM1-6	—	2.50
MS2	1974 (7)	10,740	KM12-17, 19	5.30	5.00

PROOF SETS

KM#	Date	Mintage	Identification	Issue Price	Mkt Val
PS1	1967 (7)	15,000	KM1-7	10.00	7.00
PS2	1974 (7)	5,578	KM12a-17a, 19a	53.00	30.00
PS3	1988 (3)	—	KM75-77	—	910
PS4	1991 (2)	1,000	KM83-84	—	160
PS5	1994 (3)	500	KM94-96	—	345

SAN MARINO

The Republic of San Marino, the oldest and smallest republic in the world is located in north central Italy entirely surrounded by the Province of Emilia-Romagna. It has an area of 24 sq. mi. (60 sq. km.) and a population of *23,000. Capital: San Marino. The principal economic activities are farming, livestock raising, cheese making, tourism and light manufacturing. Building stone, lime, wheat, hides and baked goods are exported. The government derives most of its revenue from the sale of postage stamps for philatelic purposes.

According to tradition, San Marino was founded about 350AD by a Christian stonecutter as a refuge against religious persecution. While gradually acquiring the institutions of an independent state, it avoided the factional fights of the Middle Ages and, except for a brief period in fief to Cesare Borgia, retained its freedom despite attacks on its sovereignty by the Papacy, the Lords of Rimini, Napoleon and Mussolini. In 1862 San Marino established a customs union with, and put itself under the protection of, Italy. A Communist-Socialist coalition controlled the Government for 12 years after World War II. The Christian Democratic Party has been the core of government since 1957. In 1978 a Communist-Socialist coalition again came into power and remained in control until 1991.

San Marino has its own coinage, but Italian and Vatican City coins and currency are also in circulation.

MINT MARKS

M - Milan
R – Rome

MONETARY SYSTEM

100 Centesimi = 1 Lira

REPUBLIC

STANDARD COINAGE

KM# 12 5 CENTESIMI
Bronze **Obv:** Crowned pointed arms within wreath **Rev:** Value and date

Date	Mintage	F	VF	XF	Unc	BU
1935R	800,000	1.25	2.00	12.00	32.00	—
1936R	400,000	1.25	2.00	12.00	32.00	—
1937R	200,000	2.00	6.00	19.00	38.00	—
1938R	200,000	2.00	6.00	19.00	38.00	—

KM# 13 10 CENTESIMI
Bronze **Obv:** Crowned pointed arms within wreath **Rev:** Value and date

Date	Mintage	F	VF	XF	Unc	BU
1935R	600,000	2.00	6.00	15.00	30.00	—
1936R	300,000	2.00	6.00	15.00	30.00	—
1937R	400,000	2.00	6.00	15.00	30.00	—
1938R	400,000	2.00	6.00	15.00	30.00	—

KM# 4 LIRA
5.0000 g., 0.8350 Silver .1342 oz. ASW **Obv:** Crowned arms within wreath **Obv. Legend:** RESPVBLICA S. MARINI **Rev:** Value, date within wreath

Date	Mintage	F	VF	XF	Unc	BU
1906R	30,000	15.00	22.50	40.00	228	—

KM# 14 LIRA
Aluminum **Obv:** Bust of Saint 1/4 left **Rev:** Value above arms without shield **Designer:** Monassi

Date	Mintage	F	VF	XF	Unc	BU
1972	291,000	—	—	0.10	0.20	—

KM# 22 LIRA
Aluminum **Obv:** Crowned shield **Rev:** Girl with national flag **Designer:** Guido Veroi

Date	Mintage	F	VF	XF	Unc	BU
1973	291,000	—	—	0.10	0.20	—

KM# 30 LIRA
Aluminum **Obv:** Smoking towers within circle **Rev:** Insect **Designer:** Luciano Minguzzi

Date	Mintage	F	VF	XF	Unc	BU
1974	276,000	—	—	0.25	1.25	1.50

KM# 40 LIRA
Aluminum **Obv:** Smoking towers within circle **Rev:** Spiders in web **Designer:** Bino Bini

Date	Mintage	F	VF	XF	Unc	BU
1975	291,000	—	—	0.25	1.25	1.50

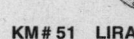

KM# 51 LIRA
Aluminum **Obv:** Smoking towers **Rev:** Crossed flags flanked by hands **Designer:** Mario Molteni

Date	Mintage	F	VF	XF	Unc	BU
1976	195,000	—	—	0.10	0.20	—

KM# 63 LIRA
Aluminum **Series:** F.A.O. **Obv:** Smoking towers within circle **Rev:** Globe in center of star wreath **Designer:** J. Vivarelli

Date	Mintage	F	VF	XF	Unc	BU
1977	1,180,000	—	—	0.10	0.20	—

KM# 76 LIRA
Aluminum **Obv:** Value below smoking towers **Rev:** Sitting figure within spider web

Date	Mintage	F	VF	XF	Unc	BU
1978	130,000	—	—	0.15	0.30	—

KM# 89 LIRA
Aluminum **Obv:** Crowned shield **Rev:** Sword handle divides value

Date	Mintage	F	VF	XF	Unc	BU
1979	125,000	—	—	0.15	0.30	—

KM# 102 LIRA
Aluminum **Series:** 1980 Olympics **Obv:** Olympic circles and date to left of smoking towers **Rev:** Ballerina

Date	Mintage	F	VF	XF	Unc	BU
1980	125,000	—	—	0.15	0.30	—

KM# 116 LIRA
Aluminum **Obv:** Crowned shield **Rev:** Value within design

Date	Mintage	F	VF	XF	Unc	BU
1981	100,000	—	—	0.15	0.30	—

KM# 131 LIRA
Aluminum **Subject:** Social conquest **Obv:** Crown above smoking towers **Rev:** Back of standing figure divides date and value

Date	Mintage	F	VF	XF	Unc	BU
1982R	78,000	—	—	0.15	0.30	—

KM# 145 LIRA
Aluminum **Subject:** Nuclear war threat **Obv:** Crowned shield above sprig **Rev:** Beast of war

Date	Mintage	F	VF	XF	Unc	BU
1983R	72,000	—	—	0.20	0.40	—

KM# 159 LIRA
Aluminum **Obv:** Castle **Rev:** Bust facing flanked by value and caduceus

Date	Mintage	F	VF	XF	Unc	BU
1984R	65,000	—	—	0.20	0.40	—

KM# 173 LIRA
Aluminum **Subject:** War on drugs **Obv:** Shield **Rev:** Supine male 1/2 length figure below value and date

Date	Mintage	F	VF	XF	Unc	BU
1985R	60,000	—	—	0.10	0.25	—

KM# 187 LIRA
Aluminum **Subject:** Revolution of technology **Obv:** Crown above smoking towers on rock **Rev:** Footprints on the moon

Date	Mintage	F	VF	XF	Unc	BU
1986R	50,000	—	—	0.10	0.25	—

KM# 201 LIRA

Aluminum **Subject:** 15th Anniversary - Resumption of Coinage **Obv:** Crowned pointed arms within sprigs **Rev:** Tree flanked by value

Date	Mintage	F	VF	XF	Unc	BU
1987R	83,000	—	—	0.10	0.25	—

KM# 218 LIRA

Aluminum **Subject:** Fortifications **Obv:** Crowned ornate arms on shield **Rev:** Corner Tower **Designer:** Sergio Giandomenico

Date	Mintage	F	VF	XF	Unc	BU
1988R	38,000	—	—	0.10	0.25	—

KM# 231 LIRA

Aluminum **Subject:** History **Obv:** Crowned shield **Rev:** Stone Age tool

Date	Mintage	F	VF	XF	Unc	BU
1989R	37,000	—	—	0.10	0.25	—

KM# 248 LIRA

Aluminum **Subject:** 1,600 Years of History **Obv:** Stylized towers **Rev:** Stylized Saint **Designer:** Magdalena Dobrucka

Date	Mintage	F	VF	XF	Unc	BU
1990R	36,000	—	—	0.10	0.25	—

KM# 261 LIRA

Aluminum **Obv:** Date to upper left of smoking towers **Rev:** Hands holding hammer and chisel below value

Date	Mintage	F	VF	XF	Unc	BU
1991R	—	—	—	0.10	0.25	—

KM# 278 LIRA

Aluminum **Subject:** Columbus **Obv:** Towers with feather-like designs above within circle **Rev:** Potatoes and plant within design with value at left

Date	Mintage	F	VF	XF	Unc	BU
ND(1992)R	—	—	—	0.10	0.25	—

KM# 293 LIRA

Aluminum **Obv:** Stylized smoking towers **Rev:** Seedling divides date and value

Date	Mintage	F	VF	XF	Unc	BU
1993R	—	—	—	0.10	0.25	—

KM# 306 LIRA

Aluminum **Obv:** Bust facing with arms holding hammer and chisel, smoking towers at left **Rev:** Mother and child

Date	Mintage	F	VF	XF	Unc	BU
1994R	40,000	—	—	0.10	0.25	—

KM# 322 LIRA

Aluminum **Obv:** Banner around design **Rev:** Child on broken sword divides sprig and value **Designer:** Loredana Pancotto

Date	Mintage	F	VF	XF	Unc	BU
1995R	—	—	—	0.10	0.25	—

KM# 349 LIRA

Aluminum **Subject:** Talete - Child of the Universe **Obv:** Bust facing with flame within hands **Rev:** Value and date at left of head facing

Date	Mintage	F	VF	XF	Unc	BU
1996	32,000	—	—	0.10	0.25	—

KM# 359 LIRA

Aluminum **Subject:** The Arts - Prehistoric **Obv:** Bust facing with flame within hands **Rev:** Elk

Date	Mintage	F	VF	XF	Unc	BU
1997	28,000	—	—	0.10	0.25	0.75

KM# 5 2 LIRE

10.0000 g., 0.8350 Silver .2684 oz. ASW, 27 mm. **Obv:** Crowned arms within wreath **Obv. Legend:** RESPVBLICA S. MARINI **Rev:** Value, date within wreath

Date	Mintage	F	VF	XF	Unc	BU
1906R	15,000	25.00	40.00	175	380	—

KM# 15 2 LIRE

Aluminum, 18 mm. **Obv:** Value above stylized smoking towers **Rev:** Bust of Saint 1/4 right **Designer:** Monassi

Date	Mintage	F	VF	XF	Unc	BU
1972	291,000	—	—	0.10	0.30	—

KM# 23 2 LIRE

Aluminum, 18 mm. **Obv:** Crowned shield **Rev:** Pelican **Designer:** Guido Veroi

Date	Mintage	F	VF	XF	Unc	BU
1973	291,000	—	—	0.20	1.00	1.50

KM# 31 2 LIRE

Aluminum, 18 mm. **Obv:** Smoking towers within circle **Rev:** Beetle **Designer:** Lucaiano Minguzzi

Date	Mintage	F	VF	XF	Unc	BU
1974	276,000	—	—	0.25	1.25	2.00

KM# 41 2 LIRE

Aluminum, 18 mm. **Obv:** Smoking towers **Rev:** Seahorses **Designer:** Bino Bini

Date	Mintage	F	VF	XF	Unc	BU
1975	291,000	—	—	0.25	1.25	1.50

KM# 52 2 LIRE

Aluminum, 18 mm. **Obv:** Smoking towers **Rev:** Stylized sun, hills and sitting figure **Designer:** Mario Molteni

Date	Mintage	F	VF	XF	Unc	BU
1976	195,000	—	—	0.10	0.30	0.50

KM# 64 2 LIRE

Aluminum, 18 mm. **Obv:** Value and smoking towers within circle **Rev:** Stars above wave-like designs within circle **Designer:** J. Vivarelli

Date	Mintage	F	VF	XF	Unc	BU
1977	180,000	—	—	0.10	0.30	—

KM# 77 2 LIRE

Aluminum, 18 mm. **Obv:** Value below smoking towers **Rev:** Standing figure working

Date	Mintage	F	VF	XF	Unc	BU
1978	130,000	—	—	0.10	0.30	—

KM# 90 2 LIRE

Aluminum, 18 mm. **Obv:** Crowned shield **Rev:** Bugle with banner divides value

Date	Mintage	F	VF	XF	Unc	BU
1979	125,000	—	—	0.10	0.30	—

KM# 103 2 LIRE

Aluminum, 18 mm. **Series:** 1980 Olympics **Obv:** Olympic rings and date to left of smoking towers **Rev:** Soccer player

Date	Mintage	F	VF	XF	Unc	BU
1980	125,000	—	—	0.25	0.75	—

KM# 117 2 LIRE
Aluminum, 18 mm. **Obv:** Crowned shield **Rev:** Small head and hand left, date and value at upper left

Date	Mintage	F	VF	XF	Unc	BU
1981	100,000	—	—	0.10	0.30	—

KM# 132 2 LIRE
Aluminum, 18 mm. **Subject:** Social Conquests **Obv:** Crown above smoking towers **Rev:** Value below stylized design

Date	Mintage	F	VF	XF	Unc	BU
1982R	78,000	—	—	0.10	0.30	—

KM# 146 2 LIRE
Aluminum, 18 mm. **Subject:** Nuclear war threat **Obv:** Crowned shield above sprig **Rev:** Two reaching arms

Date	Mintage	F	VF	XF	Unc	BU
1983R	72,000	—	—	0.20	0.40	—

KM# 160 2 LIRE
Aluminum, 18 mm. **Obv:** Castle **Rev:** Head facing

Date	Mintage	F	VF	XF	Unc	BU
1984R	65,000	—	—	0.20	0.40	—

KM# 174 2 LIRE
Aluminum, 18 mm. **Subject:** War on Drugs **Obv:** Shield **Rev:** Clenched fist

Date	Mintage	F	VF	XF	Unc	BU
1985R	60,000	—	—	0.10	0.25	—

KM# 188 2 LIRE
Aluminum, 18 mm. **Subject:** Revolution of Technology **Obv:** Crown above smoking towers on rock **Rev:** Astronaut walking in space

Date	Mintage	F	VF	XF	Unc	BU
1986R	50,000	—	—	0.10	0.25	—

KM# 202 2 LIRE
Aluminum, 18 mm. **Subject:** 15th Anniversary - Resumption of Coinage **Obv:** Crowned pointed shield within sprigs **Rev:** Flower designs

Date	Mintage	F	VF	XF	Unc	BU
1987R	83,000	—	—	0.10	0.25	—

KM# 219 2 LIRE
Aluminum, 18 mm. **Subject:** Fortifications **Obv:** Crowned ornate arms on shield **Rev:** Fortified archway **Designer:** Sergio Giandomenico

Date	Mintage	F	VF	XF	Unc	BU
1988R	38,000	—	—	0.10	0.25	—

KM# 232 2 LIRE
Aluminum, 18 mm. **Subject:** History **Obv:** Crowned shield **Rev:** Value divides wheat stalk and olive branch

Date	Mintage	F	VF	XF	Unc	BU
1989R	37,000	—	—	0.10	0.25	—

KM# 249 2 LIRE
Aluminum, 18 mm. **Subject:** 1,600 Years of History **Obv:** Stylized towers **Rev:** Stylized figure with spear **Designer:** Magdalena Dobrucka

Date	Mintage	F	VF	XF	Unc	BU
1990R	36,000	—	—	0.10	0.25	—

KM# 262 2 LIRE
Aluminum, 18 mm. **Obv:** Date to upper left of smoking towers **Rev:** Hands with interlocked fingers below value

Date	Mintage	F	VF	XF	Unc	BU
1991R	—	—	—	0.10	0.25	—

KM# 279 2 LIRE
Aluminum, 18 mm. **Subject:** Columbus **Obv:** Towers with feather-like designs on top within circle **Rev:** Ear of corn to left of value within design

Date	Mintage	F	VF	XF	Unc	BU
ND(1992)R	—	—	—	0.10	0.25	—

KM# 294 2 LIRE
Aluminum, 18 mm. **Obv:** Smoking towers **Rev:** Rose

Date	Mintage	F	VF	XF	Unc	BU
1993R	—	—	—	0.10	0.25	—

KM# 307 2 LIRE
Aluminum, 18 mm. **Obv:** Head with hands holding hammer and chisel, towers at left **Rev:** Standing stonecutter at work

Date	Mintage	F	VF	XF	Unc	BU
1994R	40,000	—	—	0.10	0.25	—

KM# 323 2 LIRE
Aluminum, 18 mm. **Obv:** Banner around bottom of design **Rev:** Child with toy castle **Designer:** Loredana Pancotto

Date	Mintage	F	VF	XF	Unc	BU
1995R	—	—	—	0.10	0.25	—

KM# 350 2 LIRE
Aluminum, 18 mm. **Obv:** Bust facing with flame within hands **Rev:** Head of Socrates

Date	Mintage	F	VF	XF	Unc	BU
1996	32,000	—	—	0.10	0.25	—

KM# 360 2 LIRE
Aluminum, 18 mm. **Subject:** The Arts - Literature **Obv:** Bust facing with flame within hands **Rev:** Dante holding Divine Comedy

Date	Mintage	F	VF	XF	Unc	BU
1997	28,000	—	—	0.10	0.25	—

KM# 9 5 LIRE
5.0000 g., 0.8350 Silver .1342 oz. ASW, 23 mm. **Obv:** Bust left within beaded circle **Rev:** Plant divides value above plow **Designer:** E. Saroldi

Date	Mintage	F	VF	XF	Unc	BU
1931R	50,000	3.50	5.50	10.00	100	—
1932R	50,000	3.50	5.50	10.00	100	—
1933R	50,000	3.50	5.50	8.50	30.00	—
1935R	200,000	3.50	5.50	8.50	20.00	—
1936R	100,000	3.50	5.50	8.50	50.00	—
1937R	100,000	3.50	5.50	8.50	50.00	—
1938R	120,000	3.50	5.50	8.50	50.00	—

KM# 16 5 LIRE
Aluminum, 20 mm. **Obv:** Bust of Saint 1/4 left **Rev:** Value above stylized smoking towers **Designer:** Monassi

Date	Mintage	F	VF	XF	Unc	BU
1972	291,000	—	—	0.10	0.35	—

KM# 24 5 LIRE
Aluminum, 20 mm. **Obv:** Crowned shield **Rev:** Heads within small circle on globe, radiant star border **Designer:** Guido Veroi

Date	Mintage	F	VF	XF	Unc	BU
1973	291,000	—	—	0.10	0.35	—

KM# 32 5 LIRE

Aluminum, 20 mm. **Obv:** Smoking towers within circle **Rev:** Porcupine **Designer:** Luciano Minguzzi

Date	Mintage	F	VF	XF	Unc	BU
1974	276,000	—	—	0.25	1.25	2.50

KM# 42 5 LIRE

Aluminum, 20 mm. **Obv:** Smoking towers **Rev:** Hedgehogs **Designer:** Bino Bini

Date	Mintage	F	VF	XF	Unc	BU
1975	291,000	—	—	0.20	1.00	2.50

KM# 53 5 LIRE

Aluminum, 20 mm. **Series:** F.A.O. **Obv:** Stylized smoking towers **Rev:** Stylized standing figures within design **Designer:** Mario Molteni

Date	Mintage	F	VF	XF	Unc	BU
1976	695,000	—	—	0.10	0.25	—

KM# 65 5 LIRE

Aluminum, 20 mm. **Obv:** Value below smoking towers within circle **Rev:** Stars within circle **Designer:** J. Vivarelli

Date	Mintage	F	VF	XF	Unc	BU
1977	180,000	—	—	0.10	0.35	—

KM# 78 5 LIRE

Aluminum, 20 mm. **Obv:** Value below smoking towers **Rev:** Standing figure holding water hose

Date	Mintage	F	VF	XF	Unc	BU
1978	130,000	—	—	0.10	0.35	—

KM# 91 5 LIRE

Aluminum, 20 mm. **Obv:** Crowned shield **Rev:** Crossbow divides value

Date	Mintage	F	VF	XF	Unc	BU
1979	125,000	—	—	0.10	0.35	—

KM# 104 5 LIRE

Aluminum, 20 mm. **Series:** 1980 Olympics **Obv:** Olympic rings and date to left of smoking towers **Rev:** Running figure right

Date	Mintage	F	VF	XF	Unc	BU
1980	125,000	—	—	0.25	0.75	—

KM# 118 5 LIRE

Aluminum, 20 mm. **Obv:** Crowned shield **Rev:** Goat divides value and date

Date	Mintage	F	VF	XF	Unc	BU
1981	100,030	—	—	0.25	0.75	2.00

KM# 133 5 LIRE

Aluminum, 20 mm. **Subject:** Social Conquests **Obv:** Crown above smoking towers **Rev:** Stylized boats and plane

Date	Mintage	F	VF	XF	Unc	BU
1982R	78,000	—	—	0.10	0.30	—

KM# 147 5 LIRE

Aluminum, 20 mm. **Subject:** Nuclear War Threat **Obv:** Crown above shield and sprig **Rev:** Pair of reaching arms within barred window

Date	Mintage	F	VF	XF	Unc	BU
1983R	72,000	—	—	0.20	0.40	—

KM# 161 5 LIRE

Aluminum, 20 mm. **Obv:** Castle **Rev:** Bust of Galileo facing

Date	Mintage	F	VF	XF	Unc	BU
1984R	65,000	—	—	0.20	0.40	—

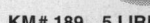

KM# 175 5 LIRE

Aluminum, 20 mm. **Subject:** War on Drugs **Obv:** Shield **Rev:** Face of addict

Date	Mintage	F	VF	XF	Unc	BU
1985R	60,000	—	—	0.10	0.30	—

KM# 189 5 LIRE

Aluminum, 20 mm. **Subject:** Revolution of Technology **Obv:** Crown above smoking towers on rock **Rev:** Human figure operating larger robot

Date	Mintage	F	VF	XF	Unc	BU
1986R	50,000	—	—	0.10	0.30	—

KM# 203 5 LIRE

Aluminum, 20 mm. **Subject:** 15th Anniversary - Resumption of Coinage **Obv:** Crowned pointed shield within sprigs **Rev:** Flowers in designed vase divide value

Date	Mintage	F	VF	XF	Unc	BU
1987R	83,000	—	—	0.10	0.30	—

KM# 220 5 LIRE

Aluminum, 20 mm. **Subject:** Fortification **Obv:** Crowned ornate arms on shield **Rev:** Round corner tower **Designer:** Sergio Giandomenico

Date	Mintage	F	VF	XF	Unc	BU
1988R	38,000	—	—	0.10	0.30	—

KM# 233 5 LIRE

Aluminum, 20 mm. **Subject:** History **Obv:** Crowned shield **Rev:** Cluster of grapes divide value

Date	Mintage	F	VF	XF	Unc	BU
1989R	37,000	—	—	0.10	0.30	—

KM# 250 5 LIRE

Aluminum, 20 mm. **Subject:** 1,600 Years of History **Obv:** Stylized towers above design **Rev:** Two stylized facing figures **Designer:** Magdalena Dobrucka

Date	Mintage	F	VF	XF	Unc	BU
1990R	36,000	—	—	0.10	0.30	—

KM# 263 5 LIRE

Aluminum, 20 mm. **Obv:** Date at upper left of smoking towers **Rev:** Hand holding quill below value

Date	Mintage	F	VF	XF	Unc	BU
1991R	—	—	—	0.10	0.30	—

KM# 280 5 LIRE

Aluminum, 20 mm. **Subject:** Columbus **Obv:** Towers with feather-like designs on top within circle **Rev:** Cotton plants and value within design

Date	Mintage	F	VF	XF	Unc	BU
ND(1992)R	—	—	—	0.10	0.30	—

KM# 295 5 LIRE

Aluminum, 20 mm. **Obv:** Stylized smoking towers **Rev:** Spade and hoe

Date	Mintage	F	VF	XF	Unc	BU
1993R	—	—	—	0.10	0.30	—

KM# 308 5 LIRE

Aluminum, 20 mm. **Obv:** Stone cutter holding hammer and chisel, towers at left **Rev:** Standing figures with tools

Date	Mintage	F	VF	XF	Unc	BU
1994R	40,000	—	—	0.10	0.30	—

KM# 324 5 LIRE
Aluminum, 20 mm. **Obv:** Banner wrapped around quills **Rev:** Child with 2 deer **Designer:** Loredana Pancotto

Date	Mintage	F	VF	XF	Unc	BU
1995R	—	—	—	0.10	0.30	—

KM# 351 5 LIRE
Aluminum, 20 mm. **Obv:** Bust facing with flame within hands **Rev:** Plato

Date	Mintage	F	VF	XF	Unc	BU
1996	32,000	—	—	0.10	0.30	—

KM# 361 5 LIRE
Aluminum, 20 mm. **Subject:** The Arts - Theater **Obv:** Bust facing with flame within hands **Rev:** Hamlet with skull

Date	Mintage	F	VF	XF	Unc	BU
1997	28,000	—	—	0.10	0.30	—

KM# 7 10 LIRE
3.2258 g., 0.9000 Gold .0933 oz. AGW **Obv:** Smoking towers within circle **Rev:** Standing Saint facing divides value **Note:** 16,000 coins melted at the mint.

Date	Mintage	F	VF	XF	Unc	BU
1925R	20,000	175	500	800	1,250	—

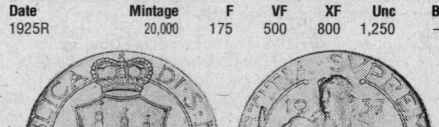

KM# 10 10 LIRE
10.0000 g., 0.8350 Silver .2684 oz. ASW **Obv:** Nine sided shield divides value within circle, crown at top divides circle **Rev:** Facing figure holding crown divides date within circle

Date	Mintage	F	VF	XF	Unc	BU
1931R	25,000	8.50	15.00	35.00	80.00	—
1932R	25,000	8.50	15.00	35.00	80.00	—
1933R	25,000	8.50	15.00	35.00	80.00	—
1935R	30,000	6.50	10.00	25.00	65.00	—
1936R	15,000	10.00	18.00	40.00	95.00	—
1937R	20,000	6.50	10.00	25.00	65.00	—
1938R	10,000	12.00	20.00	50.00	200	—

KM# 17 10 LIRE
1.6000 g., Aluminum, 23.3 mm. **Obv:** Stylized smoking towers **Rev:** Cow nursing calf

Date	Mintage	F	VF	XF	Unc	BU
1972	291,000	—	0.10	0.20	0.50	2.00

KM# 25 10 LIRE
1.6000 g., Aluminum, 23.3 mm. **Obv:** Crowned shield **Rev:** Man fighting four-headed dragon **Designer:** Guido Veroi

Date	Mintage	F	VF	XF	Unc	BU
1973	291,000	—	0.10	0.15	0.40	—

KM# 33 10 LIRE
1.6000 g., Aluminum, 23.3 mm. **Series:** F.A.O. **Obv:** Smoking towers within circle **Rev:** Bee **Designer:** Luciano Minguzzi

Date	Mintage	F	VF	XF	Unc	BU
1974	1,276,000	—	—	0.15	0.45	1.25

KM# 43 10 LIRE
1.6000 g., Aluminum, 23.3 mm. **Obv:** Smoking towers **Rev:** Rats divide value **Designer:** Bino Bini

Date	Mintage	F	VF	XF	Unc	BU
1975	291,000	—	0.10	0.25	1.00	1.50

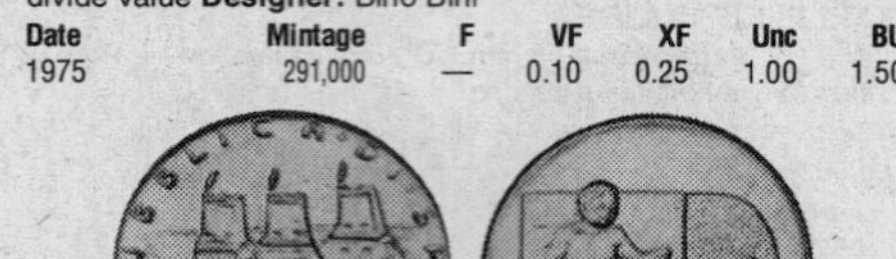

KM# 54 10 LIRE
1.6000 g., Aluminum, 23.3 mm. **Obv:** Stylized smoking towers **Rev:** Fetus within circle, standing baby at left **Designer:** Mario Molteni

Date	Mintage	F	VF	XF	Unc	BU
1976	195,000	—	0.10	0.15	0.40	—

KM# 66 10 LIRE
1.6000 g., Aluminum, 23.3 mm. **Obv:** Stylized smoking towers within circle **Rev:** Foot above 1/2 designed star wreath **Designer:** J. Varelli

Date	Mintage	F	VF	XF	Unc	BU
1977	180,000	—	0.10	0.15	0.40	—

KM# 79 10 LIRE
1.6000 g., Aluminum, 23.3 mm. **Obv:** Smoking towers above value **Rev:** Seated figure

Date	Mintage	F	VF	XF	Unc	BU
1978	130,000	—	0.10	0.15	0.40	—

KM# 92 10 LIRE
1.6000 g., Aluminum, 23.3 mm. **Obv:** Crowned shield **Rev:** Date flanked by two crowned shields on stands

Date	Mintage	F	VF	XF	Unc	BU
1979	125,000	—	0.10	0.15	0.40	—

KM# 105 10 LIRE
1.6000 g., Aluminum, 23.3 mm. **Series:** 1980 Olympics **Obv:** Olympic rings and date to left of smoking towers **Rev:** Jumping equestrian

Date	Mintage	F	VF	XF	Unc	BU
1980	125,000	—	0.25	0.50	0.80	1.00

KM# 119 10 LIRE
1.6000 g., Aluminum, 23.3 mm. **Obv:** Crowned shield **Rev:** Value surrounded by nude figure

Date	Mintage	F	VF	XF	Unc	BU
1981	100,000	—	0.10	0.20	0.50	—

KM# 134 10 LIRE
1.6000 g., Aluminum, 23.3 mm. **Subject:** Social Conquests **Obv:** Crown above smoking towers **Rev:** Stylized figures **Designer:** A. Biancini

Date	Mintage	F	VF	XF	Unc	BU
1982R	78,000	—	0.10	0.20	0.50	—

KM# 148 10 LIRE
1.6000 g., Aluminum, 23.3 mm. **Subject:** Nuclear War Threat **Obv:** Crown above shield and sprig **Rev:** Vertical line within square divides reaching arms

Date	Mintage	F	VF	XF	Unc	BU
1983R	72,000	—	0.10	0.25	0.75	—

KM# 162 10 LIRE
1.6000 g., Aluminum, 23.3 mm. **Subject:** Alessandro Volta **Obv:** Castle **Rev:** Bust 3/4 right

Date	Mintage	F	VF	XF	Unc	BU
1984R	65,000	—	0.10	0.25	0.75	—

KM# 176 10 LIRE

1.6000 g., Aluminum, 23.3 mm. **Subject:** War on Drugs **Obv:** Shield **Rev:** Mother lecturing son

Date	Mintage	F	VF	XF	Unc	BU
1985R	60,000	—	—	0.10	0.35	—

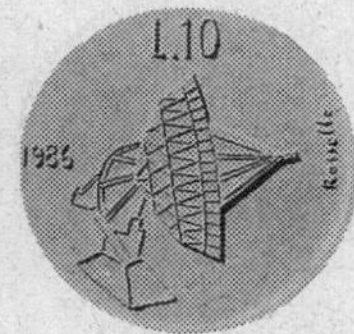

KM# 190 10 LIRE

1.6000 g., Aluminum, 23.3 mm. **Subject:** Revolution of Technology **Obv:** Crown above smoking towers on rock **Rev:** Radio receiver

Date	Mintage	F	VF	XF	Unc	BU
1986R	50,000	—	—	0.10	0.35	—

KM# 204 10 LIRE

1.6000 g., Aluminum, 23.3 mm. **Subject:** 15th Anniversary - Resumption of Coinage **Obv:** Crowned pointed shield within sprigs **Rev:** Tower divides value

Date	Mintage	F	VF	XF	Unc	BU
1987R	83,000	—	—	0.10	0.35	—

KM# 221 10 LIRE

1.6000 g., Aluminum, 23.3 mm. **Subject:** Fortifications **Obv:** Crowned ornate arms on shield **Rev:** Sloping fortress wall **Designer:** Sergio Giandomenico

Date	Mintage	F	VF	XF	Unc	BU
1988R	38,000	—	—	0.10	0.35	—

KM# 234 10 LIRE

1.6000 g., Aluminum, 23.3 mm. **Subject:** History **Obv:** Crowned shield **Rev:** Ancient pottery divides value

Date	Mintage	F	VF	XF	Unc	BU
1989R	37,000	—	—	0.10	0.35	—

KM# 251 10 LIRE

1.6000 g., Aluminum, 23.3 mm. **Subject:** 1,600 Years of History **Obv:** Stylized towers above design **Rev:** Stylized soldier **Designer:** Magdalena Dobrucka

Date	Mintage	F	VF	XF	Unc	BU
1990R	36,000	—	—	0.10	0.35	—

KM# 264 10 LIRE

1.6000 g., Aluminum, 23.3 mm. **Obv:** Date at left of smoking towers **Rev:** Value above hand holding castle tower

Date	Mintage	F	VF	XF	Unc	BU
1991R	—	—	—	0.10	0.35	—

KM# 281 10 LIRE

1.6000 g., Aluminum, 23.3 mm. **Subject:** Columbus **Obv:** Towers with feather-like designs on top within circle **Rev:** Dolphin, ship and value within globe design

Date	Mintage	F	VF	XF	Unc	BU
ND(1992)R	—	—	—	0.20	0.75	1.50

KM# 296 10 LIRE

1.6000 g., Aluminum, 23.3 mm. **Obv:** Smoking towers **Rev:** Value above corinthian column

Date	Mintage	F	VF	XF	Unc	BU
1993R	—	—	—	0.10	0.35	—

KM# 309 10 LIRE

1.6000 g., Aluminum, 23.3 mm. **Obv:** Stone cutter holding hammer and chisel, towers at left **Rev:** Marino and Leo working

Date	Mintage	F	VF	XF	Unc	BU
1994R	40,000	—	—	0.10	0.35	—

KM# 325 10 LIRE

1.6000 g., Aluminum, 23.3 mm. **Obv:** Banner wrapped around bottom of design **Rev:** Child holding two urns within square **Designer:** Loredana Pancotto

Date	Mintage	F	VF	XF	Unc	BU
1995R	—	—	—	0.10	0.35	—

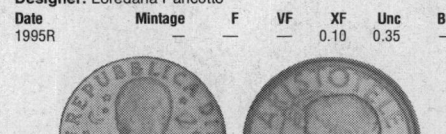

KM# 352 10 LIRE

1.6000 g., Aluminum, 23.3 mm. **Obv:** Bust facing with flame within hands **Rev:** Aristotle

Date	Mintage	F	VF	XF	Unc	BU
1996	28,000	—	—	0.10	0.35	—

KM# 362 10 LIRE

1.6000 g., Aluminum, 23.3 mm. **Subject:** The Arts - Architecture **Obv:** Bust facing with flame within hands **Rev:** Building on pillars

Date	Mintage	F	VF	XF	Unc	BU
1997	28,000	—	—	0.10	0.35	—

KM# 378 10 LIRE

1.6000 g., Aluminum, 23.3 mm. **Subject:** Mathematics **Rev:** Hand and geometric shape

Date	Mintage	F	VF	XF	Unc	BU
1998	—	—	—	0.10	0.35	—

KM# 389 10 LIRE

1.6000 g., Aluminum, 23.3 mm. **Subject:** Exploration **Obv:** Crowned shield **Rev:** Earth flat, as once envisioned

Date	Mintage	F	VF	XF	Unc	BU
1999	—	—	—	0.10	0.35	—

KM# 399 10 LIRE

1.6000 g., Aluminum, 23.3 mm. **Subject:** Love **Obv:** Bust facing with flame within hands **Rev:** Child within poinsettia and globe design **Edge:** Plain **Note:** Struck at Rome.

Date	Mintage	F	VF	XF	Unc	BU
2000	—	—	—	—	0.35	—

KM# 8 20 LIRE

6.4516 g., 0.9000 Gold .1867 oz. AGW **Obv:** Smoking towers **Rev:** Standing Saint figure divides value **Note:** 7,334 coins were melted at the mint.

Date	Mintage	F	VF	XF	Unc	BU
1925R	9,334	400	700	1,200	2,300	—

KM# 11 20 LIRE

15.0000 g., 0.8000 Silver .3858 oz. ASW **Obv:** Upright stylized feathers above value with crown above **Rev:** Half length figure holding smoking towers within circle **Designer:** Saroldi

Date	Mintage	F	VF	XF	Unc	BU
1931R	10,000	25.00	45.00	90.00	200	—
1932R	10,000	35.00	60.00	110	235	—
1933R	10,000	30.00	50.00	100	220	—
1935R	10,000	30.00	50.00	100	220	—
1936R	5,000	60.00	125	200	425	—

KM# 11a 20 LIRE
20.0000 g., 0.8000 Silver .5145 oz. ASW **Obv:** Stylized upright feathers above value with crown above **Rev:** Half length figure holding smoking towers within circle

Date	Mintage	F	VF	XF	Unc	BU
1935R Rare	2	—	—	—	—	—
1937R	5,100	100	200	435	775	—
1938R	2,500	200	400	850	1,325	—

KM# 18 20 LIRE
3.6000 g., Aluminum-Bronze, 21.25 mm. **Obv:** Stylized feathers within towers **Rev:** Standing figures

Date	Mintage	F	VF	XF	Unc	BU
1972	291,000	—	0.10	0.25	0.60	—

KM# 26 20 LIRE
3.6000 g., Aluminum-Bronze, 21.25 mm. **Obv:** Crowned shield **Rev:** Man rescuing old man and baby from fire **Designer:** Guido Veroi

Date	Mintage	F	VF	XF	Unc	BU
1973	291,000	—	0.10	0.25	0.60	—

KM# 34 20 LIRE
3.6000 g., Aluminum-Bronze, 21.25 mm. **Obv:** Smoking towers within circle **Rev:** Lobster **Designer:** Luciano Minguzzi

Date	Mintage	F	VF	XF	Unc	BU
1974	276,000	—	0.10	0.30	1.50	2.50

KM# 44 20 LIRE
3.6000 g., Aluminum-Bronze, 21.25 mm. **Series:** F.A.O. **Obv:** Smoking towers **Rev:** Bird feeding babies **Designer:** Bino Bini

Date	Mintage	F	VF	XF	Unc	BU
1975	291,000	—	0.10	0.30	0.75	1.25

KM# 55 20 LIRE
3.6000 g., Aluminum-Bronze, 21.25 mm. **Obv:** Smoking towers **Rev:** Design flanked by stylized hands **Designer:** Mario Molteni

Date	Mintage	F	VF	XF	Unc	BU
1976	195,000	—	0.10	0.25	0.60	—

KM# 67 20 LIRE
3.6000 g., Aluminum-Bronze, 21.25 mm. **Obv:** Smoking towers **Rev:** Circular pattern within stylized hand **Designer:** J. Vivarelli

Date	Mintage	F	VF	XF	Unc	BU
1977	180,000	—	0.10	0.25	0.60	—

KM# 80 20 LIRE
3.6000 g., Aluminum-Bronze, 21.25 mm. **Obv:** Value below smoking towers **Rev:** Kneeling figure **Designer:** Monassi

Date	Mintage	F	VF	XF	Unc	BU
1978	130,000	—	0.10	0.25	0.60	—

KM# 93 20 LIRE
3.6000 g., Aluminum-Bronze, 21.25 mm. **Obv:** Crowned shield **Rev:** Crowned skeleton keys divide value

Date	Mintage	F	VF	XF	Unc	BU
1979	125,000	—	0.10	0.30	0.60	—

KM# 106 20 LIRE
3.6000 g., Aluminum-Bronze, 21.25 mm. **Series:** 1980 Olympics **Obv:** Olympic rings and date to left of smoking towers **Rev:** Pole vaulter

Date	Mintage	F	VF	XF	Unc	BU
1980	125,000	—	0.25	0.50	1.00	—

KM# 120 20 LIRE
3.6000 g., Aluminum-Bronze, 21.25 mm. **Obv:** Crowned shield **Rev:** Value above bird

Date	Mintage	F	VF	XF	Unc	BU
1981	100,000	—	0.10	0.30	0.75	1.50

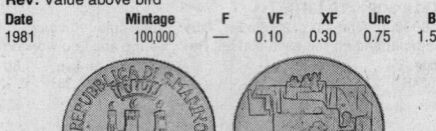

KM# 135 20 LIRE
3.6000 g., Aluminum-Bronze, 21.25 mm. **Subject:** Social conquests **Obv:** Crown above smoking towers **Rev:** Standing figures within design

Date	Mintage	F	VF	XF	Unc	BU
1982R	78,000	—	0.10	0.25	0.60	—

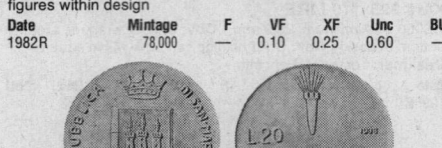

KM# 149 20 LIRE
3.6000 g., Aluminum-Bronze, 21.25 mm. **Subject:** Nuclear war threat **Obv:** Crown above shield and sprig **Rev:** Torch above man

Date	Mintage	F	VF	XF	Unc	BU
1983R	72,000	—	0.10	0.30	0.75	—

KM# 163 20 LIRE
3.6000 g., Aluminum-Bronze, 21.25 mm. **Obv:** Castle **Rev:** Bust of Louis Pasteur facing

Date	Mintage	F	VF	XF	Unc	BU
1984R	65,000	—	0.10	0.30	0.75	—

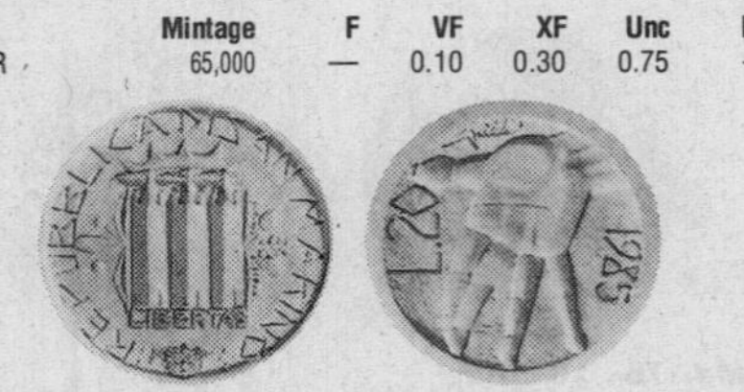

KM# 177 20 LIRE
3.6000 g., Aluminum-Bronze, 21.25 mm. **Subject:** War on drugs **Obv:** Shield **Rev:** Open hand flanked by value and date

Date	Mintage	F	VF	XF	Unc	BU
1985R	60,000	—	—	0.15	0.55	—

KM# 191 20 LIRE
3.6000 g., Aluminum-Bronze, 21.25 mm. **Subject:** Revolution of technology **Obv:** Crown above smoking towers on rock **Rev:** Stylized figure at lower right of computer flanked by value and date

Date	Mintage	F	VF	XF	Unc	BU
1986R	50,000	—	—	0.15	0.55	—

KM# 205 20 LIRE
3.6000 g., Aluminum-Bronze, 21.25 mm. **Subject:** 15th Anniversary - Resumption of Coinage **Obv:** Crowned pointed arms within sprigs **Rev:** Volcanoes

Date	Mintage	F	VF	XF	Unc	BU
1987R	83,000	—	—	0.15	0.55	—

KM# 222 20 LIRE
3.6000 g., Aluminum-Bronze, 21.25 mm. **Subject:** Fortifications **Obv:** Crowned ornate arms on shield **Rev:** Small fortified gate **Designer:** Sergio Giandomenico

Date	Mintage	F	VF	XF	Unc	BU
1988R	38,000	—	—	0.15	0.55	—

KM# 235 20 LIRE
3.6000 g., Aluminum-Bronze, 21.25 mm. **Subject:** History **Obv:** Crowned shield **Rev:** Sword with value within flag

Date	Mintage	F	VF	XF	Unc	BU
1989R	37,000	—	—	0.15	0.55	—

KM# 252 20 LIRE
3.6000 g., Aluminum-Bronze, 21.25 mm. **Subject:** 1,600 Years of History **Obv:** Stylized towers above design **Rev:** Stylized large figure straddling value **Designer:** Magdalena Dobrucka

Date	Mintage	F	VF	XF	Unc	BU
1990R	96,000	—	—	0.15	0.55	—

KM# 265 20 LIRE

3.6000 g., Aluminum-Bronze, 21.25 mm. **Obv:** Date at upper left of smoking towers **Rev:** Value above gloved hand rejecting cardinal ring

Date	Mintage	F	VF	XF	Unc	BU
1991R	—	—	—	0.15	0.55	—

KM# 282 20 LIRE

3.6000 g., Aluminum-Bronze, 21.25 mm. **Obv:** Towers with feather-like designs on top within circle **Rev:** Columbus landing on Hispaniola **Designer:** L. Cretara

Date	Mintage	F	VF	XF	Unc	BU
1992R	—	—	—	0.10	0.55	—

KM# 297 20 LIRE

3.6000 g., Aluminum-Bronze, 21.25 mm. **Rev:** Scroll and arch

Date	Mintage	F	VF	XF	Unc	BU
1993R	—	—	—	0.10	0.55	—

KM# 310 20 LIRE

3.6000 g., Aluminum-Bronze, 21.25 mm. **Obv:** Stone cutter **Rev:** Workers pulling stone

Date	Mintage	F	VF	XF	Unc	BU
1994R	40,000	—	—	0.10	0.55	—

KM# 326 20 LIRE

3.6000 g., Aluminum-Bronze, 21.25 mm. **Obv:** Banner wrapped around quills **Rev:** Child straddling cornucopia **Designer:** Loredana Pancotto

Date	Mintage	F	VF	XF	Unc	BU
1995R	—	—	—	0.10	0.55	—

KM# 353 20 LIRE

3.6000 g., Aluminum-Bronze, 21.25 mm. **Obv:** Bust of Saint Thomas facing

Date	Mintage	F	VF	XF	Unc	BU
1996	32,000	—	—	0.10	0.55	—

KM# 363 20 LIRE

3.6000 g., Aluminum-Bronze, 21.25 mm. **Subject:** The Arts - Cinema **Obv:** Bust facing with flame within hands **Rev:** Film strips

Date	Mintage	F	VF	XF	Unc	BU
1997	28,000	—	—	0.10	0.55	—

KM# 379 20 LIRE

3.6000 g., Aluminum-Bronze, 21.25 mm. **Subject:** Communications **Rev:** Two profiles in silhouette left

Date	Mintage	F	VF	XF	Unc	BU
1998	—	—	—	0.10	0.55	—

KM# 390 20 LIRE

3.6000 g., Aluminum-Bronze, 21.25 mm. **Subject:** Exploration **Obv:** Crowned shield **Rev:** Earth as known today **Designer:** Abd el-Kalik Yhia

Date	Mintage	F	VF	XF	Unc	BU
1999	—	—	—	0.10	0.55	—

KM# 400 20 LIRE

3.6000 g., Aluminum-Bronze, 21.8 mm. **Subject:** Solidarity **Obv:** Bust facing with flame within hands **Rev:** Two hands about to grasp, globe design in background **Edge:** Plain

Date	Mintage	F	VF	XF	Unc	BU
2000	—	—	—	0.10	0.55	—

KM# 19 50 LIRE

6.2000 g., Steel, 24.8 mm. **Obv:** Stylized feathers within towers **Rev:** Female kneeling before St. Marinus

Date	Mintage	F	VF	XF	Unc	BU
1972	291,000	0.15	0.25	0.50	1.00	—

KM# 27 50 LIRE

6.2000 g., Steel, 24.8 mm. **Obv:** Crowned shield **Rev:** Stylized standing figure with sword and scale **Designer:** Guido Veroi

Note: Depicts the balance of man, not as an individual but as a race

Date	Mintage	F	VF	XF	Unc	BU
1973	291,000	0.15	0.25	0.50	1.00	—

KM# 35 50 LIRE

6.2000 g., Steel, 24.8 mm. **Obv:** Smoking towers within circle **Rev:** Stylized chicken **Designer:** Luciano Minguzzi

Date	Mintage	F	VF	XF	Unc	BU
1974	276,000	0.15	0.25	0.60	1.25	2.00

KM# 45 50 LIRE

6.2000 g., Steel, 24.8 mm. **Obv:** Smoking towers **Rev:** Cluster of fish **Designer:** Bino Bini

Date	Mintage	F	VF	XF	Unc	BU
1975	831,000	0.15	0.25	0.60	1.25	2.00

KM# 56 50 LIRE

6.2000 g., Steel, 24.8 mm. **Obv:** Stylized smoking towers **Rev:** Face forward within triangle flanked by bottle-like designs **Designer:** Mario Molteni

Date	Mintage	F	VF	XF	Unc	BU
1976	195,000	0.15	0.25	0.50	1.00	—

KM# 68 50 LIRE

6.2000 g., Steel, 24.8 mm. **Obv:** Value below smoking towers within circle **Rev:** Fingers in center of circle of stars **Designer:** J. Vivarelli

Date	Mintage	F	VF	XF	Unc	BU
1977	180,000	0.15	0.25	0.50	1.00	—

KM# 81 50 LIRE

6.2000 g., Steel, 24.8 mm. **Obv:** Value below smoking towers **Rev:** Flowering plant below seated mother and child at desk

Date	Mintage	F	VF	XF	Unc	BU
1978	130,000	0.15	0.25	0.50	1.00	—

KM# 94 50 LIRE

6.2000 g., Steel, 24.8 mm. **Obv:** Crowned shield **Rev:** Liberty bell in front of building

Date	Mintage	F	VF	XF	Unc	BU
1979	125,000	0.15	0.25	0.50	1.00	—

KM# 107 50 LIRE

6.2000 g., Steel, 24.8 mm. **Series:** 1980 Olympics **Obv:** Olympic rings and date to upper left of smoking towers **Rev:** Downhill skier

Date	Mintage	F	VF	XF	Unc	BU
1980	125,000	0.25	0.50	1.00	2.00	—

KM# 121 50 LIRE

6.2000 g., Steel, 24.8 mm. **Obv:** Crowned shield **Rev:** Value at left of dancing figure

Date	Mintage	F	VF	XF	Unc	BU
1981	100,000	0.15	0.25	0.50	1.00	—

KM# 136 50 LIRE

6.2000 g., Steel, 24.8 mm. **Subject:** Social conquests **Obv:** Crown above smoking towers **Rev:** Standing figures within design

Date	Mintage	F	VF	XF	Unc	BU
1982R	78,000	0.15	0.25	0.50	1.00	—

KM# 150 50 LIRE

6.2000 g., Steel, 24.8 mm. **Subject:** Nuclear war threat **Obv:** Crown above shield and sprig **Rev:** Beast of war above woman

Date	Mintage	F	VF	XF	Unc	BU
1983R	72,000	0.20	0.40	0.80	1.50	—

KM# 164 50 LIRE

6.2000 g., Steel, 24.8 mm. **Obv:** Castle **Rev:** Pierre and Marie Curie

Date	Mintage	F	VF	XF	Unc	BU
1984R	65,000	0.20	0.40	0.80	1.50	—

KM# 178 50 LIRE

6.2000 g., Steel, 24.8 mm. **Subject:** War on drugs **Obv:** Shield **Rev:** Stylized figures

Date	Mintage	F	VF	XF	Unc	BU
1985R	110,000	—	0.10	0.20	0.85	—

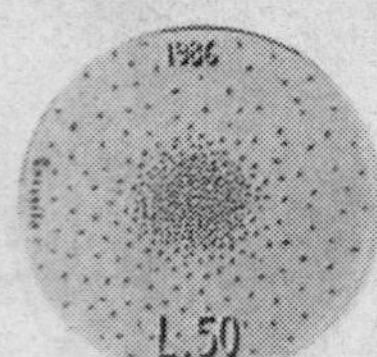

KM# 192 50 LIRE

6.2000 g., Steel, 24.8 mm. **Subject:** Revolution of technology **Obv:** Crown above smoking towers on rock **Rev:** Splitting the atom

Date	Mintage	F	VF	XF	Unc	BU
1986R	50,000	—	0.10	0.20	0.85	—

KM# 206 50 LIRE

6.2000 g., Steel, 24.8 mm. **Subject:** 15th Anniversary - Resumption of Coinage **Obv:** Crowned pointed shield within sprigs **Rev:** Animal in front of rock with tower at top

Date	Mintage	F	VF	XF	Unc	BU
1987R	93,000	—	0.10	0.20	0.85	—

KM# 223 50 LIRE

6.2000 g., Steel, 24.8 mm. **Subject:** Fortifications **Obv:** Crowned ornate arms on shield **Rev:** Ramp leading to gate house **Designer:** Sergio Giandomenico

Date	Mintage	F	VF	XF	Unc	BU
1988R	38,000	—	0.10	0.20	0.85	—

KM# 236 50 LIRE

6.2000 g., Steel, 24.8 mm. **Subject:** History **Obv:** Crowned shield **Rev:** Crossbow divides value

Date	Mintage	VG	F	VF	XF	Unc
1989R	87,000	—	—	0.10	0.20	0.85

KM# 253 50 LIRE

Steel, 17 mm. **Subject:** 1,600 Years of History **Obv:** Stylized towers above design **Rev:** Stylized bird **Designer:** Magdalena Dobrucka

Date	Mintage	F	VF	XF	Unc	BU
1990R	52,000	—	0.10	0.20	0.85	—

KM# 266 50 LIRE

Steel, 17 mm. **Obv:** Date at upper left of smoking towers **Rev:** Value above hand holding cannon barrels and wheat stalks

Date	Mintage	F	VF	XF	Unc	BU
1991R	—	—	0.10	0.20	0.85	—

KM# 283 50 LIRE

Steel, 17 mm. **Subject:** Columbus **Obv:** Towers with feather-like designs on top within circle **Rev:** Flying seagulls within radiant sun flanked by dates

Date	Mintage	F	VF	XF	Unc	BU
1992R	—	—	0.10	0.20	0.85	—

KM# 298 50 LIRE

Steel, 17 mm. **Obv:** Stylized feathers within towers **Rev:** Wheat growing through barbed wire

Date	Mintage	F	VF	XF	Unc	BU
1993R	—	—	0.10	0.20	0.85	—

KM# 311 50 LIRE

Stainless Steel, 17 mm. **Obv:** Stonecutter holding hammer and chisel, smoking towers at left **Rev:** Two stonecutters

Date	Mintage	F	VF	XF	Unc	BU
1994R	40,000	—	0.10	0.20	0.85	—

KM# 327 50 LIRE

Stainless Steel, 17 mm. **Obv:** Banner wrapped around bottom of design **Rev:** Child hugging bird **Designer:** Loredana Pancotto

Date	Mintage	F	VF	XF	Unc	BU
1995R	—	—	0.10	0.20	0.85	—

KM# 354 50 LIRE

Stainless Steel, 17 mm. **Obv:** Bust facing with flame within hands **Rev:** Descartes

Date	Mintage	F	VF	XF	Unc	BU
1996	32,000	—	0.10	0.20	0.85	—

KM# 364 50 LIRE

Stainless Steel, 19 mm. **Subject:** The Arts - Sculpture **Obv:** Bust facing with flame within hands **Rev:** Han Dynasty Horse statue

Date	Mintage	F	VF	XF	Unc	BU
1997	28,000	—	0.10	0.20	0.85	1.00

KM# 380 50 LIRE

Copper-Nickel, 19 mm. **Subject:** Engineering **Rev:** Cogwheel mind

Date	Mintage	F	VF	XF	Unc	BU
1998	—	—	0.10	0.20	0.85	—

KM# 391 50 LIRE

Copper-Nickel, 19 mm. **Subject:** Exploration **Obv:** Crowned shield **Rev:** Ship sail, sun and waves

Date	Mintage	F	VF	XF	Unc	BU
1999	—	—	0.10	0.20	0.85	—

KM# 401 50 LIRE

4.5000 g., Copper-Nickel, 19.2 mm. **Subject:** Equality **Obv:** Bust facing with flame within hands **Rev:** Five different plant leaves on 1 stem **Edge:** Plain **Note:** Struck at Rome.

Date	Mintage	F	VF	XF	Unc	BU
2000	—	—	0.10	0.20	0.85	—

KM# 20 100 LIRE

8.0000 g., Steel, 27.8 mm. **Obv:** Three smoking towers **Rev:** St. Marinus in a small boat **Designer:** Monassi

Date	Mintage	F	VF	XF	Unc	BU
1972	291,000	0.15	0.30	0.60	1.50	—

KM# 28 100 LIRE

8.0000 g., Steel, 27.8 mm. **Obv:** Crowned shield **Rev:** Ulysses passing the pillars of Hercules **Designer:** Guido Veroi

Date	Mintage	F	VF	XF	Unc	BU
1973	291,000	0.15	0.30	0.60	1.50	—

KM# 36 100 LIRE

8.0000 g., Steel, 27.8 mm. **Obv:** Smoking towers within circle **Rev:** Goat **Designer:** Luciano Minguzzi

Date	Mintage	F	VF	XF	Unc	BU
1974	276,000	0.15	0.30	0.65	1.75	3.00

KM# 46 100 LIRE

8.0000 g., Steel, 27.8 mm. **Obv:** Smoking towers **Rev:** Dog and cat lying together **Designer:** Bino Bini

Date	Mintage	F	VF	XF	Unc	BU
1975	821,000	0.15	0.30	0.65	1.75	3.00

KM# 57 100 LIRE

8.0000 g., Steel, 27.8 mm. **Obv:** Smoking towers **Rev:** Stylized seated figures within arch of building **Designer:** Mario Molteni

Date	Mintage	F	VF	XF	Unc	BU
1976	1,853,000	0.15	0.30	0.60	1.50	—

KM# 69 100 LIRE

8.0000 g., Steel, 27.8 mm. **Obv:** Value below smoking towers within circle **Rev:** Design within circular star wreath **Designer:** J. Vivarelli

Date	Mintage	F	VF	XF	Unc	BU
1977	565,000	0.15	0.30	0.60	1.50	—

KM# 70 100 LIRE

8.0000 g., Steel, 27.8 mm. **Obv:** Value below smoking towers within circle **Rev:** Stylized fish **Designer:** J. Vivarelli

Date	Mintage	F	VF	XF	Unc	BU
1977	565,000	0.15	0.30	0.60	1.50	—

KM# 82 100 LIRE

8.0000 g., Steel, 27.8 mm. **Series:** F.A.O. **Obv:** Value below smoking towers **Rev:** Standing figure using sickle

Date	Mintage	F	VF	XF	Unc	BU
1978	875,000	0.15	0.30	0.60	1.50	—

KM# 95 100 LIRE

8.0000 g., Steel, 27.8 mm. **Obv:** Crowned shield **Rev:** Design in center with assorted shields around border

Date	Mintage	F	VF	XF	Unc	BU
1979	665,000	0.15	0.30	0.60	1.50	—

KM# 108 100 LIRE

8.0000 g., Steel, 27.8 mm. **Series:** 1980 Olympics **Obv:** Olympic rings and date to upper left of smoking towers **Rev:** Archery **Designer:** Crocetti

Date	Mintage	F	VF	XF	Unc	BU
1980	350,000	0.25	0.50	1.00	2.00	—

KM# 122 100 LIRE

8.0000 g., Steel, 27.8 mm. **Obv:** Crowned shield **Rev:** Stylized draped figure to left of value **Designer:** Crilli

Date	Mintage	F	VF	XF	Unc	BU
1981	512,000	0.15	0.30	0.60	1.50	—

KM# 137 100 LIRE

8.0000 g., Steel, 27.8 mm. **Obv:** Crown above smoking towers **Rev:** Social conquests

Date	Mintage	F	VF	XF	Unc	BU
1982R	178,000	0.15	0.30	0.60	1.50	—

KM# 151 100 LIRE

8.0000 g., Steel, 27.8 mm. **Subject:** Nuclear War Threat **Obv:** Crown above shield and sprig **Rev:** Beast of war above man and woman

Date	Mintage	F	VF	XF	Unc	BU
1983R	172,000	0.15	0.30	0.60	1.50	—

KM# 165 100 LIRE

8.0000 g., Steel, 27.8 mm. **Obv:** Castle **Rev:** Bust of Guglielmo Marconi left

Date	Mintage	F	VF	XF	Unc	BU
1984R	165,000	0.15	0.30	0.60	1.50	—

KM# 179 100 LIRE

8.0000 g., Steel, 27.8 mm. **Subject:** War on Drugs **Obv:** Shield **Rev:** Three figures in discussion

Date	Mintage	F	VF	XF	Unc	BU
1985R	210,000	—	—	0.35	1.25	—

KM# 193 100 LIRE

8.0000 g., Steel, 27.8 mm. **Subject:** Revolution of Technology **Obv:** Crown above smoking towers on rock **Rev:** Satellite and receiving dishes divide date and value

Date	Mintage	F	VF	XF	Unc	BU
1986R	150,000	—	—	0.35	1.25	—

KM# 207 100 LIRE

8.0000 g., Steel, 27.8 mm. **Subject:** 15th Anniversary - Resumption of Coinage **Obv:** Crowned pointed shield within sprigs **Rev:** Sprig divides value

Date	Mintage	F	VF	XF	Unc	BU
1987R	143,000	—	—	0.35	1.25	—

KM# 224 100 LIRE

8.0000 g., Steel, 27.8 mm. **Subject:** Fortifications **Obv:** Crowned ornate arms on shield **Rev:** Gate tower **Designer:** Sergio Giandomenico

Date	Mintage	F	VF	XF	Unc	BU
1988R	38,000	—	—	0.35	1.25	—

KM# 237 100 LIRE
8.0000 g., Steel, 27.8 mm. **Subject:** History **Obv:** Crowned shield **Rev:** Teacher and student

Date	Mintage	F	VF	XF	Unc	BU
1989R	37,000	—	—	0.35	1.25	—

KM# 254 100 LIRE
Steel, 18 mm. **Subject:** 1,600 Years of History **Obv:** Towers above design **Rev:** Balance scales **Designer:** Magdalena Dobrncka

Date	Mintage	F	VF	XF	Unc	BU
1990R	1,086,000	—	—	0.35	1.25	—

KM# 267 100 LIRE
Steel, 18 mm. **Obv:** Date at upper left of smoking towers **Rev:** Value above clasped hands

Date	Mintage	F	VF	XF	Unc	BU
1991R	—	—	—	0.35	1.25	—

KM# 284 100 LIRE
Steel, 18 mm. **Subject:** Columbus **Obv:** Towers with feather-like designs on top within circle **Rev:** Value below three sailing ships

Date	Mintage	F	VF	XF	Unc	BU
1992R	—	—	—	0.35	1.25	—

KM# 299 100 LIRE
Copper-Nickel, 22 mm. **Obv:** Three towers above dentiled design **Rev:** Pan swallow above western Europe

Date	Mintage	F	VF	XF	Unc	BU
1993R	—	—	—	0.35	1.50	—

KM# 312 100 LIRE
Copper-Nickel, 22 mm. **Obv:** Stonecutter holding hammer and chisel, smoking towers at left **Rev:** Two stonecutters

Date	Mintage	F	VF	XF	Unc	BU
1994R	40,000	—	—	0.35	1.25	—

KM# 328 100 LIRE
Copper-Nickel, 22 mm. **Obv:** Banner wrapped around quills **Rev:** Three children **Designer:** Loredana Pancotto

Date	Mintage	F	VF	XF	Unc	BU
1995R	—	—	—	0.35	1.25	—

KM# 355 100 LIRE
Copper-Nickel, 22 mm. **Obv:** Bust facing with flame within hands **Rev:** Head of Rousseau 1/4 right

Date	Mintage	F	VF	XF	Unc	BU
1996	32,000	—	—	0.35	1.25	—

KM# 365 100 LIRE
Copper-Nickel, 22 mm. **Subject:** The Arts - Dance **Obv:** Bust facing with flame within hands **Rev:** Ballet dancers

Date	Mintage	F	VF	XF	Unc	BU
1997	28,000	—	—	0.35	1.25	—

KM# 381 100 LIRE
Copper-Nickel, 22 mm. **Subject:** Physics **Rev:** Human, crossbow

Date	Mintage	F	VF	XF	Unc	BU
1998	—	—	—	0.35	1.25	—

KM# 392 100 LIRE
Copper-Nickel, 22 mm. **Subject:** Exploration **Obv:** Crowned shield **Rev:** Submarine below Arctic ice-cap

Date	Mintage	F	VF	XF	Unc	BU
1999	—	—	—	0.35	1.25	—

KM# 402 100 LIRE
4.5000 g., Copper-Nickel, 22 mm. **Subject:** Ecology **Obv:** Bust facing with flame within hands **Rev:** Outline of house in center of leaf design, globe design in background **Edge:** Reeded and plain sectioned

Date	Mintage	F	VF	XF	Unc	BU
2000	—	—	—	0.35	1.25	—

KM# 83 200 LIRE
5.0000 g., Aluminum-Bronze, 24 mm. **Obv:** Value below smoking towers **Rev:** Seated figure weaving

Date	Mintage	F	VF	XF	Unc	BU
1978	530,000	—	0.25	0.75	1.75	—

KM# 96 200 LIRE
5.0000 g., Aluminum-Bronze, 24 mm. **Series:** F.A.O. **Obv:** Crowned shield **Rev:** Nude figure fighting lion flanked by value and date, F.A.O logo at upper right

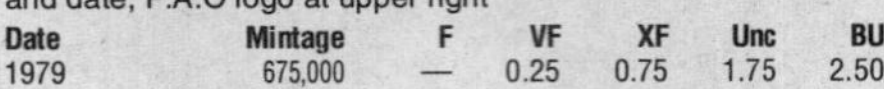

Date	Mintage	F	VF	XF	Unc	BU
1979	675,000	—	0.25	0.75	1.75	2.50

KM# 109 200 LIRE
5.0000 g., Aluminum-Bronze, 24 mm. **Series:** 1980 Olympics **Obv:** Olympic rings and date at upper left of smoking towers **Rev:** Wrestlers

Date	Mintage	F	VF	XF	Unc	BU
1980	675,000	—	0.50	1.00	2.50	—

KM# 123 200 LIRE
5.0000 g., Aluminum-Bronze, 24 mm. **Series:** F.A.O. **Obv:** Crowned shield **Rev:** Stylized animal divides date and value **Designer:** Crilli

Date	Mintage	F	VF	XF	Unc	BU
1981	700,000	—	0.25	0.75	1.75	2.50

KM# 138 200 LIRE
5.0000 g., Aluminum-Bronze, 24 mm. **Subject:** Social Conquests **Obv:** Crown above smoking towers **Rev:** Stylized figure within design

Date	Mintage	F	VF	XF	Unc	BU
1982R	178,000	—	0.25	0.75	1.75	—

KM# 152 200 LIRE
5.0000 g., Aluminum-Bronze, 24 mm. **Subject:** Nuclear War Threat **Obv:** Crown above shield and sprig **Rev:** Rider spearing victim

Date	Mintage	F	VF	XF	Unc	BU
1983	172,000	—	0.25	0.75	1.75	—

KM# 166 200 LIRE
5.0000 g., Aluminum-Bronze, 24 mm. **Obv:** Castle **Rev:** Bust of Enrico Fermi facing

Date	Mintage	F	VF	XF	Unc	BU
1984R	165,000	—	0.25	0.75	1.75	—

KM# 180 200 LIRE
5.0000 g., Aluminum-Bronze, 24 mm. **Subject:** War on Drugs **Obv:** Shield **Rev:** Family group

Date	Mintage	F	VF	XF	Unc	BU
1985R	210,000	—	—	0.40	1.50	—

KM# 194 200 LIRE
5.0000 g., Aluminum-Bronze, 24 mm. **Subject:** Revolution of Technology **Obv:** Crown above smoking towers on rock **Rev:** Stylized hand holding microchip

Date	Mintage	F	VF	XF	Unc	BU
1986R	150,000	—	—	0.40	1.50	—

KM# 208 200 LIRE
5.0000 g., Aluminum-Bronze, 24 mm. **Subject:** 15th Anniversary - Resumption of Coinage **Obv:** Crowned pointed shield within sprigs **Rev:** Building in front of smoking towers

Date	Mintage	F	VF	XF	Unc	BU
1987R	143,000	—	—	0.40	1.50	—

KM# 225 200 LIRE
5.0000 g., Aluminum-Bronze, 24 mm. **Subject:** Fortifications **Obv:** Crowned ornate arms on shield **Rev:** Tower divides value **Designer:** Sergio Giandomenico

Date	Mintage	F	VF	XF	Unc	BU
1988R	38,000	—	—	0.40	1.50	—

KM# 238 200 LIRE
5.0000 g., Aluminum-Bronze, 24 mm. **Subject:** History **Obv:** Crowned shield **Rev:** Stylized view of San Marino **Designer:** J. Asselbergs

Date	Mintage	F	VF	XF	Unc	BU
1989R	1,037,000	—	—	0.40	1.50	—

KM# 255 200 LIRE
5.0000 g., Aluminum-Bronze, 24 mm. **Subject:** 1,600 Years of History **Obv:** Towers above design **Rev:** Stylized head left **Designer:** Magdalena Dobrucka

Date	Mintage	F	VF	XF	Unc	BU
1990R	36,000	—	—	0.40	1.50	—

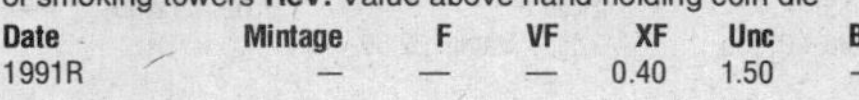

KM# 268 200 LIRE
5.0000 g., Aluminum-Bronze, 24 mm. **Obv:** Date at upper left of smoking towers **Rev:** Value above hand holding coin die

Date	Mintage	F	VF	XF	Unc	BU
1991R	—	—	—	0.40	1.50	—

KM# 285 200 LIRE
5.0000 g., Aluminum-Bronze, 24 mm. **Obv:** Stylized feathers on top of towers within circle **Rev:** Columbus navigating by the stars **Designer:** L. Cretara

Date	Mintage	F	VF	XF	Unc	BU
ND(1992)R	—	—	—	0.40	1.50	—

KM# 300 200 LIRE
5.0000 g., Aluminum-Bronze, 24 mm. **Rev:** Door and arches

Date	Mintage	F	VF	XF	Unc	BU
1993R	—	—	—	0.40	1.50	—

KM# 313 200 LIRE
5.0000 g., Aluminum-Bronze, 24 mm. **Obv:** Stonecutter holding hammer and chisel, smoking towers at left **Rev:** Man and bear

Date	Mintage	F	VF	XF	Unc	BU
1994R	40,000	—	—	0.40	1.50	—

KM# 329 200 LIRE
5.0000 g., Aluminum-Bronze, 24 mm. **Obv:** Banner wrapped around quills **Rev:** Two children playing **Designer:** Loredana Pancotto

Date	Mintage	F	VF	XF	Unc	BU
1995R	—	—	—	0.40	1.50	—

KM# 356 200 LIRE
5.0000 g., Aluminum-Bronze, 24 mm. **Subject:** Kant **Obv:** Bust facing with flame within hands **Rev:** Head of Kant right within square above value

Date	Mintage	F	VF	XF	Unc	BU
1996	32,000	—	—	0.40	1.50	—

KM# 366 200 LIRE
5.0000 g., Aluminum-Bronze, 24 mm. **Subject:** The Arts - Painting **Obv:** Bust facing with flame within hands **Rev:** Seated figure painting portrait of standing figure at left **Designer:** Galeabason

Date	Mintage	F	VF	XF	Unc	BU
1997	28,000	—	—	0.40	1.50	—

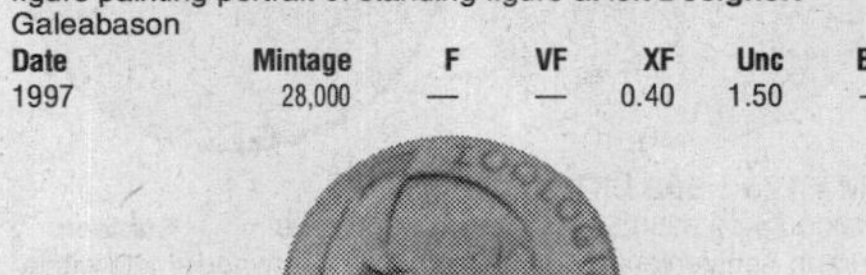

KM# 382 200 LIRE
5.0000 g., Aluminum-Bronze, 24 mm. **Subject:** Zoology **Rev:** Stylized dolphins

Date	Mintage	F	VF	XF	Unc	BU
1998	—	—	—	0.40	2.50	—

KM# 393 200 LIRE
5.0000 g., Aluminum-Bronze, 24 mm. **Subject:** Exploration **Obv:** Crowned shield **Rev:** Stonehenge beneath the sun and stars

Date	Mintage	F	VF	XF	Unc	BU
1999	—	—	—	0.40	1.50	—

KM# 403 200 LIRE
5.0000 g., Aluminum-Bronze, 24 mm. **Subject:** Knowledge **Obv:** Bust facing with flame within hands **Rev:** Allegorical female head left within globe design **Edge:** Reeded **Note:** Struck at Rome.

Date	Mintage	F	VF	XF	Unc	BU
2000	—	—	—	0.40	1.50	—

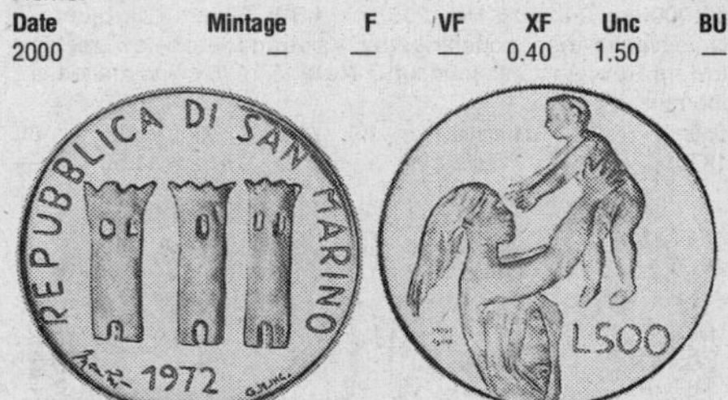

KM# 21 500 LIRE
11.0000 g., 0.8350 Silver .2953 oz. ASW, 29 mm. **Obv:** Three towers **Rev:** Mother lifting child in air **Designer:** Giacomo Manzu **Note:** 22,374 coins melted at the mint.

Date	Mintage	F	VF	XF	Unc	BU
1972	291,000	—	—	6.50	11.50	—

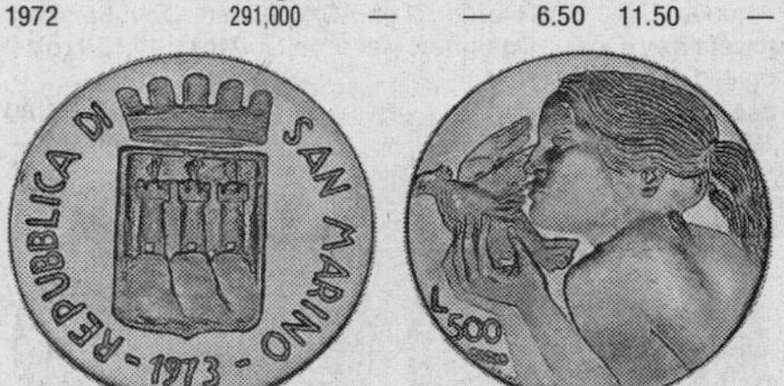

KM# 29 500 LIRE
11.0000 g., 0.8350 Silver .2953 oz. ASW, 29 mm. **Obv:** Crowned shield **Rev:** Child holding dove **Designer:** Emilio Greco **Note:** 6,544 coins melted at the mint.

Date	Mintage	F	VF	XF	Unc	BU
1973	291,000	—	—	6.50	11.50	—

KM# 37 500 LIRE
11.0000 g., 0.8350 Silver .2953 oz. ASW, 29 mm. **Obv:** Smoking towers within circle **Rev:** Two stylized pigeons **Designer:** Luciano Minguzzi **Note:** 6,295 coins melted at the mint.

Date	Mintage	F	VF	XF	Unc	BU
1974	276,000	—	—	7.00	12.50	17.00

KM# 47 500 LIRE

11.0000 g., 0.8350 Silver .2953 oz. ASW, 29 mm. **Obv:** Smoking towers **Rev:** Seagulls flying over barbed wire **Designer:** Bino Bini **Note:** 119,743 coins melted at the mint.

Date	Mintage	F	VF	XF	Unc	BU
1975	291,000	—	—	7.00	12.50	15.00

KM# 48 500 LIRE

11.0000 g., 0.8350 Silver .2953 oz. ASW, 29 mm. **Subject:** Numismatic Agency opening **Obv:** Value and date below smoking towers **Rev:** Ancient stonecutter **Note:** 47,495 coins melted at the mint.

Date	Mintage	F	VF	XF	Unc	BU
1975	200,000	—	—	6.50	11.50	—

KM# 58 500 LIRE

11.0000 g., 0.8350 Silver .2953 oz. ASW, 29 mm. **Obv:** Smoking towers **Rev:** Design **Designer:** Mario Molteni **Note:** 40,509 coins melted at the mint.

Date	Mintage	F	VF	XF	Unc	BU
1976	195,000	—	—	6.50	11.50	—

KM# 59 500 LIRE

11.0000 g., 0.8350 Silver .2953 oz. ASW, 29 mm. **Subject:** Social Security **Obv:** Stylized smoking towers **Rev:** Standing figure holding blanket to cover man **Note:** 106,604 coins melted at the mint.

Date	Mintage	F	VF	XF	Unc	BU
1976	195,000	—	—	6.50	11.50	—

KM# 71 500 LIRE

11.0000 g., 0.8350 Silver .2953 oz. ASW, 29 mm. **Obv:** Value below stylized smoking towers within circle **Rev:** Stylized upside-down bird among stars within circle **Designer:** J. Vivarelli **Note:** 45,483 coins melted at the mint.

Date	Mintage	F	VF	XF	Unc	BU
1977	180,000	—	—	6.50	11.50	—

KM# 84 500 LIRE

11.0000 g., 0.8350 Silver .2953 oz. ASW, 29 mm. **Obv:** Value below smoking towers **Rev:** Group of figures holding flags **Note:** 16,297 coins melted at the mint.

Date	Mintage	F	VF	XF	Unc	BU
1978	130,000	—	—	6.50	11.50	—

KM# 97 500 LIRE

11.0000 g., 0.8350 Silver .2953 oz. ASW, 29 mm. **Obv:** Half length figure holding three smoking towers **Rev:** Victory in a biga **Note:** 33,278 coins melted at the mint.

Date	Mintage	F	VF	XF	Unc	BU
1979	125,000	—	—	7.00	12.50	—

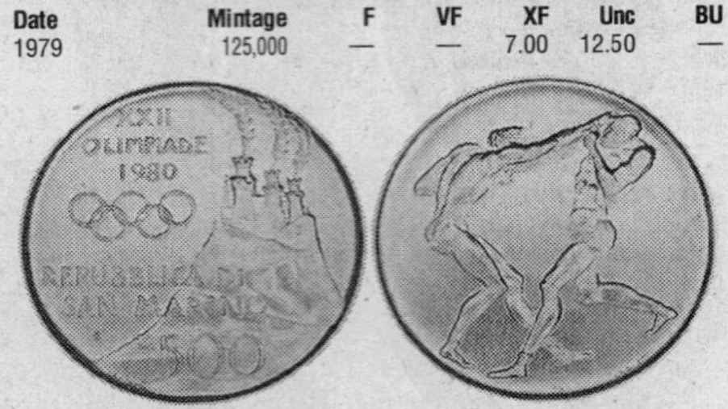

KM# 110 500 LIRE

11.0000 g., 0.8350 Silver .2953 oz. ASW, 29 mm. **Series:** 1980 Olympics **Obv:** Olympic rings and date at upper left of smoking towers **Rev:** Boxers **Note:** 47,724 coins melted at the mint.

Date	Mintage	F	VF	XF	Unc	BU
1980	125,000	—	—	7.00	12.50	—

KM# 124 500 LIRE

11.0000 g., 0.8350 Silver .2953 oz. ASW, 29 mm. **Subject:** 2000th Anniversary - Virgil's Death **Obv:** Crowned shield within sprigs **Rev:** Seated figure playing flute under tree **Note:** 9,122 coins melted at the mint.

Date	Mintage	F	VF	XF	Unc	BU
1981	75,000	—	—	7.00	12.50	—

KM# 125 500 LIRE

11.0000 g., 0.8350 Silver .2953 oz. ASW, 29 mm. **Subject:** 2,000th Anniversary - Virgil's Death **Obv:** Crowned shield within sprigs **Rev:** The seed sower **Note:** 9,122 coins melted at the mint.

Date	Mintage	F	VF	XF	Unc	BU
1981	75,000	—	—	7.00	12.50	—

KM# 126 500 LIRE

11.0000 g., 0.8350 Silver .2953 oz. ASW, 29 mm. **Obv:** Crowned shield **Rev:** Value flanked by hands below head right **Note:** 21,124 coins melted at the mint.

Date	Mintage	F	VF	XF	Unc	BU
1981	100,000	—	—	7.00	12.50	—

KM# 139 500 LIRE

11.0000 g., 0.8350 Silver .2953 oz. ASW, 29 mm. **Subject:** Centennial - Death of Garibaldi **Obv:** Crowned design above towers **Rev:** Head facing **Note:** 112 uncirculated and 369 proof coins melted at the mint.

Date	Mintage	F	VF	XF	Unc	BU
ND(1982)R	48,000	—	—	7.00	12.50	—
ND(1982)R Proof	13,000	Value: 22.50				

KM# 140 500 LIRE

6.8000 g., Bi-Metallic Aluminum-Bronze center in Stainless Steel ring, 25.8 mm. **Subject:** Social Conquests **Obv:** Crown above smoking towers within circle **Rev:** Stylized figures within circle **Designer:** A. Biancini

Date	Mintage	F	VF	XF	Unc	BU
1982R	1,900,000	—	—	2.00	4.00	—

KM# 153 500 LIRE

6.8000 g., Bi-Metallic Aluminum-Bronze center in Stainless Steel ring, 25.8 mm. **Subject:** Nuclear War Threat **Obv:** Crown above shield and sprig **Rev:** Three horses above two people **Designer:** A. Fabbri

Date	Mintage	F	VF	XF	Unc	BU
1983R	1,922,000	—	—	2.00	4.00	—

KM# 154 500 LIRE

11.0000 g., 0.8350 Silver .2953 oz. ASW, 29 mm. **Subject:** 500th Anniversary - Birth of Artist Raphael **Obv:** Head 3/4 right, smoking towers at top and to right **Rev:** Seated figure looking at portrait **Note:** 80 uncirculated and 1,939 proof coins melted at the mint.

Date	Mintage	F	VF	XF	Unc	BU
1983R	42,000	—	—	7.00	12.50	—
1983R Proof	12,000	Value: 22.50				

KM# 167 500 LIRE

6.8000 g., Bi-Metallic Aluminum-Bronze center in Stainless Steel ring, 25.8 mm. **Obv:** Castle within circle **Rev:** Bust of Albert Einstein facing within circle

Date	Mintage	F	VF	XF	Unc	BU
1984R	2,633,000	—	—	2.00	4.00	—

KM# 168 500 LIRE

11.0000 g., 0.8350 Silver .2953 oz. ASW, 29 mm. **Series:** 1984 Summer Olympics **Obv:** Stylized smoking towers **Rev:** Entwined vertical figures to left of Olympic rings, date and value **Designer:** Laura Cretara **Note:** 2,920 uncirculated and 20 proof coins melted at the mint.

Date	Mintage	F	VF	XF	Unc	BU
1984	52,000	—	—	6.50	11.50	—
1984 Proof	15,000	Value: 13.50				

KM# 181 500 LIRE

6.8000 g., Bi-Metallic Aluminum-Bronze center in Stainless Steel ring, 25.8 mm. **Subject:** War on Drugs **Obv:** Stylized bending figure within circle **Rev:** Cured addict within circle **Designer:** Crilli

Date	Mintage	F	VF	XF	Unc	BU
1985R	2,647,000	—	—	2.00	4.00	—

KM# 182 500 LIRE

11.0000 g., 0.8350 Silver .2953 oz. ASW, 29 mm. **Subject:** European Music Year, Bach Tercentenary **Rev:** Music seated at organ **Designer:** Guido Veroi **Note:** 6,704 uncirculated and 122 proof coins melted at the mint.

Date	Mintage	F	VF	XF	Unc	BU
1985	40,000	—	—	7.00	12.50	—
1985 Proof	12,000	Value: 15.00				

KM# 195 500 LIRE

6.8000 g., Bi-Metallic Aluminum-Bronze center in Stainless Steel ring, 25.8 mm. **Subject:** Revolution of Technology **Obv:** Crown above smoking towers on rock **Rev:** Human figure seated on console control panel **Designer:** Rossello

Date	Mintage	F	VF	XF	Unc	BU
1986R	3,111,000	—	—	2.00	4.00	—

KM# 196 500 LIRE

11.0000 g., 0.8350 Silver .2953 oz. ASW, 29 mm. **Subject:** Soccer **Obv:** Head left **Rev:** Field design **Note:** 5,212 uncirculated and 60 proof coins melted at the mint.

Date	Mintage	F	VF	XF	Unc	BU
1986R	45,000	—	—	—	12.50	—
1986R Proof	12,000	Value: 15.00				

KM# 209 500 LIRE

6.8000 g., Bi-Metallic Aluminum-Bronze center in Stainless Steel ring, 25.8 mm. **Subject:** 15th Anniversary - Resumption of Coinage **Obv:** Crowned pointed shield within sprigs **Rev:** Smoking towers

Date	Mintage	F	VF	XF	Unc	BU
1987R	3,063,000	—	—	2.00	4.00	—

KM# 213 500 LIRE

11.0000 g., 0.8350 Silver .2953 oz. ASW, 29 mm. **Subject:** Zagreb University Games **Rev:** Runner **Note:** 9,208 uncirculated and 1,206 proof coins melted at the mint.

Date	Mintage	F	VF	XF	Unc	BU
1987R	35,000	—	—	—	12.50	—
1987R Proof	10,000	Value: 15.00				

KM# 216 500 LIRE

11.0000 g., 0.8350 Silver .2953 oz. ASW, 29 mm. **Series:** Winter Olympics **Obv:** Stylized smoking towers **Rev:** Downhill skier, oak leaf and Olympic rings **Designer:** Maurizio Soccorsi **Note:** 146 uncirculated and 3 proof coins melted at the mint.

Date	Mintage	F	VF	XF	Unc	BU
1988R	32,000	—	—	—	9.00	—
1988R Proof	9,600	Value: 15.00				

KM# 226 500 LIRE

6.8000 g., Bi-Metallic Aluminum-Bronze center in Stainless Steel ring, 25.8 mm. **Subject:** Fortifications **Obv:** Crowned ornate arms on shield **Rev:** Hilltop fortification **Designer:** Sergio Giandomenico

Date	Mintage	F	VF	XF	Unc	BU
1988R	3,526,000	—	—	2.00	4.00	—

KM# 239 500 LIRE

6.8000 g., Bi-Metallic Aluminum-Bronze center in Stainless Steel ring, 25.8 mm. **Subject:** History **Obv:** Crowned shield **Rev:** Stone carver **Designer:** J. Asselbergs

Date	Mintage	F	VF	XF	Unc	BU
1989R	3,145,000	—	—	2.00	4.00	—

KM# 243 500 LIRE

11.0000 g., 0.8350 Silver .2953 oz. ASW, 29 mm. **Subject:** San Marino Grand Prix **Obv:** Stylized smoking towers **Rev:** Vertical horse and rider above car **Note:** 5,180 coins melted at the mint.

Date	Mintage	F	VF	XF	Unc	BU
1989R	30,000	—	—	—	10.00	—
1989R Proof	8,000	Value: 25.00				

KM# 246 500 LIRE

11.0000 g., 0.8350 Silver .2953 oz. ASW, 29 mm. **Subject:** World Cup Soccer Championship Game **Obv:** Patterned design surrounds oval shield at center **Rev:** Cluster of stylized running figures

Date	Mintage	F	VF	XF	Unc	BU
1990R	40,000	—	—	—	10.00	—
1990R Proof	19,000	Value: 20.00				

KM# 256 500 LIRE

6.8000 g., Bi-Metallic Aluminum-Bronze center in Stainless Steel ring, 25.8 mm. **Subject:** 1,600 Years of History **Obv:** Towers above design **Rev:** Birds and stamp **Designer:** Magdalena Dobrucka

Date	Mintage	F	VF	XF	Unc	BU
1990R	Est. 60,000	—	—	2.00	4.00	—

KM# 269 500 LIRE

6.8000 g., Bi-Metallic Aluminum-Bronze center in Stainless Steel ring, 25.8 mm. **Obv:** Date at left of smoking towers within circle **Rev:** Value above hand holding flowers within circle **Designer:** Aparielo

Date	Mintage	F	VF	XF	Unc	BU
1991R	3,580,563	—	—	2.00	4.00	—

KM# 271 500 LIRE

11.0000 g., 0.8350 Silver .2953 oz. ASW, 29 mm. **Series:** Barcelona Olympics **Obv:** Seated Saint facing with hammer in hand **Rev:** Priestess lighting fire with sun beam

Date	Mintage	F	VF	XF	Unc	BU
1991R	Est. 60,000	—	—	—	9.00	—
1991R Proof	Est. 8,000	Value: 20.00				

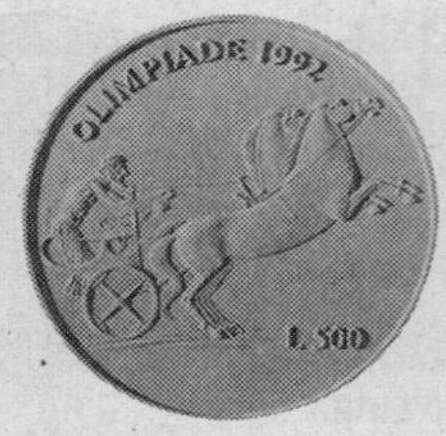

KM# 276 500 LIRE
11.0000 g., 0.8350 Silver .2953 oz. ASW, 29 mm. **Series:** Olympics **Obv:** Three smoking towers **Rev:** Chariot

Date	Mintage	F	VF	XF	Unc	BU
1992R	Est. 70,000	—	—	—	12.00	—
1992R Proof	—	Value: 20.00				

KM# 286 500 LIRE
6.8000 g., Bi-Metallic Aluminumn-Bronze center in Steel ring, 25.8 mm. **Subject:** Columbus **Obv:** Towers with feather-like designs on top within circle **Rev:** Winds blowing ship within circle

Date	Mintage	F	VF	XF	Unc	BU
1992R	4,554,864	—	—	—	3.50	—

KM# 291 500 LIRE
11.0000 g., 0.8350 Silver .2953 oz. ASW, 29 mm. **Subject:** Wildlife protection **Obv:** Crowned pointed shield within sprigs **Rev:** Two European polecats

Date	Mintage	F	VF	XF	Unc	BU
1993R	Est. 35,000	—	—	—	12.50	17.00
1993R Proof	—	Value: 24.00				

KM# 301 500 LIRE
6.8000 g., Bi-Metallic Aluminum-Bronze center in Stainless Steel ring, 25.8 mm. **Obv:** Smoking towers within circle **Rev:** Growth from a tree stump **Designer:** G.P. Malison

Date	Mintage	F	VF	XF	Unc	BU
1993R	4,200,000	—	—	—	3.50	—

KM# 314 500 LIRE
6.8000 g., Bi-Metallic Aluminum-Bronze center in Stainless Steel ring, 25.8 mm. **Obv:** Stonecutter holding hammer and chisel, smoking towers at left, all within circle **Rev:** St. Marino receiving Mount Titano within circle **Designer:** Lozica Driulli

Date	Mintage	F	VF	XF	Unc	BU
1994R	40,000	—	—	—	3.50	—

KM# 317 500 LIRE
11.0000 g., 0.8350 Silver .2953 oz. ASW, 29 mm. **Subject:** World Cup Soccer **Obv:** Crowned pointed shield within sprigs **Rev:** Fallen soccer player

Date	Mintage	F	VF	XF	Unc	BU
1994R Proof	—	Value: 15.00				

KM# 330 500 LIRE
6.8000 g., Bi-Metallic Aluminum-Bronze center in Stainless Steel ring, 25.8 mm. **Series:** F.A.O. **Subject:** 50th Anniversary - F.A.O. **Obv:** Banner wrapped around bottom of design **Rev:** Kneeling figure under sprig **Designer:** Loredana Pancotto

Date	Mintage	F	VF	XF	Unc	BU
1995R	3,000,000	—	—	—	3.50	—

KM# 357 500 LIRE
6.8000 g., Bi-Metallic Aluminum-Bronze center in Stainless Steel ring, 25.8 mm. **Obv:** Bust facing with flame within hands within circle **Obv. Designer:** Giulianelli **Rev:** Face within triangle and circle design **Rev. Designer:** Renka

Date	Mintage	F	VF	XF	Unc	BU
1996	3,911,288	—	—	—	3.50	—

KM# 367 500 LIRE
6.8000 g., Bi-Metallic Aluminum-Bronze center in Stainless Steel ring, 25.8 mm. **Subject:** The Arts - Music **Obv:** Bust facing with flame within hands within circle **Obv. Designer:** Giulianelli **Rev:** Woman playing pipes within circle

Date	Mintage	F	VF	XF	Unc	BU
1997	28,000	—	—	—	3.50	—

Note: In mint sets only

KM# 383 500 LIRE
6.8000 g., Bi-Metallic Aluminum-Bronze center in Stainless Steel ring, 25.8 mm. **Subject:** Chemistry **Obv. Designer:** Giulianelli **Rev:** Laboratory **Rev. Designer:** Magdalena Dobrucka

Date	Mintage	F	VF	XF	Unc	BU
1998	1,300,000	—	—	—	3.50	—

KM# 394 500 LIRE
6.8000 g., Bi-Metallic Aluminum-Bronze center in Stainless Steel ring, 25.8 mm. **Subject:** Exploration **Obv:** Crowned shield **Rev:** Moon's surface, radio waves and Saturn **Designer:** Y. Abd el-Kalik

Date	Mintage	F	VF	XF	Unc	BU
1999	2,000,000	—	—	—	3.50	—

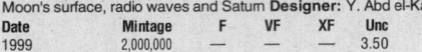

KM# 404 500 LIRE
6.8000 g., Bi-Metallic Aluminum-Bronze center in Stainless Steel ring, 25.8 mm. **Subject:** Work **Obv:** Bust facing with flames within hands within circle **Obv. Designer:** Giulianelli **Rev:** Spinning wheel design within circle **Edge:** Reeded and plain sections

Date	Mintage	VG	F	VF	XF	Unc
2000	28,000	—	—	—	—	4.00

Note: In mint sets only

KM# 72 1000 LIRE
14.6000 g., 0.8350 Silver .3919 oz. ASW, 31.4 mm. **Subject:** 600th Anniversary - Birth of Brunelleschi- architect, author **Obv:** Standing figures on railed platform **Rev:** Head 3/4 left facing **Note:** 38,145 coins melted at the mint.

Date	Mintage	F	VF	XF	Unc	BU
ND(1977)	180,000	—	—	—	10.00	—

KM# 85 1000 LIRE
14.6000 g., 0.8350 Silver .3919 oz. ASW, 31.4 mm. **Subject:** 150th Anniversary - Birth of Tolstoy **Obv:** Smoking towers **Rev:** Head left **Note:** 17,892 coins melted at the mint.

Date	Mintage	F	VF	XF	Unc	BU
ND(1978)	130,000	—	—	—	10.00	—

KM# 98 1000 LIRE
14.6000 g., 0.8350 Silver .3919 oz. ASW, 31.4 mm. **Subject:** European Unity **Obv:** Crown above stylized smoking towers **Rev:** Seagulls above figure facing right **Note:** 14,945 coins melted at the mint.

Date	Mintage	F	VF	XF	Unc	BU
1979	125,000	—	—	—	16.50	—

KM# 112 1000 LIRE
14.6000 g., 0.8350 Silver .3919 oz. ASW, 31.4 mm. **Subject:** 1,500th Anniversary - Birth of St. Benedict **Obv:** Smoking towers **Rev:** Bust facing **Note:** 49,095 coins melted at the mint.

Date	Mintage	F	VF	XF	Unc	BU
1980	125,000	—	—	—	15.00	—

KM# 127 1000 LIRE

14.6000 g., 0.8350 Silver .3919 oz. ASW, 31.4 mm. **Subject:** 200th Anniversary - Virgil's Death **Obv:** Crowned shield within sprigs **Rev:** Armored figure on horse **Note:** 9,122 coins melted at the mint.

Date	Mintage	F	VF	XF	Unc	BU
1981	75,000	—	—	—	15.00	—

KM# 141 1000 LIRE

14.6000 g., 0.8350 Silver .3919 oz. ASW, 31.4 mm. **Subject:** Centennial - Garibaldi's Death **Obv:** Crowned design above towers **Rev:** Large head facing **Note:** 112 uncirculated and 369 proof coins melted at the mint.

Date	Mintage	F	VF	XF	Unc	BU
ND(1982)R	48,000	—	—	—	15.00	—
ND(1982)R Proof	13,000	Value: 25.00				

KM# 155 1000 LIRE

14.6000 g., 0.8350 Silver .3919 oz. ASW, 31.4 mm. **Subject:** 500th Anniversary - Birth of Artist Raphael **Obv:** Head 1/4 right, towers at top and right **Rev:** Standing figure facing divides date and value **Note:** 80 uncirculated and 1,939 proof coins melted at the mint.

Date	Mintage	F	VF	XF	Unc	BU
1983R	42,000	—	—	—	15.00	—
1983R Proof	12,000	Value: 25.00				

KM# 169 1000 LIRE

14.6000 g., 0.8350 Silver .3919 oz. ASW, 31.4 mm. **Series:** 1984 Summer Olympics **Obv:** Stylized smoking towers **Rev:** Figures reaching wings of bird divide date and value with olympic rings below **Designer:** Laura Cretara **Note:** 2,920 uncirculated and 20 proof coins melted at the mint.

Date	Mintage	F	VF	XF	Unc	BU
1984R	52,000	—	—	—	12.50	—
1984R Proof	15,000	Value: 22.50				

KM# 183 1000 LIRE

14.6000 g., 0.8350 Silver .3919 oz. ASW, 31.4 mm. **Subject:** European Music Year, Bach Tercentenary **Obv:** Smoking towers within crowned shield **Rev:** J.S. Bach **Designer:** Guido Veroi **Note:** 6,704 uncirculated and 122 proof coins melted at the mint.

Date	Mintage	F	VF	XF	Unc	BU
1985R	40,000	—	—	—	15.00	—
1985R Proof	12,000	Value: 25.00				

KM# 197 1000 LIRE

14.6000 g., 0.8350 Silver .3919 oz. ASW, 31.4 mm. **Subject:** Soccer **Obv:** Head left **Rev:** Stylized flags **Designer:** Jorio Vivarelli **Note:** 5,212 uncirculated and 60 proof coins melted at the mint.

Date	Mintage	F	VF	XF	Unc	BU
1986R	45,000	—	—	—	16.00	—
1986R Proof	12,000	Value: 30.00				

KM# 210 1000 LIRE

14.6000 g., 0.8350 Silver .3919 oz. ASW, 31.4 mm. **Subject:** 15th Anniversary - Resumption of Coinage **Obv:** Crowned pointed shield within sprigs **Rev:** Standing Saint figure facing **Note:** 13 coins melted at the mint.

Date	Mintage	F	VF	XF	Unc	BU
1987R	43,000	—	—	—	18.00	—

KM# 214 1000 LIRE

14.6000 g., 0.8350 Silver .3919 oz. ASW, 31.4 mm. **Subject:** Zagreb University Games **Rev:** Pole vaulter **Note:** 9,207 uncirculated and 1,206 proof coins melted at the mint.

Date	Mintage	F	VF	XF	Unc	BU
1987R	35,000	—	—	—	16.00	—
1987R Proof	10,000	Value: 30.00				

KM# 217 1000 LIRE

14.6000 g., 0.8350 Silver .3919 oz. ASW, 31.4 mm. **Series:** Summer Olympics **Obv:** Stylized smoking towers **Rev:** Diver **Designer:** Maurizio Soccorsi **Note:** 146 uncirculated and 3 proof coins melted at the mint.

Date	Mintage	F	VF	XF	Unc	BU
1988R	32,000	—	—	—	17.50	—
1988R Proof	9,600	Value: 30.00				

KM# 227 1000 LIRE

14.6000 g., 0.8350 Silver .3919 oz. ASW, 31.4 mm. **Subject:** Fortifications **Obv:** Crowned ornate arms on shield **Rev:** Walls and towers **Designer:** Sergio Giandelmonico

Date	Mintage	F	VF	XF	Unc	BU
1988R	38,000	—	—	—	20.00	—

KM# 240 1000 LIRE

14.6000 g., 0.8350 Silver .3919 oz. ASW, 31.4 mm. **Subject:** History **Obv:** Crowned shield **Rev:** Two men standing in boat

Date	Mintage	F	VF	XF	Unc	BU
1989R	32,000	—	—	—	20.00	—

KM# 244 1000 LIRE

14.6000 g., 0.8350 Silver .3919 oz. ASW, 31.4 mm. **Subject:** San Marino Grand Prix **Obv:** Stylized smoking towers **Rev:** Date and value below race car **Note:** 5,180 coins melted at the mint.

Date	Mintage	F	VF	XF	Unc	BU
1989R	30,000	—	—	—	20.00	—
1989R Proof	8,000	Value: 35.00				

KM# 247 1000 LIRE

14.6000 g., 0.8350 Silver .3919 oz. ASW, 31.4 mm. **Subject:** World Cup Soccer Championship Games **Obv:** Patterned design surrounds oval shield at center **Rev:** Winged Victory divides value

Date	Mintage	F	VF	XF	Unc	BU
1990R	40,000	—	—	—	20.00	—
1990R Proof	19,000	Value: 30.00				

KM# 257 1000 LIRE

14.6000 g., 0.8350 Silver .3919 oz. ASW, 31.4 mm. **Subject:** 1,600 Years of History **Obv:** Towers above design **Rev:** Stylized hand and two figures **Designer:** Madgalena Dobrncka

Date	Mintage	F	VF	XF	Unc	BU
1990R	36,000	—	—	—	20.00	—

KM# 270 1000 LIRE
14.6000 g., 0.8350 Silver .3919 oz. ASW, 31.4 mm. **Obv:** Date at upper left of smoking towers **Rev:** Large value above hand holding dove

Date	Mintage	F	VF	XF	Unc	BU
1991R	—	—	—	—	20.00	—

KM# 272 1000 LIRE
14.6000 g., 0.8350 Silver .3919 oz. ASW, 31.4 mm. **Series:** Barcelona Olympics **Rev:** Stylized runner and Olympic rings

Date	Mintage	F	VF	XF	Unc	BU
1991R	Est. 60,000	—	—	—	20.00	—
1991R Proof	Est. 8,000	Value: 32.50				

KM# 277 1000 LIRE
14.6000 g., 0.8350 Silver .3919 oz. ASW, 31.4 mm. **Series:** Olympics **Obv:** Stylized smoking towers **Rev:** Athletes

Date	Mintage	F	VF	XF	Unc	BU
1992R	Est. 70,000	—	—	—	20.00	—
1992R Proof	—	Value: 32.50				

KM# 287 1000 LIRE
14.6000 g., 0.8350 Silver .3919 oz. ASW, 31.4 mm. **Obv:** Towers with feather-like designs at top within circle **Rev:** Columbus studying chart within circle

Date	Mintage	F	VF	XF	Unc	BU
ND(1992)R	—	—	—	—	22.50	—

KM# 292 1000 LIRE
14.6000 g., 0.8350 Silver .3919 oz. ASW, 31.4 mm. **Series:** Wildlife Protection **Obv:** Crowned pointed shield within sprigs **Rev:** Falcon and Woodpecker

Date	Mintage	F	VF	XF	Unc	BU
1993R	Est. 35,000	—	—	—	20.00	—
1993R Proof	—	Value: 30.00				

KM# 302 1000 LIRE
14.6000 g., 0.8350 Silver .3919 oz. ASW, 31.4 mm. **Obv:** Smoking towers **Rev:** Wing above globe

Date	Mintage	F	VF	XF	Unc	BU
1993R	—	—	—	—	22.50	—

KM# 315 1000 LIRE
14.6000 g., 0.8350 Silver .3919 oz. ASW, 31.4 mm. **Subject:** Founder Building First San Marino Church **Obv:** Stonecutter holding hammer and chisel, smoking towers at left **Rev:** Seated stone cutter

Date	Mintage	F	VF	XF	Unc	BU
1994R	40,000	—	—	—	22.50	—

KM# 316 1000 LIRE
14.6000 g., 0.8350 Silver .3919 oz. ASW, 31.4 mm. **Series:** Olympics **Obv:** Crowned pointed shield within sprigs **Rev:** Ski jumper **Designer:** Doris Waschk-Balz

Date	Mintage	F	VF	XF	Unc	BU
1994R Proof	—	Value: 18.50				

KM# 318 1000 LIRE
14.6000 g., 0.8350 Silver .3919 oz. ASW, 31.4 mm. **Subject:** World Cup Soccer **Obv:** Crowned pointed shield within sprigs **Rev:** Soccer players

Date	Mintage	F	VF	XF	Unc	BU
1994R Proof	—	Value: 27.50				

KM# 331 1000 LIRE
14.6000 g., 0.8350 Silver .3919 oz. ASW, 31.4 mm. **Obv:** Banner wrapped around quills **Rev:** Pyramid of children within value **Designer:** Loredana Pancotto

Date	Mintage	F	VF	XF	Unc	BU
1995R	—	—	—	—	22.50	—

KM# 332 1000 LIRE
14.6000 g., 0.8350 Silver .3919 oz. ASW, 31.4 mm. **Series:** 1996 Olympics **Obv:** Crowned pointed shield within sprigs **Rev:** Pole vaulting and discus

Date	Mintage	F	VF	XF	Unc	BU
1995R Proof	50,000	Value: 30.00				

KM# 358 1000 LIRE
14.6000 g., 0.8350 Silver .3919 oz. ASW, 31.4 mm. **Obv:** Bust facing with flame within hands **Obv. Designer:** Giulianelli **Rev:** Head of Popper facing

Date	Mintage	F	VF	XF	Unc	BU
1996	32,000	—	—	—	20.00	—

KM# 368 1000 LIRE
Bi-Metallic Copper-Nickel center in Aluminum-Bronze ring, 27 mm. **Obv:** Heraldic lion within circle **Rev:** Statue, building and value within circle

Date	Mintage	F	VF	XF	Unc	BU
1997	2,232,541	—	—	—	8.00	—

KM# 369 1000 LIRE
14.6000 g., 0.8350 Silver .3919 oz. ASW, 31.4 mm. **Subject:** The Arts - Interplanetary Communication **Obv:** Bust facing with flame within hands **Rev:** Nude couple from Pioneer 10 space probe plaque

Date	Mintage	F	VF	XF	Unc	BU
1997	28,000	—	—	—	25.00	—

KM# 384 1000 LIRE
Bi-Metallic Copper-Nickel center in Aluminum-Bronze ring, 27 mm. **Subject:** Geology **Obv:** Bust facing with flame within hands **Rev:** Family standing on earth **Designer:** Magdalena Dobrucka

Date	Mintage	F	VF	XF	Unc	BU
1998	2,061,275	—	—	—	8.00	—

KM# 395 1000 LIRE
Bi-Metallic Copper-Nickel center in Aluminum-Bronze ring, 27 mm. **Subject:** Exploration **Obv:** Crowned shield **Rev:** Radiant north star design **Designer:** Y. Abd el-Kalik

Date	Mintage	F	VF	XF	Unc	BU
1999	1,836,495	—	—	—	8.00	—

KM# 405 1000 LIRE
Bi-Metallic Copper-Nickel center in Aluminum-Bronze ring, 27 mm. **Subject:** Liberty **Obv:** Child of the Universe **Rev:** Barn Swallow flying over world globe **Edge:** Reeded and plain sectioned **Note:** Struck at Rome.

Date	Mintage	F	VF	XF	Unc	BU
2000	2,898,805	—	—	—	10.00	—

KM# 333 5000 LIRE
18.0000 g., 0.8350 Silver .4832 oz. ASW **Subject:** Sail Training Ship "Amerigo Vespucci" **Obv:** Crowned pointed shield within sprigs **Rev:** Sailing ship

Date	Mintage	F	VF	XF	Unc	BU
1995R Proof	Est. 35,000	Value: 17.50				

KM# 340 5000 LIRE
18.0000 g., 0.8350 Silver .4832 oz. ASW **Series:** Wildlife Protection **Obv:** Crowned pointed shield within sprigs **Rev:** Falcons

Date	Mintage	F	VF	XF	Unc	BU
1996 Proof	Est. 35,000	Value: 45.00				

KM# 370 5000 LIRE
18.0000 g., 0.8350 Silver .4832 oz. ASW **Obv:** Crowned pointed shield within sprigs **Rev:** Sailing ship and map of Africa **Rev. Legend:** VASCO DA GAMA 1497

Date	Mintage	F	VF	XF	Unc	BU
1997 Proof	—	Value: 17.50				

KM# 385 5000 LIRE
18.0000 g., 0.8350 Silver .4832 oz. ASW **Subject:** Medicine **Obv:** Child of the Universe **Rev:** Emblem within circle of face outline left

Date	Mintage	F	VF	XF	Unc	BU
1998	—	—	—	—	18.00	—

KM# 386 5000 LIRE
18.0000 g., 0.8350 Silver .4832 oz. ASW, 32 mm. **Subject:** Europe in the New Millennium **Obv:** Crowned pointed shield within sprigs **Rev:** Euro bridge with ivy, olive and oak trees **Edge:** Lettered **Edge Lettering:** RELINQUO VOS LIBEROS **Note:** Struck at Rome.

Date	Mintage	F	VF	XF	Unc	BU
1998 Proof	—	Value: 20.00				

KM# 396 5000 LIRE
18.0000 g., 0.8350 Silver .4832 oz. ASW **Subject:** Exploration **Obv:** Crowned shield **Rev:** Solar system, European map and dish in human mind

Date	Mintage	F	VF	XF	Unc	BU
1999	—	—	—	—	18.00	—

KM# 410 5000 LIRE
18.0000 g., 0.8350 Silver .4832 oz. ASW **Subject:** European Union **Obv:** Crowned pointed shield within sprigs **Rev:** Value above flags **Edge:** Lettered **Edge Lettering:** RELINQUO VOS LIBEROS

Date	Mintage	F	VF	XF	Unc	BU
1999 Proof	—	Value: 30.00				

KM# 406 5000 LIRE
18.0000 g., 0.8350 Silver .4832 oz. ASW, 32 mm. **Subject:** Peace **Obv:** Child of the Universe **Rev:** Hawk and dove with same olive branch in their beaks **Edge:** Reeded and plain sectioned **Note:** Struck at Rome.

Date	Mintage	F	VF	XF	Unc	BU
2000	—	—	—	—	25.00	—

KM# 421 5000 LIRE
18.0000 g., 0.8350 Silver .4832 oz. ASW **Subject:** First Holy Year Jubilee **Obv:** Crowned pointed shield within sprigs **Rev:** Pope Boniface VIII with two aides **Edge:** Lettered **Edge Lettering:** RELINQUO VOS LIBEROS

Date	Mintage	F	VF	XF	Unc	BU
2000 Proof	—	Value: 20.00				

KM# 334 10000 LIRE
22.0000 g., 0.8350 Silver .5907 oz. ASW **Subject:** Amerigo Vespucci **Obv:** Crowned pointed shield within sprigs **Rev:** Cameo to upper left of ship

Date	Mintage	F	VF	XF	Unc	BU
1995R Proof	Est. 35,000	Value: 22.50				

KM# 341 10000 LIRE
22.0000 g., 0.8350 Silver .5907 oz. ASW **Series:** Wildlife Protection **Obv:** Crowned pointed shield within sprigs **Rev:** Wolves

Date	Mintage	F	VF	XF	Unc	BU
1996 Proof	Est. 35,000	Value: 60.00				

KM# 342 10000 LIRE
22.0000 g., 0.8350 Silver .5907 oz. ASW **Subject:** Euro **Obv:** Crowned pointed shield within sprigs **Rev:** Parliament building and map

Date	Mintage	F	VF	XF	Unc	BU
1996 Proof	—	Value: 30.00				

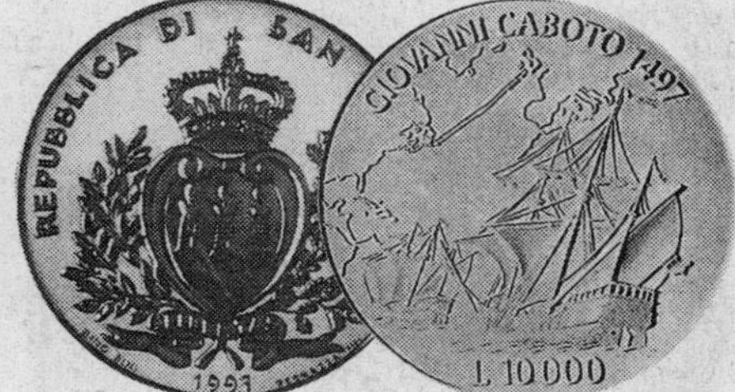

KM# 371 10000 LIRE
22.0000 g., 0.8350 Silver .5907 oz. ASW **Subject:** Giovanni Caboto 1497 **Obv:** Crowned pointed shield within sprigs **Rev:** Ship and Atlantic map

Date	Mintage	F	VF	XF	Unc	BU
1997 Proof	—	Value: 28.00				

KM# 372 10000 LIRE
22.0000 g., 0.8350 Silver .5907 oz. ASW **Subject:** Euro - "Libertas" **Obv:** National arms above the 9 Casteli arms **Rev:** Head left within oval star design

Date	Mintage	F	VF	XF	Unc	BU
1997 Proof	—	Value: 32.00				

KM# 376 10000 LIRE
22.0000 g., 0.8350 Silver .5907 oz. ASW **Subject:** Soccer World Championship **Obv:** Crowned pointed shield within sprigs **Rev:** Soccer players

Date	Mintage	F	VF	XF	Unc	BU
1998 Proof	—	Value: 30.00				

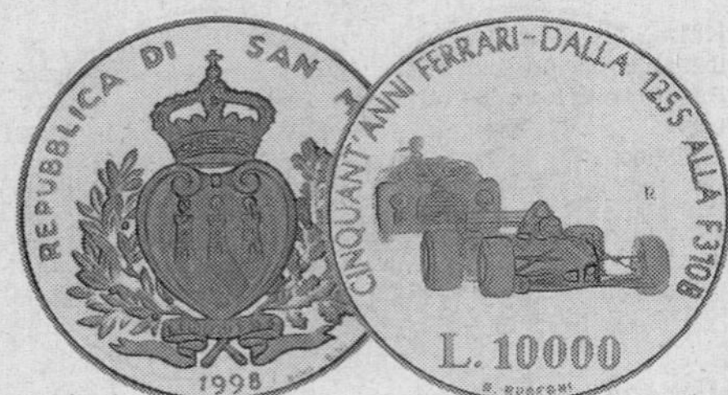

KM# 377 10000 LIRE
22.0000 g., 0.8350 Silver .5907 oz. ASW, 34 mm. **Subject:** 50th Anniversary - Ferrari **Obv:** Crowned pointed shield within sprigs **Rev:** Race cars **Edge:** Reeded and plain sections

Date	Mintage	F	VF	XF	Unc	BU
1998 Proof	30,000	Value: 27.50				

KM# 387 10000 LIRE
22.0000 g., 0.8350 Silver .5907 oz. ASW **Subject:** Europe in the New Millennium **Obv:** Crowned pointed shield within sprigs **Rev:** Child with flags

Date	Mintage	F	VF	XF	Unc	BU
1998 Proof	—	Value: 27.50				

KM# 397 10000 LIRE
22.0000 g., 0.8350 Silver .5907 oz. ASW **Subject:** III Millennium **Obv:** Crowned pointed shield within sprigs **Rev:** Allegorical portrait of DNA unraveling from human mind

Date	Mintage	F	VF	XF	Unc	BU
1999 Proof	Est. 25,000	Value: 30.00				

KM# 398 10000 LIRE
22.0000 g., 0.8350 Silver .5907 oz. ASW **Series:** 2000 Olympics **Obv:** Crowned pointed shield within sprigs **Rev:** Prone shooter

Date	Mintage	F	VF	XF	Unc	BU
1999 Proof	Est. 35,000	Value: 27.50				

KM# 411 10000 LIRE
22.0000 g., 0.8350 Silver .5907 oz. ASW **Subject:** European Union **Obv:** Crowned pointed shield within sprigs **Rev:** Circle of paper dolls above value

Date	Mintage	F	VF	XF	Unc	BU
1999 Proof	—	Value: 35.00				

KM# 419 10000 LIRE
22.0000 g., 0.8350 Silver .5907 oz. ASW, 34 mm. **Subject:** 17th Centennial of the Republic **Obv:** Crowned pointed shield within sprigs **Rev:** Bust of St. Marino facing

Date	Mintage	F	VF	XF	Unc	BU
2000 Proof	18,000	Value: 22.50				

KM# 422 10000 LIRE
22.0000 g., 0.8350 Silver .5907 oz. ASW, 34 mm. **Subject:** Holy Year **Obv:** Crowned pointed shield within sprigs **Rev:** Pope kneeling before an open door **Edge:** Reeded and plain sections

Date	Mintage	F	VF	XF	Unc	BU
2000 Proof	—	Value: 30.00				

KM# 423 10000 LIRE
22.0000 g., 0.8350 Silver .5907 oz. ASW, 34 mm. **Obv:** Crowned pointed shield within sprigs **Rev:** Michelangelo's Sacred Family Painting **Edge:** Reeded and plain sections

Date	Mintage	F	VF	XF	Unc	BU
2000 Proof	—	Value: 30.00				

KM# 416 1/2 SCUDO
1.6100 g., 0.9000 Gold .0466 oz. AGW, 14 mm. **Subject:** Ilcenacolo **Obv:** Crowned pointed shield within sprigs **Rev:** Bearded bust facing **Edge:** Reeded **Note:** 1,915 coins melted at the mint.

Date	Mintage	F	VF	XF	Unc	BU
1998	8,000	—	—	—	40.00	—

KM# 413 1/2 SCUDO
1.6100 g., 0.9000 Gold .0466 oz. AGW **Subject:** Ritratto di Agnolo Doni **Obv:** Crowned pointed shield within sprigs **Rev:** Head 3/4 right

Date	Mintage	F	VF	XF	Unc	BU
1999 Proof	8,000	Value: 37.50				

KM# 407 1/2 SCUDO
1.6100 g., 0.9000 Gold .0466 oz. AGW **Subject:** Ritratto di Giovane Donna **Obv:** Crowned pointed shield within sprigs **Rev:** Head left

Date	Mintage	F	VF	XF	Unc	BU
2000 Proof	6,000	—	—	—	37.50	—

KM# 38 SCUDO
3.0000 g., 0.9170 Gold .0883 oz. AGW **Obv:** Crowned pointed shield within sprigs **Rev:** Standing Saint facing **Note:** 2,491 coins melted at the mint.

Date	Mintage	F	VF	XF	Unc	BU
1974	87,000	—	—	—	65.00	—

KM# 49 SCUDO
3.0000 g., 0.9170 Gold .0883 oz. AGW **Obv:** Crowned pointed shield within sprigs **Rev:** Value and date within wreath **Note:** 37,668 coins melted at the mint.

Date	Mintage	F	VF	XF	Unc	BU
1975	90,000	—	—	—	70.00	—

KM# 60 SCUDO
3.0000 g., 0.9170 Gold .0883 oz. AGW **Obv:** Smoking towers **Rev:** Laureate head right **Note:** 30,026 coins melted at the mint.

Date	Mintage	F	VF	XF	Unc	BU
1976	65,000	—	—	—	65.00	—

KM# 73 SCUDO
3.0000 g., 0.9170 Gold .0883 oz. AGW **Obv:** Smoking towers **Rev:** Democrazia **Note:** 1,839 coins melted at the mint.

Date	Mintage	F	VF	XF	Unc	BU
1977	35,000	—	—	—	70.00	—

KM# 86 SCUDO

3.0000 g., 0.9170 Gold .0883 oz. AGW **Obv:** Smoking towers **Rev:** Miss Liberta **Note:** 9,021 coins melted at the mint.

Date	Mintage	F	VF	XF	Unc	BU
1978	38,000	—	—	—	70.00	—

KM# 99 SCUDO

3.0000 g., 0.9170 Gold .0883 oz. AGW **Obv:** Value within upright feathers **Rev:** Peace **Note:** 4,152 coins melted at the mint.

Date	Mintage	F	VF	XF	Unc	BU
1979	38,000	—	—	—	70.00	—

KM# 113 SCUDO

3.0000 g., 0.9170 Gold .0883 oz. AGW **Rev:** Head on hands facing, dove at left **Note:** 10,309 coins melted at the mint.

Date	Mintage	F	VF	XF	Unc	BU
1980	38,000	—	—	—	70.00	—

KM# 128 SCUDO

3.0000 g., 0.9170 Gold .0883 oz. AGW **Subject:** World Food Day **Obv:** Crowned pointed shield within sprigs above inscription **Rev:** Seated figure reading **Note:** 196 coins melted at the mint.

Date	Mintage	F	VF	XF	Unc	BU
1981	31,000	—	—	—	70.00	—

KM# 142 SCUDO

3.0000 g., 0.9170 Gold .0883 oz. AGW **Obv:** Crowned shield **Rev:** Head left **Note:** 1,192 coins melted at the mint.

Date	Mintage	F	VF	XF	Unc	BU
1982R	17,000	—	—	—	70.00	—

KM# 156 SCUDO

2.0000 g., 0.9170 Gold .059 oz. AGW **Rev:** Perpetual Liberty **Designer:** Guido Veroi **Note:** 917 coins melted at the mint.

Date	Mintage	F	VF	XF	Unc	BU
1983R	14,000	—	—	—	65.00	—

KM# 170 SCUDO

2.0000 g., 0.9170 Gold .059 oz. AGW **Subject:** Peace **Obv:** Crowned shield in front of city scene **Rev:** Half-figure holding laurel branch left **Note:** 979 coins melted at the mint.

Date	Mintage	F	VF	XF	Unc	BU
1984R	11,000	—	—	—	65.00	—

KM# 184 SCUDO

2.0000 g., 0.9170 Gold .059 oz. AGW **Subject:** International Year for Youth **Rev:** Head left **Note:** 1,162 coins melted at the mint.

Date	Mintage	F	VF	XF	Unc	BU
1985R	10,000	—	—	—	90.00	—

KM# 198 SCUDO

3.3920 g., 0.9170 Gold .1 oz. AGW **Subject:** Insects at Work **Rev:** Large ant **Note:** 1,308 coins melted at the mint.

Date	Mintage	F	VF	XF	Unc	BU
1986R	9,000	—	—	—	80.00	—

KM# 211 SCUDO

3.3920 g., 0.9170 Gold .1 oz. AGW **Subject:** European Year for Environment **Obv:** Robe-like design with seagull at right **Rev:** Nude children under sprig **Note:** 962 coins melted at the mint.

Date	Mintage	F	VF	XF	Unc	BU
1987R	8,000	—	—	—	80.00	—

KM# 228 SCUDO

3.3920 g., 0.9170 Gold .1 oz. AGW **Subject:** Disarmament **Obv:** Smoking towers **Rev:** Design within globe **Note:** 873 coins melted at the mint.

Date	Mintage	F	VF	XF	Unc	BU
1988R	7,000	—	—	—	80.00	—

KM# 241 SCUDO

3.2258 g., 0.9000 Gold .0933 oz. AGW **Subject:** French Revolution **Rev:** Standing figure holding flag **Note:** 731 coins melted at the mint.

Date	Mintage	F	VF	XF	Unc	BU
1989R	7,500	—	—	—	75.00	—

KM# 258 SCUDO

3.2258 g., 0.9000 Gold .0933 oz. AGW **Subject:** San Marino's Presidency of the European Council **Obv:** Crowned pointed shield within sprigs **Rev:** Bust facing

Date	Mintage	F	VF	XF	Unc	BU
1990R	7,300	—	—	—	75.00	—

KM# 273 SCUDO

3.2258 g., 0.9000 Gold .0933 oz. AGW **Subject:** Peace **Obv:** Crowned pointed shield within sprigs **Rev:** Child fleeing

Date	Mintage	F	VF	XF	Unc	BU
1991R Proof	Est. 7,500	Value: 75.00				

KM# 288 SCUDO

3.2258 g., 0.9000 Gold .0933 oz. AGW **Subject:** San Marino's Entry Into the United Nations **Obv:** Crowned shield within sprigs **Rev:** UN logo

Date	Mintage	F	VF	XF	Unc	BU
1992R	8,500	Value: 75.00				

KM# 303 SCUDO

3.2258 g., 0.9000 Gold .0933 oz. AGW **Series:** International Monetary Fund **Rev:** Three standing figures within pointed oblong design **Designer:** Laura Cretara **Note:** 455 coins melted at the mint.

Date	Mintage	F	VF	XF	Unc	BU
1993R	7,500	—	—	—	70.00	—
1993R Proof	—	Value: 75.00				

KM# 319 SCUDO

3.2258 g., 0.9000 Gold .0933 oz. AGW **Series:** International Year of the Family **Obv:** Crowned shield within sprigs **Rev:** Couple facing each other **Note:** Sets only. 648 coins melted at the mint.

Date	Mintage	F	VF	XF	Unc	BU
1994R Proof	7,500	Value: 80.00				

KM# 335 SCUDO

3.2258 g., 0.9000 Gold .0933 oz. AGW **Series:** 50th Anniversary - United Nations **Obv:** Crowned shield within sprigs **Rev:** Vertical dolphin and nude figure on triangle sides **Note:** Sets only. 494 coins melted at the mint.

Date	Mintage	F	VF	XF	Unc	BU
1995R Proof	6,500	Value: 75.00				

KM# 338 SCUDO

3.2258 g., 0.9000 Gold .0933 oz. AGW **Series:** 1996 Olympics **Rev:** Boxers **Note:** 664 coins melted at the mint.

Date	Mintage	F	VF	XF	Unc	BU
1996 Proof	7,000	Value: 75.00				

KM# 373 SCUDO

3.2258 g., 0.9000 Gold .0933 oz. AGW **Rev:** Michelangelo's "Kneeling Angel" **Note:** 412 coins melted at the mint.

Date	Mintage	F	VF	XF	Unc	BU
1997 Proof	6,500	Value: 75.00				

KM# 417 SCUDO

3.2258 g., 0.9000 Gold .0933 oz. AGW, 15.9 mm. **Subject:** Canone Delle Proporzioni **Obv:** Crowned pointed shield within sprigs **Rev:** Anatomical drawing **Edge:** Reeded **Note:** 312 coins melted at the mint.

Date	Mintage	F	VF	XF	Unc	BU
1998 Proof	6,000	Value: 75.00				

KM# 414 SCUDO

3.2258 g., 0.9000 Gold .0933 oz. AGW **Subject:** La Velata **Obv:** Crowned shield **Rev:** Head facing 1/4 left

Date	Mintage	F	VF	XF	Unc	BU
1999 Proof	8,000	Value: 75.00				

KM# 408 SCUDO

3.2258 g., 0.9000 Gold .0933 oz. AGW **Obv:** Crowned shield **Rev:** La Primavera

Date	Mintage	F	VF	XF	Unc	BU
2000 Proof	—	Value: 75.00				

KM# 39 2 SCUDI
6.0000 g., 0.9170 Gold .1769 oz. AGW **Obv:** Crowned pointed shield within wreath **Rev:** Standing figure facing **Note:** 1,637 coins melted at the mint.

Date	Mintage	F	VF	XF	Unc	BU
1974	77,000	—	—	—	125	—

KM# 50 2 SCUDI
6.0000 g., 0.9170 Gold .1769 oz. AGW **Obv:** Crowned pointed shield within wreath **Rev:** Value and date within wreath **Note:** 3,373 coins melted at the mint.

Date	Mintage	F	VF	XF	Unc	BU
1975	80,000	—	—	—	125	—

KM# 61 2 SCUDI
6.0000 g., 0.9170 Gold .1769 oz. AGW **Obv:** Smoking towers **Rev:** Head 3/4 right **Note:** 20,246 coins melted at the mint.

Date	Mintage	F	VF	XF	Unc	BU
1976	55,000	—	—	—	125	—

KM# 74 2 SCUDI
6.0000 g., 0.9170 Gold .1769 oz. AGW **Obv:** Date at right of smoking towers **Rev:** Democrazia **Note:** 912 coins melted at the mint.

Date	Mintage	F	VF	XF	Unc	BU
1977	34,000	—	—	—	130	—

KM# 87 2 SCUDI
6.0000 g., 0.9170 Gold .1769 oz. AGW **Obv:** Value at upper left of smoking towers **Rev:** Libertas **Note:** 8,120 coins melted at the mint.

Date	Mintage	F	VF	XF	Unc	BU
1978	37,000	—	—	—	130	—

KM# 100 2 SCUDI
6.0000 g., 0.9170 Gold .1769 oz. AGW **Subject:** Peace **Obv:** Three upright feathers **Rev:** Clasped hands **Note:** 3,238 coins melted at the mint.

Date	Mintage	F	VF	XF	Unc	BU
1979	37,000	—	—	—	130	—

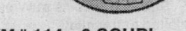

KM# 114 2 SCUDI
6.0000 g., 0.9170 Gold .1769 oz. AGW **Subject:** Justice **Obv:** Smoking towers **Rev:** Mother holding 2 children **Note:** 9,340 coins melted at the mint.

Date	Mintage	F	VF	XF	Unc	BU
1980	37,000	—	—	—	130	—

KM# 129 2 SCUDI
6.0000 g., 0.9170 Gold .1769 oz. AGW **Series:** World Food Day **Obv:** Crowned pointed arms within wreath above sprigs **Rev:** Seated nude figure with knees bent upright **Note:** 196 coins melted at the mint.

Date	Mintage	F	VF	XF	Unc	BU
1981	30,000	—	—	—	130	—

KM# 143 2 SCUDI
6.0000 g., 0.9170 Gold .1769 oz. AGW **Obv:** Crown above smoking towers flanked by sprig and design **Rev:** Stylized seated nude right **Note:** 244 coins melted at the mint.

Date	Mintage	F	VF	XF	Unc	BU
1982R	16,000	—	—	—	135	—

KM# 157 2 SCUDI
4.0000 g., 0.9170 Gold .1179 oz. AGW **Subject:** Perpetual Liberty **Obv:** Inscription above crowned shield and sprig **Rev:** Smoking towers on top of head left **Designer:** Guido Veroi **Note:** 17 coins melted at the mint.

Date	Mintage	F	VF	XF	Unc	BU
1983R	13,000	—	—	—	110	—

KM# 171 2 SCUDI
4.0000 g., 0.9170 Gold .1179 oz. AGW **Subject:** Liberty **Obv:** Crowned shield in front of city scene **Rev:** Standing figure with arms outstretched left **Note:** 12 coins melted at the mint.

Date	Mintage	F	VF	XF	Unc	BU
1984R	10,000	—	—	—	110	—

KM# 185 2 SCUDI
4.0000 g., 0.9170 Gold .1179 oz. AGW **Series:** International Year for Youth **Obv:** Crown above smoking towers on rock flanked by sprigs **Rev:** Head right divides flower and date **Note:** 200 coins melted at the mint.

Date	Mintage	F	VF	XF	Unc	BU
1985R	9,000	—	—	—	110	—

KM# 199 2 SCUDI
6.7840 g., 0.9170 Gold .2 oz. AGW **Obv:** Crowned shield above view **Rev:** Spider within web divides 2S **Note:** 329 coins melted at the mint.

Date	Mintage	F	VF	XF	Unc	BU
1986R	8,000	—	—	—	150	—

KM# 212 2 SCUDI
6.7840 g., 0.9170 Gold .2 oz. AGW **Subject:** European Year for Envrionment **Rev:** Sprig divides dancing figures **Note:** 14 coins melted at the mint.

Date	Mintage	F	VF	XF	Unc	BU
1987R	7,000	—	—	—	150	—

KM# 229 2 SCUDI
6.7840 g., 0.9170 Gold .2 oz. AGW **Subject:** Disarmament **Rev:** Value above sprig within clasped hands, all within world globe design **Note:** 7 coins melted at the mint.

Date	Mintage	F	VF	XF	Unc	BU
1988R	6,000	—	—	—	150	—

KM# 242 2 SCUDI
6.4516 g., 0.9000 Gold .1867 oz. AGW **Subject:** French Revolution **Rev:** Dates above building

Date	Mintage	F	VF	XF	Unc	BU
1989R	6,500	—	—	—	130	—

KM# 259 2 SCUDI
6.4516 g., 0.9000 Gold .1867 oz. AGW **Subject:** San Marino's Presidency of the European Council **Obv:** Crowned shield within wreath **Rev:** World globe **Designer:** Carmela Colaneri

Date	Mintage	F	VF	XF	Unc	BU
1990R	6,800	—	—	—	130	—

KM# 274 2 SCUDI
6.4516 g., 0.9000 Gold .1867 oz. AGW **Subject:** Peace **Obv:** Crowned shield within wreath **Rev:** New shoots growing from stump

Date	Mintage	F	VF	XF	Unc	BU
1991R Proof	Est. 6,500	Value: 130				

KM# 289 2 SCUDI
6.4516 g., 0.9000 Gold .1867 oz. AGW **Subject:** San Marino's

Entry Into the United Nations **Obv:** Crowned shield within wreath **Rev:** UN logo above inscription

Date	Mintage	F	VF	XF	Unc	BU
1992R Proof	7,500	Value: 130				

KM# 304 2 SCUDI
6.4516 g., 0.9000 Gold .1867 oz. AGW **Series:** International Monetary Fund **Obv:** Crowned shield within wreath **Rev:** Two stylized figures within globe design **Designer:** Laura Cretara **Note:** 106 coins melted at the mint.

Date	Mintage	F	VF	XF	Unc	BU
1993R	6,500	—	—	—	130	—
1993R Proof	—	Value: 140				

KM# 320 2 SCUDI
6.4516 g., 0.9000 Gold .1867 oz. AGW **Series:** International Year of the Family **Obv:** Crowned shield within wreath **Rev:** Family divides value **Note:** Sets only. 252 coins melted at the mint.

Date	Mintage	F	VF	XF	Unc	BU
1994R Proof	6,500	Value: 140				

KM# 336 2 SCUDI
6.4516 g., 0.9000 Gold .1867 oz. AGW **Series:** 50th Anniversary - United Nations **Obv:** Crowned shield within wreath **Rev:** Seated figure with arms outstretched below value within triangular design **Note:** Sets only.

Date	Mintage	F	VF	XF	Unc	BU
1995R Proof	Est. 7,000	Value: 140				

KM# 339 2 SCUDI
6.4516 g., 0.9000 Gold .1867 oz. AGW **Series:** 1996 Olympics **Subject:** Track and Field **Obv:** Crowned shield within wreath **Rev:** Three athletes standing left **Note:** 1 coin melted at the mint.

Date	Mintage	F	VF	XF	Unc	BU
1996 Proof	6,000	Value: 140				

KM# 374 2 SCUDI
6.4516 g., 0.9000 Gold .1867 oz. AGW **Rev:** Michelangelo's "David" **Note:** 124 coins melted at the mint.

Date	Mintage	F	VF	XF	Unc	BU
1997 Proof	5,800	Value: 140				

KM# 418 2 SCUDI
6.4516 g., 0.9000 Gold .1867 oz. AGW, 21 mm. **Subject:** Vergine Delle Rocce **Obv:** Crowned shield within wreath **Rev:** Female Saint facing **Edge:** Reeded **Note:** Struck at Rome. 334 coins melted at the mint.

Date	Mintage	F	VF	XF	Unc	BU
1998 Proof	5,500	Value: 140				

KM# 415 2 SCUDI
6.4516 g., 0.9000 Gold .1867 oz. AGW **Subject:** Sposalizio Della Vergine **Obv:** Crowned shield within wreath **Rev:** Three seated figures

Date	Mintage	F	VF	XF	Unc	BU
1999 Proof	8,000	Value: 135				

KM# 409 2 SCUDI
6.4516 g., 0.9000 Gold .1867 oz. AGW **Subject:** Madonna Della Melagrna **Obv:** Crowned shield within wreath **Rev:** Madonna and child

Date	Mintage	F	VF	XF	Unc	BU
2000 Proof	6,000	Value: 135				

KM# 62 5 SCUDI
15.0000 g., 0.9170 Gold .4422 oz. AGW **Obv:** Value below smoking towers **Rev:** Head left **Note:** 25 coins melted at mint.

Date	Mintage	F	VF	XF	Unc	BU
1976	8,000	—	—	—	625	—

KM# 75 5 SCUDI
15.0000 g., 0.9170 Gold .4422 oz. AGW **Subject:** Democrazia **Obv:** Value below smoking towers **Rev:** Stylized head left **Note:** 29 coins melted at mint.

Date	Mintage	F	VF	XF	Unc	BU
1977	16,000	—	—	—	315	—

KM# 101 5 SCUDI
15.0000 g., 0.9170 Gold .4422 oz. AGW **Subject:** Peace **Obv:** Value within upright feathers **Rev:** Stylized hands and arms **Note:** 161 coins melted at mint.

Date	Mintage	F	VF	XF	Unc	BU
1979	24,000	—	—	—	315	—

KM# 115 5 SCUDI
15.0000 g., 0.9170 Gold .4422 oz. AGW **Subject:** Justice **Obv:** Smoking towers **Rev:** Head at upper right of birds **Note:** 1,428 coins melted at mint.

Date	Mintage	F	VF	XF	Unc	BU
1980	24,000	—	—	—	315	—

KM# 130 5 SCUDI
15.0000 g., 0.9170 Gold .4422 oz. AGW **Series:** World Food Day **Obv:** Crowned shield on sprigs above inscription **Rev:** Seated nude figure with knees bent upright **Note:** 33 coins melted at mint.

Date	Mintage	F	VF	XF	Unc	BU
1981	24,000	—	—	—	315	—

KM# 144 5 SCUDI
15.0000 g., 0.9170 Gold .4422 oz. AGW **Subject:** Defense of Liberty **Obv:** Crown above smoking towers flanked by sprig and design **Rev:** Value above stylized hands **Note:** 19 coins melted at mint.

Date	Mintage	F	VF	XF	Unc	BU
1982R	15,000	—	—	—	315	—

KM# 158 5 SCUDI
10.0000 g., 0.9170 Gold .2949 oz. AGW **Subject:** Perpetual Liberty **Obv:** Inscription above crowned shield and sprig **Rev:** Standing figure and child walking right **Designer:** Guido Veroi **Note:** 25 coins melted at mint.

Date	Mintage	F	VF	XF	Unc	BU
1983R	11,000	—	—	—	250	—

KM# 172 5 SCUDI
10.0000 g., 0.9170 Gold .2949 oz. AGW **Subject:** Justice **Obv:** Crowned shield in front of castle view **Rev:** Liberty walking on parapet of castle **Designer:** Pietro Giampaoli **Note:** 28 coins melted at mint.

Date	Mintage	F	VF	XF	Unc	BU
1984R	9,000	—	—	—	300	—

KM# 186 5 SCUDI
10.0000 g., 0.9170 Gold .2949 oz. AGW **Subject:** Libertas **Obv:** Crown above smoking towers on rock flanked by sprigs **Rev:** Three nude dancing figures **Note:** 13 coins melted at mint.

Date	Mintage	F	VF	XF	Unc	BU
1985R	7,400	—	—	—	400	—

KM# 200 5 SCUDI
16.9500 g., 0.9170 Gold .5 oz. AGW **Subject:** Work **Obv:** Crowned shield above view **Rev:** Bee within honey comb design divides value **Note:** 14 coins melted at mint.

Date	Mintage	F	VF	XF	Unc	BU
1986R	7,000	—	—	—	350	—

KM# 215 5 SCUDI
16.9500 g., 0.9170 Gold .5 oz. AGW **Subject:** United Nations **Obv:** Crowned shield within wreath **Rev:** Value to left of building and tower **Note:** 49 coins melted at mint.

Date	Mintage	F	VF	XF	Unc	BU
1987R	6,000	—	—	—	350	—

KM# 230 5 SCUDI
16.9500 g., 0.9170 Gold .5 oz. AGW **Subject:** Human Rights **Obv:** Crowned shield within wreath **Obv. Designer:** Valentini **Rev:** Stylized flame within wreath, value at upper left **Rev. Designer:** Sergio Giandomenico **Note:** 11 coins melted at mint.

Date	Mintage	F	VF	XF	Unc	BU
1988R	5,000	—	—	—	350	—

KM# 245 5 SCUDI
16.9500 g., 0.9170 Gold .5 oz. AGW **Subject:** Entrance of San Marino in Common Market

Date	Mintage	F	VF	XF	Unc	BU
1989R	6,000	—	—	—	350	—

KM# 260 5 SCUDI
16.9500 g., 0.9170 Gold .5 oz. AGW **Subject:** Founding of the Republic **Obv:** Doves in front of smoking towers **Rev:** Three kneeling figures to right of standing figure **Designer:** Bino Bini

Date	Mintage	F	VF	XF	Unc	BU
1990R Proof	6,500	Value: 350				

KM# 275 5 SCUDI
16.9500 g., 0.9170 Gold .5 oz. AGW **Subject:** Peace and Freedom **Obv:** Crowned shield within wreath **Rev:** Tree divides family **Designer:** Bino Bini

Date	Mintage	F	VF	XF	Unc	BU
1991R Proof	7,000	Value: 350				

KM# 290 5 SCUDI
16.9500 g., 0.9170 Gold .5 oz. AGW **Subject:** Customer Agreement with European Economic Community **Obv:** Crowned shield within wreath **Rev:** Value and oat sprig within center of circle of stars

Date	Mintage	F	VF	XF	Unc	BU
1992R Proof	Est. 6,500	Value: 350				

KM# 305 5 SCUDI
16.9500 g., 0.9170 Gold .5 oz. AGW **Series:** International Monetary Fund **Obv:** Crowned shield within wreath **Rev:** Stylized figure holding scale above shield **Designer:** Laura Cretara **Note:** 68 coins melted at the mint.

Date	Mintage	F	VF	XF	Unc	BU
1993R Proof	5,500	Value: 350				

KM# 321 5 SCUDI
16.9500 g., 0.9170 Gold .5 oz. AGW **Series:** International Year of the Family **Obv:** Crowned shield within wreath **Rev:** Family divides value **Note:** 207 coins melted at the mint.

Date	Mintage	F	VF	XF	Unc	BU
1994R Proof	5,500	Value: 350				

KM# 337 5 SCUDI
16.9500 g., 0.9170 Gold .5 oz. AGW **Series:** 50th Anniversary - United Nations **Obv:** Crowned shield within wreath **Rev:** Seated nude figure and squirrel flanked by dates above value **Note:** 65 coins melted at the mint.

Date	Mintage	F	VF	XF	Unc	BU
1995R Proof	5,000	Value: 350				

KM# 343 5 SCUDI
16.9500 g., 0.9170 Gold .5 oz. AGW **Subject:** Pieta **Obv:** Crowned shield within wreath **Rev:** Mary receives Jesus' body **Note:** 19 coins melted at the mint.

Date	Mintage	F	VF	XF	Unc	BU
1996 Proof	5,840	Value: 350				

KM# 375 5 SCUDI
16.9500 g., 0.9170 Gold .5 oz. AGW **Subject:** The Annunciation **Obv:** Crowned shield within wreath **Rev:** Angel **Note:** 469 coins melted at the mint.

Date	Mintage	F	VF	XF	Unc	BU
1997 Proof	5,500	Value: 350				

KM# 412 5 SCUDI
16.9590 g., 0.9170 Gold .5 oz. AGW **Subject:** Madonna Della Seggiola **Obv:** Crowned shield within wreath **Rev:** Woman with 2 children **Note:** 1,151 coins melted at the mint.

Date	Mintage	F	VF	XF	Unc	BU
1998 Proof	5,000	Value: 350				

KM# 388 5 SCUDI
16.9590 g., 0.9170 Gold .5 oz. AGW **Subject:** Birth of Venus **Obv:** Crowned shield within wreath **Rev:** Venus standing in shell

Date	Mintage	F	VF	XF	Unc	BU
1999 Proof	Est. 5,500	Value: 350				

KM# 420 5 SCUDI
16.9590 g., 0.9170 Gold .5 oz. AGW **Subject:** Tiziano's painting "Rape of Europa" **Obv:** Crowned shield within wreath **Rev:** Europa on a bull's (Zeus) back

Date	Mintage	F	VF	XF	Unc	BU
2000 Proof	4,500	—	—	—	350	—

KM# 88 10 SCUDI
30.0000 g., 0.9170 Gold .8844 oz. AGW **Obv:** Smoking towers within circle **Rev:** Head left **Note:** 54 coins melted at the mint.

Date	Mintage	F	VF	XF	Unc	BU
1978	20,000	—	—	—	625	—

PROVAS

KM#	Date	Mintage	Identification	Mkt Val
Pr1	1925R	75	20 Lire. Gold. KM8.	3,300
Pr2	1931R	—	5 Lire. Silver. KM9.	265
Pr3	1931R	—	10 Lire. Silver. KM10.	225
Pr4	1931R	—	20 Lire. Silver. KM11.	525
Pr5	1932R	—	5 Lire. Silver. KM9.	900
Pr6	1932R	—	10 Lire. Silver. KM10.	525
Pr7	1933	—	5 Lire. Silver. KM9.	175
Pr8	1933	—	10 Lire. Silver. KM10.	185
Pr9	1933	—	20 Lire. Silver. KM11.	200
Pr10	1935R	—	5 Lire. Silver. KM9.	525
Pr11	1935R	—	20 Lire. Silver. KM11.	575
Pr12	1937R	—	10 Lire. Silver. KM10.	400
Pr13	1938R	—	10 Lire. 0.8350 Silver. 10.0000 g. 27 mm. Crowned arms. Allegorical woman. Lettered edge.	—

MINT SETS

KM#	Date	Mintage	Identification	Issue Price	Mkt Val
MS1	1972 (8)	—	KM14-21	5.00	12.50
MS2	1973 (8)	—	KM22-29	6.00	12.50
MS3	1974 (8)	60,000	KM30-37	9.00	15.00
MS4	1974 (2)	60,000	KM38-39	—	185
MS5	1975 (8)	—	KM40-47	6.50	15.00
MS6	1975 (5)	—	KM40-44	—	—
MS7	1975 (2)	90,000	KM49-50	—	185
MS8	1976 (8)	—	KM51-58	6.00	12.50
MS9	1976 (2)	40,000	KM60-61	—	185
MS10	1977 (9)	—	KM63-71	—	15.00
MS11	1977 (2)	30,000	KM73-74	—	185
MS12	1978 (9)	—	KM76-84	—	15.00
MS13	1978 (2)	—	KM86-87	—	160
MS14	1979 (9)	—	KM89-98	—	15.00
MS15	1979 (2)	—	KM99-100	—	160
MS16	1980 (9)	—	KM102-110	—	15.00
MS17	1980 (2)	—	KM113-114	—	160
MS18	1981 (9)	—	KM116-123, 126	—	15.00
MS19	1981 (3)	—	KM124-125, 127	—	—
MS20	1981 (2)	—	KM128-129	—	160
MS21	1982 (9)	—	KM131-138, 140	6.00	8.50
MS22	1982 (2)	—	KM139, 141	—	27.50
MS23	1982 (2)	—	KM142-143	—	170
MS24	1983 (9)	—	KM145-153	5.50	8.50
MS25	1983 (2)	—	KM154-155	—	27.50
MS26	1983 (2)	—	KM156-157	—	175
MS27	1984 (9)	—	KM159-167	—	—
MS28	1984 (2)	—	KM168-169	—	22.00
MS29	1984 (2)	—	KM170-171	—	175
MS30	1985 (9)	—	KM173-181	—	8.50
MS31	1985 (2)	—	KM182-183	—	22.00
MS32	1985 (2)	—	KM184-185	—	200
MS33	1986 (9)	—	KM187-195	7.00	8.50
MS34	1986 (2)	—	KM196-197	—	30.00
MS35	1986 (2)	—	KM198-199	—	190
MS36	1987 (10)	43,000	KM201-210	—	25.00
MS38	1987 (2)	—	KM211-212	—	190
MS37	1987 (2)	—	KM213-214	—	30.00
MS39	1988 (10)	80,000	KM218-227	22.00	26.00
MS40	1988 (2)	—	KM216-217	—	30.00
MS41	1988 (2)	—	KM228-229	—	190
MS42	1989 (10)	32,000	KM231-240	—	28.00
MS44	1989 (2)	6,500	KM241-242	—	170
MS43	1989 (2)	30,000	KM243-244	—	30.00
MS45	1990 (10)	36,000	KM248-257	—	35.00
MS46	1990 (2)	40,000	KM246-247	—	175
MS47	1990 (2)	6,800	KM258-259	—	175
MS48	1991 (10)	36,000	KM261-270	—	32.00
MS49	1991 (2)	25,000	KM271-272	—	32.00
MS50	1992 (10)	45,000	KM278-287	—	32.00
MS51	1992 (2)	—	KM276-277	34.00	40.00
MS52	1993 (10)	—	KM293-302	18.00	28.00
MS53	1993 (2)	35,000	KM291-292	26.00	30.00
MS54	1994 (10)	40,000	KM307-315	18.00	30.00
MS55	1995 (10)	—	KM322-331	—	30.00
MS56	1996 (10)	32,000	KM344, 349-357	18.00	30.00
MS57	1997 (10)	28,000	KM358-367	18.00	30.00
MS58	1998 (8)	—	KM378-385	18.00	25.00
MS59	1999 (8)	—	KM389-396	18.00	25.00
MS60	2000 (8)	28,000	KM399-406	18.00	25.00

PROOF SETS

KM#	Date	Mintage	Identification	Issue Price	Mkt Val
PS1	1989 (2)	8,000	KM243-244	55.00	60.00
PS2	1990 (2)	18,800	KM246-247	55.00	60.00
PS4	1991 (2)	6,800	KM273-274	—	175
PS3	1991 (2)	8,000	KM271-272	55.00	60.00
PS5	1993 (2)	—	KM303-304	158	160
PS6	1994 (2)	7,500	KM319-320	—	200
PS7	1995 (2)	—	KM333-334	31.00	45.00
PS8	1995 (2)	7,000	KM335-336	161	175
PS9	1996 (2)	—	KM340-341	35.00	45.00
PS10	1997 (2)	—	KM347-348	35.00	45.00
PS11	1999 (2)	—	KM410-411	—	60.00
PS12	1999 (3)	8,000	KM413-415	179	180
PS13	2000 (3)	6,000	KM407-409	179	180

SARAWAK

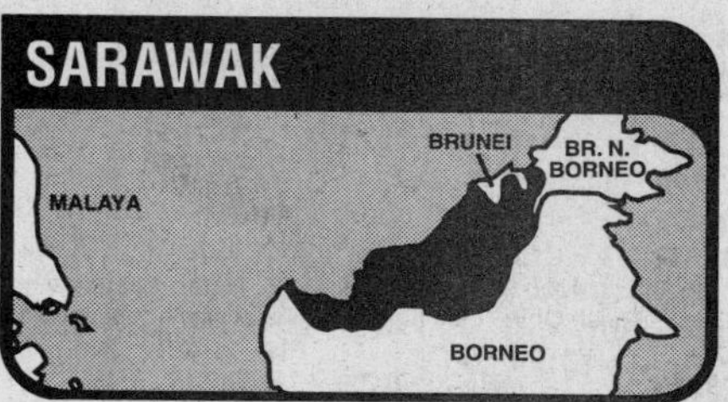

Sarawak is a former British protectorate located on the northwest coast of Borneo. The Japanese occupation during World War II so thoroughly devastated the economy that Rajah Sir Charles V. Brooke ceded it to Great Britain on July 1, 1946. In September, 1963 the colony joined the Federation of Malaysia. The capital is Kuching.

RULERS

Charles J. Brooke, Rajah, 1868-1917
Charles V. Brooke, Rajah, 1917-1946

MINT MARKS

H - Heaton, Birmingham

MONETARY SYSTEM

100 Cents = 1 Dollar

BRITISH COLONY

STANDARD COINAGE

100 Cents = 1 Dollar

KM# 20 1/2 CENT

Bronze 0 **Ruler:** Charles V. Brooke Rajah **Obv:** Head right **Rev:** Value within wreath

Date	Mintage	F	VF	XF	Unc	BU
1933H	2,000,000	5.00	8.00	20.00	30.00	—
1933H Proof	—	Value: 300				

KM# 12 CENT

Copper-Nickel **Ruler:** Charles V. Brooke Rajah **Obv:** Head right **Rev:** Value within wreath

Date	Mintage	F	VF	XF	Unc	BU
1920H	5,000,000	4.00	7.50	20.00	35.00	55.00

KM# 18 CENT

Bronze **Ruler:** Charles V. Brooke Rajah **Obv:** Head right **Rev:** Value within wreath

Date	Mintage	F	VF	XF	Unc	BU
1927H	5,000,000	1.25	3.00	6.00	12.00	—
1929H	2,000,000	1.25	3.00	6.00	12.00	—
1930H	3,000,000	1.25	3.00	6.00	12.00	—
1937H	3,000,000	1.25	3.00	6.00	12.00	—
1937H Proof	—	Value: 250				
1941H	3,000,000	320	615	950	1,450	—

Note: Estimate 50 pieces exist

KM# 8 5 CENTS

1.3500 g., 0.8000 Silver .0347 oz. ASW **Ruler:** Charles J. Brooke Rajah **Obv:** Head left **Obv. Legend:** C. BROOKE RAJAH **Rev:** Value within roped wreath

Date	Mintage	F	VF	XF	Unc	BU
1908H	40,000	45.00	120	200	300	—
1908H Proof	—	Value: 560				
1911H	40,000	45.00	120	200	300	—
1913H	100,000	50.00	95.00	190	260	—
1913H Proof	—	Value: 510				
1915H	100,000	50.00	95.00	150	260	—
1915H Proof	—	Value: 510				

KM# 13 5 CENTS

1.3500 g., 0.4000 Silver .0174 oz. ASW **Ruler:** Charles V. Brooke Rajah **Obv:** Head right **Rev:** Value within roped wreath

Date	Mintage	F	VF	XF	Unc	BU
1920H	100,000	70.00	140	215	380	—
1920H Proof	—	Value: 600				

KM# 14 5 CENTS

Copper-Nickel **Ruler:** Charles V. Brooke Rajah **Obv:** Head right **Rev:** Value within wreath

Date	Mintage	F	VF	XF	Unc	BU
1920H	400,000	2.00	4.00	10.00	25.00	—
1927H	600,000	2.00	4.00	10.00	22.00	—
1927H Proof	—	Value: 320				

KM# 9 10 CENTS

2.7100 g., 0.8000 Silver .0697 oz. ASW **Ruler:** Charles J. Brooke Rajah **Obv:** Head left **Obv. Legend:** C. BROOKE RAJAH **Rev:** Value within roped wreath

Date	Mintage	F	VF	XF	Unc	BU
1906H	50,000	35.00	50.00	95.00	210	—
1906H Proof	—	Value: 520				
1910H	50,000	35.00	50.00	95.00	210	—
1910H Proof	—	Value: 520				
1911H	100,000	28.00	45.00	85.00	190	—
1913H	100,000	28.00	45.00	85.00	190	—
1913H Proof	—	Value: 520				
1915H	100,000	70.00	120	200	350	—
1915H Proof	—	Value: 580				

KM# 15 10 CENTS

2.7100 g., 0.4000 Silver .0349 oz. ASW **Ruler:** Charles V. Brooke Rajah **Obv:** Head right **Rev:** Value within roped wreath

Date	Mintage	F	VF	XF	Unc	BU
1920H	150,000	35.00	70.00	120	200	—
1920H Proof	—	Value: 480				

KM# 16 10 CENTS

Copper-Nickel **Ruler:** Charles V. Brooke Rajah **Obv:** Head right **Rev:** Value within wreath

Date	Mintage	F	VF	XF	Unc	BU
1920H	800,000	2.00	4.00	9.00	20.00	—
1927H	1,000,000	2.00	3.00	7.00	19.00	—
1927H Proof	—	Value: 330				
1934H	2,000,000	2.00	3.00	7.00	19.00	—
1934H Proof	—	Value: 330				

KM# 10 20 CENTS

5.4300 g., 0.8000 Silver .1396 oz. ASW **Ruler:** Charles J. Brooke Rajah **Obv:** Head left **Obv. Legend:** C. BROOKE RAJAH **Rev:** Value within roped wreath

Date	Mintage	F	VF	XF	Unc	BU
1906H	25,000	60.00	120	280	480	—
1906H Proof	—	Value: 800				
1910H	25,000	60.00	120	280	480	—
1910H Proof	—	Value: 800				
1911H	15,000	60.00	120	280	480	—
1913H	25,000	60.00	120	280	480	—
1913H Proof	—	Value: 800				
1915H	25,000	310	410	620	960	—
1915H Proof	—	Value: 1,300				

KM# 17 20 CENTS

5.4300 g., 0.4000 Silver .0699 oz. ASW **Ruler:** Charles V. Brooke Rajah **Obv:** Head right **Rev:** Value within roped wreath

Date	Mintage	F	VF	XF	Unc	BU
1920H	25,000	140	280	415	760	—
1920H Proof	—	Value: 1,000				

KM# 17a 20 CENTS

5.0800 g., 0.4000 Silver .0653 oz. ASW **Ruler:** Charles V. Brooke Rajah **Obv:** Head right **Rev:** Value within roped wreath

Date	Mintage	F	VF	XF	Unc	BU
1927H	250,000	20.00	35.00	70.00	165	—
1927H Proof	—	Value: 600				

KM# 11 50 CENTS

13.5700 g., 0.8000 Silver .349 oz. ASW **Ruler:** Charles J. Brooke Rajah **Obv:** Head left **Obv. Legend:** C. BROOKE RAJAH **Rev:** Value within roped wreath

Date	Mintage	F	VF	XF	Unc	BU
1906H	10,000	500	700	1,100	1,900	—
1906H Proof	—	Value: 2,700				

KM# 19 50 CENTS

10.3000 g., 0.5000 Silver .1656 oz. ASW **Ruler:** Charles V. Brooke Rajah **Obv:** Head right **Rev:** Value within roped wreath

Date	Mintage	F	VF	XF	Unc	BU
1927H	200,000	35.00	65.00	120	200	—
1927H Proof	—	Value: 550				

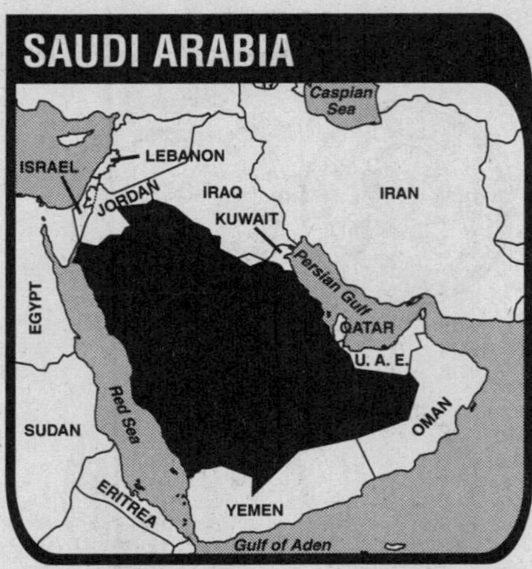

The Kingdom of Saudi Arabia, an independent and absolute hereditary monarchy comprising the former sultanate of Nejd, the old kingdom of Hejaz, Asir and Al Hasa, occupies four-fifths of the Arabian peninsula. The kingdom has an area of 830,000 sq. mi. (2,149,690 sq. km.) and a population of *16.1 million. Capital: Riyadh. The economy is based on oil, which provides 85 percent of Saudi Arabia's revenue.

Mohammed united the Arabs in the 7th century and his followers founded a great empire with its capital at Medina. The Turks established nominal rule over much of Arabia in the 16th and 17th centuries, and in the 18thcentury divided it into principalities.

The Kingdom of Saudi Arabia was created by King Abd Al-Aziz Bin Saud (1882-1953), a descendant of earlier Wahhabi rulers of the Arabian peninsula. In 1901 he seized Riyadh, capital of the Sultanate of Nejd, and in 1905 established himself as Sultan. In 1913 he captured the Turkish province of Al Hasa; took the Hejaz in 1925 and by 1926 most of Asir. In1932 he combined Nejd and Hejaz into the single kingdom of Saudi Arabia. Asir was incorporated into the kingdom a year later.

TITLES

العربية السعودية

Al-Arabiya(t) as-Sa'udiya(t)

المملكة العربية السعودية

Al-Mamlaka(t) al-'Arabiya(t) as-Sa'udiya(t)

RULERS

al Sa'ud Dynasty

Abd Al-Aziz Bin Sa'ud, (Ibn Sa'ud), AH1344-1373/1926-1953AD
Sa'ud Bin Abd Al-Aziz, AH1373-1383/1953-1964AD
Faisal Bin Abd Al-Aziz, AH1383-1395/1964-1975AD
Khalid Bin Abd Al-Aziz, AH1395-1403/1975-1982AD
Fahad Bin Abd Al-Aziz, AH1403-/1982-AD

MONETARY SYSTEM

Until 1960

20-22 Ghirsh = 1 Riyal
40 Riyals = 1 Guinea

NOTE: Copper-nickel, reeded-edge coins dated AH1356 and silver coins dated AH1354 were struck at the U. S. Mint in Philadelphia between 1944-1949.

HEJAZ & NEJD

Mecca, the metropolis of Islam and the capital of Hejaz, is located inland from the Red Sea due east of the port of Jidda. A center of non-political commercial, cultural and religious activities, Mecca remained virtually independent until 1259. Two centuries of Egyptian rule were followed by four centuries of Turkish rule which lasted until the Arab revolts which extinguished pretensions to sovereignty over any part of the Arabian peninsula.

MINT NAME

Makkah, Mecca

RULERS

Sharifs of Mecca

Ghalib b. Ma'sud, AH1219-1229
Yahya b. Surer, AH1230-1240
Abdul Muttalib and Ibn Awn, AH1240-1248

KINGDOM AND SULTANATE

Abd Al-Aziz bin Sa'ud as King of Hejaz and Sultan of Nejd

TRANSITIONAL COINAGE

Struck at the Mecca Mint during the occupation by Abd Al-Aziz Bin Sa'ud while establishing his kingdom.

KM# 1 1/4 GHIRSH
Copper Or Bronze **Obv:** Toughra **Rev:** Inscription

Date	Mintage	Good	VG	F	VF	XF
AH1343	—	—	60.00	125	175	325

Note: Several varieties exist, including reeded and plain edges; Some specimens struck over bronze Hejaz 1/4 and 1/2 Piastres (KM#23 and KM#26), and some occur with a light silver wash

KM# 2.1 1/2 GHIRSH
Copper Or Bronze **Obv:** Toughra **Obv. Inscription:** Al-Faisal al Saud **Rev:** Inscription

Date	Mintage	Good	VG	F	VF	XF
AH1343	—	—	20.00	40.00	60.00	125

KM# 2.2 1/2 GHIRSH
Copper Or Bronze **Obv:** Toughra **Obv. Inscription:** Al-Faisal **Rev:** Inscription

Date	Mintage	Good	VG	F	VF	XF
AH1343	—	—	75.00	150	300	500

KM# A3 1/2 GHIRSH
Bronze

Date	Mintage	Good	VG	F	VF	XF
AH1344//2	—	—	15.00	30.00	50.00	100

REGULAR COINAGE

KM# 4 1/4 GHIRSH
Copper-Nickel **Obv:** Legend **Rev:** Value and date below legend

Date	Mintage	Good	VG	F	VF	XF
AH1344	—	—	4.00	8.00	12.00	40.00
AH1344 Proof	—	Value: 750				

KM# 5 1/2 GHIRSH
Copper-Nickel **Obv:** Legend **Rev:** Value and date below legend

Date	Mintage	Good	VG	F	VF	XF
AH1344	—	—	8.00	15.00	30.00	75.00
AH1344 Proof	—	Value: 750				

KM# 6 GHIRSH
Copper-Nickel **Obv:** Legend **Rev:** Value and date below legend

Date	Mintage	Good	VG	F	VF	XF
AH1344	—	—	6.00	12.00	25.00	60.00
AH1344 Proof	—	Value: 750				

HEJAZ & NEJD SULTANATE

KINGDOM

REGULAR COINAGE

KM# 7 1/4 GHIRSH
Copper-Nickel **Obv:** Legend **Rev:** Value and date below legend

Date	Mintage	VG	F	VF	XF	Unc
AH1346	3,000,000	6.00	10.00	15.00	40.00	—

KM# 13 1/4 GHIRSH
Copper-Nickel **Obv:** Legend **Rev:** Value and date below legend

Date	Mintage	VG	F	VF	XF	Unc
AH1348	—	12.00	20.00	40.00	75.00	—
AH1348 Proof	1,000	—	—	—	—	—

KM# 8 1/2 GHIRSH
Copper-Nickel

Date	Mintage	VG	F	VF	XF	Unc
AH1346	3,000,000	10.00	15.00	25.00	60.00	—

KM# 14 1/2 GHIRSH
Copper-Nickel **Obv:** Legend **Rev:** Value and date below legend

Date	Mintage	VG	F	VF	XF	Unc
AH1348	—	12.00	25.00	40.00	100	—
AH1348 Proof	1,000	—	—	—	—	—

KM# 9 GHIRSH
Copper-Nickel **Obv:** Legend **Rev:** Value and date below legend

Date	Mintage	VG	F	VF	XF	Unc
AH1346	3,000,000	3.00	5.00	10.00	35.00	—

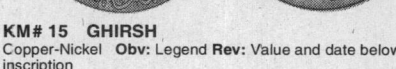

KM# 15 GHIRSH
Copper-Nickel **Obv:** Legend **Rev:** Value and date below inscription

Date	Mintage	VG	F	VF	XF	Unc
AH1348	—	12.00	20.00	30.00	75.00	—
AH1348 Proof	1,000	—	—	—	—	—

KM# 10 1/4 RIYAL
6.0500 g., 0.9170 Silver .1783 oz. ASW, 24 mm. **Obv:** Inscription within beaded circle, legend above, crossed swords below within design flanked by palms trees **Rev:** Inscription within beaded circle, legend above, value below within design flanked by palm trees

Date	Mintage	VG	F	VF	XF	Unc
AH1346	400,000	40.00	60.00	100	200	—
AH1346 Proof	—	Value: 750				
AH1348	200,000	60.00	90.00	150	350	—
AH1348 Proof	1,500	—	—	—	—	—

KM# 11 1/2 RIYAL
12.1000 g., 0.9170 Silver .3567 oz. ASW, 27 mm. **Obv:** Inscription within beaded circle, legend above, crossed swords below within design flanked by palm trees **Rev:** Inscription within beaded circle, legend above, value below within design flanked by palm trees and swords

Date	Mintage	VG	F	VF	XF	Unc
AH1346	200,000	100	175	250	500	—
AH1346 Proof	—	Value: 1,250				
AH1348	100,000	125	200	350	750	—
AH1348 Proof	2,000	—	—	—	—	—

KM# 12 RIYAL
24.1000 g., 0.9170 Silver .7105 oz. ASW, 37 mm. **Obv:** Inscription within beaded circle, legend above, crossed swords below within design flanked by palm trees **Rev:** Inscription within beaded circle, legend above, value below within design flanked by palm trees

Date	Mintage	VG	F	VF	XF	Unc
AH1346	800,000	40.00	60.00	90.00	150	—
AH1346 Proof	—	Value: 1,500				
AH1348	400,000	50.00	75.00	150	250	—
AH1348 Proof	2,000	—	—	—	—	—

UNITED KINGDOMS

STANDARD COINAGE

KM# 19.1 1/4 GHIRSH
Copper-Nickel **Obv:** Legend **Rev:** Value and date below legend
Edge: Plain

Date	Mintage	VG	F	VF	XF	Unc
AH1356 (1937)	1,000,000	2.00	5.00	10.00	35.00	—

KM# 19.2 1/4 GHIRSH
Copper-Nickel **Obv:** Legend **Rev:** Value and date below legend
Edge: Reeded

Date	Mintage	VG	F	VF	XF	Unc
AH1356 (1937)	21,500,000	0.25	0.50	1.00	2.50	7.50

Note: Struck in 1947 (AH1366-67) at Philadelphia

KM# 20.1 1/2 GHIRSH

Copper-Nickel **Obv:** Legend **Rev:** Value and date below legend **Edge:** Plain

Date	Mintage	VG	F	VF	XF	Unc
AH1356 (1937)	1,000,000	3.00	8.00	20.00	45.00	—

KM# 20.2 1/2 GHIRSH

Copper-Nickel **Obv:** Legend **Rev:** Value and date below legend **Edge:** Reeded

Date	Mintage	VG	F	VF	XF	Unc
AH1356 (1937)	10,850,000	0.20	0.50	1.50	3.00	10.00

Note: Struck in 1947 (AH1366-67) at Philadelphia

KM# 21.1 GHIRSH

Copper-Nickel **Obv:** Legend **Rev:** Value and date below legend **Edge:** Plain

Date	Mintage	VG	F	VF	XF	Unc
AH1356 (1937)	4,000,000	3.00	8.00	15.00	40.00	—

KM# 21.2 GHIRSH

Copper-Nickel **Obv:** Legend **Rev:** Value and date below legend **Edge:** Reeded

Date	Mintage	VG	F	VF	XF	Unc
AH1356 (1937)	7,150,000	0.50	1.00	2.50	5.00	12.50

Note: Struck in 1947 (AH1366-67) at Philadelphia

KM# 40 GHIRSH

Copper-Nickel, 22 mm. **Obv:** Palm above crossed swords at center of legend **Rev:** Value and date below legend **Edge:** Reeded

Date	Mintage	F	VF	XF	Unc	BU
AH1376 (1957)	10,000,000	0.15	0.25	0.50	3.00	—
AH1378 (1958)	50,000,000	0.15	0.25	0.50	2.00	—

KM# 41 2 GHIRSH

Copper-Nickel, 27 mm. **Obv:** Crossed swords below palm at center of legend **Rev:** Value and date below legend **Edge:** Reeded

Date	Mintage	F	VF	XF	Unc	BU
AH1376 (1957)	50,000,000	0.10	0.35	0.75	5.00	—
AH1379 (1959)	28,110,000	0.10	0.35	0.70	3.50	—

KM# 42 4 GHIRSH

Copper-Nickel, 30 mm. **Obv:** Crossed swords below palm at center of legend **Rev:** Value and date below legend **Edge:** Reeded

Date	Mintage	F	VF	XF	Unc	BU
AH1376 (1956)	49,100,000	0.25	0.50	1.00	6.00	—
AH1378 (1958)	10,000,000	0.25	0.50	1.00	5.00	—

KM# 16 1/4 RIYAL

3.1000 g., 0.9170 Silver .0913 oz. ASW **Obv:** Inscription within beaded circle, legend above, crossed swords below within design flanked by palm trees **Rev:** Inscription within beaded circle, legend above, value below within design flanked by palm trees

Date	Mintage	F	VF	XF	Unc	BU
AH1354 (1935)	900,000	1.75	2.50	3.00	5.50	—
AH1354 (1935) Proof	—	Value: 250				

KM# 37 1/4 RIYAL

2.9500 g., 0.9170 Silver .0869 oz. ASW **Obv:** Inscription within beaded circle, legend above, crossed swords below within design flanked by palm trees **Rev:** Inscription within beaded circle, legend above, value below within design flanked by palm trees

Date	Mintage	F	VF	XF	Unc	BU
AH1374 (1954)	4,000,000	BV	1.50	3.00	5.50	—

KM# 17 1/2 RIYAL

5.8500 g., 0.9170 Silver .1724 oz. ASW **Obv:** Inscription within beaded circle, legend above, crossed swords below within design flanked by palm trees **Rev:** Inscription within beaded circle, legend above, value below within design flanked by palm trees

Date	Mintage	F	VF	XF	Unc	BU
AH1354 (1935)	950,000	BV	3.00	8.00	20.00	—
AH1354 (1935) Proof	—	Value: 250				

KM# 38 1/2 RIYAL

5.9500 g., 0.9170 Silver .1754 oz. ASW **Obv:** Inscription within beaded circle, legend above, crossed swords below within design flanked by palm trees **Rev:** Inscription within beaded circle, legend above, value below within design flanked by palm trees

Date	Mintage	F	VF	XF	Unc	BU
AH1374 (1954)	2,000,000	BV	3.00	4.50	15.00	—

KM# 18 RIYAL

11.6000 g., 0.9170 Silver .3419 oz. ASW **Obv:** Inscription within beaded circle, legend above, crossed swords below within design flanked by palm trees **Rev:** Inscription within beaded circle, legend above, value below within design flanked by palm trees

Date	Mintage	F	VF	XF	Unc	BU
AH1354 (1935)	60,000,000	BV	5.50	6.50	12.50	—
AH1354 (1935) Proof	20,000,000	Value: 300				
AH1367 (1947)	Inc. above	BV	5.50	6.50	15.00	—
AH1370 (1950)	—	BV	5.50	6.50	17.50	—

KM# 39 RIYAL

11.6000 g., 0.9170 Silver .3419 oz. ASW **Obv:** Inscription within beaded circle, legend above, crossed swords below within design flanked by palm trees **Rev:** Inscription within beaded circle, legend above, value below within design flanked by palm trees

Date	Mintage	F	VF	XF	Unc	BU
AH1374 (1954)	48,000,000	BV	5.75	7.00	17.50	—

COUNTERMARKED COINAGE

70 = 65 Countermark

The following pieces are countermarked examples of earlier types bearing the Arabic numerals 65. They were countermarked in a move to break money changers' monopoly on small coins in AH1365 (1946AD). These countermarks vary in size and are found with the Arabic numbers raised in a circle. Incuse countermarks are considered a recent fabrication.

KM# 22 1/4 GHIRSH

Countermark: "65" **Note:** Countermark in Arabic numerals on 1/4 Ghirsh, KM#4.

CM Date	Host Date	Good	VG	F	VF	XF
AH1365	AH1344	6.00	12.00	30.00	65.00	—

KM# 23 1/4 GHIRSH

Countermark: "65" **Obv:** Countermark at center of legend **Rev:** Value and date below legend **Note:** Countermark in Arabic numerals on 1/4 Ghirsh, KM#7.

CM Date	Host Date	Good	VG	F	VF	XF
AH1365	AH1346	6.00	12.00	30.00	65.00	—

KM# 24 1/4 GHIRSH

Countermark: "65" **Note:** Countermark in Arabic numerals on 1/4 Ghirsh, KM#13.

CM Date	Host Date	Good	VG	F	VF	XF
AH1365	AH1348	20.00	30.00	50.00	100	—

KM# 25 1/4 GHIRSH

Countermark: "65" **Obv:** Countermark at center of legend **Rev:** Value and date below legend **Edge:** Plain **Note:** Countermark in Arabic numerals on 1/4 Ghirsh, KM#19.

CM Date	Host Date	Good	VG	F	VF	XF
AH1365	AH1356	2.50	5.00	15.00	30.00	—

KM# 26 1/2 GHIRSH

Countermark: "65" **Obv:** Countermark at center of legend **Rev:** Date below legend **Note:** Countermark in Arabic numerals on 1/2 Ghirsh, KM#5.

CM Date	Host Date	Good	VG	F	VF	XF
AH1365	AH1344	6.00	12.00	25.00	60.00	—

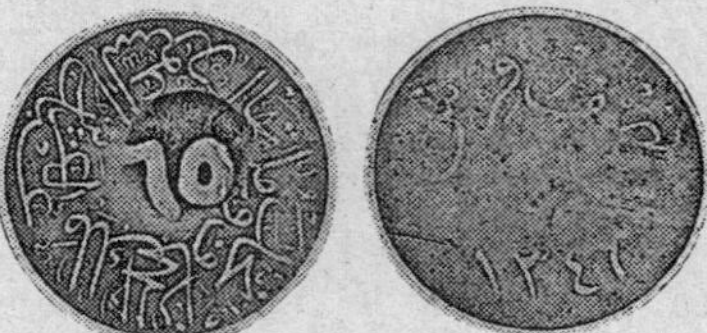

KM# 27 1/2 GHIRSH

Countermark: "65" **Obv:** Countermark at center of legend **Rev:**

Date below legend **Note:** Countermark in Arabic numerals on 1/2 Ghirsh, KM#8.

CM Date	Host Date	Good	VG	F	VF	XF
AH1365	AH1346	6.00	12.00	25.00	60.00	—

KM# 28 1/2 GHIRSH

Countermark: "65" **Note:** Countermark in Arabic numerals on 1/2 Ghirsh, KM#14.

CM Date	Host Date	Good	VG	F	VF	XF
AH1365	AH1348	6.00	12.00	25.00	60.00	—

KM# 29 1/2 GHIRSH

Copper-Nickel **Countermark:** "65" **Obv:** Countermark at center of legend **Rev:** Date below legend **Edge:** Plain **Note:** Countermark in Arabic numerals on 1/2 Ghirsh, KM#20.1.

CM Date	Host Date	Good	VG	F	VF	XF
AH1365	AH1356	5.00	10.00	25.00	40.00	—

KM# 30 GHIRSH

Countermark: "65" **Obv:** Countermark at center of legend **Rev:** Value and date below legend **Note:** Countermark in Arabic numerals on 1 Ghirsh, KM#6.

CM Date	Host Date	Good	VG	F	VF	XF
AH1365	AH1344	6.00	12.00	35.00	65.00	—

KM# 31 GHIRSH

Countermark: "65" **Note:** Countermark in Arabic numerals on 1 Ghirsh, KM#9.

CM Date	Host Date	Good	VG	F	VF	XF
AH1365	AH1346	6.00	12.00	30.00	65.00	—

KM# 32 GHIRSH

Countermark: "65" **Obv:** Countermark at center of legend **Rev:** Value and date below legend **Note:** Countermark in Arabic numerals on 1 Ghirsh, KM#15.

CM Date	Host Date	Good	VG	F	VF	XF
AH1365	AH1348	10.00	20.00	35.00	65.00	—

KM# 33 GHIRSH

Copper-Nickel **Countermark:** "65" **Edge:** Plain **Note:** Countermark in Arabic numerals on 1 Ghirsh, KM#21.

CM Date	Host Date	Good	VG	F	VF	XF
AH1365	AH1356	6.00	10.00	20.00	30.00	—

REFORM COINAGE

5 Halala = 1 Ghirsh; 100 Halala = 1 Riyal

KM# 44 HALALA

Bronze **Obv:** Crossed swords and palm tree at center, legend above and below **Rev:** Value and date below legend

Date	Mintage	F	VF	XF	Unc	BU
AH1383 (1963)	5,000,000	0.50	0.60	0.85	3.00	—

KM# 60 HALALA

Bronze **Obv:** Different legend **Rev:** Value and date below legend

Date	Mintage	F	VF	XF	Unc	BU
AH1397 (1979)	—	—	—	—	—	175

Note: Not released for circulation

KM# 45 5 HALALA (Ghirsh)

2.5000 g., Copper-Nickel, 19.5 mm. **Obv:** Crossed swords and palm tree at center, legend above and below **Rev:** Legend above inscription in circle dividing value, date below

Date	Mintage	F	VF	XF	Unc	BU
AH1392 (1972)	130,000,000	0.10	0.15	0.30	0.50	—

KM# 53 5 HALALA (Ghirsh)

2.5000 g., Copper-Nickel, 19.5 mm. **Obv:** Crossed swords and palm tree at center, legend above and below **Rev:** Legend above inscription in circle dividing value, date below

Date	Mintage	F	VF	XF	Unc	BU
AH1397 (1976)	20,000,000	0.15	0.25	0.60	2.00	—
AH1400 (1979)	—	0.15	0.25	0.60	2.00	—

KM# 57 5 HALALA (Ghirsh)

2.5000 g., Copper-Nickel, 19.5 mm. **Series:** F.A.O. **Obv:** Crossed swords and palm tree at center, legend above and below **Rev:** Legend above inscription in circle dividing value, date below

Date	Mintage	F	VF	XF	Unc	BU
AH1398 (1977)	1,500,000	—	0.30	0.50	1.00	—

KM# 61 5 HALALA (Ghirsh)

2.5000 g., Copper-Nickel, 19.5 mm. **Obv:** Crossed swords and palm tree at center, legend above and below **Rev:** Legend above inscription in circle dividing value, date below

Date	Mintage	F	VF	XF	Unc	BU
AH1408 (1987)	80,000,000	—	0.30	0.50	1.00	—
AH1408 (1987) Proof	5,000	Value: 5.00				

KM# 46 10 HALALA (2 Ghirsh)

4.0000 g., Copper-Nickel, 21 mm. **Obv:** Crossed swords and palm tree at center, legend above and below **Rev:** Legend above inscription in circle dividing value, date below **Edge:** Reeded

Date	Mintage	F	VF	XF	Unc	BU
AH1392 (1972)	55,000,000	0.10	0.20	0.35	0.50	—

KM# 54 10 HALALA (2 Ghirsh)

4.0000 g., Copper-Nickel, 21 mm. **Obv:** Crossed swords and palm tree at center, legend above and below **Rev:** Legend above inscription in circle dividing value, date below

Date	Mintage	F	VF	XF	Unc	BU
AH1397 (1976)	50,000,000	0.15	0.25	1.00	2.50	—
AH1400 (1979)	29,500,000	0.25	0.75	1.00	3.00	—

KM# 58 10 HALALA (2 Ghirsh)

4.0000 g., Copper-Nickel, 21 mm. **Series:** F.A.O. **Obv:** Crossed swords and palm tree at center, legend above and below **Rev:** Legend above inscription in circle dividing value, date below

Date	Mintage	F	VF	XF	Unc	BU
AH1398 (1977)	1,000,000	—	0.25	0.50	1.00	—

KM# 62 10 HALALA (2 Ghirsh)

4.0000 g., Copper-Nickel, 21 mm. **Ruler:** Fahad Bin Abd Al-Aziz AH1403-/1982-AD **Obv:** Crossed swords and palm tree at center, legend above and below **Rev:** Legend above inscription in circle dividing value, date below

Date	Mintage	F	VF	XF	Unc	BU
AH1408 (1987)	100,000,000	—	0.30	0.60	1.25	—
AH1408 (1987) Proof	5,000	Value: 6.00				

KM# 49 25 HALALA (1/4 Riyal)

5.0000 g., Copper-Nickel, 23 mm. **Series:** F.A.O. **Obv:** Crossed swords and palm tree at center, legend above and below **Rev:** Legend above inscription in circle dividing value, date below

Date	Mintage	F	VF	XF	Unc	BU
AH1392-1973	200,000	—	0.20	0.50	1.00	—

KM# 48 25 HALALA (1/4 Riyal)

5.0000 g., Copper-Nickel, 23 mm. **Obv:** Crossed swords and palm tree at center, legend above and below **Rev:** Legend above inscription in circle dividing value, date below **Note:** Corrected denomination; feminine gender.

Date	Mintage	F	VF	XF	Unc	BU
AH1392 (1972)	Inc. above	0.25	0.50	1.00	2.00	—

KM# 47 25 HALALA (1/4 Riyal)

5.0000 g., Copper-Nickel, 23 mm. **Obv:** Crossed swords and palm tree at center, legend above and below **Rev:** Legend above inscription in circle dividing value, date below **Note:** Error. Denomination in masculine gender.

Date	Mintage	F	VF	XF	Unc	BU
AH1392 (1972)	48,465,000	1.00	2.00	6.00	25.00	30.00

KM# 55 25 HALALA (1/4 Riyal)

5.0000 g., Copper-Nickel, 23 mm. **Obv:** Crossed swords and palm tree at center, legend above and below **Rev:** Legend above inscription in circle dividing value, date below

Date	Mintage	F	VF	XF	Unc	BU
AH1397 (1976)	20,000,000	0.35	0.50	1.00	3.00	—
AH1400 (1979)	57,000,000	0.35	0.50	0.85	2.50	—

KM# 63 25 HALALA (1/4 Riyal)
5.0000 g., Copper-Nickel, 23 mm. **Ruler:** Fahad Bin Abd Al-Aziz AH1403-/1982-AD **Obv:** Crossed swords and palm tree at center, legend above and below **Rev:** Legend above inscription in circle dividing value, date below

Date	Mintage	F	VF	XF	Unc	BU
AH1408 (1987)	100,000,000	—	0.40	0.70	1.50	—
AH1408 (1987) Proof	5,000	Value: 7.50				

KM# 50 50 HALALA (1/2 Riyal)
6.5000 g., Copper-Nickel, 26 mm. **Series:** F.A.O. **Obv:** Crossed swords and palm tree at center, legend above and below **Rev:** Legend above inscription in circle dividing value, date below

Date	Mintage	F	VF	XF	Unc	BU
AH1392 (1972)	500,000	—	0.30	0.60	2.50	—

KM# 51 50 HALALA (1/2 Riyal)
6.5000 g., Copper-Nickel, 26 mm. **Obv:** Crossed swords and palm tree at center, legend above and below **Rev:** Legend above inscription in circle dividing value, date below

Date	Mintage	F	VF	XF	Unc	BU
AH1392 (1972)	16,000,000	0.20	0.35	0.60	2.00	—

KM# 56 50 HALALA (1/2 Riyal)
6.5000 g., Copper-Nickel, 26 mm. **Obv:** Crossed swords and palm tree at center, legend above and below **Rev:** Legend above inscription in circle dividing value, date below **Edge:** Reeded

Date	Mintage	F	VF	XF	Unc	BU
AH1397 (1976)	20,000,000	0.50	0.75	1.00	3.00	—
AH1400 (1979)	21,600,000	0.75	1.00	1.50	3.50	—

KM# 64 50 HALALA (1/2 Riyal)
6.5000 g., Copper-Nickel, 26 mm. **Ruler:** Fahad Bin Abd Al-Aziz AH1403-/1982-AD **Obv:** Crossed swords and palm tree at center, legend above and below **Rev:** Legend above inscription in circle dividing value, date below

Date	Mintage	F	VF	XF	Unc	BU
AH1408 (1987)	70,000,000	0.20	0.50	2.25	3.50	—
AH1408 (1987) Proof	5,000	Value: 15.00				

KM# 52 100 HALALA (1 Riyal)
10.0000 g., Copper-Nickel, 30 mm. **Obv:** Crossed swords and palm tree at center, legend above and below **Rev:** Legend above inscription in circle dividing value, date below

Date	Mintage	F	VF	XF	Unc	BU
AH1396 (1976)	250,000	—	0.65	1.00	3.50	—
AH1400 (1980)	30,000,000	—	0.65	1.00	3.00	—

KM# 59 100 HALALA (1 Riyal)
10.0000 g., Copper-Nickel, 30 mm. **Series:** F.A.O. **Obv:** Crossed swords and palm tree at center flanked by dates, legend above and below **Rev:** Legend above inscription in circle dividing value, date below

Date	Mintage	F	VF	XF	Unc	BU
AH1397 - 1977	—	—	—	150	275	325

Note: AH1397 date was struck as samples for the Saudi Arabia government by the British Royal Mint, but some escaped into circulation

Date	Mintage	F	VF	XF	Unc	BU
AH1398 - 1978	10,000,000	—	0.75	1.50	3.50	—

KM# 65 100 HALALA (1 Riyal)
10.0000 g., Copper-Nickel, 30 mm. **Obv:** Crossed swords and palm tree at center, legend above and below **Rev:** Legend above inscription in circle dividing value, date below

Date	Mintage	F	VF	XF	Unc	BU
AH1408 (1987)	40,000,000	—	1.00	2.00	3.00	—
AH1408 (1987) Proof	5,000	Value: 22.00				
AH1414 (1993)	5,000	—	1.00	2.00	4.00	—

KM# 66 100 HALALA (1 Riyal)
Bi-Metallic Brass center in Copper-Nickel ring, 23 mm. **Obv:** Crossed swords and palm tree within circle, legend above and below **Rev:** Inscription at center, value at left, legend above, date below **Edge:** Reeded

Date	Mintage	F	VF	XF	Unc	BU
AH1419 (1999)	—	—	1.00	2.50	5.00	—

KM# 67 100 HALALA (1 Riyal)
Bi-Metallic Brass center in Copper-Nickel ring, 23 mm. **Subject:** Centennial of Kingdom **Obv:** Palm tree design and legend **Rev:** Inscription at center, legend above, value at left, date below **Edge:** Reeded

Date	Mintage	F	VF	XF	Unc	BU
AH1419 (1999)	—	—	1.50	3.50	6.50	—
AH1419 (1999) Proof	—	Value: 12.50				

TRADE COINAGE

KM# 36 GUINEA
7.9881 g., 0.9170 Gold .2354 oz. AGW **Obv:** Inscription within beaded circle, legend above, crossed swords below within design flanked by palm trees **Rev:** Inscription within beaded circle, legend above, value below within design flanked by palm trees

Date	Mintage	F	VF	XF	Unc	BU
AH1370 (1950)	2,000,000	—	—	BV	175	200

KM# 43 GUINEA
7.9881 g., 0.9170 Gold .2354 oz. AGW

Date	Mintage	F	VF	XF	Unc	BU
AH1377 (1957)	1,579,000	—	—	BV	200	250

BULLION COINAGE

Post WWII Issues

KM# 35 SOVEREIGN (Pound)
7.9881 g., 0.9170 Gold .2354 oz. AGW **Obv:** Eagle with wings open **Rev:** Three lined inscription within horizontal bars **Note:** KM#35 and KM#34 were struck at the Philadelphia Mint for a concession payment for oil to the Saudi Government. Most were melted into bullion.

Date	Mintage	F	VF	XF	Unc	BU
ND(1947)	123,000	—	300	500	750	—

KM# 34 4 POUNDS
31.9500 g., 0.9170 Gold .9420 oz. AGW **Obv:** Eagle with wings open **Rev:** Three lined inscription within horizontal bars **Note:** KM#34 and KM#35 were struck at the Philadelphia Mint for a concession payment for oil to the Saudi Government. Most were melted into bullion.

Date	Mintage	F	VF	XF	Unc	BU
ND(1945-46)	91,000	—	650	800	1,200	—

PATTERNS

Including off metal strikes

KM#	Date	Mintage	Identification	Mkt Val
Pn1	AH1373	—	1/4 Riyal. 0.9170 Silver. 2.9500 g. As KM37	—
Pn2	AH1373	—	1/2 Riyal. 0.9170 Silver. 5.9500 g. As KM38	—
Pn3	AH1373	—	Riyal. 0.9170 Silver. 11.6000 g. As KM39	—
Pn4	AH1370	—	Guinea. Aluminum. KM#36.	1,500
Pn5	AH1370	—	Guinea. Bronze. KM#36, reeded edge, with Paris privy marks.	3,500
Pn6	AH1370	—	Guinea. Gold. KM#36, reeded edge, with Paris privy marks, Rare.	—

MINT SETS

KM#	Date	Mintage	Identification	Issue Price	Mkt Val
MS1	AH1408(1988) (5)	—	KM#61-65	20.00	25.00

PROOF SETS

KM#	Date	Mintage	Identification	Issue Price	Mkt Val
PS1	AH1408(1988) (5)	5,000	KM#61-65	40.00	55.00

SENEGAL

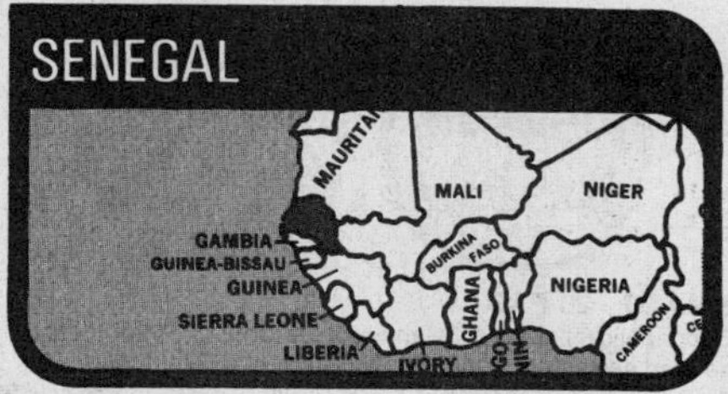

The Republic of Senegal, located on the bulge of West Africa between Mauritania and Guinea-Bissau, has an area of 75,750 sq. mi. (196,190 sq. km.) and a population of *7.5 million. Capital: Dakar. The economy is primarily agricultural. Peanuts and products, phosphates, and canned fish are exported.

An abundance of megalithic remains indicates that Senegal was inhabited in prehistoric times. The Portuguese had some trading stations on the banks of the Senegal River in the 15th century. French commercial establishments date from the 17th century. The French gradually acquired control over the interior regions, which were administered as a protectorate until 1920, and as a colony thereafter. After the 1958 French constitutional referendum, Senegal became a member of the French Community with virtual autonomy. In 1959 Senegal and the French Soudan merged to form the Mali Federation, which became fully independent on June 20, 1960. (April 4, the date the transfer of power agreement was signed with France, is celebrated as Senegal's independence day). The Federation broke up on Aug. 20, 1960, when Senegal seceded and proclaimed the Republic of Senegal. Soudan became the Republic of Mali a month later.

Senegal is a member of a monetary union of autonomous republics called the Monetary Union of West African States (*Union Monetaire Ouest-Africaine*). The other members are Ivory Coast, Benin, Burkina Faso (Upper Volta), Niger, Mauritania and Togo. Mali was a member, but seceded in1962. Some of the member countries have issued coinage in addition to the common currency issued by the Monetary Union of West African States.

REPUBLIC

STANDARD COINAGE

KM# 1 10 FRANCS
3.2000 g., 0.9000 Gold .0926 oz. AGW **Subject:** 8th Anniversary of Independence **Obv:** Star above shield within wreath **Rev:** Stars above value and date

Date	Mintage	F	VF	XF	Unc	BU
1968 Proof	—	Value: 85.00				

KM# 2 25 FRANCS
8.0000 g., 0.9000 Gold .2315 oz. AGW **Subject:** 8th Anniversary of Independence **Obv:** Star above shield within wreath **Rev:** Stars above value and date

Date	Mintage	F	VF	XF	Unc	BU
1968 Proof	—	Value: 175				

KM# 3 50 FRANCS
16.0000 g., 0.9000 Gold .463 oz. AGW **Subject:** 8th Anniversary of Independence **Obv:** Star above shield within wreath **Rev:** Stars above value and date

Date	Mintage	F	VF	XF	Unc	BU
1968 Proof	—	Value: 325				

KM# 5 50 FRANCS
28.2800 g., 0.9250 Silver .8411 oz. ASW **Subject:** 25th Anniversary of Eurafrique Program **Obv:** Sailboat at upper left of value and map **Rev:** Bust facing

Date	Mintage	F	VF	XF	Unc	BU
1975	1,968	—	—	—	220	270
1975 Proof	18,032	Value: 210				

KM# 4 100 FRANCS
32.0000 g., 0.9000 Gold .926 oz. AGW **Subject:** 8th Anniversary of Independence **Obv:** Star above shield within wreath **Rev:** Stars above value and date

Date	Mintage	F	VF	XF	Unc	BU
1968 Proof	—	Value: 650				

KM# 6 150 FRANCS
79.9700 g., 0.9250 Silver 2.3776 oz. ASW **Subject:** 25th Anniversary of Eurafrique Program **Obv:** Flying stork above value and map **Rev:** Bust facing

Date	Mintage	F	VF	XF	Unc	BU
1975	1,075	—	—	—	250	300
1975 Proof	18,925	Value: 245				

KM# 7 250 FRANCS
3.9800 g., 0.9170 Gold .1172 oz. AGW **Subject:** 25th Anniversary of Eurafrique Program **Obv:** Star above shield within wreath **Rev:** Bust facing

Date	Mintage	F	VF	XF	Unc	BU
1975	1,000	—	—	—	90.00	—
1975 Proof	1,250	Value: 90.00				

KM# 8 500 FRANCS
7.9600 g., 0.9170 Gold .2344 oz. AGW **Subject:** 25th Anniversary of Eurafrique Program **Obv:** Star above shield within wreath **Rev:** Bust facing

Date	Mintage	F	VF	XF	Unc	BU
1975	500	—	—	—	200	—
1975 Proof	1,250	Value: 165				

KM# 9 1000 FRANCS
15.9500 g., 0.9160 Gold .4697 oz. AGW **Subject:** 25th Anniversary of Eurafrique Program **Obv:** Star above shield within wreath **Rev:** Bust facing

Date	Mintage	F	VF	XF	Unc	BU
1975	217	—	—	—	375	—
1975 Proof	1,250	Value: 325				

KM# 10 2500 FRANCS
39.9300 g., 0.9160 Gold 1.176 oz. AGW **Subject:** 25th Anniversary of Eurafrique Program **Obv:** Star above shield within wreath **Rev:** Bust facing

Date	Mintage	F	VF	XF	Unc	BU
1975	195	—	—	—	875	—
1975 Proof	1,250	Value: 825				

TOKEN COINAGE

KM# Tn2 5 CENTIMES
Aluminum **Issuer:** Dakar, Chamber of Commerce

Date	Mintage	VG	F	VF	XF	Unc
1920	—	9.00	18.00	40.00	120	300

KM# Tn7 5 CENTIMES
Aluminum **Issuer:** Kayes, Upper Senegal-Niger Chamber of Commerce

Date	Mintage	VG	F	VF	XF	Unc
1920	—	12.00	22.00	45.00	125	—

KM# Tn12 5 CENTIMES
Aluminum **Issuer:** Rufisque, Chamber of Commerce **Shape:** Octagon

Date	Mintage	VG	F	VF	XF	Unc
1920	—	9.00	18.00	40.00	120	260

KM# Tn3 10 CENTIMES
Aluminum **Issuer:** Dakar, Chamber of Commerce

Date	Mintage	VG	F	VF	XF	Unc
1920	—	6.00	12.00	30.00	90.00	—

KM# Tn4 10 CENTIMES
Brass **Issuer:** Dakar, Chamber of Commerce

Date	Mintage	VG	F	VF	XF	Unc
1920	—	9.00	18.00	40.00	120	—

KM# Tn8 10 CENTIMES
Aluminum **Issuer:** Kayes, Upper Senegal-Niger Chamber of Commerce

Date	Mintage	VG	F	VF	XF	Unc
1920	—	14.00	28.00	60.00	150	300

KM# Tn13 10 CENTIMES
Aluminum **Issuer:** Rufisque, Chamber of Commerce

Date	Mintage	VG	F	VF	XF	Unc
1920	—	6.00	12.00	30.00	100	—

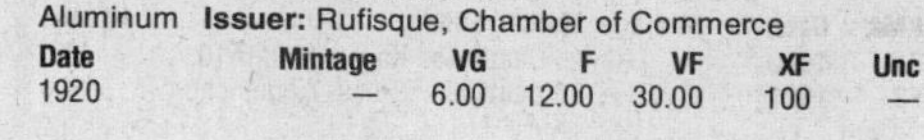

KM# Tn5 25 CENTIMES
Aluminum **Issuer:** Dakar, Chamber of Commerce

Date	Mintage	VG	F	VF	XF	Unc
1920	—	15.00	30.00	55.00	100	300

KM# Tn9 25 CENTIMES
Aluminum **Issuer:** Kayes, Upper Senegal-Niger Chamber of Commerce

Date	Mintage	VG	F	VF	XF	Unc
1920	—	15.00	30.00	65.00	180	—

KM# Tn10 25 CENTIMES
Copper-Nickel **Issuer:** Kayes, Upper Senegal-Niger Chamber of Commerce

Date	Mintage	VG	F	VF	XF	Unc
1920	—	18.00	35.00	75.00	220	—

KM# Tn14 25 CENTIMES
Aluminum **Issuer:** Rufisque, Chamber of Commerce

Date	Mintage	VG	F	VF	XF	Unc
1920	—	12.00	25.00	50.00	150	—

KM# Tn6 50 CENTIMES
Aluminum **Issuer:** Dakar, Chamber of Commerce **Shape:** Octagon

Date	Mintage	VG	F	VF	XF	Unc
1920	—	12.00	25.00	50.00	150	—

KM# Tn11 50 CENTIMES
Aluminum **Issuer:** Kayes, Upper Senegal-Niger Chamber of Commerce

Date	Mintage	VG	F	VF	XF	Unc
1920	—	20.00	40.00	85.00	200	350

KM# Tn15 50 CENTIMES
Aluminum **Issuer:** Rufisque, Chamber of Commerce

Date	Mintage	VG	F	VF	XF	Unc
1920	—	18.00	30.00	60.00	160	—

KM# Tn16 50 CENTIMES
Brass **Issuer:** Rufisque, Chamber of Commerce

Date	Mintage	VG	F	VF	XF	Unc
1920	—	20.00	35.00	70.00	175	—

KM# Tn17 50 CENTIMES
Brass **Issuer:** Ziguinchor, Chamber of Commerce

Date	Mintage	VG	F	VF	XF	Unc
1921	—	22.00	40.00	80.00	180	400

KM# Tn18 FRANC
Brass **Issuer:** Ziguinchor, Chamber of Commerce

Date	Mintage	VG	F	VF	XF	Unc
1921	—	30.00	45.00	90.00	200	—

KM# Tn19 FRANC
Aluminum **Issuer:** Ziguinchor, Chamber of Commerce

Date	Mintage	VG	F	VF	XF	Unc
1921	—	40.00	80.00	175	350	500

ESSAIS

Standard metals unless otherwise noted

KM#	Date	Mintage	Identification	Mkt Val
E1	1920	—	25 Centimes. Kayes. KM#Tn10.	250
E2	1921	—	50 Centimes. Brass. Zinguinchor. KMTn17.	300
E3	1921	—	Franc. Brass. Zinguinchor. KMTn18.	320

MINT SETS

KM#	Date	Mintage	Identification	Issue Price	Mkt Val
MS1	1975 (4)	195	KM#7-10	—	1,350

PROOF SETS

KM#	Date	Mintage	Identification	Issue Price	Mkt Val
PS1	1968 (4)	—	KM#1-4	—	1,125
PS2	1975 (2)	—	KM#5-6	—	300

SERBIA

Serbia, a former inland Balkan kingdom has an area of 34,116 sq. mi. (88,361 sq. km.). Capital: Belgrade.

Serbia emerged as a separate kingdom in the 12th century and attained its greatest expansion and political influence in the mid-14th century. After the Battle of Kosovo, 1389, Serbia became a vassal principality of Turkey and remained under Turkish suzerainty until it was re-established as an independent kingdom by the 1878 Treaty of Berlin. Following World War I, which had its immediate cause in the assassination of Austrian Archduke Francis Ferdinand by a Serbian nationalist, Serbia joined with the Croats and Slovenes to form the new Kingdom of the South Slavs with Peter I of Serbia as King. The name of the kingdom was later changed to Yugoslavia. Invaded by Germany during World War II, Serbia emerged as a constituent republic of the Socialist Federal Republic of Yugoslavia.

RULERS

Alexander I, 1889-1902
Peter I, 1903-1918

MINT MARKS

A - Paris
(a) - Paris, privy mark only
(g) - Gorham Mfg. Co., Providence, R.I.
H - Birmingham
V - Vienna
БП - (BP) Budapest

MONETARY SYSTEM

100 Para = 1 Dinara

DENOMINATIONS

ПАРА = Para
ПАРЕ = Pare
ДИНАР = Dinar
ДИНАРА = Dinara

KINGDOM

STANDARD COINAGE

KM# 23 2 PARE
Bronze **Ruler:** Peter I **Obv:** Crowned double-headed eagle **Rev:** Value **Note:** Medallic die alignment.

Date	Mintage	F	VF	XF	Unc	BU
1904	12,500,000	2.00	5.00	15.00	35.00	—

KM# 18 5 PARA
Copper-Nickel **Ruler:** Milan I as Prince **Obv:** Crowned double-headed eagle **Rev:** Value **Note:** Medallic die alignment.

Date	Mintage	F	VF	XF	Unc	BU
1904	8,000,000	1.00	2.50	6.00	17.00	—
1904 Proof	Inc. above	Value: 200				
1912	10,500,032	0.75	1.50	3.50	12.00	—
1912 Proof	—	Value: 125				
1917(g)	5,000,000	5.00	10.00	20.00	36.00	—

KM# 19 10 PARA
Copper-Nickel **Ruler:** Milan I as King **Obv:** Crowned double-headed eagle **Rev:** Value **Note:** Medallic die alignment.

Date	Mintage	F	VF	XF	Unc	BU
1904 Proof	—	Value: 350				
1912	7,700,032	0.75	1.25	4.00	14.00	—
1912 Proof	—	Value: 125				
1917(g)	5,000,000	1.00	2.50	9.00	26.00	—
1917(g) Proof	—	Value: 210				

KM# 20 20 PARA
Copper-Nickel **Ruler:** Milan I as King **Obv:** Crowned double-headed eagle **Rev:** Value **Note:** Medallic die alignment.

Date	Mintage	F	VF	XF	Unc	BU
1904 Proof	—	Value: 400				
1912	5,650,035	0.75	2.00	5.00	14.00	—
1912 Proof	—	Value: 130				
1917(g)	5,000,000	1.00	3.00	9.00	25.00	—

KM# 24.1 50 PARA
2.5000 g., 0.8350 Silver .0671 oz. ASW **Ruler:** Peter I **Obv:** Head right with designer name **Rev:** Crown above value and date within wreath **Note:** Medallic die alignment.

Date	Mintage	F	VF	XF	Unc	BU
1904	1,400,031	2.00	5.00	12.50	32.00	—
1904 Proof	—	Value: 200				
1912	800,000	2.50	6.00	15.00	34.00	—
1915(a)	12,137,928	1.25	2.50	4.50	12.00	—

KM# 24.2 50 PARA
2.5000 g., 0.8350 Silver .0671 oz. ASW **Ruler:** Peter I **Obv:** Without designer's name **Rev:** Crown above value and date within wreath **Note:** Medallic die alignment

Date	Mintage	F	VF	XF	Unc	BU
1915(a)	1,862,071	6.00	12.00	32.00	95.00	—

KM# 24.3 50 PARA
Silver **Ruler:** Peter I **Obv:** With designer's signature **Rev:** Crown above value and date within wreath **Note:** Coin die alignment.

Date	Mintage	F	VF	XF	Unc	BU
1915	—	—	—	—	—	—

KM# 24.4 50 PARA
Silver **Ruler:** Peter I **Obv:** Without designer name **Rev:** Crown above value and date within wreath **Note:** Coin die alignment

Date	Mintage	F	VF	XF	Unc	BU
1915(a)	—	—	—	—	—	—

KM# 25.1 DINAR
5.0000 g., 0.8350 Silver .1342 oz. ASW **Ruler:** Peter I **Obv:** Head right with designer's name below neck **Rev:** Crown above value and date within wreath **Note:** Medallic die alignment

Date	Mintage	F	VF	XF	Unc	BU
1904	2,000,086	4.50	12.00	25.00	75.00	—
1904 Proof	—	Value: 260				
1912	8,000,000	3.00	6.00	15.00	38.00	—
1915(a)	10,688,711	2.25	4.50	9.00	18.00	—

KM# 25.2 DINAR
5.0000 g., 0.8350 Silver .1342 oz. ASW **Ruler:** Peter I **Obv:** Without designer's name **Rev:** Crown above value and date within wreath **Note:** Medallic die alignment.

Date	Mintage	F	VF	XF	Unc	BU
1915(a)	2,312,304	5.00	15.00	35.00	95.00	—

KM# 25.3 DINAR
Silver **Ruler:** Peter I **Obv:** With designer name **Rev:** Crown above value and date within wreath **Note:** Coin die alignment

Date	Mintage	F	VF	XF	Unc	BU
1915(a)	—	—	—	—	—	—

KM# 25.4 DINAR
Silver **Ruler:** Peter I **Obv:** Without designer name **Rev:** Crown above value and date within wreath **Note:** Coin die alignment

Date	Mintage	F	VF	XF	Unc	BU
1915(a)	—	—	—	—	—	—

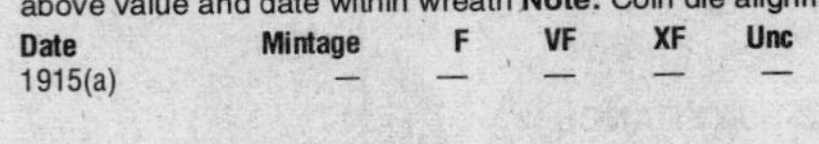

KM# 26.1 2 DINARA

10.0000 g., 0.8350 Silver .2684 oz. ASW **Ruler:** Peter I **Obv:** Head right with designer's name below neck **Rev:** Crown above value and date within wreath **Note:** Medallic die alignment

Date	Mintage	F	VF	XF	Unc	BU
1904	1,150,044	7.50	15.00	32.00	85.00	—
1904 Proof	—	Value: 325				
1912	800,016	8.00	16.00	35.00	95.00	—
1915(a)	4,174,142	5.00	10.00	18.00	35.00	—

KM# 26.2 2 DINARA

10.0000 g., 0.8350 Silver .2684 oz. ASW **Ruler:** Peter I **Obv:** Without designer's name **Rev:** Crown above value and date within wreath **Note:** Medallic die alignment.

Date	Mintage	F	VF	XF	Unc	BU
1915(a)	825,858	8.00	22.00	50.00	140	—

KM# 26.3 2 DINARA

10.0000 g., 0.8350 Silver .2684 oz. ASW **Ruler:** Peter I **Obv:** Without designer's signature **Rev:** Crown above value and date within wreath **Note:** Coin die alignment.

Date	Mintage	VG	F	VF	XF	Unc
1915(a)	Inc. above	—	5.00	10.00	18.00	36.00

KM# 26.4 2 DINARA

Silver **Ruler:** Peter I **Obv:** Without designer's name **Rev:** Crown above value and date within wreath **Note:** Coin die alignment

Date	Mintage	F	VF	XF	Unc	BU
1915A	—	—	—	—	—	—

KM# 27 5 DINARA

25.0000 g., 0.9000 Silver .7234 oz. ASW, 37 mm. **Ruler:** Peter I **Subject:** 100th Anniversary - Karageorgevich Dynasty **Obv:** Conjoined heads right with designer name below neck **Obv. Designer:** Schwartz **Rev:** Crowned double-headed eagle on shield within crowned mantle **Edge:** Lettered, Type I

Date	Mintage	F	VF	XF	Unc	BU
1904	200,000	35.00	75.00	220	675	—
1904 Proof	—	Value: 2,000				

KM# 28 5 DINARA

25.0000 g., 0.9000 Silver .7234 oz. ASW, 37 mm. **Ruler:** Peter I **Subject:** 100th Anniversary - Karageorgevich Dynasty **Edge:** Lettered, Type II

Date	Mintage	F	VF	XF	Unc	BU
1904	Inc. above	150	300	700	1,800	—

GERMAN OCCUPATION

World War II

OCCUPATION COINAGE

KM# 30 50 PARA

Zinc **Obv:** Double-headed eagle **Rev:** Value and date within oat sprigs

Date	Mintage	F	VF	XF	Unc	BU
1942БП (BP)	20,000,000	2.00	4.50	10.00	20.00	—

KM# 31 DINAR

Zinc **Obv:** Double headed eagle **Rev:** Value and date within oat sprigs

Date	Mintage	F	VF	XF	Unc	BU
1942БП (BP)	50,000,000	0.70	2.00	6.00	18.00	—

KM# 32 2 DINARA

Zinc **Obv:** Double-headed eagle **Rev:** Value and date within oat sprigs

Date	Mintage	F	VF	XF	Unc	BU
1942БП (BP)	40,000,000	0.70	2.00	7.00	20.00	—

KM# 33 10 DINARA

Zinc **Obv:** Double-headed eagle **Rev:** Value and date within oat sprigs

Date	Mintage	F	VF	XF	Unc	BU
1943БП (BP)	50,000,000	1.00	2.50	8.00	22.00	—

PATTERNS

Including off metal strikes

KM#	Date	Mintage	Identification	Mkt Val
PnC6	1904	—	2 Dinara. Bronze.	1,500
PnD6	1904	4	5 Dinara. Gold. 44.5000 g.	—
Pn6	1917	—	5 Para. Gold.	—
Pn7	1917	—	10 Para. Gold.	—
Pn8	1917	—	20 Para. Gold.	—
Pn9	1917	—	20 Dinara. Gold.	—

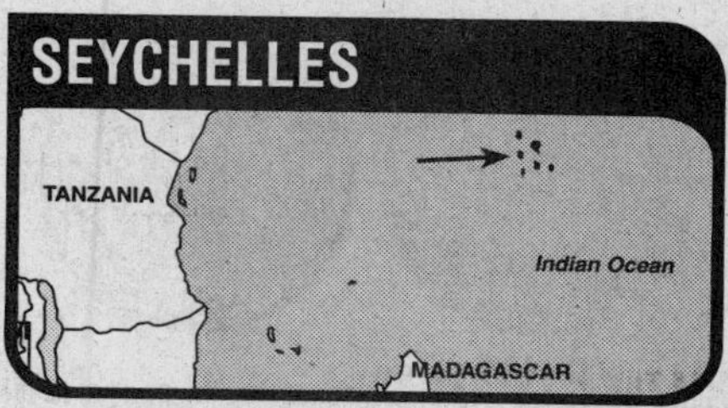

The Republic of Seychelles, an archipelago of 85 granite and coral islands situated in the Indian Ocean 600 miles (965 km.) northeast of Madagascar, has an area of 156 sq. mi. (455 sq. km.) and a population of *70,000. Among these islands are the Aldabra Islands, the Farquhar Group, and Ile Desroches, which the United Kingdom ceded to the Seychelles upon its independence. Capital: Victoria, on Mahe. The economy is based on fishing, a plantation system of agriculture, and tourism. Copra, cinnamon and vanilla are exported.

Although the Seychelles is marked on Portuguese charts of the early 16th century, the first recorded visit to the islands, by an English ship, occurred in 1609. The Seychelles were annexed to France by Captain Lazare Picault in 1743 and permanently settled in 1768, with the intention of establishing spice plantations to compete with the Dutch monopoly of the spice trade. British troops seized the islands in 1810, during the Napoleonic Wars; the Treaty of Paris, 1814, formally ceded them to Britain. The Seychelles was a dependency of Mauritius until Aug. 31, 1903, when they became a separate British Crown Colony. The colony was granted limited internal self-government in 1970, and attained independence on June 28, 1976, becoming Britain's last African possession to do so. Seychelles is a member of the Commonwealth of Nations. The president is the Head of State and of Government.

RULERS

British, until 1976

MINT MARKS

M – South African Mint Co.
M in oval – South African Mint Co. On coins dated 2000 and up in Place of PM
PM - Pobjoy Mint
None - British Royal Mint

MONETARY SYSTEM

100 Cents = 1 Rupee

BRITISH CROWN COLONY

STANDARD COINAGE

KM# 5 CENT

Bronze **Obv:** Crowned head left **Obv. Designer:** Percy Metcalfe **Rev:** Value within beaded circle

Date	Mintage	F	VF	XF	Unc	BU
1948	300,000	—	0.25	0.50	1.25	—
1948 Proof	—	Value: 50.00				

KM# 14 CENT

Bronze **Obv:** Crowned head right **Obv. Designer:** Cecil Thomas **Rev:** Value within beaded circle

Date	Mintage	F	VF	XF	Unc	BU
1959	30,000	—	0.75	1.50	3.00	—
1959 Proof	—	—	—	—	—	—
1961	30,000	—	0.50	1.00	2.25	—
1961 Proof	—	—	—	—	—	—
1963	40,000	—	0.50	1.00	1.50	—
1963 Proof	—	—	—	—	—	—
1965	20,000	—	2.00	3.00	5.00	—
1969	Est. 5,000	15.00	20.00	30.00	65.00	—

Note: Latest reports indicate only 5,000 circulation strikes have been releasesd to date in addition to proof issues

Date	Mintage	F	VF	XF	Unc	BU
1969 Proof	—	Value: 5.00				

KM# 17 CENT

Aluminum, 16 mm. **Series:** F.A.O. **Obv:** Young bust right **Obv. Designer:** Arnold Machin **Rev:** Cow head **Edge:** Plain

Date	Mintage	F	VF	XF	Unc	BU
1972	2,350,000	—	—	0.10	0.25	1.00

KM# 6 2 CENTS

Bronze **Obv:** Crowned head left **Obv. Designer:** Percy Metcalfe **Rev:** Value within beaded circle

Date	Mintage	F	VF	XF	Unc	BU
1948	350,000	—	0.35	0.60	1.50	—
1948 Proof	—	Value: 75.00				

KM# 15 2 CENTS

Bronze **Obv:** Crowned head right **Obv. Designer:** Cecil Thomas **Rev:** Value within beaded circle

Date	Mintage	F	VF	XF	Unc	BU
1959	30,000	—	0.50	1.00	2.50	—
1959 Proof	—	—	—	—	—	—
1961	30,000	—	0.50	1.00	2.75	—
1961 Proof	—	—	—	—	—	—
1963	40,000	—	0.75	1.25	2.50	—
1963 Proof	—	—	—	—	—	—
1965	20,000	—	2.00	3.00	4.00	—
1968	20,000	—	2.00	3.00	5.50	—
1969 Proof	5,000	Value: 4.00				

KM# 7 5 CENTS

Bronze **Obv:** Crowned head left **Obv. Designer:** Percy Metcalfe **Rev:** Value within circle

Date	Mintage	F	VF	XF	Unc	BU
1948	300,000	—	0.40	0.80	3.00	—
1948 Proof	—	Value: 100				

KM# 16 5 CENTS

Bronze **Obv:** Crowned head right **Obv. Designer:** Cecil Thomas **Rev:** Value within beaded circle

Date	Mintage	F	VF	XF	Unc	BU
1964	20,000	—	1.00	2.00	4.50	—
1964 Proof	—	—	—	—	—	—
1965	40,000	—	1.50	2.50	5.50	—
1967	20,000	—	1.50	3.00	8.00	—
1968	40,000	—	1.00	2.00	7.00	—
1969	100,000	—	0.50	1.00	5.00	—
1969 Proof	—	Value: 4.00				
1971	25,000	—	0.50	1.50	2.50	—

KM# 18 5 CENTS

Aluminum, 18.5 mm. **Series:** F.A.O. **Obv:** Young bust right **Obv. Designer:** Arnold Machin **Rev:** Cabbage head **Shape:** Scalloped

Date	Mintage	F	VF	XF	Unc	BU
1972	2,200,000	—	—	0.10	0.25	—
1975	1,200,000	—	—	0.10	0.25	—

KM# 1 10 CENTS

Copper-Nickel **Obv:** Crowned head left **Obv. Designer:** Percy Metcalfe **Rev:** Value within sprig above date **Shape:** Scalloped

Date	Mintage	F	VF	XF	Unc	BU
1939	36,000	—	10.00	35.00	70.00	—
1939 Proof	—	Value: 150				
1943	36,000	—	10.00	22.00	40.00	—
1944	36,000	—	10.00	22.00	40.00	—
1944 Proof	—	Value: 175				

KM# 8 10 CENTS

Copper-Nickel **Obv:** Crowned head left **Obv. Designer:** Percy Metcalfe **Rev:** Value within sprig above date **Shape:** Scalloped

Date	Mintage	F	VF	XF	Unc	BU
1951	36,000	—	6.00	15.00	30.00	—
1951 Proof	—	Value: 135				

KM# 10 10 CENTS

Nickel-Brass **Obv:** Crowned head right **Obv. Designer:** Cecil Thomas **Rev:** Value within sprig above date **Shape:** 12-sided

Date	Mintage	F	VF	XF	Unc	BU
1953	130,000	—	0.50	1.00	3.00	—
1953 Proof	—	Value: 100				
1965	40,000	—	1.00	1.50	5.00	—
1967	20,000	—	4.00	7.50	15.00	—
1968	50,000	—	1.00	4.00	12.50	—
1969	60,000	—	1.00	2.00	7.00	—
1969 Proof	—	Value: 2.00				
1970	75,000	—	0.50	1.00	4.50	—
1971	100,000	—	0.50	1.00	1.75	—
1972	120,000	—	0.30	0.50	1.00	—
1973	100,000	—	0.15	0.25	1.00	—
1974	100,000	—	0.15	0.25	0.75	—

KM# 2 25 CENTS

2.9200 g., 0.5000 Silver .0469 oz. ASW **Obv:** Crowned head left **Obv. Designer:** Percy Metcalfe **Rev:** Value within sprig above date

Date	Mintage	F	VF	XF	Unc	BU
1939	36,000	—	7.50	35.00	125	—
1939 Proof	—	Value: 200				
1943	36,000	—	5.00	25.00	100	—
1944	36,000	—	3.50	20.00	85.00	—
1944 Proof	—	Value: 300				

KM# 9 25 CENTS

Copper-Nickel **Obv:** Crowned head left **Obv. Designer:** Percy Metcalfe **Rev:** Value within sprig above date

Date	Mintage	F	VF	XF	Unc	BU
1951	36,000	—	2.00	7.50	35.00	—
1951 Proof	—	Value: 160				

KM# 11 25 CENTS

Copper-Nickel **Obv:** Crowned head right **Obv. Designer:** Cecil Thomas **Rev:** Value within sprig above date

Date	Mintage	F	VF	XF	Unc	BU
1954	124,000	—	0.75	1.25	3.50	—
1954 Proof	—	Value: 120				
1960	40,000	—	0.75	1.25	2.00	—
1960 Proof	—	—	—	—	—	—
1964	40,000	—	1.00	2.00	5.00	—
1965	40,000	—	1.00	2.00	5.00	—
1966	10,000	—	3.50	10.00	25.00	—
1967	20,000	—	2.50	4.00	15.00	—
1968	20,000	—	2.50	4.00	15.00	—
1969	100,000	—	1.00	2.00	4.00	—
1969 Proof	—	Value: 3.00				
1970	40,000	—	1.50	3.00	10.00	—
1972	120,000	—	0.50	0.75	1.50	—
1973	100,000	—	0.50	0.75	1.50	—
1974	100,000	—	0.50	0.75	1.50	—

KM# 3 1/2 RUPEE

5.8300 g., 0.5000 Silver .0937 oz. ASW **Obv:** Crowned head left **Obv. Designer:** Percy Metcalfe **Rev:** Value within sprig above date

Date	Mintage	F	VF	XF	Unc	BU
1939	36,000	—	22.00	80.00	175	—
1939 Proof	—	Value: 250				

KM# 12 1/2 RUPEE

Copper-Nickel **Obv:** Crowned head right **Obv. Designer:** Cecil Thomas **Rev:** Value within sprig above date

Date	Mintage	F	VF	XF	Unc	BU
1954	72,000	—	0.50	1.25	3.75	—
1954 Proof	—	Value: 150				
1960	60,000	—	0.50	1.00	3.00	—
1960 Proof	—	Value: 150				
1966	15,000	—	1.50	5.00	20.00	—
1967	20,000	—	3.00	8.00	25.00	—
1968	20,000	—	3.00	8.00	30.00	—
1969	60,000	—	0.75	1.00	12.00	—
1969 Proof	—	Value: 3.00				
1970	50,000	—	0.75	1.00	8.00	—
1971	100,000	—	0.75	1.00	3.00	—
1972	120,000	—	0.50	0.75	1.00	—
1974	100,000	—	0.50	0.75	1.00	—

KM# 4 RUPEE

11.6600 g., 0.5000 Silver .1874 oz. ASW, 30 mm. **Obv:** Crowned head left **Obv. Designer:** Percy Metcalfe **Rev:** Value within sprig above date **Edge:** Reeded

Date	Mintage	F	VF	XF	Unc	BU
1939	90,000	12.00	25.00	95.00	165	—
1939 Proof	—	Value: 400				

KM# 13 RUPEE

Copper-Nickel, 30 mm. **Obv:** Crowned head right **Obv. Designer:** Cecil Thomas **Rev:** Value within sprig above date

Date	Mintage	F	VF	XF	Unc	BU
1954	150,000	—	0.50	1.00	3.00	—
1954 Proof	—	Value: 200				
1960	60,000	—	0.75	1.25	3.50	—
1960 Proof	—	—	—	—	—	—
1966	45,000	—	1.25	2.25	8.50	—
1967	10,000	—	3.50	7.50	27.50	—
1968	40,000	—	2.50	5.00	20.00	—
1969	50,000	—	1.50	3.00	12.50	—
1969 Proof	—	Value: 5.00				
1970	50,000	—	1.50	2.50	10.00	—
1971	100,000	—	0.75	1.50	5.00	—
1972	120,000	—	0.75	1.50	2.00	—
1974	100,000	—	—	—	1.50	—

KM# 19 5 RUPEES
Copper-Nickel, 30 mm. **Obv:** Young bust right **Obv. Designer:** Arnold Machin **Rev:** Palm tree, sailboats,giant tortoise and value **Edge:** Plain **Shape:** 7-sided

Date	Mintage	F	VF	XF	Unc	BU
1972	220,000	—	1.50	2.50	5.00	6.00

KM# 19a 5 RUPEES
15.5000 g., 0.9250 Silver .4609 oz. ASW, 30 mm. **Obv:** Young bust right **Rev:** Palm tree, boats and value **Shape:** 7-sided

Date	Mintage	F	VF	XF	Unc	BU
1972 Proof	2,500	Value: 20.00				
1974 Proof	5,000	Value: 14.50				

KM# 20 10 RUPEES
Copper-Nickel, 38.5 mm. **Obv:** Young bust right **Obv. Designer:** Arnold Machin **Rev:** Sea turtle and value **Rev. Designer:** Suzanne Danielli

Date	Mintage	F	VF	XF	Unc	BU
1974	—	—	2.00	4.00	12.00	—

KM# 20a 10 RUPEES
28.2800 g., 0.9250 Silver .8411 oz. ASW **Obv:** Young bust right **Obv. Designer:** Arnold Machin **Rev:** Green sea turtle **Rev. Designer:** Suzanne Danielli

Date	Mintage	F	VF	XF	Unc	BU
1974 Proof	25,000	Value: 18.50				

REPUBLIC

STANDARD COINAGE

KM# 21 CENT
Aluminum, 16 mm. **Subject:** Declaration of Independence **Obv:** Head right **Rev:** Boueteur fish and value

Date	Mintage	F	VF	XF	Unc	BU
1976	109,000	—	0.10	0.20	0.75	1.00
1976 Proof	8,500	Value: 1.50				

KM# 30 CENT
0.7000 g., Aluminum, 16 mm. **Obv:** Arms with supporters **Rev:** Boueteur fish and value

Date	Mintage	F	VF	XF	Unc	BU
1977	—	—	—	0.15	0.75	1.00

KM# 46.1 CENT
Brass **Obv:** Arms with supporters **Rev:** Mud Crab and value

Date	Mintage	F	VF	XF	Unc	BU
1982	500,000	—	—	0.15	0.50	1.50
1982 Proof	—	Value: 2.25				

KM# 46.2 CENT
Brass **Obv:** Altered coat of arms **Rev:** Mud Crab

Date	Mintage	F	VF	XF	Unc	BU
1990 PM	—	—	—	0.15	0.50	1.50
1992 PM	—	—	—	0.15	0.50	1.50
1992 PM Proof	—	Value: 2.25				
1997	—	—	—	0.15	0.50	1.50

KM# 22 5 CENTS
Aluminum **Subject:** Declaration of Independence **Obv:** Head right **Rev:** Fish above value and sprigs **Shape:** Scalloped **Note:** Varieties exist.

Date	Mintage	F	VF	XF	Unc	BU
1976	209,000	—	0.10	0.20	0.75	1.25
1976 Proof	8,500	Value: 1.50				

KM# 31 5 CENTS
Aluminum **Series:** F.A.O. **Obv:** Arms with supporters **Rev:** Fish above value and sprigs **Shape:** Scalloped

Date	Mintage	F	VF	XF	Unc	BU
1977	300,000	—	—	0.15	0.75	1.25

KM# 43 5 CENTS
1.9500 g., Brass, 18 mm. **Series:** World Food Day **Obv:** Arms with supporters **Rev:** Value at lower left of tapioca plant

Date	Mintage	F	VF	XF	Unc	BU
1981	720,000	—	—	0.15	0.45	1.00

KM# 47.1 5 CENTS
1.9500 g., Brass, 18 mm. **Obv:** Arms with supporters **Rev:** Value at lower left of tapioca plant

Date	Mintage	F	VF	XF	Unc	BU
1982	1,500,000	—	—	0.10	0.30	—
1982 Proof	Inc. above	Value: 2.50				

KM# 47.2 5 CENTS
1.9500 g., Brass, 18 mm. **Obv:** Altered coat of arms **Rev:** Tapioca plant

Date	Mintage	F	VF	XF	Unc	BU
1990 PM	—	—	—	0.10	0.30	0.50
1992 PM	—	—	—	0.10	0.30	0.50
1992 PM Proof	—	Value: 2.50				
1995 PM	—	—	—	0.10	0.30	0.50
1997 PM	—	—	—	0.10	0.30	0.50
1997 PM Proof	—	Value: 2.50				
2000 m	—	—	—	0.10	0.30	0.50

KM# 23 10 CENTS
Nickel-Brass, 21 mm. **Subject:** Declaration of Independence **Obv:** Head right **Rev:** Sailfish and value **Edge:** Plain **Shape:** 12-sided

Date	Mintage	F	VF	XF	Unc	BU
1976	209,000	—	0.20	0.50	1.50	2.50
1976 Proof	8,500	Value: 2.50				

KM# 32 10 CENTS
Nickel-Brass, 21 mm. **Series:** F.A.O. **Obv:** Arms with supporters **Rev:** Sailfish and value

Date	Mintage	F	VF	XF	Unc	BU
1977	125,000	—	0.10	0.35	1.50	2.50

KM# 44 10 CENTS
3.2500 g., Brass, 21 mm. **Series:** World Food Day **Obv:** Arms with supporters **Rev:** Yellowfin tuna and value

Date	Mintage	F	VF	XF	Unc	BU
1981	145,000	—	0.10	0.25	1.00	1.50

KM# 48.1 10 CENTS
3.2500 g., Brass, 21 mm. **Obv:** Arms with supporters **Rev:** Yellowfin tuna and value

Date	Mintage	F	VF	XF	Unc	BU
1982	1,000,000	—	0.10	0.25	1.00	1.50
1982 Proof	Inc. above	Value: 2.75				

KM# 48.2 10 CENTS
3.2500 g., Brass, 21 mm. **Obv:** Altered coat of arms **Rev:** Yellowfin tuna

Date	Mintage	F	VF	XF	Unc	BU
1990	—	—	0.10	0.25	1.00	1.50
1992	—	—	0.10	0.25	1.00	1.50
1992 Proof	—	Value: 2.75				
1994	—	—	0.10	0.25	1.00	1.50
1997	—	—	0.10	0.25	1.00	1.50
2000 m	—	—	0.10	0.25	1.00	1.50

KM# 24 25 CENTS
2.9000 g., Copper-Nickel, 19 mm. **Subject:** Declaration of Independence **Obv:** Head right **Rev:** Black Parrot and value

Date	Mintage	F	VF	XF	Unc	BU
1976	209,000	—	0.50	1.00	3.00	—
1976 Proof	8,500	Value: 3.50				

KM# 33 25 CENTS
2.9000 g., Copper-Nickel, 19 mm. **Obv:** Arms with supporters **Rev:** Black Parrot and value

Date	Mintage	F	VF	XF	Unc	BU
1977	—	—	0.25	0.75	3.00	—

KM# 49.1 25 CENTS
2.9000 g., Copper-Nickel, 19 mm. **Obv:** Arms with supporters **Rev:** Black Parrot and value **Edge:** Reeded

Date	Mintage	F	VF	XF	Unc	BU
1982	375,000	—	0.25	0.75	2.50	3.00
1982 Proof	Inc. above	Value: 3.00				

KM# 49.2 25 CENTS
2.9000 g., Copper-Nickel, 19 mm. **Obv:** Arms with supporters **Rev:** Black Parrot and value

Date	Mintage	F	VF	XF	Unc	BU
1989	1,500,000	—	0.25	0.75	2.25	4.00
1992 PM	—	—	0.25	0.75	2.25	4.00
1992 PM Proof	—	Value: 5.00				
2000 m	—	—	—	0.50	2.00	4.00

KM# 49.3 25 CENTS
Nickel Clad Steel, 19 mm. **Obv:** Arms with supporters **Rev:** Black Parrot and value

Date	Mintage	F	VF	XF	Unc	BU
1993 PM	—	—	0.25	0.75	2.25	4.00
1997PM	—	—	0.25	0.75	2.25	4.00

KM# 49.4 25 CENTS
Stainless Steel, 19 mm. **Obv:** Arms with supporters **Rev:** Black Parrot and value

Date	Mintage	F	VF	XF	Unc	BU
2000 m	—	—	—	—	2.50	4.00

KM# 25 50 CENTS
5.8000 g., Copper-Nickel, 23.6 mm. **Subject:** Declaration of Independence **Obv:** Head right **Rev:** Orchid and value **Edge:** Reeded

Date	Mintage	F	VF	XF	Unc	BU
1976	209,000	—	0.50	1.00	2.50	—
1976 Proof	8,500	Value: 3.50				

KM# 34 50 CENTS
5.8000 g., Copper-Nickel, 23.6 mm. **Obv:** Arms with supporters **Rev:** Orchid and value

Date	Mintage	F	VF	XF	Unc	BU
1977	—	—	0.20	0.45	1.00	—

KM# 26 RUPEE
11.6500 g., Copper-Nickel, 30 mm. **Subject:** Declaration of Independence **Obv:** Head right **Rev:** Triton Conch shell and value **Edge:** Reeded

Date	Mintage	F	VF	XF	Unc	BU
1976	259,000	—	0.75	1.00	1.75	2.50
1976 Proof	8,500	Value: 2.50				

KM# 35 RUPEE
11.6500 g., Copper-Nickel, 30 mm. **Obv:** Arms with supporters **Rev:** Triton Conch shell and value

Date	Mintage	F	VF	XF	Unc	BU
1977	—	—	0.50	0.75	1.75	2.50

KM# 50.1 RUPEE
Copper-Nickel **Obv:** Arms with supporters **Rev:** Triton Conch shell and value

Date	Mintage	F	VF	XF	Unc	BU
1982	2,000,000	—	0.25	0.50	2.00	—
1982 Proof	Inc. above	Value: 5.00				
1983	—	—	0.50	1.00	2.00	—

KM# 50.2 RUPEE
Copper-Nickel **Obv:** Altered coat of arms **Rev:** Triton Conch Shell

Date	Mintage	F	VF	XF	Unc	BU
1992 PM	—	—	0.25	0.50	2.00	—
1992 PM Proof	—	Value: 5.00				
1995 PM	—	—	0.25	0.50	2.00	—
1997 PM	—	—	0.25	0.50	2.00	—

KM# 85 RUPEE
Copper-Nickel **Series:** Queen Elizabeth The Queen Mother **Subject:** Wedding of Lady Elizabeth Bowes-Lyon: The Duke of York, 1923 **Obv:** Arms with supporters **Rev:** Royal couple facing on steps

Date	Mintage	F	VF	XF	Unc	BU
1995	Est. 30,000	—	—	—	10.00	—

KM# 27 5 RUPEES
13.5000 g., Copper-Nickel, 30 mm. **Subject:** Declaration of Independence **Obv:** Head right **Rev:** Palm tree and value **Shape:** 7-sided

Date	Mintage	F	VF	XF	Unc	BU
1976	50,000	—	1.25	1.75	3.00	—

KM# 27a 5 RUPEES
15.5000 g., 0.9250 Silver .4609 oz. ASW, 30 mm. **Subject:** Declaration of Independence **Obv:** Head right **Rev:** Palm tree and value

Date	Mintage	F	VF	XF	Unc	BU
1976 Proof	8,500	Value: 12.50				

KM# 36 5 RUPEES
13.5000 g., Copper-Nickel, 30 mm. **Obv:** Arms with supporters **Rev:** Palm tree and value **Shape:** 7-sided

Date	Mintage	F	VF	XF	Unc	BU
1977	—	—	1.00	1.50	2.25	—

KM# 51.1 5 RUPEES
13.5000 g., Copper-Nickel, 30 mm. **Obv:** Arms with supporters **Rev:** Palm tree and value

Date	Mintage	F	VF	XF	Unc	BU
1982	300,000	—	1.00	1.50	2.00	—
1982 Proof	Inc. above	Value: 5.00				

KM# 51.2 5 RUPEES
Copper-Nickel **Obv:** Altered arms **Rev:** Fruit tree divides value

Date	Mintage	F	VF	XF	Unc	BU
1992 PM	—	—	1.00	1.50	2.00	—
1992 PM Proof	—	Value: 5.00				
1997 PM	—	—	1.00	1.50	2.00	—
2000 m	—	—	1.00	1.50	2.00	—

KM# 89 5 RUPEES
Copper-Nickel **Series:** 50th Anniversary United Nations **Obv:** Arms with supporters **Rev:** Dove in flight over UN's logo, large 50 at right

Date	Mintage	F	VF	XF	Unc	BU
ND(1995)	—	—	—	—	10.00	—

KM# 109 5 RUPEES
Copper-Nickel **Subject:** Marriage of Prince Edward **Obv:** Arms with supporters **Rev:** Tied initials and birds **Note:** Similar to 25 Rupees, KM#110.

Date	Mintage	F	VF	XF	Unc	BU
1999	—	—	—	—	9.00	—

KM# 112 5 RUPEES
Copper-Nickel **Subject:** Millennium **Obv:** Arms with supporters **Rev:** Latent image of 1999-2000 dates **Note:** Similar to 25 Rupees, KM#113.

Date	Mintage	F	VF	XF	Unc	BU
2000 m	—	—	—	—	9.00	—

KM# 114 5 RUPEES
Copper-Nickel **Subject:** British Queen Mother **Obv:** Arms with supporters **Rev:** Head with hat 1/4 right, dates at right **Edge:** Reeded

Date	Mintage	F	VF	XF	Unc	BU
2000 m	—	—	—	—	9.00	—

KM# 28 10 RUPEES

18.1000 g., Copper-Nickel, 34.5 mm. **Subject:** Declaration of Independence **Obv:** Head right **Rev:** Green sea turtle and value **Rev. Designer:** Suzanne Danielli

Date	Mintage	F	VF	XF	Unc	BU
1976	50,000	—	2.00	2.75	6.00	10.00

KM# 28a 10 RUPEES

28.2800 g., 0.9250 Silver .8411 oz. ASW, 34.5 mm. **Subject:** Declaration of Independence **Obv:** Head right **Rev:** Green sea turtle and value **Rev. Designer:** Suzanne Danielli

Date	Mintage	F	VF	XF	Unc	BU
1976 Proof	29,000	Value: 17.50				

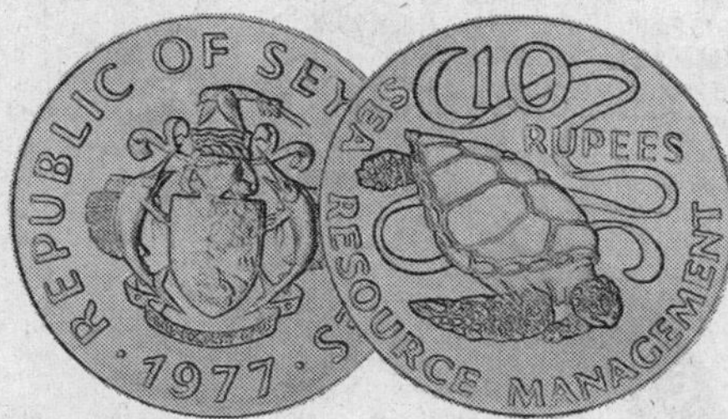

KM# 37 10 RUPEES

18.1000 g., Copper-Nickel, 34.5 mm. **Series:** F.A.O. **Obv:** Arms with supporters **Rev:** Green sea turtle and value **Rev. Designer:** Suzanne Danielli

Date	Mintage	F	VF	XF	Unc	BU
1977	—	—	2.00	3.00	6.00	10.00
1977 Proof	—	Value: 10.00				

KM# 64 10 RUPEES

10.0000 g., 0.9250 Silver .2974 oz. ASW **Series:** Endangered Wildlife **Obv:** Arms with supporters **Rev:** Magpie Robin **Note:** Similar to 25 Rupees, KM#65.

Date	Mintage	F	VF	XF	Unc	BU
1993 Proof	Est. 20,000	Value: 20.00				

KM# 87 10 RUPEES

10.0000 g., 0.5000 Silver .1607 oz. ASW **Subject:** 1996 Olympics **Obv:** Arms with supporters **Rev:** Cyclist

Date	Mintage	F	VF	XF	Unc	BU
1996	Est. 10,000	—	—	—	27.50	30.00

KM# 52 20 RUPEES

Copper-Nickel **Subject:** 5th Anniversary of Central Bank **Obv:** Arms with supporters **Rev:** Turtle at center of symbols of commerce

Date	Mintage	F	VF	XF	Unc	BU
1983	—	—	4.00	5.00	6.00	—

KM# 52a 20 RUPEES

19.4400 g., 0.9250 Silver .5781 oz. ASW **Subject:** 5th Anniversary of Central Bank **Obv:** Arms with supporters **Rev:** Turtle at center of symbols of commerce

Date	Mintage	F	VF	XF	Unc	BU
1983 Proof	5,000	Value: 50.00				

KM# 52b 20 RUPEES

33.9000 g., 0.9170 Gold .9994 oz. AGW **Subject:** 5th Anniversary of Central Bank **Obv:** Arms with supporters **Rev:** Turtle at center of symbols of commerce

Date	Mintage	F	VF	XF	Unc	BU
1983 Proof	50	Value: 1,000				

KM# 38 25 RUPEES

28.2800 g., 0.5000 Silver .4546 oz. ASW **Subject:** Queen's Silver Jubilee **Obv:** Head right **Rev:** Royal Orb at center of legends

Date	Mintage	F	VF	XF	Unc	BU
ND(1977)	17,000	—	—	—	9.00	11.50

KM# 38a 25 RUPEES

28.2800 g., 0.9250 Silver .8411 oz. ASW **Subject:** Queen's Silver Jubilee **Obv:** Head right **Rev:** Royal Orb at center of legends

Date	Mintage	F	VF	XF	Unc	BU
ND(1977) Proof	15,000	Value: 16.50				

KM# 53 25 RUPEES

Copper-Nickel **Series:** F.A.O. **Subject:** World Fisheries Conference **Obv:** Arms with supporters **Rev:** Fish trap **Rev. Designer:** Stuart Devlin

Date	Mintage	F	VF	XF	Unc	BU
1983	100,000	—	5.00	6.00	9.00	12.00

KM# 53a 25 RUPEES

28.2800 g., 0.9250 Silver .8411 oz. ASW **Series:** F.A.O. **Subject:** World Fisheries Conference **Obv:** Arms with supporters **Rev:** Fish trap **Rev. Designer:** Stuart Devlin

Date	Mintage	F	VF	XF	Unc	BU
1983 Proof	20,000	Value: 37.50				

KM# 53b 25 RUPEES

47.5400 g., 0.9170 Gold 1.4015 oz. AGW **Series:** F.A.O. **Subject:** World Fisheries Conference **Obv:** Arms with supporters **Rev:** Fish trap **Rev. Designer:** Stuart Devlin

Date	Mintage	F	VF	XF	Unc	BU
1983 Proof	100	Value: 1,100				

KM# 63 25 RUPEES

31.4700 g., 0.9250 Silver .9359 oz. ASW **Subject:** 40th Anniversary of Queen Elizabeth's Coronation **Obv:** Arms with supporters **Rev:** Royal carriage

Date	Mintage	F	VF	XF	Unc	BU
1993 Proof	Est. 10,000	Value: 45.00				

KM# 65 25 RUPEES

28.2800 g., 0.9250 Silver .8411 oz. ASW **Series:** Endangered Wildlife **Obv:** Arms with supporters **Rev:** Magpie Robin

Date	Mintage	F	VF	XF	Unc	BU
1993 Proof	Est. 20,000	Value: 30.00				

KM# 67 25 RUPEES

31.4600 g., 0.9250 Silver .9359 oz. ASW **Subject:** World Cup Soccer **Obv:** Arms with supporters **Rev:** Goalie at net

Date	Mintage	F	VF	XF	Unc	BU
1993 Proof	Est. 15,000	Value: 28.00				

KM# 68 25 RUPEES

31.4600 g., 0.9250 Silver .9359 oz. ASW **Obv:** Arms with supporters **Rev:** Space shuttle

Date	Mintage	F	VF	XF	Unc	BU
1993 Proof	Est. 10,000	Value: 25.00				

KM# 69 25 RUPEES

31.4600 g., 0.9250 Silver .9359 oz. ASW **Subject:** First French Landing **Obv:** Arms with supporters **Rev:** Figure with flag in boat, ships in background

Date	Mintage	F	VF	XF	Unc	BU
1993 Proof	Est. 10,000	Value: 22.50				

KM# 70 25 RUPEES

31.4600 g., 0.9250 Silver .9359 oz. ASW **Series:** 1992 Olympics **Obv:** Arms with supporters **Rev:** Balance beam gymnasts

Date	Mintage	F	VF	XF	Unc	BU
1993 Proof	Est. 40,000	Value: 15.00				

KM# 71 25 RUPEES

31.4600 g., 0.9250 Silver .9359 oz. ASW **Series:** Protect Our World **Obv:** Arms with supporters **Rev:** Fish and coral

Date	Mintage	F	VF	XF	Unc	BU
1993 Proof	Est. 10,000	Value: 35.00				

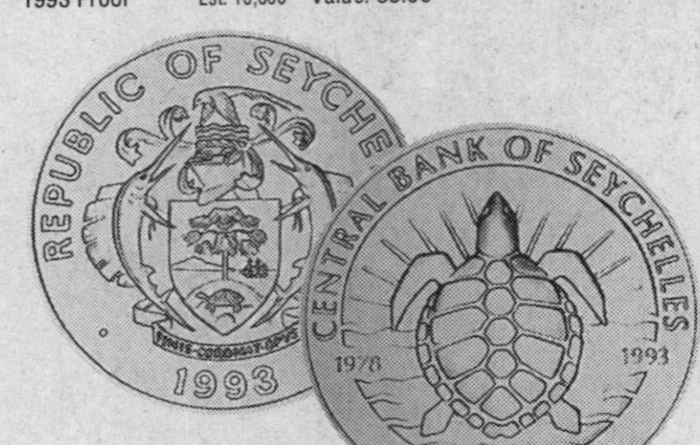

KM# 72 25 RUPEES

19.4400 g., 0.9250 Silver .5782 oz. ASW **Subject:** 15th Anniversary - Central Bank **Obv:** Arms with supporters **Rev:** Turtle flanked by dates

Date	Mintage	F	VF	XF	Unc	BU
1993 Proof	Est. 1,000	Value: 75.00				

KM# 74 25 RUPEES

19.4400 g., 0.9250 Silver .5782 oz. ASW **Series:** Endangered Wildlife **Obv:** Arms with supporters **Rev:** Butterfly and value

Date	Mintage	F	VF	XF	Unc	BU
1994PM Proof	20,000	Value: 35.00				

KM# 79 25 RUPEES

31.4700 g., 0.9250 Silver .9359 oz. ASW **Series:** Queen Elizabeth The Queen Mother **Subject:** Wedding of Lady Elizabeth Bowes-Lyon: The Duke of York, 1923 **Obv:** Arms with supporters **Rev:** Royal couple on steps

Date	Mintage	F	VF	XF	Unc	BU
1994 Proof	50,000	Value: 25.00				

KM# 78 25 RUPEES

28.2800 g., 0.9250 Silver .8411 oz. ASW **Series:** Endangered Wildlife **Obv:** Arms with supporters **Rev:** Kestrel

Date	Mintage	F	VF	XF	Unc	BU
1995 Proof	Est. 20,000	Value: 35.00				

KM# 80 25 RUPEES

28.2800 g., 0.9250 Silver .8411 oz. ASW **Series:** Olympics **Obv:** Arms with supporters **Rev:** Figures sailing

Date	Mintage	F	VF	XF	Unc	BU
1995 Proof	Est. 30,000	Value: 25.00				

KM# 81 25 RUPEES

28.2800 g., 0.9250 Silver .8411 oz. ASW **Subject:** Vasco da Gama **Obv:** Arms with supporters **Rev:** Horizontal line divides ship and palms from standing ship captain **Edge:** Reeding over lettering **Edge Lettering:** EXPLORERS OF THE WORLD

Date	Mintage	F	VF	XF	Unc	BU
1995 Proof	Est. 10,000	Value: 37.50				

KM# 108 25 RUPEES

28.2800 g., 0.9250 Silver .8411 oz. ASW **Series:** 50th Anniversary U.N. **Obv:** Arms with supporters **Rev:** Flying bird above UN logo and numeral 50

Date	Mintage	F	VF	XF	Unc	BU
1995 Proof	—	Value: 35.00				

KM# 97 25 RUPEES

31.4700 g., 0.9250 Silver .9359 oz. ASW **Series:** 1996 Olympic Games **Obv:** Arms with supporters **Rev:** Cyclist

Date	Mintage	F	VF	XF	Unc	BU
1995 Proof	—	Value: 25.00				

KM# 124 25 RUPEES

28.2800 g., 0.9250 Silver 0.841 oz. ASW, 39 mm. **Obv:** National arms **Rev:** Victoria Cross above advancing infantry **Edge:** Reeded

Date	Mintage	F	VF	XF	Unc	BU
1996 Proof	—	Value: 25.00				

KM# 88 25 RUPEES

31.4700 g., 0.9250 Silver .9359 oz. ASW **Subject:** Foundation of the Commonwealth **Obv:** Arms with supporters **Rev:** Crown and assorted flags

Date	Mintage	F	VF	XF	Unc	BU
1996	40,000	—	—	—	30.00	32.50

KM# 83 25 RUPEES

28.2800 g., 0.9250 Silver .8411 oz. ASW **Series:** Endangered Wildlife **Obv:** Arms with supporters **Rev:** Flycatcher bird feeding babies

Date	Mintage	F	VF	XF	Unc	BU
1996 Proof	Est. 20,000	Value: 45.00				

KM# 92 25 RUPEES

1.2400 g., 0.9990 Gold .0398 oz. AGW **Subject:** Diana - The People's Princess **Obv:** Arms with supporters **Rev:** Head 1/4 right **Note:** Similar to KM#91.

Date	Mintage	F	VF	XF	Unc	BU
1997 Proof	Est. 10,000	Value: 50.00				

KM# 117 25 RUPEES
19.4400 g., 0.9250 Silver 0.5781 oz. ASW, 36 mm. **Subject:** UNICEF **Obv:** Arms with supporters **Rev:** Boy fishing **Edge:** Reeded

Date	Mintage	F	VF	XF	Unc	BU
1997 Proof	25,000	Value: 25.00				

KM# 91 25 RUPEES
28.2800 g., 0.9250 Silver .8410 oz. ASW **Subject:** Diana - The People's Princess **Obv:** Arms with supporters **Rev:** Head 1/4 right

Date	Mintage	F	VF	XF	Unc	BU
1997 Proof	Est. 10,000	Value: 40.00				

KM# 95 25 RUPEES
28.2800 g., 0.9250 Silver .8410 oz. ASW **Subject:** Diana - The People's Princess **Obv:** Arms with supporters **Rev:** Diana holding baby Prince William

Date	Mintage	F	VF	XF	Unc	BU
1997 Proof	Est. 10,000	Value: 30.00				

KM# 96 25 RUPEES
1.2400 g., 0.9990 Gold .0398 oz. AGW **Subject:** Diana - The People's Princess **Obv:** Arms with supporters **Rev:** Diana holding baby Prince William

Date	Mintage	F	VF	XF	Unc	BU
1997 Proof	Est. 10,000	Value: 55.00				

KM# 99 25 RUPEES
28.2800 g., 0.9250 Silver .8410 oz. ASW **Subject:** Diana - The People's Princess **Obv:** Arms with supporters **Rev:** Bust left holding young cancer patient

Date	Mintage	F	VF	XF	Unc	BU
1997 Proof	Est. 10,000	Value: 40.00				

KM# 100 25 RUPEES
1.2400 g., 0.9990 Gold .0398 oz. AGW **Subject:** Diana - The People's Princess **Obv:** Arms with supporters **Rev:** Diana holding young cancer patient

Date	Mintage	F	VF	XF	Unc	BU
1997 Proof	Est. 10,000	Value: 55.00				

KM# 103 25 RUPEES
28.2800 g., 0.9250 Silver .8410 oz. ASW **Subject:** Diana - The People's Princess **Obv:** Arms with supporters **Rev:** Diana in summer clothes

Date	Mintage	F	VF	XF	Unc	BU
1998 Proof	Est. 10,000	Value: 42.50				

KM# 104 25 RUPEES
1.2441 g., 0.9999 Gold .0400 oz. AGW **Subject:** Diana - The People's Princess **Obv:** Arms with supporters **Rev:** Diana in summer clothes

Date	Mintage	F	VF	XF	Unc	BU
1998 Proof	Est. 10,000	Value: 60.00				

KM# 110 25 RUPEES
28.2800 g., 0.9250 Silver .8410 oz. ASW **Subject:** Marriage of Prince Edward and Miss Sophie Rhys-Jones **Obv:** Arms with supporters **Rev:** Tied vertical monograms flanked by doves

Date	Mintage	F	VF	XF	Unc	BU
1999 Proof	Est. 10,000	Value: 40.00				

KM# 113 25 RUPEES
1.2441 g., 0.9999 Gold .0400 oz. AGW **Subject:** Millennium **Obv:** Arms with supporters **Rev:** Latent image of 1999-2000 dates

Date	Mintage	F	VF	XF	Unc	BU
2000 Proof	Est. 10,000	Value: 50.00				

KM# 115 25 RUPEES
1.2441 g., 0.9999 Gold .0400 oz. AGW **Subject:** 100th Birthday - British Queen Mother **Obv:** Arms with supporters **Rev:** Head with hat 1/4 right **Edge:** Reeded

Date	Mintage	F	VF	XF	Unc	BU
2000 Proof	Est. 10,000	Value: 50.00				

KM# 39 50 RUPEES
28.2800 g., 0.9250 Silver .8411 oz. ASW **Subject:** Conservation **Obv:** Arms with supporters **Rev:** Squirrel fish, coral and value

Date	Mintage	F	VF	XF	Unc	BU
1978	4,453	—	—	—	20.00	22.50
1978 Proof	4,281	Value: 27.50				

KM# 42 50 RUPEES
19.4400 g., 0.9250 Silver .5781 oz. ASW **Series:** UNICEF and International Year of the Child **Obv:** Arms with supporters **Rev:** Figures below palm tree flanked by UNICEF logos

Date	Mintage	F	VF	XF	Unc	BU
1980 Proof	10,000	Value: 17.50				

KM# 54 50 RUPEES
19.4400 g., 0.9250 Silver .5781 oz. ASW **Series:** Decade for Women **Obv:** Arms with supporters **Rev:** Map flanked by figures above value **Rev. Designer:** Michael Rizzello

Date	Mintage	F	VF	XF	Unc	BU
1985 Proof	500	Value: 28.00				

KM# 75 50 RUPEES
1.2440 g., 0.9999 Gold .0497 oz. AGW **Series:** Endangered Wildlife **Obv:** Arms with supporters **Rev:** Milkweed Butterfly **Note:** Similar to 25 Rupees, KM#74.

Date	Mintage	F	VF	XF	Unc	BU
1994 PM Prooflike	—	—	—	—	—	45.00

KM# 107 50 RUPEES
3.1100 g., 0.5833 Gold .0583 oz. AGW **Series:** Olympics Games 2000 **Obv:** Arms with supporters **Rev:** Two divers

Date	Mintage	F	VF	XF	Unc	BU
1997 Proof	5,000	Value: 65.00				

KM# 40 100 RUPEES
31.6500 g., 0.9250 Silver .9413 oz. ASW **Subject:** Conservation **Obv:** Arms with supporters **Rev:** White-tailed Tropic bird

Date	Mintage	F	VF	XF	Unc	BU
1978	4,453	—	—	—	22.50	25.00
1978 Proof	4,075	Value: 32.50				

KM# 45 100 RUPEES
31.6500 g., 0.9250 Silver .9413 oz. ASW **Series:** World Food Day **Obv:** Arms with supporters **Rev:** Value and coconuts below seated figure flanked by palm trees

Date	Mintage	F	VF	XF	Unc	BU
1981	6,000	—	—	—	25.00	27.50
1981 Proof	5,000	Value: 37.50				

KM# 45a 100 RUPEES
35.0000 g., 0.5000 Silver .5627 oz. ASW **Subject:** World Food Day **Obv:** Arms with supporters **Rev:** Value and coconuts below seated figure flanked by palm trees

Date	Mintage	F	VF	XF	Unc	BU
1981 Proof	10,000	Value: 25.00				

KM# 55 100 RUPEES

19.4400 g., 0.9250 Silver .5781 oz. ASW **Subject:** 10th Anniversary of Independence **Obv:** Arms with supporters **Rev:** Design above shark tail design dividing dates

Date	Mintage	F	VF	XF	Unc	BU
ND(1986) Proof	1,000	Value: 45.00				

KM# 57 100 RUPEES

19.4400 g., 0.9250 Silver .5781 oz. ASW **Subject:** 10th Anniversary of Liberation **Obv:** Arms with supporters **Rev:** Standing figure divides dates

Date	Mintage	F	VF	XF	Unc	BU
ND(1987) PM Proof	1,000	Value: 40.00				

KM# 59 100 RUPEES

19.4000 g., 0.9170 Silver .5720 oz. ASW **Subject:** 10th Anniversary of Central Bank **Obv:** Arms with supporters **Rev:** Sea Turtle, dates below

Date	Mintage	F	VF	XF	Unc	BU
ND(1988) PM Proof	—	Value: 90.00				

KM# 60 100 RUPEES

1.7000 g., 0.9170 Gold .0501 oz. AGW **Subject:** 10th Anniversary of Central Bank **Obv:** Arms with supporters **Rev:** Sea turtle

Date	Mintage	F	VF	XF	Unc	BU
ND(1988) PM Proof	—	Value: 100				

KM# 76 100 RUPEES

3.1103 g., 0.9999 Gold .1000 oz. AGW **Series:** Endangered Wildlife **Obv:** Arms with supporters **Rev:** Milkweed Butterfly

Date	Mintage	F	VF	XF	Unc	BU
1994 PM Prooflike	—	—	—	—	—	100

KM# 82 100 RUPEES

7.7760 g., 0.5830 Gold .1458 oz. AGW **Series:** Olympics **Obv:** Arms with supporters **Rev:** Sailboats

Date	Mintage	F	VF	XF	Unc	BU
1995 Proof	Est. 3,000	Value: 125				

KM# 86 100 RUPEES

7.7760 g., 0.5830 Gold .1458 oz. AGW **Subject:** British Queen Mother **Obv:** Arms with supporters **Rev:** Wedding portrait

Date	Mintage	F	VF	XF	Unc	BU
1995	Est. 5,000	—	—	—	135	150

KM# 93 100 RUPEES

7.7760 g., 0.5830 Gold .1458 oz. AGW **Subject:** Diana - The People's Princess **Obv:** Arms with supporters **Rev:** Bust facing

Date	Mintage	F	VF	XF	Unc	BU
1997 Proof	Est. 7,500	Value: 120				

KM# A97 100 RUPEES

7.7760 g., 0.5830 Gold .1458 oz. AGW **Subject:** Diana - The People's Princess **Obv:** Arms with supporters **Rev:** Diana holding newborn Prince William

Date	Mintage	F	VF	XF	Unc	BU
1997	7,500	Value: 120				

KM# 101 100 RUPEES

7.7760 g., 0.5830 Gold .1458 oz. AGW **Subject:** Diana - The People's Princess **Obv:** Arms with supporters **Rev:** Diana holding young cancer patient

Date	Mintage	F	VF	XF	Unc	BU
1997 Proof	Est. 7,500	Value: 115				

KM# 105 100 RUPEES

7.7760 g., 0.5830 Gold .1458 oz. AGW **Subject:** Diana - The People's Princess **Obv:** Arms with supporters **Rev:** Diana in summer clothes

Date	Mintage	F	VF	XF	Unc	BU
1998 Proof	Est. 7,500	Value: 115				

KM# 111 100 RUPEES

6.2200 g., 0.9999 Gold .2000 oz. AGW **Subject:** Marriage of Prince Edward **Obv:** Arms with supporters **Rev:** Tied monograms and birds

Date	Mintage	F	VF	XF	Unc	BU
1999 Proof	Est. 2,000	Value: 185				

KM# 116 100 RUPEES

6.2200 g., 0.9999 Gold .2000 oz. AGW, 22 mm. **Subject:** 100th Birthday Queen Mother **Obv:** Arms with supporters **Rev:** Queen Mother's portrait **Edge:** Reeded

Date	Mintage	F	VF	XF	Unc	BU
2000 Proof	2,000	Value: 175				

KM# 66 250 RUPEES

6.2200 g., 0.9990 Gold .2000 oz. AGW **Series:** Endangered Wildlife **Obv:** Arms with supporters **Rev:** Magpie Robin

Date	Mintage	F	VF	XF	Unc	BU
1993 Proof	—	Value: 165				

KM# 77 250 RUPEES

6.2200 g., 0.9990 Gold .2000 oz. AGW **Series:** Endangered Wildlife **Obv:** Arms with supporters **Rev:** Milkweed Butterfly

Date	Mintage	F	VF	XF	Unc	BU
1993 Proof	—	Value: 200				
1994 PM Prooflike	—	—	—	—	150	—
1996PM Proof	5,000	Value: 185				

KM# 84 250 RUPEES

6.2200 g., 0.9990 Gold .2000 oz. AGW **Series:** Endangered Wildlife **Obv:** Arms with supporters **Rev:** Paradise Flycatcher Bird

Date	Mintage	F	VF	XF	Unc	BU
1996 Proof	Est. 5,000	Value: 185				

KM# 98 250 RUPEES

6.2200 g., 0.9990 Gold .2000 oz. AGW **Subject:** Diana - The People's Princess **Obv:** Arms with supporters **Rev:** Diana holding newborn Prince William

Date	Mintage	F	VF	XF	Unc	BU
1997 Proof	Est. 5,000	Value: 185				

KM# 102 250 RUPEES

6.2200 g., 0.9990 Gold .2000 oz. AGW **Subject:** Diana - The People's Princess **Obv:** Arms with supporters **Rev:** Diana holding young cancer patient

Date	Mintage	F	VF	XF	Unc	BU
1997 Proof	Est. 5,000	Value: 185				

KM# 94 250 RUPEES

6.2200 g., 0.9990 Gold .2000 oz. AGW **Subject:** Diana - The People's Princess **Obv:** Arms with supporters **Rev:** Bust facing **Note:** Similar to 25 Rupees, KM#91.

Date	Mintage	F	VF	XF	Unc	BU
1997 Proof	Est. 5,000	Value: 185				

KM# 106 250 RUPEES

6.2200 g., 0.9990 Gold .2000 oz. AGW **Subject:** Diana - The People's Princess **Obv:** Arms with supporters **Rev:** Diana in summer dress

Date	Mintage	F	VF	XF	Unc	BU
1998 Proof	Est. 5,000	Value: 185				

KM# 62 500 RUPEES

7.1300 g., 0.9000 Gold .2036 oz. AGW **Series:** Decade for Women **Obv:** Arms with supporters **Rev:** Value below standing figures

Date	Mintage	F	VF	XF	Unc	BU
1985 Proof	500	Value: 175				

KM# 29 1000 RUPEES

15.9800 g., 0.9170 Gold .4707 oz. AGW **Subject:** Declaration of Independence **Obv:** President Mancham **Rev:** Tortoise, date, value

Date	Mintage	F	VF	XF	Unc	BU
1976	5,000	—	—	—	335	—
1976 Proof	1,000	Value: 375				

KM# 56 1000 RUPEES

15.9800 g., 0.9170 Gold .4707 oz. AGW **Subject:** 10th Anniversary of Independence **Obv:** Arms with supporters **Rev:** Design above shark tail design dividing dates

Date	Mintage	F	VF	XF	Unc	BU
ND(1986) Proof	100	Value: 415				

KM# 58 1000 RUPEES

15.9800 g., 0.9170 Gold .4707 oz. AGW **Subject:** 10th Anniversary of Liberation **Obv:** Arms with supporters **Rev:** Standing figure divides dates

Date	Mintage	F	VF	XF	Unc	BU
ND(1987) PM Proof	100	Value: 400				

KM# 61 1000 RUPEES

15.9400 g., 0.9170 Gold .4698 oz. AGW **Subject:** 100th Anniversary of Central Bank **Obv:** Arms with supporters **Rev:** Sea turtle

Date	Mintage	F	VF	XF	Unc	BU
ND(1988) PM Proof	Est. 5,000	Value: 345				

KM# 73 1000 RUPEES

15.9800 g., 0.9170 Gold .4710 oz. AGW **Subject:** Central Banking

Date	Mintage	F	VF	XF	Unc	BU
1993 Proof	Est. 200	Value: 375				

KM# 41 1500 RUPEES

33.4370 g., 0.9000 Gold .9676 oz. AGW **Subject:** Conservation **Obv:** Arms with supporters **Rev:** Flycatcher birds

Date	Mintage	F	VF	XF	Unc	BU
1978	683	—	—	—	675	—
1978 Proof	201	Value: 975				

PATTERNS

Including off metal strikes

KM#	Date	Mintage	Identification	Mkt Val
Pn1	1974	—	10 Rupees. Brass. KM#20.	—
Pn2	1974	—	10 Rupees. Bronze. KM#20.	—
Pn3	1974	—	10 Rupees. Copper-Nickel. KM#20.	—
Pn4	1974	—	10 Rupees. Silver. KM#20.	—
Pn5	1976	—	10 Cents. Silver. KM#23, thick planchet.	250
Pn6	1976	—	1000 Rupees. Bronze. KM#29.	—

PIEFORTS

KM#	Date	Mintage	Identification	Mkt Val
P1	1980	78	50 Rupees. Silver. KM#42.	90.00
P2	1983	500	50 Rupees.	65.00
P3	1984	500	50 Rupees. 0.9250 Silver.	65.00
P4	1984	100	50 Rupees. 0.9000 Gold.	1,500

MINT SETS

KM#	Date	Mintage	Identification	Issue Price	Mkt Val
MS1	1972 (7)	—	KM#10-13, 17-19	—	8.50
MS2	1974 (5)	—	KM#10-13, 20	—	8.50
MS3	1976 (8)	—	KM#21-28	—	16.00
MS4	1977 (8)	—	KM#30-37	—	11.50
MS5	1982 (6)	—	KM#46.1-51.1	—	5.00
MS6	1992 (6)	—	KM#46.2, 47.2, 48.2, 49.2, 50.2, 51.2	12.00	12.00
MS7	Mixed dates (6)	—	KM#46.2 (1990), 47.2-51.2 (1997)	—	8.50

PROOF SETS

KM#	Date	Mintage	Identification	Issue Price	Mkt Val
PS1	1939 (4)	—	KM#1-4	—	1,000
PS2	1969 (7)	5,000	KM#10-16	8.40	20.00
PS3	1974 (2)	5,000	KM#19-a, 20a	37.00	32.50
PS4	1976 (9)	1,000	KM#21-26 , 27a, 28a, 29	375	375
PS5	1976 (8)	7,500	KM#21-26, 27a, 28a	42.50	42.50
PS6	1982 (6)	5,000	KM#46.1-51.1	29.95	20.00
PS7	1992 (6)	—	KM#46.2-51.2	—	20.00

SHARJAH

Sharjah is the only one of the emirates that shares boundaries with all of the others plus Oman. It has an area of 1,000 sq. mi. (2,600 sq. km.) and a population of 40,000. Sharjah was an important pirate base in the 18th and early 19th centuries. Most of the treaties and diplomatic relations were with Great Britain.

TITLES

Ash-Sharqa(t)

RULERS

Saqr Bin Khalid al-Qasimi, 1883-1914
Khalid Bin Ahmad al-Qasimi, 1914-1924
Sultan Bin Saqr al-Qasimi, 1924-1951
Saqr Bin Sultan al-Qasimi, 1951-1965
Khalid Bin Muhammad al-Qasimi, 1965-1972
Sultan Bin Muhammad al-Qasimi,1972-

EMIRATE

NON-CIRCULATING LEGAL TENDER COINAGE

KM# 2 RIYAL
3.0000 g., 1.0000 Silver .0965 oz. ASW **Ruler:** Khalid bin Muhammad al-Qasimi **Subject:** Mona Lisa **Obv:** National arms **Rev:** Bust facing

Date	Mintage	F	VF	XF	Unc	BU
AH1389-1970 Proof	3,850	Value: 17.50				

KM# 3 2 RIYALS
6.0000 g., 1.0000 Silver .1929 oz. ASW **Ruler:** Khalid bin Muhammad al-Qasimi **Subject:** Mexico World Soccer Cup **Obv:** National arms **Rev:** World soccer cup within globe design

Date	Mintage	F	VF	XF	Unc	BU
AH1389-1970 Proof	4,500	Value: 27.50				

KM# 4 5 RIYALS
15.0000 g., 1.0000 Silver .4823 oz. ASW **Ruler:** Khalid bin Muhammad al-Qasimi **Subject:** Napoleon **Obv:** National arms **Rev:** Uniformed bust facing 1/4 left divides logo and dates

Date	Mintage	F	VF	XF	Unc	BU
AH1389-1970 Proof	2,500	Value: 37.50				

KM# 5 10 RIYALS
30.0000 g., 1.0000 Silver .9646 oz. ASW **Ruler:** Khalid bin Muhammad al-Qasimi **Subject:** Bolivar **Obv:** National arms **Rev:** Head right

Date	Mintage	F	VF	XF	Unc	BU
AH1389-1970 Proof	3,200	Value: 65.00				

KM# 7 25 RIYALS
5.1800 g., 0.9000 Gold .1499 oz. AGW **Ruler:** Khalid bin Muhammad al-Qasimi **Subject:** Mona Lisa **Obv:** National arms **Rev:** Bust facing

Date	Mintage	F	VF	XF	Unc	BU
AH1389-1970 Proof	6,775	Value: 165				

KM# 8 50 RIYALS
10.3600 g., 0.9000 Gold .2998 oz. AGW **Ruler:** Khalid bin Muhammad al-Qasimi **Subject:** Mexico World Soccer Cup **Obv:** National arms **Rev:** World soccer cup within globe design

Date	Mintage	F	VF	XF	Unc	BU
AH1389-1970 Proof	1,815	Value: 275				

KM# 9 100 RIYALS
20.7300 g., 0.9000 Gold .5999 oz. AGW **Ruler:** Khalid bin Muhammad al-Qasimi **Subject:** Bicentennial - Napoleon **Obv:** National arms **Rev:** Uniformed bust facing 1/4 left divides logo and dated

Date	Mintage	F	VF	XF	Unc	BU
AH1389-1970 Proof	—	Value: 465				

KM# 10 100 RIYALS
20.7300 g., 0.9000 Gold .5999 oz. AGW **Ruler:** Khalid bin Muhammad al-Qasimi **Subject:** Bolivar **Obv:** National arms **Rev:** Head right

Date	Mintage	F	VF	XF	Unc	BU
AH1389-1970 Proof	—	Value: 450				

KM# 11 200 RIYALS
41.4600 g., 0.9000 Gold 1.1998 oz. AGW **Ruler:** Khalid bin Muhammad al-Qasimi **Subject:** Khalid III **Obv:** National arms **Rev:** Head facing

Date	Mintage	F	VF	XF	Unc	BU
AH1389-1970 Proof	435	Value: 900				

PROOF SETS

KM#	Date	Mintage	Identification	Issue Price	Mkt Val
PS1	1970 (9)	—	KM#2-5, 7-11	—	2,125
PS2	1970 (5)	—	KM#7-11	—	2,000
PS3	1970 (4)	2,500	KM#2-5	25.30	140

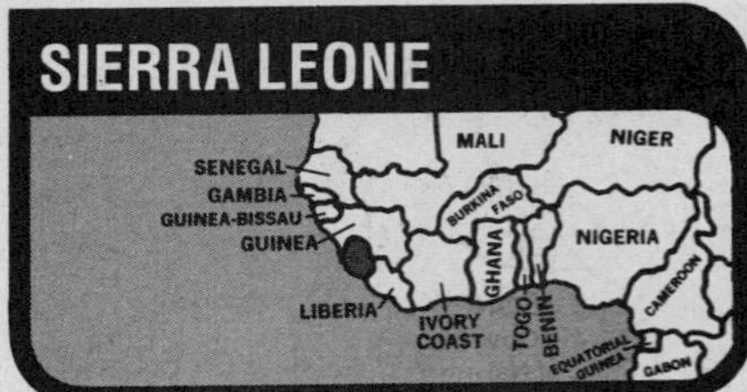

The Republic of Sierra Leone is located in western Africa between Guinea and Liberia, has an area of 27,699 sq. mi. (71,740 sq. km.) and a population of *4.1 million. Capital: Freetown. The economy is predominantly agricultural but mining contributes significantly to export revenues. Diamonds, iron ore, palm kernels, cocoa, and coffee are exported.

The coast of Sierra Leone was first visited by Portuguese and British slavers in the 15th and 16th centuries. The first settlement, at Freetown, 1787, was established as a refuge for freed slaves within the British Empire, runaway slaves from the United States and Negroes discharged from the British armed forces. The first settlers were virtually wiped out by tribal attacks and disease. The colony was re-established under the auspices of the Sierra Leone Company and transferred to the British Crown in 1807. The interior region was secured and established as a protectorate in 1896. Sierra Leone became independent on April 27, 1961, and adopted a republican constitution ten years later. It is a member of the Commonwealth of Nations. The president is Chief of State and Head of Government.

For similar coinage refer to British West Africa.

RULERS

British, until 1961

MONETARY SYSTEM

Until 1906

100 Cents = 1 Dollar

Commencing 1961

Sterling

100 Cents = 1 Leone = 1 Dollar

NOTE: Sierra Leone's official currency is the Leone.

REPUBLIC

STANDARD COINAGE

KM# 16 1/2 CENT

2.8500 g., Bronze, 20.2 mm. **Obv:** Value divides fish **Rev:** Head of right Sir Milton Margai **Edge:** Plain

Date	Mintage	F	VF	XF	Unc	BU
1964	600,000	—	—	0.15	0.25	0.75
1964 Proof	10,000	Value: 1.00				

KM# 16a 1/2 CENT

2.8300 g., 0.9250 Silver .0841 oz. ASW, 20.2 mm. **Obv:** Value divides fish **Rev:** Head of right Sir Milton Margai

Date	Mintage	F	VF	XF	Unc	BU
1964 Proof	22	Value: 650				

KM# 31 1/2 CENT

2.8500 g., Bronze, 20.2 mm. **Obv:** Value above arms **Rev:** Head of Dr. Siaka Stevens right

Date	Mintage	F	VF	XF	Unc	BU
1980	—	—	0.15	0.30	1.00	—
1980 Proof	10,000	Value: 1.50				

KM# 17 CENT

5.7000 g., Bronze, 25.45 mm. **Obv:** Value within palm sprigs **Rev:** Head of Sir Milton Margai right **Edge:** Plain

Date	Mintage	F	VF	XF	Unc	BU
1964	35,000,000	—	—	0.15	0.25	—
1964 Proof	10,000	Value: 1.25				

KM# 17a CENT

5.6700 g., 0.9250 Silver .1686 oz. ASW, 25.45 mm. **Obv:** Value within palm sprigs **Rev:** Head of Sir Milton Margai right

Date	Mintage	F	VF	XF	Unc	BU
1964 Proof	22	Value: 650				

KM# 32 CENT

5.7000 g., Bronze, 25.45 mm. **Obv:** Value above arms **Rev:** Head of Sir Milton Margai right

Date	Mintage	F	VF	XF	Unc	BU
1980	—	—	0.15	0.30	1.00	—
1980 Proof	10,000	Value: 1.50				

KM# 18 5 CENTS

2.5000 g., Copper-Nickel, 17.8 mm. **Obv:** Tree divides date within circle **Rev:** Head of right Sir Milton Margai

Date	Mintage	F	VF	XF	Unc	BU
1964	900,000	—	0.15	0.25	0.50	—
1964 Proof	10,000	Value: 1.50				

KM# 18a 5 CENTS

2.4900 g., 0.9250 Silver .0740 oz. ASW, 17.8 mm. **Obv:** Tree divides date within circle **Rev:** Head of right Sir Milton Margai

Date	Mintage	F	VF	XF	Unc	BU
1964 Proof	22	Value: 650				

KM# 33 5 CENTS

2.5000 g., Copper-Nickel, 17.8 mm. **Obv:** Value above arms **Rev:** Head of Dr. Siaka Stevens right

Date	Mintage	F	VF	XF	Unc	BU
1980	—	—	0.15	0.30	0.75	—
1980 Proof	10,000	Value: 2.50				
1984	—	—	0.15	0.30	0.75	—

KM# 19 10 CENTS

4.9000 g., Copper-Nickel, 22.9 mm. **Obv:** Value within cocoa bean wreath **Rev:** Head of right Sir Milton Margai

Date	Mintage	F	VF	XF	Unc	BU
1964	24,000,000	—	0.25	0.40	0.65	—
1964 Proof	10,000	Value: 1.25				

KM# 19a 10 CENTS

4.9200 g., 0.9250 Silver .1463 oz. ASW, 22.9 mm. **Obv:** Value within cocoa bean wreath **Rev:** Head of right Sir Milton Margai

Date	Mintage	F	VF	XF	Unc	BU
1964 Proof	22	Value: 650				

KM# 34 10 CENTS

4.9000 g., Copper-Nickel, 22.9 mm. **Obv:** Value above arms **Rev:** Head of Dr. Siaka Stevens right

Date	Mintage	F	VF	XF	Unc	BU
1978	200,000	—	0.25	0.50	1.00	—
1980	—	—	0.20	0.40	0.75	—
1980 Proof	10,000	Value: 5.00				
1984	—	—	0.20	0.40	0.75	—

KM# 20 20 CENTS

8.2500 g., Copper-Nickel, 26.95 mm. **Obv:** Lion walking left **Rev:** Head of Sir Milton Margai right **Edge:** Reeded

Date	Mintage	F	VF	XF	Unc	BU
1964	11,000,000	—	0.35	0.60	1.25	—
1964 Proof	10,000	Value: 2.00				

KM# 20a 20 CENTS

8.2200 g., 0.9250 Silver .2444 oz. ASW, 26.95 mm. **Obv:** Lion walking right **Rev:** Head of right Sir Milton Margai

Date	Mintage	F	VF	XF	Unc	BU
1964 Proof	22	Value: 650				

KM# 30 20 CENTS

8.2500 g., Copper-Nickel, 26.95 mm. **Obv:** Value above arms **Rev:** Head of Dr. Siaka Stevens right

Date	Mintage	F	VF	XF	Unc	BU
1978	2,375,000	—	0.35	0.65	1.50	—
1980	—	—	0.35	0.60	1.25	—
1980 Proof	10,000	Value: 7.00				
1984	—	—	0.35	0.60	1.25	—

KM# 25 50 CENTS

11.6000 g., Copper-Nickel, 30 mm. **Obv:** Value above arms **Rev:** Head of Dr. Siaka Stevens right

Date	Mintage	F	VF	XF	Unc	BU
1972	1,000,000	—	1.00	1.75	3.00	—
1972 Proof	2,000	Value: 5.00				
1980	—	—	1.00	1.50	2.75	—
1980 Proof	10,000	Value: 10.00				
1984	—	—	1.00	1.50	2.75	—

KM# 21 LEONE

Copper-Nickel **Obv:** Value above arms **Rev:** Head of right Sir Milton Margai

Date	Mintage	F	VF	XF	Unc	BU
1964 Proof	10,000	Value: 10.00				

KM# 21a LEONE

22.6220 g., 0.9250 Silver .6738 oz. ASW **Obv:** Value above arms **Rev:** Head of right Sir Milton Margai

Date	Mintage	F	VF	XF	Unc	BU
1964 Proof	12	Value: 1,000				

KM# 21b LEONE

0.9170 Gold **Obv:** Value above arms **Rev:** Head of right Sir Milton Margai

Date	Mintage	F	VF	XF	Unc	BU
1964 Proof	10	Value: 2,500				

KM# 26 LEONE

Copper-Nickel **Subject:** 10 Anniversary of Bank **Obv:** Lion right within circle **Rev:** Head of Dr. Siaka Stevens right

Date	Mintage	F	VF	XF	Unc	BU
ND(1974)	103,000	—	1.50	2.50	6.00	7.50

KM# 26a LEONE
28.2800 g., 0.9250 Silver .8411 oz. ASW **Obv:** Head of Dr. Siaka Stevens right **Rev:** Lion right within circle

Date	Mintage	F	VF	XF	Unc	BU
1974 Proof	22,000	Value: 17.50				

KM# 26b LEONE
Gold **Subject:** 10 Anniversary of Bank **Obv:** Head of Dr. Siaka Stevens right **Rev:** Lion right within circle

Date	Mintage	F	VF	XF	Unc	BU
1974	100	—	—	—	1,250	—

KM# 36 LEONE
Copper-Nickel **Subject:** O.A.U. Summit Conference **Obv:** Map within circle **Rev:** Head of Dr. Siaka Stevens right

Date	Mintage	F	VF	XF	Unc	BU
1980	75,000	—	1.75	2.75	6.00	—

KM# 36a LEONE
28.2800 g., 0.9250 Silver .8411 oz. ASW **Obv:** Map within circle **Rev:** Head of Dr. Siaka Stevens right

Date	Mintage	F	VF	XF	Unc	BU
1980 Proof	15,000	Value: 20.00				

KM# 40 LEONE
9.5000 g., 0.9250 Silver .2825 oz. ASW **Subject:** Freetown Bicentennial **Obv:** Numeral 200 within design **Rev:** Bust of Dr. Joseph Saidu Momoh left **Shape:** Octagon

Date	Mintage	F	VF	XF	Unc	BU
1987 Proof	3,000	Value: 25.00				

KM# 40a LEONE
16.0000 g., 0.9170 Gold .4716 oz. AGW **Subject:** Freetown Bicentennial **Obv:** Numeral 200 within design **Rev:** Bust of Dr. Joseph Saidu Momoh left **Shape:** Octagon

Date	Mintage	F	VF	XF	Unc	BU
1987 Proof	1,250	Value: 375				

KM# 43 LEONE
Nickel-Bronze **Obv:** Value above arms **Rev:** Bust of Dr. Joseph Saidu Momoh left **Shape:** Octagon

Date	Mintage	F	VF	XF	Unc	BU
1987	—	—	0.50	0.75	1.50	2.50
1988	—	—	0.50	0.75	1.50	2.50

KM# 29 2 LEONES
Copper-Nickel, 30 mm. **Series:** F.A.O. **Subject:** Regional Conference for Africa **Obv:** Farmer tilling field **Rev:** Head of Dr. Siaka Stevens right **Edge:** Plain **Shape:** 7-sided

Date	Mintage	F	VF	XF	Unc	BU
1976	20,000	—	1.00	2.50	5.50	6.50

KM# 38 10 LEONES
28.2800 g., 0.9250 Silver .8411 oz. ASW **Series:** Year of the Scout **Obv:** Seated figure with hat within plants **Rev:** Head of Dr. Siaka Stevens right

Date	Mintage	F	VF	XF	Unc	BU
ND(1983)	10,000	—	—	—	35.00	—
ND(1983) Proof	10,000	Value: 47.50				

KM# 41 10 LEONES
28.2800 g., 0.9250 Silver .8411 oz. ASW **Series:** World Wildlife Fund **Obv:** Pygmy Hippopotamus **Rev:** Bust of Dr. Joseph Saidu Momoh left

Date	Mintage	F	VF	XF	Unc	BU
1987 Proof	25,000	Value: 27.50				

KM# 44 10 LEONES
Nickel Clad Steel **Obv:** Value divides fish **Rev:** Bust of Mammy Yoko facing within circle **Designer:** Avril Vaughan

Date	Mintage	F	VF	XF	Unc	BU
1996	—	—	—	—	0.75	1.00

KM# 45 50 LEONES
Nickel Clad Steel **Obv:** Building above value **Rev:** Bust of Sir Henry Lightfoot facing **Shape:** Octagon **Designer:** Avril Vaughan

Date	Mintage	F	VF	XF	Unc	BU
1996	—	—	—	—	1.25	1.50

KM# 39 100 LEONES
15.9800 g., 0.9170 Gold .4711 oz. AGW **Series:** Year of the Scout **Obv:** Lion within shield **Rev:** Head of Dr. Siaka Stevens right

Date	Mintage	F	VF	XF	Unc	BU
ND(1983)	2,000	—	—	—	345	—
ND(1983) Proof	2,000	Value: 400				

KM# 46 100 LEONES
Nickel Clad Steel **Obv:** Cocoa pods and value within beaded circle **Rev:** Head of Naimbana facing within beaded circle **Designer:** Avril Vaughan

Date	Mintage	F	VF	XF	Unc	BU
1996	—	—	—	—	1.75	2.00

KM# 22 1/4 GOLDE
13.6360 g., 0.9000 Gold .3946 oz. AGW, 24 mm. **Subject:** 5th Anniversary of Independence **Obv:** Value within map **Rev:** Lion head facing

Date	Mintage	F	VF	XF	Unc	BU
ND(1966)	5,000	—	—	—	275	320

KM# 22a 1/4 GOLDE
15.0000 g., 0.9160 Gold .4418 oz. AGW **Subject:** 5th Anniversary of Independence **Obv:** Value within map **Rev:** Lion head facing

Date	Mintage	F	VF	XF	Unc	BU
ND(1966) Proof	600	Value: 350				

KM# 22b 1/4 GOLDE
10.3150 g., Palladium **Subject:** 5th Anniversary of Independence **Obv:** Value within map **Rev:** Lion head facing

Date	Mintage	F	VF	XF	Unc	BU
ND(1966) Proof	100	Value: 325				

KM# 23 1/2 GOLDE
27.2730 g., 0.9000 Gold .7891 oz. AGW, 32 mm. **Subject:** 5th Anniversary of Independence **Obv:** Value within map **Rev:** Lion head facing

Date	Mintage	F	VF	XF	Unc	BU
ND(1966)	2,500	—	—	—	550	575

KM# 23a 1/2 GOLDE
30.0000 g., 0.9160 Gold .8836 oz. AGW **Subject:** 5th Anniversary of Independence **Obv:** Value within map **Rev:** Lion head facing

Date	Mintage	F	VF	XF	Unc	BU
ND(1966) Proof	600	Value: 650				

KM# 23b 1/2 GOLDE
20.6290 g., Palladium **Subject:** 5th Anniversary of Independence **Obv:** Value within map **Rev:** Lion head facing

Date	Mintage	F	VF	XF	Unc	BU
ND(1966) Proof	100	Value: 600				

KM# 24 GOLDE
54.5450 g., 0.9000 Gold 1.5783 oz. AGW, 48 mm. **Subject:** 5th Anniversary of Independence **Obv:** Value within map **Rev:** Lion head facing

Date	Mintage	F	VF	XF	Unc	BU
ND(1966)	1,500	—	—	—	800	900
ND(1966)	1,500	—	—	—	1,150	1,200

KM# 24a GOLDE
60.0000 g., 0.9160 Gold 1.7672 oz. AGW **Subject:** 5th Anniversary of Independence **Obv:** Value within map **Rev:** Lion head facing

Date	Mintage	F	VF	XF	Unc	BU
ND(1966) Proof	400	Value: 1,300				

KM# 24b GOLDE
41.2590 g., Palladium **Subject:** 5th Anniversary of Independence **Obv:** Value within map **Rev:** Lion head facing

Date	Mintage	F	VF	XF	Unc	BU
ND(1966) Proof	100	Value: 1,150				

KM# 24c GOLDE
41.2590 g., Platinum APW **Subject:** 5th Anniversary of Independence **Obv:** Value within map **Rev:** Lion head facing

Date	Mintage	F	VF	XF	Unc	BU
ND(1966) Proof	—	Value: 1,750				

KM# 37 5 GOLDE

15.9800 g., 0.9170 Gold .4711 oz. AGW **Subject:** O.A.U. Summit Conference **Obv:** Head of Dr. Siaka Stevens right **Rev:** Map within circle

Date	Mintage	F	VF	XF	Unc	BU
1980	457	—	—	—	345	—
1980 Proof	325	Value: 375				

KM# 42 5 GOLDE

15.9980 g., 0.9170 Gold .4711 oz. AGW **Series:** World Wildlife Fund **Obv:** Bust of Dr. Joseph Saidu Momoh left **Rev:** Duiker Zebra

Date	Mintage	F	VF	XF	Unc	BU
1987 Proof	5,000	Value: 335				

KM# 28 10 GOLDE

57.6000 g., 0.9160 Gold 1.6965 oz. AGW **Subject:** 70th Birthday - Dr. Siaka Stevens **Obv:** Lion facing right **Rev:** Head right

Date	Mintage	F	VF	XF	Unc	BU
ND(1975)	727	—	—	—	1,200	—
ND(1975) Proof	307	Value: 1,350				

DOLLAR DENOMINATED COINAGE

KM# 47 DOLLAR

Copper-Nickel **Obv:** Arms **Rev:** Crowned lion

Date	Mintage	F	VF	XF	Unc	BU
1997	—	—	—	—	7.50	9.00

KM# 48 DOLLAR

Copper-Nickel **Obv:** Arms **Rev:** Unicorn

Date	Mintage	F	VF	XF	Unc	BU
1997	—	—	—	—	7.50	9.00

KM# 53 DOLLAR

Copper-Nickel **Subject:** Golden Wedding Anniversary **Obv:** Arms **Rev:** E and P monogram

Date	Mintage	F	VF	XF	Unc	BU
1997	—	—	—	—	10.00	12.00

KM# 56 DOLLAR

Copper-Nickel **Subject:** Golden Wedding Anniversary **Obv:** Arms **Rev:** Royal yacht

Date	Mintage	F	VF	XF	Unc	BU
1997	—	—	—	—	7.00	8.50

KM# 59 DOLLAR

Copper-Nickel **Subject:** Golden Wedding Anniversary **Obv:** Arms **Rev:** Royal couple

Date	Mintage	F	VF	XF	Unc	BU
1997	—	—	—	—	7.00	8.50

KM# 62 DOLLAR

Copper-Nickel **Subject:** Golden Wedding Anniversary **Obv:** Arms **Rev:** Fireworks above palace

Date	Mintage	F	VF	XF	Unc	BU
1997	—	—	—	—	7.00	8.50

KM# 65 DOLLAR

Copper-Nickel **Subject:** Golden Wedding Anniversary **Obv:** Arms **Rev:** Queen with two children

Date	Mintage	F	VF	XF	Unc	BU
1997	—	—	—	—	7.00	8.50

KM# 68 DOLLAR

Copper-Nickel **Subject:** Golden Wedding Anniversary **Obv:** Arms **Rev:** Royal couple with two children

Date	Mintage	F	VF	XF	Unc	BU
1997	—	—	—	—	7.00	8.50

KM# 71 DOLLAR

Copper-Nickel **Subject:** Diana - The Peoples' Princess **Obv:** Arms **Rev:** Head 1/4 right

Date	Mintage	F	VF	XF	Unc	BU
1997	—	—	—	—	8.00	9.00

KM# 77 DOLLAR

Copper-Nickel **Subject:** Diana - The Peoples' Princess **Obv:** Arms **Rev:** Diana with Mother Theresa

Date	Mintage	F	VF	XF	Unc	BU
1997	—	—	—	—	9.00	10.00

KM# 83 DOLLAR

Copper-Nickel **Subject:** Diana - The Peoples' Princess **Obv:** Arms **Rev:** Diana and AIDS patient

Date	Mintage	F	VF	XF	Unc	BU
1997	—	—	—	—	8.00	9.00

KM# 89 DOLLAR

Copper-Nickel **Subject:** Diana - The Peoples' Princess **Obv:** Arms **Rev:** Diana with sons William and Harry

Date	Mintage	F	VF	XF	Unc	BU
1997	—	—	—	—	8.00	9.00

KM# 95 DOLLAR

Copper-Nickel **Subject:** Jurassic Park **Obv:** Arms **Rev:** Velociraptor

Date	Mintage	F	VF	XF	Unc	BU
1997	—	—	—	—	15.00	—

KM# 103 DOLLAR

Copper-Nickel **Subject:** In Memoriam, Diana - The Peoples' Princess **Obv:** Arms **Rev:** Head 1/4 left

Date	Mintage	F	VF	XF	Unc	BU
1998	—	—	—	—	8.00	9.00

KM# 109 DOLLAR

Copper-Nickel **Subject:** Dr. Livingston **Obv:** Arms **Rev:** Half length bust of David Livingstone at right above natives in longboat

Date	Mintage	F	VF	XF	Unc	BU
1998	—	—	—	—	8.00	9.00

KM# 118 DOLLAR

Copper-Nickel **Subject:** China 2000 Series **Obv:** Arms **Rev:** Kneeling terracotta warrior

Date	Mintage	F	VF	XF	Unc	BU
1999	—	—	—	—	8.50	10.00

KM# 112 DOLLAR

Copper-Nickel **Subject:** Amerigo Vespucci **Obv:** Arms **Rev:** Ship and mountainous portrait

Date	Mintage	F	VF	XF	Unc	BU
1999	—	—	—	—	8.00	9.00

KM# 115 DOLLAR

Copper-Nickel **Subject:** Charles Darwin **Obv:** Arms **Rev:** Ship at left, bust at right

Date	Mintage	F	VF	XF	Unc	BU
1999	—	—	—	—	8.00	9.00

KM# 121 DOLLAR

Copper-Nickel **Subject:** China 2000 Series - Ming Dynasty **Obv:** Arms **Rev:** Temple of Heaven

Date	Mintage	F	VF	XF	Unc	BU
1999	—	—	—	—	8.50	10.00

KM# 124 DOLLAR

Copper-Nickel **Subject:** China 2000 Series **Obv:** Arms **Rev:** Portion of the Great Wall

Date	Mintage	F	VF	XF	Unc	BU
1999	—	—	—	—	8.50	10.00

KM# 127 DOLLAR

Copper-Nickel **Subject:** China 2000 Series **Obv:** Arms **Rev:** Bronze chariot

Date	Mintage	F	VF	XF	Unc	BU
1999	—	—	—	—	8.50	10.00

KM# 130 DOLLAR

Copper-Nickel **Subject:** China 2000 Series **Obv:** Arms **Rev:** First century armillary sphere

Date	Mintage	F	VF	XF	Unc	BU
1999	—	—	—	—	8.50	10.00

KM# 133 DOLLAR

Copper-Nickel **Subject:** China 2000 Series **Obv:** Arms **Rev:** Tang Dynasty Royal Horse

Date	Mintage	F	VF	XF	Unc	BU
1999	—	—	—	—	8.50	10.00

KM# 136 DOLLAR

Copper-Nickel **Subject:** Macau returns to China **Obv:** Arms **Rev:** Church, car, roulette wheel, and hands shaking

Date	Mintage	F	VF	XF	Unc	BU
1999	—	—	—	—	9.50	11.00

KM# 139 DOLLAR

Copper-Nickel **Subject:** Prince Edward's Wedding **Obv:** Arms **Rev:** Symbolic wedding design

Date	Mintage	F	VF	XF	Unc	BU
1999	—	—	—	—	8.50	10.00

KM# 152 DOLLAR

28.4300 g., Copper-Nickel, 38.7 mm. **Obv:** Arms **Rev:** Chinese unicorn within circle **Edge:** Reeded

Date	Mintage	F	VF	XF	Unc	BU
2000	—	—	—	—	10.00	12.00
1999	—	—	—	—	10.00	12.00

Note: Reported as an error date resulting from muled dies

KM# 142 DOLLAR

Copper-Nickel **Subject:** Year of the Dragon **Obv:** Arms **Rev:** Dragon

Date	Mintage	F	VF	XF	Unc	BU
2000	—	—	—	—	10.00	13.00

KM# 150 DOLLAR

28.2800 g., Copper-Nickel **Obv:** Arms **Rev:** Two Phoenix birds **Edge:** Reeded

Date	Mintage	F	VF	XF	Unc	BU
2000	—	—	—	—	10.00	13.00

KM# 151 DOLLAR

Copper-Nickel **Obv:** Arms **Rev:** Chinese dragon

Date	Mintage	F	VF	XF	Unc	BU
2000	—	—	—	—	10.00	13.00

KM# 174 DOLLAR

Copper-Nickel **Subject:** Buddha **Obv:** Arms **Rev:** Seated Buddha

Date	Mintage	F	VF	XF	Unc	BU
2000	—	—	—	—	8.50	10.00

KM# 175 DOLLAR

Copper-Nickel **Obv:** Arms **Rev:** Goddess of Mercy

Date	Mintage	F	VF	XF	Unc	BU
2000	—	—	—	—	8.50	10.00

KM# 176 DOLLAR

Copper-Nickel **Obv:** Arms **Rev:** Tzai-yen holding scroll

Date	Mintage	F	VF	XF	Unc	BU
2000	—	—	—	—	10.00	12.00

KM# 98 5 DOLLARS
15.5517 g., 0.9990 Silver .5000 oz. ASW **Subject:** Shanghai Coin and Stamp Exposition **Obv:** Arms **Rev:** Standing crowned lion right

Date	Mintage	F	VF	XF	Unc	BU
1997 Proof	Est. 10,000	Value: 30.00				

KM# 99 5 DOLLARS
15.5517 g., 0.9990 Silver .5000 oz. ASW **Subject:** Shanghai Coin and Stamp Exposition **Obv:** Arms **Rev:** Standing unicorm left

Date	Mintage	F	VF	XF	Unc	BU
1997 Proof	Est. 10,000	Value: 30.00				

KM# 101 5 DOLLARS
15.5517 g., 0.9990 Silver .5000 oz. ASW **Subject:** Visit of President Clinton to China **Obv:** Arms **Rev:** Bust 1/4 right, tower at right

Date	Mintage	F	VF	XF	Unc	BU
1998 Proof	Est. 10,000	Value: 30.00				

KM# 102 5 DOLLARS
15.5517 g., 0.9990 Silver .5000 oz. ASW **Subject:** Visit of President Clinton to Beijing **Obv:** Arms **Rev:** Great Wall at left, bust 1/4 left

Date	Mintage	F	VF	XF	Unc	BU
1998 Proof	Est. 10,000	Value: 30.00				

KM# 49 10 DOLLARS
28.2800 g., 0.9250 Silver .8411 oz. ASW **Obv:** Arms **Rev:** Standing crowned lion right

Date	Mintage	F	VF	XF	Unc	BU
1997 Proof	Est. 10,000	Value: 45.00				

KM# 50 10 DOLLARS
28.2800 g., 0.9250 Silver .8411 oz. ASW **Obv:** Arms **Rev:** Standing unicorn left

Date	Mintage	F	VF	XF	Unc	BU
1997 Proof	Est. 10,000	Value: 45.00				

KM# 54 10 DOLLARS
28.2800 g., 0.9250 Silver .8411 oz. ASW **Subject:** Golden Wedding Anniversary **Obv:** Arms **Rev:** E and P monogram within flower circle

Date	Mintage	F	VF	XF	Unc	BU
1997 Proof	Est. 10,000	Value: 47.50				

KM# 57 10 DOLLARS
28.2800 g., 0.9250 Silver .8411 oz. ASW **Subject:** Golden Wedding Anniversary **Obv:** Arms **Rev:** Royal Yacht with cameo head facing at upper left

Date	Mintage	F	VF	XF	Unc	BU
1997 Proof	Est. 10,000	Value: 47.50				

KM# 60 10 DOLLARS
28.2800 g., 0.9250 Silver .8411 oz. ASW **Subject:** Golden Wedding Anniversary **Obv:** Arms **Rev:** Royal couple

Date	Mintage	F	VF	XF	Unc	BU
1997 Proof	Est. 10,000	Value: 47.50				

KM# 63 10 DOLLARS
28.2800 g., 0.9250 Silver .8411 oz. ASW **Subject:** Golden Wedding Anniversary **Obv:** Arms **Rev:** Fireworks above palace

Date	Mintage	F	VF	XF	Unc	BU
1997 Proof	Est. 10,000	Value: 47.50				

KM# 66 10 DOLLARS
28.2800 g., 0.9250 Silver .8411 oz. ASW **Subject:** Golden Wedding Anniversary **Obv:** Arms **Rev:** Queen with two children

Date	Mintage	F	VF	XF	Unc	BU
1997 Proof	Est. 10,000	Value: 47.50				

KM# 69 10 DOLLARS
28.2800 g., 0.9250 Silver .8411 oz. ASW **Subject:** Golden Wedding Anniversary **Obv:** Arms **Rev:** Royal couple with two children

Date	Mintage	F	VF	XF	Unc	BU
1997 Proof	Est. 10,000	Value: 47.50				

KM# 72 10 DOLLARS
28.2800 g., 0.9250 Silver .8411 oz. ASW **Subject:** Diana - The Peoples' Princess **Obv:** Arms **Rev:** Head facing

Date	Mintage	F	VF	XF	Unc	BU
1997 Proof	Est. 10,000	Value: 30.00				

KM# 78 10 DOLLARS
28.2800 g., 0.9250 Silver .8411 oz. ASW **Subject:** Diana - The Peoples' Princess **Obv:** Arms **Rev:** Diana with Mother Theresa

Date	Mintage	F	VF	XF	Unc	BU
1997	Est. 10,000	Value: 42.50				

KM# 84 10 DOLLARS
28.2800 g., 0.9250 Silver .8411 oz. ASW **Subject:** Diana - The Peoples' Princess **Obv:** Arms **Rev:** Diana and AIDS patient

Date	Mintage	F	VF	XF	Unc	BU
1997 Proof	Est. 10,000	Value: 25.00				

KM# 90 10 DOLLARS
28.2800 g., 0.9250 Silver .8411 oz. ASW **Subject:** Diana - The Peoples' Princess **Obv:** Arms **Rev:** Diana with sons William and Harry

Date	Mintage	F	VF	XF	Unc	BU
1997 Proof	Est. 10,000	Value: 27.50				

KM# 96 10 DOLLARS
28.2800 g., 0.9250 Silver .8411 oz. ASW **Subject:** Jurassic Park **Obv:** Arms **Rev:** Velociraptor

Date	Mintage	F	VF	XF	Unc	BU
1997 Proof	Est. 10,000	Value: 45.00				

KM# 104 10 DOLLARS
28.2800 g., 0.9250 Silver .8411 oz. ASW **Subject:** In Memoriam, Diana - The Peoples' Princess **Obv:** Arms **Rev:** Head 1/4 left

Date	Mintage	F	VF	XF	Unc	BU
1998 Proof	Est. 10,000	Value: 37.50				

KM# A110 10 DOLLARS
28.2800 g., 0.9250 Silver .8411 oz. ASW **Subject:** Dr. Livingstone **Obv:** Arms **Rev:** Standing figures rowing ancient boat, bust 1/4 left at upper right **Note:** Prev. KM#110.

Date	Mintage	F	VF	XF	Unc	BU
1998 Proof	Est. 10,000	Value: 50.00				

KM# 113 10 DOLLARS
28.2800 g., 0.9250 Silver .8411 oz. ASW **Subject:** Amerigo Vespucci **Obv:** Arms **Rev:** Ship and Vespucci portrait

Date	Mintage	F	VF	XF	Unc	BU
1999 Proof	Est. 10,000	Value: 50.00				

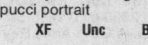

KM# 116 10 DOLLARS
28.2800 g., 0.9250 Silver .8411 oz. ASW **Subject:** Charles Darwin **Obv:** Arms **Rev:** Ship and bust facing at upper right

Date	Mintage	F	VF	XF	Unc	BU
1999 Proof	Est. 10,000	Value: 50.00				

KM# 119 10 DOLLARS
28.2800 g., 0.9250 Silver .8411 oz. ASW **Subject:** China 2000 Series **Obv:** Arms **Rev:** Kneeling Terracotta warrior

Date	Mintage	F	VF	XF	Unc	BU
1999 Proof	Est. 10,000	Value: 47.50				

KM# 122 10 DOLLARS
28.2800 g., 0.9250 Silver .8411 oz. ASW **Subject:** China 2000 Series - Ming Dynasty **Obv:** Arms **Rev:** Temple of Heaven

Date	Mintage	F	VF	XF	Unc	BU
1999 Proof	Est. 10,000	Value: 47.50				

KM# 125 10 DOLLARS
28.2800 g., 0.9250 Silver .8411 oz. ASW **Subject:** China 2000 Series **Obv:** Arms **Rev:** Portion of the Great Wall

Date	Mintage	F	VF	XF	Unc	BU
1999 Proof	Est. 10,000	Value: 47.50				

KM# 128 10 DOLLARS
28.2800 g., 0.9250 Silver .8411 oz. ASW **Subject:** China 2000 Series **Obv:** Arms **Rev:** Bronze chariot

Date	Mintage	F	VF	XF	Unc	BU
1999 Proof	Est. 10,000	Value: 47.50				

KM# 131 10 DOLLARS
28.2800 g., 0.9250 Silver .8411 oz. ASW **Subject:** China 2000 Series **Obv:** Arms **Rev:** First century armillary sphere

Date	Mintage	F	VF	XF	Unc	BU
1999 Proof	Est. 10,000	Value: 47.50				

KM# 134 10 DOLLARS
28.2800 g., 0.9250 Silver .8411 oz. ASW **Subject:** China 2000 Series **Obv:** Arms **Rev:** Tang Dynasty royal horse

Date	Mintage	F	VF	XF	Unc	BU
1999 Proof	Est. 10,000	Value: 47.50				

KM# 137 10 DOLLARS
28.2800 g., 0.9250 Silver .8411 oz. ASW **Subject:** Macau Return to China **Obv:** Arms **Rev:** Church, car, roulette wheel and clasped hands below

Date	Mintage	F	VF	XF	Unc	BU
1999 Proof	Est. 10,000	Value: 50.00				

KM# 140 10 DOLLARS
28.2800 g., 0.9250 Silver .8411 oz. ASW **Subject:** Prince Edward's Wedding **Obv:** Arms **Rev:** Symbolic wedding design

Date	Mintage	F	VF	XF	Unc	BU
1999 Proof	Est. 10,000	Value: 50.00				

KM# 143 10 DOLLARS
28.2800 g., 0.9250 Silver .8411 oz. ASW **Subject:** Year of the Dragon **Obv:** Arms **Rev:** Dragon

Date	Mintage	F	VF	XF	Unc	BU
2000 Proof	Est. 25,000	Value: 45.00				

KM# 153 10 DOLLARS
28.2800 g., 0.9250 Silver .8411 oz. ASW **Obv:** Arms **Rev:** Two Phoenix birds

Date	Mintage	F	VF	XF	Unc	BU
2000 Proof	Est. 10,000	Value: 45.00				

KM# 154 10 DOLLARS
28.2800 g., 0.9250 Silver .8411 oz. ASW **Obv:** Arms **Rev:** Chinese dragon

Date	Mintage	F	VF	XF	Unc	BU
2000 Proof	Est. 10,000	Value: 45.00				

KM# 155 10 DOLLARS
28.2800 g., 0.9250 Silver .8411 oz. ASW **Obv:** Arms **Rev:** Chinese unicorn within circle

Date	Mintage	F	VF	XF	Unc	BU
2000 Proof	Est. 10,000	Value: 45.00				

KM# 177 10 DOLLARS
28.2800 g., 0.9250 Silver .8411 oz. ASW **Obv:** Arms **Rev:** Seated Buddha

Date	Mintage	F	VF	XF	Unc	BU
2000 Proof	Est. 25,000	Value: 47.50				

KM# 178 10 DOLLARS
28.2800 g., 0.9250 Silver .8411 oz. ASW **Obv:** Arms **Rev:** Goddess of Mercy

Date	Mintage	F	VF	XF	Unc	BU
2000 Proof	Est. 25,000	Value: 47.50				

KM# 179 10 DOLLARS
28.2800 g., 0.9250 Silver .8411 oz. ASW **Obv:** Arms **Rev:** Tzai-yen holding scroll

Date	Mintage	F	VF	XF	Unc	BU
2000 Proof	Est. 25,000	Value: 47.50				

KM# 73 20 DOLLARS
1.2441 g., 0.9990 Gold .0400 oz. AGW **Subject:** Diana - The Peoples' Princess **Obv:** Arms **Rev:** Head facing

Date	Mintage	F	VF	XF	Unc	BU
1997 Proof	Est. 101,000	Value: 47.50				

KM# 79 20 DOLLARS
1.2441 g., 0.9990 Gold .0400 oz. AGW **Subject:** Diana - The Peoples' Princess **Obv:** Arms **Rev:** Lady Diana and Mother Theresa

Date	Mintage	F	VF	XF	Unc	BU
1997 Proof	Est. 101,000	Value: 55.00				

KM# 85 20 DOLLARS
1.2441 g., 0.9990 Gold .0400 oz. AGW **Subject:** Diana - The Peoples' Princess **Obv:** Arms **Rev:** Lady Diana and AIDS patient

Date	Mintage	F	VF	XF	Unc	BU
1997 Proof	Est. 101,000	Value: 42.50				

KM# 91 20 DOLLARS
1.2441 g., 0.9990 Gold .0400 oz. AGW **Subject:** Diana - The Peoples' Princess **Obv:** Arms **Rev:** With sons William and Harry

Date	Mintage	F	VF	XF	Unc	BU
1997 Proof	Est. 101,000	Value: 45.00				

KM# 105 20 DOLLARS
1.2441 g., 0.9990 Gold .0400 oz. AGW **Subject:** In Memorium **Obv:** Arms **Rev:** Lady Diana

Date	Mintage	F	VF	XF	Unc	BU
1998 Proof	Est. 10,000	Value: 50.00				

KM# 144 20 DOLLARS
1.2441 g., 0.9990 Gold .0400 oz. AGW **Subject:** Year of the Dragon **Obv:** Arms **Rev:** Dragon

Date	Mintage	F	VF	XF	Unc	BU
2000 Proof	Est. 15,000	Value: 55.00				

KM# 180 20 DOLLARS
1.2400 g., 0.9990 Gold .0399 oz. AGW **Subject:** Buddha **Obv:** Arms **Rev:** Seated Buddha **Edge:** Reeded **Note:** Struck at Pobjoy Mint.

Date	Mintage	F	VF	XF	Unc	BU
2000 Proof	Est. 5,000	Value: 55.00				

KM# 181 20 DOLLARS
1.2400 g., 0.9990 Gold .0399 oz. AGW **Obv:** Arms **Rev:** Goddess of Mercy

Date	Mintage	F	VF	XF	Unc	BU
2000 Proof	Est. 5,000	Value: 55.00				

KM# 182 20 DOLLARS
1.2400 g., 0.9990 Gold .0399 oz. AGW **Obv:** Arms **Rev:** Tzai-yen holding scroll

Date	Mintage	F	VF	XF	Unc	BU
2000 Proof	Est. 5,000	Value: 55.00				

KM# 74 50 DOLLARS
3.1100 g., 0.9990 Gold .1000 oz. AGW **Subject:** Diana - The Peoples' Princess **Obv:** Arms **Rev:** Portrait of Lady Diana

Date	Mintage	F	VF	XF	Unc	BU
1997 Proof	Est. 7,500	Value: 85.00				

KM# 80 50 DOLLARS
3.1100 g., 0.9990 Gold .1000 oz. AGW **Subject:** Diana - The Peoples' Princess **Obv:** Arms **Rev:** Lady Diana and Mother Theresa

Date	Mintage	F	VF	XF	Unc	BU
1997 Proof	Est. 7,500	Value: 90.00				

KM# 86 50 DOLLARS
3.1100 g., 0.9990 Gold .1000 oz. AGW **Subject:** Diana - The Peoples' Princess **Obv:** Arms **Rev:** Lady Diana and AIDS patient

Date	Mintage	F	VF	XF	Unc	BU
1997 Proof	Est. 7,500	Value: 80.00				

KM# 92 50 DOLLARS
3.1100 g., 0.9990 Gold .1000 oz. AGW **Subject:** Diana - The Peoples' Princess **Obv:** Arms **Rev:** With sons William and Harry

Date	Mintage	F	VF	XF	Unc	BU
1997 Proof	Est. 7,500	Value: 85.00				

KM# 106 50 DOLLARS
3.1100 g., 0.9990 Gold .1000 oz. AGW **Subject:** Diana - The Peoples' Princess **Obv:** Arms **Rev:** Portrait of Lady Diana

Date	Mintage	F	VF	XF	Unc	BU
1998 Proof	Est. 7,500	Value: 90.00				

KM# 184 50 DOLLARS
3.1100 g., 0.9990 Gold .1000 oz. AGW **Obv:** Arms **Rev:** Goddess of Mercy

Date	Mintage	F	VF	XF	Unc	BU
2000 Proof	Est. 5,000	Value: 95.00				

KM# 145 50 DOLLARS
3.1100 g., 0.9990 Gold .1000 oz. AGW **Subject:** Year of the Dragon **Obv:** Arms **Rev:** Dragon

Date	Mintage	F	VF	XF	Unc	BU
2000 Proof	Est. 20,000	Value: 90.00				

KM# 183 50 DOLLARS
3.1100 g., 0.9990 Gold .1000 oz. AGW **Obv:** Arms **Rev:** Seated Buddha **Edge:** Reeded

Date	Mintage	F	VF	XF	Unc	BU
2000 Proof	Est. 5,000	Value: 95.00				

KM# 185 50 DOLLARS
3.1100 g., 0.9990 Gold .1000 oz. AGW **Obv:** Arms **Rev:** Tzai-yen holding scroll

Date	Mintage	F	VF	XF	Unc	BU
2000 Proof	Est. 5,000	Value: 95.00				

KM# 51 100 DOLLARS
6.2200 g., 0.9999 Gold .2000 oz. AGW **Subject:** Shanghai Coin and Stamp Exposition **Obv:** Arms **Rev:** Crowned lion

Date	Mintage	F	VF	XF	Unc	BU
1997 Proof	Est. 5,000	Value: 175				

KM# 52 100 DOLLARS
6.2200 g., 0.9999 Gold .2000 oz. AGW **Subject:** Shanghai Coin and Stamp Exposition **Obv:** Arms **Rev:** Crowned lion

Date	Mintage	F	VF	XF	Unc	BU
1997 Proof	Est. 5,000	Value: 175				

KM# 55 100 DOLLARS
6.2200 g., 0.9999 Gold .2000 oz. AGW **Subject:** Golden Wedding Anniversary **Obv:** Arms **Rev:** E and P monogram

Date	Mintage	F	VF	XF	Unc	BU
1997 Proof	Est. 3,500	Value: 175				

KM# 58 100 DOLLARS
6.2200 g., 0.9999 Gold .2000 oz. AGW **Subject:** Golden Wedding Anniversary **Obv:** Arms **Rev:** Yacht

Date	Mintage	F	VF	XF	Unc	BU
1997 Proof	Est. 3,500	Value: 175				

KM# 61 100 DOLLARS
6.2200 g., 0.9999 Gold .2000 oz. AGW **Subject:** Golden Wedding Anniversary **Obv:** Arms **Rev:** Royal couple

Date	Mintage	F	VF	XF	Unc	BU
1997 Proof	Est. 10,000	Value: 175				

KM# 64 100 DOLLARS
6.2200 g., 0.9999 Gold .2000 oz. AGW **Subject:** Golden Wedding Anniversary **Obv:** Arms **Rev:** Fireworks above palace

Date	Mintage	F	VF	XF	Unc	BU
1997 Proof	Est. 3,500	Value: 175				

KM# 67 100 DOLLARS
6.2200 g., 0.9999 Gold .2000 oz. AGW **Subject:** Golden Wedding Anniversary **Obv:** Arms **Rev:** Queen with two children

Date	Mintage	F	VF	XF	Unc	BU
1997 Proof	Est. 3,500	Value: 175				

KM# 70 100 DOLLARS
6.2200 g., 0.9999 Gold .2000 oz. AGW **Subject:** Golden Wedding Anniversary **Obv:** Arms **Rev:** Royal couple with two children

Date	Mintage	F	VF	XF	Unc	BU
1997 Proof	Est. 3,500	Value: 175				

KM# 75 100 DOLLARS
6.2200 g., 0.9999 Gold .2000 oz. AGW **Subject:** Diana - The Peoples' Princess **Obv:** Arms **Rev:** Portrait of Lady Diana

Date	Mintage	F	VF	XF	Unc	BU
1997 Proof	Est. 5,000	Value: 165				

KM# 81 100 DOLLARS
6.2200 g., 0.9999 Gold .2000 oz. AGW **Subject:** Diana - The Peoples' Princess **Obv:** Arms with supporters **Rev:** Diana with Mother Theresa

Date	Mintage	F	VF	XF	Unc	BU
1997 Proof	Est. 5,000	Value: 175				

KM# 87 100 DOLLARS
6.2200 g., 0.9999 Gold .2000 oz. AGW **Subject:** Diana - The Peoples' Princess **Obv:** Arms **Rev:** Lady Diana and AIDS patient

Date	Mintage	F	VF	XF	Unc	BU
1997 Proof	Est. 5,000	Value: 155				

KM# 93 100 DOLLARS
6.2200 g., 0.9999 Gold .2000 oz. AGW **Subject:** Diana - The Peoples' Princess **Obv:** Arms **Rev:** With sons William and Harry

Date	Mintage	F	VF	XF	Unc	BU
1997 Proof	Est. 5,000	Value: 160				

KM# 97 100 DOLLARS
6.2200 g., 0.9999 Gold .2000 oz. AGW **Subject:** Jurassic Park **Obv:** Arms **Rev:** Velociraptor

Date	Mintage	F	VF	XF	Unc	BU
1997 Proof	Est. 5,000	Value: 175				

KM# 100 100 DOLLARS
6.2200 g., 0.9999 Gold .2000 oz. AGW **Subject:** Queen Victoria's Diamond Jubilee Centennial **Obv:** Arms **Rev:** Crowned bust with diamond necklace facing

Date	Mintage	F	VF	XF	Unc	BU
1997 Proof	Est. 3,500	Value: 200				

KM# 107 100 DOLLARS
6.2200 g., 0.9999 Gold .2000 oz. AGW **Subject:** Diana - The People's Princess **Obv:** Arms **Rev:** Head half left

Date	Mintage	F	VF	XF	Unc	BU
1998 Proof	Est. 5,000	Value: 165				

KM# 111 100 DOLLARS
6.2200 g., 0.9999 Gold .2000 oz. AGW **Subject:** Dr. Livingstone **Obv:** Arms **Rev:** Dr. Livingstone above figures in boat

Date	Mintage	F	VF	XF	Unc	BU
1998 Proof	Est. 5,000	Value: 170				

KM# 114 100 DOLLARS
6.2200 g., 0.9999 Gold .2000 oz. AGW **Subject:** Amerigo Vespucci **Obv:** Arms **Rev:** Ship and mountainous portrait

Date	Mintage	F	VF	XF	Unc	BU
1999 Proof	Est. 5,000	Value: 175				

KM# 117 100 DOLLARS
6.2200 g., 0.9999 Gold .2000 oz. AGW **Subject:** Charles Darwin **Obv:** Arms **Rev:** Ship and portrait

Date	Mintage	F	VF	XF	Unc	BU
1999 Proof	Est. 5,000	Value: 175				

KM# 120 100 DOLLARS
6.2200 g., 0.9999 Gold .2000 oz. AGW **Subject:** China 2000 Series **Obv:** Arms **Rev:** Kneeling terra cotta warrior

Date	Mintage	F	VF	XF	Unc	BU
1999 Proof	Est. 5,000	Value: 165				

KM# 123 100 DOLLARS
6.2200 g., 0.9999 Gold .2000 oz. AGW **Subject:** China 2000 Series - Ming Dynasty **Obv:** Arms **Rev:** Temple of Heaven

Date	Mintage	F	VF	XF	Unc	BU
1999 Proof	Est. 5,000	Value: 165				

KM# 126 100 DOLLARS
6.2200 g., 0.9999 Gold .2000 oz. AGW **Subject:** China 2000 Series **Obv:** Arms **Rev:** Portion of the Great Wall

Date	Mintage	F	VF	XF	Unc	BU
1999 Proof	Est. 5,000	Value: 165				

KM# 129 100 DOLLARS
6.2200 g., 0.9999 Gold .2000 oz. AGW **Series:** China 2000 **Obv:** Arms **Rev:** Bronze chariot

Date	Mintage	F	VF	XF	Unc	BU
1999 Proof	Est. 5,000	Value: 165				

KM# 132 100 DOLLARS
6.2200 g., 0.9999 Gold .2000 oz. AGW **Series:** China 2000 **Obv:** Arms **Rev:** First century armillary sphere

Date	Mintage	F	VF	XF	Unc	BU
1999 Proof	Est. 5,000	Value: 165				

KM# 135 100 DOLLARS
6.2200 g., 0.9999 Gold .2000 oz. AGW **Series:** China 2000 **Obv:** Arms **Rev:** Tang Dynasty royal horse

Date	Mintage	F	VF	XF	Unc	BU
1999 Proof	Est. 5,000	Value: 165				

KM# 138 100 DOLLARS
6.2200 g., 0.9999 Gold .2000 oz. AGW **Subject:** Macau Return to China **Obv:** Arms **Rev:** Church, car, roulette wheel, and hands shaking

Date	Mintage	F	VF	XF	Unc	BU
1999 Proof	Est. 5,000	Value: 175				

KM# 141 100 DOLLARS
6.2200 g., 0.9999 Gold .2000 oz. AGW **Subject:** Prince Edward's Wedding **Obv:** Arms **Rev:** Symbolic wedding design

Date	Mintage	F	VF	XF	Unc	BU
1999 Proof	Est. 5,000	Value: 175				

KM# 146 100 DOLLARS
6.2200 g., 0.9999 Gold .2000 oz. AGW **Subject:** Year of the Dragon **Obv:** Arms **Rev:** Dragon

Date	Mintage	F	VF	XF	Unc	BU
2000 Proof	Est. 20,000	Value: 165				

KM# 186 100 DOLLARS
6.2200 g., 0.9999 Gold .2000 oz. AGW **Obv:** Arms **Rev:** Seated Buddha **Edge:** Reeded

Date	Mintage	F	VF	XF	Unc	BU
2000	Est. 5,000	Value: 175				

KM# 187 100 DOLLARS
6.2200 g., 0.9999 Gold .2000 oz. AGW **Obv:** Arms **Rev:** Goddess of Mercy

Date	Mintage	F	VF	XF	Unc	BU
2000 Proof	Est. 5,000	Value: 175				

KM# 188 100 DOLLARS
6.2200 g., 0.9999 Gold .2000 oz. AGW **Obv:** Arms **Rev:** Tzai-yen holding scroll

Date	Mintage	F	VF	XF	Unc	BU
2000 Proof	Est. 5,000	Value: 175				

KM# 240 250 DOLLARS

15.5500 g., 0.9999 Gold .4999 oz. AGW, 29.9 mm. **Subject:** Centennial of Queen Victoria's Diamond Jubilee **Obv:** Arms **Rev:** Crowned bust with diamond necklace facing **Edge:** Reeded
Note: This denomination was never offered to the public. The entire issue is reported to have been commissioned by and sold to a single purchaser.

Date	Mintage	F	VF	XF	Unc	BU
1997 Proof	Est. 1,000	Value: 375				

KM# 76 250 DOLLARS

15.5000 g., 0.9990 Gold .5000 oz. AGW **Subject:** Diana - The Peoples' Princess **Obv:** Arms **Rev:** Portrait of Lady Diana

Date	Mintage	F	VF	XF	Unc	BU
1997 Proof	Est. 3,000	Value: 370				

KM# 82 250 DOLLARS

15.5000 g., 0.9990 Gold .5000 oz. AGW **Subject:** Diana - The Peoples' Princess **Obv:** Arms **Rev:** Mother Theresa and Lady Diana

Date	Mintage	F	VF	XF	Unc	BU
1997 Proof	Est. 3,000	Value: 385				

KM# 88 250 DOLLARS

15.5000 g., 0.9990 Gold .5000 oz. AGW **Subject:** Diana - The Peoples' Princess **Obv:** Arms **Rev:** Lady Diana with AIDS patient

Date	Mintage	F	VF	XF	Unc	BU
1997 Proof	Est. 3,000	Value: 360				

KM# 94 250 DOLLARS

15.5000 g., 0.9990 Gold .5000 oz. AGW **Subject:** Diana - The Peoples' Princess **Obv:** Arms **Rev:** Lady Diana with sons William and Harry

Date	Mintage	F	VF	XF	Unc	BU
1997 Proof	Est. 3,000	Value: 365				

KM# 108 250 DOLLARS

15.5000 g., 0.9990 Gold .5000 oz. AGW **Subject:** Diana - The Peoples' Princess **Obv:** Arms **Rev:** Head half left

Date	Mintage	F	VF	XF	Unc	BU
1998 Proof	Est. 3,000	Value: 370				

KM# 147 250 DOLLARS

15.5000 g., 0.9990 Gold .5000 oz. AGW **Subject:** Year of the Dragon **Obv:** Arms **Rev:** Dragon

Date	Mintage	F	VF	XF	Unc	BU
2000 Proof	Est. 5,000	Value: 370				

KM# 189 250 DOLLARS

15.5000 g., 0.9990 Gold .5000 oz. AGW **Obv:** Arms **Rev:** Seated Buddha

Date	Mintage	F	VF	XF	Unc	BU
2000 Proof	Est. 5,000	Value: 385				

KM# 190 250 DOLLARS

15.5500 g., 0.9990 Gold .5000 oz. AGW **Obv:** Arms **Rev:** Goddess of Mercy

Date	Mintage	F	VF	XF	Unc	BU
2000 Proof	Est. 5,000	Value: 385				

KM# 191 250 DOLLARS

15.5500 g., 0.9990 Gold .5000 oz. AGW **Obv:** Arms **Rev:** Tzai-yen holding scroll

Date	Mintage	F	VF	XF	Unc	BU
2000 Proof	Est. 5,000	Value: 385				

KM# 148 500 DOLLARS

31.1035 g., 0.9990 Gold 1.0000 oz. AGW **Subject:** Year of the Dragon **Obv:** Arms **Rev:** Dragon **Note:** Similar to 10 Dollars, KM#143.

Date	Mintage	F	VF	XF	Unc	BU
2000 Proof	Est. 1,000	Value: 765				

KM# 192 500 DOLLARS

31.1035 g., 0.9990 Gold 1.0000 oz. AGW **Obv:** Arms **Rev:** Seated Buddha **Edge:** Reeded **Note:** Struck at Pobjoy Mint.

Date	Mintage	F	VF	XF	Unc	BU
2000 Proof	Est. 5,000	Value: 740				

KM# 193 500 DOLLARS

31.1035 g., 0.9990 Gold 1.0000 oz. AGW **Obv:** Arms **Rev:** Goddess of Mercy

Date	Mintage	F	VF	XF	Unc	BU
2000 Proof	Est. 5,000	Value: 740				

KM# 194 500 DOLLARS

31.1035 g., 0.9990 Gold 1.0000 oz. AGW **Obv:** Arms **Rev:** Tzai-yen holding scroll

Date	Mintage	F	VF	XF	Unc	BU
2000 Proof	Est. 5,000	Value: 740				

KM# 149 2500 DOLLARS

155.5175 g., 0.9990 Gold 5.0000 oz. AGW **Subject:** Year of the Dragon **Obv:** Arms **Rev:** Dragon

Date	Mintage	F	VF	XF	Unc	BU
2000 Proof	250	Value: 3,500				

KM# 195 2500 DOLLARS

155.5175 g., 0.9990 Gold 5.0000 oz. AGW **Obv:** Arms **Rev:** Seated Buddha **Edge:** Reeded

Date	Mintage	F	VF	XF	Unc	BU
2000 Proof	Est. 250	Value: 3,500				

KM# 196 2500 DOLLARS

155.5175 g., 0.9990 Gold 5.0000 oz. AGW **Obv:** Arms **Rev:** Goddess of Mercy

Date	Mintage	F	VF	XF	Unc	BU
2000 Proof	Est. 250	Value: 3,500				

KM# 197 2500 DOLLARS

155.5175 g., 0.9990 Gold 5.0000 oz. AGW **Obv:** Arms **Rev:** Tzai-yen holding scroll

Date	Mintage	F	VF	XF	Unc	BU
2000 Proof	Est. 250	Value: 3,500				

TRIAL STRIKES

KM#	Date	Mintage	Identification	Mkt Val
TS1	ND	—	5 Centesimos. Steel. Portrait of Milton Margai, Prime Minster. Uruguay 5 Centavos design with MBLAT top, HA in number 5. Reeded edge.	135
TS2	ND(1964)	—	10 Cents. Brass. Head right. Value within wreath.	125
TS3	ND(1964)	—	10 Cents. Aluminum. Reverse of KM#19. Uruguay 10 Centesimos.	125

MINT SETS

KM#	Date	Mintage	Identification	Issue Price	Mkt Val
MS1	1966 (3)	—	KM#22-24	—	1,650

PROOF SETS

KM#	Date	Mintage	Identification	Issue Price	Mkt Val
PS1	1964 (6)	10,000	KM#16-21	—	16.50
PS2	1964 (6)	12	KM#16a-20a, 21b	—	5,750
PS3	1964 (6)	10	KM#16a-21a	—	4,250
PS4	1966 (3)	400	KM#22a-24a	—	1,950
PS5	1972 (2)	1,000	KM25 (2 pieces with 50 cent bank note (0 serial#) in plush case	—	20.00
PS6	1980 (6)	10,000	KM25, 30-34	34.00	28.00

SINGAPORE

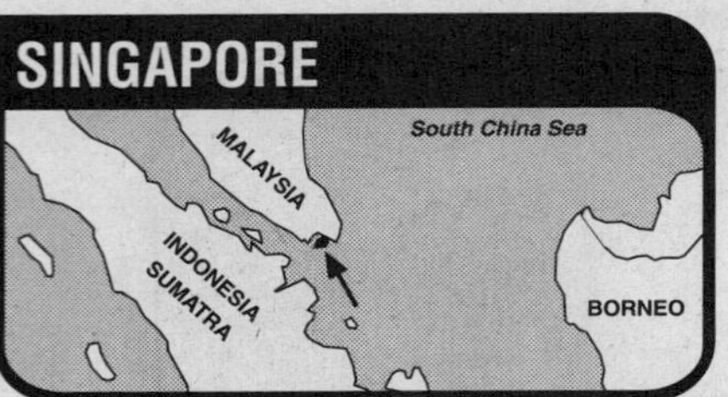

The Republic of Singapore, a member of the Commonwealth of Nations situated off the southern tip of the Malay peninsula, has an area of 224 sq. mi. (633 sq. km.) and a population of *2.7 million. Capital: Singapore. The economy is based on entrepot trade, manufacturing and oil. Rubber, petroleum products, machinery and spices are exported.

Singapore's modern history - it was an important shipping center in the 14th century before the rise of Malacca and Penang - began in 1819 when Sir Thomas Stamford Raffles, an agent for the British East India Company, founded the town of Singapore. By 1825 its trade exceeded that of Malacca and Penang combined. The opening of the Suez Canal (1869) and the demand for rubber and tin created by the automobile and packaging industries combined to make Singapore one of the major ports of the world. In 1826 Singapore, Penang and Malacca were combined to form the Straits Settlements, which was made a Crown Colony in 1867. Singapore became a separate Crown Colony in 1946 when the Straits Settlements was dissolved. It joined in the formation of Malaysia in 1963, but broke away on Aug. 9, 1965, to become an independent republic. The President is Chief of State. The prime minister is Head of Government.

For earlier coinage see Straits Settlements, Malaya, Malaya and British Borneo.

MINT MARKS

sm = ***"sm"*** - Singapore Mint monogram

MONETARY SYSTEM

100 Cents = 1 Dollar

REPUBLIC

STANDARD COINAGE

100 Cents = 1 Dollar

KM# 1 CENT

Bronze, 17.8 mm. **Obv:** Value **Rev:** Apartment building **Edge:** Plain

Date	Mintage	F	VF	XF	Unc	BU
1967	7,500,000	—	—	0.30	0.60	—
1967 Proof	2,000	Value: 2.25				
1968	2,969,000	—	—	0.30	0.60	—
1968 Proof	5,000	Value: 2.00				
1969	7,220,000	—	—	1.20	2.00	—
1969 Proof	3,000	Value: 10.00				
1970	1,402,000	—	0.25	1.00	2.00	—
1971	9,731,000	—	—	0.25	0.60	—
1972	1,665,000	—	—	0.30	0.70	—
1972 Proof	749	Value: 40.00				
1973	6,377,000	—	—	0.20	0.30	—
1973 Proof	1,000	Value: 5.00				
1974	9,421,000	—	—	—	0.30	—
1974 Proof	1,500	Value: 4.00				
1975	24,226,000	—	—	—	0.30	—
1975 Proof	3,000	Value: 1.50				
1976	2,500,000	—	0.20	1.00	2.00	—
1976sm Proof	3,500	Value: 1.25				
1977sm Proof	3,500	Value: 1.25				
1978sm Proof	4,000	Value: 1.25				
1979sm Proof	3,500	Value: 1.25				
1980sm Proof	14,000	Value: 1.00				
1982sm Proof	20,000	Value: 1.00				
1983sm Proof	15,000	Value: 1.00				
1984sm Proof	15,000	Value: 1.00				

KM# 1a CENT

1.7500 g., Copper Clad Steel, 17.8 mm. **Obv:** Value **Rev:** Apartment building

Date	Mintage	F	VF	XF	Unc	BU
1976	13,665,000	—	—	0.20	0.30	—
1977	13,940,000	—	—	0.20	0.30	—
1978	5,931,000	—	—	—	0.30	—
1979	11,986,000	—	—	—	0.25	—
1980	19,922,000	—	—	—	0.25	—
1981	38,084,000	—	—	—	0.25	—
1982	24,105,000	—	—	—	0.25	—
1983	2,204,000	—	—	—	0.25	—
1984	5,695,000	—	—	—	0.25	—
1985	148,424	—	—	—	0.45	—

Note: In sets only

KM# 1b CENT

2.9200 g., 0.9250 Silver .0869 oz. ASW, 17.8 mm. **Obv:** Value **Rev:** Apartment building

Date	Mintage	F	VF	XF	Unc	BU
1981sm Proof	30,000	Value: 5.00				

KM# 49 CENT

1.7500 g., Bronze, 17.8 mm. **Obv:** Arms with supporters **Rev:** Value divides plants **Edge:** Plain

Date	Mintage	F	VF	XF	Unc	BU
1986	20,000,000	—	—	—	0.10	0.15
1987	—	—	—	—	0.10	0.15
1988	—	—	—	—	0.10	0.15
1989	20,080,000	—	—	—	0.10	0.15
1990	10,000,000	—	—	—	0.10	0.15

KM# 49a CENT

1.8100 g., 0.9250 Silver .0538 oz. ASW, 17.8 mm. **Obv:** Arms with supporters **Rev:** Value divides plants

Date	Mintage	F	VF	XF	Unc	BU
1985sm Proof	20,000	Value: 2.25				
1986sm Proof	15,000	Value: 2.25				
1987sm Proof	15,000	Value: 2.25				
1988 Proof	15,000	Value: 2.25				
1989 Proof	15,000	Value: 2.25				
1990 Proof	15,000	Value: 2.25				
1991 Proof	15,000	Value: 2.25				

KM# 49b CENT

Copper Plated Zinc, 17.8 mm. **Obv:** Arms with supporters **Rev:** Value divides plants

Date	Mintage	F	VF	XF	Unc	BU
1991	—	—	—	—	0.10	0.15

KM# 98a CENT

1.8100 g., 0.9250 Silver .0538 oz. ASW, 17.8 mm. **Obv:** Arms with supporters **Rev:** Value divides plants

Date	Mintage	F	VF	XF	Unc	BU
1992 Proof	15,000	Value: 2.25				
1993 Proof	15,000	Value: 2.25				
1994 Proof	10,000	Value: 2.25				
1995 Proof	10,000	Value: 2.25				
1996 Proof	17,000	Value: 2.25				
1997 Proof	20,000	Value: 2.25				
1998 Proof	—	Value: 2.25				
1999 Proof	—	Value: 2.25				
2000 Proof	17,000	Value: 2.25				

KM# 98 CENT

Copper Plated Zinc, 17.8 mm. **Obv:** Arms with supporters **Rev:** Value divides plants **Edge:** Plain **Note:** Similar to KM#49 but motto ribbon on arms curves down at center.

Date	Mintage	F	VF	XF	Unc	BU
1992	20,000,000	—	—	—	0.10	0.15
1993	39,920,000	—	—	—	0.10	0.15
1994	130,810,000	—	—	—	0.10	0.15
1995	220,000,000	—	—	—	0.10	0.15
1996	—	—	—	—	0.20	0.30
1997	—	—	—	—	0.20	0.30
1998	—	—	—	—	0.20	0.30
1999	—	—	—	—	0.20	0.30
2000	50,000,000	—	—	—	0.10	0.15

KM# 2 5 CENTS

Copper-Nickel, 16.25 mm. **Obv:** Value and date **Rev:** Great White Egret **Edge:** Reeded

Date	Mintage	F	VF	XF	Unc	BU
1967	28,000,000	—	—	0.20	0.35	0.75
1967 Proof	2,000	Value: 3.25				
1968	4,217,000	—	—	0.25	0.40	0.80
1968 Proof	5,000	Value: 3.00				
1969	14,778,000	—	—	0.10	0.35	0.75
1969 Proof	3,000	Value: 15.00				
1970	4,065,000	—	—	0.20	0.40	0.80
1971	13,202,000	—	—	0.10	0.35	0.75
1972	9,817,000	—	—	0.10	0.35	0.75
1972 Proof	749	Value: 50.00				
1973	2,980,000	—	0.50	1.50	2.25	—
1973 Proof	1,000	Value: 7.50				
1974	10,868,000	—	—	0.10	0.35	0.75
1974 Proof	1,500	Value: 6.50				
1975	1,729,000	—	—	0.40	1.00	1.25
1975 Proof	3,000	Value: 2.50				
1976	15,541,000	—	—	0.10	0.35	0.75
1976sm Proof	3,500	Value: 2.25				
1977	9,956,000	—	—	0.10	0.35	0.75
1977sm Proof	3,500	Value: 2.25				
1978	5,956,000	—	—	0.10	0.35	0.75
1978sm Proof	4,000	Value: 2.25				
1979	9,974,000	—	—	—	0.35	0.75
1979sm Proof	3,500	Value: 2.25				
1980	20,534,000	—	—	—	0.35	0.75
1980sm Proof	14,000	Value: 2.00				
1981	23,866,000	—	—	—	0.35	0.75
1982	24,413,000	—	—	—	0.35	0.75
1982sm Proof	20,000	Value: 2.00				
1983	4,016,000	—	—	—	0.35	0.75
1983sm Proof	15,000	Value: 2.00				
1984	18,880,000	—	—	—	0.35	0.75
1984sm Proof	15,000	Value: 2.00				
1985 In sets only	148,424	—	—	—	0.50	0.85

KM# 2a 5 CENTS

1.3000 g., Copper-Nickel Clad Steel, 16.25 mm. **Obv:** Value **Rev:** Great White Egret **Edge:** Reeded

Date	Mintage	F	VF	XF	Unc	BU
1980	12,001,000	—	—	—	0.35	0.50
1981	23,866,000	—	—	—	0.35	0.50
1982	24,413,000	—	—	—	0.35	0.50
1983	4,016,000	—	—	—	0.35	0.50
1984	—	—	—	—	0.35	0.50

KM# 2b 5 CENTS

1.6500 g., 0.9250 Silver .0491 oz. ASW, 16.25 mm. **Obv:** Value **Rev:** Great White Egret

Date	Mintage	F	VF	XF	Unc	BU
1981 Proof	30,000	Value: 5.00				

KM# 8 5 CENTS

Aluminum **Series:** F.A.O. **Obv:** Value and date **Rev:** Pomfret fish **Edge:** Plain

Date	Mintage	F	VF	XF	Unc	BU
1971	3,049,000	—	0.10	0.30	1.00	1.25

KM# 50 5 CENTS

Aluminum-Bronze, 16.25 mm. **Obv:** Arms with supporters **Rev:** Fruit salad plant **Edge:** Reeded

Date	Mintage	F	VF	XF	Unc	BU
1985	14,840,000	—	—	—	0.20	0.30
1986	15,480,000	—	—	—	0.20	0.30
1987	31,040,000	—	—	—	0.20	0.30
1988	45,180,000	—	—	—	0.20	0.30
1989	69,988,000	—	—	—	0.20	0.30
1990	26,052,000	—	—	—	0.20	0.30
1991	—	—	—	—	0.20	0.30

KM# 50a 5 CENTS

2.0000 g., 0.9250 Silver .0595 oz. ASW, 16.25 mm. **Obv:** Arms with supporters **Rev:** Fruit salad plant

Date	Mintage	F	VF	XF	Unc	BU
1985sm Proof	20,000	Value: 2.50				
1986sm Proof	15,000	Value: 2.50				
1987sm Proof	15,000	Value: 2.50				
1988 Proof	15,000	Value: 2.50				
1989 Proof	15,000	Value: 2.50				
1990 Proof	15,000	Value: 2.50				
1991 Proof	15,000	Value: 2.50				

KM# 99a 5 CENTS

2.0000 g., 0.9250 Silver .0595 oz. ASW, 16.25 mm. **Obv:** Arms with supporters **Rev:** Fruit salad plant

Date	Mintage	F	VF	XF	Unc	BU
1992 Proof	15,000	Value: 2.50				
1993 Proof	15,000	Value: 2.50				
1994 Proof	10,000	Value: 2.50				
1995 Proof	10,000	Value: 2.50				
1996 Proof	17,000	Value: 2.50				
1997 Proof	20,000	Value: 2.50				
1998 Proof	—	Value: 2.50				
1999 Proof	—	Value: 2.50				
2000 Proof	17,000	Value: 2.50				

KM# 99 5 CENTS

Aluminum-Bronze, 16.25 mm. **Obv:** Arms with supporters **Rev:** Fruit salad plant **Edge:** Reeded **Note:** Similar to KM#50 but motto ribbon on arms curves down at center.

Date	Mintage	F	VF	XF	Unc	BU
1992	—	—	—	—	0.20	0.30
1993	5,996,000	—	—	—	0.20	0.30
1994	—	—	—	—	0.20	0.30
1995	90,000,000	—	—	—	0.20	0.30
1996	—	—	—	—	0.20	0.30
1997	60,000,000	—	—	—	0.20	0.30
1998	—	—	—	—	0.20	0.30
1999	—	—	—	—	0.20	0.30
2000	30,000,000	—	—	—	0.20	0.30

KM# 3 10 CENTS

2.8500 g., Copper-Nickel, 19.4 mm. **Obv:** Value and date **Rev:** Stylized Great Crowned Seahorse **Edge:** Reeded

Date	Mintage	F	VF	XF	Unc	BU
1967	40,000,000	—	—	0.15	0.65	1.50
1967 Proof	2,000	Value: 4.50				
1968	36,261,000	—	—	0.20	0.65	1.50
1968 Proof	5,000	Value: 4.25				
1969	25,000,000	—	—	0.10	0.65	1.50
1969 Proof	3,000	Value: 20.00				
1970	21,304,000	—	—	0.20	0.65	1.50
1971	33,040,999	—	—	0.10	0.50	1.50
1972	2,675,000	—	0.20	0.75	1.50	2.00
1972 Proof	749	Value: 60.00				
1973	14,290,000	—	0.10	0.20	0.65	1.50
1973 Proof	1,000	Value: 10.00				
1974	13,450,000	—	0.10	0.20	0.65	1.50
1974 Proof	1,500	Value: 7.50				
1975	828,000	—	0.50	1.25	2.25	3.00
1975 Proof	3,000	Value: 4.00				
1976	29,718,000	—	—	0.15	0.35	1.50
1976sm Proof	3,500	Value: 3.50				
1977	11,776,000	—	—	0.10	0.35	1.50
1977sm Proof	3,500	Value: 3.50				
1978	5,936,000	—	—	0.10	0.35	1.50
1978sm Proof	4,000	Value: 3.50				
1979	12,001,000	—	—	0.10	0.35	1.50
1979sm Proof	3,500	Value: 3.50				
1980	40,299,000	—	—	0.10	0.35	1.50
1980sm Proof	14,000	Value: 3.00				
1981	58,600,000	—	—	0.10	0.35	1.50
1982	48,514,000	—	—	0.10	0.35	1.50
1982sm Proof	20,000	Value: 3.00				
1983	10,415,000	—	—	0.10	0.35	1.50
1983sm Proof	15,000	Value: 3.00				
1984	29,700,000	—	—	0.10	0.35	1.50
1984sm Proof	15,000	Value: 3.00				
1985 In sets only	148,424	—	—	0.10	0.35	1.50

KM# 3a 10 CENTS

3.3500 g., 0.9250 Silver .0996 oz. ASW, 19.4 mm. **Obv:** Value and date **Rev:** Stylized Great Crowned Seahorse

Date	Mintage	F	VF	XF	Unc	BU
1981sm Proof	30,000	Value: 9.00				

KM# 51 10 CENTS

2.8500 g., Copper-Nickel, 19.4 mm. **Obv:** Arms with supporters **Rev:** Star Jasmine plant above value **Edge:** Reeded

Date	Mintage	F	VF	XF	Unc	BU
1985	45,040,000	—	—	—	0.20	0.30
1986	113,000,000	—	—	—	0.20	0.30
1987	90,000,000	—	—	—	0.20	0.30
1988	54,455,000	—	—	—	0.20	0.30
1989	134,190,000	—	—	—	0.20	0.30
1990	51,720,000	—	—	—	0.20	0.30
1991	159,770,000	—	—	—	0.20	0.30

KM# 51a 10 CENTS

3.0500 g., 0.9250 Silver .0907 oz. ASW, 19.4 mm. **Obv:** Arms with supporters **Rev:** Star Jasmine plant above value

Date	Mintage	F	VF	XF	Unc	BU
1985sm Proof	20,000	Value: 4.00				
1986sm Proof	15,000	Value: 4.00				
1987sm Proof	15,000	Value: 4.00				
1988 Proof	15,000	Value: 4.00				
1989 Proof	15,000	Value: 4.00				
1990 Proof	15,000	Value: 4.00				
1991 Proof	15,000	Value: 4.00				

KM# 100a 10 CENTS

3.0500 g., 0.9250 Silver .0907 oz. ASW, 19.4 mm. **Obv:** Arms with supporters **Rev:** Star Jasmine plant

Date	Mintage	F	VF	XF	Unc	BU
1992 Proof	15,000	Value: 4.00				
1993 Proof	15,000	Value: 4.00				
1994 Proof	10,000	Value: 4.00				
1995 Proof	10,000	Value: 4.00				
1996 Proof	17,000	Value: 4.00				
1997 Proof	20,000	Value: 4.00				
1998 Proof	—	Value: 4.00				
1999 Proof	—	Value: 4.00				
2000 Proof	17,000	Value: 4.00				

KM# 100 10 CENTS

2.8500 g., Copper-Nickel, 19.4 mm. **Obv:** Arms with supporters **Rev:** Star Jasmine plant **Edge:** Reeded **Note:** Similar to KM#51 but motto ribbon on arms curves down at center.

Date	Mintage	F	VF	XF	Unc	BU
1992	—	—	—	—	0.20	0.30
1993	89,855,000	—	—	—	0.20	0.30
1994	—	—	—	—	0.20	0.30
1995	—	—	—	—	0.20	0.30
1996	—	—	—	—	0.20	0.30
1997	—	—	—	—	0.20	0.30
1998	—	—	—	—	0.20	0.30
1999	—	—	—	—	0.20	0.30
2000	—	—	—	—	0.20	0.30

KM# 4 20 CENTS

5.6500 g., Copper-Nickel, 23.6 mm. **Obv:** Value and date **Rev:** Swordfish **Edge:** Reeded

Date	Mintage	F	VF	XF	Unc	BU
1967	36,500,000	—	0.15	0.35	0.75	1.50
1967 Proof	2,000	Value: 7.00				
1968	10,934,000	—	0.15	0.35	0.75	1.50
1968 Proof	5,000	Value: 6.00				
1969	8,460,000	—	0.15	0.35	0.75	1.50
1969 Proof	3,000	Value: 30.00				
1970	3,250,000	—	0.15	0.30	0.80	1.50
1971	1,732,000	—	0.15	0.70	2.00	3.00
1972	9,107,000	—	0.15	0.30	0.80	1.50
1972 Proof	749	Value: 70.00				
1973	8,838,000	—	0.15	0.30	0.80	1.50
1973 Proof	1,000	Value: 17.50				
1974	4,567,000	—	0.15	0.30	0.75	1.50
1974 Proof	1,500	Value: 12.50				
1975	1,546,000	0.15	0.35	1.20	2.00	2.50
1975 Proof	3,000	Value: 6.50				
1976	19,760,000	—	0.20	0.50	0.85	1.50
1976sm Proof	3,500	Value: 6.00				
1977	7,074,000	—	0.15	0.50	0.85	1.50
1977sm Proof	3,500	Value: 6.00				
1978	4,450,000	—	0.15	0.50	0.85	1.50
1978sm Proof	4,000	Value: 6.00				
1979	14,865,000	—	0.15	0.50	0.85	1.50
1979sm Proof	3,500	Value: 6.00				
1980	27,903,000	—	—	0.25	0.60	1.50
1980sm Proof	14,000	Value: 5.00				
1981	46,997,000	—	—	0.25	0.60	1.50
1982	25,234,000	—	—	0.25	0.60	1.50
1982sm Proof	20,000	Value: 4.00				
1983	6,424,000	—	—	0.25	0.60	1.50
1983sm Proof	15,000	Value: 4.00				
1984	9,290,000	—	—	0.25	0.60	1.50
1984sm Proof	15,000	Value: 4.00				
1985	148,424	—	—	—	0.60	1.50

Note: In sets only

KM# 4a 20 CENTS

6.5100 g., 0.9250 Silver .1936 oz. ASW, 23.6 mm. **Obv:** Value and date **Rev:** Swordfish

Date	Mintage	F	VF	XF	Unc	BU
1981sm Proof	30,000	Value: 12.50				

KM# 52 20 CENTS

5.6500 g., Copper-Nickel, 23.6 mm. **Obv:** Arms with supporters **Rev:** Powder-puff plant above value

Date	Mintage	F	VF	XF	Unc	BU
1985	25,980,000	—	—	0.20	0.50	0.70
1986	47,560,000	—	—	0.20	0.50	0.70
1987	80,010,000	—	—	0.20	0.50	0.70
1988	35,783,000	—	—	0.20	0.50	0.70
1989	51,890,000	—	—	0.20	0.50	0.70
1990	49,958,000	—	—	0.20	0.50	0.70
1991	60,000,000	—	—	0.20	0.50	0.70

KM# 52a 20 CENTS

5.2400 g., 0.9250 Silver .1559 oz. ASW, 23.6 mm. **Obv:** Arms with supporters **Rev:** Powder puff plant above value

Date	Mintage	F	VF	XF	Unc	BU
1985sm Proof	20,000	Value: 6.50				
1986sm Proof	15,000	Value: 6.50				
1987sm Proof	15,000	Value: 6.50				
1988 Proof	15,000	Value: 6.50				
1989 Proof	15,000	Value: 6.50				
1990 Proof	15,000	Value: 6.50				
1991 Proof	15,000	Value: 6.50				

KM# 101 20 CENTS

5.6500 g., Copper-Nickel, 23.6 mm. **Obv:** Arms with supporters **Rev:** Powder puff plant above value **Edge:** Reeded **Note:** Similar to KM#52 but motto ribbon on arms curves down at center.

Date	Mintage	F	VF	XF	Unc	BU
1992	—	—	—	—	0.60	0.85
1993	24,998,000	—	—	—	0.50	0.70
1994	—	—	—	—	0.60	0.85
1995	—	—	—	—	0.60	0.85
1996	45,000,000	—	—	—	0.50	0.70
1997	90,000,000	—	—	—	0.50	0.70
1998	—	—	—	—	0.60	0.85
1999	—	—	—	—	0.60	0.85
2000	—	—	—	—	0.60	0.85

KM# 101a 20 CENTS

5.2400 g., 0.9250 Silver .1936 oz. ASW, 23.6 mm. **Obv:** Arms with supporters **Rev:** Powder puff plant above value

Date	Mintage	F	VF	XF	Unc	BU
1992 Proof	15,000	Value: 6.50				
1993 Proof	15,000	Value: 6.50				
1994 Proof	10,000	Value: 6.50				
1995 Proof	10,000	Value: 6.50				
1996 Proof	17,000	Value: 6.50				
1997 Proof	20,000	Value: 6.50				
1998 Proof	—	Value: 6.50				
1999 Proof	—	Value: 6.50				
2000 Proof	17,000	Value: 6.50				

KM# 5 50 CENTS

9.3500 g., Copper-Nickel, 27.75 mm. **Obv:** Value and date **Rev:** Lion fish **Edge:** Reeded

Date	Mintage	F	VF	XF	Unc	BU
1967	11,000,000	—	0.30	0.65	2.00	2.50
1967 Proof	2,000	Value: 10.00				
1968	3,189,000	—	0.30	0.80	2.00	2.50
1968 Proof	5,000	Value: 8.50				
1969	2,008,000	—	0.30	1.00	2.00	2.50
1969 Proof	3,000	Value: 35.00				
1970	3,102,000	—	0.30	0.65	2.00	2.50
1971	3,933,000	—	0.30	0.65	1.80	2.00
1972	5,427,000	—	0.30	0.65	1.60	2.00
1972 Proof	749	Value: 90.00				
1973	4,474,000	—	0.30	0.60	1.10	1.50
1973 Proof	1,000	Value: 30.00				
1974	11,550,000	—	—	0.60	1.10	1.50
1974 Proof	1,500	Value: 22.50				
1975	1,432,000	0.25	0.60	2.00	3.00	4.00
1975 Proof	3,000	Value: 10.00				
1976	5,728,000	—	0.30	0.65	1.20	1.75
1976sm Proof	3,500	Value: 8.50				
1977	6,953,000	—	—	0.65	1.20	1.75
1977sm Proof	3,500	Value: 8.50				
1978	3,934,000	—	—	0.65	1.20	1.75
1978sm Proof	4,000	Value: 8.50				
1979	8,461,000	—	—	0.65	1.20	1.75
1979sm Proof	3,500	Value: 8.50				
1980	14,717,000	—	—	0.65	1.20	1.75
1980sm Proof	14,000	Value: 7.00				
1981	29,542,000	—	—	0.60	1.10	1.75
1982	13,756,000	—	—	0.60	1.10	1.75
1982sm Proof	20,000	Value: 5.00				
1983	4,482,000	—	—	0.85	1.50	1.85
1983sm Proof	15,000	Value: 5.00				
1984	3,658,000	—	—	0.85	1.50	1.85
1984sm Proof	15,000	Value: 5.00				
1985	148,424	—	—	—	1.50	1.85

Note: In sets only

KM# 5a 50 CENTS

10.8200 g., 0.9250 Silver .3218 oz. ASW, 27.75 mm. **Obv:** Value and date **Rev:** Lion fish

Date	Mintage	F	VF	XF	Unc	BU
1981sm Proof	30,000	Value: 15.00				

KM# 53.1 50 CENTS

Copper-Nickel **Obv:** Arms with supporters within designed circle **Rev:** Yellow Allamanda plant above value **Edge:** Reeded

Date	Mintage	F	VF	XF	Unc	BU
1985	14,960,000	—	—	0.60	1.10	1.35
1986	15,022,000	—	—	0.60	1.10	1.35
1987	30,000,000	—	—	0.60	1.10	1.35
1988	25,000,000	—	—	0.60	1.10	1.35

KM# 53.1a 50 CENTS

8.5600 g., 0.9250 Silver .2546 oz. ASW **Obv:** Arms with supporters within designed circle **Rev:** Yellow Allamanda plant above value

Date	Mintage	F	VF	XF	Unc	BU
1985sm Proof	20,000	Value: 12.00				
1986sm Proof	15,000	Value: 12.00				
1987sm Proof	15,000	Value: 12.00				
1988 Proof	15,000	Value: 12.00				

KM# 53.2 50 CENTS

Copper-Nickel **Obv:** Arms with supporters **Rev:** Yellow Allamanda plant above value **Edge Lettering:** REPUBLIC OF SINGAPORE (lion's head)

Date	Mintage	F	VF	XF	Unc	BU
1989	20,046,000	—	—	0.45	0.75	1.00
1990	19,740,000	—	—	0.45	0.75	1.00
1991	19,946,000	—	—	0.35	0.60	0.85

KM# 53.2a 50 CENTS

8.5600 g., 0.9250 Silver .2546 oz. ASW **Obv:** Arms with supporters **Rev:** Yellow Allamanda plant above value

Date	Mintage	F	VF	XF	Unc	BU
1989 Proof	15,000	Value: 12.00				
1990 Proof	—	Value: 12.00				
1991 Proof	—	Value: 12.00				

KM# 102 50 CENTS

Copper-Nickel **Obv:** Arms with supporters **Rev:** Yellow Allamanda plant above value **Edge Lettering:** REPUBLIC OF SINGAPORE (lion's head) **Note:** Similar to KM#53 but motto ribbon on arms curves down at center.

Date	Mintage	F	VF	XF	Unc	BU
1992	—	—	—	—	0.60	0.85
1993	4,878,000	—	—	—	0.60	0.85
1994	—	—	—	—	0.60	0.85
1995	49,440,000	—	—	—	0.60	0.85
1996	—	—	—	—	0.60	0.85
1997	30,000,000	—	—	—	0.60	0.85
1998	—	—	—	—	0.60	0.85
1999	—	—	—	—	0.60	0.85
2000	—	—	—	—	0.60	0.85

KM# 102a 50 CENTS

8.5600 g., 0.9250 Silver .2546 oz. ASW **Obv:** Arms with supporters **Rev:** Yellow Allamanda plant above value

Date	Mintage	F	VF	XF	Unc	BU
1992 Proof	15,000	Value: 12.00				
1993 Proof	15,000	Value: 12.00				
1994 Proof	10,000	Value: 12.00				
1995 Proof	10,000	Value: 12.00				
1996 Proof	17,000	Value: 12.00				
1997 Proof	20,000	Value: 12.00				
1998 Proof	—	Value: 12.00				
1999 Proof	—	Value: 12.00				
2000 Proof	17,000	Value: 12.00				

KM# 6 DOLLAR

16.8500 g., Copper-Nickel, 33.3 mm. **Obv:** Value and date **Rev:** Statue flanked by sprigs **Edge:** Reeded

Date	Mintage	F	VF	XF	Unc	BU
1967	3,000,000	—	0.65	1.50	3.00	—
1967 Proof	2,000	Value: 22.50				
1968	2,194,000	—	0.65	1.50	3.00	—
1968 Proof	5,000	Value: 20.00				
1969	1,871,000	—	0.65	1.75	3.25	—
1969 Proof	3,000	Value: 75.00				
1970	560,000	—	0.65	1.75	3.25	—
1971	900,000	—	0.65	1.75	3.25	—
1972	458,000	—	0.75	2.00	5.00	—
1972 Proof	749	Value: 150				
1973	341,000	—	0.75	2.00	3.50	—
1973 Proof	1,000	Value: 50.00				
1974	352,000	—	0.75	2.00	3.50	—
1974 Proof	1,500	Value: 40.00				
1975	430,000	—	0.75	2.00	3.50	—
1975 Proof	3,000	Value: 20.00				
1976	165,000	—	2.00	3.00	6.00	—
1976sm Proof	3,500	Value: 13.50				
1977	132,000	—	2.00	4.00	8.00	—
1977sm Proof	3,500	Value: 13.50				
1978	37,000	—	5.00	10.00	20.00	—
1978sm Proof	4,000	Value: 13.50				
1979	100,000	—	—	4.00	8.00	—
1979sm Proof	3,500	Value: 13.50				
1980	166,000	—	—	2.25	4.00	—
1980sm Proof	14,000	Value: 11.50				
1981	1,230,000	—	—	2.25	4.00	—
1982	1,080,000	—	—	2.25	4.00	—
1983	101,000	—	—	3.00	5.25	—
1984	170,000	—	—	3.00	4.50	—

Date	Mintage	F	VF	XF	Unc	BU
1985	148,424	—	—	0.65	1.25	—

Note: In sets only

KM# 6a DOLLAR

18.0500 g., 0.9250 Silver .5368 oz. ASW, 33.3 mm. **Obv:** Value and date **Rev:** Statue flanked by sprigs

Date	Mintage	F	VF	XF	Unc	BU
1975 Proof	3,000	Value: 140				
1976sm Proof	10,000	Value: 65.00				
1977sm Proof	10,000	Value: 65.00				
1978sm Proof	10,000	Value: 85.00				
1979sm Proof	8,000	Value: 75.00				
1980sm Proof	15,000	Value: 65.00				
1981sm Proof	30,000	Value: 12.50				
1982sm Proof	20,000	Value: 15.00				
1983sm Proof	15,000	Value: 12.50				
1984sm Proof	15,000	Value: 12.50				

KM# 28 DOLLAR

3.1100 g., 0.9990 Gold .1000 oz. AGW **Obv:** Arms with supporters **Rev:** Carp and lotus flower

Date	Mintage	F	VF	XF	Unc	BU
1983	20,000	—	—	—BV+15%		—
1984	10,000	—	—	—BV+15%		—

KM# 54 DOLLAR

Copper-Nickel **Obv:** Arms with supporters **Rev:** Periwinkle flower

Date	Mintage	F	VF	XF	Unc	BU
1985	—	—	—	—	1.75	2.50
1986	120,000	—	—	—	1.75	2.50

Note: In sets only

Date	Mintage	F	VF	XF	Unc	BU
1987	120,000	—	—	—	1.75	2.50

Note: In sets only

KM# 54a DOLLAR

9.9700 g., 0.9250 Silver .2965 oz. ASW **Obv:** Arms with supporters **Rev:** Periwinkle flower

Date	Mintage	F	VF	XF	Unc	BU
1985sm Proof	20,000	Value: 15.00				
1986sm Proof	15,000	Value: 15.00				

KM# 54b DOLLAR

Aluminum-Bronze, 22.3 mm. **Obv:** Arms with supporters **Rev:** Periwinkle flower **Edge Lettering:** REPUBLIC OF SINGAPORE (lion's head)

Date	Mintage	F	VF	XF	Unc	BU
1987	21,772,000	—	—	0.75	1.50	2.25
1988	59,332,000	—	—	0.75	1.50	2.25
1989	62,586,000	—	—	0.75	1.50	2.25
1990	37,608,000	—	—	0.75	1.50	2.25
1991	—	—	—	0.75	1.50	2.25

KM# 54c DOLLAR

8.4273 g., 0.9250 Silver .2507 oz. ASW **Obv:** Arms with supporters **Rev:** Periwinkle flower

Date	Mintage	F	VF	XF	Unc	BU
1987sm Proof	15,000	Value: 15.00				
1988 Proof	15,000	Value: 15.00				
1989 Proof	15,000	Value: 15.00				
1990 Proof	15,000	Value: 15.00				
1991 Proof	15,000	Value: 15.00				

KM# 103 DOLLAR

Aluminum-Bronze **Obv:** Arms with supporters **Rev:** Periwinkle flower **Note:** Similar to KM#54 but motto ribbon on arms curves down at center.

Date	Mintage	F	VF	XF	Unc	BU
1992	—	—	—	—	1.50	2.25
1993	—	—	—	—	1.50	2.25
1994	5,008,000	—	—	—	1.50	2.25
1995	65,000,000	—	—	—	1.50	2.25
1996	—	—	—	—	1.50	2.25
1997	129,856,000	—	—	—	1.50	2.25
1998	—	—	—	—	1.50	2.25
1999	—	—	—	—	1.50	2.25
2000	—	—	—	—	1.50	2.25

KM# 103a DOLLAR

8.4273 g., 0.9250 Silver .2507 oz. ASW **Obv:** Arms with supporters **Rev:** Periwinkle flower

Date	Mintage	F	VF	XF	Unc	BU
1992 Proof	15,000	Value: 15.00				
1993 Proof	15,000	Value: 15.00				
1994 Proof	10,000	Value: 15.00				
1995 Proof	10,000	Value: 15.00				
1996 Proof	17,000	Value: 15.00				
1997 Proof	20,000	Value: 15.00				
1998 Proof	—	Value: 15.00				
1999 Proof	—	Value: 15.00				
2000 Proof	17,000	Value: 15.00				

KM# 144 DOLLAR

1.5552 g., 0.9990 Gold .0400 oz. AGW **Subject:** Year of the Rat **Obv:** Arms with supporters **Rev:** Lion head right

Date	Mintage	F	VF	XF	Unc	BU
1996 Proof	2,688	—	—	—BV+25%		—

KM# 158 DOLLAR

1.5552 g., 0.9990 Gold .0400 oz. AGW **Subject:** Year of the Ox **Obv:** Arms with supporters **Rev:** Lion head **Note:** Similar to 20 DOllars, KM#161.

Date	Mintage	F	VF	XF	Unc	BU
1997 Proof	Est. 2,200	—	—	—BV+25%		—

KM# 29 2 DOLLARS

7.7750 g., 0.9990 Gold .2500 oz. AGW **Obv:** Arms with supporters **Rev:** Qilin **Designer:** Henry Steiner

Date	Mintage	F	VF	XF	Unc	BU
1983	20,000	—	—	—BV+12%		—
1984	10,000	—	—	—BV+12%		—

KM# 156 2 DOLLARS

20.0000 g., 0.9250 Silver .5948 oz. ASW **Series:** UNICEF **Obv:** Arms with supporters **Rev:** Children using computer below UNICEF logo within circle

Date	Mintage	F	VF	XF	Unc	BU
1997 Proof	25,000	Value: 60.00				

KM# 10 5 DOLLARS

25.0000 g., 0.5000 Silver .4019 oz. ASW **Subject:** 7th Southeast Asia Peninsular Games **Obv:** Arms with supporters **Rev:** Games logo above stadium

Date	Mintage	F	VF	XF	Unc	BU
1973	250,000	—	—	—	25.00	—
1973 Proof	5,000	Value: 160				

KM# 19 5 DOLLARS

Copper-Nickel, 33.5 mm. **Obv:** Arms with supporters **Rev:** Changi Airport **Edge:** Reeded

Date	Mintage	F	VF	XF	Unc	BU
1981	220,000	—	—	6.00	10.00	—

KM# 19a 5 DOLLARS

18.0500 g., 0.9250 Silver .5368 oz. ASW, 33.5 mm. **Obv:** Arms with supporters **Rev:** Changi airport

Date	Mintage	F	VF	XF	Unc	BU
1981sm Proof	20,000	Value: 75.00				

KM# 22 5 DOLLARS

Copper-Nickel, 33.5 mm. **Obv:** Arms with supporters **Rev:** Benjamin Shears Bridge

Date	Mintage	F	VF	XF	Unc	BU
1982	260,000	—	—	6.00	10.00	—

KM# 22a 5 DOLLARS

18.0500 g., 0.9250 Silver .5368 oz. ASW, 33.5 mm. **Obv:** Arms with supporters **Rev:** Benjamin Shears Bridge

Date	Mintage	F	VF	XF	Unc	BU
1982sm Proof	20,000	Value: 75.00				

KM# 25 5 DOLLARS

Copper-Nickel **Subject:** 12th SEA Games **Obv:** Arms with supporters **Rev:** Games logo above waves within circle, athletes around outer top half **Designer:** Lim Ching San

Date	Mintage	F	VF	XF	Unc	BU
1983	270,000	—	—	6.00	10.00	—

KM# 25a 5 DOLLARS

20.0000 g., 0.9250 Silver .5949 oz. ASW **Obv:** Arms with supporters **Rev:** Games logo above waves within circle, athletes around outer top half

Date	Mintage	F	VF	XF	Unc	BU
1983sm Proof	20,000	Value: 75.00				

KM# 30 5 DOLLARS

15.5500 g., 0.9990 Gold .5000 oz. AGW **Obv:** Arms with supporters **Rev:** Phoenix **Designer:** Henry Steiner

Date	Mintage	F	VF	XF	Unc	BU
1983	10,000	—	—	—	BV+9%	—
1984	10,000	—	—	—	BV+9%	—

KM# 32 5 DOLLARS
Copper-Nickel **Subject:** 25 Years of Nation - Building **Obv:** Arms with supporters **Rev:** Value above flowered sprigs

Date	Mintage	F	VF	XF	Unc	BU
ND(1984)	270,000	—	—	6.00	10.00	—

KM# 32a 5 DOLLARS
20.0000 g., 0.9250 Silver .5949 oz. ASW **Subject:** 25 Years of Nation - Building **Obv:** Arms with supporters **Rev:** Value above flower sprigs

Date	Mintage	F	VF	XF	Unc	BU
ND(1984)sm Proof	20,000	Value: 75.00				

KM# 48 5 DOLLARS
Copper-Nickel **Subject:** 25 Years of Public Housing **Obv:** Arms with supporters and legend **Rev:** Figures in front of buildings

Date	Mintage	F	VF	XF	Unc	BU
1985	117,000	—	—	6.00	10.00	—

KM# 48a 5 DOLLARS
20.0000 g., 0.9250 Silver .5949 oz. ASW **Obv:** Arms with supporters and legend **Rev:** Figures in front of buildings

Date	Mintage	F	VF	XF	Unc	BU
1985sm Proof	20,000	Value: 75.00				

KM# 68 5 DOLLARS
Copper-Nickel **Subject:** 100th Anniversary of National Museum **Obv:** Arms with supporters **Rev:** Museum building

Date	Mintage	F	VF	XF	Unc	BU
ND(1987)	70,000	—	—	—	10.00	—

KM# 68a 5 DOLLARS
20.0000 g., 0.9250 Silver .5949 oz. ASW **Subject:** 100th Anniversary of National Museum **Obv:** Arms with supporters **Rev:** Museum building

Date	Mintage	F	VF	XF	Unc	BU
ND(1987)sm Proof	25,000	Value: 75.00				

KM# 70 5 DOLLARS
Copper-Nickel **Subject:** 100th Anniversary of Singapore Fire Brigade **Obv:** Arms with supporters **Rev:** Pair of horses pulling wagon with equipment within circle

Date	Mintage	F	VF	XF	Unc	BU
ND(1988)	50,000	—	—	—	13.50	15.00

KM# 70a 5 DOLLARS
20.0000 g., 0.9250 Silver .5949 oz. ASW **Subject:** 100th Anniversary of Singapore Fire Brigade **Obv:** Arms with supporters **Rev:** Pair of horses pulling wagon with equipment within circle

Date	Mintage	F	VF	XF	Unc	BU
ND(1988)sm Proof	25,000	Value: 75.00				

KM# 74 5 DOLLARS
Copper-Nickel **Subject:** Rapid Transit System **Obv:** Arms with supporters **Rev:** Train in city

Date	Mintage	F	VF	XF	Unc	BU
1989	60,000	—	—	—	10.00	12.00

KM# 74a 5 DOLLARS
20.0000 g., 0.9250 Silver .5949 oz. ASW **Subject:** Rapid Transit System **Obv:** National arms **Rev:** Train in city

Date	Mintage	F	VF	XF	Unc	BU
1989 Proof	30,000	Value: 62.50				

KM# 77 5 DOLLARS
20.0000 g., 0.9250 Silver .5949 oz. ASW **Series:** Save the Children Fund **Obv:** Arms with supporters **Rev:** Children, kayak, palm tree and value

Date	Mintage	F	VF	XF	Unc	BU
1989 Proof	20,000	Value: 52.50				

KM# 79 5 DOLLARS
1.5550 g., 0.9990 Gold .0500 oz. AGW **Obv:** Arms with supporters **Rev:** Lion head

Date	Mintage	F	VF	XF	Unc	BU
1990	8,000	—	—	—BV+20%		—
1990 Proof	Est. 2,000	—	—	—BV+25%		—

KM# 94 5 DOLLARS
Copper-Aluminum-Nickel **Subject:** 25th Anniversary of Independence **Obv:** Arms with supporters **Rev:** City view from water

Date	Mintage	F	VF	XF	Unc	BU
1990	1,000,000	—	—	—	7.00	—

KM# 86 5 DOLLARS
Copper-Nickel **Subject:** Civil Defense **Obv:** Arms with supporters **Rev:** Working figures within circle

Date	Mintage	F	VF	XF	Unc	BU
1991	55,000	—	—	—	9.00	—
1991 Proof	10,000	Value: 50.00				

KM# 86a 5 DOLLARS
20.0000 g., 0.9250 Silver .4949 oz. ASW **Subject:** Civil Defense **Obv:** Arms with supporters **Rev:** Working figures within circle

Date	Mintage	F	VF	XF	Unc	BU
1991 Proof	20,000	Value: 50.00				

KM# 87 5 DOLLARS
1.5550 g., 0.9990 Gold .0500 oz. AGW **Subject:** Year of the Goat **Obv:** Arms with supporters **Rev:** Lion head

Date	Mintage	F	VF	XF	Unc	BU
1991	8,000	—	—	—BV+20%		—
1991 Proof	2,500	—	—	—BV+25%		—

KM# 104 5 DOLLARS
Bi-Metallic Aluminum-Bronze center in Copper-Nickel ring **Subject:** Vanda Miss Joaquim **Obv:** Arms with supporters **Rev:** Flower and value within beaded circle **Shape:** Scalloped

Date	Mintage	F	VF	XF	Unc	BU
1992	—	—	—	—	14.00	—
Note: In mint sets only						
1993	—	—	—	—	15.00	—
Note: In mint sets only						
1994	—	—	—	—	15.00	—
Note: In mint sets only						
1995	—	—	—	—	15.00	—
Note: In mint sets only						
1996	—	—	—	—	14.00	—
Note: In mint sets only						
1997	—	—	—	—	14.00	—
Note: In mint sets only						
1998	—	—	—	—	14.00	—
Note: In mint sets only						

KM# 104a 5 DOLLARS
20.0000 g., 0.9250 Silver .4949 oz. ASW **Subject:** Vanda Miss Joaquim **Obv:** Arms with supporters **Rev:** Flower and value within beaded circle

Date	Mintage	F	VF	XF	Unc	BU
1992 Proof	15,000	Value: 25.00				
1994 Proof	10,000	Value: 25.00				
1995 Proof	10,000	Value: 25.00				
1996 Proof	17,000	Value: 25.00				
1997 Proof	20,000	Value: 25.00				
1998 Proof	—	Value: 25.00				

KM# 108 5 DOLLARS
1.5550 g., 0.9990 Gold .0500 oz. AGW **Subject:** Year of the Monkey **Obv:** Arms with supporters

Date	Mintage	F	VF	XF	Unc	BU
1992	6,500	—	—	—BV+20%		—
1992 Proof	2,000	—	—	—BV+25%		—

KM# 115 5 DOLLARS
Copper-Nickel **Subject:** XVII Sea Games **Obv:** Arms with supporters **Rev:** Martial arts

Date	Mintage	F	VF	XF	Unc	BU
1993	23,000	—	—	—	9.00	—
1993 Proof	2,000	Value: 35.00				

KM# 115a 5 DOLLARS
20.0000 g., 0.9250 Silver .5949 oz. ASW **Subject:** XVII Sea Games **Obv:** Arms with supporters **Rev:** Martial arts

Date	Mintage	F	VF	XF	Unc	BU
1993 Proof	10,000	Value: 62.50				

KM# 117 5 DOLLARS
1.5550 g., 0.9990 Gold .0500 oz. AGW **Subject:** Year of the Rooster **Obv:** Arms with supporters **Rev:** Lion head

Date	Mintage	F	VF	XF	Unc	BU
1993	3,400	—	—	—	BV+20%	—
1993 Proof	Est. 1,500	—	—	—	BV+25%	—

Note: In proof sets only

KM# 124 5 DOLLARS
Copper-Nickel **Subject:** Year of the Family **Obv:** Arms with supporters **Rev:** Stylized family and value

Date	Mintage	F	VF	XF	Unc	BU
1994	20,000	—	—	—	14.00	—

KM# 124a 5 DOLLARS
20.0000 g., 0.9250 Silver .4949 oz. ASW **Subject:** Year of the Family **Obv:** Arms with supporters **Rev:** Stylized family and value

Date	Mintage	F	VF	XF	Unc	BU
1994 Proof	40,000	Value: 62.50				

KM# 128 5 DOLLARS
1.5550 g., 0.9990 Gold .0500 oz. AGW **Subject:** Year of the Dog **Obv:** Arms with supporters **Rev:** Lion head

Date	Mintage	F	VF	XF	Unc	BU
1994	—	—	—	—	BV+20%	—
1994 Proof	Est. 1,500	—	—	—	BV+25%	—

Note: In proof sets only

KM# 133 5 DOLLARS
1.5550 g., 0.9990 Gold .0500 oz. AGW **Subject:** Year of the Pig **Obv:** Arms with supporters

Date	Mintage	F	VF	XF	Unc	BU
1995	—	—	—	—	BV+20%	—
1995 Proof	1,500	—	—	—	BV+25%	—

KM# 138 5 DOLLARS
Bi-Metallic Aluminum-Bronze center in Copper-Nickel ring **Series:** 50th Anniversary - United Nations **Obv:** Arms with supporters within beaded circle **Rev:** UN logo within artistic design **Shape:** Scalloped

Date	Mintage	F	VF	XF	Unc	BU
1995	500,000	—	—	—	10.00	12.00

KM# 139 5 DOLLARS
20.0000 g., 0.9250 Silver .4949 oz. ASW **Series:** 50th Anniversary - United Nations **Obv:** Arms with supporters **Rev:** UN logo within artistic design

Date	Mintage	F	VF	XF	Unc	BU
1995 Proof	9,000	Value: 70.00				

KM# 150 5 DOLLARS
Copper-Nickel **Subject:** 30th Anniversary - Singapore's Independence **Obv:** Arms with supporters **Rev:** Globe on map

Date	Mintage	F	VF	XF	Unc	BU
1995	20,000	—	—	—	12.00	15.00

KM# 150a 5 DOLLARS
20.0000 g., 0.9250 Silver .4949 oz. ASW **Subject:** 30th Anniversary - Singapore's Independence **Obv:** Arms with supporters **Rev:** Globe on map

Date	Mintage	F	VF	XF	Unc	BU
1995 Proof	8,000	Value: 70.00				

KM# 149 5 DOLLARS
Copper-Nickel **Subject:** World Trade Organization Conference **Obv:** Arms with supporters **Rev:** Value within stylized lion head

Date	Mintage	F	VF	XF	Unc	BU
1996	23,800	—	—	—	8.00	—

KM# 149a 5 DOLLARS
20.0000 g., 0.9250 Silver .4949 oz. ASW **Subject:** World Trade Organization Conference **Obv:** Arms with supporters with mintmark **Rev:** Value within stylized lion head

Date	Mintage	F	VF	XF	Unc	BU
1996 Proof	16,800	Value: 62.50				

KM# 145 5 DOLLARS
3.1103 g., 0.9990 Gold .1000 oz. AGW **Subject:** Year of the Rat **Obv:** Arms with supporters **Rev:** Lion head

Date	Mintage	F	VF	XF	Unc	BU
1996 Proof	1,600	—	—	—	BV+20%	—

KM# 151 5 DOLLARS
Copper-Nickel **Subject:** 50th Anniversary - Singapore Airlines **Obv:** Arms with supporters with no mint mark **Rev:** Plane in front of numeral 50

Date	Mintage	F	VF	XF	Unc	BU
1997	20,800	—	—	—	17.00	—

KM# 151a 5 DOLLARS
20.0000 g., 0.9250 Silver .4949 oz. ASW **Subject:** 50th Anniversary - Singapore Airlines **Obv:** Arms with supporters with mint mark **Rev:** Plane in front of numeral 50

Date	Mintage	F	VF	XF	Unc	BU
1997 Proof	14,112	Value: 62.50				

KM# 157 5 DOLLARS
7.7760 g., 0.9999 Gold .2500 oz. AGW **Series:** UNICEF **Obv:** Arms with supporters **Rev:** Children using computer

Date	Mintage	F	VF	XF	Unc	BU
1997 Proof	10,000	Value: 350				

KM# 159 5 DOLLARS
3.1103 g., 0.9999 Gold .1000 oz. AGW **Subject:** Year of the Ox **Obv:** Arms with supporters **Rev:** Lion head

Date	Mintage	F	VF	XF	Unc	BU
1997 Proof	Est. 1,000	—	—	—	BV+20%	—

KM# 163 5 DOLLARS
Copper-Nickel **Subject:** Charity Work in Singapore **Obv:** Arms with supporters **Rev:** Two hands holding heart-shaped fruit

Date	Mintage	F	VF	XF	Unc	BU
1998	9,200	—	—	—	21.50	—

KM# 163a 5 DOLLARS
20.0000 g., 0.9250 Silver .5948 oz. ASW **Subject:** Charity Work in Singapore **Obv:** Arms with supporters **Rev:** Two hands holding heart-shaped fruit

Date	Mintage	F	VF	XF	Unc	BU
1998 Proof	12,000	Value: 95.00				

KM# 173 5 DOLLARS
20.0000 g., Copper-Nickel **Subject:** Parliament **Obv:** Arms with supporters **Rev:** Parliament building **Edge:** Reeded

Date	Mintage	F	VF	XF	Unc	BU
1999	10,000	—	—	—	20.00	—
1999 Proof	10,000	Value: 60.00				

KM# 104.1 5 DOLLARS
Copper-Nickel **Obv:** Arms with supporters above latent image **Rev:** Flower above value **Edge:** Plain

Date	Mintage	F	VF	XF	Unc	BU
1999sm	—	—	—	—	14.00	—

Note: In mint sets only

Date	Mintage	F	VF	XF	Unc	BU
2000sm	—	—	—	—	14.00	—

Note: In mint sets only

KM# 104.1a 5 DOLLARS
20.0000 g., 0.9250 Silver 0.5948 oz. ASW **Obv:** National arms above latent image **Rev:** Flower above value **Edge:** Plain

Date	Mintage	F	VF	XF	Unc	BU
1999sm Proof	—	Value: 25.00				
2000sm Proof	17,000	Value: 25.00				

KM# 173a 5 DOLLARS
20.0000 g., 0.9250 Silver .5948 oz. ASW **Obv:** Arms with supporters **Rev:** Parliament building

Date	Mintage	F	VF	XF	Unc	BU
1999 Proof	10,000	Value: 55.00				

KM# 171 5 DOLLARS
Bi-Metallic Aluminum-Bronze center in Copper-Nickel ring **Obv:** Arms with supporters above latent date within beaded circle **Rev:** Millennium design **Edge:** Scalloped

Date	Mintage	F	VF	XF	Unc	BU
2000	406,000	—	—	—	6.50	10.00

KM# 172 5 DOLLARS
31.1030 g., 0.9990 Gold 1.0000 oz. AGW **Subject:** Millennium **Obv:** Arms with supporters above latent date within beaded circle **Rev:** Millennium design **Edge:** Scalloped

Date	Mintage	F	VF	XF	Unc	BU
2000 Proof	3,000	Value: 1,000				

KM# 9.1 10 DOLLARS
31.1000 g., 0.9000 Silver .8999 oz. ASW **Obv:** Arms with supporters **Obv. Legend:** SINGAPORE inverted **Rev:** Hawk descending

Date	Mintage	F	VF	XF	Unc	BU
1972	80,000	—	—	—	30.00	35.00
1972 Proof	3,000	Value: 175				

KM# 9.2 10 DOLLARS

31.1000 g., 0.9000 Silver .8999 oz. ASW **Obv:** Arms with supporters **Rev:** Hawk descending

Date	Mintage	F	VF	XF	Unc	BU
1973	80,000	—	—	—	25.00	30.00
1973 Proof	5,000	Value: 170				

KM# 9.2a 10 DOLLARS

31.1000 g., 0.5000 Silver .5000 oz. ASW **Obv:** Arms with supporters **Rev:** Hawk descending

Date	Mintage	F	VF	XF	Unc	BU
1974	100,000	—	—	—	20.00	22.50
1974 Proof	6,000	Value: 120				

KM# 11 10 DOLLARS

31.1000 g., 0.5000 Silver .5000 oz. ASW **Subject:** 10th Anniversary of Independence **Obv:** Arms with supporters **Rev:** Value above ship **Designer:** William Lee

Date	Mintage	F	VF	XF	Unc	BU
ND(1975)	200,000	—	—	—	12.50	15.00
ND(1975) Proof	10,000	Value: 70.00				

KM# 15 10 DOLLARS

31.1000 g., 0.5000 Silver .5000 oz. ASW **Subject:** 10th Anniversary of Independence **Obv:** Arms with supporters **Rev:** Ship in port **Designer:** William Lee

Date	Mintage	F	VF	XF	Unc	BU
1976	150,000	—	—	—	12.50	15.00
1976sm Proof	10,000	Value: 70.00				
1977	150,000	—	—	—	12.50	15.00
1977sm Proof	10,000	Value: 70.00				

KM# 16 10 DOLLARS

31.1000 g., 0.5000 Silver .5000 oz. ASW **Subject:** ASEAN 10th Anniversary **Obv:** Arms with supporters **Rev:** Cluster of hands holding circled map

Date	Mintage	F	VF	XF	Unc	BU
ND(1977)	200,000	—	—	—	12.50	15.00
ND(1977)sm Proof	10,000	Value: 70.00				

KM# 17.1 10 DOLLARS

31.1000 g., 0.5000 Silver .5000 oz. ASW **Obv:** Arms with supporters **Rev:** Communications Satellites

Date	Mintage	F	VF	XF	Unc	BU
1978	167,000	—	—	—	12.50	15.00
1978sm Proof	10,000	Value: 70.00				
1979	168,000	—	—	—	12.50	15.00
1979sm Proof	9,000	Value: 70.00				

KM# 17.1a 10 DOLLARS

Nickel **Obv:** Arms with supporters **Rev:** Communications Satellites

Date	Mintage	F	VF	XF	Unc	BU
1980	120,000	—	—	—	13.50	16.50

KM# 17.2 10 DOLLARS

Nickel **Obv:** Arms with supporters **Rev:** Communications Satellites

Date	Mintage	F	VF	XF	Unc	BU
1980sm Proof	15,000	Value: 70.00				

KM# 20 10 DOLLARS

Nickel **Subject:** Year of the Rooster **Obv:** Arms with supporters **Rev:** Rooster within circle, value below, various animals border

Date	Mintage	F	VF	XF	Unc	BU
1981	180,000	—	—	—	68.00	70.00

KM# 20a 10 DOLLARS

31.1000 g., 0.5000 Silver .5000 oz. ASW **Obv:** Arms with supporters **Rev:** Rooster within circle, value below, various animals border

Date	Mintage	F	VF	XF	Unc	BU
1981sm Proof	20,000	Value: 220				

KM# 23 10 DOLLARS

Nickel **Subject:** Year of the Dog **Obv:** Arms with supporters **Rev:** Dog within circle, value below, various animals border

Date	Mintage	F	VF	XF	Unc	BU
1982	210,000	—	—	—	35.00	45.00

KM# 23a 10 DOLLARS

31.1000 g., 0.5000 Silver .5000 oz. ASW **Obv:** Arms with supporters **Rev:** Dog within circle, value below, various animals border

Date	Mintage	F	VF	XF	Unc	BU
1982sm Proof	20,000	Value: 140				

KM# 31 10 DOLLARS

31.1000 g., 0.9990 Gold 1.0000 oz. AGW **Subject:** Year of the Dragon **Obv:** Arms with supporters **Rev:** Dragon **Designer:** Henry Steiner

Date	Mintage	F	VF	XF	Unc	BU
1983	10,000	—	—	—	BV+10%	—
1984 Proof	10,000	—	—	—	BV+10%	—

KM# 26 10 DOLLARS

Nickel **Subject:** Year of the Pig **Obv:** Arms with supporters **Rev:** Pig within circle, value below, various animals border

Date	Mintage	F	VF	XF	Unc	BU
1983	307,000	—	—	—	20.00	30.00

KM# 26a 10 DOLLARS

31.1000 g., 0.5000 Silver .5000 oz. ASW **Obv:** Arms with supporters **Rev:** Pig within circle, value below, various animals border

Date	Mintage	F	VF	XF	Unc	BU
1983sm Proof	20,000	Value: 130				

KM# 33 10 DOLLARS

Nickel **Subject:** Year of the Rat **Obv:** Arms with supporters **Rev:** Rat within circle, value below, various animals border **Designer:** Soo Yeong

Date	Mintage	F	VF	XF	Unc	BU
1984	300,000	—	—	—	20.00	30.00

KM# 33a 10 DOLLARS

31.1000 g., 0.5000 Silver .5000 oz. ASW **Obv:** Arms with supporters **Rev:** Rat within circle, value below, various animals border

Date	Mintage	F	VF	XF	Unc	BU
1984sm Proof	20,000	Value: 100				

KM# 44 10 DOLLARS

Nickel **Subject:** Year of the Ox **Obv:** Arms with supporters **Rev:** Ox within circle, value below, various animals border

Date	Mintage	F	VF	XF	Unc	BU
1985	307,000	—	—	—	15.00	28.00

KM# 44a 10 DOLLARS

31.1000 g., 0.5000 Silver .5000 oz. ASW **Obv:** Arms with supporters **Rev:** Ox within circle, value below, various animals border

Date	Mintage	F	VF	XF	Unc	BU
1985sm Proof	20,000	Value: 110				

KM# 59 10 DOLLARS

Nickel **Subject:** Year of the Tiger **Obv:** Arms with supporters **Rev:** Tiger within circle, value below, various animals border

Date	Mintage	F	VF	XF	Unc	BU
1986	300,000	—	—	—	20.00	30.00

KM# 59a 10 DOLLARS

31.1000 g., 0.5000 Silver .5000 oz. ASW **Obv:** Arms with supporters **Rev:** Tiger within circle, value below, various animals border

Date	Mintage	F	VF	XF	Unc	BU
1986 Proof	20,000	Value: 100				

KM# 66 10 DOLLARS

Nickel **Subject:** Year of the Rabbit **Obv:** Arms with supporters **Rev:** Rabbit within circle, value below, various animals border

Date	Mintage	F	VF	XF	Unc	BU
1987	300,000	—	—	—	15.00	30.00

KM# 66a 10 DOLLARS

31.1000 g., 0.5000 Silver .5000 oz. ASW **Obv:** Arms with supporters **Rev:** Rabbit within circle, value below, various animals border

Date	Mintage	F	VF	XF	Unc	BU
1987sm Proof	25,000	Value: 70.00				

KM# 67 10 DOLLARS

Copper-Nickel **Subject:** Association of Southeast Asian Nations **Obv:** Arms with supporters above 1967-1987 **Rev:** ASEAN logo within legend above value

Date	Mintage	F	VF	XF	Unc	BU
1987	80,000	—	—	—	8.50	12.50

KM# 67a 10 DOLLARS

31.1030 g., 0.5000 Silver .5000 oz. ASW **Subject:** Association of Southeast Asian Nations **Obv:** Arms with supporters above 1967-1987 **Rev:** ASEAN logo within legend above value

Date	Mintage	F	VF	XF	Unc	BU
1987sm Proof	25,000	Value: 60.00				

KM# 69 10 DOLLARS

Nickel **Subject:** Year of the Dragon **Obv:** Arms with supporters **Rev:** Dragon within circle, value below, various animals border

Date	Mintage	F	VF	XF	Unc	BU
1988	300,000	—	—	—	25.00	30.00

KM# 69a 10 DOLLARS
31.1030 g., 0.5000 Silver .5000 oz. ASW **Subject:** Year of the Dragon **Obv:** Arms with supporters **Rev:** Dragon within circle, value below, various animals border

Date	Mintage	F	VF	XF	Unc	BU
1988 Proof	25,000	Value: 110				

KM# 71 10 DOLLARS
Nickel **Subject:** Year of the Snake **Obv:** Arms with supporters **Rev:** Snake within circle, value below, various animals border

Date	Mintage	F	VF	XF	Unc	BU
1989	250,000	—	—	—	20.00	25.00

KM# 71a 10 DOLLARS
31.1030 g., 0.9250 Silver .9250 oz. ASW **Subject:** Year of the Snake **Obv:** Arms with supporters **Rev:** Snake within circle, value below, various animals border

Date	Mintage	F	VF	XF	Unc	BU
1989 Proof	25,000	Value: 95.00				

KM# 75 10 DOLLARS
Nickel **Subject:** Year of the Horse **Obv:** Arms with supporters **Rev:** Horse within circle with value and assorted animal border

Date	Mintage	F	VF	XF	Unc	BU
1990	330,000	—	—	—	20.00	25.00

KM# 75a 10 DOLLARS
31.1030 g., 0.9250 Silver .9250 oz. ASW **Subject:** Year of the Horse **Obv:** Arms with supporters **Rev:** Horse within circle, value below, various animals border

Date	Mintage	F	VF	XF	Unc	BU
1990sm Proof	30,000	Value: 70.00				

KM# 80 10 DOLLARS
3.1103 g., 0.9990 Gold .1000 oz. AGW **Obv:** Arms with supporters **Rev:** Lion head

Date	Mintage	F	VF	XF	Unc	BU
1990	Est. 5,000	—	—	—BV+15%		—
1990 Proof	Est. 2,000	—	—	—BV+20%		—

KM# 95 10 DOLLARS
31.1030 g., 0.9250 Silver **Subject:** 25th Anniversary of Independence **Obv:** Arms with supporters **Rev:** Stylized numeral 25 above city view and dates with value at right

Date	Mintage	F	VF	XF	Unc	BU
1990 Proof	50,000	Value: 70.00				

KM# 84 10 DOLLARS
Nickel **Subject:** Year of the Goat **Obv:** Arms with supporters **Rev:** Goat within circle, value below, various animals border

Date	Mintage	F	VF	XF	Unc	BU
1991	300,000	—	—	—	15.00	25.00

KM# 84a 10 DOLLARS
31.1030 g., 0.9250 Silver .9250 oz. ASW **Subject:** Year of the Goat **Obv:** Arms with supporters **Rev:** Goat within circle, value below, various animals border

Date	Mintage	F	VF	XF	Unc	BU
1991sm Proof	30,000	Value: 70.00				

KM# 88 10 DOLLARS
3.1103 g., 0.9990 Gold .1000 oz. AGW **Subject:** Year of the Goat **Obv:** Arms with supporters **Rev:** Lion head with goat privy mark at lower left

Date	Mintage	F	VF	XF	Unc	BU
1991	5,500	—	—	—BV+15%		—
1991 Proof	2,500	—	—	—BV+20%		—

KM# 92 10 DOLLARS
Nickel **Subject:** Year of the Monkey **Obv:** Arms with supporters **Rev:** Monkey below value **Note:** Similar to 500 Dollars, KM#93.

Date	Mintage	F	VF	XF	Unc	BU
1992	300,000	—	—	—	20.00	22.50

KM# 92a 10 DOLLARS
31.1030 g., 0.9250 Silver .9250 oz. ASW **Obv:** Arms with supporters **Rev:** Monkey below value

Date	Mintage	F	VF	XF	Unc	BU
1992 Proof	30,000	Value: 75.00				

KM# 105 10 DOLLARS
0.9250 Silver .0550 oz. ASW **Subject:** 25th Anniversary - Board of Commissioners of Currency **Obv:** Arms with supporters **Rev:** Stylized dollar sign within circle

Date	Mintage	F	VF	XF	Unc	BU
1992 Proof	15,000	Value: 85.00				

KM# 109 10 DOLLARS
3.1103 g., 0.9990 Gold .1000 oz. AGW **Obv:** Arms with supporters **Rev:** Lion head **Note:** Year of the Monkey privy mark.

Date	Mintage	F	VF	XF	Unc	BU
1992	4,000	—	—	—BV+15%		—
1992 Proof	2,000	—	—	—BV+20%		—

KM# 118 10 DOLLARS
3.1103 g., 0.9990 Gold .1000 oz. AGW **Obv:** Arms with supporters **Rev:** Lion head with rooster privy mark at lower left **Note:** Lion/Year of the Rooster privy mark.

Date	Mintage	F	VF	XF	Unc	BU
1993	Est. 1,500	—	—	—BV+20%		—
Note: In proof sets only						
1993	3,100	—	—	—BV+15%		—

KM# 113 10 DOLLARS
Copper-Nickel **Subject:** Year of the Rooster **Obv:** Arms with supporters **Rev:** Stylized rooster

Date	Mintage	F	VF	XF	Unc	BU
1993 Prooflike	209,000	—	—	—	25.00	30.00

KM# 113a 10 DOLLARS
62.2070 g., 0.9990 Silver 2.0000 oz. ASW **Subject:** Year of the Rooster **Obv:** Arms with supporters **Rev:** Stylized rooster

Date	Mintage	F	VF	XF	Unc	BU
1993 Proof	40,000	Value: 85.00				

KM# 122 10 DOLLARS
Copper-Nickel **Subject:** Year of the Dog **Obv:** Arms with supporters **Rev:** Stylized dog within designs

Date	Mintage	F	VF	XF	Unc	BU
1994 Prooflike	215,000	—	—	—	28.00	30.00

KM# 122a 10 DOLLARS
62.2070 g., 0.9990 Silver 2.0000 oz. ASW **Subject:** Year of the Dog **Obv:** Arms with supporters **Rev:** Stylized dog within designs

Date	Mintage	F	VF	XF	Unc	BU
1994 Proof	35,000	Value: 85.00				

KM# 129 10 DOLLARS
3.1103 g., 0.9990 Gold .1000 oz. AGW **Obv:** Arms with supporters **Rev:** Lion head with dog privy mark at lower left **Note:** Lion/Year of the Dog privy mark.

Date	Mintage	F	VF	XF	Unc	BU
1994 Proof	Est. 1,500	—	—	—BV+20%		—
Note: In proof sets only						
1994	—	—	—	—BV+15%		—

KM# 125 10 DOLLARS
Copper-Nickel **Subject:** Year of the Pig **Obv:** Arms with supporters **Rev:** Stylized pig

Date	Mintage	F	VF	XF	Unc	BU
1995 Prooflike	210,000	—	—	—	17.50	20.00

KM# 125a 10 DOLLARS
62.2070 g., 0.9990 Silver 2.0000 oz. ASW **Subject:** Year of the Pig **Obv:** Arms with supporters **Rev:** Stylized pig

Date	Mintage	F	VF	XF	Unc	BU
1995 Proof	8,000	Value: 90.00				

KM# 134 10 DOLLARS
3.1103 g., 0.9990 Gold .1000 oz. AGW **Obv:** Arms with supporters **Rev:** Lion head with pig privy mark at lower left **Note:** Lion/Year of the Pig privy mark.

Date	Mintage	F	VF	XF	Unc	BU
1995	—	—	—	—BV+15%		—
1995 Proof	—	BV+20%				

KM# 141 10 DOLLARS
Copper-Nickel **Subject:** Year of the Rat **Obv:** Arms with supporters **Rev:** Stylized rat within designs

Date	Mintage	F	VF	XF	Unc	BU
1996 Prooflike	245,000	—	—	—	16.00	20.00

KM# 141a 10 DOLLARS
62.2070 g., 0.9990 Silver 2.0000 oz. ASW **Subject:** Year of the Rat **Obv:** Arms with supporters **Rev:** Stylized rat within designs

Date	Mintage	F	VF	XF	Unc	BU
1996 Proof	35,000	Value: 90.00				

KM# 146 10 DOLLARS
7.7759 g., 0.9990 Gold .2500 oz. AGW **Obv:** Arms with supporters **Note:** Year of the Rat privy mark.

Date	Mintage	F	VF	XF	Unc	BU
1996 Proof	2,688	—	—	—BV+10%		—

KM# 153 10 DOLLARS
Copper-Nickel **Subject:** Year of the Ox **Obv:** Arms with supporters **Rev:** Stylized ox within designs **Note:** Similar to KM#154.

Date	Mintage	F	VF	XF	Unc	BU
1997 Prooflike	251,000	—	—	—	15.00	18.00

KM# 160 10 DOLLARS
7.7759 g., 0.9999 Gold .2500 oz. AGW **Obv:** Arms with supporters **Rev:** Lion head with ox privy marks at lower left **Note:** Lion/Year of the Ox privy mark. Similar to KM#154.

Date	Mintage	F	VF	XF	Unc	BU
1997 Proof	Est. 2,200	—	—	—BV+10%		—

KM# 154 10 DOLLARS
62.2070 g., 0.9990 Silver 2.0000 oz. ASW **Subject:** Year of the Ox **Obv:** Arms with supporters **Rev:** Stylized Ox within designs

Date	Mintage	F	VF	XF	Unc	BU
1997 Proof	38,000	Value: 95.00				

KM# 165 10 DOLLARS
62.2070 g., 0.9990 Silver 1.9980 oz. ASW **Subject:** Year of the Tiger **Obv:** Arms with supporters **Rev:** Stylized tiger within designs

Date	Mintage	F	VF	XF	Unc	BU
1998 Proof	38,000	Value: 90.00				

KM# 164 10 DOLLARS
Copper-Nickel **Subject:** Year of the Tiger **Obv:** Arms with supporters **Rev:** Stylized tiger **Note:** Similar to KM#165.

Date	Mintage	F	VF	XF	Unc	BU
1998 Prooflike	220,000	—	—	—	16.00	20.00

KM# 167 10 DOLLARS
28.0000 g., Copper-Nickel **Subject:** Year of the Rabbit **Obv:** Arms with supporters **Rev:** Stylized rabbit within designs **Edge:** Reeded

Date	Mintage	F	VF	XF	Unc	BU
1999	—	—	—	—	15.00	20.00

KM# 168 10 DOLLARS
62.2070 g., 0.9990 Silver 1.9980 oz. ASW **Subject:** Year of the Rabbit **Obv:** Arms with supporters **Rev:** Rabbit

Date	Mintage	F	VF	XF	Unc	BU
1999 Proof	38,000	Value: 100				

KM# 174 10 DOLLARS
Copper-Nickel **Subject:** Year of the Dragon **Obv:** Arms with supporters **Rev:** Dragon **Edge:** Reeded

Date	Mintage	F	VF	XF	Unc	BU
2000 Prooflike	225,000	—	—	—	20.00	25.00

KM# 175 10 DOLLARS
62.2060 g., 0.9990 Silver 1.9980 oz. ASW, 40.7 mm. **Subject:** Year of the Dragon **Obv:** Arms with supporters **Rev:** Dragon **Edge:** Reeded **Note:** Piefort thickness.

Date	Mintage	F	VF	XF	Unc	BU
2000 Proof	38,000	Value: 100				

KM# 147 20 DOLLARS
15.5517 g., 0.9990 Gold .5000 oz. AGW **Obv:** Arms with supporters **Rev:** Lion head with rat privy mark at lower left **Note:** Lion/Year of the Rat privy mark.

Date	Mintage	F	VF	XF	Unc	BU
1996 Proof	2,688	—	—	—BV+15%		—

KM# 161 20 DOLLARS
15.5517 g., 0.9999 Gold :5000 oz. AGW **Obv:** Arms with supporters **Rev:** Lion head with ox privy mark at lower left **Note:** Lion/Year of the Ox privy mark.

Date	Mintage	F	VF	XF	Unc	BU
1997 Proof	Est. 2,200	—	—	—BV+15%		—

KM# 81 25 DOLLARS
7.7757 g., 0.9990 Gold .2500 oz. AGW **Obv:** Arms with supporters **Rev:** Lion head

Date	Mintage	F	VF	XF	Unc	BU
1990	Est. 5,000	—	—	—BV+12%		—
1990 Proof	Est. 2,000	—	—	—BV+15%		—

KM# 89 25 DOLLARS
7.7757 g., 0.9990 Gold .2500 oz. AGW **Obv:** Arms with supporters **Rev:** Lion head with goat privy mark at lower left **Note:** Year of the Goat privy mark.

Date	Mintage	F	VF	XF	Unc	BU
1991	5,500	—	—	—BV+12%		—
1991 Proof	2,500	—	—	—BV+15%		—

KM# 110 25 DOLLARS
7.7757 g., 0.9990 Gold .2500 oz. AGW **Obv:** Arms with supporters **Rev:** Lion head with monkey privy mark at lower left **Note:** Year of the Monkey privy mark.

Date	Mintage	F	VF	XF	Unc	BU
1992	4,000	—	—	—BV+12%		—
1992 Proof	2,000	—	—	—BV+15%		—

KM# 119 25 DOLLARS
7.7757 g., 0.9990 Gold .2500 oz. AGW **Obv:** Arms with supporters **Rev:** Lion head with rooster privy mark at lower left **Note:** Year of the Rooster privy mark.

Date	Mintage	F	VF	XF	Unc	BU
1993	3,000	—	—	—BV+12%		—
1993	Est. 1,500	—	—	—BV+15%		—

Note: In proof sets only

KM# 130 25 DOLLARS
7.7757 g., 0.9990 Gold .2500 oz. AGW **Obv:** Arms with supporters **Rev:** Lion head with dog privy mark at lower left **Note:** Year of the Dog privy mark.

Date	Mintage	F	VF	XF	Unc	BU
1994	—	—	—	—BV+12%		—
1994	Est. 1,500	—	—	—BV+15%		—

Note: In proof sets only

KM# 135 25 DOLLARS
7.7757 g., 0.9990 Gold .2500 oz. AGW **Obv:** Arms with supporters **Rev:** Lion head with pig privy mark at lower left **Note:** Year of the Pig privy mark.

Date	Mintage	F	VF	XF	Unc	BU
1995	—	—	—	—BV+12%		—
1995 Proof	1,500	—	—	—BV+15%		—

KM# 18 50 DOLLARS
31.1000 g., 0.5000 Silver .5000 oz. ASW **Subject:** International Financial Center **Obv:** Arms with supporters **Rev:** Stylized letters and dollar sign

Date	Mintage	F	VF	XF	Unc	BU
1980	25,000	—	—	—	45.00	—
1980sm Proof	15,000	Value: 90.00				
1981	50,000	—	—	—	45.00	—
1981sm Proof	20,000	Value: 90.00				

KM# 78 50 DOLLARS
10.0000 g., 0.9160 Gold .2945 oz. AGW **Series:** Save the Children Fund **Obv:** Arms with supporters **Rev:** Children, kayak, palm tree and value

Date	Mintage	F	VF	XF	Unc	BU
1989 Proof	3,000	Value: 420				

KM# 82 50 DOLLARS
15.5500 g., 0.9990 Gold .5000 oz. AGW **Obv:** Arms with supporters **Rev:** Lion head

Date	Mintage	F	VF	XF	Unc	BU
1990	Est. 5,000	—	—	—	BV+10%	—
1990 Proof	Est. 2,000	—	—	—	BV+12%	—

KM# 90 50 DOLLARS
15.5500 g., 0.9990 Gold .5000 oz. AGW **Obv:** Arms with supporters **Rev:** Lion head with goat privy mark at lower left **Note:** Year of the Goat privy mark.

Date	Mintage	F	VF	XF	Unc	BU
1991	5,500	—	—	—	BV+10%	—
1991 Proof	2,500	—	—	—	BV+12%	—

KM# 111 50 DOLLARS
15.5500 g., 0.9990 Gold .5000 oz. AGW **Obv:** Arms with supporters **Rev:** Lion head with monkey privy mark at lower left **Note:** Year of the Monkey privy mark.

Date	Mintage	F	VF	XF	Unc	BU
1992	4,000	—	—	—	BV+10%	—
1992 Proof	2,000	—	—	—	BV+12%	—

KM# 120 50 DOLLARS
15.5500 g., 0.9990 Gold .5000 oz. AGW **Obv:** Arms with supporters **Rev:** Lion head with rooster privy mark at lower left **Note:** Year of the Rooster privy mark.

Date	Mintage	F	VF	XF	Unc	BU
1993	2,600	—	—	—	BV+10%	—
1993	Est. 1,500	—	—	—	BV+12%	—

Note: In proof sets only

KM# 131 50 DOLLARS
15.5500 g., 0.9990 Gold .5000 oz. AGW **Obv:** Arms with supporters **Rev:** Lion head with dog privy mark at lower left **Note:** Year of the Dog privy mark.

Date	Mintage	F	VF	XF	Unc	BU
1994	—	—	—	—	BV+10%	—
1994	Est. 1,500	—	—	—	BV+12%	—

Note: In proof sets only

KM# 136 50 DOLLARS
15.5500 g., 0.9990 Gold .5000 oz. AGW **Obv:** Arms with supporters **Rev:** Lion head with pig privy marks at lower left **Note:** Year of the Pig privy mark.

Date	Mintage	F	VF	XF	Unc	BU
1995	—	—	—	—	BV+10%	—
1995 Proof	1,500	—	—	—	BV+12%	—

KM# 140 50 DOLLARS
31.1035 g., 0.9999 Gold 1.0000 oz. AGW **Series:** 50th Anniversary - United Nations **Obv:** Arms with supporters **Rev:** UN logo within design

Date	Mintage	F	VF	XF	Unc	BU
1995 Proof	1,000	Value: 950				

KM# 148 50 DOLLARS
31.1035 g., 0.9999 Gold 1.0000 oz. AGW **Obv:** Arms with supporters **Rev:** Lion head with rat privy mark at lower left **Note:** Lion/Year of the Rat privy mark.

Date	Mintage	F	VF	XF	Unc	BU
1996 Proof	2,688	—	—	—	BV+9%	—

KM# 152 50 DOLLARS
31.1035 g., 0.9999 Gold 1.0000 oz. AGW **Subject:** 50th Anniversary - Singapore Airlines **Obv:** Arms with supporters **Rev:** Airplane in front of numeral 50

Date	Mintage	F	VF	XF	Unc	BU
1997 Proof	1,800	Value: 1,100				

KM# 162 50 DOLLARS
31.1035 g., 0.9999 Gold 1.0000 oz. AGW **Obv:** Arms with supporters **Rev:** Lion head with ox privy mark at lower left **Note:** Lion/Year of the Ox privy mark.

Date	Mintage	F	VF	XF	Unc	BU
1997 Proof	Est. 2,200	—	—	—	BV+9%	—

KM# 170 50 DOLLARS
31.1035 g., 0.9999 Gold 1.0000 oz. AGW **Subject:** Parliament **Obv:** Arms with supporters **Rev:** Parliament buildings

Date	Mintage	F	VF	XF	Unc	BU
1999 Proof	1,000	Value: 1,480				

KM# 12 100 DOLLARS
6.9119 g., 0.9000 Gold .2000 oz. AGW **Subject:** 10th Anniversary of Independence **Obv:** Arms with supporters **Rev:** Building **Designer:** Ng Ah Kuan

Date	Mintage	F	VF	XF	Unc	BU
1975	100,000	—	—	—	120	130
1975 Proof	3,000	Value: 330				

KM# 83 100 DOLLARS
31.1000 g., 0.9990 Gold 1.0000 oz. AGW **Obv:** Arms with supporters **Rev:** Lion head

Date	Mintage	F	VF	XF	Unc	BU
1990	Est. 5,000	—	—	—	BV+7%	—
1990 Proof	Est. 2,000	—	—	—	BV+9%	—

KM# 91 100 DOLLARS
31.1000 g., 0.9990 Gold 1.0000 oz. AGW **Obv:** Arms with supporters **Rev:** Lion head with goat privy marks at lower left **Note:** Year of the Goat privy mark.

Date	Mintage	F	VF	XF	Unc	BU
1991	13,000	—	—	—	BV+7%	—
1991 Proof	2,500	—	—	—	BV+9%	—

KM# 112 100 DOLLARS
31.1000 g., 0.9990 Gold 1.0000 oz. AGW **Obv:** Arms with supporters **Rev:** Lion head with monkey privy marks at lower left **Note:** Year of the Monkey privy mark.

Date	Mintage	F	VF	XF	Unc	BU
1992	4,000	—	—	—	BV+7%	—
1992 Proof	2,000	—	—	—	BV+9%	—

KM# 106 100 DOLLARS
31.1000 g., 0.9990 Gold 1.0000 oz. AGW **Subject:** 25th Anniversary - Board of Commissioners of Currency **Obv:** Arms with supporters **Rev:** Stylized dollar sign and value within circle

Date	Mintage	F	VF	XF	Unc	BU
1992 Proof	800	Value: 860				

KM# 121 100 DOLLARS
31.1000 g., 0.9990 Gold 1.0000 oz. AGW **Obv:** Arms with supporters **Rev:** Lion head with rooster privy mark at lower left **Note:** Year of the Rooster privy mark.

Date	Mintage	F	VF	XF	Unc	BU
1993	3,100	—	—	—	BV+7%	—
1993 Proof	Est. 1,500	—	—	—	BV+9%	—

Note: In proof sets only

KM# 132 100 DOLLARS
31.1000 g., 0.9990 Gold 1.0000 oz. AGW **Obv:** Arms with supporters **Rev:** Lion head with dog privy mark at lower left **Note:** Year of the Dog privy mark.

Date	Mintage	F	VF	XF	Unc	BU
1994	—	—	—	—	BV+7%	—
1994 Proof	Est. 1,500	—	—	—	BV+9%	—

Note: In proof sets only

KM# 137 100 DOLLARS
31.1000 g., 0.9990 Gold 1.0000 oz. AGW **Obv:** Arms with supporters **Rev:** Lion head with pig privy marks at lower left **Note:** Year of the Pig privy mark.

Date	Mintage	F	VF	XF	Unc	BU
1995	—	—	—	—	BV+7%	—
1995 Proof	1,500	—	—	—	BV+9%	—

KM# 7 150 DOLLARS
24.8830 g., 0.9160 Gold .7360 oz. AGW **Subject:** 150th Anniversary - Founding of Singapore **Obv:** Arms with supporters **Rev:** Lighthouse and value

Date	Mintage	F	VF	XF	Unc	BU
ND(1969)	198,000	—	—	—	700	750
ND(1969) Proof	500	Value: 2,400				

KM# 107 200 DOLLARS
31.1035 g., 0.9990 Platinum 1.0000 oz. APW **Subject:** 25th Anniversary - Board of Commissioners of Currency **Obv:** Arms with supporters **Rev:** Stylized dollar sign and value within circle **Note:** Similar to KM#106.

Date	Mintage	F	VF	XF	Unc	BU
1992 Proof	300	Value: 1,380				

KM# 13 250 DOLLARS
17.2797 g., 0.9000 Gold .5000 oz. AGW **Subject:** 10th Anniversary of Independence **Obv:** Arms with supporters **Rev:** Four grasped hands below value **Designer:** Tan Huay Peng

Date	Mintage	F	VF	XF	Unc	BU
ND(1975)	30,000	—	—	—	370	390
ND(1975) Proof	2,000	Value: 750				

KM# 96 250 DOLLARS
31.1040 g., 0.9990 Gold 1.0000 oz. AGW **Subject:** 25th Anniversary of Independence **Obv:** Arms with supporters **Rev:** Stylized numeral 25 above city view with value at lower right

Date	Mintage	F	VF	XF	Unc	BU
1990 Proof	6,000	Value: 900				

KM# 114 250 DOLLARS
31.1035 g., 0.9990 Gold 1.0000 oz. AGW **Subject:** Year of the Rooster **Obv:** Arms with supporters **Rev:** Stylized rooster

Date	Mintage	F	VF	XF	Unc	BU
1993 Proof	10,000	Value: 1,000				

KM# 123 250 DOLLARS
31.1035 g., 0.9990 Gold 1.0000 oz. AGW **Subject:** Year of the Dog **Obv:** Arms with supporters **Rev:** Stylized dog within designs

Date	Mintage	F	VF	XF	Unc	BU
1994 Proof	7,500	Value: 900				

KM# 127 250 DOLLARS
31.1035 g., 0.9990 Gold 1.0000 oz. AGW **Subject:** Year of the Pig **Obv:** Arms with supporters **Rev:** Stylized pig within design

Date	Mintage	F	VF	XF	Unc	BU
1995 Proof	7,500	Value: 900				

KM# 143 250 DOLLARS
31.1035 g., 0.9990 Gold 1.0000 oz. AGW **Subject:** Year of the Rat **Obv:** Arms with supporters **Rev:** Stylized rat within designs

Date	Mintage	F	VF	XF	Unc	BU
1996 Proof	7,500	Value: 900				

KM# 155 250 DOLLARS
31.1035 g., 0.9990 Gold 1.0000 oz. AGW **Subject:** Year of the Ox **Obv:** Arms with supporters **Rev:** Stylized ox within designs

Date	Mintage	F	VF	XF	Unc	BU
1997 Proof	7,800	Value: 800				

KM# 166 250 DOLLARS
31.1035 g., 0.9990 Gold 1.0000 oz. AGW **Subject:** Year of the Tiger **Obv:** Arms with supporters **Rev:** Stylized tiger

Date	Mintage	F	VF	XF	Unc	BU
1998 Proof	7,600	Value: 900				

KM# 169 250 DOLLARS
31.1035 g., 0.9990 Gold 1.0000 oz. AGW **Obv:** Arms with supporters **Rev:** Stylized rabbit within designs **Edge:** Reeded

Date	Mintage	F	VF	XF	Unc	BU
1999 Proof	7,600	Value: 900				

KM# 176 250 DOLLARS
31.1035 g., 0.9990 Gold 1.0000 oz. AGW, 32.12 mm. **Subject:** Year of the Dragon **Obv:** Arms with supporters **Rev:** Stylized dragon **Edge:** Reeded

Date	Mintage	F	VF	XF	Unc	BU
2000 Proof	7,600	Value: 1,000				

KM# 14 500 DOLLARS
34.5594 g., 0.9000 Gold 1.0000 oz. AGW **Subject:** 10th Anniversary of Independence **Obv:** Arms with supporters **Rev:** Lion head **Designer:** Tan Huay Peng

Date	Mintage	F	VF	XF	Unc	BU
ND(1975)	30,000	—	—	—	900	950
ND(1975) Proof	2,000	Value: 2,000				

KM# 21 500 DOLLARS
16.9650 g., 0.9160 Gold .5000 oz. AGW **Subject:** Year of the Rooster **Obv:** Arms with supporters **Rev:** Rooster

Date	Mintage	F	VF	XF	Unc	BU
1981sm Proof	12,000	Value: 900				

KM# 24 500 DOLLARS
16.9650 g., 0.9160 Gold .5000 oz. AGW **Subject:** Year of the Dog **Obv:** Arms with supporters **Rev:** Dog

Date	Mintage	F	VF	XF	Unc	BU
1982sm Proof	5,500	Value: 850				

KM# 27 500 DOLLARS
16.9650 g., 0.9160 Gold .5000 oz. AGW **Subject:** Year of the Pig **Obv:** Arms with supporters **Rev:** Pig

Date	Mintage	F	VF	XF	Unc	BU
1983sm Proof	5,000	Value: 850				

KM# 34 500 DOLLARS
16.9650 g., 0.9160 Gold .5000 oz. AGW **Subject:** Year of the Rat **Obv:** Arms with supporters **Rev:** Rat

Date	Mintage	F	VF	XF	Unc	BU
1984sm Proof	4,000	Value: 800				

KM# 45 500 DOLLARS
16.9650 g., 0.9160 Gold .5000 oz. AGW **Subject:** Year of the Ox **Obv:** Arms with supporters **Rev:** Ox

Date	Mintage	F	VF	XF	Unc	BU
1985sm Proof	4,000	Value: 700				

KM# 60 500 DOLLARS
16.9650 g., 0.9160 Gold .5000 oz. AGW **Subject:** Year of the Tiger **Obv:** Arms with supporters **Rev:** Tiger

Date	Mintage	F	VF	XF	Unc	BU
1986sm Proof	3,000	Value: 1,200				

KM# 64 500 DOLLARS
16.9650 g., 0.9160 Gold .5000 oz. AGW **Subject:** Year of the Rabbit **Obv:** Arms with supporters **Rev:** Rabbit

Date	Mintage	F	VF	XF	Unc	BU
1987sm Proof	2,400	Value: 1,950				

KM# 73 500 DOLLARS
16.9650 g., 0.9160 Gold .5000 oz. AGW **Subject:** Year of the Dragon **Obv:** Arms with supporters **Rev:** Dragon

Date	Mintage	F	VF	XF	Unc	BU
1988sm Proof	4,000	Value: 970				

KM# 72 500 DOLLARS
16.9650 g., 0.9160 Gold .5000 oz. AGW **Subject:** Year of the Snake **Obv:** Arms with supporters **Rev:** Snake

Date	Mintage	F	VF	XF	Unc	BU
1989sm Proof	2,500	Value: 1,500				

KM# 76 500 DOLLARS
16.9650 g., 0.9160 Gold .5000 oz. AGW **Subject:** Year of the Horse **Obv:** Arms with supporters **Rev:** Horse

Date	Mintage	F	VF	XF	Unc	BU
1990sm Proof	5,000	Value: 750				

KM# 97 500 DOLLARS
31.1040 g., 0.9990 Platinum 1.0000 oz. APW **Subject:** 25th Anniversary of Independence **Obv:** Arms with supporters **Rev:** Numeral 25 and value above city view

Date	Mintage	F	VF	XF	Unc	BU
1990 Proof	2,000	Value: 1,150				

KM# 85 500 DOLLARS
16.9650 g., 0.9160 Gold .5000 oz. AGW **Subject:** Year of the Goat **Obv:** Arms with supporters **Rev:** Goat

Date	Mintage	F	VF	XF	Unc	BU
1991sm Proof	5,000	Value: 700				

KM# 93 500 DOLLARS
16.9650 g., 0.9160 Gold .5000 oz. AGW **Subject:** Year of the Monkey **Obv:** Arms with supporters **Rev:** Monkey

Date	Mintage	F	VF	XF	Unc	BU
1992sm Proof	5,000	Value: 700				

MINT SETS

KM#	Date	Mintage	Identification	Issue Price	Mkt Val
MS1	1967 (6)	8,000	KM#1-6	1.50	45.00
MS2	1968 (6)	16,000	KM#1-6	1.50	40.00
MS3	1969 (6)	14,000	KM#1-6	1.50	45.00
MS4	1970 (6)	13,000	KM#1-6	1.50	80.00
MS5	1970 (6)	27,000	KM#1-6 Issued only in package of 3 sets plus KM#11, each set in plastic wallet for Expo'97 Osaka Japan	1.75	80.00
MS7	1972 (6)	13,000	KM#1-6	3.00	95.00
MS8	1973 (6)	15,000	KM#1-6	2.00	20.00
MS9	1974 (6)	20,000	KM#1-6	2.00	40.00
MS10	1975 (6)	30,000	KM#1-6	12.00	20.00
MS11	1975 (3)	30,000	KM#12-14	—	1,100
MS12	1976 (6)	35,000	KM#1-6	2.00	13.00
MS13	1977 (6)	40,000	KM#1a, 2-6	2.00	13.00
MS14	1978 (6)	55,000	KM#1a, 2-6	—	25.00
MS15	1979 (6)	65,000	KM#1a, 2-6	—	12.00
MS16	1980 (6)	70,000	kM#1a, 2-6	—	10.00
MS17	1981 (6)	110,000	KM#1a, 2-6	5.00	7.50
MS18	1982 (6)	160,000	KM#1a, 2-6	5.00	7.50
MS19	1983 (6)	40,000	KM#1a, 2-6 with Medallion, I.A.P.N.	—	9.00
MS20	1983 (6)	150,000	KM#1a, 2-6	5.00	8.00
MS21	1984 (6)	160,000	KM#1a, 2-6	3.75	7.50
MS22	1985 (6)	148,424	KM#1a, 2-6	—	22.00
MS23	1986 (6)	120,000	KM#49-52, 53.1, 54	—	14.50
MS24	1987 (6)	120,000	KM#49-52, 53.1, 54	—	15.00
MS25	1988 (6)	120,000	KM#49-52, 53.1, 54b	—	7.50
MS26	1989 (6)	100,000	KM#49-52, 53.2, 54b	—	7.50
MS27	1990 (6)	100,000	KM#49-52, 53.2, 54b	—	7.50
MS28	1990 (5)	5,000	KM#79-83	—	900
MS29	1991 (7)	70,000	KM#49b, 50-52, 53.2, 54b (1991), 94 (1990)	—	12.00
MS30	1992 (7)	55,000	KM#98-104	—	12.00
MS31	1993 (7)	—	KM#98-104	—	12.00
MS32	1994 (7)	100,000	KM#98-104	—	12.00
MS33	1995 (7)	124,000	KM#98-104	—	12.00
MS34	1996 (7)	180,000	KM#98-104	—	12.00
MS35	1997 (7)	—	KM#98-104	—	12.00
MS36	1998 (7)	—	KM#98-104	—	12.00
MS37	1999 (7)	—	KM#98-104.1	—	12.00
MS38	2000 (7)	—	KM#98-104.1	—	12.00

PROOF SETS

KM#	Date	Mintage	Identification	Issue Price	Mkt Val
PS1	1967 (6)	2,000	KM#1-6	25.00	85.00
PS2	1968 (6)	5,000	KM#1-6	25.00	65.00
PS3	1969 (6)	3,000	KM#1-6	25.00	280
PS4	1972 (6)	749	KM#1-6	25.00	475
PS5	1973 (6)	1,000	KM#1-6	32.00	200
PS6	1974 (6)	1,500	KM#1-6	34.00	170
PS7	1975 (6)	3,000	KM#1-6	35.00	60.00
PS8	1975 (3)	2,000	KM#12-14	—	1,600
PS9	1976 (6)	3,500	KM#1-6	37.00	60.00
PS10	1977 (6)	3,500	kM#1-6	—	60.00
PS11	1978 (6)	4,000	KM#1-6	—	60.00
PS12	1979 (7)	3,500	KM#1-6, 17.1	—	120
PS13	1980 (7)	14,000	KM#1-6, 17.2	64.00	60.00
PS14	1981 (6)	30,000	KM#1b-2b, 3a-6a, .925 Silver	82.00	80.00
PS15	1982 (6)	20,000	KM#1-5, 6a	52.00	55.00
PS16	1983 (6)	15,000	KM#1-5, 6a	52.00	50.00
PS17	1984 (6)	15,000	KM#1-5, 6a	52.00	50.00
PS18	1985 (6)	20,000	KM#49a-52a, 53.1a, 54a	40.00	50.00
PS19	1986 (6)	15,000	KM#49a-52a, 53.1a, 54a	—	48.00
PS20	1987 (6)	15,000	KM#49a-52a, 53.1a, 54c	42.00	48.00
PS21	1987 (5)	1,000	KM-MB28-MB32	1,400	1,650
PS22	1988 (6)	15,000	KM#49a-52a, 53.1a, 54c	—	45.00
PS23	1988 (5)	500	KM-MB41-45	—	1,650
PS24	1989 (6)	15,000	KM#49a-52a, 53.2a, 54c	—	60.00
PS25	1989 (5)	200	KM-MB51-55	—	1,975
PS26	1990 (6)	15,000	KM#49a-52a, 53.2a, 54c	—	55.00
PS27	1990 (5)	2,000	KM#79-83	—	850
PSA28	1990 (3)	1,000	KM#95-97	—	1,700
PS28	1991 (7)	15,000	KM#49a-52a, 53.2a, 54c, 86a	—	65.00
PS29	1991 (5)	2,500	KM#87-91	—	850
PS30	1991 (2)	5,000	KM#86, 86a	—	65.00
PS31	1992 (7)	15,000	KM#98a-104a	—	80.00
PS32	1992 (5)	2,000	KM#108-112 Ingot	—	850
PS33	1992 (3)	200	KM#105-107	—	1,600
PS34	1993 (7)	15,000	KM#98a-104a	—	80.00
PS35	1993 (5)	1,500	KM#117-121 Ingot	—	875
PS36	1993 (2)	2,000	KM#115, 115a	—	85.00
PS37	1994 (7)	10,000	KM#98a-104a	—	80.00
PS38	1994 (5)	1,500	KM#128-132 Ingot	—	875
PS39	1995 (7)	10,000	KM#98a-104a	—	75.00
PS41	1995 (5)	1,500	KM#133-137 Ingot	1,718	875
PS42	1995 (3)	2,689	KM#138-140	1,052	750
PS43	1996 (7)	17,000	KM#98a-104a Ingot	—	75.00
PS44	1996 (5)	2,688	KM#144-148 Ingot	—	900
PS45	1996 (2)	2,800	KM#149, 149a	66.00	70.00
PS46	1997 (7)	20,000	KM#98a-104a Ingot	90.00	120
PS47	1997 (2)	3,800	KM#151, 151a Ingot	—	65.00
PS48	1997 (3)	888	KM#151, 151a, 152 Ingot	—	625
PS49	1997 (5)	2,200	KM#158-162	—	1,000
PS50	1998 (3)	1,998	KM#164-166 Ingot	—	675
PS51	1998 (7)	—	KM#98a-104a	—	100
PS52	1999 (7)	—	KM#98a-104.1a	—	100
PS53	2000 (7)	17,000	KM#98a-104.1a	74.25	100
PS54	2000 (3)	2,000	KM#174-176 Plus Ingot	—	685

The Republic of Slovakia has an area of 18,923 sq. mi. (49,035 sq. km.) and a population of 4.9 million. Capital: Bratislava. Textiles, steel, and wood products are exported.

The Slovak lands were united with the Czechs and the Czechoslovak State came into existence on Oct. 28, 1918 upon the dissolution of Austro-Hungarian Empire at the close of World War I. In March 1939, the German-influenced Slovak government proclaimed Slovakia independent and Germany incorporated the Czech lands into the Third Reich as the "Protectorate of Bohemia and Moravia". A Czechoslovak government-in-exile was setup in London in July 1940. The Soviet and USA forces liberated the area by May, 1945. At the close of World War II, Communist influence increased steadily while pressure for liberalization culminated in the overthrow of the Stalinist leader Antonin Novotn'y and his associates in 1968.The Communist Party then introduced far reaching reforms which received warnings from Moscow, followed by occupation by Warsaw Pact forces resulting in stationing of Soviet forces. Mass civilian demonstrations for reform began in Nov.1989 and the Federal Assembly abolished the Communist Party's sole right to govern. New governments followed on Dec. 3 and Dec. 10 and the Czech and Slovak Federal Republic was formed. The Movement for Democratic Slovakia was apparent in the June 1992 elections with the Slovak National Council adopting a declaration of sovereignty. Later, a constitution for an independent Slovakia with the Federal Assembly voting for the dissolution of the Republic came into effect on Dec. 31, 1992, and two new republics came into being on Jan. 1, 1993.

MINT MARK

Kremnica Mint

REPUBLIC
1939-45
STANDARD COINAGE

100 Halierov = 1 Koruna Slovenska (Ks)

KM# 8 5 HALIEROV
0.9400 g., Zinc, 14 mm. **Obv:** Double cross within shield **Obv. Designer:** Anton Ham **Rev:** Large value **Rev. Designer:** S. Grosch **Edge:** Plain

Date	Mintage	F	VF	XF	Unc	BU
1942	1,000,000	3.00	5.00	15.00	30.00	—

KM# 1 10 HALIEROV
1.6600 g., Bronze, 16 mm. **Obv:** Double cross within shield above sprigs **Rev:** Castle and large value **Rev. Designer:** A. Peter

Date	Mintage	F	VF	XF	Unc	BU
1939	15,000,000	1.50	2.00	4.00	8.00	—
1942	7,000,000	3.00	2.00	8.00	16.00	—

KM# 4 20 HALIEROV
2.5000 g., Bronze, 18 mm. **Obv:** Double cross on shield within flower sprig **Obv. Designer:** A. Ham **Rev:** Nitra Castle, large value **Rev. Designer:** A. Peter **Edge:** Plain

Date	Mintage	F	VF	XF	Unc	BU
1940	10,972,000	1.25	2.00	3.00	6.00	—
1941	4,028,000	2.50	6.00	10.00	30.00	—
1942	6,474,000	10.00	15.00	30.00	60.00	—

KM# 4a 20 HALIEROV

0.6500 g., Aluminum, 18 mm. **Obv:** Double cross on shield within flower sprigs **Obv. Designer:** A. Ham **Rev:** Nitra castle and large value **Rev. Designer:** A. Peter **Edge:** Plain **Note:** Varieties exist.

Date	Mintage	F	VF	XF	Unc	BU
1942	Inc. above	1.00	1.50	4.00	9.00	—
1943	15,000,000	1.00	1.50	4.00	9.00	—

KM# 5 50 HALIEROV

3.3300 g., Copper-Nickel, 20 mm. **Obv:** Double cross on shield and date **Rev:** Value above plow **Edge:** Plain **Designer:** Anton Ham, Andrej Peter, G. Angyal

Date	Mintage	F	VF	XF	Unc	BU
1940	Inc. above	30.00	40.00	50.00	100	—
1941	8,000,000	1.00	2.00	3.00	6.00	—

KM# 5a 50 HALIEROV

1.0000 g., Aluminum, 20 mm. **Obv:** Double cross on shield and date **Rev:** Value above plow **Edge:** Milled **Designer:** Anton ham, Andrej Peter, G. Angyal

Date	Mintage	F	VF	XF	Unc	BU
1943	4,400,000	1.00	1.50	2.50	5.00	—
1944	2,621,000	5.00	10.00	15.00	30.00	—

KM# 6 KORUNA

5.0000 g., Copper-Nickel, 22 mm. **Obv:** Double cross on shield within circle above date **Rev:** Value within oat sprigs and stalks **Edge:** Milled **Designer:** Gejza Angyal, Anton Ham, Andrej Peter

Date	Mintage	F	VF	XF	Unc	BU
1940	2,350,000	0.75	1.25	2.25	6.00	—
1941	11,650,000	0.50	1.00	2.00	5.00	—
1942	6,000,000	0.50	1.00	2.00	5.00	—
Note: Varieties exist of 1942, in the numeral 4						
1944	884,000	10.00	15.00	30.00	60.00	—
1945	3,321,000	0.75	1.25	2.25	6.00	—

KM# 2 5 KORUN

Nickel, 27 mm. **Obv:** Double cross on shield within wheat sprigs below value with date below **Rev:** Head left **Edge:** Milled **Designer:** Anton Ham, Andrej Peter **Note:** Two varieties exist in the letter A in NAROD.

Date	Mintage	F	VF	XF	Unc	BU
1939	5,101,000	1.50	2.00	3.50	10.00	—
Note: Approximately 2,000,000 pieces were melted down by the Czechoslovak National Bank in 1947						

KM# 9.1 10 KORUN

7.0000 g., 0.5000 Silver .1125 oz. ASW, 29 mm. **Obv:** Double cross on shield within radiant circle **Rev:** Standing figures facing divide value **Edge:** Plain **Designer:** Ladislav Majersky **Note:** Variety 1 - Cross atop church held by left figure.

Date	Mintage	F	VF	XF	Unc	BU
1944	1,381,000	2.00	4.00	5.00	12.00	—

KM# 9.2 10 KORUN

7.0000 g., 0.5000 Silver .1125 oz. ASW **Obv:** Double cross on shield within radiant circle **Rev:** Standing figure facing divides value **Designer:** Ladislav Majersky **Note:** Variety 2 - Without cross atop church held by left figure.

Date	Mintage	F	VF	XF	Unc	BU
1944	Inc. above	2.50	5.00	7.00	15.00	—

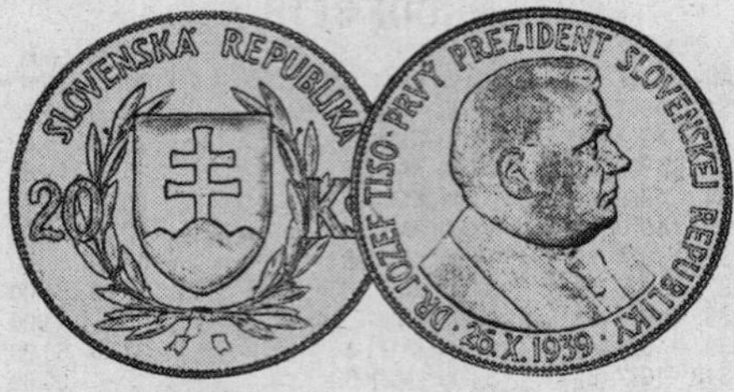

KM# 3 20 KORUN

15.0000 g., 0.5000 Silver .2411 oz. ASW, 31 mm. **Obv:** Double cross on shield within wreath flanked by value **Rev:** Head right **Edge:** Milled **Designer:** Anton Ham, Andrej Peter

Date	Mintage	F	VF	XF	Unc	BU
1939	200,000	5.00	10.00	20.00	40.00	—

KM# 7.1 20 KORUN

15.0000 g., 0.5000 Silver .2411 oz. ASW, 31 mm. **Subject:** St. Kyrill and St. Methodius **Obv:** Double cross on shield within sprigs **Rev:** Standing figures flanked by value **Edge:** Milled **Designer:** Frano Stefunko

Date	Mintage	F	VF	XF	Unc	BU
1941	2,500,000	4.00	5.00	7.00	16.00	—

KM# 7.2 20 KORUN

15.0000 g., 0.5000 Silver .2411 oz. ASW **Subject:** St. Kyrill and St. Methodius **Obv:** Double cross on shield within sprigs **Rev:** Variety 2 - Double bar cross **Designer:** Frano Stefunko

Date	Mintage	F	VF	XF	Unc	BU
1941	Inc. above	4.50	6.50	20.00	50.00	—

KM# 10 50 KORUN

16.5000 g., 0.7000 Silver .3713 oz. ASW, 34 mm. **Subject:** 5th Anniversary of Independence **Obv:** Double cross on shield within wreath flanked by value **Rev:** Head right **Edge:** Milled **Designer:** Anton Ham, Andrej Peter

Date	Mintage	F	VF	XF	Unc	BU
1944	2,000,000	6.00	7.00	9.00	18.00	—

REPUBLIC

STANDARD COINAGE

100 Halierov = 1 Slovak Koruna (Sk)

KM# 17 10 HALIEROV

0.7000 g., Aluminum, 17 mm. **Obv:** Double cross on shield above inscription **Rev:** Church steeple **Edge:** Plain **Designer:** Drahomir Zobek

Date	Mintage	F	VF	XF	Unc	BU
1993	80,320,000	—	—	—	0.35	—
Note: Varieties of cross on state emblem						
1994	65,000,000	—	—	—	0.35	—
1995	12,000	—	—	—	1.00	—
Note: In sets only						
1996	31,540,000	—	—	—	0.35	—
1997	10,000,000	—	—	—	0.35	—
1998	30,260,000	—	—	—	0.35	—
1999	31,420,000	—	—	—	0.35	—
2000	30,600,000	—	—	—	0.35	—
2000 Proof	900	Value: 5.00				

KM# 18 20 HALIEROV

0.9500 g., Aluminum, 19.5 mm. **Obv:** Double cross on shield above inscription **Rev:** Mountain peak and value **Edge:** Reeded **Designer:** Drahomir Zobek

Date	Mintage	F	VF	XF	Unc	BU
1993	80,830,000	—	—	—	0.45	—
1994	59,990,000	—	—	—	0.45	—
1995	12,000	—	—	—	1.00	—
Note: In sets only						
1996	19,800,000	—	—	—	0.45	—
1997	10,000,000	—	—	—	0.45	—
1998	21,000,000	—	—	—	0.45	—
1999	15,710,000	—	—	—	0.45	—
2000	31,120,000	—	—	—	0.45	—
2000 Proof	900	Value: 5.00				

KM# 15 50 HALIEROV

1.2000 g., Aluminum, 22 mm. **Obv:** Double cross on shield above inscription **Rev:** Watch tower and value **Edge:** Plain **Designer:** Drahomir Zobek

Date	Mintage	F	VF	XF	Unc	BU
1993	54,160,000	—	—	—	0.55	—
1994	19,900	—	—	—	1.50	—
Note: In sets only						
1995	12,000	—	—	—	1.50	—
Note: In sets only						

KM# 35 50 HALIEROV

2.8000 g., Copper Plated Steel, 18.7 mm. **Obv:** Double cross on shield above inscription **Rev:** Watch tower and value **Edge:** Milled and plain **Designer:** Drahomir Zobek

Date	Mintage	F	VF	XF	Unc	BU
1996	39,640,000	—	—	—	0.60	—
1997	11,500	—	—	—	1.50	—
Note: In sets only						
1998	15,000,000	—	—	—	0.60	—
1999	11,500	—	—	—	1.50	—
Note: In sets only						
2000	20,212,000	—	—	—	0.60	—
2000 Proof	900	Value: 5.00				

KM# 12 KORUNA

3.8000 g., Bronze Clad Steel, 21 mm. **Subject:** 15th Century of Madonna and Child **Obv:** Double cross on shield above inscription **Rev:** Madonna holding child and value **Edge:** Milled **Designer:** Drahomir Zobek

Date	Mintage	F	VF	XF	Unc	BU
1993	80,263,000	—	—	—	0.75	—
1994	30,000,000	—	—	—	0.75	—
1995	21,000,000	—	—	—	0.75	—
1996	15,000	—	—	—	1.50	—
Note: In sets only						
1997	15,000	—	—	—	1.50	—
Note: In sets only						
1998	12,000	—	—	—	1.50	—
Note: In sets only						
1999	11,500	—	—	—	1.50	—
Note: In sets only						
2000	12,500	—	—	—	1.50	—
Note: In sets only						
2000 Proof	900	Value: 10.00				

KM# 13 2 KORUNA

4.4000 g., Nickel Clad Steel, 21.5 mm. **Obv:** Double cross on shield above inscription **Rev:** Venus statue and value **Designer:** Drahomir Zobek

Date	Mintage	F	VF	XF	Unc	BU
1993	51,982,000	—	—	—	0.85	—
Note: Varieties of artist's initials						
1994	19,062,000	—	—	—	0.85	—
1995	20,998,000	—	—	—	0.85	—
1996	15,000	—	—	—	2.00	—
Note: In sets only						
1997	15,000	—	—	—	2.00	—
Note: In sets only						
1998	12,000	—	—	—	2.00	—
Note: In sets only						
1999	11,500	—	—	—	2.00	—
Note: In sets only						
2000	12,500	—	—	—	2.00	—
Note: In sets only						
2000 Proof	900	Value: 10.00				

KM# 14 5 KORUNA

5.4000 g., Nickel Clad Steel, 24.75 mm. **Obv:** Double cross on shield above inscription **Rev:** Celtic coin of BIATEC at upper left of value **Edge:** Milled **Designer:** Drahomir Zobek

Date	Mintage	F	VF	XF	Unc	BU
1993	48,914,000	—	—	—	1.25	—
Note: Varieties in artist's initials						
1994	19,556,000	—	—	—	1.25	—
1995	10,400,000	—	—	—	1.25	—
1996	15,000	—	—	—	2.00	—
Note: In sets only						
1997	15,000	—	—	—	2.00	—
Note: In sets only						
1998	11,500	—	—	—	2.00	—
Note: In sets only						
1999	12,500	—	—	—	2.00	—
Note: In sets only						
2000	12,500	—	—	—	2.00	—
Note: In sets only						
2000 Proof	900	Value: 20.00				

KM# 11.1 10 KORUNA

6.6000 g., Brass, 26.5 mm. **Obv:** Double cross on shield above inscription **Rev:** Bronze cross and value **Designer:** Drahomir Zobek

Date	Mintage	F	VF	XF	Unc	BU
1993	41,169,000	—	—	—	2.50	—
1994	25,000,000	—	—	—	2.50	—
1995	32,204,000	—	—	—	2.50	—
1996	15,000	—	—	—	4.00	—
Note: In sets only						
1997	15,000	—	—	—	4.00	—
Note: In sets only						
1998	12,000	—	—	—	4.00	—
Note: In sets only						
1999	11,500	—	—	—	4.00	—
Note: In sets only						
2000	12,500	—	—	—	4.00	—
Note: In sets only						
2000 Proof	900	Value: 35.00				

KM# 11.2 10 KORUNA

8.5000 g., 0.7500 Silver .2527 oz. ASW, 26.5 mm. **Obv:** Double cross on shield abov inscription **Rev:** Bronze cross and value **Designer:** Drahomir Zobek

Date	Mintage	F	VF	XF	Unc	BU
1993 Proof	1,000	Value: 350				
Note: These coins are numbered and punched with an R						

KM# 16 100 KORUN

13.0000 g., 0.7500 Silver .3135 oz. ASW, 29 mm. **Subject:** National Independence **Obv:** Double cross on shield above inscription and value **Rev:** Three doves below double cross within clouds **Edge:** Milled **Designer:** Stefan Novotny **Note:** 7,450 uncirculated pieces melted in 2002.

Date	Mintage	F	VF	XF	Unc	BU
1993MK	65,000	—	—	—	9.00	—
1993MK Proof	5,000	Value: 18.00				

KM# 20 200 KORUN

20.0000 g., 0.7500 Silver .4823 oz. ASW, 34 mm. **Subject:** 200th Anniversary - Birth of Jan Kollar **Obv:** Double cross on shield above inscription, value at left **Rev:** Windswept head facing, name and dates at bottom **Edge Lettering:** SLAVME SLAVNE SLAVU SLAVOV SLAVNYCH **Designer:** Vojtech Pohanka **Note:** 10,065 uncirculated pieces melted in 2002.

Date	Mintage	F	VF	XF	Unc	BU
1993MK	35,000	—	—	—	15.00	—
1993MK Proof	2,000	Value: 35.00				

KM# 19 200 KORUN

20.0000 g., 0.7500 Silver .4823 oz. ASW, 34 mm. **Subject:** 150th Anniversary of Slovak Language **Obv:** Double cross on shield above value **Rev:** Three heads facing above dates **Edge:** Plain with ornament **Designer:** Miroslav Rona **Note:** 5,682 uncirculated pieces melted in 2002.

Date	Mintage	F	VF	XF	Unc	BU
1993MK	35,000	—	—	—	15.00	—
1993MK Proof	2,000	Value: 30.00				

KM# 23 200 KORUN

20.0000 g., 0.7500 Silver .4823 oz. ASW, 34 mm. **Subject:** 50th Anniversary - D-Day **Obv:** Double cross on shield within stylized leaves flanked by dates and value **Rev:** Crowned emblem within v-shaped design divides dates and symbol **Edge Lettering:** SLOVACI PROTI FASISMU **Designer:** Imrich Svitana **Note:** 10,150 uncirculated pieces melted in 2002.

Date	Mintage	F	VF	XF	Unc	BU
1994	35,000	—	—	—	20.00	—
1994 Proof	2,600	Value: 100				

KM# 21 200 KORUN

20.0000 g., 0.7500 Silver .4823 oz. ASW, 34 mm. **Subject:** 100th Anniversary - Olympic Committee **Obv:** Olympic rings and double cross on shield within design, dates at upper left **Rev:** Value, hockey player and snow flake design below **Edge:** Snowflakes **Designer:** Miroslav Ronai **Note:** 15,775 uncirculated pieces melted in 2002.

Date	Mintage	F	VF	XF	Unc	BU
1994	45,000	—	—	—	15.00	—
1994 Proof	3,000	Value: 32.50				

KM# 22 200 KORUN

20.0000 g., 0.7500 Silver .4823 oz. ASW, 34 mm. **Subject:** 100th Anniversary - Birth of Poet and Painter Janko Alexy **Obv:** Small double cross on shield below value and head of young girl in winter **Rev:** Head 3/4 right **Edge:** Plain with ornament **Designer:** Stefan Novotny **Note:** 12,400 uncirculated pieces melted in 2002.

Date	Mintage	F	VF	XF	Unc	BU
1994MK	31,500	—	—	—	15.00	—
1994MK Proof	2,500	Value: 35.00				

KM# 26 200 KORUN

20.0000 g., 0.7500 Silver .4823 oz. ASW, 34 mm. **Subject:** European Environmental Protection **Obv:** Double cross on shield above woodpecker feeding young **Rev:** Two storks and a flying swallow at right of flowers above value **Edge Lettering:** ENCY 1995 (3 fish) **Designer:** Miroslav Ronai **Note:** 11,100 uncirculated pieces melted in 2002.

Date	Mintage	F	VF	XF	Unc	BU
1995	28,000	—	—	—	25.00	—
1995 Proof	2,000	Value: 40.00				

KM# 25 200 KORUN

20.0000 g., 0.7500 Silver .4823 oz. ASW, 34 mm. **Subject:** 100th Anniversary - Birth of Mikulas Galanda **Obv:** Double cross on shield to left of mother with child **Rev:** Head facing 3/4 right, dates diagonally at right, value at lower right **Edge Lettering:** MIKULAS GALANDA - MALIAR A GRAFIK **Designer:** Vojtech Pohanka **Note:** 10,200 uncirculated pieces melted in 2002.

Date	Mintage	F	VF	XF	Unc	BU
1995	23,500	—	—	—	15.00	—
1995 Proof	1,500	Value: 30.00				

KM# 27 200 KORUN
20.0000 g., 0.7500 Silver .4823 oz. ASW, 34 mm. **Subject:** Centennial of Bratislava Electric Tram **Obv:** Double cross on shield and date in center of inscription and value as a triangular design **Rev:** Two tram cars within triangular design **Edge Lettering:** HLAVNE NADRAZIE TEREZIANSKA STVRT **Designer:** Patrik Kovacovsky **Note:** 10,500 uncirculated pieces melted in 2002.

Date	Mintage	F	VF	XF	Unc	BU
1995	27,500	—	—	—	15.00	—
1995 Proof	1,600	Value: 40.00				

KM# 24 200 KORUN
20.0000 g., 0.7500 Silver .4823 oz. ASW, 34 mm. **Subject:** 200th Anniversary - Birth of Pavol Jozef Safarik **Obv:** Double cross on shield in center of inscription **Rev:** Head facing within inscription, value at bottom, dates diagonally at left **Edge Lettering:** ZAKLADATEL VEDECKEJ SLAVISTIKY **Designer:** Patrik Kovacovsky **Note:** 8,700 uncirculated pieces melted in 2002.

Date	Mintage	F	VF	XF	Unc	BU
1995MK	23,500	—	—	—	15.00	—
1995MK Proof	1,500	Value: 37.50				

KM# 34 200 KORUN
20.0000 g., 0.7500 Silver .4823 oz. ASW, 34 mm. **Subject:** 200th Anniversary - Birth of Moric Benovsky **Obv:** Small double cross on shield at left of ship **Rev:** Bust facing **Edge Lettering:** IN ADVERSIS ET PROSPERIS **Designer:** Miroslav Ronai **Note:** 5,050 uncirculated pieces melted in 2002.

Date	Mintage	F	VF	XF	Unc	BU
1996	21,400	—	—	—	15.00	—
1996 Proof	2,000	Value: 40.00				

KM# 33 200 KORUN
20.0000 g., 0.7500 Silver .4823 oz. ASW, 34 mm. **Subject:** Centennial - Mountain Railway to Strba Lake **Obv:** Double cross on shield above value, inscription and date **Rev:** Train and passenger car above dates and inscription **Edge Lettering:** VYSOKE TATRY VYSOKE TATRY **Designer:** Vojtech Pohanka **Note:** 5,850 uncirculated pieces melted in 2002.

Date	Mintage	F	VF	XF	Unc	BU
1996	22,000	—	—	—	15.00	—
1996 Proof	1,500	Value: 32.50				

KM# 31 200 KORUN
20.0000 g., 0.7500 Silver .4823 oz. ASW, 34 mm. **Subject:** Olympic Games **Obv:** Double cross on shield and Olympic rings within square, date and inscription below **Rev:** Greek column within oval track, value below **Edge Lettering:** V DUCHU ODKAZU PIERRA DE COUBERTINA **Designer:** Imrich Svitana **Note:** 7,300 uncirculated pieces melted in 2002.

Date	Mintage	F	VF	XF	Unc	BU
1996MK	23,000	—	—	—	16.50	—
1996MK Proof	1,700	Value: 35.00				

KM# 30 200 KORUN
20.0000 g., 0.7500 Silver .4823 oz. ASW, 34 mm. **Subject:** 200th Anniversary - Birth of Samuel Jurkovic **Obv:** Double cross on shield to left of design within lined square **Rev:** Half of head facing at left of lined square design **Edge Lettering:** V SLUZBACH NARODA **Designer:** Patrik Kovacovsky **Note:** 10,700 uncirculated pieces melted in 2002.

Date	Mintage	F	VF	XF	Unc	BU
1996MK	26,000	—	—	—	15.00	—
1996MK Proof	1,600	Value: 37.50				

KM# 32 200 KORUN
20.0000 g., 0.7500 Silver .4823 oz. ASW, 34 mm. **Subject:** 100th Anniversary - Birth of Jozef Ciger Hronsky **Obv:** Small double cross on shield within last O of value within square **Rev:** Half face with glasses and stylized sun within small squares flanked by dates and inscription **Edge Lettering:** NIET KRAJSICH SLOV AKO SKUTKY **Designer:** Patrik Kovacovsky **Note:** 10,700 uncirculated pieces melted in 2002.

Date	Mintage	F	VF	XF	Unc	BU
1996MK	21,000	—	—	—	15.00	—
1996MK Proof	1,500	Value: 32.50				

KM# 37 200 KORUN
20.0000 g., 0.7500 Silver .4823 oz. ASW, 34 mm. **Subject:** 150th Anniversary - Birth of Svetozar Hurban Vajansky 1847-1916 **Obv:** Double cross on shield **Rev:** Large head with beard and mustache **Edge Lettering:** POLITIK SPISOVATEL KRITIK NOVINAR **Designer:** Miroslav Tomasek **Note:** 4,000 uncirculated pieces melted in 2002.

Date	Mintage	F	VF	XF	Unc	BU
1997	17,400	—	—	—	15.00	—
1997 Proof	1,800	Value: 35.00				

KM# 38 200 KORUN
20.0000 g., 0.7500 Silver .4823 oz. ASW, 34 mm. **Subject:** Banska Stiavnica - UNESCO **Obv:** Small double cross on shield at right of tower **Rev:** Baroque buildings **Edge Lettering:** PATRIMOINE MODIAL **Designer:** Milan Vircik

Date	Mintage	F	VF	XF	Unc	BU
1997	16,500	—	—	—	15.00	—
1997 Proof	1,700	Value: 37.50				

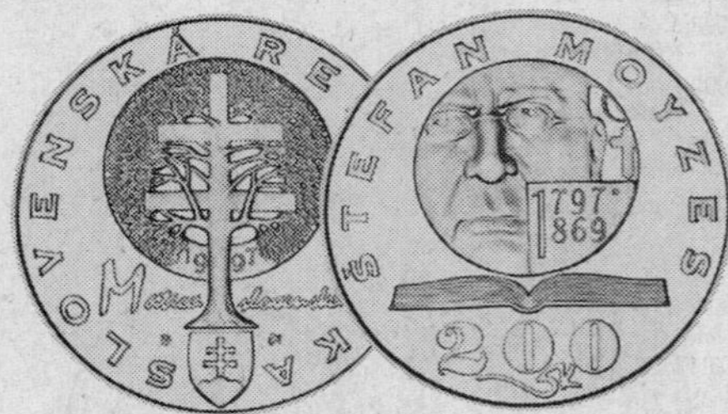

KM# 40 200 KORUN
20.0000 g., 0.7500 Silver .4823 oz. ASW, 34 mm. **Subject:** 200th Anniversary - Birth of Stefan Moyzes, 1797-1997 **Obv:** Stylized double cross in tree form with small double cross on shield below **Rev:** Head with glasses facing within circle above book and value **Edge Lettering:** PRVY PREDSEDA MATICE SLOVENSKEJ

Date	Mintage	F	VF	XF	Unc	BU
1997	14,900	—	—	—	15.00	—
1997 Proof	1,500	Value: 35.00				

KM# 41 200 KORUN
20.0000 g., 0.7500 Silver .4823 oz. ASW, 34 mm. **Subject:** 50th Anniversary - Slovak National Gallery **Obv:** Crowned Madonna and child **Rev:** Daughters of King Lycomed **Edge Lettering:** GOTIKA A BAROK V ZBIERKACH SNG **Designer:** Milan Vircik

Date	Mintage	F	VF	XF	Unc	BU
1998	15,000	—	—	—	15.00	—
1998 Proof	1,600	Value: 30.00				

KM# 42 200 KORUN
20.0000 g., 0.7500 Silver .4823 oz. ASW **Subject:** 150th Anniversary - 1st Railroad in Slovakia **Obv:** Small double cross on shield to right of train emerging from tunnel **Rev:** Bratislava Castle and locomotive **Edge Lettering:** 150 ROKOV ZELEZNIC NA SLOVENSKU **Designer:** Milan Vircik

Date	Mintage	F	VF	XF	Unc	BU
1998	14,000	—	—	—	15.00	—
1998 Proof	1,800	Value: 32.50				

KM# 43 200 KORUN

20.0000 g., 0.7500 Silver .4823 oz. ASW **Subject:** 150th Anniversary - Slovak Revolt of 1848 **Obv:** Small double cross on shield divides date above emblem within circle flanked by vertical inscriptions **Rev:** Standing figure flanked by vertical inscriptions and dates **Edge Lettering:** ZA NARODNU SLOBODU **Designer:** Patrik Kovacovsky

Date	Mintage	F	VF	XF	Unc	BU
1998	13,400	—	—	—	15.00	—
1998 Proof	1,500	Value: 37.50				

KM# 44 200 KORUN

20.0000 g., 0.7500 Silver .4823 oz. ASW, 34 mm. **Subject:** UNESCO World Heritage site **Obv:** Cathedral towers **Rev:** Castle and gothic window arch **Edge Lettering:** PATRIMONIE MONDIAL WORLD HERITAGE **Designer:** Milan Vircik

Date	Mintage	F	VF	XF	Unc	BU
1998	13,500	—	—	—	15.00	—
1998 Proof	1,500	Value: 35.00				

KM# 45 200 KORUN

20.0000 g., 0.7500 Silver .4823 oz. ASW, 34 mm. **Subject:** Centennial - Birth of Jan Smrek **Obv:** Stylized seated female figure **Rev:** Half figure outline facing left **Edge Lettering:** BASNIK JAN SMREK 100 VYROCIE NARODENIA **Designer:** Maria Poldaufova

Date	Mintage	F	VF	XF	Unc	BU
1998	13,400	—	—	—	15.00	—
1998 Proof	1,500	Value: 35.00				

KM# 48 200 KORUN

20.0000 g., 0.7500 Silver .4823 oz. ASW, 34 mm. **Subject:** 150th Anniversary - Birth of Pavol Orszagh Hviezdoslav **Obv:** Portrait of face made with treetops **Rev:** Portrait of the artist **Edge Lettering:** HEROLD SVITAJUCICH CASOV **Designer:** Patrik Kovacovsky

Date	Mintage	F	VF	XF	Unc	BU
1999	12,700	—	—	—	15.00	—
1999 Proof	1,400	Value: 35.00				

KM# 49 200 KORUN

20.0000 g., 0.7500 Silver .4823 oz. ASW, 34 mm. **Subject:** 50th Anniversary - Slovac Philharmonic **Obv:** Pipe organ above double cross on shield flanked by value and date **Rev:** Reduta building bay window **Edge Lettering:** HUDBA-UNIVERZALNA REC LUDSTVA **Designer:** Michal Gavula

Date	Mintage	F	VF	XF	Unc	BU
1999MK	12,700	—	—	—	15.00	—
1999MK Proof	1,400	Value: 35.00				

KM# 55 200 KORUN

20.0000 g., 0.7500 Silver .4823 oz. ASW, 33.9 mm. **Subject:** Juraj Fandly **Obv:** Radiant book above double cross on shield within design **Rev:** Half figure writing in book facing right **Edge Lettering:** NIE SILOU ANI MOCOU, ALE MOJIM DUCHM **Designer:** Michal Gavula

Date	Mintage	F	VF	XF	Unc	BU
2000	10,600	—	—	—	15.00	—
2000 Proof	1,600	Value: 35.00				

KM# 28 500 KORUN

33.6300 g., 0.9250 Silver 1.0001 oz. ASW, 40 mm. **Subject:** Slovensky Raj National Park **Obv:** Double cross on shield, date, value and flowers **Rev:** Waterfall **Edge Lettering:** OCHRANA PRIRODY A. KRAJINY **Designer:** Imrich Svitana **Note:** 11,200 Uncirculated pieces melted in 2002.

Date	Mintage	F	VF	XF	Unc	BU
1994	27,500	—	—	—	35.00	—
1994 Proof	2,400	Value: 45.00				

KM# 39 500 KORUN

33.6300 g., 0.9250 Silver 1.0001 oz. ASW, 40 mm. **Subject:** Pieninsky National Park **Obv:** Double cross on shield above butterfly within circle **Rev:** Park scene in circle within butterfly wings **Edge Lettering:** OCHRANA PRIRODY A KRAJINY **Designer:** Patrik Kovacovsky

Date	Mintage	F	VF	XF	Unc	BU
1997	14,500	—	—	—	50.00	—
1997 Proof	1,700	Value: 65.00				

KM# 47 500 KORUN

33.6300 g., 0.9250 Silver 1.0001 oz. ASW, 40 mm. **Subject:** Tatransky National Park **Obv:** Value, mountains, flowers and dates **Rev:** Mountain goats above flowers, date and double cross on shield **Edge Lettering:** OCHRANA PRIRODY A KRAJINY **Designer:** Milan Vircak

Date	Mintage	F	VF	XF	Unc	BU
1999	12,000	—	—	—	40.00	—
1999 Proof	1,400	Value: 250				

KM# 50 500 KORUN

33.6300 g., 0.9250 Silver 1.0001 oz. ASW, 40 mm. **Subject:** 500th Anniversary - First Thalers of Kremnica **Obv:** Mining scene within beaded circle **Rev:** Old coin designs and city view within beaded circle **Edge Lettering:** GULDINER-PREDCHODCA TOLIARA **Designer:** Milan Vircik

Date	Mintage	F	VF	XF	Unc	BU
1999	12,000	—	—	—	45.00	—
1999 Proof	1,400	Value: 400				

KM# 53 500 KORUN

33.6300 g., 0.9250 Silver 1.0001 oz. ASW, 40 mm. **Subject:** 250th Anniversary - Death of Samuel Mikovini **Obv:** Armored bust right and cartographic instruments **Rev:** Allegorical scene and map **Edge Lettering:** KARTOGRAF - MATEMATIK - STAVITEL **Designer:** Milan Vircik

Date	Mintage	F	VF	XF	Unc	BU
2000	10,100	—	—	—	37.50	—
2000 Proof	1,500	Value: 60.00				

KM# 51 2000 KORUN

124.4140 g., 0.9990 Silver 3.9960 oz. ASW, 65 mm. **Subject:** 2000 Bi-millennium **Obv:** Small double cross on shield, value and historical scenes **Rev:** Jesus within churches and value **Edge:** Plain **Shape:** Octagon **Designer:** Stefan Novotny

Date	Mintage	F	VF	XF	Unc	BU
MM(2000) Proof	4,000	Value: 450				

KM# 29 5000 KORUN

7.0000 g., 0.9000 Gold .2025 oz. AGW, 24 mm. **Subject:** 1100th Anniversary - Death of Great Moravian King Svatopluk **Obv:** Double cross on shield, value and date **Rev:** Head of Svatopluk and ruin of castle Devin **Edge:** Milled **Designer:** Vojtech Pohanka

Date	Mintage	F	VF	XF	Unc	BU
1994 Proof	5,000	Value: 500				

KM# 36 5000 KORUN

9.5000 g., 0.9000 Gold .2749 oz. AGW, 26 mm. **Subject:** Banska Stiavnica Historical Mines - UNESCO **Obv:** Double cross on shield, value, date and upright design **Rev:** Steepled buildings **Edge:** Milled **Designer:** Milan Vircik

Date	Mintage	F	VF	XF	Unc	BU
1997 Proof	8,000	Value: 325				

KM# 46 5000 KORUN

9.5000 g., 0.9000 Gold .2749 oz. AGW, 26 mm. **Subject:** Spissky Castle - UNESCO **Obv:** Double cross on shield and lion within design above date **Rev:** Scenic design and value **Edge:** Milled **Designer:** Pavel Karoly

Date	Mintage	F	VF	XF	Unc	BU
1998 Proof	6,000	Value: 325				

KM# 54 5000 KORUN

9.5000 g., 0.9000 Gold .2749 oz. AGW, 26 mm. **Subject:** 500th Anniversary - Kremnica Mint **Obv:** Hungarian coin design **Rev:** Hungarian coin design **Edge:** Reeded **Designer:** Jan Cernaj

Date	Mintage	F	VF	XF	Unc	BU
ND(1999) Proof	5,500	Value: 325				

KM# 52 10000 KORUN

19.0000 g., 0.9000 Gold .5498 oz. AGW, 34 mm. **Subject:** 2000 Bi-millennium **Obv:** Double cross on shield, value and historical scenes **Rev:** Jesus with churches **Edge:** Milled **Designer:** Stefan Novotny **Note:** Similar to 2000 Korun, KM#51.

Date	Mintage	F	VF	XF	Unc	BU
MM(2000) Proof	Est. 3,500	Value: 600				

ESSAIS

KM#	Date	Mintage	Identification	Mkt Val
E1	1939	—	20 Korun. 0.5000 Silver. KM#7	—
E2	1941	—	10 Korun. 0.5000 Silver. KM#9.1	—

MINT SETS

KM#	Date	Mintage	Identification	Issue Price	Mkt Val
MS1	1993 (7)	28,800	KM#11.1-15, 17-18, plus medal	—	12.00
MS2	1994 (7)	19,000	KM#11.1-15, 17-18, plus medal	—	12.00
MS3	1995 (7)	12,000	KM#11.1-15, 17-18, plus medal	—	12.00
MS4	1996 (7)	15,000	KM#11.1-14, 17-18, 35, plus medal	—	12.00
MS5	1997 (7)	15,000	KM#11.1-14, 17-18, 35, plus medal	—	12.00
MS6	1998 (7)	12,000	KM#11.1-14, 17-18, 35, plus medal	—	12.00
MS7	1999 (7)	11,500	KM#11.1-14, 17-18, 35, plus medal	—	12.00
MS8	2000 (7)	13,000	KM#11.1-14, 17-18, 35, plus medal	—	12.00

PROOF SETS

KM#	Date	Mintage	Identification	Issue Price	Mkt Val
PS1	2000 (7)	900	KM#11.1-14, 17-18, 35	—	85.00

The Republic of Slovenia is located northwest of Yugoslavia in the valleys of the Danube River. It has an area of 7,819 sq. mi. and a population of *1.9 million. Capital: Ljubljana. Agriculture is the main industry with large amounts of hops and fodder crops grown as well as many varieties of fruit trees. Sheep raising, timber production and the mining of mercury from one of the country's oldest mines are also very important to the economy.

Slovenia was important as a land route between Europe and the eastern Mediterranean region. The Roman Catholic Austro-Hungarian Empire gained control of the area during the 14th century and retained its dominance until World War I. The United Kingdom of the Serbs, Croats and Slovenes (Yugoslavia) was founded in 1918 and consisted of various groups of South Slavs.

In 1929, King Alexander declared his assumption of power temporarily, however he was assassinated in 1934. His son Peter's regent, Prince Paul tried to settle internal problems, however, the Slovenes denounced the agreement he made. He resigned in 1941 and Peter assumed the throne. Peter was forced to flee when Yugoslavia was occupied. Slovenia was divided between Germany and Italy. Even though Yugoslavia attempted to remain neutral, the Nazis occupied the country and were resisted by guerilla armies, most notably Marshal Josif Broz Tito.

Under Marshal Tito, the Constitution of 1946 established 6 constituent republics which made up Yugoslavia. Each republic was permitted Liberties under supervision of the Communist Party.

In Oct. 1989 the Slovene Assembly voted a constitutional amendment giving it the right to secede from Yugoslavia. A referendum on Dec. 23, 1990 resulted in a majority vote for independence, which was formally declared on Dec. 26.

On June 25 Slovenia declared independence, but agreed to suspend this for 3 months at peace talks sponsored by the EC. Federal troops moved into Slovenia on June 27 to secure Yugoslavia's external borders, but after some fighting withdrew by the end of July. The 3-month moratorium agreed at the EC having expired, Slovenia (and Croatia) declared their complete independence of the Yugoslav federation on Oct.8, 1991.

MINT MARKS

Based on last digit in date.

(K) - Kremnitz (Slovakia): open 4, upturned 5

(BP) - Budapest (Hungary): closed 4, downturned 5

MONETARY SYSTEM

100 Stotinov = 1 Tolar

REPUBLIC

STANDARD COINAGE

100 Stotinow = 1 Tolar

KM# 7 10 STOTINOV

0.5500 g., Aluminum, 16 mm. **Obv:** Value within square **Rev:** Salamander **Edge:** Plain **Note:** Varieties exist.

Date	Mintage	F	VF	XF	Unc	BU
1992	2,515,000	—	—	—	0.35	0.75
1992 Proof	1,000	Value: 3.00				
1993	2,515,000	—	—	—	0.35	0.75
1993 Proof	1,000	Value: 3.00				
1994	1,000	—	—	—	—	3.00
Note: In sets only						
1994 Proof	1,000	Value: 3.00				
1995	1,000	—	—	—	—	3.00
Note: In sets only						
1995 Proof	1,000	Value: 3.00				
2000 Proof	—	Value: 3.00				

KM# 8 20 STOTINOV

0.7000 g., Aluminum, 18.05 mm. **Obv:** Value within square **Rev:** Small owl and value **Edge:** Plain

Date	Mintage	F	VF	XF	Unc	BU
1992	2,515,000	—	—	—	0.50	1.00
Note: Minor reverse varieties exist						
1992 Proof	1,000	Value: 4.00				
1993	2,515,000	—	—	—	0.50	1.00
Note: Minor reverse varieties exist						
1993 Proof	1,000	Value: 4.00				

Date	Mintage	F	VF	XF	Unc	BU
1994	1,000	—	—	—	—	4.00
Note: In sets only						
1994 Proof	1,000	Value: 4.00				
1995	1,000	—	—	—	—	4.00
Note: In sets only						
1995 Proof	1,000	Value: 4.00				
2000 Proof	—	Value: 4.00				

KM# 3 50 STOTINOV

0.8500 g., Aluminum, 19.9 mm. **Obv:** Value within square **Rev:** Bee and value **Edge:** Plain

Date	Mintage	F	VF	XF	Unc	BU
1992	5,015,000	—	—	0.10	0.50	0.75
Note: Minor reverse varieties exist						
1992 Proof	1,000	Value: 6.00				
1993	18,315,000	—	—	0.10	0.50	0.75
1993 Proof	1,000	Value: 6.00				
1994	1,000	—	—	—	—	6.00
Note: In sets only						
1994 Proof	1,000	Value: 6.00				
1995	3,000,000	—	—	0.10	0.50	0.75
1995	1,000	—	—	—	—	6.00
Note: In sets only						
1995 Proof	1,000	Value: 6.00				
1996	3,000,000	—	—	0.10	0.50	0.75
1996 Proof	Est. 3,000	Value: 6.00				
2000 Proof	—	Value: 6.00				

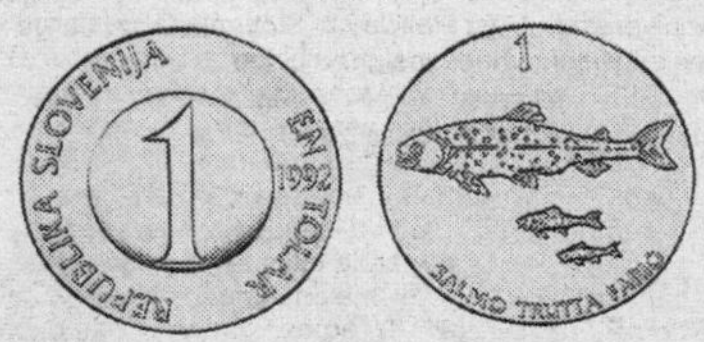

KM# 4 TOLAR

4.5000 g., Brass, 21.9 mm. **Obv:** Value within circle **Rev:** Three brown trout **Edge:** Reeded **Note:** Date varieties exist: 1994 = closed or open "4"; 1995 = serif up and serif down in "5".

Date	Mintage	F	VF	XF	Unc	BU
1992	10,015,000	—	—	0.20	0.85	1.35
1992 Proof	1,000	Value: 5.00				
1993	30,015,000	—	—	0.20	0.85	1.35
1993 Proof	1,000	Value: 5.00				
1994 (K)	10,000,000	—	—	—	0.75	1.25
Note: 4 open to the top						
1994 (K)	1,000	—	—	—	—	5.00
Note: 4 open to right; in sets only						
1994 (K) Proof	1,000	Value: 5.00				
Note: 4 open to right						
1994 (BP)	5,000,000	—	—	—	0.75	1.25
1995 (K)	10,000,000	—	—	—	0.75	1.25
1995 (K)	1,000	—	—	—	—	5.00
Note: In sets only						
1995 (K) Proof	1,000	Value: 5.00				
1995 (BP)	10,000,000	—	—	—	0.75	1.25
1996	Est. 21,800,000	—	—	—	0.75	1.25
1996 Proof	Est. 3,000	Value: 5.00				
1997	8,000,000	—	—	—	0.75	1.25
1998	12,000,000	—	—	—	0.75	1.25
1999	8,000,000	—	—	—	0.75	1.25
2000	Est. 15,000,000	—	—	—	0.75	1.25
2000 Proof	—	Value: 5.00				

KM# 5 2 TOLARJA

5.4000 g., Brass, 24 mm. **Obv:** Value within circle **Rev:** Barn swallow in flight **Edge:** Reeded **Note:** Date varieties exist: 1994 = closed or open "4"; 1995 = serif up and serif down in "5".

Date	Mintage	F	VF	XF	Unc	BU
1992	5,015,000	—	—	0.25	0.85	1.60
1992 Proof	1,000	Value: 7.00				
1993	10,015,000	—	—	0.25	0.85	1.60
1993 Proof	1,000	Value: 7.00				
1994 (K)	10,000,000	—	—	—	0.75	1.50
Note: 4 open to the top						
1994 (K)	1,000	—	—	—	—	7.00
Note: 4 open to right; in sets only						
1994 (K) Proof	1,000	Value: 7.00				
Note: 4 open to right						
1994 (BP)	5,000,000	—	—	—	0.75	1.50
1995 (K)	10,000,000	—	—	—	0.75	1.50
1995 (K)	1,000	—	—	—	—	7.00
Note: In sets only						
1995 (K) Proof	1,000	Value: 7.00				
1995 (BP)	10,000,000	—	—	—	0.75	1.50
1996	Est. 16,600,000	—	—	—	0.75	1.50
1996 Proof	1,000	Value: 7.00				
1997	6,060,000	—	—	—	0.75	1.50
1998	5,000,000	—	—	—	0.75	1.50
1999	5,200,000	—	—	—	0.75	1.50
2000	Est. 15,000,000	—	—	—	0.75	1.50
2000 Proof	—	Value: 7.00				

KM# 6 5 TOLARJEV

6.0500 g., Brass, 26 mm. **Obv:** Value within circle **Rev:** Head and horns of ibex **Edge:** Reeded **Note:** Date varieties exist: 1994 = closed or open "4"; 1995 = serif up and serif down in "5".

Date	Mintage	F	VF	XF	Unc	BU
1992	10,015,000	—	—	0.35	1.00	1.75
1992 Proof	1,000	Value: 8.00				
1993	10,015,000	—	—	0.35	1.00	1.75
1993 Proof	1,000	Value: 8.00				
1994 (K)	10,000,000	—	—	—	0.85	1.50
Note: 4 open to the top						
1994 (K)	1,000	—	—	—	—	8.00
Note: 4 open to right; in sets only						
1994 (K) Proof	1,000	Value: 8.00				
Note: 4 open to right						
1994 (BP)	5,000,000	—	—	—	0.85	1.50
1995	5,000,000	—	—	—	0.85	1.50
1995 2 tip	—	—	—	—	0.85	1.50
1996	6,000,000	—	—	—	0.85	1.50
1996 Proof	Est. 3,000	Value: 8.00				
1997	8,000,000	—	—	—	0.85	1.50
1998	10,000,000	—	—	—	0.85	1.50
1999	6,403,000	—	—	—	0.85	1.50
2000	—	—	—	—	0.85	1.50
2000 Proof	—	Value: 8.00				

KM# 9 5 TOLARJEV

6.4000 g., Brass, 26 mm. **Subject:** 400th Anniversary - Battle of Sisek **Obv:** Value and date **Rev:** City view, arms, date, Andrej G. Turjaski **Edge:** Reeded **Designer:** Danilo Riznar

Date	Mintage	F	VF	XF	Unc	BU
1993	100,000	—	—	—	1.65	—

KM# 12 5 TOLARJEV

6.4000 g., Brass, 26 mm. **Subject:** 300th Anniversary - Establishment of Operosorum Labacensium Academy **Obv:** Value and date **Rev:** Beehive and bees **Edge:** Reeded **Designer:** Danilo Riznar

Date	Mintage	F	VF	XF	Unc	BU
1993	100,000	—	—	—	1.75	4.00

KM# 15 5 TOLARJEV

Brass, 26 mm. **Subject:** 50th Anniversary - Slovenian Bank **Obv:** Value and date **Rev:** Linden leaf and seed pod **Edge:** Reeded

Date	Mintage	F	VF	XF	Unc	BU
1994	100,000	—	—	—	1.65	2.25

KM# 16 5 TOLARJEV

Brass, 26 mm. **Subject:** 1,000th Anniversary - Glagolitic Alphabet **Obv:** Value and date **Rev:** Feather **Edge:** Reeded

Date	Mintage	F	VF	XF	Unc	BU
1994	200,000	—	—	—	1.65	2.25

KM# 21 5 TOLARJEV

Brass, 26 mm. **Series:** F.A.O. **Subject:** 50th Anniversary - F.A.O. **Obv:** Value within circle **Rev:** Hands holding F.A.O. logo **Edge:** Reeded

Date	Mintage	F	VF	XF	Unc	BU
ND(1995)	500,000	—	—	—	1.65	2.25

KM# 22 5 TOLARJEV

Brass, 26 mm. **Subject:** 50th Anniversary - Defeat of Fascism **Obv:** Value **Rev:** Vertical chain link design and dates **Edge:** Reeded

Date	Mintage	F	VF	XF	Unc	BU
1995	200,000	—	—	—	1.65	2.25

KM# 26 5 TOLARJEV

Brass, 26 mm. **Subject:** Aljazev Stolp **Obv:** Value within triangle design **Rev:** Head facing in front of mountains **Edge:** Reeded

Date	Mintage	F	VF	XF	Unc	BU
1995	200,000	—	—	—	1.65	2.25

KM# 29 5 TOLARJEV

Brass, 26 mm. **Subject:** 100th Anniversary - First Railway in Slovenia **Obv:** Date within design at upper right, value at far left **Rev:** Dates above train **Edge:** Reeded

Date	Mintage	F	VF	XF	Unc	BU
1996	Est. 300,000	—	—	—	1.65	2.25
1996 Proof	Inc. above	Value: 8.00				

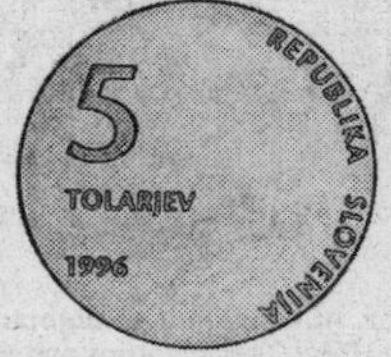

KM# 32 5 TOLARJEV

Brass, 26 mm. **Subject:** 5th Anniversary of Independence **Obv:** Value and date at left **Rev:** Pink Carnation and dates **Edge:** Reeded

Date	Mintage	F	VF	XF	Unc	BU
1996	200,000	—	—	—	1.65	2.25
1996 Proof	—	Value: 8.00				

KM# 33 5 TOLARJEV
Brass, 26 mm. **Series:** Olympics **Subject:** Olympics Centennial **Obv:** Value above olympic rings and flag **Rev:** Gymnast above dates **Edge:** Reeded

Date	Mintage	F	VF	XF	Unc	BU
1996	200,000	—	—	—	1.65	2.25
1996 Proof	Est. 3,000	Value: 8.00				

KM# 38 5 TOLARJEV
Brass, 26 mm. **Subject:** Ziga Zois **Obv:** Value and date **Rev:** Zois ziga written within outline of face above dates **Edge:** Reeded

Date	Mintage	F	VF	XF	Unc	BU
1997	200,000	—	—	—	1.65	2.25

KM# 41 10 TOLARJEV
5.7500 g., Copper Nickel, 22 mm. **Obv:** Value within circle **Rev:** Stylized rearing horse **Edge:** Reeded

Date	Mintage	F	VF	XF	Unc	BU
2000	—	—	—	—	3.00	4.00
2000 Proof	—	Value: 10.00				

KM# 1 500 TOLARJEV
15.0000 g., 0.9250 Silver .4461 oz. ASW **Subject:** 1st Anniversary of Independence **Obv:** Value within circle at left, date at right **Rev:** Leaf, design and value **Note:** Eight minor obverse and reverse varieties exist.

Date	Mintage	F	VF	XF	Unc	BU
1991 Proof	50,000	Value: 35.00				

KM# 10 500 TOLARJEV
15.0000 g., 0.9250 Silver .4461 oz. ASW, 32 mm. **Subject:** Battle of Sisek **Obv:** Value and date **Rev:** City view, arms and date

Date	Mintage	F	VF	XF	Unc	BU
1993 Proof	Est. 5,000	Value: 28.50				

KM# 13 500 TOLARJEV
15.0000 g., 0.9250 Silver .4461 oz. ASW, 32 mm. **Subject:** 300th Anniversary - Establishment of Operasorum Labacensium Academy **Obv:** Value and date **Rev:** Dates above angel

Date	Mintage	F	VF	XF	Unc	BU
1993 Proof	5,000	Value: 28.50				

KM# 17 500 TOLARJEV
15.0000 g., 0.9250 Silver .4461 oz. ASW, 32 mm. **Subject:** 50th Anniversary - Slovenian Bank **Obv:** Value **Rev:** Leaf and dates

Date	Mintage	F	VF	XF	Unc	BU
1994 Proof	5,000	Value: 28.50				

KM# 19 500 TOLARJEV
15.0000 g., 0.9250 Silver .4461 oz. ASW **Subject:** 1000th Anniversary - Bishop Abraham - Glagolistic Alphabet **Obv:** Value and date **Rev:** Feather and dates

Date	Mintage	F	VF	XF	Unc	BU
1994 Proof	3,000	Value: 28.50				

KM# 23 500 TOLARJEV
15.0000 g., 0.9250 Silver .4461 oz. ASW, 32 mm. **Subject:** 50th Anniversary - Defeat of Fascism **Obv:** Stylized design **Rev:** Stylized design, dates and value

Date	Mintage	F	VF	XF	Unc	BU
1995 Proof	3,000	Value: 28.50				

KM# 25 500 TOLARJEV
15.0000 g., 0.9250 Silver .4461 oz. ASW, 25 mm. **Series:** F.A.O. **Subject:** 50th Anniversary - F.A.O. **Obv:** Vertical value **Rev:** F.A.O. logo above weeds

Date	Mintage	F	VF	XF	Unc	BU
1995 Proof	3,000	Value: 28.50				

KM# 27 500 TOLARJEV
15.0000 g., 0.9250 Silver .4461 oz. ASW, 32 mm. **Subject:** 100th Anniversary - Aljazev Stolp **Obv:** Value within triangle design below date **Rev:** Head facing in front of mountains

Date	Mintage	F	VF	XF	Unc	BU
1995 Proof	3,000	Value: 28.50				

KM# 30 500 TOLARJEV
15.0000 g., 0.9250 Silver .4461 oz. ASW, 32 mm. **Subject:** 100th Anniversary - First Railway in Slovenia **Obv:** Large value **Rev:** Design within wheel designed circle

Date	Mintage	F	VF	XF	Unc	BU
1996 Proof	3,000	Value: 28.50				

KM# 34 500 TOLARJEV
15.0000 g., 0.9250 Silver .4461 oz. ASW, 32 mm. **Subject:** 5th Anniversary of Independence **Obv:** Map of Slovenia divides date and value **Rev:** World globe and dates

Date	Mintage	F	VF	XF	Unc	BU
1996 Proof	3,000	Value: 28.50				

KM# 36 500 TOLARJEV
15.0000 g., 0.9250 Silver .4461 oz. ASW, 32 mm. **Series:** Olympics **Obv:** Value above olympic rings and flag **Rev:** Gymnast and dates

Date	Mintage	F	VF	XF	Unc	BU
1996 Proof	3,000	Value: 27.50				

KM# 39 500 TOLARJEV
15.0000 g., 0.9250 Silver .4461 oz. ASW, 32 mm. **Subject:** Zois Ziga

Date	Mintage	F	VF	XF	Unc	BU
1997 Proof	3,000	Value: 28.50				

KM# 2.1 5000 TOLARJEV
7.0000 g., 0.9000 Gold .2025 oz. AGW **Subject:** 1st Anniversary of Independence **Obv:** Value within circle at left, date at right **Rev:** Bird's beak at center of spiral

Date	Mintage	F	VF	XF	Unc	BU
1991 Proof	4,000	Value: 235				

KM# 2.2 5000 TOLARJEV
7.0000 g., 0.9000 Gold .2025 oz. AGW **Obv:** Value within circle at left, date at right **Rev:** Bird's beak lower center of spiral

Date	Mintage	F	VF	XF	Unc	BU
1991 Proof	Inc. above	Value: 200				

KM# 11 5000 TOLARJEV
7.0000 g., 0.9000 Gold .2025 oz. AGW, 24 mm. **Subject:** Battle of Sisek **Obv:** Value below date **Rev:** City view, arms and date

Date	Mintage	F	VF	XF	Unc	BU
1993 Proof	Est. 2,000	Value: 200				

KM# 14 5000 TOLARJEV
7.0000 g., 0.9000 Gold .2025 oz. AGW, 24 mm. **Subject:** 300th Anniversary - Establishment of Operosorum Labacensium Academy **Obv:** Value below date **Rev:** Beehive among bees

Date	Mintage	F	VF	XF	Unc	BU
1993 Proof	2,000	Value: 215				

KM# 18 5000 TOLARJEV
7.0000 g., 0.9000 Gold .2025 oz. AGW, 24 mm. **Subject:** 50th Anniversary - Slovenian Bank **Obv:** Value and vertical date **Rev:** Leaf and dates

Date	Mintage	F	VF	XF	Unc	BU
1994 Proof	2,000	Value: 200				

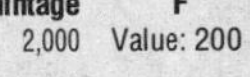

KM# 20 5000 TOLARJEV
7.0000 g., 0.9000 Gold .2025 oz. AGW **Subject:** 1000th Anniversary - Bishop Abraham - Glagolitic Alphabet **Obv:** Value **Rev:** Feather

Date	Mintage	F	VF	XF	Unc	BU
1994 Proof	1,000	Value: 210				

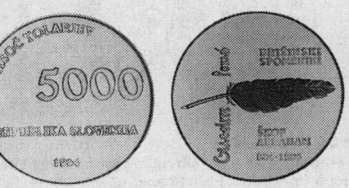

KM# 24 5000 TOLARJEV
7.0000 g., 0.9000 Gold .2025 oz. AGW, 24 mm. **Subject:** 50th Anniversary - Defeat of Fascism **Obv:** Value **Rev:** Vertical chain link design and dates

Date	Mintage	F	VF	XF	Unc	BU
1995 Proof	1,000	Value: 210				

KM# 28 5000 TOLARJEV
7.0000 g., 0.9000 Gold .2025 oz. AGW, 24 mm. **Subject:** Aljazev Stolp and Mountain Summit **Obv:** Value within triangle design **Rev:** Head facing in front of mountains

Date	Mintage	F	VF	XF	Unc	BU
1995 Proof	1,000	Value: 210				

KM# 31 5000 TOLARJEV
7.0000 g., 0.9000 Gold .2025 oz. AGW, 24 mm. **Subject:** 100th Anniversary - First Railway in Slovenia **Obv:** Date within design at upper right, value at left **Rev:** Train below dates

Date	Mintage	F	VF	XF	Unc	BU
1996 Proof	1,000	Value: 215				

KM# 35 5000 TOLARJEV
7.0000 g., 0.9000 Gold .2025 oz. AGW, 24 mm. **Subject:** 5th Anniversary of Independence **Obv:** Value above date **Rev:** Pink carnation above dates

Date	Mintage	F	VF	XF	Unc	BU
1996 Proof	1,000	Value: 210				

KM# 37 5000 TOLARJEV
7.0000 g., 0.9000 Gold .2025 oz. AGW, 24 mm. **Series:** Olympics **Obv:** Value above olympic rings and flag **Rev:** Gymnast above dates

Date	Mintage	F	VF	XF	Unc	BU
1996 Proof	1,000	Value: 225				

KM# 40 5000 TOLARJEV
7.0000 g., 0.9000 Gold .2025 oz. AGW, 24 mm. **Subject:** Zois Ziga

Date	Mintage	F	VF	XF	Unc	BU
1997 Proof	1,000	Value: 210				

MINT SETS

KM#	Date	Mintage	Identification	Issue Price	Mkt Val
MS1	1992 (6)	—	KM#3-8	—	8.00
MS2	1992 (5)	15,000	KM#4-8	—	7.00
MS3	1993 (6)	—	KM#3-8	—	8.00
MS4	1993 (5)	15,000	KM#4-8	—	7.00
MS5	1996 (9)	300	KM#4-6, 29-30, 32-34, 36	—	45.00
MS6	1994	1,000	KM#3-8	—	35.00
MS7	1995	1,000	KM#3-8	—	35.00

PROOF SETS

KM#	Date	Mintage	Identification	Issue Price	Mkt Val
PS1	1991 (2)	—	KM#1, 2.2	—	325
PS2	1992 (6)	1,000	KM#3-8	—	35.00
PS3	1992 (5)	1,000	KM#4-8	—	30.00
PS4	1993 (6)	1,000	KM#3-8	—	35.00
PS5	1993 (5)	1,000	KM#4-8	—	30.00
PS6	1994 (6)	1,000	KM#3-8	—	35.00
PS7	1995 (6)	1,000	KM#3-8	—	35.00
PS8	1996 (9)	3,000	KM#4-6, 29-30, 32-34, 36	—	125
PS12	2000 (7)	—	KM#3, 4, 5, 6, 7, 8, 41	—	45.00

SOLOMON ISLANDS

The Solomon Islands, located in the southwest Pacific east of Papua New Guinea, has an area of 10,983 sq. mi. (28,450 sq. km.) and a population of *324,000. Capital: Honiara. The most important islands of the Solomon chain are Guadalcanal (scene of some of the fiercest fighting of World War II), Malaitia, New Georgia, Florida, Vella Lavella, Choiseul, Rendova, San Cristobal, the Lord Howe group, the Santa Cruz islands, and the Duff group. Copra is the only important cash crop but it is hoped that timber will become an economic factor.

The Solomon Islands were discovered by Spanish navigator Alvaro de Mendana in 1567, and in 1569 he made an unsuccessful attempt to colonize them. European knowledge of the group would not be completed until the end of the 19th century. Germany declared a protectorate over the northern Solomon's in 1885. The British protectorate over the southern Solomons was established in 1893. In 1899 Germany transferred its claim to all Solomon Islands except Buka and Bougainville to Great Britain in exchange for recognition of German claims in Western Samoa. Australia occupied the two German islands in 1914, and administered them after 1920.

The Japanese invaded the Solomons during 1942-43, but were driven out by an American counteroffensive after a series of bloody clashes.

Following World War II, the islands returned to the status of a British protectorate. In 1976 the protectorate was abolished, and the Solomons became a self-governing dependency. Full independence was achieved on July 7,1978. Solomon Islands is a member of the Commonwealth of Nations. Queen Elizabeth II is Head of State, as Queen of the Solomon Islands.

RULERS
British, until 1978

MINT MARKS
FM - Franklin Mint, U.S.A.*

NOTE: From 1977-1985 the Franklin Mint produced coinage in up to 3 different qualities. Qualities of issue are designated in ( ) after each date and are defined as follows:

(M) MATTE - Normal circulation strike or a dull finish produced by sandblasting special uncirculated (polish finish) or proof quality dies.

(U) SPECIAL UNCIRCULATED - Polished or proof-like in appearance without any frosted features.

(P) PROOF - The highest quality obtainable having mirror-like fields and frosted features.

MONETARY SYSTEM
100 Cents = 1 Dollar

COMMONWEALTH NATION

STANDARD COINAGE

KM# 1 CENT
2.6000 g., Bronze, 17.53 mm. **Series:** F.A.O. **Obv:** Young bust right **Rev:** Food bowl divides value **Edge:** Plain

Date	Mintage	F	VF	XF	Unc	BU
1977	1,828,000	—	—	0.10	0.15	0.35
1977FM (M)	6,000	—	—	—	0.50	0.75
1977FM (U)	—	—	—	—	1.25	2.00
1977FM (P)	14,000	Value: 1.00				
1978FM (M)	6,000	—	—	—	0.50	0.75
1978FM (U)	544	—	—	—	1.25	2.00
1978FM (P)	5,122	Value: 1.00				
1979FM (M)	6,000	—	—	—	0.50	0.75
1979FM (U)	677	—	—	—	1.25	2.00
1979FM (P)	2,845	Value: 1.50				
1980FM (M)	6,000	—	—	—	0.50	0.75
1980FM (U)	624	—	—	—	1.25	2.00
1980FM (P)	1,031	Value: 1.50				
1981	—	—	—	—	0.50	0.75
1981FM (M)	6,000	—	—	—	0.50	0.75
1981FM (U)	212	—	—	—	2.00	3.00
1981FM (P)	448	Value: 1.50				
1982FM (U)	—	—	—	—	1.25	2.00
1982FM (P)	—	Value: 1.50				
1983FM (M)	—	—	—	—	0.50	0.75
1983FM (U)	200	—	—	—	2.00	3.00
1983FM (P)	—	Value: 1.50				

KM# 1a CENT
Bronze Plated Steel, 17.53 mm. **Series:** F.A.O. **Obv:** Young bust right **Rev:** Food bowl divides value **Edge:** Plain

Date	Mintage	F	VF	XF	Unc	BU
1985	—	—	—	—	0.25	0.50

KM# 24 CENT

Bronze Plated Steel, 17.53 mm. **Series:** F.A.O. **Obv:** Crowned head right **Rev:** Food bowl divides value **Edge:** Plain

Date	Mintage	F	VF	XF	Unc	BU
1987	—	—	—	—	0.35	0.75
1996	—	—	—	—	0.35	0.75

KM# 2 2 CENTS

5.2000 g., Bronze, 21.59 mm. **Subject:** Eagle Spirit of Malaita **Obv:** Young bust right **Rev:** Eagle spirit below value **Edge:** Plain

Date	Mintage	F	VF	XF	Unc	BU
1977	2,400,000	—	—	0.10	0.25	0.50
1977FM (M)	6,000	—	—	—	0.75	1.25
1977FM (U)	—	—	—	—	1.50	2.50
1977FM (P)	14,000	Value: 1.50				
1978FM (M)	6,000	—	—	—	0.75	1.25
1978FM (U)	544	—	—	—	1.50	2.50
1978FM (P)	5,122	Value: 1.50				
1979FM (M)	6,000	—	—	—	0.75	1.25
1979FM (U)	677	—	—	—	1.50	2.50
1979FM (P)	2,845	Value: 1.75				
1980FM (M)	6,000	—	—	—	0.75	1.25
1980FM (U)	624	—	—	—	1.50	2.50
1980FM (P)	1,031	—	—	—	1.25	2.00
1981FM (M)	6,000	—	—	—	0.75	1.25
1981FM (U)	212	—	—	—	1.50	2.50
1981FM (P)	448	Value: 2.00				
1982FM (U)	—	—	—	—	1.50	2.50
1982FM (P)	—	Value: 2.00				
1983FM (M)	—	—	—	—	0.75	1.25
1983FM (U)	200	—	—	—	1.50	2.50
1983FM (P)	—	Value: 2.00				

KM# 2a 2 CENTS

Bronze Plated Steel, 21.6 mm. **Subject:** Eagle Spirit of Malaita **Obv:** Crowned bust right **Rev:** Eagle spirit below value **Edge:** Plain

Date	Mintage	F	VF	XF	Unc	BU
1985	—	—	—	—	0.30	0.50

KM# 25 2 CENTS

Bronze Plated Steel, 21.6 mm. **Obv:** Crowned head right **Rev:** Eagle spirit below value **Edge:** Plain

Date	Mintage	F	VF	XF	Unc	BU
1987	—	—	—	—	0.35	0.75
1996	—	—	—	—	0.35	0.75

KM# 3 5 CENTS

2.8000 g., Copper-Nickel, 19.4 mm. **Subject:** Santa Ysabel **Obv:** Young bust right **Rev:** Native mask and value **Edge:** Reeded

Date	Mintage	F	VF	XF	Unc	BU
1977	1,200,000	—	—	0.15	0.35	0.75
1977FM (U)	—	—	—	—	1.50	2.50
1977FM (M)	6,000	—	—	—	1.00	1.50
1977FM (P)	14,000	Value: 1.75				
1978FM (M)	6,000	—	—	—	1.00	1.50
1978FM (U)	544	—	—	—	1.50	2.50
1978FM (P)	5,122	Value: 2.00				
1979FM (M)	6,000	—	—	—	1.00	1.50
1979FM (U)	677	—	—	—	1.50	2.50
1979FM (P)	2,845	Value: 2.25				
1980	—	—	—	—	—	—
1980FM (M)	6,000	—	—	—	1.00	1.50
1980FM (U)	624	—	—	—	1.50	2.50
1980FM (P)	1,031	Value: 2.50				
1981	—	—	—	—	—	—
1981FM (M)	6,000	—	—	—	1.00	1.50
1981FM (U)	212	—	—	—	1.50	2.50
1981FM (P)	448	Value: 2.50				
1982FM (U)	—	—	—	—	1.50	2.50
1982FM (P)	—	Value: 2.50				
1983FM (M)	—	—	—	—	1.00	1.50
1983FM (U)	200	—	—	—	2.00	3.50
1983FM (P)	—	Value: 2.50				
1985	—	—	—	—	0.30	0.50

KM# 26 5 CENTS

2.8000 g., Copper-Nickel, 19.4 mm. **Obv:** Crowned head right **Rev:** Native mask and value **Edge:** Reeded

Date	Mintage	F	VF	XF	Unc	BU
1988	—	—	—	—	0.50	1.00
1993	—	—	—	—	0.50	1.00
1996	—	—	—	—	0.50	1.00

KM# 4 10 CENTS

5.6500 g., Copper-Nickel, 23.6 mm. **Subject:** Ngorieru **Obv:** Young bust right **Rev:** Sea spirit divides value **Edge:** Reeded

Date	Mintage	F	VF	XF	Unc	BU
1977	3,600,000	—	—	0.20	0.50	0.75
1977FM (M)	6,000	—	—	—	1.25	2.00
1977FM (U)	—	—	—	—	2.50	4.00
1977FM (P)	14,000	Value: 2.50				
1978FM (M)	6,000	—	—	—	1.25	2.00
1978FM (U)	544	—	—	—	2.50	4.00
1978FM (P)	5,122	Value: 2.75				
1979FM (M)	6,000	—	—	—	1.25	2.00
1979FM (U)	677	—	—	—	2.50	4.00
1979FM (P)	2,845	Value: 3.50				
1980FM (M)	6,000	—	—	—	1.25	2.00
1980FM (U)	624	—	—	—	2.50	4.00
1980FM (P)	1,031	Value: 4.00				
1981FM (M)	6,000	—	—	—	1.25	2.00
1981FM (U)	212	—	—	—	2.50	4.00
1981FM (P)	448	Value: 4.00				
1982FM (U)	—	—	—	—	2.50	4.00
1982FM (P)	—	Value: 4.00				
1983FM (M)	—	—	—	—	1.25	2.00
1983FM (U)	200	—	—	—	3.50	5.00
1983FM (P)	—	Value: 4.00				

KM# 27 10 CENTS

5.6500 g., Copper-Nickel, 23.6 mm. **Subject:** Ngorieru **Obv:** Crowned head right **Rev:** Sea spirit divides value **Edge:** Reeded

Date	Mintage	F	VF	XF	Unc	BU
1988	—	—	—	—	0.65	1.00

KM# 27a 10 CENTS

Nickel Plated Steel, 23.6 mm. **Subject:** Ngorieru **Obv:** Crowned head right **Rev:** Sea spirit divides value **Edge:** Reeded

Date	Mintage	F	VF	XF	Unc	BU
1990	—	—	—	—	0.65	1.00
1993	—	—	—	—	0.65	1.00
1996	—	—	—	—	0.65	1.00
2000	—	—	—	—	0.65	1.00

KM# 5 20 CENTS

11.2500 g., Copper-Nickel, 28.5 mm. **Obv:** Young bust right **Rev:** Malaita pendant design within circle, denomination appears twice in legend **Edge:** Reeded

Date	Mintage	F	VF	XF	Unc	BU
1977	3,000,000	—	0.15	0.35	0.80	1.25
1977FM (M)	5,000	—	—	—	2.50	3.50
1977FM (P)	14,000	Value: 3.50				
1978	293,000	—	0.25	0.50	1.00	1.75
1978FM (M)	5,000	—	—	—	2.50	3.50
1978FM (U)	544	—	—	—	3.50	5.50
1978FM (P)	5,122	Value: 3.75				
1979FM (M)	5,000	—	—	—	2.50	3.50
1979FM (U)	677	—	—	—	3.50	5.00
1979FM (P)	2,845	Value: 3.75				
1980FM (M)	5,000	—	—	—	2.50	3.50
1980FM (U)	624	—	—	—	3.50	5.00
1980FM (P)	1,031	Value: 3.75				
1981FM (M)	5,000	—	—	—	2.50	3.50
1981FM (U)	212	—	—	—	4.00	6.00
1981FM (P)	448	Value: 4.00				
1982FM (U)	—	—	—	—	4.00	6.00
1982FM (P)	—	Value: 4.00				
1983FM (M)	—	—	—	—	2.50	3.50
1983FM (U)	200	—	—	—	5.00	7.00
1983FM (P)	—	Value: 4.00				

KM# 28 20 CENTS

11.2500 g., Nickel Plated Steel, 28.5 mm. **Obv:** Crowned head right **Rev:** Malaita pendant design within circle, denomination appears twice in legend **Edge:** Reeded

Date	Mintage	F	VF	XF	Unc	BU
1989	—	—	—	—	0.85	1.25
1996	—	—	—	—	0.85	1.25
1997	—	—	—	—	0.85	1.25
2000	—	—	—	—	0.85	1.25

KM# 82 20 CENTS

Nickel Plated Steel, 26 mm. **Obv:** Crowned bust right **Rev:** Native woman with basket on head **Edge:** Reeded

Date	Mintage	F	VF	XF	Unc	BU
1995	20,200	—	—	—	3.00	4.00

KM# 23 50 CENTS

Copper-Nickel, 29.5 mm. **Subject:** 10th Anniversary of Independence **Obv:** Crowned head right **Rev:** Arms with supporters **Edge:** Plain **Shape:** 12-sided

Date	Mintage	F	VF	XF	Unc	BU
1988	—	—	—	—	2.00	3.00

KM# 29 50 CENTS

Copper-Nickel, 29.5 mm. **Obv:** Crowned head right **Rev:** Arms with supporters **Edge:** Plain **Shape:** 12-sided **Note:** Circulation type.

Date	Mintage	F	VF	XF	Unc	BU
1990	—	—	—	—	2.00	3.00
1996	—	—	—	—	2.00	3.00
1997	—	—	—	—	2.00	3.00

KM# 6 DOLLAR

13.4000 g., Copper-Nickel, 30 mm. **Subject:** Nusu-Nusu head **Obv:** Young bust right **Rev:** Sea spirit statue divides value **Edge:** Plain **Shape:** 7-sided

Date	Mintage	F	VF	XF	Unc	BU
1977	1,500,000	—	—	1.00	2.00	3.00

Date	Mintage	F	VF	XF	Unc	BU
1977FM (M)	3,000	—	—	—	3.00	5.00
1977FM (P)	14,000	Value: 4.50				
1978FM (M)	3,000	—	—	—	3.00	5.00
1978FM (U)	544	—	—	—	4.50	6.00
1978FM (P)	5,122	Value: 4.50				
1979FM (M)	3,000	—	—	—	3.00	5.00
1979FM (U)	677	—	—	—	4.50	6.00
1979FM (P)	2,845	Value: 5.00				
1980FM (M)	3,000	—	—	—	3.00	5.00
1980FM (U)	624	—	—	—	4.50	6.00
1980FM (P)	1,031	Value: 5.50				
1981FM (M)	3,000	—	—	—	3.00	5.00
1981FM (U)	212	—	—	—	7.00	10.00
1981FM (P)	448	Value: 6.00				
1982FM (U)	—	—	—	—	4.50	6.00
1982FM (P)	—	Value: 6.00				
1983FM (M)	—	—	—	—	3.00	5.00
1983FM (U)	200	—	—	—	7.00	10.00
1983FM (P)	—	Value: 5.50				

KM# 19 DOLLAR
Copper-Nickel **Series:** 1984 Olympics **Obv:** Young bust right **Rev:** Runners above torch and value **Rev. Designer:** E.W. Roberts

Date	Mintage	F	VF	XF	Unc	BU
1984	5,000	—	—	—	4.50	6.00

KM# 30 DOLLAR
Copper-Nickel **Subject:** 50th Anniversary of Pearl Harbor **Obv:** Crowned head right **Rev:** Pearl Harbor war scene within circle **Rev. Designer:** Willem Vis

Date	Mintage	F	VF	XF	Unc	BU
1991	—	—	—	—	3.00	5.00

KM# 30a DOLLAR
28.2800 g., 0.9250 Silver .8411 oz. ASW **Subject:** 50th Anniversary of Pearl Harbor **Obv:** Crowned head right **Rev:** Pearl Harbor war scene

Date	Mintage	F	VF	XF	Unc	BU
1991 Proof	Est. 25,000	Value: 13.50				

KM# 35 DOLLAR
Copper-Nickel **Subject:** 50th Anniversary - Battle of the Coral Sea **Obv:** Crowned head right **Rev:** Planes bombing ship within circle **Rev. Designer:** Willem Vis

Date	Mintage	F	VF	XF	Unc	BU
1992	—	—	—	—	3.00	5.00

KM# 35a DOLLAR
28.2800 g., 0.9250 Silver .8411 oz. ASW **Subject:** 50th Anniversary - Battle of the Coral Sea **Obv:** Crowned head right **Rev:** War planes bombing ships within circle

Date	Mintage	F	VF	XF	Unc	BU
1992 Proof	Est. 25,000	Value: 15.00				

KM# 41 DOLLAR
Copper-Nickel **Subject:** 50th Anniversary - Battle of Guadalcanal **Obv:** Crowned head right **Rev:** Uniformed soldiers within circle **Rev. Designer:** Willem Vis

Date	Mintage	F	VF	XF	Unc	BU
1992	—	—	—	—	4.00	6.00

KM# 41a DOLLAR
28.2800 g., 0.9250 Silver .8411 oz. ASW **Subject:** 50th Anniversary - Battle of Guadalcanal **Obv:** Crowned head right **Rev:** Uniformed soldiers within circle

Date	Mintage	F	VF	XF	Unc	BU
1992 Proof	Est. 25,000	Value: 14.00				

KM# 77 DOLLAR
28.3000 g., Copper Nickel, 38.6 mm. **Subject:** Queen Mother **Obv:** Crowned head right **Rev:** Queen Mother's Coronation within beaded circle **Edge:** Reeded

Date	Mintage	F	VF	XF	Unc	BU
1995	30,000	—	—	—	6.00	8.00

KM# 72 DOLLAR
13.4500 g., Copper-Nickel, 30 mm. **Obv:** Crowned head right **Rev:** Sea spirit statue divides value **Edge:** Plain **Shape:** 7-sided

Date	Mintage	F	VF	XF	Unc	BU
1996	—	—	—	—	2.50	4.00

KM# 64 DOLLAR
Copper-Nickel **Subject:** World Wildlife Fund - Conserving Nature **Obv:** Crowned head right **Rev:** Eagle descending on fish **Rev. Designer:** Willem Vis

Date	Mintage	F	VF	XF	Unc	BU
1998	—	—	—	—	7.00	9.00

KM# 64a DOLLAR
28.2800 g., 0.9250 Silver .8411 oz. ASW **Subject:** World Wildlife Fund - Conserving Nature **Obv:** Crowned head right **Rev:** Eagle descending on fish

Date	Mintage	F	VF	XF	Unc	BU
1998 Proof	—	Value: 20.00				

KM# 65 DOLLAR
32.3200 g., Silver, 38.6 mm. **Series:** Olympics 2000 **Obv:** Head with tiara right **Rev:** Multicolor koala swimming below torch within map **Edge:** Reeded **Note:** Struck at Valcambi.

Date	Mintage	F	VF	XF	Unc	BU
2000 Proof	50,000	Value: 12.50				

KM# 66 DOLLAR
32.3200 g., Silver **Series:** Olympics 2000 **Obv:** Head with tiara right **Rev:** Multicolor kangaroo sail boarding

Date	Mintage	F	VF	XF	Unc	BU
2000 Proof	50,000	Value: 12.50				

KM# 7 5 DOLLARS
28.2800 g., 0.9250 Silver .8411 oz. ASW, 40 mm. **Obv:** Young bust right **Rev:** Fossilized clam shell on top of circle **Edge:** Reeded

Date	Mintage	F	VF	XF	Unc	BU
1977FM (U)	200	—	—	—	40.00	—
1977FM (P)	15,000	Value: 12.50				
1978FM (P)	5,148	Value: 14.00				
1979FM (P)	2,845	Value: 16.00				
1980FM (P)	1,031	Value: 18.00				
1981FM (P)	448	Value: 22.50				
1983FM (P)	339	Value: 25.00				

KM# 7a 5 DOLLARS
Copper-Nickel, 40 mm. **Obv:** Young bust right **Rev:** Fossilized clam shell on top of circle **Edge:** Reeded

Date	Mintage	F	VF	XF	Unc	BU
1978FM (M)	200	—	—	—	25.00	—
1978FM (U)	544	—	—	—	15.00	—
1979FM (M)	200	—	—	—	25.00	—
1979FM (U)	677	—	—	—	13.50	—
1980FM (M)	200	—	—	—	25.00	—
1980FM (U)	624	—	—	—	13.50	—
1981FM (M)	200	—	—	—	25.00	—
1981FM (U)	212	—	—	—	25.00	—
1983FM (U)	202	—	—	—	25.00	—

KM# 8 5 DOLLARS
28.2800 g., 0.9250 Silver .8411 oz. ASW **Subject:** Coronation Jubilee **Obv:** Young bust right **Rev:** Crown flanked by supporters

Date	Mintage	F	VF	XF	Unc	BU
1978	8,886	Value: 13.50				

KM# 13 5 DOLLARS
Copper-Nickel, 40 mm. **Subject:** Battle of Guadalcanal **Obv:** Young bust right **Rev:** Uniformed soldiers

Date	Mintage	F	VF	XF	Unc	BU
1982FM (U)	—	—	—	—	10.00	12.00

KM# 13a 5 DOLLARS
28.2800 g., 0.9250 Silver .8411 oz. ASW, 40 mm. **Subject:** Battle of Guadalcanal **Obv:** Young bust right **Rev:** Uniformed soldiers

Date	Mintage	F	VF	XF	Unc	BU
1982FM (P)	1,368	Value: 20.00				

KM# 15 5 DOLLARS
30.2800 g., 0.5000 Silver .4868 oz. ASW **Subject:** 30th Anniversary of Coronation **Obv:** Young bust right **Rev:** Crossed scepters divides dates, crown and cross on globe design

Date	Mintage	F	VF	XF	Unc	BU
1983FM (P)	2,944	Value: 8.50				

KM# 16 5 DOLLARS
28.2800 g., 0.9250 Silver .8411 oz. ASW **Series:** International Year of the Child **Obv:** Young bust right **Rev:** Figures rowing boat divides emblems

Date	Mintage	F	VF	XF	Unc	BU
1983 Proof	5,775	Value: 13.50				

KM# 22 5 DOLLARS
28.2800 g., 0.9250 Silver .8589 oz. ASW **Series:** Decade for Women **Obv:** Crowned head right **Rev:** Teacher and student reading within circle

Date	Mintage	F	VF	XF	Unc	BU
1985 Proof	1,050	Value: 16.50				

KM# 63 5 DOLLARS
10.0000 g., 0.5000 Silver .1607 oz. ASW **Subject:** Alvaro Mendana de Neyra **Obv:** Crowned head right **Rev:** Bust with hat facing, palm tree and ancient boat at left

Date	Mintage	F	VF	XF	Unc	BU
1994 Proof	Est. 20,000	Value: 6.00				

KM# 54 5 DOLLARS
Copper-Nickel **Subject:** MacArthur Accepting Japanese Surrender **Obv:** Crowned head right **Rev:** Uniformed bust left at far right **Rev. Designer:** Willem Vis

Date	Mintage	F	VF	XF	Unc	BU
1995	—	—	—	—	5.00	7.00

KM# 54a 5 DOLLARS
28.2800 g., 0.9250 Silver .8411 oz. ASW **Subject:** MacArthur Accepting Japanese Surrender **Obv:** Crowned head right **Rev:** Uniformed bust left at far right **Rev. Designer:** Willem Vis **Note:** Similar to 50 Dollars, KM#57.

Date	Mintage	F	VF	XF	Unc	BU
1995 Proof	Est. 10,000	Value: 16.50				

KM# 78 5 DOLLARS
28.2000 g., 0.9250 Silver 0.8387 oz. ASW, 38.6 mm. **Subject:** Queen's 70th Birthday **Obv:** Crowned bust right **Rev:** Royal yacht **Edge:** Reeded

Date	Mintage	F	VF	XF	Unc	BU
1996 Proof	—	Value: 20.00				

KM# 80 5 DOLLARS
9.9400 g., 0.5250 Silver 0.1678 oz. ASW, 29.9 mm. **Obv:** Crowned head right **Rev:** Queen and Diana at the races **Edge:** Reeded

Date	Mintage	F	VF	XF	Unc	BU
1998 Proof	—	Value: 7.50				

KM# 69 5 DOLLARS
20.1000 g., 0.8000 Silver .5170 oz. ASW, 33.9 mm. **Subject:** Ship of Death **Obv:** Crowned head right **Rev:** Sailing ship **Edge:** Reeded

Date	Mintage	F	VF	XF	Unc	BU
1999 Proof	Est. 20,000	Value: 10.00				

KM# 70 5 DOLLARS
32.2000 g., Copper-Nickel, 38.6 mm. **Obv:** Head with tiara right **Obv. Inscription:** Portrait from dies of Solomon Islands KM# 67-68 **Rev:** Pied Cormorant **Rev. Inscription:** From dies from New Zealand KM#125 **Edge:** Reeded **Note:** Mule.

Date	Mintage	F	VF	XF	Unc	BU
2000 Proof	—	Value: 650				

Note: This coin is included in a New Zealand Proof set dated 2000

KM# 67 5 DOLLARS
24.9100 g., 0.9250 Silver .7408 oz. ASW, 38.7 mm. **Series:** Olympics 2000 **Obv:** Head with tiara right **Rev:** Stylized multicolor koala tennis player below torch within map **Edge:** Reeded **Note:** Struck at Valcambi.

Date	Mintage	F	VF	XF	Unc	BU
2000 Proof	15,000	Value: 12.50				

KM# 68 5 DOLLARS
24.9100 g., 0.9250 Silver .7408 oz. ASW **Series:** Olympics 2000 **Obv:** Crowned head right **Rev:** Stylized multicolored kangaroo bicyclist below torch within map

Date	Mintage	F	VF	XF	Unc	BU
2000 Proof	15,000	Value: 12.50				

KM# 10 10 DOLLARS
Copper-Nickel, 45 mm. **Obv:** Young bust right **Rev:** Flying frigate bird above value **Edge:** Reeded

Date	Mintage	F	VF	XF	Unc	BU
1979FM (M)	100	—	—	—	35.00	—
1979FM (U)	777	—	—	—	15.00	—
1980FM (M)	100	—	—	—	35.00	—
1980FM (U)	624	—	—	—	15.00	—
1981FM (M)	100	—	—	—	35.00	—
1981FM (U)	212	—	—	—	18.50	—
1982FM (U)	—	—	—	—	15.00	—

KM# 10a 10 DOLLARS

42.2700 g., 0.9250 Silver 1.2571 oz. ASW, 45 mm. **Obv:** Young bust right **Rev:** Frigate bird above value **Edge:** Reeded

Date	Mintage	F	VF	XF	Unc	BU
1979FM (P)	4,670	Value: 20.00				
1980FM (P)	1,569	Value: 22.50				
1981FM (P)	593	Value: 32.50				
1982FM (P)	579	Value: 32.50				

KM# 17 10 DOLLARS

Copper-Nickel, 45 mm. **Subject:** 5th Anniversary of Independence **Obv:** Young bust right **Rev:** Arms with supporters in front of flag

Date	Mintage	F	VF	XF	Unc	BU
1983FM (U)	202	—	—	—	16.50	—

KM# 17a 10 DOLLARS

40.5000 g., 0.9250 Silver 1.2045 oz. ASW, 45 mm. **Subject:** 5th Anniversary of Independence **Obv:** Young bust right **Rev:** Arms with supporters in front of flag

Date	Mintage	F	VF	XF	Unc	BU
1983FM (P)	425	Value: 32.50				

KM# 20 10 DOLLARS

33.4400 g., 0.9250 Silver .9946 oz. ASW **Series:** 1984 Olympics **Obv:** Young bust right **Rev:** Runners above torch and value **Rev. Designer:** E.W. Roberts

Date	Mintage	F	VF	XF	Unc	BU
1984 Proof	2,500	Value: 20.00				

KM# 47 10 DOLLARS

31.8000 g., 0.9250 Silver .9457 oz. ASW **Subject:** Alvaro de Neyra **Obv:** Crowned head right **Rev:** Half figure with hat facing

Date	Mintage	F	VF	XF	Unc	BU
1991 Proof	—	Value: 16.00				

KM# 31 10 DOLLARS

3.1300 g., 0.9990 Gold .1006 oz. AGW, 16.5 mm. **Subject:** 50th Anniversary of Pearl Harbor **Obv:** Crowned head right **Rev:** Map of Pearl Harbor **Rev. Designer:** Willem Vis

Date	Mintage	F	VF	XF	Unc	BU
1991 Proof	Est. 500	Value: 70.00				

KM# 48 10 DOLLARS

31.4200 g., 0.9250 Silver .9359 oz. ASW **Series:** 1992 Olympics **Obv:** Crowned head right **Rev:** Runner

Date	Mintage	F	VF	XF	Unc	BU
1991 Proof	Est. 40,000	Value: 14.50				

KM# 36 10 DOLLARS

3.1300 g., 0.9990 Gold .1006 oz. AGW, 16.5 mm. **Subject:** 50th Anniversary - Battle of the Coral Sea **Rev:** Planes dropping bombs within circle **Rev. Designer:** Willem Vis

Date	Mintage	F	VF	XF	Unc	BU
1992 Proof	500	Value: 70.00				

KM# 40 10 DOLLARS

31.4700 g., 0.9250 Silver .9359 oz. ASW **Subject:** First Lunar Vehicle **Obv:** Crowned head right **Rev:** First lunar vehicle with astronaut

Date	Mintage	F	VF	XF	Unc	BU
1992 Proof	Est. 10,000	Value: 15.00				

KM# 42 10 DOLLARS

3.1300 g., 0.9990 Gold .1006 oz. AGW, 16.5 mm. **Subject:** 50th Anniversary - Battle of Guadalcanal **Rev:** Battle scene within circle **Rev. Designer:** Willem Vis

Date	Mintage	F	VF	XF	Unc	BU
1992 Proof	500	Value: 70.00				

KM# 46 10 DOLLARS

31.4700 g., 0.9250 Silver .9359 oz. ASW **Subject:** 40th Anniversary - Queen Elizabeth's Coronation **Obv:** Crowned head right **Rev:** Crowned figure on throne facing

Date	Mintage	F	VF	XF	Unc	BU
1992 Proof	Est. 50,000	Value: 15.00				

KM# 50 10 DOLLARS

31.4700 g., 0.9250 Silver .9359 oz. ASW **Series:** 1992 Olympics **Obv:** Crowned head right **Rev:** Boxer

Date	Mintage	F	VF	XF	Unc	BU
1992 Proof	40,000	Value: 14.50				

KM# 51 10 DOLLARS

31.4700 g., 0.9250 Silver .9359 oz. ASW **Series:** Endangered Wildlife **Obv:** Crowned head right **Rev:** Saltwater crocodile

Date	Mintage	F	VF	XF	Unc	BU
1992 Proof	Est. 10,000	Value: 30.00				

KM# 49 10 DOLLARS

28.2800 g., 0.9250 Silver .8411 oz. ASW **Subject:** 100 Years as British Protectorate **Obv:** Crowned head right **Rev:** Cameo to upper left of ship

Date	Mintage	F	VF	XF	Unc	BU
1993 Proof	5,000	Value: 20.00				

KM# 59 10 DOLLARS

31.4700 g., 0.9250 Silver .9359 oz. ASW **Subject:** Protect Our World **Obv:** Crowned head right **Rev:** Orchid and butterfly

Date	Mintage	F	VF	XF	Unc	BU
1993 Proof	Est. 10,000	Value: 18.50				

KM# 52 10 DOLLARS
28.2800 g., 0.9250 Silver .8411 oz. ASW **Subject:** Sailing ship "Swallow" **Obv:** Crowned head right **Rev:** Ship divides cameos

Date	Mintage	F	VF	XF	Unc	BU
1994 Proof	Est. 15,000	Value: 14.50				

KM# 53 10 DOLLARS
28.2800 g., 0.9250 Silver .8411 oz. ASW **Series:** 1996 Olympics **Obv:** Crowned head right **Rev:** Relay runners

Date	Mintage	F	VF	XF	Unc	BU
1994 Proof	Est. 30,000	Value: 13.50				

KM# 55 10 DOLLARS
3.1300 g., 0.9990 Gold 0.1006 oz. AGW, 16.5 mm. **Rev:** Marine and armored tank within circle **Rev. Designer:** Willem Vis

Date	Mintage	F	VF	XF	Unc	BU
1995 Proof	Est. 500	Value: 75.00				

KM# 71 10 DOLLARS
31.4400 g., 0.9250 Silver 0.935 oz. ASW, 38.5 mm. **Subject:** Queen Mother **Obv:** Crowned head right **Rev:** Coronation scene within beaded circle **Edge:** Reeded

Date	Mintage	F	VF	XF	Unc	BU
1995 Proof	—	Value: 16.50				

KM# 79 10 DOLLARS
31.6000 g., 0.9250 Silver 0.9398 oz. ASW, 38.6 mm. **Obv:** Crowned head right **Rev:** Queen Elizabeth and Diana at the races **Edge:** Reeded

Date	Mintage	F	VF	XF	Unc	BU
1998 Proof	—	Value: 18.50				

KM# 73 10 DOLLARS
28.3200 g., 0.9250 Silver with gilt outer ring 0.8422 oz. ASW, 38.5 mm. **Subject:** Queen Mother **Obv:** Crowned head right within beaded circle **Rev:** Inspecting the bombing of Buckingham Palace **Edge:** Reeded

Date	Mintage	F	VF	XF	Unc	BU
2000 Proof	—	Value: 17.50				

KM# 74 10 DOLLARS
31.5500 g., 0.9250 Silver 0.9383 oz. ASW, 38.7 mm. **Obv:** Crowned head right **Rev:** Missionary ship **Edge:** Reeded

Date	Mintage	F	VF	XF	Unc	BU
2000 Proof	—	Value: 20.00				

KM# 32 25 DOLLARS
7.8100 g., 0.9990 Gold .2514 oz. AGW, 22 mm. **Subject:** 50th Anniversary - Pearl Harbor **Obv:** Crowned head right **Rev:** Pearl Harbor battle scene within circle **Rev. Designer:** Willem Vis

Date	Mintage	F	VF	XF	Unc	BU
1991 Proof	Est. 3,000	Value: 170				

KM# 37 25 DOLLARS
7.8100 g., 0.9990 Gold .2514 oz. AGW, 22 mm. **Subject:** 50th Anniversary - Battle of the Coral Sea **Rev:** Pearl Harbor battle scene within circle **Rev. Designer:** Willem Vis

Date	Mintage	F	VF	XF	Unc	BU
1992 Proof	Est. 3,000	Value: 170				

KM# 43 25 DOLLARS
7.8100 g., 0.9990 Gold .2514 oz. AGW, 22 mm. **Subject:** 50th Anniversary - Battle of Guadalcanal **Rev:** Uniformed soldiers and armored tank in woods within circle **Rev. Designer:** Willem Vis

Date	Mintage	F	VF	XF	Unc	BU
1992 Proof	Est. 3,000	Value: 170				

KM# 56 25 DOLLARS
7.8100 g., 0.9990 Gold .2514 oz. AGW, 22 mm. **Subject:** 50th Anniversary - Iwo Jima Flag Raising **Rev:** Uniformed soldiers raising flag within circle **Rev. Designer:** Willem Vis

Date	Mintage	F	VF	XF	Unc	BU
1995 Proof	Est. 2,500	Value: 175				

KM# 81 25 DOLLARS
500.0000 g., 0.9990 Silver 16.0593 oz. ASW, 89 mm. **Subject:** Discovery of the Solomon Islands by Kermadec **Obv:** Crowned head right **Rev:** Sailing ship **Edge:** Reeded

Date	Mintage	F	VF	XF	Unc	BU
2000 Proof	—	Value: 245				

KM# 33 50 DOLLARS
15.6000 g., 0.9990 Gold .5016 oz. AGW, 27 mm. **Subject:** 50th Anniversary - Pearl Harbor **Obv:** Crowned head right **Rev:** Pearl Harbor battle scene within circle **Rev. Designer:** Willem Vis

Date	Mintage	F	VF	XF	Unc	BU
1991 Proof	Est. 500	Value: 340				

KM# 38 50 DOLLARS
15.6000 g., 0.9990 Gold .5016 oz. AGW, 27 mm. **Subject:** 50th Anniversary - Battle of the Coral Sea **Rev:** Planes bombing ship within circle **Rev. Designer:** Willem Vis

Date	Mintage	F	VF	XF	Unc	BU
1992 Proof	Est. 500	Value: 340				

KM# 44 50 DOLLARS
15.6000 g., 0.9990 Gold .5016 oz. AGW, 27 mm. **Subject:** 50th Anniversary - Battle of Guadalcanal **Rev:** Uniformed soldiers within circle **Rev. Designer:** Willem Vis

Date	Mintage	F	VF	XF	Unc	BU
1992 Proof	Est. 500	Value: 340				

KM# 60 50 DOLLARS
7.7600 g., 0.5830 Gold .1458 oz. AGW **Series:** Endangered Wildlife **Obv:** Crowned head right **Rev:** Descending eagle

Date	Mintage	F	VF	XF	Unc	BU
1993 Proof	Est. 3,000	Value: 125				

KM# 61 50 DOLLARS
155.5175 g., 0.9990 Silver 5 oz. ASW, 65 mm. **Subject:** Johannes Kepler **Obv:** Crowned bust right **Rev:** Bust 1/4 right **Note:** Photo reduced.

Date	Mintage	F	VF	XF	Unc	BU
1994 Proof	Est. 2,000	Value: 90.00				

KM# 62 50 DOLLARS
31.4700 g., 0.9250 Silver .9359 oz. ASW **Rev:** MacArthur accepting Japanese surrender **Rev. Designer:** Willem Vis **Note:** Similar to 5 Dollars, KM#54.

Date	Mintage	F	VF	XF	Unc	BU
1995 Proof	—	Value: 27.50				

KM# 57 50 DOLLARS
15.6100 g., 0.9990 Gold .5016 oz. AGW, 27 mm. **Rev:** MacArthur accepting Japanese surrender **Rev. Designer:** Willem Vis

Date	Mintage	F	VF	XF	Unc	BU
1995 Proof	500	Value: 345				

Note: In proof sets only

KM# 9 100 DOLLARS
9.3700 g., 0.9000 Gold .2711 oz. AGW **Subject:** Attainment of Sovereignty **Obv:** Young bust right **Rev:** Arms with supporters

Date	Mintage	F	VF	XF	Unc	BU
1978FM (M)	50	—	—	—	245	—
1978FM (U)	213	—	—	—	200	—
1978FM (P)	3,159	Value: 185				

KM# 11 100 DOLLARS
7.6400 g., 0.5000 Gold .1228 oz. AGW **Subject:** Native Art **Obv:** Young bust right **Rev:** Artistic design in center of designed circles

Date	Mintage	F	VF	XF	Unc	BU
1980FM (U)	50	—	—	—	185	—
1980FM (P) Proof	7,500	Value: 90.00				

KM# 12 100 DOLLARS
7.6400 g., 0.5000 Gold .1228 oz. AGW **Obv:** Young bust right **Rev:** Shark

Date	Mintage	F	VF	XF	Unc	BU
1981 Proof	675	Value: 145				

KM# 14 100 DOLLARS
9.3700 g., 0.9000 Gold .2711 oz. AGW **Subject:** Battle of Guadalcanal **Obv:** Young bust right **Rev:** Uniformed soldiers

Date	Mintage	F	VF	XF	Unc	BU
1982FM (P)	311	Value: 220				

KM# 18 100 DOLLARS
9.3700 g., 0.9000 Gold .2711 oz. AGW **Subject:** 5th Anniversary of Independence **Obv:** Young bust right within circle, radiant border **Rev:** Arms with supporters in front of flag within circle, radiant border **Shape:** Pentagon

Date	Mintage	F	VF	XF	Unc	BU
1983FM (P)	268	Value: 225				

KM# 21 100 DOLLARS
7.5000 g., 0.9170 Gold .2211 oz. AGW **Series:** 1984 Olympics **Rev:** Weightlifter **Rev. Designer:** E.W. Roberts

Date	Mintage	F	VF	XF	Unc	BU
1984 Proof	500	Value: 160				

KM# 34 100 DOLLARS
31.2100 g., 0.9990 Gold 1.0035 oz. AGW, 32.69 mm. **Subject:** 50th Anniversary of Pearl Harbor **Obv:** Crowned head right **Rev:** Pearl Harbor battle scene within circle **Rev. Designer:** Willem Vis

Date	Mintage	F	VF	XF	Unc	BU
1991 Proof	Est. 500	Value: 675				

KM# 39 100 DOLLARS
31.2100 g., 0.9990 Gold 1.0035 oz. AGW, 32.69 mm. **Subject:** 50th Anniversary - Battle of Coral Sea **Rev:** Soldiers in lifeboats, burning building and boat, all within circle **Rev. Designer:** Willem Vis

Date	Mintage	F	VF	XF	Unc	BU
1992 Proof	Est. 500	Value: 675				

KM# 45 100 DOLLARS
31.2100 g., 0.9990 Gold 1.0035 oz. AGW, 32.69 mm. **Subject:** 50th Anniversary - Battle of Guadalcanal **Rev:** Planes bombing ship within circle **Rev. Designer:** Willem Vis

Date	Mintage	F	VF	XF	Unc	BU
1992 Proof	Est. 500	Value: 675				

KM# 58 100 DOLLARS
31.2100 g., 0.9990 Gold 1.0035 oz. AGW, 32.69 mm. **Rev:** B-25 bomber and mushroom cloud within circle **Rev. Designer:** Willem Vis

Date	Mintage	F	VF	XF	Unc	BU
1995 Proof	Est. 500	Value: 685				

Note: In proof sets only

PIEFORTS

KM#	Date	Mintage	Identification	Mkt Val
P1	1983	62	5 Dollars. Silver. KM16.	100

PATTERNS

Including off metal strikes

KM#	Date	Mintage	Identification	Mkt Val
Pn1	2000	1	Dollar. Copper-Nickel. 32.3000 g. 38.6 mm. Head with tiara right with italic legends. Cartoon kangaroo on sailboard. Reeded edge.	—
Pn2	2000	30	Dollar. Copper-Nickel. 32.3000 g. 38.6 mm. Head with tiara right italic legends. Cartoon kangaroo on sailboard. Reeded edge.	—
Pn3	2000	—	Dollar. Copper-Nickel. 32.3000 g. 38.6 mm. Head with tiara right with italic legend. Multicolor cartoon kangaroo on sailboard. Reeded edge.	—
			Note: Mintage included in Pn2	
Pn4	2000	30	Dollar. Copper-Nickel. 32.3000 g. 38.6 mm. Head with tiara right with italic legends. Cartoon koala swimming. Reeded edge.	—
Pn5	2000	—	Dollar. Copper-Nickel. 32.3000 g. 38.6 mm. Head with tiara right. Multicolor cartoon koala swimming. Reeded edge.	—
			Note: mintage included with Pn4	
Pn6	2000	1	5 Dollars. Copper-Nickel. 32.3000 g. 38.6 mm. Head with tiara right with italic legends. Cartoon koala playing tennis. Reeded edge.	—
Pn7	2000	30	5 Dollars. 0.9250 Silver. 32.0000 g. 38.6 mm. Head with tiara right. Cartoon koala playing tennis. Reeded edge.	—
Pn8	2000	—	5 Dollars. 0.9250 Silver. 32.0000 g. 38.6 mm. Head with tiara right with italic legends. Multicolor cartoon koala playing tennis. Reeded edge.	—
			Note: mintage included with Pn7	
Pn9	2000	30	5 Dollars. 0.9250 Silver. 32.0000 g. 38.6 mm. Head with tiara right with italic legends. Cartoon kangaroo on bicycle. Reeded edge.	—
Pn10	2000	—	5 Dollars. 0.9250 Silver. 32.0000 g. 38.6 mm. Head with tiara right with italic legends. Multicolor cartoon kangaroo on bicycle. Reeded edge.	—
			Note: mintage included with Pn9	
Pn11	2000	30	50 Dollars. 0.5833 Gold. 7.7600 g. 25 mm. Head with tiara right with italic legends. Multicolor cartoon emu running. Reeded edge.	—

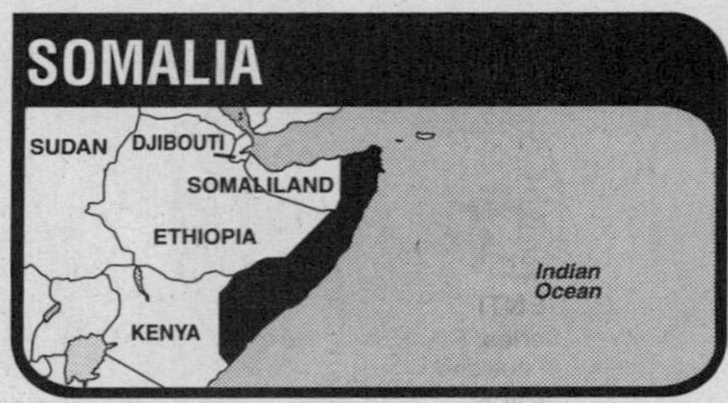

The Somali Democratic Republic, comprised of the former Italian Somaliland, is located on the coast of the eastern projection of the African continent commonly referred to as the "Horn". It has an area of 178,201 sq. mi. (461,657 sq. km.) and a population of *8.2 million. Capital: Mogadishu. The economy is pastoral and agricultural. Livestock, bananas and hides are exported.

The area of the British Somaliland Protectorate was known to the Egyptians at least 1,500 years B.C., and was occupied by the Arabs and Portuguese before British sea captains obtained trading and anchorage rights in 1827. The land of sandy clay and sporadic rainfall acquired a strategic importance with the opening of the Suez Canal in1869. After negotiating treaties with the tribes, Britain declared the area a protectorate in 1888. Italy acquired Italian Somaliland in 1895 by purchase from the Sultan of Zanzibar. Britain occupied Italian Somaliland in 1941 and administered it until April 1, 1950, when it was returned to Italy as a U.N. trusteeship. The British Somaliland protectorate became independent on June 26, 1960. Five days later it joined with Italian Somaliland to form the Somali Republic. The country was under a revolutionary military regime installed Oct. 21, 1969. After eleven years of civil war rebel forces fought their way into the capital. A.M. Muhammad became president in Aug. 1991,but inter-factional fighting continued. A UN-sponsored truce was signed in March 1992 and a peace plan and pact was signed Jan. 15, 1993.

The Northern Somali National Movement (SNM) declared a secession of the northwestern Somaliland Republic on May 17, 1991, which is not recognized by the Somali Democratic Republic.

TITLES

Al-Jumhuriya(t)as - Somaliya(t)

RULERS

Italian, until 1941
British, until 1950

MINT MARKS

Az - Arezzo (Italy)
R – Rome

U. N. TRUSTEESHIP UNDER ITALY

STANDARD COINAGE

100 Centesimi = 1 Somalo

KM# 1 CENTESIMO
Copper, 21 mm. **Obv:** African elephant **Rev:** Value within circle with star flanked by crescents above **Edge:** Plain

Date	Mintage	F	VF	XF	Unc	BU
AH1369-1950	4,000,000	—	0.20	0.50	2.00	4.00

KM# 2 5 CENTESIMI
Copper **Obv:** African elephant **Rev:** Value within circle with star flanked by crescents above

Date	Mintage	F	VF	XF	Unc	BU
AH1369-1950	6,800,000	—	0.30	1.00	3.50	7.50

KM# 3 10 CENTESIMI
Copper **Rev:** Value within circle with star flanked by crescents above **Edge:** African elephant

Date	Mintage	F	VF	XF	Unc	BU
AH1369-1950	7,400,000	—	0.50	2.00	6.00	12.00

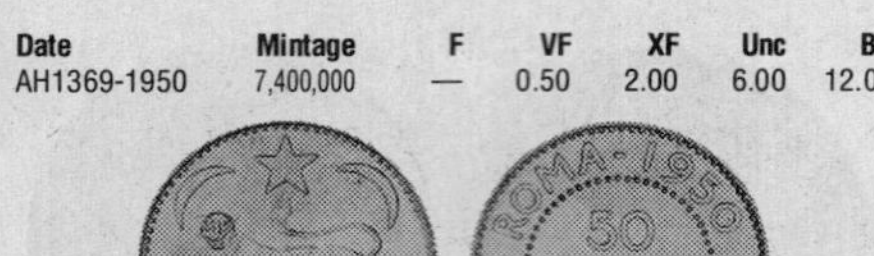

KM# 4 50 CENTESIMI
3.8000 g., 0.2500 Silver .0305 oz. ASW **Obv:** Star flanked by crescents above lion **Rev:** Value within beaded circle

Date	Mintage	F	VF	XF	Unc	BU
AH1369-1950	1,800,000	—	1.25	3.75	10.00	15.00

KM# 5 SOMALO
7.6000 g., 0.2500 Silver .0610 oz. ASW **Obv:** Star flanked by crescents above lion **Rev:** Value within beaded circle

Date	Mintage	F	VF	XF	Unc	BU
AH1369-1950	11,480,000	—	2.25	4.75	12.50	18.00

SOMALI REPUBLIC

STANDARD COINAGE

100 Centesimi = 1 Somalo

KM# 6 5 CENTESIMI
Brass **Obv:** Crowned arms with supporters **Rev:** Value and star within circle **Designer:** Michael Rizzello

Date	Mintage	F	VF	XF	Unc	BU
1967	10,000,000	—	—	0.20	0.60	1.00

KM# 7 10 CENTESIMI
Brass **Obv:** Crowned arms with supporters **Rev:** Value and star within circle **Designer:** Michael Rizzello

Date	Mintage	F	VF	XF	Unc	BU
1967	15,000,000	—	0.15	0.25	0.70	1.25

KM# 8 50 CENTESIMI
Copper-Nickel **Obv:** Crowned arms with supporters **Rev:** Value and star within beaded circle **Designer:** Michael Rizzello

Date	Mintage	F	VF	XF	Unc	BU
1967	5,100,000	—	0.50	1.00	2.50	4.00

KM# 9 SCELLINO / SHILLING
Copper-Nickel **Obv:** Arms with supporters **Rev:** Value within beaded circle

Date	Mintage	F	VF	XF	Unc	BU
1967	8,150,000	—	1.00	3.00	6.00	9.00

KM# 10 20 SHILLINGS / SCELLINI
2.8000 g., 0.9000 Gold .0810 oz. AGW **Subject:** 5th Anniversary of Independence **Obv:** Bust facing **Rev:** Crowned arms with supporters

Date	Mintage	F	VF	XF	Unc	BU
1965Az Proof	6,325	Value: 65.00				
1966Az Proof	—	Value: 65.00				

KM# 11 50 SHILLINGS
7.0000 g., 0.9000 Gold .2025 oz. AGW **Subject:** 5th Anniversary of Independence **Obv:** Bust facing **Rev:** Crowned arms with supporters

Date	Mintage	F	VF	XF	Unc	BU
1965Az Proof	6,325	Value: 145				
1966Az Proof	—	Value: 145				

KM# 12 100 SHILLINGS
14.0000 g., 0.9000 Gold .4051 oz. AGW **Subject:** 5th Anniversary of Independence **Obv:** Bust facing **Rev:** Crowned arms with supporters

Date	Mintage	F	VF	XF	Unc	BU
1965Az Proof	6,325	Value: 285				
1966Az Proof	—	Value: 285				

KM# 13 200 SHILLINGS
28.0000 g., 0.9000 Gold .8102 oz. AGW **Subject:** 5th Anniversary of Independence **Obv:** Bust facing **Rev:** Arms with supporters **Note:** Similar to 100 Shillings, KM#12.

Date	Mintage	F	VF	XF	Unc	BU
1965Az Proof	6,325	Value: 575				
1966Az Proof	—	Value: 575				

KM# 14 500 SHILLINGS
70.0000 g., 0.9000 Gold 2.0257 oz. AGW **Subject:** 5th Anniversary of Independence **Obv:** Bust facing **Rev:** Arms with supporters **Note:** Similar to 100 Shillings, KM#12.

Date	Mintage	F	VF	XF	Unc	BU
1965Az Proof	6,325	Value: 1,425				
1966Az Proof	—	Value: 1,425				

DEMOCRATIC REPUBLIC

STANDARD COINAGE

100 Centesimi = 1 Somalo

KM# 15 5 SHILLINGS
Copper-Nickel, 38 mm. **Subject:** 2nd F.A.O. Conference **Obv:** Crowned arms with supporters **Rev:** Cow and goats **Rev. Designer:** Christopher Ironside **Edge:** Reeded

Date	Mintage	F	VF	XF	Unc	BU
1970	100,000	—	1.50	2.50	6.00	7.00
1970 Proof	1,000	Value: 16.50				

KM# 16 20 SHILLINGS
2.8000 g., 0.9000 Gold .0810 oz. AGW **Subject:** 10th Anniversary of Independence **Obv:** Crowned arms with supporters **Rev:** Star-like design within circle

Date	Mintage	F	VF	XF	Unc	BU
ND(1970) Proof	8,000	Value: 90.00				

KM# 17 50 SHILLINGS
7.0000 g., 0.9000 Gold .2025 oz. AGW **Subject:** 10th Anniversary of Independence **Obv:** Crowned arms with supporters **Rev:** Half-figure with bowl right

Date	Mintage	F	VF	XF	Unc	BU
ND(1970) Proof	8,000	Value: 175				

KM# 18 50 SHILLINGS
7.0000 g., 0.9000 Gold .2025 oz. AGW **Subject:** 1st Anniversary of 1969 Revolution **Obv:** Crowned arms with supporters **Rev:** Wheat sprig

Date	Mintage	F	VF	XF	Unc	BU
ND(1970) Proof	—	Value: 175				

KM# 19 100 SHILLINGS
14.0000 g., 0.9000 Gold .4051 oz. AGW **Subject:** 10th Anniversary of Independence **Obv:** Crowned arms with supporters flanked by dates **Rev:** Bust with headscarf and fruit basket on back left

Date	Mintage	F	VF	XF	Unc	BU
ND(1970) Proof	8,000	Value: 320				

KM# 20 100 SHILLINGS
14.0000 g., 0.9000 Gold .4051 oz. AGW **Subject:** 1st Anniversary of the 1969 Revolution **Obv:** Crowned arms with supporters **Rev:** Hand, helmet and gun in front of design

Date	Mintage	F	VF	XF	Unc	BU
ND(1970) Proof	—	Value: 300				

KM# 21 200 SHILLINGS
28.0000 g., 0.9000 Gold .8102 oz. AGW **Subject:** 10th Anniversary of Independence **Obv:** Crowned arms with supporters **Rev:** Supplies on camel

Date	Mintage	F	VF	XF	Unc	BU
ND(1970) Proof	8,000	Value: 675				

KM# 22 200 SHILLINGS
28.0000 g., 0.9000 Gold .8102 oz. AGW **Subject:** 1st Anniversary of 1969 Revolution **Obv:** Crowned arms with supporters **Rev:** Monument

Date	Mintage	F	VF	XF	Unc	BU
ND(1970) Proof	—	Value: 645				

KM# 23 500 SHILLINGS
70.0000 g., 0.9000 Gold 2.0257 oz. AGW **Subject:** 10th Anniversary of Independence **Obv:** Crowned arms with supporters **Rev:** Building within map

Date	Mintage	F	VF	XF	Unc	BU
ND(1970) Proof	8,000	Value: 1,450				

REFORM COINAGE

100 Senti = 1 Shilling

KM# A24 5 SENTI
Aluminum **Series:** F.A.O. **Obv:** Value within circle **Rev:** Corn ears and flower flanked by dates **Shape:** Round

Date	Mintage	F	VF	XF	Unc	BU
1976	—	—	—	—	200	—

KM# 24 5 SENTI
Aluminum, 20 mm. **Series:** F.A.O. **Obv:** Crowned arms with supporters **Rev:** Value above fruit, grains and bread **Shape:** 12-sided

Date	Mintage	F	VF	XF	Unc	BU
1976	18,500,000	—	0.10	0.20	0.35	0.50

KM# 25 10 SENTI
Aluminum, 23.5 mm. **Series:** F.A.O. **Obv:** Crowned arms with supporters **Rev:** Lamb flanked by dates below value **Edge:** Plain **Shape:** 12-sided

Date	Mintage	F	VF	XF	Unc	BU
1976	40,500,000	—	0.10	0.20	0.50	1.00

KM# 26 50 SENTI
Copper-Nickel **Series:** F.A.O. **Obv:** Crowned arms with supporters **Rev:** Value above grains and dates

Date	Mintage	F	VF	XF	Unc	BU
1976	10,080,000	—	0.15	0.25	0.75	1.00

KM# 26a 50 SENTI
Nickel Plated Steel **Series:** F.A.O. **Obv:** Crowned arms with supporters **Rev:** Value above grains and dates

Date	Mintage	F	VF	XF	Unc	BU
1984	—	—	1.00	2.00	5.00	—

KM# 27 SHILLING
Copper-Nickel **Series:** F.A.O. **Obv:** Crowned arms with supporters **Rev:** Lamb flanked by dates below value

Date	Mintage	F	VF	XF	Unc	BU
1976	20,040,000	—	0.35	0.65	2.25	2.50

KM# 27a SHILLING
Nickel Plated Steel **Series:** F.A.O. **Obv:** Crowned arms with supporters **Rev:** Lamb flanked by dates below value

Date	Mintage	F	VF	XF	Unc	BU
1984	—	—	2.00	4.00	10.00	—

KM# 28 10 SHILLINGS
Copper-Nickel **Subject:** 10th Anniversary of Republic **Obv:** Crowned arms with supporters **Rev:** Workers

Date	Mintage	F	VF	XF	Unc	BU
ND(1979)	—	—	—	—	7.00	8.00

KM# 28a 10 SHILLINGS
28.2800 g., 0.9250 Silver .8411 oz. ASW **Subject:** 10th Anniversary of Republic **Obv:** Crowned arms with supporters **Rev:** Workers

Date	Mintage	F	VF	XF	Unc	BU
ND(1979) Proof	Est. 5,000	Value: 37.50				

KM# 29 10 SHILLINGS
Copper-Nickel **Subject:** 10th Anniversary of Republic **Obv:** Crowned arms with supporters **Rev:** Seated figures in front of tents

Date	Mintage	F	VF	XF	Unc	BU
ND(1979)	—	—	—	—	7.00	8.00

KM# 29a 10 SHILLINGS
28.2800 g., 0.9250 Silver .8411 oz. ASW **Subject:** 10th Anniversary of Republic **Obv:** Crowned arms with supporters **Rev:** Seated figures in front of tents

Date	Mintage	F	VF	XF	Unc	BU
ND(1979) Proof	Est. 5,000	Value: 38.50				

KM# 30 10 SHILLINGS
Copper-Nickel **Subject:** 10th Anniversary of Republic **Obv:** Crowned arms with supporters **Rev:** Lab workers

Date	Mintage	F	VF	XF	Unc	BU
ND(1979)	—	—	—	—	7.00	8.00

KM# 30a 10 SHILLINGS
28.2800 g., 0.9250 Silver .8411 oz. ASW **Subject:** 10th Anniversary of Republic **Obv:** Crowned arms with supporters **Rev:** Lab workers

Date	Mintage	F	VF	XF	Unc	BU
ND(1979) Proof	Est. 5,000	Value: 36.50				

KM# 31 10 SHILLINGS
Copper-Nickel **Subject:** 10th Anniversary of Republic **Obv:** Crowned arms with supporters **Rev:** Dancers

Date	Mintage	F	VF	XF	Unc	BU
ND(1979)	—	—	—	—	7.00	8.00

KM# 31a 10 SHILLINGS
28.2800 g., 0.9250 Silver .8411 oz. ASW **Subject:** 10th Anniversary of Republic **Obv:** Crowned arms with supporters **Rev:** Dancers

Date	Mintage	F	VF	XF	Unc	BU
ND(1979) Proof	Est. 5,000	Value: 37.50				

KM# 32 10 SHILLINGS
Copper-Nickel **Subject:** 10th Anniversary of Republic **Obv:** Crowned arms with supporters **Rev:** Man and woman

Date	Mintage	F	VF	XF	Unc	BU
ND(1979)	—	—	—	—	7.00	8.00

KM# 32a 10 SHILLINGS
28.2800 g., 0.9250 Silver .8411 oz. ASW **Subject:** 10th Anniversary of Republic **Obv:** Crowned arms with supporters **Rev:** Man and woman

Date	Mintage	F	VF	XF	Unc	BU
ND(1979) Proof	Est. 5,000	Value: 37.50				

KM# 40 25 SHILLINGS
Copper-Nickel **Subject:** World Fisheries Conference **Obv:** Crowned arms with supporters **Rev:** Green sea turtle **Rev. Designer:** Stuart Devlin

Date	Mintage	F	VF	XF	Unc	BU
ND(1984)	100,000	—	—	12.00	35.00	45.00

KM# 40a 25 SHILLINGS
28.2800 g., 0.9250 Silver .8411 oz. ASW **Subject:** World Fisheries Conference **Obv:** Crowned arms with supporters **Rev:** Green sea turtle

Date	Mintage	F	VF	XF	Unc	BU
ND(1984) Proof	20,000	Value: 75.00				

KM# 40b 25 SHILLINGS
47.5400 g., 0.9170 Gold 1.4011 oz. AGW **Subject:** World Fisheries Conference **Obv:** Crowned arms with supporters **Rev:** Green sea turtle

Date	Mintage	F	VF	XF	Unc	BU
ND(1984) Proof	200	Value: 1,100				

KM# 38 150 SHILLINGS
28.2800 g., 0.9250 Silver .8411 oz. ASW **Series:** International Year of Disabled Persons **Obv:** Crowned arms with supporters **Rev:** Head left, emblem at lower left

Date	Mintage	F	VF	XF	Unc	BU
1983	5,500	—	—	—	40.00	45.00
1983 Proof	5,500	Value: 50.00				

KM# 33 1500 SHILLINGS
15.9800 g., 0.9170 Gold .4711 oz. AGW **Subject:** 10th Anniversary of Republic **Obv:** Crowned arms with supporters **Rev:** Workers facing

Date	Mintage	F	VF	XF	Unc	BU
ND(1979)	500	—	—	—	345	350
ND(1979) Proof	500	Value: 360				

KM# 34 1500 SHILLINGS
15.9800 g., 0.9170 Gold .4711 oz. AGW **Subject:** 10th Anniversary of Republic **Obv:** Crowned arms with supporters **Rev:** Seated figures in front of tents

Date	Mintage	F	VF	XF	Unc	BU
ND(1979)	500	—	—	—	345	350
ND(1979) Proof	500	Value: 360				

KM# 35 1500 SHILLINGS
15.9800 g., 0.9170 Gold .4711 oz. AGW **Subject:** 10th Anniversary of Republic **Obv:** Crowned arms with supporters **Rev:** Lab workers

Date	Mintage	F	VF	XF	Unc	BU
ND(1979)	500	—	—	—	345	350
ND(1979) Proof	500	Value: 360				

KM# 36 1500 SHILLINGS
15.9800 g., 0.9170 Gold .4711 oz. AGW **Subject:** 10th Anniversary of Republic **Obv:** Crowned arms with supporters **Rev:** Dancers

Date	Mintage	F	VF	XF	Unc	BU
ND(1979)	500	—	—	—	345	350
ND(1979) Proof	500	Value: 360				

KM# 37 1500 SHILLINGS
15.9800 g., 0.9170 Gold .4711 oz. AGW **Subject:** 10th Anniversary of Republic **Obv:** Crowned arms with supporters **Rev:** Man and woman

Date	Mintage	F	VF	XF	Unc	BU
1979	500	—	—	—	345	350
1979 Proof	500	Value: 360				

KM# 39 1500 SHILLINGS
15.9800 g., 0.9170 Gold .4711 oz. AGW **Series:** International Year of Disabled Persons **Obv:** Crowned arms with supporters **Rev:** Emblem above busts facing

Date	Mintage	F	VF	XF	Unc	BU
1983	—	—	—	—	350	375
1983 Proof	—	Value: 400				

REPUBLIC OF SOMALIA

STANDARD COINAGE

100 Centesimi = 1 Somalo

KM# 45 5 SHILLING / SCELLINI
Aluminum **Series:** F.A.O. **Obv:** Crowned arms with supporters **Rev:** Elephant

Date	Mintage	F	VF	XF	Unc	BU
2000	—	—	—	—	1.50	1.75

KM# 46 10 SHILLINGS / SCELLINI
Aluminum, 22 mm. **Series:** F.A.O. **Obv:** Crowned arms with supporters **Rev:** Camel

Date	Mintage	F	VF	XF	Unc	BU
1999	—	—	—	—	2.00	2.25
2000(1999)	—	—	—	—	2.00	2.25

KM# 90 10 SHILLINGS / SCELLINI
4.8200 g., Nickel Clad Steel, 25 mm. **Series:** Asian Astrology **Obv:** Crowned arms with supporters **Rev:** Rat **Edge:** Plain

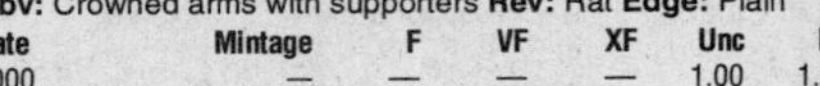

Date	Mintage	F	VF	XF	Unc	BU
2000	—	—	—	—	1.00	1.25

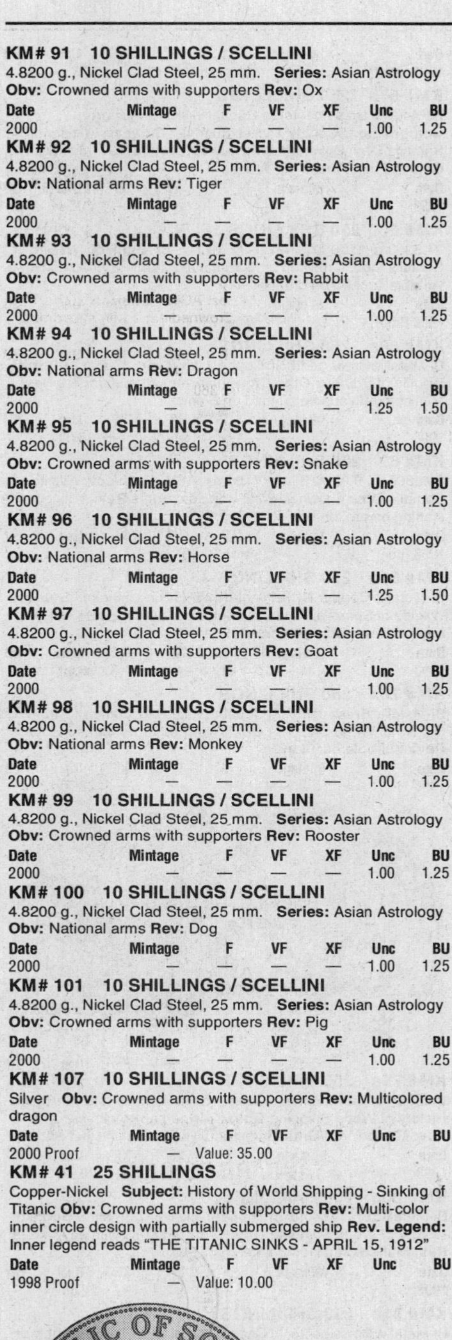

KM# 91 10 SHILLINGS / SCELLINI

4.8200 g., Nickel Clad Steel, 25 mm. **Series:** Asian Astrology **Obv:** Crowned arms with supporters **Rev:** Ox

Date	Mintage	F	VF	XF	Unc	BU
2000	—	—	—	—	1.00	1.25

KM# 92 10 SHILLINGS / SCELLINI

4.8200 g., Nickel Clad Steel, 25 mm. **Series:** Asian Astrology **Obv:** National arms **Rev:** Tiger

Date	Mintage	F	VF	XF	Unc	BU
2000	—	—	—	—	1.00	1.25

KM# 93 10 SHILLINGS / SCELLINI

4.8200 g., Nickel Clad Steel, 25 mm. **Series:** Asian Astrology **Obv:** Crowned arms with supporters **Rev:** Rabbit

Date	Mintage	F	VF	XF	Unc	BU
2000	—	—	—	—	1.00	1.25

KM# 94 10 SHILLINGS / SCELLINI

4.8200 g., Nickel Clad Steel, 25 mm. **Series:** Asian Astrology **Obv:** National arms **Rev:** Dragon

Date	Mintage	F	VF	XF	Unc	BU
2000	—	—	—	—	1.25	1.50

KM# 95 10 SHILLINGS / SCELLINI

4.8200 g., Nickel Clad Steel, 25 mm. **Series:** Asian Astrology **Obv:** Crowned arms with supporters **Rev:** Snake

Date	Mintage	F	VF	XF	Unc	BU
2000	—	—	—	—	1.00	1.25

KM# 96 10 SHILLINGS / SCELLINI

4.8200 g., Nickel Clad Steel, 25 mm. **Series:** Asian Astrology **Obv:** National arms **Rev:** Horse

Date	Mintage	F	VF	XF	Unc	BU
2000	—	—	—	—	1.25	1.50

KM# 97 10 SHILLINGS / SCELLINI

4.8200 g., Nickel Clad Steel, 25 mm. **Series:** Asian Astrology **Obv:** Crowned arms with supporters **Rev:** Goat

Date	Mintage	F	VF	XF	Unc	BU
2000	—	—	—	—	1.00	1.25

KM# 98 10 SHILLINGS / SCELLINI

4.8200 g., Nickel Clad Steel, 25 mm. **Series:** Asian Astrology **Obv:** National arms **Rev:** Monkey

Date	Mintage	F	VF	XF	Unc	BU
2000	—	—	—	—	1.00	1.25

KM# 99 10 SHILLINGS / SCELLINI

4.8200 g., Nickel Clad Steel, 25 mm. **Series:** Asian Astrology **Obv:** Crowned arms with supporters **Rev:** Rooster

Date	Mintage	F	VF	XF	Unc	BU
2000	—	—	—	—	1.00	1.25

KM# 100 10 SHILLINGS / SCELLINI

4.8200 g., Nickel Clad Steel, 25 mm. **Series:** Asian Astrology **Obv:** National arms **Rev:** Dog

Date	Mintage	F	VF	XF	Unc	BU
2000	—	—	—	—	1.00	1.25

KM# 101 10 SHILLINGS / SCELLINI

4.8200 g., Nickel Clad Steel, 25 mm. **Series:** Asian Astrology **Obv:** Crowned arms with supporters **Rev:** Pig

Date	Mintage	F	VF	XF	Unc	BU
2000	—	—	—	—	1.00	1.25

KM# 107 10 SHILLINGS / SCELLINI

Silver **Obv:** Crowned arms with supporters **Rev:** Multicolored dragon

Date	Mintage	F	VF	XF	Unc	BU
2000 Proof	—	Value: 35.00				

KM# 41 25 SHILLINGS

Copper-Nickel **Subject:** History of World Shipping - Sinking of Titanic **Obv:** Crowned arms with supporters **Rev:** Multi-color inner circle design with partially submerged ship **Rev. Legend:** Inner legend reads "THE TITANIC SINKS - APRIL 15, 1912"

Date	Mintage	F	VF	XF	Unc	BU
1998 Proof	—	Value: 10.00				

KM# 47 25 SHILLINGS

2.0000 g., Copper-Nickel, 37.9 mm. **Subject:** Wildlife of Somalia **Obv:** Crowned arms with supporters **Rev:** Multicolored hippopotamus **Edge:** Plain

Date	Mintage	F	VF	XF	Unc	BU
1998	—	—	—	—	15.00	—

KM# 50 25 SHILLINGS

Copper-Nickel **Subject:** History of World Shipping - Cutty Sark **Obv:** Crowned arms with supporters **Rev:** Multicolored Ship **Edge:** Plain **Note:** Weight varies 18.42-20.2g.

Date	Mintage	F	VF	XF	Unc	BU
1998 Proof	—	Value: 10.00				

KM# 51 25 SHILLINGS

Copper-Nickel **Subject:** History of World Shipping - Caravel Nina **Obv:** Crowned arms with supporters **Rev:** Multicolored ship

Date	Mintage	F	VF	XF	Unc	BU
1998 Proof	—	Value: 10.00				

KM# 52 25 SHILLINGS

Copper-Nickel **Subject:** History of World Shipping **Obv:** Crowned arms with supporters **Rev:** Multicolored Greek Trireme **Note:** Weight varies 18.42-20.2g.

Date	Mintage	VG	F	VF	XF	Unc
1998 Proof	—	Value: 10.00				

KM# 53 25 SHILLINGS

Copper-Nickel **Subject:** History of World Shipping **Obv:** Crowned arms with supporters **Rev:** Multicolored Roman merchant ship **Note:** Weight varies 18.42-20.2g.

Date	Mintage	F	VF	XF	Unc	BU
1998 Proof	—	Value: 10.00				

KM# 54 25 SHILLINGS

Copper-Nickel **Subject:** History of World Shipping **Obv:** Crowned arms with supporters **Rev:** Multicolored Hansa Trading Cog **Note:** Weight varies 18.42-20.2g.

Date	Mintage	F	VF	XF	Unc	BU
1998 Proof	—	Value: 10.00				

KM# 55 25 SHILLINGS

Copper-Nickel **Subject:** History of World Shipping **Obv:** Crowned arms with supporters **Rev:** Multicolored Titanic **Note:** Weight varies 18.42-20.2g.

Date	Mintage	F	VF	XF	Unc	BU
1998 Proof	—	Value: 10.00				

KM# 56 25 SHILLINGS

Copper-Nickel **Subject:** Wildlife of Somalia **Obv:** Crowned arms with supporters **Rev:** Multicolored Ostrich **Note:** Weight varies 18.42-20.2g.

Date	Mintage	F	VF	XF	Unc	BU
1998	—	—	—	—	17.50	20.00

KM# 57 25 SHILLINGS

Copper-Nickel **Subject:** Wildlife of Somalia **Obv:** Crowned arms with supporters **Rev:** Multicolored running Eland **Note:** Weight varies 18.42-20.2g.

Date	Mintage	F	VF	XF	Unc	BU
1998	—	—	—	—	17.50	20.00

KM# 58 25 SHILLINGS

Copper-Nickel **Subject:** Wildlife of Somalia **Obv:** Crowned arms with supporters **Rev:** Multicolored Spurfowl in grass **Note:** Weight varies 18.42-20.2g.

Date	Mintage	F	VF	XF	Unc	BU
1998	—	—	—	—	17.50	20.00

KM# 59 25 SHILLINGS

Copper-Nickel **Subject:** Wildlife of Somalia **Obv:** Crowned arms with supporters **Rev:** Multicolored Leopard **Note:** Weight varies 18.42-20.2g.

Date	Mintage	F	VF	XF	Unc	BU
1998	—	—	—	—	17.50	20.00

KM# 60 25 SHILLINGS

Copper-Nickel **Subject:** Wildlife of Somalia **Obv:** Crowned arms with supporters **Rev:** Multicolored bird on branch **Note:** Weight varies 18.42-20.2g.

Date	Mintage	F	VF	XF	Unc	BU
1998	—	—	—	—	17.50	24.00

KM# 61 25 SHILLINGS

Copper-Nickel **Subject:** Wildlife of Somalia **Obv:** Crowned arms with supporters **Rev:** Multicolored variable sunbird on branch **Note:** Weight varies 18.42-20.2g.

Date	Mintage	F	VF	XF	Unc	BU
1998	—	—	—	—	17.50	24.00

KM# 62 25 SHILLINGS

Copper-Nickel **Subject:** Wildlife of Somalia **Obv:** Crowned arms with supporters **Rev:** Multicolored starling on broken branch **Note:** Weight varies 18.42-20.2g.

Date	Mintage	F	VF	XF	Unc	BU
1998	—	—	—	—	17.50	24.00

KM# 141 25 SHILLINGS

20.0000 g., Copper-Nickel, 38 mm. **Subject:** 100th Birthday - British Queen Mother **Obv:** Crowned arms with supporters above value **Rev:** Queen Mother **Edge:** Plain

Date	Mintage	F	VF	XF	Unc	BU
ND (1999)	—	—	—	—	10.00	12.00

KM# 106 25 SHILLINGS

Copper-Nickel **Subject:** Fall of Berlin Wall **Obv:** Crowned arms with supporters **Rev:** Berlin wall destruction scene

Date	Mintage	F	VF	XF	Unc	BU
1999	—	—	—	—	8.00	—

KM# 108 25 SHILLINGS

Silver **Obv:** Crowned arms with supporters **Rev:** Multicolored penguins

Date	Mintage	F	VF	XF	Unc	BU
2000 Proof	—	Value: 30.00				

KM# 70 25 SHILLINGS

Copper-Nickel, 38 mm. **Subject:** Winston Churchill **Obv:** Crowned arms with supporters **Rev:** Bust facing **Edge:** Plain

Date	Mintage	F	VF	XF	Unc	BU
2000	—	—	—	—	5.00	6.00

KM# 71 25 SHILLINGS

Copper-Nickel, 38 mm. **Subject:** Pope John Paul II **Obv:** Crowned arms with supporters **Rev:** Bust facing **Edge:** Plain

Date	Mintage	F	VF	XF	Unc	BU
2000	—	—	—	—	5.00	6.00

KM# 72 25 SHILLINGS

20.0000 g., Copper-Nickel, 38 mm. **Subject:** Nelson Mandela **Obv:** Crowned arms with supporters **Rev:** Bust facing **Edge:** Reeded

Date	Mintage	F	VF	XF	Unc	BU
2000	—	—	—	—	5.00	6.00

KM# 73 25 SHILLINGS
Copper-Nickel **Subject:** Che Guevara **Obv:** Crowned arms with supporters **Rev:** Bust with hat facing

Date	Mintage	F	VF	XF	Unc	BU
2000	—	—	—	—	5.00	6.00

KM# 74 25 SHILLINGS
Copper-Nickel, 37.9 mm. **Subject:** Emperor Hirohito **Obv:** Crowned arms with supporters **Rev:** Bust facing **Edge:** Plain

Date	Mintage	F	VF	XF	Unc	BU
2000 Prooflike	—	—	—	—	7.00	8.50

KM# 75 25 SHILLINGS
Copper-Nickel **Subject:** Mao Tse-Tung **Obv:** Crowned arms with supporters **Rev:** Bust facing

Date	Mintage	F	VF	XF	Unc	BU
2000 Prooflike	—	—	—	—	7.00	8.50

KM# 76 25 SHILLINGS
Copper-Nickel **Subject:** Berlin **Obv:** Crowned arms with supporters **Rev:** Berlin wall destruction scene

Date	Mintage	F	VF	XF	Unc	BU
ND(2000) Prooflike	—	—	—	—	7.00	8.50

KM# 113 150 SHILLINGS
15.0000 g., 0.9990 Silver 0.4818 oz. ASW, 34.25 mm. **Subject:** Millennium **Obv:** Crowned arms with supporters **Rev:** World globe **Edge:** Reeded

Date	Mintage	F	VF	XF	Unc	BU
2000	—	Value: 25.00				

KM# 77 150 SHILLINGS
14.8100 g., 0.9990 Silver .4757 oz. ASW, 34.25 mm. **Subject:** Christopher Columbus **Obv:** Crowned arms with supporters **Rev:** Cameo above 3 ships **Edge:** Reeded

Date	Mintage	F	VF	XF	Unc	BU
2000 Proof	—	Value: 25.00				

KM# 42 250 SHILLINGS
23.5000 g., 0.9250 Silver .6989 oz. ASW **Subject:** History of World Shipping - Sinking of Titanic **Obv:** Crowned arms with supporters **Rev:** Multicolored sinking ship

Date	Mintage	F	VF	XF	Unc	BU
1998 Proof	20,000	Value: 35.00				

KM# 42a 250 SHILLINGS
Bi-Metallic Copper-Nickel center in Brass ring **Subject:** Historic Ships **Obv:** Crowned arms with supporters **Rev:** Multicolor sinking ship

Date	Mintage	F	VF	XF	Unc	BU
1998	—	—	—	—	22.50	—

KM# 48 250 SHILLINGS
23.7000 g., 0.9250 Silver .7048 oz. ASW, 38.1 mm. **Subject:** Wildlife of Somalia **Obv:** Crowned arms with supporters **Rev:** Multicolored Hippopotamus **Edge:** Reeded

Date	Mintage	F	VF	XF	Unc	BU
1998 Proof	—	Value: 25.00				

KM# 48a 250 SHILLINGS
Bi-Metallic Copper-Nickel center in Brass ring, 38 mm. **Subject:** Wildlife of Somalia **Obv:** Crowned arms with supporters **Rev:** Multicolored Hippopotamus **Edge:** Reeded

Date	Mintage	F	VF	XF	Unc	BU
1998	—	—	—	—	25.00	—

KM# 49 250 SHILLINGS
23.7000 g., 0.9250 Silver .7048 oz. ASW **Subject:** Wildlife of Somalia **Obv:** Crowned arms with supporters **Rev:** Multicolored Ostrich

Date	Mintage	F	VF	XF	Unc	BU
1998 Proof	—	Value: 35.00				

KM# 49a 250 SHILLINGS
Bi-Metallic Brass center in Copper-nickel ring, 38 mm. **Subject:** Wildlife of Somalia **Obv:** Crowned arms with supporters **Rev:** Multicolored Ostrich

Date	Mintage	F	VF	XF	Unc	BU
1998	—	—	—	—	30.00	—

KM# 64 250 SHILLINGS
24.8300 g., 0.9000 Silver .7185 oz. ASW, 37.2 mm. **Subject:** Wildlife of Somalia **Obv:** Crowned arms with supporters **Rev:** Multicolored Yellow-necked Spurfowl in grass **Edge:** Reeded

Date	Mintage	F	VF	XF	Unc	BU
1998 Proof	—	Value: 30.00				

KM# 64a 250 SHILLINGS
Bi-Metallic Brass center in Copper-nickel ring, 38 mm. **Subject:** Wildlife of Somalia **Obv:** Crowned arms with supporters **Rev:** Multicolored Yellow-necked Spurfowl in grass

Date	Mintage	F	VF	XF	Unc	BU
1998	—	—	—	—	30.00	—

KM# 65 250 SHILLINGS
24.8300 g., 0.9000 Silver .7185 oz. ASW **Subject:** Wildlife of Somalia **Obv:** Crowned arms with supporters **Rev:** Multicolored running Eland

Date	Mintage	F	VF	XF	Unc	BU
1998 Proof	—	Value: 32.50				

KM# 66 250 SHILLINGS
24.8300 g., 0.9000 Silver .7185 oz. ASW **Subject:** Wildlife of Somalia **Obv:** Crowned arms with supporters **Rev:** Multicolored Leopard

Date	Mintage	F	VF	XF	Unc	BU
1998 Proof	—	Value: 35.00				

KM# 66a 250 SHILLINGS
Bi-Metallic Brass center in Copper-nickel ring, 38 mm. **Subject:** Wildlife of Somalia **Obv:** Crowned arms with supporters **Rev:** Multicolored Leopard

Date	Mintage	F	VF	XF	Unc	BU
1998	—	—	—	—	24.00	—

KM# 67 250 SHILLINGS
24.8300 g., 0.9000 Silver .7185 oz. ASW **Subject:** Wildlife of Somalia **Obv:** Crowned arms with supporters **Rev:** Multicolored Golden Palm Weaver on branch

Date	Mintage	F	VF	XF	Unc	BU
1998 Proof	—	Value: 35.00				

KM# 67a 250 SHILLINGS
Bi-Metallic Brass center in Copper-nickel ring **Ring Composition:** Copper-Nickel, 38 mm. **Subject:** Wildlife of Somalia **Obv:** Crowned arms with supporters **Rev:** Multicolored Golden Palm Weaver on branch

Date	Mintage	F	VF	XF	Unc	BU
1998	—	—	—	—	30.00	—

KM# 68 250 SHILLINGS
24.8300 g., 0.9000 Silver .7185 oz. ASW **Subject:** Wildlife of Somalia **Obv:** Crowned arms with supporters **Rev:** Multicolored variable sunbird on branch

Date	Mintage	F	VF	XF	Unc	BU
1998 Proof	—	Value: 35.00				

KM# 68a 250 SHILLINGS
Bi-Metallic Brass center in Copper-nickel ring, 38 mm. **Subject:** Wildlife of Somalia **Obv:** Crowned arms with supporters **Rev:** Multicolored variable sunbird on branch

Date	Mintage	F	VF	XF	Unc	BU
1998	—	—	—	—	35.00	—

KM# 69 250 SHILLINGS
24.8300 g., 0.9000 Silver .7185 oz. ASW **Subject:** Wildlife of Somalia **Obv:** Crowned arms with supporters **Rev:** Multicolored starling on broken branch

Date	Mintage	F	VF	XF	Unc	BU
1998 Proof	—	Value: 35.00				

KM# 69a 250 SHILLINGS
Bi-Metallic Copper-Nickel center in Brass ring, 38 mm. **Subject:** Wildlife of Somalia **Obv:** Crowned arms with supporters **Rev:** Multicolored starling on broken branch

Date	Mintage	F	VF	XF	Unc	BU
1998	—	—	—	—	30.00	—

KM# 78a 250 SHILLINGS
Bi-Metallic Brass center in Copper-nickel ring, 38 mm. **Subject:** History of World Shipping **Obv:** Crowned arms with supporters **Rev:** Multicolored Titanic

Date	Mintage	F	VF	XF	Unc	BU
1998	—	—	—	—	22.50	—

KM# 79a 250 SHILLINGS
Bi-Metallic Brass center in Copper-nickel ring, 38 mm. **Subject:** History of World Shipping **Obv:** Crowned arms with supporters **Rev:** Multicolored Greek trirema

Date	Mintage	F	VF	XF	Unc	BU
1998	—	—	—	—	22.50	—

KM# 80a 250 SHILLINGS
Bi-Metallic Brass center in Copper-nickel ring, 38 mm. **Subject:** History of World Shipping **Obv:** Crowned arms with supporters **Rev:** Multicolored Roman merchant ship

Date	Mintage	F	VF	XF	Unc	BU
1998	—	—	—	—	22.50	—

KM# 81a 250 SHILLINGS
Bi-Metallic Brass center in Copper-nickel ring, 38 mm. **Subject:** History of World Shipping **Obv:** Crowned arms with supporters **Rev:** Multicolored Hanseatic Trading Cog

Date	Mintage	F	VF	XF	Unc	BU
1998	—	—	—	—	22.50	—

KM# 82a 250 SHILLINGS
Bi-Metallic Brass center in Copper-nickel ring, 38 mm. **Subject:** History of World Shipping **Obv:** Crowned arms with supporters **Rev:** Multicolored Caravel "Nina" **Edge:** Reeded

Date	Mintage	F	VF	XF	Unc	BU
1998	—	—	—	—	22.50	—

KM# 83a 250 SHILLINGS
Bi-Metallic Brass center in Copper-nickel ring, 38 mm. **Subject:**

History of World Shipping **Obv:** Crowned arms with supporters **Rev:** Multicolored Clipper "Cutty Sark"

Date	Mintage	F	VF	XF	Unc	BU
1998	—	—	—	—	22.50	—

KM# 102 250 SHILLINGS
24.0000 g., 0.9000 Silver .6945 oz. ASW, 38.1 mm. **Subject:** Olympics **Obv:** Crowned arms with supporters **Rev:** Multicolor skier **Edge:** Reeded

Date	Mintage	F	VF	XF	Unc	BU
1998 Proof	—	Value: 40.00				

KM# 142 250 SHILLINGS
22.0000 g., Tri-Metallic Gold Plated Brass center in Silver Plated Brass inner ring within a Gold Plated Brass outer ring, 38 mm. **Subject:** 100th Birthday - British Queen Mother **Obv:** Crowned arms with supporters above value **Rev:** Queen Mother **Edge:** Reeded

Date	Mintage	F	VF	XF	Unc	BU
ND (1999)	—	—	—	—	35.00	40.00

KM# 105 250 SHILLINGS
23.1000 g., 0.9250 Silver 0.841 oz. ASW, 38.6 mm. **Obv:** Crowned arms with supporters **Rev:** Two giraffes **Edge:** Reeded

Date	Mintage	F	VF	XF	Unc	BU
1999 Proof	—	Value: 35.00				

KM# 114 250 SHILLINGS
23.0000 g., 0.9250 Silver 0.684 oz. ASW, 38 mm. **Subject:** Winston Churchill **Obv:** Crowned arms with supporters **Rev:** Bust facing **Edge:** Reeded

Date	Mintage	F	VF	XF	Unc	BU
2000	—	—	—	—	40.00	42.50

KM# 115 250 SHILLINGS
23.0000 g., 0.9250 Silver 0.684 oz. ASW, 38 mm. **Subject:** Pope John Paul II **Obv:** Crowned arms with supporters **Rev:** Bust facing **Edge:** Reeded

Date	Mintage	F	VF	XF	Unc	BU
2000	—	—	—	—	40.00	42.50

KM# 116 250 SHILLINGS
23.0000 g., 0.9250 Silver 0.684 oz. ASW, 38 mm. **Subject:** Nelson Mandela **Obv:** Crowned arms with supporters **Rev:** Bust facing **Edge:** Reeded

Date	Mintage	F	VF	XF	Unc	BU
2000	—	—	—	—	40.00	42.50

KM# 117 250 SHILLINGS
23.0000 g., 0.9250 Silver 0.684 oz. ASW, 38 mm. **Obv:** Crowned arms with supporters **Rev:** Bust of Emperor Hirohito facing **Edge:** Reeded

Date	Mintage	F	VF	XF	Unc	BU
2000	—	—	—	—	42.50	45.00

KM# 118 250 SHILLINGS
23.0000 g., 0.9250 Silver 0.684 oz. ASW, 38 mm. **Obv:** Crowned arms with supporters **Rev:** Head Of Mao Tse-Tung right **Edge:** Reeded

Date	Mintage	F	VF	XF	Unc	BU
2000	—	—	—	—	42.50	45.00

KM# 119 250 SHILLINGS
23.0000 g., 0.9250 Silver 0.684 oz. ASW, 38 mm. **Obv:** Crowned arms with supporters **Rev:** Bust Of Che Guevara facing **Edge:** Reeded

Date	Mintage	F	VF	XF	Unc	BU
2000	—	—	—	—	40.00	42.50

KM# 104 250 SHILLINGS
22.1000 g., Bi-Metallic Brass center in Copper-nickel ring, 38 mm. **Obv:** Crowned arms with supporters **Rev:** Bust of Che Guevara facing **Edge:** Reeded

Date	Mintage	F	VF	XF	Unc	BU
2000	—	—	—	—	30.00	—

KM# 63 250 SHILLINGS
24.8300 g., 0.9000 Silver .7185 oz. ASW, 37.2 mm. **Subject:** Marine Life Protection **Obv:** Crowned arms with supporters **Rev:** Multicolor penguins **Edge:** Reeded

Date	Mintage	F	VF	XF	Unc	BU
2000 Proof	—	Value: 45.00				

KM# 84 5000 SHILLINGS / SCELLINI
7.0600 g., 0.9990 Silver .2268 oz. ASW, 29.7 mm. **Subject:** Tall Ship Series: Amerigo Vespucci **Obv:** Crowned arms with supporters **Rev:** Sailing ship **Edge:** Plain

Date	Mintage	F	VF	XF	Unc	BU
1998 Proof	—	Value: 25.00				

KM# 85 5000 SHILLINGS / SCELLINI
7.0600 g., 0.9990 Silver .2268 oz. ASW **Subject:** Tall Ships Series: Sedov **Obv:** Crowned arms with supporters **Rev:** Sailing ship

Date	Mintage	F	VF	XF	Unc	BU
1998 Proof	—	Value: 25.00				

KM# 86 5000 SHILLINGS / SCELLINI
7.0600 g., 0.9990 Silver .2268 oz. ASW **Subject:** Tall Ships Series: Gorch Fock **Obv:** Crowned arms with supporters **Rev:** Sailing ship

Date	Mintage	F	VF	XF	Unc	BU
1998 Proof	—	Value: 25.00				

KM# 87 5000 SHILLINGS / SCELLINI
7.0600 g., 0.9990 Silver .2268 oz. ASW **Subject:** Tall Ships Series: Libertad **Obv:** Crowned arms with supporters **Rev:** Sailing ship

Date	Mintage	F	VF	XF	Unc	BU
1998 Proof	—	Value: 25.00				

KM# 88 5000 SHILLINGS / SCELLINI
7.0600 g., 0.9990 Silver .2268 oz. ASW **Subject:** Tall Ships Series: Alexander von Humboldt **Obv:** Crowned arms with supporters **Rev:** Sailing ship

Date	Mintage	F	VF	XF	Unc	BU
1998 Proof	—	Value: 25.00				

KM# 89 5000 SHILLINGS / SCELLINI
7.0600 g., 0.9990 Silver .2268 oz. ASW **Subject:** Tall Ship Series: Eagle **Obv:** Crowned arms with supporters **Rev:** Sailing ship

Date	Mintage	F	VF	XF	Unc	BU
1998 Proof	—	Value: 25.00				

KM# 43 10000 SHILLINGS / SCELLINI
15.0000 g., 0.9990 Silver .4818 oz. ASW **Subject:** Fauna of Africa **Obv:** Crowned arms with supporters **Rev:** Ostriches

Date	Mintage	F	VF	XF	Unc	BU
1998 Proof	—	Value: 40.00				

KM# 44 10000 SHILLINGS / SCELLINI
15.0000 g., 0.9990 Silver .4818 oz. ASW **Subject:** Fauna of Africa **Obv:** Crowned arms with supporters **Rev:** Three Dammah Oryx

Date	Mintage	F	VF	XF	Unc	BU
1998 Proof	—	Value: 50.00				

PIEFORTS

KM#	Date	Mintage	Identification	Mkt Val
P1	1983	500	150 Shillings. 0.9250 Silver.	115
P2	1983	—	1500 Shillings. Gold. KM39.	875
P3	ND(1984)	500	25 Shillings. 0.9250 Silver.	100
P4	1998	2,500	250 Shillings. 0.9250 Silver. 47.5400 g. Skier.	135
P5	1998	—	250 Shillings. Silver. Titanic. KM42.	70.00
P6	1998	—	250 Shillings. 0.9250 Silver. Ostrich. KM49.	50.00

PROVAS

KM#	Date	Mintage	Identification	Mkt Val
Pr1	1950	—	Centesimo.	50.00
Pr2	1950	—	5 Centesimi.	50.00
Pr3	1950	—	10 Centesimi.	50.00
Pr4	1950	—	50 Centesimi.	75.00
Pr5	1950	—	Somalo.	100

MINT SETS

KM#	Date	Mintage	Identification	Issue Price	Mkt Val
MS1	1979 (5)	—	KM33-37	2,375	1,400

PROOF SETS

KM#	Date	Mintage	Identification	Issue Price	Mkt Val
PS1	1965 (5)	6,325	KM10-14	—	2,150
PS2	1965 (5)	—	KM10-14. Giilt copper nickel.	—	—
PS3	1970 (5)	8,000	KM16, 17, 19, 21, 23	335	2,500
PS4	1970 (3)	14,500	KM18, 20, 22	—	1,100
PS5	1979 (5)	5,000	KM28a-32a	325	150
PS6	1979 (5)	—	KM33-37	3,125	1,500

SOMALILAND

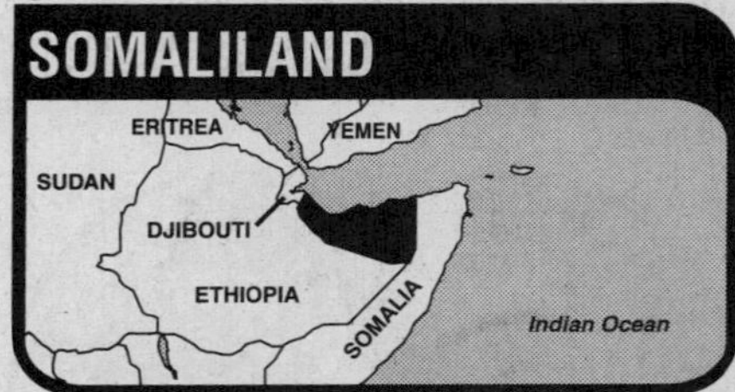

The Somaliland Republic, comprised of the former British Somaliland Protectorate is located on the coast of the northeastern projection of the African continent commonly referred to as the "Horn" on the southwestern end of the Gulf of Aden.

Bordered by Ethiopia to west and south and Somalia to the east. It has an area of 68,000* sq. mi. (176,000* sq. km). Capital: Hargeysa. It is mostly arid and mountainous except for the gulf shoreline.

The Protectorate of British Somaliland was established in 1888 and from 1905 a commissioner under the British Colonial Office administered the territory. Italian Somaliland was administered as a colony from1893 to 1941, when British forces occupied the territory. In 1950 the United Nations allowed Italy to resume control of Italian Somaliland under a trusteeship. In 1960 British and Italian Somaliland were united as Somalia, an independent republic outside the Commonwealth.

Civil war erupted in the late 1970's and continued until the capital of Somalia was taken in 1990. The United Nations provided aid and peacekeeping. A UN sponsored truce was signed in March 1992 and a peace plan and pact was signed Jan. 15, 1993. The northern Somali National Movement (SNM) declared a secession of the Somaliland Republic on May 17, 1991, which is not recognized by the Somali Democratic Republic.

The currency issued by the East African Currency Board was used in British Somaliland from 1945 to 1961; Somali currency was used later until 1995.

REPUBLIC

SHILLING COINAGE

KM# 1 SHILLING
1.0700 g., Aluminum, 20.5 mm. **Issuer:** Bank of Somaliland **Obv:** Bird **Obv. Legend:** REPUBLIC OF SOMALILAND **Rev:** Value **Rev. Legend:** • BAANKA SOMALILAND • **Edge:** Reeded

Date	Mintage	F	VF	XF	Unc	BU
1994	—	—	—	1.50	3.00	5.00

SOUTH AFRICA

The Republic of South Africa, located at the southern tip of Africa, has an area of 471,445 sq. mi. (1,221,043 sq. km.) and a population of *30.2 million. Capitals: Administrative, Pretoria; Legislative, Cape Town; Judicial, Bloemfontein. Manufacturing, mining and agriculture are the principal industries. Exports include wool, diamonds, gold, and metallic ores.

Portuguese navigator Bartholomew Diaz became the first European to sight the region of South Africa when he rounded the Cape of Good Hope in 1488, but throughout the 16th century the only white men to come ashore were the survivors of ships wrecked while attempting the stormy Cape passage. Jan van Riebeeck of the Dutch East India Company established the first permanent settlement in 1652. In subsequent decades additional Dutch, German and Huguenot refugees from France settled in the Cape area to form the Afrikaner segment of today's population.

Great Britain captured the Cape colony in 1795, and again in 1806, receiving permanent title in 1814. To escape British political rule and cultural dominance, many Afrikaner farmers (Boers) migrated northward (the Great Trek) beginning in 1836, and established the independent Boer Republics of the Transvaal (the South African Republic, Zuid Afrikaansche Republic) in 1852, and the Orange Free State in 1854. British political intrigues against the two republics, coupled with the discovery of diamonds and gold in the Boer-settled regions, led to the bitter Boer Wars (1880-81, 1899-1902) and the incorporation of the Boer republics into the British Empire.

On May 31, 1910, the two former Boer Republics (Transvaal and Orange Free State) were joined with the British colonies of Cape of Good Hope and Natal to form the Union of South Africa, a dominion of the British Empire. In 1934 the Union achieved status as a sovereign state within the British Empire.

Political integration of the various colonies did not still the conflict between the Afrikaners and the English-speaking groups, which continued to have a significant impact on political developments. A resurgence of Afrikaner nationalism in the 1940s and 1950s led to a referendum in the white community authorizing the relinquishment of dominion status and the establishment of a republic. The decision took effect on May 31, 1961. The Republic of South Africa withdrew from the British Commonwealth in Oct. 1961.

The apartheid era ended April 27, 1994 with the first democratic election for all people of South Africa. Nelson Mandela was inaugurated President May 10, 1994, and South Africa was readmitted into the Commonwealth of Nations. Walvis Bay, former enclave of Cape Province, transferred to Namibia.

South African coins and currency bear inscriptions in tribal languages, Afrikaans and English.

RULERS
British, until 1934

MONETARY SYSTEM

Until 1961
12 Pence = 1 Shilling
2 Shillings = 1 Florin
20 Shillings = 1 Pound (Pond)

Commencing 1961
100 Cents = 1 Rand

REPUBLIK

Zuid-Afrikaansche Republiek

STANDARD COINAGE

12 Pence = 1 Shilling; 20 Shillings = 1 Pond

KM# 11 1/2 POND
0.9990 Gold **Subject:** Veld-Boer War Siege Issue **Obv:** Monogram and date **Rev:** Inscription

Date	Mintage	F	VF	XF	Unc	BU
1902	986	750	1,350	2,750	5,000	—

UNION OF SOUTH AFRICA

Dominion under Great Britain

STANDARD COINAGE

12 Pence = 1 Shilling; 2 Shillings = 1 Florin; 20 Shillings 1 Pound

KM# 12.1 1/4 PENNY (Farthing)
Bronze **Ruler:** George V **Obv:** Crowned bust left **Obv. Designer:** E.B. MacKennal **Rev:** Wheat sprig and berries divide birds within circle **Rev. Designer:** G.T. Kruger-Gray

Date	Mintage	F	VF	XF	Unc	BU
1923	33,000	2.00	5.00	10.00	20.00	—
1923 Proof	1,402	Value: 30.00				
1924	95,000	1.50	2.50	5.00	10.00	—

KM# 12.2 1/4 PENNY (Farthing)
Bronze **Ruler:** George V **Obv:** Crowned bust left **Obv. Designer:** E.B. MacKennal **Rev:** Oat sprigs and berries divide birds within circle **Rev. Designer:** G.T. Kruger-Gray

Date	Mintage	F	VF	XF	Unc	BU
1926 Proof	16	Value: 6,000				
1928	64,000	1.50	3.00	5.00	12.50	—
1930	6,560	30.00	60.00	120	200	—
1930 Proof	14	Value: 1,200				
1931	154,000	1.00	1.50	4.00	6.00	—

KM# 12.3 1/4 PENNY (Farthing)
Bronze **Ruler:** George V **Obv:** Crowned bust left **Obv. Designer:** E.B. MacKennal **Rev:** Oat sprig and berries divide birds within circle **Rev. Designer:** G.T. Kruger-Gray

Date	Mintage	F	VF	XF	Unc	BU
1931	Inc. above	5.00	10.00	15.00	35.00	—
1931 Proof	62	Value: 200				
1932	105,000	1.00	1.50	3.50	7.00	—
1932 Proof	12	Value: 375				
1933	76	750	1,450	2,200	3,250	—
1933 Proof	20	Value: 4,000				
1934	52	750	1,450	2,200	3,250	—
1934 Proof	24	Value: 3,750				
1935	61,000	1.00	1.50	3.50	8.00	—
1935 Proof	20	Value: 3,000				
1936	43	350	750	1,100	2,000	—
1936 Proof	40	Value: 3,000				

KM# 23 1/4 PENNY (Farthing)
Bronze **Ruler:** George VI **Obv:** Head left **Obv. Designer:** T.H. Paget **Rev:** Oat sprig and berries divide birds within circle **Rev. Designer:** G.T. Kruger-Gray

Date	Mintage	F	VF	XF	Unc	BU
1937	38,000	1.50	3.00	6.00	12.50	—
1937 Proof	116	Value: 40.00				
1938	51,000	1.00	2.00	4.00	8.00	—
1938 Proof	44	Value: 100				
1939	102,000	0.50	1.50	3.00	7.50	—
1939 Proof	30	Value: 125				
1941	91,000	0.50	1.50	3.00	7.50	—
1942	3,756,000	0.25	0.50	1.00	2.00	—
1943	9,918,000	0.25	0.50	0.75	1.50	—
1943 Proof	104	Value: 40.00				
1944	4,468,000	0.25	0.50	0.75	2.00	—
1944 Proof	150	Value: 35.00				
1945	5,297,000	0.25	0.50	1.50	3.00	—
1945 Proof	150	Value: 35.00				
1946	4,378,000	0.25	0.50	1.50	4.00	—
1946 Proof	150	Value: 35.00				
1947	3,895,000	0.25	0.50	1.50	4.00	—
1947 Proof	2,600	Value: 4.00				

KM# 32.1 1/4 PENNY (Farthing)
Bronze **Ruler:** George VI **Obv:** Head left **Obv. Designer:** T.H. Paget **Rev:** Oat sprig and berries divide birds within circle **Rev. Designer:** G.T. Kruger-Gray

Date	Mintage	F	VF	XF	Unc	BU
1948	2,415,000	0.25	0.50	1.00	2.00	—
1948 Proof	1,120	Value: 3.00				
1949	3,568,000	0.25	0.50	1.00	2.50	—
1949 Proof	800	Value: 5.00				
1950	8,694,000	0.25	0.50	0.75	1.50	—
1950 Proof	500	Value: 8.00				

KM# 32.2 1/4 PENNY (Farthing)
Bronze, 20.5 mm. **Ruler:** Edward VIII **Obv:** Head left **Obv. Designer:** T.H. Paget **Rev:** Oat sprig and berries divide birds within circle **Rev. Legend:** SUID AFRIKA-SOUTH AFRICA **Rev. Designer:** G.T. Kruger-Gray

Date	Mintage	F	VF	XF	Unc	BU
1951	3,511,000	0.15	0.35	0.75	2.50	—
1951 Proof	2,000	Value: 2.00				
1952	2,805,000	0.15	0.35	0.75	2.00	—
1952 Proof	16,000	Value: 2.00				

KM# 44 1/4 PENNY (Farthing)
Bronze **Ruler:** Elizabeth II **Obv:** Laureate head right **Obv. Designer:** Mary Gillick **Rev:** Oat sprig and berries divide birds within circle **Rev. Designer:** G.T. Kruger-Gray

Date	Mintage	F	VF	XF	Unc	BU
1953	7,193,000	0.15	0.25	0.50	1.50	—
1953 Proof	5,000	Value: 2.00				
1954	6,568,000	0.15	0.25	0.50	1.50	—
1954 Proof	3,150	Value: 2.00				
1955	11,798,000	0.15	0.25	0.50	1.50	—
1955 Proof	2,850	Value: 2.00				
1956	1,287,000	0.15	0.25	0.50	2.50	—
1956 Proof	1,700	Value: 3.00				
1957	3,065,000	0.15	0.25	0.50	1.50	—
1957 Proof	1,130	Value: 4.00				
1958	5,452,000	0.15	0.25	0.50	1.50	—
1958 Proof	985	Value: 5.00				
1959	1,567,000	0.15	0.25	0.50	1.50	—
1959 Proof	900	Value: 6.00				
1960	1,022,999	0.15	0.25	0.50	2.00	—
1960 Proof	3,360	Value: 1.50				

KM# 13.1 1/2 PENNY
Bronze **Ruler:** George V **Subject:** Dromedaris (ship) **Obv:** Crowned bust left **Obv. Designer:** E.B. MacKennal **Rev:** Sailing ship **Rev. Designer:** G.T. Kruger-Gray

Date	Mintage	F	VF	XF	Unc	BU
1923	12,000	25.00	40.00	70.00	100	—
1923 Proof	1,402	Value: 100				
1924	64,000	7.50	12.50	30.00	60.00	—
1925	69,000	7.50	12.50	30.00	80.00	—
1926	65,000	10.00	15.00	35.00	100	—

KM# 13.2 1/2 PENNY
Bronze **Ruler:** George V **Subject:** Dromedaris (ship) **Obv:** Crowned bust left **Obv. Designer:** E.B. MacKennal **Rev:** Sailing ship **Rev. Designer:** G.T. Kruger-Gray

Date	Mintage	F	VF	XF	Unc	BU
1928	105,000	5.00	12.50	35.00	75.00	—
1929	272,000	2.50	5.00	15.00	35.00	—
1930	147,000	3.50	7.00	20.00	40.00	—
1930 Proof	14	Value: 400				
1930	Inc. above	4.00	8.00	25.00	50.00	—
Note: Without star after date						
1931	145,000	3.50	7.00	25.00	50.00	—

KM# 13.3 1/2 PENNY
Bronze **Ruler:** George V **Subject:** Dromedaris (ship) **Obv:** Crowned bust left **Obv. Designer:** E.B. MacKennal **Rev:** Sailing ship **Rev. Designer:** G.T. Kruger-Gray

Date	Mintage	F	VF	XF	Unc	BU
1931 Proof	62	Value: 1,000				
1932	106,000	5.00	10.00	30.00	75.00	—
1932 Proof	12	Value: 1,000				
1933	63,000	8.00	25.00	55.00	100	—
1933 Proof	20	Value: 500				
1934	326,000	1.50	5.00	15.00	45.00	—
1934 Proof	24	Value: 500				
1935	405,000	1.50	5.00	15.00	40.00	—
1935 Proof	20	Value: 500				
1936	407,000	1.50	5.00	15.00	30.00	—
1936 Proof	40	Value: 200				

KM# 24 1/2 PENNY
Bronze **Ruler:** George VI **Subject:** Dromedaris (ship) **Obv:** Head left **Obv. Designer:** T.H. Paget **Rev:** Sailing ship **Rev. Designer:** G.T. Kruger-Gray

Date	Mintage	F	VF	XF	Unc	BU
1937	638,000	1.00	2.00	9.00	15.00	—
1937 Proof	116	Value: 50.00				
1938	560,000	1.00	2.00	6.00	15.00	—
1938 Proof	44	Value: 125				
1939	271,000	2.50	5.00	10.00	20.00	—
1939 Proof	30	Value: 175				
1940	1,535,000	0.30	0.75	3.00	8.00	—
1941	2,053,000	0.30	0.75	3.00	8.00	—
1942	8,382,000	0.25	0.60	2.00	6.00	—
1943	5,135,000	0.25	0.60	2.00	6.00	—
1943 Proof	104	Value: 45.00				
1944	3,920,000	0.25	0.75	3.00	8.00	—
1944 Proof	150	Value: 35.00				
1945	2,357,000	0.25	0.60	2.50	7.00	—
1945 Proof	150	Value: 35.00				
1946	1,022,000	0.25	0.75	3.00	9.00	—
1946 Proof	150	Value: 35.00				
1947	258,000	1.00	3.00	6.00	17.50	—
1947 Proof	2,600	Value: 10.00				

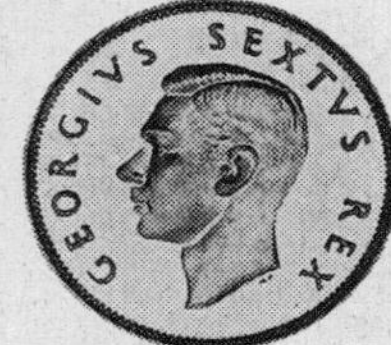

KM# 33 1/2 PENNY
Bronze, 25 mm. **Ruler:** George VI **Subject:** Dromedaris (ship) **Obv:** Head left **Obv. Designer:** T.H. Paget **Rev:** Sailing ship **Rev. Designer:** G.T. Kruger-Gray

Date	Mintage	F	VF	XF	Unc	BU
1948	685,000	0.50	1.00	4.00	9.00	—
1948 Proof	1,120	Value: 15.00				
1949	1,850,000	0.25	0.50	1.75	4.00	—
1949 Proof	800	Value: 15.00				
1950	2,186,000	0.25	0.50	1.50	3.00	—
1950 Proof	500	Value: 6.00				
1951	3,746,000	0.25	0.50	1.25	3.00	—
1951 Proof	2,000	Value: 5.00				
1952	4,174,000	0.25	0.50	1.00	2.50	—
1952 Proof	1,550	Value: 4.00				

KM# 45 1/2 PENNY
Bronze **Ruler:** Elizabeth II **Subject:** Dromedaris (ship) **Obv:** Laureate head right **Obv. Designer:** Mary Gillick **Rev:** Sailing ship **Rev. Designer:** G.T. Kruger-Gray

Date	Mintage	F	VF	XF	Unc	BU
1953	5,572,000	0.15	0.35	1.00	3.00	—
1953 Proof	5,000	Value: 4.00				
1954	101,000	2.00	4.00	7.50	12.50	—
1954 Proof	3,150	Value: 15.00				
1955	3,774,000	0.15	0.35	1.00	3.00	—
1955 Proof	2,850	Value: 4.00				
1956	1,305,000	0.15	0.35	1.00	3.00	—
1956 Proof	1,700	Value: 4.00				
1957	2,025,000	0.15	0.35	1.00	3.00	—
1957 Proof	1,130	Value: 4.00				
1958	2,171,000	0.15	0.35	1.00	2.50	—
1958 Proof	985	Value: 5.00				
1959	2,397,000	0.15	0.25	0.75	2.00	—
1959 Proof	900	Value: 6.00				
1960	2,552,000	0.15	0.25	0.75	2.00	—
1960 Proof	3,360	Value: 1.50				

KM# 14.1 PENNY
Bronze, 30.8 mm. **Ruler:** George V **Subject:** Dromedaris (ship) **Obv:** Crowned bust left **Obv. Designer:** E.B. MacKennal **Rev:** Sailing ship **Rev. Designer:** G.T. Kruger-Gray

Date	Mintage	F	VF	XF	Unc	BU
1923	91,000	3.00	7.00	17.50	35.00	—
1923 Proof	1,402	Value: 50.00				
1924	134,000	4.00	10.00	25.00	50.00	—

KM# 14.2 PENNY
Bronze, 30.8 mm. **Ruler:** George V **Subject:** Dromedaris (ship) **Obv:** Crowned bust left **Obv. Designer:** E.B. MacKennal **Rev:** Sailing ship **Rev. Designer:** G.T. Kruger-Gray

Date	Mintage	F	VF	XF	Unc	BU
1926	393,000	3.00	10.00	40.00	100	—
1926 Proof	16	Value: 600				
1927	285,000	3.00	10.00	40.00	90.00	—
1928	386,000	3.00	10.00	40.00	90.00	—
1929	1,093,000	1.00	5.00	15.00	35.00	—
1930	754,000	1.00	5.00	20.00	40.00	—
1930 Proof	14	Value: 600				

KM# 14.3 PENNY
Bronze, 30.8 mm. **Ruler:** George V **Subject:** Dromedaris (ship) **Obv:** Crowned bust left **Obv. Designer:** T.H. Paget **Rev:** Sailing ship **Rev. Designer:** G.T. Kruger-Gray

Date	Mintage	F	VF	XF	Unc	BU
1931	284,000	1.00	5.00	17.50	40.00	—
1931 Proof	62	Value: 400				
1932	260,000	1.00	5.00	20.00	50.00	—
1932 Proof	12	Value: 800				
1933	225,000	2.00	10.00	30.00	45.00	—
1933 Proof	20	Value: 500				
1933	Inc. above	4.00	10.00	30.00	50.00	—
Note: Without star after date						
1934	2,089,999	0.50	1.50	8.00	22.50	—
1934 Proof	24	Value: 600				
1935	2,295,000	0.50	1.50	8.00	22.50	—
1935 Proof	20	Value: 600				
1936	1,819,000	0.35	1.00	5.00	20.00	—
1936 Proof	40	Value: 300				

KM# 25 PENNY
Bronze, 30.8 mm. **Ruler:** George VI **Subject:** Dromedaris (ship) **Obv:** Head left **Rev:** Sailing ship **Rev. Designer:** G.T. Kruger-Gray

Date	Mintage	F	VF	XF	Unc	BU
1937	3,281,000	0.50	1.50	10.00	25.00	—
1937 Proof	116	Value: 75.00				
1938	1,840,000	0.50	1.50	8.00	30.00	—
1938 Proof	44	Value: 100				
1939	1,506,000	0.50	1.50	10.00	25.00	—
1939 Proof	30	Value: 175				
1940	3,592,000	0.35	1.00	4.00	10.00	—
1940	Inc. above	1.50	3.00	6.00	15.00	—
Note: Without star after date						
1941	7,871,000	0.25	0.75	2.50	7.00	—
1942	14,428,000	0.25	0.75	2.00	6.00	—
1942	Inc. above	3.00	6.00	12.50	30.00	—
Note: Without star after date						
1943	4,010,000	0.25	0.75	2.50	6.00	—
1943 Proof	104	Value: 55.00				
1944	6,425,000	0.25	0.75	2.50	7.00	—
1944 Proof	150	Value: 45.00				
1945	4,810,000	0.25	0.75	2.50	7.00	—
1945 Proof	150	Value: 45.00				
1946	2,605,000	0.25	0.75	3.00	8.00	—
1946 Proof	150	Value: 45.00				
1947	135,000	2.50	4.00	7.50	17.50	—
1947 Proof	2,600	Value: 7.00				

KM# 34.1 PENNY
Bronze, 30.8 mm. **Ruler:** George VI **Subject:** Dromedaris (ship) **Obv:** Head left **Obv. Designer:** T.H. Paget **Rev:** Sailing ship **Rev. Designer:** G.T. Kruger-Gray

Date	Mintage	F	VF	XF	Unc	BU
1948	2,398,000	0.25	0.75	2.50	6.00	—
1948 Proof	1,120	Value: 5.00				
1948	Inc. above	1.00	2.00	5.00	10.00	—
Note: Without star after date						
1949	3,634,000	0.25	0.75	2.00	6.00	—
1949 Proof	800	Value: 12.00				
1950	4,890,000	0.25	0.75	2.00	5.00	—
1950 Proof	500	Value: 10.00				

KM# 34.2 PENNY
Bronze, 30.8 mm. **Ruler:** George VI **Subject:** Dromedaris (ship) **Obv:** Head left **Obv. Designer:** T.H. Paget **Rev:** Sailing ship **Rev. Legend:** SUID AFRIKA-SOUTH AFRICA **Rev. Designer:** G.T. Kruger-Gray

Date	Mintage	F	VF	XF	Unc	BU
1951	3,787,000	0.25	0.75	1.50	4.00	—
1951 Proof	2,000	Value: 5.00				
1952	12,674,000	0.25	0.50	1.00	2.50	—
1952 Proof	16,000	Value: 4.00				

KM# 46 PENNY
Bronze, 30.8 mm. **Ruler:** Elizabeth II **Subject:** Dromedaris (ship) **Obv:** Laureate head right **Obv. Designer:** Mary Gillick **Rev:** Sailing ship **Rev. Designer:** G.T. Kruger-Gray

Date	Mintage	F	VF	XF	Unc	BU
1953	5,491,000	0.20	0.35	0.75	2.00	—
1953 Proof	5,000	Value: 2.00				
1954	6,665,000	1.00	2.00	5.00	10.00	—
1954 Proof	3,150	Value: 15.00				
1955	6,508,000	0.20	0.35	0.75	3.00	—
1955 Proof	2,850	Value: 2.00				
1956	4,390,000	0.20	0.35	1.00	4.00	—
1956 Proof	1,700	Value: 3.00				
1957	3,973,000	0.20	0.35	0.75	3.00	—
1957 Proof	1,130	Value: 5.00				
1958	5,311,000	0.20	0.35	0.75	3.00	—
1958 Proof	985	Value: 6.00				
1959	5,066,000	0.20	0.35	0.75	2.00	—
1959 Proof	900	Value: 7.00				
1960	5,106,000	0.20	0.35	0.75	2.00	—
1960 Proof	3,360	Value: 2.00				

KM# 15A 3 PENCE
1.4100 g., 0.8000 Silver .0362 oz. ASW, 16.5 mm. **Ruler:** George V **Obv:** Crowned bust left **Obv. Designer:** E.B. MacKennal **Rev:** Value within wreath

Date	Mintage	F	VF	XF	Unc	BU
1923	302,000	4.00	8.00	20.00	45.00	—
1923 Proof	1,402	Value: 50.00				
1924	501,000	4.00	10.00	25.00	50.00	—
1925	—	10.00	35.00	200	475	—

KM# 15.1 3 PENCE
1.4100 g., 0.8000 Silver .0362 oz. ASW, 16.5 mm. **Ruler:** George V **Obv:** Crowned bust left **Obv. Designer:** E.B. MacKennal **Rev:** Protea flower in center, value as 3 PENCE **Rev. Designer:** G.T. Kruger-Gray

Date	Mintage	F	VF	XF	Unc	BU
1925	358,000	5.00	25.00	90.00	175	—
1926	1,572,000	1.00	3.50	20.00	50.00	—
1926 Proof	16	Value: 2,000				
1927	2,285,000	1.00	2.50	15.00	45.00	—
1928	919,000	1.50	3.50	20.00	50.00	—
1929	1,948,000	1.00	2.50	15.00	45.00	—
1930	981,000	1.00	3.50	20.00	50.00	—
1930 Proof	14	Value: 800				

KM# 15.2 3 PENCE
1.4100 g., 0.8000 Silver .0362 oz. ASW, 16.5 mm. **Ruler:** George V **Obv:** Crowned bust left **Obv. Designer:** E.B. MacKennal **Rev:** Protea flower in center, value as 3D **Rev. Designer:** G.T. Kruger-Gray

Date	Mintage	F	VF	XF	Unc	BU
1931	66	750	1,000	1,750	3,500	—
1931 Proof	62	Value: 3,500				
1932	2,622,000	1.00	2.50	15.00	30.00	—
1932 Proof	12	Value: 1,000				
1933	5,135,000	1.00	2.50	15.00	30.00	—
1933 Proof	20	Value: 1,000				
1934	2,357,000	1.00	2.50	15.00	30.00	—
1934 Proof	24	Value: 1,000				
1935	1,655,000	1.00	2.50	15.00	30.00	—
1935 Proof	20	Value: 1,000				
1936	1,095,000	1.00	2.50	15.00	35.00	—
1936 Proof	40	Value: 250				

KM# 26 3 PENCE
1.4100 g., 0.8000 Silver .0362 oz. ASW, 16.5 mm. **Ruler:** George VI **Obv:** Head left **Obv. Designer:** T.H. Paget **Rev:** Protea flower in center of designed bars shaped as a triangle **Rev. Designer:** G.T. Kruger-Gray

Date	Mintage	F	VF	XF	Unc	BU
1937	3,576,000	0.60	1.00	3.00	10.00	—
1937 Proof	116	Value: 80.00				
1938	2,394,000	0.60	1.50	7.00	20.00	—
1938 Proof	44	Value: 100				
1939	3,224,000	0.60	1.50	5.00	12.50	—
1939 Proof	30	Value: 250				
1940	4,887,000	0.60	1.00	3.00	12.50	—
1941	8,968,000	0.60	1.00	3.00	9.00	—
1942	8,055,999	0.60	1.00	3.00	9.00	—
1943	14,827,000	0.60	1.00	2.50	6.00	—
1943 Proof	104	Value: 70.00				
1944	3,331,000	0.60	1.00	3.00	9.00	—
1944 Proof	150	Value: 60.00				
1945/3	4,094,000	1.00	3.00	10.00	20.00	—
1945	Inc. above	0.60	1.00	3.00	9.00	—
1945 Proof	150	Value: 60.00				
1946	2,219,000	0.60	1.00	3.00	10.00	—
1946 Proof	150	Value: 65.00				
1947	1,127,000	0.60	1.00	2.50	8.00	—
1947 Proof	2,600	Value: 8.00				

KM# 35.1 3 PENCE
1.4100 g., 0.8000 Silver .0362 oz. ASW, 16.5 mm. **Ruler:** George VI **Obv:** Head left **Obv. Designer:** T.H. Paget **Rev:** Protea flower in center of designed bars shaped as a triangle **Rev. Designer:** G.T. Kruger-Gray

Date	Mintage	F	VF	XF	Unc	BU
1948	2,720,000	0.60	1.00	3.00	7.00	—
1948 Proof	1,120	Value: 5.00				
1949	1,904,000	0.60	1.00	3.00	7.00	—
1949 Proof	800	Value: 5.00				
1950	4,096,000	0.60	1.00	2.50	5.00	—
1950 Proof	500	Value: 7.00				

KM# 35.2 3 PENCE
1.4100 g., 0.5000 Silver .0226 oz. ASW, 16.5 mm. **Ruler:** George VI **Obv:** Head left **Obv. Designer:** T.H. Paget **Rev:** Protea flower in center of designed bars shaped as a triangle **Rev. Designer:** G.T. Kruger-Gray **Note:** Many varieties exist of George VI 3 Pence.

Date	Mintage	F	VF	XF	Unc	BU
1951	6,323,000	BV	0.50	1.00	3.00	—
1951 Proof	2,000	Value: 4.00				
1952	13,057,000	BV	0.50	1.00	2.00	—
1952 Proof	16,000	Value: 2.00				

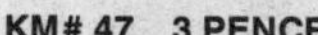

KM# 47 3 PENCE
1.4100 g., 0.5000 Silver .0226 oz. ASW, 16.5 mm. **Ruler:** Elizabeth II **Obv:** Laureate head right **Obv. Designer:** Mark Gillick **Rev:** Protea flower in center of designed bars shaped as a triangle **Rev. Designer:** G.T. Kruger-Gray

Date	Mintage	F	VF	XF	Unc	BU
1953	5,483,000	BV	0.50	1.00	3.00	—
1953 Proof	5,000	Value: 3.00				
1954	3,898,000	BV	0.50	1.00	3.50	—
1954 Proof	3,150	Value: 4.00				
1955	4,720,000	BV	0.50	1.00	3.00	—
1955 Proof	2,850	Value: 3.00				
1956	6,189,000	BV	0.50	1.00	3.00	—
1956 Proof	1,700	Value: 4.00				
1957	1,893,000	BV	0.50	1.00	3.00	—
1957 Proof	1,130	Value: 5.00				
1958	3,227,000	BV	0.50	1.00	3.00	—
1958 Proof	985	Value: 6.00				
1959	2,552,000	BV	0.50	1.00	2.00	—
1959 Proof	900	Value: 7.00				
1959	Inc. above	2.00	3.00	5.00	10.00	—
Note: No K-G on reverse						
1960	18,000	1.00	2.50	4.00	7.00	—
1960 Proof	3,360	Value: 3.00				

KM# 16A 6 PENCE
2.8300 g., 0.8000 Silver .0727 oz. ASW, 19.5 mm. **Ruler:** George V **Obv:** Crowned bust left **Obv. Designer:** E.B. MacKennal **Rev:** Value within wreath

Date	Mintage	F	VF	XF	Unc	BU
1923	208,000	4.00	15.00	35.00	80.00	—
1923 Proof	1,402	Value: 80.00				
1924	326,000	3.50	12.50	30.00	70.00	—

KM# 16.1 6 PENCE
2.8300 g., 0.8000 Silver .0727 oz. ASW, 19.5 mm. **Ruler:** George V **Obv:** Crowned bust left **Obv. Designer:** E.B. MacKennal **Rev:** Protea flower in center, value as 6 PENCE **Rev. Designer:** G.T. Kruger-Gray

Date	Mintage	F	VF	XF	Unc	BU
1925	79,000	5.00	15.00	55.00	125	—
1926	722,000	2.00	10.00	45.00	100	—
1926 Proof	16	Value: 3,000				
1927	1,548,000	1.50	4.00	25.00	50.00	—
1929	784,000	2.00	8.00	30.00	60.00	—
1930	448,000	2.00	8.00	35.00	70.00	—
1930 Proof	14	Value: 1,000				

KM# 16.2 6 PENCE
2.8300 g., 0.8000 Silver .0727 oz. ASW, 19.5 mm. **Ruler:** George V **Obv:** Crowned bust left **Obv. Designer:** E.B. MacKennal **Rev:** Protea flower in center, value as 6D **Rev. Designer:** G.T. Kruger-Gray

Date	Mintage	F	VF	XF	Unc	BU
1931	4,743	75.00	150	250	550	—
1931 Proof	62	Value: 1,000				
1932	1,525,000	1.50	5.00	17.50	35.00	—
1932 Proof	12	Value: 1,200				
1933	2,819,000	1.50	5.00	17.50	35.00	—
1933 Proof	20	Value: 1,200				
1934	1,519,000	1.50	7.00	20.00	40.00	—
1934 Proof	24	Value: 1,200				
1935	573,000	2.00	8.00	30.00	100	—
1935 Proof	20	Value: 1,200				
1936	627,000	1.50	7.00	20.00	40.00	—
1936 Proof	40	Value: 275				

KM# 27 6 PENCE
2.8300 g., 0.8000 Silver .0727 oz. ASW, 19.5 mm. **Ruler:** George VI **Obv:** Head left **Obv. Designer:** T.H. Paget **Rev:** Protea flower in center of designed bars **Rev. Designer:** G.T. Kruger-Gray

Date	Mintage	F	VF	XF	Unc	BU
1937	1,696,000	1.20	2.00	7.00	17.50	—
1937 Proof	116	Value: 90.00				
1938	1,725,000	1.20	2.00	7.00	17.50	—
1938 Proof	44	Value: 125				
1939 Proof	30	Value: 3,750				
1940	1,629,000	1.20	1.50	5.00	10.00	—
1941	2,263,000	1.20	1.50	5.00	10.00	—
1942	4,936,000	BV	1.25	3.00	8.00	—
1943	3,776,000	BV	1.25	3.00	8.00	—
1943 Proof	104	Value: 85.00				
1944	228,000	2.00	7.00	15.00	30.00	—
1944 Proof	150	Value: 75.00				
1945	420,000	1.50	5.00	15.00	35.00	—
1945 Proof	150	Value: 75.00				
1946	290,000	1.50	6.00	15.00	30.00	—
1946 Proof	150	Value: 80.00				
1947	577,000	1.20	1.50	5.00	10.00	—
1947 Proof	2,600	Value: 10.00				

KM# 36.1 6 PENCE
2.8300 g., 0.8000 Silver .0727 oz. ASW, 19.5 mm. **Ruler:** George VI **Obv:** Head left **Obv. Designer:** T.H. Paget **Rev:** Protea flower in center of designed bars **Rev. Designer:** G.T. Kruger-Gray

Date	Mintage	F	VF	XF	Unc	BU
1948	2,266,000	BV	1.25	2.50	6.00	—
1948 Proof	1,120	Value: 10.00				
1949	196,000	3.00	7.50	15.00	30.00	—
1949 Proof	800	Value: 15.00				
1950	2,122,000	BV	1.20	2.00	5.00	—
1950 Proof	500	Value: 15.00				

KM# 36.2 6 PENCE
2.8300 g., 0.5000 Silver .0454 oz. ASW, 19.5 mm. **Ruler:** George VI **Obv:** Head left **Obv. Designer:** T.H. Paget **Rev:** Protea flower in center of designed bars **Rev. Designer:** G.T. Kruger-Gray

Date	Mintage	F	VF	XF	Unc	BU
1951	2,602,000	BV	1.00	2.00	4.00	—
1951 Proof	2,000	Value: 4.00				
1952	4,265,000	BV	0.75	1.25	3.00	—
1952 Proof	16,000	Value: 2.00				

KM# 48 6 PENCE
2.8300 g., 0.5000 Silver .0454 oz. ASW, 19 mm. **Ruler:** Elizabeth II **Obv:** Laureate head right **Obv. Designer:** Mary Gillick **Rev:** Protea flower in center of designed bars **Rev. Designer:** G.T. Kruger-Gray

Date	Mintage	F	VF	XF	Unc	BU
1953	2,496,000	BV	0.75	1.75	4.50	—
1953 Proof	5,000	Value: 3.00				
1954	2,196,000	BV	1.00	2.00	4.50	—
1954 Proof	3,150	Value: 4.00				
1955	1,969,000	BV	1.00	2.00	4.50	—
1955 Proof	2,850	Value: 3.00				
1956	1,772,000	BV	1.00	2.00	5.00	—
1956 Proof	1,700	Value: 4.00				
1957	3,288,000	BV	0.75	1.75	4.50	—
1957 Proof	1,130	Value: 6.00				
1958	1,172,000	BV	1.00	2.00	4.50	—
1958 Proof	985	Value: 6.00				
1959	261,000	1.00	2.00	4.00	12.00	—
1959 Proof	900	Value: 8.00				
1960	1,587,000	BV	0.75	1.25	2.50	—
1960 Proof	3,360	Value: 2.50				

KM# 17.1 SHILLING
5.6600 g., 0.8000 Silver .1455 oz. ASW, 23.5 mm. **Ruler:** George V **Obv:** Crowned bust left **Obv. Designer:** E.B. MacKennal **Rev:** Value as 1 SHILLING 1 **Rev. Designer:** G.T. Kruger-Gray

Date	Mintage	F	VF	XF	Unc	BU
1923	808,000	4.00	15.00	35.00	75.00	—
1923 Proof	1,402	Value: 80.00				
1924	1,269,000	3.50	12.50	30.00	75.00	—

KM# 17.2 SHILLING
5.6600 g., 0.8000 Silver .1455 oz. ASW, 23.5 mm. **Ruler:** George V **Obv:** Crowned bust left **Obv. Designer:** E.B. MacKennal **Rev:** Value as SHILLING **Rev. Designer:** G.T. Kruger-Gray

Date	Mintage	F	VF	XF	Unc	BU
1926	238,000	15.00	75.00	400	1,150	—
1926 Proof	16	Value: 3,000				
1927	488,000	10.00	25.00	150	375	—
1928	889,000	8.00	25.00	100	250	—
1929	926,000	5.00	10.00	30.00	175	—
1930	422,000	6.00	15.00	60.00	150	—
1930 Proof	14	Value: 1,000				

KM# 17.3 SHILLING
5.6600 g., 0.8000 Silver .1455 oz. ASW, 23.5 mm. **Ruler:** George V **Obv:** Crowned bust left **Obv. Designer:** E.B. MacKennal **Rev:** Standing female figure leaning on large anchor **Rev. Designer:** G.T. Kruger-Gray

Date	Mintage	F	VF	XF	Unc	BU
1931	6,541	80.00	165	375	600	—
1931 Proof	62	Value: 1,200				
1932	2,537,000	2.50	5.00	15.00	50.00	—
1932 Proof	12	Value: 1,400				
1933	1,463,000	3.50	7.00	30.00	70.00	—
1933 Proof	20	Value: 1,400				
1934	821,000	3.50	7.00	35.00	80.00	—
1934 Proof	24	Value: 1,400				
1935	685,000	4.00	8.50	45.00	90.00	—
1935 Proof	20	Value: 1,400				
1936	693,000	3.50	7.00	25.00	60.00	—
1936 Proof	40	Value: 500				

KM# 28 SHILLING
5.6600 g., 0.8000 Silver .1455 oz. ASW, 23.5 mm. **Ruler:** George VI **Obv:** Head left **Obv. Designer:** T.H. Paget **Rev:** Standing female figure leaning on large anchor **Rev. Designer:** G.T. Kruger-Gray

Date	Mintage	F	VF	XF	Unc	BU
1937	1,194,000	BV	3.00	10.00	25.00	—
1937 Proof	116	Value: 120				
1938	1,160,000	BV	3.00	10.00	25.00	—
1938 Proof	44	Value: 250				
1939 Proof	30	Value: 4,000				
1940	1,365,000	BV	2.50	7.50	17.50	—
1941	1,826,000	BV	2.50	7.50	17.50	—
1942	3,867,000	BV	2.50	7.50	17.50	—
1943	4,187,999	BV	2.00	5.00	10.00	—
1943 Proof	104	Value: 165				
1944	48,000	8.00	20.00	40.00	70.00	—
1944 Proof	160	Value: 150				
1945	54,000	8.00	20.00	40.00	70.00	—
1945 Proof	150	Value: 150				
1946	27,000	10.00	30.00	60.00	120	—

Date	Mintage	F	VF	XF	Unc	BU
1946 Proof	150	Value: 165				
1947	7,184	10.00	20.00	35.00	65.00	—
1947 Proof	2,600	Value: 70.00				

KM# 37.1 SHILLING

5.6600 g., 0.8000 Silver .1455 oz. ASW, 23.5 mm. **Ruler:** George VI **Obv:** Head left **Obv. Designer:** T.H. Paget **Rev:** Standing female figure leaning on large anchor **Rev. Designer:** G.T. Kruger-Gray

Date	Mintage	F	VF	XF	Unc	BU
1948	4,974	10.00	20.00	35.00	65.00	—
1948 Proof	1,120	Value: 70.00				
1949 Proof	800	Value: 225				
1950	1,704,000	BV	2.50	4.00	8.00	—
1950 Proof	500	Value: 40.00				

KM# 37.2 SHILLING

5.6600 g., 0.5000 Silver .0909 oz. ASW, 23.5 mm. **Ruler:** George VI **Obv:** Head left **Obv. Designer:** T.H. Paget **Rev:** Standing female figure, value as 1S **Rev. Designer:** G.T. Kruger-Gray

Date	Mintage	F	VF	XF	Unc	BU
1951	2,405,000	BV	1.50	4.00	8.00	—
1951 Proof	2,000	Value: 4.00				
1952	1,934,000	BV	1.50	3.50	7.00	—
1952 Proof	1,550	Value: 3.00				

KM# 49 SHILLING

5.6600 g., 0.5000 Silver .0909 oz. ASW, 23.5 mm. **Ruler:** Elizabeth II **Obv:** Laureate head right **Obv. Designer:** Mary Gillick **Rev:** Standing female figure leaning on large anchor **Rev. Designer:** G.T. Kruger-Gray

Date	Mintage	F	VF	XF	Unc	BU
1953	2,672,000	BV	1.50	2.50	5.50	—
1953 Proof	5,000	Value: 4.00				
1954	3,576,000	BV	1.50	2.50	5.50	—
1954 Proof	3,150	Value: 4.00				
1955	2,206,000	BV	1.50	2.50	5.50	—
1955 Proof	2,850	Value: 5.50				
1956	2,142,000	BV	1.50	2.50	6.00	—
1956 Proof	1,700	Value: 6.00				
1957	791,000	BV	2.50	5.00	10.00	—
1957 Proof	1,130	Value: 6.00				
1958	4,067,000	BV	1.50	2.50	5.50	—
1958 Proof	985	Value: 8.00				
1959	205,000	1.50	3.00	5.00	10.00	—
1959 Proof	900	Value: 10.00				
1960	2,187,000	BV	1.50	2.50	5.50	—
1960 Proof	3,360	Value: 3.00				

KM# 18 FLORIN

11.3100 g., 0.8000 Silver .2909 oz. ASW, 28.3 mm. **Ruler:** George V **Obv:** Crowned bust left **Obv. Designer:** E.B. MacKennal **Rev:** Shield divides date **Rev. Designer:** G.T. Kruger-Gray

Date	Mintage	F	VF	XF	Unc	BU
1923	695,000	6.00	20.00	40.00	80.00	—
1923 Proof	1,402	Value: 120				
1924	1,513,000	5.00	15.00	40.00	150	—
1925	50,000	125	350	1,000	2,200	—
1926	324,000	7.50	40.00	250	650	—

Date	Mintage	F	VF	XF	Unc	BU
1927	399,000	7.50	35.00	200	600	—
1928	1,092,000	5.00	10.00	100	200	—
1929	648,000	6.00	15.00	120	225	—
1930	267,000	6.00	15.00	75.00	150	—
1930 Proof	14	Value: 1,200				

KM# 22 2 SHILLINGS

11.3100 g., 0.8000 Silver .2909 oz. ASW, 28.3 mm. **Ruler:** George V **Obv:** Crowned bust left **Obv. Designer:** E.B. MacKennal **Rev:** Shield divides date **Rev. Designer:** G.T. Kruger-Gray

Date	Mintage	F	VF	XF	Unc	BU
1931	383	250	450	700	1,200	—
1931 Proof	62	Value: 1,500				
1932	1,315,000	BV	6.00	18.00	75.00	—
1932 Proof	12	Value: 2,000				
1933	891,000	4.75	8.00	25.00	85.00	—
1933 Proof	20	Value: 2,000				
1934	559,000	4.75	8.00	25.00	60.00	—
1934 Proof	24	Value: 1,650				
1935	554,000	5.00	9.00	25.00	90.00	—
1935 Proof	20	Value: 1,650				
1936	669,000	4.75	8.00	25.00	65.00	—
1936 Proof	40	Value: 650				

KM# 29 2 SHILLINGS

11.3100 g., 0.8000 Silver .2909 oz. ASW, 28.3 mm. **Ruler:** George VI **Obv:** Head left **Obv. Designer:** T.H. Paget **Rev:** Shield divides date **Rev. Designer:** G.T. Kruger-Gray

Date	Mintage	F	VF	XF	Unc	BU
1937	1,495,000	BV	5.00	10.00	30.00	—
1937 Proof	116	Value: 150				
1938	214,000	5.00	10.00	20.00	50.00	—
1938 Proof	44	Value: 325				
1939	279,000	5.00	10.00	20.00	50.00	—
1939 Proof	30	Value: 1,000				
1940	2,600,000	BV	4.75	8.00	20.00	—
1941	1,764,000	BV	4.75	8.00	20.00	—
1942	2,847,000	—	BV	5.00	10.00	—
1943	3,125,000	—	BV	5.00	10.00	—
1943 Proof	104	Value: 135				
1944	225,000	4.75	7.00	17.50	40.00	—
1945	473,000	BV	6.00	15.00	35.00	—
1945 Proof	150	Value: 120				
1946	14,000	7.50	20.00	40.00	90.00	—
1946 Proof	150	Value: 135				
1947	2,892	15.00	25.00	40.00	85.00	—
1947 Proof	2,600	Value: 70.00				

KM# 38.1 2 SHILLINGS

11.3100 g., 0.8000 Silver .2909 oz. ASW, 28.3 mm. **Ruler:** George VI **Obv:** Head left **Obv. Designer:** T.H. Paget **Rev:** Shield divides date **Rev. Designer:** G.T. Kruger-Gray

Date	Mintage	F	VF	XF	Unc	BU
1948	6,773	10.00	15.00	30.00	70.00	—
1948 Proof	1,120	Value: 70.00				
1949	203,000	5.00	10.00	15.00	35.00	—
1949 Proof	800	Value: 60.00				
1950	4,945	20.00	40.00	80.00	140	—
1950 Proof	500	Value: 160				

KM# 38.2 2 SHILLINGS

11.3100 g., 0.5000 Silver .1818 oz. ASW, 28.3 mm. **Ruler:** George VI **Obv:** Head left **Obv. Designer:** T.H. Paget **Rev:** Shield, value as 2S **Rev. Designer:** G.T. Kruger-Gray

Date	Mintage	F	VF	XF	Unc	BU
1951	730,000	BV	3.50	5.00	10.00	—
1951 Proof	2,000	Value: 15.00				
1952	3,570,000	—	BV	3.50	6.50	—
1952 Proof	16,000	Value: 8.00				

KM# 50 2 SHILLINGS

11.3100 g., 0.5000 Silver .1818 oz. ASW, 28.3 mm. **Ruler:** Elizabeth II **Obv:** Laureate head right **Obv. Designer:** Mary Gillick **Rev:** Shield **Rev. Designer:** G.T. Kruger-Gray

Date	Mintage	F	VF	XF	Unc	BU
1953	3,274,000	BV	3.00	5.00	8.50	—
1953 Proof	5,000	Value: 6.50				
1954	5,866,000	BV	3.00	4.00	7.00	—
1954 Proof	3,150	Value: 6.50				
1955	3,745,000	BV	3.00	4.00	7.50	—
1955 Proof	2,850	Value: 6.50				
1956	2,549,000	BV	3.00	5.00	9.00	—
1956 Proof	1,700	Value: 7.50				
1957	2,507,000	BV	3.00	5.00	10.00	—
1957 Proof	1,130	Value: 7.50				
1958	2,821,000	BV	3.00	5.00	10.00	—
1958 Proof	985	Value: 15.00				
1959	1,219,000	BV	3.00	5.00	10.00	—
1959 Proof	900	Value: 20.00				
1960	1,951,000	BV	3.00	4.00	6.00	—
1960 Proof	3,360	Value: 4.00				

KM# 19.1 2-1/2 SHILLINGS

14.1400 g., 0.8000 Silver .3637 oz. ASW, 32.3 mm. **Ruler:** George V **Obv:** Crowned bust left **Obv. Designer:** E.B. MacKennal **Rev:** Value as 2-1/2 SHILLINGS 2-1/2 **Rev. Legend:** ZUID-AFRIKA **Rev. Designer:** G.T. Kruger-Gray

Date	Mintage	F	VF	XF	Unc	BU
1923	1,227,000	6.00	15.00	35.00	70.00	—
1923 Proof	1,402	Value: 125				
1924	2,556,000	BV	10.00	50.00	120	—
1925	460,000	9.00	30.00	180	600	—

KM# 19.2 2-1/2 SHILLINGS

14.1400 g., 0.8000 Silver .3637 oz. ASW, 32.3 mm. **Ruler:** George V **Obv:** Crowned bust left **Obv. Designer:** E.B. MacKennal **Rev:** Value as 2-1/2 SHILLINGS **Rev. Designer:** G.T. Kruger-Gray

Date	Mintage	F	VF	XF	Unc	BU
1926	205,000	10.00	40.00	250	650	—
1926 Proof	16	Value: 4,000				
1927	194,000	10.00	40.00	350	850	—

Date	Mintage	F	VF	XF	Unc	BU
1928	984,000	6.50	25.00	125	325	—
1929	617,000	6.50	25.00	175	350	—
1930	324,000	6.50	15.00	100	250	—
1930 Proof	14	Value: 1,650				

KM# 19.3 2-1/2 SHILLINGS

14.1400 g., 0.8000 Silver .3637 oz. ASW, 32.3 mm. **Ruler:** George V **Obv:** Crowned bust left **Obv. Designer:** E.B. MacKennal **Rev:** Crowned shield divides date **Rev. Legend:** SUID. AFRIKA **Rev. Designer:** G.T. Kruger-Gray

Date	Mintage	F	VF	XF	Unc	BU
1931	790	225	450	700	1,300	—
1931 Proof	62	Value: 1,800				
1932	1,028,999	6.00	8.00	22.50	85.00	—
1932 Proof	12	Value: 2,400				
1933	136,000	9.00	40.00	185	300	—
1933 Proof	20	Value: 2,400				
1934	416,000	6.00	9.00	30.00	100	—
1934 Proof	24	Value: 1,650				
1935	345,000	6.50	12.50	32.50	125	—
1935 Proof	20	Value: 1,650				
1936	553,000	6.00	8.50	25.00	90.00	—
1936 Proof	40	Value: 800				

KM# 30 2-1/2 SHILLINGS

14.1400 g., 0.8000 Silver .3637 oz. ASW, 32.3 mm. **Ruler:** George VI **Obv:** Head left **Obv. Designer:** T.H. Paget **Rev:** G.T. Kruger-Gray

Date	Mintage	F	VF	XF	Unc	BU
1937	1,154,000	BV	6.00	15.00	32.50	—
1937 Proof	116	Value: 175				
1938	534,000	6.00	8.00	20.00	60.00	—
1938 Proof	44	Value: 400				
1939	133,000	7.00	15.00	40.00	80.00	—
1939 Proof	30	Value: 800				
1940	2,976,000	BV	6.00	8.00	20.00	—
1941	1,988,000	BV	6.00	8.00	20.00	—
1942	3,180,000	BV	6.00	8.00	20.00	—
1943	2,098,000	BV	6.00	8.00	20.00	—
1943 Proof	104	Value: 150				
1944	1,360,000	BV	6.50	10.00	25.00	—
1944 Proof	150	Value: 130				
1945	183,000	BV	8.00	25.00	60.00	—
1945 Proof	150	Value: 130				
1946	11,000	15.00	30.00	50.00	90.00	—
1946 Proof	150	Value: 150				
1947	3,582	20.00	35.00	60.00	100	—
1947 Proof	2,600	Value: 110				

KM# 39.1 2-1/2 SHILLINGS

14.1400 g., 0.8000 Silver .3637 oz. ASW, 32.3 mm. **Ruler:** George VI **Obv:** Head left **Obv. Designer:** T.H. Paget **Rev:** Crowned shield divides date

Date	Mintage	F	VF	XF	Unc	BU
1948	1,600	25.00	45.00	75.00	100	—
1948 Proof	1,120	Value: 110				
1949	1,891	25.00	45.00	75.00	110	—
1949 Proof	800	Value: 120				
1950	5,076	25.00	45.00	75.00	140	—
1950 Proof	500	Value: 200				

KM# 39.2 2-1/2 SHILLINGS

14.1400 g., 0.5000 Silver .2273 oz. ASW, 32.3 mm. **Ruler:** George VI **Obv:** Head left **Obv. Designer:** T.H. Paget **Rev:** Crowned shield, value as 2-1/2 S **Rev. Designer:** G.T. Kruger-Gray

Date	Mintage	F	VF	XF	Unc	BU
1951	783,000	3.75	4.50	6.00	15.00	—
1951 Proof	2,000	Value: 9.00				
1952	1,996,000	BV	3.75	4.50	8.50	—
1952 Proof	16,000	Value: 5.00				

KM# 51 2-1/2 SHILLINGS

14.1400 g., 0.5000 Silver .2273 oz. ASW, 32.3 mm. **Ruler:** Elizabeth II **Obv:** Laureate head right **Obv. Designer:** Mary Gillick **Rev:** Crowned shield **Rev. Designer:** G.T. Kruger-Gray

Date	Mintage	F	VF	XF	Unc	BU
1953	2,513,000	BV	3.75	4.50	8.50	—
1953 Proof	6,000	Value: 6.00				
1954	4,249,000	BV	3.75	4.50	8.50	—
1954 Proof	3,150	Value: 7.50				
1955	3,863,000	BV	3.75	4.50	8.50	—
1955 Proof	2,850	Value: 7.50				
1956	2,437,000	BV	3.75	4.50	8.50	—
1956 Proof	1,700	Value: 8.50				
1957	2,137,000	BV	3.75	4.50	8.50	—
1957 Proof	1,130	Value: 8.50				
1958	2,260,000	BV	3.75	4.50	9.00	—
1958 Proof	985	Value: 14.00				
1959	46,000	3.75	4.50	7.00	12.50	—
1959 Proof	900	Value: 18.00				
1960	12,000	3.75	5.00	7.50	12.50	—
1960 Proof	3,360	Value: 5.00				

KM# 31 5 SHILLINGS

28.2800 g., 0.8000 Silver .7274 oz. ASW, 38.8 mm. **Ruler:** George VI **Subject:** Royal Visit **Obv:** Head left **Obv. Designer:** T.H. Paget **Rev:** Springbok **Rev. Designer:** Coert L. Steynberg

Date	Mintage	F	VF	XF	Unc	BU
1947	300,000	BV	12.50	15.00	20.00	—
1947 Proof	5,600	Value: 45.00				

KM# 40.1 5 SHILLINGS

28.2800 g., 0.8000 Silver .7274 oz. ASW, 38.8 mm. **Ruler:** George VI **Obv:** Head left **Obv. Designer:** T.H. Paget **Rev:** Springbok **Rev. Designer:** Coert L. Steynberg

Date	Mintage	F	VF	XF	Unc	BU
1948	780,000	—	BV	13.50	20.00	—
1948 Prooflike	1,000	—	—	—	22.50	—
1948 Proof	1,120	Value: 30.00				
1949	535,000	—	BV	13.50	20.00	—
1949 Prooflike	2,000	—	—	—	35.00	—
1949 Proof	800	Value: 50.00				
1950	83,000	BV	15.00	17.50	25.00	—
1950 Prooflike	1,200	—	—	—	60.00	—
1950 Proof	500	Value: 75.00				

KM# 40.2 5 SHILLINGS

28.2800 g., 0.5000 Silver .4546 oz. ASW, 38.8 mm. **Ruler:** George VI **Obv:** Head left **Obv. Designer:** T.H. Paget **Rev:** Springbok **Rev. Designer:** Coert L. Steynberg

Date	Mintage	F	VF	XF	Unc	BU
1951	363,000	BV	7.50	10.00	18.00	—
1951 Prooflike	1,483	—	—	—	25.00	—
1951 Proof	2,000	Value: 35.00				

KM# 41 5 SHILLINGS

28.2800 g., 0.5000 Silver .4546 oz. ASW, 38.8 mm. **Ruler:** George VI **Subject:** 300th Anniversary - Founding of Capetown **Obv:** Head left **Obv. Designer:** T.H. Paget **Rev:** Schooner in harbor **Rev. Designer:** Marion Walgate **Edge:** Reeded

Date	Mintage	F	VF	XF	Unc	BU
ND(1952)	1,698,000	BV	7.50	9.00	12.00	—
ND(1952) Prooflike	12,000	—	—	—	13.50	—
ND(1952) Proof	16,000	Value: 16.50				

KM# 52 5 SHILLINGS

28.2800 g., 0.5000 Silver .4546 oz. ASW, 38.8 mm. **Ruler:** Elizabeth II **Obv:** Laureate head right **Obv. Designer:** Mary Gillick **Rev:** Springbok **Rev. Designer:** Coert L. Steynberg

Date	Mintage	F	VF	XF	Unc	BU
1953	250,000	BV	7.50	10.00	16.00	—
1953 Prooflike	8,000	—	—	—	18.00	—
1953 Proof	5,000	Value: 22.00				
1953 Matte Proof	—	Value: 700				
1954	10,000	BV	8.50	12.50	20.00	—
1954 Prooflike	3,890	—	—	—	22.50	—
1954 Proof	3,150	Value: 25.00				
1955	40,000	BV	7.50	10.00	16.00	—
1955 Prooflike	2,230	—	—	—	20.00	—
1955 Proof	2,850	Value: 22.50				
1956	100,000	BV	7.00	9.00	12.50	—
1956 Prooflike	2,200	—	—	—	20.00	—
1956 Proof	1,700	Value: 25.00				
1957	154,000	BV	7.00	9.00	12.50	—
1957 Prooflike	1,600	—	—	—	25.00	—
1957 Proof	1,130	Value: 30.00				
1958	233,000	BV	7.00	9.00	12.50	—
1958 Prooflike	1,500	—	—	—	25.00	—
1958 Proof	985	Value: 30.00				
1959	2,989	20.00	35.00	65.00	100	—
1959 Prooflike	2,200	—	—	—	110	—
1959 Proof	950	Value: 120				

KM# 55 5 SHILLINGS

28.2800 g., 0.5000 Silver .4546 oz. ASW, 38.8 mm. **Ruler:** Elizabeth II **Subject:** 50th Anniversary - South African Union **Obv:** Shield **Obv. Designer:** G.T. Kruger-Gray **Rev:** Building and ship divides dates **Rev. Designer:** Hilda Mason **Edge:** Reeded **Note:** Many varieties exist of letters HM below building.

Date	Mintage	F	VF	XF	Unc	BU
1960	396,000	BV	7.00	8.50	11.50	—
1960 Prooflike	22,000	—	—	—	13.50	—
1960 Proof	3,360	Value: 16.50				

KM# 20 1/2 SOVEREIGN

3.9940 g., 0.9170 Gold .1177 oz. AGW **Ruler:** George V **Obv:** Head left **Rev:** Armored figure on rearing horse **Note:** British type with Pretoria mint mark: SA.

Date	Mintage	F	VF	XF	Unc	BU
1923 Proof	655	Value: 525				
1925	947,000	—	BV	90.00	150	—
1926	809,000	—	BV	90.00	150	—

KM# 42 1/2 POUND

3.9940 g., 0.9170 Gold .1177 oz. AGW **Ruler:** George V **Obv:** Head left **Obv. Designer:** T.H. Paget **Rev:** Springbok **Rev. Designer:** Coert L. Steynberg **Note:** Similar to 1 Pound, KM#43.

Date	Mintage	F	VF	XF	Unc	BU
1952	4,002	—	—	—	100	—
1952 Proof	12,000	Value: 110				

KM# 53 1/2 POUND

3.9940 g., 0.9170 Gold .1177 oz. AGW **Ruler:** Elizabeth II **Obv:** Laureate head right **Obv. Designer:** Mary Gillick **Rev. Designer:** Coert L. Steynberg

Date	Mintage	F	VF	XF	Unc	BU
1953 Proof	4,000	Value: 110				
1954 Proof	1,275	Value: 115				
1955 Proof	900	Value: 120				
1956 Proof	508	Value: 210				
1957 Proof	560	Value: 180				
1958 Proof	515	Value: 195				
1959	500	—	—	—	100	—
1959 Proof	630	Value: 165				
1960	1,052	—	—	—	90.00	—
1960 Proof	1,950	Value: 100				

KM# 21 SOVEREIGN

7.9881 g., 0.9170 Gold .2354 oz. AGW **Ruler:** George V **Obv:** Head left **Rev:** Armored figure on rearing horse **Note:** British type with Pretoria mint mark: SA.

Date	Mintage	F	VF	XF	Unc	BU
1923	64	200	300	400	700	—
1923 Proof	655	Value: 650				
1924	3,184	700	1,350	2,250	4,500	—
1925	6,086,000	—	—	BV	170	—
1926	11,108,000	—	—	BV	170	—
1927	16,379,999	—	—	BV	170	—
1928	18,235,000	—	—	BV	170	—

KM# A22 SOVEREIGN

7.9881 g., 0.9170 Gold .2354 oz. AGW **Ruler:** George V **Obv:** Modified effigy, slightly smaller bust

Date	Mintage	F	VF	XF	Unc	BU
1929	12,024,000	—	—	BV	165	—
1930	10,028,000	—	—	BV	165	—
1931	8,512,000	—	—	BV	165	—
1932	1,067,000	—	—	BV	175	—

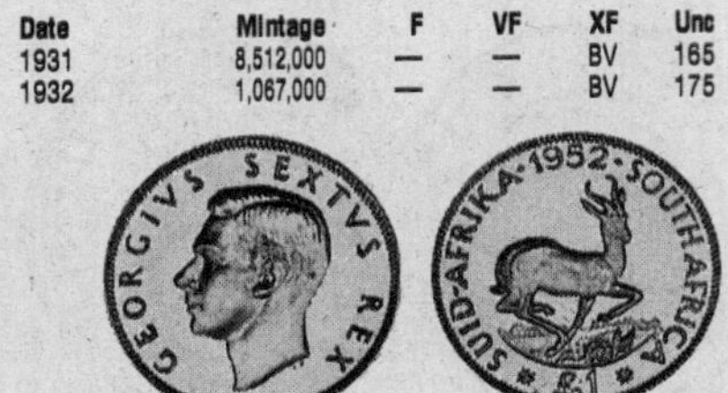

KM# 43 POUND

7.9881 g., 0.9170 Gold .2354 oz. AGW **Ruler:** George VI **Obv:** Head left **Obv. Designer:** T.H. Paget **Rev:** Springbok **Rev. Designer:** Coert L. Steynberg

Date	Mintage	F	VF	XF	Unc	BU
1952	4,508	—	—	—	180	—
1952 Proof	12,000	Value: 195				

KM# 54 POUND

7.9881 g., 0.9170 Gold .2354 oz. AGW **Ruler:** Elizabeth II **Obv:** Laureate head right **Obv. Designer:** Mary Gillick **Rev:** Springbok **Rev. Designer:** Coert L. Steynberg

Date	Mintage	F	VF	XF	Unc	BU
1953 Proof	4,000	Value: 190				
1954 Proof	1,275	Value: 200				
1955 Proof	900	Value: 210				
1956 Proof	508	Value: 250				
1957 Proof	560	Value: 235				
1958 Proof	515	Value: 240				
1959	502	—	—	—	175	—
1959 Proof	630	Value: 230				
1960	1,161	—	—	—	170	—
1960 Proof	1,950	Value: 170				

STANDARD COINAGE

100 Cents = 1 Rand

KM# 56 1/2 CENT

Brass **Obv:** Oat sprig and berries divide birds **Obv. Designer:** G.T. Kruger-Gray **Rev:** Bust facing 1/4 right

Date	Mintage	F	VF	XF	Unc	BU
1961	39,189,000	—	0.15	0.25	1.25	1.50
1961 Proof	7,530	Value: 1.00				
1962	17,895,000	—	0.15	0.25	1.25	1.50
1962 Proof	3,844	Value: 1.00				
1963	11,611,000	—	0.15	0.25	2.00	2.50
1963 Proof	4,025	Value: 1.00				
1964	9,258,000	—	0.15	0.25	1.25	1.50
1964 Proof	16,000	Value: 1.00				

KM# 81 1/2 CENT

Bronze **Obv:** Arms with supporters **Rev:** Sparrows below value **Designer:** Tommy Sasseen **Note:** Bilingual.

Date	Mintage	F	VF	XF	Unc	BU
1970	Est. 57,721,000	—	0.10	0.25	0.50	—

Note: Coins dated 1970 were also struck for circulation in 1971, 1972 and 1973

Date	Mintage	F	VF	XF	Unc	BU
1970 Proof	10,000	Value: 2.50				
1971	8,000	—	—	—	2.50	—
1971 Proof	12,000	Value: 2.50				
1972	8,000	—	—	—	2.50	—
1972 Proof	12,000	Value: 2.50				
1973	20,000	—	0.10	0.20	2.50	—
1973 Proof	11,000	Value: 2.50				
1974	20,000	—	0.20	0.40	2.50	—
1974 Proof	15,000	Value: 2.50				
1975	20,000	—	0.10	0.20	2.50	—
1975 Proof	18,000	Value: 2.50				
1977	20,000	—	0.10	0.20	2.50	—
1977 Proof	19,000	Value: 2.50				
1978	18,000	—	0.10	0.20	2.50	—
1978 Proof	19,000	Value: 2.50				
1980 Proof	15,000	Value: 2.50				
1981 Proof	10,000	Value: 2.50				
1983 Proof	14,000	Value: 2.50				

KM# 90 1/2 CENT

Bronze **Obv:** President Fouche left **Rev:** Birds on branches **Note:** Similar to 1 Cent, KM#91.

Date	Mintage	F	VF	XF	Unc	BU
1976	20,000	—	—	—	1.00	—
1976 Proof	21,000	Value: 1.50				

KM# 97 1/2 CENT

Bronze **Obv:** Head of President Diederichs left **Rev:** Sparrows below value **Rev. Designer:** Tommy Sasseen

Date	Mintage	F	VF	XF	Unc	BU
1979	18,000	—	—	—	1.00	—
1979 Proof	17,000	Value: 1.50				

KM# 108 1/2 CENT

Bronze **Obv:** Head of President Vorster 1/4 right **Rev:** Sparrows below value **Rev. Designer:** Tommy Sasseen

Date	Mintage	F	VF	XF	Unc	BU
1982 Proof	12,000	Value: 1.50				

KM# 57 CENT

Brass **Obv:** Covered wagon **Rev:** Bust 1/4 right

Date	Mintage	F	VF	XF	Unc	BU
1961	52,266,000	—	0.15	0.40	1.50	—
1961 Proof	7,530	Value: 0.75				
1962	21,929,000	—	0.15	0.40	1.50	—
1962 Proof	3,844	Value: 1.00				
1963	9,081,000	—	0.15	0.50	3.00	—
1963 Proof	4,025	Value: 1.00				
1964	14,265,000	—	0.15	0.40	1.50	—
1964 Proof	16,000	Value: 2.00				

KM# 65.1 CENT

3.0000 g., Bronze, 19 mm. **Obv:** Head of Jan van Riebeeck right **Obv. Legend:** English legend **Rev:** Sparrows below value **Designer:** Tommy Sasseen

Date	Mintage	F	VF	XF	Unc	BU
1965	26,000	—	—	—	2.00	—
1965 Proof	25,000	Value: 2.50				
1966	50,157,000	—	—	0.10	0.50	—
1967	21,114,000	—	—	0.10	0.50	—
1969	10,196,000	—	—	0.10	0.50	—

KM# 65.2 CENT

3.0000 g., Bronze, 19 mm. **Obv:** Head of Jan van Riebeeck right **Obv. Legend:** Afrikaans legend **Rev:** Sparrows below value **Designer:** Tommy Sasseen

Date	Mintage	F	VF	XF	Unc	BU
1965	846	—	100	200	300	—
1965 Proof	185	Value: 350				
1966	50,157,000	—	—	0.10	0.50	—
1966 Proof	25,000	Value: 1.00				
1967	21,114,000	—	—	0.10	0.50	—
1967 Proof	25,000	Value: 1.00				
1969	10,196,000	—	—	0.10	0.50	—
1969 Proof	12,000	Value: 1.50				

KM# 74.1 CENT

3.0000 g., Bronze, 19 mm. **Subject:** President Charles Swart **Obv:** Head left **Obv. Legend:** English legend **Rev:** Sparrows below value **Designer:** Tommy Sasseen

Date	Mintage	F	VF	XF	Unc	BU
1968	6,000,000	—	—	0.10	0.50	—
1968 Proof	25,000	Value: 1.00				

KM# 74.2 CENT

3.0000 g., Bronze, 19 mm. **Subject:** President Charles Swart **Obv:** Head left **Obv. Legend:** Afrikaans legend **Rev:** Sparrows below value **Designer:** Tommy Sasseen

Date	Mintage	F	VF	XF	Unc	BU
1968	6,000,000	—	—	0.10	0.50	—

KM# 82 CENT

3.0000 g., Bronze, 19 mm. **Obv:** Arms with supporters **Obv. Legend:** Bilingual legend **Rev:** Sparrows below value **Designer:** Tommy Sasseen

Date	Mintage	F	VF	XF	Unc	BU
1970	37,072,000	—	—	—	0.30	0.50
1970 Proof	10,000	Value: 1.00				
1971	34,053,000	—	—	—	0.30	0.50
1971 Proof	12,000	Value: 1.00				
1972	35,662,000	—	—	—	0.30	0.50
1972 Proof	10,000	Value: 1.00				
1973	35,898,000	—	0.10	0.20	0.40	0.60
1973 Proof	11,000	Value: 1.00				
1974	54,940,000	—	—	—	0.25	0.50
1974 Proof	15,000	Value: 1.00				
1975	62,982,000	—	—	—	0.25	0.50
1975 Proof	18,000	Value: 1.00				
1977	72,444,000	—	—	—	0.25	0.50
1977 Proof	19,000	Value: 1.00				
1978	70,152,000	—	—	—	0.25	0.50
1978 Proof	17,000	Value: 0.50				
1980	63,432,000	—	—	—	0.25	0.50
1980 Proof	15,000	Value: 0.50				
1981	63,444,000	—	—	—	0.25	0.50
1981 Proof	10,000	Value: 0.50				
1983	182,131,000	—	—	—	0.25	0.50
1983 Proof	14,000	Value: 0.50				
1984	107,155,000	—	—	—	0.25	0.50
1984 Proof	11,000	Value: 0.50				
1985	186,042,000	—	—	—	0.25	0.50
1985 Proof	9,859	Value: 0.50				
1986	169,734,000	—	—	—	0.25	0.50
1986 Proof	7,000	Value: 0.50				
1987	120,674,000	—	—	—	0.25	0.50
1987 Proof	6,781	Value: 0.50				
1988	240,272,000	—	—	—	0.25	0.50
1988 Proof	7,250	Value: 0.50				
1989	—	—	—	—	0.25	0.50
1989 Proof	—	Value: 0.50				

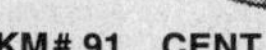

KM# 91 CENT

3.0000 g., Bronze, 19 mm. **Obv:** Head of President Fouche right **Rev:** Sparrows below value **Rev. Designer:** Tommy Sasseen

Date	Mintage	F	VF	XF	Unc	BU
1976	91,860,000	—	—	0.30	0.50	—
1976 Proof	21,000	Value: 0.75				

KM# 98 CENT

3.0000 g., Bronze, 19 mm. **Obv:** Head of President Diederichs left **Rev:** Sparrows below value **Rev. Designer:** Tommy Sasseen

Date	Mintage	F	VF	XF	Unc	BU
1979	63,432,000	—	—	0.30	0.50	—
1979 Proof	15,000	Value: 0.75				

KM# 109 CENT

3.0000 g., Bronze, 19 mm. **Obv:** Head of President Vorster 1/4 right **Rev:** Sparrows below value **Rev. Designer:** Tommy Sasseen

Date	Mintage	F	VF	XF	Unc	BU
1982	145,954,000	—	—	0.30	0.50	—
1982 Proof	12,000	Value: 0.75				

KM# 132 CENT

1.5000 g., Copper-Plated-Steel, 15 mm. **Obv:** Arms with supporters **Obv. Designer:** A.L. Sutherland **Rev:** Value divides sparrows **Rev. Designer:** W. Lumley

Date	Mintage	F	VF	XF	Unc	BU
1990	—	—	—	—	0.25	0.35
1990 Proof	—	Value: 0.50				
1991	—	—	—	—	0.25	0.35
1991 Proof	—	Value: 0.50				
1992	—	—	—	—	0.25	0.35
1992 Proof	—	Value: 0.50				
1993	—	—	—	—	0.25	0.35
1993 Proof	7,790	Value: 0.50				
1994	—	—	—	—	0.25	0.35
1994 Proof	5,804	Value: 0.50				
1995	—	—	—	—	0.25	0.35
1995 Proof	—	Value: 0.50				

KM# 158 CENT

1.5000 g., Copper-Plated-Steel, 15 mm. **Obv:** Arms with supporters **Obv. Legend:** Zulu legend **Obv. Designer:** A.L. Sutherland **Rev:** Value divides sparrows **Rev. Designer:** W. Lumley

Date	Mintage	F	VF	XF	Unc	BU
1996	—	—	—	—	0.25	0.35
1996 Proof	10,000	Value: 0.50				

KM# 170 CENT

1.5000 g., Copper Plated Steel, 15 mm. **Obv:** Arms with supporters **Obv. Legend:** Ndebele legend **Obv. Designer:** A.L. Sutherland **Rev:** Value divides sparrows **Rev. Designer:** W. Lumley

Date	Mintage	F	VF	XF	Unc	BU
1997	—	—	—	—	0.25	0.35
1997 Proof	3,596	Value: 0.50				
1998	—	—	—	—	0.25	0.35
1998 Proof	—	Value: 0.50				
1999	—	—	—	—	0.25	0.35
1999 Proof	—	Value: 0.50				
2000	—	Value: 0.25				

KM# 221 CENT

1.5000 g., Copper Plated Steel, 15 mm. **Obv:** Crowned arms **Obv. Designer:** A.L. Sutherland **Rev:** Value divides sparrows **Rev. Designer:** W. Lumley **Edge:** Plain

Date	Mintage	F	VF	XF	Unc	BU
2000	—	—	—	—	0.35	0.50

KM# 66.1 2 CENTS

4.0000 g., Bronze, 22.45 mm. **Obv:** English legend **Obv. Designer:** Tommy Sasseen **Rev:** Black Wildebeest

Date	Mintage	F	VF	XF	Unc	BU
1965	29,887,000	—	—	0.10	0.35	1.00
1966	9,267,000	—	—	0.10	0.40	1.00
1966 Proof	25,000	Value: 0.50				
1967	11,862,000	—	—	0.10	0.35	1.00
1967 Proof	25,000	Value: 0.50				
1969	5,817,000	—	—	0.10	0.40	1.00
1969 Proof	12,000	Value: 0.50				

KM# 66.2 2 CENTS

4.0000 g., Bronze, 22.45 mm. **Obv:** Afrikaans legend **Obv. Designer:** Tommy Sasseen **Rev:** Black Wildebeest

Date	Mintage	F	VF	XF	Unc	BU
1965	29,887,000	—	—	0.10	0.35	1.00
1965 Proof	25,000	Value: 0.50				
1966	9,267,000	—	—	0.10	0.35	1.00
1967	11,862,000	—	—	0.10	0.35	1.00
1969	5,817,000	—	—	0.10	0.40	1.00

KM# 75.1 2 CENTS

4.0000 g., Bronze, 22.45 mm. **Obv:** Head of President Charles Swart left **Obv. Legend:** English legend **Obv. Designer:** Tommy Sasseen **Rev:** Wildebeest

Date	Mintage	F	VF	XF	Unc	BU
1968	5,500,000	—	—	0.20	0.50	1.00

KM# 75.2 2 CENTS

4.0000 g., Bronze, 22.45 mm. **Obv:** Head of President Charles Swart left **Obv. Legend:** Afrikaans legend **Obv. Designer:** Tommy Sasseen **Rev:** Wildebeest

Date	Mintage	F	VF	XF	Unc	BU
1968	5,525,000	—	—	0.20	0.50	1.00
1968 Proof	25,000	Value: 1.00				

KM# 83 2 CENTS

4.0000 g., Bronze, 22.45 mm. **Obv:** Arms with supporters **Obv. Legend:** Bilingual legend **Obv. Designer:** Tommy Sasseen **Rev:** Wildebeest

Date	Mintage	F	VF	XF	Unc	BU
1970	35,217,000	—	—	0.15	0.50	1.00
1970 Proof	10,000	Value: 0.75				
1971	24,093,000	—	—	0.15	0.50	1.00
1971 Proof	12,000	Value: 0.75				
1972	7,304,000	—	—	0.15	0.50	1.00
1972 Proof	10,000	Value: 0.75				
1973	18,685,000	—	—	0.15	0.50	1.00
1973 Proof	11,000	Value: 0.75				
1974	25,301,000	—	—	0.15	0.50	1.00
1974 Proof	15,000	Value: 0.75				
1975	24,982,000	—	—	0.15	0.50	1.00
1975 Proof	18,000	Value: 0.75				
1977	45,116,000	—	—	0.15	0.50	1.00
1977 Proof	19,000	Value: 0.75				
1978	50,527,000	—	—	0.15	0.50	1.00

Date	Mintage	F	VF	XF	Unc	BU
1978 Proof	17,000	Value: 0.75				
1980	37,795,000	—	—	0.15	0.50	1.00
1980 Proof	15,000	Value: 0.75				
1981	79,350,000	—	—	0.15	0.50	1.00
1981 Proof	10,000	Value: 0.75				
1983	112,575,000	—	—	0.15	0.50	1.00
1983 Proof	14,000	Value: 0.75				
1984	101,497,000	—	—	0.15	0.50	1.00
1984 Proof	11,000	Value: 0.75				
1985	102,708,000	—	—	0.15	0.50	1.00
1985 Proof	9,859	Value: 0.75				
1986	683,294,000	—	—	0.15	0.50	1.00
1986 Proof	7,100	Value: 0.75				
1987	104,981,000	—	—	0.15	0.50	1.00
1987 Proof	6,781	Value: 0.75				
1988	182,036,000	—	—	0.15	0.50	1.00
1988 Proof	7,250	Value: 0.75				
1989	—	—	—	0.15	0.50	1.00
1989 Proof	—	Value: 0.75				
1990	215,192,000	—	—	0.15	0.50	1.00

KM# 92 2 CENTS
4.0000 g., Bronze, 22.45 mm. **Obv:** Head of President Fouche right **Rev:** Wildebeest

Date	Mintage	F	VF	XF	Unc	BU
1976	51,474,000	—	—	0.25	0.50	0.75
1976 Proof	21,000	Value: 0.75				

KM# 99 2 CENTS
4.0000 g., Bronze, 22.45 mm. **Obv:** Head of President Diederichs left **Rev:** Wildebeest

Date	Mintage	F	VF	XF	Unc	BU
1979	40,043,000	—	—	0.25	0.50	0.75
1979 Proof	15,000	Value: 0.75				

KM# 110 2 CENTS
4.0000 g., Bronze, 22.45 mm. **Obv:** Head of President Vorster 1/4 right **Rev:** Wildebeest

Date	Mintage	F	VF	XF	Unc	BU
1982	53,962,000	—	—	0.25	0.50	0.75
1982 Proof	12,000	Value: 0.75				

KM# 133 2 CENTS
3.0000 g., Copper-Plated-Steel, 18 mm. **Obv:** Arms with supporters **Rev:** Eagle with fish in talons divides value **Designer:** A.L. Sutherland

Date	Mintage	F	VF	XF	Unc	BU
1990	—	—	—	—	1.50	1.75
1990 Proof	—	Value: 2.00				
1991	—	—	—	—	1.50	1.75
1991 Proof	12,000	Value: 2.00				
1992	—	—	—	—	0.50	0.75
1992 Proof	—	Value: 2.00				
1993	—	—	—	—	0.50	0.75
1993 Proof	7,790	Value: 2.00				
1994	—	—	—	—	0.50	0.75
1994 Proof	5,804	Value: 2.00				
1995	—	—	—	—	0.50	0.75
1995 Proof	—	Value: 2.00				

KM# 159 2 CENTS
3.0000 g., Copper-Plated-Steel, 18 mm. **Obv:** Arms with supporters **Obv. Legend:** AFURIKA TSHIPEMBE, Venda legend **Rev:** Eagle with fish in talons divides value **Designer:** A.L. Sutherland

Date	Mintage	F	VF	XF	Unc	BU
1996	—	—	—	—	0.50	0.75
1996 Proof	—	Value: 1.00				
1997	—	—	—	—	0.50	0.75
1997 Proof	3,596	Value: 1.00				
1998	—	—	—	—	0.50	0.75
1998 Proof	—	Value: 1.00				
1999	—	—	—	—	0.50	0.75
1999 Proof	—	Value: 1.00				
2000	—	—	—	—	0.50	0.75

KM# 222 2 CENTS
3.0000 g., Copper Plated Steel, 17.9 mm. **Obv:** Crowned arms **Rev:** Eagle with fish in talons divides value **Edge:** Plain **Designer:** A.L. Sutherland

Date	Mintage	F	VF	XF	Unc	BU
2000	—	—	—	—	0.50	0.75

KM# 58 2-1/2 CENTS
1.4100 g., 0.5000 Silver .0226 oz. ASW **Obv:** Protea flower **Rev:** Bust facing

Date	Mintage	F	VF	XF	Unc	BU
1961	292,000	—	0.50	1.00	2.00	—
1961 Proof	7,530	Value: 4.00				
1962	8,745	—	2.00	4.00	8.00	—
1962 Proof	3,844	Value: 8.00				
1963	33,000	—	1.50	2.50	4.00	—
1963 Proof	4,025	Value: 6.00				
1964	14,000	—	2.00	4.00	6.00	—
1964 Proof	16,000	Value: 4.00				

KM# 174 2-1/2 CENTS
1.4140 g., 0.9250 Silver .0420 oz. ASW **Obv:** Protea flower **Rev:** Knysna seahorse below value

Date	Mintage	F	VF	XF	Unc	BU
1997 Proof	Est. 2,627	Value: 20.00				

KM# 176 2-1/2 CENTS
1.4140 g., 0.9250 Silver .0420 oz. ASW **Obv:** Protea flower **Rev:** Jackass Penguin

Date	Mintage	F	VF	XF	Unc	BU
1998 Proof	Est. 5,000	Value: 25.00				

KM# 217 2-1/2 CENTS
1.4100 g., 0.9250 Silver .0419 oz. ASW **Obv:** Protea flower **Rev:** Great White Shark

Date	Mintage	F	VF	XF	Unc	BU
1999 Proof	5,000	Value: 25.00				

KM# 233 2-1/2 CENTS
1.4140 g., 0.9250 Silver 0.0421 oz. ASW, 16.3 mm. **Obv:** Protea flower **Rev:** Octopus **Edge:** Reeded

Date	Mintage	F	VF	XF	Unc	BU
2000 Proof	—	Value: 25.00				

KM# 59 5 CENTS
2.8300 g., 0.5000 Silver .0454 oz. ASW, 17.35 mm. **Obv:** Protea flower in center of designed bars **Rev:** Bust 1/4 right

Date	Mintage	F	VF	XF	Unc	BU
1961	1,479,000	—	BV	1.00	2.00	—
1961 Proof	7,530	Value: 2.50				
1962	4,187,999	—	BV	0.85	1.50	—
1962 Proof	3,844	Value: 3.00				
1963	8,054,000	—	BV	0.75	1.25	—
1963 Proof	4,025	Value: 3.00				
1964	3,567,000	—	BV	0.75	1.25	—
1964 Proof	16,000	Value: 1.50				

KM# 67.1 5 CENTS
2.5000 g., Nickel, 17.35 mm. **Obv:** English legend **Rev:** Blue Crane **Designer:** Tommy Sasseen

Date	Mintage	F	VF	XF	Unc	BU
1965	32,689,999	—	—	0.15	0.75	1.00
1965 Proof	25,000	Value: 0.80				
1966	4,101,000	—	—	0.15	0.75	1.00
1967	4,590,000	—	—	0.15	0.75	1.00
1969	5,020,000	—	—	0.15	0.75	1.00

KM# 67.2 5 CENTS
2.5000 g., Nickel, 17.35 mm. **Obv:** Afrikaans legend **Rev:** Blue Crane **Designer:** Tommy Sasseen

Date	Mintage	F	VF	XF	Unc	BU
1965	32,689,999	—	—	0.15	0.75	1.00
1966	4,101,000	—	—	0.15	0.75	1.00
1966 Proof	25,000	Value: 0.80				
1967	4,590,000	—	—	0.15	0.75	1.00
1967 Proof	25,000	Value: 0.80				
1969	5,020,000	—	—	0.15	0.75	1.00
1969 Proof	12,000	Value: 0.80				

KM# 76.1 5 CENTS
2.5000 g., Nickel, 17.35 mm. **Subject:** President Charles Swart **Obv:** Head left **Obv. Legend:** English legend **Rev:** Blue Crane **Designer:** Tommy Sasseen

Date	Mintage	F	VF	XF	Unc	BU
1968	6,000,000	—	—	0.15	0.75	1.00
1968 Proof	25,000	Value: 0.80				

KM# 76.2 5 CENTS
2.5000 g., Nickel, 17.35 mm. **Subject:** President Charles Swart **Obv:** Afrikaans legend **Rev:** Blue Crane **Designer:** Tommy Sasseen

Date	Mintage	F	VF	XF	Unc	BU
1968	6,000,000	—	—	0.15	0.75	1.00

KM# 84 5 CENTS
2.5000 g., Nickel, 17.35 mm. **Obv:** Arms with supporters **Obv. Legend:** Bilingual legend **Rev:** Blue Crane

Date	Mintage	F	VF	XF	Unc	BU
1970	6,652,000	—	—	0.15	0.75	1.00
1970 Proof	10,000	Value: 0.80				
1971	20,329,000	—	—	0.15	0.75	1.00
1971 Proof	12,000	Value: 0.80				
1972	3,117,000	—	—	0.15	0.75	1.00
1972 Proof	9,000	Value: 0.80				
1973	17,092,000	—	—	0.15	0.75	1.00
1973 Proof	11,000	Value: 0.80				
1974	19,978,000	—	—	0.15	0.75	1.00
1974 Proof	15,000	Value: 0.80				
1975	21,982,000	—	—	0.15	0.75	1.00
1975 Proof	18,000	Value: 0.80				
1977	51,729,000	—	—	0.15	0.75	1.00
1977 Proof	19,000	Value: 0.80				
1978	30,050,000	—	—	0.15	0.75	1.00
1978 Proof	19,000	Value: 0.80				
1980	46,665,000	—	—	0.15	0.75	1.00
1980 Proof	15,000	Value: 0.80				

Date	Mintage	F	VF	XF	Unc	BU
1981	40,351,000	—	—	0.15	0.75	1.00
1981 Proof	10,000	Value: 0.80				
1983	57,487,000	—	—	0.15	0.75	1.00
1983 Proof	14,000	Value: 0.80				
1984	67,345,000	—	—	0.15	0.75	1.00
1984 Proof	11,000	Value: 0.80				
1985	57,167,000	—	—	0.15	0.75	1.00
1985 Proof	9,859	Value: 0.80				
1986	54,226,000	—	—	0.15	0.75	1.00
1986 Proof	7,100	Value: 0.80				
1987	42,786,000	—	—	0.15	0.75	1.00
1987 Proof	5,297	Value: 0.80				
1988	110,164,000	—	—	0.15	0.75	1.00
1988 Proof	7,250	Value: 0.80				
1989	35,540,000	—	—	0.15	0.75	1.00
1989 Proof	Inc. above	Value: 1.50				

KM# 93 5 CENTS

2.5000 g., Nickel, 17.35 mm. **Obv:** Head of President Fouche right **Rev:** Blue Crane **Rev. Designer:** Tommy Sasseen

Date	Mintage	F	VF	XF	Unc	BU
1976	48,972,000	—	—	0.30	0.75	1.00
1976 Proof	19,000	Value: 1.50				

KM# 100 5 CENTS

2.5000 g., Nickel, 17.35 mm. **Obv:** Head of President Diederichs left **Rev:** Tommy Sasseen

Date	Mintage	F	VF	XF	Unc	BU
1979	17,533,000	—	—	0.30	0.75	1.00
1979 Proof	17,000	Value: 1.50				

KM# 111 5 CENTS

2.5000 g., Nickel, 17.35 mm. **Obv:** Head of President Vorster 1/4 right **Rev:** Blue Crane **Rev. Designer:** Tommy Sasseen

Date	Mintage	F	VF	XF	Unc	BU
1982	47,236,000	—	—	0.30	0.75	1.00
1982 Proof	12,000	Value: 1.50				

KM# 134 5 CENTS

4.5000 g., Copper-Plated-Steel, 21 mm. **Obv:** Arms with supporters **Obv. Designer:** A.L. Sutherland **Rev:** Blue crane **Rev. Designer:** G. Richard

Date	Mintage	F	VF	XF	Unc	BU
1990	—	—	—	0.15	1.00	—
1990 Proof	—	Value: 1.25				
1991	—	—	—	0.15	1.00	—
1991 Proof	12,000	Value: 1.25				
1992	—	—	—	0.15	1.00	—
1992 Proof	—	Value: 1.25				
1993	—	—	—	0.15	1.00	—
1993 Proof	7,790	Value: 1.25				
1994	—	—	—	0.15	1.00	—
1994 Proof	5,804	Value: 1.25				
1995	—	—	—	0.15	1.00	—
1995 Proof	—	Value: 1.25				

KM# 160 5 CENTS

4.5000 g., Copper Plated Steel, 21 mm. **Obv:** Arms with supporters **Obv. Legend:** AFRIKA DZONGA, Tsonga legend **Obv. Designer:** A.L. Sutherland **Rev:** Blue crane **Rev. Designer:** G. Richard

Date	Mintage	F	VF	XF	Unc	BU
1996	—	—	—	0.15	0.75	1.00
1996 Proof	—	Value: 1.25				

Date	Mintage	F	VF	XF	Unc	BU
1997	—	—	—	0.15	0.75	1.00
1997 Proof	3,596	Value: 1.25				
1998	—	—	—	0.15	0.75	1.00
1998 Proof	—	Value: 1.50				
1999	—	—	—	0.15	0.75	1.00
1999 Proof	—	Value: 1.50				
2000	—	—	—	0.15	0.75	1.00

KM# 234 5 CENTS

8.4560 g., 0.9250 Silver 0.2515 oz. ASW, 26.7 mm. **Obv:** Lion and country name **Rev:** Lions and value **Edge:** Reeded

Date	Mintage	F	VF	XF	Unc	BU
ND(2000) Proof	—	Value: 20.00				

KM# 223 5 CENTS

4.4300 g., Copper Plated Steel, 21 mm. **Obv:** Crowned arms **Obv. Designer:** A.L. Sutherland **Rev:** Blue crane **Rev. Designer:** G. Richard **Edge:** Plain

Date	Mintage	F	VF	XF	Unc	BU
2000	—	—	—	—	0.50	1.00

KM# 60 10 CENTS

5.6600 g., 0.5000 Silver .0909 oz. ASW **Obv:** Standing female figure leaning on large anchor **Rev:** Bust 1/4 right **Designer:** G.E. Kruger-Gray

Date	Mintage	F	VF	XF	Unc	BU
1961	1,136,000	—	BV	1.50	2.50	—
1961 Proof	7,530	Value: 2.50				
1962	2,447,000	—	BV	1.50	2.50	—
1962 Proof	3,844	Value: 3.50				
1963	3,327,000	—	BV	1.50	2.50	—
1963 Proof	4,025	Value: 3.50				
1964	4,152,999	—	BV	1.50	2.00	—
1964 Proof	16,000	Value: 2.50				

KM# 68.1 10 CENTS

4.0000 g., Nickel, 20.7 mm. **Obv:** Head of Jan van Riebeeck right **Rev:** Aloe plant and value **Designer:** Tommy Sasseen

Date	Mintage	F	VF	XF	Unc	BU
1965	29,210,000	—	—	0.10	0.35	—
1966	3,685,000	—	—	0.10	0.45	—
1966 Proof	25,000	Value: 0.60				
1967	50,000	—	—	—	1.00	—
1967 Proof	25,000	Value: 0.60				
1969	558,000	—	—	0.10	0.50	—
1969 Proof	12,000	Value: 1.00				

KM# 68.2 10 CENTS

4.0000 g., Nickel, 20.7 mm. **Obv:** Head of Jan van Riebeeck right **Rev:** Aloe plant and value **Designer:** Tommy Sasseen

Date	Mintage	F	VF	XF	Unc	BU
1965	29,210,000	—	—	0.10	0.35	—
1965 Proof	25,000	Value: 0.60				
1966	3,685,000	—	—	0.10	0.45	—
1967	50,000	—	—	—	1.00	—
1969	558,000	—	0.10	0.20	2.50	—

KM# 77.1 10 CENTS

4.0000 g., Nickel, 20.7 mm. **Obv:** Head of President Charles Swart left **Rev:** Aloe plant and value **Designer:** Tommy Sasseen

Date	Mintage	F	VF	XF	Unc	BU
1968	50,000	—	—	—	2.00	—

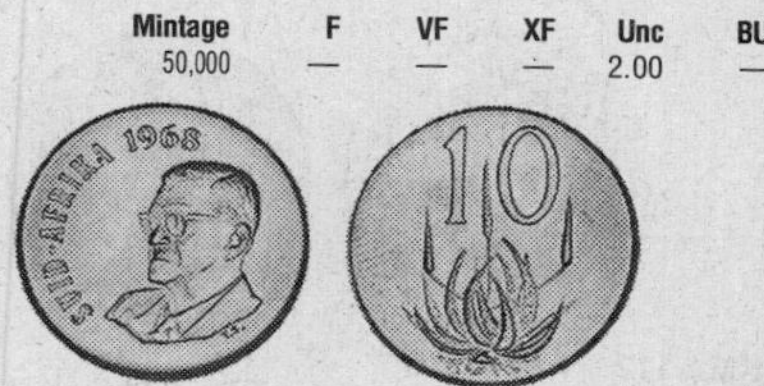

KM# 77.2 10 CENTS

4.0000 g., Nickel, 20.7 mm. **Obv:** Afrikaans legend **Rev:** Aloe plant and value **Designer:** Tommy Sasseen

Date	Mintage	F	VF	XF	Unc	BU
1968	50,000	—	—	—	1.50	—
1968 Proof	25,000	Value: 0.60				

KM# 85 10 CENTS

4.0000 g., Nickel, 20.7 mm. **Obv:** Arms with supporters **Rev:** Aloe plant and value **Designer:** Tommy Sasseen

Date	Mintage	F	VF	XF	Unc	BU
1970	7,598,000	—	—	0.10	0.35	—
1970 Proof	10,000	Value: 0.60				
1971	6,440,000	—	—	0.10	0.35	—
1971 Proof	12,000	Value: 0.60				
1972	10,028,000	—	—	0.10	0.35	—
1972 Proof	10,000	Value: 0.60				
1973	1,760,000	—	—	0.10	0.35	—
1973 Proof	11,000	Value: 0.60				
1974	9,897,000	—	—	0.10	0.35	—
1974 Proof	15,000	Value: 0.60				
1975	12,982,000	—	—	0.10	0.35	—
1975 Proof	18,000	Value: 0.60				
1977	28,851,000	—	—	0.10	0.35	—
1977 Proof	19,000	Value: 0.60				
1978	25,008,000	—	—	0.10	0.35	—
1978 Proof	19,000	Value: 0.60				
1980	5,040,000	—	—	0.10	0.35	—
1980 Proof	15,000	Value: 0.60				
1981	9,604,000	—	—	0.10	0.35	—
1981 Proof	10,000	Value: 0.60				
1983	26,495,000	—	—	0.10	0.35	—
1983 Proof	14,000	Value: 0.60				
1984	35,465,000	—	—	0.10	0.35	—
1984 Proof	11,000	Value: 0.60				
1985	29,270,000	—	—	0.10	0.35	—
1985 Proof	9,859	Value: 0.60				
1986	24,480,000	—	—	0.10	0.35	—
1986 Proof	7,100	Value: 0.60				
1987	43,234,000	—	—	0.10	0.35	—
1987 Proof	6,781	Value: 0.60				
1988	48,267,000	—	—	0.10	0.35	—
1988 Proof	7,250	Value: 0.60				
1989	—	—	—	—	0.35	—
1989 Proof	—	Value: 0.60				

KM# 94 10 CENTS

4.0000 g., Nickel, 20.7 mm. **Obv:** Head of President Fouche right **Rev:** Aloe plant and value **Rev. Designer:** Tommy Sasseen

Date	Mintage	F	VF	XF	Unc	BU
1976	30,986,000	—	—	0.40	1.00	—
1976 Proof	21,000	Value: 1.50				

KM# 101 10 CENTS

4.0000 g., Nickel, 20.7 mm. **Obv:** Head of President Diederichs left **Rev:** Aloe plant and value **Rev. Designer:** Tommy Sasseen

Date	Mintage	F	VF	XF	Unc	BU
1979	5,042,000	—	—	0.40	1.00	—
1979 Proof	17,000	Value: 1.50				

KM# 112 10 CENTS
4.0000 g., Nickel, 20.7 mm. **Obv:** Head of President Vorster 1/4 right **Rev:** Aloe plant and value **Rev. Designer:** Tommy Sasseen

Date	Mintage	F	VF	XF	Unc	BU
1982	15,806,000	—	—	0.40	1.00	—
1982 Proof	12,000	Value: 1.50				

KM# 135 10 CENTS
Brass Plated Steel, 16 mm. **Obv:** Arms with supporters **Obv. Designer:** A.L. Sutherland **Rev:** Arum lily and value **Rev. Designer:** R.C. McFarlane

Date	Mintage	F	VF	XF	Unc	BU
1990	—	—	—	—	0.40	—
1990 Proof	—	Value: 0.60				
1991	—	—	—	—	0.40	—
1991 Proof	12,000	Value: 0.60				
1992	—	—	—	—	0.40	—
1992 Proof	—	Value: 0.60				
1993	—	—	—	—	0.40	—
1993 Proof	7,790	Value: 0.60				
1994	—	—	—	—	0.40	—
1994 Proof	5,804	Value: 0.60				
1995	—	—	—	—	0.40	—
1995 Proof	—	Value: 0.60				

KM# 161 10 CENTS
Brass Plated Steel, 16 mm. **Obv:** English legend **Obv. Designer:** A.L. Sutherland **Rev:** Arum lily and value **Rev. Designer:** R.C. McFarlane

Date	Mintage	F	VF	XF	Unc	BU
1996	—	—	—	—	0.40	0.60
1996 Proof	—	Value: 0.75				
1997	—	—	—	—	0.40	0.60
1997 Proof	3,596	Value: 0.75				
1998	—	—	—	—	0.40	0.60
1998 Proof	—	Value: 1.75				
1999	—	—	—	—	0.40	0.60
1999 Proof	—	Value: 1.75				
2000	—	—	—	—	0.40	0.60

KM# 235 10 CENTS
16.8630 g., 0.9250 Silver 0.5015 oz. ASW, 32.7 mm. **Obv:** Lion and country name **Rev:** Lions and value **Edge:** Reeded

Date	Mintage	F	VF	XF	Unc	BU
ND(2000) Proof	—	Value: 25.00				

KM# 224 10 CENTS
2.0000 g., Brass Plated Steel, 16 mm. **Obv:** Crowned arms **Obv. Designer:** A.L. Sutherland **Rev:** Arum Lily and value **Rev. Designer:** R.C. McFarlane **Edge:** Reeded

Date	Mintage	F	VF	XF	Unc	BU
2000	—	—	—	—	0.60	0.85

KM# 61 20 CENTS
11.3100 g., 0.5000 Silver .1818 oz. ASW **Obv:** Shield **Obv. Designer:** G.E. Kruger-Gray **Rev:** Bust of Jan van Riebeeck 1/4 right

Date	Mintage	F	VF	XF	Unc	BU
1961	2,954,000	—	BV	3.00	3.50	—
1961 Proof	7,530	Value: 4.00				
1962 Small 2	3,568,000	—	BV	3.00	3.50	—
1962 Large 2	Inc. above	—	—	—	—	—
1962 Small 2; Proof	3,844	Value: 5.00				
1963	4,380,000	—	BV	3.00	3.50	—
1963 Proof	4,025	Value: 5.00				
1964	4,335,000	—	BV	3.00	3.50	—
1964 Proof	16,000	Value: 3.50				

KM# 69.1 20 CENTS
6.0000 g., Nickel, 24.2 mm. **Obv:** Head of Jan van Riebeeck, English legend **Obv. Legend:** English legend **Rev:** Protea flower within sprigs, value at left

Date	Mintage	F	VF	XF	Unc	BU
1965	29,210,000	—	0.15	0.20	0.40	—
1965 Proof	25,000	Value: 0.60				
1966	4,049,000	—	0.15	0.20	0.50	—
1967	58,000	—	—	—	1.00	—
1969	9,952	—	—	—	10.00	—

KM# 69.2 20 CENTS
6.0000 g., Nickel, 24.2 mm. **Obv:** Head of Jan van Riebeeck, Africaans legend **Obv. Legend:** Afrikaans legend **Rev:** Protea flower within sprigs, value at left

Date	Mintage	F	VF	XF	Unc	BU
1965	29,210,000	—	0.15	0.20	0.40	—
1966	4,049,000	—	0.15	0.20	0.50	—
1966 Proof	25,000	Value: 0.60				
1967	58,000	—	—	—	1.00	—
1967 Proof	25,000	Value: 0.60				
1969	9,952	—	—	—	6.00	—
1969 Proof	12,000	Value: 4.00				

KM# 78.1 20 CENTS
6.0000 g., Nickel, 24.2 mm. **Obv:** Head of President Charles Swart left, English legend **Obv. Designer:** Tommy Sasseen **Rev:** Protea flower within sprigs, value at left

Date	Mintage	F	VF	XF	Unc	BU
1968	50,000	—	—	—	3.00	—
1968 Proof	25,000	Value: 0.60				

KM# 78.2 20 CENTS
6.0000 g., Nickel, 24.2 mm. **Obv:** Africaans legend **Obv. Designer:** Tommy Sasseen **Rev:** Protea flower within sprigs, value at left

Date	Mintage	F	VF	XF	Unc	BU
1968	50,000	—	—	—	3.50	—

KM# 86 20 CENTS
6.0000 g., Nickel, 24.2 mm. **Obv:** Arms with supporters, bilingual legend **Obv. Legend:** Bilingual legend **Obv. Designer:** Tommy Sasseen **Rev:** Protea flower within sprigs, value at left **Note:** Varieties exist.

Date	Mintage	F	VF	XF	Unc	BU
1970	14,000	—	—	—	10.00	—
1970 Proof	10,000	Value: 1.50				
1971	5,893,000	—	0.15	0.25	0.60	—
1971 Proof	12,000	Value: 1.50				
1972	9,069,000	—	0.15	0.25	0.60	—
1972 Proof	10,000	Value: 1.50				
1973	20,000	—	—	—	5.00	—
1973 Proof	11,000	Value: 1.50				
1974	2,436,000	—	0.15	0.35	0.75	—
1974 Proof	15,000	Value: 1.50				
1975	12,982,000	—	—	0.20	0.60	—
1975 Proof	18,000	Value: 1.00				
1977	30,650,000	—	—	0.20	0.60	—
1977 Proof	19,000	Value: 0.75				
1978	10,049,000	—	—	0.20	0.60	—
1978 Proof	19,000	Value: 0.75				
1980	13,335,000	—	—	0.20	0.60	—
1980 Proof	15,000	Value: 0.75				
1981	8,534,000	—	—	0.20	0.60	—
1981 Proof	10,000	Value: 0.75				
1983	25,667,000	—	—	0.20	0.60	—
1983 Proof	14,000	Value: 0.75				
1984	31,607,000	—	—	0.20	0.60	—
1984 Proof	11,000	Value: 0.75				
1985	29,329,000	—	—	0.20	0.60	—
1985 Proof	9,859	Value: 0.75				
1986	11,408,000	—	—	0.20	0.60	—
1986 Proof	7,100	Value: 0.75				
1987	36,904,000	—	—	0.20	0.60	—
1987 Proof	6,781	Value: 0.75				
1988	43,115,000	—	—	0.20	0.60	—
1988 Proof	7,250	Value: 0.75				
1989	—	—	—	0.20	0.60	—
1989 Proof	—	Value: 0.75				
1990	98,512,000	—	—	0.20	0.60	—

KM# 95 20 CENTS
6.0000 g., Nickel, 24.2 mm. **Obv:** Head of President Fouche right **Rev:** Protea flower within sprigs, value at left

Date	Mintage	F	VF	XF	Unc	BU
1976	18,826,000	—	—	0.70	1.50	—
1976 Proof	21,000	Value: 2.50				

KM# 102 20 CENTS
6.0000 g., Nickel, 24.2 mm. **Obv:** Head of President Diederichs left **Rev:** Protea flower within sprigs, value at left

Date	Mintage	F	VF	XF	Unc	BU
1979	5,032,000	—	—	0.70	1.50	—
1979 Proof	15,000	Value: 2.50				

KM# 113 20 CENTS
6.0000 g., Nickel, 24.2 mm. **Obv:** Head of President Vorster 1/4 right **Rev:** Protea flower within sprigs, value at left

Date	Mintage	F	VF	XF	Unc	BU
1982	18,083,000	—	—	0.70	1.50	—
1982 Proof	12,000	Value: 2.50				

KM# 136 20 CENTS
Brass Plated Steel, 19 mm. **Obv:** Arms with supporters **Obv. Designer:** A.L. Sutherland **Rev:** Protea flower within sprigs, value at upper right **Rev. Designer:** S. Erasmus

Date	Mintage	F	VF	XF	Unc	BU
1990	—	—	—	—	4.00	—
1990 Proof	—	Value: 8.00				
1991	—	—	—	—	4.00	—
1991 Proof	11,800	Value: 8.00				

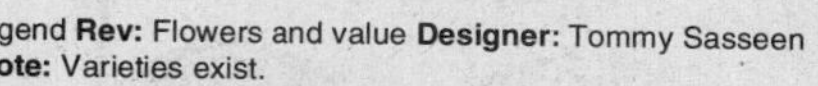

Date	Mintage	F	VF	XF	Unc	BU
1992	—	—	—	—	0.60	—
1992 Proof	—	Value: 8.00				
1993	—	—	—	—	0.60	—
1993 Proof	7,790	Value: 8.00				
1994	—	—	—	—	0.60	—
1994 Proof	5,804	Value: 8.00				
1995	—	—	—	—	0.60	—
1995 Proof	—	Value: 8.00				

KM# 162 20 CENTS

Brass Plated Steel, 19 mm. **Obv:** Arms with supporters **Obv. Legend:** AFERIKA BORWA, Tswana legend above arms **Obv. Designer:** A.L. Sutherland **Rev:** Protea flower within sprigs, value at upper right **Rev. Designer:** S. Erasmus

Date	Mintage	F	VF	XF	Unc	BU
1996	—	—	—	—	0.60	0.85
1996 Proof	—	Value: 4.00				
1997	—	—	—	—	0.60	0.85
1997 Proof	3,596	Value: 4.00				
1998	—	—	—	—	0.60	0.85
1998 Proof	—	Value: 4.00				
1999	—	—	—	—	0.60	0.85
1999 Proof	—	Value: 4.00				
2000	—	—	—	—	0.60	0.85

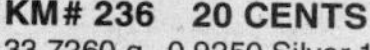

KM# 236 20 CENTS

33.7260 g., 0.9250 Silver 1.003 oz. ASW, 38.3 mm. **Obv:** Lion and country name **Rev:** Lions and value **Edge:** Reeded

Date	Mintage	F	VF	XF	Unc	BU
ND(2000) Proof	—	Value: 35.00				

KM# 225 20 CENTS

3.4500 g., Brass Plated Steel, 19 mm. **Obv:** Crowned arms **Obv. Designer:** A.L. Sutherland **Rev:** Protea flower within sprigs and value **Edge:** Reeded

Date	Mintage	F	VF	XF	Unc	BU
2000	—	—	—	—	0.75	1.00

KM# 62 50 CENTS

28.2800 g., 0.5000 Silver .4546 oz. ASW **Obv:** Springbok **Obv. Designer:** C.L. Steynberg **Rev:** Bust of Jan van Riebeeck 1/4 right **Note:** Varieties exist with narrow, high relief and wide, low letters.

Date	Mintage	F	VF	XF	Unc	BU
1961	26,000	—	BV	7.50	10.00	—
1961 Prooflike	20,000	—	—	—	10.00	—
1961 Proof	8,530	Value: 18.00				
1962	15,000	—	BV	7.50	10.00	—
1962 Prooflike	6,024	—	—	—	12.50	—
1962 Proof	3,844	Value: 20.00				
1963	143,000	—	BV	7.50	10.00	—
1963 Prooflike	10,000	—	—	—	12.50	—
1963 Proof	4,025	Value: 20.00				
1964	86,000	—	BV	7.50	9.00	—
1964 Prooflike	25,000	—	—	—	10.00	—
1964 Proof	16,000	Value: 10.00				

KM# 70.1 50 CENTS

9.5000 g., Nickel, 27.8 mm. **Obv:** Head of Jan van Riebeeck right, English legend **Rev:** Flower and value **Designer:** Tommy Sasseen

Date	Mintage	F	VF	XF	Unc	BU
1965 Proof	—	Value: 3,500				
1966	8,055,999	—	—	0.50	2.50	—
1966 Proof	25,000	Value: 4.00				
1967	52,000	—	—	—	1.50	—
Note: In sets only						
1967 Proof	25,000	Value: 4.00				
1969	7,968	—	—	—	10.00	—
Note: In sets only						
1969 Proof	12,000	Value: 10.00				

KM# 70.2 50 CENTS

9.5000 g., Nickel, 27.8 mm. **Obv:** Head of Jan van Riebeeck right, Afrikaans legend **Rev:** Flower and value **Designer:** Tommy Sasseen

Date	Mintage	F	VF	XF	Unc	BU
1965	28,000	—	—	—	6.00	—
1965 Proof	25,000	Value: 6.00				
1966	8,055,999	—	—	0.50	2.50	—
1967	52,000	—	—	—	3.50	—
Note: In sets only						
1969	7,968	—	—	—	15.00	—
Note: In sets only						

KM# 79.1 50 CENTS

9.5000 g., Nickel, 27.8 mm. **Obv:** Head of President Charles Swart left, English legend **Rev:** Flowers and value **Designer:** Tommy Sasseen

Date	Mintage	F	VF	XF	Unc	BU
1968	750,000	—	—	0.50	1.50	—

KM# 79.2 50 CENTS

9.5000 g., Nickel, 27.8 mm. **Obv:** Head of President Charles Swart left, Afrikaans legend **Rev:** Flowers and value **Designer:** Tommy Sasseen

Date	Mintage	F	VF	XF	Unc	BU
1968	750,000	—	—	0.50	2.00	—
1968 Proof	25,000	Value: 3.50				

KM# 87 50 CENTS

9.5000 g., Nickel, 27.8 mm. **Obv:** Arms with supporters, bilingual legend **Rev:** Flowers and value **Designer:** Tommy Sasseen **Note:** Varieties exist.

Date	Mintage	F	VF	XF	Unc	BU
1970	4,098,000	—	—	0.50	1.50	—
1970 Proof	10,000	Value: 2.00				
1971	5,062,000	—	—	0.50	1.50	—
1971 Proof	12,000	Value: 2.00				
1972	771,000	—	—	0.50	1.50	—
1972 Proof	10,000	Value: 2.00				
1973	1,042,999	—	—	0.50	1.50	—
1973 Proof	11,000	Value: 2.00				
1974	1,942,000	—	—	0.50	1.50	—
1974 Proof	15,000	Value: 2.00				
1975	4,888,000	—	—	0.50	1.50	—
1975 Proof	18,000	Value: 2.00				
1977	10,196,000	—	—	0.50	1.50	—
1977 Proof	19,000	Value: 2.00				
1978	5,071,000	—	—	0.50	1.50	—
1978 Proof	17,000	Value: 2.00				
1980	4,268,000	—	—	0.50	1.50	—
1980 Proof	15,000	Value: 2.00				
1981	5,681,000	—	—	0.50	1.50	—
1981 Proof	10,000	Value: 2.00				
1983	5,150,000	—	—	0.40	1.00	—
1983 Proof	14,000	Value: 1.50				
1984	9,687,000	—	—	0.40	1.00	—
1984 Proof	11,000	Value: 1.50				
1985	13,339,000	—	—	0.40	1.00	—
1985 Proof	9,859	Value: 1.50				
1986	2,294,000	—	—	0.40	1.00	—
1986 Proof	7,100	Value: 1.50				
1987	19,071,000	—	—	0.40	1.00	—
1987 Proof	6,781	Value: 1.50				
1988	27,698,000	—	—	0.40	1.00	—
1988 Proof	7,250	Value: 1.50				
1989	—	—	—	0.40	1.00	—
1989 Proof	—	Value: 1.50				
1990	29,442,000	—	—	0.40	1.00	—

KM# 96 50 CENTS

9.5000 g., Nickel, 27.8 mm. **Obv:** Head of President Fouche right **Rev:** Flowers and value **Rev. Designer:** Tommy Sasseen

Date	Mintage	F	VF	XF	Unc	BU
1976	9,632,000	—	0.75	1.50	3.00	—
1976 Proof	21,000	Value: 5.00				

KM# 103 50 CENTS

9.5000 g., Nickel, 27.8 mm. **Obv:** Head of President Diederichs left **Rev:** Flowers and value **Rev. Designer:** Tommy Sasseen

Date	Mintage	F	VF	XF	Unc	BU
1979	5,051,000	—	0.75	1.50	3.50	—
1979 Proof	15,000	Value: 5.00				

KM# 114 50 CENTS

9.5000 g., Nickel, 27.8 mm. **Obv:** Head of President Vorster 1/4 right **Obv. Designer:** Tommy Sasseen **Rev:** Flowers and value

Date	Mintage	F	VF	XF	Unc	BU
1982	2,069,999	—	0.75	1.50	3.50	—
1982 Proof	12,000	Value: 5.00				

KM# 137 50 CENTS
5.0000 g., Brass Plated Steel, 22 mm. **Obv:** Arms with supporters **Obv. Designer:** A.L. Sutherland **Rev:** Plant and value **Rev. Designer:** C. Cogle

Date	Mintage	F	VF	XF	Unc	BU
1990	—	—	—	—	5.00	—
1990 Proof	—	Value: 10.00				
1991	—	—	—	—	5.00	—
1991 Proof	12,000	Value: 10.00				
1992	—	—	—	—	1.00	—
1992 Proof	—	Value: 10.00				
1993	—	—	—	—	1.00	—
1993 Proof	7,790	Value: 10.00				
1994	—	—	—	—	1.00	—
1994 Proof	5,804	Value: 10.00				
1995	—	—	—	—	1.00	—
1995 Proof	—	Value: 10.00				

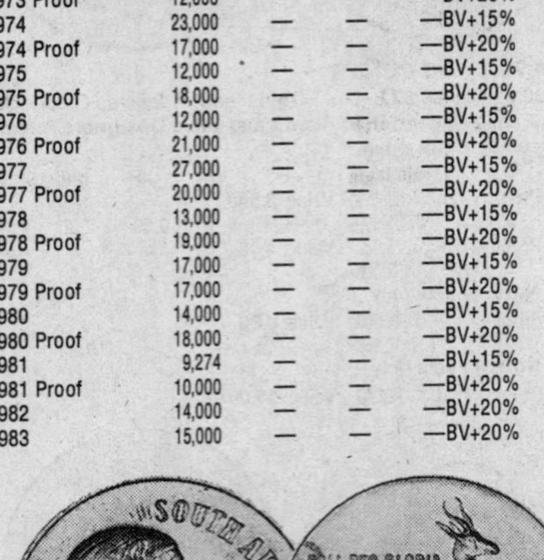

KM# 163 50 CENTS
5.0000 g., Bronze Plated Steel, 22 mm. **Obv:** Arms with supporters **Obv. Legend:** AFRIKA BORWA, Sotho legend **Obv. Designer:** A.L. Sutherland **Rev:** Plant and value **Rev. Designer:** C. Cogle

Date	Mintage	F	VF	XF	Unc	BU
1996	—	—	—	—	1.00	1.25
1996 Proof	—	Value: 5.00				
1997	—	—	—	—	1.00	1.25
1997 Proof	—	Value: 5.00				
1998	—	—	—	—	1.00	1.25
1998 Proof	—	Value: 5.00				
1999	—	—	—	—	1.00	1.25
1999 Proof	—	Value: 5.00				
2000	—	—	—	—	1.00	1.25

KM# 237 50 CENTS
76.4020 g., 0.9250 Silver 2.2722 oz. ASW, 50 mm. **Obv:** Lion and country name **Rev:** Lion and value **Edge:** Reeded

Date	Mintage	F	VF	XF	Unc	BU
2000 Proof	—	Value: 65.00				

KM# 226 50 CENTS
4.9000 g., Brass Plated Steel, 22 mm. **Obv:** Crowned arms **Obv. Designer:** A.L. Sutherland **Rev:** Plant and value **Rev. Designer:** C. Cogle **Edge:** Reeded

Date	Mintage	F	VF	XF	Unc	BU
2000	—	—	—	—	1.00	1.25

KM# 63 RAND
3.9940 g., 0.9170 Gold .1177 oz. AGW **Obv:** Springbok **Rev:** Bust of Jan van Riebeeck 1/4 right

Date	Mintage	F	VF	XF	Unc	BU
1961	4,246	—	—	—	BV+15%	—
1961 Proof	4,932	—	—	—	BV+20%	—
1962	3,955	—	—	—	BV+15%	—
1962 Proof	2,344	—	—	—	BV+20%	—
1963	4,023	—	—	—	BV+15%	—
1963 Proof	2,508	—	—	—	BV+20%	—
1964	5,866	—	—	—	BV+15%	—
1964 Proof	4,000	—	—	—	BV+20%	—
1965	10,000	—	—	—	BV+15%	—
1965 Proof	6,024	—	—	—	BV+20%	—
1966	10,000	—	—	—	BV+15%	—
1966 Proof	11,000	—	—	—	BV+20%	—
1967	10,000	—	—	—	BV+15%	—
1967 Proof	11,000	—	—	—	BV+20%	—
1968	10,000	—	—	—	BV+15%	—
1968 Proof	11,000	—	—	—	BV+20%	—
1969	10,000	—	—	—	BV+15%	—
1969 Proof	8,000	—	—	—	BV+20%	—
1970	10,000	—	—	—	BV+15%	—
1970 Proof	7,000	—	—	—	BV+20%	—
1971	10,000	—	—	—	BV+15%	—
1971 Proof	7,650	—	—	—	BV+20%	—
1972	12,000	—	—	—	BV+15%	—
1972 Proof	7,500	—	—	—	BV+20%	—
1973	15,000	—	—	—	BV+15%	—
1973 Proof	12,000	—	—	—	BV+20%	—
1974	23,000	—	—	—	BV+15%	—
1974 Proof	17,000	—	—	—	BV+20%	—
1975	12,000	—	—	—	BV+15%	—
1975 Proof	18,000	—	—	—	BV+20%	—
1976	12,000	—	—	—	BV+15%	—
1976 Proof	21,000	—	—	—	BV+20%	—
1977	27,000	—	—	—	BV+15%	—
1977 Proof	20,000	—	—	—	BV+20%	—
1978	13,000	—	—	—	BV+15%	—
1978 Proof	19,000	—	—	—	BV+20%	—
1979	17,000	—	—	—	BV+15%	—
1979 Proof	17,000	—	—	—	BV+20%	—
1980	14,000	—	—	—	BV+15%	—
1980 Proof	18,000	—	—	—	BV+20%	—
1981	9,274	—	—	—	BV+15%	—
1981 Proof	10,000	—	—	—	BV+20%	—
1982	14,000	—	—	—	BV+20%	—
1983	15,000	—	—	—	BV+20%	—

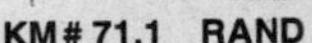

KM# 71.1 RAND
15.0000 g., 0.8000 Silver .3858 oz. ASW **Obv:** Head of Jan van Riebeeck right **Rev:** Springbok above value

Date	Mintage	F	VF	XF	Unc	BU
1965	—	—	—	BV	7.00	—
1965 Proof	25,000	Value: 20.00				
1966	1,434,000	—	—	BV	6.50	—
1966 Proof	20	Value: 1,250				
1968	50,000	—	—	BV	6.50	—
Note: In sets only						
1968 Proof	25,000	Value: 6.50				

KM# 71.2 RAND
15.0000 g., 0.8000 Silver .3858 oz. ASW **Obv:** Head of Jan van Riebeeck right, Afrikaans legend **Rev:** Springbok above value

Date	Mintage	F	VF	XF	Unc	BU
1965 V.I.P. Proof	—	—	—	—	1,000	—
1966	1,434,000	—	—	BV	6.50	—
1966 Proof	25,000	Value: 7.00				
1968	50,000	—	—	—	8.00	—
Note: In sets only						
1968 Proof	Est. 20	Value: 1,250				

KM# 72.1 RAND
15.0000 g., 0.8000 Silver .3858 oz. ASW **Subject:** 1st Anniversary - Death of Dr. Verwoerd **Obv:** Bust right, English legend **Obv. Designer:** Tommy Sasseen **Rev:** Springbok above value

Date	Mintage	F	VF	XF	Unc	BU
1967	1,544,000	—	—	BV	6.50	—
1967 Proof	Est. 20	Value: 1,250				

KM# 72.2 RAND
15.0000 g., 0.8000 Silver .3858 oz. ASW **Subject:** 1st Anniversary - Death of Dr. Verwoerd **Obv:** Bust right, Afrikaans legend **Obv. Designer:** Tommy Sasseen **Rev:** Springbok above value

Date	Mintage	F	VF	XF	Unc	BU
1967	1,544,000	—	—	BV	6.50	—
1967 Proof	25,000	Value: 7.50				

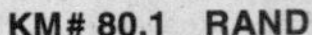

KM# 80.1 RAND
15.0000 g., 0.8000 Silver .3858 oz. ASW, 32.6 mm. **Subject:** Dr. T.E. Donges **Obv:** Bust right, English legend **Rev:** Springbok above value **Designer:** Tommy Sasseen **Note:** The South African mint does not acknowledge the existence of these 1 Rand pieces struck in proof.

Date	Mintage	F	VF	XF	Unc	BU
1969	506,000	—	—	BV	6.50	—
1969 Proof	Est. 20	Value: 1,250				

KM# 80.2 RAND
15.0000 g., 0.8000 Silver .3858 oz. ASW, 32.6 mm. **Subject:** Dr. T.E. Donges **Obv:** Bust right, Afrikaans legend **Rev:** Springbok above value **Designer:** Tommy Sasseen

Date	Mintage	F	VF	XF	Unc	BU
1969	506,000	—	—	BV	6.50	—
1969 Proof	12,000	Value: 7.50				

KM# 89 RAND
15.0000 g., 0.8000 Silver .3858 oz. ASW **Subject:** 50th Anniversary of Pretoria Mint **Obv:** Arms with supporters **Rev:** 4 Coin designs surround brick door at center **Designer:** Tommy Sasseen

Date	Mintage	F	VF	XF	Unc	BU
1974	20,000	—	—	—	12.50	—
1974 Proof	15,000	Value: 15.00				

KM# 88 RAND

15.0000 g., 0.8000 Silver .3858 oz. ASW **Obv:** Arms with supporters, bilingual legend **Obv. Designer:** Tommy Sasseen **Rev:** Springbok

Date	Mintage	F	VF	XF	Unc	BU
1970	14,000	—	—	BV	6.50	—
1970 Proof	10,000	Value: 8.00				
1971	20,000	—	—	BV	6.50	—
1971 Proof	12,000	Value: 8.00				
1972	20,000	—	—	BV	6.50	—
1972 Proof	10,000	Value: 8.00				
1973	20,000	—	—	BV	6.50	—
1973 Proof	11,000	Value: 8.00				
1975	20,000	—	—	BV	6.50	—
1975 Proof	18,000	Value: 8.00				
1976	20,000	—	—	BV	6.50	—
1976 Proof	21,000	Value: 8.00				
1977 Proof	19,000	Value: 9.00				
1978 Proof	17,000	Value: 9.00				
1979 Proof	15,000	Value: 9.00				
1980 Proof	15,000	Value: 9.00				
1981 Proof	12,000	Value: 12.50				
1982 Proof	10,000	Value: 12.50				
1983 Proof	14,000	Value: 12.50				
1984 Proof	11,000	Value: 12.50				
1987	4,526	—	—	BV	15.00	—
1987 Proof	13,000	Value: 12.50				
1988	21	—	—	—	—	—
1988 Proof	7,250	Value: 15.00				
1989	3,684	—	—	BV	15.00	—
1989 Proof	15,000	Value: 12.50				
1990 Proof	—	Value: 25.00				

KM# 88a RAND

12.0000 g., Nickel, 31 mm. **Obv:** Arms with supporters, bilingual legend **Obv. Designer:** Tommy Sasseen **Rev:** Springbok above value

Date	Mintage	F	VF	XF	Unc	BU
1977	29,871,000	—	—	0.75	2.00	—
1977 Proof	10	Value: 1,500				
1978	12,021,000	—	—	0.75	2.00	—
1978 Proof	10	Value: 1,500				
1980	2,690,000	—	—	0.75	2.00	—
1981	2,035,000	—	—	0.75	2.00	—
1983	7,182,000	—	—	0.75	2.00	—
1983 Proof	10	Value: 1,500				
1984	5,736,000	—	—	0.75	2.00	—
1984 Proof	11,000	Value: 5.00				
1986	1,570,000	—	—	0.75	2.00	—
1986 Proof	7,000	Value: 5.00				
1987	12,152,000	—	—	0.75	2.00	—
1987 Proof	6,781	Value: 5.00				
1988	21,335,000	—	—	0.75	2.00	—
1988 Proof	7,250	Value: 5.00				
1989	—	—	—	—	2.00	—
1989 Proof	—	Value: 5.00				

KM# 104 RAND

12.0000 g., Nickel, 31 mm. **Obv:** Head of President Diederichs left **Rev:** Springbok above value

Date	Mintage	F	VF	XF	Unc	BU
1979	13,466,000	—	2.00	4.00	10.00	—
1979 Proof	5	Value: 2,000				

KM# 115 RAND

Nickel .3858 oz. **Obv:** Head of President Vorster 1/4 right **Rev:** Springbok above value

Date	Mintage	F	VF	XF	Unc	BU
1982	7,685,000	—	2.50	5.00	10.00	—
1982 Proof	15	Value: 1,500				

KM# 116 RAND

15.0000 g., 0.8000 Silver .3858 oz. ASW **Subject:** 75th Anniversary of Parliament **Obv:** Crossed scepters divides shield and lion **Rev:** Parliament building

Date	Mintage	F	VF	XF	Unc	BU
1985	8,731	—	—	—	11.50	—
1985 Proof	26,000	Value: 18.50				

KM# 117 RAND

Nickel **Obv:** Head of President Marais Viljoen left **Obv. Designer:** A.L. Sutherland **Rev:** Springbok above value

Date	Mintage	F	VF	XF	Unc	BU
1985	3,983,000	—	2.50	5.00	10.00	—
1985 Proof	9,859	Value: 5.00				

KM# 119 RAND

15.0000 g., 0.8000 Silver .3858 oz. ASW **Subject:** 100th Anniversary of Johannesburg **Obv:** Arms with supporters **Obv. Designer:** A.L. Sutherland **Rev:** View of city

Date	Mintage	F	VF	XF	Unc	BU
1986	7,501	—	—	—	13.50	—
1986 Proof	5,683	Value: 22.50				

KM# 120 RAND

15.0000 g., 0.8000 Silver .3858 oz. ASW **Series:** Year of the Disabled **Obv:** Arms with supporters **Obv. Designer:** A.L. Sutherland **Rev:** Stylized standing figure and figure in wheelchair, value at left

Date	Mintage	F	VF	XF	Unc	BU
1986	1,005	—	—	—	40.00	—
1986 Proof	5,150	Value: 22.50				

KM# 122 RAND

15.0000 g., 0.8000 Silver .3858 oz. ASW **Subject:** Bartolomeu Dias **Obv:** Arms with supporters **Obv. Designer:** A.L. Sutherland **Rev:** Crown above point of star design to left of map

Date	Mintage	F	VF	XF	Unc	BU
1988	7,091	—	—	—	12.50	—
1988 Proof	9,640	Value: 16.50				

KM# 125 RAND

15.0000 g., 0.8000 Silver .3858 oz. ASW **Subject:** Huguenots **Obv:** Arms with supporters **Obv. Designer:** A.L. Sutherland **Rev:** Descending dove and design divide dates below small cross, all within circle **Rev. Designer:** Tommy Sasseen

Date	Mintage	F	VF	XF	Unc	BU
1988	5,497	—	—	—	12.50	—
1988 Proof	9,028	Value: 16.50				

KM# 128 RAND

15.0000 g., 0.8000 Silver .3858 oz. ASW **Subject:** The Great Trek **Obv:** Arms with supporters **Obv. Designer:** A.L. Sutherland **Rev:** Stylized wheel and arrow design

Date	Mintage	F	VF	XF	Unc	BU
1988	6,555	—	—	—	12.50	—
1988 Proof	7,941	Value: 17.50				

KM# 141 RAND

Nickel **Obv:** Head of President Botha facing **Rev:** Springbok above value

Date	Mintage	F	VF	XF	Unc	BU
1990	25,323,000	—	—	1.75	3.50	—
1990 Proof	15,000	Value: 10.00				

KM# 148 RAND

Nickel Plated Copper **Obv:** Head of President Botha facing **Obv. Designer:** A.L. Sutherland **Rev:** Springbok below value **Rev. Designer:** L. Lotriet

Date	Mintage	F	VF	XF	Unc	BU
1990	12,000	—	—	—	10.00	—
1990 Proof	10,000	Value: 15.00				

KM# 138 RAND
Nickel Plated Copper **Obv:** Arms with supporters **Obv. Designer:** A.L. Sutherland **Rev:** Springbok below value **Rev. Designer:** L. Lotriet

Date	Mintage	F	VF	XF	Unc	BU
1991	20,765,000	—	—	—	2.50	—
1991 Proof	12,000	Value: 15.00				
1992	59,571,000	—	—	—	2.50	—
1992 Proof	10,000	Value: 15.00				
1993	37,977,000	—	—	—	2.50	—
1993 Proof	7,790	Value: 20.00				
1994	54,633,000	—	—	—	2.50	—
1994 Proof	5,804	Value: 20.00				
1995	28,012,000	—	—	—	2.50	—
1995 Proof	5,816	Value: 20.00				

KM# 142 RAND
14.9700 g., 0.9250 Silver .4452 oz. ASW **Subject:** South African Nursing Schools **Obv:** Protea flower **Obv. Designer:** A.L. Sutherland **Rev:** Aladdin lamp divides dates within cross design

Date	Mintage	F	VF	XF	Unc	BU
1991	4,901	—	—	—	12.50	—
1991 Proof	8,675	Value: 17.50				

KM# 143 RAND
14.9700 g., 0.9250 Silver .4452 oz. ASW **Subject:** Coinage Centennial **Obv:** Protea flower **Obv. Designer:** A.L. Sutherland **Rev:** Assorted coin designs

Date	Mintage	F	VF	XF	Unc	BU
1992	5,826	—	—	—	12.50	—
1992 Proof	8,094	Value: 17.50				

KM# 168 RAND
14.9700 g., 0.9250 Silver .4452 oz. ASW **Subject:** 200 Years of Banking **Obv:** Protea flower **Obv. Designer:** A.L. Sutherland **Rev:** Tower divides lion head and coin designs **Rev. Designer:** L. Lotriet

Date	Mintage	F	VF	XF	Unc	BU
1993	3,677	—	—	—	17.50	—
1993 Proof	3,907	Value: 27.50				

KM# 149 RAND
14.9700 g., 0.8000 Silver .3858 oz. ASW **Subject:** Presidential Inauguration **Obv:** Arms with supporters **Obv. Designer:** A.L. Sutherland **Rev:** Building below value

Date	Mintage	F	VF	XF	Unc	BU
1994 Proof	6,269	Value: 22.50				

KM# 167 RAND
15.0000 g., 0.9250 Silver .4461 oz. ASW **Subject:** Conservation **Obv:** Protea flower **Obv. Designer:** A.L. Sutherland **Rev:** Assorted animals within stylized design

Date	Mintage	F	VF	XF	Unc	BU
1994	6,404	—	—	—	12.50	—
1994 Proof	4,706	Value: 17.50				

KM# 152 RAND
15.0000 g., 0.9250 Silver .4461 oz. ASW **Subject:** Railway Centennial **Obv:** Protea flower **Obv. Designer:** A.L. Sutherland **Rev:** Train and value

Date	Mintage	F	VF	XF	Unc	BU
1995	3,515	—	—	—	15.00	—
1995 Proof	4,491	Value: 22.50				

KM# 164 RAND
Nickel Plated Copper, 20 mm. **Obv:** Arms with supporters, Afrikaans legend **Obv. Designer:** A.L. Sutherland **Rev:** Springbok and value **Rev. Designer:** L. Lotriet

Date	Mintage	F	VF	XF	Unc	BU
1996	12,199,000	—	—	—	1.75	—
1996 Proof	4,827	Value: 6.00				
1997	38,876,000	—	—	—	1.75	—
1997 Proof	3,596	Value: 6.00				
1998	—	—	—	—	1.75	—
1998 Proof	—	Value: 6.00				
1999	—	—	—	—	1.75	—
1999 Proof	—	Value: 6.00				
2000	—	—	—	—	1.75	—

KM# 169 RAND
15.0000 g., 0.9250 Silver .4461 oz. ASW **Subject:** Constitution **Rev:** Hand writing in book

Date	Mintage	F	VF	XF	Unc	BU
1996	2,585	—	—	—	15.00	—
1996 Proof	2,474	Value: 25.00				

KM# 181 RAND
15.0000 g., 0.9250 Silver .4461 oz. ASW **Subject:** Women of South Africa **Obv:** Protea flower **Obv. Designer:** A.L. Sutherland **Rev:** Stylized 1/2 head facing within map

Date	Mintage	F	VF	XF	Unc	BU
1997	1,983	—	—	—	17.50	—
1997 Proof	2,329	Value: 28.50				

KM# 182 RAND
3.1103 g., 0.9999 Gold .1000 oz. AGW **Subject:** 30th Anniversary - First Heart Transplant **Rev:** Doctor working on heart

Date	Mintage	F	VF	XF	Unc	BU
1997 Proof	1,000	Value: 115				

KM# 177 RAND
15.0000 g., 0.9250 Silver .4461 oz. ASW **Obv:** Protea flower **Rev:** Assorted designs divided into 16 sections

Date	Mintage	F	VF	XF	Unc	BU
1998	—	—	—	—	16.50	—
1998 Proof	—	Value: 28.00				

KM# 178 RAND
3.1103 g., 0.9999 Gold .1000 oz. AGW **Subject:** San Tribe **Rev:** Tribesman hunting

Date	Mintage	F	VF	XF	Unc	BU
1998 Proof	—	Value: 115				

KM# 219 RAND
3.1103 g., 0.9999 Gold .1000 oz. AGW, 16.5 mm. **Obv:** National arms **Rev:** Zulu warrior **Edge:** Reeded

Date	Mintage	F	VF	XF	Unc	BU
1999 Proof	1,000	Value: 115				

KM# 232 RAND
15.0000 g., 0.9250 Silver 0.4461 oz. ASW, 32.7 mm. **Obv:** Protea flower **Rev:** Mine tower **Edge:** Reeded

Date	Mintage	F	VF	XF	Unc	BU
1999 Proof	1,500	Value: 22.50				

KM# 238 RAND
15.0000 g., 0.9250 Silver 0.4461 oz. ASW, 32.7 mm. **Obv:** Protea flower **Rev:** Wine barrels, grapes and leaves **Edge:** Reeded

Date	Mintage	F	VF	XF	Unc	BU
2000 Proof	—	Value: 25.00				

KM# 239 RAND
3.1103 g., 0.9999 Gold 0.1 oz. AGW, 16.5 mm. **Obv:** National arms **Rev:** Three Xhosa tribe members **Edge:** Reeded

Date	Mintage	F	VF	XF	Unc	BU
2000 Proof	—	Value: 115				

KM# 227 RAND
4.0000 g., Nickel Plated Steel, 20 mm. **Obv:** Crowned arms **Obv. Designer:** A.L. Sutherland **Rev:** Springbok and value **Rev. Designer:** L. Lotriet **Edge:** Reeded and plain sections

Date	Mintage	F	VF	XF	Unc	BU
2000	—	—	—	—	1.75	2.75

KM# 64 2 RAND
7.9881 g., 0.9170 Gold .2354 oz. AGW **Obv:** Springbok **Obv. Designer:** C.L. Steynberg **Rev:** Bust of Jan van Riebeeck 1/4 right

Date	Mintage	F	VF	XF	Unc	BU
1961	3,014	—	—	—	BV+10%	—
1961 Proof	3,932	—	—	—	BV+15%	—
1962	10,000	—	—	—	BV+10%	—
1962 Proof	2,344	—	—	—	BV+15%	—
1963	3,179	—	—	—	BV+10%	—
1963 Proof	2,508	—	—	—	BV+15%	—
1964	3,994	—	—	—	BV+10%	—
1964 Proof	4,000	—	—	—	BV+15%	—
1965	10,000	—	—	—	BV+10%	—
1965 Proof	6,024	—	—	—	BV+15%	—
1966	10,000	—	—	—	BV+10%	—
1966 Proof	11,000	—	—	—	BV+15%	—
1967	10,000	—	—	—	BV+10%	—
1967 Proof	11,000	—	—	—	BV+15%	—
1968	10,000	—	—	—	BV+10%	—
1968 Proof	11,000	—	—	—	BV+15%	—
1969	10,000	—	—	—	BV+10%	—
1969 Proof	8,000	—	—	—	BV+15%	—
1970	10,000	—	—	—	BV+10%	—
1970 Proof	7,000	—	—	—	BV+15%	—
1971	10,000	—	—	—	BV+10%	—
1971 Proof	7,650	—	—	—	BV+15%	—
1972	18,000	—	—	—	BV+10%	—
1972 Proof	7,500	—	—	—	BV+15%	—
1973	14,000	—	—	—	BV+10%	—
1973 Proof	13,000	—	—	—	BV+15%	—
1974	13,000	—	—	—	BV+10%	—
1974 Proof	17,000	—	—	—	BV+15%	—
1975	12,000	—	—	—	BV+10%	—
1975 Proof	18,000	—	—	—	BV+15%	—
1976	12,000	—	—	—	BV+10%	—
1976 Proof	21,000	—	—	—	BV+15%	—
1977	12,000	—	—	—	BV+10%	—
1977 Proof	20,000	—	—	—	BV+15%	—
1978	11,000	—	—	—	BV+10%	—
1978 Proof	19,000	—	—	—	BV+15%	—
1979	12,000	—	—	—	BV+10%	—
1979 Proof	20,000	—	—	—	BV+15%	—
1980	12,000	—	—	—	BV+10%	—
1980 Proof	18,000	—	—	—	BV+15%	—
1981	8,538	—	—	—	BV+10%	—
1981 Proof	10,000	—	—	—	BV+15%	—
1982	2,030	—	—	—	BV+10%	—
1982 Proof	12,000	—	—	—	BV+15%	—
1983	15,000	—	—	—	BV+15%	—

KM# 139 2 RAND
Nickel Plated Copper, 23 mm. **Obv:** Arms with supporters **Rev:** Greater Kudu **Designer:** A.L. Sutherland

Date	Mintage	F	VF	XF	Unc	BU
1989	65,233,000	—	—	—	2.00	—
1989 Proof	13,000	Value: 10.00				
1990	70,655,000	—	—	—	2.00	—
1990 Proof	10,000	Value: 7.50				
1991	39,243,000	—	—	—	2.00	—
1991 Proof	12,000	Value: 7.50				
1992	2,115,000	—	—	—	2.00	—
1992 Proof	10,000	Value: 7.50				
1993	92,000	—	—	—	2.00	—
1993 Proof	7,790	Value: 7.50				
1994	994,000	—	—	—	2.00	—
1994 Proof	5,804	Value: 7.50				
1995	13,213,000	—	—	—	2.00	—
1995 Proof	5,816	Value: 7.50				

KM# 145 2 RAND
33.4700 g., 0.9250 Silver .9954 oz. ASW **Subject:** Coin Minting **Obv:** Arms with supporters **Rev:** Assorted coins and design above value

Date	Mintage	F	VF	XF	Unc	BU
1992	50	—	—	—	—	—
1992 Proof	6,688	Value: 35.00				

KM# 147 2 RAND
33.4700 g., 0.9250 Silver .9954 oz. ASW **Series:** Barcelona Olympics **Obv:** Arm holding torch in front of map **Rev:** Three event athletes

Date	Mintage	F	VF	XF	Unc	BU
1992	1,670	—	—	—	—	—
1992 Proof	15,000	Value: 27.50				

KM# 151 2 RAND
33.4700 g., 0.9250 Silver .9954 oz. ASW **Subject:** Peace **Obv:** Arms with supporters **Rev:** Stylized doves and figures within globe design

Date	Mintage	F	VF	XF	Unc	BU
1993	828	—	—	—	—	—
1993 Proof	4,800	Value: 42.50				

KM# 156 2 RAND
33.6750 g., 0.9250 Silver 1.0014 oz. ASW **Subject:** World Cup Soccer **Obv:** Stylized figure and soccer ball **Rev:** Soccer ball and North American map

Date	Mintage	F	VF	XF	Unc	BU
1994	288	—	—	—	—	—
1994 Proof	3,210	Value: 40.00				

KM# 153 2 RAND
33.6260 g., 0.9250 Silver 1.0000 oz. ASW **Subject:** Rugby World Cup **Rev. Designer:** L. Lotriet

Date	Mintage	F	VF	XF	Unc	BU
1995 Proof	3,981	Value: 40.00				

KM# 154 2 RAND
33.6260 g., 0.9250 Silver 1.0000 oz. ASW **Series:** 50th Anniversary - F.A.O. **Obv:** Arms with supporters **Rev:** Two children in bird nest, sparrow and F.A.O. logo

Date	Mintage	F	VF	XF	Unc	BU
1995 Proof	1,743	Value: 45.00				

KM# 155 2 RAND
33.6260 g., 0.9250 Silver 1.0000 oz. ASW **Series:** 50th Anniversary - United Nations **Obv:** Arms with supporters **Rev:** Numeral 50 and UN emblem above world globe and map

Date	Mintage	F	VF	XF	Unc	BU
1995 Proof	1,412	Value: 42.50				

KM# 157 2 RAND
33.6260 g., 0.9250 Silver 1.0000 oz. ASW **Obv:** Arms with supporters **Rev:** Soccer player within soccerball design

Date	Mintage	F	VF	XF	Unc	BU
1996 Proof	2,690	Value: 40.00				

KM# 165 2 RAND
Nickel Plated Copper, 23 mm. **Obv:** Arms with supporters **Obv. Legend:** UMZANSTI AFRIKA, Xhosa legend **Rev:** Greater Kudu **Designer:** A.L. Sutherland

Date	Mintage	F	VF	XF	Unc	BU
1996	123,000	—	—	—	2.50	—
1996 Proof	4,827	Value: 8.00				
1997	1,804,000	—	—	—	2.50	—
1997 Proof	3,596	Value: 8.00				
1998	—	—	—	—	2.50	—
1998 Proof	—	Value: 8.00				
1999	—	—	—	—	2.50	—
1999 Proof	—	Value: 8.00				
2000	—	—	—	—	2.50	—

KM# 175 2 RAND
33.6260 g., 0.9250 Silver 1.0000 oz. ASW **Obv:** Arms with supporters **Rev:** Knysna Seahorse

Date	Mintage	F	VF	XF	Unc	BU
1997 Proof	3,000	Value: 45.00				

KM# 183 2 RAND
7.7700 g., 0.9999 Gold .2500 oz. AGW **Subject:** Early Man **Obv:** Arms with supporters **Rev:** Australopithecus Africanus

Date	Mintage	F	VF	XF	Unc	BU
1997 Proof	1,000	Value: 185				

KM# 179 2 RAND
33.6200 g., 0.9250 Silver 1.0000 oz. ASW **Obv:** Arms with supporters **Rev:** Jackass Penguin

Date	Mintage	F	VF	XF	Unc	BU
1998 Proof	Est. 3,000	Value: 45.00				

KM# 180 2 RAND
7.7770 g., 0.9999 Gold .2500 oz. AGW **Obv:** Arms with supporters **Rev:** Coelacanth fish and fossil

Date	Mintage	F	VF	XF	Unc	BU
1998 Proof	—	Value: 195				

KM# 220 2 RAND
7.7759 g., 0.9999 Gold .2500 oz. AGW **Obv:** Arms with supporters **Rev:** Thrinaxodon dinosaur

Date	Mintage	F	VF	XF	Unc	BU
1999 Proof	1,000	Value: 200				

KM# 218 2 RAND
33.6000 g., 0.9250 Silver .9992 oz. ASW, 38.7 mm. **Obv:** Arms with supporters **Rev:** Great white shark **Edge:** Reeded **Note:** Struck at Pretoria.

Date	Mintage	F	VF	XF	Unc	BU
1999 Proof	3,000	Value: 60.00				

KM# 240 2 RAND
33.6260 g., 0.9250 Silver 1 oz. ASW, 38.7 mm. **Obv:** Protea flower **Rev:** Octopus **Edge:** Reeded

Date	Mintage	F	VF	XF	Unc	BU
2000 Proof	—	Value: 60.00				

KM# 241 2 RAND
7.7770 g., 0.9999 Gold 0.25 oz. AGW, 22 mm. **Obv:** Arms with supporters **Rev:** "Little Foot" skeleton find **Edge:** Reeded

Date	Mintage	F	VF	XF	Unc	BU
2000 Proof	—	Value: 185				

KM# 140 5 RAND
7.0000 g., Nickel Plated Copper, 26 mm. **Obv:** Arms with supporters **Rev:** Wildebeest **Designer:** A.L. Sutherland

Date	Mintage	F	VF	XF	Unc	BU
1994	45,212,000	—	—	—	4.50	5.50
1994 Proof	5,804	Value: 10.00				
1995	41,238,000	—	—	—	4.50	5.50
1995 Proof	5,816	Value: 10.00				

KM# 150 5 RAND
7.0000 g., Nickel Plated Copper, 26 mm. **Subject:** Presidential Inauguration **Obv:** Arms with supporters **Obv. Designer:** A.L. Sutherland **Rev:** Building below value **Rev. Designer:** S. Erasmus

Date	Mintage	F	VF	XF	Unc	BU
1994	10,095,000	—	—	—	5.50	6.50
1994 Proof	10,000	Value: 8.50				

KM# 166 5 RAND
7.0000 g., Nickel Plated Copper, 26 mm. **Obv:** Arms with supporters **Obv. Legend:** ININGIZIMU AFRIKA, Zulu/Swati legend **Rev:** Wildebeest **Designer:** A.L. Sutherland

Date	Mintage	F	VF	XF	Unc	BU
1996	15,435,000	—	—	—	4.50	—
1996 Proof	4,827	Value: 10.00				
1997	1,276,000	—	—	—	4.50	—
1997 Proof	3,596	Value: 10.00				
1998	—	—	—	—	4.50	—
1998 Proof	—	Value: 10.00				
1999	—	—	—	—	4.50	—
1999 Proof	—	Value: 10.00				
2000	—	—	—	—	4.50	—

KM# 230 5 RAND
6.9400 g., Nickel Plated Steel, 25.9 mm. **Obv:** Head of Nelson Mandela 1/4 right **Obv. Legend:** ININGIZIMU AFRIKA, Zulu legend **Rev:** Wildebeest **Edge:** Reeded and plain sections **Designer:** A.L. Sutherland

Date	Mintage	F	VF	XF	Unc	BU
2000	—	—	—	—	4.50	5.50
2000 Proof	—	Value: 10.00				

BULLION COINAGE

Mint mark: GRC - Gold Reef City

KM# 105 1/10 KRUGERRAND
3.3900 g., 0.9170 Gold .1000 oz. AGW

Date	Mintage	F	VF	XF	Unc	BU
1980	857,000	—	—	—	BV+15%	—
1980 Proof	60	Value: 2,500				
1981	1,321,000	—	—	—	BV+15%	—
1981 Proof	7,500	Value: 90.00				
1982	1,065,000	—	—	—	BV+15%	—
1982 Proof	11,000	Value: 85.00				
1983	508,000	—	—	—	BV+15%	—
1983 Proof	12,000	Value: 85.00				
1984	898,000	—	—	—	BV+15%	—
1984 Proof	13,000	Value: 85.00				
1985	282,000	—	—	—	BV+15%	—
1985 Proof	6,700	Value: 85.00				
1986	87,000	—	—	—	BV+15%	—
1986 Proof	8,001	Value: 85.00				
1987	53,000	—	—	—	BV+15%	—
1987 Proof	6,065	Value: 85.00				
1987 GRC Proof	1,126	Value: 400				
1988	87,000	—	—	—	BV+15%	—
1988 Proof	2,056	Value: 90.00				
1988 GRC Proof	949	Value: 400				
1989	—	—	—	—	BV+15%	—
1989 Proof	3,316	Value: 90.00				
1989 GRC Proof	377	Value: 1,000				
1990	—	—	—	—	BV+15%	—
1990 Proof	3,459	Value: 90.00				
1990 GRC Proof	1,096	Value: 275				
1991 Proof	3,524	Value: 90.00				
1991 GRC Proof	426	Value: 275				
1992 Proof	1,789	Value: 90.00				
1993	54,000	—	—	—	BV+15%	—
1993 Proof	3,811	Value: 90.00				
1994	86,000	—	—	—	BV+15%	—
1994 Proof	—	Value: 90.00				
1995	25,000	—	—	—	BV+15%	—
1995 Proof	750	Value: 120				
1996 Proof	4,000	Value: 90.00				
1997 Proof	3,410	Value: 90.00				
1997 Proof	30	Value: 300				

Note: 30th Anniversary of Krugerrand privy mark

Date	Mintage	F	VF	XF	Unc	BU
1998 Proof	—	Value: 90.00				
1999 Proof	—	Value: 90.00				

KM# 106 1/4 KRUGERRAND
8.4800 g., 0.9170 Gold .2500 oz. AGW **Obv:** Bust left **Rev:** Springbok divides date **Rev. Designer:** Coert L. Steynberg

Date	Mintage	F	VF	XF	Unc	BU
1980	534,000	—	—	—	BV+10%	—
1980 Proof	60	Value: 3,000				
1981	726,000	—	—	—	BV+10%	—
1981 Proof	7,500	Value: 195				
1982	1,269,000	—	—	—	BV+10%	—
1982 Proof	11,000	Value: 195				
1983	64,000	—	—	—	BV+10%	—
1983 Proof	12,000	Value: 195				
1984	503,000	—	—	—	BV+10%	—
1984 Proof	13,000	Value: 195				
1985	594,000	—	—	—	BV+10%	—
1985 Proof	6,700	Value: 195				
1986 Proof	8,001	Value: 195				
1987 Proof	6,050	Value: 195				
1987 GRC Proof	1,121	Value: 500				
1988	5,946	—	—	—	BV+10%	—
1988 Proof	2,056	Value: 200				
1988 GRC Proof	835	Value: 500				
1989	5,943	—	—	—	BV+10%	—
1989 Proof	3,316	Value: 200				
1989 GRC Proof	318	Value: 1,400				
1990 Proof	2,750	Value: 200				
1990 GRC Proof	1,066	Value: 400				
1991 Proof	1,626	Value: 200				
1991 GRC Proof	426	Value: 400				
1992 Proof	1,629	Value: 200				
1993 Proof	3,061	Value: 200				
1994	39,000	—	—	—	BV+10%	—
1994 Proof	1,874	Value: 200				
1995	13,000	—	—	—	BV+10%	—
1995 Proof	1,095	Value: 215				
1996 Proof	1,853	Value: 200				
1997 Proof	1,440	Value: 200				
1997 Proof	30	Value: 450				

Note: 30th Anniversary of Krugerrand privy mark

Date	Mintage	F	VF	XF	Unc	BU
1998 Proof	—	Value: 200				
1999 Proof	—	Value: 200				

KM# 107 1/2 KRUGERRAND

16.9700 g., 0.9170 Gold .5000 oz. AGW **Obv:** Bust left **Rev:** Springbok divides date **Rev. Designer:** Coert L. Steynberg

Date	Mintage	F	VF	XF	Unc	BU
1980	374,000	—	—	—	BV+8%	—
1980 Proof	60	Value: 3,500				
1981	178,000	—	—	—	BV+8%	—
1981 Proof	9,000	Value: 375				
1982	429,000	—	—	—	BV+8%	—
1982 Proof	13,000	Value: 375				
1983	60,000	—	—	—	BV+8%	—
1983 Proof	14,000	Value: 375				
1984	187,000	—	—	—	BV+8%	—
1984 Proof	9,900	Value: 375				
1985	104,000	—	—	—	BV+8%	—
1985 Proof	5,945	Value: 375				
1986 Proof	8,002	Value: 375				
1987 Proof	5,389	Value: 375				
1987 GRC Proof	1,186	Value: 800				
1988	5,454	—	—	—	BV+8%	—
1988 Proof	2,282	Value: 400				
1988 GRC Proof	1,026	Value: 800				
1989	4,980	—	—	—	BV+8%	—
1989 Proof	3,727	Value: 400				
1989 GRC Proof	399	Value: 1,500				
1990 Proof	2,850	Value: 400				
1990 GRC Proof	1,066	Value: 500				
1991 Proof	3,459	Value: 400				
1991 GRC Proof	426	Value: 500				
1992 Proof	1,501	Value: 400				
1993	11,000	—	—	—	BV+8%	—
1993 Proof	2,439	Value: 400				
1994	16,000	—	—	—	BV+8%	—
1994 Proof	2,146	Value: 400				
1995	10,000	—	—	—	BV+8%	—
1995 Proof	1,012	Value: 400				
1996 Proof	1,788	Value: 400				
1997 Proof	2,000	Value: 400				
1997 Proof	30	Value: 550				
Note: 30th Anniversary of Krugerrand privy mark						
1998 Proof	—	Value: 375				
1999 Proof	—	Value: 400				

KM# 73 KRUGERRAND

33.9305 g., 0.9170 Gold 1.0000 oz. AGW **Obv:** Bust left **Rev:** Springbok divides date **Rev. Designer:** Coert L. Steynberg

Date	Mintage	F	VF	XF	Unc	BU
1967	40,000	—	—	—	BV+5%	—
1967 Proof	10,000	Value: 725				
1968	20,000	—	—	—	BV+5%	—
1968 Proof	5,000	Value: 1,000				
Note: Frosted bust and frosted reverse						
1968 Proof	8,956	Value: 745				
1969	20,000	—	—	—	BV+5%	—
1969 Proof	10,000	Value: 725				
1970	211,000	—	—	—	BV+5%	—
1970 Proof	10,000	Value: 720				
1971	550,000	—	—	—	BV+5%	—
1971 Proof	6,000	Value: 720				
1972	544,000	—	—	—	BV+5%	—
1972 Proof	6,625	Value: 720				
1973	859,000	—	—	—	BV+5%	—
1973 Proof	10,000	Value: 720				
1974	3,204,000	—	—	—	BV+5%	—
1974 Proof	6,352	Value: 720				
1975	4,804,000	—	—	—	BV+5%	—
1975 Proof	5,600	Value: 720				
1976	3,005,000	—	—	—	BV+5%	—
1976 Proof	6,600	Value: 720				
1977	3,331,000	—	—	—	BV+5%	—
Note: 188 serrations on edge						
1977 Proof	8,500	Value: 720				
Note: 188 serrations on edge						
1977	Inc. above	—	—	—	BV+5%	—
Note: 220 serrations on edge						
1977 Proof	Inc. above	Value: 720				
Note: 220 serrations on edge						
1978	6,012,000	—	—	—	BV+5%	—

Date	Mintage	F	VF	XF	Unc	BU
1978 Proof	10,000	Value: 720				
1979	4,941,000	—	—	—	BV+5%	—
1979 Proof	12,000	Value: 720				
1980	3,143,000	—	—	—	BV+5%	—
1980 Proof	12,000	Value: 720				
1981	3,560,000	—	—	—	BV+5%	—
1981 Proof	13,000	Value: 720				
1982	2,566,000	—	—	—	BV+5%	—
1982 Proof	17,000	Value: 720				
1983	3,368,000	—	—	—	BV+5%	—
1983 Proof	19,000	Value: 720				
1984	2,070,000	—	—	—	BV+5%	—
1984 Proof	14,000	Value: 720				
1985	875,000	—	—	—	BV+5%	—
1985 Proof	10,000	Value: 720				
1986 Proof	20,000	Value: 720				
1987	11,000	—	—	—	BV+5%	—
1987 Proof	11,000	Value: 720				
1987 GRC Proof	1,160	Value: 1,200				
1988	615,000	—	—	—	BV+5%	—
1988 Proof	4,268	Value: 725				
1988 GRC Proof	1,220	Value: 1,200				
1989	194,000	—	—	—	BV+5%	—
1989 Proof	5,070	Value: 725				
1989 GRC Proof	987	Value: 1,600				
1990	391,000	—	—	—	BV+5%	—
1990 Proof	3,032	Value: 725				
1990 GRC Proof	1,066	Value: 1,600				
1991	283,000	—	—	—	BV+5%	—
1991 Proof	2,181	Value: 725				
1991 GRC Proof	426	Value: 1,600				
1992	1,803	—	—	—	BV+5%	—
1992 Proof	2,067	Value: 725				
1993	162,000	—	—	—	BV+5%	—
1993 Proof	3,963	Value: 725				
1994	130,000	—	—	—	BV+5%	—
1994 Proof	1,761	Value: 725				
1995	59,000	—	—	—	BV+5%	—
1995 Proof	1,678	Value: 725				
1996 Proof	2,188	Value: 725				
1997 Proof	1,663	Value: 725				
1997 SS Proof	72	Value: 850				
1997 Proof	30	Value: 1,250				
Note: 30th Anniversary of Krugerrand privy mark						
1998 Proof	—	Value: 725				
1999 Proof	—	Value: 725				

KM# 118 OUNCE

33.9305 g., 0.9170 Gold 1.0000 oz. AGW **Subject:** 75th Anniversary of Parliament **Obv:** Crossed scepters divide lion and shield **Rev:** Parliament building

Date	Mintage	F	VF	XF	Unc	BU
1985 Proof	3,019	Value: 1,200				

KM# 184 OUNCE

31.1070 g., 0.9999 Gold 1.0000 oz. AGW **Subject:** Presidential Inauguration

Date	Mintage	F	VF	XF	Unc	BU
1994 Proof	1,742	Value: 750				

KM# 185 OUNCE

31.1070 g., 0.9999 Gold 1.0000 oz. AGW **Subject:** Rugby

Date	Mintage	F	VF	XF	Unc	BU
1995 Proof	406	Value: 775				

KM# 131 1/10 PROTEA

3.3900 g., 0.9170 Gold .1000 oz. AGW **Subject:** 100th Anniversary of Johannesburg

Date	Mintage	F	VF	XF	Unc	BU
1986 Proof	5,212	Value: 115				

KM# 123 1/10 PROTEA

3.3900 g., 0.9170 Gold .1000 oz. AGW **Subject:** Bartolomeu Dias **Obv:** Protea flower **Rev:** Crown above point of radiant star, map of Africa at right

Date	Mintage	F	VF	XF	Unc	BU
1988 Proof	2,199	Value: 115				

KM# 126 1/10 PROTEA

3.3900 g., 0.9170 Gold .1000 oz. AGW **Subject:** Huguenots **Obv:** Protea flowers **Rev:** Descending dove and design divide dates below small cross, all within circle

Date	Mintage	F	VF	XF	Unc	BU
1988 Proof	2,060	Value: 115				

KM# 129 1/10 PROTEA

3.3900 g., 0.9170 Gold .1000 oz. AGW **Subject:** The Great Trek **Obv:** Protea flower **Rev:** Stylized wheel and arrow design

Date	Mintage	F	VF	XF	Unc	BU
1988 Proof	2,999	Value: 115				

KM# 171 1/10 PROTEA

3.3900 g., 0.9170 Gold .1000 oz. AGW **Subject:** South African Nursing Schools **Obv:** Protea Flower **Rev:** Aladdin lamp divides dates within cross design **Note:** Similar to 1 Rand, KM#142.

Date	Mintage	F	VF	XF	Unc	BU
1991 Proof	3,950	Value: 115				

KM# 144 1/10 PROTEA

3.3900 g., 0.9170 Gold .1000 oz. AGW **Subject:** Coinage Centennial **Obv:** Protea flower **Rev:** Assorted coin designs

Date	Mintage	F	VF	XF	Unc	BU
1992 Proof	2,503	Value: 115				

KM# 172 1/10 PROTEA

3.3900 g., 0.9170 Gold .1000 oz. AGW **Subject:** 200 Years of Banking **Obv:** Protea flower **Rev:** Towers divide lion head and coin designs **Note:** Similar to 1 Rand, KM#168.

Date	Mintage	F	VF	XF	Unc	BU
1993 Proof	5,064	Value: 100				
1993 Proof	5,064	Value: 115				

KM# 187 1/10 PROTEA

3.3900 g., 0.9170 Gold .1000 oz. AGW **Subject:** Conservation

Date	Mintage	F	VF	XF	Unc	BU
1994 Proof	1,485	Value: 125				

KM# 193 1/10 PROTEA

3.3900 g., 0.9170 Gold .1000 oz. AGW **Subject:** Railways

Date	Mintage	F	VF	XF	Unc	BU
1995 Proof	1,217	Value: 125				

KM# 199 1/10 PROTEA

3.3900 g., 0.9170 Gold .1000 oz. AGW **Subject:** Constitution

Date	Mintage	F	VF	XF	Unc	BU
1996 Proof	946	Value: 125				

KM# 205 1/10 PROTEA

3.3900 g., 0.9170 Gold .1000 oz. AGW **Subject:** Women of South Africa **Designer:** Natanya van Niekerk

Date	Mintage	F	VF	XF	Unc	BU
1997 Proof	648	Value: 130				

KM# 211 1/10 PROTEA

3.3900 g., 0.9170 Gold .1000 oz. AGW **Subject:** Year of the Child

Date	Mintage	F	VF	XF	Unc	BU
1998 Proof	—	Value: 130				

KM# 250 1/10 PROTEA

3.1103 g., 0.9999 Gold 0.1 oz. AGW, 16.5 mm. **Obv:** Protea flower **Rev:** Mine cart and entrance **Edge:** Reeded

Date	Mintage	F	VF	XF	Unc	BU
1999 Proof	—	Value: 115				

KM# 256 1/10 PROTEA

3.1103 g., 0.9999 Gold 0.1 oz. AGW, 16.5 mm. **Obv:** Protea flower **Rev:** Grape vines and building **Edge:** Reeded

Date	Mintage	F	VF	XF	Unc	BU
2000 Proof	—	Value: 115				

KM# 121 PROTEA

33.9300 g., 0.9170 Gold 1.0000 oz. AGW **Subject:** 100th Anniversary of Johannesburg

Date	Mintage	F	VF	XF	Unc	BU
1986 Proof	4,701	Value: 735				

KM# 124 PROTEA
33.9300 g., 0.9170 Gold 1.0000 oz. AGW **Subject:** Bartolomeu Dias **Obv:** Protea flower **Rev:** Crown above point of radiant star design, map of Africa at right

Date	Mintage	F	VF	XF	Unc	BU
1988 Proof	3,776	Value: 735				

KM# 127 PROTEA
33.9300 g., 0.9170 Gold 1.0000 oz. AGW **Subject:** Huguenots **Obv:** Protea flowers **Obv. Designer:** A.L. Sutherland **Rev:** Descending dove and design divide dates below small cross, all within circle

Date	Mintage	F	VF	XF	Unc	BU
1988 Proof	3,391	Value: 735				

KM# 130 PROTEA
33.9300 g., 0.9170 Gold 1.0000 oz. AGW **Subject:** The Great Trek **Obv:** Protea flower **Rev:** Wheel and arrow design

Date	Mintage	F	VF	XF	Unc	BU
1988 Proof	2,956	Value: 735				

KM# 186 PROTEA
33.9300 g., 0.9170 Gold 1.0000 oz. AGW **Subject:** Nursing

Date	Mintage	F	VF	XF	Unc	BU
1991 Proof	3,004	Value: 735				

KM# 146 PROTEA
33.9300 g., 0.9170 Gold 1.0000 oz. AGW **Subject:** Coinage Centennial **Obv:** Protea flower **Obv. Designer:** A.L. Sutherland **Rev:** Assorted coin designs

Date	Mintage	F	VF	XF	Unc	BU
1992 Proof	1,752	Value: 750				

KM# 173 PROTEA
33.9300 g., 0.9170 Gold 1.0000 oz. AGW **Subject:** 200 Years of Banking **Note:** Similar to 1 Rand, KM#168.

Date	Mintage	F	VF	XF	Unc	BU
1993 Proof	2,032	Value: 735				
1993 GRC Proof	500	Value: 800				

KM# 188 PROTEA
33.9300 g., 0.9170 Gold 1.0000 oz. AGW **Subject:** Conservation

Date	Mintage	F	VF	XF	Unc	BU
1994 Proof	1,187	Value: 735				
1994 Proof	600	Value: 800				

Note: PTA.ZOO

KM# 194 PROTEA
33.9300 g., 0.9170 Gold 1.0000 oz. AGW **Subject:** Railway

Date	Mintage	F	VF	XF	Unc	BU
1995 Proof	694	Value: 800				

KM# 200 PROTEA
33.9300 g., 0.9170 Gold 1.0000 oz. AGW **Subject:** Constitution

Date	Mintage	F	VF	XF	Unc	BU
1996 Proof	641	Value: 800				

KM# 206 PROTEA
33.9300 g., 0.9170 Gold 1.0000 oz. AGW **Subject:** Women of South Africa **Designer:** Natanya van Niekerk

Date	Mintage	F	VF	XF	Unc	BU
1997 Proof	207	Value: 825				

KM# 212 PROTEA
33.9300 g., 0.9170 Gold 1.0000 oz. AGW **Subject:** Year of the Child

Date	Mintage	F	VF	XF	Unc	BU
1998 Proof	—	Value: 825				

KM# 251 PROTEA
31.1035 g., 0.9999 Gold 0.9999 oz. AGW, 32.7 mm. **Obv:** Protea flower **Rev:** Miner **Edge:** Reeded

Date	Mintage	F	VF	XF	Unc	BU
1999 Proof	—	Value: 735				

KM# 257 PROTEA
31.1035 g., 0.9999 Gold 0.9999 oz. AGW, 32.7 mm. **Obv:** Protea flower **Rev:** Worker holding basket **Edge:** Reeded

Date	Mintage	F	VF	XF	Unc	BU
2000 Proof	—	Value: 735				

NATURA GOLD BULLION COINAGE

KM# 189 1/10 OUNCE
3.1104 g., 0.9990 Gold .1000 oz. AGW **Rev:** Lions drinking

Date	Mintage	F	VF	XF	Unc	BU
1994 Proof	6,660	Value: 115				

KM# 195 1/10 OUNCE
3.1104 g., 0.9990 Gold .1000 oz. AGW **Rev:** Rhinocerous drinking

Date	Mintage	F	VF	XF	Unc	BU
1995 Proof	2,703	Value: 115				

KM# 201 1/10 OUNCE
3.1104 g., 0.9990 Gold .1000 oz. AGW **Rev:** Elephant **Rev. Designer:** Natanya van Niekerk

Date	Mintage	F	VF	XF	Unc	BU
1996 Proof	9,014	Value: 115				

KM# 207 1/10 OUNCE
3.1104 g., 0.9990 Gold .1000 oz. AGW **Rev:** Buffalo **Rev. Designer:** Natanya van Niekerk

Date	Mintage	F	VF	XF	Unc	BU
1997 Proof	3,590	Value: 115				

KM# 213 1/10 OUNCE
3.1104 g., 0.9990 Gold .1000 oz. AGW **Rev:** Leopard **Rev. Designer:** Natanya van Niekerk

Date	Mintage	F	VF	XF	Unc	BU
1998 Proof	—	Value: 115				

KM# 252 1/10 OUNCE
3.1103 g., 0.9999 Gold 0.1 oz. AGW, 16.5 mm. **Obv:** Greater Kudu head **Rev:** Koodoo herd drinking **Edge:** Reeded

Date	Mintage	F	VF	XF	Unc	BU
1999 Proof	—	Value: 115				

KM# 258 1/10 OUNCE
3.1103 g., 0.9999 Gold 0.1 oz. AGW, 16.5 mm. **Obv:** Ibex head **Rev:** Ibex drinking **Edge:** Reeded

Date	Mintage	F	VF	XF	Unc	BU
2000 Proof	—	Value: 115				

KM# 190 1/4 OUNCE
7.7770 g., 0.9999 Gold .2500 oz. AGW **Rev:** Lions

Date	Mintage	F	VF	XF	Unc	BU
1994 Proof	4,159	Value: 200				

KM# 196 1/4 OUNCE
7.7770 g., 0.9999 Gold .2500 oz. AGW **Rev:** Rhinoceros

Date	Mintage	F	VF	XF	Unc	BU
1995 Proof	1,752	Value: 200				

KM# 202 1/4 OUNCE
7.7770 g., 0.9999 Gold .2500 oz. AGW **Rev:** Elephant **Rev. Designer:** Natanya van Niekerk

Date	Mintage	F	VF	XF	Unc	BU
1996 Proof	3,740	Value: 200				

KM# 208 1/4 OUNCE
7.7770 g., 0.9999 Gold .2500 oz. AGW **Rev:** Buffalo **Rev. Designer:** Natanya van Niekerk

Date	Mintage	F	VF	XF	Unc	BU
1997 Proof	2,164	Value: 200				

KM# 214 1/4 OUNCE
7.7770 g., 0.9999 Gold .2500 oz. AGW **Rev:** Leopard **Rev. Designer:** Natanya van Niekerk

Date	Mintage	F	VF	XF	Unc	BU
1998 Proof	—	Value: 200				

KM# 253 1/4 OUNCE
7.7770 g., 0.9999 Gold 0.25 oz. AGW, 22 mm. **Obv:** Kudu heads within circle below value **Rev:** Two Kudu fighting **Edge:** Reeded

Date	Mintage	F	VF	XF	Unc	BU
1999 Proof	—	Value: 200				

KM# 259 1/4 OUNCE
7.7770 g., 0.9999 Gold 0.25 oz. AGW, 22 mm. **Obv:** Ibex head **Rev:** Two Ibexe males facing off **Edge:** Reeded

Date	Mintage	F	VF	XF	Unc	BU
2000 Proof	—	Value: 200				

KM# 191 1/2 OUNCE
15.5530 g., 0.9999 Gold .5000 oz. AGW **Rev:** Lions

Date	Mintage	F	VF	XF	Unc	BU
1994 Proof	3,999	Value: 365				

KM# 197 1/2 OUNCE
15.5530 g., 0.9999 Gold .5000 oz. AGW **Rev:** Rhinocerous

Date	Mintage	F	VF	XF	Unc	BU
1995 Proof	1,551	Value: 365				

KM# 203 1/2 OUNCE
15.5530 g., 0.9999 Gold .5000 oz. AGW **Rev:** Elephant **Rev. Designer:** Natanya van Niekerk

Date	Mintage	F	VF	XF	Unc	BU
1996 Proof	3,457	Value: 365				

KM# 209 1/2 OUNCE
15.5530 g., 0.9999 Gold .5000 oz. AGW **Rev:** Buffalo **Rev. Designer:** Natanya van Niekerk

Date	Mintage	F	VF	XF	Unc	BU
1997 Proof	1,912	Value: 365				

KM# 215 1/2 OUNCE
15.5530 g., 0.9999 Gold .5000 oz. AGW **Rev:** Leopard **Rev. Designer:** Natanya van Niekerk

Date	Mintage	F	VF	XF	Unc	BU
1998 Proof	—	Value: 365				

KM# 254 1/2 OUNCE
15.5518 g., 0.9990 Gold 0.4995 oz. AGW, 27 mm. **Obv:** Greater Kudu head **Rev:** Kudu attacked by lion **Edge:** Reeded

Date	Mintage	F	VF	XF	Unc	BU
1999 Proof	—	Value: 365				

KM# 260 1/2 OUNCE
15.5518 g., 0.9990 Gold 0.4995 oz. AGW, 27 mm. **Obv:** Ibex head **Rev:** Ibex head **Edge:** Reeded

Date	Mintage	F	VF	XF	Unc	BU
2000 Proof	—	Value: 365				

KM# 192 OUNCE
31.1070 g., 0.9999 Gold 1.0000 oz. AGW **Rev:** Lions

Date	Mintage	F	VF	XF	Unc	BU
1994 Proof	2,902	Value: 700				
1994 Pre.Zoo Proof	775	Value: 750				

KM# 198 OUNCE
31.1070 g., 0.9999 Gold 1.0000 oz. AGW **Rev:** Rhinoceros

Date	Mintage	F	VF	XF	Unc	BU
1995 Proof	1,800	Value: 700				
1995 Hluhuwe Proof	350	Value: 750				

KM# 204 OUNCE
31.1070 g., 0.9999 Gold 1.0000 oz. AGW **Rev:** Elephant **Rev. Designer:** Natanya van Niekerk

Date	Mintage	F	VF	XF	Unc	BU
1996 Proof	4,472	Value: 700				
1996 Mandleve Proof	—	Value: 750				

KM# 210 OUNCE
31.1070 g., 0.9999 Gold 1.0000 oz. AGW **Rev:** Buffalo **Rev. Designer:** Natanya van Niekerk

Date	Mintage	F	VF	XF	Unc	BU
1997 Proof	2,472	Value: 700				
1997 SS Proof	220	Value: 750				

KM# 216 OUNCE
31.1070 g., 0.9999 Gold 1.0000 oz. AGW **Rev:** Leopard **Rev. Designer:** Natanya van Niekerk

Date	Mintage	F	VF	XF	Unc	BU
1998 Proof	—	Value: 700				

KM# 255 OUNCE
31.1035 g., 0.9990 Gold 0.999 oz. AGW, 32.7 mm. **Obv:** Greater Kudu head **Rev:** Kudu eating tree leaves **Edge:** Reeded

Date	Mintage	F	VF	XF	Unc	BU
1999 Proof	—	Value: 700				

KM# 261 OUNCE

31.1035 g., 0.9990 Gold 0.999 oz. AGW, 32.7 mm. **Obv:** Ibex head **Rev:** Ibex head **Edge:** Reeded

Date	Mintage	F	VF	XF	Unc	BU
2000 Proof	—	Value: 700				

PATTERNS

Including off metal strikes

KM#	Date	Mintage	Identification	Mkt Val
Pn1	1925	—	1/4 Penny. Lead.	—
Pn3	1942	—	1/4 Penny. Bronze. Smaller head of George VI.	—

TRIAL STRIKES

KM#	Date	Mintage	Identification	Mkt Val
TS1	1925	—	2 Shilling 6 Pence. Lead. Uniface. 2s6d.	—

MINT SETS

KM#	Date	Mintage	Identification	Issue Price	Mkt Val
MS1	1967 (7)	50,000	KM#65.1-70.1, 72.1	7.50	10.00
MS2	1967 (7)	50,000	KM#65.2-70.2, 72.2	7.50	10.00
MS3	1968 (7)	50,000	KM#71.1, 74.1-79.1	7.50	12.00
MS4	1968 (7)	50,000	KM#71.2, 74.2-79.2	7.50	12.00
MS5	1969 (7)	7,500	KM#65.1-70.1, 80.1	7.50	50.00
MS6	1969 (7)	7,500	KM#65.2-70.2, 80.2	7.50	50.00
MS7	1970 (8)	16,000	KM#81-88	7.50	12.00
MS8	1971 (8)	20,000	KM#81-88	7.50	8.00
MS9	1972 (8)	20,000	KM#81-88	7.50	8.00
MS10	1973 (8)	20,000	KM#81-88	7.50	8.00
MS11	1974 (8)	20,000	KM#81-87, 89	7.50	17.50
MS12	1975 (8)	20,000	KM#81-88	7.50	8.00
MS13	1976 (8)	20,000	KM#88, 90-96	5.65	8.00
MS14	1977 (8)	20,000	KM#81-87, 88a	—	8.00
MS15	1978 (8)	20,000	KM#81-87, 88a	—	8.00
MS16	1979 (8)	20,000	KM#97-104	—	25.00
MS17	1980 (7)	20,000	KM#82-87, 88a	—	8.00
MS18	1981 (7)	10,000	KM#82-87, 88a	—	10.00
MS19	1982 (7)	10,000	KM#109-115	—	25.00
MS20	1983 (7)	23,000	KM#82-87, 88a	—	8.00
MS21	1984 (7)	13,875	KM#82-87, 88a	—	10.00
MS22	1985 (7)	10,200	KM#82-87, 117	—	17.50
MS23	1986 (7)	9,100	KM#82-87, 88a	—	12.00
MS24	1987 (7)	7,642	KM#82-87, 88a	—	12.00
MS25	1988 (7)	6,250	KM#82-87, 88a	—	25.00
MS26	1989 (7)	13,000	KM#82-87, 88a	—	15.00
MS27	1990 (8)	12,000	KM#132-137, 139, 148	—	30.00
MS28	1991 (8)	15,000	KM#132-139	—	30.00
MSA29	1992 (8)	15,000	KM#132-139	—	30.00
MS29	1993 (8)	11,000	KM#132-139	—	30.00
MS30	1994 (9)	6,786	KM#132-140	—	35.00
MS31	1995 (9)	8,477	KM#132-140 Plastic holder	—	35.00
MS32	1995 (9)	—	KM#132-140 Cardboard holder	—	30.00
MS33	1996 (9)	12,000	KM#158-166	12.50	15.00
MS34	1997 (9)	7,515	KM#159-166, 170	—	30.00
MS35	1998 (9)	—	KM#159-166, 170	—	30.00
MS36	1999 (9)	10,000	KM#159-166, 170	19.50	30.00
MS37	2000 (9)	—	KM#159-166, 170	—	30.00

PROOF SETS

KM#	Date	Mintage	Identification	Issue Price	Mkt Val
PS1	1923 (10)	655	KM#12.1-17.1, 18, 19.1, 20-21	—	1,500
PS2	1923 (8)	747	KM#12.1-17.1, 18, 19.1	—	600
PS3	1926 (6)	3	KM#12.2, 14-2-17.2, 19.2	—	20,000
PS4	1930 (8)	14	KM#12.2-17.2, 18, 19.2	—	7,500
PS5	1930 (8)	—	KM#12.2 (dated 1928), 13.2-17.2, 18, 19.2	—	15,000
PS6	1931 (8)	62	KM#12.3-17.3, 19.3, 22	—	9,000
PS7	1932 (8)	12	KM#12.3-17.3, 19.3, 22	—	7,500
PS8	1933 (8)	20	KM#12.3-17.3, 19.3, 22	—	9,000
PS9	1934 (8)	24	KM#12.3-17.3, 19.3, 22	—	7,500
PS10	1935 (8)	20	KM#12.3-17.3, 19.3, 22	—	6,500
PS11	1936 (8)	40	KM#12.3-17.3, 19.3, 22	—	3,500
PS12	1937 (8)	116	KM#23-30	—	750
PS13	1938 (8)	44	KM#23-30	—	1,500
PS14	1939 (8)	30	KM#23-30	—	8,000
PS15	1943 (8)	104	KM#23-30	—	700
PS16	1944 (8)	150	KM#23-30	—	600
PS17	1945 (8)	150	KM#23-30	—	600
PS18	1946 (8)	150	KM#23-30	—	700
PS19	1947 (9)	2,600	KM#23-31	—	225
PS20	1948 (9)	1,120	KM#32.1, 33, 34.1-40.1	—	250
PS21	1949 (9)	800	KM#32.1, 33, 34.1-40.1	—	350
PS22	1950 (9)	500	KM#32.1, 33, 34.1-40.1	—	375
PS23	1951 (9)	2,000	KM#32.2, 33, 34.2-40.2	—	60.00
PS24	1952 (11)	12,000	KM#32.2, 33, 34.2-39.2, 41-43	—	300
PS25	1952 (9)	3,500	KM#32.2, 33, 34.2-39.2, 41	—	35.00
PS26	1953 (11)	3,000	KM#44-54	29.40	300
PS27	1953 (9)	2,000	KM#44-52	4.35	35.00
PS28	1953 (2)	1,000	KM#53-54	25.20	270
PS29	1954 (11)	875	KM#44-54	29.40	325
PS30	1954 (9)	2,275	KM#44-52	4.35	40.00
PS31	1954 (2)	350	KM#53-54	25.20	280
PS32	1955 (11)	600	KM#44-54	29.40	350
PS33	1955 (9)	2,250	KM#44-52	4.35	30.00
PS34	1955 (2)	300	KM#53-54	25.20	310
PS35	1956 (11)	350	KM#44-54	29.40	450
PS36	1956 (9)	1,350	KM#44-52	4.35	45.00
PS37	1956 (2)	158	KM#53-54	25.20	400
PS38	1957 (11)	380	KM#44-54	29.40	440
PS39	1957 (9)	750	KM#44-52	4.35	70.00
PS40	1957 (2)	180	KM#53-54	25.20	400
PS41	1958 (11)	360	KM#44-54	29.40	450
PS42	1958 (9)	625	KM#44-52	4.35	80.00
PS43	1958 (2)	155	KM#53-54	25.20	400
PS44	1959 (11)	390	KM#44-54	29.40	525
PS45	1959 (9)	560	KM#44-52	4.35	275
PS46	1959 (2)	240	KM#53-54	25.20	400
PS47	1960 (11)	1,500	KM#44-51, 53-55	29.40	300
PS48	1960 (9)	1,860	KM#44-51, 55	4.35	20.00
PS49	1960 (2)	450	KM#53-54	25.20	275
PS50	1961 (9)	3,139	KM#56-64	—	200
PS51	1961 (7)	4,391	KM#56-62	—	20.00
PS52	1961 (2)	793	KM#63-64 BV + 20%	—	—
PS53	1962 (9)	1,544	KM#56-64	—	210
PS54	1962 (7)	2,300	KM#56-62	—	15.00
PS55	1962 (2)	800	KM#63-64 BV+20%	—	—
PS56	1963 (9)	1,500	KM#56-64	—	200
PS57	1963 (7)	2,525	KM#56-62	—	12.00
PS58	1963 (2)	1,008	KM#63-64 BV+20%	—	—
PS59	1964 (9)	3,000	KM#56-64	—	190
PS60	1964 (7)	13,000	KM#56-62	—	10.00
PS61	1964 (2)	1,000	KM#63-64 BV+20%	—	—
PS62	1965 (9)	5,099	KM#63-64, 65.1, 66.2, 67.1, 68.2, 69.1, 70.2, 71.1	23.50	185
PS63	1965 (9)	85	KM#63-64, 65.1-66.2, 67.1, 68.2, 69.1, 70.2, 71.2 V.I.P.	—	1,200
PS64	1965 (7)	19,889	KM#65.1, 66.2, 67.1, 68.2, 69.1, 70.2, 71.1	5.00	12.00
PS65	1965 (2)	925	KM#63-64 BV+20%	18.15	—
PS66	1966 (9)	10,000	KM#63-64, 65.2, 66.1, 67.2, 68.1, 69.2, 70.1, 71.2	24.10	185
PS67	1966 (7)	15,000	KM#65.2, 66.1, 67.2, 68.1, 69.2, 70.1, 71.2	5.00	8.00
PS68	1966 (2)	1,000	KM#63-64 BV+20%	18.15	—
PS69	1967 (9)	10,000	KM#63-64, 65.2, 66.1, 67.2, 68.1, 69.2, 70.1, 72.2	24.10	185
PS70	1967 (7)	15,000	KM#65.2, 66.1, 67.2, 68.1, 69.2, 70.1, 72.2	5.00	8.00
PS71	1967 (2)	1,000	KM#63-64 BV+20%	18.15	—
PS72	1968 (9)	10,000	KM#63-64, 71.1, 74.1, 75.2, 76.1, 77.2, 78.1, 79.2	35.00	185
PS73	1968 (7)	15,000	KM#71.1, 74.1, 75.2, 76.1, 77.2, 78.1, 79.2	16.00	8.00
PS74	1968 (2)	1,000	KM#63-64 BV+20%	28.00	—
PS75	1969 (9)	7,000	KM#63-64, 65.2, 66.1, 67.2, 68.1, 69.2, 70.1, 80.2	34.85	185
PS76	1969 (7)	5,000	KM#65.2, 66.1, 67.2, 68.1, 69.2, 70.1, 80.2	13.95	8.00
PS77	1969 (2)	1,000	KM#63-64 BV+20%	27.85	—
PS78	1970 (10)	6,000	KM#63-64, 81-88	35.05	185
PS79	1970 (8)	4,000	KM#81-88	14.00	9.00
PS80	1970 (2)	1,000	KM#63-64 BV+20%	28.05	—
PS81	1971 (10)	7,000	KM#63-64, 81-88	35.00	185
PS82	1971 (8)	5,000	KM#81-88	14.00	9.00
PS83	1971 (2)	650	KM#63-64 BV+20%	28.00	—
PS84	1972 (10)	6,000	KM#63-64, 81-88	32.80	185
PS85	1972 (8)	4,000	KM#81-88	13.10	9.00
PS86	1972 (2)	1,500	KM#63-64 BV+20%	26.25	—
PS87	1973 (10)	6,850	KM#63-64, 81-88	32.00	185
PS88	1973 (8)	4,000	KM#81-88	12.80	9.00
PS89	1973 (2)	6,088	KM#63-64 BV+20%	25.60	—
PS90	1974 (10)	11,000	KM#63-64, 81-87, 89	52.50	185
PS91	1974 (8)	4,000	KM#81-87, 89	15.00	9.00
PS92	1974 (2)	5,600	KM#63-64 BV+20%	45.00	—
PS93	1975 (10)	12,500	KM#63-64, 81-87, 88	116	185
PS94	1975 (8)	5,500	KM#81-88	14.55	9.00
PS95	1975 (2)	7,000	KM#63-64 BV+20%	102	—
PS96	1976 (10)	14,000	KM#63-64, 88, 90-96	92.00	185
PS97	1976 (8)	7,000	KM#88, 90-96	11.50	9.00
PS98	1976 (2)	8,000	KM#63-64 BV+20%	80.50	—
PS99	1977 (10)	12,000	KM#63-64, 81-88	92.00	185
PS100	1977 (8)	7,000	KM#81-88	11.50	12.00
PS101	1977 (2)	8,000	KM#63-64 BV+20%	80.50	—
PS102	1978 (10)	10,000	KM#63-64, 81-88	—	185
PS103	1978 (8)	7,000	KM#81-88	—	12.00
PS104	1978 (2)	9,000	KM#63-64 BV+20%	—	—
PS105	1979 (10)	10,000	KM#63-64, 97-103, 104a	—	185
PS106	1979 (8)	5,000	KM#88, 97-103	—	22.00
PS107	1979 (2)	10,000	KM#63-64 BV+20%	—	—
PS108	1980 (10)	10,000	KM#63-64, 81-88	—	185
PS109	1980 (8)	5,000	KM#81-88	—	22.00
PS110	1980 (2)	8,000	kM#63-64 BV+20%	—	—
PS111	1980 (2)	8,000	KM#63-64	—	—
PS112	1980 (3)	60	KM#105-107	—	9,000
PS113	1981 (10)	6,000	KM#63-64, 81-88	—	185
PS114	1981 (8)	4,900	KM#81-88	—	22.00
PS115	1981 (2)	6,238	KM#63-64 BV+20%	—	—
PS116	1982 (10)	7,100	KM#63-64, 108-115	—	190
PS117	1982 (8)	4,900	KM#88, 108-114	—	22.00
PS118	1982 (2)	6,930	KM#63-64 BV+20%	—	—
PS119	1983 (10)	7,300	KM#63-64, 81-88	—	185
PS120	1983 (8)	6,835	KM#81-88	—	22.00
PS121	1983 (2)	7,300	KM#63-64 BV+20%	—	—
PS122	1984 (8)	11,250	KM#82-88, 88a	—	15.00
PS123	1985 (8)	9,859	KM#82-87, 116, 117	—	25.00
PS124	1986 (8)	7,000	KM#82-87, 88a, 119	—	25.00
PS125	1986 (2)	428	KM#73, 121 Plus large gold plated Silver #1	—	1,400
PS126	1986 (2)	750	KM#121, 131	—	700
PS127	1986 (3)	500	KM#119, 121, 131	—	725
PS128	1987 (8)	6,781	KM#82-88, 88a	—	25.00
PS129	1987 (4)	750	KM#73, 105-107	—	1,050
PS130	1987 GRC (4)	1,121	KM#73, 105-107	—	2,900
PS131	1988 (8)	7,250	KM#82-88, 88a	—	50.00
PS132	1988 (4)	806	KM#73, 105-107	—	1,050
PS133	1988 GRC (4)	835	KM#73, 105-107	—	2,900
PS134	1988 (3)	3,388	KM#122, 125, 128	—	70.00
PS135	1988 (3)	600	KM#124, 127, 130	—	2,750
PS136	1989 (8)	9,571	KM#82-88, 88a	—	50.00
PS137	1989 (4)	—	KM#73, 105-107	—	1,050
PS138	1989 GRC (4)	318	KM#73, 105-107	—	5,500
PS139	1990 (8)	10,000	KM#132-137, 139, 148	—	70.00
PS140	1990 (4)	—	KM#73, 105-107	—	1,050
PS141	1990 GRC (4)	1,066	KM#73, 105-107	—	2,775
PS142	1991 (8)	12,000	KM#132-139	—	70.00
PSA143	1991 GRC (4)	426	KM#73, 105-107	—	2,775
PS143	1992 (8)	10,000	KM#132-139	—	50.00
PS144	1993 (8)	—	KM#132-139	—	50.00
PS145	1994 (9)	5,804	KM#132-140	—	60.00
PS146	1994 (4)	168	KM#189-192 Wood case	—	1,200
PS147	1994 (4)	1,750	KM#189-192 Velvet case	—	1,175
PS148	1994 (3)	420	KM#167, 187-188	—	750
PS149	1995 (9)	5,816	KM#132-140	—	65.00
PS150	1995 (4)	750	KM#73, 105-107	—	1,400
PS151	1995	—	KM#73, 105-107 Wooden box	—	1,425
PS152	1995 (4)	89	KM#195-198 Wood case	—	1,200
PS153	1995 (4)	925	KM#195-198 Velvet case	—	1,175
PS154	1995 (3)	210	KM#152, 193-194	—	755
PS155	1996 (9)	4,827	KM#158-166	30.00	36.00
PS156	1996 (4)	368	KM#201-402 Wood case	—	1,200
PS157	1996 (4)	1,677	KM#201-204 Velvet case	—	1,175
PS158	1996 (3)	346	KM#169, 199-200	—	760
PS159	1997 (4)	500	KM#73, 105-107	—	1,100
PS160	1997 (4)	500	KM#207-210 Wood case	—	1,200
PS161	1997 (4)	1,015	KM#207-210 Velvet case	—	1,175
PS162	1997 (3)	144	KM#181, 205-206	—	780
PS163	1997 (4)	30	KM#73, 105-107, 30 Year Wine set with privy marks	—	2,550
PS164	1997 (9)	3,596	KM#159-166, 170	—	40.00
PS165	1998 (9)	—	KM#159-166, 170	—	40.00
PS166	1998 (4)	—	KM#213-216 Wood case	—	1,200
PS167	1998 (4)	—	KM#213-216 Velvet case	—	1,175
PS168	1998 (3)	—	KM#177, 211-212	—	780
PS169	1999 (9)	6,000	KM#159-166, 170	39.50	40.00

SPECIMEN SETS (SS)

KM#	Date	Mintage	Identification	Issue Price	Mkt Val
SS1	1994 (9)	5,508	KM#132-140	—	25.00
SS2	1995 (9)	4,956	KM#132-140	—	25.00
SS3	1996 (9)	5,766	KM#158-166	19.50	25.00
SS4	1997 (9)	4,236	KM#159-166, 170	—	25.00
SS5	1998 (9)	—	KM#159-166, 170	—	25.00
SS6	1999 (9)	—	KM#159-166, 170	—	25.00

Fifteen of the sixteen Western Protectorate States, the Wahidi State of the Eastern Protectorate, and Aden Colony joined to form the Federation of South Arabia.

In 1959, Britain agreed to prepare South Arabia for full independence, which was achieved on Nov. 30, 1967, at which time South Arabia, including Aden, changed its name to the Peoples Republic of Southern Yemen. On Dec. 1, 1970, following the overthrow of the new government by the National Liberation Front, Southern Yemen changed its name to the Peoples Democratic Republic of Yemen.

TITLES
Al-Junubiya(t) al-Arabiya(t)

MONETARY SYSTEM
1000 Fils = 1 Dinar

FEDERATION

STANDARD COINAGE

KM# 1 FILS
Aluminum, 20 mm. **Obv:** Snowflake design **Rev:** Crossed swords

Date	Mintage	F	VF	XF	Unc	BU
1964	10,000,000	—	—	0.10	0.15	0.25
1964 Proof	—	Value: 1.50				

KM# 2 5 FILS
Bronze **Obv:** Snowflake design **Rev:** Crossed swords

Date	Mintage	F	VF	XF	Unc	BU
1964	10,000,000	—	0.15	0.25	0.50	0.65
1964 Proof	—	Value: 2.00				

KM# 3 25 FILS
Copper-Nickel **Obv:** Snowflake design **Rev:** Sailboat

Date	Mintage	F	VF	XF	Unc	BU
1964	4,000,000	—	0.25	0.45	0.85	1.00
1964 Proof	—	Value: 2.75				

KM# 4 50 FILS
Copper-Nickel **Obv:** Snowflake design **Rev:** Sailboat

Date	Mintage	F	VF	XF	Unc	BU
1964	6,000,000	—	0.45	0.65	1.25	1.50
1964 Proof	—	Value: 3.75				

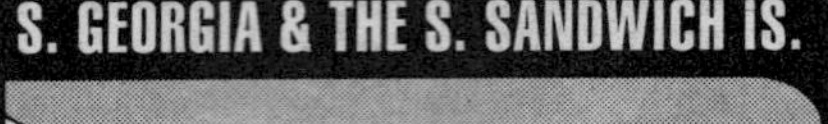

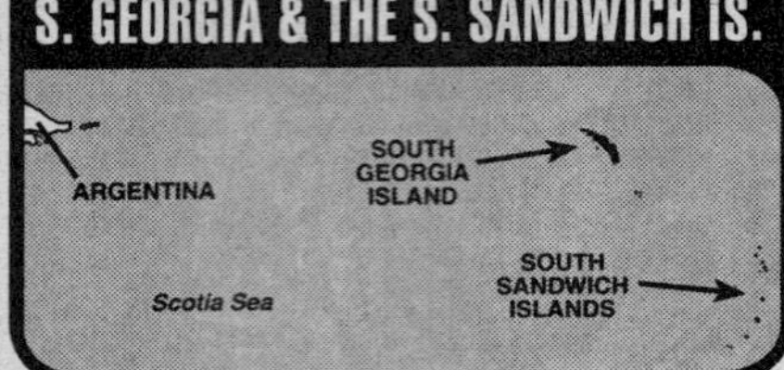

South Georgia and the South Sandwich Islands are a dependency of the Falkland Islands, and located about 800 miles east of them. South Georgia is 1,450 sq. mi. (1,770 sq. km.), South Sandwich Islands is 120 sq. mi. (311 sq. km.) Fishing and Antarctic research are the main industries. The islands were claimed for Great Britain in 1775 by Captain James Cook.

RULERS
British since 1775

BRITISH ADMINISTRATION

STANDARD COINAGE

KM# 1a.1 2 POUNDS
28.2800 g., 0.9250 Silver 0.841 oz. ASW, 38.6 mm. **Mint:** Pobjoy **Subject:** Queen Mother **Obverse:** Bust with tiara right **Reverse:** Crowned arms with supporters with a tiny black sapphire mounted below **Edge:** Reeded

Date	Mintage	F	VF	XF	Unc
2000 Proof	1,000	Value: 55.00			

KM# 1 2 POUNDS
28.2800 g., Copper-Nickel, 38.7 mm. **Mint:** Pobjoy **Subject:** 100th Birthday - Queen Mother **Obverse:** Crowned bust of Queen Elizabeth II right **Obv. Designer:** Ian Rank-Broadley **Reverse:** Crowned arms with supporters **Edge:** Reeded

Date	Mintage	F	VF	XF	Unc
2000	—	—	—	—	10.00

KM# 1a 2 POUNDS
28.2800 g., 0.9250 Silver .841 oz. ASW **Mint:** Pobjoy **Subject:** 100th Birthday - Queen Mother **Obverse:** Crowned bust of Queen Elizabeth II right **Reverse:** Crowned arms with supporters **Edge:** Reeded

Date	Mintage	F	VF	XF	Unc
2000 Proof	—	Value: 50.00			

KM# 3 2 POUNDS
28.2800 g., Copper-Nickel, 38.6 mm. **Mint:** Pobjoy **Obverse:** Crowned bust of Queen Elizabeth II right **Obv. Designer:** Ian Rank-Broadley **Reverse:** Standing figure on deck of ship within inner circle **Edge:** Reeded

Date	Mintage	F	VF	XF	Unc
2000	—	—	—	—	8.50

KM# 3a 2 POUNDS
28.2800 g., 0.9250 Silver .841 oz. ASW, 38.7 mm. **Mint:** Pobjoy **Obverse:** Crowned bust of Queen Elizabeth II right **Reverse:** Standing figure on the deck of the ship within inner circle **Edge:** Reeded

Date	Mintage	F	VF	XF	Unc
2000 Proof	—	Value: 47.50			

KM# 4 2 POUNDS
28.2800 g., Copper-Nickel **Mint:** Pobjoy **Subject:** 225th Anniversary - Possession by Captain Cook **Obverse:** Crowned bust of Queen Elizabeth II right **Reverse:** Bust right

Date	Mintage	F	VF	XF	Unc
2000	—	—	—	—	8.50

KM# 4a 2 POUNDS
28.2800 g., 0.9250 Silver .841 oz. ASW **Mint:** Pobjoy **Subject:** 225th Anniversary - Possession by Captain Cook **Obverse:** Crowned bust of Queen Elizabeth II right **Reverse:** Bust right

Date	Mintage	F	VF	XF	Unc
2000 Proof	—	Value: 47.50			

KM# 2.2 20 POUNDS
6.2200 g., 0.9990 Gold 0.1998 oz. AGW, 22 mm. **Mint:** Pobjoy **Obverse:** Crowned bust of Queen Elizabeth II right **Obv. Designer:** Ian Rank-Broadley **Reverse:** Crowned arms with supporters with a tiny black sapphire mounted below **Edge:** Reeded

Date	Mintage	F	VF	XF	Unc
2000 Proof	1,000	Value: 190			

KM# 2.1 20 POUNDS
6.2200 g., 0.9999 Gold .2 oz. AGW **Mint:** Pobjoy **Subject:** 100th Birthday - Queen Mother **Obverse:** Crowned bust of Queen Elizabeth II right **Obv. Designer:** Ian Rank-Broadley **Reverse:** Crowned arms with supporters **Edge:** Reeded

Date	Mintage	F	VF	XF	Unc
2000 Proof	—	Value: 185			

KM# 5 20 POUNDS
6.2200 g., 0.9999 Gold .2 oz. AGW, 22 mm. **Mint:** Pobjoy **Obverse:** Crowned bust of Queen Elizabeth II right **Reverse:** Standing figure on the deck of the ship within circle **Edge:** Reeded

Date	Mintage	F	VF	XF	Unc
2000 Proof	—	Value: 175			

KM# 6 20 POUNDS
6.2200 g., 0.9999 Gold .2 oz. AGW **Mint:** Pobjoy **Subject:** 225th Anniversary - Possession by Captain Cook **Obverse:** Crowned bust of Queen Elizabeth II right **Reverse:** Bust right

Date	Mintage	F	VF	XF	Unc
2000 Proof	—	Value: 175			

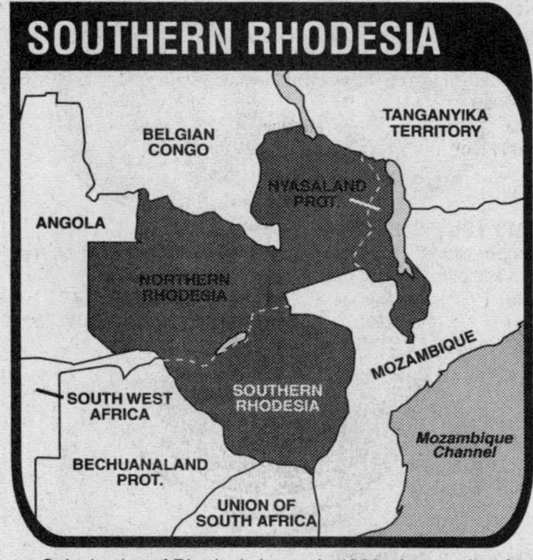

Colonization of Rhodesia began in 1890 when settlers forcibly acquired Shona lands and then Ndebele lands in 1893. It was named as Rhodesia, after Cecil Rhodes who led the build-up of the Colony.

Rhodesia became a self-governing colony under the name of Southern Rhodesia in 1923. Consequent upon later political difficulties and disagreement with the British authorities over common emancipation of the people, a unilateral declaration of independence (UDI) was declared on November 11, 1965.

Following United Nations sanctions against the country, various renamings as Rhodesia and Rhodesia-Zimbabwe, and elections in February 1980, the country became independent on April 18, 1980, as the Republic of Zimbabwe as a member of the Commonwealth of Nations.

RULERS

British, until 1966

MONETARY SYSTEM

12 Pence = 1 Shilling
2 Shillings = 1 Florin
5 Shillings = 1 Crown
20 Shillings = 1 Pound

BRITISH COLONY

POUND COINAGE

KM# 6 1/2 PENNY

Copper-Nickel **Ruler:** George V **Obv:** Crowned flower design within circle, hole in center **Rev:** Value written within sprigs, hole in center

Date	Mintage	F	VF	XF	Unc	BU
1934	240,000	1.00	6.00	20.00	40.00	—
1934 Proof	—	Value: 125				
1936	240,000	5.00	40.00	80.00	150	—
1936 Proof	—	—	—	—	—	—

KM# 14 1/2 PENNY

Copper-Nickel **Ruler:** George VI **Obv:** Crowned flower design within circle, hole in center **Rev:** Value written within sprigs, hole in center

Date	Mintage	F	VF	XF	Unc	BU
1938	240,000	0.75	1.75	10.00	20.00	30.00
1938 Proof	—	—	—	—	—	—
1939	480,000	1.00	2.00	30.00	60.00	85.00
1939 Proof	—	—	—	—	—	—

KM# 14a 1/2 PENNY

Bronze **Ruler:** George VI **Obv:** Crowned flower design within circle, hole in center **Rev:** Value within sprigs, hole in center

Date	Mintage	F	VF	XF	Unc	BU
1942	480,000	0.60	1.50	13.50	25.00	—
1942 Proof	—	—	—	—	—	—
1943	960,000	0.35	0.75	2.25	6.50	18.00
1944	960,000	0.35	0.75	2.50	8.00	—
1944 Proof	—	—	—	—	—	—

KM# 26 1/2 PENNY

Bronze **Ruler:** George VI **Obv:** Crowned flower design within circle, hole in center **Obv. Legend:** KING GEORGE THE SIXTH **Rev:** Value witten within sprigs, hole in center

Date	Mintage	F	VF	XF	Unc	BU
1951	480,000	0.75	1.25	2.25	6.50	18.00
1951 Proof	—	—	—	—	—	—
1952	480,000	0.75	1.25	5.00	10.00	—
1952 Proof	—	—	—	—	—	—

KM# 28 1/2 PENNY

Bronze **Ruler:** Elizabeth II **Obv:** Crowned flower design within circle, hole in center **Rev:** Value written within sprigs, hole in center

Date	Mintage	F	VF	XF	Unc	BU
1954	960,000	0.75	2.00	35.00	65.00	—
1954 Proof	20	Value: 350				

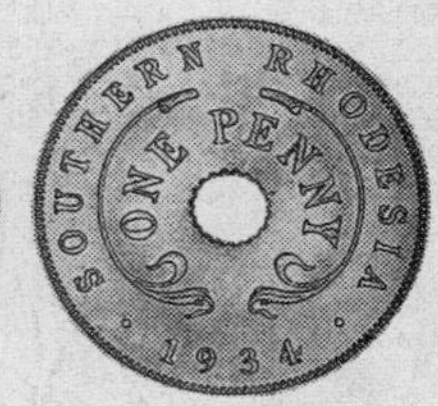

KM# 7 PENNY

Copper-Nickel **Ruler:** George V **Obv:** Crowned flower design within circle, hole in center **Rev:** Value written within sprigs, hole in center

Date	Mintage	F	VF	XF	Unc	BU
1934	360,000	0.75	1.50	13.50	25.00	—
1934 Proof	—	Value: 125				
1935	492,000	1.50	15.00	75.00	125	250
1935 Proof	—	—	—	—	—	—
1936	1,044,000	0.60	1.25	13.50	30.00	—
1936 Proof	—	—	—	—	—	—

KM# 8 PENNY

Copper-Nickel **Ruler:** George VI **Obv:** Crowned flower design within circle, hole in center **Rev:** Value written within sprigs, hole in center

Date	Mintage	F	VF	XF	Unc	BU
1937	908,000	0.60	1.25	13.50	25.00	—
1937 Proof	—	Value: 300				
1938	240,000	1.50	3.00	27.50	50.00	—
1938 Proof	—	—	—	—	—	—
1939	1,284,000	0.45	1.00	23.50	37.50	—
1939 Proof	—	—	—	—	—	—
1940	1,080,000	0.45	1.00	23.50	37.50	—
1940 Proof	—	—	—	—	—	—
1941	720,000	0.50	1.25	24.50	40.00	—
1941 Proof	—	—	—	—	—	—
1942	960,000	0.50	1.25	34.50	65.00	—
1942 Proof	—	—	—	—	—	—

KM# 8a PENNY

Bronze **Ruler:** George VI **Obv:** Crowned flower design within circle, hole in center **Rev:** Written value within sprigs, hole in center

Date	Mintage	F	VF	XF	Unc	BU
1942	480,000	4.00	6.50	42.50	100	—
1942 Proof	—	Value: 400				
1943	3,120,000	0.50	0.80	6.50	15.00	30.00
1944	2,400,000	0.50	0.80	8.50	20.00	40.00
1944 Proof	—	—	—	—	—	—
1947	3,600,000	0.75	1.25	8.50	20.00	40.00
1947 Proof	—	—	—	—	—	—

KM# 25 PENNY

Bronze **Ruler:** George VI **Obv:** Crowned flower design within circle, hole in center **Rev:** Value written within sprigs, hole in center

Date	Mintage	F	VF	XF	Unc	BU
1949	1,440,000	0.50	1.00	12.50	25.00	—
1949 Proof	—	Value: 125				
1950	720,000	1.00	1.75	25.00	40.00	—
1950 Proof	—	Value: 125				
1951	4,896,000	0.50	0.75	3.25	10.00	18.00
1951 Proof	—	Value: 125				
1952	2,400,000	0.50	0.75	1.75	12.50	—
1952 Proof	—	—	—	—	—	—

KM# 29 PENNY

Bronze **Ruler:** Elizabeth II **Obv:** Crowned flower design within circle, hole in center **Rev:** Value written within sprigs, hole in center

Date	Mintage	F	VF	XF	Unc	BU
1954	960,000	4.00	27.50	115	250	350
1954 Proof	20	Value: 450				

KM# 1 3 PENCE

1.4100 g., 0.9250 Silver .0419 oz. ASW, 16 mm. **Ruler:** George V **Obv:** Crowned bust left **Obv. Designer:** E.B. MacKennal **Rev:** Three spearheads divide date **Rev. Designer:** G.E. Kruger-Gray

Date	Mintage	F	VF	XF	Unc	BU
1932	688,000	0.85	1.50	16.50	32.00	—
1932 Proof	—	Value: 60.00				
1934	628,000	0.85	2.00	40.00	60.00	—
1934 Proof	—	—	—	—	—	—
1935	840,000	0.85	2.00	27.50	45.00	—
1935 Proof	—	—	—	—	—	—
1936	1,052,000	0.85	2.00	27.50	45.00	65.00
1936 Proof	—	—	—	—	—	—

KM# 9 3 PENCE

1.4100 g., 0.9250 Silver .0419 oz. ASW, 16 mm. **Ruler:** George VI **Obv:** Crowned head left **Obv. Designer:** Percy Metcalfe **Rev:** Three spearheads divide date **Rev. Designer:** G.E. Kruger-Gray

Date	Mintage	F	VF	XF	Unc	BU
1937	1,228,000	0.85	2.00	20.00	40.00	—
1937 Proof	—	Value: 225				

KM# 16 3 PENCE

1.4100 g., 0.9250 Silver .0419 oz. ASW, 16 mm. **Ruler:** George VI **Obv:** Crowned head left **Obv. Designer:** Percy Metcalfe **Rev:** Three spearheads divide date **Rev. Designer:** G.E. Kruger-Gray

Date	Mintage	F	VF	XF	Unc	BU
1939	160,000	6.00	10.00	80.00	150	—
1939 Proof	—	Value: 300				
1940	1,200,000	0.85	2.00	27.50	40.00	—
1940 Proof	—	—	—	—	—	—

Date	Mintage	F	VF	XF	Unc	BU
1941	600,000	2.50	5.00	30.00	50.00	—
1941 Proof	—	—	—	—	—	—
1942	2,000,000	0.75	1.50	16.50	30.00	—
1942 Proof	—	—	—	—	—	—

KM# 16a 3 PENCE

1.4100 g., 0.5000 Silver .0226 oz. ASW, 16 mm. **Ruler:** George VI **Obv:** Crowned head left **Obv. Designer:** Percy Metcalfe **Rev:** Three spearheads divide date **Rev. Designer:** G.E. Kruger-Gray **Edge:** Plain

Date	Mintage	F	VF	XF	Unc	BU
1944	1,600,000	0.65	1.50	30.00	60.00	—
1945	800,000	1.00	3.00	30.00	60.00	—
1945 Proof	—	—	—	—	—	—
1946	2,400,000	0.65	1.50	17.00	35.00	—
1946 Proof	—	—	—	—	—	—

KM# 16b 3 PENCE

Copper-Nickel, 16 mm. **Ruler:** George VI **Obv:** Crowned head left **Rev:** Three spearheads divide date

Date	Mintage	F	VF	XF	Unc	BU
1947	8,000,000	0.40	0.80	8.00	20.00	—
1947 Proof	—	Value: 250				

KM# 20 3 PENCE

Copper-Nickel, 16 mm. **Ruler:** George VI **Obv:** Crowned head left **Obv. Designer:** Percy Metcalfe **Rev:** Three spearheads divide date **Rev. Designer:** G.E. Kruger-Gray

Date	Mintage	F	VF	XF	Unc	BU
1948	2,000,000	0.40	2.00	13.50	30.00	45.00
1948 Proof	—	—	—	—	—	—
1949	4,000,000	0.40	2.00	13.00	25.00	—
1949 Proof	—	Value: 150				
1951	5,600,000	0.40	5.00	40.00	75.00	125
1951 Proof	—	—	—	—	—	—
1952	4,800,000	0.40	5.00	32.50	60.00	110
1952 Proof	—	Value: 150				

KM# 2 6 PENCE

2.8300 g., 0.9250 Silver .0841 oz. ASW **Ruler:** George V **Obv:** Crowned bust left **Obv. Designer:** E.B. MacKennal **Rev:** Crossed axes divide date and value **Rev. Designer:** G.E. Kruger-Gray

Date	Mintage	F	VF	XF	Unc	BU
1932	544,000	2.00	13.00	30.00	55.00	—
1932 Proof	—	Value: 65.00				
1934	214,000	3.00	17.00	55.00	90.00	—
1935	380,000	2.00	16.00	45.00	75.00	—
1935 Proof	—	—	—	—	—	—
1936	675,000	1.50	13.00	35.00	60.00	—
1936 Proof	—	—	—	—	—	—

KM# 10 6 PENCE

2.8300 g., 0.9250 Silver .0841 oz. ASW **Ruler:** George VI **Obv:** Crowned head left **Obv. Designer:** Percy Metcalfe **Rev:** Crossed axes divide date and value **Rev. Designer:** G.E. Kruger-Gray

Date	Mintage	F	VF	XF	Unc	BU
1937	823,000	2.50	15.00	30.00	55.00	—
1937 Proof	—	Value: 300				

KM# 17 6 PENCE

2.8300 g., 0.9250 Silver .0841 oz. ASW **Ruler:** George VI **Obv:** Crowned head left **Obv. Designer:** Percy Metcalfe **Rev:** Crossed axes divide date and value **Rev. Designer:** G.E. Kruger-Gray

Date	Mintage	F	VF	XF	Unc	BU
1939	200,000	3.00	27.00	125	200	300
1939 Proof	—	Value: 450				
1940	600,000	1.75	13.00	45.00	75.00	—
1940 Proof	—	—	—	—	—	—
1941	300,000	2.00	14.00	40.00	65.00	—
1941 Proof	—	—	—	—	—	—
1942	1,200,000	1.50	12.00	27.00	55.00	140
1942 Proof	—	Value: 200				

KM# 17a 6 PENCE

2.8300 g., 0.5000 Silver .0454 oz. ASW **Ruler:** George VI **Obv:** Crowned head left **Obv. Designer:** Percy Metcalfe **Rev:** Crossed axes divide date and value **Rev. Designer:** G.E. Kruger-Gray

Date	Mintage	F	VF	XF	Unc	BU
1944	800,000	1.25	2.50	55.00	90.00	150
1945	400,000	15.00	25.00	85.00	150	—
1945 Proof	—	—	—	—	—	—
1946	1,600,000	1.25	12.50	35.00	60.00	135
1946 Proof	—	—	—	—	—	—

KM# 17b 6 PENCE

Copper-Nickel **Ruler:** George VI **Obv:** Crowned head left **Obv. Designer:** Percy Metcalfe **Rev:** Crossed axes divide date and value **Rev. Designer:** G.E. Kruger-Gray

Date	Mintage	F	VF	XF	Unc	BU
1947	5,000,000	0.50	1.00	10.00	20.00	50.00
1947 Proof	—	Value: 250				

KM# 21 6 PENCE

Copper-Nickel **Ruler:** George VI **Obv:** Crowned head left **Obv. Designer:** Percy Metcalfe **Rev:** Crossed axes divide date and value **Rev. Designer:** G.E. Kruger-Gray

Date	Mintage	F	VF	XF	Unc	BU
1948	1,000,000	0.50	1.25	14.00	27.50	50.00
1948 Proof	—	—	—	—	—	—
1949	2,000,000	0.50	5.00	18.00	30.00	60.00
1949 Proof	—	Value: 250				
1950	2,000,000	0.50	6.00	24.00	55.00	95.00
1950 Proof	—	Value: 250				
1951	2,800,000	0.50	1.00	8.00	27.50	50.00
1951 Proof	—	—	—	—	—	—
1952	1,200,000	0.50	1.50	23.00	45.00	80.00
1952 Proof	—	—	—	—	—	—

KM# 3 SHILLING

5.6600 g., 0.9250 Silver .1683 oz. ASW **Ruler:** George V **Obv:** Crowned bust left **Obv. Designer:** E.B. MacKennal **Rev:** Bird sculpture divides date **Rev. Designer:** G.E. Kruger-Gray

Date	Mintage	F	VF	XF	Unc	BU
1932	896,000	2.75	20.00	42.00	80.00	—
1932 Proof	—	Value: 90.00				
1934	333,000	4.00	40.00	100	175	—
1935	830,000	2.75	24.00	70.00	120	—
1935 Proof	—	Value: 220				
1936	1,663,000	2.75	23.00	60.00	115	—
1936 Proof	—	—	—	—	—	—

KM# 11 SHILLING

5.6600 g., 0.9250 Silver .1683 oz. ASW **Ruler:** George VI **Obv:** Crowned head left **Obv. Designer:** Percy Metcalfe **Rev:** Bird sculpture divides date **Rev. Designer:** G.E. Kruger-Gray

Date	Mintage	F	VF	XF	Unc	BU
1937	1,700,000	2.75	24.00	55.00	90.00	—
1937 Proof	—	Value: 300				

KM# 18 SHILLING

5.6600 g., 0.9250 Silver .1683 oz. ASW **Ruler:** George VI **Obv:** Crowned head left **Obv. Designer:** Percy Metcalfe **Rev:** Bird sculpture divides date **Rev. Designer:** G.E. Kruger-Gray

Date	Mintage	F	VF	XF	Unc	BU
1939	420,000	7.00	45.00	150	275	—
1939 Proof	—	Value: 500				
1940	750,000	5.50	35.00	90.00	165	—
1940 Proof	—	—	—	—	—	—
1941	800,000	6.50	32.00	80.00	140	—
1941 Proof	—	—	—	—	—	—
1942	2,100,000	2.75	5.00	25.00	55.00	—
1942 Proof	—	—	—	—	—	—

KM# 18a SHILLING

5.6600 g., 0.5000 Silver .0909 oz. ASW **Ruler:** George VI **Obv:** Crowned head left **Rev:** Bird sculpture divides date

Date	Mintage	F	VF	XF	Unc	BU
1944	1,600,000	2.00	14.00	45.00	80.00	—
1946	1,700,000	3.50	18.00	70.00	120	—
1946 Proof	—	—	—	—	—	—

KM# 18b SHILLING

Copper-Nickel **Ruler:** George VI **Obv:** Crowned head left **Rev:** Bird sculpture divides date

Date	Mintage	F	VF	XF	Unc	BU
1947	8,000,000	0.75	1.50	24.00	40.00	80.00
1947 Proof	—	Value: 300				

KM# 22 SHILLING

Copper-Nickel **Ruler:** George VI **Obv:** Crowned head left **Obv. Designer:** Percy Metcalfe **Rev:** Bird sculpture divides date **Rev. Designer:** G.E. Kruger-Gray

Date	Mintage	F	VF	XF	Unc	BU
1948	1,500,000	0.75	1.50	16.00	30.00	60.00
1948 Proof	—	—	—	—	—	—
1949	4,000,000	0.75	8.00	18.00	35.00	65.00
1949 Proof	—	Value: 250				
1950	2,000,000	1.00	13.00	30.00	55.00	90.00
1950 Proof	—	Value: 225				
1951	3,000,000	0.75	4.00	14.00	20.00	40.00
1951 Proof	—	—	—	—	—	—
1952	2,600,000	0.75	8.00	30.00	55.00	90.00
1952 Proof	—	—	—	—	—	—

KM# 4 2 SHILLINGS

11.3100 g., 0.9250 Silver .3363 oz. ASW **Ruler:** George V **Obv:** Crowned bust left **Obv. Designer:** E.B. MacKennal **Rev:** Sable antelope **Rev. Designer:** G.E. Kruger-Gray

Date	Mintage	F	VF	XF	Unc	BU
1932	498,000	5.50	20.00	55.00	110	—
1932 Proof	—	Value: 125				
1934	154,000	12.50	40.00	140	225	—
1935	365,000	6.50	25.00	70.00	120	200
1935 Proof	—	—	—	—	—	—
1936	683,000	5.50	25.00	65.00	120	—
1936 Proof	—	—	—	—	—	—

KM# 12 2 SHILLINGS

11.3100 g., 0.9250 Silver .3363 oz. ASW **Ruler:** George VI **Obv:** Crowned head left **Obv. Designer:** Percy Metcalfe **Rev:** Sable antelope **Rev. Designer:** G.E. Kruger-Gray

Date	Mintage	F	VF	XF	Unc	BU
1937	552,000	7.50	30.00	75.00	135	—
1937 Proof	—	Value: 400				

KM# 19 2 SHILLINGS

11.3100 g., 0.9250 Silver .3363 oz. ASW **Ruler:** George VI **Obv:** Crowned head left **Obv. Designer:** Percy Metcalfe **Rev:** Sable antelope **Rev. Designer:** G.E. Kruger-Gray

Date	Mintage	F	VF	XF	Unc	BU
1939	120,000	50.00	225	450	650	—
1939 Proof	—	Value: 750				
1940	525,000	8.00	55.00	150	250	—
1940 Proof	—	—	—	—	—	—
1941	400,000	8.00	25.00	175	300	—
1941 Proof	—	—	—	—	—	—
1942	850,000	5.50	10.00	45.00	90.00	—

KM# 19a 2 SHILLINGS

11.3100 g., 0.5000 Silver .1818 oz. ASW **Ruler:** George VI **Obv:** Crowned head left **Rev:** Sable antelope

Date	Mintage	F	VF	XF	Unc	BU
1944	1,300,000	6.00	22.00	60.00	135	—
1946	700,000	100	300	400	650	—
1946 Proof	—	—	—	—	—	—

KM# 19b 2 SHILLINGS

Copper-Nickel **Ruler:** George VI **Obv:** Crowned head left **Rev:** Sable antelope

Date	Mintage	F	VF	XF	Unc	BU
1947	3,750,000	1.75	4.00	22.50	45.00	90.00
1947 Proof	—	Value: 300				

KM# 23 2 SHILLINGS

Copper-Nickel **Ruler:** George VI **Obv:** Crowned head left **Obv. Designer:** Percy Metcalfe **Rev:** Sable antelope **Rev. Designer:** G.E. Kruger-Gray

Date	Mintage	F	VF	XF	Unc	BU
1948	750,000	1.00	3.00	30.00	60.00	110
1948 Proof	—	—	—	—	—	—
1949	2,000,000	1.00	3.00	30.00	80.00	—
1949 Proof	—	Value: 350				
1950	1,000,000	1.00	4.00	35.00	115	—
1950 Proof	—	Value: 350				
1951	2,600,000	1.00	3.00	16.00	47.00	—
1951 Proof	—	—	—	—	—	—
1952	1,800,000	1.00	3.00	40.00	75.00	175
1952 Proof	—	—	—	—	—	—

KM# 30 2 SHILLINGS

Copper-Nickel **Ruler:** Elizabeth II **Obv:** Laureate bust right **Obv. Designer:** Mary Gillick **Rev:** Sable antelope **Rev. Designer:** G.E. Kruger-Gray

Date	Mintage	F	VF	XF	Unc	BU
1954	300,000	25.00	55.00	375	900	—
1954 Proof	20	Value: 1,250				

KM# 5 1/2 CROWN

14.1400 g., 0.9250 Silver .4205 oz. ASW, 32 mm. **Ruler:** George V **Obv:** Crowned bust left **Obv. Designer:** E.B. MacKennal **Rev:** Crowned shield **Rev. Designer:** G.E. Kruger-Gray

Date	Mintage	F	VF	XF	Unc	BU
1932	634,000	7.00	10.00	50.00	115	—
1932 Proof	—	Value: 125				

Date	Mintage	F	VF	XF	Unc	BU
1934	419,000	7.50	30.00	145	240	—
1934 Proof	—	—	—	—	—	—
1935	512,000	7.00	25.00	85.00	175	—
1935 Proof	—	—	—	—	—	—
1936	518,000	7.00	28.00	70.00	145	260
1936 Proof	—	—	—	—	—	—

KM# 13 1/2 CROWN

14.1400 g., 0.9250 Silver .4205 oz. ASW, 32 mm. **Ruler:** George VI **Obv:** Crowned head left **Obv. Designer:** Percy Metcalfe **Rev:** Crowned shield **Rev. Designer:** G.E. Kruger-Gray

Date	Mintage	F	VF	XF	Unc	BU
1937	1,174,000	7.00	28.00	70.00	130	200
1937 Proof	—	Value: 350				

KM# 15 1/2 CROWN

14.1400 g., 0.9250 Silver .4205 oz. ASW, 32 mm. **Ruler:** George VI **Obv:** Crowned head left **Obv. Designer:** Percy Metcalfe **Rev:** Crowned shield **Rev. Designer:** G.E. Kruger-Gray

Date	Mintage	F	VF	XF	Unc	BU
1938	400,000	7.00	28.00	75.00	150	260
1938 Proof	—	—	—	—	—	—
1939	224,000	10.00	30.00	160	300	550
1939 Proof	—	Value: 500				
1940	800,000	7.00	10.00	37.50	80.00	—
1940 Proof	—	—	—	—	—	—
1941	1,240,000	BV	7.00	35.00	65.00	—
1941 Proof	—	—	—	—	—	—
1942	2,008,000	BV	7.00	35.00	70.00	140
1942 Proof	—	—	—	—	—	—

KM# 15a 1/2 CROWN

14.1400 g., 0.5000 Silver .2273 oz. ASW **Ruler:** George VI **Obv:** Crowned head left **Rev:** Crowned shield

Date	Mintage	F	VF	XF	Unc	BU
1944	800,000	3.75	7.00	40.00	90.00	—
1946	1,400,000	4.00	10.00	75.00	135	200
1946 Proof	—	—	—	—	—	—

KM# 15b 1/2 CROWN

Copper-Nickel, 32 mm. **Ruler:** George VI **Obv:** Crowned head left **Obv. Designer:** Percy Metcalfe **Rev:** Crowned shield **Rev. Designer:** G.E. Kruger-Gray

Date	Mintage	F	VF	XF	Unc	BU
1947	6,000,000	1.25	2.50	5.00	20.00	50.00
1947 Proof	—	Value: 300				

KM# 24 1/2 CROWN

Copper-Nickel, 32 mm. **Ruler:** George VI **Obv:** Crowned head left **Obv. Designer:** Percy Metcalfe **Rev:** Crowned shield **Rev. Designer:** G.E. Kruger-Gray

Date	Mintage	F	VF	XF	Unc	BU
1948	800,000	1.25	2.50	30.00	60.00	—
1948 Proof	—	—	—	—	—	—
1949	1,600,000	1.25	2.50	25.00	65.00	—
1949 Proof	—	Value: 450				
1950	1,200,000	1.25	2.50	35.00	75.00	—
1950 Proof	—	Value: 450				
1951	3,200,000	1.25	2.50	27.50	50.00	90.00
1951 Proof	—	Value: 350				
1952	2,800,000	1.25	2.50	30.00	70.00	100
1952 Proof	—	Value: 350				

KM# 31 1/2 CROWN

Copper-Nickel, 32 mm. **Ruler:** Elizabeth II **Obv:** Laureate bust right **Obv. Designer:** Mary Gillick **Rev:** Crowned shield **Rev. Designer:** G.E. Kruger-Gray

Date	Mintage	F	VF	XF	Unc	BU
1954	1,200,000	8.00	16.00	45.00	95.00	130
1954 Proof	20	Value: 450				

KM# 27 CROWN

28.2800 g., 0.5000 Silver .4546 oz. ASW, 38.5 mm. **Ruler:** Elizabeth II **Subject:** Birth of Cecil Rhodes Centennial **Obv:** Larueate bust right **Obv. Designer:** Mary Gillick **Rev:** Cameo flanked by sprigs with ribbon above assorted shields **Rev. Designer:** T.H. Paget **Edge Lettering:** 1853 OUT OF VISION CAME REALITY 1953 **Note:** Both upright and inverted edge varieties exist.

Date	Mintage	F	VF	XF	Unc	BU
1953	124,000	7.50	15.00	30.00	40.00	85.00
1953 Proof	1,500	Value: 85.00				
1953 Matte Proof	—	Value: 350				

TRIAL STRIKES

KM#	Date	Mintage	Identification	Mkt Val
TS1	1932	—	3 Pence. White Metal. Plain edge. Rev. KM#1.	500
TS2	1932	—	6 Pence. White Metal. Plain edge. Rev. KM#2.	500
TS3	1932	—	Shilling. White Metal. Plain edge. Rev. KM#3.	600

KM#	Date	Mintage	Identification	Mkt Val
TS4	1932	—	Florin. White Metal. Plain edge. Rev. KM#4.	800
TS5	1932	—	1/2 Crown. White Metal. Plain edge. Rev. KM#5.	1,000
TS6	1934	—	3 Pence. White Metal. Plain edge. Rev. KM#1, Thick flan.	500
TS7	1934	—	1/2 Crown. White Metal. Plain edge. Rev. KM#5. Thick flan.	1,000

PROOF SETS

KM#	Date	Mintage	Identification	Issue Price	Mkt Val
PS1	1932 (5)	496	KM#1-5	—	450
PS2	1937 (6)	40	KM#8-13	—	2,000
PS3	1939 (5)	10	KM#15-19	—	2,500
PS6	1947 (5)	10	KM#15b-19b	—	1,500
PS4	1953 (2)	3	KM#27 Double set; Rare	—	—
PS5	1954 (4)	20	KM#28-31	—	2,500

The Spanish State, forming the greater part of the Iberian Peninsula of southwest Europe, has an area of 195,988 sq. mi. (504,714 sq. km.) and a population of 39.4 million including the Balearic and the Canary Islands. Capital: Madrid. The economy is based on agriculture, industry and tourism. Machinery, fruit, vegetables and chemicals are exported.

Discontent against the mother country increased after 1808 as colonists faced new imperialist policies from Napoleon or Spanish liberals. The revolutionary movement was established which resulted in the eventual independence of the Vice-royalties of New Spain, New Granada and Rio de la Plata within 2 decades.

The doomed republic was trapped in a tug-of-war between the right and left wing forces inevitably resulting in the Spanish Civil War of 1936-38. The leftist Republicans were supported by the U.S.S.R. and the International Brigade, which consisted of mainly communist volunteers from all over the western world. The right wing Nationalists were supported by the Fascist governments of Italy and Germany. Under the leadership of Gen. Francisco Franco, the Nationalists emerged victorious and immediately embarked on a program of reconstruction and neutrality as dictated by the new "Caudillo"(leader) Franco.

The monarchy was reconstituted in 1947 under the regency of General Francisco Franco; the king designate to be crowned after Franco's death. Franco died on Nov. 20, 1975. Two days after his passing, Juan Carlos de Borbon, the grandson of Alfonso XIII, was proclaimed King of Spain.

RULERS

Alfonso XIII, 1886-1931
2nd Republic and Civil War, 1931-1939
Francisco Franco, 1939-1947
as Caudillo and regent, 1947-1975
Juan Carlos I, 1975-

NOTE: From 1868 to 1982, two dates may be found on most Spanish coinage. The larger date is the year of authorization and the smaller date incused on the two 6-pointed-stars found on most types is the year of issue. The latter appears in parentheses in these listings.

MINT MARKS

Until 1980
6-pointed star - Madrid

NOTE: Letters after date are initials of mint officials.

After 1982
Crowned M – Madrid

KINGDOM

DECIMAL COINAGE

Peseta System

100 Centimos = 1 Peseta

KM# 726 CENTIMO

Bronze **Ruler:** Alfonso XIII **Obv:** Head right **Rev:** Crowned shield divides value within beaded circle **Note:** Mint mark: 6-pointed star.

Date	Mintage	F	VF	XF	Unc	BU
1906 (6) SL-V	7,500,000	0.35	0.75	1.50	3.50	5.00
1906 (6) SM-V	Inc. above	225	400	600	800	900

KM# 731 CENTIMO

Bronze **Ruler:** Alfonso XIII **Obv:** Head left **Rev:** Crowned shield divides value within beaded circle **Note:** Mint mark: 6-pointed star.

Date	Mintage	F	VF	XF	Unc	BU
1911 (1) PC-V	1,462,000	30.00	50.00	80.00	110	130
1912 (2) PC-V	2,109,000	2.00	3.50	6.00	12.00	16.00
1913 (3) PC-V	1,429,000	3.50	6.50	12.00	20.00	25.00

KM# 722 2 CENTIMOS

Copper **Ruler:** Alfonso XIII **Obv:** Head right **Rev:** Crowned shield divides value within beaded circle **Note:** Mint mark: 6-pointed star.

Date	Mintage	F	VF	XF	Unc	BU
1904 (04) SM-V	10,000,000	0.65	1.75	5.00	9.00	16.00
1905 (05) SM-V	5,000,000	0.65	1.75	6.50	11.50	20.00

KM# 732 2 CENTIMOS

Copper **Ruler:** Alfonso XIII **Obv:** Head left **Rev:** Crowned shield divides value within beaded circle **Note:** Mint mark: 6-pointed star.

Date	Mintage	F	VF	XF	Unc	BU
1911 (11) PC-V	2,284,000	0.65	1.75	4.50	12.00	16.50
1912 (12) PC-V	5,216,000	0.65	1.75	5.00	12.00	15.00

KM# 740 25 CENTIMOS

Copper-Nickel **Ruler:** Alfonso XIII **Obv:** Sailing ship **Rev:** Crowned value flanked by sprigs

Date	Mintage	F	VF	XF	Unc	BU
1925 PC-S	8,001,000	0.50	1.50	8.50	25.00	60.00

KM# 742 25 CENTIMOS

Copper-Nickel **Ruler:** Alfonso XIII **Obv:** Vine entwined on cross, crown and date, hole in center **Rev:** Value above oat sprigs, hole in center

Date	Mintage	F	VF	XF	Unc	BU
1927 PC-S	12,000,000	0.45	1.00	8.50	25.00	70.00

KM# 723 50 CENTIMOS

2.5000 g., 0.8350 Silver .0671 oz. ASW **Ruler:** Alfonso XIII **Obv:** Head left **Rev:** Crowned shield flanked by pillars with banner **Note:** Mint mark: 6-pointed star.

Date	Mintage	F	VF	XF	Unc	BU
1904 (04) SM-V	4,851,000	2.00	3.00	7.00	13.50	15.00
1904 (10) PC-V	1,303,000	2.00	3.50	7.50	15.00	20.00

KM# 730 50 CENTIMOS

2.5000 g., 0.8350 Silver .0671 oz. ASW **Ruler:** Alfonso XIII **Obv:** Head left **Rev:** Crowned shield flanked by pillars with banner **Note:** Mint mark: 6-pointed star.

Date	Mintage	F	VF	XF	Unc	BU
1910 (10) PC-V	4,526,000	2.00	3.50	6.50	20.00	25.00

KM# 741 50 CENTIMOS

2.5000 g., 0.8350 Silver .0671 oz. ASW **Ruler:** Alfonso XIII **Obv:** Head left **Rev:** Crowned shield within wreath

Date	Mintage	F	VF	XF	Unc	BU
1926 PC-S	4,000,000	2.00	3.00	4.50	9.00	16.00

KM# 706 PESETA

5.0000 g., 0.8350 Silver .1342 oz. ASW **Ruler:** Alfonso XIII **Obv:** Child's head left **Obv. Legend:** ALFONSO XIII... **Rev:** Crowned arms, pillars, value below **Rev. Legend:** REYCONST... **Note:** Mint mark: 6-pointed star. Prices are for coins with full right star dates. Partial right star dates sell for less. Examples with no visable right star date have limited collector appeal.

Date	Mintage	F	VF	XF	Unc	BU
1901 (01) SM-V	8,449,000	5.00	12.50	45.00	120	145
1902 (02) SM-V	2,599,000	13.50	40.00	125	250	300

KM# 721 PESETA

5.0000 g., 0.8350 Silver .1342 oz. ASW **Ruler:** Alfonso XIII **Obv:** Head left **Rev:** Crowned shield flanked by pillars with banner **Note:** Mint mark 6-pointed star.

Date	Mintage	F	VF	XF	Unc	BU
1903 (03) SM-V	10,602,000	2.25	7.00	25.00	65.00	80.00
1904 (04) SM-V	5,294,000	3.00	9.50	30.00	75.00	90.00
1905 (05) SM-V	492,000	35.00	125	550	950	1,100

KM# 725 2 PESETAS

10.0000 g., 0.8350 Silver .2685 oz. ASW **Ruler:** Alfonso XIII **Obv:** Head left **Rev:** Crowned shield flanked by pillars with banner **Note:** Mint mark: 6-pointed star.

Date	Mintage	F	VF	XF	Unc	BU
1905 (05) SM-V	3,589,000	4.50	7.50	18.00	27.00	35.00

KM# 724 20 PESETAS

6.4516 g., 0.9000 Gold .1867 oz. AGW **Obv:** Head right **Rev:** Crowned and mantled shield **Note:** Mint mark: 6-pointed star.

Date	Mintage	F	VF	XF	Unc	BU
1904 (04) SM-V	3,814	850	1,650	2,250	3,000	—

REPUBLIC

1931 - 1939

DECIMAL COINAGE

Peseta System

100 Centimos = 1 Peseta

KM# 752 5 CENTIMOS

Iron **Obv:** Head left **Rev:** Value and date within wreath

Date	Mintage	F	VF	XF	Unc	BU
1937	10,000,000	0.35	1.00	2.00	5.00	10.00

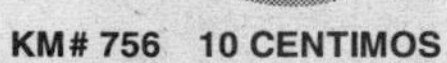

KM# 756 10 CENTIMOS

Iron **Obv:** Crowned shield **Rev:** Value and date within wreath

Date	Mintage	F	VF	XF	Unc	BU
1938	1,000	—	600	1,050	2,100	4,000

Note: This coin was never released into circulation

KM# 751 25 CENTIMOS

Copper-Nickel **Obv:** Bust right holding sprig, hole in center **Rev:** Value above oat sprig and gear, hole in center

Date	Mintage	F	VF	XF	Unc	BU
1934	12,272,000	0.30	0.75	3.50	12.00	25.00

KM# 753 25 CENTIMOS

Copper-Nickel, 25 mm. **Obv:** Inscription, date and arrow design, hole in center **Rev:** Crowned shield, value and sprig, hole in center

Date	Mintage	F	VF	XF	Unc	BU
1937	42,000,000	0.20	0.40	1.00	4.00	5.00

Note: This coin was issued by way of decree April 5, 1938, by the Governmant in Burgos. Franco and the Nationalist forces controlled the majority of Spain by this point in time

KM# 757 25 CENTIMOS

Copper **Obv:** Chain links around center hole **Rev:** Value and center hole divide sprigs

Date	Mintage	F	VF	XF	Unc	BU
1938	45,500,000	0.75	1.50	3.50	8.00	10.00

KM# 754.1 50 CENTIMOS

Copper **Obv:** Seated figure holding sprig **Rev:** Value within beaded circle **Note:** Mint mark: 6-pointed star. Several varieties exist.

Date	Mintage	F	VF	XF	Unc	BU
1937 (34)	50,000,000	0.50	1.00	3.50	11.50	15.00
1937 (36)	1,000,000	0.65	1.50	4.50	9.50	16.00

KM# 754.2 50 CENTIMOS

Copper **Obv:** Seated allegorical figure left **Rev:** Border of rectangles **Note:** Mint mark: 6-pointed star.

Date	Mintage	F	VF	XF	Unc	BU
1937 (36)	Inc. above	1.50	3.00	8.00	20.00	30.00

KM# 750 PESETA

5.0000 g., 0.8350 Silver .1342 oz. ASW **Obv:** Seated figure holding sprig **Rev:** Crowned shield flanked by pillars with banner **Note:** Mint mark: 6-pointed star.

Date	Mintage	F	VF	XF	Unc	BU
1933 (3-4)	2,000,000	5.00	10.00	18.00	25.00	32.00

Note: Rotated reverse varieties exist, with values increasing by the degree of rotation.

KM# 755 PESETA

Brass **Obv:** Head left **Rev:** Value and grapes on vine

Date	Mintage	F	VF	XF	Unc	BU
1937	50,000,000	0.35	0.85	2.00	7.50	10.00

NATIONALIST GOVERNMENT

1939 - 1947

DECIMAL COINAGE

Peseta System

100 Centimos = 1 Peseta

KM# 765 5 CENTIMOS

Aluminum **Obv:** Armored figure on rearing horse **Rev:** Crowned shield within eagle flanked by pillars with banner **Note:** Mint mark: 6-pointed star. To realize the values below all Unc. and BU coins must have full strike including letters.

Date	Mintage	F	VF	XF	Unc	BU
1940 PLVS	175,000,000	0.75	2.00	9.00	35.00	55.00
1941	202,107,000	0.35	1.25	3.50	15.00	18.00
1945	221,500,000	—	0.25	1.00	8.00	11.00
1953	31,573,000	5.50	12.00	22.00	65.00	80.00

KM# 766 10 CENTIMOS

Aluminum, 22.5 mm. **Obv:** Armored figure on rearing horse **Rev:** Crowned shield within eagle flanked by pillars with banner **Designer:** Reeded **Note:** Varieties exist. To realize the values below all Unc. and BU coins must have full strike including letters.

Date	Mintage	F	VF	XF	Unc	BU
1940 PLUS	225,000,000	0.40	2.00	11.00	45.00	60.00
1940 PLVS	Inc. above	15.00	30.00	60.00	125	175
1941 PLUS	247,981,000	0.50	2.00	5.00	12.50	16.50
1941 PLVS	Inc. above	10.00	15.00	35.00	75.00	100
1945	250,000,000	—	0.60	2.50	8.00	10.00
1953	865,850,000	—	0.35	1.25	4.00	5.00

KM# 767 PESETA

Aluminum-Bronze **Obv:** Crowned shield within eagle flanked by pillars with banner **Rev:** Value in center of design **Note:** To realize the values below all Unc. and BU coins must have full strike including letters.

Date	Mintage	F	VF	XF	Unc	BU
1944	150,000,000	—	0.45	3.50	22.50	30.00

KINGDOM

1949 - Present

DECIMAL COINAGE

Peseta System

100 Centimos = 1 Peseta

KM# 790 10 CENTIMOS

Aluminum, 18 mm. **Ruler:** Caudillo and regent **Obv:** Head right **Rev:** Value within designed wreath **Edge:** Reeded

Date	Mintage	F	VF	XF	Unc	BU
1959	900,000,000	—	—	—	0.55	0.75
1959 Proof	101,000	Value: 1.50				

KM# 776 50 CENTIMOS

Copper-Nickel, 21 mm. **Ruler:** Caudillo and regent **Obv:** Anchor, date and part of captains wheel, hole in center **Rev:** Value, design with arrows pointing down and hole in center divide assorted shields **Edge:** Plain **Note:** Mint mark: 6-pointed star.

Date	Mintage	F	VF	XF	Unc	BU
1949 (51)	990,000	3.50	6.50	12.50	25.00	35.00

Note: Minting date "51" in incused star

KM# 777 50 CENTIMOS

Copper-Nickel, 21 mm. **Ruler:** Caudillo and regent **Obv:** Anchor, date and part of captains wheel, hole in center **Rev:** Value, design with arrows pointing up and hole in center divide assorted shields **Edge:** Plain **Note:** Mint mark: 6-pointed star.

Date	Mintage	F	VF	XF	Unc	BU
1949 (51)	8,010,000	—	2.00	3.00	18.50	30.00
1949 (E51)	Est. 5,000	—	—	—	500	600

Note: Issued to commemorate a numismatic exposition December 2, 1951; An "E" replaces the "19" on the lower star

Date	Mintage	F	VF	XF	Unc	BU
1949 (52)	18,567,000	—	0.25	2.00	12.00	18.00
1949 (53)	17,500,000	—	0.50	5.00	25.00	30.00
1949 (54)	37,000,000	—	0.60	4.00	15.00	20.00
1949 (56)	38,000,000	—	0.15	2.00	12.00	18.00
1949 (62)	31,000,000	—	0.20	1.50	7.00	10.00
1963 (63)	4,000,000	1.50	5.50	9.00	30.00	35.00
1963 (64)	20,000,000	—	0.10	0.25	2.50	3.50
1963 (65)	14,000,000	—	0.10	0.20	1.50	2.50

KM# 795 50 CENTIMOS

1.1000 g., Aluminum, 20.1 mm. **Ruler:** Caudillo and regent **Obv:** Head right **Rev:** Sprig divides value **Edge:** Reeded **Note:** Mint mark: 6-pointed star. These coins generally suffer from oxidation and the values given are for perfect proof specimens.

Date	Mintage	F	VF	XF	Unc	BU
1966 (67)	80,000,000	—	—	0.15	0.75	1.00
1966 (68)	100,000,000	—	—	0.15	0.60	1.00
1966 (69)	50,000,000	—	—	0.25	1.25	2.00
1966 (70) Prooflike	—	—	—	5.00	70.00	165
1966 (71)	99,000,000	—	—	0.15	0.35	0.75
1966 (72)	2,283,000	—	—	0.60	1.50	4.00
1966 (72) Proof	30,000	Value: 5.00				
1966 (73)	10,000,000	—	—	0.15	0.35	0.75
1966 (73) Proof	25,000	Value: 4.00				
1966 (74) Proof	23,000	Value: 50.00				
1966 (75) Proof	75,000	Value: 8.00				

KM# 805 50 CENTIMOS
Copper-Nickel **Ruler:** Juan Carlos I **Obv:** Head left **Rev:** Sprig divides value **Note:** Mint mark: 6-pointed star.

Date	Mintage	F	VF	XF	Unc	BU
1975 (76)	4,060,000	—	—	0.10	0.20	0.50
1975 (76) Proof	—	Value: 0.85				

KM# 815 50 CENTIMOS
Center Composition: Aluminum, 20 mm. **Ruler:** Juan Carlos I **Subject:** World Cup Soccer Games **Obv:** Head left **Rev:** Soccer balls above value **Edge:** Reeded **Note:** Mint mark: 6-pointed star.

Date	Mintage	F	VF	XF	Unc	BU
1980 (80)	15,000,000	—	—	0.10	0.20	0.35
1980 (80) Proof	—	Value: 0.75				

KM# 775 PESETA
Aluminum-Bronze, 21 mm. **Ruler:** Francisco Franco, caudillo **Obv:** Head right **Rev:** Crowned shield within eagle flanked by pillars with banner **Edge:** Reeded **Note:** Mint mark: 6-pointed star.

Date	Mintage	F	VF	XF	Unc	BU
1946 (48)	Est. 5,000	750	1,200	2,000	3,000	—
1947 (48)	15,000,000	—	1.00	15.00	120	170
1947 (49)	27,600,000	—	0.75	15.00	110	160
1947 (50)	4,000,000	1.50	6.00	50.00	300	500
1947 (51)	9,185,000	2.00	4.00	40.00	200	400
1947 (E51)	Est. 5,000	—	—	—	600	700

Note: Issued to commemorate the Second National Numismatic Exposition December 2, 1951; An "E" replaces the "19" on the lower star

Date	Mintage	F	VF	XF	Unc	BU
1947 (52)	19,195,000	—	1.00	10.00	60.00	100
1947 (53)	34,000,000	—	0.75	10.00	50.00	100
1947 (54)	50,000,000	—	1.00	15.00	60.00	120
1947 (56)	—	10.00	30.00	85.00	400	700
1953 (54)	40,272,000	—	3.00	30.00	250	325
1953 (56)	118,000,000	—	0.10	1.00	5.00	8.00
1953 (60)	45,160,000	—	0.70	10.50	60.00	110
1953 (61)	25,830,000	—	0.60	10.00	50.00	90.00
1953 (62)	66,252,000	—	0.10	1.00	3.00	7.00
1953 (63)	37,000,000	—	0.25	1.50	15.00	30.00
1963 (63)	36,000,000	—	0.35	2.25	20.00	25.00
1963 (64)	80,000,000	—	0.10	1.00	3.00	5.00
1963 (65)	70,000,000	—	0.10	1.00	3.00	5.00
1963 (66)	63,000,000	—	0.10	1.00	5.00	10.00
1963 (67)	11,300,000	—	2.00	10.00	50.00	80.00

KM# 796 PESETA
Aluminum-Bronze, 21 mm. **Ruler:** Caudillo and regent **Obv:** Head right **Rev:** Crowned shield within eagle flanked by pillars with banner **Edge:** Reeded **Note:** Mint mark: 6-pointed star.

Date	Mintage	F	VF	XF	Unc	BU
1966 (67)	59,000,000	—	0.15	0.30	1.50	4.50
1966 (68)	120,000,000	—	0.10	0.20	1.00	1.50
1966 (69)	120,000,000	—	0.10	0.20	1.00	1.50
1966 (70)	75,000,000	—	0.10	0.20	2.00	3.00
1966 (71)	115,270,000	—	0.10	0.15	0.75	1.50
1966 (72)	106,000,000	—	—	0.10	0.50	0.75
1966 (72) Proof	30,000	Value: 2.00				
1966 (73)	152,000,000	—	—	0.10	0.35	0.65
1966 (73) Proof	25,000	Value: 2.00				
1966 (74)	181,000,000	—	—	0.10	0.35	0.65
1966 (74) Proof	23,000	Value: 2.00				
1966 (75)	227,580,000	—	—	0.10	0.25	0.35
1966 (75) Proof	75,000	Value: 1.00				

KM# 806 PESETA
Aluminum-Bronze, 21 mm. **Ruler:** Juan Carlos I **Obv:** Head left **Rev:** Crowned shield within eagle flanked by pillars with banner **Edge:** Reeded

Date	Mintage	F	VF	XF	Unc	BU
1975 (76)	170,380,000	—	—	0.10	0.25	0.35
1975 (76) Proof	—	Value: 0.75				
1975 (77)	243,380,000	—	—	0.10	0.25	0.35
1975 (77) Proof	—	Value: 0.75				
1975 (78)	Est. 603,320,000	—	—	0.10	0.25	0.35
1975 (79)	507,000,000	—	—	0.10	0.25	0.35

Note: Two varieties of tilde size for the n in España exist of this date; Large is Madrid mint, small is Santiago de Chile

Date	Mintage	F	VF	XF	Unc	BU
1975 (79) Proof	—	Value: 0.75				
1975 (80)	590,000,000	—	—	0.10	0.25	0.50

KM# 816 PESETA
Aluminum-Bronze, 21 mm. **Ruler:** Juan Carlos I **Subject:** World Cup Soccer Games **Obv:** Head left **Rev:** Small crowned shield within eagle at left of value

Date	Mintage	F	VF	XF	Unc	BU
1980 (80)	—	—	—	0.10	0.15	0.30
1980 (80) Proof	—	Value: 0.75				
1980 (81)	385,000,000	—	—	0.10	0.25	0.35
1980 (82)	333,000,000	—	—	0.10	0.25	0.35

KM# 821 PESETA
1.2000 g., Aluminum, 21 mm. **Ruler:** Juan Carlos I **Obv:** Head left **Rev:** Crowned shield flanked by pillars with banner to right of value **Designer:** Plain

Date	Mintage	F	VF	XF	Unc	BU
1982	—	—	—	0.10	0.20	0.35

Note: Mintage included in KM#816, 1980 (82)

Date	Mintage	F	VF	XF	Unc	BU
1983	52,000,000	—	—	0.10	0.50	0.75
1984	131,000,000	—	—	0.10	0.20	0.35
1985	220,065,000	—	—	0.10	0.20	0.35
1986	299,960,000	—	—	0.10	0.20	0.35
1987	299,550,000	—	—	0.10	0.20	0.35
1987 Proof	60,000	Value: 55.00				
1988	223,460,000	—	—	0.10	0.20	0.35
1989	—	—	—	0.10	0.60	1.00

Note: Mintage included in KM#832, 1989

KM# 828 PESETA
Aluminum, 21 mm. **Ruler:** Juan Carlos I **Subject:** 3rd National Numismatic Exposition - Madrid **Obv:** Head left **Rev:** Crowned shield flanked by pillars with banner at right of value

Date	Mintage	F	VF	XF	Unc	BU
1987/E-87 Proof	60,000	Value: 50.00				

KM# 832 PESETA
Aluminum, 14 mm. **Ruler:** Juan Carlos I **Obv:** Vertical line divides head left from value **Rev:** Crowned shield flanked by pillars with banner **Edge:** Plain

Date	Mintage	F	VF	XF	Unc	BU
1989	198,415,000	—	—	0.10	0.25	0.50
1990	197,700,000	—	—	0.10	0.25	0.50
1991	173,780,000	—	—	0.10	0.25	0.50
1992	168,870,000	—	—	0.10	0.20	0.25
1993	300,013,000	—	—	0.10	0.20	0.25
1994	162,860,000	—	—	0.10	0.20	0.25
1995	183,175,000	—	—	0.10	0.20	0.25
1996	101,885,000	—	—	0.10	0.20	0.25
1997	342,620,000	—	—	0.10	0.20	0.25
1998	411,614,000	—	—	0.10	0.20	0.25
1999	84,946,000	—	—	0.10	0.20	0.25
2000	—	—	—	0.10	0.20	0.25

KM# 822 2 PESETAS
2.0000 g., Aluminum, 24 mm. **Ruler:** Juan Carlos I **Obv:** Head left **Rev:** Value within map

Date	Mintage	F	VF	XF	Unc	BU
1982	21,500,000	—	—	0.20	0.50	0.75
1984	47,650,000	—	—	0.20	0.45	0.65

KM# 785 2-1/2 PESETAS
Aluminum-Bronze **Ruler:** Caudillo and regent **Obv:** Head right **Rev:** Crowned shield within eagle flanked by pillars with banner

Date	Mintage	F	VF	XF	Unc	BU
1953 (54)	22,729,000	—	0.25	1.00	4.50	6.00
1953 (56)	30,322,000	—	0.25	1.00	4.50	6.00
1953 (56) Proof	—	Value: 100				
1953 (68)	1,000	—	—	—	—	900

Note: In sets only

Date	Mintage	F	VF	XF	Unc	BU
1953 (69)	2,000	—	—	—	—	1,000

Note: In sets only

Date	Mintage	F	VF	XF	Unc	BU
1953 (70)	6,000	—	—	—	—	100

Note: In sets only

Date	Mintage	F	VF	XF	Unc	BU
1953 (71)	10,000	—	—	—	—	100

Note: In sets only

KM# 778 5 PESETAS
Nickel, 32 mm. **Ruler:** Caudillo and regent **Obv:** Head right **Rev:** Crowned shield within eagle flanked by pillars with banner **Edge:** Reeded

Date	Mintage	F	VF	XF	Unc	BU
1949 (49)	612,000	—	2.50	10.00	20.00	30.00
1949 (50)	21,000,000	—	0.85	2.00	5.00	10.00
1949 (E51)	Est. 6,000	—	—	—	900	1,200

Note: Issued to commemorate the Second National Numismatic Exposition December 2, 1951; An "E" replaces the "19" on the lower star

Date	Mintage	F	VF	XF	Unc	BU
1949 (51) Rare	145,000	—	—	—	—	—
1949 (52) Rare	Est. 200,000	—	—	—	—	—

KM# 786 5 PESETAS
5.7500 g., Copper-Nickel, 23 mm. **Ruler:** Caudillo and regent **Obv:** Head right **Rev:** Crowned shield within flying bird **Edge:** Reeded **Note:** Values in uncirculated drop by 50% or more when the PLUS in legend is not readable. This defect is most often seen on coins struck before 1968.

Date	Mintage	F	VF	XF	Unc	BU
1957 BA	Est. 43,000	—	50.00	100	150	200

Note: Issued to commemorate the 1958 2nd Ibero-American Numismatic Exposition in Barcelona with "BA" replacing the star on left side of reverse

Date	Mintage	F	VF	XF	Unc	BU
1957 (58)	13,000,000	—	0.45	3.00	40.00	80.00
1957 (59)	107,000,000	—	0.10	1.00	20.00	25.00
1957 (60)	26,000,000	—	0.10	1.00	10.00	20.00
1957 (61)	78,992,000	—	0.15	3.50	25.00	35.00
1957 (62)	40,963,000	—	0.20	2.25	7.50	27.00

Date	Mintage	F	VF	XF	Unc	BU
1957 (63)	50,000,000	—	2.00	15.00	80.00	175
1957 (64)	51,000,000	—	0.10	1.00	10.00	20.00
1957 (65)	25,000,000	—	0.15	0.75	8.00	15.00
1957 (66)	28,000,000	—	0.15	3.50	20.00	30.00
1957 (67)	30,000,000	—	0.15	0.75	5.00	10.00
1957 (68)	60,000,000	—	0.20	0.60	3.00	4.00
1957 (69)	40,000,000	—	0.20	0.60	3.00	5.00
1957 (70)	43,000,000	—	0.20	0.60	3.00	9.00
1957 (71)	77,000,000	—	0.20	0.60	1.50	3.00
1957 (72)	70,000,000	—	—	0.55	3.00	8.00
1957 (72) Proof	30,000	Value: 5.00				
1957 (73)	78,000,000	—	—	0.10	0.75	2.00
1957 (73) Proof	25,000	Value: 3.00				
1957 (74)	100,000,000	—	—	0.10	0.45	1.00
1957 (74) Proof	23,000	Value: 3.00				
1957 (75)	139,047,000	—	—	0.10	0.25	0.50
1957 (75) Proof	75,000	Value: 1.00				

KM# 811 5 PESETAS
Copper-Nickel **Ruler:** Juan Carlos I **Obv:** Head left **Rev:** World globe, soccerball, value and star with numeral 80 **Note:** Mule.

Date	Mintage	F	VF	XF	Unc	BU
1975 (80)	Est. 30,000	—	—	175	300	350

KM# 807 5 PESETAS
5.7500 g., Copper-Nickel, 23 mm. **Ruler:** Juan Carlos I **Obv:** Head left **Rev:** Crossed scepters and shield within wreath divides value, crown on top **Edge:** Reeded

Date	Mintage	F	VF	XF	Unc	BU
1975 (76)	150,560,000	—	—	0.10	0.25	0.35
1975 (76) Proof	—	Value: 1.00				
1975 (77)	154,982,000	—	—	0.10	0.25	0.35
1975 (77) Proof	Inc. above	Value: 1.00				
1975 (78)	412,610,000	—	—	0.10	0.35	0.50
1975 (79)	436,000,000	—	—	0.10	0.25	0.35
1975 (79) Proof	—	Value: 1.00				
1975 (80)	322,000,000	—	—	0.10	0.50	1.00

KM# 817 5 PESETAS
5.7500 g., Copper-Nickel, 23 mm. **Ruler:** Juan Carlos I **Subject:** World Cup Soccer Games **Obv:** Head left **Rev:** Numeral 82 on world globe, soccer ball above value

Date	Mintage	F	VF	XF	Unc	BU
1980 (80)	75,000,000	—	—	0.10	0.25	0.35
1980 (80) Proof	—	Value: 1.00				
1980 (81)	294,000,000	—	—	0.10	0.25	0.50
1980 (82)	291,000,000	—	—	0.10	0.25	0.50

KM# 823 5 PESETAS
5.7500 g., Copper-Nickel, 23 mm. **Ruler:** Juan Carlos I **Obv:** Head left **Rev:** Crossed scepters and shield within wreath divide value, crown on top **Note:** Mint mark: Crowned M.

Date	Mintage	F	VF	XF	Unc	BU
1982	—	—	—	0.10	1.00	1.50
Note: Mintage included in KM#817, 1980 (82)						
1983	200,000,000	—	—	0.10	0.50	0.65
1984	169,000,000	—	—	0.10	0.60	0.80
1989	—	—	—	0.10	0.75	1.00

KM# 833 5 PESETAS
Aluminum-Bronze, 18 mm. **Ruler:** Juan Carlos I **Obv:** Stylized design and date **Rev:** Value above above stylized sailboats **Edge:** Plain

Date	Mintage	F	VF	XF	Unc	BU
1989	109,270,000	—	—	0.10	0.30	0.50
1990	191,740,000	—	—	0.10	0.50	1.00

Date	Mintage	F	VF	XF	Unc	BU
1991	313,820,000	—	—	0.10	0.45	0.85
1992	493,224,000	—	—	0.10	0.35	0.50
1998	923,978,000	—	—	0.10	0.25	0.35
2000	—	—	—	0.10	0.25	0.35

KM# 919 5 PESETAS
Nickel-Brass, 17.5 mm. **Ruler:** Juan Carlos I **Subject:** Jacobeo **Obv:** Standing figure with staff at left of design **Rev:** Value, dates and design **Edge:** Plain **Note:** Coins with extra metal in the denomination 5 sell for a premium.

Date	Mintage	F	VF	XF	Unc	BU
1993	372,746,000	—	—	—	0.25	0.35

KM# 931 5 PESETAS
Nickel-Brass, 17.5 mm. **Ruler:** Juan Carlos I **Subject:** Aragon **Obv:** Front view of building **Rev:** Ballerina **Edge:** Plain **Note:** Wide rim variety exists.

Date	Mintage	F	VF	XF	Unc	BU
1994	199,678,000	—	—	—	0.25	0.40

KM# 946 5 PESETAS
Aluminum-Bronze, 17.5 mm. **Ruler:** Juan Carlos I **Subject:** Asturias **Obv:** Cross and date **Rev:** Value and design **Edge:** Plain

Date	Mintage	F	VF	XF	Unc	BU
1995	301,756,000	—	—	—	0.25	0.40

KM# 960 5 PESETAS
Aluminum-Bronze, 17.5 mm. **Ruler:** Juan Carlos I **Subject:** La Rioja **Obv:** Front view of building **Rev:** Figure on stilts, value and grapes **Edge:** Plain

Date	Mintage	F	VF	XF	Unc	BU
1996	674,168,000	—	—	—	0.15	0.25

KM# 981 5 PESETAS
Brass, 17.5 mm. **Ruler:** Juan Carlos I **Subject:** Balearic Islands **Obv:** Stone monument **Rev:** Figure on rearing horse **Edge:** Plain

Date	Mintage	F	VF	XF	Unc	BU
1997	709,006,000	—	—	—	0.15	0.25

KM# 1008 5 PESETAS
Brass, 17.5 mm. **Ruler:** Juan Carlos I **Obv:** Crowned shield with supporters on arch **Rev:** Murcia waterwheel **Edge:** Plain

Date	Mintage	F	VF	XF	Unc	BU
1999	216,230,000	—	—	—	0.15	0.25

KM# 827 10 PESETAS
4.0000 g., Copper-Nickel, 18.5 mm. **Ruler:** Juan Carlos I **Obv:** Head left **Rev:** Crowned shield flanked by pillars with banner **Note:** Denomination "DIEZ".

Date	Mintage	F	VF	XF	Unc	BU
1983	149,000,000	—	—	0.25	0.35	0.40

Date	Mintage	F	VF	XF	Unc	BU
1984	66,000,000	—	—	0.50	0.80	1.00
1985	45,706,000	—	—	0.25	0.50	0.60

KM# 903 10 PESETAS
4.0000 g., Copper-Nickel, 18.5 mm. **Ruler:** Juan Carlos I **Obv:** Head left **Rev:** Crowned shield flanked by pillars with banner **Edge:** Reeded

Date	Mintage	F	VF	XF	Unc	BU
1992	51,820,000	—	—	0.25	0.40	0.50

KM# 918 10 PESETAS
4.0000 g., Copper-Nickel, 18.5 mm. **Ruler:** Juan Carlos I **Subject:** Juan Miro **Obv:** Value, dates and inscription **Rev:** Head 3/4 right **Edge:** Plain

Date	Mintage	F	VF	XF	Unc	BU
1993	53,845,000	—	—	0.25	0.60	1.00

KM# 932 10 PESETAS
4.0000 g., Copper-Nickel, 18.5 mm. **Ruler:** Juan Carlos I **Subject:** Musician P. Sarasate **Obv:** Head right **Rev:** Violin **Edge:** Reeded

Date	Mintage	F	VF	XF	Unc	BU
1994	3,050,000	—	—	0.35	1.25	2.50

KM# 947 10 PESETAS
4.0000 g., Copper-Nickel, 18.5 mm. **Ruler:** Juan Carlos I **Subject:** Don Francisco de Quevedo **Obv:** Bust 1/4 left **Rev:** Quill in ink, book, glasses and value **Edge:** Reeded

Date	Mintage	F	VF	XF	Unc	BU
1995	1,050,000	—	—	0.55	2.25	4.00

KM# 961 10 PESETAS
4.0000 g., Copper-Nickel, 18.5 mm. **Ruler:** Juan Carlos I **Subject:** Emilia Pardo Bazan **Obv:** Monument and value **Rev:** Half length figure facing **Edge:** Reeded

Date	Mintage	F	VF	XF	Unc	BU
1996	1,060,000	—	—	0.30	1.75	3.50

KM# 982 10 PESETAS
4.0000 g., Copper-Nickel, 18.5 mm. **Ruler:** Juan Carlos I **Subject:** Seneca **Obv:** Head facing **Rev:** Castle gate

Date	Mintage	F	VF	XF	Unc	BU
1997	—	—	—	0.25	0.45	0.65

KM# 1012 10 PESETAS
4.0000 g., Copper-Nickel, 18.5 mm. **Ruler:** Juan Carlos I **Obv:** Head left **Rev:** Value above national arms **Edge:** Reeded **Note:** Older portrait.

Date	Mintage	F	VF	XF	Unc	BU
1998	14,965,000	—	—	0.25	0.75	1.00
1999	2,125,000	—	—	0.35	0.85	1.00
2000	—	—	—	0.25	0.65	0.75

KM# 787 25 PESETAS
8.5000 g., Copper-Nickel, 26.5 mm. **Ruler:** Caudillo and regent **Obv:** Head right **Rev:** Crowned shield within flying bird **Edge Lettering:** UNA GRANDE LIBRE **Note:** Values in uncirculated drop by 50% or more when the "PLUS" in legend is not readable. This defect is most often seen on coins struck before 1968.

Date	Mintage	F	VF	XF	Unc	BU
1957 (58)	8,635,000	—	0.35	5.00	60.00	90.00
1957(BA)	43,000	—	25.00	55.00	85.00	100
Note: Issued to commemorate the 1958 Barcelona Exposition with "BA" replacing the star on left side of the reverse						
1957 (59)	42,185,000	—	0.30	1.50	25.00	45.00
1957 (61)	24,120,000	—	2.50	30.00	125	175
1957 (64)	42,200,000	—	0.15	1.50	18.00	25.00
1957 (65)	20,000,000	—	0.20	1.00	3.50	10.00
1957 (66)	15,000,000	—	0.20	1.00	5.00	10.00
1957 (67)	20,000,000	—	0.15	1.50	12.00	20.00
1957 (68)	30,000,000	—	0.20	1.00	2.50	5.00
1957 (69)	24,000,000	—	0.30	0.75	2.00	3.00
1957 (70)	25,000,000	—	0.20	1.00	5.00	7.00
1957 (71)	7,800,000	—	1.00	10.00	35.00	50.00
1957 (72)	4,733,000	—	0.20	0.75	4.00	8.00
1957 (72) Proof	30,000	Value: 10.00				
	23,000	Value: 10.00				
1957 (73) Proof	25,000	Value: 80.00				
1957 (74)	5,000,000	—	0.30	0.65	4.00	6.00
1957 (74) Proof	23,000	Value: 10.00				
1957 (75)	10,270,000	—	0.30	0.65	2.25	3.00
1957 (75) Proof	75,000	Value: 3.50				

KM# 808 25 PESETAS
8.5000 g., Copper-Nickel, 26.5 mm. **Ruler:** Juan Carlos I **Obv:** Head left **Rev:** Crown above value **Edge Lettering:** UNA GRANDE LIBRE

Date	Mintage	F	VF	XF	Unc	BU
1975 (76)	35,707,000	—	0.20	0.25	0.75	1.00
1975 (76) Proof	—	Value: 1.00				
1975 (77)	46,690,000	—	0.20	0.25	0.75	1.00
1975 (77) Proof	Inc. above	Value: 1.00				
1975 (78)	97,555,000	—	0.20	0.25	2.00	3.00
1975 (79)	172,000,000	—	0.20	0.25	0.75	1.00
1975 (79) Proof	—	Value: 1.00				
1975 (80)	136,000,000	—	0.20	0.25	2.50	5.00

KM# 818 25 PESETAS
8.5000 g., Copper-Nickel, 26.5 mm. **Ruler:** Juan Carlos I **Subject:** World Cup Soccer Games **Obv:** Head left **Rev:** Soccer ball on net above value **Edge Lettering:** UNA GRANDE LIBRE

Date	Mintage	F	VF	XF	Unc	BU
1980 (80)	35,000,000	—	0.20	0.30	0.60	0.75
1980 (80) Proof	—	Value: 1.50				
1980 (81)	117,000,000	—	0.20	0.30	0.75	1.00
1980 (82)	100,000,000	—	0.20	0.30	1.00	2.00

KM# 824 25 PESETAS
8.5000 g., Copper-Nickel, 26.5 mm. **Ruler:** Juan Carlos I **Obv:** Head left **Rev:** Crown above value **Edge:** Reeded **Note:** Mint mark: Crowned M; Similar to KM#808.

Date	Mintage	F	VF	XF	Unc	BU
1982	146,000,000	—	0.20	0.30	2.00	3.00
1983	248,000,000	—	0.30	0.45	1.50	2.25
1984	242,000,000	—	0.20	0.30	3.50	5.00

KM# 850 25 PESETAS
Nickel-Bronze, 19.5 mm. **Ruler:** Juan Carlos I **Subject:** 1992 Olympics **Obv:** Discus thrower to right of center hole **Rev:** Center hole divides value, Olympic rings below

Date	Mintage	F	VF	XF	Unc	BU
1990	150,000,000	—	0.25	0.30	1.25	1.50
1991	Inc. above	—	0.20	0.25	3.50	6.50

KM# 851 25 PESETAS
Nickel-Bronze, 19.5 mm. **Ruler:** Juan Carlos I **Subject:** 1992 Olympics **Obv:** Center hole divides letters and bust left **Rev:** High jumper to upper right of center hole **Edge:** Plain

Date	Mintage	F	VF	XF	Unc	BU
1990	Inc. above	—	—	—	0.95	1.50
1991	87,000,000	—	—	—	2.50	3.00

KM# 904 25 PESETAS
Nickel-Bronze, 19.5 mm. **Ruler:** Juan Carlos I **Subject:** Giralda Tower of Sevilla **Obv:** Center hole divides letters and bust left **Rev:** Center hole divides tower and value

Date	Mintage	F	VF	XF	Unc	BU
1992	179,833,000	—	—	—	2.50	3.00

KM# 905 25 PESETAS
Nickel-Bronze, 19.5 mm. **Ruler:** Juan Carlos I **Subject:** Tower of Gold in Seville **Obv:** Globe design around center hole **Rev:** Center hole divides tower and vertical letters **Edge:** Plain

Date	Mintage	F	VF	XF	Unc	BU
1992	Inc. above	—	—	—	1.00	1.25

KM# 920 25 PESETAS
Nickel-Bronze, 19.5 mm. **Ruler:** Juan Carlos I **Subject:** Vasc Country **Obv:** Center hole divides inscription, date and design **Rev:** Center hole divides value and buildings

Date	Mintage	F	VF	XF	Unc	BU
1993	150,012,000	—	—	—	0.80	1.00

KM# 933 25 PESETAS
Nickel-Bronze, 19.5 mm. **Ruler:** Juan Carlos I **Subject:** Canary Islands **Obv:** Center hole divides inscription, date and flowers **Rev:** Center hole divides value, design and inscription **Edge:** Plain

Date	Mintage	F	VF	XF	Unc	BU
1994	242,566,000	—	—	—	0.60	0.75

KM# 948 25 PESETAS
Brass, 19.5 mm. **Ruler:** Juan Carlos I **Subject:** Castilla and Leon **Obv:** Center hole divides tower and inscription **Rev:** Center hole divides stylized animal figures, value and inscription **Edge:** Plain

Date	Mintage	F	VF	XF	Unc	BU
1995	221,963,000	—	—	—	1.00	1.25
1995 without Y	Inc. above	—	—	45.00	65.00	80.00

KM# 962 25 PESETAS
Copper-Zinc-Nickel, 19.5 mm. **Ruler:** Juan Carlos I **Subject:** Castilla - La Mancha - Don Quiote **Obv:** Center hole divides figure on horse, design and inscription **Rev:** Center hole divides design, inscription and value **Edge:** Plain

Date	Mintage	F	VF	XF	Unc	BU
1996	37,403,000	—	—	—	0.45	0.70

KM# 983 25 PESETAS
Brass, 19.5 mm. **Ruler:** Juan Carlos I **Subject:** Melilla **Obv:** Center hole divides towered buildings **Rev:** Center hole divides ancient amphora and dates **Edge:** Plain

Date	Mintage	F	VF	XF	Unc	BU
1997	461,688,000	—	—	—	0.45	0.70

KM# 990 25 PESETAS
Copper-Zinc-Nickel, 19.5 mm. **Ruler:** Juan Carlos I **Subject:** Ceuta **Obv:** Center hole right of ornamented building corner **Rev:** Center hole divides statue on wall shelf and value **Edge:** Plain

Date	Mintage	F	VF	XF	Unc	BU
1998	184,360,000	—	—	—	0.50	0.80

KM# 1007 25 PESETAS
Nickel-Brass, 19.5 mm. **Ruler:** Juan Carlos I **Subject:** Navarra **Obv:** Center hole between castle towers **Rev:** Man running from bull, value and shield, all around center hole **Edge:** Plain

Date	Mintage	F	VF	XF	Unc	BU
1999	2,130,000	—	—	—	2.00	3.00

KM# 1013 25 PESETAS
Nickel-Brass, 19.5 mm. **Ruler:** Juan Carlos I **Subject:** Navarra **Obv:** Center hole divides bust left and vertical letters **Rev:** Crowned above center hole, order collar at right, value at left **Edge:** Plain

Date	Mintage	F	VF	XF	Unc	BU
2000	—	—	—	—	1.00	1.50

KM# 788 50 PESETAS
12.3500 g., Copper-Nickel, 30 mm. **Ruler:** Caudillo and regent **Obv:** Head right **Rev:** Crowned shield within flying bird **Edge Lettering:** UNA GRANDE LIBRE

Date	Mintage	F	VF	XF	Unc	BU
1957 (BA)	Est. 43,000	—	22.00	40.00	60.00	100
Note: Issued to commemorate the 1958 Barcelona Exposition with "BA" replacing the star on left side of reverse						
1957 (58)	21,471,000	—	0.50	0.75	2.50	3.50
1957 (58)	Inc. above	—	—	250	500	700
Note: Edge variety with UNA - LIBRE - GRANDE						
1957 (59)	28,000,000	—	0.50	0.75	2.50	3.50
1957 (60)	24,800,000	—	0.50	0.75	2.50	3.50
1957 (67)	850,000	—	0.50	2.00	8.00	10.00
1957 (68)	1,000	—	—	—	—	1,000
Note: In sets only						
1957 (69)	1,200	—	—	—	—	1,000
Note: In sets only						
1957 (70)	19,000	—	—	—	—	200
Note: In sets only						
1957(71)	4,400,000	—	0.65	2.50	18.50	35.00
1957 (72) Proof	23,000	Value: 35.00				
1957 (73) Proof	28,000	Value: 60.00				
1957 (74) Proof	25,000	Value: 60.00				
1957 (75) Proof	75,000	Value: 12.00				

KM# 809 50 PESETAS
12.3500 g., Copper-Nickel, 30 mm. **Ruler:** Juan Carlos I **Obv:** Head left **Rev:** Crossed scepters and shield within order collar, crown above

Date	Mintage	F	VF	XF	Unc	BU
1975 (76)	4,400,000	—	0.50	0.65	1.20	1.50
1975 (76) Proof	—	Value: 2.00				
1975 (78)	17,555,000	—	0.50	0.75	2.50	3.00
1975 (79)	33,000,000	—	0.50	0.60	1.00	1.50
1975 (79) Proof	—	Value: 2.00				
1975 (80)	34,000,000	—	0.50	0.60	3.50	4.50

KM# 819 50 PESETAS
12.3500 g., Copper-Nickel, 30 mm. **Ruler:** Juan Carlos I **Subject:** World Cup Soccer Games **Obv:** Head left **Rev:** Soccer ball above value **Edge Lettering:** UNA GRANDE LIBRE

Date	Mintage	F	VF	XF	Unc	BU
1980 (80)	15,000,000	—	0.50	0.60	0.75	0.85
1980 (80) Proof	—	Value: 2.00				
1980 (81)	38,300,000	—	0.50	0.60	1.35	1.50
1980 (82)	30,950,000	—	0.50	0.60	2.00	2.50

KM# 825 50 PESETAS
12.3500 g., Copper-Nickel, 30 mm. **Ruler:** Juan Carlos I **Obv:** Head left **Rev:** Crossed scepters and shield within order collar, crown above **Note:** Mint mark: Crowned M.

Date	Mintage	F	VF	XF	Unc	BU
1982	27,000,000	—	0.50	1.00	2.50	4.50
1983	93,000,000	—	0.50	1.00	2.00	3.00
1984	17,500,000	5.00	12.00	20.00	40.00	70.00

KM# 852 50 PESETAS
Copper-Nickel, 20.3 mm. **Ruler:** Juan Carlos I **Subject:** Expo '92 **Obv:** Bust left **Rev:** Globe and value **Edge:** Notched

Date	Mintage	F	VF	XF	Unc	BU
1990	25,234,000	—	—	—	1.00	1.25

KM# 853 50 PESETAS
Copper-Nickel, 20.3 mm. **Ruler:** Juan Carlos I **Subject:** Expo '92 **Obv:** City view **Rev:** Globe and value **Edge:** Notched

Date	Mintage	F	VF	XF	Unc	BU
1990	7,916,000	—	—	—	1.00	1.25

KM# 906 50 PESETAS
Copper-Nickel, 20.3 mm. **Ruler:** Juan Carlos I **Subject:** 1992 Olympics **Obv:** "La Pedrera" building **Rev:** Pointed designs above Olympic rings, value at left **Edge:** Notched

Date	Mintage	F	VF	XF	Unc	BU
1992	40,370,000	—	—	—	1.00	1.25

KM# 907 50 PESETAS
Copper-Nickel, 20.3 mm. **Ruler:** Juan Carlos I **Subject:** 1992 Olympics **Obv:** Bust left **Rev:** Cathedral Sagrada Famillia (Gaudi) **Edge:** Notched

Date	Mintage	F	VF	XF	Unc	BU
1992	Inc. above	—	—	—	1.00	1.25

KM# 921 50 PESETAS
Copper-Nickel, 20.3 mm. **Ruler:** Juan Carlos I **Subject:** Extremadura **Obv:** Bridge **Rev:** Tower **Edge:** Notched

Date	Mintage	F	VF	XF	Unc	BU
1993	24,314,000	—	—	—	1.00	1.25

KM# 934 50 PESETAS
Copper-Nickel, 20.3 mm. **Ruler:** Juan Carlos I **Subject:** Altamira Cave Paintings **Obv:** Building **Rev:** Stylized design above value **Edge:** Notched

Date	Mintage	F	VF	XF	Unc	BU
1994	3,002,000	—	—	—	2.25	3.00

KM# 949 50 PESETAS
Copper-Nickel, 20.3 mm. **Ruler:** Juan Carlos I **Subject:** Alcala Gate **Obv:** Partial building and date **Rev:** Steepled buildings **Edge:** Notched

Date	Mintage	F	VF	XF	Unc	BU
1995	1,001,000	—	—	—	4.00	5.00

KM# 963 50 PESETAS
Copper-Nickel, 20.3 mm. **Ruler:** Juan Carlos I **Subject:** Philip V **Obv:** Head facing **Rev:** Shield divides value and letters, crown above divides date **Edge:** Notched

Date	Mintage	F	VF	XF	Unc	BU
1996	11,047,000	—	—	—	0.75	1.00

KM# 985 50 PESETAS
Copper-Nickel, 20.3 mm. **Ruler:** Juan Carlos I **Subject:** Juan De Herrera **Obv:** Head left **Rev:** Escorial Monastery **Edge:** Notched

Date	Mintage	F	VF	XF	Unc	BU
1997	17,496,000	—	—	—	1.00	1.25

KM# 991 50 PESETAS
Copper-Nickel, 20.3 mm. **Ruler:** Juan Carlos I **Obv:** Bust left **Rev:** Crossed scepters and shield within order chain, crown above, value at left **Edge:** Notched

Date	Mintage	F	VF	XF	Unc	BU
1998	17,496,000	—	—	—	1.00	1.50
1999	2,100,000	—	—	—	2.25	3.00
2000	—	—	—	—	2.00	2.50

KM# 797 100 PESETAS
19.0000 g., 0.8000 Silver .4887 oz. ASW **Ruler:** Caudillo and regent **Obv:** Head right **Rev:** Assorted emblems within flower design, crown on top **Edge Lettering:** UNA GRANDE LIBRE

Date	Mintage	F	VF	XF	Unc	BU
1966 (66)	15,045,000	—	BV	BV	7.50	9.00
1966 (67)	15,000,000	—	BV	BV	7.50	9.00
1966 (68)	24,000,000	—	BV	BV	7.50	9.00
1966 (69)	1,000,000	—	—	175	350	450
Note: 69 with straight 9 in star						
1966 (69)	Inc. above	—	—	75.00	125	150
Note: 69 with curved 9 in star						
1966 (70)	995,000	BV	7.50	10.00	20.00	25.00
Note: 1966(69) coins heavily altered; authentication recommended						

KM# 810 100 PESETAS
Copper-Nickel **Ruler:** Juan Carlos I **Obv:** Head left **Rev:** Crowned shield flanked by pillars with banner

Date	Mintage	F	VF	XF	Unc	BU
1975 (76)	4,400,000	—	0.75	1.00	1.50	2.00
1975 (76) Proof	—	Value: 3.00				

KM# 820 100 PESETAS
Copper-Nickel **Ruler:** Juan Carlos I **Subject:** World Cup Soccer Games - Spain '82 **Obv:** Head left **Rev:** Value in center of assorted emblems

Date	Mintage	F	VF	XF	Unc	BU
1980 (80)	20,000,000	—	—	0.75	1.00	1.50
1980 (80) Proof	—	Value: 3.00				

KM# 826 100 PESETAS
9.3000 g., Aluminum-Bronze, 24.5 mm. **Ruler:** Juan Carlos I **Obv:** Head left **Rev:** Crowned shield flanked by pillars with banner **Edge:** Fleur-de-lis repeated

Date	Mintage	F	VF	XF	Unc	BU
1982	117,600,000	—	0.75	1.25	3.50	5.00
1982 Proof	—	Value: 5.00				
1983	—	—	0.75	1.25	30.00	50.00
1984	208,000,000	—	0.75	1.25	6.00	10.00
1985	118,000,000	—	0.75	1.25	10.00	15.00
1986	160,000,000	—	0.75	1.25	3.00	4.00
1988	125,674,000	—	0.75	1.25	4.00	6.00
1989	80,877,000	—	0.75	1.25	2.50	3.00
1990	25,636,000	—	0.75	1.25	5.00	7.00

Note: Varieties exist

KM# 834 100 PESETAS
1.6800 g., 0.9250 Silver .0500 oz. ASW **Ruler:** Juan Carlos I **Subject:** Discovery of America **Obv:** Crown within beaded circle **Rev:** Mayan pyramid within beaded circle

Date	Mintage	F	VF	XF	Unc	BU
1989	43,000	—	—	—	—	5.00
1989 Proof	57,000	Value: 6.00				

KM# 854 100 PESETAS
1.6800 g., 0.9250 Silver .0500 oz. ASW **Ruler:** Juan Carlos I **Obv:** Bust of Brother Juniper Serra 3/4 right **Rev:** Mission ruins within legend

Date	Mintage	F	VF	XF	Unc	BU
1990	24,000	—	—	—	—	6.00
1990 Proof	27,000	Value: 6.00				

KM# 882 100 PESETAS
1.6800 g., 0.9250 Silver .0500 oz. ASW **Ruler:** Juan Carlos I **Obv:** bust of Celestino Mutis 1/4 right **Rev:** Flower plant within beaded circle

Date	Mintage	F	VF	XF	Unc	BU
1991	14,000	—	—	—	—	8.00
1991 Proof	—	Value: 8.50				

KM# 908 100 PESETAS
9.3000 g., Aluminum-Bronze, 24.5 mm. **Ruler:** Juan Carlos I **Rev:** Crowned shield flanked by pillars with banner

Date	Mintage	F	VF	XF	Unc	BU
1992	22,661,000	—	—	—	4.00	5.00

Note: Edge varieties exist with positioning of fleur-de-lis

KM# 993 100 PESETAS
1.6800 g., 0.9250 Silver .0500 oz. ASW **Ruler:** Juan Carlos I **Subject:** Seville Expo '92 **Obv:** Arched bridge **Rev:** Bridge

Date	Mintage	F	VF	XF	Unc	BU
1992	16,000	—	—	—	—	9.50
1992 Proof	16,000	Value: 10.00				

KM# 922 100 PESETAS
9.3000 g., Nickel-Brass, 24.5 mm. **Ruler:** Juan Carlos I **Subject:** European unity **Obv:** Value within map **Rev:** Radiant sun within star circle

Date	Mintage	F	VF	XF	Unc	BU
1993	39,723,000	—	—	—	3.00	5.00

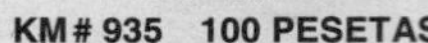

KM# 935 100 PESETAS
9.3000 g., Nickel-Brass, 24.5 mm. **Ruler:** Juan Carlos I **Subject:** Museo del Prado **Obv:** Head left **Rev:** Statue in front of museum **Edge:** Fleur-de-lis repeated

Date	Mintage	F	VF	XF	Unc	BU
1994	24,853,000	—	—	—	2.50	3.50

KM# 950 100 PESETAS
9.3000 g., Copper-Nickel, 24.5 mm. **Ruler:** Juan Carlos I **Series:** F.A.O. **Obv:** Head left **Rev:** Oat sprig, value and F.A.O. logo **Edge:** Fleur-de-lis repeated

Date	Mintage	F	VF	XF	Unc	BU
1995	71,957,000	—	—	—	2.00	3.00

KM# 964 100 PESETAS
9.3000 g., Copper-Zinc-Nickel, 24.5 mm. **Ruler:** Juan Carlos I **Obv:** Head left **Rev:** National Library **Edge:** Fleur-de-lis repeated

Date	Mintage	F	VF	XF	Unc	BU
1996	21,466,000	—	—	—	2.50	3.50

KM# 984 100 PESETAS
9.3000 g., Copper-Zinc-Nickel, 24.5 mm. **Ruler:** Juan Carlos I **Subject:** Royal Theatre **Obv:** Head left **Rev:** Building

Date	Mintage	F	VF	XF	Unc	BU
1997	29,480,000	—	—	—	2.00	3.00

KM# 989 100 PESETAS
9.3000 g., Aluminum-Bronze, 24.5 mm. **Ruler:** Juan Carlos I **Obv:** Head left **Rev:** Crowned shield flanked by pillars with banner **Edge:** Fleur-de-lis repeated

Date	Mintage	F	VF	XF	Unc	BU
1998	—	—	—	—	1.50	2.00
2000	—	—	—	—	2.00	2.50

KM# 1006 100 PESETAS
9.3000 g., Brass, 24.5 mm. **Ruler:** Juan Carlos I **Obv:** Head left **Rev:** Design above sprig and value **Edge:** Fleur-de-lis repeated

Date	Mintage	F	VF	XF	Unc	BU
1999	60,332,000	—	—	—	1.50	2.00

KM# 829 200 PESETAS
Copper-Nickel, 21.7 mm. **Ruler:** Juan Carlos I **Obv:** Head left **Rev:** Value divides sprigs

Date	Mintage	F	VF	XF	Unc	BU
1986	43,576,000	—	—	2.00	6.00	8.00
1987	66,718,000	—	—	2.00	12.00	16.00
1988	37,190,000	—	—	2.00	12.00	16.00

KM# 830 200 PESETAS
Copper-Nickel, 21.7 mm. **Ruler:** Juan Carlos I **Subject:** Madrid Numismatic Exposition **Obv:** Head left **Rev:** Value divides sprigs

Date	Mintage	F	VF	XF	Unc	BU
1987 (E87) Proof	60,000	Value: 55.00				

KM# 835 200 PESETAS
3.3700 g., 0.9250 Silver .1000 oz. ASW **Ruler:** Juan Carlos I **Subject:** Discovery of America **Obv:** Crown above monogram within beaded circle **Rev:** Astrolobe within beaded circle

Date	Mintage	F	VF	XF	Unc	BU
1989	43,000	—	—	—	—	7.00
1989 Proof	57,000	Value: 8.00				

KM# 855 200 PESETAS
Copper-Nickel, 25.5 mm. **Ruler:** Juan Carlos I **Obv:** Conjoined busts of King and Crown Prince right **Rev:** Pair of lions pulling seated figure on barrel within circle

Date	Mintage	F	VF	XF	Unc	BU
1990	8,000,000	—	—	—	7.00	8.00

KM# 856 200 PESETAS
3.3700 g., 0.9250 Silver .1000 oz. ASW **Ruler:** Juan Carlos I **Subject:** History in Common-Alonso de Frcilla **Obv:** Bust left **Rev:** Hand writing in a book within inner circle

Date	Mintage	F	VF	XF	Unc	BU
1990	24,000	—	—	—	—	8.00
1990 Proof	27,000	Value: 8.00				

KM# 883 200 PESETAS
3.3700 g., 0.9250 Silver .1000 oz. ASW **Ruler:** Juan Carlos I **Subject:** Las Casas **Obv:** Bust left within beaded circle **Rev:** 3 Indian figures within beaded circle

Date	Mintage	F	VF	XF	Unc	BU
1991	14,000	—	—	—	—	9.50
1991 Proof	14,000	Value: 10.00				

KM# 884 200 PESETAS
Copper-Nickel, 25.5 mm. **Ruler:** Juan Carlos I **Subject:** Madrid - European Culture Capital **Obv:** Conjoined busts of King and Crown Prince right **Rev:** Pair of lions pulling seated figure on barrel within circle

Date	Mintage	F	VF	XF	Unc	BU
1991	11,400,000	—	—	—	2.00	3.00

KM# 884a 200 PESETAS
12.2500 g., 0.9250 Silver .3643 oz. ASW **Ruler:** Juan Carlos I **Subject:** Madrid - European Culture Capital **Obv:** Conjoined busts of King and Crown Prince right **Rev:** Pair of lions pulling seated figure on barrel within circle

Date	Mintage	F	VF	XF	Unc	BU
1992 Proof	38,000	Value: 150				

KM# 909 200 PESETAS
Copper-Nickel, 25.5 mm. **Ruler:** Juan Carlos I **Subject:** Madrid - European Culture Capital **Obv:** Conjoined busts of King and Crown Prince right **Rev:** Equestrian within circle

Date	Mintage	F	VF	XF	Unc	BU
1992	Inc. above	—	—	—	3.00	3.50

KM# 910 200 PESETAS
Copper-Nickel, 25.5 mm. **Ruler:** Juan Carlos I **Subject:** Madrid - European Culture Capital **Obv:** Conjoined busts of King and Crown Prince right **Rev:** Upright bear by tree within circle

Date	Mintage	F	VF	XF	Unc	BU
1992	Inc. above	—	—	—	3.00	3.50

KM# 994 200 PESETAS
3.3700 g., 0.9250 Silver .1000 oz. ASW **Ruler:** Juan Carlos I **Subject:** Seville Expo '92 **Obv:** Hydro-electric dam within beaded circle **Rev:** Tower of Seville within beaded circle

Date	Mintage	F	VF	XF	Unc	BU
1992	17,000	—	—	—	—	12.00
1992	16,000	Value: 12.50				

KM# 923 200 PESETAS
Copper-Nickel, 25.5 mm. **Ruler:** Juan Carlos I **Subject:** Juan Luis Vives **Obv:** Feather and designs within circle **Rev:** Bust facing and crowned design within circle

Date	Mintage	F	VF	XF	Unc	BU
1993	2,811,000	—	—	—	6.00	7.00

KM# 936 200 PESETAS
Copper-Nickel, 25.5 mm. **Ruler:** Juan Carlos I **Subject:** Velasquez and Goya Paintings **Obv:** Three figures within circle **Rev:** Kneeling figures with umbrella within circle

Date	Mintage	F	VF	XF	Unc	BU
1994	2,997,000	—	—	—	4.00	5.00

KM# 951 200 PESETAS
Copper-Nickel, 25.5 mm. **Ruler:** Juan Carlos I **Subject:** Murillo and El Greco paintings **Obv:** Standing figures within circle **Rev:** Child and lamb within circle

Date	Mintage	F	VF	XF	Unc	BU
1995	1,022,000	—	—	—	12.00	24.00

KM# 965 200 PESETAS
Copper-Nickel, 25.5 mm. **Ruler:** Juan Carlos I **Subject:** Fortuny and Balleau paintings **Obv:** Seated figure blowing on instrument within circle **Rev:** Seated figure playing guitar within circle

Date	Mintage	F	VF	XF	Unc	BU
1996	9,206,000	—	—	—	2.00	3.00

KM# 986 200 PESETAS
Copper-Nickel, 25.5 mm. **Ruler:** Juan Carlos I **Subject:** Jacinto Benavente **Obv:** Stylized books within circle **Rev:** Bust left within circle

Date	Mintage	F	VF	XF	Unc	BU
1997	6,845,000	—	—	—	3.00	4.00

KM# 992 200 PESETAS
Copper-Nickel, 25.5 mm. **Ruler:** Juan Carlos I **Obv:** Conjoined busts of King and Crown Prince right **Rev:** Value within circle

Date	Mintage	F	VF	XF	Unc	BU
1998	5,008,000	—	—	—	2.00	3.50
1999	—	—	—	—	4.00	6.00
2000	—	—	—	—	5.00	7.00

KM# 831 500 PESETAS
Copper-Aluminum-Nickel **Ruler:** Juan Carlos I **Obv:** Conjoined heads of Juan Carlos and Sofia left **Rev:** Crowned shield flanked by pillars with banner, vertical value at right

Date	Mintage	F	VF	XF	Unc	BU
1987	400,000,000	—	—	3.50	10.00	12.00
1987 Proof	Inc. above	Value: 10.00				
1988	81,309,000	—	—	3.50	9.00	11.00
1989	103,861,000	—	—	3.50	5.00	6.00
1990	28,372,000	—	—	2.25	7.00	12.00

KM# 836 500 PESETAS
6.7500 g., 0.9250 Silver .2008 oz. ASW **Ruler:** Juan Carlos I **Subject:** Discovery of America - Juego De Pelota Game **Obv:** Head facing within beaded circle **Rev:** Kneeling masked figure within beaded circle

Date	Mintage	F	VF	XF	Unc	BU
1989	43,000	—	—	—	—	10.00
1989 Proof	57,000	Value: 10.00				

KM# 857 500 PESETAS
6.7500 g., 0.9250 Silver .2008 oz. ASW **Ruler:** Juan Carlos I **Subject:** Juan de la Cosa **Obv:** Bust with hat facing within beaded circle **Rev:** Ocean navigation map within legend

Date	Mintage	F	VF	XF	Unc	BU
1990	24,000	—	—	—	—	12.00
1990 Proof	27,000	Value: 12.00				

KM# 885 500 PESETAS
6.7500 g., 0.9250 Silver .2008 oz. ASW **Ruler:** Juan Carlos I **Obv:** Bust of Jorge Juan 1/4 left within beaded circle **Rev:** World globe map within beaded circle

Date	Mintage	F	VF	XF	Unc	BU
1991	14,000	—	—	—	—	16.00
1991 Proof	14,000	Value: 16.00				

KM# 995 500 PESETAS
6.7500 g., 0.9250 Silver .2008 oz. ASW **Ruler:** Juan Carlos I **Subject:** Seville Expo '92 **Obv:** Church within beaded circle **Rev:** Palace portal within beaded circle

Date	Mintage	F	VF	XF	Unc	BU
1992	17,000	—	—	—	—	20.00
1992 Proof	16,000	Value: 20.00				

KM# 924 500 PESETAS
Copper-Aluminum-Nickel **Ruler:** Juan Carlos I **Obv:** Conjoined heads of Juan Carlos and Sofia left **Rev:** Crowned shield flanked by pillars with banner, vertical value at right

Date	Mintage	F	VF	XF	Unc	BU
1993	3,059,000	—	—	—	16.50	30.00
1994	3,041,000	—	—	—	23.00	40.00
1995	1,015,000	—	—	—	18.00	35.00
1996	1,031,000	—	—	—	10.50	20.00
1997	4,881,000	—	—	—	6.00	8.00
1998	5,161,000	—	—	—	7.00	9.00
1999	2,030,000	—	—	—	8.00	10.00
2000	—	—	—	—	8.00	10.00

KM# 837 1000 PESETAS
13.5000 g., 0.9250 Silver .4015 oz. ASW **Ruler:** Juan Carlos I **Subject:** Discovery of America - Capture of Granada **Obv:** Standing figure divides date and beaded circle **Rev:** Armored figures on horses within beaded circle

Date	Mintage	F	VF	XF	Unc	BU
1989	43,000	—	—	—	—	12.50
1989 Proof	57,000	Value: 12.50				

KM# 858 1000 PESETAS
13.5000 g., 0.9250 Silver .4015 oz. ASW **Ruler:** Juan Carlos I **Subject:** Magallanes and Elcano **Obv:** Busts facing above ships wheel **Rev:** Primitive global world map within legend

Date	Mintage	F	VF	XF	Unc	BU
1990	24,000	—	—	—	—	15.00
1990 Proof	27,000	Value: 15.00				

KM# 886 1000 PESETAS
13.5000 g., 0.9250 Silver .4015 oz. ASW **Ruler:** Juan Carlos I **Subject:** Simon Bolivar and San Martin **Obv:** Figure on horse within beaded circle **Rev:** Bust facing within beaded circle

Date	Mintage	F	VF	XF	Unc	BU
1991	14,000	—	—	—	—	20.00
1991 Proof	14,000	Value: 20.00				

KM# 996 1000 PESETAS
13.5000 g., 0.9250 Silver .4015 oz. ASW **Ruler:** Juan Carlos I **Subject:** Seville Expo '92 **Obv:** Expo buildings within beaded circle **Rev:** India's archives building within beaded circle

Date	Mintage	F	VF	XF	Unc	BU
1992	17,000	—	—	—	—	25.00
1992 Proof	16,000	Value: 25.00				

KM# 952 1000 PESETAS
13.6600 g., 0.9250 Silver .4062 oz. ASW **Ruler:** Juan Carlos I **Subject:** 1996 Olympics **Obv:** Head left **Rev:** Stylized figure, torch and value

Date	Mintage	F	VF	XF	Unc	BU
1995 Proof	67,743	Value: 25.00				

KM# 973 1000 PESETAS
13.6600 g., 0.9250 Silver .4062 oz. ASW **Ruler:** Juan Carlos I **Subject:** Olympics **Obv:** Head left **Rev:** Three divers

Date	Mintage	F	VF	XF	Unc	BU
1996 Proof	30,000	Value: 25.00				

KM# 988 1000 PESETAS
13.5000 g., 0.9250 Silver .4015 oz. ASW **Ruler:** Juan Carlos I **Subject:** Soccer World Championship - France '98 **Obv:** Head left **Rev:** Two soccer players

Date	Mintage	F	VF	XF	Unc	BU
1998 Proof	30,000	Value: 30.00				

KM# 1000 1000 PESETAS
13.5000 g., 0.9250 Silver .4015 oz. ASW **Ruler:** Juan Carlos I **Subject:** Expo '98 Lisbon **Obv:** Head left **Rev:** Sailing ship

Date	Mintage	F	VF	XF	Unc	BU
1998 Proof	50,000	Value: 22.50				

KM# 1034 1000 PESETAS
13.5000 g., 0.9250 Silver 0.4015 oz. ASW, 32.9 mm. **Ruler:** Juan Carlos I **Subject:** Constitution **Obv:** Head left **Rev:** Building **Edge:** Reeded

Date	Mintage	F	VF	XF	Unc	BU
1998Crowned M Proof	75,000	Value: 25.00				

KM# 1009 1000 PESETAS
13.5000 g., 0.9250 Silver .4015 oz. ASW **Ruler:** Juan Carlos I **Subject:** Olympics - Sidney 2000 **Obv:** Head left **Rev:** Water polo players **Rev. Designer:** Esther Gonzalez **Edge:** Plain

Date	Mintage	F	VF	XF	Unc	BU
1999 Proof	50,000	Value: 22.50				

KM# 1010 1500 PESETAS
19.8300 g., 0.9250 Silver .5897 oz. ASW **Ruler:** Juan Carlos I **Subject:** Millennium **Obv:** Head left within beaded border **Rev:** Space walking astronaut above Columbus's ships **Edge:** Plain **Shape:** Octagon

Date	Mintage	F	VF	XF	Unc	BU
1999 Proof	50,000	Value: 25.00				

KM# 1039 1500 PESETAS
20.0000 g., 0.9250 Silver 0.5948 oz. ASW, 33 mm. **Ruler:** Juan Carlos I **Subject:** Millennium **Obv:** Head left **Rev:** Dove above Atlantic Ocean **Edge:** Plain **Shape:** Octagon

Date	Mintage	F	VF	XF	Unc	BU
2000Crowned M Proof	30,000	Value: 30.00				

KM# 1035 1500 PESETAS
20.0000 g., 0.9250 Silver, 33 mm. **Ruler:** Juan Carlos I **Subject:** Printing **Obv:** Head left **Rev:** Antique printing press **Edge:** Plain **Shape:** Octagon

Date	Mintage	F	VF	XF	Unc	BU
2000Crowned M Proof	30,000	Value: 30.00				

KM# 838 2000 PESETAS
27.0000 g., 0.9250 Silver .8031 oz. ASW **Ruler:** Juan Carlos I **Subject:** Discovery of America **Obv:** Busts facing each other within beaded circle **Rev:** Head of Columbus 1/4 left within beaded circle

Date	Mintage	F	VF	XF	Unc	BU
1989	43,000	—	—	—	—	22.50
1989 Proof	57,000	Value: 22.50				

KM# 859 2000 PESETAS
27.0000 g., 0.9250 Silver .8031 oz. ASW **Ruler:** Juan Carlos I
Subject: 1992 Olympics **Obv:** Conjoined busts of King and Crown Prince right **Rev:** Symbols

Date	Mintage	F	VF	XF	Unc	BU
1990	52,524	—	—	—	—	20.00
1990 Proof	130,993	Value: 20.00				

Note: See note below KM#914

KM# 861 2000 PESETAS
26.7000 g., 0.9250 Silver .7940 oz. ASW **Ruler:** Juan Carlos I
Subject: 1992 Olympics **Obv:** Conjoined busts of King and Crown Prince right **Rev:** Archer

Date	Mintage	F	VF	XF	Unc	BU
1990	26,843	—	—	—	—	20.00
1990 Proof	87,655	Value: 20.00				

Note: Uncirculated strikes have medallic die alignment and edges with reeded and plain sections; Proof strikes have coin die alignment and reeded edges

KM# 862 2000 PESETAS
26.7000 g., 0.9250 Silver .7940 oz. ASW **Ruler:** Juan Carlos I
Subject: 1992 Olympics **Obv:** Conjoined busts of King and Crown Prince right **Rev:** Soccer player

Date	Mintage	F	VF	XF	Unc	BU
1990	Est. 19,638	—	—	—	—	20.00
1990 Proof	Est. 104,351	Value: 20.00				

Note: Uncirculated strikes have medallic die alignment and edges with reeded and plain sections; Proof strikes have coin die alignment and reeded edges

KM# 863 2000 PESETAS
26.7000 g., 0.9250 Silver .7940 oz. ASW **Ruler:** Juan Carlos I
Subject: 1992 Olympics **Obv:** Conjoined busts of King and Crown Prince right **Rev:** Human pyramid

Date	Mintage	F	VF	XF	Unc	BU
1990	Est. 16,332	—	—	—	—	22.50
1990 Proof	Est. 73,510	Value: 22.50				

Note: Uncirculated strikes have medallic die alignment and edges with reeded and plain sections; Proof strikes have coin die alignment and reeded edges

KM# 864 2000 PESETAS
26.7000 g., 0.9250 Silver .7940 oz. ASW **Ruler:** Juan Carlos I
Subject: 1992 Olympics **Obv:** Conjoined busts of King and Crown Prince right **Rev:** Greek runner

Date	Mintage	F	VF	XF	Unc	BU
1990	Est. 15,407	—	—	—	—	25.00
1990 Proof	Est. 73,469	Value: 25.00				

Note: Uncirculated strikes have medallic die alignment and edges with reeded and plain sections; Proof strikes have coin die alignment and reeded edges

KM# 865 2000 PESETAS
26.7000 g., 0.9250 Silver .7940 oz. ASW **Ruler:** Juan Carlos I
Subject: 1992 Olympics **Obv:** Conjoined busts of King and Crown Prince right **Rev:** Ancient boat

Date	Mintage	F	VF	XF	Unc	BU
1990	Est. 14,223	—	—	—	—	25.00
1990 Proof	Est. 53,835	Value: 25.00				

Note: Uncirculated strikes have medallic die alignment and edges with reeded and plain sections; Proof strikes have coin die alignment and reeded edges

KM# 866 2000 PESETAS
26.7000 g., 0.9250 Silver .7940 oz. ASW **Ruler:** Juan Carlos I
Subject: 1992 Olympics **Obv:** Conjoined busts of King and Crown Prince right **Rev:** Basketball players

Date	Mintage	F	VF	XF	Unc	BU
1990	Est. 14,395	—	—	—	—	25.00
1990 Proof	Est. 56,356	Value: 25.00				

Note: Uncirculated strikes have medallic die alignment and edges with reeded and plain sections; Proof strikes have coin die alignment and reeded edges

KM# 867 2000 PESETAS
26.7000 g., 0.9250 Silver .7940 oz. ASW **Ruler:** Juan Carlos I
Subject: 1992 Olympics **Obv:** Conjoined busts of King and Crown Prince right **Rev:** Pelota player

Date	Mintage	F	VF	XF	Unc	BU
1990	Est. 12,554	—	—	—	—	25.00
1990 Proof	Est. 45,219	Value: 25.00				

Note: Uncirculated strikes have medallic die alignment and edges with reeded and plain sections; Proof strikes have coin die alignment and reeded edges

KM# 868 2000 PESETAS
26.7000 g., 0.9250 Silver .7940 oz. ASW **Ruler:** Juan Carlos I
Subject: Hidalgo, Morelos and Juarez **Obv:** Three busts facing **Rev:** Aztec pictorial design within legend

Date	Mintage	F	VF	XF	Unc	BU
1990	24,000	—	—	—	—	27.50
1990 Proof	27,000	Value: 27.50				

KM# 860 2000 PESETAS
26.7000 g., 0.9250 Silver .7940 oz. ASW **Ruler:** Juan Carlos I
Counterstamp: INUTILIZACION/OCTOBRE 1992 **Obv:** Conjoined busts of King and Crown Prince right **Rev:** Symbols and Olympic rings **Note:** Counterstamp on reverse below Olympic rings

Date	Mintage	F	VF	XF	Unc	BU
1990 "1992"; Proof	—	Value: 35.00				

Note: Uncirculated strikes have medallic die alignment and edges with reeded and plain sections; Proof strikes have coin die alignment and reeded edges

KM# 887 2000 PESETAS
26.7000 g., 0.9250 Silver .7940 oz. ASW **Ruler:** Juan Carlos I
Subject: Olympics **Obv:** Conjoined busts of King and Crown Prince right **Rev:** Torch, flag and Olympic rings

Date	Mintage	F	VF	XF	Unc	BU
1991	18,545	—	—	—	—	40.00
1991 Proof	78,192	Value: 40.00				

KM# 888 2000 PESETAS
26.7000 g., 0.9250 Silver .7940 oz. ASW **Ruler:** Juan Carlos I
Subject: Olympics **Obv:** Conjoined busts of King and Crown Prince right **Rev:** Tennis player

Date	Mintage	F	VF	XF	Unc	BU
1991	12,350	—	—	—	—	40.00
1991 Proof	38,905	Value: 40.00				

Note: Medal rotation

KM# 889 2000 PESETAS
26.7000 g., 0.9250 Silver .7940 oz. ASW **Ruler:** Juan Carlos I
Subject: Olympics **Obv:** Conjoined busts of King and Crown Prince right **Rev:** Medieval rider

Date	Mintage	F	VF	XF	Unc	BU
1991	15,056	—	—	—	—	40.00
1991 Proof	31,317	Value: 40.00				

Note: Medal rotation

KM# 890 2000 PESETAS
26.7000 g., 0.9250 Silver .7940 oz. ASW **Ruler:** Juan Carlos I
Subject: Olympics **Obv:** Conjoined busts of King and Crown Prince right **Rev:** Bowling

Date	Mintage	F	VF	XF	Unc	BU
1991	10,561	—	—	—	—	40.00
1991 Proof	35,447	Value: 40.00				

Note: Medal rotation

KM# 891 2000 PESETAS
26.7000 g., 0.9250 Silver .7940 oz. ASW **Ruler:** Juan Carlos I
Subject: Ibero - American Series **Obv:** Crowned shield flanked by pillars with banner in center of assorted shields **Rev:** Crown divides beaded circle with assorted designs in center

Date	Mintage	F	VF	XF	Unc	BU
(19)91 Proof	20,000	Value: 90.00				

KM# 892 2000 PESETAS
26.7000 g., 0.9250 Silver .7940 oz. ASW **Ruler:** Juan Carlos I
Subject: Federman, Quesada and Benalcazar **Obv:** Armored busts left within beaded circle **Rev:** Standing figures around armored figure on horse within beaded circle

Date	Mintage	F	VF	XF	Unc	BU
1991	14,000	—	—	—	—	25.00
1991 Proof	14,000	Value: 25.00				

KM# 911 2000 PESETAS
26.7000 g., 0.9250 Silver .7940 oz. ASW **Ruler:** Juan Carlos I
Subject: Olympics **Obv:** Conjoined busts of King and Crown Prince right **Rev:** Tug-of-war

Date	Mintage	F	VF	XF	Unc	BU
1992	9,043	—	—	—	—	50.00
1992 Proof	33,980	Value: 50.00				

Note: Uncirculated strikes have medallic die alignment and edges with reeded and plain sections; Proof strikes have coin die alignment and reeded edges

KM# 912 2000 PESETAS
26.7000 g., 0.9250 Silver .7940 oz. ASW **Ruler:** Juan Carlos I
Subject: Olympics **Obv:** Conjoined busts of King and Crown Prince right **Rev:** Wheelchair basketball

Date	Mintage	F	VF	XF	Unc	BU
1992	8,997	—	—	—	—	50.00
1992 Proof	27,886	Value: 50.00				

Note: Uncirculated strikes have medallic die alignment and edges with reeded and plain sections; Proof strikes have coin die alignment and reeded edges

KM# 913 2000 PESETAS
26.7000 g., 0.9250 Silver .7940 oz. ASW **Ruler:** Juan Carlos I
Subject: Olympics **Obv:** Conjoined busts of King and Crown Prince right **Rev:** Sprinters

Date	Mintage	F	VF	XF	Unc	BU
1992	16,000	—	—	—	—	40.00
1992 Proof	42,000	Value: 40.00				

Note: Uncirculated strikes have medallic die alignment and edges with reeded and plain sections; Proof strikes have coin die alignment and reeded edges

KM# 914 2000 PESETAS
26.7000 g., 0.9250 Silver .7940 oz. ASW **Ruler:** Juan Carlos I
Subject: Olympics **Obv:** Conjoined busts of King and Crown Prince right **Rev:** Chariot racing

Date	Mintage	F	VF	XF	Unc	BU
1992	13,000	—	—	—	—	50.00
1992 Proof	37,000	Value: 50.00				

Note: Uncirculated strikes have medallic die alignment and edges with reeded and plain sections; Proof strikes have coin die alignment and reeded edges

KM# 980 2000 PESETAS
26.7000 g., 0.9250 Silver .7940 oz. ASW **Ruler:** Juan Carlos I
Subject: Seville Expo '92 **Obv:** Exposition building and date within beaded circle **Rev:** Tower of Seville within beaded circle

Date	Mintage	F	VF	XF	Unc	BU
1992	17,000	—	—	—	—	35.00
1992 Proof	16,000	Value: 35.00				

KM# 925 2000 PESETAS
26.7000 g., 0.9250 Silver .7940 oz. ASW **Ruler:** Juan Carlos I
Subject: Holy Jacobean Year **Obv:** Head left **Rev:** German Jacobean Pilgrims within square and beaded circle

Date	Mintage	F	VF	XF	Unc	BU
1993 Proof	10,000	Value: 75.00				

KM# 926 2000 PESETAS
26.7000 g., 0.9250 Silver .7940 oz. ASW **Ruler:** Juan Carlos I
Subject: Holy Jacobean Year **Obv:** Head left **Rev:** Santiago cross and scallop shell within beaded circle

Date	Mintage	F	VF	XF	Unc	BU
1993 Proof	17,000	Value: 75.00				

KM# 937 2000 PESETAS
18.0000 g., 0.9250 Silver .5353 oz. ASW **Ruler:** Juan Carlos I
Subject: International Monetary Fund and Bank **Obv:** Head left **Rev:** Designs above building

Date	Mintage	F	VF	XF	Unc	BU
1994	8,669,000	—	—	—	15.00	20.00

KM# 938 2000 PESETAS
27.0000 g., 0.9250 Silver .8031 oz. ASW **Ruler:** Juan Carlos I
Subject: Courtyard of the Lions **Rev:** Courtyard scene

Date	Mintage	F	VF	XF	Unc	BU
1994 Proof	7,312	Value: 40.00				

KM# 939 2000 PESETAS
27.0000 g., 0.9250 Silver .8031 oz. ASW **Ruler:** Juan Carlos I
Subject: Environmental Protection **Rev:** Spanish lynx within circle

Date	Mintage	F	VF	XF	Unc	BU
1994 Proof	20,000	Value: 100				

KM# 940 2000 PESETAS
27.0000 g., 0.9250 Silver .8031 oz. ASW **Ruler:** Juan Carlos I
Obv: Head left **Rev:** Purple herons in swamp

Date	Mintage	F	VF	XF	Unc	BU
1994 Proof	6,555	Value: 45.00				

KM# 941 2000 PESETAS
27.0000 g., 0.9250 Silver .8031 oz. ASW **Ruler:** Juan Carlos I
Obv: Head left **Rev:** Two bulls fighting

Date	Mintage	F	VF	XF	Unc	BU
1994 Proof	10,388	Value: 50.00				

KM# 953 2000 PESETAS
27.0000 g., 0.9250 Silver .8031 oz. ASW **Ruler:** Juan Carlos I
Obv: Head left **Rev:** Capercaillie bird

Date	Mintage	F	VF	XF	Unc	BU
1995 Proof	13,859	Value: 50.00				

KM# 954 2000 PESETAS
27.0000 g., 0.9250 Silver .8031 oz. ASW **Ruler:** Juan Carlos I
Subject: Presidential Council - V.E **Obv:** Head left **Rev:** Designs above building

Date	Mintage	F	VF	XF	Unc	BU
1995	—	—	—	—	15.00	20.00

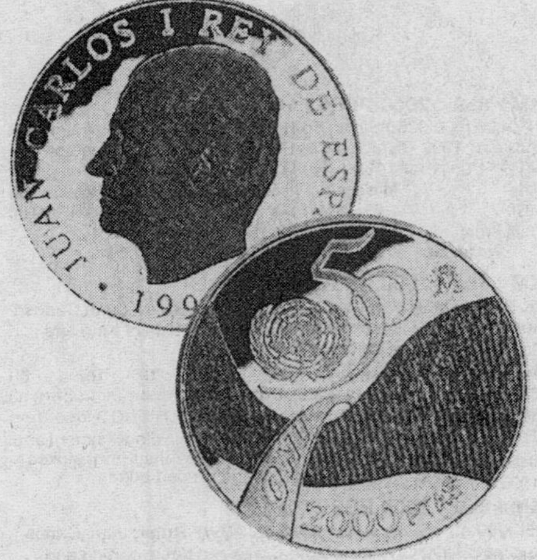

KM# 955 2000 PESETAS
27.0000 g., 0.9250 Silver .8031 oz. ASW **Ruler:** Juan Carlos I
Subject: 50th Anniversary - United Nations **Obv:** Head left **Rev:** Numeral 50 and UN logo above design

Date	Mintage	F	VF	XF	Unc	BU
1995 Proof	26,049	Value: 100				

KM# 966 2000 PESETAS
27.0000 g., 0.9250 Silver .8031 oz. ASW **Ruler:** Juan Carlos I
Obv: Head left **Rev:** Wolves

Date	Mintage	F	VF	XF	Unc	BU
1996 Proof	35,000	Value: 75.00				

KM# 967 2000 PESETAS
27.0000 g., 0.9250 Silver .8031 oz. ASW **Ruler:** Juan Carlos I
Obv: Head left **Rev:** Bears

Date	Mintage	F	VF	XF	Unc	BU
1996 Proof	35,000	Value: 50.00				

KM# 968 2000 PESETAS
18.0000 g., 0.9250 Silver .5353 oz. ASW **Ruler:** Juan Carlos I **Subject:** Francisco de Goya **Obv:** Head left **Rev:** Reclining nude female figure

Date	Mintage	F	VF	XF	Unc	BU
1996	—	—	—	—	16.50	21.50

KM# 974 2000 PESETAS
27.0000 g., 0.9250 Silver .8031 oz. ASW **Ruler:** Juan Carlos I **Series:** Patrimonio de la Humanidad **Obv:** UNESCO logo **Rev:** Taj Mahal, India

Date	Mintage	F	VF	XF	Unc	BU
1996 Proof	30,000	Value: 35.00				

KM# 975 2000 PESETAS
27.0000 g., 0.9250 Silver .8031 oz. ASW **Ruler:** Juan Carlos I **Series:** Patrimonio de la Humanidad **Obv:** Crowned shield with value as II **Rev:** Djenne, Mali

Date	Mintage	F	VF	XF	Unc	BU
1996 Proof	30,000	Value: 35.00				

KM# 976 2000 PESETAS
27.0000 g., 0.9250 Silver .8031 oz. ASW **Ruler:** Juan Carlos I **Series:** Patrimonio de la Humanidad **Obv:** Crowned shield with value as II **Rev:** Abu Simbel, Egypt

Date	Mintage	F	VF	XF	Unc	BU
1996 Proof	30,000	Value: 35.00				

KM# 977 2000 PESETAS
27.0000 g., 0.9250 Silver .8031 oz. ASW **Ruler:** Juan Carlos I **Series:** Patrimonio de la Humanidad **Obv:** Crowned shield with value as II **Rev:** Palenque, Mexico

Date	Mintage	F	VF	XF	Unc	BU
1996 Proof	30,000	Value: 35.00				

KM# 978 2000 PESETAS
27.0000 g., 0.9250 Silver .8031 oz. ASW **Ruler:** Juan Carlos I **Series:** Patrimonio de la Humanidad **Obv:** Crowned shield with value as II **Rev:** Merida, Spain

Date	Mintage	F	VF	XF	Unc	BU
1996 Proof	30,000	Value: 35.00				

KM# 999 2000 PESETAS
18.0000 g., 0.9250 Silver .5353 oz. ASW **Ruler:** Juan Carlos I **Subject:** Don Quixote **Obv:** Head left **Rev:** Quixote and friend plus cameo of Cervantes

Date	Mintage	F	VF	XF	Unc	BU
1997	—	—	—	—	17.50	22.50

KM# 1018 2000 PESETAS
27.0000 g., 0.9250 Silver .8031 oz. ASW, 40 mm. **Ruler:** Juan Carlos I **Series:** "Patrimono de la Humanidad" UNESCO **Obv:** UNESCO logo **Rev:** Abomey lion **Edge:** Reeded

Date	Mintage	F	VF	XF	Unc	BU
1997 Proof	30,000	Value: 30.00				

KM# 1019 2000 PESETAS
27.0000 g., 0.9250 Silver .8031 oz. ASW **Ruler:** Juan Carlos I **Series:** "Patrimono de la Humanidad" UNESCO **Obv:** UNESCO logo **Rev:** Easter Island statues

Date	Mintage	F	VF	XF	Unc	BU
1997 Proof	30,000	Value: 30.00				

KM# 1020 2000 PESETAS
27.0000 g., 0.9250 Silver .8031 oz. ASW **Ruler:** Juan Carlos I **Series:** "Patrimono de la Humanidad" UNESCO **Obv:** UNESCO logo **Rev:** Temple at Petra

Date	Mintage	F	VF	XF	Unc	BU
1997 Proof	30,000	Value: 30.00				

KM# 1021 2000 PESETAS
27.0000 g., 0.9250 Silver .8031 oz. ASW **Ruler:** Juan Carlos I **Series:** "Patrimono de la Humanidad" UNESCO **Obv:** UNESCO logo **Rev:** Acropolis

Date	Mintage	F	VF	XF	Unc	BU
1997 Proof	30,000	Value: 30.00				

KM# 1022 2000 PESETAS
27.0000 g., 0.9250 Silver .8031 oz. ASW **Ruler:** Juan Carlos I **Series:** "Patrimono de la Humanidad" UNESCO **Obv:** UNESCO logo **Rev:** Horyu-Ji pagoda

Date	Mintage	F	VF	XF	Unc	BU
1997 Proof	30,000	Value: 30.00				

KM# 1024 2000 PESETAS
27.0000 g., 0.9250 Silver .8031 oz. ASW, 40 mm. **Ruler:** Juan Carlos I **Subject:** House of Borbon **Obv:** Bust of Philip V facing within beaded border **Rev:** Figural sculpture within beaded border **Edge:** Reeded

Date	Mintage	F	VF	XF	Unc	BU
1997 Proof	—	Value: 30.00				

KM# 1025 2000 PESETAS
27.0000 g., 0.9250 Silver .8031 oz. ASW **Ruler:** Juan Carlos I **Subject:** House of Borbon **Obv:** Bust of Louis I left within beaded border **Rev:** Crowned arms in order chain within beaded border

Date	Mintage	F	VF	XF	Unc	BU
1997 Proof	—	Value: 30.00				

KM# 1026 2000 PESETAS
27.0000 g., 0.9250 Silver .8031 oz. ASW **Ruler:** Juan Carlos I **Subject:** House of Borbon **Obv:** Bust of Ferdinand VI 1/4 right within beaded circle **Rev:** Spanish galleon within beaded circle

Date	Mintage	F	VF	XF	Unc	BU
1997 Proof	—	Value: 30.00				

KM# 1036 2000 PESETAS
27.3000 g., 0.9250 Silver 0.8119 oz. ASW, 39.9 mm. **Ruler:** Juan Carlos I **Subject:** House of Borbon **Obv:** Bust of Ferdinand VII 1/4 right **Rev:** Prado Museum **Edge:** Reeded

Date	Mintage	F	VF	XF	Unc	BU
1998Crowned M Proof	30,000	Value: 30.00				

KM# 987 2000 PESETAS
18.0000 g., 0.9250 Silver .5353 oz. ASW **Ruler:** Juan Carlos I **Subject:** Philip II **Obv:** Head left within beaded circle **Rev:** Head left, design above steepled building within beaded circle

Date	Mintage	F	VF	XF	Unc	BU
1998	—	—	—	—	18.00	23.00

KM# 1011 2000 PESETAS
18.0000 g., 0.9250 Silver .5353 oz. ASW **Ruler:** Juan Carlos I
Subject: St. Jacob **Obv:** Head left within beaded circle **Rev:** St. Jacob, value and dagger

Date	Mintage	F	VF	XF	Unc	BU
1999	—	—	—	—	27.00	30.00

KM# 1029 2000 PESETAS
27.0000 g., 0.9250 Silver .8031 oz. ASW **Ruler:** Juan Carlos I
Subject: Barcelona City Government 750 Years **Obv:** Head left **Rev:** Stylized city arms

Date	Mintage	F	VF	XF	Unc	BU
1999 Proof	30,000	Value: 30.00				

KM# 1030 2000 PESETAS
27.0000 g., 0.9250 Silver .8031 oz. ASW **Ruler:** Juan Carlos I
Subject: House of Borbon **Obv:** Bust of Isabel II 1/4 right within beaded circle

Date	Mintage	F	VF	XF	Unc	BU
1999 Proof	—	Value: 30.00				

KM# 1031 2000 PESETAS
27.0000 g., 0.9250 Silver .8031 oz. ASW **Ruler:** Juan Carlos I
Subject: House of Borbon **Obv:** Head of Alfonso XII 1/4 right within beaded circle **Rev:** Train within beaded circle

Date	Mintage	F	VF	XF	Unc	BU
1999 Proof	—	Value: 32.50				

KM# 1032 2000 PESETAS
27.0000 g., 0.9250 Silver .8031 oz. ASW **Ruler:** Juan Carlos I
Subject: House of Borbon - Alfonso XIII **Obv:** Childhood portrait of Alfonso XIII within circle and beaded border

Date	Mintage	F	VF	XF	Unc	BU
1999 Proof	—	Value: 30.00				

KM# 1033 2000 PESETAS
27.0000 g., 0.9250 Silver .8031 oz. ASW **Ruler:** Juan Carlos I
Subject: House of Borbon - Alfonso XIII **Obv:** Adult portrait of Alfonso XIIII within beaded border

Date	Mintage	F	VF	XF	Unc	BU
1999 Proof	—	Value: 30.00				

KM# 1015 2000 PESETAS
18.0000 g., 0.9250 Silver .5353 oz. ASW, 33 mm. **Ruler:** Juan Carlos I **Subject:** Charles V **Obv:** Head left within beaded border **Rev:** Laureate Head right within beaded border **Edge:** Plain

Date	Mintage	F	VF	XF	Unc	BU
2000	—	—	—	—	28.00	32.00

KM# 1037 2000 PESETAS
27.0000 g., 0.9250 Silver .8031 oz. ASW, 40 mm. **Ruler:** Juan Carlos I **Obv:** Head left **Rev:** Bilbao city arms **Edge:** Reeded

Date	Mintage	F	VF	XF	Unc	BU
2000Crowned M Proof	30,000	Value: 30.00				

KM# 839 5000 PESETAS
54.0000 g., 0.9250 Silver 1.6059 oz. ASW **Ruler:** Juan Carlos I
Subject: Discovery of America **Obv:** Crowned shield flanked by pillars with banner within beaded circle **Rev:** Santa Maria

Date	Mintage	F	VF	XF	Unc	BU
1989	24,000	—	—	—	—	45.00
1989 Proof	33,000	Value: 45.00				

KM# 840 5000 PESETAS
1.6800 g., 0.9990 Gold .0540 oz. AGW **Ruler:** Juan Carlos I
Subject: Discovery of America **Obv:** Crown within beaded circle **Rev:** Crown above compass face within beaded circle

Date	Mintage	F	VF	XF	Unc	BU
1989	6,000	—	—	—	—	60.00
1989 Proof	8,000	Value: 60.00				

KM# 869 5000 PESETAS
54.0000 g., 0.9250 Silver 1.6059 oz. ASW **Ruler:** Juan Carlos I
Subject: Cortes, Montezuma and Marina **Obv:** Three busts facing within beaded circle **Rev:** Scene from Aztec mythology within legend

Date	Mintage	F	VF	XF	Unc	BU
1990	11,000	—	—	—	—	60.00
1990 Proof	13,000	Value: 60.00				

KM# 870 5000 PESETAS
1.6800 g., 0.9990 Gold .0540 oz. AGW **Ruler:** Juan Carlos I
Obv: Bust of Philip V facing **Rev:** Compass face

Date	Mintage	F	VF	XF	Unc	BU
1990	3,000	—	—	—	—	65.00
1990 Proof	4,000	Value: 65.00				

KM# 893 5000 PESETAS
54.0000 g., 0.9250 Silver 1.6059 oz. ASW **Ruler:** Juan Carlos I
Obv: Pizarro and Atahualpa facing right within circle **Rev:** Incan ruins in mountains within beaded circle

Date	Mintage	F	VF	XF	Unc	BU
1991	8,000	—	—	—	—	85.00
1991 Proof	8,145	Value: 85.00				

KM# 894 5000 PESETAS
1.6800 g., 0.9990 Gold .0540 oz. AGW **Ruler:** Juan Carlos I
Obv: Bust of Fernando VI 1/4 right **Rev:** Crown above compass face within beaded circle

Date	Mintage	F	VF	XF	Unc	BU
1991	1,000	—	—	—	—	90.00
1991 Proof	2,000	Value: 90.00				

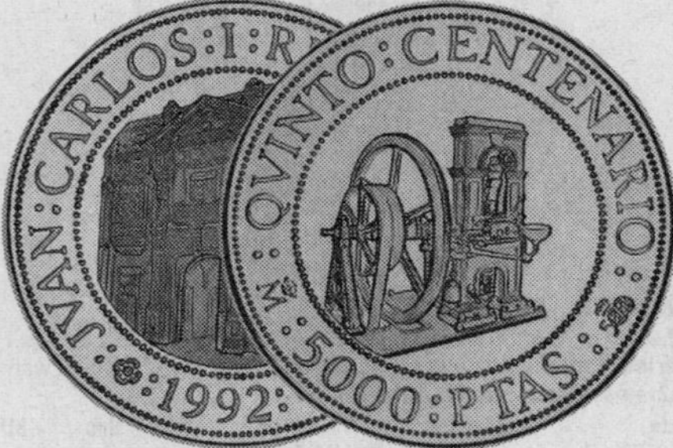

KM# 997 5000 PESETAS
54.0000 g., 0.9250 Silver 1.6059 oz. ASW **Ruler:** Juan Carlos I
Subject: Seville Expo '92 **Obv:** Mint building within beaded circle **Rev:** Old coin press within beaded circle

Date	Mintage	F	VF	XF	Unc	BU
1992	8,000	—	—	—	—	100
1992 Proof	7,000	Value: 100				

KM# 1001 5000 PESETAS
54.0000 g., 0.9250 Silver 1.6059 oz. ASW **Ruler:** Juan Carlos I
Obv: Crown within beaded circle **Rev:** Screw press

Date	Mintage	F	VF	XF	Unc	BU
1992	1,000	—	—	—	—	110
1992 Proof	—	Value: 110				

KM# 942 5000 PESETAS

54.0000 g., 0.9250 Silver 1.6059 oz. ASW **Ruler:** Juan Carlos I **Rev:** Imperial Eagle

Date	Mintage	F	VF	XF	Unc	BU
1994 Proof	30,000	Value: 70.00				

KM# 956 5000 PESETAS

54.0000 g., 0.9250 Silver 1.6059 oz. ASW **Ruler:** Juan Carlos I **Rev:** Spanish Ibex

Date	Mintage	F	VF	XF	Unc	BU
1995 Proof	25,000	Value: 75.00				

KM# 969 5000 PESETAS

54.0000 g., 0.9250 Silver 1.6059 oz. ASW **Ruler:** Juan Carlos I **Rev:** Gaudi sculpture

Date	Mintage	F	VF	XF	Unc	BU
1996 Proof	Est. 20,000	Value: 65.00				

KM# 842 10000 PESETAS

3.3700 g., 0.9990 Gold .1084 oz. AGW **Ruler:** Juan Carlos I **Subject:** Discovery of America **Obv:** Crown above monogram within beaded circle **Rev:** Armillary sphere within beaded circle

Date	Mintage	F	VF	XF	Unc	BU
1989	5,000	—	—	—	—	95.00
1989 Proof	7,000	Value: 95.00				

KM# 841 10000 PESETAS

168.7500 g., 0.9250 Silver 5.0191 oz. ASW, 73 mm. **Ruler:** Juan Carlos I **Subject:** Regional Autonomy **Obv:** Royal family depicted in circular frames **Rev:** Crowned arms at center of crowned provincial arms **Note:** Photo reduced.

Date	Mintage	F	VF	XF	Unc	BU
1989	47,000	—	—	—	—	120
1989 Proof	—	Value: 120				

KM# 873 10000 PESETAS

168.7500 g., 0.9250 Silver 5.0191 oz. ASW, 73 mm. **Ruler:** Juan Carlos I **Subject:** Spanish Royal Family **Obv:** Royal family depicted in circular frames within beaded circle **Rev:** Center circle depicts men holding up world within beaded circle, busts of discoverers and liberators surround **Note:** Photo reduced.

Date	Mintage	F	VF	XF	Unc	BU
1990	26,000	—	—	—	—	140
1990 Proof	—	Value: 140				

KM# 871 10000 PESETAS

3.3700 g., 0.9990 Gold .1084 oz. AGW **Ruler:** Juan Carlos I **Series:** 1992 Olympics **Obv:** Bust right **Rev:** Stylized field hockey player

Date	Mintage	F	VF	XF	Unc	BU
1990	3,000	—	—	—	—	95.00
1990 Proof	5,000	Value: 95.00				

Note: Uncirculated strikes have medallic die alignment and edges with reeded and plain sections; Proof strikes have coin die alignment and reeded edges

KM# 872 10000 PESETAS

3.3700 g., 0.9990 Gold .1084 oz. AGW **Ruler:** Juan Carlos I **Series:** 1992 Olympics **Obv:** Bust right **Rev:** Stylized gymnast

Date	Mintage	F	VF	XF	Unc	BU
1990	2,000	—	—	—	—	100
1990 Proof	3,000	Value: 100				

Note: Uncirculated strikes have medallic die alignment and edges with reeded and plain sections; Proof strikes have coin die alignment and reeded edges

KM# 874 10000 PESETAS

3.3700 g., 0.9990 Gold .1084 oz. AGW **Ruler:** Juan Carlos I **Obv:** Quauchtemoc within beaded circle **Rev:** Crown above compass face within beaded circle

Date	Mintage	F	VF	XF	Unc	BU
1990	9,000	—	—	—	—	100
1990 Proof	2,000	Value: 100				

KM# 895 10000 PESETAS

3.3700 g., 0.9990 Gold .1084 oz. AGW **Ruler:** Juan Carlos I **Series:** Olympics **Obv:** Bust 3/4 right within circle **Rev:** Tae Kwon Do participant within circle

Date	Mintage	F	VF	XF	Unc	BU
1991	2,000	—	—	—	—	180
1991 Proof	3,000	Value: 180				

Note: Uncirculated strikes have medallic die alignment and edges with reeded and plain sections; Proof strikes have coin die alignment and reeded edges.

KM# 897 10000 PESETAS

3.3700 g., 0.9990 Gold .1084 oz. AGW **Ruler:** Juan Carlos I **Obv:** Tupac Amaru II within beaded circle **Rev:** Armillary sphere within beaded circle

Date	Mintage	F	VF	XF	Unc	BU
1991	1,000	—	—	—	—	150
1991 Proof	2,000	Value: 150				

KM# 896 10000 PESETAS

168.7500 g., 0.9250 Silver 5.0191 oz. ASW, 73 mm. **Ruler:** Juan Carlos I **Subject:** Discoverers and Liberators **Obv:** Royal family depicted in circular frames within beaded circle **Rev:** Center circle depicts men holding up world within beaded circle, busts of discoverers and liberators surround **Note:** Photo reduced.

Date	Mintage	F	VF	XF	Unc	BU
1991	17,000	—	—	—	—	175
1991 Proof	—	Value: 175				

KM# 1002 10000 PESETAS

3.3700 g., 0.9990 Gold .1084 oz. AGW **Ruler:** Juan Carlos I **Obv:** Crowned monogram **Rev:** Worker operating screw press

Date	Mintage	F	VF	XF	Unc	BU
1992	1,000	—	—	—	—	180
1992 Proof	—	Value: 180				

KM# 915 10000 PESETAS

3.3700 g., 0.9990 Gold .1084 oz. AGW **Ruler:** Juan Carlos I **Series:** Olympics **Obv:** Bust 1/4 right within circle **Rev:** Baseball player within circle

Date	Mintage	F	VF	XF	Unc	BU
1992	1,000	—	—	—	—	180
1992 Proof	6,000	Value: 180				

Note: Uncirculated strikes have medallic die alignment and edges with reeded and plain sections; Proof strikes have coin die alignment and reeded edges

KM# 998 10000 PESETAS

168.7500 g., 0.9250 Silver 5.0191 oz. ASW **Ruler:** Juan Carlos I **Series:** Seville Expo '92 - Nobel Prize winners **Obv:** Royal family depicted in circular frames **Rev:** Nobel winners depicted in oval frames, hand with quill encircled below

Date	Mintage	F	VF	XF	Unc	BU
1992 Proof	14,000	Value: 235				

KM# 928 10000 PESETAS

168.7500 g., 0.9250 Silver 5.0191 oz. ASW, 75 mm. **Ruler:** Juan Carlos I **Subject:** Holy Jacobean Year **Obv:** Crowned cameo above cathedral within beaded circle **Rev:** Pilgrims within beaded circle, crown at top **Note:** Photo reduced.

Date	Mintage	F	VF	XF	Unc	BU
1993 Proof	7,000	Value: 265				

KM# 943 10000 PESETAS
167.7500 g., 0.9250 Silver 4.9888 oz. ASW, 73 mm. **Ruler:** Juan Carlos I **Subject:** Goya's paintings **Obv:** "The Parasol" **Rev:** Bull fighting scene **Note:** Photo reduced.

Date	Mintage	F	VF	XF	Unc	BU
1994 Proof	15,000	Value: 200				

KM# 957 10000 PESETAS
168.7500 g., 0.9250 Silver 5.0018 oz. ASW, 73 mm. **Ruler:** Juan Carlos I **Subject:** Velazguez's paintings **Obv:** Cameo to right of figure on horse **Rev:** Radiant sun and three standing figures **Note:** Photo reduced.

Date	Mintage	F	VF	XF	Unc	BU
1995 Proof	5,368	Value: 185				

KM# 970 10000 PESETAS
168.7500 g., 0.9250 Silver 5.0018 oz. ASW **Ruler:** Juan Carlos I **Subject:** Velazguez's paintings **Obv:** "The Naked Maja" **Rev:** Family picking flowers

Date	Mintage	F	VF	XF	Unc	BU
1996 Proof	15,000	Value: 150				

KM# 1027 10000 PESETAS
168.7500 g., 0.9250 Silver 5.0185 oz. ASW, 73 mm. **Ruler:** Juan Carlos I **Subject:** House of Borbon - Juan Carlos I **Obv:** King standing and Queen seated **Rev:** Crowned provincial arms within circle at center of family heads separated by fleur de lis **Edge:** Reeded **Note:** Photo reduced.

Date	Mintage	F	VF	XF	Unc	BU
1997 Proof	10,000	Value: 150				

KM# 1068 10000 PESETAS
169.1000 g., 0.9250 Silver 5.0289 oz. ASW, 73 mm. **Ruler:** Juan Carlos I **Subject:** 500th Birthday of Charles I **Obv:** Uniformed half-figure facing **Rev:** Uniformed figure seated on an eagle with pillars in background **Edge:** Plain

Date	Mintage	F	VF	XF	Unc	BU
ND (2000)Crowned M Proof	—	Value: 150				

KM# 843 20000 PESETAS
6.7500 g., 0.9990 Gold .2170 oz. AGW **Ruler:** Juan Carlos I **Subject:** Discovery of America **Obv:** Head facing within beaded circle **Rev:** Pinzon Brother within beaded circle

Date	Mintage	F	VF	XF	Unc	BU
1989	5,000	—	—	—	—	160
1989 Proof	6,500	Value: 160				

KM# 875 20000 PESETAS
6.7500 g., 0.9990 Gold .2170 oz. AGW **Ruler:** Juan Carlos I **Subject:** 1992 Olympics - La Sagrada Familia **Obv:** Bust 1/4 right within beaded circle **Rev:** Cathedral towers within beaded circle

Date	Mintage	F	VF	XF	Unc	BU
1990	4,000	—	—	—	—	180
1990 Proof	10,000	Value: 180				

Note: Uncirculated strikes have medallic die alignment and edges with reeded and plain sections; Proof strikes have coin die alignment and reeded edges

KM# 876 20000 PESETAS
6.7500 g., 0.9990 Gold .2170 oz. AGW **Ruler:** Juan Carlos I **Series:** 1992 Olympics **Obv:** Bust 1/4 right within beaded circle **Rev:** Ruins of Empuries within beaded circle

Date	Mintage	F	VF	XF	Unc	BU
1990	2,000	—	—	—	—	180
1990 Proof	4,000	Value: 180				

Note: Uncirculated strikes have medallic die alignment and edges with reeded and plain sections; Proof strikes have coin die alignment and reeded edges

KM# 877 20000 PESETAS
6.7500 g., 0.9990 Gold .2170 oz. AGW **Ruler:** Juan Carlos I **Subject:** Tupac Amaru I **Obv:** Bust 1/4 right within beaded circle **Rev:** Stylized standing figure with hat and scepter within beaded circle

Date	Mintage	F	VF	XF	Unc	BU
1990	2,000	—	—	—	—	180
1990 Proof	3,000	Value: 180				

KM# 898 20000 PESETAS
6.7500 g., 0.9990 Gold .2170 oz. AGW **Ruler:** Juan Carlos I **Series:** Olympics **Obv:** Bust 1/4 right within circle **Rev:** Montjuic Stadium within circle

Date	Mintage	F	VF	XF	Unc	BU
1991	2,000	—	—	—	—	270
1991 Proof	3,000	Value: 270				

Note: Uncirculated strikes have medallic die alignment and edges with reeded and plain sections; Proof strikes have coin die alignment and reeded edges

KM# 899 20000 PESETAS
6.7500 g., 0.9990 Gold .2170 oz. AGW **Ruler:** Juan Carlos I **Subject:** Huascar **Obv:** Bust facing within beaded circle **Rev:** Armored bust with spear within beaded circle

Date	Mintage	F	VF	XF	Unc	BU
1991	1,000	—	—	—	—	240
1991 Proof	2,000	Value: 240				

KM# 916 20000 PESETAS
6.7500 g., 0.9990 Gold .2170 oz. AGW **Ruler:** Juan Carlos I **Series:** Olympics **Obv:** Bust 1/4 right within circle **Rev:** Dome building within circle

Date	Mintage	F	VF	XF	Unc	BU
1992	1,000	—	—	—	—	270
1992 Proof	3,000	Value: 270				

Note: Uncirculated strikes have medallic die alignment and edges with reeded and plain sections; Proof strikes have coin die alignment and reeded edges

KM# 1003 20000 PESETAS
6.7500 g., 0.9990 Gold .2170 oz. AGW **Ruler:** Juan Carlos I **Obv:** Bust facing within beaded circle **Rev:** Worker feeding screw press

Date	Mintage	F	VF	XF	Unc	BU
1992	1,000	—	—	—	—	270
1992 Proof	—	Value: 270				

KM# 929 20000 PESETAS
6.7500 g., 0.9990 Gold .2170 oz. AGW **Ruler:** Juan Carlos I **Subject:** Holy Jacobean Year **Rev:** Conveyance of Santiago's body

Date	Mintage	F	VF	XF	Unc	BU
1993 Proof	2,000	Value: 240				

KM# 944 20000 PESETAS
6.7500 g., 0.9990 Gold .2170 oz. AGW **Ruler:** Juan Carlos I **Subject:** Paleolithic Cave Painting **Rev:** Stylized animal cave paintings

Date	Mintage	F	VF	XF	Unc	BU
1994 Proof	8,000	Value: 260				

KM# 958 20000 PESETAS
6.7500 g., 0.9990 Gold .2170 oz. AGW **Ruler:** Juan Carlos I **Subject:** Ancient Sculpture - Dama de Elche **Rev:** Hooded bust left

Date	Mintage	F	VF	XF	Unc	BU
1995 Proof	8,000	Value: 220				

KM# 971 20000 PESETAS
6.7500 g., 0.9990 Gold .2170 oz. AGW **Ruler:** Juan Carlos I **Rev:** Pillars and arches

Date	Mintage	F	VF	XF	Unc	BU
1996 Proof	Est. 6,000	Value: 220				

KM# 844 40000 PESETAS
13.5000 g., 0.9990 Gold .4341 oz. AGW **Ruler:** Juan Carlos I **Subject:** Discovery of America **Obv:** Standing figure divides date and beaded circle **Rev:** Sea monster attacking ship within beaded circle

Date	Mintage	F	VF	XF	Unc	BU
1989	4,500	—	—	—	—	325
1989 Proof	6,000	Value: 325				

KM# 878 40000 PESETAS
13.5000 g., 0.9990 Gold .4341 oz. AGW **Ruler:** Juan Carlos I **Subject:** Felipe II **Obv:** Standing figure divides date and beaded circle **Rev:** King seated on throne within beaded circle

Date	Mintage	F	VF	XF	Unc	BU
1990	2,000	—	—	—	—	350
1990 Proof	3,000	Value: 350				

KM# 900 40000 PESETAS
13.5000 g., 0.9990 Gold .4341 oz. AGW **Ruler:** Juan Carlos I **Obv:** Standing figure divides beaded circle and dates **Rev:** Imperial double eagle

Date	Mintage	F	VF	XF	Unc	BU
1991	1,000	—	—	—	—	450
1991 Proof	2,000	Value: 450				

KM# 1004 40000 PESETAS
13.5000 g., 0.9990 Gold .4341 oz. AGW **Ruler:** Juan Carlos I **Obv:** Standing figure divides beaded circle and dates **Rev:** Horse-powered coin press

Date	Mintage	F	VF	XF	Unc	BU
1992	1,000	—	—	—	—	500
1992 Proof	—	Value: 500				

KM# 979 40000 PESETAS
13.5000 g., 0.9990 Gold .4341 oz. AGW **Ruler:** Juan Carlos I **Subject:** Patrimonio de la Humanidad **Obv:** UNESCO logo **Rev:** Statues at Abu Simbel

Date	Mintage	F	VF	XF	Unc	BU
1996 Proof	4,000	Value: 425				

KM# 1023 40000 PESETAS
13.5000 g., 0.9990 Gold .4341 oz. AGW, 30 mm. **Ruler:** Juan Carlos I **Series:** "Patrimonio de la Humanidad - UNESCO" **Obv:** UNESCO logo **Rev:** Horyu-Ji pagoda **Edge:** Reeded

Date	Mintage	F	VF	XF	Unc	BU
1997 Proof	4,000	Value: 425				

KM# 845 80000 PESETAS
27.0000 g., 0.9990 Gold .8682 oz. AGW **Ruler:** Juan Carlos I **Subject:** Discovery of America **Obv:** Crowned busts of Juan Carlos and Sofia facing each other within beaded circle **Rev:** Crowned busts of Ferdinand and Isabella facing each other within beaded circle

Date	Mintage	F	VF	XF	Unc	BU
1989	6,000	—	—	—	—	640
1989 Proof	7,000	Value: 640				

KM# 879 80000 PESETAS
27.0000 g., 0.9990 Gold .8682 oz. AGW **Ruler:** Juan Carlos I **Series:** 1992 Olympics **Obv:** Royal family facing within circle **Rev:** Discus thrower within circle

Date	Mintage	F	VF	XF	Unc	BU
1990	3,000	—	—	—	—	640
1990 Proof	5,000	Value: 640				

Note: Uncirculated strikes have medallic die alignment and edges with reeded and plain sections; Proof strikes have coin die alignment and reeded edges

KM# 880 80000 PESETAS
27.0000 g., 0.9990 Gold .8682 oz. AGW **Ruler:** Juan Carlos I **Series:** 1992 Olympics **Obv:** Royal family facing **Rev:** Prince Balthasar Carlos on horseback

Date	Mintage	F	VF	XF	Unc	BU
1990	1,000	—	—	—	—	675
1990 Proof	4,000	Value: 675				

Note: Uncirculated strikes have medallic die alignment and edges with reeded and plain sections; Proof strikes have coin die alignment and reeded edges

KM# 881 80000 PESETAS
27.0000 g., 0.9990 Gold .8682 oz. AGW **Ruler:** Juan Carlos I **Subject:** Carlos V **Obv:** Crowned heads of Juan Carlos and Sofia facing each other within beaded circle **Rev:** Armored half-figure facing within beaded circle

Date	Mintage	F	VF	XF	Unc	BU
1990	2,000	—	—	—	—	675
1990 Proof	3,000	Value: 675				

KM# 901 80000 PESETAS
27.0000 g., 0.9990 Gold .8682 oz. AGW **Ruler:** Juan Carlos I **Series:** Olympics **Obv:** Royal family facing **Rev:** Women tossing man on blanket within circle

Date	Mintage	F	VF	XF	Unc	BU
1991	1,000	—	—	—	—	1,000
1991 Proof	2,000	Value: 1,000				

Note: Uncirculated strikes have medallic die alignment and edges with reeded and plain sections; Proof strikes have coin die alignment and reeded edges

KM# 902 80000 PESETAS
27.0000 g., 0.9990 Gold .8682 oz. AGW **Ruler:** Juan Carlos I **Subject:** Carlos III **Obv:** Crowned busts of Juan Carlos and Sofia facing each other within beaded circle **Rev:** Armored bust right within beaded circle

Date	Mintage	F	VF	XF	Unc	BU
1991	1,000	—	—	—	—	925
1991 Proof	2,000	Value: 925				

KM# 917 80000 PESETAS
27.0000 g., 0.9990 Gold .8682 oz. AGW **Ruler:** Juan Carlos I **Series:** Olympics **Rev:** Two children playing within circle

Date	Mintage	F	VF	XF	Unc	BU
1992	1,000	—	—	—	—	1,000
1992 Proof	2,000	Value: 1,000				

Note: Uncirculated strikes have medallic die alignment and edges with reeded and plain sections; Proof strikes have coin die alignment and reeded edges

KM# 1005 80000 PESETAS
27.0000 g., 0.9990 Gold .8682 oz. AGW **Ruler:** Juan Carlos I **Obv:** Crowned busts of Juan Carlos and Sofia facing each other within beaded circle **Rev:** Hammer minting scene

Date	Mintage	F	VF	XF	Unc	BU
1992	1,000	—	—	—	—	1,000
1992 Proof	—	Value: 1,000				

KM# 930 80000 PESETAS
27.0000 g., 0.9990 Gold .8682 oz. AGW **Ruler:** Juan Carlos I **Subject:** Holy Jacobean Year **Obv:** Head left **Rev:** French Fraternity of Santiago Medallion within beaded circle

Date	Mintage	F	VF	XF	Unc	BU
1993 Proof	1,500	Value: 850				

KM# 945 80000 PESETAS
27.0000 g., 0.9990 Gold .8682 oz. AGW **Ruler:** Juan Carlos I **Rev:** Iberian Lynx

Date	Mintage	F	VF	XF	Unc	BU
1994 Proof	5,000	Value: 750				

KM# 959 80000 PESETAS
27.0000 g., 0.9990 Gold .8682 oz. AGW **Ruler:** Juan Carlos I **Rev:** Leda and the Swan

Date	Mintage	F	VF	XF	Unc	BU
1995 Proof	5,000	Value: 800				

KM# 972 80000 PESETAS
27.0000 g., 0.9990 Gold .8682 oz. AGW **Ruler:** Juan Carlos I **Rev:** Folk dancers

Date	Mintage	F	VF	XF	Unc	BU
1996 Proof	Est. 3,500	Value: 800				

KM# 1028 80000 PESETAS
27.0000 g., 0.9990 Gold .8672 oz. AGW, 38 mm. **Ruler:** Juan Carlos I **Subject:** House of Borbon **Obv:** Head of Ferdinand VI right within circle and beaded border **Rev:** Crowned shield within circle and beaded border **Edge:** Reeded

Date	Mintage	F	VF	XF	Unc	BU
1997 Proof	4,000	Value: 800				

EURO COINAGE

European Union Issues

KM# 1040 EURO CENT
2.2700 g., Copper Plated Steel, 16.2 mm. **Ruler:** Juan Carlos I **Obv:** Cathedral of Santiago de Compostela **Obv. Designer:** Garcilano Rollan **Rev:** Value and globe **Rev. Designer:** Luc Luycx **Edge:** Plain

Date	Mintage	F	VF	XF	Unc	BU
1999	716,494,385	—	—	—	0.25	0.35
2000	70,473,000	—	—	—	1.00	1.25

KM# 1041 2 EURO CENTS
3.0300 g., Copper Plated Steel, 18.7 mm. **Ruler:** Juan Carlos I **Obv:** Cathedral of Santiago de Compostela **Obv. Designer:** Garcilano Rollan **Rev:** Value and globe **Rev. Designer:** Luc Luycx **Edge:** Grooved

Date	Mintage	F	VF	XF	Unc	BU
1999	114,704,000	—	—	—	0.75	1.00
2000	819,290,000	—	—	—	0.25	0.35

KM# 1042 5 EURO CENTS
3.8600 g., Copper Plated Steel, 21.2 mm. **Ruler:** Juan Carlos I **Obv:** Cathedral of Santiago de Compostela **Obv. Designer:** Garcilano Rollan **Rev:** Value and globe **Rev. Designer:** Luc Luycx **Edge:** Plain

Date	Mintage	F	VF	XF	Unc	BU
1999	378,191,385	—	—	—	0.65	0.75
2000	472,195,000	—	—	—	0.65	0.75

KM# 1043 10 EURO CENTS
4.0700 g., Brass, 19.7 mm. **Ruler:** Juan Carlos I **Obv:** Head of Cervantes with ruffed collar 1/4 left within star border **Rev:** Value and map **Edge:** Reeded

Date	Mintage	F	VF	XF	Unc	BU
1999	484,985,385	—	—	—	0.65	0.75
2000	281,491,000	—	—	—	0.65	0.75

KM# 1044 20 EURO CENTS
5.7300 g., Brass, 22.1 mm. **Ruler:** Juan Carlos I **Obv:** Head of Cervantes with ruffed collar 1/4 left within star border **Obv. Designer:** Begoña Castellanos **Rev:** Value and map **Rev. Designer:** Luc Luycx **Edge:** Notched

Date	Mintage	F	VF	XF	Unc	BU
1999	691,458,385	—	—	—	0.85	1.00
2000	77,452,000	—	—	—	2.75	3.50

KM# 1045 50 EURO CENTS
7.8100 g., Brass, 24.2 mm. **Ruler:** Juan Carlos I **Obv:** Head of Cervantes with ruffed collar 1/4 left within star border **Obv. Designer:** Begoña Castellanos **Rev:** Value and map **Rev. Designer:** Luc Luycx **Edge:** Reeded

Date	Mintage	F	VF	XF	Unc	BU
1999	78,974,000	—	—	—	1.50	1.75
2000	773,124,000	—	—	—	1.25	1.50

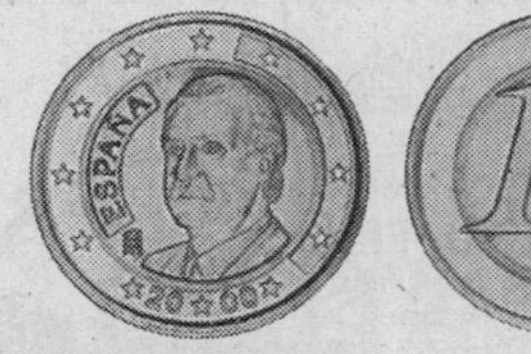

KM# 1046 EURO
7.5000 g., Bi-Metallic Copper-Nickel center in Brass ring, 23.2 mm. **Ruler:** Juan Carlos I **Obv:** Head 1/4 left within circle and star border **Obv. Designer:** Luiz Jose Diaz **Rev:** Value and map within circle **Rev. Designer:** Luc Luycx **Edge:** Reeded and plain sections

Date	Mintage	F	VF	XF	Unc	BU
1999	100,200,000	—	—	—	3.00	3.50
2000	132,474,000	—	—	—	4.00	4.50

KM# 1047 2 EUROS
8.5200 g., Bi-Metallic Brass center in Copper-Nickel ring, 25.7 mm. **Ruler:** Juan Carlos I **Obv:** Head 1/4 left within circle and star border **Obv. Designer:** Luis Jose Diaz **Rev:** Value and map within circle **Rev. Designer:** Luc Luycx **Edge:** Reeded **Edge Lettering:** 2's and stars

Date	Mintage	F	VF	XF	Unc	BU
1999	60,500,000	—	—	—	5.00	6.00
2000	65,098,000	—	—	—	5.00	6.00

TRIAL STRIKES

KM#	Date	Mintage	Identification	Mkt Val
TS1	1987	—	500 Pesetas. Silver. Conjoined heads left. Inscription divides crown, letter and star. KM#831.	12.50
TS3	1987	—	500 Pesetas. Silver. Inscription divides crown, letter and star. Crown above monogram within banner.	12.50
TS4	1987	—	500 Pesetas. Stainless Steel. Inscription divides crown, letter and star. Value above design and crown.	10.00
TS2	1987	—	500 Pesetas. Stainless Steel.	10.00
TS5	ND	—	2000 Pesetas. Silver. KM#859.	175

PATTERNS

Including off metal strikes

KM#	Date	Mintage	Identification	Mkt Val
Pn16	1937	—	10 Centimos. Zinc. Denomination. Crowned arms on eagle. III Año Triunfal.	1,000
Pn17	ND	—	5 Euro Cents. Bronze. 4.7200 g. 23.4 mm. Sumpol, mint mark and denomination. Denomination. Plain edge.	—
Pn18	ND	—	10 Euro Cents. Brass. 4.6400 g. 23 mm. Symbol, mint mark and denomination. Denomination. Plain edge.	—

MINT SETS

KM#	Date	Mintage	Identification	Issue Price	Mkt Val
MS1	1949 (E51) (3)	5,000	KM#776, 777-778	—	3,500
MS2	1958Ba (3)	—	KM#786-788	—	400
MS3	1964 (7)	—	KM#785-788, 790, 795-796; Set contains KM#790, dated 1959 with added 'strike date' to match the set. In cardboard holder.	3.60	100
MS4	1965 (7)	—	KM#785-788, 790, 795-796; Set contains KM#790, dated 1959 with added 'strike date' to match the set. In cardboard holder.	3.60	100
MS5	1966 (8)	—	KM#775, 777, 785-788, 790, 797; Set contains KM#790, dated 1959 with added 'strike date' to match the set. In cardboard holder.	—	200
MS6	1966 (8)	—	KM#775, 777, 785-788, 790, 797; Set contains KM#790, dated 1959 with added 'strike date' to match the set. In plastic sleeve.	—	100
MS7	1968 (8)	1,000	KM#785-788, 790, 795-797; Set contains KM#790, dated 1959 with added 'strike date' to match the set	3.60	2,500
MS8	1969 (8)	1,200	KM#785-788, 790, 795-797; Set contains KM#790, dated 1959 with added 'strike date' to match the set	3.60	2,200
MS9	1970 (8)	6,000	KM#785-788, 790, 795-797; Set contains KM#790, dated 1959 with added 'strike date' to match the set	3.60	500
MS10	1971 (7)	10,000	KM#785-788, 790, 795-797; Set contains KM#790, dated 1959 with added 'strike date' to match the set	3.60	225
MS11	1980(80) (6)	—	KM#815-820. Released in 1987, only in sets.	2.50	5.00
MSA12	1980//82 (4)	—	KM#816, 817, 818, 819	—	6.50
MS12	1982 (4)	—	KM#823, 824, 825, 826	—	15.00
MS13	1990 (U) (5)	—	KM#854, 856-858, 868	—	60.00
MS15	1991 (U) (5)	—	KM#882-883, 885-886, 892	—	85.00
MS18	1992 (10)	—	KM#832-833, 903-910	12.00	60.00
MS19	1993 (8)	—	KM#832, 918-919, 920-924, labeled as proof	15.00	45.00
MS20	1994 (8)	—	KM#832, 924, 931-936	12.00	70.00
MS21	1995 (8)	—	KM#832, 924, 946-951	13.50	175
MS22	1996 (8)	—	KM#832, 924, 960-965	14.00	50.00
MS23	1997 (8)	—	KM#832, 924, 981-986	15.50	20.00
MS24	1998 (8)	—	KM#832-833, 924, 989-992, 1012	15.50	25.00
MS25	1999 (8)	—	KM#832, 924, 991-992, 1006-1008, 1012	15.50	30.00
MSA25	1999 (8)	—	KM#832-833, 924, 989-992, 1012	15.50	80.00
MSA26	2000 (8)	—	KM#832-833, 924, 989-992, 1012	—	45.00
MS26	2000 (8)	—	KM#832-833, 924, 989, 991-992, 1012-1013	15.50	30.00
MS27	2000-2001 (8)	—	KM#832-833, 924, 991-992 (both dated 2000), 1012-1013, 1016	15.50	20.00

PROOF SETS

KM#	Date	Mintage	Identification	Issue Price	Mkt Val
PS1	1972 (6)	30,000	KM#786-788, 790, 795-796	5.00	50.00
PS2	1973 (6)	25,000	KM#786-788, 790, 795-796	5.00	150
PS3	1974 (6)	23,000	KM#786-788, 790, 795-796	5.00	125
PS4	1975 (6)	75,000	KM#786-788, 790, 795-796	5.00	25.00
PS5	1976 (6)	400,000	KM#805-810	5.00	3.50
PS6	1977 (3)	300,000	KM#806-808	0.35	1.50
PS7	1979 (4)	300,000	KM#806-809	0.90	2.50
PS8	1987 (6)	—	KM#831, Pn4, Pn4a, Pn5-6	25.00	35.00
PS9	1987 (2)	—	KM#828, 830	—	50.00
PS10	1989 (7)	—	KM#834-839, 841	—	250
PS11	1989 (5)	—	KM#M1-M5	—	950
PS12	1989 (5)	—	KM#840, 842-845	3,177	1,775
PS13	1990 (7)	—	KM#854, 856-858, 868-869, 873	—	250
PS14	1991 (7)	—	KM#882-883, 885-886, 892-893, 896	—	375
PS15	1992 (7)	—	KM#980, 993-998	—	450
PS16	1995 (6)	I.A.	KM#938, 953, 956-959	—	1,350
PS17	1995 (4)	25,000	KM#938, 953, 956-959	—	300
PS18	1996 (6)	—	KM#966-967, 969-972	1,675	1,300
PS19	1996 (6)	—	KM#966-967, 969-972	1,650	1,300
PS20	1996 (4)	—	KM#966-967, 969-972	—	240
PS21	1996 (4)	—	KM#966-967, 969-970	—	240
PS22	1996 (5)	—	KM#973-978	198	160
PS23	1996 (6)	—	KM#973-979	702	600

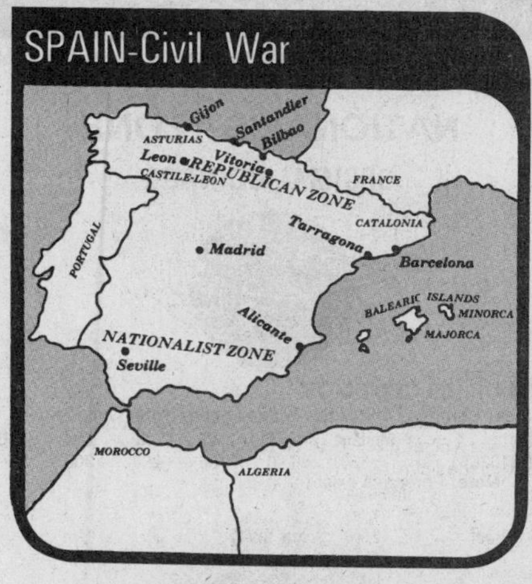

With the loss of her American empire, Spain drifted into chaotic times. Stung by their defeats in Cuba, the army blamed the Socialists for what they considered to be mismanagement at home. Additional political complications were derived from the successful Russian Revolution which gave impetus to an already thriving Socialist party and trade union movement. Finally, King Alphonso XIII committed the fatal mistake of encouraging a reckless general to start a campaign in Morocco that ended in the virtual extermination of the Spanish army. Fearing that the inevitable parliamentary investigation would incriminate the crown, he offered no objection when General Primo de Rivera seized the government and established himself as dictator in 1926. Rivera fell from power in 1930, and the government was taken over by an alliance of Liberals and Socialists who tried to separate the Church and State, take the army out of politics, and introduce effective labor and agrarian reforms despite numerous strikes and street riots. The election of 1936 brought to power a coalition of Socialists, Liberals and Communists, to the dismay of the traditionalists and landowners.

A number of right-wing generals, including the young and clever Francisco Franco, began preparations for a military coup which erupted into a civil war in July of 1936.The destructive conflict, in which more than a million died, lasted three years. During the struggle, areas under control of both the Nationalists (rebels) and the Republicans (Loyalists) issued coinages that circulated to whatever extent the political and military situation permitted. The war ended defeat for the Loyalists when Madrid fell to Franco on March 28, 1939.

During the Spanish Civil War (1936-1939) a great many coins and tokens were minted in the provincial districts. The coins are grouped here under the heading of the district in which they most commonly circulated.

CAUTIONARY NOTE: Many counterfeits of the Civil War coinage exist. Authentication has been recommended by leading experts in this field.

AMETLLA DEL VALLES

A town in the province of Tarragona in northeastern Spain. The town adopted the name L'Ametlla del Valles in 1933. Before that the name was La Ametlla.

REPUBLICAN ZONE

DECIMAL COINAGE

KM# 1 25 CENTIMOS

Brass, 25 mm.

Date	Mintage	F	VF	XF	Unc	BU
ND (1937)	50,000	12.00	25.00	35.00	50.00	—

KM# 2.1 50 CENTIMOS

Aluminum, 20 mm.

Date	Mintage	F	VF	XF	Unc	BU
ND (1937)	3,000	100	200	250	300	—

KM# 2.2 50 CENTIMOS

Aluminum, 20 mm. **Obv:** Without legend

Date	Mintage	F	VF	XF	Unc	BU
ND (1937)	30,000	25.00	50.00	70.00	100	—

KM# 3.1 PESETA

Aluminum, 26 mm.

Date	Mintage	F	VF	XF	Unc	BU
ND (1937)	3,000	75.00	100	125	150	—

KM# 3.2 PESETA

Aluminum, 26 mm. **Obv:** Without legend

Date	Mintage	F	VF	XF	Unc	BU
ND (1937)	30,000	15.00	30.00	40.00	50.00	—

ARAHAL

A town 30 miles east of Seville. Issued 3 undated types of coins in 1936.

NATIONALIST ZONE

DECIMAL COINAGE

KM# 1 50 CENTIMOS
Brass, 19 mm. **Obv:** Value within legend **Note:** Uniface.

Date	Mintage	F	VF	XF	Unc	BU
ND (1936)	3,000	50.00	100	200	300	—

Note: Forgeries exist

KM# 2 PESETA
Brass, 25 mm. **Obv:** Value within legend **Note:** Uniface.

Date	Mintage	F	VF	XF	Unc	BU
ND (1936)	10,000	20.00	30.00	50.00	75.00	—

Note: Forgeries exist

KM# 3 2 PESETAS
Brass, 30 mm. **Obv:** Value within legend **Note:** Uniface.

Date	Mintage	F	VF	XF	Unc	BU
ND (1936)	10,000	20.00	30.00	50.00	75.00	—

Note: Forgeries exist

ARENYS DE MAR

A resort village on the Mediterranean shore that is 20 miles north of Barcelona. One of the villages in the area of operations of General Mola at the beginning of the war.

REPUBLICAN ZONE

DECIMAL COINAGE

KM# 1 50 CENTIMOS
Aluminum, 21 mm. **Obv:** Shield divides value **Note:** Uniface.

Date	Mintage	F	VF	XF	Unc	BU
ND (1937)	6,000	50.00	90.00	110	150	—

Note: Forgeries exist

KM# 2 PESETA
Aluminum, 29 mm. **Obv:** Shield divides value **Note:** Uniface.

Date	Mintage	F	VF	XF	Unc	BU
ND (1937)	3,500	55.00	100	120	160	—

Note: Forgeries exist

ASTURIAS AND LEON

Asturias is a province on the northern coast of Spain with the province of Leon just to its south. The councils of these adjoining provinces decided to mint coins in 1937 for use in the area due to lack of other circulating coins in the north.

REPUBLICAN ZONE

DECIMAL COINAGE

KM# 1 50 CENTIMOS
Copper-Nickel, 21 mm. **Obv:** Crossed tools and gear in back of upright design **Rev:** Value and date

Date	Mintage	F	VF	XF	Unc	BU
1937	200,000	15.00	20.00	30.00	35.00	40.00

KM# 2 PESETA
Copper, 23 mm. **Obv:** Standing figure with hat facing left **Rev:** Value and date

Date	Mintage	F	VF	XF	Unc	BU
1937	100,000	15.00	25.00	35.00	50.00	—

KM# 3 2 PESETAS
Copper-Nickel **Obv:** Standing figure with hand on gear **Rev:** Value and date **Note:** Varieties exist with differences in the leaves.

Date	Mintage	F	VF	XF	Unc	BU
1937	400,000	5.00	7.50	10.00	20.00	25.00

CAZALLA DE LA SIERRA

A town 43 miles north of Seville that issued a 10 Centimos in brass in 1936 (undated).

NATIONALIST ZONE

DECIMAL COINAGE

KM# 1 10 CENTIMOS
Brass, 23 mm. **Obv:** Crowned shield to right of legend **Rev:** Legend and value, single sprig at left

Date	Mintage	F	VF	XF	Unc	BU
ND (1936)	10,000	30.00	45.00	70.00	125	—

EUZKADI

Euzkadi or the Viscayan Republic was located in north central Spain adjoining the southeast corner of France. It was made up of 3 provinces - Guipuzcoa, Alava, and Viscaya. These Basque provinces declared autonomy on October 8, 1936. The 2 nickel coins were made in Brussels, Belgium and saw some circulation before the end of the Republic on June 18, 1937.

VISCAYAN REPUBLIC

DECIMAL COINAGE

KM# 1 PESETA
Nickel, 22 mm. **Obv:** Liberty head right **Rev:** Value and date within wreath

Date	Mintage	F	VF	XF	Unc	BU
1937	7,000,000	2.50	5.00	7.00	10.00	12.50

KM# 2 2 PESETAS
Nickel, 26 mm. **Obv:** Liberty head right **Rev:** Value and date within wreath

Date	Mintage	F	VF	XF	Unc	BU
1937	6,000,000	3.00	6.00	8.00	12.00	15.00

IBI

A village north and west of Alicante on the east coast of Spain. The isolation of the area in comparison with other contending areas made the maintaining of this area during the war very difficult.

REPUBLICAN ZONE

DECIMAL COINAGE

KM# 1.1 25 CENTIMOS
Copper, 24 mm. **Obv:** Legend and value **Rev:** Liberty head left flanked by sprigs **Note:** Varieties exist.

Date	Mintage	F	VF	XF	Unc	BU
1937	30,000	20.00	35.00	50.00	60.00	—

KM# 1.2 25 CENTIMOS
Copper, 24 mm. **Obv:** Value and map of Spain in field **Rev:** Liberty head left flanked by sprigs

Date	Mintage	F	VF	XF	Unc	BU
1937	7,000	65.00	100	150	200	—

KM# 2 PESETA
Nickel-Brass, 24 mm. **Obv:** Legend and date **Rev:** Value

Date	Mintage	F	VF	XF	Unc	BU
1937	5,000	50.00	85.00	125	200	—

LORA DEL RIO

A town 35 miles northeast of Seville. Issued an undated 25 Centimos in 1936.

NATIONALIST ZONE

DECIMAL COINAGE

KM# 1 25 CENTIMOS
Brass, 23 mm. **Obv:** Crowned shield within cross **Rev:** Legend and value, wheat sprig at right

Date	Mintage	F	VF	XF	Unc	BU
ND (1936)	1,500	225	375	450	950	—

MARCHENA

A village 30 miles east of Seville. It was the last issuer in Seville province. Two varieties of undated coins were produced in 1936.

NATIONALIST ZONE

DECIMAL COINAGE

KM# 1.1 25 CENTIMOS
Brass, 40 mm. **Obv:** Value at center of Legend **Note:** Uniface; denomination: 25C.

Date	Mintage	F	VF	XF	Unc	BU
ND (1936)	5,000	30.00	75.00	125	225	—

KM# 1.2 25 CENTIMOS
Brass, 40 mm. **Obv:** Value at center of legend **Note:** Uniface; denomination: 025C.

Date	Mintage	F	VF	XF	Unc	BU
ND (1936)	500	400	600	900	1,200	—

Note: Forgeries exist

MENORCA

Menorca is the smaller of the 2 major islands in the Balearic Islands. A serious coin and supply shortage developed during the war because of the isolation of the island from the mainland.

REPUBLICAN ZONE

DECIMAL COINAGE

KM# 1 5 CENTIMOS
Brass, 13 mm. **Obv:** Emblem within beaded circle **Rev:** Value above star, single sprig at left **Note:** Varieties exist.

Date	Mintage	F	VF	XF	Unc	BU
1937	42,000	—	40.00	50.00	60.00	—

KM# 2 10 CENTIMOS
Brass, 16 mm. **Obv:** Emblem within beaded circle **Rev:** Value above star, single sprig at left **Note:** Varieties exist.

Date	Mintage	F	VF	XF	Unc	BU
1937	32,000	—	25.00	35.00	45.00	—

KM# 3 25 CENTIMOS
Brass, 18 mm. **Obv:** Emblem within beaded circle **Rev:** Value above star, single sprig at left

Date	Mintage	F	VF	XF	Unc	BU
1937	38,000	—	20.00	25.00	30.00	—

KM# 4 PESETA
Brass, 20 mm. **Obv:** Emblem within beaded circle **Rev:** Value above star, single sprig at left

Date	Mintage	F	VF	XF	Unc	BU
1937	37,000	—	20.00	25.00	30.00	—

KM# 5 2-1/2 PESETAS
Brass, 22 mm. **Obv:** Emblem within beaded circle **Rev:** Value above star, single sprig at left

Date	Mintage	F	VF	XF	Unc	BU
1937	24,000	—	60.00	100	125	—

NULLES

Nulles is a mountain village in the province of Tarragona. The mountainous terrain of the area isolated the village from friendly forces and normal commerce. Therefore, in 1937, an undated series of 5 denominations were issued.

REPUBLICAN ZONE

DECIMAL COINAGE

KM# 1 5 CENTIMOS
Zinc, 23 mm. **Obv:** Value at center of legend **Shape:** Octagonal **Note:** Uniface, legends similar to 10 Centimos, KM#2.

Date	Mintage	F	VF	XF	Unc	BU
ND (1937)	5,000	200	350	500	650	—

KM# 2 10 CENTIMOS
Zinc, 21 mm. **Obv:** Value at center of legend **Note:** Uniface.

Date	Mintage	F	VF	XF	Unc	BU
ND (1937)	3,000	250	400	600	900	—

KM# 3 25 CENTIMOS
Brass, 20 mm. **Obv:** Value at center of legend **Shape:** Square **Note:** Uniface. Legends similar to 10 Centimos, KM#2.

Date	Mintage	F	VF	XF	Unc	BU
ND (1937)	5,000	200	350	500	600	—

KM# 4 50 CENTIMOS
Brass, 22 mm. **Obv:** Value at center of legend **Shape:** Octagonal **Note:** Uniface, legends similar to 10 Centimos, KM#2.

Date	Mintage	F	VF	XF	Unc	BU
ND (1937)	1,000	250	400	550	700	—

KM# 5 PESETA
Brass, 22 mm. **Obv:** Value at center of legend **Note:** Uniface.

Date	Mintage	F	VF	XF	Unc	BU
ND (1937)	5,000	150	200	250	350	—

OLOT

A village in the province of Gerona in northeastern Spain near the French border. The village council authorized 2 denominations of coins on September 24, 1937.

REPUBLICAN ZONE

DECIMAL COINAGE

KM# 1 10 CENTIMOS
Iron, 24 mm. **Obv:** Vertical lines and eagle wing within design **Rev:** Caduceus divides value

Date	Mintage	F	VF	XF	Unc	BU
1937	25,000	45.00	65.00	100	175	—

KM# 2 15 CENTIMOS
Iron, 30 mm. **Obv:** Vertical lines and eagle wing within design **Rev:** Stylized factory scene and value

Date	Mintage	F	VF	XF	Unc	BU
1937	100	1,600	1,850	3,700	7,400	—

Note: Forgeries exist

PUEBLA DE CAZALLA

A village only a few miles east of El Arahal and some 40 miles from Sevilla. Undated coins of 2 values were issued in 1936.

NATIONALIST ZONE

DECIMAL COINAGE

KM# 1 10 CENTIMOS
Brass, 23 mm. **Obv:** Tied arrows with banner to left of legend **Rev:** Value **Note:** Counterstamped varieties exist.

Date	Mintage	F	VF	XF	Unc	BU
ND (1936)	1,500	175	350	450	650	—

KM# 2 25 CENTIMOS
Brass, 25 mm. **Obv:** Tied arrows with banner to left of legend **Rev:** Value **Note:** Counterstamped varieties exist.

Date	Mintage	F	VF	XF	Unc	BU
ND (1936)	5,000	150	325	425	600	—

SANTANDER, PALENCIA & BURGOS

REPUBLICAN ZONE

DECIMAL COINAGE

KM# 1.1 50 CENTIMOS
Copper-Nickel, 20 mm. **Obv:** Standing 1/2 length figure with hammer **Rev:** Value above crossed sprigs

Date	Mintage	F	VF	XF	Unc	BU
1937	100,000	—	25.00	35.00	45.00	55.00

KM# 1.2 50 CENTIMOS
Copper-Nickel, 20 mm. **Obv:** Blacksmith with factory in background **Rev:** Letters PR or PJR below CTS

Date	Mintage	F	VF	XF	Unc	BU
1937	10,000	—	30.00	40.00	50.00	60.00

KM# 2 PESETA
Copper-Nickel, 23 mm. **Obv:** Crowned shield to left of legend **Rev:** Value within 1/2 wreath

Date	Mintage	F	VF	XF	Unc	BU
1937	300,000	—	15.00	20.00	30.00	—

SEGARRA DE GAIA

A village in the southern part of the province of Tarragona. A single denomination of coin was authorized in 1937.

REPUBLICAN ZONE

DECIMAL COINAGE

KM# 1 PESETA
Copper-Nickel, 23 mm. **Obv:** Value over bars of Aragon in circle

Date	Mintage	F	VF	XF	Unc	BU
ND (1937)	5,000	15.00	25.00	35.00	40.00	—

KM# 1a PESETA
Copper, 23 mm. **Obv:** Value over bars of Aragon in circle **Note:** Uniface. Value over bars of Aragon in circle.

Date	Mintage	F	VF	XF	Unc	BU
ND (1937)	20,000	75.00	125	150	200	—

SPITZBERGEN

Spitzbergen (Svalbard), a Norwegian territory, is a group of mountainous islands in the Arctic Ocean 360 miles (579 km.) north of Norway. The islands have an area of 23,957 sq. mi. (62,050 sq. km.) and a population of about 4,000. West Spitzbergen, the largest island, is the seat of administration. Sealing and fishing are economically important. Despite rich carboniferous and tertiary coal deposits, coal mining, which was started on a commercial scale by the Arctic Coal Co. of Boston, Mass. in 1904, produces only small quantities.

Spitzbergen was probably discovered in 1194, but modern knowledge of it dates from its discovery by William Barents in 1596. Quarrels among the various nationalities involved in the whaling industry, which was set up in 1611, resulted in a de facto division of the coast, but despite diverse interests in, and claims to the islands by British, Dutch, Norwegians, Swedes, Danes, Russians and Americans, the question of sovereignty was not resolved until 1920, when a treaty agreed to by the claimants awarded the islands to Norway.

In 1932, the Russian mining company Arktikugol began operations in the islands. The tokens listed here were minted in Leningrad for use by the company in Spitzbergen.

RULERS
Norwegian, 1920-

LEGENDS
ШПИЦБЕРГЕН = Spitzbergen
АРКТИКУГОЛЬ = Artikugol = Arctic Coal Co.
РАЗМѢННЫЙ ЗНАК = Exchange Tokens

NORWEGIAN TERRITORY

TOKEN COINAGE

Catastrophe Memorial Issues

KM# Tn1 10 KOPEKS
Aluminum-Bronze **Obv:** Star below date, legend around **Rev:** Value, legend

Date	Mintage	F	VF	XF	Unc	BU
1946	—	18.00	30.00	65.00	125	—

KM# Tn2 15 KOPEKS
Aluminum-Bronze **Obv:** Star below date, legend around **Rev:** Value, legend

Date	Mintage	F	VF	XF	Unc	BU
1946	—	22.00	35.00	70.00	140	—

KM# Tn3 20 KOPEKS
Copper-Nickel **Obv:** Star below date, legend around **Rev:** Value, legend

Date	Mintage	F	VF	XF	Unc	BU
1946	—	25.00	45.00	75.00	150	—

KM# Tn4.1 50 KOPEKS
Copper-Nickel **Obv:** Larger star below date, legend around **Rev:** Value, legend

Date	Mintage	F	VF	XF	Unc	BU
1946	—	30.00	50.00	80.00	160	—

KM# Tn4.2 50 KOPEKS
Copper-Nickel **Obv:** Smaller star below date, legend around **Rev:** Value, legend

Date	Mintage	F	VF	XF	Unc	BU
1946	—	30.00	50.00	80.00	160	—

KM# Tn5 10 ROUBLES
Copper-Nickel Clad Steel **Obv:** Polar bear seated on 1/2 world globe **Rev:** Value within circle, legend around with date below

Date	Mintage	F	VF	XF	Unc	BU
1993	—	—	—	—	3.50	5.00

KM# Tn6 25 ROUBLES
Copper-Nickel Clad Steel **Obv:** Polar bear seated on 1/2 world globe **Rev:** Value within circle, legend around with date below

Date	Mintage	F	VF	XF	Unc	BU
1993	—	—	—	—	4.50	6.00

KM# Tn7 50 ROUBLES
Copper-Nickel Clad Steel **Obv:** Polar bear seated on 1/2 world globe **Rev:** Value within circle, legend around with date below

Date	Mintage	F	VF	XF	Unc	BU
1993	—	—	—	—	6.50	8.00

KM# Tn8 100 ROUBLES
Aluminum-Bronze **Obv:** Polar bear seated on 1/2 world globe **Rev:** Value within circle, legend around with date below

Date	Mintage	F	VF	XF	Unc	BU
1993	—	—	—	—	9.00	11.00

SRI (SHRI) LANKA

The Democratic Socialist Republic of Sri Lanka (formerly Ceylon) situated in the Indian Ocean 18 miles (29 km.) southeast of India, has an area of 25,332 sq. mi.(65,610 sq. km.) and a population of *16.9 million. Capital: Colombo. The economy is chiefly agricultural. Tea, coconut products and rubber are exported.

Sri Lanka remains a member of the Commonwealth of Nations. The president is Chief of State. The prime minister is Head of Government. The present leaders of the country have reverted the country name back to Sri Lanka.

RULERS

British, 1796-1948

DEMOCRATIC SOCIALIST REPUBLIC

DECIMAL COINAGE

100 Cents = 1 Rupee

KM# 137 CENT

Aluminum **Obv:** Value above designs within wreath **Rev:** Navy emblem

Date	Mintage	F	VF	XF	Unc	BU
1975	52,778,000	—	—	0.10	0.25	0.45
1978	34,006,000	—	—	0.10	0.25	0.45
1978 Proof	20,000	Value: 2.50				
1989	6,000,000	—	—	0.10	0.25	0.45
1994	5,000,000	—	—	0.10	0.25	0.45

KM# 138 2 CENTS

Aluminum **Obv:** Value above designs within wreath **Rev:** Navy emblem **Shape:** Scalloped

Date	Mintage	F	VF	XF	Unc	BU
1975	62,503,000	—	—	0.10	0.25	0.45
1978	23,425,000	—	—	0.10	0.25	0.45
1978 Proof	20,000	Value: 3.00				

KM# 139 5 CENTS

Nickel-Brass **Obv:** Value above designs within wreath **Rev:** Navy emblem **Shape:** Round-edged square

Date	Mintage	F	VF	XF	Unc	BU
1975	19,584,000	—	—	0.10	0.25	0.45

KM# 139a 5 CENTS

Aluminum **Obv:** Value above designs within wreath **Rev:** Navy emblem **Shape:** Round-edged square

Date	Mintage	F	VF	XF	Unc	BU
1978	272,308,000	—	—	0.10	0.25	0.45
1978 Proof	20,000	Value: 3.00				
1988	40,000,000	—	—	0.10	0.25	0.45
1991	50,000,000	—	—	0.10	0.25	0.45

KM# 140 10 CENTS

Nickel-Brass **Obv:** Value above designs within wreath **Rev:** Navy emblem **Shape:** Scalloped

Date	Mintage	F	VF	XF	Unc	BU
1975	10,800,000	—	—	0.10	0.25	0.45

KM# 140a 10 CENTS

Aluminum **Obv:** Value above designs within wreath **Rev:** Navy emblem **Shape:** Scalloped

Date	Mintage	F	VF	XF	Unc	BU
1978	188,820,000	—	—	0.10	0.25	0.45
1978 Proof	20,000	Value: 3.50				
1988	40,000,000	—	—	0.10	0.25	0.45
1991	50,000,000	—	—	0.10	0.25	0.45

KM# 141.1 25 CENTS

Copper-Nickel **Obv:** Value above designs within wreath **Rev:** Navy emblem **Edge:** Security

Date	Mintage	F	VF	XF	Unc	BU
1975	39,600,000	—	—	0.10	0.25	0.45
1975 Proof	1,431	Value: 4.00				
1978	65,009,000	—	—	0.10	0.25	0.45
1978 Proof	20,000	Value: 3.50				

KM# 141.2 25 CENTS

Copper-Nickel **Obv:** Value above designs within wreath **Rev:** Navy emblem **Edge:** Reeded

Date	Mintage	F	VF	XF	Unc	BU
1982	90,000,000	—	—	0.10	0.25	0.45
1989	45,000,000	—	—	0.10	0.25	0.45
1991	50,000,000	—	—	0.10	0.25	0.45
1994	50,000,000	—	—	0.10	0.25	0.45

KM# 141.2a 25 CENTS

Nickel Clad Steel **Obv:** Value above designs within wreath **Rev:** Navy emblem **Edge:** Reeded

Date	Mintage	F	VF	XF	Unc	BU
1996	50,000,000	—	—	0.10	0.25	0.45

KM# 135.1 50 CENTS

Copper-Nickel **Obv:** Value above designs within wreath **Rev:** Navy emblem **Edge:** Security

Date	Mintage	F	VF	XF	Unc	BU
1972	11,000,000	—	0.15	0.30	0.75	1.25
1975	34,000,000	—	0.15	0.30	0.75	1.25
1978	66,010,000	—	0.15	0.30	0.75	1.25
1978 Proof	20,000	Value: 4.50				

KM# 135.2 50 CENTS

Copper-Nickel **Obv:** Value above designs within wreath **Rev:** Navy emblem **Edge:** Reeded

Date	Mintage	F	VF	XF	Unc	BU
1982	65,000,000	—	0.10	0.25	0.65	1.00
1991	40,000,000	—	0.10	0.25	0.65	1.00
1994	40,000,000	—	0.10	0.25	0.65	1.00

KM# 135.2a 50 CENTS

Nickel Clad Steel **Obv:** Value above designs within wreath **Rev:** Navy emblem **Edge:** Reeded

Date	Mintage	F	VF	XF	Unc	BU
1996	50,000,000	—	0.10	0.25	0.65	1.00

KM# 136.1 RUPEE

Copper-Nickel **Obv:** Inscription below designs within wreath **Rev:** Navy emblem **Edge:** Security

Date	Mintage	F	VF	XF	Unc	BU
1972	7,000,000	—	0.30	0.60	1.25	1.75
1975	31,500,000	—	0.25	0.50	1.00	1.50
1978	37,018,000	—	0.25	0.50	1.00	1.50
1978 Proof	20,000	Value: 6.50				

KM# 136.2 RUPEE

Copper-Nickel **Obv:** Inscriptions below designs within wreath **Rev:** Navy emblem **Edge:** Reeded

Date	Mintage	F	VF	XF	Unc	BU
1982	75,000,000	—	0.25	0.50	1.00	1.50
1994	50,000,000	—	0.25	0.50	1.00	1.50

KM# 136.2a RUPEE

Nickel Clad Steel **Obv:** Inscription below designs within wreath **Rev:** Navy emblem **Edge:** Reeded

Date	Mintage	F	VF	XF	Unc	BU
1996	50,000,000	—	0.25	0.50	1.00	1.50
2000	30,000,000	—	0.25	0.50	1.00	1.50

KM# 144 RUPEE

Copper-Nickel **Subject:** Inauguration of President Jayewardene **Obv:** Head left **Rev:** Navy emblem

Date	Mintage	F	VF	XF	Unc	BU
1978	1,997,400	—	0.30	0.60	1.25	1.75
1978	2,600	—	—	—	—	50.00

Note: Right shoulder straight

Date	Mintage	F	VF	XF	Unc	BU
1978 Proof	20,000	Value: 6.50				

Note: In sets only

KM# 144a RUPEE

Gold **Subject:** Inauguration of President Jayawardene **Obv:** Head left **Rev:** Navy emblem

Date	Mintage	F	VF	XF	Unc	BU
1978 Proof	40	—	—	—	—	—

KM# 151 RUPEE

Copper-Nickel **Subject:** 3rd anniversary of 2nd Executive President Premadusa **Obv:** Facing lions with swords above rectangular design **Rev:** Bust facing within wreath

Date	Mintage	F	VF	XF	Unc	BU
1992	25,000,000	—	0.30	0.65	1.75	2.50
1992 Proof	2,000	Value: 10.00				

KM# 151a RUPEE

0.9250 Silver **Subject:** 3rd Anniversary of 2nd Executive President Premadusa **Obv:** Facing lions with swords above rectangular design **Rev:** Bust facing within wreath

Date	Mintage	F	VF	XF	Unc	BU
1992 Frosted Proof	2,500	Value: 50.00				

KM# 151b RUPEE

0.9167 Gold **Subject:** 3rd Anniversary of 2nd Executive President Premadusa **Obv:** Lions with swords above rectangular design **Rev:** Bust facing within wreath

Date	Mintage	F	VF	XF	Unc	BU
1992 Proof	100	—	—	—	—	—

KM# 157 RUPEE

Copper-Nickel **Series:** UNICEF **Subject:** UNICEF 50th Anniversary **Obv:** Inscription and value below designs within wreath **Rev:** Numeral 50 and UNICEF logo within circle

Date	Mintage	F	VF	XF	Unc	BU
1996	5,000,000	—	—	—	1.75	2.50

KM# 162 RUPEE

7.1300 g., Nickel Plated Steel, 25.4 mm. **Subject:** Army's 50th Anniversary **Obv:** Navy emblem on crossed swords above dates within beaded circle **Rev:** Soldier giving dove to boy **Edge:** Reeded

Date	Mintage	F	VF	XF	Unc	BU
1999 Proof	8,000	Value: 10.00				
1999 Prooflike	127,000	—	—	—	—	6.00

KM# 164 RUPEE
7.1300 g., Nickel Plated Steel, 25.4 mm. **Subject:** Sri Lankan Navy 50 Years **Obv:** Patrol boat within circle **Rev:** Navy emblem within circle **Edge:** Reeded

Date	Mintage	F	VF	XF	Unc	BU
2000	20,000	—	—	—	—	6.00

KM# 164a RUPEE
Copper Nickel, 25.4 mm. **Subject:** Sri Lankan Navy 50 Years **Obv:** Patrol boat within circle **Rev:** Navy emblem within circle **Edge:** Reeded

Date	Mintage	F	VF	XF	Unc	BU
2000 Proof	2,000	Value: 10.00				

KM# 142 2 RUPEES
Copper-Nickel, 30 mm. **Subject:** Non-Aligned Nations Conference **Obv:** Value within inscription, legend around border **Rev:** Conference building **Edge:** Plain **Shape:** 7-sided

Date	Mintage	F	VF	XF	Unc	BU
1976	2,000,000	—	0.50	1.50	2.25	3.50
1976 Proof	500	Value: 10.00				

KM# 145 2 RUPEES
Copper-Nickel **Subject:** Mahaweli Dam **Obv:** Numeral value within inscription, legend around border **Rev:** Dam within circle

Date	Mintage	F	VF	XF	Unc	BU
1981	45,000,000	—	0.35	0.75	2.50	3.75

KM# 147 2 RUPEES
Copper-Nickel **Obv:** Value within inscription above date **Rev:** Navy emblem

Date	Mintage	F	VF	XF	Unc	BU
1984	25,000,000	—	0.25	0.50	1.00	1.50
1993	40,000,000	—	0.30	0.60	1.35	1.75
1996	50,000,000	—	0.30	0.60	1.35	1.75

KM# 155 2 RUPEES
Copper-Nickel **Series:** F.A.O. **Subject:** F.A.O. 50th Anniversary **Obv:** Value within inscription, legend around border **Rev:** F.A.O. logo and dates within circle

Date	Mintage	F	VF	XF	Unc	BU
1995	40,000,000	—	—	—	2.25	3.25

KM# 143 5 RUPEES
Nickel **Subject:** Non-Aligned Nations Conference **Obv:** Value within inscription, legend around border **Rev:** Conference building **Shape:** 10-sided

Date	Mintage	F	VF	XF	Unc	BU
1976	1,000,000	—	0.75	1.50	3.00	4.50
1976 Proof	500	Value: 12.00				

KM# 146 5 RUPEES
Copper-Nickel **Subject:** 50th Anniversary - Universal Adult Franchise **Obv:** Value within inscription, legend around border **Rev:** Building with flag **Shape:** 10-sided

Date	Mintage	F	VF	XF	Unc	BU
1981	2,000,000	—	0.75	1.50	3.00	4.50

KM# 148.1 5 RUPEES
Aluminum-Bronze **Obv:** Value within inscription, legend around border **Rev:** Navy emblem **Edge:** Lettered **Edge Lettering:** CBC - Central Bank of Ceylon

Date	Mintage	F	VF	XF	Unc	BU
1984	25,000,000	—	0.35	0.75	2.25	3.00

KM# 148.2 5 RUPEES
Aluminum-Bronze **Obv:** Value within inscription, legend around border **Rev:** Navy emblem **Edge:** Lettered **Edge Lettering:** CBSL - Central Bank of Sri Lanka

Date	Mintage	F	VF	XF	Unc	BU
1986	60,000,000	—	0.35	0.75	2.25	3.00
1991	40,000,000	—	0.35	0.75	2.25	3.00
1994	50,000,000	—	0.35	0.65	2.00	2.75

KM# 156 5 RUPEES
Aluminum-Bronze **Subject:** 50th Anniversary - United Nations **Obv:** Value within inscription, legend around border **Rev:** Numeral 50 and UN logo within circle

Date	Mintage	F	VF	XF	Unc	BU
1995	50,000,000	—	—	—	2.50	3.50
1995 Proof	5,000	—	—	—	—	—

KM# 161 5 RUPEES
Aluminum-Bronze **Subject:** World Cricket Champions **Obv:** Trophy **Rev:** Batsman within circle

Date	Mintage	F	VF	XF	Unc	BU
1999	50,000,000	—	—	—	2.75	4.00

KM# 149 10 RUPEES
Copper-Nickel **Subject:** International Year of Shelter for Homeless **Obv:** Value within inscription, legend around border **Rev:** Logo, legend around border **Shape:** 4-sided

Date	Mintage	F	VF	XF	Unc	BU
1987	2,000,000	—	—	—	3.50	5.00
1987 Proof	200	—	—	—	—	—

KM# 158 10 RUPEES
Bi-Metallic Brass center in Copper-Nickel ring, 27 mm. **Subject:** 50th Anniversary of Independence **Obv:** Value and dates within designed wreath **Rev:** Building within and outside of circle **Edge:** CBSL, (4 times) reeded

Date	Mintage	F	VF	XF	Unc	BU
1998	50,000,000	—	—	—	4.50	5.50

KM# 152 100 RUPEES
10.2000 g., 0.9250 Silver .3033 oz. ASW **Subject:** 5th South Asian Federation Games **Obv:** Sunface above lion, elephant and rabbit, crescent below **Rev:** Logo above inscription, date and value **Shape:** Square

Date	Mintage	F	VF	XF	Unc	BU
1991 Proof	20,000	Value: 35.00				

KM# 150 500 RUPEES
28.2800 g., 0.9250 Silver .8411 oz. ASW, 38.6 mm. **Subject:** 40th Anniversary of Central Bank **Obv:** National arms within circle **Rev:** Central Bank building within circle **Edge:** Reeded **Designer:** Ian Rank-Broadley

Date	Mintage	F	VF	XF	Unc	BU
1990	10,000	—	—	—	—	32.50
1990 frosted Proof	2,200	Value: 60.00				

KM# 153 500 RUPEES
1.6000 g., 0.5000 Gold .0257 oz. AGW **Subject:** 5th South Asian Federation Games **Obv:** Stylized seated figure **Rev:** Value above logo and inscription

Date	Mintage	F	VF	XF	Unc	BU
1991 Proof	8,000	Value: 50.00				

KM# 154 500 RUPEES
28.2800 g., 0.9250 Silver .8411 oz. ASW **Subject:** 2,300th Anniversary - Buddha's Teachings in Sri Lanka **Obv:** Large stylized leaf within circle **Rev:** Kneeling figure praying within forest, design above, all within circle **Note:** This is the only coin on which the country name SHRI LANKA appears. Shri Lanka was used only from June 1992 to December 1993, without constitutional authority, by decision of President Premadasa.

Date	Mintage	F	VF	XF	Unc	BU
1993 Proof	30,000	Value: 55.00				

KM# 159 1000 RUPEES
28.2800 g., 0.9250 Silver .841 oz. ASW **Subject:** 50 Years of Independence **Obv:** Flag and value within wreath **Rev:** Lion statue within circle

Date	Mintage	F	VF	XF	Unc	BU
1998 Proof	25,000	Value: 60.00				

KM# 163 1000 RUPEES
28.2800 g., 0.9250 Silver 8410 oz. ASW, 38.6 mm. **Subject:** 1996 Cricket Champions **Obv:** Trophy **Rev:** Two players **Edge:** Reeded **Note:** Struck at British Royal Mint.

Date	Mintage	F	VF	XF	Unc	BU
1999 Proof	25,000	Value: 45.00				

KM# 165 1000 RUPEES
28.2800 g., 0.9250 Silver .8410 oz. ASW, 38.6 mm. **Subject:** Central Bank 50 Years **Obv:** Sunface in center circle of designs **Rev:** Building and value within circle **Edge:** Milled **Note:** Struck at British Royal Mint.

Date	Mintage	F	VF	XF	Unc	BU
2000 Proof	10,000	Value: 50.00				

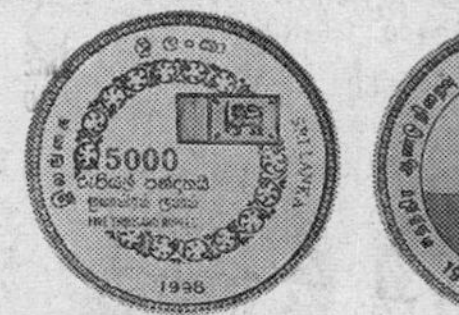

KM# 160 5000 RUPEES
7.9800 g., 0.9167 Gold .2352 oz. AGW **Subject:** 50 Years of Independence **Obv:** Flag and value within wreath **Rev:** Avalokitheshvara, an aspirant Buddha, seated in a graceful stance within circle

Date	Mintage	F	VF	XF	Unc	BU
1998 Proof	5,000	Value: 245				

PATTERNS

Including off metal strikes

KM#	Date	Mintage	Identification	Mkt Val
Pn1	1971	—	5 Cents. Nickel-Brass Plated Steel. Similar to KM#129, with TRIAL in raised letters on obverse.	—
Pn2	1971	—	5 Cents. Steel. Similar to KM#129, with TRIAL in raised letters on obverse.	—
Pn3	1971	—	5 Cents. Aluminum. Similar to #KM129, with TRIAL in raised letters on obverse.	—
Pn4	1971	—	10 Cents. Nickel-Brass Plated Steel. Similar to KM#130, with TRIAL in raised letters on obverse.	—
Pn5	1971	—	10 Cents. Steel. Similar to KM#130, with TRIAL in raised letters on obverse.	—
Pn6	1971	—	10 Cents. Aluminum. Similar to KM#130, with TRIAL in raised letters on obverse.	—
Pn7	1975	—	5 Cents. Aluminum. KM#139a	—
Pn8	1975	—	10 Cents. Aluminum. KM#140a	—

PROOF SETS

KM#	Date	Mintage	Identification	Issue Price	Mkt Val
PS1	1978 (8)	20,000	KM135.1, 136.1, 137, 138, 139a, 140a, 141.1, 144	26.00	35.00

STRAITS SETTLEMENTS

Straits Settlements, a former British crown colony situated on the Malay Peninsula of Asia, was formed in 1826 by combining the territories of Singapore, Penang and Malacca. The colony was administered by the East India Company until its abolition in 1858. Straits Settlements was a part of British India from 1858 to 1867 at which time it became a Crown Colony.

The Straits Settlements coinage gradually became acceptable legal tender in the neighboring Federated as well as the Unfederated Malay States. The Straits Settlements were dissolved in 1946, while the coinage continued to circulate until demonetized at the end of 1952.

RULERS
British

MINT MARKS
H - Heaton, Birmingham
W - Soho Mint
B - Bombay

MONETARY SYSTEM
100 Cents = 1 Dollar

BRITISH COLONY
1867-1939

STANDARD COINAGE

KM# 14 1/4 CENT
Bronze **Ruler:** Victoria **Obv:** Crowned head left **Obv. Legend:** VICTORIA QUEEN **Obv. Designer:** G.W. DeSaulles **Rev:** Value within beaded circle **Rev. Legend:** STRAITS SETTLEMENTS.. **Edge:** Reeded

Date	Mintage	F	VF	XF	Unc	BU
1901	2,000,000	10.00	20.00	70.00	220	—

KM# 17 1/4 CENT
Bronze **Ruler:** Edward VII **Obv:** Crowned bust right **Obv. Designer:** E.B. MacKennal **Rev:** Value within beaded circle

Date	Mintage	F	VF	XF	Unc	BU
1904 Proof	—	Value: 900				
Note: Plain edge						
1905	2,008,000	10.00	25.00	70.00	155	—
1905 Proof	—	Value: 520				
1908	1,200,000	10.00	25.00	70.00	155	—

KM# 27 1/4 CENT
Bronze **Ruler:** George V **Obv:** Crowned bust left **Rev:** Value within beaded circle

Date	Mintage	F	VF	XF	Unc	BU
1916	4,000,000	6.00	12.50	22.00	35.00	—
1916 Proof	—	Value: 350				

KM# 18 1/2 CENT
Bronze **Ruler:** Edward VII **Obv:** Crowned bust right **Obv. Designer:** G.W. DeSaulles **Rev:** Value within beaded circle

Date	Mintage	F	VF	XF	Unc	BU
1904 Proof	—	Value: 1,700				
1908	2,000,000	15.00	27.50	80.00	180	—

KM# 28 1/2 CENT

Bronze **Ruler:** George V **Obv:** Crowned bust left **Obv. Designer:** E.B. MacKennal **Rev:** Value within beaded circle

Date	Mintage	F	VF	XF	Unc	BU
1916	3,000,000	6.00	10.00	20.00	32.00	—
1916 Proof	—	Value: 420				

KM# 37 1/2 CENT

Bronze **Ruler:** George V **Obv. Designer:** E.B. MacKennal **Rev:** Value within beaded circle **Edge:** Crowned bust left **Shape:** 4-sided

Date	Mintage	F	VF	XF	Unc	BU
1932	5,000,000	3.50	6.50	14.00	26.00	—
1932 Proof	—	Value: 330				

KM# 16 CENT

Bronze **Ruler:** Victoria **Obv:** Crowned head left **Obv. Legend:** VICTORIA QUEEN **Rev:** Value within beaded circle **Rev. Legend:** STRAITS SETTLEMENTS **Edge:** Reeded

Date	Mintage	F	VF	XF	Unc	BU
1901	15,230,000	1.25	10.00	50.00	180	—

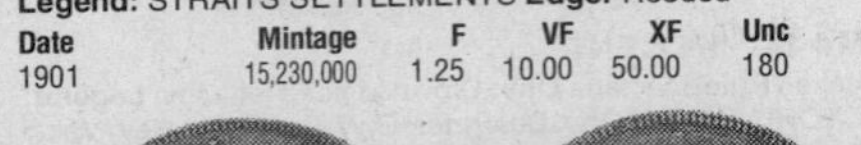

KM# 19 CENT

Bronze **Ruler:** Edward VII **Obv:** Crowned bust right **Obv. Designer:** G.W. DeSaulles **Rev:** Value within beaded circle

Date	Mintage	F	VF	XF	Unc	BU
1903	7,053,000	2.00	10.00	50.00	180	—
1903 Proof	—	Value: 520				
1904	6,647,000	2.00	10.00	50.00	180	—
1904 Proof	—	Value: 520				
1906	7,504,000	8.00	42.00	100	210	—
1907	5,015,000	2.00	10.00	50.00	165	—
1908	Inc. above	2.00	6.00	26.00	120	—
1908 Proof	—	Value: 520				

KM# 32 CENT

Bronze, 21 mm. **Obv:** Crowned bust left **Obv. Designer:** E.B. MacKennal **Rev:** Value within beaded circle **Edge:** Plain **Shape:** 4-sided

Date	Mintage	F	VF	XF	Unc	BU
1919	20,165,000	0.50	1.50	10.00	42.00	—
1919 Proof	—	Value: 330				
1920	55,000,000	0.50	1.50	6.00	30.00	—
1920 Proof	—	Value: 320				
1926	5,000,000	0.50	1.50	6.00	55.00	—

KM# 10 5 CENTS

1.3600 g., 0.8000 Silver .0349 oz. ASW **Ruler:** Victoria **Obv:** Crowned head left **Obv. Legend:** VICTORIA QUEEN **Rev:** Value within beaded circle **Rev. Legend:** STRAITS SETTLEMENTS

Date	Mintage	F	VF	XF	Unc	BU
1901	3,000,000	6.00	9.00	35.00	175	—
1901 Proof	—	Value: 900				

KM# 20 5 CENTS

1.3600 g., 0.8000 Silver .0349 oz. ASW **Ruler:** Edward VII **Obv:** Crowned bust right **Obv. Designer:** G.W. DeSaulles **Rev:** Value within beaded circle

Date	Mintage	F	VF	XF	Unc	BU
1902	1,920,000	10.00	25.00	130	190	—
1902 Proof	—	Value: 650				
1903	2,270,000	10.00	25.00	130	190	—
1903 Proof	—	Value: 650				

KM# 20a 5 CENTS

1.3600 g., 0.6000 Silver .0262 oz. ASW **Ruler:** Edward VII **Obv:** Crowned bust right **Obv. Designer:** G.W. DeSaulles **Rev:** Value within beaded circle

Date	Mintage	F	VF	XF	Unc	BU
1910B	13,012,000	1.25	3.00	14.00	26.00	—
1910B Proof	—	Value: 650				

KM# 31 5 CENTS

1.3600 g., 0.4000 Silver .0174 oz. ASW **Ruler:** George V **Obv:** Crowned bust left **Obv. Designer:** E.B. MacKennal **Rev:** Value within beaded circle

Date	Mintage	F	VF	XF	Unc	BU
1918	3,100,000	0.50	2.00	14.00	25.00	—
1919	6,900,000	0.50	2.00	14.00	25.00	—
1920	4,000,000	370	700	1,600	3,500	—

KM# 34 5 CENTS

Copper-Nickel **Ruler:** George V **Obv:** Crowned bust left **Obv. Designer:** E.B. MacKennal **Rev:** Value within beaded circle

Date	Mintage	F	VF	XF	Unc	BU
1920	20,000,000	1.50	15.00	72.00	150	—
1920 Proof	—	Value: 900				

KM# 36 5 CENTS

1.3600 g., 0.6000 Silver .0262 oz. ASW **Ruler:** George V **Obv:** Smaller bust, broader rim **Obv. Designer:** E.B. MacKennal **Rev:** Value within beaded circle

Date	Mintage	F	VF	XF	Unc	BU
1926	10,000,000	0.65	1.00	7.20	14.00	—
1926 Proof	—	Value: 430				
1935	3,000,000	0.65	1.00	4.00	10.00	—
1935 Proof	—	Value: 430				

KM# 11 10 CENTS

2.7100 g., 0.8000 Silver .0697 oz. ASW **Ruler:** Victoria **Obv:** Crowned head left **Obv. Legend:** VICTORIA QUEEN **Rev:** Value within beaded circle **Rev. Legend:** STRAITS SETTLEMENTS

Date	Mintage	F	VF	XF	Unc	BU
1901	2,700,000	6.00	8.50	38.00	140	—

KM# 21 10 CENTS

2.7100 g., 0.8000 Silver .0697 oz. ASW **Ruler:** Edward VII **Obv:** Crowned bust right **Obv. Designer:** G.W. DeSaulles **Rev:** Value within beaded circle

Date	Mintage	F	VF	XF	Unc	BU
1902	6,118,000	7.00	23.00	70.00	180	—
1902 Proof	—	Value: 600				
1903	1,401,000	7.00	23.00	70.00	180	—
1903 Proof	—	Value: 600				

KM# 21a 10 CENTS

2.7100 g., 0.6000 Silver .0522 oz. ASW **Ruler:** Edward VII **Obv:** Crowned bust right **Obv. Designer:** G.W. DeSaulles **Rev:** Value within beaded circle

Date	Mintage	F	VF	XF	Unc	BU
1909B	11,088,000	15.00	40.00	120	335	—
1910B	1,657,000	2.00	5.00	10.00	22.00	—
1910B Proof	—	Value: 470				

KM# 29 10 CENTS

2.7100 g., 0.6000 Silver .0522 oz. ASW **Ruler:** George V **Obv:** Crowned bust left **Obv. Designer:** E.B. MacKennal **Rev:** Value within beaded circle

Date	Mintage	F	VF	XF	Unc	BU
1916	600,000	5.00	12.00	50.00	130	—
1917	5,600,000	1.00	2.00	15.00	95.00	—

KM# 29a 10 CENTS

2.7100 g., 0.4000 Silver .0348 oz. ASW **Ruler:** George V **Obv:** Crowned bust left **Obv. Designer:** E.B. MacKennal **Rev:** Value within beaded circle

Date	Mintage	F	VF	XF	Unc	BU
1918	7,500,000	1.00	2.50	15.00	95.00	—
1919	11,500,000	1.00	2.50	15.00	90.00	—
1920	4,000,000	14.00	35.00	165	320	—

KM# 29b 10 CENTS

2.7100 g., 0.6000 Silver .0522 oz. ASW **Ruler:** George V **Obv:** Crowned bust left **Obv. Designer:** E.B. MacKennal **Rev:** Value within beaded circle

Date	Mintage	F	VF	XF	Unc	BU
1926	20,000,000	1.25	1.75	8.00	19.00	—
1926 Proof	—	Value: 350				
1927	23,000,000	1.00	1.50	3.00	5.50	—
1927 Proof	—	Value: 350				

KM# 12 20 CENTS

5.4300 g., 0.8000 Silver .1396 oz. ASW, 23 mm. **Ruler:** Victoria **Obv:** Crowned head left **Obv. Legend:** VICTORIA QUEEN **Rev:** Value within beaded circle **Rev. Legend:** STRAITS SETTLEMENTS

Date	Mintage	F	VF	XF	Unc	BU
1901	600,000	7.00	12.00	32.00	138	—

KM# 22 20 CENTS

5.4300 g., 0.8000 Silver .1396 oz. ASW, 23 mm. **Ruler:** Edward VII **Obv:** Crowned bust right **Obv. Designer:** G.W. DeSaulles **Rev:** Value within beaded circle

Date	Mintage	F	VF	XF	Unc	BU
1902	1,105,000	18.00	38.00	165	350	—
1902 Proof	—	Value: 1,000				
1903	1,150,000	18.00	38.00	165	350	—
1903 Proof	—	Value: 1,000				

KM# 22a 20 CENTS

5.4300 g., 0.6000 Silver .1047 oz. ASW, 23 mm. **Ruler:** Edward VII **Obv:** Crowned bust right **Obv. Designer:** G.W. DeSaulles **Rev:** Value within beaded circle

Date	Mintage	F	VF	XF	Unc	BU
1910B	3,276,000	5.00	7.00	28.00	95.00	—
1910B Proof	—	Value: 1,000				

KM# 30 20 CENTS

5.4300 g., 0.6000 Silver .1047 oz. ASW, 23 mm. **Ruler:** George V **Obv:** Crowned bust left **Obv. Designer:** E.B. MacKennal **Rev:** Value within beaded circle

Date	Mintage	F	VF	XF	Unc	BU
1916B	545,000	10.00	20.00	95.00	200	—
1916B Proof	—	Value: 430				
1917B	652,000	4.50	12.00	70.00	155	—

KM# 30a 20 CENTS
5.4300 g., 0.4000 Silver .0698 oz. ASW, 23 mm. **Ruler:** George V **Obv:** Crowned bust left **Obv. Designer:** E.B. MacKennal **Rev:** Value within beaded circle

Date	Mintage	F	VF	XF	Unc	BU
1919B	2,500,000	3.00	7.00	32.50	110	—
1919B Proof	—	Value: 430				

KM# 30b 20 CENTS
5.4300 g., 0.6000 Silver .1047 oz. ASW, 23 mm. **Ruler:** George V **Obv:** Crowned bust left **Obv. Designer:** E.B. MacKennal **Rev:** Value within beaded circle

Date	Mintage	F	VF	XF	Unc	BU
1926	2,500,000	1.75	3.50	20.00	100	—
1926 Proof	—	Value: 430				
1927	3,000,000	1.75	3.50	9.00	25.00	—
1927 Proof	—	Value: 430				
1935 Round-top 3	1,000,000	1.75	2.75	7.00	14.00	—
1935 Flat-top 3	Inc. above	1.75	2.75	7.00	14.00	—

KM# 13 50 CENTS
13.5769 g., 0.8000 Silver .3492 oz. ASW **Ruler:** Victoria **Obv:** Crowned head left **Obv. Legend:** VICTORIA QUEEN **Rev:** Value within beaded circle **Rev. Legend:** STRAITS SETTLEMENTS

Date	Mintage	F	VF	XF	Unc	BU
1901	120,000	52.00	80.00	300	550	—

KM# 23 50 CENTS
13.5769 g., 0.8000 Silver .3492 oz. ASW, 31 mm. **Ruler:** Edward VII **Obv:** Crowned bust right **Obv. Designer:** G.W. DeSaulles **Rev:** Value within beaded circle

Date	Mintage	F	VF	XF	Unc	BU
1902	148,000	100	190	450	760	—
1902 Proof	—	Value: 1,450				
1903	193,000	100	190	450	760	—
1903 Proof	—	Value: 1,450				
1905B Raised	498,000	95.00	165	330	460	—
1905B Proof, raised	—	Value: 1,450				
1905B Proof, incuse	—	Value: 1,450				

KM# 24 50 CENTS
10.1000 g., 0.9000 Silver .2922 oz. ASW, 28 mm. **Ruler:** Edward VII **Obv:** Crowned bust right **Obv. Designer:** G.W. DeSaulles **Rev:** Value within beaded circle

Date	Mintage	F	VF	XF	Unc	BU
1907	464,000	17.50	28.00	70.00	165	—
1907H	2,667,000	17.50	28.00	70.00	165	—
1908	2,869,000	17.50	28.00	70.00	165	—
1908H	Inc. above	17.50	35.00	100	185	—

Note: Mintage included with 1907H

KM# 35.1 50 CENTS
8.4200 g., 0.5000 Silver .1353 oz. ASW **Ruler:** George V **Obv:** Crowned bust left **Obv. Designer:** E.B. MacKennal **Rev:** Value within beaded circle

Date	Mintage	F	VF	XF	Unc	BU
1920	3,900,000	4.00	5.00	7.00	15.00	—
1920 Proof	—	Value: 430				

Date	Mintage	F	VF	XF	Unc	BU
1921	2,579,000	4.00	5.00	9.00	18.00	—
1921 Proof	—	Value: 430				

KM# 35.2 50 CENTS
8.4200 g., 0.5000 Silver .1353 oz. ASW **Ruler:** George V **Obv:** Crowned bust left with dot below bust **Obv. Designer:** E.B. MacKennal **Rev:** Value within beaded circle

Date	Mintage	F	VF	XF	Unc	BU
1920	Inc. above	200	350	560	1,000	—

KM# 25 DOLLAR
26.9500 g., 0.9000 Silver .7799 oz. ASW, 37 mm. **Ruler:** Edward VII **Obv:** Crowned bust right **Obv. Designer:** G.W. DeSaulles **Rev:** Artistic design within circle

Date	Mintage	F	VF	XF	Unc	BU
1903 Proof	—	Value: 1,450				
1903B Incuse	15,010,000	40.00	62.50	165	260	—
1903B Raised	Inc. above	140	250	450	960	—
1903B Proof, raised	—	Value: 1,800				
1904B	20,365,000	28.00	38.00	97.50	190	—
1904B Proof	—	Value: 1,450				

KM# 26 DOLLAR
20.2100 g., 0.9000 Silver .5848 oz. ASW, 34.5 mm. **Ruler:** Edward VII **Obv:** Crowned bust right **Obv. Designer:** G.W. DeSaulles **Rev:** Artistic design within circle **Note:** Reduced size.

Date	Mintage	F	VF	XF	Unc	BU
1907	6,842,000	10.00	20.00	50.00	100	—
1907H	4,000,000	10.00	20.00	50.00	100	—
1907H Proof	—	Value: 720				
1908	4,152,000	10.00	18.00	42.00	95.00	—
1908 Proof	—	Value: 720				
1909	1,014,000	12.00	25.00	55.00	160	—
1909 Proof	—	Value: 7,200				

KM# 33 DOLLAR
16.8500 g., 0.5000 Silver .2709 oz. ASW **Ruler:** George V **Obv:** Crowned bust left **Obv. Designer:** E.B. MacKennal **Rev:** Artistic design within circle

Date	Mintage	F	VF	XF	Unc	BU
1919	6,000,000	60.00	110	200	300	—
1919 Proof	—	Value: 175				
Note: Restrike						
1920	8,164,000	20.00	40.00	80.00	160	—
1920 Proof	—	Value: 175				
Note: Restrike						
1925	—	—	—	6,900	—	—
1925 Proof	—	Value: 9,100				
1925 Proof	—	Value: 2,000				
Note: Restrike						
1926	—	—	—	5,500	—	—
1926 Proof	—	Value: 9,000				
1926 Proof	—	Value: 2,000				
Note: Restrike						

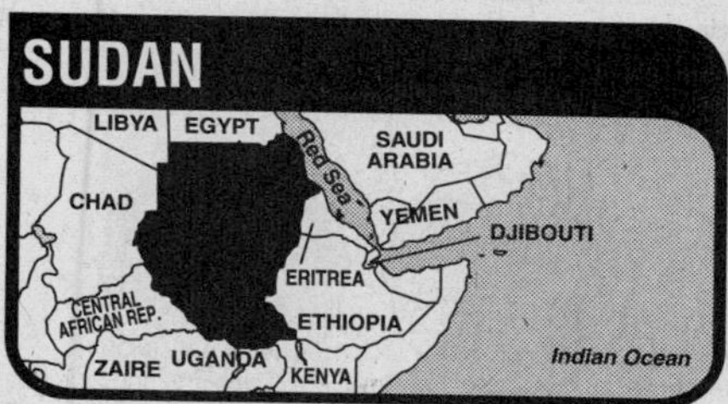

The Democratic Republic of the Sudan, located in northeast Africa on the Red Sea between Egypt and Ethiopia, has an area of 967,500 sq. mi. (2,505,810 sq. km.) and a population of *24.5 million. Capital: Khartoum. Agriculture and livestock raising are the chief occupations. Cotton, gum arabic and peanuts are exported.

The Sudan, site of the powerful Nubian kingdom of Roman times, was a collection of small independent states from the 14th century until 1820-22 when it was conquered and united by Mohammed Ali, Pasha of Egypt. Egyptian forces were driven from the area during the Mahdist revolt, 1881-98, but the Sudan was retaken by Anglo-Egyptian expeditions, 1896-98, and established as an Anglo-Egyptian condominium in 1899. Britain supplied the administrative apparatus and personnel, but the appearance of joint Anglo-Egyptian administration was continued until Jan. 9, 1954, when the first Sudanese self-government parliament was inaugurated. The Sudan achieved independence on Jan. 1, 1956 with the consent of the British and Egyptian government.

TITLES

جمهورية السودان

Jumhuriya(t) as-Sudan

الجمهورية السودان
الد ميقرا طية

Al-Arabiya(t) as-Sa'udiya(t)al-Jumhuriya(t) as-Sudan ad-Dimiqratiya(t)

MINT NAME

مالناپور

Omdurman

REPUBLIC

STANDARD COINAGE

KM# 29.1 MILLIM
Bronze **Obv:** Large legend and value above flower sprigs **Rev:** Camel with rider running left

Date	Mintage	F	VF	XF	Unc	BU
AH1376-1956	5,000,000	—	—	0.15	0.30	0.50
AH1379-1960	1,300,000	—	—	0.15	0.35	0.60
AH1386-1966 Proof	—	—	—	—	—	—
AH1387-1967	—	—	—	0.15	0.30	0.50
AH1388-1968	—	—	—	0.15	0.30	0.50
AH1389-1969	—	—	—	0.15	0.30	0.50

KM# 29.2 MILLIM
Bronze **Obv:** Small legend and value above flower sprigs **Rev:** Camel with rider running left **Note:** Except for proof sets, mintage figures have generally not been released since 1967.

Date	Mintage	F	VF	XF	Unc	BU
AH1387-1967 Proof	7,834	Value: 0.75				
AH1388-1968 Proof	5,251	Value: 0.75				
AH1389-1969 Proof	2,149	Value: 0.75				

KM# 39 MILLIM
Bronze **Obv:** New Arabic legend and value above flower sprigs **Rev:** Camel with rider running left

Date	Mintage	F	VF	XF	Unc	BU
AH1390-1970	—	—	—	—	—	—
AH1390-1970 Proof	1,646	Value: 1.00				
AH1391-1971 Proof	1,772	Value: 1.00				

KM# 30.1 2 MILLIM

Bronze **Obv:** Large written value with legend above flower sprigs **Rev:** Camel with rider running left **Edge:** Plain **Shape:** Scalloped

Date	Mintage	F	VF	XF	Unc	BU
AH1376-1956	5,000,000	—	—	0.15	0.50	1.00
AH1386-1966 Proof	—	Value: 1.00				
AH1387-1967	—	—	—	0.15	0.50	1.00
AH1388-1968	—	—	—	0.15	0.50	1.00
AH1389-1969	—	—	—	0.15	0.50	1.00

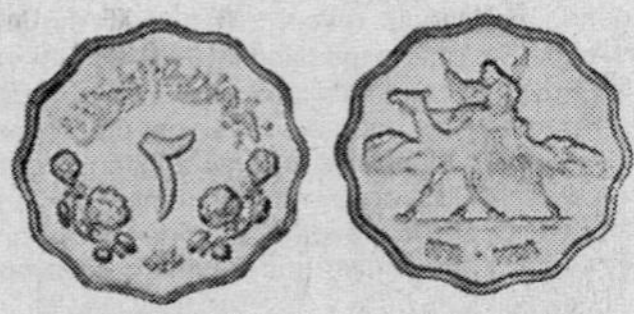

KM# 30.2 2 MILLIM

Bronze, 20.5 mm. **Obv:** Small written value with legend above flower sprigs **Rev:** Camel with rider running left **Edge:** Plain **Shape:** Scalloped

Date	Mintage	F	VF	XF	Unc	BU
AH1387-1967 Proof	7,834	Value: 1.00				
AH1388-1968 Proof	5,251	Value: 1.00				
AH1389-1969 Proof	2,149	Value: 1.25				

KM# 40 2 MILLIM

Bronze **Obv:** New Arabic legend and value above flower sprigs **Rev:** Camel with rider running left **Shape:** Scalloped

Date	Mintage	F	VF	XF	Unc	BU
AH1390-1970 Proof	1,646	Value: 1.50				
AH1391-1971 Proof	1,772	Value: 1.50				

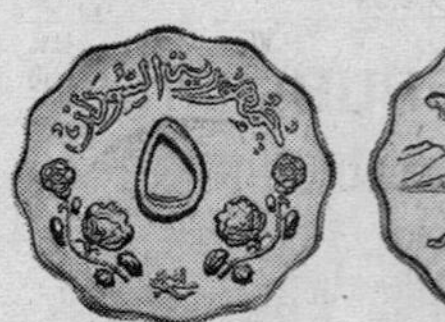

KM# 31.1 5 MILLIM

Bronze **Obv:** Thin legend and narrow 5 **Rev:** Camel with rider running left **Shape:** Scalloped **Note:** Camel and rider, date size varieties exist, and with or without outlined bare line.

Date	Mintage	F	VF	XF	Unc	BU
AH1376-1956	30,000,000	—	0.10	0.20	0.50	1.00
AH1382-1962	6,000,000	—	0.10	0.20	0.50	1.00
AH1386-1966	4,000,000	—	0.10	0.15	0.50	1.00
AH1386-1966 Proof	—	—	—	—	—	—
AH1387-1967	4,000,000	—	0.10	0.15	0.35	1.00
AH1388-1968	—	—	0.10	0.15	0.35	1.00
AH1389-1969	—	—	0.10	0.15	0.35	1.00

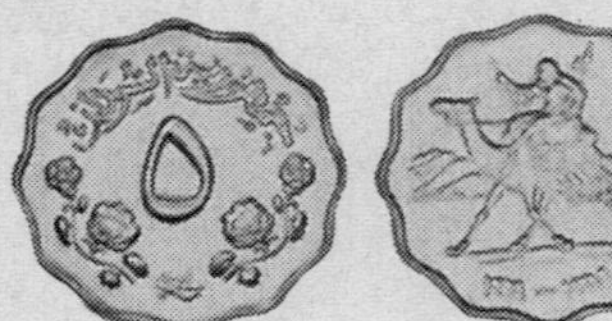

KM# 31.2 5 MILLIM

Bronze **Obv:** Thick legend and small value **Rev:** Camel with rider running left **Shape:** Scalloped

Date	Mintage	F	VF	XF	Unc	BU
AH1387-1967 Proof	7,834	Value: 1.00				
AH1388-1968 Proof	5,251	Value: 1.25				
AH1389-1969 Proof	2,149	Value: 1.50				

KM# 41.1 5 MILLIM

Bronze **Obv:** New large Arabic legend narrow 5 **Rev:** Camel with rider running left **Shape:** Scalloped **Note:** Date heighth and size varieties exist

Date	Mintage	F	VF	XF	Unc	BU
AH1390-1970	—	—	0.20	0.45	1.25	1.75
AH1391-1971	3,000,000	—	0.20	0.45	1.25	1.75

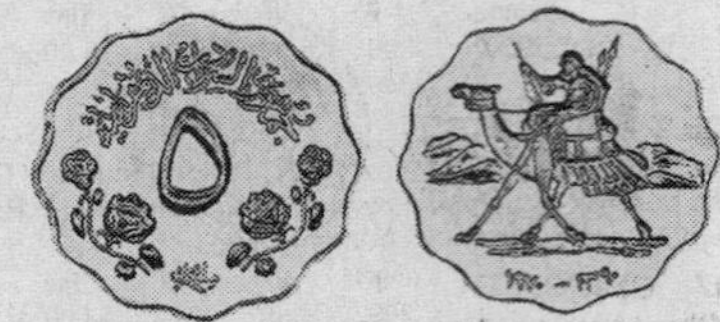

KM# 41.2 5 MILLIM

Bronze **Obv:** Small legend and wide 5 **Rev:** Camel with rider running left **Shape:** Scalloped

Date	Mintage	F	VF	XF	Unc	BU
AH1390-1970 Proof	1,646	Value: 2.50				
AH1391-1971 Proof	1,772	Value: 2.50				

KM# 47 5 MILLIM

Bronze **Subject:** 2nd Anniversary of Revolution **Obv:** Legend and value above flower sprigs **Rev:** Eagle divides dates below legend

Date	Mintage	F	VF	XF	Unc	BU
AH1391-1971	500,000	—	0.15	0.25	0.50	1.00

KM# 53 5 MILLIM

Bronze, 21.5 mm. **Series:** F.A.O. **Obv:** Legend and value above flower sprigs **Rev:** Eagle divides dates below legend **Edge:** Plain

Date	Mintage	F	VF	XF	Unc	BU
AH1392-1972	6,000,000	—	—	0.15	0.35	—
AH1393-1973	9,000,000	—	—	0.15	0.35	—

KM# 54 5 MILLIM

Bronze **Obv:** Legend and value **Rev:** Eagle divides AH and CE dates **Note:** Similar to 10 Millim, KM#55, but round.

Date	Mintage	F	VF	XF	Unc	BU
AH1392-1972	—	—	—	0.20	0.45	—

KM# 54a.1 5 MILLIM

Brass **Obv:** Thick legend and written value **Rev:** Ribbon with 3 equal sections

Date	Mintage	F	VF	XF	Unc	BU
AH1395-1975	4,132,000	—	—	0.20	0.40	—
AH1398-1978	—	—	—	0.20	0.40	—

KM# 54a.2 5 MILLIM

Brass **Obv:** Large legend and large 5 **Rev:** Eagle divides dates, ribbon with long center section

Date	Mintage	F	VF	XF	Unc	BU
AH1398-1978	—	—	—	0.20	0.40	—

KM# 54a.3 5 MILLIM

Brass **Obv:** Thin legend and narrow 5, different style **Rev:** Eagle divides dates, ribbon with 3 equal sections

Date	Mintage	F	VF	XF	Unc	BU
AH1400-1980 Proof	—	Value: 1.00				

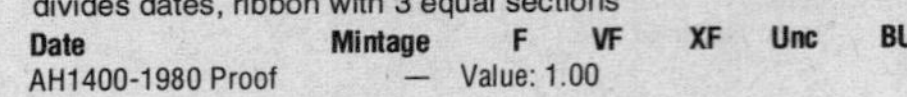

KM# 60 5 MILLIM

Brass **Series:** F.A.O. **Obv:** Legend and value above flower sprigs **Rev:** Eagle within sprigs divide legend and dates **Note:** Size varies 21.4 - 22.5 mm.

Date	Mintage	F	VF	XF	Unc	BU
AH1396-1976	7,868,000	—	—	0.10	0.20	—
AH1398-1978	7,000,000	—	—	0.10	0.20	—

KM# 94 5 MILLIM

Brass **Subject:** 20th Anniversary of Independence **Obv:** Legend and value above flower sprigs **Rev:** Eagle divides dates below legend

Date	Mintage	F	VF	XF	Unc	BU
AH1396-1976	—	—	0.15	0.20	0.25	—

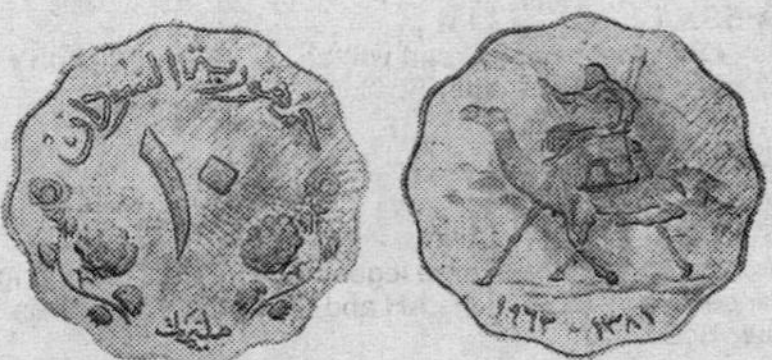

KM# 32.1 10 MILLIM

Bronze **Obv:** Large written value **Rev:** Camel with rider running left **Shape:** Scalloped **Note:** Camel, rider and date size varieties exist.

Date	Mintage	F	VF	XF	Unc	BU
AH1376-1956	15,000,000	—	0.15	0.25	0.85	1.25
AH1380-1960	12,250,000	—	0.15	0.20	0.75	1.00
AH1381-1962 High date	—	—	0.15	0.20	0.75	1.00
AH1381-1962 Low date	—	—	0.15	0.20	0.75	1.00
AH1386-1966	1,000,000	—	0.15	0.25	0.85	1.25
AH1386-1966 Proof	—	—	—	—	—	—
AH1387-1967	1,000,000	—	0.15	0.20	0.75	1.00
AH1388-1968	—	—	0.15	0.20	0.75	1.25
AH1389-1969	—	—	0.15	0.20	0.75	1.25

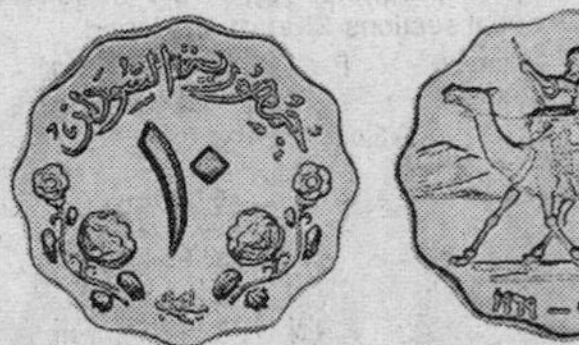

KM# 32.2 10 MILLIM

Bronze **Obv:** Small written value **Rev:** Camel with rider running left **Shape:** Scalloped

Date	Mintage	F	VF	XF	Unc	BU
AH1387-1967 Proof	7,834	Value: 1.25				
AH1388-1968 Proof	5,251	Value: 1.50				
AH1389-1969 Proof	2,149	Value: 1.75				

KM# 42.1 10 MILLIM

Bronze **Obv:** New large Arabic legend and written value **Rev:** Camel with rider running left **Shape:** Scalloped

Date	Mintage	F	VF	XF	Unc	BU
AH1390-1970	—	—	0.20	0.40	1.00	1.50
AH1391-1971	3,000,000	—	0.20	0.40	1.00	1.50

KM# 42.2 10 MILLIM

Bronze **Obv:** Small legend and written value **Rev:** Camel with rider running left **Shape:** Scalloped

Date	Mintage	F	VF	XF	Unc	BU
AH1390-1970 Proof	1,646	Value: 1.50				
AH1391-1971 Proof	1,772	Value: 1.50				

KM# 48 10 MILLIM
Bronze **Subject:** 2nd Anniversary of the Revolution **Obv:** Legend and value above flower sprigs **Rev:** Eagle divides dates below legend

Date	Mintage	F	VF	XF	Unc	BU
AH1391-1971	500,000	—	10.00	15.00	25.00	—

KM# 55 10 MILLIM
Bronze **Obv:** Legend and value above flower sprigs **Rev:** Eagle divides dates **Shape:** Scalloped

Date	Mintage	F	VF	XF	Unc	BU
AH1392-1972	6,500,000	—	0.15	0.25	0.50	—

KM# 55a.1 10 MILLIM
Brass **Obv:** Large legend and written value **Rev:** Ribbon with three equal sections **Shape:** Scalloped

Date	Mintage	F	VF	XF	Unc	BU
AH1395-1975	12,000,000	—	0.25	0.35	0.75	—
AH1398-1978	9,410,000	—	0.25	0.45	1.00	—

KM# 55a.2 10 MILLIM
Brass, 25.5 mm. **Obv:** Large legend **Rev:** Ribbon with long center section, eagle divides AH and CE dates **Edge:** Plain **Shape:** Scalloped

Date	Mintage	F	VF	XF	Unc	BU
AH1398-1978	—	—	0.75	1.75	4.25	—

KM# 55a.3 10 MILLIM
Brass **Obv:** Small legend and written value **Rev:** Eagle divides dates, ribbon with 3 equal sections **Shape:** Scalloped

Date	Mintage	F	VF	XF	Unc	BU
AH1400-1980	2,490,000	—	0.25	0.45	1.00	—
AH1400-1980 Proof	—	Value: 2.50				

KM# 61 10 MILLIM
Brass **Series:** F.A.O. **Obv:** Legend and value above flower sprigs **Rev:** Eagle within sprigs divides date and legend **Shape:** Scalloped

Date	Mintage	F	VF	XF	Unc	BU
AH1396-1976	3,000,000	—	0.10	0.15	0.25	—
AH1398-1978	—	—	0.10	0.15	0.25	—

KM# 62 10 MILLIM
Brass **Subject:** 20th Anniversary of Independence **Obv:** Legend and value above flower sprigs **Rev:** Eagle divides dates below legend **Shape:** Scalloped

Date	Mintage	F	VF	XF	Unc	BU
AH1396-1976	3,610,000	—	0.10	0.20	0.40	—

KM# 111 10 MILLIM
Brass, 24.5 mm. **Obv:** Legend and value above flower sprigs **Rev:** Eagle divides dates **Shape:** Round

Date	Mintage	F	VF	XF	Unc	BU
AH1400-1980	—	—	1.25	3.75	7.50	—

KM# 97 GHIRSH
Brass **Obv:** Legend and value above flower sprigs **Rev:** Eagle divides dates, ribbon with 3 equal sections

Date	Mintage	F	VF	XF	Unc	BU
AH1403-1983	1,140,000	—	0.25	0.65	2.00	—

KM# 99 GHIRSH
Aluminum-Bronze **Obv:** Legend and value above flower sprigs **Rev:** Building above inscription and crossed sprigs

Date	Mintage	F	VF	XF	Unc	BU
AH1408-1987	—	—	0.30	0.80	3.00	—

KM# 33 2 GHIRSH
Copper-Nickel, 17.5 mm. **Obv:** Legend and value above flower sprigs **Rev:** Camel with rider running left

Date	Mintage	F	VF	XF	Unc	BU
AH1376-1956	5,000,000	—	0.15	0.35	0.75	1.00
AH1381-1962	—	—	0.15	0.35	0.75	1.00

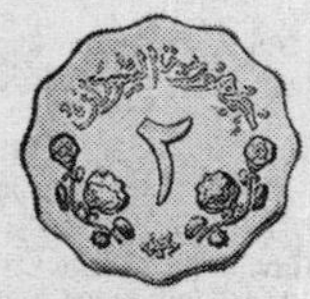

KM# 36 2 GHIRSH
Copper-Nickel, 20 mm. **Obv:** Legend and value above flower sprigs **Rev:** Camel with rider running left

Date	Mintage	F	VF	XF	Unc	BU
AH1382-1963	1,250,000	—	0.15	0.35	0.75	1.00
AH1386-1966 Proof	—	—	—	—	—	—
AH1387-1967	7,834	—	0.15	0.35	0.75	1.00
AH1387-1967 Proof	7,834	Value: 1.50				
AH1388-1968	5,251	—	0.15	0.35	0.75	1.00
AH1388-1968 Proof	5,251	Value: 1.50				
AH1389-1969	2,149	—	0.15	0.35	0.75	1.00
AH1389-1969 Proof	2,149	Value: 1.75				

KM# 43.1 2 GHIRSH
Copper-Nickel **Obv:** New large Arabic legend and written value **Rev:** Camel with rider running left

Date	Mintage	F	VF	XF	Unc	BU
AH1390-1970	—	—	0.30	0.60	1.25	1.50

KM# 43.2 2 GHIRSH
Copper-Nickel **Obv:** New small legend and written value **Rev:** Camel with rider running left

Date	Mintage	F	VF	XF	Unc	BU
AH1390-1970 Proof	1,646	Value: 1.50				
AH1391-1971 Proof	1,772	Value: 1.50				

KM# 49 2 GHIRSH
Copper-Nickel **Subject:** 2nd Anniversary of Revolution **Obv:** Legend and value above flower sprigs **Rev:** Eagle divides dates below legend

Date	Mintage	F	VF	XF	Unc	BU
AH1391-1971	500,000	—	0.25	0.45	0.80	—

KM# 57.1 2 GHIRSH
Copper-Nickel **Obv:** Thick legend and value above flower sprigs **Rev:** Eagle divides dates, ribbon with 3 equal sections

Date	Mintage	F	VF	XF	Unc	BU
AH1395-1975	1,000,000	—	0.20	0.35	0.75	—
AH1398-1978	1,250,000	—	0.20	0.35	0.75	—

KM# 57.2 2 GHIRSH
Copper-Nickel **Obv:** Large legend **Rev:** Ribbon with long center section, eagle divides AH and AD dates

Date	Mintage	F	VF	XF	Unc	BU
AH1398-1978	—	—	0.20	0.35	0.75	—
AH1400-1980	—	—	0.20	0.35	0.75	—

KM# 57.3 2 GHIRSH
Copper-Nickel, 20 mm. **Obv:** Thin legend and value above flower sprig **Rev:** Eagle divides dates, ribbon with 3 equal sections **Edge:** Reeded

Date	Mintage	F	VF	XF	Unc	BU
AH1399-1979	2,000,000	—	0.20	0.35	0.75	—
AH1400-1980	6,825,000	—	0.20	0.35	0.75	—
AH1400-1980 Proof	Inc. above	Value: 2.00				

KM# 57.2a 2 GHIRSH
Brass **Obv:** Legend with different style and value above flower sprigs **Rev:** Eagle divides dates

Date	Mintage	F	VF	XF	Unc	BU
AH1403-1983	100,000	—	0.75	1.50	3.50	—

KM# 63.1 2 GHIRSH
Copper-Nickel **Series:** F.A.O. **Obv:** Thick value **Rev:** Eagle within sprigs divides dates and legend

Date	Mintage	F	VF	XF	Unc	BU
AH1396-1976	500,000	—	0.20	0.35	0.75	—
AH1398-1978	Inc. above	—	0.20	0.35	0.75	—

KM# 63.2 2 GHIRSH
Copper-Nickel **Series:** F.A.O. **Obv:** Thin value **Rev:** Eagle divides AH and AD dates **Note:** Like KM#63.1.

Date	Mintage	F	VF	XF	Unc	BU
AH1398-1978	Inc. above	—	5.00	7.00	10.00	—

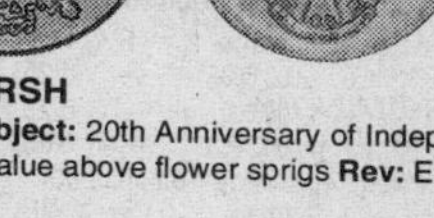

KM# 64 2 GHIRSH
Copper-Nickel **Subject:** 20th Anniversary of Independence **Obv:** Legend and value above flower sprigs **Rev:** Eagle divides dates below legend

Date	Mintage	F	VF	XF	Unc	BU
AH1396-1976	1,750,000	—	0.20	0.30	0.60	—

KM# 34.1 5 GHIRSH

Copper-Nickel, 24 mm. **Obv:** Large written value **Rev:** Camel with rider running left **Edge:** Reeded

Date	Mintage	F	VF	XF	Unc	BU
AH1376-1956	40,000,000	—	0.20	0.40	1.20	1.50
AH1386-1966 Proof	—	Value: 1.50				
AH1387-1967	—	—	0.20	0.30	1.00	1.25
AH1388-1968	—	—	0.20	0.30	1.00	1.25
AH1389-1969	—	—	0.20	0.30	1.00	1.25

KM# 34.2 5 GHIRSH

Copper-Nickel **Obv:** Small written value **Rev:** Camel with rider running left

Date	Mintage	F	VF	XF	Unc	BU
AH1387-1967 Proof	7,834	Value: 1.50				
AH1388-1968 Proof	5,251	Value: 1.75				
AH1389-1969 Proof	2,149	Value: 2.50				

KM# 44 5 GHIRSH

Copper-Nickel **Obv:** New Arabic legend, value above flower sprigs **Rev:** Camel with rider running left

Date	Mintage	F	VF	XF	Unc	BU
AH1390-1970 Proof	1,646	Value: 2.50				
AH1391-1971 Proof	1,772	Value: 2.50				

KM# 51 5 GHIRSH

Copper-Nickel **Subject:** 2nd Anniversary of Revolution **Obv:** Legend and value above flower sprigs **Rev:** Eagle divides dates below legend

Date	Mintage	F	VF	XF	Unc	BU
AH1391-1971	500,000	—	0.30	0.60	1.20	—

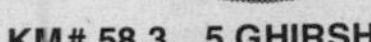

KM# 58.3 5 GHIRSH

Copper-Nickel, 23.5 mm. **Obv:** Small legend with different style and value above flower sprigs **Rev:** Ribbon with 3 equal sections, eagle divides dates **Edge:** Reeded

Date	Mintage	F	VF	XF	Unc	BU
AH1397-1977	2,000,000	—	0.25	0.45	0.85	—
AH1398-1978	1,000,000	—	0.25	0.45	0.85	—
AH1400-1980	1,000,000	—	0.25	0.45	0.85	—
AH1400-1980 Proof	Inc. above	Value: 3.00				

KM# 58.1 5 GHIRSH

Copper-Nickel **Obv:** Large legend and value **Rev:** Eagle divides dates, ribbon with 3 equal sections

Date	Mintage	F	VF	XF	Unc	BU
AH1395-1975	1,600,000	—	0.25	0.45	0.85	—

KM# 58.2 5 GHIRSH

Copper-Nickel **Obv:** Large legend style change, small value **Rev:** Eagle divides dates, ribbon with long center section **Note:** Edge varieties exist.

Date	Mintage	F	VF	XF	Unc	BU
AH1400-1980	—	—	0.25	0.45	0.85	—

Note: Mintage included with KM#58.1.

KM# 58.4 5 GHIRSH

Copper-Nickel **Obv:** Large legend in different style **Rev:** Ribbon with long center section, eagle divides AH and AD dates **Note:** Edge varieties exist.

Date	Mintage	F	VF	XF	Unc	BU
AH1400-1980	—	—	0.25	0.45	0.85	—

Note: Mintage included with KM#58.1.

KM# 65 5 GHIRSH

Copper-Nickel **Series:** F.A.O. **Obv:** Legend and value above flower sprigs **Rev:** Eagle within sprigs divides dates and legend

Date	Mintage	F	VF	XF	Unc	BU
AH1396-1976	500,000	—	0.20	0.30	0.65	—
AH1398-1978	—	—	0.20	0.30	0.65	—

KM# 66 5 GHIRSH

Copper-Nickel **Subject:** 20th Anniversary of Independence **Obv:** Legend and value above flower sprigs **Rev:** Eagle divides dates below legend

Date	Mintage	F	VF	XF	Unc	BU
AH1396-1976	3,940,000	—	0.25	0.50	1.00	—

KM# 74 5 GHIRSH

Copper-Nickel **Subject:** Council of Arab Economic Unity **Obv:** Clasped hands and legend within wreath **Rev:** Eagle divides dates **Note:** Edge varieties exist.

Date	Mintage	F	VF	XF	Unc	BU
AH1398-1978	5,040,000	—	0.15	0.25	0.50	—

KM# 84 5 GHIRSH

Copper-Nickel **Series:** F.A.O. **Obv:** Cow and calf flanked by designs **Rev:** Eagle divides dates **Note:** Edge varieties exist.

Date	Mintage	F	VF	XF	Unc	BU
AH1401-1981	1,000,000	—	0.20	0.40	0.75	—

KM# 110.1 5 GHIRSH

Brass **Obv:** Large value **Rev:** Ribbon with three equal sections, eagle divides AH and AD dates

Date	Mintage	F	VF	XF	Unc	BU
AH1403-1983	—	—	0.25	0.60	1.55	—

KM# 110.2 5 GHIRSH

Brass **Obv:** Legend and value above flower sprigs **Rev:** Eagle divides dates, ribbon with long center section

Date	Mintage	F	VF	XF	Unc	BU
AH1403-1983	—	—	0.50	1.25	2.25	—

KM# 110.3 5 GHIRSH

Brass **Obv:** Small value, legend in different style **Rev:** Ribbon with three equal sections, eagle divides AH and AD dates

Date	Mintage	F	VF	XF	Unc	BU
AH1403-1983	—	—	5.00	7.00	10.00	—

KM# 110.4 5 GHIRSH

Brass **Obv:** Large value and legend **Rev:** Ribbon with long center section, eagle divides AH and AD dates

Date	Mintage	F	VF	XF	Unc	BU
AH1403-1983	—	—	1.50	4.50	7.50	—

KM# 100 5 GHIRSH

Aluminum-Bronze **Obv:** Legend and value above flower sprigs **Rev:** Central bank building above inscription and crossed sprigs

Date	Mintage	F	VF	XF	Unc	BU
AH1408-1987	—	—	0.40	1.00	2.00	—

KM# 35.1 10 GHIRSH

Copper-Nickel, 28 mm. **Obv:** Large written value **Rev:** Camel with rider running left

Date	Mintage	F	VF	XF	Unc	BU
AH1376-1956	15,000,000	—	0.35	0.75	2.00	2.50
AH1386-1966 Proof	—	—	—	—	—	—
AH1387-1967	—	—	0.30	0.60	1.50	2.00
AH1388-1968	—	—	0.30	0.60	1.50	2.00
AH1389-1969	—	—	0.30	0.60	1.50	2.00

KM# 35.2 10 GHIRSH

Copper-Nickel, 28 mm. **Obv:** Small written value **Rev:** Camel with rider running left

Date	Mintage	F	VF	XF	Unc	BU
AH1387-1967 Proof	7,834	Value: 2.50				
AH1388-1968 Proof	5,251	Value: 2.50				
AH1389-1969 Proof	2,149	Value: 3.00				

KM# 45.1 10 GHIRSH
Copper-Nickel, 28 mm. **Obv:** New large Arabic legend and written value **Rev:** Camel with rider running left

Date	Mintage	F	VF	XF	Unc	BU
AH1390-1970	—	—	0.60	1.25	2.50	—
AH1391-1971	385,000	—	0.60	1.25	2.50	—

KM# 45.2 10 GHIRSH
Copper-Nickel, 28 mm. **Obv:** New small Arabic legend and written value **Rev:** Camel with rider running left

Date	Mintage	F	VF	XF	Unc	BU
AH1390-1970 Proof	1,646	Value: 3.00				
AH1391-1971 Proof	1,772	Value: 3.00				

KM# 52 10 GHIRSH
Copper-Nickel, 28 mm. **Subject:** 2nd Anniversary of Revolution **Obv:** Legend and value above flower sprigs **Rev:** Eagle divides dates below legend

Date	Mintage	F	VF	XF	Unc	BU
AH1391-1971	500,000	—	0.60	1.25	3.00	—

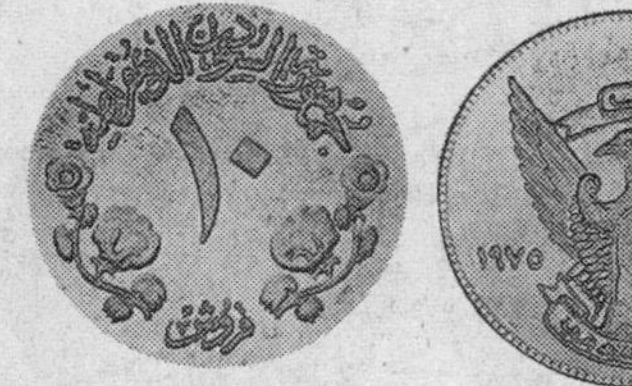

KM# 59.1 10 GHIRSH
Copper-Nickel, 28 mm. **Obv:** Legend and value above flower sprigs **Rev:** Eagle divides dates, ribbon with 3 equal sections **Edge:** Reeded

Date	Mintage	F	VF	XF	Unc	BU
AH1395-1975	1,000,000	—	0.50	1.00	2.50	—

KM# 59.2 10 GHIRSH
Copper-Nickel, 28 mm. **Obv:** Legend and value above flower sprigs **Rev:** Eagle divides dates, ribbon with long center section **Note:** Edge varieties exist.

Date	Mintage	F	VF	XF	Unc	BU
AH1400-1980	—	—	0.50	1.00	2.50	—

KM# 59.3 10 GHIRSH
Copper-Nickel **Obv:** Legend and value above flower sprigs **Rev:** Eagle divides dates **Note:** Reduced size. Edge varieties exist.

Date	Mintage	F	VF	XF	Unc	BU
AH1403-1983	—	—	0.50	1.00	2.50	—

KM# 59.4 10 GHIRSH
Copper-Nickel **Obv:** Value within flower sprigs below legend **Rev:** Ribbon with three equal sections, eagle divides AH and AD dates

Date	Mintage	F	VF	XF	Unc	BU
AH1403-1983	1,100,000	—	7.00	10.00	20.00	—

KM# 59.5 10 GHIRSH
Copper-Nickel, 28 mm. **Obv:** Thin legend, different style and value above flower sprigs **Rev:** Eagle divides dates **Edge:** Reeded

Date	Mintage	F	VF	XF	Unc	BU
AH1397-1977	1,000,000	—	0.50	1.00	2.75	—
AH1400-1980	2,965,000	—	0.50	1.00	2.75	—
AH1400-1980 Proof	—	Value: 4.50				

KM# 67 10 GHIRSH
Copper-Nickel, 28 mm. **Series:** F.A.O. **Obv:** Legend and value above flower sprigs **Rev:** Eagle within sprigs divides dates and legend

Date	Mintage	F	VF	XF	Unc	BU
AH1396-1976	500,000	—	0.30	0.65	1.50	—
AH1398-1978	—	—	0.30	0.65	1.50	—

KM# 68 10 GHIRSH
Copper-Nickel, 28 mm. **Subject:** 20th Anniversary of Independence **Obv:** Legend and value above flower sprigs **Rev:** Eagle divides dates below legend **Edge:** Reeded **Note:** Edge varieties exist.

Date	Mintage	F	VF	XF	Unc	BU
AH1396-1976	5,540,000	—	0.25	0.60	1.25	—

KM# 95 10 GHIRSH
Copper-Nickel, 28 mm. **Subject:** Council of Arab Economic Unity **Obv:** Clasped hands below inscription within wreath **Rev:** Eagle divides dates **Note:** Edge varieties exist.

Date	Mintage	F	VF	XF	Unc	BU
AH1398-1978	1,000,000	—	0.60	1.25	2.50	—

KM# 85 10 GHIRSH
Copper-Nickel, 28 mm. **Series:** F.A.O. **Obv:** Cow and calf flanked by designs **Rev:** Eagle divides dates **Edge:** Reeded **Note:** Edge varieties exist.

Date	Mintage	F	VF	XF	Unc	BU
AH1401-1981	1,000,000	—	0.60	1.25	2.50	—

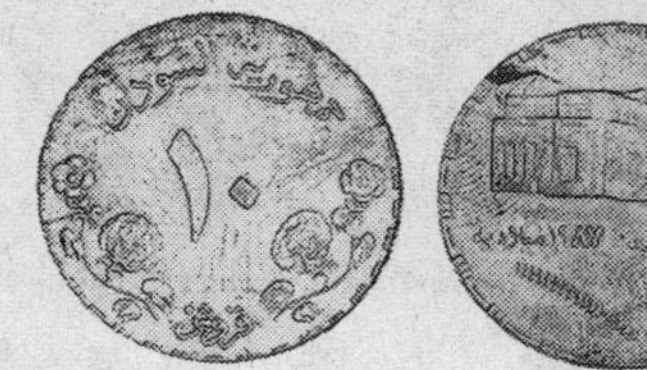

KM# 107 10 GHIRSH
Aluminum-Bronze **Obv:** Legend and value above flower sprigs **Rev:** Central bank building above inscription and crossed sprigs

Date	Mintage	F	VF	XF	Unc	BU
AH1408-1987	—	—	0.75	1.50	3.00	—

KM# 37 20 GHIRSH
Copper-Nickel **Obv:** Legend and value above flower sprigs **Rev:** Camel with rider running left

Date	Mintage	F	VF	XF	Unc	BU
AH1387-1967 Proof	7,834	Value: 4.00				
AH1388-1968 Proof	5,251	Value: 4.00				
AH1389-1969 Proof	2,149	Value: 7.00				

KM# 46 20 GHIRSH
Copper-Nickel **Obv:** New Arabic legend and value above flower sprigs **Rev:** Camel with rider running left

Date	Mintage	F	VF	XF	Unc	BU
AH1390-1970 Proof	1,646	Value: 9.00				
AH1391-1971 Proof	1,772	Value: 10.00				

KM# 98 20 GHIRSH
Copper-Nickel, 26.5 mm. **Obv:** Legend and value above flower sprigs **Rev:** Eagle divides dates

Date	Mintage	F	VF	XF	Unc	BU
AH1403-1983	72,000	—	—	—	5.00	—

KM# 96 20 GHIRSH
Copper-Nickel **Series:** F.A.O. **Obv:** Designs, value and F.A.C. letters **Rev:** Eagle divides dates

Date	Mintage	F	VF	XF	Unc	BU
AH1405-1985	—	—	—	—	3.00	—

KM# 101.1 20 GHIRSH
Aluminum-Bronze **Obv:** Small value **Rev:** Central bank building above inscription and crossed sprigs **Note:** Denomination is 8 mm high.

Date	Mintage	F	VF	XF	Unc	BU
AH1408-1987	—	—	0.60	1.25	2.50	—

KM# 101.2 20 GHIRSH
Aluminum-Bronze **Obv:** Large value **Rev:** Central bank building **Note:** Denomination is 9.5 mm high.

Date	Mintage	F	VF	XF	Unc	BU
AH1408-1988	—	—	0.60	1.25	2.50	—

KM# 38 25 GHIRSH
Copper-Nickel **Series:** F.A.O. **Obv:** Legend and value above flower sprigs **Rev:** Camel with rider running left

Date	Mintage	F	VF	XF	Unc	BU
AH1388-1968	Inc. below	—	—	—	35.00	—
AH1388-1968 Prooflike	224,000	—	—	—	—	15.00

KM# 102.1 25 GHIRSH
Aluminum-Bronze **Obv:** Legend and value above flower sprigs **Rev:** Central bank building, inner ring of dashes only visible on the corners **Shape:** Square

Date	Mintage	F	VF	XF	Unc	BU
AH1408-1987	—	—	0.85	1.75	3.50	—

KM# 102.2 25 GHIRSH
Aluminum-Bronze **Obv:** Value **Rev:** Inner ring of dashes completely visible **Shape:** Square

Date	Mintage	F	VF	XF	Unc	BU
AH1408-1987	—	—	1.00	2.00	4.00	—

KM# 108 25 GHIRSH
Copper-Nickel Plated Steel **Obv:** Legend, value and dates **Rev:** Central bank building

Date	Mintage	F	VF	XF	Unc	BU
AH1409-1989	—	—	0.50	1.00	2.25	—

KM# 56.1 50 GHIRSH
Copper-Nickel **Series:** F.A.O. **Obv:** Eagle divides dates **Rev:** Largen design

Date	Mintage	F	VF	XF	Unc	BU
AH1392-1972	1,000,000	—	1.50	3.00	6.50	—

KM# 56.2 50 GHIRSH
Copper-Nickel **Series:** F.A.O. **Obv:** Eagle divides dates **Rev:** Small design **Note:** Struck in 1976.

Date	Mintage	F	VF	XF	Unc	BU
AH1392-1972	30,000	—	5.00	10.00	20.00	—

KM# 69 50 GHIRSH
Copper-Nickel **Subject:** Establishment of Arab Cooperative **Obv:** Shield and value **Rev:** Legend above eagle and dates

Date	Mintage	F	VF	XF	Unc	BU
AH1396-1976	—	—	1.00	2.25	4.50	—

KM# 73 50 GHIRSH
Copper-Nickel **Subject:** 8th Anniversary of 1969 Revolt **Obv:** Eagle divides dates **Rev:** Cogwheel design with inscription on circular design at bottom

Date	Mintage	F	VF	XF	Unc	BU
AH1397-1977	100,000	—	1.00	2.25	4.50	—

KM# 103 50 GHIRSH
Aluminum-Bronze **Obv:** Legend and value above flower sprigs **Rev:** Central bank building above inscription and crossed sprigs **Shape:** 8-sided

Date	Mintage	F	VF	XF	Unc	BU
AH1408-1987	—	—	0.75	1.75	3.75	—

KM# 105 50 GHIRSH
Aluminum-Bronze **Subject:** 33rd Anniversary of Independence **Obv:** Legend and value above flower sprigs **Rev:** Inscription within map flanked by dates, designs below and legend above **Shape:** 8-sided

Date	Mintage	F	VF	XF	Unc	BU
AH1409-1989	—	—	0.75	1.75	3.75	—

KM# 109 50 GHIRSH
Copper-Nickel Plated Steel **Obv:** Value **Rev:** Central Bank building

Date	Mintage	F	VF	XF	Unc	BU
AH1409-1989	—	—	0.65	1.25	2.75	—

KM# 75 POUND
Copper-Nickel **Series:** F.A.O. **Subject:** Rural women **Obv:** Eagle divides dates **Rev:** Stylized designs **Shape:** 10-sided

Date	Mintage	F	VF	XF	Unc	BU
AH1398-1978	456,000	—	2.50	4.00	8.00	—

KM# 104 POUND
Aluminum-Bronze **Obv:** Legend and value above flower sprigs **Rev:** Central bank building

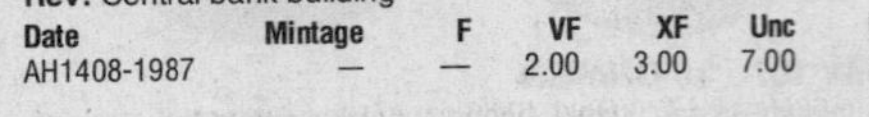

Date	Mintage	F	VF	XF	Unc	BU
AH1408-1987	—	—	2.00	3.00	7.00	—

KM# 106 POUND
Copper-Nickel Plated Steel **Obv:** Value **Rev:** Central Bank building

Date	Mintage	F	VF	XF	Unc	BU
AH1409-1989	—	—	0.75	1.50	3.75	—

KM# 70 2-1/2 POUNDS
28.2800 g., 0.9250 Silver .841 oz. ASW **Subject:** Conservation **Obv:** Eagle divides date **Rev:** Shoebill Stork

Date	Mintage	F	VF	XF	Unc	BU
AH1396-1976	5,183	—	—	—	22.50	25.00
AH1396-1976 Proof	5,590	Value: 30.00				

KM# 71 5 POUNDS
35.0000 g., 0.9250 Silver 1.0409 oz. ASW **Subject:** Conservation **Obv:** Eagle divides dates **Rev:** Hippopotamus with young one

Date	Mintage	F	VF	XF	Unc	BU
AH1396-1976	5,087	—	—	—	25.00	27.50
AH1396-1976 Proof	5,393	Value: 35.00				

KM# 76 5 POUNDS
17.5000 g., 0.9250 Silver .5205 oz. ASW **Subject:** Khartoum meeting of O.A.U. **Obv:** Eagle divides value **Rev:** African map within circle

Date	Mintage	F	VF	XF	Unc	BU
AH1398-1978	21	—	—	—	—	—
AH1398-1978 Proof	1,423	Value: 22.50				

Note: Without countermarks

Date	Mintage	F	VF	XF	Unc	BU
AH1398-1978 Proof	2,000	Value: 16.50				

Note: AH1398 with countermarks of B23 in hexagon and bell between dates

KM# 80 5 POUNDS
17.5000 g., 0.9250 Silver .5205 oz. ASW **Subject:** 1,400th

Anniversary of Islam **Obv:** Eagle divides value below legend **Rev:** Monument

Date	Mintage	F	VF	XF	Unc	BU
AH1400-1980	7,500	—	—	—	17.50	20.00
AH1400-1980 Proof	5,500	Value: 22.50				

KM# 86 5 POUNDS
28.2800 g., 0.9250 Silver .841 oz. ASW **Subject:** 25th Anniversary of Independence **Obv:** Bust 3/4 right **Rev:** Monument **Shape:** Hexagonal

Date	Mintage	F	VF	XF	Unc	BU
AH1401-1981	20,000	—	—	—	40.00	45.00
AH1401-1981 Proof	20,000	Value: 50.00				

KM# 87 5 POUNDS
19.4400 g., 0.9250 Silver .5781 oz. ASW **Series:** UNICEF, International Year of the Child **Obv:** Eagle divides value **Rev:** Children playing in front of building with logos below

Date	Mintage	F	VF	XF	Unc	BU
AH1401-1981 Proof	35,000	Value: 13.50				

KM# 92 5 POUNDS
19.4400 g., 0.9250 Silver .5781 oz. ASW **Series:** Decade for Women **Obv:** Eagle divides value **Rev:** Dancing female within map

Date	Mintage	F	VF	XF	Unc	BU
AH1404-1984 Proof	20,000	Value: 22.50				

KM# 77 10 POUNDS
35.0000 g., 0.9250 Silver 1.0409 oz. ASW **Subject:** Khartoum Meeting of O.A.U. **Obv:** Eagle divides value **Rev:** African map within circle

Date	Mintage	F	VF	XF	Unc	BU
AH1398-1978	21	—	—	—	—	350
AH1398-1978 Proof	1,417	Value: 45.00				

Note: Without countermarks

Date	Mintage	F	VF	XF	Unc	BU
AH1398-1978 Proof	2,000	Value: 37.50				

Note: AH1398 with countermarks of B23 in hexagon and bell between dates

KM# 81 10 POUNDS
35.0000 g., 0.9250 Silver 1.0409 oz. ASW **Subject:** 1,400th Anniversary of Islam **Obv:** Eagle divides value **Rev:** Buildings and upright design

Date	Mintage	F	VF	XF	Unc	BU
AH1400-1980	3,000	—	—	—	32.50	35.00
AH1400-1980 Proof	2,000	Value: 42.50				

KM# 88 10 POUNDS
28.2800 g., 0.9250 Silver .8411 oz. ASW **Series:** Year of the Disabled Person **Obv:** Eagle divides legend and dates **Rev:** Rope entwined on post and tree trunk

Date	Mintage	F	VF	XF	Unc	BU
AH1401-1981	Est. 10,000	—	—	—	35.00	37.50
AH1401-1981 Proof	10,000	Value: 42.50				

KM# 78 25 POUNDS
8.2500 g., 0.9170 Gold .2432 oz. AGW **Subject:** Khartoum Meeting of O.A.U. **Obv:** Eagle divides value **Rev:** African map within circle

Date	Mintage	F	VF	XF	Unc	BU
AH1398-1978	15	—	—	—	600	—
AH1398-1978 Proof	467	Value: 225				

Note: Without countermarks

Date	Mintage	F	VF	XF	Unc	BU
AH1398-1978 Proof	350	Value: 180				

Note: With countermarks of B23 in hexagon and bell between dates

KM# 82 25 POUNDS
8.2500 g., 0.9170 Gold .2432 oz. AGW **Subject:** 1,400th Anniversary of Islam **Obv:** Eagle divides value **Rev:** Buildings and upright design

Date	Mintage	F	VF	XF	Unc	BU
AH1400-1980	7,500	—	—	—	170	175
AH1400-1980 Proof	5,500	Value: 180				

KM# 79 50 POUNDS
17.5000 g., 0.9170 Gold .5160 oz. AGW **Subject:** Khartoum Meeting of O.A.U. **Obv:** Eagle divides value **Rev:** African map within circle

Date	Mintage	F	VF	XF	Unc	BU
AH1398-1978	11	—	—	—	1,500	—
AH1398-1978 Proof	211	Value: 420				

Note: Without countermarks

Date	Mintage	F	VF	XF	Unc	BU
AH1398-1978 Proof	350	Value: 380				

Note: With countermarks of B23 in hexagon and bell between dates

KM# 83 50 POUNDS
17.5000 g., 0.9170 Gold .5160 oz. AGW **Subject:** 1,400th Anniversary of Islam **Obv:** Eagle divides value **Rev:** Buildings and upright design

Date	Mintage	F	VF	XF	Unc	BU
AH1400-1979	3,000	—	—	—	365	380
AH1400-1979 Proof	2,000	Value: 400				

KM# 89 50 POUNDS
7.9900 g., 0.9170 Gold .2353 oz. AGW **Subject:** 25th Anniversary of Independence

Date	Mintage	F	VF	XF	Unc	BU
AH1401-1981	5,000	—	—	—	165	175
AH1401-1981 Proof	5,000	Value: 185				

KM# 72 100 POUNDS
33.4370 g., 0.9000 Gold .9676 oz. AGW **Subject:** Conservation **Obv:** Eagle divides dates **Rev:** Scimitar-horned oryx

Date	Mintage	F	VF	XF	Unc	BU
AH1396-1976	872	—	—	—	700	725
AH1396-1976 Proof	251	Value: 750				

KM# 90 100 POUNDS
15.9800 g., 0.9170 Gold .4706 oz. AGW **Subject:** 25th Anniversary of Independence

Date	Mintage	F	VF	XF	Unc	BU
AH1401-1981	2,500	—	—	—	325	350
AH1401-1981 Proof	2,500	Value: 375				

KM# 91 100 POUNDS
15.9800 g., 0.9170 Gold .4706 oz. AGW **Series:** Year of the Disabled Person **Obv:** Eagle **Rev:** Stylized arrowhead within wreath

Date	Mintage	F	VF	XF	Unc	BU
AH1401-1981	2,000	—	—	—	375	400
AH1401-1981 Proof	2,000	Value: 475				

KM# 93 100 POUNDS
8.1000 g., 0.9170 Gold .2388 oz. AGW **Series:** Decade for Women **Obv:** Eagle divides value **Rev:** Half female figure facing right

Date	Mintage	F	VF	XF	Unc	BU
AH1404-1984 Proof	513	Value: 225				

REFORM COINAGE

100 Qurush (Piastres) = 1 Dinar

10 Pounds = 1 Dinar

KM# 117 1/4 DINAR

3.0000 g., Brass Plated Steel, 18 mm. **Obv:** Value **Rev:** Central Bank building **Edge:** Plain

Date	Mintage	F	VF	XF	Unc	BU
AH1415-1994 Rare	—	—	—	—	—	—

KM# 118 1/2 DINAR

4.0000 g., Brass-Plated Steel, 20 mm. **Obv:** Value **Rev:** Central Bank building **Edge:** Plain

Date	Mintage	F	VF	XF	Unc	BU
AH1415-1994 Rare	—	—	—	—	—	—

KM# 112 DINAR

Brass **Obv:** Value **Rev:** Central Bank building **Edge:** Plain

Date	Mintage	F	VF	XF	Unc	BU
AH1415-1994	—	—	0.25	0.50	1.00	2.00

KM# 113 2 DINAR

Brass Plated Steel **Obv:** Value **Rev:** Central Bank building **Edge:** Plain **Note:** Varieties exist in lines and size of the 2.

Date	Mintage	F	VF	XF	Unc	BU
AH1415-1994	—	—	0.45	0.75	1.00	3.00

KM# 114 5 DINARS

Brass **Obv:** Value **Rev:** Central Bank building **Edge:** Plain

Date	Mintage	F	VF	XF	Unc	BU
AH1417-1996	—	—	1.00	2.00	4.50	7.00

KM# 115.1 10 DINARS

Brass **Obv:** Legend and value above designs **Rev:** Central Bank building, thin inscription below **Edge:** Plain

Date	Mintage	F	VF	XF	Unc	BU
AH1417-1996	—	—	1.00	2.00	3.50	6.00

KM# 115.2 10 DINARS

Brass **Obv:** Legend and value **Rev:** Central Bank building, thick inscription below **Edge:** Plain

Date	Mintage	F	VF	XF	Unc	BU
AH1417-1996	—	—	1.00	2.00	3.50	6.00

KM# 116.2 20 DINARS

Copper-Nickel **Obv:** Legend and value **Rev:** Small bank building, "A" above "N" in Sudan **Note:** 64 beads in border; legend below building is away from the rim.

Date	Mintage	F	VF	XF	Unc	BU
AH1417-1996	—	—	1.25	2.25	4.00	7.00
AH1419-1999	—	—	1.25	2.25	4.00	7.00

KM# 116.1 20 DINARS

Copper-Nickel, 22 mm. **Obv:** Value **Rev:** Central Bank building **Edge:** Plain **Note:** 72 beads in border; legend below building touches rim.

Date	Mintage	F	VF	XF	Unc	BU
AH1417-1996	—	—	1.25	2.25	4.00	7.00

PATTERNS

Including off metal strikes

KM#	Date	Mintage	Identification	Mkt Val
Pn1	1956AD-1375AH	—	Millim. Copper. 19.6 mm. "HAKUMAT AS-SUDAN"	—
Pn2	1956AD-1375AH	—	5 Millim. Copper. 24.9 mm. "HAKUMAT AS-SUDAN"	—
Pn3	1956AD-1375AH	—	5 Ghirsh. Copper-Nickel. 23.9 mm. "HAKUMAT AS-SUDAN"	—
Pn4	1956AD-1375AH	—	10 Ghirsh. Copper-Nickel. 30.9 mm. "HAKUMAT AS-SUDAN"	—

ESSAIS

KM#	Date	Mintage	Identification	Mkt Val
E1	1978	25	5 Pounds. Aluminum.	40.00
E2	1978	15	5 Pounds. Copper.	85.00

KM#	Date	Mintage	Identification	Mkt Val
E3	1978	25	10 Pounds. Aluminum. 40.6 mm.	40.00
E4	1978	21	10 Pounds. Copper. KM77.	125
E5	1978	25	25 Pounds. Aluminum.	40.00
E6	1978	21	25 Pounds. Copper.	75.00
E7	1978	25	50 Pounds. Aluminum.	40.00
E8	1978	21	50 Pounds. Copper.	85.00
E9	1979	15	5 Pounds. Copper. KM817.	85.00

KM#	Date	Mintage	Identification	Mkt Val
E10	1979	40	10 Pounds. Aluminum. 40.7 mm. KM81.	40.00
E11	1979	21	10 Pounds. Copper. KM81.	125
E12	1979	21	50 Pounds. Copper. KM83.	85.00
E13	1980	25	5 Pounds. Aluminum.	40.00
E14	1980	15	5 Pounds. Copper.	85.00
E15	1980	25	10 Pounds. Aluminum.	40.00
E16	1980	21	10 Pounds. Copper.	125
E17	1980	25	25 Pounds. Aluminum.	40.00
E18	1980	20	25 Pounds. Copper.	75.00
E19	1980	25	50 Pounds. Aluminum.	40.00
E20	1980	21	50 Pounds. Copper.	85.00

PIEFORTS

KM#	Date	Mintage	Identification	Mkt Val
P1	1978	5	5 Pounds. Copper. KM76.	185
P2	1978	10	5 Pounds. 0.9250 Silver. KM76.	—
P3	1978	5	10 Pounds. Copper.	225
P4	1978	10	10 Pounds. 0.9250 Silver. KM77.	—
P5	1978	5	25 Pounds. Copper.	185
P6	1979	5	5 Pounds. Copper. KM80.	185
P7	1979	10	5 Pounds. 0.9250 Silver. KM80.	—
P8	1979	5	10 Pounds. Copper. KM81.	225
P9	1979	10	10 Pounds. 0.9250 Silver. KM81.	—
P10	1979	—	25 Pounds. Brass. KM83.	185

KM#	Date	Mintage	Identification	Mkt Val
P11	1979	10	25 Pounds. Silver. 22.5 mm. KM83.	185

KM#	Date	Mintage	Identification	Mkt Val
PA12	1979	—	50 Pounds. Silver. 26.1 mm. KM#83.	—
P12	1979	—	50 Pounds. Copper. KM83. Gold plated.	—
P13	1980	5	5 Pounds. Copper.	185
P14	1980	5	10 Pounds. Copper.	225
P15	1980	5	25 Pounds. Copper.	185
P16	1979	—	50 Pounds. Gold. KM83.	—
P17	1981	2,587	5 Pounds. Silver. KM87.	40.00
P18	1981	1,000	10 Pounds. Silver. KM88.	75.00
P19	1981	—	100 Pounds. Gold. KM91.	1,350

MINT SETS

KM#	Date	Mintage	Identification	Issue Price	Mkt Val
MS1	1976 (2)	—	KM70-71	—	40.00

PROOF SETS

KM#	Date	Mintage	Identification	Issue Price	Mkt Val
PS1	1967 (8)	7,834	KM29-32, 34-37	12.25	7.50
PS2	1968 (8)	5,251	KM29-32, 34-37	15.25	8.00
PS3	1969 (8)	2,149	KM29-32, 34-37	15.25	10.00
PS4	1970 (8)	1,646	KM39-46	15.25	15.00
PS5	1971 (8)	1,772	KM39-46	15.25	15.00
PS6	1976 (2)	—	KM70-71	—	50.00
PS7	1978 (4)	—	KM76-79	—	600
PS9	1980 (4)	—	KM80-83	—	535
PS8	1980 (5)	—	KM54, 55a, 57-59	12.00	—

DARFUR

Darfur had been an independent Sultanate until taken over by Egypt in 1874, and subsequently by the Mahdists. After the latter's defeat in 1898 by the British, 'Ali Dinar re-established the Sultanate which ended in 1916 with his demise. His coins copied the Ottoman coins of Egypt. The mint was located at El Fasher, the Sultanate capital, and was active from 1909 to 1914.

MINT

الفشير

al-Fasher

RULER

Ali Dinar, AH1316-1335/1898-1916AD

SULTANATE

HAMMERED COINAGE

KM# 4 1/2 PIASTRE

Billon **Ruler:** Ali Dinar AH1316-35/1898-1916AD **Obv:** Toughra within circle **Rev:** Value and date within circle

Date	Mintage	Good	VG	F	VF	XF
AH1328/8 Rare	—	—	—	—	—	—

Note: Due to the low denomination and little demand, this coin was only struck for a very short time, though varieties do exist

KM# 1 PIASTRE

Copper-Nickel-Zinc **Obv:** Toughra within circle **Rev:** Inscription, date and value within circle

Date	Mintage	Good	VG	F	VF	XF
AH1223 (sic)/23 Rare	—	—	—	—	—	—

Date	Mintage	Good	VG	F	VF	XF
AH1223 (sic)/13 Rare	—	—	—	—	—	—

Note: Due to a shortage of small change, debased, unmilled imitations of Egyptian Qirsh (Piastre) KM#181, which had been produced outside of Sudan were brought into circulation in Darfur from AH1323-1325/1905-1907AD, privately struck in agreement with the Sultan

KM# 2 PIASTRE

Billon **Obv:** Toughra within circle **Rev:** Inscription, date and value within circle **Note:** Struck at al-Fasher mint from 1909-1914. Flan size varies and most appear crude due to thinness of flan. Off center and double strikes exist. Those bearing the date AH1327, regnal year 17 are probably the sultan's approved type. Other hejira and regnal years are engraving errors of filled dies.

Date	Mintage	Good	VG	F	VF	XF
AH1227(sic)/5	—	—	—	—	—	—
AH1237(sic)/71	—	—	—	—	—	—
Note: With retrograde 3						
AH1321(sic)/71	—	—	—	—	—	—
AH1323(sic)/65	—	—	—	—	—	—
AH1327/7	—	—	—	—	—	—
AH1327/17	—	30.00	80.00	160	190	—
AH1327/26	—	—	—	—	—	—
AH3127/71	—	—	—	—	—	—
AH1327/71	—	15.00	30.00	45.00	60.00	—
AH1327/71	—	—	—	—	—	—
Note: Retrograde 3						
AH1327/76	—	—	—	—	—	—
AH1327/77	—	—	—	—	—	—
AHx321(sic)/17	—	—	—	—	—	—
AH3167/7x	—	—	—	—	—	—
AH1387(sic)/17	—	—	—	—	—	—
AH7132(sic)/x	—	—	—	—	—	—

KM# 5 5 PIASTRES

Copper-Nickel-Zinc **Ruler:** Ali Dinar AH1316-35/1898-1916AD **Obv:** Toughra within design **Rev:** Inscription, value and date within design **Note:** Size varies: 21.6-24.4 mm.

Date	Mintage	Good	VG	F	VF	XF
AH1328 Rare	—	—	—	—	—	—

Note: Copied from Ottoman Mejidiye coinage; about 800 are reported having been put into circulation; further striking was discontinued as the coin was unpopular due to low silver content. Specimens dated 8231 are contemporary forgeries.

COUNTERMARKED COINAGE

KM# 3 PIASTRE

Copper-Nickel-Zinc **Countermark:** "Ali" 1312 **Obv:** Inscription, date and value within circle **Rev:** Toughra within circle **Note:** Countermark on KM#1.

CM Date	Host Date	Good	VG	F	VF	XF
ND	AH1223/13 Rare	—	—	—	—	—
Note: In a move to control import and circulation of KM#1, the Sultan ordered the countermarking; AH1312 is the year 'Ali Dinar used as the official beginning of his Sultanate. The countermark can be on the obverse or reverse. Counterfeit (contemporary) may exist. AH1327/17 approximates 1312, the year 'Ali Dinar officially used as the beginning of his dynasty as per noted historian O'Fahey.						
ND	AH1223/23 Rare	—	—	—	—	—

SURINAME

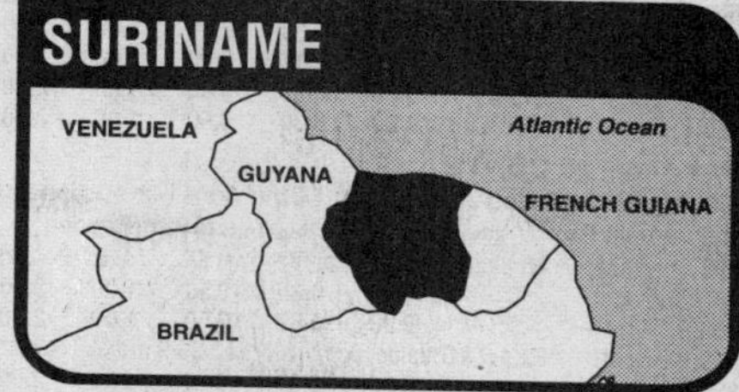

The Republic of Suriname also known as Dutch Guiana, located on the north central coast of South America between Guyana and French Guiana has an area of 63,037 sq. mi. (163,270 sq. km.) and a population of *433,000. Capital: Paramaribo. The country is rich in minerals and forests, and self-sufficient in rice, the staple food crop. The mining, processing and exporting of bauxite is the principal economic activity.

Lieutenants of Amerigo Vespucci sighted the Guiana coast in 1499. Spanish explorers of the 16th century, disappointed at finding no gold, departed leaving the area to be settled by the British in 1652. The colony prospered and the Netherlands acquired it in 1667 in exchange for the Dutch rights in Nieuw Nederland (state of New York). During the European wars of the 18th and 19th centuries, which were fought in part in the new world, Suriname was occupied by the British from 1781-1784 and 1796-1814. Suriname became an autonomous part of the Kingdom of the Netherlands on Dec. 15, 1954. Full independence was achieved on Nov. 25, 1975. In 1980, a coup installed a military government, which has since been dissolved.

RULERS

Dutch, until 1975

MINT MARKS

(B) - British Royal Mint, no mint mark
FM - Franklin Mint, U.S.A.**
P - Philadelphia, U.S.A.
S - Sydney
(u) - Utrecht (privy marks only)

****NOTE**: From 1975-1985 the Franklin Mint produced coinage in up to 3 different qualities. Qualities of issue are designated in ( ) after each date and are defined as follows:

(M) MATTE - Normal circulation strike or a dull finish produced by sandblasting special uncirculated (polish finish) or proof quality dies.

(U) SPECIAL UNCIRCULATED - Polished or prooflike in appearance without any frosted features.

(P) PROOF - The highest quality obtainable having mirror-like fields and frosted features.

MONETARY SYSTEM

100 Cents = 1 Gulden (Guilders)

After January, 2004

1 Dollar = 100 Cents

DUTCH ADMINISTRATION

WORLD WAR II COINAGE

The 1942-1943 issues that follow are homeland coinage types of the Netherlands. KM#152, KM#163 and KM#164 were executed expressly for use in Suriname. Related issues produced for use in Curacao and Suriname are listed under Curacao. They are distinguished by a palm tree (acorn on homeland issues) and a mint mark (P-Philadelphia, D-Denver, S-San Francisco) flanking the date. See the Netherlands for similar issues. See Curacao for similar coins dated 1941-P, 1942-P and 1943-P.

KM# 10 CENT

2.5000 g., Brass, 18 mm. **Obv:** Upright lion with sword within beaded circle **Rev:** Value within orange wreath **Edge:** Reeded

Date	Mintage	F	VF	XF	Unc	BU
1943P Palm	4,000,000	0.85	3.75	7.50	15.00	20.00

KM# 10a CENT

2.5000 g., Bronze, 19 mm. **Obv:** Upright lion with sword within beaded circle **Rev:** Value within orange wreath **Edge:** Reeded

Date	Mintage	F	VF	XF	Unc	BU
1957(u)	1,200,000	—	1.25	2.50	5.00	9.00
1957(u) Proof	—	Value: 20.00				
1959(u)	1,800,000	—	1.25	2.50	5.00	9.00
1959(u) Proof	—	Value: 20.00				

Date	Mintage	F	VF	XF	Unc	BU
1960(u)	1,200,000	—	1.25	2.50	5.00	7.50
1960(u) Proof	—	Value: 20.00				

KM# 9 10 CENTS

1.4000 g., 0.6400 Silver .0288 oz. ASW **Obv:** Head of Queen Wilhelmina left **Obv. Legend:** Value and date within orange wreath **Edge:** Reeded

Date	Mintage	F	VF	XF	Unc	BU
1942P Palm	1,500,000	6.00	12.50	15.00	30.00	35.00

REPUBLIC

MODERN COINAGE

KM# 11 CENT

2.5000 g., Bronze, 18 mm. **Obv:** Arms with supporters within wreath **Rev:** Value divides date within circle **Edge:** Plain

Date	Mintage	F	VF	XF	Unc	BU
1962(u) Fish	6,000,000	—	0.25	0.50	1.00	0.90
1962(u) S Proof	650	Value: 28.00				
1966(u)	6,500,000	—	0.25	0.50	1.00	0.90
1966(u) Proof	—	Value: 42.00				
1970(u) Cock	5,000,000	—	0.25	0.50	1.00	0.90
1972(u)	6,000,000	—	0.25	0.50	1.00	0.90

KM# 11a CENT

0.8000 g., Aluminum, 18 mm. **Obv:** Arms with supporters within wreath **Rev:** Value divides date within circle **Edge:** Plain

Date	Mintage	F	VF	XF	Unc	BU
1972 Proof	—	Value: 45.00				
1974(u)	1,000,000	—	0.10	0.20	0.50	1.00
1975(u)	1,000,000	—	0.10	0.20	0.50	1.00
1976(u)	3,000,000	—	0.10	0.15	0.30	0.80
1976 Proof	Est. 10	Value: 55.00				
1977(u)	10,000,000	—	—	0.15	0.30	0.80
1978(u)	6,000,000	—	—	0.15	0.30	0.30
1979(u)	10,000,000	—	—	0.15	0.30	0.30
1980(u)	8,000,000	—	—	0.15	0.30	0.80
Note: Cock and star privy marks						
1982(u) Anvil	8,000,000	—	—	0.15	0.30	0.80
1984	5,000,000	—	—	0.15	0.30	0.80
1985	2,000,000	—	—	0.20	0.40	0.80
1986	3,000,000	—	—	0.20	0.40	0.80

KM# 11b CENT

2.5000 g., Copper Plated Steel, 18 mm. **Obv:** Arms with supporters within wreath **Rev:** Value divides date within circle **Edge:** Plain

Date	Mintage	F	VF	XF	Unc	BU
1987(B)	—	—	—	0.20	0.40	0.90
1988(B)	—	—	—	0.20	0.40	0.90
1988(B) Proof	Est. 1,500	Value: 2.00				
1989(B)	—	—	—	0.20	0.40	0.90

KM# 12.1 5 CENTS

4.0000 g., Nickel-Brass, 22 mm. **Obv:** Arms with supporters within circle **Rev:** Value divides date within circle **Shape:** 4-sided

Date	Mintage	F	VF	XF	Unc	BU
1962(u) Fish	2,200,000	—	0.50	1.00	2.00	4.00
1962(u) S Proof	650	Value: 20.00				
1966(u)	2,300,000	—	0.50	1.00	2.00	4.00
Note: With mint mark and mintmaster's mark						
1966(u) Proof	—	Value: 50.00				
1966(u)	400,000	—	1.75	3.50	7.00	10.00
Note: Without mint mark and mint master's mark						

Date	Mintage	F	VF	XF	Unc	BU
1971(u) Cock	500,000	—	1.25	2.50	5.00	10.00
1972(u)	1,500,000	—	0.50	1.00	2.00	4.00

KM# 12.2 5 CENTS

4.0000 g., Nickel-Brass, 18 mm. **Obv:** Arms with supporters within circle **Rev:** Value divides date within circle **Shape:** Square **Note:** Medal turn.

Date	Mintage	F	VF	XF	Unc	BU
1966(u)	—	—	6.00	12.50	25.00	35.00
1966(u) Proof	—	Value: 450				

KM# 12.1a 5 CENTS

1.2000 g., Aluminum, 18 mm. **Obv:** Arms with supporters within circle **Rev:** Value divides date within circle **Shape:** Square

Date	Mintage	F	VF	XF	Unc	BU
1976(u)	5,500,000	—	0.10	0.25	0.50	1.00
1976 Proof	Est. 10	Value: 75.00				
1978(u)	3,000,000	—	0.10	0.25	0.50	1.00
1979(u)	2,000,000	—	0.10	0.25	0.50	1.00
1980(u)	1,000,000	—	0.10	0.25	0.50	1.00
Note: Cock and star privy marks						
1982(u) Anvil	1,000,000	—	0.10	0.25	0.50	1.00
1985(u)	1,000,000	—	0.10	0.25	0.50	1.00
1986(u)	1,500,000	—	0.10	0.25	0.50	1.00

KM# 12.1b 5 CENTS

4.0000 g., Copper Plated Steel, 18 mm. **Obv:** Arms with supporters within circle **Rev:** Value divides date within circle **Shape:** Square

Date	Mintage	F	VF	XF	Unc	BU
1987(B)	—	—	—	0.30	0.60	1.00
1988(B)	—	—	—	0.30	0.60	1.00
1988(B) Proof	Est. 1,500	Value: 2.00				
1989(B)	—	—	—	0.30	0.60	1.00

KM# 13 10 CENTS

2.0000 g., Copper-Nickel, 16 mm. **Obv:** Arms with supporters within wreath **Rev:** Value and date within circle

Date	Mintage	F	VF	XF	Unc	BU
1962(u) Fish	3,000,000	—	0.25	0.50	1.00	2.00
1962(u) S Proof	650	Value: 25.00				
1966(u)	2,500,000	—	0.25	0.50	1.00	2.00
1966(u) Proof	—	Value: 50.00				
1971(u) Cock	500,000	—	0.75	1.50	3.00	4.00
1972(u)	1,500,000	—	0.25	0.50	1.00	2.00
1974(u)	1,500,000	—	0.25	0.50	1.00	2.00
1976(u)	5,000,000	—	0.15	0.30	0.60	1.50
1976 Proof	Est. 10	Value: 100				
1978(u)	2,000,000	—	0.15	0.30	0.60	1.50
1979(u)	2,000,000	—	0.15	0.30	0.60	1.50
1982(u) Anvil	1,000,000	—	0.15	0.30	0.60	1.50
1985(u)	1,000,000	—	0.15	0.30	0.60	1.50
1986(u)	1,500,000	—	0.15	0.30	0.60	1.50

KM# 13a 10 CENTS

2.0000 g., Nickel Plated Steel, 15 mm. **Obv:** Arms with supporters within wreath **Rev:** Value and date within circle **Edge:** Reeded

Date	Mintage	F	VF	XF	Unc	BU
1987(B)	—	—	0.15	0.35	0.75	1.50
1988(B) Proof	Est. 1,500	Value: 3.00				
1989(B)	—	—	0.10	0.35	0.75	1.50

KM# 14 25 CENTS

3.5000 g., Copper-Nickel, 20 mm. **Obv:** Arms with supporters within wreath **Rev:** Value and date within circle **Edge:** Reeded

Date	Mintage	F	VF	XF	Unc	BU
1962(u) Fish	2,300,000	0.25	0.30	0.50	1.00	2.00
1962(u) S Proof	650	Value: 20.00				
1966(u)	2,300,000	0.25	0.30	0.50	1.00	2.00
1966(u) Proof	—	Value: 50.00				
1972(u) Cock	1,800,000	0.25	0.30	0.50	1.00	2.50
1974(u)	1,500,000	0.30	0.30	0.50	1.00	2.50
1976(u)	5,000,000	0.20	0.30	0.50	1.00	2.00
1976 Proof	Est. 10	Value: 125				

Date	Mintage	F	VF	XF	Unc	BU
1979(u)	2,000,000	0.20	0.30	0.50	1.00	2.00
1982(u) Anvil	2,000,000	0.20	0.30	0.50	1.00	2.00
1985(u)	1,000,000	0.20	0.30	0.50	1.00	2.50
1986(u)	1,500,000	0.20	0.30	0.50	1.00	2.50

KM# 14a 25 CENTS

3.5000 g., Nickel Plated Steel, 20 mm. **Obv:** Arms with supporters within wreath **Rev:** Value and date within circle **Edge:** Reeded

Date	Mintage	F	VF	XF	Unc	BU
1987(B)	—	0.20	0.30	0.50	1.00	2.00
1988(B)	—	0.20	0.30	0.50	1.00	2.00
1988(B) Proof	Est. 1,500	Value: 5.00				
1989(B)	—	0.20	0.35	0.65	1.25	2.50

KM# 23 100 CENTS

Copper-Nickel, 23 mm. **Obv:** Arms with supporters within wreath **Rev:** Value and date within circle **Edge:** Reeded

Date	Mintage	F	VF	XF	Unc	BU
1987(B)	—	—	0.40	0.80	1.75	3.00
1988(B)	—	—	0.40	0.80	1.75	3.00
1988(B) Proof	Est. 1,500	Value: 12.00				
1989(B)	—	—	0.40	0.80	1.75	3.00

KM# 24 250 CENTS

Copper-Nickel, 28 mm. **Obv:** Arms with supporters within wreath **Rev:** Value and date within circle

Date	Mintage	F	VF	XF	Unc	BU
1987(B)	—	—	0.80	1.75	3.50	5.00
1988(B)	—	—	0.80	1.75	3.50	5.00
1988(B) Proof	Est. 1,500	Value: 17.50				
1989(B)	—	—	0.80	1.75	3.50	5.00

KM# 15 GULDEN

10.0000 g., 0.7200 Silver .2315 oz. ASW, 28 mm. **Obv:** Head of Queen Juliana right **Rev:** Arms with supporters within wreath **Edge Lettering:** JUSTITIA * PIETAS * FIDES *

Date	Mintage	F	VF	XF	Unc	BU
1962(u)	150,000	—	BV	5.00	10.00	12.50
1962(u) S Proof	650	Value: 40.00				
1966(u)	100,000	—	—	—	125	130
Note: Never officially released to circulation						
1966(u) Proof	—	Value: 150				

KM# 16 10 GULDEN

15.9500 g., 0.9250 Silver .4743 oz. ASW **Subject:** 1st Anniversary of Independence **Obv:** Flag, Surinam map, rising sun **Rev:** Arms with supporters divide date **Edge Lettering:** JUSTITIA * PIETAS * FIDES *

Date	Mintage	F	VF	XF	Unc	BU
1976(u)	100,000	—	—	—	12.50	13.50
1976(u) Proof	5,711	Value: 15.00				

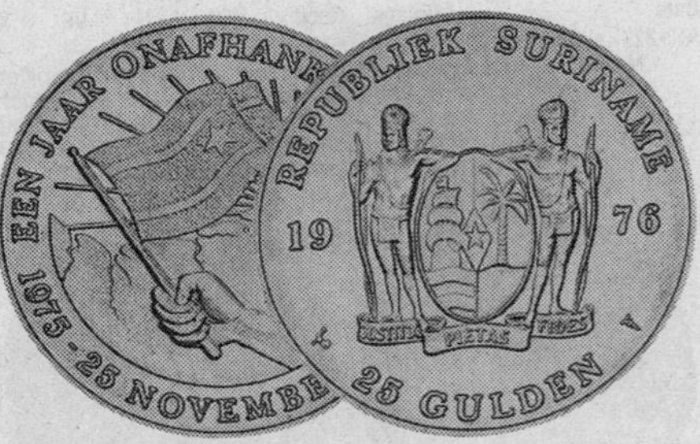

KM# 17 25 GULDEN

26.2000 g., 0.9250 Silver .779 oz. ASW **Subject:** 1st Anniversary of Independence **Obv:** Flag, Surinam map, rising sun **Rev:** Arms with supporters divide date

Date	Mintage	F	VF	XF	Unc	BU
1976(u)	75,000	—	—	—	17.50	20.00
1976(u) F Proof	5,503	Value: 16.50				

KM# 19 25 GULDEN

15.5000 g., 0.9250 Silver .461 oz. ASW **Subject:** 1st Anniversary of Revolution **Obv:** Revolution monument **Rev:** Allegorical group of revolutionaries **Edge:** Reeded

Date	Mintage	F	VF	XF	Unc	BU
1981FM (U)	10,000	—	—	—	30.00	35.00
1981FM (P)	800	Value: 75.00				

KM# 21 25 GULDEN

25.1000 g., 0.9250 Silver .7435 oz. ASW **Subject:** 5th Anniversary of Revolution **Obv:** Peace dove, flag superimposed on Surinam map **Rev:** Stylized fist and 5 on star within designed circle **Edge Lettering:** JUSTITIA * PIETAS * FIDES *

Date	Mintage	F	VF	XF	Unc	BU
ND(1985)(u)	4,800	—	—	—	60.00	65.00
ND(1985)(u) Proof	200	Value: 90.00				

KM# 32 25 GUILDER

28.2800 g., 0.9250 Silver .8411 oz. ASW **Subject:** World Cup Soccer **Obv:** Arms with supporters within wreath **Rev:** Player R. Gullit, stadium and half globe **Rev. Designer:** Willem Vis

Date	Mintage	F	VF	XF	Unc	BU
1990(B) Proof	50,000	Value: 60.00				

KM# 36 25 GUILDER
28.2800 g., 0.9250 Silver .8411 oz. ASW **Series:** Save the Children **Obv:** Arms with supporters **Rev:** Children **Rev. Designer:** Willem Vis **Edge:** Reeded

Date	Mintage	F	VF	XF	Unc	BU
1991(B) Proof	30,000	Value: 50.00				

KM# 27 30 GULDEN
14.3000 g., 0.9250 Silver .425 oz. ASW **Subject:** 30th Anniversary of Central Bank **Obv:** Arms with supporters divide date **Rev:** Central Bank building

Date	Mintage	F	VF	XF	Unc	BU
1987(u)	7,000	—	—	30.00	40.00	55.00

KM# 28 50 GUILDER
28.2800 g., 0.9250 Silver .8411 oz. ASW **Series:** Seoul Olympics **Subject:** Anthony Nesty, Butterfly gold medalist **Obv:** Arms with supporters within wreath **Rev:** Conjoined swimmers left within circle **Edge:** Reeded

Date	Mintage	F	VF	XF	Unc	BU
1988(B) Proof	Est. 25,000	Value: 45.00				

KM# 30 50 GUILDER
28.2800 g., 0.9250 Silver .8411 oz. ASW **Subject:** 125th Anniversary of De Surinaamsche Bank **Obv:** Arms with supporters within wreath **Rev:** Designs and horizontal lines within circle **Rev. Designer:** Robert Elderton **Edge:** Reeded

Date	Mintage	F	VF	XF	Unc	BU
ND(1990)(B) Proof	Est. 7,500	Value: 50.00				

KM# 34 50 GUILDER
26.0000 g., 0.9250 Silver .7733 oz. ASW **Subject:** 15th Anniversary of Independence **Obv:** Arms with supporters **Rev:** Stylized design **Edge:** Reeded **Note:** Similar to 500 Guilders, KM#35.

Date	Mintage	F	VF	XF	Unc	BU
ND(1990)(B) Proof	Est. 5,000	Value: 45.00				

KM# 38 50 GUILDER
26.0000 g., 0.9250 Silver .7733 oz. ASW **Subject:** 35th Anniversary of Central Bank **Obv:** Arms with supporters within wreath **Rev:** Geometric arrow design divides date at top and bottom within circle **Edge:** Reeded

Date	Mintage	F	VF	XF	Unc	BU
ND(1992) Proof	Est. 1,500	Value: 60.00				

KM# 18a 100 GULDEN
6.7200 g., 0.9000 Yellow Gold .1945 oz. AGW **Subject:** 1st Anniversary of Independence **Obv:** Flag, Surinam map, rising sun within circle **Rev:** Arms with supporters divide date

Date	Mintage	F	VF	XF	Unc	BU
1976(u)	19,100	—	—	—	—	135
1976(u) Proof	4,749	Value: 145				

KM# 18b 100 GULDEN
6.7200 g., 0.9000 Red Gold 0.1944 oz. AGW **Subject:** 1st Anniversary of Independence **Obv:** Flag, Surinam map, rising sun within circle **Rev:** Arms with supporters divide date

Date	Mintage	F	VF	XF	Unc	BU
1976(u)	900	—	—	—	175	200

KM# 52 100 GULDEN
20.0000 g., 0.9990 Silver 0.6424 oz. ASW, 36.9 mm. **Subject:** 700th Anniversary of the Helvetic Confederation and 125th Anniversary of the Red Cross **Obv:** Arms with supporters **Rev:** Wilhelm Tell, maps, flags and arms **Edge:** Reeded

Date	Mintage	F	VF	XF	Unc	BU
ND(1991) Proof	—	Value: 90.00				

KM# 40 100 GUILDER
20.0000 g., 0.9990 Silver .642 oz. ASW **Series:** Barcelona Olympics **Subject:** Basketball **Obv:** Arms with supporters within wreath **Rev:** Four basketball players within circle **Edge:** Reeded **Note:** Struck at Nova Mint, Barcelona.

Date	Mintage	F	VF	XF	Unc	BU
1992 Proof	Est. 15,000	Value: 50.00				

KM# 41 100 GUILDER
20.0000 g., 0.9990 Silver .642 oz. ASW **Series:** Barcelona Olympics **Subject:** Cyclists **Obv:** Arms with supporters **Rev:** Three cyclists **Edge:** Reeded **Note:** Struck at Nova Mint, Barcelona.

Date	Mintage	F	VF	XF	Unc	BU
1992 Proof	Est. 15,000	Value: 50.00				

KM# 42.1 100 GUILDER
20.0000 g., 0.9990 Silver .642 oz. ASW **Series:** Barcelona Olympics **Subject:** Anthony Nesty **Obv:** Arms with supporters **Rev:** Swimmer within circle **Edge:** Reeded **Note:** Struck at Kaapstad (Capetown, South Africa).

Date	Mintage	F	VF	XF	Unc	BU
ND(1992) Proof	2,500	Value: 65.00				

KM# 42.2 100 GUILDER
20.0000 g., 0.9990 Silver **Series:** Barcelona Olympics **Obv:** Arms with supporters **Rev:** Swimmer Antony Nesty, "200 M" above swimmer **Edge:** Reeded **Note:** Struck at Kaapstad (Capetown, South Africa).

Date	Mintage	F	VF	XF	Unc	BU
ND(1992) Proof	2,500	Value: 75.00				

KM# 43.1 100 GUILDER
19.7000 g., 0.9990 Silver .642 oz. ASW **Subject:** World Cup soccer **Obv:** Arms with supporters **Rev:** 2 soccer players, "999 E.P." at right **Edge:** Reeded

Date	Mintage	F	VF	XF	Unc	BU
ND(1994) Proof	—	Value: 50.00				

KM# 43.2 100 GUILDER
19.7000 g., 0.9990 Silver .6330 oz. ASW **Subject:** World Cup soccer **Obv:** Arms with supporters **Rev:** 2 soccer players, "999 E.P." at left **Edge:** Reeded

Date	Mintage	F	VF	XF	Unc	BU
ND(1994) Proof	—	Value: 85.00				

KM# 44 100 GUILDER
20.0000 g., 0.9990 Silver .6430 oz. ASW **Subject:** World Cup soccer **Obv:** Arms with supporters within wreath **Rev:** Soccer player in stadium, Brazil winner **Edge:** Reeded **Note:** Struck at Capetown.

Date	Mintage	F	VF	XF	Unc	BU
ND(1994) Proof	—	Value: 45.00				

KM# 46 100 GUILDER
28.5000 g., Copper-Nickel **Obv:** Arms with supporters **Rev:** 1956 Ford Thunderbird **Edge:** Reeded

Date	Mintage	F	VF	XF	Unc	BU
1996 Proof	500	Value: 75.00				

KM# 47 100 GUILDER
28.5000 g., Copper-Nickel **Obv:** Arms with supporters **Rev:** 1957 Ford Thunderbird **Edge:** Reeded

Date	Mintage	F	VF	XF	Unc	BU
1996 Proof	500	Value: 75.00				

KM# 49 100 GUILDER
28.3000 g., 0.9990 Copper-Nickel **Series:** Olympics **Obv:** Arms with supporters within wreath **Rev:** Discus thrower flanked by sprigs within pillars **Edge:** Reeded

Date	Mintage	F	VF	XF	Unc	BU
1996 Proof	—	Value: 140				

KM# 20 200 GULDEN
7.1200 g., 0.5000 Gold .1144 oz. AGW **Subject:** 1st Anniversary of Revolution **Obv:** Revolution monument **Rev:** Allegorical group of revolutionaries **Edge:** Reeded

Date	Mintage	F	VF	XF	Unc	BU
1981FM (U)	11,000	—	—	—	130	—
1981FM (P) Proof	1,363	Value: 175				

KM# 22 250 GUILDER
6.7200 g., 0.9000 Gold .1945 oz. AGW **Subject:** 5th Anniversary of Revolution **Obv:** Dove and "10" on map-shaped flag **Rev:** Stylized fist on star design **Edge:** Reeded

Date	Mintage	F	VF	XF	Unc	BU
1985(u)	5,000	—	—	—	150	160
1985(u) Proof	200	Value: 225				

KM# 33 250 GUILDER
7.9800 g., 0.9170 Gold .2353 oz. AGW **Subject:** World Cup Soccer **Obv:** Arms with supporters within wreath **Rev:** Soccer player R. Gullit, stadium and half-globe **Rev. Designer:** Willem Vis **Edge:** Reeded

Date	Mintage	F	VF	XF	Unc	BU
1990(B) Proof	1,000	Value: 225				

KM# 37 250 GUILDER
7.9800 g., 0.9170 Gold .2353 oz. AGW **Series:** Save the Children **Obv:** Arms with supporters within wreath **Rev:** Children looking at spider web **Rev. Designer:** Willem Vis **Edge:** Reeded

Date	Mintage	F	VF	XF	Unc	BU
1991 Proof	3,000	Value: 200				
1992	—	—	—	—	165	—

KM# 25 500 GUILDER
7.9800 g., 0.9170 Gold .2353 oz. AGW **Subject:** 43rd General Assembly, Military Sports Organization CISM **Obv:** Arms with supporters **Rev:** Globe, laurel wreath, rings and sword within flower design **Edge:** Reeded

Date	Mintage	F	VF	XF	Unc	BU
ND(1988)(B) Proof	2,500	Value: 200				

KM# 29 500 GUILDER
7.9800 g., 0.9170 Gold .2353 oz. AGW **Series:** Seoul Olympics **Subject:** Anthony Nesty, butterfly gold medalist **Obv:** Arms with supporters within wreath **Rev:** Swimmer within circle **Edge:** Reeded

Date	Mintage	F	VF	XF	Unc	BU
1988(B) Proof	Est. 2,000	Value: 225				

KM# 31 500 GUILDER
7.9800 g., 0.9170 Gold .2353 oz. AGW **Subject:** 125th Anniversary - De Surinaamsche Bank **Obv:** Arms with supporters **Rev:** Abstract design **Edge:** Reeded **Designer:** Robert Elderton

Date	Mintage	F	VF	XF	Unc	BU
1990(B) Proof	Est. 2,000	Value: 250				

KM# 35 500 GUILDER
7.9800 g., 0.9170 Gold .2353 oz. AGW **Subject:** 15th Anniversary of Independence **Obv:** Arms with supporters within wreath **Rev:** Floral design **Edge:** Reeded

Date	Mintage	F	VF	XF	Unc	BU
ND(1990)(B) Proof	Est. 1,250	Value: 275				

KM# 39 500 GUILDER
7.9800 g., 0.9170 Gold .2353 oz. AGW **Subject:** 35th Anniversary of Central Bank **Obv:** Arms with supporters **Rev:** Symetric arrow design and dates within circle and legend **Edge:** Reeded

Date	Mintage	F	VF	XF	Unc	BU
1992(B) Proof	Est. 300	Value: 325				

KM# 26 1000 GUILDER
15.9800 g., 0.9170 Gold .4708 oz. AGW **Subject:** 40th Anniversary - Military Sports Organization CISM **Obv:** Arms with supporters **Rev:** Globe, laurel wreath, rings and sword within flower design **Edge:** Reeded

Date	Mintage	F	VF	XF	Unc	BU
ND(1988)(B) Proof	1,250	Value: 375				

KM# 48 1000 GUILDER
4.8000 g., Gold Plated Brass .4708 oz. **Series:** Olympics **Obv:** Arms with supporters **Rev:** Three cyclists **Edge:** Reeded **Note:** Struck at Capetown.

Date	Mintage	F	VF	XF	Unc	BU
1992	—	—	—	—	—	—

KM# 48a 1000 GUILDER
7.9800 g., 0.9170 Gold .2355 oz. AGW **Series:** Olympics **Obv:** Arms with supporters **Rev:** Three cyclists **Edge:** Reeded **Note:** Struck at Capetown.

Date	Mintage	F	VF	XF	Unc	BU
1992 Proof	400	Value: 250				

KM# 50 12500 GULDEN
28.2800 g., 0.9250 Silver .8410 oz. ASW **Subject:** Hindu Immigration **Obv:** Arms with supporters within wreath **Rev:** Standing figures in front of ship **Edge:** Reeded

Date	Mintage	F	VF	XF	Unc	BU
ND(1999)(B) Proof	Est. 1,000	Value: 70.00				

KM# 51 50000 GULDEN
7.9800 g., 0.9170 Gold .2353 oz. AGW **Subject:** Hindu Immigration **Obv:** Arms with supporters **Rev:** Hindu couple with ship in background **Edge:** Reeded

Date	Mintage	F	VF	XF	Unc	BU
ND(1998)(B) Proof	Est. 1,000	Value: 350				

KM# 53 75000 GULDEN
7.9800 g., 0.9170 Gold .2353 oz. AGW **Subject:** Coppename Bridge **Edge:** Reeded

Date	Mintage	F	VF	XF	Unc	BU
1999 Proof	1,000	Value: 375				

KM# 54 100000 GULDEN
7.9800 g., 0.9170 Gold 0.2353 oz. AGW **Subject:** 25th Anniversary of Independence **Obv:** Arms with supporters **Edge:** Reeded

Date	Mintage	F	VF	XF	Unc	BU
2000 Proof	1,000	Value: 400				

KM# 55 100000 GULDEN
7.9800 g., 0.9170 Gold 0.2353 oz. AGW **Subject:** River Bridge **Obv:** Arms with supporters **Rev:** Bridge over Suriam River **Edge:** Reeded

Date	Mintage	F	VF	XF	Unc	BU
2000 Proof	1,000	Value: 400				

KM# 56 100000 GULDEN
7.9800 g., 0.9170 Gold 0.2353 oz. AGW **Subject:** Millennium 2000-2001 **Obv:** Arms with supporters **Rev:** Circles **Edge:** Reeded

Date	Mintage	F	VF	XF	Unc	BU
2000 Proof	1,500	Value: 450				

KM# 57 125,000 GULDEN
15.0000 g., 0.5850 Gold 0.2821 oz. AGW **Subject:** Millennium 2000-2001 **Obv:** Arms with supporters **Rev:** Circles **Edge:** Reeded

Date	Mintage	F	VF	XF	Unc	BU
2000 Proof	2,500	Value: 400				

PATTERNS

Including off metal strikes

KM#	Date	Mintage	Identification	Mkt Val
Pn1	1962	—	Gulden. Bronze. KM#15. Nickel coated.	60.00
Pn2	ND(1994)	—	100 Guilder. Copper-Nickel. KM#44.	60.00
Pn3	ND(1994)	—	100 Guilder. Silver. KM#44.	80.00

TRIAL STRIKES

KM#	Date	Mintage	Identification	Mkt Val
TS1	1984	—	10 Guilders. Silver. Arms with supporters. Shot put thrower and torch.	—

PROOF SETS

KM#	Date	Mintage	Identification	Issue Price	Mkt Val
PS1	1962 (5)	650	KM11-15	—	130
PS2	1966 (5)	—	KM11-15	—	250
PS3	1976 (4)	10	KM11a, 12.1a, 13, 14	—	300
PS4	1976 (3)	—	KM16-18	145	130
PS5	1976 (2)	—	KM16-17	50.00	50.00
PS6	1988 (6)	1,500	KM11b, 12.1b, 13a, 14a, 23, 24	42.00	50.00

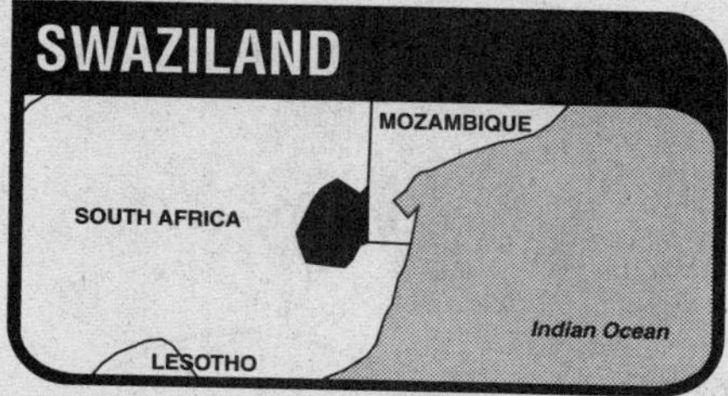

The Kingdom of Swaziland, located in southeastern Africa, has an area of 6,704 sq. mi. (17,360 sq. km.) and a population of *756,000. Capital: Mbabane (administrative); Lobamba (legislative). The diversified economy includes mining, agriculture, and light industry. Asbestos, iron ore, wood pulp, and sugar are exported.

The people of the present Swazi nation established themselves in an area including what is now Swaziland in the early 1800s. The first Swazi contact with the British came early in the reign of the extremely able Swazi leader Mswati when he asked the British for aid against Zulu raids into Swaziland. The British and Transvaal responded by guaranteeing the independence of Swaziland, 1881. South Africa assumed the power of protection and administration in 1894 and Swaziland continued under this administration until the conquest of the Transvaal during the Anglo-Boer War, when administration was transferred to the British government. After World War II, Britain began to prepare Swaziland for independence, which was achieved on Sept. 6, 1968. The Kingdom is a member of the Commonwealth of Nations. King Mswati III is Head of State. The prime minister is Head of Government.

RULERS

Sobhuza II, 1968-1982
Queen Dzeliwe, Regent for Prince Makhosetive, 1982-1986
King Msawati III, 1986-

MONETARY SYSTEM

100 Cents = 1 Luhlanga
25 Luhlanga = 1 Lilangeni
(plural - Emalangeni)

KINGDOM

STANDARD COINAGE

100 Cents = 1 Luhlanga; 25 Luhlanga = 1 Lilangeni

KM# 1 5 CENTS

2.7500 g., 0.8000 Silver .0707 oz. ASW **Ruler:** Sobhuza II **Subject:** Independence Commemorative **Obv:** Head 3/4 left **Rev:** Shield and three spears **Designer:** Tommy Sasseen

Date	Mintage	F	VF	XF	Unc	BU
1968 Proof	10,000	Value: 5.00				

KM# 2 10 CENTS

4.3800 g., 0.8000 Silver .1126 oz. ASW **Ruler:** Sobhuza II **Subject:** Independence Commemorative **Obv:** Head 3/4 left **Rev:** Shield and three spears **Designer:** Tommy Sasseen

Date	Mintage	F	VF	XF	Unc	BU
1968 Proof	10,000	Value: 7.00				

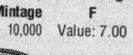

KM# 3 20 CENTS

6.6300 g., 0.8000 Silver .1705 oz. ASW **Ruler:** Sobhuza II **Subject:** Independence Commemorative **Obv:** Head 3/4 left **Rev:** Shield and three spears **Designer:** Tommy Sasseen

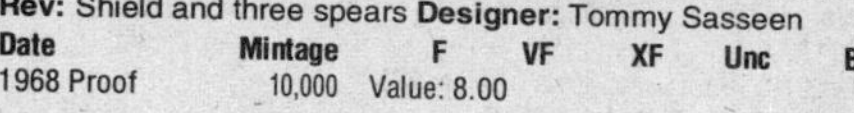

Date	Mintage	F	VF	XF	Unc	BU
1968 Proof	10,000	Value: 8.00				

KM# 4 50 CENTS

10.3900 g., 0.8000 Silver .2672 oz. ASW **Ruler:** Sobhuza II **Subject:** Independence Commemorative **Obv:** Head 3/4 left **Rev:** Shield and three spears **Designer:** Tommy Sasseen

Date	Mintage	F	VF	XF	Unc	BU
1968 Proof	10,000	Value: 9.00				

KM# 5 LUHLANGA

15.0000 g., 0.8000 Silver .3858 oz. ASW **Ruler:** Sobhuza II **Subject:** Independence Commemorative **Obv:** Head 3/4 left **Rev:** Shield with three spears divides date **Designer:** Tommy Sasseen

Date	Mintage	VG	F	VF	XF	Unc
1968 Proof	10,000	Value: 12.00				

KM# 6 LILANGENI

33.9305 g., 0.9170 Gold 1 oz. AGW **Ruler:** Sobhuza II **Subject:** Independence Commemorative **Obv:** Head 3/4 left **Rev:** Arms with supporters **Designer:** Tommy Sasseen **Note:** Approximately 1,450 melted.

Date	Mintage	F	VF	XF	Unc	BU
1968 Proof	2,000	Value: 675				

DECIMAL COINAGE

100 Cents = 1 Lilangeni (plural emelangeni)

KM# 7 CENT

2.0000 g., Bronze, 18.3 mm. **Ruler:** Sobhuza II **Obv:** Head 1/4 right **Rev:** Pineapple and value **Designer:** Michael Rizzello

Date	Mintage	F	VF	XF	Unc	BU
1974	6,002,000	—	—	0.10	0.20	—
1974 Proof	13,000	Value: 0.75				
1979	500,000	—	—	0.10	0.25	—
1979 Proof	10,000	Value: 0.75				
1982	—	—	—	0.10	0.25	—
1983	1,100,000	—	—	0.10	0.25	—

KM# 21 CENT

2.0000 g., Bronze, 18.3 mm. **Ruler:** Sobhuza II **Series:** F.A.O. **Obv:** Head 1/4 right **Rev:** Pineapple and value **Shape:** 12-sided **Designer:** Michael Rizzello

Date	Mintage	F	VF	XF	Unc	BU
1975	2,500,000	—	—	0.10	0.25	—

KM# 39 CENT

Copper Plated Steel **Ruler:** Queen Dzeliwe Regent for Prince Makhosetive **Obv:** Bust facing **Rev:** Pineapple

Date	Mintage	F	VF	XF	Unc	BU
1986	12,000,000	—	—	0.10	0.25	—

KM# 39a CENT

Bronze **Ruler:** Queen Dzeliwe Regent for Prince Makhosetive **Obv:** Bust facing **Rev:** Pineapple

Date	Mintage	F	VF	XF	Unc	BU
1986	—	—	—	1.00	2.50	—

KM# 51 CENT

Bronze **Ruler:** King Msawati III **Obv:** Head 1/4 right **Rev:** Pineapple and value

Date	Mintage	F	VF	XF	Unc	BU
1995	—	—	—	—	0.25	—

KM# 8 2 CENTS

2.8000 g., Bronze, 18.6 mm. **Ruler:** Sobhuza II **Obv:** Head 1/4 right **Rev:** Trees and value **Shape:** Square **Designer:** Michael Rizzello

Date	Mintage	F	VF	XF	Unc	BU
1974	2,252,000	—	—	0.15	0.30	—
1974 Proof	13,000	Value: 0.75				
1979	1,000,000	—	—	0.15	0.30	—
1979 Proof	10,000	Value: 1.00				
1982	500,000	—	—	0.15	0.30	—

KM# 22 2 CENTS

2.8000 g., Bronze, 18.6 mm. **Ruler:** Sobhuza II **Series:** F.A.O **Obv:** Head 1/4 right **Rev:** Trees and value **Edge:** Plain **Shape** 4-sided **Designer:** Michael Rizzello

Date	Mintage	F	VF	XF	Unc	BU
1975	1,500,000	—	—	0.15	0.30	—

KM# 9 5 CENTS

2.1500 g., Copper-Nickel, 18.5 mm. **Ruler:** Sobhuza II **Obv:** Head 1/4 right **Rev:** Arum lily and value **Shape:** Scalloped **Designer:** Michael Rizzello

Date	Mintage	F	VF	XF	Unc	BU
1974	1,252,000	—	0.10	0.20	0.40	—
1974 Proof	13,000	Value: 1.00				
1975	1,500,000	—	0.10	0.20	0.40	—
1979	1,680,000	—	0.10	0.20	0.40	—
1979 Proof	10,000	Value: 1.75				

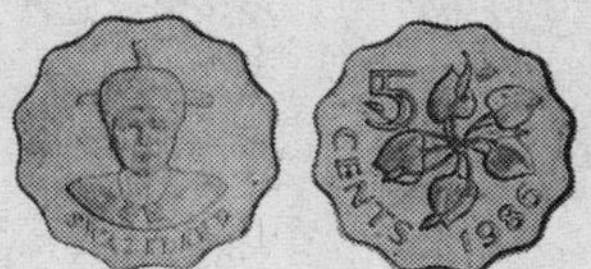

KM# 40.1 5 CENTS

2.1500 g., Copper-Nickel, 18.5 mm. **Ruler:** Queen Dzeliwe Regent for Prince Makhosetive **Obv:** Bust facing **Rev:** Arum lily and value **Edge:** Plain **Shape:** Scalloped

Date	Mintage	F	VF	XF	Unc	BU
1986	—	—	0.15	0.25	0.50	—

KM# 40.2 5 CENTS

Nickel Plated Steel, 18.5 mm. **Ruler:** King Msawati III **Obv:** Bust facing **Rev:** Arum lily **Edge:** Plain **Shape:** Scalloped

Date	Mintage	F	VF	XF	Unc	BU
1992	—	—	0.15	0.25	0.50	—

KM# 48 5 CENTS
Nickel Plated Steel, 18.5 mm. **Ruler:** King Msawati III **Obv:** Head 1/4 right **Rev:** Arum lily and value **Shape:** Scalloped

Date	Mintage	F	VF	XF	Unc	BU
1995	—	—	—	—	0.50	0.75
1996	—	—	—	—	0.50	0.75
1998	—	—	—	—	0.50	0.75
1999	—	—	—	—	0.50	0.75
2000	—	—	—	—	0.50	0.75
Note: Thick inscription						
2000	—	—	—	—	0.50	0.75
Note: Thin inscription						

KM# 48a 5 CENTS
Copper-Nickel, 18.5 mm. **Ruler:** King Msawati III **Obv:** Bust 1/4 right **Rev:** Arum lily and value

Date	Mintage	F	VF	XF	Unc	BU
1999	—	—	—	—	0.50	0.75

KM# 10 10 CENTS
Copper-Nickel, 22 mm. **Ruler:** Sobhuza II **Obv:** Head 1/4 right **Rev:** Sugar cane and value **Shape:** Scalloped **Designer:** Michael Rizzello

Date	Mintage	F	VF	XF	Unc	BU
1974	752,000	—	0.15	0.25	0.50	—
1974 Proof	13,000	Value: 1.00				
1979	500,000	—	0.15	0.25	0.50	—
1979 Proof	4,231	Value: 2.50				

KM# 23 10 CENTS
Copper-Nickel, 22 mm. **Ruler:** Sobhuza II **Series:** F.A.O. **Obv:** Head 1/4 right **Rev:** Sugar cane and value **Shape:** Scalloped

Date	Mintage	F	VF	XF	Unc	BU
1975	1,500,000	—	0.15	0.25	0.50	—

KM# 41 10 CENTS
Copper-Nickel, 22 mm. **Ruler:** King Msawati III **Obv:** Head facing **Rev:** Sugar cane and value **Edge:** Plain **Shape:** Scalloped

Date	Mintage	F	VF	XF	Unc	BU
1986	—	—	0.15	0.25	0.50	—
1992	—	—	0.15	0.25	0.50	—

KM# 49 10 CENTS
Copper-Nickel, 22 mm. **Ruler:** King Msawati III **Obv:** Head 1/4 right **Rev:** Sugar cane and value **Shape:** Scalloped

Date	Mintage	F	VF	XF	Unc	BU
1995	—	—	—	—	0.50	0.75
1996	—	—	—	—	0.50	0.75
1998	—	—	—	—	0.50	0.75
2000	—	—	—	—	0.50	0.75

KM# 11 20 CENTS
5.6000 g., Copper-Nickel, 25.2 mm. **Ruler:** Sobhuza II **Obv:** Head 1/4 right **Rev:** Elephant head and value **Shape:** Scalloped **Designer:** Michael Rizzello

Date	Mintage	F	VF	XF	Unc	BU
1974	502,000	—	0.35	0.75	2.50	4.50
1974 Proof	13,000	Value: 3.00				
1975	1,000,000	—	0.35	0.75	2.50	4.50
1979	—	—	0.35	0.75	2.50	4.50
1979 Proof	—	Value: 4.00				

KM# 31 20 CENTS
5.6000 g., Copper-Nickel, 25.2 mm. **Ruler:** Sobhuza II **Series:** F.A.O. **Obv:** Head 1/4 right **Rev:** Sprigs and logo **Shape:** Scalloped

Date	Mintage	F	VF	XF	Unc	BU
1981	150,000	—	0.40	0.80	1.75	—

KM# 42 20 CENTS
5.6000 g., Copper-Nickel, 25.2 mm. **Ruler:** Queen Dzeliwe Regent for Prince Makhosetive **Obv:** Head facing **Rev:** Elephant head and value **Edge:** Plain **Shape:** Scalloped

Date	Mintage	F	VF	XF	Unc	BU
1986	—	—	0.40	0.80	2.50	4.50

KM# 50 20 CENTS
5.6000 g., Copper-Nickel, 25.2 mm. **Ruler:** King Msawati III **Obv:** Head 1/4 right **Rev:** Elephant head and value **Shape:** Scalloped **Note:** "Lg bust and legend": right tusk closer to rim; "Sm bust and legend": right tusk further from rim.

Date	Mintage	F	VF	XF	Unc	BU
1996	—	—	0.40	0.80	2.50	4.50
Note: Large bust and legend						
1998	—	—	0.40	0.80	2.50	4.50
Note: Small bust and legend						
2000	—	—	0.40	0.80	2.50	4.50
Note: Large bust and legend						

KM# 12 50 CENTS
8.9000 g., Copper-Nickel, 29.45 mm. **Ruler:** Sobhuza II **Obv:** Head 1/4 right **Rev:** Arms with supporters **Shape:** 12-sided **Designer:** Michael Rizzello

Date	Mintage	F	VF	XF	Unc	BU
1974	252,000	—	1.00	1.50	2.75	—
1974 Proof	13,000	Value: 3.00				
1975	500,000	—	1.00	1.50	2.75	—
1979	—	—	0.50	1.00	2.50	—
1979 Proof	10,000	Value: 5.00				
1981	1,150,000	—	0.50	1.00	2.50	

KM# 43 50 CENTS
8.9000 g., Copper-Nickel, 29.45 mm. **Ruler:** King Msawati III **Obv:** Head facing **Rev:** Arms with supporters **Edge:** Plain

Date	Mintage	F	VF	XF	Unc	BU
1986	1,000,000	—	0.50	1.50	3.50	—
1993	—	—	0.50	1.50	3.50	—

KM# 52 50 CENTS
8.9000 g., Copper-Nickel, 29.45 mm. **Ruler:** King Msawati III **Obv:** Head 1/4 right **Rev:** Arms with supporters

Date	Mintage	F	VF	XF	Unc	BU
1996	—	—	—	—	3.75	4.50
1998	—	—	—	—	3.75	4.50

KM# 13 LILANGENI
11.6500 g., Copper-Nickel, 30 mm. **Ruler:** Sobhuza II **Obv:** Head 1/4 right **Rev:** Female and child facing **Designer:** Michael Rizzello

Date	Mintage	F	VF	XF	Unc	BU
1974	127,000	—	1.50	2.50	4.50	—
1974 Proof	13,000	Value: 6.00				
1979	—	—	1.00	2.00	4.50	—
1979 Proof	110,000	Value: 7.50				

KM# 24 LILANGENI
Copper-Nickel, 30.5 mm. **Ruler:** Sobhuza II **Series:** F.A.O., International Women's Year **Obv:** Head 1/4 right **Rev:** Female and child facing

Date	Mintage	F	VF	XF	Unc	BU
1975	100,000	—	1.50	2.75	6.50	—

KM# 28 LILANGENI
11.6500 g., Copper-Nickel, 30 mm. **Ruler:** Sobhuza II **Series:** F.A.O. **Obv:** Head 1/4 right **Rev:** Female and child facing

Date	Mintage	F	VF	XF	Unc	BU
1976	100,000	—	1.50	2.75	6.50	—

KM# 29.1 LILANGENI
15.5500 g., 0.9990 Gold .5 oz. AGW **Ruler:** Sobhuza II **Subject:** 80th Anniversary - Birth of King Sobhuza II **Obv:** Head 1/4 right **Rev:** Arms with supporters

Date	Mintage	F	VF	XF	Unc	BU
ND(1979)	1,250	—	—	—	350	—
ND(1979) Proof	Inc. above	Value: 375				

KM# 29.2 LILANGENI
15.5500 g., 0.9990 Gold .5 oz. AGW **Ruler:** Sobhuza II **Subject:** 80th Anniversary - Birth of King Sobhuza II **Obv:** Head 1/4 right **Rev:** Dates 1923-1979 above arms with supporters

Date	Mintage	F	VF	XF	Unc	BU
ND(1979)	—	—	—	—	400	—

KM# 32 LILANGENI
11.6500 g., Copper-Nickel, 30 mm. **Ruler:** Sobhuza II **Series:** F.A.O. **Obv:** Head 1/4 right **Rev:** Half length figure husking corn

Date	Mintage	F	VF	XF	Unc	BU
1981	871,000	—	1.50	3.00	7.00	—

KM# 32a LILANGENI
11.6600 g., 0.9250 Silver .3468 oz. ASW **Ruler:** Sobhuza II **Series:** F.A.O. **Obv:** Head 1/4 right **Rev:** Half length figure husking corn

Date	Mintage	F	VF	XF	Unc	BU
1981	5,000	—	—	—	22.50	—
1981 Proof	5,000	Value: 32.50				

KM# 44.1 LILANGENI
9.5000 g., Nickel-Brass, 22.5 mm. **Ruler:** Queen Dzeliwe Regent for Prince Makhosetive **Obv:** Head facing **Rev:** Bust facing **Edge:** Reeded

Date	Mintage	F	VF	XF	Unc	BU
1986	1,025,000	—	—	2.00	4.00	—

KM# 44.2 LILANGENI
Nickel-Brass Plated Steel, 22.5 mm. **Ruler:** King Msawati III **Obv:** Head facing **Rev:** Bust facing **Edge:** Reeded

Date	Mintage	F	VF	XF	Unc	BU
1992	—	—	—	1.50	3.50	—

KM# 45 LILANGENI
Brass, 22.5 mm. **Ruler:** King Msawati III **Obv:** Head 1/4 right **Rev:** Bust facing

Date	Mintage	F	VF	XF	Unc	BU
1995	—	—	—	1.50	3.50	4.00
1996	—	—	—	1.50	3.50	4.00
1998	—	—	—	1.50	3.50	4.00

KM# 33 2 EMALANGENI
17.0000 g., 0.9250 Silver .5056 oz. ASW, 34 mm. **Ruler:** Sobhuza II **Subject:** Diamond Jubilee of King Sobhuza II **Obv:** Head 1/4 right **Rev:** Lilies and value

Date	Mintage	F	VF	XF	Unc	BU
1981 Proof	—	Value: 32.50				

KM# 33a 2 EMALANGENI
Copper-Nickel **Ruler:** Sobhuza II **Subject:** Diamond Jubilee of King Sobhuza II **Obv:** Head 1/4 right **Rev:** Lilies and value

Date	Mintage	F	VF	XF	Unc	BU
1981	50,000	—	2.00	3.50	7.50	—

KM# 46 2 EMALANGENI
Brass **Ruler:** King Msawati III **Obv:** Head 1/4 right **Rev:** Lilies and value

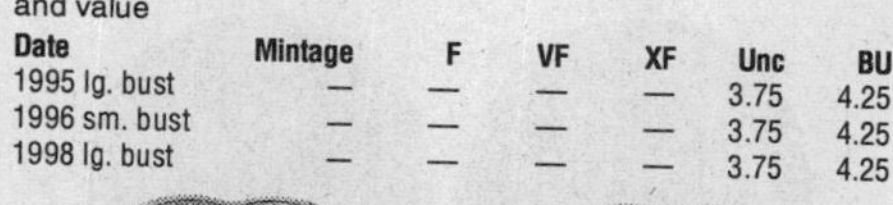

Date	Mintage	F	VF	XF	Unc	BU
1995 lg. bust	—	—	—	—	3.75	4.25
1996 sm. bust	—	—	—	—	3.75	4.25
1998 lg. bust	—	—	—	—	3.75	4.25

KM# 14 5 EMALANGENI
10.3000 g., 0.9250 Silver .3063 oz. ASW **Ruler:** Sobhuza II **Subject:** 75th Anniversary - Birth of King Sobhuza II **Obv:** Head 1/4 right **Rev:** Building and emblem **Shape:** Scalloped

Date	Mintage	F	VF	XF	Unc	BU
1974 Proof	—	Value: 50.00				

KM# 15 5 EMALANGENI
5.5600 g., 0.9000 Gold .1609 oz. AGW **Ruler:** Sobhuza II **Subject:** 75th Anniversary - Birth of King Sobhuza II **Obv:** Head 1/4 right **Rev:** Arms with supporters within circle

Date	Mintage	F	VF	XF	Unc	BU
1974 Proof	60,000	Value: 120				

KM# 47 5 EMALANGENI
Brass **Ruler:** King Msawati III **Obv:** Head 1/4 right **Rev:** Arms with supporters above value that divides date

Date	Mintage	F	VF	XF	Unc	BU
1995 sm. bust	—	—	—	—	6.00	7.00
1996 sm. bust	—	—	—	—	6.00	7.00
1998 lg. bust	—	—	—	—	6.00	7.00
1999	—	—	—	—	6.00	7.00

KM# 53 5 EMALANGENI
Brass **Ruler:** King Msawati III **Subject:** Central Bank's 25th Anniversary **Obv:** Head 1/4 right **Rev:** Bank seal within circle

Date	Mintage	F	VF	XF	Unc	BU
ND(1999)	—	—	—	—	5.50	6.50

KM# 16 7-1/2 EMALANGENI
16.2000 g., 0.9250 Silver .4818 oz. ASW **Ruler:** Sobhuza II **Subject:** 75th Anniversary - Birth of King Sobhuza II **Obv:** Head 1/4 right **Rev:** Bird **Shape:** 10-sided

Date	Mintage	F	VF	XF	Unc	BU
1974 Proof	—	Value: 65.00				

KM# 17 10 EMALANGENI
11.1200 g., 0.9000 Gold .3218 oz. AGW **Ruler:** Sobhuza II **Subject:** 75th Anniversary - Birth of King Sobhuza II **Obv:** Head 1/4 right **Rev:** Standing figure divides date and value within circle **Shape:** Scalloped

Date	Mintage	F	VF	XF	Unc	BU
1974 Proof	Est. 40,000	Value: 275				

KM# 25 10 EMALANGENI
25.5000 g., 0.9250 Silver .7584 oz. ASW **Ruler:** Sobhuza II **Subject:** 75th Anniversary - Birth of King Sobhuza II **Obv:** Head 1/4 right **Rev:** Heron

Date	Mintage	F	VF	XF	Unc	BU
1975	Est. 1,000	—	—	—	50.00	55.00
1975 Proof	Est. 1,500	Value: 60.00				

KM# 18 15 EMALANGENI
32.6000 g., 0.9250 Silver .9696 oz. ASW **Ruler:** Sobhuza II **Subject:** 75th Anniversary - Birth of King Sobhuza II **Obv:** Head 1/4 right **Rev:** Uniformed bust right saluting army with flags

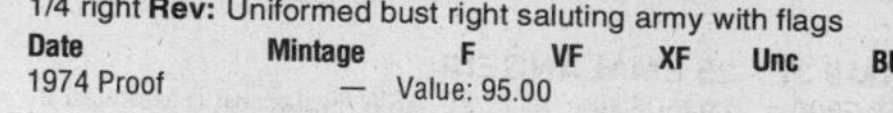

Date	Mintage	F	VF	XF	Unc	BU
1974 Proof	—	Value: 95.00				

KM# 19 20 EMALANGENI
22.2300 g., 0.9000 Gold .6433 oz. AGW **Ruler:** Sobhuza II **Subject:** 75th Anniversary - Birth of King Sobhuza II **Obv:** Head 1/4 right **Rev:** Child facing and UNICEF emblem **Shape:** 10-sided

Date	Mintage	F	VF	XF	Unc	BU
1974 Proof	Est. 25,000	Value: 450				

KM# 20 25 EMALANGENI
27.7800 g., 0.9000 Gold .8039 oz. AGW **Ruler:** Sobhuza II **Subject:** 75th Anniversary - Birth of King Sobhuza II **Obv:** Head 1/4 right **Rev:** Conjoined busts facing within circle

Date	Mintage	F	VF	XF	Unc	BU
1974	Est. 15,000	—	—	—	—	565

KM# 34 25 EMALANGENI
28.2800 g., 0.9250 Silver .8411 oz. ASW, 38.61 mm. **Ruler:** Sobhuza II **Subject:** Diamond Jubilee of King Sobhuza II **Obv:** Head 1/4 right **Rev:** Bird and value

Date	Mintage	F	VF	XF	Unc	BU
1981	Est. 10,000	—	—	—	35.00	40.00
1981 Proof	Est. 10,000	Value: 50.00				

KM# 37 25 EMALANGENI
28.2800 g., 0.9250 Silver .8411 oz. ASW **Ruler:** King Msawati III **Subject:** Accession of King Makhosetive **Obv:** Bust facing **Rev:** Bust facing

Date	Mintage	F	VF	XF	Unc	BU
ND(1986) Proof	Est. 2,500	Value: 45.00				

KM# 26 50 EMALANGENI
4.3100 g., 0.9000 Gold .1247 oz. AGW **Ruler:** Sobhuza II **Subject:** 75th Anniversary - Birth of King Sobhuza II **Obv:** Head 1/4 right **Rev:** Antelope

Date	Mintage	F	VF	XF	Unc	BU
1975	3,510	—	—	—	95.00	100
1975 Proof	3,262	Value: 110				

KM# 27 100 EMALANGENI
8.6400 g., 0.9000 Gold .25 oz. AGW **Ruler:** Sobhuza II **Subject:** 75th Anniversary - Birth of King Sobhuza II **Obv:** Head 1/4 right **Rev:** Bust 1/4 left

Date	Mintage	F	VF	XF	Unc	BU
ND(1975)	1,000	—	—	—	185	195
ND(1975) Proof	1,000	Value: 225				

KM# 35 250 EMALANGENI
15.9800 g., 0.9170 Gold .4711 oz. AGW **Ruler:** Sobhuza II **Subject:** Diamond Jubilee of King Sobhuza II **Obv:** Head 1/4 right **Rev:** Elephant

Date	Mintage	F	VF	XF	Unc	BU
1981	2,000	—	—	—	325	345
1981 Proof	2,000	Value: 375				

KM# 38 250 EMALANGENI
15.9800 g., 0.9170 Gold .4711 oz. AGW **Ruler:** King Msawati III **Subject:** Accession of King Makhosetive **Obv:** Bust facing **Rev:** Bust facing

Date	Mintage	F	VF	XF	Unc	BU
ND(1986)	250	—	—	—	345	365
ND(1986) Proof	250	Value: 400				

GOLD BULLION COINAGE

KM# 30 2 EMALANGENI
31.1000 g., 0.9990 Gold 1 oz. AGW **Ruler:** Sobhuza II **Subject:** 80th Anniversary - Birth of King Sobhuza II **Obv:** Head 1/4 right **Rev:** Young bust of Queen Elizabeth II right

Date	Mintage	F	VF	XF	Unc	BU
ND(1979)	1,250	—	—	—	675	700
ND(1979) Proof	Inc. above	Value: 725				

KM# 36 5 EMALANGENI
31.1000 g., 0.9990 Gold 1 oz. AGW **Ruler:** Sobhuza II **Subject:** Queen Elizabeth II's Silver Jubilee **Obv:** Head 1/4 right within circle **Rev:** Crowned bust of Queen Elizabeth II facing divides dates within circle

Date	Mintage	F	VF	XF	Unc	BU
ND(1978) Proof	—	Value: 725				

SWEDEN

The Kingdom of Sweden, a limited constitutional monarchy located in northern Europe between Norway and Finland, has an area of 173,732 sq. mi. (449,960 sq. km.) and a population of *8.5 million. Capital: Stockholm. Mining, lumbering and a specialized machine industry dominate the economy. Machinery, paper, iron and steel, motor vehicles and wood pulp are exported.

Olaf Skottkonung founded Sweden as a Christian stronghold late in the 10th century. After conquering Finland late in the 13th century, Sweden, together with Norway, came under the rule of Denmark, 1397-1523, in an association known as the Union of Kalmar. Modern Sweden had its beginning in 1523 when Gustaf Vasa drove the Danes out of Sweden and was himself chosen king. Under Gustaf Adolphus II and Charles XII, Sweden was one of the great powers of 17th century Europe – until Charles invaded Russia in 1708, and was defeated at the Battle of Pultowa in June, 1709. Early in the 18th century, a coalition of Russia, Poland and Denmark took away Sweden's Baltic empire and in 1809 Sweden was forced to cede Finland to Russia. The Treaty of Kiel ceded Norway to Sweden in January 1814. The Norwegians resisted for a time but later signed the Act of Union at the Convention of Moss in August 1814,The Union was dissolved in 1905 and Norway became independent. A new constitution that took effect on Jan. 1, 1975, restricts the function of the king largely to a ceremonial role.

RULERS
Oscar II, 1872-1907
Gustaf V, 1907-1950
Gustaf VI, 1950-1973
Carl XVI Gustaf, 1973-

MINT OFFICIALS' INITIALS

Letter	Date	Name
AL	1898-1916	Adolf Lindberg, engraver
B	1992-2005	Stefan Ingves
D	1986-1992	Bengt Dennis
EB	1876-1908	Emil Brusewitz
EL	1916-1944	Erik Lindberg, engraver
G	1927-1945	Alf Grabe
LH	1944-1974	Leo Holmberg, engraver
SI	2005-	Stefan Ingves
TS	1945-1961	Torsten Swensson
U	1961-1986	Benkt Ulvfot
W	1908-1927	Karl-August Wallroth

MONETARY SYSTEM
100 Ore = 1 Krona

KINGDOM

REFORM COINAGE

1873 - present

KM# 750 ORE
Bronze, 16 mm. **Ruler:** Oscar II **Obv:** Monogram within crowned shield, legend lengthened **Rev:** Value and date flanked by 3 crowns

Date	Mintage	F	VF	XF	Unc	BU
1901	3,074,700	1.00	2.50	4.50	20.00	—
1902	2,685,400	1.00	2.50	4.50	22.50	—
1903	2,695,600	1.00	2.50	4.50	22.50	—
1904	2,032,700	1.00	2.50	4.50	20.00	—
1905	3,556,000	0.85	2.25	3.50	16.50	—

KM# 768 ORE
Bronze, 16 mm. **Ruler:** Oscar II **Obv:** Crowned shield **Rev:** Value and date flanked by crowns

Date	Mintage	F	VF	XF	Unc	BU
1906	1,783,300	2.00	4.00	10.00	65.00	—
1907	8,250,500	0.20	0.50	2.00	12.50	—

KM# 777.1 ORE
Bronze, 16 mm. **Ruler:** Gustaf V **Obv:** Crowned monogram with small cross on crown **Rev:** Value and crowns

Date	Mintage	F	VF	XF	Unc	BU
1909	3,805,600	6.00	9.00	18.00	100	—

KM# 777.2 ORE

Bronze, 16 mm. **Ruler:** Gustaf V **Obv:** Large cross **Rev:** Value and crowns **Edge:** Plain

Date	Mintage	F	VF	XF	Unc	BU
1909	Inc. above	2.00	3.00	8.00	30.00	—
1910	1,582,600	3.00	6.00	10.00	50.00	—
1911	3,149,000	0.75	1.50	3.00	15.00	—
1912/1	3,170,000	8.50	20.00	47.50	250	—
1912	Inc. above	0.75	1.50	3.00	15.00	—
1913/12	3,197,300	4.00	10.00	22.50	125	—
1913	Inc. above	0.75	1.50	3.00	15.00	—
Note: Long and short-tailed 9						
1914 Open 4	2,214,050	35.00	60.00	125	435	—
1914 Closed 4	Inc. above	0.75	1.50	5.00	30.00	—
1915/3	4,471,300	2.25	6.00	10.00	37.50	—
1915	Inc. above	0.25	0.50	1.75	7.00	—
1916 Short 6	7,615,500	0.25	0.50	1.75	7.00	—
1916 Long 6	Inc. above	0.30	0.75	2.50	10.00	—
1919 Unique	—	—	—	—	—	—
1920	5,547,600	0.25	0.50	1.25	5.00	—
1921	7,441,510	0.25	0.50	1.25	5.00	—
1922	1,165,700	2.00	4.00	6.00	30.00	—
1923	4,511,800	0.35	0.75	1.75	7.00	—
1924	2,578,900	0.25	0.75	1.75	8.00	—
1925	4,714,900	0.15	0.35	0.60	3.00	—
1926	7,739,300	0.15	0.35	0.60	3.00	—
1927	3,601,600	0.15	0.35	0.60	3.00	—
1928	2,380,800	0.25	0.75	2.50	10.00	—
1929 Curved 2	6,090,500	0.20	0.35	0.85	4.00	—
1929 Straight 2	Inc. above	0.40	0.60	2.00	9.00	—
1930	5,477,300	0.20	0.35	0.85	4.00	—
1931	5,678,500	0.20	0.35	0.85	4.00	—
1932	3,339,000	—	0.45	1.75	7.00	—
1933	3,426,800	—	0.45	0.85	6.00	—
1934	6,120,500	—	0.30	0.60	3.00	—
1935	4,599,800	—	0.30	0.60	3.00	—
1936 Long 6	6,166,100	0.20	0.45	1.25	3.50	—
1936 Short 6	Inc. above	0.10	0.30	0.60	3.00	—
1937	7,738,200	0.10	0.25	0.60	1.75	—
1938	6,992,900	0.10	0.25	0.60	1.75	—
1939	6,562,300	0.10	0.25	0.60	1.75	—
1940	4,059,900	0.10	0.25	0.50	1.50	—
1941	11,599,090	0.10	0.25	0.50	1.50	—
1942	3,992,000	0.10	0.25	0.60	1.75	—
1950	22,421,200	0.10	0.25	0.50	1.50	—

KM# 789 ORE

Iron, 16 mm. **Ruler:** Gustaf V **Obv:** Crowned monogram divides date **Rev:** Value and crowns **Note:** World War I issues.

Date	Mintage	F	VF	XF	Unc	BU
1917	8,127,700	0.50	1.50	4.00	20.00	—
1918	9,706,100	1.00	2.25	6.50	27.50	—
1919	7,169,500	1.50	3.00	8.00	40.00	—

KM# 810 ORE

Iron, 16 mm. **Ruler:** Gustaf V **Obv:** Crowned monogram divides date **Rev:** Value and crowns **Note:** World War II issues. Similar to KM#777.

Date	Mintage	F	VF	XF	Unc	BU
1942	10,053,000	0.10	0.25	0.75	3.50	—
1943	10,714,000	0.10	0.25	0.85	4.50	—
1944	8,648,500	0.10	0.25	0.75	4.50	—
1945	9,527,000	0.10	0.25	0.75	4.50	—
1945 Serif 4	Inc. above	3.50	6.50	15.00	30.00	—
1946	6,611,000	—	0.25	1.00	4.50	—
1947	14,244,500	—	0.20	0.40	1.50	—
1948	15,442,000	—	0.20	0.40	1.50	—
1949	11,778,900	—	0.20	0.40	1.50	—
1950	14,431,500	—	0.20	0.40	1.50	—

KM# 820 ORE

Bronze, 16 mm. **Ruler:** Gustaf VI **Obv:** Crown above inscription **Rev:** Value within circle divides date below crown **Edge:** Plain **Note:** Varieties exist.

Date	Mintage	F	VF	XF	Unc	BU
1952 TS	3,819,000	—	0.20	0.75	3.50	—
1953 TS	22,635,800	—	—	0.30	2.00	—
1954 TS	15,492,000	—	—	0.30	2.00	—
1955 TS	24,008,000	—	—	0.30	2.00	—
1956 TS	20,792,000	—	—	0.30	2.00	—
1957 TS	21,018,500	—	—	0.30	2.00	—
1958 TS	20,220,000	—	—	0.30	2.00	—
1959 TS	14,027,500	—	—	0.30	2.00	—
1960 TS	21,840,000	—	—	0.25	2.00	—
1961 TS	11,457,500	—	—	0.35	2.25	—
1961 U	4,927,500	—	0.20	0.50	3.50	—
1962 U	19,692,500	—	—	0.30	2.00	—
1963 U	26,070,000	—	—	0.15	0.65	—
1964 U	19,290,000	—	—	0.15	0.65	—
1965 U	22,335,000	—	—	0.15	0.65	—
1966 U	24,092,500	—	—	0.15	0.30	—
1967 U	30,420,000	—	—	0.10	0.30	—
1968 U	20,760,000	—	—	0.10	0.30	—
1969 U	20,197,500	—	—	0.10	0.30	—
1970 U	44,400,000	—	—	0.10	0.30	—
1971 U	16,490,000	—	—	0.10	0.30	—

KM# 746 2 ORE

Bronze, 21 mm. **Ruler:** Oscar II **Obv:** Large lettering **Rev:** Value, date and crowns within circle

Date	Mintage	F	VF	XF	Unc	BU
1901	1,415,200	0.50	1.25	3.50	22.50	—
1902	2,035,550	0.50	1.25	3.50	22.50	—
1904	698,050	0.50	1.25	4.50	30.00	—
1905	1,429,900	0.50	1.25	3.50	22.50	—

KM# 769 2 ORE

Bronze, 21 mm. **Ruler:** Oscar II **Obv:** Crowned shield **Rev:** Value, date and crowns within circle

Date	Mintage	F	VF	XF	Unc	BU
1906/5	994,250	100	200	420	875	—
1906	Inc. above	2.75	8.00	25.00	90.00	—
1907	3,807,350	0.30	0.60	2.50	15.00	—

KM# 778 2 ORE

Bronze, 21 mm. **Ruler:** Gustaf V **Obv:** Crowned monogram divides date **Rev:** Value and crowns

Date	Mintage	F	VF	XF	Unc	BU
1909	1,584,550	0.50	2.00	8.00	47.50	—
1910	809,400	2.00	8.00	22.50	90.00	—
1912	445,750	2.50	10.00	32.50	100	—
1913	805,650	0.30	2.00	10.00	47.50	—
1914	1,196,900	0.30	2.00	10.00	47.50	—
1915/4	813,850	4.50	12.50	35.00	110	—
1915	Inc. above	0.30	2.00	10.00	47.50	—
1916/5	2,815,450	2.75	8.00	27.50	90.00	—
1916 Short 6	Inc. above	0.25	0.60	5.00	30.00	—
1916 Long 6	Inc. above	0.25	0.60	5.00	30.00	—
1919	1,202,700	0.25	0.60	4.00	22.50	—
1920	3,464,750	0.30	0.50	2.00	10.00	—
1921	2,958,250	0.30	0.50	2.00	10.00	—
1922	521,600	0.70	1.75	6.00	37.50	—
1923	769,200	1.00	2.50	7.00	47.50	—
1924	1,283,000	0.30	0.75	3.50	27.50	—
1925	3,903,350	0.20	0.50	1.75	15.00	—
1926	3,573,950	0.20	0.50	1.75	15.00	—
1927	2,190,250	0.20	0.50	1.75	15.00	—
1928	832,250	0.40	1.00	4.00	30.00	—
1929	2,384,350	0.20	0.30	1.75	10.00	—
1930	2,589,850	0.20	0.30	1.75	10.00	—
1931	2,295,200	0.20	0.30	1.75	10.00	—
1932	1,179,150	0.35	0.85	4.00	30.00	—
1933	1,721,300	0.20	0.35	1.75	10.00	—
1934	1,794,950	0.20	0.35	1.75	10.00	—
1935	3,677,750	0.20	0.30	1.25	7.00	—
1936 Short 6	2,244,100	0.20	0.30	1.00	6.00	—
1936 Long 6	Inc. above	0.65	1.25	3.75	18.50	—
1937	2,980,950	0.10	0.25	1.25	6.00	—
1938	3,224,800	0.10	0.25	0.75	6.00	—
1939	4,014,200	0.10	0.25	0.75	4.50	—
1940	3,304,750	0.10	0.25	0.75	4.50	—
1941	7,337,198	0.10	0.25	0.75	4.50	—
1942	1,614,000	0.30	0.75	1.50	10.00	—
1950	5,823,000	0.10	0.20	0.65	4.50	—

KM# 790 2 ORE

Iron, 21 mm. **Ruler:** Gustaf V **Obv:** Crowned monogram divides date **Rev:** Value and crowns **Note:** World War I issues. Similar to KM#553.

Date	Mintage	F	VF	XF	Unc	BU
1917	4,576,200	2.00	3.00	8.50	42.50	—
1918	4,981,750	2.50	5.00	12.50	57.50	—
1919	2,923,100	6.50	12.50	27.50	90.00	—
1920	1	—	—	—	—	—

KM# 811 2 ORE

Iron, 21 mm. **Ruler:** Gustaf V **Obv:** Crowned monogram divides date **Rev:** Value and crowns **Note:** World War II issues.

Date	Mintage	F	VF	XF	Unc	BU
1942	9,343,350	0.15	0.30	1.50	10.00	—
1943	6,999,300	0.15	0.30	1.50	10.00	—
1944	6,125,900	0.15	0.30	1.50	10.00	—
1945	4,773,400	0.20	0.40	1.50	11.50	—
1946	5,854,000	0.15	0.30	1.50	10.00	—
1947	9,535,750	0.15	0.30	0.75	7.00	—
1948	11,424,250	0.15	0.30	0.75	7.00	—
1949 Long 9	10,599,750	0.15	0.30	0.75	7.00	—
1949 Short 9	Inc. above	0.15	0.30	0.75	7.00	—
1950	13,323,000	0.15	0.30	0.75	7.00	—

KM# 821 2 ORE

Bronze, 21 mm. **Ruler:** Gustaf VI **Obv:** Crown above inscription **Rev:** Value within circle divides date below crown **Edge:** Plain **Note:** Varieties exist.

Date	Mintage	F	VF	XF	Unc	BU
1952 TS	3,011,000	0.20	0.50	0.85	6.00	—
1953 TS	15,619,900	0.10	0.20	0.75	4.50	—
1954 TS	10,086,000	0.10	0.20	0.75	4.50	—
1955 TS	12,963,400	0.10	0.20	0.75	4.50	—
1956 TS	13,890,250	0.10	0.20	0.75	4.50	—
1957 TS	9,991,300	0.10	0.20	0.75	4.50	—
1958 TS	10,105,500	0.10	0.20	0.75	4.50	—
1959 TS	11,571,750	0.10	0.20	0.75	4.50	—
1960 TS	11,092,500	0.10	0.20	0.75	4.50	—
1961 TS	9,672,500	0.10	0.20	0.75	4.50	—
1961 U	1,075,000	0.70	1.50	3.00	15.00	—
1962 U	9,568,750	—	0.10	0.45	2.00	—
1963 U	13,337,500	—	0.10	0.45	2.00	—
1964 U	19,346,250	—	0.10	0.20	2.00	—
1964 U	Inc. above	0.60	1.25	2.50	10.00	—
Note: O in crown: first dot in crown on left with hollow center						
1965 U	23,356,000	—	0.10	0.20	0.75	—
1966 U	18,278,000	—	0.10	0.20	0.75	—
1967 U	23,931,000	—	—	0.10	0.45	—
1968 U	26,238,000	—	—	0.10	0.45	—
1969 U	16,843,000	—	—	0.10	0.45	—
1970 U	31,254,000	—	—	0.10	0.45	—
1971 U	19,179,000	—	—	0.10	0.45	—

KM# 757 5 ORE

Bronze, 27 mm. **Ruler:** Oscar II **Obv:** Large lettering **Rev:** Value, date and crowns within beaded circle

Date	Mintage	F	VF	XF	Unc	BU
1901	441,660	1.00	4.00	12.50	60.00	—
1902	652,420	1.00	4.00	12.50	60.00	—

Date	Mintage	F	VF	XF	Unc	BU
1903	243,000	1.75	5.00	18.00	70.00	—
1904	414,240	1.00	4.00	12.50	50.00	—
1905	545,080	1.00	4.00	15.00	55.00	—

KM# 770 5 ORE

Bronze, 27 mm. **Ruler:** Oscar II **Obv:** Crowned shield **Rev:** Value, date and crowns within beaded circle

Date	Mintage	F	VF	XF	Unc	BU
1906	565,280	0.75	3.50	12.50	47.50	—
1907	1,953,260	0.50	2.00	6.00	25.00	—

KM# 779.1 5 ORE

Bronze, 27 mm. **Ruler:** Gustaf V **Obv:** Small cross **Rev:** Value above crowns

Date	Mintage	F	VF	XF	Unc	BU
1909	917,230	2.00	6.00	30.00	175	—

KM# 779.2 5 ORE

Bronze, 27 mm. **Ruler:** Gustaf V **Obv:** Largen cross **Rev:** Value above crowns **Note:** Varieties exist.

Date	Mintage	F	VF	XF	Unc	BU
1909	Inc. above	7.00	45.00	265	875	—
1910	30,630	115	265	545	1,325	—
1911	778,000	0.85	3.50	25.00	135	—
Note: Narrow base mint mark						
1911	Inc. above	3.00	12.00	50.00	200	—
Note: Wide base mint mark						
1912	547,480	1.00	3.50	35.00	190	—
1913	761,780	0.85	2.25	22.50	125	—
1914	400,100	2.50	5.50	42.50	235	—
1915	1,122,820	0.50	2.50	18.50	65.00	—
1916/5	955,440	10.00	20.00	40.00	165	—
1916 Short 6	Inc. above	0.50	2.50	15.00	70.00	—
1916 Long 6	Inc. above	0.50	2.50	15.00	70.00	—
1917	1	—	—	—	—	—
1919	1,129,380	0.25	1.00	13.50	60.00	—
1920	2,360,920	0.25	1.00	8.00	35.00	—
1921	1,878,500	0.20	0.75	12.00	50.00	—
1922	763,420	0.25	2.50	27.50	125	—
1923	505,580	0.85	4.50	65.00	245	—
1924	899,500	0.25	1.50	17.50	90.00	—
1925	1,943,500	0.20	0.75	8.50	50.00	—
1926	1,742,100	0.20	0.75	8.50	50.00	—
1927	36,380	80.00	175	525	1,200	—
1928	987,900	0.20	1.00	12.00	65.00	—
1929	1,668,560	0.20	0.50	8.50	50.00	—
1930	1,716,040	0.20	0.50	8.50	50.00	—
1931	1,130,960	0.20	0.50	8.50	55.00	—
1932	1,165,220	0.20	0.50	8.50	55.00	—
1933	574,340	0.65	2.50	27.50	135	—
1934	1,710,260	0.20	0.40	5.00	37.50	—
1935	1,682,020	0.20	0.40	5.00	37.50	—
1936 Short 6	1,625,700	0.20	0.40	6.00	37.50	—
1936	Inc. above	0.25	0.75	7.00	47.50	—
1937	2,637,260	—	0.30	4.00	22.50	—
1938	2,354,240	—	0.30	4.00	22.50	—
1939	2,591,500	—	0.45	6.00	22.50	—
1940	2,729,580	—	0.35	3.50	20.00	—
1940 Serif 4	Inc. above	—	0.45	4.00	25.00	—
1941	2,054,540	—	0.35	2.50	17.50	—
1942	395,400	2.00	4.00	22.50	90.00	—
1950	12,559,100	—	0.25	0.75	6.00	—

KM# 791 5 ORE

Iron **Ruler:** Gustaf V **Obv:** Crowned monogram **Rev:** Value above crowns **Note:** World War I issues

Date	Mintage	F	VF	XF	Unc	BU
1917	2,953,320	4.00	8.00	18.00	70.00	—
1918	2,457,840	10.00	20.00	32.50	125	—
1919	2,302,480	10.00	20.00	32.50	120	—

KM# 812 5 ORE

Iron, 27 mm. **Ruler:** Gustaf V **Obv:** Crowned monogram divides date **Rev:** Value above crowns **Note:** World War II issues.

Date	Mintage	F	VF	XF	Unc	BU
1942	4,343,420	0.20	0.75	4.00	30.00	—
1943	5,570,180	0.20	0.75	4.00	30.00	—
1944	4,561,980	0.20	0.75	4.00	30.00	—
1945	3,771,100	0.20	0.75	4.00	30.00	—
1946	2,375,080	—	0.50	3.00	20.00	—
1947	6,034,840	—	0.50	3.00	20.00	—
1948	6,246,000	—	0.50	3.00	20.00	—
1949	7,839,640	—	0.50	2.00	16.50	—
1950	5,289,500	—	0.50	2.00	16.50	—

KM# 822 5 ORE

Bronze, 27 mm. **Ruler:** Gustaf VI **Obv:** Crown above inscription **Rev:** Value within circle divides date below crown **Edge:** Plain

Date	Mintage	F	VF	XF	Unc	BU
1952 TS	3,065,400	0.20	0.50	1.75	8.50	—
1953 TS	12,329,320	0.20	0.50	1.75	8.50	—
1954 TS	7,232,100	0.20	0.50	1.75	8.50	—
1955 TS	8,464,620	0.20	0.50	1.75	8.50	—
1956 TS	7,997,120	0.20	0.50	2.00	9.00	—
1957 TS	6,275,600	0.20	0.50	1.75	8.50	—
1958 TS	9,498,400	0.20	0.50	2.00	9.00	—
1959 TS	8,370,500	0.20	0.50	2.00	9.00	—
1960 TS	10,542,300	0.20	0.40	1.25	7.50	—
1961 TS	3,909,000	0.20	0.40	1.25	7.50	—
1961 U	2,451,500	0.20	0.50	1.25	8.50	—
1962 U	22,305,500	—	0.10	0.50	3.50	—
1963 U	17,156,500	—	0.10	0.50	3.50	—
1964 U	10,922,500	—	0.10	0.75	7.00	—
1964 U	Inc. above	2.75	5.50	11.50	30.00	—
Note: O in crown: first dot in crown on left with hollow center						
1965 U	22,635,000	—	0.10	0.20	1.00	—
1966 U	18,213,000	—	0.10	0.20	1.00	—
1967 U	20,776,000	—	0.10	0.20	1.00	—
1968 U	27,093,500	—	0.10	0.20	1.00	—
1969 U	26,886,500	—	0.10	0.20	1.00	—
1970 U	29,419,500	—	0.10	0.20	1.00	—
1971 U	15,749,000	—	0.10	0.20	1.00	—

KM# 845 5 ORE

2.7000 g., Bronze, 18 mm. **Ruler:** Gustaf VI **Obv:** Large crown above smaller crown **Rev:** Value divides date

Date	Mintage	F	VF	XF	Unc	BU
1972 U	107,894,000	—	—	0.10	0.25	0.60
1973 U	193,037,580	—	—	0.10	0.25	0.60

KM# 849 5 ORE

Copper-Tin-Zinc, 18 mm. **Ruler:** Carl XVI Gustaf **Obv:** Value **Rev:** Crowned monogram divides date **Edge:** Plain **Designer:** Lars Englund

Date	Mintage	F	VF	XF	Unc	BU
1976 U	4,672,350	—	—	0.10	0.40	0.60
1977 U	31,037,129	—	—	0.10	0.30	0.60
1978 U	46,021,707	—	—	0.10	0.30	0.60
1979 U	65,833,193	—	—	0.10	0.30	0.60
1980 U	60,996,699	—	—	0.10	0.25	0.60
1981 U	19,791,000	—	—	0.10	0.25	0.60

KM# 849a 5 ORE

Copper-Zinc, 18 mm. **Ruler:** Carl XVI Gustaf **Obv:** Value **Rev:** Crowned monogram divides date **Designer:** Lars Englund

Date	Mintage	F	VF	XF	Unc	BU
1981 U	34,960,593	—	—	0.10	0.20	0.60
1982 U	40,471,115	—	—	0.10	0.20	0.60
1983 U	36,304,042	—	—	0.10	0.20	0.60
1984 U	13,449,245	—	—	0.10	0.20	0.60

KM# 755 10 ORE

1.4500 g., 0.4000 Silver .0186 oz. ASW, 15 mm. **Ruler:** Oscar II **Obv:** Large lettering **Rev:** Value, date **Note:** Varieties exist.

Date	Mintage	F	VF	XF	Unc	BU
1902 EB	1,945,600	1.00	3.50	12.50	32.50	—
1903 EB	1,508,930	1.00	3.50	12.50	32.50	—
1904 EB	3,279,520	0.75	1.50	8.50	25.00	—

KM# 774 10 ORE

1.4500 g., 0.4000 Silver .0186 oz. ASW, 15 mm. **Ruler:** Oscar II **Obv:** Crowned shield flanked by crowns **Rev:** Value and date

Date	Mintage	F	VF	XF	Unc	BU
1907 EB	7,319,040	0.45	1.25	5.00	20.00	—

KM# 780 10 ORE

1.4500 g., 0.4000 Silver .0186 oz. ASW, 15 mm. **Ruler:** Gustaf V **Obv:** Three small crowns within crowned shield divides date **Rev:** Value

Date	Mintage	F	VF	XF	Unc	BU
1909 W	1,610,400	1.25	4.00	13.50	70.00	—
1911 W	3,180,650	0.35	2.00	8.50	32.50	—
1913 W	1,580,910	1.00	2.50	11.50	50.00	—
1914 W	1,571,330	0.75	3.00	8.50	32.50	—
1914 Serif 4	Inc. above	0.75	2.25	10.00	50.00	—
1915 W	1,546,950	0.50	2.25	8.00	47.50	—
1916/5 W	3,034,880	2.50	7.00	22.50	110	—
1916 W	Inc. above	0.75	1.75	6.50	32.50	—
1917 W	4,996,139	0.35	0.75	2.50	18.50	—
1918 W	4,114,180	0.35	0.75	2.50	18.50	—
1919 W	5,737,020	0.35	0.75	2.50	18.50	—
1927 W	2,509,590	0.30	0.60	2.50	22.50	—
1928 G	2,901,150	0.30	0.60	2.50	22.50	—
1929 G	5,505,200	0.30	0.60	1.75	11.50	—
1930 G	3,222,710	0.30	0.60	1.75	11.50	—
1931 G	4,272,073	0.30	0.60	1.75	11.50	—
1933 G	1,948,090	0.80	1.75	3.25	25.00	—
1934 G	4,059,293	0.30	0.50	1.25	6.50	—
1935 G	2,426,283	0.30	0.50	1.25	6.50	—
1936 G Short 6	5,099,270	1.75	4.50	20.00	60.00	—
1936 G Long 6	Inc. above	0.30	0.45	1.50	9.00	—
1937 G	5,116,920	0.30	0.40	1.00	6.50	—
1938 G	7,428,140	0.30	0.40	1.00	6.50	—
1938 G Proof	—	Value: 12.50				
1939/29 G	2,020,670	3.75	8.00	22.00	55.00	—
1939 G	Inc. above	0.30	0.60	2.25	13.50	—
1939 G Proof	—	Value: 17.50				
1940 G	3,017,320	0.30	0.50	1.25	6.00	—
1941 G	9,106,380	0.30	0.50	1.25	6.00	—
1942 G	3,691,640	0.30	0.50	1.25	6.00	—

KM# 795 10 ORE

Nickel-Bronze, 15 mm. **Ruler:** Gustaf V **Obv:** Crowned monogram divides date **Rev:** Value

Date	Mintage	F	VF	XF	Unc	BU
1920 W	3,612,250	0.50	1.00	5.00	40.00	—
1920 W Large W	Inc. above	13.50	28.00	60.00	300	—
1921 W	2,269,950	0.50	1.25	6.00	40.00	—
1923 W	2,143,560	0.50	1.25	7.00	50.00	—
1924 W	1,600,000	0.50	1.50	8.00	70.00	—
1925 W	1,472,340	0.75	3.25	16.50	85.00	—
1940 G	3,373,200	0.20	0.50	2.00	16.00	—
1941	815,880	0.75	1.50	4.00	30.00	—
1946 TS	4,115,940	0.10	0.30	0.75	6.00	—
1947 TS	4,132,950	0.10	0.30	0.75	6.00	—

KM# 813 10 ORE

1.4400 g., 0.4000 Silver .0185 oz. ASW, 15 mm. **Ruler:** Gustaf V **Obv:** Crown **Rev:** Value **Note:** Varieties exist.

Date	Mintage	F	VF	XF	Unc	BU
1942 G	1,600,000	0.25	0.40	1.25	6.50	—
1942 G Proof	—	Value: 35.00				
1943 G	7,661,100	0.25	0.40	1.25	6.50	—
1944 G	12,276,900	BV	0.35	0.85	5.00	—
1945 G	11,702,510	BV	0.35	0.85	5.00	—
1945 TS	Inc. above	BV	0.35	0.85	5.00	—
1945 TS/G	Inc. above	BV	0.35	1.25	6.50	—
1946/5 TS Open 6	3,575,500	5.50	13.00	25.00	70.00	—
1946 TS Open 6	Inc. above	0.30	0.75	2.50	22.50	—
1946 TS Closed 6	Inc. above	BV	0.35	1.75	12.50	—
1947 TS	7,293,250	BV	0.30	0.85	5.00	—
1948 TS	10,418,650	BV	0.30	0.75	5.00	—
1949 TS	12,044,000	BV	0.30	0.75	5.00	—
1950 TS	31,823,870	BV	0.30	0.75	4.00	—

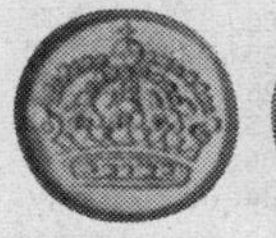

KM# 823 10 ORE

1.4400 g., 0.4000 Silver .0185 oz. ASW, 15 mm. **Ruler:** Gustaf VI **Obv:** Crown **Rev:** Value

Date	Mintage	F	VF	XF	Unc	BU
1952 TS	4,659,700	BV	0.40	0.85	4.50	—
1953 TS	28,484,040	—	BV	0.85	4.50	—
1954 TS	15,913,250	—	BV	0.85	4.50	—
1955 TS	16,687,200	—	BV	0.85	4.50	—
1956 TS	21,985,600	—	BV	0.60	3.50	—
1957 TS	21,294,400	—	BV	0.60	3.50	—
1958 TS	19,605,400	—	BV	0.60	3.50	—
1959 TS	18,523,000	—	BV	0.60	3.50	—
1960 TS	16,605,000	—	BV	0.60	3.50	—
1961 TS	8,283,000	—	BV	0.60	3.50	—
1961 U	7,843,000	—	BV	0.60	3.50	—
1962 U	8,619,000	—	BV	0.60	3.50	—

KM# 835 10 ORE

1.4000 g., Copper-Nickel, 15 mm. **Ruler:** Gustaf VI **Obv:** Crowned monogram divides date **Rev:** Value

Date	Mintage	F	VF	XF	Unc	BU
1962 U	8,814,000	0.10	0.25	0.60	3.50	7.50
1963 U	28,170,000	—	—	0.15	0.60	3.50
1964 U	36,895,000	—	—	0.15	0.60	3.50
1965 U	29,870,000	—	—	0.15	0.60	3.50
1966 U	20,435,000	—	—	0.15	0.60	3.50
1967 U	18,245,000	—	—	0.15	0.60	3.50
1968 U	51,490,000	—	—	0.15	0.50	3.50
1969 U	55,880,000	—	—	0.15	0.50	1.75
1970 U	60,910,000	—	—	0.15	0.50	1.75
1971 U	27,075,000	—	—	0.15	0.50	1.75
1972 U	36,766,500	—	—	0.15	0.25	1.00
1973 U	160,740,000	—	—	0.15	0.25	1.00

KM# 850 10 ORE

1.4000 g., Copper-Nickel, 15 mm. **Ruler:** Carl XVI Gustaf **Obv:** Crowned monogram divides date **Rev:** Value **Edge:** Plain **Designer:** Lars Englund

Date	Mintage	F	VF	XF	Unc	BU
1976 U	4,172,790	—	—	0.15	0.50	1.00
1977 U	44,517,287	—	—	0.10	0.35	0.75
1978 U	74,341,720	—	—	0.10	0.35	0.75
1979 U	75,305,608	—	—	0.10	0.15	0.40
1980 U	108,293,811	—	—	0.10	0.15	0.40
1981 U	102,453,931	—	—	0.10	0.15	0.30
1982 U	103,905,592	—	—	0.10	0.15	0.30
1983 U	773,149,400	—	—	0.10	0.15	0.40
1984 U	122,128,092	—	—	0.10	0.15	0.30
1985 U	79,154,951	—	—	0.10	0.15	0.40
1986 U	48,945,396	—	—	0.10	0.15	0.40
1986 D	48,945,220	—	—	0.10	0.15	0.40
1987 D	146,877,318	—	—	0.10	0.15	0.40
1988 D	194,986,479	—	—	0.10	0.15	0.30
1989 D	245,180,644	—	—	0.10	0.15	0.30
1990 D	139,298,404	—	—	0.10	0.15	0.30
1991 D	5,176,842	—	—	0.15	0.50	1.00

KM# 739 25 ORE

2.4200 g., 0.6000 Silver 0.0467 oz. ASW, 17 mm. **Ruler:** Oscar II **Obv:** Large lettering **Rev:** Value within wreath, date below

Date	Mintage	F	VF	XF	Unc	BU
1902 EB	1,259,039	2.00	7.00	22.50	80.00	—
1904 EB	691,888	2.00	7.00	22.50	82.00	—
1905 EB	732,000	1.75	5.50	18.50	70.00	—

KM# 775 25 ORE

2.4200 g., 0.6000 Silver 0.0467 oz. ASW, 17 mm. **Ruler:** Oscar II **Obv:** Crowned shield flanked by crowns **Rev:** Value within wreath

Date	Mintage	F	VF	XF	Unc	BU
1907 EB	3,222,580	0.80	2.00	6.00	42.50	—

KM# 785 25 ORE

2.4200 g., 0.6000 Silver 0.0467 oz. ASW, 17 mm. **Ruler:** Gustaf V **Obv:** Small crowns within crowned shield divides date **Rev:** Value above sprigs

Date	Mintage	F	VF	XF	Unc	BU
1910 W Large cross	2,043,936	0.75	2.00	6.00	50.00	—
1910 W Small cross	Inc. above	7.00	27.50	75.00	475	—
1912 W	1,013,740	0.75	2.75	15.00	70.00	—
1914 W	3,719,232	0.75	2.75	15.00	40.00	—
1916 W	1,269,120	0.75	2.75	15.00	70.00	—
1917 W	1,657,312	0.75	2.25	5.50	40.00	—
1918 W Small 8	2,364,784	0.75	2.25	7.50	50.00	—
1918 W Wide 8	Inc. above	0.75	2.25	9.50	58.00	—
1919 W	3,205,164	0.75	1.50	5.00	35.00	—
1927 W	1,687,984	0.75	1.75	5.00	35.00	—
1928 G	836,899	0.75	2.00	9.50	58.00	—
1929 G	1,124,932	0.75	1.75	6.00	40.00	—
1930 G	3,489,628	BV	1.50	3.00	18.50	—
1931 G	1,391,938	BV	1.50	3.00	18.50	—
1932 G	1,133,344	BV	1.50	3.00	18.50	—
1933 G	964,340	BV	1.50	8.00	35.00	—
1934 G	1,403,648	BV	1.50	3.00	11.50	—
1936 G	1,852,000	BV	1.50	3.00	11.50	—
1937 G Large G	Inc. above	0.75	2.00	4.50	18.50	—
1937 G Proof	Inc. above	Value: 20.00				
1937 G Small G	3,258,956	BV	1.50	4.50	12.50	—
1938	3,678,876	BV	1.25	2.75	7.50	—
1939	2,136,600	BV	1.00	2.75	7.50	—
1940	2,301,788	BV	1.00	2.50	7.00	—
1941	1,995,200	BV	1.00	2.50	7.00	—

KM# 798 25 ORE

Nickel-Bronze, 17 mm. **Ruler:** Gustaf V **Obv:** Crowned monogram divides date **Rev:** Value within oat sprigs

Date	Mintage	F	VF	XF	Unc	BU
1921 W	1,354,656	1.50	3.00	13.50	85.00	—
1940 G	2,333,040	0.15	0.50	3.00	18.50	—
1941 G	1,056,680	0.15	0.50	3.00	27.50	—
1946 TS	2,066,048	0.15	0.30	1.25	9.00	—
1947 TS	1,594,200	0.15	0.30	1.25	9.00	—

KM# 816 25 ORE

2.3200 g., 0.4000 Silver .0298 oz. ASW, 17 mm. **Ruler:** Gustaf V **Obv:** Crown **Rev:** Value and date

Date	Mintage	F	VF	XF	Unc	BU
1943 G	9,854,640	BV	0.50	1.25	7.50	—
1944 G	9,532,148	BV	0.50	1.25	7.50	—
1945 G	5,362,800	BV	0.50	1.25	7.50	—
1945 TS	Inc. above	BV	0.75	2.50	11.50	—
1945 G/TS	Inc. above	BV	0.60	3.50	16.50	—
1946 TS	2,249,600	—	BV	2.50	11.50	—
1946 TS serif 6	Inc. above	2.00	4.00	14.50	42.50	—
1947 TS	5,332,800	—	BV	1.25	4.50	—
1948 TS	3,191,000	—	BV	1.25	4.50	—
1949 TS	5,812,180	—	BV	1.25	4.50	—
1950 TS	12,059,144	—	BV	1.25	3.50	—

KM# 824 25 ORE

2.3200 g., 0.4000 Silver .0298 oz. ASW, 17 mm. **Ruler:** Gustaf VI **Obv:** Value and date **Rev:** Crown

Date	Mintage	F	VF	XF	Unc	BU
1952 TS	2,113,890	—	BV	1.25	4.50	—
1953 TS	18,177,420	—	BV	1.00	2.50	—
1954 TS	9,491,740	—	BV	1.00	2.50	—
1955 TS	7,663,100	—	BV	1.25	4.00	—
1956 TS	10,930,800	—	BV	1.00	3.50	—
1957 TS	12,497,200	—	BV	1.00	3.50	—
1958 TS	6,883,940	—	BV	1.00	3.50	—
1959 TS	4,772,000	—	BV	1.00	3.50	—
1960 TS	4,374,000	BV	0.50	2.00	10.00	—
1961 TS	8,380,800	—	BV	1.00	3.50	—

KM# 836 25 ORE

2.2000 g., Copper-Nickel, 17 mm. **Ruler:** Gustaf VI **Obv:** Crowned monogram divides date **Rev:** Value

Date	Mintage	F	VF	XF	Unc	BU
1962 U	4,426,000	—	0.25	1.00	3.25	—
1963 U	26,710,000	—	0.20	0.50	2.50	—
1964 U	17,300,000	—	0.20	0.50	2.50	—
1965 U	6,884,000	—	0.20	0.50	2.50	—
1966 U	12,932,000	—	—	0.25	1.25	—
1967 U	28,038,000	—	—	0.20	0.65	—
1968 U	14,366,000	—	—	0.20	0.65	—
1969 U	20,214,000	—	—	0.20	0.65	—
1970 U	23,780,000	—	—	0.20	0.65	—
1971 U	8,606,000	—	—	0.20	0.65	—
1972 U	1,323,200	—	—	0.20	0.65	—
1973 U	76,993,000	—	—	0.15	0.45	—

KM# 851 25 ORE

2.2000 g., Copper-Nickel, 17 mm. **Ruler:** Carl XVI Gustaf **Obv:** Crowned monogram divides date **Rev:** Value **Designer:** Lars Englund

Date	Mintage	F	VF	XF	Unc	BU
1976 U	2,515,285	—	—	0.15	0.65	—
1977 U	5,509,491	—	—	0.15	0.50	—
1978 U	54,593,293	—	—	0.10	0.30	—
1979 U	48,423,422	—	—	0.10	0.30	—
1980 U	38,889,325	—	—	0.10	0.30	—
1981 U	46,371,204	—	—	0.10	0.30	—
1982 U	43,212,638	—	—	0.10	0.30	—
1983 U	28,954,257	—	—	0.10	0.30	—
1984 U	7,293,722	—	—	0.10	0.30	—

KM# 771 50 ORE

5.0000 g., 0.6000 Silver .0965 oz. ASW, 22 mm. **Ruler:** Oscar II **Obv:** Crowned shield flanked by crowns **Rev:** Value and date within wreath

Date	Mintage	F	VF	XF	Unc	BU
1906 EB	319,452	2.75	8.00	35.00	190	—
1907 EB	803,340	2.00	5.00	32.50	125	—

KM# 788 50 ORE
5.0000 g., 0.6000 Silver .0965 oz. ASW, 22 mm. **Ruler:** Gustaf V **Obv:** Three small crowns within crowned shield divides date **Rev:** Value above sprigs

Date	Mintage	F	VF	XF	Unc	BU
1911 W	472,534	3.25	7.00	28.00	140	—
1912 W	483,062	4.50	8.50	30.00	165	—
1914 W	378,448	4.50	8.50	30.00	165	—
1916 W	536,718	3.25	7.00	25.00	135	—
1919 W	458,296	3.25	7.00	28.00	120	—
1927 W	671,596	1.50	3.00	15.00	80.00	—
1928 G	1,135,054	BV	2.00	7.00	45.00	—
1929 G	470,990	1.50	3.00	15.00	80.00	—
1930 G	547,920	1.50	3.00	15.00	75.00	—
1931 G	671,457	BV	2.00	12.50	55.00	—
1933 G	547,606	BV	2.00	12.50	55.00	—
1934 G	613,124	BV	2.00	7.00	40.00	—
1935 G	690,792	BV	2.00	7.00	40.00	—
1936 G Short 6	823,176	BV	2.00	7.00	40.00	—
1936 G Long 6	Inc. above	BV	3.50	12.50	70.00	—
1938 G	441,546	BV	1.50	4.50	25.00	—
1939 G	921,750	—	BV	2.50	18.00	—
1939 G Proof	—	Value: 35.00				

KM# 796 50 ORE
Nickel-Bronze, 22 mm. **Ruler:** Gustaf V **Obv:** Crowned monogram divides date **Rev:** Value within oat sprigs **Note:** Varieties exist.

Date	Mintage	F	VF	XF	Unc	BU
1920 W Oval 0	479,500	1.75	8.00	40.00	200	—
1920 W Round 0	Inc. above	35.00	70.00	230	645	—
1921 W	214,922	2.75	20.00	110	385	—
1924 W	645,368	1.25	10.00	45.00	275	—
1940 G	1,340,750	0.25	1.00	4.50	35.00	—
1940 G large G	Inc. above	5.50	15.00	40.00	90.00	—
1946 TS	1,425,990	0.25	1.00	4.00	20.00	—
1947 TS	1,031,800	0.25	1.00	4.00	20.00	—

KM# 817 50 ORE
4.8000 g., 0.4000 Silver .0617 oz. ASW, 22 mm. **Ruler:** Gustaf V **Obv:** Crown **Rev:** Value and date

Date	Mintage	F	VF	XF	Unc	BU
1943 G	784,700	1.50	3.00	10.00	55.00	—
1944 G	1,540,296	BV	1.00	2.00	12.00	—
1945 G	2,584,800	BV	1.00	2.00	12.00	—
1946 TS	1,091,000	BV	1.00	2.00	12.00	—
1947 TS	1,770,500	BV	1.00	2.00	12.00	—
1948 TS	1,731,400	BV	1.00	2.00	12.00	—
1949 TS	1,883,100	BV	1.00	2.00	12.00	—
1950 TS	3,353,620	BV	1.00	1.50	10.00	—

KM# 825 50 ORE
4.8000 g., 0.4000 Silver .0617 oz. ASW, 22 mm. **Ruler:** Gustaf VI **Obv:** Value and date **Rev:** Crown

Date	Mintage	F	VF	XF	Unc	BU
1952 TS	1,197,760	BV	1.00	3.00	22.50	—
1953 TS	4,395,620	BV	1.00	2.50	20.00	—
1954 TS	5,778,850	BV	1.00	2.50	20.00	—
1955 TS	2,699,700	BV	1.00	4.00	18.50	—
1956 TS	7,056,670	—	BV	1.50	8.50	—
1957 TS	2,404,700	—	BV	2.50	18.50	—
1958 TS	1,659,800	—	BV	2.50	18.50	—
1961 TS	2,775,000	—	BV	1.50	11.50	—

KM# 837 50 ORE
4.5000 g., Copper-Nickel, 22 mm. **Ruler:** Gustaf VI **Obv:** Crowned monogram divides date **Rev:** Value

Date	Mintage	F	VF	XF	Unc	BU
1962 U	1,400,000	0.50	0.75	3.25	21.50	—
1963 U	5,808,000	0.15	0.25	1.25	11.50	—
1964 U	5,325,000	0.15	0.25	1.25	11.50	—
1965 U	6,453,000	0.15	0.25	0.60	7.50	—
1966 U	6,309,000	0.15	0.25	0.50	6.00	—
1967 U	7,890,000	0.15	0.25	0.50	6.00	—
1968 U	9,198,000	—	0.15	0.25	1.25	—
1969 U	7,265,000	—	0.15	0.25	1.25	—
1970 U	9,426,000	—	0.15	0.25	1.25	—
1971 U	7,218,000	—	0.15	0.25	1.25	—
1972 U	7,388,000	—	0.15	0.25	1.25	—
1973 U	52,467,000	—	0.15	0.20	0.60	—

KM# 855 50 ORE
4.5000 g., Copper-Nickel, 22 mm. **Ruler:** Carl XVI Gustaf **Obv:** Crowned monogram divides date **Rev:** Value **Edge:** Plain
Designer: Lars Englund

Date	Mintage	F	VF	XF	Unc	BU
1976 U	2,588,575	—	0.15	0.25	1.00	—
1977 U	10,359,708	—	—	0.15	0.40	—
1978 U	33,282,476	—	—	0.15	0.40	—
1979 U	30,723,730	—	—	0.15	0.40	—
1980 U	28,665,662	—	—	0.15	0.40	—
1981 U	15,516,559	—	—	0.15	0.40	—
1982 U	14,778,358	—	—	0.15	0.40	—
1983 U	17,528,777	—	—	0.15	0.40	—
1984 U	27,527,534	—	—	0.15	0.40	—
1985 U	14,078,477	—	—	0.15	0.40	—
1986 U	937,214	—	—	0.20	0.75	—
1987 D	1,077,317	—	—	0.20	0.70	—
1988 D	531,669	—	—	0.20	0.75	—
1989 D	605,780	—	—	0.20	0.75	—
1990 D	31,934,675	—	—	0.10	0.20	—
1991 D	16,315,160	—	—	0.10	0.20	—

KM# 878 50 ORE
Bronze **Ruler:** Carl XVI Gustaf **Obv:** Value **Rev:** Three crowns and date

Date	Mintage	F	VF	XF	Unc	BU
1992 B	39,531,000	—	—	0.15	0.40	—
1992 D	39,531,000	—	—	0.15	0.30	—
1992 B	39,530,810	—	—	0.15	0.40	0.50
1993 B	643,520	—	—	0.20	0.65	0.85
1994 B	517,575	—	—	0.20	0.65	0.85
1995 B	486,538	—	—	0.10	0.20	0.35
1996 B	247,620	—	—	0.10	0.20	0.35
1997 B	69,995	—	—	0.10	0.20	0.35
1998 B	5,064,956	—	—	0.10	0.15	0.25
1999 B	22,076,128	—	—	0.10	0.15	0.25
2000 B	33,060,252	—	—	0.10	0.15	0.25

KM# 760 KRONA
7.5000 g., 0.8000 Silver .1929 oz. ASW **Ruler:** Oscar II **Obv:** Head left **Obv. Legend:** OSCAR II SVERIGES... **Rev:** Crowned arms with supporters

Date	Mintage	F	VF	XF	Unc	BU
1901/898 EB	270,960	9.00	30.00	150	560	—
1901 EB	Inc. above	7.00	28.00	140	485	—
1903 EB	473,386	6.00	25.00	95.00	365	—
1904 EB	563,586	5.00	15.00	90.00	325	—

KM# 772 KRONA
7.5000 g., 0.8000 Silver .1929 oz. ASW **Ruler:** Oscar II **Obv:** Head left **Rev:** Crowned arms with supporters

Date	Mintage	F	VF	XF	Unc	BU
1906 EB	426,939	5.00	20.00	85.00	270	—
1907 EB	1,058,286	3.50	14.00	60.00	245	—

KM# 786.1 KRONA
7.5000 g., 0.8000 Silver .1929 oz. ASW **Ruler:** Gustaf V **Obv:** Head left **Rev:** Crowned arms within order chain

Date	Mintage	F	VF	XF	Unc	BU
1.9.1.0 W	643,065	3.25	12.50	45.00	175	—
1.9.1.2 W	303,420	7.00	22.50	110	420	—
1.9.1.3 W	353,051	3.50	12.50	42.50	190	—
1.9.1.4 W	622,217	3.25	11.50	40.00	180	—
1.9.1.5 W	1,415,956	3.00	7.00	25.00	145	—
1.9.1.6/5 W	1,139,245	4.00	13.50	55.00	230	—
1.9.1.6 W	Inc. above	3.25	11.50	40.00	190	—
1.9.1.8 W	258,091	3.25	8.50	30.00	200	—
1.9.2.3 W	746,277	3.00	8.00	27.50	135	—
1.9.2.4 W	2,066,155	BV	6.50	17.50	100	—

KM# 786.2 KRONA
7.5000 g., 0.8000 Silver .1929 oz. ASW **Ruler:** Gustaf V **Obv:** Head left **Rev:** Crowned arms within order chain

Date	Mintage	F	VF	XF	Unc	BU
1924 W	Inc. above	BV	4.50	22.50	90.00	—
1925 W	369,919	3.00	8.50	45.00	200	—
1926 W	465,467	3.00	7.50	28.00	135	—
1927 G	401,167	3.00	8.00	40.00	180	—
1928 G	739,189	BV	3.50	22.50	80.00	—
1929 G	1,345,647	BV	3.00	12.50	50.00	—
1930 G	1,743,783	—	BV	6.50	37.50	—
1931 G	1,007,523	—	BV	6.50	37.50	—
1932 G	1,035,877	—	BV	6.50	37.50	—
1933 G	1,044,634	—	BV	6.50	37.50	—
1934 G	585,673	—	3.00	12.50	60.00	—
1935 G	1,604,343	—	BV	3.00	12.50	—
1936 G	3,222,312	—	BV	3.00	10.00	—
1937 G	2,666,998	—	BV	3.00	10.00	—
1938 G	1,911,464	—	BV	3.00	10.00	—
1938 G Proof	—	Value: 25.00				
1939 G	7,589,316	—	BV	3.00	6.00	—
1940 G	6,917,460	—	BV	3.00	6.00	—
1941 G	Inc. above	—	BV	3.50	10.00	—
1941/4 G	2,183,338	BV	6.00	18.00	45.00	—
1942 G	240,000	20.00	40.00	90.00	345	—

KM# 814 KRONA
7.0000 g., 0.4000 Silver .0900 oz. ASW, 25 mm. **Ruler:** Gustaf V **Obv:** Head left **Rev:** Crowned arms within order chain divide value

Date	Mintage	F	VF	XF	Unc	BU
1942 G	5,644,990	—	BV	3.00	18.50	—
1943 G Plain 4	7,915,850	—	BV	3.00	18.50	—
1943 G Crosslet 4	Inc. above	—	BV	3.00	18.50	—
1944 G	7,423,463	—	BV	2.00	8.00	—
1945 G	7,359,360	—	BV	2.00	8.00	—
1945 TS	Inc. above	BV	1.50	2.75	15.00	—
1945 TS/G	Inc. above	BV	1.60	3.00	20.00	—
1946 TS	19,170,454	—	BV	1.75	6.00	—
1947 TS	9,124,335	—	BV	1.75	6.00	—
1948 TS	10,430,588	—	BV	1.75	6.00	—
1949 TS	7,981,162	—	BV	1.75	6.00	—
1950 TS	5,310,141	—	BV	1.75	8.00	—

KM# 826 KRONA

7.0000 g., 0.4000 Silver .0900 oz. ASW, 25 mm. **Ruler:** Gustaf VI **Obv:** Head left **Rev:** Crowned shield divides value

Date	Mintage	F	VF	XF	Unc	BU
1952 TS	1,101,625	—	BV	3.00	22.50	—
1953/2 TS	Inc. above	BV	1.50	4.50	20.00	—
1953 TS	3,305,843	—	BV	3.00	20.00	—
1954 TS	6,460,770	—	BV	3.00	15.00	—
1955 TS	4,140,904	—	BV	3.00	15.00	—
1956 TS	6,226,705	—	BV	3.00	8.00	—
1957 TS	3,544,268	—	BV	3.00	9.00	—
1958 TS	1,438,940	BV	1.50	4.50	20.00	—
1959 TS	1,187,000	1.50	2.75	7.50	35.00	—
1960 TS	4,085,250	—	BV	2.00	6.00	—
1961 TS	4,283,000	—	BV	2.00	6.00	—
1961 U	2,973,275	BV	1.50	3.00	20.00	—
1962 U	6,838,550	—	BV	2.00	6.00	—
1963 U	14,227,500	—	BV	1.50	3.50	—
1964 U	15,972,500	—	BV	1.50	3.00	—
1965 U	18,638,500	—	BV	1.50	3.00	—
1966 U	22,396,500	—	—	BV	2.25	—
1967 U	17,234,500	—	—	BV	2.25	—
1968 U	12,325,500	—	—	BV	2.25	—

KM# 826a KRONA

7.0000 g., Copper-Nickel Clad Copper, 25 mm. **Ruler:** Gustaf VI **Obv:** Head left **Rev:** Crowned shield divides value

Date	Mintage	F	VF	XF	Unc	BU
1968 U	5,177,000	—	0.30	1.00	3.50	—
1969 U	30,855,500	—	0.30	0.40	1.50	—
1970 U	25,314,500	—	0.30	0.40	1.50	—
1971 U	18,342,000	—	0.30	0.40	1.50	—
1972 U	21,941,000	—	0.30	0.40	1.50	—
1973 U	142,000,000	—	0.30	0.40	1.50	—

KM# 852 KRONA

7.0000 g., Copper-Nickel Clad Copper, 25 mm. **Ruler:** Carl XVI Gustaf **Obv:** Head left **Rev:** Three small crowns within crowned shield **Designer:** Lars Englund

Date	Mintage	F	VF	XF	Unc	BU
1976 U	4,320,811	—	0.30	0.50	1.25	—
1977 U	80,477,822	—	0.30	0.40	0.75	—
1978 U	81,407,892	—	0.30	0.40	0.75	—
1979 U	47,450,148	—	0.30	0.40	0.75	—
1980 U	51,694,323	—	0.30	0.40	0.75	—
1981 U	62,078,991	—	0.30	0.40	0.75	—

KM# 852a KRONA

7.0000 g., Copper-Nickel, 25 mm. **Ruler:** Carl XVI Gustaf **Obv:** Head left **Rev:** Three small crowns within crowned shield **Designer:** Lars Englund

Date	Mintage	F	VF	XF	Unc	BU
1982 U	24,836,789	—	—	0.30	0.65	—
1983 U	23,530,222	—	—	0.30	0.65	—
1984 U	37,811,592	—	—	0.30	0.65	—
1985 U	4,909,279	—	—	0.30	0.70	—
1986 U	901,095	—	—	0.50	1.25	—
1987 D	21,543,317	—	—	0.30	0.65	—
1988 D	30,341,842	—	—	0.30	0.45	—
1989 D	55,963,148	—	—	—	0.30	—
1990 D	54,469,545	—	—	—	0.30	—
1991 D	34,249,994	—	—	—	0.30	—
1992 B	16,770,810	—	—	—	0.30	—
1993 B	407,208	—	0.30	0.50	1.00	—
1994 B	567,137	—	0.30	0.50	1.00	—
1995 B	499,758	—	0.30	0.50	1.00	—
1996 B	323,656	—	—	1.00	2.00	—
1997 B	25,042,398	—	—	—	0.25	—
1998 B	39,747,941	—	—	—	0.25	—
1999 B	55,018,508	—	—	—	0.25	—
2000 B	104,213,074	—	—	—	0.25	—

KM# 897 KRONA

6.9800 g., Copper-Nickel, 24.9 mm. **Ruler:** Carl XVI Gustaf **Subject:** Millennium **Obv:** Head left **Rev:** Crowned monogram **Edge:** Reeded

Date	Mintage	F	VF	XF	Unc	BU
2000	2,978,113	—	—	—	2.00	3.00

KM# 761 2 KRONOR

15.0000 g., 0.8000 Silver .3858 oz. ASW, 31 mm. **Ruler:** Oscar II **Obv:** Head left **Obv. Legend:** OSCAR II SVERIGES... **Rev:** Crowned arms with supporters

Date	Mintage	F	VF	XF	Unc	BU
1903 EB	64,308	25.00	85.00	240	865	—
1904 EB	175,029	12.00	40.00	145	465	—

KM# 773 2 KRONOR

15.0000 g., 0.8000 Silver .3858 oz. ASW, 31 mm. **Ruler:** Oscar II **Obv:** Head left **Rev:** Crowned arms with supporters

Date	Mintage	F	VF	XF	Unc	BU
1906 EB	112,468	9.00	22.50	90.00	320	—
1907 EB	300,573	6.50	18.50	75.00	320	—

KM# 776 2 KRONOR

15.0000 g., 0.8000 Silver .3858 oz. ASW, 31 mm. **Ruler:** Oscar II **Subject:** Golden Wedding Anniversary **Obv:** Busts of King Oscar II and Queen Sofia right **Rev:** Crowned arms within order chain **Edge:** Reeded **Designer:** Adolph Lindberg

Date	Mintage	F	VF	XF	Unc	BU
1907	251,000	BV	6.50	11.50	22.50	—

KM# 787 2 KRONOR

15.0000 g., 0.8000 Silver .3858 oz. ASW, 31 mm. **Ruler:** Gustaf V **Obv:** Head left **Rev:** Crowned arms within order chain

Date	Mintage	F	VF	XF	Unc	BU
1910 W Initial far from date	374,725	6.00	16.00	70.00	220	—
1910 W	Inc. above	37.50	100	365	900	—
1912 W	156,912	6.50	25.00	90.00	320	—
1913 W	304,616	BV	10.00	50.00	220	—
1914 W	191,905	6.00	13.50	68.00	240	—
1915 W	155,965	6.00	18.00	70.00	245	—
1922 W	201,821	BV	7.00	30.00	110	—
1924 W	199,314	BV	8.00	30.00	120	—
1926 W	221,577	BV	6.50	25.00	100	—
1928 G	160,319	BV	7.00	30.00	175	—
1929 G	184,458	BV	6.50	25.00	110	—
1930 G	178,387	BV	6.00	20.00	95.00	—
1931 G	210,576	—	BV	10.00	30.00	—
1934 G	273,419	—	BV	10.00	30.00	—
1935 G	211,059	—	BV	10.00	30.00	—
1936 G	491,296	—	BV	8.00	20.00	—
1937 G	129,760	—	BV	16.50	70.00	—
1937 G Proof	—	Value: 200				
1938 G	638,970	—	BV	7.00	18.00	—
1938 G Proof	—	Value: 30.00				
1939 G	1,200,329	—	BV	6.00	14.00	—
1939 G Proof	—	Value: 30.00				
1940 G	517,740	—	BV	7.00	15.00	—
1940 G Serif 4	Inc. above	BV	6.00	9.00	30.00	—

KM# 799 2 KRONOR

15.0000 g., 0.8000 Silver .3858 oz. ASW, 31 mm. **Ruler:** Gustaf V **Subject:** 400th Anniversary of Political Liberty **Obv:** Head right within decorative inner circle **Rev:** Crowned shield divides date within decorative inner circle **Designer:** Eric Lindberg

Date	Mintage	F	VF	XF	Unc	BU
1921 W	265,943	BV	6.00	8.50	20.00	—

KM# 805 2 KRONOR

15.0000 g., 0.8000 Silver .3858 oz. ASW, 31 mm. **Ruler:** Gustaf V **Subject:** 300th Anniversary - Death of Gustaf II Adolf **Obv:** Inscription within square with three small crowns within shield below **Rev:** Laureate bust right **Designer:** Eric Lindberg

Date	Mintage	F	VF	XF	Unc	BU
1932 G	253,770	BV	6.00	10.00	27.50	—

KM# 807 2 KRONOR

15.0000 g., 0.8000 Silver .3858 oz. ASW, 31 mm. **Ruler:** Gustaf V **Subject:** 300th Anniversary - Settlement of Delaware **Obv:** Head left **Rev:** The ship "Calmare Nyckel"

Date	Mintage	F	VF	XF	Unc	BU
ND(1938) G	508,815	BV	6.00	9.00	20.00	—

KM# 815 2 KRONOR

14.0000 g., 0.4000 Silver .1800 oz. ASW **Ruler:** Gustaf V **Obv:** Head left **Rev:** Crowned arms divides value

Date	Mintage	F	VF	XF	Unc	BU
1942 G	200,000	BV	3.75	6.50	32.50	—
1943 G	271,824	3.00	5.50	14.50	70.00	—
1944 G	627,200	BV	3.00	5.00	20.00	—
1945 G	969,675	BV	2.75	4.00	15.00	—
1945 G	Inc. above	6.50	13.50	28.00	90.00	—

Note: Without dots in motto

Date	Mintage	F	VF	XF	Unc	BU
1945 TS	Inc. above	BV	3.00	5.00	20.00	—
1945 TS/G	Inc. above	BV	3.50	7.00	27.50	—
1946 TS	978,000	—	BV	3.50	14.50	—
1947 TS	1,465,975	—	BV	3.50	14.50	—
1948 TS	281,660	BV	3.00	5.00	20.00	—
1949 TS	331,715	BV	3.00	5.00	20.00	—
1950/1 TS	3,727,465	—	BV	3.50	14.50	—
1950 TS	Inc. above	—	BV	3.50	8.50	—

KM# 827 2 KRONOR

14.0000 g., 0.4000 Silver .1800 oz. ASW **Ruler:** Gustaf VI **Obv:** Head left **Rev:** Crowned shield divides value

Date	Mintage	F	VF	XF	Unc	BU
1952 TS	315,325	BV	2.75	4.00	16.50	—
1953 TS	1,009,380	—	BV	3.00	8.00	—
1954 TS	2,300,835	—	BV	3.00	7.00	—
1955 TS	1,137,734	—	BV	3.50	9.00	—
1956 TS	1,709,468	—	BV	3.00	7.00	—
1957 TS	688,900	—	BV	3.50	15.00	—
1958 TS	1,104,555	—	BV	3.00	7.00	—
1959 TS	581,330	—	BV	3.50	15.00	—
1961 TS	533,220	—	BV	3.00	13.50	—
1963 U	1,468,750	—	—	BV	5.00	—
1964 U	1,212,750	—	—	BV	4.50	—
1965 U	1,189,500	—	—	BV	4.50	—
1966 U	989,250	—	—	BV	5.00	—

KM# 827a 2 KRONOR

Copper-Nickel **Ruler:** Gustaf VI **Obv:** Head left **Rev:** Crowned shield divides value

Date	Mintage	F	VF	XF	Unc	BU
1968 U	1,170,750	0.45	0.55	1.25	4.00	—
1969 U	1,148,250	0.45	0.55	0.70	2.25	—
1970 U	1,159,000	0.45	0.55	0.70	2.25	—
1971 U	1,213,250	0.45	0.55	0.85	2.75	—

KM# 766 5 KRONOR

2.2402 g., 0.9000 Gold .0648 oz. AGW **Ruler:** Oscar II **Obv:** Head right **Rev:** Value and crowns within wreath

Date	Mintage	F	VF	XF	Unc	BU
1901 EB	109,186	BV	50.00	70.00	100	—

KM# 797 5 KRONOR

2.2402 g., 0.9000 Gold .0648 oz. AGW **Ruler:** Gustaf V **Obv:** Head right **Rev:** Value and crowns above sprigs

Date	Mintage	F	VF	XF	Unc	BU
1920 W	103,000	BV	50.00	70.00	100	—

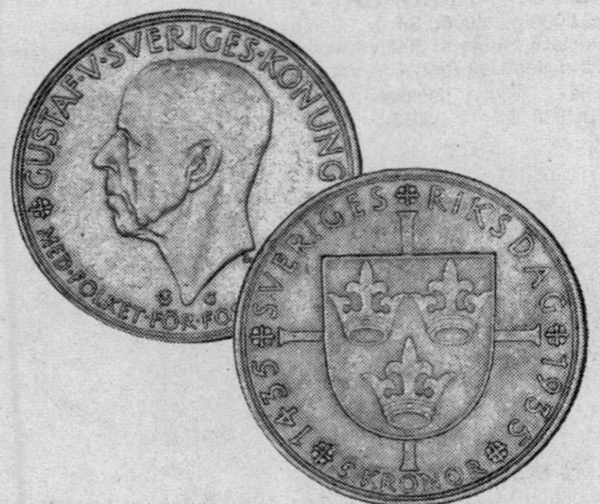

KM# 806 5 KRONOR

25.0000 g., 0.9000 Silver .7234 oz. ASW, 36 mm. **Ruler:** Gustaf V **Subject:** 500th Anniversary of Riksdag **Obv:** Head left **Rev:** Three small crowns within shield in center of cross design **Designer:** Eric Lindberg

Date	Mintage	F	VF	XF	Unc	BU
ND(1935) G	663,819	BV	11.50	14.50	22.50	—

KM# 828 5 KRONOR

22.7000 g., 0.4000 Silver .2920 oz. ASW, 36 mm. **Ruler:** Gustaf VI **Subject:** 70th Birthday of Gustaf VI Adolf **Obv:** Head left **Rev:** Crowned monogram divides value **Edge:** Plain **Designer:** Leo Holmgren

Date	Mintage	F	VF	XF	Unc	BU
ND(1952) TS	219,237	4.50	7.50	13.50	30.00	—

KM# 829 5 KRONOR

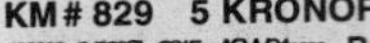

18.0000 g., 0.4000 Silver .2315 oz. ASW, 34 mm. **Ruler:** Gustaf VI **Obv:** Head left **Rev:** Crowned shield divides value **Edge Lettering:** PLIKTEN FRAMFÖR ALLT **Note:** Regular issue

Date	Mintage	F	VF	XF	Unc	BU
1954 TS	1,510,316	—	BV	3.75	7.00	—
1955 TS	3,568,985	—	BV	3.50	6.00	—
1971 U	712,500	—	BV	3.50	6.00	—

KM# 830 5 KRONOR

18.0000 g., 0.4000 Silver .2315 oz. ASW, 34 mm. **Ruler:** Gustaf VI **Subject:** Constitution Sesquicentennial **Obv:** Head left **Rev:** Standing figures with hats facing **Designer:** Leo Holmgren

Date	Mintage	F	VF	XF	Unc	BU
1959 TS	504,150	—	BV	4.50	8.50	—

KM# 838 5 KRONOR

18.0000 g., 0.4000 Silver .2315 oz. ASW, 34 mm. **Ruler:** Gustaf VI **Subject:** 80th Birthday of Gustaf VI Adolf **Obv:** Head left **Rev:** Pallas Athena left holding shield and owl

Date	Mintage	F	VF	XF	Unc	BU
ND(1962) U	256,000	4.00	7.50	13.50	35.00	—

Note: An additional 96,525 melted

KM# 839 5 KRONOR

18.0000 g., 0.4000 Silver .2315 oz. ASW, 34 mm. **Ruler:** Gustaf VI **Subject:** 100th Anniversary of Constitution Reform **Obv:** Head left **Rev:** Inscription within square flanked by sprigs **Edge:** Horizontal wavy lines **Designer:** Leo Holmgren

Date	Mintage	F	VF	XF	Unc	BU
1966 U	1,023,500	—	BV	3.50	6.00	—

KM# 846 5 KRONOR

Copper-Nickel Clad Nickel **Ruler:** Gustaf VI **Obv:** Head left **Rev:** Crowned shield divides value

Date	Mintage	F	VF	XF	Unc	BU
1972 U	21,736,000	—	—	1.25	2.00	—
1973 U	1,139,000	—	1.25	1.50	2.75	—

KM# 853 5 KRONOR

9.5000 g., Copper-Nickel, 28.5 mm. **Ruler:** Carl XVI Gustaf **Obv:** Crowned monogram **Rev:** Value **Designer:** Lars Englund

Date	Mintage	F	VF	XF	Unc	BU
1976 U	2,252,923	—	—	1.00	1.75	—
1977 U	3,985,381	—	—	1.00	1.75	—
1978 U	3,952,352	—	—	1.00	1.75	—
1979 U	3,164,051	—	—	1.00	1.75	—
1980 U	2,221,846	—	—	1.00	1.75	—
1981 U	5,507,222	—	—	1.00	1.75	—
1982 U	36,603,696	—	—	0.75	1.25	—
1983 U	31,364,320	—	—	0.85	1.50	—
1984 U	27,689,251	—	—	0.85	1.50	—
1985 U	10,603,060	—	—	0.75	1.25	—
1986 U	714,132	—	—	1.25	4.00	—
1987 D	15,117,317	—	—	0.75	1.25	—
1988 D	18,643,957	—	—	0.85	1.50	—
1989 D	960,667	—	—	1.25	3.50	—
1990 D	10,557,882	—	—	0.75	1.25	—
1991 D	15,792,139	—	—	0.75	1.25	—
1991 U	Est. 25,000	16.50	27.50	55.00	110	—
1992 D	5,350,810	—	—	1.00	1.50	—

KM# 853a 5 KRONOR

Copper-Nickel Clad Nickel, 28.5 mm. **Ruler:** Carl XVI Gustaf **Obv:** Crowned monogram **Rev:** Value

Date	Mintage	F	VF	XF	Unc	BU
1993 B	274,932	—	—	—	1.75	2.00
1994 B	173,438	—	—	—	2.00	2.25
1995 B	186,687	—	—	—	1.00	1.25
1996 B	180,405	—	—	—	1.00	1.25
1997 B	174,455	—	—	—	1.00	1.25
1998 B	84,991	—	—	—	1.00	1.25
1999 B	96,035	—	—	—	1.00	1.25
2000 B	3,851,326	—	—	—	1.00	1.25

KM# 885 5 KRONOR

Copper-Nickel Clad Nickel, 28.5 mm. **Ruler:** Carl XVI Gustaf **Subject:** 50th Anniversary - United Nations **Obv:** Crowned monogram **Rev:** Numeral 50 and UN emblem

Date	Mintage	F	VF	XF	Unc	BU
ND(1995) B	300,000	—	—	1.00	3.50	4.50

KM# 767 10 KRONOR

4.4803 g., 0.9000 Gold .1296 oz. AGW **Ruler:** Oscar II **Obv:** Large head right **Rev:** Crowned and mantled arms

Date	Mintage	F	VF	XF	Unc	BU
1901 EB	213,286	—	BV	90.00	125	—
1901 EB Proof	Inc. above	Value: 525				

KM# 847 10 KRONOR

18.0000 g., 0.8300 Silver .4803 oz. ASW, 32 mm. **Ruler:** Gustaf VI **Subject:** 90th Birthday of Gustaf VI Adolf **Obv:** Head left **Rev:** Inscription and value

Date	Mintage	F	VF	XF	Unc	BU
1972 U	2,000,000	—	BV	7.50	9.50	—

Note: 652,907 were returned to the mint.

KM# 877 10 KRONOR

Copper-Aluminum-Zinc **Ruler:** Carl XVI Gustaf **Obv:** Head left **Rev:** Three crowns within value

Date	Mintage	F	VF	XF	Unc	BU
1991 D Medal	106,548,000	—	—	2.00	3.00	—
1991 D Coin	Inc. above	20.00	30.00	40.00	60.00	—
1992 D	42,506,792	—	—	—	1.75	—
1993 B	20,107,110	—	—	—	1.75	—
1994 B	573,243	—	—	—	2.00	—
1995 B	523,685	—	—	—	2.00	—
1996 B	295,053	—	—	—	2.00	—
1997 B	332,450	—	—	—	2.00	—
1998	—	—	—	—	2.00	—
B	332,000	—	—	—	2.00	—
1999 B	81,430	—	—	—	2.00	—
2000 B	8,520,983	—	—	—	1.75	—

KM# 765 20 KRONOR

8.9606 g., 0.9000 Gold .2593 oz. AGW **Ruler:** Oscar II **Obv:** Head right **Obv. Legend:** OSCAR II SVERIGES... **Rev:** Crowned and mantled arms

Date	Mintage	F	VF	XF	Unc	BU
1901 EB	226,679	—	BV	180	245	—
1902 EB	113,810	—	BV	190	265	—

KM# 800 20 KRONOR

8.9606 g., 0.9000 Gold .2593 oz. AGW **Ruler:** Gustaf V **Obv:** Head right **Rev:** Crowned arms within order chain divide value

Date	Mintage	F	VF	XF	Unc	BU
1925 W	387,257	185	320	465	765	—

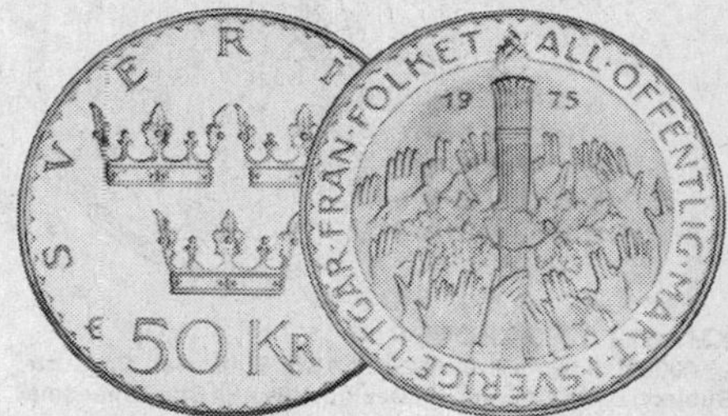

KM# 848 50 KRONOR

27.0000 g., 0.9250 Silver .8029 oz. ASW **Ruler:** Carl XVI Gustaf **Subject:** Constitutional Reform **Obv:** Three crowns above value **Rev:** Flaming torch divides date within cluster of reaching hands, all within inner circle

Date	Mintage	F	VF	XF	Unc	BU
1975 U	500,000	—	BV	12.50	15.00	—

KM# 854 50 KRONOR

27.0000 g., 0.9250 Silver .8029 oz. ASW **Ruler:** Carl XVI Gustaf **Subject:** Wedding of King Carl XVI Gustaf and Queen Silvia **Obv:** Heads facing **Rev:** Crowned arms with supporters

Date	Mintage	F	VF	XF	Unc	BU
ND(1976) U	2,000,000	—	BV	12.50	14.50	—

KM# 861 100 KRONOR

16.0000 g., 0.9250 Silver .4759 oz. ASW **Ruler:** Carl XVI Gustaf **Subject:** Parliament **Obv:** Front view of radiant arched building **Rev:** Three crowns within brick designed circle

Date	Mintage	F	VF	XF	Unc	BU
1983	400,000	—	—	—	18.50	20.00

KM# 863 100 KRONOR

16.0000 g., 0.9250 Silver .4759 oz. ASW **Ruler:** Carl XVI Gustaf **Subject:** Stockholm Conference **Obv:** Three crowns on thin upright branch within waved circle **Rev:** Design and arch within circle

Date	Mintage	F	VF	XF	Unc	BU
1984	300,000	—	—	—	18.50	20.00

KM# 864 100 KRONOR

16.0000 g., 0.9250 Silver .4759 oz. ASW **Ruler:** Carl XVI Gustaf **Subject:** International Youth Year **Obv:** Three small crowns within crowned shield **Rev:** Three conjoined lined profiles left within wreath, inner circle surrounds **Designer:** Bo Thoren

Date	Mintage	F	VF	XF	Unc	BU
1985	120,000	—	—	—	20.00	22.50

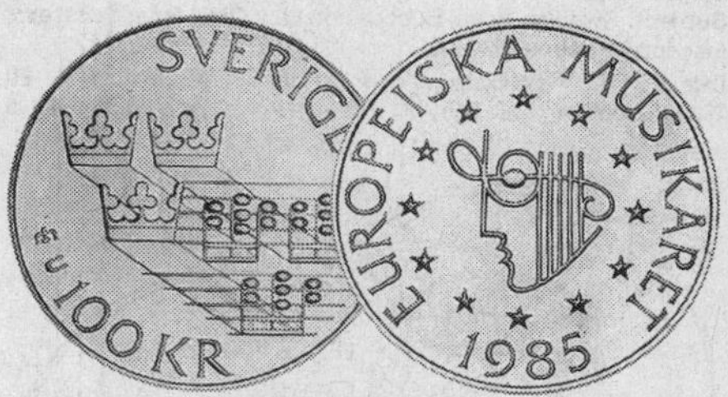

KM# 865 100 KRONOR

16.0000 g., 0.9250 Silver .4759 oz. ASW **Ruler:** Carl XVI Gustaf **Subject:** European Music Year **Obv:** Three crowns at upper left of music notes **Rev:** Stylized profile left within circle of stars

Date	Mintage	F	VF	XF	Unc	BU
1985	120,000	—	—	—	20.00	22.50

KM# 866 100 KRONOR

16.0000 g., 0.9250 Silver .4759 oz. ASW **Ruler:** Carl XVI Gustaf **Subject:** International Year of the Forest **Obv:** Three crowns on tree ring design **Rev:** Standing figures under tree within circle flanked by small trees

Date	Mintage	F	VF	XF	Unc	BU
1985	120,000	—	—	—	22.50	25.00

KM# 867.1 100 KRONOR

16.0000 g., 0.9250 Silver .4759 oz. ASW **Ruler:** Carl XVI Gustaf **Subject:** 350th Anniversary of Swedish Colony in Delaware **Obv:** Large head left **Rev:** Three small crowns, map and ship

Date	Mintage	F	VF	XF	Unc	BU
ND(1988)	32,000	—	—	—	27.50	30.00

KM# 867.2 100 KRONOR

16.0000 g., 0.9250 Silver .4759 oz. ASW **Ruler:** Carl XVI Gustaf **Subject:** 350th Anniversary of Swedish Colony in Delaware **Obv:** Small head left **Rev:** Three small crowns, map and ship

Date	Mintage	F	VF	XF	Unc	BU
ND(1988)	118,000	—	—	—	22.50	25.00

KM# 860 200 KRONOR
27.0000 g., 0.9250 Silver .8029 oz. ASW **Ruler:** Carl XVI Gustaf **Subject:** Swedish Royal Succession Law **Obv:** Head left **Rev:** Inscription, date and value

Date	Mintage	F	VF	XF	Unc	BU
1980 U Prooflike	500,000	—	—	—	30.00	40.00

KM# 862 200 KRONOR
27.0000 g., 0.9250 Silver .8029 oz. ASW **Ruler:** Carl XVI Gustaf **Subject:** 10th Anniversary of Reign **Obv:** Head left **Rev:** Crowned arms with supporters

Date	Mintage	F	VF	XF	Unc	BU
1983	100,000	—	—	—	35.00	42.50

KM# 869 200 KRONOR
27.0000 g., 0.9250 Silver .8029 oz. ASW **Ruler:** Carl XVI Gustaf **Subject:** Ice Hockey **Obv:** Three small crowns within patterned circle **Rev:** Hockey goalie within circle **Designer:** Bo Thoren

Date	Mintage	F	VF	XF	Unc	BU
1989	Est. 80,000	—	—	—	32.50	40.00

KM# 875 200 KRONOR
27.0000 g., 0.9250 Silver .8029 oz. ASW **Ruler:** Carl XVI Gustaf **Subject:** Warship - Vasa **Obv:** Head left **Rev:** Ship

Date	Mintage	F	VF	XF	Unc	BU
1990	50,000	—	—	—	35.00	40.00

KM# 879 200 KRONOR
27.0000 g., 0.9250 Silver .8029 oz. ASW **Ruler:** Carl XVI Gustaf **Subject:** 200th Anniversary - Death of Gustaf III **Obv:** Three small crowns within mantle **Rev:** Head right

Date	Mintage	F	VF	XF	Unc	BU
ND(1992)	50,000	—	—	—	35.00	40.00

KM# 881 200 KRONOR
27.0000 g., 0.9250 Silver .8029 oz. ASW **Ruler:** Carl XVI Gustaf **Subject:** 20th Anniversary of Reign **Obv:** Head left **Rev:** Crown

Date	Mintage	F	VF	XF	Unc	BU
1993	50,000	—	—	—	35.00	40.00

KM# 882 200 KRONOR
27.0000 g., 0.9250 Silver .8029 oz. ASW **Ruler:** Carl XVI Gustaf **Subject:** 50th Birthday of Queen Silvia **Obv:** Crowned head right **Rev:** Crowned arms with supporters

Date	Mintage	F	VF	XF	Unc	BU
ND(1993)	49,000	—	—	—	35.00	40.00
ND(1993) Prooflike	1,000	—	—	—	—	75.00

KM# 886 200 KRONOR
27.0000 g., 0.9250 Silver .8029 oz. ASW **Ruler:** Carl XVI Gustaf **Subject:** 1000th Anniversary - Swedish Coinage **Obv:** Head left **Rev:** Coin designs within circle

Date	Mintage	F	VF	XF	Unc	BU
ND(1995)	49,000	—	—	—	35.00	40.00
ND(1995) Prooflike	1,000	—	—	—	—	75.00

KM# 888 200 KRONOR
27.0000 g., 0.9250 Silver .8029 oz. ASW **Ruler:** Carl XVI Gustaf **Subject:** 50th Birthday - King Carl XVI Gustaf **Obv:** Head left **Rev:** Crowned arms with supporters

Date	Mintage	F	VF	XF	Unc	BU
ND(1996)	49,000	—	—	—	35.00	40.00
ND(1996) Prooflike	1,000	—	—	—	—	75.00

KM# 890 200 KRONOR
27.0000 g., 0.9250 Silver .8029 oz. ASW **Ruler:** Carl XVI Gustaf **Subject:** Kalmar Union **Obv:** Head left **Rev:** Queen Margareta's head left and castle

Date	Mintage	F	VF	XF	Unc	BU
1997	Est. 50,000	—	—	—	35.00	45.00

KM# 892 200 KRONOR
27.0000 g., 0.9250 Silver .8029 oz. ASW **Ruler:** Carl XVI Gustaf **Subject:** 25th Anniversary - Reign of Carl XVI **Obv:** Head 1/4 left **Rev:** Crown above sceptre, crowned monogram and orb

Date	Mintage	F	VF	XF	Unc	BU
1998	50,000	—	—	—	35.00	40.00

KM# 898 200 KRONOR
27.0300 g., 0.9250 Silver 0.8039 oz. ASW, 36 mm. **Ruler:** Carl XVI Gustaf **Subject:** Millennium **Obv:** Conjoined heads of King Gustaf and Crown Princess Victoria left **Rev:** Crowned and mantled arms **Edge:** Plain

Date	Mintage	F	VF	XF	Unc	BU
1999	98,000	—	—	—	30.00	—
1999 Prooflike	2,000	—	—	—	—	40.00

KM# 868 1000 KRONOR
5.8000 g., 0.9000 Gold .1678 oz. AGW **Ruler:** Carl XVI Gustaf **Subject:** 350th Anniversary of Swedish Colony in Delaware **Obv:** Head left **Rev:** Ship at sea

Date	Mintage	F	VF	XF	Unc	BU
ND(1988)	10,000	—	—	—	235	285

KM# 870 1000 KRONOR
5.8000 g., 0.9000 Gold .1678 oz. AGW **Ruler:** Carl XVI Gustaf

Subject: Ice Hockey **Obv:** Three small crowns within designed circle **Rev:** Hockey goalie within circle **Designer:** Bo Thoren

Date	Mintage	F	VF	XF	Unc	BU
1989	20,000	—	—	—	175	225

KM# 876 1000 KRONOR

5.8000 g., 0.9000 Gold .1678 oz. AGW **Ruler:** Carl XVI Gustaf **Subject:** The Vasa - Arms **Obv:** Head left **Rev:** The Vasa - Arms

Date	Mintage	F	VF	XF	Unc	BU
1990	15,000	—	—	—	185	250

KM# 880 1000 KRONOR

5.8000 g., 0.9000 Gold .1678 oz. AGW **Ruler:** Carl XVI Gustaf **Subject:** 200th Anniversary - Death of Gustaf III **Obv:** Crowned arms within order chain **Rev:** Head right

Date	Mintage	F	VF	XF	Unc	BU
ND(1992)	15,000	—	—	—	185	250

KM# 883 1000 KRONOR

5.8000 g., 0.9000 Gold .1678 oz. AGW **Ruler:** Carl XVI Gustaf **Subject:** 20th Anniversary of Reign **Obv:** Head left **Rev:** Crown

Date	Mintage	F	VF	XF	Unc	BU
1993	15,000	—	—	—	175	225

KM# 884 1000 KRONOR

5.8000 g., 0.9000 Gold .1678 oz. AGW **Ruler:** Carl XVI Gustaf **Subject:** 50th Birthday of Queen Silvia **Obv:** Crowned head right **Rev:** Crowned arms with supporters

Date	Mintage	F	VF	XF	Unc	BU
ND(1993)	14,000	—	—	—	175	225
ND(1993) Prooflike	1,000	—	—	—	—	385

KM# 887 1000 KRONOR

5.8000 g., 0.9000 Gold .1678 oz. AGW **Ruler:** Carl XVI Gustaf **Subject:** 100th Anniversary - Swedish Coinage **Obv:** Head left **Rev:** Coin designs within circle

Date	Mintage	F	VF	XF	Unc	BU
ND(1995)	14,000	—	—	—	175	225
ND(1995) Prooflike	1,000	—	—	—	—	350

KM# 889 1000 KRONOR

5.8000 g., 0.9000 Gold .1678 oz. AGW **Ruler:** Carl XVI Gustaf **Subject:** 50th Birthday - King Carl XVI Gustaf **Obv:** Head left **Rev:** Crowned arms with supporters

Date	Mintage	F	VF	XF	Unc	BU
ND(1996)	14,000	—	—	—	175	225
ND(1996) Prooflike	1,000	—	—	—	—	350

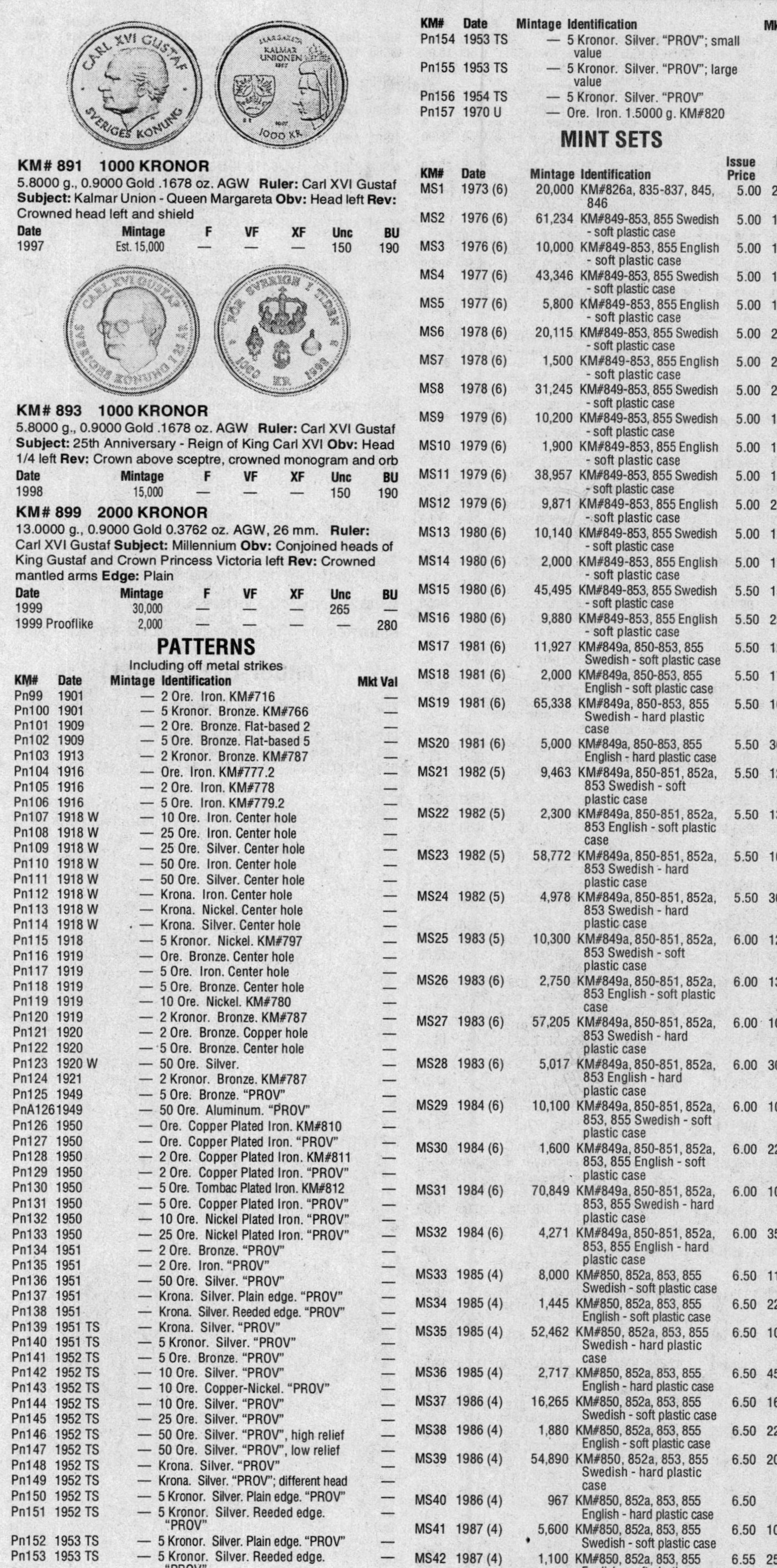

KM# 891 1000 KRONOR

5.8000 g., 0.9000 Gold .1678 oz. AGW **Ruler:** Carl XVI Gustaf **Subject:** Kalmar Union - Queen Margareta **Obv:** Head left **Rev:** Crowned head left and shield

Date	Mintage	F	VF	XF	Unc	BU
1997	Est. 15,000	—	—	—	150	190

KM# 893 1000 KRONOR

5.8000 g., 0.9000 Gold .1678 oz. AGW **Ruler:** Carl XVI Gustaf **Subject:** 25th Anniversary - Reign of King Carl XVI **Obv:** Head 1/4 left **Rev:** Crown above sceptre, crowned monogram and orb

Date	Mintage	F	VF	XF	Unc	BU
1998	15,000	—	—	—	150	190

KM# 899 2000 KRONOR

13.0000 g., 0.9000 Gold 0.3762 oz. AGW, 26 mm. **Ruler:** Carl XVI Gustaf **Subject:** Millennium **Obv:** Conjoined heads of King Gustaf and Crown Princess Victoria left **Rev:** Crowned mantled arms **Edge:** Plain

Date	Mintage	F	VF	XF	Unc	BU
1999	30,000	—	—	—	265	—
1999 Prooflike	2,000	—	—	—	—	280

PATTERNS

Including off metal strikes

KM#	Date	Mintage	Identification	Mkt Val
Pn99	1901	—	2 Ore. Iron. KM#716	—
Pn100	1901	—	5 Kronor. Bronze. KM#766	—
Pn101	1909	—	2 Ore. Bronze. Flat-based 2	—
Pn102	1909	—	5 Ore. Bronze. Flat-based 5	—
Pn103	1913	—	2 Kronor. Bronze. KM#787	—
Pn104	1916	—	Ore. Iron. KM#777.2	—
Pn105	1916	—	2 Ore. Iron. KM#778	—
Pn106	1916	—	5 Ore. Iron. KM#779.2	—
Pn107	1918 W	—	10 Ore. Iron. Center hole	—
Pn108	1918 W	—	25 Ore. Iron. Center hole	—
Pn109	1918 W	—	25 Ore. Silver. Center hole	—
Pn110	1918 W	—	50 Ore. Iron. Center hole	—
Pn111	1918 W	—	50 Ore. Silver. Center hole	—
Pn112	1918 W	—	Krona. Iron. Center hole	—
Pn113	1918 W	—	Krona. Nickel. Center hole	—
Pn114	1918 W	—	Krona. Silver. Center hole	—
Pn115	1918	—	5 Kronor. Nickel. KM#797	—
Pn116	1919	—	Ore. Bronze. Center hole	—
Pn117	1919	—	5 Ore. Iron. Center hole	—
Pn118	1919	—	5 Ore. Bronze. Center hole	—
Pn119	1919	—	10 Ore. Nickel. KM#780	—
Pn120	1919	—	2 Kronor. Bronze. KM#787	—
Pn121	1920	—	2 Ore. Bronze. Copper hole	—
Pn122	1920	—	5 Ore. Bronze. Center hole	—
Pn123	1920 W	—	50 Ore. Silver.	—
Pn124	1921	—	2 Kronor. Bronze. KM#787	—
Pn125	1949	—	5 Ore. Bronze. "PROV"	—
PnA126	1949	—	50 Ore. Aluminum. "PROV"	—
Pn126	1950	—	Ore. Copper Plated Iron. KM#810	—
Pn127	1950	—	Ore. Copper Plated Iron. "PROV"	—
Pn128	1950	—	2 Ore. Copper Plated Iron. KM#811	—
Pn129	1950	—	2 Ore. Copper Plated Iron. "PROV"	—
Pn130	1950	—	5 Ore. Tombac Plated Iron. KM#812	—
Pn131	1950	—	5 Ore. Copper Plated Iron. "PROV"	—
Pn132	1950	—	10 Ore. Nickel Plated Iron. "PROV"	—
Pn133	1950	—	25 Ore. Nickel Plated Iron. "PROV"	—
Pn134	1951	—	2 Ore. Bronze. "PROV"	—
Pn135	1951	—	2 Ore. Iron. "PROV"	—
Pn136	1951	—	50 Ore. Silver. "PROV"	—
Pn137	1951	—	Krona. Silver. Plain edge. "PROV"	—
Pn138	1951	—	Krona. Silver. Reeded edge. "PROV"	—
Pn139	1951 TS	—	Krona. Silver. "PROV"	—
Pn140	1951 TS	—	5 Kronor. Silver. "PROV"	—
Pn141	1952 TS	—	5 Ore. Bronze. "PROV"	—
Pn142	1952 TS	—	10 Ore. Silver. "PROV"	—
Pn143	1952 TS	—	10 Ore. Copper-Nickel. "PROV"	—
Pn144	1952 TS	—	10 Ore. Silver. "PROV"	—
Pn145	1952 TS	—	25 Ore. Silver. "PROV"	—
Pn146	1952 TS	—	50 Ore. Silver. "PROV", high relief	—
Pn147	1952 TS	—	50 Ore. Silver. "PROV", low relief	—
Pn148	1952 TS	—	Krona. Silver. "PROV"	—
Pn149	1952 TS	—	Krona. Silver. "PROV"; different head	—
Pn150	1952 TS	—	5 Kronor. Silver. Plain edge. "PROV"	—
Pn151	1952 TS	—	5 Kronor. Silver. Reeded edge. "PROV"	—
Pn152	1953 TS	—	5 Kronor. Silver. Plain edge. "PROV"	—
Pn153	1953 TS	—	5 Kronor. Silver. Reeded edge. "PROV"	—
Pn154	1953 TS	—	5 Kronor. Silver. "PROV"; small value	—
Pn155	1953 TS	—	5 Kronor. Silver. "PROV"; large value	—
Pn156	1954 TS	—	5 Kronor. Silver. "PROV"	—
Pn157	1970 U	—	Ore. Iron. 1.5000 g. KM#820	175

MINT SETS

KM#	Date	Mintage	Identification	Issue Price	Mkt Val
MS1	1973 (6)	20,000	KM#826a, 835-837, 845, 846	5.00	22.50
MS2	1976 (6)	61,234	KM#849-853, 855 Swedish - soft plastic case	5.00	11.00
MS3	1976 (6)	10,000	KM#849-853, 855 English - soft plastic case	5.00	11.00
MS4	1977 (6)	43,346	KM#849-853, 855 Swedish - soft plastic case	5.00	12.00
MS5	1977 (6)	5,800	KM#849-853, 855 English - soft plastic case	5.00	13.50
MS6	1978 (6)	20,115	KM#849-853, 855 Swedish - soft plastic case	5.00	20.00
MS7	1978 (6)	1,500	KM#849-853, 855 English - soft plastic case	5.00	22.50
MS8	1978 (6)	31,245	KM#849-853, 855 Swedish - soft plastic case	5.00	27.50
MS9	1979 (6)	10,200	KM#849-853, 855 Swedish - soft plastic case	5.00	12.00
MS10	1979 (6)	1,900	KM#849-853, 855 English - soft plastic case	5.00	17.50
MS11	1979 (6)	38,957	KM#849-853, 855 Swedish - soft plastic case	5.00	16.50
MS12	1979 (6)	9,871	KM#849-853, 855 English - soft plastic case	5.00	25.00
MS13	1980 (6)	10,140	KM#849-853, 855 Swedish - soft plastic case	5.00	12.00
MS14	1980 (6)	2,000	KM#849-853, 855 English - soft plastic case	5.00	17.50
MS15	1980 (6)	45,495	KM#849-853, 855 Swedish - soft plastic case	5.50	15.00
MS16	1980 (6)	9,880	KM#849-853, 855 English - soft plastic case	5.50	25.00
MS17	1981 (6)	11,927	KM#849a, 850-853, 855 Swedish - soft plastic case	5.50	12.00
MS18	1981 (6)	2,000	KM#849a, 850-853, 855 English - soft plastic case	5.50	17.50
MS19	1981 (6)	65,338	KM#849a, 850-853, 855 Swedish - hard plastic case	5.50	10.00
MS20	1981 (6)	5,000	KM#849a, 850-853, 855 English - hard plastic case	5.50	30.00
MS21	1982 (5)	9,463	KM#849a, 850-851, 852a, 853 Swedish - soft plastic case	5.50	12.00
MS22	1982 (5)	2,300	KM#849a, 850-851, 852a, 853 English - soft plastic case	5.50	13.50
MS23	1982 (5)	58,772	KM#849a, 850-851, 852a, 853 Swedish - hard plastic case	5.50	10.00
MS24	1982 (5)	4,978	KM#849a, 850-851, 852a, 853 Swedish - hard plastic case	5.50	30.00
MS25	1983 (5)	10,300	KM#849a, 850-851, 852a, 853 Swedish - soft plastic case	6.00	12.00
MS26	1983 (6)	2,750	KM#849a, 850-851, 852a, 853 English - soft plastic case	6.00	13.50
MS27	1983 (6)	57,205	KM#849a, 850-851, 852a, 853 Swedish - hard plastic case	6.00	10.00
MS28	1983 (6)	5,017	KM#849a, 850-851, 852a, 853 English - hard plastic case	6.00	30.00
MS29	1984 (6)	10,100	KM#849a, 850-851, 852a, 853, 855 Swedish - soft plastic case	6.00	10.00
MS30	1984 (6)	1,600	KM#849a, 850-851, 852a, 853, 855 English - soft plastic case	6.00	22.50
MS31	1984 (6)	70,849	KM#849a, 850-851, 852a, 853, 855 Swedish - hard plastic case	6.00	10.00
MS32	1984 (6)	4,271	KM#849a, 850-851, 852a, 853, 855 English - hard plastic case	6.00	35.00
MS33	1985 (4)	8,000	KM#850, 852a, 853, 855 Swedish - soft plastic case	6.50	11.50
MS34	1985 (4)	1,445	KM#850, 852a, 853, 855 English - soft plastic case	6.50	22.50
MS35	1985 (4)	52,462	KM#850, 852a, 853, 855 Swedish - hard plastic case	6.50	10.00
MS36	1985 (4)	2,717	KM#850, 852a, 853, 855 English - hard plastic case	6.50	45.00
MS37	1986 (4)	16,265	KM#850, 852a, 853, 855 Swedish - soft plastic case	6.50	16.50
MS38	1986 (4)	1,880	KM#850, 852a, 853, 855 English - soft plastic case	6.50	22.50
MS39	1986 (4)	54,890	KM#850, 852a, 853, 855 Swedish - hard plastic case	6.50	20.00
MS40	1986 (4)	967	KM#850, 852a, 853, 855 English - hard plastic case	6.50	100
MS41	1987 (4)	5,600	KM#850, 852a, 853, 855 Swedish - soft plastic case	6.50	10.00
MS42	1987 (4)	1,100	KM#850, 852a, 853, 855 English - soft plastic case	6.55	25.00

KM#	Date	Mintage	Identification	Issue Price	Mkt Val
MS43	1987 (4)	70,060	KM#850, 852a, 853, 855 Swedish - hard plastic case	6.50	10.00
MS44	1987 (4)	557	KM#850, 852a, 853, 855 Swedish and English - hard plastic case	6.50	200
MS45	1988 (4)	4,815	KM#850, 852a, 853, 855 Swedish - soft plastic case	6.50	15.00
MS46	1988 (4)	2,456	KM#850, 852a, 853, 855 English - soft plastic case	6.50	16.50
MS47	1988 (4)	56,753	KM#850, 852a, 853, 855 Swedish - hard plastic case	6.50	15.00
MS48	1988 (4)	1,777	KM#850, 852a, 853, 855 English - hard plastic case	6.50	47.50
MS49	1989 (4)	7,170	KM#850, 852a, 853, 855 Swedish - soft plastic case	6.50	16.00
MS50	1989 (4)	56,895	KM#850, 852a, 853, 855 Swedish - hard plastic case	6.50	15.00
MS51	1989 (4)	2,780	KM#850, 852a, 853, 855 English - hard plastic case	—	17.50
MS52	1989 (4)	1,000	KM#850, 852a, 853, 855 English - hard plastic case	—	32.50
MS53	1990 (4)	6,503	KM#850, 852a, 853, 855 Swedish - soft plastic case	6.50	12.50
MS54	1990 (4)	55,265	KM#850, 852a, 853, 855 Swedish - hard plastic case	6.50	13.50
MS55	1990 (4)	2,440	KM#850, 852a, 853, 855 English - hard plastic case	—	13.50
MS56	1990 (4)	2,492	KM#850, 852a, 853, 855 English - hard plastic case	—	11.50
MS57	1991 (5)	8,079	KM#850, 852a, 853, 855, 877 Swedish - soft plastic case	—	17.50
MS58	1991 (5)	1,680	KM#850, 852a, 853, 855, 877 English - soft plastic case	—	17.50
MS59	1991 (5)	62,517	KM#850, 852a, 853, 855, 877 Swedish - hard plastic case	—	18.50
MS60	1991 (5)	2,884	KM#850, 852a, 853, 855, 877 English - hard plastic case	—	20.00
MS61	1991 (5)	5,000	KM#850 (3), 855 (2), medal	—	12.00
MS62	1992 (4)	5,600	KM#852a, 853, 877-878 Swedish - soft plastic case	6.50	11.50
MS63	1992 (4)	1,840	KM#852a, 853, 877-878 English - soft plastic case	6.50	11.50
MS64	1992 (4)	61,183	KM#852a, 853, 877-878 Swedish - hard plastic case	6.50	11.00
MS65	1992 (4)	2,187	KM#852a, 853, 877-878 English - hard plastic case	6.50	13.50
MS66	1993 (4)	4,784	KM#852a, 853a, 877, 878 Swedish - soft plastic case	6.50	16.50
MS67	1993 (4)	2,016	KM#852a, 853a, 877, 878 English - soft plastic case	6.50	11.00
MS68	1993 (4)	57,700	KM#852a, 853a, 877, 878 Swedish - hard plastic case	6.50	16.50
MS69	1993 (4)	2,164	KM#852a, 853a, 877, 878 English - hard plastic case	6.50	17.50
MS70	1993 (4)	4,956	KM#852a, 853a, 877, 878 Souvenir folder	—	22.50
MS71	1994 (4)	5,360	KM#852a, 853a, 877, 878 Swedish - soft plastic case	—	16.50
MS72	1994 (4)	2,240	KM#852a, 853a, 877, 878 English - soft plastic case	—	15.00
MS73	1994 (4)	48,881	KM#852a, 853a, 877, 878, mint medal Swedish - hard plastic case	—	16.50
MS74	1994 (4)	1,966	KM#852a, 853a, 877, 878, mint medal English - hard plastic case	—	17.50
MS75	1994 (4)	9,950	KM#852a, 853a, 877, 878, mint medal Souvenir folder	—	13.50
MS76	1995 (5)	10,000	KM#852a, 853a, 877, 878, 885 Swedish - soft plastic case	14.00	32.50
MS77	1995 (4)	45,836	KM#852a, 877, 878, 885, medal Swedish - hard plastic case	20.00	16.50
MS78	1995 (5)	4,650	KM#852a, 853a, 877, 878, 885 English - soft plastic case	—	15.00
MS79	1995 (4)	2,479	KM#852a, 853a, 877, 878, 885, medal English - hard plastic case	—	18.50
MS80	1995 (4)	5,000	KM#852a, 877, 878, 885, medal Souvenir folder	—	32.50
MS81	1996 (4)	42,729	KM#852a, 853a, 877, 878 Swedish - hard plastic case	11.05	13.50
MS82	1996 (4)	2,000	KM#852a, 853a, 877, 878 English - hard plastic case	11.05	16.50
MS83	1996 (4)	7,100	KM#852a, 853a, 877, 878 Swedish - soft plastic case	7.55	11.50
MS84	1996 (4)	2,500	KM#852a, 853a, 877, 878 English - soft plastic case	7.55	12.50
MS85	1996 (4)	5,481	KM#852a, 853a, 877, 878 Souvenir folder	11.05	14.50
MS86	1997 (4)	39,470	KM#852a, 853a, 877, 878 Swedish - hard plastic case	11.05	18.50
MS87	1997 (4)	1,997	KM#852a, 853a, 877, 878 English - hard plastic case	11.05	22.50
MS88	1997 (4)	5,100	KM#852a, 853a, 877, 878 Swedish - soft plastic case	7.55	15.00
MS89	1997 (4)	2,200	KM#852a, 853a, 877, 878 English - soft plastic case	7.55	16.50
MS90	1997 (4)	4,954	KM#852a, 853a, 877, 878 Souvenir folder	11.05	16.50
MS91	1998 (4)	7,067	KM#852a, 853a, 877, 878 Souvenir folder	13.34	13.50
MS92	1998 (4)	5,170	KM#852a, 853a, 877, 878 Swedish - soft plastic case	—	15.00
MS93	1998 (4)	2,000	KM#852a, 853a, 877, 878 English - soft plastic case	—	16.50
MS94	1998 (4)	34,750	KM#852a, 853a, 877, 878 Swedish - hard plastic case	—	18.50
MS95	1998 (4)	1,980	KM#852a, 853a, 877, 878 English - hard plastic case	—	20.00
MS96	1999 (4)	4,480	KM#852a, 853a, 877, 878 Swedish - hard plastic case	—	11.50
MS97	1999 (4)	2,080	KM#852a, 853a, 877, 878 English - soft plastic case	—	12.50
MS98	1999 (4)	33,334	KM#852a, 853a, 877, 878 Swedish - hard plastic case	—	16.50
MS99	1999 (4)	1,970	KM#852a, 853a, 877, 878 English - hard plastic case	—	17.50
MS100	1999 (4)	8,045	KM#852a, 853a, 877, 878 Souvenir folder	—	13.50
MS101	2000 (4)	5,000	KM#852a, 853a, 877, 878 Swedish - hard plastic case	—	8.00
MS102	2000 (4)	1,000	KM#852a, 853a, 877, 878 English - soft plastic case	—	8.00
MS103	2000 (4)	30,912	KM#852a, 853a, 877, 878 Swedish - hard plastic case	—	13.50
MS104	2000 (4)	1,801	KM#852a, 853a, 877, 878 English - hard plastic case	—	13.50
MS105	2000 (4)	7,209	KM#852a, 853a, 877, 878 Souvenir folder	—	13.50
MS106	2000 (4)	14,300	KM#852a, 853a, 877, 878 Special Millennium set	—	20.00

PROOF-LIKE SETS (PL)

KM#	Date	Mintage	Identification	Issue Price	Mkt Val
PL1	1993 (2)	1,000	KM#882, 884	—	460
PL2	1995 (2)	1,000	KM#886, 887	—	425
PL3	ND(1996) (2)	1,000	KM#888, 889	—	425
PL4	1999 (2)	2,000	KM#898-899	—	300

SWITZERLAND

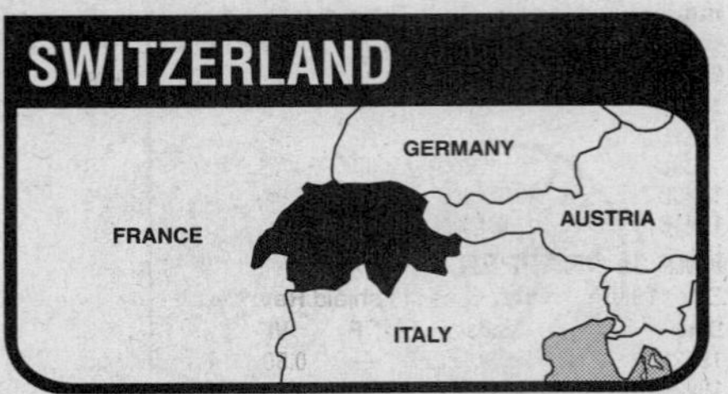

The Swiss Confederation, located in central Europe north of Italy and south of Germany, has an area of 15,941 sq. mi. (41,290 sq. km.) and a population of *6.6 million. Capital: Bern. The economy centers about a well developed manufacturing industry. Machinery, chemicals, watches and clocks, and textiles are exported.

Switzerland, the habitat of lake dwellers in prehistoric times, was peopled by the Celtic Helvetians when Julius Caesar made it a part of the Roman Empire in 58 B.C. After the decline of Rome, Switzerland was invaded by Teutonic tribes, who established small temporal holdings which in the Middle Ages, became a federation of fiefs of the Holy Roman Empire. As a nation, Switzerland originated in 1291 when the districts of Nidwalden, Schwyz and Uri united to defeat Austria and attain independence as the Swiss Confederation. After acquiring new cantons in the 14th century, Switzerland was made independent from the Holy Roman Empire by the 1648 Treaty of Westphalia. The revolutionary armies of Napoleonic France occupied Switzerland and set up the Helvetian Republic, 1798-1803. After the fall of Napoleon, the Congress of Vienna, 1815, recognized the independence of Switzerland and guaranteed its neutrality. The Swiss Constitutions of 1848 and 1874 established a union modeled upon that of the United States.

MINT MARKS

B - Bern
BA - Basel
BB - Strasbourg
S – Solothurn

NOTE: The coinage of Switzerland has been struck at the Bern Mint since 1853 with but a few exceptions. All coins minted there carry a B mint mark through 1969, except for the 2-Centime and 2-Franc values where the mint mark was discontinued after 1968. In 1968 and 1969 some issues were struck at both Bern (B) and in London (no mint mark).

NOTE: The Swiss Shooting Fest coins, KM#S18-S68 previously listed here are actually medallic issues without legal tender status and as such are now listed in ***Unusual World Coins, 4th Edition***, by Krause Publications.

CONFEDERATION

Confoederatio Helvetica

MONETARY SYSTEM

100 Rappen (Centimes) = 1 Franc

DECIMAL COINAGE

KM# 3.2 RAPPEN

1.5000 g., Bronze, 16 mm. **Obv:** Thin cross in shield within sprigs **Rev:** Value within wreath

Date	Mintage	F	VF	XF	Unc	BU
1902B	950,000	20.00	45.00	100	150	250
1903B	1,000,000	15.00	25.00	35.00	55.00	120
1904B	1,000,000	15.00	22.00	40.00	60.00	115
1905B	2,000,000	5.00	8.00	12.00	18.00	28.00
1906B	1,000,000	10.00	20.00	30.00	55.00	100
1907B	2,000,000	3.00	6.00	12.00	20.00	30.00
1908B	3,000,000	2.00	4.00	7.00	13.00	18.00
1909B	1,000,000	7.00	12.50	20.00	32.00	48.00
1910B	1,500,000	5.00	9.00	14.00	24.00	35.00
1911B	1,500,000	5.00	9.00	14.00	24.00	35.00
1912B	2,000,000	2.00	4.00	7.00	14.00	21.00
1913B	3,000,000	0.50	2.00	3.00	5.00	8.00
1914B	3,500,000	0.50	2.50	6.00	13.00	20.00
1915B	3,000,000	1.00	3.50	7.00	20.00	25.00
1917B	2,000,000	1.50	5.00	10.00	16.00	22.00
1918B	3,000,000	0.50	2.00	4.00	9.00	14.00
1919B	3,000,000	0.50	2.00	4.00	9.00	14.00
1920B	1,000,000	1.50	5.00	8.00	15.00	21.00
1921B	3,000,000	0.50	2.00	3.50	9.00	14.00
1924B	2,000,000	1.00	5.00	10.00	20.00	28.00
1925/4B	2,500,000	1.50	6.00	12.00	25.00	35.00
1925B	Inc. above	0.50	2.50	5.00	9.00	14.00
1926B	2,000,000	0.50	2.50	5.00	10.00	16.00
1927B	1,500,000	2.00	6.00	9.00	16.00	23.00
1928B	2,000,000	0.50	3.00	5.00	9.00	14.00
1929B	4,000,000	0.25	0.75	1.50	3.00	6.00
1930B	2,500,000	1.00	2.50	5.00	14.00	21.00
1931B	5,000,000	0.25	1.00	1.50	4.00	7.00
1932B	5,000,000	0.25	1.00	1.50	4.00	7.00
1933B	3,000,000	0.25	1.00	3.00	6.00	10.00

Date	Mintage	F	VF	XF	Unc	BU
1934B	3,000,000	0.25	1.00	2.50	6.00	10.00
1936B	2,000,000	0.50	2.50	5.00	9.00	14.00
1937B	2,400,000	0.25	1.50	2.50	4.00	7.00
1938B	5,300,000	0.25	1.50	2.50	4.00	7.00
1939B	10,000	18.00	28.00	40.00	60.00	85.00
1940B	3,027,000	0.50	3.00	5.00	9.00	14.00
1941B	12,794,000	—	0.50	1.00	3.00	6.00

KM# 3a RAPPEN

Zinc, 16 mm. **Obv:** Cross in shield **Rev:** Value within wreath

Date	Mintage	F	VF	XF	Unc	BU
1942B	17,969,000	—	0.50	1.50	6.00	10.00
1943B	8,647,000	0.25	0.75	1.50	7.00	12.00
1944B	11,825,000	—	0.50	1.50	6.50	11.00
1945B	2,800,000	2.50	6.00	12.00	20.00	30.00
1946B	12,063,000	—	0.50	1.50	4.00	7.00

KM# 46 RAPPEN

1.5000 g., Bronze, 16 mm. **Obv:** Cross **Rev:** Value and oat sprig **Edge:** Plain

Date	Mintage	F	VF	XF	Unc	BU
1948B	10,500,000	—	0.10	0.35	2.00	4.00
1949B	11,100,000	—	0.10	0.35	2.00	4.00
1950B	3,610,000	—	0.75	2.50	5.00	8.00
1951B	22,624,000	—	0.10	0.30	2.00	4.00
1952B	11,520,000	—	0.10	0.30	2.00	4.00
1953B	5,947,000	—	0.10	0.30	2.00	4.00
1954B	5,175,000	—	0.10	0.30	2.00	4.00
1955B	5,282,000	—	0.20	0.60	2.25	4.50
1956B	4,960,000	—	0.10	0.30	2.00	4.00
1957B	15,226,000	—	0.10	0.15	1.00	1.50
1958B	20,142,000	—	0.10	0.15	1.00	1.50
1959B	5,582,000	—	0.10	0.25	1.25	2.00
1962B	5,010,000	—	0.10	0.25	1.25	2.00
1963B	15,920,000	—	—	0.10	0.50	1.00
1966B	5,030,000	—	—	0.10	0.50	1.00
1967B	3,020,000	—	—	0.10	0.50	1.00
1968B	4,920,000	—	—	0.10	0.50	1.00
1969B	4,810,000	—	—	0.10	0.50	1.00
1970	7,810,000	—	—	0.10	0.50	1.00
1971	5,030,000	—	—	0.10	0.50	1.00
1973	3,000,000	—	—	0.10	0.50	1.00
1974	3,007,000	—	—	0.10	0.50	1.00
1974 Proof	2,400	Value: 35.00				
1975	3,010,000	—	—	0.10	0.50	1.00
1975 Proof	10,000	Value: 2.50				
1976	3,005,000	—	—	0.10	0.50	1.00
1976 Proof	5,130	Value: 3.00				
1977	2,007,000	—	—	0.10	0.50	1.00
1977 Proof	7,030	Value: 3.00				
1978	2,010,000	—	—	0.10	0.50	1.00
1978 Proof	10,000	Value: 2.50				
1979	1,025,000	—	—	0.10	0.50	1.00
1979 Proof	10,000	Value: 2.50				
1980	1,030,000	—	—	0.10	0.50	1.00
1980 Proof	10,000	Value: 2.50				
1981	4,935,000	—	—	0.10	0.50	1.00
1981 Proof	10,000	Value: 2.50				
1982	6,655,000	—	—	0.10	0.50	1.00
1982 Proof	10,000	Value: 2.50				
1983	4,031,000	—	—	0.10	0.50	1.00
1983 Proof	11,000	Value: 2.50				
1984	3,995,000	—	—	0.10	0.50	1.00
1984 Proof	14,000	Value: 2.50				
1985	3,027,000	—	—	0.10	0.50	1.00
1985 Proof	12,000	Value: 2.50				
1986B	2,031,000	—	—	0.10	0.50	1.00
1986B Proof	10,000	Value: 2.50				
1987B	1,028,000	—	—	0.10	0.50	1.00
1987B Proof	8,800	Value: 3.00				
1988B	2,029,000	—	—	0.10	0.50	1.00
1988B Proof	9,000	Value: 3.00				
1989B	2,031,000	—	—	0.10	0.50	1.00
1989B Proof	8,800	Value: 3.00				
1990B	1,032,000	—	—	—	0.50	1.00
1990B Proof	8,900	Value: 3.00				
1991B	536,000	—	—	—	1.50	2.50
1991B Proof	9,900	Value: 3.00				
1992B	528,000	—	—	—	1.50	2.50
1992B Proof	7,450	Value: 3.00				
1993B	523,000	—	—	—	1.50	2.50
1993B Proof	6,200	Value: 3.00				
1994B	2,023,000	—	—	—	0.50	1.00
1994B Proof	6,100	Value: 3.00				
1995B	6,024,000	—	—	—	0.50	1.00
1995B Proof	6,100	Value: 3.00				
1996B	1,023,000	—	—	—	0.50	1.00
1996B Proof	6,100	Value: 3.00				
1997B	1,022,000	—	—	—	0.50	1.00
1997B Proof	5,500	Value: 3.00				
1998B	1,021,000	—	—	—	0.50	1.00
1998B Proof	4,800	Value: 3.00				
1999B	1,021,000	—	—	—	0.50	1.00
1999B Proof	5,000	Value: 3.00				
2000B	1,026,000	—	—	—	0.50	1.00
2000B Proof	5,500	Value: 3.00				

KM# 4.2a 2 RAPPEN

Bronze **Obv:** Cross in shield within sprigs **Rev:** Value within wreath

Date	Mintage	F	VF	XF	Unc	BU
1902B	500,000	12.00	30.00	50.00	90.00	200
1903B	500,000	10.00	22.00	35.00	65.00	125
1904B	500,000	10.00	21.00	40.00	60.00	110
1906B	500,000	10.00	21.00	40.00	65.00	125
1907B	1,000,000	2.50	8.00	10.00	22.00	28.00
1908B	1,000,000	2.50	6.00	9.00	22.00	28.00
1909B	1,000,000	2.50	6.00	9.00	18.00	25.00
1910B	500,000	10.00	22.00	32.00	45.00	70.00
1912B	1,000,000	4.50	6.00	12.00	20.00	30.00
1913B	1,000,000	5.00	10.00	12.50	30.00	50.00
1914B	1,000,000	5.00	10.00	12.50	28.00	45.00
1915B	1,000,000	4.00	7.00	12.50	25.00	35.00
1918B	1,000,000	3.50	5.00	9.00	14.00	21.00
1919B	2,000,000	1.00	2.50	3.00	9.00	14.00
1920B	500,000	15.00	28.00	45.00	75.00	115
1925B	1,250,000	0.50	2.50	4.00	7.00	10.00
1926B	750,000	7.00	17.50	30.00	50.00	75.00
1927B	500,000	10.00	25.00	35.00	50.00	75.00
1928B	500,000	10.00	20.00	30.00	50.00	75.00
1929B	750,000	2.00	7.50	10.00	18.00	28.00
1930B	1,000,000	2.00	7.00	10.00	18.00	28.00
1931B	1,288,000	1.50	5.00	8.00	16.00	25.00
1932B	1,500,000	1.00	2.00	3.00	6.00	10.00
1933B	1,000,000	1.00	3.50	6.00	15.00	21.00
1934B	500,000	4.00	12.50	20.00	35.00	55.00
1936B	500,000	2.00	5.00	9.00	15.00	22.00
1937B	1,200,000	0.50	2.00	3.50	6.50	10.00
1938B	1,369,000	0.50	3.00	6.00	15.00	21.00
1941B	3,448,000	—	1.00	1.50	2.50	4.00

KM# 4.2b 2 RAPPEN

Zinc **Obv:** Cross on shield within sprigs **Rev:** Value within wreath

Date	Mintage	F	VF	XF	Unc	BU
1942B	8,954,000	—	0.75	1.50	7.00	10.00
1943B	4,499,000	—	1.00	3.00	11.00	16.00
1944B	8,086,000	—	0.75	1.50	7.00	10.00
1945B	3,640,000	0.50	4.00	7.00	20.00	28.00
1946B	1,393,000	1.00	15.00	28.00	35.00	50.00

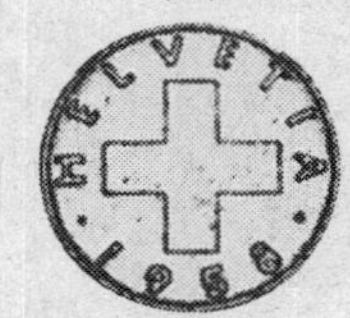

KM# 47 2 RAPPEN

Bronze **Obv:** Cross **Rev:** Value and oat sprig

Date	Mintage	F	VF	XF	Unc	BU
1948B	10,197,000	—	0.25	0.50	3.50	5.50
1951B	9,622,000	—	0.25	0.50	3.50	5.50
1952B	1,916,000	—	0.50	1.00	4.50	7.00
1953B	2,007,000	—	0.50	1.00	3.50	5.50
1954B	2,539,000	—	0.50	1.00	3.00	5.00
1955B	2,493,000	—	0.25	1.00	3.00	5.00
1957B	8,099,000	—	0.10	0.25	1.75	2.50
1958B	6,078,000	—	0.10	0.25	1.75	2.50
1963B	10,065,000	—	0.10	0.25	1.00	2.50
1966B	2,510,000	—	0.10	0.25	1.00	1.50
1967B	1,510,000	—	0.20	0.60	1.50	1.50
1968B	2,865,000	—	0.10	0.25	0.75	1.50
1969	6,200,000	—	0.10	0.25	0.75	1.00
1970	3,115,000	—	0.10	0.25	0.50	1.00
1974	3,540,000	—	0.10	0.25	0.50	1.00
1974 Proof	2,400	Value: 50.00				

KM# 26 5 RAPPEN

Copper-Nickel, 17.1 mm. **Obv:** Crowned head right **Obv. Legend:** CONFOEDERATIO HELVETICA **Rev:** Value within wreath **Edge:** Plain

Date	Mintage	F	VF	XF	Unc	BU
1901B	3,000,000	0.50	2.00	5.00	25.00	50.00
1902B	1,000,000	5.00	10.00	28.00	75.00	175
1902B	Inc. above	6.00	12.00	32.00	100	200
Note: "T" over "L" in HELVETICA						
1902B	Inc. above	5.00	10.00	30.00	100	175
Note: "I" over tilted "I" in Helvetica						
1903B	2,000,000	1.00	2.50	12.00	45.00	110
1904B	1,000,000	4.00	10.00	28.00	110	200
1905B	1,000,000	3.00	7.00	12.00	60.00	120
1906B	3,000,000	0.50	2.00	6.00	20.00	35.00
1907B	5,000,000	0.50	1.50	3.50	9.00	14.00
1908B	3,000,000	0.50	2.00	4.00	12.00	18.00
1909B	2,000,000	0.50	2.00	5.00	15.00	25.00
1910B	1,000,000	2.00	5.00	10.00	50.00	75.00
1911B	2,000,000	0.50	1.00	3.00	12.00	20.00
1912B	3,000,000	0.50	1.00	3.00	10.00	20.00
1913B	3,000,000	0.50	1.00	3.00	12.50	22.00
1914B	3,000,000	0.50	1.00	7.00	75.00	125
1915B	3,000,000	0.50	1.00	12.50	110	225
1917B	1,000,000	1.50	2.50	10.00	100	200
1919B	6,000,000	—	0.50	2.50	15.00	25.00
1920B	5,000,000	—	0.50	2.50	12.00	25.00
1921B	3,000,000	—	0.50	2.50	12.00	20.00
1922B	4,000,000	—	0.50	1.50	10.00	18.00
1925B	3,000,000	—	0.50	2.00	12.00	20.00
1926B	3,000,000	—	0.50	2.00	12.00	20.00
1927B	2,000,000	—	0.50	3.00	14.00	22.00
1928B	2,000,000	—	0.50	1.50	12.00	20.00
1929B	2,000,000	—	0.50	1.50	12.00	20.00
1930B	3,000,000	—	0.50	1.50	12.00	20.00
1931B	5,037,000	—	0.50	1.00	9.00	15.00
1940B	1,416,000	—	0.50	5.00	50.00	150
1942B	5,078,000	—	0.25	0.50	12.50	17.50
1943B	6,591,000	—	0.25	0.50	12.00	17.00
1944B	9,981,000	—	0.25	0.50	12.50	17.50
1945B	985,000	—	1.00	12.00	100	250
1946B	6,179,000	—	0.25	0.50	12.50	20.00
1947B	5,125,000	—	0.25	0.50	12.50	20.00
1948B	4,710,000	—	0.25	0.50	4.50	6.50
1949B	4,589,000	—	0.25	0.50	3.00	5.00
1950B	920,000	—	0.50	1.50	4.00	6.50
1951B	2,141,000	—	0.50	2.50	40.00	60.00
1952B	4,690,000	—	0.20	0.35	3.50	5.00
1953B	9,131,000	—	0.20	0.35	3.00	5.00
1954B	8,038,000	—	0.20	0.35	3.00	5.00
1955B	19,943,000	—	0.20	0.30	1.50	4.00
1957B	10,147,000	—	0.20	0.30	1.50	4.00
1958B	10,217,000	—	0.20	0.30	1.50	4.00
1959B	11,085,000	—	0.20	0.30	1.50	4.00
1962B	23,840,000	—	0.10	0.20	0.50	2.00
1963B	29,730,000	—	0.10	0.20	0.50	2.00
1964B	17,080,000	—	0.10	0.20	0.50	2.00
1965B	1,430,000	—	0.25	1.00	1.50	2.25
1966B	10,010,000	—	—	0.15	0.50	1.00
1967B	13,010,000	—	—	0.25	0.75	1.25
1968B	10,020,000	—	—	0.15	0.50	1.00
1969B	32,990,000	—	—	0.10	0.50	1.00
1970	34,800,000	—	—	0.10	0.50	1.00
1971	40,020,000	—	—	0.10	0.50	1.00
1974	30,002,000	—	—	0.10	0.50	1.00
1974 Proof	2,400	Value: 35.00				
1975	34,005,000	—	—	0.10	0.50	1.00
1975 Proof	10,000	Value: 3.00				
1976	12,005,000	—	—	0.10	0.50	1.00
1976 Proof	5,130	Value: 4.00				
1977	14,012,000	—	—	0.10	0.50	1.00
1977 Proof	7,030	Value: 4.00				
1978	16,415,000	—	—	0.10	0.50	1.00
1978 Proof	10,000	Value: 3.00				
1979	27,010,000	—	—	0.10	0.50	1.00
1979 Proof	10,000	Value: 3.00				
1980	15,500,000	—	—	0.10	0.50	1.00
1980 Proof	10,000	Value: 3.00				

KM# 26a 5 RAPPEN

Brass, 17.1 mm. **Obv:** Crowned head right **Rev:** Value within wreath

Date	Mintage	F	VF	XF	Unc	BU
1918B	6,000,000	4.00	7.00	13.00	20.00	30.00

KM# 26b 5 RAPPEN

Nickel, 17.1 mm. **Obv:** Crowned head right **Rev:** Value within wreath **Edge:** Plain **Note:** Retired legal tender status as of January 1, 2004, removed from circulation.

Date	Mintage	F	VF	XF	Unc	BU
1932B	6,000,000	—	0.50	1.50	7.00	15.00
1933B	3,000,000	—	0.50	1.50	7.50	15.00
1934B	4,000,000	—	0.50	1.50	7.00	15.00
1936B	1,000,000	—	0.75	2.50	8.50	18.00
1937B	2,000,000	—	0.50	1.00	9.00	18.00
1938B	1,000,000	—	0.50	1.50	9.00	18.00
1939B	10,048,000	—	0.50	1.00	7.00	10.00
1941B	3,087,000	—	1.00	5.00	60.00	90.00

KM# 26c 5 RAPPEN

2.0000 g., Aluminum-Brass, 17.1 mm. **Obv:** Crowned head right **Rev:** Value within wreath

Date	Mintage	F	VF	XF	Unc	BU
1981	79,020,000	—	—	—	0.50	1.00

Date	Mintage	F	VF	XF	Unc	BU
1981 Proof	10,000	Value: 3.00				
1982	75,340,000	—	—	—	0.50	1.00
1982 Proof	10,000	Value: 3.00				
1983	92,746,000	—	—	—	0.50	1.00
1983 Proof	11,000	Value: 3.00				
1984	69,960,000	—	—	—	0.50	1.00
1984 Proof	14,000	Value: 3.00				
1985	60,032,000	—	—	—	0.50	1.00
1985 Proof	12,000	Value: 3.00				
1986B	55,041,000	—	—	—	0.50	1.00
1986B Proof	10,000	Value: 3.00				
1987B	39,828,000	—	—	—	0.50	1.00
1987B Proof	8,800	Value: 4.00				
1988B	55,044,000	—	—	—	0.50	1.00
1988B Proof	9,000	Value: 4.00				
1989B	45,031,000	—	—	—	0.50	1.00
1989B Proof	8,800	Value: 4.00				
1990B	16,042,000	—	—	—	0.50	1.00
1990B Proof	8,900	Value: 4.00				
1991B	35,036,000	—	—	—	0.50	1.00
1991B Proof	9,900	Value: 3.00				
1992B	35,028,000	—	—	—	0.50	1.00
1992B Proof	7,450	Value: 4.00				
1993B	38,023,000	—	—	—	0.50	1.00
1993B Proof	6,200	Value: 4.00				
1994B	35,023,000	—	—	—	0.50	1.00
1994B Proof	6,100	Value: 4.00				
1995B	20,024,000	—	—	—	0.50	1.00
1995B Proof	6,100	Value: 4.00				
1996B	25,023,000	—	—	—	0.50	1.00
1996B Proof	6,100	Value: 4.00				
1997B	25,022,000	—	—	—	0.50	1.00
1997B Proof	5,500	Value: 4.00				
1998B	10,021,000	—	—	—	0.50	1.00
1998B Proof	4,800	Value: 4.00				
1999B	8,021,000	—	—	—	0.50	1.00
1999B Proof	5,000	Value: 4.00				
2000B	5,026,000	—	—	—	0.50	1.00
2000B Proof	5,500	Value: 4.00				

KM# 27 10 RAPPEN

3.0000 g., Copper-Nickel, 19.1 mm. **Obv:** Crowned head right **Obv. Legend:** CONFOEDERATIO HELVETICA **Rev:** Value within wreath **Edge:** Plain **Note:** Retired from legal tender status as of January 1, 2004, and removed from circulation

Date	Mintage	F	VF	XF	Unc	BU
1901B	1,000,000	1.50	5.00	12.00	65.00	125
1902B	1,000,000	1.50	5.00	12.00	60.00	100
1903B	1,000,000	1.50	4.50	10.00	60.00	130
1904B	1,000,000	1.50	5.00	16.00	140	300
1906B	1,000,000	1.50	5.00	10.00	40.00	90.00
1907B	2,000,000	1.00	2.00	5.00	24.00	40.00
1908B	2,000,000	1.00	2.00	5.00	24.00	40.00
1909B	2,000,000	1.00	2.00	5.00	24.00	35.00
1911B	1,000,000	1.50	3.00	8.00	40.00	60.00
1912B	1,500,000	0.50	1.50	5.00	38.00	60.00
1913B	2,000,000	0.50	1.00	5.00	45.00	75.00
1914B	2,000,000	0.50	1.50	7.00	70.00	150
1915B	1,200,000	0.50	2.00	25.00	190	325
1919B	3,000,000	—	0.50	2.50	25.00	36.00
1920B	3,500,000	—	0.50	2.50	18.00	28.00
1921B	3,000,000	—	0.50	2.50	18.00	28.00
1922B	2,000,000	—	0.50	2.50	22.00	35.00
1924B	2,000,000	—	0.50	2.50	22.00	35.00
1925B	3,000,000	—	0.50	2.00	18.00	28.00
1926B	3,000,000	—	0.50	2.00	16.00	25.00
1927B	2,000,000	—	0.50	2.50	16.00	25.00
1928B	2,000,000	—	0.50	2.50	16.00	25.00
1929B	2,000,000	—	0.50	2.50	16.00	25.00
1930B	2,000,000	—	0.50	2.50	22.00	35.00
1931B	2,244,000	—	0.50	2.50	22.00	35.00
1940B	2,000,000	—	0.75	10.00	75.00	250
1942B	2,110,000	—	0.75	10.00	50.00	80.00
1943B	3,176,000	—	0.50	5.00	37.50	56.00
1944B	6,133,000	—	0.50	2.50	10.00	16.00
1945B	993,000	—	1.00	12.00	120	200
1946B	4,010,000	—	0.50	2.50	24.00	35.00
1947B	3,152,000	—	0.50	2.50	24.00	35.00
1948B	1,000,000	0.50	1.00	15.00	200	350
1949B	2,269,000	—	0.50	1.00	22.00	35.00
1950B	3,200,000	—	0.50	1.00	2.50	3.50
1951B	3,430,000	—	0.50	1.00	7.00	10.00
1952B	4,451,000	—	0.50	1.00	7.00	10.00
1953B	6,149,000	—	0.50	1.00	7.00	10.00
1954B	3,200,000	—	0.50	1.00	15.00	22.00
1955B	11,795,000	—	0.50	1.00	4.50	7.00
1957B	10,092,000	—	0.50	1.00	6.00	10.00
1958B	10,040,000	—	0.50	1.00	4.50	7.00
1959B	13,053,000	—	0.50	1.00	3.50	5.00
1960B	4,040,000	—	0.50	1.00	3.50	5.00
1961B	7,949,000	—	—	0.50	2.00	3.00
1962B	34,965,000	—	—	0.25	1.00	1.50
1964B	16,340,000	—	—	0.25	1.00	1.50
1965B	14,190,000	—	—	0.25	1.00	1.50
1966B	4,025,000	—	—	0.50	1.00	1.50
1967B	10,000,000	—	—	0.50	1.00	1.50
1968B	14,065,000	—	—	0.25	0.50	1.00
1969B	28,855,000	—	—	0.25	0.50	1.00
1970	40,020,000	—	—	0.25	0.50	1.00
1972	7,877,000	—	—	0.25	0.50	1.00
1973	30,350,000	—	—	—	0.40	0.75
1974	30,007,000	—	—	—	0.40	0.75
1974 Proof	2,400	Value: 60.00				
1975	25,002,000	—	—	—	0.40	0.75
1975 Proof	10,000	Value: 4.00				
1976	19,012,000	—	—	—	0.40	0.75
1976 Proof	5,130	Value: 5.00				
1977	10,007,000	—	—	—	0.40	0.75
1977 Proof	7,030	Value: 5.00				
1978	19,957,000	—	—	—	0.40	0.75
1978 Proof	10,000	Value: 4.00				
1979	18,010,000	—	—	—	0.40	0.75
1979 Proof	10,000	Value: 4.00				
1980	18,005,000	—	—	—	0.50	1.00
1980 Proof	10,000	Value: 4.00				
1981	30,140,000	—	—	—	0.50	1.00
1981 Proof	10,000	Value: 4.00				
1982	50,110,000	—	—	—	0.50	1.00
1982 Proof	10,000	Value: 4.00				
1983	40,033,000	—	—	—	0.50	1.00
1983 Proof	11,000	Value: 4.00				
1984	22,022,000	—	—	—	0.50	1.00
1984 Proof	14,000	Value: 4.00				
1985	3,032,000	—	—	—	0.50	1.00
1985 Proof	12,000	Value: 4.00				
1986B	2,324,000	—	—	—	0.50	1.00
1986B Proof	10,000	Value: 4.00				
1987B	5,028,000	—	—	—	0.50	1.00
1987B Proof	8,800	Value: 5.00				
1988B	5,029,000	—	—	—	0.50	1.00
1988B Proof	9,000	Value: 5.00				
1989B	41,031,000	—	—	—	0.50	1.00
1989B Proof	8,800	Value: 5.00				
1990B	40,032,000	—	—	—	0.50	1.00
1990B Proof	8,900	Value: 5.00				
1991B	35,046,000	—	—	—	0.50	1.00
1991B Proof	9,900	Value: 4.00				
1992B	18,028,000	—	—	—	0.50	1.00
1992B Proof	7,450	Value: 5.00				
1993B	27,022,000	—	—	—	0.50	1.00
1993B Proof	6,200	Value: 5.00				
1994B	18,023,000	—	—	—	0.50	1.00
1994B Proof	6,100	Value: 5.00				
1995B	5,024,000	—	—	—	0.50	1.00
1995B Proof	6,100	Value: 5.00				
1996B	18,023,000	—	—	—	0.50	1.00
1996B Proof	6,100	Value: 5.00				
1997B	15,022,000	—	—	—	0.50	1.00
1997B Proof	5,500	Value: 5.00				
1998B	10,021,000	—	—	—	0.50	1.00
1998B Proof	4,800	Value: 5.00				
1999B	7,021,000	—	—	—	0.50	1.00
1999B Proof	5,000	Value: 5.00				
2000B	5,026,000	—	—	—	0.50	1.00
2000B Proof	5,500	Value: 5.00				

KM# 27a 10 RAPPEN

Brass, 19.1 mm. **Obv:** Crowned head right **Rev:** Value within wreath

Date	Mintage	F	VF	XF	Unc	BU
1918B	6,000,000	5.00	12.00	20.00	30.00	45.00
1919B	3,000,000	20.00	48.00	60.00	100	150

KM# 27b 10 RAPPEN

Nickel, 19.1 mm. **Obv:** Crowned head right **Rev:** Value within wreath **Edge:** Plain **Note:** Retired legal tender status as of January 1, 2004, removed from circulation.

Date	Mintage	F	VF	XF	Unc	BU
1932B	3,500,000	—	0.50	1.00	9.00	18.00
1933B	2,000,000	—	0.50	1.00	12.50	20.00
1934B	3,000,000	—	0.50	1.00	12.00	20.00
1936B	1,500,000	—	0.50	1.00	14.00	22.00
1937B	1,000,000	0.40	0.75	1.50	15.00	25.00
1938B	1,000,000	0.40	0.75	1.50	10.00	20.00
1939B	10,022,000	—	0.50	1.00	8.00	15.00

KM# 29 20 RAPPEN

Nickel, 21 mm. **Obv:** Crowned head right **Obv. Legend:** CONFOEDERATIO HELVETICA **Rev:** Value within wreath **Note:** Retired legal tender status as of January 1, 2004, removed from circulation.

Date	Mintage	F	VF	XF	Unc	BU
1901B	1,000,000	0.50	1.00	8.00	100	300
1902B	1,000,000	0.50	1.00	8.00	55.00	150
1903B	1,000,000	0.50	1.00	8.00	50.00	160
1906B	1,000,000	0.50	1.00	8.00	50.00	130
1907B	1,000,000	0.50	1.00	7.00	32.00	70.00
1908B	1,500,000	0.50	1.00	5.00	38.00	75.00
1909B	2,000,000	0.50	1.00	5.00	32.00	45.00
1911B	1,000,000	0.50	1.00	6.00	65.00	150
1912B	2,000,000	0.25	0.75	5.00	45.00	90.00
1913B	1,500,000	0.25	0.75	5.00	70.00	150
1919B	1,500,000	0.25	0.75	5.00	38.00	55.00
1920B	3,100,000	—	0.50	2.00	22.00	37.00
1921B	2,500,000	—	0.50	2.00	22.00	35.00
1924B	1,100,000	—	0.50	2.00	40.00	85.00
1925B	1,500,000	—	0.50	2.00	20.00	32.00
1926B	1,500,000	—	0.50	2.00	20.00	32.00
1927B	500,000	1.00	2.50	12.00	110	200
1929B	2,000,000	—	0.50	1.00	20.00	30.00
1930B	2,000,000	—	0.50	1.00	20.00	30.00
1931B	2,250,000	—	0.50	1.00	20.00	30.00
1932B	2,000,000	—	0.50	1.00	20.00	55.00
1933B	1,500,000	—	0.50	1.00	28.00	55.00
1934B	2,000,000	—	0.50	1.00	20.00	60.00
1936B	1,000,000	0.50	1.00	2.00	32.00	85.00
1938B	2,805,000	—	0.50	1.50	32.00	85.00

KM# 29a 20 RAPPEN

4.2000 g., Copper-Nickel, 21 mm. **Obv:** Crowned head right **Rev:** Value within wreath **Edge:** Plain

Date	Mintage	F	VF	XF	Unc	BU
1939B	8,100,000	—	0.50	10.00	110	300
1943B	10,173,000	—	0.50	1.00	28.00	42.00
1944B	7,139,000	—	0.50	1.00	10.00	16.00
1945B	1,992,000	—	1.00	10.00	75.00	250
1947B	5,131,000	—	0.50	0.75	15.00	45.00
1947B	Inc. above	1.00	2.00	4.00	24.00	50.00
Note: Dot over 4 in date						
1950B	5,970,000	—	0.50	0.75	6.00	10.00
1951B	3,640,000	—	0.50	0.75	8.00	16.00
1952B	3,075,000	—	0.50	0.75	9.00	18.00
1953B	6,958,000	—	0.50	0.75	6.00	10.00
1954B	1,504,000	—	1.00	4.00	32.00	125
1955B	9,103,000	—	0.50	0.75	9.00	18.00
1956B	5,111,000	—	0.50	0.75	9.00	18.00
1957B	2,535,000	—	0.50	1.25	28.00	100
1958B	5,037,000	—	0.50	0.75	9.00	18.00
1959B	10,136,000	—	—	0.50	2.50	8.00
1960B	15,469,000	—	—	0.50	2.50	5.00
1961B	8,234,000	—	—	0.50	2.50	5.00
1962B	30,145,000	—	—	0.50	2.00	5.00
1963B	9,020,000	—	—	0.50	2.00	5.00
1964B	14,370,000	—	—	0.50	2.00	3.00
1965B	15,005,000	—	—	0.50	2.00	3.00
1966B	10,785,000	—	—	0.50	1.00	2.00
1967B	8,995,000	—	—	0.50	1.00	2.00
1968B	10,540,000	—	—	0.50	1.00	2.00
1969B	39,875,000	—	—	0.40	1.00	2.00
1970	45,605,000	—	—	—	1.00	2.00
1971	25,160,000	—	—	—	1.00	2.00
1974	30,025,000	—	—	—	1.00	2.00
1974 Proof	2,400	Value: 75.00				
1975	50,060,000	—	—	—	1.00	2.00
1975 Proof	10,000	Value: 5.00				
1976	23,150,000	—	—	—	1.00	2.00
1976 Proof	5,130	Value: 6.00				
1977	14,012,000	—	—	—	1.00	2.00
1977 Proof	7,030	Value: 6.00				
1978	14,815,000	—	—	—	1.00	2.00
1978 Proof	10,000	Value: 5.00				
1979	18,378,000	—	—	—	1.00	2.00
1979 Proof	10,000	Value: 5.00				
1980	24,560,000	—	—	—	1.00	2.00
1980 Proof	10,000	Value: 5.00				
1981	22,020,000	—	—	—	1.00	2.00
1981 Proof	10,000	Value: 5.00				
1982	25,035,000	—	—	—	1.00	2.00
1982 Proof	10,000	Value: 5.00				
1983	10,026,000	—	—	—	1.00	2.00
1983 Proof	11,000	Value: 5.00				
1984	22,055,000	—	—	—	1.00	2.00
1984 Proof	14,000	Value: 5.00				
1985	40,027,000	—	—	—	1.00	2.00
1985 Proof	12,000	Value: 5.00				
1986B	10,299,000	—	—	—	1.00	1.50
1986B Proof	10,000	Value: 5.00				
1987B	10,028,000	—	—	—	1.00	1.50
1987B Proof	8,800	Value: 6.00				
1988B	25,029,000	—	—	—	1.00	1.50
1988B Proof	9,000	Value: 6.00				
1989B	20,031,000	—	—	—	1.00	1.50
1989B Proof	8,800	Value: 6.00				
1990B	6,534,000	—	—	—	1.00	1.50
1990B Proof	8,900	Value: 6.00				
1991B	48,076,000	—	—	—	1.00	1.50
1991B Proof	9,900	Value: 6.00				
1992B	12,628,000	—	—	—	1.00	1.50
1992B Proof	7,450	Value: 6.00				
1993B	32,523,000	—	—	—	1.00	1.50
1993B Proof	6,200	Value: 6.00				

Date	Mintage	F	VF	XF	Unc	BU
1994B	20,023,000	—	—	—	1.00	1.50
1994B Proof	6,100	Value: 6.00				
1995B	8,024,000	—	—	—	1.00	1.50
1995B Proof	6,100	Value: 6.00				
1996B	4,023,000	—	—	—	1.00	1.50
1996B Proof	6,100	Value: 6.00				
1997B	6,022,000	—	—	—	1.00	1.50
1997B Proof	5,500	Value: 6.00				
1998B	7,021,000	—	—	—	1.00	1.50
1998B Proof	4,800	Value: 6.00				
1999B	4,021,000	—	—	—	1.00	1.50
1999B Proof	5,000	Value: 6.00				
2000B	3,026,000	—	—	—	1.00	1.50
2000B Proof	5,500	Value: 6.00				

KM# 23 1/2 FRANC

2.5000 g., 0.8350 Silver .0671 oz. ASW, 18.1 mm. **Obv:** Standing Helvetia with lance and shield within star border **Rev:** Value, date within wreath **Edge:** Reeded **Designer:** A. Bovy

Date	Mintage	F	VF	XF	Unc	BU
1901B	200,000	15.00	50.00	175	750	1,750
1901B Specimen	—	—	—	—	—	3,000
1903B	800,000	1.00	2.50	15.00	70.00	175
1903B Specimen	—	—	—	—	—	1,000
1904B	400,000	2.00	5.00	75.00	600	1,200
1904B Specimen	—	—	—	—	—	3,000
1905B	600,000	1.00	2.50	15.00	125	225
1905B Specimen	—	—	—	—	—	900
1906B	1,000,000	1.00	2.50	15.00	125	200
1906B Specimen	—	—	—	—	—	900
1907B	1,200,000	1.00	2.50	15.00	100	180
1907B Specimen	—	—	—	—	—	750
1908B	800,000	1.00	2.50	15.00	125	200
1908B Specimen	—	—	—	—	—	750
1909B	1,000,000	1.00	2.50	10.00	75.00	150
1909B Specimen	—	—	—	—	—	750
1910B	1,000,000	1.00	2.50	10.00	65.00	125
1910B Specimen	—	—	—	—	—	750
1913B	800,000	1.00	2.50	7.50	65.00	100
1913B Specimen	—	—	—	—	—	600
1914B	2,000,000	1.00	2.50	5.00	32.00	50.00
1914B Specimen	—	—	—	—	—	360
1916B	800,000	1.00	2.50	5.00	60.00	125
1916B Specimen	—	—	—	—	—	450
1920B	5,400,000	1.00	2.00	4.00	14.00	25.00
1920B Specimen	—	—	—	—	—	150
1921B	6,000,000	1.00	2.00	4.00	14.00	25.00
1921B Specimen	—	—	—	—	—	150
1928B	1,000,000	1.00	2.50	6.00	55.00	110
1928B Specimen	—	—	—	—	—	300
1929B	2,000,000	1.00	2.50	5.00	14.00	28.00
1929B Specimen	—	—	—	—	—	180
1931B	1,000,000	1.00	2.00	6.00	32.00	50.00
1931B Specimen	—	—	—	—	—	240
1932B	1,000,000	1.00	2.00	4.00	22.00	40.00
1932B Specimen	—	—	—	—	—	240
1934B	2,000,000	1.00	2.00	4.00	14.00	25.00
1934B Specimen	—	—	—	—	—	120
1936B	400,000	1.50	3.00	6.00	32.00	70.00
1936B Specimen	—	—	—	—	—	240
1937B	1,000,000	1.00	2.00	5.00	14.00	30.00
1937B Specimen	—	—	—	—	—	180
1939B	1,001,000	1.00	2.00	5.00	15.00	30.00
1939B Specimen	—	—	—	—	—	120
1940B	2,002,000	—	2.00	4.00	12.00	25.00
1940B Specimen	—	—	—	—	—	120
1941B	200,000	1.50	3.00	8.00	20.00	30.00
1941B Specimen	—	—	—	—	—	90.00
1942B	2,969,000	—	1.50	2.50	5.00	10.00
1942B Specimen	—	—	—	—	—	90.00
1943B	4,573,000	—	1.50	2.50	5.00	10.00
1943B Specimen	—	—	—	—	—	90.00
1944B	7,455,000	—	1.50	2.50	5.00	10.00
1944B Specimen	—	—	—	—	—	90.00
1945B	4,928,000	—	1.50	2.50	5.00	10.00
1945B Specimen	—	—	—	—	—	90.00
1946B	6,817,000	—	1.50	2.50	4.00	8.00
1946B	Inc. above	50.00	110	160	250	400
Note: Medal alignment						
1946B Specimen	—	—	—	—	—	90.00
1948B	6,113,000	—	1.50	2.50	4.00	7.00
1948B Specimen	—	—	—	—	—	90.00
1950B	7,148,000	—	1.50	2.50	4.00	7.00
1950B Specimen	—	—	—	—	—	90.00
1951B	8,530,000	—	1.50	2.50	4.00	7.00
1951B Specimen	—	—	—	—	—	90.00
1952B	14,023,000	—	1.50	2.50	4.00	7.00
1952B Specimen	—	—	—	—	—	75.00
1953B	3,567,000	—	1.50	2.50	4.50	7.50
1953B Specimen	—	—	—	—	—	90.00
1955B	1,320,000	—	1.50	3.00	8.00	12.00
1955B Specimen	—	—	—	—	—	110
1956B	4,250,000	—	1.50	2.50	4.50	7.50
1956B Specimen	—	—	—	—	—	60.00
1957B	12,085,000	—	1.50	2.50	4.00	7.00
1957B Specimen	—	—	—	—	—	30.00
1958B	11,558,000	—	1.50	2.50	4.00	7.00
1958B Specimen	—	—	—	—	—	30.00
1959B	12,581,000	—	1.50	2.50	4.00	7.00
1959B Specimen	—	—	—	—	—	30.00
1960B	14,528,000	—	1.50	2.50	4.00	7.00
1960B Specimen	—	—	—	—	—	30.00
1961B	6,906,000	—	1.50	2.50	4.00	7.00
1961B Specimen	—	—	—	—	—	30.00
1962B	18,272,000	—	1.50	2.50	3.50	6.00
1962B Specimen	—	—	—	—	—	30.00
1963B	25,168,000	—	1.50	2.50	3.50	6.00
1963B Specimen	—	—	—	—	—	30.00
1964B	22,720,000	—	1.50	2.50	3.50	6.00
1964B Specimen	—	—	—	—	—	30.00
1965B	17,920,000	—	1.50	2.50	3.50	6.00
1965B Specimen	—	—	—	—	—	30.00
1966B	10,008,000	—	1.50	2.50	3.50	6.00
1966B Specimen	—	—	—	—	—	30.00
1967B	16,096,000	—	1.50	2.50	3.50	6.00
1967B Specimen	—	—	—	—	—	30.00

KM# 23a.1 1/2 FRANC

2.2000 g., Copper-Nickel, 18.1 mm. **Obv:** Standing Helvetia with lance and shield within star border **Rev:** Value within wreath

Date	Mintage	F	VF	XF	Unc	BU
1968	20,000,000	—	—	—	2.50	4.00
1968B	44,920,000	—	—	—	2.50	4.00
1969	31,400,000	—	—	—	2.50	4.00
1969B	51,704,000	—	—	—	2.50	4.00
1970	52,620,000	—	—	—	2.50	4.00
1971	34,472,000	—	—	—	2.50	4.00
1972	9,996,000	—	—	—	2.50	4.00
1973	5,000,000	—	—	—	4.00	7.00
1974	45,006,000	—	—	—	2.50	4.00
1974 Proof	2,400	Value: 85.00				
1975	27,234,000	—	—	—	2.50	3.50
1975 Proof	10,000	Value: 6.00				
1976	10,009,000	—	—	—	2.50	3.50
1976 Proof	5,130	Value: 6.00				
1977	19,011,000	—	—	—	2.50	3.50
1977 Proof	7,030	Value: 6.00				
1978	20,818,000	—	—	—	2.50	3.50
1978 Proof	10,000	Value: 6.00				
1979	27,014,000	—	—	—	2.50	3.50
1979 Proof	10,000	Value: 6.00				
1980	31,064,000	—	—	—	2.50	3.50
1980 Proof	10,000	Value: 6.00				
1981	30,155,000	—	—	—	2.50	3.50
1981 Proof	10,000	Value: 6.00				

KM# 23a.2 1/2 FRANC

2.2000 g., Copper-Nickel, 18.1 mm. **Obv:** 22 Stars around figure **Rev:** Value within wreath **Note:** Medal alignment.

Date	Mintage	F	VF	XF	Unc	BU
1982	30,151,000	—	—	—	2.50	3.50
1982 Proof	10,000	Value: 6.00				

KM# 23a.3 1/2 FRANC

2.2000 g., Copper-Nickel, 18.1 mm. **Obv:** 23 Stars around figure **Rev:** Value within wreath

Date	Mintage	F	VF	XF	Unc	BU
1983	22,020,000	—	—	—	1.75	2.75
1983 Proof	11,000	Value: 6.00				
1984	22,036,000	—	—	—	1.75	2.75
1984 Proof	14,000	Value: 6.00				
1985	6,026,000	—	—	—	2.50	3.50
1985 Proof	12,000	Value: 6.00				
1986B	5,031,000	—	—	—	2.50	3.50
1986B Proof	10,000	Value: 6.00				
1987B	10,028,000	—	—	—	1.75	2.75
1987B Proof	8,800	Value: 6.00				
1988B	5,029,000	—	—	—	2.50	3.50
1988B Proof	9,000	Value: 6.00				
1989B	10,031,000	—	—	—	1.75	2.75
1989B Proof	8,800	Value: 6.00				
1990B	20,032,000	—	—	—	1.75	2.75
1990B Proof	8,900	Value: 6.00				
1991B	10,036,000	—	—	—	1.75	2.75
1991B Proof	9,900	Value: 6.00				
1992B	30,028,000	—	—	—	1.75	2.75
1992B Proof	7,450	Value: 7.00				
1993B	13,023,000	—	—	—	1.75	2.75
1993B Proof	6,200	Value: 7.00				
1994B	15,023,000	—	—	—	1.75	3.00
1994B Proof	6,100	Value: 7.00				
1995B	10,024,000	—	—	—	2.50	3.50
1995B Proof	6,000	Value: 7.00				
1996B	8,023,000	—	—	—	2.50	3.50
1996B Proof	6,100	Value: 7.00				
1997B	6,022,000	—	—	—	2.50	3.50
1997B Proof	5,500	Value: 8.00				
1998B	6,021,000	—	—	—	2.50	3.50
1998B Proof	4,800	Value: 8.00				
1999B	5,021,000	—	—	—	2.50	3.50
1999B Proof	5,000	Value: 8.00				
2000B	4,026,000	—	—	—	2.50	3.50
2000B Proof	5,500	Value: 8.00				

KM# 24 FRANC

5.0000 g., 0.8350 Silver .1342 oz. ASW **Obv:** Standing Helvetia with lance and shield within star border **Rev:** Value, date within wreath **Edge:** A. Bovy

Date	Mintage	F	VF	XF	Unc	BU
1901B	400,000	3.00	8.00	75.00	400	1,250
1901B Specimen	—	—	—	—	—	3,000
1903B	1,000,000	2.00	3.50	20.00	120	250
1903B Specimen	—	—	—	—	—	1,200
1904B	400,000	5.00	10.00	150	900	2,500
1904B Specimen	—	—	—	—	—	4,800
1905B	700,000	2.00	3.50	25.00	180	350
1905B Specimen	—	—	—	—	—	1,200
1906B	700,000	2.00	3.50	40.00	275	500
1906B Specimen	—	—	—	—	—	1,200
1907B	800,000	2.00	3.50	40.00	275	500
1907B Specimen	—	—	—	—	—	1,200
1908B	1,200,000	2.00	3.50	10.00	110	225
1908B Specimen	—	—	—	—	—	1,200
1909B	900,000	2.00	3.50	10.00	110	200
1909B Specimen	—	—	—	—	—	1,200
1910B	1,000,000	2.00	3.50	9.00	100	200
1910B Specimen	—	—	—	—	—	1,200
1911B	1,200,000	2.00	3.50	8.00	70.00	120
1911B Specimen	—	—	—	—	—	900
1912B	1,200,000	2.00	3.50	6.00	60.00	110
1912B Specimen	—	—	—	—	—	750
1913B	1,200,000	2.00	3.50	6.00	60.00	110
1913B Specimen	—	—	—	—	—	900
1914B	4,200,000	2.00	3.50	5.00	25.00	50.00
1914B Specimen	—	—	—	—	—	600
1916B	1,000,000	2.00	3.50	7.00	60.00	100
1916B Specimen	—	—	—	—	—	1,050
1920B	3,300,000	2.00	3.00	5.00	20.00	40.00
1920B Specimen	—	—	—	—	—	180
1921B	3,800,000	2.00	3.00	5.00	20.00	40.00
1921B Specimen	—	—	—	—	—	180
1928B	1,500,000	2.00	3.00	5.00	20.00	30.00
1928B Specimen	—	—	—	—	—	240
1931B	1,000,000	2.00	3.00	5.00	30.00	50.00
1931B Specimen	—	—	—	—	—	240
1932B	500,000	2.00	3.50	7.00	65.00	175
1932B Specimen	—	—	—	—	—	480
1934B	500,000	2.00	3.50	7.50	65.00	175
1934B Specimen	—	—	—	—	—	480
1936B	500,000	2.00	3.50	6.50	45.00	100
1936B Specimen	—	—	—	—	—	360
1937B	1,000,000	2.00	3.00	5.00	20.00	35.00
1937B Specimen	—	—	—	—	—	240
1939B	2,106,000	2.00	3.00	5.00	10.00	15.00
1939B Specimen	—	—	—	—	—	150
1940B	2,003,000	2.00	3.00	5.00	10.00	18.00
1940B Specimen	—	—	—	—	—	150
1943B	3,526,000	2.00	3.00	4.00	7.00	10.00
1943B Specimen	—	—	—	—	—	150
1944B	6,225,000	2.00	3.00	4.00	7.00	10.00
1944B Specimen	—	—	—	—	—	150
1945B	7,794,000	2.00	3.00	4.00	7.00	10.00
1945B Specimen	—	—	—	—	—	150
1946B	2,539,000	2.00	3.00	4.00	9.00	13.00
1946B Specimen	—	—	—	—	—	150
1947B	624,000	2.50	3.00	5.00	15.00	25.00
1947B Specimen	—	—	—	—	—	150
1952B	2,853,000	2.00	3.00	4.00	6.00	9.00
1952B Specimen	—	—	—	—	—	120
1953B	786,000	2.50	3.00	5.00	15.00	25.00
1953B Specimen	—	—	—	—	—	120
1955B	194,000	3.00	4.00	10.00	20.00	30.00
1955B Specimen	—	—	—	—	—	120
1956B	2,500,000	—	—	3.00	4.50	7.00
1956B Specimen	—	—	—	—	—	90.00
1957B	6,421,000	—	—	3.00	4.50	7.00
1957B Specimen	—	—	—	—	—	45.00
1958B	3,580,000	—	—	3.00	4.50	7.00
1958B Specimen	—	—	—	—	—	45.00
1959B	1,859,000	—	—	3.00	4.50	7.00
1959B Specimen	—	—	—	—	—	45.00
1960B	3,523,000	—	—	2.00	4.50	7.00
1960B Specimen	—	—	—	—	—	45.00
1961B	6,549,000	—	—	2.50	4.00	6.00
1961B Specimen	—	—	—	—	—	45.00
1962B	6,220,000	—	—	2.50	4.00	6.00
1962B Specimen	—	—	—	—	—	45.00
1963B	13,476,000	—	—	2.50	3.50	5.50
1963B Specimen	—	—	—	—	—	45.00
1964B	12,560,000	—	—	2.50	3.50	5.50
1964B Specimen	—	—	—	—	—	45.00

Date	Mintage	F	VF	XF	Unc	BU
1965B	5,032,000	—	—	2.50	4.00	6.00
1965B Specimen	—	—	—	—	—	45.00
1966B	3,032,000	—	—	2.50	4.50	7.00
1966B Specimen	—	—	—	—	—	45.00
1967B	2,088,000	—	—	2.50	4.50	7.00
1967B Specimen	—	—	—	—	—	45.00

KM# 24a.1 FRANC

4.4000 g., Copper-Nickel, 23.1 mm. **Obv:** Standing Helvetia with lance and shield within star border **Rev:** Value within wreath **Edge:** Reeded **Designer:** A. Bovy

Date	Mintage	F	VF	XF	Unc	BU
1968	15,000,000	—	—	1.00	3.00	5.00
1968B	40,864,000	—	—	—	3.00	5.00
1969B	37,598,000	—	—	—	3.00	5.00
1970	24,240,000	—	—	—	3.00	5.00
1971	11,496,000	—	—	—	3.00	5.00
1973	5,000,000	—	—	—	4.00	7.00
1974	15,012,000	—	—	—	3.00	5.00
1974 Proof	2,400	Value: 85.00				
1975	13,012,000	—	—	—	3.00	5.00
1975 Proof	10,000	Value: 7.00				
1976	5,009,000	—	—	—	4.00	7.00
1976 Proof	5,130	Value: 8.00				
1977	6,019,000	—	—	—	4.00	7.00
1977 Proof	7,030	Value: 8.00				
1978	13,548,000	—	—	—	3.00	5.00
1978 Proof	10,000	Value: 7.00				
1979	10,800,000	—	—	—	3.00	5.00
1979 Proof	10,000	Value: 7.00				
1980	11,002,000	—	—	—	3.00	5.00
1980 Proof	10,000	Value: 7.00				
1981	18,013,000	—	—	—	3.00	5.00
1981 Proof	10,000	Value: 7.00				

KM# 24a.2 FRANC

4.4000 g., Copper-Nickel, 23.1 mm. **Obv:** 22 Stars around figure **Rev:** Value and date within wreath **Note:** Medal alignment.

Date	Mintage	F	VF	XF	Unc	BU
1982	15,039,000	—	—	—	3.50	6.00
1982 Proof	10,000	Value: 8.00				

KM# 24a.3 FRANC

4.4000 g., Copper-Nickel, 23.1 mm. **Obv:** 23 Stars around figure **Rev:** Value and date within wreath **Edge:** Reeded **Designer:** A. Bovy

Date	Mintage	F	VF	XF	Unc	BU
1983	7,018,000	—	—	—	3.00	5.00
1983 Proof	11,000	Value: 7.00				
1984	3,028,000	—	—	—	3.00	5.00
1984 Proof	14,000	Value: 7.00				
1985	20,042,000	—	—	—	3.00	5.00
1985 Proof	12,000	Value: 7.00				
1986B	17,997,000	—	—	—	3.00	5.00
1986B Proof	10,000	Value: 7.00				
1987B	17,028,000	—	—	—	3.00	5.00
1987B Proof	8,800	Value: 7.00				
1988B	18,029,000	—	—	—	3.00	5.00
1988B Proof	9,000	Value: 7.00				
1989B	15,031,000	—	—	—	3.00	5.00
1989B Proof	8,800	Value: 7.00				
1990B	2,032,000	—	—	—	4.00	7.00
1990B Proof	8,900	Value: 7.00				
1991B	9,036,000	—	—	—	3.00	5.00
1991B Proof	9,900	Value: 7.00				
1992B	12,028,000	—	—	—	3.00	5.00
1992B Proof	7,450	Value: 7.00				
1993B	12,023,000	—	—	—	3.00	5.00
1993B Proof	6,200	Value: 8.00				
1994B	10,023,000	—	—	—	3.00	5.00
1994B Proof	6,100	Value: 8.00				
1995B	13,024,000	—	—	—	3.00	5.00
1995B Proof	6,100	Value: 8.00				
1996B	3,023,000	—	—	—	3.50	6.00
1996B Proof	6,100	Value: 8.00				
1997B	3,022,000	—	—	—	3.50	6.00
1997B Proof	5,500	Value: 8.00				
1998B	3,021,000	—	—	—	3.50	6.00
1998B Proof	4,800	Value: 8.00				
1999B	3,021,000	—	—	—	3.50	6.00
1999B Proof	5,000	Value: 8.00				
2000B	4,026,000	—	—	—	3.50	6.00
2000B Proof	5,500	Value: 8.00				

KM# 21 2 FRANCS

10.0000 g., 0.8350 Silver .2685 oz. ASW **Obv:** Standing Helvetia with lance and shield within star border **Rev:** Value, date within wreath **Edge:** Reeded **Designer:** A. Bovy

Date	Mintage	F	VF	XF	Unc	BU
1901B	50,000	80.00	135	1,600	9,000	15,000
1901B Specimen; Rare	—	—	—	—	—	—
1903B	300,000	4.50	10.00	80.00	600	1,250
1903B Specimen	—	—	—	—	—	2,700
1904B	200,000	6.00	15.00	225	1,250	2,750
1904B Specimen	—	—	—	—	—	5,700
1905B	300,000	4.50	10.00	75.00	600	1,500
1905B Specimen	—	—	—	—	—	2,700
1906B	400,000	4.00	8.00	75.00	500	1,400
1906B Specimen	—	—	—	—	—	3,000
1907B	300,000	4.50	12.00	160	1,000	2,000
1907B Specimen	—	—	—	—	—	3,000
1908B	200,000	6.00	15.00	300	1,500	3,000
1908B Specimen	—	—	—	—	—	5,400
1909B	300,000	4.50	10.00	65.00	450	1,350
1909B Specimen	—	—	—	—	—	3,900
1910B	250,000	5.00	7.00	130	650	1,500
1910B Specimen	—	—	—	—	—	4,200
1911B	400,000	4.00	6.00	30.00	175	450
1911B Specimen	—	—	—	—	—	1,800
1912B	400,000	4.00	6.00	30.00	110	350
1912B Specimen	—	—	—	—	—	1,500
1913B	300,000	4.00	6.00	45.00	160	325
1913B Specimen	—	—	—	—	—	2,100
1914B	1,000,000	4.00	5.00	20.00	100	200
1914B Specimen	—	—	—	—	—	1,200
1916B	250,000	4.00	6.00	110	425	1,250
1916B Specimen	—	—	—	—	—	2,400
1920B	2,300,000	4.00	5.00	10.00	30.00	60.00
1920B Specimen	—	—	—	—	—	450
1921B	2,000,000	4.00	5.00	10.00	30.00	60.00
1921B Specimen	—	—	—	—	—	450
1922B	400,000	4.00	6.00	27.50	175	350
1922B Specimen	—	—	—	—	—	1,200
1928B	750,000	4.00	5.00	10.00	30.00	60.00
1928B Specimen	—	—	—	—	—	450
1931B	500,000	4.00	5.00	10.00	40.00	75.00
1931B Specimen	—	—	—	—	—	450
1932B	250,000	4.00	5.00	30.00	185	400
1932B Specimen	—	—	—	—	—	1,050
1936B	250,000	4.00	5.00	20.00	100	180
1936B Specimen	—	—	—	—	—	600
1937B	250,000	4.00	5.00	14.00	65.00	125
1937B Specimen	—	—	—	—	—	450
1939B	1,455,000	—	4.00	6.00	12.00	20.00
1939B Specimen	—	—	—	—	—	600
1940B	2,503,000	—	4.00	6.00	11.00	18.00
1940B Specimen	—	—	—	—	—	180
1941B	1,192,000	—	4.00	6.00	15.00	25.00
1941B Specimen	—	—	—	—	—	180
1943B	2,089,000	—	4.00	5.00	14.00	20.00
1943B Specimen	—	—	—	—	—	180
1944B	6,276,000	—	4.00	5.00	9.00	15.00
1944B Specimen	—	—	—	—	—	180
1945B	1,134,000	—	4.00	10.00	21.00	35.00
1945B Specimen	—	—	—	—	—	180
1946B	1,629,000	—	4.00	8.00	14.00	20.00
1946B Specimen	—	—	—	—	—	180
1947B	500,000	4.00	5.00	10.00	30.00	45.00
1947B Specimen	—	—	—	—	—	180
1948B	920,000	—	4.00	7.00	15.00	25.00
1948B Specimen	—	—	—	—	—	180
1953B	438,000	4.00	5.00	10.00	32.00	55.00
1953B Specimen	—	—	—	—	—	180
1955B	1,032,000	—	4.00	5.00	10.00	18.00
1955B Specimen	—	—	—	—	—	150
1957B	2,298,000	—	4.00	5.00	7.00	12.00
1957B Specimen	—	—	—	—	—	60.00
1958B	650,000	—	4.00	5.00	7.00	12.00
1958B Specimen	—	—	—	—	—	60.00
1959B	2,905,000	—	4.00	4.50	7.00	12.00
1959B Specimen	—	—	—	—	—	60.00
1960B	1,980,000	—	—	4.00	7.00	12.00
1960B Specimen	—	—	—	—	—	60.00
1961B	4,653,000	—	—	4.00	6.00	9.00
1961B Specimen	—	—	—	—	—	60.00
1963B	8,030,000	—	—	4.00	6.00	9.00
1963B Specimen	—	—	—	—	—	60.00
1964B	4,558,000	—	—	4.00	6.00	9.00
1964B Specimen	—	—	—	—	—	60.00
1965B	8,526,000	—	—	4.00	6.00	9.00
1965B Specimen	—	—	—	—	—	60.00
1967B	4,132,000	—	—	4.00	6.00	9.00
1967B Specimen	—	—	—	—	—	60.00

KM# 21a.1 2 FRANCS

8.8000 g., Copper-Nickel, 27.4 mm. **Obv:** Standing Helvetia with lance and shield within star border **Rev:** Value within wreath **Edge:** Reeded **Designer:** A. Bovy

Date	Mintage	F	VF	XF	Unc	BU
1968	10,000,000	—	—	—	5.00	8.00
1968B	31,588,000	—	—	—	4.50	7.50
1969B	17,296,000	—	—	—	4.50	7.50
1970	10,350,000	—	—	—	4.50	7.50
1972	5,003,000	—	—	—	4.50	7.50
1973	5,996,000	—	—	—	4.50	7.50
1974	15,009,000	—	—	—	5.00	8.00
1974 Proof	2,400	Value: 85.00				
1975	7,061,000	—	—	—	5.00	8.00
1975 Proof	10,000	Value: 12.00				
1976	5,011,000	—	—	—	5.00	8.00
1976 Proof	5,130	Value: 15.00				
1977	2,010,000	—	—	—	6.00	10.00
1977 Proof	7,030	Value: 15.00				
1978	12,812,000	—	—	—	5.00	8.00
1978 Proof	10,000	Value: 12.00				
1979	10,995,000	—	—	—	5.00	8.00
1979 Proof	10,000	Value: 12.00				
1980	10,001,000	—	—	—	5.00	6.00
1980 Proof	10,000	Value: 12.00				
1981	13,852,000	—	—	—	5.00	8.00
1981 Proof	10,000	Value: 12.00				

KM# 21a.2 2 FRANCS

8.8000 g., Copper-Nickel, 27.4 mm. **Obv:** 22 Stars around figure **Rev:** Value within wreath **Note:** Medal alignment.

Date	Mintage	F	VF	XF	Unc	BU
1982	5,912,000	—	—	—	4.50	7.50
1982 Proof	10,000	Value: 15.00				

KM# 21a.3 2 FRANCS

8.8000 g., Copper-Nickel, 27.4 mm. **Obv:** 23 Stars around figure **Rev:** Value within wreath

Date	Mintage	F	VF	XF	Unc	BU
1983	3,023,000	—	—	—	5.00	8.00
1983 Proof	11,000	Value: 12.00				
1984	2,029,000	—	—	—	5.00	8.00
1984 Proof	14,000	Value: 12.00				
1985	2,022,000	—	—	—	5.00	8.00
1985 Proof	12,000	Value: 12.00				
1986B	3,032,000	—	—	—	5.00	8.00
1986B Proof	10,000	Value: 12.00				
1987B	8,028,000	—	—	—	3.50	6.00
1987B Proof	8,800	Value: 15.00				
1988B	10,029,000	—	—	—	3.50	6.00
1988B Proof	9,000	Value: 12.00				
1989B	8,031,000	—	—	—	3.50	6.00
1989B Proof	8,800	Value: 12.00				
1990B	5,045,000	—	—	—	4.00	7.00
1990B Proof	8,900	Value: 12.00				
1991B	12,036,000	—	—	—	3.50	6.00
1991B Proof	9,900	Value: 12.00				
1992B	10,028,000	—	—	—	3.50	6.00
1992B Proof	7,450	Value: 15.00				
1993B	13,050,000	—	—	—	3.50	6.00
1993B Proof	6,200	Value: 15.00				
1994B	16,023,000	—	—	—	3.50	6.00
1994B Proof	6,100	Value: 15.00				
1995B	7,024,000	—	—	—	3.50	6.00
1995B Proof	6,100	Value: 15.00				
1996B	5,023,000	—	—	—	4.00	7.00
1996B Proof	6,100	Value: 15.00				
1997B	5,022,000	—	—	—	4.00	7.00
1997B Proof	5,500	Value: 15.00				
1998B	4,021,000	—	—	—	4.00	7.00
1998B Proof	4,800	Value: 15.00				
1999B	3,021,000	—	—	—	5.00	8.00
1999B Proof	5,000	Value: 15.00				
2000B	3,026,000	—	—	—	5.00	8.00
2000B Proof	5,500	Value: 15.00				

KM# 34 5 FRANCS
25.0000 g., 0.9000 Silver .7234 oz. ASW **Obv:** Laureate head left **Obv. Legend:** CONFOEDERATIO HELVETICA **Rev:** Shield divides value within wreath, star above

Date	Mintage	F	VF	XF	Unc	BU
1904B	40,000	225	600	900	3,000	5,500
1904B Specimen	—	—	—	—	—	9,000
1907B	277,000	60.00	100	200	800	2,000
1907B Specimen	—	—	—	—	—	4,500
1908B	200,000	75.00	125	250	800	2,000
1908B Specimen	—	—	—	—	—	4,500
1909B	120,000	100	180	300	850	2,100
1909B Specimen	—	—	—	—	—	4,500
1912B	11,000	1,500	2,200	3,500	7,000	10,000
1912B Specimen	—	—	—	—	—	15,000
1916B	22,000	500	900	1,250	2,500	4,000
1916B Specimen	—	—	—	—	—	7,500

KM# 37 5 FRANCS
25.0000 g., 0.9000 Silver .7234 oz. ASW **Obv:** William Tell right **Rev:** Shield flanked by sprigs

Date	Mintage	F	VF	XF	Unc	BU
1922B	2,400,000	40.00	55.00	90.00	275	400
1922B	Inc. above	—	—	1,500	2,000	2,500
Note: Dot between Confoederatio and Helvetica						
1922B Specimen	—	—	—	—	—	2,000
1923B	11,300,000	25.00	35.00	70.00	120	325
1923B Specimen	—	—	—	—	—	3,000

KM# 38 5 FRANCS
25.0000 g., 0.9000 Silver .7234 oz. ASW **Obv:** William Tell right **Rev:** Shield flanked by sprigs

Date	Mintage	F	VF	XF	Unc	BU
1924B	182,000	150	250	400	900	2,000
1924B Specimen	—	—	—	—	—	3,000
1925B	2,830,000	40.00	60.00	90.00	225	450
1925B Specimen	—	—	—	—	—	1,500
1926B	2,000,000	50.00	90.00	125	250	475
1926B Specimen	—	—	—	—	—	1,500
1928B	24,000	3,500	6,500	8,500	14,000	20,000
1928B Specimen; Rare	—	—	—	—	—	—

KM# 40 5 FRANCS
15.0000 g., 0.8350 Silver .4027 oz. ASW, 31.5 mm. **Obv:** William Tell right **Rev:** Shield flanked by sprigs **Edge:** Lettered; two variations **Edge Lettering:** Lettering starts with vertical dividing line and group of three stars. Type I; "3 stars/DOMINUS/PROVIDEBIT/10 stars" Type II; "3 stars/DOMINUS/10 stars/PROVIDEBIT" **Note:** Raised edge lettering.

Date	Mintage	F	VF	XF	Unc	BU
1931B	3,520,000	5.50	8.00	25.00	100	130
Note: Edge lettering type I starts at 6 o'clock						
1931B	Inc. above	—	10.00	30.00	75.00	110
Note: Edge lettering type II starts at 6 o'clock						
1931B Specimen	Inc. above	—	—	—	—	900
Note: Edge lettering type I starts at 6 o'clock						
1931B	Inc. above	—	25.00	50.00	200	350
Note: Edge lettering type I starts at 2 o'clock						
1931B Edge word	Inc. above	—	800	1,200	1,500	2,500
Note: Edge lettering type II starts at 10 o'clock						
1932B	10,580,000	5.50	6.00	10.00	16.00	30.00
1932B Specimen	—	—	—	—	—	450
1933B	5,900,000	5.50	7.00	10.00	22.00	40.00
1933B Specimen	—	—	—	—	—	450
1935B	3,000,000	5.50	6.00	12.00	30.00	50.00
1935B Specimen	—	—	—	—	—	450
1937B	645,000	6.00	9.00	15.00	60.00	110
1937B Specimen	—	—	—	—	—	900
1939B	2,197,000	5.50	7.00	12.00	22.00	40.00
1939B Specimen	—	—	—	—	—	450
1940B	1,601,000	5.50	7.00	18.00	40.00	70.00
1940B Specimen	—	—	—	—	—	600
1948B	416,000	6.00	9.00	18.00	50.00	80.00
1948B Specimen	—	—	—	—	—	600
1949B	407,000	6.00	9.00	18.00	55.00	90.00
1949B Specimen	—	—	—	—	—	600
1950B	482,000	6.00	9.00	18.00	45.00	70.00
1950B Specimen	—	—	—	—	—	600
1951B	1,096,000	5.50	8.00	16.00	30.00	50.00
1951B Specimen	—	—	—	—	—	300
1952B	155,000	10.00	50.00	90.00	170	300
1952B Specimen	—	—	—	—	—	750
1953B	3,403,000	5.50	6.00	9.00	15.00	25.00
1953B Specimen	—	—	—	—	—	150
1954B	6,600,000	5.50	5.75	7.00	14.00	22.00
1954B Specimen	—	—	—	—	—	150
1965B	5,021,000	5.50	5.75	6.00	9.00	16.00
1965B Specimen	—	—	—	—	—	120
1966B	9,016,000	5.50	5.75	6.00	7.00	15.00
1966B Specimen	—	—	—	—	—	120
1967B	13,817,000	5.50	5.75	6.00	7.00	15.00
Note: Edge lettering type I starts at 6 o'clock						
1967B Specimen	—	—	—	—	—	120
Note: Edge lettering type I starting at 6 o'clock						
1967B Three stars group of edge in front of face	Inc. above	15.00	40.00	70.00	125	200
Note: Edge lettering type II starts at 2 o'clock						
1969B	8,637,000	5.50	5.75	6.00	8.00	14.00
1969B Specimen	—	—	—	—	—	120

KM# A48 5 FRANCS
Gold

Date	Mintage	F	VF	XF	Unc	BU
1948B	Est. 50	—	—	—	15,000	—

KM# 40a.1 5 FRANCS
13.2000 g., Copper-Nickel, 31.3 mm. **Obv:** William Tell right **Rev:** Shield flanked by sprigs **Edge Lettering:** DOMINUS PROVIDEBIT

Date	Mintage	F	VF	XF	Unc	BU
1968B	33,871,000	—	—	—	7.00	10.00
1970	6,306,000	—	—	—	8.00	12.00
1973	5,002,000	—	—	—	8.00	12.00
1974	6,007,000	—	—	—	8.00	12.00
1974 Proof	2,400	Value: 125				
1975	4,015,000	—	—	—	8.00	12.00
1975 Proof	10,000	Value: 20.00				
1976	3,007,000	—	—	—	8.00	12.00
1976 Proof	5,130	Value: 20.00				
1977	2,009,000	—	—	5.00	9.00	14.00
1977 Proof	7,030	Value: 20.00				
1978	4,411,000	—	—	—	8.00	12.00
1978 Proof	10,000	Value: 16.00				
1979	4,011,000	—	—	—	8.00	12.00
1979 Proof	10,000	Value: 16.00				
1980	4,026,000	—	—	—	8.00	12.00
1980 Proof	10,000	Value: 16.00				
1981	6,018,000	—	—	—	8.00	12.00
1981 Proof	10,000	Value: 16.00				

KM# 40a.2 5 FRANCS
13.2000 g., Copper-Nickel, 31.3 mm. **Obv:** William Tell right **Rev:** Cross on shield flanked by sprigs **Note:** Medal alignment.

Date	Mintage	F	VF	XF	Unc	BU
1982	5,050,000	—	—	—	8.00	12.00
1982 Proof	10,000	Value: 20.00				
1983	4,033,000	—	—	—	8.00	12.00
1983 Proof	11,000	Value: 20.00				
1984	3,953,000	—	—	—	8.00	12.00
1984 Proof	14,000	Value: 16.00				

KM# 40a.3 5 FRANCS
13.2000 g., Copper-Nickel, 31.3 mm. **Obv:** William Tell right **Rev:** Shield flanked by sprigs **Note:** Incuse edge lettering. Retired legal tender status as of January 1, 2004, 1985-1993 removed from circulation.

Date	Mintage	F	VF	XF	Unc	BU
1985	4,050,000	—	—	—	8.00	12.00
1985 Proof	12,000	Value: 16.00				
1986B	7,083,000	—	—	—	8.00	12.00
1986B Proof	10,000	Value: 16.00				
1987B	7,028,000	—	—	—	8.00	12.00
1987B Proof	8,800	Value: 20.00				
1988B	7,029,000	—	—	—	8.00	12.00
1988B Proof	9,000	Value: 20.00				
1989B	5,031,000	—	—	—	8.00	12.00
1989B Proof	8,800	Value: 20.00				
1990B	1,049,000	—	—	5.00	10.00	12.00
1990B Proof	8,900	Value: 20.00				
1991B	37,000	—	—	—	—	130
Note: In sets only						
1991B Proof	9,900	Value: 135				
1992B	5,035,000	—	—	—	8.00	12.00
1992B Proof	7,450	Value: 20.00				
1993B Variety 2 open shirt	Inc. above	—	—	—	—	135
1993B Variety 1 closed shirt	22,700	—	—	—	—	135
Note: In sets only; 5,000,000 were minted and destroyed						
1993B Proof	6,200	Value: 140				

KM# 40a.4 5 FRANCS
13.2000 g., Copper-Nickel, 31.3 mm. **Obv:** William Tell right **Rev:** Shield flanked by sprigs **Edge:** Raised lettering

Date	Mintage	F	VF	XF	Unc	BU
1994B	12,023,000	—	—	—	7.00	10.00
1994B Proof	6,100	Value: 20.00				
1995B	12,024,000	—	—	—	7.00	10.00
1995B Proof	6,100	Value: 20.00				
1996B	12,023,000	—	—	—	7.00	10.00
1996B Proof	6,100	Value: 20.00				
1997B	9,022,000	—	—	—	7.00	10.00
1997B Proof	5,500	Value: 20.00				
1998B	9,021,000	—	—	—	7.00	10.00
1998B Proof	4,800	Value: 22.50				
1999B	9,021,000	—	—	—	7.00	10.00
1999B Proof	5,000	Value: 22.50				
2000B	7,026,000	—	—	—	7.00	10.00
2000B Proof	5,500	Value: 20.00				

KM# 36 10 FRANCS
3.2258 g., 0.9000 Gold .0933 oz. AGW **Obv:** Young bust left **Rev:** Radiant cross above date and sprigs **Designer:** Fritz Ulysse Landry

Date	Mintage	F	VF	XF	Unc	BU
1911B	100,000	75.00	150	250	350	500
1912B	200,000	—	BV	75.00	125	175
1913B	600,000	—	BV	70.00	95.00	150
1914B	200,000	—	BV	75.00	115	160
1915B	400,000	—	BV	70.00	100	125
1916B	130,000	—	BV	75.00	115	160
1922B	1,020,000	—	—	BV	70.00	95.00

KM# 35.1 20 FRANCS
6.4516 g., 0.9000 Gold .1867 oz. AGW **Obv:** Young head left **Obv. Legend:** HELVETIA **Rev:** Shield within oak branches divides value **Designer:** Fritz Ulysse Landry

Date	Mintage	F	VF	XF	Unc	BU
1901B	500,000	—	—	BV	140	175
1902B	600,000	—	—	BV	140	175
1903B	200,000	—	—	BV	145	190
1904B	100,000	—	BV	150	200	225
1905B	100,000	—	BV	150	200	225
1906B	100,000	—	BV	150	200	225
1907B	150,000	—	—	BV	140	185
1908B	355,000	—	—	—	135	175
1909B	400,000	—	—	—	135	175
1910B	375,000	—	—	—	135	175
1911B	350,000	—	—	—	135	175
1912B	450,000	—	—	—	135	175
1913B	700,000	—	—	—	135	175
1914B	700,000	—	—	—	135	175
1915B	750,000	—	—	—	135	175
1916B	300,000	—	—	—	135	175
1922B	2,783,678	—	—	—	BV	135
1925B	400,000	—	—	—	135	150
1926B	50,000	BV	125	150	165	210
1927B	5,015,000	—	—	—	BV	150
1930B	3,371,764	—	—	—	BV	150
1935B	175,000	—	—	BV	150	185
1935L-B	20,008,813	—	—	—	BV	135

Note: The 1935L-B issue was struck in 1945, 1946 and 1947

KM# 35.2 20 FRANCS
6.4516 g., 0.9000 Gold .1867 oz. AGW **Obv:** Bust left **Rev:** Shield within oak branches divides value **Edge Lettering:** AD LEGEM ANNI MCMXXXI

Date	Mintage	F	VF	XF	Unc	BU
1947B	9,200,000	—	—	—	BV	145
1949B	10,000,000	—	—	—	BV	145

KM# 49 25 FRANCS
5.6450 g., 0.9000 Gold .1634 oz. AGW **Obv:** Value above small cross **Rev:** William Tell with bow **Note:** Not available in commercial channels.

Date	Mintage	F	VF	XF	Unc	BU
1955B	5,000,000	—	—	—	—	—
1958B	5,000,000	—	—	—	—	—
1959B	5,000,000	—	—	—	—	—

KM# 50 50 FRANCS
11.2900 g., 0.9000 Gold .3267 oz. AGW **Obv:** Value above small cross **Rev:** Three standing figures facing **Note:** Not available in commercial channels.

Date	Mintage	F	VF	XF	Unc	BU
1955B	2,000,000	—	—	—	—	—
1958B	2,000,000	—	—	—	—	—
1959B	2,000,000	—	—	—	—	—

KM# 39 100 FRANCS
32.2581 g., 0.9000 Gold .9334 oz. AGW **Obv:** Young bust left **Rev:** Radiant cross above value, date and sprigs **Designer:** Fritz Ulysse Landry

Date	Mintage	F	VF	XF	Unc	BU
1925B	5,000	—	4,000	6,000	7,500	10,000

COMMEMORATIVE COINAGE

KM# 41 5 FRANCS
15.0000 g., 0.8350 Silver .4027 oz. ASW, 31 mm. **Subject:** Confederation Armament Fund **Obv:** Kneeling female figure holding sword and dove right **Rev:** Inscription within square flanked by oak leaves **Edge:** DOMINUS PROVIDEBIT (stars) **Designer:** Max Weber

Date	Mintage	F	VF	XF	Unc	BU
1936B	130,000	—	10.00	15.00	25.00	40.00
1936B Specimen	—	—	—	—	—	300

KM# 42 5 FRANCS
15.0000 g., 0.8350 Silver .4027 oz. ASW, 31 mm. **Subject:** 600th Anniversary - Battle of Laupen **Obv:** Seated hooded figure facing right **Rev:** Cross, date and value **Edge Lettering:** DOMINUS PROVIDEBIT (stars) **Designer:** Remo Rossi

Date	Mintage	F	VF	XF	Unc	BU
1939B	30,600	—	150	250	350	500

KM# 43 5 FRANCS
15.0000 g., 0.8350 Silver .4027 oz. ASW, 31 mm. **Subject:** Zurich Exposition **Obv:** Small cross on shield above inscription **Rev:** Shaking hands below standing figures with horse

Date	Mintage	F	VF	XF	Unc	BU
1939B	60,000	—	30.00	50.00	70.00	100
Note: Minted at Huguenin, Le Locle						
1939 Specimen	—	—	—	—	—	900
1939B Matte	Est. 250	—	—	1,500	1,850	2,250

KM# 44 5 FRANCS
15.0000 g., 0.8350 Silver .4027 oz. ASW, 31 mm. **Subject:** 650th Anniversary of Confederation **Obv:** Three standing figures representing the original cantons of Uri, Schwyz and Unterwalden **Rev:** Small cross divides dates above inscription **Edge Lettering:** DOMINUS PROVIDEBIT (stars) **Designer:** Ernst Suter

Date	Mintage	F	VF	XF	Unc	BU
ND(1941)B	100,150	9.00	20.00	30.00	45.00	70.00
ND(1941)B Specimen	—	—	—	—	—	360

KM# 45 5 FRANCS
15.0000 g., 0.8350 Silver .4027 oz. ASW, 31 mm. **Subject:** 500th Anniversary - Battle of St. Jakob An Der Birs **Obv:** Kneeling figure looking right **Rev:** Small cross above inscription **Edge Lettering:** DOMINUS PROVIDEBIT (stars) **Designer:** E. Wiederkehr

Date	Mintage	F	VF	XF	Unc	BU
1944B	101,680	10.00	20.00	28.00	40.00	60.00
1944B Specimen	—	—	—	—	—	360

KM# 48 5 FRANCS
15.0000 g., 0.8350 Silver .4027 oz. ASW, 31 mm. **Subject:** Swiss Constitution Centennial **Obv:** Seated woman and child facing left **Rev:** Small cross divides date below inscription **Designer:** Max Weber

Date	Mintage	F	VF	XF	Unc	BU
1948B	500,400	5.50	5.75	7.00	10.00	15.00
1948B Specimen	—	—	—	—	—	150

KM# 51 5 FRANCS
Silver, 31 mm. **Subject:** Red Cross Centennial **Obv:** Value **Rev:** Nurse standing, patient on stretcher, motif forming a cross

Date	Mintage	F	VF	XF	Unc	BU
ND(1963)B	623,000	5.50	5.75	6.00	9.00	15.00
ND(1963)B Specimen	—	—	—	—	—	120

KM# 52 5 FRANCS
13.2000 g., Copper-Nickel, 31.3 mm. **Subject:** 100th Anniversary - Revision of Constitution **Obv:** Dates flanked by vertical inscriptions **Rev:** Three standing female figures and cross **Designer:** Max Weber

Date	Mintage	F	VF	XF	Unc	BU
ND(1974)	3,709,000	—	—	—	7.00	10.00
ND(1974) Proof	130,000	Value: 14.00				

KM# 53 5 FRANCS
13.2000 g., Copper-Nickel, 31.3 mm. **Subject:** European Monument Protection Year **Obv:** Value and inscription **Rev:** Date above inscription flanked by hands

Date	Mintage	F	VF	XF	Unc	BU
1975	2,500,000	—	—	—	7.00	10.00
1975 Proof	60,000	Value: 15.00				

KM# 54 5 FRANCS
13.2000 g., Copper-Nickel, 31.3 mm. **Subject:** 500th Anniversary - Battle of Murten **Obv:** Value **Rev:** Stylized figures

Date	Mintage	F	VF	XF	Unc	BU
1976	1,506,000	—	—	—	7.00	10.00
1976 Proof	100,900	Value: 14.00				

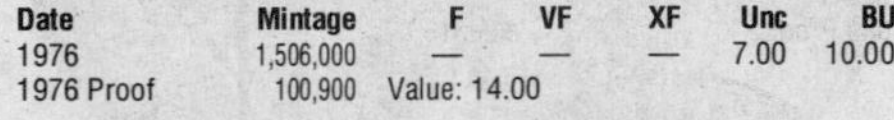

KM# 55 5 FRANCS
13.2000 g., Copper-Nickel, 31.3 mm. **Subject:** 150th Anniversary - Death of Johann Pestalozzi **Obv:** Value and cross at center **Rev:** Hooded head left

Date	Mintage	F	VF	XF	Unc	BU
1977	802,000	—	—	—	7.00	10.00
1977 Proof	50,260	Value: 15.00				

KM# 56 5 FRANCS
13.2000 g., Copper-Nickel, 31.3 mm. **Subject:** 150th Anniversary - Birth of Henry Dunant, founder of the International Red Cross **Obv:** Value and date **Rev:** Head facing

Date	Mintage	F	VF	XF	Unc	BU
1978	903,000	—	—	—	7.00	10.00
1978 Proof	60,000	Value: 14.00				

KM# 57 5 FRANCS
13.2000 g., Copper-Nickel, 31.3 mm. **Subject:** Centennial - Birth of Albert Einstein **Obv:** Inscription, value and date **Rev:** Head facing

Date	Mintage	F	VF	XF	Unc	BU
1979	900,000	—	—	—	7.00	10.00
1979 Proof	35,000	Value: 50.00				

KM# 58 5 FRANCS
13.2000 g., Copper-Nickel, 31.3 mm. **Subject:** Centennial - Birth of Albert Einstein **Obv:** Inscription above value **Rev:** Formulas

Date	Mintage	F	VF	XF	Unc	BU
1979	902,000	—	—	—	7.00	10.00
1979 Proof	35,000	Value: 50.00				

KM# 59 5 FRANCS
13.2000 g., Copper-Nickel, 31.3 mm. **Subject:** Ferdinand Hodler - Painter **Obv:** Value above legend and date **Rev:** Head facing

Date	Mintage	F	VF	XF	Unc	BU
1980	951,000	—	—	—	7.00	10.00
1980 Proof	50,000	Value: 15.00				

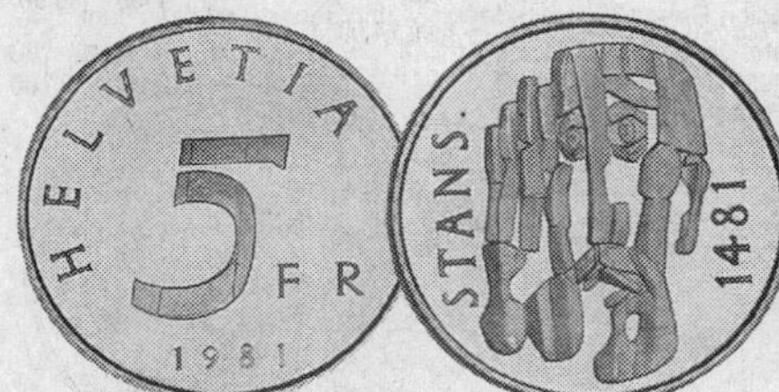

KM# 60 5 FRANCS
13.2000 g., Copper-Nickel, 31.3 mm. **Subject:** 500th Anniversary - Stans Convention of 1481 **Obv:** Value and date **Rev:** Stylized design

Date	Mintage	F	VF	XF	Unc	BU
1981	950,000	—	—	—	7.00	10.00
1981 Proof	50,260	Value: 14.00				

KM# 61 5 FRANCS
13.2000 g., Copper-Nickel, 31.3 mm. **Subject:** 100th Anniversary - Gotthard Railway **Obv:** Value and date above sprigs **Rev:** Stylized design **Edge:** Lettering in relief **Edge Lettering:** DOMINUS PROVIDEBIT (stars)

Date	Mintage	F	VF	XF	Unc	BU
1982	1,105,000	—	—	—	8.00	12.00
1982 Proof	65,110	Value: 18.00				

KM# 62 5 FRANCS
13.2000 g., Copper-Nickel, 31.3 mm. **Subject:** 100th Anniversary - Birth of Ernest Ansermet **Obv:** Value and date **Rev:** Music notes within head right **Designer:** Jean Lacoultre

Date	Mintage	F	VF	XF	Unc	BU
1983	951,000	—	—	—	8.00	12.00
1983 Proof	60,160	Value: 16.00				

KM# 63 5 FRANCS
13.2000 g., Copper-Nickel, 31.3 mm. **Subject:** Centennial - Birth of Auguste Piccard **Obv:** Value and date **Rev:** Stylized designs **Designer:** Hugo Suter

Date	Mintage	F	VF	XF	Unc	BU
1984	1,012,000	—	—	—	8.00	12.00
1984 Proof	75,000	Value: 16.00				

KM# 64 5 FRANCS
13.2000 g., Copper-Nickel, 31.3 mm. **Subject:** European Year of Music **Obv:** Value and vertical inscription **Rev:** Sphere design **Edge Lettering:** DOMINUS PROVIDEBIT (stars) **Designer:** Angela Baccini

Date	Mintage	F	VF	XF	Unc	BU
1985	1,156,000	—	—	—	8.00	12.00
1985 Proof	84,000	Value: 16.00				

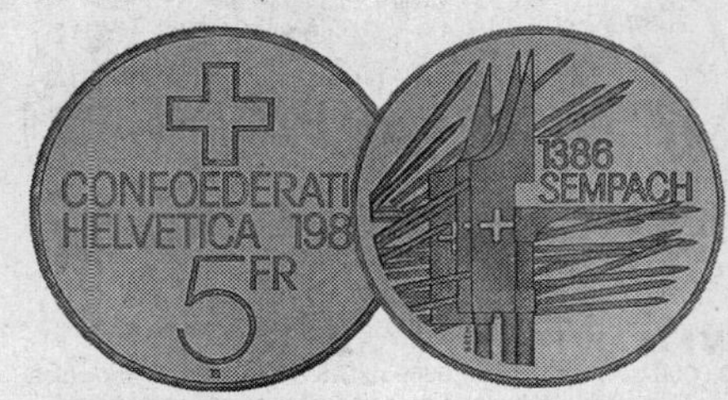

KM# 65 5 FRANCS
13.2000 g., Copper-Nickel, 31.3 mm. **Subject:** 500th Anniversary - Battle of Sempach **Obv:** Cross above inscription and date **Rev:** Stylized design

Date	Mintage	F	VF	XF	Unc	BU
1986B	1,082,000	—	—	—	8.00	12.00
1986B Proof	75,000	Value: 16.00				

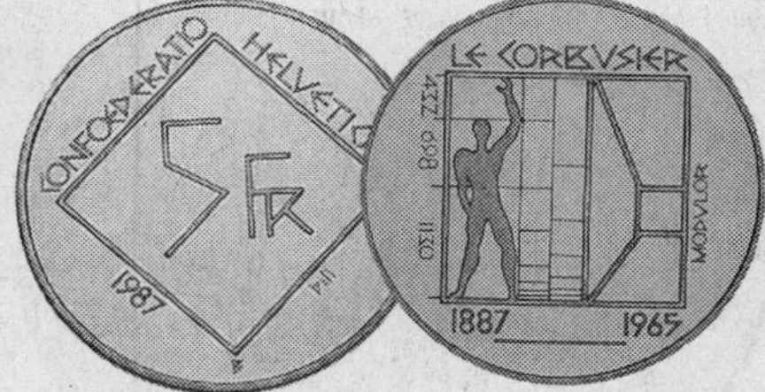

KM# 66 5 FRANCS
13.2000 g., Copper-Nickel, 31.3 mm. **Subject:** 100th Anniversary - Birth of Le Corbusier **Obv:** Value within diamond shape **Rev:** Standing figure within squared design **Designer:** Max Bill

Date	Mintage	F	VF	XF	Unc	BU
1987B	960,000	—	—	—	8.00	12.00
1987B Proof	62,000	Value: 16.00				

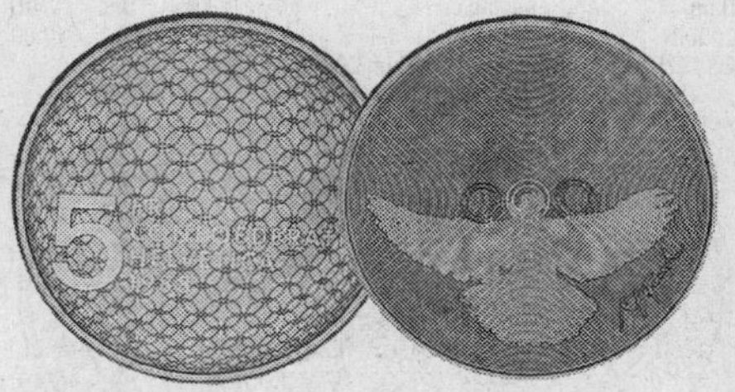

KM# 67 5 FRANCS
13.2000 g., Copper-Nickel, 31.3 mm. **Subject:** Olympics - Dove and Rings **Obv:** Value within entwined circles **Rev:** Stylized dove and circles

Date	Mintage	F	VF	XF	Unc	BU
1988B	1,026,000	—	—	—	8.00	14.00
1988B Proof	68,500	Value: 18.00				

KM# 68 5 FRANCS
13.2000 g., Copper-Nickel, 31.3 mm. **Subject:** General Guisan - 1939 Mobilization **Obv:** Value within cluster of small crosses **Rev:** Stylized head with cap facing 1/4 left

Date	Mintage	F	VF	XF	Unc	BU
1989B	1,270,000	—	—	—	10.00	16.00
1989B Proof	69,000	Value: 20.00				

KM# 69 5 FRANCS
13.2000 g., Copper-Nickel, 31.3 mm. **Subject:** Gottfried Keller **Obv:** Value, inscription and date **Rev:** Bust left

Date	Mintage	F	VF	XF	Unc	BU
1990B	1,100,000	—	—	—	8.00	12.00
1990B Proof	69,400	Value: 16.00				

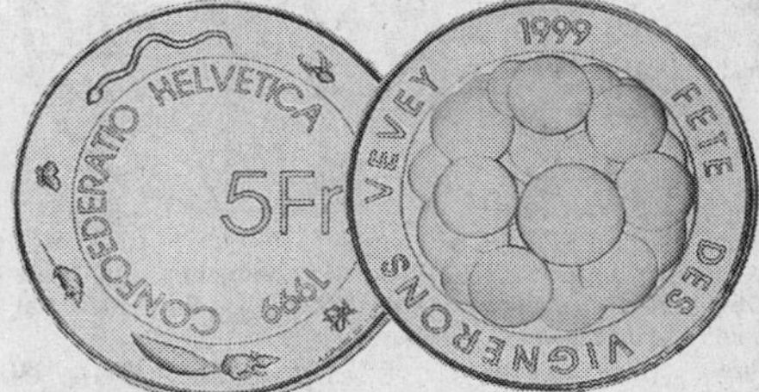

KM# 86 5 FRANCS
14.9100 g., Bi-Metallic Gold center in Copper-Nickel ring, 33 mm.

Subject: Wine Festival **Obv:** Value and inscription within circle, assorted rodents around border **Rev:** Grapes within circle

Date	Mintage	F	VF	XF	Unc	BU
1999B	160,000	—	—	—	8.00	12.00
1999B Proof	16,000	Value: 20.00				

KM# 89 5 FRANCS

15.0000 g., Bi-Metallic Brass center in Copper-Nickel ring, 33 mm. **Subject:** Basler Fasnacht **Obv:** Value within circle **Rev:** Costumed flutists within circle **Edge:** Reeded

Date	Mintage	F	VF	XF	Unc	BU
2000B	170,000	—	—	—	8.00	12.00
2000B Proof	20,000	Value: 20.00				

KM# 91 5 FRANCS

15.0000 g., Bi-Metallic Gold center in Copper-Nickel ring, 33 mm. **Subject:** Swiss National Coinage, 150 Years **Obv:** Value within detailed leaf surface showing vein structure **Rev:** Honeycomb design within circle **Edge:** Reeded

Date	Mintage	F	VF	XF	Unc	BU
2000B	150,000	—	—	—	8.00	12.00
2000B Proof	15,000	Value: 25.00				

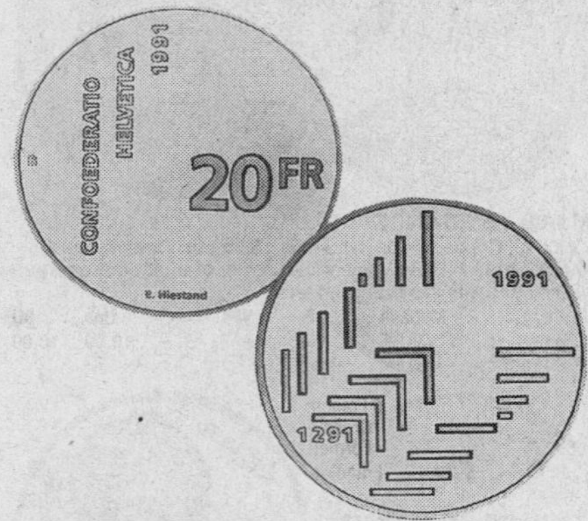

KM# 70 20 FRANCS

20.0000 g., 0.8350 Silver .5369 oz. ASW **Subject:** 700 Years of Confederation **Obv:** Value **Rev:** Dates and designs

Date	Mintage	F	VF	XF	Unc	BU
1991B	2,440,000	—	—	—	20.00	25.00
1991B Proof	100,000	Value: 30.00				

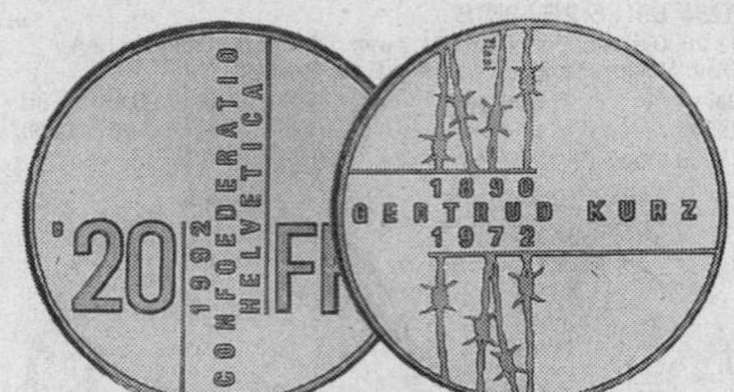

KM# 72 20 FRANCS

20.0000 g., 0.8350 Silver .5369 oz. ASW **Subject:** Gertrud Kurz **Obv:** Vertical inscription and date divides value **Rev:** Horizontal dates and inscription divides barbed wire

Date	Mintage	F	VF	XF	Unc	BU
1992B	325,000	—	—	—	20.00	25.00
1992B Proof	36,000	Value: 33.00				

KM# 73 20 FRANCS

20.0000 g., 0.8350 Silver .5369 oz. ASW **Subject:** 500th Anniversary - Birth of Paracelsus **Obv:** Value and date **Rev:** Head 1/4 left

Date	Mintage	F	VF	XF	Unc	BU
1993B	260,000	—	—	—	20.00	25.00
1993B Proof	30,000	Value: 35.00				

KM# 74 20 FRANCS

20.0000 g., 0.8350 Silver .5369 oz. ASW **Subject:** Devil's Bridge - Teufelsbrucke **Obv:** Value and date at center of large cross **Rev:** Stylized devil within trees **Edge Lettering:** DOMINUS PROVIDEBEIT

Date	Mintage	F	VF	XF	Unc	BU
1994B	240,000	—	—	—	22.00	28.00
1994B Proof	32,200	Value: 35.00				

KM# 75 20 FRANCS

20.0000 g., 0.8350 Silver .5369 oz. ASW **Subject:** Mythological White Snake Queen **Obv:** Value and date at center of large cross **Rev:** Crowned snake **Edge Lettering:** DOMINUS PROVIDEBIT (13 stars)

Date	Mintage	F	VF	XF	Unc	BU
1995B	235,000	—	—	—	22.00	28.00
1995B Proof	30,700	Value: 35.00				

KM# 76 20 FRANCS

20.0000 g., 0.8350 Silver .5369 oz. ASW **Subject:** Mythological Giant Boy **Obv:** Value and date at center of large cross **Rev:** Giant's bust facing above trees

Date	Mintage	F	VF	XF	Unc	BU
1996B	206,000	—	—	—	20.00	26.00
1996B Proof	30,000	Value: 32.00				

KM# 77 20 FRANCS

20.0000 g., 0.8350 Silver .5369 oz. ASW **Subject:** Mythological Dragon of Breno **Obv:** Value and date at center of large cross **Rev:** Dragon above mountains and water

Date	Mintage	F	VF	XF	Unc	BU
1996B	190,000	—	—	—	20.00	26.00
1996B Proof	26,700	Value: 32.00				

KM# 78 20 FRANCS

20.0000 g., 0.8350 Silver .5369 oz. ASW **Subject:** 150th Anniversary - Swiss Railway **Obv:** Modern train wheel **Rev:** Ancient train wheel **Designer:** Georg Staehelin

Date	Mintage	F	VF	XF	Unc	BU
1997B	215,000	—	—	—	22.00	28.00
1997B Proof	19,000	Value: 40.00				

KM# 79 20 FRANCS

20.0000 g., 0.8350 Silver .5369 oz. ASW **Subject:** 200th Anniversary - Birth of Jeremias Gotthelf **Obv:** Stylized numeral value and date **Rev:** Bust facing

Date	Mintage	F	VF	XF	Unc	BU
1997B	160,000	—	—	—	22.00	28.00
1997B Proof	20,000	Value: 40.00				

KM# 80 20 FRANCS

20.0000 g., 0.8350 Silver .5369 oz. ASW **Subject:** 200th Anniversary - Helvetian Republic **Obv:** Value and boxed crosses design **Rev:** 1798 coin design within square, crosses flank

Date	Mintage	F	VF	XF	Unc	BU
1998B	108,000	—	—	—	24.00	30.00
1998B Proof	15,500	Value: 60.00				

KM# 82 20 FRANCS

20.0000 g., 0.8350 Silver .5369 oz. ASW **Subject:** 150th

Anniversary - Confederation **Obv:** Boxed crosses design and value **Rev:** 1848 coin design within square flanked by crosses

Date	Mintage	F	VF	XF	Unc	BU
1998B	109,000	—	—	—	24.00	30.00
1998B Proof	15,500	Value: 60.00				

KM# 84 20 FRANCS
20.0000 g., 0.8350 Silver .5369 oz. ASW **Subject:** Death of C.F. Meyer **Obv:** Value and date **Rev:** Large head 3/4 right with signature across face

Date	Mintage	F	VF	XF	Unc	BU
1998B	108,000	—	—	—	22.00	28.00
1998B Proof	14,500	Value: 50.00				

KM# 85 20 FRANCS
20.0000 g., 0.8350 Silver .5369 oz. ASW **Subject:** 150th Anniversary Swiss Postal Service **Obv:** Value, country name and date within wreath **Rev:** Cartoon-like postal carrier on top half of globe

Date	Mintage	F	VF	XF	Unc	BU
1999B	171,000	—	—	—	22.00	28.00
1999B Proof	12,000	Value: 50.00				

KM# 87 20 FRANCS
20.0000 g., 0.8350 Silver .5369 oz. ASW **Subject:** Battle of Dornach **Obv:** Value and cross design **Rev:** Sword splitting an eagle, boxed crosses around border **Edge Lettering:** DOMINUS PROVIDEBIT (13 stars)

Date	Mintage	F	VF	XF	Unc	BU
1999B	85,000	—	—	—	22.00	28.00
1999B Proof	11,000	Value: 50.00				

KM# 90 20 FRANCS
20.0000 g., 0.8350 Silver .5369 oz. ASW, 32.7 mm. **Subject:** Year 2000 - Peace on Earth **Obv:** Olive branch **Rev:** Angel floating above people

Date	Mintage	F	VF	XF	Unc	BU
2000B	100,000	—	—	—	22.00	28.00
2000B Proof	15,000	Value: 45.00				

KM# 97 20 FRANCS
20.0000 g., 0.8350 Silver .5369 oz. ASW, 32.7 mm. **Subject:** Lumen Christi **Obv:** Inscription above value **Rev:** Jesus preaching within design

Date	Mintage	F	VF	XF	Unc	BU
2000B	85,000	—	—	—	22.00	28.00
2000B Proof	14,000	Value: 45.00				

KM# 81 100 FRANCS
22.5800 g., 0.9000 Gold .6534 oz. AGW **Subject:** 200th Anniversary of Helvetian Republic **Obv:** Value and boxed crosses design **Rev:** 1798 coin design within square flanked by crosses

Date	Mintage	F	VF	XF	Unc	BU
1998B Proof	2,500	Value: 750				

KM# 83 100 FRANCS
22.5800 g., 0.9000 Gold .6534 oz. AGW **Subject:** 150th Anniversary of Swiss Confederation **Obv:** Value and boxed crosses design **Rev:** 1848 coin design within square flanked by crosses

Date	Mintage	F	VF	XF	Unc	BU
1998B Proof	2,500	Value: 750				

KM# 88 100 FRANCS
22.5800 g., 0.9000 Gold .6534 oz. AGW **Subject:** Wine Festival **Obv:** Value and small fox looking up at grapes **Rev:** Small fox eating grapes and crescent

Date	Mintage	F	VF	XF	Unc	BU
1999B Proof	3,000	Value: 575				

KM# 96 100 FRANCS
22.5800 g., 0.9000 Gold .6534 oz. AGW, 28 mm. **Subject:** 2000 Years of Christianity **Obv:** Inscription and date divides value **Rev:** Stylized baby **Edge:** Lettered

Date	Mintage	F	VF	XF	Unc	BU
2000B Proof	3,000	Value: 575				

KM# 71.1 250 FRANCS
8.0000 g., 0.9000 Gold .2315 oz. AGW **Subject:** 700 Years of Confederation **Obv:** Diagonal and horizontal inscription to right of value **Rev:** Dates **Edge:** Plus sign (+) between dates

Date	Mintage	F	VF	XF	Unc	BU
1991B	296,741	—	—	—	225	275

Note: 200,000 recalled and melted due to poor quality

KM# 71.2 250 FRANCS
8.0000 g., 0.9000 Gold .2315 oz. AGW **Subject:** 700 Years of Confederation **Edge:** Elongated plus sign between dates

Date	Mintage	F	VF	XF	Unc	BU
1991B	193,259	—	—	—	225	275

COMMEMORATIVE COINAGE

Shooting Festival

Shooting Festival coinage is now in ***Unusual World Coins.***

ESSAIS

KM#	Date	Mintage	Identification	Mkt Val
E4	1911	—	10 Francs. Gold.	12,500
E5	1925B	—	100 Francs. Bronze. 16.0800 g. Young head left. Radiant cross above value, date and sprigs.	2,750
E6	1925B	—	100 Francs. Bronze. 14.3800 g. Head left.	2,250
E7	1998	250	5 Francs. Silver.	500

KM#	Date	Mintage	Identification	Mkt Val
EA8	1930B	—	5 Francs. Silver. Hooded bust right. Cross on shield flanked by sprigs. Formerly Pn63.	12,000
E8	1930	—	Franc. Nickel.	5,000

KM#	Date	Mintage	Identification	Mkt Val
E9	1998	250	20 Francs. Silver. KM#80.	500

KM#	Date	Mintage	Identification	Mkt Val
E10	1998	250	20 Francs. Silver. KM#82.	500

KM#	Date	Mintage	Identification	Mkt Val
E11	1998	500	20 Francs. Silver. KM#84.	360
EA12	1999	765	5 Francs. Copper-Nickel. KM#86	180
E12	2000	—	20 Francs. Silver. KM#97	240
E17	1928B	—	100 Francs. Brass. Plain edge. Prev. KM#E5.	6,000
E18	1930B	—	100 Francs. Brass. Lettered edge. Prev. KM#E6.	6,500

PATTERNS

Including off metal strikes

KM#	Date	Mintage	Identification	Mkt Val
Pn40	1910	56	10 Francs. Gold. Reeded edge.	15,000
Pn41	1910	I.A.	10 Francs. Gold. Plain edge.	22,500
Pn42	1917	6	5 Rappen. Brass.	4,000
Pn43	1918	—	10 Rappen. Nickel.	—
Pn44	1922B	—	5 Francs. Silver.	3,500
Pn45	1924B	—	5 Francs.	20,000
Pn46	1925B	—	10 Francs. Silver.	6,000
Pn47	1925B	—	100 Francs. Copper.	5,000
Pn48	1927B	—	20 Rappen. Nickel.	4,500
Pn49	1928B	—	20 Rappen. Nickel.	4,500
Pn50	1928B	—	Franc. Nickel.	4,500
Pn51	1928B	—	2 Francs. Nickel.	4,500
Pn52	1928B	—	5 Francs. Silver.	15,000
Pn53	1928B	—	5 Francs. Nickel.	12,500
Pn54	1929B	—	5 Rappen. Bronze.	—
Pn55	1929B	—	50 Rappen. Nickel.	3,500
Pn56	1929	—	5 Francs. Silver.	20,000
Pn57	1930B	—	10 Rappen. Nickel.	2,500
Pn58	1930B	—	20 Rappen. Nickel.	2,500
Pn59	1930B	—	50 Rappen. Nickel.	3,500
Pn60	1930	—	50 Rappen. Nickel. Triangle.	3,000
Pn61	19xxB	—	Franc. Nickel.	—
Pn62	19xxB	—	5 Francs. Silver.	20,000
Pn64	1931	—	5 Rappen. Copper-Nickel.	—
Pn65	1931	—	50 Rappen. Nickel.	2,000
Pn66	1935	—	20 Francs. Copper.	—
Pn67	1937B	—	Franc. Copper-Nickel.	5,000
Pn68	1937B	—	2 Francs. Copper-Nickel.	5,000
Pn69	1937	—	5 Francs. Aluminum.	4,000
Pn70	1938B	—	20 Rappen. Zinc.	2,500
Pn71	1938B	—	Franc. Copper-Nickel.	3,500
Pn72	1938B	—	2 Francs. Copper-Nickel.	4,000
Pn73	1939B	—	5 Rappen. Zinc. KM#26.	1,600
Pn74	1939	—	5 Francs. Silver.	6,000
Pn75	1940B	—	5 Rappen. Aluminum. KM#26.	3,500
PnA76	1940B	—	20 Rappen. Copper-Nickel. KM#29a.	2,850
Pn76	1940B	—	10 Rappen. Zinc. KM#27.	2,000
Pn77	1940B	—	10 Rappen. Aluminum. KM#27.	4,200
Pn78	1941B	—	2 Francs. Silver-Zinc.	2,500
Pn79	1941B	—	Rappen. Aluminum. KM#3.	2,500
Pn80	1941B	—	2 Rappen. Aluminum. KM#4.	3,000
Pn81	1947	—	20 Francs. Gold.	—
Pn82	1948B	—	5 Francs. Copper Gilt.	3,500
Pn83	1955B	—	25 Francs. Silver. KM#49.	14,000
Pn84	1955B	—	50 Francs. Silver. KM#50.	14,000
Pn85	1959B	—	50 Francs. Aluminum. 4.0300 g. KM#50.	6,000
Pn86	1979	—	5 Rappen. Aluminum-Bronze. Prev. Pn.#85.	2,000

TRIAL STRIKES

KM#	Date	Mintage	Identification	Mkt Val
TS3	1935	—	20 Francs. Copper.	3,250

MINT SETS

KM#	Date	Mintage	Identification	Issue Price	Mkt Val
MS2	1970 (9)	10,000	KM#21a.1, 23a.1-24a.1, 26-27, 29a, 40a.1, 46-47	6.40	35.00
MS3	1971 (5)	5,000	KM#23a.1-24a.1, 26, 29a, 46	2.40	30.00
MS4	1972 (3)	5,000	KM#21a.1, 23a.1, 27	2.40	20.00
MS5	1973 (6)	10,000	KM#21a.1, 23a.1-24a.1, 27, 40a.1, 46	6.40	30.00
MS6	1974 (9)	10,000	KM#21a.1, 23a.1-24a.1, 26-27, 29a, 40a.1, 46-47	6.40	55.00
MS7	1975 (8)	10,000	KM#21a.1, 23a.1-24a.1, 26-27, 29a, 40a.1, 46	6.40	30.00
MS8	1976 (8)	10,000	KM#21a.1, 23a.1-24a.1, 26-27, 29a, 40a.1, 46	9.00	45.00
MS9	1977 (8)	10,000	KM#21a.1, 23a.1-24a.1, 26-27, 29a, 40a.1, 46	9.00	31.00
MS10	1978 (8)	10,000	KM#21a.1, 23a.1-24a.1, 26-27, 29a, 40a.1, 46	9.00	24.00
MS11	1979 (8)	10,000	KM#21a.1, 23a.1-24a.1, 26-27, 29a, 40a.1, 46	9.00	24.00
MS12	1980 (8)	15,000	KM#21a.1, 23a.1-24a.1, 26-27, 29a, 40a.1, 46	9.00	42.00
MS13	1981 (8)	15,000	KM#21a.1, 23a.1-24a.1, 26c, 27, 29a, 40a.1, 46	9.00	28.00
MS14	1982 (8)	15,000	KM#21a.2, 23a.2-24a.2, 26c, 27, 29a, 40a.2, 46	9.00	45.00
MS15	1983 (8)	15,740	KM#21a.3, 23a.3-24a.3, 26c, 27, 29a, 40a.2, 46	9.00	30.00
MS16	1984 (8)	20,000	KM#21a.3, 23a.3-24a.3, 26c, 27, 29a, 40a.2, 46	9.00	30.00
MS17	1985 (8)	22,140	KM#21a.3, 23a.3-24a.3, 26c, 27, 29a, 40a.3, 46	9.00	30.00
MS18	1986 (8)	21,400	KM#21a.3, 23a.3-24a.3, 26c, 27, 29a, 40a.3, 46	9.00	26.00
MS19	1987 (8)	19,100	KM#21a.3, 23a.3-24a.3, 26c, 27, 29a, 40a.3, 46	9.00	42.00
MS20	1988 (8)	20,700	KM#21a.3, 23a.3-24a.3, 26c, 27, 29a, 40a.3, 46	—	30.00
MS21	1989 (8)	22,700	KM#21a.3, 23a.3-24a.3, 26c, 27, 29a, 40a.3, 46	11.00	21.00
MS22	1990 (8)	23,100	KM#21a.3, 23a.3-24a.3, 26c, 27, 29a, 40a.3, 46	—	21.00
MS23	1991 (8)	26,100	KM#21a.3, 23a.3-24a.3, 26c, 27, 29a, 40a.3, 46	—	150
MS24	1991 (2)	110,000	KM#70-71	210	240
MS25	1992 (8)	20,300	KM#21a.3, 23a.3-24a.3, 26c, 27, 29a, 40a.3, 46	—	21.00
MS26	1993 (8)	16,200	KM#21a.3, 23a.3-24a.3, 26c, 27, 29a, 40a.3, 46	—	150
MS27	1994 (8)	17,300	KM#21a.3, 23a.3-24a.3, 26c, 27, 29a, 40a.4, 46	—	25.00
MS28	1995 (8)	18,000	KM#21a.3, 23a.3-24a.3, 26c, 27, 29a, 40a.4, 46	—	25.00
MS29	1996 (8)	17,300	KM#21a.3, 23a.3-24a.3, 26c, 27, 29a, 40a.3, 46	—	25.00
MS30	1997 (8)	16,500	KM#21a.3, 23a.3, 24a.3, 26c, 27, 29a, 40a.4, 46	—	25.00
MS31	1998 (8)	16,000	KM#21a.3, 23a.3, 24a.3, 26c, 27, 29a, 40a.4, 46	—	25.00
MS32	1999 (8)	16,000	KM#21a.3, 23a.3, 24a.3, 26c, 27, 29a, 40a.4, 46	—	55.00
MS33	2000 (9)	18,000	KM#21a.3, 23a.3, 24a.3, 26c, 27, 29a, 40a.4, 46, 89 Fasnacht	—	40.00
MS34	2000 (9)	2,000	KM#21a.3, 23a.3, 24a.3, 26c, 27, 29a, 40a.4, 46, 91 150 Years of the Swiss Franken	—	185

PROOF SETS

KM#	Date	Mintage	Identification	Issue Price	Mkt Val
PS1	1974 (9)	2,400	KM#21a.1, 23a.1, 24a.1, 26, 27, 29a, 40a.1, 46-47	12.80	525
PS2	1975 (8)	10,000	KM#21a.1, 23a.1, 24a.1, 26, 27, 29a, 40a.1, 46	16.75	40.00
PS3	1976 (8)	5,130	KM#21a.1, 23a.1, 24a.1, 26, 27, 29a, 40a.1, 46	16.75	55.00
PS4	1977 (8)	7,030	KM#21a.1, 23a.1, 24a.1, 26, 27, 29a, 40a.1, 46	16.75	30.00
PS5	1978 (8)	10,090	KM#21a.1, 23a.1, 24a.1, 26, 27, 29a, 40a.1, 46	28.00	30.00
PS6	1979 (8)	10,150	KM#21a.1, 23a.1, 24a.1, 26, 27, 29a, 40a.1, 46	28.00	30.00
PS7	1980 (8)	10,010	KM#21a.1, 23a.1, 24a.1, 26, 27, 29a, 40a.1, 46	30.00	45.00
PS8	1981 (8)	10,280	KM#21a.1, 23a.1, 24a.1, 26c, 27, 29a, 40a.1, 46	30.00	25.00
PS9	1982 (8)	10,090	KM#21a.2, 23a.2, 24a.2, 26c, 27, 29a, 40a.2, 46	30.00	60.00
PS10	1983 (8)	11,390	KM#21a.3, 23a.3, 24a.3, 26c, 27, 29a, 40a.2, 46	30.00	30.00
PS11	1984 (8)	14,100	KM#21a.3, 23a.3, 24a.3, 26c, 27, 29a, 40a.2, 46	30.00	30.00
PS12	1985 (8)	12,060	KM#21a.3, 23a.3-24a.3, 26c, 27, 29a, 40a.3, 46	30.00	30.00
PS13	1986 (8)	10,000	KM#21a.3, 23a.3, 24a.3, 26c, 27, 29a, 40a.3, 46	30.00	30.00
PS14	1987 (8)	8,800	KM#21a.3, 23a.3, 24a.3, 26c, 27, 29a, 40a.3, 46	30.00	50.00
PS15	1988 (8)	9,150	KM#21a.3, 23a.3, 24a.3, 26c, 27, 29a, 40a.3, 46	—	40.00
PS16	1989 (8)	8,800	KM#21a.3, 23a.3, 24a.3, 26c, 27, 29a, 40a.3, 46	36.50	30.00
PS17	1990 (8)	8,900	KM#21a.3, 23a.3, 24a.3, 26c, 27, 29a, 40a.3, 46	—	30.00
PS18	1991 (8)	9,900	KM#21a.3, 23a.3, 24a.3, 26c, 27, 29a, 40a.3, 46	—	175
PS19	1992 (8)	7,450	KM#21a.3, 23a.3, 24a.3, 26c, 27, 29a, 40a.3, 46	—	45.00
PS20	1993 (8)	6,200	KM#21a.3, 23a.3, 24a.3, 26c, 27, 29a, 40a.3, 46	—	160
PS21	1994 (8)	6,100	KM#21a.3, 23a.3, 24a.3, 26c, 27, 29a, 40a.4, 46	—	60.00
PS22	1995 (8)	6,100	KM#21a.3, 23a.3, 24a.3, 26c, 27, 29a, 40a.4, 46	42.50	60.00
PS23	1994-1996 (4)	6,000	KM#74-77	—	125
PS24	1996 (8)	6,100	KM#21a.3, 23a.3, 24a.3, 26c, 27, 29a, 40a.4, 46	—	60.00
PS25	1997 (8)	5,500	KM#21a.3, 23a.3, 24a.3, 26c, 27, 29a, 40a.4, 46	—	60.00
PS26	1998 (8)	4,800	KM#21a.3, 23a.3, 24a.3, 26c, 27, 29a, 40a.4, 46	—	60.00
PS27	1999 (9)	5,000	KM#21a.3, 23a.3, 24a.3, 26c, 27, 29a, 40a.4, 46, 86	—	100
PS28	2000 (9)	5,500	KM#21a.3, 23a.3, 24a.3, 26c, 27, 29a, 40a.4, 46, 89 Fasnacht	—	85.00
PS29	2000 (9)	500	KM#21a.3, 23a.3, 24a.3, 26c, 27, 29a, 40a.4, 46, 91 150 Years of the Swiss Franken	—	825

SYRIA

The Syrian Arab Republic, located in the Near East at the eastern end of the Mediterranean Sea, has an area of 71,498 sq. mi. (185,180 sq. km.) and a population of *12 million. Capital: Greater Damascus. Agriculture and animal breeding are the chief industries. Cotton, crude oil and livestock are exported.

Ancient Syria, a land bridge connecting Europe, Africa and Asia, has spent much of its history in thrall to the conqueror's whim. Its subjection by Egypt about 1500 B.C. was followed by successive conquests by the Hebrews, Phoenicians, Babylonians, Assyrians, Persians, Macedonians, Romans, Byzantines and finally, in 636 A.D., by the Moslems. The Arabs made Damascus, one of the oldest continuously inhabited cities of the world, the trade center and capital of an empire stretching from India to Spain. In 1516, following the total destruction of Damascus by the Mongols of Tamerlane, Syria fell to the Ottoman Turks and remained a part of Turkey until the end of World War I. The League of Nations gave France a mandate to the Levant states of Syria and Lebanon in 1920. In 1930, following a series of uprisings, France recognized Syria as an independent republic, but still subject to the mandate. Lebanon became fully independent on Nov. 22, 1943, and Syria on Jan. 1,1944.

TITLES

الجمهورية السورية

al-Jumhuriya(t) al-Suriya(t)

الجمهورية لعربية السورية

al-Jumhuriya(t) al-Arabiya(t) as-Suriya(t)

RULERS

Ottoman, until 1918
Faysal, 1918-1920

MINT MARK

(a)- Paris, privy marks only

MINT NAMES

دمشق

Damascus (Dimask)

حلب

Haleb (Aleppo)

KINGDOM

STANDARD COINAGE

KM# 67 DINAR

6.7000 g., Gold **Obv:** Crowned shield within sprigs **Rev:** Design within wreath

Date	Mintage	F	VF	XF	Unc	BU
AH1338 (1919)	Est. 12	—	—	—	8,000	—

FRENCH PROTECTORATE

STANDARD COINAGE

KM# 68 1/2 PIASTRE

Copper-Nickel **Obv:** Value within roped wreath flanked by oat sprigs **Rev:** Value within wreath

Date	Mintage	F	VF	XF	Unc	BU
1921(a)	4,000,000	0.50	2.00	5.00	15.00	—

KM# 75 1/2 PIASTRE
Nickel-Brass **Obv:** Value within roped circle **Rev:** Value within oat sprigs

Date	Mintage	F	VF	XF	Unc	BU
1935(a)	600,000	1.00	4.00	12.00	42.50	—
1936(a)	800,000	1.00	4.00	9.00	30.00	—

KM# 71 PIASTRE
Nickel-Brass **Obv:** Hole in center of wreath flanked by stars **Rev:** Hole in center of sprigs flanked by lion heads

Date	Mintage	F	VF	XF	Unc	BU
1929(a)	750,000	1.00	3.00	7.00	32.50	—
1933(a)	600,000	1.50	4.00	10.00	40.00	—
1935(a)	1,900,000	0.75	2.50	5.00	22.50	—
1936(a)	1,400,000	0.75	2.50	7.00	25.00	—

KM# 71a PIASTRE
Zinc **Obv:** Hole in center of wreath flanked by stars **Rev:** Hole in center flanked by lion heads

Date	Mintage	F	VF	XF	Unc	BU
1940(a)	2,000,000	2.00	5.00	15.00	60.00	—

KM# 69 2 PIASTRES
Aluminum-Bronze **Obv:** Inscription divides dates within design **Rev:** Crossed oat sprigs divide value

Date	Mintage	F	VF	XF	Unc	BU
1926(a)	600,000	5.00	10.00	25.00	75.00	—
1926	Inc. above	5.00	10.00	25.00	75.00	—

Note: Without privy marks by date

KM# 76 2-1/2 PIASTRES
Aluminum-Bronze **Obv:** Hole in center of wreath flanked by stars **Rev:** Hole in center of sprigs flanked by lion heads

Date	Mintage	F	VF	XF	Unc	BU
1940(a)	2,000,000	1.25	4.00	8.00	27.50	—

KM# 70 5 PIASTRES
Aluminum-Bronze **Obv:** Inscription divides dates within design **Rev:** Crossed oat sprigs divide value

Date	Mintage	F	VF	XF	Unc	BU
1926(a)	300,000	0.75	2.00	8.00	25.00	—
1926	600,000	0.75	3.00	12.00	35.00	—
1933(a)	1,200,000	0.40	2.00	12.50	40.00	—
1935(a)	2,000,000	0.30	1.50	8.00	25.00	—
1936(a)	900,000	0.50	2.00	10.00	30.00	—
1940(a)	500,000	0.50	1.50	4.00	15.00	—

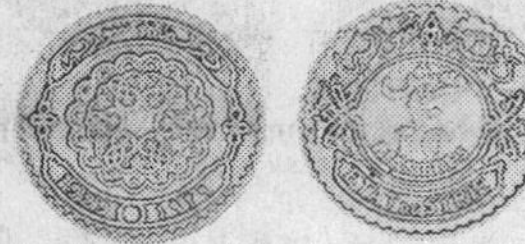

KM# 72 10 PIASTRES
2.0000 g., 0.6800 Silver .0437 oz. ASW **Obv:** Star in center of flower design **Rev:** Value within circle

Date	Mintage	F	VF	XF	Unc	BU
1929	1,000,000	4.00	12.00	28.00	90.00	—

KM# 73 25 PIASTRES
5.0000 g., 0.6800 Silver .1093 oz. ASW **Obv:** Value within circle **Rev:** Star in center of flower design

Date	Mintage	F	VF	XF	Unc	BU
1929	1,000,000	3.00	5.00	27.50	85.00	—
1933(a)	500,000	4.00	12.00	40.00	160	—
1936(a)	897,000	3.50	7.00	30.00	100	—
1937(a)	393,000	5.00	10.00	35.00	140	—

KM# 74 50 PIASTRES
10.0000 g., 0.6800 Silver .2186 oz. ASW **Obv:** Value within circle **Rev:** Star in center of flower design

Date	Mintage	F	VF	XF	Unc	BU
1929	880,000	4.00	8.00	35.00	140	—
1933(a)	250,000	6.00	10.00	45.00	190	—
1936(a)	400,000	5.00	10.00	40.00	160	—
1937(a)	Inc. above	7.00	12.00	50.00	200	—

WORLD WAR II EMERGENCY COINAGE

KM# 77 PIASTRE
Brass **Obv:** English value **Rev:** Arabic value

Date	Mintage	F	VF	XF	Unc	BU
ND	—	2.50	5.00	10.00	20.00	—

KM# 78 2-1/2 PIASTRES
Aluminum **Obv:** English value **Rev:** Arabic value

Date	Mintage	F	VF	XF	Unc	BU
ND	—	10.00	20.00	35.00	65.00	—

REPUBLIC

STANDARD COINAGE

KM# 81 2-1/2 PIASTRES
Copper-Nickel **Obv:** Imperial eagle **Rev:** Inscription within rectangle below value

Date	Mintage	F	VF	XF	Unc	BU
AH1367-1948	2,500,000	0.75	1.50	3.00	6.00	—
AH1375-1956	5,000,000	0.75	1.50	3.00	6.00	—

KM# 82 5 PIASTRES
Copper-Nickel **Obv:** Imperial eagle **Rev:** Value within diamond shape above design flanked by stars **Designer:** Gilroy Roberts

Date	Mintage	F	VF	XF	Unc	BU
AH1367-1948	8,000,000	0.75	1.50	3.00	6.00	—
AH1375-1956	4,000,000	0.75	1.50	3.00	6.00	—

KM# 83 10 PIASTRES
Copper-Nickel **Obv:** Imperial eagle **Rev:** Value above 1/2 designed wreath **Designer:** Gilroy Roberts

Date	Mintage	F	VF	XF	Unc	BU
AH1367-1948	—	0.75	1.50	3.00	6.00	—
AH1375-1956	4,000,000	0.75	1.50	3.00	6.00	—

KM# 79 25 PIASTRES
2.5000 g., 0.6000 Silver .0482 oz. ASW **Obv:** Imperial eagle **Rev:** Value within circle of design flanked by oat sprigs

Date	Mintage	F	VF	XF	Unc	BU
AH1366-1947	6,300,000	1.50	2.50	6.00	20.00	—

KM# 80 50 PIASTRES
5.0000 g., 0.6000 Silver .0965 oz. ASW **Obv:** Imperial eagle **Rev:** Value in center circle of design

Date	Mintage	F	VF	XF	Unc	BU
AH1366-1947	4,500,000	2.50	5.00	10.00	25.00	—

KM# 84 1/2 POUND
3.3793 g., 0.9000 Gold .0978 oz. AGW **Obv:** Imperial eagle **Rev:** Inscription within rectangle above sprigs

Date	Mintage	F	VF	XF	Unc	BU
AH1369-1950	100,000	BV	70.00	80.00	125	175

KM# 85 LIRA
10.0000 g., 0.6800 Silver .2186 oz. ASW **Obv:** Imperial eagle **Rev:** Inscription and value within center of rectangle and sprigs

Date	Mintage	F	VF	XF	Unc	BU
AH1369-1950	7,000,000	3.50	6.50	12.50	25.00	—

KM# 86 POUND
6.7586 g., 0.9000 Gold .1956 oz. AGW **Obv:** Imperial eagle **Rev:** Inscription and value within rectangle above sprigs

Date	Mintage	F	VF	XF	Unc	BU
AH1369-1950	250,000	—	BV	145	175	225

UNITED ARAB REPUBLIC

STANDARD COINAGE

KM# 90 2-1/2 PIASTRES
2.0000 g., Aluminum-Bronze, 17 mm. **Obv:** Imperial eagle flanked by dates **Rev:** Inscription within rectangle below value

Date	Mintage	F	VF	XF	Unc	BU
AH1380-1960	1,100,000	0.10	0.20	0.35	0.75	—

KM# 91 5 PIASTRES
3.0000 g., Aluminum-Bronze, 19 mm. **Obv:** Imperial eagle **Rev:** Value, inscription

Date	Mintage	F	VF	XF	Unc	BU
AH1380-1960	4,240,000	0.10	0.20	0.35	0.75	—

KM# 92 10 PIASTRES
4.0000 g., Aluminum-Bronze, 21 mm. **Obv:** Imperial eagle flanked by dates **Rev:** Value in center of 1/2 wreath

Date	Mintage	F	VF	XF	Unc	BU
AH1380-1960	2,800,000	0.10	0.20	0.40	1.00	—

KM# 87 25 PIASTRES
0.3500 g., 0.6000 Silver .0482 oz. ASW, 20.3 mm. **Obv:** Imperial eagle **Rev:** Value flanked by oat sprigs in center of gear

Date	Mintage	F	VF	XF	Unc	BU
AH1377-1958	2,300,000	1.00	2.00	3.00	7.00	—

KM# 88 50 PIASTRES
5.0000 g., 0.6000 Silver .0965 oz. ASW, 23.4 mm. **Obv:** Imperial eagle **Rev:** Sword divides value within wreath

Date	Mintage	F	VF	XF	Unc	BU
AH1377-1958	120,000	2.00	3.50	7.00	18.00	—

KM# 89 50 PIASTRES
5.0000 g., 0.6000 Silver .0965 oz. ASW **Subject:** 1st Anniversary - Founding of United Arab Republic **Obv:** Imperial eagle **Rev:** Value

Date	Mintage	F	VF	XF	Unc	BU
AH1378-1959	1,500,000	1.75	2.75	5.00	12.00	—

SYRIAN ARAB REPUBLIC

STANDARD COINAGE

KM# 93 2-1/2 PIASTRES
2.0000 g., Aluminum-Bronze, 17 mm. **Obv:** Imperial eagle **Rev:** Inscription within rectangle below value

Date	Mintage	F	VF	XF	Unc	BU
AH1382-1962	8,000,000	—	0.10	0.20	0.50	—
AH1385-1965	8,000,000	—	0.10	0.20	0.50	—

KM# 104 2-1/2 PIASTRES
2.0000 g., Aluminum-Bronze, 17 mm. **Obv:** Imperial eagle **Rev:** Inscription within rectangle below value

Date	Mintage	F	VF	XF	Unc	BU
AH1393-1973	10,000,000	—	0.10	0.15	0.25	—

KM# 94 5 PIASTRES
3.0000 g., Aluminum-Bronze, 19 mm. **Obv:** Imperial eagle **Rev:** Value within diamond shape above design flanked by stars

Date	Mintage	F	VF	XF	Unc	BU
AH1382-1962	7,000,000	—	0.10	0.15	0.35	—
AH1385-1965	18,000,000	—	0.10	0.15	0.35	—

KM# 100 5 PIASTRES
3.0000 g., Aluminum-Bronze, 19 mm. **Series:** F.A.O. **Obv:** Imperial eagle **Rev:** Upright oat sprig within sprigs **Rev. Designer:** Khalid Asali

Date	Mintage	F	VF	XF	Unc	BU
AH1391-1971	15,000,000	—	0.10	0.15	0.25	—

KM# 105 5 PIASTRES
3.0000 g., Aluminum-Bronze, 19 mm. **Obv:** Imperial eagle **Rev:** Value within diamond shape above design flanked by stars

Date	Mintage	F	VF	XF	Unc	BU
AH1394-1974	—	—	0.10	0.15	0.25	—

KM# 110 5 PIASTRES
3.0000 g., Aluminum-Bronze, 19 mm. **Series:** F.A.O. **Obv:** Imperial eagle **Rev:** Euphrates dam within 1/2 gear and 1/2 oat sprig

Date	Mintage	F	VF	XF	Unc	BU
AH1396-1976	2,000,000	—	0.10	0.15	0.25	—

KM# 116 5 PIASTRES
3.0000 g., Aluminum-Bronze, 19 mm. **Obv:** Imperial eagle with heavy neck feathers **Rev:** Value within diamond shape above design flanked by stars **Note:** Similar to KM#94 but heavier neck feathers

Date	Mintage	F	VF	XF	Unc	BU
AH1399-1979	—	—	0.10	0.15	0.25	—

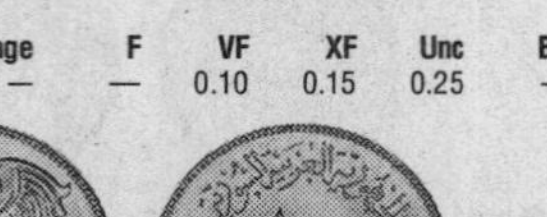

KM# 95 10 PIASTRES
4.0000 g., Aluminum-Bronze, 21 mm. **Obv:** Imperial eagle **Rev:** Value within 1/2 designed wreath **Note:** Varieties exist with fine (narrow) and course (widely spaced) reeding.

Date	Mintage	F	VF	XF	Unc	BU
AH1382-1962	6,000,000	—	0.10	0.20	0.45	—
AH1385-1965	22,000,000	—	0.10	0.20	0.45	—

Note: Reeding varieties exist

KM# 106 10 PIASTRES
4.0000 g., Aluminum-Bronze, 21 mm. **Obv:** Imperial eagle **Rev:** Value within 1/2 designed wreath

Date	Mintage	F	VF	XF	Unc	BU
AH1394-1974	—	—	0.10	0.15	0.30	—

KM# 111 10 PIASTRES
4.0000 g., Brass, 21 mm. **Series:** F.A.O. **Obv:** Imperial eagle with heavy neck feathers **Rev:** Euphrates dam within 1/2 gear and 1/2 oat sprig **Note:** Similar to 5 Piastres, KM#110.

Date	Mintage	F	VF	XF	Unc	BU
AH1396-1976	500,000	—	0.10	0.15	0.25	—

KM# 117 10 PIASTRES
4.0000 g., Copper-Nickel, 21 mm. **Obv:** Imperial eagle **Rev:** Value within 1/2 designed wreath

Date	Mintage	F	VF	XF	Unc	BU
AH1399-1979	—	—	0.10	0.15	0.30	—

KM# 96 25 PIASTRES
3.5000 g., Nickel, 20.3 mm. **Obv:** Imperial eagle **Rev:** Inscription within rectangle flanked by dates below value

Date	Mintage	F	VF	XF	Unc	BU
AH1387-1968	15,000,000	—	0.20	0.30	0.60	—

KM# 101 25 PIASTRES
3.5000 g., Nickel, 20.3 mm. **Subject:** 25th Anniversary - Al-Ba'ath Party **Obv:** Imperial eagle **Rev:** Flaming torch divides value within oat sprigs

Date	Mintage	F	VF	XF	Unc	BU
AH1392-1972	—	—	0.15	0.25	0.60	—

KM# 107 25 PIASTRES
3.5000 g., Nickel, 20.3 mm. **Obv:** Imperial eagle **Rev:** Inscription within rectangle below value

Date	Mintage	F	VF	XF	Unc	BU
AH1394-1974	—	—	0.10	0.25	0.50	—

KM# 112 25 PIASTRES
3.5000 g., Nickel, 20.5 mm. **Series:** F.A.O. **Obv:** Imperial eagle **Rev:** Euphrates dam within 1/2 gear and 1/2 oat sprig

Date	Mintage	F	VF	XF	Unc	BU
AH1396-1976	1,000,000	—	0.10	0.25	0.50	—

KM# 118 25 PIASTRES
3.5000 g., Copper-Nickel, 20.3 mm. **Obv:** Imperial eagle **Rev:** Inscription within rectangle below value

Date	Mintage	F	VF	XF	Unc	BU
AH1399-1979	—	—	0.10	0.25	0.50	—

KM# 97 50 PIASTRES
5.0000 g., Nickel, 23.4 mm. **Obv:** Imperial eagle **Rev:** Value in center square of design above dates and oat sprigs

Date	Mintage	F	VF	XF	Unc	BU
AH1387-1968	10,000,000	—	0.25	0.50	0.85	—

KM# 102 50 PIASTRES
5.0000 g., Nickel, 23.4 mm. **Subject:** 25th Anniversary - Al-Ba'ath Party **Obv:** Imperial eagle **Rev:** Inscription, dates, value and flames

Date	Mintage	F	VF	XF	Unc	BU
AH1392-1972	—	—	0.50	1.00	2.00	—

KM# 108 50 PIASTRES
5.0000 g., Nickel, 23.4 mm. **Obv:** Imperial eagle **Rev:** Value within center square of design above sprigs

Date	Mintage	F	VF	XF	Unc	BU
AH1394-1974	—	—	0.20	0.30	0.75	—

KM# 113 50 PIASTRES
5.0000 g., Nickel, 23.4 mm. **Series:** F.A.O. **Obv:** Imperial eagle **Rev:** Euphrates dam within 1/2 gear and 1/2 oat sprig

Date	Mintage	F	VF	XF	Unc	BU
AH1396-1976	1,000,000	—	0.20	0.50	1.00	—

KM# 119 50 PIASTRES
5.0000 g., Copper-Nickel, 23.4 mm. **Obv:** Imperial eagle **Rev:** Value in center square of design above sprigs

Date	Mintage	F	VF	XF	Unc	BU
AH1399-1979	—	—	0.20	0.30	0.75	—

KM# 98 POUND
7.5000 g., Nickel, 27 mm. **Obv:** Imperial eagle **Rev:** Value in diamond shape within rectangle **Edge:** Reeded

Date	Mintage	F	VF	XF	Unc	BU
AH1387-1968	10,000,000	—	0.30	0.75	1.25	—
AH1391-1971	10,000,000	—	0.30	0.75	1.25	—

KM# 99 POUND
7.5000 g., Nickel, 27 mm. **Series:** F.A.O. **Obv:** Imperial eagle **Rev:** Hands holding rectangle, oat sprig bouquet above **Designer:** Khalid Asali

Date	Mintage	F	VF	XF	Unc	BU
AH1388-1968	500,000	—	1.00	2.00	3.50	—

KM# 103 POUND
7.5000 g., Nickel, 27 mm. **Subject:** 25th Anniversary - Al-Ba'ath Party **Obv:** Imperial eagle **Rev:** Stylized map and flaming torch

Date	Mintage	F	VF	XF	Unc	BU
AH1392-1972	10,000,000	—	0.50	1.00	2.50	—

KM# 109 POUND
7.5000 g., Nickel, 27 mm. **Obv:** Imperial eagle **Rev:** Value in diamond shape at center of rectangle

Date	Mintage	F	VF	XF	Unc	BU
AH1394-1974	—	—	0.30	0.75	2.00	—

KM# 114 POUND
7.5000 g., Nickel, 27 mm. **Series:** F.A.O. **Obv:** Imperial eagle **Rev:** Euphrates dam within 1/2 gear and 1/2 oat sprig

Date	Mintage	F	VF	XF	Unc	BU
AH1396-1976	500,000	—	0.50	1.00	2.50	—

KM# 115 POUND
7.5000 g., Nickel, 27 mm. **Subject:** Re-election of President **Obv:** Imperial eagle within circle **Rev:** Head left within circle

Date	Mintage	F	VF	XF	Unc	BU
AH1398-1978	—	—	1.50	2.50	5.00	—

KM# 120.1 POUND
7.5000 g., Copper-Nickel, 27 mm. **Obv:** Imperial eagle **Rev:** Value in diamond shape at center of rectangle **Edge:** Reeded

Date	Mintage	F	VF	XF	Unc	BU
AH1399-1979	—	—	0.30	0.70	1.50	—

KM# 120.2 POUND
Stainless Steel **Obv:** Imperial eagle **Rev:** Value in diamond shape at center of rectangle **Note:** Reduced size and weight.

Date	Mintage	F	VF	XF	Unc	BU
AH1412-1991	—	—	0.30	0.70	1.50	2.00

KM# 121 POUND
Stainless Steel **Obv:** Imperial eagle **Rev:** Value in diamond shape at center of rectangle

Date	Mintage	F	VF	XF	Unc	BU
AH1414-1994	—	—	0.30	0.70	1.50	2.00
AH1416 1996	—	—	0.30	0.75	1.50	2.00

KM# 132 POUND
5.0000 g., Stainless Steel, 25.4 mm. **Obv:** Flowers to left of dates below heraldic bird **Rev:** Value and ornamentation **Edge:** Reeded

Date	Mintage	F	VF	XF	Unc	BU
AH1416-1996	—	—	—	—	1.50	2.00

KM# 125 2 POUNDS
Stainless Steel **Obv:** Imperial eagle flanked by dates **Rev:** Ancient ruins and value

Date	Mintage	F	VF	XF	Unc	BU
AH1416-1996	—	—	—	0.85	1.75	2.50

KM# 123 5 POUNDS
Copper-Nickel **Obv:** Imperial eagle within birdhouse design **Rev:** Palace above value within birdhouse design

Date	Mintage	F	VF	XF	Unc	BU
AH1416-1996	—	—	—	1.00	2.00	3.00

KM# 124 10 POUNDS
Copper-Nickel **Obv:** Imperial eagle within circle **Rev:** Ancient ruins above value within circle

Date	Mintage	F	VF	XF	Unc	BU
AH1416-1996	—	—	—	1.25	2.50	3.50
AH1417-1997(a)	—	—	—	1.25	2.50	3.50

KM# 128 10 POUNDS
7.0000 g., Copper-Nickel, 26.5 mm. **Subject:** 50th Anniversary of Al Ba'ath Party **Obv:** Imperial eagle within circle **Rev:** Map and flag above sprigs within circle **Edge:** Reeded

Date	Mintage	F	VF	XF	Unc	BU
AH1417-1997	100,000	—	—	1.25	2.50	3.50

KM# 122 25 POUNDS
Bi-Metallic Stainless Steel center in Bronze ring **Obv:** Imperial eagle within circle **Rev:** Head left within circle

Date	Mintage	F	VF	XF	Unc	BU
ND(1995)	—	—	—	2.50	7.00	9.00

KM# 126 25 POUNDS
Bi-Metallic Stainless Steel center in Bronze ring **Obv:** Imperial eagle within designed wreath **Rev:** Central Bank building within circle

Date	Mintage	F	VF	XF	Unc	BU
AH1416-1996	—	—	—	2.00	6.00	7.50

ESSAIS

KM#	Date	Mintage	Identification	Issue Price	Mkt Val
E1	1926(a)	—	2 Piastres. Aluminum-Bronze. KM69.	—	200
E2	1926(a)	—	5 Piastres. Aluminum-Bronze. KM70.	—	220

KM#	Date	Mintage	Identification	Issue Price	Mkt Val
E3	1929(a)	—	Piastre. Nickel-Brass. Hole in center of wreath. Value and dates below hole in center flanked by lion heads. KM71.	—	115
E4	1929(a)	—	10 Piastres. Silver. KM72.	—	200
E5	1929(a)	—	25 Piastres. Silver. KM73.	—	250

KM#	Date	Mintage	Identification	Issue Price	Mkt Val
E6	1929(a)	—	50 Piastres. Silver. Value within circle. Star in center of flower design. KM74.	—	265
E7	AH1350(a)	—	50 Piastres.	—	350
E8	1935(a)	—	1/2 Piastre. Nickel-Brass. KM75.	—	60.00

MINT SETS

KM#	Date	Mintage	Identification	Issue Price	Mkt Val
MS1	1968 (3)	—	KM96-98	—	5.50
MS2	1978-79 (6)	—	KM115 (1978), 116-120.1 (1979)	—	8.50

TAJIKISTAN

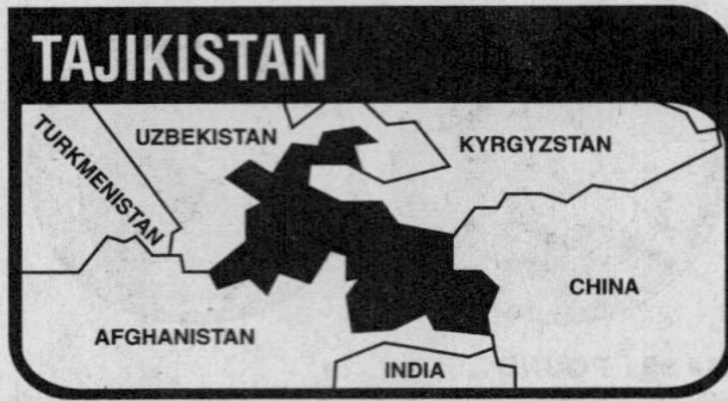

The Republic of Tajikistan (Tadjiquistan), was formed from those regions of Bukhara and Turkestan where the population consisted mainly of Tajiks. Is bordered in the north and west by Uzbekistan and Kyrgyzstan, in the east by China and in the south by Afghanistan. It has an area of 55,240 sq. miles (143,100 sq. km.) and a population of 5.95 million. It includes 2 provinces of Khudzand and Khatlon together with the Gorno-Badakhshan Autonomous Region with a population of 5,092,603. Capital: Dushanbe. Tajikistan was admitted as a constituent republic of the Soviet Union on Dec. 5, 1929. In August 1990 the Tajik Supreme Soviet adopted a declaration of republican sovereignty, and in Dec. 1991 the republic became a member of the CIS.

After demonstrations and fighting, the Communist government was replaced by a Revolutionary Coalition Council on May 7, 1992. Following further demonstrations President Nabiev was ousted on Sept. 7, 1992. Civil war broke out, and the government resigned on Nov. 10, 1992. On Nov. 30, 1992 it was announced that a CIS peacekeeping force would be sent to Tajikistan. A state of emergency was imposed in Jan. 1993. A ceasefire was signed in 1996 and a peace agreement signed in June 1997.

MONETARY SYSTEM
1 Ruble = 100 Tanga

REPUBLIC

DECIMAL COINAGE

KM# 1 20 ROUBLES
20.0000 g., 0.9250 Silver .5948 oz. ASW, 35.1 mm. **Subject:** Medal without denomination **Obv:** Radiant Royal device within circle **Rev:** Crowned bust 1/4 right **Edge:** Reeded **Note:** Medallic.

Date	Mintage	F	VF	XF	Unc	BU
1999 Proof	—	Value: 75.00				

TANNU TUVA

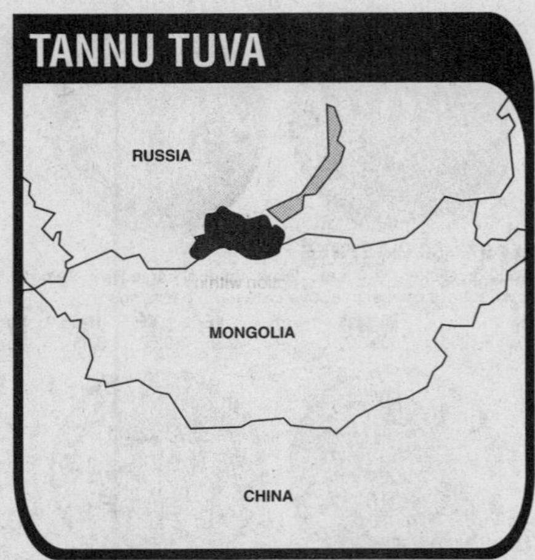

The Tannu-Tuva Peoples Republic (Tuva), an autonomous part of Russia located in central Asia on the northwest border of Outer Mongolia, has an area of 64,000 sq. mi. (165,760 sq. km.) and a population of about 175,000. Capital: Kyzyl. The economy is based on herding, forestry and mining.

As Urianghi, Tuva was part of Outer Mongolia of the Chinese Empire when tsarist Russia, after fomenting a separatist movement, extended its protection to the mountainous country in 1914. Tuva declared its independence as the Tannu-Tuva Peoples Republic in 1921 under the auspices of the Tuva Peoples Revolutionary Party. In 1926, following Russia's successful mediation of the resultant Tuvinian-Mongolian territorial dispute, Tannu-Tuva and Outer Mongolia formally recognized each other's independence. The Tannu-Tuva Peoples Republic became an autonomous region of the U.S.S.R. on Oct. 13, 1944.

MONETARY SYSTEM
100 Kopejek (Kopeks) = 1 Aksha

REPUBLIC

STANDARD COINAGE

KM# 1 KOPEJEK
Aluminum-Bronze **Obv:** Inscription within circle **Rev:** Value and date

Date	Mintage	VG	F	VF	XF	Unc
1934	—	20.00	30.00	50.00	85.00	—

KM# 2 2 KOPEJEK
Aluminum-Bronze **Obv:** Inscription within circle **Rev:** Value and date

Date	Mintage	VG	F	VF	XF	Unc
1933	—	—	—	—	—	—
1934	—	22.50	35.00	65.00	100	—

KM# 3 3 KOPEJEK
Aluminum-Bronze **Obv:** Inscription within circle **Rev:** Value and date

Date	Mintage	VG	F	VF	XF	Unc
1933	—	—	—	—	—	—
1934	—	20.00	30.00	50.00	85.00	—

KM# 4 5 KOPEJEK
Aluminum-Bronze **Obv:** Inscription within circle **Rev:** Value and date

Date	Mintage	VG	F	VF	XF	Unc
1934	—	22.50	35.00	65.00	100	—

KM# 5 10 KOPEJEK
Copper-Nickel **Obv:** Inscription within circle **Rev:** Value and date

Date	Mintage	VG	F	VF	XF	Unc
1934	—	22.50	35.00	65.00	100	—

KM# 6 15 KOPEJEK
Copper-Nickel **Obv:** Inscription within circle **Rev:** Value and date

Date	Mintage	VG	F	VF	XF	Unc
1934	—	22.50	35.00	65.00	100	—

KM# 7 20 KOPEJEK
Copper-Nickel **Obv:** Inscription within circle **Rev:** Value and date

Date	Mintage	VG	F	VF	XF	Unc
1934	—	22.50	35.00	65.00	100	—

TANZANIA

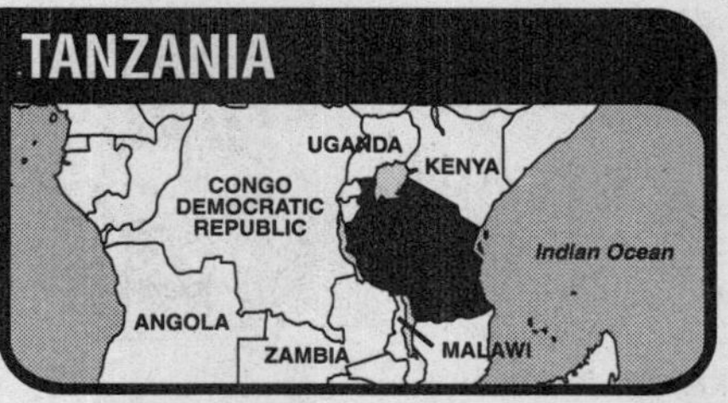

The United Republic of Tanzania, located on the east coast of Africa between Kenya and Mozambique, consists of Tanganyika and the islands of Zanzibar and Pemba. It has an area of 364,900 sq. mi. (945,090 sq. km.) and a population of *25.2 million. Capital: Dar es Salaam (Haven of Peace). The chief exports are cotton, coffee, diamonds, sisal, cloves, petroleum products, and cashew nuts.

Tanzania is a member of the Commonwealth of Nations. The President is Chief of State.

NOTE: For earlier coinage see East Africa.

REPUBLIC

STANDARD COINAGE

100 Senti = 1 Shilingi

KM# 1 5 SENTI
4.0000 g., Bronze, 22.5 mm. **Obv:** Head of President J.K. Nyerere left **Rev:** Sailfish above value **Shape:** 12-sided **Designer:** Christopher Ironside

Date	Mintage	F	VF	XF	Unc	BU
1966	55,250,000	—	0.10	0.20	0.50	1.25
1966 Proof	5,500	Value: 1.25				
1971	5,000,000	—	0.10	0.20	0.50	1.25
1972	—	—	0.10	0.20	0.50	1.25
1973	20,000,000	—	0.10	0.20	0.50	1.25
1974	12,500,000	—	0.10	0.20	0.50	1.25
1975	—	—	0.10	0.20	0.50	1.25
1976	37,500,000	—	0.10	0.20	0.50	1.25
1977	10,000,000	—	0.10	0.20	0.50	1.25
1979	7,200,000	—	0.10	0.20	0.50	1.25
1980	10,000,000	—	0.10	0.20	0.50	1.25
1981	13,650,000	—	0.10	0.20	0.50	1.25
1982	—	—	0.10	0.20	0.50	1.25
1983	18,000	—	0.10	0.20	0.50	1.25
1984	—	—	0.10	0.20	0.50	1.25

KM# 11 10 SENTI
5.0000 g., Nickel-Brass, 25 mm. **Obv:** Head of President J.K. Nyerere left **Rev:** Zebra running right **Shape:** Scalloped **Designer:** Christopher Ironside

Date	Mintage	F	VF	XF	Unc	BU
1977	19,505,000	—	0.75	1.50	4.00	6.00
1979	8,000,000	—	0.75	1.50	4.00	6.00
1980	10,000,000	—	0.75	1.50	4.00	6.00
1981	10,000,000	—	0.75	1.50	4.00	6.00
1984	—	—	0.75	1.50	4.00	6.00

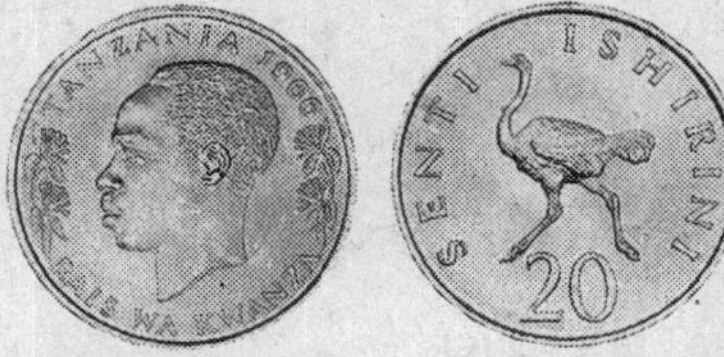

KM# 2 20 SENTI
5.0000 g., Nickel-Brass, 24 mm. **Obv:** Head of President J.K. Nyerere left **Rev:** Ostrich running left **Designer:** Christopher Ironside

Date	Mintage	F	VF	XF	Unc	BU
1966	26,500,000	—	0.20	0.40	1.50	2.00
1966 Proof	5,500	Value: 2.25				
1970	5,000,000	—	0.20	0.40	1.50	2.00
1973	20,100,000	—	0.20	0.40	1.50	2.00
1975	—	—	0.20	0.40	1.50	2.00
1976	10,000,000	—	0.20	0.40	1.50	2.00
1977	10,000,000	—	0.20	0.40	1.50	2.00
1979	10,000,000	—	0.20	0.40	1.50	2.00
1980	10,000,000	—	0.20	0.40	1.50	2.00
1981	10,000,000	—	0.20	0.40	1.50	2.00
1982	—	—	0.20	0.40	1.50	2.00
1983	50,000	—	0.20	0.40	1.50	2.00
1984	—	—	0.20	0.40	1.50	2.00

KM# 3 50 SENTI
4.0000 g., Copper-Nickel, 21 mm. **Obv:** Head of President J.K. Nyerere left **Rev:** Rabbit left **Designer:** Christopher Ironside

Date	Mintage	F	VF	XF	Unc	BU
1966	6,250,000	—	0.20	0.40	2.00	2.50
1966 Proof	5,500	Value: 3.00				
1970	10,000,000	—	0.20	0.40	2.00	2.50
1973	10,000,000	—	0.25	0.50	2.00	2.50
1980	10,000,000	—	0.25	0.50	2.00	2.50
1981	—	—	0.25	0.50	2.00	2.50
1982	10,000,000	—	0.25	0.50	2.00	2.50
1983	—	—	0.25	0.50	2.00	2.50
1984	10,000,000	—	0.25	0.50	2.00	2.50

KM# 26 50 SENTI
Nickel Clad Steel, 21 mm. **Obv:** President Mwinyi right flanked by flowers **Rev:** Rabbit left **Edge:** Reeded

Date	Mintage	F	VF	XF	Unc	BU
1988	10,000,000	—	0.25	0.75	1.50	2.00
1989	—	—	0.25	0.75	1.50	2.00
1990	—	—	0.25	0.75	1.50	2.00

KM# 4 SHILINGI
Copper-Nickel, 27.5 mm. **Obv:** Head of President J.K. Nyerere left **Rev:** Hand holding torch **Designer:** Christopher Ironside

Date	Mintage	F	VF	XF	Unc	BU
1966	48,000,000	—	0.25	0.50	1.50	2.00
1966 Proof	5,500	Value: 5.00				
1972	10,000,000	—	0.25	0.50	1.50	2.00
1974	15,000,000	—	0.30	0.60	1.75	2.25
1975	—	—	0.30	0.60	1.75	2.25
1977	5,000,000	—	0.30	0.60	1.75	2.25
1980	10,000,000	—	0.25	0.50	1.50	2.00
1981	—	—	0.30	0.60	1.75	2.25
1982	10,000,000	—	0.30	0.60	1.75	2.25
1983	10,000,000	—	0.30	0.60	1.75	2.25
1984	10,000,000	—	0.30	0.60	1.75	2.25

KM# 22 SHILINGI
6.5000 g., Nickel Clad Steel, 23.5 mm. **Obv:** President Mwinyi right flanked by flowers **Rev:** Hand holding torch

Date	Mintage	F	VF	XF	Unc	BU
1987	5,000,000	—	0.40	0.80	2.00	2.50
1988	10,000,000	—	0.40	0.80	2.00	2.50
1989	—	—	0.40	0.80	2.00	2.50
1990	—	—	0.20	0.40	1.25	1.75
1991	—	—	0.20	0.40	1.25	1.75
1992	—	—	0.20	0.40	1.25	1.75

KM# 5 5 SHILINGI

Copper-Nickel, 31.5 mm. **Series:** F.A.O. **Subject:** 10th Anniversary of Independence **Obv:** Head of President J.K. Nyerere left **Rev:** Value in center circle, food sources in frames surround **Shape:** 10-sided **Designer:** Christopher Ironside

Date	Mintage	F	VF	XF	Unc	BU
ND(1971)	1,000,000	—	0.75	1.50	3.50	4.50

KM# 6 5 SHILINGI

Copper-Nickel, 31.5 mm. **Series:** F.A.O. **Obv:** Head of President J.K. Nyerere left **Rev:** Value in center circle, food sources in frames surround **Shape:** 10-sided **Designer:** Christopher Ironside

Date	Mintage	F	VF	XF	Unc	BU
1972	8,000,000	—	0.75	1.50	3.50	4.00
1973	5,000,000	—	0.75	1.75	4.00	4.50
1980	5,000,000	—	0.75	1.75	4.00	4.50

KM# 10 5 SHILINGI

Copper-Nickel, 31.5 mm. **Subject:** 10th Anniversary - Bank of Tanzania **Obv:** Head of President J.K. Nyerere left **Rev:** Bank building above sprigs and value **Shape:** 10-sided **Designer:** Christopher Ironside

Date	Mintage	F	VF	XF	Unc	BU
ND(1976)	1,000,000	—	0.75	1.50	3.50	4.50
ND(1976) Proof	200	Value: 40.00				

KM# 12 5 SHILINGI

Copper-Nickel, 31.5 mm. **Series:** F.A.O. **Subject:** Regional Conference for Africa **Obv:** President J.K. Nyerere left flanked by oat sprigs **Rev:** Farmer working with tractor **Shape:** 10-sided **Designer:** Christopher Ironside

Date	Mintage	F	VF	XF	Unc	BU
1978	50,000	—	0.75	1.50	2.75	3.75
1978 Proof	2,000	Value: 11.50				

KM# 23 5 SHILINGI

Copper-Nickel **Obv:** President Mwinyi right flanked by flowers **Rev:** Value within center circle, food sources in frames surround **Shape:** 10-sided

Date	Mintage	F	VF	XF	Unc	BU
1987	5,000,000	—	0.75	1.50	3.00	3.50
1988	10,000,000	—	0.75	1.50	3.00	3.50
1989	—	—	0.75	1.50	3.00	3.50

KM# 23a.1 5 SHILINGI

8.5000 g., Nickel Clad Steel, 26.5 mm. **Obv:** Small (17mm) head right flanked by flowers **Rev:** Value within center circle, food sources in frames surround **Edge:** Reeded

Date	Mintage	F	VF	XF	Unc	BU
1990	—	—	0.60	1.20	1.85	2.25

KM# 23a.2 5 SHILINGI

8.5000 g., Nickel Clad Steel, 26.5 mm. **Obv:** Large (18mm) head right flanked by flowers **Rev:** Value within center circle, food sources in frames surround

Date	Mintage	F	VF	XF	Unc	BU
1991	—	—	0.60	1.20	1.85	2.25
1992	—	—	0.50	1.00	1.50	2.00
1993	—	—	0.50	1.00	1.50	2.00

KM# 20 10 SHILINGI

Copper-Nickel, 29 mm. **Obv:** President J.K. Nyerere 1/4 left within circle **Rev:** National arms **Designer:** Philip Nathan

Date	Mintage	F	VF	XF	Unc	BU
1987	10,000,000	—	1.00	1.50	3.25	3.75
1988	10,000,000	—	1.00	1.50	3.25	3.75
1989	—	—	1.00	1.50	3.25	3.75

KM# 20a 10 SHILINGI

10.0000 g., Nickel Clad Steel, 29 mm. **Obv:** Bust of President J.K. Nyerere 1/4 left within circle **Rev:** National arms

Date	Mintage	F	VF	XF	Unc	BU
1990	—	—	1.00	1.50	2.25	2.75
1991	—	—	1.00	1.50	2.25	2.75
1992	—	—	0.85	1.25	2.00	2.50
1993	—	—	0.85	1.25	2.00	2.50

KM# 20a.1 10 SHILINGI

10.0000 g., Nickel Clad Steel, 29 mm. **Obv:** Bust of President J.K. Nyerere 1/4 left within circle **Rev:** 4 mm "10"; inscription near edge

Date	Mintage	F	VF	XF	Unc	BU
1990	—	—	0.60	1.20	1.85	2.25

KM# 20a.2 10 SHILINGI

10.0000 g., Nickel Clad Steel, 29 mm. **Obv:** Bust of President J.K. Nyerere 1/4 left within circle **Rev:** 3 mm "10"; inscription away from edge

Date	Mintage	F	VF	XF	Unc	BU
1991	—	—	0.60	1.20	1.85	2.25
1992	—	—	0.60	1.20	1.85	2.25
1993	—	—	0.60	1.20	1.85	2.25

KM# 13 20 SHILINGI

Copper-Nickel **Subject:** 20th Anniversary of Independence **Obv:** President J.K. Nyerere 1/4 left within circle **Rev:** National arms **Designer:** Philip Nathan

Date	Mintage	F	VF	XF	Unc	BU
ND(1981)	997,000	—	2.50	4.50	10.00	12.00

KM# 13a 20 SHILINGI

16.0000 g., 0.9250 Silver .4759 oz. ASW **Obv:** Bust of President J.K. Nyerere 1/4 left within circle **Rev:** National arms

Date	Mintage	F	VF	XF	Unc	BU
ND(1981) Proof	20,000	Value: 42.50				

KM# 21 20 SHILINGI

Copper-Nickel **Subject:** 20th Anniversary of Central Bank **Obv:** President Mwinyi right **Rev:** Torch within sprigs

Date	Mintage	F	VF	XF	Unc	BU
ND(1986)	—	—	—	—	45.00	65.00

KM# 21a 20 SHILINGI

16.0000 g., 0.9250 Silver .4759 oz. ASW **Obv:** Head of President Mwinyi right **Rev:** Torch within sprigs

Date	Mintage	F	VF	XF	Unc	BU
ND(1986) Proof	5,000	Value: 110				

KM# 27.1 20 SHILINGI

Nickel Bonded Steel **Obv:** President Mwinyi right flanked by flowers **Rev:** Elephants **Shape:** 7-sided

Date	Mintage	F	VF	XF	Unc	BU
1990	—	—	1.50	2.00	3.50	3.75
1991	—	—	1.50	2.00	3.50	3.75

KM# 27.2 20 SHILINGI

13.0000 g., Nickel Bonded Steel, 31 mm. **Obv:** President Mwinyi right flanked by flowers **Rev:** Elephant with calf **Shape:** 7-sided **Note:** Reduced size.

Date	Mintage	F	VF	XF	Unc	BU
1992	—	—	1.25	1.75	3.25	4.00

KM# 7 25 SHILINGI

25.4000 g., 0.5000 Silver .4083 oz. ASW **Subject:** Conservation **Obv:** Head of President J.K. Nyerere left **Rev:** Giraffes running right **Designer:** Christopher Ironside

Date	Mintage	F	VF	XF	Unc	BU
1974	8,848	—	—	—	18.00	22.00

KM# 7a 25 SHILINGI

28.2800 g., 0.9250 Silver .8411 oz. ASW **Obv:** Head of President J.K. Nyerere left **Rev:** Giraffes running right

Date	Mintage	F	VF	XF	Unc	BU
1974 Proof	13,000	Value: 35.00				

KM# 28 25 SHILINGI

Nickel Bonded Steel **Subject:** 25th Anniversary of Central Bank **Obv:** President Mwinyi right **Rev:** Building within sprigs

Date	Mintage	F	VF	XF	Unc	BU
ND(1991)	—	—	—	—	3.00	4.00

KM# 28a 25 SHILINGI
13.0400 g., 0.9250 Silver .3878 oz. ASW **Obv:** Head of President Mwinyi right **Rev:** Building within sprigs

Date	Mintage	F	VF	XF	Unc	BU
ND(1991) Proof	Est. 2,000	Value: 65.00				

KM# 30 25 SHILINGI
Copper-Nickel **Subject:** 25 Years of Independence **Obv:** President J.K. Nyerere 1/4 left within circle **Rev:** National arms **Designer:** Philip Nathan

Date	Mintage	F	VF	XF	Unc	BU
ND(1985) Proof	—	Value: 260				

KM# 8 50 SHILINGI
31.8500 g., 0.5000 Silver .5120 oz. ASW **Subject:** Conservation **Obv:** Head of President J.K. Nyerere left **Rev:** Black Rhinoceros facing **Designer:** Christopher Ironside

Date	Mintage	F	VF	XF	Unc	BU
1974	8,826	—	—	—	24.00	26.00

KM# 8a 50 SHILINGI
35.0000 g., 0.9250 Silver 1.0409 oz. ASW **Obv:** Head of President J.K. Nyerere left **Rev:** Black Rhinoceros facing **Designer:** Christopher Ironside

Date	Mintage	F	VF	XF	Unc	BU
1974 Proof	12,000	Value: 28.00				

KM# 33 50 SHILINGI
Brass Plated Steel **Subject:** Conservation **Obv:** Head of Ali Nassan Mwinyi right within circle **Rev:** Mother rhino and calf **Shape:** 7-sided **Designer:** Philip Nathan

Date	Mintage	F	VF	XF	Unc	BU
1996	—	—	—	—	4.00	5.00

KM# 16 100 SHILINGI
23.3300 g., 0.9250 Silver .6938 oz. ASW **Series:** Decade for Women **Obv:** Head of President J.K. Nyerere left **Obv. Designer:** Christopher Ironside **Rev:** Kneeling nurse holding baby in air

Date	Mintage	F	VF	XF	Unc	BU
1984 Proof	1,000	Value: 42.50				

KM# 18 100 SHILINGI
Copper-Nickel **Subject:** Conservation **Obv:** President J.K. Nyerere left flanked by flowers **Obv. Designer:** Christopher Ironside **Rev:** Elephant mother and calf

Date	Mintage	F	VF	XF	Unc	BU
1986	—	—	—	—	6.50	9.00

KM# 18a 100 SHILINGI
19.4400 g., 0.9250 Silver .5782 oz. ASW **Obv:** Head of President J.K. Nyerere left **Rev:** Elephant mother and calf **Designer:** Christopher Ironside

Date	Mintage	F	VF	XF	Unc	BU
1986 Proof	25,000	Value: 30.00				

KM# 24 100 SHILINGI
19.4400 g., 0.9250 Silver .5782 oz. ASW **Series:** Save the Children Fund **Rev:** Two girls with clubs mashing grain in pail within circle

Date	Mintage	F	VF	XF	Unc	BU
1990 Proof	Est. 20,000	Value: 22.50				

KM# 32 100 SHILINGI
Brass Plated Steel **Subject:** Conservation **Obv:** Bust of President J.K. Nyerere left **Obv. Designer:** Philip Nathan **Rev:** Four Impalas running right

Date	Mintage	F	VF	XF	Unc	BU
1993	—	—	—	—	4.00	5.00
1994	—	—	—	—	4.00	5.00

KM# 14 200 SHILINGI
28.2800 g., 0.9250 Silver .8411 oz. ASW **Subject:** 20th Anniversary of Independence **Obv:** Bust of President J.K. Nyerere left **Rev:** National arms

Date	Mintage	F	VF	XF	Unc	BU
ND(1981)	110	—	—	—	135	145
ND(1981) Proof	Inc. above	Value: 160				

KM# 41 200 SHILINGI
20.0000 g., 0.5000 Silver .3214 oz. ASW, 34 mm. **Subject:** Wildlife of Africa **Obv:** National arms **Rev:** Adult and baby rhino **Edge:** Reeded

Date	Mintage	F	VF	XF	Unc	BU
1997 Proof	—	Value: 25.00				

KM# 34 200 SHILINGI
Copper-Nickel-Zinc **Obv:** Head of Sheikh Karume 1/4 left within circle **Rev:** Two lions **Edge:** Plain and reeded sections

Date	Mintage	F	VF	XF	Unc	BU
1998	—	—	—	—	5.00	6.50

KM# 40 200 SHILINGI
15.4000 g., 0.9250 Silver .4580 oz. ASW, 33.9 mm. **Subject:** Pan Troglodytes **Obv:** National arms **Rev:** Chimpanzee family **Edge:** Reeded

Date	Mintage	F	VF	XF	Unc	BU
1999 Proof	—	Value: 30.00				

KM# 59 200 SHILINGI
15.4000 g., 0.9250 Silver 0.458 oz. ASW, 33.9 mm. **Obv:** National arms **Rev:** Water Buffalo **Edge:** Reeded

Date	Mintage	F	VF	XF	Unc	BU
1999 Proof	—	Value: 30.00				

KM# 29 250 SHILINGI
28.1600 g., 0.9250 Silver .8374 oz. ASW **Subject:** 25th Anniversary of Independence **Obv:** Bust of President J.K. Nyerere left **Obv. Designer:** Philip Nathan **Rev:** National arms

Date	Mintage	F	VF	XF	Unc	BU
ND(1985) Proof	—	Value: 250				

KM# 57 250 SHILINGI
19.3400 g., 0.9250 Silver 0.5752 oz. ASW, 26.9 mm. **Subject:** Serengeti Wildlife **Obv:** National arms **Rev:** Lion, Cheetah and Zebra **Edge:** Reeded

Date	Mintage	F	VF	XF	Unc	BU
1998 Proof	—	Value: 35.00				

KM# 44 500 SHILINGI
20.0000 g., 0.9990 Silver .6424 oz. ASW **Subject:** Visit of Richard von Weizsacker **Obv:** National arms **Rev:** Weizsacker and elephant

Date	Mintage	F	VF	XF	Unc	BU
1992 Proof	Est. 20,000	Value: 35.00				

KM# 48 500 SHILINGI
33.6300 g., 0.9250 Silver 1.0001 oz. ASW, 38.4 mm. **Subject:** Serengeti Wildlife **Obv:** National arms **Rev:** Leopard head and full body portraits **Edge:** Reeded

Date	Mintage	F	VF	XF	Unc	BU
1998 Proof	—	Value: 40.00				

KM# 49 500 SHILINGI
33.6300 g., 0.9250 Silver 1.0001 oz. ASW, 38.4 mm. **Subject:** Serengeti Wildlife **Obv:** National arms **Rev:** Cheetah head and full body portraits **Edge:** Reeded

Date	Mintage	F	VF	XF	Unc	BU
1998 Proof	—	Value: 40.00				

KM# 50 500 SHILINGI
33.6300 g., 0.9250 Silver 1.0001 oz. ASW, 38.4 mm. **Subject:** Serengeti Wildlife **Obv:** National arms **Rev:** Hyena head and full body portraits **Edge:** Reeded

Date	Mintage	F	VF	XF	Unc	BU
1998 Proof	—	Value: 40.00				

KM# 51 500 SHILINGI
33.6300 g., 0.9250 Silver 1.0001 oz. ASW, 38.4 mm. **Subject:** Serengeti Wildlife **Obv:** National arms **Rev:** Crocodile head and full body portraits **Edge:** Reeded

Date	Mintage	F	VF	XF	Unc	BU
1998 Proof	—	Value: 40.00				

KM# 43 500 SHILINGI
33.8000 g., 0.9250 Silver 1.0052 oz. ASW, 38.5 mm. **Subject:** Serengeti Wildlife **Obv:** National arms **Rev:** Lions **Edge:** Reeded

Date	Mintage	F	VF	XF	Unc	BU
1998 Proof	—	Value: 40.00				

KM# 17 1000 SHILINGI
8.1000 g., 0.9000 Gold .2344 oz. AGW **Series:** Decade for Women **Obv:** President J.K. Nyerere left flanked by flowers **Obv. Designer:** Christopher Ironside **Rev:** Half figure separating grain

Date	Mintage	F	VF	XF	Unc	BU
1984 Proof	500	Value: 200				

KM# 45 1000 SHILINGI
6.0000 g., 0.9990 Gold .1927 oz. AGW **Subject:** Visit of Richard von Weizsacker **Obv:** National arms **Rev:** Weizsacker and elephant

Date	Mintage	F	VF	XF	Unc	BU
1992 Proof	Est. 8,000	Value: 145				

KM# 9 1500 SHILINGI
33.4370 g., 0.9000 Gold .9676 oz. AGW **Subject:** Conservation **Obv:** President J.K. Nyerere left flanked by flowers **Obv. Designer:** Christopher Ironside **Rev:** Cheetahs

Date	Mintage	F	VF	XF	Unc	BU
1974	2,779	—	—	—	685	725
1974 Proof	866	Value: 775				

KM# 15 2000 SHILINGI
15.9800 g., 0.9170 Gold .4712 oz. AGW **Subject:** 20th Anniversary of Independence **Obv:** President J.K. Nyerere **Obv. Designer:** Philip Nathan **Rev:** National arms

Date	Mintage	F	VF	XF	Unc	BU
ND(1981)	110	—	—	—	375	400
ND(1981) Proof	Inc. above	Value: 425				

KM# 19 2000 SHILINGI
15.9800 g., 0.9170 Gold .4712 oz. AGW **Subject:** Conservation **Obv:** President J.K. Nyerere left flanked by flowers **Obv. Designer:** Christopher Ironside **Rev:** Banded Green Sunbird

Date	Mintage	F	VF	XF	Unc	BU
1986 Proof	5,000	Value: 335				

KM# 25 2000 SHILINGI
10.0000 g., 0.9170 Gold .2948 oz. AGW **Series:** Save the Children Fund **Obv:** President Mwinyi right flanked by small sprigs **Rev:** Child and calf within circle

Date	Mintage	F	VF	XF	Unc	BU
1990 Proof	Est. 3,000	Value: 235				

KM# 46 2000 SHILINGI
10.0000 g., 0.9990 Gold .3212 oz. AGW **Subject:** Visit of Richard von Weizsacker **Obv:** National arms **Rev:** Weizsacker and elephant

Date	Mintage	F	VF	XF	Unc	BU
1992 Proof	Est. 5,000	Value: 225				

KM# 31 2500 SHILINGI
46.8500 g., 0.9170 Gold 1.3808 oz. AGW **Subject:** 25 Years of Independence **Obv:** President J.K. Nyerere 1/4 left within circle **Obv. Designer:** Philip Nathan **Rev:** National arms

Date	Mintage	F	VF	XF	Unc	BU
ND(1985) Proof	—	Value: 1,000				

KM# 35 2500 SHILINGI
155.3600 g., 0.9990 Silver 4.9899 oz. ASW, 65 mm. **Subject:** Serengeti Wildlife **Obv:** National arms **Rev:** Zebra head and full body zebra **Edge:** Reeded **Note:** Photo reduced.

Date	Mintage	F	VF	XF	Unc	BU
1998 Proof	—	Value: 100				

KM# 36 2500 SHILINGI
155.3600 g., 0.9990 Silver 4.9899 oz. ASW, 65 mm. **Subject:** Serengeti Wildlife **Obv:** National arms **Rev:** Giraffe head and full body giraffe

Date	Mintage	F	VF	XF	Unc	BU
1998 Proof	—	Value: 100				

KM# 37 2500 SHILINGI
155.3600 g., 0.9990 Silver 4.9899 oz. ASW, 65 mm. **Subject:** Serengeti Wildlife **Obv:** National arms **Rev:** Cheetah head and full body portrait

Date	Mintage	F	VF	XF	Unc	BU
1998 Proof	—	Value: 115				

KM# 38 2500 SHILINGI
155.3600 g., 0.9990 Silver 4.9899 oz. ASW, 65 mm. **Subject:** Serengeti Wildlife **Obv:** National arms **Rev:** Wildebeast herd **Note:** Photo reduced.

Date	Mintage	F	VF	XF	Unc	BU
1998 Proof	—	Value: 100				

KM# 39 2500 SHILINGI
155.3600 g., 0.9990 Silver 4.9899 oz. ASW, 65 mm. **Subject:** Serengeti Wildlife **Obv:** National arms **Rev:** Gazelle head and full body portrait

Date	Mintage	F	VF	XF	Unc	BU
1998 Proof	—	Value: 100				

KM# 54 2500 SHILINGI
155.3600 g., 0.9990 Silver 4.9899 oz. ASW, 65 mm. **Subject:** Serengeti Wildlife **Obv:** National arms **Rev:** Hyena head and full body portraits **Edge:** Reeded

Date	Mintage	F	VF	XF	Unc	BU
1998 Proof	—	Value: 110				

KM# 55 2500 SHILINGI
155.3600 g., 0.9990 Silver 4.9899 oz. ASW, 65 mm. **Subject:** Serengeti Wildlife **Obv:** National arms **Rev:** Crocodile head and full body portraits **Edge:** Reeded

Date	Mintage	F	VF	XF	Unc	BU
1998 Proof	—	Value: 110				

KM# 52 2500 SHILINGI
155.3600 g., 0.9990 Silver 4.9899 oz. ASW, 65 mm. **Subject:** Serengeti Wildlife **Obv:** National arms **Rev:** Lion head and full body lion **Edge:** Reeded

Date	Mintage	F	VF	XF	Unc	BU
1998 Proof	—	Value: 100				

KM# 53 2500 SHILINGI
155.3600 g., 0.9990 Silver 4.9899 oz. ASW, 65 mm. **Subject:** Serengeti Wildlife **Obv:** National arms **Rev:** Leopard head and full body portraits **Edge:** Reeded **Note:** Photo reduced.

Date	Mintage	F	VF	XF	Unc	BU
1998 Proof	—	Value: 100				

KM# 42 10000 SHILINGI
31.1035 g., 0.9999 Gold 1.0000 oz. AGW, 32.5 mm. **Subject:** Serengeti Wildlife **Obv:** National arms **Rev:** Lion, Cheetah and Zebra **Edge:** Reeded

Date	Mintage	F	VF	XF	Unc	BU
1998 Proof	Est. 1,000	Value: 735				

KM# 58 50000 SHILINGI
155.5100 g., 0.9990 Gold 4.9948 oz. AGW **Subject:** Serengeti Wildlife **Obv:** National arms **Rev:** Lion, Cheetah and Zebra

Date	Mintage	F	VF	XF	Unc	BU
1998 Proof	—	Value: 5,800				

KM# 47 500 SHILLINGS
31.2200 g., 0.9250 Silver 0.9285 oz. ASW, 38.5 mm. **Subject:** British Queen Mother **Obv:** National arms **Rev:** Scene from Queen Mother's African tour **Edge:** Reeded

Date	Mintage	F	VF	XF	Unc	BU
1997 Proof	—	Value: 40.00				

TRIAL STRIKES

KM#	Date	Mintage	Identification	Mkt Val
TS1	1981	—	50 Senti. Copper-Nickel. KM#3.	85.00
TS2	1980	—	Shilingi. Copper-Nickel. KM#4.	115
TS3	1980	—	5 Senti. Copper-Nickel. KM#6.	145

PATTERNS

Including off metal strikes

KM#	Date	Mintage	Identification	Mkt Val
Pn1	1973	—	50 Senti. Nickel-Bronze. KM#3.	75.00

PROOF SETS

KM#	Date	Mintage	Identification	Issue Price	Mkt Val
PS1	1966 (4)	5,500	KM#1-4	10.20	10.00
PS2	1974 (2)	30,000	KM#7a-8a	50.00	50.00
PS3	1985 (3)	—	KM#29-31	—	12.00

TATARSTAN

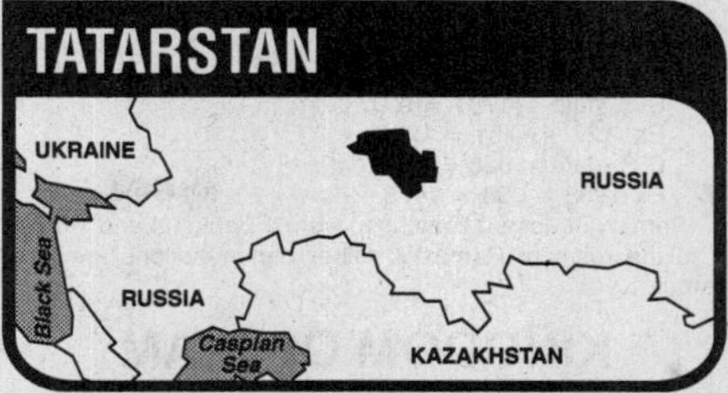

Tatarstan, an autonomous republic in the Russian Federation, is situated between the middle of the Volga river and its tributary Kama, extends east to the Ural mountains, covering 26,500 sq. mi. (68,000 sq. km.) and as of the 1970 census, has a population of 3,743,600. Capital: Kazan. Tatarstan's economy combines its ancient traditions in the craftmanship of wood, leather, cloth, and ceramics with modern engineering, chemical, and food industries.

Colonized by the Bulgars in the 5th century, the territory of the Volga-Kama Bulgar State was inhabited by Turks. In the 13th century, Ghengis Khan conquered the area and established control until the 15th century, when residual Mongol influence left Tatarstan as the Tatar Khanate, seat of the Kazan (Tatar) Khans. In 1552, under Ivan IV (The Terrible), Russia conquered, absorbed and controlled Tatarstan until the dissolution of the U.S.S.R. in the late 20th century.

Constituted as an autonomous republic on May 27,1990, and as a sovereign state equal with Russia April, 1992, Tatarstan, with Russia's president, signed a treaty in Feb. 1994 defining Tatarstan as a state united with Russia (Commonwealth of Independent States).

RULERS
President Mintimir Shaimiev

RUSSIAN STATE

TOKEN COINAGE

KM# Tn1 KILO (Bread)
Bronze **Ruler:** President Mintimir Shaimiev **Obv:** Arms **Rev:** Wheat stalks **Edge:** Reeded

Date	Mintage	F	VF	XF	Unc	BU
ND (1993)	—	2.00	3.00	6.00	12.00	—

KM# Tn2 10 LITRES (Petrol)
Bronze **Ruler:** President Mintimir Shaimiev **Obv:** Arms **Rev:** Oil derrick **Edge:** Reeded **Note:** The bronze 10 Litres token was withdrawn from circulation because it was nickel plated in large numbers and passed off as the higher valued copper-nickel version KM-Tn3.

Date	Mintage	F	VF	XF	Unc	BU
ND (1993)	—	3.00	5.00	10.00	18.00	—

KM# Tn3 20 LITRES (Petrol)
Copper Nickel **Ruler:** President Mintimir Shaimiev **Obv:** Arms **Rev:** Oil derrick **Edge:** Reeded **Note:** The copper-nickel Tn3 are often found with test file notches, because of the nickel plating problems of the bronze Tn2.

Date	Mintage	F	VF	XF	Unc	BU
ND (1993)	—	3.50	6.00	12.00	20.00	—

THAILAND

The Kingdom of Thailand (formerly Siam), a constitutional monarchy located in the center of mainland Southeast Asia between Burma and Laos, has an area of 198,457 mi. (514,000 sq. km.) and a population of *55.5 million. Capital: Bangkok. The economy is based on agriculture and mining. Rubber, rice, teakwood, tin and tungsten are exported.

The history of The Kingdom of Siam, the only country in south and Southeast Asia that was never colonized by an European power, dates from the 6th century A.D. when Thai people started to migrate into the area a process that accelerated with the Mongol invasion of China in the 13th century. After 400 years of sporadic warfare with the neighboring Burmese, King Taskin won the last battle in 1767. He founded a new capital, Dhonburi, on the west bank of the Chao Praya River. King Rama I moved the capital to Bangkok in 1782, thus initiating the so-called Bangkok Period of Siamese coinage characterized by Pot Duang money (bullet coins) stamped with regal symbols.

The Portuguese, who were followed by the Dutch, British and French, introduced the Thai to the Western world. Rama III of the present ruling dynasty negotiated a treaty of friendship and commerce with Britain in 1826, and in 1896 the independence of the kingdom was guaranteed by an Anglo-French accord.

In 1909 Siam ceded to Great Britain its suzerain rights over the dependencies of Kedah, Kelantan, Trengganu and Perlis, Malay states situated in southern Siam just north of British Malaya, which eliminated any British jurisdiction in Siam proper.

The absolute monarchy was changed into a constitutional monarchy in 1932.

On Dec. 8, 1941, after five hours of fighting, Thailand agreed to permit Japanese troops passage through the country to invade Northern British Malaysia. This eventually led to increased Japanese intervention and finally occupation of the country. On Jan. 25, 1942, Thailand declared war on Great Britain and the United States. A free Thai guerilla movement was soon organized to counteract the Japanese. In July 1943 Japan transferred the four northern Malay States back to Thailand. These were returned to Great Britain after peace treaties were signed in 1946.

RULERS
Rama V (Phra Maha Chulalongkorn), 1868-1910
Rama VI (Phra Maha Vajiravudh), 1910-1925
Rama VII (Phra Maha Prajadhipok), 1925-1935
Rama VIII (Phra Maha Ananda Mahidol), 1935-1946
Rama IX (Phra Maha Bhumifhol Adulyadej), 1946-

MONETARY SYSTEM

Old currency system

2 Solos = 1 Att
2 Att = 1 Sio (Pai)
2 Sio = 1 Sik
2 Sik = 1 Fuang
2 Fuang = 1 Salung (not Sal'ung)
4 Salung = 1 Baht
4 Baht = 1 Tamlung
20 Tamlung = 1 Chang

UNITS OF OLD THAI CURRENCY

Chang -	ชั่ง	Sik -	ซีก
Tamlung -	ตำลึง	Sio (Pai) -	เสี้ยว
Baht -	บาท	Att -	อัฐ
Salung -	สลึง	Solos -	โสฬส
Fuang -	เฟื้อง		

MINT MARKS
H-Heaton Birmingham

DATING

Typical BE Dating

Typical CS Dating

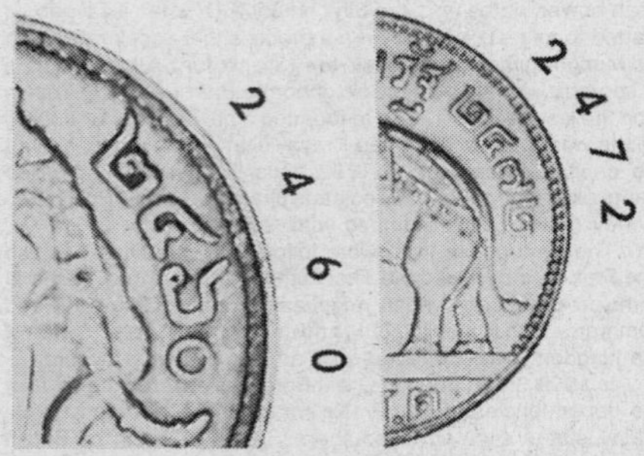

NOTE: Sometimes the era designator *BE* or *CS* will actually appear on the coin itself.

Denomination

2-1/2 (Satang) RS Dating

DATE CONVERSION TABLES

B.E. date - 543 = A.D. date
Ex: 2516 - 543 = 1973
R.S. date + 1781 = A.D. date
Ex: 127 + 1781 = 1908
C.S. date + 638 = A.D. date
Ex 1238 + 638 = 1876

Primary denominations used were 1 Baht, 1/4 and 1/8 Baht up to the reign of Rama IV. Other denominations are much scarcer.

KINGDOM OF SIAM
until 1939
STANDARD COINAGE

Y# 21 1/2 ATT (1 Solot)
Bronze **Ruler:** Rama V **Obv:** Uniformed bust left **Rev:** Crowned seated figure right

Date	Mintage	F	VF	XF	Unc	BU
RS124 (1905)	—	1.50	2.50	8.50	85.00	—

Note: These coins were also minted in RS114, RS115, RS121 and RS122. The last year had a mintage of 5,120,000. Coins with these dates have not been observed and were probably additional mintings of coins dated RS109 and RS118. A nickel pattern dated RS114 does exist. Varieties in numeral size and rotated dies exist

Y# 22 ATT
Bronze **Ruler:** Rama V **Obv:** Uniformed bust left **Rev:** Crowned seated figure right **Note:** Full red uncirculated coins of this type carry a substantial premium.

Date	Mintage	F	VF	XF	Unc	BU
RS121 (1902)	11,251,000	3.50	5.00	30.00	170	—
RS122 (1903)	4,109,000	4.50	10.00	50.00	200	—
Note: Exists with large (greater than 1mm) and small (less than 1mm) numerals						
RS124 (1905)	—	3.50	5.00	30.00	170	—

Y# 23 2 ATT (1/32 Baht = 1 Sio)
Bronze **Ruler:** Rama V **Obv:** Uniformed bust left **Rev:** Crowned seated figure right **Note:** Varieties in numeral size and rotated dies exist. Full red uncirculated coins of this type carry a substantial premium.

Date	Mintage	F	VF	XF	Unc	BU
RS121 (1902)	2,797,000	1.50	3.00	25.00	160	—
RS122 (1903)	2,323,000	1.50	3.00	25.00	160	—
RS124 (1905)	—	1.50	3.00	25.00	160	—

Y# 32a FUANG (1/8 Baht)
Silver **Ruler:** Rama V **Obv:** Bust left **Rev:** National arms **Note:** Weight range: 1.7-2.01 g.

Date	Mintage	F	VF	XF	Unc	BU
RS120 (1901)	—	3.00	15.00	50.00	100	—
RS121 (1902)	380,000	3.00	15.00	50.00	100	—
RS122 (1903)	460,000	3.00	15.00	60.00	120	—
RS123 (1904)	310,000	3.00	15.00	50.00	100	—
RS124 (1905)	410,000	3.00	15.00	60.00	120	—
RS125 (1906)	—	3.00	15.00	50.00	100	—
RS126 (1907)	—	3.00	15.00	50.00	100	—
RS127 (1908)	480,000	3.00	15.00	80.00	180	—

Y# 32c FUANG (1/8 Baht)
Gold **Ruler:** Rama V **Obv:** Bust left **Rev:** National arms

Date	Mintage	F	VF	XF	Unc	BU
RS122 (1903)	—	500	1,000	1,500	2,500	—
RS123 (1904)	—	1,500	3,000	5,000	7,000	—
RS124 (1905)	—	1,500	3,000	5,000	7,000	—
RS125 (1906)	—	1,500	3,000	5,000	7,000	—
RS126 (1907)	—	1,500	3,000	5,000	7,000	—
RS127 (1908)	—	1,500	3,000	5,000	7,000	—
RS128 (1909)	—	1,500	3,000	5,000	7,000	—
RS129 (1910)	—	1,500	3,000	5,000	7,000	—

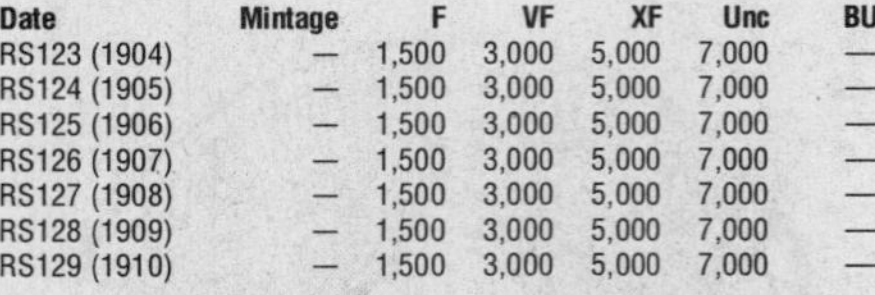

Y# 33a SALUNG = 1/4 BAHT
Silver **Ruler:** Rama V **Obv:** Bust left **Rev:** National arms **Note:** Weight range: 3.60-4.02g.

Date	Mintage	F	VF	XF	Unc	BU
RS120 (1901)	—	80.00	120	160	4,000	—
RS121 (1902)	560,000	20.00	40.00	60.00	180	—
RS122 (1903)	340,000	30.00	60.00	80.00	240	—
RS123 (1904)	190,000	30.00	40.00	60.00	180	—
RS125 (1906)	—	20.00	40.00	60.00	180	—
RS126 (1907)	—	20.00	40.00	60.00	180	—
RS127 (1908)	270,000	20.00	60.00	80.00	200	—

Y# 43 SALUNG = 1/4 BAHT
3.7500 g., 0.8000 Silver .0965 oz. ASW **Ruler:** Rama VI **Obv:** Bust right **Rev:** Elephant heads flank facing elephant

Date	Mintage	F	VF	XF	Unc	BU
BE2458 (1915)	2,040,000	—	5.00	10.00	20.00	—

Y# 43a SALUNG = 1/4 BAHT
3.7500 g., 0.6500 Silver .0784 oz. ASW **Ruler:** Rama VI **Obv:** Bust right **Rev:** Elephant heads flank facing elephant

Date	Mintage	F	VF	XF	Unc	BU
BE2460 (1917)	1,100,000	—	4.00	8.00	18.50	—
BE2461 (1918)	2,170,000	—	4.00	8.00	18.50	—
BE2462 (1919)	7,860,000	—	3.00	6.50	15.00	—
BE2467 (1924)	2,100,000	—	4.00	8.00	18.50	—
BE2468 (1925)	—	—	4.00	8.00	18.50	—

Y# 43b SALUNG = 1/4 BAHT
3.7500 g., 0.5000 Silver .0603 oz. ASW **Ruler:** Rama VI **Obv:** Bust right **Rev:** Elephant heads flank facing elephant

Date	Mintage	F	VF	XF	Unc	BU
BE2462 (1919) Dot after legend	Inc. above	—	40.00	65.00	120	—

Y# 34a BAHT
Silver, 31.5 mm. **Ruler:** Rama V **Obv:** Bust left **Rev:** National arms, flags flanking **Edge:** Plain

Date	Mintage	F	VF	XF	Unc	BU
RS120 (1901)	—	100	200	400	1,500	—
RS121 (1902)	4,070,000	20.00	40.00	90.00	300	—
Note: There are two varieties, large and small date						
RS122 (1903)	19,150,000	30.00	50.00	80.00	240	—
RS123 (1904)	4,790,000	20.00	40.00	60.00	180	—
RS124 (1905)	6,770,000	20.00	40.00	60.00	180	—
RS125 (1906)	—	20.00	40.00	60.00	180	—
RS126 (1907)	—	40.00	60.00	150	380	—

DECIMAL COINAGE

25 Satang = 1 Salung; 100 Satang = 1 Baht

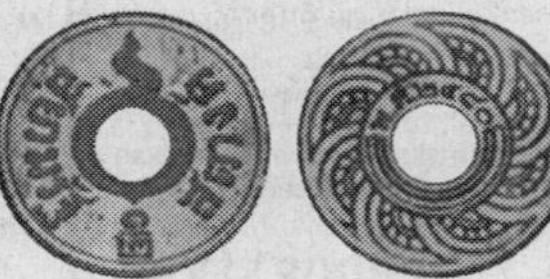

Y# 50 1/2 SATANG
Bronze **Ruler:** Rama VIII **Obv:** Hole in center divides inscription **Rev:** Hole in center of design

Date	Mintage	F	VF	XF	Unc	BU
BE2480 (1937)	—	—	0.75	1.75	3.50	—

Y# 35 SATANG

Bronze **Ruler:** Rama VI **Obv:** Hole in center divides inscription **Rev:** Hole in center of design **Edge:** Plain **Note:** Variations in lettering exist.

Date	Mintage	F	VF	XF	Unc	BU
RS127 (1908)	17,000,000	—	2.50	35.00	100	—
RS128 (1909)	150,000	—	3.50	35.00	100	—
RS129 (1910)	9,000,000	—	1.50	35.00	100	—
RS130 (1911)	30,000,000	—	1.50	25.00	50.00	—
RS132 (1913) Rare	—	—	—	—	—	—
BE2456 (1913)	10,000,000	—	1.00	1.50	4.00	—
BE2457 (1914)	1,000,000	—	2.00	4.00	12.50	—
BE2458 (1915)	5,000,000	—	0.75	1.00	2.75	—
BE2461 (1918)	18,880,000	—	0.65	1.25	3.00	—
BE2462 (1919)	6,400,000	—	0.65	1.00	2.75	—
BE2463 (1920)	17,240,000	—	1.00	1.50	3.50	—
BE2464 (1921)	6,360,000	—	15.00	25.00	100	—
BE2466 (1923)	14,000,000	—	0.75	1.00	2.75	—
BE2467 (1924)	Inc. above	—	1.00	1.50	3.50	—
BE2469 (1926)	20,000,000	—	0.50	0.75	2.50	—
BE2470 (1927)	—	—	0.50	0.75	2.50	—
BE2472 (1929)	—	—	0.50	1.00	2.75	—
BE2478 (1935)	—	—	0.50	0.70	2.00	—
BE2480 (1937)	—	—	0.50	0.70	2.00	—

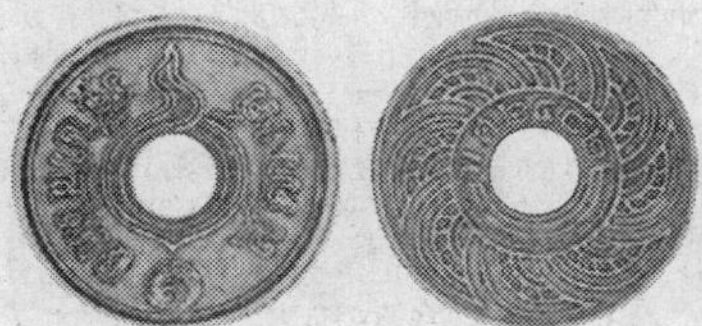

Y# 51 SATANG

Bronze **Ruler:** Rama VIII **Obv:** Hole in center divides inscription **Rev:** Hole in center of design **Edge:** Plain

Date	Mintage	F	VF	XF	Unc	BU
BE2482 (1939)	24,400,000	—	1.50	3.00	6.00	—

Y# 36 5 SATANG

Nickel, 18 mm. **Ruler:** Rama VI **Obv:** Hole in center divides inscription **Rev:** Center hole within design

Date	Mintage	F	VF	XF	Unc	BU
RS127 (1908)	7,000,000	—	3.00	35.00	100	—
RS128 (1909)	4,000,000	—	3.50	35.00	100	—
RS129 (1910)	4,000,000	—	1.50	35.00	100	—
RS131 (1912)	2,000,000	—	1.50	25.00	50.00	—
RS132 (1913) Rare	—	—	—	—	—	—
BE2456 (1913)	2,000,000	—	1.50	2.50	6.00	—
BE2457 (1914)	2,000,000	—	1.50	2.50	6.00	—
BE2461 (1918)	2,000,000	—	1.50	2.50	6.00	—
BE2462 (1919)	2,000,000	—	1.00	2.00	6.00	—
BE2463 (1920)	9,900,000	—	1.00	1.50	4.50	—
BE2464 (1921)	13,000,000	—	0.60	1.25	3.00	—
BE2469 (1926)	20,000,000	—	0.60	1.25	3.00	—
BE2478 (1935)	10,000,000	—	0.60	1.25	3.00	—
BE2480 (1937)	20,000,000	—	0.60	1.25	3.00	—

Y# 37 10 SATANG

Nickel **Ruler:** Rama VI **Obv:** Hole in center divides inscription **Rev:** Hole in center of design **Edge:** Plain **Note:** Variations in lettering exist.

Date	Mintage	F	VF	XF	Unc	BU
RS127 (1908)	7,000,000	—	1.50	35.00	100	—
RS129 (1910)	5,000,000	—	1.50	35.00	100	—
RS130 (1911)	500,000	—	2.00	5.00	12.00	—
RS131 (1912)	1,500,000	—	1.50	3.00	10.00	—
BE2456 (1913)	1,000,000	—	1.25	2.00	6.00	—
BE2457 (1914)	1,000,000	—	1.25	2.00	6.00	—
BE2461 (1918)	770,000	—	2.50	3.50	9.00	—
BE2462 (1919)	774,000	—	1.25	1.50	3.50	—
BE2463 (1920)	Inc. above	—	1.25	1.50	3.50	—
BE2464 (1921)	21,727,000	—	1.00	1.25	3.00	—

Date	Mintage	F	VF	XF	Unc	BU
BE2478 (1935)	5,000,000	—	1.00	1.25	3.00	—
BE2480 (1937)	5,000,000	—	0.75	1.00	2.50	—

Y# 48 25 SATANG = 1/4 BAHT

3.7500 g., 0.6500 Silver .0784 oz. ASW **Ruler:** Rama VII **Obv:** Uniformed bust left **Rev:** Elephant

Date	Mintage	F	VF	XF	Unc	BU
BE2472 (1929)	—	—	4.50	9.00	22.50	—

Y# 49 50 SATANG = 1/2 BAHT

7.5000 g., 0.6500 Silver .1567 oz. ASW **Ruler:** Rama VII **Obv:** Uniformed bust left **Rev:** Elephant

Date	Mintage	F	VF	XF	Unc	BU
BE2472 (1929)	17,008,000	—	7.00	16.50	35.00	—

Y# 44 2 SALUNG = 1/2 BAHT

7.5000 g., 0.8000 Silver .1929 oz. ASW **Ruler:** Rama VI **Obv:** Uniformed bust right **Rev:** Elephant heads flank facing elephant

Date	Mintage	F	VF	XF	Unc	BU
BE2458 (1915)	2,740,000	—	7.50	18.50	40.00	—

Y# 44a 2 SALUNG = 1/2 BAHT

7.5000 g., 0.6500 Silver .1568 oz. ASW **Ruler:** Rama VI **Obv:** Uniformed bust right **Rev:** Elephant heads flank facing elephant **Note:** Date varieties exist.

Date	Mintage	F	VF	XF	Unc	BU
BE2462 (1919)	3,230,000	—	6.00	14.00	30.00	—
BE2463 (1920)	4,970,000	—	6.00	14.00	30.00	—
BE2464 (1921)	—	—	6.00	14.00	30.00	—

Y# 44b 2 SALUNG = 1/2 BAHT

7.5000 g., 0.5000 Silver .1206 oz. ASW **Ruler:** Rama VI **Obv:** Uniformed bust right **Rev:** Elephant heads flank facing elephant

Date	Mintage	F	VF	XF	Unc	BU
BE2462 (1919)	Inc. above	—	7.50	16.50	32.50	—
Note: Large dot after legend						
BE2462 (1919)	Inc. above	—	7.50	16.50	32.50	—
Note: Small dot after legend						

Y# 39 BAHT

15.0000 g., 0.9000 Silver .4340 oz. ASW **Ruler:** Rama V **Obv:** Uniformed bust left **Rev:** Elephant heads flank facing elephant

Date	Mintage	F	VF	XF	Unc	BU
RS127 (1908)	1,037,000	—	2,500	3,750	6,750	—

Y# 45 BAHT

15.0000 g., 0.9000 Silver .4340 oz. ASW **Ruler:** Rama VI **Obv:** Uniformed bust right **Rev:** Elephant heads flank facing elephant

Date	Mintage	F	VF	XF	Unc	BU
BE2456 (1913)	2,690,000	—	12.50	18.50	40.00	—
Note: BE2456 is often found weakly struck so it does appear similar to a counterfeit						
BE2457 (1914)	490,000	—	14.50	25.00	50.00	—
BE2458 (1915)	5,000,000	—	12.50	18.50	40.00	—
BE2459 (1916)	9,080,000	—	12.50	18.50	32.00	—
BE2460 (1917)	14,340,000	—	12.50	18.50	32.00	—
BE2461 (1918)	3,840,000	—	12.50	18.50	45.00	—

KINGDOM OF THAILAND

1939-

DECIMAL COINAGE

25 Satang = 1 Salung; 100 Satang = 1 Baht

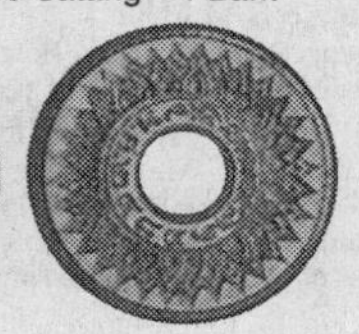

Y# 54 SATANG

Bronze **Ruler:** Rama VIII **Obv:** Hole in center of design **Rev:** Hole in center of design **Edge:** Plain

Date	Mintage	F	VF	XF	Unc	BU
BE2484 (1941)	—	—	0.50	1.50	3.00	—

Y# 57 SATANG

Tin **Ruler:** Rama VIII **Obv:** Center hole within design **Rev:** Center hole within design **Edge:** Plain **Note:** BE date and denomination in Thai numerals, without hole.

Date	Mintage	F	VF	XF	Unc	BU
BE2485 (1942)	20,700,000	—	0.30	0.50	1.00	—
Note: Approximately 790,000 coins were struck for circulation 1967-73						

Y# 60 SATANG

Tin **Ruler:** Rama VIII **Obv:** Hole in center of design **Rev:** Hole in center of design **Edge:** Plain **Note:** BE date and denomination in Western numerals. No hole.

Date	Mintage	F	VF	XF	Unc	BU
BE2487 (1944)	500,000	—	0.10	0.20	0.50	—

Y# 186 SATANG

Aluminum **Ruler:** Rama IX **Obv:** Head left **Rev:** Steepled building

Date	Mintage	F	VF	XF	Unc	BU
BE2530 (1987)	93,000	—	—	—	0.10	—
BE2531 (1988)	200,000	—	—	—	0.10	—
BE2533 (1990)	—	—	—	—	0.10	—
BE2534 (1991)	—	—	—	—	0.10	—
BE2535 (1992)	—	—	—	—	0.10	—
BE2536 (1993)	—	—	—	—	0.10	—
BE2537 (1994)	—	—	—	—	0.10	—

Y# 342 SATANG

Aluminum **Ruler:** Rama IX **Subject:** 50th Anniversary - Reign of King Rama IX **Obv:** Uniformed bust facing **Rev:** Arms

Date	Mintage	F	VF	XF	Unc	BU
BE2539 (1996)	—	—	—	—	0.15	—

Y# 55 5 SATANG

1.5000 g., 0.6500 Silver .0313 oz. ASW **Ruler:** Rama VIII **Obv:** Center hole within design **Rev:** Center hole within design

Date	Mintage	F	VF	XF	Unc	BU
BE2484 (1941)	—	—	1.50	3.00	4.50	—

Y# 58 5 SATANG

Tin **Ruler:** Rama VIII **Obv:** Hole in center of design **Rev:** Hole in center of design **Note:** BE date and denomination in Thai numerals.

Date	Mintage	F	VF	XF	Unc	BU
BE2485 (1942)	—	—	0.50	1.50	3.00	—

Y# 61 5 SATANG
Tin **Ruler:** Rama VIII **Obv:** Hole in center of design **Rev:** Hole in center of design **Note:** Thick (2.2mm) planchet. BE date and denomination in Western numerals.

Date	Mintage	F	VF	XF	Unc	BU
BE2487 (1944)	—	—	0.50	1.25	3.00	—
BE2488 (1945)	—	—	0.50	1.25	3.00	—

Y# 61a 5 SATANG
Tin **Ruler:** Rama VIII **Obv:** Hole in center of design **Rev:** Hole in center of design **Note:** Thin (2mm) planchet.

Date	Mintage	F	VF	XF	Unc	BU
BE2488 (1945)	—	—	0.50	1.25	3.00	—

Y# 61b 5 SATANG
Tin **Ruler:** Rama VIII **Obv:** Hole in center of design **Rev:** Hole in center of design **Note:** Medium planchet.

Date	Mintage	F	VF	XF	Unc	BU
BE2488 (1945)	—	—	0.50	1.25	3.00	—

Y# 64 5 SATANG
Tin **Ruler:** Rama VIII **Obv:** King Ananda, youth head left **Rev:** Mythical creature "Garuda"

Date	Mintage	F	VF	XF	Unc	BU
BE2489 (1946)	—	—	0.50	1.00	2.00	—

Y# 68 5 SATANG
Tin **Ruler:** Rama VIII **Obv:** King Ananda, youth head left **Rev:** Mythical creature "Garuda"

Date	Mintage	F	VF	XF	Unc	BU
BE2489 (1946)	24,480,000	—	0.15	0.50	1.00	—

Y# 72 5 SATANG
Tin **Ruler:** Rama IX **Obv:** Uniformed bust left with one medal **Rev:** Mantled arms

Date	Mintage	F	VF	XF	Unc	BU
BE2493 (1950)	Est. 6,480,000	—	0.50	0.75	1.25	—

Note: Coins bearing this date were also struck in 1954, 58, 59, and 73. Mintages are included here

Y# 72a 5 SATANG
Aluminum-Bronze **Ruler:** Rama IX **Obv:** Uniformed bust left **Rev:** Mantled arms **Edge:** Plain

Date	Mintage	F	VF	XF	Unc	BU
BE2493 (1950)	15,500,000	—	0.25	1.00	2.00	—

Y# 78 5 SATANG
Aluminum-Bronze **Ruler:** Rama IX **Obv:** Smaller head, 3 medals on uniform **Rev:** Mantled arms **Edge:** Plain

Date	Mintage	F	VF	XF	Unc	BU
BE2500 (1957)	Est. 46,440,000	—	—	0.10	0.25	—

Note: Minted without date change until 1987

Y# 78a 5 SATANG
Bronze **Ruler:** Rama IX **Obv:** Uniformed bust left **Rev:** Mantled arms **Edge:** Plain

Date	Mintage	F	VF	XF	Unc	BU
BE2500 (1957)	Est. 6,240,000	—	0.50	1.50	2.00	—

Y# 78b 5 SATANG
Tin **Ruler:** Rama IX **Obv:** Uniformed bust left **Rev:** Mantled arms

Date	Mintage	F	VF	XF	Unc	BU
BE2500 (1957)	—	—	1.75	3.00	5.00	—

Note: The above coins were struck to replace Y#72 in mint sets

Y# 208 5 SATANG
Aluminum **Ruler:** Rama IX **Obv:** Bust left **Rev:** Steepled building

Date	Mintage	F	VF	XF	Unc	BU
BE2530 (1987)	—	—	—	—	20.00	—
BE2531 (1988)	704,000	—	—	—	0.10	—
BE2533 (1990)	—	—	—	—	0.10	—
BE2534 (1991)	—	—	—	—	0.10	—
BE2535 (1992)	—	—	—	—	0.10	—
BE2536 (1993)	—	—	—	—	0.10	—
BE2537 (1994)	—	—	—	—	0.10	—

Y# 343 5 SATANG
Aluminum **Ruler:** Rama IX **Subject:** 50th Anniversary - Reign of King Rama IX **Obv:** Bust facing **Rev:** Arms

Date	Mintage	F	VF	XF	Unc	BU
BE2539 (1996)	—	—	—	—	0.25	—

Y# 56 10 SATANG
2.5000 g., 0.6500 Silver .0522 oz. ASW **Ruler:** Rama VIII **Obv:** Hole in center of design **Rev:** Hole in center of design **Edge:** Plain

Date	Mintage	F	VF	XF	Unc	BU
BE2484 (1941)	—	—	2.00	4.00	8.00	—

Y# 59 10 SATANG
Tin **Ruler:** Rama VIII **Obv:** Hole in center of design **Rev:** Hole in center of design **Note:** BE date and denomination in Thai numerals.

Date	Mintage	F	VF	XF	Unc	BU
BE2485 (1942)	230,000	—	1.00	2.00	5.00	—

Y# 62 10 SATANG
Tin **Ruler:** Rama VIII **Obv:** Hole in center of design **Rev:** Hole in center of design **Note:** Thick (2.5mm) planchet. BE date and denomination in Western numerals.

Date	Mintage	F	VF	XF	Unc	BU
BE2487 (1944)	—	—	1.00	2.00	3.50	—
BE2488 (1945)	—	—	3.50	7.00	15.00	—

Y# 62a 10 SATANG
Tin **Ruler:** Rama IX **Obv:** Hole in center of design **Rev:** Hole in center of design **Note:** Thin (2mm) planchet.

Date	Mintage	F	VF	XF	Unc	BU
BE2488 (1945)	—	—	1.00	2.50	4.00	—

Y# 65 10 SATANG
Tin **Ruler:** Rama IX **Obv:** King Ananda, child head **Rev:** Mythical creature "Garuda"

Date	Mintage	F	VF	XF	Unc	BU
BE2489 (1946)	—	—	0.50	1.25	2.25	—

Y# 69 10 SATANG
Tin **Ruler:** Rama IX **Obv:** Youth head **Rev:** Mythical creature "Garuda" **Edge:** Plain

Date	Mintage	F	VF	XF	Unc	BU
BE2489 (1946)	40,470,000	—	0.50	1.25	2.00	—

Y# 73 10 SATANG
Tin **Ruler:** Rama IX **Obv:** King Bhumiphol, one medal on uniform **Rev:** Arms **Edge:** Plain

Date	Mintage	F	VF	XF	Unc	BU
BE2493 (1950)	139,695,000	—	0.40	1.00	1.50	—

Note: These coins were also struck in 1954-1973 and the mintages are also included here

Y# 73a 10 SATANG
Aluminum-Bronze **Ruler:** Rama IX **Obv:** King Bhumiphol left **Rev:** Arms

Date	Mintage	F	VF	XF	Unc	BU
BE2493 (1950)	4,060,000	—	0.75	1.50	2.50	—

Y# 79 10 SATANG
Aluminum-Bronze **Ruler:** Rama IX **Obv:** Smaller head, 3 medals on uniform **Rev:** Mantled arms with thin style legend

Date	Mintage	F	VF	XF	Unc	BU
BE2500 (1957)	Est. 55,410,000	—	0.10	0.25	0.50	—

Note: Minted without date change until 1987

Y# 79a 10 SATANG
Bronze **Ruler:** Rama IX **Obv:** Uniformed bust left **Rev:** Mantled arms with thick style legend **Edge:** Plain

Date	Mintage	F	VF	XF	Unc	BU
BE2500 (1957)	13,365,000	—	0.25	0.75	1.25	—
BE2501 (1958)	—	—	0.25	0.75	1.25	—

Y# 79b 10 SATANG
Tin **Ruler:** Rama IX **Obv:** Uniformed bust left **Rev:** Mantled arms with thick style legend

Date	Mintage	F	VF	XF	Unc	BU
BE2500 (1957)	—	—	—	—	20.00	—

Y# 79c 10 SATANG
Bronze **Ruler:** Rama IX **Obv:** Uniformed bust left **Rev:** Mantled arms with thin style legend

Date	Mintage	F	VF	XF	Unc	BU
BE2500 (1957)	Inc. above	—	100	200	400	—

Y# 79d 10 SATANG
Aluminum-Bronze **Ruler:** Rama IX **Obv:** Uniformed bust left **Rev:** Mantled arms with thick style legend **Edge:** Plain

Date	Mintage	F	VF	XF	Unc	BU
BE2500 (1957)	—	—	0.10	0.25	0.50	—

Y# 209 10 SATANG
Aluminum **Ruler:** Rama IX **Obv:** Young bust left **Rev:** Steepled building

Date	Mintage	F	VF	XF	Unc	BU
BE2530 (1987)	—	—	—	—	20.00	—
BE2531 (1988)	900,000	—	—	—	0.10	—
BE2533 (1990)	—	—	—	—	0.10	—
BE2534 (1991)	—	—	—	—	0.10	—
BE2535 (1992)	—	—	—	—	0.10	—
BE2536 (1993)	—	—	—	—	0.10	—
BE2537 (1994)	—	—	—	—	0.10	—

Y# 344 10 SATANG
Aluminum **Ruler:** Rama IX **Subject:** 50th Anniversary - Reign of King Rama IX **Obv:** Bust facing **Rev:** Arms

Date	Mintage	F	VF	XF	Unc	BU
BE2539 (1996)	—	—	—	—	0.35	—

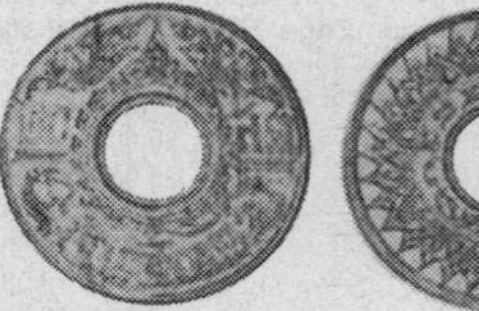
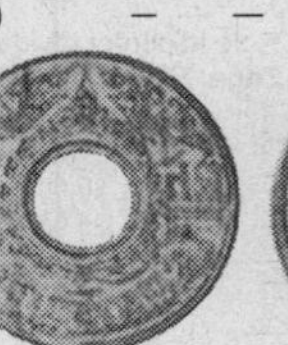

Y# A56 20 SATANG
3.0000 g., 0.6500 Silver .0627 oz. ASW **Ruler:** Rama VIII **Obv:** Hole in center of design **Rev:** Hole in center of design **Note:** BE date and denomination in Thai numerals

Date	Mintage	F	VF	XF	Unc	BU
BE2485 (1942)	—	—	3.00	6.00	12.00	—

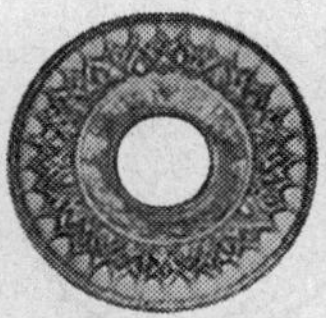

Y# 63 20 SATANG

Tin **Ruler:** Rama VIII **Obv:** Hole in center of design **Rev:** Hole in center of design **Edge:** Plain **Note:** BE date and denomination in Western numerals.

Date	Mintage	F	VF	XF	Unc	BU
BE2488 (1945)	—	—	1.00	2.50	5.00	—

Y# 66 25 SATANG = 1/4 BAHT

Tin **Ruler:** Rama VIII **Obv:** King Ananda, childs head **Rev:** Mythical creature "Garuda"

Date	Mintage	F	VF	XF	Unc	BU
BE2489 (1946)	—	—	2.50	4.50	12.50	—

Y# 70 25 SATANG = 1/4 BAHT

Tin **Ruler:** Rama VIII **Obv:** Youth's head left **Rev:** Mythical creature "Garuda" **Edge:** Reeded

Date	Mintage	F	VF	XF	Unc	BU
BE2489 (1946)	Est. 226,348,000	—	0.20	0.40	0.75	—

Note: These coins were also struck 1954-64 and mintage figure is a total

Y# 76 25 SATANG = 1/4 BAHT

Aluminum-Bronze **Ruler:** Rama IX **Obv:** Young bust left, one medal on uniform **Rev:** Mantled arms

Date	Mintage	F	VF	XF	Unc	BU
BE2493 (1950)	23,170,000	—	0.75	1.75	4.00	—

Y# 80 25 SATANG = 1/4 BAHT

Aluminum-Bronze **Ruler:** Rama IX **Obv:** Smaller head, 3 medals on uniform **Rev:** Mantled arms **Edge:** Reeded **Note:** Dot after the letters for "Satang" are found with raised and incuse varieties.

Date	Mintage	F	VF	XF	Unc	BU
BE2500 (1957)	620,480,000	—	0.10	0.15	0.25	—

Note: Minted without date change and with and without reeded edges until 1987

Y# 109 25 SATANG = 1/4 BAHT

Brass **Ruler:** Rama IX **Obv:** Bust left **Rev:** Value and inscription **Note:** Date varieties exist.

Date	Mintage	F	VF	XF	Unc	BU
BE2520 (1977)	183,356,000	—	—	0.10	0.15	—

Y# 187 25 SATANG = 1/4 BAHT

Aluminum-Bronze **Ruler:** Rama IX **Obv:** Head left **Rev:** Steepled building **Edge:** Reeded

Date	Mintage	F	VF	XF	Unc	BU
BE2530 (1987)	5,108,000	—	—	—	0.20	—
BE2531 (1988)	42,096,000	—	—	—	0.10	—
BE2532 (1989)	—	—	—	—	0.10	—
BE2533 (1990)	—	—	—	—	0.10	—
BE2534 (1991)	—	—	—	—	0.10	—
BE2535 (1992)	—	—	—	—	0.10	—
BE2536 (1993)	—	—	—	—	0.10	—
BE2537 (1994)	—	—	—	—	0.10	—
BE2538 (1995)	—	—	—	—	0.10	—
BE2540 (1997)	—	—	—	—	0.10	—
BE2541 (1998)	—	—	—	—	0.10	—

Y# 345 25 SATANG = 1/4 BAHT

Brass **Ruler:** Rama IX **Subject:** Golden Jubilee - Reign of King Rama IX **Obv:** Bust facing **Rev:** Arms with supporters

Date	Mintage	F	VF	XF	Unc	BU
BE2539 (1996)	—	—	—	—	0.50	—

Y# 67 50 SATANG = 1/2 BAHT

Tin **Ruler:** Rama VIII **Obv:** King Ananda, child's head left **Rev:** Mythical creature "Garuda"

Date	Mintage	F	VF	XF	Unc	BU
BE2489 (1946)	—	—	40.00	75.00	180	—

Y# 71 50 SATANG = 1/2 BAHT

Tin **Ruler:** Rama VIII **Obv:** Youth's head left **Rev:** Mythical creature "Garuda" **Edge:** Reeded

Date	Mintage	F	VF	XF	Unc	BU
BE2489 (1946)	17,008,000	—	0.75	1.50	4.00	—

Note: These coins were minted from 1954-1957 and mintage figure is a total

Y# 77 50 SATANG = 1/2 BAHT

Aluminum-Bronze **Ruler:** Rama IX **Obv:** Young bust left, 1 medal on uniform **Rev:** Mantled arms

Date	Mintage	F	VF	XF	Unc	BU
BE2493 (1950)	20,710,000	—	—	—	20.00	—

Y# 81 50 SATANG = 1/2 BAHT

Aluminum-Bronze **Ruler:** Rama IX **Obv:** Smaller head, 3 medals on uniform **Rev:** Mantled arms **Edge:** Reeded

Date	Mintage	F	VF	XF	Unc	BU
BE2500 (1957)	439,874,000	—	0.10	0.15	0.25	—

Note: Minted without date change until 1987

Y# 168 50 SATANG = 1/2 BAHT

Aluminum-Bronze **Ruler:** Rama IX **Obv:** Bust left **Rev:** Value and inscription **Edge:** Plain

Date	Mintage	F	VF	XF	Unc	BU
BE2523 (1980)	122,260,000	—	0.10	0.15	0.25	—

Y# 203 50 SATANG = 1/2 BAHT

Brass **Ruler:** Rama IX **Obv:** Head left **Rev:** Steepled building divides value

Date	Mintage	F	VF	XF	Unc	BU
BE2530 (1987)	—	—	—	—	15.00	—
BE2531 (1988)	23,776,000	—	—	—	0.10	—
BE2532 (1989)	—	—	0.20	0.30	1.00	—
BE2533 (1990)	—	—	—	—	0.10	—
BE2534 (1991)	—	—	—	—	0.10	—
BE2535 (1992)	—	—	—	—	0.10	—
BE2536 (1993)	—	—	—	—	0.10	—
BE2537 (1994)	—	—	—	—	0.10	—
BE2538 (1995)	—	—	—	—	0.10	—
BE2539 (1996)	—	—	—	—	0.10	—
BE2543 (2000)	—	—	—	—	0.10	—

Y# 329 50 SATANG = 1/2 BAHT

Aluminum-Bronze **Ruler:** Rama IX **Subject:** 50th Year of Reign - King Rama IX **Obv:** Bust facing **Rev:** Arms

Date	Mintage	F	VF	XF	Unc	BU
BE2539 (1996)	—	—	—	—	0.35	—

Y# 82.1 BAHT

Copper-Nickel-Silver-Zinc, 26.9 mm. **Ruler:** Rama IX **Obv:** Bust left, three medals on uniform **Rev:** National arms **Edge:** Reeded

Date	Mintage	F	VF	XF	Unc	BU
BE2500 (1957)	3,143,000	—	0.75	1.50	6.00	—

Note: These coins were minted from 1958-60 and mintage figure is a total

Y# 82.2 BAHT

Copper-Nickel, 26.9 mm. **Ruler:** Rama IX **Obv:** Bust left, one medal on uniform **Rev:** National arms

Date	Mintage	F	VF	XF	Unc	BU
BE2500 (1957)	—	—	0.75	1.50	6.00	—

Y# 82a BAHT

Silver, 26.9 mm. **Ruler:** Rama IX **Obv:** Bust left **Rev:** National arms

Date	Mintage	F	VF	XF	Unc	BU
BE2500 (1957) Rare	—	—	—	—	—	—

Y# 83 BAHT

Copper-Nickel, 26.9 mm. **Ruler:** Rama IX **Subject:** King Rama IX and Queen Sirikit return from abroad **Obv:** Conjoined busts left flanked by diamonds **Rev:** Mantled arms **Edge:** Reeded

Date	Mintage	F	VF	XF	Unc	BU
BE2504 (1961)	4,430,000	—	0.40	0.75	2.00	—

Y# 84 BAHT

Copper-Nickel, 26.9 mm. **Ruler:** Rama IX **Obv:** Young bust left **Rev:** Mantled arms **Edge:** Reeded

Date	Mintage	F	VF	XF	Unc	BU
BE2505 (1962)	883,086,000	—	0.10	0.15	0.50	—

Note: These coins were minted from 1962-82 and mintage figure is a total

Y# 85 BAHT

Copper-Nickel, 26.9 mm. **Ruler:** Rama IX **Subject:** 36th Birthday - King Rama IX **Obv:** Uniformed bust left **Rev:** Design in center circle of design **Edge:** Reeded

Date	Mintage	F	VF	XF	Unc	BU
ND(1963)	3,000,000	—	0.25	0.75	2.00	—

Y# 87 BAHT

Copper-Nickel, 26.9 mm. **Ruler:** Rama IX **Subject:** 5th Asian Games Bangkok **Obv:** Conjoined busts right **Rev:** Star design **Edge:** Reeded

Date	Mintage	F	VF	XF	Unc	BU
BE2509 (1966)	9,000,000	—	0.25	0.75	3.00	—

Y# 91 BAHT

Copper-Nickel, 26.9 mm. **Ruler:** Rama IX **Subject:** 6th Asian Games Bangkok **Obv:** Conjoined busts right **Rev:** Star design **Edge:** Reeded

Date	Mintage	F	VF	XF	Unc	BU
BE2513 (1970)	9,000,000	—	0.25	0.75	1.50	—

Y# 96 BAHT

Copper-Nickel, 26.9 mm. **Ruler:** Rama IX **Series:** F.A.O. **Obv:** Head left **Rev:** State ploughing ceremony **Edge:** Reeded **Note:** Released on May 7, 1973.

Date	Mintage	F	VF	XF	Unc	BU
BE2515 (1972)	9,000,000	—	0.10	0.25	0.75	—

Y# 97 BAHT

Copper-Nickel, 26.9 mm. **Ruler:** Rama IX **Subject:** Prince Vajiralongkorn Investiture **Obv:** Young head left **Rev:** Crowned monogram **Edge:** Reeded

Date	Mintage	F	VF	XF	Unc	BU
BE2515 (1972)	9,000,000	—	0.15	0.40	1.00	—

Y# 99 BAHT

Copper-Nickel, 26.9 mm. **Ruler:** Rama IX **Subject:** 25th Anniversary - World Health Organization **Obv:** Head left **Rev:** Arms within wreath **Edge:** Reeded

Date	Mintage	F	VF	XF	Unc	BU
BE2516 (1973)	1,000,000	—	0.25	0.65	1.25	—

Y# 100 BAHT

Copper-Nickel, 25 mm. **Ruler:** Rama IX **Obv:** Head left **Rev:** Mythical creature "Garuda" **Edge:** Reeded

Date	Mintage	F	VF	XF	Unc	BU
BE2517 (1974)	248,978,000	—	0.15	0.40	1.00	—

Y# 105 BAHT

7.0000 g., Copper-Nickel, 25 mm. **Ruler:** Rama IX **Subject:** 8th SEAP Games **Obv:** Conjoined heads right **Rev:** Flower design within center circle of poinsettia design

Date	Mintage	F	VF	XF	Unc	BU
BE2518 (1975)	3,000,000	—	0.25	0.65	1.25	—

Y# 107 BAHT

7.0000 g., Copper-Nickel, 25 mm. **Ruler:** Rama IX **Subject:** 75th Birthday of Princess Mother October 21st **Obv:** Bust facing **Rev:** Monogram **Edge:** Reeded

Date	Mintage	F	VF	XF	Unc	BU
BE2518 (1975)	9,000,000	—	0.15	0.40	1.00	—

Y# 110 BAHT

7.0000 g., Copper-Nickel **Ruler:** Rama IX **Obv:** Head left **Rev:** Suphannahong, with Wat Aran Temple **Edge:** Reeded **Note:** Varieties exist.

Date	Mintage	F	VF	XF	Unc	BU
BE2520 (1977)	506,460,000	—	0.10	0.20	0.50	—

Y# 112 BAHT

7.0000 g., Copper-Nickel, 25 mm. **Ruler:** Rama IX **Series:** F.A.O. **Obv:** Figures scattering rice **Rev:** Seated female figure left

Date	Mintage	F	VF	XF	Unc	BU
BE2520 (1977)	2,000,000	—	0.15	0.40	1.00	—

Y# 114 BAHT

7.0000 g., Copper-Nickel, 25 mm. **Ruler:** Rama IX **Subject:** Princess Sirindhorn, 1st Thai Royal graduate of a great university **Obv:** Bust left **Rev:** Radiant crown **Edge:** Reeded

Date	Mintage	F	VF	XF	Unc	BU
BE2520 (1977)	8,998,000	—	0.15	0.40	1.00	—

Y# 114a BAHT

Bronze, 25 mm. **Ruler:** Rama IX **Subject:** Princess Sirindhorn, 1st Thai Royal graduate of a great university **Obv:** Bust left **Rev:** Radiant crown

Date	Mintage	F	VF	XF	Unc	BU
BE2520 (1977)	—	—	—	—	—	—

Y# 124 BAHT

7.0000 g., Copper-Nickel **Ruler:** Rama IX **Subject:** Investiture of Princess Sirindhorn, May 12, female counterpart to the crown prince **Obv:** Bust right **Rev:** Crowned monogram

Date	Mintage	F	VF	XF	Unc	BU
BE2520 (1977)	5,000,000	—	0.15	0.40	1.00	—

Y# 127 BAHT

7.0000 g., Copper-Nickel, 25 mm. **Ruler:** Rama IX **Subject:** Graduation of Crown Prince Vajiralongkorn September 15, with the rank of "Panturi" **Obv:** Bust left **Rev:** Crown within oval design **Edge:** Reeded

Date	Mintage	F	VF	XF	Unc	BU
BE2521 (1978)	5,000,000	—	0.10	0.20	0.50	—

Y# 130 BAHT

7.0000 g., Copper-Nickel, 25 mm. **Ruler:** Rama IX **Subject:** 8th Asian Games **Obv:** Conjoined busts right **Rev:** Small radiant sun within design **Edge:** Reeded

Date	Mintage	F	VF	XF	Unc	BU
BE2521 (1978)	5,000,000	—	0.10	0.20	0.50	—

Y# 157 BAHT

7.0000 g., Copper-Nickel, 25 mm. **Ruler:** Rama IX **Series:** World Food Day October 16 **Obv:** Bust left **Rev:** F.A.O. logo above wheat sprigs

Date	Mintage	F	VF	XF	Unc	BU
BE2525 (1982)	1,500,000	—	0.10	0.20	0.50	—

Y# 159.1 BAHT

7.0000 g., Copper-Nickel, 25 mm. **Ruler:** Rama IX **Obv:** Large bust with collar touching hairline **Rev:** The Grand Palace **Edge:** Reeded **Note:** 2527 and 2528 are frozen dates, with the Thai numerals for 27 and 28 in the Finance Ministry decal at the bottom of the reverse.

Date	Mintage	F	VF	XF	Unc	BU
BE2525 (1982)	123,585,000	—	0.10	0.20	0.50	—
BE2525 (1984)	—	—	0.10	0.20	0.50	—
BE2525 (1985)	—	—	0.10	0.20	0.50	—

Y# 159.2 BAHT

7.0000 g., Copper-Nickel **Ruler:** Rama IX **Obv:** Small bust with space between collar and lower hairline **Rev:** The Grand Palace **Edge:** Reeded

Date	Mintage	F	VF	XF	Unc	BU
BE2525 (1982)	Inc. above	—	2.50	5.00	10.00	—

Y# 183 BAHT

Copper-Nickel, 20 mm. **Ruler:** Rama IX **Obv:** Head left **Rev:** Palace **Edge:** Reeded **Note:** Circulation coinage. Varieties exist.

Date	Mintage	F	VF	XF	Unc	BU
BE2529 (1986)	—	—	0.20	0.30	1.00	—
BE2530 (1987)	325,271,000	—	—	—	0.10	—
BE2531 (1988)	391,442,000	—	—	—	0.10	—
BE2532 (1989)	—	—	—	—	0.10	—
BE2533 (1990)	—	—	—	—	0.10	—
BE2534 (1991)	—	—	—	—	0.10	—
BE2535 (1992)	—	—	—	—	0.10	—
BE2536 (1993)	—	—	—	—	0.10	—
BE2537 (1994)	—	—	—	—	0.10	—
BE2538 (1995)	—	—	—	—	0.10	—
BE2539 (1996)	—	—	—	—	0.10	—
BE2540 (1997)	—	—	—	—	0.10	—
BE2541 (1998)	—	—	—	—	0.10	—
BE2542 (1999)	—	—	—	—	0.10	—
BE2543 (2000)	—	—	—	—	0.10	—

Y# 330 BAHT

Copper-Nickel, 20 mm. **Ruler:** Rama IX **Subject:** 50th Anniversary - Reign of King Rama IX June 8 **Obv:** Bust facing **Rev:** Arms with supporters **Edge:** Reeded

Date	Mintage	F	VF	XF	Unc	BU
BE2539 (1996)	—	—	—	—	0.35	—

Y# 134 2 BAHT

Copper-Nickel, 27 mm. **Ruler:** Rama IX **Subject:** Graduation of Princess Chulabhorn from Gusaehit University July 19 **Obv:** Bust 1/4 left **Rev:** Design within circle **Edge:** Plain **Note:** Science of Agriculture University.

Date	Mintage	F	VF	XF	Unc	BU
BE2522 (1979)	5,000,000	—	0.20	0.40	1.00	—

Y# 176 2 BAHT

Copper-Nickel Clad Copper, 22 mm. **Ruler:** Rama IX **Subject:** International Youth Year **Obv:** Bust left **Rev:** Conjoined profiles right within wreath **Edge:** Reeded

Date	Mintage	F	VF	XF	Unc	BU
BE2528 (1985)	10,000,000	—	0.20	0.40	1.00	—

Y# 177 2 BAHT

Copper-Nickel Clad Copper, 22 mm. **Ruler:** Rama IX **Subject:** XII SEAP Games Bangkok December 8-17 **Obv:** Half length bust facing **Rev:** Games logo flanked by value **Edge:** Reeded

Date	Mintage	F	VF	XF	Unc	BU
BE2528 (1985)	5,000,000	—	0.20	0.40	1.00	—

Y# 178 2 BAHT

Copper-Nickel Clad Copper, 22 mm. **Ruler:** Rama IX **Subject:** National Years of the Trees 2528-2531 **Obv:** Bust left **Rev:** Inscription within tree flanked by emblems below **Edge:** Reeded

Date	Mintage	F	VF	XF	Unc	BU
ND (1986)	3,000,000	—	0.50	1.00	3.50	—

Y# 180 2 BAHT

Copper-Nickel Clad Copper, 22 mm. **Ruler:** Rama IX **Subject:** Year of Peace **Obv:** Bust left **Rev:** Dove divides wreath below inscription **Note:** Australia, Russia and Mongolia issued coins with identical motif.

Date	Mintage	F	VF	XF	Unc	BU
BE2529 (1986)	5,000,000	—	—	—	0.50	—

Y# 191 2 BAHT

Copper-Nickel Clad Copper, 22 mm. **Ruler:** Rama IX **Subject:** Princess Chulabhorn Awarded Einstein Medal for research October 24 **Obv:** Bust in cap and gown 1/4 left **Rev:** Head left within center circle of hexagon design

Date	Mintage	F	VF	XF	Unc	BU
BE2529 (1986)	3,000,000	—	—	—	0.50	—

Y# 188 2 BAHT

Copper-Nickel Clad Copper, 22 mm. **Ruler:** Rama IX **Subject:** 100th Year of "Nairoi" Chulalongkorn Military Academy **Obv:** Conjoined busts left **Rev:** Flagged arms

Date	Mintage	F	VF	XF	Unc	BU
BE2530 (1987)	3,000,000	—	—	—	0.50	—

Y# 194 2 BAHT

Copper-Nickel Clad Copper, 22 mm. **Ruler:** Rama IX **Subject:** 60th Birthday - King Rama IX, December 5 **Obv:** Bust facing **Rev:** Radiant crown

Date	Mintage	F	VF	XF	Unc	BU
BE2530 (1987)	10,000	—	—	—	0.50	—

Y# 204 2 BAHT

Copper-Nickel Clad Copper, 22 mm. **Ruler:** Rama IX **Subject:** 72nd Anniversary of Thai Cooperatives February 26 **Obv:** Conjoined busts left **Rev:** Inscription **Edge:** Reeded

Date	Mintage	F	VF	XF	Unc	BU
BE2531 (1988)	3,000,000	—	—	—	0.50	—

Y# 210 2 BAHT

Copper-Nickel Clad Copper, 22 mm. **Ruler:** Rama IX **Subject:** 42nd Anniversary - Reign of King Rama IX July 2 **Obv:** Bust facing **Rev:** Crowned monogram **Edge:** Reeded

Date	Mintage	F	VF	XF	Unc	BU
BE2531 (1988)	5,000,000	—	—	—	0.50	—

Y# 220 2 BAHT

Copper-Nickel Clad Copper, 22 mm. **Ruler:** Rama IX **Subject:** 100th Anniversary of Siriraj Hospital April 26 **Obv:** Conjoined busts left **Rev:** Radiant crown above design

Date	Mintage	F	VF	XF	Unc	BU
BE2531 (1988)	3,412,000	—	—	—	0.50	—

Y# 222 2 BAHT

Copper-Nickel Clad Copper, 22 mm. **Ruler:** Rama IX **Subject:** Crown Prince's 36th birthday **Obv:** Head 1/4 left **Rev:** Crowned monogram within lightning bolts

Date	Mintage	F	VF	XF	Unc	BU
BE2531 (1988)	2,000,000	—	—	—	0.50	—

Y# 225 2 BAHT

Copper-Nickel Clad Copper, 22 mm. **Ruler:** Rama IX **Subject:** 72nd Anniversary of Chulalongkorn University March 26 **Obv:** Conjoined busts left **Rev:** Radiant crown **Edge:** Reeded

Date	Mintage	F	VF	XF	Unc	BU
BE2532 (1989)	3,000,000	—	—	—	0.50	—

Y# 230 2 BAHT

Copper-Nickel Clad Copper, 22 mm. **Ruler:** Rama IX **Subject:** Centennial of First Medical College, Siriraj, September 5 2433-2533 **Obv:** Conjoined uniformed busts facing **Rev:** First medical college **Edge:** Reeded

Date	Mintage	F	VF	XF	Unc	BU
BE2533 (1990)	1,000,000	—	—	—	0.50	—

Y# 232 2 BAHT

Copper-Nickel Clad Copper, 22 mm. **Ruler:** Rama IX **Subject:** 90th Birthday of Queen Mother October 21 **Obv:** Crown on stand flanked by others **Rev:** Bust 1/4 left **Edge:** Reeded

Date	Mintage	F	VF	XF	Unc	BU
BE2533 (1990)	2,000,000	—	—	—	0.50	—

Y# 235 2 BAHT

Copper-Nickel Clad Copper, 22 mm. **Ruler:** Rama IX **Subject:** 100th Anniversary - Office of the Comptroller General 2433-2533 **Obv:** Conjoined uniformed busts 1/4 left **Rev:** Building above computer, typewriter and phone **Edge:** Reeded

Date	Mintage	F	VF	XF	Unc	BU
BE2533 (1990)	1,000,000	—	—	—	0.50	—

Y# 243 2 BAHT

Copper-Nickel Clad Copper, 22 mm. **Ruler:** Rama IX **Subject:** World Health Organization **Obv:** Bust of Queen Mother 1/4 left **Rev:** Gold medal for good health, December 17 **Edge:** Reeded

Date	Mintage	F	VF	XF	Unc	BU
BE2533 (1990)	2,000,000	—	—	—	1.00	—

Y# 237 2 BAHT

Copper-Nickel Clad Copper, 22 mm. **Ruler:** Rama IX **Subject:** 36th Birthday of Princess Sirindhorn April 2 **Obv:** Uniformed bust 1/4 left **Rev:** Crowned monogram flanked by stars above sprigs **Edge:** Reeded

Date	Mintage	F	VF	XF	Unc	BU
BE2534 (1991)	2,300,000	—	—	—	0.50	—

Y# 240 2 BAHT

Copper-Nickel Clad Copper, 22 mm. **Ruler:** Rama IX **Subject:** 80th Anniversary of Thai Boy Scouts July 1 2454-2534 **Obv:** Conjoined young busts 1/4 left in scout uniforms **Rev:** Scouting emblem and phrase "Better to die than to lie" **Edge:** Reeded

Date	Mintage	F	VF	XF	Unc	BU
BE2534 (1991)	2,000,000	—	—	—	1.50	—

Y# 255 2 BAHT

Copper-Nickel Clad Copper, 22 mm. **Ruler:** Rama IX **Subject:** Princess Sirindhorn's Magsaysay Foundation Award for public administration August 31 **Obv:** Seated figures within circle **Rev:** Shield within sprig and circle below cameo **Edge:** Reeded

Date	Mintage	F	VF	XF	Unc	BU
BE2534 (1991)	12,000,000	—	—	—	0.50	—

Y# 248 2 BAHT

Copper-Nickel Clad Copper, 22 mm. **Ruler:** Rama IX **Subject:** Centenary Celebration of Mahitorn - Father of King Rama IX, January 1 **Obv:** Head facing **Rev:** Crown on stand flanked by others **Edge:** Reeded

Date	Mintage	F	VF	XF	Unc	BU
BE2535 (1992)	2,308,000	—	—	—	0.50	—

Y# 251 2 BAHT

Copper-Nickel Clad Copper, 22 mm. **Ruler:** Rama IX **Subject:** Ministry of Justice Centennial March 25 **Obv:** Conjoined busts left **Rev:** Balance scales within design **Edge:** Reeded

Date	Mintage	F	VF	XF	Unc	BU
BE2535 (1992)	1,500,000	—	—	—	0.50	—

Y# 253 2 BAHT

Copper-Nickel Clad Copper, 22 mm. **Ruler:** Rama IX **Subject:** Ministry of Justice Centennial April 1 2435-2535 **Obv:** Conjoined busts facing **Rev:** Mythical animal within circle **Edge:** Reeded

Date	Mintage	F	VF	XF	Unc	BU
1992 (1992)	1,500,000	—	—	—	0.50	—

Y# 259 2 BAHT

Copper-Nickel Clad Copper, 22 mm. **Ruler:** Rama IX **Subject:** Queen's 60th Birthday August 12 (Thai Mother's Day) **Obv:** Crowned bust facing **Rev:** Crowned monogram **Edge:** Reeded

Date	Mintage	F	VF	XF	Unc	BU
BE2535 (1992)	1,700,000	—	—	—	0.50	—

Y# 268 2 BAHT

Copper-Nickel Clad Copper, 22 mm. **Ruler:** Rama IX **Subject:** 60th Anniversary of the National Assembly - June 28 **Obv:** Conjoined busts left **Rev:** Anatasamakhom Throne Hall **Edge:** Reeded

Date	Mintage	F	VF	XF	Unc	BU
BE2535 (1992)	1,000,000	—	—	—	0.50	—

Y# 270 2 BAHT

Copper-Nickel Clad Copper, 22 mm. **Ruler:** Rama IX **Subject:** 100th Anniversary Ministry of Agriculture April 1 2435-2535 **Obv:** Conjoined busts 1/4 left **Rev:** Emblem within sprigs **Edge:** Reeded

Date	Mintage	F	VF	XF	Unc	BU
BE2535 (1992)	1,000,000	—	—	—	0.50	—

Y# 276 2 BAHT

Copper-Nickel Clad Copper, 22 mm. **Ruler:** Rama IX **Subject:** Centennial of Thai Teacher Training October 12 **Obv:** Conjoined busts left **Rev:** Emblem **Edge:** Reeded

Date	Mintage	F	VF	XF	Unc	BU
BE2535 (1992)	1,200,000	—	—	—	0.50	—

Y# 277 2 BAHT

Copper-Nickel Clad Copper, 22 mm. **Ruler:** Rama IX **Subject:** 50th Year of Thai National Bank December 10 **Obv:** Conjoined busts facing **Rev:** Seated figure

Date	Mintage	F	VF	XF	Unc	BU
BE2535 (1992)	1,000,000	—	—	—	0.50	—

Y# 272 2 BAHT

Copper-Nickel Clad Copper, 22 mm. **Ruler:** Rama IX **Subject:** King's 64th Birthday November 18 **Obv:** Conjoined busts 1/4 left **Rev:** Crowned monograms **Edge:** Reeded **Note:** In honor of the King reaching the lifespan of his great-grandfather.

Date	Mintage	F	VF	XF	Unc	BU
BE2535 (1992)	1,000,000	—	—	—	0.50	—

Y# 278 2 BAHT

Copper-Nickel Clad Copper, 22 mm. **Ruler:** Rama IX **Subject:** Centennial of Attorney General's Office April 1 2436-2536 **Obv:** Conjoined busts facing **Rev:** Crowned balance scale **Edge:** Reeded

Date	Mintage	F	VF	XF	Unc	BU
BE2536 (1993)	1,000,000	—	—	—	0.50	—

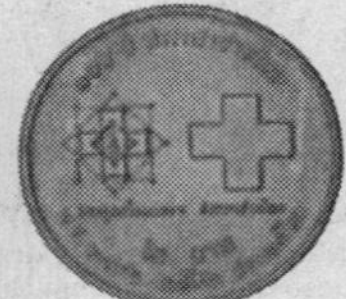

Y# 279 2 BAHT

Copper-Nickel Clad Copper, 22 mm. **Ruler:** Rama IX **Subject:** Centennial of Thai Red Cross 2436-2536 **Obv:** Conjoined busts 1/4 left **Rev:** Symbols **Edge:** Reeded

Date	Mintage	F	VF	XF	Unc	BU
BE2536 (1993)	1,200,000	—	—	—	0.50	—

Y# 282 2 BAHT

Copper-Nickel Clad Copper, 22 mm. **Ruler:** Rama IX **Subject:** 60th Year of the Treasury Department May 23 **Obv:** Conjoined busts left **Rev:** Emblem within circle **Edge:** Reeded

Date	Mintage	F	VF	XF	Unc	BU
BE2536 (1993)	1,200,000	—	—	—	0.50	—

Y# 288 2 BAHT

Copper-Nickel Clad Copper, 22 mm. **Ruler:** Rama IX **Subject:** 100th Anniversary of Rama VII November 8 **Obv:** Bust left **Rev:** Crown and designs within oval circle **Edge:** Reeded

Date	Mintage	F	VF	XF	Unc	BU
BE2536 (1993)	1,500,000	—	—	—	0.50	—

Y# 292 2 BAHT

Copper-Nickel Clad Copper, 22 mm. **Ruler:** Rama IX **Subject:** 60th Anniversary - Royal Thai Language Academy March 31 **Obv:** Conjoined busts left **Rev:** Crowned emblem **Edge:** Reeded

Date	Mintage	F	VF	XF	Unc	BU
BE2537 (1994)	1,200,000	—	—	—	0.50	—

Y# 294 2 BAHT

Copper-Nickel Clad Copper, 22 mm. **Ruler:** Rama IX **Subject:** 120th Anniversary - Council of Advisors to the King - Royal decree 2417-2537 **Obv:** Conjoined busts facing **Rev:** Building **Edge:** Reeded

Date	Mintage	F	VF	XF	Unc	BU
BE2537 (1994)	1,200,000	—	—	—	0.50	—

Y# 296 2 BAHT

Copper-Nickel Clad Copper, 22 mm. **Ruler:** Rama IX **Subject:** 60th Anniversary - Thammasat University June 27 **Obv:** Conjoined busts left **Rev:** University emblem within circle **Edge:** Reeded

Date	Mintage	F	VF	XF	Unc	BU
BE2537 (1994)	1,250,000	—	—	—	0.50	—

Y# 307 2 BAHT

Copper-Nickel Clad Copper, 22 mm. **Ruler:** Rama IX **Series:** F.A.O. 50th Year, 1945-1995 **Obv:** Bust left **Rev:** Emblem and dates **Edge:** Reeded

Date	Mintage	F	VF	XF	Unc	BU
BE2538 (1995)	—	—	—	—	0.65	—

Y# 313 2 BAHT

Copper-Nickel Clad Copper, 22 mm. **Ruler:** Rama IX **Subject:** Information Technology Year **Obv:** Bust 3/4 left **Rev:** Symbols on globe background **Edge:** Reeded

Date	Mintage	F	VF	XF	Unc	BU
BE2538 (1995)	—	—	—	—	0.50	—

Y# 315 2 BAHT

Copper-Nickel Clad Copper, 22 mm. **Ruler:** Rama IX **Subject:** ASEAN Environment Year "Greenland Clean" **Obv:** Conjoined busts left **Rev:** Design within circle flanked by sprig and arrow **Edge:** Reeded

Date	Mintage	F	VF	XF	Unc	BU
BE2538 (1995)	—	—	—	—	0.50	—

Y# 317 2 BAHT

Copper-Nickel Clad Copper, 22 mm. **Ruler:** Rama IX **Subject:** Siriraj Nursing and Midwifery School Centennial January 12 **Obv:** Bust facing **Rev:** Crowned monogram **Edge:** Reeded

Date	Mintage	F	VF	XF	Unc	BU
BE2539 (1996)	—	—	—	—	0.65	—

Y# 319 2 BAHT

Copper-Nickel Clad Copper, 22 mm. **Ruler:** Rama IX **Subject:** King's 50th Year of Reign June 9 **Obv:** Bust facing **Rev:** National arms **Edge:** Reeded

Date	Mintage	F	VF	XF	Unc	BU
BE2539 (1996)	—	—	—	—	1.25	—

Y# 98 5 BAHT

Copper-Nickel **Ruler:** Rama IX **Obv:** Head left **Rev:** Mythical creature "Garuda" **Edge:** Plain **Shape:** 9-sided

Date	Mintage	F	VF	XF	Unc	BU
BE2515 (1972)	30,016,000	—	0.30	0.60	1.20	—

Y# 111 5 BAHT

Copper-Nickel Clad Copper **Ruler:** Rama IX **Obv:** Head left **Rev:** Mythical creature "Garuda" **Edge:** Lettered

Date	Mintage	F	VF	XF	Unc	BU
BE2520 (1977)	27,257,000	—	0.30	0.60	1.20	—
BE2522 (1979)	72,740,000	—	0.30	0.60	1.20	—

Y# 120 5 BAHT

Copper-Nickel Clad Copper, 29.5 mm. **Ruler:** Rama IX **Subject:** 50th Birthday - Rama IX December 5 **Obv:** Head left **Obv. Legend:** PRATHET THAI **Rev:** Crowned monogram **Edge:** Reeded

Date	Mintage	F	VF	XF	Unc	BU
BE2520 (1977)	500,000	—	0.35	0.75	1.50	—

Y# 121 5 BAHT

Copper-Nickel Clad Copper, 29.5 mm. **Ruler:** Rama IX **Subject:** 50th Birthday - Rama IX December 5 **Obv:** Bust left **Obv. Legend:** "SIAM MINTA" **Rev:** Crowned monogram **Edge:** Reeded **Note:** Error legend

Date	Mintage	F	VF	XF	Unc	BU
BE2520 (1977)	—	—	7.00	15.00	30.00	—

Y# 131 5 BAHT

Copper-Nickel Clad Copper, 30 mm. **Ruler:** Rama IX **Subject:** 8th ASEAN Games Bangkok **Obv:** Conjoined busts right **Rev:** Small radiant sun within designs **Edge:** Reeded

Date	Mintage	F	VF	XF	Unc	BU
BE2521 (1978)	500,000	—	1.50	3.50	6.50	—

Y# 132 5 BAHT

Copper-Nickel Clad Copper, 30 mm. **Ruler:** Rama IX **Subject:** Royal Cradle Ceremony January 11 **Obv:** Small child head right **Rev:** Inscription within designed wreath **Edge:** Reeded

Date	Mintage	F	VF	XF	Unc	BU
BE2522 (1979)	1,000,000	—	0.50	1.00	2.00	—

Y# 137 5 BAHT

Copper-Nickel Clad Copper, 30 mm. **Ruler:** Rama IX **Subject:** Queen's Birthday August 12 and F.A.O. Ceres Medal **Obv:** Crowned head 1/4 left **Rev:** Figures working within football-like designs **Edge:** Reeded

Date	Mintage	F	VF	XF	Unc	BU
BE2523 (1980)	9,000,000	—	0.25	0.50	1.50	—

Y# 140 5 BAHT

Copper-Nickel Clad Copper, 30 mm. **Ruler:** Rama IX **Subject:** 80th Birthday of King's Mother October 21 **Obv:** Bust with hat left **Rev:** Crown on stand flanked by others **Edge:** Reeded

Date	Mintage	F	VF	XF	Unc	BU
BE2523 (1980)	3,504,000	—	0.25	0.50	1.50	—

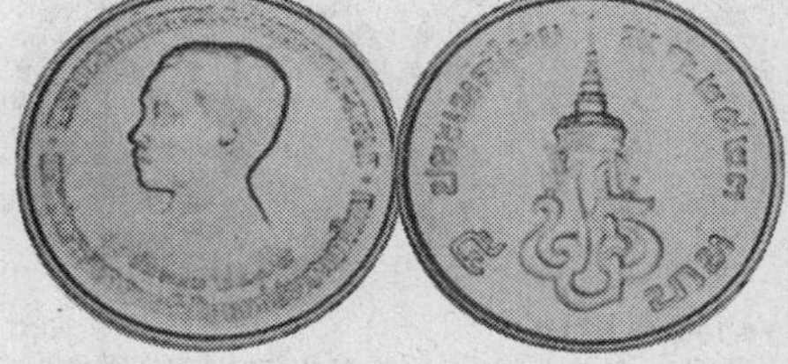

Y# 144 5 BAHT

Copper-Nickel Clad Copper, 30 mm. **Ruler:** Rama IX **Subject:** Rama VII Constitutional Monarchy December 10 2475-2523 **Obv:** Head left **Rev:** Crowned monogram **Edge:** Reeded

Date	Mintage	F	VF	XF	Unc	BU
BE2523 (1980)	2,113,000	—	0.25	0.50	1.50	—

Y# 142 5 BAHT

Copper-Nickel Clad Copper, 30 mm. **Ruler:** Rama IX **Subject:** Centennial - Birth of King Rama VI January 3 **Obv:** Bust right **Rev:** Design **Edge:** Reeded

Date	Mintage	F	VF	XF	Unc	BU
BE2524 (1981)	2,222,000	—	0.25	0.50	1.50	—

Y# 149 5 BAHT

Copper-Nickel Clad Copper, 30 mm. **Ruler:** Rama IX **Subject:** Bicentennial of the Chakri Dynasty **Obv:** Conjoined busts left **Rev:** Emblem **Edge:** Reeded

Date	Mintage	F	VF	XF	Unc	BU
BE2525 (1982)	5,000,000	—	0.25	0.50	1.50	—

Y# 158 5 BAHT

Copper-Nickel Clad Copper, 30 mm. **Ruler:** Rama IX **Series:** World Food Day **Obv:** Uniformed bust left **Rev:** Emblem above wheat sprigs **Edge:** Reeded

Date	Mintage	F	VF	XF	Unc	BU
BE2525 (1982)	400,000	—	0.35	0.75	1.50	—

Y# 161 5 BAHT

Copper-Nickel Clad Copper, 30 mm. **Ruler:** Rama IX **Subject:** 75th Anniversary of Boy Scouts **Obv:** Bust left in scout uniform **Rev:** Stylized banner and flag

Date	Mintage	F	VF	XF	Unc	BU
BE2525 (1982)	206,000	—	1.50	3.50	6.50	—

Y# 160 5 BAHT

12.0000 g., Copper-Nickel Clad Copper **Ruler:** Rama IX **Obv:** Bust left **Rev:** Mythical creature "Garuda" **Note:** 2525 is a frozen date, with the Thai numerals for the first 2 digits of the actual year (25, 28, 29) in the Finance Ministry decal at the bottom of the reverse

Date	Mintage	F	VF	XF	Unc	BU
BE2525 (25) (1982)	200,000	—	0.50	1.00	2.00	—
BE2526 (1983)	—	—	0.60	1.25	2.25	—
BE2527 (1984)	—	—	0.60	1.25	2.25	—
BE2525 (1985)	—	—	5.00	10.00	25.00	—
BE2528 (1985)	—	—	1.00	2.00	5.00	—
BE2525 (1986)	—	—	0.20	0.50	1.00	—
BE2529 (1986)	—	—	0.20	0.50	1.00	—

Y# 171 5 BAHT

Copper-Nickel Clad Copper **Ruler:** Rama IX **Subject:** 84th Birthday of King's Mother October 21 **Obv:** Crown on stand flanked by others **Rev:** Bust 3/4 left

Date	Mintage	F	VF	XF	Unc	BU
BE2527 (1984)	600,000	—	1.00	2.00	4.50	—

Y# 184 5 BAHT

Copper-Nickel Clad Copper, 24 mm. **Ruler:** Rama IX **Subject:** 200th Anniversary - Birth of Rama III 2330-2530 **Obv:** Bust facing **Rev:** Design within circle **Edge:** Reeded

Date	Mintage	F	VF	XF	Unc	BU
BE2530 (1987)	2,000,000	—	—	—	0.75	—

Y# 195 5 BAHT

Copper-Nickel Clad Copper, 30 mm. **Ruler:** Rama IX **Subject:** 60th Birthday - King Rama IX December 5 **Obv:** Uniformed bust facing **Rev:** Crowned emblem within lightning bolts **Edge:** Reeded

Date	Mintage	F	VF	XF	Unc	BU
BE2530 (1987)	1,500,000	—	—	—	2.00	—

Y# 185 5 BAHT

Copper-Nickel Clad Copper **Ruler:** Rama IX **Obv:** Head left **Rev:** Suphannahong, royal grand palace **Note:** Circulation coinage.

Date	Mintage	F	VF	XF	Unc	BU
BE2530 (1987)	14,000,000	—	—	—	0.75	—
BE2531 (1988)	—	—	—	—	0.75	—

Y# 219 5 BAHT

Copper-Nickel Clad Copper, 24 mm. **Ruler:** Rama IX **Obv:** Head left **Rev:** Penjahwat **Edge:** Reeded **Note:** Circulation coinage.

Date	Mintage	F	VF	XF	Unc	BU
BE2531 (1988)	—	—	—	—	0.50	—
BE2532 (1989)	—	—	—	—	0.50	—
BE2533 (1990)	—	—	—	—	0.50	—
BE2534 (1991)	—	—	—	—	0.50	—
BE2535 (1992)	—	—	—	—	0.50	—
BE2536 (1993)	—	—	—	—	0.50	—
BE2537 (1994)	—	—	—	—	0.50	—
BE2538 (1995)	—	—	—	—	0.50	—
BE2539 (1996)	—	—	—	—	0.50	—
BE2540 (1997)	—	—	—	—	0.50	—
BE2541 (1998)	—	—	—	—	0.50	—
BE2542 (1999)	—	—	—	—	0.50	—
BE2543 (2000)	—	—	—	—	0.50	—

Y# 211 5 BAHT

Copper-Nickel, 30 mm. **Ruler:** Rama IX **Subject:** 42nd Anniversary - Reign of King Rama IX July 2 **Obv:** Uniformed bust facing **Rev:** Crowned monogram **Edge:** Reeded

Date	Mintage	F	VF	XF	Unc	BU
BE2531 (1988)	1,500,000	—	—	—	2.00	—

Y# 260 5 BAHT

Copper-Nickel Clad Copper, 24 mm. **Ruler:** Rama IX **Subject:** Queen's 60th Birthday August 12 **Obv:** Crowned bust facing **Rev:** Crowned monogram **Edge:** Reeded

Date	Mintage	F	VF	XF	Unc	BU
BE2535 (1992)	1,000,000	—	—	—	1.25	—

Y# 306 5 BAHT

Copper-Nickel Clad Copper, 24 mm. **Ruler:** Rama IX **Subject:** 18th SEA Games December 9-17 held at Ching My **Obv:** Half length bust facing **Rev:** Designs and inscription within circle above designed sprigs **Edge:** Reeded

Date	Mintage	F	VF	XF	Unc	BU
BE2538 (1995)	—	—	—	—	1.25	—

Y# 320 5 BAHT

Copper-Nickel Clad Copper, 24 mm. **Ruler:** Rama IX **Subject:** King's 50th Year of Reign June 9 **Obv:** Bust facing **Rev:** National arms **Edge:** Reeded

Date	Mintage	F	VF	XF	Unc	BU
BE2539 (1996)	—	—	—	—	1.50	—

Y# 92 10 BAHT

5.0000 g., 0.8000 Silver .1286 oz. ASW, 20 mm. **Ruler:** Rama IX **Subject:** 25th Anniversary - Reign of King Rama IX June 9 **Obv:** Head right **Rev:** Radiant crowned monogram **Edge:** Reeded

Date	Mintage	F	VF	XF	Unc	BU
BE2514 (1971)	2,000,000	—	BV	2.50	4.50	—

Y# 115 10 BAHT

Nickel, 32 mm. **Ruler:** Rama IX **Subject:** Graduation of Princess

Sirindhorn 1st royal graduate **Obv:** Bust left **Rev:** Radiant crown **Edge:** Reeded

Date	Mintage	F	VF	XF	Unc	BU
BE2520 (1977)	2,097,000	—	0.50	1.00	2.50	—

Y# 115a 10 BAHT

Bronze, 32 mm. **Ruler:** Rama IX **Subject:** Graduation of Princess Sirindhorn 1st royal graduate **Obv:** Bust left **Rev:** Radiant crown

Date	Mintage	F	VF	XF	Unc	BU
BE2520 (1977)	—	—	—	—	20.00	—

Y# 117 10 BAHT

Nickel, 32 mm. **Ruler:** Rama IX **Subject:** Crown Prince Vajiralongkom and Princess Soamsawali Wedding January 3 **Obv:** Conjoined busts right **Rev:** Crowned monogram **Edge:** Reeded

Date	Mintage	F	VF	XF	Unc	BU
BE2520 (1977)	1,890,000	—	0.50	1.00	2.50	—

Y# 135 10 BAHT

Nickel, 32 mm. **Ruler:** Rama IX **Subject:** Graduation of Princess Chulabhorn **Obv:** Bust 3/4 left **Rev:** Graduation emblem within circle

Date	Mintage	F	VF	XF	Unc	BU
BE2522 (1979)	1,196,000	—	0.50	1.00	2.50	—

Y# 141 10 BAHT

Nickel, 32 mm. **Ruler:** Rama IX **Subject:** 80th Birthday of King's Mother October 21 **Obv:** Bust with hat left **Rev:** Crown on stand flanked by others **Edge:** Reeded

Date	Mintage	F	VF	XF	Unc	BU
BE2523 (1980)	1,288,000	—	0.50	1.00	2.50	—

Y# 145 10 BAHT

Nickel, 32 mm. **Ruler:** Rama IX **Subject:** 30th Anniversary of Buddhist Fellowship **Obv:** Bust left **Rev:** Design within circle and wreath **Edge:** Reeded

Date	Mintage	F	VF	XF	Unc	BU
BE2523 (1980)	1,035,000	—	0.50	1.00	2.50	—

Y# 146 10 BAHT

Nickel, 32 mm. **Ruler:** Rama IX **Subject:** King Rama IX Anniversary of Reign, twice as long on the throne - June 19 **Obv:** Conjoined busts left **Rev:** Crowns and emblems **Edge:** Reeded

Date	Mintage	F	VF	XF	Unc	BU
BE2524 (1981)	2,039,000	—	0.50	1.00	2.50	—

Y# 154 10 BAHT

Nickel, 32 mm. **Ruler:** Rama IX **Subject:** 50th Birthday of Queen Sirikit August 12 **Obv:** Crowned head 1/4 left **Rev:** Crowned monogram **Edge:** Reeded

Date	Mintage	F	VF	XF	Unc	BU
BE2525 (1982)	500,000	—	0.75	1.50	3.50	—
BE2525 (1982) Proof	9,999	Value: 22.50				

Y# 162 10 BAHT

Nickel, 32 mm. **Ruler:** Rama IX **Subject:** 75th Anniversary of Boy Scouts **Obv:** Bust left in scouting uniform **Rev:** Stylized banner and flag **Edge:** Reeded **Note:** Similar to 5 Baht, Y#161.

Date	Mintage	F	VF	XF	Unc	BU
BE2525 (1982)	100,000	—	1.25	2.50	5.00	—
BE2525 (1982) Proof	1,500	Value: 45.00				

Y# 163 10 BAHT

Nickel, 32 mm. **Ruler:** Rama IX **Subject:** 100th Anniversary of Postal Service August 4 **Obv:** Bust left **Rev:** Radiant crown above inscription

Date	Mintage	F	VF	XF	Unc	BU
BE2526 (1983)	300,000	—	0.75	1.50	3.50	—
BE2526 (1983) Proof	5,000	Value: 27.50				

Y# 165 10 BAHT

Nickel, 32 mm. **Ruler:** Rama IX **Subject:** 700th Anniversary of Thai Alphabet **Obv:** Seated figure, Ramkamhaeng the Great, pre-Bangkok era **Rev:** Six-line inscription

Date	Mintage	F	VF	XF	Unc	BU
BE2526 (1983)	500,000	—	0.75	1.50	3.50	—
BE2526 (1983) Proof	5,167	Value: 25.00				

Y# 172 10 BAHT

Nickel, 32 mm. **Ruler:** Rama IX **Subject:** 84th Birthday of King's Mother October 21 **Obv:** Three crowns on stands **Rev:** Bust left **Note:** Similar to 5 Baht, Y#171.

Date	Mintage	F	VF	XF	Unc	BU
BE2527 (1984)	200,000	—	1.25	2.50	5.50	—
BE2527 (1984) Proof	3,492	Value: 37.50				

Y# 175 10 BAHT

Nickel, 32 mm. **Ruler:** Rama IX **Subject:** 72nd Anniversary of Government Savings Bank April 1 **Obv:** Conjoined uniformed busts 1/4 left **Rev:** Designs within sectioned circle **Edge:** Reeded

Date	Mintage	F	VF	XF	Unc	BU
BE2528 (1985)	500,000	—	0.50	1.00	2.50	—
BE2528 (1985) Proof	3,000	Value: 37.50				

Y# 179 10 BAHT

Nickel, 32 mm. **Ruler:** Rama IX **Subject:** National Years of the Trees 2528-2531 **Obv:** Bust left **Rev:** Circular design below inscription within tree, emblems flank tree below

Date	Mintage	F	VF	XF	Unc	BU
ND (1986)	100,000	—	4.00	9.00	18.00	—
ND (1986) Proof	2,100	Value: 45.00				

Y# 181 10 BAHT

Nickel, 32 mm. **Ruler:** Rama IX **Subject:** 6th ASEAN Orchid Congress November 7-14 **Obv:** Bust left **Rev:** Symbols of congress meeting **Edge:** Reeded

Date	Mintage	F	VF	XF	Unc	BU
BE2529 (1986)	200,000	—	—	—	2.50	—
BE2529 (1986) Proof	3,000	Value: 37.50				

Y# 192 10 BAHT

Nickel, 32 mm. **Ruler:** Rama IX **Subject:** Princess Chulabhorn Awarded Einstein Medal October 24 **Obv:** Graduate's bust 1/4 left **Rev:** Head left within center circle of hexagon design

Date	Mintage	F	VF	XF	Unc	BU
BE2529 (1986)	200,000	—	—	—	2.50	—
BE2529 (1986) Proof	1,080	Value: 50.00				

Y# 196 10 BAHT
Nickel, 32 mm. **Ruler:** Rama IX **Subject:** 60th Birthday of King Rama IX December 5 **Obv:** Uniformed bust facing **Rev:** Crowned emblem within lightning bolts **Edge:** Reeded

Date	Mintage	F	VF	XF	Unc	BU
BE2530 (1987)	500,000	—	—	—	2.50	—
BE2530 (1987) Proof	5,000	Value: 32.50				

Y# 189 10 BAHT
Nickel, 32 mm. **Ruler:** Rama IX **Subject:** Chulachomklao Royal Military Academy August 5 **Obv:** Conjoined busts left **Rev:** Flagged arms

Date	Mintage	F	VF	XF	Unc	BU
BE2530 (1987)	300,000	—	—	—	2.50	—
BE2530 (1987) Proof	2,060	Value: 45.00				

Y# 190 10 BAHT
Nickel, 32 mm. **Ruler:** Rama IX **Subject:** Rural Development Leadership July 21 **Obv:** Kneeling figure facing left talking to seated figures **Rev:** Emblem above inscription **Edge:** Reeded

Date	Mintage	F	VF	XF	Unc	BU
BE2530 (1987)	300,000	—	—	—	2.50	—
BE2530 (1987) Proof	2,100	Value: 45.00				

Y# 205 10 BAHT
Nickel, 32 mm. **Ruler:** Rama IX **Subject:** 72nd Anniversary of Thai Cooperatives February 26 **Obv:** Conjoined busts left **Rev:** Inscription

Date	Mintage	F	VF	XF	Unc	BU
BE2531 (1988)	143,000	—	—	—	2.50	—
BE2530 (1988) Proof	3,000	Value: 32.50				

Y# 212 10 BAHT
Nickel, 32 mm. **Ruler:** Rama IX **Subject:** 42nd Anniversary - Reign of King Rama IX July 2 **Obv:** Bust facing **Rev:** Crowned monogram

Date	Mintage	F	VF	XF	Unc	BU
BE2531 (1988)	500,000	—	—	—	2.50	—

Date	Mintage	F	VF	XF	Unc	BU
BE2531 (1988) Proof	8,110	Value: 25.00				

Y# 221 10 BAHT
Nickel, 32 mm. **Ruler:** Rama IX **Subject:** 100th Anniversary of Siriraj Hospital April 26 **Obv:** Crowned busts left **Rev:** Crown above design

Date	Mintage	F	VF	XF	Unc	BU
BE2531 (1988)	290,000	—	—	—	2.50	—
BE2531 (1988) Proof	5,000	Value: 27.50				

Y# 223 10 BAHT
Nickel, 32 mm. **Ruler:** Rama IX **Subject:** Crown Prince's Birthday **Obv:** Head 1/4 left **Rev:** Crowned monogram within lightning bolts **Edge:** Reeded

Date	Mintage	F	VF	XF	Unc	BU
BE2531 (1988)	200,000	—	—	—	2.50	—
BE2531 (1988) Proof	3,000	Value: 32.50				

Y# 227 10 BAHT
Bi-Metallic Aluminum-bronze center in Stainless steel ring, 26 mm. **Ruler:** Rama IX **Obv:** Head left within circle **Rev:** Temple of the Dawn within circle **Note:** Varieties exist.

Date	Mintage	F	VF	XF	Unc	BU
BE2531 (1988) Prooflike; Rare	100,000	—	—	—	—	—

Note: The BE2531 (1988) pieces were not released to general circulation and are very scarce in the numismatic community

Date	Mintage	F	VF	XF	Unc	BU
BE2532 (1989)	200,000,000	—	—	—	2.50	—
BE2533 (1990)	100	—	—	—	2,500	—
BE2534 (1991)	—	—	—	—	2.50	—
BE2535 (1992)	—	—	—	—	2.50	—
BE2536 (1993)	—	—	—	—	2.50	—
BE2537 (1994)	—	—	—	—	3.00	—
BE2538 (1995)	—	—	—	—	3.00	—
BE2539 (1996)	—	—	—	—	3.00	—

Y# 228 10 BAHT
Nickel, 32 mm. **Ruler:** Rama IX **Subject:** 72nd Anniversary Chulalongkorn University March 26 **Obv:** 3 Conjoined busts left **Rev:** Radiant crown

Date	Mintage	F	VF	XF	Unc	BU
BE2532 (1989)	500,000	—	—	—	2.50	—

Y# 231 10 BAHT
Copper-Nickel, 32 mm. **Ruler:** Rama IX **Subject:** Centennial of First Medical College September 5 2433 to September 5 2533 **Obv:** Conjoined busts facing **Rev:** Building **Edge:** Reeded

Date	Mintage	F	VF	XF	Unc	BU
BE2533 (1990)	300,000	—	—	—	2.50	—
BE2533 (1990) Proof	3,772	Value: 32.50				

Y# 233 10 BAHT
Copper-Nickel, 32 mm. **Ruler:** Rama IX **Subject:** 90th Birthday of the King's Mother October 21 **Obv:** Crown on stand flanked by others **Rev:** Bust 1/4 left **Edge:** Reeded

Date	Mintage	F	VF	XF	Unc	BU
BE2533 (1990)	500,000	—	—	—	2.50	—
BE2533 (1991) Proof	6,076	Value: 32.50				

Y# 236 10 BAHT
Copper-Nickel, 32 mm. **Ruler:** Rama IX **Subject:** 100th Anniversary - Office of Comptroller General **Obv:** Conjoined busts 1/4 left **Rev:** Building above computer, typewriter and phone

Date	Mintage	F	VF	XF	Unc	BU
BE2533 (1990)	300,000	—	—	—	2.50	—

Y# 244 10 BAHT
Copper-Nickel, 32 mm. **Ruler:** Rama IX **Subject:** World Health Organization December 17 **Obv:** Bust 1/4 left **Rev:** W.H.O. Medal **Edge:** Reeded

Date	Mintage	F	VF	XF	Unc	BU
BE2533 (1990)	800,000	—	—	—	3.00	—
BE2533 (1990) Proof	34,041	Value: 45.00				

Y# 238 10 BAHT
Copper-Nickel, 32 mm. **Ruler:** Rama IX **Subject:** 36th Birthday of Princess Sirindhorn April 2 **Obv:** Uniformed bust 1/4 left **Rev:** Crowned monogram flanked by stars above sprigs **Edge:** Reeded

Date	Mintage	F	VF	XF	Unc	BU
BE2534 (1991)	1,100,000	—	—	—	2.50	—

Date	Mintage	F	VF	XF	Unc	BU
BE2534 (1991) Proof	3,300	Value: 35.00				

Y# 241 10 BAHT
Copper-Nickel, 32 mm. **Ruler:** Rama IX **Subject:** 80th Anniversary of Thai Boy Scouts July 1 2454-2534 **Obv:** Conjoined busts 1/4 left in scouting uniform **Rev:** Scout emblem and motto "Better to die than to lie" **Edge:** Reeded

Date	Mintage	F	VF	XF	Unc	BU
BE2534 (1991)	650,000	—	—	—	3.00	—
BE2534 (1991) Proof	3,237	Value: 35.00				

Y# 256 10 BAHT
Copper-Nickel, 32 mm. **Ruler:** Rama IX **Subject:** Princess Sirindhorn's Magsaysay Foundation Award August 31 **Obv:** Seated and kneeling figures within circle **Rev:** Foundation Award medal below cameo **Edge:** Reeded

Date	Mintage	F	VF	XF	Unc	BU
BE2534 (1991)	800,000	—	—	—	2.50	—
BE2534 (1991) Proof	2,111	Value: 37.50				

Y# 249 10 BAHT
Copper-Nickel, 32 mm. **Ruler:** Rama IX **Subject:** Centenary Celebration - Father of King Rama IX Mahidon - January 1 **Obv:** Crown on stand flanked by others **Rev:** Bust facing **Edge:** Reeded

Date	Mintage	F	VF	XF	Unc	BU
BE2535 (1992)	800,000	—	—	—	2.50	—
BE2535 (1992) Proof	5,314	Value: 25.00				

Y# 252 10 BAHT
Copper-Nickel, 32 mm. **Ruler:** Rama IX **Subject:** Ministry of Justice Centennial March 25 **Obv:** Conjoined busts left **Rev:** Balance scales within design **Edge:** Reeded

Date	Mintage	F	VF	XF	Unc	BU
BE2535 (1992)	800,000	—	—	—	2.50	—
BE2535 (1992) Proof	—	Value: 22.50				

Y# 254 10 BAHT
Copper-Nickel, 32 mm. **Ruler:** Rama IX **Subject:** Ministry of Interior Centennial April 1 2435 to 2535 **Obv:** Conjoined uniformed busts facing **Rev:** Mythical animal within circle **Edge:** Reeded

Date	Mintage	F	VF	XF	Unc	BU
BE2535 (1992)	800,000	—	—	—	2.50	—
BE2535 (1992) Proof	10,000	Value: 17.50				

Y# 261 10 BAHT
Copper-Nickel, 32 mm. **Ruler:** Rama IX **Subject:** Queen's 60th Birthday August 12 (Thai Mother's Day) **Obv:** Crowned bust facing **Rev:** Crowned monogram **Edge:** Reeded

Date	Mintage	F	VF	XF	Unc	BU
BE2535 (1992)	1,100,000	—	—	—	3.00	—
BE2535 (1992) Proof	18,000	Value: 17.50				

Y# 269 10 BAHT
Copper-Nickel, 32 mm. **Ruler:** Rama IX **Subject:** 60th Anniversary of National Assembly June 28 **Obv:** Conjoined busts left **Rev:** Ratasapa - Paraliment building **Edge:** Reeded

Date	Mintage	F	VF	XF	Unc	BU
BE2535 (1992)	44,000	—	—	—	2.50	—

Y# 271 10 BAHT
Copper-Nickel, 32 mm. **Ruler:** Rama IX **Subject:** Ministry of Agriculture April 1 **Obv:** Conjoined busts 1/4 left **Rev:** Emblem above designed sprigs **Edge:** Reeded

Date	Mintage	F	VF	XF	Unc	BU
BE2535 (1992)	550,000	—	—	—	2.50	—
BE2535 (1992) Proof	—	Value: 25.00				

Y# 284 10 BAHT
Copper-Nickel, 32 mm. **Ruler:** Rama IX **Subject:** Centennial of Thai Teacher Training October 12 **Obv:** Conjoined busts left **Rev:** Emblem **Edge:** Reeded

Date	Mintage	F	VF	XF	Unc	BU
BE2535 (1992)	700,000	—	—	—	2.50	—

Y# 285 10 BAHT
Copper-Nickel, 32 mm. **Ruler:** Rama IX **Subject:** Centennial of Thai National Bank December 10 **Obv:** Conjoined busts facing **Rev:** Seated figure **Edge:** Reeded

Date	Mintage	F	VF	XF	Unc	BU
BE2535 (1992)	700,000	—	—	—	2.50	—
BE2535 (1992) Proof	6,927	Value: 20.00				

Y# 273 10 BAHT
Copper-Nickel, 32 mm. **Ruler:** Rama IX **Subject:** King's 64th Birthday November 18 **Obv:** Conjoined busts 1/4 left **Rev:** Crowned monograms **Edge:** Reeded **Note:** In honor of the King reaching the life span of his great grandfather.

Date	Mintage	F	VF	XF	Unc	BU
BE2535 (1992)	550,000	—	—	—	2.50	—
BE2535 (1992) Proof	3,711	Value: 25.00				

Y# 280 10 BAHT
Copper-Nickel, 32 mm. **Ruler:** Rama IX **Subject:** Centennial of Thai Red Cross 2436-2536 **Obv:** Conjoined busts 1/4 left **Rev:** Symbols **Edge:** Reeded

Date	Mintage	F	VF	XF	Unc	BU
BE2536 (1993)	700,000	—	—	—	2.50	—
BE2535 (1993) Proof	14,000	Value: 18.50				

Y# 283 10 BAHT
Copper-Nickel, 32 mm. **Ruler:** Rama IX **Subject:** 60th Anniversary Treasury Department May 23 **Obv:** Conjoined busts left **Rev:** Emblem within circle **Edge:** Reeded

Date	Mintage	F	VF	XF	Unc	BU
BE2536 (1993)	600,000	—	—	—	2.50	—
BE2535 (1993) Proof	10,000	Value: 22.50				

Y# 286 10 BAHT
Copper-Nickel, 32 mm. **Ruler:** Rama IX **Subject:** Centennial of

Attorney General's Office April 1 2436-2536 **Obv:** Conjoined busts facing **Rev:** Crowned balance scales above sprigs **Edge:** Reeded

Date	Mintage	F	VF	XF	Unc	BU
BE2536 (1993)	700,000	—	—	—	2.50	—

Y# 289 10 BAHT

Copper-Nickel, 32 mm. **Ruler:** Rama IX **Subject:** 100th Anniversary of Rama VII November 8 **Obv:** Bust left **Rev:** Crown and designs within oval circle **Edge:** Reeded

Date	Mintage	F	VF	XF	Unc	BU
BE2536 (1993)	800,000	—	—	—	2.50	—
BE2536 (1993) Proof	10,000	Value: 22.50				

Y# 293 10 BAHT

Copper-Nickel, 32 mm. **Ruler:** Rama IX **Subject:** 60th Anniversary - Royal Thai Language Academy March 31 **Obv:** Conjoined busts left **Rev:** Crowned emblem **Edge:** Reeded

Date	Mintage	F	VF	XF	Unc	BU
BE2537 (1994)	700,000	—	—	—	2.50	—
BE2537 (1994) Proof	10,000	Value: 22.50				

Y# 295 10 BAHT

Copper-Nickel, 32 mm. **Ruler:** Rama IX **Subject:** 120th Anniversary Council of Advisors to the King - Royal decree 2417-2537 **Obv:** Conjoined busts facing **Rev:** Building **Edge:** Reeded

Date	Mintage	F	VF	XF	Unc	BU
BE2537 (1994)	800,000	—	—	—	2.50	—
BE2537 (1994) Proof	12,000	Value: 22.50				

Y# 297 10 BAHT

Copper-Nickel, 32 mm. **Ruler:** Rama IX **Subject:** 60th Anniversary - Thammasat University June 27 **Obv:** Conjoined busts left **Rev:** Emblem within circle and wreath **Edge:** Reeded

Date	Mintage	F	VF	XF	Unc	BU
BE2537 (1994)	800,000	—	—	—	2.50	—
BE2537 (1994) Proof	12,000	Value: 22.50				

Y# 339 10 BAHT

Bi-Metallic Brass center in Copper-Nickel ring, 26 mm. **Ruler:** Rama IX **Subject:** International Rice Award June 5 **Obv:** Half length figure with camera left within circle **Rev:** Rice plant within circle **Edge:** Alternating reeded and plain

Date	Mintage	F	VF	XF	Unc	BU
BE2538 (1996)	—	—	—	—	3.50	—

Y# 328.1 10 BAHT

Bi-Metallic Brass center in Copper-Nickel ring, 26 mm. **Ruler:** Rama IX **Subject:** 50th Anniversary - Reign of King Rama IX June 9 **Obv:** Bust facing within circle **Rev:** National arms within circle **Edge:** Alternating reeded and plain

Date	Mintage	F	VF	XF	Unc	BU
BE2539 (1996)	—	—	—	—	3.00	—

Y# 328.2 10 BAHT

Bi-Metallic Brass center in Copper-Nickel ring, 26 mm. **Ruler:** Rama IX **Subject:** 50th Anniversary - Reign of King Rama IX June 9 **Obv:** Bust facing within circle **Rev:** National arms within circle **Edge:** Alternating reeded and plain

Date	Mintage	F	VF	XF	Unc	BU
BE2539 (1996)	—	—	—	—	3.00	—

Y# 334 10 BAHT

Bi-Metallic Brass center in Copper-Nickel ring, 26 mm. **Ruler:** Rama IX **Subject:** F.A.O. World Summit December 2 **Obv:** Bust left within circle **Rev:** Seated and kneeling figures within circle **Edge:** Alternating reeded and plain

Date	Mintage	F	VF	XF	Unc	BU
BE2538 (1996)	—	—	—	—	3.50	—

Y# 347 10 BAHT

Bi-Metallic Brass center in Copper-Nickel ring, 26 mm. **Ruler:** Rama IX **Subject:** 100th Anniversary of Chulalongkorn's European Tour **Obv:** Bust right within circle **Rev:** Design and inscription divides circle **Edge:** Alternating reeded and plain

Date	Mintage	F	VF	XF	Unc	BU
BE2540 (1997)	—	—	—	—	2.50	—

Y# 346 10 BAHT

Bi-Metallic Brass center in Copper-Nickel ring, 26 mm. **Ruler:** Rama IX **Subject:** 100th Anniversary - Central General Hospital - Medication Office 2441-2541 **Obv:** Conjoined busts facing within circle **Rev:** Figure seated on facing elephant within circle **Edge:** Alternating reeded and plain

Date	Mintage	F	VF	XF	Unc	BU
BE2541 (1998)	—	—	—	—	4.00	—

Y# 348 10 BAHT

Bi-Metallic Brass center in Copper-Nickel ring, 26 mm. **Ruler:** Rama IX **Subject:** 13th Asian Games Bangkok December 6-20 **Obv:** Bust left within circle **Rev:** Symbols within circle **Edge:** Alternating reeded and plain

Date	Mintage	F	VF	XF	Unc	BU
BE2541 (1998)	10,000,000	—	—	—	2.50	—

Y# 352 10 BAHT

Bi-Metallic Brass center in Copper-Nickel ring, 26 mm. **Ruler:** Rama IX **Subject:** Rama III honored with the title "Great" March 31 **Obv:** Head facing within circle **Rev:** Crowned arms within circle **Edge:** Alternating reeded and plain

Date	Mintage	F	VF	XF	Unc	BU
BE2541 (1998)	—	—	—	—	2.50	—

Y# 349 10 BAHT

Bi-Metallic Brass center in Copper-Nickel ring, 26 mm. **Ruler:** Rama IX **Subject:** 125th Anniversary of the Customer's Department July 4 **Obv:** Conjoined busts 1/4 right **Rev:** Buildings below emblem **Edge:** Alternating reeded and plain

Date	Mintage	F	VF	XF	Unc	BU
BE2542 (1999)	—	—	—	—	2.50	—

Y# 350 10 BAHT

Bi-Metallic Brass center in Copper-Nickel ring, 26 mm. **Ruler:** Rama IX **Subject:** King's 72nd Birthday December 5 **Obv:** Head left within circle **Rev:** Crowned emblem within circle **Edge:** Alternating reeded and plain

Date	Mintage	F	VF	XF	Unc	BU
BE2542 (1999)	10,000,000	—	—	—	1.75	—

Y# 354 10 BAHT

Bi-Metallic Brass center in Copper-Nickel ring, 26 mm. **Ruler:** Rama IX **Subject:** 100th Anniversary Army Medical Department January 7 2443-2543 **Obv:** Conjoined busts facing **Rev:** Emblem within circle **Edge:** Alternating reeded and plain

Date	Mintage	F	VF	XF	Unc	BU
ND (2000)	—	—	—	—	2.00	—

Y# 358 10 BAHT

Bi-Metallic Brass center in Copper-Nickel ring, 26 mm. **Ruler:** Rama IX **Subject:** 80th Anniversary - Commerce Ministry August 20 **Obv:** Head facing within circle **Rev:** Ministry logo within square and circle **Edge:** Alternating reeded and plain

Date	Mintage	F	VF	XF	Unc	BU
BE2543 (2000)	—	—	—	—	2.00	—

Y# 361 10 BAHT

Bi-Metallic Brass center in Copper-Nickel ring, 26 mm. **Ruler:** Rama IX **Subject:** 100th Birthday - King's Mother October 21 **Obv:** Bust left within circle **Rev:** Emblem within circle **Edge:** Alternating reeded and plain

Date	Mintage	F	VF	XF	Unc	BU
BE2543 (2000)	—	—	—	—	2.00	—

Y# 371 10 BAHT

8.4500 g., Bi-Metallic Brass center in Copper-Nickel ring, 26 mm. **Ruler:** Rama IX **Subject:** National Economic and Social Development Board February 15 **Obv:** Bust 3/4 left **Rev:** Three seated figures within circle **Edge:** Alternating reeded and plain

Date	Mintage	F	VF	XF	Unc	BU
BE2543(2000)	—	—	—	—	2.00	—

Y# 86 20 BAHT

19.6000 g., 0.7500 Silver .4726 oz. ASW, 34.5 mm. **Ruler:** Rama IX **Subject:** 36th Birthday - Rama IX **Obv:** Uniformed bust left **Rev:** Crown and emblem divided by crossed scepter and spear

Date	Mintage	F	VF	XF	Unc	BU
ND (1963)	1,000,000	—	—	7.50	9.50	12.50

Y# 298 20 BAHT

Copper-Nickel, 32 mm. **Ruler:** Rama IX **Subject:** 120th Anniversary - Ministry of Finance 2418-2538 **Obv:** Conjoined busts right **Rev:** Stylized eagle **Edge:** Reeded

Date	Mintage	F	VF	XF	Unc	BU
BE2538 (1994)	800,000	—	—	—	3.50	—
BE2538 (1994) Proof	1,920	Value: 35.00				

Y# 300 20 BAHT

Copper-Nickel, 32 mm. **Ruler:** Rama IX **Subject:** 108th Anniversary - Ministry of Defense April 8 **Obv:** Conjoined uniformed busts facing **Rev:** Mythical animal within circle **Edge:** Reeded

Date	Mintage	F	VF	XF	Unc	BU
BE2538 (1994)	800,000	—	—	—	3.50	—
BE2538 (1994) Proof	2,000	Value: 35.00				

Y# 302 20 BAHT

Copper-Nickel **Ruler:** Rama IX **Subject:** 120th Anniversary - Ministry of Foreign Affairs April 14 **Obv:** Conjoined busts facing **Rev:** Seated figure within designed circle and wreath **Edge:** Reeded

Date	Mintage	F	VF	XF	Unc	BU
BE2538 (1994)	800,000	—	—	—	3.50	—
BE2538 (1994) Proof	740	Value: 55.00				

Y# 308 20 BAHT

Copper-Nickel, 32 mm. **Ruler:** Rama IX **Series:** F.A.O. 1945-1995 **Obv:** Bust left **Rev:** F.A.O. logo and dates **Edge:** Reeded

Date	Mintage	F	VF	XF	Unc	BU
BE2538 (1995)	400,000	—	—	—	3.50	—
BE2538 (1995) Proof	—	Value: 25.00				

Y# 309 20 BAHT

Copper-Nickel **Ruler:** Rama IX **Subject:** 80th Anniversary - Department of Revenue September 2 **Obv:** Conjoined busts 1/4 left **Rev:** Seated figure within circle **Edge:** Reeded

Date	Mintage	F	VF	XF	Unc	BU
BE2538 (1995)	800,000	—	—	—	3.50	—
BE2538 (1995) Proof	—	Value: 20.00				

Y# 311 20 BAHT

Copper-Nickel, 32 mm. **Ruler:** Rama IX **Subject:** 120th Anniversary - Audit Council 2418-2538 **Obv:** Conjoined uniformed busts facing **Rev:** Balance scales **Edge:** Reeded

Date	Mintage	F	VF	XF	Unc	BU
BE2538 (1995)	800,000	—	—	—	3.50	—
BE2538 (1995) Proof	—	Value: 20.00				

Y# 314 20 BAHT

Copper-Nickel, 32 mm. **Ruler:** Rama IX **Subject:** Information Technology Year **Obv:** Bust left **Rev:** Design and inscription within world globe **Edge:** Reeded

Date	Mintage	F	VF	XF	Unc	BU
BE2538 (1995)	—	—	—	—	3.50	—
BE2538 (1995) Proof	—	Value: 20.00				

Y# 316 20 BAHT

Copper-Nickel, 32 mm. **Ruler:** Rama IX **Subject:** Asean Environment Year **Obv:** Conjoined busts right **Rev:** Symbol within center circle, grain sprig and arrow surround

Date	Mintage	F	VF	XF	Unc	BU
BE2538 (1995)	—	—	—	—	3.50	—
BE2538 (1995) Proof	—	Value: 20.00				

Y# 331 20 BAHT

Copper-Nickel, 32 mm. **Ruler:** Rama IX **Subject:** Ministry of Commerce **Obv:** Conjoined uniformed busts facing **Rev:** Seal within circle **Edge:** Reeded

Date	Mintage	F	VF	XF	Unc	BU
BE2538 (1995)	—	—	—	—	4.00	—

Y# 338 20 BAHT

Copper-Nickel, 32 mm. **Ruler:** Rama IX **Subject:** 50 Years of Peace August 16 **Obv:** Uniformed busts of Rama VIII and Rama IX facing **Rev:** Busts left with flag and doves within center circle **Edge:** Reeded

Date	Mintage	F	VF	XF	Unc	BU
ND(BE2538) (1995)	—	—	—	—	3.50	—

Y# 304 20 BAHT

Copper-Nickel, 32 mm. **Ruler:** Rama IX **Subject:** 72nd Birthday of Princess May 6 **Obv:** Uniformed bust 3/4 facing **Rev:** Crowned arms **Edge:** Reeded **Note:** Similar to 600 Baht, Y#305.

Date	Mintage	F	VF	XF	Unc	BU
BE2538 (1995)	800,000	—	—	—	3.50	—
BE2538 (1995) Proof	1,560	Value: 27.50				

Y# 318 20 BAHT

Copper-Nickel, 32 mm. **Ruler:** Rama IX **Subject:** Siriraj Nursing and Midwife School Centennial January 12 **Obv:** Uniformed bust facing **Rev:** Crowned monogram flanked by sprigs **Edge:** Reeded

Date	Mintage	F	VF	XF	Unc	BU
BE2539 (1996)	—	—	—	—	3.50	—

Y# 321.1 20 BAHT

Copper-Nickel, 32 mm. **Ruler:** Rama IX **Subject:** 50th Anniversary - Reign of King Rama IX June 9 **Obv:** Bust facing **Rev:** National arms **Edge:** Reeded

Date	Mintage	F	VF	XF	Unc	BU
BE2539 (1996)	—	—	—	—	4.00	—
BE2539 (1996) Proof	—	Value: 30.00				

Y# 321.2 20 BAHT

Copper-Nickel, 32 mm. **Ruler:** Rama IX **Subject:** 50th Anniversary - Reign of King Rama IX June 9 **Obv:** Bust facing **Rev:** National arms

Date	Mintage	F	VF	XF	Unc	BU
BE2539 (1996)	—	—	—	—	4.00	—
BE2539 (1996) Proof	—	Value: 30.00				

Y# 335 20 BAHT
Copper-Nickel, 32 mm. **Ruler:** Rama IX **Subject:** F.A.O. World Food Summit **Obv:** Bust left within circle **Rev:** Seated and kneeling figures within circle **Edge:** Reeded

Date	Mintage	F	VF	XF	Unc	BU
BE2539 (1996)	—	—	—	—	3.50	—
BE2539 (1996) Proof	—	Value: 25.00				

Y# 340 20 BAHT
Copper-Nickel, 32 mm. **Ruler:** Rama IX **Subject:** International Rice Award June 5 **Obv:** Half length bust left within circle **Rev:** Inscription and sprigs within circle **Edge:** Reeded

Date	Mintage	F	VF	XF	Unc	BU
BE2539 (1996)	—	—	—	—	3.50	—
BE2539 (1996) Proof	—	Value: 25.00				

Y# 332 20 BAHT
Copper-Nickel, 32 mm. **Ruler:** Rama IX **Subject:** 100th Anniversary - Thai Railway March 26 **Obv:** Conjoined busts 1/4 left **Rev:** Radiant crown above stylized eagle **Edge:** Reeded

Date	Mintage	F	VF	XF	Unc	BU
BE2540 (1997)	—	—	—	—	3.50	—
BE2540 (1997) Proof	—	Value: 30.00				

Y# 333 20 BAHT
Copper-Nickel, 32 mm. **Ruler:** Rama IX **Subject:** 90th Anniversary - Thai Savings Bank April 1 **Obv:** Uniformed bust facing **Rev:** Designs within sectioned circle **Edge:** Reeded

Date	Mintage	F	VF	XF	Unc	BU
BE2540 (1997)	—	—	—	—	3.50	—
BE2540 (1997) Proof	—	Value: 28.00				

Y# 341 20 BAHT
Copper-Nickel, 32 mm. **Ruler:** Rama IX **Subject:** 50th Anniversary - Thai Veterans Organization; Veteran's Day February 3 **Obv:** Uniformed bust facing **Rev:** Armored figures within circle **Edge:** Reeded

Date	Mintage	F	VF	XF	Unc	BU
BE2541 (1998)	—	—	—	—	3.50	—
BE2541 (1998) Proof	—	Value: 18.50				

Y# 351 20 BAHT
Copper Nickel, 32 mm. **Ruler:** Rama IX **Subject:** 72nd Birthday of the King December 5 **Obv:** Bust left **Rev:** Crowned emblem **Edge:** Reeded

Date	Mintage	F	VF	XF	Unc	BU
BE2542 (1999)	—	—	—	—	2.50	—
BE2542 (1999) Proof	5,000	Value: 17.50				

Y# 355 20 BAHT
14.9100 g., Copper Nickel, 32 mm. **Ruler:** Rama IX **Subject:** 84th Anniversary - Audit Council Bureau September 18 **Obv:** Uniformed bust facing **Rev:** Balance scale **Edge:** Reeded

Date	Mintage	F	VF	XF	Unc	BU
BE2542 (1999)	—	—	—	—	3.50	—

Y# 376 20 BAHT
15.0000 g., Copper-Nickel, 32 mm. **Ruler:** Rama IX **Subject:** The 9th King reaches the age of the 1st King May 23 **Obv:** Conjoined busts facing **Rev:** Two royal symbols **Edge:** Reeded

Date	Mintage	F	VF	XF	Unc	BU
BE2543(2000)	—	—	—	—	3.50	—

Y# 357 20 BAHT
Copper-Nickel, 32 mm. **Ruler:** Rama IX **Subject:** Asian Development Bank Board Meeting **Obv:** Bust 1/4 right **Rev:** Chieng money illustration **Edge:** Reeded

Date	Mintage	F	VF	XF	Unc	BU
ND (2000)	—	—	—	—	4.00	—

Y# 362 20 BAHT
Copper-Nickel, 32 mm. **Ruler:** Rama IX **Subject:** 100th Birthday - King's Mother **Obv:** Bust left **Rev:** Emblem divides date **Edge:** Reeded

Date	Mintage	F	VF	XF	Unc	BU
BE2543 (2000)	—	—	—	—	3.50	—
BE2543 (2000) Proof	—	Value: 17.50				

Y# 95 50 BAHT
24.7000 g., 0.9000 Silver .7147 oz. ASW, 40 mm. **Ruler:** Rama IX **Subject:** 20th Year Buddhist Fellowship **Obv:** Bust 1/4 left **Rev:** The Buddhist wheel of law, Dhamachakr **Edge:** Reeded

Date	Mintage	F	VF	XF	Unc	BU
BE2514 (1971)	200,000	—	BV	12.00	14.00	—
BE2514 (1971) Prooflike	60,000	—	—	—	—	22.00

Y# 101 50 BAHT
24.8500 g., 0.4000 Silver .3195 oz. ASW **Ruler:** Rama IX **Subject:** National Museum Centennial **Obv:** Conjoined busts left **Rev:** Crowns within designed wreath

Date	Mintage	F	VF	XF	Unc	BU
BE2517 (1974)	200,000	—	—	8.00	14.00	—

Y# 102 50 BAHT
25.5500 g., 0.5000 Silver .4173 oz. ASW **Ruler:** Rama IX **Series:** Conservation **Obv:** Bust 1/4 left **Rev:** Rhinoceros **Rev. Designer:** Bernard Sindall

Date	Mintage	F	VF	XF	Unc	BU
BE2517 (1974)	20,000	—	—	—	32.00	35.00

Y# 102a 50 BAHT
28.2800 g., 0.9250 Silver .8411 oz. ASW **Ruler:** Rama IX **Series:** Conservation **Obv:** Bust 1/4 left **Rev:** Rhinoceros **Rev. Designer:** Bernard Sindall

Date	Mintage	F	VF	XF	Unc	BU
BE2517 (1974) Proof	9,885	Value: 60.00				

Y# 336 50 BAHT
Nickel, 36 mm. **Ruler:** Rama IX **Subject:** F.A.O. World Food Summit December 2 **Obv:** Bust left within circle **Rev:** Seated and kneeling figures within circle **Edge:** Reeded **Note:** Similar to 20 Baht, Y#335.

Date	Mintage	F	VF	XF	Unc	BU
BE2538 (1995)	—	—	—	—	12.50	—

Y# 363 50 BAHT
20.0000 g., 0.9250 Silver .5948 oz. ASW, 38.7 mm. **Ruler:** Rama IX **Subject:** Year of the Dragon **Obv:** Bust 1/4 left **Rev:** Dragon and latent image date pearl **Edge:** Reeded

Date	Mintage	F	VF	XF	Unc	BU
BE2543 (2000) Proof	8,500	Value: 55.00				

Y# 364 50 BAHT
20.0000 g., 0.9250 Silver .5948 oz. ASW **Ruler:** Rama IX **Subject:** Year of the Dragon **Obv:** Bust 1/4 left **Rev:** Two dragons with pearl hologram

Date	Mintage	F	VF	XF	Unc	BU
BE2543 (2000) Proof	8,500	Value: 150				

Y# 365 50 BAHT
20.0000 g., 0.9250 Silver .5948 oz. ASW **Ruler:** Rama IX **Subject:** Year of the Dragon **Obv:** Bust 1/4 left **Rev:** Dragon with gold-plated pearl

Date	Mintage	F	VF	XF	Unc	BU
BE2543 (2000) Proof	8,500	Value: 55.00				

Y# 103 100 BAHT
31.9000 g., 0.5000 Silver .5128 oz. ASW **Ruler:** Rama IX **Series:** Conservation **Obv:** Bust 1/4 left **Rev:** Brown-antlered deer **Rev. Designer:** Bernard Sindall

Date	Mintage	F	VF	XF	Unc	BU
BE2517 (1974)	20,000	—	—	—	37.50	40.00

Y# 103a 100 BAHT
35.0000 g., 0.9250 Silver 1.0409 oz. ASW **Ruler:** Rama IX **Series:** Conservation **Obv:** Bust 1/4 left **Rev:** Brown-antlered deer **Rev. Designer:** Bernard Sindall

Date	Mintage	F	VF	XF	Unc	BU
BE2517 (1974) Proof	9,294	Value: 70.00				

Y# 106 100 BAHT
25.0000 g., 0.9000 Silver .7234 oz. ASW **Ruler:** Rama IX **Subject:** 100th Anniversary - Ministry of Finance **Obv:** Conjoined busts facing **Rev:** Building within circle

Date	Mintage	F	VF	XF	Unc	BU
BE2518 (1975)	30,000	—	—	12.50	20.00	—

Y# 242 100 BAHT
Copper-Nickel, 38 mm. **Ruler:** Rama IX **Subject:** World Bank - International Monetary Fund **Obv:** Conjoined busts right **Rev:** Emblem

Date	Mintage	F	VF	XF	Unc	BU
BE2534 (1991)	500,000	—	—	—	12.50	—
BE2534 (1991) Proof	60,000	Value: 27.50				

Y# 287 100 BAHT
Copper-Nickel, 38 mm. **Ruler:** Rama IX **Subject:** 33rd World Scount Conference **Obv:** Conjoined busts right **Rev:** Crowned emblem

Date	Mintage	F	VF	XF	Unc	BU
BE2536 (1993)	200,000	—	—	—	17.50	—
BE2536 (1993) Proof	30,000	Value: 32.50				

Y# 359 100 BAHT
15.0000 g., 0.9250 Silver .4461 oz. ASW, 30 mm. **Ruler:** Rama IX **Series:** World Wildlife Fund **Obv:** Bust left **Rev:** Tiger head and value **Note:** Thickness of coin is 4.7mm.

Date	Mintage	F	VF	XF	Unc	BU
BE2540 (1997) Proof	50,000	Value: 25.00				

Y# 366 100 BAHT
7.7759 g., 0.9999 Gold .2500 oz. AGW, 22 mm. **Ruler:** Rama IX **Subject:** Year of the Dragon **Obv:** Bust 1/4 left **Rev:** Dragon with golden plated pearl **Edge:** Reeded

Date	Mintage	F	VF	XF	Unc	BU
BE2543 (2000) Proof	1,800	Value: 200				

Y# 88 150 BAHT
3.7500 g., 0.9000 Gold .1085 oz. AGW **Ruler:** Rama IX **Subject:** Queen Sirikit 36th Birthday **Obv:** Bust right **Rev:** Crowned monogram

Date	Mintage	F	VF	XF	Unc	BU
BE2511 (1968)	202,000	—	—	—	100	—

Y# 108 150 BAHT
22.0000 g., 0.9250 Silver .6543 oz. ASW **Ruler:** Rama IX **Subject:** 75th Birthday of King's Mother October 21 **Obv:** Bust with hat facing **Rev:** Emblem

Date	Mintage	F	VF	XF	Unc	BU
BE2518 (1975)	200,000	—	—	12.00	18.50	—

Y# 113 150 BAHT
22.0000 g., 0.9250 Silver .6543 oz. ASW **Ruler:** Rama IX **Series:** F.A.O. **Obv:** Standing half length figures scattering rice **Rev:** Elephants within circle

Date	Mintage	F	VF	XF	Unc	BU
BE2520 (1977)	50,000	—	—	12.00	20.00	25.00

Y# 118 150 BAHT
22.0000 g., 0.9250 Silver .6543 oz. ASW **Ruler:** Rama IX **Subject:** Crown Prince Vajiralongkorn and Princess Soamsawali Wedding January 3 **Obv:** Conjoined busts right **Rev:** Crowned monogram within designs

Date	Mintage	F	VF	XF	Unc	BU
BE2520 (1977)	200,000	—	—	11.50	15.00	—

Y# 116 150 BAHT
22.0000 g., 0.9250 Silver .6543 oz. ASW **Ruler:** Rama IX **Subject:** Graduation of Princess Sirindhorn; 1st royal graduate of a Thai University **Obv:** Bust left **Rev:** Radiant crown

Date	Mintage	F	VF	XF	Unc	BU
BE2520 (1977)	100,000	—	—	11.50	15.00	—

Y# 125 150 BAHT
22.0000 g., 0.9250 Silver .6543 oz. ASW **Ruler:** Rama IX **Subject:** Investiture of Princess Sirindhorn May 12 **Obv:** Bust right **Rev:** Crowned monogram

Date	Mintage	F	VF	XF	Unc	BU
BE2520 (1977)	50,000	—	—	13.50	28.50	—

Y# 123 150 BAHT
22.0000 g., 0.9250 Silver .6543 oz. ASW **Ruler:** Rama IX **Subject:** 9th World Orchid Conference **Obv:** Uniformed bust 1/4 left **Rev:** Orchids

Date	Mintage	F	VF	XF	Unc	BU
BE2521 (1978)	30,000	—	—	12.50	25.00	—

Y# 128 150 BAHT
22.0000 g., 0.9250 Silver .6543 oz. ASW **Ruler:** Rama IX **Subject:** Graduation of Crown Prince Vajiralongkorn **Obv:** Bust left **Rev:** Crowned elephant head facing within frame

Date	Mintage	F	VF	XF	Unc	BU
BE2521 (1978)	50,000	—	—	12.00	18.50	—

Y# 197 150 BAHT
7.5000 g., 0.9250 Silver .2230 oz. ASW **Ruler:** Rama IX **Subject:** 60th Birthday - King Rama IX **Obv:** Uniformed bust facing **Rev:** Crowned radiant emblem **Note:** Similar to 6000 Baht, Y#202.

Date	Mintage	F	VF	XF	Unc	BU
BE2530 (1987)	12,000	—	—	—	25.00	—
BE2530 (1987) Proof	1,100	Value: 125				

Y# 213 150 BAHT
7.5000 g., 0.9250 Silver .2230 oz. ASW **Ruler:** Rama IX **Subject:** 42nd Anniversary - Reign of King Rama IX **Obv:** Uniformed bust facing **Rev:** Crowned monogram **Note:** Similar to 10 Baht, Y#212.

Date	Mintage	F	VF	XF	Unc	BU
BE2531 (1988)	20,000	—	—	—	25.00	—
BE2531 (1988) Proof	2,454	Value: 135				

Y# 262 150 BAHT
7.5000 g., 0.9250 Silver .2230 oz. ASW **Ruler:** Rama IX **Subject:** Queen's 60th Birthday **Obv:** Crowned bust facing **Rev:** Crowned monogram **Note:** Similar to 10 Baht, Y#261.

Date	Mintage	F	VF	XF	Unc	BU
BE2535 (1992)	25,000	—	—	—	25.00	—
BE2535 (1992) Proof	5,600	Value: 45.00				

Y# 322 150 BAHT
7.5000 g., 0.9250 Silver .2230 oz. ASW **Ruler:** Rama IX **Subject:** 50th Anniversary - Reign of King Rama IX **Obv:** Bust facing **Rev:** National arms **Note:** Similar to 20 Baht, Y#321.1.

Date	Mintage	F	VF	XF	Unc	BU
BE2539 (1996)	—	—	—	—	17.50	—
BE2539 (1996) Proof	—	Value: 45.00				

Y# 133 200 BAHT
22.0000 g., 0.9250 Silver .6544 oz. ASW **Ruler:** Rama IX **Subject:** Royal Cradle Ceremony **Obv:** Infant head 1/4 right **Rev:** Inscription within designed wreath

Date	Mintage	F	VF	XF	Unc	BU
BE2522 (1979)	50,000	—	—	11.50	16.50	—

Y# 152 200 BAHT
23.3200 g., 0.9250 Silver .6935 oz. ASW **Ruler:** Rama IX **Series:** International Year of the Child **Obv:** Bust lęft **Rev:** Dancing figure flanked by emblems below

Date	Mintage	F	VF	XF	Unc	BU
BE2524 (1981) Proof	9,525	Value: 75.00				

Y# 206 200 BAHT
23.1800 g., 0.9250 Silver .6894 oz. ASW **Ruler:** Rama IX **Series:** 25th Anniversary of World Wildlife Fund **Obv:** Bust left **Rev:** Siamese Fireback pheasant

Date	Mintage	F	VF	XF	Unc	BU
BE2530 (1987) Proof	25,000	Value: 30.00				

Y# 379 200 BAHT
23.3300 g., 0.9250 Silver 0.6938 oz. ASW, 38.6 mm. **Ruler:** Rama IX **Subject:** UNICEF **Obv:** Bust left **Rev:** Three seated children **Edge:** Reeded

Date	Mintage	F	VF	XF	Unc	BU
BE2540-1997 Proof	2,900	Value: 27.50				

Y# 399 200 BAHT
23.2600 g., 0.9250 Silver 0.6917 oz. ASW, 38.5 mm. **Ruler:** Rama IX **Subject:** World Wildlife Fund **Obv:** Bust left **Rev:** Elephants right **Edge:** Reeded

Date	Mintage	F	VF	XF	Unc	BU
BE2541-1998 Proof	—	Value: 120				

Y# 360 200 BAHT
23.1800 g., 0.9250 Silver .6894 oz. ASW, 38.5 mm. **Ruler:** Rama IX **Series:** World Wildlife Fund **Obv:** Bust left **Rev:** Two tigers above value **Edge:** Reeded **Note:** Thickness of coin is 4.7mm.

Date	Mintage	F	VF	XF	Unc	BU
BE2541-1998 Proof	15,000	Value: 75.00				

Y# 372 200 BAHT
23.1800 g., 0.9250 Silver .6894 oz. ASW **Ruler:** Rama IX **Series:** World Wildlife Fund **Obv:** Bust left **Rev:** Elephants

Date	Mintage	F	VF	XF	Unc	BU
BE2541-1998 Proof	—	Value: 60.00				

Y# 367 200 BAHT
155.5175 g., 0.9250 Silver 4.625 oz. ASW, 65 mm. **Ruler:** Rama IX **Subject:** Year of the Dragon **Obv:** Bust left **Rev:** Two dragons around silver pearl within orange circle **Edge:** Reeded

Date	Mintage	F	VF	XF	Unc	BU
BE2543-2000 Proof	2,000	Value: 185				

Y# 169 250 BAHT
28.2800 g., 0.9250 Silver .8411 oz. ASW **Ruler:** Rama IX **Series:** International Year of Disabled Persons **Obv:** Bust left **Rev:** Emblem within sprigs

Date	Mintage	F	VF	XF	Unc	BU
BE2526 (1983)	307	—	—	—	275	—
BE2526 (1983) Proof	233	Value: 550				

Y# 368 250 BAHT
15.5510 g., 0.9999 Gold .5000 oz. AGW, 27 mm. **Ruler:** Rama IX **Subject:** Year of the Dragon **Obv:** Bust left **Rev:** Dragon with latent image pearl **Edge:** Reeded

Date	Mintage	F	VF	XF	Unc	BU
BE2543-2000 Proof	2,800	Value: 385				

Y# 89 300 BAHT
7.5000 g., 0.9000 Gold .2170 oz. AGW **Ruler:** Rama IX **Subject:** Queen Sirikit 36th Birthday **Obv:** Bust right **Rev:** Crowned monogram

Date	Mintage	F	VF	XF	Unc	BU
BE2511 (1968)	101,000	—	—	—	175	—

Y# 136 300 BAHT
22.0000 g., 0.9250 Silver .6543 oz. ASW **Ruler:** Rama IX **Subject:** Graduation of Princess Chulabhorn **Obv:** Bust 1/4 left **Rev:** Graduation emblem within circle **Note:** Similar to 10 Baht, Y#135.

Date	Mintage	F	VF	XF	Unc	BU
BE2522 (1979)	20,000	—	—	15.00	20.00	—

Y# 198 300 BAHT
15.0000 g., 0.9250 Silver .4461 oz. ASW **Ruler:** Rama IX **Subject:** 60th Birthday - King Rama IX **Obv:** Uniformed bust facing **Rev:** Radiant crowned emblem

Date	Mintage	F	VF	XF	Unc	BU
BE2530 (1987)	6,680	—	—	—	25.00	—
BE2530 (1987) Proof	800	Value: 50.00				

Y# 214 300 BAHT
15.0000 g., 0.9250 Silver .4461 oz. ASW **Ruler:** Rama IX **Subject:** 42nd Anniversary - Reign of King Rama IX **Obv:** Uniformed bust facing **Rev:** Crowned monogram

Date	Mintage	F	VF	XF	Unc	BU
BE2531 (1988)	11,000	—	—	—	20.00	—
BE2531 (1988) Proof	2,391	Value: 50.00				

Y# 263 300 BAHT
15.0000 g., 0.9250 Silver .4461 oz. ASW **Ruler:** Rama IX **Subject:** Queen's 60th Birthday **Obv:** Crowned bust facing **Rev:** Crowned monogram

Date	Mintage	F	VF	XF	Unc	BU
BE2535 (1992)	25,000	—	—	—	35.00	—
BE2535 (1992) Proof	4,000	Value: 45.00				

Y# 323 300 BAHT
15.0000 g., 0.9250 Silver .4461 oz. ASW **Ruler:** Rama IX **Subject:** 50th Anniversary - Reign of King Rama IX **Obv:** Bust facing **Rev:** National arms

Date	Mintage	F	VF	XF	Unc	BU
BE2539 (1996)	—	—	—	—	22.50	—
BE2539 (1996) Proof	—	Value: 50.00				

Y# 93 400 BAHT
10.0000 g., 0.9000 Gold .2893 oz. AGW **Ruler:** Rama IX **Subject:** 25th Anniversary - Reign of King Rama IX **Obv:** Head right **Rev:** Radiant crowned monogram

Date	Mintage	F	VF	XF	Unc	BU
BE2514 (1971)	47,000	—	—	—	225	280

Y# 90 600 BAHT
15.0000 g., 0.9000 Gold .4340 oz. AGW **Ruler:** Rama IX **Subject:** Queen Sirikit 36th Birthday **Obv:** Crowned bust right **Rev:** Crowned monogram within wreath

Date	Mintage	F	VF	XF	Unc	BU
BE2511 (1968)	46,000	—	—	—	325	380

Y# 138 600 BAHT
14.9000 g., 0.9250 Silver .4432 oz. ASW **Ruler:** Rama IX **Subject:** Queen's Anniversary and F.A.O. Ceres Medal **Obv:** Crowned bust 1/4 left **Rev:** Figures working within football-like frames

Date	Mintage	F	VF	XF	Unc	BU
BE2523 (1980)	23,000	—	—	18.00	28.00	—

Y# 143 600 BAHT
14.9000 g., 0.9250 Silver .4432 oz. ASW **Ruler:** Rama IX **Subject:** Centennial - Birth of Rama VI **Obv:** Bust right **Rev:** Emblem

Date	Mintage	F	VF	XF	Unc	BU
BE2524 (1981)	19,000	—	—	15.00	25.00	—

Y# 147 600 BAHT
22.0000 g., 0.9250 Silver .6543 oz. ASW **Ruler:** Rama IX **Subject:** 35th Anniversary - Reign of King Rama IX **Obv:** Conjoined busts left **Rev:** Crowns and emblem

Date	Mintage	F	VF	XF	Unc	BU
BE2524 (1981)	15,000	—	—	20.00	30.00	—

Y# 150 600 BAHT
22.0000 g., 0.9250 Silver .6543 oz. ASW **Ruler:** Rama IX **Subject:** Bicentennial of Bangkok **Obv:** Conjoined busts left **Rev:** Emblem

Date	Mintage	F	VF	XF	Unc	BU
BE2525 (1982)	15,000	—	—	20.00	30.00	—

Y# 155 600 BAHT
22.0000 g., 0.9250 Silver .6543 oz. ASW **Ruler:** Rama IX **Subject:** 50th Birthday of Queen Sirikit **Obv:** Crowned bust 1/4 left **Rev:** Crowned monogram

Date	Mintage	F	VF	XF	Unc	BU
BE2525 (1982)	3,895	—	—	28.00	55.00	—
BE2525 (1982) Proof	1,011	Value: 225				

Y# 164 600 BAHT
22.0000 g., 0.9250 Silver .6543 oz. ASW **Ruler:** Rama IX **Subject:** 100th Anniversary of Postage Stamps **Obv:** Conjoined busts left **Rev:** Stamps

Date	Mintage	F	VF	XF	Unc	BU
BE2526 (1983)	5,000	—	—	28.00	55.00	—
BE2526 (1983) Proof	1,400	Value: 165				

Y# 166 600 BAHT
22.0000 g., 0.9250 Silver .6543 oz. ASW **Ruler:** Rama IX **Subject:** 700th Anniversary of Thai Alphabet **Obv:** Seated figure left **Rev:** Inscription

Date	Mintage	F	VF	XF	Unc	BU
BE2526 (1983)	4,300	—	—	28.00	55.00	—
BE2526 (1983) Proof	1,000	Value: 200				

Y# 173 600 BAHT
22.0000 g., 0.9250 Silver .6543 oz. ASW **Ruler:** Rama IX **Subject:** 84th Birthday of Princess Mother **Obv:** Bust 1/4 left **Rev:** Crown on stand flanked by others

Date	Mintage	F	VF	XF	Unc	BU
BE2527 (1984)	3,530	—	—	28.00	45.00	—
BE2527 (1984) Proof	520	Value: 260				

Y# 193 600 BAHT
22.0000 g., 0.9250 Silver .6543 oz. ASW **Ruler:** Rama IX **Subject:** Princess Chulabhorn Awarded Einstein Medal **Obv:** Head of Albert Einstein left within circle at center of hexagon **Rev:** Graduate's bust left **Note:** Similar to 10 Baht, Y#192.

Date	Mintage	F	VF	XF	Unc	BU
BE2529 (1986)	2,400	—	—	—	55.00	—
BE2529 (1986) Proof	212	Value: 225				

Y# 182 600 BAHT
22.0000 g., 0.9250 Silver .6543 oz. ASW **Ruler:** Rama IX **Subject:** 6th ASEAN Orchid Congress **Obv:** Uniformed bust left **Rev:** Symbols of congress **Note:** Similar to 10 Baht, Y#181.

Date	Mintage	F	VF	XF	Unc	BU
BE2529 (1986)	5,000	—	—	—	45.00	—
BE2529 (1986) Proof	300	Value: 200				

Y# 229 600 BAHT
30.0000 g., 0.9250 Silver .8922 oz. ASW **Ruler:** Rama IX **Subject:** Asian Institute of Technology **Obv:** Kneeling figure left with students **Rev:** Symbol above inscription **Note:** Similar to 10 Baht, Y#190.

Date	Mintage	F	VF	XF	Unc	BU
BE2530 (1987)	2,700	—	—	—	40.00	—
BE2530 (1987) Proof	400	Value: 175				

Y# 199 600 BAHT
30.0000 g., 0.9250 Silver .8922 oz. ASW **Ruler:** Rama IX **Subject:** 60th Birthday - King Rama IX **Obv:** Uniformed bust facing **Rev:** Radiant crowned emblem **Note:** Similar to 6000 Baht, Y#202.

Date	Mintage	F	VF	XF	Unc	BU
BE2530 (1987)	5,000	—	—	—	100	—
BE2530 (1987) Proof	750	Value: 350				

Y# 215 600 BAHT
30.0000 g., 0.9250 Silver .8922 oz. ASW **Ruler:** Rama IX **Subject:** 42nd Anniversary - Reign of King Rama IX **Obv:** Uniformed bust facing **Rev:** Crowned monogram **Note:** Similar to 10 Baht, Y#212.

Date	Mintage	F	VF	XF	Unc	BU
BE2531 (1988)	8,840	—	—	—	45.00	—
BE2531 (1988) Proof	1,110	Value: 135				

Y# 224 600 BAHT
30.0000 g., 0.9250 Silver .8922 oz. ASW **Ruler:** Rama IX **Subject:** Crown Prince's Birthday **Obv:** Head 1/4 left **Rev:** Crowned monogram within lightning bolts

Date	Mintage	F	VF	XF	Unc	BU
BE2531 (1988)	5,000	—	—	—	45.00	—
BE2531 (1988) Proof	1,000	Value: 145				

Y# 226 600 BAHT
30.0000 g., 0.9000 Silver .8682 oz. ASW **Ruler:** Rama IX **Subject:** 72nd Anniversary of Chulalongkorn University **Obv:** Conjoined busts left **Rev:** Radiant crown

Date	Mintage	F	VF	XF	Unc	BU
BE2532 (1989)	10,000	—	—	—	50.00	—

Y# 234 600 BAHT
30.0000 g., 0.9250 Silver .8922 oz. ASW **Ruler:** Rama IX **Subject:** 90th Birthday of Princess Mother **Obv:** Bust 1/4 left **Rev:** Crown on stand flanked by others

Date	Mintage	F	VF	XF	Unc	BU
BE2533 (1990)	20,000	—	—	—	35.00	—
BE2533 (1990) Proof	2,000	Value: 130				

Y# 245 600 BAHT
30.0000 g., 0.9250 Silver .8922 oz. ASW **Ruler:** Rama IX **Subject:** World Health Organization **Obv:** Bust facing **Rev:** Medal with small emblem above **Note:** Similar to 10 Baht, Y#244.

Date	Mintage	F	VF	XF	Unc	BU
BE2533 (1990)	25,000	—	—	—	32.50	—
BE2533 (1990) Proof	596	Value: 275				

Y# 239 600 BAHT
30.0000 g., 0.9000 Silver .8682 oz. ASW **Ruler:** Rama IX **Subject:** 36th Birthday of Princess Sirindhorn **Obv:** Uniformed bust 1/4 left **Rev:** Crowned monogram flanked by stars above sprigs

Date	Mintage	F	VF	XF	Unc	BU
BE2534 (1991)	30,000	—	—	—	32.50	—
BE2534 (1991) Proof	2,583	Value: 125				

Y# 257 600 BAHT
30.0000 g., 0.9250 Silver .8922 oz. ASW **Ruler:** Rama IX **Subject:** Princess Sirindhorn's Magsaysay Foundation Award **Obv:** Seated and kneeling figures within circle **Rev:** Inscription within sprigs and circle below cameo

Date	Mintage	F	VF	XF	Unc	BU
BE2534 (1991)	15,000	—	—	—	35.00	—
BE2534 (1991) Proof	10,000	Value: 115				

Y# 264 600 BAHT
30.0000 g., 0.9250 Silver .8922 oz. ASW **Ruler:** Rama IX **Subject:** Queen's 60th Birthday **Obv:** Crowned bust facing **Rev:** Crowned monogram

Date	Mintage	F	VF	XF	Unc	BU
BE2535 (1992)	25,000	—	—	—	32.50	—
BE2535 (1992) Proof	3,500	Value: 120				

Y# 274 600 BAHT
30.0000 g., 0.9250 Silver .8922 oz. ASW **Ruler:** Rama IX **Subject:** 64th Birthday - King Rama IX **Obv:** Conjoined busts 1/4 left **Rev:** Crowned monograms

Date	Mintage	F	VF	XF	Unc	BU
BE2535 (1992)	10,000	—	—	—	37.50	—
BE2535 (1992) Proof	511	Value: 320				

Y# 250 600 BAHT
30.0000 g., 0.9250 Silver .8922 oz. ASW **Ruler:** Rama IX **Subject:** Centenary Celebration - Father of King Rama IX **Obv:** Three crowns on stands **Rev:** Bust facing

Date	Mintage	F	VF	XF	Unc	BU
BE2535 (1992)	19,000	—	—	—	35.00	—
BE2535 (1992) Proof	11,000	Value: 115				

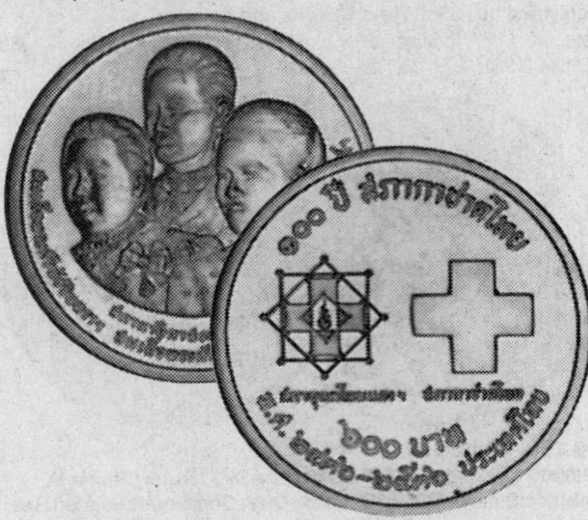

Y# 281 600 BAHT
30.0000 g., 0.9250 Silver .8922 oz. ASW **Ruler:** Rama IX **Subject:** Centennial of Thai Red Cross **Obv:** Conjoined busts 1/4 left **Rev:** Emblems

Date	Mintage	F	VF	XF	Unc	BU
BE2536 (1993)	13,000	—	—	—	37.50	—

Y# 290 600 BAHT
30.0000 g., 0.9250 Silver .8922 oz. ASW **Ruler:** Rama IX **Subject:** 100th Anniversary of Rama VII **Obv:** Uniformed bust left **Rev:** Crown and designs within oval

Date	Mintage	F	VF	XF	Unc	BU
BE2536 (1993)	12,000	—	—	—	37.50	—
BE2536 (1993) Proof	1,000	Value: 100				

Y# 299 600 BAHT
22.1500 g., 0.9250 Silver .6587 oz. ASW **Ruler:** Rama IX **Subject:** 120th Anniversary - Ministry of Finance **Obv:** Conjoined busts right **Rev:** Stylized eagle within circle

Date	Mintage	F	VF	XF	Unc	BU
BE2538 (1995)	17,000	—	—	—	35.00	—
BE2538 (1995) Proof	491	Value: 85.00				

Y# 301 600 BAHT
22.1500 g., 0.9250 Silver .6587 oz. ASW **Ruler:** Rama IX **Subject:** Ministry of Defense **Obv:** Conjoined uniformed busts facing **Rev:** Mythical animal within circle

Date	Mintage	F	VF	XF	Unc	BU
BE2538 (1995)	18,000	—	—	—	32.50	—
BE2538 (1995) Proof	2,960	Value: 75.00				

Y# 303 600 BAHT
22.1500 g., 0.9250 Silver .6587 oz. ASW **Ruler:** Rama IX **Subject:** Ministry of Foreign Affairs **Obv:** Conjoined busts facing **Rev:** Seated figure within designed circle and wreath

Date	Mintage	F	VF	XF	Unc	BU
BE2538 (1995)	14,000	—	—	—	35.00	—
BE2538 (1995) Proof	627	Value: 85.00				

Y# 305 600 BAHT
22.1500 g., 0.9250 Silver .6587 oz. ASW **Ruler:** Rama IX **Subject:** 72nd Birthday of Princess **Obv:** Uniformed bust 3/4 facing **Rev:** Crowned arms

Date	Mintage	F	VF	XF	Unc	BU
BE2538 (1995)	12,000	—	—	—	35.00	—
BE2538 (1995) Proof	600	Value: 75.00				

Y# 310 600 BAHT
22.0000 g., 0.9250 Silver .6543 oz. ASW **Ruler:** Rama IX **Subject:** 80th Anniversary - Department of Revenue **Obv:** Conjoined busts 1/4 left **Rev:** Seated figure within circle

Date	Mintage	F	VF	XF	Unc	BU
BE2538 (1995)	4,000	—	—	—	37.50	—
BE2538 (1995) Proof	—	Value: 75.00				

Y# 312 600 BAHT

22.0000 g., 0.9250 Silver .6543 oz. ASW **Ruler:** Rama IX **Subject:** 120th Anniversary - Audit Council **Obv:** Conjoined busts facing **Rev:** Balance scale

Date	Mintage	F	VF	XF	Unc	BU
BE2538 (1995)	6,000	—	—	—	35.00	—
BE2538 (1995) Proof	—	Value: 75.00				

Y# 324 600 BAHT

30.0000 g., 0.9250 Silver .8922 oz. ASW **Ruler:** Rama IX **Subject:** 50th Anniversary - Reign of King Rama IX **Obv:** Bust facing **Rev:** National arms **Note:** Similar to 20 Baht, Y#321.1.

Date	Mintage	F	VF	XF	Unc	BU
BE2539 (1996)	—	—	—	—	32.50	—
BE2539 (1996) Proof	—	Value: 75.00				

Y# 356 600 BAHT

22.1500 g., 0.9250 Silver .6587 oz. ASW, 35 mm. **Ruler:** Rama IX **Subject:** King's 6th Cycle Birthday Anniversary **Obv:** Bust facing **Rev:** Radiant arms **Edge:** Reeded

Date	Mintage	F	VF	XF	Unc	BU
BE2542 (1999)	100,000	—	—	—	20.00	—
BE2542 (1999) Proof	30,000	Value: 40.00				

Y# 377 600 BAHT

22.1500 g., 0.9250 Silver .6587 oz. ASW, 35 mm. **Ruler:** Rama IX **Subject:** King's 72nd Birthday **Obv:** King and Rama I portraits **Rev:** Two royal symbols **Edge:** Reeded

Date	Mintage	F	VF	XF	Unc	BU
BE2543(2000) Proof	—	Value: 75.00				

Y# 94 800 BAHT

20.0000 g., 0.9000 Gold .5787 oz. AGW **Ruler:** Rama IX **Subject:** 25th Anniversary - Reign of King Rama IX **Obv:** Head right **Rev:** Radiant crowned monogram flanked by sprigs

Date	Mintage	F	VF	XF	Unc	BU
BE2514 (1971)	22,000	—	—	—	425	485

Y# 200 1500 BAHT

3.7500 g., 0.9000 Gold .1085 oz. AGW **Ruler:** Rama IX **Subject:** 60th Birthday - King Rama IX **Obv:** Bust facing **Rev:** Radiant crowned emblem

Date	Mintage	F	VF	XF	Unc	BU
BE2530 (1987)	5,000	—	—	—	95.00	—
BE2530 (1987) Proof	400	Value: 175				

Y# 216 1500 BAHT

3.7500 g., 0.9000 Gold .1085 oz. AGW **Ruler:** Rama IX **Subject:** 42nd Anniversary - Reign of King Rama IX **Obv:** Bust facing **Rev:** Crowned monogram

Date	Mintage	F	VF	XF	Unc	BU
BE2531 (1988)	11,000	—	—	—	90.00	—
BE2531 (1988) Proof	995	Value: 160				

Y# 265 1500 BAHT

3.7500 g., 0.9000 Gold .1085 oz. AGW **Ruler:** Rama IX **Subject:** Queen's 60th Birthday **Obv:** Crowned bust facing **Rev:** Crowned monogram **Note:** Similar to 10 Baht, Y#261.

Date	Mintage	F	VF	XF	Unc	BU
BE2535 (1992)	10,000	—	—	—	90.00	—
BE2535 (1992) Proof	1,500	Value: 150				

Y# 380 2000 BAHT

6.2200 g., 0.9990 Gold 0.1998 oz. AGW, 22 mm. **Ruler:** Rama IX **Subject:** UNICEF **Obv:** Bust 3/4 left **Rev:** Girl with Thai desk **Edge:** Reeded

Date	Mintage	F	VF	XF	Unc	BU
BE2540-1997 Proof	1,700	Value: 175				

Y# 119 2500 BAHT

15.0000 g., 0.9000 Gold .4340 oz. AGW **Ruler:** Rama IX **Subject:** Crown Prince Vajiralongkorn and Princess Soamsawali Wedding **Obv:** Conjoined busts right **Rev:** Crowned monogram within lightning bolts

Date	Mintage	F	VF	XF	Unc	BU
BE2520 (1977)	20,000	—	—	—	300	325

Y# 126 2500 BAHT

15.0000 g., 0.9000 Gold .4340 oz. AGW **Ruler:** Rama IX **Subject:** Investiture of Princess Sirindhorn **Obv:** Bust 1/4 right **Rev:** Crowned monogram

Date	Mintage	F	VF	XF	Unc	BU
BE2520 (1977)	5,000	—	—	—	320	350

Y# 170 2500 BAHT

15.0000 g., 0.9000 Gold .4340 oz. AGW **Ruler:** Rama IX **Series:** International Year of Disabled Persons **Obv:** Bust left **Rev:** Emblem within sprigs

Date	Mintage	F	VF	XF	Unc	BU
BE2526 (1983)	92	—	—	—	1,400	—
BE2526 (1983) Proof	793	Value: 1,250				

Y# 207 2500 BAHT

15.9800 g., 0.9000 Gold .4625 oz. AGW **Ruler:** Rama IX **Series:** 25th Anniversary of World Wildlife Fund **Obv:** Bust left **Rev:** Elephant left within circle

Date	Mintage	F	VF	XF	Unc	BU
BE2530 (1987) Proof	Est. 5,000	Value: 350				

Y# 325 2500 BAHT

3.7500 g., 0.9000 Gold .1085 oz. AGW **Ruler:** Rama IX **Subject:** 50th Anniversary - Reign of King Rama IX **Obv:** Bust facing **Rev:** National arms **Note:** Similar to 20 Baht, Y#321.1.

Date	Mintage	F	VF	XF	Unc	BU
BE2539 (1996)	—	—	—	—	85.00	—
BE2539 (1996) Proof	—	Value: 135				

Y# 369 2500 BAHT

155.5175 g., 0.9999 Gold 5.0000 oz. AGW, 55 mm. **Ruler:** Rama IX **Subject:** Year of the Dragon **Obv:** Bust left **Rev:** Two dragons with pearl hologram **Edge:** Reeded

Date	Mintage	F	VF	XF	Unc	BU
BE2543 (2000) In sets only	500	—	—	—	3,500	—

Y# 129 3000 BAHT

15.0000 g., 0.9000 Gold .4340 oz. AGW **Ruler:** Rama IX **Subject:** Graduation of Crown Prince Vijiralongkorn **Obv:** Bust left **Rev:** Crowned elephant head facing within frame

Date	Mintage	F	VF	XF	Unc	BU
BE2521 (1978)	10,000	—	—	—	320	340

Y# 201 3000 BAHT

7.5000 g., 0.9000 Gold .2170 oz. AGW **Ruler:** Rama IX **Subject:** 60th Birthday - King Rama IX **Obv:** Uniformed bust facing **Rev:** Radiant crowned emblem

Date	Mintage	F	VF	XF	Unc	BU
BE2530 (1987)	3,000	—	—	—	165	—
BE2530 (1987) Proof	400	Value: 275				

Y# 217 3000 BAHT

7.5000 g., 0.9000 Gold .2170 oz. AGW **Ruler:** Rama IX **Subject:** 42nd Anniversary - Reign of King Rama IX **Obv:** Uniformed bust facing **Rev:** Radiant crowned monogram

Date	Mintage	F	VF	XF	Unc	BU
BE2531 (1988)	7,904	—	—	—	175	—
BE2531 (1988) Proof	780	Value: 325				

Y# 266 3000 BAHT

7.5000 g., 0.9000 Gold .2170 oz. AGW **Ruler:** Rama IX **Subject:** Queen's 60th Birthday **Obv:** Crowned bust facing **Rev:** Crowned monogram

Date	Mintage	F	VF	XF	Unc	BU
BE2535 (1992)	7,000	—	—	—	175	—
BE2535 (1992) Proof	1,100	Value: 330				

Y# 326 3000 BAHT

7.5000 g., 0.9000 Gold .2170 oz. AGW **Ruler:** Rama IX **Subject:** 50th Anniversary - Reign of King Rama IX **Obv:** Uniformed bust facing **Rev:** National arms

Date	Mintage	F	VF	XF	Unc	BU
BE2539 (1996)	—	—	—	—	185	—
BE2539 (1996) Proof	—	Value: 325				

Y# 153 4000 BAHT

17.1700 g., 0.9000 Gold .4969 oz. AGW **Ruler:** Rama IX **Series:** International Year of the Child **Obv:** Bust left **Rev:** Two children playing

Date	Mintage	F	VF	XF	Unc	BU
BE2524 (1981) Proof	3,963	Value: 365				

Y# 104 5000 BAHT

33.4370 g., 0.9000 Gold .9676 oz. AGW **Ruler:** Rama IX **Series:** Conservation **Obv:** Bust 1/4 left **Rev:** White-eyed River Martin

Date	Mintage	F	VF	XF	Unc	BU
BE2517 (1974)	2,602	—	—	—	685	725
BE2517 (1974) Proof	623	Value: 1,800				

Y# 122 5000 BAHT

30.0000 g., 0.9000 Gold .8681 oz. AGW **Ruler:** Rama IX **Subject:** 50th Birthday - King Rama IX **Obv:** Bust left **Rev:** Radiant crowned monogram

Date	Mintage	F	VF	XF	Unc	BU
BE2520 (1977)	6,400	—	—	—	620	650

Y# 156 6000 BAHT

15.0000 g., 0.9000 Gold .4341 oz. AGW **Ruler:** Rama IX **Subject:** 50th Birthday - Queen Sirikit **Obv:** Crowned bust 1/4 left **Rev:** Crowned monogram

Date	Mintage	F	VF	XF	Unc	BU
BE2525 (1982)	1,471	—	—	—	450	500
BE2525 (1982) Proof	99	Value: 4,000				

Y# 167 6000 BAHT

15.0000 g., 0.9000 Gold .4341 oz. AGW **Ruler:** Rama IX **Subject:** 700th Anniversary - Thai Alphabet **Obv:** Seated figure left **Rev:** Inscription

Date	Mintage	F	VF	XF	Unc	BU
BE2526 (1983)	700	—	—	—	350	380
BE2526 (1983) Proof	235	Value: 620				

Y# 174 6000 BAHT

15.0000 g., 0.9000 Gold .4341 oz. AGW **Ruler:** Rama IX **Subject:** 84th Birthday - Princess Mother **Obv:** Bust left **Rev:** Crown on stand flanked by others

Date	Mintage	F	VF	XF	Unc	BU
BE2527 (1984)	835	—	—	—	350	380
BE2527 (1984) Proof	246	Value: 650				

Y# 202 6000 BAHT

15.0000 g., 0.9000 Gold .4341 oz. AGW **Ruler:** Rama IX **Subject:** 60th Birthday - King Rama IX **Obv:** Uniformed bust facing **Rev:** Radiant crowned emblem

Date	Mintage	F	VF	XF	Unc	BU
BE2530 (1987)	2,000	—	—	—	325	350
BE2530 (1987) Proof	350	Value: 475				

Y# 247 6000 BAHT

15.0000 g., 0.9000 Gold .4341 oz. AGW **Ruler:** Rama IX **Subject:** Asian Institute of Technology **Obv:** Kneeling and seated figures within circle **Rev:** Emblem

Date	Mintage	F	VF	XF	Unc	BU
BE2530 (1987)	700	—	—	—	350	380
BE2530 (1987) Proof	100	Value: 650				

Y# 218 6000 BAHT

15.0000 g., 0.9000 Gold .4341 oz. AGW **Ruler:** Rama IX **Subject:** 42nd Anniversary - Reign of King Rama IX **Obv:** Uniformed bust facing **Rev:** Radiant crowned monogram

Date	Mintage	F	VF	XF	Unc	BU
BE2531 (1988)	6,067	—	—	—	320	340
BE2531 (1988) Proof	670	Value: 500				

Y# 246 6000 BAHT

15.0000 g., 0.9000 Gold .4341 oz. AGW **Ruler:** Rama IX **Subject:** World Health Organization

Date	Mintage	F	VF	XF	Unc	BU
BE2534 (1991)	5,000	—	—	—	350	380
BE2534 (1991) Proof	591	Value: 600				

Y# 258 6000 BAHT

15.0000 g., 0.9000 Gold .4341 oz. AGW **Ruler:** Rama IX **Subject:** Princess Sirindhorn's Magsaysay Foundation Award **Obv:** Princess seated with children **Rev:** Obverse of medal above larger reverse with inscription

Date	Mintage	F	VF	XF	Unc	BU
BE2535 (1992)	1,600	—	—	—	350	380
BE2535 (1992) Proof	500	Value: 650				

Y# 267 6000 BAHT

15.0000 g., 0.9000 Gold .4341 oz. AGW **Ruler:** Rama IX **Subject:** Queen's 60th Birthday **Obv:** Crowned bust facing **Rev:** Crowned monogram

Date	Mintage	F	VF	XF	Unc	BU
BE2535 (1992)	7,000	—	—	—	320	340
BE2535 (1992) Proof	1,200	Value: 450				

Y# 275 6000 BAHT

15.0000 g., 0.9000 Gold .4341 oz. AGW **Ruler:** Rama IX **Subject:** 64th Birthday - King Rama IX **Obv:** Conjoined busts left **Rev:** Crowned monograms

Date	Mintage	F	VF	XF	Unc	BU
BE2535 (1992)	3,000	—	—	—	330	350
BE2535 (1992) Proof	500	Value: 600				

Y# 291 6000 BAHT

15.0000 g., 0.9000 Gold .4341 oz. AGW **Ruler:** Rama IX **Subject:** 100th Anniversary of Rama VII **Obv:** Bust left **Rev:** Royal crown and accoutrements

Date	Mintage	F	VF	XF	Unc	BU
BE2536 (1993)	2,484	—	—	—	330	350
BE2536 (1993) Proof	300	Value: 600				

Y# 327 6000 BAHT

15.0000 g., 0.9000 Gold .4341 oz. AGW **Ruler:** Rama IX **Subject:** King's 50th Year of Reign **Obv:** Uniformed bust facing **Rev:** National arms

Date	Mintage	F	VF	XF	Unc	BU
BE2539 (1996)	—	—	—	—	320	340
BE2539 (1996) Proof	—	Value: 550				

Y# 337 6000 BAHT

15.0000 g., 0.9000 Gold .4341 oz. AGW **Ruler:** Rama IX **Series:** F.A.O. **Subject:** 50th Anniversary - Reign of King Rama IX and World Food Summit **Obv:** Bust left within circle **Rev:** King planting seedlings before adoring crowd

Date	Mintage	F	VF	XF	Unc	BU
BE2539 (1996)	—	—	—	—	320	340
BE2539 (1996) Proof	—	Value: 550				

Y# 370 6000 BAHT

15.0000 g., 0.9000 Gold .4341 oz. AGW **Ruler:** Rama IX **Subject:** King's 72nd Birthday **Obv:** King's portrait **Rev:** Crowned emblem

Date	Mintage	F	VF	XF	Unc	BU
BE2542 (1999)	20,000	—	—	—	300	320
BE2542 (1999) Proof	10,000	Value: 400				

Y# 378 6000 BAHT

15.0000 g., 0.9000 Gold .4340 oz. AGW, 26 mm. **Ruler:** Rama IX **Subject:** King's 72nd Birthday **Obv:** King and Rama I portraits **Rev:** Two royal symbols **Edge:** Reeded

Date	Mintage	F	VF	XF	Unc	BU
BE2543(2000) Proof	—	Value: 375				

Y# 139 9000 BAHT

12.0000 g., 0.9000 Gold .3472 oz. AGW **Ruler:** Rama IX **Series:** F.A.O. Ceres Medal **Subject:** Queen's Anniversary **Obv:** Crowned bust 3/4 facing **Rev:** Medal design

Date	Mintage	F	VF	XF	Unc	BU
BE2523 (1980)	3,900	—	—	—	375	400

Y# A143 9000 BAHT

12.0000 g., 0.9000 Gold .3472 oz. AGW **Ruler:** Rama IX **Subject:** Centennial - Birth of King Rama VI **Obv:** Uniformed bust right **Rev:** Radiant crown on stand flanked by others

Date	Mintage	F	VF	XF	Unc	BU
BE2524 (1981)	2,600	—	—	—	375	400

Y# 148 9000 BAHT

15.0000 g., 0.9000 Gold .4340 oz. AGW **Ruler:** Rama IX **Subject:** King Rama IX Anniversary of Reign

Date	Mintage	F	VF	XF	Unc	BU
BE2524 (1981)	4,000	—	—	—	375	400

Y# 151 9000 BAHT

15.0000 g., 0.9000 Gold .4340 oz. AGW **Ruler:** Rama IX **Subject:** Bicentennial of Bangkok **Obv:** Uniformed conjoined busts left **Rev:** Emblem

Date	Mintage	F	VF	XF	Unc	BU
BE2525 (1982)	3,290	—	—	—	375	400

OCCUPATION COINAGE

These coins were to be circulated in the four occupied provinces of Malaya during World War II. They were not put into circulation there but were later used in Japanese military service clubs in Bangkok before Japan's surrender in 1945.

KM# 5 SEN

Tin **Ruler:** Rama VIII **Obv:** Mythical creature "Garuda" **Rev:** Value

Date	Mintage	F	VF	XF	Unc	BU
BE2486	—	—	—	7,000	—	—

KM# 10 5 SEN

Tin **Ruler:** Rama VIII **Obv:** Mythical creature "Garuda" **Rev:** Value within beaded circle

Date	Mintage	F	VF	XF	Unc	BU
BE2486	—	—	—	5,000	—	—

KM# 15 10 SEN

Tin **Ruler:** Rama VIII **Obv:** Mythical creature "Garuda" **Rev:** Value within beaded circle

Date	Mintage	F	VF	XF	Unc	BU
BE2486	—	—	—	4,000	—	—

BULLION COINAGE

In 1943, the government of Thailand made an internal loan by virtue of the Royal Act of Internal Loan related regulation of the Ministry of Finance, both dated 17th May, 1943.

Eight years later another Regulation of the Ministry of Finance dated 11th June, 1951 related to the actual redemption of the loan above mentioned was proclaimed with the following effect: Bond holders have the choice to be paid either in gold coins or gold bars or in other forms, all of which should bear the Garuda emblem and the specific inscription as to its weight and gold purity.

KM# 1 50 BAHT
8.6930 g., 0.9950 Gold .2781 oz. AGW **Ruler:** Rama IX **Obv:** Mythical creature "Garuda" flanked by sprigs **Rev:** Inscription

Date	Mintage	F	VF	XF	Unc	BU
ND(1951)	—	—	225	275	375	—

KM# 2 100 BAHT
17.3870 g., 0.9950 Gold .5562 oz. AGW **Ruler:** Rama IX **Obv:** Mythical creature "Garuda" flanked by sprigs **Rev:** Inscription

Date	Mintage	F	VF	XF	Unc	BU
ND(1951)	—	—	425	500	650	—

KM# 3 1000 BAHT
173.8790 g., 0.9950 Gold 5.5620 oz. AGW **Ruler:** Rama IX **Obv:** Mythical creature "Garuda" flanked by sprigs **Rev:** Inscription

Date	Mintage	F	VF	XF	Unc	BU
ND(1951)	—	—	6,000	9,000	14,000	—

TRIAL STRIKES

KM#	Date	Mintage	Identification	Mkt Val
TS1	ND (1963)	—	20 Baht. Copper. Trial strike in copper of 20 Baht, Y#86.	—

ESSAIS

KM#	Date	Mintage	Identification	Mkt Val
E1	RS127	—	Baht. Silver. Y#39.	23,000

KM#	Date	Mintage	Identification	Mkt Val
E2	RS128	—	1/4 Baht. Silver.	10,000
E3	RS129	—	1/2 Baht. Silver.	—

Note: Struck at the Paris Mint. Taisei-Baldwin-Gillio Hong Kong sale 25 9-97 BU realized $23,000. Spink-Taisei Singapore Auction 14 3-93 Unc set of E 1, 2 and 2 realized $190,000

PATTERNS

Including off metal strikes

KM#	Date	Mintage	Identification	Mkt Val
Pn47	RS124	—	2 Att. Copper. Facing bust.	10,000
Pn48	RS126	—	Baht. Silver. Y#39. Vishnu and Garuda.	40,000
Pn49	RS127	—	Satang. Nickel. Y#35.	3,000
Pn50	RS127	—	Satang. Gold. Y#35a.	10,000
Pn51	RS127	—	5 Satang. Gold. Y#36a.	10,000
Pn52	RS127	—	10 Satang. Gold. Y#37a.	10,000
Pn53	RS129	—	Baht. Silver. Y#39.	—
PnA54	BE2488	—	Baht. Tin. 10.0000 g. 30 mm. "Child's head" of King Rama VIII (Ananda Mahidol) facing left. National arms.	—
Pn54	BE2489	—	Baht. Tin. Y#67.	—
Pn55	BE2505	—	Baht. Copper-Nickel. Y#84.	—
Pn56	BE2515	—	5 Baht. Copper-Nickel. Small bust, Y#28.	—
Pn57	BE2515	—	5 Baht. Copper-Nickel. Royal parasol.	—
Pn58	BE2515	—	5 Baht. Copper-Nickel. Different bust.	100

PIEFORTS

KM#	Date	Mintage	Identification	Mkt Val
P1	BE2524	126	200 Baht. I.Y.O.C.	850
P2	BE2524	61	4000 Baht. Gold. I.Y.O.C.	2,200
P3	BE2526	500	250 Baht. 0.9250 Silver. I.Y.D.P.	1,250
P4	BE2526	—	2500 Baht. Gold. I.Y.D.P.	6,500
P5	BE2540	—	100 Baht. 0.9250 Silver. 30.0000 g. WWF Tiger.	75.00
P6	BE2541	—	200 Baht. 0.9250 Silver. 46.3600 g. WWF Tigers.	110
P7	BE2541	—	200 Baht. 0.9250 Silver. 46.3600 g. WWF Elephants.	125

MINT SETS

KM#	Date	Mintage	Identification	Issue Price	Mkt Val
MS2	Mixed (32)	—	Two each Y#57, 70, 72, 73, 78a, 78-87, 91	22.00	45.00
MS3	Mixed (30)	100,000	Two each Y#60, 70, 72, 73, 78, 78a, 79, 79a, 80-86	20.00	30.00
MS4	Mixed (10)	—	Y#70, 72, 73, 78, 78a, 79, 79a, 80-82	—	12.00
MS5	Mixed (10)	—	Y#70, 78, 78a, 78b, 79a, 79b, 79d, 80, 81, 82	—	12.00
MS6	Mixed (8)	—	Y#83, 85-87, 91, 92, 95, 97	11.00	35.00
MS7	1975 (2)	—	Y#102-103	32.50	70.00
MS8	1988 (7)	—	Y#183, 185-187, 203, 208-209	—	3.50
MS9	1991 (8)	—	Y#183, 186-187, 203, 208-209, 219, 227	4.00	10.00
MS10	1992 (8)	—	Y#183, 186-187, 203, 208-209, 219, 227	—	10.00
MS11	1993 (8)	—	Y#183, 186-187, 203, 208-209, 219, 227	—	10.00
MS12	1994 (8)	—	Y#183, 186-187, 203, 208-209, 219, 227	—	10.00
MS13	Mixed (34)	—	Two each Y#57, 70, 72-73, 78, 78a, 79, 79a, 80-87, 91	—	60.00
MS14	Mixed (29)	—	Y#86 plus two each Y#57, 68, 73, 78, 78a, 79, 79a, 80-85, 87	—	35.00

PROOF SETS

KM#	Date	Mintage	Identification	Issue Price	Mkt Val
PS1	1974 (2)	—	Y#102a-103a	50.00	160
PS2	2000 (3)	3,500	Y#363-365	115	115
PS3	2000 (5)	500	Y#363-365, 367, 369	3,480	3,650
PS4	2000 (2)	1,800	Y#366, 368	446	450

TIBET

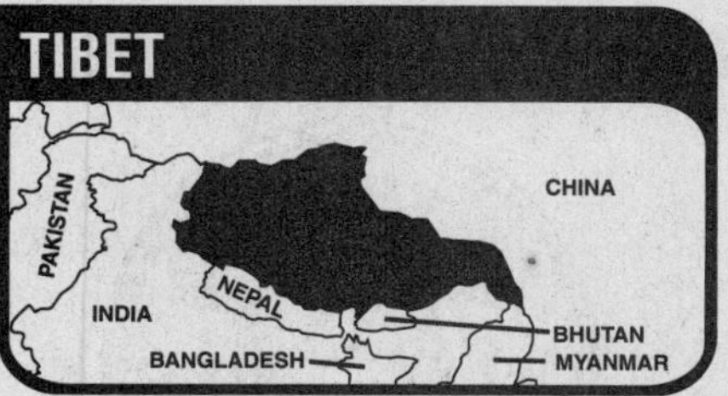

Tibet, an autonomous region of China located in central Asia between the Himalayan and Kunlun Mns. has an area of 471,660 sq. mi. (1,221,599 sq. km.) and a population of *1.9 million. Capital: Lhasa. The economy is based on agriculture and livestock raising. Wool, livestock, salt and hides are exported.

Lamaism, a form of Buddhism, developed in Tibet in the 8th century. From that time until the 1900s, the Tibetan rulers virtually isolated the country from the outside world. The British in India achieved some influence in the early 20th century. British troops were sent with the Young Husband mission to extend trade in the north of India in December 1903; leaving during September 1904. The 13th Dalai Lama had fled to Urga where he remained until 1907. In April 1905 a revolt broke out and spread through southwestern Szechuan and northwestern Yunnan. Chao Erh-feng was appointed to subdue this rebellion and entered Lhasa in January 1910 with 2,000 troops. The Dalai Lama fled to India until he returned in June 1912., The British encouraged Tibet to declare its independence from China in 1913. The Communist revolution in China marked a new era in Tibetan history. Chinese Communist troops invaded Tibet in Oct., 1950. After a token resistance, Tibet signed an agreement with China in which China recognized the spiritual and temporal leadership of the Dalai Lama, and Tibet recognized the suzerainty of China. In 1959, a nationwide revolt triggered by Communist-initiated land reform broke out. The revolt was ruthlessly crushed. The dalai lama fled to India, and on Sept. 1,1965, the Chinese made Tibet an autonomous region of China.

The first coins to circulate in Tibet were those of neighboring Nepal from about 1570. Shortly after 1720, the Nepalese government began striking specific issues for use in Tibet. These coins had a lower silver content than those struck for use in Nepal and were exchanged with the Tibetans for an equal weight in silver bullion. Around 1763 the Tibetans struck their own coins for the first time in history. The number of coins struck at that time must have been very small. Larger quantities of coins were struck by the Tibetan government mint, which opened in 1791 with the permission of the Chinese. Operations of this mint however were suspended two years later. The Chinese opened a second mint in Lhasa in 1792. It produced a coinage until 1836. Shortly thereafter, the Tibetan mint was reopened and the government of Tibet continued to strike coins until 1953.

DATING

Based on the Tibetan calendar, Tibetan coins are dated by the cycle which contains 60 years. To calculate the western date use the following formula: Number of cycles -1, x 60 + number of years + 1026. Example 15th cycle 25th year = 1891 AD. Example: 15th cycle, 25th year 15 - 1 x 60 + 25 + 1026 = 1891AD.

13/30 = 1776	14/30 = 1836	15/30 = 1896
13/40 = 1786	14/40 = 1846	15/40 = 1906
13/50 = 1796	14/50 = 1856	15/50 = 1916
13/60 = 1806	14/60 = 1866	15/60 = 1926
14/10 = 1816	15/10 = 1876	16/10 = 1936
14/20 = 1826	15/20 = 1886	16/20 = 1946

Certain Sino-Tibetan issues are dated in the year of reign of the Emperor of China.

MONETARY SYSTEM

15 Skar = 1-1/2 Sho = 1 Tangka
10 Sho = 1 Srang

TANGKA

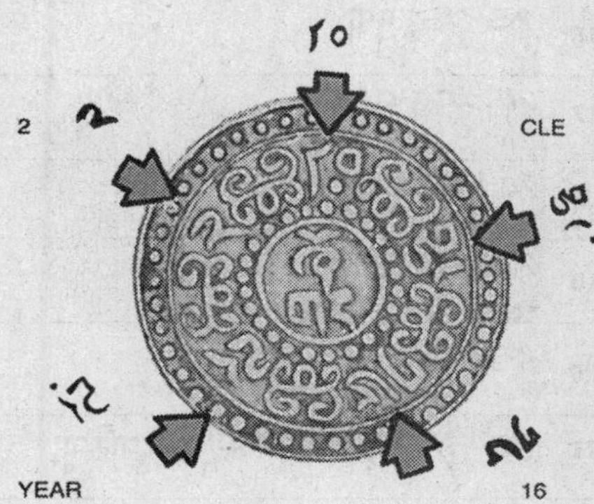

16(th)CYCLE 2(nd)YEAR = 1928AD

16(th) CYCLE 7(th) YEAR = 1933AD

NUMERALS

1	༡	གཅིག
2	༢	གཉིས
3	༣	གསུམ
4	༤	བཞི
5	༥	ལྔ
6	༦	དྲུག
7	༧	བདུན
8	༨	བརྒྱད
9	༩	དགུ
10	༡༠	བཅུ or བཅུ་ཐམ་པ
11	༡༡	བཅུག or བཅུ་གཅིག
12	༡༢	བཅུས or བཅུ་གཉིས
13	༡༣	བཅུ་མ or བཅུ་གསུམ
14	༡༤	བཅུ་བཞི
15	༡༥	བཅོ་ལྔ
16	༡༦	བཅུ་དྲུག
17	༡༧	བཅུ་བདུན
18	༡༨	བཅོ་བརྒྱད
19	༡༩	བཅུ་དགུ
20	༢༠	ཉི་ཤུ
21	༢༡	ཉི་ཤུ་རྩ་གཅིག or ཉེར་གཅིག
22	༢༢	ཉེར་གཉིས
23	༢༣	ཉེར་གསུམ
24	༢༤	ཉེར་བཞི
25	༢༥	ཉེར་ལྔ
26	༢༦	ཉེར་དྲུག
27	༢༧	ཉེར་བདུན
28	༢༨	ཉེར་བརྒྱད

CHINESE AUTHORITY

SINO-TIBETAN COINAGE

Milled

Y# A4 1/2 SKAR

Copper **Ruler:** Hsüan-t'ung **Edge:** Plain **Note:** Weight varies: 3.10-3.60 grams.

Date	Mintage	Good	VG	F	VF	XF
ND(1910)	—	300	500	700	1,000	—

Y# 4 SKAR

Copper, 27 mm. **Ruler:** Hsüan-t'ung **Rev. Inscription:** Hsüan-t'ung.... **Edge:** Plain **Note:** Weight varies: 5.40-6.60 grams. Varieties exist. Modern counterfeits exist.

Date	Mintage	Good	VG	F	VF	XF
ND(1910)	—	90.00	150	250	400	—

Y# 5 SHO

Silver, 22 mm. **Ruler:** Hsüan-t'ung **Rev. Inscription:** Hsüan-t'ung.... **Edge:** Reeded **Note:** Weight varies: 3.30-4.10 grams. Varieties exist, one having the inner circle of dots, on the Chinese side, connected by lines. Modern counterfeits exist.

Date	Mintage	Good	VG	F	VF	XF
ND(1910)	—	20.00	30.00	50.00	75.00	125

Y# 6 2 SHO

Silver, 25 mm. **Ruler:** Hsüan-t'ung **Rev. Inscription:** Hsüan-t'ung.... **Edge:** Reeded **Note:** Weight varies: 5.20-8.40 grams. Varieties with different dragon claws and lotus exist. Modern counterfeits exist.

Date	Mintage	Good	VG	F	VF	XF
ND(1910)	—	25.00	40.00	80.00	125	175

TANGKA COINAGE

Kong-par Tangka

The legend of this so called Ranjana Tangka appears to be in ornamental Lansa script and represents a mantra alluding to wealth and luck. The type is a copy of the Nepalese debased Tangka of Pratap Simha. Struck unofficially by Nepalese traders in Tibet between 1880 and 1912, it was legal tender, due to an edict issued in 1881 ordering that no distinction be made between false and genuine coins. The Tangka, C#27 was cut in parts of 3, 4, and 5 petals to make change and the resulting fractions are occasionally encountered.

C# 27.1 TANGKA

Silver **Obv:** Crescent and moon at top **Note:** Weight varies: 4.60-5.40 grams. Prev. #C27.

Date	Mintage	Good	VG	F	VF	XF
BE15-40 (1906)	—	8.00	15.00	25.00	40.00	70.00

Note: In addition to the meaningful dates, the following meaningless ones exist: 13-16, 13-31, 13-92, 15-40, 16-16, 16-61, 16-64, 16-69, 16-92, 16-93, 92-34, 92-39, 96-61 (sixes may be reversed threes and nines reversed ones); These are of silver, varying from 3.9 to 5.2 grams

C# 27.2 TANGKA

Silver **Obv:** Crescent and swastika at top **Note:** Weight varies: 4.60-5.40 grams. See note for C#27.1.

Date	Mintage	Good	VG	F	VF	XF
BE15-46 (1912)	—	60.00	80.00	100	150	225

GA-DEN TANGKA COINAGE

Hammered

The Ga-den Tangkas are among the most common and perhaps most beautiful of all Tibetan silver coins. The obverse shows a stylized Lotus flower within a circle surrounded by the 8 Buddhist lucky symbols in radiating petals. The reverse shows an 8-petalled wheel (flower) within a star surrounded by a Tibetan inscription (reading Ga-den Palace, victorious in all directions), which is broken up into 8 oval frames. The Ga-den Palace is the former residence of the Dala Lamas, located in Drepung Monastery near Lhasa. On Tibetan coins the name "Ga-den Palace" is used as epithet for "Tibetan Government". Compass directions indicate the location of the Buddhist emblems.

Numbers for Obverse Types A & B

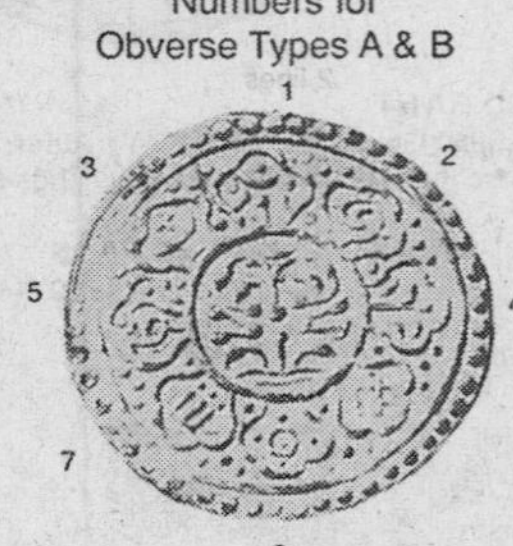

Numbers for Obverse Types C thru H

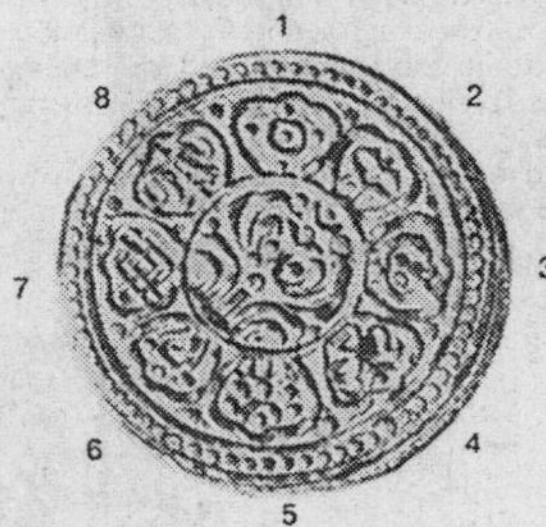

1. Umbrella of sovereignty.
2. Two golden fish of good fortune.
3. Amphora of ambrosia.
4. Lotus.
5. Conch shell.
6. Emblem of endless birth.
7. Banner of victory.
8. Wheel of empire.

Reverse - All Types

དགའ་	dGa'	"Ga-"
ལྡན་	lDan	"den"
ཕོ་	Pho	Po-
བྲང་	Braṅ	dang
ཕྱོགས་	Phyogs	Tschog-
ལས་	Las	le
རྣམ་	rNam	Nam-
རྒྱལ་	rGyal	gyel

Based on the ornamentation in the outer angles between the petals on both sides of the coin, the Ga-Den Tangkas can be differentiated in the following 8 types, A-H.

Type	Outer Obv.	Water-line	Outer Rev.	Rev. Ctr.
A	∵	None	〰	Pellet
B	∵	2 lines	〰	3 Crescents
C	∵	1 line	〰	2 Crescents
D	∵	1 line	∵	2 Crescents
E	〰	1 line	∵	2 Crescents
F	•	1 line	∵	2 Crescents
G	None	1 line	None	2 Crescents
H	•	1 line	•	3 Crescents

Within these types, changes in the order, design, and style of the 8 lucky signs or significant errors constitute subtypes. The sutypes appearing in this catalog are not the only ones. Some subtypes show a wide range of styles and die varieties. Weights given include 95 percent of the indicated types.

Error strikes with muled reverses exist. Specimens of Types D, E, and F with lumps are known, reportedly containing gold, probably used by high lamas in their offerings.

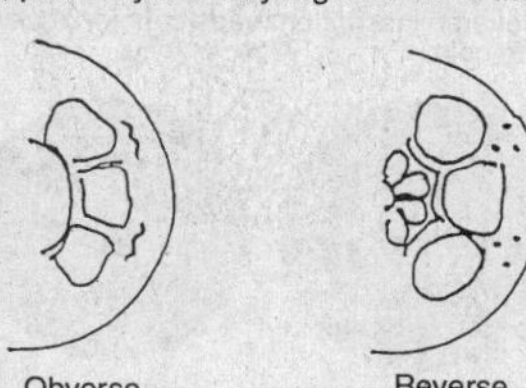

Obverse Reverse

Obverse has wavy water line in outer angles. New style lotus without three small leaves to left and right. Reverse has three dots in outer angles, wheel with spokes.

Y# E13.1 TANGKA

Silver **Obv:** Dot to left and right of lotus **Edge:** Plain **Note:** Weight varies: 4.60-4.80 grams. Prev. Y#13.4.

Date	Mintage	VG	F	VF	XF	Unc
ND(ca.1899-1907)	—	3.00	4.00	7.00	12.00	35.00

Y# E13.2 TANGKA

Silver **Obv:** Dot to left and right of lotus **Edge:** Plain

Date	Mintage	Good	VG	F	VF	XF
ND(ca.1899-1907)	—	150	250	400	600	1,000

Y# E13.3 TANGKA

Silver **Obv:** Four dots (NE), one dot (E) **Edge:** Plain **Note:** Weight varies: 3.80-5.70 grams. Similar to Y#E13.1 but obverse emblems rotated by one position clockwise (error).

Date	Mintage	Good	VG	F	VF	XF
ND(ca.1899-1907)	—	75.00	100	150	200	300

Y# E13.4 TANGKA

3.8000 g., Silver **Obv:** 7.5-8.0mm lotus circle, no dot at left and right of lotus **Edge:** Plain **Note:** Prev. Y#E13.8 (Y#13.5).

Date	Mintage	VG	F	VF	XF	Unc
ND(ca.1904)	—	60.00	85.00	120	180	250

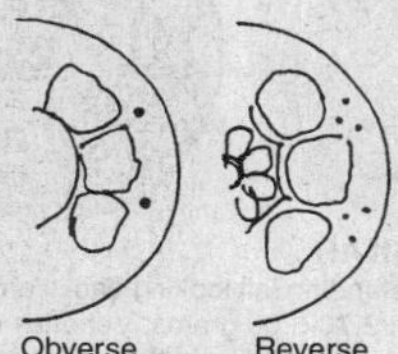

Obverse Reverse

Obverse has one dot in outer angles.
The reverse has three dots in outer angles.

Y# F13.1 TANGKA

Billon **Obv:** Nine dots within lotus circle **Rev:** Flower buds full or outlined **Edge:** Plain **Note:** Six varieties exist. Weight varies: 4.10-4.70 grams. Prev. Y#13.6.

Date	Mintage	VG	F	VF	XF	Unc
ND(ca.1907-09)	—	4.00	6.00	10.00	16.00	40.00

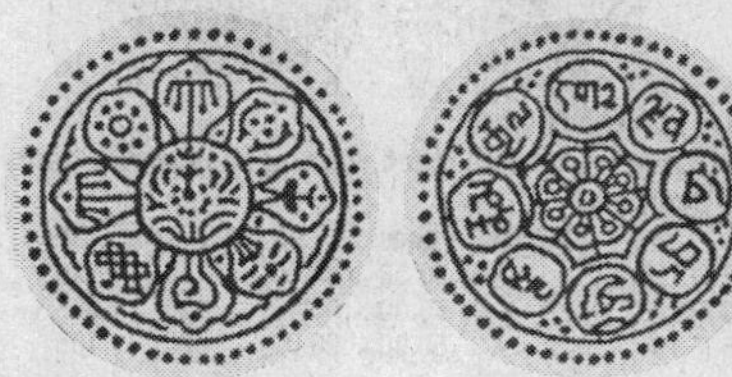

Y# F13.2 TANGKA

Billon **Obv:** Northwest symbol circle with dots; no dot at left and right of lotus; lotus circle varies 10-12mm **Rev:** Central lotus buds hollow **Edge:** Plain **Note:** Weight varies: 4.10-4.70. Four varieties exist.

Date	Mintage	Good	VG	F	VF	XF
ND(1910-15)	—	6.00	9.00	15.00	25.00	45.00

Y# F13.3 TANGKA

Billon **Obv:** 11mm lotus circle **Rev:** Solid lotus buds **Edge:** Plain **Note:** Machine struck. Similar to Y#F13.2 and 2 Tangka, Y#15. Weight varies: 5.20-5.60 grams.

Date	Mintage	Good	VG	F	VF	XF
ND(ca.1912)	—	100	150	200	275	500

Y# F13.6 TANGKA

Billon, 27 mm. **Obv:** Dots to left and right of base of lotus in the water line; northwest symbol a circle with dots; northeast symbol two fish with dots; south symbol very ornate with two side hooks and a dot **Edge:** Plain **Note:** Weight varies: 4.10-4.70 grams.

Date	Mintage	Good	VG	F	VF	XF
ND(ca.1909)	—	8.00	12.00	18.00	30.00	50.00

Y# F13.5 TANGKA

Billon **Obv:** Dot to left and right of lotus; northeast symbol double hook between two fish and dots; northwest symbol circle with two hooks, dots south symbol has three dots **Edge:** Plain **Note:** Weight varies: 4.10-4.70 grams. Varieties exist including 34-78 dots for outer circle. Prev. Y#13.8.

Date	Mintage	Good	VG	F	VF	XF
ND(1912-22)	—	8.00	12.00	20.00	32.00	60.00

Y# F13.4 TANGKA

Billon **Obv:** Dot to left and right of lotus; northeast symbol two fish with dots; south symbol with 3 dots; northwest symbol circle with 4 dots around center dot **Edge:** Plain **Note:** Weight varies: 4.10-4.70 grams. Varieties exist including 34-78 dots for outer circles. Prev. Y#13.7.

Date	Mintage	VG	F	VF	XF	Unc
ND(ca.1912-22)	—	8.00	12.00	20.00	32.00	60.00

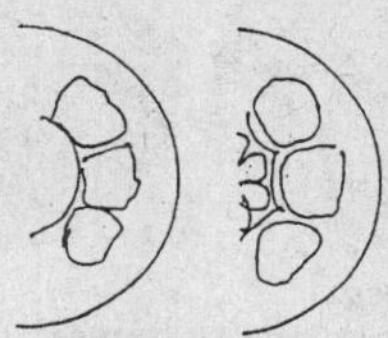

Obverse Reverse

The obverse and reverse have no outer angle symbols.
The petals are joined on the obverse.

Y# G13 TANGKA

Billon **Rev:** No outer angles at inner circle **Edge:** Plain **Note:** Weight varies: 3.30-4.60 grams. Prev. Y#13.9.

Date	Mintage	VG	F	VF	XF	Unc
ND(ca.1921)	—	4.00	6.00	9.00	15.00	45.00

Y# F13.7 TANGKA

Billon, 31 mm. **Edge:** Plain **Note:** Similar to Y#F13.6.

Date	Mintage	Good	VG	F	VF	XF
ND(ca.1924-25) Rare	—	—	—	—	—	—

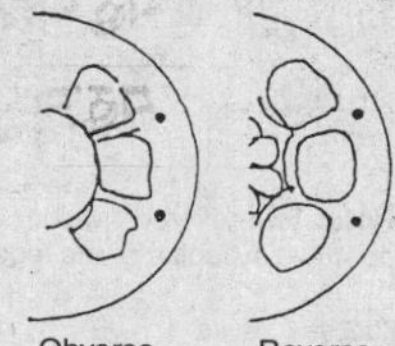

Obverse Reverse

The obverse and reverse have one dot in outer angles.
The obverse petals are joined.

Y# H13.1 TANGKA

Billon **Obv:** Dot between symbols at inner circle, lotus petals joined **Rev:** Dot between characters at inner circle **Edge:** Plain **Note:** Weight varies: 4.00-4.20 grams. Two minor die varieties exist. Prev. Y#13.10.

Date	Mintage	VG	F	VF	XF	Unc
ND(1929)	—	10.00	14.00	20.00	30.00	50.00

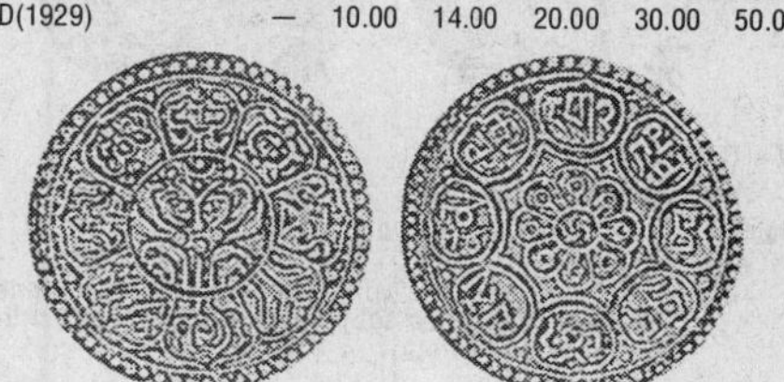

Y# H13.2 TANGKA

Billon **Obv:** Similar to Y#H13.1 **Rev:** Similar to Y#H13.1 but Northeast character in retrograde **Edge:** Plain **Note:** Weight varies: 4.00-4.20 grams. Machine struck.

Date	Mintage	VG	F	VF	XF	Unc
ND(ca.1929-30)	—	60.00	90.00	120	150	—

Y# 15 2 TANGKA
Billon **Note:** Weight varies: 7.80-10.50 grams. Varieties exist.

Date	Mintage	VG	F	VF	XF	Unc
ND(ca.1912)	—	125	200	400	500	—

PRESENTATION TANGKA COINAGE

Y# 14 TANGKA
Silver **Edge:** Plain **Note:** Weight varies: 2.70-5.00 grams. Fifteen obverse varieties exist with combinations of none or up to two dots inside trapezoids enclosing the legend.

Date	Mintage	VG	F	VF	XF	Unc
ND(1910)	600,000	10.00	15.00	25.00	50.00	60.00

Y# 31 TANGKA
Silver **Edge:** Reeded **Note:** Weight varies: 3.10-5.30 grams. Varieties exist, the two "commas" in central circle are in either vertical or horizontal alignment.

Date	Mintage	VG	F	VF	XF	Unc
ND(1953)	—	7.00	10.00	15.00	22.00	—
ND(1953)	331,292	7.00	10.00	15.00	22.00	40.00

Note: Struck for presentation to Monks; Circulated later but briefly with value of 5 and then 10 Srang

SHO-SRANG COINAGE

Y# A7 1/8 SHO
Copper, 22 mm. **Note:** Two reverse varieties exist, one with a dot between the upper two syllables of the legend, the other is without a dot.

Date	Mintage	Good	VG	F	VF	XF
1 (1909)	—	85.00	150	225	350	—

Note: A silver striking of this type exists (rare), possibly a pattern; Year 1 of the reign of Hsuan T'ung

Y# B7 1/4 SHO
Copper, 26 mm.

Date	Mintage	Good	VG	F	VF	XF
1(1909)	—	50.00	100	150	250	—

Note: This coin struck in silver is a forgery; Modern forgeries struck in copper and copper-nickel exist; Year 1 of the reign of Husan T'ung

Y# 10 2-1/2 SKAR
Copper, 22 mm. **Obv:** Lion standing left, looking backwards **Edge:** Plain **Note:** Lion varieties exist.

Date	Mintage	Good	VG	F	VF	XF
BE15-43 (1909)	—	150	250	350	500	—

Y# 16.1 2-1/2 SKAR
Copper **Obv:** Lion crouching and looking upwards **Edge:** Plain **Note:** Weight varies: 3.70-6.00 grams. Varieties exist.

Date	Mintage	Good	VG	F	VF	XF
BE15-47 (1913)	—	5.00	12.00	20.00	50.00	—
BE15-48 (1914)	—	5.00	12.00	20.00	50.00	—
BE15-49 (1915)	—	15.00	30.00	60.00	120	—
BE15-50 (1916)	—	8.00	16.00	30.00	70.00	—
BE15-51 (1917)	—	30.00	60.00	120	240	—
BE15-52 (1918)	—	6.50	14.00	25.00	60.00	—

Y# 16.2 2-1/2 SKAR
Copper **Obv:** Lion standing left looking backwards **Edge:** Plain **Note:** Weight varies: 3.70-6.00 grams. Varieties exist, one with retrograde syllable on reverse top in the word "gsum" (three)(error); the other variety has the letter corrected. With and without rays from sun.

Date	Mintage	Good	VG	F	VF	XF
BE15-48 (1914)	—	8.00	16.00	30.00	70.00	—

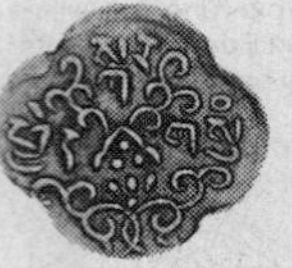

Y# A19 2-1/2 SKAR
Copper **Obv:** Lion standing left, looking back and upwards **Shape:** Scalloped

Date	Mintage	Good	VG	F	VF	XF
BE15-52 (1918)	—	50.00	85.00	110	150	—
BE15-53 (1918)	—	50.00	90.00	120	165	—
BE15-55 (1921)	—	50.00	90.00	120	165	—

Y# A10 5 SKAR
Copper, 25 mm. **Obv:** Lion standing left, looking back and upwards **Edge:** Plain

Date	Mintage	Good	VG	F	VF	XF
BE15-43 (1909)	—	150	250	350	500	—

Y# 17 5 SKAR
Copper **Obv:** Lion standing left and looking upward **Edge:** Plain

Date	Mintage	Good	VG	F	VF	XF
BE15-47 (1913)	—	6.00	10.00	25.00	55.00	—
BE15-48 (1914)	—	4.00	7.00	15.00	35.00	—
BE15-49 (1915)	—	5.00	8.00	18.00	40.00	—
BE15-50 (1916)	—	5.00	8.00	18.00	40.00	—
BE15-51 (1917)	—	3.50	6.00	12.00	30.00	—
BE15-52 (1918)	—	25.00	55.00	120	250	—

Y# 17.1 5 SKAR
Copper **Obv:** Lion standing left, looking back **Edge:** Plain **Note:** Size of obverse circle and weight of coin vary considerably.

Date	Mintage	Good	VG	F	VF	XF
BE15-49 (1914)	—	4.00	7.00	15.00	32.00	—
Note: Obverse varieties (lion) exist						
BE15-50 (1916)	—	4.00	7.00	15.00	32.00	—
BE15-51 (1917)	—	4.00	7.00	15.00	32.00	—
BE15-52 (1918)	—	5.00	8.00	18.00	40.00	—

Y# 17.2 5 SKAR
Copper **Obv:** Lion standing left looking back and upwards **Edge:** Plain

Date	Mintage	Good	VG	F	VF	XF
BE15-48 (1914)	—	5.00	9.00	20.00	45.00	—
BE15-49 (1915)	—	8.00	14.00	35.00	70.00	—

Y# 17.3 5 SKAR
Copper **Obv:** Lion standing left looking back and upwards **Rev:** Flower with eight petals rather than wheel with eight spokes **Edge:** Plain

Date	Mintage	Good	VG	F	VF	XF
BE15-48 (1914)	—	6.00	10.00	25.00	55.00	—

Y# 19 5 SKAR
Copper **Obv:** Lion standing left **Edge:** Reeded **Note:** Varieties exist.

Date	Mintage	Good	VG	F	VF	XF
BE15-52 (1918)	—	2.25	3.50	6.00	12.00	—
BE15-53 (1919)	—	2.00	3.00	5.50	11.00	—
BE15-54 (1920)	—	1.50	2.50	5.00	10.00	—
BE15-55 (1921)	—	5.00	10.00	20.00	40.00	—
BE15-56 (1922)	—	1.50	2.50	5.00	10.00	—
BE56-15 (1922) Error	—	25.00	40.00	70.00	110	—

Note: Reverse inscription reads counterclockwise on error date coin

Y# 19.1 5 SKAR
Copper **Obv:** Lion standing left **Rev:** Dot added above center **Edge:** Reeded

Date	Mintage	Good	VG	F	VF	XF
BE15-55 (1921)	—	10.00	20.00	35.00	65.00	—
BE15-56 (1922)	—	4.00	8.00	15.00	25.00	—

Y# 11 7-1/2 SKAR

Copper, 28 mm. **Obv:** Lion standing left, looking back and upwards **Edge:** Plain **Note:** Modern counterfeits exist.

Date	Mintage	Good	VG	F	VF	XF
BE15-43 (1909)	—	150	250	350	500	—

Y# 20 7-1/2 SKAR

Copper **Edge:** Plain **Note:** Some 15-52, 15-53, and 15-55 specimens have the reverse central "whirlwind" in a counterclockwise direction. Many varieties exist with size of inner circle on reverse.

Date	Mintage	Good	VG	F	VF	XF
BE15-52 (1918)	—	2.00	3.00	5.00	8.50	—
BE15-53 (1919)	—	1.50	2.50	4.00	7.00	—
BE15-54 (1920)	—	1.50	2.50	4.00	7.00	—
BE15-55 (1921)	—	1.50	2.50	4.00	7.00	—
BE15-56 (1922)	—	1.50	2.50	4.00	7.00	—
BE15-60 (1926)	—	20.00	30.00	50.00	100	—

Y# 21 SHO

Copper **Obv:** Lion standing left, looking upwards **Rev:** Central legend horizontal

Date	Mintage	Good	VG	F	VF	XF
BE15-52 (1918)	—	30.00	45.00	75.00	120	—

Y# 21.1 SHO

Copper, 24 mm. **Obv:** Lion standing left, looking backwards, without dot in reverse arabesque **Note:** Weight varies: 3.95-7.13 grams. Varieties exist.

Date	Mintage	Good	VG	F	VF	XF
BE15-52 (1918)	—	1.50	2.00	3.25	7.00	—
BE15-53/52 (1919)	—	—	—	—	—	—
BE15-53 (1919)	—	1.00	1.50	2.50	5.00	—
BE15-54 (1920)	—	1.00	1.50	2.50	5.00	—
BE15-55 (1921)	—	1.00	1.50	2.50	5.00	—
BE15-56 (1922)	—	1.00	1.50	2.50	5.00	—
BE15-57 (1923)	—	1.50	2.00	3.25	7.00	—
BE15-57 (1923) Without dots (obverse)	—	5.00	10.00	20.00	30.00	—
BE15-58 (1924)	—	1.00	1.50	2.50	5.00	—
BE58-15 (1924) (error) year and cycle transposed	—	—	—	—	—	—
BE15-59 (1925)	—	1.00	1.50	2.50	5.00	—
BE15-59 (1925) Without dots (obverse)	—	5.00	10.00	20.00	30.00	—
BE15-60 (1926)	—	1.00	1.50	2.50	5.00	—
BE15-6 (1926) (error) for 15-60	—	—	—	—	—	—
BE16-1 (1927)	—	1.00	1.50	2.50	5.00	—
BE16-2 (1928)	—	1.00	1.50	2.50	5.00	—

Y# 21.2 SHO

Copper **Obv:** Lion looking upwards, with dot in reverse arabesque. **Note:** Varieties exist.

Date	Mintage	Good	VG	F	VF	XF
BE15-54 (1920)	—	2.00	3.00	5.00	9.00	—

Note: Specimens dated 15-54 may all be contemporary forgeries

Date	Mintage	Good	VG	F	VF	XF
BE54-15 (1920) (Error) year and cycle transposed	—	25.00	40.00	65.00	100	—
BE15/51-54 (1920) (error) cycle transposed	—	25.00	40.00	65.00	100	—
BE15-55 (1921)	—	1.50	2.50	4.50	7.00	—
BE55-15 (1921) Error; "year" and "cycle" transposed	—	25.00	40.00	65.00	100	—
BE15-56/5 (1921)	—	1.00	1.50	2.50	5.00	—
BE15-56 (1922)	—	1.00	1.50	2.50	5.00	—
BE15-57 (1923)	—	1.25	1.75	3.25	7.00	—
BE15-58 (1924)	—	1.00	1.50	2.50	5.00	—
BE15-59 (1925)	—	1.00	1.50	2.50	5.00	—
BE15-60 (1926)	—	1.00	1.50	2.50	5.00	—
BE16-1/15-60 (1927)	—	15.00	25.00	40.00	65.00	—
BE16-1 (1927)	—	1.00	1.50	2.50	5.00	—
BE16-2/1 (1928)	—	1.00	1.50	2.50	5.00	—
BE16-2 (1928)	—	1.00	1.50	2.50	5.00	—

Y# 21a SHO

Copper **Rev:** Central legend vertical **Note:** Two varieties (lion) exist for each of the following dates: 15-56, 15-57, 15-58, and 16-2. Overstrikes on 5 Skar, Y#17 exist.

Date	Mintage	VG	F	VF	XF	Unc
BE15-56 (1922)	—	8.00	13.50	20.00	30.00	—
BE15-57 (1923)	—	2.00	3.50	6.00	10.00	—
BE57-15 (1923) Error; year and cycle transposed	—	25.00	40.00	65.00	100	—
BE15-58 (1924)	—	2.00	3.50	6.00	10.00	—
BE15-59/8 (1925)	—	1.25	2.25	4.00	8.00	—
BE15-59 (1925)	—	1.25	2.25	4.00	8.00	—
BE15-60 (1925)	—	1.25	2.25	4.00	8.00	—
BE15-60/59 (1926)	—	1.25	2.25	4.00	8.00	—
BE16-1 (1927)	—	1.25	2.25	4.00	8.00	—
BE16-1 (1927) Dot below 0 above denomination	—	1.25	2.25	4.00	8.00	—
BE(16-2/1) (1927) Reported, not confirmed	—	—	—	—	—	—
BE16-2 (1928)	—	2.00	3.50	6.00	10.00	—

Note: A scarce 16-2 variety features a reversed 2

Date	Mintage	VG	F	VF	XF	Unc
BE16-2 (1928) dot below syllable "rab"	—	—	—	—	—	—

Y# 21b SHO

Copper **Obv:** Lion looking backwards

Date	Mintage	Good	VG	F	VF	XF
BE15-52 (1923)	—	40.00	60.00	80.00	140	—

Y# 23 SHO

Copper **Edge:** Reeded **Note:** Weight varies: 4.02-6.09 grams. Dates 16-10, 16-11, 16-12, and 16-16 exist struck on thick and thin planchets and many lion obverse varieties. Several mint marks are known in reverse.

Date	Mintage	VG	F	VF	XF	Unc
BE16-6 (1932) (a)	6,000,000	3.00	5.00	9.00	15.00	—
BE16-7 (1933) (a)	Inc. above	3.00	5.00	9.00	15.00	—
BE16-8 (1934) (a)	Inc. above	3.00	5.00	9.00	15.00	—

Note: Two varieties exist

Date	Mintage	VG	F	VF	XF	Unc
BE16-9 (1935) (a)	Inc. above	2.00	3.50	6.00	11.00	—

Note: Two varieties exist

Date	Mintage	VG	F	VF	XF	Unc
BE16-9 (1935) (b)	Inc. above	1.50	3.00	5.00	10.00	—

Note: A scarce 16-9 variety features a hook ("bird") on the Sengi's (lion's) back

Date	Mintage	VG	F	VF	XF	Unc
BE16-10 (1936) (a)	Inc. above	5.00	10.00	15.00	25.00	—
BE16-10 (1936) (b)	Inc. above	5.00	10.00	15.00	25.00	—
BE16-10 (1936) (c)	Inc. above	1.50	3.00	5.00	10.00	—
BE16-11 (1937) (a)	Inc. above	2.50	4.00	9.00	15.00	—
BE16-11 (1937) (b)	Inc. above	5.00	10.00	15.00	25.00	—
BE16-11 (1937) (c)	Inc. above	2.50	4.00	9.00	15.00	—
BE16-11 (1937) (d)	Inc. above	2.50	4.00	9.00	15.00	—
BE16-11 (1937) (e)	Inc. above	1.50	3.00	5.00	10.00	—
BE16-11 (1937) (f)	Inc. above	5.00	10.00	15.00	25.00	—
BE16-11 (1937) (g)	Inc. above	5.00	10.00	15.00	25.00	—
BE16-12 (1938) (c)	Inc. above	5.00	10.00	15.00	25.00	—
BE16-12 (1938) (d)	Inc. above	5.00	10.00	15.00	25.00	—
BE16-12 (1938) (f)	Inc. above	4.00	8.00	12.00	20.00	—
BE16-12 (1938) (g)	Inc. above	4.00	8.00	12.00	20.00	—
BE16-16 (1942) (f) Rare	Inc. above	—	—	—	—	—

Y# 27.1 3 SHO

Copper **Note:** Single cloud line. Four varieties of conch shell on reverse.

Date	Mintage	VG	F	VF	XF	Unc
BE16-20 (1946)	—	8.00	15.00	25.00	50.00	—

Y# 27.2 3 SHO

Copper **Note:** Double cloud line.

Date	Mintage	VG	F	VF	XF	Unc
BE16-20 (1946)	—	15.00	30.00	50.00	85.00	—

Y# 8 5 SHO

Silver **Ruler:** Hsüan-t'ung **Edge:** Reeded **Note:** Weight varies: 9.4-9.7 grams.

Date	Mintage	VG	F	VF	XF	Unc
BE1 (1909)	—	600	1,200	2,000	2,500	—

Note: A forgery exists with some of the stars blundered and letters inaccurate

Y# 18 5 SHO

Silver **Obv:** Lion looking upwards **Edge:** Reeded **Note:** Weight varies: 8.4-11.4 grams.

Date	Mintage	VG	F	VF	XF	Unc
BE15-47 (1913)	—	50.00	70.00	100	150	—
BE15-48 (1914)	—	35.00	50.00	80.00	125	—
BE15-49 (1915)	—	35.00	50.00	80.00	125	—
BE15-50 (1916)	—	35.00	50.00	80.00	125	—

Note: Two BE15-50 varieties exist; small and large lions, or 13.5mm vs. 14.5mm obverse circle, short or long flowers on reverse

Date	Mintage	VG	F	VF	XF	Unc
BE15-58 (1924) Rare	—	—	—	—	—	—
BE15-59 (1925)	—	150	250	350	500	—
BE15-60 (1926)	—	125	240	400	600	—

Y# 18.1 5 SHO

Silver **Obv:** Lion looking backwards **Edge:** Reeded **Note:** Weight varies: 7.40-9.80 grams. Varieties exist.

Date	Mintage	VG	F	VF	XF	Unc
BE15-49 (1915)	—	35.00	50.00	80.00	125	—
BE15-50 (1916)	—	35.00	50.00	80.00	125	—
BE15-51 (1917)	—	35.00	50.00	80.00	125	—
BE15-52 (1918)	—	35.00	50.00	80.00	125	—
BE15-53 (1919)	—	100	175	275	400	—
BE15-56 (1922)	—	100	175	275	400	—
BE15-59 (1925)	—	350	450	600	800	—
BE15-60 (1926)	—	200	350	500	700	—
BE16-1 (1927)	—	125	225	350	500	—

Y# 18.1a 5 SHO

Copper **Note:** Some specimens are silver plated or silver washed.

Date	Mintage	VG	F	VF	XF	Unc
BE15-53 (1919)	—	225	300	400	500	—

Y# 18.2 5 SHO

Silver **Edge:** Reeded **Note:** Weight varies: 8.00-9.70 grams.

Date	Mintage	VG	F	VF	XF	Unc
BE15-52 (1920)	—	125	175	250	350	—

Y# 32 5 SHO

Silver **Edge:** Reeded **Note:** Weight varies: 5.43-6.55 grams. Two obverse varieties exist. Considered a pattern by some authorities.

Date	Mintage	VG	F	VF	XF	Unc
ND(1928-29)	—	500	750	1,000	1,400	—

a. "CYCLE"

b. "YEAR"

c. "16"

Y# 28 5 SHO

Copper **Obv:** Two mountains with two suns **Edge:** Reeded **Note:** Three lion die varieties exist. Modern counterfiets made of yellowish copper exist.

Date	Mintage	VG	F	VF	XF	Unc
BE16-21 (1947)	—	4.00	7.50	10.00	20.00	—

Y# 28.1 5 SHO

Copper **Obv:** Three mountains with two suns **Edge:** Reeded **Note:** Die varieties involving tail hairs (5-8), leg hairs (2-5) and yin-yang features (S, reversed S or the incuse of either) include 5 of 16-21, 38 of 16-22 and 30 of 16-23.

Date	Mintage	VG	F	VF	XF	Unc
BE16-21 (1947)	—	2.00	3.50	6.00	10.00	—
Note: A modern medallic series dated 16-21 (1947) exists struck in copper, silver, and gold which were authorized by the Dalai Lama while in exile; Refer to Unusual World Coins, 4th edition, KP Books, 2005						
BE16-22 (1948)	—	2.50	4.00	7.50	12.50	—
Note: Dots a and c						
BE16-22 (1948)	—	23.00	30.00	40.00	50.00	—
Note: Without dot after "16"						
BE16-23 (1949)	—	5.00	8.00	14.00	25.00	—
Note: With 8 sun rays						
BE16-23 (1949)	—	1.50	3.00	5.00	8.50	—
Note: With dot after 16; Unclear overdates and varieties of BE16-23 exist						
BE16-24 (1950)	—	30.00	40.00	50.00	65.00	—
BE16-24/3 (1950)	—	40.00	60.00	80.00	100	—

Y# 28.2 5 SHO

Copper **Obv:** Cloud above middle mountain missing **Edge:** Reeded

Date	Mintage	VG	F	VF	XF	Unc
BE16-22 (1948)	—	35.00	60.00	95.00	150	—

Y# 28a 5 SHO

Copper **Obv:** Moon and sun above 3 mountains **Rev:** Regular inscription has dots after the word cycle and before the years **Edge:** Reeded **Note:** Lion and edge varieties exist.

Date	Mintage	VG	F	VF	XF	Unc
BE16-23 (1949)	—	20.00	28.00	38.00	50.00	—
BE16-24/3 (1950)	—	40.00	60.00	80.00	100	—
BE16-24 (1950)	—	2.00	3.50	6.50	11.00	—
BE16-24 (1950)	—	10.00	15.00	22.00	30.00	—
Note: Cloud merged with mountain as in illustration						
BE16-24 (1950)	—	15.00	22.00	30.00	40.00	—
Note: Moon engraved over sun						
BE16-25/24 (1951)	—	4.00	7.00	12.50	20.00	—
BE16-25 (1951)	—	2.00	3.50	6.50	11.00	—
BE16-25 (1951)	—	6.00	10.00	16.00	25.00	—
Note: Moon over engraved sun; Unclear overdates exist for BE16-25						
BE16-26 (1952)	—	4.00	7.00	12.00	20.00	—
BE16-26 (1952)	—	4.00	7.00	12.00	20.00	—
Note: Without dot after "26"						
BE16-27 (1953)	—	6.00	10.00	18.00	30.00	—
BE16-27 (1953)	—	23.00	30.00	40.00	50.00	—
Note: Without dot after "27" or after "Cycle"						

Y# 9 SRANG

Silver **Edge:** Reeded **Note:** 17.2-19.9 g. Obverse varieties exist

Date	Mintage	VG	F	VF	XF	Unc
BE1 (1909)	—	125	185	275	425	—

Y# 12 SRANG

Silver **Obv:** Lion standing left, looking backwards **Edge:** Plain **Note:** Weight varies: 18.00-18.30 grams. Varieties exist.

Date	Mintage	VG	F	VF	XF	Unc
BE15-43 (1909)	—	140	225	325	475	—

Y# A18 SRANG

18.1000 g., Silver **Obv:** Lion standing left looking back and upwards **Edge:** Reeded **Note:** Varieties exist.

Date	Mintage	VG	F	VF	XF	Unc
BE15-48 (1914)	—	400	700	1,200	1,750	—

Y# A18.1 SRANG

Silver **Obv:** Lion looking backwards **Edge:** Reeded **Note:** Weight varies: 17.80-18.30 grams

Date	Mintage	VG	F	VF	XF	Unc
BE15-52 (1918)	—	350	650	850	1,200	—
BE15-53 (1919)	—	275	450	700	1,000	—

Y# 24 1-1/2 SRANG

5.0000 g., Silver **Edge:** Reeded **Note:** Dates are written in words, not numerals. Obverse varieties exist.

Date	Mintage	F	VF	XF	Unc	BU
BE16-10 (1936)	—	3.50	6.00	10.00	20.00	—
BE16-11 (1937)	—	3.00	5.00	9.00	17.00	—
BE16-12 (1938)	—	3.50	6.00	10.00	20.00	—
BE16-20 (1946)	—	20.00	40.00	70.00	90.00	—

Y# 25 3 SRANG

11.3000 g., Silver **Edge:** Reeded **Note:** Dates are written in words, not numerals. Varieties exist in lion.

Date	Mintage	F	VF	XF	Unc	BU
BE16-7 (1933)	—	8.00	12.00	20.00	35.00	—
Note: 7 or 8-tail plume variety						
BE16-8 (1934)	—	8.00	12.00	20.00	35.00	—

Y# 26 3 SRANG

Silver **Edge:** Reeded **Note:** Dates are written in words, not numerals. Varieties in circular obverse and reverse legends exist.

Date	Mintage	F	VF	XF	Unc	BU
BE16-9 (1935)	—	7.00	10.00	18.00	30.00	—
BE16-10 (1936)	—	6.00	9.00	15.00	25.00	—
BE16-10/9 (1936)	—	7.00	10.00	18.00	30.00	—
BE16-11 (1937)	—	6.00	9.00	15.00	25.00	—
BE16-12 (1938)	—	6.00	9.00	15.00	25.00	—
BE16-20 (1946)	—	20.00	40.00	70.00	110	—

Y# 29 10 SRANG

Billon **Obv:** Two suns **Rev:** Numerals for denomination at center right **Edge:** Reeded

Date	Mintage	F	VF	XF	Unc	BU
BE16-22 (1948)	—	4.50	9.00	18.00	40.00	—

Y# 29a 10 SRANG

Billon **Obv:** Moon and sun **Edge:** Reeded **Note:** The "dot" is after the denomination. A modern medallic series dated 16-24 (1950) exists struck in copper-nickel, silver, and gold which were authorized by the Dalai Lama while in exile. Refer to "Unusual World Coins", 4th edition, KP Books, 2005.

Date	Mintage	F	VF	XF	Unc	BU
BE16-23 (1949)	—	20.00	45.00	100	175	—
Note: With dot						
BE16-24/23 (1950)	—	7.00	15.00	30.00	60.00	—
Note: With dot						
BE16-24/23 (1950)	—	20.00	40.00	80.00	140	—
Note: With dot and moon cut over sun						
BE16-24/22 (1950)	—	9.00	18.00	35.00	70.00	—
BE16-24 (1950)	—	10.00	20.00	40.00	70.00	—
Note: Moon cut over sun, denomination in words						
BE16-24 (1950)	—	12.00	22.00	50.00	90.00	—
Note: With dot						
BE16-25/24 (1951)	—	7.00	15.00	30.00	60.00	—
Note: With dot						
BE16-25/24 (1951)	—	10.00	20.00	40.00	70.00	—
Note: Without dot						
BE16-25 (1951)	—	7.00	15.00	30.00	60.00	—
Note: With dot						
BE16-26/25 (1952)	—	7.00	15.00	30.00	60.00	—
Note: Without dot						
BE16-26 (1952)	—	7.00	15.00	30.00	60.00	—
Note: With dot						

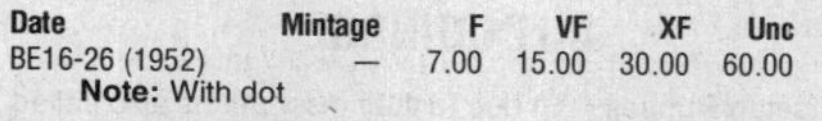

Y# 29.1 10 SRANG

Billon **Rev:** Words for denomination at center right

Date	Mintage	F	VF	XF	Unc	BU
BE16-23 (1949)	—	6.00	10.00	20.00	40.00	—
Note: With dot before and after ten						
BE16-23 (1949)	—	6.00	10.00	20.00	40.00	—
Note: Without dot after ten						
BE16-23/22 (1949)	—	12.00	20.00	35.00	70.00	—

Y# 30 10 SRANG

Billon **Rev:** Cycle and year in words **Edge:** Reeded **Note:** Said to be struck for payment of Tibetan Army members

Date	Mintage	F	VF	XF	Unc	BU
BE16-24 (1950)	—	6.00	12.00	25.00	55.00	—
Note: Without dot after year						
BE16-24 (1950)	—	7.00	15.00	30.00	65.00	—
Note: With dot						
BE16-25/4 (1951)	—	5.00	10.00	20.00	45.00	—
Note: With dot						
BE16-25 (1951)	—	5.00	10.00	20.00	45.00	—
Note: With dot						

Y# 22 20 SRANG

Gold **Obv:** Eight Buddhist lucky symbols in outer circle **Edge:** Reeded

Date	Mintage	F	VF	XF	Unc	BU
BE15-52 (1918)	—	425	575	825	1,150	—
Note: With dot in reverse center						
BE15-53 (1919)	—	425	575	825	1,150	—
Note: With large circle in reverse center; Silver strikings for 15-53 exist and are believed to be forgeries						
BE15-53 (1919)	—	425	575	825	1,150	—
Note: With small circle in reverse center						
BE15-54 (1920)	—	425	575	825	1,100	—
Note: Silver strikings for 15-54 exist and are believed to be forgeries; Deceptive forgeries struck in high grade gold also exist; without dot in reverse center						
BE15-54 (1920)	—	425	575	825	1,150	—
Note: With dot in reverse center						
BE15-55 (1921)	—	700	1,000	1,500	2,000	—

TRADE COINAGE

1 Rupee = 3 Tangka

Total mintage of the 1 Rupee between 1902 and 1942 was between 25.5 and 27.5 million according to Chinese sources. In addition to the types illustrated above, large quantities of the following coins also circulated in Tibet: China Dollars, Y#318a, 329, and 345 plus Szechuan issues Y#449 and 459, and Indian Rupees, KM#473, 492, and 508.

Rupees exist with local merchant countermarks in Chinese, Tibetan, and other scripts. Examples of crown-size rupees struck in silver (26.30-27.50 grams) and gold (36.30 grams) are considered fantasies.

Y# 1 1/4 RUPEE

2.8000 g., 0.9350 Silver, 19 mm. **Edge:** Reeded **Note:** Varieties exist

Date	Mintage	F	VF	XF	Unc	BU
ND(1904-05)	120,000	40.00	60.00	90.00	150	—
ND(1904-05, 1912)	120,000	45.00	65.00	100	175	—

Y# 1a 1/4 RUPEE

5.4500 g., Gold

Date	Mintage	F	VF	XF	Unc	BU
ND(1905)	—	1,150	1,900	2,650	3,450	—

Y# 2 1/2 RUPEE

5.6000 g., 0.9350 Silver, 24 mm. **Edge:** Reeded **Note:** Varieties exist

Date	Mintage	F	VF	XF	Unc	BU
ND(1904-05, 1907, 1912)	130,000	60.00	85.00	145	250	—

Y# 2a 1/2 RUPEE

9.3800 g., Gold

Date	Mintage	F	VF	XF	Unc	BU
ND(1905)	—	1,250	2,000	2,750	3,500	—

Y# A1.1 RUPEE

11.5000 g., Silver **Ruler:** Hsüan-t'ung **Edge:** Plain **Note:** Prev. #C20.

Date	Mintage	Good	VG	F	VF	XF
ND(1902-03)	—	750	1,000	1,500	2,250	—
Note: Struck in or near Tachienlu (today Kang Ting) and known as Lu Kuan Rupee. It was meant to replace the Indian Rupee which was used in eastern Tibet and western Szechuan (Sichuan) in the 19th century and is considered the forerunner of the Szechuan Rupee (Y#3). Varieties exist.						

Y# A1.2 RUPEE

Silver **Ruler:** Hsüan-t'ung **Note:** Obverse and reverse inscriptions deviating in style. Kann#1285

Date	Mintage	Good	VG	F	VF	XF
ND(1902-03)	—	750	1,000	1,500	2,250	—

Y# 3 RUPEE

Silver **Obv:** Small bust without collar **Rev:** Vertical rosette **Edge:** Reeded **Note:** Two reverse varieties exist. Weight varies: .8800-.9350 grams.

Date	Mintage	F	VF	XF	Unc	BU
ND(1902-11)	—	30.00	50.00	80.00	125	—

Y# 3.1 RUPEE

Silver **Rev:** Horizontal rosette **Edge:** Reeded **Note:** Two reverse varieties exist. Weight varies: .8800-.9350 grams.

Date	Mintage	F	VF	XF	Unc	BU
ND(1902-11)	—	20.00	40.00	60.00	100	—

Y# 3.2 RUPEE

0.7000 Silver **Obv:** Small bust with collar **Rev:** Vertical rosette **Note:** Struck at Chengdu (Szechuan) Mint before 1930, then at Kangding (Tachienlu) Mint after 1930. Two reverse varieties exist.

Date	Mintage	F	VF	XF	Unc	BU
ND(1911-16, 1930-33)	—	15.00	25.00	45.00	75.00	—

Note: An example with two obverses exists

Y# 3.2a RUPEE

20.6700 g., Gold **Note:** Prev. Y#3b.

Date	Mintage	F	VF	XF	Unc	BU
ND(ca. 1903-05)	—	900	1,200	1,750	—	—

Note: An example with two obverses exists (20.40 grams)

Y# 3b RUPEE

Gold

Date	Mintage	F	VF	XF	Unc	BU
ND(ca.1930)	—	—	—	—	—	—

Y# 3.3 RUPEE

Silver **Obv:** Large bust **Rev:** Vertical rosette **Note:** Finenesses vary .4200-.5000. Varieties exist.

Date	Mintage	F	VF	XF	Unc	BU
ND(1939-42)	—	20.00	35.00	65.00	110	—

Y# 3.4 RUPEE

Silver **Obv:** Small bust with flat nose, revised non-floral gown. **Rev:** Vertical rosette **Note:** .650-.500 silver

Date	Mintage	F	VF	XF	Unc	BU
ND(1933-39)	—	20.00	35.00	65.00	110	—

Y# 3.5 RUPEE

Silver **Obv:** Small bust similar to Y#3.4 **Rev:** Horizontal rosette **Note:** .650-.500 silver.

Date	Mintage	F	VF	XF	Unc	BU
ND(1933-39)	—	30.00	50.00	90.00	160	—

Y# 3a RUPEE

Debased Silver/Billon

Date	Mintage	F	VF	XF	Unc	BU
ND(1939-42)	—	10.00	20.00	40.00	70.00	—

Note: Coins with copper base and silver wash exist

CUT COINAGE

Tibetan Rupees (Y3) due to their inscriptions also called Szechuan Rupees, have been cut in half and quarter for use as small change. The process of cutting the rupee frequently allowed customers to chip away from the coin's middle. In 1934 the treasury made cutting of the rupee illegal. To enforce this decree, all official payments had to be made with uncut coins; payment of smaller values was to be made with copper coins. However, the shortage of coinage made this decree impractical.

Y# A5 1/4 RUPEE

Silver **Note:** 1/4 segment of 1 Rupee, Y#3.

Date	Mintage	VG	F	VF	XF	Unc
ND (1902-42)	—	—	—	—	—	—

Y# B5 1/2 RUPEE

Silver **Note:** 1/2 segment of 1 Rupee, Y#3.

Date	Mintage	VG	F	VF	XF	Unc
ND (1902-42)	—	15.00	20.00	35.00	60.00	—

TOKEN COINAGE

KM# Tn1 4 SHO

Copper **Note:** 8.23-8.98 grams. Struck over 3 Sho, Y#27 and 5 Sho, Y#28a

Date	Mintage	VG	F	VF	XF	Unc
ND(1959-60) Rare	—	—	—	—	—	—

KM# Tn2 4 SHO

Copper **Note:** Struck over 5 Sho, Y#28a and Y#28.1

Date	Mintage	VG	F	VF	XF	Unc
ND	—	75.00	100	200	400	600

PATTERNS

Including off metal strikes

KM#	Date	Mintage	Identification	Mkt Val
Pn3	ND (1909)	—	10 Tam. Silver. 27.6700 g.	—
Pn4	ND (1910)	—	Shokang. Silver. 3.6000 g. Y5	—
Pn5	BE15-57 (1923)	—	Sho. Copper.	—
Pn6	BE15-57 (1923)	—	Sho. Brass.	—
Pn8	BE15-57 (1923)	—	20 Srang. Brass. 7.2300 g.	—
Pn9	BE16-1 (1928)	—	Sho. Brass. 5.2600 g.	—
Pn10	ND (1928)	—	Srang. Silver.	—
Pn11	ND (1928)	—	10 Tam. Silver. 12.6100 g.	—
Pn12	ND (1929-30)	—	10 Tam. Silver. 8.3000 g.	—
Pn13	BE16-4 (1931)	—	5 Sho. Silver. 5.0000 g.	—
Pn14	Yr.925 (1951)	—	25 Srang. Silver. 13.5200 g.	—
Pn15	Yr.925 (1951)	—	50 Srang. Copper. 17.3000 g.	—
Pn16	Yr.925 (1951)	—	50 Srang. Silver. 26.0000 g.	—
Pn17	Yr.925 (1951)	—	50 Srang. Silver. 26.0000 g.	—
Pn18	ND (1951)	—	50 Srang. Silver. 25.1000 g.	—
Pn20	Yr.927 (1953)	—	5 Srang. Copper. 6.2000 g.	600

Note: Some specimens of Pn20 seem to have entered circulation.

KM#	Date	Mintage	Identification	Mkt Val
Pn21	Yr. 927 (1953)	—	5 Srang. Silver. 5.0000 g.	—

TIMOR

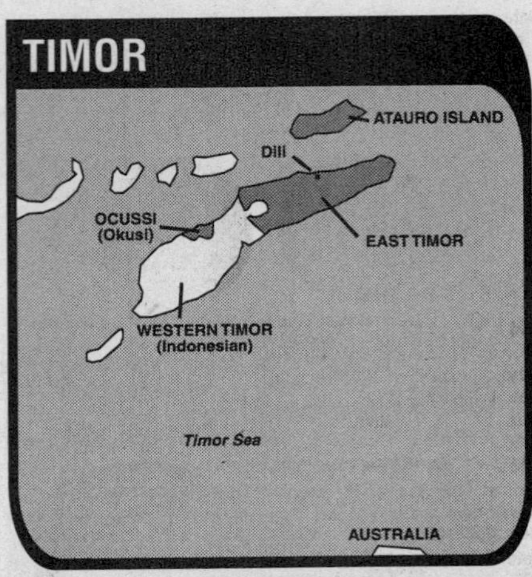

East Timor, population: 522,433, area: 7332 sq. miles, capital: Dili, is primarily located on the eastern half of the island of Timor, just northwest of Australia at the eastern end of the Indonesian archipelago. Formerly a Portuguese colony, Timor declared its independence from Portugal on November 28, 1975. After nine short days of fledgling autonomy, a guerilla faction sympathetic to the Indonesian territorial claim to East Timor seized the government. On July 17, 1976 the Provisional government enacted a law, which dissolved the free republic and made East Timor the 24th province of Indonesia. Violent rule and civil unrest plagued the province, with great loss of life and extreme damage to property and natural resources until independence was again achieved with United Nations assistance during a period from 1999 to 2002. Emerging as the Democratic Republic of Timor-Leste and commonly known as East Timor the country has worked, with international assistance to rebuild its decimated infrastructure. Natural resources waiting to be tapped include rich oil reserves, though current exports are most dependent on coffee, sandalwood and marble. The first coins of the new republic were issued in 2003.

For earlier Portuguese Colonial coinage, see Timor.

PORTUGUESE COLONY

MILLED COINAGE

100 Avos = 1 Pataca

KM# 5 10 AVOS

Bronze **Obv:** Small circles within cross design **Obv. Legend:** REPUBLICA PORTUGUESA **Rev:** Value above sprigs **Rev. Legend:** COLONIA DE TIMOR

Date	Mintage	F	VF	XF	Unc	BU
1945	50,000	120	220	400	1,000	—
1948	500,000	3.50	8.00	17.00	35.00	—
1951	6,250,000	1.50	3.50	7.50	15.00	—

KM# 6 20 AVOS

Nickel-Bronze **Obv:** Laureate liberty head right **Obv. Legend:** REPUBLICA PORTUGUESA **Rev:** Shield within globe and wreath **Rev. Legend:** COLONIA DE TIMOR

Date	Mintage	F	VF	XF	Unc	BU
1945	50,000	16.00	35.00	70.00	175	—

KM# 7 50 AVOS

3.5000 g., 0.6500 Silver .0731 oz. ASW **Obv:** Shield within globe on maltese cross **Obv. Legend:** REPUBLICA PORTUGUESA **Rev:** Value above sprigs **Rev. Legend:** COLONIA DE TIMOR

Date	Mintage	F	VF	XF	Unc	BU
1945	100,000	45.00	90.00	135	275	—

Date	Mintage	F	VF	XF	Unc	BU
1948	500,000	3.00	5.50	12.00	30.00	—
1951	6,250,000	2.00	4.00	9.00	18.00	—

1958 REFORM COINAGE

100 Centavos = 1 Escudo

KM# 10 10 CENTAVOS

Bronze **Obv:** Value **Obv. Legend:** REPUBLICA PORTUGUESA **Rev:** Shield within crowned globe, flowers in legend, date below **Rev. Legend:** TIMOR

Date	Mintage	F	VF	XF	Unc	BU
1958	1,000,000	1.00	3.00	15.00	35.00	—

KM# 17 20 CENTAVOS

Bronze **Obv:** Value **Obv. Legend:** REPUBLICA PORTUGUESA **Rev:** Shield within crowned globe, flowers in legend, date below **Rev. Legend:** TIMOR

Date	Mintage	F	VF	XF	Unc	BU
1970	1,000,000	0.45	1.00	2.50	5.00	7.50

KM# 11 30 CENTAVOS

Bronze **Obv:** Value **Obv. Legend:** REPUBLICA PORTUGUESA **Rev:** Shield within crowned globe, flowers in legend, date below **Rev. Legend:** TIMOR

Date	Mintage	F	VF	XF	Unc	BU
1958	2,000,000	0.75	1.50	12.00	30.00	—

KM# 18 50 CENTAVOS

Bronze **Obv:** Value **Obv. Legend:** REPUBLICA PORTUGUESA **Rev:** Shield within crowned globe, flowers in legend, date below **Rev. Legend:** TIMOR

Date	Mintage	F	VF	XF	Unc	BU
1970	1,000,000	0.45	1.00	2.00	4.50	6.50

KM# 12 60 CENTAVOS

Copper-Nickel-Zinc **Obv:** Shield within globe on maltese cross, date below **Obv. Legend:** REPUBLICA PORTUGUESA **Rev:** Shield within crowned globe, flowers in legend, value below **Rev. Legend:** TIMOR

Date	Mintage	F	VF	XF	Unc	BU
1958	1,000,000	1.25	2.75	12.00	30.00	—

KM# 13 ESCUDO

Copper-Nickel-Zinc **Obv:** Shield within globe on maltese cross, date below **Obv. Legend:** REPUBLICA PORTUGUESA **Rev:** Shield within crowned globe, flowers in legend, value below **Rev. Legend:** TIMOR

Date	Mintage	F	VF	XF	Unc	BU
1958	1,200,000	2.00	4.00	40.00	75.00	—

KM# 19 ESCUDO

Bronze **Obv:** Value **Obv. Legend:** REPUBLICA PORTUGUESA **Rev:** Shield within crowned globe, flowers in legend, date below **Rev. Legend:** TIMOR

Date	Mintage	F	VF	XF	Unc	BU
1970	1,200,000	1.50	3.00	7.00	15.00	—

KM# 20 2-1/2 ESCUDOS

Copper-Nickel **Obv:** Shield within globe on maltese cross, date below **Obv. Legend:** REPUBLICA PORTUGUESA **Rev:** Shield within crowned globe, flowers in legend, value below **Rev. Legend:** TIMOR

Date	Mintage	F	VF	XF	Unc	BU
1970	1,000,000	0.75	1.50	3.50	8.00	14.00

KM# 14 3 ESCUDOS

3.5000 g., 0.6500 Silver .0731 oz. ASW **Obv:** Shield within globe on maltese cross, date below **Obv. Legend:** REPUBLICA PORTUGUESA **Rev:** Shield within crowned globe, flowers in legend, value below **Rev. Legend:** TIMOR

Date	Mintage	F	VF	XF	Unc	BU
1958	1,000,000	3.00	5.00	10.00	25.00	—

KM# 21 5 ESCUDOS

Copper-Nickel **Obv:** Shield within globe on maltese cross, date below **Obv. Legend:** REPUBLICA PORTUGUESA **Rev:** Shield within crowned globe, flowers in legend, value below **Rev. Legend:** TIMOR

Date	Mintage	F	VF	XF	Unc	BU
1970	1,200,000	1.50	3.00	6.50	12.00	—

KM# 15 6 ESCUDOS

7.0000 g., 0.6500 Silver .1463 oz. ASW **Obv:** Shield within globe on maltese cross, date below **Obv. Legend:** REPUBLICA PORTUGUESA **Rev:** Shield within crowned globe, flowers in legend, value below **Rev. Legend:** TIMOR

Date	Mintage	F	VF	XF	Unc	BU
1958	1,000,000	3.50	6.00	12.50	25.00	—

KM# 16 10 ESCUDOS

7.0000 g., 0.6500 Silver .1463 oz. ASW **Obv:** Shield within globe on maltese cross, date below **Obv. Legend:** REPUBLICA PORTUGUESA **Rev:** Shield within crowned globe, flowers in legend, value below **Rev. Legend:** TIMOR

Date	Mintage	F	VF	XF	Unc	BU
1964	600,000	3.50	6.00	12.50	25.00	—

KM# 22 10 ESCUDOS

Copper-Nickel **Obv:** Shield within globe on maltese cross, date below **Obv. Legend:** REPUBLICA PORTUGUESA **Rev:** Shield within crowned globe, flowers in legend, value below **Rev. Legend:** TIMOR

Date	Mintage	F	VF	XF	Unc	BU
1970	700,000	3.00	5.50	12.00	24.00	—

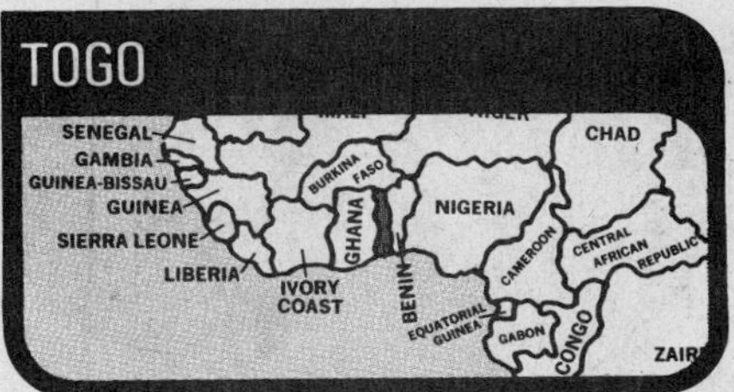

The Republic of Togo (formerly part of German Togoland), situated on the Gulf of Guinea in West Africa between Ghana and Dahomey, has an area of 21,622 sq.mi. (56,790 sq. km.) and a population of *3.4 million. Capital: Lome. Agriculture and herding, the production of dyewoods, and the mining of phosphates and iron ore are the chief industries. Copra, phosphates and coffee are exported.

Although Brazilians were the first traders to settle in Togo, Germany achieved possession, in 1884, by inducing coastal chiefs to place their territories under German protection. The German protectorate was extended international recognition at the Berlin conference of 1885 and its ultimate boundaries delimited by treaties with France in 1897 and with Britain in 1904. Anglo-French forces occupied Togoland in 1914, subsequently becoming a League of Nations mandate and a U.N. trusteeship divided, for administrative purpose, between Great Britain and France. The British portion voted in 1957 for incorporation with Ghana. The French portion became the independent Republic of Togo on April 27, 1960.

RULERS

German, 1884-1914
Anglo - French, 1914-1957
French, 1957-1960

MINT MARKS

(a) - Paris, privy marks only

MONETARY SYSTEM

100 Centimes = 1 Franc

FRENCH COLONIAL

U.N. Trusteeship

STANDARD COINAGE

100 Centimes = 1 Franc

KM# 1 50 CENTIMES

Aluminum-Bronze **Obv:** Laureate head left **Rev:** Value within upright sprigs **Designer:** A. Patay

Date	Mintage	F	VF	XF	Unc	BU
1924(a)	3,691,000	4.00	20.00	50.00	80.00	—
1925(a)	2,064,000	5.00	22.00	55.00	100	—
1926(a)	445,000	20.00	50.00	100	300	—

KM# 2 FRANC

Aluminum-Bronze **Obv:** Laureat head left **Rev:** Value within upright sprigs **Designer:** A. Patay

Date	Mintage	F	VF	XF	Unc	BU
1924(a)	3,472,000	3.50	27.50	60.00	125	—
1925(a)	2,768,000	4.00	19.00	65.00	140	—

KM# 4 FRANC

Aluminum **Obv:** Winged head left **Rev:** Slender-horned gazelle head divides value within sprigs **Designer:** G.B.L. Bazor

Date	Mintage	F	VF	XF	Unc	BU
1948(a)	5,000,000	5.00	12.00	30.00	70.00	125

KM# 3 2 FRANCS
Aluminum-Bronze **Obv:** Laureate head left **Rev:** Value within upright sprigs **Designer:** A. Patay

Date	Mintage	F	VF	XF	Unc	BU
1924(a)	750,000	6.00	35.00	110	250	—
1925(a)	580,000	7.00	38.00	120	275	—

KM# 5 2 FRANCS
Aluminum **Obv:** Winged head left **Rev:** Slender-horned gazelle head divides value within sprigs **Designer:** G.B.L. Bazor **Note:** Similar to 1 Franc, KM#4.

Date	Mintage	F	VF	XF	Unc	BU
1948(a)	5,000,000	6.00	15.00	35.00	80.00	150

KM# 6 5 FRANCS
Aluminum-Bronze, 20 mm. **Obv:** Head left **Rev:** Slender-horned gazelle head divides value within sprigs

Date	Mintage	F	VF	XF	Unc	BU
1956(a)	10,000,000	3.00	6.00	12.00	25.00	—

FRENCH WEST AFRICA - TOGO

STANDARD COINAGE

100 Centimes = 1 Franc

KM# A8 10 FRANCS
Aluminum-Bronze **Note:** Issued for circulation in French West Africa, including Togo.

Date	Mintage	F	VF	XF	Unc	BU
1957(a)	30,000,000	0.50	1.00	1.50	3.00	—

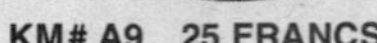

KM# A9 25 FRANCS
Aluminum-Bronze **Obv:** "Taku", a symbol of prosperity divides value **Rev:** Slender-horned gazelle head divides value within sprigs **Note:** Issued for circulation in French West Africa, including Togo.

Date	Mintage	F	VF	XF	Unc	BU
1957(a)	30,000,000	0.50	1.00	2.00	5.00	—

REPUBLIC

STANDARD COINAGE

100 Centimes = 1 Franc

KM# 13 500 FRANCS
7.0000 g., 0.9990 Silver 0.2248 oz. ASW, 30 mm. **Obv:** Arms with supporters **Rev:** Apollo 11 launch scene **Edge:** Plain

Date	Mintage	F	VF	XF	Unc	BU
ND(1999) Proof	—	Value: 35.00				

KM# 14 500 FRANCS
7.0000 g., 0.9990 Silver 0.2248 oz. ASW **Obv:** Arms with supporters **Rev:** Three astronauts, moon and space capsule

Date	Mintage	F	VF	XF	Unc	BU
ND(1999) Proof	—	Value: 35.00				

KM# 15 500 FRANCS
7.0000 g., 0.9990 Silver 0.2248 oz. ASW **Obv:** Arms with supporters **Rev:** Moon-walking astronaut

Date	Mintage	F	VF	XF	Unc	BU
ND(1999) Proof	—	Value: 35.00				

KM# 19 500 FRANCS
6.9300 g., 0.9990 Silver 0.2226 oz. ASW, 27.9 mm. **Obv:** Arms with supporters **Rev:** Head of Albert Einstein facing **Edge:** Plain

Date	Mintage	F	VF	XF	Unc	BU
ND Proof	—	Value: 35.00				

KM# 16 1000 FRANCS
14.9700 g., 0.9990 Silver 0.4808 oz. ASW, 35 mm. **Obv:** Arms with supporters **Rev:** Bust of Martin Luther 3/4 right **Edge:** Plain

Date	Mintage	F	VF	XF	Unc	BU
1999 Proof	—	Value: 50.00				

KM# 28 1000 FRANCS
14.9500 g., 0.9990 Silver 0.4802 oz. ASW, 35 mm. **Obv:** Arms with supporters **Rev:** Lion **Edge:** Plain

Date	Mintage	F	VF	XF	Unc	BU
2000 Proof	5,000	Value: 40.00				

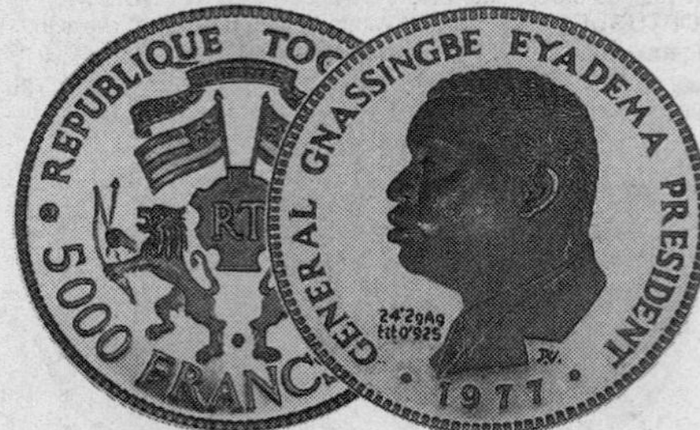

KM# 8 5000 FRANCS
24.3600 g., 0.9250 Silver .7245 oz. ASW **Subject:** 10th Year of General Gnassingbe Eyadema as President **Obv:** Arms with supporters **Rev:** Head left

Date	Mintage	F	VF	XF	Unc	BU
1977 Proof	150	Value: 150				

KM# 9 10000 FRANCS
49.3200 g., 0.9250 Silver 1.4669 oz. ASW **Subject:** 10th Year of General Gnassingbe Eyadema as President **Obv:** Arms with supporters **Rev:** Head left

Date	Mintage	F	VF	XF	Unc	BU
1977 Proof	150	Value: 350				

KM# 10 15000 FRANCS
4.4800 g., 0.9170 Gold .1320 oz. AGW **Subject:** 10th Year of General Gnassingbe Eyadema as President **Obv:** Arms with supporters **Rev:** Head facing

Date	Mintage	F	VF	XF	Unc	BU
1977 Proof	75	Value: 150				

KM# 11 25000 FRANCS
9.0000 g., 0.9170 Gold .2653 oz. AGW **Subject:** 10th Year of General Gnassingbe Eyadema as President **Obv:** Arms with supporters **Rev:** Head facing

Date	Mintage	F	VF	XF	Unc	BU
1977 Proof	75	Value: 275				

KM# 12 50000 FRANCS
18.0000 g., 0.9170 Gold .5306 oz. AGW **Subject:** 10th Year of General Gnassingbe Eyadema as President **Obv:** Arms with supporters **Rev:** Head facing **Note:** Similar to 25,000 Francs, KM#11.

Date	Mintage	F	VF	XF	Unc	BU
1977 Proof	50	Value: 525				

ESSAIS

KM#	Date	Mintage	Identification	Mkt Val
E1	1924(a)	—	50 Centimes. Aluminum-Bronze. KM#1.	150

KM#	Date	Mintage	Identification	Mkt Val
E2	1924(a)	—	Franc. Aluminum-Bronze. Head laureate left. Value within upright sprigs. KM#2.	150
E3	1924(a)	—	2 Francs. Aluminum-Bronze. KM#3.	200
E4	1948(a)	2,000	Franc. Copper-Nickel. KM#4.	30.00
E5	1948(a)	2,000	2 Francs. Copper-Nickel. KM#5.	37.50
E6	1956(a)	2,300	5 Francs. Aluminum-Bronze. KM#6.	15.00
E7	1956(a)	2,300	10 Francs. KM#7.	37.50
E8	1956(a)	2,300	25 Francs.	45.00
EA8	1957	2,300	10 Francs. Aluminum-Bronze. KM#A8.	25.00
EB8	1957	2,300	25 Francs. Aluminum-Bronze. KM#A9.	30.00
E9	1977	25	5000 Francs. Aluminum. KM#8.	200
E10	1977	20	5000 Francs. Copper. KM#8.	200
E11	1977	25	10000 Francs. Aluminum. KM#9.	275
E12	1977	20	10000 Francs. Copper. KM#9.	275
E13	1977	25	15000 Francs. Aluminum. KM#10.	100
E14	1977	20	15000 Francs. Copper. KM#10.	100
E15	1977	25	25000 Francs. Aluminum. KM#11.	150

KM#	Date	Mintage	Identification	Mkt Val
E16	1977	20	25000 Francs. Copper. KM#11.	150
E17	ND(2003)	2	150000 Cfa Francs - 100 Africa. Bi-Metallic. President and map. Elephant head on map.	250

PIEFORTS

KM#	Date	Mintage	Identification	Mkt Val
P1	1977	5	5000 Francs. Copper. KM#8.	400
P2	1977	10	5000 Francs. Silver. 48.7200 g. KM#8.	400
P3	1977	5	10000 Francs. Copper. KM#9.	500
P4b	1977	2	15000 Francs. Gold. KM#10.	800
P5b	1977	2	25000 Francs. Gold. KM#11.	1,000
P3a	1977	10	10000 Francs. Silver. KM#9.	500
P4	1977	5	15000 Francs. Copper. KM#10.	200
P4a	1977	10	15000 Francs. Silver. KM#10.	200
P5	1977	5	25000 Francs. Copper. KM#11.	300
P5a	1977	10	25000 Francs. Silver. KM#11.	300

PIEFORTS WITH ESSAIS

KM#	Date	Mintage	Identification	Mkt Val
PE1	1948(a)	104	Franc. Aluminum. KM#4.	85.00
PE2	1948(a)	104	2 Francs. Aluminum. KM#5.	95.00

TRIAL STRIKES

KM#	Date	Mintage	Identification	Mkt Val
TS1	1977	10	5000 Francs. Copper. Obverse of KM#8. PRUEBA.	200
TS2	1977	10	5000 Francs. Copper. Reverse of KM#8. PRUEBA.	200
TS3	1977	10	5000 Francs. Silver. Obverse of KM#8. PRUEBA.	250
TS4	1977	10	5000 Francs. Silver. Reverse of KM#8. PRUEBA.	250
TS5	1977	10	10000 Francs. Copper. Obverse of KM#9. PRUEBA.	250
TS6	1977	10	10000 Francs. Copper. Reverse of KM#9. PRUEBA.	250
TS7	1977	10	10000 Francs. Silver. Obverse of KM#9. PRUEBA.	300
TS8	1977	10	10000 Francs. Silver. Obverse of KM#9. PRUEBA.	300
TS9	1977	10	15000 Francs. Copper. Obverse of KM#10. PRUEBA.	100
TS10	1977	10	15000 Francs. Copper. Reverse of KM#10. PRUEBA.	100
TS11	1977	10	15000 Francs. Silver. Obverse of KM#10. PRUEBA.	125
TS12	1977	10	15000 Francs. Silver. Reverse of KM#10. PRUEBA.	125
TS13	1977	10	25000 Francs. Copper. Obverse of KM#11. PRUEBA.	150
TS14	1977	10	25000 Francs. Copper. Reverse of KM11. PRUEBA.	150
TS15	1977	10	25000 Francs. Silver. Obverse of KM#11. PRUEBA.	175
TS16	1977	10	25000 Francs. Silver. Reverse of KM#11. PRUEBA.	175

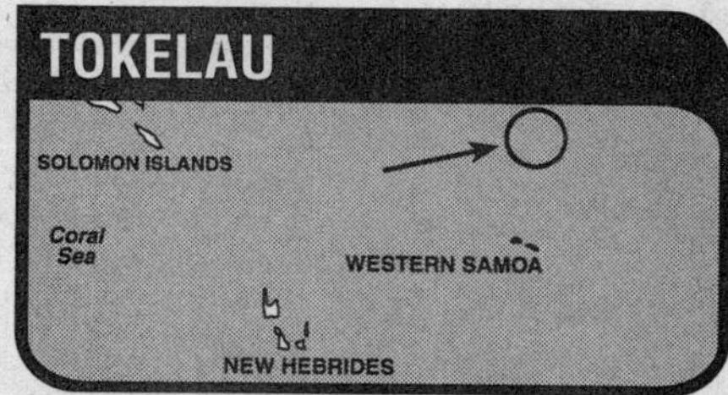

Tokelau or Union Islands, a New Zealand Territory located in the South Pacific 2,100 miles (3,379 km.) northeast of New Zealand and 300 miles (483 km.) north of Samoa, has an area of 4 sq. mi. (10 sq. km.) and a population of *2,000. Geographically, the group consists of four atolls - Atafu, Nukunono, Fakaofo and Swains – but the last belongs to American Samoa (and the United States claims the other three). The people are of Polynesian origin; Samoan is the official language. The New Zealand Minister for Foreign Affairs governs the islands; councils of family elders handle local government at the village level. The chief settlement is Fenuafala, on Fakaofo. It is connected by wireless with the offices of the New Zealand Administrative Center, located at Apia, Western Samoa. Subsistence farming and the production of copra for export are the main occupations. Revenue is also derived from the sale of postage stamps and, since 1978,coins.

Great Britain annexed the group of islands in 1889. They were added to the Gilbert and Ellice Islands colony in 1916. In 1926, they were brought under the jurisdiction of Western Samoa, which was held as a mandate of the League of Nations by New Zealand. They were declared a part of New Zealand in 1948.

Tokelau Islands issued its first coin in 1978, a "$1 TahiTala," Tokelauan for "One Dollar."

RULERS
British

MINT MARKS
PM - Pobjoy

NEW ZEALAND TERRITORY

STANDARD COINAGE

KM# 1 TALA
Copper-Nickel, 38.5 mm. **Ruler:** Elizabeth II **Obv:** Young bust right **Obv. Designer:** Arnold Machin **Rev:** Coconut and value **Edge:** Reeded

Date	Mintage	F	VF	XF	Unc	BU
1978	10,000	—	—	3.00	12.00	17.50

KM# 1a TALA
27.2500 g., 0.9250 Silver .8104 oz. ASW, 38.5 mm. **Ruler:** Elizabeth II **Obv:** Young bust right **Obv. Designer:** Arnold Machin **Rev:** Coconut and value

Date	Mintage	F	VF	XF	Unc	BU
1978 Proof	5,000	Value: 22.50				

KM# 2 TALA
Copper-Nickel, 38.5 mm. **Ruler:** Elizabeth II **Obv:** Young bust right **Obv. Designer:** Arnold Machin **Rev:** V-shaped tool, bucket, rope and value

Date	Mintage	F	VF	XF	Unc	BU
1979	—	—	—	2.50	10.00	15.00

KM# 2a TALA
27.2500 g., 0.9250 Silver .8104 oz. ASW, 38.5 mm. **Ruler:** Elizabeth II **Obv:** Young bust right **Obv. Designer:** Arnold Machin **Rev:** V-shaped tool, bucket, rope and value

Date	Mintage	F	VF	XF	Unc	BU
1979 Proof	—	Value: 20.00				

KM# 3 TALA
Copper-Nickel **Ruler:** Elizabeth II **Obv:** Young bust right **Obv. Designer:** Arnold Machin **Rev:** Coconut crab and value **Edge:** Reeded

Date	Mintage	F	VF	XF	Unc	BU
1980	10,000	—	—	4.00	15.00	18.50

KM# 3a TALA
27.2500 g., 0.9250 Silver .8104 oz. ASW, 38.5 mm. **Ruler:** Elizabeth II **Obv:** Young bust right **Rev:** Coconut Crab and value

Date	Mintage	F	VF	XF	Unc	BU
1980 Proof	6,004	Value: 22.50				

KM# 4 TALA
Copper-Nickel **Ruler:** Elizabeth II **Obv:** Young bust right **Obv. Designer:** Arnold Machin **Rev:** Frigate bird and value **Rev. Designer:** Faraimo Paulo

Date	Mintage	F	VF	XF	Unc	BU
1981	6,500	—	—	4.00	15.00	18.50

KM# 4a TALA
27.2500 g., 0.9250 Silver .8104 oz. ASW, 38.5 mm. **Ruler:** Elizabeth II **Obv:** Arnold Machin **Obv. Designer:** Arnold Machin **Rev:** Frigate bird and value **Rev. Designer:** Faraimo Paulo

Date	Mintage	F	VF	XF	Unc	BU
1981 Proof	6,500	Value: 22.50				

KM# 5 TALA
Copper-Nickel, 38.5 mm. **Ruler:** Elizabeth II **Obv:** Young bust right **Obv. Designer:** Arnold Machin **Rev:** Outrigger canoe **Rev. Designer:** Faraimo Paulo **Edge:** Reeded

Date	Mintage	F	VF	XF	Unc	BU
1982	10,000	—	—	5.00	18.00	22.50

KM# 5a TALA
27.2500 g., 0.9250 Silver .8104 oz. ASW, 38.5 mm. **Ruler:** Elizabeth II **Obv:** Young bust right **Obv. Designer:** Arnold Machin **Rev:** Outrigger canoe **Rev. Designer:** Faraimo Paulo

Date	Mintage	F	VF	XF	Unc	BU
1982 Proof	5,000	Value: 27.50				

KM# 6 TALA
Copper-Nickel, 38.5 mm. **Ruler:** Elizabeth II **Subject:** Water Conservation **Obv:** Young bust right **Obv. Designer:** Arnold Machin **Rev:** Seated and standing figure next to ancient water barrel

Date	Mintage	F	VF	XF	Unc	BU
1983	2,000	—	—	—	30.00	50.00

KM# 7 5 TALA
28.2800 g., 0.9250 Silver .8411 oz. ASW **Ruler:** Elizabeth II **Subject:** Water Conservation **Obv:** Young bust right **Obv. Designer:** Arnold Machin **Rev:** Seated and standing figure next to ancient water barrel **Note:** Similar to 1 Tala, KM#6.

Date	Mintage	F	VF	XF	Unc	BU
1983 Proof	1,000	Value: 65.00				

KM# 8.1 5 TALA
27.0500 g., 0.9250 Silver .8045 oz. ASW **Ruler:** Elizabeth II **Obv:** Young bust right **Obv. Designer:** Arnold Machin **Rev:** Fishermen in sailboat **Rev. Designer:** Faraimo Paulo **Edge:** Plain

Date	Mintage	F	VF	XF	Unc	BU
1984	1,500	—	—	—	35.00	55.00

KM# 8.2 5 TALA
27.0500 g., 0.9250 Silver .8045 oz. ASW **Ruler:** Elizabeth II **Obv:** Young bust right **Obv. Designer:** Arnold Machin **Rev:** Fishermen in sailboat **Rev. Designer:** Faraimo Paulo **Edge:** Reeded

Date	Mintage	F	VF	XF	Unc	BU
1984 Proof	500	Value: 75.00				

KM# 10 5 TALA
27.0500 g., 0.9250 Silver .8045 oz. ASW **Ruler:** Elizabeth II **Series:** Olympics **Obv:** Young bust right **Obv. Designer:** Arnold Machin **Rev:** Javelin thrower

Date	Mintage	F	VF	XF	Unc	BU
1988	20,000	—	—	—	13.50	17.50

KM# 9 5 TALA
27.2100 g., 0.9250 Silver .8093 oz. ASW **Ruler:** Elizabeth II **Obv:** Crowned head right **Obv. Designer:** Raphael Maklouf **Rev:** Captain John Byron and HMS Dolphin **Edge:** Reeded

Date	Mintage	F	VF	XF	Unc	BU
1989 Proof	500	Value: 25.00				

KM# 11 5 TALA
Copper-Nickel **Ruler:** Elizabeth II **Subject:** 50th Anniversary of Attack on Pearl Harbor **Obv:** Crowned bust right **Obv. Designer:** Raphael Maklouf **Rev:** Pearl Harbor scene within circle

Date	Mintage	F	VF	XF	Unc	BU
1991 Prooflike	—	—	—	—	5.00	7.00

KM# 13 5 TALA
Copper-Nickel **Ruler:** Elizabeth II **Obv:** Crowned bust right **Obv. Designer:** Raphael Maklouf **Rev:** Battle of Guadal canal scene within circle

Date	Mintage	F	VF	XF	Unc	BU
1991 Proof-like	—	—	—	—	5.00	7.00

KM# 14 5 TALA
Copper-Nickel **Ruler:** Elizabeth II **Obv:** Crowned bust right **Obv. Designer:** Raphael Maklouf **Rev:** General Dwight Eisenhower saluting left

Date	Mintage	F	VF	XF	Unc	BU
1991 Proof-like	—	—	—	—	5.00	7.00

KM# 15 5 TALA
Copper-Nickel **Ruler:** Elizabeth II **Obv:** Crowned bust right **Obv. Designer:** Raphael Maklouf **Rev:** Raising the flag on Iwo Jima scene

Date	Mintage	F	VF	XF	Unc	BU
1991 Proof-like	—	—	—	—	5.00	7.00

KM# 16 5 TALA
31.4700 g., 0.9250 Silver .9359 oz. ASW **Ruler:** Elizabeth II **Obv:** Crowned head right **Obv. Designer:** Raphael Maklouf **Rev:** Scene of first lunar orbit

Date	Mintage	F	VF	XF	Unc	BU
1993 Proof	10,000	Value: 25.00				

KM# 17 5 TALA
31.4700 g., 0.9250 Silver .9359 oz. ASW **Ruler:** Elizabeth II **Series:** Endangered Wildlife **Obv:** Crowned head right **Obv. Designer:** Raphael Maklouf **Rev:** Iguana

Date	Mintage	F	VF	XF	Unc	BU
1993 Proof	15,000	Value: 27.50				

KM# 18 5 TALA
31.4700 g., 0.9250 Silver .9359 oz. ASW **Ruler:** Elizabeth II **Obv:** Crowned head right **Obv. Designer:** Raphael Maklouf **Rev:** H.M.S. Pandora

Date	Mintage	F	VF	XF	Unc	BU
1993 Proof	15,000	Value: 25.00				

KM# 19 5 TALA
31.4700 g., 0.9250 Silver .9359 oz. ASW **Ruler:** Elizabeth II **Series:** Olympics **Obv:** Crowned head right **Obv. Designer:** Raphael Maklouf **Rev:** Swimmers

Date	Mintage	F	VF	XF	Unc	BU
1994 Proof	40,000	Value: 16.50				

KM# 20 5 TALA
31.4700 g., 0.9250 Silver .9359 oz. ASW **Ruler:** Elizabeth II **Subject:** World Cup Soccer **Obv:** Crowned head right **Obv. Designer:** Raphael Maklouf **Rev:** Soccer player and flying bird within globe design

Date	Mintage	F	VF	XF	Unc	BU
1994 Proof	25,000	Value: 16.50				

KM# 21 5 TALA
31.4700 g., 0.9250 Silver .9359 oz. ASW **Ruler:** Elizabeth II **Series:** Protect Our World **Obv:** Crowned head right **Obv. Designer:** Raphael Maklouf **Rev:** Swamp scene

Date	Mintage	F	VF	XF	Unc	BU
1994 Proof	10,000	Value: 22.50				

KM# 22 5 TALA
31.4700 g., 0.9250 Silver .9359 oz. ASW **Ruler:** Elizabeth II **Series:** Olympics **Obv:** Crowned head right **Obv. Designer:** Raphael Maklouf **Rev:** Sailboarding

Date	Mintage	F	VF	XF	Unc	BU
1994 Proof	50,000	Value: 16.50				

KM# 23 5 TALA
31.4700 g., 0.9250 Silver .9359 oz. ASW **Ruler:** Elizabeth II **Series:** Queen Elizabeth The Queen Mother **Obv:** Crowned head right **Obv. Designer:** Raphael Maklouf **Rev:** Queen Mother, daughter and son

Date	Mintage	F	VF	XF	Unc	BU
1995 Proof	30,000	Value: 16.50				

KM# 27 5 TALA
31.5500 g., 0.9250 Silver 0.9383 oz. ASW, 38.5 mm. **Ruler:** Elizabeth II **Series:** Queen Elizabeth The Queen Mother **Subject:** VE Day Celebrations, 8th of May **Obv:** Crowned head right **Obv. Designer:** Raphael Maklouf **Rev:** 1/2 Figures of royal couple facing within beaded circle **Edge:** Reeded

Date	Mintage	F	VF	XF	Unc	BU
1997 Proof	—	Value: 25.00				

KM# 25 5 TALA
31.4700 g., 0.9250 Silver .9359 oz. ASW, 38.5 mm. **Ruler:** Elizabeth II **Obv:** Crowned head right **Obv. Designer:** Raphael Maklouf **Rev:** H.M.S. Dolphin **Edge:** Reeded

Date	Mintage	F	VF	XF	Unc	BU
1998 Proof	—	Value: 16.50				

KM# 29 5 TALA
31.5200 g., 0.9250 Silver 0.9374 oz. ASW, 38.6 mm. **Ruler:** Elizabeth II **Subject:** Diana Princess Of Wales **Obv:** Crowned head right **Rev:** Diana and young dancers **Edge:** Reeded

Date	Mintage	F	VF	XF	Unc	BU
1999 Proof	—	Value: 35.00				

KM# 26 5 TALA
28.1200 g., 0.9250 Silver 0.8363 oz. ASW, 38.4 mm. **Ruler:** Elizabeth II **Subject:** Queen Mother **Obv:** Crowned head right **Rev:** Queen Mother celebrating "VE" day **Edge:** Reeded

Date	Mintage	F	VF	XF	Unc	BU
2000 Proof	10,000	Value: 17.50				

Note: With gold gilt outer ring

KM# 12 50 TALA
31.1030 g., 0.9990 Silver 1 oz. ASW **Ruler:** Elizabeth II **Subject:** 50th Anniversary of Attack on Pearl Harbor **Obv:** Crowned bust right **Obv. Designer:** Raphael Maklouf **Rev:** Pearl Harbor scene

Date	Mintage	F	VF	XF	Unc	BU
1991 Proof	50,000	Value: 22.50				

KM# 28 50 TALA
31.2500 g., 0.9990 Silver 1.0037 oz. ASW, 38.6 mm. **Ruler:** Elizabeth II **Subject:** Anne Frank **Obv:** Crowned bust right **Obv. Designer:** Raphael Maklouf **Rev:** Building arch and head facing within circle **Edge:** Reeded

Date	Mintage	F	VF	XF	Unc	BU
1993 Proof	—	Value: 20.00				

KM# 24 100 TALA
32.1480 g., 0.9990 Silver 1 oz. ASW, 100 mm. **Ruler:** Elizabeth II **Subject:** Warships; H.M.S. Dolphin, Pandora and General Jackson **Obv:** Crowned head right **Obv. Designer:** Raphael Maklouf **Rev:** Three sailing warships and compass face **Note:** Photo reduced.

Date	Mintage	F	VF	XF	Unc	BU
1996 Proof	1,500	Value: 35.00				

TONGA

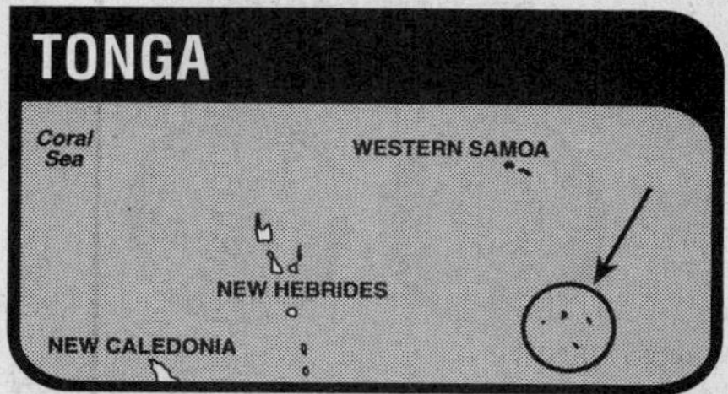

The Kingdom of Tonga (or Friendly Islands) is an archipelago situated in the southern Pacific Ocean south of Western Samoa and east of Fiji comprised of 150 islands. Tonga has an area of 270 sq. mi. (748 sq. km.) and a population of *100,000. Capital: Nuku'alofa. Primarily agricultural, the kingdom exports bananas and copra.

Dutch navigators Willem Schouten and Jacob Lemaire were the first Europeans to visit Tonga in 1616. The noted Dutch explorer Abel Tasman who visited the Tongatapu group in 1643 followed them. No further European contact was made until 1773 when British navigator Capt. James Cook arrived and, impressed by the peaceful deportment of the natives, named the islands the Friendly Islands. Within a few years of Cook's visit, Tonga was embroiled in a civil war that lasted until the great chief Taufa'ahau, who reigned as Siasoi Tupou I (1845-93), was converted to Christianity and brought unity and peace to the islands. Tonga became a self-governing protectorate of Great Britain in 1900 and a fully independent state on June 4, 1970. The monarchy is a member of the Commonwealth of Nations. King Taufa'ahau is Head of State and Government.

RULERS
Queen Salote, 1918-1965
King Taufa'ahau IV, 1967—2006

MONETARY SYSTEM
12 Pence = 1 Shilling
20 Shillings = 1 Pound

KINGDOM

STANDARD COINAGE

16 Pounds = 1 Koula

KM# 1 1/4 KOULA
8.1250 g., 0.9160 Gold .2395 oz. AGW **Ruler:** Queen Salote **Obv:** Head right **Rev:** Crowned arms

Date	Mintage	F	VF	XF	Unc	BU
1962	—	—	—	—	165	—
1962 Proof	6,300	Value: 175				

KM# 1a 1/4 KOULA
Platinum APW **Ruler:** Queen Salote **Obv:** Head right **Rev:** Crowned arms

Date	Mintage	F	VF	XF	Unc	BU
1962 Proof	—	Value: 600				

KM# 2 1/2 KOULA
16.2500 g., 0.9160 Gold .4789 oz. AGW **Ruler:** Queen Salote **Obv:** Crowned arms **Rev:** Standing female half left

Date	Mintage	F	VF	XF	Unc	BU
1962	—	—	—	—	335	—
1962 Proof	3,000	Value: 350				

KM# 2a 1/2 KOULA
Platinum APW **Ruler:** Queen Salote **Obv:** Crowned arms **Rev:** Standing female half left

Date	Mintage	F	VF	XF	Unc	BU
1962 Proof	—	Value: 850				

KM# 3 KOULA
32.5000 g., 0.9160 Gold .9278 oz. AGW **Ruler:** Queen Salote **Obv:** Crowned arms below value **Rev:** Standing figure half left

Date	Mintage	F	VF	XF	Unc	BU
1962	1,500	—	—	—	650	—
1962 Proof	—	Value: 675				

KM# 3a KOULA
Platinum APW **Ruler:** Queen Salote **Obv:** Crowned arms below value **Rev:** Standing figure half left

Date	Mintage	F	VF	XF	Unc	BU
1962 Proof	—	Value: 1,350				

DECIMAL COINAGE

100 Senti = 1 Pa'anga; 100 Pa'anga = 1 Hau

KM# 4 SENITI
1.8500 g., Bronze, 17.5 mm. **Ruler:** King Taufa'ahau IV **Obv:** Head right **Rev:** Giant Tortoise **Edge:** Plain

Date	Mintage	F	VF	XF	Unc	BU
1967	500,000	—	0.10	0.15	1.00	2.00
1967 Proof	—	Value: 2.00				

KM# 27 SENITI
1.8500 g., Bronze, 17.5 mm. **Ruler:** King Taufa'ahau IV **Obv:** Head right **Rev:** Giant tortoise **Edge:** Plain

Date	Mintage	F	VF	XF	Unc	BU
1968	500,000	—	0.10	0.15	1.00	2.00
1968 Proof	—	Value: 2.00				

KM# 27a SENITI
Brass, 17.5 mm. **Ruler:** King Taufa'ahau IV **Obv:** Head right **Rev:** Giant tortoise **Edge:** Plain

Date	Mintage	F	VF	XF	Unc	BU
1974	500,000	—	0.10	0.15	0.75	1.50

KM# 42 SENITI
1.8500 g., Bronze, 17.5 mm. **Ruler:** King Taufa'ahau IV **Series:** F.A.O. **Obv:** Ear of corn **Rev:** Sow right **Edge:** Plain

Date	Mintage	F	VF	XF	Unc	BU
1975	1,000,000	—	—	0.10	0.45	1.00
1979	1,000,000	—	—	0.10	0.45	1.00

KM# 66 SENITI
1.8500 g., Bronze, 17.5 mm. **Ruler:** King Taufa'ahau IV **Series:** World Food Day **Obv:** Ear of corn **Rev:** Vanilla plant **Edge:** Plain

Date	Mintage	F	VF	XF	Unc	BU
1981	1,544,000	—	—	0.10	0.45	0.80
1990	—	—	—	0.10	0.35	0.75
1991	—	—	—	0.10	0.35	0.75
1994	500,000	—	—	0.10	0.35	0.75
1996	—	—	—	0.10	0.35	0.75

KM# 5 2 SENITI
3.9000 g., Bronze, 21 mm. **Ruler:** King Taufa'ahau IV **Obv:** Head right **Rev:** Giant Tortoise **Edge:** Plain

Date	Mintage	F	VF	XF	Unc	BU
1967	500,000	—	0.10	0.20	1.50	2.75
1967 Proof	—	Value: 3.00				

KM# 28 2 SENITI
3.9000 g., Bronze, 21 mm. **Ruler:** King Taufa'ahau IV **Obv:** Head right **Rev:** Giant tortoise **Edge:** Plain

Date	Mintage	F	VF	XF	Unc	BU
1968	200,000	—	0.10	0.20	1.75	2.75
1968 Proof	—	Value: 2.50				
1974	25,000	—	0.10	0.20	1.75	2.75

KM# 43 2 SENITI
3.9000 g., Bronze, 21 mm. **Ruler:** King Taufa'ahau IV **Series:** F.A.O. **Obv:** Two watermelons **Rev:** Paper doll cutouts form design in center circle of wreath **Edge:** Plain

Date	Mintage	F	VF	XF	Unc	BU
1975	400,000	—	—	0.15	0.65	1.50
1979	500,000	—	—	0.15	0.65	1.50

KM# 67 2 SENITI
3.9000 g., Bronze, 21 mm. **Ruler:** King Taufa'ahau IV **Series:** World Food Day **Obv:** Taro Plants **Rev:** Paper doll cutouts form design in center circle of wreath **Edge:** Plain

Date	Mintage	F	VF	XF	Unc	BU
1981	1,102,000	—	—	0.15	0.65	1.35
1990	—	—	—	0.15	0.50	1.25
1991	—	—	—	0.15	0.50	1.25
1994	250,000	—	—	0.15	0.50	1.25
1996	—	—	—	0.15	0.50	1.25

KM# 6 5 SENITI
2.8000 g., Copper-Nickel, 19.5 mm. **Ruler:** King Taufa'ahau IV **Obv:** Head right **Rev:** Value and stars flanked by sprigs **Edge:** Plain

Date	Mintage	F	VF	XF	Unc	BU
1967	300,000	—	0.10	0.25	1.75	2.50
1967 Proof	—	Value: 3.50				

KM# 29 5 SENITI
2.8000 g., Copper-Nickel, 19.5 mm. **Ruler:** King Taufa'ahau IV **Obv:** Head right **Rev:** Value and stars flanked by sprigs

Date	Mintage	F	VF	XF	Unc	BU
1968	100,000	—	0.10	0.25	1.50	2.25
1968 Proof	—	Value: 2.50				
1974	75,000	—	0.10	0.25	1.50	2.25

KM# 44 5 SENITI
2.8000 g., Copper-Nickel, 19.5 mm. **Ruler:** King Taufa'ahau IV **Series:** F.A.O. **Obv:** Hen with chicks **Rev:** Bunch of bananas

Date	Mintage	F	VF	XF	Unc	BU
1975	100,000	—	0.10	0.25	1.00	1.75
1977	110,000	—	0.10	0.25	1.00	1.75
1979	100,000	—	0.10	0.25	1.00	1.75

KM# 68 5 SENITI
2.8000 g., Copper-Nickel, 19.5 mm. **Ruler:** King Taufa'ahau IV **Series:** World Food Day **Obv:** Hen with chicks **Rev:** Coconuts above sprig **Edge:** Reeded

Date	Mintage	F	VF	XF	Unc	BU
1981	941,000	—	0.10	0.25	0.85	1.50
1990	—	—	0.10	0.25	0.85	1.50
1991	—	—	—	0.25	0.85	1.50
1994	200,000	—	0.10	0.25	0.85	1.50
1996	—	—	0.10	0.25	0.75	1.25

KM# 7 10 SENITI
5.6500 g., Copper-Nickel, 23.5 mm. **Ruler:** King Taufa'ahau IV **Obv:** Head right **Rev:** Value and stars flanked by sprigs

Date	Mintage	F	VF	XF	Unc	BU
1967	300,000	—	0.20	0.35	1.85	2.50
1967 Proof	—	Value: 3.50				

KM# 30 10 SENITI
5.6500 g., Copper-Nickel, 23.5 mm. **Ruler:** King Taufa'ahau IV **Obv:** Head right **Rev:** Value and stars flanked by sprigs

Date	Mintage	F	VF	XF	Unc	BU
1968	100,000	—	0.20	0.40	1.75	2.25
1968 Proof	—	Value: 3.00				
1974	50,000	—	0.25	0.50	1.75	2.25

KM# 45 10 SENITI
5.6500 g., Copper-Nickel, 23.5 mm. **Ruler:** King Taufa'ahau IV **Series:** F.A.O. **Obv:** Uniformed bust facing **Rev:** Cows in pasture

Date	Mintage	F	VF	XF	Unc	BU
1975	75,000	—	0.20	0.30	1.25	2.00
1977	25,000	—	0.20	0.30	1.25	2.00
1979	100,000	—	0.20	0.30	1.25	2.00

KM# 69 10 SENITI
5.6500 g., Copper-Nickel, 23.5 mm. **Ruler:** King Taufa'ahau IV **Series:** World Food Day **Obv:** Uniformed bust facing **Rev:** Banana tree **Edge:** Reeded

Date	Mintage	F	VF	XF	Unc	BU
1981	712,000	—	0.20	0.30	1.25	2.00
1990	—	—	0.20	0.30	1.00	1.75
1991	—	—	0.20	0.30	1.00	1.75
1994	140,000	—	0.20	0.30	1.00	1.75
1996	—	—	0.20	0.30	1.00	1.75

KM# 8 20 SENITI
11.3000 g., Copper-Nickel, 28.5 mm. **Ruler:** King Taufa'ahau IV **Obv:** Head right **Rev:** Crowned arms

Date	Mintage	F	VF	XF	Unc	BU
1967	150,000	—	0.25	0.50	2.25	3.50
1967 Proof	—	Value: 4.50				

KM# 13 20 SENITI

11.3000 g., Copper-Nickel, 28.5 mm. **Ruler:** King Taufa'ahau IV **Subject:** Coronation of Taufa'ahau Tupou IV **Obv:** Head right, small crowns around border **Obv. Designer:** Maurice Meers **Rev:** Crowned arms **Rev. Designer:** Ernest Hyde **Edge:** Reeded

Date	Mintage	F	VF	XF	Unc	BU
ND(1967)	15,000	—	0.50	1.25	2.25	3.50
ND(1967) Proof	—	Value: 3.50				

KM# 31 20 SENITI

11.3000 g., Copper-Nickel, 28.5 mm. **Ruler:** King Taufa'ahau IV **Obv:** Head right **Rev:** Crowned arms

Date	Mintage	F	VF	XF	Unc	BU
1968	35,000	—	0.25	0.50	2.00	2.75
1968 Proof	—	Value: 3.00				
1974	50,000	—	0.25	0.50	2.00	2.75

KM# 46 20 SENITI

11.3000 g., Copper-Nickel, 28.5 mm. **Ruler:** King Taufa'ahau IV **Series:** F.A.O. **Obv:** Uniformed bust facing **Rev:** Box hive and 20 bees

Date	Mintage	F	VF	XF	Unc	BU
1975	75,000	—	0.25	0.60	1.50	2.50
1977	25,000	—	0.25	0.60	1.50	2.50
1979	50,000	—	0.25	0.60	1.50	2.50

KM# 70 20 SENITI

11.3000 g., Copper-Nickel, 28.5 mm. **Ruler:** King Taufa'ahau IV **Series:** World Food Day **Obv:** Uniformed bust facing **Rev:** Yams **Edge:** Reeded

Date	Mintage	F	VF	XF	Unc	BU
1981	610,000	—	0.25	0.50	1.50	2.50
1990	610,000	—	0.25	0.50	1.25	2.25
1991	—	—	0.25	0.50	1.25	2.25
1994	680,000	—	0.25	0.50	1.25	2.00
1996	—	—	0.25	0.50	1.25	2.00

KM# 9 50 SENITI

Copper-Nickel, 34.5 mm. **Ruler:** King Taufa'ahau IV **Obv:** Head right **Rev:** Crowned arms

Date	Mintage	F	VF	XF	Unc	BU
1967	75,000	—	0.75	1.25	2.75	4.00
1967 Proof	—	Value: 5.00				

KM# 15 50 SENITI

Copper-Nickel, 34.5 mm. **Ruler:** King Taufa'ahau IV **Subject:** Coronation of Taufa'ahau Tupou IV **Obv:** Head right **Obv. Designer:** Maurice Meers **Rev:** Crowned arms **Rev. Designer:** Ernest Hyde

Date	Mintage	F	VF	XF	Unc	BU
ND(1967)	15,000	—	1.00	1.75	3.00	4.50
ND(1967) Proof	—	Value: 6.00				

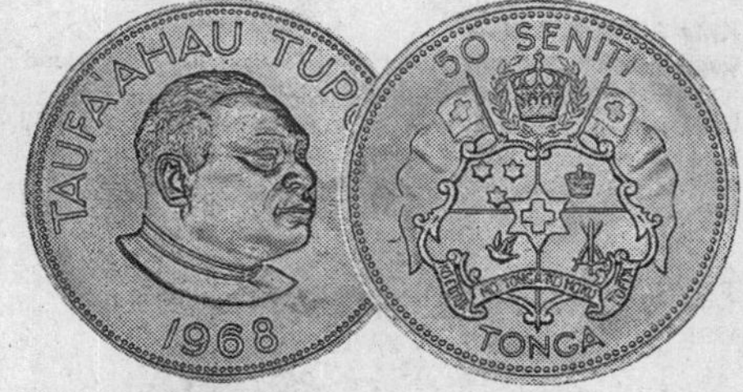

KM# 32 50 SENITI

Copper-Nickel, 34.5 mm. **Ruler:** King Taufa'ahau IV **Obv:** Head right **Rev:** Crowned arms

Date	Mintage	F	VF	XF	Unc	BU
1968	25,000	—	0.75	1.25	2.25	3.50
1968 Proof	—	Value: 4.00				

KM# 41 50 SENITI

14.6000 g., Copper-Nickel, 32.5 mm. **Ruler:** King Taufa'ahau IV **Obv:** Head right **Rev:** Crowned arms **Edge:** Plain **Shape:** 12-sided

Date	Mintage	F	VF	XF	Unc	BU
1974	50,000	—	0.75	1.25	2.00	3.50

KM# 47 50 SENITI

14.6000 g., Copper-Nickel, 32.5 mm. **Ruler:** King Taufa'ahau IV **Series:** F.A.O. **Obv:** Uniformed bust facing **Rev:** 50 Fish swimming in circle formation **Edge:** Plain **Shape:** 12-sided

Date	Mintage	F	VF	XF	Unc	BU
1975	40,000	—	0.50	1.00	2.25	3.00
1977	20,000	—	0.75	1.25	2.75	3.25
1978	60,000	—	0.50	1.00	2.25	3.00

KM# 71 50 SENITI

14.6000 g., Copper-Nickel, 32.5 mm. **Ruler:** King Taufa'ahau IV **Series:** World Food Day **Obv:** Uniformed bust facing **Rev:** Tomatoe plants **Edge:** Plain **Shape:** 12-sided

Date	Mintage	F	VF	XF	Unc	BU
1981	555,000	—	0.45	0.75	1.75	3.00
1990	—	—	0.45	0.75	1.50	3.00
1991	—	—	0.45	0.75	1.50	2.75
1994	41,000	—	0.45	0.75	1.50	2.75
1996	—	—	0.45	0.75	1.50	2.50

KM# 82 50 SENITI

Copper-Nickel, 38.5 mm. **Ruler:** King Taufa'ahau IV **Subject:** 100th Anniversary of Automobile Industry **Obv:** Head right **Rev:** Silver Ghost and Camargue by Rolls-Royce **Edge:** Reeded

Date	Mintage	F	VF	XF	Unc	BU
1985	Est. 20,000	—	—	—	3.50	4.00

KM# 83 50 SENITI

Copper-Nickel, 38.5 mm. **Ruler:** King Taufa'ahau IV **Subject:** 100th Anniversary of Automobile Industry **Obv:** Head right **Rev:** Range Rover and Land Rover **Edge:** Reeded

Date	Mintage	F	VF	XF	Unc	BU
1985	Est. 20,000	—	—	—	3.50	4.00

KM# 84 50 SENITI

Copper-Nickel, 38.5 mm. **Ruler:** King Taufa'ahau IV **Subject:** 100th Anniversary of Automobile Industry **Obv:** Head right **Rev:** Cowley Touring Car and Morris Mini **Edge:** Reeded

Date	Mintage	F	VF	XF	Unc	BU
1985	Est. 20,000	—	—	—	3.50	4.00

KM# 85 50 SENITI

Copper-Nickel, 38.5 mm. **Ruler:** King Taufa'ahau IV **Subject:** 100th Anniversary of Automobile Industry **Obv:** Head right **Rev:** MGB GT and MG TA **Edge:** Reeded

Date	Mintage	F	VF	XF	Unc	BU
1985	Est. 20,000	—	—	—	3.50	4.00

KM# 98 50 SENITI

Copper-Nickel, 38.5 mm. **Ruler:** King Taufa'ahau IV **Subject:** 85th Birthday of Queen Mother **Obv:** Head right **Rev:** Queen Mother as a young girl **Edge:** Reeded

Date	Mintage	F	VF	XF	Unc	BU
1985	Est. 20,000	—	—	—	3.00	3.50

KM# 99 50 SENITI

Copper-Nickel, 38.5 mm. **Ruler:** King Taufa'ahau IV **Subject:** 85th Birthday of Queen Mother **Obv:** Head right **Rev:** Wedding of King George VI and Elizabeth **Edge:** Reeded

Date	Mintage	F	VF	XF	Unc	BU
1985	Est. 20,000	—	—	—	3.00	3.50

KM# 100 50 SENITI

Copper-Nickel, 38.5 mm. **Ruler:** King Taufa'ahau IV **Subject:** 85th Birthday of Queen Mother **Obv:** Head right **Rev:** King George VI and Elizabeth **Edge:** Reeded

Date	Mintage	F	VF	XF	Unc	BU
1985	Est. 20,000	—	—	—	3.00	3.50

KM# 101 50 SENITI

Copper-Nickel, 38.5 mm. **Ruler:** King Taufa'ahau IV **Subject:** 85th Birthday of Queen Mother **Obv:** Head right **Rev:** Queen Mother holding Queen Elizabeth II **Edge:** Reeded

Date	Mintage	F	VF	XF	Unc	BU
1985	Est. 20,000	—	—	—	3.00	3.50

KM# 102 50 SENITI
Copper-Nickel, 38.5 mm. **Ruler:** King Taufa'ahau IV **Subject:** 85th Birthday of Queen Mother **Obv:** Head right **Rev:** Queen Mother facing **Edge:** Reeded

Date	Mintage	F	VF	XF	Unc	BU
1985	Est. 20,000	—	—	—	3.00	3.50

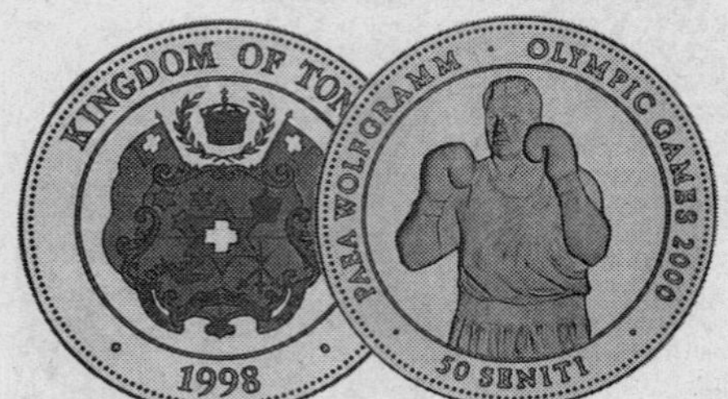

KM# 171 50 SENITI
20.0000 g., 0.9250 Silver .5948 oz. ASW, 34 mm. **Ruler:** King Taufa'ahau IV **Subject:** Olympics **Obv:** Crowned arms within circle **Rev:** Boxer within circle **Edge:** Reeded

Date	Mintage	F	VF	XF	Unc	BU
1998 Proof	50,000	Value: 16.50				

KM# 11 PA'ANGA
Copper-Nickel, 38.5 mm. **Ruler:** King Taufa'ahau IV **Obv:** Head right **Rev:** Crowned arms **Edge:** Reeded

Date	Mintage	F	VF	XF	Unc	BU
1967	78,000	—	1.00	2.00	3.75	5.00
1967 Proof	—	Value: 6.00				

KM# 17 PA'ANGA
Copper-Nickel, 38.5 mm. **Ruler:** King Taufa'ahau IV **Subject:** Coronation of Taufa'ahau Tupou IV **Obv:** Head right, small crowns around border **Obv. Designer:** Maurice Meers **Rev:** Crowned arms **Rev. Designer:** Ernest Hyde **Edge:** Reeded

Date	Mintage	F	VF	XF	Unc	BU
ND(1967)	13,000	—	1.00	2.00	4.00	5.50
ND(1967) Proof	1,923	Value: 6.50				

KM# 33 PA'ANGA
Copper-Nickel, 38.5 mm. **Ruler:** King Taufa'ahau IV **Obv:** Head right **Rev:** Crowned arms **Edge:** Reeded

Date	Mintage	F	VF	XF	Unc	BU
1968	14,000	—	1.00	2.00	4.00	5.50
1968 Proof	—	Value: 6.50				
1974	10,000	—	1.00	2.00	4.00	4.00

KM# 48 PA'ANGA
Copper-Nickel, 38.5 mm. **Ruler:** King Taufa'ahau IV **Series:** F.A.O. **Obv:** Uniformed bust facing **Rev:** 100 Palm trees **Edge:** Reeded

Date	Mintage	F	VF	XF	Unc	BU
1975	13,000	—	1.25	2.50	4.50	6.00

KM# 57 PA'ANGA
Copper-Nickel, 48x27 mm. **Ruler:** King Taufa'ahau IV **Series:** F.A.O **Obv:** Uniformed bust facing **Rev:** 100 Palm trees **Edge:** Plain **Shape:** Rectangular

Date	Mintage	F	VF	XF	Unc	BU
1977	25,000	—	2.00	3.50	7.50	12.50

KM# 58 PA'ANGA
Copper-Nickel, 48x27 mm. **Ruler:** King Taufa'ahau IV **Series:** F.A.O. **Subject:** 60th Birthday **Obv:** Uniformed bust facing flanked by stars and dates **Rev:** 100 Palm trees **Edge:** Plain **Shape:** Rectangular

Date	Mintage	F	VF	XF	Unc	BU
1978	10,000	—	2.00	3.50	7.50	12.50

KM# 58a PA'ANGA
24.5000 g., 0.9990 Silver .7869 oz. ASW, 48x27 mm. **Ruler:** King Taufa'ahau IV **Obv:** Uniformed bust facing flanked by stars and dates **Rev:** 100 Palm trees **Shape:** Rectangular

Date	Mintage	F	VF	XF	Unc	BU
1978 Proof	750	Value: 25.00				

KM# 60 PA'ANGA
Copper-Nickel, 48x27 mm. **Ruler:** King Taufa'ahau IV **Series:** F.A.O. **Subject:** Technical Cooperation Program **Obv:** Uniformed bust facing divides circular inscriptions **Rev:** 100 Palm trees **Shape:** Rectangular

Date	Mintage	F	VF	XF	Unc	BU
1979	26,000	—	1.50	3.00	5.50	8.50

KM# 60a PA'ANGA
24.5000 g., 0.9990 Silver .7869 oz. ASW, 48x27 mm. **Ruler:** King Taufa'ahau IV **Obv:** Uniformed bust facing divides circular inscriptions **Rev:** 100 Palm trees **Shape:** Rectangular

Date	Mintage	F	VF	XF	Unc	BU
1979 Proof	850	Value: 20.00				

KM# 62 PA'ANGA
Copper-Nickel, 48x27 mm. **Ruler:** King Taufa'ahau IV **Series:** F.A.O. **Subject:** Rural Women's Advancement **Obv:** Bust facing **Rev:** Kneeling figure in front of hut and palm trees **Edge:** Plain **Shape:** Rectangular

Date	Mintage	F	VF	XF	Unc	BU
1980	8,000	—	—	2.50	5.50	8.50

KM# 62a PA'ANGA
24.5000 g., 0.9990 Silver .7869 oz. ASW, 48x27 mm. **Ruler:** King Taufa'ahau IV **Subject:** Rural Women's Adnancement **Obv:** Bust facing **Rev:** Kneeling figure in front of hut and palm trees **Rev. Legend:** F.A.O. **Shape:** Rectangular

Date	Mintage	F	VF	XF	Unc	BU
1980 Proof	2,200	Value: 17.50				

KM# 72 PA'ANGA
Copper-Nickel, 48x27 mm. **Ruler:** King Taufa'ahau IV **Series:** World Food Day **Obv:** Uniformed bust facing **Rev:** Sailboat **Edge:** Plain **Shape:** Rectangular

Date	Mintage	F	VF	XF	Unc	BU
1981	485,000	—	—	2.50	5.50	8.50

KM# 72a PA'ANGA
24.5000 g., 0.9990 Silver .7869 oz. ASW, 48x27 mm. **Ruler:** King Taufa'ahau IV **Subject:** World Food Day **Obv:** Uniformed bust facing **Rev:** Sailboat **Shape:** Rectangular

Date	Mintage	F	VF	XF	Unc	BU
1981 Proof	3,500	Value: 17.50				

KM# 77 PA'ANGA
Copper-Nickel, 30 mm. **Ruler:** King Taufa'ahau IV **Subject:** Christmas **Obv:** Head right **Rev:** Praying hands **Edge:** Plain **Shape:** 7-sided

Date	Mintage	F	VF	XF	Unc	BU
1982	5,000	—	—	1.00	3.00	4.00
1982 Proof	—	Value: 5.00				

KM# 77a PA'ANGA
15.5000 g., 0.9250 Silver .4610 oz. ASW, 30 mm. **Ruler:** King Taufa'ahau IV **Subject:** Christmas **Obv:** Head right **Rev:** Praying hands **Shape:** 7-sided

Date	Mintage	F	VF	XF	Unc	BU
1982 Proof	2,500	Value: 8.50				

KM# 77b PA'ANGA
26.0000 g., 0.9170 Gold .7666 oz. AGW, 30 mm. **Ruler:** King Taufa'ahau IV **Subject:** Christmas **Obv:** Head right **Rev:** Praying hands **Shape:** 7-sided

Date	Mintage	F	VF	XF	Unc	BU
1982 Proof	250	Value: 550				

KM# 77c PA'ANGA
30.4000 g., 0.9500 Platinum .9286 oz. APW, 30 mm. **Ruler:** King Taufa'ahau IV **Subject:** Christmas **Obv:** Head right **Rev:** Praying hands **Shape:** 7-sided

Date	Mintage	F	VF	XF	Unc	BU
1982 Proof	25	Value: 1,200				

KM# 80 PA'ANGA

Copper-Nickel, 30 mm. **Ruler:** King Taufa'ahau IV **Subject:** Christmas **Obv:** Head right **Rev:** Kneeling Joseph and Mary **Edge:** Plain **Shape:** 7-sided

Date	Mintage	F	VF	XF	Unc	BU
1983	5,000	—	—	1.00	3.00	4.00

KM# 80a PA'ANGA

15.5000 g., 0.9250 Silver .4610 oz. ASW, 30 mm. **Ruler:** King Taufa'ahau IV **Subject:** Christmas **Obv:** Head right **Rev:** Kneeling Joseph and Mary **Shape:** 7-sided

Date	Mintage	F	VF	XF	Unc	BU
1983 Proof	2,500	Value: 8.50				

KM# 80b PA'ANGA

26.0000 g., 0.9170 Gold .7666 oz. AGW, 30 mm. **Ruler:** King Taufa'ahau IV **Subject:** Christmas **Obv:** Head right **Rev:** Kneeling Joseph and Mary **Shape:** 7-sided

Date	Mintage	F	VF	XF	Unc	BU
1983 Proof	250	Value: 550				

KM# 80c PA'ANGA

30.4000 g., 0.9500 Platinum .9286 oz. APW, 30 mm. **Ruler:** King Taufa'ahau IV **Subject:** Christmas **Obv:** Head right **Rev:** Kneeling Joseph and Mary **Shape:** 7-sided

Date	Mintage	F	VF	XF	Unc	BU
1983 Proof	25	Value: 1,200				

KM# 81 PA'ANGA

Copper-Nickel, 30 mm. **Ruler:** King Taufa'ahau IV **Subject:** Christmas **Obv:** Head right **Rev:** After Bellini's Madonna & Child **Rev. Designer:** Leslie Lindsay **Edge:** Plain **Shape:** 7-sided

Date	Mintage	F	VF	XF	Unc	BU
1984	5,000	—	—	1.00	3.00	4.00

KM# 81a PA'ANGA

15.5000 g., 0.9250 Silver .4610 oz. ASW, 30 mm. **Ruler:** King Taufa'ahau IV **Subject:** Christmas **Obv:** Head right **Rev:** After Bellini's Madonna & Child **Rev. Designer:** Leslie Lindsay **Shape:** 7-sided

Date	Mintage	F	VF	XF	Unc	BU
1984 Proof	2,500	Value: 8.50				

KM# 81b PA'ANGA

26.0000 g., 0.9170 Gold .7666 oz. AGW, 30 mm. **Ruler:** King Taufa'ahau IV **Subject:** Christmas **Obv:** Head right **Rev:** After Bellini's Madonna & Child **Rev. Designer:** Leslie Lindsay **Shape:** 7-sided

Date	Mintage	F	VF	XF	Unc	BU
1984 Proof	250	Value: 550				

KM# 81c PA'ANGA

30.4000 g., 0.9500 Platinum .9286 oz. APW, 30 mm. **Ruler:** King Taufa'ahau IV **Subject:** Christmas **Obv:** Head right **Rev:** After Bellini's Madonna & Child **Rev. Designer:** Leslie Lindsay **Shape:** 7-sided

Date	Mintage	F	VF	XF	Unc	BU
1984 Proof	25	Value: 1,200				

KM# 86 PA'ANGA

Silver Clad Copper-Nickel **Ruler:** King Taufa'ahau IV **Subject:** 100th Anniversary of Automobile Industry **Obv:** Head right **Rev:** Rolls-Royce and Silver Ghost

Date	Mintage	F	VF	XF	Unc	BU
1985 Proof	—	Value: 5.00				

KM# 86a PA'ANGA

28.2800 g., 0.9250 Silver .8411 oz. ASW **Ruler:** King Taufa'ahau IV **Subject:** 100th Anniversary of Automobile Industry **Obv:** Head right **Rev:** Rolls Royce and Silver Ghost

Date	Mintage	F	VF	XF	Unc	BU
1985 Proof	5,000	Value: 22.50				

KM# 87 PA'ANGA

Silver Clad Copper-Nickel **Ruler:** King Taufa'ahau IV **Subject:** 100th Anniversary of Automobile Industry **Obv:** Head right **Rev:** Range Rover and Land Rover

Date	Mintage	F	VF	XF	Unc	BU
1985 Proof	—	Value: 5.00				

KM# 87a PA'ANGA

28.2800 g., 0.9250 Silver .8411 oz. ASW **Ruler:** King Taufa'ahau IV **Subject:** 100th Anniversary of Automobile Industry **Obv:** Head right **Rev:** Range Rover and Land Rover

Date	Mintage	F	VF	XF	Unc	BU
1985 Proof	5,000	Value: 16.50				

KM# 88 PA'ANGA

Silver Clad Copper-Nickel **Ruler:** King Taufa'ahau IV **Subject:** 100th Anniversary of Automobile Industry **Obv:** Head right **Rev:** Mini Morris Cowley and Touring Car

Date	Mintage	F	VF	XF	Unc	BU
1985 Proof	—	Value: 5.00				

KM# 88a PA'ANGA

28.2800 g., 0.9250 Silver .8411 oz. ASW **Ruler:** King Taufa'ahau IV **Subject:** 100th Anniversary of Automobile Industry **Obv:** Head right **Rev:** Mini Morris Cowley and Touring Car

Date	Mintage	F	VF	XF	Unc	BU
1985 Proof	5,000	Value: 16.50				

KM# 89 PA'ANGA

Silver Clad Copper-Nickel **Ruler:** King Taufa'ahau IV **Subject:** 100th Anniversary of Automobile Industry **Obv:** Head right **Rev:** MGB GT and MG TA **Note:** Similar to 50 Seniti, KM#85.

Date	Mintage	F	VF	XF	Unc	BU
1985 Proof	—	Value: 5.00				

KM# 89a PA'ANGA

28.2800 g., 0.9250 Silver .8411 oz. ASW **Ruler:** King Taufa'ahau IV **Subject:** 100th Anniversary of Automobile Industry **Obv:** Head right **Rev:** MGB GT and MG TA

Date	Mintage	F	VF	XF	Unc	BU
1985 Proof	5,000	Value: 16.50				

KM# 103 PA'ANGA

Silver Clad Copper-Nickel **Ruler:** King Taufa'ahau IV **Subject:** 85th Birthday of Queen Mother **Obv:** Head right **Rev:** Queen Mother as a young girl **Note:** Similar to 50 Seniti, KM#98.

Date	Mintage	F	VF	XF	Unc	BU
1985 Proof	—	Value: 4.50				

KM# 103a PA'ANGA

28.2800 g., 0.9250 Silver .8411 oz. ASW **Ruler:** King Taufa'ahau IV **Subject:** 85th Birthday of Queen Mother **Obv:** Head right **Rev:** Queen Mother as a young girl

Date	Mintage	F	VF	XF	Unc	BU
1985 Proof	5,000	Value: 13.50				

KM# 104 PA'ANGA

Silver Clad Copper-Nickel **Ruler:** King Taufa'ahau IV **Subject:** 85th Birthday of Queen mother **Obv:** Head right **Rev:** Wedding of King George VI and Elizabeth **Note:** Similar to 50 Seniti, KM#99.

Date	Mintage	F	VF	XF	Unc	BU
1985 Proof	—	Value: 4.50				

KM# 104a PA'ANGA

28.2800 g., 0.9250 Silver .8411 oz. ASW **Ruler:** King Taufa'ahau IV **Subject:** 85th Birthday of Queen Mother **Obv:** Head right **Rev:** Wedding of King George VI and Elizabeth

Date	Mintage	F	VF	XF	Unc	BU
1985 Proof	5,000	Value: 13.50				

KM# 105 PA'ANGA

Silver Clad Copper-Nickel **Ruler:** King Taufa'ahau IV **Subject:** 85th Birthday of Queen Mother **Obv:** Head right **Rev:** King George VI and Elizabeth **Note:** Similar to 50 Seniti, KM#100.

Date	Mintage	F	VF	XF	Unc	BU
1985 Proof	—	Value: 4.50				

KM# 105a PA'ANGA

28.2800 g., 0.9250 Silver .8411 oz. ASW **Ruler:** King Taufa'ahau IV **Subject:** 85th Birthday of Queen mother **Obv:** Head right **Rev:** King George VI and Elizabeth

Date	Mintage	F	VF	XF	Unc	BU
1985 Proof	5,000	Value: 13.50				

KM# 106 PA'ANGA

Silver Clad Copper-Nickel **Ruler:** King Taufa'ahau IV **Subject:** 85th Birthday of Queen Mother **Obv:** Head right **Rev:** Queen Mother holding Queen Elizabeth II **Note:** Similar to 50 Seniti, KM#101.

Date	Mintage	F	VF	XF	Unc	BU
1985 Proof	—	Value: 4.50				

KM# 106a PA'ANGA

28.2800 g., 0.9250 Silver .8411 oz. ASW **Ruler:** King Taufa'ahau IV **Subject:** 85th Birthday of Queen Mother **Obv:** Head right **Rev:** Queen Mother holding Queen Elizabeth II

Date	Mintage	F	VF	XF	Unc	BU
1985 Proof	5,000	Value: 13.50				

KM# 107 PA'ANGA

Silver Clad Copper-Nickel **Ruler:** King Taufa'ahau IV **Subject:** 85th Birthday of Queen Mother **Obv:** Head right **Rev:** Queen Mother facing **Note:** Similar to 50 Seniti, KM#102.

Date	Mintage	F	VF	XF	Unc	BU
1985 Proof	—	Value: 4.50				

KM# 107a PA'ANGA

28.2800 g., 0.9250 Silver .8411 oz. ASW **Ruler:** King Taufa'ahau IV **Subject:** 85th Birthday of the Queen Mother **Obv:** Head right **Rev:** Queen Mother facing

Date	Mintage	F	VF	XF	Unc	BU
1985 Proof	5,000	Value: 13.50				

KM# 118 PA'ANGA

Copper-Nickel, 30 mm. **Ruler:** King Taufa'ahau IV **Subject:** Christmas **Obv:** Head right **Rev:** Dove with laurel branch **Rev. Designer:** Barry Stanton **Edge:** Plain **Shape:** 7-sided

Date	Mintage	F	VF	XF	Unc	BU
1985	—	—	—	1.00	2.75	4.00

KM# 118a PA'ANGA

15.5000 g., 0.9250 Silver .4610 oz. ASW **Ruler:** King Taufa'ahau IV **Subject:** Christmas **Obv:** Head right **Rev:** Dove with laurel branch **Rev. Designer:** Barry Stanton

Date	Mintage	F	VF	XF	Unc	BU
1985 Proof	250	Value: 17.50				

KM# 118b PA'ANGA

26.0000 g., 0.9170 Gold .7666 oz. AGW **Ruler:** King Taufa'ahau IV **Subject:** Christmas **Obv:** Head right **Rev:** Dove with laurel branch **Rev. Designer:** Barry Stanton

Date	Mintage	F	VF	XF	Unc	BU
1985 Proof	250	Value: 550				

KM# 118c PA'ANGA

30.4000 g., 0.9500 Platinum .9286 oz. APW **Ruler:** King Taufa'ahau IV **Subject:** Christmas **Obv:** Head right **Rev:** Dove with laurel branch **Rev. Designer:** Barry Stanton

Date	Mintage	F	VF	XF	Unc	BU
1985 Proof	—	Value: 1,200				

KM# 123 PA'ANGA

Copper-Nickel **Ruler:** King Taufa'ahau IV **Subject:** Christmas **Obv:** Head right **Rev:** Three Wise Men

Date	Mintage	F	VF	XF	Unc	BU
1986	—	—	—	1.00	2.75	4.00

KM# 123a PA'ANGA

15.5000 g., 0.9250 Silver .4610 oz. ASW **Ruler:** King Taufa'ahau IV **Subject:** Christmas **Obv:** Head right **Rev:** Three Wise Men

Date	Mintage	F	VF	XF	Unc	BU
1986 Proof	—	Value: 16.50				

KM# 123b PA'ANGA

26.0000 g., 0.9170 Gold .7666 oz. AGW **Ruler:** King Taufa'ahau IV **Subject:** Christmas **Obv:** Head right **Rev:** Three Wise Men

Date	Mintage	F	VF	XF	Unc	BU
1986 Proof	—	Value: 550				

KM# 123c PA'ANGA

30.4000 g., 0.9500 Platinum .9286 oz. APW **Ruler:** King Taufa'ahau IV **Subject:** Christmas **Obv:** Head right **Rev:** Three Wise Men

Date	Mintage	F	VF	XF	Unc	BU
1986 Proof	—	Value: 1,200				

KM# 128 PA'ANGA

Copper-Nickel **Ruler:** King Taufa'ahau IV **Series:** 25th Anniversary of World Wildlife Fund **Obv:** Head right **Rev:** Humpback whale cow and calf within circle **Edge:** Reeded

Date	Mintage	F	VF	XF	Unc	BU
1986	—	—	—	—	7.00	12.00

KM# 139 PA'ANGA

Copper-Nickel **Ruler:** King Taufa'ahau IV **Subject:** Christmas **Obv:** Head right **Rev:** Madonna and child

Date	Mintage	F	VF	XF	Unc	BU
1987	—	—	—	—	2.75	4.00
1987 Proof	—	Value: 5.00				

KM# 127 PA'ANGA
Copper-Nickel, 30 mm. **Ruler:** King Taufa'ahau IV **Subject:** Christmas **Obv:** Head right **Rev:** After Albrecht Durer, Madonna and child **Edge:** Plain **Shape:** 7-sided

Date	Mintage	F	VF	XF	Unc	BU
1988	—	—	—	—	2.75	4.00
1988 Proof	—	Value: 5.00				

KM# 127a PA'ANGA
15.5000 g., 0.9250 Silver .4610 oz. ASW **Ruler:** King Taufa'ahau IV **Subject:** Christmas **Obv:** Head right **Rev:** After Albrecht Durer, Madonna and child

Date	Mintage	F	VF	XF	Unc	BU
1988 Proof	—	Value: 16.50				

KM# 127b PA'ANGA
26.0000 g., 0.9170 Gold .7666 oz. AGW **Ruler:** King Taufa'ahau IV **Subject:** Christmas **Obv:** Head right **Rev:** After Albrecht Durer, Madonna and child

Date	Mintage	F	VF	XF	Unc	BU
1988 Proof	—	Value: 550				

KM# 127c PA'ANGA
30.4000 g., 0.9500 Platinum .9286 oz. APW **Ruler:** King Taufa'ahau IV **Subject:** Christmas **Obv:** Head right **Rev:** After Albrecht Durer, Madonna and child

Date	Mintage	F	VF	XF	Unc	BU
1988 Proof	—	Value: 1,200				

KM# 133 PA'ANGA
31.7300 g., 0.9250 Silver .9437 oz. ASW **Ruler:** King Taufa'ahau IV **Series:** Olympics **Obv:** Head right **Rev:** Javelin thrower within circle

Date	Mintage	F	VF	XF	Unc	BU
1988 Proof	—	Value: 16.50				

KM# 134 PA'ANGA
31.7300 g., 0.9250 Silver .9437 oz. ASW **Ruler:** King Taufa'ahau IV **Series:** Olympics **Obv:** Head right **Rev:** Swimmers within circle

Date	Mintage	F	VF	XF	Unc	BU
1988 Proof	—	Value: 16.50				

KM# 135 PA'ANGA
31.7300 g., 0.9250 Silver .9437 oz. ASW **Ruler:** King Taufa'ahau IV **Series:** Olympics **Obv:** Head right **Rev:** Boxers

Date	Mintage	F	VF	XF	Unc	BU
1988 Proof	—	Value: 16.50				

KM# 136 PA'ANGA
31.7300 g., 0.9250 Silver .9437 oz. ASW **Ruler:** King Taufa'ahau IV **Series:** Olympics **Obv:** Head right **Rev:** Discus thrower within circle

Date	Mintage	F	VF	XF	Unc	BU
1988 Proof	—	Value: 16.50				

KM# 137 PA'ANGA
31.7300 g., 0.9250 Silver .9437 oz. ASW **Ruler:** King Taufa'ahau IV **Series:** Olympics **Obv:** Head right **Rev:** Shotput thrower

Date	Mintage	F	VF	XF	Unc	BU
1988 Proof	—	Value: 16.50				

KM# 138 PA'ANGA
31.7300 g., 0.9250 Silver .9437 oz. ASW **Ruler:** King Taufa'ahau IV **Series:** Olympics **Obv:** Head right **Rev:** Runners within circle

Date	Mintage	F	VF	XF	Unc	BU
1988 Proof	—	Value: 16.50				

KM# 145 PA'ANGA
31.7300 g., 0.9250 Silver .9437 oz. ASW **Ruler:** King Taufa'ahau IV **Series:** Olympics **Obv:** Head right **Rev:** Bicycling within circle

Date	Mintage	F	VF	XF	Unc	BU
1988 Proof	—	Value: 16.50				

KM# 146 PA'ANGA
31.7300 g., 0.9250 Silver .9437 oz. ASW **Ruler:** King Taufa'ahau IV **Series:** Olympics **Obv:** Head right **Rev:** Gymnast on rings within circle

Date	Mintage	F	VF	XF	Unc	BU
1988 Proof	—	Value: 16.50				

KM# 147 PA'ANGA
31.7300 g., 0.9250 Silver .9437 oz. ASW **Ruler:** King Taufa'ahau IV **Series:** Olympics **Obv:** Head right **Rev:** Diver

Date	Mintage	F	VF	XF	Unc	BU
1988 Proof	—	Value: 22.50				

KM# 148 PA'ANGA
31.7300 g., 0.9250 Silver .9437 oz. ASW **Ruler:** King Taufa'ahau IV **Series:** Olympics **Obv:** Head right **Rev:** Judo

Date	Mintage	F	VF	XF	Unc	BU
1988 Proof	—	Value: 16.50				

KM# 149 PA'ANGA
31.7300 g., 0.9250 Silver .9437 oz. ASW **Ruler:** King Taufa'ahau IV **Series:** Olympics **Obv:** Head right **Rev:** Broad jumper

Date	Mintage	F	VF	XF	Unc	BU
1988 Proof	—	Value: 16.50				

KM# 150 PA'ANGA
31.7300 g., 0.9250 Silver .9437 oz. ASW **Ruler:** King Taufa'ahau IV **Series:** Olympics **Obv:** Head right **Rev:** Weight lifter

Date	Mintage	F	VF	XF	Unc	BU
1988 Proof	—	Value: 16.50				

KM# 175 PA'ANGA
31.8000 g., 0.9250 Silver .9457 oz. ASW **Ruler:** King Taufa'ahau IV **Subject:** 25th Anniversary of Reign **Obv:** Crowned arms **Rev:** Radiant sun rising through stone structure

Date	Mintage	F	VF	XF	Unc	BU
ND(1990) Proof	—	Value: 20.00				

KM# 140 PA'ANGA
31.6000 g., 0.9250 Silver .9398 oz. ASW **Ruler:** King Taufa'ahau IV **Series:** Olympics **Obv:** National arms **Rev:** Diver

Date	Mintage	F	VF	XF	Unc	BU
1991 Proof	Est. 40,000	Value: 14.50				

KM# 141 PA'ANGA
31.6000 g., 0.9250 Silver .9398 oz. ASW **Ruler:** King Taufa'ahau IV **Subject:** Explorers **Rev:** William Schouten and Jakob LeMaire and ship

Date	Mintage	F	VF	XF	Unc	BU
1991 Proof	Est. 10,000	Value: 15.00				

KM# 143 PA'ANGA
31.6000 g., 0.9250 Silver .9398 oz. ASW **Ruler:** King Taufa'ahau IV **Subject:** Endangered Wildlife **Rev:** Pritchard's Megapode Birds

Date	Mintage	F	VF	XF	Unc	BU
1991 Proof	—	Value: 17.50				

KM# 156 PA'ANGA
31.6000 g., 0.9250 Silver .9398 oz. ASW **Ruler:** King Taufa'ahau IV **Series:** 1996 Olympics **Obv:** National arms **Rev:** Sailing

Date	Mintage	F	VF	XF	Unc	BU
1992 Proof	40,000	Value: 14.50				

KM# 157 PA'ANGA
31.6000 g., 0.9250 Silver .9398 oz. ASW **Ruler:** King Taufa'ahau IV **Subject:** Soccer **Rev:** Players

Date	Mintage	F	VF	XF	Unc	BU
1992 Proof	10,000	Value: 15.00				

KM# 158 PA'ANGA
31.6000 g., 0.9250 Silver .9398 oz. ASW **Ruler:** King Taufa'ahau IV **Subject:** Space Flight **Obv:** National arms within circle **Rev:** Saturn V on launchpad at right, US map at left

Date	Mintage	F	VF	XF	Unc	BU
1992 Proof	10,000	Value: 15.00				

KM# 168 PA'ANGA
31.6000 g., 0.9250 Silver .9398 oz. ASW **Ruler:** King Taufa'ahau IV **Subject:** 25th Anniversary - Coronation of Tupou IV **Obv:** National arms within circle **Rev:** Coronation scene

Date	Mintage	F	VF	XF	Unc	BU
1992 Proof	Est. 5,000	Value: 16.50				

KM# 144 PA'ANGA
31.4700 g., 0.9250 Silver .9359 oz. ASW **Ruler:** King Taufa'ahau IV **Subject:** 40th Anniversary of Queen Elizabeth's Coronation **Obv:** National arms within circle **Rev:** Symbols of royalty

Date	Mintage	F	VF	XF	Unc	BU
1993 Proof	Est. 10,000	Value: 14.50				

KM# 151 PA'ANGA
31.4700 g., 0.9250 Silver .9359 oz. ASW **Ruler:** King Taufa'ahau IV **Subject:** Hermann Oberth 1894-1989 **Obv:** Crowned arms within circle **Rev:** Bust facing left to right of standing figures and rockets

Date	Mintage	F	VF	XF	Unc	BU
1993 Proof	Est. 10,000	Value: 15.00				

KM# 152 PA'ANGA
31.4700 g., 0.9250 Silver .9359 oz. ASW **Ruler:** King Taufa'ahau IV **Subject:** Johannes Gutenberg 1400-1468 **Obv:** Crowned arms within circle **Rev:** Half-length bust at left, stack of printed pages and press at right

Date	Mintage	F	VF	XF	Unc	BU
1993 Proof	Est. 10,000	Value: 15.00				

KM# 153 PA'ANGA
31.4700 g., 0.9250 Silver .9359 oz. ASW **Ruler:** King Taufa'ahau IV **Subject:** Protect Our World **Obv:** Crowned arms within circle **Rev:** Alexander von Humboldt

Date	Mintage	F	VF	XF	Unc	BU
1993 Proof	Est. 10,000	Value: 15.00				

KM# 154 PA'ANGA
31.4700 g., 0.9250 Silver .9359 oz. ASW **Ruler:** King Taufa'ahau IV **Obv:** Crowned arms within circle **Rev:** Sailing ship - "La Princesa"

Date	Mintage	F	VF	XF	Unc	BU
1993 Proof	Est. 15,000	Value: 15.00				
1994 Proof	—	Value: 15.00				

KM# 160 PA'ANGA
31.4700 g., 0.9250 Silver .9359 oz. ASW **Ruler:** King Taufa'ahau IV **Subject:** Richard Wagner **Obv:** Crowned arms within circle **Rev:** Bust at right, dancers at upper left

Date	Mintage	F	VF	XF	Unc	BU
1993 Proof	Est. 10,000	Value: 15.00				

KM# 169 PA'ANGA
31.4700 g., 0.9250 Silver .9359 oz. ASW **Ruler:** King Taufa'ahau IV **Subject:** 75th Birthday, July 4, 1993 **Obv:** Uniformed bust facing **Rev:** Siu'a'alo rowers

Date	Mintage	F	VF	XF	Unc	BU
1993 Proof	Est. 2,000	Value: 18.00				

KM# 159.1 PA'ANGA
31.5500 g., 0.9250 Silver .9383 oz. ASW **Ruler:** King Taufa'ahau IV **Series:** 1996 Olympics **Obv:** Crowned arms within circle **Rev:** Javelin thrower within circle **Note:** Prev. KM#159.

Date	Mintage	F	VF	XF	Unc	BU
1994 Proof	40,000	Value: 14.50				

KM# 159.2 PA'ANGA

31.4700 g., 0.9250 Silver 0.9359 oz. ASW, 38.7 mm. **Ruler:** King Taufa'ahau IV **Subject:** Olympics **Obv:** Crowned arms within circle **Rev:** Javelin thrower within circle **Edge:** Reeded **Note:** Smaller letters in legend than the KM-159.1 version

Date	Mintage	F	VF	XF	Unc	BU
1994 Proof	—	Value: 30.00				

KM# 161 PA'ANGA

31.4700 g., 0.9250 Silver .9359 oz. ASW **Ruler:** King Taufa'ahau IV **Subject:** World Cup Soccer **Obv:** Crowned arms within circle **Rev:** Two soccer players

Date	Mintage	F	VF	XF	Unc	BU
1994 Proof	Est. 10,000	Value: 16.50				

KM# 162 PA'ANGA

31.4700 g., 0.9250 Silver .9359 oz. ASW **Ruler:** King Taufa'ahau IV **Series:** Endangered Wildlife **Obv:** Crowned arms within circle **Rev:** Humpback whale cow and calf

Date	Mintage	F	VF	XF	Unc	BU
1994 Proof	Est. 10,000	Value: 30.00				

KM# 166 PA'ANGA

31.4700 g., 0.9250 Silver .9359 oz. ASW **Ruler:** King Taufa'ahau IV **Series:** Queen Elizabeth The Queen Mother **Obv:** Crowned arms within circle **Rev:** Crown within beaded circle

Date	Mintage	F	VF	XF	Unc	BU
1996	Est. 40,000	—	—	—	15.00	—

KM# 170 PA'ANGA

31.4700 g., 0.9250 Silver .9359 oz. ASW **Ruler:** King Taufa'ahau IV **Subject:** 70th Birthday - Queen Mata'aho, May 25, 1996 **Obv:** National arms within circle **Rev:** Crown above bust of Queen Mata'aho facing within wreath

Date	Mintage	F	VF	XF	Unc	BU
1996 Proof	Est. 5,000	Value: 16.50				

KM# 177 PA'ANGA

31.4100 g., 0.9250 Silver 0.9341 oz. ASW, 38.6 mm. **Ruler:** King Taufa'ahau IV **Series:** Queen Elizabeth The Queen Mother **Subject:** The Coronation of Elizabeth **Obv:** Crowned arms within circle **Rev:** Queen seated on throne within beaded circle **Edge:** Reeded

Date	Mintage	F	VF	XF	Unc	BU
1996 Proof	—	Value: 22.50				

KM# 174 PA'ANGA

31.4700 g., 0.9250 Silver .9359 oz. ASW **Ruler:** King Taufa'ahau IV **Obv:** National arms within circle **Rev:** Polynesian sailing catamaran

Date	Mintage	F	VF	XF	Unc	BU
1998 Proof	20,000	Value: 16.00				

KM# 176 PA'ANGA

31.1100 g., 0.9250 Silver .9252 oz. ASW, 35.5 mm. **Ruler:** King Taufa'ahau IV **Subject:** Millennium 2000 **Obv:** Crowned arms within circle and beaded border **Rev:** Stone archway **Edge:** Reeded **Shape:** Scalloped

Date	Mintage	F	VF	XF	Unc	BU
1999 Proof	—	Value: 35.00				

KM# 19 2 PA'ANGA

Copper-Nickel, 44.5 mm. **Ruler:** King Taufa'ahau IV **Subject:** Coronation of Taufa'ahau Tupou IV **Obv:** Head right **Obv. Designer:** Maurice Meers **Rev:** National arms **Rev. Designer:** Ernest Hyde

Date	Mintage	F	VF	XF	Unc	BU
ND(1967)	10,000	—	1.25	2.75	5.50	6.50
ND(1967) Proof	—	Value: 10.00				

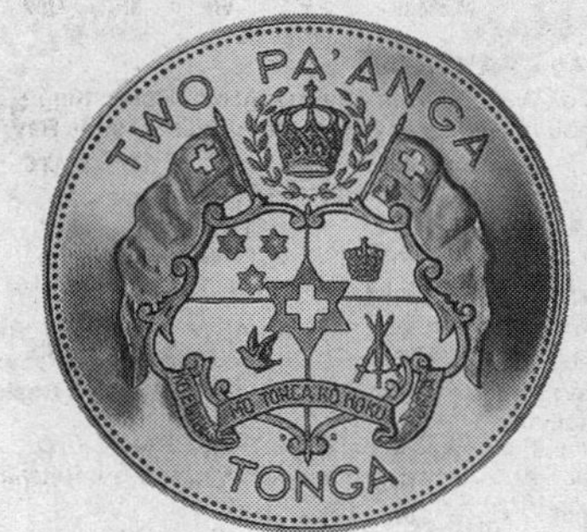

KM# 37 2 PA'ANGA

Copper-Nickel, 44.5 mm. **Ruler:** King Taufa'ahau IV **Obv:** Head right **Rev:** National arms **Edge:** Reeded

Date	Mintage	F	VF	XF	Unc	BU
1968	14,000	—	1.25	2.25	5.00	6.00
1968 Proof	—	Value: 8.00				
1974	10,000	—	1.25	3.00	5.50	6.50

KM# 49 2 PA'ANGA

Copper-Nickel, 44.5 mm. **Ruler:** King Taufa'ahau IV **Series:** F.A.O. **Obv:** Uniformed bust facing **Rev:** Palm tree in center of assorted animals, grains and fruit **Edge:** Reeded

Date	Mintage	F	VF	XF	Unc	BU
1975	13,000	—	1.25	2.75	5.50	6.50
1977	12,000	—	1.25	2.75	5.50	6.50

KM# 59 2 PA'ANGA

Copper-Nickel, 44.5 mm. **Ruler:** King Taufa'ahau IV **Series:** F.A.O. **Subject:** 60th Birthday **Obv:** Uniformed bust facing **Rev:** Palm tree in center of assorted animals and grains **Edge:** Reeded

Date	Mintage	F	VF	XF	Unc	BU
1978	10,000	—	1.25	2.75	5.50	6.50

KM# 59a 2 PA'ANGA

42.1000 g., 0.9990 Silver 1.3523 oz. ASW, 44.5 mm. **Ruler:** King Taufa'ahau IV **Series:** F.A.O. **Subject:** 60th Birthday **Obv:** Uniformed bust facing **Rev:** Palm tree in center of assorted animals and grains

Date	Mintage	F	VF	XF	Unc	BU
1978 Proof	750	Value: 25.00				

KM# 61 2 PA'ANGA

Copper-Nickel, 44.5 mm. **Ruler:** King Taufa'ahau IV **Series:** F.A.O. **Subject:** SEA Resource Management **Obv:** Uniformed bust facing **Rev:** Humpback whale - bull in breach **Edge:** Reeded

Date	Mintage	F	VF	XF	Unc	BU
1979	8,000	—	—	3.00	7.00	9.00

KM# 61a 2 PA'ANGA

42.1000 g., 0.9990 Silver 1.3523 oz. ASW, 44.5 mm. **Ruler:** King Taufa'ahau IV **Series:** F.A.O. **Subject:** SEA Resource Management **Obv:** Uniformed bust facing **Rev:** Humpback whale - bull in breach

Date	Mintage	F	VF	XF	Unc	BU
1979 Proof	850	Value: 25.00				

KM# 63 2 PA'ANGA

Copper-Nickel, 44.5 mm. **Ruler:** King Taufa'ahau IV **Series:** F.A.O. **Subject:** SEA Resource Management **Obv:** Uniformed bust facing **Rev:** Humpback whale - bull in breach **Edge:** Reeded

Date	Mintage	F	VF	XF	Unc	BU
1980	8,000	—	—	3.00	7.00	9.00

KM# 63a 2 PA'ANGA

42.1000 g., 0.9990 Silver 1.3523 oz. ASW, 44.5 mm. **Ruler:** King Taufa'ahau IV **Series:** F.A.O. **Subject:** SEA Resource Management **Obv:** Uniformed bust facing **Rev:** Humpback whale - bull in breach

Date	Mintage	F	VF	XF	Unc	BU
1980 Proof	2,200	Value: 22.50				

KM# 73 2 PA'ANGA

Copper-Nickel, 44.5 mm. **Ruler:** King Taufa'ahau IV **Series:** World Food Day **Obv:** Uniformed bust facing **Rev:** Pigs, chickens and nursing calf, logo at top **Edge:** Reeded

Date	Mintage	F	VF	XF	Unc	BU
1981	485,000	—	—	1.75	4.50	7.50

KM# 73a 2 PA'ANGA

42.1000 g., 0.9990 Silver 1.3523 oz. ASW, 44.5 mm. **Ruler:** King Taufa'ahau IV **Series:** World Food Day **Obv:** Uniformed bust facing **Rev:** Chickens, pig and nursing calf, logo at top

Date	Mintage	F	VF	XF	Unc	BU
1981 Proof	3,500	Value: 24.00				

KM# 120 2 PA'ANGA

28.2800 g., 0.5000 Silver .4546 oz. ASW, 38.61 mm. **Ruler:** King Taufa'ahau IV **Subject:** Commonwealth Games **Obv:** Head right **Rev:** Boxing match

Date	Mintage	F	VF	XF	Unc	BU
1986	50,000	—	—	BV	8.50	—

KM# 120a 2 PA'ANGA
28.2800 g., 0.9250 Silver .8411 oz. ASW, 38.61 mm. **Ruler:** King Taufa'ahau IV **Subject:** Commonwealth Games **Obv:** Head right **Rev:** Boxing match

Date	Mintage	F	VF	XF	Unc	BU
1986 Proof	20,000	Value: 16.50				

KM# 121 2 PA'ANGA
28.2800 g., 0.9250 Silver .8411 oz. ASW, 38.61 mm. **Ruler:** King Taufa'ahau IV **Subject:** Wildlife **Obv:** Uniformed bust facing **Rev:** Humpback whales - cow and calf within circle

Date	Mintage	F	VF	XF	Unc	BU
1986 Proof	25,000	Value: 27.50				

KM# 124 2 PA'ANGA
155.5200 g., 0.9990 Silver 5.0000 oz. ASW, 65 mm. **Ruler:** King Taufa'ahau IV **Subject:** America's Cup **Rev:** Sailing ship in front of map within circle **Note:** Photo reduced.

Date	Mintage	F	VF	XF	Unc	BU
1987 Proof	7,500	Value: 80.00				

KM# 129 2 PA'ANGA
155.5200 g., 0.9990 Silver 5.0000 oz. ASW, 65 mm. **Ruler:** King Taufa'ahau IV **Series:** Olympics **Obv:** Head right **Rev:** Swimmers within circle **Note:** Photo reduced.

Date	Mintage	F	VF	XF	Unc	BU
1988 Proof	2,000	Value: 85.00				

KM# 50 5 PA'ANGA
31.0000 g., 0.9990 Silver .9957 oz. ASW **Ruler:** King Taufa'ahau IV **Subject:** Constitution Centennial **Obv:** Uniformed bust left above open scroll **Rev:** Crowned arms **Designer:** Norman Sillman

Date	Mintage	F	VF	XF	Unc	BU
ND(1975)	2,118	—	—	—	15.00	16.50
ND(1975) Proof	418	Value: 22.50				

KM# 51 10 PA'ANGA
62.0000 g., 0.9990 Silver 1.9915 oz. ASW **Ruler:** King Taufa'ahau IV **Subject:** Constitution Centennial **Obv:** Uniformed bust left above stone arch **Rev:** Crowned arms **Designer:** Norman Sillman

Date	Mintage	F	VF	XF	Unc	BU
ND(1975)	1,116	—	—	—	30.00	32.00
ND(1975) Proof	420	Value: 35.00				

KM# 64 10 PA'ANGA
4.0000 g., 0.9170 Gold .0117 oz. AGW **Ruler:** King Taufa'ahau IV **Series:** F.A.O. **Subject:** Rural Women's Advancement **Obv:** Queen Salote **Rev:** Female symbol on dove

Date	Mintage	F	VF	XF	Unc	BU
1980	750	—	—	—	12.50	16.00
1980 Proof	2,000	Value: 18.50				

KM# 78 10 PA'ANGA
28.2800 g., 0.9250 Silver .8411 oz. ASW, 38.61 mm. **Ruler:** King Taufa'ahau IV **Subject:** Commonwealth Games **Obv:** Head right **Rev:** Two runners at finish line **Edge:** Reeded **Designer:** Philip Nathan

Date	Mintage	F	VF	XF	Unc	BU
1982	500	—	—	—	12.50	16.50
1982 Proof	1,000	Value: 20.00				

KM# 90 10 PA'ANGA
5.1000 g., 0.3750 Gold .0615 oz. AGW **Ruler:** King Taufa'ahau IV **Subject:** 100th Anniversary of Automobile Industry **Obv:** Head right **Rev:** Rolls Royce and Silver Ghost **Note:** Similar to 50 Seniti, KM#82

Date	Mintage	F	VF	XF	Unc	BU
1985 Proof	1,000	Value: 45.00				

KM# 90a 10 PA'ANGA
7.9600 g., 0.9170 Gold .2347 oz. AGW **Ruler:** King Taufa'ahau IV **Subject:** 100th Anniversary of Automobile Industry **Obv:** Head right **Rev:** Rolls Royce and Silver Ghost

Date	Mintage	F	VF	XF	Unc	BU
1985 Proof	500	Value: 165				

KM# 91 10 PA'ANGA
5.1000 g., 0.3750 Gold .0615 oz. AGW **Ruler:** King Taufa'ahau IV **Subject:** 100th Anniversary of Automobile Industry **Obv:** Head right **Rev:** Range Rover and Land Rover **Note:** Similar to 50 Seniti, KM#83.2

Date	Mintage	F	VF	XF	Unc	BU
1985 Proof	1,000	Value: 45.00				

KM# 91a 10 PA'ANGA
7.9600 g., 0.9170 Gold .2347 oz. AGW **Ruler:** King Taufa'ahau IV **Subject:** 100th Anniversary of Automobile Industry **Obv:** Head right **Rev:** Range Rover and Land Rover

Date	Mintage	F	VF	XF	Unc	BU
1985 Proof	500	Value: 165				

KM# 92 10 PA'ANGA
5.1000 g., 0.3750 Gold .0615 oz. AGW **Ruler:** King Taufa'ahau IV **Subject:** 100th Anniversary of Automobile Industry **Obv:** Head right **Rev:** Mini Morris Cowley and Touring Car **Note:** Similar to 50 Seniti, KM#84.

Date	Mintage	F	VF	XF	Unc	BU
1985 Proof	1,000	Value: 45.00				

KM# 92a 10 PA'ANGA
7.9600 g., 0.9170 Gold .2347 oz. AGW **Ruler:** King Taufa'ahau IV **Subject:** 100th Anniversary of Automobile Industry **Obv:** Head right **Rev:** Mini Morris Cowley and Touring Car

Date	Mintage	F	VF	XF	Unc	BU
1985 Proof	500	Value: 165				

KM# 93 10 PA'ANGA
5.1000 g., 0.3750 Gold .0615 oz. AGW **Ruler:** King aufa'ahau IV **Subject:** 100th Anniversary of Automobile Industry **Obv:** Head right **Rev:** MGB GT and MG TA **Note:** Similar to 50 Seniti, KM#85.

Date	Mintage	F	VF	XF	Unc	BU
1985 Proof	1,000	Value: 45.00				

KM# 93a 10 PA'ANGA
7.9600 g., 0.9170 Gold .2347 oz. AGW **Ruler:** King Taufa'ahau IV **Subject:** 100th Anniversary of Automobile Industry **Obv:** Head right **Rev:** MGB GT and MG TA

Date	Mintage	F	VF	XF	Unc	BU
1985 Proof	500	Value: 165				

KM# 108 10 PA'ANGA
5.1000 g., 0.3750 Gold .0615 oz. AGW **Ruler:** King Taufa'ahau IV **Subject:** 85th Birthday of Queen Mother **Obv:** Head right **Rev:** Queen Mother as a young girl **Note:** Similar to 50 Seniti, KM#98.

Date	Mintage	F	VF	XF	Unc	BU
1985 Proof	1,000	Value: 45.00				

KM# 108a 10 PA'ANGA
7.9600 g., 0.9170 Gold .2347 oz. AGW **Ruler:** King Taufa'ahau IV **Subject:** 85th Birthday of Queen Mother **Obv:** Head right **Rev:** Queen Mother as a young girl

Date	Mintage	F	VF	XF	Unc	BU
1985 Proof	500	Value: 165				

KM# 109 10 PA'ANGA
5.1000 g., 0.3750 Gold .0615 oz. AGW **Ruler:** King Taufa'ahau IV **Subject:** 85th Birthday of Queen Mother **Obv:** Head right **Rev:** Wedding of King George VI and Elizabeth **Note:** Similar to 50 Seniti, KM#99.

Date	Mintage	F	VF	XF	Unc	BU
1985 Proof	1,000	Value: 45.00				

KM# 109a 10 PA'ANGA
7.9600 g., 0.9170 Gold .2347 oz. AGW **Ruler:** King Taufa'ahau IV **Subject:** 85th Birthday of Queen Mother **Obv:** Head right **Rev:** Wedding of King George VI and Elizabeth

Date	Mintage	F	VF	XF	Unc	BU
1985 Proof	500	Value: 165				

KM# 110 10 PA'ANGA
5.1000 g., 0.3750 Gold .0615 oz. AGW **Ruler:** King Taufa'ahau IV **Subject:** 85th Birthday of Queen Mother **Obv:** Head right **Rev:** King George VI and Elizabeth **Note:** Similar to 50 Seniti, KM#100.

Date	Mintage	F	VF	XF	Unc	BU
1985 Proof	1,000	Value: 45.00				

KM# 110a 10 PA'ANGA
7.9600 g., 0.9170 Gold .2347 oz. AGW **Ruler:** King Taufa'ahau IV **Subject:** 85th Birthday of Queen Mother **Obv:** Head right **Rev:** King George VI and Elizabeth

Date	Mintage	F	VF	XF	Unc	BU
1985 Proof	500	Value: 165				

KM# 111 10 PA'ANGA
5.1000 g., 0.3750 Gold .0615 oz. AGW **Ruler:** King Taufa'ahau IV **Subject:** 85th Birthday of Queen Mother **Obv:** Head right **Rev:** Queen Mother holding Queen Elizabeth II **Note:** Similar to 50 Seniti, KM#101.

Date	Mintage	F	VF	XF	Unc	BU
1985 Proof	1,000	Value: 45.00				

KM# 111a 10 PA'ANGA
7.9600 g., 0.9170 Gold .2347 oz. AGW **Ruler:** King Taufa'ahau IV **Subject:** 85th Birthday of Queen Mother **Obv:** Head right **Rev:** Queen Mother holding Queen Elizabeth II

Date	Mintage	F	VF	XF	Unc	BU
1985 Proof	500	Value: 165				

KM# 112 10 PA'ANGA
5.1000 g., 0.3750 Gold .0615 oz. AGW **Ruler:** King Taufa'ahau IV **Subject:** 85th Birthday of Queen Mother **Obv:** Head right **Rev:** Queen Mother facing **Note:** Similar to 50 Seniti, KM#102.

Date	Mintage	F	VF	XF	Unc	BU
1985 Proof	1,000	Value: 45.00				

KM# 112a 10 PA'ANGA
7.9600 g., 0.9170 Gold .2347 oz. AGW **Ruler:** King Taufa'ahau IV **Subject:** 85th Birthday of Queen Mother **Obv:** Head right **Rev:** Queen Mother facing

Date	Mintage	F	VF	XF	Unc	BU
1985 Proof	500	Value: 165				

KM# 126 10 PA'ANGA
Copper-Nickel **Ruler:** King Taufa'ahau IV **Subject:** America's Cup **Obv:** Head right **Rev:** National flags and sailboat

Date	Mintage	F	VF	XF	Unc	BU
1987	—	—	—	—	5.00	6.00

KM# 126a 10 PA'ANGA
31.1030 g., 0.9990 Palladium 1.0000 oz. **Ruler:** King Taufa'ahau IV **Subject:** America's Cup **Obv:** Head right **Rev:** National flags and sailboat

Date	Mintage	F	VF	XF	Unc	BU
1987 Proof	25,000	Value: 365				

KM# 125 10 PA'ANGA
311.0400 g., 0.9990 Silver 10.0000 oz. ASW, 75 mm. **Ruler:** King Taufa'ahau IV **Subject:** America's Cup **Obv:** Head right **Rev:** Sailboat and map **Note:** Photo reduced.

Date	Mintage	F	VF	XF	Unc	BU
1987 Proof	5,000	Value: 160				

KM# 130 10 PA'ANGA
15.5500 g., 0.9990 Gold .5000 oz. AGW **Ruler:** King Taufa'ahau IV **Subject:** Summer Olympics **Obv:** Head right **Rev:** Boxing match within circle

Date	Mintage	F	VF	XF	Unc	BU
1988 Proof	Est. 2,000	Value: 350				

KM# 131 10 PA'ANGA
31.1000 g., 0.9990 Palladium 1.0000 oz. **Ruler:** King Taufa'ahau IV **Series:** Summer Olympics **Obv:** Head right **Rev:** Shot putter within circle

Date	Mintage	F	VF	XF	Unc	BU
1988 Proof	Est. 2,000	Value: 375				

KM# 132 10 PA'ANGA
15.6300 g., 0.9500 Palladium .5000 oz. **Ruler:** King Taufa'ahau IV **Series:** Summer Olympics **Obv:** Head right **Rev:** Discus thrower within circle

Date	Mintage	F	VF	XF	Unc	BU
1988 Proof	Est. 2,000	Value: 195				

KM# 173 10 PA'ANGA
1.2441 g., 0.9999 Gold .0400 oz. AGW, 13.92 mm. **Ruler:** King Taufa'ahau IV **Subject:** Destruction of the English Privateer "Port-au-Prince" **Obv:** Crowned arms **Rev:** Looted shipwreck and native **Edge:** Reeded

Date	Mintage	F	VF	XF	Unc	BU
1998 Proof	—	Value: 40.00				

KM# 172 10 PA'ANGA
1.2441 g., 0.9999 Gold .0400 oz. AGW, 13.92 mm. **Ruler:** King Taufa'ahau IV **Subject:** King's 80th Birthday July 3, 1998 **Obv:** National arms within circle **Rev:** Bust 3/4 left **Edge:** Reeded **Note:** Struck at Valcambi Mint.

Date	Mintage	F	VF	XF	Unc	BU
1998 Proof	—	Value: 40.00				

KM# 52 20 PA'ANGA
140.0000 g., 0.9990 Silver 4.4971 oz. ASW **Ruler:** King Taufa'ahau IV **Subject:** Constitution Centennial **Obv:** Heads of various Monarchs **Rev:** National arms **Designer:** Norman Sillman

Date	Mintage	F	VF	XF	Unc	BU
1975	1,170	—	—	—	65.00	70.00
1975 Proof	800	Value: 75.00				

KM# 65 20 PA'ANGA
0.8000 g., 0.9170 Gold .0235 oz. AGW **Ruler:** King Taufa'ahau IV **Series:** F.A.O. **Subject:** Rural Women's Advancement **Obv:** Head of Queen Salote right **Rev:** Female symbol on dove

Date	Mintage	F	VF	XF	Unc	BU
1980	750	—	—	BV	20.00	—
1980 Proof	2,000	Value: 18.50				

KM# 53 25 PA'ANGA
5.0000 g., 0.9170 Gold .1474 oz. AGW **Ruler:** King Taufa'ahau IV **Subject:** Constitution Centennial **Obv:** Head facing **Rev:** National arms **Designer:** Norman Sillman

Date	Mintage	F	VF	XF	Unc	BU
1975	405	—	—	—	110	—
1975 Proof	105	Value: 120				

KM# 54 50 PA'ANGA
10.0000 g., 0.9170 Gold .2948 oz. AGW **Ruler:** King Taufa'ahau IV **Subject:** Constitution Centennial **Obv:** Head facing **Rev:** National arms **Designer:** Norman Sillman

Date	Mintage	F	VF	XF	Unc	BU
1975	205	—	—	—	220	—
1975 Proof	105	Value: 230				

KM# 55 75 PA'ANGA
15.0000 g., 0.9170 Gold .4423 oz. AGW **Ruler:** King Taufa'ahau IV **Subject:** Constitution Centennial **Obv:** Queen Salote Tupou III **Rev:** National arms **Designer:** Norman Sillman

Date	Mintage	F	VF	XF	Unc	BU
1975	204	—	—	—	325	—
1975 Proof	105	Value: 335				

KM# 56 100 PA'ANGA
20.0000 g., 0.9170 Gold .5897 oz. AGW **Ruler:** King Taufa'ahau IV **Subject:** Constitution Centennial **Obv:** Uniformed bust left **Rev:** National arms **Designer:** Norman Sillman

Date	Mintage	F	VF	XF	Unc	BU
ND(1975)	205	—	—	—	425	—
ND(1975) Proof	105	Value: 435				

KM# 167 100 PA'ANGA
17.7000 g., 0.5833 Gold .3319 oz. AGW **Ruler:** King Taufa'ahau IV **Subject:** 25th Jubilee of Accession **Obv:** Head left at center of circle with dove, crown and stars **Rev:** National arms within circle

Date	Mintage	F	VF	XF	Unc	BU
ND(1990) Proof	Est. 5,000	Value: 235				

KM# 155 100 PA'ANGA
17.7000 g., 0.5833 Gold .3319 oz. AGW **Ruler:** King Taufa'ahau IV **Series:** Olympics **Obv:** Crowned arms within circle **Rev:** Gymnast on rings

Date	Mintage	F	VF	XF	Unc	BU
1993 Proof	3,000	Value: 235				

KM# 163 100 PA'ANGA
17.7000 g., 0.5833 Gold .3319 oz. AGW **Ruler:** King Taufa'ahau IV **Subject:** World Cup Soccer **Obv:** Crowned arms within circle **Rev:** Goalie

Date	Mintage	F	VF	XF	Unc	BU
1994 Proof	Est. 3,000	Value: 235				

KM# 164 100 PA'ANGA
17.7000 g., 0.5833 Gold .3319 oz. AGW **Ruler:** King Taufa'ahau IV **Series:** 1996 Olympic Games **Obv:** Crowned arms within circle **Rev:** High jumper

Date	Mintage	F	VF	XF	Unc	BU
1994 Proof	Est. 3,000	Value: 235				

KM# 165 100 PA'ANGA
17.7000 g., 0.5833 Gold .3319 oz. AGW **Ruler:** King Taufa'ahau IV **Series:** Endangered Wildlife **Obv:** Crowned arms within circle **Rev:** Leguan Lizard

Date	Mintage	F	VF	XF	Unc	BU
1994 Proof	Est. 2,000	Value: 235				

KM# 21 1/4 HAU
16.0000 g., 0.9800 Palladium .5041 oz. **Ruler:** King Taufa'ahau IV **Subject:** Coronation of Taufa'ahau Tupou IV **Obv:** Head right, small crowns around border **Obv. Designer:** Maurice Meers **Rev:** Crowned arms **Rev. Designer:** Ernest Hyde **Edge Lettering:** HISTORICALLY THE FIRST PALLADIUM COINAGE

Date	Mintage	F	VF	XF	Unc	BU
1967	1,700	—	—	—	200	—

KM# 23 1/2 HAU
32.0000 g., 0.9800 Palladium 1.0082 oz. **Ruler:** King Taufa'ahau IV **Subject:** Coronation of Taufa'ahau Tupou IV **Obv. Designer:** Maurice Meers **Rev:** National arms **Rev. Designer:** Ernest Hyde **Edge Lettering:** HISTORICALLY THE FIRST PALLADIUM COINAGE

Date	Mintage	F	VF	XF	Unc	BU
1967	1,650	—	—	—	385	—

KM# 74 1/2 HAU
28.2800 g., 0.9250 Silver .8411 oz. ASW **Ruler:** King Taufa'ahau IV **Subject:** Wedding and Treaty of Friendship **Obv:** Head right **Rev:** Wedding of Prince Charles and Lady Diana

Date	Mintage	F	VF	XF	Unc	BU
1981	1,000	—	—	—	22.50	—
1981 Proof	15,000	Value: 18.50				

KM# 122 1/2 HAU
10.0000 g., 0.9170 Gold .2948 oz. AGW **Ruler:** King Taufa'ahau IV **Subject:** Wildlife **Obv:** Head right **Rev:** Ground dwelling birds

Date	Mintage	F	VF	XF	Unc	BU
1986 Proof	5,000	Value: 210				

KM# 25 HAU
64.0000 g., 0.9800 Palladium 2.0164 oz. **Ruler:** King Taufa'ahau IV **Subject:** Coronation of Taufa'ahau Tupou IV **Obv:** Head right, small crowns around border **Obv. Designer:** Maurice Meers **Rev:** National arms **Rev. Designer:** Ernest Hyde **Edge Lettering:** HISTORICALLY THE FIRST PALLADIUM COINAGE

Date	Mintage	F	VF	XF	Unc	BU
1967	1,500	—	—	—	775	—

KM# 75 HAU
7.9900 g., 0.9170 Gold .2356 oz. AGW **Ruler:** King Taufa'ahau IV **Subject:** Wedding and Treaty of Friendship **Obv:** Head right **Rev:** Wedding of Prince Charles and Lady Diana

Date	Mintage	F	VF	XF	Unc	BU
1981	500	—	—	—	175	—
1981 Proof	2,500	Value: 165				

KM# 79 HAU
7.9900 g., 0.9170 Gold .2356 oz. AGW **Ruler:** King Taufa'ahau IV **Subject:** Commonwealth Games **Obv:** Head right **Rev:** Runners and emblem **Designer:** Philip Nathan

Date	Mintage	F	VF	XF	Unc	BU
1982	500	—	—	—	175	—
1982 Proof	500	Value: 175				

KM# 94 HAU
52.0000 g., 0.9500 Platinum 1.5884 oz. APW **Ruler:** King Taufa'ahau IV **Subject:** 100th Anniversary of Automobile Industry **Obv:** Head right **Rev:** Rolls Royce and Silver Ghost **Note:** Similar to 50 Seniti, KM#82.

Date	Mintage	F	VF	XF	Unc	BU
1985 Proof	—	Value: 2,150				

KM# 95 HAU
52.0000 g., 0.9500 Platinum 1.5884 oz. APW **Ruler:** King Taufa'ahau IV **Subject:** 100th Anniversary of Automobile Industry **Obv:** Head right **Rev:** Range Rover and Land Rover **Note:** Similar to 50 Seniti, KM#83.

Date	Mintage	F	VF	XF	Unc	BU
1985 Proof	—	Value: 2,150				

KM# 96 HAU
52.0000 g., 0.9500 Platinum 1.5884 oz. APW **Ruler:** King Taufa'ahau IV **Subject:** 100th Anniversary of Automobile Industry **Obv:** Head right **Rev:** Mini Morris Cowley and Touring Car **Note:** Similar to 50 Seniti, KM#84.

Date	Mintage	F	VF	XF	Unc	BU
1985 Proof	—	Value: 2,150				

KM# 97 HAU
52.0000 g., 0.9500 Platinum 1.5884 oz. APW **Ruler:** King Taufa'ahau IV **Subject:** 100th Anniversary of Automobile Industry **Obv:** Head right **Rev:** MGB GT and MG TA **Note:** Similar to 50 Seniti, KM#85.

Date	Mintage	F	VF	XF	Unc	BU
1985 Proof	—	Value: 2,150				

KM# 113 HAU
52.0000 g., 0.9500 Platinum 1.5884 oz. APW **Ruler:** King Taufa'ahau IV **Subject:** 85th Birthday of Queen Mother **Obv:** Head right **Rev:** Queen Mother as a young girl **Note:** Similar to 50 Seniti, KM#98.

Date	Mintage	F	VF	XF	Unc	BU
1985 Proof	—	Value: 2,150				

KM# 114 HAU
52.0000 g., 0.9500 Platinum 1.5884 oz. APW **Ruler:** King Taufa'ahau IV **Subject:** 85th Birthday of Queen Mother **Obv:** Head right **Rev:** Wedding of King George VI and Elizabeth **Note:** Similar to 50 Seniti, KM#99.

Date	Mintage	F	VF	XF	Unc	BU
1985 Proof	—	Value: 2,150				

KM# 115 HAU
52.0000 g., 0.9500 Platinum 1.5884 oz. APW **Ruler:** King Taufa'ahau IV **Subject:** 85th Birthday of Queen Mother **Obv:** Head right **Rev:** King George VI and Elizabeth **Note:** Similar to 50 Seniti, KM#100.

Date	Mintage	F	VF	XF	Unc	BU
1985 Proof	—	Value: 2,150				

KM# 116 HAU
52.0000 g., 0.9500 Platinum 1.5884 oz. APW **Ruler:** King Taufa'ahau IV **Subject:** 85th Birthday of Queen Mother **Obv:** Head right **Rev:** Queen Mother holding Queen Elizabeth II **Note:** Similar to 50 Seniti, KM#101.

Date	Mintage	F	VF	XF	Unc	BU
1985 Proof	—	Value: 2,150				

KM# 117 HAU
52.0000 g., 0.9500 Platinum 1.5884 oz. APW **Ruler:** King Taufa'ahau IV **Subject:** 85th Birthday of Queen Mother **Obv:** Head right **Rev:** Queen Mother facing **Note:** Similar to 50 Seniti, KM#102.

Date	Mintage	F	VF	XF	Unc	BU
1985 Proof	—	Value: 2,150				

KM# 76 5 HAU
15.9800 g., 0.9170 Gold .4711 oz. AGW **Ruler:** King Taufa'ahau IV **Subject:** Wedding and Treaty of Friendship **Obv:** Head right **Rev:** Wedding of Prince Charles and Lady Diana

Date	Mintage	F	VF	XF	Unc	BU
1981	250	—	—	—	350	—
1981 Proof	1,000	Value: 335				

COUNTERMARKED COMMEMORATIVE COINAGE

Commemorative coins which contain a countermark creating a new commemorative representation. The Date listed refers to the original date the coin was struck.

KM# 14 20 SENITI
Copper-Nickel, 28.5 mm. **Ruler:** King Taufa'ahau IV **Countermark:** 1918/TTIV/1968 **Obv:** Head right, small crowns around border **Note:** Countermark on KM#13.

Date	Mintage	F	VF	XF	Unc	BU
ND(1967) Proof	1,577	Value: 6.00				

KM# 10 50 SENITI
Gold Plated Copper-Nickel, 34.5 mm. **Ruler:** King Taufa'ahau IV **Countermark:** IN MEMORIAM/1965+1970 **Obv:** Head right **Edge:** Reeded **Note:** Countermark on KM#9.

Date	Mintage	F	VF	XF	Unc	BU
1967	Inc. above	—	—	—	5.00	—

KM# 16 50 SENITI
Copper-Nickel, 34.5 mm. **Ruler:** King Taufa'ahau IV **Countermark:** 1918/TTIV/1968 **Obv:** Head right, small crowns around border **Note:** Countermark on KM#15.

Date	Mintage	F	VF	XF	Unc	BU
ND(1967) Proof	1,577	Value: 7.00				

KM# 12 PA'ANGA
Gold Plated Copper-Nickel, 38.5 mm. **Ruler:** King Taufa'ahau IV **Countermark:** IN MEMORIAM/1965+1970 **Obv:** Head right **Note:** Countermark on KM#11.

Date	Mintage	F	VF	XF	Unc	BU
1967	Inc. above	—	—	—	6.50	—

KM# 18 PA'ANGA
Copper-Nickel, 38.5 mm. **Ruler:** King Taufa'ahau IV **Countermark:** 1918/TTIV/1968 **Obv:** Head right, small crowns around border **Note:** Countermark on KM#17.

Date	Mintage	F	VF	XF	Unc	BU
1967 Proof	1,577	Value: 8.00				

KM# 34 PA'ANGA
Gold Plated Copper-Nickel, 38.5 mm. **Ruler:** King Taufa'ahau IV **Countermark:** Oil rig 1969 OIL SEARCH **Obv:** Head right **Edge:** Reeded **Note:** Countermark on KM#17.

Date	Mintage	F	VF	XF	Unc	BU
1968	5,017	—	1.50	2.50	5.50	—

KM# 35 PA'ANGA
Gold Plated Copper-Nickel, 38.5 mm. **Countermark:** COMMONWEALTH MEMBER/1970 **Obv:** Head right **Edge:** Reeded **Note:** Countermark on KM#17.

Date	Mintage	F	VF	XF	Unc	BU
1968	3,000	—	1.50	3.00	6.50	—

KM# 36 PA'ANGA
Gold Plated Copper-Nickel, 38.5 mm. **Ruler:** King Taufa'ahau IV **Countermark:** INVESTITURE/1971 **Obv:** Head right **Edge:** Reeded **Note:** Countermark on KM#17.

Date	Mintage	F	VF	XF	Unc	BU
1968	3,000	—	1.50	3.00	6.50	—
1968 Proof	1,000	Value: 9.00				

KM# 20 2 PA'ANGA
Copper-Nickel, 44.5 mm. **Ruler:** King Taufa'ahau IV **Countermark:** 1918/TTIV/1968 **Obv:** Head right, small crowns around border **Note:** Countermark on KM#19.

Date	Mintage	F	VF	XF	Unc	BU
ND(1967) Proof	1,577	Value: 10.00				

KM# 38 2 PA'ANGA
Gold Plated Copper-Nickel, 44.5 mm. **Ruler:** King Taufa'ahau IV **Countermark:** Oil rig 1969 OIL SEARCH **Obv:** Head right **Edge:** Reeded **Note:** Countermark on KM#37.

Date	Mintage	F	VF	XF	Unc	BU
1968	5,039	—	2.00	4.00	7.50	—

KM# 39 2 PA'ANGA
Gold Plated Copper-Nickel, 44.5 mm. **Ruler:** King Taufa'ahau IV **Countermark:** COMMONWEALTH MEMBER/1970 **Obv:** Head right **Edge:** Reeded **Note:** Countermark on KM#37.

Date	Mintage	F	VF	XF	Unc	BU
1968	3,006	—	2.00	4.50	8.50	—

KM# 40 2 PA'ANGA

Gold Plated Copper-Nickel, 44.5 mm. **Ruler:** King Taufa'ahau IV **Countermark:** INVESTITURE/1971 **Obv:** Head right **Note:** Countermark on KM#37.

Date	Mintage	F	VF	XF	Unc	BU
1968	3,000	—	2.00	4.50	8.50	—
1968 Proof	1,000	Value: 15.00				

KM# 22 1/4 HAU

16.0000 g., 0.9800 Palladium .5040 oz. **Ruler:** King Taufa'ahau IV **Countermark:** 1918/TTIV/1968 **Edge Lettering:** HISTORICALLY THE FIRST PALLADIUM COINAGE **Note:** Countermark on KM#21.

Date	Mintage	F	VF	XF	Unc	BU
1967	400	—	—	—	225	—

KM# 24 1/2 HAU

32.0000 g., 0.9800 Palladium 1.0082 oz. **Ruler:** King Taufa'ahau IV **Countermark:** 1918/TTIV/1968 **Obv:** Head right, small crowns around border **Rev:** Crowned arms **Edge Lettering:** HISTORICALLY THE FIRST PALLADIUM COINAGE **Note:** Countermark on KM#23.

Date	Mintage	F	VF	XF	Unc	BU
ND(1967)	513	—	—	—	450	—

KM# 26 HAU

64.0000 g., 0.9800 Palladium 2.0164 oz. **Ruler:** King Taufa'ahau IV **Countermark:** 1918/TTIV/1968 **Edge Lettering:** HISTORICALLY THE FIRST PALLADIUM COINAGE **Note:** Countermark on KM#25.

Date	Mintage	F	VF	XF	Unc	BU
ND(1967)	400	—	—	—	875	—

MINT SETS

KM#	Date	Mintage	Identification	Issue Price	Mkt Val
MS1	1962 (3)	—	KM#1-3	—	1,000
MS2	1967 (3)	1,500	KM#21, 23, 25	207	1,275
MS3	1968 (3)	400	KM#22, 24, 26	—	1,650
MS4	1970 (2)	10,000	KM#10, 12	2.30	11.50
MS5	1969 (2)	10,000	KM#34, 38	13.68	12.50
MS6	1970 (2)	3,000	KM#35, 39	13.68	15.00
MS7	1971 (2)	3,000	KM#36, 40	4.80	15.00
MS8	1974 (8)	10,000	KM#27-33, 37	7.60	20.00
MS9	1975 (8)	—	KM#42-49	7.75	18.00
MS10	1975 (4)	—	KM#53-56	385	885
MS11	1975 (3)	—	KM#50-52	59.60	85.00
MS12	1977 (5)	—	KM#44-47	0.85	7.00
MS13	1977 (2)	—	KM#49, 57	3.00	10.00
MS14	1978 (2)	—	KM#58-59	3.00	11.50
MS15	1978 (5)	—	KM#42-46	—	5.50
MS16	1979 (2)	8,008	KM#60-61	3.00	10.00
MS17	1980 (2)	8,000	KM#62-63	3.00	12.00
MS18	1980 (2)	750	KM#64-65, Gold	30.00	45.00
MS19	1981 (8)	15,000	KM#66-73	5.38	18.00
MS20	1985 (5)	20,000	KM#98-102	25.25	10.00
MS21	1985 (4)	20,000	KM#82-85. Auto Industry.	21.00	15.00
MS22	1991 (6)	—	KM#66-71	—	6.00

PROOF SETS

KM#	Date	Mintage	Identification	Issue Price	Mkt Val
PS1	1962 (3)	250	KM#1-3	—	1,070
PS2	1962 (3)	25	KM#1a-3a. Platinum.	—	2,400
PS3	1967 (7)	5,000	KM#4-9, 11	15.00	22.50
PS4	1967 (4)	1,923	KM#13, 15, 17, 19	17.25	25.00
PS5	1968 (8)	2,500	KM#27-33, 37	22.50	32.00
PS6	1968 (4)	1,577	KM#14, 16, 18, 20	22.80	32.50
PS8	1971 (2)	1,000	KM#36, 40	13.40	25.00
PS9	1975 (3)	418	KM#50-52	82.00	120
PS10	1975 (4)	105	KM#53-56	538	950
PS11	1978 (2)	750	KM#58a-59a	—	55.00
PS12	1979 (2)	854	KM#60a-61a	45.00	50.00
PS13	1980 (2)	400	KM#62a-63a	80.00	40.00
PS14	1980 (2)	200	KM#64-65	60.00	45.00
PS15	1981 (2)	3,500	KM#72a-73a	88.00	40.00
PSA15	1981 (3)	—	KM#74-76	—	450
PS16	1985 (5)	20,000	KM#98-102, Copper-nickel	26.25	18.00
PS17	1985 (5)	10,000	KM#103-107, Silver clad copper-nickel	55.00	22.00
PS18	1985 (5)	5,000	KM#103a-107a, .925 Silver	180	75.00
PS19	1985 (5)	1,000	KM#108-112, .374 Gold	315	200
PS20	1985 (5)	500	KM#108a-112a, .917 Gold	775	725
PS21	1985 (5)	50	KM#113-117, .950 Platinum. BV+15%.	5,850	—
PS22	1985 (4)	10,000	KM#86-89	44.00	20.00
PS23	1985 (4)	5,000	KM#86a-89a, .925 Silver	144	75.00
PS24	1985 (4)	1,000	KM#90-93, .374 Gold	252	170
PS25	1985 (4)	500	KM#90a-93a, .917 Gold	620	580
PS26	1985 (4)	50	KM#94-97, .950 Platinum. BV+15%.	4,680	—
PS28	1988 (4)	2,000	KM#129-132	—	950

TONKIN

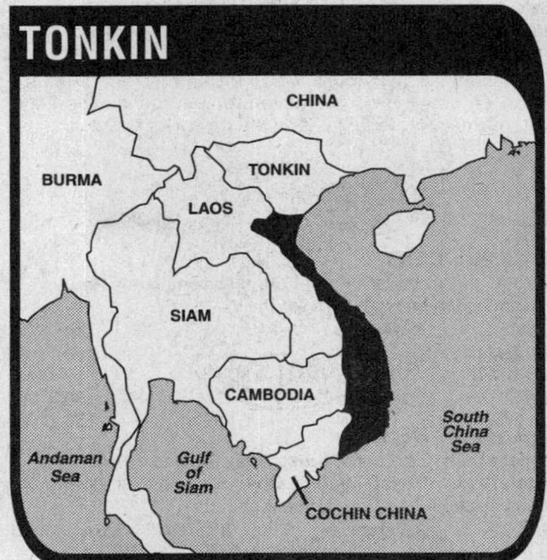

FRENCH PROTECTORATE

MILLED COINAGE

KM# 1 1/600 PIASTRE

2.1000 g., Zinc **Obv:** Legend around square center hole **Obv. Legend:** PROTECTORAT DU TONKIN **Rev:** Value above and below, "Thong-bao" at left and right **Note:** 0.9 mm thick planchet.

Date	Mintage	F	VF	XF	Unc	BU
1905(a)	60,000,000	3.50	7.50	18.00	45.00	—

ESSAIS

KM#	Date	Mintage	Identification	Mkt Val
E1	1905(a)	—	1/600 Piastre. Zinc. 2.1000 g. Legend around center squared hole. PROTECTORAT DU TONKIN. Value above and below squared hole in center flanked by thong-bao. 0.9 mm thick planchet.	300

PIEFORTS

KM#	Date	Mintage	Identification	Mkt Val
P1	1905(a)	—	1/600 Piastre. Zinc. 4.8000 g. PROTECTORAT DU TONKIN. Value above and below, "Thong-bao" at left and right. 1.5 mm thick planchet.	700

TRANSNISTRIA

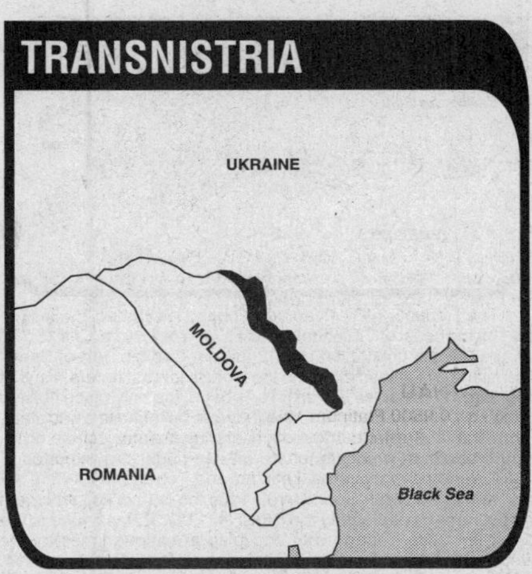

The Transnistria Moldavian Republic was formed in 1990, even before the separation of Moldavia from Russia. It has an area of 11,544 sq. mi. (29,900 sq. km.) and a population of 700,000. Capital: Tiraspol.

The area was conquered from the Turks in the last half of the 18th century, and in 1792 the capital city of Bessarabia (present Moldova and part of the Ukraine) became part of the Russian Empire. During the Russian Revolution, in 1918, the area was taken by Romanian troops, and in 1924 the Moldavian Autonomous SSR was formed on the left bank of the Dniester River. On June 22, 1941, Romania declared war on the U.S.S.R. and Romanian troops fought alongside the Germans up to Stalingrad. A Romanian occupation area between the Dniester and Bug Rivers called Transnistria was established in October 1941. Its center was the port of Odessa.

Once the Moldavian SSR declared independence in August 1991, Transnistria did not want to be part of Moldavia. In 1992, Moldova tried to solve the issue militarily with battles in Bendery and Doubossary. The conflict was ended with Russian mediation and Russian peacekeeping forces were stationed there.

Transnistria has a president, parliament, army and police forces, but as yet it is lacking international recognition.

MOLDAVIAN REPUBLIC

STANDARD COINAGE

1 Rublei = 100 Kopeek

KM# 1 KOPEEK

0.6200 g., Aluminum, 15.9 mm. **Obv:** State arms **Rev:** Value between wheat stalks **Edge:** Plain

Date	Mintage	F	VF	XF	Unc	BU
2000	—	—	—	—	0.25	0.40

KM# 2 5 KOPEEK

0.7000 g., Aluminum, 17.9 mm. **Obv:** State arms **Rev:** Value between wheat stalks **Edge:** Plain

Date	Mintage	F	VF	XF	Unc	BU
2000	—	—	—	—	0.50	0.65

KM# 3 10 KOPEEK

1.0000 g., Aluminum, 20 mm. **Obv:** State arms **Rev:** Value between wheat stalks **Edge:** Plain

Date	Mintage	F	VF	XF	Unc	BU
2000	—	—	—	—	0.75	0.90

KM# 4 50 KOPEEK

2.7500 g., Brass, 19 mm. **Obv:** State arms **Rev:** Value between wheat stalks **Edge:** Plain

Date	Mintage	F	VF	XF	Unc	BU
2000	—	—	—	—	1.25	1.50

KM# 6 50 RUBLEI

14.3700 g., Copper-Nickel, 32.75 mm. **Subject:** 10th Anniversary **Obv:** State arms above value **Rev:** Statue **Edge:** Plain

Date	Mintage	F	VF	XF	Unc	BU
(ND)2000 Proof	—	Value: 40.00				

TRINIDAD & TOBAGO

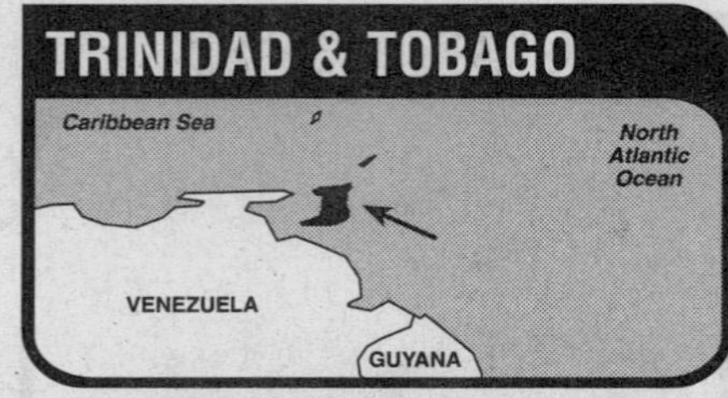

The Republic of Trinidad and Tobago is situated 7 miles (11 km.) off the coast of Venezuela, has an area of 1,981 sq. mi. (5,130 sq. km.) and a population of *1.2 million. Capital: Port-of-Spain. The island of Trinidad contains the world's largest natural asphalt bog. Birds of Paradise live on little Tobago, the only place outside of their native New Guinea where they can be found in a wild state. Petroleum and petroleum products are the mainstay of the economy. Petroleum products, crude oil and sugar are exported.

Columbus discovered Trinidad and Tobago in 1498. Trinidad remained under Spanish rule from the time of its settlement in 1592 until its capture by the British in 1797. It was ceded to the British in 1802. Tobago was occupied at various times by the French, Dutch and English before being ceded to Britain in 1814. Trinidad and Tobago were merged into a single colony in 1888. The colony was part of the Federation of the West Indies until Aug. 31, 1962, when it became independent. A new constitution establishing a republican form of government was adopted on Aug. 1, 1976. Trinidad and Tobago is a member of the Commonwealth of Nations. The President is Chief of State. The Prime Minister is Head of Government.

RULERS

British, until 1976

MINT MARKS

FM - Franklin Mint, U.S.A.*

*NOTE: From 1975-1985 the Franklin Mint produced coinage in up to 3 different qualities. Qualities of issue are designated in ( ) after each date and are defined as follows:

(M) MATTE - Normal circulation strike or a dull finish produced by sandblasting special uncirculated (polish finish) or proof quality dies.

(U) SPECIAL UNCIRCULATED - Polished or proof-like in appearance without any frosted features.

(P) PROOF - The highest quality obtainable having mirror-like fields and frosted features.

MONETARY SYSTEM

100 Cents = 1 Dollar

COLONIAL

STANDARD COINAGE

KM# 1 CENT

1.9500 g., Bronze, 17.8 mm. **Obv:** Value **Rev:** National arms **Edge:** Plain

Date	Mintage	F	VF	XF	Unc	BU
1966	24,500,000	—	—	—	0.15	0.30
1966 Proof	8,000	Value: 1.00				
1967	4,000,000	—	—	—	0.25	0.50
1968	5,000,000	—	—	—	0.25	0.50
1970	5,000,000	—	—	—	0.25	0.50
1970 Proof	2,104	Value: 1.50				
1971	10,600,000	—	—	—	0.15	0.30
1971FM (M)	286,000	—	—	—	0.20	0.40
1971FM (P)	12,000	Value: 0.50				
1972	16,500,000	—	—	—	0.15	0.30
1973	10,000,000	—	—	—	0.15	0.30

KM# 9 CENT

1.9500 g., Bronze, 17.8 mm. **Subject:** 10th Anniversary of Independence **Obv:** Value and date **Rev:** National arms **Edge:** Plain

Date	Mintage	F	VF	XF	Unc	BU
1972	5,000,000	—	—	0.10	0.15	0.30
1972FM (M)	125,000	—	—	—	0.25	0.50
1972FM (P)	16,000	Value: 0.50				

KM# 17 CENT

1.9500 g., Bronze, 17.8 mm. **Obv:** Value and date **Rev:** National arms **Edge:** Plain

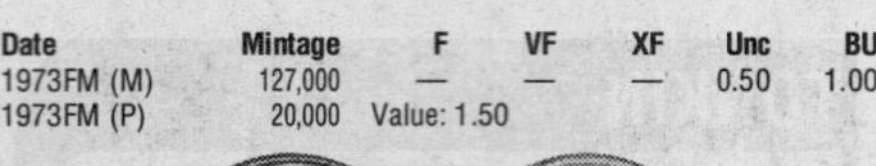

Date	Mintage	F	VF	XF	Unc	BU
1973FM (M)	127,000	—	—	—	0.50	1.00
1973FM (P)	20,000	Value: 1.50				

KM# 25 CENT

1.9500 g., Bronze, 17.8 mm. **Obv:** National arms **Rev:** Hummingbird and value **Edge:** Plain

Date	Mintage	F	VF	XF	Unc	BU
1974FM (M)	128,000	—	—	—	0.50	1.00
1974FM (P)	14,000	Value: 0.80				
1975	10,000,000	—	—	—	0.50	1.00
1975FM (M)	125,000	—	—	—	0.50	1.00
1975FM (U)	1,111	—	—	—	1.25	2.50
1975FM (P)	24,000	Value: 0.80				
1976	15,050,000	—	—	—	0.50	1.00

KM# 2 5 CENTS

3.2500 g., Bronze, 21.15 mm. **Obv:** Value **Rev:** National arms

Date	Mintage	F	VF	XF	Unc	BU
1966	7,500,000	—	—	0.10	0.25	0.50
1966 Proof	8,000	Value: 1.25				
1967	3,000,000	—	—	0.10	0.50	1.00
1970 Proof	2,104	Value: 1.75				
1971	2,400,000	—	—	0.10	0.50	1.00
1971FM (M)	57,000	—	—	—	0.15	0.30
1971FM (P)	12,000	Value: 0.75				
1972	2,250,000	—	—	0.10	0.50	1.00

KM# 10 5 CENTS

3.2500 g., Bronze, 21.15 mm. **Subject:** 10th Anniversary of Independence **Obv:** Value and date **Rev:** National arms

Date	Mintage	F	VF	XF	Unc	BU
1972	15,000	—	—	—	0.35	0.70
1972FM (M)	25,000	—	—	—	0.25	0.50
1972FM (P)	16,000	Value: 0.75				

KM# 57 5 CENTS

3.2500 g., Bronze, 21.15 mm. **Obv:** Value **Rev:** National arms

Date	Mintage	F	VF	XF	Unc	BU
1973FM (M)	27,000	—	—	—	0.50	1.00
1973FM (P)	20,000	Value: 1.50				

KM# 26 5 CENTS

3.2500 g., Bronze, 21.15 mm. **Obv:** National arms **Rev:** Bird of Paradise and value

Date	Mintage	F	VF	XF	Unc	BU
1974FM (M)	28,000	—	—	—	0.50	1.00
1974FM (P)	14,000	Value: 0.75				
1975	1,500,000	—	—	0.10	0.45	0.90
1975FM (M)	25,000	—	—	—	0.45	0.90
1975FM (U)	1,111	—	—	—	2.50	5.00
1975FM (P)	24,000	Value: 0.75				
1976	7,500,000	—	—	0.10	0.45	0.90

KM# 3 10 CENTS

1.4000 g., Copper-Nickel, 16.3 mm. **Obv:** Value and date **Rev:** National arms **Edge:** Reeded

Date	Mintage	F	VF	XF	Unc	BU
1966	7,800,000	—	—	0.10	0.30	0.60
1966 Proof	8,000	Value: 1.50				
1967	4,000,000	—	—	0.10	0.45	0.90
1970 Proof	2,104	Value: 2.00				
1971	—	—	—	0.10	0.45	0.90
1971FM (M)	29,000	—	—	—	0.35	0.70
1971FM (P)	12,000	Value: 1.00				
1972	4,000,000	—	—	0.10	0.30	0.60

KM# 11 10 CENTS

1.4000 g., Copper-Nickel, 16.3 mm. **Subject:** 10th Anniversary of Independence **Obv:** Value **Rev:** National arms **Edge:** Reeded

Date	Mintage	F	VF	XF	Unc	BU
1972	41,000	—	—	—	0.40	0.80
1972FM (M)	13,000	—	—	—	0.60	1.20
1972FM (P)	16,000	Value: 1.00				

KM# 58 10 CENTS

1.4000 g., Copper-Nickel, 16.3 mm. **Obv:** Value **Rev:** National arms **Edge:** Reeded

Date	Mintage	F	VF	XF	Unc	BU
1973FM (M)	14,000	—	—	—	1.00	2.00
1973FM (P)	20,000	Value: 2.50				

KM# 27 10 CENTS

1.4000 g., Copper-Nickel, 16.3 mm. **Obv:** National arms **Rev:** Flaming Hibiscus and value **Edge:** Reeded

Date	Mintage	F	VF	XF	Unc	BU
1974FM (M)	16,000	—	—	—	1.00	2.00
1974FM (P)	14,000	Value: 1.00				
1975	4,000,000	—	—	0.10	0.25	0.50
1975FM (M)	13,000	—	—	—	0.50	1.00
1975FM (U)	1,111	—	—	—	2.50	5.00
1975FM (P)	24,000	Value: 1.00				
1976	14,720,000	—	—	0.10	0.20	0.40

KM# 4 25 CENTS

3.5000 g., Copper-Nickel, 20 mm. **Obv:** Value **Rev:** National arms **Edge:** Reeded

Date	Mintage	F	VF	XF	Unc	BU
1966	7,200,000	—	0.10	0.15	0.35	0.70
1966 Proof	8,000	Value: 1.75				
1967	1,800,000	—	0.10	0.15	0.50	1.00
1970 Proof	2,014	Value: 2.50				
1971	1,500,000	—	0.10	0.15	0.50	1.00
1971FM (M)	11,000	—	—	—	0.65	1.30
1971FM (P)	12,000	Value: 1.25				
1972	3,000,000	—	0.10	0.15	0.35	0.70

KM# 12 25 CENTS

3.5000 g., Copper-Nickel, 20 mm. **Subject:** 10th Anniversary of Independence **Obv:** Value and date **Rev:** National arms **Edge:** Reeded

Date	Mintage	F	VF	XF	Unc	BU
1972	14,000	—	0.20	0.65	1.00	2.00

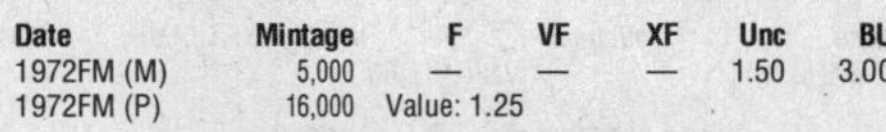

Date	Mintage	F	VF	XF	Unc	BU
1972FM (M)	5,000	—	—	—	1.50	3.00
1972FM (P)	16,000	Value: 1.25				

KM# 59 25 CENTS
3.5000 g., Copper-Nickel, 20 mm. **Obv:** Value **Rev:** National arms **Edge:** Reeded

Date	Mintage	F	VF	XF	Unc	BU
1973FM (M)	6,575	—	—	—	2.25	4.50
1973FM (P)	20,000	Value: 3.00				

KM# 28 25 CENTS
3.5000 g., Copper-Nickel, 20 mm. **Obv:** National arms **Rev:** Chaconia and value **Edge:** Reeded

Date	Mintage	F	VF	XF	Unc	BU
1974FM (M)	8,258	—	—	—	1.75	3.50
1974FM (P)	14,000	Value: 1.25				
1975	3,000,000	—	0.10	0.15	0.30	0.60
1975FM (M)	5,000	—	—	—	1.50	3.00
1975FM (U)	1,111	—	—	—	2.00	4.00
1975FM (P)	24,000	Value: 1.25				
1976	9,000,000	—	0.10	0.15	0.30	0.60

KM# 5 50 CENTS
7.0000 g., Copper-Nickel, 26 mm. **Obv:** Value **Rev:** National arms **Edge:** Reeded

Date	Mintage	F	VF	XF	Unc	BU
1966	975,000	—	0.25	0.60	1.50	3.00
1966 Proof	8,000	Value: 2.50				
1967	750,000	—	0.25	0.50	1.25	2.50
1970 Proof	2,104	Value: 3.00				
1971FM (M)	5,714	—	—	—	2.50	5.00
1971FM (P)	12,000	Value: 1.75				

KM# 13 50 CENTS
7.0000 g., Copper-Nickel, 26 mm. **Subject:** 10th Anniversary of Independence **Obv:** Value **Rev:** National arms **Edge:** Reeded

Date	Mintage	F	VF	XF	Unc	BU
1972	375,000	—	0.50	0.75	1.50	3.00
1972FM (M)	2,500	—	—	—	5.00	10.00
1972FM (P)	16,000	Value: 1.75				

KM# 22 50 CENTS
7.0000 g., Copper-Nickel, 26 mm. **Obv:** National arms **Rev:** Kettle drums and value **Edge:** Reeded

Date	Mintage	F	VF	XF	Unc	BU
1973FM (M)	4,075	—	—	—	2.50	5.00
1973FM (P)	20,000	Value: 2.25				
1974FM (M)	5,758	—	—	—	2.50	5.00
1974FM (P)	14,000	Value: 2.25				
1975FM (M)	2,500	—	—	—	4.00	8.00
1975FM (U)	1,111	—	—	—	2.50	5.00
1975FM (P)	24,000	Value: 2.00				
1976	750,000	—	0.50	0.75	1.50	3.00

KM# 6 DOLLAR
12.7000 g., Nickel, 32 mm. **Series:** F.A.O. **Obv:** National arms **Rev:** Value in front of leaves

Date	Mintage	F	VF	XF	Unc	BU
1969	250,000	—	0.75	1.50	3.50	7.00

KM# 7 DOLLAR
12.7000 g., Copper-Nickel, 32 mm. **Obv:** Value **Rev:** National arms

Date	Mintage	F	VF	XF	Unc	BU
1971FM (M)	2,857	—	—	—	5.00	10.00
1971FM (P)	12,000	Value: 3.00				

KM# 7a DOLLAR
Nickel, 36 mm. **Obv:** Value **Rev:** National arms

Date	Mintage	F	VF	XF	Unc	BU
1970 Proof	2,014	Value: 6.00				

KM# 14 DOLLAR
Copper-Nickel, 36 mm. **Subject:** 10th Anniversary of Independence **Obv:** National arms **Rev:** Bird on branch and value

Date	Mintage	F	VF	XF	Unc	BU
1972	9,700	—	—	—	6.00	10.00
1972FM (M)	1,250	—	—	—	12.50	20.00
1972FM (P)	16,000	Value: 4.00				

KM# 23 DOLLAR
Copper-Nickel, 36 mm. **Obv:** National arms **Rev:** Bird on branch and value

Date	Mintage	F	VF	XF	Unc	BU
1973FM (M)	2,825	—	—	—	5.50	9.00
1973FM (P)	20,000	Value: 4.00				
1974FM (M)	4,508	—	—	—	5.50	9.00
1974FM (P)	14,000	Value: 4.00				
1975FM (M)	1,250	—	—	—	6.50	12.00
1975FM (U)	1,111	—	—	—	6.50	12.00
1975FM (P)	24,000	Value: 4.00				

KM# 8 5 DOLLARS
29.7000 g., 0.9250 Silver .8833 oz. ASW, 40 mm. **Obv:** National arms **Rev:** Scarlet Ibis and value

Date	Mintage	F	VF	XF	Unc	BU
1971FM (M)	571	—	—	—	25.00	30.00
1971FM (P)	11,000	Value: 18.00				
1973FM (M)	1,825	—	—	—	20.00	25.00
1973FM (P)	25,000	Value: 15.00				
1974FM (P)	16,000	Value: 15.00				
1975FM (P)	26,000	Value: 15.00				

KM# 8a 5 DOLLARS
Copper-Nickel, 40 mm. **Obv:** National arms **Rev:** Scarlet Ibis and value

Date	Mintage	F	VF	XF	Unc	BU
1974FM (M)	3,508	—	—	—	10.00	15.00
1975FM (M)	250	—	—	—	20.00	25.00
1975FM (U)	1,111	—	—	—	9.00	12.50

KM# 15 5 DOLLARS
29.7000 g., 0.9250 Silver .8833 oz. ASW, 40 mm. **Subject:** 10th Anniversary of Independence **Obv:** National arms **Rev:** Scarlet Ibis and value

Date	Mintage	F	VF	XF	Unc	BU
1972	10,000	—	—	—	14.50	16.50
1972FM	250	—	—	—	40.00	45.00
1972FM Proof	19,000	Value: 14.50				

KM# 16 10 DOLLARS
35.0000 g., 0.9250 Silver 1.0409 oz. ASW, 42 mm. **Subject:** 10th Anniversary of Independence **Obv:** National arms **Rev:** Fish, ship, map and value within waves

Date	Mintage	F	VF	XF	Unc	BU
1972	—	—	—	—	17.50	20.00
1972FM (M)	125	—	—	—	125	130
1972FM (P)	26,000	Value: 18.00				

KM# 24 10 DOLLARS
Copper-Nickel, 42 mm. **Obv:** National arms **Rev:** Fish, ship, map and value within waves

Date	Mintage	F	VF	XF	Unc	BU
1974FM (M)	3,632	—	—	—	12.50	15.00
1975FM (M)	125	—	—	—	50.00	60.00
1975FM (U)	1,111	—	—	—	15.00	20.00

KM# 24a 10 DOLLARS
35.0000 g., 0.9250 Silver 1.0409 oz. ASW, 42 mm. **Obv:** National arms **Rev:** Fish, ship, map and value within waves

Date	Mintage	F	VF	XF	Unc	BU
1973FM (M)	1,700	—	—	—	22.50	25.00
1973FM (U)	—	—	—	—	20.00	22.50
1973FM (P)	24,000	Value: 18.50				
1974FM (P)	21,000	Value: 18.50				
1975FM (P)	28,000	Value: 18.50				

REPUBLIC

STANDARD COINAGE

KM# 29 CENT

1.9500 g., Bronze, 17.8 mm. **Obv:** National arms **Rev:** Hummingbird and value **Edge:** Plain

Date	Mintage	F	VF	XF	Unc	BU
1976	—	—	—	—	—	—
1976FM (M)	150,000	—	—	0.20	0.35	1.00
1976FM (U)	582	—	—	1.00	2.50	3.50
1976FM (P)	10,000	Value: 0.60				
1977	25,000,000	—	—	0.20	0.35	1.00
1977FM (M)	150,000	—	—	0.20	0.35	1.00
1977FM (U)	633	—	—	1.00	2.50	3.50
1977FM (P)	5,337	Value: 0.60				
1978	12,500,000	—	—	0.20	0.35	1.00
1978FM (M)	150,000	—	—	0.20	0.35	1.00
1978FM (U)	472	—	—	1.00	2.50	3.50
1978FM (P)	4,845	Value: 1.00				
1979	30,200,000	—	—	0.20	0.35	1.00
1979FM (M)	150,000	—	—	0.20	0.35	1.00
1979FM (U)	518	—	—	1.00	2.50	3.50
1979FM (P)	3,270	Value: 1.00				
1980	12,500,000	—	—	0.20	0.35	1.00
1980FM (M)	75,000	—	—	0.20	0.35	1.00
1980FM (U)	796	—	—	1.00	2.50	3.50
1980FM (P)	2,393	Value: 1.00				
1981	—	—	—	0.20	0.35	1.00
1981FM (M)	—	—	—	0.20	0.35	1.00
1981FM (U)	—	—	—	1.00	2.50	3.50
1981FM (P)	—	Value: 1.00				
1982	—	—	—	0.20	0.35	1.00
1983	—	—	—	0.20	0.35	1.00
1984	—	—	—	0.20	0.35	1.00
1985	25,400,000	—	—	0.20	0.35	1.00
1986	10,000,000	—	—	0.20	0.35	1.00
1987	10,000,000	—	—	0.20	0.35	1.00
1988	5,000,000	—	—	0.20	0.35	1.00
1989	—	—	—	0.20	0.35	1.00
1990	—	—	—	0.20	0.35	1.00
1991	—	—	—	0.20	0.35	1.00
1993	—	—	—	0.20	0.35	1.00
1994	—	—	—	0.20	0.35	1.00
1995	—	—	—	0.20	0.35	1.00
1996	—	—	—	0.20	0.35	1.00
1997	—	—	—	0.20	0.35	1.00
1998	—	—	—	0.20	0.35	1.00
1999	—	—	—	0.20	0.35	1.00
1999 Proof	3,000	Value: 0.60				
2000	—	—	—	0.20	0.35	1.00

KM# 29a CENT

2.0000 g., 0.9250 Silver .0594 oz. ASW, 17.8 mm. **Obv:** National arms **Rev:** Hummingbird and value

Date	Mintage	F	VF	XF	Unc	BU
1981FM (P)	898	Value: 10.00				

KM# 42 CENT

1.9500 g., Bronze, 17.8 mm. **Subject:** 20th Anniversary of Independence **Obv:** National arms **Rev:** Flaming hibiscus and value **Edge:** Plain

Date	Mintage	F	VF	XF	Unc	BU
1982FM (M)	—	—	—	—	0.15	0.30
1982FM (U)	—	—	—	—	1.50	3.00
1982FM (P)	—	Value: 1.00				

KM# 42a CENT

2.0000 g., 0.9250 Silver .0594 oz. ASW, 17.8 mm. **Obv:** National arms **Rev:** Flaming hibiscus and value

Date	Mintage	F	VF	XF	Unc	BU
1982FM (P)	699	Value: 10.00				

KM# 51 CENT

1.9500 g., Bronze, 17.8 mm. **Obv:** National arms **Rev:** Flaming hibiscus and value **Edge:** Plain

Date	Mintage	F	VF	XF	Unc	BU
1983FM (M)	—	—	—	—	1.50	3.00
1983FM (P)	—	Value: 1.00				
1984FM (P)	—	Value: 1.00				

KM# 51a CENT

2.0000 g., 0.9250 Silver .0594 oz. ASW, 17.8 mm. **Obv:** National arms **Rev:** Flaming hibiscus and value

Date	Mintage	F	VF	XF	Unc	BU
1983FM (P)	1,344	Value: 10.00				
1984FM (P)	—	Value: 10.00				

KM# 30 5 CENTS

3.2500 g., Bronze, 21.15 mm. **Obv:** National arms **Rev:** Bird of paradise and value

Date	Mintage	F	VF	XF	Unc	BU
1976FM (M)	30,000	—	—	—	0.25	1.00
1976FM (U)	582	—	—	—	1.75	3.50
1976FM (P)	10,000	Value: 0.75				
1977	12,000,000	—	—	0.10	0.25	1.00
1977FM (M)	30,000	—	—	—	0.25	1.00
1977FM (U)	633	—	—	—	1.75	3.50
1977FM (P)	5,337	Value: 0.75				
1978	1,500,000	—	—	0.10	0.25	1.00
1978FM (M)	30,000	—	—	—	0.25	1.00
1978FM (U)	472	—	—	—	1.75	3.50
1978FM (P)	4,845	Value: 1.25				
1979	—	—	—	0.10	0.25	1.00
1979FM (M)	30,000	—	—	—	0.25	1.00
1979FM (U)	518	—	—	—	1.75	3.50
1979FM (P)	3,270	Value: 1.25				
1980	15,000,000	—	—	0.10	0.25	1.00
1980FM (M)	15,000	—	—	—	0.25	1.00
1980FM (U)	796	—	—	—	5.00	7.50
1980FM (P)	2,393	Value: 1.25				
1981	—	—	—	0.10	0.25	1.00
1981FM (M)	—	—	—	—	0.25	1.00
1981FM (U)	—	—	—	—	1.75	2.50
1981FM (P)	—	Value: 1.25				
1983	—	—	—	0.10	0.25	1.00
1984	4,094,999	—	—	0.10	1.00	1.25
1988	20,000,000	—	—	0.10	0.25	1.00
1990	—	—	—	0.10	0.25	1.00
1992	—	—	—	0.10	0.25	1.00
1995	—	—	—	0.10	0.25	1.00
1996	—	—	—	0.10	0.25	1.00
1997	—	—	—	0.10	0.25	1.00
1998	—	—	—	0.10	0.25	1.00
1999	—	—	—	0.10	0.25	1.00
1999 Proof	3,000	Value: 1.00				
2000	—	—	—	0.10	0.25	1.00

KM# 30a 5 CENTS

3.5000 g., 0.9250 Silver .1040 oz. ASW, 21.15 mm. **Obv:** National arms **Rev:** Bird of paradise and value

Date	Mintage	F	VF	XF	Unc	BU
1981FM (P)	898	Value: 13.50				

KM# 43 5 CENTS

3.2500 g., Bronze, 21.15 mm. **Subject:** 20th Anniversary of Independence **Obv:** National arms **Rev:** Butterfly and value

Date	Mintage	F	VF	XF	Unc	BU
1982FM (M)	—	—	—	—	1.50	4.00
1982FM (U)	—	—	—	—	3.00	5.00
1982FM (P)	—	Value: 3.00				

KM# 43a 5 CENTS

3.5000 g., 0.9250 Silver .1040 oz. ASW, 21.15 mm. **Obv:** National arms **Rev:** Butterfly and value

Date	Mintage	F	VF	XF	Unc	BU
1982FM (P)	699	Value: 15.00				

KM# 52 5 CENTS

3.2500 g., Bronze, 21.15 mm. **Obv:** National arms **Rev:** Butterfly

Date	Mintage	F	VF	XF	Unc	BU
1983FM (M)	—	—	—	—	2.50	5.00
1983FM (P)	—	Value: 5.00				
1984FM (P)	—	Value: 5.00				

KM# 52a 5 CENTS

3.5000 g., 0.9250 Silver .1040 oz. ASW, 21.15 mm. **Obv:** National arms **Rev:** Butterfly and value

Date	Mintage	F	VF	XF	Unc	BU
1983FM (P)	1,324	Value: 15.00				
1984FM (P)	—	Value: 15.00				

KM# 31 10 CENTS

1.4000 g., Copper-Nickel, 16.3 mm. **Obv:** National arms **Rev:** Hibiscus and value **Edge:** Reeded

Date	Mintage	F	VF	XF	Unc	BU
1976FM (M)	15,000	—	—	—	0.50	1.00
1976FM (U)	582	—	—	5.00	7.50	10.00
1976FM (P)	10,000	Value: 1.00				
1977	17,280,000	—	—	0.10	0.20	0.40
1977FM (M)	15,000	—	—	—	0.50	1.00
1977FM (U)	633	—	—	5.00	7.50	10.00
1977FM (P)	5,337	Value: 1.00				
1978	10,000,000	—	—	0.10	0.20	0.40
1978FM (M)	15,000	—	—	—	0.50	1.00
1978FM (U)	472	—	—	5.00	7.50	9.00
1978FM (P)	4,845	Value: 1.50				
1979	1,970,000	—	—	0.10	0.30	0.60
1979FM (M)	15,000	—	—	—	0.50	1.00
1979FM (U)	518	—	—	5.00	7.50	9.00
1979FM (P)	3,270	Value: 1.50				
1980	20,000,000	—	—	0.10	0.30	0.60
1980FM (M)	7,500	—	—	—	0.50	1.00
1980FM (U)	796	—	—	5.00	7.50	9.00
1980FM (P)	2,393	Value: 1.50				
1981	—	—	—	0.10	0.30	0.60
1981FM (M)	—	—	—	—	0.50	1.00
1981FM (U)	—	—	—	5.00	7.50	9.00
1981FM (P)	—	Value: 1.50				
1990	—	—	—	0.10	0.30	0.60
1997	—	—	—	—	0.50	1.00
1998	—	—	—	—	0.50	1.00
1999	—	—	—	—	0.50	1.00
1999 Proof	—	Value: 2.00				
2000	—	—	—	—	0.50	1.00

KM# 31a 10 CENTS

1.5000 g., 0.9250 Silver .0446 oz. ASW, 16.3 mm. **Obv:** National arms **Rev:** Hibiscus and value

Date	Mintage	F	VF	XF	Unc	BU
1981FM (P)	898	Value: 15.00				

KM# 44 10 CENTS

1.4000 g., Copper-Nickel, 16.3 mm. **Subject:** 20th Anniversary of Independence **Obv:** National arms **Rev:** Hummingbird and value **Edge:** Reeded

Date	Mintage	F	VF	XF	Unc	BU
1982FM (M)	—	—	—	—	2.50	5.00
1982FM (U)	—	—	—	—	4.00	8.00
1982FM (P)	—	Value: 2.50				

KM# 44a 10 CENTS

1.5000 g., 0.9250 Silver .0446 oz. ASW, 16.3 mm. **Obv:** National arms **Rev:** Hummingbird and value

Date	Mintage	F	VF	XF	Unc	BU
1982FM (P)	699	Value: 15.00				

KM# 53 10 CENTS

1.4000 g., Copper-Nickel, 16.3 mm. **Obv:** National arms **Rev:** Hummingbird and value

Date	Mintage	F	VF	XF	Unc	BU
1983FM (M)	—	—	—	—	3.00	6.00
1983FM (P)	—	Value: 2.00				
1984FM (P)	—	Value: 2.00				

KM# 53a 10 CENTS

1.5000 g., 0.9250 Silver .0446 oz. ASW, 16.3 mm. **Obv:** National arms **Rev:** Hummingbird and value

Date	Mintage	F	VF	XF	Unc	BU
1983FM (P)	—	Value: 10.00				
1984FM (P)	—	Value: 10.00				

KM# 32 25 CENTS

3.5000 g., Copper-Nickel, 20 mm. **Obv:** National arms **Rev:** Chaconia and value **Edge:** Reeded

Date	Mintage	F	VF	XF	Unc	BU
1976FM (M)	6,000	—	—	—	1.00	2.00

Date	Mintage	F	VF	XF	Unc	BU
1976FM (U)	582	—	—	5.00	7.50	10.00
1976FM (P)	10,000	Value: 1.25				
1977	9,000,000	—	0.10	0.15	0.30	0.60
1977FM (M)	6,000	—	—	—	1.00	2.00
1977FM (U)	633	—	—	5.00	7.50	10.00
1977FM (P)	5,337	Value: 1.25				
1978	5,470,000	—	0.10	0.15	0.30	0.60
1978FM (M)	6,000	—	—	—	1.00	2.00
1978FM (U)	472	—	—	5.00	7.50	10.00
1978FM (P)	4,845	Value: 1.75				
1979	—	—	0.10	0.15	0.40	0.80
1979FM (M)	6,000	—	—	—	1.00	2.00
1979FM (U)	518	—	—	5.00	7.50	10.00
1979FM (P)	3,270	Value: 2.00				
1980	15,000,000	—	0.10	0.15	0.40	0.80
1980FM (M)	3,000	—	—	—	1.00	2.00
1980FM (U)	796	—	—	5.00	7.50	10.00
1980FM (P)	2,393	Value: 2.00				
1981	—	—	0.10	0.15	0.40	0.80
1981FM (M)	—	—	—	—	1.00	2.00
1981FM (U)	—	—	—	5.00	7.50	10.00
1981FM (P)	—	Value: 2.00				
1983	—	—	0.10	0.15	0.40	0.80
1983FM (M)	—	—	—	—	2.00	4.00
1983FM (P)	—	Value: 2.00				
1984	—	—	0.10	0.15	0.40	0.80
1984	—	Value: 2.00				
1993	—	—	—	0.15	0.40	0.80
1997	—	—	—	0.15	0.40	0.80
1998	—	—	—	0.15	0.40	0.80
1999	—	—	—	0.15	0.40	0.80
1999 Proof	—	Value: 3.00				

KM# 32a 25 CENTS

3.6000 g., 0.9250 Silver .1070 oz. ASW, 20 mm. **Obv:** National arms **Rev:** Chaconia and value

Date	Mintage	F	VF	XF	Unc	BU
1981FM (P)	898	Value: 12.00				
1983FM (P)	—	Value: 12.00				
1984FM (P)	—	Value: 12.00				

KM# 45 25 CENTS

3.5000 g., Copper-Nickel, 20 mm. **Subject:** 20th Anniversary of Independence **Obv:** National arms **Rev:** Chaconia and value **Edge:** Reeded

Date	Mintage	F	VF	XF	Unc	BU
1982FM (M)	—	—	—	—	1.00	2.00
1982FM (U)	—	—	—	—	2.25	4.50
1982FM (P)	—	Value: 2.00				

KM# 45a 25 CENTS

3.6000 g., 0.9250 Silver .1070 oz. ASW, 20 mm. **Obv:** National arms **Rev:** Chaconia and value

Date	Mintage	F	VF	XF	Unc	BU
1982FM (P)	699	Value: 15.00				

KM# 33 50 CENTS

7.0000 g., Copper-Nickel, 26 mm. **Obv:** National arms **Rev:** Kettle drums and value **Edge:** Reeded

Date	Mintage	F	VF	XF	Unc	BU
1976FM (M)	3,000	—	—	—	3.25	5.00
1976FM (U)	582	—	—	5.00	7.50	15.00
1976FM (P)	10,000	Value: 1.50				
1977	1,500,000	—	0.25	0.50	1.00	2.00
1977FM (M)	3,000	—	—	—	3.00	6.00
1977FM (U)	633	—	—	5.00	7.50	15.00
1977FM (P)	5,337	Value: 1.50				
1978	563,000	—	0.50	0.75	1.50	3.50
1978FM (M)	3,000	—	—	—	3.00	6.00
1978FM (U)	472	—	—	5.00	7.50	15.00
1978FM (P)	4,845	Value: 2.00				
1979	750,000	—	0.50	0.75	1.50	3.50
1979FM (M)	3,000	—	—	—	3.25	6.00
1979FM (U)	518	—	—	5.00	7.50	15.00
1979FM (P)	3,270	Value: 2.00				
1980	3,750,000	—	0.25	0.50	1.00	2.00
1980FM (M)	1,500	—	—	—	3.00	6.00
1980FM (U)	796	—	—	5.00	7.50	15.00
1980FM (P)	2,393	Value: 2.00				
1981FM (M)	—	—	—	—	3.00	6.00
1981FM (U)	—	—	—	5.00	7.50	10.00
1981FM (P)	—	Value: 2.00				
1999	—	—	—	—	2.00	4.00
1999 Proof	3,000	Value: 4.00				

KM# 33a 50 CENTS

7.2500 g., 0.9250 Silver .2156 oz. ASW, 26 mm. **Obv:** National arms **Rev:** Kettle drums and value

Date	Mintage	F	VF	XF	Unc	BU
1981FM (P)	898	Value: 18.00				

KM# 46 50 CENTS

7.0000 g., Copper-Nickel, 26 mm. **Subject:** 20th Anniversary of Independence **Obv:** National arms **Rev:** Kettle drums and player **Edge:** Reeded

Date	Mintage	F	VF	XF	Unc	BU
1982FM (M)	—	—	—	—	3.00	6.00
1982FM (U)	—	—	—	—	2.50	5.00
1982FM (P)	—	Value: 2.00				

KM# 46a 50 CENTS

7.2500 g., 0.9250 Silver .2156 oz. ASW, 26 mm. **Obv:** National arms **Rev:** Kettle drums and player

Date	Mintage	F	VF	XF	Unc	BU
1982FM (P)	699	Value: 20.00				

KM# 54 50 CENTS

7.0000 g., Copper-Nickel, 26 mm. **Obv:** National arms **Rev:** Kettle drums and player

Date	Mintage	F	VF	XF	Unc	BU
1983FM (M)	—	—	—	—	4.00	8.00
1983FM (P)	—	Value: 2.00				
1984FM (P)	—	Value: 2.00				

KM# 54a 50 CENTS

7.2500 g., 0.9250 Silver .2156 oz. ASW, 26 mm. **Obv:** National arms **Rev:** Kettle drums and player

Date	Mintage	F	VF	XF	Unc	BU
1983FM (P)	1,325	Value: 17.00				
1984FM (P)	—	Value: 17.00				

KM# 34 DOLLAR

Copper-Nickel, 36 mm. **Obv:** National arms **Rev:** Bird on branch and value

Date	Mintage	F	VF	XF	Unc	BU
1976FM (M)	1,500	—	—	—	6.00	10.00
1976FM (U)	582	—	—	8.00	10.00	15.00
1976FM (P)	10,000	Value: 2.00				
1977FM (M)	1,500	—	—	—	6.00	10.00
1977FM (U)	633	—	—	8.00	10.00	15.00
1977FM (P)	5,337	Value: 2.00				
1978FM (M)	1,500	—	—	—	6.00	10.00
1978FM (U)	472	—	—	8.00	10.00	15.00
1978FM (P)	4,845	Value: 3.00				
1979FM (M)	1,500	—	—	—	6.00	10.00
1979FM (U)	518	—	—	8.00	10.00	15.00
1979FM (P)	3,270	Value: 3.00				
1980FM (M)	750	—	—	8.00	10.00	15.00
1980FM (U)	796	—	—	8.00	10.00	15.00
1980FM (P)	2,393	Value: 5.00				
1981FM (M)	—	—	—	—	5.00	10.00
1981FM (U)	—	—	—	—	3.00	6.00
1981FM (P)	—	Value: 2.50				
1983FM (M)	—	—	—	—	6.00	10.00
1983FM (P)	—	Value: 2.50				
1984FM (P)	—	Value: 2.50				

KM# 34a DOLLAR

18.6000 g., 0.9250 Silver .5532 oz. ASW, 36 mm. **Obv:** National arms **Rev:** Bird on branch and value

Date	Mintage	F	VF	XF	Unc	BU
1981FM (P)	898	Value: 20.00				
1983FM (P)	2,544	Value: 16.50				
1984FM (P)	—	Value: 16.50				

KM# 38 DOLLAR

12.7000 g., Copper Nickel, 32 mm. **Series:** F.A.O. **Obv:** National arms **Rev:** Value in front of leaves

Date	Mintage	F	VF	XF	Unc	BU
1979	—	—	0.75	1.50	3.50	6.50

KM# 47 DOLLAR

Copper-Nickel, 36 mm. **Subject:** 20th Anniversary of Independence **Obv:** National arms **Rev:** Bird on branch and value within circle

Date	Mintage	F	VF	XF	Unc	BU
1982FM (M)	—	—	—	—	9.00	12.50
1982FM (U)	—	—	—	—	6.00	9.00
1982FM (P)	—	Value: 5.00				

KM# 47a DOLLAR

18.6000 g., 0.9250 Silver .5532 oz. ASW, 36 mm. **Obv:** National arms **Rev:** Bird on branch and value within circle

Date	Mintage	F	VF	XF	Unc	BU
1982FM (P)	699	Value: 20.00				

KM# 61 DOLLAR

Copper-Nickel **Subject:** 50th Anniversary - F.A.O. **Obv:** National arms **Rev:** Sprig, value and logo

Date	Mintage	F	VF	XF	Unc	BU
1995	—	—	—	1.00	1.75	2.75
1999	—	—	—	1.00	1.75	2.75
1999 Proof	3,000	Value: 5.00				

KM# 35a 5 DOLLARS

29.7000 g., 0.9250 Silver .8833 oz. ASW, 40 mm. **Obv:** National arms **Rev:** Bird on branch and value

Date	Mintage	F	VF	XF	Unc	BU
1976FM (P)	11,000	Value: 13.50				
1977FM (P)	6,107	Value: 16.00				
1978FM (P)	5,460	Value: 16.00				
1979FM (P)	3,755	Value: 18.50				
1980FM (P)	2,393	Value: 20.00				
1981FM (P)	—	Value: 30.00				
1983FM (P)	—	Value: 30.00				
1984FM (P)	—	Value: 30.00				

KM# 35 5 DOLLARS

Copper-Nickel, 40 mm. **Obv:** National arms **Rev:** Bird on branch and value

Date	Mintage	F	VF	XF	Unc	BU
1976FM (M)	300	—	—	—	20.00	25.00
1976FM (U)	582	—	—	—	20.00	25.00

Date	Mintage	F	VF	XF	Unc	BU
1977FM (M)	300	—	—	—	20.00	25.00
1977FM (U)	633	—	—	—	17.00	20.00
1978FM (M)	300	—	—	—	20.00	25.00
1978FM (U)	472	—	—	—	20.00	25.00
1979FM (M)	300	—	—	—	20.00	25.00
1979FM (U)	518	—	—	—	20.00	25.00
1980FM (M)	150	—	—	—	25.00	30.00
1980FM (U)	796	—	—	—	17.00	20.00
1981FM (M)	—	—	—	—	20.00	25.00
1981FM (U)	—	—	—	—	17.00	20.00
1981FM (P)	—	Value: 20.00				
1983FM (U)	—	—	—	—	20.00	25.00
1983FM (P)	1,312	Value: 20.00				
1984FM (P)	—	Value: 20.00				

KM# 35a.1 5 DOLLARS

11.0000 g., Copper Nickel, 30 mm. **Obv:** National arms **Rev:** Bird on branch and value **Note:** Reduced size.

Date	Mintage	F	VF	XF	Unc	BU
1999 Proof	—	Value: 20.00				

KM# 48 5 DOLLARS

Copper-Nickel, 40 mm. **Subject:** 20th Anniversary of Independence **Obv:** National arms **Rev:** Bird on branch and value

Date	Mintage	F	VF	XF	Unc	BU
1982FM (M)	—	—	—	—	20.00	25.00
1982FM (U)	—	—	—	—	12.50	15.00
1982FM (P)	—	Value: 17.00				

KM# 48a 5 DOLLARS

30.0000 g., 0.9250 Silver .8922 oz. ASW, 40 mm. **Obv:** National arms **Rev:** Bird on branch and value

Date	Mintage	F	VF	XF	Unc	BU
1982FM (P)	699	Value: 30.00				

KM# 36a 10 DOLLARS

35.0000 g., 0.9250 Silver 1.0409 oz. ASW, 42 mm. **Obv:** National arms **Rev:** Fish, ship, map and value within waves

Date	Mintage	F	VF	XF	Unc	BU
1976FM (P)	13,000	Value: 16.00				
1977FM (P)	6,643	Value: 17.50				
1978FM (P)	7,449	Value: 17.50				
1979FM (P)	4,994	Value: 22.00				
1980FM (P)	3,726	Value: 25.00				

KM# 36 10 DOLLARS

Copper-Nickel, 42 mm. **Obv:** National arms **Rev:** Fish, ship, value and map within waves

Date	Mintage	F	VF	XF	Unc	BU
1976FM (M)	150	—	—	—	40.00	45.00
1976FM (U)	582	—	—	—	30.00	35.00
1977FM (M)	150	—	—	—	40.00	45.00
1977FM (U)	633	—	—	—	30.00	35.00
1978FM (M)	150	—	—	—	40.00	45.00
1978FM (U)	472	—	—	—	30.00	35.00
1979FM (M)	150	—	—	—	40.00	45.00
1979FM (U)	518	—	—	—	30.00	35.00
1980FM (M)	—	—	—	—	40.00	45.00
1980FM (U)	—	—	—	—	30.00	35.00

KM# 40 10 DOLLARS

Copper-Nickel, 42 mm. **Subject:** 5th Anniversary of the Republic **Obv:** National arms **Rev:** Fish, ship, map and value in waves within circle

Date	Mintage	F	VF	XF	Unc	BU
1981FM (U)	—	—	—	—	20.00	25.00

KM# 40a 10 DOLLARS

35.0000 g., 0.9250 Silver 1.0409 oz. ASW, 42 mm. **Obv:** National arms **Rev:** Fish, boat, map and value in waves within circle

Date	Mintage	F	VF	XF	Unc	BU
1981FM (P)	2,374	Value: 27.50				

KM# 49 10 DOLLARS

Copper-Nickel, 42 mm. **Subject:** 20th Anniversary of Independence **Obv:** National arms **Rev:** Flag and value

Date	Mintage	F	VF	XF	Unc	BU
1982FM (M)	—	—	—	—	20.00	25.00
1982FM (U)	—	—	—	—	20.00	25.00
1982FM (P)	—	Value: 20.00				

KM# 49a 10 DOLLARS

35.0000 g., 0.9250 Silver 1.0409 oz. ASW, 42 mm. **Obv:** National arms **Rev:** Flag and value

Date	Mintage	F	VF	XF	Unc	BU
1982FM (P)	1,682	Value: 37.50				

KM# 55 10 DOLLARS

Copper-Nickel, 42 mm. **Obv:** National arms **Rev:** Ships and value

Date	Mintage	F	VF	XF	Unc	BU
1983FM (U)	288	—	—	—	55.00	65.00

KM# 55a 10 DOLLARS

35.0000 g., 0.9250 Silver 1.0409 oz. ASW, 42 mm. **Obv:** National arms **Rev:** Ships and value

Date	Mintage	F	VF	XF	Unc	BU
1983FM (P)	1,565	Value: 40.00				
1984FM (P)	—	Value: 40.00				

KM# 60 10 DOLLARS

28.2800 g., 0.9250 Silver .8411 oz. ASW, 38.61 mm. **Subject:** 30th Anniversary - Central Bank **Obv:** National arms **Rev:** Bird and sprigs **Designer:** Robert Elderton

Date	Mintage	F	VF	XF	Unc	BU
1994 Proof	Est. 5,000	Value: 40.00				

KM# 62 10 DOLLARS

Bi-Metallic Silver center in Gold-plated ring, 28.4 mm. **Subject:** Central Bank 35 Years **Obv:** National arms within circle **Rev:** Bank building within circle **Edge:** Reeded **Shape:** Octagonal

Date	Mintage	F	VF	XF	Unc	BU
1999 Proof	6,500	Value: 42.50				

KM# 39 25 DOLLARS

30.2800 g., 0.5000 Silver .4868 oz. ASW **Subject:** 10th Anniversary of Caribbean Development Bank **Obv:** National arms **Rev:** Map on globe above flag, beaded border

Date	Mintage	F	VF	XF	Unc	BU
ND(1980)FM (P)	3,039	Value: 20.00				

KM# 37 100 DOLLARS

6.2100 g., 0.5000 Gold .0998 oz. AGW **Obv:** National arms **Rev:** Flying birds and value

Date	Mintage	F	VF	XF	Unc	BU
1976FM (M)	200	—	—	—	110	120
1976FM (P)	29,000	Value: 70.00				

KM# 41 100 DOLLARS

6.2100 g., 0.5000 Gold .0998 oz. AGW **Subject:** 5th Anniversary of the Republic **Obv:** National arms **Rev:** Hummingbird and flower

Date	Mintage	F	VF	XF	Unc	BU
1981FM (U)	100	—	—	—	175	195
1981FM (P)	400	Value: 150				

KM# 50 100 DOLLARS

6.2100 g., 0.5000 Gold .0998 oz. AGW **Subject:** 20th Anniversary of Independence **Obv:** National arms **Rev:** Building within circle

Date	Mintage	F	VF	XF	Unc	BU
1982FM (P)	1,380	Value: 100				

KM# 56 200 DOLLARS

11.1700 g., 0.5000 Gold .1796 oz. AGW **Subject:** 20th Anniversary of Central Bank **Obv:** National arms **Rev:** Building below value

Date	Mintage	F	VF	XF	Unc	BU
1984FM (P)	1,200	Value: 145				

MINT SETS

KM#	Date	Mintage	Identification	Issue Price	Mkt Val
MS1	1973 (8)	1,575	KM#8, 18-24	24.00	22.00
MS2	1974 (8)	3,258	KM#8a, 22-23, 24a, 25-28	25.00	15.00
MS3	1975 (8)	1,111	KM#8a, 22-23, 24a, 25-28	27.50	20.00
MS4	1976 (8)	582	KM#29-34, 35a-36a	27.50	30.00
MS5	1977 (8)	632	KM#29-34, 35a-36a	27.50	30.00
MS6	1978 (8)	472	KM#29-34, 35a-36a	27.50	30.00
MS7	1979 (8)	518	KM#29-34, 35a-36a	28.50	40.00
MS8	1980 (8)	796	KM#29-34, 35a-36a	28.50	30.00
MS9	1981 (8)	—	KM#29-34, 35a, 40	28.50	45.00
MS10	1982 (8)	—	KM#42-49	28.50	45.00
MS11	1983 (8)	281	KM#32, 34, 35a, 51-55	37.00	80.00
MS12	1999 (6)	—	KM#29-33, 61	35.00	35.00

PROOF SETS

KM#	Date	Mintage	Identification	Issue Price	Mkt Val
PS1	1966 (5)	8,000	KM#1-5	12.50	10.00
PS2	1970 (6)	2,104	KM#1-5, 7	15.25	12.50
PS3	1971 (7)	11,039	KM#1-5, 7a, 8	21.00	15.00
PS4	1971 (6)	488	KM#1-6	15.00	12.50
PS5	1972 (8)	13,874	KM#9-16	35.00	20.00
PS6	1972 (7)	15,957	KM#9-15	22.00	12.50
PS7	1973 (8)	14,615	KM#8, 17, 22-23, 24a, 57-59	35.00	20.00
PS8	1973 (7)	5,050	KM#8,17,22-23, 57-59	22.00	15.00
PS9	1974 (8)	13,991	KM#8, 22-28	50.00	20.00
PS10	1975 (8)	24,472	KM#8, 22-28	55.00	22.00
PS11	1976 (8)	10,099	KM#29-36	55.00	25.00
PS12	1977 (8)	5,337	KM#29-36	55.00	35.00
PS13	1978 (8)	4,845	KM#29-36	55.00	35.00
PS14	1979 (8)	3,270	KM#29-36	57.00	40.00
PS15	1980 (8)	2,393	KM#29-36	66.00	55.00
PS16	1981 (8)	—	KM#29-34, 35a, 40a	87.00	65.00
PS17	1981 (8)	—	KM#29a-34a, 35, 40a	222	125
PS18	1982 (8)	—	KM#42-49	87.00	65.00
PS19	1982 (8)	—	KM#42a-49a	222	135
PS20	1983 (8)	461	KM#32, 34, 35a, 51-54, 55a	87.00	85.00
PS21	1983 (8)	753	KM#32a, 34a, 35, 51a-55a	197	100
PS22	1984 (8)	—	KM#32, 34, 35a, 51-54, 55a	87.00	75.00
PS23	1984 (8)	—	KM#32a, 34a, 35, 51a-55a	197	100
PS24	1999 (8)	3,000	KM#29-33, 35a.1, 61-62	90.00	95.00

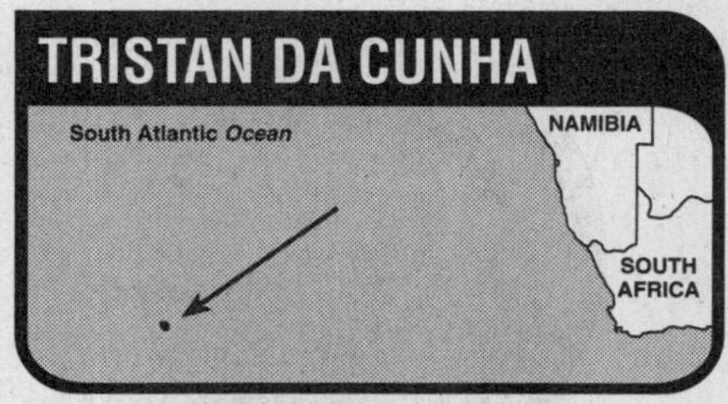

Tristan da Cunha is the principal island and group name of a small cluster of volcanic islands located in the South Atlantic midway between the Cape of Good Hope and South America, and 1,500 miles (2,414 km.) south-southwest of the British colony of St. Helena. The other islands are Inaccessible, Gough, and the three Nightingale Islands. The group, which comprises a dependency of St. Helena, has a total area of 40 sq. mi. (104 sq. km.) and a population of less than 300. There is a village of 60 houses called Edinburgh. Potatoes are the staple subsistence crop.

Portuguese admiral Tristao da Cunha discovered Tristan da Cunha in 1506. Unsuccessful attempts to colonize the islands were made by the Dutch in 1656, but the first permanent inhabitant didn't arrive until 1810. During the exile of Napoleon on St. Helena, Britain placed a temporary garrison on Tristan da Cunha to prevent any attempt to rescue Napoleon from his island prison. The islands were formally annexed to Britain in 1816 and became a dependency of St. Helena in 1938.

RULERS
British

MINT MARKS
PM - Pobjoy Mint

MONETARY SYSTEM
Sterling until 1961
1961 – South African Rand
1963 – Reverted to Sterling
25 Pence = 1 Crown
4 Crowns = 1 Pound

ST. HELENA DEPENDENCY

STANDARD COINAGE

KM# 1 25 PENCE

Copper-Nickel, 38.5 mm. **Ruler:** Elizabeth II **Subject:** Queen's Silver Jubilee **Obv:** Young bust right **Obv. Designer:** Arnold Machin **Rev:** Boat and rock **Edge:** Reeded

Date	Mintage	F	VF	XF	Unc	BU
ND(1977)	50,000	—	1.00	2.00	5.00	6.00

KM# 1a 25 PENCE

28.2800 g., 0.9250 Silver .8411 oz. ASW, 38.5 mm. **Ruler:** Elizabeth II **Subject:** Queen's Silver Jubilee **Obv:** Young bust right **Obv. Designer:** Arnold Machin **Rev:** Boat and rock

Date	Mintage	F	VF	XF	Unc	BU
ND(1977) Proof	25,000	Value: 14.50				

KM# 3 25 PENCE

Copper-Nickel, 38.5 mm. **Ruler:** Elizabeth II **Subject:** 80th Birthday of Queen Mother **Obv:** Young bust right **Obv. Designer:** Arnold Machin **Rev:** Queen Mother 1/4 left above sprig **Edge:** Reeded

Date	Mintage	F	VF	XF	Unc	BU
ND(1980)	65,000	—	1.00	1.75	3.50	4.50

KM# 3a 25 PENCE

28.2800 g., 0.9250 Silver .8411 oz. ASW, 38.5 mm. **Ruler:** Elizabeth II **Subject:** 80th Birthday of Queen Mother **Obv:** Young bust right **Obv. Designer:** Arnold Machin **Rev:** Queen Mother 1/4 left above sprig

Date	Mintage	F	VF	XF	Unc	BU
ND(1980) Proof	25,000	Value: 14.50				

KM# 4 25 PENCE

Copper-Nickel, 38.5 mm. **Ruler:** Elizabeth II **Subject:** Wedding of Prince Charles and Lady Diana **Obv:** Young bust right **Obv. Designer:** Arnold Machin **Rev:** Design in center divides cameo heads facing each other **Edge:** Reeded

Date	Mintage	F	VF	XF	Unc	BU
ND(1981)PM	—	—	1.00	1.75	3.50	4.50

KM# 4a 25 PENCE

28.2800 g., 0.9250 Silver .8411 oz. ASW, 38.5 mm. **Ruler:** Elizabeth II **Subject:** Wedding of Prince Charles and Lady Diana **Obv:** Young bust right **Obv. Designer:** Arnold Machin **Rev:** Design in center divides cameo heads facing each other

Date	Mintage	F	VF	XF	Unc	BU
ND(1981)PM Proof	30,000	Value: 17.50				

KM# 5 25 PENCE

28.2800 g., 0.9250 Silver .8411 oz. ASW, 38.5 mm. **Ruler:** Elizabeth II **Series:** International Year of the Scout **Obv:** Young bust right **Rev:** Scouting emblem within roped wreath

Date	Mintage	F	VF	XF	Unc	BU
ND(1983)	10,000	—	—	—	32.50	35.00
ND(1983) Proof	10,000	Value: 47.50				

KM# 7 50 PENCE

28.2800 g., 0.9250 Silver .8411 oz. ASW, 38.5 mm. **Ruler:** Elizabeth II **Subject:** 40th Wedding Anniversary of Queen Elizabeth and Prince Philip **Obv:** Crowned bust right **Rev:** Crowned initials at center of flower design **Rev. Designer:** Ronald Dutton **Edge:** Reeded

Date	Mintage	F	VF	XF	Unc	BU
ND(1987) Proof	2,000	Value: 25.00				

KM# 7a 50 PENCE

47.5400 g., 0.9170 Gold 1.4001 oz. AGW, 38.5 mm. **Ruler:** Elizabeth II **Subject:** 40th Wedding Anniversary of Queen Elizabeth and Prince Philip **Obv:** Crowned head right **Rev:** Crowned initials at center of flower design **Rev. Designer:** Ronald Dutton

Date	Mintage	F	VF	XF	Unc	BU
ND(1987) Proof	75	Value: 985				

KM# 7b 50 PENCE

Copper-Nickel, 38.5 mm. **Ruler:** Elizabeth II **Subject:** 40th Wedding Anniversary of Queen Elizabeth and Prince Philip **Obv:** Crowned bust right **Rev:** Crowned initials at center of flower design **Rev. Designer:** Ronald Dutton

Date	Mintage	F	VF	XF	Unc	BU
ND(1987)	—	—	—	—	4.50	6.00

KM# 9 50 PENCE
28.2800 g., Copper-Nickel, 38.6 mm. **Ruler:** Elizabeth II **Subject:** Winston Churchill **Obv:** Crowned bust right **Obv. Designer:** Raphael Maklouf **Rev:** Uniformed bust 1/4 left and two fighter planes **Edge:** Reeded **Note:** Struck at British Royal Mint.

Date	Mintage	F	VF	XF	Unc	BU
1999	—	—	—	—	7.00	9.00

KM# 9a 50 PENCE
28.2800 g., 0.9250 Silver .8411 oz. ASW, 38.6 mm. **Subject:** Winston Churchill **Obv:** Crowned head right **Rev:** Uniformed bust 1/4 left and two fighter planes

Date	Mintage	F	VF	XF	Unc	BU
1999 Proof	2,500	Value: 42.50				

KM# 9b 50 PENCE
47.5400 g., 0.9170 Gold 1.4001 oz. AGW, 38.6 mm. **Ruler:** Elizabeth II **Subject:** Winston Churchill **Obv:** Crowned bust right **Rev:** Uniformed bust 1/4 left and two fighter planes

Date	Mintage	F	VF	XF	Unc	BU
1999	Est. 125	Value: 985				

KM# 11 50 PENCE
28.6400 g., Copper-Nickel, 38.6 mm. **Ruler:** Elizabeth II **Subject:** Princess Anne's 50th Birthday **Obv:** Crowned bust right **Obv. Designer:** Raphael Maklouf **Rev:** Bust of Princess Anne facing **Edge:** Reeded

Date	Mintage	F	VF	XF	Unc	BU
ND(2000)	—	—	—	—	6.50	7.50

KM# 10a 50 PENCE
28.4000 g., 0.9250 Silver 0.8446 oz. ASW, 38.6 mm. **Ruler:** Elizabeth II **Subject:** Queen Mother's Centennial Birthday **Obv:** Crowned bust right **Obv. Designer:** Raphael Maklouf **Rev:** Bust of Queen Mother right

Date	Mintage	F	VF	XF	Unc	BU
ND(2000)	—	—	—	—	—	—
ND(2000) Proof	10,000	Value: 50.00				

KM# 10b 50 PENCE
47.5400 g., 0.9166 Gold 1.401 oz. AGW, 38.6 mm. **Ruler:** Elizabeth II **Subject:** Queen Mother's 100th Birthday **Obv:** Crowned bust right **Obv. Designer:** Raphael Maklouf **Rev:** Bust of Queen Mother right **Edge:** Reeded

Date	Mintage	F	VF	XF	Unc	BU
ND(2000) Proof	100	Value: 985				

KM# 11a 50 PENCE
28.2800 g., 0.9250 Silver 0.841 oz. ASW, 38.6 mm. **Ruler:** Elizabeth II **Subject:** Princess Anne's 50th Birthday **Obv:** Crowned bust right **Obv. Designer:** Raphael Maklouf **Rev:** Bust of Princess Anne facing **Edge:** Reeded

Date	Mintage	F	VF	XF	Unc	BU
ND(2000) Proof	2,500	Value: 50.00				

KM# 11b 50 PENCE
47.5400 g., 0.9166 Gold 1.401 oz. AGW, 38.6 mm. **Ruler:** Elizabeth II **Subject:** Princess Anne's 50th Birthday **Obv:** Crowned bust right **Obv. Designer:** Raphael Maklouf **Rev:** Bust of Princess Anne facing **Edge:** Reeded

Date	Mintage	F	VF	XF	Unc	BU
ND(2000) Proof	50	Value: 1,000				

KM# 10 50 PENCE
28.6400 g., Copper-Nickel, 38.6 mm. **Ruler:** Elizabeth II **Subject:** Queen Mother's Centennial Birthday **Obv:** Crowned bust right **Obv. Designer:** Raphael Maklouf **Rev:** Bust of Queen Mother right **Edge:** Reeded

Date	Mintage	F	VF	XF	Unc	BU
ND(2000)	—	—	—	—	6.50	7.50

KM# 2 CROWN
Copper-Nickel, 38.5 mm. **Ruler:** Elizabeth II **Subject:** 25th Anniversary of Coronation **Obv:** Young bust right **Obv. Designer:** Arnold Machin **Rev:** Tristan rock lobster on coat of arms **Edge:** Reeded

Date	Mintage	F	VF	XF	Unc	BU
1978PM	—	—	1.00	1.75	3.50	4.50

KM# 2a CROWN
28.2800 g., 0.9250 Silver .8411 oz. ASW, 38.5 mm. **Ruler:** Elizabeth II **Obv:** Young bust right **Obv. Designer:** Arnold Machin **Rev:** Tristan rock lobster on coat of arms

Date	Mintage	F	VF	XF	Unc	BU
1978PM	70,000	—	—	—	13.50	15.00
1978PM Proof	25,000	Value: 18.50				

KM# 6 2 POUNDS
15.9800 g., 0.9170 Gold .4712 oz. AGW **Ruler:** Elizabeth II **Series:** International Year of the Scout **Obv:** Young bust right **Rev:** Sailboat

Date	Mintage	F	VF	XF	Unc	BU
1983	2,000	—	—	—	350	375
1983 Proof	2,000	Value: 500				

KM# 8 2 POUNDS
Copper-Nickel, 38.5 mm. **Ruler:** Elizabeth II **Subject:** 90th Anniversary of Queen Mother **Obv:** Crowned bust right **Rev:** Crowned monogram flanked by flower sprigs **Rev. Designer:** Robert Elderton **Edge:** Reeded

Date	Mintage	F	VF	XF	Unc	BU
ND(1990)	—	—	—	—	12.50	13.50

KM# 8a 2 POUNDS
28.2800 g., 0.9250 Silver .8411 oz. ASW, 38.5 mm. **Ruler:** Elizabeth II **Subject:** 90th Anniversary of Queen Mother **Obv:** Crowned bust right **Rev:** Crowned monogram flanked by flower sprigs **Rev. Designer:** Robert Elderton

Date	Mintage	F	VF	XF	Unc	BU
ND(1990) Proof	Est. 10,000	Value: 55.00				

The Republic of Tunisia, located on the northern coast of Africa between Algeria and Libya, has an area of 63,170sq. mi. (163,610 sq. km.) and a population of *7.9 million. Capital: Tunis. Agriculture is the backbone of the economy. Crude oil, phosphates, olive oil, and wine are exported.

Tunisia, settled by the Phoenicians in the 12th century B.C., was the center of the seafaring Carthaginian Empire. After the total destruction of Carthage, Tunisia became part of Rome's African province. It remained a part of the Roman Empire (except for the 439-533 interval of Vandal conquest) until taken by the Arabs, 648, who administered it until the Turkish invasion of 1570. Under Turkish control, the public revenue was heavily dependent upon the piracy of Mediterranean shipping, an endeavor that wasn't abandoned until 1819 when a coalition of powers threatened appropriate reprisal. Deprived of its major source of income, Tunisia underwent a financial regression that ended in bankruptcy, enabling France to establish a protectorate over the country in 1881. National agitation and guerrilla fighting forced France to grant Tunisia internal autonomy in 1955 and to recognize Tunisian independence on March 20, 1956. Tunisia abolished the monarchy and established a republic on July 25, 1957.

TITLES

المملكة التونسية

al-Mamlaka al-Tunisiya

الجمهورية العراقية

al-Jumhuriya al-Tunisiya

al-Amala al-Tunisiya
(Tunisian Protectorate)

MINT MARKS
A - Paris, AH1308/1891-AH1348/1928
(a) - Paris, privy marks, AH1349/1929-AH1376/1957
FM - Franklin Mint, Franklin Center, PA
Numismatic Italiana, Arezzo, Italy

TUNIS

Tunis, the capital and major seaport of Tunisia, existed in the Carthaginian era, but its importance dates only from the Moslem conquest, following which it became a major center of Arab power and prosperity. Spain seized it in 1535, lost it in 1564, retook it in 1573 and ceded it to the Turks in 1574. Thereafter the history of Tunis merged with that of Tunisia.

Local Rulers
Ali Bey, AH1299-1320/1882-1902AD
Muhammad Al-Hadi Bey, AH1320-1324/1902-1906AD
Muhammad Al-Nasir Bey, AH1324-1340/1906-1922AD
Muhammad Al-Habib Bey, AH1340-1348/1922-1929AD
Ahmad Pasha Bey, AH1348-1361/1929-1942AD
Muhammad Al-Munsif Bey, AH1361-1362/1942-1943AD
Muhammad Al-Amin Bey, AH1362-1376/1943-1957AD

NOTE: All coins struck until AH1298/1881AD bear the name of the Ottoman Sultan; the name of the Bey of Tunis was added in AH1272/1855AD. After AH1298, when the French established their protectorate, only the Bey's name appears on the coin until AH1376/1956AD.

TUNISIA

FRENCH PROTECTORATE

Ali Bey
"Struck in his name"

DECIMAL COINAGE
100 Centimes = 1 Franc

The following coins all bear French inscriptions on one side, Arabic on the other, and usually have both AH and AD dates. Except for KM#246-48, they are struck in the name of the Tunisian Bey.

KM# 223 50 CENTIMES

2.5000 g., 0.8350 Silver .0671 oz. ASW **Obv:** Legend flanked by sprigs **Obv. Legend:** ALI **Rev:** Value, date in center circle of ornate design

Date	Mintage	F	VF	XF	Unc
AH1319/1901A	1,000	—	—	150	250
AH1320/1902A	1,000	—	—	150	250

KM# 224 FRANC

5.0000 g., 0.8350 Silver .1342 oz. ASW **Obv:** Legend flanked by sprigs **Obv. Legend:** ALI **Rev:** Value, date in center circle of ornate design

Date	Mintage	F	VF	XF	Unc
AH1319/1901A	700	—	—	175	275
AH1320/1902A	703	—	—	175	275

KM# 225 2 FRANCS

10.0000 g., 0.8350 Silver .2685 oz. ASW **Obv:** Legend flanked by sprigs **Obv. Legend:** ALI **Rev:** Value, date within center circle of ornate design

Date	Mintage	F	VF	XF	Unc
AH1319/1901A	300	—	—	200	350
AH1320/1902A	300	—	—	200	350

KM# 226 10 FRANCS

3.2258 g., 0.9000 Gold .0933 oz. AGW **Obv:** Legend flanked by sprigs **Obv. Legend:** ALI **Rev:** Value, date in center circle of ornate design

Date	Mintage	F	VF	XF	Unc
AH1319/1901A	80	—	—	450	850
AH1319/1901A	80	—	—	450	850
AH1320/1902A	83	—	—	450	850

KM# 227 20 FRANCS

6.4516 g., 0.9000 Gold .1867 oz. AGW **Obv:** Legend flanked by sprigs **Obv. Legend:** ALI **Rev:** Value, date in center circle of ornate design

Date	Mintage	F	VF	XF	Unc
AH1319/1901A	150,000	—	—	BV	145
AH1319/1901A	150,000	—	—	BV	145
AH1320/1902A	20	—	—	550	1,000

Muhammad al-Hadi Bey

"Struck in his name"

DECIMAL COINAGE

100 Centimes = 1 Franc

The following coins all bear French inscriptions on one side, Arabic on the other, and usually have both AH and AD dates. Except for KM#246-48, they are struck in the name of the Tunisian Bey.

KM# 228 5 CENTIMES

Bronze **Obv:** Inscription within sprigs **Obv. Legend:** MUHAMMAD AL-HADI **Rev:** Value and date within center circle

Date	Mintage	F	VF	XF	Unc
AH1321/1903A	500,000	—	8.00	12.00	25.00
AH1322/1904A	1,000,000	—	8.00	12.00	25.00

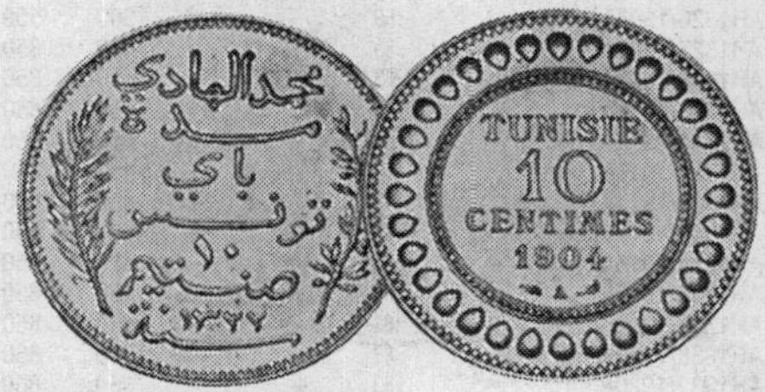

KM# 229 10 CENTIMES

Bronze **Obv:** Inscription within sprigs **Obv. Legend:** MUHAMMAD AL-HADI **Rev:** Value and date within center circle

Date	Mintage	F	VF	XF	Unc
AH1321/1903A	250,000	—	10.00	20.00	30.00
AH1322/1904A	500,000	—	10.00	20.00	30.00

KM# 230 50 CENTIMES

2.5000 g., 0.8350 Silver .0671 oz. ASW **Obv. Legend:** MUHAMMAD AL-HADI

Date	Mintage	F	VF	XF	Unc
AH1321/1903A	1,003	—	—	150	250
AH1322/1904A	1,003	—	—	150	250
AH1323/1905A	1,003	—	—	150	250
AH1324/1906A	1,003	—	—	150	250

KM# 231 FRANC

5.0000 g., 0.8350 Silver .1342 oz. ASW **Obv. Legend:** MUHAMMAD AL-HADI

Date	Mintage	F	VF	XF	Unc
AH1321/1903A	703	—	—	150	250
AH1322/1904A	300,000	—	75.00	100	150
AH1323/1905A	703	—	—	150	250
AH1324/1906A	703	—	—	150	250

KM# 232 2 FRANCS

10.0000 g., 0.8350 Silver .2685 oz. ASW **Obv. Legend:** MUHAMMAD AL-HADI

Date	Mintage	F	VF	XF	Unc
AH1321/1903A	303	—	—	150	250
AH1322/1904A	150,000	—	100	150	220
AH1323/1905A	303	—	—	150	250
AH1324/1906A	303	—	—	150	250

KM# 233 10 FRANCS

3.2258 g., 0.9000 Gold .0933 oz. AGW **Obv. Legend:** MUHAMMAD AL-HADI

Date	Mintage	F	VF	XF	Unc
AH1321/1903A	83	—	—	450	900
AH1322/1904A	83	—	—	450	900
AH1323/1905A	83	—	—	450	900
AH1324/1906A	83	—	—	450	900

KM# 234 20 FRANCS

6.4516 g., 0.9000 Gold .1867 oz. AGW **Obv:** Inscription within sprigs **Obv. Legend:** MUHAMMAD AL-HADI **Rev:** Value and date within center circle

Date	Mintage	F	VF	XF	Unc
AH1321/1903A	300,000	—	—	BV	135
AH1321/1904A	600,000	—	—	BV	135
AH1322/1904A	Inc. above	—	—	BV	135
AH1323/1905A	23	—	—	550	1,000
AH1324/1906A	23	—	—	550	1,000

Muhammad al-Nasir Bey

"Struck in his name"

DECIMAL COINAGE

100 Centimes = 1 Franc

The following coins all bear French inscriptions on one side, Arabic on the other, and usually have both AH and AD dates. Except for KM#246-48, they are struck in the name of the Tunisian Bey.

KM# 235 5 CENTIMES

Bronze, 26 mm. **Obv:** Inscription within sprigs **Obv. Legend:** MUHAMMAD AL-NASIR **Rev:** Value and date within center circle **Edge:** Plain

Date	Mintage	F	VF	XF	Unc
AH1325/1907A	1,000,000	—	3.00	6.00	17.00
AH1326/1908A	1,000,000	—	3.00	6.00	17.00
AH1330/1912A	1,000,000	—	3.00	6.00	17.00
AH1332/1914A	1,000,000	—	3.00	6.00	17.00
AH1334/1916A	2,000,000	—	3.00	6.00	12.00
AH1336/1917A	2,021,000	—	3.00	6.00	12.00

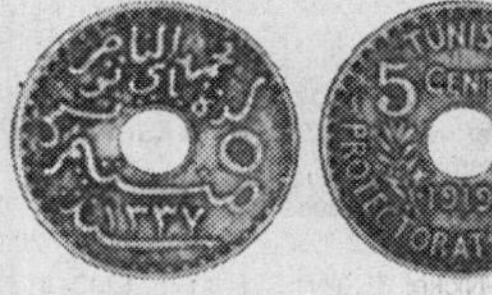

KM# 242 5 CENTIMES

Nickel-Bronze, 19 mm. **Obv:** Hole in center of inscription **Obv. Legend:** MOHAMMED AL-NASIR **Rev:** Value above hole in center, date and sprigs

Date	Mintage	F	VF	XF	Unc
AH1337/1918(a)	1,549,000	—	4.00	10.00	25.00
AH1337/1919(a)	4,451,000	—	3.00	8.00	20.00
AH1338/6/1920(a)	2,206,000	—	4.00	10.00	25.00
AH1338/7/1920(a)	Inc. above	—	4.00	10.00	25.00
AH1338/1920(a)	Inc. above	—	3.00	8.00	20.00
AH1339/1920(a)	Inc. above	—	3.00	8.00	20.00

KM# 245 5 CENTIMES

Nickel-Bronze, 17 mm. **Obv:** Hole in center of inscription **Rev:** Value above hole in center, date and sprigs **Note:** Reduced size.

Date	Mintage	F	VF	XF	Unc
AH1339/1920(a)	1,794,000	—	20.00	40.00	75.00

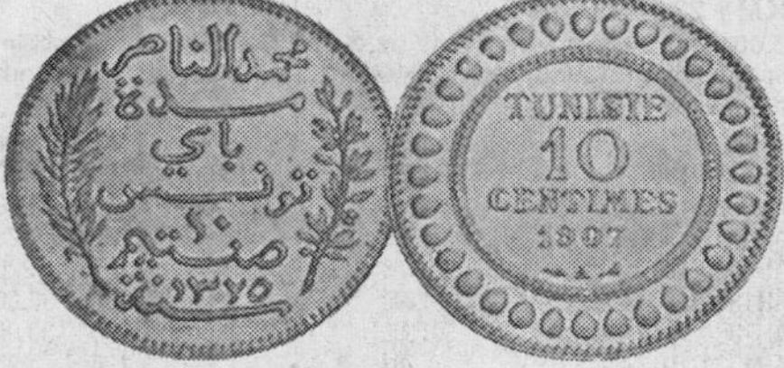

KM# 236 10 CENTIMES

Bronze **Obv:** Inscription within sprigs **Obv. Legend:** MUHAMMAD AL-NASIR **Rev:** Value and date within center circle

Date	Mintage	F	VF	XF	Unc
AH1325/1907A	500,000	—	3.00	8.00	20.00
AH1326/1908A	500,000	—	3.00	8.00	20.00
AH1329/1911A	500,000	—	3.00	8.00	20.00
AH1330/1912A	500,000	—	3.00	8.00	20.00
AH1332/1914A	500,000	—	3.00	8.00	20.00
AH1334/1916A	1,000,000	—	3.00	8.00	20.00
AH1336/1917A	1,050,000	—	3.00	8.00	20.00

KM# 243 10 CENTIMES

Nickel-Bronze **Obv:** Hole in center of inscription **Obv. Legend:** MUHAMMAD AL-NASIR **Rev:** Value above hole in center, date and sprigs

Date	Mintage	F	VF	XF	Unc
AH1337/1918(a)	1,288,000	—	3.00	8.00	25.00
AH1337/1919(a)	2,712,000	—	3.00	8.00	20.00
AH1338/1920(a)	3,000,000	—	3.00	8.00	20.00

KM# 244 25 CENTIMES

Nickel-Bronze **Obv:** Hole in center of inscription **Obv. Legend:** MUHAMMAD AL-NASIR **Rev:** Value above hole in center, date and sprigs

Date	Mintage	F	VF	XF	Unc
AH1337/1918(a)	2,000,000	—	5.00	12.00	35.00

Date	Mintage	F	VF	XF	Unc
AH1337/1919(a)	Inc. above	—	4.00	10.00	25.00
AH1338/1920(a)	2,000,000	—	4.00	10.00	25.00

KM# 237 50 CENTIMES
2.5000 g., 0.8350 Silver .0671 oz. ASW **Obv:** Inscription within sprigs **Obv. Legend:** MUHAMMAD AL-NASIR **Rev:** Value and date within center circle

Date	Mintage	F	VF	XF	Unc
AH1325/1907A	201,000	—	10.00	20.00	40.00
AH1326/1908A	2,006	—	—	100	150
AH1327/1909A	1,003	—	—	100	175
AH1328/1910A	1,003	—	—	100	175
AH1329/1911A	1,003	—	—	100	175
AH1330/1912A	201,000	—	10.00	20.00	40.00
AH1331/1913A	1,003	—	—	100	175
AH1332/1914A	201,000	—	10.00	20.00	40.00
AH1334/1915A	707,000	—	8.00	15.00	30.00
AH1334/1916A	3,614,000	—	7.00	12.00	25.00
AH1335/1916A	Inc. above	—	7.00	12.00	25.00
AH1335/1917A	2,139,000	—	7.00	12.00	25.00
AH1336/1917A	Inc. above	—	7.00	12.00	25.00
AH1337/1918A	1,003	—	—	100	175
AH1338/1919A	1,003	—	—	100	175
AH1339/1920A	1,003	—	—	100	175
AH1340/1921A	1,003	—	—	100	175

KM# 238 FRANC
5.0000 g., 0.8350 Silver .1342 oz. ASW **Obv:** Inscription within sprigs **Obv. Legend:** MUHAMMAD AL-NASIR **Rev:** Value and date within center circle

Date	Mintage	F	VF	XF	Unc
AH1325/1907A	301,000	—	10.00	20.00	35.00
AH1326/1908A	401,000	—	10.00	15.00	35.00
AH1327/1909A	703	—	—	135	225
AH1328/1910A	703	—	—	135	225
AH1329/1911A	1,051,000	—	7.00	12.00	30.00
AH1330/1912A	501,000	—	8.00	15.00	30.00
AH1331/1913A	703	—	—	135	225
AH1332/1914A	201,000	—	8.00	15.00	25.00
AH1333/1914A	Inc. above	—	8.00	15.00	25.00
AH1334/1915A	1,060,000	—	7.00	12.00	20.00
AH1334/1916A	3,270,000	—	7.00	12.00	20.00
AH1335/1916A	Inc. above	—	7.00	12.00	20.00
AH1335/1917A	1,628,000	—	7.00	12.00	20.00
AH1336/1918A	804,000	—	7.00	12.00	18.00
AH1337/1918A	Inc. above	—	7.00	12.00	18.00
AH1338/1919A	703	—	—	135	225
AH1339/1920A	703	—	—	135	225
AH1340/1921A	703	—	—	135	225

KM# 239 2 FRANCS
10.0000 g., 0.8350 Silver .2685 oz. ASW **Obv:** Inscription within sprigs **Obv. Legend:** MUHAMMAD AL-NASIR **Rev:** Value and date within center circle

Date	Mintage	F	VF	XF	Unc
AH1325/1907A	306	—	—	150	250
AH1326/1908A	101,000	—	20.00	40.00	100
AH1327/1909A	303	—	—	150	250
AH1328/1910A	303	—	—	150	250
AH1329/1911A	475,000	—	20.00	30.00	50.00
AH1330/1912A	200,000	—	20.00	30.00	50.00
AH1331/1913A	303	—	—	150	250
AH1332/1914A	100,000	—	20.00	30.00	50.00
AH1333/1914A	Inc. above	—	20.00	30.00	50.00
AH1334/1915A	408,000	—	20.00	30.00	50.00
AH1334/1916A	1,000,000	—	20.00	30.00	50.00
AH1335/1916A	Inc. above	—	20.00	30.00	50.00
AH1336/1917A	303	—	—	150	250
AH1337/1918A	303	—	—	150	250
AH1338/1919A	303	—	—	150	250
AH1339/1920A	303	—	—	150	250
AH1340/1921A	303	—	—	150	250

KM# 240 10 FRANCS
3.2258 g., 0.9000 Gold .0933 oz. AGW **Obv. Legend:** MUHAMMAD AL-NASIR

Date	Mintage	F	VF	XF	Unc
AH1325/1907A	36	—	—	500	900
AH1326/1908A	166	—	—	300	500
AH1327/1909A	83	—	—	450	850
AH1328/1910A	83	—	—	450	850
AH1329/1911A	83	—	—	450	850
AH1330/1912A	83	—	—	450	850
AH1331/1913A	83	—	—	450	850
AH1332/1914A	83	—	—	450	850
AH1334/1915A	83	—	—	450	850
AH1334/1916A	83	—	—	450	850
AH1336/1917A	83	—	—	450	850
AH1337/1918A	83	—	—	450	850
AH1338/1919A	83	—	—	450	850
AH1339/1920A	83	—	—	450	850
AH1340/1921A	83	—	—	450	850

KM# 241 20 FRANCS
6.4516 g., 0.9000 Gold .1867 oz. AGW **Obv. Legend:** MUHAMMAD AL-NASIR

Date	Mintage	F	VF	XF	Unc
AH1325/1907A	26	—	—	550	1,000
AH1326/1908A	46	—	—	450	850
AH1327/1909A	23	—	—	550	1,000
AH1328/1910A	23	—	—	550	1,000
AH1329/1911A	23	—	—	550	1,000
AH1330/1912A	23	—	—	550	1,000
AH1331/1913A	23	—	—	550	1,000
AH1332/1914A	23	—	—	550	1,000
AH1334/1915A	23	—	—	550	1,000
AH1334/1916A	23	—	—	550	1,000
AH1336/1917A	23	—	—	550	1,000
AH1337/1918A	23	—	—	550	1,000
AH1338/1919A	23	—	—	550	1,000
AH1339/1920A	23	—	—	550	1,000
AH1340/1921A	23	—	—	550	1,000

Muhammad al-Habib Bey
"Struck in his name"

DECIMAL COINAGE
100 Centimes = 1 Franc

The following coins all bear French inscriptions on one side, Arabic on the other, and usually have both AH and AD dates. Except for KM#246-48, they are struck in the name of the Tunisian Bey.

KM# 254 10 CENTIMES
Nickel-Bronze **Obv:** Hole in center of inscription **Obv. Legend:** MUHAMMAD AL-HABIB **Rev:** Value above hole in center, date and sprigs

Date	Mintage	F	VF	XF	Unc
AH1345/1926(a)	1,000,000	—	20.00	50.00	100

KM# 249 50 CENTIMES
2.5000 g., 0.8350 Silver .0671 oz. ASW **Obv:** Inscription within sprigs **Obv. Legend:** MUHAMMAD AL-HABIB **Rev:** Value and date within center circle

Date	Mintage	F	VF	XF	Unc
AH1341/1922A	1,003	—	—	100	200
AH1342/1923A	2,009	—	—	100	200
AH1343/1924A	1,003	—	—	100	200
AH1344/1925A	1,003	—	—	100	200
AH1345/1926A	1,003	—	—	100	200
AH1346/1927A	1,003	—	—	100	200
AH1347/1928A	1,003	—	—	100	200

KM# 250 FRANC
5.0000 g., 0.8350 Silver .1342 oz. ASW **Obv. Legend:** MUHAMMAD AL-HABIB

Date	Mintage	F	VF	XF	Unc
AH1341/1922A	703	—	—	135	275
AH1342/1923A	1,409	—	—	100	250
AH1343/1924A	703	—	—	135	275
AH1344/1925A	703	—	—	135	275
AH1345/1926A	703	—	—	135	275
AH1346/1927A	703	—	—	135	275
AH1347/1928A	703	—	—	135	275

KM# 250a FRANC
5.5000 g., 0.8350 Silver .1476 oz. ASW

Date	Mintage	F	VF	XF	Unc
AH1347/1928A	Inc. above	—	—	135	275

KM# 251 2 FRANCS
10.0000 g., 0.8350 Silver .2685 oz. ASW **Obv. Legend:** MUHAMMAD AL-HABIB

Date	Mintage	F	VF	XF	Unc
AH1341/1922A	303	—	—	150	325
AH1342/1923A	690	—	—	135	275
AH1343/1924A	303	—	—	150	325
AH1344/1925A	303	—	—	150	325
AH1345/1926A	303	—	—	150	325
AH1346/1927A	303	—	—	150	325

KM# 251a 2 FRANCS
8.6000 g., 0.8350 Silver 0.2309 oz. ASW

Date	Mintage	F	VF	XF	Unc
AH1347/1928A	303	—	—	150	325

KM# 252 10 FRANCS
3.2258 g., 0.9000 Gold .0933 oz. AGW **Obv. Legend:** MUHAMMAD AL-HABIB BEY

Date	Mintage	F	VF	XF	Unc
AH1341/1922A	83	—	—	450	850
AH1342/1923A	169	—	—	300	500
AH1343/1924A	83	—	—	450	850
AH1344/1925A	83	—	—	450	850
AH1345/1926A	83	—	—	450	850
AH1346/1927A	83	—	—	450	850
AH1347/1928A	83	—	—	450	850

KM# 253 20 FRANCS
6.4516 g., 0.9000 Gold .1867 oz. AGW **Obv. Legend:** MUHAMMAD AL-HABIB

Date	Mintage	F	VF	XF	Unc
AH1341/1922A	23	—	—	650	1,100
AH1342/1923A	49	—	—	450	850
AH1343/1924A	23	—	—	550	1,000
AH1344/1925A	23	—	—	550	1,000
AH1345/1926A	23	—	—	550	1,000
AH1346/1927A	23	—	—	550	1,000
AH1347/1928A	23	—	—	550	1,000

Ahmad Pasha Bey
"Struck in his name"

DECIMAL COINAGE
100 Centimes = 1 Franc

The following coins all bear French inscriptions on one side, Arabic on the other, and usually have both AH and AD dates. Except for KM#246-48, they are struck in the name of the Tunisian Bey.

KM# 258 5 CENTIMES
Nickel-Bronze **Obv:** Hole in center of inscription **Obv. Legend:** AHMAD **Rev:** Value above hole in center, date and sprigs

Date	Mintage	F	VF	XF	Unc
AH1350/1931(a)	2,000,000	—	4.00	10.00	25.00
AH1352/1933(a)	1,000,000	—	5.00	12.00	30.00
AH1357/1938(a)	1,200,000	—	4.00	10.00	25.00

KM# 259 10 CENTIMES
Nickel-Bronze **Obv:** Hole in center of inscription **Obv. Legend:** AHMAD **Rev:** Value above hole in center, date and sprigs

Date	Mintage	F	VF	XF	Unc
AH1350/1931(a)	750,000	—	6.00	15.00	35.00
AH1352/1933(a)	1,000,000	—	6.00	15.00	35.00
AH1357/1938(a)	1,200,000	—	5.00	12.00	25.00

KM# 267 10 CENTIMES
Zinc **Obv. Legend:** AHMAD

Date	Mintage	F	VF	XF	Unc
AH1360/1941(a)	5,000,000	—	2.50	6.00	25.00
AH1361/1942(a)	10,000,000	—	1.50	4.00	20.00

KM# 268 20 CENTIMES
Zinc **Obv:** Hole in center of inscription **Obv. Legend:** AHMAD **Rev:** Value above hole in center, date and sprigs

Date	Mintage	F	VF	XF	Unc
AH1361/1942A	5,000,000	—	20.00	35.00	50.00

KM# 260 25 CENTIMES
Nickel-Aluminum-Bronze **Obv:** Hole in center of inscription **Obv. Legend:** AHMAD **Rev:** Value above hole in center, date and sprigs

Date	Mintage	F	VF	XF	Unc
AH1350/1931(a)	300,000	—	8.00	15.00	35.00
AH1352/1933(a)	400,000	—	8.00	15.00	35.00
AH1357/1938(a)	480,000	—	4.00	10.00	25.00

KM# 261 5 FRANCS
5.0000 g., 0.6800 Silver .1093 oz. ASW **Obv:** Inscription and date within sprigs **Obv. Legend:** AHMAD **Rev:** Value flanked by designs

Date	Mintage	F	VF	XF	Unc
AH1353/1934(a)	2,000,000	—	10.00	18.00	25.00
AH1355/1936(a)	2,000,000	—	10.00	18.00	25.00

KM# 264 5 FRANCS
5.0000 g., 0.6800 Silver .1093 oz. ASW **Obv:** Inscription and date within sprigs **Obv. Legend:** AHMAD **Rev:** Value in center of circular inscription and design

Date	Mintage	F	VF	XF	Unc
AH1358/1939(a)	1,600,000	—	15.00	25.00	40.00

KM# 255 10 FRANCS
10.0000 g., 0.6800 Silver .2186 oz. ASW **Obv:** Inscription within oblong design flanked by sprigs **Obv. Legend:** AHMAD **Rev:** Value and date within center circle of design

Date	Mintage	F	VF	XF	Unc
AH1349/1930(a)	60,000	—	45.00	70.00	110
AH1350/1931(a)	1,103	—	150	250	350
AH1351/1932(a)	60,000	—	60.00	100	200
AH1352/1933(a)	1,103	—	150	250	350
AH1353/1934(a)	30,000	—	45.00	70.00	110

KM# 262 10 FRANCS
10.0000 g., 0.6800 Silver .2186 oz. ASW **Obv:** Inscription and date within sprigs **Rev:** Value flanked by designs

Date	Mintage	F	VF	XF	Unc
AH1353/1934(a)	1,501,000	—	10.00	20.00	35.00
AH1354/1935(a)	1,103	—	—	225	350
AH1355/1936(a)	2,006	—	—	225	350
AH1356/1937(a)	1,103	—	—	225	350
AH1357/1938	—	—	—	400	600
AH1358/1939	—	—	—	400	600

KM# 265 10 FRANCS
10.0000 g., 0.6800 Silver .2186 oz. ASW **Obv:** Inscription and date within sprigs **Rev:** Value and date within circular inscription and design

Date	Mintage	F	VF	XF	Unc
AH1358/1939(a)	501,000	—	7.00	15.00	35.00
AH1359/1940(a)	—	—	—	225	350
AH1360/1941(a)	1,103	—	—	225	350
AH1361/1942(a)	1,103	—	—	225	350

KM# 256 20 FRANCS
20.0000 g., 0.6800 Silver .4372 oz. ASW **Obv:** Inscription within oblong design flanked by sprigs **Obv. Legend:** AHMAD **Rev:** Value and date within center circle of design

Date	Mintage	F	VF	XF	Unc
AH1349/1930(a)	20,000	—	60.00	100	175
AH1350/1931(a)	53	—	200	300	500
AH1351/1932(a)	20,000	—	75.00	150	275
AH1352/1933(a)	53	—	200	300	500
AH1353/1934(a)	9,500	—	60.00	100	175

Note: It is believed that an additional number of coins dated AH1353/1934(a) were struck and included in mintage figures of KM#263 of the same date

KM# 263 20 FRANCS
20.0000 g., 0.6800 Silver .4372 oz. ASW **Obv:** Inscription and date within sprigs **Rev:** Value flanked by designs

Date	Mintage	F	VF	XF	Unc
AH1353/1934(a)	1,250,000	—	12.00	25.00	60.00
AH1354/1935(a)	53	—	—	275	450
AH1355/1936(a)	106	—	—	225	375
AH1356/1937(a)	53	—	—	275	450

KM# 266 20 FRANCS
20.0000 g., 0.6800 Silver .4372 oz. ASW **Obv:** Inscription and date within sprigs **Rev:** Value and date within circular inscription and design

Date	Mintage	F	VF	XF	Unc
AH1358/1939(a)	100,000	—	20.00	40.00	90.00
AH1359/1940(a)	—	—	—	—	—
Note: Reported, not confirmed					
AH1360/1941(a)	53	—	—	275	450
AH1361/1942(a)	53	—	—	275	450

KM# 257 100 FRANCS
6.5500 g., 0.9000 Gold .1895 oz. AGW **Obv:** Inscription within oblong design flanked by sprigs **Obv. Legend:** AHMAD **Rev:** Value and date within center circle of design

Date	Mintage	F	VF	XF	Unc
AH1349/1930(a)	3,000	—	—	BV	145
AH1350/1931(a)	33	—	—	500	900
AH1351/1932(a)	3,000	—	—	BV	145
AH1352/1933(a)	33	—	—	500	900
AH1353/1934(a)	133	—	—	300	400
AH1354/1935(a)	3,000	—	—	BV	145
AH1355/1936(a)	33	—	—	500	900
AH1356/1937(a)	33	—	—	500	900

Muhammad al-Amin Bey

"Struck in his name"

DECIMAL COINAGE

100 Centimes = 1 Franc

The following coins all bear French inscriptions on one side, Arabic on the other, and usually have both AH and AD dates. Except for KM#246-48, they are struck in the name of the Tunisian Bey.

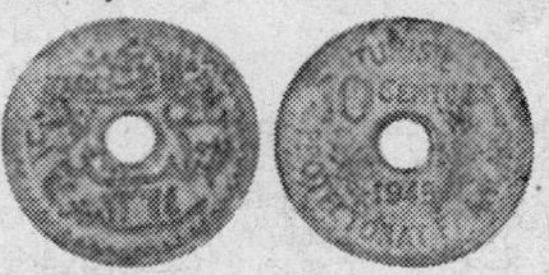

KM# 271 10 CENTIMES
Nickel-Aluminum-Bronze **Obv:** Hole in center of inscription **Obv. Legend:** MUHAMMAD AL AMIN **Rev:** Value above hole in center, date and sprigs

Date	Mintage	F	VF	XF	Unc
AH1364/1945(a)	10,000,000	—	40.00	75.00	140

Note: Most were probably melted

KM# 272 20 CENTIMES
Zinc **Obv:** Hole in center of inscription **Obv. Legend:** MUHAMMAD AL-AMIN **Rev:** Value above hole in center, date and sprigs

Date	Mintage	F	VF	XF	Unc
AH1364/1945(a)	5,205,000	—	60.00	120	200

Note: A large quantity was remelted

KM# 273 5 FRANCS
Aluminum-Bronze **Obv:** Inscription and date within sprigs **Obv. Legend:** MUHAMMAD AL-AMIN **Rev:** Value and date within circular inscription and design

Date	Mintage	F	VF	XF	Unc
AH1365/1946(a)	10,000,000	—	1.50	5.00	10.00

KM# 277 5 FRANCS
Copper-Nickel **Obv:** Dates within crescent below design **Rev:** Value and date within upper circle

Date	Mintage	F	VF	XF	Unc
AH1373/1954(a)	18,000,000	—	1.00	2.50	5.00
AH1376/1957(a)	4,000,000	—	2.00	4.00	7.00

KM# 269 10 FRANCS
10.0000 g., 0.6800 Silver .2186 oz. ASW **Obv:** Inscription and date within sprigs **Rev:** Value and date within circular inscription and design

Date	Mintage	F	VF	XF	Unc
AH1363/1943(a)	1,503	—	—	225	350
AH1364/1944(a)	2,206	—	—	200	300

KM# 270 20 FRANCS
20.0000 g., 0.6800 Silver .4372 oz. ASW **Obv. Legend:** MUHAMMAD AL-AMIN

Date	Mintage	F	VF	XF	Unc
AH1363/1943(a)	103	—	—	300	500
AH1364/1944(a)	106	—	—	300	500

KM# 274 20 FRANCS
Copper-Nickel **Obv:** Dates within crescent below design **Rev:** Value and date within upper circle

Date	Mintage	F	VF	XF	Unc
AH1370/1950(a)	10,000,000	—	0.60	2.25	6.50
AH1376/1957(a)	4,000,000	—	0.45	1.25	4.50

KM# 275 50 FRANCS
Copper-Nickel **Obv:** Dates within crescent below design **Obv. Legend:** MUHAMMAD AL-AMIN **Rev:** Value and date within upper circle

Date	Mintage	F	VF	XF	Unc
AH1370/1950(a)	5,000,000	—	0.60	2.25	6.50
AH1376/1957(a)	600,000	—	1.25	2.75	6.50

KM# 276 100 FRANCS
Copper-Nickel **Obv:** Dates within crescent below design **Obv. Legend:** MUHAMMAD AL-AMIN **Rev:** Value and date within upper circle

Date	Mintage	F	VF	XF	Unc
AH1370/1950(a)	8,000,000	—	2.25	5.50	11.50
AH1376/1957(a)	1,000,000	—	2.25	4.50	10.00

Anonymous Ruler

TOKEN COINAGE

KM# 246 50 CENTIMES
Aluminum-Bronze, 18 mm. **Obv:** Date within wreath **Rev:** Value within wreath **Rev. Inscription:** BON POUR (Good For) 50 CENTIMES

Date	Mintage	F	VF	XF	Unc
AH1340/1921(a)	4,000,000	—	2.00	7.00	20.00
AH1345/1926(a)	1,000,000	—	3.00	10.00	25.00
AH1352/1933(a)	500,000	—	6.00	17.00	50.00
AH1360/1941(a)	4,646,000	—	1.00	3.00	10.00
AH1364/1945(a)	11,180,000	—	1.00	2.00	10.00

KM# 247 FRANC
Aluminum-Bronze, 23.5 mm. **Obv:** Date within wreath **Rev:** Value within wreath **Rev. Inscription:** BON POUR (Good For) 1 FRANC

Date	Mintage	F	VF	XF	Unc
AH1340/1921(a)	5,000,000	—	2.00	7.00	20.00
AH1344/1926(a)	1,000,000	—	2.00	15.00	35.00
AH1345/1926(a)	1,000,000	—	4.00	17.00	40.00
AH1360/1941(a)	6,612,000	—	1.00	4.00	10.00
AH1364/1945(a)	10,699,000	—	1.00	3.00	10.00

KM# 248 2 FRANCS
Aluminum-Bronze **Obv:** Date within wreath **Rev:** Value within wreath **Rev. Inscription:** BON POUR (Good For) 2 FRANCS

Date	Mintage	F	VF	XF	Unc
AH1340/1921(a)	1,500,000	—	3.00	15.00	35.00
AH1343/1924(a)	500,000	—	8.00	20.00	50.00
AH1345/1926(a)	500,000	—	8.00	20.00	50.00
AH1360/1941(a)	1,976,000	—	3.00	8.00	15.00
AH1364/1945(a)	6,464,000	—	3.00	6.00	15.00

REPUBLIC

DECIMAL COINAGE

100 Centimes = 1 Franc

The following coins all bear French inscriptions on one side, Arabic on the other, and usually have both AH and AD dates. Except for KM#246-48, they are struck in the name of the Tunisian Bey.

KM# 351 DINAR
18.0000 g., 0.6800 Silver 0.3935 oz. ASW, 32 mm. **Subject:** F.A.O. 50th Anniversary **Obv:** F.A.O. logo **Rev:** Orchard workers with ladder **Edge:** Reeded

Date	Mintage	F	VF	XF	Unc
ND (1995) Proof	5,000	Value: 40.00			

DECIMAL COINAGE

1000 Millim = 1 Dinar

KM# 280 MILLIM
0.6500 g., Aluminum, 18 mm. **Obv:** Oak tree and date **Rev:** Value within sprigs

Date	Mintage	F	VF	XF	Unc
1960	—	—	—	0.10	0.25
1983	—	—	—	0.10	0.25

KM# 349 MILLIM
Aluminum **Series:** F.A.O. **Obv:** Oak tree and date **Rev:** Value within sprigs

Date	Mintage	F	VF	XF	Unc
2000(1999)	—	—	—	—	0.75

KM# 281 2 MILLIM
1.0000 g., Aluminum, 21 mm. **Obv:** Oak tree and date **Rev:** Value within sprigs

Date	Mintage	F	VF	XF	Unc
1960	—	—	—	0.10	0.25
1983	—	—	—	0.10	0.25

KM# 282 5 MILLIM
1.5000 g., Aluminum, 24 mm. **Obv:** Oak tree and date **Rev:** Value within sprigs

Date	Mintage	F	VF	XF	Unc
1960	—	—	—	0.10	0.25
1983	—	—	—	0.10	0.25
1993	—	—	—	0.10	0.25
1996	—	—	—	0.10	0.25

KM# 348 5 MILLIM
Aluminum **Obv:** Oak tree and dates **Rev:** Value within sprigs

Date	Mintage	F	VF	XF	Unc
AH1418-1997	—	—	—	—	0.50

KM# 306 10 MILLIM
3.5000 g., Brass, 19 mm. **Obv:** Inscription and dates within inner circle of design **Rev:** Value in center of design **Edge:** Reeded

Date	Mintage	F	VF	XF	Unc
AH1380-1960	—	—	0.15	0.25	0.50
AH1403-1983	—	—	0.15	0.25	0.50
Note: Large and small date varieties exist.					
AH1414-1993	—	—	0.15	0.25	0.50
AH1416-1996	—	—	0.15	0.25	0.50
AH1418-1997	—	—	0.15	0.50	0.50

KM# 307 20 MILLIM
4.5000 g., Brass, 22 mm. **Obv:** Inscription and dates within center circle of design **Rev:** Value within center of design

Date	Mintage	F	VF	XF	Unc
AH1380-1960	—	—	0.30	0.50	0.80
AH1403-1983	—	—	0.30	0.50	0.80
Note: Large and small date varieties exist.					
AH1414-1993	—	—	0.30	0.50	0.80
AH1416-1996	—	—	0.30	0.50	0.80
AH1418-1997	—	—	0.30	0.50	0.80

KM# 308 50 MILLIM
6.0000 g., Brass, 25 mm. **Obv:** Inscription and dates within center circle of design **Rev:** Value in center of design

Date	Mintage	F	VF	XF	Unc
AH1380-1960	—	—	0.65	0.85	1.25
AH1403-1983	—	—	0.65	0.85	1.25
Note: Large and small date varieties exist.					
AH1414-1993	—	—	0.65	0.85	1.25
AH1416-1996	—	—	0.65	0.85	1.25
AH1417-1997	—	—	0.65	0.85	1.25
AH1418-1997	—	—	0.65	0.85	1.25

KM# 309 100 MILLIM
7.5000 g., Brass, 27 mm. **Obv:** Inscription and dates within center circle of design **Rev:** Value in center of design

Date	Mintage	F	VF	XF	Unc
AH1380-1960	—	—	1.25	1.50	2.00
AH1403-1983	—	—	1.25	1.50	2.00
Note: Large and small date varieties exist.					
AH1414-1993	—	—	1.25	1.50	2.00
AH1416-1996	—	—	1.25	1.50	2.00
AH1418-1997	—	—	1.25	1.50	2.00
AH1421-2000	—	—	1.25	1.50	2.00

KM# 291 1/2 DINAR
Nickel **Obv:** Head left **Rev:** Value and date

Date	Mintage	F	VF	XF	Unc
1968(a)	500,000	—	1.00	2.00	4.50

KM# 303 1/2 DINAR
Copper-Nickel **Series:** F.A.O. **Obv:** Head left **Rev:** 2 Hands with fruit and wheat sprig

Date	Mintage	F	VF	XF	Unc
1976	700,000	—	1.50	3.50	6.50
Note: Variations exist with large and small designer's name					
1983	400,000	—	1.50	3.50	6.50

KM# 318 1/2 DINAR
Copper-Nickel **Series:** F.A.O. **Obv:** Map and date **Rev:** 2 Hands with fruit and wheat sprig

Date	Mintage	F	VF	XF	Unc
1988	—	—	1.00	3.00	5.50
1990	300,000	—	1.00	3.00	5.50

KM# 346 1/2 DINAR
Copper-Nickel **Obv:** Shield within circle **Rev:** 2 Hands with fruit and wheat sprig

Date	Mintage	F	VF	XF	Unc
AH1416-1996 (1996)	—	—	1.00	2.50	4.50
AH1418-1997 (1997)	—	—	1.00	2.50	4.50
AH1418-1998 (1998)	—	—	1.00	2.50	4.50

KM# 292 DINAR
20.0000 g., 0.9250 Silver .5949 oz. ASW **Obv:** Head of Habib Bourguiba left **Rev:** Standing armored figure of Hannibal among elephant heads and designs

Date	Mintage	F	VF	XF	Unc
1969FM NI Proof	15,000	Value: 16.50			
1969 NI Proof	5,000	Value: 42.50			

KM# 293 DINAR
20.0000 g., 0.9250 Silver .5949 oz. ASW **Obv:** Head of Habib Bourguiba left **Rev:** Stylized armored figure on horse and head of Masinissa left

Date	Mintage	F	VF	XF	Unc
1969FM NI Proof	15,000	Value: 12.00			
1969 NI Proof	5,000	Value: 40.00			

KM# 294 DINAR
20.0000 g., 0.9250 Silver .5949 oz. ASW **Obv:** Head of Habib Bourguiba left **Rev:** Stylized head of Jugurtha left in center of balance scale

Date	Mintage	F	VF	XF	Unc
1969FM NI Proof	15,000	Value: 12.00			
1969 NI Proof	5,000	Value: 40.00			

KM# 295 DINAR
20.0000 g., 0.9250 Silver .5949 oz. ASW **Obv:** Head of Habib Bourguiba left **Rev:** Seated figure of Virgil flanked by standing figures

Date	Mintage	F	VF	XF	Unc
1969FM NI Proof	15,000	Value: 12.00			
1969 NI Proof	5,000	Value: 40.00			

KM# 296 DINAR
20.0000 g., 0.9250 Silver .5949 oz. ASW **Obv:** Head of Habib Bourguiba left **Rev:** Seated figure of St. Augustine at desk and bust facing

Date	Mintage	F	VF	XF	Unc
1969FM NI Proof	15,000	Value: 12.00			
1969 NI Proof	5,000	Value: 40.00			

KM# 297 DINAR
20.0000 g., 0.9250 Silver .5949 oz. ASW **Obv:** Head of Habib Bourguiba left **Rev:** Phoenician Ship

Date	Mintage	F	VF	XF	Unc
1969FM NI Proof	15,000	Value: 17.50			
1969 NI Proof	5,000	Value: 50.00			

KM# 298 DINAR
20.0000 g., 0.9250 Silver .5949 oz. ASW **Obv:** Head of Habib Bourguiba left **Rev:** Standing Neptune surrounded by mermaids and sea horses

Date	Mintage	F	VF	XF	Unc
1969FM NI Proof	15,000	Value: 12.50			
1969 NI Proof	5,000	Value: 40.00			

KM# 299 DINAR
20.0000 g., 0.9250 Silver .5949 oz. ASW **Obv:** Head of Habib Bourguiba left **Rev:** Venus, with the ribbon of love

Date	Mintage	F	VF	XF	Unc
1969FM NI Proof	15,000	Value: 16.50			
1969 NI Proof	5,000	Value: 50.00			

KM# 300 DINAR
20.0000 g., 0.9250 Silver .5949 oz. ASW **Obv:** Head of Habib Bourguiba left **Rev:** Thysdrus-El Djem, Africa's Colosseum

Date	Mintage	F	VF	XF	Unc
1969FM NI Proof	15,000	Value: 12.00			
1969 NI Proof	5,000	Value: 40.00			

KM# 301 DINAR
20.0000 g., 0.9250 Silver .5949 oz. ASW **Obv:** Head of Habib Bourguiba left **Rev:** Building - Sbeitla-Sufetula

Date	Mintage	F	VF	XF	Unc
1969FM NI Proof	15,000	Value: 12.00			
1969 NI Proof	5,000	Value: 40.00			

KM# 302 DINAR
18.0000 g., 0.6800 Silver .3935 oz. ASW **Series:** F.A.O. **Obv:** Head of Habib Bourguiba left **Rev:** Coconut tree, oxen and figure, tractor in background at left

Date	Mintage	F	VF	XF	Unc
1970(a)	100,000	—	6.00	8.00	12.00
1970(a) Proof	1,250	Value: 40.00			

KM# 304 DINAR
Copper-Nickel **Series:** F.A.O. **Obv:** Head of Habib Bourguiba left **Rev:** Female half figure right **Note:** Varieties exist. Coins dated 1976 exist with or without dots (error) below iy of Tunisiya.

Date	Mintage	F	VF	XF	Unc
1976	12,000,000	—	2.00	4.00	8.00
1983	4,000,000	—	2.00	4.00	8.00

KM# 319 DINAR
Copper-Nickel **Series:** F.A.O. **Obv:** Map and date **Rev:** Female half figure right

Date	Mintage	F	VF	XF	Unc
1988	—	—	2.00	4.00	8.00
1989	—	—	2.00	4.00	8.00
1990	8,000,000	—	2.00	4.00	8.00

KM# 347 DINAR
Copper-Nickel **Series:** F.A.O. **Obv:** Shield within circle **Rev:** Female half figure right

Date	Mintage	F	VF	XF	Unc
AH1416-1996	—	—	2.00	4.00	7.50
AH1417-1997	—	—	2.00	4.00	7.50
AH1418-1997	—	—	2.00	4.00	7.50

KM# 286 2 DINARS
3.8000 g., 0.9000 Gold .1099 oz. AGW **Subject:** 10th Anniversary of Republic **Obv:** Head of Habib Bourguiba left **Rev:** Towered building flanked by dates

Date	Mintage	F	VF	XF	Unc
ND(1967) NI Proof	7,259	Value: 85.00			

KM# 283 5 DINARS
11.7900 g., 0.9000 Gold .3412 oz. AGW **Obv:** Head of Habib Bourguiba left, French legend **Rev:** Shield above sprigs, value and banner, French legend

Date	Mintage	F	VF	XF	Unc
1962 Proof	—	Value: 550			

KM# 320 5 DINARS
11.7900 g., 0.9000 Gold .3412 oz. AGW **Obv:** Arabic legends **Rev:** Arabic legends

Date	Mintage	F	VF	XF	Unc
1962 Proof	—	Value: 550			

KM# 284 5 DINARS
11.7900 g., 0.9000 Gold .3412 oz. AGW **Obv:** Head of Habib Bourguiba left, French legends **Rev:** Shield above value, French legends

Date	Mintage	F	VF	XF	Unc
1963 Proof	—	Value: 550			

KM# 321 5 DINARS
9.3600 g., 0.9000 Gold .2708 oz. AGW **Obv:** Arabic legends **Rev:** Arabic legends

Date	Mintage	F	VF	XF	Unc
1963 Proof	—	Value: 550			

KM# 287 5 DINARS
9.5000 g., 0.9000 Gold .2749 oz. AGW **Subject:** 10th Anniversary of Republic **Obv:** Head of Habib Bourguiba left **Rev:** Minaret

Date	Mintage	F	VF	XF	Unc
ND(1967) NI Proof	7,259	Value: 200			

KM# 305 5 DINARS
24.0000 g., 0.6800 Silver .5247 oz. ASW **Subject:** 20th Anniversary of Independence **Obv:** Head of Habib Bourguiba left **Rev:** Design and value

Date	Mintage	F	VF	XF	Unc
1976	200,000	—	—	—	20.00
1976 Proof	1,000	Value: 45.00			

KM# 284a 5 DINARS
9.3600 g., 0.9000 Gold .2708 oz. AGW **Obv:** Head of Habib Bourguiba left **Rev:** Shield above value

Date	Mintage	F	VF	XF	Unc
1976 Proof	—	Value: 500			

KM# 310 5 DINARS
9.4120 g., 0.9000 Gold .2723 oz. AGW **Obv:** Head of Habib Bourguiba left **Rev:** President's return

Date	Mintage	F	VF	XF	Unc
1981 Proof	1,450	Value: 215			

KM# 313 5 DINARS
27.2200 g., 0.9250 Silver .8096 oz. ASW **Series:** International Year of the Child **Obv:** Head of Habib Bourguiba left **Rev:** Seated child playing Designer: Philip Nathan

Date	Mintage	F	VF	XF	Unc
1982	7,575	—	—	—	13.50
1982 Proof	1,108	Value: 20.00			

KM# 326 5 DINARS
9.4120 g., 0.9000 Gold .2723 oz. AGW **Rev:** Arabic legends

Date	Mintage	F	VF	XF	Unc
AH1402 Proof	725	Value: 225			

KM# 325 5 DINARS
9.4120 g., 0.9000 Gold .2723 oz. AGW **Obv:** President **Rev:** Coat of arms **Note:** French legends.

Date	Mintage	F	VF	XF	Unc
1982 Proof	725	Value: 225			

KM# 327 5 DINARS
9.4120 g., 0.9000 Gold .2723 oz. AGW **Subject:** 25th Anniversary of Republic **Note:** French legends.

Date	Mintage	F	VF	XF	Unc
1983-85 Proof	—	Value: 225			

KM# 328 5 DINARS
9.4120 g., 0.9000 Gold .2723 oz. AGW **Note:** Arabic legends.

Date	Mintage	F	VF	XF	Unc
AH1403-05 Proof	—	Value: 225			

KM# 330 5 DINARS
9.4120 g., 0.9000 Gold .2723 oz. AGW **Note:** Arabic legends.

Date	Mintage	F	VF	XF	Unc
AH1408	375	—	—	—	275
AH1409	Inc. above	—	—	—	275

KM# 329 5 DINARS
9.4120 g., 0.9000 Gold .2723 oz. AGW **Obv:** Map **Rev:** Allegorical design **Note:** French legends.

Date	Mintage	F	VF	XF	Unc
1988	375	—	—	—	275
1989	Inc. above	—	—	—	275

KM# 322 10 DINARS
23.4800 g., 0.9000 Gold .6795 oz. AGW **Obv:** French legends **Rev:** French legends

Date	Mintage	F	VF	XF	Unc
1962 Proof	—	Value: 850			

KM# 285 10 DINARS

23.4800 g., 0.9000 Gold .6795 oz. AGW **Obv:** Head of Habib Bourguiba left, Arabic legends **Rev:** Shield above value, Arabic legends

Date	Mintage	F	VF	XF	Unc
AH1382-1962 Proof	—	Value: 850			
AH1384-1964 Proof	—	Value: 850			

KM# 288 10 DINARS

19.0000 g., 0.9000 Gold .5498 oz. AGW **Subject:** 10th Anniversary of Republic **Obv:** Head of Habib Bourguiba left **Rev:** Towered building flanked by dates

Date	Mintage	F	VF	XF	Unc
ND(1967) NI Proof	6,480	Value: 400			

KM# 324 10 DINARS

0.9000 Gold **Subject:** 20th Anniversary of Independence **Obv:** Head of Habib Bourguiba left **Rev:** Shield

Date	Mintage	F	VF	XF	Unc
1976	Est. 2,000	—	—	—	750

KM# 345 10 DINARS

18.8080 g., 0.9000 Gold .5442 oz. AGW **Subject:** 20th Anniversary - Central Bank

Date	Mintage	F	VF	XF	Unc
1978	2,000	—	—	—	700

KM# 344 10 DINARS

38.0000 g., 0.9000 Silver 1.0995 oz. ASW **Subject:** 20th Anniversary - Central Bank **Obv:** Head of Habib Bourguiba left **Rev:** Large old-style bank building

Date	Mintage	F	VF	XF	Unc
1978	—	—	—	—	35.00

KM# 343 10 DINARS

18.7700 g., 0.9000 Gold .5431 oz. AGW **Obv:** Head of Habib Bourguiba left, Arabic legends **Rev:** Shield, Arabic legends

Date	Mintage	F	VF	XF	Unc
AH1399 (1979)	—	—	—	—	900

KM# 342 10 DINARS

18.7700 g., 0.9000 Gold .5431 oz. AGW **Obv:** Head of Habib Bourguiba left, French legends **Rev:** Stylized head facing, French legends

Date	Mintage	F	VF	XF	Unc
1979	—	—	—	—	900

KM# 311 10 DINARS

18.8240 g., 0.9000 Gold .5447 oz. AGW **Obv:** Habib Bourguiba **Rev:** President's return

Date	Mintage	F	VF	XF	Unc
1981 Proof	2,000	Value: 550			

KM# 312 10 DINARS

18.8080 g., 0.9000 Gold .5442 oz. AGW **Subject:** 25th Anniversary of Independence **Obv:** Head of Habib Bourguiba left **Rev:** Silhouette of girl

Date	Mintage	F	VF	XF	Unc
1981 Proof	2,000	Value: 550			

KM# 314 10 DINARS

38.0000 g., 0.9000 Silver 1.0995 oz. ASW **Subject:** Gabes Bank **Obv:** Head left **Rev:** Gabes branch bank building

Date	Mintage	F	VF	XF	Unc
1982 Proof	2,500	Value: 40.00			

KM# 315 10 DINARS

38.0000 g., 0.9000 Silver 1.0995 oz. ASW **Subject:** Central Bank of Nabeul **Obv:** Head left **Rev:** Nabeul bank building

Date	Mintage	F	VF	XF	Unc
1982 Proof	1,000	Value: 45.00			

KM# 316 10 DINARS

38.0000 g., 0.9000 Silver 1.0995 oz. ASW **Subject:** Sfax Branch Office **Obv:** Head left **Rev:** Sfax branch bank building

Date	Mintage	F	VF	XF	Unc
1982 Proof	1,000	Value: 45.00			

KM# 331 10 DINARS

38.0000 g., 0.9000 Silver 1.0995 oz. ASW **Obv:** President **Rev:** Coat of arms **Note:** French legends.

Date	Mintage	F	VF	XF	Unc
1982 Proof	700	Value: 55.00			

KM# 332 10 DINARS

38.0000 g., 0.9000 Silver 1.0995 oz. ASW **Note:** Arabic legends.

Date	Mintage	F	VF	XF	Unc
AH1402 Proof	700	Value: 55.00			

KM# 333 10 DINARS

38.0000 g., 0.9000 Silver 1.0995 oz. ASW **Note:** Tunisian girl.

Date	Mintage	F	VF	XF	Unc
1982 Proof	2,000	Value: 40.00			

KM# 335 10 DINARS

38.0000 g., 0.9000 Silver 1.0995 oz. ASW **Note:** Arabic legends.

Date	Mintage	F	VF	XF	Unc
AH1403-05 Proof	—	Value: 45.00			

KM# 334 10 DINARS

38.0000 g., 0.9000 Silver 1.0995 oz. ASW **Subject:** 25th Anniversary of Republic **Note:** French legends.

Date	Mintage	F	VF	XF	Unc
1983-85 Proof	—	Value: 45.00			

KM# 336 10 DINARS

38.0000 g., 0.9000 Silver 1.0995 oz. ASW **Subject:** 50th Anniversary of the Socialist Party

Date	Mintage	F	VF	XF	Unc
1984 Proof	—	Value: 45.00			

KM# 323 10 DINARS

18.8080 g., 0.9000 Gold .5442 oz. AGW **Obv:** Head left **Rev:** Statue of Burgiba

Date	Mintage	F	VF	XF	Unc
AH1405 (1985) Proof	2,000	Value: 550			

KM# 337 10 DINARS

18.8080 g., 0.9000 Gold .5442 oz. AGW **Subject:** 30th Anniversary of Independence

Date	Mintage	F	VF	XF	Unc
1986 Proof	—	Value: 550			

KM# 338 10 DINARS

18.8080 g., 0.9000 Gold .5442 oz. AGW **Subject:** 30th Anniversary of Republic

Date	Mintage	F	VF	XF	Unc
1987 Proof	2,000	Value: 550			

KM# 339 10 DINARS

38.0000 g., 0.9000 Silver 1.0995 oz. ASW **Obv:** Picture of country

Date	Mintage	F	VF	XF	Unc
1988 Proof	4,000	Value: 40.00			

KM# 340 10 DINARS

18.8080 g., 0.9000 Gold .5442 oz. AGW **Obv:** Map **Rev:** Allegorical design **Note:** French legends.

Date	Mintage	F	VF	XF	Unc
1988	375	—	—	—	650
1989	Inc. above	—	—	—	650

KM# 341 10 DINARS

18.8080 g., 0.9000 Gold .5442 oz. AGW **Note:** Arabic legends.

Date	Mintage	F	VF	XF	Unc
AH1408	375	—	—	—	650
AH1409	Inc. above	—	—	—	650

KM# 289 20 DINARS

38.0000 g., 0.9000 Gold 1.0996 oz. AGW **Subject:** 10th Anniversary of Republic **Rev:** Minaret

Date	Mintage	F	VF	XF	Unc
ND(1967) NI	3,536	—	—	—	775

KM# 290 40 DINARS

76.0000 g., 0.9000 Gold 2.1991 oz. AGW **Subject:** 10th Anniversary of Republic **Obv:** Head left **Rev:** Minaret **Note:** Similar to 20 Dinars, KM#289.

Date	Mintage	F	VF	XF	Unc
ND(1967) NI Proof	3,031	Value: 1,550			

KM# 353 50 DINARS

0.9000 Gold, 34 mm. **Obv:** National arms **Rev:** Two interlocked currycombs, each with the number 21 **Note:** 13th Anniversary of the Bloodless November 7, 1987 Coup

Date	Mintage	F	VF	XF	Unc
2000-1421 Proof	—	Value: 750			

KM# 317 75 DINARS

15.5500 g., 0.9000 Gold .4500 oz. AGW **Series:** International Year of the Child **Obv:** Head of Habib Bourguiba left **Rev:** Standing figures facing left

Date	Mintage	F	VF	XF	Unc
1982 Proof	4,518	Value: 325			

ESSAIS

Standard metals unless otherwise noted

KM#	Date	Mintage	Identification	Mkt Val
E1	1918(a)	—	5 Centimes. Nickel-Bronze. KM#242.	80.00
E2	1918(a)	—	10 Centimes. Nickel-Bronze. KM#243.	85.00
E3	1918(a)	—	25 Centimes. Nickel-Bronze. KM#244.	90.00
E4	1920(a)	—	5 Centimes. Nickel-Bronze. KM#245.	125
E5	1921(a)	—	50 Centimes. Aluminum-Bronze. KM#246.	90.00
E6	1921(a)	—	Franc. Aluminum-Bronze. KM#247.	120
E7	1921(a)	—	Franc. Aluminum. KM#247.	130
E8	1928A	—	Franc. Nickel-Bronze. KM#250a.	250
E9	1928	—	2 Francs. Silver-Bronze. KM#251.	260
E10	1930(a)	—	10 Francs. Silver. KM#255, uniface.	170
E11	1930(a)	—	20 Francs. Silver. KM#256, uniface.	350
E12	1930(a)	—	100 Francs. Gold. KM#257, uniface.	375
E13	1931(a)	—	5 Centimes. Nickel-Bronze. KM#258.	75.00
E14	1931(a)	—	10 Centimes. Nickel-Bronze. KM#259.	80.00
E15	1931(a)	—	25 Centimes. Nickel-Aluminum-Bronze. KM#260.	85.00
E16	1353(a)	—	5 Francs. Silver. KM#261.	90.00
E17	1353(a)	—	10 Francs. Silver. KM#255.	100
E18	1353(a)	—	20 Francs. Silver. KM#256.	175

KM#	Date	Mintage	Identification	Mkt Val
E-A19	1354(a)	—	100 Francs. Gilt Bronze. KM#257.	—
E19	1938(a)	—	100 Francs. Gilt Bronze. KM-M1.	110
E20	1938(a)	—	100 Francs. Gold. KM-M1.	950
E21	1939(a)	—	5 Francs. Silver. KM#264.	60.00
E22	1939(a)	—	10 Francs. Silver. KM#265.	80.00
E23	1939(a)	—	20 Francs. Silver. KM#266.	150
E24	1942(a)	—	20 Centimes. Zinc. KM#268.	50.00
E25	1945(a)	1,100	10 Centimes. Nickel-Aluminum-Bronze. KM#271.	50.00
E26	1945(a)	1,100	20 Centimes. Zinc. KM#272.	60.00

KM#	Date	Mintage	Identification	Mkt Val
E27	1946(a)	1,100	5 Francs. Aluminum-Bronze. Inscription and date within sprigs. Value and date within circular inscription and design. KM#273.	35.00
E28	1950(a)	1,100	20 Francs. Copper-Nickel. KM#274.	35.00
E29	1950(a)	1,100	50 Francs. Copper-Nickel. KM#275.	35.00
E30	1950(a)	1,100	100 Francs. Copper-Nickel. KM#276.	35.00
E31	1954(a)	1,100	5 Francs. Copper-Nickel. KM#277.	20.00
E32	1968(a)	1,260	1/2 Dinar. Nickel. KM#291.	35.00
E33	1968(a)	70	1/2 Dinar. Gold.	550

KM#	Date	Mintage	Identification	Mkt Val

KM#	Date	Mintage	Identification	Mkt Val
E34	1970(a)	1,250	Dinar. Silver. Head left. Coconut tree in center of oxen, tractor and figure. KM#302.	45.00
E35	1976	2,050	1/2 Dinar. Copper-Nickel. KM#303.	30.00
E36	1976	2,050	Dinar. Copper-Nickel. KM#304.	40.00

PIEFORTS

Double thickness; standard metals unless otherwise noted

KM#	Date	Mintage	Identification	Issue Price	Mkt Val
P1	1968(a)	500	1/2 Dinar. Nickel. KM#291	—	35.00
P2	1982	96	5 Dinars. Silver. KM#313.	—	165
P3	1982	55	75 Dinars. Gold. KM#317.	—	1,250

PIEFORTS WITH ESSAI

Double thickness

KM#	Date	Mintage	Identification	Mkt Val
PE1	1945(a)	104	20 Centimes. Zinc. . KM#272.	100

KM#	Date	Mintage	Identification	Mkt Val
PE2	1945(a)	104	50 Centimes. Aluminum-Bronze. KM#246.	100
PE3	1945(a)	104	Franc. Aluminum-Bronze. KM#247.	100

KM#	Date	Mintage	Identification	Mkt Val
PE4	1945(a)	104	2 Francs. Aluminum-Bronze. Date within wreath. Value flanked by sprigs. KM#248.	100
PE5	1946(a)	104	5 Francs. Aluminum-Bronze. KM#273.	120
PE6	1954(a)	104	5 Francs. Copper-Nickel. KM#277.	90.00

MINT SETS

KM#	Date	Mintage	Identification	Issue Price	Mkt Val
MS1	1960 (7)	—	KM#280-282, 306-309	—	5.50
MS2	1996 (7)	—	KM#282, 306-309, 346-347	—	16.50

PROOF SETS

KM#	Date	Mintage	Identification	Issue Price	Mkt Val
PS2	1967 (5)	3,031	KM#286-290	—	2,000
PS3	1969FM-NI (10)	15,202	KM#292-301	77.00	120
PS4	1969NI (10)	5,000	KM#292-301	—	475

TURKEY

The Republic of Turkey, a parliamentary democracy of the Near East located partially in Europe and partially in Asia between the Black and the Mediterranean Seas, has an area of 301,382 sq. mi. (780,580 sq. km.) and a population of *55.4 million. Capital: Ankara. Turkey exports cotton, hazelnuts, and tobacco, and enjoys a virtual monopoly in meerschaum.

The Ottoman Turks, a tribe from Central Asia, first appeared in the early 13th century, and by the 17th century had established the Ottoman Empire which stretched from the Persian Gulf to the southern frontier of Poland, and from the Caspian Sea to the Algerian plateau. The defeat of the Turkish navy by the Holy League in 1571, and of the Turkish forces besieging Vienna in 1683, began the steady decline of the Ottoman Empire which, accelerated by the rise of nationalism, contracted its European border, and by the end of World War I deprived it of its Arab lands. The present Turkish boundaries were largely fixed by the Treaty of Lausanne in 1923. The sultanate and caliphate, the political and spiritual ruling institutions of the old empire, were separated and the sultanate abolished in 1922. On Oct. 29, 1923, Turkey formally became a republic.

RULERS

Abdul Hamid II, AH1293-1327/1876-1909AD
Muhammad V, AH1327-1336/1909-1918AD
Muhammad VI, AH1336-1341/1918-1923AD
Republic, AH1341/AD1923-

MINT NAMES

قسطنطنية

Constantinople
(Qustantiniyah)

مصر

Misr
See Egypt

MONETARY EQUIVALENTS

3 Akche = 1 Para
5 Para = Beshlik (Beshparalik)
10 Para = Onluk
20 Para = Yirmilik
30 Para = Zolota
40 Para = Kurush (Piastre)
1-1/2 Kurush (Piastres) = Altmishlik

MONETARY SYSTEM

Silver Coinage

40 Para = 1 Kurush (Piastre)
2 Kurush (Piastres) = 1 Ikilik
2-1/2 Kurush (Piastres) = Yuzluk
3 Kurush (Piastres) = Uechlik
5 Kurush (Piastres) = Beshlik
6 Kurush (Piastres) = Altilik

Gold Coinage

100 Kurush (Piastres) = 1 Turkish Pound (Lira)

This system has remained essentially unchanged since its introduction by Ahmad III in 1688, except that the Asper and Para have long since ceased to be coined. The Piastre, established as a crown-sized silver coin approximately equal to the French Ecu of Louis XIV, has shrunk to a tiny copper coin, worth about 1/15 of a U.S. cent. Since the establishment of the Republic in 1923, the Turkish terms, Kurus and Lira, have replaced the European names Piastres and Turkish Pounds.

MINT VISIT ISSUES

From time to time, certain cities of the Ottoman Empire, such as Bursa, Edirne, Kosova, Manistir and Salonika were honored by having special coins struck at Istanbul, but with inscriptions stating that they were struck in the city of honor. These were produced on the occasion of the Sultan's visit to that city. The coins were struck in limited, but not small quantities, and were probably intended for distribution to the notables of the city and the Sultan's own followers. Because they were of the same size and type as the regular circulation issues struck at Istanbul, many specimens found their way into circulation and worn or mounted specimens are found today, although some have been preserved in XF or better condition. Mintage statistics are not known.

MONNAIE DE LUXE

In the 23rd year of the reign of Abdul Hamid II, two parallel series of gold coins were produced, regular mint issues and monnaies de luxe', which were intended primarily for presentation and jewelry purposes. The Monnaie de Luxe' were struck to a slightly less weight and the same fineness as regular issues, but were broader and thinner, and from more ornate dies.

Coins are listed by type, followed by a list of reported years. Most of the reported years have never been confirmed and other years may also exist. Mintage figures are known for the AH1293 and 1327 series, but are unreliable and of little utility.

Although some years are undoubtedly much rarer than others, there is at present no date collecting of Ottoman gold and therefore little justification for higher prices for rare dates.

There is no change in design in the regular series. Only the toughra, accessional date and regnal year vary. The deluxe series show ornamental changes. The standard coins generally do not bear the denomination.

HONORIFIC TITLES

El Ghazi

Reshat

The first coinage of Abdul Hamid II has a flower right of the toughra while the second coinage has *el Ghazi* (The Victorious). The first coinage of Mohammad Reshat Vhas *Reshat* right of the toughra while his second coinage has *el Ghazi.*

SULTANATE

Abdul Hamid II

AH1293-1327/1876-1909AD

MILLED COINAGE

Gold Issues

KM# 745 12-1/2 KURUSH

0.8770 g., 0.9170 Gold .0258 oz. AGW **Series:** Monnaie de Luxe **Obverse:** Toughra **Mint:** Qustantiniyah

Date	Mintage	VG	F	VF	XF	Unc
AH1293//27 (1901)	720	—	—	—	—	—
AH1293//28 (1902)	800	40.00	120	200	300	—
AH1293//29 (1903)	11,696	30.00	70.00	150	220	—
AH1293//30 (1904)	13,208	30.00	70.00	150	220	—
AH1293//31 (1905)	24,504	30.00	70.00	150	220	—
AH1293//32 (1906)	14,392	30.00	70.00	150	220	—
AH1293//33 (1907)	13,032	30.00	70.00	150	220	—
AH1293//34 (1908)	—	40.00	120	200	300	—

KM# 729 25 KURUSH

1.8040 g., 0.9170 Gold .0532 oz. AGW **Obverse:** Toughra; "el-Ghazi" to right **Reverse:** Text, value and date within wreath, star above **Mint:** Qustantiniyah

Date	Mintage	VG	F	VF	XF	Unc
AH1293//27 (1901)	99,500	—	BV	45.00	70.00	—
AH1293//28 (1902)	77,300	—	BV	45.00	70.00	—
AH1293//29 (1903)	101,548	—	BV	45.00	70.00	—
AH1293//30 (1904)	156,280	—	BV	45.00	70.00	—
AH1293//31 (1905)	58,404	—	BV	45.00	70.00	—
AH1293//32 (1906)	112,000	—	BV	45.00	70.00	—
AH1293//33 (1907)	15,535	—	BV	45.00	70.00	—
AH1293//34 (1908)	115,484	—	BV	45.00	70.00	—

KM# 739 25 KURUSH

1.7540 g., 0.9170 Gold .0517 oz. AGW **Series:** Monnaie de Luxe **Obverse:** Toughra; "el-Ghazi" to right **Reverse:** Text, value and date in beaded circle within circular text **Mint:** Qustantiniyah

Date	Mintage	VG	F	VF	XF	Unc
AH1293//27 (1901)	7,620	50.00	70.00	120	180	—
AH1293//28 (1902)	9,268	50.00	70.00	120	180	—
AH1293//29 (1903)	29,056	50.00	70.00	120	180	—
AH1293//30 (1904)	27,964	50.00	70.00	120	180	—
AH1293//31 (1905)	39,192	50.00	70.00	120	180	—
AH1293//32 (1906)	41,696	50.00	70.00	120	180	—
AH1293//33 (1907)	17,728	50.00	70.00	120	180	—
AH1293//34 (1908)	—	50.00	95.00	150	200	—

KM# 731 50 KURUSH

3.6080 g., 0.9170 Gold .1064 oz. AGW **Obverse:** Toughra; "el-Ghazi" to right **Reverse:** Text, value and date within wreath, star above **Mint:** Qustantiniyah

Date	Mintage	VG	F	VF	XF	Unc
AH1293//27 (1901)	14,200	—	BV	75.00	95.00	—
AH1293//28 (1902)	33,450	—	BV	75.00	92.00	—
AH1293//29 (1903)	24,244	—	BV	75.00	92.00	—
AH1293//30 (1904)	66,000	—	BV	75.00	92.00	—
AH1293//31 (1905)	58,612	—	BV	75.00	92.00	—
AH1293//32 (1906)	48,000	—	BV	75.00	92.00	—
AH1293//33 (1907)	16,145	—	BV	75.00	92.00	—
AH1293//34 (1908)	6,276	—	BV	90.00	150	—

KM# 740 50 KURUSH

3.5080 g., 0.9170 Gold .1034 oz. AGW **Series:** Monnaie de Luxe **Obverse:** Toughra; "el-Ghazi" to right **Reverse:** Text, value and date in beaded circle within circular text **Mint:** Qustantiniyah

Date	Mintage	VG	F	VF	XF	Unc
AH1293//27 (1901)	6,630	BV	75.00	140	200	—
AH1293//28 (1902)	8,660	BV	75.00	140	200	—
AH1293//29 (1903)	14,924	BV	75.00	140	200	—
AH1293//30 (1904)	18,812	BV	75.00	140	200	—
AH1293//31 (1905)	22,460	BV	75.00	140	200	—
AH1293//32 (1906)	27,542	BV	75.00	140	200	—
AH1293//33 (1907)	12,886	BV	75.00	140	200	—
AH1293//34 (1908)	—	BV	75.00	180	250	—

KM# 730 100 KURUSH

7.2160 g., 0.9170 Gold .2128 oz. AGW **Obverse:** Toughra; "el-Ghazi" to right **Reverse:** Text, value and date within wreath, star above **Mint:** Qustantiniyah

Date	Mintage	VG	F	VF	XF	Unc
AH1293//27 (1901)	48,200	—	—	BV	160	—
AH1293//28 (1902)	865,011	—	—	BV	150	—
AH1293//29 (1903)	1,026,275	—	—	BV	150	—
AH1293//30 (1904)	1,643,795	—	—	BV	150	—
AH1293//31 (1905)	2,748,448	—	—	BV	150	—
AH1293//32 (1906)	1,951,611	—	—	BV	150	—
AH1293//33 (1907)	962,672	—	—	BV	150	—
AH1293//34 (1908)	1,715,274	—	BV	200	250	—

KM# 741 100 KURUSH

7.0160 g., 0.9170 Gold .2068 oz. AGW **Series:** Monnaie de Luxe **Obverse:** Toughra; "el-Ghazi" to right **Reverse:** Text, value and date in beaded circle within circular text **Mint:** Qustantiniyah

Date	Mintage	VG	F	VF	XF	Unc
AH1293//27 (1901)	9,580	—	BV	150	220	—
AH1293//28 (1902)	13,638	—	BV	150	220	—
AH1293//29 (1903)	18,129	—	BV	150	220	—
AH1293//30 (1904)	22,796	—	BV	150	220	—
AH1293//31 (1905)	31,126	—	BV	150	220	—
AH1293//32 (1906)	42,662	—	BV	150	220	—
AH1293//33 (1907)	18,716	—	BV	150	220	—
AH1293//34 (1908)	—	—	BV	180	250	—

KM# 732 250 KURUSH

18.0400 g., 0.9170 Gold .5319 oz. AGW **Obverse:** Toughra; "el-Ghazi" to right **Reverse:** Text, value and date within wreath, star above **Mint:** Qustantiniyah

Date	Mintage	VG	F	VF	XF	Unc
AH1293//27 (1901)	1,450	—	BV	375	450	—
AH1293//28 (1902)	7,027	—	BV	375	450	—
AH1293//29 (1903)	7,522	—	BV	375	450	—
AH1293//30 (1904)	4,900	—	BV	375	450	—
AH1293//31 (1905)	8,552	—	BV	375	450	—
AH1293//32 (1906)	8,729	—	BV	375	450	—
AH1293//33 (1907)	2,669	—	BV	375	450	—
AH1293//34 (1908)	6,478	—	BV	400	600	—

KM# 742 250 KURUSH

17.5400 g., 0.9170 Gold .5169 oz. AGW **Series:** Monnaie de Luxe **Obverse:** Toughra; "el-Ghazi" to right **Reverse:** Text, value and date within beaded circle, designed wreath **Mint:** Qustantiniyah

Date	Mintage	VG	F	VF	XF	Unc
AH1293//27 (1901)	1,770	BV	360	500	750	—
AH1293//28 (1902)	1,520	BV	360	500	750	—
AH1293//29 (1903)	1,631	BV	360	500	750	—
AH1293//30 (1904)	1,922	BV	360	500	750	—
AH1293//31 (1905)	1,778	BV	360	500	750	—
AH1293//32 (1906)	2,650	BV	360	500	750	—
AH1293//33 (1907)	931	BV	450	800	1,000	—
AH1293//34 (1908) Rare	—	—	—	—	—	—

KM# 733 500 KURUSH

36.0800 g., 0.9170 Gold 1.0638 oz. AGW **Obverse:** Toughra; "el-Ghazi" to right **Reverse:** Text, value and date within wreath, star above **Mint:** Qustantiniyah

Date	Mintage	VG	F	VF	XF	Unc
AH1293//27 (1901)	22,450	—	BV	745	850	—
AH1293//28 (1902)	35,918	—	BV	745	850	—
AH1293//29 (1903)	16,621	—	BV	745	850	—
AH1293//30 (1904)	33,129	—	BV	745	850	—
AH1293//31 (1905)	40,953	—	BV	745	850	—
AH1293//32 (1906)	32,516	—	BV	745	850	—
AH1293//33 (1907)	16,403	—	BV	745	850	—
AH1293//34 (1908)	39,028	—	BV	745	850	—

KM# 746 500 KURUSH

35.0800 g., 0.9170 Gold 1.0338 oz. AGW **Series:** Monnaie de Luxe **Obverse:** Radiant Toughra above crossed flags, ornamental base **Reverse:** Inscription and date within star and designed border **Mint:** Qustantiniyah

Date	Mintage	Good	VG	F	VF	XF
AH1293//27 (1901)	1,428	—	725	800	900	1,200
AH1293//28 (1902)	858	—	725	800	900	1,200
AH1293//29 (1903)	804	—	725	800	900	1,200
AH1293//30 (1904)	1,204	—	725	800	900	1,200
AH1293//31 (1905)	1,021	—	725	800	900	1,200
AH1293//32 (1906)	1,334	—	725	800	900	1,200
AH1293//33 (1907)	812	—	725	800	900	1,200
AH1293//34 (1908)	—	—	725	800	900	1,200

STANDARD COINAGE

KM# 743 5 PARA

1.0023 g., 0.1000 Silver .0032 oz. ASW **Obverse:** Toughra; "el-Ghazi" to right **Reverse:** Text within crescent below value, date and star **Mint:** Qustantiniyah

Date	Mintage	VG	F	VF	XF	Unc
AH1293//27 (1901)	—	0.25	0.50	1.25	4.00	—
AH1293//28 (1902)	—	0.50	1.00	3.00	12.00	—
AH1293//30 (1904)	—	6.00	12.00	20.00	40.00	—

KM# 744 10 PARA

2.0046 g., 0.1000 Silver .0064 oz. ASW **Obverse:** Toughra; "el-Ghazi" to right **Reverse:** Text within crescent below date, value and star **Mint:** Qustantiniyah

Date	Mintage	VG	F	VF	XF	Unc
AH1293//27 (1901)	—	0.25	0.50	1.00	4.00	—
Note: Varieties exist in size of regnal year 27						
AH1293//28 (1902)	—	0.25	0.50	1.50	6.00	—
AH1293//30 (1904)	—	1.00	2.00	5.00	15.00	—

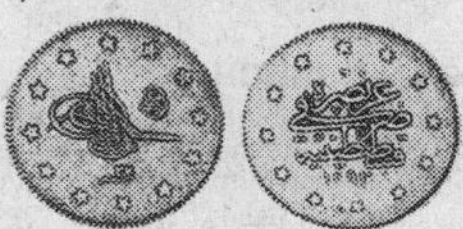

KM# 735 KURUSH

1.2027 g., 0.8300 Silver .0321 oz. ASW **Obverse:** Toughra; "el-Ghazi" to right **Reverse:** Text, value and date within circle of stars **Mint:** Qustantiniyah **Note:** Varieties exist in the size of year and inscription.

Date	Mintage	VG	F	VF	XF	Unc
AH1293//27 (1901)	9,945,000	1.00	2.00	3.00	5.00	—
AH1293//28 (1902)	16,139,000	1.00	2.00	3.00	5.00	—
AH1293//29 (1903)	7,076,000	1.00	2.00	3.00	5.00	—
AH1293//30 (1904)	707,000	2.00	4.00	8.00	15.00	—
AH1293//31 (1905)	1,366,000	1.00	2.00	3.00	5.00	—
AH1293//32 (1906)	1,140,000	1.00	2.00	3.00	5.00	—
AH1293//33 (1907)	1,700,000	1.00	2.00	3.00	5.00	—
AH1293//34 (1908)	—	150	200	230	260	—

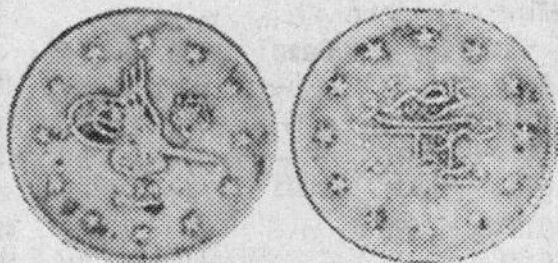

KM# 736 2 KURUSH

2.4055 g., 0.8300 Silver .0642 oz. ASW **Obverse:** Toughra; "el-Ghazi" to right **Reverse:** Text, value and date within circle of stars **Mint:** Qustantiniyah **Note:** Varieties exist in the size of toughra and year.

Date	Mintage	VG	F	VF	XF	Unc
AH1293//27 (1901)	4,689,000	1.50	2.00	4.00	7.00	—
AH1293//28 (1902)	7,567,000	1.50	2.00	4.00	7.00	—
AH1293//29 (1903)	7,775,000	1.50	2.00	4.00	7.00	—
AH1293//30 (1904)	1,366,000	1.50	2.00	4.00	7.00	—
AH1293//31 (1905)	3,014,000	1.50	2.00	4.00	7.00	—
AH1293//32 (1906)	1,625,000	1.50	2.00	4.00	7.00	—
AH1293//33 (1907)	2,173,000	1.50	2.00	4.00	7.00	—
AH1293//34 (1908)	—	150	225	250	300	—

KM# 737 5 KURUSH

6.0130 g., 0.8300 Silver .1605 oz. ASW **Obverse:** Toughra; "el-Ghazi" to right **Reverse:** Text, value and date within circle of stars and crescent border **Mint:** Qustantiniyah **Note:** Varieties exist in the size of toughra, inscription, and date.

Date	Mintage	VG	F	VF	XF	Unc
AH1293//27 (1901)	16,000	15.00	30.00	45.00	75.00	—
AH1293//28 (1902)	6,000	100	150	175	200	—

Date	Mintage	VG	F	VF	XF	Unc
AH1293//29 (1903)	7,000	100	150	175	200	—
AH1293//30 (1904)	38,000	5.00	10.00	15.00	30.00	—
AH1293//31 (1905)	Inc. above	3.50	4.50	7.00	15.00	—
AH1293//31/0 (1905)	3,175,000	6.00	13.00	25.00	35.00	—
AH1293//32 (1906)	3,334,000	2.50	3.75	5.00	9.50	—
AH1293//33 (1907)	907,000	3.00	5.00	9.00	16.00	—
AH1293//34 (1908)	—	200	225	275	350	—

KM# 738 10 KURUSH

12.0270 g., 0.8300 Silver .3210 oz. ASW **Obverse:** Toughra; "el-Ghazi" to right **Reverse:** Text, value and date within circle of stars and crescent border

Date	Mintage	VG	F	VF	XF	Unc
AH1293//31 (1905)	51,000	60.00	100	120	150	—
AH1293//32 (1906)	575,000	7.50	12.50	18.00	30.00	—
AH1293//33 (1907)	274,000	6.50	11.50	20.00	35.00	—

Muhammad V

AH1327-36/1909-18AD

MILLED COINAGE

Gold Issues

KM# 762 12-1/2 KURUSH

0.9020 g., 0.9170 Gold .0266 oz. AGW **Series:** Monnaie de Luxe **Obverse:** Toughra; "Reshat" to right **Reverse:** Value and date within designed wreath **Mint:** Qustantiniyah

Date	Mintage	Good	VG	F	VF	XF
AH1327//2 (1910)	43,568	—	30.00	50.00	90.00	130
AH1327//3 (1911)	50,368	—	30.00	50.00	90.00	130
AH1327//4 (1912)	19,344	—	30.00	50.00	90.00	130
AH1327//5 (1913)	9,160	—	30.00	50.00	90.00	130
AH1327//6 (1914)	11,880	—	30.00	50.00	90.00	130

KM# 752 25 KURUSH

1.8040 g., 0.9170 Gold .0532 oz. AGW **Obverse:** Toughra; "Reshat" to right **Reverse:** Inscription and date within wreath, star on top **Mint:** Qustantiniyah

Date	Mintage	Good	VG	F	VF	XF
AH1327//1 (1909)	115,484	—	—	BV	40.00	50.00
AH1327//2 (1910)	194,740	—	—	BV	40.00	50.00
AH1327//3 (1911)	249,416	—	—	BV	40.00	50.00
AH1327//4 (1912)	338,172	—	—	BV	40.00	50.00
AH1327//5 (1913)	167,592	—	—	BV	40.00	50.00
AH1327//6 (1914)	72,872	—	—	BV	40.00	50.00

KM# 763 25 KURUSH

1.7540 g., 0.9170 Gold .0517 oz. AGW **Series:** Monnaie de Luxe **Obverse:** Toughra within designed wreath **Reverse:** Inscription and date within designed wreath **Mint:** Qustantiniyah

Date	Mintage	Good	VG	F	VF	XF
AH1327//2 (1910)	47,788	—	BV	60.00	90.00	120
AH1327//3 (1911)	70,775	—	BV	60.00	90.00	120
AH1327//4 (1912)	47,088	—	BV	60.00	90.00	120
AH1327//5 (1913)	25,964	—	50.00	80.00	110	140
AH1327//6 (1914)	23,348	—	50.00	80.00	110	140

KM# 773 25 KURUSH

1.8040 g., 0.9170 Gold .0532 oz. AGW **Obverse:** Toughra; "el-Ghazi" to right **Reverse:** Inscription and date within wreath, star on top **Mint:** Qustantiniyah

Date	Mintage	Good	VG	F	VF	XF
AH1327//7 (1915)	22,420	—	—	BV	45.00	75.00

Date	Mintage	Good	VG	F	VF	XF
AH1327//8 (1916)	5,926	—	—	BV	45.00	75.00
AH1327//9 (1917)	4,060	—	—	BV	45.00	75.00
AH1327//10 (1918)	53,524	—	1,000	1,500	2,000	—

KM# 774 25 KURUSH

1.7540 g., 0.9170 Gold .0517 oz. AGW **Series:** Monnaie de Luxe **Obverse:** Toughra **Mint:** Qustantiniyah

Date	Mintage	Good	VG	F	VF	XF
AH1327//8 (1916)	10,612	—	1,750	2,500	3,500	5,000

KM# 753 50 KURUSH

3.6080 g., 0.9170 Gold .1064 oz. AGW **Obverse:** Toughra; "Reshat" to right **Reverse:** Inscription and date within wreath, star on top **Mint:** Qustantiniyah

Date	Mintage	Good	VG	F	VF	XF
AH1327//1 (1909)	6,276	—	1,000	1,500	2,000	3,000
AH1327//2 (1910)	89,712	—	—	BV	75.00	95.00
AH1327//3 (1911)	75,442	—	—	BV	75.00	95.00
AH1327//4 (1912)	96,030	—	—	BV	75.00	95.00
AH1327//5 (1913)	40,618	—	—	BV	75.00	95.00
AH1327//6 (1914)	26,408	—	—	BV	80.00	110

KM# 764 50 KURUSH

3.5080 g., 0.9170 Gold .1034 oz. AGW **Series:** Monnaie de Luxe **Obverse:** Toughra within designed wreath **Reverse:** Inscription and date within designed wreath **Mint:** Qustantiniyah

Date	Mintage	Good	VG	F	VF	XF
AH1327//2 (1910)	25,224	—	BV	75.00	140	180
AH1327//3 (1911)	23,971	—	BV	75.00	140	180
AH1327//4 (1912)	15,716	—	BV	75.00	140	180
AH1327//5 (1913)	17,118	—	BV	75.00	140	180
AH1327//6 (1914)	8,706	—	BV	75.00	180	250

KM# 775 50 KURUSH

3.6080 g., 0.9170 Gold .1064 oz. AGW **Obverse:** Toughra; "el-Ghazi" to right **Mint:** Qustantiniyah

Date	Mintage	Good	VG	F	VF	XF
AH1327//7 (1915)	9,175	—	BV	75.00	150	250
AH1327//8 (1916)	7,330	—	BV	75.00	150	250
AH1327//9 (1917)	2,000	—	BV	75.00	150	250
AH1327//10 (1918)	53,524	—	1,000	1,500	2,000	3,000

KM# 781 50 KURUSH

3.5080 g., 0.9170 Gold .1034 oz. AGW **Series:** Monnaie de Luxe **Obverse:** Toughra **Mint:** Qustantiniyah

Date	Mintage	Good	VG	F	VF	XF
AH1327//8 (1916)	3,291	—	250	500	800	1,200

KM# 754 100 KURUSH

7.2160 g., 0.9170 Gold .2125 oz. AGW **Obverse:** Toughra; "Reshat" to right **Reverse:** Inscription and date within wreath, star on top **Mint:** Qustantiniyah

Date	Mintage	Good	VG	F	VF	XF
AH1327//1 (1909)	1,715,274	—	—	BV	150	165
AH1327//2 (1910)	3,376,679	—	—	BV	150	165
AH1327//3 (1911)	4,627,115	—	—	BV	150	165
AH1327//4 (1912)	3,591,676	—	—	BV	150	165
AH1327//5 (1913)	881,895	—	—	BV	150	165
AH1327//6 (1914)	3,769,100	—	—	BV	150	165
AH1327//7 (1915)	2,989,609	—	—	BV	150	165

KM# 755 100 KURUSH

7.0160 g., 0.9170 Gold .2068 oz. AGW **Series:** Monnaie de Luxe **Obverse:** Toughra within designed wreath **Reverse:** Inscription and date within designed wreath

Date	Mintage	Good	VG	F	VF	XF
AH1327//1 (1909)	—	—	—	BV	180	250
AH1327//2 (1910)	37,110	—	—	BV	180	250
AH1327//3 (1911)	53,738	—	—	BV	180	250
AH1327//4 (1912)	41,507	—	—	BV	180	250
AH1327//5 (1913)	58,819	—	—	BV	180	250
AH1327//6 (1914)	19,768	—	—	BV	180	250

KM# 776 100 KURUSH

7.2160 g., 0.9170 Gold .2128 oz. AGW **Obverse:** Toughra; "el-Ghazi" to right **Reverse:** Inscription and date within wreath, star on top **Mint:** Qustantiniyah

Date	Mintage	Good	VG	F	VF	XF
AH1327//7 (1915)	1,232,090	—	—	BV	150	170
AH1327//8 (1916)	Inc. above	—	—	BV	150	170
AH1327//9 (1917)	3,582,005	—	—	BV	150	170
AH1327//10 (1918)	—	—	—	BV	160	200

KM# 782 100 KURUSH

7.0160 g., 0.9170 Gold .2068 oz. AGW **Series:** Monnaie de Luxe **Obverse:** Toughra **Mint:** Qustantiniyah

Date	Mintage	Good	VG	F	VF	XF
AH1327//8 (1916)	13,250	—	250	400	600	1,000

KM# 756 250 KURUSH

18.0400 g., 0.9170 Gold .5319 oz. AGW **Obverse:** Toughra; "Reshat" to right **Reverse:** Inscription and date within wreath, star on top **Mint:** Qustantiniyah

Date	Mintage	Good	VG	F	VF	XF
AH1327//1 (1909)	6,878	—	—	BV	400	500
AH1327//2 (1910)	9,207	—	—	BV	400	500
AH1327//3 (1911)	9,990	—	—	BV	400	500
AH1327//4 (1912)	13,400	—	—	BV	400	500
AH1327//5 (1913)	18,143	—	—	BV	400	500
AH1327//6 (1914)	6,155	—	—	BV	400	500

KM# 757 250 KURUSH

17.5400 g., 0.9170 Gold .5619 oz. AGW **Series:** Monnaie de Luxe **Obverse:** Toughra within designed wreath **Reverse:** Inscription and date within designed wreath **Mint:** Qustantiniyah

Date	Mintage	Good	VG	F	VF	XF
AH1327//1 (1909)	—	—	BV	400	600	800
AH1327//2 (1910)	6,995	—	BV	400	600	800
AH1327//3 (1911)	12,084	—	BV	400	600	800
AH1327//4 (1912)	10,250	—	BV	400	600	800
AH1327//5 (1913)	16,879	—	BV	400	600	800
AH1327//6 (1914)	9,039	—	BV	400	600	800

KM# 777 250 KURUSH

18.0400 g., 0.9170 Gold .5319 oz. AGW **Obverse:** Toughra; "el-Ghazi" to right **Reverse:** Inscription and date within wreath, star on top **Mint:** Qustantiniyah

Date	Mintage	Good	VG	F	VF	XF
AH1327//7 (1915)	30	—	1,250	1,750	2,800	4,000
AH1327//8 (1916)	21	—	1,750	2,500	3,500	5,000
AH1327//9 (1917)	28	—	1,750	2,500	3,500	5,000

KM# 783 250 KURUSH

17.5400 g., 0.9170 Gold .5619 oz. AGW **Series:** Monnaie de Luxe **Obverse:** Toughra within designed wreath **Reverse:** Inscription and date within designed wreath **Mint:** Qustantiniyah

Date	Mintage	Good	VG	F	VF	XF
AH1327//8 (1916)	3,107	—	1,250	1,750	2,500	3,500

KM# 758 500 KURUSH

17.5400 g., 0.9170 Gold .5619 oz. AGW **Obverse:** Toughra; "Reshat" to right **Reverse:** Inscription and date within wreath, star on top **Mint:** Qustantiniyah

Date	Mintage	Good	VG	F	VF	XF
AH1327//1 (1909)	39,028	—	—	BV	525	650
AH1327//2 (1910)	37,474	—	—	BV	525	650
AH1327//3 (1911)	53,900	—	—	BV	525	650
AH1327//4 (1912)	41,863	—	—	BV	525	650
AH1327//5 (1913)	36,996	—	—	BV	525	650
AH1327//6 (1914)	17,792	—	—	BV	525	650

KM# 765 500 KURUSH

35.0800 g., 0.9170 Gold 1.0338 oz. AGW **Series:** Monnaie de Luxe **Obverse:** Radiant Toughra above crossed flags, ornamental base **Reverse:** Inscription and date within designed wreath **Mint:** Qustantiniyah

Date	Mintage	Good	VG	F	VF	XF
AH1327//2 (1910)	1,718	—	BV	750	900	1,350
AH1327//3 (1911)	4,631	—	BV	750	900	1,350
AH1327//4 (1912)	3,887	—	BV	750	900	1,350
AH1327//5 (1913)	5,145	—	BV	750	900	1,350
AH1327//6 (1914)	2,401	—	BV	750	900	1,350

KM# 784 500 KURUSH

36.0800 g., 0.9170 Gold 1.0638 oz. AGW **Obverse:** Toughra; "el-Ghazi" to right **Reverse:** Inscription and date within wreath, star on top **Mint:** Qustantiniyah

Date	Mintage	Good	VG	F	VF	XF
AH1327//7 (1915)	484	—	1,750	2,500	3,500	5,000
AH1327//8 (1916)	19	—	1,750	2,750	4,250	6,000
AH1327//9 (1917)	22	—	1,750	2,750	4,250	6,000
AH1327//10 (1918)	—	—	1,750	2,500	3,500	5,000

KM# 778 500 KURUSH

35.0800 g., 0.9170 Gold 1.0338 oz. AGW **Series:** Monnaie de Luxe **Obverse:** Radiant Toughra above crossed flags, ornamental base **Reverse:** Inscription and date within designed wreath **Mint:** Qustantiniyah **Note:** Struck at Qustantiniyah.

Date	Mintage	Good	VG	F	VF	XF
AH1327//7 (1915)	295	—	1,200	1,750	2,500	3,500
AH1327//8 (1916)	1,618	—	1,000	1,500	2,200	3,000

MILLED COINAGE

Gold Mint Visit Issues

Muhammad V's visit to Bursa

KM# 787 25 KURUSH

1.8040 g., 0.9170 Gold .0532 oz. AGW **Obverse:** Toughra in center of sprigs and stars **Reverse:** Inscription and date within wreath, star on top **Mint:** Bursa

Date	Mintage	F	VF	XF	Unc
AH1327//1 (1909)	—	185	275	400	800

KM# 788 50 KURUSH

3.6080 g., 0.9170 Gold .1064 oz. AGW **Obverse:** Toughra in center of sprigs and stars **Reverse:** Inscription and date within wreath, star on top **Mint:** Bursa

Date	Mintage	F	VF	XF	Unc
AH1327//1 (1909)	—	165	275	350	650

KM# 789 100 KURUSH

7.2160 g., 0.9170 Gold .2128 oz. AGW **Obverse:** Toughra in center of sprigs and stars **Reverse:** Inscription and date within wreath, star on top **Mint:** Bursa

Date	Mintage	F	VF	XF	Unc
AH1327//1 (1909)	—	215	325	400	700

MILLED COINAGE

Gold Mint Visit Issues

Muhammad V visit to Edirne

KM# 793 50 KURUSH

3.6080 g., 0.9170 Gold .1064 oz. AGW **Obverse:** Toughra in center of sprigs and stars **Reverse:** Inscription and date within wreath, star on top **Mint:** Edirne

Date	Mintage	F	VF	XF	Unc
AH1327//2 (1910)	—	200	275	350	600

KM# 794 100 KURUSH

7.2160 g., 0.9170 Gold .2128 oz. AGW **Obverse:** Toughra in center of sprigs and stars **Reverse:** Inscription and date within wreath, star on top **Mint:** Edirne

Date	Mintage	F	VF	XF	Unc
AH1327//2 (1910)	—	250	350	475	700

KM# 795 500 KURUSH

36.0800 g., 0.9170 Gold 1.0638 oz. AGW **Obverse:** Toughra in center of sprigs and stars **Reverse:** Inscription and date within wreath, star on top **Mint:** Edirne

Date	Mintage	F	VF	XF	Unc
AH1327//2 (1910)	—	1,500	2,500	3,500	4,000

MILLED COINAGE

Gold Mint Visit Issues

Muhammad Vs visit to Kosova

KM# 799 50 KURUSH

3.6080 g., 0.9170 Gold .1064 oz. AGW **Obverse:** Toughra in center of sprigs and stars **Reverse:** Inscription and date within wreath, star on top **Mint:** Kosova

Date	Mintage	F	VF	XF	Unc
AH1327//3 (1911)	1,200	225	275	400	700

KM# 800 100 KURUSH

7.2160 g., 0.9170 Gold .2128 oz. AGW **Obverse:** Toughra in center of stars and sprigs **Reverse:** Inscription and date within wreath, star on top **Mint:** Kosova

Date	Mintage	F	VF	XF	Unc
AH1327//3 (1911)	750	250	300	450	750

KM# 801 500 KURUSH
36.0800 g., 0.9170 Gold 1.0638 oz. AGW **Obverse:** Toughra in center of stars and sprigs **Reverse:** Inscription and date within wreath, star on top **Mint:** Kosova

Date	Mintage	F	VF	XF	Unc
AH1327//3 (1911)	20	3,000	4,000	5,000	6,000

MILLED COINAGE

Gold Mint Visit Issues

Muhammad V's visit to Manastir

KM# 805 50 KURUSH
3.6080 g., 0.9170 Gold .1064 oz. AGW **Obverse:** Toughra in center of sprigs and stars **Reverse:** Inscription and date within wreath, star on top **Mint:** Manastir

Date	Mintage	F	VF	XF	Unc
AH1327//3 (1911)	1,200	200	325	450	700

KM# 806 100 KURUSH
7.2160 g., 0.9170 Gold .2128 oz. AGW **Obverse:** Toughra in center of sprigs and stars **Reverse:** Inscription and date within wreath, star on top **Mint:** Manastir

Date	Mintage	F	VF	XF	Unc
AH1327//3 (1911)	750	225	350	450	750

KM# 807 500 KURUSH
36.0800 g., 0.9170 Gold 1.0638 oz. AGW **Obverse:** Toughra in center of sprigs and stars **Reverse:** Inscription and date within wreath, star on top **Mint:** Manastir

Date	Mintage	F	VF	XF	Unc
AH1327//3 (1911)	20	2,500	4,000	5,000	6,250

MILLED COINAGE

Gold Mint Visit Issues

Muhammad V's visit to Salonika

KM# 811 50 KURUSH
3.6080 g., 0.9170 Gold .1064 oz. AGW **Obverse:** Toughra in center of sprigs and stars **Reverse:** Inscription and date within wreath, star on top **Mint:** Salonika

Date	Mintage	F	VF	XF	Unc
AH1327//3 (1911)	1,200	200	325	400	700

KM# 812 100 KURUSH
7.2160 g., 0.9170 Gold .2128 oz. AGW **Obverse:** Toughra in center of sprigs and stars **Reverse:** Inscription and date within wreath, star on top **Mint:** Salonika

Date	Mintage	F	VF	XF	Unc
AH1327//3 (1911)	750	225	350	450	750

KM# 813 500 KURUSH
36.0800 g., 0.9170 Gold 1.0638 oz. AGW **Obverse:** Toughra in center of sprigs and stars **Reverse:** Inscription and date within wreath, star on top **Mint:** Salonika

Date	Mintage	F	VF	XF	Unc
AH1327//3 (1911)	20	2,500	4,000	5,250	6,750

STANDARD COINAGE

KM# 759 5 PARA
Nickel **Obverse:** Toughra; "Reshat" to right **Reverse:** Value within beaded circle above sprigs **Mint:** Qustantiniyah

Date	Mintage	Good	VG	F	VF	XF
AH1327//2 (1910)	1,664,000	—	2.00	4.00	6.00	9.00
AH1327//3 (1911)	21,760,000	—	0.50	1.00	2.00	4.00
AH1327//4 (1912)	21,392,000	—	0.50	1.00	2.00	4.00
AH1327//5 (1913)	30,579,000	—	0.50	1.00	2.00	4.00
AH1327//6 (1914)	15,751,000	—	0.50	1.00	2.00	4.00
AH1327//7 (1915)	2,512,000	—	10.00	15.00	20.00	30.00

KM# 767 5 PARA
Nickel **Obverse:** Toughra; "el-Ghazi" to right **Reverse:** Value within beaded circle above sprigs **Mint:** Qustantiniyah

Date	Mintage	Good	VG	F	VF	XF
AH1327//7 (1915)	740,000	—	10.00	12.50	15.00	20.00

KM# 760 10 PARA
Nickel **Obverse:** Toughra; "Reshat" to right **Reverse:** Value within beaded circle above sprigs **Mint:** Qustantiniyah

Date	Mintage	Good	VG	F	VF	XF
AH1327//2 (1910)	2,576,000	—	0.25	0.50	2.00	5.00
AH1327//3 (1911)	18,992,000	—	0.15	0.25	1.00	3.00
AH1327//4 (1912)	18,576,000	—	0.15	0.25	1.00	3.00
AH1327//5 (1913)	31,799,000	—	0.15	0.25	1.00	3.00
AH1327//6 (1914)	17,024,000	—	0.15	0.25	1.00	3.00
AH1327//7 (1915)	21,680,000	—	0.30	0.65	1.50	4.00

KM# 768 10 PARA
Nickel **Obverse:** Toughra; "el-Ghazi" to right **Reverse:** Value within beaded circle above sprigs **Mint:** Qustantiniyah

Date	Mintage	Good	VG	F	VF	XF
AH1327//7 (1915)	—	—	0.30	0.60	1.50	4.00
Note: Mintage included in KM760						
AH1327//8 (1916)	7,590,000	—	0.50	1.00	4.00	10.00

KM# 761 20 PARA
Nickel **Obverse:** Toughra; "Reshat" to right **Reverse:** Value within beaded circle above sprigs **Mint:** Qustantiniyah

Date	Mintage	Good	VG	F	VF	XF
AH1327 (1909) No regnal year	—	—	5.00	8.50	15.00	25.00
AH1327//2 (1910)	1,524,000	—	0.25	0.50	2.00	8.00
AH1327//3 (1911)	11,418,000	—	0.15	0.35	1.50	6.00
AH1327//4 (1912)	10,848,000	—	0.15	0.25	1.00	5.00
AH1327//5 (1913)	24,350,000	—	0.15	0.25	1.00	5.00
AH1327//6 (1914)	20,663,000	—	0.15	0.25	1.00	5.00
AH1327//7 (1915) Rare	—	—	500	700	900	1,200

KM# 769 20 PARA
Nickel **Obverse:** Toughra; "el-Ghazi" to right **Mint:** Qustantiniyah

Date	Mintage	Good	VG	F	VF	XF
AH1327//7 (1915) Rare	—	—	400	600	750	1,000

KM# 766 40 PARA
Nickel **Obverse:** Toughra; "el-Ghazi" to right **Mint:** Qustantiniyah **Note:** Struck at Qustantiniyah.

Date	Mintage	Good	VG	F	VF	XF
AH1327//3 (1910)	1,992,000	—	0.50	1.00	3.00	10.00
AH1327//4 (1911)	8,716,000	—	0.15	0.30	2.00	5.00
AH1327//5 (1912)	9,248,000	—	0.15	0.30	2.00	5.00

KM# 779 40 PARA
Copper-Nickel **Obverse:** Toughra; "el-Ghazi" to right **Reverse:** Value within beaded circle above sprigs **Mint:** Qustantiniyah

Date	Mintage	Good	VG	F	VF	XF
AH1327//8 (1916)	16,339,000	—	0.15	0.30	2.00	5.00
AH1327//9 (1917)	3,034,000	—	1.00	2.00	10.00	25.00

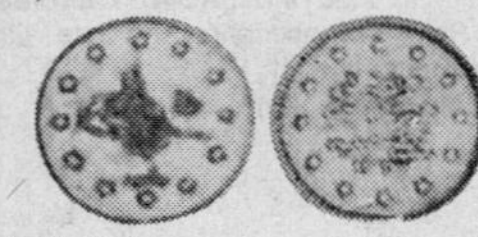

KM# 748 KURUSH
1.2027 g., 0.8300 Silver .0321 oz. ASW **Obverse:** Toughra within star border **Reverse:** Inscription and date within star border **Mint:** Qustantiniyah

Date	Mintage	Good	VG	F	VF	XF
AH1327//1 (1909)	1,270,000	—	1.25	2.50	3.50	6.00
AH1327//2 (1910)	8,770,000	—	1.00	2.00	3.00	5.00
AH1327//3 (1911)	840,000	—	1.50	3.00	6.00	12.50

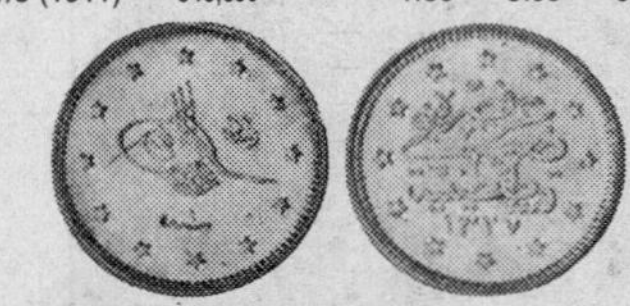

KM# 749 2 KURUSH
2.4055 g., 0.8300 Silver .0642 oz. ASW **Obverse:** Toughra; "Reshat" to right **Reverse:** Inscription and date within star border **Mint:** Qustantiniyah **Note:** Varieties exist in the size of date.

Date	Mintage	Good	VG	F	VF	XF
AH1327//1 (1909)	5,157,000	—	1.75	2.25	3.50	7.50
AH1327//2 (1910)	11,120,000	—	1.50	2.00	3.00	6.50
AH1327//3 (1911)	6,110,000	—	1.50	2.00	3.00	6.50
AH1327//4 (1912)	4,031,000	—	1.50	2.00	3.00	6.50
AH1327//5 (1913)	301,000	—	2.50	5.00	10.00	20.00
AH1327//6 (1914)	1,884,000	—	2.00	2.50	4.00	8.00
AH1327//6/2 (1914)	Inc. above	—	2.00	2.50	4.00	8.00

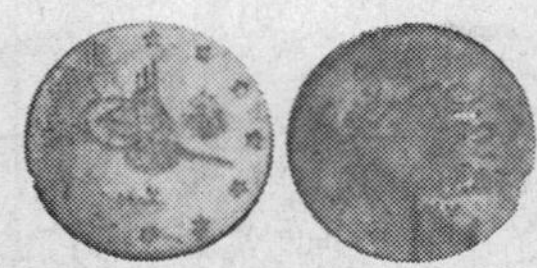

KM# 770 2 KURUSH

2.4055 g., 0.8300 Silver .0642 oz. ASW **Obverse:** Toughra; "el-Ghazi" to right **Reverse:** Inscription and date within star border **Mint:** Qustantiniyah **Note:** Varieties exist in the size of date.

Date	Mintage	Good	VG	F	VF	XF
AH1327//7 (1915)	17,000	—	12.50	25.00	40.00	75.00
AH1327//8 (1916)	398,000	—	20.00	30.00	50.00	100
AH1327//9 (1917)	8,000	—	250	350	450	600

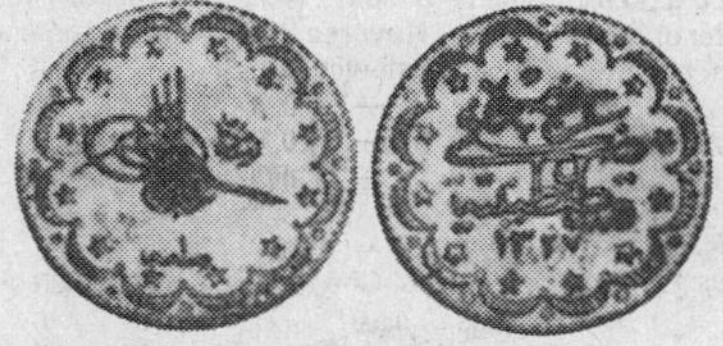

KM# 750 5 KURUSH

6.0130 g., 0.8300 Silver .1605 oz. ASW **Obverse:** Toughra; "Reshat" to right **Reverse:** Inscription and date within star border and design **Mint:** Qustantiniyah

Date	Mintage	Good	VG	F	VF	XF
AH1327//1 (1909)	1,558,000	—	BV	3.50	6.00	10.00
AH1327//2 (1910)	1,886,000	—	BV	3.50	6.00	10.00
AH1327//3 (1911)	1,273,000	—	BV	3.50	6.00	10.00
AH1327//4 (1912)	1,635,000	—	BV	3.50	6.00	10.00
AH1327//5 (1913)	194,000	—	6.00	9.00	15.00	28.00
AH1327//6 (1914)	664,000	—	3.00	3.50	5.00	9.00
AH1327//7 (1915)	834,000	—	3.00	3.50	5.00	9.00

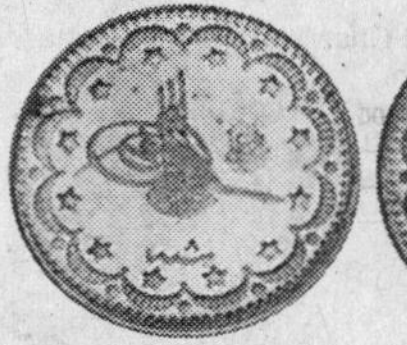

KM# 771 5 KURUSH

6.0130 g., 0.8300 Silver .1605 oz. ASW **Obverse:** Toughra; "el-Ghazi" to right **Reverse:** Inscription and date within star border and design **Mint:** Qustantiniyah

Date	Mintage	Good	VG	F	VF	XF
AH1327//7 (1915)	—	—	3.50	4.50	7.00	10.00
Note: Mintage included in KM750						
AH1327//8 (1916)	648,000	—	4.00	7.00	10.00	20.00
AH1327//9 (1917)	3,938	—	100	200	250	350

KM# 751 10 KURUSH

12.0270 g., 0.8300 Silver .3210 oz. ASW **Obverse:** Toughra; "Reshat" to right **Reverse:** Inscription and date within star border and design **Mint:** Qustantiniyah

Date	Mintage	Good	VG	F	VF	XF
AH1327//1 (1909)	110,000	—	12.50	25.00	50.00	100
AH1327//2 (1910)	Inc. above	—	10.00	20.00	50.00	100
AH1327//3 (1911)	8,000	—	70.00	125	1,000	1,600
AH1327//4 (1912)	96,000	—	5.00	8.00	15.00	25.00
AH1327//5 (1913)	34,000	—	10.00	20.00	50.00	100
AH1327//6 (1914)	81,000	—	7.50	12.50	17.50	30.00
AH1327//7 (1915)	582,000	—	6.00	10.00	16.50	32.00

KM# 772 10 KURUSH

12.0270 g., 0.8300 Silver .3210 oz. ASW **Obverse:** Toughra; "el-Ghazi" to right **Reverse:** Inscription and date within star border and design **Mint:** Qustantiniyah

Date	Mintage	Good	VG	F	VF	XF
AH1327//7 (1915)	—	—	5.00	8.00	15.00	28.00
Note: Mintage included in KM751						
AH1327//8 (1916)	408,000	—	7.00	9.00	17.50	32.00

Date	Mintage	Good	VG	F	VF	XF
AH1327//9 (1917)	299,000	—	10.00	20.00	35.00	50.00
AH1327//10 (1918)	666,000	—	12.50	25.00	50.00	85.00

KM# 780 20 KURUSH

24.0550 g., 0.8300 Silver .6419 oz. ASW **Obverse:** Toughra within star border and cresent wreath **Reverse:** Inscription and date within star border and crescent wreath **Mint:** Qustantiniyah

Date	Mintage	Good	VG	F	VF	XF
AH1327//8 (1916)	713,000	—	10.00	12.00	20.00	35.00
AH1327//9 (1917)	5,962,000	—	BV	10.00	15.00	30.00
AH1327//10 (1918)	11,025,000	—	10.00	12.00	20.00	35.00

MINT VISIT COINAGE

KM# 785 2 KURUSH

2.4055 g., 0.8300 Silver .0642 oz. ASW **Obverse:** Toughra within star border **Reverse:** Inscription and date within star border **Mint:** Bursa

Date	Mintage	F	VF	XF	Unc
AH1327//1 (1909)	—	15.00	30.00	75.00	125

KM# 790 2 KURUSH

2.4055 g., 0.8300 Silver .0642 oz. ASW **Obverse:** Toughra within star border **Reverse:** Inscription and date within star border **Mint:** Edirne

Date	Mintage	F	VF	XF	Unc
AH1327//2 (1910)	—	15.00	30.00	75.00	125

KM# 796 2 KURUSH

2.4055 g., 0.8300 Silver .0642 oz. ASW **Obverse:** Toughra within star border **Reverse:** Inscription and date within star border **Mint:** Kosova

Date	Mintage	F	VF	XF	Unc
AH1327//3 (1911)	13,000	15.00	30.00	100	150

KM# 802 2 KURUSH

2.4055 g., 0.8300 Silver .0642 oz. ASW **Obverse:** Toughra within star border **Reverse:** Inscription and date within star border **Mint:** Manastir

Date	Mintage	F	VF	XF	Unc
AH1327//3 (1911)	13,000	15.00	30.00	100	150

KM# 808 2 KURUSH

2.4055 g., 0.8300 Silver .0642 oz. ASW **Obverse:** Toughra within star border **Reverse:** Inscription and date within star border **Mint:** Salonika

Date	Mintage	F	VF	XF	Unc
AH1327//3 (1911)	13,000	15.00	30.00	100	150

KM# 786 5 KURUSH

6.0130 g., 0.8300 Silver .1605 oz. ASW **Obverse:** Toughra within star border and design **Reverse:** Inscription and date within star border and design **Mint:** Bursa

Date	Mintage	F	VF	XF	Unc
AH1327//1 (1909)	—	20.00	40.00	90.00	165

KM# 791 5 KURUSH

6.0130 g., 0.8300 Silver .1605 oz. ASW **Obverse:** Toughra within star border and design **Reverse:** Inscription and date within star border and design **Mint:** Edirne

Date	Mintage	F	VF	XF	Unc
AH1327//2 (1910)	—	20.00	40.00	90.00	165

KM# 797 5 KURUSH

6.0130 g., 0.8300 Silver .1605 oz. ASW **Obverse:** Toughra within star border and design **Reverse:** Inscription and date within star border and design **Mint:** Kosova

Date	Mintage	F	VF	XF	Unc
AH1327//3 (1911)	3,000	20.00	40.00	125	185

KM# 803 5 KURUSH

6.0130 g., 0.8300 Silver .1605 oz. ASW **Obverse:** Toughra within star border and design **Reverse:** Inscription and date within star border and design **Mint:** Manastir

Date	Mintage	F	VF	XF	Unc
AH1327//3 (1911)	3,000	20.00	40.00	125	185

KM# 809 5 KURUSH

6.0130 g., 0.8300 Silver .1605 oz. ASW **Obverse:** Toughra within star border and design **Reverse:** Inscription and date within star border and design **Mint:** Salonika

Date	Mintage	F	VF	XF	Unc
AH1327//3 (1911)	3,000	20.00	40.00	125	185

KM# 792 10 KURUSH

12.0270 g., 0.8300 Silver .3210 oz. ASW **Obverse:** Toughra within star border and design **Reverse:** Inscription and date within star border and design **Mint:** Edirne

Date	Mintage	F	VF	XF	Unc
AH1327//2 (1910)	—	90.00	150	250	455

KM# 798 10 KURUSH
12.0270 g., 0.8300 Silver .3210 oz. ASW **Obverse:** Toughra within star border and crescent wreath **Reverse:** Inscription and date within star border and crescent wreath **Mint:** Kosova

Date	Mintage	F	VF	XF	Unc
AH1327//3 (1911)	1,500	100	175	300	525

KM# 804 10 KURUSH
12.0270 g., 0.8300 Silver .3210 oz. ASW **Obverse:** Toughra within star border and design **Reverse:** Inscription and date within star border and design **Mint:** Manastir

Date	Mintage	F	VF	XF	Unc
AH1327//3 (1911)	1,500	100	200	350	550

KM# 810 10 KURUSH
12.0270 g., 0.8300 Silver .3210 oz. ASW **Obverse:** Toughra within star border and design **Reverse:** Inscription and date within star border and design **Mint:** Salonika

Date	Mintage	F	VF	XF	Unc
AH1327//3 (1911)	1,500	100	200	350	550

Muhammad VI
AH1336-41/1918-23AD

MILLED COINAGE

Gold Issues

KM# 819 25 KURUSH
1.8040 g., 0.9170 Gold .0532 oz. AGW **Obverse:** Toughra in center of sprigs and stars **Reverse:** Inscription and date within wreath, star on top **Mint:** Qustantiniyah

Date	Mintage	Good	VG	F	VF	XF
AH1336//1 (1917)	53,524	—	37.50	45.00	60.00	100
AH1336//2 (1918)	62,253	—	37.50	45.00	60.00	100
AH1336//3 (1919)	52,421	—	40.00	75.00	150	200
AH1336//4 (1920)	400	—	50.00	90.00	200	300
AH1336//5 (1921)	819	—	80.00	140	240	375

KM# 825 25 KURUSH
1.7540 g., 0.9170 Gold .0517 oz. AGW **Series:** Monnaie de Luxe **Obverse:** Toughra **Mint:** Qustantiniyah

Date	Mintage	Good	VG	F	VF	XF
AH1336//2 (1918)	8,400	—	60.00	80.00	100	150
AH1336//3 (1919)	11,179	—	60.00	80.00	100	150

KM# 820 50 KURUSH
3.6080 g., 0.9170 Gold .1064 oz. AGW **Obverse:** Toughra in center of sprigs and stars **Reverse:** Inscription and date within wreath, star on top **Mint:** Qustantiniyah

Date	Mintage	Good	VG	F	VF	XF
AH1336//1 (1917)	162,363	—	100	125	150	300
AH1336//2 (1918)	346	—	100	125	150	300
AH1336//3 (1919)	447	—	150	200	250	500

Date	Mintage	Good	VG	F	VF	XF
AH1336//4 (1920)	200	—	250	450	750	1,500
AH1336//5 (1921)	204	—	200	300	450	1,000

KM# 821 100 KURUSH
7.2160 g., 0.9170 Gold .2128 oz. AGW **Obverse:** Toughra in center of sprigs and stars **Reverse:** Inscription and date within wreath, star on top **Mint:** Qustantiniyah

Date	Mintage	Good	VG	F	VF	XF
AH1336//1 (1917)	5,036,830	—	BV	150	165	185
AH1336//2 (1918)	37,634	—	BV	150	165	185
AH1336//3 (1919)	30,313	—	160	185	225	450
AH1336/4 (1920)	200	—	400	600	800	1,000
AH1336//5 (1921)	—	—	400	600	800	1,000

KM# 826 100 KURUSH
7.0160 g., 0.9170 Gold .2068 oz. AGW **Series:** Monnaie de Luxe **Obverse:** Toughra in center of legend **Reverse:** Inscription and date in center of legend **Mint:** Qustantiniyah

Date	Mintage	Good	VG	F	VF	XF
AH1336//2 (1918)	33,077	—	250	300	325	375
AH1336//3 (1919)	20,248	—	250	300	325	375

KM# 822 250 KURUSH
18.0400 g., 0.9170 Gold .5319 oz. AGW **Obverse:** Toughra in center of sprigs and stars **Reverse:** Inscription and date within wreath, star on top **Mint:** Qustantiniyah

Date	Mintage	Good	VG	F	VF	XF
AH1336//1 (1917)	39	—	1,750	3,000	4,500	6,500
AH1336//2 (1918)	26	—	1,750	3,000	4,500	6,500
AH1336//3 (1919)	31	—	1,750	3,000	4,500	6,500
AH1336/4 (1920)	20	—	1,750	3,000	4,500	6,500
AH1336/5 (1921)	21	—	1,750	3,000	4,500	6,500

KM# 827 250 KURUSH
17.5400 g., 0.9170 Gold .5169 oz. AGW **Series:** Monnaie de Luxe **Obverse:** Toughra within beaded circle **Reverse:** Inscription and date within beaded circle **Mint:** Qustantiniyah

Date	Mintage	Good	VG	F	VF	XF
AH1336//2 (1918)	5,995	—	BV	500	700	900
AH1336//3 (1919)	12,739	—	BV	425	600	800

KM# 823 500 KURUSH
36.0800 g., 0.9170 Gold 1.0638 oz. AGW **Obverse:** Toughra in center of sprigs and stars **Reverse:** Inscription and date within wreath, star on top **Mint:** Qustantiniyah

Date	Mintage	Good	VG	F	VF	XF
AH1336//1 (1917)	26,984	—	1,000	1,200	1,450	1,800
AH1336//2 (1918)	22,192	—	1,000	1,200	1,450	1,800
AH1336//3 (1919)	16,424	—	1,000	1,200	1,450	1,800
AH1336//4 (1920)	23	—	2,000	4,000	6,000	8,000
AH1336//5 (1921)	22	—	2,000	4,000	6,000	8,000

KM# 824 500 KURUSH
35.0800 g., 0.9170 Gold 1.0338 oz. AGW **Series:** Monnaie de Luxe **Obverse:** Radiant Toughra above crossed flags, ornamental base **Reverse:** Inscription and date within designed wreath **Mint:** Qustantiniyah

Date	Mintage	Good	VG	F	VF	XF
AH1336//1 (1917)	—	—	1,000	1,250	1,750	2,400
AH1336//2 (1918)	—	—	BV	750	950	1,300
AH1336//3 (1919)	5,207	—	BV	750	950	1,300
AH1336//4 (1920)	88	—	1,500	2,000	2,500	3,200

STANDARD COINAGE

KM# 828 40 PARA
Copper-Nickel **Obverse:** Toughra within beaded circle above sprigs **Reverse:** Value within beaded circle above sprigs **Mint:** Qustantiniyah

Date	Mintage	Good	VG	F	VF	XF
AH1336//4 (1920)	6,520,000	—	1.75	2.50	4.00	10.00

KM# 815 2 KURUSH
2.4055 g., 0.8300 Silver .0642 oz. ASW **Obverse:** Toughra within star border **Reverse:** Inscription and date within star border **Mint:** Qustantiniyah

Date	Mintage	Good	VG	F	VF	XF
AH1336//1 (1918)	25,000	—	50.00	100	150	220
AH1336//2 (1918)	3,000	—	75.00	125	200	350

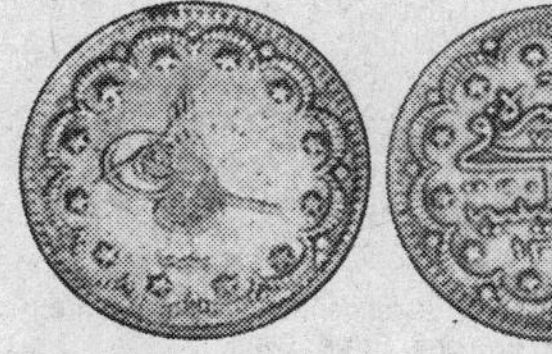

KM# 816 5 KURUSH
6.0130 g., 0.8300 Silver .1605 oz. ASW **Obverse:** Toughra within star border and crescent wreath **Reverse:** Inscription and date within star border and crescent wreath **Mint:** Qustantiniyah

Date	Mintage	Good	VG	F	VF	XF
AH1336//1 (1917)	10,000	—	50.00	125	175	265
AH1336//2 (1918)	2,000	—	75.00	150	225	385

KM# 817 10 KURUSH
12.0270 g., 0.8300 Silver .3210 oz. ASW **Obverse:** Toughra within star border and crescent wreath **Reverse:** Inscription and date within star border and crescent wreath **Mint:** Qustantiniyah

Date	Mintage	Good	VG	F	VF	XF
AH1336//1 (1917)	10,000	—	120	250	400	600
AH1336//2 (1918)	2,000	—	200	400	600	1,000

KM# 818 20 KURUSH
24.0550 g., 0.8300 Silver .6419 oz. ASW **Obverse:** Toughra within star bordr and crescent wreath **Reverse:** Inscription and date within star border and crescent wreath **Mint:** Qustantiniyah

Date	Mintage	Good	VG	F	VF	XF
AH1336//1 (1917)	—	—	30.00	60.00	125	185
AH1336//2 (1918)	1,530	—	350	525	650	925

REPUBLIC

STANDARD COINAGE

Old Monetary System

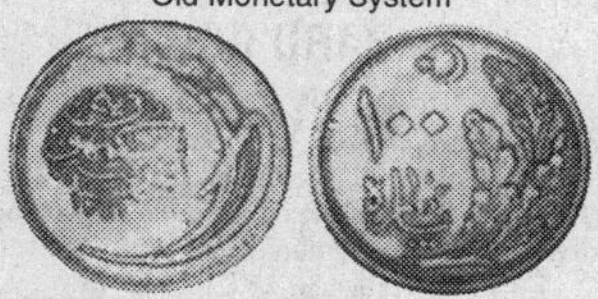

KM# 830 100 PARA
Aluminum-Bronze **Obverse:** Inscription and date to left of oat sprig **Reverse:** Value to left of sprig, crescent and star at top

Date	Mintage	F	VF	XF	Unc
AH1340 (1921)	1,798,026	3.00	5.00	10.00	60.00
AH1341 (1922)	5,582,846	1.00	2.50	5.00	30.00

KM# 834 100 PARA
Aluminum-Bronze **Obverse:** Inscription and date to left of oat sprig **Reverse:** Value to left of sprig, crescent and star on top

Date	Mintage	F	VF	XF	Unc
1926 (1926)	4,388,266	1.00	2.50	6.00	32.00
AH1347 (1928)	—	150	225	400	600
1928 (1928)	4,000	150	225	400	600

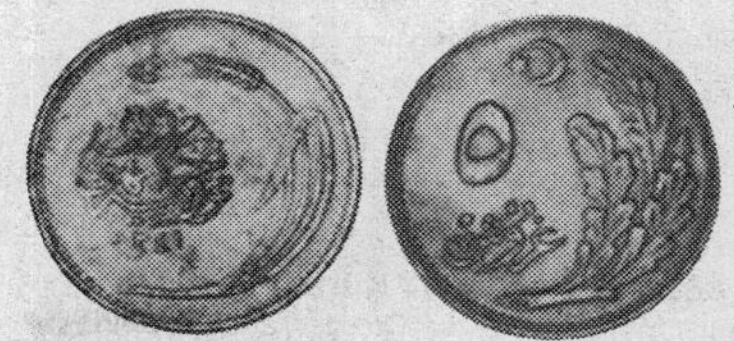

KM# 831 5 KURUS
Aluminum-Bronze **Obverse:** Inscription and date to left of oat sprig **Reverse:** Value to left of sprig, crescent and star on top

Date	Mintage	F	VF	XF	Unc
AH1340 (1921)	5,023,238	1.00	2.50	7.00	32.00
AH1341 (1922)	23,544,591	1.00	2.50	7.00	32.00

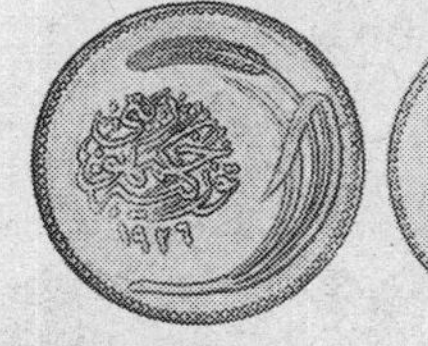

KM# 835 5 KURUS
Aluminum-Bronze **Obverse:** Inscription and date to left of oat sprig **Reverse:** Value to left of sprig, crescent and star on top

Date	Mintage	F	VF	XF	Unc
1926 (1926)	355,910	1.00	2.50	7.00	32.00
1928 (1928)	2,000	175	250	500	700

KM# 832 10 KURUS
Aluminum-Bronze **Obverse:** Inscription and date to left of oat sprig **Reverse:** Value to left of sprig, crescent and star on top **Note:** Varieties exist.

Date	Mintage	F	VF	XF	Unc
AH1340 (1921)	4,836,483	1.50	3.00	8.00	35.00
AH1341 (1922)	14,223,098	1.50	3.00	8.00	35.00

KM# 836 10 KURUS
Aluminum-Bronze **Obverse:** Inscription and date to left of oat sprig **Reverse:** Value to left of sprigs, crescent and star on top

Date	Mintage	F	VF	XF	Unc
1926	855,982	1.50	3.00	8.00	35.00
1928	1,000	125	200	375	575

KM# 833 25 KURUS
Nickel **Obverse:** Inscription and date to left of oat sprig **Reverse:** Value to left of sprigs, crescent and star on top

Date	Mintage	F	VF	XF	Unc
AH1341 (1922)	4,972,686	2.00	4.00	10.00	30.00

KM# 837 25 KURUS
Nickel **Obverse:** Inscription and date to left of oat sprig **Reverse:** Value to left of sprigs, crescent and star on top **Note:** Varieties exist.

Date	Mintage	F	VF	XF	Unc
1926	26,869	175	275	475	675
1928	5,794,000	1.50	3.00	8.00	30.00

KM# 840 25 KURUSH
1.8040 g., 0.9170 Gold .0532 oz. AGW **Obverse:** Inscription and date within wreath **Reverse:** Star divides inner circle above inscription and date

Date	Mintage	F	VF	XF	Unc
1926	4,539	40.00	75.00	140	175
1927	14,000	40.00	75.00	120	150
1928	8,424	40.00	75.00	130	165
1929	—	40.00	75.00	120	150

KM# 844 25 KURUSH
1.7540 g., 0.9170 Gold .0517 oz. AGW, 23 mm. **Series:** Monnaie de Luxe **Obverse:** Radiant star and crescent above inscription within sprigs **Reverse:** Value and date within designed wreath

Date	Mintage	F	VF	XF	Unc
1927	4,103	50.00	80.00	150	200
1928	4,549	50.00	80.00	150	200

KM# 841 50 KURUSH
3.6080 g., 0.9170 Gold .1064 oz. AGW **Obverse:** Inscription and date within wreath **Reverse:** Star divides circle above inscription and date

Date	Mintage	F	VF	XF	Unc
1926	2,168	100	150	200	275
1927	2,116	100	150	200	275
1928	2,431	100	150	200	275
1929	—	100	150	200	275

KM# 845 50 KURUSH
3.5080 g., 0.9170 Gold .1034 oz. AGW, 28 mm. **Series:** Monnaie de Luxe **Obverse:** Radiant star and crescent above inscription within sprigs **Reverse:** Inscription and date within designed wreath

Date	Mintage	F	VF	XF	Unc
1927	3,903	75.00	150	250	375
1928	3,620	75.00	150	250	375

KM# 842 100 KURUSH
7.2160 g., 0.9170 Gold .2128 oz. AGW **Obverse:** Inscription and date within wreath **Reverse:** Star divides circle above inscription and date

Date	Mintage	F	VF	XF	Unc
1926	1,073	BV	175	250	350
1927	—	BV	175	250	350
1928	920	BV	175	250	350
1929	—	BV	175	250	350

KM# 846 100 KURUSH
7.0160 g., 0.9170 Gold .2069 oz. AGW, 35 mm. **Series:** Monnaie de Luxe

Date	Mintage	F	VF	XF	Unc
1927	8,676	BV	150	250	350
1928	6,092	BV	150	250	350

KM# 843 250 KURUSH
18.0400 g., 0.9170 Gold .5319 oz. AGW **Obverse:** Inscription and date within wreath **Reverse:** Star divides circle above inscription and date

Date	Mintage	F	VF	XF	Unc
1926	604	375	450	600	750
1927	886	375	450	600	750
1928	110	375	450	600	750
1929	—	375	450	600	750

KM# 847 250 KURUSH
17.5400 g., 0.9170 Gold .5169 oz. AGW, 45 mm. **Series:** Monnaie de Luxe **Obverse:** Radiant star and crescent above inscription within sprigs **Reverse:** Inscription and date within designed wreath

Date	Mintage	F	VF	XF	Unc
1927	7,411	—	BV	450	650
1928	5,045	—	BV	450	650

KM# 839 500 KURUSH
36.0800 g., 0.9170 Gold 1.0638 oz. AGW **Obverse:** Inscription and date within wreath **Reverse:** Star divides circle above inscription and date

Date	Mintage	F	VF	XF	Unc
1925	226	BV	750	1,000	1,500
1926	2,268	—	BV	725	875
1927	4,011	—	BV	725	875
1928	375	BV	750	1,000	1,500
1929	—	BV	750	1,000	1,500

KM# 848 500 KURUSH
35.0800 g., 0.9170 Gold 1.0344 oz. AGW, 49 mm. **Series:** Monnaie de Luxe **Obverse:** Radiant star and crescent above inscription within sprigs **Reverse:** Inscription and date within designed wreath

Date	Mintage	F	VF	XF	Unc
1927	5,097	—	BV	725	875
1928	2,242	—	BV	725	875

DECIMAL COINAGE

Western numerals and Latin alphabet

40 Para = 1 Kurus; 100 Kurus = 1 Lira

Mintage figures of the 1930s and early 1940s may not be exact. It is suspected that in some cases, figures for a particular year may include quantities struck with the previous year's date.

KM# 868 10 PARA (1/4 Kurus)
Aluminum-Bronze **Obverse:** Crescent and star **Reverse:** Value and date

Date	Mintage	VG	F	VF	XF	Unc
1940	30,800,000	0.25	0.75	2.50	5.00	—
1941	22,400,000	0.25	0.75	2.50	5.00	—
1942	26,800,000	0.25	0.75	2.50	5.00	—

KM# 884 1/2 KURUS (20 Para)
Brass **Obverse:** Center hole and date **Reverse:** Center hole divides oat sprig and value

Date	Mintage	F	VF	XF	Unc
1948	150	—	—	300	550

Note: Not released to circulation

KM# 884a 1/2 KURUS (20 Para)
3.9000 g., 0.9160 Gold .1149 oz. AGW, 16 mm. **Series:** Nostalgia **Obverse:** Center hole and date **Reverse:** Center hole divides value and sprig **Edge:** Plain **Mint:** Istanbul

Date	Mintage	F	VF	XF	Unc
1948	441	—	—	—	85.00

KM# 861 KURUS
Copper-Nickel **Obverse:** Star above crescent **Reverse:** Value within designed sprigs

Date	Mintage	VG	F	VF	XF	Unc
1935	784,000	2.00	4.00	6.00	15.00	—
1936	5,300,000	2.50	3.50	5.00	10.00	—
1937	4,500,000	2.50	3.50	5.00	10.00	—

KM# 867 KURUS
Copper-Nickel **Obverse:** Star above crescent **Reverse:** Value within designed sprigs

Date	Mintage	VG	F	VF	XF	Unc
1938	16,400,000	0.25	0.50	1.50	4.00	—
1939	21,600,000	0.25	0.50	1.50	4.00	—
1940	8,800,000	0.50	1.00	2.00	8.00	—
1941	6,700,000	0.25	0.75	1.75	5.00	—
1942	10,800,000	0.25	0.50	1.50	4.00	—
1943	4,000,000	0.25	0.75	1.75	5.00	—
1944	6,000,000	0.25	0.75	1.75	5.00	—

KM# 881 KURUS
Brass, 18.5 mm. **Obverse:** Date below hole in center **Reverse:** Hole in center flanked by oat sprig and value **Edge:** Plain

Date	Mintage	F	VF	XF	Unc
1947	890,000	1.00	1.50	2.50	5.00
1948	35,470,000	0.15	0.25	0.50	1.50
1949	29,530,000	0.15	0.25	0.50	1.25
1950	32,800,000	0.15	0.25	0.50	1.25
1951	6,310,000	0.15	0.30	0.75	2.25

KM# 881a KURUS
4.9000 g., 0.9160 Gold .1443 oz. AGW, 18 mm. **Series:** Nostalgia **Obverse:** Date below hole in center **Reverse:** Hole in center flanked by oat sprig and value **Edge:** Plain **Mint:** Istanbul

Date	Mintage	F	VF	XF	Unc
1949	441	—	—	—	110

KM# 895 KURUS
Brass **Obverse:** Crescent and star **Reverse:** Olive branch divides value and date

Date	Mintage	F	VF	XF	Unc
1961	1,180,000	—	—	0.10	5.00
1962	3,620,000	—	—	0.10	5.00
1963	1,085,000	—	—	0.10	5.00

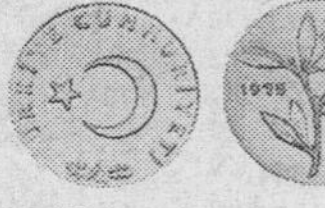

KM# 895a KURUS
Bronze, 14 mm. **Obverse:** Crescent and star **Reverse:** Olive branch divides value and date **Edge:** Plain

Date	Mintage	F	VF	XF	Unc
1963	1,180,000	—	—	0.10	1.50
1964	2,520,000	—	—	0.10	1.50
1965	1,860,000	—	—	0.10	1.50
1966	1,820,000	—	—	0.10	1.50
1967	2,410,000	—	—	0.10	1.50
1968	1,040,000	—	—	0.10	1.50
1969	900,000	—	—	0.10	1.50
1970	1,960,000	—	—	0.10	1.50
1971	2,940,000	—	—	0.10	1.50
1972	720,000	—	—	0.10	1.50
1973	540,000	—	—	0.10	1.50
1974	510,000	—	—	0.10	1.50

KM# 895b KURUS
Aluminum, 14 mm. **Obverse:** Crescent and star **Reverse:** Olive branch divides date and value

Date	Mintage	F	VF	XF	Unc
1975	690,000	—	0.10	0.25	1.00
1976	200,000	—	0.10	0.25	1.50
1977	110,000	—	0.10	0.25	4.00

KM# 924 KURUS
Bronze **Series:** F.A.O. **Obverse:** Anatolic bride's head left **Reverse:** Olive branch divides value and date

Date	Mintage	F	VF	XF	Unc
1979	15,000	—	0.25	1.00	3.00

KM# 924a KURUS
Aluminum **Series:** F.A.O. **Obverse:** Head left **Reverse:** Olive branch divides date and value

Date	Mintage	F	VF	XF	Unc
1979	15,000	—	0.25	1.00	3.00

KM# 885 2-1/2 KURUS
Brass, 21 mm. **Obverse:** Date below center hole **Reverse:** Center hole divides oat sprig and value

Date	Mintage	F	VF	XF	Unc
1948	24,720,000	0.25	0.50	1.00	3.00
1949	23,720,000	0.25	0.50	1.00	3.00
1950	11,560,000	3.00	5.00	8.00	15.00
1951	2,000,000	12.50	25.00	50.00	100

KM# 885a 2-1/2 KURUS
6.9000 g., 0.9160 Gold .2032 oz. AGW, 21 mm. **Series:** Nostalgia **Obverse:** Date below center hole **Reverse:** Hole in center divides oat sprig and value **Edge:** Plain **Mint:** Istanbul

Date	Mintage	F	VF	XF	Unc
1950	441	—	—	—	150

KM# 862 5 KURUS
Copper-Nickel **Obverse:** Star within crescent **Reverse:** Value within designed sprigs

Date	Mintage	VG	F	VF	XF	Unc
1935	100,000	2.00	5.00	10.00	50.00	100
1936	2,900,000	0.50	1.00	2.00	8.00	25.00
1937	4,060,000	0.30	0.75	1.50	8.00	22.50
1938	13,380,000	0.25	0.50	1.00	5.00	12.50
1939	12,520,000	0.25	0.50	1.00	5.00	12.50
1940	4,340,000	0.30	0.75	1.50	5.00	15.00
1942	10,160,000	0.20	0.40	1.00	5.00	12.50
1943	15,360,000	0.20	0.40	1.00	5.00	12.50

KM# 887 5 KURUS

Brass, 16.3 mm. **Obverse:** Crescent, star and date **Reverse:** Value within wreath **Edge:** TURMITE CUMHURITETI

Date	Mintage	F	VF	XF	Unc
1949	4,500,000	0.25	0.50	1.00	4.00
1950	45,900,000	0.15	0.35	0.75	3.00
1951	29,600,000	0.15	0.35	0.75	3.00
1955	15,300,000	0.15	0.35	0.75	3.00
1956	21,380,000	0.15	0.35	0.75	3.00
1957	3,320,000	0.25	0.50	1.00	4.00

KM# 890.1 5 KURUS

2.5000 g., Bronze **Obverse:** Crescent and star **Reverse:** Oak branch divides value and date

Date	Mintage	F	VF	XF	Unc
1958	25,870,000	0.10	0.25	0.50	20.00
1959	21,580,000	—	—	0.10	20.00
1960	17,150,000	—	—	0.10	15.00
1961	11,110,000	—	—	0.10	15.00
1962	15,280,000	—	—	0.10	6.00
1963	17,680,000	—	—	0.10	6.00
1964	18,190,000	—	—	0.10	5.00
1965	19,170,000	—	—	0.10	3.00
1966	19,840,000	—	—	0.10	3.00
1967	16,170,000	—	—	0.10	2.00
1968	26,050,000	—	—	0.10	2.00

KM# 890.2 5 KURUS

2.0000 g., Bronze **Obverse:** Crescent and star **Reverse:** Oak branch divides value and date **Note:** Reduced weight.

Date	Mintage	F	VF	XF	Unc
1969	33,630,000	—	—	0.10	2.00
1970	29,360,000	—	—	0.10	1.00
1971	17,440,000	—	—	0.10	1.00
1972	22,670,000	—	—	0.10	1.00
1973	17,370,000	—	—	0.10	1.00

KM# 890.3 5 KURUS

1.3500 g., Bronze **Obverse:** Crescent and star **Reverse:** Oak branch divides value and date **Note:** Varieties exist.

Date	Mintage	F	VF	XF	Unc
1974	13,540,000	—	—	0.10	1.00

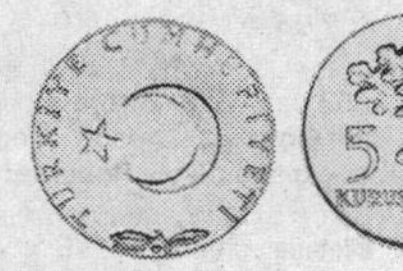

KM# 890a 5 KURUS

Aluminum **Obverse:** Crescent and star **Reverse:** Oak branch divides value and date

Date	Mintage	F	VF	XF	Unc
1975	1,560,000	—	—	0.10	1.00
1976	1,321,000	—	—	0.10	1.00
1977	190,000	—	0.10	0.20	5.00

KM# 906 5 KURUS

Aluminum **Series:** F.A.O. **Obverse:** Anatolic bride's head left **Reverse:** Oak branch divides date and value

Date	Mintage	F	VF	XF	Unc
1975	1,019,000	—	0.50	1.50	3.00

KM# 907 5 KURUS

Aluminum **Series:** F.A.O. **Obverse:** Mother breastfeading infant **Reverse:** Oak branch divides value and date

Date	Mintage	F	VF	XF	Unc
1976	17,000	—	0.50	1.50	10.00

KM# 934 5 KURUS

Bronze **Series:** F.A.O. **Obverse:** Fisherman within flounder **Reverse:** Oak branch divides value and date

Date	Mintage	F	VF	XF	Unc
1980	13,000	—	0.25	0.75	7.00

KM# 863 10 KURUS

Copper-Nickel **Obverse:** Star within crescent **Reverse:** Star above value and date within designed sprigs

Date	Mintage	VG	F	VF	XF	Unc
1935	60,000	2.00	5.00	8.00	20.00	—
1936	3,580,000	0.75	2.00	5.00	12.50	—
1937	3,020,000	0.50	1.00	4.00	8.00	—
1938	6,610,000	0.50	1.00	4.00	8.00	—
1939	4,610,000	0.50	1.00	2.50	5.00	—
1940	6,960,000	0.50	1.00	2.50	5.00	—

KM# 888 10 KURUS

Brass **Obverse:** Star, crescent and date **Reverse:** Value within wreath

Date	Mintage	F	VF	XF	Unc
1949	27,000,000	0.10	0.25	0.75	3.00
1951	6,200,000	0.10	0.25	0.75	3.00
1955	10,090,000	0.10	0.25	0.75	3.00
1956	9,910,000	0.10	0.25	0.75	3.00

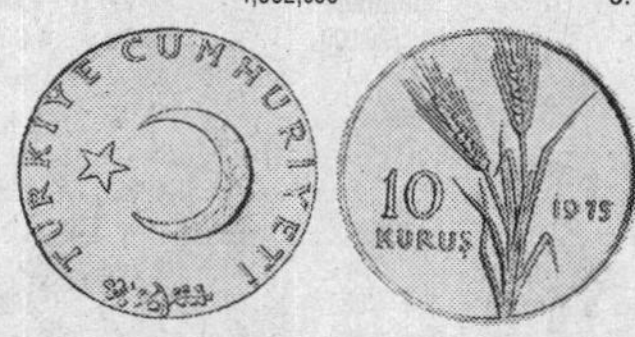

KM# 891.1 10 KURUS

4.0000 g., Bronze, 21.3 mm. **Obverse:** Star and crescent **Reverse:** Oat stalks divide date and value

Date	Mintage	F	VF	XF	Unc
1958	14,770,000	—	0.10	0.25	30.00
1959	11,160,000	—	—	0.10	30.00
1960	9,450,000	—	—	0.10	20.00
1961	5,370,000	—	—	0.10	20.00
1962	9,250,000	—	—	0.10	10.00
1963	10,390,000	—	—	0.10	4.00
1964	9,890,000	—	—	0.10	4.00
1965	10,480,000	—	—	0.10	3.00
1966	12,200,000	—	—	0.10	3.00
1967	11,410,000	—	—	0.10	2.00
1968	1,862,000	—	—	0.10	2.00

KM# 891a 10 KURUS

Aluminum **Obverse:** Star and crescent **Reverse:** Oat stalks divide date and value

Date	Mintage	F	VF	XF	Unc
1975	2,165,000	—	—	0.10	1.00
1976	559,000	—	0.10	0.20	1.00
1977	106,000	—	0.10	0.50	10.00

KM# 891.2 10 KURUS

3.5000 g., Bronze **Obverse:** Star and crescent **Reverse:** Oat stalks divide date and value **Note:** Reduced weight.

Date	Mintage	F	VF	XF	Unc
1969	21,190,000	—	—	0.10	2.00
1970	19,930,000	—	—	0.10	1.00
1971	14,780,000	—	—	0.10	1.00
1972	17,960,000	—	—	0.10	1.00
1973	11,930,000	—	—	0.10	1.00

KM# 891.3 10 KURUS

2.5000 g., Bronze **Obverse:** Star and crescent **Reverse:** Oat stalks divide date and value **Note:** Varieties exist.

Date	Mintage	F	VF	XF	Unc
1974	9,280,000	—	—	1.00	1.50

KM# 898.1 10 KURUS

3.5000 g., Bronze **Series:** F.A.O. **Obverse:** Atatürk driving a tractor **Obv. Designer:** M. Duyer **Reverse:** Oat stalks divide value and date

Date	Mintage	F	VF	XF	Unc
1971	1,140,000	—	0.50	1.00	2.00
1972	500,000	—	1.00	2.00	4.00
1973	10,000	—	100	250	500

KM# 898.2 10 KURUS

2.5000 g., Bronze **Obverse:** Atatürk driving tractor **Reverse:** Oat stalks divide date and value

Date	Mintage	F	VF	XF	Unc
1974	605,000	—	1.00	2.00	4.00

KM# 898a 10 KURUS

Aluminum **Obverse:** Atatürk driving tractor **Reverse:** Oat stalks divide date and value

Date	Mintage	F	VF	XF	Unc
1975	517,000	—	0.50	1.00	2.00

KM# 908 10 KURUS

Aluminum **Series:** F.A.O. **Obverse:** Mother breastfeading infant **Reverse:** Oat stalks divide value and date

Date	Mintage	F	VF	XF	Unc
1976	17,000	—	0.50	2.00	10.00

KM# 935 10 KURUS

Bronze **Series:** F.A.O. **Obverse:** Anatolic bride's head left **Reverse:** Oat stalks divide date and value

Date	Mintage	F	VF	XF	Unc
1980	13,000	—	0.25	1.00	6.00

KM# 864 25 KURUS

3.0000 g., 0.8300 Silver .0801 oz. ASW **Obverse:** Head of Kemal Atatürk left **Reverse:** Oat sprig divides date, value at left

Date	Mintage	VG	F	VF	XF	Unc
1935	888,000	1.35	2.25	6.00	15.00	—
1936	10,576,000	1.35	2.50	10.00	20.00	—
1937	8,536,000	1.35	2.50	10.00	20.00	—

KM# 880 25 KURUS

Nickel-Bronze **Obverse:** Crescent and star **Reverse:** Oat sprig divides date, value at left

Date	Mintage	VG	F	VF	XF	Unc
1944	20,000,000	0.25	0.50	1.00	2.50	—
1945	5,328,000	0.50	1.00	1.50	3.00	—
1946	2,672,000	0.50	1.25	2.00	4.00	—

KM# 886 25 KURUS
Brass **Obverse:** Crescent and star **Reverse:** Value within wreath

Date	Mintage	F	VF	XF	Unc
1948	18,000,000	0.10	0.20	0.40	1.25
1949	21,000,000	0.10	0.20	0.40	1.25
1951	2,000,000	5.00	10.00	25.00	50.00
1955	9,624,000	0.10	0.20	0.40	1.25
1956	14,376,000	0.10	0.20	0.40	1.25

KM# 886a 25 KURUS
10.0000 g., 0.9160 Gold .2945 oz. AGW, 22.6 mm. **Series:** Nostalgia **Obverse:** Crescent and star **Reverse:** Value within wreath **Edge:** Plain **Mint:** Istanbul

Date	Mintage	F	VF	XF	Unc
1951	441	—	—	—	215

KM# 892.1 25 KURUS
5.0000 g., Stainless Steel, 22.5 mm. **Obverse:** Smooth ground under standing figure facing **Reverse:** Value within wreath

Date	Mintage	F	VF	XF	Unc
1959	21,864,000	0.10	0.15	0.30	10.00

KM# 892.2 25 KURUS
5.0000 g., Stainless Steel, 22.5 mm. **Obverse:** Rough ground under standing figure facing **Reverse:** Value within wreath

Date	Mintage	F	VF	XF	Unc
1960	14,778,000	—	0.10	0.15	10.00
1961	7,248,000	—	0.10	0.15	15.00
1962	10,722,000	—	0.10	0.15	10.00
1963	11,016,000	—	0.10	0.15	10.00
1964	13,962,000	—	0.10	0.15	8.00
1965	9,816,000	—	0.10	0.15	5.00
1966	2,424,000	—	0.10	0.15	5.00

KM# 892.3 25 KURUS
4.0000 g., Stainless Steel **Obverse:** Standing figure facing **Reverse:** Value within wreath **Note:** Reduced weight

Date	Mintage	F	VF	XF	Unc
1966	7,596,000	—	—	0.10	5.00
1967	17,022,000	—	—	0.10	4.00
1968	31,482,000	—	—	0.10	3.00
1969	34,566,000	—	—	0.10	3.00
1970	32,960,000	—	—	0.10	2.00
1973	20,496,000	—	—	0.10	2.00
1974	16,602,000	—	—	0.10	1.00
1977	10,204,000	—	—	0.10	1.00
1978	185,000	0.35	0.75	1.25	3.00

KM# 865 50 KURUS
6.0000 g., 0.8300 Silver .1601 oz. ASW **Obverse:** Head of Kemal Atatürk left **Reverse:** Oat sprig divides date, value at left

Date	Mintage	VG	F	VF	XF	Unc
1935	630,000	3.25	6.50	10.00	25.00	—
1936	5,082,000	2.75	5.00	8.00	17.00	—
1937	4,270,000	12.00	30.00	50.00	100	—

KM# 882 50 KURUS
4.0000 g., 0.6000 Silver .0772 oz. ASW **Obverse:** Crescent, star and date **Reverse:** Value within wreath **Note:** Edge varieties exist.

Date	Mintage	F	VF	XF	Unc
1947	9,296,000	1.25	2.50	3.50	6.00
1948	12,704,000	1.25	2.50	3.50	6.00

KM# 899 50 KURUS
Stainless Steel, 24 mm. **Obverse:** Anatolic bride's head left **Reverse:** Value within wreath

Date	Mintage	F	VF	XF	Unc
1971	16,756,000	—	0.10	0.15	1.00
1972	22,152,000	—	0.10	0.15	1.00
1973	18,928,000	—	0.10	0.15	1.00
1974	14,480,000	—	0.10	0.15	1.00
1975	27,714,000	—	0.10	0.15	1.00
1976	27,476,000	—	0.10	0.15	1.00
1977	5,062,000	—	0.10	0.15	1.00
1979	3,714,000	—	0.10	0.15	1.00

KM# 913 50 KURUS
Stainless Steel, 24 mm. **Series:** F.A.O. **Obverse:** Mother breastfeeding child **Reverse:** Value and date within wreath

Date	Mintage	F	VF	XF	Unc
1978	10,000	—	2.00	4.00	6.00

KM# 925 50 KURUS
Stainless Steel, 24 mm. **Series:** F.A.O. **Obverse:** Atatürk driving tractor **Obv. Designer:** M. Duyer **Reverse:** Value and date within wreath

Date	Mintage	F	VF	XF	Unc
1979	20,000	—	2.00	4.00	6.00

KM# 936 50 KURUS
Stainless Steel, 24 mm. **Series:** F.A.O. **Obverse:** Anatolic bride's head left **Reverse:** Value and date within wreath

Date	Mintage	F	VF	XF	Unc
1980	13,000	—	2.00	4.00	6.00

KM# 860.2 100 KURUS (Lira)
12.0000 g., 0.8300 Silver .3203 oz. ASW **Obverse:** Head of Kemal Atatürk left **Reverse:** Low star above value within crescent, date below

Date	Mintage	VG	F	VF	XF	Unc
1934	Inc. above	15.00	30.00	50.00	80.00	—

KM# 860.1 100 KURUS (Lira)
12.0000 g., 0.8300 Silver .3203 oz. ASW **Obverse:** Head of Kemal Atatürk left **Reverse:** High star above value within crescent, date below

Date	Mintage	VG	F	VF	XF	Unc
1934	718,000	30.00	40.00	75.00	150	—

KM# 860.1a 100 KURUS (Lira)
13.5000 g., 0.9250 Silver .4015 oz. ASW, 29.5 mm. **Series:** Nostalgia **Obverse;** Head of Kemal Atatürk left **Reverse:** High star above value within crescent, date below **Edge:** Plain **Mint:** Istanbul

Date	Mintage	F	VF	XF	Unc
1934 Matte	684	—	—	—	40.00

KM# 941 1/2 LIRA
7.8600 g., 0.9250 Silver .2337 oz. ASW **Subject:** 100th Anniversary of Atatürk's Birth **Obverse:** Crescent and star at top of mountain, signature above globe below **Reverse:** Head of Kemal Atatürk right

Date	Mintage	F	VF	XF	Unc
ND(1981)	7,555	—	—	—	20.00

KM# 941a 1/2 LIRA
8.0000 g., 0.9170 Gold .2358 oz. AGW **Subject:** 100th Anniversary of Atatürk's Birth **Obverse:** Crescent and star at top of mountain, signature above globe below **Reverse:** Head of Kemal Atatürk right

Date	Mintage	F	VF	XF	Unc
ND(1981)	25,000	—	—	—	165

KM# 866 LIRA
12.0000 g., 0.8300 Silver .3203 oz. ASW **Obverse:** Head of Kemal Atatürk left **Reverse:** Value and date within crescent below star

Date	Mintage	VG	F	VF	XF	Unc
1937	1,624,000	5.50	10.00	15.00	32.00	—
1938	8,282,000	25.00	50.00	75.00	150	—
1939	376,000	5.50	10.00	15.00	32.00	—

KM# 869 LIRA
12.0000 g., 0.8300 Silver .3203 oz. ASW **Obverse:** Head of Ismet Inonu left **Reverse:** Star above value and date within crescent

Date	Mintage	VG	F	VF	XF	Unc
1940	253,000	7.50	12.50	15.00	25.00	—
1941	6,167,000	5.00	10.00	12.50	22.50	—

KM# 883 LIRA

7.5000 g., 0.6000 Silver .1447 oz. ASW **Obverse:** Crescent, star and date **Reverse:** Value within wreath **Note:** Edge varieties exist.

Date	Mintage	F	VF	XF	Unc
1947	11,104,000	BV	3.50	5.00	8.50
1948	16,896,000	BV	3.00	4.00	7.50

KM# 889 LIRA

Copper-Nickel **Obverse:** Head of Kemal Atatürk left **Reverse:** Value and date within wreath

Date	Mintage	F	VF	XF	Unc
1957	25,000,000	0.25	0.50	1.00	7.00

KM# 889a.1 LIRA

8.0000 g., Stainless Steel **Obverse:** Head of Kemal Atatürk left **Reverse:** Value and date within wreath

Date	Mintage	F	VF	XF	Unc
1959	7,452,000	—	0.10	0.20	25.00
1960	11,436,000	—	0.10	0.20	25.00
1961	2,100,000	—	0.10	0.20	75.00
1962	4,228,000	—	0.10	0.20	20.00
1963	4,316,000	—	0.10	0.20	20.00
1964	4,976,000	—	0.10	0.20	15.00
1965	5,348,000	—	0.10	0.20	10.00
1966	8,040,000	—	0.10	0.20	10.00
1967	—	—	0.10	0.20	50.00

KM# 889a.2 LIRA

7.0000 g., Stainless Steel, 27 mm. **Obverse:** Head of Kemal Atatürk left **Reverse:** Value and date within wreath **Note:** Reduced weight.

Date	Mintage	F	VF	XF	Unc
1967	10,444,000	—	0.10	0.20	10.00
1968	12,728,000	—	0.10	0.20	5.00
1969	6,612,000	—	0.10	0.20	5.00
1970	8,652,000	—	0.10	0.20	3.00
1971	10,504,000	—	0.10	0.20	3.00
1972	26,512,000	—	0.10	0.20	3.00
1973	12,596,000	—	0.10	0.20	3.00
1974	11,596,000	—	0.10	0.20	3.00
1975	20,348,000	—	0.10	0.20	2.00
1976	23,144,000	—	0.10	0.20	1.00
1977	30,244,000	—	0.10	0.20	1.00
1978	22,156,000	—	0.10	0.20	1.00
1979	9,289,000	—	0.10	0.20	1.00
1980	3,585,000	—	0.10	0.20	1.00

KM# 914 LIRA

8.0000 g., Stainless Steel **Series:** F.A.O. **Obverse:** Mother breastfeeding infant **Reverse:** Value and date within wreath

Date	Mintage	F	VF	XF	Unc
1978	20,000	—	2.00	4.00	6.00

KM# 926 LIRA

8.0000 g., Stainless Steel **Series:** F.A.O. **Obverse:** Atatürk driving tractor **Reverse:** Value and date within wreath

Date	Mintage	F	VF	XF	Unc
1979	20,000	—	2.00	4.00	6.00

KM# 937 LIRA

8.0000 g., Stainless Steel **Series:** F.A.O. **Obverse:** Anatolic bride's head left **Reverse:** Value and date within wreath

Date	Mintage	F	VF	XF	Unc
1980	13,000	—	2.00	4.00	6.00

KM# 942 LIRA

16.0000 g., 0.9250 Silver **Subject:** 100th Anniversary of Ataturk's Birth **Obverse:** Crescent and star at top of mountain, signature above globe below **Reverse:** Head of Kemal Atatürk right

Date	Mintage	F	VF	XF	Unc
ND(1981)	7,580	—	—	—	30.00

KM# 942a LIRA

16.0000 g., 0.9170 Gold .4716 oz. AGW **Subject:** 100th Anniversary of Atatürk's Birth **Obverse:** Crescent and star at top of mountain, signature above globe below **Reverse:** Head of Kemal Atatürk right

Date	Mintage	F	VF	XF	Unc
ND(1981)	25,000	—	—	—	335

KM# 943 LIRA

1.1000 g., Aluminum, 17 mm. **Obverse:** Head of Kemal Atatürk left **Reverse:** Value and date within wreath

Date	Mintage	F	VF	XF	Unc
1981	14,432,000	—	—	0.10	0.50

KM# 990 LIRA

1.1000 g., Aluminum, 17 mm. **Obverse:** Head of Kemal Atatürk left **Reverse:** Crescent opens right with thin "1"

Date	Mintage	F	VF	XF	Unc
1982	799,000	—	—	1.00	2.00

KM# 962.1 LIRA

1.1000 g., Aluminum, 17 mm. **Obverse:** Head of Kemal Atatürk left **Reverse:** Large (5mm) "1"

Date	Mintage	F	VF	XF	Unc
1984	498,000	—	—	0.10	0.50

KM# 962.2 LIRA

1.1000 g., Aluminum, 17 mm. **Obverse:** Head of Kemal Atatürk left **Reverse:** Small (3.5mm) "1" **Note:** Varieties exist.

Date	Mintage	F	VF	XF	Unc
1985	712,000	—	—	0.10	0.50
1986	504,000	—	—	0.10	0.50
1987	500,000	—	—	0.10	0.50
1988	75,000	—	—	0.10	0.50
1989	10,000	—	—	0.10	4.00

KM# 893.1 2-1/2 LIRA

12.0000 g., Stainless Steel, 30 mm. **Obverse:** Standing figure facing right **Reverse:** Value and date within wreath

Date	Mintage	F	VF	XF	Unc
1960	4,015,000	—	0.25	1.00	100
1961	1,222,000	—	0.25	1.00	150
1962	3,636,000	—	0.25	1.00	150
1963	3,108,000	—	0.25	1.00	100
1964	2,710,000	—	0.25	1.00	50.00
1965	1,246,000	—	0.25	1.00	10.00
1966	1,788,000	—	0.25	1.00	40.00
1967	5,333,000	—	0.25	1.00	20.00
1968	2,707,000	—	0.25	1.00	10.00

KM# 893.1a 2-1/2 LIRA

11.8000 g., 0.9250 Silver .3509 oz. ASW, 30 mm. **Series:** Nostalgia **Obverse:** Standing figure facing right **Reverse:** Value and date within wreath **Edge:** Plain **Mint:** Istanbul

Date	Mintage	F	VF	XF	Unc
1965	684	—	—	—	20.00

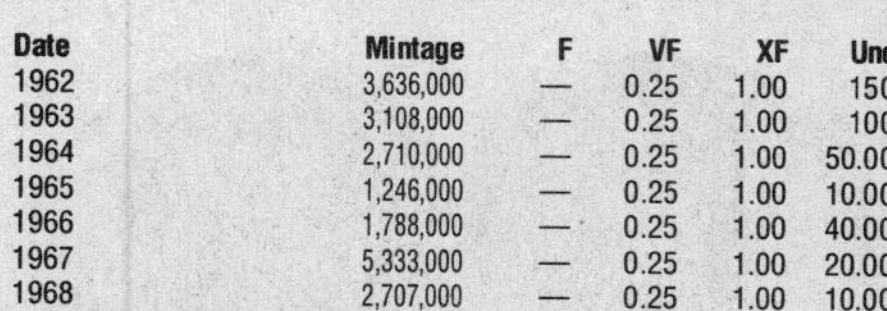

KM# 893.2 2-1/2 LIRA

9.0000 g., Stainless Steel, 30 mm. **Obverse:** Standing figure facing right **Reverse:** Value and date within wreath **Note:** Reduced weight. Varieties exist with landscape and number of beads in laurel.

Date	Mintage	F	VF	XF	Unc
1969	1,378,000	—	0.15	0.75	10.00
1970	3,777,000	—	0.15	0.75	5.00
1971	2,170,000	—	0.15	0.75	4.00
1972	9,147,000	—	0.15	0.50	4.00
1973	4,348,000	—	0.15	0.50	4.00
1974	3,816,000	—	0.15	0.50	4.00
1975	9,811,000	—	0.15	0.50	2.50
1976	3,952,000	—	0.15	0.50	2.50
1977	21,473,000	—	0.10	0.25	2.00
1978	15,738,000	—	0.10	0.25	2.00
1979	6,074,000	—	0.10	0.25	2.00
1980	2,621,000	—	0.10	0.25	2.00

KM# 896 2-1/2 LIRA

Stainless Steel, 30 mm. **Series:** F.A.O. **Obverse:** Atatürk driving tractor **Obv. Designer:** M. Duyer **Reverse:** Value and date within wreath

Date	Mintage	F	VF	XF	Unc
1970	200,000	—	0.75	1.00	1.50

KM# 910 2-1/2 LIRA

Stainless Steel, 30 mm. **Series:** F.A.O. **Obverse:** Stylized standing figures **Reverse:** Value and date within wreath

Date	Mintage	F	VF	XF	Unc
1977	25,000	—	1.00	1.50	2.00

KM# 915 2-1/2 LIRA

Stainless Steel, 30 mm. **Series:** F.A.O. **Obverse:** Mother breastfeeding infant **Reverse:** Value and date within wreath

Date	Mintage	F	VF	XF	Unc
1978	10,000	—	2.50	5.00	10.00

KM# 927 2-1/2 LIRA
Stainless Steel, 30 mm. **Series:** F.A.O. **Obverse:** Head of Kemal Atatürk left **Reverse:** Value and date within wreath

Date	Mintage	F	VF	XF	Unc
1979	20,000	—	4.00	6.00	8.00

KM# 938 2-1/2 LIRA
Stainless Steel, 30 mm. **Series:** F.A.O. **Obverse:** Fisherman within flounder **Reverse:** Value and date within wreath

Date	Mintage	F	VF	XF	Unc
1980	13,000	—	3.00	5.00	10.00

KM# 905 5 LIRA
Stainless Steel, 32.5 mm. **Obverse:** Atatürk on horseback **Reverse:** Value and date within wreath

Date	Mintage	F	VF	XF	Unc
1974	2,842,000	—	0.15	0.75	5.00
1975	10,855,000	—	0.15	0.25	2.00
1976	17,532,000	—	0.15	0.25	2.00
1977	6,172,000	—	0.15	0.75	3.00
1978	76,000	1.50	2.50	3.50	8.00
1979	6,054,000	—	0.15	0.30	1.00

KM# 905a 5 LIRA
14.7000 g., 0.9250 Silver .4372 oz. ASW, 32.5 mm. **Series:** Nostalgia **Obverse:** Atatürk on horseback **Reverse:** Value and date within wreath **Edge:** Plain **Mint:** Istanbul

Date	Mintage	F	VF	XF	Unc
1975	684	—	—	—	20.00

KM# 909 5 LIRA
Stainless Steel **Series:** International Women's Year; F.A.O. **Obverse:** Mother breastfeeding infant **Reverse:** Value and date within wreath

Date	Mintage	F	VF	XF	Unc
1976	17,000	—	3.00	6.00	12.00

KM# 911 5 LIRA
Stainless Steel **Series:** F.A.O. **Obverse:** Stylized standing figures **Reverse:** Value and date within wreath

Date	Mintage	F	VF	XF	Unc
1977	25,000	—	1.75	2.50	3.50

KM# 916 5 LIRA
Stainless Steel **Series:** F.A.O. **Obverse:** Atatürk driving tractor **Obv. Designer:** M. Duyer **Reverse:** Value and date within wreath

Date	Mintage	F	VF	XF	Unc
1978	10,000	—	5.00	8.00	12.00

KM# 928 5 LIRA
Stainless Steel **Series:** F.A.O. **Obverse:** Anatolic bride's head left **Reverse:** Value and date within wreath

Date	Mintage	F	VF	XF	Unc
1979	20,000	—	3.00	6.00	12.00

KM# 939 5 LIRA
Stainless Steel **Series:** F.A.O. **Obverse:** Fisherman within flounder **Reverse:** Value and date within wreath

Date	Mintage	F	VF	XF	Unc
1980	13,000	—	6.00	8.00	12.00

KM# 944 5 LIRA
Aluminum **Obverse:** Atatürk on horseback **Reverse:** Crescent opens left

Date	Mintage	F	VF	XF	Unc
1981	61,605,000	—	—	0.15	1.00

KM# 949.1 5 LIRA
Aluminum **Obverse:** Atatürk on horseback **Reverse:** Crescent opens right

Date	Mintage	F	VF	XF	Unc
1982	69,975,000	—	—	0.15	1.00

KM# 949.2 5 LIRA
Aluminum **Obverse:** Atatürk on horseback **Reverse:** Smaller, bolder "5"

Date	Mintage	F	VF	XF	Unc
1983	90,310,000	—	—	0.15	1.00

KM# 963 5 LIRA
1.7000 g., Aluminum, 21 mm. **Obverse:** Head left **Reverse:** Value and date within wreath **Note:** Varieties exist.

Date	Mintage	F	VF	XF	Unc
1984	17,316,000	—	—	0.15	1.00
1985	9,405,000	—	—	0.15	1.00
1986	9,575,000	—	—	0.20	1.00
1987	500,000	—	—	0.20	1.00
1988	100,000	—	—	0.20	1.00
1989	10,000	—	—	0.20	4.00

KM# 894 10 LIRA
15.0000 g., 0.8300 Silver .4003 oz. ASW **Subject:** 27th May Revolution **Obverse:** Head of Atatürk left **Reverse:** Radiant crescent and star above torch, balance scales, crossed flag and wing

Date	Mintage	F	VF	XF	Unc
ND(1960)	4,000,000	—	BV	6.50	10.00
ND(1960) Prooflike	—	—	—	—	12.50

KM# 945 10 LIRA
Aluminum **Obverse:** Half-length figure right **Reverse:** Value and date within wreath, crescent opens left

Date	Mintage	F	VF	XF	Unc
1981	25,520,000	—	0.10	0.25	0.50

KM# 950.1 10 LIRA
Aluminum **Obverse:** Half-length figure right **Reverse:** Value and date within wreath, crescent opens right

Date	Mintage	F	VF	XF	Unc
1982	17,092,000	—	0.10	0.25	0.50

KM# 950.2 10 LIRA
Aluminum **Obverse:** Half-length figure right **Reverse:** Value and date within wreath

Date	Mintage	F	VF	XF	Unc
1983	2,228,000	—	0.10	1.00	4.00

KM# 964 10 LIRA
2.3000 g., Aluminum, 25 mm. **Obverse:** Head of Atatürk left **Reverse:** Value and date within wreath **Note:** Varieties exist.

Date	Mintage	F	VF	XF	Unc
1984	23,360,000	—	0.10	0.25	0.50
1985	41,736,000	—	—	0.15	0.50
1986	78,224,000	—	—	0.15	0.50
1987	62,340,000	—	—	0.15	0.50
1988	17,620,000	—	—	0.15	1.00
1989	10,000	—	—	0.15	4.00

KM# 946 20 LIRA
Aluminum **Series:** World Food Day **Obverse:** Value and date within wreath **Reverse:** Stylized design below sprig

Date	Mintage	F	VF	XF	Unc
1981	10,000	—	—	2.50	4.00

KM# 965 20 LIRA
Copper-Nickel **Obverse:** Head of Atatürk left **Reverse:** Value and date within wreath

Date	Mintage	F	VF	XF	Unc
1984	1,644,000	—	0.10	0.25	2.00
1989	—	—	0.10	0.25	2.00

KM# 897 25 LIRA
14.6000 g., 0.8300 Silver .3896 oz. ASW **Subject:** 50th Anniversary of National Assembly in Ankara **Obverse:** Bust facing **Reverse:** Building above value

Date	Mintage	F	VF	XF	Unc
ND(1970)	23,000	—	—	8.00	12.00
ND(1970) Proof	Inc. above	Value: 14.00			

KM# 975 25 LIRA
2.8500 g., Aluminum, 27 mm. **Obverse:** Head of Atatürk left **Reverse:** Value and date within wreath **Note:** Varieties exist.

Date	Mintage	F	VF	XF	Unc
1985	37,014,000	—	—	0.15	0.50
1986	49,611,000	—	—	0.15	0.50
1987	61,335,000	—	—	0.15	0.50
1988	39,540,000	—	—	0.15	1.00
1989	10,000	—	—	0.15	4.00

KM# 900 50 LIRA
19.0000 g., 0.8300 Silver .5070 oz. ASW **Subject:** 900th Anniversary - Battle of Malazgirt, Alparslan **Obverse:** Armored bust 1/4 left **Obv. Designer:** A. Kumuk **Reverse:** Map of Turkey

Date	Mintage	F	VF	XF	Unc
ND(1971)	33,000	—	—	9.00	13.00
ND(1971) Proof	Inc. above	Value: 15.00			

KM# 901 50 LIRA
20.1000 g., 0.8300 Silver .5363 oz. ASW **Subject:** Kemal Atatürk's Entry into Smyrna **Obverse:** Atatürk on horse left **Obv. Designer:** A. Kumuk **Reverse:** Uniformed figures in battle

Date	Mintage	F	VF	XF	Unc
ND(1972)	172,000	—	—	8.00	12.00
ND(1972) Proof	—	Value: 13.50			

KM# 902 50 LIRA
13.0000 g., 0.9000 Silver .3761 oz. ASW **Subject:** 50th Anniversary of Republic **Obverse:** Radiant head on torch facing divides profiles **Reverse:** Cascading star within flower at upper right of inscription

Date	Mintage	F	VF	XF	Unc
ND(1973)	70,000	—	—	7.50	10.00
ND(1973) Proof	Inc. above	Value: 12.00			

KM# 912 50 LIRA
8.8500 g., 0.8300 Silver .2361 oz. ASW **Series:** F.A.O. **Obverse:** Stylized standing figures **Reverse:** Value and date within wreath

Date	Mintage	F	VF	XF	Unc
1977	25,000	—	—	7.50	11.50

KM# 966 50 LIRA
Copper-Nickel-Zinc, 26.8 mm. **Obverse:** Head of Atatürk left **Reverse:** Value and date within wreath **Edge:** Reeded **Note:** Varieties exist.

Date	Mintage	F	VF	XF	Unc
1984	14,731,000	—	0.10	0.25	0.60
1985	52,658,000	—	0.10	0.20	0.50
1986	80,656,000	—	0.10	0.20	0.50
1987	32,078,000	—	0.10	0.20	0.50

KM# 987 50 LIRA
3.2500 g., Aluminum-Bronze, 18.7 mm. **Obverse:** Head of Atatürk left **Reverse:** Value and date within wreath **Note:** Varieties exist.

Date	Mintage	F	VF	XF	Unc
1988	3,396,000	—	—	—	0.15
1989	25,463,000	—	—	—	0.15
1990	500,000	—	—	—	0.15
1991	10,000	—	—	—	0.15
1992	10,000	—	—	—	0.15
1993	5,000	—	—	—	0.35
1994	2,500	—	—	—	0.50

KM# 903 100 LIRA
22.0000 g., 0.9000 Silver .6367 oz. ASW **Subject:** 50th Anniversary of Republic **Obverse:** Radiant head on torch facing divides profiles **Reverse:** Cascading star within flower to upper right of inscription

Date	Mintage	F	VF	XF	Unc
1973	65,000	—	—	12.00	18.00
1973 Prooflike	—	—	—	—	25.00

KM# 951 100 LIRA
Copper-Nickel, 38.5 mm. **Subject:** World Championship Soccer - Madrid **Obverse:** Soccer player **Obv. Designer:** Reeded **Reverse:** Date within soccer ball

Date	Mintage	F	VF	XF	Unc
1982	100,000	0.75	1.50	3.00	6.00

KM# 967 100 LIRA
Copper-Nickel-Zinc **Obverse:** Head of Atatürk left **Reverse:** Value and date within wreath **Note:** Varieties exist.

Date	Mintage	F	VF	XF	Unc
1984	758,000	—	0.20	0.40	0.85
1985	866,000	—	0.20	0.40	0.85
1986	12,064,000	—	0.20	0.40	0.85
1987	91,400,000	—	0.15	0.25	0.65
1988	16,184,000	—	0.15	0.25	0.65

KM# 988 100 LIRA
4.1500 g., Aluminum-Bronze, 20.8 mm. **Obverse:** Head of Atatürk left **Reverse:** Value and date within wreath **Note:** Varieties exist.

Date	Mintage	F	VF	XF	Unc
1988	10,000,000	—	—	—	0.20
1989	233,750,000	—	—	—	0.20
1990	152,230,000	—	—	—	0.20
1991	49,160,000	—	—	—	0.20
1992	22,930,000	—	—	—	0.20
1993	3,700,000	—	—	—	0.20
1994	2,500	—	—	—	0.50

KM# 988a 100 LIRA
5.1000 g., 0.9250 Silver 0.1517 oz. ASW, 21 mm. **Obverse:** Head of Atatürk left **Reverse:** Value and date within wreath **Edge:** Reeded **Mint:** Mexico City

Date	Mintage	F	VF	XF	Unc
1988 Proof	998	Value: 75.00			

KM# 917 150 LIRA
9.0000 g., 0.8000 Silver .2314 oz. ASW **Subject:** World Cup Soccer Championship **Obverse:** Soccer player and net **Reverse:** Various maps divide emblem and value

Date	Mintage	F	VF	XF	Unc
1978	5,000	—	—	—	30.00

KM# 918.1 150 LIRA

9.0000 g., 0.8000 Silver .2314 oz. ASW **Series:** F.A.O. **Obverse:** Atatürk driving tractor **Obv. Designer:** M. Duyer **Reverse:** Value and date within wreath **Edge:** Reeded

Date	Mintage	F	VF	XF	Unc
1978	10,000	—	—	—	15.00

KM# 918.2 150 LIRA

9.0000 g., 0.8000 Silver .2314 oz. ASW **Series:** F.A.O. **Obverse:** Atatürk driving tractor **Reverse:** Value and date within wreath **Edge:** Lettered

Date	Mintage	F	VF	XF	Unc
1978 Proof	2,500	Value: 80.00			

KM# 929.1 150 LIRA

9.0000 g., 0.8000 Silver .2314 oz. ASW **Series:** F.A.O. **Obverse:** Anatolic bride's head left **Reverse:** Value and date within wreath **Edge:** Reeded

Date	Mintage	F	VF	XF	Unc
1979	10,000	—	—	—	15.00

KM# 929.2 150 LIRA

9.0000 g., 0.8000 Silver .2314 oz. ASW **Series:** F.A.O. **Obverse:** Anatolic bride's head left **Reverse:** Value and date within wreath **Edge:** Lettered

Date	Mintage	F	VF	XF	Unc
1979 Proof	2,500	Value: 40.00			

KM# 919 200 LIRA

9.0000 g., 0.8300 Silver .2402 oz. ASW **Subject:** 705th Anniversary - Death of Jalaladdin Rumi, Poet **Obverse:** Bust with headdress facing 1/4 left **Reverse:** Steepled and dome buildings

Date	Mintage	F	VF	XF	Unc
1978	10,000	—	—	—	17.50
1978 Proof	1,000	Value: 35.00			

KM# 904 500 LIRA

6.0000 g., 0.9170 Gold .1769 oz. AGW **Subject:** 50th Anniversary of Republic **Obverse:** Bust facing **Reverse:** Cascading star within flower to upper right of inscription

Date	Mintage	F	VF	XF	Unc
1973	30,000	—	—	—	135

KM# 920 500 LIRA

8.0000 g., 0.9170 Gold .2358 oz. AGW **Series:** F.A.O. **Obverse:** Mother breastfeeding infant **Reverse:** Value and date within wreath

Date	Mintage	F	VF	XF	Unc
1978 Proof	650	Value: 210			

KM# 921 500 LIRA

8.0000 g., 0.9170 Gold .2358 oz. AGW **Subject:** 705th Anniversary - Death of Jalaladdin Rumi, Poet

Date	Mintage	F	VF	XF	Unc
1978 Proof	900	Value: 475			

KM# 930 500 LIRA

8.0000 g., 0.9170 Gold .2358 oz. AGW **Series:** F.A.O.

Date	Mintage	F	VF	XF	Unc
1979 Proof	783	Value: 210			

KM# 931 500 LIRA

23.3300 g., 0.9250 Silver .6938 oz. ASW **Subject:** UNICEF and I.Y.C. **Obverse:** Value within wreath **Reverse:** Multiracial children dancing, city view above, logos and date below

Date	Mintage	F	VF	XF	Unc
1979(1981) Proof	10,000	Value: 30.00			

KM# 940.1 500 LIRA

9.0000 g., 0.9000 Silver .2604 oz. ASW **Series:** F.A.O. **Obverse:** Mother breastfeeding infant **Reverse:** Value and date within wreath **Edge:** Reeded

Date	Mintage	F	VF	XF	Unc
1980	13,000	—	—	—	15.00

KM# 940.2 500 LIRA

9.0000 g., 0.9000 Silver .2604 oz. ASW **Obverse:** Mother breastfeeding infant **Reverse:** Value and date within wreath **Edge:** Lettered

Date	Mintage	F	VF	XF	Unc
1980 Proof	4,000	Value: 40.00			

KM# 952 500 LIRA

23.3300 g., 0.9250 Silver .6938 oz. ASW **Subject:** World Championship Soccer - Madrid **Obverse:** Soccer player **Reverse:** Soccer ball and map in front of lined globe design

Date	Mintage	F	VF	XF	Unc
1982 Proof	12,000	Value: 30.00			

KM# 953 500 LIRA

23.3300 g., 0.9250 Silver .6938 oz. ASW **Subject:** World Championship Soccer - Madrid **Obverse:** Soccer ball in inner circle **Reverse:** Goalie blocking shot

Date	Mintage	F	VF	XF	Unc
1982 Proof	12,000	Value: 20.00			

KM# 957 500 LIRA

Copper-Nickel **Subject:** Lydia - First Coin in the World **Obverse:** Value and date within oat sprigs **Reverse:** Animal heads at center of circular inscriptions

Date	Mintage	F	VF	XF	Unc
1983	3,542	—	—	6.50	12.50

KM# 968 500 LIRA

Copper-Nickel **Series:** F.A.O. **Subject:** World Fisheries Conference **Obverse:** Value **Reverse:** Turbot fish **Rev. Designer:** Stuart Devlin

Date	Mintage	F	VF	XF	Unc
ND(1984)	3,000	—	—	10.00	25.00

KM# 968a 500 LIRA

28.2800 g., 0.9250 Silver .8411 oz. ASW **Series:** World Fisheries Conference **Obverse:** Value **Reverse:** Turbot fish **Rev. Designer:** Stuart Devlin

Date	Mintage	F	VF	XF	Unc
ND(1984) Proof	763,000	Value: 75.00			

KM# 968b 500 LIRA

47.5400 g., 0.9170 Gold 1.4009 oz. AGW **Subject:** World Fisheries Conference **Obverse:** Value **Reverse:** Turbot fish **Rev. Designer:** Stuart Devlin

Date	Mintage	F	VF	XF	Unc
ND(1984) Proof	74	Value: 1,250			

KM# 979 500 LIRA

Copper-Nickel **Subject:** 40th Anniversary of F.A.O. **Obverse:** Value within wreath **Reverse:** Leafy produce in bowl in front of FAO logo, dates on bottom

Date	Mintage	F	VF	XF	Unc
ND(1986) Proof	3,000	Value: 12.00			

KM# 989 500 LIRA

6.1500 g., Aluminum-Bronze, 24 mm. **Obverse:** Head of Atatürk left **Reverse:** Value and date within wreath **Edge:** Reeded **Note:** Varieties exist.

Date	Mintage	F	VF	XF	Unc
1989	141,813,000	—	—	—	0.60
1990	100,114,000	—	—	—	0.60
1991	30,006,000	—	—	—	0.60
1992	10,000	—	—	—	0.60
1993	5,000	—	—	—	0.75
1994	2,500	—	—	—	0.85
1995	2,500	—	—	—	0.85
1996	10,000	—	—	—	0.60
1997	—	—	—	—	0.60

KM# 989a 500 LIRA

7.6000 g., 0.9250 Silver 0.226 oz. ASW, 24 mm. **Obverse:** Head of Atatürk left **Reverse:** Value and date within wreath **Edge:** Reeded **Mint:** Mexico City

Date	Mintage	F	VF	XF	Unc
1989 Proof	998	Value: 75.00			

KM# 922 1000 LIRA

16.0000 g., 0.9170 Gold .4717 oz. AGW **Series:** F.A.O. **Obverse:** Anatolic bride's head left **Reverse:** Value and date within wreath

Date	Mintage	F	VF	XF	Unc
1978 Proof	650	Value: 500			

KM# 923 1000 LIRA

16.0000 g., 0.9170 Gold .4717 oz. AGW **Subject:** 705th Anniversary - Death of Jalaladdin Rumi, Poet

Date	Mintage	F	VF	XF	Unc
1978 Proof	450	Value: 1,000			

KM# 932 1000 LIRA

16.0000 g., 0.9170 Gold .4717 oz. AGW **Series:** F.A.O.

Date	Mintage	F	VF	XF	Unc
1979 Proof	900	Value: 400			

KM# 985 1000 LIRA

Nickel-Bronze **Subject:** Peace **Obverse:** Value within wreath **Reverse:** Doves within diamond shape

Date	Mintage	F	VF	XF	Unc
1986 Proof	—	Value: 12.50			

KM# 980 1000 LIRA

Copper-Nickel **Subject:** Shelter for the Homeless **Obverse:** Value within wreath **Reverse:** Emblem within center of window design

Date	Mintage	F	VF	XF	Unc
ND(1987) Proof	—	Value: 12.50			

KM# 991 1000 LIRA

Copper-Nickel **Subject:** 400th Anniversary - Death of Architect Sinan **Obverse:** Value within wreath **Reverse:** Arched city view

Date	Mintage	F	VF	XF	Unc
ND(1988) Proof	—	Value: 15.00			

KM# 996 1000 LIRA

Copper-Zinc-Nickel, 25.8 mm. **Subject:** Environmental Protection **Obverse:** Value and date within oat sprigs **Reverse:** Fence surrounds tree trunk

Date	Mintage	F	VF	XF	Unc
1990	500,000	—	—	—	8.50

KM# 997 1000 LIRA

Copper-Zinc-Nickel, 25.8 mm. **Obverse:** Head of Atatürk left **Reverse:** Value and date within oat sprigs **Edge:** Reeded

Date	Mintage	F	VF	XF	Unc
1990	136,480,000	—	0.15	0.25	2.00
1991	110,245,000	—	0.15	0.25	2.00
1992	15,820,000	—	0.15	0.25	2.00
1993	11,675,000	—	0.15	0.25	2.00
1994	61,515,000	—	0.15	0.25	2.00

KM# 1028 1000 LIRA

Bronze Clad Brass **Obverse:** Head of Atatürk left **Reverse:** Value and date within oat sprigs

Date	Mintage	F	VF	XF	Unc
1995	36,820,000	—	—	—	1.00
1996	3,900,000	—	—	—	1.00
1997	—	—	—	—	1.00

KM# 947 1500 LIRA

16.0000 g., 0.9250 Silver .4758 oz. ASW **Series:** F.A.O. **Obverse:** Value and date within wreath **Reverse:** Stylized design below sprig

Date	Mintage	F	VF	XF	Unc
1981	6,000	—	—	—	18.50
1982	500	—	—	—	47.50

KM# 958 1500 LIRA

16.0000 g., 0.9250 Silver .4758 oz. ASW **Series:** World Food Day **Obverse:** Value and date within wreath **Reverse:** Nursing goat within designed wreath

Date	Mintage	F	VF	XF	Unc
1983 Proof	1,552	Value: 45.00			

KM# 1015 2500 LIRA

Nickel-Bronze, 26.5 mm. **Obverse:** Head of Atatürk left **Reverse:** Value to lower right of oak leaf branch **Edge Lettering:** TURKIYC CUMHURIYETI

Date	Mintage	F	VF	XF	Unc
1991	22,938,000	0.10	0.25	0.50	3.00
1992	48,784,000	0.10	0.25	0.50	3.00
1993	2,310,000	0.10	0.25	0.50	3.00
1994	2,500	0.10	0.25	0.50	4.50
1995	2,500	0.10	0.25	0.50	4.50
1996	10,000	0.10	0.25	0.50	3.00
1997	—	0.10	0.25	0.50	3.00

KM# 948 3000 LIRA

28.2800 g., 0.9250 Silver .8411 oz. ASW **Series:** International Year of Disabled Persons **Obverse:** Stylized design divides top and bottom emblems **Reverse:** Value within wreath

Date	Mintage	F	VF	XF	Unc
1981	14,000	—	—	—	45.00
1981 Proof	16,000	Value: 55.00			

KM# 959 3000 LIRA

28.2800 g., 0.9250 Silver .8411 oz. ASW **Series:** International Year of the Scout **Obverse:** Value within wreath **Reverse:** Mountain campsite scene

Date	Mintage	F	VF	XF	Unc
ND(1982)	12,000	—	—	—	45.00
ND(1982) Proof	14,000	Value: 55.00			

KM# 960 3000 LIRA

16.0000 g., 0.9250 Silver .4758 oz. ASW **Subject:** 60th Anniversary of the Republic **Obverse:** Head of Atatürk left within circle **Reverse:** Stylized reaching and standing figures within circle

Date	Mintage	F	VF	XF	Unc
ND(1983) Proof	4,000	Value: 35.00			

KM# 954 5000 LIRA

7.1300 g., 0.5000 Gold .1146 oz. AGW **Subject:** World Championship Soccer - Madrid **Obverse:** Soccer player kicking the ball **Reverse:** Soccer ball as world globe with SPANYA'82 across middle

Date	Mintage	F	VF	XF	Unc
ND(1982) Proof	2,400	Value: 145			

KM# 969 5000 LIRA

23.3300 g., 0.9250 Silver .6939 oz. ASW **Subject:** Decade for Women **Obverse:** Value and date within wreath **Reverse:** Stylized woman holding dove **Rev. Designer:** Suat Ozyonum

Date	Mintage	F	VF	XF	Unc
1984 Proof	20,000	Value: 35.00			

KM# 970 5000 LIRA

23.3300 g., 0.9250 Silver .6939 oz. ASW **Series:** 1984 Summer Olympics **Obverse:** Value within wreath **Reverse:** Olympic athletes around center circle with stylized flame

Date	Mintage	F	VF	XF	Unc
ND(1984) Proof	5,343	Value: 40.00			

KM# 971 5000 LIRA

23.3300 g., 0.9250 Silver .6939 oz. ASW **Series:** 1984 Winter Olympics **Obverse:** Value within wreath **Reverse:** Stylized slalom, bobsledder, ski jumper, and figure skater in inner circle, legend around

Date	Mintage	F	VF	XF	Unc
1984 Proof	4,657	Value: 50.00			

KM# 972 5000 LIRA

23.3300 g., 0.9250 Silver .6939 oz. ASW **Subject:** 50th Anniversary of Women's Suffrage **Obverse:** Value within wreath **Reverse:** Three standing women facing in front of building

Date	Mintage	F	VF	XF	Unc
ND(1984) Proof	1,000	Value: 80.00			

KM# 976 5000 LIRA

23.3300 g., 0.9250 Silver .6939 oz. ASW **Subject:** 500th Anniversary of Turkish Navy **Obverse:** Value within wreatzh **Reverse:** Bust with Turkish headdress at right, fleet of masted ships at left

Date	Mintage	F	VF	XF	Unc
ND(1985) Proof	1,000	Value: 80.00			

KM# 977 5000 LIRA

23.3300 g., 0.9250 Silver .6939 oz. ASW **Subject:** Forestry Conference - Mexico **Obverse:** Value within wreath **Reverse:** Trees

Date	Mintage	F	VF	XF	Unc
1985 Proof	2,000	Value: 45.00			

KM# 978 5000 LIRA

23.3300 g., 0.9250 Silver .6939 oz. ASW **Subject:** Youth Year **Obverse:** Value within wreath **Reverse:** Stylized head facing

Date	Mintage	F	VF	XF	Unc
1985 Proof	2,000	Value: 40.00			

KM# 1011 5000 LIRA

23.3300 g., 0.9250 Silver .6939 oz. ASW **Subject:** Architect - Sinan

Date	Mintage	F	VF	XF	Unc
ND(1988) Proof	—	Value: 40.00			

KM# 1005 5000 LIRA

Copper-Nickel **Subject:** Yunus Emre Sevgi Yili **Obverse:** Value within wreath **Reverse:** Inscription and arched design

Date	Mintage	F	VF	XF	Unc
1991 Proof	—	Value: 7.50			

KM# 1018 5000 LIRA

Copper-Nickel **Subject:** Turkish Jews **Obverse:** Value within wreath **Reverse:** Standing figures below ship

Date	Mintage	F	VF	XF	Unc
ND(1992) Proof	—	Value: 8.50			

KM# 1025 5000 LIRA
Nickel-Bronze, 28.5 mm. **Obverse:** Head of Atatürk left **Reverse:** Flower sprigs to left of value and date

Date	Mintage	F	VF	XF	Unc
1992	24,904,000	0.10	0.25	0.50	3.00
1992 Proof	—	Value: 6.50			
1993	15,872,000	0.10	0.25	0.50	3.00
1994	69,504,000	0.10	0.25	0.50	3.00

KM# 1029.1 5000 LIRA
5.9800 g., Brass, 19.5 mm. **Obverse:** Head of Atatürk left **Reverse:** Flower sprigs to left of value and date

Date	Mintage	F	VF	XF	Unc
1995 Large date	69,550,000	—	—	—	1.50
1995 Small date	Inc. above	—	—	—	0.75
1996	80,506,000	—	—	—	0.75
1997	—	—	—	—	0.75
1998	—	—	—	—	0.75
1999	—	—	—	—	0.75

KM# 1029.2 5000 LIRA
3.4800 g., Brass, 19.5 mm. **Obverse:** Head of Atatürk left **Reverse:** Flower sprigs to left of value and date **Edge:** Reeded **Note:** Reduced weight version of KM#1029.1

Date	Mintage	F	VF	XF	Unc
1999	—	—	—	—	0.75

KM# 933 10000 LIRA (10 Bin Lira)
17.1700 g., 0.9000 Gold .4900 oz. AGW **Subject:** UNICEF and I.Y.C. **Obverse:** Value within wreath **Reverse:** Multiracial children dancing, city view above, logos and date below **Note:** Similar to 500 Lira, KM#931

Date	Mintage	F	VF	XF	Unc
1979(1981) Proof	4,450	Value: 350			

KM# 986 10000 LIRA (10 Bin Lira)
23.3300 g., 0.9250 Silver .6939 oz. ASW **Subject:** 1986 World Cup Soccer - Mexico **Reverse:** Soccer player in center of soccer ball

Date	Mintage	F	VF	XF	Unc
1986 Proof	5,000	Value: 22.50			

KM# 1009 10000 LIRA (10 Bin Lira)
23.3300 g., 0.9250 Silver .6939 oz. ASW **Subject:** 1986 World Cup Soccer **Reverse:** Cactus

Date	Mintage	F	VF	XF	Unc
1986 Proof	7,000	Value: 20.00			

KM# 1010 10000 LIRA (10 Bin Lira)
23.3300 g., 0.9250 Silver .6939 oz. ASW **Subject:** A. Ersoy - Poet

Date	Mintage	F	VF	XF	Unc
1986 Proof	—	Value: 35.00			

KM# 1022 10000 LIRA (10 Bin Lira)
23.3300 g., 0.9250 Silver .6939 oz. ASW **Subject:** World Peace **Obverse:** Value within wreath **Reverse:** Doves within diamond shape

Date	Mintage	F	VF	XF	Unc
1986 Proof	Est. 1,200	Value: 60.00			

KM# 981 10000 LIRA (10 Bin Lira)
22.9700 g., 0.9250 Silver .6832 oz. ASW **Subject:** Shelter for the Homeless **Obverse:** Value within wreath **Reverse:** Emblem within center of window design

Date	Mintage	F	VF	XF	Unc
ND(1987) Proof	—	Value: 35.00			

KM# 982 10000 LIRA (10 Bin Lira)
22.9700 g., 0.9250 Silver .6832 oz. ASW **Subject:** 130 Years of Turkish Forestry **Obverse:** Value within wreath **Reverse:** Bird on top of globe design above pine trees

Date	Mintage	F	VF	XF	Unc
ND(1987) Proof	5,000	Value: 40.00			

KM# 983 10000 LIRA (10 Bin Lira)
23.3300 g., 0.9250 Silver .6939 oz. ASW **Series:** Winter Olympics **Obverse:** Value within wreath **Reverse:** Stylized upright bear holding torch at left of totem pole

Date	Mintage	F	VF	XF	Unc
1988 Proof	Est. 10,000	Value: 40.00			

KM# 984 10000 LIRA (10 Bin Lira)
23.3300 g., 0.9250 Silver .6939 oz. ASW **Series:** 1988 Summer Olympics **Obverse:** Value within wreath **Reverse:** Stylized torch and designs

Date	Mintage	F	VF	XF	Unc
1988	1,000	—	—	—	35.00
1988 Proof	Est. 10,000	Value: 40.00			

KM# 1027.1 10000 LIRA (10 Bin Lira)
9.7500 g., Copper-Nickel-Zinc, 23.5 mm. **Obverse:** Head of Atatürk left **Reverse:** Value to left of flower sprig **Edge:** Reeded with legend **Edge Lettering:** TURKIYE CUMHURIYETI

Date	Mintage	F	VF	XF	Unc
1994	17,319,000	—	0.10	0.25	3.00
1995	56,584,000	—	0.10	0.25	3.00
1996	119,572,000	—	0.10	0.25	3.00
1997	—	—	0.10	0.25	3.00

KM# 1042 10000 LIRA (10 Bin Lira)
Copper-Nickel-Zinc, 23.5 mm. **Series:** 1994 Olympics **Obverse:** Value to left of flower sprig **Reverse:** Radiant Olympic rings

Date	Mintage	F	VF	XF	Unc
1994	500,000	—	—	—	3.75

KM# 1027.2 10000 LIRA (10 Bin Lira)
6.9200 g., Copper-Nickel-Zinc, 23.5 mm. **Obverse:** Head of Atatürk left **Reverse:** Value to left of flower sprig **Edge:** "TC" six times between reeded sections **Note:** Thin planchet. Edge varieties exist.

Date	Mintage	F	VF	XF	Unc
1998	—	—	0.10	0.25	3.00
1999	—	—	0.10	0.25	3.00

KM# 1027.3 10000 LIRA (10 Bin Lira)
Copper-Nickel-Zinc, 23.5 mm. **Obverse:** Head of Atatürk left **Reverse:** Value to left of flower sprig **Note:** Like KM#1027.2 but edge: "T.C." repeated twice in groups of three.

Date	Mintage	F	VF	XF	Unc
1998	—	—	—	—	—

KM# 998 20000 LIRA (20 Bin Lira)
23.3200 g., 0.9250 Silver .6938 oz. ASW **Subject:** Environmental Protection **Obverse:** Value within wreath **Reverse:** Designs

Date	Mintage	F	VF	XF	Unc
1988 Proof	Est. 5,000	Value: 40.00			

KM# 1001 20000 LIRA (20 Bin Lira)
23.3200 g., 0.9250 Silver .6938 oz. ASW **Subject:** 400th Anniversary - Death of Architect Sinan **Obverse:** Value within wreath **Reverse:** City view

Date	Mintage	F	VF	XF	Unc
ND(1988) Proof	1,239	Value: 37.50			

KM# 1003 20000 LIRA (20 Bin Lira)
23.3200 g., 0.9250 Silver .6938 oz. ASW **Subject:** Teacher's Day **Obverse:** Value within wreath **Reverse:** Stylized design divides date below

Date	Mintage	F	VF	XF	Unc
1989 Proof	1,013	Value: 37.50			

KM# 1013 20000 LIRA (20 Bin Lira)
23.3200 g., 0.9250 Silver .6938 oz. ASW **Subject:** Istanbul Metro **Obverse:** Value within wreath **Reverse:** City view

Date	Mintage	F	VF	XF	Unc
ND(1989) Proof	Est. 5,000	Value: 75.00			

KM# 992 20000 LIRA (20 Bin Lira)
23.3200 g., 0.9250 Silver .6938 oz. ASW **Subject:** 1990 World Cup Soccer **Obverse:** Value within wreath **Reverse:** Stylized football player kicking ball **Rev. Legend:** 1990 DUNYA FUTBOL SAMPIYONASI ITALYA

Date	Mintage	F	VF	XF	Unc
1990 Proof	12,959	Value: 35.00			

KM# 993 20000 LIRA (20 Bin Lira)
23.3200 g., 0.9250 Silver .6938 oz. ASW **Subject:** 75th Anniversary - Battle of Gallipoli **Obverse:** Value within wreath **Reverse:** Armored figure facing, holding flag and weapon in front of monument

Date	Mintage	F	VF	XF	Unc
ND(1990) Proof	1,963	Value: 40.00			

KM# 995 20000 LIRA (20 Bin Lira)
23.3200 g., 0.9250 Silver .6938 oz. ASW **Subject:** Soccer **Obverse:** Value within wreath **Reverse:** Soccer ball above stylized wolf

Date	Mintage	F	VF	XF	Unc
1990 Proof	8,796	Value: 37.50			

KM# 1014 20000 LIRA (20 Bin Lira)
23.3200 g., 0.9250 Silver .6938 oz. ASW **Subject:** 70th Anniversary of Parliament **Reverse:** Parliament building

Date	Mintage	F	VF	XF	Unc
1990 Proof	1,163	Value: 40.00			

KM# 1057 20000 LIRA (20 Bin Lira)
23.3200 g., 0.9250 Silver .6938 oz. ASW **Series:** Summer Olympics **Obverse:** Value within wreath **Reverse:** Bicyclist

Date	Mintage	F	VF	XF	Unc
ND(1990) Proof	—	Value: 40.00			

KM# 1077 20000 LIRA (20 Bin Lira)
23.4200 g., 0.9250 Silver .6965 oz. ASW **Series:** Olympics **Subject:** Speed Skating **Obverse:** Value within wreath **Reverse:** Speed skater

Date	Mintage	F	VF	XF	Unc
ND(1990) Proof	—	Value: 30.00			

KM# 1041 25000 LIRA (25 Bin Lira)
Copper-Nickel-Zinc, 26.5 mm. **Obverse:** Head of Atatürk left **Reverse:** Value to left of rose **Edge:** Lettered TC and flower five times

Date	Mintage	F	VF	XF	Unc
1995	13,740,000	0.20	0.30	0.50	3.00
1996	59,742,000	0.20	0.30	0.50	3.00
1997	—	0.20	0.30	0.50	3.00
1998	—	0.20	0.30	0.50	3.00
1999	—	0.20	0.30	0.50	3.00
2000	—	0.20	0.30	0.50	3.00

KM# 1043 25000 LIRA (25 Bin Lira)
Copper-Nickel-Zinc, 26.5 mm. **Series:** Environmental Protection **Obverse:** Small head facing divides profiles with birds and nest on top of heads **Reverse:** Value to left of rose

Date	Mintage	F	VF	XF	Unc
1995	500,000	—	—	—	5.00

KM# 955 30000 LIRA
15.9800 g., 0.9170 Gold .4712 oz. AGW **Series:** International Year of Disabled Persons **Obverse:** Value within wreath **Reverse:** Stylized seated figure missing legs and globe design

Date	Mintage	F	VF	XF	Unc
1981	140	—	—	—	420
1981 Proof	3,000	Value: 460			

KM# 961 30000 LIRA
15.9800 g., 0.9170 Gold .4712 oz. AGW **Series:** International Year of the Scout **Obverse:** Value within wreath **Reverse:** Emblems within circle

Date	Mintage	F	VF	XF	Unc
ND(1983)	2,000	—	—	—	450
ND(1983) Proof	2,000	Value: 500			

KM# 973 50000 LIRA (50 Bin Lira)
7.1300 g., 0.9000 Gold .2063 oz. AGW **Series:** Decade for Women **Obverse:** Value and date within wreath **Reverse:** Half-figure of female facing **Rev. Designer:** Suat Ozyonum

Date	Mintage	F	VF	XF	Unc
1984 Proof	800	Value: 160			

KM# 999 50000 LIRA (50 Bin Lira)
28.2800 g., 0.9250 Silver .8411 oz. ASW **Series:** Winter Olympics **Obverse:** Value within wreath **Reverse:** Speed skater

Date	Mintage	F	VF	XF	Unc
ND(1990) Proof	15,000	Value: 30.00			

KM# 1000 50000 LIRA (50 Bin Lira)
28.2800 g., 0.9250 Silver .8411 oz. ASW **Series:** 1990 Summer Olympics **Obverse:** Value within wreath **Reverse:** Bicyclist

Date	Mintage	F	VF	XF	Unc
ND(1990) Proof	15,000	Value: 30.00			

KM# 1006 50000 LIRA (50 Bin Lira)
22.8700 g., 0.9250 Silver .6801 oz. ASW **Subject:** Yunus Emre Sevgi Yili **Obverse:** Value within wreath **Reverse:** Inscription and arched brick facade

Date	Mintage	F	VF	XF	Unc
1991 Proof	1,578	Value: 40.00			

KM# 1007 50000 LIRA (50 Bin Lira)
22.8700 g., 0.9250 Silver .6801 oz. ASW **Subject:** Mozart Opera **Obverse:** Value within wreath **Reverse:** Cameo within curtains above theater, circle surrounds all

Date	Mintage	F	VF	XF	Unc
ND(1991) Proof	1,614	Value: 40.00			

KM# 1019 50000 LIRA (50 Bin Lira)
22.7700 g., 0.9250 Silver .6772 oz. ASW **Subject:** Ahmet Adnan Saygun - Musician **Obverse:** Value within wreath **Reverse:** Bust facing in front of music sheet

Date	Mintage	F	VF	XF	Unc
ND(1991) Proof	1,021	Value: 45.00			

KM# 1016 50000 LIRA (50 Bin Lira)
23.3300 g., 0.9250 Silver .6858 oz. ASW **Subject:** Turkish Jews **Obverse:** Value within wreath **Reverse:** Similar to 5000 Lira, KM#1018

Date	Mintage	F	VF	XF	Unc
ND(1992) Proof	2,813	Value: 60.00			

KM# 1023 50000 LIRA (50 Bin Lira)
23.0800 g., 0.9250 Silver .6184 oz. ASW **Subject:** 200th Birthday of Rossini **Obverse:** Value within wreath **Reverse:** Bust 1/4 right to left of building within circle

Date	Mintage	F	VF	XF	Unc
ND(1992) Proof	945	Value: 70.00			

KM# 1136 50000 LIRA (50 Bin Lira)
23.1600 g., 0.9250 Silver 0.6888 oz. ASW, 38.6 mm. **Subject:** 30th Anniversary - Constitution **Obverse:** Value within wreath **Reverse:** Flame above open book within circle **Edge:** Reeded **Mint:** Istanbul

Date	Mintage	F	VF	XF	Unc
ND(1992) Proof	1,134	Value: 65.00			

KM# 1020 50000 LIRA (50 Bin Lira)
23.0800 g., 0.9250 Silver .6184 oz. ASW **Subject:** 1994 World Cup Soccer **Obverse:** Value within wreath **Reverse:** Soccer ball on top of torch

Date	Mintage	F	VF	XF	Unc
ND(1993) Proof	3,724	Value: 30.00			

KM# 1021.1 50000 LIRA (50 Bin Lira)
23.0800 g., 0.9250 Silver .6184 oz. ASW **Subject:** 1994 World Cup Soccer **Obverse:** Value within wreath **Reverse:** Bridge behind soccer player, fuzzy looking rock under bridge

Date	Mintage	F	VF	XF	Unc
ND(1993)	6,038	—	—	—	75.00
ND(1993) Proof	Inc. above	Value: 25.00			

KM# 1021.2 50000 LIRA (50 Bin Lira)
23.0800 g., 0.9250 Silver .6184 oz. ASW **Subject:** 1994 World Cup Soccer **Obverse:** Value within wreath **Reverse:** Sharp looking rock under bridge

Date	Mintage	F	VF	XF	Unc
ND(1993) Proof	550	Value: 45.00			

KM# 1044 50000 LIRA (50 Bin Lira)
23.0800 g., 0.9250 Silver .6184 oz. ASW **Subject:** 125 Years - Turkish Supreme Court **Obverse:** Value within wreath **Reverse:** Balance scales within circle

Date	Mintage	F	VF	XF	Unc
ND(1993) Proof	1,052	Value: 40.00			

KM# 1024 50000 LIRA (50 Bin Lira)
23.0800 g., 0.9250 Silver .6184 oz. ASW **Subject:** 25th Anniversary of Turkish Red Crescent **Obverse:** Value within wreath **Reverse:** Aerial country view below world globe

Date	Mintage	F	VF	XF	Unc
ND(1993) Proof	938	Value: 70.00			

KM# 1026 50000 LIRA (50 Bin Lira)
22.8400 g., 0.9250 Silver .6793 oz. ASW **Series:** Olympics **Obverse:** Value within wreath **Reverse:** Flag and Olympic rings

Date	Mintage	F	VF	XF	Unc
ND(1994) Proof	1,821	Value: 60.00			

KM# 1030 50000 LIRA (50 Bin Lira)
31.4700 g., 0.9250 Silver .9359 oz. ASW **Series:** Endangered Wildlife **Obverse:** Value within wreath **Reverse:** Bald Ibis

Date	Mintage	F	VF	XF	Unc
ND(1994) Proof	6,807	Value: 45.00			

KM# 1031 50000 LIRA (50 Bin Lira)
23.3300 g., 0.9250 Silver .6938 oz. ASW **Subject:** Tschaikovsky **Obverse:** Value within wreath **Reverse:** Head facing at upper right of ballet scene

Date	Mintage	F	VF	XF	Unc
ND(1994) Proof	1,237	Value: 35.00			

KM# 1033 50000 LIRA (50 Bin Lira)
23.3300 g., 0.9250 Silver .6938 oz. ASW **Subject:** 75th Anniversary - Turkish National Assembly **Obverse:** Value within wreath **Reverse:** Upright designs above building

Date	Mintage	F	VF	XF	Unc
1995 Proof	3,000	Value: 25.00			

KM# 1035 50000 LIRA (50 Bin Lira)
23.3300 g., 0.9250 Silver .6938 oz. ASW **Subject:** 150th Anniversary - National Police **Obverse:** Value within wreath **Reverse:** Police badge above dates

Date	Mintage	F	VF	XF	Unc
1995 Proof	1,262	Value: 45.00			

KM# 1037 50000 LIRA (50 Bin Lira)
Brass **Obverse:** Value within wreath **Reverse:** Swimming sea turtle **Note:** Oxidized finish.

Date	Mintage	F	VF	XF	Unc
1995	1,235	—	—	—	45.00

KM# 1037a 50000 LIRA (50 Bin Lira)
23.3300 g., 0.9250 Silver .6938 oz. ASW **Obverse:** Value within wreath **Reverse:** Swimming sea turtle

Date	Mintage	F	VF	XF	Unc
1995 Proof	2,961	Value: 40.00			

KM# 1038 50000 LIRA (50 Bin Lira)
23.3300 g., 0.9250 Silver .6938 oz. ASW **Obverse:** Value within wreath **Reverse:** Sailing ship - "Piri Reis"

Date	Mintage	F	VF	XF	Unc
1995 Proof	13,923	Value: 40.00			

KM# 1040 50000 LIRA (50 Bin Lira)
23.3300 g., 0.9250 Silver .6938 oz. ASW **Series:** 50th Anniversary - F.A.O. **Obverse:** Value within wreath **Reverse:** Anniversary date above logo within design

Date	Mintage	F	VF	XF	Unc
1995 Proof	3,798	Value: 22.50			

KM# 1045 50000 LIRA (50 Bin Lira)
31.4700 g., 0.9250 Silver .9359 oz. ASW **Series:** Summer Olympics **Obverse:** Value and date within wreath **Reverse:** Wrestlers

Date	Mintage	F	VF	XF	Unc
1995 Proof	12,476	Value: 30.00			

KM# 1050 50000 LIRA (50 Bin Lira)
Copper-Nickel-Zinc **Series:** F.A.O. **Obverse:** Globe within center of designs, single sprig at left **Reverse:** Value **Edge:** "T.C." and four fleur-de-lis repeated four times

Date	Mintage	F	VF	XF	Unc
ND(1996)	500,000	—	—	—	4.50

KM# 1056 50000 LIRA (50 Bin Lira)
Copper-Nickel-Zinc **Obverse:** Head of Atatürk left **Reverse:** Value

Date	Mintage	F	VF	XF	Unc
1996	11,916,000	—	—	—	3.50
1997	—	—	—	—	3.50
1998	—	—	—	—	3.50
1999	—	—	—	—	3.50
2000	—	—	—	—	3.50

KM# 1103 50000 LIRA (50 Bin Lira)
Aluminum, 20 mm. **Series:** F.A.O **Obverse:** Value and date within wreath **Reverse:** Ancient vintner **Edge:** Plain **Mint:** Istanbul

Date	Mintage	F	VF	XF	Unc
1999	—	—	—	—	1.00

KM# 956 100000 LIRA (100 Bin Lira)
33.8200 g., 0.9170 Gold .9972 oz. AGW **Subject:** Islamic World 15th Century **Reverse:** City view above value within circle

Date	Mintage	F	VF	XF	Unc
1982 Proof	12,000	Value: 675			

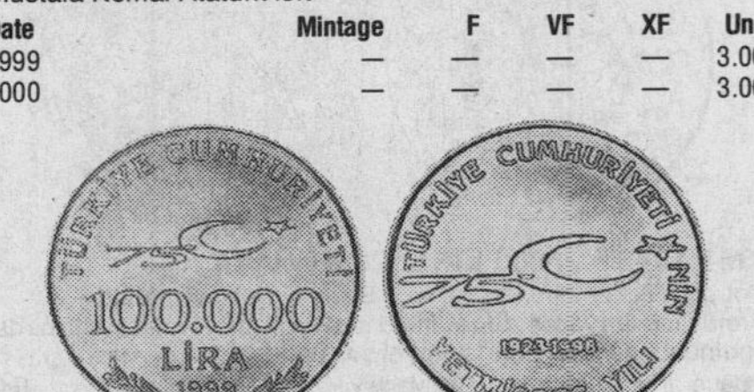

KM# 1078 100000 LIRA (100 Bin Lira)
Copper-Nickel-Zinc **Subject:** 75th Anniversary of Republic **Obverse:** Value below crescent and star **Reverse:** Bust of Mustafa Kemal Atatürk left

Date	Mintage	F	VF	XF	Unc
1999	—	—	—	—	3.00
2000	—	—	—	—	3.00

KM# 1079 100000 LIRA (100 Bin Lira)

Copper-Nickel-Zinc **Subject:** 75th Anniversary of Republic **Obverse:** Value below crescent and star **Reverse:** Anniversary logo and dates

Date	Mintage	F	VF	XF	Unc
1999	—	—	—	—	4.00
2000	—	—	—	—	4.00

KM# 974 200000 LIRA

33.8200 g., 0.9170 Gold .9972 oz. AGW **Subject:** 50th Anniversary of Women's Suffrage

Date	Mintage	F	VF	XF	Unc
ND(1984) Proof	62	Value: 1,850			

KM# 1002 200000 LIRA

7.2160 g., 0.9170 Gold .2126 oz. AGW **Subject:** 400th Anniversary - Death of Architect Sinan **Obverse:** Value within wreath **Reverse:** Arched city view

Date	Mintage	F	VF	XF	Unc
ND(1988) Proof	244	Value: 325			

KM# 1004 200000 LIRA

7.2160 g., 0.9170 Gold .2126 oz. AGW **Subject:** Teacher's Day **Obverse:** Value within wreath **Reverse:** Stylized design divides date

Date	Mintage	F	VF	XF	Unc
1989 Proof	197	Value: 350			

KM# 994 200000 LIRA

7.2160 g., 0.9170 Gold .2126 oz. AGW **Subject:** 75th Anniversary - Battle of Gallipoli

Date	Mintage	F	VF	XF	Unc
ND(1990) Proof	Est. 494	Value: 325			

KM# 1051 400000 LIRA

Bronze **Subject:** Habitat II **Obverse:** City view **Reverse:** Conference logo

Date	Mintage	F	VF	XF	Unc
1996	2,402	—	—	—	12.50

KM# 1008 500000 LIRA

7.1300 g., 0.9000 Gold .2063 oz. AGW **Subject:** Yunus Emre **Obverse:** Value within wreath **Reverse:** Inscription and arched brick facade

Date	Mintage	F	VF	XF	Unc
1991 Proof	288	Value: 320			

KM# 1017 500000 LIRA

7.1400 g., 0.9000 Gold .2066 oz. AGW **Subject:** 100 Years of Peace and Harmony - Turkish Jews **Obverse:** Value within wreath **Reverse:** Standing figures next to ship

Date	Mintage	F	VF	XF	Unc
ND(1992) Proof	485	Value: 320			

KM# 1032 500000 LIRA

7.2160 g., 0.9166 Gold .2126 oz. AGW **Subject:** Southeast Anatolian Project **Obverse:** Value within wreath **Reverse:** Design within wreath

Date	Mintage	F	VF	XF	Unc
ND(1994) Proof	950	Value: 300			

KM# 1034 500000 LIRA

7.2160 g., 0.9166 Gold .2126 oz. AGW **Subject:** 75th Anniversary - Turkish National Assembly **Obverse:** Value and date within wreath **Reverse:** Building in front of upright designs

Date	Mintage	F	VF	XF	Unc
1995 Proof	255	Value: 300			

KM# 1036 500000 LIRA

7.2160 g., 0.9166 Gold .2126 oz. AGW **Subject:** Istanbul Gold Exchange **Obverse:** Value and date within wreath **Reverse:** AR above inscription and date

Date	Mintage	F	VF	XF	Unc
1995 Proof	271	Value: 300			

KM# 1039 500000 LIRA

7.2160 g., 0.9166 Gold .2126 oz. AGW **Obverse:** Value and date within wreath **Reverse:** Sailing ship - "Piri Reis"

Date	Mintage	F	VF	XF	Unc
1995 Proof	1,904	Value: 300			

KM# 1138 500000 LIRA

12.1000 g., Copper Nickel, 32 mm. **Subject:** Lira to Euro Transition **Obverse:** Value and date within wreath **Reverse:** Head of Atatürk left **Edge:** Reeded **Mint:** Istanbul **Note:** Dual denomination: 500,000 lira-2 euro

Date	Mintage	F	VF	XF	Unc
1998	12,660	—	—	—	15.00

KM# 1081 500000 LIRA

11.9100 g., Copper-Nickel **Subject:** Trojan Horse **Obverse:** Value and date within wreath **Reverse:** Ancient Greek soldier and wooden horse **Edge:** Reeded **Note:** Struck at Istanbul.

Date	Mintage	F	VF	XF	Unc
1999	6,243	—	—	—	15.00

KM# 1046 750000 LIRA

31.4700 g., 0.9250 Silver .9359 oz. ASW **Subject:** Europa **Obverse:** Value and date within wreath **Reverse:** Various landmarks

Date	Mintage	F	VF	XF	Unc
1996 Proof	Est. 35,000	Value: 30.00			

KM# 1048.1 750000 LIRA

23.2000 g., 0.9250 Silver .6899 oz. ASW **Series:** F.A.O. **Obverse:** Value within wreath **Reverse:** World globe with corn stalks at left

Date	Mintage	F	VF	XF	Unc
1996 Proof	—	Value: 20.00			

KM# 1048.2 750000 LIRA

23.2000 g., 0.9250 Silver .6899 oz. ASW **Series:** F.A.O. **Obverse:** Value within wreath **Reverse:** World globe with corn stalks at right

Date	Mintage	F	VF	XF	Unc
1996 Proof	2,010	Value: 22.50			

KM# 1049 750000 LIRA

23.4100 g., 0.9250 Silver .6962 oz. ASW **Subject:** Turkish European Customs Union **Obverse:** Flying plane and hills **Reverse:** Clasped hands divide circle of stars

Date	Mintage	F	VF	XF	Unc
1996 Proof	3,947	Value: 22.50			

KM# 1052 750000 LIRA

23.3700 g., 0.9250 Silver .6950 oz. ASW **Subject:** Nasreddin Hoca **Obverse:** Stylized figure with headdress on donkey facing **Reverse:** Stylized figure with headdress on donkey walking away

Date	Mintage	F	VF	XF	Unc
1996 Proof	4,300	Value: 20.00			

KM# 1063 750000 LIRA

31.4700 g., 0.9250 Silver .9359 oz. ASW **Subject:** World Cup Soccer **Obverse:** Value and date within wreath **Reverse:** Goalie catching ball

Date	Mintage	F	VF	XF	Unc
1996 Proof	6,848	Value: 30.00			

KM# 1058 750000 LIRA

Bronze **Subject:** First World Air Games - Manned Flight **Obverse:** Value within wreath **Reverse:** Figure with bat-like wings flying over city, all within circle

Date	Mintage	F	VF	XF	Unc
1997	1,733	—	—	—	10.00

KM# 1059 750000 LIRA

Bronze **Subject:** XI World Forestry Congress **Obverse:** Value within wreath **Reverse:** Stylized dove left below tree

Date	Mintage	F	VF	XF	Unc
1997	1,778	—	—	—	12.50

KM# 1068 750000 LIRA
Bronze **Subject:** Forestry - "TEMA" **Obverse:** Value within wreath **Reverse:** Wheel of trees design

Date	Mintage	F	VF	XF	Unc
1998	1,950	—	—	—	12.50

KM# 1047 1000000 LIRA
31.7200 g., 0.9250 Silver .9433 oz. ASW **Series:** Endangered Wildlife **Obverse:** Ocean view within circle **Reverse:** Mediterranean seal

Date	Mintage	F	VF	XF	Unc
1996 Proof	3,594	Value: 35.00			

KM# 1053 1000000 LIRA
31.4600 g., 0.9250 Silver .9356 oz. ASW **Series:** Endangered Wildlife **Obverse:** Value and date within wreath **Reverse:** Galathus Elwesii flowers

Date	Mintage	F	VF	XF	Unc
1996 Proof	3,100	Value: 25.00			

KM# 1054 1000000 LIRA
31.4600 g., 0.9250 Silver .9356 oz. ASW **Subject:** Habitat II **Obverse:** Steepled buildings **Reverse:** Conference logo

Date	Mintage	F	VF	XF	Unc
1996 Proof	3,968	Value: 25.00			

KM# 1055 1000000 LIRA
31.7700 g., 0.9250 Silver .9448 oz. ASW **Obverse:** Value and date within oat sprigs **Reverse:** Bust of Hulusi Behcet facing

Date	Mintage	F	VF	XF	Unc
1996 Proof	2,250	Value: 22.50			

KM# 1060 1000000 LIRA
31.5700 g., 0.9250 Silver .9389 oz. ASW **Subject:** Chinese History - Excavation of the Terra Cotta Army **Obverse:** Great Wall of China **Reverse:** Excavation site

Date	Mintage	F	VF	XF	Unc
1997	4,273	—	—	—	22.50

Note: This coin does not have any national identification other than the mintmark and denomination

KM# 1066 1000000 LIRA
1.2441 g., 0.9990 Gold .0400 oz. AGW **Obverse:** Value in wreath **Reverse:** Head of King Croesus of Lydia right **Edge:** Reeded **Mint:** Istanbul

Date	Mintage	F	VF	XF	Unc
1997 Proof	10,465	Value: 45.00			

KM# 1067 1000000 LIRA
1.2441 g., 0.9990 Gold **Obverse:** Value and date within wreath **Reverse:** Ancient Lydian coin portraying lion

Date	Mintage	F	VF	XF	Unc
1997 Proof	3,848	Value: 45.00			

KM# 1069 1000000 LIRA
31.4400 g., 0.9250 Silver .9350 oz. ASW **Subject:** Mehmed Akif Ersoy **Obverse:** Spiral inscription **Reverse:** Bust facing

Date	Mintage	F	VF	XF	Unc
1997 Proof	Est. 2,250	Value: 30.00			

KM# 1098 1000000 LIRA
1.2200 g., 0.9990 Gold 0.0392 oz. AGW, 13.9 mm. **Obverse:** Value and date within wreath **Reverse:** Sailing ship - "Piri Reis" **Edge:** Reeded **Mint:** Istanbul

Date	Mintage	F	VF	XF	Unc
1997 Proof	10,655	Value: 45.00			

KM# 1061 1500000 LIRA
31.4400 g., 0.9250 Silver .9350 oz. ASW **Subject:** First World Air Games - Manned Flight **Obverse:** Value and date within wreath **Reverse:** Figure with bat-like wings flying over city

Date	Mintage	F	VF	XF	Unc
1997 Proof	2,300	Value: 28.00			

KM# 1062 1500000 LIRA
31.4400 g., 0.9250 Silver .9350 oz. ASW **Subject:** XI World Forestry Conference **Obverse:** Value within wreath **Reverse:** Stylized dove left below tree

Date	Mintage	F	VF	XF	Unc
1997 Proof	2,255	Value: 28.00			

KM# 1082 1500000 LIRA
31.3300 g., 0.9250 Silver .9317 oz. ASW **Subject:** Barbaros Hayreddin **Obverse:** Value and date within wreath **Reverse:** Two war ships **Edge:** Reeded **Mint:** Istanbul

Date	Mintage	F	VF	XF	Unc
1997 Proof	7,062	Value: 30.00			

KM# 1100 1500000 LIRA
31.3700 g., 0.9250 Silver .9329 oz. ASW, 38.6 mm. **Subject:** Myra'li Aziz Noel Baba and Euro **Obverse:** Value and date within wreath **Reverse:** Statue and tower within 1/2 star wreath **Edge:** Reeded **Mint:** Istanbul

Date	Mintage	F	VF	XF	Unc
1997 Proof	10,492	Value: 25.00			

KM# 1064 2500000 LIRA
31.1500 g., 0.9250 Silver .9264 oz. ASW **Obverse:** Value and date within wreath **Reverse:** Bust of Hasan-Ali Yücel 1/4 right

Date	Mintage	F	VF	XF	Unc
1998 Proof	2,030	Value: 37.50			

KM# 1065 2500000 LIRA
31.5800 g., 0.9250 Silver .9392 oz. ASW **Subject:** Forestry - "TEMA" **Obverse:** Value and date within wreath **Reverse:** Wheel of trees design, similar to 750000 Lira, KM#1068

Date	Mintage	F	VF	XF	Unc
1998 Proof	Est. 4,537	Value: 22.50			

KM# 1070 2500000 LIRA
31.4400 g., 0.9250 Silver .9350 oz. ASW **Subject:** 75 Years of Peace **Obverse:** Value and date within wreath **Reverse:** Doves, treaty, and radiant sun

Date	Mintage	F	VF	XF	Unc
1998 Proof	2,394	Value: 30.00			

KM# 1084 2500000 LIRA
23.3000 g., 0.9250 Silver .6929 oz. ASW **Obverse:** Value and date within wreath **Reverse:** Head of Atatürk left **Edge:** Reeded **Mint:** Istanbul

Date	Mintage	F	VF	XF	Unc
1998 Proof	4,694	Value: 30.00			

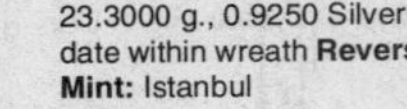

KM# 1083 2500000 LIRA

31.3500 g., 0.9250 Silver .9323 oz. ASW **Series:** 2000 Olympics **Obverse:** Value and date within wreath **Reverse:** Weight lifter and mosque **Edge:** Reeded **Note:** Struck at Istanbul.

Date	Mintage	F	VF	XF	Unc
1998 Proof	4,983	Value: 27.50			

KM# 1071 3000000 LIRA

31.3233 g., 0.9250 Silver .9315 oz. ASW **Subject:** 75 Years of Peace **Obverse:** 75th Anniversary logo above inscription, value below flanked by sprigs **Reverse:** Doves, treaty, and radiant sun

Date	Mintage	F	VF	XF	Unc
ND(1998) Proof	4,352	Value: 30.00			

KM# 1072 3000000 LIRA

31.3233 g., 0.9250 Silver .9315 oz. ASW **Subject:** 75th Anniversary Republic **Obverse:** 75th Anniversary logo **Reverse:** Atatürk's revolution

Date	Mintage	F	VF	XF	Unc
ND(1998) Proof	3,513	Value: 32.50			

KM# 1073 3000000 LIRA

31.3233 g., 0.9250 Silver .9315 oz. ASW **Subject:** 75th Anniversary of Republic **Obverse:** 75th Anniversary logo **Reverse:** Couple dancing, people in background

Date	Mintage	F	VF	XF	Unc
ND(1998) Proof	4,150	Value: 30.00			

KM# 1074 3000000 LIRA

31.3233 g., 0.9250 Silver .9315 oz. ASW **Obverse:** 75th Anniversary logo **Reverse:** Ataturk with children

Date	Mintage	F	VF	XF	Unc
ND(1998) Proof	3,701	Value: 32.50			

KM# 1075 3000000 LIRA

31.3233 g., 0.9250 Silver .9315 oz. ASW **Obverse:** 75th Anniversary logo **Reverse:** Atatürk with cane before crowd

Date	Mintage	F	VF	XF	Unc
ND(1998) Proof	6,199	Value: 30.00			

KM# 1076 3000000 LIRA

31.3233 g., 0.9250 Silver .9315 oz. ASW **Obverse:** 75th Anniversary logo **Reverse:** Depictions of arts and sciences in Turkey

Date	Mintage	F	VF	XF	Unc
ND(1998) Proof	3,522	Value: 30.00			

KM# 1086 3000000 LIRA

31.3600 g., 0.9250 Silver .9326 oz. ASW **Subject:** Galata Kulesi **Obverse:** Value and date within wreath **Reverse:** Tower and city view above "EURO"

Date	Mintage	F	VF	XF	Unc
1998 Proof	7,843	Value: 30.00			

KM# 1080 3000000 LIRA

31.3600 g., 0.9250 Silver .9326 oz. ASW **Subject:** Dolmabahce Sarayi Palace **Obverse:** Value within wreath **Reverse:** Building above "EURO" with stars above **Edge:** Reeded **Note:** Struck at Istanbul.

Date	Mintage	F	VF	XF	Unc
1998 Proof	1,710	Value: 50.00			

KM# 1107 3000000 LIRA

31.4700 g., 0.9250 Silver .9359 oz. ASW, 38.6 mm. **Series:** Olympics **Obverse:** Value and date within wreath **Reverse:** Long jumper and logo **Edge:** Reeded **Mint:** Istanbul

Date	Mintage	F	VF	XF	Unc
1999 Proof	31,000	Value: 32.50			

KM# 1108 4000000 LIRA

31.4700 g., 0.9250 Silver .9359 oz. ASW, 38.6 mm. **Subject:** Ataturk **Obverse:** Value and date within wreath **Reverse:** Half length bust right below "EURO" flanked by stars **Edge:** Reeded **Mint:** Istanbul

Date	Mintage	F	VF	XF	Unc
1999 Proof	4,596	Value: 32.50			

KM# 1087 4000000 LIRA

31.4000 g., 0.9250 Silver .9338 oz. ASW **Subject:** Fethiye **Obverse:** Value within wreath **Reverse:** Two sailing ships **Edge:** Reeded **Mint:** Istanbul

Date	Mintage	F	VF	XF	Unc
1999 Proof	3,857	Value: 35.00			

KM# 1088 4000000 LIRA

31.4000 g., 0.9250 Silver .9338 oz. ASW **Subject:** 80th Anniversary - Atatürk's Landing at Samsun **Obverse:** Value and date within wreath **Reverse:** Bust right above steamship

Date	Mintage	F	VF	XF	Unc
1999 Proof	1,632	Value: 45.00			

KM# 1089 4000000 LIRA

31.4000 g., 0.9250 Silver .9338 oz. ASW **Subject:** Istanbul Culture Capital **Obverse:** Value and date within wreath **Reverse:** Capital building

Date	Mintage	F	VF	XF	Unc
1999 Proof	1,180	Value: 55.00			

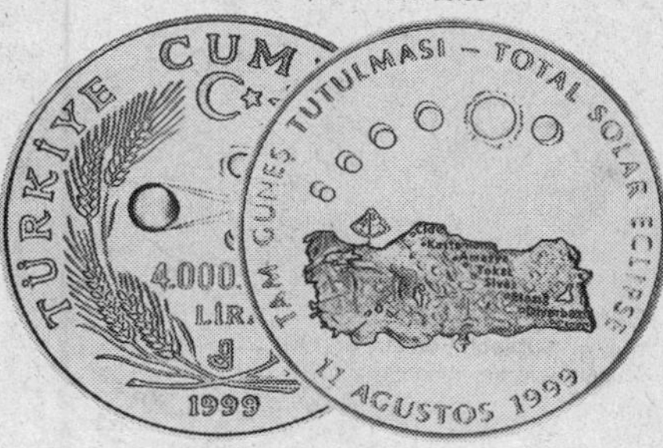

KM# 1090 4000000 LIRA

31.4000 g., 0.9250 Silver .9338 oz. ASW **Subject:** Solar Eclipse **Obverse:** Value within wreath **Reverse:** Eclipse stages above map

Date	Mintage	F	VF	XF	Unc
1999 Proof	2,520	Value: 50.00			

KM# 1091 4000000 LIRA

31.4000 g., 0.9250 Silver .9338 oz. ASW **Subject:** Solar Eclipse **Obverse:** Value and date within wreath **Reverse:** People watching eclipse

Date	Mintage	F	VF	XF	Unc
1999 Proof	2,327	Value: 50.00			

KM# 1092 4000000 LIRA

31.4000 g., 0.9250 Silver .9338 oz. ASW **Subject:** Silk Road **Obverse:** Scroll design with landmarks **Reverse:** Mounted archer hunting lion **Note:** Antiqued finish.

Date	Mintage	F	VF	XF	Unc
1999 Proof	1,263	Value: 55.00			

KM# 1093 4000000 LIRA

31.4000 g., 0.9250 Silver .9338 oz. ASW **Subject:** Osman Gazi **Obverse:** Value within wreath **Reverse:** Turbaned 1/2-length bust facing

Date	Mintage	F	VF	XF	Unc
1999 Proof	2,408	Value: 50.00			

KM# 1094 4000000 LIRA

31.4000 g., 0.9250 Silver .9338 oz. ASW **Obverse:** Value within wreath **Reverse:** Gazi leading mounted troops

Date	Mintage	F	VF	XF	Unc
1999 Proof	2,483	Value: 45.00			

KM# 1095 4000000 LIRA
31.4000 g., 0.9250 Silver .9338 oz. ASW **Obverse:** Value within wreath **Reverse:** Mounted archers and prey

Date	Mintage	F	VF	XF	Unc
1999 Proof	2,336	Value: 45.00			

KM# 1099 4000000 LIRA
31.4100 g., 0.9250 Silver .9341 oz. ASW, 38.6 mm. **Subject:** Lacerta Clarkorum **Obverse:** Value and date within wreath **Reverse:** Two Clark's lizards **Edge:** Reeded **Mint:** Istanbul

Date	Mintage	F	VF	XF	Unc
1999 Proof	2,608	Value: 55.00			

KM# 1096 4000000 LIRA
31.4000 g., 0.9250 Silver .9338 oz. ASW **Obverse:** Value within wreath **Reverse:** 700-year-old Islamic coin design

Date	Mintage	F	VF	XF	Unc
1999 Proof	2,483	Value: 45.00			

KM# 1109 4000000 LIRA
31.4700 g., 0.9250 Silver .9359 oz. ASW, 38.6 mm. **Subject:** "Bogazici" (Bosphorus) **Obverse:** Value within wreath **Reverse:** Water front mosque above "EURO" **Edge:** Reeded **Mint:** Istanbul

Date	Mintage	F	VF	XF	Unc
1999 Proof	5,692	Value: 35.00			

KM# 1097 60000000 LIRA
15.0000 g., 0.9167 Gold .4921 oz. AGW **Subject:** 700th Anniversary - The Ottoman Empire **Obverse:** Value within wreath **Reverse:** Ottoman coat of arms **Edge:** Reeded **Mint:** Istanbul

Date	Mintage	F	VF	XF	Unc
1999 Proof	1,904	Value: 400			

KM# 1101 7500000 LIRA
31.4000 g., 0.9250 Silver .9338 oz. ASW, 38.6 mm. **Subject:** 34th World Chess Olympiad **Obverse:** World globe with chess pieces within circle **Reverse:** Logo and horse head **Edge:** Reeded **Mint:** Istanbul

Date	Mintage	F	VF	XF	Unc
2000 Proof	1,318	Value: 62.50			

KM# 1102 7500000 LIRA
23.3300 g., 0.9250 Silver .6938 oz. ASW, 38.6 mm. **Subject:** UNICEF **Obverse:** Value within wreath **Reverse:** Two children candle dancing **Edge:** Reeded **Mint:** Istanbul

Date	Mintage	F	VF	XF	Unc
2000 Proof	—	Value: 50.00			

KM# 1111 7500000 LIRA
31.4700 g., 0.9250 Silver .9359 oz. ASW, 38.6 mm. **Subject:** Ephesus' Celcius Library **Obverse:** Mint logo and value within circle **Reverse:** Building **Edge:** Reeded **Mint:** Istanbul

Date	Mintage	F	VF	XF	Unc
2000 Matte	1,042	—	—	—	40.00
2000 Proof	1,171	Value: 40.00			

KM# 1112 7500000 LIRA
31.4700 g., 0.9250 Silver .9359 oz. ASW **Subject:** Traditional Turkish Theater **Obverse:** Mint logo and value within circle **Reverse:** Marionette theater scene **Mint:** Istanbul

Date	Mintage	F	VF	XF	Unc
2000 Proof	1,183	Value: 40.00			

KM# 1113 7500000 LIRA
31.4700 g., 0.9250 Silver .9359 oz. ASW **Subject:** United Nations Summit **Obverse:** Coiled rope design within circle **Reverse:** UN logo and stylized 2000 **Mint:** Istanbul

Date	Mintage	F	VF	XF	Unc
2000 Proof	1,026	Value: 40.00			

KM# 1114 7500000 LIRA
31.4700 g., 0.9250 Silver .9359 oz. ASW **Subject:** Turkish European Union Candidacy **Obverse:** Inscription within circular design **Reverse:** Cluster of flags behind star and crescent within star border **Mint:** Istanbul

Date	Mintage	F	VF	XF	Unc
2000 Proof	1,202	Value: 40.00			

KM# 1115 7500000 LIRA
31.4700 g., 0.9250 Silver .9359 oz. ASW **Subject:** First Female Pilots **Obverse:** Turkish pilot's badge within circle **Reverse:** Early female pilot saluting **Mint:** Istanbul

Date	Mintage	F	VF	XF	Unc
2000 Proof	1,148	Value: 40.00			

KM# 1116 7500000 LIRA
31.4700 g., 0.9990 Silver 1.0108 oz. ASW **Subject:** President Clinton's Turkish Visit **Obverse:** Mint logo within circle **Reverse:** Clinton holding baby

Date	Mintage	F	VF	XF	Unc
2000 Proof	1,490	Value: 40.00			

KM# 1119 150000000 LIRA
Bi-Metallic 0.916 Gold center in 0.925 Silver ring, 38.6 mm. **Subject:** President Clinton's Turkish Visit **Obverse:** Mint logo **Reverse:** Clinton holding baby **Edge:** Reeded **Mint:** Istanbul

Date	Mintage	F	VF	XF	Unc
2000 Proof	444	Value: 750			

GOLD BULLION COINAGE

Since 1943, the Turkish government has issued regular and deluxe gold coins in five denominations corresponding to the old traditional 25, 50, 100, 250, and 500 Kurus of the Ottoman period. The regular coins are all dated 1923, plus the year of the republic (e.g. 1923/40 = 1963), de Luxe coins bear actual AD dates. For a few years, 1944-1950, the bust of Ismet Inonu replaced that of Kemal Ataturk.

KM# 850 25 KURUSH
1.8041 g., 0.9170 Gold .0532 oz. AGW, 15 mm. **Obverse:** Head of Ismet Inonu

Date	Mintage	F	VF	XF	Unc
1923/20	—	BV	50.00	65.00	90.00
1923/22	3,228	BV	50.00	75.00	120
1923/23	2,757	BV	50.00	75.00	120
1923/24	46,000	BV	50.00	65.00	90.00
1923/25	20,000	BV	50.00	70.00	110
1923/26	11,000	BV	50.00	70.00	110

KM# 851 25 KURUSH
1.8041 g., 0.9170 Gold .0532 oz. AGW **Obverse:** Head of Atatürk left **Reverse:** Legend and date within wreath

Date	Mintage	F	VF	XF	Unc
1923/20	14,000	—	BV	40.00	55.00
1923/27	18,000	—	BV	40.00	55.00
1923/28	15,000	—	BV	40.00	55.00
1923/29	15,000	—	BV	40.00	55.00
1923/30	17,000	—	BV	40.00	55.00
1923/31	19,000	—	BV	40.00	55.00
1923/32	5,455	—	BV	40.00	55.00
1923/33	11,000	—	BV	40.00	55.00
1923/34	20,000	—	BV	40.00	55.00
1923/35	25,000	—	BV	40.00	55.00
1923/36	34,000	—	BV	40.00	55.00
1923/37	31,000	—	BV	40.00	55.00
1923/38	35,000	—	BV	40.00	55.00
1923/39	46,000	—	BV	40.00	55.00
1923/40	49,000	—	BV	40.00	55.00
1923/41	59,000	—	BV	40.00	55.00
1923/42	74,000	—	BV	40.00	55.00
1923/43	90,000	—	BV	40.00	55.00
1923/44	85,000	—	BV	40.00	55.00

Date	Mintage	F	VF	XF	Unc
1923/45	73,000	—	BV	40.00	55.00
1923/46	89,000	—	BV	40.00	55.00
1923/47	119,000	—	BV	40.00	55.00
1923/48	112,000	—	BV	40.00	55.00
1923/49	112,000	—	BV	40.00	55.00
1923/50	67,000	—	BV	40.00	55.00
1923/51	40,000	—	BV	40.00	55.00
1923/52	71,000	—	BV	40.00	55.00
1923/53	124,000	—	BV	40.00	55.00
1923/54	196	—	BV	40.00	55.00
1923/55	112,000	—	BV	40.00	55.00
1923/56	—	—	BV	40.00	55.00
1923/57	—	—	BV	40.00	55.00
1923/60	—	—	BV	40.00	55.00
1923/64	—	—	BV	40.00	55.00
1923/65	—	—	BV	40.00	55.00
1923/66	—	—	BV	40.00	55.00

KM# 870 25 KURUSH

1.7540 g., 0.9170 Gold .0517 oz. AGW **Series:** Monnaie de Luxe **Obverse:** Head of Atatürk left **Reverse:** Country name and date in ornate monogram within circle of stars, floral border surrounds

Date	Mintage	F	VF	XF	Unc
1942	138	—	50.00	75.00	150
1943	386	—	50.00	75.00	125
1944	811	—	50.00	75.00	125
1946	235	—	50.00	75.00	150
1950	2,053	—	BV	45.00	60.00
1951	2,035	—	BV	45.00	60.00
1952	3,374	—	BV	45.00	60.00
1953	1,944	—	BV	45.00	60.00
1954	2,244	—	BV	45.00	60.00
1955	2,573	—	BV	45.00	60.00
1956	4,004	—	BV	45.00	60.00
1957	8,842	—	BV	45.00	60.00
1958	9,546	—	BV	45.00	60.00
1959	17,000	—	BV	40.00	55.00
1960	19,000	—	BV	40.00	55.00
1961	35,000	—	BV	40.00	55.00
1962	31,000	—	BV	40.00	55.00
1963	47,000	—	BV	40.00	55.00
1964	57,000	—	BV	40.00	55.00
1965	78,000	—	BV	40.00	55.00
1966	106,000	—	BV	40.00	55.00
1967	114,000	—	BV	40.00	55.00
1968	152,000	—	BV	40.00	55.00
1969	163,000	—	BV	40.00	55.00
1970	224,000	—	BV	40.00	55.00
1971	306,000	—	BV	40.00	55.00
1972	271,000	—	BV	40.00	55.00
1973	162,000	—	BV	40.00	55.00
1974	141,000	—	BV	40.00	55.00
1975	202,000	—	BV	40.00	55.00
1976	583,000	—	BV	40.00	55.00
1977	1,089,000	—	BV	40.00	55.00
1978	238,000	—	BV	40.00	55.00
1980	—	—	BV	40.00	55.00

KM# 875 25 KURUSH

1.7540 g., 0.9170 Gold .0517 oz. AGW **Series:** Monnaie de Luxe **Obverse:** Head of Ismet Inonu left

Date	Mintage	F	VF	XF	Unc
1943	—	70.00	90.00	140	200
Note: Mintage included in KM#870					
1944	—	70.00	90.00	140	200
Note: Mintage included in KM#870					
1945	592	70.00	90.00	140	200
1946	—	70.00	90.00	140	200
Note: Mintage included in KM#870					
1947	3,443	70.00	90.00	125	185
1948	714	70.00	90.00	140	200
1949	552	70.00	90.00	140	200

KM# 852 50 KURUSH

3.6083 g., 0.9170 Gold .1063 oz. AGW, 18 mm. **Obverse:** Head of Ismet Inonu left

Date	Mintage	F	VF	XF	Unc
1923/20	—	BV	95.00	125	175
1923/22	1,093	BV	95.00	125	175
1923/23	897	BV	120	140	200
1923/24	11,000	BV	95.00	125	175
1923/25	3,004	BV	95.00	125	175
1923/26	817	BV	120	140	200
1923/27	5,228	BV	95.00	125	175

KM# 853 50 KURUSH

3.6083 g., 0.9170 Gold .1063 oz. AGW **Obverse:** Head of Atatürk left **Reverse:** Legend and date within wreath

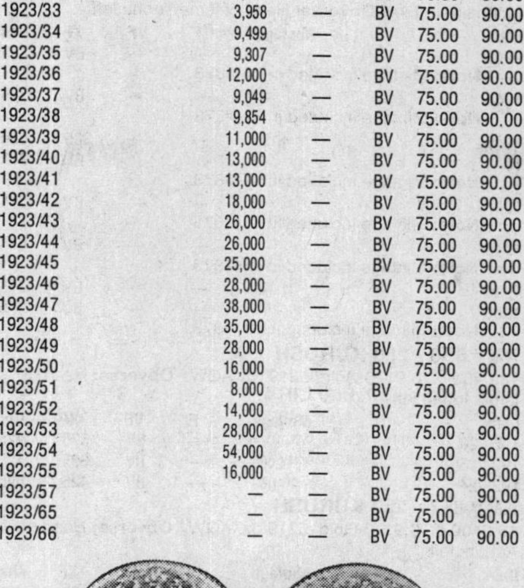

Date	Mintage	F	VF	XF	Unc
1923/20	12,000	—	BV	75.00	90.00
1923/27	Inc. above	—	BV	75.00	90.00
1923/28	3,300	—	BV	75.00	90.00
1923/29	6,384	—	BV	75.00	90.00
1923/30	4,590	—	BV	75.00	90.00
1923/31	9,068	—	BV	75.00	90.00
1923/32	4,344	—	BV	75.00	90.00
1923/33	3,958	—	BV	75.00	90.00
1923/34	9,499	—	BV	75.00	90.00
1923/35	9,307	—	BV	75.00	90.00
1923/36	12,000	—	BV	75.00	90.00
1923/37	9,049	—	BV	75.00	90.00
1923/38	9,854	—	BV	75.00	90.00
1923/39	11,000	—	BV	75.00	90.00
1923/40	13,000	—	BV	75.00	90.00
1923/41	13,000	—	BV	75.00	90.00
1923/42	18,000	—	BV	75.00	90.00
1923/43	26,000	—	BV	75.00	90.00
1923/44	26,000	—	BV	75.00	90.00
1923/45	25,000	—	BV	75.00	90.00
1923/46	28,000	—	BV	75.00	90.00
1923/47	38,000	—	BV	75.00	90.00
1923/48	35,000	—	BV	75.00	90.00
1923/49	28,000	—	BV	75.00	90.00
1923/50	16,000	—	BV	75.00	90.00
1923/51	8,000	—	BV	75.00	90.00
1923/52	14,000	—	BV	75.00	90.00
1923/53	28,000	—	BV	75.00	90.00
1923/54	54,000	—	BV	75.00	90.00
1923/55	16,000	—	BV	75.00	90.00
1923/57	—	—	BV	75.00	90.00
1923/65	—	—	BV	75.00	90.00
1923/66	—	—	BV	75.00	90.00

KM# 871 50 KURUSH

3.5080 g., 0.9170 Gold .1034 oz. AGW **Series:** Monnaie de Luxe **Obverse:** Head of Kemal Atatürk left within circle of stars, wreath surrounds **Reverse:** Country name and date in ornate monogram within circle of stars, floral border surrounds

Date	Mintage	F	VF	XF	Unc
1942	115	100	150	200	250
1943	91	100	150	200	250
1944	950	80.00	120	140	175
1946	565	80.00	120	140	175
1950	1,971	—	BV	80.00	140
1951	1,780	—	BV	80.00	140
1952	2,557	—	BV	80.00	140
1953	2,392	—	BV	80.00	140
1954	1,714	—	BV	80.00	140
1955	4,143	—	BV	75.00	115
1956	2,956	—	BV	75.00	115
1957	6,855	—	BV	75.00	115
1958	6,381	—	BV	75.00	115
1959	12,000	—	—	BV	75.00
1960	12,000	—	—	BV	75.00
1961	15,000	—	—	BV	75.00
1962	22,000	—	—	BV	75.00
1963	29,000	—	—	BV	75.00
1964	34,000	—	—	BV	75.00
1965	44,000	—	—	BV	75.00
1966	58,000	—	—	BV	75.00
1967	64,000	—	—	BV	75.00
1968	82,000	—	—	BV	75.00
1969	79,000	—	—	BV	75.00
1970	109,000	—	—	BV	75.00
1971	154,000	—	—	BV	75.00
1972	110,000	—	—	BV	75.00
1973	73,000	—	—	BV	75.00
1974	45,000	—	—	BV	75.00
1975	72,000	—	—	BV	75.00
1976	196,000	—	—	BV	75.00
1977	361,000	—	—	BV	75.00
1978	161,000	—	—	BV	75.00
1980	—	—	—	BV	75.00

KM# 876 50 KURUSH

3.5080 g., 0.9170 Gold .1034 oz. AGW **Series:** Monnaie de Luxe **Obverse:** Head of Ismet Inonu left

Date	Mintage	F	VF	XF	Unc
1943	—	—	150	200	250
Note: Mintage included in KM#871					
1944	—	—	120	170	220
Note: Mintage included in KM#871					
1946	—	—	90.00	140	190
Note: Mintage included in KM#871					
1947	3,481	—	90.00	140	190
1948	773	—	90.00	140	190
1949	582	—	90.00	140	190

KM# 872 100 KURUSH

7.0160 g., 0.9170 Gold .2069 oz. AGW **Series:** Monnaie de Luxe **Obverse:** Head of Atatürk left within circle of stars, wreath surrounds **Reverse:** Country name and date in ornate monogram within circle of stars, floral border surrounds

Date	Mintage	F	VF	XF	Unc
1942	8,659	—	145	160	225
1943	6,594	—	145	160	225
1944	7,160	—	145	160	225
1948	14,000	—	145	160	200
1950	25,000	—	145	160	200
1951	35,000	—	145	160	185
1952	41,000	—	145	160	185
1953	32,000	—	145	160	185
1954	24,000	—	145	160	185
1955	4,881	—	145	160	200
1956	11,000	—	BV	145	160
1957	49,000	—	BV	145	160
1958	67,000	—	BV	145	160
1959	89,000	—	BV	145	160
1960	57,000	—	BV	145	160
1961	77,000	—	BV	145	160
1962	108,000	—	BV	145	160
1963	146,000	—	BV	145	160
1964	128,000	—	BV	145	160
1965	157,000	—	BV	145	160
1966	190,000	—	BV	145	160
1967	177,000	—	BV	145	160
1968	143,000	—	BV	145	160
1969	206,000	—	BV	145	160
1970	253,000	—	BV	145	160
1971	293,000	—	BV	145	160
1972	222,000	—	BV	145	160
1973	140,000	—	BV	145	160
1974	82,000	—	BV	145	160
1975	142,000	—	BV	145	160
1976	265,000	—	BV	145	160
1977	277,000	—	BV	145	160
1978	86,000	—	BV	145	160
1980	—	—	BV	145	160

KM# 877 100 KURUSH

7.0160 g., 0.9170 Gold .2069 oz. AGW, 22 mm. **Series:** Monnaie de Luxe **Obverse:** Head of Ismet Inonu left

Date	Mintage	F	VF	XF	Unc
1943	—	150	190	265	325
Note: Mintage included in KM#872					
1944	—	150	190	265	375
Note: Mintage included in KM#872					
1945	2,202	150	190	265	400
1946	8,863	150	190	265	325
1947	28,000	150	190	265	325
1948	—	150	190	265	325
Note: Mintage included in KM#872					
1949	6,578	150	190	265	325
1950	—	150	190	265	325
Note: Mintage included in KM#872					

KM# 854 100 KURUSH

7.2160 g., 0.9170 Gold .2126 oz. AGW **Obverse:** Head of Ismet Inonu left **Reverse:** legend and date within wreath

Date	Mintage	F	VF	XF	Unc
1923/20	—	—	BV	150	165
1923/22 Rare	3	—	—	—	—
1923/23	381,000	—	BV	150	165
1923/24	2,274	—	BV	155	175
1923/25	28,000	—	BV	150	165
1923/26	2,097	—	BV	155	175
1923/27	17,000	—	BV	150	165

KM# 855 100 KURUSH

7.2160 g., 0.9170 Gold .2126 oz. AGW **Obverse:** Head of Atatürk left **Reverse:** Legend and date within wreath

Date	Mintage	F	VF	XF	Unc
1923/20	29,000	—	—	BV	150
1923/27	Inc. above	—	—	BV	150
1923/28 Rare	3	—	—	—	—
1923/29	2,111	—	—	BV	150
1923/30	13,000	—	—	BV	150
1923/31	109,000	—	—	BV	150
1923/32	134,000	—	—	BV	150
1923/33	216,000	—	—	BV	150
1923/34	463,000	—	—	BV	150
1923/35	405,000	—	—	BV	150
1923/36	25,000	—	—	BV	150
1923/37	131,000	—	—	BV	150
1923/38	159,000	—	—	BV	150
1923/39	85,000	—	—	BV	150
1923/40	10,000	—	—	BV	150
1923/41	164,000	—	—	BV	150
1923/42	63,000	—	—	BV	150
1923/43	56,000	—	—	BV	150
1923/44	198,000	—	—	BV	150
1923/45	176,000	—	—	BV	150
1923/46	1,290,000	—	—	BV	150
1923/47	513,000	—	—	BV	150
1923/48	600	—	—	BV	165
1923/49	1,300	—	—	BV	165
1923/50	47,000	—	—	BV	150
1923/51	240,000	—	—	BV	150
1923/52	1,046,999	—	—	BV	150
1923/53	550,000	—	—	BV	150
1923/54	18,000	—	—	BV	150
1923/55	309,000	—	—	BV	150
1923/57	—	—	—	BV	150
1923/58	—	—	—	BV	150
1923/59	—	—	—	BV	150
1923/60	—	—	—	BV	150
1923/61	—	—	—	BV	150
1923/62	—	—	—	BV	150
1923/63	—	—	—	BV	150
1923/64	—	—	—	BV	150
1923/65	—	—	—	BV	150

KM# 873 250 KURUSH

17.5400 g., 0.9170 Gold .5169 oz. AGW **Series:** Monnaie de Luxe **Obverse:** Head of Atatürk left within circle of stars, wreath surrounds **Reverse:** Country name and date in ornate monogram within circle of stars, floral border surrounds

Date	Mintage	F	VF	XF	Unc
1942	10,000	—	385	425	600
1943	11,000	—	385	425	600
1944	15,000	—	385	650	900
1946	16,000	—	385	650	900
1947	42,000	—	385	425	600
1948	13,000	—	385	425	600
1950	45,000	—	385	425	600
1951	41,000	—	—	BV	375
1952	59,000	—	—	BV	375
1953	45,000	—	—	BV	375
1954	40,000	—	—	BV	375
1955	7,067	—	—	BV	375
1956	14,000	—	—	BV	375
1957	47,000	—	—	BV	375
1958	75,000	—	—	BV	375
1959	93,000	—	—	BV	375
1960	50,000	—	—	BV	375
1961	65,000	—	—	BV	375
1962	99,000	—	—	BV	375
1963	137,000	—	—	BV	375
1964	152,000	—	—	BV	375
1965	194,000	—	—	BV	375
1966	218,000	—	—	BV	375
1967	201,000	—	—	BV	375
1968	150,000	—	—	BV	375
1969	262,000	—	—	BV	375
1970	301,000	—	—	BV	375
1971	356,000	—	—	BV	375
1972	305,000	—	—	BV	375
1973	198,000	—	—	BV	375
1974	142,000	—	—	BV	375
1975	223,000	—	—	BV	375
1976	345,000	—	—	BV	375
1977	227,000	—	—	BV	375
1978	311,000	—	—	BV	375
1980	—	—	—	BV	375

KM# 878 250 KURUSH

17.5400 g., 0.9170 Gold .5169 oz. AGW, 27 mm. **Series:** Monnaie de Luxe **Obverse:** Head of Ismet Inonu left

Date	Mintage	F	VF	XF	Unc
1943	—	—	—	BV	375
Note: Mintage included in KM#873					
1944	—	—	—	BV	375
Note: Mintage included in KM#873					
1945	4,135	—	—	385	550
1946	—	—	—	BV	375
Note: Mintage included in KM#873					
1947	—	—	—	BV	375
Note: Mintage included in KM#873					
1948	—	—	—	BV	375
Note: Mintage included in KM#873					
1949	11,000	—	—	BV	375
1950	—	—	—	BV	375
Note: Mintage included in KM#873					

KM# 856 250 KURUSH

18.0400 g., 0.9170 Gold .5319 oz. AGW **Obverse:** Head of Ismet Inonu left

Date	Mintage	F	VF	XF	Unc
1923/20	—	—	BV	395	425
1923/23	14,000	—	BV	395	425
1923/24	60	—	BV	425	525

KM# 857 250 KURUSH

18.0400 g., 0.9170 Gold .5319 oz. AGW **Obverse:** Head of Atatürk left

Date	Mintage	F	VF	XF	Unc
1923/20	10,000	—	—	BV	400
1923/29 Rare	3	—	—	—	—
1923/30	130	—	450	700	900
1923/31	—	—	450	700	900
1923/38	245	—	395	425	600
1923/39	389	—	395	425	600
1923/40	435	—	395	425	600
1923/41	349	—	395	425	600
1923/42	460	—	395	425	600
1923/43	1,008	—	BV	395	425
1923/44	712	—	BV	395	425
1923/45	1,034	—	BV	395	425
1923/46	1,035	—	BV	395	425
1923/47	1,408	—	BV	395	425
1923/48	904	—	BV	395	425
1923/49	1,066	—	BV	395	425
1923/50	975	—	BV	395	425
1923/51	298	—	BV	395	425
1923/52	610	—	BV	395	425
1923/53	586	—	BV	395	425
1923/54	289	—	BV	395	425
1923/55	267	—	BV	395	425
1923/57	—	—	BV	395	425
1923/70	—	—	BV	395	425

KM# 858 500 KURUSH

36.0800 g., 0.9170 Gold 1.0638 oz. AGW, 35 mm. **Obverse:** Head of Ismet Inonu left **Reverse:** Legend and date within wreath

Date	Mintage	F	VF	XF	Unc
1923/20	—	—	BV	750	850
1923/23	9,006	—	BV	750	850
1923/24	7,923	—	750	850	1,000
1923/25	272	—	800	950	1,100

KM# 859 500 KURUSH

36.0800 g., 0.9170 Gold 1.0638 oz. AGW **Obverse:** Head of Atatürk left **Reverse:** Legend and date within wreath

Date	Mintage	F	VF	XF	Unc
1923/20	12,000	—	BV	750	800
1923/27	615	—	BV	850	1,000
1923/28	34	—	BV	850	1,000
1923/29	137	—	BV	800	950
1923/30	45	—	BV	800	950
1923/31	100	—	BV	800	950
1923/32	74	—	BV	800	950
1923/33	268	—	BV	750	850
1923/34	758	—	BV	750	850
1923/35	1,586	—	—	BV	750
1923/36	765	—	—	BV	750
1923/37	983	—	—	BV	750
1923/38	1,738	—	—	BV	750
1923/39	2,629	—	—	BV	750
1923/40	2,763	—	—	BV	750
1923/41	3,440	—	—	BV	750
1923/42	3,335	—	—	BV	750
1923/43	4,914	—	—	BV	750
1923/44	4,308	—	—	BV	750
1923/45	3,488	—	—	BV	750
1923/46	5,636	—	—	BV	750
1923/47	7,588	—	—	BV	750
1923/48	6,060	—	—	BV	750
1923/49	4,235	—	—	BV	750
1923/50	4,733	—	—	BV	750
1923/51	2,757	—	—	BV	750
1923/52	2,041	—	—	BV	750
1923/53	4,819	—	—	BV	750
1923/54	1,401	—	—	BV	750
1923/55	1,484	—	—	BV	750
1923/57	—	—	—	BV	750
1923/69	—	—	—	BV	750

KM# 874 500 KURUSH

35.0800 g., 0.9170 Gold 1.0338 oz. AGW **Series:** Monnaie de Luxe **Obverse:** Head of Atatürk left within circle of stars, wreath surrounds **Reverse:** Country name and date in ornate monogram within circle of stars, floral border surrounds

Date	Mintage	F	VF	XF	Unc
1942	2,949	—	—	BV	745
1943	1,210	—	—	BV	745
1944	1,254	—	—	BV	745
1947	3,699	—	—	BV	745
1950	59	—	—	BV	760
1951	21	—	—	BV	760
1952	26	—	—	BV	760
1953	35	—	—	BV	760
1954	182	—	—	BV	760
1955	14	—	—	BV	760
1956	13	—	—	BV	760
1957	68	—	—	BV	760
1958	121	—	—	BV	760
1959	294	—	—	BV	760
1960	208	—	—	BV	760
1961	619	—	—	BV	745
1962	1,228	—	—	BV	745
1963	1,985	—	—	BV	745
1964	2,787	—	—	BV	745
1965	4,631	—	—	BV	745
1966	5,572	—	—	BV	745
1967	6,637	—	—	BV	745
1968	5,983	—	—	BV	745
1969	7,152	—	—	BV	745
1970	11,000	—	—	BV	745
1971	15,000	—	—	BV	745
1972	15,000	—	—	BV	745
1973	7,939	—	—	BV	745
1974	5,412	—	—	BV	745
1975	6,205	—	—	BV	745
1976	11,000	—	—	BV	745
1977	6,931	—	—	BV	745
1978	5,740	—	—	BV	745
1980	—	—	—	BV	745

KM# 879 500 KURUSH
35.0800 g., 0.9170 Gold 1.0338 oz. AGW **Series:** Monnaie de Luxe **Obverse:** Head of Ismet Inonu left within circle of stars **Reverse:** Country name and date in ornate monogram within circle of stars, floral border surrounds

Date	Mintage	F	VF	XF	Unc
1943	—	—	—	BV	745
Note: Mintage included in KM#874					
1944	—	—	—	BV	745
Note: Mintage included in KM#874					
1945	115	—	—	BV	745
1946	298	—	—	BV	745
1947	—	—	—	BV	745
Note: Mintage included in KM#874					
1948	40	—	—	BV	745

PATTERNS

Including off metal strikes

KM#	Date	Mintage	Identification	Mkt Val
Pn9	1948	—	5 Kurus. Brass. . KM#887. Prev. KM#Pn2.	500
Pn10	1948	—	10 Kurus. Brass. . KM#888. Prev. KM#Pn3.	500

PIEFORTS

KM#	Date	Mintage	Identification	Mkt Val
P1	1981	2,500	500 Lira. 0.9250 Silver. . KM#931	165
P2	1981	1,200	3000 Lira. 0.9250 Silver. . KM#948	180
P3	1981	—	30000 Lira. Gold. . KM#955	1,350
P4	1982	600	3000 Lira. 0.9250 Silver. . KM#959	125

MINT SETS

KM#	Date	Mintage	Identification	Issue Price	Mkt Val
MSA1	1949 (8)	—	KM#881-888	—	—
MS1	1962 (7)	—	KM#889a.1, 890.1, 891.1, 892.2, 893.1, 894 (1960), 895	—	—
MSA2	1963 (6)	—	KM#889a.1, 890.1, 891.1, 892.2, 893.1, 895a	—	—
MS2	1964 (6)	—	KM#889a.1, 890.1, 891.1, 892.2, 893.1, 895a	—	4.50
MS3	1965 (6)	—	KM#889a.1, 890.1, 891.1, 892.2, 893.1, 895a	—	4.50
MS4	1966 (6)	—	KM#889a.1, 890.1, 891.1, 892.2, 893.1, 895a	—	4.50
MSA5	1967 (6)	—	KM#889a.2, 890.1, 891.1, 892.3, 893.1, 895a	—	—
MS5	1968 (6)	—	KM#889a.2, 890.1, 891.1, 892.3, 893.1, 895a	—	4.50
MS6	1969 (6)	—	KM#889a.2, 890.2, 891.2, 892.3, 893.2, 895a	—	3.50
MS7	1970 (6)	—	KM#889a.2, 890.2, 891.2, 892.3, 893.2, 895a	—	3.50
MS8	1971 (6)	—	KM#889a.2, 890.2, 891.2, 893.2, 895a, 899	—	3.50
MS9	1972 (6)	—	KM#889a.2, 890.2, 891.2, 893.2, 895a, 899	—	3.50
MS10	1973 (7)	—	KM#889a.2, 890.2, 891.2, 892.3, 893.2, 895a, 899	—	3.00
MS11	1974 (7)	—	KM#889a.2, 890.3-892.3, 893.2, 895a, 899	—	3.00
MS12	1975 (7)	—	KM#889a.2, 890a, 891a, 893.2, 895c, 899, 905	—	3.00
MS13	1976 (7)	—	KM#889a.2, 890a, 891a, 893.2, 895c, 899, 905	—	3.00
MS14	1977 (8)	—	KM#889a.2, 890a, 891a, 892.3, 893.2, 895c, 899, 905	—	3.50
MS15	1978 (4)	—	KM#889a.2, 892.3, 893.2, 905	—	3.00
MS16	1979 (4)	—	KM#889a.2, 893.2, 899, 905	—	3.00
MS17	1980 (2)	—	KM#889a.2, 893.2	—	2.00
MS18	1981 (3)	—	KM#943-945	—	3.00
MS19	1982 (3)	—	KM#943, 949.1, 950.1	—	3.00
MS20	1983 (2)	—	KM#949.2, 950.2	—	3.00
MS21	1984 (6)	—	KM#962-967	—	5.50
MS22	1985 (6)	—	KM#962-964, 966, 967, 975	—	5.00
MS23	1986 (5)	—	KM#963-967	—	4.00
MS24	1989 (7)	9,350	KM#962-964, 975, 987, 988, and medal	2.00	2.00
MS25	1990 (5)	5,300	KM#987-989, 996, 997, and medal	4.00	8.50
MS26	1991 (5)	2,250	KM#987-989, 997, 1015, and mint medal	—	20.00
MS27	1992 (6)	2,240	KM#987-989, 997, 1015, 1025, and mint medal	—	20.00
MS28	1993 (6)	1,750	KM#987-989, 997, 1015, 1025, and mint medal	—	20.00
MS29	1994 (8)	2,500	KM#987-989, 997, 1015, 1025, 1027, 1042, plus mint medal	—	20.00
MS30	1995 (7)	2,500	KM#989, 1015, 1027-1029, 1041, 1043, plus mint medal	—	15.00
MS31	1996 (8)	10,000	KM#989, 1015, 1027-1029, 1041, 1050, 1056, plus mint medal	—	8.00
MS32	1997 (7)	—	KM#989, 1015, 1027.2, 1028, 1029, 1041, 1056, plus silver mint medal	—	20.00
MS33	2000 (3)	10,000	KM#860.1a, 893.1a, 905a Mixed dates; Silver Coin Nostalgia Set	60.00	—
MS34	2000 (4)	25,000	KM#881a, 884a, 885a, 886a Mixed dates; Gold Coin Nostalgia Set	325	—
MS35	2000 (7)	10,000	KM#860.1a, 881a, 884a, 885a, 886a, 893.1a, 905a Mixed dates; Silver and Gold Nostalgia Set	350	—

TURKMENISTAN

The Turkmenistan Republic (formerly the Turkmen Soviet Socialist Republic) covers the territory of the Trans-Caspian Region of Turkestan, the Charjiui Vilayet of Bukhara and the part of Khiva located on the right bank of the Oxus. Bordered on the north by the Autonomous Kara-Kalpak Republic (a constituent of Uzbekistan), by Iran and Afghanistan on the south, by the Usbek Republic on the east and the Caspian Sea on the west. It has an area of 186,400 sq. mi. (488,100 sq. km.) and a population of 3.5 million. Capital: Ashkhabad (formerly Poltoratsk). Main occupation is agricultural products including cotton and maize. It is rich in minerals, oil, coal, sulphur and salt and is also famous for its carpets, Turkoman horses and Karakui sheep.

The Turkomans arrived in Trancaspia as nomadic Seluk Turks in the 11th century. It often became subjected to one of the neighboring states. Late in the 19th century the Czarist Russians invaded with their first victory at Kyzyl Arvat in 1877, arriving in Ashkhabad in 1882 resulting in submission of the Turkmen tribes. By March 18,1884 the Transcaspian province of Russian Turkestan was formed. During WW I the Czarist government tried to conscript the Turkmen; this led to a revolt in Oct. 1916 under the leadership of Aziz Chapykov. In 1918 the Turks captured Baku from the Red army and the British sent a contingent to Merv to prevent a German-Turkish offensive toward Afghanistan and India. In mid-1919 a Bureau of Turkestan Moslem Communist Organization was formed in Moscow hoping to develop one large republic including all surrounding Turkic areas within a Soviet federation. A Turkestan Autonomous Soviet Socialist Republic was formed and plans to partition Turkestan into five republics according to the principle of nationalities was quickly implemented by Joseph Stalin. On Oct. 27, 1924 Turkmenistan became a Soviet Socialist Republic and was accepted as a member of the U.S.S.R. on Jan. 29, 1925. The Bureau of T.M.C.O. was disbanded in 1934. In Aug. 1990 the Turkmen Supreme Soviet adopted a declaration of sovereignty followed by a declaration of independence in Oct. 1991 joining the Commonwealth of Independent States in Dec. A new constitution was adopted in 1992 providing for an executive presidency.

REPUBLIC

STANDARD COINAGE

100 Tenge = 1 Manat

KM# 1 TENGE
1.9000 g., Copper Plated Steel, 16 mm. **Obv:** Value in center of flower-like design within circle **Rev:** Head of President Saparmyrat Nyyazow left **Edge:** Plain

Date	Mintage	F	VF	XF	Unc	BU
1993	—	—	—	—	0.25	0.35

KM# 2 5 TENGE
3.0000 g., Copper Plated Steel, 19.5 mm. **Obv:** Value in center of flower-like design within circle **Rev:** Head of President Saparmyrat Nyyazow left **Edge:** Plain

Date	Mintage	F	VF	XF	Unc	BU
1993	—	—	—	—	0.35	0.45

KM# 3 10 TENGE
4.5000 g., Copper Plated Steel, 22.5 mm. **Obv:** Value in center of designs within circle **Rev:** Head of President Saparmyrat Nyyazow left **Edge:** Plain

Date	Mintage	F	VF	XF	Unc	BU
1993	—	—	—	—	0.60	0.75

KM# 4 20 TENGE
3.6000 g., Nickel Plated Steel, 20.9 mm. **Obv:** Value within ornate circle **Rev:** Head of President Saparmyrat Nyyazow left **Edge:** Plain

Date	Mintage	F	VF	XF	Unc	BU
1993	—	—	—	—	1.25	1.50

KM# 5 50 TENGE
4.9000 g., Nickel Plated Steel, 24 mm. **Obv:** Value above animal leaning on horn at right **Rev:** Head of President Saparmyrat Nyyazow left **Edge:** Plain

Date	Mintage	F	VF	XF	Unc	BU
1993	—	—	—	—	2.75	3.00

KM# 6 500 MANAT
28.2800 g., 0.9250 Silver .8410 oz. ASW **Series:** Endangered Wildlife **Obv:** Head of President Saparmyrat Nyyazow left **Rev:** Goitered gazelle

Date	Mintage	F	VF	XF	Unc	BU
1996 Proof	Est. 5,000	Value: 60.00				

KM# 7 500 MANAT
28.2800 g., 0.9250 Silver .8410 oz. ASW **Series:** Endangered Wildlife **Obv:** Head of President Saparmyrat Nyyazow left **Rev:** Purple Swamphen

Date	Mintage	F	VF	XF	Unc	BU
1996 Proof	Est. 5,000	Value: 60.00				

KM# 8 500 MANAT
28.2800 g., 0.9250 Silver .8410 oz. ASW **Series:** Endangered Wildlife **Subject:** Kaspi Ular **Obv:** Head of President Saparmyrat Nyyazow left **Rev:** Pair of Caspian Ular snowcock

Date	Mintage	F	VF	XF	Unc	BU
1996 Proof	Est. 5,000	Value: 60.00				

KM# 9 500 MANAT
28.2800 g., 0.9250 Silver .8410 oz. ASW **Series:** Endangered Wildlife **Subject:** Manul **Obv:** Head of President Saparmyrat Nyyazow left **Rev:** Pallas' cat

Date	Mintage	F	VF	XF	Unc	BU
1996 Proof	Est. 5,000	Value: 65.00				

KM# 10 500 MANAT
28.2800 g., 0.9250 Silver .8410 oz. ASW **Series:** Endangered Wildlife **Subject:** Gulan **Obv:** Head of President Saparmyrat Nyyazow left **Rev:** Asian wild ass

Date	Mintage	F	VF	XF	Unc	BU
1996 Proof	Est. 5,000	Value: 60.00				

KM# 11 500 MANAT
28.2800 g., 0.9250 Silver .8410 oz. ASW **Series:** Endangered Wildlife **Subject:** Turkmen Eublefary **Obv:** Head of President Saparmyrat Nyyazow left **Rev:** Gecko

Date	Mintage	F	VF	XF	Unc	BU
1996 Proof	Est. 5,000	Value: 65.00				

KM# 12 500 MANAT
Nickel Clad Steel **Obv:** Head of President Saparmyrat Nyyazow left **Rev:** Crown and value within circle **Edge:** Reeded

Date	Mintage	F	VF	XF	Unc	BU
1999	Est. 5,000	—	—	—	1.25	1.50

KM# 14 500 MANAT
28.2800 g., 0.9250 Silver .8410 oz. ASW **Series:** Wildlife Series **Subject:** Jaculus Turkmenicus **Obv:** Head of President Saparmyrat Nyyazow left **Rev:** Two Turkmenic Jerboa **Edge:** Reeded

Date	Mintage	F	VF	XF	Unc	BU
1999 Proof	Est. 5,000	Value: 65.00				

KM# 15 500 MANAT
28.2800 g., 0.9250 Silver .8410 oz. ASW **Series:** Wildlife Series **Subject:** Chlamydotis Undulata **Obv:** Head of President Saparmyrat Nyyazow left **Rev:** Two Houbara Bustards

Date	Mintage	F	VF	XF	Unc	BU
1999 Proof	Est. 5,000	Value: 60.00				

KM# 16 500 MANAT
28.2800 g., 0.9250 Silver .8410 oz. ASW **Series:** Wildlife Series **Subject:** Falco cherrug **Obv:** Head of President Saparmyrat Nyyazow left **Rev:** Saker falcon on branch and falconer at left

Date	Mintage	F	VF	XF	Unc	BU
1999 Proof	Est. 5,000	Value: 65.00				

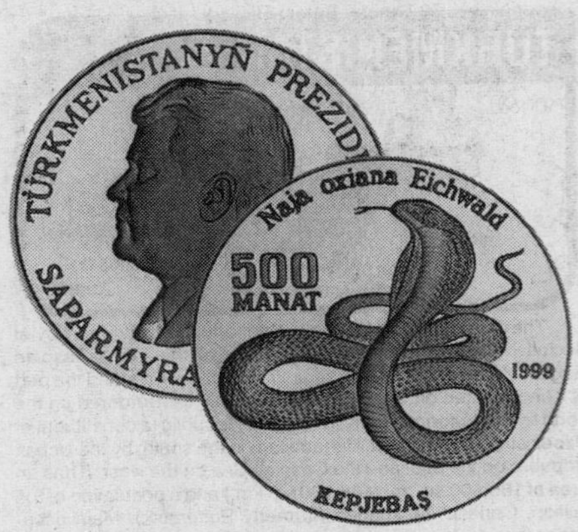

KM# 17 500 MANAT
28.2800 g., 0.9250 Silver .8410 oz. ASW **Series:** Wildlife Series **Subject:** Naja Oxiana **Obv:** Head of President Saparmyrat Nyyazow left **Rev:** Cobra

Date	Mintage	F	VF	XF	Unc	BU
1999 Proof	Est. 5,000	Value: 65.00				

KM# 18 500 MANAT
28.2800 g., 0.9250 Silver .8410 oz. ASW **Series:** Wildlife Series **Subject:** Felis Caracal **Obv:** Head of President Saparmyrat Nyyazow left **Rev:** Seated caracal

Date	Mintage	F	VF	XF	Unc	BU
1999 Proof	Est. 5,000	Value: 65.00				

KM# 19 500 MANAT
28.2800 g., 0.9250 Silver .8410 oz. ASW **Series:** Wildlife Series **Subject:** Panthera tigris **Obv:** Head of President Saparmyrat Nyyazow left **Rev:** Tiger

Date	Mintage	F	VF	XF	Unc	BU
1999 Proof	Est. 5,000	Value: 65.00				

KM# 20 500 MANAT
28.2800 g., 0.9250 Silver 0.841 oz. ASW, 38.5 mm. **Subject:** 5th Anniversary of Neutrality **Obv:** Head of President Saparmyrat Nyyazow left within circle **Rev:** Map and monument within sprigs and circle **Edge:** Reeded

Date	Mintage	F	VF	XF	Unc	BU
ND Proof	5,000	Value: 45.00				

KM# 21 500 MANAT
28.2800 g., 0.9250 Silver 0.841 oz. ASW, 38.5 mm. **Subject:** 5th Anniversary of Neutrality **Obv:** Head of President Saparmyrat Nyyazow left within circle **Rev:** Astanbaba Mausoleum within circle **Edge:** Reeded

Date	Mintage	F	VF	XF	Unc	BU
2000 Proof	5,000	Value: 45.00				

KM# 22 500 MANAT
28.2800 g., 0.9250 Silver 0.841 oz. ASW, 38.5 mm. **Obv:** Head of President Saparmyrat Nyyazow left within circle **Rev:** Square based Soltan Sanjar Mausoleum within circle **Edge:** Reeded

Date	Mintage	F	VF	XF	Unc	BU
2000 Proof	5,000	Value: 45.00				

KM# 23 500 MANAT
28.2800 g., 0.9250 Silver 0.841 oz. ASW, 38.5 mm. **Obv:** Head of President Saparmyrat Nyyazow left within circle **Rev:** Shirkebir Mausoleum - Mosque within circle **Edge:** Reeded

Date	Mintage	F	VF	XF	Unc	BU
2000 Proof	5,000	Value: 45.00				

KM# 24 500 MANAT
28.2800 g., 0.9250 Silver 0.841 oz. ASW, 38.5 mm. **Obv:** Head left within circle **Rev:** Nisa Fortress, statue with mountaintop in background **Edge:** Reeded

Date	Mintage	F	VF	XF	Unc	BU
2000 Proof	5,000	Value: 45.00				

KM# 25 500 MANAT
28.2800 g., 0.9250 Silver 0.841 oz. ASW, 38.5 mm. **Subject:** 10th Anniversary of Independence **Obv:** Head of President Saparmyrat Nyyazow left within circle **Rev:** Monument divides dates within circle **Edge:** Reeded

Date	Mintage	F	VF	XF	Unc	BU
2000 Proof	5,000	Value: 45.00				

KM# 13 1000 MANAT
Nickel Clad Steel **Obv:** Head of President Saparmyrat Nyyazow left within circle **Rev:** Value within circle **Edge:** Reeded

Date	Mintage	F	VF	XF	Unc	BU
1999 Proof	—	—	—	—	2.50	3.00

PROOF SETS

KM#	Date	Mintage	Identification	Issue Price	Mkt Val
PS1	1996 (6)	5,000	KM#6-11	—	210

TURKS & CAICOS ISLANDS

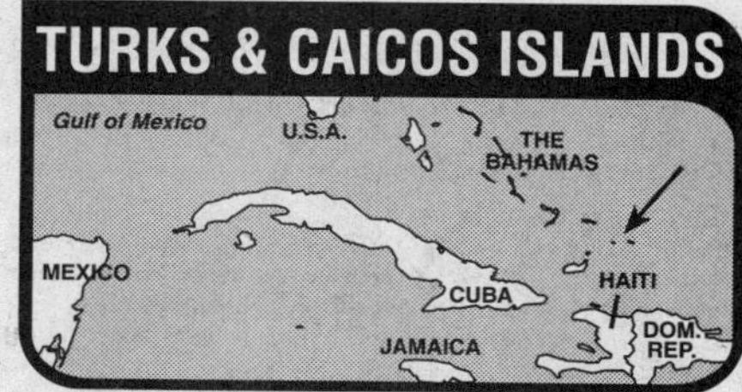

The Colony of the Turks and Caicos Islands, a British colony situated in the West Indies at the eastern end of the Bahama Islands, has an area of 166 sq. mi. (430 sq.km.) and a population of *10,000. Capital: Cockburn Town, on Grand Turk. The principal industry of the colony is the production of salt, which is gathered by raking. Salt, crayfish, and conch shells are exported.

The Turks and Caicos Islands were discovered by Juan Ponce de Leon in 1512, but were not settled until 1678 when Bermudians arrived to rake salt from the salt ponds. The Spanish drove the British settlers from the island in 1710, during the long War of the Spanish Succession. They returned and throughout the remaining years of the war repulsed repeated attacks by France and Spain. In 1799 the islands were granted representation in the Bahamian assembly, but in 1848, on petition of the inhabitants, they were made a separate colony under Jamaica. They were annexed by Jamaica in 1873 and remained a dependency until 1959 when they became a unit territory of the Federation of the West Indies. When the Federation was dissolved in 1962, the Turks and Caicos Islands became a separate Crown Colony.

RULERS

British

MONETARY SYSTEM

100 Cents = 1 East Caribbean Dollar
1 Crown = 1 Dollar U.S.A.

CROWN COLONY

STANDARD COINAGE

KM# 51 1/4 CROWN

Copper-Nickel, 24.3 mm. **Ruler:** Elizabeth II **Obv:** Young bust right **Obv. Designer:** Arnold Machin **Rev:** Spiny Lobster

Date	Mintage	F	VF	XF	Unc	BU
1981	—	—	—	0.75	1.50	2.50

KM# 52 1/2 CROWN

11.3500 g., Copper-Nickel, 30.65 mm. **Ruler:** Elizabeth II **Obv:** Young bust right **Obv. Designer:** Arnold Machin **Rev:** Windmill

Date	Mintage	F	VF	XF	Unc	BU
1981	—	—	—	1.00	2.00	3.00

KM# 1 CROWN

Copper-Nickel, 38.5 mm. **Ruler:** Elizabeth II **Obv:** Young bust right **Obv. Designer:** Arnold Machin **Rev:** National arms

Date	Mintage	F	VF	XF	Unc	BU
1969	50,000	—	—	2.00	4.50	5.50
1969 Proof	6,000	Value: 12.50				

KM# 5 CROWN

Copper-Nickel, 36 mm. **Ruler:** Elizabeth II **Obv:** Young bust right **Obv. Designer:** Arnold Machin **Rev:** Map **Edge Lettering:** REDEEMABLE AT TURKS AND CAICOS FOR US CURRENCY

Date	Mintage	F	VF	XF	Unc	BU
1975 Matte	590	—	—	—	12.00	14.00
1975 Proof	1,370	Value: 13.50				
1976	1,960	—	—	—	7.00	9.00
1976 Proof	2,270	Value: 13.50				
1977 Proof	1,420	Value: 13.50				

KM# 60 CROWN

Copper-Nickel, 38.5 mm. **Ruler:** Elizabeth II **Subject:** Prince Andrew's Marriage **Obv:** Young bust right **Obv. Designer:** Arnold Machin **Rev:** Conjoined heads right

Date	Mintage	F	VF	XF	Unc	BU
1986	20,000	—	—	2.00	4.50	6.50

KM# 60a CROWN

28.2800 g., 0.9250 Silver .8411 oz. ASW, 38.5 mm. **Ruler:** Elizabeth II **Subject:** Prince Andrew's Marriage **Obv:** Young bust right **Rev:** Conjoined heads right

Date	Mintage	F	VF	XF	Unc	BU
1986 Proof	5,000	Value: 13.50				

KM# 122 CROWN

Copper-Nickel, 38.5 mm. **Ruler:** Elizabeth II **Obv:** Young bust right **Obv. Designer:** Arnold Machin **Rev:** National arms

Date	Mintage	F	VF	XF	Unc	BU
1986	—	—	—	2.00	4.00	5.00

KM# 64 CROWN

Copper-Nickel, 38.5 mm. **Ruler:** Elizabeth II **Series:** World Wildlife Fund **Obv:** Young bust right **Obv. Designer:** Arnold Machin **Rev:** Iguana within circle

Date	Mintage	F	VF	XF	Unc	BU
1988	—	—	—	3.00	7.50	12.00

KM# 64a CROWN

28.2800 g., 0.9250 Silver .8411 oz. ASW, 38.5 mm. **Ruler:** Elizabeth II **Series:** World Wildlife Fund **Obv:** Young bust right **Obv. Designer:** Arnold Machin **Rev:** Iguana within circle

Date	Mintage	F	VF	XF	Unc	BU
1988 Proof	Est. 25,000	Value: 25.00				

KM# 66 CROWN

Copper-Nickel, 38.5 mm. **Ruler:** Elizabeth II **Subject:** Queen Mother's 90th Birthday **Obv:** Crowned head right **Obv. Designer:** Raphael Maklouf **Rev:** Crowned monogram flanked by thistle stems **Rev. Designer:** Robert Elderton

Date	Mintage	F	VF	XF	Unc	BU
ND(1990)	—	—	—	2.00	5.50	6.50

KM# 66a CROWN

28.2800 g., 0.9250 Silver .8411 oz. ASW, 38.5 mm. **Ruler:** Elizabeth II **Subject:** Queen Mother's 90th Birthday **Obv:** Crowned head right **Obv. Designer:** Raphael Maklouf **Rev:** Crowned monogram flanked by thistle stems **Rev. Designer:** Robert Elderton

Date	Mintage	F	VF	XF	Unc	BU
ND(1990) Proof	Est. 10,000	Value: 22.50				

KM# 74 CROWN

Copper-Nickel **Ruler:** Elizabeth II **Subject:** Royal Birthdays **Obv:** Crowned head right **Rev:** Conjoined heads of Queen Elizabeth II and Prince Philip facing

Date	Mintage	F	VF	XF	Unc	BU
1991	—	—	—	2.00	4.50	6.50

KM# 74a CROWN

31.1200 g., 0.9990 Silver 0.9995 oz. ASW, 39.1 mm. **Ruler:** Elizabeth II **Subject:** Royal Birthdays **Obv:** Crowned head right **Rev:** Conjoined heads of Queen Elizabeth II and Prince Philip facing **Edge:** Reeded with plain section containing fineness

Date	Mintage	F	VF	XF	Unc	BU
1991 Proof	—	Value: 27.50				

KM# 76 CROWN

Copper-Nickel **Ruler:** Elizabeth II **Subject:** 10th Wedding Anniversary - Prince and Princess of Wales **Obv:** Crowned head right **Rev:** Head of Princess Diana facing

Date	Mintage	F	VF	XF	Unc	BU
1991	—	—	—	2.00	4.00	5.00

KM# 76a CROWN

31.1200 g., 0.9990 Silver 0.9995 oz. ASW, 39.1 mm. **Ruler:** Elizabeth II **Subject:** 10th Wedding Anniversary - Prince Charles and Princess Diana **Obv:** Crowned head right **Rev:** Head of Princess Diana facing **Edge:** Reeded with plain section containing fineness

Date	Mintage	F	VF	XF	Unc	BU
1991 Proof	—	Value: 40.00				

KM# 121 CROWN

Copper-Nickel **Ruler:** Elizabeth II **Subject:** 10th Wedding Anniversary - Prince and Princess of Wales **Obv:** Crowned head right **Rev:** Head of Prince Charles facing

Date	Mintage	F	VF	XF	Unc	BU
1991	—	—	—	2.00	4.00	5.00

KM# 121a CROWN

31.2100 g., 0.9250 Silver .9282 oz. ASW **Ruler:** Elizabeth II **Subject:** 10th Wedding Anniversary of Prince Charles and Princess Diana **Obv:** Crowned head right **Rev:** Head of Prince Charles facing

Date	Mintage	F	VF	XF	Unc	BU
1991 Proof	—	Value: 35.00				

KM# 143 DOLLAR

Copper-Nickel **Ruler:** Elizabeth II **Series:** Steam Locomotive **Subject:** City of Truro **Obv:** Crowned head right **Rev:** Locomotive train **Note:** Similar to 20 Dollars, KM#145.

Date	Mintage	F	VF	XF	Unc	BU
1996	—	—	—	2.00	5.00	6.50

KM# 146 DOLLAR

Copper-Nickel **Ruler:** Elizabeth II **Series:** Steam Locomotive **Subject:** Flying Scotsman **Obv:** Crowned head right **Rev:** Locomotive train **Note:** Similar to 20 Dollars, KM#148.

Date	Mintage	F	VF	XF	Unc	BU
1996	—	—	—	2.00	5.00	6.50

KM# 149 DOLLAR

Copper-Nickel **Ruler:** Elizabeth II **Series:** Steam Locomotive **Subject:** Rocket **Obv:** Crowned head right **Rev:** Locomotive train **Note:** Similar to 20 Dollars, KM#151.

Date	Mintage	F	VF	XF	Unc	BU
1996	—	—	—	2.00	5.00	6.50

KM# 152 DOLLAR

Copper-Nickel **Ruler:** Elizabeth II **Series:** Steam Locomotive **Subject:** Evening Star **Obv:** Crowned head right **Rev:** Locomotive train **Note:** Similar to 20 Dollars, KM#154.

Date	Mintage	F	VF	XF	Unc	BU
1996	—	—	—	2.00	5.00	6.50

KM# 155 DOLLAR

Copper-Nickel **Ruler:** Elizabeth II **Series:** Steam Locomotive **Subject:** Mallard **Obv:** Crowned head right **Rev:** Locomotive train **Note:** Similar to 20 Dollars, KM#157.

Date	Mintage	F	VF	XF	Unc	BU
1996	—	—	—	2.00	5.00	6.50

KM# 158 DOLLAR

Copper-Nickel **Ruler:** Elizabeth II **Series:** Steam Locomotive **Subject:** Princess Elizabeth **Obv:** Crowned head right **Rev:** Locomotive train **Note:** Similar to 20 Dollars, KM#160.

Date	Mintage	F	VF	XF	Unc	BU
1996	—	—	—	2.00	5.00	6.50

KM# 161 DOLLAR

Copper-Nickel **Ruler:** Elizabeth II **Series:** Steam Locomotive **Subject:** Southern Pacific Lines - Class GS4 **Obv:** Crowned head right **Rev:** Locomotive train **Note:** Similar to 20 Dollars, KM#163.

Date	Mintage	F	VF	XF	Unc	BU
1996	—	—	—	2.00	5.00	6.50

KM# 164 DOLLAR

Copper-Nickel **Ruler:** Elizabeth II **Series:** Steam Locomotive **Subject:** German States Railway Class 05 **Obv:** Crowned head right **Rev:** Locomotive train **Note:** Similar to 20 Dollars, KM#166.

Date	Mintage	F	VF	XF	Unc	BU
1996	—	—	—	2.00	5.00	6.50

KM# 167 DOLLAR

Copper-Nickel **Ruler:** Elizabeth II **Series:** Steam Locomotive **Subject:** Japanese National Railways Class 62 **Obv:** Crowned head right **Rev:** Locomotive train **Note:** Similar to 20 Dollars, KM#169.

Date	Mintage	F	VF	XF	Unc	BU
1996	—	—	—	2.00	5.00	6.50

KM# 170 DOLLAR

Copper-Nickel **Ruler:** Elizabeth II **Series:** Steam Locomotive **Subject:** Chinese State Railways Class RM **Obv:** Crowned head right **Rev:** Locomotive train **Note:** Similar to 20 Dollars, KM#171.

Date	Mintage	F	VF	XF	Unc	BU
1996	—	—	—	2.00	5.00	6.50

KM# 6 5 CROWNS

24.2400 g., 0.5000 Silver .3897 oz. ASW **Ruler:** Elizabeth II **Obv:** Young bust right **Obv. Designer:** Arnold Machin **Rev:** Turks-head cactus

Date	Mintage	F	VF	XF	Unc	BU
1975 Matte	440	—	—	9.00	18.00	20.00
1975 Proof	1,320	Value: 13.50				
1976	1,760	—	—	6.00	11.50	13.50
1976 Proof	2,220	Value: 11.50				
1977 Proof	1,370	Value: 13.50				

KM# 47 5 CROWNS

14.5800 g., 0.5000 Silver .2344 oz. ASW **Ruler:** Elizabeth II **Subject:** Lord Mountbatten **Obv:** Young bust right **Rev:** Uniformed head left above crossed flag and sword

Date	Mintage	F	VF	XF	Unc	BU
1980 Proof	—	Value: 9.50				

KM# 75 5 CROWNS

Copper-Nickel **Ruler:** Elizabeth II **Subject:** Discovery of America **Obv:** Young bust right **Obv. Designer:** Arnold Machin **Rev:** Columbus before Ferdinand and Isabella

Date	Mintage	F	VF	XF	Unc	BU
1991	—	—	—	3.00	7.50	9.00

KM# 68 5 CROWNS

Copper-Nickel **Ruler:** Elizabeth II **Series:** Olympics **Obv:** National arms **Rev:** Equestrian and 3 events

Date	Mintage	F	VF	XF	Unc	BU
1992	—	—	—	2.00	4.50	6.50

KM# 69 5 CROWNS

Copper-Nickel **Ruler:** Elizabeth II **Series:** Olympics **Obv:** National arms **Rev:** Gymnast on rings and 5 events

Date	Mintage	F	VF	XF	Unc	BU
1992	—	—	—	2.00	4.50	6.50

KM# 70 5 CROWNS

Copper-Nickel **Ruler:** Elizabeth II **Series:** Olympics **Obv:** National arms **Rev:** Weightlifting and 3 events

Date	Mintage	F	VF	XF	Unc	BU
1992	—	—	—	2.00	4.50	6.50

KM# 71 5 CROWNS

Copper-Nickel **Ruler:** Elizabeth II **Series:** Olympics **Obv:** National arms **Rev:** Rifle shooting and 3 events

Date	Mintage	F	VF	XF	Unc	BU
1992	—	—	—	2.00	4.50	6.50

KM# 72 5 CROWNS

Copper-Nickel **Ruler:** Elizabeth II **Series:** Olympics **Obv:** National arms **Rev:** Sail boarding and 3 events

Date	Mintage	F	VF	XF	Unc	BU
1992	—	—	—	2.00	4.50	6.50

KM# 73 5 CROWNS

Copper-Nickel **Ruler:** Elizabeth II **Series:** Olympics **Obv:** National arms **Rev:** Ski jumper and 4 events

Date	Mintage	F	VF	XF	Unc	BU
1992	—	—	—	2.00	4.50	6.50

KM# 77 5 CROWNS

Copper-Nickel **Ruler:** Elizabeth II **Subject:** 40th Anniversary - Reign of Elizabeth II **Obv:** National arms **Rev:** Crowned bust facing

Date	Mintage	F	VF	XF	Unc	BU
1992	—	—	—	3.00	6.75	7.25

KM# 77a 5 CROWNS

28.0400 g., 0.9250 Silver .8339 oz. ASW **Ruler:** Elizabeth II **Subject:** 40th Anniversary - Reign of Elizabeth II **Obv:** National arms **Rev:** Crowned bust facing

Date	Mintage	F	VF	XF	Unc	BU
1992 Proof	—	Value: 40.00				

KM# 84 5 CROWNS

Copper-Nickel **Ruler:** Elizabeth II **Subject:** 40th Anniversary - Reign of Elizabeth II **Obv:** Crowned head right **Rev:** Conjoined busts of Queen Elizabeth II and Prince Philip facing

Date	Mintage	F	VF	XF	Unc	BU
1992	—	—	—	3.00	6.75	7.25

KM# 84a 5 CROWNS

28.0400 g., 0.9250 Silver .8339 oz. ASW **Ruler:** Elizabeth II **Subject:** 40th Anniversary - Reign of Elizabeth II **Obv:** Crowned head right **Rev:** Conjoined busts of Queen Elizabeth II and Prince Philip facing

Date	Mintage	F	VF	XF	Unc	BU
1992 Proof	—	Value: 40.00				

KM# 85 5 CROWNS

Copper-Nickel **Ruler:** Elizabeth II **Subject:** 40th Anniversary - Reign of Elizabeth II **Obv:** Crowned head right **Rev:** Head of King George VI facing

Date	Mintage	F	VF	XF	Unc	BU
1992	—	—	—	3.00	6.75	7.25

KM# 85a 5 CROWNS

28.0400 g., 0.9250 Silver .8339 oz. ASW **Ruler:** Elizabeth II **Subject:** 40th Anniversary - Reign of Elizabeth II **Obv:** Crowned head right **Rev:** Head of King George VI facing

Date	Mintage	F	VF	XF	Unc	BU
1992 Proof	—	Value: 40.00				

KM# 86 5 CROWNS

Copper-Nickel **Ruler:** Elizabeth II **Subject:** 40th Anniversary - Reign of Elizabeth II **Obv:** Crowned head right **Rev:** Windsor Castle

Date	Mintage	F	VF	XF	Unc	BU
1992	—	—	—	3.00	6.75	7.25

KM# 86a 5 CROWNS

28.2800 g., 0.9250 Silver .8339 oz. ASW **Ruler:** Elizabeth II **Subject:** 40th Anniversary - Reign of Elizabeth II **Obv:** Crowned head right **Rev:** Windsor Castle

Date	Mintage	F	VF	XF	Unc	BU
1992 Proof	—	Value: 40.00				

KM# 87 5 CROWNS

Copper-Nickel **Ruler:** Elizabeth II **Subject:** World Cup '94 **Obv:** Crowned head right **Rev:** Jules Rimet and trophy

Date	Mintage	F	VF	XF	Unc	BU
ND(1993)	—	—	—	3.00	6.50	7.50

KM# 88 5 CROWNS

Copper-Nickel **Ruler:** Elizabeth II **Subject:** World Cup '94 - Uruguay Winners **Obv:** Crowned head right **Rev:** Soccer players shaking hands

Date	Mintage	F	VF	XF	Unc	BU
ND(1993)	—	—	—	3.00	6.50	7.50

KM# 89 5 CROWNS

Copper-Nickel **Ruler:** Elizabeth II **Subject:** World Cup '94 - Italy Winners **Obv:** Crowned head right **Rev:** Dino Zoff holding trophy

Date	Mintage	F	VF	XF	Unc	BU
ND(1993)	—	—	—	3.00	6.50	7.50

KM# 90 5 CROWNS

Copper-Nickel **Ruler:** Elizabeth II **Subject:** World Cup '94 - West Germany winners **Obv:** Crowned head right **Rev:** Franz Beckenbauer

Date	Mintage	F	VF	XF	Unc	BU
ND(1993)	—	—	—	3.00	6.50	7.50

KM# 91 5 CROWNS

Copper-Nickel **Ruler:** Elizabeth II **Subject:** World Cup '94 - Brazil Winners **Obv:** Crowned head right **Rev:** Pelé with arm raised

Date	Mintage	F	VF	XF	Unc	BU
ND(1993)	—	—	—	3.00	6.50	7.50

KM# 92 5 CROWNS

Copper-Nickel **Ruler:** Elizabeth II **Subject:** World Cup '94 - England Winners **Obv:** Crowned head right **Rev:** Bobby Moore with trophy on teammates shoulders

Date	Mintage	F	VF	XF	Unc	BU
ND(1993)	—	—	—	3.00	6.50	7.50

KM# 93 5 CROWNS

Copper-Nickel **Ruler:** Elizabeth II **Subject:** World Cup '94 - Argentina winners **Obv:** Crowned head right **Rev:** Mario Kempes running right

Date	Mintage	F	VF	XF	Unc	BU
ND(1993)	—	—	—	3.00	6.50	7.50

KM# 94 5 CROWNS

Copper-Nickel **Ruler:** Elizabeth II **Subject:** World Cup '94 - USA Host **Obv:** Crowned head right **Rev:** Stylized flag and trophy

Date	Mintage	F	VF	XF	Unc	BU
ND(1993)	—	—	—	3.00	6.50	7.50

KM# 103 5 CROWNS

Copper-Nickel **Ruler:** Elizabeth II **Subject:** 40th Anniversary of Coronation **Obv:** Crowned head right **Rev:** Westminster Abbey

Date	Mintage	F	VF	XF	Unc	BU
ND(1993)	—	—	—	3.50	7.50	8.50

KM# 104 5 CROWNS

Copper-Nickel **Ruler:** Elizabeth II **Subject:** 40th Anniversary of Coronation **Obv:** Crowned head right **Rev:** Crown jewels

Date	Mintage	F	VF	XF	Unc	BU
ND(1993)	—	—	—	3.50	7.50	8.50

KM# 105 5 CROWNS

Copper-Nickel **Ruler:** Elizabeth II **Subject:** 40th Anniversary of Coronation **Obv:** Crowned head right **Rev:** Queen, clergy and maids of honor

Date	Mintage	F	VF	XF	Unc	BU
ND(1993)	—	—	—	3.50	7.50	8.50

KM# 106 5 CROWNS

Copper-Nickel **Ruler:** Elizabeth II **Subject:** 40th Anniversary of Coronation **Obv:** Crowned head right **Rev:** Consort's Homage

Date	Mintage	F	VF	XF	Unc	BU
ND(1993)	—	—	—	3.50	7.50	8.50

KM# 107 5 CROWNS

Copper-Nickel **Ruler:** Elizabeth II **Subject:** 40th Anniversary of Coronation **Obv:** Crowned head right **Rev:** Enthroned Queen

Date	Mintage	F	VF	XF	Unc	BU
ND(1993)	—	—	—	3.50	7.50	8.50

KM# 108 5 CROWNS

Copper-Nickel **Ruler:** Elizabeth II **Subject:** 40th Anniversary of Coronation **Obv:** Crowned head right **Rev:** Queen in coach

Date	Mintage	F	VF	XF	Unc	BU
ND(1993)	—	—	—	3.50	7.50	8.50

KM# 123 5 CROWNS

Copper-Nickel **Ruler:** Elizabeth II **Series:** 1994 Winter Olympics - Lillehammer **Obv:** Crowned head right **Rev:** Speed skater within circle

Date	Mintage	F	VF	XF	Unc	BU
1993 Prooflike	—	—	—	2.00	4.75	5.50

KM# 124 5 CROWNS

Copper-Nickel **Ruler:** Elizabeth II **Series:** 1994 Winter Olympics - Lillehammer **Obv:** Crowned head right **Rev:** Figure skater

Date	Mintage	F	VF	XF	Unc	BU
1993 Prooflike	—	—	—	2.00	4.75	5.50

KM# 125 5 CROWNS

Copper-Nickel **Ruler:** Elizabeth II **Series:** 1994 Winter Olympics - Lillehammer **Obv:** Arms with supporters **Rev:** Hockey player within circle

Date	Mintage	F	VF	XF	Unc	BU
1993 Prooflike	—	—	—	2.00	4.75	5.50

KM# 126 5 CROWNS

Copper-Nickel **Ruler:** Elizabeth II **Series:** 1994 Winter Olympics - Lillehammer **Obv:** Crowned head right **Rev:** Slalom skier within circle

Date	Mintage	F	VF	XF	Unc	BU
1993 Prooflike	—	—	—	2.00	4.75	5.50

KM# 127 5 CROWNS
Copper-Nickel **Ruler:** Elizabeth II **Series:** 1994 Winter Olympics - Lillehammer **Obv:** Crowned head right **Rev:** Ski jumper

Date	Mintage	F	VF	XF	Unc	BU
1993 Prooflike	—	—	—	2.00	4.75	5.50

KM# 128 5 CROWNS
Copper-Nickel **Ruler:** Elizabeth II **Series:** 1994 Winter Olympics - Lillehammer **Obv:** Crowned head right **Rev:** Bobsled and team within circle

Date	Mintage	F	VF	XF	Unc	BU
1993 Prooflike	—	—	—	2.00	4.75	5.50

KM# 177 5 CROWNS
Copper-Nickel **Ruler:** Elizabeth II **Subject:** 25th Anniversary 1969-1994 - Apollo 11 **Obv:** Crowned head right **Rev:** Launching rocket

Date	Mintage	F	VF	XF	Unc	BU
1993	—	—	—	3.00	6.75	7.50

KM# 178 5 CROWNS
Copper-Nickel **Ruler:** Elizabeth II **Subject:** 25th Anniversary 1969-1994 - Apollo 11 **Obv:** Crowned head right **Rev:** Lunar landing

Date	Mintage	F	VF	XF	Unc	BU
1993	—	—	—	3.00	6.75	7.50

KM# 179 5 CROWNS
Copper-Nickel **Ruler:** Elizabeth II **Subject:** 25th Anniversary 1969-1994 - Apollo 11 **Obv:** Crowned head right **Rev:** Astronaut descending ladder

Date	Mintage	F	VF	XF	Unc	BU
1993	—	—	—	3.00	6.75	7.50

KM# 181 5 CROWNS
Copper-Nickel **Ruler:** Elizabeth II **Subject:** 25th Anniversary 1969-1994 - Apollo 11 **Obv:** Crowned head right **Rev:** Astronaut walking on moon

Date	Mintage	F	VF	XF	Unc	BU
1993	—	—	—	3.00	6.75	7.50

KM# 182 5 CROWNS
Copper-Nickel **Ruler:** Elizabeth II **Subject:** 25th Anniversary 1969-1994 - Apollo 11 **Obv:** Crowned head right **Rev:** Ocean recovery

Date	Mintage	F	VF	XF	Unc	BU
1993	—	—	—	3.00	6.75	7.50

KM# 180 5 CROWNS
Copper-Nickel **Ruler:** Elizabeth II **Subject:** 25th Anniversary 1969-1994 - Apollo 11 **Obv:** Crowned head right **Rev:** Astronauts raising flag on moon

Date	Mintage	F	VF	XF	Unc	BU
1993	—	—	—	3.00	6.75	7.50

KM# 234 5 CROWNS
3.1104 g., 0.9995 Platinum 0.1 oz. APW, 16.5 mm. **Ruler:** Elizabeth II **Subject:** ANA Salute to Coin Collecting **Obv:** Crowned head right **Rev:** Astronaut on the moon **Edge:** Reeded

Date	Mintage	F	VF	XF	Unc	BU
1994 Proof	200	Value: 145				

KM# 132 5 CROWNS
Copper-Nickel **Ruler:** Elizabeth II **Subject:** 25th Anniversary 1969-1994 - Apollo 11 **Obv:** Crowned head right **Rev:** Salute to ANA and coin collecting **Rev. Designer:** Don Everhart II **Edge Lettering:** PEACE on a smooth section of alternating smooth and reeded

Date	Mintage	F	VF	XF	Unc	BU
1994 Prooflike	10,000	—	—	5.00	10.00	12.00

KM# 173 5 CROWNS
Copper-Nickel **Ruler:** Elizabeth II **Subject:** 50th Anniversary - Normandy Landing **Obv:** Crowned head right **Rev:** Bust of Sir Bertram II Ramsay left

Date	Mintage	F	VF	XF	Unc	BU
1994	—	—	—	4.50	9.50	11.00

KM# 174 5 CROWNS
Copper-Nickel **Ruler:** Elizabeth II **Subject:** 50th Anniversary - Normandy Landing **Obv:** Crowned head right **Rev:** Bust of Bernard L. Montgomery left

Date	Mintage	F	VF	XF	Unc	BU
1994	—	—	—	4.50	9.50	11.00

KM# 175 5 CROWNS
Copper-Nickel **Ruler:** Elizabeth II **Subject:** 50th Anniversary - Normandy Landing **Obv:** Crowned head right **Rev:** Bust of Omar N. Bradley right

Date	Mintage	F	VF	XF	Unc	BU
1994	—	—	—	4.50	9.50	11.00

KM# 176 5 CROWNS
Copper-Nickel **Ruler:** Elizabeth II **Subject:** 50th Anniversary - Normandy Landing **Obv:** Crowned head right **Rev:** Bust of Dwight D. Eisenhower right

Date	Mintage	F	VF	XF	Unc	BU
1994	—	—	—	4.50	9.50	11.00

KM# 133 5 CROWNS
Copper-Nickel **Ruler:** Elizabeth II **Subject:** 50th Anniversary - VE Day **Obv:** National arms **Rev:** Heads of Churchill, Roosevelt and Stalin facing

Date	Mintage	F	VF	XF	Unc	BU
1995	—	—	—	4.50	9.50	11.00

KM# 134 5 CROWNS
Copper-Nickel **Ruler:** Elizabeth II **Subject:** 50th Anniversary - VE Day **Obv:** National arms **Rev:** Planes

Date	Mintage	F	VF	XF	Unc	BU
1995	—	—	—	3.00	7.50	8.50

KM# 135 5 CROWNS
Copper-Nickel **Ruler:** Elizabeth II **Subject:** 50th Anniversary - VE Day **Obv:** Arms with supporters **Rev:** U.S. and Soviet troops meet

Date	Mintage	F	VF	XF	Unc	BU
1995	—	—	—	3.00	7.50	8.50

KM# 136 5 CROWNS
Copper-Nickel **Ruler:** Elizabeth II **Subject:** 50th Anniversary - VE Day **Obv:** Arms with supporters **Rev:** London, Washington and Paris

Date	Mintage	F	VF	XF	Unc	BU
1995	—	—	—	3.00	7.50	8.50

KM# 188 5 CROWNS
10.0000 g., 0.9990 Silver .3212 oz. ASW **Ruler:** Elizabeth II **Series:** XXVI Summer Olympics **Obv:** Crowned head right **Rev:** Hurdlers

Date	Mintage	F	VF	XF	Unc	BU
1995 Proof	—	Value: 12.50				

KM# 190 5 CROWNS
10.0000 g., 0.9990 Silver .3212 oz. ASW **Ruler:** Elizabeth II **Series:** XXVI Summer Olympics **Obv:** Crowned head right **Rev:** Cyclist

Date	Mintage	F	VF	XF	Unc	BU
1995 Proof	—	Value: 12.50				

KM# 192 5 CROWNS
10.0000 g., 0.9990 Silver .3212 oz. ASW **Ruler:** Elizabeth II **Series:** XXVI Summer Olympics **Obv:** Crowned head right **Rev:** Fencers

Date	Mintage	F	VF	XF	Unc	BU
1995 Proof	—	Value: 12.50				

KM# 194 5 CROWNS
10.0000 g., 0.9990 Silver .3212 oz. ASW **Ruler:** Elizabeth II **Series:** XXVI Summer Olympics **Obv:** Crowned head right **Rev:** Equestrian

Date	Mintage	F	VF	XF	Unc	BU
1995 Proof	—	Value: 12.50				

KM# 196 5 CROWNS
10.0000 g., 0.9990 Silver .3212 oz. ASW **Ruler:** George VI **Series:** XXVI Summer Olympics **Obv:** Crowned head right **Rev:** Pole vaulter

Date	Mintage	F	VF	XF	Unc	BU
1995 Proof	—	Value: 12.50				

KM# 198 5 CROWNS
10.0000 g., 0.9990 Silver .3212 oz. ASW **Ruler:** Elizabeth II **Series:** XXVI Summer Olympics **Obv:** Crowned head right **Rev:** Runners

Date	Mintage	F	VF	XF	Unc	BU
1995 Proof	—	Value: 12.50				

KM# 200 5 CROWNS

10.0000 g., 0.9990 Silver .3212 oz. ASW **Ruler:** Elizabeth II **Series:** XXVI Summer Olympics **Obv:** Crowned head right **Rev:** Gymnast

Date	Mintage	F	VF	XF	Unc	BU
1995 Proof	—	Value: 12.50				

KM# 202 5 CROWNS

10.0000 g., 0.9990 Silver .3212 oz. ASW **Ruler:** Elizabeth II **Series:** XXVI Summer Olympics **Obv:** Crowned head right **Rev:** Swimmer

Date	Mintage	F	VF	XF	Unc	BU
1995 Proof	—	Value: 12.50				

KM# 204 5 CROWNS

10.0000 g., 0.9990 Silver .3212 oz. ASW **Ruler:** Elizabeth II **Series:** XXVI Summer Olympics **Obv:** Crowned head right **Rev:** Diver

Date	Mintage	F	VF	XF	Unc	BU
1995 Proof	—	Value: 12.50				

KM# 206 5 CROWNS

10.0000 g., 0.9990 Silver .3212 oz. ASW **Ruler:** Elizabeth II **Series:** XXVI Summer Olympics **Obv:** Crowned head right **Rev:** Sprinter within circle **Designer:** Raphael Maklouf

Date	Mintage	F	VF	XF	Unc	BU
1995 Proof	—	Value: 12.50				

KM# 225 5 CROWNS

26.2000 g., Brass, 39.1 mm. **Ruler:** Elizabeth II **Subject:** Mother Theresa **Obv:** National arms **Rev:** Bust 1/4 left and star design within globe **Edge:** Reeded

Date	Mintage	F	VF	XF	Unc	BU
1997	—	—	—	—	10.00	12.50

KM# 238 5 CROWNS

1.5600 g., 0.9999 Gold 0.0502 oz. AGW, 13.7 mm. **Ruler:** Elizabeth II **Obv:** Crowned head right **Rev:** Two Bottle-nosed Dolphins **Edge:** Reeded

Date	Mintage	F	VF	XF	Unc	BU
1998 Proof	—	Value: 50.00				

KM# 232 5 CROWNS

26.4300 g., Copper-Nickel, 39.2 mm. **Ruler:** Elizabeth II **Subject:** Year of the Tiger **Obv:** Crowned head right **Obv. Designer:** Raphael Maklouf **Rev:** Stylized tiger within circle **Edge:** Reeded

Date	Mintage	F	VF	XF	Unc	BU
1998	—	—	—	3.00	7.50	8.50

KM# 144 5 DOLLARS

10.0000 g., 0.9990 Silver .3212 oz. ASW **Ruler:** Elizabeth II **Series:** Steam Locomotive **Subject:** City of Truro **Obv:** Crowned head right **Rev:** Locomotive train **Note:** Similar to 20 Dollars, KM#145.

Date	Mintage	F	VF	XF	Unc	BU
1996 Proof	Est. 25,000	Value: 22.00				

KM# 147 5 DOLLARS

10.0000 g., 0.9990 Silver .3212 oz. ASW **Ruler:** Elizabeth II **Series:** Steam Locomotive **Subject:** Flying Scotsman **Obv:** Crowned head right **Rev:** Locomotive train **Note:** Similar to 20 Dollars, KM#148.

Date	Mintage	F	VF	XF	Unc	BU
1996 Proof	Est. 25,000	Value: 22.00				

KM# 150 5 DOLLARS

10.0000 g., 0.9990 Silver .3212 oz. ASW **Ruler:** Elizabeth II **Series:** Steam Locomotive **Subject:** Rocket **Obv:** Crowned head right **Rev:** Locomotive train **Note:** Similar to 20 Dollars, KM#151.

Date	Mintage	F	VF	XF	Unc	BU
1996 Proof	Est. 25,000	Value: 22.00				

KM# 153 5 DOLLARS

10.0000 g., 0.9990 Silver .3212 oz. ASW **Ruler:** Elizabeth II **Series:** Steam Locomotive **Subject:** Evening Star **Obv:** Crowned head right **Rev:** Locomotive train **Note:** Similar to 20 Dollars, KM#154.

Date	Mintage	F	VF	XF	Unc	BU
1996 Proof	Est. 25,000	Value: 22.00				

KM# 156 5 DOLLARS

10.0000 g., 0.9990 Silver .3212 oz. ASW **Ruler:** Elizabeth II **Series:** Steam Locomotive **Subject:** Mallard **Obv:** Crowned head right **Rev:** Locomotive train **Note:** Similar to 20 Dollars, KM#157.

Date	Mintage	F	VF	XF	Unc	BU
1996 Proof	Est. 25,000	Value: 22.00				

KM# 159 5 DOLLARS

10.0000 g., 0.9990 Silver .3212 oz. ASW **Ruler:** Elizabeth II **Series:** Steam Locomotive **Subject:** Princess Elizabeth **Obv:** Crowned head right **Rev:** Locomotive train **Note:** Similar to 20 Dollars, KM#160.

Date	Mintage	F	VF	XF	Unc	BU
1996 Proof	Est. 25,000	Value: 22.00				

KM# 162 5 DOLLARS

10.0000 g., 0.9990 Silver .3212 oz. ASW **Ruler:** Elizabeth II **Series:** Steam Locomotive **Subject:** Southern Pacific Lines - Class GS4 **Obv:** Crowned head right **Rev:** Locomotive train **Note:** Similar to 20 Dollars, KM#163.

Date	Mintage	F	VF	XF	Unc	BU
1996 Proof	Est. 25,000	Value: 22.00				

KM# 165 5 DOLLARS

10.0000 g., 0.9990 Silver .3212 oz. ASW **Ruler:** Elizabeth II **Series:** Steam Locomotive **Subject:** German States Railway - Class 05 **Obv:** Crowned head right **Rev:** Locomotive train **Note:** Similar to 20 Dollars, KM#166.

Date	Mintage	F	VF	XF	Unc	BU
1996 Proof	Est. 25,000	Value: 22.00				

KM# 168 5 DOLLARS

10.0000 g., 0.9990 Silver .3212 oz. ASW **Ruler:** Elizabeth II **Series:** Steam Locomotive **Subject:** Japanese National Railways - Class 62 **Obv:** Crowned head right **Rev:** Locomotive train **Note:** Similar to 20 Dollars, KM#169.

Date	Mintage	F	VF	XF	Unc	BU
1996 Proof	Est. 25,000	Value: 22.00				

KM# 171 5 DOLLARS

10.0000 g., 0.9990 Silver .3212 oz. ASW **Ruler:** Elizabeth II **Series:** Steam Locomotive **Subject:** Chinese State Railways - Class RM **Obv:** Crowned head right **Rev:** Locomotive train **Note:** Similar to 20 Dollars, KM#172.

Date	Mintage	F	VF	XF	Unc	BU
1996 Proof	Est. 25,000	Value: 22.00				

KM# 7 10 CROWNS

29.9800 g., 0.9250 Silver .8916 oz. ASW **Ruler:** Elizabeth II **Subject:** Age of Exploration **Obv:** Young bust right **Obv. Designer:** Arnold Machin **Rev:** Spacecraft's orbital paths

Date	Mintage	F	VF	XF	Unc	BU
1975 Matte	1,250	—	—	—	16.50	20.00
1975 Proof	2,935	Value: 14.50				

KM# 12 10 CROWNS

29.9800 g., 0.9250 Silver .8916 oz. ASW **Ruler:** Elizabeth II **Obv:** Young bust right **Obv. Designer:** Arnold Machin **Rev:** Salt windmill

Date	Mintage	F	VF	XF	Unc	BU
1976	4,185	—	—	—	13.50	16.00
1976 Proof	2,220	Value: 16.00				
1977 Proof	1,370	Value: 17.50				

KM# 45 10 CROWNS

29.7000 g., 0.9250 Silver .8832 oz. ASW **Ruler:** Elizabeth II **Subject:** 10th Anniversary - Prince Charles' Investiture **Obv:** Young bust right **Rev:** Head of Prince Charles left above crossed scepter and sword, with crown and ring

Date	Mintage	F	VF	XF	Unc	BU
1979 Proof	25,000	Value: 12.50				

KM# 48 10 CROWNS

23.3300 g., 0.5000 Silver .3750 oz. ASW **Ruler:** Elizabeth II **Subject:** Lord Mountbatten **Obv:** Young bust right **Rev:** Uniformed bust right and crowned shield

Date	Mintage	F	VF	XF	Unc	BU
1980 Proof	—	Value: 13.50				

KM# 53 10 CROWNS

29.7000 g., 0.9250 Silver .8832 oz. ASW **Ruler:** Elizabeth II **Subject:** Wedding of Prince Charles and Lady Diana **Obv:** Young bust right **Obv. Designer:** Arnold Machin **Rev:** Conjoined busts 1/4 left **Note:** Similar to 100 Crowns, KM#54.

Date	Mintage	F	VF	XF	Unc	BU
1981 Proof	40,000	Value: 18.50				

KM# 55 10 CROWNS

23.2800 g., 0.9250 Silver .6923 oz. ASW **Ruler:** Elizabeth II **Series:** International Year of the Child **Obv:** Young bust right **Obv. Designer:** Arnold Machin **Rev:** Child holding shell, palm trees at left and right **Rev. Designer:** Michael Rizzello

Date	Mintage	F	VF	XF	Unc	BU
1982 Proof	7,928	Value: 20.00				

KM# 56 10 CROWNS

23.2800 g., 0.9250 Silver .6923 oz. ASW **Ruler:** Elizabeth II **Subject:** World Football Championship **Obv:** Young bust right **Rev:** Soccer player

Date	Mintage	F	VF	XF	Unc	BU
1982 Proof	7,865	Value: 16.50				

KM# 57 10 CROWNS

23.2800 g., 0.9250 Silver .6923 oz. ASW **Ruler:** Elizabeth II **Subject:** World Football Championship **Obv:** Young bust right **Obv. Designer:** Arnold Machin **Rev:** Two players

Date	Mintage	F	VF	XF	Unc	BU
1982 Proof	7,165	Value: 16.50				

KM# 58 10 CROWNS

23.2800 g., 0.9250 Silver .6923 oz. ASW **Ruler:** Elizabeth II **Series:** Summer Olympics **Obv:** Young bust right **Obv. Designer:** Arnold Machin **Rev:** Javelin thrower

Date	Mintage	F	VF	XF	Unc	BU
1984 Proof	2,160	Value: 20.00				

KM# 63 10 CROWNS
23.2800 g., 0.9250 Silver .6923 oz. ASW **Ruler:** Elizabeth II
Series: Decade for Women **Obv:** Young bust right **Obv. Designer:** Arnold Machin **Rev:** Female figure facing holding shell and stylized dove within circle

Date	Mintage	F	VF	XF	Unc	BU
1985 Proof	1,001	Value: 35.00				

KM# 2 20 CROWNS
38.7000 g., 0.9250 Silver 1.1509 oz. ASW **Ruler:** Elizabeth II
Subject: Centenary - Birth of Winston Churchill **Obv:** National arms **Rev:** Bust 1/4 left **Rev. Designer:** Michael Rizzello

Date	Mintage	F	VF	XF	Unc	BU
1974 Matte	268,000	—	—	—	18.00	20.00
1974 Proof	8,400	Value: 22.50				

Note: 4,100 issued individually; 4,300 issued in binational sets with Cayman Islands 25 Dollars, KM#10.

KM# 8 20 CROWNS
38.7000 g., 0.9250 Silver 1.1509 oz. ASW **Ruler:** Elizabeth II
Subject: Age of Exploration **Obv:** Young bust right **Obv. Designer:** Arnold Machin **Rev:** Bust of Christopher Columbus right and three ships

Date	Mintage	F	VF	XF	Unc	BU
1975 Matte	1,037	—	—	—	20.00	22.50
1975 Proof	2,769	Value: 18.50				

KM# 13 20 CROWNS
38.7000 g., 0.9250 Silver 1.1509 oz. ASW **Ruler:** Elizabeth II
Subject: U.S. Bicentennial **Obv:** Young bust right **Rev:** Two cameos facing each other below flags and crossed scepters

Date	Mintage	F	VF	XF	Unc	BU
1976 Matte	5,022	—	—	—	17.50	20.00
1976 Proof	4,474	Value: 22.50				

KM# 14 20 CROWNS
38.7000 g., 0.9250 Silver 1.1509 oz. ASW **Ruler:** Elizabeth II
Obv: Young bust right **Rev:** 4 Victoria cameos left

Date	Mintage	F	VF	XF	Unc	BU
1976	25,000	—	—	—	17.50	20.00
1976 Proof	22,000	Value: 20.00				
1977 Proof	1,934	Value: 27.50				

KM# 18 20 CROWNS
38.7000 g., 0.9250 Silver 1.1509 oz. ASW **Ruler:** Elizabeth II
Obv: Young bust right **Rev:** 4 George III cameos right

Date	Mintage	F	VF	XF	Unc	BU
1977	—	—	—	—	27.50	30.00
1977 Proof	1,973	Value: 32.50				

KM# 23 20 CROWNS
38.7000 g., 0.9250 Silver 1.1509 oz. ASW **Ruler:** Elizabeth II
Subject: XI Commonwealth Games **Obv:** Young bust right **Obv. Designer:** Arnold Machin **Rev:** Javelin thrower and runner

Date	Mintage	F	VF	XF	Unc	BU
1978 Proof	10,000	Value: 18.00				

KM# 49 20 CROWNS
29.8100 g., 0.5000 Silver .4792 oz. ASW **Ruler:** Elizabeth II
Subject: Lord Mountbatten **Obv:** Young bust right **Obv. Designer:** Arnold Machin **Rev:** Uniformed bust 1/4 right divides dates

Date	Mintage	F	VF	XF	Unc	BU
1980 Proof	—	Value: 22.50				

KM# 131.1 20 CROWNS
28.0400 g., 0.9250 Silver .8339 oz. ASW **Ruler:** Elizabeth II
Subject: 500th Anniversary - Discovery of America **Obv:** Crude bust right **Rev:** Columbus and Indians exchange gifts

Date	Mintage	F	VF	XF	Unc	BU
1989 Proof	—	Value: 25.00				

KM# 67.1 20 CROWNS
28.0400 g., 0.9250 Silver .8339 oz. ASW **Ruler:** Elizabeth II
Subject: 500th Anniversary - Discovery of America **Obv:** Crude young bust right **Rev:** Sailing ship - Santa Maria

Date	Mintage	F	VF	XF	Unc	BU
1989 Proof	—	Value: 25.00				

KM# 67.2 20 CROWNS
28.0400 g., 0.9250 Silver .8339 oz. ASW **Ruler:** Elizabeth II
Subject: 500th Anniversary - Discovery of America **Obv:** Refined young bust right **Rev:** Sailing ship - Santa Maria

Date	Mintage	F	VF	XF	Unc	BU
1991 Proof	—	Value: 27.50				

KM# 67.3 20 CROWNS
28.0400 g., 0.9250 Silver .8339 oz. ASW **Ruler:** Elizabeth II
Subject: 500th Anniversary - Discovery of America **Obv:** Refined young bust right #2 **Rev:** Sailing ship - Santa Maria

Date	Mintage	F	VF	XF	Unc	BU
1992 Proof	—	Value: 27.50				

KM# 115.1 20 CROWNS
28.0400 g., 0.9250 Silver .8339 oz. ASW **Ruler:** Elizabeth II
Subject: 500th Anniversary - Discovery of America **Obv:** Crude young bust right **Rev:** Ship - The Nina

Date	Mintage	F	VF	XF	Unc	BU
1989 Proof	—	Value: 25.00				

KM# 115.2 20 CROWNS
28.0400 g., 0.9250 Silver .8339 oz. ASW **Ruler:** Elizabeth II
Subject: 500th Anniversary - Discovery of America **Obv:** Refined young bust right **Rev:** Ship - The Nina

Date	Mintage	F	VF	XF	Unc	BU
1991 Proof	—	Value: 27.50				

KM# 115.3 20 CROWNS
28.0400 g., 0.9250 Silver .8339 oz. ASW **Ruler:** Elizabeth II **Subject:** 500th Anniversary - Discovery of America **Obv:** Refined young bust #2 right **Rev:** Ship - The Nina

Date	Mintage	F	VF	XF	Unc	BU
1992 Proof	—	Value: 27.50				

KM# 116.1 20 CROWNS
28.0400 g., 0.9250 Silver .8339 oz. ASW **Ruler:** Elizabeth II **Subject:** 500th Anniversary - Discovery of America **Obv:** Crude young bust right **Rev:** The Pinta

Date	Mintage	F	VF	XF	Unc	BU
1989 Proof	—	Value: 25.00				

KM# 116.2 20 CROWNS
28.0400 g., 0.9250 Silver .8339 oz. ASW **Ruler:** Elizabeth II **Subject:** 500th Anniversary - Discovery of America **Obv:** Refined young bust right **Rev:** The Pinta

Date	Mintage	F	VF	XF	Unc	BU
1991 Proof	—	Value: 27.50				

KM# 116.3 20 CROWNS
28.0400 g., 0.9250 Silver .8339 oz. ASW **Ruler:** Elizabeth II **Subject:** 500th Anniversary - Discovery of America **Obv:** Refined young bust right #2 **Rev:** The Pinta

Date	Mintage	F	VF	XF	Unc	BU
1992 Proof	—	Value: 27.50				

KM# 117.1 20 CROWNS
28.0400 g., 0.9250 Silver .8339 oz. ASW **Ruler:** Elizabeth II **Subject:** 500th Anniversary - Discovery of America **Obv:** Crude young bust right **Rev:** Ships set sail

Date	Mintage	F	VF	XF	Unc	BU
1989 Proof	—	Value: 27.50				

KM# 117.2 20 CROWNS
28.0400 g., 0.9250 Silver .8339 oz. ASW **Ruler:** Elizabeth II **Subject:** 500th Anniversary - Discovery of America **Obv:** Refined young bust right **Rev:** Ships set sail

Date	Mintage	F	VF	XF	Unc	BU
1991 Proof	—	Value: 27.50				

KM# 117.3 20 CROWNS
28.0400 g., 0.9250 Silver .8339 oz. ASW **Ruler:** Elizabeth II **Subject:** 500th Anniversary - Discovery of America **Obv:** Refined young bust #2 right **Rev:** Ships set sail

Date	Mintage	F	VF	XF	Unc	BU
1992 Proof	—	Value: 27.50				

KM# 118.1 20 CROWNS
28.0400 g., 0.9250 Silver .8339 oz. ASW **Ruler:** Elizabeth II **Subject:** 500th Anniversary _ Discovery of America **Obv:** Crude young bust right **Rev:** Ships crossing the Atlantic

Date	Mintage	F	VF	XF	Unc	BU
1989 Proof	—	Value: 25.00				

KM# 118.2 20 CROWNS
28.0400 g., 0.9250 Silver .8339 oz. ASW **Ruler:** Elizabeth II **Subject:** 500th Anniversary _ Discovery of America **Obv:** Refined young bust right **Rev:** Ships crossing the Atlantic

Date	Mintage	F	VF	XF	Unc	BU
1991 Proof	—	Value: 27.50				

KM# 118.3 20 CROWNS
28.0400 g., 0.9250 Silver .8339 oz. ASW **Ruler:** Elizabeth II **Subject:** 500th Anniversary _ Discovery of America **Obv:** Refined young bust #2 right **Rev:** Ships crossing the Atlantic

Date	Mintage	F	VF	XF	Unc	BU
1992 Proof	—	Value: 27.50				

KM# 119.1 20 CROWNS
28.0400 g., 0.9250 Silver .8339 oz. ASW **Ruler:** Elizabeth II **Subject:** 500th Anniversary _ Discovery of America **Obv:** Crude young bust right **Rev:** Sighting land

Date	Mintage	F	VF	XF	Unc	BU
1989 Proof	—	Value: 25.00				

KM# 119.2 20 CROWNS
28.0400 g., 0.9250 Silver .8339 oz. ASW **Ruler:** Elizabeth II **Subject:** 500th Anniversary _ Discovery of America **Obv:** Refined young bust right **Rev:** Sighting land

Date	Mintage	F	VF	XF	Unc	BU
1991 Proof	—	Value: 27.50				

KM# 119.3 20 CROWNS
28.0400 g., 0.9250 Silver .8339 oz. ASW **Ruler:** Elizabeth II **Subject:** 500th Anniversary _ Discovery of America **Obv:** Refined young bust #2 right **Rev:** Sighting land

Date	Mintage	F	VF	XF	Unc	BU
1992 Proof	—	Value: 27.50				

KM# 120.1 20 CROWNS
28.0400 g., 0.9250 Silver .8339 oz. ASW **Ruler:** Elizabeth II **Subject:** 500th Anniversary _ Discovery of America **Obv:** Crude young bust right **Rev:** Columbus explores the Caribbean

Date	Mintage	F	VF	XF	Unc	BU
1989 Proof	—	Value: 25.00				

KM# 120.2 20 CROWNS
28.0400 g., 0.9250 Silver .8339 oz. ASW **Ruler:** Elizabeth II **Subject:** 500th Anniversary - Discovery of America **Obv:** Refined young bust right **Rev:** Columbus explores the Caribbean

Date	Mintage	F	VF	XF	Unc	BU
1991 Proof	—	Value: 27.50				

KM# 120.3 20 CROWNS
28.0400 g., 0.9250 Silver .8339 oz. ASW **Ruler:** Elizabeth II **Subject:** 500th Anniversary - Discovery of America **Obv:** Refined young bust #2 right **Rev:** Columbus explores the Caribbean

Date	Mintage	F	VF	XF	Unc	BU
1992 Proof	—	Value: 27.50				

KM# 129.1 20 CROWNS
28.0400 g., 0.9250 Silver .8339 oz. ASW **Ruler:** Elizabeth II **Subject:** 500th Anniversary - Discovery of America **Obv:** Crude bust right **Rev:** Columbus sights New World

Date	Mintage	F	VF	XF	Unc	BU
1989 Proof	—	Value: 25.00				

KM# 129.2 20 CROWNS
28.0400 g., 0.9250 Silver .8339 oz. ASW **Ruler:** Elizabeth II **Subject:** 500th Anniversary - Discovery of America **Obv:** Refined bust right **Rev:** Columbus sights New World

Date	Mintage	F	VF	XF	Unc	BU
1991 Proof	—	Value: 27.50				

KM# 129.3 20 CROWNS
28.0400 g., 0.9250 Silver .8339 oz. ASW **Ruler:** Elizabeth II **Subject:** 500th Anniversary - Discovery of America **Obv:** Refined bust #2 right **Rev:** Columbus sights New World

Date	Mintage	F	VF	XF	Unc	BU
1992 Proof	—	Value: 27.50				

KM# 130.1 20 CROWNS
28.0400 g., 0.9250 Silver .8339 oz. ASW **Ruler:** Elizabeth II **Subject:** 500th Anniversary - Discovery of America **Obv:** Crude bust right **Rev:** Columbus claims land for Spain

Date	Mintage	F	VF	XF	Unc	BU
1989 Proof	—	Value: 25.00				

KM# 130.2 20 CROWNS
28.0400 g., 0.9250 Silver .8339 oz. ASW **Ruler:** Elizabeth II **Subject:** 500th Anniversary - Discovery of America **Obv:** Refined bust right **Rev:** Columbus claims land for Spain

Date	Mintage	F	VF	XF	Unc	BU
1991 Proof	—	Value: 27.50				

KM# 130.3 20 CROWNS
28.0400 g., 0.9250 Silver .8339 oz. ASW **Ruler:** Elizabeth II **Subject:** 500th Anniversary - Discovery of America **Obv:** Refined bust #2 right **Rev:** Columbus claims land for Spain

Date	Mintage	F	VF	XF	Unc	BU
1992 Proof	—	Value: 27.50				

KM# 131.2 20 CROWNS
28.0400 g., 0.9250 Silver .8339 oz. ASW **Ruler:** Elizabeth II **Subject:** 500th Anniversary - Discovery of America **Obv:** Refined bust right **Rev:** Columbus and Indians exchange gifts

Date	Mintage	F	VF	XF	Unc	BU
1991 Proof	—	Value: 27.50				

KM# 226 20 CROWNS
31.1700 g., 0.9990 Silver 1.0011 oz. ASW, 38.9 mm. **Ruler:** Elizabeth II **Subject:** 40th Anniversary of Accession **Obv:** National arms **Rev:** Crowned bust facing **Edge:** Reeded

Date	Mintage	F	VF	XF	Unc	BU
ND(1992) Proof	—	Value: 30.00				
1993 Proof	—	Value: 30.00				

KM# 227.1 20 CROWNS
31.1700 g., 0.9990 Silver 1.0011 oz. ASW, 38.9 mm. **Ruler:** Elizabeth II **Subject:** 40th Anniversary of the Accession **Obv:** Crowned head right with wavy truncation **Rev:** Head of H.M. King George VI facing **Edge:** Reeded

Date	Mintage	F	VF	XF	Unc	BU
ND(1992) Proof	—	Value: 30.00				

KM# 228.1 20 CROWNS
31.1700 g., 0.9990 Silver 1.0011 oz. ASW, 38.9 mm. **Ruler:** Elizabeth II **Subject:** 40th Anniversary of the Accession **Obv:** Crowned head right with wavy truncation **Rev:** Windsor castle **Edge:** Reeded

Date	Mintage	F	VF	XF	Unc	BU
ND(1992) Proof	—	Value: 30.00				

KM# 229.1 20 CROWNS
31.1700 g., 0.9990 Silver 1.0011 oz. ASW, 38.9 mm. **Ruler:** Elizabeth II **Subject:** 40th Anniversary of the Accession **Obv:** Crowned head right with wavy truncation **Rev:** Conjoined busts of the Queen and Prince Philip facing **Edge:** Reeded

Date	Mintage	F	VF	XF	Unc	BU
ND(1992) Proof	—	Value: 30.00				

KM# 229.2 20 CROWNS
31.1700 g., 0.9990 Silver 1.0011 oz. ASW, 38.9 mm. **Ruler:** Elizabeth II **Subject:** 40th Anniversary of the Accession **Obv:** Crowned head right with smooth truncation **Obv. Designer:** Raphael Maklouf **Rev:** Conjoined busts of the Queen and Prince Philip facing **Edge:** Reeded

Date	Mintage	F	VF	XF	Unc	BU
ND(1992) Proof	—	Value: 30.00				

KM# 131.3 20 CROWNS
28.0400 g., 0.9250 Silver .8339 oz. ASW **Ruler:** Elizabeth II **Subject:** 500th Anniversary - Discovery of America **Obv:** Refined bust #2 right **Rev:** Columbus and Indians exchange gifts

Date	Mintage	F	VF	XF	Unc	BU
1992 Proof	—	Value: 30.00				

KM# 78 20 CROWNS
31.1000 g., 0.9990 Silver 1 oz. ASW **Ruler:** Elizabeth II **Series:** Olympics **Obv:** National arms **Rev:** Equestrian and 3 events

Date	Mintage	F	VF	XF	Unc	BU
1992 Proof	20,000	Value: 21.50				

KM# 79 20 CROWNS
31.1000 g., 0.9990 Silver 1 oz. ASW **Ruler:** Elizabeth II **Series:** Olympics **Obv:** National arms **Rev:** Gymnast on rings and 5 events

Date	Mintage	F	VF	XF	Unc	BU
1992 Proof	Est. 20,000	Value: 21.50				

KM# 80 20 CROWNS
31.1000 g., 0.9990 Silver 1 oz. ASW **Ruler:** Elizabeth II **Series:** Olympics **Obv:** National arms **Rev:** Weightlifting and 3 events

Date	Mintage	F	VF	XF	Unc	BU
1992 Proof	Est. 20,000	Value: 21.50				

KM# 81 20 CROWNS
31.1000 g., 0.9990 Silver 1 oz. ASW **Ruler:** Elizabeth II **Series:** Olympics **Obv:** National arms **Rev:** Rifle shooting and 3 events

Date	Mintage	F	VF	XF	Unc	BU
1992 Proof	Est. 20,000	Value: 21.50				

KM# 82 20 CROWNS
31.1000 g., 0.9990 Silver 1 oz. ASW **Ruler:** Elizabeth II **Series:** Olympics **Obv:** National arms **Rev:** Sail boarding and 3 events

Date	Mintage	F	VF	XF	Unc	BU
1992 Proof	Est. 20,000	Value: 21.50				

KM# 83 20 CROWNS
31.1000 g., 0.9990 Silver 1 oz. ASW **Ruler:** Elizabeth II **Series:** Olympics **Obv:** National arms **Rev:** Ski jumper and 4 events

Date	Mintage	F	VF	XF	Unc	BU
1992 Proof	Est. 20,000	Value: 21.50				

KM# 184 20 CROWNS
28.0400 g., 0.9250 Silver .8339 oz. ASW **Ruler:** Elizabeth II **Series:** Apollo II **Obv:** Crowned head right **Rev:** Lunar landing scene

Date	Mintage	F	VF	XF	Unc	BU
1993 Proof	—	Value: 30.00				
1994 Mule?	—	—	—	—	—	—

Note: Re-engraved number 4 in date

KM# 239 20 CROWNS
28.0400 g., 0.9250 Silver **Ruler:** Elizabeth II **Series:** Lillehamer Winter Olympics **Obv:** Crowned head right **Rev:** Olympic skier

Date	Mintage	F	VF	XF	Unc	BU
1993 Proof	—	Value: 27.50				

KM# 187 20 CROWNS
28.0400 g., 0.9250 Silver 0.8339 oz. ASW, 38.9 mm. **Ruler:** Elizabeth II **Series:** Apollo 11 **Obv:** Crowned head right **Rev:** Astronaut walking on the moon **Edge:** Reeded

Date	Mintage	F	VF	XF	Unc	BU
1993 Proof	—	Value: 30.00				

KM# 95 20 CROWNS
31.1000 g., 0.9990 Silver 1 oz. ASW **Ruler:** Elizabeth II **Subject:** World Cup '94 **Obv:** Crowned bust right **Rev:** Bust of Jules Rimet right and trophy

Date	Mintage	F	VF	XF	Unc	BU
ND(1993) Proof	Est. 10,000	Value: 27.50				

KM# 96 20 CROWNS
31.1000 g., 0.9990 Silver 1 oz. ASW **Ruler:** Elizabeth II **Subject:** World Cup '94 - Uruguay Winners **Obv:** Crowned head right **Rev:** Two players

Date	Mintage	F	VF	XF	Unc	BU
ND(1993) Proof	Est. 10,000	Value: 30.00				

KM# 97 20 CROWNS
31.1000 g., 0.9990 Silver 1 oz. ASW **Ruler:** Elizabeth II **Subject:** World Cup '94 - Italy Winners **Obv:** Crowned head right **Rev:** Dino Zoff

Date	Mintage	F	VF	XF	Unc	BU
ND(1993) Proof	Est. 10,000	Value: 30.00				

KM# 98 20 CROWNS
31.1000 g., 0.9990 Silver 1 oz. ASW **Ruler:** Elizabeth II **Subject:** World Cup '94 - West German Winners **Obv:** Crowned head right **Rev:** Franz Breckenbauer

Date	Mintage	F	VF	XF	Unc	BU
ND(1993) Proof	Est. 10,000	Value: 30.00				

KM# 99 20 CROWNS
31.1000 g., 0.9990 Silver 1 oz. ASW **Ruler:** Elizabeth II **Subject:** World Cup '94 - Brazil Winners **Obv:** Crowned head right **Rev:** Pelé

Date	Mintage	F	VF	XF	Unc	BU
ND(1993) Proof	Est. 10,000	Value: 27.50				

KM# 100 20 CROWNS
31.1000 g., 0.9990 Silver 1 oz. ASW **Ruler:** Elizabeth II **Subject:** World Cup '94 - England Winners **Obv:** Crowned head right **Rev:** Bobby Moore

Date	Mintage	F	VF	XF	Unc	BU
ND(1993) Proof	Est. 10,000	Value: 30.00				

KM# 110.1 20 CROWNS
31.1000 g., 0.9990 Silver 1 oz. ASW **Ruler:** Elizabeth II **Subject:** 40th Anniversary of Coronation **Obv:** Crowned head right with wavy truncation **Rev:** Crown jewels

Date	Mintage	F	VF	XF	Unc	BU
ND(1993) Proof	Est. 10,000	Value: 30.00				

KM# 101 20 CROWNS
31.1000 g., 0.9990 Silver 1 oz. ASW **Ruler:** Elizabeth II **Subject:** World Cup '94 - Argentina Winners **Obv:** Crowned head right **Rev:** Mario Kempes

Date	Mintage	F	VF	XF	Unc	BU
ND(1993) Proof	Est. 10,000	Value: 30.00				

KM# 110.2 20 CROWNS
31.1700 g., 0.9990 Silver 1.0011 oz. ASW, 38.9 mm. **Ruler:** Elizabeth II **Subject:** 40th Anniversary of Coronation **Obv:** Crowned head right with smooth truncation **Rev:** Crown jewels **Edge:** Reeded

Date	Mintage	F	VF	XF	Unc	BU
1993 Proof	—	Value: 30.00				

KM# 102 20 CROWNS
31.1000 g., 0.9990 Silver 1 oz. ASW **Ruler:** Elizabeth II **Subject:** World Cup '94 - USA Host **Obv:** Crowned head right **Rev:** Trophy and flag

Date	Mintage	F	VF	XF	Unc	BU
ND(1993) Proof	Est. 10,000	Value: 27.50				

KM# 111.1 20 CROWNS
31.1000 g., 0.9990 Silver 1 oz. ASW **Ruler:** Elizabeth II **Subject:** 40th Anniversary of Coronation **Obv:** Crowned head right with wavy truncation **Rev:** Queen, clergy and maids of honor

Date	Mintage	F	VF	XF	Unc	BU
ND(1993) Proof	Est. 10,000	Value: 30.00				

KM# 109 20 CROWNS
31.1000 g., 0.9990 Silver 1 oz. ASW **Ruler:** Elizabeth II **Subject:** 40th Anniversary of Coronation **Obv:** Crowned head right **Rev:** Westminster Abbey

Date	Mintage	F	VF	XF	Unc	BU
ND(1993) Proof	Est. 10,000	Value: 30.00				

KM# 111.2 20 CROWNS
31.1700 g., 0.9990 Silver 1.0011 oz. ASW, 38.9 mm. **Ruler:** Elizabeth II **Subject:** 40th Anniversary of Coronation **Obv:** Crowned head right with smooth truncation **Rev:** Queen, clergy and maids of honor **Edge:** Reeded

Date	Mintage	F	VF	XF	Unc	BU
1993 Proof	—	Value: 30.00				

KM# 112.1 20 CROWNS
31.1000 g., 0.9990 Silver 1 oz. ASW **Ruler:** Elizabeth II **Subject:** 40th Anniversary of Coronation **Obv:** Crowned head right with wavy truncation **Rev:** Consort's homage

Date	Mintage	F	VF	XF	Unc	BU
ND(1993) Proof	Est. 10,000	Value: 30.00				

KM# 112.2 20 CROWNS
31.1700 g., 0.9990 Silver 1.0011 oz. ASW, 38.9 mm. **Ruler:** Elizabeth II **Subject:** Coronation Anniversary **Obv:** Crowned head right with smooth truncation **Rev:** Consort's homage **Edge:** Reeded

Date	Mintage	F	VF	XF	Unc	BU
1993 Proof	—	Value: 30.00				

KM# 113.1 20 CROWNS
31.1000 g., 0.9990 Silver 1 oz. ASW **Ruler:** Elizabeth II **Subject:** 40th Anniversary of Coronation **Obv:** Crowned head right with wavy truncation **Rev:** Enthroned Queen seated left facing

Date	Mintage	F	VF	XF	Unc	BU
ND(1993) Proof	Est. 10,000	Value: 30.00				

KM# 113.2 20 CROWNS
31.1700 g., 0.9990 Silver 1.0011 oz. ASW, 38.9 mm. **Ruler:** Elizabeth II **Subject:** Coronation Anniversary **Obv:** Crowned head right with smooth truncation **Rev:** Enthroned Queen seated left facing **Edge:** Reeded

Date	Mintage	F	VF	XF	Unc	BU
1993 Proof	—	Value: 30.00				

KM# 114.1 20 CROWNS
31.1000 g., 0.9990 Silver 1 oz. ASW **Ruler:** Elizabeth II **Subject:** 40th Anniversary of Coronation **Obv:** Crowned head right with wavy truncation **Rev:** Queen in coach

Date	Mintage	F	VF	XF	Unc	BU
ND(1993) Proof	Est. 10,000	Value: 30.00				

KM# 114.2 20 CROWNS
31.1700 g., 0.9990 Silver 1.0011 oz. ASW, 38.9 mm. **Ruler:** Elizabeth II **Subject:** Coronation Anniversary **Obv:** Crowned head right with smooth truncation **Rev:** Queen in coach **Edge:** Reeded

Date	Mintage	F	VF	XF	Unc	BU
1993 Proof	—	Value: 30.00				

KM# 141 20 CROWNS
31.1000 g., 0.9990 Silver 1 oz. ASW **Ruler:** Elizabeth II **Series:** 1994 Olympics **Obv:** Crowned head right **Rev:** Bobsled and team within circle

Date	Mintage	F	VF	XF	Unc	BU
1993 Proof	—	Value: 27.50				

KM# 142 20 CROWNS
31.1000 g., 0.9990 Silver 1 oz. ASW **Ruler:** Elizabeth II **Subject:** 25th Anniversary - Apollo 11 Moon Landing **Obv:** Crowned head right **Rev:** Astronaut descending ladder on moon

Date	Mintage	F	VF	XF	Unc	BU
1993 Proof	—	Value: 30.00				

KM# 183 20 CROWNS
28.0400 g., 0.9250 Silver .8339 oz. ASW **Ruler:** Elizabeth II **Series:** Apollo II **Obv:** Crowned head right **Rev:** Rocket launch scene **Note:** Similar to 5 Crowns, KM#177.

Date	Mintage	F	VF	XF	Unc	BU
1993 Proof	—	Value: 35.00				

KM# 185 20 CROWNS
28.0400 g., 0.9250 Silver .8339 oz. ASW **Ruler:** Elizabeth II **Series:** Apollo II - Leaving Lunar Landing Module **Obv:** Crowned head right **Rev:** Astronaut descending ladder

Date	Mintage	F	VF	XF	Unc	BU
1993 Proof	—	Value: 35.00				

KM# 186 20 CROWNS
28.0400 g., 0.9250 Silver .8339 oz. ASW **Ruler:** Elizabeth II **Series:** Apollo II **Obv:** Crowned head right **Rev:** Astronauts planting flag on moon

Date	Mintage	F	VF	XF	Unc	BU
1993 Proof	—	Value: 30.00				

KM# 228.2 20 CROWNS
31.1700 g., 0.9990 Silver 1.0011 oz. ASW, 38.9 mm. **Ruler:** Elizabeth II **Subject:** 40th Anniversary of the Accession **Obv:** Crowned head right with smooth truncation **Rev:** Windsor Castle **Edge:** Reeded

Date	Mintage	F	VF	XF	Unc	BU
1993 Proof	—	Value: 30.00				

KM# 227.2 20 CROWNS
31.1700 g., 0.9990 Silver 1.0011 oz. ASW, 38.9 mm. **Ruler:** Elizabeth II **Subject:** 40th Anniversary of the Accession **Obv:** Crowned head right with smooth truncation **Rev:** Head of H.M. King George VI facing **Edge:** Reeded

Date	Mintage	F	VF	XF	Unc	BU
1993 Proof	—	Value: 30.00				

KM# 218 20 CROWNS
31.1035 g., 0.9990 Silver 1.0000 oz. ASW, 39.1 mm. **Ruler:** Elizabeth II **Series:** D-Day **Subject:** General Omar Bradley **Obv:** Crowned head right **Rev:** Helmeted bust 1/4 right **Edge:** Reeded

Date	Mintage	F	VF	XF	Unc	BU
1994 Proof	—	Value: 35.00				

Note: Due to poor die work, KM#218-221 appear to be dated 1991 at first glance

KM# 219 20 CROWNS
31.1035 g., 0.9990 Silver 1.0000 oz. ASW, 39.1 mm. **Ruler:** Elizabeth II **Series:** D-Day **Subject:** General Montgomery **Obv:** Crowned head right **Rev:** Uniformed bust left **Edge:** Reeded

Date	Mintage	F	VF	XF	Unc	BU
1994 Proof	—	Value: 35.00				

KM# 220 20 CROWNS
31.1035 g., 0.9990 Silver 1.0000 oz. ASW, 39.1 mm. **Ruler:** Elizabeth II **Series:** D-Day **Subject:** Normandy Landing **Obv:** Crowned head right **Rev:** Sir Bertram Ramsay left **Edge:** Reeded

Date	Mintage	F	VF	XF	Unc	BU
1994 Proof	—	Value: 35.00				

KM# 221 20 CROWNS
31.1035 g., 0.9990 Silver 1.0000 oz. ASW, 39.1 mm. **Ruler:** Elizabeth II **Series:** D-Day **Subject:** Normandy Landing **Obv:** Crowned head right **Rev:** General Dwight Eisenhower right **Edge:** Reeded

Date	Mintage	F	VF	XF	Unc	BU
1994 Proof	—	Value: 35.00				

KM# 208 20 CROWNS
21.1300 g., 0.9990 Silver .9999 oz. ASW **Ruler:** Elizabeth II **Series:** XVII Winter Olympics **Obv:** Crowned head right **Rev:** Figure skater within circle **Note:** Reportedly a mule or pattern.

Date	Mintage	F	VF	XF	Unc	BU
1994 Proof	—	Value: 125				

KM# 137 20 CROWNS
31.1035 g., 0.9990 Silver 1 oz. ASW **Ruler:** Elizabeth II **Subject:** 50th Anniversary - VE Day **Obv:** Arms with supporters **Rev:** Heads of Churchill, Roosevelt and Stalin facing

Date	Mintage	F	VF	XF	Unc	BU
1995 Proof	15,000	Value: 32.50				

KM# 230 20 CROWNS
31.1700 g., 0.9990 Silver 1.0011 oz. ASW, 38.9 mm. **Ruler:** Elizabeth II **Subject:** The Lady of the Century - The Queen Mother **Obv:** Crowned head right with smooth truncation **Rev:** Bust 1/4 right **Edge:** Reeded

Date	Mintage	F	VF	XF	Unc	BU
1995 Proof	—	Value: 30.00				

KM# 138 20 CROWNS
31.1035 g., 0.9990 Silver 1 oz. ASW **Ruler:** Elizabeth II **Subject:** 50th Anniversary - VE Day **Obv:** Arms with supporters **Rev:** Three fighter planes

Date	Mintage	F	VF	XF	Unc	BU
1995 Proof	15,000	Value: 32.50				

KM# 139 20 CROWNS
31.1035 g., 0.9990 Silver 1 oz. ASW **Ruler:** Elizabeth II **Subject:** 50th Anniversary - VE Day **Obv:** Arms with supporters **Rev:** U.S. and Soviet troops meet

Date	Mintage	F	VF	XF	Unc	BU
1995 Proof	15,000	Value: 32.50				

KM# 140 20 CROWNS
31.1035 g., 0.9990 Silver 1 oz. ASW **Ruler:** Elizabeth II **Subject:** 50th Anniversary - VE Day **Obv:** Arms with supporters **Rev:** London, Washington, Moscow and Paris

Date	Mintage	F	VF	XF	Unc	BU
1995 Proof	15,000	Value: 40.00				

KM# 189 20 CROWNS
31.1035 g., 0.9990 Silver 1 oz. ASW **Ruler:** Elizabeth II **Series:** XXVI Summer Olympics **Obv:** Crowned head right **Rev:** Hurdlers within circle

Date	Mintage	F	VF	XF	Unc	BU
1995 Proof	—	Value: 22.50				

KM# 191 20 CROWNS
31.1035 g., 0.9990 Silver 1 oz. ASW **Ruler:** Elizabeth II **Series:** XXVI Summer Olympics **Obv:** Crowned head right **Rev:** Cyclist within circle

Date	Mintage	F	VF	XF	Unc	BU
1995 Proof	—	Value: 22.50				

KM# 193 20 CROWNS
31.1035 g., 0.9990 Silver 1 oz. ASW **Ruler:** Elizabeth II **Series:** XXVI Summer Olympics **Obv:** Crowned head right **Rev:** Fencers within circle

Date	Mintage	F	VF	XF	Unc	BU
1995 Proof	—	Value: 22.50				

KM# 195 20 CROWNS
31.1035 g., 0.9990 Silver 1 oz. ASW **Ruler:** Elizabeth II **Series:** XXVI Summer Olympics **Obv:** Crowned head right **Rev:** Equestrian

Date	Mintage	F	VF	XF	Unc	BU
1995 Proof	—	Value: 22.50				

KM# 197 20 CROWNS
31.1035 g., 0.9990 Silver 1 oz. ASW **Ruler:** Elizabeth II **Series:** XXVI Summer Olympics **Obv:** Crowned head right **Rev:** Pole vaulter

Date	Mintage	F	VF	XF	Unc	BU
1995 Proof	—	Value: 22.50				

KM# 199 20 CROWNS
31.1035 g., 0.9990 Silver 1 oz. ASW **Ruler:** Elizabeth II **Series:** XXVI Summer Olympics **Obv:** Crowned head right **Rev:** Runners within circle

Date	Mintage	F	VF	XF	Unc	BU
1995 Proof	—	Value: 22.50				

KM# 201 20 CROWNS
31.1035 g., 0.9990 Silver 1 oz. ASW **Ruler:** Elizabeth II **Series:** XXVI Summer Olympics **Obv:** Crowned head right **Rev:** Gymnast

Date	Mintage	F	VF	XF	Unc	BU
1995 Proof	—	Value: 22.50				

KM# 203 20 CROWNS
31.1035 g., 0.9990 Silver 1 oz. ASW **Ruler:** Elizabeth II **Series:** XXVI Summer Olympics **Obv:** Crowned head right **Rev:** Swimmer within circle

Date	Mintage	F	VF	XF	Unc	BU
1995 Proof	—	Value: 22.50				

KM# 205 20 CROWNS
31.1035 g., 0.9990 Silver 1 oz. ASW **Ruler:** Elizabeth II **Series:** XXVI Summer Olympics **Obv:** Crowned head right **Rev:** Diver

Date	Mintage	F	VF	XF	Unc	BU
1995 Proof	—	Value: 22.50				

KM# 207 20 CROWNS
31.1035 g., 0.9990 Silver 1 oz. ASW **Ruler:** Elizabeth II **Series:** XXVI Summer Olympics **Obv:** Crowned head right **Rev:** Sprinter within circle

Date	Mintage	F	VF	XF	Unc	BU
1995 Proof	—	Value: 22.50				

KM# 231 20 CROWNS
31.1100 g., 0.9990 Silver 0.9992 oz. ASW, 38.9 mm. **Ruler:** Elizabeth II **Subject:** The 70th Birthday of H. M. Queen Elizabeth II **Obv:** National arms **Rev:** Seated Queen with her pet Corgi's on either side **Edge:** Reeded

Date	Mintage	F	VF	XF	Unc	BU
1996 Proof	—	Value: 30.00				

KM# 222 20 CROWNS
31.1035 g., 0.9990 Silver 1.0000 oz. ASW, 38.9 mm. **Ruler:** Elizabeth II **Subject:** Hong Kong's Return to China **Obv:** Crowned head right **Rev:** City view below flower design **Edge:** Reeded

Date	Mintage	F	VF	XF	Unc	BU
1997 Proof	—	Value: 28.50				

KM# 243 20 CROWNS
31.1600 g., 0.9990 Silver 1.0008 oz. ASW, 39 mm. **Ruler:** Elizabeth II **Subject:** Return of Hong Kong **Obv:** Crowned head right **Rev:** Sailing junk in harbor **Edge:** Reeded

Date	Mintage	F	VF	XF	Unc	BU
1997 Proof	—	Value: 40.00				

KM# 217 20 CROWNS
31.2400 g., 0.9990 Silver 1.0034 oz. ASW, 39 mm. **Ruler:** Elizabeth II **Obv:** Crowned head right **Obv. Designer:** Raphael Maklouf **Rev:** Dolphins **Edge:** Reeded

Date	Mintage	F	VF	XF	Unc	BU
1998 Proof	—	Value: 30.00				

KM# 240 20 CROWNS
31.2300 g., 0.9990 Silver 1.0031 oz. ASW, 38.9 mm. **Ruler:** Elizabeth II **Obv:** Crowned head right **Rev:** Ship - R.M.S. Titanic **Edge:** Reeded

Date	Mintage	F	VF	XF	Unc	BU
1998 Proof	—	Value: 50.00				

KM# 241 20 CROWNS
31.2300 g., 0.9990 Silver 1.0031 oz. ASW **Ruler:** Elizabeth II **Subject:** 80th Anniveresary of the British Royal Air Force **Obv:** Crowned head right **Obv. Designer:** Raphael Maklouf **Rev:** Spitfire in flight **Edge:** Reeded

Date	Mintage	F	VF	XF	Unc	BU
1998 Proof	—	Value: 50.00				

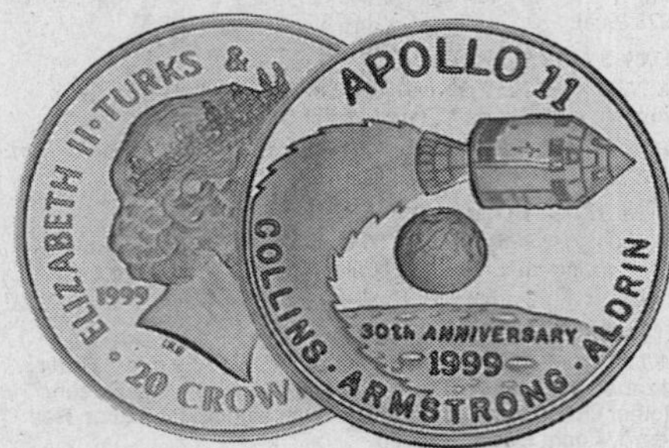

KM# 242 20 CROWNS
33.3700 g., 0.9990 Silver 1.0718 oz. ASW, 39.9 mm. **Ruler:** Elizabeth II **Obv:** National arms **Rev:** Three marlins jumping out of water **Edge:** Reeded

Date	Mintage	F	VF	XF	Unc	BU
1999FM Proof	—	Value: 40.00				

KM# 244 20 CROWNS
31.1600 g., 0.9990 Silver 1.0008 oz. ASW, 39 mm. **Ruler:** Elizabeth II **Obv:** Crowned head right **Rev:** Queen Mother **Edge:** Reeded

Date	Mintage	F	VF	XF	Unc	BU
1999 Proof	—	Value: 40.00				

KM# 223 20 CROWNS
31.1035 g., 0.9990 Silver 1.0000 oz. ASW, 38.9 mm. **Ruler:** Elizabeth II **Subject:** Apollo 11 **Obv:** Head with tiara right **Rev:** Spacecraft in flight above world globe **Edge:** Reeded **Designer:** Ian Rank-Broadley

Date	Mintage	F	VF	XF	Unc	BU
1999 Proof	—	Value: 30.00				

KM# 224 20 CROWNS
31.1035 g., 0.9990 Silver 1.0000 oz. ASW, 38.9 mm. **Ruler:** Elizabeth II **Subject:** Apollo 11 **Obv:** Head with tiara right **Obv. Designer:** Ian Rank-Broadley **Rev:** Heads of Collins, Armstrong and Aldrin left **Edge:** Reeded

Date	Mintage	F	VF	XF	Unc	BU
1999 Proof	—	Value: 30.00				

KM# 235 20 CROWNS
31.2000 g., 0.9990 Silver 1.0021 oz. ASW, 38.9 mm. **Ruler:** Elizabeth II **Subject:** Prince Edward's Wedding **Obv:** Head with tiara right **Obv. Designer:** Ian Rank-Broadley **Rev:** Conjoined busts of Edward and Sophie facing **Edge:** Reeded

Date	Mintage	F	VF	XF	Unc	BU
1999 Proof	—	Value: 40.00				

KM# 145 20 DOLLARS
31.1035 g., 0.9990 Silver 1 oz. ASW **Ruler:** Elizabeth II **Subject:** Steam Locomotive **Obv:** Crowned head right **Rev:** City of Truro

Date	Mintage	F	VF	XF	Unc	BU
1996 Proof	Est. 20,000	Value: 32.50				

KM# 148 20 DOLLARS
31.1035 g., 0.9990 Silver 1 oz. ASW **Ruler:** Elizabeth II **Subject:** Steam Locomotive **Obv:** Crowned head right **Rev:** Flying Scotsman

Date	Mintage	F	VF	XF	Unc	BU
1996 Proof	Est. 20,000	Value: 32.50				

KM# 151 20 DOLLARS
31.1035 g., 0.9990 Silver 1 oz. ASW **Ruler:** Elizabeth II **Subject:** Steam Locomotive **Obv:** Crowned head right **Rev:** Rocket

Date	Mintage	F	VF	XF	Unc	BU
1996 Proof	Est. 20,000	Value: 35.00				

KM# 154 20 DOLLARS
31.1035 g., 0.9990 Silver 1 oz. ASW **Ruler:** Elizabeth II **Subject:** Steam Locomotive **Obv:** Crowned head right **Rev:** Evening Star

Date	Mintage	F	VF	XF	Unc	BU
1996 Proof	Est. 20,000	Value: 35.00				

KM# 157 20 DOLLARS
31.1035 g., 0.9990 Silver 1 oz. ASW **Ruler:** Elizabeth II **Subject:** Steam Locomotive **Obv:** Crowned head right **Rev:** Mallard

Date	Mintage	F	VF	XF	Unc	BU
1996 Proof	Est. 20,000	Value: 35.00				

KM# 160 20 DOLLARS
31.1035 g., 0.9990 Silver 1 oz. ASW **Ruler:** Elizabeth II **Subject:** Steam Locomotive **Obv:** Crowned head right **Rev:** Princess Elizabeth

Date	Mintage	F	VF	XF	Unc	BU
1996 Proof	Est. 20,000	Value: 32.50				

KM# 163 20 DOLLARS
31.1035 g., 0.9990 Silver 1 oz. ASW **Ruler:** Elizabeth II **Subject:** Steam Locomotive **Obv:** Crowned head right **Rev:** South Pacific Line - Class GS4

Date	Mintage	F	VF	XF	Unc	BU
1996 Proof	Est. 20,000	Value: 35.00				

KM# 166 20 DOLLARS
31.1035 g., 0.9990 Silver 1 oz. ASW **Ruler:** Elizabeth II **Subject:** Steam Locomotive **Obv:** Crowned head right **Rev:** German State railway - Class 05

Date	Mintage	F	VF	XF	Unc	BU
1996 Proof	Est. 20,000	Value: 32.50				

KM# 169 20 DOLLARS
31.1035 g., 0.9990 Silver 1 oz. ASW **Ruler:** Elizabeth II **Subject:** Steam Locomotive **Obv:** Crowned head right **Rev:** Japanese Railway - Class 62

Date	Mintage	F	VF	XF	Unc	BU
1996 Proof	Est. 20,000	Value: 35.00				

KM# 172 20 DOLLARS
31.1035 g., 0.9990 Silver 1 oz. ASW **Ruler:** Elizabeth II **Subject:** Steam Locomotive **Obv:** Crowned head right **Rev:** Chinese Stat Railways Class RM

Date	Mintage	F	VF	XF	Unc	BU
1996 Proof	Est. 20,000	Value: 35.00				

KM# 9.1 25 CROWNS
4.5000 g., 0.5000 Gold .0723 oz. AGW **Ruler:** Elizabeth II **Obv:** Young bust right **Obv. Designer:** Arnold Machin **Rev:** National arms

Date	Mintage	F	VF	XF	Unc	BU
1975	1,272	—	—	—	50.00	60.00
1975 Proof	2,096	Value: 60.00				

KM# 9.2 25 CROWNS
4.5000 g., 0.5000 Gold .0723 oz. AGW, 19 mm. **Ruler:** Elizabeth II **Obv:** Young bust right **Obv. Designer:** Arnold Machin **Rev:** National arms

Date	Mintage	F	VF	XF	Unc	BU
1976	—	—	—	—	50.00	60.00
1976 Proof	2,185	Value: 60.00				
1977 Proof	2,125	Value: 60.00				

KM# 19 25 CROWNS
43.7500 g., 0.9250 Silver 1.3012 oz. ASW **Ruler:** Elizabeth II **Subject:** Queen's Silver Jubilee **Obv:** Young bust right **Rev:** Crown and date within sprigs above banner

Date	Mintage	F	VF	XF	Unc	BU
1977 Matte	—	—	—	—	22.50	25.00
1977 Proof	13,000	Value: 28.00				

KM# 24 25 CROWNS
43.7500 g., 0.9250 Silver 1.3012 oz. ASW **Ruler:** Elizabeth II **Subject:** 25th Anniversary of Coronation **Obv:** Young bust right **Rev:** Lion of England

Date	Mintage	F	VF	XF	Unc	BU
1978 Proof	—	Value: 32.00				

KM# 25 25 CROWNS
43.7500 g., 0.9250 Silver 1.3012 oz. ASW **Ruler:** Elizabeth II **Obv:** Young bust right **Rev:** Griffin of Edward III left

Date	Mintage	F	VF	XF	Unc	BU
1978 Proof	—	Value: 32.00				

KM# 26 25 CROWNS
43.7500 g., 0.9250 Silver 1.3012 oz. ASW **Ruler:** Elizabeth II **Obv:** Young bust right **Rev:** Red Dragon of Wales left

Date	Mintage	F	VF	XF	Unc	BU
1978 Proof	—	Value: 32.00				

KM# 27 25 CROWNS
43.7500 g., 0.9250 Silver 1.3012 oz. ASW **Ruler:** Elizabeth II **Obv:** Young bust right **Rev:** White Greyhound of Richmond left

Date	Mintage	F	VF	XF	Unc	BU
1978 Proof	—	Value: 32.00				

KM# 28 25 CROWNS
43.7500 g., 0.9250 Silver 1.3012 oz. ASW **Ruler:** Elizabeth II **Obv:** Young bust right **Rev:** Unicorn of Scotland right

Date	Mintage	F	VF	XF	Unc	BU
1978 Proof	—	Value: 37.50				

KM# 29 25 CROWNS
43.7500 g., 0.9250 Silver 1.3012 oz. ASW **Ruler:** Elizabeth II **Obv:** Young bust right **Rev:** The White Horse of Hannover

Date	Mintage	F	VF	XF	Unc	BU
1978 Proof	—	Value: 32.00				

KM# 30 25 CROWNS
43.7500 g., 0.9250 Silver 1.3012 oz. ASW **Ruler:** Elizabeth II **Obv:** Young bust right **Obv. Designer:** Arnold Machin **Rev:** Black Bull of Clarence left

Date	Mintage	F	VF	XF	Unc	BU
1978 Proof	—	Value: 32.00				

KM# 31 25 CROWNS
43.7500 g., 0.9250 Silver 1.3012 oz. ASW **Ruler:** Elizabeth II **Obv:** Young bust right **Rev:** Yale of Beaufort left

Date	Mintage	F	VF	XF	Unc	BU
1978 Proof	—	Value: 32.00				

KM# 32 25 CROWNS
43.7500 g., 0.9250 Silver 1.3012 oz. ASW **Ruler:** Elizabeth II **Obv:** Young bust right **Rev:** Falcon of the Plantagenets right

Date	Mintage	F	VF	XF	Unc	BU
1978 Proof	—	Value: 32.00				

KM# 33 25 CROWNS
43.7500 g., 0.9250 Silver 1.3012 oz. ASW **Ruler:** Elizabeth II **Obv:** Young bust right **Rev:** White Lion of Mortimer left

Date	Mintage	F	VF	XF	Unc	BU
1978 Proof	—	Value: 32.00				

KM# 209 25 CROWNS
155.4400 g., 0.9990 Silver 4.9925 oz. ASW, 63 mm. **Ruler:** Elizabeth II **Obv:** Crowned bust right **Obv. Designer:** Raphael Maklouf **Rev:** Multicolor purple-throated Carib bird within flowers **Note:** Photo reduced.

Date	Mintage	F	VF	XF	Unc	BU
1995 Matte	—	—	—	—	100	125
1995 Proof	—	Value: 90.00				

KM# 210 25 CROWNS
155.4400 g., 0.9990 Silver 4.9925 oz. ASW, 63 mm. **Ruler:** Elizabeth II **Obv:** Crowned bust right **Rev:** Multicolor Streamertail bird **Note:** Photo reduced.

Date	Mintage	F	VF	XF	Unc	BU
1995 Matte	—	—	—	—	100	125
1995 Proof	—	Value: 90.00				

KM# 211 25 CROWNS
155.4400 g., 0.9990 Silver 4.9925 oz. ASW, 63 mm. **Ruler:** Elizabeth II **Obv:** Crowned bust right **Rev:** Multicolor Woodstar bird **Note:** Photo reduced.

Date	Mintage	F	VF	XF	Unc	BU
1995	—	—	—	—	100	125
1995 Proof	—	Value: 90.00				

KM# 3 50 CROWNS
9.0000 g., 0.5000 Gold .1447 oz. AGW **Ruler:** Elizabeth II **Subject:** Centenary - Birth of Churchill **Obv:** National arms **Rev:** Bust 1/4 left **Rev. Designer:** Michael Rizzello **Edge Lettering:** REDEEMABLE AT TURKS AND CAICOS FOR U.S. CURRENCY

Date	Mintage	F	VF	XF	Unc	BU
1974 Matte	30,000	—	—	—	100	110
1974 Proof	4,000	Value: 120				

KM# 10 50 CROWNS
6.2200 g., 0.5000 Gold .1 oz. AGW **Ruler:** Elizabeth II **Subject:** Age of Exploration **Obv:** Young bust right **Obv. Designer:** Arnold Machin **Rev:** Head od Christopher Columbus right and 3 ships

Date	Mintage	F	VF	XF	Unc	BU
1975	2,863	—	—	—	80.00	90.00
1975 Proof	1,577	Value: 100				

KM# 15 50 CROWNS
6.2200 g., 0.5000 Gold .1 oz. AGW **Ruler:** Elizabeth II **Subject:** U.S. Bicentennial **Obv:** Young bust right **Obv. Designer:** Arnold Machin **Rev:** Cameos facing each other below flags and crossed scepter and sword

Date	Mintage	F	VF	XF	Unc	BU
1976	905	—	—	—	100	110
1976 Proof	2,421	Value: 90.00				

KM# 16 50 CROWNS
55.1800 g., 0.9250 Silver 1.6412 oz. ASW **Ruler:** Elizabeth II **Obv:** Young bust right **Obv. Designer:** Arnold Machin **Rev:** 4 Victoria cameos left

Date	Mintage	F	VF	XF	Unc	BU
1976 Matte	3,500	—	—	—	40.00	45.00
1976 Proof	2,908	Value: 45.00				
1977 Proof	940	Value: 50.00				

KM# 20 50 CROWNS
9.0000 g., 0.5000 Gold .1447 oz. AGW **Ruler:** Elizabeth II **Subject:** Queen's Silver Jubilee **Obv:** Young bust right **Obv. Designer:** Arnold Machin **Rev:** Crown and date within sprigs above banner

Date	Mintage	F	VF	XF	Unc	BU
1977	—	—	—	—	100	110
1977 Proof	2,903	Value: 120				

KM# 21 50 CROWNS
55.1800 g., 0.9250 Silver 1.6412 oz. ASW **Ruler:** Elizabeth II **Obv:** Young bust right **Rev:** 4 George III cameos right

Date	Mintage	F	VF	XF	Unc	BU
1977	—	—	—	—	50.00	55.00
1977 Proof	958	Value: 60.00				

KM# 34 50 CROWNS
9.0000 g., 0.5000 Gold .1447 oz. AGW **Ruler:** Elizabeth II **Subject:** 25th Anniversary of Coronation **Obv:** Young bust right **Rev:** Lion of England right

Date	Mintage	F	VF	XF	Unc	BU
1978 Proof	261	Value: 175				

KM# 35 50 CROWNS
9.0000 g., 0.5000 Gold .1447 oz. AGW **Ruler:** Elizabeth II **Obv:** Young bust right **Rev:** Griffin of Edward III left

Date	Mintage	F	VF	XF	Unc	BU
1978 Proof	266	Value: 175				

KM# 36 50 CROWNS
9.0000 g., 0.5000 Gold .1447 oz. AGW **Ruler:** Elizabeth II **Obv:** Young bust right **Rev:** Red Dragon of Wales left

Date	Mintage	F	VF	XF	Unc	BU
1978 Proof	266	Value: 175				

KM# 37 50 CROWNS
9.0000 g., 0.5000 Gold .1447 oz. AGW **Ruler:** Elizabeth II **Obv:** Young bust right **Rev:** White Greyhound of Richmond

Date	Mintage	F	VF	XF	Unc	BU
1978 Proof	270	Value: 175				

KM# 38 50 CROWNS
9.0000 g., 0.5000 Gold .1447 oz. AGW **Ruler:** Elizabeth II **Obv:** Young bust right **Rev:** The Unicorn of Scotland right

Date	Mintage	F	VF	XF	Unc	BU
1978 Proof	268	Value: 175				

KM# 39 50 CROWNS
9.0000 g., 0.5000 Gold .1447 oz. AGW **Ruler:** Elizabeth II **Obv:** Young bust right **Rev:** White Horse of Hannover left

Date	Mintage	F	VF	XF	Unc	BU
1978 Proof	266	Value: 175				

KM# 40 50 CROWNS
9.0000 g., 0.5000 Gold .1447 oz. AGW **Ruler:** Elizabeth II **Obv:** Young bust right **Rev:** Black Bull of Clarence Left

Date	Mintage	F	VF	XF	Unc	BU
1978 Proof	269	Value: 175				

KM# 41 50 CROWNS
9.0000 g., 0.5000 Gold .1447 oz. AGW **Ruler:** Elizabeth II **Obv:** Young bust right **Rev:** Yale of Beaufort left

Date	Mintage	F	VF	XF	Unc	BU
1978 Proof	254	Value: 175				

KM# 42 50 CROWNS
9.0000 g., 0.5000 Gold .1447 oz. AGW **Ruler:** Elizabeth II **Obv:** Young bust right **Obv. Designer:** Arnold Machin **Rev:** Falcon of the Plantagenets right

Date	Mintage	F	VF	XF	Unc	BU
1978 Proof	265	Value: 175				

KM# 43 50 CROWNS
9.0000 g., 0.5000 Gold .1447 oz. AGW **Ruler:** Elizabeth II **Obv:** Young bust right **Obv. Designer:** Arnold Machin **Rev:** White Lion of Mortimer left

Date	Mintage	F	VF	XF	Unc	BU
1978 Proof	265	Value: 175				

KM# 61 50 CROWNS
136.0800 g., 0.9250 Silver 4.0699 oz. ASW, 63 mm. **Ruler:** Elizabeth II **Subject:** Columbus proposes Atlantic voyage to Ferdinand and Isabella **Obv:** Young bust right **Obv. Designer:** Arnold Machin **Rev:** 3 Wreathed cameos and ship **Note:** Photo reduced.

Date	Mintage	F	VF	XF	Unc	BU
1986 Proof	20,000	Value: 85.00				

KM# 4 100 CROWNS
18.0150 g., 0.5000 Gold .2896 oz. AGW **Ruler:** Elizabeth II **Subject:** Birth of Churchill Centenary **Obv:** National arms **Rev:** Bust 1/4 left

Date	Mintage	F	VF	XF	Unc	BU
1974	4,500	—	—	—	200	210
1974 Proof	5,100	Value: 210				

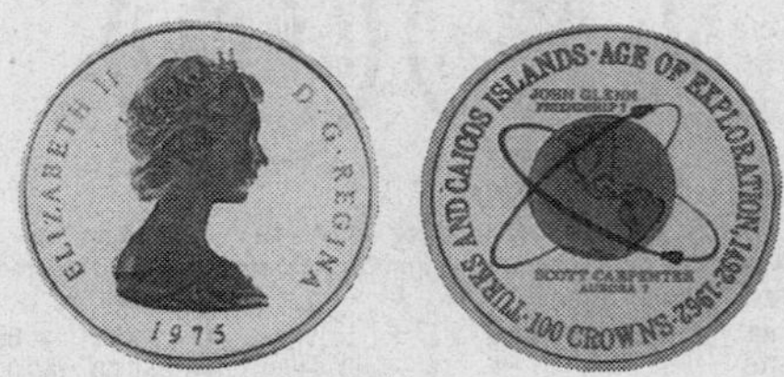

KM# 11 100 CROWNS
12.4400 g., 0.5000 Gold .2000 oz. AGW **Ruler:** Elizabeth II **Subject:** Age of Exploration **Obv:** Young bust right **Obv. Designer:** Arnold Machin **Rev:** Spacecraft flying around globe

Date	Mintage	F	VF	XF	Unc	BU
1975	756	—	—	—	145	150
1975 Proof	1,508	Value: 135				

KM# 17 100 CROWNS
18.0150 g., 0.5000 Gold .2896 oz. AGW **Ruler:** Elizabeth II **Obv:** Young bust right **Obv. Designer:** Arnold Machin **Rev:** 4 Vicoria cameos left

Date	Mintage	F	VF	XF	Unc	BU
1976	250	—	—	—	215	220
1976 Proof	350	Value: 225				

Date	Mintage	F	VF	XF	Unc	BU
1977	1,655	—	—	—	210	215
1977 Proof	2,648	Value: 220				

KM# 22 100 CROWNS
18.0150 g., 0.5000 Gold .2896 oz. AGW **Ruler:** Elizabeth II **Obv:** Young bust right **Obv. Designer:** Arnold Machin **Rev:** 4 George III cameos right

Date	Mintage	F	VF	XF	Unc	BU
1977	—	—	—	—	215	220
1977 Proof	844	Value: 225				

KM# 44 100 CROWNS
18.0150 g., 0.5000 Gold .2896 oz. AGW **Ruler:** Elizabeth II **Subject:** XI Commonwealth Games

Date	Mintage	F	VF	XF	Unc	BU
1978 Proof	540	Value: 250				

KM# 46 100 CROWNS
18.0150 g., 0.5000 Gold .2896 oz. AGW **Ruler:** Elizabeth II **Subject:** 10th Anniversary - Prince Charles' Investiture **Obv:** Young bust right **Obv. Designer:** Arnold Machin **Rev:** Head of Prince Charles facing left at right with crown, crossed sword and sceptre at left

Date	Mintage	F	VF	XF	Unc	BU
1979	10,000	—	—	—	210	215

KM# 50 100 CROWNS
12.9600 g., 0.5000 Gold .2083 oz. AGW **Ruler:** Elizabeth II **Subject:** Lord Mountbatten **Obv:** Crowned bust right **Rev:** Bust 1/4 right flanked by dates

Date	Mintage	F	VF	XF	Unc	BU
1980 Proof	—	Value: 155				

KM# 54 100 CROWNS
6.4800 g., 0.9000 Gold .1875 oz. AGW **Ruler:** Elizabeth II **Subject:** Wedding of Princes Charles and Lady Diana **Rev:** Conjoined busts left

Date	Mintage	F	VF	XF	Unc	BU
1981 Proof	1,205	Value: 135				

KM# 59 100 CROWNS
6.4800 g., 0.9000 Gold .1875 oz. AGW **Ruler:** Elizabeth II **Subject:** World Football Championship **Obv:** Young bust right **Obv. Designer:** Arnold Machin **Rev:** Football players

Date	Mintage	F	VF	XF	Unc	BU
1982 Proof	565	Value: 225				

KM# 62 100 CROWNS
7.1300 g., 0.9000 Gold .2063 oz. AGW **Ruler:** Elizabeth II **Series:** Decade for Women **Rev:** Half-length figure right

Date	Mintage	F	VF	XF	Unc	BU
1985 Proof	313	Value: 275				

KM# 65 100 CROWNS
10.00 g., 0.9170 Gold .2949 oz. AGW **Ruler:** Elizabeth II **Series:** World Wildlife Fund **Obv:** Crowned bust right **Rev:** Spiny lobster

Date	Mintage	F	VF	XF	Unc	BU
1988 Proof	Est. 5,000	Value: 220				

KM# 237 100 CROWNS
155.51 g., 0.9990 Gold Plated Silver 4.995 oz. ASW AGW, 63.7 mm. **Ruler:** Elizabeth II **Subject:** Queen's Golden Wedding Anniversary **Obv:** National arms **Rev:** Wedding portrait of Queen and Prince Philip **Edge:** Reeded and numbered **Note:** Photo reduced.

Date	Mintage	F	VF	XF	Unc	BU
1997 Proof	3,000	Value: 175				

PATTERNS

Standard metals unless noted otherwise

KM#	Date	Mintage	Identification	Issue Price	Mkt Val
Pn1	ND(1993)	50	20 Crowns. Silver. Bobsledders.	—	75.00
Pn2	ND(1993)	50	20 Crowns. Silver. Skier.	—	75.00
Pn3	ND(1993)	50	20 Crowns. Silver. Ski jumper.	—	75.00
Pn4	ND(1993)	50	20 Crowns. Silver. Figure skater.	—	75.00
Pn5	ND(1993)	50	20 Crowns. Silver. Hockey player.	—	75.00
Pn6	ND(1993)	50	20 Crowns. Silver. Speed skater.	—	75.00

PIEFORTS

KM#	Date	Mintage	Identification	Issue Price	Mkt Val
P1	1980	500	5 Crowns. Silver. KM47.	79.50	32.00
P2	1980	400	10 Crowns. Silver. KM48.	95.00	38.00
P3	1980	300	20 Crowns. Silver. KM49.	115	40.00
P4	1980	250	100 Crowns. Gold. KM50.	825	275
P5	1982	80	10 Crowns. Silver. KM55.	—	135
P6	1991	—	Crown. Silver. KM76.	—	40.00
P7	1991	400	Crown. Silver. KM121.	—	30.00

MINT SETS

KM#	Date	Mintage	Identification	Issue Price	Mkt Val
MS1	1975 (7)	440	KM5-11	214	350
MS2	ND(1993) (8)	—	KM87-94	67.20	45.00
MS3	ND(1993) (6)	—	KM103-108	49.95	35.00
MS4	1995 (4)	—	KM133-136	33.50	33.50
MS5	1996 (10)	—	KM143, 146, 149, 152, 155, 158, 161, 164, 167, 170	33.50	33.50

PROOF SETS

KM#	Date	Mintage	Identification	Issue Price	Mkt Val
PS1	1974 (2)	1,600	KM2, 4	—	170
PS2	1975 (7)	1,270	KM5-8, 9.1, 10-11	313	385
PS3	1976 (4)	2,185	KM5, 6, 9.2, 12	78.00	85.00
PS4	1976 (3)	—	KM14, 16, 17	280	270
PS5	1976 (2)	1,951	KM13, 15	108	115
PS6	1977 (4)	1,370	KM5, 6, 9.2, 12	87.50	100
PS8	1977 (2)	—	KM14, 18	62.00	115
PS7	1977 (3)	—	KM18, 21, 22	280	380
PS10	1978 (10)	—	KM34-43	1,120	1,650
PS9	1978 (10)	—	KM24-33	560	320
PS11	1979 (2)	—	KM45, 46	228	160
PS12	1980 (4)	—	KM47-50	458	195
PS13	1980 (3)	—	KM47-49	108	45.00
PS15	ND(1993) (8)	—	KM95-102	320	325
PS17	ND(1993) (6)	—	KM109-114	234	255
PS18	1995 (4)	15,000	KM137-140	160	160
PS19	1996 (10)	20,000	KM144, 147, 150, 153, 156, 159, 162, 165, 168, 171	220	220
PS20	1996 (10)	20,000	KM145, 148, 151, 154, 157, 160, 163, 166, 169, 172	350	350

TUVALU

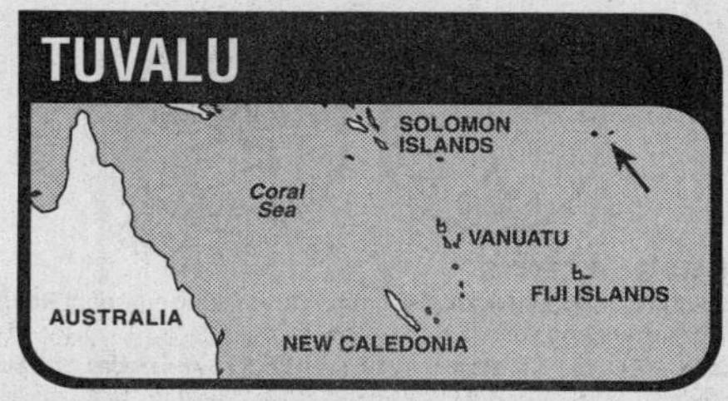

Tuvalu (formerly the Ellice or Lagoon Islands of the Gilbert and Ellice Islands), located in the South Pacific north of the Fiji Islands, has an area of 10 sq. mi. (26 sq.km.) and a population of *9,000. Capital: Funafuti. The independent state includes the islands of Nanumanga, Nanumea, Nui, Niutao, Viatupa, Funafuti, Nukufetau, Nukulailai and Nurakita. The latter four islands were claimed by the United States until relinquished by the Feb. 7, 1979, Treaty of Friendship signed by the United States and Tuvalu. The principal industries are copra production and phosphate mining.

The islands were discovered in 1764 by John Byron, a British navigator, and annexed by Britain in 1892. In 1915 they became part of the crown colony of the Gilbert and Ellice Islands. In 1974 the islanders voted to separate from the Gilberts, becoming on Jan. 1, 1976, the separate constitutional dependency of Tuvalu. Full independence was attained on Oct. 1, 1978. Tuvalu is a member of the Commonwealth of Nations. Elizabeth II is Head of State as Queen of Tuvalu.

RULERS
British, until 1978

MONETARY SYSTEM
100 Cents = 1 Dollar

PARLIMENTARY DEMOCRACY

STANDARD COINAGE

KM# 1 CENT
2.6000 g., Bronze, 17.5 mm. **Obv:** Young bust right **Rev:** Sea shell and value

Date	Mintage	F	VF	XF	Unc	BU
1976	93,000	—	—	0.10	0.35	0.75
1976 Proof	20,000	Value: 1.00				
1981	—	—	—	0.10	0.35	0.75
1981 Proof	—	Value: 1.00				
1985	—	—	—	0.10	0.35	0.75

KM# 26 CENT
2.6000 g., Bronze, 17.5 mm. **Obv:** Crowned head right **Obv. Designer:** Raphael Maklouf **Rev:** Sea shell and value

Date	Mintage	F	VF	XF	Unc	BU
1994	—	—	—	—	0.25	0.75

KM# 2 2 CENTS
5.2000 g., Bronze, 21.6 mm. **Obv:** Young bust right **Rev:** Stingray and value

Date	Mintage	F	VF	XF	Unc	BU
1976	51,000	—	0.10	0.15	0.50	1.50
1976 Proof	20,000	Value: 1.75				
1981	—	—	0.10	0.15	0.50	1.50
1981 Proof	—	Value: 1.75				
1985	—	—	0.10	0.15	0.50	1.50

KM# 30 2 CENTS
5.2000 g., Bronze, 21.6 mm. **Obv:** Crowned head right **Obv. Designer:** Raphael Maklouf

Date	Mintage	F	VF	XF	Unc	BU
1994	—	—	—	—	0.35	1.00

KM# 3 5 CENTS
2.8000 g., Copper-Nickel, 19.4 mm. **Obv:** Young bust right **Rev:** Tiger shark and value

Date	Mintage	F	VF	XF	Unc	BU
1976	26,000	—	0.10	0.25	1.25	3.50
1976 Proof	20,000	Value: 4.00				
1981	—	—	0.10	0.25	1.25	3.50
1981 Proof	—	Value: 4.00				
1985	—	—	0.10	0.25	1.25	3.50

KM# 31 5 CENTS
2.8000 g., Copper-Nickel, 19.4 mm. **Obv:** Crowned head right **Obv. Designer:** Raphael Maklouf

Date	Mintage	F	VF	XF	Unc	BU
1994	—	—	—	—	1.50	4.00

KM# 4 10 CENTS
5.6000 g., Copper-Nickel, 23.5 mm. **Obv:** Young bust right **Rev:** Crab and value

Date	Mintage	F	VF	XF	Unc	BU
1976	26,000	0.15	0.20	0.35	1.25	3.50
1976 Proof	20,000	Value: 4.00				
1981	—	0.15	0.20	0.35	1.25	3.50
1981 Proof	—	Value: 4.00				
1985	—	0.15	0.20	0.35	1.25	3.50

KM# 32 10 CENTS
5.6000 g., Copper-Nickel, 23.5 mm. **Obv:** Crowned head right **Obv. Designer:** Raphael Maklouf

Date	Mintage	F	VF	XF	Unc	BU
1994	—	—	—	—	1.50	4.00

KM# 5 20 CENTS
11.2500 g., Copper-Nickel, 28.45 mm. **Obv:** Young bust right **Rev:** Flying fish and value

Date	Mintage	F	VF	XF	Unc	BU
1976	36,000	0.30	0.40	0.60	2.50	4.50
1976 Proof	20,000	Value: 6.00				
1981	—	0.30	0.40	0.60	2.50	4.50
1981 Proof	—	Value: 6.00				
1985	—	0.30	0.40	0.60	2.50	4.50

KM# 33 20 CENTS
11.2500 g., Copper-Nickel, 28.45 mm. **Obv:** Crowned head right **Obv. Designer:** Raphael Maklouf

Date	Mintage	F	VF	XF	Unc	BU
1994	—	—	—	—	1.25	3.50

KM# 6 50 CENTS
15.5000 g., Copper-Nickel, 31.65 mm. **Obv:** Young bust right **Rev:** Octopus and value

Date	Mintage	F	VF	XF	Unc	BU
1976	19,000	0.50	0.75	1.50	4.50	7.50
1976 Proof	20,000	Value: 8.00				
1981	—	0.50	0.75	1.50	4.50	7.50
1981 Proof	—	Value: 8.00				
1985	—	0.50	0.75	1.50	4.50	7.50

KM# 34 50 CENTS
15.5000 g., Copper-Nickel, 31.65 mm. **Obv:** Crowned head right **Obv. Designer:** Raphael Maklouf

Date	Mintage	F	VF	XF	Unc	BU
1994	—	—	—	—	4.25	7.50

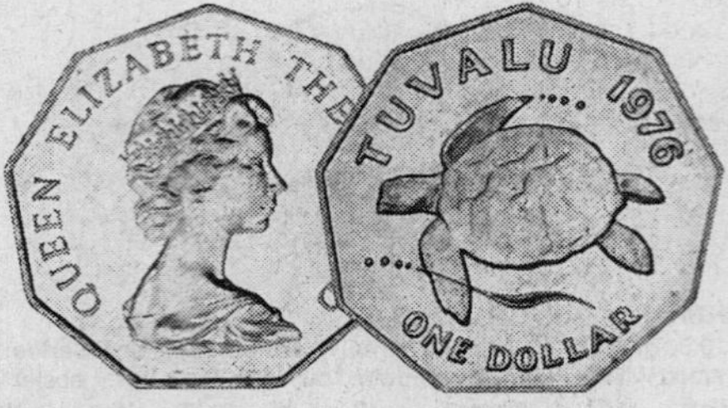

KM# 7 DOLLAR
16.0000 g., Copper-Nickel, 33 mm. **Obv:** Young bust right **Rev:** Sea turtle and value **Shape:** 9-sided

Date	Mintage	F	VF	XF	Unc	BU
1976	21,000	1.00	1.50	2.00	5.50	9.00
1976 Proof	20,000	Value: 11.50				
1981	—	1.00	1.50	2.00	5.50	9.00
1981 Proof	—	Value: 11.50				
1985	—	1.00	1.50	2.00	5.50	9.00

KM# 35 DOLLAR
16.0000 g., Copper-Nickel, 33 mm. **Obv:** Crowned head right **Obv. Designer:** Raphael Maklouf

Date	Mintage	F	VF	XF	Unc	BU
1994	—	—	—	—	4.50	9.00

KM# 37 2 DOLLARS
10.0000 g., 0.5000 Silver .1608 oz. ASW, 30 mm. **Series:** Olympics **Obv:** Crowned head right **Rev:** Swimmer **Edge:** Reeded

Date	Mintage	F	VF	XF	Unc	BU
1996 Proof	—	Value: 6.50				

KM# 48 2 DOLLARS
15.8500 g., 0.9250 Silver 0.4714 oz. ASW, 28.3 mm. **Obv:** Crowned head right **Rev:** Queen Mother receiving honorary Doctor of Music degree **Edge:** Reeded

Date	Mintage	F	VF	XF	Unc	BU
1997 Proof	—	Value: 12.50				

KM# 8 5 DOLLARS
28.2800 g., 0.9250 Silver .8411 oz. ASW **Obv:** Young bust right **Rev:** Outrigger canoe

Date	Mintage	F	VF	XF	Unc	BU
1976 Proof	20,000	Value: 13.50				

KM# 12 5 DOLLARS
Copper-Nickel **Subject:** Wedding of Prince Charles and Lady Diana **Obv:** Young bust right **Obv. Designer:** Arnold Machin **Rev:** Three plumes within crown, value at right

Date	Mintage	F	VF	XF	Unc	BU
1981	—	—	—	—	5.00	6.50

KM# 12a 5 DOLLARS
28.2800 g., 0.9250 Silver .8411 oz. ASW **Subject:** Wedding of Prince Charles and Lady Diana **Obv:** Young bust right **Rev:** Three plumes within crown, value at right

Date	Mintage	F	VF	XF	Unc	BU
1981 Proof	35,000	Value: 13.50				

KM# 38 5 DOLLARS
31.6400 g., 0.9250 Silver 0.941 oz. ASW, 38.6 mm. **Subject:** Victorian Age **Obv:** Crowned head right **Rev:** 3/4 Standing figure at left, SS Great Britain in back at right **Edge:** Reeded

Date	Mintage	F	VF	XF	Unc	BU
1997 Proof	—	Value: 18.50				

KM# 45 5 DOLLARS
31.5500 g., 0.9250 Silver 0.9383 oz. ASW, 38.6 mm. **Subject:** Queen Mother - Opening of the Federal Parliament at Canberra **Obv:** Crowned head right **Rev:** Cameo of the Queen Mother and King George VI above the Australian Parliament building **Edge:** Reeded

Date	Mintage	F	VF	XF	Unc	BU
1997 Proof	—	Value: 18.50				

KM# 46 5 DOLLARS
31.5500 g., 0.9250 Silver 0.9383 oz. ASW, 38.6 mm. **Subject:** Queen Mother **Obv:** Crowned head right **Rev:** Queen Mother being granted an Honorary Doctor of Music degree **Edge:** Reeded

Date	Mintage	F	VF	XF	Unc	BU
1997 Proof	—	Value: 18.50				

KM# 47 5 DOLLARS
31.5200 g., 0.9250 Silver 0.9374 oz. ASW, 38.7 mm. **Subject:** Princess Diana **Obv:** Crowned head right **Rev:** Diana **Edge:** Reeded

Date	Mintage	F	VF	XF	Unc	BU
1998 Proof	—	Value: 20.00				

KM# 36 5 DOLLARS
31.2200 g., 0.9250 Silver .9285 oz. ASW, 30.2 mm. **Subject:** Millennium 2000 **Obv:** Crowned head right **Rev:** Seashell, stars and stylized waves above value **Edge:** Reeded, square

Date	Mintage	F	VF	XF	Unc	BU
1998 Proof	—	Value: 18.50				

KM# 44 5 DOLLARS
31.2000 g., 0.9250 Silver 0.9279 oz. ASW, 30.2 mm. **Subject:** Millennium **Obv:** Crowned head right **Rev:** Seashell and value **Edge:** Reeded

Date	Mintage	F	VF	XF	Unc	BU
2000 Proof	—	Value: 18.50				

KM# 10 10 DOLLARS
35.0000 g., 0.5000 Silver .5627 oz. ASW **Subject:** 1st Anniversary of Independence **Obv:** Young bust right **Rev:** Brigantine "Rebecca"

Date	Mintage	F	VF	XF	Unc	BU
1979	5,000	—	—	—	11.50	13.50

KM# 10a 10 DOLLARS
35.0000 g., 0.9250 Silver 1.0409 oz. ASW **Obv:** Young bust right **Rev:** Brigantine "Rebecca"

Date	Mintage	F	VF	XF	Unc	BU
1979 Proof	2,500	Value: 20.00				

KM# 11 10 DOLLARS
35.0000 g., 0.5000 Silver .5627 oz. ASW **Subject:** 80th Birthday of Queen Mother **Obv:** Young bust right **Rev:** Crowned bust of the Queen Mother left

Date	Mintage	F	VF	XF	Unc	BU
1980	—	—	—	—	10.00	12.00

KM# 11a 10 DOLLARS
35.0000 g., 0.9250 Silver 1.0409 oz. ASW **Obv:** Young bust right **Rev:** Crowned bust of the Queen Mother left

Date	Mintage	F	VF	XF	Unc	BU
1980 Proof	—	Value: 18.00				

KM# 13 10 DOLLARS
35.0000 g., 0.5000 Silver .5627 oz. ASW **Subject:** Duke of Edinburgh Award **Obv:** Young bust right **Rev:** Head left

Date	Mintage	F	VF	XF	Unc	BU
1981	5,000	—	—	—	10.00	12.00

KM# 13a 10 DOLLARS
35.0000 g., 0.9250 Silver 1.0409 oz. ASW **Subject:** Duke of Edinburgh Award **Obv:** Young bust right **Rev:** Head left

Date	Mintage	F	VF	XF	Unc	BU
1981 Proof	3,000	Value: 17.50				

KM# 15 10 DOLLARS
35.0000 g., 0.5000 Silver .5627 oz. ASW **Subject:** Royal Visit **Obv:** Young bust right **Rev:** Conjoined busts of the Queen and Prince Philip right within circle

Date	Mintage	F	VF	XF	Unc	BU
1982	2,500	—	—	—	10.00	12.00

KM# 15a 10 DOLLARS
35.0000 g., 0.9250 Silver 1.0409 oz. ASW **Subject:** Royal Visit **Obv:** Young bust right **Rev:** Conjoined busts of the Queen and Prince Philip right within circle

Date	Mintage	F	VF	XF	Unc	BU
1982 Proof	2,500	Value: 20.00				

KM# 16 20 DOLLARS
31.4700 g., 0.9250 Silver .9359 oz. ASW **Subject:** 40th Anniversary of Coronation **Obv:** Crowned head right **Rev:** Coronation scene

Date	Mintage	F	VF	XF	Unc	BU
1993 Proof	10,000	Value: 16.00				

KM# 17 20 DOLLARS
31.4700 g., 0.9250 Silver .9359 oz. ASW **Subject:** Sir Isaac Newton **Obv:** Crowned head right

Date	Mintage	F	VF	XF	Unc	BU
1993 Proof	10,000	Value: 16.00				

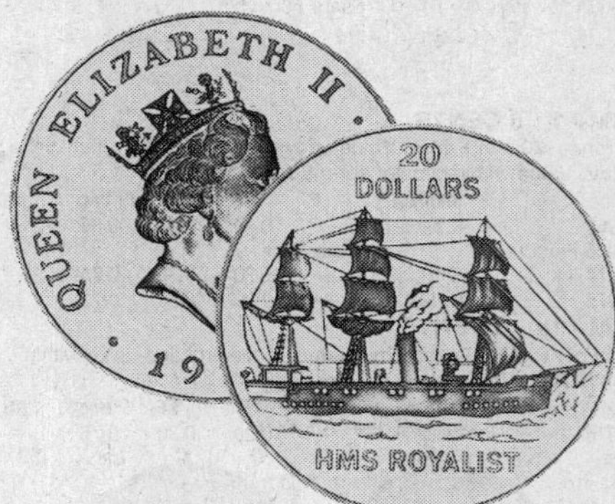

KM# 18 20 DOLLARS
31.4700 g., 0.9250 Silver .9359 oz. ASW **Obv:** Crowned head right **Rev:** HMS Royalist

Date	Mintage	F	VF	XF	Unc	BU
1993 Proof	15,000	Value: 16.00				

KM# 19 20 DOLLARS
31.4700 g., 0.9250 Silver .9359 oz. ASW **Obv:** Crowned head right **Rev:** Leatherback Turtle

Date	Mintage	F	VF	XF	Unc	BU
1993 Proof	Est. 10,000	Value: 30.00				

KM# 20 20 DOLLARS
31.4700 g., 0.9250 Silver .9359 oz. ASW **Obv:** Crowned head right **Rev:** Dugong - Manatee-like animal

Date	Mintage	F	VF	XF	Unc	BU
1994 Proof	Est. 10,000	Value: 35.00				

KM# 22 20 DOLLARS
31.4700 g., 0.9250 Silver .9359 oz. ASW **Subject:** 1994 World Cup Soccer **Obv:** Crowned head right **Rev:** Soccer ball within circles of world flags

Date	Mintage	F	VF	XF	Unc	BU
1994 Proof	Est. 30,000	Value: 16.00				

KM# 24 20 DOLLARS
31.4700 g., 0.9250 Silver .9359 oz. ASW **Series:** Olympics **Obv:** Crowned head right **Rev:** Swimming event

Date	Mintage	F	VF	XF	Unc	BU
1994 Proof	Est. 50,000	Value: 16.00				

KM# 25 20 DOLLARS
31.4700 g., 0.9250 Silver .9359 oz. ASW **Series:** Olympics **Obv:** Crowned head right **Rev:** Javelin thrower

Date	Mintage	F	VF	XF	Unc	BU
1994 Proof	Est. 50,000	Value: 16.00				

KM# 27 20 DOLLARS
31.7000 g., 0.9250 Silver .9427 oz. ASW **Series:** Protect Our World **Obv:** Crowned head right **Rev:** Blue Coral seascape

Date	Mintage	F	VF	XF	Unc	BU
1994 Proof	—	Value: 16.50				

KM# 39 20 DOLLARS
155.5000 g., 0.9990 Silver 4.9944 oz. ASW, 65 mm. **Subject:** Birthday of Queen Elizabeth - The Queen Mother **Obv:** Crowned head right **Rev:** Queen Mother and grandchildren **Edge:** Reeded **Note:** Photo reduced.

Date	Mintage	F	VF	XF	Unc	BU
1996 Proof	3,000	Value: 80.00				

KM# 9 50 DOLLARS
15.9800 g., 0.9170 Gold .4710 oz. AGW **Obv:** Young bust right **Rev:** Native meeting hut

Date	Mintage	F	VF	XF	Unc	BU
1976 Proof	2,074	Value: 345				

KM# 14 50 DOLLARS
15.9800 g., 0.9170 Gold .4710 oz. AGW **Subject:** Wedding of Prince Charles and Lady Diana **Obv:** Young bust right **Rev:** Three plumes within crown, value at right

Date	Mintage	F	VF	XF	Unc	BU
1981 Proof	5,000	Value: 335				

KM# 29 100 DOLLARS
7.7760 g., 0.5833 Gold .1458 oz. AGW **Subject:** 40th Anniversary of Coronation **Obv:** Crowned head right **Rev:** Coronation scene

Date	Mintage	F	VF	XF	Unc	BU
1993 Proof	—	Value: 110				

KM# 21 100 DOLLARS
7.7760 g., 0.5833 Gold .1458 oz. AGW **Subject:** Todos Los Santos

Date	Mintage	F	VF	XF	Unc	BU
1994 Proof	3,000	Value: 115				

KM# 23 100 DOLLARS
7.7760 g., 0.5833 Gold .1458 oz. AGW **Subject:** 1994 World Cup Soccer **Obv:** Crowned head right **Rev:** Soccer ball to upper left of eagle head and wing

Date	Mintage	F	VF	XF	Unc	BU
1994 Proof	3,000	Value: 120				

MINT SETS

KM#	Date	Mintage	Identification	Issue Price	Mkt Val
MS1	1985 (7)	—	KM#1-7	10.00	20.00

PROOF SETS

KM#	Date	Mintage	Identification	Issue Price	Mkt Val
PS1	1976 (7)	20,000	KM#1-7	13.00	25.00
PS2	1981 (7)	—	KM#1-7	—	25.00

UGANDA

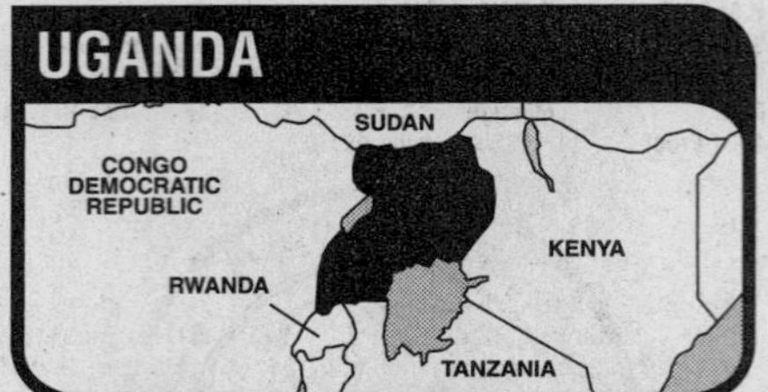

The Republic of Uganda, a former British protectorate located astride the equator in east-central Africa, has an area of 91,134 sq. mi. (236,040 sq. km.) and a population of *17 million. Capital: Kampala. Agriculture, including livestock, is the basis of the economy; there is some mining of copper, tin, gold and lead. Coffee, cotton, copper and tea are exported.

Uganda was first visited by Arab slavers in the 1830s. They were followed in the 1860s by British explorers searching for the headwaters of the Nile. The explorers, and the missionaries who followed them into the Lake Victoria region of south central Africa in 1877-79, found well-developed African kingdoms dating back several centuries. In 1894 the local native Kingdom of Buganda was established as a British protectorate that was extended in 1896 to encompass an area substantially the same as the present Republic of Uganda. The protectorate was given a ministerial form of government in 1955, full internal self-government on March 1, 1962, and complete independence on Oct. 9, 1962. Uganda is a member of the Commonwealth of Nations. The president is Chief of State and Head of Government.

For earlier coinage refer to East Africa.

RULERS
British, until 1962

MONETARY SYSTEM
100 Cents = 1 Shilling

REPUBLIC

STANDARD COINAGE

KM# 1 5 CENTS
Bronze, 20 mm. **Obv:** Value above crossed tusks within circle **Rev:** Value within circular sprig **Edge:** Plain

Date	Mintage	F	VF	XF	Unc	BU
1966	41,000,000	—	0.10	0.15	0.30	—
1966 Proof	—	Value: 1.00				
1974	8,624,000	—	0.20	0.30	0.75	—
1975	14,784,000	—	0.20	0.30	0.75	—

KM# 1a 5 CENTS
Copper Plated Steel **Obv:** Value above crossed tusks within circle **Rev:** Value within circular sprig

Date	Mintage	F	VF	XF	Unc	BU
1976	10,000,000	—	0.20	0.30	0.75	—

KM# 2 10 CENTS
Bronze **Obv:** Value above crossed tusks within circle **Rev:** Value within circular sprig

Date	Mintage	F	VF	XF	Unc	BU
1966	19,100,000	—	0.10	0.15	0.35	—
1966 Proof	—	Value: 1.00				
1968	20,000,000	—	0.10	0.15	0.35	—
1970	6,000,000	—	0.20	0.30	0.75	—
1972	6,000,000	—	0.20	0.30	0.75	—
1974	4,110,000	—	0.20	0.30	0.75	—
1975	14,000,000	—	0.20	0.30	0.75	—

KM# 2a 10 CENTS
Copper-Plated-Steel **Obv:** Value above crossed tusks within circle **Rev:** Value within circular sprig

Date	Mintage	F	VF	XF	Unc	BU
1976	10,000,000	—	0.20	0.30	0.75	—

KM# 3 20 CENTS
Bronze **Obv:** Value above crossed tusks within circle **Rev:** Value within circular sprig

Date	Mintage	F	VF	XF	Unc	BU
1966	7,000,000	—	0.30	0.70	1.65	—
1966 Proof	—	Value: 2.00				
1974	2,000,000	—	0.50	1.00	2.25	—

KM# 4 50 CENTS
Copper-Nickel **Obv:** National arms **Rev:** East African crowned crane, mountains and value

Date	Mintage	F	VF	XF	Unc	BU
1966	16,000,000	—	0.20	0.40	2.00	3.00
1966 Proof	—	Value: 3.50				
1970	3,000,000	—	0.25	0.75	3.00	3.50
1974	10,000,000	—	0.25	0.65	2.00	3.00

KM# 4a 50 CENTS
Copper-Nickel Plated Steel **Obv:** National arms **Rev:** East African crowned crane within circular sprig above value and date

Date	Mintage	F	VF	XF	Unc	BU
1976	10,000,000	—	0.25	0.65	2.00	2.50

KM# 5 SHILLING
Copper-Nickel **Obv:** National arms **Rev:** East African crowned crane within circular sprig above date and value

Date	Mintage	F	VF	XF	Unc	BU
1966	24,500,000	—	0.25	0.50	2.50	4.00
1966 Proof	—	Value: 4.50				
1968	10,000,000	—	0.35	0.85	2.75	4.00
1972	4,040,000	—	0.35	0.85	2.75	4.00
1975	15,500,000	—	0.35	0.85	2.50	4.00

KM# 5a SHILLING
Copper-Nickel Plated Steel **Obv:** National arms **Rev:** East African crowned crane within circular sprig above date and value

Date	Mintage	F	VF	XF	Unc	BU
1976	10,000,000	—	0.35	0.85	2.50	3.00

KM# 27 SHILLING
4.3000 g., Copper Plated Steel, 19.5 mm. **Obv:** National arms **Rev:** Value in center circle of flowered sprigs **Edge:** Plain **Shape:** 12-sided

Date	Mintage	F	VF	XF	Unc	BU
1987	—	—	—	—	0.25	0.40
1987 Proof	—	Value: 2.50				

KM# 6 2 SHILLINGS
Copper-Nickel **Obv:** National arms **Rev:** East African crowned crane within circular sprig above date and value

Date	Mintage	F	VF	XF	Unc	BU
1966	4,000,000	—	1.00	2.00	5.00	7.50
1966 Proof	—	Value: 9.00				

KM# 8 2 SHILLINGS
4.0000 g., 0.9990 Silver .1284 oz. ASW **Subject:** Visit of Pope Paul VI **Obv:** National arms **Rev:** Head right

Date	Mintage	F	VF	XF	Unc	BU
1969 Proof	8,170	Value: 8.50				
1970 Proof	Inc. above	Value: 8.50				

KM# 28 2 SHILLINGS
8.0000 g., Copper Plated Steel, 24 mm. **Obv:** National arms **Rev:** Value in center circle of flowered sprigs **Shape:** 12-sided

Date	Mintage	F	VF	XF	Unc	BU
1987	—	—	—	—	1.00	1.50
1987 Proof	—	Value: 4.00				

KM# 7 5 SHILLINGS
Copper-Nickel, 37.8 mm. **Series:** F.A.O. **Obv:** National arms **Rev:** Cow and calf

Date	Mintage	F	VF	XF	Unc	BU
ND(1968)	100,000	—	1.50	2.50	5.00	6.50
ND(1968) Proof	5,000	Value: 8.50				

KM# 9 5 SHILLINGS
10.0000 g., 0.9990 Silver .3212 oz. ASW **Subject:** Visit of Pope Paul VI **Obv:** National arms **Rev:** Crested cranes within circle

Date	Mintage	F	VF	XF	Unc	BU
1969 Proof	7,670	Value: 16.50				
1970 Proof	Inc. above	Value: 16.50				

KM# 18 5 SHILLINGS
Copper-Nickel, 30 mm. **Obv:** National arms **Rev:** East African crowned crane within circular sprig **Edge:** Plain **Shape:** 7-sided **Note:** Withdrawn from circulation. Almost entire mintage was melted.

Date	Mintage	F	VF	XF	Unc	BU
1972	Est. 8,000,000	—	25.00	45.00	80.00	125

KM# 29 5 SHILLINGS
3.5000 g., Stainless Steel, 22 mm. **Obv:** National arms **Rev:** Value within center circle of sprigs **Edge:** Plain **Shape:** 7-sided

Date	Mintage	F	VF	XF	Unc	BU
1987	—	—	—	—	2.50	3.00
1987 Proof	—	Value: 6.50				

KM# 10 10 SHILLINGS
20.0000 g., 0.9990 Silver .6424 oz. ASW **Subject:** Visit of Pope Paul VI **Obv:** National arms **Rev:** Martyrs' shrine within circle

Date	Mintage	F	VF	XF	Unc	BU
1969 Proof	6,720	Value: 22.50				
1970 Proof	Inc. above	Value: 22.50				

KM# 21 10 SHILLINGS
Copper-Nickel **Subject:** Wedding of Prince Charles and Lady Diana **Obv:** National arms **Rev:** Conjoined heads right

Date	Mintage	F	VF	XF	Unc	BU
1981	10,000	—	—	—	7.00	8.00

KM# 30 10 SHILLINGS
5.7000 g., Stainless Steel, 26 mm. **Obv:** National arms **Rev:** Value in center circle of sprigs **Edge:** Plain **Shape:** 7-sided

Date	Mintage	F	VF	XF	Unc	BU
1987	—	—	—	—	3.50	4.50
1987 Proof	—	Value: 12.50				

KM# 11 20 SHILLINGS
40.0000 g., 0.9990 Silver 1.2848 oz. ASW **Subject:** Visit of Pope Paul VI **Obv:** National arms **Rev:** Bust right within map and circle

Date	Mintage	F	VF	XF	Unc	BU
1969 Proof	6,670	Value: 30.00				
1970 Proof	Inc. above	Value: 32.50				

KM# 12 25 SHILLINGS
50.0000 g., 0.9990 Silver 1.6061 oz. ASW **Subject:** Visit of Pope Paul VI **Obv:** National arms **Rev:** Half-length figure facing, right arm raised in blessing superimposed on world globe

Date	Mintage	F	VF	XF	Unc	BU
1969 Proof	6,070	Value: 32.50				
1970 Proof	Inc. above	Value: 35.00				

KM# 13 30 SHILLINGS
60.0000 g., 0.9990 Silver 1.9273 oz. ASW, 60 mm. **Subject:** Visit of Pope Paul VI **Obv:** National arms **Rev:** Head right **Note:** Photo reduced.

Date	Mintage	F	VF	XF	Unc	BU
1969 Proof	6,720	Value: 37.50				
1970 Proof	Inc. above	Value: 40.00				

KM# 14 50 SHILLINGS
6.9100 g., 0.9000 Gold .1999 oz. AGW **Subject:** Visit of Pope Paul VI **Obv:** National arms **Rev:** Martyrs' shrine within circle

Date	Mintage	F	VF	XF	Unc	BU
1969 Proof	4,390	Value: 145				
1970 Proof	Inc. above	Value: 150				

KM# 66 50 SHILLINGS
Nickel Plated Steel **Obv:** National arms **Rev:** Antelope head facing

Date	Mintage	F	VF	XF	Unc	BU
1998	—	—	—	—	1.00	1.25

KM# 15 100 SHILLINGS
13.8200 g., 0.9000 Gold .3999 oz. AGW **Subject:** Visit of Pope Paul VI **Obv:** National arms **Rev:** Bust right within map and circle

Date	Mintage	F	VF	XF	Unc	BU
1969 Proof	4,190	Value: 295				
1970 Proof	Inc. above	Value: 300				

KM# 22 100 SHILLINGS
31.4700 g., 0.9250 Silver .9360 oz. ASW **Subject:** Wedding of Prince Charles and Lady Diana **Obv:** National arms **Rev. Designer:** Conjoined heads right

Date	Mintage	F	VF	XF	Unc	BU
1981 Proof	5,000	Value: 20.00				

KM# 67 100 SHILLINGS
Copper-Nickel **Obv:** National arms **Rev:** African bull

Date	Mintage	F	VF	XF	Unc	BU
1998	—	—	—	—	1.50	1.75

KM# 26 200 SHILLINGS
28.2800 g., 0.9250 Silver .8411 oz. ASW **Series:** International Year of Disabled Persons **Obv:** National arms **Rev:** Wooden cane divides emblem within wreath

Date	Mintage	F	VF	XF	Unc	BU
1981	10,000	—	—	—	25.00	27.50
1981 Proof	10,000	Value: 37.50				

KM# 68 200 SHILLINGS
Copper-Nickel **Obv:** National arms **Rev:** Cichlid fish above value and date

Date	Mintage	F	VF	XF	Unc	BU
1998	—	—	—	—	2.00	2.25

KM# 16 500 SHILLINGS
69.1200 g., 0.9000 Gold 2.0002 oz. AGW **Subject:** Visit of Pope Paul VI **Obv:** National arms **Rev:** Bust with hat facing within world globe

Date	Mintage	F	VF	XF	Unc	BU
1969 Proof	1,680	Value: 1,425				
1970 Proof	Inc. above	Value: 1,450				

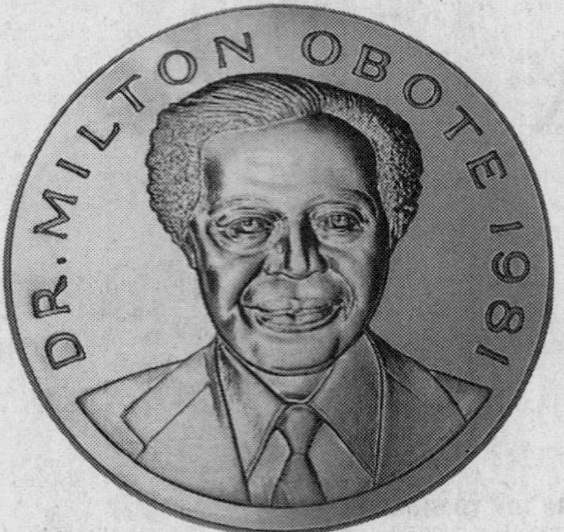

KM# 23 500 SHILLINGS
136.0000 g., 0.5000 Silver 2.1864 oz. ASW **Series:** Wildlife **Obv:** Bust of Dr. Milton Obote facing **Rev:** Elephants

Date	Mintage	F	VF	XF	Unc	BU
1981	700	—	—	—	110	125

KM# 23a 500 SHILLINGS
136.0000 g., 9.2500 Silver 4.045 oz. ASW **Series:** Wildlife **Obv:** Bust of Dr. Milton Obote facing **Rev:** Elephants

Date	Mintage	F	VF	XF	Unc	BU
1981 Proof	700	Value: 185				

KM# 69 500 SHILLINGS
Nickel-Brass **Obv:** National arms **Rev:** East African crowned crane head left

Date	Mintage	F	VF	XF	Unc	BU
1998	—	—	—	—	2.50	3.00

KM# 17 1000 SHILLINGS
138.2400 g., 0.9000 Gold 4.0005 oz. AGW **Subject:** Visit of Pope John Paul VI **Obv:** National arms **Rev:** Head right

Date	Mintage	F	VF	XF	Unc	BU
1969 Proof	1,390	Value: 2,825				
1970 Proof	Inc. above	Value: 2,850				

KM# 24 1000 SHILLINGS
10.0000 g., 0.5000 Gold .1607 oz. AGW **Subject:** Wedding of Prince Charles and Lady Diana **Obv:** National arms **Rev:** Conjoined busts right **Rev. Designer:** E.W. Roberts

Date	Mintage	F	VF	XF	Unc	BU
1981 Proof	1,500	Value: 125				

KM# 35 1000 SHILLINGS
Copper-Nickel **Series:** Famous Places **Subject:** Matterhorn Mountain **Obv:** National arms **Rev:** Multicolor plastic applique

Date	Mintage	F	VF	XF	Unc	BU
1993 Proof	15,000	Value: 17.50				

KM# 49 1000 SHILLINGS
Copper-Nickel **Series:** Famous Places **Subject:** Munich **Obv:** National arms

Date	Mintage	F	VF	XF	Unc	BU
1994 Proof	—	Value: 17.50				

KM# 40 1000 SHILLINGS
Copper-Nickel **Series:** 50th Anniversary - United Nations **Obv:** National arms **Rev:** Monument divides sprigs within circle

Date	Mintage	F	VF	XF	Unc	BU
1995 Proof	—	Value: 20.00				

KM# 50 1000 SHILLINGS
Copper-Nickel **Subject:** Year of the Pig **Obv:** Sow and piglets left **Rev:** Stylized pig left

Date	Mintage	F	VF	XF	Unc	BU
1995 Proof	—	Value: 17.50				

KM# 41 1000 SHILLINGS
Copper-Nickel **Series:** Endangered Wildlife **Obv:** National arms **Rev:** Multicolor zebra applique

Date	Mintage	F	VF	XF	Unc	BU
1996 Proof	—	Value: 20.00				

KM# 56 1000 SHILLINGS
Copper-Nickel **Subject:** Michael Schumacher **Obv:** National arms **Rev:** Multicolor applique head facing, car and flags

Date	Mintage	F	VF	XF	Unc	BU
1996 Proof	—	Value: 22.50				
1997 Proof	—	Value: 16.50				

KM# 44 1000 SHILLINGS
Copper-Nickel **Series:** Endangered Wildlife **Obv:** National arms **Rev:** Rhinoceros

Date	Mintage	F	VF	XF	Unc	BU
1996 Proof	15,000	Value: 22.50				

KM# 45 1000 SHILLINGS
Copper-Nickel **Series:** Endangered Wildlife **Obv:** National arms **Rev:** Lion

Date	Mintage	F	VF	XF	Unc	BU
1996 Proof	15,000	Value: 22.50				

KM# 52 1000 SHILLINGS
Copper-Nickel **Subject:** Hong Kong's return to China **Obv:** National arms **Rev:** City view

Date	Mintage	F	VF	XF	Unc	BU
1996	—	—	—	—	18.00	—

KM# 54 1000 SHILLINGS
Copper-Nickel **Subject:** Year of the rat **Obv:** Pair of rats flanking Chinese symbol **Rev:** Multicolor rat applique

Date	Mintage	F	VF	XF	Unc	BU
1996	—	—	—	—	22.50	—

KM# 55 1000 SHILLINGS
Copper-Nickel **Subject:** Africa - Protection of Endangered Wildlife **Obv:** National arms **Rev:** Multicolor elephant applique

Date	Mintage	F	VF	XF	Unc	BU
1996 Proof	—	Value: 22.50				

KM# 74 1000 SHILLINGS
28.5200 g., Copper-Nickel, 38.15 mm. **Subject:** Birth of Jesus and the Modern Dating System **Obv:** National arms **Rev:** Head of Jesus facing **Edge:** Reeded

Date	Mintage	F	VF	XF	Unc	BU
1996 Proof	—	Value: 20.00				

KM# 57 1000 SHILLINGS
Copper-Nickel **Subject:** Princess Diana - Queen of Hearts **Obv:** National arms **Rev:** Multicolor applique of Princess Diana

Date	Mintage	F	VF	XF	Unc	BU
1997 Proof	—	Value: 28.00				

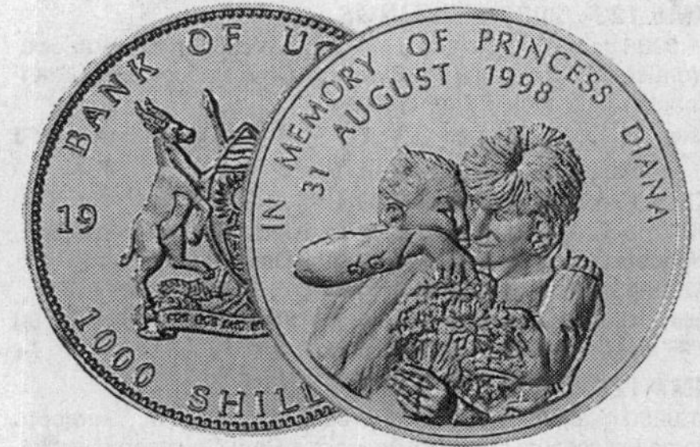

KM# 119 1000 SHILLINGS
28.7400 g., Copper-Nickel, 38 mm. **Obv:** National arms **Rev:** Princess Diana hugging child **Edge:** Reeded

Date	Mintage	F	VF	XF	Unc	BU
1998	—	—	—	—	15.00	17.50

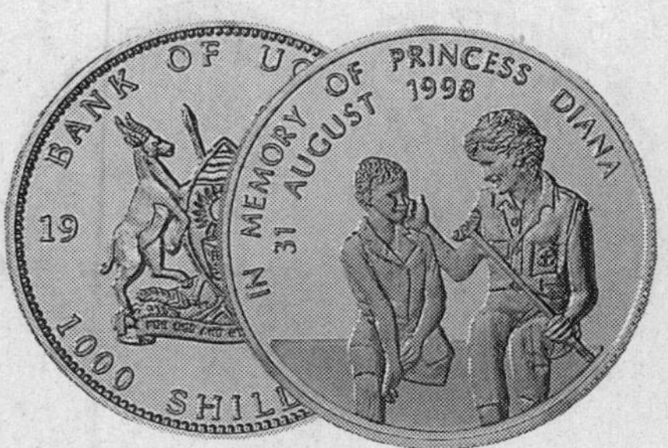

KM# 120 1000 SHILLINGS
28.7400 g., Copper-Nickel, 38 mm. **Obv:** National arms **Rev:** Diana holding one-legged child's crutch **Edge:** Reeded

Date	Mintage	F	VF	XF	Unc	BU
1998	—	—	—	—	15.00	17.50

KM# 118 1000 SHILLINGS
31.5600 g., 0.9250 Silver 0.9386 oz. ASW, 38.7 mm. **Subject:** Princess Diana **Obv:** National arms **Rev:** Charles and Diana engagement portrait **Edge:** Reeded

Date	Mintage	F	VF	XF	Unc	BU
1999 Proof	—	Value: 45.00				

KM# 70 1000 SHILLINGS
14.9700 g., 0.9990 Silver .4808 oz. ASW **Series:** XXVII Olympic Games **Obv:** National arms **Rev:** Javelin thrower

Date	Mintage	F	VF	XF	Unc	BU
1999 Proof	—	Value: 25.00				

KM# 116 1000 SHILLINGS
22.1300 g., Copper-Nickel, 38.6 mm. **Subject:** Euro Currency **Obv:** National arms **Rev:** European map with paper applique illustrating the Netherlands 10 Euro cent coin KM-237 **Edge:** Reeded

Date	Mintage	F	VF	XF	Unc	BU
1999	—	—	—	—	18.00	20.00

KM# 31 2000 SHILLINGS
15.9800 g., 0.9170 Gold .4710 oz. AGW **Series:** International Year of Disabled Persons **Obv:** National arms **Rev:** Stylized standing figure with cane

Date	Mintage	F	VF	XF	Unc	BU
1981	2,005	—	—	—	550	600
1981 Proof	2,005	Value: 700				

KM# 38 2000 SHILLINGS
19.8000 g., 0.9990 Silver .6359 oz. ASW **Subject:** World Cup Soccer **Obv:** Arms with supporters **Rev:** Soccer player

Date	Mintage	F	VF	XF	Unc	BU
1993 Proof	—	Value: 47.50				

KM# 39 2000 SHILLINGS
19.8000 g., 0.9990 Silver .6359 oz. ASW **Subject:** World Cup Soccer **Obv:** National arms **Rev:** Player kicking ball down field

Date	Mintage	F	VF	XF	Unc	BU
1993 Proof	—	Value: 47.50				

KM# 42 2000 SHILLINGS
19.9200 g., 0.9990 Silver .6398 oz. ASW **Series:** Famous Places **Subject:** Matterhorn Mountain **Note:** With multicolor applique.

Date	Mintage	F	VF	XF	Unc	BU
1993 Proof	10,000	Value: 30.00				

KM# 64 2000 SHILLINGS
30.4600 g., 0.9990 Silver .9783 oz. ASW **Subject:** Protection of the African elephant **Obv:** National arms **Rev:** Elephant head facing

Date	Mintage	F	VF	XF	Unc	BU
1993 Proof	—	Value: 50.00				

KM# 43 2000 SHILLINGS
19.9200 g., 0.9990 Silver .6398 oz. ASW **Series:** Famous Places **Subject:** Munich's Frauen Kirche **Obv:** National arms **Rev:** Towers

Date	Mintage	F	VF	XF	Unc	BU
1994 Proof	10,000	Value: 27.50				

KM# 53 2000 SHILLINGS
Copper-Nickel **Subject:** Nations United for Peace **Obv:** National arms **Rev:** United Nations 50th Anniversary

Date	Mintage	F	VF	XF	Unc	BU
ND(1995)	—	—	—	—	8.50	10.00

KM# 58 2000 SHILLINGS
30.8400 g., 0.9990 Silver .9904 oz. ASW **Obv:** Sow and piglets **Rev:** Multicolor pig applique

Date	Mintage	F	VF	XF	Unc	BU
1995 Proof	—	Value: 27.50				

KM# 46 2000 SHILLINGS
19.9200 g., 0.9990 Silver .6398 oz. ASW **Series:** Endangered Wildlife **Obv:** National arms **Rev:** Zebra

Date	Mintage	F	VF	XF	Unc	BU
1996 Proof	10,000	Value: 27.50				

KM# 93 2000 SHILLINGS
19.9200 g., 0.9990 Silver .6398 oz. ASW **Obv:** National arms **Rev:** Multicolor leaning Tower of Pisa

Date	Mintage	F	VF	XF	Unc	BU
1996 Proof	10,000	Value: 35.00				

KM# 94 2000 SHILLINGS
19.9000 g., 0.9990 Silver 0.6392 oz. ASW, 37.9 mm. **Subject:** Christian Dating System **Obv:** National arms **Rev:** Head of Jesus facing **Edge:** Reeded

Date	Mintage	F	VF	XF	Unc	BU
1996 Proof	—	Value: 35.00				

KM# 122 2000 SHILLINGS
31.0200 g., 0.9990 Silver 0.9963 oz. ASW, 38.5 mm. **Subject:** Wonders of the World - Leaning Tower of Pisa **Obv:** National arms **Rev:** Leaning tower within circle **Edge:** Reeded

Date	Mintage	F	VF	XF	Unc	BU
1996 Proof	—	Value: 50.00				

KM# 123 2000 SHILLINGS
31.0200 g., 0.9990 Silver 0.9963 oz. ASW, 38.5 mm. **Subject:** Wonders of the World - The Pyramids **Obv:** National arms **Rev:** Sphinx within circle **Edge:** Reeded

Date	Mintage	F	VF	XF	Unc	BU
1996 Proof	—	Value: 50.00				

KM# 124 2000 SHILLINGS
31.0200 g., 0.9990 Silver 0.9963 oz. ASW, 38.5 mm. **Subject:** Wonders of the World - The Parthenon **Obv:** National arms **Rev:** Building within circle **Edge:** Reeded

Date	Mintage	F	VF	XF	Unc	BU
1996 Proof	—	Value: 50.00				

KM# 125 2000 SHILLINGS
31.0200 g., 0.9990 Silver 0.9963 oz. ASW, 38.5 mm. **Subject:** Rome Colosseum **Obv:** National arms **Rev:** Colosseum within circle **Edge:** Reeded

Date	Mintage	F	VF	XF	Unc	BU
1996 Proof	—	Value: 50.00				

KM# 126 2000 SHILLINGS
31.0200 g., 0.9990 Silver 0.9963 oz. ASW, 38.5 mm. **Subject:** Wonders of the World - Taj Mahal **Obv:** National arms **Rev:** Taj Mahal within circle **Edge:** Reeded

Date	Mintage	F	VF	XF	Unc	BU
1996 Proof	—	Value: 50.00				

KM# 127 2000 SHILLINGS
31.0200 g., 0.9990 Silver 0.9963 oz. ASW, 38.5 mm. **Subject:** Wonders of the World - Yungang Grottoes **Obv:** National arms **Rev:** Half figures facing in front of mountain **Edge:** Reeded

Date	Mintage	F	VF	XF	Unc	BU
1996 Proof	—	Value: 50.00				

KM# 47 2000 SHILLINGS
19.9200 g., 0.9990 Silver .6398 oz. ASW **Series:** Endangered Wildlife **Obv:** National arms **Rev:** Rhinocerous within circle

Date	Mintage	F	VF	XF	Unc	BU
1996 Proof	10,000	Value: 45.00				

KM# 48 2000 SHILLINGS
19.9200 g., 0.9990 Silver .6398 oz. ASW **Series:** Endangered Wildlife **Obv:** National arms **Rev:** Lion

Date	Mintage	F	VF	XF	Unc	BU
1996 Proof	10,000	Value: 50.00				

KM# 59 2000 SHILLINGS
30.8400 g., 0.9990 Silver .9904 oz. ASW **Obv:** Pair of rats flanking Chinese symbols **Rev:** Multicolor rat applique

Date	Mintage	F	VF	XF	Unc	BU
1996 Proof	—	Value: 35.00				

KM# 60 2000 SHILLINGS
7.1000 g., 0.9990 Silver .228 oz. ASW **Subject:** 1998 World Championship Football **Obv:** National arms **Rev:** Soccer player and Eiffel Tower within circle

Date	Mintage	F	VF	XF	Unc	BU
1996 Proof	—	Value: 22.50				

KM# 61 2000 SHILLINGS
Copper-Nickel **Series:** XXVI Summer Olympic Games **Obv:** National arms **Rev:** German Olympic stamp

Date	Mintage	F	VF	XF	Unc	BU
1996 Proof	—	Value: 20.00				

KM# 62 2000 SHILLINGS
Copper-Nickel **Series:** Olympics **Obv:** National arms **Rev:** Spanish postal stamp design

Date	Mintage	F	VF	XF	Unc	BU
1996 Proof	—	Value: 20.00				

KM# 65 2000 SHILLINGS
20.2600 g., 0.9990 Silver .6507 oz. ASW **Series:** Endangered Wildlife **Obv:** National arms **Rev:** Multicolor elephant

Date	Mintage	F	VF	XF	Unc	BU
1996 Proof	—	Value: 40.00				

KM# 63 2000 SHILLINGS
Copper-Nickel **Subject:** Queen's Golden Wedding Anniversary **Obv:** National arms **Rev:** Queen Elizabeth and Prince Philip on horseback

Date	Mintage	F	VF	XF	Unc	BU
ND(1997)	—	—	—	—	8.00	10.00

KM# 51 2000 SHILLINGS
19.7400 g., 0.9990 Silver .6346 oz. ASW **Subject:** Hong Kong's return to China **Obv:** National arms **Rev:** City view below head left

Date	Mintage	F	VF	XF	Unc	BU
1997 Proof	—	Value: 35.00				

KM# 95 2000 SHILLINGS
31.3200 g., 0.9990 Silver 1.006 oz. ASW, 38.8 mm. **Subject:** Zebras **Obv:** National arms **Rev:** Zebra and nursing colt **Edge:** Reeded

Date	Mintage	F	VF	XF	Unc	BU
1999 Proof	—	Value: 42.50				

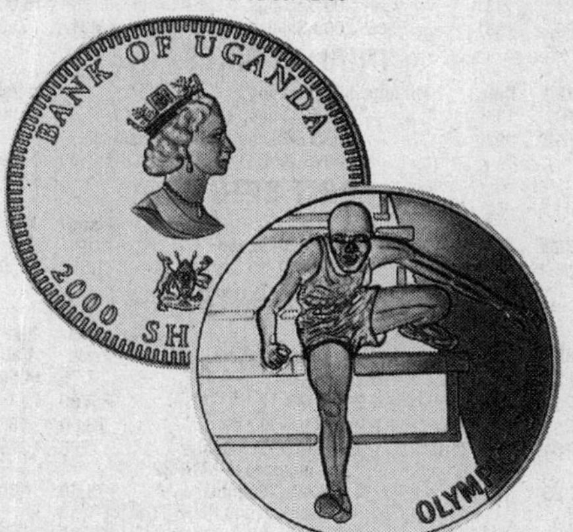

KM# 71 2000 SHILLINGS
26.0000 g., 0.9990 Silver .8351 oz. ASW, 40.1 mm. **Series:** Olympics 2000 **Obv:** Crowned head right above national arms **Rev:** Hurdler **Edge:** Reeded

Date	Mintage	F	VF	XF	Unc	BU
2000 Proof	5,000	Value: 32.50				

KM# 72 2000 SHILLINGS
15.7500 g., 0.9250 Silver .4684 oz. ASW, 45.2x23.2 mm. **Series:** Millennium **Obv:** National arms above crowned head right **Rev:** Pythagoras **Edge:** Plain **Shape:** Triangular

Date	Mintage	F	VF	XF	Unc	BU
2000 Proof	10,000	Value: 30.00				

KM# 73 2000 SHILLINGS
25.0000 g., 0.9250 Silver .7435 oz. ASW, 37.9 mm. **Subject:** Wildlife protection **Obv:** National arms below crowned head right **Rev:** Three zebras drinking in reflective water **Edge:** Reeded

Date	Mintage	F	VF	XF	Unc	BU
2000 Proof	5,000	Value: 35.00				

KM# 25 5000 SHILLINGS
33.9300 g., 0.9170 Gold 1 oz. AGW **Subject:** Wildlife **Obv:** Bust of Dr. Milton Obote facing **Rev:** East African crowned crane

Date	Mintage	F	VF	XF	Unc	BU
1981	100	—	—	—	700	750
1981 Proof	100	Value: 775				

KM# 32 5000 SHILLINGS
12.0000 g., 0.9990 Silver .3858 oz. ASW **Subject:** Soccer **Obv:** National arms **Rev:** Soccer ball and net

Date	Mintage	F	VF	XF	Unc	BU
1992	Est. 10,000	—	—	—	22.50	25.00

KM# 36 5000 SHILLINGS
500.0000 g., 0.9990 Silver 16.0753 oz. ASW **Series:** Endangered Wildlife **Obv:** African map **Rev:** 2 Leopards on branches

Date	Mintage	F	VF	XF	Unc	BU
1993 Proof	2,500	Value: 275				

KM# 36.1 5000 SHILLINGS
10.4800 g., 0.9990 Silver 0.3366 oz. ASW, 38 mm. **Subject:** Reduced Size **Obv:** African map **Rev:** Two lions in tree **Edge:** Reeded

Date	Mintage	F	VF	XF	Unc	BU
1993 Proof	—	Value: 35.00				

KM# 128 5000 SHILLINGS
28.2000 g., Silver, 38 mm. **Subject:** FAO - Food for All **Obv:** National arms **Rev:** Bananas

Date	Mintage	F	VF	XF	Unc	BU
1995	—	—	—	—	—	40.00

KM# 33 10000 SHILLINGS
20.0000 g., 0.9990 Silver .6430 oz. ASW **Subject:** Soccer **Obv:** National arms **Rev:** Mount Rushmore behind soccer players

Date	Mintage	F	VF	XF	Unc	BU
ND(1992) Proof	Est. 10,000	Value: 45.00				

KM# 34 10000 SHILLINGS
20.0000 g., 0.9990 Silver .6430 oz. ASW **Subject:** Papal visit **Obv:** National arms **Rev:** Half-length figure facing

Date	Mintage	F	VF	XF	Unc	BU
1993 Proof	—	Value: 37.50				

KM# 37.1 10000 SHILLINGS
12.9420 g., 0.9990 Silver 0.4157 oz. ASW, 38 mm. **Subject:** Reduced Size **Obv:** African map **Rev:** Two rhinos **Edge:** Reeded

Date	Mintage	F	VF	XF	Unc	BU
1993 Proof	—	Value: 35.00				

KM# 37 10000 SHILLINGS
1000.0000 g., 0.9990 Silver 32.1507 oz. ASW **Series:** Endangered Wildlife **Obv:** African map **Rev:** Rhinoceros

Date	Mintage	F	VF	XF	Unc	BU
1993 Proof	2,000	Value: 500				

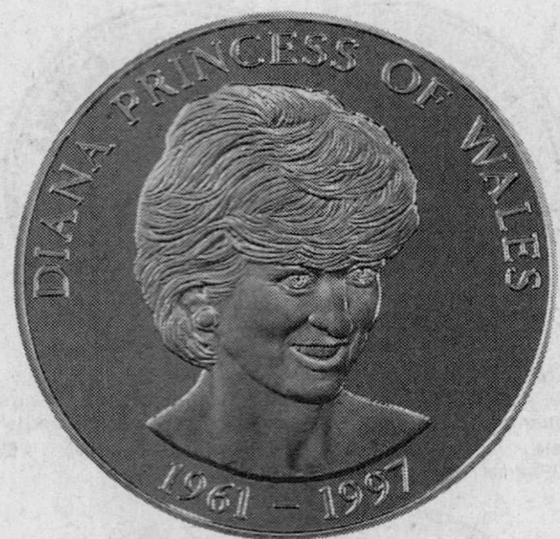

KM# 92 10000 SHILLINGS
155.5000 g., 0.9990 Silver 4.9944 oz. ASW, 65 mm. **Subject:** Diana Princess of Wales **Obv:** National arms **Rev:** Head 1/4 right **Edge:** Reeded **Note:** Photo reduced.

Date	Mintage	F	VF	XF	Unc	BU
1998 Proof	2,500	Value: 150				

PATTERNS

Including off metal strikes

KM#	Date	Mintage	Identification	Mkt Val
Pn1	1994	—	1000 Shillings. Copper-Nickel. Soccer player, 999.	—
Pn2	1994	—	1000 Shillings. Copper-Nickel. 3 soccer players, 999 CuNi.	—
Pn3	1994	—	1000 Shillings. Copper-Nickel. 4 soccer players, 999.	—
Pn4	1996	—	1000 Shillings. Gilt Bronze. Surinam. 100 Guilders.	—

PIEFORTS

KM#	Date	Mintage	Identification	Mkt Val
P1	1981	—	200 Shillings. 0.9250 Silver. KM26.	75.00
P2	1981	505	2000 Shillings. 0.9170 Gold. KM31.	750

TRIAL STRIKES

KM#	Date	Mintage	Identification	Mkt Val
TS1	1969	—	500 Shillings. Goldine. KM16.	100
TS2	1970	—	1000 Shillings. Goldine. National arms. KM17.	125

MINT SETS

KM#	Date	Mintage	Identification	Issue Price	Mkt Val
MS1	1987 (4)	—	KM27-30	10.50	11.50

PROOF SETS

KM#	Date	Mintage	Identification	Issue Price	Mkt Val
PS1	1966 (6)	8,250	KM1-6	7.75	14.50
PS2	1969 (10)	1,390	KM8-17	790	4,175
PS3	1969 (6)	6,070	KM8-13	78.50	160
PS4	1970 (10)	I.A.	KM8-17, mintage included in KM-PS2	790	4,275
PS5	1970 (6)	I.A.	KM8-13, mintage included in KM-PS3	78.50	170
PS6	1987 (4)	2,500	KM27-30	25.00	27.50

UKRAINE

Ukraine (formerly the Ukrainian Soviet Socialist Republic) is bordered by Russia to the east, Russia and Belarus to the north, Poland, Slovakia and Hungary to the west, Romania and Moldova to the southwest and in the south by the Black Sea and the Sea of Azov. It has an area of 233,088 sq. mi. (603,700 sq. km.) and a population of 51.9 million. Capital: Kyiv (Kiev). Coal, grain, vegetables and heavy industrial machinery are major exports.

The territory of Ukraine has been inhabited for over 30,000 years. As the result of its location, Ukraine has served as the gateway to Europe for millennia and its early history has been recorded by Arabic, Greek, Roman, as well as Ukrainian historians.

Ukraine, which was known as *Rus'* until the sixteenth century (and from which the name Russia was derived in the 17th century) became the major political and cultural center of Eastern Europe in the 9th century. The Rus' Kingdom, under a dynasty of Varangian origin, due to its position on the intersection of the north-south Scandinavia to Byzantium and the east-west Orient to Europe trade routes, became a focal point of world trade. At its apex Rus' stretched from the Baltic to the Black Sea and from the upper Volga River in the east, almost to the Vistula River in the west. It has family ties to many European dynasties. In 988 knyaz (king) Volodymyr adopted Christianity from Byzantium. With it came church books written in the Cyrillic alphabet, which originated in Bulgaria. The Mongol invasion in 1240 brought an end to the might of the Rus' Kingdom.

In the seventeenth century, after almost four hundred years of Mongol, Lithuanian, Polish, and Turkish domination, the Cossack State under Hetman Bohdan Khmelnytsky regained Ukrainian independence. The Hetman State lasted until the mid-eighteenth century and was followed by a period of foreign rule. Eastern Ukraine was controlled by Russia, which enforced russification through introduction of the Russian language and prohibiting the use of the Ukrainian language in schools, books and public life. Western Ukraine came under relatively benign Austro-Hungarian rule.

With the disintegration of the Russian and Austro-Hungarian Empires in 1917 and 1918. Eastern Ukraine declared its full independence on January 22,1918 and Western Ukraine followed suit on November 1 of that year. On January 22, 1919 both parts united into one state that had to defend itself on three fronts: from the "Red Bolsheviks"and their puppet Ukrainian Soviet Republic formed in Kharkiv, from the "White" czarist Russian forces, and from Poland. Ukraine lost the war. In 1920 Eastern Ukraine was occupied by the Bolsheviks and in 1922 was incorporated into the Soviet Union. There followed a brief resurgence of Ukrainian language and culture which Stalin suppressed in 1928. The artificial famine-genocide of 1932-33 killed 7-10 million Ukrainians, and Stalinist purges in the mid-1930s took a heavy toll. Western Ukraine was partitioned between Poland, Romania, Hungary and Czechoslovakia.

On August 24, 1991 Ukraine once again declared its independence. On December 1, 1991 over 90% of Ukraine's electorate approved full independence from the Soviet Union. On December 5, 1991 the Ukrainian Parliament abrogated the 1922 treaty which incorporated Ukraine into the Soviet Union. Later, Leonid Kravchuk was elected president by a 65% majority.

Ukraine is a charter member of the United Nations and has inherited the third largest nuclear arsenal in the world.

RULERS
Russian (Eastern, Northern, Southern, Central Ukraine), 1654-1917
Austrian (Western Ukraine), 1774-1918

MINT
w/o mm - Lugansk; Kiev (1997-1998)

MONETARY SYSTEM
(1) Kopiyka
(2) Kopiyky КОПІИКН
(5 and up) Kopiyok КОПИОК
100 Kopiyok = 1 Hrynia ГРИВЕНЬ
100,000 Karbovanetsiv = 1 Hryni or Hryven)

REPUBLIC

STANDARD COINAGE

KM# 9 200000 KARBOVANTSIV
14.3500 g., Copper-Nickel, 33 mm. **Obv:** National arms **Rev:** Bohdan Khmelnytsky Monument **Edge:** Reeded

Date	Mintage	F	VF	XF	Unc	BU
1995 Prooflike	250,000	—	—	—	6.00	7.00

KM# 10.1 200000 KARBOVANTSIV
14.3500 g., Copper-Nickel, 33 mm. **Subject:** 50th Anniversary - End of World War II **Obv:** Ukranian letter "Y" looks similar to "X" **Rev:** Ukranian letter "Y" looks similar to "X" **Edge:** Reeded

Date	Mintage	F	VF	XF	Unc	BU
1995 Prooflike	10,000	—	—	—	20.00	22.50

KM# 10.2 200000 KARBOVANTSIV
14.3500 g., Copper-Nickel, 33 mm. **Subject:** 50th Anniversary - End of World War II **Obv:** Ukranian letter "Y" like Y/2 in legends **Rev:** Ukranian letter "Y" like Y/2 in legends **Edge:** Reeded

Date	Mintage	F	VF	XF	Unc	BU
1995 Prooflike	240,000	—	—	—	5.00	6.00

KM# 11 200000 KARBOVANTSIV
14.3500 g., Copper-Nickel, 33 mm. **Subject:** World War II - Monument at Kerch **Obv:** National arms **Rev:** Monument and ship **Edge:** Reeded

Date	Mintage	F	VF	XF	Unc	BU
1995 Prooflike	50,000	—	—	—	13.50	15.00

KM# 12 200000 KARBOVANTSIV
14.3500 g., Copper-Nickel, 33 mm. **Subject:** World War II - Monument at Odessa **Obv:** National arms **Rev:** Monument divides ship and lighthouse **Edge:** Reeded

Date	Mintage	F	VF	XF	Unc	BU
1995 Prooflike	75,000	—	—	—	6.00	7.00

KM# 13 200000 KARBOVANTSIV
14.3500 g., Copper-Nickel, 33 mm. **Subject:** World War II - Monument at Kiev **Obv:** National arms **Rev:** Monument and city scene **Edge:** Reeded

Date	Mintage	F	VF	XF	Unc	BU
1995 Prooflike	100,000	—	—	—	6.00	7.00

KM# 14 200000 KARBOVANTSIV
14.3500 g., Copper-Nickel, 33 mm. **Subject:** World War II - Monument at Sevastopol **Obv:** National arms **Rev:** Monuments and ship **Edge:** Reeded

Date	Mintage	F	VF	XF	Unc	BU
1995 Prooflike	75,000	—	—	—	7.00	8.00

KM# 15 200000 KARBOVANTSIV
28.2800 g., Copper-Nickel, 38.61 mm. **Series:** 50th Anniversary - United Nations **Obv:** National arms **Rev:** Numeral 50 and emblem on top of assorted flag globe **Edge:** Reeded

Date	Mintage	F	VF	XF	Unc	BU
1995	100,000	—	—	—	5.50	6.50

KM# 17 200000 KARBOVANTSIV
14.3500 g., Copper-Nickel, 33 mm. **Subject:** Lesya Ukrainka **Obv:** National arms **Rev:** Half-length Poetess facing **Edge:** Reeded

Date	Mintage	F	VF	XF	Unc	BU
1996 Prooflike	100,000	—	—	—	6.50	7.50

KM# 21 200000 KARBOVANTSIV
14.3500 g., Copper-Nickel, 33 mm. **Subject:** 10th Anniversary - Chernobyl Disaster **Obv:** National arms **Rev:** Bell with cross at top **Edge:** Reeded

Date	Mintage	F	VF	XF	Unc	BU
1996 Prooflike	250,000	—	—	—	6.00	7.00

KM# 23 200000 KARBOVANTSIV
14.3500 g., Copper-Nickel, 33 mm. **Series:** 1st Participation in Summer Olympics **Obv:** National arms **Rev:** Athletes around octagon **Edge:** Reeded

Date	Mintage	F	VF	XF	Unc	BU
1996 Prooflike	100,000	—	—	—	5.50	6.50

KM# 24 200000 KARBOVANTSIV
14.3500 g., Copper-Nickel, 33 mm. **Series:** Centennial of Modern Olympics **Obv:** National arms **Rev:** Flame and logo **Edge:** Reeded

Date	Mintage	F	VF	XF	Unc	BU
1996 Prooflike	100,000	—	—	—	5.50	6.50

KM# 27 200000 KARBOVANTSIV
14.3500 g., Copper-Nickel, 33 mm. **Subject:** Mikhailo Hrushevsky - 1866-1934 **Obv:** National arms **Rev:** Half-length figure facing **Edge:** Reeded

Date	Mintage	F	VF	XF	Unc	BU
1996 Prooflike	75,000	—	—	—	7.00	8.00

KM# 16 1000000 KARBOVANETS
16.8110 g., 0.9250 Silver .5 oz. ASW, 33 mm. **Subject:** Bohdan Khmelnytsky Monument **Obv:** National arms **Rev:** Bohdan Khmelnytsky Monument **Edge:** Reeded

Date	Mintage	F	VF	XF	Unc	BU
1996 Proof	10,000	Value: 42.50				

KM# 18 1000000 KARBOVANETS
16.8110 g., 0.9250 Silver .5 oz. ASW, 33 mm. **Subject:** Lesya Ukrainka **Obv:** National arms **Rev:** Half-length Poetess facing **Edge:** Reeded

Date	Mintage	F	VF	XF	Unc	BU
1996 Proof	10,000	Value: 40.00				

KM# 20 1000000 KARBOVANETS
16.8110 g., 0.9250 Silver .5 oz. ASW, 33 mm. **Subject:** Hryhoriy Skovoroda **Obv:** National arms **Rev:** Bust facing **Edge:** Reeced

Date	Mintage	F	VF	XF	Unc	BU
1996 Proof	10,000	Value: 37.50				

KM# 32 1000000 KARBOVANETS
16.8110 g., 0.9250 Silver .5 oz. ASW, 33 mm. **Subject:** Mykhaylo Hrushevsky **Obv:** National arms **Rev:** Half-length figure facing **Edge:** Reeded

Date	Mintage	F	VF	XF	Unc	BU
1996 Proof	10,000	Value: 37.50				

KM# 19 2000000 KARBOVANETS
33.6220 g., 0.9250 Silver 1 oz. ASW, 38.61 mm. **Series:** 50 Years - United Nations **Obv:** National arms **Rev:** Numeral 50 and emblem on top of assorted flag globe **Edge:** Reeded **Note:** Minted in 1995, issued on March 7, 1996.

Date	Mintage	F	VF	XF	Unc	BU
1995 Proof	10,000	Value: 40.00				

KM# 22 2000000 KARBOVANETS
33.6220 g., 0.9250 Silver 1 oz. ASW, 38.61 mm. **Subject:** 10th Anniversary - Chernobyl Disaster **Obv:** National arms **Rev:** Bell with cross at top **Edge:** Reeded

Date	Mintage	F	VF	XF	Unc	BU
1996 Proof	10,000	Value: 42.50				

KM# 25 2000000 KARBOVANETS
33.6220 g., 0.9250 Silver 1 oz. ASW, 38.61 mm. **Series:** 1st Participation in Summer Olympics **Obv:** National arms **Rev:** Head right within octagon surrounded by athletes **Edge:** Reeded

Date	Mintage	F	VF	XF	Unc	BU
1995 Proof	10,000	Value: 40.00				

KM# 26 2000000 KARBOVANETS
33.6220 g., 0.9250 Silver 1 oz. ASW, 38.61 mm. **Series:** Centennial of Modern Olympics **Obv:** National arms **Rev:** Olympic flame and logo **Edge:** Reeded

Date	Mintage	F	VF	XF	Unc	BU
1996 Proof	10,000	Value: 40.00				

KM# 33 2000000 KARBOVANETS
33.6220 g., 0.9250 Silver 1 oz. ASW, 39 mm. **Subject:** Independence **Obv:** National arms **Rev:** Standing female figure holding sprig and wreath to left of flag and map **Edge:** Reeded

Date	Mintage	F	VF	XF	Unc	BU
1996 Proof	10,000	Value: 150				

REFORM COINAGE

September 2, 1996

100,000 Karbovanets = 1 Hryvnia; 100 Kopiyok = 1 Hryvnia; The Kopiyok has replaced the Karbovanet

KM# 6 KOPIYKA
1.5000 g., Stainless Steel, 16 mm. **Obv:** National arms **Rev:** Value within wreath **Edge:** Plain

Date	Mintage	F	VF	XF	Unc	BU
1992	—	—	—	0.15	0.35	—
1994	—	—	—	5.00	10.00	—
1996	—	—	—	2.00	5.00	—
2000	—	—	—	0.35	0.75	—

KM# 4a 2 KOPIYKY
0.6400 g., Aluminum, 17.3 mm. **Obv:** National arms **Rev:** Value within wreath **Edge:** Plain **Note:** Prev. KM#4.

Date	Mintage	F	VF	XF	Unc	BU
1993	—	—	0.20	0.50	1.00	—
1994	—	—	0.20	0.50	1.00	—
1996	—	—	0.40	2.00	3.00	—

KM# 7 5 KOPIYOK
4.3000 g., Stainless Steel, 24 mm. **Obv:** National arms **Rev:** Value within wreath **Edge:** Reeded

Date	Mintage	F	VF	XF	Unc	BU
1992	—	—	—	0.35	0.65	—
1996	—	—	0.50	3.00	6.00	—

KM# 1.1a 10 KOPIYOK
1.7000 g., Brass, 16.3 mm. **Obv:** National arms **Rev:** Five dots right of final "K" in value **Edge:** Reeded **Note:** Fine or coarse reeded edge varieties exist. Prev. KM#1.1.

Date	Mintage	F	VF	XF	Unc	BU
1992	—	—	0.50	1.00	2.25	—
1994	—	—	0.50	1.00	2.25	—
1996	—	—	0.60	1.25	2.50	—

KM# 1.2 10 KOPIYOK
Brass **Obv:** National arms **Rev:** Six dots right of "K"

Date	Mintage	F	VF	XF	Unc	BU
1992	—	—	0.50	1.00	2.25	—

KM# 2.1a 25 KOPIYOK
2.9000 g., Brass, 20.8 mm. **Obv:** National arms **Rev:** Value within wreath **Note:** Prev. KM#2.1.

Date	Mintage	F	VF	XF	Unc	BU
1992	—	—	0.60	1.25	2.50	—
1994	—	—	0.60	1.25	2.50	—
1995	—	—	1.50	3.00	6.00	—
1996	—	—	0.80	2.25	4.00	—

KM# 2.2 25 KOPIYOK
Brass **Obv:** National arms **Rev:** Berries with dots inside

Date	Mintage	F	VF	XF	Unc	BU
1992	—	—	0.60	1.25	2.50	—

KM# 3.1 50 KOPIYOK
4.2000 g., Brass, 23 mm. **Obv:** National arms **Rev:** Five dots grouped i wreath to right of final letter "K" in value **Edge:** Reeded sections of 16 grooves each

Date	Mintage	F	VF	XF	Unc	BU
1992	—	—	0.85	1.75	3.50	—
1994	—	—	0.85	1.75	3.50	—

KM# 3.3a 50 KOPIYOK
Brass **Obv:** National arms **Rev:** Five dots grouped in wreath to right of final letter "K" in value **Note:** Prev. KM#3.3.

Date	Mintage	F	VF	XF	Unc	BU
1992	—	—	0.85	1.75	3.50	—
1994	—	—	0.85	1.75	3.50	—
1995	—	—	3.00	5.00	10.00	—
1996	—	—	1.00	2.50	4.50	—

KM# 3.2 50 KOPIYOK
Brass **Obv:** National arms **Rev:** Four dots grouped in wreath to right of final letter "K" in value **Edge:** Reeded sections of seven grooves each

Date	Mintage	F	VF	XF	Unc	BU
1992	—	—	0.85	1.75	3.50	—

KM# 8a HRYVNIA
7.1000 g., Brass, 26 mm. **Obv:** National arms **Rev:** Value, sprigs and designs **Note:** Prev. KM#8.

Date	Mintage	F	VF	XF	Unc	BU
1992	—	—	—	80.00	200	—
1995	—	—	—	4.00	8.00	—
1996	—	—	—	2.50	4.50	—

KM# 30 2 HRYVNI
Copper-Nickel-Zinc **Subject:** Modern Ukrainian coinage **Obv:** National arms within beaded circle **Rev:** Assorted coins

Date	Mintage	F	VF	XF	Unc	BU
1996	—	—	—	—	8.00	—
1997 (Lugansk Mint)	200,000	—	—	—	9.50	—
1998 (Kiev Mint)	50,000	—	—	—	10.00	—

KM# 28 2 HRYVNI
14.3500 g., Copper-Nickel-Zinc, 33 mm. **Subject:** 200th Anniversary - Sophiyivka Dendrological Park **Obv:** National arms **Rev:** Partially overgrown stone face **Edge:** Reeded

Date	Mintage	F	VF	XF	Unc	BU
1996 Prooflike	30,000	—	—	—	—	40.00

KM# 29 2 HRYVNI
14.3500 g., Copper-Nickel-Zinc, 33 mm. **Subject:** Desiatynna Church **Obv:** National arms above Madonna and child, vines surround **Rev:** Church **Edge:** Reeded

Date	Mintage	F	VF	XF	Unc	BU
1996 Prooflike	30,000	—	—	—	—	70.00

KM# 39 2 HRYVNI
14.3500 g., Copper-Nickel-Zinc, 33 mm. **Subject:** Yuri Kondratiuk **Obv:** National arms on astrological design **Rev:** Scientific drawing to right of bust facing **Edge:** Reeded

Date	Mintage	F	VF	XF	Unc	BU
1997 Prooflike	20,000	—	—	—	—	90.00

KM# 40 2 HRYVNI
14.3500 g., Copper-Nickel-Zinc, 33 mm. **Subject:** 1st Anniversary of the Constitution **Obv:** National arms **Rev:** Scroll below design within beaded circle **Edge:** Reeded

Date	Mintage	F	VF	XF	Unc	BU
1997 Prooflike	20,000	—	—	—	—	120

KM# 41 2 HRYVNI
14.3500 g., Copper-Nickel-Zinc, 33 mm. **Subject:** Solomiya Krushelnytska - 1872-1952 **Obv:** National arms within beaded circle **Rev:** Bust with hat left **Edge:** Reeded

Date	Mintage	F	VF	XF	Unc	BU
1997 Prooflike	20,000	—	—	—	—	70.00

KM# 42 2 HRYVNI
12.8000 g., Copper-Nickel-Zinc, 31 mm. **Subject:** 80 Years of Nationhood **Obv:** National arms and people above value **Rev:** Outreached arm with army on forearm to right of Cossacks **Edge:** Reeded

Date	Mintage	F	VF	XF	Unc	BU
ND(1998)	150,000	—	—	—	7.50	—
ND(1998) Prooflike	50,000	—	—	—	10.00	—

Note: Encapsulated

KM# 47 2 HRYVNI
12.8000 g., Copper-Nickel-Zinc, 31 mm. **Subject:** 80 Years of Nationhood **Obv:** National arms and family group **Rev:** Soldiers on guard **Edge:** Reeded

Date	Mintage	F	VF	XF	Unc	BU
1998	150,000	—	—	—	7.50	—
1998 Prooflike	50,000	—	—	—	12.50	—

Note: Encapsulated

KM# 49 2 HRYVNI
12.8000 g., Copper-Nickel-Zinc, 31 mm. **Subject:** 100th Anniversary - Askania-Nova Wildlife Preserve **Obv:** National arms, value, wild animals and plants **Rev:** Standing half-length figure to lower left of animals running right **Edge:** Reeded

Date	Mintage	F	VF	XF	Unc	BU
1998	90,000	—	—	—	22.50	—
1998 Prooflike	10,000	—	—	—	45.00	—

Note: Encapsulated

KM# 51 2 HRYVNI
12.8000 g., Copper-Nickel-Zinc, 31 mm. **Subject:** 100th Anniversary - Kiev Polytechnical Institute **Obv:** National arms in circular design **Rev:** Building within circle **Edge:** Reeded

Date	Mintage	F	VF	XF	Unc	BU
1998	40,000	—	—	—	40.00	—
1998 Prooflike	10,000	—	—	—	70.00	—

Note: Encapsulated

KM# 43 2 HRYVNI
12.8000 g., Copper-Nickel-Zinc, 31 mm. **Subject:** Volodimir Sosura - 1898-1965 **Obv:** National arms within beaded circle **Rev:** Head facing 1/4 left **Edge:** Reeded

Date	Mintage	F	VF	XF	Unc	BU
1998 Prooflike	20,000	—	—	—	—	140

Note: Encapsulated

KM# 48 2 HRYVNI
12.8000 g., Copper-Nickel-Zinc, 31 mm. **Subject:** European Bank of Reconstruction and Development **Obv:** National arms and value **Rev:** Legendary founders at Kiev monument, emblem of the ERRD **Edge:** Reeded

Date	Mintage	F	VF	XF	Unc	BU
1998	10,000	—	—	—	300	—

KM# 72 2 HRYVNI

12.8000 g., Copper-Nickel-Zinc, 31 mm. **Subject:** 50 Years - United Nations Human Rights Declaration **Obv:** National arms and value **Rev:** Logo on globe within circle **Edge:** Reeded

Date	Mintage	F	VF	XF	Unc	BU
1998	100,000	—	—	—	11.50	—

KM# 73 2 HRYVNI

12.8000 g., Copper-Nickel-Zinc, 31 mm. **Subject:** Steppe Eagle **Obv:** National arms and date divide wreath, value in center **Rev:** Eagle in flight **Edge:** Reeded

Date	Mintage	F	VF	XF	Unc	BU
1999	50,000	—	—	—	140	—

KM# 75 2 HRYVNI

12.8000 g., Copper-Nickel-Zinc, 31 mm. **Subject:** 80th Anniversary - Ukranian State **Obv:** National arms divides date **Rev:** Seated woman in front of two shields **Edge:** Reeded

Date	Mintage	F	VF	XF	Unc	BU
1999	50,000	—	—	—	25.00	—

KM# 76 2 HRYVNI

12.8000 g., Copper-Nickel-Zinc, 31 mm. **Subject:** Panas Myrny, (P.Y. Rudchenko, 1849-1920), writer **Obv:** National arms within beaded circle **Rev:** Half length figure facing divides dates divides beaded circle **Edge:** Reeded

Date	Mintage	F	VF	XF	Unc	BU
1999 Prooflike	50,000	—	—	—	10.00	—

KM# 78 2 HRYVNI

12.8000 g., Copper-Nickel-Zinc, 31 mm. **Subject:** Anatoliy Solovianenko (opera singer) **Obv:** National arms within beaded circle **Rev:** Head left **Edge:** Reeded

Date	Mintage	F	VF	XF	Unc	BU
1999 Prooflike	25,000	—	—	—	10.00	—

KM# 81 2 HRYVNI

12.8000 g., Copper-Nickel-Zinc, 31 mm. **Subject:** Platanthera Bifolia **Obv:** National arms and date divide wreath, value in center **Rev:** Flower **Edge:** Reeded

Date	Mintage	F	VF	XF	Unc	BU
1999	50,000	—	—	—	70.00	—

KM# 82 2 HRYVNI

12.8000 g., Copper-Nickel-Zinc, 31 mm. **Subject:** 100 Years - Ukraine's National Mining Academy **Obv:** National arms within beaded circle **Rev:** Building within circle **Edge:** Reeded

Date	Mintage	F	VF	XF	Unc	BU
1999	20,000	—	—	—	30.00	—

KM# 83 2 HRYVNI

12.8000 g., Copper-Nickel-Zinc, 31 mm. **Obv:** National arms and date divide wreath, value in center **Rev:** Mouse **Edge:** Reeded

Date	Mintage	F	VF	XF	Unc	BU
1999	50,000	—	—	—	10.00	—

KM# 79 2 HRYVNI

12.8000 g., Copper-Nickel-Zinc, 31 mm. **Subject:** 55th Annivesary - Freedom From Nazi Occupation **Obv:** National arms divides date at center of grain sprig wreath **Rev:** Stylized sword design **Edge:** Reeded

Date	Mintage	F	VF	XF	Unc	BU
1999	50,000	—	—	—	15.00	—

KM# 91 2 HRYVNI

12.8000 g., Copper-Nickel-Zinc, 31 mm. **Subject:** 55th Annivesary - Victory in World War II **Obv:** National arms and ribbon divide wreath, value and date within **Rev:** Symbolic "Peace" figure **Edge:** Reeded

Date	Mintage	F	VF	XF	Unc	BU
2000	50,000	—	—	—	10.00	—

KM# 92 2 HRYVNI

12.8000 g., Copper-Nickel-Zinc, 31 mm. **Subject:** Archaeologist V. Hvoika **Obv:** National arms within circles and artifacts **Rev:** Head facing **Edge:** Reeded

Date	Mintage	F	VF	XF	Unc	BU
2000	20,000	—	—	—	10.00	—

KM# 93 2 HRYVNI

12.8000 g., Copper-Nickel-Zinc, 31 mm. **Series:** Sydney 2000 Olympics **Obv:** Horizontal stylized figures divides arms and value **Rev:** Stylized broad jumper **Edge:** Reeded

Date	Mintage	F	VF	XF	Unc	BU
2000	50,000	—	—	—	7.00	—

KM# 94 2 HRYVNI

12.8000 g., Copper-Nickel-Zinc **Series:** Sydney 2000 Olympics **Obv:** Horizontal stylized figures divide arms and value **Rev:** Stylized gymnast on parallel bars

Date	Mintage	F	VF	XF	Unc	BU
2000	50,000	—	—	—	7.00	—

KM# 96 2 HRYVNI

12.8000 g., Copper-Nickel-Zinc, 31 mm. **Subject:** Musician Ivan Kozlovsky **Obv:** Head left **Rev:** Value within lyre, shield at top divides date, all within cluster of sprigs **Edge:** Reeded

Date	Mintage	F	VF	XF	Unc	BU
2000	20,000	—	—	—	10.00	—

KM# 97 2 HRYVNI

12.8000 g., Copper-Nickel-Zinc, 31 mm. **Series:** Sydney 2000 Olympics **Obv:** Horizontal stylized sports figures divide arms and value **Rev:** Stylized sailing scene **Edge:** Reeded

Date	Mintage	F	VF	XF	Unc	BU
2000	50,000	—	—	—	7.00	—

KM# 98 2 HRYVNI
12.8000 g., Copper-Nickel-Zinc, 31 mm. **Subject:** Oles' Honchar (writer) **Obv:** National arms, flowers and value **Rev:** Head facing to right of stylized buildings, dates below **Edge:** Reeded

Date	Mintage	F	VF	XF	Unc	BU
2000	20,000	—	—	—	10.00	—

KM# 99 2 HRYVNI
12.8000 g., Copper-Nickel-Zinc, 31 mm. **Obv:** Arms and date divide wreath, value within **Rev:** Crab **Edge:** Reeded

Date	Mintage	F	VF	XF	Unc	BU
2000	50,000	—	—	—	15.00	—

KM# 100 2 HRYVNI
12.8000 g., Copper-Nickel-Zinc, 31 mm. **Subject:** 125th Anniversary - Chernivtsy National University **Obv:** Arms divide circular designs **Rev:** University viewed through arch **Edge:** Reeded

Date	Mintage	F	VF	XF	Unc	BU
2000	50,000	—	—	—	11.50	—

KM# 101 2 HRYVNI
12.8000 g., Copper-Nickel-Zinc, 31 mm. **Series:** Sydney 2000 Olympics **Obv:** National arms, athletes and value **Rev:** Gymnast doing floor exercise **Edge:** Reeded

Date	Mintage	F	VF	XF	Unc	BU
2000	50,000	—	—	—	7.00	—

KM# 110 2 HRYVNI
12.8000 g., Copper-Nickel-Zinc, 31 mm. **Subject:** Kateryna Bilokour (People's Artist of Ukraine) **Obv:** Shield divides date above flowers and value **Rev:** Half-figure facing right **Edge:** Reeded

Date	Mintage	F	VF	XF	Unc	BU
2000	30,000	—	—	—	15.00	—

KM# 66 5 HRYVEN
16.5400 g., Copper-Nickel-Zinc, 35 mm. **Subject:** St. Michaels Cathedral **Obv:** Arms, value and date within beaded star **Rev:** Cathedral behind human silhouettes **Edge:** Reeded

Date	Mintage	F	VF	XF	Unc	BU
1998	200,000	—	—	—	12.00	—

KM# 69 5 HRYVEN
16.5400 g., Copper-Nickel-Zinc, 35 mm. **Subject:** Kiev-Pechersk Assumption Cathedral **Obv:** Shield, value and date within beaded star **Rev:** Cathedral behind carved ruins **Edge:** Reeded

Date	Mintage	F	VF	XF	Unc	BU
1998	200,000	—	—	—	12.00	—

KM# 74 5 HRYVEN
16.5400 g., Copper-Nickel-Zinc, 35 mm. **Subject:** 900th Anniversary - Novgorod-Siversky Principality **Obv:** Value in center of stylized sun with doves left and right **Rev:** Armored horsemen **Edge:** Reeded

Date	Mintage	F	VF	XF	Unc	BU
1999	50,000	—	—	—	22.50	—

KM# 80 5 HRYVEN
16.5400 g., Copper-Nickel-Zinc, 35 mm. **Subject:** 500th Anniversary - Kiev Magdeburg Law **Obv:** Arms above value and date in center of design **Rev:** Monument to the Law **Edge:** Reeded

Date	Mintage	F	VF	XF	Unc	BU
1999	50,000	—	—	—	16.50	—

KM# 84 5 HRYVEN
16.5400 g., Copper-Nickel-Zinc, 35 mm. **Subject:** Birth of Jesus **Obv:** National arms, value and angels **Rev:** Nativity scene **Edge:** Reeded

Date	Mintage	F	VF	XF	Unc	BU
1999	100,000	—	—	—	12.00	—

KM# 95 5 HRYVEN
16.5400 g., Copper-Nickel-Zinc, 35 mm. **Subject:** 2,500 Years - Bilgorod-Dnestrovski **Obv:** Arms above value and date within design **Rev:** Castle above city arms and ancient coins **Edge:** Reeded

Date	Mintage	F	VF	XF	Unc	BU
2000	50,000	—	—	—	12.00	—

KM# 104 5 HRYVEN
9.4000 g., Bi-Metallic Brass center in Copper-Nickel ring, 28 mm. **Subject:** Third Millennium **Obv:** National arms **Rev:** Figure sowing seeds within circle **Edge:** Reeded and plain sections

Date	Mintage	F	VF	XF	Unc	BU
2000	50,000	—	—	—	25.00	—

KM# 102 5 HRYVEN
16.5400 g., Copper-Nickel-Zinc, 35 mm. **Subject:** Russian Conversion to Christianity **Obv:** National arms and angels **Rev:** Standing bearded figure facing and crowd **Edge:** Reeded

Date	Mintage	F	VF	XF	Unc	BU
2000	100,000	—	—	—	10.00	—

KM# 103 5 HRYVEN
16.5400 g., Copper-Nickel-Zinc, 35 mm. **Subject:** Centennial - Lviv's Opera House **Obv:** Vase divides seated figures below shield **Rev:** Opera house **Edge:** Reeded

Date	Mintage	F	VF	XF	Unc	BU
2000	50,000	—	—	—	11.50	—

KM# 105 5 HRYVEN
16.5400 g., Copper-Nickel-Zinc, 35 mm. **Subject:** 2600th Anniversary - City of Kerch's **Obv:** National arms above value and bracelet **Rev:** Ancient coins above pillar **Edge:** Reeded

Date	Mintage	F	VF	XF	Unc	BU
2000	50,000	—	—	—	10.00	—

KM# 34 10 HRYVEN
16.8110 g., 0.9250 Silver .5 oz. ASW, 33 mm. **Subject:** Petro Mohyla, 1596-1647 **Obv:** National arms, people and building **Rev:** Bust1/4n right holding scepter **Edge:** Reeded

Date	Mintage	F	VF	XF	Unc	BU
1996 Proof	5,000	Value: 500				

KM# 44 10 HRYVEN
33.6220 g., 0.9250 Silver 1 oz. ASW, 38.61 mm. **Series:** Nagano Olympics **Obv:** National arms divide large snow flake designs **Rev:** Cross-country skier **Edge:** Reeded

Date	Mintage	F	VF	XF	Unc	BU
1998 Proof	7,500	Value: 40.00				

KM# 45 10 HRYVEN
33.6220 g., 0.9250 Silver 1 oz. ASW, 38.61 mm. **Series:** Nagano Olympics **Obv:** National arms divide larg snowflake designs **Rev:** Biathlon shooter **Edge:** Reeded

Date	Mintage	F	VF	XF	Unc	BU
1998 Proof	7,500	Value: 40.00				

KM# 50 10 HRYVEN
33.6220 g., 0.9250 Silver 1 oz. ASW, 38.61 mm. **Subject:** 100th Anniversary - Ascania National Park **Obv:** National arms within cluster of plants and animals above value **Rev:** Standing half length figure to lower left of animals running right **Edge:** Reeded

Date	Mintage	F	VF	XF	Unc	BU
1998 Proof	10,000	Value: 42.50				

KM# 52 10 HRYVEN
33.6220 g., 0.9250 Silver 1 oz. ASW, 38.61 mm. **Series:** Nagano Olympics **Obv:** National arms and value **Rev:** Figure skater **Edge:** Reeded

Date	Mintage	F	VF	XF	Unc	BU
1998 Proof	7,500	Value: 40.00				

KM# 53 10 HRYVEN
33.6220 g., 0.9250 Silver 1 oz. ASW, 38.61 mm. **Subject:** Prince Kiy - Founder of Kiev **Obv:** Value and arms within ornamental frame **Rev:** Head facing and armored equestrians **Edge:** Reeded

Date	Mintage	F	VF	XF	Unc	BU
1998 Proof	10,000	Value: 42.50				

KM# 64 10 HRYVEN
33.6220 g., 0.9250 Silver 1 oz. ASW, 38.61 mm. **Subject:** Prince Danylo of Halych **Obv:** National arms and value within ornamental frame **Rev:** Half-length bust holding sword, castle at left and army at right **Edge:** Reeded

Date	Mintage	F	VF	XF	Unc	BU
1998 Proof	10,000	Value: 50.00				

KM# 67 10 HRYVEN
33.6220 g., 0.9250 Silver 1 oz. ASW, 38.61 mm. **Subject:** St. Michael's Golden-Domed Cathedral **Obv:** Arms, value and date within ornamental frame **Rev:** Human silhouettes in front of cathedral **Edge:** Reeded

Date	Mintage	F	VF	XF	Unc	BU
1998 Proof	10,000	Value: 50.00				

KM# 70 10 HRYVEN
33.6220 g., 0.9250 Silver 1 oz. ASW, 38.61 mm. **Subject:** The Kyiv-Pechersk Assumption Cathedral **Obv:** Arms, value and date within beaded star **Rev:** Cathedral behind carved ruins **Edge:** Reeded

Date	Mintage	F	VF	XF	Unc	BU
1998 Proof	10,000	Value: 50.00				

KM# 77 10 HRYVEN
33.6220 g., 0.9250 Silver 1 oz. ASW, 38.61 mm. **Subject:** Dmytro Vyshnevetsky - BAYDA (Cossack leader) **Obv:** National arms with angel and crowned lion within beaded circle **Rev:** 3/4-length figure facing with bow and arrow **Edge:** Reeded

Date	Mintage	F	VF	XF	Unc	BU
1999 Proof	10,000	Value: 50.00				

KM# 85 10 HRYVEN
33.9000 g., 0.9250 Silver 1.0082 oz. ASW, 38.6 mm. **Subject:** Birth of Jesus **Obv:** National arms, value and angels **Rev:** Nativity scene **Edge:** Reeded

Date	Mintage	F	VF	XF	Unc	BU
1999 Proof	10,000	Value: 100				

KM# 86 10 HRYVEN
33.9000 g., 0.9250 Silver 1.0082 oz. ASW, 38.61 mm. **Subject:** Prince Askold **Obv:** Shield and value within Viking carvings **Rev:** Viking and ships **Edge:** Reeded

Date	Mintage	F	VF	XF	Unc	BU
1999 Proof	10,000	Value: 50.00				

KM# 87 10 HRYVEN
33.6200 g., 0.9250 Silver 1.0082 oz. ASW, 38.61 mm. **Subject:** 500th Anniversary - Magdeburg Law **Obv:** National arms, value and date within design **Rev:** Monument **Edge:** Reeded

Date	Mintage	F	VF	XF	Unc	BU
1999 Proof	5,000	Value: 50.00				

KM# 88 10 HRYVEN
33.6200 g., 0.9250 Silver 1.0082 oz. ASW, 38.61 mm. **Subject:** Petro Doroshenko (Cossack leader) **Obv:** National arms, angel and crowned lion within beaded circle **Rev:** Armored equestrian divides beaded circle **Edge:** Reeded

Date	Mintage	F	VF	XF	Unc	BU
1999 Proof	10,000	Value: 50.00				

KM# 89 10 HRYVEN
33.6200 g., 0.9250 Silver 1.0082 oz. ASW, 38.6 mm. **Obv:** Arms and date divide wreath with bird, value within **Rev:** Dormouse **Edge:** Reeded

Date	Mintage	F	VF	XF	Unc	BU
1999 Proof	5,000	Value: 52.50				

KM# 90 10 HRYVEN
33.6200 g., 0.9250 Silver 1.0082 oz. ASW, 38.61 mm. **Obv:** Arms and date divide wreath with bird, value within **Rev:** Eagle in flight **Edge:** Reeded

Date	Mintage	F	VF	XF	Unc	BU
1999 Proof	5,000	Value: 85.00				

KM# 116 10 HRYVEN
33.6220 g., 0.9250 Silver .9998 oz. ASW, 38.61 mm. **Series:** Olympics **Obv:** National arms, value and Olympic motto **Rev:** Stylized broad jumper **Edge:** Reeded

Date	Mintage	F	VF	XF	Unc	BU
1999 Proof	15,000	Value: 40.00				

KM# 117 10 HRYVEN
33.6220 g., 0.9250 Silver .9998 oz. ASW, 38.61 mm. **Series:** Olympics **Obv:** National arms, value and Olympic motto **Rev:** Stylized gymnast on parallel bars **Edge:** Reeded

Date	Mintage	F	VF	XF	Unc	BU
1999 Proof	15,000	Value: 40.00				

KM# 118 10 HRYVEN
33.6220 g., 0.9250 Silver .9998 oz. ASW, 38.61 mm. **Subject:** Platanthera Bifolia **Obv:** Arms and date divide wreath, value within **Rev:** Flower **Edge:** Reeded

Date	Mintage	F	VF	XF	Unc	BU
1999 Proof	5,000	Value: 45.00				

KM# 108 10 HRYVEN
33.6220 g., 0.9250 Silver .9998 oz. ASW, 38.61 mm. **Subject:** 55th Anniversary - End of WWII **Obv:** Arms and ribbon divide wreath, value and date within **Rev:** Standing figure holding palm branch above head in front of globe within 1/2 wreath **Edge:** Reeded

Date	Mintage	F	VF	XF	Unc	BU
2000 Proof	3,000	Value: 600				

KM# 109 10 HRYVEN
33.6220 g., 0.9250 Silver .9998 oz. ASW, 38.61 mm. **Subject:** Conversion of the Russ to Christianity **Obv:** Arms and value divide angels **Rev:** Mass baptism scene **Edge:** Reeded

Date	Mintage	F	VF	XF	Unc	BU
2000 Proof	3,000	Value: 47.50				

KM# 119 10 HRYVEN
33.6220 g., 0.9250 Silver .9998 oz. ASW, 38.61 mm. **Subject:** Princess Olga **Obv:** Arms, date and value within ornamental frame **Rev:** Princess and court scene **Edge:** Reeded

Date	Mintage	F	VF	XF	Unc	BU
2000 Proof	10,000	Value: 60.00				

KM# 120 10 HRYVEN
33.6220 g., 0.9250 Silver .9998 oz. ASW, 38.61 mm. **Subject:** Petro Sahaidachny (Cossack leader) **Obv:** National arms, angel and crowned lion within beaded circle **Rev:** Cameo to upper right of ship within beaded circle **Edge:** Reeded

Date	Mintage	F	VF	XF	Unc	BU
2000 Proof	10,000	Value: 50.00				

KM# 121 10 HRYVEN
33.6220 g., 0.9250 Silver .9998 oz. ASW, 38.61 mm. **Obv:** Arms and date divide wreath with bird, value within **Rev:** Crab **Edge:** Reeded

Date	Mintage	F	VF	XF	Unc	BU
2000 Proof	5,000	Value: 50.00				

KM# 122 10 HRYVEN
33.6220 g., 0.9250 Silver .9998 oz. ASW, 38.61 mm. **Subject:** Prince Volodymyr the Great **Obv:** Arms divide ornamental frame, value within **Rev:** Crowned bust with raised hands **Designer:** Reeded

Date	Mintage	F	VF	XF	Unc	BU
2000 Proof	5,000	Value: 400				

KM# 123 10 HRYVEN
33.6220 g., 0.9250 Silver .9998 oz. ASW, 38.61 mm. **Subject:** 100 Years of L'viv Opera and Ballet Theatre **Obv:** Vase divides seated figures below shield **Rev:** Opera House **Edge:** Reeded

Date	Mintage	F	VF	XF	Unc	BU
2000 Proof	3,000	Value: 65.00				

KM# 35 20 HRYVEN
33.6220 g., 0.9250 Silver 1 oz. ASW, 38.61 mm. **Subject:** The Tithe Church **Obv:** Madonna and child in center circle, vines surround **Rev:** Church **Edge:** Reeded

Date	Mintage	F	VF	XF	Unc	BU
1996 Proof	5,000	Value: 300				

KM# 36 20 HRYVEN
33.6220 g., 0.9250 Silver 1 oz. ASW, 38.61 mm. **Subject:** The Savior Cathedral in Chernihiv **Obv:** Arms above Madonna and child **Rev:** Cathedral **Edge:** Reeded

Date	Mintage	F	VF	XF	Unc	BU
1997 Proof	5,000	Value: 250				

KM# 46 20 HRYVEN
33.6220 g., 0.9250 Silver 1 oz. ASW, 38.61 mm. **Obv:** National arms **Rev:** Cossacks in revolt

Date	Mintage	F	VF	XF	Unc	BU
1997 Proof	5,000	Value: 150				

KM# 54 20 HRYVEN
33.6220 g., 0.9250 Silver 1 oz. ASW, 38.61 mm. **Subject:** Cossacks Mamay **Obv:** National arms supported by St. Michael and lion **Rev:** Cossack playing a bandre in center of assorted designs **Edge:** Reeded

Date	Mintage	F	VF	XF	Unc	BU
1997 Proof	5,000	Value: 450				

KM# 57 20 HRYVEN

33.6220 g., 0.9250 Silver 1 oz. ASW, 38.61 mm. **Subject:** 200th Anniversary - Kiev Commodity Futures Market **Obv:** National arms within center of scrolls **Rev:** Steepled building, sailboat and balance scale **Edge:** Reeded

Date	Mintage	F	VF	XF	Unc	BU
1997 Proof	5,000	Value: 120				

KM# 58 20 HRYVEN

33.6220 g., 0.9250 Silver 1 oz. ASW, 38.61 mm. **Subject:** 350th Anniversary - Cossack Revolt **Obv:** National arms supported by St. Michael and lion **Rev:** Cossacks attacking Polish cavalryman **Edge:** Reeded

Date	Mintage	F	VF	XF	Unc	BU
1998 Proof	10,000	Value: 60.00				

KM# 126 20 HRYVEN

Bi-Metallic Gold center in Silver ring, 31 mm. **Subject:** Paleolithic Age **Obv:** Eagle on captains wheel **Rev:** Pottery and petroglyphs **Edge:** Reeded and plain sections

Date	Mintage	F	VF	XF	Unc	BU
2000 Proof	3,000	Value: 200				

KM# 127 20 HRYVEN

Bi-Metallic Gold center in silver ring **Subject:** Trypolean Culture **Obv:** Eagle on captains wheel **Rev:** Ancient sculptures **Edge:** Reeded and plain alternating

Date	Mintage	F	VF	XF	Unc	BU
2000 Proof	3,000	Value: 200				

KM# 128 20 HRYVEN

Bi-Metallic Gold center in Silver ring **Subject:** The Olbian City State **Obv:** Eagle on captains wheel **Rev:** Ancient coin in center circle of Greek figures

Date	Mintage	F	VF	XF	Unc	BU
2000 Proof	3,000	Value: 225				

KM# 59 50 HRYVEN

3.1104 g., 0.9999 Gold .1 oz. AGW, 16 mm. **Subject:** St. Sophia Cathedral in Kiev **Obv:** Cathedral **Rev:** Mother of God Mossaic **Edge:** Segmented reeding **Note:** Minted in 1996, issued on July 28, 1997.

Date	Mintage	F	VF	XF	Unc	BU
1996	2,000	—	—	—	450	—

KM# 124 50 HRYVEN

17.6300 g., 0.9000 Gold .5101 oz. AGW, 25 mm. **Subject:** Birth of Jesus **Obv:** Two angels, arms and value **Rev:** Nativity scene **Edge:** Plain

Date	Mintage	F	VF	XF	Unc	BU
1999 Proof	3,000	Value: 600				

KM# 125 50 HRYVEN

17.6300 g., 0.9000 Gold .5101 oz. AGW, 25 mm. **Subject:** Conversion of the Russ to Christianity **Obv:** National arms, angels and value **Rev:** Baptism scene **Edge:** Plain

Date	Mintage	F	VF	XF	Unc	BU
2000 Proof	3,000	Value; 600				

KM# 63 100 HRYVEN

17.2797 g., 0.9000 Gold .5 oz. AGW, 25 mm. **Subject:** Kyiv Psalm book **Obv:** Open book divides shield and value **Rev:** Monk writing book **Edge:** Plain **Note:** Minted in 1997, issued in January 1998.

Date	Mintage	F	VF	XF	Unc	BU
1997 Proof	2,000	Value: 600				

KM# 65 100 HRYVEN

17.2797 g., 0.9000 Gold .5 oz. AGW **Subject:** Poem "Eneida" by Ivan P. Kotlyarevsky **Obv:** Helmet and musical instruments divide shield and value **Rev:** Seated helmeted figure playing a bandre

Date	Mintage	F	VF	XF	Unc	BU
1998 Proof	2,000	Value: 600				

KM# 68 100 HRYVEN

17.2797 g., 0.9000 Gold .5 oz. AGW, 25 mm. **Subject:** St. Michael's Cathedral **Obv:** Arms, value and date in center of design **Rev:** Cathedral behind human silhouettes **Edge:** Plain

Date	Mintage	F	VF	XF	Unc	BU
1998 Proof	3,000	Value: 600				

KM# 71 100 HRYVEN

17.2797 g., 0.9000 Gold .5 oz. AGW, 25 mm. **Subject:** Kyiv-Pechersk Assumption Cathedral **Obv:** Arms, value and date within beaded star **Rev:** Cathedral behind carved ruins **Edge:** Plain

Date	Mintage	F	VF	XF	Unc	BU
1998 Proof	3,000	Value: 600				

KM# 60 125 HRYVEN

7.7759 g., 0.9999 Gold .25 oz. AGW, 20 mm. **Obv:** St. Sophia Cathedral in Kiev **Rev:** Ornate Mosaic of the Mother of God - "Ozanta" **Edge:** Segmented reeding **Note:** Minted in 1996, issued on July 28, 1997.

Date	Mintage	F	VF	XF	Unc	BU
1996	4,000	—	—	—	400	—

KM# 37 200 HRYVEN

17.5000 g., 0.9000 Gold .5 oz. AGW, 25 mm. **Obv:** National arms within beaded circle **Rev:** Bust of Taras G. Shevchenko facing **Edge:** Plain **Note:** Minted in 1996, issued on March 12, 1997.

Date	Mintage	F	VF	XF	Unc	BU
1996 Proof	10,000	Value: 600				

KM# 38 200 HRYVEN

17.5000 g., 0.9000 Gold .5 oz. AGW, 25 mm. **Subject:** Pecherska Lavra **Obv:** Church above date and value within beaded circle **Rev:** Standing angelic figure with radiant dove within cloud-like wings **Edge:** Plain **Note:** Minted in 1996, issued on April 10, 1997.

Date	Mintage	F	VF	XF	Unc	BU
1996 Proof	20,000	Value: 600				

KM# 61 250 HRYVEN

15.5518 g., 0.9999 Gold .5 oz. AGW, 25 mm. **Obv:** St. Sophia Cathedral in Kiev **Rev:** St. Sophia **Edge:** Segmented reeding **Note:** Minted in 1996, issued on July 28, 1997.

Date	Mintage	F	VF	XF	Unc	BU
1996	3,000	—	—	—	650	—

KM# 62 500 HRYVEN

31.1035 g., 0.9999 Gold 1 oz. AGW, 32 mm. **Obv:** St. Sophia Cathedral in Kiev **Rev:** St. Sophia **Edge:** Segmented reeding **Note:** Minted in 1996, issued on July 28, 1997.

Date	Mintage	F	VF	XF	Unc	BU
1996	1,000	—	—	—	3,500	—

PATTERNS

Including off metal strikes

KM#	Date	Mintage	Identification	Mkt Val
Pn1	1992	—	Kopiyka. Aluminum.	—
Pn2	1922	—	2 Kopiyky. Aluminum.	—
Pn3	1992	—	5 Kopiyok. White Brass.	—
Pn4	1992	—	10 Kopiyok. Brass. Incuse shield.	20.00
Pn5	1992	—	15 Kopiyok. Brass.	35.00
Pn6	1992	—	15 Kopiyok. Bronze.	35.00
Pn7	1992	—	25 Kopiyok. Brass. Incuse shield.	20.00
Pn8	1992	—	50 Kopiyok. Copper-Nickel.	—
Pn9	1992	—	50 Kopiyok. Brass. Incuse shield.	20.00
Pn10	1992	—	50 Kopiyok. Brass Clad Steel.	—
Pn11	1993	—	2 Kopiyky. Brass.	—
Pn12	1993	—	2 Kopiyky. Aluminum-Zinc.	—
Pn13	1993	—	15 Kopiyok. Aluminum.	35.00
Pn14	1994	—	Kopiyka. 0.6000 Silver. Specific gravity: 9.8.	—
Pn15	1994	—	2 Kopiyky. Bronze. 3.7500 g. Piefort.	—
Pn16	1996	—	Kopiyka. 0.3500 Silver. Specific gravity: 9.43.	—
Pn17	1996	—	25 Kopiyok. Aluminum.	—
Pn18	1998	—	100 Hryvnias. Brass.	—
Pn19	ND(1998)	—	100 Hryvnias. Brass.	—
Pn20	1998	—	100 Hryvnias. Brass.	—
Pn21	ND(1998)	—	100 Hryvnias. Brass.	—
Pn22	1998	—	100 Hryvnias. Brass.	—
Pn23	ND(1998)	—	100 Hryvnias. Brass.	—

MINT SETS

KM#	Date	Mintage	Identification	Issue Price	Mkt Val
MS1	1996 (8)	—	KM#1, 2, 3.3, 4, 6, 7, 8, 30	—	100

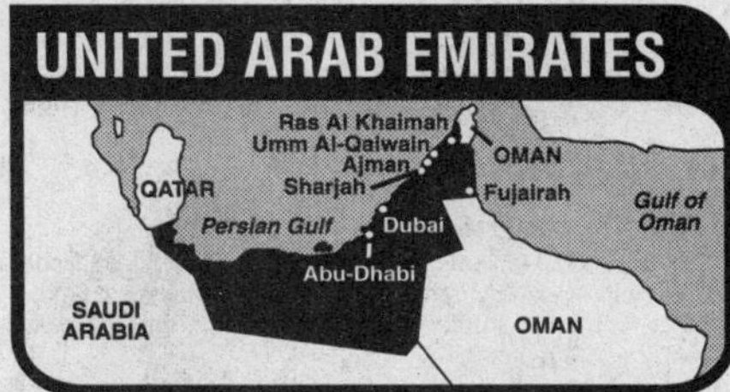

The seven United Arab Emirates (formerly known as the Trucial Sheikhdoms or States), located along the southern shore of the Persian Gulf, are comprised of the Sheikhdoms of Abu Dhabi, Dubai, al-Sharjah, Ajman, Umm al Qaiwain, Ras al-Khaimah and al-Fujairah. They have a combined area of about 32,000 sq. mi. (83,600 sq. km.) and a population of *2.1 million. Capital: Abu Zaby (Abu Dhabi). Since the oil strikes of 1958-60, the economy has centered about petroleum.

The Trucial States came under direct British influence in 1892 when the Maritime Truce Treaty enacted after the supression of pirate activity along the Trucial Coast was enlarged to enjoin the states from disposing of any territory, or entering into any foreign agreements, without British consent in return for British protection from external aggression. In March of 1971 Britain reaffirmed its decision to terminate its treaty relationships with the Trucial Sheikhdoms, whereupon the seven states joined with Bahrain and Qatar in an effort to form a union of Arab Emirates under British protection. When the prospective members failed to agree on terms of union, Bahrain and Qatar declared their respective independence, Aug. and Sept. of 1971. Six of the sheikhdoms united to form the United Arab Emirates on Dec. 2, 1971. Ras al-Khaimah joined a few weeks later.

TITLE

الامارات العربية المتحدة

al-Imara(t) al-Arabiya(t) al-Muttahida(t)

MONETARY SYSTEM

Falus, Fulus — Fals, Fils — Falsan

100 Fils = 1 Dirham

UNITED EMIRATES

STANDARD COINAGE

KM# 1 FILS
1.5000 g., Bronze, 15 mm. **Series:** F.A.O. **Obv:** Value **Rev:** Date palms above dates **Edge:** Plain **Designer:** Geoffrey Colley

Date	Mintage	F	VF	XF	Unc	BU
AH1393-1973	4,000,000	—	0.10	0.20	0.45	0.75
AH1395-1975	—	—	0.20	0.30	0.50	0.75
AH1409-1989	—	—	0.20	0.30	0.50	0.75
AH1418-1997	—	—	0.20	0.30	0.50	0.75

KM# 2.1 5 FILS
3.7500 g., Bronze, 22 mm. **Series:** F.A.O. **Obv:** Value **Rev:** Fish above dates **Edge:** Plain **Designer:** Geoffrey Colley

Date	Mintage	F	VF	XF	Unc	BU
AH1393-1973	11,400,000	—	0.10	0.15	0.30	1.00
AH1402-1982	—	—	0.10	0.20	0.35	1.00
AH1407-1987	—	—	0.10	0.20	0.35	1.00
AH1408-1988	—	—	0.10	0.20	0.35	1.00
AH1409-1989	—	—	0.10	0.20	0.35	1.00

KM# 2.2 5 FILS
Bronze **Series:** F.A.O. **Obv:** Value **Rev:** Fish above dates **Note:** Reduced size.

Date	Mintage	F	VF	XF	Unc	BU
AH1416-1996	—	—	0.10	0.15	0.30	1.00

KM# 3.1 10 FILS
7.5000 g., Bronze, 27 mm. **Obv:** Value **Rev:** Arab dhow above dates

Date	Mintage	F	VF	XF	Unc	BU
AH1393-1973	6,400,000	—	0.25	0.40	0.95	1.25
AH1402-1982	—	—	0.25	0.45	1.00	1.25
AH1404-1984	—	—	0.25	0.45	1.00	1.25
AH1407-1987	—	—	0.25	0.45	1.00	1.25
AH1408-1988	—	—	0.25	0.45	1.00	1.25
AH1409-1989	—	—	0.25	0.45	1.00	1.25

KM# 3.2 10 FILS
Bronze **Obv:** Value **Rev:** Arab dhow above dates **Note:** Reduced size.

Date	Mintage	F	VF	XF	Unc	BU
AH1416-1996	—	—	0.20	0.35	0.80	1.20

KM# 4 25 FILS
3.5000 g., Copper-Nickel, 20 mm. **Obv:** Value **Rev:** Gazelle above dates

Date	Mintage	F	VF	XF	Unc	BU
AH1393-1973	10,400,000	—	0.15	0.35	0.70	1.00
AH1402-1982	—	—	0.20	0.40	0.75	1.00
AH1403-1983	—	—	0.20	0.40	0.75	1.00
AH1404-1984	—	—	0.20	0.40	0.75	1.00
AH1406-1986	—	—	0.20	0.40	0.75	1.00
AH1407-1987	—	—	0.20	0.40	0.75	1.00
AH1408-1988	—	—	0.20	0.40	0.75	1.00
AH1409-1989	—	—	0.20	0.40	0.75	1.00
AH1410-1990	—	—	0.20	0.40	0.75	1.00
AH1415-1995	—	—	0.20	0.40	0.75	1.00
AH1416-1996	—	—	0.20	0.40	0.75	1.00
AH1419-1998	—	—	0.20	0.40	0.75	1.00

KM# 5 50 FILS
Copper-Nickel, 24.8 mm. **Obv:** Value **Rev:** Oil derricks above dates **Edge:** Reeded

Date	Mintage	F	VF	XF	Unc	BU
AH1393-1973	8,400,000	—	0.35	0.50	1.50	2.00
AH1402-1982	—	—	0.35	0.55	1.65	2.00
AH1404-1984	—	—	0.35	0.55	1.65	2.00
AH1407-1987	—	—	0.35	0.55	1.65	2.00
AH1408-1988	—	—	0.35	0.55	1.65	2.00
Note: Coarser edge reeding						
AH1409-1989	—	—	0.35	0.55	1.65	2.00

KM# 16 50 FILS
Copper-Nickel, 21 mm. **Obv:** Value **Rev:** Oil derricks above dates **Shape:** 7-sided **Note:** Reduced size.

Date	Mintage	F	VF	XF	Unc	BU
AH1415-1995	—	—	0.25	0.45	1.35	1.85
AH1419-1998	—	—	0.25	0.45	1.35	1.85

KM# 6.1 DIRHAM
11.3000 g., Copper-Nickel, 28.5 mm. **Obv:** Value **Rev:** Jug above dates **Edge:** Reeded

Date	Mintage	F	VF	XF	Unc	BU
AH1393-1973	13,000,000	—	0.50	0.75	2.00	2.50
AH1402-1982	—	—	0.50	0.80	2.25	2.75
AH1404-1984	—	—	0.50	0.80	2.25	2.75
AH1406-1986	—	—	0.50	0.80	2.25	2.75
AH1407-1987	—	—	0.50	0.80	2.25	2.75

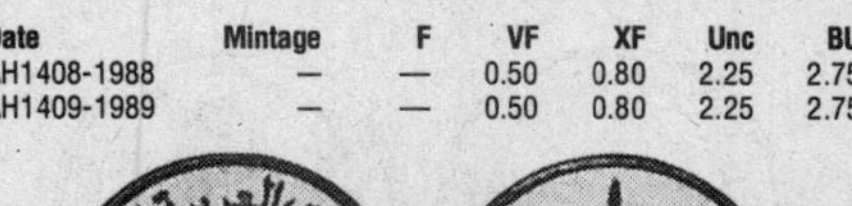

Date	Mintage	F	VF	XF	Unc	BU
AH1408-1988	—	—	0.50	0.80	2.25	2.75
AH1409-1989	—	—	0.50	0.80	2.25	2.75

KM# 6.2 DIRHAM
Copper-Nickel, 24 mm. **Obv:** Value **Rev:** Jug above dates **Edge:** Reeded **Note:** Reduced size.

Date	Mintage	F	VF	XF	Unc	BU
AH1415-1995	—	—	0.35	0.65	1.85	2.25
AH1419-1998	—	—	0.35	0.65	1.85	2.25

KM# 14 DIRHAM
Copper-Nickel, 28.5 mm. **Subject:** 10th Anniversary - al-Ain University **Obv:** Value **Rev:** Emblem above map and book within radiant design

Date	Mintage	F	VF	XF	Unc	BU
ND(1987)	200,000	—	1.75	4.00	8.00	—

KM# 10 DIRHAM
11.3100 g., Copper-Nickel, 28.5 mm. **Subject:** 27th Chess Olympiad in Dubai **Obv:** Value **Rev:** Chess pieces and olympic rings

Date	Mintage	F	VF	XF	Unc	BU
ND(1987)	200,000	—	2.00	4.50	9.00	—

KM# 11 DIRHAM
Copper-Nickel, 28.5 mm. **Subject:** 25th Anniversary - Offshore Oil Drilling **Obv:** Value **Rev:** Offshore oil drilling rig

Date	Mintage	F	VF	XF	Unc	BU
ND(1987)	300,000	—	2.00	4.50	9.00	—

KM# 15 DIRHAM
Copper-Nickel, 28.5 mm. **Subject:** U.A.E. Soccer Team - Qualification for WC - 1990 **Obv:** Value **Rev:** Stylized winged soccer player

Date	Mintage	F	VF	XF	Unc	BU
ND(1991)	250,000	—	1.50	3.00	6.50	—

KM# 32 DIRHAM

Copper-Nickel, 24 mm. **Subject:** Bank of Dubai 35th Anniversary **Obv:** Value **Rev:** Towered bank building divides dates

Date	Mintage	F	VF	XF	Unc	BU
ND(1998)	500,000	—	—	—	3.50	—

KM# 35 DIRHAM

Copper-Nickel, 24 mm. **Subject:** 10th Anniversary - College of Technology **Obv:** Value **Rev:** Bird viewed through window frame

Date	Mintage	F	VF	XF	Unc	BU
ND(1998)	250,000	—	—	—	3.50	—

KM# 38 DIRHAM

Copper-Nickel, 24 mm. **Subject:** 15th Anniversary - Rashid bin Humaid Award for Culture **Obv:** Value **Rev:** Logo within circle

Date	Mintage	F	VF	XF	Unc	BU
ND(1998)	250,000	—	—	—	3.50	—

KM# 39 DIRHAM

Copper-Nickel, 24 mm. **Subject:** Sharjah Cultural City **Obv:** Value **Rev:** Stylized flame within beaded circle

Date	Mintage	F	VF	XF	Unc	BU
ND(1998)	—	—	—	—	3.50	—
ND(1999)	200,000	—	—	—	3.50	—

KM# 40 DIRHAM

6.3700 g., Copper-Nickel, 24 mm. **Subject:** 25 Years - Oil Production on Abu Al Bukhoosh Oil Field **Obv:** Value **Rev:** Offshore oil drilling rig **Edge:** Reeded

Date	Mintage	F	VF	XF	Unc	BU
ND(1999)	200,000	—	—	—	3.50	—

KM# 41 DIRHAM

6.3700 g., Copper-Nickel, 24 mm. **Subject:** Islamic Personality of 1999 - Sheikh Zayed **Obv:** Value **Rev:** Square design

Date	Mintage	F	VF	XF	Unc	BU
ND(2000)	500,000	—	—	—	3.50	—

KM# 43 DIRHAM

6.3700 g., Copper-Nickel, 24 mm. **Subject:** 25th Anniversary - Dubai Islamic Bank **Obv:** Value **Rev:** Bank name within circle

Date	Mintage	F	VF	XF	Unc	BU
ND(2000)	250,000	—	—	—	3.50	—

KM# 46 DIRHAM

6.3700 g., Copper-Nickel, 24 mm. **Subject:** 25th Anniversary - General Women's Union (1975-2000) **Obv:** Value **Rev:** Stylized gazelle

Date	Mintage	F	VF	XF	Unc	BU
ND(2001)	500,000	—	—	—	3.50	—

KM# 9 5 DIRHAMS

Copper-Nickel **Subject:** 1500th Anniversary - al-Hegira **Obv:** Value flanked by dates **Rev:** Perched eagle **Shape:** 15-sided

Date	Mintage	F	VF	XF	Unc	BU
AH1401-1981	2,000,000	—	2.00	4.00	15.00	—

KM# 33 25 DIRHAMS

20.0000 g., 0.9250 Silver .5948 oz. ASW **Subject:** Dubai National Bank - 35 Years **Obv:** Value **Rev:** Towered bank building divides dates

Date	Mintage	F	VF	XF	Unc	BU
ND(1998) Proof	5,000	Value: 35.00				

KM# 55 25 DIRHAMS

20.0000 g., 0.9250 Silver 0.5948 oz. ASW **Subject:** 25th Anniversary - Al Bukhoosh Oil Field's Production

Date	Mintage	F	VF	XF	Unc	BU
ND(1999) Proof	2,000	Value: 45.00				

KM# 44 25 DIRHAMS

20.0000 g., 0.9250 Silver, 27.9 mm. **Subject:** 25th Anniversary - Dubai Islamic Bank **Obv:** Value **Rev:** Bank name within circle **Edge:** Reeded

Date	Mintage	F	VF	XF	Unc	BU
ND(2000) Proof	1,000	Value: 35.00				

KM# 7 50 DIRHAMS

27.2200 g., 0.9250 Silver .8095 oz. ASW **Subject:** IYC and UNICEF **Obv:** Value **Rev:** Conjoined standing figures, emblems at sides

Date	Mintage	F	VF	XF	Unc	BU
AH1400-1980 Proof	8,031	Value: 21.50				

KM# 17 50 DIRHAMS

40.0000 g., 0.9250 Silver 1.1896 oz. ASW, 40 mm. **Subject:** Death of Shaikh Rashid Bin Saeed Al-Maktoum **Obv:** Bust facing **Rev:** International Trade Center **Edge:** Reeded

Date	Mintage	F	VF	XF	Unc	BU
ND(1992) (1990) Proof	4,000	Value: 70.00				

KM# 18 50 DIRHAMS

40.0000 g., 0.9250 Silver 1.1896 oz. ASW, 40 mm. **Subject:** 10th Anniversary - UAE Central Bank **Obv:** Bust of Shaikh Zayed Bin Sultan Al-Nahyan right **Rev:** Bank **Edge:** Reeded

Date	Mintage	F	VF	XF	Unc	BU
ND(1992) (1992) Proof	2,000	Value: 70.00				

KM# 19 50 DIRHAMS

40.0000 g., 0.9250 Silver 1.1896 oz. ASW, 40 mm. **Subject:** 50th Anniversary of the Arab League **Obv:** Eagle **Rev:** Inscription in center circle of wreath **Edge:** Reeded

Date	Mintage	F	VF	XF	Unc	BU
ND(1996) (1995) Proof	2,000	Value: 70.00				

KM# 21 50 DIRHAMS

40.0000 g., 0.9250 Silver 1.1896 oz. ASW, 40 mm. **Subject:** 25th Anniversary of the UAE - National Day Issue **Obv:** Bust of Shaikh Zayed Bin Sultan Al-Nahyan right **Rev:** Eagle within circle **Edge:** Reeded

Date	Mintage	F	VF	XF	Unc	BU
1996 (1996) Proof	8,000	Value: 65.00				

KM# 22 50 DIRHAMS

40.0000 g., 0.9250 Silver 1.1896 oz. ASW, 40 mm. **Subject:** 30th Anniversary - Reign of Shaikh Zayed **Obv:** Bust of Shaikh Zayed Bin Sultan Al-Nahyan right **Rev:** Circular design of Arabic lettering **Edge:** Reeded

Date	Mintage	F	VF	XF	Unc	BU
1996 (1996) Proof	8,000	Value: 65.00				

KM# 34 50 DIRHAMS

40.0000 g., 0.9250 Silver 1.1896 oz. ASW, 40 mm. **Subject:** Dubai National Bank - 35 Years **Obv:** Value **Rev:** Towered bank building divides dates **Edge:** Reeded

Date	Mintage	F	VF	XF	Unc	BU
ND(1998) Proof	5,000	Value: 65.00				

KM# 36 50 DIRHAMS

40.0000 g., 0.9250 Silver 1.1896 oz. ASW, 40 mm. **Subject:** Colleges of Technology: 10 Years **Obv:** Bust of Shaikh Zayed Bin Sultan Al-Nahyan right **Rev:** Bird viewed through window frame **Edge:** Reeded

Date	Mintage	F	VF	XF	Unc	BU
ND(1998) Proof	6,000	Value: 65.00				

KM# 37 50 DIRHAMS

27.5000 g., 0.9250 Silver .8178 oz. ASW **Series:** UNICEF **Obv:** Value **Rev:** Two children, dates at left and right

Date	Mintage	F	VF	XF	Unc	BU
AH1419-1998 Proof	25,000	Value: 37.50				

KM# 56 50 DIRHAMS

40.0000 g., 0.9250 Silver 1.1896 oz. ASW, 40 mm. **Subject:** 30th Anniversary - Abu Dhabi Chamber of Commerce **Edge:** Reeded

Date	Mintage	F	VF	XF	Unc	BU
ND(1999) Proof	5,000	Value: 65.00				

KM# 42 50 DIRHAMS

40.2200 g., 0.9250 Silver 1.1961 oz. ASW, 40 mm. **Subject:** Islamic Personality of 1999 - Sheikh Zayed **Obv:** Bust of Shaikh Zayed Bin Sultan Al-Nahyan right **Rev:** Square design **Edge:** Reeded

Date	Mintage	F	VF	XF	Unc	BU
ND(2000) Proof	5,000	Value: 90.00				

KM# 57 50 DIRHAMS

40.0000 g., 0.9250 Silver 1.1896 oz. ASW, 40 mm. **Subject:** Sharjah Cultural City **Obv:** Value **Rev:** Stylized flame within beaded circle **Edge:** Reeded **Note:** Similar to 1 Dirham, KM#39.

Date	Mintage	F	VF	XF	Unc	BU
ND(1999) Proof	4,000	Value: 65.00				

KM# 45 50 DIRHAMS

40.2200 g., 0.9250 Silver 1.1961 oz. ASW, 40 mm. **Subject:** 25th Anniversary - Dubai Islamic Bank **Obv:** Value **Rev:** Bank name within circle **Edge:** Reeded

Date	Mintage	F	VF	XF	Unc	BU
ND(2000) Proof	2,000	Value: 55.00				

KM# 48 50 DIRHAMS

40.0000 g., 0.9250 Silver 1.1896 oz. ASW, 40 mm. **Subject:** Dubai Airport - Sheikh Rashid Terminal **Obv:** Bust facing **Rev:** Airport scene **Edge:** Reeded

Date	Mintage	F	VF	XF	Unc	BU
ND(2001) Proof	5,000	Value: 50.00				

KM# 58 50 DIRHAMS

40.0000 g., 0.9250 Silver 1.1896 oz. ASW, 40 mm. **Subject:** 100th Anniversary - Dubai's Dept. of Ports and Customs **Edge:** Reeded

Date	Mintage	F	VF	XF	Unc	BU
ND(2000) Proof	5,000	Value: 65.00				

KM# 12 500 DIRHAMS

19.9700 g., 0.9170 Gold .5886 oz. AGW, 25 mm. **Subject:** 5th Anniversary - United Arab Emirates **Obv:** Head /4 right, inscription above **Rev:** Dates

Date	Mintage	F	VF	XF	Unc	BU
ND(1976) Proof	13,450	Value: 425				

KM# 23 500 DIRHAMS

19.9700 g., 0.9170 Gold .5886 oz. AGW, 25 mm. **Subject:** Commemoration - Death of Sheikh Rashid Bin Saeed Al Maktoum **Obv:** Bust right **Rev:** Dubai International Trade Center **Note:** Similar to 50 Dirhams, KM#17.

Date	Mintage	F	VF	XF	Unc	BU
ND(1992) Proof	2,000	Value: 475				

KM# 24 500 DIRHAMS

19.9700 g., 0.9170 Gold .5886 oz. AGW, 25 mm. **Subject:** 10th Anniversary - U.A.E. Central Bank **Obv:** Bust of Shaikh Zayed Bin Sultan Al-Nahyan right **Rev:** Bank building **Note:** Similar to 50 Dirhams, KM#18.

Date	Mintage	F	VF	XF	Unc	BU
ND(1992) Proof	1,000	Value: 500				

KM# 25 500 DIRHAMS

19.9700 g., 0.9170 Gold .5886 oz. AGW, 25 mm. **Subject:** 20th Anniversary - Women's Union **Obv:** Heraldic eagle **Rev:** Seal in wreath **Note:** Similar to 1000 Dirhams, KM#28.

Date	Mintage	F	VF	XF	Unc	BU
ND(1996) Proof	1,000	Value: 500				

KM# 8 750 DIRHAMS

17.1700 g., 0.9000 Gold .4969 oz. AGW, 25 mm. **Subject:** IYC and UNICEF **Obv:** Value **Rev:** Armored horseman divides emblems

Date	Mintage	F	VF	XF	Unc	BU
AH1400-1980 Proof	3,063	Value: 375				

KM# 13 1000 DIRHAMS

39.9400 g., 0.9170 Gold 1.1771 oz. AGW, 40 mm. **Subject:** 5th

Anniversary - United Arab Emirates **Obv:** Head 1/4 right **Rev:** Dates

Date	Mintage	F	VF	XF	Unc	BU
ND(1976) Proof	12,500	Value: 850				

KM# 26 1000 DIRHAMS
39.9400 g., 0.9170 Gold 1.1771 oz. AGW, 40 mm. **Subject:** Death of Shaikh Rashid Bin Saeed Al Maktoum **Obv:** Bust right **Rev:** Dubai International Trade Center **Note:** Similar to 50 Dirhams, KM#17.

Date	Mintage	F	VF	XF	Unc	BU
ND(1992) Proof	2,000	Value: 875				

KM# 27 1000 DIRHAMS
39.9400 g., 0.9170 Gold 1.1771 oz. AGW, 40 mm. **Subject:** 10th Anniversary - U.A.E. Central Bank **Obv:** Bust half right **Rev:** Bank building **Note:** Similar to 50 Dirhams, KM#18.

Date	Mintage	F	VF	XF	Unc	BU
ND(1992) Proof	1,000	Value: 900				

KM# 28 1000 DIRHAMS
39.9400 g., 0.9170 Gold 1.1771 oz. AGW, 40 mm. **Subject:** 20th Anniversary - General Women's Union **Obv:** Bust right **Rev:** Seal in wreath

Date	Mintage	F	VF	XF	Unc	BU
ND(1996) Proof	1,000	Value: 900				

PIEFORTS

KM#	Date	Mintage	Identification	Mkt Val
P1	1980	75	50 Dirhams. 0.9250 Silver. KM#7.	75.00
P2	1981	100	750 Dirhams. 0.9000 Gold. KM#8.	800

MINT SETS

KM#	Date	Mintage	Identification	Issue Price	Mkt Val
MS1	AH1409/1989 (6)	—	KM#1, 2.1-3.1, 4-5, 6.1	—	15.00
MS2	Mixed dates (5)	—	KM#10-11 1987, KM#14 1988, KM#15 1991, KM#9 1981	—	—

This emirate, one of the original members of the United Arab Emirates, is the second smallest, least developed and lowest in population. The area is 300 sq. mi. (800 sq. km.) and the population is 5,000. The first recognition by the West was in 1820. Most of the emirate is uninhabited desert. Native boat building is an important activity.

TITLE

Umm al Qaiwain

RULERS
Ahmad Bin Abdullah al-Mualla, 1872-1904
Rashid Bin Ahmad al-Mualla, 1904-1929
Ahmad Bin Rashid al-Mualla, 1929-1981
Rashid Bin Ahmad al-Mualla, 1981-

EMIRATE

NON-CIRCULATING LEGAL TENDER COINAGE

KM# 1 RIYAL
3.0000 g., 1.0000 Silver .0965 oz. ASW **Ruler:** Ahmad bin Rashid al-Mualla **Obv:** Dates within crossed flags, sprigs within circle **Rev:** Old cannon within wreath

Date	Mintage	F	VF	XF	Unc	BU
AH1389 (1969) Proof	2,050	Value: 17.50				

KM# 2 2 RIYALS
6.0000 g., 1.0000 Silver .1929 oz. ASW **Ruler:** Ahmad bin Rashid al-Mualla **Obv:** Dates within crossed flags, sprigs at left and right within circle **Rev:** Fort of the 19th Century

Date	Mintage	F	VF	XF	Unc	BU
AH1389 (1969) Proof	2,050	Value: 27.50				

KM# 3 5 RIYALS
15.0000 g., 1.0000 Silver .4823 oz. ASW **Ruler:** Ahmad bin Rashid al-Mualla **Obv:** Dates within crossed flags, sprigs at left and right within circle **Rev:** Two gazelles

Date	Mintage	F	VF	XF	Unc	BU
AH1389 (1969) Proof	2,100	Value: 40.00				

KM# 4 10 RIYALS
30.0000 g., 1.0000 Silver .9646 oz. ASW **Ruler:** Ahmad bin Rashid al-Mualla **Obv:** Dates within crossed flags, sprigs at left and right within circle **Rev:** Facade of the great Rock Temple

Date	Mintage	F	VF	XF	Unc	BU
AH1389 (1969) Proof	2,000	Value: 225				

KM# 6 25 RIYALS
5.1800 g., 0.9000 Gold .1499 oz. AGW **Ruler:** Ahmad bin Rashid al-Mualla **Obv:** Dates within crossed flags, sprigs at left and right within circle **Rev:** Old cannon within wreath

Date	Mintage	F	VF	XF	Unc	BU
AH1389 (1969) Proof	500	Value: 175				

KM# 7 50 RIYALS
10.3600 g., 0.9000 Gold .2998 oz. AGW **Ruler:** Ahmad bin Rashid al-Mualla **Obv:** Dates within crossed flags, sprigs at left and right within circle **Rev:** Fort of the 19th Century

Date	Mintage	F	VF	XF	Unc	BU
AH1389 (1969) Proof	420	Value: 285				

KM# 8 100 RIYALS
20.7300 g., 0.9000 Gold .5999 oz. AGW **Ruler:** Ahmad bin Rashid al-Mualla **Obv:** Dates within crossed flags, sprigs at left and right within circle **Rev:** Gazelles

Date	Mintage	F	VF	XF	Unc	BU
AH1389 (1969) Proof	300	Value: 485				

KM# 9 200 RIYALS
41.46 g., 0.90 Gold 1.1998 oz. AGW **Ruler:** Ahmad bin Rashid al-Mualla **Obv:** Dates within crossed flags, sprigs at left and right within circle **Rev:** Head of Sheik Ahmed Ben Rashid as Moalia left

Date	Mintage	F	VF	XF	Unc	BU
AH1389 (1969) Proof	230	Value: 900				

UNITED STATES OF AMERICA

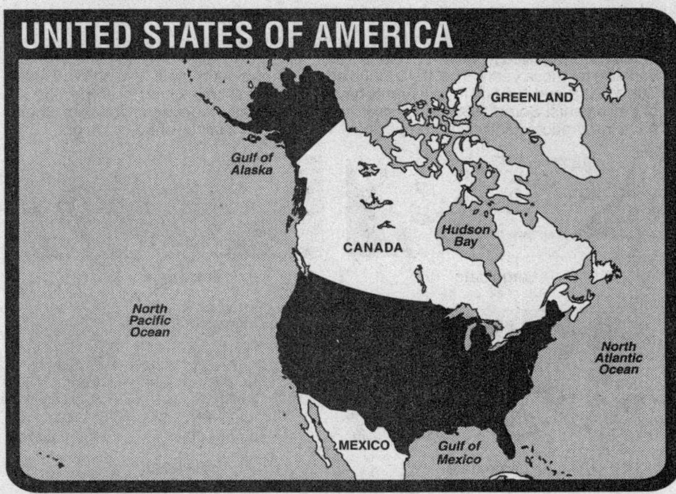

The United States of America as politically organized, under the Articles of Confederation consisted of the 13 original British-American colonies; New Hampshire, Massachusetts, Rhode Island, Connecticut, New York, New Jersey, Pennsylvania, Delaware, Virginia, North Carolina, South Carolina, Georgia and Maryland. Clustered along the eastern seaboard of North American between the forests of Maine and the marshes of Georgia. Under the Article of Confederation, the United States had no national capital: Philadelphia, where the "United States in Congress Assembled", was the "seat of government". The population during this political phase of America's history (1781-1789) was about 3 million, most of whom lived on self-sufficient family farms. Fishing, lumbering and the production of grains for export were major economic endeavors. Rapid strides were also being made in industry and manufacturing by 1775, the (then) colonies were accounting for one-seventh of the world's production of raw iron.

On the basis of the voyage of John Cabot to the North American mainland in 1497, England claimed the entire continent. The first permanent English settlement was established at Jamestown, Virginia, in 1607. France and Spain also claimed extensive territory in North America. At the end of the French and Indian Wars (1763), England acquired all of the territory east of the Mississippi River, including East and West Florida. From 1776 to 1781, the States were governed by the Continental Congress. From 1781 to 1789, they were organized under the Articles of Confederation, during which period the individual States had the right to issue money. Independence from Great Britain was attained with the American Revolution in 1776. The Constitution organized and governs the present United States. It was ratified on Nov. 21, 1788.

MINT MARKS

D – Denver, CO, 1906-present
O – New Orleans, LA, 1838-1909
P – Philadelphia, PA, 1793-present
S – San Francisco, CA, 1854-present
W – West Point, NY, 1984-present

MONETARY SYSTEM

Nickel = 5 Cents
Dime = 10 Cents
Quarter = 25 Cents
Half Dollar = 50 Cents
Dollar = 100 Cents
Quarter Eagle = $2.50 Gold
Half Eagle = $5.00 Gold
Eagle = $10.00 Gold
Double Eagle = $20.00 Gold

BULLION COINS

Silver Eagle = $1.00
Gold 1/10 Ounce = $5.00
Gold ¼ Ounce = $10.00
Gold ½ Ounce = $25.00
Gold Ounce = $50.00
Platinum 1/10 Ounce = $10.00
Platinum ¼ Ounce = $25.00
Platinum ½ Ounce = $50.00
Platinum Ounce = $100.00

CIRCULATION COINAGE

CENT

Indian Head Cent

KM# 90a BRONZE 19 mm. 3.1100 g. **Designer:** James B. Longacre **Notes:** The 1864 "L" variety has the designer's initial in Liberty's hair to the right of her neck.

Date	Mintage	G-4	VG-8	F-12	VF-20	XF-40	AU-50	MS-60	MS-65	Prf-65
1901	79,611,143	1.85	2.20	2.50	4.00	11.00	23.00	30.00	200	425
1902	87,376,722	1.85	2.20	2.50	4.00	10.00	22.00	30.00	200	425
1903	85,094,493	1.85	2.20	2.50	4.00	10.00	21.00	30.00	200	425
1904	61,328,015	1.75	2.20	2.50	4.00	10.00	21.00	30.00	200	475
1905	80,719,163	1.75	2.20	2.50	3.50	9.00	20.00	30.00	175	475
1906	96,022,255	1.75	2.20	2.50	3.50	9.00	21.00	30.00	175	395
1907	108,138,618	1.75	2.20	2.50	3.50	8.50	20.00	30.00	175	485
1908	32,327,987	1.75	2.30	2.50	3.50	9.00	20.00	30.00	145	395
1908S	1,115,000	62.50	65.00	75.00	88.00	150	185	300	750	—
1909	14,370,645	7.50	8.00	8.50	9.00	17.00	23.50	30.00	150	400
1909S	309,000	500	535	575	595	650	725	800	2,000	—

Lincoln Cent

Wheat Ears

KM# 132 BRONZE 19 mm. 3.1100 g. **Designer:** Victor D. Brenner **Notes:** The 1909 "VDB" varieties have the designer's initials inscribed at the 6 o'clock position on the reverse. The initials were removed until 1918, when they were restored on the obverse.

Date	Mintage	G-4	VG-8	F-12	VF-20	XF-40	AU-50	MS-60	MS-65	Prf-65
1909 VDB	27,995,000	10.00	10.25	10.50	10.75	11.00	11.50	11.00	100.00	6,000
1909 VDB Doubled Die Obverse	Inc. above	—	—	—	75.00	100.00	120	—	—	—
1909S VDB	484,000	750	800	850	1,050	1,200	1,250	1,500	7,500	—
1909	72,702,618	1.75	2.00	2.60	3.00	4.50	11.00	15.00	80.00	520
1909S	1,825,000	75.00	82.00	95.00	140	195	225	295	1,300	—
1909S/S S over horizontal S	Inc. above	90.00	105	115	160	225	260	—	—	—
1910	146,801,218	.50	.60	.75	1.00	4.00	9.00	17.50	250	700
1910S	6,045,000	8.50	11.00	12.00	14.00	32.00	60.00	65.00	800	—
1911	101,177,787	.60	.80	2.00	2.50	4.50	9.00	19.00	375	600
1911D	12,672,000	5.25	6.00	10.00	15.00	40.00	65.00	80.00	1,350	—
1911S	4,026,000	18.00	20.00	26.00	32.00	50.00	90.00	160	3,300	—
1912	68,153,060	1.75	2.00	2.50	6.00	12.00	21.00	30.00	550	950
1912D	10,411,000	7.00	8.50	10.00	23.50	55.00	85.00	150	2,800	—
1912S	4,431,000	14.00	17.00	20.00	26.00	55.00	90.00	130	4,400	—
1913	76,532,352	1.00	1.20	1.75	3.25	13.50	20.00	33.50	415	550
1913D	15,804,000	3.00	3.50	4.00	10.50	28.00	61.00	90.00	2,100	—
1913S	6,101,000	6.50	7.75	9.00	14.00	33.50	75.00	150	5,500	—
1914	75,238,432	.75	1.10	2.25	5.50	14.00	34.00	47.50	415	600
1914D	1,193,000	210	250	385	440	665	1,300	1,900	22,000	—
1914S	4,137,000	14.00	16.50	18.00	28.00	62.00	150	285	10,000	—
1915	29,092,120	1.75	2.00	3.75	13.00	42.00	67.50	80.00	1,150	600
1915D	22,050,000	1.75	2.00	3.50	6.50	19.00	40.00	67.50	1,250	—
1915S	4,833,000	9.00	11.00	13.50	20.00	48.00	75.00	160	4,800	—
1916	131,833,677	.35	.60	1.25	2.60	6.00	11.50	18.00	415	1,650
1916D	35,956,000	1.75	2.25	3.00	6.00	13.00	27.50	65.00	3,000	—
1916S	22,510,000	2.25	3.25	4.50	7.00	17.00	36.00	71.00	8,500	—
1917	196,429,785	.35	.45	.55	2.00	4.50	10.00	16.00	450	—
1917 Doubled Die Obverse	Inc. above	90.00	110	175	350	900	1,750	—	—	—
1917D	55,120,000	1.50	1.75	2.50	5.50	16.00	30.00	60.00	3,000	—
1917S	32,620,000	.80	1.20	1.75	2.50	9.50	22.00	58.50	7,200	—
1918	288,104,634	.35	.40	.50	1.25	4.50	8.00	12.50	415	—
1918D	47,830,000	1.60	2.00	2.65	5.50	15.00	29.00	70.00	3,550	—
1918S	34,680,000	.50	1.20	1.75	3.65	10.00	32.00	61.00	7,800	—
1919	392,021,000	.30	.40	.50	.80	1.75	4.25	8.00	100.00	—
1919D	57,154,000	1.25	1.60	2.00	4.00	10.00	30.00	50.00	2,700	—
1919S	139,760,000	.40	.70	1.80	2.65	6.00	16.00	41.50	4,300	—
1920	310,165,000	.35	.40	.90	1.50	2.80	7.00	13.50	205	—
1920D	49,280,000	1.25	1.65	2.80	5.50	16.00	31.00	62.50	2,750	—
1920S	46,220,000	.90	1.00	1.50	2.75	10.00	32.50	90.00	9,000	—
1921	39,157,000	.60	1.00	1.25	2.80	10.00	20.00	41.50	375	—
1921S	15,274,000	1.65	2.10	2.85	6.00	25.00	68.00	100.00	6,700	—
1922D	7,160,000	12.50	14.00	16.00	20.00	27.50	55.00	90.00	2,350	—
1922D Weak Rev	Inc. above	12.00	13.50	15.00	18.00	25.00	50.00	—	—	—
1922D Weak D	Inc. above	35.00	48.00	70.00	150	275	400	—	—	—
1922 No D Die 2 Strong Rev	Inc. above	560	725	1,200	1,700	3,300	6,600	9,600	180,000	—
1922 No D Die 3 Weak Rev	Inc. above	175	245	440	675	1,450	3,500	—	—	—
1923	74,723,000	.60	.80	1.00	1.35	4.50	8.00	13.50	480	—
1923S	8,700,000	2.50	3.50	4.50	7.75	30.00	80.00	195	15,000	—
1924	75,178,000	.35	.50	.60	1.00	4.50	8.00	20.00	390	—
1924D	2,520,000	25.00	28.50	35.00	44.00	92.00	150	235	8,500	—
1924S	11,696,000	1.75	2.00	2.80	5.00	18.00	66.00	115	11,000	—
1925	139,949,000	.30	.40	.50	.70	2.50	6.00	8.50	100.00	—
1925D	22,580,000	1.50	2.00	3.00	5.00	15.00	27.50	60.00	5,000	—
1925S	26,380,000	1.20	1.50	2.00	2.75	11.00	30.00	80.00	9,000	—
1926	157,088,000	.25	.40	.50	.70	1.65	4.40	7.00	66.00	—
1926D	28,020,000	1.50	1.70	2.80	4.50	13.50	32.50	80.00	4,350	—
1926S	4,550,000	5.00	6.00	8.00	10.00	20.00	56.00	110	10,500	—
1927	144,440,000	.20	.30	.40	.70	1.60	4.50	7.00	6,000	—
1927D	27,170,000	1.50	1.75	2.25	3.35	7.00	23.00	58.50	1,850	—
1927S	14,276,000	1.50	1.85	3.00	4.65	11.50	32.50	62.50	6,000	—
1928	134,116,000	.20	.30	.40	.70	1.25	3.75	7.50	90.00	—
1928D	31,170,000	1.10	1.40	2.00	3.00	6.50	14.00	34.00	1,100	—
1928S Small S	17,266,000	1.20	1.65	2.60	3.50	8.00	25.00	71.50	4,800	—
1928S Large S	Inc. above	1.75	2.50	4.00	6.00	15.00	40.00	—	—	—
1929	185,262,000	.20	.30	.40	.60	1.00	4.25	6.00	85.00	—
1929D	41,730,000	.70	1.20	1.50	2.35	4.65	11.00	21.50	550	—
1929S	50,148,000	.80	1.25	1.75	2.50	4.00	6.75	17.50	415	—
1930	157,415,000	.20	.30	.40	.60	1.25	2.25	3.75	32.50	—
1930D	40,100,000	.35	.45	.65	.90	2.00	4.00	10.50	95.00	—
1930S	24,286,000	.35	.45	.60	.80	1.50	6.00	10.00	50.00	—
1931	19,396,000	.70	.80	1.30	2.00	2.75	8.00	19.00	130	—
1931D	4,480,000	4.50	5.75	6.00	7.00	12.50	37.50	52.00	815	—
1931S	866,000	80.00	85.00	90.00	95.00	100.00	105	120	750	—
1932	9,062,000	1.50	1.85	2.75	3.50	5.75	12.50	19.00	83.50	—
1932D	10,500,000	1.40	2.00	2.50	2.85	4.15	9.60	17.50	96.00	—
1933	14,360,000	1.40	1.80	2.50	2.85	4.25	9.50	17.50	80.00	—
1933D	6,200,000	3.25	4.00	4.75	6.25	11.50	16.00	23.00	100.00	—
1934	219,080,000	.20	.30	.40	.60	1.25	4.00	4.00	28.50	—
1934D	28,446,000	.35	.50	.80	1.50	3.00	9.00	16.50	52.00	—

Date	Mintage	G-4	VG-8	F-12	VF-20	XF-40	AU-50	MS-60	MS-65	Prf-65
1935	245,338,000	.20	.30	.40	.55	.90	1.50	2.50	13.00	—
1935D	47,000,000	.15	.20	.30	.40	.95	2.50	5.50	9.50	—
1935S	38,702,000	.25	.35	.60	1.75	3.00	5.00	12.00	52.50	—
1936 (Proof in Satin Finish)	309,637,569	.20	.30	.40	.55	.85	1.40	2.00	6.00	1,200
1936 Brilliant Proof	Inc. above	—	—	—	—	—	—	—	—	—
1936D	40,620,000	.20	.30	.40	.55	.90	1.50	2.75	11.00	—
1936S	29,130,000	.20	.30	.45	.60	1.00	1.75	2.75	13.50	—
1937	309,179,320	.20	.30	.40	.55	.85	1.40	1.75	7.00	125
1937D	50,430,000	.20	.30	.40	.60	.95	1.00	2.50	11.00	—
1937S	34,500,000	.20	.30	.40	.55	.90	1.25	3.00	9.50	—
1938	156,696,734	.20	.30	.40	.55	.85	1.20	2.00	8.00	85.00
1938D	20,010,000	.20	.30	.45	.60	1.00	1.50	3.50	13.50	—
1938S	15,180,000	.30	.40	.50	.70	1.00	2.00	2.80	9.50	—
1939	316,479,520	.20	.30	.40	.55	.75	.90	1.00	5.75	78.00
1939D	15,160,000	.35	.45	.50	.60	.85	1.90	2.25	9.50	—
1939S	52,070,000	.30	.40	.50	.60	.80	1.10	1.35	13.50	—
1940	586,825,872	.10	.20	.30	.40	.50	.75	1.00	5.75	70.00
1940D	81,390,000	.20	.30	.40	.55	.75	.50	1.20	9.50	—
1940S	112,940,000	.20	.30	.40	.55	.90	1.25	1.25	7.50	—
1941	887,039,100	.10	.20	.30	.40	.50	.70	.85	5.75	65.00
1941 Doubled Die Obv	Inc. above	35.00	50.00	70.00	80.00	95.00	135	—	—	—
1941D	128,700,000	.20	.30	.40	.55	.75	1.25	2.00	8.50	—
1941S	92,360,000	.20	.30	.40	.55	.75	1.75	2.25	12.50	—
1942	657,828,600	.10	.20	.30	.40	.50	.70	.50	4.00	78.00
1942D	206,698,000	.20	.25	.30	.35	.40	.50	.50	7.50	—
1942S	85,590,000	.25	.35	.45	.85	1.25	2.50	3.50	19.00	—

KM# 132a ZINC COATED STEEL 19 mm. 2.7000 g. **Designer:** Victor D. Brenner

Date	Mintage	G-4	VG-8	F-12	VF-20	XF-40	AU-50	MS-60	MS-65	Prf-65
1943	684,628,670	.25	.30	.35	.45	.60	.85	1.25	4.75	—
1943D	217,660,000	.35	.40	.45	.50	.70	1.00	1.25	8.50	—
1943D/D RPM	—	30.00	38.00	50.00	65.00	90.00	125	200	—	—
1943S	191,550,000	.45	.45	.50	.65	.90	1.40	3.00	13.50	—

KM# A132 COPPER-ZINC 19 mm. 3.1100 g. **Designer:** Victor D. Brenner **Notes:** KM#132 design and composition resumed.

Date	Mintage	XF-40	MS-65	Prf-65
1944	1,435,400,000	.40	2.00	—
1944D	430,578,000	.50	2.00	—
1944D/S Type 1	—	235	1,700	—
1944D/S Type 2	Inc. above	175	—	—
1944S	282,760,000	.40	5.50	—
1945	1,040,515,000	.40	2.00	—
1945D	226,268,000	.40	2.00	—
1945S	181,770,000	.40	5.50	—
1946	991,655,000	.30	2.00	—
1946D	315,690,000	.30	4.50	—
1946S	198,100,000	.30	4.60	—
1946S/D	—	70.00	—	—
1947	190,555,000	.45	2.25	—
1947D	194,750,000	.40	2.00	—
1947S	99,000,000	.35	5.50	—
1948	317,570,000	.40	2.00	—
1948D	172,637,000	.40	2.25	—
1948S	81,735,000	.40	5.50	—
1949	217,775,000	.40	3.50	—
1949D	153,132,000	.40	3.50	—
1949S	64,290,000	.50	6.00	—
1950	272,686,386	.40	1.75	40.00
1950D	334,950,000	.35	1.50	—
1950S	118,505,000	.40	2.50	—
1951	295,633,500	.40	2.00	40.00
1951D	625,355,000	.30	1.65	—
1951S	136,010,000	.40	3.00	—
1952	186,856,980	.40	3.00	34.00
1952D	746,130,000	.30	1.60	—
1952S	137,800,004	.60	5.00	—
1953	256,883,800	.30	1.25	28.00
1953D	700,515,000	.30	1.25	—
1953S	181,835,000	.40	1.75	—
1954	71,873,350	.25	1.25	9.00
1954D	251,552,500	.25	.50	—
1954S	96,190,000	.25	.75	—
1955	330,958,000	.25	.75	13.00
1955 doubled die	—	1,425	37,500	—

Note: The 1955 "doubled die" has distinct doubling of the date and lettering on the obverse.

Date	Mintage	XF-40	MS-65	Prf-65
1955D	563,257,500	.20	.75	—
1955S	44,610,000	.35	1.00	—
1956	421,414,384	.20	.50	3.00
1956D	1,098,201,100	.20	.50	—
1957	283,787,952	.20	.50	2.00
1957D	1,051,342,000	.20	.50	—
1958	253,400,652	.20	.50	3.00
1958D	800,953,300	.20	.50	—

Lincoln Memorial

KM# 201 COPPER-ZINC 3.1100 g. **Rev. Designer:** Frank Gasparro **Notes:** The dates were modified in 1960, 1970 and 1982, resulting in large-date and small-date varieties for those years. The 1972 "doubled die" shows doubling of "In God We Trust." The 1979-S and 1981-S Type II proofs have a clearer mint mark than the Type I proofs of those years. Some 1982 cents have the predominantly copper composition; others have the predominantly zinc composition. They can be distinguished by weight.

Large date

Small date

Large date

Small date

Date	Mintage	XF-40	MS-65	Prf-65
1959	610,864,291	—	.50	1.50
1959D	1,279,760,000	—	.50	—
1960 small date	588,096,602	2.10	7.00	16.00
1960 large date	Inc. above	—	.30	1.25
1960D small date	1,580,884,000	—	.30	—
1960D large date	Inc. above	—	.30	—
1961	756,373,244	—	.30	1.00
1961D	1,753,266,700	—	.30	—
1962	609,263,019	—	.30	1.00
1962D	1,793,148,400	—	.30	—
1963	757,185,645	—	.30	1.00
1963D	1,774,020,400	—	.30	—
1964	2,652,525,762	—	.30	1.00
1964D	3,799,071,500	—	.30	—
1965	1,497,224,900	—	.30	—
1966	2,188,147,783	—	.30	—
1967	3,048,667,100	—	.50	—
1968	1,707,880,970	—	.30	—
1968D	2,886,269,600	—	.40	—
1968S	261,311,510	—	.40	1.00
1969	1,136,910,000	—	.60	—
1969D	4,002,832,200	—	.40	—
1969S	547,309,631	—	.40	1.10
1970	1,898,315,000	—	.40	—
1970D	2,891,438,900	—	.40	—
1970S	693,192,814	—	.40	1.20
1970S small date	Inc. above	—	55.00	60.00
1971	1,919,490,000	—	.35	—
1971D	2,911,045,600	—	.40	—
1971S	528,354,192	—	.25	1.20
1972	2,933,255,000	—	.25	—
1972 doubled die	—	285	800	—
1972D	2,665,071,400	—	.25	—
1972S	380,200,104	—	.25	1.15
1973	3,728,245,000	—	.25	—
1973D	3,549,576,588	—	.25	—
1973S	319,937,634	—	.25	0.80
1974	4,232,140,523	—	.25	—
1974D	4,235,098,000	—	.25	—
1974S	412,039,228	—	.25	0.75
1975	5,451,476,142	—	.25	—
1975D	4,505,245,300	—	.25	—
1975S	(2,845,450)	—	—	5.50
1976	4,674,292,426	—	.25	—
1976D	4,221,592,455	—	.25	—
1976S	(4,149,730)	—	—	5.00
1977	4,469,930,000	—	.25	—
1977D	4,149,062,300	—	.25	—
1977S	(3,251,152)	—	—	3.00
1978	5,558,605,000	—	.25	—
1978D	4,280,233,400	—	.25	—
1978S	(3,127,781)	—	—	3.50
1979	6,018,515,000	—	.25	—
1979D	4,139,357,254	—	.25	—
1979S type I, proof	(3,677,175)	—	—	4.00
1979S type II, proof	Inc. above	—	—	4.25
1980	7,414,705,000	—	.25	—
1980D	5,140,098,660	—	.25	—
1980S	(3,554,806)	—	—	2.25
1981	7,491,750,000	—	.25	—
1981S type II, proof	Inc. above	—	—	60.00
1981D	5,373,235,677	—	.25	—
1981S type I, proof	(4,063,083)	—	—	3.50
1982 large date	10,712,525,000	—	.25	—
1982 small date	—	—	.25	—

Date	Mintage	XF-40	MS-65	Prf-65
1982D large date	6,012,979,368	—	.25	—

KM# 201a COPPER PLATED ZINC 19 mm. 2.5000 g.

Date	Mintage	XF-40	MS-65	Prf-65
1982 large date	—	—	.50	—
1982 small date	—	—	2.00	—
1982D large date	—	—	.30	—
1982D small date	—	—	.25	—

KM#201b COPPER PLATED ZINC 19 mm. **Notes:** The 1983 "doubled die reverse" shows doubling of "United States of America." The 1984 "doubled die" shows doubling of Lincoln's ear on the obverse.

Date	Mintage	XF-40	MS-65	Prf-65
1982S	(3,857,479)	—	—	3.00
1983	7,752,355,000	—	.25	—
1983 doubled die	—	—	400	—
1983D	6,467,199,428	—	.50	—
1983S	(3,279,126)	—	—	4.00
1984	8,151,079,000	—	.25	—
1984 doubled die	—	—	275	—
1984D	5,569,238,906	—	.75	—
1984S	(3,065,110)	—	—	4.50
1985	5,648,489,887	—	.25	—
1985D	5,287,399,926	—	.25	—
1985S	(3,362,821)	—	—	6.00
1986	4,491,395,493	—	1.50	—
1986D	4,442,866,698	—	1.25	—
1986S	(3,010,497)	—	—	7.50
1987	4,682,466,931	—	.25	—
1987D	4,879,389,514	—	.25	—
1987S	(4,227,728)	—	—	5.00
1988	6,092,810,000	—	.25	—
1988D	5,253,740,443	—	.25	—
1988S	(3,262,948)	—	—	4.00
1989	7,261,535,000	—	.25	—
1989D	5,345,467,111	—	.25	—
1989S	(3,220,194)	—	—	6.00
1990	6,851,765,000	—	.25	—
1990D	4,922,894,533	—	.25	—
1990S	(3,299,559)	—	—	5.00
1990 no S	—	—	—	2,750
1991	5,165,940,000	—	.25	—
1991D	4,158,442,076	—	.25	—
1991S	(2,867,787)	—	—	5.00
1992	4,648,905,000	—	.25	—
1992D	4,448,673,300	—	.25	—
1992S	(4,176,560)	—	—	5.00
1993	5,684,705,000	—	.25	—
1993D	6,426,650,571	—	.25	—
1993S	(3,394,792)	—	—	7.00
1994	6,500,850,000	—	.25	—
1994D	7,131,765,000	—	.25	—
1994S	(3,269,923)	—	—	4.00
1995	6,411,440,000	—	.25	—
1995 doubled die	—	20.00	50.00	—
1995D	7,128,560,000	—	.25	—
1995S	(2,707,481)	—	—	9.50
1996	6,612,465,000	—	.25	—
1996D	6,510,795,000	—	.25	—
1996S	(2,915,212)	—	—	6.50
1997	4,622,800,000	—	.25	—
1997D	4,576,555,000	—	.25	—
1997S	(2,796,678)	—	—	11.50
1998	5,032,155,000	—	.25	—
1998D	5,255,353,500	—	.25	—
1998S	(2,957,286)	—	—	9.50
1999	5,237,600,000	—	.25	—
1999D	6,360,065,000	—	.25	—
1999S	(3,362,462)	—	—	5.00
2000	5,503,200,000	—	.25	—
2000D	8,774,220,000	—	.25	—
2000S	(4,063,361)	—	—	4.00

5 CENTS

Liberty Nickel

KM# 112 COPPER-NICKEL 5.0000 g.

Date	Mintage	G-4	VG-8	F-12	VF-20	XF-40	AU-50	MS-60	MS-65	Prf-65
1901	26,480,213	1.70	2.50	7.00	15.00	32.50	60.00	75.00	720	560
1902	31,480,579	1.70	2.50	4.00	15.00	30.00	60.00	77.50	720	560
1903	28,006,725	1.70	2.50	5.00	15.00	30.00	57.50	80.00	725	560
1904	21,404,984	1.70	2.50	5.00	11.00	27.50	55.00	72.50	750	725
1905	29,827,276	1.70	2.00	4.00	11.00	27.50	55.00	72.50	720	560
1906	38,613,725	1.70	2.00	4.00	11.00	27.50	55.00	70.00	950	560
1907	39,214,800	1.70	2.00	4.00	11.00	27.50	55.00	72.50	1,400	625
1908	22,686,177	1.70	2.00	4.00	11.00	27.50	55.00	72.50	1,250	560
1909	11,590,526	2.50	3.00	5.00	12.50	30.00	62.50	82.50	1,300	560
1910	30,169,353	1.70	2.00	4.00	10.00	27.50	48.50	65.00	750	560
1911	39,559,372	1.70	2.00	4.00	10.00	27.50	48.50	65.00	720	560
1912	26,236,714	1.70	2.00	4.00	10.00	27.50	48.50	65.00	720	575
1912D	8,474,000	2.50	4.00	10.00	35.00	68.50	150	290	2,500	—
1912S	238,000	160	220	280	500	850	1,350	1,550	7,500	—
1913 5 known	—	—	—	—	—	—	—	—	—	—

Note: 1913, Superior Sale, March 2001, Proof, $1,840,000.

Buffalo Nickel

Buffalo standing on a mound

KM# 133 COPPER-NICKEL 21.2 mm. 5.0000 g. **Designer:** James Earle Fraser

Date	Mintage	G-4	VG-8	F-12	VF-20	XF-40	AU-50	MS-60	MS-65	Prf-65
1913	30,993,520	8.00	11.00	11.25	12.00	18.50	23.50	32.50	185	3,500
1913D	5,337,000	12.50	15.00	19.00	25.00	35.00	50.00	62.50	330	—
1913S	2,105,000	35.00	42.00	50.00	60.00	75.00	100.00	125	700	—

American Bison standing on a line

KM# 134 COPPER-NICKEL 21.2 mm. 5.0000 g. **Designer:** James Earle Fraser **Notes:** In 1913 the reverse design was modified so the ground under the buffalo was represented as a line rather than a mound. On the 1937D 3-legged variety, the buffalo's right front leg is missing, the result of a damaged die.

1918/17D

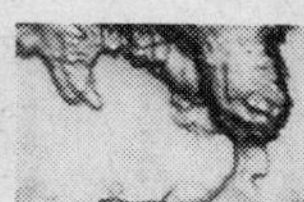
1937D 3-legged

Date	Mintage	G-4	VG-8	F-12	VF-20	XF-40	AU-50	MS-60	MS-65	Prf-65
1913	29,858,700	8.00	11.00	11.50	12.50	18.50	25.00	34.00	375	2,600
1913D	4,156,000	110	140	155	170	195	225	285	1,575	—
1913S	1,209,000	325	395	415	475	575	675	850	4,300	—
1914	20,665,738	15.00	17.50	19.00	21.50	27.50	37.50	49.00	450	2,350
1914D	3,912,000	80.00	110	155	220	315	395	450	1,850	—
1914S	3,470,000	26.00	37.50	45.00	62.50	90.00	135	150	2,350	—
1915	20,987,270	4.75	6.00	6.75	11.00	21.50	38.50	50.00	325	2,100
1915D	7,569,500	16.00	25.00	41.50	66.00	115	150	225	2,500	—
1915S	1,505,000	40.00	60.00	90.00	185	320	490	625	3,400	—
1916	63,498,066	4.00	5.90	6.00	7.50	13.50	22.50	43.50	350	3,850
1916/16	Inc. above	2,000	4,250	8,000	12,000	17,000	38,000	55,000	395,000	—
1916D	13,333,000	12.00	18.50	25.00	38.50	82.50	110	150	2,500	—
1916S	11,860,000	11.00	13.50	20.00	35.00	75.00	115	175	2,650	—
1917	51,424,029	4.00	5.90	6.25	9.75	15.00	32.50	60.00	580	—
1917D	9,910,800	16.00	23.00	47.50	80.00	135	255	345	4,400	—
1917S	4,193,000	23.00	35.00	70.00	110	180	285	395	5,250	—
1918	32,086,314	4.00	5.90	6.75	15.00	31.00	48.50	110	1,700	—
1918/17D	8,362,314	1,050	1,550	2,850	6,250	10,000	11,500	28,500	285,000	—
1918D	Inc. above	18.50	32.50	50.00	130	220	330	430	5,000	—
1918S	4,882,000	14.00	27.50	47.50	100.00	175	300	495	32,500	—
1919	60,868,000	1.75	2.75	3.25	7.00	15.00	30.00	60.00	595	—
1919D	8,006,000	12.50	23.50	57.50	115	235	335	570	8,000	—
1919S	7,521,000	8.00	20.00	50.00	110	225	360	540	19,000	—
1920	63,093,000	1.35	2.10	3.00	7.50	15.00	30.00	59.00	850	—
1920D	9,418,000	8.50	15.00	35.00	125	275	340	555	7,800	—
1920S	9,689,000	4.50	10.00	30.00	100.00	200	300	525	28,500	—
1921	10,663,000	3.75	6.25	8.50	25.00	53.50	70.00	125	850	—
1921S	1,557,000	67.50	120	200	545	845	1,100	1,500	8,000	—
1923	35,715,000	1.70	3.00	4.25	7.00	13.50	37.50	60.00	750	—
1923S	6,142,000	7.50	10.00	25.00	125	260	335	595	12,500	—
1924	21,620,000	1.00	2.10	4.15	9.60	19.00	41.00	73.50	950	—
1924D	5,258,000	7.50	11.00	30.00	85.00	215	315	375	5,600	—
1924S	1,437,000	18.00	34.00	96.00	470	1,100	1,700	2,300	12,000	—
1925	35,565,100	2.00	2.50	3.75	8.50	17.50	30.00	44.00	525	—
1925D	4,450,000	8.00	16.00	40.00	80.00	160	240	380	6,600	—
1925S	6,256,000	4.50	9.00	17.50	77.50	170	240	445	45,000	—
1926	44,693,000	.90	1.25	2.80	5.40	11.50	20.00	31.50	185	—
1926D	5,638,000	7.50	13.50	28.50	100.00	170	295	315	6,400	—
1926S	970,000	20.00	35.00	85.00	465	915	2,850	5,250	115,000	—
1927	37,981,000	.90	1.25	2.15	4.15	12.50	20.00	35.00	300	—
1927D	5,730,000	2.00	4.00	5.50	27.50	75.00	110	150	9,000	—
1927S	3,430,000	2.00	3.00	6.00	31.00	80.00	160	485	22,500	—
1928	23,411,000	.85	1.25	2.20	4.15	12.50	23.00	32.50	325	—
1928D	6,436,000	1.20	2.10	3.45	15.00	40.00	45.00	50.00	1,000	—
1928S	6,936,000	1.35	1.50	2.20	11.50	27.50	100.00	215	5,500	—
1929	36,446,000	.90	1.25	2.15	4.15	12.50	20.00	35.00	375	—
1929D	8,370,000	1.00	1.35	3.00	6.75	32.50	42.50	55.00	2,000	—
1929S	7,754,000	.90	1.35	2.25	5.00	11.50	25.00	47.50	525	—
1930	22,849,000	.90	1.40	2.15	4.15	11.50	20.00	32.50	250	—
1930S	5,435,000	1.00	1.40	2.75	4.25	15.00	34.00	52.50	500	—
1931S	1,200,000	16.00	18.00	20.00	22.00	33.00	50.00	65.00	315	—
1934	20,213,003	.90	1.40	2.15	4.15	10.00	19.00	48.50	440	—
1934D	7,480,000	1.75	2.75	4.40	9.60	22.00	50.00	82.50	1,000	—

Date	Mintage	G-4	VG-8	F-12	VF-20	XF-40	AU-50	MS-60	MS-65	Prf-65
1935	58,264,000	.90	1.00	1.10	1.40	2.75	8.50	20.00	135	—
1935D	12,092,000	1.35	2.20	2.80	8.00	20.00	46.00	75.00	540	—
1935S	10,300,000	.90	1.00	1.10	1.50	3.15	16.00	50.00	260	—
1936	119,001,420	.90	1.00	1.10	1.40	2.00	6.50	15.00	100.00	1,100
1936D	24,814,000	.90	1.00	1.10	1.85	3.85	11.50	35.00	110	—
1936S	14,930,000	.90	1.00	1.10	1.50	3.15	10.00	35.00	110	—
1937	79,485,769	.90	1.00	1.10	1.40	2.00	6.50	14.50	70.00	850
1937D	17,826,000	.90	1.00	1.10	1.50	3.15	9.00	30.00	75.00	—
1937D 3-legged	Inc. above	550	600	850	1,000	1,200	1,475	2,700	29,500	—
1937S	5,635,000	.90	1.20	1.40	1.80	4.00	11.00	27.50	67.50	—
1938D	7,020,000	3.50	3.75	3.90	4.00	4.25	8.00	20.00	70.00	—
1938D/D	—	2.50	4.50	6.00	8.00	10.00	17.00	20.00	52.50	—
1938D/S	Inc. above	4.50	6.75	9.00	12.50	19.00	32.50	50.00	185	—

Jefferson Nickel

Monticello, mint mark to right side

KM# 192 COPPER-NICKEL 21.2 mm. 5.0000 g. **Designer:** Felix Schlag **Notes:** Some 1939 strikes have doubling of the word "Monticello" on the reverse.

Date	Mintage	VG-8	F-12	VF-20	XF-40	MS-60	MS-65	-65FS	Prf-65
1938	19,515,365	.30	.50	.80	1.25	4.00	8.50	125	130
1938D	5,376,000	.90	1.00	1.25	1.75	3.50	8.00	95.00	—
1938S	4,105,000	1.75	2.00	2.50	3.00	4.75	8.50	165	—
1939 T I	—	—	—	—	—	—	—	300	70.00
1939 T II	120,627,535	—	.20	.25	.30	1.75	3.50	40.00	130
1939 doubled Monticello T II	—	30.00	50.00	80.00	140	250	750	900	—
1939D T I	—	—	—	—	—	—	—	275	—
1939D T II	3,514,000	3.50	4.00	5.00	10.00	42.00	125	250	—
1939S T I	—	—	—	—	—	—	—	250	—
1939S T II	6,630,000	.45	.60	1.50	2.75	15.00	45.00	275	—
1940	176,499,158	—	—	—	.25	1.00	3.00	35.00	135
1940D	43,540,000	—	.20	.30	.40	1.50	2.75	25.00	—
1940S	39,690,000	—	.20	.25	.50	2.50	6.00	45.00	—
1941	203,283,720	—	—	—	.20	.75	2.50	40.00	130
1941D	53,432,000	—	.20	.30	.50	2.50	6.00	25.00	—
1941S	43,445,000	—	.20	.30	.50	3.75	6.75	60.00	—
1942	49,818,600	—	—	—	.40	5.00	8.50	75.00	115
1942D	13,938,000	.30	.40	1.00	2.00	27.00	60.00	70.00	—

Note: Fully Struck Full Step nickels command higher prices. Bright, Fully Struck coins command even higher prices. 1938 thru 1989 - 5 Full Steps. 1990 to date - 6 Full Steps. Without bag marks or nicks on steps.

Monticello, mint mark above

KM# 192a 0.3500 **COPPER-SILVER-MANGANESE** .0563 oz. 21.2 mm. **Designer:** Felix Schlag **Notes:** War-time composition nickels have the mint mark above Monticello on the reverse.

1943/2

Date	Mintage	VG-8	F-12	VF-20	XF-40	MS-60	MS-65	-65FS	Prf-65
1942P	57,900,600	.65	.85	1.00	1.75	6.00	22.50	70.00	205
1942S	32,900,000	.70	1.00	1.10	1.75	6.00	20.00	125	—
1943P	271,165,000	.50	.85	1.00	1.50	2.75	15.00	35.00	—
1943/2P	Inc. above	35.00	50.00	75.00	110	250	650	1,000	—
1943D	15,294,000	.90	1.20	1.50	1.75	4.00	13.00	30.00	—
1943S	104,060,000	.55	.70	1.00	1.50	3.00	13.00	55.00	—
1944P	119,150,000	.50	.70	1.00	1.50	4.00	22.50	100.00	—
1944D	32,309,000	.60	.80	1.00	1.75	6.50	17.50	30.00	—
1944S	21,640,000	.70	1.00	1.25	2.00	3.50	14.00	185	—
1945P	119,408,100	.50	.70	1.00	1.50	3.50	13.50	125	—
1945D	37,158,000	.55	.75	1.00	1.50	3.50	13.00	40.00	—
1945S	58,939,000	.50	.70	.80	.90	3.00	14.00	250	—

Note: Fully Struck Full Step nickels command higher prices. Bright, Fully Struck coins command even higher prices. 1938 thru 1989 - 5 Full Steps. 1990 to date - 6 Full Steps. Without bag marks or nicks on steps.

Pre-war design resumed

KM# A192 COPPER-NICKEL 21.2 mm. 5.0000 g. **Designer:** Felix Schlag **Notes:** KM#192 design and composition resumed. The 1979-S and 1981-S Type II proofs have clearer mint marks than the Type I proofs of those years.

Date	Mintage	VG-8	F-12	VF-20	XF-40	MS-60	MS-65	-65FS	Prf-65
1946	161,116,000	—	—	.20	.25	.80	3.50	40.00	—
1946D	45,292,200	—	—	.25	.35	.95	3.50	30.00	—
1946S	13,560,000	—	—	.30	.40	.50	2.00	45.00	—
1947	95,000,000	—	—	.20	.25	.75	2.00	30.00	—
1947D	37,822,000	—	—	.20	.30	.90	2.50	30.00	—
1947S	24,720,000	—	—	.20	.25	1.00	2.25	55.00	—
1948	89,348,000	—	—	.20	.25	.50	2.50	60.00	—
1948D	44,734,000	—	—	.25	.35	1.20	4.50	30.00	—
1948S	11,300,000	—	—	.25	.50	1.20	3.50	45.00	—
1949	60,652,000	—	—	.25	.30	2.25	6.00	200	—
1949D	36,498,000	—	—	.30	.40	1.25	5.00	75.00	—
1949D/S	Inc. above	—	35.00	40.00	65.00	170	325	1,750	—
1949S	9,716,000	.25	.35	.45	.90	1.50	3.50	145	—
1950	9,847,386	.20	.30	.35	.75	1.50	4.75	150	70.00
1950D	2,630,030	11.00	11.50	12.00	12.50	22.00	30.00	45.00	—
1951	28,609,500	—	—	.40	.50	1.50	9.00	90.00	70.00
1951D	20,460,000	.25	.30	.40	.50	3.00	10.00	45.00	—
1951S	7,776,000	.30	.40	.50	1.10	1.75	5.00	150	—
1952	64,069,980	—	—	.20	.25	.85	4.50	125	37.50
1952D	30,638,000	—	—	.30	.45	2.00	7.00	65.00	—
1952S	20,572,000	—	—	.20	.25	.75	3.50	195	—
1953	46,772,800	—	—	.20	.25	.40	1.50	200	37.50
1953D	59,878,600	—	—	.20	.25	.40	1.50	100.00	—
1953S	19,210,900	—	—	.20	.25	.60	2.50	1,750	—
1954	47,917,350	—	—	—	—	.60	2.00	95.00	20.00
1954D	117,136,560	—	—	—	—	.35	2.00	175	—
1954S	29,384,000	—	—	—	.20	1.00	3.00	1,000	—
1954S/D	Inc. above	—	6.00	9.00	13.00	22.00	65.00	—	—
1955	8,266,200	.25	.35	.40	.45	.75	2.00	85.00	13.50
1955D	74,464,100	—	—	—	—	.20	1.00	150	—
1955D/S	Inc. above	—	5.00	8.50	13.00	33.00	75.00	—	—
1956	35,885,384	—	—	—	—	.30	.70	35.00	2.50
1956D	67,222,940	—	—	—	—	.25	.60	90.00	—
1957	39,655,952	—	—	—	—	.25	.60	40.00	1.50
1957D	136,828,900	—	—	—	—	.25	.60	55.00	—
1958	17,963,652	—	—	.15	.20	.30	.65	80.00	7.00
1958D	168,249,120	—	—	—	—	.25	.60	30.00	—

Note: Fully Struck Full Step nickels command higher prices. Bright, Fully Struck coins command even higher prices. 1938 thru 1989 - 5 Full Steps. 1990 to date - 6 Full Steps. Without bag marks or nicks on steps.

Date	Mintage	MS-65	-65FS	Prf-65
1959	28,397,291	.65	30.00	1.25
1959D	160,738,240	.55	45.00	—
1960	57,107,602	2.00	60.00	1.00
1960D	192,582,180	.55	650	—
1961	76,668,244	.55	100.00	1.00
1961D	229,342,760	.55	800	—
1962	100,602,019	1.50	75.00	1.00
1962D	280,195,720	.55	600	—
1963	178,851,645	.55	45.00	1.00
1963D	276,829,460	.55	650	—
1964	1,028,622,762	.55	55.00	1.00
1964D	1,787,297,160	.50	500	—
1965	136,131,380	.50	225	—
1966	156,208,283	.50	350	—
1967	107,325,800	.50	275	—
1968 none minted	—	—	—	—
1968D	91,227,880	.50	750	—
1968S	103,437,510	.50	300	0.75
1969 none minted	—	—	—	—
1969D	202,807,500	.50	—	—
1969S	123,099,631	.50	450	0.75
1970 none minted	—	—	—	—
1970D	515,485,380	.50	500	—
1970S	241,464,814	.50	125	0.75
1971	106,884,000	2.00	35.00	—
1971D	316,144,800	.50	25.00	—
1971S	(3,220,733)	—	—	2.00
1972	202,036,000	.50	35.00	—
1972D	351,694,600	.50	25.00	—
1972S	(3,260,996)	—	—	2.00
1973	384,396,000	.50	20.00	—
1973D	261,405,000	.50	20.00	—
1973S	(2,760,339)	—	—	1.75
1974	601,752,000	.50	75.00	—
1974D	277,373,000	.50	50.00	—
1974S	(2,612,568)	—	—	2.00
1975	181,772,000	.75	65.00	—
1975D	401,875,300	.50	60.00	—
1975S	(2,845,450)	—	—	2.25
1976	367,124,000	.75	150	—
1976D	563,964,147	.60	55.00	—
1976S	(4,149,730)	—	—	2.00
1977	585,376,000	.40	65.00	—
1977D	297,313,460	.55	35.00	—
1977S	(3,251,152)	—	—	1.75
1978	391,308,000	.40	40.00	—
1978D	313,092,780	.40	35.00	—
1978S	(3,127,781)	—	—	1.75
1979	463,188,000	.40	95.00	—
1979D	325,867,672	.40	35.00	—
1979S type I, proof	(3,677,175)	—	—	1.50
1979S type II, proof	Inc. above	—	—	1.75
1980P	593,004,000	.40	30.00	—
1980D	502,323,448	.40	25.00	—
1980S	(3,554,806)	—	—	1.50
1981P	657,504,000	.40	70.00	—
1981D	364,801,843	.40	40.00	—
1981S type I, proof	(4,063,083)	—	—	2.00
1981S type II, proof	Inc. above	—	—	2.50
1982P	292,355,000	12.50	80.00	—
1982D	373,726,544	3.50	45.00	—
1982S	(3,857,479)	—	—	3.50

Date	Mintage	MS-65	-65FS	Prf-65
1983P	561,615,000	4.00	45.00	—
1983D	536,726,276	2.50	35.00	—
1983S	(3,279,126)	—	—	4.00
1984P	746,769,000	3.00	65.00	—
1984D	517,675,146	.85	30.00	—
1984S	(3,065,110)	—	—	5.00
1985P	647,114,962	.75	60.00	—
1985D	459,747,446	.75	35.00	—
1985S	(3,362,821)	—	—	4.00
1986P	536,883,483	1.00	70.00	—
1986D	361,819,140	2.00	60.00	—
1986S	(3,010,497)	—	—	7.00
1987P	371,499,481	.75	30.00	—
1987D	410,590,604	.75	25.00	—
1987S	(4,227,728)	—	—	3.50
1988P	771,360,000	.75	30.00	—
1988D	663,771,652	.75	25.00	—
1988S	(3,262,948)	—	—	6.50
1989P	898,812,000	.75	75.00	—
1989D	570,842,474	.75	25.00	—
1989S	(3,220,194)	—	—	5.50
1990P	661,636,000	.75	25.00	—
1990D	663,938,503	.75	25.00	—
1990S	(3,299,559)	—	—	5.50
1991P	614,104,000	.75	25.00	—
1991D	436,496,678	.75	25.00	—
1991S	(2,867,787)	—	—	5.00
1992P	399,552,000	2.00	25.00	—
1992D	450,565,113	.75	25.00	—
1992S	(4,176,560)	—	—	4.00
1993P	412,076,000	.75	25.00	—
1993D	406,084,135	.75	25.00	—
1993S	(3,394,792)	—	—	4.50
1994P	722,160,000	.75	25.00	—
1994P matte proof	(167,703)	—	—	75.00
1994D	715,762,110	.75	25.00	—
1994S	(3,269,923)	—	—	4.00
1995P	774,156,000	.75	25.00	—
1995D	888,112,000	.85	25.00	—
1995S	(2,707,481)	—	—	7.50
1996P	829,332,000	.75	25.00	—
1996D	817,736,000	.75	25.00	—
1996S	(2,915,212)	—	—	4.00
1997P	470,972,000	.75	25.00	—
1997P matte proof	(25,000)	—	—	200
1997D	466,640,000	2.00	25.00	—
1997S	(1,975,000)	—	—	5.00
1998P	688,272,000	.80	25.00	—
1998D	635,360,000	.80	25.00	—
1998S	(2,957,286)	—	—	4.50
1999P	1,212,000,000	.80	20.00	—
1999D	1,066,720,000	.80	20.00	—
1999S	(3,362,462)	—	—	3.50
2000P	846,240,000	.80	20.00	—
2000D	1,509,520,000	.80	20.00	—
2000S	(4,063,361)	—	—	2.00

DIME

Barber Dime

KM# 113 0.9000 **SILVER** 0.0724 oz. ASW. 17.9 mm. 2.5000 g. **Designer:** Charles E. Barber

Date	Mintage	G-4	VG-8	F-12	VF-20	XF-40	AU-50	MS-60	MS-65	Prf-65
1901	18,860,478	2.50	3.75	6.50	10.00	27.50	65.00	110	850	1,450
1901O	5,620,000	3.75	5.25	16.00	27.50	67.50	180	450	4,500	—
1901S	593,022	80.00	150	360	450	520	675	1,000	5,500	—
1902	21,380,777	3.00	3.75	5.50	8.00	23.00	65.00	100.00	700	1,450
1902O	4,500,000	3.45	5.25	15.00	32.50	62.50	135	340	4,650	—
1902S	2,070,000	8.00	21.00	55.00	85.00	135	200	385	4,000	—
1903	19,500,755	2.50	3.75	4.40	8.00	25.00	65.00	110	1,150	1,450
1903O	8,180,000	3.50	5.00	13.50	23.50	50.00	110	250	5,100	—
1903S	613,300	84.00	130	340	490	770	845	1,150	3,750	—
1904	14,601,027	2.50	3.75	6.25	9.50	25.00	65.00	110	1,950	1,450
1904S	800,000	45.00	75.00	160	240	345	480	750	4,500	—
1905	14,552,350	2.80	3.45	5.60	8.00	25.00	65.00	110	700	1,450
1905O	3,400,000	4.00	10.00	34.00	57.50	96.00	155	285	1,900	—
1905S	6,855,199	3.50	3.85	9.00	18.50	45.00	100.00	220	800	—
1906	19,958,406	1.75	2.20	3.75	6.75	22.00	62.50	100.00	700	1,450
1906D	4,060,000	2.75	3.85	7.00	15.00	36.00	80.00	175	1,600	—
1906O	2,610,000	5.50	13.00	47.50	75.00	100.00	135	200	1,300	—
1906S	3,136,640	2.80	5.25	12.50	22.00	46.00	115	240	1,300	—
1907	22,220,575	1.75	2.20	3.40	6.75	22.00	62.50	110	700	1,450
1907D	4,080,000	2.50	4.00	8.50	17.50	45.00	115	280	4,600	—
1907O	5,058,000	3.45	6.75	31.50	47.50	62.50	110	210	1,350	—
1907S	3,178,470	3.45	5.50	16.00	27.50	67.50	150	420	2,500	—
1908	10,600,545	2.20	2.50	3.40	6.75	22.00	62.50	110	700	1,450
1908D	7,490,000	2.15	2.50	4.65	9.50	30.00	62.50	130	1,150	—
1908O	1,789,000	5.00	11.00	42.50	61.00	96.00	150	300	1,700	—
1908S	3,220,000	3.45	5.25	11.50	22.00	47.50	175	325	2,750	—
1909	10,240,650	2.20	2.50	3.40	6.75	22.00	62.50	110	700	1,700
1909D	954,000	7.50	19.50	60.00	96.00	135	230	500	3,600	—
1909O	2,287,000	4.00	7.50	12.50	22.00	50.00	96.00	190	2,000	—
1909S	1,000,000	9.00	20.00	85.00	125	190	330	535	3,200	—
1910	11,520,551	1.85	2.20	3.40	9.50	23.00	62.50	110	700	1,450
1910D	3,490,000	2.50	4.00	8.50	19.50	47.50	110	220	1,550	—
1910S	1,240,000	5.25	10.00	50.00	71.00	110	200	435	2,600	—
1911	18,870,543	1.75	2.10	3.40	6.75	22.00	62.50	110	700	1,700
1911D	11,209,000	1.75	2.10	3.40	6.75	25.00	62.50	110	750	—
1911S	3,520,000	2.80	3.75	8.50	19.00	41.50	110	200	1,300	—
1912	19,350,700	1.75	2.10	3.40	6.75	22.00	62.50	110	700	1,700
1912D	11,760,000	1.75	2.10	3.75	6.75	22.00	62.50	110	700	—
1912S	3,420,000	2.20	2.75	5.60	12.50	34.00	96.00	160	850	—
1913	19,760,622	1.75	2.10	3.00	6.50	22.00	62.50	110	700	1,450
1913S	510,000	22.00	32.00	85.00	135	240	330	480	1,350	—
1914	17,360,655	1.75	2.10	3.00	6.50	22.00	62.50	110	700	1,700
1914D	11,908,000	1.75	2.10	3.40	6.50	22.00	62.50	110	700	—
1914S	2,100,000	3.00	4.00	8.00	17.50	41.50	80.00	150	1,350	—
1915	5,620,450	2.20	2.50	3.00	7.00	22.00	62.50	110	700	2,000
1915S	960,000	7.00	12.00	32.50	47.50	70.00	135	250	1,600	—
1916	18,490,000	1.75	2.15	3.40	8.00	22.00	62.50	110	700	—
1916S	5,820,000	1.75	2.65	4.00	8.00	23.50	65.00	110	850	—

Mercury Dime

KM# 140 0.9000 **SILVER** 0.0724 oz. ASW. 17.9 mm. 2.5000 g. **Designer:** Adolph A. Weinman **Notes:** All specimens listed as -65FSB are for fully struck MS-65 coins with fully split and rounded horizontal bands on the fasces.

Mint mark

1942/41

Date	Mintage	G-4	VG-8	F-12	VF-20	XF-40	AU-50	MS-60	MS-63	MS-65	-65FSB
1916	22,180,080	3.45	4.70	6.25	7.00	10.00	22.50	30.00	40.00	90.00	120
1916D	264,000	825	1,500	2,600	3,850	6,200	9,250	13,500	17,500	25,000	44,500
1916S	10,450,000	4.00	4.75	9.75	12.50	20.00	26.00	35.00	55.00	155	600
1917	55,230,000	1.85	2.00	2.50	5.00	7.50	12.50	30.00	60.00	155	400
1917D	9,402,000	4.00	5.00	10.00	21.50	42.00	92.50	120	300	1,100	6,000
1917S	27,330,000	1.80	2.00	3.50	5.75	10.00	26.50	62.00	170	470	1,150
1918	26,680,000	2.40	2.75	5.50	10.00	25.00	42.00	70.00	95.00	420	1,150
1918D	22,674,800	2.65	3.00	4.50	10.00	21.50	44.00	105	210	600	33,500
1918S	19,300,000	2.40	2.75	3.50	8.50	16.00	37.00	90.00	230	660	6,600
1919	35,740,000	1.90	2.00	3.00	5.00	10.00	22.50	37.00	100.00	320	700
1919D	9,939,000	3.35	6.00	11.00	21.50	35.00	72.00	175	420	1,400	38,500
1919S	8,850,000	2.75	3.00	8.00	15.00	31.00	72.00	175	450	1,000	13,000
1920	59,030,000	1.45	1.60	2.00	3.50	6.50	13.50	27.50	70.00	235	515
1920D	19,171,000	2.40	2.75	4.00	7.00	18.00	44.00	105	310	750	4,000
1920S	13,820,000	2.40	2.75	4.00	7.50	15.00	40.00	110	300	1,300	8,000
1921	1,230,000	54.00	75.00	125	280	565	900	1,250	1,500	3,200	4,400
1921D	1,080,000	68.00	115	200	380	650	1,150	1,350	1,650	3,200	5,600
1923	50,130,000	1.45	1.75	2.00	3.50	6.00	14.00	27.50	40.00	110	295
1923S	6,440,000	2.40	2.75	7.00	12.50	65.00	100.00	160	370	1,150	6,900
1924	24,010,000	1.45	1.75	2.50	4.25	12.00	26.50	42.00	88.00	175	520
1924D	6,810,000	2.75	4.00	6.00	16.00	49.00	100.00	160	300	950	1,400
1924S	7,120,000	2.75	3.50	4.00	8.75	44.00	95.00	170	450	1,100	14,000
1925	25,610,000	1.45	1.50	2.00	3.75	7.50	16.00	27.00	78.00	195	1,000
1925D	5,117,000	4.00	4.25	11.50	38.00	110	190	350	700	1,750	3,500
1925S	5,850,000	2.40	2.75	7.00	12.50	65.00	100.00	175	460	1,400	4,400
1926	32,160,000	1.45	1.60	1.70	2.75	4.25	12.00	25.00	60.00	240	525
1926D	6,828,000	2.75	4.00	4.50	8.50	24.00	43.00	125	260	550	2,650
1926S	1,520,000	11.00	12.00	25.00	55.00	225	420	900	1,475	3,000	6,500
1927	28,080,000	1.45	1.60	1.75	3.50	4.50	11.00	26.00	48.00	125	400
1927D	4,812,000	2.75	5.00	7.25	18.50	65.00	92.50	175	360	1,200	8,500
1927S	4,770,000	2.10	3.50	4.75	8.00	23.00	48.00	280	550	1,400	7,700
1928	19,480,000	1.45	1.60	1.75	3.50	4.00	16.00	27.50	48.00	110	300
1928D	4,161,000	3.75	4.00	8.00	18.50	44.00	85.00	170	310	875	2,500
1928S Large S	740,000	3.25	4.50	6.75	10.00	20.00	52.00	185	350	750	—
1928S Small S	Inc. above	1.80	2.10	2.75	5.50	16.00	37.00	125	260	425	1,900
1929	25,970,000	1.45	1.60	1.95	2.75	4.00	9.50	20.00	30.00	60.00	265
1929D	5,034,000	1.80	3.00	3.50	6.25	14.50	20.00	26.00	30.00	70.00	225
1929S	4,730,000	1.45	1.60	2.00	4.00	7.00	20.00	32.50	42.00	120	525
1930	6,770,000	1.45	1.60	2.00	3.50	7.00	13.00	26.00	48.00	115	525
1930S	1,843,000	2.50	3.50	4.80	6.25	15.00	45.00	75.00	115	200	565
1931	3,150,000	2.10	2.90	3.35	4.25	8.75	22.50	35.00	62.50	135	—
1931D	1,260,000	9.00	11.00	15.00	18.00	32.50	56.00	85.00	100.00	225	350
1931S	1,800,000	3.00	3.50	5.00	9.00	16.00	43.50	85.00	90.00	225	2,100
1934	24,080,000	—	1.45	1.75	3.00	5.00	10.00	21.50	26.50	40.00	150
1934D	6,772,000	1.60	2.10	2.75	4.00	8.00	18.50	50.00	57.50	72.00	360
1935	58,830,000	—	—	1.50	2.15	4.25	7.50	8.00	13.00	30.00	70.00
1935D	10,477,000	1.25	1.75	2.50	3.75	7.50	18.00	34.00	42.00	72.00	600
1935S	15,840,000	1.00	1.50	1.75	3.00	5.50	14.00	24.00	25.00	31.50	500
1936	87,504,130	—	—	1.50	2.25	3.50	6.50	8.00	13.00	25.00	90.00
1936D	16,132,000	—	1.25	1.50	3.00	6.50	14.00	26.00	31.50	42.00	295
1936S	9,210,000	—	1.25	1.50	2.50	3.00	8.00	20.00	26.00	31.50	85.00
1937	56,865,756	—	—	1.50	2.00	3.25	6.00	8.00	12.00	23.00	42.00
1937D	14,146,000	—	1.25	1.50	3.00	5.50	9.50	21.00	26.00	43.00	100.00
1937S	9,740,000	—	1.25	1.50	3.00	5.50	7.50	24.00	26.00	34.00	195
1938	22,198,728	—	—	1.50	2.25	3.50	5.00	13.00	22.00	27.50	80.00
1938D	5,537,000	1.50	1.75	2.00	3.50	6.00	9.50	16.00	24.00	28.00	65.00
1938S	8,090,000	1.35	1.55	1.75	2.35	3.75	9.00	20.00	27.50	35.00	135
1939	67,749,321	—	—	1.50	2.00	3.25	5.00	8.50	13.50	25.00	170
1939D	24,394,000	—	1.25	1.50	2.00	3.50	6.00	7.50	12.00	26.00	45.00
1939S	10,540,000	1.25	1.50	2.00	3.00	6.00	13.00	23.00	28.00	40.00	750
1940	65,361,827	—	—	—	1.50	2.50	4.00	6.00	10.00	26.00	57.50
1940D	21,198,000	—	—	—	1.75	2.25	5.00	8.00	14.00	30.00	55.00
1940S	21,560,000	—	—	—	1.75	2.25	4.50	8.50	12.50	30.00	95.00
1941	175,106,557	—	—	—	1.40	1.75	3.00	5.00	8.00	30.00	42.00
1941D	45,634,000	—	—	—	1.50	2.00	4.00	8.00	14.00	23.00	40.00

Date	Mintage	G-4	VG-8	F-12	VF-20	XF-40	AU-50	MS-60	MS-63	MS-65	-65FSB
1941S	43,090,000	—	—	—	1.50	2.00	4.50	7.00	9.50	30.00	50.00
1942	205,432,329	—	—	—	1.40	1.75	3.00	5.50	9.00	24.00	52.50
1942/41	Inc. above	525	525	625	715	835	1,250	2,100	4,000	12,500	38,500
1942D	60,740,000	—	—	—	1.50	2.00	4.00	8.00	12.75	27.50	40.00
1942/41D	Inc. above	500	595	650	780	920	1,400	2,600	4,450	6,700	19,500
1942S Large S	49,300,000	—	—	—	1.50	2.00	4.50	9.50	16.00	24.00	140
1942S Small S	Inc. above	—	—	—	2.00	2.75	6.00	15.00	24.00	40.00	—
1943	191,710,000	—	—	—	1.40	1.75	3.00	5.50	9.00	30.00	50.00
1943D	71,949,000	—	—	—	1.50	2.00	4.00	7.50	10.00	27.50	40.00
1943S	60,400,000	—	—	—	1.50	2.00	4.50	8.25	12.50	25.00	66.00
1944	231,410,000	—	—	—	1.40	1.75	3.00	5.50	9.00	23.00	80.00
1944D	62,224,000	—	—	—	1.50	2.00	4.00	6.50	11.00	23.00	40.00
1944S	49,490,000	—	—	—	1.50	2.00	4.00	6.50	10.00	30.00	50.00
1945	159,130,000	—	—	—	1.40	1.75	3.00	5.50	9.00	23.00	8,000
1945D	40,245,000	—	—	—	1.50	2.00	4.00	6.00	9.00	24.00	40.00
1945S	41,920,000	—	—	—	1.50	2.00	4.00	6.50	9.50	24.00	135
1945S micro S	Inc. above	2.00	2.50	3.50	5.00	13.50	20.00	26.00	37.00	100.00	650

Roosevelt Dime

KM# 195 0.9000 **SILVER** 0.0724 oz. ASW. 17.9 mm. 2.5000 g. **Designer:** John R. Sinnock

Mint mark 1946-64

Date	Mintage	G-4	VG-8	F-12	VF-20	XF-40	AU-50	MS-60	MS-65	Prf-65
1946	225,250,000	—	—	—	—	1.10	1.45	2.00	14.00	—
1946D	61,043,500	—	—	—	—	1.10	1.50	2.25	15.00	—
1946S	27,900,000	—	—	—	—	1.20	1.55	2.35	17.00	—
1947	121,520,000	—	—	—	—	1.30	2.00	4.00	15.00	—
1947D	46,835,000	—	—	—	—	1.50	2.25	5.00	17.00	—
1947S	34,840,000	—	—	—	—	1.30	2.00	5.00	16.00	—
1948	74,950,000	—	—	—	—	1.40	2.00	4.50	15.00	—
1948D	52,841,000	—	—	—	—	1.60	2.50	6.00	17.00	—
1948S	35,520,000	—	—	—	—	1.50	2.25	5.00	14.00	—
1949	30,940,000	—	—	1.50	2.00	3.00	8.00	16.00	50.00	—
1949D	26,034,000	—	—	1.35	1.50	2.25	5.00	9.00	22.00	—
1949S	13,510,000	—	1.60	2.00	3.50	7.50	14.00	40.00	65.00	—
1950	50,181,500	—	—	—	1.40	2.25	3.50	10.00	25.00	55.00
1950D	46,803,000	—	—	—	—	—	2.50	5.00	12.00	—
1950S	20,440,000	—	1.10	1.40	2.00	3.75	9.00	32.00	60.00	—
1951	102,937,602	—	—	—	—	—	1.60	2.50	10.00	60.00
1951D	56,529,000	—	—	—	—	—	1.45	2.50	8.00	—
1951S	31,630,000	—	—	—	1.20	2.00	4.00	10.00	26.00	—
1952	99,122,073	—	—	—	—	—	1.35	2.50	9.00	40.00
1952D	122,100,000	—	—	—	—	—	1.25	2.50	10.00	—
1952S	44,419,500	—	—	—	.75	1.50	2.75	5.50	15.00	—
1953	53,618,920	—	—	—	—	—	1.35	2.25	8.00	45.00
1953D	136,433,000	—	—	—	—	—	1.35	2.00	8.00	—
1953S	39,180,000	—	—	—	—	—	1.75	3.00	15.00	—
1954	114,243,503	—	—	—	—	—	1.10	1.50	7.00	20.00
1954D	106,397,000	—	—	—	—	—	1.10	1.50	7.00	—
1954S	22,860,000	—	—	—	—	—	1.25	1.60	10.00	—
1955	12,828,381	—	—	—	1.20	1.40	1.70	2.75	10.00	18.00
1955D	13,959,000	—	—	—	1.30	1.50	1.85	2.75	10.00	—
1955S	18,510,000	—	—	—	1.25	1.45	1.75	2.25	9.00	—
1956	109,309,384	—	—	—	—	—	1.35	1.50	9.00	8.00
1956D	108,015,100	—	—	—	—	—	1.45	1.60	10.00	—
1957	161,407,952	—	—	—	—	—	1.35	1.50	8.00	6.00
1957D	113,354,330	—	—	—	—	—	1.35	1.50	8.00	—
1958	32,785,652	—	—	—	—	—	1.35	1.50	8.50	6.00
1958D	136,564,600	—	—	—	—	—	1.35	1.50	9.00	—
1959	86,929,291	—	—	—	—	—	1.35	1.50	8.00	5.00
1959D	164,919,790	—	—	—	—	—	1.35	1.50	8.00	—
1960	72,081,602	—	—	—	—	—	1.35	1.50	7.50	5.00
1960D	200,160,400	—	—	—	—	—	1.35	1.50	7.50	—
1961	96,758,244	—	—	—	—	—	1.35	1.50	6.50	4.50
1961D	209,146,550	—	—	—	—	—	1.35	1.50	6.50	—
1962	75,668,019	—	—	—	—	—	1.35	1.50	7.00	4.50
1962D	334,948,380	—	—	—	—	—	1.35	1.50	7.00	—
1963	126,725,645	—	—	—	—	—	1.35	1.50	6.50	4.00
1963D	421,476,530	—	—	—	—	—	1.35	1.50	6.50	—
1964	933,310,762	—	—	—	—	—	1.35	1.50	6.00	4.00
1964D	1,357,517,180	—	—	—	—	—	1.35	1.50	6.00	—

KM# 195a COPPER-NICKEL CLAD COPPER 17.9 mm. 2.2700 g. **Designer:** John R. Sinnock **Notes:** The 1979-S and 1981-S Type II proofs have clearer mint marks than the Type I proofs of those years. On the 1982 no-mint-mark variety, the mint mark was inadvertently left off.

Mint mark 1968-present

No mint mark

Date	Mintage	MS-65	Prf-65
1965	1,652,140,570	1.00	—
1966	1,382,734,540	1.00	—
1967	2,244,007,320	1.50	—
1968	424,470,000	1.00	—
1968D	480,748,280	1.00	—
1968S	(3,041,506)	—	1.00
1969	145,790,000	3.00	—
1969D	563,323,870	1.00	—
1969S	(2,934,631)	—	0.80
1970	345,570,000	1.00	—
1970S No S	—	—	1,300
1970D	754,942,100	1.00	—
1970S	(2,632,810)	—	1.00
1971	162,690,000	2.00	—
1971D	377,914,240	1.00	—
1971S	(3,220,733)	—	1.00
1972	431,540,000	1.00	—
1972D	330,290,000	1.00	—
1972S	(3,260,996)	—	1.00
1973	315,670,000	1.00	—
1973D	455,032,426	1.00	—
1973S	(2,760,339)	—	1.00
1974	470,248,000	1.00	—
1974D	571,083,000	1.00	—
1974S	(2,612,568)	—	1.00
1975	585,673,900	1.00	—
1975D	313,705,300	1.00	—
1975S	(2,845,450)	—	2.00
1976	568,760,000	1.50	—
1976D	695,222,774	1.00	—
1976S	(4,149,730)	—	1.00
1977	796,930,000	1.00	—
1977D	376,607,228	1.00	—
1977S	(3,251,152)	—	2.00
1978	663,980,000	1.00	—
1978D	282,847,540	1.00	—
1978S	(3,127,781)	—	1.00
1979	315,440,000	1.00	—
1979D	390,921,184	1.00	—
1979 type I	—	—	1.00
1979S type I	(3,677,175)	—	1.00
1979S type II	Inc. above	—	2.00
1980P	735,170,000	1.00	—
1980D	719,354,321	.70	—
1980S	(3,554,806)	—	1.00
1981P	676,650,000	1.00	—
1981D	712,284,143	1.00	—
1981S type I	—	—	1.00
1981S type II	—	—	2.00
1982P	519,475,000	8.50	—
1982 no mint mark	—	300	—
1982D	542,713,584	3.00	—
1982S	(3,857,479)	—	2.00
1983P	647,025,000	7.00	—
1983D	730,129,224	2.50	—
1983S	(3,279,126)	—	2.00
1984P	856,669,000	1.00	—
1984D	704,803,976	2.00	—
1984S	(3,065,110)	—	2.00
1985P	705,200,962	1.00	—
1985D	587,979,970	1.00	—
1985S	(3,362,821)	—	1.00
1986P	682,649,693	2.00	—
1986D	473,326,970	2.00	—
1986S	(3,010,497)	—	2.75
1987P	762,709,481	1.00	—
1987D	653,203,402	1.00	—
1987S	(4,227,728)	—	1.00
1988P	1,030,550,000	1.00	—
1988D	962,385,488	1.00	—
1988S	(3,262,948)	—	3.00
1989P	1,298,400,000	1.00	—
1989D	896,535,597	1.00	—
1989S	(3,220,194)	—	4.00
1990P	1,034,340,000	1.00	—
1990D	839,995,824	1.00	—
1990S	(3,299,559)	—	2.00
1991P	927,220,000	1.00	—
1991D	601,241,114	1.00	—
1991S	(2,867,787)	—	3.00
1992P	593,500,000	1.00	—
1992D	616,273,932	1.00	—
1992S	(2,858,981)	—	4.00
1993P	766,180,000	1.00	—
1993D	750,110,166	1.50	—
1993S	(2,633,439)	—	7.00
1994P	1,189,000,000	1.00	—
1994D	1,303,268,110	1.00	—
1994S	(2,484,594)	—	5.00
1995P	1,125,500,000	1.50	—
1995D	1,274,890,000	2.00	—
1995S	(2,010,384)	—	20.00
1996P	1,421,163,000	1.00	—
1996D	1,400,300,000	1.00	—
1996W	1,457,949	25.00	—
1996S	(2,085,191)	—	2.50
1997P	991,640,000	2.00	—
1997D	979,810,000	1.00	—
1997S	(1,975,000)	—	11.00
1998P	1,163,000,000	1.00	—
1998D	1,172,250,000	1.25	—
1998S	(2,078,494)	—	4.00
1999P	2,164,000,000	1.00	—
1999D	1,397,750,000	1.00	—
1999S	(2,557,897)	—	4.00
2000P	1,842,500,000	1.00	—
2000D	1,818,700,000	1.00	—
2000S	(3,097,440)	—	1.00

KM# A195 SILVER

Date	Mintage	Prf-65
1992S	(1,317,579)	5.00
1993S	(761,353)	9.00
1994S	(785,329)	9.00
1995S	(838,953)	25.00
1996S	(830,021)	9.00
1997S	(821,678)	25.00
1998S	(878,792)	9.00
1999S	(804,565)	6.50
2000S	(965,921)	4.00

QUARTER

Barber Quarter

KM# 114 0.9000 **SILVER** 0.1809 oz. ASW. 24.3 mm. 6.2500 g. **Designer:** Charles E. Barber

Date	Mintage	G-4	VG-8	F-12	VF-20	XF-40	AU-50	MS-60	MS-65	Prf-65
1901	8,892,813	11.00	13.00	25.00	41.50	80.00	135	215	2,250	2,200
1901O	1,612,000	40.00	60.00	135	275	470	685	900	5,750	—
1901S	72,664	7,000	11,000	16,500	21,000	28,500	38,000	42,000	100,000	—
1902	12,197,744	6.00	8.00	19.50	33.50	70.00	125	220	1,300	2,100
1902O	4,748,000	8.50	16.00	52.50	82.50	150	245	485	5,000	—
1902S	1,524,612	13.50	22.00	55.00	95.00	170	260	540	3,600	—
1903	9,670,064	6.75	8.00	19.00	33.50	66.00	115	215	2,600	2,000
1903O	3,500,000	8.00	12.50	41.50	65.00	125	260	450	5,800	—
1903S	1,036,000	15.50	25.00	46.00	80.00	145	285	450	2,900	—
1904	9,588,813	8.00	9.75	20.00	36.00	72.50	125	225	1,475	2,000
1904O	2,456,000	11.00	21.50	62.50	100.00	225	460	850	3,250	—
1905	4,968,250	11.00	13.00	27.50	41.50	75.00	125	215	1,650	2,000
1905O	1,230,000	18.50	32.50	82.50	160	260	375	515	6,600	—
1905S	1,884,000	11.00	15.00	43.50	66.00	115	225	350	3,650	—
1906	3,656,435	6.75	8.00	19.00	33.50	70.00	115	215	1,300	2,000
1906D	3,280,000	7.00	8.00	25.00	42.50	71.50	155	220	2,200	—
1906O	2,056,000	7.00	9.00	41.50	60.00	105	200	300	1,400	—
1907	7,192,575	5.25	8.00	17.50	33.50	66.00	115	215	1,300	2,000
1907D	2,484,000	6.00	9.00	29.00	52.50	80.00	180	250	2,750	—
1907O	4,560,000	5.25	8.00	19.00	38.50	70.00	135	220	2,600	—
1907S	1,360,000	10.00	18.50	47.50	75.00	135	275	480	3,500	—
1908	4,232,545	5.00	6.25	18.50	33.50	70.00	115	215	1,300	2,200
1908D	5,788,000	5.00	6.25	17.50	32.50	70.00	120	250	1,750	—
1908O	6,244,000	5.00	8.50	17.50	38.50	75.00	125	215	1,300	—

Date	Mintage	G-4	VG-8	F-12	VF-20	XF-40	AU-50	MS-60	MS-65	Prf-65
1908S	784,000	20.00	40.00	92.50	160	320	520	775	5,100	—
1909	9,268,650	5.00	6.25	17.50	33.50	66.00	115	215	1,300	2,000
1909D	5,114,000	6.25	8.00	22.00	41.50	90.00	160	215	2,350	—
1909O	712,000	25.00	60.00	175	400	900	1,250	1,700	9,000	—
1909S	1,348,000	8.00	11.00	37.50	57.50	96.00	200	300	2,400	—
1910	2,244,551	7.75	10.00	30.00	46.00	80.00	140	215	1,300	2,000
1910D	1,500,000	8.00	11.00	47.50	75.00	130	260	375	2,250	—
1911	3,720,543	5.25	8.00	17.50	33.50	72.50	125	215	1,300	2,000
1911D	933,600	8.00	19.00	95.00	215	330	500	700	6,250	—
1911S	988,000	7.00	12.00	51.50	80.00	160	300	400	1,500	—
1912	4,400,700	5.75	8.00	17.50	33.50	70.00	115	215	1,300	2,000
1912S	708,000	10.00	13.00	46.00	77.50	125	230	390	2,750	—
1913	484,613	15.00	25.00	75.00	185	415	535	960	5,000	2,200
1913D	1,450,800	12.50	13.50	38.50	58.50	94.00	185	275	1,400	—
1913S	40,000	1,500	2,350	3,800	5,750	6,500	7,250	9,000	25,000	—
1914	6,244,610	5.00	6.25	17.50	30.00	57.50	115	215	1,300	2,200
1914D	3,046,000	5.00	6.25	17.50	30.00	57.50	115	215	1,300	—
1914S	264,000	70.00	105	200	315	520	700	940	3,550	—
1915	3,480,450	5.00	6.25	17.50	30.00	66.00	115	215	1,300	2,200
1915D	3,694,000	5.00	6.25	17.50	30.00	66.00	115	215	1,300	—
1915S	704,000	9.00	13.00	35.00	57.50	110	220	285	1,300	—
1916	1,788,000	5.00	9.50	17.50	27.50	57.50	115	215	1,300	—
1916D	6,540,800	5.00	6.25	17.50	30.00	57.50	115	215	1,300	—
1916D/D	—	15.00	22.00	30.00	50.00	125	—	—	—	—

Standing Liberty Quarter

Right breast exposed; Type 1

KM# 141 0.9000 **SILVER** 0.1809 oz. ASW. 24.3 mm. 6.2500 g. **Designer:** Hermon A. MacNeil

Bare bust

Date	Mintage	G-4	VG-8	F-12	VF-20	XF-40	AU-50	MS-60	MS-65	-65FH
1916	52,000	3,500	6,350	9,500	13,000	14,500	16,500	18,500	30,000	37,500
1917	8,792,000	24.00	40.00	52.00	70.00	95.00	175	200	750	1,500
1917D	1,509,200	28.00	42.00	55.00	85.00	125	195	235	950	2,550
1917S	1,952,000	30.00	44.00	60.00	90.00	160	210	240	1,200	4,100

Standing Liberty Quarter

Right breast covered; Type 2 Three stars below eagle

KM# 145 0.9000 **SILVER** 0.1809 oz. ASW. 24.3 mm. 6.2500 g. **Designer:** Hermon A. MacNeil

Mailed bust

Mint mark

Date	Mintage	G-4	VG-8	F-12	VF-20	XF-40	AU-50	MS-60	MS-65	-65FH
1917	13,880,000	22.00	33.00	42.50	54.00	75.00	105	165	575	950
1917D	6,224,400	40.00	45.00	65.00	78.00	110	160	225	1,325	3,500
1917S	5,522,000	40.00	45.00	63.00	75.00	108	155	215	1,100	3,650
1918	14,240,000	17.00	21.00	29.00	35.00	46.00	80.00	135	560	1,750
1918D	7,380,000	26.00	36.00	66.00	78.00	122	195	250	1,485	4,850
1918S	11,072,000	17.00	21.00	32.00	35.00	48.00	95.00	185	1,250	13,500
1918/17S	Inc. above	1,550	2,250	3,850	5,200	7,500	13,500	17,850	110,000	320,000
1919	11,324,000	33.00	44.00	55.00	74.00	80.00	118	175	600	1,650
1919D	1,944,000	85.00	110	195	345	565	695	825	2,950	28,500
1919S	1,836,000	80.00	105	185	285	510	585	750	4,200	30,000
1920	27,860,000	15.00	18.00	25.00	37.00	51.00	90.00	165	600	2,100
1920D	3,586,400	48.00	65.00	88.00	120	160	215	325	2,250	7,200
1920S	6,380,000	19.00	25.00	30.00	37.00	57.00	110	235	2,650	24,000
1921	1,916,000	185	220	450	625	750	1,100	1,500	3,850	5,500
1923	9,716,000	15.00	18.00	35.00	37.00	55.00	95.00	155	620	4,000
1923S	1,360,000	300	425	675	985	1,250	1,650	2,300	4,750	6,500
1924	10,920,000	15.00	18.00	25.00	34.00	45.00	90.00	170	585	1,650
1924D	3,112,000	56.00	68.00	108	135	185	220	300	610	5,750
1924S	2,860,000	27.00	32.00	43.00	57.00	105	220	315	1,850	6,500
1925	12,280,000	4.00	4.75	7.00	18.50	44.00	90.00	150	575	950
1926	11,316,000	3.50	4.00	6.00	14.00	37.00	80.00	140	585	2,250
1926D	1,716,000	6.50	10.00	20.00	40.00	75.00	118	170	545	22,500
1926S	2,700,000	4.50	5.40	11.00	30.00	110	225	325	2,175	28,000
1927	11,912,000	3.50	4.00	6.00	12.00	32.00	70.00	105	550	1,300
1927D	976,400	14.00	19.00	32.00	70.00	140	210	250	600	2,650
1927S	396,000	35.00	48.00	110	285	1,000	2,650	4,750	12,000	165,000
1928	6,336,000	3.50	4.75	6.00	12.00	32.00	65.00	100.00	540	2,150
1928D	1,627,600	4.75	6.00	7.50	20.00	42.50	90.00	135	540	5,650
1928S Large S	2,644,000	6.00	7.50	10.00	25.00	65.00	115	200	—	—
1928S Small S	Inc. above	4.50	5.50	6.50	16.50	38.00	79.00	125	560	900
1929	11,140,000	3.50	4.75	6.00	12.00	32.00	65.00	100.00	540	900
1929D	1,358,000	4.25	5.50	6.75	16.00	38.50	79.00	135	540	5,850
1929S	1,764,000	4.00	5.50	6.50	15.00	34.00	75.00	120	540	875
1930	5,632,000	3.50	4.00	6.00	12.00	32.00	65.00	100.00	540	875
1930S	1,556,000	4.00	5.50	6.50	15.00	34.00	70.00	115	550	925

Washington Quarter

KM# 164 0.9000 **SILVER** 0.1809 oz. ASW. 24.3 mm. 6.2500 g. **Designer:** John Flanagan

Mint mark 1932-64

Date	Mintage	G-4	VG-8	F-12	VF-20	XF-40	AU-50	MS-60	MS-65	Prf-65
1932	5,404,000	4.00	5.50	6.25	7.50	9.75	15.00	26.00	450	—
1932D	436,800	175	195	215	240	315	550	1,000	26,500	—
1932S	408,000	175	185	202.5	215	285	300	500	7,700	—
1934 Medium Motto	31,912,052	3.00	3.40	3.60	4.00	6.00	10.00	27.50	110	—
1934D Heavy motto	Inc. above	—	4.50	5.00	7.00	14.00	24.00	50.00	225	—
1934D Light motto	Inc. above	—	—	—	—	—	35.00	—	—	—
1934D	3,527,200	4.40	6.25	7.50	12.50	23.50	90.00	250	1,550	—
1935	32,484,000	3.00	3.20	3.30	3.50	3.50	8.00	21.50	130	—
1935D	5,780,000	3.00	3.75	7.00	13.50	30.00	130	260	975	—
1935S	5,660,000	3.00	3.75	4.80	6.50	15.00	38.50	100.00	370	—
1936	41,303,837	3.00	3.20	3.30	3.50	3.25	8.50	21.50	110	1,050
1936D	5,374,000	4.50	5.25	7.00	22.00	55.00	275	625	1,900	—
1936S	3,828,000	3.00	3.75	4.40	6.25	13.50	52.50	115	4.40	—
1937	19,701,542	3.00	3.20	3.30	3.50	4.50	16.00	23.50	94.00	380
1937D	7,189,600	3.00	3.20	3.75	6.25	13.50	34.00	70.00	175	—
1937S	1,652,000	4.00	5.00	7.00	15.00	34.00	100.00	170	415	—
1938	9,480,045	4.00	4.75	5.25	6.25	16.00	46.00	96.00	250	225
1938S	2,832,000	4.75	5.25	6.00	9.75	22.50	57.50	115	300	—
1939	33,548,795	3.00	3.20	3.30	3.50	3.25	7.00	16.00	56.00	150
1939D	7,092,000	3.00	3.20	3.50	5.25	11.00	20.00	45.00	125	—
1939S	2,628,000	4.00	4.40	5.25	9.00	22.00	60.00	110	375	—
1940	35,715,246	3.00	3.20	3.30	3.50	3.25	5.50	18.50	57.50	150
1940D	2,797,600	3.25	3.75	7.00	12.50	27.50	70.00	135	350	—
1940S	8,244,000	3.00	3.20	5.00	6.50	9.00	18.00	25.00	62.50	—
1941	79,047,287	—	—	—	—	3.00	4.40	9.75	45.00	110
1941D	16,714,800	—	—	—	3.00	4.50	15.00	35.00	70.00	—
1941S	16,080,000	—	—	—	2.50	3.50	12.50	31.00	70.00	—
1942	102,117,123	—	—	—	—	3.00	3.50	5.50	37.50	110
1942D	17,487,200	—	—	—	2.50	3.75	11.00	19.00	45.00	—
1942S	19,384,000	—	—	—	3.00	5.00	24.00	80.00	180	—
1943	99,700,000	—	—	—	—	3.00	3.25	5.00	44.00	—
1943D	16,095,600	—	—	—	3.50	6.00	16.50	31.00	52.50	—
1943S	21,700,000	—	—	3.00	5.00	7.50	15.00	28.00	55.00	—
1944	104,956,000	—	—	—	—	3.00	3.25	5.00	37.50	—
1944D	14,600,800	—	—	—	—	3.75	10.00	20.00	37.50	—
1944S	12,560,000	—	—	—	3.00	4.00	9.00	15.00	37.50	—
1945	74,372,000	—	—	—	—	3.00	3.25	5.00	45.00	—
1945D	12,341,600	—	—	—	3.50	6.50	11.50	19.00	47.50	—
1945S	17,004,001	—	—	—	3.00	3.50	6.00	9.00	38.50	—
1946	53,436,000	—	—	—	—	3.00	3.50	5.00	47.50	—
1946D	9,072,800	—	—	—	—	2.50	5.25	10.00	47.50	—
1946S	4,204,000	—	—	—	3.00	4.00	5.00	9.00	50.00	—
1947	22,556,000	—	—	—	—	3.00	5.00	11.50	47.50	—
1947D	15,338,400	—	—	—	—	3.00	4.50	11.00	44.00	—
1947S	5,532,000	—	—	—	—	3.00	4.50	10.00	40.00	—
1948	35,196,000	—	—	—	—	3.00	4.00	5.50	45.00	—
1948D	16,766,800	—	—	—	—	3.00	7.00	13.50	62.50	—
1948S	15,960,000	—	—	—	—	3.00	5.00	8.00	50.00	—
1949	9,312,000	—	—	—	3.00	6.50	15.00	38.50	65.00	—
1949D	10,068,400	—	—	—	3.00	5.00	10.00	18.00	50.00	—
1950	24,971,512	—	—	—	—	2.25	3.00	5.50	30.00	55.00
1950D	21,075,600	—	—	—	—	2.50	3.00	5.00	32.00	—
1950D/S	Inc. above	30.00	33.00	40.00	60.00	140	215	275	2,250	—
1950S	10,284,004	—	—	—	—	3.25	4.50	9.00	40.00	—
1950S/D	Inc. above	32.00	36.00	44.00	70.00	180	315	400	850	—
1951	43,505,602	—	—	—	—	2.25	3.50	6.00	32.00	40.00
1951D	35,354,800	—	—	—	—	2.50	3.50	7.00	38.00	—
1951S	9,048,000	—	—	3.00	4.50	6.00	9.00	24.00	52.00	—
1952	38,862,073	—	—	—	—	2.75	3.50	5.50	35.00	37.00
1952D	49,795,200	—	—	—	—	2.75	3.25	5.00	32.00	—
1952S	13,707,800	—	—	—	4.00	6.00	9.00	21.00	42.00	—
1953	18,664,920	—	—	—	—	—	3.00	5.50	30.00	25.00
1953D	56,112,400	—	—	—	—	—	2.75	4.25	29.00	—
1953S	14,016,000	—	—	—	—	2.25	2.75	5.00	30.00	—
1954	54,645,503	—	—	—	—	—	2.75	5.00	30.00	13.00
1954D	42,305,500	—	—	—	—	—	2.75	4.75	30.00	—
1954S	11,834,722	—	—	—	—	—	2.75	4.00	25.00	—
1955	18,558,381	—	—	—	—	—	2.75	3.50	25.00	14.00
1955D	3,182,400	—	—	—	—	2.50	2.75	3.25	45.00	—
1956	44,813,384	—	—	—	—	—	2.75	4.00	22.00	4.00
1956 Double Bar 5	—	—	3.00	4.00	5.00	6.50	9.00	20.00	—	—
1956 Type B rev, proof rev die	—	—	—	8.00	12.00	20.00	30.00	40.00	100.00	—
1956D	32,334,500	—	—	—	—	—	2.50	3.00	26.00	—
1957	47,779,952	—	—	—	—	—	2.25	3.50	23.00	4.00
1957 Type B rev, proof rev die	—	—	—	5.00	7.00	10.00	16.00	30.00	—	—
1957D	77,924,160	—	—	—	—	—	2.25	2.25	26.00	—
1958	7,235,652	—	—	—	—	2.25	2.50	2.75	20.00	6.00
1958 Type B rev, proof rev die	—	—	—	—	—	—	40.00	60.00	150	—
1958D	78,124,900	—	—	—	—	—	2.25	2.50	20.00	—
1959	25,533,291	—	—	—	—	—	2.25	2.75	20.00	4.25

Date	Mintage	G-4	VG-8	F-12	VF-20	XF-40	AU-50	MS-60	MS-65	Prf-65
1959 Type B rev, proof rev die	—	—	—	4.00	6.00	10.00	—	—	—	—
1959D	62,054,232	—	—	—	—	—	2.25	2.75	25.00	—
1960	30,855,602	—	—	—	—	—	2.25	2.50	17.00	3.75
1960 Type B rev, proof rev die	—	—	—	4.00	6.00	10.00	—	—	60.00	—
1960D	63,000,324	—	—	—	—	—	2.25	2.50	17.00	—
1961	40,064,244	—	—	—	—	—	2.25	2.75	19.00	3.50
1961 Type B rev, proof rev die	—	—	—	—	—	—	—	—	—	—
1961D	83,656,928	—	—	—	—	—	2.25	2.50	16.00	—
1962	39,374,019	—	—	—	—	—	2.25	2.50	18.00	3.50
1962 Type B rev, proof rev die	—	—	—	—	—	—	—	—	—	—
1962D	127,554,756	—	—	—	—	—	2.25	2.50	16.00	—
1963	77,391,645	—	—	—	—	—	2.25	2.50	15.00	3.50
1963 Type B rev, proof rev die	—	—	—	—	—	—	—	—	—	—
1963D	135,288,184	—	—	—	—	—	2.25	2.50	15.00	—
1964	564,341,347	—	—	—	—	—	2.25	2.50	15.00	3.50
1964 Type B rev, proof rev die	—	—	—	—	—	—	—	—	—	—
1964D	704,135,528	—	—	—	1.50	—	2.25	2.50	15.00	—

KM# 164a COPPER-NICKEL CLAD COPPER 24.3 mm. 5.6700 g. **Designer:** John Flanagan

Date	Mintage	MS-65	Prf-65	Date	Mintage	MS-65	Prf-65
1965	1,819,717,540	8.00	—	1972	215,048,000	4.00	—
1966	821,101,500	4.50	—	1972D	311,067,732	5.50	—
1967	1,524,031,848	6.50	—	1972S	(3,260,996)	—	3.00
1968	220,731,500	7.50	—	1973	346,924,000	7.00	—
1968D	101,534,000	5.00	—	1973D	232,977,400	9.00	—
1968S	(3,041,506)	—	3.50	1973S	(2,760,339)	—	3.00
1969	176,212,000	7.50	—	1974	801,456,000	6.50	—
1969D	114,372,000	6.50	—	1974D	353,160,300	10.00	—
1969S	(2,934,631)	—	3.50	1974S	(2,612,568)	—	3.00
1970	136,420,000	6.50	—	1975 none minted	—	—	—
1970D	417,341,364	6.00	—	1975D none minted	—	—	—
1970S	(2,632,810)	—	3.00				
1971	109,284,000	6.00	—	1975S none minted	—	—	—
1971D	258,634,428	2.50	—				
1971S	(3,220,733)	—	3.00				

Bicentennial design, drummer boy

KM# 204 COPPER-NICKEL CLAD COPPER 24.3 mm. 5.6700 g. **Rev. Designer:** Jack L. Ahr

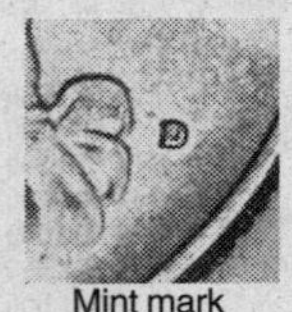

Mint mark 1968-present

Date	Mintage	G-4	VG-8	F-12	VF-20	XF-40	MS-60	MS-65	Prf-65
1976	809,784,016	—	—	—	—	—	.60	3.50	—
1976D	860,118,839	—	—	—	—	—	.60	4.00	—
1976S	(4,149,730)	—	—	—	—	—	—	—	3.00

Bicentennial design, drummer boy

KM# 204a SILVER CLAD 0.074 oz. 24.3 mm. 5.7500 g. **Rev. Designer:** Jack L. Ahr

Date	Mintage	G-4	VG-8	F-12	VF-20	XF-40	MS-60	MS-65	Prf-65
1976S	4,908,319	—	—	—	—	—	1.25	3.00	3.00
1976S	(3,998,621)	—	—	—	—	—	—	—	3.00

Regular design resumed

KM# A164a COPPER-NICKEL CLAD COPPER 24.3 mm. 5.6700 g. **Notes:** KM#164 design and composition resumed. The 1979-S and 1981 Type II proofs have clearer mint marks than the Type I proofs for those years.

Date	Mintage	MS-65	Prf-65	Date	Mintage	MS-65	Prf-65
1977	468,556,000	6.50	—	1985S	(3,362,821)	5.00	1.75
1977D	256,524,978	4.00	—	1986P	551,199,333	7.00	—
1977S	(3,251,152)	—	1.50	1986D	504,298,660	10.00	—
1978	521,452,000	6.00	—	1986S	(3,010,497)	—	3.00
1978D	287,373,152	8.00	—	1987P	582,499,481	7.00	—
1978S	(3,127,781)	—	3.00	1987D	655,594,696	5.00	—
1979	515,708,000	6.00	—	1987S	(4,227,728)	—	1.75
1979D	489,789,780	4.00	—	1988P	562,052,000	9.00	—
1979S T-I	—	—	2.00	1988D	596,810,688	8.00	—
1979S T-II	—	—	3.00	1988S	(3,262,948)	—	2.25
1980P	635,832,000	5.00	—	1989P	512,868,000	9.00	—
1980D	518,327,487	4.75	—	1989D	896,535,597	3.00	—
1980S	(3,554,806)	—	2.00	1989S	(3,220,194)	—	2.25
1981P	601,716,000	6.00	—	1990P	613,792,000	9.00	—
1981D	575,722,833	4.00	—	1990D	927,638,181	3.00	—
1981S T-I	—	—	1.75	1990S	(3,299,559)	—	6.00
1981S T-II	—	—	5.00	1991P	570,968,000	8.00	—
1982P	500,931,000	18.50	—	1991D	630,966,693	7.00	—
1982D	480,042,788	10.00	—	1991S	(2,867,787)	—	2.50
1982S	(3,857,479)	—	2.75	1992P	384,764,000	12.00	—
1983P	673,535,000	45.00	—	1992D	389,777,107	15.00	—
1983D	617,806,446	30.00	—	1992S	(2,858,981)	—	3.00
1983S	(3,279,126)	—	2.75	1993P	639,276,000	6.00	—
1984P	676,545,000	10.00	—	1993D	645,476,128	7.50	—
1984D	546,483,064	7.00	—	1993S	(2,633,439)	—	4.50
1984S	(3,065,110)	—	2.75	1994P	825,600,000	12.00	—
1985P	775,818,962	10.00	—	1994D	880,034,110	7.00	—
1985D	519,962,888	6.00	—	1994S	(2,484,594)	—	4.00

Date	Mintage	MS-65	Prf-65	Date	Mintage	MS-65	Prf-65
1995P	1,004,336,000	10.00	—	1997P	595,740,000	4.00	—
1995D	1,103,216,000	9.00	—	1997D	599,680,000	4.00	—
1995S	(2,010,384)	—	16.50	1997S	(1,975,000)	—	9.50
1996P	925,040,000	5.00	—	1998P	896,268,000	4.00	—
1996D	906,868,000	5.00	—	1998D	821,000,000	4.00	—
1996S	—	—	4.00	1998S	—	—	11.00

KM# A164b SILVER Notes: Resumption of silver.

Date	Mintage	Prf-65	Date	Mintage	Prf-65
1992S	(1,317,579)	3.50	1996S	—	11.50
1993S	(761,353)	6.50	1997S	—	19.00
1994S	(785,329)	12.50	1998S	—	10.00
1995S	(838,953)	18.00			

50 State Quarters

Connecticut

KM# 297 COPPER-NICKEL CLAD COPPER

Date	Mintage	MS-63	MS-65	Prf-65
1999P	688,744,000	.75	.75	—
1999D	657,480,000	.75	.75	—
1999S	(3,713,359)	—	—	10.00

KM# 297a 0.9000 **SILVER** .1808 oz. ASW. 6.2500 g.

Date	Mintage	MS-63	MS-65	Prf-65
1999S	(804,565)	—	—	40.00

Delaware

KM# 293 COPPER-NICKEL CLAD COPPER 24.3 mm. 5.6700 g.

Date	Mintage	MS-63	MS-65	Prf-65
1999P	373,400,000	1.25	1.25	—
1999D	401,424,000	1.25	1.25	—
1999S	(3,713,359)	—	—	10.00

KM# 293a 0.9000 **SILVER** .1808 oz. ASW. 6.2500 g.

Date	Mintage	MS-63	MS-65	Prf-65
1999S	(804,565)	—	—	40.00

Georgia

KM# 296 COPPER-NICKEL CLAD COPPER

Date	Mintage	MS-63	MS-65	Prf-65
1999P	451,188,000	.75	.75	—
1999D	488,744,000	.75	.75	—
1999S	(3,713,359)	—	—	10.00

KM# 296a 0.9000 **SILVER** .1808 oz. ASW. 6.2500 g.

Date	Mintage	MS-63	MS-65	Prf-65
1999S	(804,565)	—	—	40.00

New Jersey

KM# 295 COPPER-NICKEL CLAD COPPER

Date	Mintage	MS-63	MS-65	Prf-65
1999P	363,200,000	1.00	1.00	—
1999D	299,028,000	1.00	1.00	—
1999S	(3,713,359)	—	—	10.00

KM# 295a 0.9000 **SILVER** .1808 oz. ASW. 6.2500 g.

Date	Mintage	MS-63	MS-65	Prf-65
1999S	(804,565)	—	—	40.00

Pennsylvania

KM# 294 **COPPER-NICKEL CLAD COPPER** 24.3 mm. 5.6700 g.

Date	Mintage	MS-63	MS-65	Prf-65
1999P	349,000,000	1.50	1.50	—
1999D	358,332,000	1.25	1.25	—
1999S	(3,713,359)	—	—	10.00

KM# 294a 0.9000 **SILVER** .1808 oz. ASW. 6.2500 g.

Date	Mintage	MS-63	MS-65	Prf-65
1999S	(804,565)	—	—	40.00

Maryland

KM# 306 **COPPER-NICKEL CLAD COPPER**

Date	Mintage	MS-63	MS-65	Prf-65
2000P	678,200,000	.75	.75	—
2000D	556,526,000	.75	.75	—
2000S	(4,078,747)	—	—	5.00

KM# 306a 0.9000 **SILVER** .1808 oz. ASW. 6.2500 g.

Date	Mintage	MS-63	MS-65	Prf-65
2000S	(965,921)	—	—	7.50

Massachusetts

KM# 305 **COPPER-NICKEL CLAD COPPER**

Date	Mintage	MS-63	MS-65	Prf-65
2000P	629,800,000	.75	.75	—
2000D	535,184,000	.75	.75	—
2000S	(4,078,747)	—	—	5.00

KM# 305a 0.9000 **SILVER** .1808 oz. ASW. 6.2500 g.

Date	Mintage	MS-63	MS-65	Prf-65
2000S	(965,921)	—	—	7.50

New Hampshire

KM# 308 **COPPER-NICKEL CLAD COPPER**

Date	Mintage	MS-63	MS-65	Prf-65
2000P	673,040,000	.75	.75	—
2000D	495,976,000	.75	.75	—
2000S	(4,078,747)	—	—	5.00

KM# 308a 0.9000 **SILVER** .1808 oz. ASW. 6.2500 g.

Date	Mintage	MS-63	MS-65	Prf-65
2000S	(965,921)	—	—	7.50

South Carolina

KM# 307 **COPPER-NICKEL CLAD COPPER**

Date	Mintage	MS-63	MS-65	Prf-65
2000P	742,756,000	.75	.75	—
2000D	566,208,000	.75	.75	—
2000S	(4,078,747)	—	—	5.00

KM# 307a 0.9000 **SILVER** .1808 oz. ASW. 6.2500 g.

Date	Mintage	MS-63	MS-65	Prf-65
2000S	(965,921)	—	—	7.50

Virginia

KM# 309 **COPPER-NICKEL CLAD COPPER**

Date	Mintage	MS-63	MS-65	Prf-65
2000P	943,000,000	.75	.75	—
2000D	651,616,000	.75	.75	—
2000S	(4,078,747)	—	—	5.00

KM# 309a 0.9000 **SILVER** .1808 oz. ASW. 6.2500 g.

Date	Mintage	MS-63	MS-65	Prf-65
2000S	(965,921)	—	—	7.50

HALF DOLLAR

Barber Half Dollar

KM# 116 0.9000 **SILVER** 0.3618 oz. ASW. 30.6 mm. 12.5000 g. **Designer:** Charles E. Barber

Mint mark

Date	Mintage	G-4	VG-8	F-12	VF-20	XF-40	AU-50	MS-60	MS-65	Prf-65
1901	4,268,813	13.50	16.00	38.50	96.00	180	300	510	4,500	3,500
1901O	1,124,000	16.50	27.50	80.00	205	350	475	1,350	17,000	—
1901S	847,044	34.00	55.00	160	355	625	1,050	1,850	20,000	—
1902	4,922,777	12.50	13.50	32.50	85.00	210	295	485	4,250	3,700
1902O	2,526,000	13.50	17.00	52.50	105	225	360	725	14,000	—
1902S	1,460,670	16.00	19.00	62.50	150	250	430	750	9,350	—
1903	2,278,755	13.50	16.00	47.50	100.00	205	340	500	11,000	3,825
1903O	2,100,000	13.00	17.00	55.00	115	215	345	680	10,000	—
1903S	1,920,772	15.00	18.00	55.00	125	235	380	610	5,750	—
1904	2,992,670	12.00	13.50	34.00	85.00	155	300	475	6,000	4,100
1904O	1,117,600	20.00	32.50	80.00	220	400	600	1,100	13,300	—
1904S	553,038	38.50	70.00	260	550	1,075	1,800	6,250	37,500	—
1905	662,727	22.50	27.50	95.00	180	270	345	575	8,250	3,900
1905O	505,000	30.00	50.00	125	235	340	440	760	5,250	—
1905S	2,494,000	15.50	16.50	50.00	125	235	380	565	9,800	—
1906	2,638,675	12.00	16.00	31.00	85.00	170	300	485	3,800	3,300
1906D	4,028,000	12.00	13.50	34.00	93.50	160	300	485	4,700	—
1906O	2,446,000	12.00	13.50	44.00	100.00	180	325	625	3,750	—
1906S	1,740,154	13.00	16.00	57.50	110	220	310	610	3,800	—
1907	2,598,575	12.00	13.50	30.00	85.00	155	300	485	4,000	4,000
1907D	3,856,000	12.00	13.50	30.00	78.50	155	300	485	3,400	—
1907O	3,946,000	12.00	13.50	31.00	93.50	155	325	595	3,700	—
1907S	1,250,000	16.00	22.00	80.00	170	325	650	1,275	13,500	—
1908	1,354,545	12.00	13.50	30.00	85.00	155	295	485	4,500	4,000
1908D	3,280,000	12.00	13.50	30.00	85.00	155	295	485	3,800	—
1908O	5,360,000	12.00	13.50	30.00	93.50	155	325	550	3,800	—
1908S	1,644,828	18.00	25.00	75.00	160	285	435	850	6,850	—
1909	2,368,650	12.50	16.00	32.50	85.00	160	295	485	3,800	4,000
1909O	925,400	16.00	23.00	60.00	140	300	525	775	3,800	—
1909S	1,764,000	12.00	13.50	38.50	100.00	200	350	595	5,000	—
1910	418,551	20.00	28.50	90.00	170	330	420	625	4,000	4,250
1910S	1,948,000	13.50	17.00	37.50	100.00	190	350	650	6,850	—
1911	1,406,543	12.00	13.50	30.00	85.00	155	300	485	3,800	3,300
1911D	695,080	14.00	16.00	41.00	96.00	200	295	575	3,800	—
1911S	1,272,000	13.50	17.00	41.00	100.00	180	330	580	6,250	—
1912	1,550,700	12.00	13.50	30.00	85.00	160	300	485	4,200	4,000

Date	Mintage	G-4	VG-8	F-12	VF-20	XF-40	AU-50	MS-60	MS-65	Prf-65
1912D	2,300,800	13.00	13.50	30.00	85.00	155	325	485	3,800	—
1912S	1,370,000	15.00	20.00	41.50	100.00	200	340	550	6,000	—
1913	188,627	75.00	90.00	235	420	600	850	1,150	4,850	3,800
1913D	534,000	17.00	21.00	46.00	100.00	200	315	500	5,250	—
1913S	604,000	22.00	26.00	55.00	110	230	375	625	5,250	—
1914	124,610	150	170	325	550	775	1,025	1,400	7,500	4,300
1914S	992,000	15.00	19.00	41.00	100.00	190	315	580	5,000	—
1915	138,450	115	165	270	380	575	900	1,250	6,250	4,250
1915D	1,170,400	12.00	13.50	30.00	78.50	155	295	485	3,800	—
1915S	1,604,000	15.00	20.00	41.50	99.00	170	295	485	3,800	—

Walking Liberty Half Dollar

KM# 142 0.9000 **SILVER** 0.3618 oz. ASW. 30.6 mm. 12.5000 g. **Designer:** Adolph A. Weinman **Notes:** The mint mark appears on the obverse below the word "Trust" on 1916 and some 1917 issues. Starting with some 1917 issues and continuing through the remainder of the series, the mint mark was changed to the reverse, at about the 8 o'clock position near the rim.

Obverse mint mark

Reverse mint mark

Date	Mintage	G-4	VG-8	F-12	VF-20	XF-40	AU-50	MS-60	MS-65	Prf-65
1916	608,000	45.00	52.50	100.00	180	250	285	350	1,800	—
1916D	1,014,400	45.00	52.50	80.00	140	225	265	375	2,400	—
1916S	508,000	110	130	285	470	650	750	1,100	6,250	—
1917D obv.	765,400	22.00	31.50	80.00	160	235	350	640	8,000	—
1917S obv.	952,000	27.50	44.00	135	375	720	1,225	2,300	19,500	—
1917	12,292,000	7.00	7.25	9.00	20.00	44.00	75.00	135	1,000	—
1917D rev.	1,940,000	10.00	16.50	45.00	135	275	575	975	18,500	—
1917S rev.	5,554,000	7.00	8.00	16.50	33.00	65.00	160	345	13,000	—
1918	6,634,000	7.00	7.25	16.00	70.00	160	275	580	3,800	—
1918D	3,853,040	8.00	13.00	36.00	96.00	235	500	1,350	25,000	—
1918S	10,282,000	7.00	7.25	15.00	35.00	65.00	200	525	18,000	—
1919	962,000	19.00	32.50	78.50	275	550	920	1,350	7,500	—
1919D	1,165,000	18.00	38.50	100.00	325	765	1,550	6,250	130,000	—
1919S	1,552,000	17.50	30.00	75.00	325	850	1,800	3,450	20,500	—
1920	6,372,000	7.00	7.25	16.00	44.00	75.00	160	350	5,250	—
1920D	1,551,000	12.00	20.00	70.00	250	475	960	1,550	12,000	—
1920S	4,624,000	7.00	7.50	20.00	80.00	235	520	850	12,500	—
1921	246,000	175	220	350	780	1,550	2,750	4,350	18,000	—
1921D	208,000	285	360	550	940	2,200	3,400	5,300	27,500	—
1921S	548,000	46.00	70.00	220	750	4,800	8,600	14,000	105,000	—
1923S	2,178,000	8.50	11.50	27.50	115	315	700	1,400	15,000	—
1927S	2,392,000	7.00	7.50	13.50	47.50	160	415	1,050	10,000	—
1928S	1,940,000	7.00	7.50	15.00	70.00	200	480	1,050	10,500	—
1929D	1,001,200	8.00	12.00	19.00	60.00	110	210	415	3,500	—
1929S	1,902,000	7.00	7.50	12.50	28.50	115	230	425	3,550	—
1933S	1,786,000	8.50	11.00	12.50	20.00	60.00	260	625	4,500	—
1934	6,964,000	7.00	7.25	7.50	7.00	11.00	26.00	85.00	625	—
1934D	2,361,400	7.00	7.50	8.00	10.00	29.00	90.00	155	1,700	—
1934S	3,652,000	7.00	7.50	8.00	8.50	27.00	105	395	5,200	—
1935	9,162,000	7.00	7.25	7.50	8.00	8.50	22.50	45.00	585	—
1935D	3,003,800	7.00	7.50	8.00	10.00	32.50	70.00	140	3,150	—
1935S	3,854,000	7.00	7.50	8.00	8.50	29.00	100.00	295	3,700	—
1936	12,617,901	7.00	7.25	7.50	8.00	8.50	21.50	38.50	300	6,600
1936D	4,252,400	7.00	7.50	8.00	8.50	20.00	55.00	80.00	700	—
1936S	3,884,000	7.00	7.50	8.00	8.50	21.50	62.50	135	1,050	—
1937	9,527,728	7.00	7.00	7.50	8.00	8.50	22.50	40.00	335	1,700
1937D	1,676,000	7.00	7.75	8.50	14.00	33.50	110	225	850	—
1937S	2,090,000	7.00	7.50	8.00	8.50	25.50	65.00	175	850	—
1938	4,118,152	7.00	7.50	8.00	8.50	9.50	41.50	70.00	550	1,275
1938D	491,600	125	135	155	175	220	260	525	1,550	—
1939	6,820,808	7.00	7.25	7.50	8.00	8.50	22.50	42.50	230	1,150
1939D	4,267,800	7.00	7.25	7.50	8.00	8.50	26.00	47.50	275	—
1939S	2,552,000	7.00	7.50	8.00	9.00	25.00	80.00	150	370	—
1940	9,167,279	7.00	7.25	7.50	8.00	8.50	11.00	30.00	200	1,000
1940S	4,550,000	7.00	7.25	7.50	8.00	11.00	22.00	52.50	450	—
1941	24,207,412	7.00	7.25	7.50	8.00	8.50	11.00	32.50	160	850
1941D	11,248,400	7.00	7.25	7.50	8.00	8.50	18.00	38.50	275	—
1941S	8,098,000	7.00	7.25	7.50	8.00	8.50	27.50	75.00	1,300	—
1942	47,839,120	7.00	7.25	7.50	8.00	8.50	11.00	32.50	150	850
1942D	10,973,800	7.00	7.25	7.50	8.00	8.50	19.00	38.50	345	—
1942S	12,708,000	7.00	7.25	7.50	8.00	8.50	17.50	38.50	700	—
1943	53,190,000	7.00	7.25	7.50	8.00	8.50	11.00	33.50	150	—
1943D	11,346,000	7.00	7.25	7.50	8.00	8.50	25.00	43.50	310	—
1943S	13,450,000	7.00	7.25	7.50	8.00	8.50	18.50	43.50	495	—
1944	28,206,000	7.00	7.25	7.50	8.00	8.50	11.00	33.50	165	—
1944D	9,769,000	7.00	7.25	7.50	8.00	8.50	20.00	37.50	195	—
1944S	8,904,000	7.00	7.25	7.50	8.00	8.50	16.00	38.50	600	—
1945	31,502,000	7.00	7.25	7.50	8.00	8.50	11.00	32.50	160	—
1945D	9,966,800	7.00	7.25	7.50	8.00	8.50	19.00	34.00	160	—
1945S	10,156,000	7.00	7.25	7.50	8.00	8.50	17.50	35.00	220	—

Date	Mintage	G-4	VG-8	F-12	VF-20	XF-40	AU-50	MS-60	MS-65	Prf-65
1946	12,118,000	7.00	7.25	7.50	8.00	8.50	11.00	32.50	250	—
1946D	2,151,000	7.00	7.25	7.50	8.00	25.50	38.50	50.00	150	—
1946S	3,724,000	7.00	7.25	7.50	8.00	8.50	19.00	43.50	165	—
1947	4,094,000	7.00	6.25	7.50	8.00	9.50	22.00	52.50	230	—
1947D	3,900,600	7.00	7.25	7.50	8.00	12.50	31.50	52.50	150	—

Franklin Half Dollar

KM# 199 0.9000 **SILVER** 0.3618 oz. ASW. 30.6 mm. 12.5000 g. **Designer:** John R. Sinnock

Mint mark

Date	Mintage	G-4	VG-8	F-12	VF-20	XF-40	AU-50	MS-60	MS-65	-65FBL	-65CAM
1948	3,006,814	—	5.00	6.00	7.00	8.50	11.50	15.50	75.00	190	—
1948D	4,028,600	—	5.00	6.00	7.00	8.00	11.00	15.00	125	260	—
1949	5,614,000	—	—	—	—	6.00	12.00	38.50	145	300	—
1949D	4,120,600	—	—	—	—	8.00	25.00	43.50	900	1,750	—
1949S	3,744,000	—	—	—	7.00	11.00	30.00	62.50	155	650	—
1950	7,793,509	—	—	—	—	6.00	10.00	26.00	110	250	3,700
1950D	8,031,600	—	—	—	—	7.50	11.50	22.00	425	1,150	—
1951	16,859,602	—	—	—	—	—	6.50	11.00	75.00	235	2,200
1951D	9,475,200	—	—	—	—	7.50	17.50	26.00	170	525	—
1951S	13,696,000	—	—	—	—	—	15.00	23.50	125	775	—
1952	21,274,073	—	—	—	—	—	6.50	8.50	80.00	200	1,100
1952D	25,395,600	—	—	—	—	—	6.50	7.75	135	450	—
1952S	5,526,000	—	—	6.00	12.00	20.00	32.00	50.00	100.00	1,500	—
1953	2,796,920	—	—	—	—	8.00	16.00	25.00	125	850	475
1953D	20,900,400	—	—	—	—	—	6.50	8.00	160	400	—
1953S	4,148,000	—	—	—	—	—	15.00	25.00	65.00	16,000	—
1954	13,421,503	—	—	—	—	—	6.50	7.00	80.00	250	250
1954D	25,445,580	—	—	—	—	—	6.50	7.00	110	200	—
1954S	4,993,400	—	—	—	—	—	8.50	13.50	105	425	—
1955	2,876,381	—	18.00	20.00	21.00	22.00	23.00	24.00	65.00	185	195
1955 Bugs Bunny	—	—	20.00	22.00	23.00	25.00	26.00	28.00	100.00	750	—
1956	4,701,384	—	7.00	7.50	8.00	8.50	9.00	13.50	50.00	95.00	75.00
1957	6,361,952	—	—	—	—	—	6.50	7.00	62.50	95.00	135
1957D	19,966,850	—	—	—	—	—	6.50	7.00	65.00	100.00	—
1958	4,917,652	—	—	—	—	—	6.50	7.00	60.00	100.00	250
1958D	23,962,412	—	—	—	—	—	6.50	7.00	62.50	75.00	—
1959	7,349,291	—	—	—	—	—	6.50	7.00	105	250	475
1959D	13,053,750	—	—	—	—	—	6.50	7.00	135	190	—
1960	7,715,602	—	—	—	—	—	6.50	7.00	135	350	75.00
1960D	18,215,812	—	—	—	—	—	6.50	7.00	475	1,250	—
1961	11,318,244	—	—	—	—	—	6.50	7.00	145	1,750	75.00
1961D	20,276,442	—	—	—	—	—	6.50	7.00	200	875	—
1962	12,932,019	—	—	—	—	—	6.50	7.00	160	1,850	50.00
1962D	35,473,281	—	—	—	—	—	6.50	7.00	225	775	—
1963	25,239,645	—	—	—	—	—	6.50	7.00	55.00	775	50.00
1963D	67,069,292	—	—	—	—	—	6.50	7.00	70.00	125	—

Kennedy Half Dollar

KM# 202 0.9000 **SILVER** 0.3618 oz. ASW. 30.6 mm. 12.5000 g. **Obv. Designer:** Gilroy Roberts **Rev. Designer:** Frank Gasparro

Mint mark 1964

Date	Mintage	G-4	VG-8	F-12	VF-20	XF-40	MS-60	MS-65	Prf-65
1964	277,254,766	—	—	—	—	—	4.60	20.00	10.00
1964D	156,205,446	—	—	—	—	—	5.00	24.00	—

KM# 202a 0.4000 **SILVER** 0.1480 oz. ASW. 30.6 mm. 11.5000 g. **Obv. Designer:** Gilroy Roberts **Rev. Designer:** Frank Gasparro

Mint mark 1968-present

Date	Mintage	G-4	VG-8	F-12	VF-20	XF-40	MS-60	MS-65	Prf-65
1965	65,879,366	—	—	—	—	—	2.00	15.00	—
1965 SMS	2,360,000	—	—	—	—	—	—	10.00	—
1966	108,984,932	—	—	—	—	—	2.00	12.00	—
1966 SMS	2,261,583	—	—	—	—	—	—	11.00	—
1967	295,046,978	—	—	—	—	—	2.00	18.00	—
1967 SMS	18,633,440	—	—	—	—	—	—	13.00	—
1968D	246,951,930	—	—	—	—	—	2.00	18.00	—
1968S	3,041,506	—	—	—	—	—	—	—	9.00
1969D	129,881,800	—	—	—	—	—	2.00	20.00	—
1969S	2,934,631	—	—	—	—	—	—	—	9.00

Date	Mintage	G-4	VG-8	F-12	VF-20	XF-40	MS-60	MS-65	Prf-65
1970D	2,150,000	—	—	—	—	—	—	32.00	—
1970S	2,632,810	—	—	—	—	—	—	—	22.00

KM# 202b COPPER-NICKEL CLAD COPPER 30.6 mm. 11.3400 g. **Obv. Designer:** Gilroy Roberts **Rev. Designer:** Frank Gasparro

Date	Mintage	G-4	VG-8	F-12	VF-20	XF-40	MS-60	MS-65	Prf-65
1971	155,640,000	—	—	—	—	—	1.50	12.00	—
1971D	302,097,424	—	—	—	—	—	1.00	5.00	—
1971S	3,244,183	—	—	—	—	—	—	—	3.00
1972	153,180,000	—	—	—	—	—	1.00	9.00	—
1972D	141,890,000	—	—	—	—	—	1.00	6.00	—
1972S	3,267,667	—	—	—	—	—	—	—	2.50
1973	64,964,000	—	—	—	—	—	1.00	6.00	—
1973D	83,171,400	—	—	—	—	—	—	5.50	—
1973S	(2,769,624)	—	—	—	—	—	—	—	2.50
1974	201,596,000	—	—	—	—	—	1.00	5.00	—
1974D	79,066,300	—	—	—	—	—	1.00	6.00	—
1974S	(2,617,350)	—	—	—	—	—	—	—	3.00
1975 none minted	—	—	—	—	—	—	—	—	—
1975D none minted	—	—	—	—	—	—	—	—	—
1975S none minted	—	—	—	—	—	—	—	—	—

Bicentennial design, Independence Hall

KM# 205 COPPER-NICKEL CLAD COPPER Rev. Designer: Seth Huntington

Date	Mintage	G-4	VG-8	F-12	VF-20	XF-40	MS-60	MS-65	Prf-65
1976	234,308,000	—	—	—	—	—	1.00	10.00	—
1976D	287,565,248	—	—	—	—	—	1.00	7.00	—
1976S	(7,059,099)	—	—	—	—	—	—	—	2.00

KM# 205a 0.4000 **SILVER** 0.1480 oz. ASW. 11.5000 g. **Rev. Designer:** Seth Huntington

Date	Mintage	G-4	VG-8	F-12	VF-20	XF-40	MS-60	MS-65	Prf-65
1976S	4,908,319	—	—	—	—	—	—	13.00	—
1976S	(3,998,625)	—	—	—	—	—	—	—	5.00

Regular design resumed

KM# A202b COPPER-NICKEL CLAD COPPER 30.6 mm. 11.3400 g. **Notes:** KM#202b design and composition resumed. The 1979-S and 1981-S Type II proofs have clearer mint marks than the Type I proofs of those years.

Date	Mintage	MS-65	Prf-65
1977	43,598,000	6.50	—
1977D	31,449,106	6.00	—
1977S	(3,251,152)	—	2.00
1978	14,350,000	6.50	—
1978D	13,765,799	6.50	—
1978S	(3,127,788)	—	2.00
1979	68,312,000	5.50	—
1979D	15,815,422	6.00	—
1979S type I, proof	(3,677,175)	—	2.00
1979S type II, proof	Inc. above	—	18.00
1980P	44,134,000	5.00	—
1980D	33,456,449	4.50	—
1980S	(3,547,030)	—	2.00
1981P	29,544,000	6.00	—
1981D	27,839,533	5.50	—
1981S type I, proof	(4,063,083)	—	2.00
1981S type II, proof	Inc. above	—	14.50
1982P	10,819,000	5.00	—
1982D	13,140,102	7.00	—
1982S	(38,957,479)	—	3.50
1983P	34,139,000	10.00	—
1983D	32,472,244	10.00	—
1983S	(3,279,126)	—	3.00
1984P	26,029,000	6.50	—
1984D	26,262,158	7.00	—
1984S	(3,065,110)	—	4.00
1985P	18,706,962	10.00	—
1985D	19,814,034	12.00	—
1985S	(3,962,138)	—	4.50
1986P	13,107,633	16.00	—
1986D	15,336,145	12.00	—
1986S	(2,411,180)	—	7.50
1987P	2,890,758	12.00	—

Date	Mintage	MS-65	Prf-65
1987D	2,890,758	10.00	—
1987S	(4,407,728)	—	3.50
1988P	13,626,000	10.00	—
1988D	12,000,096	10.00	—
1988S	(3,262,948)	—	7.00
1989P	24,542,000	10.00	—
1989D	23,000,216	8.00	—
1989S	(3,220,194)	—	7.00
1990P	22,780,000	15.00	—
1990D	20,096,242	15.00	—
1990S	(3,299,559)	—	5.00
1991P	14,874,000	10.00	—
1991D	15,054,678	12.00	—
1991S	(2,867,787)	—	11.50
1992P	17,628,000	7.00	—
1992D	17,000,106	8.00	—
1992S	(2,858,981)	—	10.00
1993P	15,510,000	8.00	—
1993D	15,000,006	12.00	—
1993S	(2,633,439)	—	14.00
1994P	23,718,000	6.00	—
1994D	23,828,110	6.00	—
1994S	(2,484,594)	—	8.00
1995P	26,496,000	6.00	—
1995D	26,288,000	6.00	—
1995S	(2,010,384)	—	47.50
1996P	24,442,000	6.00	—
1996D	24,744,000	6.00	—
1996S	(2,085,191)	—	10.00
1997P	20,882,000	7.00	—
1997D	19,876,000	6.00	—
1997S	(1,975,000)	—	25.00
1998P	15,646,000	9.00	—
1998D	15,064,000	8.00	—
1998S	(2,078,494)	—	14.00
1999P	8,900,000	6.00	—

Date	Mintage	MS-65	Prf-65
1999D	10,682,000	6.00	—
1999S	(2,557,897)	—	10.00
2000P	22,600,000	6.00	—
2000D	19,466,000	6.00	—
2000S	(3,082,944)	—	4.50

KM# B202b SILVER

Date	Mintage	Prf-65
1992S	(1,317,579)	15.00
1993S	(761,353)	25.00
1994S	(785,329)	35.00
1995S	(838,953)	100.00
1996S	(830,021)	50.00
1997S	(821,678)	100.00
1998S	(878,792)	30.00
1998S Matte Proof	(62,350)	400
1999S	(804,565)	15.00
2000S	(965,921)	12.50

DOLLAR

Morgan Dollar

KM# 110 0.9000 **SILVER** 0.7736 oz. ASW. 38.1 mm. 26.7300 g. **Designer:** George T. Morgan **Notes:** "65DMPL" values are for coins grading MS-65 deep-mirror prooflike. The 1878 "8 tail feathers" and "7 tail feathers" varieties are distinguished by the number of feathers in the eagle's tail. On the "reverse of 1878" varieties, the top of the top feather in the arrows held by the eagle is straight across and the eagle's breast is concave. On the "reverse of 1879 varieties," the top feather in the arrows held by the eagle is slanted and the eagle's breast is convex. The 1890-CC "tail-bar variety has a bar extending from the arrow feathers to the wreath on the reverse, the result of a die gouge.

Date	Mintage	VG-8	F-12	VF-20	XF-40	AU-50	MS-60	MS-63	MS-64	MS-65	65DMPL	Prf-65
1901	6,962,813	27.50	36.00	57.50	110	375	2,150	17,000	56,000	220,000	220,000	6,500
1901O	13,320,000	20.00	20.00	21.00	22.50	23.00	36.00	53.50	80.00	235	3,800	—
1901S	2,284,000	20.00	20.00	31.50	46.00	220	470	700	1,075	4,100	12,500	—
1902	7,994,777	20.00	20.00	20.50	21.50	23.50	44.00	100.00	150	485	15,750	5,900
1902O	8,636,000	20.00	20.00	21.00	21.50	23.00	36.00	53.50	80.00	230	3,600	—
1902S	1,530,000	62.50	85.00	160	220	315	425	625	1,135	3,150	15,000	—
1903	4,652,755	50.00	51.00	53.50	60.00	65.00	77.50	93.50	130	280	9,150	5,900
1903O	4,450,000	350	375	400	425	440	450	475	500	700	4,650	—
1903S	1,241,000	55.00	82.50	155	335	1,800	4,250	7,000	8,500	10,500	40,000	—
1904	2,788,650	24.00	25.00	26.00	27.50	34.00	82.50	270	715	4,200	38,000	5,900
1904O	3,720,000	24.00	25.00	26.00	27.50	28.00	35.00	52.50	72.50	230	550	—
1904S	2,304,000	35.00	47.50	85.00	230	560	1,150	4,250	6,250	8,500	19,000	—
1921	44,690,000	15.00	16.00	16.50	17.00	18.00	21.00	35.00	44.00	175	8,800	—
1921D	20,345,000	15.00	16.00	16.50	17.00	18.00	44.00	60.00	135	300	15,000	—
1921S	21,695,000	15.00	16.00	16.50	17.00	18.00	31.00	66.00	160	950	22,000	—

Peace Dollar

KM# 150 0.9000 **SILVER** 0.7736 oz. ASW. 38.1 mm. 26.7300 g. **Designer:** Anthony DeFrancisci **Notes:** Commonly called Peace dollars.

Mint mark

Date	Mintage	G-4	VG-8	F-12	VF-20	XF-40	AU-50	MS-60	MS-63	MS-64	MS-65
1921	1,006,473	70.00	130	135	140	150	170	245	460	850	2,500
1922	51,737,000	8.00	16.00	16.25	16.50	17.00	17.50	18.00	33.50	60.00	225
1922D	15,063,000	8.00	16.00	16.25	16.50	17.00	17.50	26.50	48.00	92.50	400
1922S	17,475,000	8.00	16.00	16.25	16.50	17.00	17.50	26.50	66.00	300	2,500
1923	30,800,000	8.00	16.00	16.25	16.50	17.00	17.50	18.50	33.50	60.00	225
1923D	6,811,000	8.00	16.00	16.25	16.50	17.00	18.00	55.00	120	265	1,050

Date	Mintage	G-4	VG-8	F-12	VF-20	XF-40	AU-50	MS-60	MS-63	MS-64	MS-65
1923S	19,020,000	8.00	16.00	16.25	16.50	17.00	17.50	28.00	70.00	340	6,000
1924	11,811,000	8.00	16.00	16.25	16.50	17.00	17.50	18.50	33.50	60.00	225
1924S	1,728,000	12.00	25.00	27.50	34.00	44.00	68.50	200	625	1,500	9,500
1925	10,198,000	8.00	16.00	16.25	16.50	17.00	17.50	18.50	32.50	60.00	225
1925S	1,610,000	10.00	17.50	19.00	25.00	30.00	47.50	75.00	185	825	21,000
1926	1,939,000	9.00	17.00	17.25	17.50	18.50	23.00	41.50	78.50	120	375
1926D	2,348,700	8.00	17.00	17.50	18.00	22.00	32.50	66.00	150	300	600
1926S	6,980,000	8.00	16.00	16.25	16.50	18.00	19.00	41.50	90.00	280	1,000
1927	848,000	15.00	27.50	30.00	31.50	32.50	55.00	70.00	165	450	2,700
1927D	1,268,900	12.00	26.00	27.50	28.50	29.00	84.00	150	340	975	5,000
1927S	866,000	16.00	26.00	28.50	30.00	32.50	80.00	135	425	1,450	11,700
1928	360,649	300	460	475	490	500	505	550	925	1,450	4,500
1928S	1,632,000	16.00	33.50	35.00	38.50	45.00	67.50	155	580	1,575	19,500
1934	954,057	14.00	20.50	21.50	22.00	22.50	47.50	120	245	480	900
1934D	1,569,500	11.00	20.00	20.50	21.50	22.00	47.50	135	480	700	2,100
1934S	1,011,000	12.00	33.00	45.00	85.00	200	500	1,800	4,000	6,250	8,500
1935	1,576,000	11.00	17.50	20.00	21.50	22.00	30.00	62.50	100.00	190	640
1935S	1,964,000	11.00	17.50	18.50	19.00	23.00	96.00	250	385	625	1,325

Eisenhower Dollar

KM# 203 COPPER-NICKEL CLAD COPPER 38.1 mm. 22.6800 g. **Designer:** Frank Gasparro

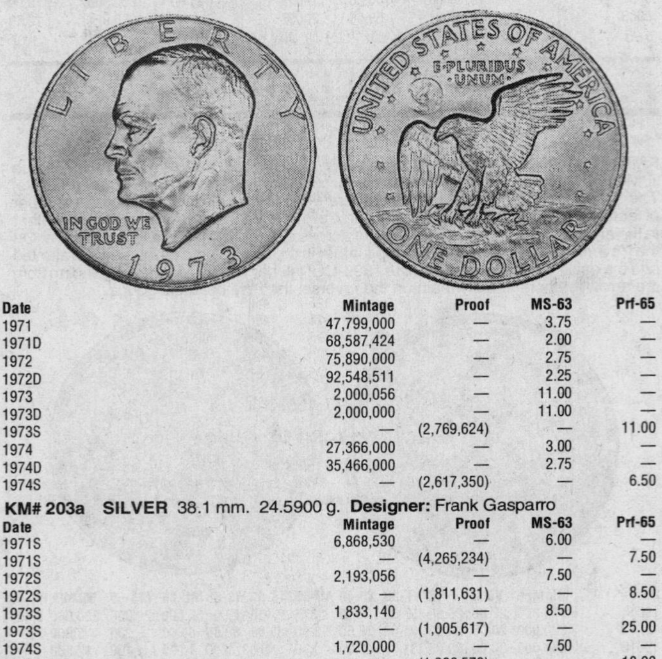

Date	Mintage	Proof	MS-63	Prf-65
1971	47,799,000	—	3.75	—
1971D	68,587,424	—	2.00	—
1972	75,890,000	—	2.75	—
1972D	92,548,511	—	2.25	—
1973	2,000,056	—	11.00	—
1973D	2,000,000	—	11.00	—
1973S	—	(2,769,624)	—	11.00
1974	27,366,000	—	3.00	—
1974D	35,466,000	—	2.75	—
1974S	—	(2,617,350)	—	6.50

KM# 203a SILVER 38.1 mm. 24.5900 g. **Designer:** Frank Gasparro

Date	Mintage	Proof	MS-63	Prf-65
1971S	6,868,530	—	6.00	—
1971S	—	(4,265,234)	—	7.50
1972S	2,193,056	—	7.50	—
1972S	—	(1,811,631)	—	8.50
1973S	1,833,140	—	8.50	—
1973S	—	(1,005,617)	—	25.00
1974S	1,720,000	—	7.50	—
1974S	—	(1,306,579)	—	18.00

Bicentennial design, moon behind Liberty Bell

KM# 206 COPPER-NICKEL CLAD COPPER 38.1 mm. 22.6800 g. **Rev. Designer:** Dennis R. Williams **Notes:** In 1976 the lettering on the reverse was changed to thinner letters, resulting in the Type II variety for that year. The Type I variety was minted 1975 and dated 1976.

Date	Mintage	Proof	MS-63	Prf-65
1976 type I	117,337,000	—	4.00	—
1976 type II	Inc. above	—	2.00	—
1976D type I	103,228,274	—	3.25	—
1976D type II	Inc. above	—	2.00	—
1976S type I	—	(2,909,369)	—	5.75
1976S type II	—	(4,149,730)	—	5.75

Bicentennial design, moon behind Liberty Bell

KM# 206a 0.4000 **SILVER** 0.3162 oz. ASW. 24.5900 g. **Rev. Designer:** Dennis R. Williams

Date	Mintage	Proof	MS-63	Prf-65
1976S	4,908,319	—	14.00	—
1976S	—	(3,998,621)	—	12.50

Regular design resumed

KM# A203 COPPER-NICKEL CLAD COPPER 38.1 mm.

Date	Mintage	Proof	MS-63	Prf-65
1977	12,596,000	—	4.25	—
1977D	32,983,006	—	3.25	—
1977S	—	(3,251,152)	—	8.00
1978	25,702,000	—	2.75	—
1978D	33,012,890	—	3.00	—
1978S	—	(3,127,788)	—	10.00

Susan B. Anthony Dollar

KM# 207 COPPER-NICKEL CLAD COPPER 0 oz. 26.5 mm. 8.1000 g. **Designer:** Frank Gasparro **Notes:** The 1979-S and 1981-S Type II coins have a clearer mint mark than the Type I varieties for those years.

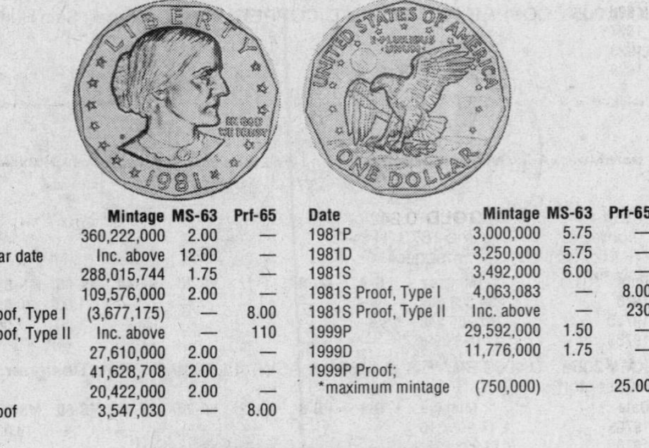

Date	Mintage	MS-63	Prf-65
1979P	360,222,000	2.00	—
1979P Near date	Inc. above	12.00	—
1979D	288,015,744	1.75	—
1979S	109,576,000	2.00	—
1979S Proof, Type I	(3,677,175)	—	8.00
1979S Proof, Type II	Inc. above	—	110
1980P	27,610,000	2.00	—
1980D	41,628,708	2.00	—
1980S	20,422,000	2.00	—
1980S Proof	3,547,030	—	8.00
1981P	3,000,000	5.75	—
1981D	3,250,000	5.75	—
1981S	3,492,000	6.00	—
1981S Proof, Type I	4,063,083	—	8.00
1981S Proof, Type II	Inc. above	—	230
1999P	29,592,000	1.50	—
1999D	11,776,000	1.75	—
1999P Proof; *maximum mintage	(750,000)	—	25.00

Sacagawea Dollar

Sacagawea bust right, with baby on back **Eagle in flight left**

KM# 310 COPPER-ZINC-MANGANESE-NICKEL CLAD COPPER 26.4 mm. 8.0700 g.

Date	Mintage	MS-63	Prf-65
2000P	767,140,000	2.00	—
2000D	518,916,000	2.00	—
2000S	(4,048,865)	—	10.00

$2.50 (QUARTER EAGLE)

GOLD

Coronet Head

KM# 72 0.9000 **GOLD** 0.121 oz. AGW. 18 mm. 4.1800 g. **Designer:** Christian Gobrecht **Notes:** Varieties for 1843 are distinguished by the size of the numerals in the date. One 1848 variety has "Cal." inscribed on the reverse, indicating it was made from California gold. The 1873 "closed-3" and "open-3" varieties are distinguished by the amount of space between the upper left and lower left serifs in the 3 in the date.

Date	Mintage	F-12	VF-20	XF-40	AU-50	MS-60	Prf-65
1901	91,322	150	175	200	235	275	12,500
1902	133,733	150	170	200	235	275	12,500
1903	201,257	150	170	200	235	275	13,000
1904	160,960	150	170	200	240	275	12,500
1905	217,944	150	170	200	240	275	12,500
1906	176,490	150	170	200	240	275	12,500
1907	336,448	150	170	200	240	275	12,500

Indian Head

KM# 128 0.9000 **GOLD** 0.121 oz. AGW. 18 mm. 4.1800 g. **Designer:** Bela Lyon Pratt

Date	Mintage	VF-20	XF-40	AU-50	MS-60	MS-63	MS-65	Prf-65
1908	565,057	165	220	230	275	1,800	8,500	16,000
1909	441,899	175	220	230	275	2,600	11,000	30,000
1910	492,682	175	220	230	275	2,600	12,500	18,000
1911	704,191	175	220	230	280	1,600	12,500	16,000
1911D	55,680	2,700	3,650	5,000	10,500	24,500	90,000	16,000
1912	616,197	175	220	230	275	2,800	16,000	16,000
1913	722,165	175	220	230	280	1,725	14,000	16,500
1914	240,117	175	235	260	480	8,500	34,000	16,500
1914D	448,000	175	220	230	300	2,650	40,000	23,000
1915	606,100	175	220	230	275	1,650	13,500	15,250
1925D	578,000	175	220	230	275	1,450	7,000	—
1926	446,000	175	220	230	275	1,450	7,000	—
1927	388,000	175	220	230	275	1,450	7,000	—
1928	416,000	175	220	230	275	1,450	7,000	—
1929	532,000	180	230	250	340	1,600	10,000	—

$5 (HALF EAGLE)

Coronet Head

KM# 101 0.9000 **GOLD** 0.242 oz. AGW. 21.6 mm. 8.3590 g. **Designer:** Christian Gobrecht **Notes:** The 1873 "closed-3" and "open-3" varieties are known and are distinguished by the amount of space between the upper left and lower left serifs of the 3 in the date.

Date	Mintage	VF-20	XF-40	AU-50	MS-60	MS-63	MS-65	Prf-65
1901	616,040	215	220	225	235	750	3,650	27,000
1901S	3,648,000	215	220	225	235	730	3,600	—
1902	172,562	215	220	225	235	730	4,400	27,000
1902S	939,000	215	220	225	235	730	3,600	—
1903	227,024	215	220	225	235	730	4,000	27,000
1903S	1,855,000	215	220	225	235	730	3,600	—
1904	392,136	215	220	225	235	730	3,600	27,000
1904S	97,000	215	240	285	900	3,850	9,600	—
1905	302,308	215	220	225	235	740	4,000	27,000
1905S	880,700	215	225	250	235	1,500	9,600	—
1906	348,820	215	220	225	235	745	3,600	26,000
1906D	320,000	215	220	225	235	930	3,200	—
1906S	598,000	215	220	230	240	900	4,400	—
1907	626,192	215	220	225	235	730	3,400	23,000
1907D	888,000	215	220	225	235	730	3,400	—
1908	421,874	215	220	225	235	730	3,400	—

Indian Head

KM# 129 0.9000 **GOLD** .2420 oz. AGW. 21.6 mm. 8.3590 g. **Designer:** Bela Lyon Pratt

Date	Mintage	VF-20	XF-40	AU-50	MS-60	MS-63	MS-65	Prf-65
1908	578,012	330	355	385	460	4,350	25,000	25,500
1908D	148,000	330	355	385	460	4,350	27,500	—
1908S	82,000	330	415	430	1,275	4,350	24,000	—
1909	627,138	330	355	385	460	4,350	25,000	36,000
1909D	3,423,560	330	355	385	460	4,350	25,000	—
1909O	34,200	2,000	3,400	6,000	21,000	66,000	260,000	—
1909S	297,200	330	355	385	1,400	11,000	45,000	—
1910	604,250	330	355	385	460	4,350	25,000	37,000
1910D	193,600	330	355	385	460	4,350	42,500	—
1910S	770,200	330	355	385	1,000	6,000	44,000	—
1911	915,139	330	355	385	460	4,350	25,000	28,500
1911D	72,500	475	535	515	4,500	37,000	241,500	—
1911S	1,416,000	340	355	385	560	4,350	41,500	—
1912	790,144	330	355	385	460	4,350	25,000	28,500
1912S	392,000	330	365	400	1,700	13,500	93,500	—
1913	916,099	330	355	385	460	4,350	25,000	28,000
1913S	408,000	340	350	385	1,400	11,500	120,000	—
1914	247,125	330	355	385	460	4,350	25,000	28,500
1914D	247,000	335	355	385	460	4,350	26,000	—
1914S	263,000	340	365	400	1,375	13,500	100,000	—
1915	588,075	330	355	385	460	4,350	25,000	39,000

Date	Mintage	VF-20	XF-40	AU-50	MS-60	MS-63	MS-65	Prf-65
1915S	164,000	340	400	385	2,000	17,000	110,000	—
1916S	240,000	330	355	385	560	4,350	25,000	—
1929	662,000	4,200	9,600	10,500	13,250	17,500	45,000	—

$10 (EAGLE)

Coronet Head

KM# 102 0.9000 **GOLD** 0.4839 oz. AGW. 27 mm. 16.7180 g. **Designer:** Christian Gobrecht **Notes:** The 1873 "closed-3" and "open-3" varieties are distinguished by the amount of space between the upper left and lower left serifs of the 3 in the date.

Date	Mintage	VF-20	XF-40	AU-50	MS-60	MS-63	MS-65	Prf-65
1901	1,718,825	420	425	450	465	1,400	22,000	30,500
1901O	72,041	420	425	450	465	3,700	—	—
1901S	2,812,750	420	425	450	465	1,400	22,000	—
1902	82,513	420	425	450	465	2,450	—	30,500
1902S	469,500	420	425	450	465	1,400	22,000	—
1903	125,926	420	425	450	465	2,500	—	30,000
1903O	112,771	420	425	450	465	3,250	—	—
1903S	538,000	420	425	450	465	1,400	22,000	—
1904	162,038	420	425	450	465	2,400	—	31,500
1904O	108,950	420	425	450	465	3,700	—	—
1905	201,078	420	425	450	465	1,450	22,000	30,000
1905S	369,250	420	425	450	1,100	4,500	—	—
1906	165,497	420	425	450	465	2,275	22,000	30,000
1906D	981,000	420	425	450	465	1,450	22,000	—
1906O	86,895	420	425	450	470	3,400	—	—
1906S	457,000	420	425	450	515	4,400	22,000	—
1907	1,203,973	420	425	450	465	1,400	—	30,000
1907D	1,030,000	420	425	450	465	1,400	—	—
1907S	210,500	420	425	450	600	4,650	—	—

Indian Head

No motto next to eagle

KM# 125 0.9000 **GOLD** 0.4839 oz. AGW. 27 mm. 16.7180 g. **Designer:** Augustus Saint-Gaudens **Notes:** 1907 varieties are distinguished by whether the edge is rolled or wired, and whether the legend "E Pluribus Unum" has periods between each word.

Date	Mintage	VF-20	XF-40	AU-50	MS-60	MS-63	MS-65	Prf-65
1907 wire edge, periods before and after legend	500	9,500	14,900	16,900	22,000	36,500	65,000	—
1907 same, without stars on edge, unique	—	—	—	—	—	—	—	—
1907 rolled edge, periods	42	26,000	38,500	49,000	66,500	98,500	250,000	—
1907 without periods	239,406	470	480	530	625	2,950	9,800	—
1908 without motto	33,500	470	480	530	735	4,650	14,500	—
1908D without motto	210,000	475	485	535	635	6,250	38,500	—

"In God We Trust" left of eagle

KM# 130 0.9000 **GOLD** 0.4839 oz. AGW. 27 mm. 16.7180 g. **Designer:** Augustus Saint-Gaudens

Date	Mintage	VF-20	XF-40	AU-50	MS-60	MS-63	MS-65	Prf-65
1908	341,486	470	480	530	595	4,450	14,500	52,500
1908D	836,500	475	485	540	625	6,850	29,000	—
1908S	59,850	485	495	620	2,950	8,500	25,500	—
1909	184,863	470	480	530	595	2,450	10,000	54,500
1909D	121,540	475	485	535	675	4,150	34,500	—

Date	Mintage	VF-20	XF-40	AU-50	MS-60	MS-63	MS-65	Prf-65
1909S	292,350	475	485	535	675	4,350	13,900	—
1910	318,704	470	480	530	595	2,350	8,500	54,500
1910D	2,356,640	465	475	525	595	2,185	8,600	—
1910S	811,000	475	485	535	675	7,250	55,000	—
1911	505,595	465	475	525	590	2,185	8,600	52,500
1911D	30,100	595	675	950	4,200	21,500	120,000	—
1911S	51,000	530	555	645	1,050	7,750	14,500	—
1912	405,083	470	480	530	595	2,350	9,350	52,500
1912S	300,000	475	485	535	675	5,300	48,500	—
1913	442,071	470	480	530	595	2,350	8,400	52,500
1913S	66,000	525	600	775	3,900	27,500	100,000	—
1914	151,050	470	480	530	595	2,400	9,000	52,500
1914D	343,500	470	480	530	595	2,450	15,500	—
1914S	208,000	480	490	540	715	6,350	32,500	—
1915	351,075	470	480	530	595	2,350	8,500	55,000
1915S	59,000	600	725	775	3,150	14,500	65,000	—
1916S	138,500	495	510	570	675	4,850	18,500	—
1920S	126,500	7,800	11,000	14,500	28,500	69,000	275,000	—
1926	1,014,000	465	475	525	575	1,485	5,500	—
1930S	96,000	5,500	7,000	8,500	14,500	31,500	67,500	—
1932	4,463,000	465	475	525	575	1,485	5,500	—
1933	312,500	110,000	140,000	150,000	185,000	245,000	650,000	—

$20 (DOUBLE EAGLE)

Liberty

KM# 74.3 0.9000 **GOLD** 0.9677 oz. AGW. 33.4360 g.

Date	Mintage	VF-20	XF-40	AU-50	MS-60	MS-63	MS-65	Prf-65
1901	111,526	825	830	840	850	1,000	6,500	—
1901S	1,596,000	825	830	840	850	3,850	—	—
1902	31,254	825	830	840	850	10,000	—	—
1902S	1,753,625	825	830	840	850	4,000	—	—
1903	287,428	825	830	840	850	1,000	6,000	51,500
1903S	954,000	825	830	840	850	1,800	12,000	—
1904	6,256,797	825	830	840	850	1,000	5,000	50,000
1904S	5,134,175	825	830	840	850	1,000	6,600	—
1905	59,011	825	830	840	850	15,000	—	—
1905S	1,813,000	825	830	840	850	3,850	16,500	—
1906	69,690	825	830	840	850	6,600	15,000	52,500
1906D	620,250	825	830	840	850	2,350	15,000	—
1906S	2,065,750	825	830	840	850	2,300	19,000	—
1907	1,451,864	825	830	840	850	1,000	7,500	—
1907D	842,250	825	830	840	850	2,350	7,000	—
1907S	2,165,800	825	830	840	850	2,400	17,000	—

Saint-Gaudens

Roman numerals in date No motto below eagle

KM# 126 0.9000 **GOLD** 0.9677 oz. AGW. 34 mm. 33.4360 g. **Designer:** Augustus Saint-Gaudens

Date	Mintage	VF-20	XF-40	AU-50	MS-60	MS-63	MS-65	Prf-65
MCMVII (1907) high relief, unique, AU-55, $150,000	—	—	—	—	—	—	—	—
MCMVII (1907) high relief, wire rim	11,250	7,000	9,750	11,000	13,500	23,500	49,500	—
MCMVII (1907) high relief, flat rim	Inc. above	7,250	10,250	11,500	15,000	27,650	55,000	—

Arabic numerals in date No motto below eagle

KM# 127 0.9000 **GOLD** 0.9677 oz. AGW. 34 mm. 33.4360 g. **Designer:** Augustus Saint-Gaudens

Date	Mintage	VF-20	XF-40	AU-50	MS-60	MS-63	MS-65	Prf-65
1907 large letters on edge, unique	—	—	—	—	—	—	—	—
1907 small letters on edge	361,667	670	685	730	805	935	3,350	—
1908	4,271,551	660	675	710	765	825	1,400	—
1908D	663,750	670	685	720	790	935	9,000	—

"In God We Trust" below eagle

KM# 131 0.9000 **GOLD** 0.9677 oz. AGW. 34 mm. 33.4360 g. **Designer:** Augustus Saint-Gaudens

Date	Mintage	VF-20	XF-40	AU-50	MS-60	MS-63	MS-65	Prf-65
1908	156,359	665	680	720	815	1,750	21,500	49,500
1908 Roman finish; Prf64 Rare	—	—	—	—	—	—	—	—
1908D	349,500	670	685	730	805	955	5,350	—
1908S	22,000	1,450	2,000	4,350	8,250	20,000	43,000	—
1909/8	161,282	670	685	770	1,375	5,400	32,500	—
1909	Inc. above	680	705	740	865	3,350	42,500	49,000
1909D	52,500	710	725	865	1,950	8,250	37,500	—
1909S	2,774,925	670	685	730	785	910	5,250	—
1910	482,167	665	680	720	815	925	7,350	49,000
1910D	429,000	665	680	720	790	895	2,600	—
1910S	2,128,250	670	685	735	795	960	8,000	—
1911	197,350	670	685	740	805	1,875	15,500	39,500
1911D	846,500	665	680	720	790	895	1,500	—
1911S	775,750	665	680	720	795	895	6,200	—
1912	149,824	670	685	735	830	1,675	19,500	44,000
1913	168,838	670	685	735	835	2,850	33,000	44,000
1913D	393,500	665	680	720	790	935	6,500	—
1913S	34,000	720	735	770	1,450	4,200	42,500	—
1914	95,320	680	695	770	1,275	3,900	25,000	41,500
1914D	453,000	665	680	720	790	905	3,250	—
1914S	1,498,000	665	680	720	790	895	2,000	—
1915	152,050	670	685	730	795	2,150	28,500	47,500
1915S	567,500	665	680	720	790	895	2,000	—
1916S	796,000	670	685	730	830	925	2,450	—
1920	228,250	660	675	710	790	955	62,500	—
1920S	558,000	12,500	14,500	22,500	41,500	88,000	210,000	—
1921	528,500	13,500	24,800	35,000	100,000	240,000	950,000	—
1922	1,375,500	660	675	710	765	845	2,450	—
1922S	2,658,000	835	925	1,250	2,150	4,200	39,500	—
1923	566,000	660	675	710	765	845	4,650	—
1923D	1,702,250	670	685	720	775	845	1,500	—
1924	4,323,500	660	675	710	765	825	1,400	—
1924D	3,049,500	950	1,500	1,800	2,950	8,250	75,000	—
1924S	2,927,500	935	1,550	1,850	3,000	8,000	44,500	—
1925	2,831,750	660	675	710	765	825	1,400	—
1925D	2,938,500	1,550	2,100	2,375	4,450	11,500	96,000	—
1925S	3,776,500	1,350	1,950	3,450	9,000	26,500	90,000	—
1926	816,750	660	675	710	765	825	1,400	—
1926D	481,000	7,500	11,000	13,500	26,500	41,500	115,000	—
1926S	2,041,500	1,050	1,550	1,725	2,600	4,950	35,000	—
1927	2,946,750	660	675	710	765	825	1,400	—
1927D	180,000	155,000	220,000	265,000	340,000	1,500,000	2,100,000	—
1927S	3,107,000	5,000	7,850	12,750	26,500	57,500	130,000	—
1928	8,816,000	660	675	710	765	825	1,400	—
1929	1,779,750	5,750	9,000	12,500	18,500	39,500	105,000	—
1930S	74,000	15,500	26,500	30,000	39,000	125,000	235,000	—
1931	2,938,250	9,800	14,500	18,850	30,000	68,500	110,000	—
1931D	106,500	9,000	11,850	21,500	32,500	95,000	130,000	—
1932	1,101,750	8,000	14,500	16,000	25,000	72,500	110,000	—
1933	445,500	—	—	—	—	—	9,000,000	—

Note: Sotheby/Stack's Sale, July 2002. Eleven known, only one currently available.

COMMEMORATIVE COINAGE

1901-1954

All commemorative half dollars of 1892-1954 have the following specifications: diameter -- 30.6 millimeters; weight -- 12.5000 grams; composition -- 0.9000 silver, 0.3617 ounces actual silver weight. Values for PDS sets contain one example each from the Philadelphia, Denver and San Francisco mints. Type coin prices are the most inexpensive single coin available from the date and mint-mark combinations listed.

HALF DOLLAR

PANAMA-PACIFIC EXPOSITION. KM# 135 Designer: Charles E. Barber.

Date	Mintage	AU-50	MS-60	MS-63	MS-64	MS-65
1915S	27,134	465	550	825	1,550	2,650

LINCOLN-ILLINOIS. KM# 143 Obv. Designer: George T. Morgan **Rev. Designer:** John R. Sinnock

Date	Mintage	AU-50	MS-60	MS-63	MS-64	MS-65
1918	100,058	135	155	170	250	525

MAINE CENTENNIAL. KM# 146 Designer: Anthony de Francisci.

Date	Mintage	AU-50	MS-60	MS-63	MS-64	MS-65
1920	50,028	135	165	195	310	585

PILGRIM TERCENTENARY. KM# 147.1 Designer: Cyrus E. Dallin.

Date	Mintage	AU-50	MS-60	MS-63	MS-64	MS-65
1920	152,112	85.00	110	122	160	465

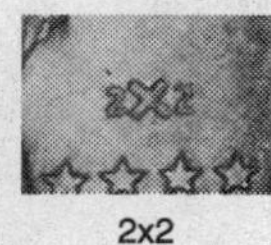

2x2

ALABAMA CENTENNIAL. KM# 148.1 Designer: Laura G. Fraser. **Obverse:** "2x2" at right above stars **Notes:** "Fake 2x2" counterstamps exist.

Date	Mintage	AU-50	MS-60	MS-63	MS-64	MS-65
1921	6,006	315	330	600	950	1,975

ALABAMA CENTENNIAL. KM# 148.2 Obv. Designer: Laura G. Fraser

Date	Mintage	AU-50	MS-60	MS-63	MS-64	MS-65
1921	59,038	190	215	525	685	1,800

MISSOURI CENTENNIAL. KM# 149.1 Designer: Robert Aitken.

Date	Mintage	AU-50	MS-60	MS-63	MS-64	MS-65
1921	15,428	410	725	925	1,775	5,000

2★4

MISSOURI CENTENNIAL. KM# 149.2 Designer: Robert Aitken. **Obverse:** 2 star 4 in field at left **Notes:** "Fake "2*4" counterstamps exist.

Date	Mintage	AU-50	MS-60	MS-63	MS-64	MS-65
1921	5,000	650	800	1,100	1,900	5,000

PILGRIM TERCENTENARY. KM# 147.2 Designer: Cyrus E. Dallin. **Obverse:** 1921 date next to Pilgrim

Date	Mintage	AU-50	MS-60	MS-63	MS-64	MS-65
1921	20,053	175	200	225	285	600

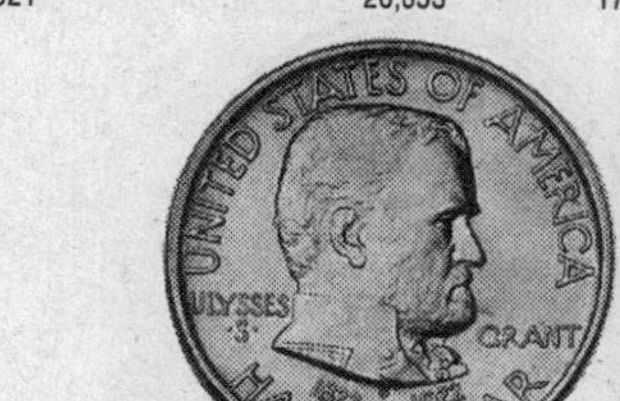

GRANT MEMORIAL. KM# 151.1 Designer: Laura G. Fraser.

Date	Mintage	AU-50	MS-60	MS-63	MS-64	MS-65
1922	67,405	115	125	160	290	800

GRANT MEMORIAL. KM# 151.2 Designer: Laura G. Fraser. **Obverse:** Star above the word "Grant" **Notes:** "Fake star" counterstamps exist.

Date	Mintage	AU-50	MS-60	MS-63	MS-64	MS-65
1922	4,256	950	1,300	2,100	2,850	7,250

MONROE DOCTRINE CENTENNIAL. **KM# 153** **Designer:** Chester Beach.

Date	Mintage	AU-50	MS-60	MS-63	MS-64	MS-65
1923S	274,077	58.00	75.00	145	525	2,950

HUGUENOT-WALLOON TERCENTENARY. **KM# 154** **Designer:** George T. Morgan. **Obverse:** Huguenot leader Gaspard de Coligny and William I of Orange

Date	Mintage	AU-50	MS-60	MS-63	MS-64	MS-65
1924	142,080	135	155	175	250	550

CALIFORNIA DIAMOND JUBILEE. **KM# 155** **Designer:** Jo Mora.

Date	Mintage	AU-50	MS-60	MS-63	MS-64	MS-65
1925S	86,594	215	240	280	520	1,125

FORT VANCOUVER CENTENNIAL. **KM# 158** **Designer:** Laura G. Fraser.

Date	Mintage	AU-50	MS-60	MS-63	MS-64	MS-65
1925	14,994	335	415	475	600	1,450

LEXINGTON-CONCORD SESQUICENTENNIAL. **KM# 156** **Designer:** Chester Beach.

Date	Mintage	AU-50	MS-60	MS-63	MS-64	MS-65
1925	162,013	96.00	110	120	185	485

STONE MOUNTAIN MEMORIAL. **KM# 157.1** **Designer:** Gutzon Borglum.

Date	Mintage	AU-50	MS-60	MS-63	MS-64	MS-65
1925	1,314,709	70.00	77.00	85.00	90.00	285

OREGON TRAIL MEMORIAL. **KM# 159** **Designer:** James E. and Laura G. Fraser.

Date	Mintage	AU-50	MS-60	MS-63	MS-64	MS-65
1926	47,955	140	170	190	210	335
1926S	83,055	140	170	185	205	335
1928	6,028	220	245	280	290	390
1933D	5,008	375	400	410	420	540
1934D	7,006	205	220	230	240	365
1936	10,006	150	190	200	210	325
1936S	5,006	170	190	210	220	360
1937D	12,008	180	205	210	215	325
1938	6,006	160	175	210	215	335
1938D	6,005	160	175	215	235	335
1938S	6,006	160	175	210	220	335
1939	3,004	525	620	630	655	720
1939D	3,004	525	620	640	675	735
1939S	3,005	525	620	630	655	725

U.S. SESQUICENTENNIAL. **KM# 160** **Designer:** John R. Sinnock.

Date	Mintage	AU-50	MS-60	MS-63	MS-64	MS-65
1926	141,120	88.00	115	150	600	4,400

VERMONT SESQUICENTENNIAL. **KM# 162** **Obv. Designer:** Charles Keck

Date	Mintage	AU-50	MS-60	MS-63	MS-64	MS-65
1927	28,142	255	290	305	350	990

HAWAIIAN SESQUICENTENNIAL. **KM# 163** **Designer:** Juliette M. Fraser. **Notes:** Counterfeits exist.

Date	Mintage	AU-50	MS-60	MS-63	MS-64	MS-65
1928	10,008	1,750	2,650	3,500	4,500	6,850

DANIEL BOONE BICENTENNIAL. **KM# 165.1** **Designer:** Augustus Lukeman.

Date	Mintage	AU-50	MS-60	MS-63	MS-64	MS-65
1934	10,007	125	135	140	150	275
1935 PDS set	10,010	120	135	140	150	275
1935D	5,005	375	415	430	485	860
1935S	5,005	375	415	430	450	890

DANIEL BOONE BICENTENNIAL. KM# 165.2 Designer: Augustus Lukeman. **Reverse:** "1934" added above the word "Pioneer."

Date	Mintage	AU-50	MS-60	MS-63	MS-64	MS-65
1935	10,008	400	415	440	460	735
Type coin	—	130	135	145	150	240
1935D	2,003	—	—	—	—	—
1935S	2,004	—	—	—	—	—
1936	12,012	400	415	440	460	735
1936D	5,005	—	—	—	—	—
1936S	5,006	—	—	—	—	—
1937	9,810	860	965	975	980	1,400
1937D	2,506	—	—	—	—	—
1937S	2,506	—	—	—	—	—
1938	2,100	1,150	1,250	1,275	1,290	1,825
1938D	2,100	—	—	—	—	—
1938S	2,100	—	—	—	—	—

MARYLAND TERCENTENARY. KM# 166 Designer: Hans Schuler.

Date	Mintage	AU-50	MS-60	MS-63	MS-64	MS-65
1934	25,015	168	185	195	220	400

TEXAS CENTENNIAL. KM# 167 Designer: Pompeo Coppini.

Date	Mintage	AU-50	MS-60	MS-63	MS-64	MS-65
1934	61,463	145	158	163	165	260
Type coin	—	145	158	163	165	260
1935 PDS set	9,994	435	475	495	500	790
1936 PDS set	8,911	435	475	495	500	790
1937 PDS set	6,571	435	475	495	500	790
1938 PDS set	3,775	750	840	960	960	1,575

ARKANSAS CENTENNIAL. KM# 168 Designer: Edward E. Burr.

Date	Mintage	AU-50	MS-60	MS-63	MS-64	MS-65
Type coin	—	110	115	125	130	210
1935 PDS set	5,505	335	350	380	405	825
1936 PDS set	9,600	335	350	380	405	850
1937 PDS set	5,505	335	350	380	415	1,050
1938 PDS set	3,155	510	590	610	625	2,000
1939 PDS set	—	1,000	1,200	1,300	1,315	3,500

CONNECTICUT TERCENTENARY. KM# 169 Designer: Henry Kreiss.

Date	Mintage	AU-50	MS-60	MS-63	MS-64	MS-65
1935	25,018	260	305	315	385	645

HUDSON, N.Y., SESQUICENTENNIAL. KM# 170 Designer: Chester Beach.

Date	Mintage	AU-50	MS-60	MS-63	MS-64	MS-65
1935	10,008	770	960	1,200	1,550	2,200

OLD SPANISH TRAIL. KM# 172 Designer: L.W. Hoffecker.

Date	Mintage	AU-50	MS-60	MS-63	MS-64	MS-65
1935	10,008	1,250	1,400	1,550	1,600	2,000

SAN DIEGO, CALIFORNIA - PACIFIC EXPOSITION. KM# 171 Designer: Robert Aitken.

Date	Mintage	AU-50	MS-60	MS-63	MS-64	MS-65
1935S	70,132	105	140	150	153	180
1936D	30,092	105	150	155	160	185

ALBANY, N.Y., CHARTER ANNIVERSARY. KM# 173 Designer: Gertrude K. Lathrop.

Date	Mintage	AU-50	MS-60	MS-63	MS-64	MS-65
1936	17,671	340	350	380	375	430

ARKANSAS CENTENNIAL. KM# 187 Obv. Designer: Henry Kreiss **Rev. Designer:** Edward E. Burr **Obverse:** Sen. Joseph T. Robinson

Date	Mintage	AU-50	MS-60	MS-63	MS-64	MS-65
1936	25,265	155	165	175	178	450

BATTLE OF GETTYSBURG 75TH ANNIVERSARY. KM# 181 Designer: Frank Vittor.

Date	Mintage	AU-50	MS-60	MS-63	MS-64	MS-65
1936	26,928	435	475	505	525	775

BRIDGEPORT, CONN., CENTENNIAL. KM# 175 Designer: Henry Kreiss.

Date	Mintage	AU-50	MS-60	MS-63	MS-64	MS-65
1936	25,015	180	185	210	220	315

CINCINNATI MUSIC CENTER. KM# 176 Designer: Constance Ortmayer.

Date	Mintage	AU-50	MS-60	MS-63	MS-64	MS-65
Type coin	—	335	345	375	560	700
1936 PDS set	5,005	1,000	1,025	1,125	1,700	2,850

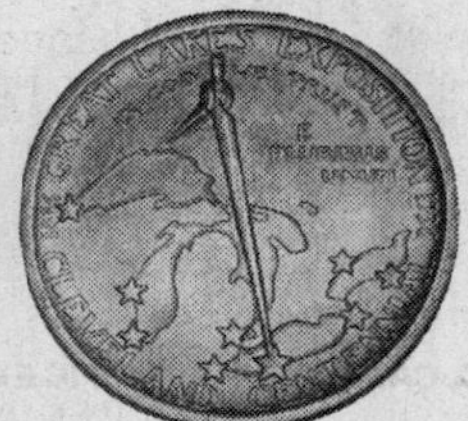

CLEVELAND-GREAT LAKES EXPOSITION. KM# 177 Designer: Brenda Putnam.

Date	Mintage	AU-50	MS-60	MS-63	MS-64	MS-65
1936	50,030	143	145	160	165	268

COLUMBIA, S.C., SESQUICENTENNIAL. KM# 178 Designer: A. Wolfe Davidson.

Date	Mintage	AU-50	MS-60	MS-63	MS-64	MS-65
1936 PDS set	9,007	785	800	880	900	920
Type coin	—	280	290	330	335	385

DELAWARE TERCENTENARY. KM# 179 Designer: Carl L. Schmitz.

Date	Mintage	AU-50	MS-60	MS-63	MS-64	MS-65
1936	20,993	340	360	385	395	500

ELGIN, ILL., CENTENNIAL. KM# 180 Designer: Trygve Rovelstad.

Date	Mintage	AU-50	MS-60	MS-63	MS-64	MS-65
1936	20,015	245	275	290	300	340

LONG ISLAND TERCENTENARY. KM# 182 Designer: Howard K. Weinman.

Date	Mintage	AU-50	MS-60	MS-63	MS-64	MS-65
1936	81,826	96.00	103	115	125	450

LYNCHBURG, VA., SESQUICENTENNIAL. KM# 183 Designer: Charles Keck.

Date	Mintage	AU-50	MS-60	MS-63	MS-64	MS-65
1936	20,013	255	285	295	298	375

NORFOLK, VA., BICENTENNIAL. KM# 184 Designer: William M. and Marjorie E. Simpson.

Date	Mintage	AU-50	MS-60	MS-63	MS-64	MS-65
1936	16,936	555	575	615	625	650

RHODE ISLAND TERCENTENARY. KM# 185 Designer: Arthur G. Carey and John H. Benson.

Date	Mintage	AU-50	MS-60	MS-63	MS-64	MS-65
1936 PDS set	15,010	320	335	375	385	870
Type coin	—	105	110	125	128	290

SAN FRANCISCO-OAKLAND BAY BRIDGE. KM# 174 Designer: Jacques Schnier.

Date	Mintage	AU-50	MS-60	MS-63	MS-64	MS-65
1936	71,424	180	185	220	225	360

WISCONSIN TERRITORIAL CENTENNIAL. KM# 188 Designer: David Parsons.

Date	Mintage	AU-50	MS-60	MS-63	MS-64	MS-65
1936	25,015	250	270	295	325	420

YORK COUNTY, MAINE, TERCENTENARY. KM# 189 Designer: Walter H. Rich.

Date	Mintage	AU-50	MS-60	MS-63	MS-64	MS-65
1936	25,015	235	250	270	280	350

BATTLE OF ANTIETAM 75TH ANNIVERSARY. KM# 190 Designer: William M. Simpson.

Date	Mintage	AU-50	MS-60	MS-63	MS-64	MS-65
1937	18,028	750	775	800	830	940

ROANOKE ISLAND, N.C.. KM# 186 Designer: William M. Simpson.

Date	Mintage	AU-50	MS-60	MS-63	MS-64	MS-65
1937	29,030	265	310	325	330	375

NEW ROCHELLE, N.Y.. KM# 191 Designer: Gertrude K. Lathrop.

Date	Mintage	AU-50	MS-60	MS-63	MS-64	MS-65
1938	15,266	430	450	470	475	585

BOOKER T. WASHINGTON. KM# 198 Designer: Isaac S. Hathaway.

Date	Mintage	AU-50	MS-60	MS-63	MS-64	MS-65
1946 PDS set	200,113	45.00	50.00	70.00	75.00	160
Type coin	—	15.00	16.00	17.50	18.50	56.00
1947 PDS set	100,017	52.50	75.00	85.00	120	300
1948 PDS set	8,005	85.00	150	160	165	225
1949 PDS set	6,004	160	230	245	250	355
1950 PDS set	6,004	75.00	135	140	150	250
1951 PDS set	7,004	84.00	115	155	160	225

IOWA STATEHOOD CENTENNIAL. KM# 197 Designer: Adam Pietz.

Date	Mintage	AU-50	MS-60	MS-63	MS-64	MS-65
1946	100,057	115	125	134	135	240

BOOKER T. WASHINGTON AND GEORGE WASHINGTON CARVER. KM# 200 Designer: Isaac S. Hathaway.

Date	Mintage	AU-50	MS-60	MS-63	MS-64	MS-65
1951 PDS set	10,004	70.00	85.00	105	125	585
Type coin	—	14.00	16.00	18.50	20.00	52.50
1952 PDS set	8,006	58.50	82.50	110	135	600
1953 PDS set	8,003	58.50	82.50	110	135	600
1954 PDS set	12,006	55.00	80.00	105	125	445

DOLLAR

LOUISIANA PURCHASE EXPOSITION. KM# 120 0.9000 Gold 0.0484 oz. AGW. 15 mm. 1.6720 g. **Obverse:** William McKinley **Obv. Designer:** Charles E. Barber

Date	Mintage	AU-50	MS-60	MS-63	MS-64	MS-65
1903	17,500	730	780	975	2,450	3,600

LOUISIANA PURCHASE EXPOSITION. KM# 119 0.9000 Gold 0.0484 oz. AGW. 15 mm. 1.6720 g. **Obverse:** Jefferson **Designer:** Charles E. Barber

Date	Mintage	AU-50	MS-60	MS-63	MS-64	MS-65
1903	17,500	725	780	1,100	2,600	3,800

LEWIS AND CLARK EXPOSITION. KM# 121 0.9000 Gold 0.7736 oz, AGW. 15 mm. 1.6720 g. **Obv. Designer:** Charles E. Barber

Date	Mintage	AU-50	MS-60	MS-63	MS-64	MS-65
1904	10,025	1,075	1,125	2,300	6,400	12,250
1905	10,041	1,300	1,550	2,800	8,000	18,500

PANAMA-PACIFIC EXPOSITION. KM# 136 0.9000 Gold 0.0484 oz. AGW. 15 mm. 1.6720 g. **Obv. Designer:** Charles Keck

Date	Mintage	AU-50	MS-60	MS-63	MS-64	MS-65
1915S	15,000	675	770	950	1,600	3,000

MCKINLEY MEMORIAL. KM# 144 0.9000 Gold 0.0484 oz. AGW. 15 mm. 1.6720 g. **Obv. Designer:** Charles E. Barber **Rev. Designer:** George T. Morgan

Date	Mintage	AU-50	MS-60	MS-63	MS-64	MS-65
1916	9,977	650	705	850	1,550	3,000
1917	10,000	800	850	1,200	2,700	4,250

GRANT MEMORIAL. KM# 152.1 0.9000 Gold 0.0484 oz. AGW. 15 mm. 1.6720 g. **Obv. Designer:** Laura G. Fraser **Notes:** Without an incuse "star" above the word GRANT on the obverse.

Date	Mintage	AU-50	MS-60	MS-63	MS-64	MS-65
1922	5,016	1,800	1,900	2,400	4,200	5,000

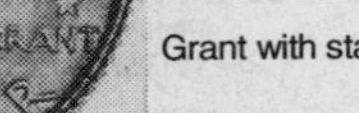

Grant with star

GRANT MEMORIAL. KM# 152.2 0.9000 Gold 0.0484 oz. AGW. 15 mm. 1.6720 g. **Obv. Designer:** Laura G. Fraser **Notes:** Variety with an incuse "star" above the word GRANT on the obverse.

Date	Mintage	AU-50	MS-60	MS-63	MS-64	MS-65
1922	5,000	1,900	2,000	2,300	3,500	4,250

$2.50 (QUARTER EAGLE)

PANAMA-PACIFIC EXPOSITION. KM# 137 0.9000 Gold 0.121 oz. AGW. 18 mm. 4.1800 g. **Obv. Designer:** Charles E. Barber **Rev. Designer:** George T. Morgan

Date	Mintage	AU-50	MS-60	MS-63	MS-64	MS-65
1915S	6,749	1,750	2,100	4,200	6,300	8,000

PHILADELPHIA SESQUICENTENNIAL. KM# 161 0.9000 Gold 0.121 oz. AGW. 18 mm. 4.1800 g. **Obv. Designer:** John R. Sinnock

Date	Mintage	AU-50	MS-60	MS-63	MS-64	MS-65
1926	46,019	585	600	900	1,600	4,850

$50

PANAMA-PACIFIC EXPOSITION. KM# 138 0.9000 Gold 2.419 oz. AGW. 44 mm. 83.5900 g. **Obv. Designer:** Robert Aitken

Date	Mintage	AU-50	MS-60	MS-63	MS-64	MS-65
1915S	483	41,500	52,500	78,000	95,000	155,000

PANAMA-PACIFIC EXPOSITION. KM# 139 0.9000 Gold 2.419 oz. AGW. 44 mm. 83.5900 g. **Obv. Designer:** Robert Aitken

Date	Mintage	AU-50	MS-60	MS-63	MS-64	MS-65
1915S	645	39,500	50,000	69,000	90,000	140,000

COMMEMORATIVE COINAGE 1982-2000

All commemorative silver dollar coins of 1982-present have the following specifications: diameter -- 38.1 millimeters; weight -- 26.7300 grams; composition -- 0.9000 silver, 0.7736 ounces actual silver weight. All commemorative $5 coins of 1982-present have the following specificiations: diameter -- 21.6 millimeters; weight -- 8.3590 grams; composition: 0.9000 gold, 0.242 ounces actual gold weight.

Note: In 1982, after a hiatus of nearly 20 years, coinage of commemorative half dollars resumed. Those designated with a 'W' were struck at the West Point Mint. Some issues were struck in copper--nickel. Those struck in silver have the same size, weight and composition as the prior commemorative half--dollar series.

HALF DOLLAR

GEORGE WASHINGTON, 250TH BIRTH ANNIVERSARY. KM# 208 0.9000 Silver 0.3618 oz. ASW. 30.6 mm. 12.5000 g. **Obv. Designer:** Elizabeth Jones

Date	Mintage	Proof	MS-65	Prf-65
1982D	2,210,458	—	6.50	—
1982S	—	(4,894,044)	—	6.50

STATUE OF LIBERTY CENTENNIAL. KM# 212 Copper-Nickel Clad Copper 11.3400 g. **Obv. Designer:** Edgar Z. Steever **Rev. Designer:** Sherl Joseph Winter

Date	Mintage	Proof	MS-65	Prf-65
1986D	928,008	—	5.50	—
1986S	—	(6,925,627)	—	5.50

BICENTENNIAL OF THE CONGRESS. KM# 224 Copper-Nickel Clad Copper 11.3400 g. **Obv. Designer:** Patricia L. Verani **Rev. Designer:** William Woodward and Edgar Z. Steever

Date	Mintage	Proof	MS-65	Prf-65
1989D	163,753	—	8.00	—
1989S	—	—	—	8.00

MOUNT RUSHMORE 50TH ANNIVERSARY. KM# 228 Copper-Nickel Clad Copper 11.3400 g. **Obv. Designer:** Marcel Jovine **Rev. Designer:** T. James Ferrell

Date	Mintage	Proof	MS-65	Prf-65
1991D	172,754	—	21.50	—
1991S	—	—	—	20.00

1992 OLYMPICS. KM# 233 Copper-Nickel Clad Copper 11.3400 g. **Obv. Designer:** William Cousins **Rev. Designer:** Steven M. Bieda

Date	Mintage	Proof	MS-65	Prf-65
1992P	161,607	—	8.50	—
1992S	—	(519,645)	—	8.50

500TH ANNIVERSARY OF COLUMBUS DISCOVERY. KM# 237 Copper-Nickel Clad Copper 11.3400 g. **Designer:** T. James Ferrell

Date	Mintage	Proof	MS-65	Prf-65
1992D	135,702	—	11.50	—
1992S	—	(390,154)	—	11.50

JAMES MADISON AND BILL OF RIGHTS. KM# 240 0.9000 Silver 0.3618 oz. ASW. 12.5000 g. **Obv. Designer:** T. James Ferrell **Rev. Designer:** Dean McMullen

Date	Mintage	Proof	MS-65	Prf-65
1993W	173,224	—	20.00	—
1993S	—	(559,758)	—	16.50

WORLD WAR II 50TH ANNIVERSARY. KM# 243 Copper-Nickel Clad Copper 11.3400 g. **Obv. Designer:** George Klauba **Rev. Designer:** William J. Leftwich

Date	Mintage	Proof	MS-65	Prf-65
(1993)P	192,968	—	29.00	—
(1993)P	—	(290,343)	—	26.50

1994 WORLD CUP SOCCER. KM# 246 Copper-Nickel Clad Copper 11.3400 g. **Obv. Designer:** Richard T. LaRoche **Rev. Designer:** Dean McMullen

Date	Mintage	Proof	MS-65	Prf-65
1994D	168,208	—	9.75	—
1994P	122,412	—	10.25	—
1994P	—	(609,354)	—	8.50

ATLANTA OLYMPICS. KM# 257 Copper-Nickel Clad Copper 11.3400 g. **Obverse:** Basketball

Date	Mintage	Proof	MS-65	Prf-65
1995S	—	(169,655)	—	18.00
1995S	171,001	—	22.50	—

ATLANTA OLYMPICS. KM# 262 Copper-Nickel Clad Copper 11.3400 g. **Obverse:** Baseball **Obv. Designer:** Edgar Z. Steever

Date	Mintage	Proof	MS-65	Prf-65
1995S	164,605	—	22.50	—
1995S	—	(118,087)	—	19.00

CIVIL WAR. KM# 254 Copper-Nickel Clad Copper 11.3400 g. **Obv. Designer:** Don Troiani **Rev. Designer:** T. James Ferrell

Date	Mintage	Proof	MS-65	Prf-65
1995S	119,510	—	42.50	—
1995S	—	(330,099)	—	41.50

ATLANTA OLYMPICS. KM# 271 Copper-Nickel Clad Copper 11.3400 g. **Obverse:** Soccer

Date	Mintage	Proof	MS-65	Prf-65
1996S	52,836	—	110	—
1996S	—	(122,412)	—	105

ATLANTA OLYMPICS. KM# 267 Copper-Nickel Clad Copper 11.3400 g. **Obverse:** Swimming

Date	Mintage	Proof	MS-65	Prf-65
1996S	49,533	—	165	—
1996S	—	(114,315)	—	36.00

DOLLAR

LOS ANGELES XXIII OLYMPIAD. KM# 209 Obv. Designer: Elizabeth Jones

Date	Mintage	Proof	MS-65	Prf-65
1983P	294,543	—	13.50	—
1983D	174,014	—	13.50	—
1983S	174,014	—	13.50	—
1983S	—	(1,577,025)	—	13.50

LOS ANGELES XXIII OLYMPIAD. KM# 210 Obv. Designer: Robert Graham

Date	Mintage	Proof	MS-65	Prf-65
1984P	217,954	—	13.50	—
1984D	116,675	—	14.50	—
1984S	116,675	—	14.50	—
1984S	—	(1,801,210)	—	13.50

STATUE OF LIBERTY CENTENNIAL. KM# 214 Obv. Designer: John Mercanti **Rev. Designer:** John Mercanti and Matthew Peloso

Date	Mintage	Proof	MS-65	Prf-65
1986P	723,635	—	13.50	—
1986S	—	(6,414,638)	—	13.50

CONSTITUTION BICENTENNIAL. KM# 220 Obv. Designer: Patricia L. Verani

Date	Mintage	Proof	MS-65	Prf-65
1987P	451,629	—	13.50	—
1987S	—	(2,747,116)	—	13.50

OLYMPICS. KM# 222 Obv. Designer: Patricia L. Verani **Rev. Designer:** Sherl Joseph Winter

Date	Mintage	Proof	MS-65	Prf-65
1988D	191,368	—	13.50	—
1988S	—	(1,359,366)	—	13.50

BICENTENNIAL OF THE CONGRESS. KM# 225 Designer: William Woodward and Chester Y. Martin.

Date	Mintage	Proof	MS-65	Prf-65
1989D	135,203	—	16.50	—
1989S	—	(762,198)	—	18.50

EISENHOWER CENTENNIAL. KM# 227 Obv. Designer: John Mercanti **Rev. Designer:** Marcel Jovine and John Mercanti

Date	Mintage	Proof	MS-65	Prf-65
1990W	241,669	—	15.50	—
1990P	—	(638,335)	—	17.00

KOREAN WAR. KM# 231 Obv. Designer: John Mercanti **Rev. Designer:** T. James Ferrell

Date	Mintage	Proof	MS-65	Prf-65
1991D	213,049	—	16.50	—
1991P	—	(618,488)	—	20.50

MOUNT RUSHMORE GOLDEN ANNIVERSARY. KM# 229 Obv. Designer: Marika Somogyi **Rev. Designer:** Frank Gasparro

Date	Mintage	Proof	MS-65	Prf-65
1991P	133,139	—	32.50	—
1991S	—	(738,419)	—	30.00

USO 50TH ANNIVERSARY. KM# 232 Obv. Designer: Robert Lamb **Rev. Designer:** John Mercanti

Date	Mintage	Proof	MS-65	Prf-65
1991D	124,958	—	14.00	—
1991S	—	(321,275)	—	19.50

COLUMBUS QUINCENTENARY. KM# 238 Obv. Designer: John Mercanti **Rev. Designer:** Thomas D. Rogers, Sr.

Date	Mintage	Proof	MS-65	Prf-65
1992D	106,949	—	29.00	—
1992P	—	(385,241)	—	39.00

OLYMPICS. KM# 234 Obv. Designer: John R. Deecken and Chester Y. Martin **Rev. Designer:** Marcel Jovine

Date	Mintage	Proof	MS-65	Prf-65
1992D	187,552	—	24.50	—
1992S	—	(504,505)	—	26.00

WHITE HOUSE BICENTENNIAL. KM# 236 Obv. Designer: Edgar Z. Steever **Rev. Designer:** Chester Y. Martin

Date	Mintage	Proof	MS-65	Prf-65
1992D	123,803	—	31.50	—
1992W	—	(375,851)	—	31.50

JAMES MADISON AND BILL OF RIGHTS. KM# 241 Obv. Designer: William Krawczewicz and Thomas D. Rogers, Sr. **Rev. Designer:** Dean McMullen and Thomas D. Rogers, Sr.

Date	Mintage	Proof	MS-65	Prf-65
1993D	98,383	—	19.50	—
1993S	—	(534,001)	—	20.00

THOMAS JEFFERSON 250TH BIRTH ANNIVERSARY. KM# 249 Designer: T. James Ferrell.

Date	Mintage	Proof	MS-65	Prf-65
1993P	266,927	—	23.00	—
1993S	—	(332,891)	—	28.00

WORLD WAR II 50TH ANNIVERSARY. KM# 244 Designer: Thomas D. Rogers, Sr..

Date	Mintage	Proof	MS-65	Prf-65
1993D	94,708	—	31.50	—
1993W	—	(322,422)	—	40.00

NATIONAL PRISONER OF WAR MUSEUM. KM# 251 Obv. Designer: Thomas Nielson and Alfred Maletsky **Rev. Designer:** Edgar Z. Steever

Date	Mintage	Proof	MS-65	Prf-65
1994W	54,790	—	96.00	—
1994P	—	(220,100)	—	46.50

U.S. CAPITOL BICENTENNIAL. KM# 253

Date	Mintage	Proof	MS-65	Prf-65
1994D	68,352	—	23.00	—
1994S	—	(279,416)	—	25.00

VIETNAM VETERANS MEMORIAL. KM# 250 Obv. Designer: John Mercanti **Rev. Designer:** Thomas D. Rogers, Sr.

Date	Mintage	Proof	MS-65	Prf-65
1994W	57,317	—	85.00	—
1994P	—	(226,262)	—	69.00

WOMEN IN MILITARY SERVICE MEMORIAL. KM# 252 Obv. Designer: T. James Ferrell **Rev. Designer:** Thomas D. Rogers, Sr.

Date	Mintage	Proof	MS-65	Prf-65
1994W	53,054	—	39.50	—
1994P	—	(213,201)	—	36.00

WORLD CUP SOCCER. KM# 247 Obv. Designer: Dean McMullen and T. James Ferrell

Date	Mintage	Proof	MS-65	Prf-65
1994D	81,698	—	26.00	—
1994S	—	(576,978)	—	29.00

ATLANTA OLYMPICS. KM# 260 Obverse: Gymnastics

Date	Mintage	Proof	MS-65	Prf-65
1995D	42,497	—	75.00	—
1995P	—	(182,676)	—	58.00

ATLANTA OLYMPICS. KM# 264 Obv. Designer: John Mercanti **Obverse:** Track and field

Date	Mintage	Proof	MS-65	Prf-65
1995D	24,796	—	98.00	—
1995P	—	(136,935)	—	53.00

ATLANTA OLYMPICS. KM# 263 Obv. Designer: John Mercanti **Obverse:** Cycling

Date	Mintage	Proof	MS-65	Prf-65
1995D	19,662	—	150	—
1995P	—	(118,795)	—	47.50

ATLANTA OLYMPICS, PARALYMPICS. KM# 259 Obverse: Blind runner

Date	Mintage	Proof	MS-65	Prf-65
1995D	28,649	—	93.00	—
1995P	—	(138,337)	—	64.00

CIVIL WAR. KM# 255 Obv. Designer: Don Troiani and Edgar Z. Steever **Rev. Designer:** John Mercanti

Date	Mintage	Proof	MS-65	Prf-65
1995P	45,866	—	74.00	—
1995S	—	(437,114)	—	78.00

SPECIAL OLYMPICS WORLD GAMES. KM# 266 Obv. Designer: Jamie Wyeth and T. James Ferrell **Rev. Designer:** Thomas D. Rogers, Sr.

Date	Mintage	Proof	MS-65	Prf-65
1995W	89,301	—	31.00	—
1995P	—	(351,764)	—	26.50

ATLANTA OLYMPICS. KM# 272A Rev. Designer: Thomas D. Rogers, Sr. **Obverse:** High jumper

Date	Mintage	Proof	MS-65	Prf-65
1996D	15,697	—	400	—
1996P	—	(124,502)	—	60.00

ATLANTA OLYMPICS. KM# 269 Rev. Designer: Thomas D. Rogers, Sr. **Obverse:** Tennis

Date	Mintage	Proof	MS-65	Prf-65
1996D	15,983	—	330	—
1996P	—	(92,016)	—	92.00

ATLANTA OLYMPICS. KM# 272 Rev. Designer: Thomas D. Rogers, Sr. **Obverse:** Rowing

Date	Mintage	Proof	MS-65	Prf-65
1996D	16,258	—	345	—
1996P	—	(151,890)	—	75.00

ATLANTA OLYMPICS, PARALYMPICS. KM# 268 Rev. Designer: Thomas D. Rogers, Sr. **Obverse:** Wheelchair racer

Date	Mintage	Proof	MS-65	Prf-65
1996D	14,497	—	385	—
1996P	—	(84,280)	—	90.00

NATIONAL COMMUNITY SERVICE. KM# 275 Obv. Designer: Thomas D. Rogers, Sr. **Rev. Designer:** William C. Cousins

Date	Mintage	Proof	MS-65	Prf-65
1996S	23,500	—	235	—
1996S	—	(101,543)	—	82.00

SMITHSONIAN INSTITUTION 150TH ANNIVERSARY. KM# 276 Obv. Designer: Thomas D. Rogers, Sr. **Rev. Designer:** John Mercanti

Date	Mintage	Proof	MS-65	Prf-65
1996D	31,230	—	150	—
1996P	—	(129,152)	—	69.00

JACKIE ROBINSON 50TH ANNIVERSARY. KM# 279 Obv. Designer: Alfred Maletsky **Rev. Designer:** T. James Ferrell

Date	Mintage	Proof	MS-65	Prf-65
1997S	30,007	—	103	—
1997S	—	(110,495)	—	85.00

NATIONAL LAW ENFORCEMENT OFFICERS MEMORIAL. KM# 281 Designer: Alfred Maletsky.

Date	Mintage	Proof	MS-65	Prf-65
1997P	—	(110,428)	—	170
1997P	28,575	—	165	—

U.S. BOTANIC GARDENS 175TH ANNIVERSARY. KM# 278 Designer: Edgar Z. Steever.

Date	Mintage	Proof	MS-65	Prf-65
1997P	57,272	—	45.00	—
1997P	—	(264,528)	—	44.00

BLACK REVOLUTIONARY WAR PATRIOTS. KM# 288 Obv. Designer: John Mercanti **Rev. Designer:** Ed Dwight **Obverse:** Crispus Attucks

Date	Mintage	Proof	MS-65	Prf-65
1998S	37,210	—	175	—
1998S	—	(75,070)	—	123

ROBERT F. KENNEDY. KM# 287 Obv. Designer: Thomas D. Rogers, Sr. **Rev. Designer:** James M. Peed and Thomas D. Rogers, Sr.

Date	Mintage	Proof	MS-65	Prf-65
1998S	106,422	—	32.50	—
1998S	—	(99,020)	—	43.00

DOLLEY MADISON. KM# 298 Designer: Tiffany & Co.. **Obv. Designer:** T. James Ferrell **Rev. Designer:** Thomas D. Rogers, Sr.

Date	Mintage	Proof	MS-65	Prf-65
1999P	22,948	—	50.00	—
1999P	—	(158,247)	—	48.00

YELLOWSTONE. KM# 299 Obv. Designer: Edgar Z. Steever **Rev. Designer:** William C. Cousins

Date	Mintage	Proof	MS-65	Prf-65
1999P	23,614	—	56.00	—
1999P	—	(128,646)	—	58.00

LEIF ERICSON. KM# 313 Obv. Designer: John Mercanti **Rev. Designer:** T. James Ferrell

Date	Mintage	Proof	MS-65	Prf-65
2000P	28,150	—	92.50	—
2000 Iceland	—	(15,947)	—	25.00
2000P	—	(58,612)	—	70.00

LIBRARY OF CONGRESS BICENTENNIAL. KM# 311 Obv. Designer: Thomas D. Rogers, Sr. **Rev. Designer:** John Mercanti

Date	Mintage	Proof	MS-65	Prf-65
2000P	52,771	—	43.00	—
2000P	—	(196,900)	—	41.00

$5 (HALF EAGLE)

STATUE OF LIBERTY CENTENNIAL. KM# 215 Designer: Elizabeth Jones.

Date	Mintage	Proof	MS-65	Prf-65
1986W	95,248	—	190	—
1986W	—	(404,013)	—	190

CONSTITUTION BICENTENNIAL. KM# 221 Designer: Marcel Jovine.

Date	Mintage	Proof	MS-65	Prf-65
1987W	214,225	—	190	—
1987W	—	(651,659)	—	190

OLYMPICS. KM# 223 Obv. Designer: Elizabeth Jones **Rev. Designer:** Marcel Jovine

Date	Mintage	Proof	MS-65	Prf-65
1988W	62,913	—	190	—
1988W	—	(281,456)	—	190

BICENTENNIAL OF THE CONGRESS. KM# 226 Obv. Designer: John Mercanti

Date	Mintage	Proof	MS-65	Prf-65
1989W	46,899	—	190	—
1989W	—	(164,690)	—	190

MOUNT RUSHMORE 50TH ANNIVERSARY. KM# 230 Obv. Designer: John Mercanti **Rev. Designer:** Robert Lamb and William C. Cousins

Date	Mintage	Proof	MS-65	Prf-65
1991W	31,959	—	285	—
1991W	—	(111,991)	—	225

COLUMBUS QUINCENTENARY. KM# 239 Obv. Designer: T. James Ferrell **Rev. Designer:** Thomas D. Rogers, Sr.

Date	Mintage	Proof	MS-65	Prf-65
1992W	—	(79,730)	—	285
1992W	24,329	—	320	—

OLYMPICS. KM# 235 Obv. Designer: James C. Sharpe and T. James Ferrell **Rev. Designer:** James M. Peed

Date	Mintage	Proof	MS-65	Prf-65
1992W	27,732	—	310	—
1992W	—	(77,313)	—	240

JAMES MADISON AND BILL OF RIGHTS. KM# 242 Obv. Designer: Scott R. Blazek **Rev. Designer:** Joseph D. Peña

Date	Mintage	Proof	MS-65	Prf-65
1993W	—	(78,651)	—	265
1993W	22,266	—	325	—

WORLD WAR II 50TH ANNIVERSARY. KM# 245 Obv. Designer: Charles J. Madsen **Rev. Designer:** Edward S. Fisher

Date	Mintage	Proof	MS-65	Prf-65
1993W	—	(65,461)	—	330
1993W	23,089	—	360	—

WORLD CUP SOCCER. KM# 248 Obv. Designer: William J. Krawczewicz **Rev. Designer:** Dean McMullen

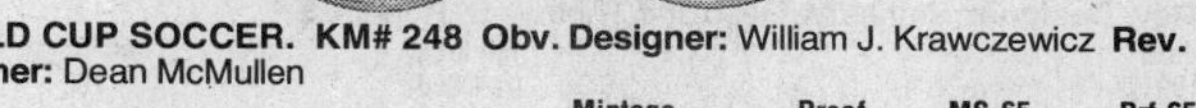

Date	Mintage	Proof	MS-65	Prf-65
1994W	22,464	—	325	—

Date	Mintage	Proof	MS-65	Prf-65
1994W	—	(89,619)	—	265

CIVIL WAR. KM# 256 Obv. Designer: Don Troiani **Rev. Designer:** Alfred Maletsky

Date	Mintage	Proof	MS-65	Prf-65
1995W	12,735	—	900	—
1995W	—	(55,246)	—	535

OLYMPICS. KM# 261 Obverse: Torch runner

Date	Mintage	Proof	MS-65	Prf-65
1995W	—	(57,442)	—	410
1995W	14,675	—	775	—

OLYMPICS. KM# 265 Obverse: Stadium

Date	Mintage	Proof	MS-65	Prf-65
1995W	—	(43,124)	—	535
1995W	10,579	—	1,200	—

1996 ATLANTA OLYMPICS. KM# 270 Obverse: Cauldron

Date	Mintage	Proof	MS-65	Prf-65
1996W	—	(38,555)	—	650
1996W	9,210	—	1,000	—

OLYMPICS. KM# 274 Obverse: Flag bearer

Date	Mintage	Proof	MS-65	Prf-65
1996W	—	(32,886)	—	615
1996W	9,174	—	1,050	—

SMITHSONIAN INSTITUTION 150TH ANNIVERSARY. KM# 277 Obv. Designer: Alfred Maletsky **Rev. Designer:** T. James Ferrell

Date	Mintage	Proof	MS-65	Prf-65
1996W	9,068	—	1,500	—
1996W	—	(29,474)	—	720

FRANKLIN DELANO ROOSEVELT. KM# 282 Obv. Designer: T. James Ferrell **Rev. Designer:** James M. Peed and Thomas D. Rogers, Sr.

Date	Mintage	Proof	MS-65	Prf-65
1997W	11,894	—	1,100	—
1997W	—	(29,474)	—	565

JACKIE ROBINSON 50TH ANNIVERSARY. KM# 280 Obv. Designer: William C. Cousins **Rev. Designer:** James M. Peed

Date	Mintage	Proof	MS-65	Prf-65
1997W	5,202	—	5,750	—
1997W	—	(24,546)	—	900

GEORGE WASHINGTON DEATH BICENTENNIAL. KM# 300 Designer: Laura G. Fraser.

Date	Mintage	Proof	MS-65	Prf-65
1999W	22,511	—	475	—
1999W	—	(41,693)	—	475

$10 (EAGLE)

LOS ANGELES XXIII OLYMPIAD. KM# 211 0.9000 Gold 0.4839 oz. AGW. 27 mm. 16.7180 g. **Obv. Designer:** James M. Peed and John Mercanti **Rev. Designer:** John Mercanti

Date	Mintage	Proof	MS-65	Prf-65
1984W	75,886	—	365	—
1984P	—	(33,309)	—	365
1984D	—	(34,533)	—	365
1984S	—	(48,551)	—	365
1984W	—	(381,085)	—	355

LIBRARY OF CONGRESS. KM# 312 Platinum-Gold-Alloy 16.2590 g. **Obv. Designer:** John Mercanti **Rev. Designer:** Thomas D. Rogers, Sr. **Notes:** Composition is 48 percent platinum, 48 percent gold, and 4 percent alloy.

Date	Mintage	Proof	MS-65	Prf-65
2000W	6,683	—	3,600	—
2000W	—	(27,167)	—	1,350

AMERICAN EAGLE BULLION COINS

SILVER DOLLAR

KM# 273 0.9993 **SILVER** 1 oz. 40.6mm. 31.1010 g. **Obv. Designer:** Adolph A. Weinman **Rev. Designer:** John Mercanti

Date	Mintage	Unc	Prf.
1986	5,393,005	20.00	—
1986S	(1,446,778)	—	32.00
1987	11,442,335	12.50	—
1987S	(904,732)	—	32.00
1988	5,004,646	16.50	—
1988S	(557,370)	—	60.00
1989	5,203,327	12.50	—
1989S	(617,694)	—	37.50
1990	5,840,210	16.50	—
1990S	(695,510)	—	35.00
1991	7,191,066	13.00	—
1991S	(511,924)	—	55.00
1992	5,540,068	15.50	—
1992S	(498,552)	—	50.00
1993	6,763,762	13.00	—
1993P	(403,625)	—	195
1994	4,227,319	16.50	—
1994P	(372,168)	—	250
1995	4,672,051	15.50	—
1995P	(395,400)	—	225
1995W 10th Anniversary	(30,125)	—	5,500
1996	3,603,386	47.50	—
1996P	(473,021)	—	70.00
1997	4,295,004	21.00	—
1997P	(429,682)	—	100.00
1998	4,847,549	13.00	—
1998P	(452,319)	—	60.00
1999	7,408,640	13.00	—
1999P	(549,769)	—	65.00
2000P	(600,000)	—	32.00
2000	9,239,132	12.50	—

GOLD $5

KM# 216 0.9167 **GOLD** 0.1 oz. 16.5mm. 3.3930 g. **Obv. Designer:** Augustus Saint-Gaudens **Rev. Designer:** Miley Busiek

Date	Mintage	Unc	Prf.
MCMLXXXVI (1986)	912,609	85.00	—
MCMLXXXVII (1987)	580,266	80.00	—
MCMLXXXVIII (1988)	159,500	200	—
MCMLXXXVIII (1988)P	(143,881)	—	80.00
MCMLXXXIX (1989)	264,790	85.00	—
MCMLXXXIX (1989)P	(82,924)	—	80.00
MCMXC (1990)	210,210	90.00	—
MCMXC (1990)P	(99,349)	—	80.00
MCMXCI (1991)	165,200	110	—
MCMXCI (1991)P	(70,344)	—	80.00
1992	209,300	95.00	—
1992P	(64,902)	—	80.00
1993	210,709	90.00	—
1993P	(58,649)	—	80.00
1994	206,380	90.00	—
1994W	(62,100)	—	80.00
1995	223,025	80.00	—
1995W	(62,650)	—	80.00
1996	401,964	80.00	—
1996W	(58,440)	—	80.00
1997	528,515	80.00	—
1997W	(35,000)	—	91.00
1998	1,344,520	70.00	—
1998W	(39,653)	—	80.00
1999	2,750,338	70.00	—
1999W	(48,426)	—	80.00
2000	569,153	85.00	—
2000W	(50,000)	—	90.00

GOLD $10

KM# 217 0.9167 **GOLD** 0.25 oz. 22mm. 8.4830 g. **Obv. Designer:** Augustus Saint-Gaudens **Rev. Designer:** Miley Busiek

Date	Mintage	Unc	Prf.
MCMLXXXVI (1986)	726,031	175	—
MCMLXXXVII (1987)	269,255	175	—
MCMLXXXVIII (1988)	49,000	175	—
MCMLXXXVIII (1988)P	(98,028)	—	200
MCMLXXXIX (1989)	81,789	175	—
MCMLXXXIX (1989P)	(53,593)	—	200
MCMXC (1990)	41,000	175	—
MCMXC (1990)P	(62,674)	—	200
MCMXCI (1991)	36,100	425	—
MCMXCI (1991)P	(50,839)	—	200
1992	59,546	175	—
1992P	(46,290)	—	200
1993	71,864	175	—
1993P	(46,271)	—	200
1994	72,650	175	—
1994W	(47,600)	—	200
1995	83,752	175	—
1995W	(47,545)	—	200
1996	60,318	175	—
1996W	(39,190)	—	200
1997	108,805	175	—
1997W	(29,800)	—	200
1998	309,829	175	—
1998W	(29,733)	—	200
1999	564,232	175	—
1999W	(34,416)	—	200
2000	128,964	175	—
2000W	(36,000)	—	200

GOLD $25

KM# 218 0.9167 **GOLD** 0.5 oz. 27mm. 16.9660 g. **Obv. Designer:** Augustus Saint-Gaudens **Rev. Designer:** Miley Busiek

Date	Mintage	Unc	Prf.
MCMLXXXVI (1986)	599,566	500	—
MCMLXXXVII (1987)	131,255	350	—
MCMLXXXVII (1987)P	(143,398)	—	400
MCMLXXXVIII (1988)	45,000	550	—
MCMLXXXVIII (1988)P	(76,528)	—	400
MCMLXXXIX (1989)	44,829	650	—
MCMLXXXIX (1989)P	(44,264)	—	400
MCMXC (1990)	31,000	800	—
MCMXC (1990)P	(51,636)	—	400
MCMXCI (1991)	24,100	1,300	—
MCMXCI (1991)P	(53,125)	—	400
1992	54,404	500	—
1992P	(40,982)	—	400
1993	73,324	350	—
1993P	(43,319)	—	400
1994	62,400	350	—
1994W	(44,100)	—	400
1995	53,474	385	—
1995W	(45,511)	—	400

Date	Mintage	Unc	Prf.
1996	39,287	525	—
1996W	(35,937)	—	400
1997	79,605	350	—
1997W	(26,350)	—	400
1998	169,029	350	—
1998W	(25,896)	—	400
1999	263,013	350	—
1999W	(30,452)	—	400
2000	79,287	350	—
2000W	(32,000)	—	400

GOLD $50

KM# 219 0.9167 **GOLD** 1 oz. 32.7mm. 33.9310 g. **Obv. Designer:** Augustus Saint-Gaudens **Rev. Designer:** Miley Busiek

Date	Mintage	Unc	Prf.
MCMLXXXVI (1986)	1,362,650	715	—
MCMLXXXVI (1986)W	(446,290)	—	725
MCMLXXXVII (1987)	1,045,500	715	—
MCMLXXXVII (1987)W	(147,498)	—	725
MCMLXXXVIII (1988)	465,000	715	—
MCMLXXXVIII (1988)W	(87,133)	—	725
MCMLXXXIX (1989)	415,790	715	—
MCMLXXXIX (1989)W	(53,960)	—	725
MCMXC (1990)	373,210	715	—
MCMXC (1990)W	(62,401)	—	725
MCMXCI (1991)	243,100	715	—
MCMXCI (1991)W	(50,411)	—	725
1992	275,000	715	—
1992W	(44,835)	—	725
1993	480,192	715	—
1993W	(34,389)	—	725
1994	221,633	715	—
1994W	(36,300)	—	725
1995	200,636	715	—
1995W	(46,553)	—	725
1996	189,148	715	—
1996W	(37,302)	—	725
1997	664,508	715	—
1997W	(28,000)	—	725
1998	1,468,530	710	—
1998W	(26,060)	—	725
1999	1,505,026	710	—
1999W	(31,446)	—	725
2000	433,319	715	—
2000W	(33,000)	—	725

PLATINUM $10

KM# 283 0.9995 **PLATINUM** .1000 oz. 3.1100 g. **Obv. Designer:** John Mercanti **Rev. Designer:** Thomas D. Rogers Sr

Date	Mintage	Unc	Prf.
1997	70,250	150	—
1997W	(36,996)	—	150
1998	39,525	150	—
1999	55,955	145	—
2000	34,027	145	—

KM# 289 0.9995 **PLATINUM** .1000 oz. 3.1100 g. **Obv. Designer:** John Mercanti

Date	Mintage	Unc	Prf.
1998W	(19,832)	—	150

KM# 301 0.9995 **PLATINUM** .1000 oz. 3.1100 g. **Obv. Designer:** John Mercanti

Date	Mintage	Unc	Prf.
1999W	(19,123)	—	145

KM# 314 0.9995 **PLATINUM** .1000 oz. 3.1100 g. **Obv. Designer:** John Mercanti

Date	Mintage	Unc	Prf.
2000W	(15,651)	—	145

PLATINUM $25

KM# 284 0.9995 **PLATINUM** 0.2500 oz. 7.7857 g. **Obv. Designer:** John Mercanti **Rev. Designer:** Thomas D. Rogers Sr

Date	Mintage	Unc	Prf.
1997	27,100	365	—
1997W	(18,628)	—	365
1998	38,887	350	—
1999	39,734	350	—
2000	20,054	350	—

KM# 290 0.9995 **PLATINUM** .2500 oz. 7.7857 g. **Obv. Designer:** John Mercanti

Date	Mintage	Unc	Prf.
1998W	(14,860)	—	350

KM# 302 0.9995 **PLATINUM** .2500 oz. 7.7857 g. **Obv. Designer:** John Mercanti

Date	Mintage	Unc	Prf.
1999W	(13,514)	—	350

KM# 315 0.9995 **PLATINUM** .2500 oz. 7.7857 g. **Obv. Designer:** John Mercanti

Date	Mintage	Unc	Prf.
2000W	(11,995)	—	350

PLATINUM $50

KM# 285 0.9995 **PLATINUM** 0.5000 oz. 15.5520 g. **Obv. Designer:** John Mercanti **Rev. Designer:** Thomas D. Rogers Sr

Date	Mintage	Unc	Prf.
1997	20,500	660	—

Date	Mintage	Unc	Prf.
1997W	(15,432)	—	660
1998	32,415	660	—
1999	32,309	660	—
2000	18,892	660	—

KM# 291 0.9995 **PLATINUM** .5000 oz. 15.5520 g. **Obv. Designer:** John Mercanti

Date	Mintage	Unc	Prf.
1998W	(13,821)	—	660

KM# 303 0.9995 **PLATINUM** .5000 oz. 15.5520 g. **Obv. Designer:** John Mercanti

Date	Mintage	Unc	Prf.
1999W	(11,098)	—	660

KM# 316 0.9995 **PLATINUM** .5000 oz. 15.5520 g. **Obv. Designer:** John Mercanti

Date	Mintage	Unc	Prf.
2000W	(11,049)	—	660

PLATINUM $100

KM# 286 0.9995 **PLATINUM** 1.000 oz. 31.1050 g. **Obv. Designer:** John Mercanti **Rev. Designer:** Thomas D. Rogers Sr

Date	Mintage	Unc	Prf.
1997	56,000	1,275	—
1997W	(15,885)	—	1,275
1998	133,002	1,275	—
1999	56,707	1,275	—
2000	18,892	1,275	—

KM# 292 0.9995 **PLATINUM** 1.000 oz. 31.1050 g. **Obv. Designer:** John Mercanti

Date	Mintage	Unc	Prf.
1998W	(14,203)	—	1,275

KM# 304 0.9995 **PLATINUM** 1.000 oz. 31.1050 g. **Obv. Designer:** John Mercanti

Date	Mintage	Unc	Prf.
1999W	—	—	1,275

KM# 317 0.9995 **PLATINUM** 1.000 oz. 31.1050 g. **Obv. Designer:** John Mercanti

Date	Mintage	Unc	Prf.
2000W	—	—	1,275

UNCIRCULATED ROLLS

Listings are for rolls containing uncirculated coins. Large date and small date varieties for 1960 and 1970 apply to the one cent coins.

Date	Cents	Nickels	Dimes	Quarters	Halves
1938	400	260	1,050	3,300	1,900
1938D	475	250	900	—	—
1938S	425	360	1,250	3,500	—
1939	130	80.00	600	1,000	1,250
1939D	265	3,600	550	1,850	2,000
1939S	205	1,200	1,500	3,300	2,400
1940	165	130	500	1,700	1,000
1940D	185	110	640	4,500	—
1940S	180	200	650	1,300	1,200
1941	115	92.00	390	800	750
1941D	215	180	650	2,950	1,200
1941S	375	180	415	2,500	3,250
1942	70.00	260	400	440	700
1942P	—	500	—	—	—
1942D	50.00	1,700	590	1,000	1,300
1942S	675	480	900	5,500	1,400
1943	130	270	400	425	700
1943D	200	280	485	2,250	1,800
1943S	500	280	580	2,000	1,400
1944	40.00	660	400	425	700
1944D	40.00	520	515	800	1,250
1944S	45.00	360	415	850	1,300
1945	50.00	300	400	380	700
1945D	60.00	280	415	1,100	1,050
1945S	38.00	270	400	650	950
1946	30.00	92.00	155	440	1,050
1946D	32.00	96.00	180	440	850
1946S	40.00	42.00	200	415	900
1947	150	48.00	290	850	1,000
1947D	30.00	60.00	340	750	950
1947S	155	60.00	180	660	—
1948	60.00	60.00	190	300	500
1948D	80.00	110	300	675	375
1948S	140	90.00	190	470	—
1949	128	180	1,400	2,250	1,750
1949D	100.00	160	550	1,650	1,440
1949S	200	92.00	2,200	—	2,500
1950	50.00	120	460	385	960
1950D	40.00	600	230	360	960
1950S	60.00	—	1,800	530	—
1951	65.00	220	130	460	430
1951D	25.00	360	100.00	440	850
1951S	61.00	160	550	1,300	800
1952	135	120	110	440	420
1952D	25.00	240	115	370	265
1952S	175	48.00	275	1,100	875
1953	30.00	20.00	140	575	400
1953D	25.00	18.00	140	240	200
1953S	42.00	60.00	60.00	350	750
1954	20.00	50.00	55.00	350	250
1954D	20.00	30.00	48.50	350	180
1954S	25.00	72.00	37.50	200	490
1955	22.00	30.00	40.00	150	500
1955D	20.00	11.00	40.00	100.00	—
1955S	25.00	—	35.00	—	—
1956	12.00	8.40	35.00	225	340
1956D	12.00	8.00	35.00	170	—
1957	12.00	12.00	36.00	140	175
1957D	12.00	6.00	41.50	85.00	175

Date	Cents	Nickels	Dimes	Quarters	Halves
1958	12.00	10.00	35.00	70.00	140
1958D	12.00	4.50	35.00	70.00	140
1959	2.00	7.00	35.00	72.50	135
1959D	2.00	7.00	35.00	70.00	160
1960 large date	2.00	7.00	35.00	70.00	135
1960 small date	240	—	—	—	—
1960D large date	2.00	7.00	35.00	70.00	135
1960D small date	2.50	—	—	—	—
1961	2.00	7.00	35.00	70.00	140
1961D	2.00	7.00	35.00	75.00	125
1962	2.00	6.00	35.00	75.00	120
1962D	2.00	7.00	35.00	70.00	105
1963	2.00	5.25	35.00	70.00	110
1963D	2.00	5.50	35.00	75.00	110
1964	2.00	4.50	35.00	66.00	75.00
1964D	2.00	4.50	35.00	66.00	75.00
1965	3.00	5.75	8.50	30.00	30.00
1966	6.00	5.00	11.00	28.00	30.00
1967	12.00	10.00	16.00	27.00	30.00
1968	5.00	—	8.50	40.00	—
1968D	3.00	7.00	10.00	35.00	28.00
1968S	4.00	6.25	—	—	—
1969	10.00	—	44.00	110	—
1969D	2.00	5.50	15.00	60.00	28.00
1969S	4.00	5.25	—	—	—
1970	5.00	—	8.00	30.00	—
1970D	4.00	4.50	8.50	16.00	375
1970S	4.00	4.50	—	—	—
1970S small date	2,500	—	—	—	—
1971	8.00	30.00	16.00	42.50	30.00
1971D	8.00	6.00	9.50	22.50	19.00
1971S	6.00	—	—	—	—
1972	3.00	6.00	10.00	25.00	38.00
1972D	3.00	4.50	11.00	22.50	32.00
1972S	4.00	—	—	—	—
1973	2.00	4.50	11.50	25.00	40.00
1973D	2.00	6.00	12.00	27.00	26.00
1973S	4.00	—	—	—	—
1974	1.50	4.50	8.50	22.00	22.00
1974D	1.50	6.00	10.00	18.00	24.00
1974S	4.00	—	—	—	—
1975	2.00	11.00	14.00	—	—
1975D	2.00	4.50	12.50	—	—
1976	2.00	15.00	20.00	22.50	22.00
1976D	5.00	14.00	19.00	23.00	22.00
1977	2.00	4.50	12.50	17.00	30.00
1977D	2.00	6.00	8.50	18.50	36.00
1978	3.00	4.50	10.00	16.00	48.00
1978D	3.00	5.00	8.00	17.00	90.00
1979	2.00	5.00	8.50	17.00	30.00
1979D	2.00	5.50	8.00	24.00	32.00
1980	2.00	4.50	10.00	17.00	22.00
1980D	2.00	4.50	8.00	19.00	23.00
1981	2.00	4.50	10.00	19.00	33.00
1981D	2.00	4.50	10.00	19.00	28.00
1982	2.00	275	250	220	85.00
1982D	2.00	76.00	60.00	90.00	60.00
1983	6.00	85.00	240	1,500	80.00
1983D	18.00	36.00	45.00	480	80.00
1984	8.00	34.00	10.00	20.00	40.00
1984D	25.00	5.00	25.00	30.00	52.00
1985	10.00	10.00	11.00	40.00	80.00
1985D	6.00	8.00	9.50	24.00	75.00
1986	40.00	8.00	27.50	125	145
1986D	50.00	42.00	26.00	275	115
1987	5.00	6.00	10.00	19.00	95.00
1987D	6.00	4.50	10.00	19.00	95.00
1988	9.00	5.50	10.25	41.50	98.00
1988D	9.00	8.00	9.50	24.00	63.00
1989	4.00	5.50	20.00	22.50	63.00
1989D	4.00	8.00	13.50	21.00	46.00
1990	3.00	10.00	15.00	29.00	56.00
1990D	3.00	11.00	12.50	30.00	76.00
1991	3.00	12.50	15.00	35.00	80.00
1991D	3.00	12.50	20.00	35.00	120
1992	3.00	48.00	10.00	26.00	36.00
1992D	5.00	8.50	10.00	34.00	65.00
1993	4.00	11.50	9.50	45.00	50.00
1993D	4.50	12.50	15.00	37.50	65.00
1994	3.00	7.00	12.50	45.00	18.00
1994D	3.00	6.00	12.50	45.00	32.50
1995	2.25	7.50	17.50	45.00	18.00
1995D	2.25	20.00	21.00	45.00	13.00
1996	2.00	5.50	11.00	22.00	15.00
1996D	2.50	7.50	11.50	28.00	20.00
1997	2.00	13.50	31.00	24.00	20.00
1997D	2.00	32.50	8.50	40.00	14.50
1998	2.25	12.50	10.50	30.00	14.50
1998D	2.25	13.50	9.00	24.00	15.00
1999P	2.50	6.00	25.00	—	18.00
1999D	2.50	5.50	12.00	—	17.50
2000P	2.00	6.00	10.00	—	14.50
2000D	2.00	3.50	10.00	—	20.00

MINT SETS

Mint, or uncirculated, sets contain one uncirculated coin of each denomination from each mint produced for circulation that year. Values listed here are only for those sets sold by the U.S. Mint. Sets were not offered in years not listed. In years when the Mint did not offer the sets, some private companies compiled and marketed uncirculated sets. Mint sets from 1947 through 1958 contained two examples of each coin mounted in cardboard holders, which caused the coins to tarnish. Beginning in 1959, the sets have been packaged in sealed Pliofilm packets and include only one specimen of each coin struck for that year (both P & D mints). Listings for 1965, 1966 and 1967 are for "special mint sets," which were of higher quality than regular mint sets and were prooflike. They were packaged in plastic cases. The 1970 large-date and small-date varieties are distinguished by the size of the date on the coin. The 1976 three-piece set contains the quarter, half dollar and dollar with the Bicentennial design. The 1971 and 1972 sets do not include a dollar coin; the 1979 set does not include an S-mint-marked dollar. Mint sets issued prior to 1959 were double sets (containing two of each coin) packaged in cardboard with a paper overlay. Origional sets will always be toned and can bring large premiums if nicely preserved with good color.

Date	Sets Sold	Issue Price	Value
1947 Est. 5,000	—	4.87	1,325
1948 Est. 6,000	—	4.92	625
1949 Est. 5,200	—	5.45	875
1950 None issued	—	—	—
1951	8,654	6.75	950
1952	11,499	6.14	850
1953	15,538	6.14	535
1954	25,599	6.19	285
1955	49,656	3.57	170
1956	45,475	3.34	165
1957	32,324	4.40	285
1958	50,314	4.43	155
1959	187,000	2.40	58.00
1960	260,485	2.40	32.00
1961	223,704	2.40	50.00
1962	385,285	2.40	20.00
1963	606,612	2.40	20.00
1964	1,008,108	2.40	20.00
1965 Special Mint Set	2,360,000	4.00	10.00
1966 Special Mint Set	2,261,583	4.00	9.75
1967 Special Mint Set	1,863,344	4.00	18.50
1968	2,105,128	2.50	6.50
1969	1,817,392	2.50	9.25
1970 large date	2,038,134	2.50	16.00
1970 small date	Inc. above	2.50	65.00
1971	2,193,396	3.50	8.00
1972	2,750,000	3.50	7.50
1973	1,767,691	6.00	18.00
1974	1,975,981	6.00	8.00
1975	1,921,488	6.00	10.50
1976 3 coins	4,908,319	9.00	13.50
1976	1,892,513	6.00	8.50
1977	2,006,869	7.00	8.75
1978	2,162,609	7.00	8.00
1979	2,526,000	8.00	7.50
1980	2,815,066	9.00	7.75
1981	2,908,145	11.00	15.00
1982 & 1983 None issued	—	—	—
1984	1,832,857	7.00	7.00
1985	1,710,571	7.00	7.50
1986	1,153,536	7.00	14.50
1987	2,890,758	7.00	8.00
1988	1,646,204	7.00	7.50
1989	1,987,915	7.00	7.00
1990	1,809,184	7.00	7.75
1991	1,352,101	7.00	8.75
1992	1,500,143	7.00	7.50
1993	1,297,094	8.00	8.50
1994	1,234,813	8.00	9.00
1995	1,038,787	8.00	16.50
1996	1,457,949	8.00	24.50
1997	950,473	8.00	21.50
1998	1,187,325	8.00	8.50
1999	1,421,625	14.95	26.00
2000	1,490,160	14.95	10.00

MODERN COMMEMORATIVE COIN SETS

Olympic, 1983-1984

Date	Price
1983S & 1984S 2 coin set: proof dollars.	22.50
1983 collectors 3 coin set: 1983 PDS uncirculated dollars; KM209.	36.50
1983 & 1984 3 coin set: 1983 and one 1984 uncirculated dollar and 1984W uncirculated gold $10; KM209, 210, 211.	360
1983S & 1984S 3 coin set: proof 1983 and 1984 dollar and 1984W gold $10; KM209, 210, 211.	360
1983 & 1984 6 coin set: 1983S and 1984S uncirculated and proof dollars, 1984W uncirculated and proof gold $10; KM209, 210, 211.	700
1984 collectors 3 coin set: 1984 PDS uncirculated dollars; KM210.	38.50

Statue of Liberty

Date	Price
1986 3 coin set: proof silver dollar, clad half dollar and gold $5; KM212, 214, 215.	195
1986 6 coin set: 1 each of the proof and uncirculated issues; KM212, 214, 215.	390
1986 2 coin set: uncirculated silver dollar and clad half dollar; KM212, 214.	17.00
1986 2 coin set: proof silver dollar and clad half dollar; KM212, 214.	17.00
1986 3 coin set: uncirculated silver dollar, clad half dollar and gold $5; KM212, 214, 215.	190

Constitution

Date	Price
1987 2 coin set: uncirculated silver dollar and gold $5; KM220, 221.	185
1987 2 coin set: proof silver dollar and gold $5; KM220, 221.	185
1987 4 coin set: silver dollar and $5 gold proof and uncirculated issues; KM220, 221.	380

Olympic, 1988

Date	Price
1988 2 coin set: uncirculated silver dollar and gold $5; KM222, 223.	185
1988 2 coin set: proof silver dollar and gold $5; KM222, 223.	195
1988 4 coin set: silver dollar and $5 gold proof and uncirculated issues; KM222, 223.	380

Congress

Date	Price
1989 2 coin set: uncirculated silver dollar and clad half dollar; KM224, 225.	20.00
1989 2 coin set: proof silver dollar and clad half dollar; KM224, 225.	21.00
1989 3 coin set: uncirculated silver dollar, clad half and gold $5; KM224, 225, 226.	195
1989 3 coin set: proof silver dollar, clad half and gold $5; KM224, 225, 226.	195
1989 6 coin set: 1 each of the proof and uncirculated issues; KM224, 225, 226.	380

Mt. Rushmore

Date	Price
1991 2 coin set: uncirculated half dollar and silver dollar; KM228, 229.	45.00
1991 2 coin set: proof half dollar and silver dollar; KM228, 229.	45.00
1991 3 coin set: uncirculated half dollar, silver dollar and gold $5; KM228, 229, 230.	300
1991 3 coin set: proof half dollar, silver dollar and gold $5; KM228, 229, 230.	225
1991 6 coin set: 1 each of proof and uncirculated issues; KM228, 229, 230.	480

Olympic, 1992

Date	Price
1992 2 coin set: uncirculated half dollar and silver dollar; KM233, 234.	28.00
1992 2 coin set: proof half dollar and silver dollar; KM233, 234.	28.00
1992 3 coin set: uncirculated half dollar, silver dollar and gold $5; KM233, 234, 235.	275
1992 3 coin set: proof half dollar, silver dollar and gold $5; KM233, 234, 235.	240
1992 6 coin set: 1 each of proof and uncirculated issues; KM233, 234, 235.	520

Columbus Quincentenary

Date	Price
1992 2 coin set: uncirculated half dollar and silver dollar; KM237, 238.	35.00
1992 2 coin set: proof half dollar and silver dollar; KM237, 238.	43.00
1992 3 coin set: uncirculated half dollar, silver dollar and gold $5; KM237, 238, 239.	320
1992 3 coin set: proof half dollar, silver dollar and gold $5; KM237, 238, 239.	275
1992 6 coin set: 1 each of proof and uncirculated issues; KM237, 238, 239.	600

Jefferson

Date	Price
1993 Jefferson: dollar, 1994 matte proof nickel and $2 note; KM249, 192.	100.00

Madison / Bill of Rights

Date	Price
1993 2 coin set: uncirculated half dollar and silver dollar; KM240, 241.	28.00
1993 2 coin set: proof half dollar and silver dollar; KM240, 241.	29.00
1993 3 coin set: uncirculated half dollar, silver dollar and gold $5; KM240, 241, 242.	310
1993 3 coin set: proof half dollar, silver dollar and gold $5; KM240, 241, 242.	250
1993 6 coin set: 1 each of proof and uncirculated issues; KM240, 241, 242.	550

World War II

Date	Price
1993 2 coin set: uncirculated half dollar and silver dollar; KM243, 244.	49.00
1993 2 coin set: proof half dollar and silver dollar; KM243, 244.	55.00
1993 3 coin set: uncirculated half dollar, silver dollar and gold $5; KM243, 244, 245.	350
1993 3 coin set: proof half dollar, silver dollar and gold $5; KM243, 244, 245.	340
1993 6 coin set: 1 each of proof and uncirculated issues; KM243, 244, 245.	560

World Cup

Date	Price
1994 2 coin set: uncirculated half dollar and silver dollar; KM246, 247.	32.00
1994 2 coin set: proof half dollar and silver dollar; KM246, 247.	38.00
1994 3 coin set: uncirculated half dollar, silver dollar and gold $5; KM246, 247, 248.	290
1994 3 coin set: proof half dollar, silver dollar and gold $5; KM246, 247, 248.	250
1994 6 coin set: 1 each of proof and uncirculated issues; KM246, 247, 248.	525

U.S. Veterans

Date	Price
1994 3 coin set: uncirculated POW, Vietnam, Women dollars; KM250, 251, 252.	170
1994 3 coin set: proof POW, Vietnam, Women dollars; KM250, 251, 252.	125

Olympic, 1995-96

Date	Price
1995 4 coin set: uncirculated basketball half, $1 gymnast & blind runner, $5 torch runner; KM257, 259, 260, 261.	725
1995 4 coin set: proof basketball half, $1 gymnast & blind runner, $5 torch runner; KM257, 259, 260, 261.	425
1995P 2 coin set: proof $1 gymnast & blind runner; KM259, 260.	110
1995P 2 coin set: proof $1 track & field, cycling; KM263, 264.	95.00
1995-96 4 coin set: proof halves, basketball, baseball, swimming, soccer; KM257, 262, 267, 271.	140
1995 & 96 8 coins in cherry wood case: proof silver dollars: blind runner, gymnast, cycling, track & field, wheelchair, tennis, rowing, high jump; KM259, 260, 263, 264, 268, 269, 272, 272A.	475
1995 & 96 16 coins in cherry wood case: bu and proof silver dollars: blind runner, gymnast, cycling, track & field, wheelchair, tennis, rowing, high jump; KM259, 260, 263, 264, 268, 269, 272, 272A.	2,450
1995 & 96 16 coins in cherry wood case: proof half dollars: basketball, baseball, swimming, soccer, KM257, 262, 267, 271. Proof silver dollars: blind runner, gymnast, cycling, track & field, wheelchair, tennis, rowing, high jump, KM259, 260, 263, 264, 268, 269, 272, 272A. Proof $5 gold: torch runner, stadium, cauldron, flag bearer, KM 261, 265, 270, 274.	2,400
1995 & 96 32 coins in cherry wood case: bu & proof half dollars: basketball, baseball, swimming, soccer, KM257, 262, 267, 271. BU & proof silver dollars: blind runner, gymnast, cycling, track & field, wheelchair, tennis, rowing, high jump, KM259, 260, 263, 264, 268, 269, 272, 272A. BU & proof $5 gold: torch runner, stadium, cauldron, flag bearer, KM261, 265, 270, 274.	6,600
1996P 2 coin set: proof $1 wheelchair & tennis; KM268, 269.	160
1996P 2 coin set: proof $1 rowing & high jump; KM272, 272A.	135

Civil War

Date	Price
1995 2 coin set: uncirculated half and dollar; KM254, 255.	95.00
1995 2 coin set: proof half and dollar; KM254, 255.	105
1995 3 coin set: uncirculated half, dollar and gold $5; KM254, 255, 256.	800
1995 3 coin set: proof half, dollar and gold $5; KM254, 255, 256.	560
1995 6 coin set: 1 each of proof and uncirculated issues; KM254, 255, 256.	1,350

Smithsonian

Date	Price
1996 2 coin set: proof dollar and $5 gold; KM276, 277.	620
1996 4 coin set: proof and B.U. ; KM276, 277.	2,200

Jackie Robinson

Date	Price
1997 2 coin set: proof dollar & $5 gold; KM279, 280.	900
1997 4 coin set: proof & BU; KM279, 280.	5,850
1997 legacy set.	950

Botanic Garden

Date	Price
1997 2 coin set: dollar, Jefferson nickel and $1 note; KM278, 192.	230

Franklin Delano Roosevelt

Date	Price
1997W 2 coin set: uncirculated and proof; KM282.	1,250

Kennedy

Date	Price
1998 2 coin set: proof; KM287.	70.00
1998 2 coin collectors set: Robert Kennedy dollar and John Kennedy half dollar; KM287, 202b. Matte finished.	345

Black Patriots

Date	Price
1998S 2 coin set: uncirculated and proof; KM288.	215

George Washington

Date	Price
1999 2 coin set: proof and uncirculated gold $5; KM300.	840

Dolley Madison

Date	Price
1999 2 coin set: proof and uncirculated silver dollars; KM298.	80.00

Yellowstone National Park

Date	Price
1999 2 coin set: proof and uncirculated silver dollars; KM299.	92.00

Millennium Coin & Currency

Date	Price
2000 2 coin set: uncirculated Sacagewea $1, silver Eagle & $1 note.	70.00

Leif Ericson

Date	Price
2000 2 coin set: proof and uncirculated silver dollars; KM313.	80.00

PROOF SETS

Proof coins are produced through a special process involving specially selected, highly polished planchets and dies. They usually receive two strikings from the coin press at increased pressure. The result is a coin with mirrorlike surfaces and, in recent years, a cameo effect on its raised design surfaces. Proof sets have been sold off and on by the U.S. Mint since 1858. Listings here are for sets from what is commonly called the modern era, since 1936. Values for earlier proofs are included in regular date listings. Sets were not offered in years not listed. Since 1968, proof coins have been produced at the San Francisco Mint; before that they were produced at the Philadelphia Mint. In 1942 the five-cent coin was struck in two compositions. Some proof sets for that year contain only one type (five-coin set); others contain both types. Two types of packaging were used in 1955 -- a box and a flat, plastic holder. The 1960 large-date and small-date sets are distinguished by the size of the date on the cent. Some 1968 sets are missing the mint mark on the dime, the result of an error in the preparation of an obverse die. The 1970 large-date and small-date sets are distinguished by the size of the date on the cent. Some 1970 sets are missing the mint mark on the dime, the result of an error in the preparation of an obverse die. Some 1971 sets are missing the mint mark on the five-cent piece, the result of an error in the preparation of an obverse die. The 1976 three-piece set contains the quarter, half dollar and dollar with the Bicentennial designs. The 1979 and 1981 Type II sets have clearer mint marks than the Type I sets for those years. Some 1983 sets are missing the mint mark on the dime, the result of an error in the preparation of an obverse die. Prestige sets contain the five regular-issue coins plus a commemorative silver dollar from that year. Sets issued prior to 1956 came in transparent envelopes stapled together in a small square box. In mid 1955 sets were changed to a flat clear cellophane envelope. In 1968 sets were changed to a clear hard plastic case as they still are currently issued.

Date	Sets Sold	Issue Price	Value
1936	3,837	1.89	7,500
1937	5,542	1.89	4,350
1938	8,045	1.89	1,900
1939	8,795	1.89	1,800
1940	11,246	1.89	1,450
1941	15,287	1.89	1,425
1942 6 coins	21,120	1.89	1,450
1942 5 coins	Inc. above	1.89	1,350
1950	51,386	2.10	775
1951	57,500	2.10	675
1952	81,980	2.10	345
1953	128,800	2.10	310
1954	233,300	2.10	135
1955 box	378,200	2.10	130
1955 flat pack	Inc. above	2.10	145
1956	669,384	2.10	62.00
1957	1,247,952	2.10	24.00
1958	875,652	2.10	50.00
1959	1,149,291	2.10	24.50
1960 large date	1,691,602	2.10	21.00
1960 small date	Inc. above	2.10	32.50
1961	3,028,244	2.10	13.75
1962	3,218,019	2.10	13.75
1963	3,075,645	2.10	15.50
1964	3,950,762	2.10	12.50
1968S	3,041,509	5.00	7.75
1968S no mint mark dime	Inc. above	5.00	18,500
1969S	2,934,631	5.00	7.50
1970S large date	2,632,810	5.00	11.00
1970S small date	Inc. above	5.00	95.00
1970S no mint mark dime	Inc. above	5.00	1,350
1971S	3,224,138	5.00	6.00
1971S no mint mark nickel Est. 1,655	1,655	5.00	1,475
1972S	3,267,667	5.50	5.50
1973S	2,769,624	7.00	9.00
1974S	2,617,350	7.00	11.75
1975S	2,909,369	7.00	11.00
1975S no mint mark dime	Inc. above	7.00	50,000
1976S 3 coins	3,998,621	12.00	18.50
1976S	4,149,730	7.00	10.75
1977S	3,251,152	9.00	8.00
1978S	3,127,788	9.00	9.00
1979S Type I	3,677,175	9.00	8.50
1979S Type II	Inc. above	9.00	125
1980S	3,547,030	10.00	8.25
1981S Type I	4,063,083	11.00	8.00
1981S Type II	Inc. above	11.00	440
1982S	3,857,479	11.00	5.25
1983S	3,138,765	11.00	7.50
1983S Prestige Set	140,361	59.00	95.00
1983S no mint mark dime	Inc. above	11.00	1,175
1984S	2,748,430	11.00	7.00
1984S Prestige Set	316,680	59.00	26.00
1985S	3,362,821	11.00	6.00
1986S	2,411,180	11.00	10.50
1986S Prestige Set	599,317	48.50	33.00
1987S	3,972,233	11.00	7.00
1987S Prestige Set	435,495	45.00	22.00
1988S	3,031,287	11.00	7.50
1988S Prestige Set	231,661	45.00	31.50
1989S	3,009,107	11.00	7.50
1989S Prestige Set	211,087	45.00	40.00
1990S	2,793,433	11.00	8.50
1990S no S 1¢	3,555	11.00	7,500
1990S Prestige Set	506,126	45.00	25.00
1990S Prestige Set, no S 1¢	Inc. above	45.00	8,000
1991S	2,610,833	11.00	14.00
1991S Prestige Set	256,954	59.00	65.00
1992S	2,675,618	12.00	7.50
1992S Prestige Set	183,285	59.00	84.00
1992S Silver	1,009,585	21.00	15.00
1992S Silver premier	308,055	37.00	15.00
1993S	2,337,819	12.50	13.75
1993S Prestige Set	224,045	57.00	35.00
1993S Silver	570,213	21.00	35.00
1993S Silver premier	191,140	37.00	35.00
1994S	2,308,701	13.00	14.00
1994S Prestige Set	175,893	57.00	57.00
1994S Silver	636,009	21.00	42.50
1994S Silver premier	149,320	37.50	42.50
1995S	2,010,384	12.50	42.50
1995S Prestige Set	107,112	57.00	135
1995S Silver	549,878	21.00	90.00
1995S Silver premier	130,107	37.50	90.00
1996S	2,085,191	16.00	18.50
1996S Prestige Set	55,000	57.00	525
1996S Silver	623,655	21.00	42.50
1996S Silver premier	151,366	37.50	42.50
1997S	1,975,000	12.50	37.00
1997S Prestige Set	80,000	57.00	175
1997S Silver	605,473	21.00	66.00
1997S Silver premier	136,205	37.50	66.00
1998S	2,078,494	12.50	24.00
1998S Silver	638,134	21.00	30.00
1998S Silver premier	240,658	37.50	30.00
1999S	2,557,899	19.95	67.00
1999S 5 quarter set	1,169,958	13.95	60.00
1999S Silver	804,565	31.95	365
2000S	3,097,442	19.95	20.00
2000S 5 quarter set	995,803	13.95	11.50
2000S Silver	965,421	31.95	28.50

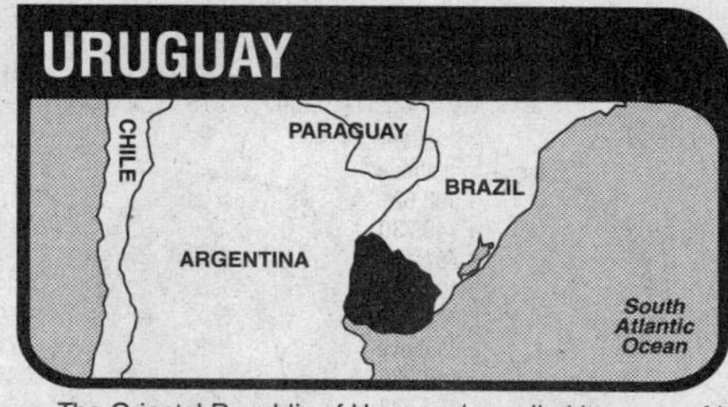

The Oriental Republic of Uruguay (so called because of its location on the east bank of the Uruguay River) is situated on the Atlantic coast of South America between Argentina and Brazil. This South American country has an area of 68,536 sq. mi. (176,220 sq. km.) and a population of *3 million. Capital: Montevideo. Uruguay's chief economic assets are the rich, rolling grassy plains. Meat, wool, hides and skins are exported.

Uruguay was discovered in 1516 by Juan Diaz de Solis, a Spaniard, but settled by the Portuguese who founded Colonia in 1680. Spain contested Portuguese possession and, after a long struggle, gained control of the country in 1778. During the general South American struggle for independence, Uruguay 's first attempt was led by Gaucho soldier Jose Gervasio Artigas leading the Banda Oriental which was quelled by Spanish and Portuguese forces in 1811. The armistice was soon broken and Argentine force from Buenos Aires cast off the Spanish bond in the Plata region in 1814 only to be conquered again by the Portuguese from Brazil in the struggle of 1816-20. Revolt flared anew in 1825 and independence was reasserted in 1828 with the help of Argentina. The Uruguayan Republic was established in 1830.

MINT MARKS

A - Paris, Berlin, Vienna
(a) Paris, privy marks only
D - Lyon (France)
H - Birmingham
Mx, Mo - Mexico City
(p) - Poissy, France
So - Santiago (Small O above S)
(u) – Utrecht

MONETARY SYSTEM

100 Centesimo = 1 Peso
1975-1993
1000 Old Pesos = 1 Nuevo (New) Peso
Commencing 1994
1000 Nuevos Pesos = 1 Peso Uruguayo

REPUBLIC

DECIMAL COINAGE

KM# 19 CENTESIMO

2.0000 g., Copper-Nickel **Obv:** Radiant sun design **Rev:** Value within wreath

Date	Mintage	F	VF	XF	Unc	BU
1901A	6,000,000	1.00	5.00	20.00	50.00	—
1901A Proof	—	Value: 225				
1909A	5,000,000	0.50	2.00	6.00	15.00	—
1924(p)	3,000,000	0.50	2.00	8.00	20.00	—
1936A	2,000,000	0.50	2.00	8.00	20.00	—

KM# 32 CENTESIMO

1.5000 g., Copper-Nickel **Obv:** Artigas bust right, 'HP' below **Obv. Designer:** T.H. Paget **Rev:** Value within wreath **Rev. Designer:** Gilroy Roberts **Note:** Medal rotation.

Date	Mintage	F	VF	XF	Unc	BU
1953	5,000,000	0.25	0.50	1.00	3.00	—
1953 Proof	—	Value: 150				

KM# 20 2 CENTESIMOS

3.5000 g., Copper-Nickel **Obv:** Radiant sun design **Rev:** Value within wreath

Date	Mintage	F	VF	XF	Unc	BU
1901A	7,500,000	1.00	4.00	12.00	30.00	—
1909A	10,000,000	1.00	2.00	9.00	20.00	—
1924(p)	11,000,000	1.00	2.00	7.00	15.00	—

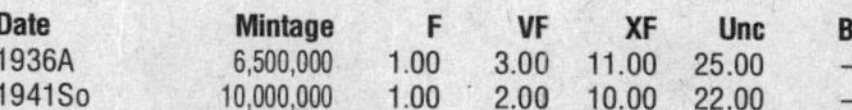

Date	Mintage	F	VF	XF	Unc	BU
1936A	6,500,000	1.00	3.00	11.00	25.00	—
1941So	10,000,000	1.00	2.00	10.00	22.00	—

KM# 20a 2 CENTESIMOS

3.5000 g., Copper **Obv:** Radiant sun design **Rev:** Value within wreath

Date	Mintage	F	VF	XF	Unc	BU
1943So	5,000,000	0.25	1.00	3.00	10.00	—
1944So	3,500,000	0.25	1.00	3.00	10.00	—
1945So	2,500,000	0.25	1.00	3.00	10.00	—
1946So	2,500,000	0.25	0.50	3.00	10.00	—
1947So	5,000,000	0.25	0.50	1.50	7.00	—
1948So	7,500,000	0.25	0.50	1.00	6.00	—
1949So	7,400,000	0.25	0.50	1.00	6.00	—
1951So	12,500,000	0.25	0.50	1.00	6.00	—

KM# 33 2 CENTESIMOS

2.5000 g., Nickel-Brass **Obv:** Artigas, 'HP' below **Obv. Designer:** T.H. Paget **Rev:** Value within wreath **Rev. Designer:** Gilroy Roberts **Note:** Medal rotation.

Date	Mintage	F	VF	XF	Unc	BU
1953	50,000,000	0.15	0.30	1.00	5.00	—
1953 Proof	—	Value: 65.00				

KM# 37 2 CENTESIMOS

2.0000 g., Nickel-Brass **Obv:** Artigas, 'HP' below **Obv. Designer:** T.H. Paget **Rev:** Value within wreath **Rev. Designer:** Gilroy Roberts **Note:** Medal rotation.

Date	Mintage	F	VF	XF	Unc	BU
1960	17,500,000	—	0.15	0.25	1.00	—
1960 Proof	—	Value: 40.00				

KM# 21 5 CENTESIMOS

5.0000 g., Copper-Nickel, 23.3 mm. **Obv:** Radiant sun design **Rev:** Value within wreath

Date	Mintage	F	VF	XF	Unc	BU
1901A	6,000,000	1.00	4.00	12.00	30.00	—
1901A Proof	—	Value: 325				
1909A	5,000,000	1.00	3.00	10.00	22.00	—
1909A Proof	—	Value: 175				
1924(p)	5,000,000	0.50	2.00	6.00	15.00	—
1936A	3,000,000	0.50	2.00	6.00	15.00	—
1941So	2,400,000	0.25	1.00	4.00	10.00	—
1941So Proof	—	Value: 200				

KM# 21a 5 CENTESIMOS

5.0000 g., Copper **Obv:** Radiant sun design **Rev:** Value within wreath

Date	Mintage	F	VF	XF	Unc	BU
1944So	4,000,000	0.25	1.00	3.00	10.00	—
1946So	2,000,000	0.20	1.00	4.00	12.00	—
1947So	2,000,000	0.20	1.00	4.00	12.00	—
1948So	3,000,000	0.20	0.75	3.00	10.00	—
1949So	2,800,000	0.20	0.75	3.00	10.00	—
1951So	15,000,000	0.20	0.50	2.00	7.00	—

KM# 34 5 CENTESIMOS

3.5000 g., Copper-Nickel **Obv:** Artigas, 'HP' below **Obv. Designer:** T.H. Paget **Rev:** Value within wreath **Rev. Designer:** Gilroy Roberts **Note:** Medal rotation.

Date	Mintage	F	VF	XF	Unc	BU
1953	17,500,000	0.20	0.30	0.50	1.00	—
1953 Proof	—	Value: 75.00				

KM# 38 5 CENTESIMOS

3.5000 g., Nickel-Brass **Obv:** Artigas, 'HP' below **Obv. Designer:** T.H. Paget **Rev:** Value within wreath **Rev. Designer:** Gilroy Roberts **Note:** Medal rotation.

Date	Mintage	F	VF	XF	Unc	BU
1960	88,000,000	—	0.15	0.25	1.00	—
1960 Proof	—	Value: 75.00				

KM# 25 10 CENTESIMOS

8.0000 g., Aluminum-Bronze, 27 mm. **Subject:** Constitutional Centennial **Obv:** MORLON behind neck **Rev:** Puma walking left in front of sun rays above value

Date	Mintage	F	VF	XF	Unc	BU
1930(a)	5,000,000	2.00	4.00	12.00	40.00	—

KM# 28 10 CENTESIMOS

6.0000 g., Aluminum-Bronze, 25 mm. **Obv:** Head laureate right **Rev:** Puma walking left in front of sunrays above value

Date	Mintage	F	VF	XF	Unc	BU
1936A	2,000,000	1.50	3.50	10.00	45.00	—

KM# 35 10 CENTESIMOS

4.5000 g., Copper-Nickel **Obv:** Artigas, 'HP' below **Obv. Designer:** T.H. Paget **Rev:** Value within wreath **Rev. Designer:** Gilroy Roberts **Note:** Medal rotation.

Date	Mintage	F	VF	XF	Unc	BU
1953	28,250,000	0.15	0.20	0.30	1.00	—
1953 Proof	—	Value: 75.00				
1959	10,000,000	0.20	0.30	1.00	3.00	—

KM# 39 10 CENTESIMOS

4.5000 g., Nickel-Brass **Obv:** Artigas, 'HP' below **Obv. Designer:** T.H. Paget **Rev:** Value within wreath **Rev. Designer:** Gilroy Roberts **Note:** Medal rotation.

Date	Mintage	F	VF	XF	Unc	BU
1960	72,500,000	0.15	0.20	0.30	1.00	—
1960 Proof	—	Value: 100				

KM# 24 20 CENTESIMOS
5.0000 g., 0.8000 Silver .1286 oz. ASW **Obv:** Radiant sun peeks out over arms within wreath **Rev:** Head left

Date	Mintage	F	VF	XF	Unc	BU
1920	2,500,000	2.50	5.50	12.00	35.00	—

KM# 26 20 CENTESIMOS
5.0000 g., 0.8000 Silver .1286 oz. ASW, 25 mm. **Subject:** Constitutional Centennial **Obv:** Seated figure left above date **Rev:** Wheat stalks divide value, mint marks flank stems

Date	Mintage	F	VF	XF	Unc	BU
1930(a)	2,500,000	2.25	4.50	10.00	30.00	—

KM# 29 20 CENTESIMOS
3.0000 g., 0.7200 Silver .0694 oz. ASW, 19 mm. **Obv:** Head laureate right **Rev:** Wheat stalks divide value

Date	Mintage	F	VF	XF	Unc	BU
1942So	18,000,000	1.50	2.50	4.50	7.00	—

KM# 36 20 CENTESIMOS
3.0000 g., 0.7200 Silver .0694 oz. ASW, 19 mm. **Obv:** Head right **Rev:** Wheat stalks divide value

Date	Mintage	F	VF	XF	Unc	BU
1954(u)	10,000,000	1.25	1.75	2.50	5.00	—

KM# 44 20 CENTESIMOS
Aluminum **Obv:** Head right **Rev:** Value within wreath **Note:** Medal rotation.

Date	Mintage	F	VF	XF	Unc	BU
1965So	40,000,000	0.15	0.20	0.35	1.00	—

KM# 40 25 CENTESIMOS
Copper-Nickel **Obv:** 'HP' below bust **Rev:** Radiant sun peeking out above arms within wreath, value divides circle of stars **Note:** Medal rotation.

Date	Mintage	F	VF	XF	Unc	BU
1960	48,000,000	0.20	0.35	0.50	1.00	—
1960 Proof	—	Value: 80.00				

KM# 22 50 CENTESIMOS
12.5000 g., 0.9000 Silver .3617 oz. ASW

Date	Mintage	F	VF	XF	Unc	BU
1916	400,000	8.50	20.00	50.00	300	—
1917	5,600,000	6.50	12.00	30.00	150	—

KM# 31 50 CENTESIMOS
7.0000 g., 0.7000 Silver .1620 oz. ASW **Obv:** Head right **Rev:** Date below value

Date	Mintage	F	VF	XF	Unc	BU
1943So	10,800,000	BV	2.75	4.75	12.00	—

KM# 41 50 CENTESIMOS
Copper-Nickel **Obv:** Artigas bust right, 'HP' below **Rev:** Radiant sun peeking out above arms within wreath, value divides circle of stars **Note:** Medal rotation.

Date	Mintage	F	VF	XF	Unc	BU
1960	18,000,000	0.20	0.50	1.00	2.00	—
1960 Proof	—	Value: 80.00				

KM# 45 50 CENTESIMOS
Aluminum **Obv:** Artigas head right **Rev:** Value within wreath **Note:** Medal rotation.

Date	Mintage	F	VF	XF	Unc	BU
1965So	50,000,000	0.15	0.25	0.40	1.00	—

KM# 23 PESO
25.0000 g., 0.9000 Silver .7235 oz. ASW **Obv:** Radiant sun peeking out above arms within wreath **Rev:** Bust left

Date	Mintage	F	VF	XF	Unc	BU
1917	2,000,000	12.00	20.00	50.00	250	—

KM# 30 PESO
9.0000 g., 0.7200 Silver .2083 oz. ASW **Obv:** Artigas head right **Rev:** Puma walking left, sunrays behind

Date	Mintage	F	VF	XF	Unc	BU
1942So	9,000,000	BV	4.50	10.00	30.00	—

KM# 42 PESO
Copper-Nickel **Obv:** Artigas head right **Rev:** Radiant sun peeking out above arms within wreath, value divides circle of stars **Note:** Medal rotation.

Date	Mintage	F	VF	XF	Unc	BU
1960	8,000,000	0.25	0.50	0.75	2.00	—
1960 Proof	—	Value: 75.00				

KM# 46 PESO
Aluminum-Bronze **Obv:** Artigas head right **Rev:** Radiant sun peeking out above arms within wreath, value divides circle of stars **Note:** Medal rotation.

Date	Mintage	F	VF	XF	Unc	BU
1965So	60,000,000	—	0.15	0.35	1.00	—
1965So Proof	25	Value: 65.00				

KM# 49 PESO
Nickel-Brass, 17.3 mm. **Obv:** Artigas head right **Rev:** Flower and value **Note:** Medal rotation.

Date	Mintage	F	VF	XF	Unc	BU
1968So	103,200,000	—	—	0.15	0.75	—
1968So Proof	50	Value: 50.00				

KM# 52 PESO
Aluminum-Brass **Obv:** Radiant sun with face **Rev:** Flower and value **Note:** Medal rotation.

Date	Mintage	F	VF	XF	Unc	BU
1969So	51,800,000	—	—	0.15	0.75	—

KM# 27 5 PESOS
8.4850 g., 0.9170 Gold .2501 oz. AGW, 22 mm. **Subject:** Constitution Centennial **Obv:** Artigas head right, L. BAZOR in left field behind neck **Rev:** Date flanked by sprigs below value

Date	Mintage	F	VF	XF	Unc	BU
1930(a)	Est. 100,000	—	—	170	180	200

Note: Only 14,415 were released; Remainder withheld

KM# 47 5 PESOS
Aluminum-Bronze **Obv:** Artigas head right **Rev:** Radiant sun peeking out above arms within wreath, value divides circle of stars **Note:** Medal rotation.

Date	Mintage	F	VF	XF	Unc	BU
1965So	18,000,000	0.20	0.30	0.50	1.00	—
1965So Proof	25	Value: 75.00				

KM# 50 5 PESOS
Nickel-Brass **Obv:** Artigas head right **Rev:** Flower and value **Note:** Medal rotation.

Date	Mintage	F	VF	XF	Unc	BU
1968So	42,680,000	0.10	0.20	0.30	0.40	—
1968So Proof	50	Value: 65.00				

KM# 53 5 PESOS
Aluminum-Bronze **Obv:** Radiant sun with face **Rev:** Flower and value **Note:** Medal rotation.

Date	Mintage	F	VF	XF	Unc	BU
1969So	42,320,000	—	—	0.10	0.30	—

KM# 43 10 PESOS
12.5000 g., 0.9000 Silver .3617 oz. ASW **Subject:** Sesquicentennial of Revolution Against Spain **Obv:** M.G. Rizzello bust right with hat **Rev:** Value within wreath

Date	Mintage	F	VF	XF	Unc	BU
1961	3,000,000	—	BV	9.00	8.00	10.00
1961 Proof	—	Value: 600				

KM# 48 10 PESOS
Aluminum-Bronze **Obv:** Artigas head right **Rev:** Radiant sun peeking out above arms within wreath, value divides circle of stars **Note:** Medal rotation.

Date	Mintage	F	VF	XF	Unc	BU
1965So	18,000,000	0.15	0.20	0.35	1.00	—

KM# 51 10 PESOS
Nickel-Brass, 23 mm. **Obv:** Artigas head right **Rev:** Flower and value **Note:** Medal rotation.

Date	Mintage	F	VF	XF	Unc	BU
1968So	90,000,000	0.15	0.20	0.35	0.65	—
1968So Proof	50	Value: 80.00				

KM# 54 10 PESOS
Aluminum-Bronze, 23 mm. **Obv:** Radiant sun with face **Rev:** Flower and value **Note:** Medal rotation.

Date	Mintage	F	VF	XF	Unc	BU
1969So	10,000,000	0.15	0.20	0.35	0.65	—

KM# 56 20 PESOS
Copper-Nickel **Obv:** Radiant sun peeking out above arms within wreath **Rev:** Spears of wheat and value **Note:** Medal rotation.

Date	Mintage	F	VF	XF	Unc	BU
1970So	50,000,000	0.15	0.25	0.40	0.75	—
1970So Proof	—	Value: 80.00				

KM# 57 50 PESOS
Copper-Nickel **Obv:** Radiant sun peeking out above arms within wreath **Rev:** Spears of wheat and value **Note:** Medal rotation.

Date	Mintage	F	VF	XF	Unc	BU
1970So	20,000,000	0.20	0.40	0.60	1.50	—
1970So Proof	—	Value: 80.00				

KM# 58 50 PESOS
Nickel-Brass **Subject:** Centennial - Birth of Rodo **Obv:** Rodo facing **Rev:** Feather, value and date **Note:** Medal rotation.

Date	Mintage	F	VF	XF	Unc	BU
1971So	15,000,000	0.20	0.50	1.00	2.00	—

KM# 58a 50 PESOS
6.0200 g., 0.9000 Silver .1742 oz. ASW **Subject:** Centennial - Birth of Rodo **Obv:** Rodo facing **Rev:** Feather, value and date

Date	Mintage	F	VF	XF	Unc	BU
1971So Proof	1,000	Value: 17.50				

KM# 58b 50 PESOS
Gold **Subject:** Centennial - Birth of Rodo **Obv:** Rodo facing **Rev:** Feather, value and date

Date	Mintage	F	VF	XF	Unc	BU
1971So Proof	100	Value: 375				

KM# 59 100 PESOS
Copper-Nickel **Obv:** Artigas head 1/4 left **Rev:** Value, date and sprig **Note:** Coin rotation.

Date	Mintage	F	VF	XF	Unc	BU
1973Mx	20,000,000	0.25	0.50	1.00	2.50	—

KM# 55 1000 PESOS
25.0000 g., 0.9000 Silver .7234 oz. ASW **Series:** F.A.O. **Obv:** Stylized radiant sun with face **Rev:** Assorted stylized designs within circle **Edge Lettering:** REPUBLICA ORIENTAL DEL URUGUAY **Designer:** Francisco Matta Vilaro **Note:** Medal rotation.

Date	Mintage	F	VF	XF	Unc	BU
1969So	500,000	—	BV	12.50	15.00	20.00
1969So Proof	350	Value: 150				

KM# 55a 1000 PESOS
Bronze **Series:** F.A.O. **Obv:** Stylized radiant sun with face **Rev:** Assorted stylized designs within circle

Date	Mintage	F	VF	XF	Unc	BU
1969So	11,000	—	—	15.00	20.00	30.00

KM# 55b 1000 PESOS
Gold **Series:** F.A.O. **Obv:** Stylized radiant sun with face **Rev:** Assorted stylized designs within circle

Date	Mintage	F	VF	XF	Unc	BU
1969So	450	—	—	—	800	850

REFORM COINAGE

1000 Old Pesos = 1 Nuevo (New) Peso

KM# 71 CENTESIMO
Aluminum, 19 mm. **Obv:** Radiant sun with face **Rev:** Value in front of supine wheat stalk **Shape:** 12-sided **Note:** Medal rotation.

Date	Mintage	F	VF	XF	Unc	BU
1977So	10,000,000	—	—	0.15	0.25	—

KM# 71a CENTESIMO
3.7000 g., 0.9000 Silver .1071 oz. ASW, 19 mm. **Obv:** Radiant sun with face **Rev:** Value in front of supine wheat stalk

Date	Mintage	F	VF	XF	Unc	BU
1979So Proof	202	Value: 15.00				

KM# 71b CENTESIMO
6.2600 g., 0.9000 Gold .1811 oz. AGW, 19 mm. **Obv:** Radiant sun with face **Rev:** Value in front of supine wheat stalk

Date	Mintage	F	VF	XF	Unc	BU
1979So Proof	50	Value: 185				

KM# 72 2 CENTESIMOS
Aluminum, 21 mm. **Obv:** Radiant sun with face **Rev:** Value in front of supine wheat stalk **Shape:** 12-sided **Note:** Medal rotation.

Date	Mintage	F	VF	XF	Unc	BU
1977So	17,000,000	—	—	0.15	0.25	—
1978So	3,000,000	—	—	0.15	0.25	—

KM# 72a 2 CENTESIMOS
5.2000 g., 0.9000 Silver .1505 oz. ASW, 21 mm. **Obv:** Radiant sun with face **Rev:** Value in front of supine wheat stalk

Date	Mintage	F	VF	XF	Unc	BU
1979So Proof	202	Value: 20.00				

KM# 72b 2 CENTESIMOS
9.2500 g., 0.9000 Gold .2676 oz. AGW, 21 mm. **Obv:** Radiant sun with face **Rev:** Value in front of supine wheat stalk

Date	Mintage	F	VF	XF	Unc	BU
1979So Proof	52	Value: 285				

KM# 73 5 CENTESIMOS
Aluminum, 23 mm. **Obv:** Steer left **Rev:** Value in front of supine wheat stalk **Shape:** 12-sided **Note:** Medal rotation.

Date	Mintage	F	VF	XF	Unc	BU
1977So	11,000,000	—	—	0.15	0.50	—
1978So	19,000,000	—	—	0.15	0.50	—

KM# 73a 5 CENTESIMOS
7.4000 g., 0.9000 Silver .2141 oz. ASW, 23 mm. **Obv:** Steer left **Rev:** Value in front of supine wheat stalk

Date	Mintage	F	VF	XF	Unc	BU
1979So Proof	202	Value: 20.00				

KM# 73b 5 CENTESIMOS
12.5500 g., 0.9000 Gold .3631 oz. AGW, 23 mm. **Obv:** Steer left **Rev:** Value in front of supine wheat stalk

Date	Mintage	F	VF	XF	Unc	BU
1979So Proof	52	Value: 365				

KM# 66a 10 CENTESIMOS
3.8000 g., 0.9000 Silver .1100 oz. ASW, 19 mm. **Obv:** Horse left **Rev:** Value flanked by sprigs

Date	Mintage	F	VF	XF	Unc	BU
1976So Proof	200	Value: 20.00				
1977So Proof	200	Value: 20.00				

KM# 66 10 CENTESIMOS
3.1000 g., Aluminum-Bronze, 19 mm. **Obv:** Horse left **Rev:** Value flanked by sprigs **Shape:** 12-sided **Note:** Medal rotation.

Date	Mintage	F	VF	XF	Unc	BU
1976So	127,400,000	—	—	0.30	0.80	1.50
1976So Proof	—	—	—	—	—	—
1977So	12,700,000	—	—	0.35	0.85	1.50

Date	Mintage	F	VF	XF	Unc	BU
1978So	19,900,000	—	—	0.35	0.85	1.50
1981So	—	—	—	0.35	0.85	1.50

KM# 66b 10 CENTESIMOS
6.0000 g., 0.9000 Gold .1736 oz. AGW, 19 mm. **Obv:** Horse left **Rev:** Value flanked by sprigs

Date	Mintage	F	VF	XF	Unc	BU
1976So Proof	50	Value: 175				

KM# 67 20 CENTESIMOS
5.1000 g., Aluminum-Bronze, 22 mm. **Obv:** Small building on top of hill **Rev:** Value flanked by sprigs **Shape:** 12-sided **Note:** Medal rotation.

Date	Mintage	F	VF	XF	Unc	BU
1976So	40,000,000	—	—	0.20	0.45	0.85
1976So Proof	—	—	—	—	—	—
1977So	4,700,000	—	—	0.20	0.60	1.00
1978So	15,300,000	—	—	0.20	0.45	0.85
1981So	—	—	—	0.20	0.45	0.85

KM# 67a 20 CENTESIMOS
6.4000 g., 0.9000 Silver .1852 oz. ASW, 22 mm. **Obv:** Small building on top of hill **Rev:** Value flanked by sprigs

Date	Mintage	F	VF	XF	Unc	BU
1976So Proof	200	Value: 22.50				
1977So Proof	200	Value: 22.50				

KM# 67b 20 CENTESIMOS
10.5000 g., 0.9000 Gold .3038 oz. AGW, 22 mm. **Obv:** Small building on top of hill **Rev:** Value flanked by sprigs

Date	Mintage	F	VF	XF	Unc	BU
1976So Proof	50	Value: 350				

KM# 68 50 CENTESIMOS
7.0000 g., Aluminum-Bronze, 25.5 mm. **Obv:** Scale **Rev:** Value flanked by sprigs **Shape:** 12-sided

Date	Mintage	F	VF	XF	Unc	BU
1976So	30,000,000	—	—	0.20	0.50	1.00
1976So Proof	—	—	—	—	—	—
1977So	9,800,000	—	—	0.20	0.50	1.00
1981So	200,000	—	—	0.25	0.60	1.25

KM# 68a 50 CENTESIMOS
9.0000 g., 0.9000 Silver .2604 oz. ASW, 25.5 mm. **Obv:** Scale **Rev:** Value flanked by sprigs

Date	Mintage	F	VF	XF	Unc	BU
1976So Proof	200	Value: 35.00				
1977So Proof	200	Value: 35.00				

KM# 68b 50 CENTESIMOS
15.0000 g., 0.9000 Gold .4340 oz. AGW, 25.5 mm. **Obv:** Scale **Rev:** Value flanked by sprigs

Date	Mintage	F	VF	XF	Unc	BU
1976So Proof	50	Value: 500				

KM# 69 NUEVO PESO
Aluminum-Bronze, 30 mm. **Obv:** Head of Jose Gervasio Artigas left **Rev:** Value in front of supine wheat stalk **Edge:** Plain **Shape:** 12-sided **Note:** Medal rotation.

Date	Mintage	F	VF	XF	Unc	BU
1976So	65,540,000	—	—	0.30	0.60	1.25
1976So Proof	—	—	—	—	—	—
1977So	7,360,000	—	—	0.30	0.65	1.45
1978So	27,100,000	—	—	0.30	0.65	1.45

KM# 69a NUEVO PESO
13.5000 g., 0.9000 Silver .3906 oz. ASW, 30 mm. **Obv:** Head of Jose Gervasio Artigas left **Rev:** Value in front of supine wheat stalk

Date	Mintage	F	VF	XF	Unc	BU
1976So Proof	200	Value: 40.00				

KM# 69b NUEVO PESO
23.0000 g., 0.9000 Gold .6655 oz. AGW, 30 mm. **Obv:** Head of Jose Gervasio Artigas left **Rev:** Value in front of supine wheat stalk

Date	Mintage	F	VF	XF	Unc	BU
1976So Proof	50	Value: 625				

KM# 74 NUEVO PESO
5.9000 g., Copper-Nickel, 24 mm. **Obv:** Radiant sun peeking over arms within wreath **Rev:** Flower and value **Note:** Medal rotation.

Date	Mintage	F	VF	XF	Unc	BU
1980So	50,000,000	—	0.20	0.35	0.65	1.00

KM# 74a NUEVO PESO
7.0000 g., 0.9000 Silver .2026 oz. ASW, 24 mm. **Obv:** Radiant sun peeking over arms within wreath **Rev:** Flower and value

Date	Mintage	F	VF	XF	Unc	BU
1980So Proof	300	Value: 25.00				

KM# 74b NUEVO PESO
11.6500 g., 0.9000 Gold .3371 oz. AGW, 24 mm. **Obv:** Radiant sun peeking over arms within wreath **Rev:** Flower and value

Date	Mintage	F	VF	XF	Unc	BU
1980So Proof	100	Value: 325				

KM# 76 NUEVO PESO
6.9400 g., 0.9000 Silver .2008 oz. ASW **Obv:** National flag

Date	Mintage	F	VF	XF	Unc	BU
1981 Proof	100	Value: 30.00				

KM# 95 NUEVO PESO
Stainless Steel **Obv:** Radiant sun **Rev:** Value within wreath **Note:** Medal rotation.

Date	Mintage	F	VF	XF	Unc	BU
1989	—	—	—	0.15	0.35	0.65

KM# 77 2 NUEVO PESOS
7.1000 g., Copper-Nickel-Zinc, 25 mm. **Subject:** World Food Day **Obv:** Wheat stalks divide date country name **Rev:** Value **Edge:** Plain **Shape:** 12-sided

Date	Mintage	F	VF	XF	Unc	BU
1981	95,000,000	—	0.25	0.50	1.00	1.50

KM# 77a 2 NUEVO PESOS
14.5300 g., 0.9000 Gold .4204 oz. AGW, 25 mm. **Subject:** World Food Day **Obv:** Wheat stalks divide date country name **Rev:** Value

Date	Mintage	F	VF	XF	Unc	BU
1981 Proof	100	Value: 425				

KM# 65 5 NUEVO PESOS
Copper-Nickel-Aluminum **Subject:** 150th Anniversary - Revolutionary Movement **Obv:** Artigas head facing within square above inscription **Rev:** Upright design **Note:** Medal rotation.

Date	Mintage	F	VF	XF	Unc	BU
ND(1975)So	3,000,000	0.50	0.75	1.25	3.50	5.00

KM# 65a 5 NUEVO PESOS
18.4300 g., 0.9000 Silver .5332 oz. ASW **Subject:** 150th Anniversary - Revolutionary Movement **Obv:** Artigas head facing within square above inscription **Rev:** Upright design

Date	Mintage	F	VF	XF	Unc	BU
ND(1975)So Proof	2,000	Value: 15.00				

KM# 65b 5 NUEVO PESOS
Gold **Subject:** 150th Anniversary - Revolutionary Movement **Obv:** Artigas head facing within square above inscription **Rev:** Upright design

Date	Mintage	F	VF	XF	Unc	BU
ND(1975)So Proof	1,000	Value: 550				

Note: 50 pieces each in aluminum, alpaca and copper are reported to have been struck

KM# 70 5 NUEVO PESOS
Copper-Aluminum **Subject:** 250th Anniversary - Founding of Montevideo **Obv:** Head facing to left of value **Rev:** Crowned shield within wreath **Note:** Medal rotation.

Date	Mintage	F	VF	XF	Unc	BU
1976So	300,000	0.75	1.00	1.50	4.00	5.50

KM# 70a 5 NUEVO PESOS
30.0000 g., 0.9000 Gold .8681 oz. AGW **Subject:** 250th Anniversary - Founding of Montevideo **Obv:** Head facing to left of value **Rev:** Crowned shield within wreath

Date	Mintage	F	VF	XF	Unc	BU
1976So Proof	100	Value: 675				

KM# 70b 5 NUEVO PESOS
Silver **Subject:** 250th Anniversary - Founding of Montevideo **Obv:** Head facing to left of value **Rev:** Crowned shield within wreath

Date	Mintage	F	VF	XF	Unc	BU
1976So	—	—	—	—	175	—

KM# 75 5 NUEVO PESOS
7.9000 g., Copper-Nickel, 26.15 mm. **Obv:** National flag **Rev:** Flower and value **Note:** Medal rotation.

Date	Mintage	F	VF	XF	Unc	BU
1980So	50,000,000	—	0.20	0.40	1.50	2.00
1981So	—	—	0.20	0.40	1.50	2.00

KM# 75a 5 NUEVO PESOS
9.3000 g., 0.9000 Silver .2691 oz. ASW, 26.15 mm. **Obv:** National flag **Rev:** Flower and value

Date	Mintage	F	VF	XF	Unc	BU
1980So Proof	300	Value: 30.00				

KM# 75b 5 NUEVO PESOS
15.6000 g., 0.9000 Gold .4514 oz. AGW, 26.15 mm. **Obv:** National flag **Rev:** Flower and value

Date	Mintage	F	VF	XF	Unc	BU
1980So Proof	100	Value: 450				

KM# 78 5 NUEVO PESOS
9.3000 g., 0.9000 Silver .2691 oz. ASW **Obv:** Coat of arms

Date	Mintage	F	VF	XF	Unc	BU
1981 Proof	100	Value: 30.00				

KM# 92 5 NUEVO PESOS
Stainless Steel **Obv:** Radiant sun **Rev:** Value and date within wreath **Note:** Medal rotation.

Date	Mintage	F	VF	XF	Unc	BU
1989	65,000,000	—	—	0.15	0.35	0.65

KM# 79 10 NUEVO PESOS
9.8000 g., Copper-Nickel, 28 mm. **Obv:** Bust of Jose Gervasio Artigas half left **Rev:** Flower and value **Note:** Medal rotation.

Date	Mintage	F	VF	XF	Unc	BU
1981So	—	—	0.20	0.50	1.75	2.25

KM# 79a 10 NUEVO PESOS
11.6300 g., 0.9000 Silver .3365 oz. ASW, 28 mm. **Obv:** Bust of Jose Gervasio Artigas half left **Rev:** Flower and value

Date	Mintage	F	VF	XF	Unc	BU
1981So Proof	100	Value: 35.00				

KM# 79b 10 NUEVO PESOS
19.4800 g., 0.9000 Gold .5637 oz. AGW, 28 mm. **Obv:** Bust of Jose Gervasio Artigas half left **Rev:** Flower and value

Date	Mintage	F	VF	XF	Unc	BU
1981So Proof	100	Value: 525				

KM# 93 10 NUEVO PESOS
Stainless Steel **Obv:** Radiant sun **Rev:** Value and date within wreath **Note:** Medal rotation.

Date	Mintage	F	VF	XF	Unc	BU
1989	79,000,000	—	—	0.20	0.45	0.75

KM# 86 20 NUEVO PESOS

Copper-Nickel, 30 mm. **Subject:** World Fisheries Conference **Obv:** Radiant sun peeking out above arms within wreath **Rev:** Fish **Rev. Designer:** Stuart Devtin **Edge:** Reeded **Note:** Medal rotation.

Date	Mintage	F	VF	XF	Unc	BU
1984	3,771	—	—	—	20.00	22.50

KM# 86a 20 NUEVO PESOS

11.6600 g., 0.9250 Silver .3468 oz. ASW, 30 mm. **Subject:** World Fisheries Conference **Obv:** Radiant sun peeking out above arms within wreath **Rev:** Fish

Date	Mintage	F	VF	XF	Unc	BU
1984 Proof	25,000	Value: 32.00				

KM# 86b 20 NUEVO PESOS

19.6000 g., 0.9170 Gold .5776 oz. AGW, 30 mm. **Subject:** World Fisheries Conference **Obv:** Radiant sun peeking out above arms within wreath **Rev:** Fish

Date	Mintage	F	VF	XF	Unc	BU
1984 Proof	100	Value: 550				

KM# 94 50 NUEVO PESOS

Stainless Steel **Obv:** Radiant sun **Rev:** Value and date within wreath **Note:** Medal rotation.

Date	Mintage	F	VF	XF	Unc	BU
1989	—	—	—	0.20	0.50	0.85

KM# 80 100 NUEVO PESOS

12.0000 g., 0.9000 Silver .3472 oz. ASW **Obv:** Hydroelectric dam **Rev:** Conjoined arms with radiant sun peeking out above arms within wreath

Date	Mintage	F	VF	XF	Unc	BU
1981So	25,000	—	—	—	7.50	9.00

KM# 96 100 NUEVO PESOS

Stainless Steel **Obv:** Gaucho with hat right **Rev:** Value and date within wreath **Note:** Medal rotation.

Date	Mintage	F	VF	XF	Unc	BU
1989	—	—	—	0.35	0.75	1.50

KM# 97 200 NUEVO PESOS

Copper-Nickel **Obv:** Unchained Liberty **Rev:** Value and date within wreath **Note:** Medal rotation.

Date	Mintage	F	VF	XF	Unc	BU
1989	—	—	—	—	1.50	2.50

KM# 82 500 NUEVO PESOS

12.0000 g., 0.9000 Silver .3472 oz. ASW **Obv:** Hydroelectric dam **Rev:** Radiant sun peeking out above arms within wreath above date

Date	Mintage	F	VF	XF	Unc	BU
1983So	15,000	—	—	—	7.50	9.00

KM# 90 500 NUEVO PESOS

12.0000 g., 0.9000 Silver .3473 oz. ASW **Obv:** Head of General Leandro Gomez half left **Rev:** Building above value and date

Date	Mintage	F	VF	XF	Unc	BU
1986Mo Proof	6,000	Value: 21.50				

KM# 98 500 NUEVO PESOS

Copper Nickel **Obv:** Bust of Jose Gervasio Artigas half right **Rev:** Value and date within wreath **Note:** Medal rotation.

Date	Mintage	F	VF	XF	Unc	BU
1989	—	—	—	—	3.00	4.50

KM# 87 2000 NUEVO PESOS

25.0000 g., 0.9000 Silver .7235 oz. ASW **Subject:** 140th Anniversary of Silver Coinage and 25th Meeting of Inter-American Bank Governors **Obv:** Radiant sun peeking over arms within wreath **Rev:** Map within U-shaped design below inscription **Note:** Coin rotation.

Date	Mintage	F	VF	XF	Unc	BU
1984 Proof	15,000	Value: 18.50				

KM# 88 2000 NUEVO PESOS

25.0000 g., 0.9000 Silver .7235 oz. ASW **Subject:** 25th Meeting of Inter-American Bank Governors **Obv:** Radiant sun peeking over arms within wreath **Rev:** Map within U-shaped design below inscription **Note:** Coin rotation.

Date	Mintage	F	VF	XF	Unc	BU
1984 Proof	15,000	Value: 18.50				

KM# 81 5000 NUEVO PESOS

12.0000 g., 0.9000 Silver .3472 oz. ASW **Obv:** Hydroelectric dam **Rev:** Conjoined arms with radiant sun peeking out above arms within wreath

Date	Mintage	F	VF	XF	Unc	BU
1981So Proof	15,000	Value: 15.00				

KM# 91 5000 NUEVO PESOS

25.0000 g., 0.9000 Silver .7235 oz. ASW **Subject:** 20th Anniversary of Central Bank **Obv:** Double wheel design **Rev:** Snowflake design

Date	Mintage	F	VF	XF	Unc	BU
1987So Proof	10,000	Value: 16.50				

KM# 91a 5000 NUEVO PESOS

42.7600 g., Gold **Obv:** Double wheel design **Rev:** Snowflake design

Date	Mintage	F	VF	XF	Unc	BU
1987	—	—	—	—	—	—

KM# 99 5000 NUEVO PESOS

25.0000 g., 0.9000 Silver .7235 oz. ASW **Subject:** Latin America Presidents' Assembly **Obv:** Value and date within circle **Rev:** Assorted arms

Date	Mintage	F	VF	XF	Unc	BU
1988 Proof	—	Value: 20.00				

KM# 85 20000 NUEVO PESOS

20.0000 g., 0.9000 Gold .5787 oz. AGW **Obv:** Hydroelectric dam **Rev:** Radiant sun peeking out above arms within wreath

Date	Mintage	F	VF	XF	Unc	BU
1983So Proof	2,500	Value: 425				

KM# 89 20000 NUEVO PESOS
19.8700 g., 0.9000 Gold .5750 oz AGW oz. AGW, 33.1 mm. **Subject:** 130th Anniversary of Gold Coinage and 25th Meeting of Inter-American Bank Governors **Obv:** Radiant sun peeking out above arms within wreath of assorted flags **Rev:** Map within U-shaped design below value and inscription **Edge:** Reeded

Date	Mintage	F	VF	XF	Unc	BU
1984 Proof	1,500	Value: 425				

KM# 101 25000 PESOS
12.5000 g., 0.9000 Silver .3617 oz. ASW **Subject:** 25th Anniversary of Central Bank **Obv:** Bell design above value **Rev:** Towered bank building to lower right of arms

Date	Mintage	F	VF	XF	Unc	BU
1992	—	—	—	—	16.50	18.50

KM# 100 50000 NUEVO PESOS
27.0000 g., 0.9250 Silver .8029 oz. ASW **Subject:** Ibero - American Series **Obv:** Arms within center circle of value, country name and assorted arms **Rev:** Crossed flags and crowned shield divides dates **Note:** Coin rotation.

Date	Mintage	F	VF	XF	Unc	BU
1991 Proof	70,000	Value: 37.50				

REFORM COINAGE

March 1993

1,000 Nuevos Pesos = 1 Uruguayan Peso; 100 Centesimos = 1 Uruguayan Peso (UYP)

KM# 102 10 CENTESIMOS
Stainless Steel **Obv:** Artigas head right **Rev:** Value, date and sprig **Note:** Coin rotation.

Date	Mintage	F	VF	XF	Unc	BU
1994	—	—	—	0.25	0.50	0.65

KM# 105 20 CENTESIMOS
Stainless Steel **Obv:** Artigas head right **Rev:** Value, date and sprig **Note:** Coin rotation.

Date	Mintage	F	VF	XF	Unc	BU
1994	—	—	—	0.30	0.60	0.75

KM# 106 50 CENTESIMOS
Stainless Steel **Obv:** Artigas head right **Rev:** Value, date and sprig **Note:** Coin rotation.

Date	Mintage	F	VF	XF	Unc	BU
1994	—	—	—	0.35	0.75	1.00
1998	—	—	—	0.35	0.75	1.00

KM# 121 10 PESOS
10.3000 g., Bi-Metallic Brass center in Stainless Steel ring, 28 mm. **Obv:** Artigas head right within circle **Rev:** Value above signature within circle **Edge:** Plain

Date	Mintage	F	VF	XF	Unc	BU
2000	—	—	—	—	3.50	5.00

KM# 103.1 UN PESO URUGUAYO
Brass **Obv:** Artigas head right **Rev:** Value and date **Note:** Left point of bust shoulder points at "U" in Republic.

Date	Mintage	F	VF	XF	Unc	BU
1994	—	—	—	—	0.60	1.00

KM# 103.2 UN PESO URUGUAYO
3.5200 g., Brass, 20 mm. **Obv:** Artigas head right **Rev:** Value and date **Edge:** Plain **Note:** Medal rotation; left point of bust shoulder points at "P" in Republic.

Date	Mintage	F	VF	XF	Unc	BU
1994	—	—	—	—	0.50	0.75
1998	—	—	—	—	0.50	0.75

KM# 104 2 DOS PESOS URUGUAYOS
Brass **Obv:** Artigas head right **Rev:** Value and date **Note:** Medal rotation.

Date	Mintage	F	VF	XF	Unc	BU
1994	—	—	—	0.75	1.50	2.00
1998S	—	—	—	0.75	1.50	2.00

Note: Mint mark under bust

KM# 113 50 PESOS URUGUAYOS
12.5000 g., 0.9000 Silver .3617 oz. ASW **Subject:** Bicentennial - City of Melo **Obv:** Map and date **Rev:** City arms, value and date

Date	Mintage	F	VF	XF	Unc	BU
1996 Proof	10,000	Value: 20.00				

KM# 111 100 PESOS URUGUAYOS
25.0000 g., 0.9990 Silver .7234 oz. ASW **Subject:** 50th Anniversary - F.A.O. **Obv:** Wheat stalks divide value **Rev:** F.A.O logo and dates within circle

Date	Mintage	F	VF	XF	Unc	BU
ND1995 Proof	—	Value: 20.00				

KM# 112 100 PESOS URUGUAYOS
25.0000 g., 0.9990 Silver .7234 oz. ASW **Subject:** Centennial - Central Bank **Obv:** Radiant sun face **Rev:** Central Bank building

Date	Mintage	F	VF	XF	Unc	BU
1996 Proof	50,000	Value: 22.50				

KM# 107 200 PESOS URUGUAYOS
27.0000 g., 0.9250 Silver .8030 oz. ASW **Subject:** Environmental Protection **Obv:** Arms in wreath within center circle of assorted arms **Rev:** Pampas deer right

Date	Mintage	F	VF	XF	Unc	BU
1994 Proof	20,000	Value: 35.00				

KM# 116 200 PESOS URUGUAYOS
28.2800 g., 0.9250 Silver .8410 oz. ASW **Subject:** 50th Anniversary - United Nations

Date	Mintage	F	VF	XF	Unc	BU
1995 Proof	—	Value: 42.50				

KM# 115 200 PESOS URUGUAYOS
25.0000 g., 0.9000 Silver .7234 oz. ASW **Subject:** Millennium Change **Obv:** Southern Cross stars within design **Rev:** Stylized symbols of mankinds connection to the stars **Edge Lettering:** "CAMBIO DE MILENIO" twice

Date	Mintage	F	VF	XF	Unc	BU
1999	50,000	—	—	—	25.00	30.00

KM# 114 250 PESOS URUGUAYOS
27.0000 g., 0.9000 Silver .8030 oz. ASW **Subject:** Ibero - American Series **Obv:** Arms in wreath within center circle of assorted arms **Rev:** Standing figures leaning on wooden gate

Date	Mintage	F	VF	XF	Unc	BU
1997 Proof	11,000	Value: 45.00				

KM# 117 250 PESOS URUGUAYOS
27.0000 g., 0.9000 Silver .8030 oz. ASW, 40 mm. **Series:** Ibero-American **Obv:** Arms in wreath within center circle of assorted arms **Rev:** Man and woman on horseback **Edge:** Reeded

Date	Mintage	F	VF	XF	Unc	BU
2000 Proof	8,000	Value: 47.50				

GOLD BULLION COINAGE

KM# 108 1/4 GAUCHO
8.6400 g., 0.9000 Gold .2500 oz. AGW **Obv:** Head of Gaucho right **Rev:** Value within wreath

Date	Mintage	F	VF	XF	Unc	BU
1992 Proof	—	Value: 225				

KM# 109 1/2 GAUCHO
17.2800 g., 0.9000 Gold .5000 oz. AGW **Obv:** Head of Gaucho right **Rev:** Value "1/2" within wreath

Date	Mintage	F	VF	XF	Unc	BU
1992 Proof	—	Value: 375				

KM# 110 GAUCHO
34.5590 g., 0.9000 Gold 1.0000 oz. AGW **Obv:** Head of Gaucho right **Rev:** Value within wreath

Date	Mintage	F	VF	XF	Unc	BU
1992 Proof	—	Value: 700				

ESSAIS

KM#	Date	Mintage	Identification	Mkt Val
E5	1924(p)	12	Centesimo. Nickel. KM19.	250
E6	1924(p)	12	2 Centesimos. Nickel. KM20.	275
E7	1924(p)	12	5 Centesimos. Nickel. KM21.	300
E8	1930(a)	70	10 Centesimos. Aluminum-Bronze. KM25.	100
E10	1930(a)	60	10 Centesimos. Gold. 18.3200 g. Head laureate right. Puma walking left in front of sun rays. KM25.	2,500
E11	1930(a)	—	20 Centesimos. Aluminum-Bronze. Seated figure left above date. Wheat stalks divides value. KM24.	100
EA12	1930	—	20 Centesimos. Silver. 4.9000 g.	—
E12	1930(a)	60	20 Centesimos. Gold. 8.9500 g. KM24.	2,750
E13	1930(a)	70	5 Pesos. Aluminum-Bronze. KM27.	225
E14	1930(a)	60	5 Pesos. Gold. KM27.	1,850
E15	1983	100	500 Pesos. Gold. ENSAYO, KM82.	425
E16	1983	200	2000 Pesos. Copper. KM83.	95.00
E17	1983	20	2000 Pesos. Gold. KM83	2,750
E18	1983	200	20000 Pesos. Silver. ENSAYO, KM85.	65.00
E19	1983	1,500	20000 Pesos. Gold. ENSAYO, KM85.	475
E20	1984	20,500	20 Pesos. Silver. ENSAYO, KM86a.	22.50
E21	1984	600	20 Pesos. Gold. ENSAYO, KM86b.	375
E22	1984	1,500	20000 Pesos. Gold. ENSAYO, KM89.	425

PATTERNS

Including off metal strikes

KM#	Date	Mintage	Identification	Mkt Val
Pn38	ND(1904)	—	4 Centesimos. Copper-Nickel. Radiant sun face. Value below banner in center.	275
PnA39	1916	—	50 Centesimos. Silver.	—
Pn39	1916	45	50 Centesimos. Silver.	—
Pn40	1917	20	Peso. Silver.	—
PnA41	1920	—	20 Centesimos. Copper-Nickel. Similar to KM#24.	—
Pn41	1942	10	20 Centesimos. Copper Gilt.	—
PnA42	1942	20	20 Centesimos. Silver Gilt.	—
Pn42	1942	—	20 Centesimos. Gold. KM29.	475
Pn43	1942So	—	Peso. Gold. KM30.	1,000
Pn44	1943So	—	2 Centesimos. Gold. KM20a.	950
Pn45	1943So	—	50 Centesimos. Gold. KM31	1,000
Pn46	1953	100	Centesimo. 0.9160 Gold. KM32.	—
Pn47	1953	—	2 Centesimos. Aluminum. KM33.	—
Pn48	1953	100	2 Centesimos. 0.9160 Gold. KM33.	—
Pn49	1953	100	5 Centesimos. 0.9160 Gold. KM34.	—
Pn50	1953	100	10 Centesimos. 0.9160 Gold. KM35.	—
PnB51	1953	—	Peso. Brass. Similar to PNA51.	—
PnC51	1953	—	Peso. Copper-Nickel. Similar to PNA51.	—
PnD51	1953	—	Peso. Silver. Similar to PNA51.	—
Pn51	1954	100	20 Centesimos. 0.9830 Gold. KM36.	550
Pn52	1959	—	10 Centesimos. 0.9160 Gold. KM35.	—
Pn53	1960	100	2 Centesimos. Gold. KM37.	—
Pn54	1960	100	5 Centesimos. Gold. KM38.	—
PnA54	ND(1960)	—	5 Centesimos. Nickel. Similar to KM#34 and KM#38 reverses. WIth a "Z" inside the base of the 5.	—
PnB54	ND(1960)	—	5 Centesimos. Aluminum. Similar to KM#34 and KM#38 reverses. With "HA" in the base of the 5 and "MBL" above the 5.	—
Pn55	1960	100	10 Centesimos. Gold. KM39.	—
Pn56	1960	100	25 Centesimos. Gold. KM40.	—
Pn57	1960	100	50 Centesimos. Gold. KM41.	—
Pn58	1960	—	Peso. Gold. KM42.	—
Pn59	1960	—	10 Pesos. Gold.	—
PnA60	1961	—	10 Pesos. Gold. KM43.	—
Pn60	1965So	10	20 Centesimos. Copper. KM44.	—
Pn61	1965So	—	20 Centesimos. Silver. KM44.	—
Pn62	1965So	—	20 Centesimos. Gold. KM44.	—
Pn63	1965So	25	50 Centesimos. Aluminum-Bronze. KM45.	—
Pn64	1965So	10	50 Centesimos. Copper. KM45.	—
Pn65	1965So	25	50 Centesimos. Copper-Nickel. KM45.	—
Pn66	1965So	—	50 Centesimos. Silver. KM45.	—
Pn67	1965So	—	50 Centesimos. Gold. KM45.	—
Pn68	1965So	10	Peso. Copper. KM46.	—
PnA69	1965	—	Peso. Aluminum-Bronze. 24 mm. Similar to KM#46. Planchet is 5 Pesos.	—
Pn69	1965So	25	Peso. Copper-Nickel. KM46.	—
Pn70	1965So	—	Peso. Silver. KM46.	—
Pn71	1965So	—	Peso. Gold. KM46.	—
Pn72	1965So	10	5 Pesos. Copper. KM47.	—
PnA73	1965	—	5 Pesos. Copper-Nickel. 29 mm. Similar to KM#47. Planchet is 10 Pesos.	—
Pn73	1965So	25	5 Pesos. Copper-Nickel. KM47.	—
Pn74	1965So	—	5 Pesos. Silver. KM47.	—
Pn75	1965So	—	5 Pesos. Gold. KM47.	—
Pn76	1965So	10	10 Pesos. Copper. KM48.	—
Pn77	1965So	—	10 Pesos. Silver. KM48.	—
Pn78	1968So	100	Peso. Copper-Nickel. KM49.	35.00
Pn79	1968So	1,000	Peso. Silver. KM49.	18.00
Pn80	1968So	100	5 Pesos. Copper-Nickel. KM50.	35.00
Pn81	1968So	1,000	5 Pesos. Silver. KM50.	20.00
Pn82	1968So	100	10 Pesos. Copper-Nickel. KM51.	35.00
Pn83	1968So	1,000	10 Pesos. Silver. KM51.	22.00
PnA84	1968S	—	20 Pesos. Yellow Metal.	—

KM#	Date	Mintage	Identification	Mkt Val
PnB84	1968	—	20 Pesos. Copper-Nickel. Similar to KM#56; Proof.	—
PnC84	1968	—	20 Pesos. Silver. Star. Similar to KM#56.	—
Pn84	1968So	1,000	20 Pesos. Silver.	25.00
PnA85	1968S	—	50 Pesos. Yellow Metal.	—
PnB85	1968	—	50 Pesos. Copper-Nickel. Similar to KM#57; Proof.	—
PnC85	1968	—	50 Pesos. Silver. Star. Similar to KM#57.	—
Pn85	1968So	1,000	50 Pesos. Silver.	30.00
Pn86	1969So	50	Peso. Copper-Nickel. KM52.	35.00
Pn87	1969So	1,000	Peso. 0.9000 Silver. KM52.	18.00
PnA88	1969So	—	Peso. 0.7500 Gold. 4.0700 g. KM52.	250
Pn88	1969So	50	5 Pesos. Copper-Nickel. KM53.	30.00
Pn89	1969So	1,000	5 Pesos. 0.9000 Silver. KM53.	18.00
PnA90	1969So	—	5 Pesos. 0.7500 Gold. 5.8600 g. KM53.	300
Pn90	1969So	50	10 Pesos. Copper-Nickel. KM54.	30.00
Pn91	1969So	1,000	10 Pesos. 0.9000 Silver. KM54.	18.00
PnA92	1969	—	10 Pesos. 0.7500 Gold. 7.8700 g. 22.9 mm. Similar to KM#54; Proof.	—
Pn92	1969	20,000	1000 Pesos. Copper.	30.00
Pn93	1969	250	1000 Pesos. Silver.	45.00
Pn95	1970So	—	20 Pesos. Silver. Star on reverse. KM56.	—
Pn96	1970So	—	20 Pesos. Silver. No star on reverse. KM56.	18.00
Pn97	1970So	1,000	20 Pesos. Gold. KM56.	300
Pn98	1970So	—	50 Pesos. Silver. KM57.	18.00
Pn99	1970So	1,000	50 Pesos. Gold. KM57.	350
Pn100	1971So	—	50 Pesos. Copper Nickel. KM58.	55.00
Pn101	1971So	80	50 Pesos. Copper Nickel. With F. ORRELLANA, P., KM58	55.00
Pn102	1971So	2,000	50 Pesos. Silver. KM58.	25.00
Pn103	1971So	200	50 Pesos. Gold. KM58.	375
Pn104	1972So	3	100 Pesos.	—
Pn105	1972So	12	100 Pesos. Alpaca.	—
Pn106	1973	—	100 Pesos. Silver. KM59.	30.00
PnA107	1973	—	100 Pesos. Gold. Similar to KM#59.	—
PnB107	1973	50	100 Pesos. Aluminum.	—
PnC107	1975	50	5 Pesos. Alpaca. Similar to KM#65.	—
PnD107	1973	50	100 Pesos. Copper.	—
Pn107	1976	—	5 Nuevo Pesos. Aluminum. KM70.	75.00
PnA108	1976	—	10 Centesimos. Copper. Similar to KM#66.	—
PnB108	1976	—	10 Centesimos. Aluminum. Similar to KM#66.	—
PnC108	1976	—	20 Centesimos. Copper. Similar to KM#67.	—
PnD108	1976	—	20 Centesimos. Aluminum. Similar to KM#67.	—
PnE108	1976	—	50 Centesimos. Copper. Similar to KM#68.	—
PnF108	1976	—	50 Centesimos. Aluminum. Similar to KM#68.	—
PnG108	1976	—	Nuevo Peso. Copper. Similar to KM#69.	—
PnH108	1976	—	Nuevo Peso. Aluminum. Similar to KM#69.	—
Pn108	1976	—	5 Nuevo Pesos. Copper-Aluminum. KM70.	75.00
Pn109	1976	—	5 Nuevo Pesos. Copper-Nickel. KM70.	100
Pn110	1976	—	5 Nuevo Pesos. Silver. KM70.	150
PnA111	1977	—	Centesimo. Gold. Similar to KM#71.	—
PnB111	1977	—	Centesimo. Nickel. Similar to KM#71.	—
PnC111	1977	—	Centesimo. Copper. Similar to KM#71.	—
PnD111	1977	—	Centesimo. Aluminum-Bronze. Similar to KM#71.	—
PnE111	1977	—	2 Centesimos. Gold. Similar to KM#72.	—
PnF111	1977	—	2 Centesimos. Nickel. Similar to KM#72.	—
PnG111	1977	—	2 Centesimos. Copper. Similar to KM#72.	—
PnH111	1977	—	2 Centesimos. Aluminum-Bronze. Similar to KM#72.	—
PnI111	1977	—	5 Centesimos. Gold. Similar to KM#73.	—
PnJ111	1977	—	5 Centesimos. Nickel. Similar to KM#73.	—
PnK111	1977	—	5 Centesimos. Copper. Similar to KM#73.	—
PnL111	1977	—	5 Centesimos. Aluminum-Bronze. Similar to KM#73.	—
PnM111	1980	—	Nuevo Peso. Aluminum. Similar to KM#74.	—
PnN111	1980	—	Nuevo Peso. Copper. Similar to KM#74.	—
PnA112	1980	—	5 Nuevo Pesos. Aluminum. Similar to KM#75.	—
PnB112	1980	—	5 Nuevo Pesos. Copper. Similar to KM#75.	—
Pn111	1980	—	Peso. Brass. KM74.	—
Pn112	1980	—	5 Pesos. Brass. KM75.	—
PnA113	1981	—	2 Nuevo Pesos. Silver. Similar to KM#77; Proof.	—
PnB113	1981	—	2 Nuevo Pesos. Aluminum-Bronze. Similar to KM#77; Proof.	—
PnC113	1981	—	10 Nuevo Pesos. Copper. Similar to KM#79.	—
PnD113	1981	—	10 Nuevo Pesos. Aluminum. Similar to KM#79.	—
Pn113	1981	—	10 Pesos. Brass. KM79.	—
PnA114	1981So	—	100 Nuevo Pesos. 0.9000 Gold. 20.0000 g. KM80.	425
PnB114	1981So	—	5000 Nuevo Pesos. 0.9000 Gold. 20.0000 g. KM81.	375
PnC114	1983So	—	500 Nuevo Pesos. 0.9000 Gold. 20.0000 g. KM82.	550
PnA118	1984	40	2000 Nuevo Pesos. Silver. 40.6 mm. Similar to KM#88. Different obverse and reverse; Proof.	—
PnA119	1984	—	20000 Nuevo Pesos. Silver. 40.6 mm. Similar to KM#89.	—
PnB119	1984	—	20000 Nuevo Pesos. Copper. Similar to KM#89.	—
PnC119	1984	—	20000 Nuevo Pesos. Brass. Similar to KM#89.	—
Pn114	1984	—	2000 Nuevo Pesos. Copper. Thick reeded edge. KM87.	—
Pn115	1984	—	2000 Nuevo Pesos. Aluminum. Thick reeded edge. KM87.	—
Pn116	1984	—	2000 Nuevo Pesos. Aluminum. Thick reeded edge. KM88.	—
Pn117	1984	—	2000 Nuevo Pesos. Aluminum. Thick reeded edge. KM88.	—
Pn118	1984	—	20000 Nuevo Pesos. Aluminum. KM89.	—
Pn119	1984	—	20000 Nuevo Pesos. Gold. 32.5 mm. KM89.	—
Pn120	1987	—	5000 Pesos. Alpaca. KM91; Alpaca	—
Pn121	1987	—	5000 Pesos. Copper. KM91.	—
Pn122	1987	—	5000 Pesos. Bronze. KM91.	—
Pn123	1988	—	5000 Nuevo Pesos. Copper. Similar to KM#99.	—
Pn124	1988	—	5000 Nuevo Pesos. Alpaca. Similar to KM#99.	—

TRIAL STRIKES

KM#	Date	Mintage	Identification	Mkt Val
TS9	1984	—	20000 Nuevo Pesos. Silver. 25.4700 g. Radiant sun peeking over shield of arms in wreath within inner circle. PRUEBA.	100
TS10	1984	—	2000 Nuevo Pesos. Silver. 25.6700 g. PRUEBA. Map of Uruguay at right, map of North and South America above rising sun at lower left.	100
TS11	1984	—	2000 Nuevo Pesos. Copper. Radiant sun peeking over shield of arms in wreath within inner circle. PRUEBA.	85.00
TS12	1984	—	2000 Nuevo Pesos. Copper. PRUEBA. Map of Uruguay at right, map of North and South America above rising sun at lower left.	85.00
TS13	1984	—	2000 Nuevo Pesos. Copper Gilt. Radiant sun peeking over shield of arms in wreath within inner circle. PRUEBA.	100
TS14	1984	—	2000 Nuevo Pesos. Copper Gilt. PRUEBA. Map of Uruguay at right, map of North and South America above rising sun at lower left.	100
TS15	1984	—	2000 Nuevo Pesos. Aluminum. Radiant sun peeking over shield of arms in wreath within inner circle. PRUEBA.	85.00
TS16	1984	—	2000 Nuevo Pesos. Aluminum. PRUEBA. Map of Uruguay at right, map of North and South America above rising sun.	85.00
TS17	1984	—	2000 Nuevo Pesos. Silver. 25.0000 g. Radiant sun peeking over shield of arms within wreath. PRUEBA.	,100
TS18	1984	—	2000 Nuevo Pesos. Silver. 24.7200 g. PRUEBA. Map of Uruguay at right, map of North and South America above rising sun.	100
TS19	1984	—	2000 Nuevo Pesos. Copper. Radiant sun peeking over arms within wreath. Winged Liberty divides value.	85.00
TS20	1984	—	2000 Nuevo Pesos. Copper. PRUEBA. Map of Uruguay at right, map of North and South America above rising sun at lower left.	85.00
TS21	1984	—	2000 Nuevo Pesos. Copper Gilt. Radiant sun peeking over shield of arms within wreath. PRUEBA.	100
TS22	1984	—	2000 Nuevo Pesos. Copper Gilt. PRUEBA. Map of Uruguay at right, map of North and South America above rising sun at lower left.	100
TS23	1984	—	2000 Nuevo Pesos. Aluminum. Radiant sun peeking over shield of arms within wreath. PRUEBA.	85.00
TS24	1984	—	2000 Nuevo Pesos. Aluminum. PRUEBA. Map of Uruguay at right, map of North and South America above rising sun at lower left.	85.00
TS25	1984	—	20000 Nuevo Pesos. Silver. 19.4400 g. Shield of arms flanked by flags in inner circle. PRUEBA.	110
TS26	1984	—	20000 Nuevo Pesos. Silver. 20.2700 g. PRUEBA. Map of Uruguay at right, map of North and South America above rising sun at lower left.	110
TS27	1984	—	20000 Nuevo Pesos. Copper. Shield of arms flanked by flags in inner circle. PRUEBA.	80.00
TS28	1984	—	20000 Nuevo Pesos. Copper. PRUEBA. Map of Uruguay at right, map of North and South America above rising sun at lower left.	80.00
TS29	1984	—	20000 Nuevo Pesos. Copper Gilt. Shield of arms flanked by flags in inner circle. PRUEBA.	90.00
TS30	1984	—	20000 Nuevo Pesos. Copper Gilt. PRUEBA. Map of Uruguay at right, map of North and South America above rising sun at lower left.	90.00

PIEFORTS

Double Thickness

KM#	Date	Mintage	Identification	Mkt Val
P1	1870	—	20 Centesimos. Copper.	375
P6	1984	600	20 Pesos. Silver. KM86a.	60.00
P7	1984	—	2000 Nuevo Pesos. Silver. 50.0000 g. Plain edge. KM87.	185
P8	1984	—	2000 Nuevo Pesos. Copper. Thick plain edge. KM87.	65.00
P9	1984	—	2000 Nuevo Pesos. Copper Gilt. Thick plain edge. KM87.	75.00
P10	1984	—	2000 Nuevo Pesos. Silver. 50.4800 g. Plain edge. KM88.	125
P11	1984	—	2000 Nuevo Pesos. Copper. Thick plain edge. KM88.	65.00
P12	1984	—	2000 Nuevo Pesos. Copper Gilt. Thick plain edge. KM88.	75.00
P13	1984	—	20000 Nuevo Pesos. Silver. 20.7500 g. Reeded edge. KM89.	125
P14	1984	—	20000 Nuevo Pesos. Silver. 40.1700 g. Reeded edge. KM89.	200
P15	1984	—	20000 Nuevo Pesos. Silver. 40.4400 g. Plain edge. KM89.	200
P16	1984	—	20000 Nuevo Pesos. Copper. Thick reeded edge. KM89.	80.00
P17	1984	—	20000 Nuevo Pesos. Copper. Reeded edge. KM89.	80.00
P18	1984	—	20000 Nuevo Pesos. Copper Gilt. KM89.	100

MINT SETS

KM#	Date	Mintage	Identification	Issue Price	Mkt Val
MS1	1969/70 (5)	—	KM52-54, 56-57 KM#MS1 was issued under the law no. 13,637 of December 21, 1967.	—	3.50
MS2	1969/70 (5)	—	KM52-54, 56-57 KM#MS2 was issued for the 11th Assembly of the Interamerica Bank.	—	3.50
MS3	1976 (4)	—	KM66-69	—	2.50
MS4	1976 (4)	—	KM#Pn107-110	—	400

PROOF SETS

KM#	Date	Mintage	Identification	Issue Price	Mkt Val
PS1	1953 (4)	100	KM32-35	—	275
PS2	1968 (5)	1,000	KM#Pn79, 81, 83-85	—	78.00
PS3	1968 (3)	50	KM49-51	—	200
PS4	1968 (3)	100	KM#Pn78, 80, 82	—	90.00
PS5	1969 (3)	50	KM#Pn86, 88, 90	—	75.00
PS6	1969 (3)	1,000	KM#Pn87, 89, 91	—	30.00
PS7	1969/70 (5)	1,000	KM#Pn87, 89, 91, 96, 98	—	50.00
PS8	1976 (4)	—	KM#66a-69a	—	125

UZBEKISTAN

The Republic of Uzbekistan (formerly the Uzbek S.S.R.), is bordered on the north by Kazakhstan, to the east by Kirghizia and Tajikistan, on the south by Afghanistan and on the west by Turkmenistan. The republic is comprised of the regions of Andizhan, Bukhara, Dzhizak, Ferghana, Kashkadar, Khorezm (Khiva), Namangan, Navoi, Samarkand, Surkhan-.Darya, Syr-Darya, Tashkent and the Karakalpak Autonomous Republic. It has an area of 172,741 sq. mi. (447,400 sq. km.) and a population of 20.3 million. Capital: Tashkent.

Crude oil, natural gas, coal, copper, and gold deposits make up the chief resources, while intensive farming, based on artificial irrigation, provides an abundance of cotton.

On the eve of WW I, Khiva and Bukhara were enclaves within a Russian Turkestan divided into five provinces or oblasti. The czarist government did not attempt to Russify the indigenous Turkic or Tajik populations. The revolution of March 1917 created a confused situation in the area. In Tashkent there was a Turkestan committee of the provisional government; a Communist-controlled council of workers', soldiers' and peasants' deputies; also a Moslem Turkic movement, Shuro-i-Islamiya, and a young Turkestan or Jaddidi (Renovation) party. The last named party claimed full political autonomy for Turkestan and the abolition of the emirate of Bukhara and the khanate of Khiva. After the Communist *coup d'etat in* Petrograd, the council of people's commissars on Nov. 24 (Dec. 7), 1917, published an appeal to "all toiling Moslems in Russia and in the east" proclaiming their right to build their national life "freely and unhindered". In response, the Moslem and Jaddidi organizations in Dec. 1917 convoked a national congress in Khokand, which appointed a provisional government headed by Mustafa Chokayev (or Chokaigolu; 1890-1941) and resolved to elect a constituent assembly to decide whether Turkestan should remain within a Russian federal state or proclaim its independence. In the spring of 1919 a Red army group defeated Kolchak and in September its commander, M.V. Frunze, arrived in Tashkent with V.V.Kuibyshev as political commissar. The Communists were still much too weak in Turkestan to proclaim the country part of Soviet Russia. Faizullah Khojayev organized a young Bukhara movement, which on Sept. 14, 1920, proclaimed the dethronement of Emir Mir Alim. Bukhara was then made a S.S.R. In 1920 the Tashkent Communist government declared war on Junaid, who took to flight, and Khiva became another S.S.R. In Oct. 1921, Enver Pasha, the former leader of the young Turks, appeared in Bukhara and assumed command of the Basmachi movement. In Aug. 1922 he was forced to retreat into Tajikistan and died on Aug. 4, in a battle near Baljuvan. Khiva concluded a treaty of alliance with the Russian S.F.S.R. in Sept. 1920, and Bukhara followed suit in March 1921. Theoretically, a Turkestan Autonomous Soviet Socialist Republic had existed since May 1, 1918; in 1920 this "Turk republic", as it was called, was proclaimed part of the R.S.F.S.R. On Sept. 18, 1924, the Uzbek and Turkmen peoples were authorized to form S.S.R.'s of their own, and the Kazakhs, Kirghiz, and Tajiks to form autonomous S.S.R.'s. On Oct.27, 1924, the Uzbek and Turkmen S.S.R. were officially constituted and the former was formally accepted on Jan.15, 1925, as a member of the U.S.S.R. Tajikistan was an autonomous soviet republic within Uzbekistan until Dec.5, 1929, when it became a S.S.R. On Dec. 5, 1936, incorporating the Kara-Kalpak A.S.S.R., which had belonged to Kazakhstan until 1930 and afterward had come under direct control of the R.S.F.S.R, increased the Uzbekistan territory.

On June 20, 1990 the Uzbek Supreme Soviet adopted a declaration of sovereignty, and in Aug. 1991, following an unsuccessful coup, declared itself independent as the "Republic of Uzbekistan", which was confirmed by referendum in Dec. That same month Uzbekistan became a member of the CIS.

Monetary System
100 Tiyin = 1 Som

REPUBLIC

STANDARD COINAGE

KM# 1.1 TIYIN

1.7500 g., Brass Clad Steel, 16.9 mm. **Obv:** Arms within wreath below stars **Rev:** Value and date flanked by sprigs **Edge:** Plain

Date	Mintage	F	VF	XF	Unc
1994	—	—	—	—	0.30

KM# 1.2 TIYIN

1.7500 g., Brass Clad Steel, 16.9 mm. **Obv:** Arms within wreath below stars **Rev:** Value and date flanked by sprigs **Edge:** Plain

Date	Mintage	F	VF	XF	Unc
1994	—	—	—	—	0.30

KM# 2.1 3 TIYIN

2.7000 g., Brass Plated Steel, 19.9 mm. **Obv:** Arms within wreath below stars **Rev:** Value and date flanked by sprigs **Edge:** Reeded

Date	Mintage	F	VF	XF	Unc
1994	—	—	—	—	3.00

KM# 2.2 3 TIYIN

2.7000 g., Brass Plated Steel, 19.9 mm. **Obv:** Arms within wreath below stars **Rev:** Value and date flanked by sprigs **Edge:** Reeded

Date	Mintage	F	VF	XF	Unc
1994	—	—	—	—	1.00

KM# 3.1 5 TIYIN

3.4000 g., Brass Plated Steel, 21.4 mm. **Obv:** Arms within wreath below stars **Rev:** Value and date flanked by sprigs **Edge:** Reeded

Date	Mintage	F	VF	XF	Unc
1994	—	—	—	—	2.00

KM# 3.2 5 TIYIN

3.4000 g., Brass Plated Steel, 21.4 mm. **Obv:** Arms within wreath below stars **Rev:** Value and date flanked by sprigs **Edge:** Reeded

Date	Mintage	F	VF	XF	Unc
1994	—	—	—	—	0.50

KM# 4.1 10 TIYIN

2.8500 g., Nickel Clad Steel, 18.7 mm. **Obv:** Arms within wreath below stars **Rev:** Value and date flanked by sprigs **Edge:** Reeded **Note:** Two varieties of sunray arrangements exist; die varieties exist with slightly larger or smaller denomination.

Date	Mintage	F	VF	XF	Unc
1994	—	—	—	—	0.60
1994PM Rare	—	—	—	—	—

KM# 4.2 10 TIYIN

2.8500 g., Nickel Clad Steel, 18.7 mm. **Obv:** Arms within wreath below stars **Rev:** Value and date flanked by sprigs **Edge:** Reeded

Date	Mintage	F	VF	XF	Unc
1994	—	—	—	—	5.00

KM# 5.1 20 TIYIN

4.0000 g., Nickel Clad Steel, 22 mm. **Obv:** Arms within wreath below stars **Rev:** Date and value flanked by sprigs **Edge:** Lettering in Cyrillic

Date	Mintage	F	VF	XF	Unc
1994	—	—	—	—	0.75

KM# 5.1a 20 TIYIN

4.0000 g., Nickel Clad Steel, 22 mm. **Obv:** Arms within wreath below stars **Rev:** Date and value flanked by sprigs **Note:** Two sun ray varieties exist, varieties exist with wide and narrow edge lettering.

Date	Mintage	F	VF	XF	Unc
1994	—	—	—	—	1.00
1994PM Rare	—	—	—	—	—

KM# 5.1b 20 TIYIN

4.0000 g., Nickel Clad Steel, 22 mm. **Obv:** Arms within wreath below stars **Rev:** Date and value flanked by sprigs **Edge:** Lettering in Cyrillic **Note:** Two varieties of sunray arrangements exist.

Date	Mintage	F	VF	XF	Unc
1994	—	—	—	—	0.75

KM# 5.2 20 TIYIN

4.0000 g., Nickel Clad Steel, 22 mm. **Obv:** Arms within wreath below stars **Rev:** Date and value flanked by sprigs **Edge:** Lettering in Cyrillic

Date	Mintage	F	VF	XF	Unc
1994 Scarce	—	—	—	—	20.00

KM# 6.1 50 TIYIN

4.8000 g., Nickel Clad Steel, 23.9 mm. **Obv:** Arms within wreath below stars **Rev:** Value and date flanked by sprigs **Edge:** Lettering in Cyrillic **Note:** 2 varieties of sunray arrangements exist; all coins show orthographic error in 1st letter of "ellik" within edge inscription.

Date	Mintage	F	VF	XF	Unc
1994	—	—	—	—	1.00
1994PM	—	—	—	—	50.00

KM# 6.2 50 TIYIN

4.8000 g., Nickel Clad Steel, 23.9 mm. **Obv:** Arms within wreath below stars **Rev:** Value and date flanked by sprigs **Edge:** Lettering in Cyrillic **Note:** All coins show orthographic error in 1st letter of "ellik" within edge inscription.

Date	Mintage	F	VF	XF	Unc
1994	—	—	—	—	1.00

KM# 8 SOM

Nickel Clad Steel **Obv:** Arms within wreath below stars **Rev:** Value and date flanked by sprigs

Date	Mintage	F	VF	XF	Unc
1997	—	—	—	—	1.35
1999	—	—	—	—	1.35
2000	—	—	—	—	1.35

KM# 12 SOM

2.8300 g., Nickel-Clad Steel, 18.8 mm. **Obv:** National arms **Rev:** Value and map **Edge:** Reeded

Date	Mintage	F	VF	XF	Unc
2000	—	—	—	—	1.00

KM# 9 5 SOM

Nickel Clad Steel **Obv:** Arms within wreath below stars **Rev:** Value and date flanked by sprigs

Date	Mintage	F	VF	XF	Unc
1997	—	—	—	—	1.50
1999	—	—	—	—	1.50

KM# 7 10 SOM

31.1000 g., 0.9990 Silver .9988 oz. ASW **Subject:** 3rd Anniversary of Independence **Obv:** Arms within wreath **Rev:** Equestrian above value

Date	Mintage	F	VF	XF	Unc
1994 Proof	Est. 1,000	Value: 65.00			

KM# 10 10 SOM

Nickel Clad Steel **Obv:** Arms within wreath below stars **Rev:** Value and date flanked by sprigs

Date	Mintage	F	VF	XF	Unc
1997	—	—	—	—	2.00
1999	—	—	—	—	2.00
2000	—	—	—	—	2.00

KM# 11 25 SOM

Nickel Clad Steel, 27 mm. **Subject:** Jaloliddin Manguberdi **Obv:** Arms within wreath **Rev:** Bust with headdress facing 1/4 right **Edge:** Plain

Date	Mintage	F	VF	XF	Unc
1999	—	—	—	—	3.50

PATTERNS

Including off metal strikes

KM#	Date	Mintage	Identification	Mkt Val
Pn1	1994	—	Som. Gold-Plated Bronze. 15.1300 g. 31 mm. National arms. Muhammad Taragay Ulugbek (1394-1449). Reeded edge. Proof	100
Pn2	1995	—	Tiyin. 0.8000 Gold Plated Silver. 15.2200 g. 31 mm. National arms. Samarkand building. Reeded edge. Proof	200

VANUATU

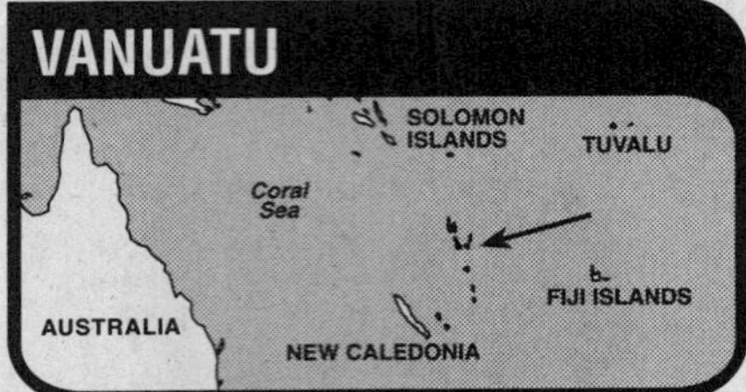

The Republic of Vanuatu, formerly New Hebrides Condominium, a group of islands located in the South Pacific 500 miles (800 km.) west of Fiji, were under the joint sovereignty of Great Britain and France. The islands have an area of 5,700 sq. mi. (14,760 sq. km.) and a population of 165,000, mainly Melanesians of mixed blood. Capital: Port-Vila. The volcanic and coral islands, while malarial land subject to frequent earthquakes, are extremely fertile, and produce copra, coffee, tropical fruits and timber for export.

The New Hebrides were discovered by Portuguese navigator Pedro de Quiros (sailing under orders by the King of Spain) in 1606, visited by French explorer Bougainville in 1768, and named by British navigator Capt. James Cook in 1774. Ships of all nations converged on the islands to trade for sandalwood, prompting France and Britain to relinquish their individual claims and declare the islands a neutral zone in 1878. The New Hebrides were placed under the control of a mixed Anglo-French commission of naval officers during the native uprisings of 1887, and established as a condominium under the joint sovereignty of France and Great Britain in 1906.

Vanuatu became an independent republic within the Commonwealth in July 1980. A president is Head of State and the Prime Minister is Head of Government.

MINT MARKS

(a) - Paris, privy marks only

MONETARY SYSTEM

Francs until 1983

Vatu to Present

REPUBLIC

STANDARD COINAGE

KM# 3 VATU

2.1000 g., Nickel-Brass, 16.95 mm. **Obv:** National arms **Rev:** Shell and value **Edge:** Plain

Date	Mintage	F	VF	XF	Unc	BU
1983	—	—	—	0.10	0.50	0.75
1983 Proof	—	Value: 1.00				
1990	—	—	—	0.10	0.50	0.75
1999	—	—	—	0.10	0.50	0.75

KM# 4 2 VATU

3.0000 g., Nickel-Brass, 20 mm. **Obv:** National arms **Rev:** Shell and value **Edge:** Plain

Date	Mintage	F	VF	XF	Unc	BU
1983	—	—	—	0.15	0.50	1.00
1983 Proof	—	Value: 1.50				
1990	—	—	—	0.15	0.50	1.00
1995	—	—	—	0.15	0.50	1.00

KM# 5 5 VATU

4.1000 g., Nickel-Brass, 23.5 mm. **Obv:** National arms **Rev:** Shell and value **Edge:** Plain

Date	Mintage	F	VF	XF	Unc	BU
1983	—	—	—	0.20	0.75	1.25
1983 Proof	—	Value: 1.75				
1990	—	—	—	0.20	0.75	1.25
1995	—	—	—	0.20	0.75	1.25

KM# 6 10 VATU

6.1000 g., Copper-Nickel, 23.95 mm. **Series:** F.A.O. **Obv:** National arms **Rev:** Crab and value, palm trees **Edge:** Plain

Date	Mintage	F	VF	XF	Unc	BU
1983	—	—	—	0.25	1.00	1.50
1983 Proof	—	Value: 2.00				
1990	—	—	—	0.25	1.00	1.50
1995	—	—	—	0.25	1.00	1.50

KM# 25 10 VATU

Copper-Nickel **Subject:** End of Victorian Era - Queen Victoria **Obv:** Arms **Rev:** Seated half figure of Queen Mother left within beaded circle

Date	Mintage	F	VF	XF	Unc	BU
1995	Est. 30,000	—	—	—	2.00	3.00

KM# 28 10 VATU

10.0000 g., 0.5000 Silver .1607 oz. ASW **Series:** Olympics **Obv:** Arms **Rev:** Gymnast

Date	Mintage	F	VF	XF	Unc	BU
1996	Est. 10,000	—	—	—	4.00	5.00

KM# 7 20 VATU

10.2000 g., Copper-Nickel, 28.45 mm. **Series:** F.A.O. **Obv:** National arms **Rev:** Crab, value, palm trees **Edge:** Reeded **Note:** Similar 10 Vatu, KM#6.

Date	Mintage	F	VF	XF	Unc	BU
1983	—	—	—	0.35	1.50	2.50
1983 Proof	—	Value: 3.00				
1990	—	—	—	0.35	1.50	2.50
1995	—	—	—	0.35	1.50	2.50

KM# 19 20 VATU

20.0000 g., 0.5000 Silver .3215 oz. ASW **Subject:** Captain James Cook **Obv:** National arms **Rev:** Seated half figure facing right

Date	Mintage	F	VF	XF	Unc	BU
1994 Proof	Est. 25,000	Value: 10.00				

KM# 20 20 VATU
20.0000 g., 0.9250 Silver .5948 oz. ASW **Series:** Endangered Wildlife **Obv:** National arms **Rev:** Kingfisher

Date	Mintage	F	VF	XF	Unc	BU
1994 Proof	Est. 25,000	Value: 28.00				

KM# 1 50 VATU
15.0000 g., Nickel, 32.9 mm. **Subject:** 1st Anniversary of Independence **Obv:** National arms **Rev:** Figures working in fields

Date	Mintage	F	VF	XF	Unc	BU
1981	—	—	—	0.75	2.00	3.00

KM# 1a 50 VATU
15.0000 g., 0.9250 Silver .4461 oz. ASW **Obv:** National arms **Rev:** Figures working in field

Date	Mintage	F	VF	XF	Unc	BU
1981 Proof	846	Value: 16.50				

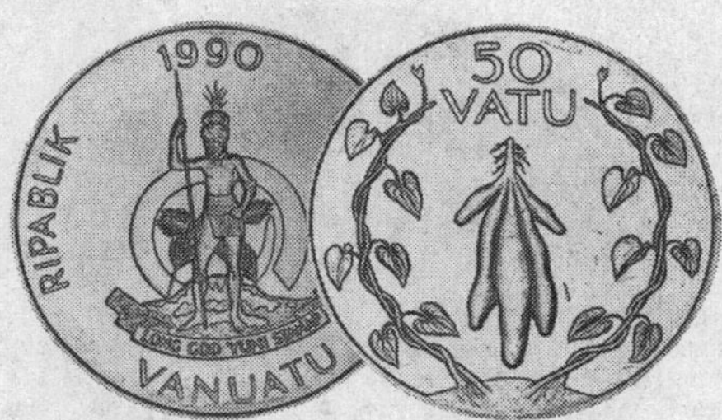

KM# 8 50 VATU
15.0000 g., Copper-Nickel, 32.9 mm. **Series:** F.A.O. **Obv:** National arms **Rev:** Vegetable within vined sprig

Date	Mintage	F	VF	XF	Unc	BU
1983	—	—	—	0.75	2.00	3.00
1983 Proof	—	Value: 5.00				
1990	—	—	—	0.75	2.00	3.00
1995	—	—	—	0.75	2.00	3.00
1999	—	—	—	0.75	2.00	3.00

KM# 10 50 VATU
34.0000 g., 0.9250 Silver 1.0111 oz. ASW **Series:** Seoul Olympics **Subject:** Boxing **Obv:** National arms **Rev:** Boxers

Date	Mintage	F	VF	XF	Unc	BU
1988 Proof	15,000	Value: 15.50				

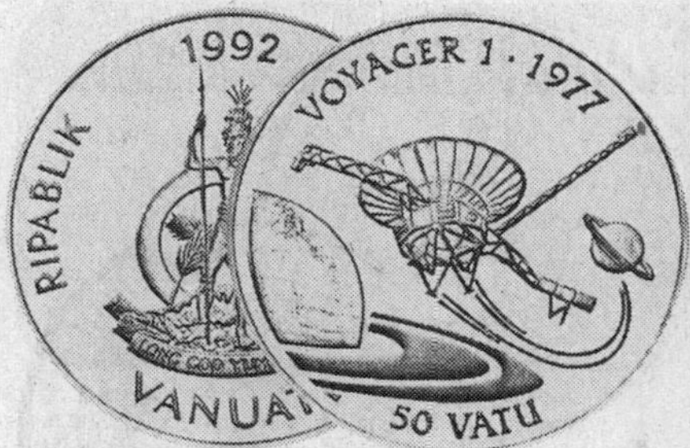

KM# 11 50 VATU
31.4700 g., 0.9250 Silver .9359 oz. ASW **Subject:** Voyager I **Obv:** National arms **Rev:** Space shuttle and planets

Date	Mintage	F	VF	XF	Unc	BU
1992 Proof	10,000	Value: 14.50				

KM# 12 50 VATU
31.4700 g., 0.9250 Silver .9359 oz. ASW **Subject:** Pedro Fernandez De Quiros **Obv:** National arms **Rev:** Kneeling figure facing, boat and ship

Date	Mintage	F	VF	XF	Unc	BU
1992 Proof	—	Value: 14.50				

KM# 13 50 VATU
31.4700 g., 0.9250 Silver .9359 oz. ASW **Series:** Endangered Wildlife **Subject:** Earth Pigeons **Obv:** National arms **Rev:** Birds

Date	Mintage	F	VF	XF	Unc	BU
1992 Proof	—	Value: 25.00				

KM# 14 50 VATU
31.4700 g., 0.9250 Silver .9359 oz. ASW **Series:** Olympics **Subject:** Canoes **Obv:** National arms **Rev:** Canoers

Date	Mintage	F	VF	XF	Unc	BU
1992 Proof	Est. 40,000	Value: 14.50				

KM# 15 50 VATU
31.4700 g., 0.9250 Silver .9359 oz. ASW **Subject:** 40th Anniversary of Coronation **Obv:** National arms

Date	Mintage	F	VF	XF	Unc	BU
1993 Proof	Est. 10,000	Value: 15.50				

KM# 16 50 VATU
31.4700 g., 0.9250 Silver .9359 oz. ASW **Subject:** The Boudeuse **Obv:** National arms **Rev:** Ship to left of half figure right

Date	Mintage	F	VF	XF	Unc	BU
1993 Proof	Est. 15,000	Value: 14.50				

KM# 17 50 VATU
31.4700 g., 0.9250 Silver .9359 oz. ASW **Subject:** Protect Our World **Obv:** National arms **Rev:** Whale and ship

Date	Mintage	F	VF	XF	Unc	BU
1993 Proof	Est. 10,000	Value: 25.00				

KM# 18 50 VATU
31.4700 g., 0.9250 Silver .9359 oz. ASW **Subject:** World Cup Soccer **Obv:** National arms **Rev:** Soccer player

Date	Mintage	F	VF	XF	Unc	BU
1994 Proof	Est. 10,000	Value: 14.50				

KM# 21 50 VATU
31.4700 g., 0.9250 Silver .9359 oz. ASW **Subject:** De Bougainville **Obv:** National arms **Rev:** Bust facing at left of book, globe and ship

Date	Mintage	F	VF	XF	Unc	BU
1994 Proof	Est. 10,000	Value: 14.50				

KM# 22 50 VATU
31.4700 g., 0.9250 Silver .9359 oz. ASW **Subject:** Queen Victoria **Obv:** National arms **Rev:** Seated half figure of Queen Mother right within beaded circle

Date	Mintage	F	VF	XF	Unc	BU
1994 Proof	Est. 20,000	Value: 14.50				

KM# 24 50 VATU
31.4700 g., 0.9250 Silver .9359 oz. ASW **Series:** Olympics **Obv:** National arms **Rev:** Swimmers

Date	Mintage	F	VF	XF	Unc	BU
1994 Proof	Est. 40,000	Value: 14.50				

KM# 30 50 VATU
31.4700 g., 0.9250 Silver .9359 oz. ASW **Series:** Olympic Games 1996 **Obv:** National arms **Rev:** Gymnast

Date	Mintage	F	VF	XF	Unc	BU
1994 Proof	40,000	Value: 14.50				

KM# 26 50 VATU
31.4700 g., 0.9250 Silver .9359 oz. ASW **Subject:** Birth of Great Grandson Prince William **Obv:** National arms **Rev:** Conjoined busts facing holding infant within beaded circle

Date	Mintage	F	VF	XF	Unc	BU
1995 Proof	Est. 30,000	Value: 15.50				

KM# 29 50 VATU
31.4700 g., 0.9250 Silver .9359 oz. ASW **Subject:** Queen Victoria and Prince Albert **Obv:** National arms **Rev:** Conjoined standing figures in front of building within circle

Date	Mintage	F	VF	XF	Unc	BU
1996 Proof	Est. 10,000	Value: 15.50				

KM# 35 50 VATU
28.3100 g., Silver, 38.5 mm. **Subject:** 50th Anniversary - Elizabeth and Philip **Obv:** National arms **Rev:** Family members gazing at baby Prince Andrew **Edge:** Reeded **Note:** Gold-plated shield on reverse reads: Prince Andrew 1960

Date	Mintage	F	VF	XF	Unc	BU
1997 Proof	—	Value: 17.50				

KM# 31 50 VATU
1.2441 g., 0.9990 Gold .0400 oz. AGW **Obv:** National arms **Rev:** Spanish 1704 gold coin design

Date	Mintage	F	VF	XF	Unc	BU
1998 Proof	—	Value: 30.00				

KM# 32 50 VATU
1.2441 g., 0.9990 Gold .0400 oz. AGW **Obv:** National arms **Rev:** Boar tusk necklace

Date	Mintage	F	VF	XF	Unc	BU
1998 Proof	—	Value: 30.00				

KM# 33 50 VATU
30.9700 g., 0.9250 Silver .9210 oz. ASW **Subject:** Millennium 2000 **Obv:** National arms **Rev:** Gold-plated shell

Date	Mintage	F	VF	XF	Unc	BU
1998 Proof	—	Value: 60.00				

KM# 36 50 VATU
31.4700 g., 0.9250 Silver 0.9359 oz. ASW, 37 mm. **Obv:** Standing native **Rev:** Three masted corvette Zelee **Edge:** Reeded **Shape:** Octagonal

Date	Mintage	F	VF	XF	Unc	BU
1999 Proof	—	Value: 45.00				

KM# 37 50 VATU
31.4700 g., 0.9250 Silver 0.9359 oz. ASW, 37 mm. **Obv:** Standing native **Rev:** Three masted corvette Astrolabe **Edge:** Reeded **Shape:** Octagonal

Date	Mintage	F	VF	XF	Unc	BU
1999 Proof	—	Value: 45.00				

KM# 9 100 VATU
Nickel-Brass **Obv:** National arms **Rev:** Sprouting bulbs

Date	Mintage	F	VF	XF	Unc	BU
1988	—	—	—	—	3.00	4.00
1995	—	—	—	—	3.00	4.00

KM# 23 100 VATU
7.7760 g., 0.5830 Gold .1458 oz. AGW **Series:** Endangered Wildlife **Obv:** National arms **Rev:** Kingfisher

Date	Mintage	F	VF	XF	Unc	BU
1994 Proof	Est. 2,000	Value: 140				

KM# 27 100 VATU
155.5000 g., 0.9250 Silver 4.6245 oz. ASW, 65 mm. **Obv:** National arms **Rev:** Crowned standing figures facing within beaded circle **Note:** Photo reduced.

Date	Mintage	F	VF	XF	Unc	BU
1995 Proof	Est. 2,000	Value: 75.00				

KM# 34 100 VATU
155.5000 g., 0.9250 Silver 4.6245 oz. ASW, 65.7 mm. **Subject:** H.M.S. Resolution **Obv:** National arms **Rev:** Sailing ship and carvings **Edge:** Reeded **Note:** Photo reduced.

Date	Mintage	F	VF	XF	Unc	BU
1996 Proof	5,000	Value: 75.00				

KM# 2 10000 VATU
15.9800 g., 0.9170 Gold .4712 oz. AGW **Subject:** 1st Anniversary of Independence **Obv:** National arms **Rev:** Crab flanked by palm trees

Date	Mintage	F	VF	XF	Unc	BU
1981	538	—	—	—	345	—
1981 Proof	1,054	Value: 325				

VATICAN CITY

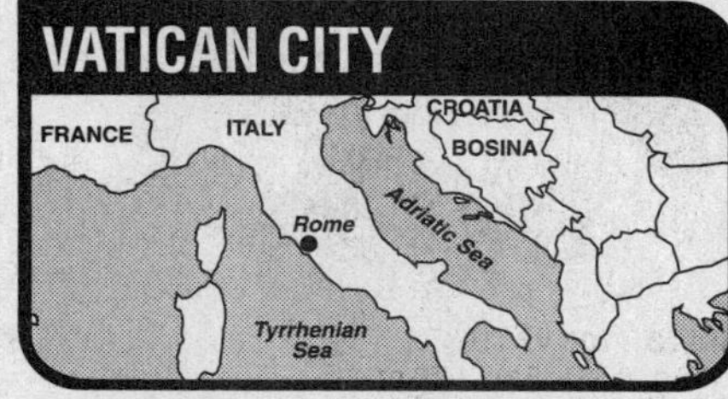

The State of the Vatican City, a papal state on the right bank of the Tiber River within the boundaries of Rome, has an area of 0.17 sq. mi. (0.44 sq. km.) and a population of *775. Capital: Vatican City.

Vatican City State, comprising the Vatican, St. Peter's, extra-territorial right to Castel Gandolfo and 13 buildings throughout Rome, is all that remains of the extensive Papal States over which the Pope exercised temporal power in central Italy. During the struggle for Italian unification, the Papal States, including Rome, were forcibly incorporated into the Kingdom of Italy in 1870. The resultant confrontation of crozier and sword remained unresolved until the signing of the Lateran Treaty, Feb. 11, 1929, between the Vatican and the Kingdom of Italy which recognized the independence and sovereignty of the State of the Vatican City, defined the relationship between the government and the church within Italy, and financially compensated the Holy See for the territorial losses from 1870.

Today the Pope exercises supreme legislative, executive and judicial power within the Vatican City, and the State of the Vatican City is recognized by many nations as an independent sovereign state under the temporal jurisdiction of the Pope, even to the extent of ambassadorial exchange. The Pope, is of course, the head of the Roman Catholic Church.

PONTIFFS

Pius XI, 1922-1939
  Sede Vacante, Feb. 10 - Mar. 2, 1939
Pius XII, 1939-1958
  Sede Vacante, Oct. 9 - 28, 1958
John XXIII, 1958-1963
  Sede Vacante, June 3 - 21,1963
Paul VI, 1963-1978
  Sede Vacante, Aug. 6 - 26, 1978
John Paul I, Aug. 26 - Sept. 28, 1978
  Sede Vacante, Sept. 28 - Oct. 16, 1978
John Paul II, 1978-2005
  Sede Vacante, April 2 - 19, 2005
Benedict XVI, 2005-

MINT MARKS

Commencing 1981

R – Rome

MONETARY SYSTEM

100 Centesimi = 1 Lira (thru 2002)
100 Euro Cent = 1 Euro

DATING

Most Vatican coins indicate the regnal year of the pope preceded by the word *Anno* (or an abbreviation), even if the *anno domini* date is omitted.

CITY STATE

Pius XI

STANDARD COINAGE

100 Centesimi = 1 Lira

Y# 1 5 CENTESIMI

Bronze **Obverse:** Crowned shield divides date **Reverse:** Olive branch divides value **Designer:** Aurelio Mistruzzi

Date	Mintage	F	VF	XF	Unc
1929/VIII	10,000	—	5.00	10.00	20.00
1930/IX	100,000	—	2.50	4.00	6.50
1931/X	100,000	—	2.50	4.00	6.50
1932/XI	100,000	—	2.50	4.00	6.50
1934/XIII	100,000	—	2.50	4.00	6.50
1935/XIV	44,000	—	5.00	10.00	20.00
1936/XV	62,000	—	2.50	4.00	6.50
1937/XVI	62,000	—	2.50	4.00	6.50
1938/XVII Rare	—	—	—	—	—

Y# 11 5 CENTESIMI

Bronze, 20 mm. **Subject:** Jubilee **Obverse:** Crowned shield flanked by date **Reverse:** Olive branch divides value **Designer:** Aurelio Mistruzzi

Date	Mintage	F	VF	XF	Unc
1933-34	100,000	—	5.00	10.00	20.00

Y# 2 10 CENTESIMI

Bronze **Obverse:** Crowned shield divides date **Reverse:** St. Peter bust right **Designer:** Aurelio Mistruzzi

Date	Mintage	F	VF	XF	Unc
1929/VIII	10,000	—	5.00	10.00	20.00
1930/IX	90,000	—	2.50	4.00	6.00
1931/X	90,000	—	2.50	4.00	6.00
1932/XI	90,000	—	2.50	4.00	6.00
1934/XIII	90,000	—	2.50	4.00	6.00
1935/XIV	90,000	—	2.50	4.00	6.00
1936/XV	81,000	—	2.50	4.00	6.00
1937/XVI	81,000	—	2.50	4.00	8.00
1938/XVII	—	—	450	900	1,500

Y# 12 10 CENTESIMI

Bronze, 22 mm. **Subject:** Jubilee **Obverse:** Crowned shield flanked by dates **Reverse:** St. Peter bust right **Designer:** Aurelio Mistruzzi

Date	Mintage	F	VF	XF	Unc
1933-34	90,000	—	5.00	10.00	20.00

Y# 3 20 CENTESIMI

Nickel **Obverse:** Crowned Arms **Reverse:** St. Paul bust left **Designer:** Aurelio Mistruzzi

Date	Mintage	F	VF	XF	Unc
1929/VIII	10,000	—	5.00	10.00	20.00
1930/IX	80,000	—	2.50	4.00	6.50
1931/X	80,000	—	2.50	4.00	6.50
1932/XI	80,000	—	2.50	4.00	6.50
1934/XIII	80,000	—	2.50	4.00	6.50
1935/XIV	11,000	—	25.00	50.00	75.00
1936/XV	64,000	—	2.50	4.00	6.50
1937/XVI	64,000	—	2.50	4.00	6.50

Y# 13 20 CENTESIMI

Nickel, 21 mm. **Subject:** Jubilee **Obverse:** Crowned Arms **Reverse:** St. Paul bust left **Designer:** Aurelio Mistruzzi

Date	Mintage	F	VF	XF	Unc
1933-34	80,000	—	5.00	10.00	20.00

Y# 4 50 CENTESIMI

Nickel **Obverse:** Crowned Arms **Reverse:** Archangel Michael divides value **Designer:** Aurelio Mistruzzi

Date	Mintage	F	VF	XF	Unc
1929/VIII	10,000	—	5.00	10.00	20.00
1930/IX	80,000	—	2.50	4.00	6.50
1931/X	80,000	—	2.50	4.00	6.50
1932/XI	80,000	—	2.50	4.00	6.50
1934/XIII	80,000	—	2.50	4.00	6.50
1935/XIV	14,000	—	6.00	12.00	25.00
1936/XV	52,000	—	2.50	4.00	6.50
1937/XVI	52,000	—	2.50	4.00	6.50

Y# 14 50 CENTESIMI

Nickel, 24 mm. **Subject:** Jubilee **Obverse:** Crowned Arms **Reverse:** Archangel Michael divides value **Designer:** Aurelio Mistruzzi

Date	Mintage	F	VF	XF	Unc
1933-34	80,000	—	4.00	8.00	17.50

Y# 5 LIRA

Nickel **Obverse:** Crowned Arms **Reverse:** Virgin Mary standing on globe and crescent **Designer:** Aurelio Mistruzzi

Date	Mintage	F	VF	XF	Unc
1929/VIII	10,000	—	5.00	10.00	20.00
1930/IX	80,000	—	2.50	4.00	6.50
1931/X	80,000	—	2.50	4.00	6.50
1932/XI	80,000	—	2.50	4.00	6.50
1934/XIII	80,000	—	2.50	4.00	6.50
1935/XIV	40,000	—	2.50	4.00	6.50
1936/XV	40,000	—	2.50	4.00	6.50
1937/XVI	70,000	—	2.50	4.00	6.50

Y# 15 LIRA

Nickel, 27 mm. **Subject:** Jubilee **Obverse:** Crowned Arms **Reverse:** Virgin Mary standing on globe and crescent **Designer:** Aurelio Mistruzzi **Note:** Enlargement of date area.

Date	Mintage	F	VF	XF	Unc
1933-34	80,000	—	5.00	12.50	25.00

Y# 6 2 LIRE

Nickel, 29 mm. **Obverse:** Crowned Arms **Reverse:** Lamb on shoulders of young shepard **Designer:** Aurelio Mistruzzi

Date	Mintage	F	VF	XF	Unc
1929/VIII	10,000	—	5.00	12.50	25.00
1930/IX	50,000	—	2.00	4.00	6.50
1931/X	50,000	—	2.00	4.00	6.50
1932/XI	50,000	—	2.00	4.00	6.50
1934/XIII	50,000	—	2.00	4.00	6.50
1935/XIV	70,000	—	2.00	4.00	6.50
1936/XV	40,000	—	2.00	4.00	6.50
1937/XVI	70,000	—	2.00	4.00	6.50

Y# 16 2 LIRE

Nickel, 30 mm. **Subject:** Jubilee **Obverse:** Crowned Arms **Reverse:** Lamb on shoulders of young shepard

Date	Mintage	F	VF	XF	Unc
1933-34	50,000	—	4.00	6.00	10.00

Y# 7 5 LIRE

5.0000 g., 0.8350 Silver .1342 oz. ASW **Obverse:** Bust left **Reverse:** St. Peter in a boat **Designer:** Aurelio Mistruzzi

Date	Mintage	F	VF	XF	Unc
1929/VIII	10,000	—	7.50	15.00	30.00
1930/IX	50,000	—	5.00	9.00	20.00
1931/X	50,000	—	5.00	9.00	20.00
1932/XI	50,000	—	5.00	9.00	20.00
1934/XIII	30,000	—	5.00	9.00	20.00
1935/XIV	20,000	—	6.00	12.00	22.50
1936/XV	40,000	—	5.00	9.00	20.00
1937/XVI	40,000	—	5.00	9.00	20.00

Y# 17 5 LIRE

5.0000 g., 0.8350 Silver .1342 oz. ASW, 23 mm. **Subject:** Jubilee **Obverse:** Bust left **Reverse:** St. Peter in a boat **Designer:** Aurelio Mistruzzi

Date	Mintage	F	VF	XF	Unc
1933-34	50,000	—	6.00	12.00	22.50

Y# 8 10 LIRE

10.0000 g., 0.8350 Silver .2684 oz. ASW **Obverse:** Bust left **Reverse:** Mary, Queen of Peace holding infant **Designer:** Aurelio Mistruzzi

Date	Mintage	F	VF	XF	Unc
1929/VIII	10,000	—	7.50	15.00	35.00
1930/IX	50,000	—	10.00	15.00	25.00
1931/X	50,000	—	10.00	15.00	25.00
1932/XI	50,000	—	10.00	15.00	25.00
1934/XIII	60,000	—	10.00	15.00	25.00
1935/XIV	50,000	—	10.00	15.00	25.00
1936/XV	40,000	—	10.00	15.00	25.00
1937/XVI	40,000	—	10.00	15.00	25.00

Y# 18 10 LIRE

10.0000 g., 0.8350 Silver .2684 oz. ASW, 27 mm. **Subject:** Jubilee **Obverse:** Bust left **Reverse:** Seated crowned figure of Mary, Queen of peace facing holding infant **Designer:** Aurelio Mistruzzi

Date	Mintage	F	VF	XF	Unc
1933-34	50,000	—	10.00	17.50	30.00

Y# 9 100 LIRE

8.8000 g., 0.9000 Gold .2546 oz. AGW, 23.5 mm. **Obverse:** Bust right **Reverse:** Standing Jesus facing with child at feet **Designer:** Aurelio Mistruzzi

Date	Mintage	F	VF	XF	Unc
1929/VIII	10,000	—	200	400	500
1930/IX	2,621	—	300	500	800
1931/X	3,343	—	180	325	500
1932/XI	5,073	—	175	250	375
1934/XIII	2,533	—	180	325	500
1935/XIV	2,015	—	180	325	500

Y# 19 100 LIRE

8.8000 g., 0.9000 Gold .2546 oz. AGW, 23.5 mm. **Subject:** Jubilee **Obverse:** Bust right **Reverse:** Standing Jesus facing with child at feet **Designer:** Aurelio Mistruzzi

Date	Mintage	F	VF	XF	Unc
1933-34	23,000	—	180	325	500

Y# 10 100 LIRE

5.1900 g., 0.9000 Gold .1501 oz. AGW, 20.5 mm. **Obverse:** Bust right **Reverse:** Standing Jesus facing with child at feet

Date	Mintage	F	VF	XF	Unc
1936/XV	8,239	—	—	325	500
1937/XVI	2,000	—	—	2,000	3,000
1938 Rare	6	—	—	—	—

Sede Vacante

STANDARD COINAGE

100 Centesimi = 1 Lira

Y# 20 5 LIRE

5.0000 g., 0.8350 Silver .1342 oz. ASW **Subject:** Sede Vacante **Obverse:** Arms of Cardinal Pacelli **Reverse:** Dove within 1/2 sun

Date	Mintage	F	VF	XF	Unc
1939	40,000	—	10.00	20.00	35.00

Y# 21 10 LIRE

10.0000 g., 0.8350 Silver .2684 oz. ASW **Obverse:** Arms of Cardinal Eugenio Pacelli **Reverse:** Dove within 1/2 sun

Date	Mintage	F	VF	XF	Unc
1939	30,000	—	15.00	30.00	45.00

Pius XII

STANDARD COINAGE

100 Centesimi = 1 Lira

Y# 22 5 CENTESIMI

Aluminum-Bronze **Obverse:** Crowned shield divides date

Date	Mintage	F	VF	XF	Unc
1939/I	62,000	—	2.50	4.00	7.50
1940/II	62,000	—	2.50	4.00	7.50
1941/III	5,000	—	7.50	15.00	27.00

Y# 31 5 CENTESIMI

Brass **Obverse:** Bust left **Reverse:** Dove

Date	Mintage	F	VF	XF	Unc
1942/IV	5,000	—	15.00	27.50	55.00
1943/V	1,000	—	25.00	45.00	95.00
1944/VI	1,000	—	35.00	55.00	110
1945/VII	1,000	—	35.00	55.00	110
1946/VIII	1,000	—	35.00	55.00	110

Y# 23 10 CENTESIMI

Aluminum-Bronze **Obverse:** Crowned shield divides date **Reverse:** St. Peter bust right **Rev. Designer:** Aurelio Mistruzzi

Date	Mintage	F	VF	XF	Unc
1939/I	81,000	—	2.50	5.00	10.00
1940/II	81,000	—	2.50	5.00	10.00
1941/III	7,500	—	7.50	15.00	27.00

Y# 32 10 CENTESIMI

Brass **Obverse:** Bust left **Reverse:** Dove **Designer:** Aurelio Mistruzzi

Date	Mintage	F	VF	XF	Unc
1942/IV	7,500	—	15.00	27.50	55.00
1943/V	1,000	—	40.00	60.00	110
1944/VI	1,000	—	40.00	60.00	110
1945/VII	1,000	—	40.00	60.00	110
1946/VIII	1,000	—	40.00	60.00	110

Y# 24 20 CENTESIMI

Nickel **Obverse:** Crowned Arms **Reverse:** St. Paul bust left **Rev. Designer:** Aurelio Mistruzzi

Date	Mintage	F	VF	XF	Unc
1939/I	64,000	—	2.00	4.00	6.00

Y# 24a 20 CENTESIMI

Stainless Steel **Obverse:** Crowned Arms **Reverse:** St. Pual bust left

Date	Mintage	F	VF	XF	Unc
1940/II	64,000	—	2.00	4.00	6.00
1941/III	125,000	—	2.00	4.00	6.00

Y# 33 20 CENTESIMI

Stainless Steel **Obverse:** Crowned shield divides date and beaded circle **Reverse:** Justice seated with tablets of the Law **Designer:** Aurelio Mistruzzi

Date	Mintage	F	VF	XF	Unc
1942/IV	125,000	—	2.00	3.00	4.50
1943/V	1,000	—	40.00	60.00	110
1944/VI	1,000	—	40.00	60.00	110
1945/VII	1,000	—	40.00	60.00	110
1946/VIII	1,000	—	40.00	60.00	110

Y# 25 50 CENTESIMI

Nickel **Obverse:** Crowned Arms **Reverse:** Archangel Michael facing, divides value **Rev. Designer:** Aurelio Mistruzzi

Date	Mintage	F	VF	XF	Unc
1939/I	52,000	—	2.50	4.00	6.00

Y# 25a 50 CENTESIMI

Stainless Steel **Obverse:** Crowned Arms **Reverse:** Archangel Michael facing, divides value

Date	Mintage	F	VF	XF	Unc
1940/II	52,000	—	2.00	4.00	6.00
1941/III	180,000	—	2.00	4.00	6.00

Y# 34 50 CENTESIMI

Stainless Steel **Obverse:** Crowned shield divides date and beaded circle **Reverse:** Justice seated with tablets of the Law **Designer:** Aurelio Mistruzzi

Date	Mintage	F	VF	XF	Unc
1942/IV	180,000	—	2.00	3.25	4.50
1943/V	1,000	—	40.00	60.00	110
1944/VI	1,000	—	40.00	60.00	110
1945/VII	1,000	—	40.00	60.00	110
1946/VIII	1,000	—	40.00	60.00	110

Y# 26 LIRA

Nickel **Reverse:** Virgin Mary standing on globe and crescent **Rev. Designer:** Aurelio Mistruzzi

Date	Mintage	F	VF	XF	Unc
1939/I	70,000	—	5.00	10.00	20.00

Y# 26a LIRA

Stainless Steel

Date	Mintage	F	VF	XF	Unc
1940/II	70,000	—	3.00	5.00	7.50
1941/III	284,000	—	1.00	2.00	4.50

Y# 35 LIRA

Stainless Steel **Obverse:** Crowned shield divides date and beaded circle **Reverse:** Justice seated with tablets of the Law **Designer:** Aurelio Mistruzzi

Date	Mintage	F	VF	XF	Unc
1942/IV	284,000	—	1.00	2.00	4.50
1943/V	1,000	—	40.00	60.00	110
1944/VI	1,000	—	40.00	60.00	110
1945/VII	1,000	—	40.00	60.00	110
1946/VIII	1,000	—	40.00	60.00	110

Y# 40 LIRA

Aluminum **Obverse:** Crowned shield divides date and beaded circle **Reverse:** Justice seated with tablet of the Law **Designer:** Aurelio Mistruzzi

Date	Mintage	F	VF	XF	Unc
1947/IX	120,000	—	1.00	2.00	4.00
1948/X	10,000	—	2.00	4.00	7.00
1949/XI	10,000	—	2.00	4.00	7.00

Y# 44 LIRA

Aluminum **Subject:** Holy Year **Obverse:** Crowned shield **Reverse:** Holy Year Door **Designer:** Giampaoli

Date	Mintage	F	VF	XF	Unc
1950	50,000	—	1.00	2.00	3.50

Y# 49.1 LIRA

Aluminum, 17 mm. **Obverse:** Crowned shield **Obv. Legend:** ANNO **Reverse:** Temperance standing pouring libation in bowl **Edge:** Plain **Designer:** Giampaoli

Date	Mintage	F	VF	XF	Unc
1951/XIII	400,000	—	0.25	0.50	1.50
1952/XIV	400,000	—	0.25	0.50	1.50
1953/XV	400,000	—	0.25	0.50	1.50
1955/XVII	10,000	—	1.50	3.00	6.00
1957/XIX	30,000	—	0.75	2.00	3.50
1958/XX	30,000	—	0.75	2.00	3.50

Y# 49.2 LIRA

Aluminum, 17 mm. **Obverse:** Crowned shield **Obv. Legend:** A **Edge:** Plain

Date	Mintage	F	VF	XF	Unc
1956/XVIII	10,000	—	1.50	3.00	6.00

Y# 27 2 LIRE

Nickel, 29 mm. **Obverse:** Crowned Arms **Reverse:** Lamb on shoulders of shepard **Rev. Designer:** Aurelio Mistruzzi

Date	Mintage	F	VF	XF	Unc
1939/I	40,000	—	4.00	6.00	12.50

Y# 27a 2 LIRE

Stainless Steel, 29 mm. **Obverse:** Crowned Arms **Reverse:** Lamb on shoulders of shepard

Date	Mintage	F	VF	XF	Unc
1940/II	40,000	—	0.75	1.50	4.00
1941/III	270,000	—	0.50	1.00	3.00

Y# 36 2 LIRE

Stainless Steel, 29 mm. **Obverse:** Crowned shield divides date and beaded circle **Reverse:** Justice seated with tablets of the Law **Designer:** Aurelio Mistruzzi

Date	Mintage	F	VF	XF	Unc
1942/IV	270,000	—	0.50	1.00	3.00
1943/V	1,000	—	40.00	60.00	110
1944/VI	1,000	—	40.00	60.00	110
1945/VII	1,000	—	40.00	60.00	110
1946/VIII	1,000	—	40.00	60.00	110

Y# 41 2 LIRE

Aluminum **Obverse:** Crowned shield divides date and beaded circle **Reverse:** Justice seated with tablets of the Law **Designer:** Aurelio Mistruzzi

Date	Mintage	F	VF	XF	Unc
1947/IX	65,000	—	2.00	4.00	8.00
1948/X	110,000	—	1.50	3.50	5.00
1949/XI	10,000	—	4.00	8.00	17.50

Y# 45 2 LIRE

Aluminum **Subject:** Holy Year **Obverse:** Bust right **Reverse:** Dove and St. Peter's Basilica Dome **Designer:** Giampaoli

Date	Mintage	F	VF	XF	Unc
1950	50,000	—	1.25	2.50	4.00

Y# 50 2 LIRE

Aluminum **Obverse:** Crowned shield **Reverse:** Fortude standing with lion at feet **Designer:** Giampaoli

Date	Mintage	F	VF	XF	Unc
1951/XIII	400,000	—	0.25	0.50	1.50
1952/XIV	400,000	—	0.25	0.50	1.50
1953/XV	400,000	—	0.25	0.50	1.50
1955/XVII	20,000	—	1.00	2.00	4.00
1956/XVIII	20,000	—	1.00	2.00	4.00
1957/XIX	30,000	—	0.75	1.25	3.00
1958/XX	30,000	—	0.75	1.25	3.00

Y# 28 5 LIRE

5.0000 g., 0.8350 Silver .1342 oz. ASW **Obverse:** Bust left **Reverse:** St. Peter in a boat **Designer:** Aurelio Mistruzzi

Date	Mintage	F	VF	XF	Unc
1939/I	100,000	—	4.00	10.00	20.00
1940/II	100,000	—	4.00	10.00	20.00
1941/III	4,000	—	25.00	40.00	65.00

Y# 37 5 LIRE

5.0000 g., 0.8350 Silver .1342 oz. ASW **Obverse:** Bust left **Reverse:** Caritas figure facing flanked by children **Designer:** Aurelio Mistruzzi

Date	Mintage	F	VF	XF	Unc
1942/IV	4,000	—	25.00	40.00	65.00
1943/V	1,000	—	50.00	75.00	120
1944/VI	1,000	—	50.00	75.00	120
1945/VII	1,000	—	50.00	75.00	120
1946/VIII	1,000	—	50.00	75.00	120

Y# 42 5 LIRE

Aluminum **Obverse:** Bust left **Reverse:** Caritas figure facing flanked by children **Designer:** Aurelio Mistruzzi

Date	Mintage	F	VF	XF	Unc
1947/IX	50,000	—	2.00	4.00	7.50
1948/X	74,000	—	2.00	4.00	7.50
1949/XI	74,000	—	2.00	4.00	7.50

Y# 46 5 LIRE

Aluminum **Subject:** Holy Year **Obverse:** Bust left **Reverse:** Standing Pope with staff flanked by figures within Holy Year Door **Designer:** Giampaoli

Date	Mintage	F	VF	XF	Unc
1950	50,000	—	3.00	5.00	10.00

Y# 51.1 5 LIRE

Aluminum, 20 mm. **Obverse:** Bust right **Obv. Legend:** AN **Reverse:** Justice standing with sword and scales **Designer:** Giampaoli

Date	Mintage	F	VF	XF	Unc
1951/XIII	1,500,000	—	0.25	0.50	1.50
1952/XIV	1,500,000	—	0.25	0.50	1.50
1953/XV	1,500,000	—	0.25	0.50	1.50
1955/XVII	30,000	—	0.50	0.75	2.00
1956/XVIII	60,000	—	0.50	0.75	2.00
1957/XIX	30,000	—	0.50	0.75	2.00
1958/XX	30,000	—	0.50	0.75	2.00

Y# 51.2 5 LIRE

Aluminum, 20 mm. **Obverse:** Bust right **Obv. Legend:** A

Date	Mintage	F	VF	XF	Unc
1956/XVIII	30,000	—	0.50	1.00	2.50
1957/XIX	30,000	—	0.50	1.00	2.50
1958/XX	30,000	—	0.50	1.00	2.50

Y# 29 10 LIRE

10.0000 g., 0.8350 Silver .2684 oz. ASW **Obverse:** Bust left **Reverse:** Mary, Queen of Peace holding child **Designer:** Aurelio Mistruzzi

Date	Mintage	F	VF	XF	Unc
1939/I	10,000	—	12.00	25.00	45.00
1940/II	10,000	—	12.00	25.00	45.00
1941/III	4,000	—	20.00	40.00	80.00

Y# 38 10 LIRE

10.0000 g., 0.8350 Silver .2684 oz. ASW **Obverse:** Bust left **Reverse:** Caritas figure facing flanked by children **Designer:** Aurelio Mistruzzi

Date	Mintage	F	VF	XF	Unc
1942/IV	4,000	—	25.00	50.00	90.00
1943/V	1,000	—	60.00	75.00	110
1944/VI	1,000	—	60.00	75.00	110
1945/VII	1,000	—	60.00	75.00	110
1946/VIII	1,000	—	60.00	75.00	110

Y# 43 10 LIRE

Aluminum **Obverse:** Bust left **Reverse:** Caritas figure facing flanked by children **Designer:** Aurelio Mistruzzi

Date	Mintage	F	VF	XF	Unc
1947/IX	50,000	—	3.00	5.00	8.00
1948/X	60,000	—	3.00	5.00	8.00
1949/XI	60,000	—	3.00	5.00	8.00

Y# 47 10 LIRE

Aluminum **Subject:** Holy Year **Obverse:** Bust right **Reverse:** Procession thru Holy Year door

Date	Mintage	F	VF	XF	Unc
1950	60,000	—	3.00	5.00	8.00

Y# 52.1 10 LIRE

Aluminum, 23 mm. **Obverse:** Bust left **Obv. Legend:** AN **Reverse:** Prudence standing and date divides value **Designer:** Giampaoli

Date	Mintage	F	VF	XF	Unc
1951/XIII	1,130,000	—	0.50	0.75	1.50
1952/XIV	1,130,000	—	0.50	0.75	1.50
1953/XV	1,130,000	—	0.50	0.75	1.50
1955/XVII	80,000	—	0.75	1.50	3.00

Y# 52.2 10 LIRE

Aluminum, 23 mm. **Obverse:** Bust left **Obv. Legend:** A **Reverse:** Prudence standing date divides value

Date	Mintage	F	VF	XF	Unc
1956/XVIII	80,000	—	0.75	1.50	3.00
1957/XIX	36,000	—	0.75	1.50	3.50
1958/XX	30,000	—	0.75	1.50	3.50

Y# A52.1 20 LIRE

3.6000 g., Aluminum-Bronze, 21.25 mm. **Obverse:** Bust left **Obv. Legend:** A **Reverse:** Caritas standing holding child with another at feet

Date	Mintage	F	VF	XF	Unc
1957/XIX	20,000	—	0.75	1.25	2.50

Y# A52.2 20 LIRE

5.6000 g., Aluminum-Bronze, 21.25 mm. **Obverse:** Bust left **Obv. Legend:** AN **Reverse:** Caritas standing holding child with another at feet

Date	Mintage	F	VF	XF	Unc
1958/XX	60,000	—	0.75	1.25	2.50

Y# 54.1 50 LIRE

6.2000 g., Stainless Steel, 24.8 mm. **Obverse:** Bust right **Obv. Legend:** AN **Reverse:** Spes standing with large anchor which divides date and value

Date	Mintage	F	VF	XF	Unc
1955/XVII	180,000	—	1.00	1.50	3.00
1956/XVIII	—	—	1.00	1.50	3.00
1957/XIX	—	—	1.00	1.50	3.00
1958/XX	—	—	1.00	1.50	3.00

Y# 54.2 50 LIRE

6.2000 g., Stainless Steel, 24.8 mm. **Obverse:** Bust right **Obv. Legend:** A **Reverse:** Spes standing facing with large anchor which divides date and value

Date	Mintage	F	VF	XF	Unc
1956/XVIII	180,000	—	1.00	1.50	3.00
1957/XIX	180,000	—	1.00	1.50	3.00
1958/XX	60,000	—	1.00	1.50	3.00

Y# 30.1 100 LIRE

5.1900 g., 0.9000 Gold .1501 oz. AGW **Obverse:** Head right **Obv. Legend:** AN **Reverse:** Standing Jesus divides value **Designer:** Aurelio Mistruzzi

Date	Mintage	F	VF	XF	Unc
1939/I	2,700	—	—	300	500
1940/II	2,000	—	—	300	500

Y# 30.2 100 LIRE

5.1900 g., 0.9000 Gold .1501 oz. AGW **Obverse:** Head right **Obv. Legend:** A **Reverse:** Standing Jesus divides value

Date	Mintage	F	VF	XF	Unc
1941/III	2,000	—	—	300	550

Y# 39 100 LIRE

5.1900 g., 0.9000 Gold .1501 oz. AGW **Obverse:** Head right **Reverse:** Caritas seated facing flanked by children

Date	Mintage	F	VF	XF	Unc
1942/IV	2,000	—	—	300	550
1943/V	1,000	—	—	350	600
1944/VI	1,000	—	—	350	600
1945/VII	1,000	—	—	350	600
1946/VIII	1,000	—	—	350	600
1947/IX	1,000	—	—	350	600
1948/X	5,000	—	—	300	500
1949/XI	1,000	—	—	350	600

Y# 48 100 LIRE

5.1900 g., 0.9000 Gold .1501 oz. AGW **Subject:** Holy Year **Obverse:** Crowned bust left **Reverse:** Opening of the Holy Year Door

Date	Mintage	F	VF	XF	Unc
MCML (1950)	20,000	—	—	300	500

Y# 53.1 100 LIRE
5.1900 g., 0.9000 Gold .1501 oz. AGW **Obverse:** Bust right **Obv. Legend:** AN **Reverse:** Caritas standing facing holding child with another at feet

Date	Mintage	F	VF	XF	Unc
1951/XIII	1,000	—	—	350	550
1952/XIV	1,000	—	—	350	550
1953/XV	1,000	—	—	350	550
1954/XVI	1,000	—	—	350	550
1955/XVII	1,000	—	—	350	550

Y# 53.2 100 LIRE
5.1900 g., 0.9000 Gold .1501 oz. AGW **Obverse:** Bust right **Obv. Legend:** A **Reverse:** Caritas standing facing holding child with another at feet

Date	Mintage	F	VF	XF	Unc
1956/XVIII	1,000	—	—	350	550

Y# 55 100 LIRE
8.0000 g., Stainless Steel, 27.75 mm. **Obverse:** Bust left **Reverse:** Fides standing with large cross divides value and date **Designer:** Giampaoli

Date	Mintage	F	VF	XF	Unc
1955/XVII	1,300,000	—	0.50	1.00	2.00
1956/XVII	1,400,000	—	0.50	1.00	2.00
1957/XIX	900,000	—	0.50	1.00	2.00
1958/XX	852,000	—	0.50	1.00	2.00

Y# A53 100 LIRE
5.1900 g., 0.9000 Gold .1501 oz. AGW **Obverse:** Bust right **Reverse:** Crowned shield divides value

Date	Mintage	F	VF	XF	Unc
1957/XIX	2,000	—	—	300	450
1958/XX	3,000	—	—	300	450

Y# 56 500 LIRE
11.0000 g., 0.8350 Silver .2953 oz. ASW, 29 mm. **Obverse:** Bust left **Reverse:** Crowned shield divides value **Designer:** Pietro Giampaoli

Date	Mintage	F	VF	XF	Unc
1958/XX	20,000	—	7.50	15.00	25.00

Sede Vacante

STANDARD COINAGE

100 Centesimi = 1 Lira

Y# 57 500 LIRE
11.0000 g., 0.8350 Silver .2953 oz. ASW, 29.3 mm. **Obverse:** Descending dove divides sun above value **Reverse:** Arms of Cardinal Benedetto Aloisi-Masella **Designer:** Pietro Giampaoli

Date	Mintage	F	VF	XF	Unc
1958	100,000	—	8.00	16.00	45.00

John XXIII

STANDARD COINAGE

100 Centesimi = 1 Lira

Y# 58.1 LIRA
Aluminum, 17 mm. **Obverse:** Crowned shield **Obv. Legend:** AN **Reverse:** Temperance kneeling pouring libation into bowl **Edge:** Plain **Designer:** Giampaoli

Date	Mintage	F	VF	XF	Unc
1959/I	25,000	—	1.00	3.00	6.00
1960/II	25,000	—	1.00	2.00	4.00

Y# 58.2 LIRA
Aluminum, 17 mm. **Obverse:** Crowned shield **Obv. Legend:** A **Reverse:** Temperance kneeling pouring libation into bowl **Edge:** Plain

Date	Mintage	F	VF	XF	Unc
1961/III	25,000	—	1.00	2.00	4.00
1962/IV	25,000	—	1.00	2.00	4.00

Y# 67 LIRA
Aluminum, 17 mm. **Subject:** Second Ecumenical Council **Obverse:** Crowned shield **Reverse:** Radiant dove in rays **Edge:** Plain

Date	Mintage	F	VF	XF	Unc
1962/IV	50,000	—	1.00	1.50	3.00

Y# 59.1 2 LIRE
Aluminum, 18 mm. **Obverse:** Crowned shield **Obv. Legend:** AN **Reverse:** Fortude seated facing and lion divides value and date

Date	Mintage	F	VF	XF	Unc
1959/I	25,000	—	1.50	4.00	6.00
1960/II	25,000	—	1.50	4.00	6.00

Y# 59.2 2 LIRE
Aluminum, 18 mm. **Obverse:** Crowned shield **Obv. Legend:** A **Reverse:** Fortude seated facing and lion divides value and date

Date	Mintage	F	VF	XF	Unc
1961/III	25,000	—	1.50	4.00	6.00
1962/IV	25,000	—	1.50	4.00	6.00

Y# 68 2 LIRE
Aluminum, 18 mm. **Subject:** Second Ecumenical Council **Obverse:** Crowned shield **Reverse:** Radiant dove in rays

Date	Mintage	F	VF	XF	Unc
1962/IV	50,000	—	1.00	1.50	3.00

Y# 60.1 5 LIRE
Aluminum, 20 mm. **Obverse:** Bust right **Obv. Legend:** AN **Reverse:** Kneeling figure holding sword and scales divides value and date

Date	Mintage	F	VF	XF	Unc
1959/I	25,000	—	1.50	4.00	7.00

Y# 60.2 5 LIRE
Aluminum, 20 mm. **Obverse:** Bust right **Obv. Legend:** A **Reverse:** Kneeling figure holding sword and scales divides date and value

Date	Mintage	F	VF	XF	Unc
1960/II	25,000	—	1.50	4.00	7.00
1961/III	25,000	—	1.50	4.00	7.00
1962/IV	25,000	—	1.00	2.00	4.00

Y# 69 5 LIRE
Aluminum, 20 mm. **Subject:** Second Ecumenical Council **Obverse:** Bust right **Reverse:** Radiant dove

Date	Mintage	F	VF	XF	Unc
1962/IV	50,000	—	0.40	0.75	1.50

Y# 61.1 10 LIRE
Aluminum, 23 mm. **Obverse:** Bust left **Obv. Legend:** AN **Reverse:** Prudence kneeling holding snake and object divides value and date

Date	Mintage	F	VF	XF	Unc
1959/I	50,000	—	1.00	3.00	6.00

Y# 61.2 10 LIRE
Aluminum, 23 mm. **Obverse:** Bust left **Obv. Legend:** A **Reverse:** Prudence kneeling

Date	Mintage	F	VF	XF	Unc
1960/II	50,000	—	1.00	3.00	6.00
1961/III	50,000	—	1.00	3.00	6.00
1962/IV	50,000	—	1.00	2.00	4.00

Y# 70 10 LIRE
Aluminum, 23 mm. **Subject:** Second Ecumenical Council **Obverse:** Bust left **Reverse:** Radiant dove

Date	Mintage	F	VF	XF	Unc
1962/IV	100,000	—	1.00	2.00	4.00

Y# 62.1 20 LIRE
3.6000 g., Aluminum-Bronze, 21.25 mm. **Obverse:** Helmeted bust left **Obv. Legend:** AN **Reverse:** Caritas seated facing flanked by children

Date	Mintage	F	VF	XF	Unc
1959/I	50,000	—	0.75	1.25	2.50

Y# 62.2 20 LIRE
3.6000 g., Aluminum-Bronze, 21.25 mm. **Obverse:** Helmeted bust left **Obv. Legend:** A **Reverse:** Seated figure with children

Date	Mintage	F	VF	XF	Unc
1960/II	50,000	—	0.75	1.25	2.50
1961/III	50,000	—	0.75	1.00	2.50
1962/IV	50,000	—	0.75	1.00	2.50

Y# 71 20 LIRE
3.6000 g., Aluminum-Bronze, 21.25 mm. **Subject:** Second Ecumenical Council **Obverse:** Helmeted bust left **Reverse:** Radiant dove

Date	Mintage	F	VF	XF	Unc
1962/IV	100,000	—	0.75	1.00	2.00

Y# 63.1 50 LIRE
6.2000 g., Stainless Steel, 24.8 mm. **Obverse:** Bust right **Reverse:** Spes standing facing with large anchor divides date and value

Date	Mintage	F	VF	XF	Unc
1959/I	100,000	—	1.00	2.50	6.50

Y# 63.2 50 LIRE
6.2000 g., Stainless Steel, 24.8 mm. **Obverse:** Bust right **Reverse:** Spes standing facing and large anchor divides date and value

Date	Mintage	F	VF	XF	Unc
1960/II	100,000	—	1.00	2.50	5.50
1961/III	100,000	—	1.00	2.00	4.50
1962/IV	100,000	—	1.00	2.00	4.50

Y# 72 50 LIRE
6.2000 g., Stainless Steel, 24.8 mm. **Subject:** Second Ecumenical Council **Obverse:** Bust right **Reverse:** Bishops at council meeting with radiant dove above **Designer:** Giampaoli

Date	Mintage	F	VF	XF	Unc
1962/IV	200,000	—	0.50	1.25	3.00

Y# 66 100 LIRE
5.1900 g., 0.9000 Gold .1501 oz. AGW **Obverse:** Bust right **Reverse:** Crowned shield divides value

Date	Mintage	F	VF	XF	Unc
1959/I	3,000	—	1,100	1,500	2,280

Y# 64.1 100 LIRE
8.0000 g., Stainless Steel, 27.75 mm. **Obverse:** Bust left **Reverse:** Fides standing, cross divides value and date **Designer:** Giampaoli

Date	Mintage	F	VF	XF	Unc
1959/I	783,000	—	1.25	2.00	4.00

Y# 64.2 100 LIRE
8.0000 g., Stainless Steel, 27.75 mm. **Obverse:** Regnal year under bust facing left **Reverse:** Fides standing, cross divides value and date

Date	Mintage	F	VF	XF	Unc
1960/II	783,000	—	1.75	3.00	6.50
1961/III	783,000	—	0.75	1.00	2.50
1962/IV	783,000	—	0.75	1.00	2.50

Y# 73 100 LIRE
8.0000 g., Stainless Steel, 27.75 mm. **Subject:** Second Ecumenical Council **Obverse:** Bust left **Reverse:** Bishops at council meeting with radiant doves **Designer:** Giampaoli

Date	Mintage	F	VF	XF	Unc
1962/IV	1,566,000	—	0.40	0.75	1.50

Y# 65.1 500 LIRE
11.0000 g., 0.8350 Silver .2953 oz. ASW, 29.3 mm. **Obverse:** Bust left with continuous legend **Reverse:** Crowned shield divides value **Designer:** Pietro Giampaoli

Date	Mintage	F	VF	XF	Unc
1959/I	30,000	—	7.50	15.00	30.00

Y# 65.2 500 LIRE
11.0000 g., 0.8350 Silver .2953 oz. ASW, 29.3 mm. **Obverse:** Regnal year under bust facing left **Reverse:** Crowned shield divides value

Date	Mintage	F	VF	XF	Unc
1960/II	30,000	—	10.00	20.00	35.00
1961/III	30,000	—	7.00	15.00	30.00
1962/IV	30,000	—	7.00	15.00	30.00

Y# 74 500 LIRE
11.0000 g., 0.8350 Silver .2953 oz. ASW, 29.3 mm. **Subject:** Second Ecumenical Council **Obverse:** Crowned bust left **Reverse:** Bishops at council meeting with radiant doves

Date	Mintage	F	VF	XF	Unc
1962/IV	60,000	—	7.00	15.00	25.00

Sede Vacante

STANDARD COINAGE

100 Centesimi = 1 Lira

Y# 75 500 LIRE
11.0000 g., 0.8350 Silver .2953 oz. ASW, 29.3 mm. **Obverse:** Descending dove divides sun above value **Reverse:** Arms of Cardinal Benedetto Aloisi-Masella

Date	Mintage	F	VF	XF	Unc
1963	200,000	—	6.00	10.00	17.50

Paul VI

STANDARD COINAGE

100 Centesimi = 1 Lira

Y# 76.1 LIRA
Aluminum, 17 mm. **Obverse:** Crowned shield **Obv. Legend:** AN **Reverse:** Temperance seated pouring libation divides value and date **Edge:** Plain

Date	Mintage	F	VF	XF	Unc
1963/I	60,000	—	0.75	2.00	3.50

Y# 76.2 LIRA
Aluminum, 17 mm. **Obverse:** Crowned shield **Obv. Legend:** A **Reverse:** Temperance seated pouring libation divides value and date **Edge:** Plain

Date	Mintage	F	VF	XF	Unc
1964/II	60,000	—	0.50	1.00	2.00
1965/III	60,000	—	0.50	1.00	2.00

Y# 84 LIRA
Aluminum, 17 mm. **Obverse:** Crowned head left **Reverse:** Sheep on shoulders of shepard **Edge:** Plain **Designer:** E. Greco

Date	Mintage	F	VF	XF	Unc
1966/IV	90,000	—	0.25	0.75	1.25

Y# 92 LIRA
Aluminum, 17 mm. **Obverse:** Crowned shield **Reverse:** Crossed keys within radiant sword **Edge:** Plain

Date	Mintage	F	VF	XF	Unc
1967/V	100,000	—	0.25	0.75	1.25

Y# 100 LIRA
Aluminum, 17 mm. **Series:** F.A.O. **Obverse:** Bust left **Reverse:** Wheat ears forming radiant cross **Edge:** Plain **Designer:** G. Pirrone

Date	Mintage	F	VF	XF	Unc
ND(1968)/VI	100,000	—	0.25	0.75	1.25

Y# 108 LIRA

Aluminum, 17 mm. **Series:** F.A.O. **Obverse:** Crowned head 1/4 left divides inscription **Reverse:** Stylized angel in flight **Edge:** Plain **Designer:** C. Ruffini

Date	Mintage	F	VF	XF	Unc
1969/VII	100,000	—	0.25	0.75	1.25

Y# 116 LIRA

Aluminum, 17 mm. **Series:** F.A.O. **Obverse:** Crowned shield **Reverse:** Palm sprigs **Designer:** Tomaso Gismondi

Date	Mintage	F	VF	XF	Unc
1970/VIII	100,000	—	0.25	0.50	1.00
1971/IX	110,000	—	0.25	0.50	1.00
1972/X	110,000	—	0.25	0.50	1.00
1973/XI	132,000	—	0.25	0.50	1.00
1974/XII	132,000	—	0.25	0.50	1.00
1975/XIII	150,000	—	0.25	0.50	1.00
1976/XIV	150,000	—	0.25	0.50	1.00
1977/XV	135,000	—	0.25	0.50	1.00

Y# 124 LIRA

Aluminum, 17 mm. **Subject:** Holy Year - Faith in the Lord on Part of Man Afflicted by Evil **Obverse:** Crowned shield **Reverse:** Mother and child playing **Designer:** Guido Veroi

Date	Mintage	F	VF	XF	Unc
1975	170,000	—	0.25	0.50	1.00

Y# 77.1 2 LIRE

Aluminum, 18 mm. **Obverse:** Crowned shield **Obv. Legend:** AN **Reverse:** Fortude standing with shield, lion at side, value

Date	Mintage	F	VF	XF	Unc
1963/I	60,000	—	0.75	2.00	3.00

Y# 77.2 2 LIRE

Aluminum, 18 mm. **Obverse:** Crowned shield **Obv. Legend:** A **Reverse:** Fortude standing with shield, lion at side, value

Date	Mintage	F	VF	XF	Unc
1964/II	60,000	—	0.75	2.00	3.00
1965/III	60,000	—	0.75	3.00	3.00

Y# 85 2 LIRE

Aluminum, 18 mm. **Obverse:** Crowned head left **Reverse:** Sheep on shoulder of shepard **Designer:** E. Greco

Date	Mintage	F	VF	XF	Unc
1966/IV	90,000	—	0.25	0.75	1.25

Y# 93 2 LIRE

Aluminum, 18 mm. **Obverse:** Crowned shield **Reverse:** Papal tiara above inverted cross, keys flanking

Date	Mintage	F	VF	XF	Unc
1967/V	100,000	—	0.25	0.75	1.25

Y# 101 2 LIRE

Aluminum, 18 mm. **Series:** F.A.O. **Subject:** Feeding of the 5,000 **Obverse:** Bust right **Reverse:** Standing figure flanked by others **Designer:** G. Pirrone

Date	Mintage	F	VF	XF	Unc
ND(1968)/VI	100,000	—	0.25	0.75	1.25

Y# 109 2 LIRE

Aluminum, 18 mm. **Obverse:** Crowned head 1/4 left divides inscription **Reverse:** Stylized angel in flight **Designer:** C. Ruffini

Date	Mintage	F	VF	XF	Unc
1969/VII	100,000	—	0.25	0.75	1.25

Y# 117 2 LIRE

Aluminum, 18 mm. **Obverse:** Crowned shield **Reverse:** Lamb standing **Designer:** Tomaso Gismondi

Date	Mintage	F	VF	XF	Unc
1970/VIII	100,000	—	0.25	0.50	1.00
1971/IX	110,000	—	0.25	0.50	1.00
1972/X	110,000	—	0.25	0.50	1.00
1973/XI	132,000	—	0.25	0.50	1.00
1974/XII	132,000	—	0.25	0.50	1.00
1975/XIII	150,000	—	0.25	0.50	1.00
1976/XIV	150,000	—	0.25	0.50	1.00
1977/XV	135,000	—	0.25	0.50	1.00

Y# 125 2 LIRE

Aluminum, 18 mm. **Subject:** Holy Year - Reconciliation among brothers **Obverse:** Crowned shield **Reverse:** Two men embracing **Designer:** Guido Veroi

Date	Mintage	F	VF	XF	Unc
1975	180,000	—	0.25	0.50	1.00

Y# 78.1 5 LIRE

Aluminum, 20 mm. **Obverse:** Bust right **Obv. Legend:** AN **Reverse:** Justice seated with sword and scales

Date	Mintage	F	VF	XF	Unc
1963/I	60,000	—	1.00	2.00	4.00

Y# 78.2 5 LIRE

Aluminum, 20 mm. **Obverse:** Bust right **Obv. Legend:** A **Reverse:** Justice seated with sword and scales

Date	Mintage	F	VF	XF	Unc
1964/II.	60,000	—	8.00	16.00	32.00
1965/III	60,000	—	8.00	16.00	32.00

Y# 86 5 LIRE

Aluminum, 20 mm. **Obverse:** Crowned head left **Reverse:** Sheep on shoulder of shepard

Date	Mintage	F	VF	XF	Unc
1966/IV	90,000	—	0.25	0.50	1.00

Y# 94 5 LIRE

Aluminum, 20 mm. **Obverse:** Bust right **Reverse:** Crossed keys within radiant sword

Date	Mintage	F	VF	XF	Unc
1967/V	100,000	—	0.25	0.50	1.00

Y# 102 5 LIRE

Aluminum, 20 mm. **Series:** F.A.O. **Subject:** Lady of the Harvest **Obverse:** Bust right **Reverse:** Our Lady of the Harvest within wheat sprigs **Designer:** G. Pirrone

Date	Mintage	F	VF	XF	Unc
ND(1968)/VI	100,000	—	0.25	0.50	1.00

Y# 110 5 LIRE

Aluminum, 20 mm. **Obverse:** Crowned head 1/4 left divides inscription **Reverse:** Stylized angel in flight **Designer:** G. Ruffini

Date	Mintage	F	VF	XF	Unc
1969/VII	100,000	—	0.25	0.50	1.00

Y# 118 5 LIRE

Aluminum, 20 mm. **Obverse:** Crowned shield **Reverse:** Pelican feeding young **Designer:** Tomaso Gismondi

Date	Mintage	F	VF	XF	Unc
1970/VIII	100,000	—	0.25	0.60	1.25
1971/IX	110,000	—	0.25	0.60	1.25
1972/X	110,000	—	0.25	0.60	1.25
1973/XI	132,000	—	0.25	0.60	1.25
1974/XII	132,000	—	0.25	0.60	1.25
1975/XIII	150,000	—	0.25	0.60	1.25
1976/XIV	150,000	—	0.25	0.60	1.25
1977/XV	135,000	—	0.25	0.60	1.25

Y# 126 5 LIRE

Aluminum, 20 mm. **Subject:** Holy Year - Redemption of the Woman of Bethany **Obverse:** Crowned shield **Reverse:** Female kneeling receiving blessing from seated figure **Designer:** Guido Veroi

Date	Mintage	F	VF	XF	Unc
1975	380,000	—	0.25	0.50	1.00

Y# 133 5 LIRE

Aluminum, 20 mm. **Obverse:** Crowned shield **Reverse:** Stylized standing figure divides value **Designer:** Nicola Morelli

Date	Mintage	F	VF	XF	Unc
1978/XVI	120,000	—	0.25	0.50	1.00

Y# 79.1 10 LIRE

Aluminum, 23 mm. **Obverse:** Bust left **Obv. Legend:** AN **Reverse:** Prudence standing dividing date and value

Date	Mintage	F	VF	XF	Unc
1963/I	90,000	—	1.00	1.50	3.00

Y# 79.2 10 LIRE

Aluminum, 23 mm. **Obverse:** Bust left **Obv. Legend:** A **Reverse:** Prudence standing dividing date and value

Date	Mintage	F	VF	XF	Unc
1964/II	90,000	—	0.75	1.00	2.00
1965/III	90,000	—	0.75	1.00	2.00

Y# 87 10 LIRE

Aluminum, 23 mm. **Obverse:** Crowned head left **Reverse:** Shepard with sheep on his shoulders

Date	Mintage	F	VF	XF	Unc
1966/IV	100,000	—	0.25	1.00	2.00

Y# 95 10 LIRE

Aluminum, 23 mm. **Obverse:** Bust left **Reverse:** Papal taira above inverted cross, keys flanking

Date	Mintage	F	VF	XF	Unc
ND(1967)/V	110,000	—	0.25	0.75	1.25

Y# 103 10 LIRE

Aluminum, 23 mm. **Series:** F.A.O. **Obverse:** Bust left **Reverse:** Feeding of the 5,000 **Designer:** G. Pirrone

Date	Mintage	F	VF	XF	Unc
ND(1968)/VI	110,000	—	0.25	0.75	1.50

Y# 111 10 LIRE

Aluminum, 23 mm. **Obverse:** Crowned head 1/4 left divides inscription **Reverse:** Stylized angel in flight **Designer:** G. Ruffini

Date	Mintage	F	VF	XF	Unc
1969/VII	110,000	—	0.25	0.50	1.25

Y# 119 10 LIRE

Aluminum, 23 mm. **Obverse:** Crowned shield **Reverse:** Fish **Designer:** Tomaso Gismondi

Date	Mintage	F	VF	XF	Unc
1970/VIII	110,000	—	0.25	0.50	1.25
1971/IX	160,000	—	0.25	0.50	1.25
1972/X	160,000	—	0.25	0.50	1.25
1973/XI	170,000	—	0.25	0.50	1.25
1974/XII	170,000	—	0.25	0.50	1.25
1975/XIII	200,000	—	0.25	0.50	1.25
1976/XIV	200,000	—	0.25	0.50	1.25
1977/XV	200,000	—	0.25	0.50	1.25

Y# 127 10 LIRE

Aluminum, 23 mm. **Subject:** Holy Year - Reconciliation between God and man **Obverse:** Crowned shield **Reverse:** Noah's ark **Designer:** Guido Veroi

Date	Mintage	F	VF	XF	Unc
1975	400,000	—	0.25	0.75	1.50

Y# 134 10 LIRE

Aluminum, 23 mm. **Obverse:** Crowned shield **Reverse:** Figure kneeling left **Designer:** Nicola Morelli

Date	Mintage	F	VF	XF	Unc
1978/XVI	250,000	—	0.25	0.50	1.00

Y# 80.1 20 LIRE

3.6000 g., Aluminum-Bronze, 21.25 mm. **Obverse:** Bust left **Obv. Legend:** AN **Reverse:** Caritas seated flanked by children

Date	Mintage	F	VF	XF	Unc
1963/I	90,000	—	1.00	2.00	4.00
1964/II	90,000	—	1.00	2.00	4.00

Y# 80.2 20 LIRE

3.6000 g., Aluminum-Bronze, 21.25 mm. **Obverse:** Bust left **Obv. Legend:** A **Reverse:** Caritas seated flanked by children

Date	Mintage	F	VF	XF	Unc
1965/III	90,000	—	0.75	1.00	2.00

Y# 88 20 LIRE

3.6000 g., Aluminum-Bronze, 21.25 mm. **Obverse:** Crowned head left **Reverse:** Shepard with sheep on his shoulders

Date	Mintage	F	VF	XF	Unc
1966/IV	100,000	—	0.25	0.75	1.25

Y# 96 20 LIRE

3.6000 g., Aluminum-Bronze, 21.25 mm. **Obverse:** Bust right **Reverse:** Saints Peter and Paul, sword between **Designer:** G. Pirrone

Date	Mintage	F	VF	XF	Unc
ND(1967)/V	105,000	—	0.25	0.75	1.25

Y# 104 20 LIRE

3.6000 g., Aluminum-Bronze, 21.25 mm. **Series:** F.A.O. **Obverse:** Bust right **Reverse:** Wheat ears forming radiant cross **Designer:** G. Pirrone

Date	Mintage	F	VF	XF	Unc
ND(1968)/VI	105,000	—	0.25	0.75	1.50

Y# 112 20 LIRE

3.6000 g., Aluminum-Bronze, 21.25 mm. **Obverse:** Crowned head 1/4 left divides inscription **Reverse:** Stylized angel in flight **Designer:** C. Ruffini

Date	Mintage	F	VF	XF	Unc
1969/VII	105,000	—	0.25	0.60	1.25

Y# 120 20 LIRE

3.6000 g., Aluminum-Bronze, 21.25 mm. **Obverse:** Crowned shield **Reverse:** Red deer **Designer:** Tomas Gismondi

Date	Mintage	F	VF	XF	Unc
1970/VIII	105,000	—	0.25	0.50	1.25
1971/IX	170,000	—	0.25	0.50	1.25
1972/X	170,000	—	0.25	0.50	1.25
1973/XI	—	—	0.25	0.50	1.25
1974/XII	—	—	0.25	0.50	1.25
1975/XIII	250,000	—	0.25	0.50	1.25
1976/XIV	250,000	—	0.25	0.50	1.25
1977/XV	250,000	—	0.25	0.50	1.25

Y# 128 20 LIRE

3.6000 g., Aluminum-Bronze, 21.25 mm. **Subject:** Holy Year - Man's Confidence in the Lord **Obverse:** Crowned shield **Reverse:** Standing figure facing right and value **Designer:** Guido Veroi

Date	Mintage	F	VF	XF	Unc
1975	400,000	—	0.25	0.50	1.25

Y# 135 20 LIRE

3.6000 g., Aluminum-Bronze, 21.25 mm. **Subject:** Prodigal Son Parable **Obverse:** Crowned shield **Reverse:** Standing figures facing each other above value **Designer:** Nicola Morelli

Date	Mintage	F	VF	XF	Unc
1978/XVI	120,000	—	0.25	0.50	1.25

Y# 81.1 50 LIRE

6.2000 g., Stainless Steel, 24.8 mm. **Subject:** Spes standing with anchor **Obverse:** Bust right **Obv. Legend:** AN **Reverse:** Spes standing with anchor date and value are divided

Date	Mintage	F	VF	XF	Unc
1963/I	120,000	—	1.00	2.00	4.00
1964/II	120,000	—	0.75	1.50	3.00

Y# 81.2 50 LIRE

6.2000 g., Stainless Steel, 24.8 mm. **Obverse:** Bust right **Obv. Legend:** A **Reverse:** Spes standing with anchor, date and value divided

Date	Mintage	F	VF	XF	Unc
1965/III	120,000	—	0.50	1.00	2.00

Y# 89 50 LIRE

6.2000 g., Stainless Steel, 24.8 mm. **Obverse:** Crowned head left **Reverse:** Shepard with sheep on shoulders

Date	Mintage	F	VF	XF	Unc
1966/IV	150,000	—	0.50	1.00	2.00

Y# 97 50 LIRE

6.2000 g., Stainless Steel, 24.8 mm. **Subject:** Conversion of Saint Paul **Obverse:** Bust right **Reverse:** Rearing equestrian **Designer:** G. Pirrone

Date	Mintage	F	VF	XF	Unc
1967/V	190,000	—	0.50	1.00	2.00

Y# 105 50 LIRE

6.2000 g., Stainless Steel, 24.8 mm. **Series:** F.A.O. **Obverse:** Bust right **Reverse:** Our Lady of Harvest standing within wheat sprigs **Designer:** G. Pirrone

Date	Mintage	F	VF	XF	Unc
ND(1968)/VI	190,000	—	0.50	1.00	2.00

Y# 113 50 LIRE

6.2000 g., Stainless Steel, 24.8 mm. **Obverse:** Crowned head 1/4 left divides inscription **Reverse:** Stylized angel

Date	Mintage	F	VF	XF	Unc
1969/VII	190,000	—	0.50	1.00	2.00

Y# 121 50 LIRE

6.2000 g., Stainless Steel, 24.8 mm. **Obverse:** Crowned shield **Reverse:** Olive branch **Designer:** Tomas Gismondi

Date	Mintage	F	VF	XF	Unc
1970/VIII	190,000	—	0.25	0.75	1.75
1971/IX	700,000	—	0.25	0.75	1.50
1972/X	700,000	—	0.25	0.75	1.50
1973/XI	750,000	—	0.25	0.75	1.50
1974/XII	750,000	—	0.25	0.75	1.50
1975/XIII	600,000	—	0.25	0.75	1.50
1976/XIV	600,000	—	0.25	0.75	1.50

Y# 129 50 LIRE

6.2000 g., Stainless Steel, 24.8 mm. **Subject:** Holy Year - The Peace of the Lord **Obverse:** Crowned shield **Reverse:** Stylized figure in fetal position within design with hand above **Designer:** Guido Veroi

Date	Mintage	F	VF	XF	Unc
1975	500,000	—	0.40	0.75	1.50

Y# A121 50 LIRE

6.2000 g., Stainless Steel, 24.8 mm. **Obverse:** Crowned shield **Reverse:** Wheat and grapes

Date	Mintage	F	VF	XF	Unc
1977/XV	600,000	—	0.25	0.50	1.25

Y# 136 50 LIRE

6.2000 g., Stainless Steel, 24.8 mm. **Obverse:** Crowned shield **Reverse:** Child and kneeling adult **Designer:** Nicola Morelli

Date	Mintage	F	VF	XF	Unc
1978/XVI	223,000	—	0.25	0.50	1.25

Y# 82.1 100 LIRE

8.0000 g., Stainless Steel, 27.75 mm. **Obverse:** Bust left **Obv. Legend:** AN **Reverse:** Fides standing figure divides value and date

Date	Mintage	F	VF	XF	Unc
1963/I	558,000	—	1.00	2.00	3.75

Y# 82.2 100 LIRE

8.0000 g., Stainless Steel, 27.75 mm. **Obverse:** Bust left **Obv. Legend:** A **Reverse:** Fides standing figure divides value and date

Date	Mintage	F	VF	XF	Unc
1964/II	558,000	—	0.50	1.00	2.50
1965/III	558,000	—	0.50	1.00	2.50

Y# 90 100 LIRE

8.0000 g., Stainless Steel, 27.75 mm. **Obverse:** Crowned head left **Reverse:** Shepard with sheep on shoulders **Designer:** E. Greco

Date	Mintage	F	VF	XF	Unc
1966/IV	388,000	—	0.50	1.00	2.50

Y# 98 100 LIRE

8.0000 g., Stainless Steel, 27.75 mm. **Obverse:** Bust left **Reverse:** St. Peter seated on throne facing **Designer:** G. Pirrone

Date	Mintage	F	VF	XF	Unc
1967/V	315,000	—	0.50	1.00	2.50

Y# 106 100 LIRE

8.0000 g., Stainless Steel, 27.75 mm. **Series:** F.A.O. **Obverse:** Bust left **Reverse:** Feeding of the 5,000 **Designer:** G. Pirrone

Date	Mintage	F	VF	XF	Unc
ND(1968)/VI	315,000	—	0.50	1.00	2.50

Y# 114 100 LIRE

8.0000 g., Stainless Steel, 27.75 mm. **Obverse:** Crowned head 1/4 left divides inscription **Reverse:** Stylized angel in flight **Designer:** C. Ruffini

Date	Mintage	F	VF	XF	Unc
1969/VII	315,000	—	0.50	1.00	2.50

Y# 122 100 LIRE

8.0000 g., Stainless Steel, 27.75 mm. **Obverse:** Crowned shield **Reverse:** Dove in flight with olive branch **Designer:** Tomas Gismondi

Date	Mintage	F	VF	XF	Unc
1970/VIII	315,000	—	0.50	1.00	2.50
1971/IX	966,000	—	0.40	0.75	1.50
1972/X	966,000	—	0.40	0.75	1.50
1973/XI	830,000	—	0.40	0.75	1.50
1974/XII	830,000	—	0.40	0.75	1.50
1975/XIII	808,000	—	0.40	0.75	1.50
1976/XIV	808,000	—	0.40	0.75	1.50
1977/XV	819,000	—	0.40	0.75	1.50

Y# 130 100 LIRE

8.0000 g., Stainless Steel, 27.75 mm. **Subject:** Holy Year - Symbolic Baptism of Man **Obverse:** Crowned shield **Reverse:** Hands pulling up net filled with fish **Designer:** Guido Veroi

Date	Mintage	F	VF	XF	Unc
1975	605,000	—	0.60	1.25	2.00

Y# 137 100 LIRE

8.0000 g., Stainless Steel, 27.75 mm. **Obverse:** Crowned shield **Reverse:** Stylized figure standing in courtyard **Designer:** Niccla Morelli

Date	Mintage	F	VF	XF	Unc
1978/XVI	399,000	—	0.50	1.00	2.00

Y# 138 200 LIRE

5.0000 g., Aluminum-Bronze, 24 mm. **Obverse:** Crowned shield **Reverse:** Stylized figure above value

Date	Mintage	F	VF	XF	Unc
1978/XVI	355,000	—	0.50	1.00	2.50

Y# 83.1 500 LIRE

11.0000 g., 0.8350 Silver .2953 oz. ASW, 29.3 mm. **Obverse:** Bust right **Obv. Legend:** AN **Reverse:** Crowned shield divides value **Designer:** Pietro Giampaoli

Date	Mintage	F	VF	XF	Unc
1963/I	70,000	—	8.00	16.00	32.00

Y# 83.2 500 LIRE

11.0000 g., 0.8350 Silver .2953 oz. ASW, 29.3 mm. **Obverse:** Bust right **Obv. Legend:** A **Reverse:** Crowned shield divides value

Date	Mintage	F	VF	XF	Unc
1964/II	70,000	—	7.00	15.00	25.00
1965/III	70,000	—	7.00	15.00	25.00

Y# 91 500 LIRE

11.0000 g., 0.8350 Silver .2953 oz. ASW, 29.3 mm. **Obverse:** Crowned head left **Reverse:** Shepard with sheep on shoulders **Designer:** E. Greco

Date	Mintage	F	VF	XF	Unc
1966/IV	100,000	—	7.00	15.00	25.00

Y# 99 500 LIRE

11.0000 g., 0.8350 Silver .2953 oz. ASW, 29.3 mm. **Obverse:** Bust left **Reverse:** Saint Peter and Paul, cross between, keys below **Designer:** G. Pirrone

Date	Mintage	F	VF	XF	Unc
ND(1967)/V	110,000	—	6.00	12.00	18.00

Y# 107 500 LIRE

11.0000 g., 0.8350 Silver .2953 oz. ASW, 29.3 mm. **Series:** F.A.O. **Obverse:** Bust left **Reverse:** Wheat ears forming radiant cross **Designer:** G. Pirrone

Date	Mintage	F	VF	XF	Unc
ND(1968)/VI	110,000	—	6.00	12.00	18.00

Y# 115 500 LIRE

11.0000 g., 0.8350 Silver .2953 oz. ASW, 29.3 mm. **Obverse:** Crowned head 1/4 left divides inscription **Reverse:** Stylized angel in flight **Designer:** C. Ruffini

Date	Mintage	F	VF	XF	Unc
1969/VII	110,000	—	6.00	12.00	18.00

Y# 123 500 LIRE

11.0000 g., 0.8350 Silver .2953 oz. ASW, 29.3 mm. **Obverse:** Crowned shield **Reverse:** Wheat and grapes **Designer:** Tomas Gismondi

Date	Mintage	F	VF	XF	Unc
1970/VIII	110,000	—	—	6.00	15.00
1971/IX	125,000	—	—	6.00	15.00
1972/X	125,000	—	—	6.00	15.00
1973/XI	145,000	—	—	6.00	15.00
1974/XII	145,000	—	—	6.00	15.00
1975/XIII	162,000	—	—	6.00	15.00
1976/XIV	162,000	—	—	6.00	15.00

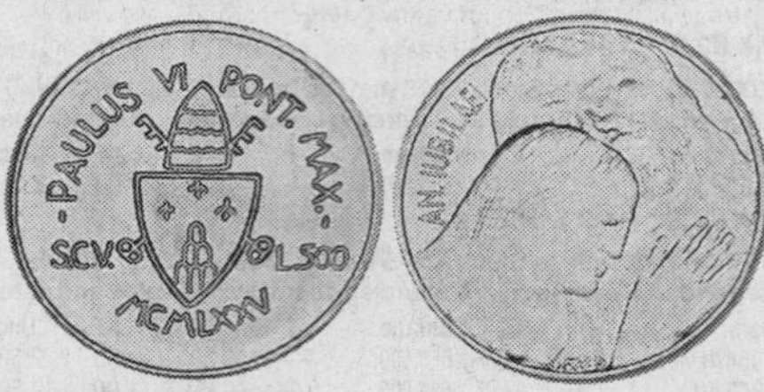

Y# 131 500 LIRE

11.0000 g., 0.8350 Silver .2953 oz. ASW, 29.3 mm. **Subject:** Holy Year - Forgiveness **Obverse:** Crowned shield **Reverse:** Stylized father embracing son **Designer:** Guido Veroi

Date	Mintage	F	VF	XF	Unc
1975	200,000	—	—	7.00	16.00

Y# 132 500 LIRE

11.0000 g., 0.8350 Silver .2953 oz. ASW, 29.3 mm. **Subject:** Book of the Evangelists **Obverse:** Crowned shield **Reverse:** Assorted animal heads within cross window frame

Date	Mintage	F	VF	XF	Unc
1977/XV	160,000	—	—	8.00	16.50

Y# 139 500 LIRE

11.0000 g., 0.8350 Silver .2953 oz. ASW, 29.3 mm. **Obverse:** Crowned shield **Reverse:** Stylized Jesus walking on water reaching for figure in boat

Date	Mintage	F	VF	XF	Unc
1978/XVI	145,000	—	—	8.00	16.50

John Paul I

STANDARD COINAGE

100 Centesimi = 1 Lira

Y# 142 1000 LIRE

14.6000 g., 0.8350 Silver .3920 oz. ASW **Obverse:** Bust left **Reverse:** Crowned shield **Designer:** Guido Veroi

Date	Mintage	F	VF	XF	Unc
1978	200,000	—	—	15.00	32.00

Sede Vacante

STANDARD COINAGE

100 Centesimi = 1 Lira

Y# 140 500 LIRE

11.0000 g., 0.8350 Silver .2953 oz. ASW, 29.3 mm. **Obverse:** Descending stylized dove above value **Reverse:** Arms of Cardinal Jean Villot **Rev. Legend:** SEDE VACANTE MCMLXXVIII **Designer:** Cismondi **Note:** First 1978 Sede Vacante issue

Date	Mintage	F	VF	XF	Unc
1978	500,000	—	—	10.00	20.00

Y# 141 500 LIRE

11.0000 g., 0.8350 Silver .2953 oz. ASW **Obverse:** Descending radiant dove **Reverse:** Arms of Cardinal Jean Villot **Rev. Legend:** SEDE VACANTE SEPTEMBER MCMLXXVIII **Note:** Second 1978 Sede Vacante issue

Date	Mintage	F	VF	XF	Unc
1978	—	—	6.00	10.00	20.00

Note: Mintage included with Y#140

John Paul II

STANDARD COINAGE

100 Centesimi = 1 Lira

Y# 143 10 LIRE

Aluminum, 23 mm. **Obverse:** Bust left **Reverse:** Cardinal Virtues - Temperance **Designer:** Guido Veroi

Date	Mintage	F	VF	XF	Unc
1979/I	250,000	—	0.25	0.50	1.00
1980/II	170,000	—	0.25	0.50	1.00

Y# 155 10 LIRE

Aluminum, 23 mm. **Obverse:** Head left **Reverse:** Jesus given water at the well **Designer:** Guido Veroi

Date	Mintage	F	VF	XF	Unc
1981/III	170,000	—	0.25	0.50	1.00

Y# 161 10 LIRE

Aluminum, 23 mm. **Subject:** Creation of Woman **Obverse:** Bust right **Reverse:** Standing figure facing to right of value **Designer:** Enrico Manfrini

Date	Mintage	F	VF	XF	Unc
1982/IV	220,000	—	0.25	0.50	1.00

Y# 170 10 LIRE

Aluminum, 23 mm. **Subject:** Work and Teaching **Obverse:** Head left at lower right of cross **Reverse:** Teacher, student and value **Designer:** Nicola Morelli

Date	Mintage	F	VF	XF	Unc
1983/V	110,000	—	0.25	0.50	1.00

Y# 177 10 LIRE

Aluminum, 23 mm. **Subject:**.Year of Peace **Obverse:** Bust left **Reverse:** Hand holding bouquet **Designer:** Ennio Tesei

Date	Mintage	F	VF	XF	Unc
1984/VI	110,000	—	0.25	0.50	1.00

Y# 185 10 LIRE

Aluminum, 23 mm. **Obverse:** Head left **Reverse:** Angel with gospel of St. Matthew **Designer:** Guido Veroi

Date	Mintage	F	VF	XF	Unc
1985/VII	90,000	—	0.25	0.50	1.00

Y# 192 10 LIRE

Aluminum, 23 mm. **Reverse:** Seated figure and value **Designer:** Guido Veroi

Date	Mintage	F	VF	XF	Unc
1986/VIII	90,000	—	0.25	0.50	1.00

Y# 199 10 LIRE

Aluminum, 23 mm. **Obverse:** Bust right **Reverse:** Basilica behind Pieta Statue **Designer:** Angelo Canevari

Date	Mintage	F	VF	XF	Unc
1987/IX	—	—	0.25	0.50	1.00

Y# 206 10 LIRE

Aluminum, 23 mm. **Subject:** Temptation of Adam and Eve **Obverse:** Bust right **Reverse:** Tree with snake divides standing figures **Designer:** Guido Veroi

Date	Mintage	F	VF	XF	Unc
1988/X	—	—	0.25	0.50	1.00

Y# 213 10 LIRE

Aluminum, 23 mm. **Subject:** Jesus the Teacher **Reverse:** Seated figure facing standing figure **Designer:** Enrico Manfrini

Date	Mintage	F	VF	XF	Unc
1989/XI	—	—	0.25	0.50	1.00

Y# 220 10 LIRE

Aluminum, 23 mm. **Subject:** Saints Peter and Paul **Obverse:** Bust 3/4 left **Reverse:** Saints Peter and Paul facing **Designer:** Angelo Canevari

Date	Mintage	F	VF	XF	Unc
1990/XII	—	—	0.25	0.50	1.00

Y# 228 10 LIRE

Aluminum, 23 mm. **Obverse:** Head left **Reverse:** Standing figure with book to right of value **Designer:** Nicola Morelli

Date	Mintage	F	VF	XF	Unc
1991/XIII	—	—	0.25	0.50	1.00

Y# 236 10 LIRE

Aluminum, 23 mm. **Obverse:** Bust right **Reverse:** Bee on flower **Designer:** Sergio Giandomenico

Date	Mintage	F	VF	XF	Unc
1992/XIV	—	—	0.25	0.50	1.00

Y# 244 10 LIRE

Aluminum, 23 mm. **Obverse:** Head facing **Reverse:** Sailboat divides inscription **Designer:** Guido Veroi

Date	Mintage	F	VF	XF	Unc
1993/XV	—	—	0.25	0.50	1.00

Y# 252 10 LIRE

Aluminum, 23 mm. **Obverse:** Bust left **Reverse:** Figures planting trees **Designer:** Angelo Canevari

Date	Mintage	F	VF	XF	Unc
1994/XVI	—	—	0.25	0.50	1.00

Y# 262 10 LIRE

Aluminum, 23 mm. **Reverse:** Preaching **Designer:** Enrico Manfrini

Date	Mintage	F	VF	XF	Unc
1995	—	—	0.25	0.50	1.00

Y# 272 10 LIRE

Aluminum, 23 mm. **Subject:** Child Carried to Peace **Obverse:** Head left **Reverse:** Stylized standing figure holding infant walking left **Designer:** Orietta Rossi

Date	Mintage	F	VF	XF	Unc
1996	—	—	0.25	0.50	1.00

Y# 280 10 LIRE

Aluminum, 23 mm. **Obverse:** Head right **Reverse:** Angel blowing horn to upper right of man sowing seeds **Designer:** Gabriella Titotto

Date	Mintage	F	VF	XF	Unc
1997/XIX	—	—	0.50	0.75	2.00

Y# 293 10 LIRE

1.6000 g., Aluminum, 23 mm. **Obverse:** Bust right holding crucifix **Reverse:** Standing figure flanked by seated figures **Designer:** Paolo Borghi

Date	Mintage	F	VF	XF	Unc
1998	—	—	0.50	0.75	2.00

Y# 305 10 LIRE

1.6000 g., Aluminum, 23.3 mm. **Subject:** Right to Life - Motherhood **Obverse:** Bust right **Reverse:** Mother with baby and child below tree **Edge:** Plain **Mint:** Rome **Designer:** Angelo Canevari

Date	Mintage	F	VF	XF	Unc
1999	—	—	0.50	0.75	2.00

Y# 323 10 LIRE

1.6000 g., Aluminum, 23.2 mm. **Obverse:** Papal arms within circle **Reverse:** Pope lifting child **Edge:** Plain **Mint:** Rome **Designer:** Cecco Bonanotte

Date	Mintage	F	VF	XF	Unc
XXII(2000)	—	—	0.50	0.75	2.00

Y# 144 20 LIRE

3.6000 g., Aluminum-Bronze, 21.25 mm. **Reverse:** Fortitude **Designer:** Guido Veroi

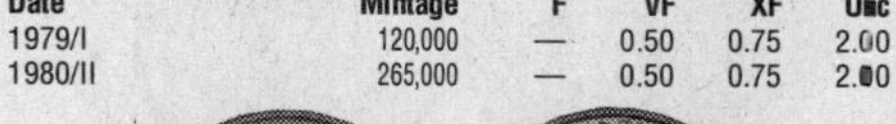

Date	Mintage	F	VF	XF	Unc
1979/I	120,000	—	0.50	0.75	2.00
1980/II	265,000	—	0.50	0.75	2.00

Y# 156 20 LIRE

3.6000 g., Aluminum-Bronze, 21.25 mm. **Obverse:** Head left **Reverse:** Open door flanked by standing figures **Designer:** Guido Veroi

Date	Mintage	F	VF	XF	Unc
1981/III	265,000	—	0.50	0.75	2.00

Y# 162 20 LIRE

3.6000 g., Aluminum-Bronze, 21.25 mm. **Subject:** Marriage **Obverse:** Bust right **Reverse:** Standing figures shaking hands **Designer:** Enrico Manfrini

Date	Mintage	F	VF	XF	Unc
1982/IV	360,000	—	0.50	0.75	2.00

Y# 171 20 LIRE

3.6000 g., Aluminum-Bronze, 21.25 mm. **Subject:** Incarnation of the Word **Obverse:** Head left to lower right of cross **Reverse:** Radiant dove above stylized kneeling figures within triangle shape **Designer:** Nicola Morelli

Date	Mintage	F	VF	XF	Unc
1983/V	170,000	—	0.50	0.75	2.00

Y# 178 20 LIRE

3.6000 g., Aluminum-Bronze, 21.25 mm. **Subject:** Year of Peace **Obverse:** Bust left **Reverse:** Child and sheep **Designer:** Ennio Tesei

Date	Mintage	F	VF	XF	Unc
1984/VI	170,000	—	0.50	0.75	2.00

Y# 186 20 LIRE

3.6000 g., Aluminum-Bronze, 21.25 mm. **Obverse:** Head left **Reverse:** Stylized eagle holding gospel of St. John **Designer:** Guido Veroi

Date	Mintage	F	VF	XF	Unc
1985/VII	255,000	—	0.50	0.75	2.00

Y# 193 20 LIRE

3.6000 g., Aluminum-Bronze, 21.25 mm. **Obverse:** Bust right **Reverse:** Stylized standing figure with wing **Designer:** Guido Veroi

Date	Mintage	F	VF	XF	Unc
1986/VIII	100,000	—	0.50	0.75	2.00

Y# 200 20 LIRE

3.6000 g., Aluminum-Bronze, 21.25 mm. **Obverse:** Bust right **Reverse:** Assumption of Mother Mary into heaven **Designer:** Angelo Canevari

Date	Mintage	F	VF	XF	Unc
1987/IX	—	—	0.50	0.75	2.00

Y# 207 20 LIRE

3.6000 g., Aluminum-Bronze, 21.25 mm. **Subject:** Temptation of Adam and Eve **Reverse:** Apple tree flanked by standing figures and pair of hands **Designer:** Guido Veroi **Note:** Similar to 200 Lire, Y#210.

Date	Mintage	F	VF	XF	Unc
1988/X	—	—	0.50	0.75	2.00

Y# 214 20 LIRE

3.6000 g., Aluminum-Bronze, 21.25 mm. **Subject:** The Harvest **Reverse:** Standing and kneeling figures **Designer:** Enrico Manfrini

Date	Mintage	F	VF	XF	Unc
1989/XI	—	—	0.50	0.75	2.00

Y# 221 20 LIRE

3.6000 g., Aluminum-Bronze, 21.25 mm. **Obverse:** Bust 3/4 left **Reverse:** Pope John Paul II and Eastern Rite Bishop **Designer:** Angelo Canevari

Date	Mintage	F	VF	XF	Unc
1990/XII	—	—	0.50	0.75	2.00

Y# 229 20 LIRE

3.6000 g., Aluminum-Bronze, 21.25 mm. **Obverse:** Head left **Reverse:** Crane and buildings **Designer:** Nicola Morelli

Date	Mintage	F	VF	XF	Unc
1991/XIII	—	—	0.50	0.75	2.00

Y# 237 20 LIRE

3.6000 g., Aluminum-Bronze, 21.25 mm. **Obverse:** Bust right **Reverse:** Three children above value **Designer:** Sergio Giandomenico

Date	Mintage	F	VF	XF	Unc
1992/XIV	—	—	0.50	0.75	2.00

Y# 245 20 LIRE

3.6000 g., Aluminum-Bronze, 21.25 mm. **Obverse:** Head facing **Reverse:** Crucifix, as on papal croizer **Designer:** Guido Veroi

Date	Mintage	F	VF	XF	Unc
1993/XV	—	—	0.50	0.75	2.00

Y# 253 20 LIRE

3.6000 g., Aluminum-Bronze, 21.25 mm. **Obverse:** Bust left **Reverse:** Hospital patient with visitors **Designer:** Angelo Canaveri

Date	Mintage	F	VF	XF	Unc
1994/XVI	—	—	0.50	0.75	2.00

Y# 263 20 LIRE

3.6000 g., Aluminum-Bronze, 21.25 mm. **Subject:** Euthanasia **Designer:** Enrico Manfrini

Date	Mintage	F	VF	XF	Unc
1995	—	—	0.50	0.75	2.00

Y# 273 20 LIRE

3.6000 g., Aluminum-Bronze, 21.25 mm. **Obverse:** Head left **Reverse:** Parents praising child **Designer:** Orietta Rossi

Date	Mintage	F	VF	XF	Unc
1996	—	—	0.50	0.75	2.00

Y# 281 20 LIRE

3.6000 g., Aluminum-Bronze, 21.25 mm. **Obverse:** Bust right **Reverse:** Jesus teaching with book **Designer:** Gabriella Titotto

Date	Mintage	F	VF	XF	Unc
1997/XIX	—	—	0.50	0.75	2.00

Y# 294 20 LIRE

3.6000 g., Aluminum-Bronze, 21.25 mm. **Obverse:** Bust right holding crucifix **Reverse:** Family and sun **Designer:** Paolo Borghi

Date	Mintage	F	VF	XF	Unc
1998	—	—	0.50	0.75	2.00

Y# 306 20 LIRE

3.6000 g., Aluminum-Bronze, 21.3 mm. **Subject:** Work - The Right to Fulfill One's Potential **Obverse:** Bust right **Reverse:** Workers **Edge:** Plain **Mint:** Rome **Designer:** Angelo Canevari

Date	Mintage	F	VF	XF	Unc
1999	—	—	0.50	0.75	2.00

Y# 324 20 LIRE

3.5700 g., Brass, 21.2 mm. **Obverse:** Papal arms within circle **Reverse:** Head of Pope stargazing **Edge:** Plain **Mint:** Rome **Designer:** Cecco Bonanotte

Date	Mintage	F	VF	XF	Unc
XXII(2000)	—	—	0.50	0.75	2.00

Y# 145 50 LIRE

6.2000 g., Stainless Steel, 24.8 mm. **Obverse:** Bust left **Reverse:** Justice seated right with sword and scales **Designer:** Guido Veroi

Date	Mintage	F	VF	XF	Unc
1979/I	223,000	—	0.50	0.75	2.00
1980/II	250,000	—	0.50	0.75	2.00

Y# 157 50 LIRE

6.2000 g., Stainless Steel, 24.8 mm. **Obverse:** Head left **Reverse:** Upright design flanked by standing figures **Designer:** Guido Veroi

Date	Mintage	F	VF	XF	Unc
1981/III	240,000	—	0.50	0.75	2.00

Y# 163 50 LIRE

6.2000 g., Stainless Steel, 24.8 mm. **Subject:** Motherhood **Obverse:** Bust right **Reverse:** Seated figure with infant on lap **Designer:** Enrico Manfrini

Date	Mintage	F	VF	XF	Unc
1982/IV	400,000	—	0.50	0.75	2.00

Y# 172 50 LIRE

6.2000 g., Stainless Steel, 24.8 mm. **Subject:** Banishment of Adam and Eve **Obverse:** Head left to lower right of cross **Reverse:** Stylized figure **Designer:** Nicola Morelli

Date	Mintage	F	VF	XF	Unc
1983/V	300,000	—	0.50	0.75	2.00

Y# 179 50 LIRE

6.2000 g., Stainless Steel, 24.8 mm. **Subject:** Year of Peace **Obverse:** Bust left **Reverse:** Doves **Designer:** Ennio Tesei

Date	Mintage	F	VF	XF	Unc
1984/VI	300,000	—	0.50	0.75	2.00

Y# 187 50 LIRE

6.2000 g., Stainless Steel, 24.8 mm. **Obverse:** Head left **Reverse:** Winged lion holding gospel of St. Mark **Designer:** Guido Veroi

Date	Mintage	F	VF	XF	Unc
1985/VII	360,000	—	0.50	0.75	2.00

Y# 194 50 LIRE

6.2000 g., Stainless Steel, 24.8 mm. **Obverse:** Bust right **Reverse:** Seated figure on rock **Designer:** Guido Veroi

Date	Mintage	F	VF	XF	Unc
1986/VIII	100,000	—	0.50	0.75	2.00

Y# 201 50 LIRE

6.2000 g., Stainless Steel, 24.8 mm. **Obverse:** Bust right **Reverse:** Mother Mary protecting kneeling sinners **Designer:** Angelo Canevari

Date	Mintage	F	VF	XF	Unc
1987/IX	—	—	0.50	0.75	2.00

Y# 208 50 LIRE

6.2000 g., Stainless Steel, 24.8 mm. **Subject:** Creation of Eve From Adam's Rib **Obverse:** Bust right **Reverse:** Face profile to right of female figure rising out of male figure on ground **Designer:** Guido Veroi

Date	Mintage	F	VF	XF	Unc
1988	—	—	0.50	0.75	2.00

Y# 215 50 LIRE

6.2000 g., Stainless Steel, 24.8 mm. **Subject:** Human Solidarity **Reverse:** Standing figures **Designer:** Enrico Manfrini

Date	Mintage	F	VF	XF	Unc
1989/XI	—	—	0.50	0.75	2.00

Y# 222 50 LIRE

Stainless Steel, 16.3 mm. **Obverse:** Bust 3/4 left **Reverse:** Radiant cross in open door **Designer:** Angelo Canevari

Date	Mintage	F	VF	XF	Unc
1990/XII	—	—	0.50	0.75	2.00

Y# 230 50 LIRE

Stainless Steel, 16.3 mm. **Obverse:** Head left **Reverse:** Baptism scene **Designer:** Nicola Morelli

Date	Mintage	F	VF	XF	Unc
1991/XIII	—	—	0.50	0.75	2.00

Y# 238 50 LIRE

Stainless Steel, 16.3 mm. **Obverse:** Bust right **Reverse:** Cross as balance scale between agriculture and industry **Designer:** Sergio Giandomenico

Date	Mintage	F	VF	XF	Unc
1992/XIV	—	—	0.50	0.75	2.00

Y# 246 50 LIRE

Stainless Steel, 16.3 mm. **Obverse:** Head facing **Reverse:** Chalice divides inscription **Designer:** Guido Veroi

Date	Mintage	F	VF	XF	Unc
1993/XV	—	—	0.50	0.75	2.00

Y# 254 50 LIRE

Stainless Steel, 16.3 mm. **Obverse:** Bust left **Reverse:** Hands and prison bars **Designer:** Angelo Canevari

Date	Mintage	F	VF	XF	Unc
1994/XVI	—	—	0.50	0.75	2.00

Y# 264 50 LIRE

Stainless Steel, 16.3 mm. **Reverse:** Dragon on Prone Woman (Abortion) **Designer:** Enrico Manfrini

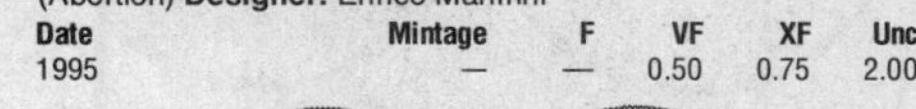

Date	Mintage	F	VF	XF	Unc
1995	—	—	0.50	0.75	2.00

Y# 274 50 LIRE

Copper-Nickel, 19.2 mm. **Obverse:** Head left **Reverse:** Guardian angel protecting child **Designer:** Orietta Rossi

Date	Mintage	F	VF	XF	Unc
1996	—	—	0.50	0.75	2.00

Y# 282 50 LIRE

Copper-Nickel, 19.2 mm. **Obverse:** Head right **Reverse:** One man with lowered sword, the other with dove **Designer:** Gabriella Titotto

Date	Mintage	F	VF	XF	Unc
1997/XIX	—	—	0.50	0.75	2.00

Y# 295 50 LIRE

Copper-Nickel, 19.2 mm. **Obverse:** Pope with crucifix croizer **Reverse:** Two figures and hand **Designer:** Paolo Borghi

Date	Mintage	F	VF	XF	Unc
1998	—	—	0.50	0.75	2.00

Y# 307 50 LIRE

4.4600 g., Copper-Nickel, 19.2 mm. **Subject:** Ecosystem - Agriculture **Obverse:** Bust right **Reverse:** Agricultural workers **Edge:** Plain **Mint:** Rome **Designer:** Angelo Canevari

Date	Mintage	F	VF	XF	Unc
1999	—	—	0.50	0.75	2.00

Y# 325 50 LIRE

4.5000 g., Copper-Nickel, 19.2 mm. **Obverse:** Papal arms within circle **Reverse:** Pope about to kiss ground **Edge:** Plain **Mint:** Rome **Designer:** Cecco Bonanotte

Date	Mintage	F	VF	XF	Unc
XXII(2000)	—	—	0.50	0.75	2.00

Y# 146 100 LIRE

8.0000 g., Stainless Steel, 27.75 mm. **Obverse:** Bust left **Reverse:** Prudence seated **Designer:** Guido Veroi

Date	Mintage	F	VF	XF	Unc
1979/I	399,000	—	0.75	1.25	2.50
1980/II	485,000	—	0.75	1.25	2.50

Y# 158 100 LIRE

8.0000 g., Stainless Steel, 27.75 mm. **Obverse:** Head left **Reverse:** Angel offering food to seated figure **Designer:** Guido Veroi

Date	Mintage	F	VF	XF	Unc
1981/III	550,000	—	0.75	1.25	2.50

Y# 164 100 LIRE

8.0000 g., Stainless Steel, 27.75 mm. **Subject:** Family Unit **Obverse:** Bust right **Reverse:** Standing and seated figure divides value **Designer:** Enrico Manfrini

Date	Mintage	F	VF	XF	Unc
1982/IV	656,000	—	0.75	1.25	2,50

Y# 173 100 LIRE

8.0000 g., Stainless Steel, 27.75 mm. **Subject:** God Gives World to Mankind **Obverse:** Head left to lower right of cross **Reverse:** Design flanked by hand and kneeling figure **Designer:** Nicola Morelli

Date	Mintage	F	VF	XF	Unc
1983/V	455,000	—	0.75	1.25	2.50

Y# 180 100 LIRE

8.0000 g., Stainless Steel, 27.75 mm. **Subject:** Year of Peace **Obverse:** Bust left **Reverse:** Cross divides lamb and value **Designer:** Ennio Tesei

Date	Mintage	F	VF	XF	Unc
1984/VI	400,000	—	0.75	1.25	2.50

Y# 188 100 LIRE

8.0000 g., Stainless Steel, 27.75 mm. **Obverse:** Head left **Reverse:** Small airplane in flight over map **Designer:** Guido Veroi

Date	Mintage	F	VF	XF	Unc
1985/VII	800,000	—	0.75	1.25	2.50

Y# 195 100 LIRE

8.0000 g., Stainless Steel, 27.75 mm. **Obverse:** Bust right **Reverse:** Seated figure on rocks **Designer:** Guido Veroi

Date	Mintage	F	VF	XF	Unc
1986/VIII	100,000	—	0.75	1.25	2.50

Y# 202 100 LIRE

8.0000 g., Stainless Steel, 27.75 mm. **Subject:** Angel and Mary, The Annunciation **Obverse:** Bust right **Reverse:** Dove above angel and seated figure **Designer:** Angelo Canevari

Date	Mintage	F	VF	XF	Unc
1987/IX	—	—	0.75	1.25	2.50

Y# 209 100 LIRE

8.0000 g., Stainless Steel, 27.75 mm. **Subject:** Adam naming the Animals **Obverse:** Bust right **Reverse:** Standing figure in palm of hand to left of assorted animals **Designer:** Guido Veroi

Date	Mintage	F	VF	XF	Unc
1988/X	—	—	0.75	1.25	2.50

Y# 216 100 LIRE

8.0000 g., Stainless Steel, 27.75 mm. **Reverse:** Pelican feeding young **Designer:** Enrico Manfrini

Date	Mintage	F	VF	XF	Unc
1989/XI	—	—	0.75	1.25	2.50

Y# 223 100 LIRE

Stainless Steel, 18 mm. **Subject:** Early Bishop **Obverse:** Bust 3/4 left **Reverse:** Hooded half-figure facing **Designer:** Angelo Canevari

Date	Mintage	F	VF	XF	Unc
1990/XII	—	—	0.75	1.25	2.50

Y# 231 100 LIRE

Stainless Steel, 18 mm. **Obverse:** Head left **Reverse:** Depiction of the risen Christ **Designer:** Nicola Morelli

Date	Mintage	F	VF	XF	Unc
1991/XIII	—	—	0.75	1.25	2.50

Y# 239 100 LIRE

Stainless Steel, 18 mm. **Obverse:** Bust right **Reverse:** Open book above value **Designer:** Sergio Giandomenico

Date	Mintage	F	VF	XF	Unc
1992/XIV	—	—	0.75	1.25	2.50

Y# 247 100 LIRE

Copper-Nickel, 21.8 mm. **Obverse:** Head facing **Reverse:** Portrait of Jesus facing divides inscription above value **Designer:** Guido Veroi

Date	Mintage	F	VF	XF	Unc
1993/XV	—	—	0.75	1.25	2.50

Y# 255 100 LIRE

Copper-Nickel, 21.8 mm. **Obverse:** Bust left **Reverse:** Basketball players with one in wheelchair **Designer:** Angelo Canevari

Date	Mintage	F	VF	XF	Unc
1994/XVI	—	—	0.75	1.25	2.50

Y# 265 100 LIRE

Copper-Nickel, 21.8 mm. **Reverse:** Guard and prisoners **Designer:** Enrico Manfrini

Date	Mintage	F	VF	XF	Unc
1995	—	—	0.75	1.25	2.50

Y# 275 100 LIRE

Copper-Nickel, 21.8 mm. **Obverse:** Head left **Reverse:** Women helping children **Designer:** Orietta Rossi

Date	Mintage	F	VF	XF	Unc
1996	—	—	0.75	1.25	2.50

Y# 283 100 LIRE

Copper-Nickel, 21.8 mm. **Obverse:** Bust right **Reverse:** Woman filling birdbath and doves **Designer:** Gabriella Titotto

Date	Mintage	F	VF	XF	Unc
1997/XIX	—	—	0.75	1.25	2.50

Y# 296 100 LIRE

Copper-Nickel, 21.8 mm. **Obverse:** Pope with crucifix croizer **Reverse:** Female figure in front of globe **Designer:** Paolo Borghi

Date	Mintage	F	VF	XF	Unc
1998	—	—	0.75	1.25	2.50

Y# 308 100 LIRE

4.5000 g., Copper-Nickel, 22 mm. **Subject:** The Right to Peace **Obverse:** Bust right within circle **Reverse:** Children of the world gathered in peace **Edge:** Reeded and plain sections **Mint:** Rome **Designer:** Angelo Canevari

Date	Mintage	F	VF	XF	Unc
1999	—	—	0.75	1.25	2.50

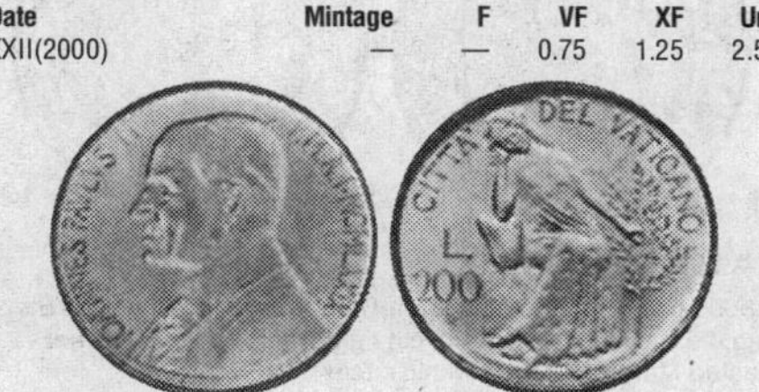

Y# 326 100 LIRE

4.5000 g., Copper-Nickel, 22 mm. **Obverse:** Papal arms within circle **Reverse:** Pope resting head on hand within window frame design **Edge:** Plain and reeded sections **Mint:** Rome **Designer:** Cecco Bonanotte

Date	Mintage	F	VF	XF	Unc
XXII(2000)	—	—	0.75	1.25	2.50

Y# 147 200 LIRE

5.0000 g., Aluminum-Bronze, 24 mm. **Obverse:** Bust left **Reverse:** Peace seated flanked by value and sprig **Designer:** Guido Veroi

Date	Mintage	F	VF	XF	Unc
1979/I	355,000	—	0.50	1.00	2.50
1980/II	200,000	—	0.50	1.00	2.50

Y# 159 200 LIRE

5.0000 g., Aluminum-Bronze, 24 mm. **Subject:** Corporal acts of Mercy - Bury the dead **Obverse:** Head left **Reverse:** Standing figures carrying supine figure **Designer:** Guido Veroi

Date	Mintage	F	VF	XF	Unc
1981/III	170,000	—	0.50	1.00	2.50

Y# 165 200 LIRE

5.0000 g., Aluminum-Bronze, 24 mm. **Subject:** Farm labor **Obverse:** Bust right **Reverse:** Workers and ox **Designer:** Enrico Manfrini

Date	Mintage	F	VF	XF	Unc
1982/IV	500,000	—	0.50	1.00	2.50

Y# 174 200 LIRE

5.0000 g., Aluminum-Bronze, 24 mm. **Subject:** Creation of Man **Obverse:** Head left to lower right of cross **Reverse:** Stylized figure above hands **Designer:** Nicola Morelli

Date	Mintage	F	VF	XF	Unc
1983/V	300,000	—	0.50	1.00	2.25

Y# 181 200 LIRE

5.0000 g., Aluminum-Bronze, 24 mm. **Subject:** Year of Peace **Obverse:** Bust left **Reverse:** Sailboat and cross **Designer:** Ennio Tesei

Date	Mintage	F	VF	XF	Unc
1984/VI	250,000	—	0.50	1.00	2.25

Y# 189 200 LIRE

5.0000 g., Aluminum-Bronze, 24 mm. **Obverse:** Head left **Reverse:** Winged Ox holding gospel **Designer:** Guido Veroi

Date	Mintage	F	VF	XF	Unc
1985/VII	300,000	—	0.50	1.00	2.25

Y# 196 200 LIRE

5.0000 g., Aluminum-Bronze, 24 mm. **Subject:** Michael the Archangel **Obverse:** Bust right **Reverse:** Archangel Michael and value **Designer:** Guido Veroi

Date	Mintage	F	VF	XF	Unc
1986/VIII	100,000	—	0.50	1.00	2.25

Y# 203 200 LIRE

5.0000 g., Aluminum-Bronze, 24 mm. **Subject:** Mary, Queen of Peace **Obverse:** Bust right **Reverse:** Seated figure in front of trees **Designer:** Angelo Canevari

Date	Mintage	F	VF	XF	Unc
1987/IX	—	—	0.50	1.00	2.25

Y# 210 200 LIRE

5.0000 g., Aluminum-Bronze, 24 mm. **Subject:** Creation of Adam **Obverse:** Bust right **Reverse:** Face profile at left of figure within palm of hand **Designer:** Guido Veroi

Date	Mintage	F	VF	XF	Unc
1988/X	—	—	0.50	1.00	2.25

Y# 217 200 LIRE

5.0000 g., Aluminum-Bronze, 24 mm. **Obverse:** Bust 3/4 right **Reverse:** Group of standing figures **Designer:** Enrico Manfrini

Date	Mintage	F	VF	XF	Unc
1989/XI	—	—	0.50	1.00	2.25

Y# 224 200 LIRE

5.0000 g., Aluminum-Bronze, 24 mm. **Subject:** Blessed Virgin Mary **Obverse:** Bust 3/4 left **Reverse:** Standing figure facing and value **Designer:** Angelo Canevari

Date	Mintage	F	VF	XF	Unc
1990/XII	—	—	0.50	1.00	2.25

Y# 232 200 LIRE

5.0000 g., Aluminum-Bronze, 24 mm. **Obverse:** Head left **Reverse:** Stylized figure to left of city **Designer:** Nicola Morelli

Date	Mintage	F	VF	XF	Unc
1991/XIII	—	—	0.50	1.00	2.25

Y# 240 200 LIRE

5.0000 g., Aluminum-Bronze, 24 mm. **Obverse:** Bust right **Reverse:** Mother nursing child **Designer:** Sergio Giandomenico

Date	Mintage	F	VF	XF	Unc
1992/XIV	—	—	0.50	1.00	2.25

Y# 248 200 LIRE

5.0000 g., Aluminum-Bronze, 24 mm. **Subject:** Ten Commandments **Obverse:** Head facing **Reverse:** 10 commandment stone divides name above value **Designer:** Guido Veroi

Date	Mintage	F	VF	XF	Unc
1993/XV	—	—	0.50	1.00	2.25

Y# 256 200 LIRE

5.0000 g., Aluminum-Bronze, 24 mm. **Subject:** Helping Victims of Drug Abuse **Obverse:** Bust left **Reverse:** Group of standing figures **Designer:** Angelo Canevari

Date	Mintage	F	VF	XF	Unc
1994/XVI	—	—	0.50	1.00	2.25

Y# 266 200 LIRE

5.0000 g., Aluminum-Bronze, 24 mm. **Reverse:** Family and farming scene **Designer:** Enrico Manfrini

Date	Mintage	F	VF	XF	Unc
1995	—	—	0.50	1.00	2.25

Y# 276 200 LIRE

5.0000 g., Aluminum-Bronze, 24 mm. **Obverse:** Head left **Reverse:** Display of family togetherness **Designer:** Orietta Rossi

Date	Mintage	F	VF	XF	Unc
1996	—	—	0.50	1.00	2.25

Y# 284 200 LIRE

5.0000 g., Aluminum-Bronze, 24 mm. **Obverse:** Bust right **Reverse:** Angel guiding two people **Designer:** Gabriella Titotto

Date	Mintage	F	VF	XF	Unc
1997/XIX	—	—	0.50	1.00	2.25

Y# 297 200 LIRE

5.0000 g., Aluminum-Bronze, 24 mm. **Obverse:** Bust left **Reverse:** Group of standing figures **Designer:** Paolo Borghi

Date	Mintage	F	VF	XF	Unc
1998	—	—	0.50	1.00	2.25

Y# 309 200 LIRE

5.0000 g., Aluminum-Bronze, 24 mm. **Obverse:** Bust right **Reverse:** Christ among the poor and outcast **Edge:** Reeded **Mint:** Rome **Designer:** Angelo Canevari

Date	Mintage	F	VF	XF	Unc
1999	—	—	0.50	1.00	2.25

Y# 327 200 LIRE

5.0000 g., Brass, 22 mm. **Obverse:** Papal arms within circle **Reverse:** Pope praying **Edge:** Reeded **Mint:** Rome **Designer:** Cecco Bonanotte

Date	Mintage	F	VF	XF	Unc
XXII(2000)	—	—	0.50	1.00	2.25

Y# 148 500 LIRE

11.0000 g., 0.8350 Silver .2953 oz. ASW, 29.3 mm. **Obverse:** Head left **Reverse:** Crowned shield **Designer:** Celestino Giampaoli

Date	Mintage	F	VF	XF	Unc
1979/I	145,000	—	—	10.00	22.50
1980/II	184,000	—	—	10.00	22.50

Y# 160 500 LIRE

11.0000 g., 0.8350 Silver .2953 oz. ASW, 29.3 mm. **Obverse:** Head left **Reverse:** Crowned shield **Designer:** Guido Veroi

Date	Mintage	F	VF	XF	Unc
1981/III	184,000	—	—	10.00	22.50

Y# 166 500 LIRE

6.8000 g., Bi-Metallic Aluminum-Bronze center in Stainless Steel ring, 25.8 mm. **Subject:** Education **Obverse:** Bust right within circle **Reverse:** Seated figure flanked by children within circle **Designer:** Enrico Manfrini

Date	Mintage	F	VF	XF	Unc
1982/IV	1,852,000	—	—	3.50	7.00

Y# 168 500 LIRE

11.0000 g., 0.8350 Silver .2953 oz. ASW, 29.3 mm. **Subject:** Extraordinary Holy Year **Obverse:** Crowned shield **Reverse:** Kneeling figure facing, people and buildings in background **Designer:** Enrico Manfrini

Date	Mintage	F	VF	XF	Unc
1983-84	130,000	—	—	15.00	30.00

Y# 175 500 LIRE

6.8000 g., Bi-Metallic Aluminum-Bronze center in Stainless Steel ring, 25.8 mm. **Subject:** Creation of the Universe **Obverse:** Head left to lower right of cross within circle **Reverse:** Hand reaching in globe within circle **Designer:** Nicola Morelli

Date	Mintage	F	VF	XF	Unc
1983/V	—	—	—	3.50	7.00

Y# 182 500 LIRE

6.8000 g., Bi-Metallic Aluminum-Bronze center in Stainless Steel ring, 25.8 mm. **Subject:** Year of Peace **Obverse:** Head left within circle **Reverse:** Sprig within clasped hands within circle **Designer:** Ennio Tesei

Date	Mintage	F	VF	XF	Unc
1984/VI	270,000	—	—	3.50	7.00

Y# 184 500 LIRE

11.0000 g., 0.8350 Silver .2953 oz. ASW, 29.3 mm. **Subject:** 2000th Anniversary - Birth of Blessed Virgin Mary **Obverse:** Crowned shield **Reverse:** Standing and kneeling figures, crosses and domed building **Designer:** Angelo Canerari

Date	Mintage	F	VF	XF	Unc
1984/VI	105,000	—	—	20.00	35.00

Y# 190 500 LIRE

6.8000 g., Bi-Metallic Aluminum-Bronze center in Stainless Steel ring, 25.8 mm. **Obverse:** Head left within circle **Reverse:** St. Paul in boat within circle **Designer:** Guido Veroi

Date	Mintage	F	VF	XF	Unc
1985/VII	300,000	—	—	2.50	6.00

Y# 197 500 LIRE

6.8000 g., Bi-Metallic Aluminum-Bronze center in Stainless Steel ring, 25.8 mm. **Obverse:** Bust right within circle **Reverse:** Seated Mary and Jesus within circle

Date	Mintage	F	VF	XF	Unc
1986/VIII	300,000	—	—	2.50	6.00

Y# 204 500 LIRE

6.8000 g., Bi-Metallic Aluminum-Bronze center in Stainless Steel ring, 25.8 mm. **Obverse:** Bust left within circle **Reverse:** Mary before Crucified Jesus within circle **Designer:** Angelo Canevari

Date	Mintage	F	VF	XF	Unc
1987/IX	—	—	—	2.50	6.00

Y# 211 500 LIRE

6.8000 g., Bi-Metallic Aluminum-Bronze center in Stainless Steel ring, 25.8 mm. **Obverse:** Head right within circle **Reverse:** Dove at center, conjoined busts within circle **Designer:** Guido Veroi

Date	Mintage	F	VF	XF	Unc
1988/X	—	—	—	2.50	6.00

Y# 218 500 LIRE

6.8000 g., Bi-Metallic Aluminum-Bronze center in Stainless Steel ring, 25.8 mm. **Obverse:** Bust right within circle **Reverse:** Grapevine within circle **Designer:** Enrico Manfrini

Date	Mintage	F	VF	XF	Unc
1989/XI	—	—	—	2.50	6.00

Y# 225 500 LIRE

6.8000 g., Bi-Metallic Aluminum-Bronze center in Stainless Steel ring, 25.8 mm. **Obverse:** Bust left within circle **Reverse:** Jesus flanked by kneeling figures within circle **Designer:** Angelo Canevari

Date	Mintage	F	VF	XF	Unc
1990/XII	—	—	—	2.00	4.00

Y# 227 500 LIRE

11.0000 g., 0.8350 Silver .2953 oz. ASW, 29.3 mm. **Subject:** Social doctrine **Obverse:** Bust right **Reverse:** Stylized figures within circle **Designer:** Nicola Morelli

Date	Mintage	F	VF	XF	Unc
1991	—	—	—	20.00	35.00

Y# 233 500 LIRE

6.8000 g., Bi-Metallic Aluminum-Bronze center in Stainless Steel ring, 25.8 mm. **Obverse:** Head left within circle **Reverse:** Redeemer sending out missionaries within circle **Designer:** Nicola Morelli

Date	Mintage	F	VF	XF	Unc
1991/XIII	—	—	—	2.00	4.00

Y# 235 500 LIRE

11.0000 g., 0.8350 Silver .2953 oz. ASW, 29.3 mm. **Subject:** Evangelization of America **Obverse:** Crowned bust left to right of world globe **Reverse:** Three ships in center of map **Designer:** Giovani Contri

Date	Mintage	F	VF	XF	Unc
1992/XIV	—	—	—	20.00	35.00

Y# 241 500 LIRE

6.8000 g., Bi-Metallic Aluminum-Bronze center in Stainless Steel ring, 25.8 mm. **Obverse:** Bust right within circle **Reverse:** Hands holding loaf of bread within globe **Designer:** Sergio Giandomenico

Date	Mintage	F	VF	XF	Unc
1992/XIV	—	—	—	2.00	4.00

Y# 243 500 LIRE

11.0000 g., 0.8350 Silver .2953 oz. ASW, 29.3 mm. **Subject:** World Peace **Reverse:** Seated figure with infant **Designer:** Guido Veroi

Date	Mintage	F	VF	XF	Unc
1993/XV	—	—	—	17.50	30.00

Y# 249 500 LIRE

6.8000 g., Bi-Metallic Aluminum-Bronze center in Stainless Steel ring, 25.8 mm. **Subject:** Thurible **Designer:** Guido Veroi

Date	Mintage	F	VF	XF	Unc
1993/XV	—	—	—	2.00	4.00

Y# 251 500 LIRE

11.0000 g., 0.8350 Silver .2953 oz. ASW, 29.3 mm. **Subject:** Veritatis Splendor **Obverse:** Sunrays above bust right holding crucifix **Reverse:** Sunrays divide circle with standing figure within map **Designer:** Giovani Contri

Date	Mintage	F	VF	XF	Unc
1994/XVI	—	—	—	18.00	30.00
1994/XVI Proof	—	Value: 40.00			

Y# 257 500 LIRE

6.8000 g., Bi-Metallic Aluminum-Bronze center in Stainless Steel ring, 25.8 mm. **Obverse:** Bust left within circle **Reverse:** People meeting, Golgotha in background **Designer:** Angelo Caevari

Date	Mintage	F	VF	XF	Unc
1994/XVI	—	—	—	2.00	4.00

Y# 259 500 LIRE

11.0000 g., 0.8350 Silver .2953 oz. ASW, 29.3 mm. **Series:** International Women's Year **Obverse:** Pope resting head on hand with crucifix to right of crowned shield **Reverse:** Half length figure holding infant to left of 1/2 designed globe **Edge Lettering:** INTERNATIONALIS ANNUS MELIEREI DICATUS **Designer:** Maria Carmella Perrini

Date	Mintage	F	VF	XF	Unc
1995	20,000	—	—	30.00	45.00
1995 Proof	7,000	Value: 65.00			

Y# 267 500 LIRE

6.8000 g., Bi-Metallic, 25.8 mm. **Subject:** Cain Slaying Abel **Reverse:** Cain slaying Abel within circle **Designer:** Enrico Manfrini

Date	Mintage	F	VF	XF	Unc
1995	460,000	—	—	2.00	4.00

Y# 269 500 LIRE

11.0000 g., 0.8350 Silver .2953 oz. ASW, 29.3 mm. **Subject:** 50th Anniversary - Ordination of Pope John Paul II **Obverse:** Bust right **Reverse:** Sheep, lamb on shepards shoulder and flying figure holding infant **Designer:** Enrico Manfrini

Date	Mintage	F	VF	XF	Unc
1996	33,000	—	—	25.00	43.00
1996 Proof	7,000	Value: 65.00			

Y# 277 500 LIRE

6.8000 g., Bi-Metallic Aluminum-Bronze center in Stainless Steel ring, 25.8 mm. **Obverse:** Head left within circle **Reverse:** Seated figures within circle, serpent at left of circle **Designer:** Orietta Rossi

Date	Mintage	F	VF	XF	Unc
1996	100,000	—	—	2.00	4.00

Y# 279 500 LIRE

11.0000 g., 0.8350 Silver .2953 oz. ASW, 29.3 mm. **Subject:** XII World Youth Conference **Obverse:** Bust right **Reverse:** Six children with Jesus **Edge Lettering:** IUVENTUTIS XII UNIVERSALIS DIES PARISIIS **Designer:** Enrico Manfrini

Date	Mintage	F	VF	XF	Unc
1997	18,000	—	—	30.00	40.00
1997 Proof	—	Value: 65.00			

Y# 285 500 LIRE

6.8000 g., Bi-Metallic Aluminum-Bronze center in Stainless Steel ring, 25.8 mm. **Obverse:** Head right within circle **Reverse:** One man freeing another from thorns **Designer:** Gabriella Titotto

Date	Mintage	F	VF	XF	Unc
1997/XIX	160,000	—	—	2.00	4.00

Y# 292 500 LIRE

11.0000 g., 0.8350 Silver .2953 oz. ASW, 29.3 mm. **Subject:** Shroud of Turin **Obverse:** Crowned bust right **Reverse:** Stylized head facing **Edge Lettering:** SACRA SINDON OSTENTATUR AVG. TAVR. MCMXCVIII **Designer:** Floriano Bodini

Date	Mintage	F	VF	XF	Unc
1998/XX	23,000	—	—	30.00	45.00
1998R Proof	—	Value: 65.00			

Y# 298 500 LIRE

6.8000 g., Bi-Metallic Aluminum-Bronze center in Stainless Steel ring, 25.8 mm. **Obverse:** Bust right holding crucifix within circle **Reverse:** Two figures within circle **Designer:** Paolo Borghi

Date	Mintage	F	VF	XF	Unc
1998	103,500	—	—	2.00	4.00

Y# 310 500 LIRE

6.7000 g., Bi-Metallic Aluminum-Bronze center in Stainless Steel ring, 25.9 mm. **Subject:** Time of Choices, Time of Hope **Obverse:** Bust right within circle **Reverse:** God's hand above young parent's with baby **Edge:** Reeded **Mint:** Rome **Designer:** Angelo Canevari

Date	Mintage	F	VF	XF	Unc
1999	161,000	—	—	2.00	4.00

Y# 322 500 LIRE

11.0000 g., 0.8350 Silver .2953 oz. ASW, 29.3 mm. **Subject:** 70th Anniversary - Vatican City Arms of Six Popes **Obverse:** Bust right **Reverse:** Dates in center of assorted crowned shields

Date	Mintage	F	VF	XF	Unc
1999	—	—	—	30.00	40.00
1999 Proof	—	Value: 65.00			

Y# 328 500 LIRE

6.7700 g., Bi-Metallic Aluminum-Bronze center in Stainless Steel ring, 25.7 mm. **Obverse:** Papal arms within circle **Reverse:** Bust right turning a page within circle **Edge:** Reeded and plain sections **Mint:** Rome **Designer:** Cecco Bonanotte

Date	Mintage	F	VF	XF	Unc
XXII(2000)	—	—	—	—	4.00

Y# 167 1000 LIRE

14.6000 g., 0.8350 Silver .3920 oz. ASW **Obverse:** Bust right **Reverse:** Crowned shield divides value **Designer:** Enrico Manfrini

Date	Mintage	F	VF	XF	Unc
1982/IV	210,000	—	—	15.00	25.00

Y# 169 1000 LIRE

14.6000 g., 0.8350 Silver .3920 oz. ASW **Subject:** Extraordinary Holy Year **Obverse:** Crowned half figure left **Reverse:** Crowned shield divides value **Designer:** Enrico Manfrini

Date	Mintage	F	VF	XF	Unc
1983-84	130,000	—	—	15.00	25.00

Y# 176 1000 LIRE

14.6000 g., 0.8350 Silver .3920 oz. ASW **Subject:** Prayer **Obverse:** Crowned bust left holding crucifix **Reverse:** Crowned shield **Designer:** Nicola Morelli

Date	Mintage	F	VF	XF	Unc
1983/V	110,000	—	—	15.00	25.00

Y# 183 1000 LIRE

14.6000 g., 0.8350 Silver .3920 oz. ASW **Subject:** Year of Peace **Obverse:** Bust left **Reverse:** Crowned shield **Designer:** Ennio Tesei

Date	Mintage	F	VF	XF	Unc
1984/VI	105,000	—	—	15.00	25.00

Y# 191 1000 LIRE

14.6000 g., 0.8350 Silver .3920 oz. ASW **Obverse:** Pope standing, vestments blowing in the wind **Reverse:** Crowned shield **Designer:** Guido Veroi

Date	Mintage	F	VF	XF	Unc
1985/VII	86,000	—	—	15.00	25.00

Y# 198 1000 LIRE

14.6000 g., 0.8350 Silver .3920 oz. ASW **Obverse:** Crowned shield **Reverse:** Pope seated at microphone **Designer:** Guido Veroi

Date	Mintage	F	VF	XF	Unc
1986/VIII	80,000	—	—	15.00	25.00

Y# 205 1000 LIRE

14.6000 g., 0.8350 Silver .3920 oz. ASW **Obverse:** Crowned shield **Reverse:** Pope in prayer and seated figure with infant **Designer:** Angelo Canevari

Date	Mintage	F	VF	XF	Unc
1987/IX	—	—	—	15.00	25.00

Y# 212 1000 LIRE

14.6000 g., 0.8350 Silver .3920 oz. ASW **Reverse:** Pope seated at desk **Designer:** Guido Veroi

Date	Mintage	F	VF	XF	Unc
1988/X	—	—	—	15.00	25.00

Y# 219 1000 LIRE

14.6000 g., 0.8350 Silver .3920 oz. ASW **Obverse:** Crowned shield **Reverse:** Pope with Prelates and worshippers **Designer:** Enrico Manfrini

Date	Mintage	F	VF	XF	Unc
1989/XI	—	—	—	15.00	25.00

Y# 226 1000 LIRE

14.6000 g., 0.8350 Silver .3920 oz. ASW **Obverse:** Crowned shield **Reverse:** Pope walking over destroyed barbed-wire fence **Designer:** Angelo Canevari

Date	Mintage	F	VF	XF	Unc
1990/XII	—	—	—	15.00	25.00

Y# 234 1000 LIRE

14.6000 g., 0.8350 Silver .3920 oz. ASW **Obverse:** Crowned shield **Reverse:** Pope handing missionary cross to two young people **Designer:** Nicola Morelli

Date	Mintage	F	VF	XF	Unc
1991/XIII	—	—	—	15.00	25.00

Y# 242 1000 LIRE

11.0000 g., 0.8350 Silver .2953 oz. ASW **Obverse:** Bust right **Reverse:** Pope's coat-of-arms **Designer:** Sergio Giandomenico

Date	Mintage	F	VF	XF	Unc
1992/XIV	—	—	—	15.00	25.00

Y# 250 1000 LIRE

14.6000 g., 0.8350 Silver .3919 oz. ASW **Obverse:** Head facing **Reverse:** Papal coat-of-arms divides inscription **Designer:** Guido Veroi

Date	Mintage	F	VF	XF	Unc
1993/XV	—	—	—	15.00	25.00

Y# 258 1000 LIRE

14.6000 g., 0.8350 Silver .3919 oz. ASW **Subject:** The Good Samaritan **Obverse:** Kneeling figure reaching for standing Pope **Reverse:** Horse behind figures **Designer:** Angelo Canevarai

Date	Mintage	F	VF	XF	Unc
1994/XVI	—	—	—	15.00	25.00

Y# 268 1000 LIRE

14.6000 g., 0.8350 Silver .3919 oz. ASW **Subject:** Radiant Virgin Mary **Obverse:** Head left **Reverse:** Radiant figure within stylized dragon **Designer:** Enrico Manfrini

Date	Mintage	F	VF	XF	Unc
1995/XVII	—	—	—	15.00	25.00

Y# 278 1000 LIRE

14.6000 g., 0.8350 Silver .3919 oz. ASW **Obverse:** John Paul II releasing doves from balcony **Reverse:** Jesus welcomes the little children **Designer:** Orietto Rossi

Date	Mintage	F	VF	XF	Unc
1996	—	—	—	15.00	25.00

Y# 287 1000 LIRE

14.0000 g., 0.8350 Silver .3919 oz. ASW **Obverse:** John Paul II teaching people **Reverse:** Saint cradling ill man **Edge Lettering:** TOTVS TVVS MCMXCVII

Date	Mintage	F	VF	XF	Unc
1997/XIX	—	—	—	15.00	25.00

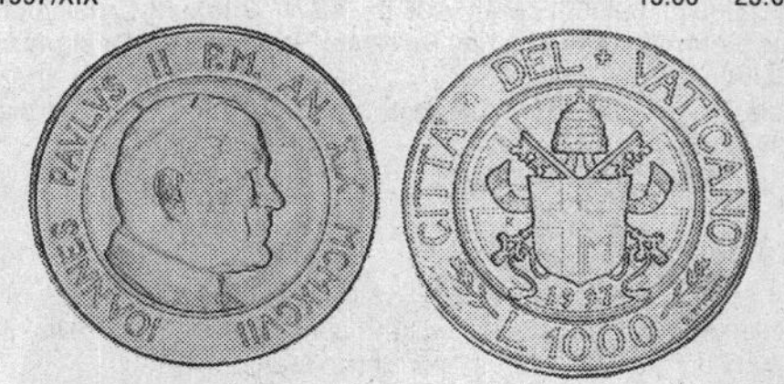

Y# 286 1000 LIRE

Bi-Metallic Stainless Steel center in Aluminum-Bronze ring, 26.9 mm. **Obverse:** Head right within circle **Reverse:** Crowned shield within circle **Designer:** Gabriella Titotto

Date	Mintage	F	VF	XF	Unc
1997/XIX	270,000	—	—	3.50	7.00

Y# 299 1000 LIRE

Bi-Metallic Stainless Steel center in Aluminum-Bronze ring, 26.9 mm. **Obverse:** Head left within circle **Reverse:** Papal coat-of-arms within circle **Designer:** Paolo Borghi

Date	Mintage	F	VF	XF	Unc
1998/XX	306,500	—	—	3.50	8.50

Y# 300 1000 LIRE

14.0000 g., 0.8350 Silver .3919 oz. ASW **Obverse:** Pope with crucifix croizer within sun rays **Reverse:** Jesus on globe **Edge Lettering:** TOTVS TVVS MCMXCVIII **Designer:** Paolo Borghi

Date	Mintage	F	VF	XF	Unc
1998/XX	—	—	—	15.00	25.00

Y# 311 1000 LIRE

8.8500 g., Bi-Metallic Stainless Steel center in Aluminum-Bronze ring, 26.9 mm. **Obverse:** Pope's arms within circle **Reverse:** Couple at base of Christ on cross within circle **Edge:** Reeded and plain sections **Mint:** Rome **Designer:** Angelo Canevari

Date	Mintage	F	VF	XF	Unc
1999/XXI	126,100	—	—	4.00	8.50

Y# 312 1000 LIRE

14.0000 g., 0.8350 Silver :3919 oz. ASW **Subject:** The Right to Religous Freedom **Obverse:** Bust right **Reverse:** Family at altar **Edge:** TOTVS TVVS ++ ++ ++ ++ MCMXCIX ++ ++ ++ ++ **Mint:** Rome **Designer:** Angelo Canevari

Date	Mintage	F	VF	XF	Unc
1999/XXI	—	—	—	20.00	40.00

Y# 329 1000 LIRE

8.8500 g., Bi-Metallic Stainless Steel center in Aluminum-Bronze ring, 26.9 mm. **Obverse:** Papal arms within circle **Reverse:** Pope and Eastern Orthodox Patriarch within circle **Edge:** Reeded and plain sections **Mint:** Rome **Designer:** Cecco Bonanotte

Date	Mintage	F	VF	XF	Unc
2000/XXII	—	—	—	4.00	8.50

Y# 330 1000 LIRE

14.6000 g., 0.8350 Silver .3919 oz. ASW, 31.4 mm. **Obverse:** Papal arms within circle **Reverse:** Praying Pope divides assorted figures within circle **Edge Lettering:** TOTVS TVVS +++MM+++ **Mint:** Rome **Designer:** Cecco Bonanotte

Date	Mintage	F	VF	XF	Unc
2000/XXII	—	—	—	15.00	25.00

Y# 313 2000 LIRE

16.0000 g., 0.8350 Silver .4295 oz. ASW **Subject:** Holy Year **Obverse:** Pope standing by open door **Reverse:** Three seated figures **Edge:** Reeded **Mint:** Rome **Designer:** Paolo Borghi

Date	Mintage	F	VF	XF	Unc
2000	60,000	—	—	20.00	40.00
2000 Proof	10,000	Value: 200			

Y# 353 2000 LIRE

16.0000 g., 0.8350 Silver 0.4295 oz. ASW, 31.4 mm. **Subject:** 2000th Birthday of Jesus **Obverse:** Bust of Pope in prayer **Reverse:** Baby divides value **Edge:** Reeded **Mint:** Rome **Designer:** Daniela Longo

Date	Mintage	F	VF	XF	Unc
2000	—	—	—	20.00	30.00
2000R Proof	22,000	Value: 75.00			

Y# 260 10000 LIRE

22.0000 g., 0.8350 Silver .5906 oz. ASW **Subject:** The Annunciation **Obverse:** Bust right **Reverse:** Angel and seated figure below radiant dove **Designer:** Enrico Manfrini

Date	Mintage	F	VF	XF	Unc
1995 Proof	30,000	Value: 80.00			

Note: Proof sets only

Y# 261 10000 LIRE

22.0000 g., 0.8350 Silver .5906 oz. ASW **Subject:** The Nativity **Obverse:** Bust right **Reverse:** Donkey heads and baby at center, standing figures at sides **Designer:** Enrico Manfrini

Date	Mintage	F	VF	XF	Unc
1995 Proof	30,000	Value: 80.00			

Note: Proof sets only

Y# 270 10000 LIRE

22.0000 g., 0.8350 Silver .5906 oz. ASW **Subject:** Holy Year 2000 - Baptism in River Jordan **Obverse:** Bust right **Reverse:** Baptism scene **Designer:** Enrico Manfrini

Date	Mintage	F	VF	XF	Unc
1996 Proof	30,000	Value: 80.00			

Note: Proof sets only

Y# 271 10000 LIRE

22.0000 g., 0.8350 Silver .5906 oz. ASW **Subject:** Holy Year 2000 - Jesus Teaching **Obverse:** Bust right **Reverse:** Seated figure above group of people **Designer:** Enrico Manfrini

Date	Mintage	F	VF	XF	Unc
1996 Proof	30,000	Value: 80.00			

Note: Proof sets only

Y# 318 10000 LIRE

22.0000 g., 0.8350 Silver .5906 oz. ASW **Subject:** Cure of the Paralytic **Obverse:** Bust left **Reverse:** Two kneeling figures on roof above figure helping ill person **Designer:** Guido Veroi

Date	Mintage	F	VF	XF	Unc
1997 Proof	—	Value: 80.00			

Note: Proof sets only

Y# 319 10000 LIRE

22.0000 g., 0.8350 Silver .5906 oz. ASW **Subject:** Calming of the Storm **Obverse:** Bust left **Reverse:** Figures in boat **Designer:** Guido Veroi

Date	Mintage	F	VF	XF	Unc
1997 Proof	—	Value: 80.00			

Note: Proof sets only

Y# 290 10000 LIRE

22.0000 g., 0.8350 Silver .5906 oz. ASW **Subject:** Last Supper **Obverse:** Bust left **Reverse:** Seated figures at long table **Designer:** Guido Veroi

Date	Mintage	F	VF	XF	Unc
1998 Proof	30,000	Value: 80.00			

Y# 291 10000 LIRE

22.0000 g., 0.8350 Silver .5906 oz. ASW **Subject:** Crucifixion of Jesus **Obverse:** Bust left **Reverse:** Jesus on cross flanked by standing figures **Designer:** Guido Veroi

Date	Mintage	F	VF	XF	Unc
1998 Proof	30,000	Value: 80.00			

Y# 303 10000 LIRE

22.0000 g., 0.8350 Silver .5906 oz. ASW, 34 mm. **Obverse:** Bust right **Reverse:** Group with flames above head **Mint:** Rome **Designer:** Enrico Manfrini

Date	Mintage	F	VF	XF	Unc
1999 Proof	30,000	Value: 80.00			

Y# 304 10000 LIRE

22.0000 g., 0.8350 Silver .5906 oz. ASW **Reverse:** Jesus rising from his tomb **Mint:** Rome **Designer:** Enrico Manfrini

Date	Mintage	F	VF	XF	Unc
1999 Proof	30,000	Value: 80.00			

Y# 314 10000 LIRE

22.0000 g., 0.8350 Silver .5906 oz. ASW **Obverse:** Bust right **Reverse:** Seated angel holding church above "GERUSALEMME" **Designer:** Guido Veroi

Date	Mintage	F	VF	XF	Unc
2000 Proof	30,000	Value: 80.00			

Y# 315 10000 LIRE

22.0000 g., 0.8350 Silver .5906 oz. ASW **Obverse:** Bust right **Reverse:** Seated angel holding church above "ROMA" **Mint:** Rome **Designer:** Guido Veroi

Date	Mintage	F	VF	XF	Unc
2000 Proof	30,000	Value: 80.00			

Y# 356 50000 LIRE

7.5000 g., 0.9170 Gold 0.2211 oz. AGW **Obverse:** Pope and Holy Year Door **Reverse:** John the Baptist and St. John the Evangelist facing each other **Designer:** Giovani Contri

Date	Mintage	F	VF	XF	Unc
1996R Proof	6,000	Value: 300			

Y# 288 50000 LIRE

7.5000 g., 0.9170 Gold .2211 oz. AGW **Obverse:** Pope and Holy Year Door **Reverse:** St. Paul facing **Designer:** Giovani Contri

Date	Mintage	F	VF	XF	Unc
1997/XIX Proof	6,000	Value: 300			

Y# 301 50000 LIRE

7.5000 g., 0.9170 Gold .2211 oz. AGW, 23 mm. **Obverse:** Pope and Holy Year Door **Reverse:** Madonna and child **Edge:** Reeded **Mint:** Rome **Designer:** Giovani Contri

Date	Mintage	F	VF	XF	Unc
1998 Proof	6,000	Value: 300			

Y# 320 50000 LIRE

7.5000 g., 0.9170 Gold .2211 oz. AGW **Obverse:** Pope and Holy Year Door **Reverse:** Statue of St. Peter **Designer:** Giovani Contri

Date	Mintage	F	VF	XF	Unc
1999 Proof	—	Value: 300			

Y# 316 50000 LIRE

7.5000 g., 0.9170 Gold .2211 oz. AGW **Subject:** Prodigal Son **Obverse:** Bust right **Reverse:** Jesus on cross, standing figures at sides **Mint:** Rome **Designer:** Enrico Manfrini

Date	Mintage	F	VF	XF	Unc
2000/XXII Proof	6,000	Value: 300			

Y# 357 100000 LIRE

15.0000 g., 0.9170 Gold 0.4422 oz. AGW **Obverse:** Pope and Holy Year Door **Reverse:** Basilica of St. John Lateran **Designer:** Giovani Contri

Date	Mintage	F	VF	XF	Unc
1996R Proof	6,000	Value: 550			

Y# 289 100000 LIRE

15.0000 g., 0.9170 Gold .4422 oz. AGW **Obverse:** Pope and Holy Year Door **Reverse:** Basilica of St. Paul outside the walls **Designer:** Giovani Contri

Date	Mintage	F	VF	XF	Unc
1997/XIX Proof	6,000	Value: 550			

Y# 302 100000 LIRE

15.0000 g., 0.9170 Gold .4422 oz. AGW, 28 mm. **Obverse:** Pope and Holy Year Door **Reverse:** Basilica of St. Mary Major **Edge:** Reeded **Mint:** Rome **Designer:** Giovani Contri

Date	Mintage	F	VF	XF	Unc
1998 Proof	6,000	Value: 550			

Y# 321 100000 LIRE

15.0000 g., 0.9170 Gold .4422 oz. AGW **Obverse:** Pope and Holy Year Door **Reverse:** St. Peter's Basilica **Designer:** Giovani Contri

Date	Mintage	F	VF	XF	Unc
1999 Proof	—	Value: 550			

Y# 317 100000 LIRE

15.0000 g., 0.9170 Gold .4422 oz. AGW **Obverse:** Bust right **Reverse:** Crucifixion scene **Mint:** Rome **Designer:** Enrico Manfrini

Date	Mintage	F	VF	XF	Unc
2000/XXII Proof	6,000	Value: 550			

PROVAS

KM#	Date	Mintage	Identification	Mkt Val
Pr1	1951	103	Lira. Silver. . Y#49.	50.00
Pr2	1951	103	2 Lire. Silver. . Y#50.	65.00
Pr3	1951	103	5 Lire. Silver. . Y#51.	85.00
Pr4	1951	103	10 Lire. Silver. . Y#52.	100
Pr5	1952	103	Lira. Silver. . Y#49.	50.00
Pr6	1952	103	2 Lire. Silver. . Y#50.	65.00
Pr7	1952	103	5 Lire. Silver. . Y#51.	85.00
Pr8	1952	103	10 Lire. Silver. . Y#52.	100
Pr9	1953	103	Lira. Silver. . Y#49.	50.00
Pr10	1953	103	2 Lire. Silver. . Y#50.	65.00
Pr11	1953	103	5 Lire. Silver. . Y#51.	85.00
Pr12	1953	103	10 Lire. Silver. . Y#52.	100
Pr13	1955	103	Lira. Silver. . Y#49.	40.00
Pr14	1955	103	2 Lire. Silver. . Y#50.	55.00
Pr15	1955	103	5 Lire. Silver. . Y#51.	65.00
Pr16	1955	103	10 Lire. Silver. . Y#52.	75.00
Pr17	1955	103	50 Lire. Silver. . Y#54.	90.00
Pr18	1955	103	100 Lire. Silver. . Y#55.	100
Pr19	1956	103	Lira. Silver. . Y#49.	40.00
Pr20	1956	103	2 Lire. Silver. . Y#50.	55.00
Pr21	1956	103	5 Lire. Silver. . Y#51.	65.00
Pr22	1956	103	10 Lire. Silver. . Y#52.	75.00
Pr23	1956	103	50 Lire. Silver. . Y#54.	90.00
Pr24	1956	103	100 Lire. Silver. . Y#55.	100
Pr25	1957	103	Lira. Silver. . Y#49.	40.00
Pr26	1957	103	2 Lire. Silver. . Y#50.	50.00
Pr27	1957	103	5 Lire. Silver. . Y#51.	60.00
Pr28	1957	103	10 Lire. Silver. . Y#52.	70.00
Pr29	1957	103	20 Lire. Silver. . Y-A52.	80.00
Pr30	1957	103	50 Lire. Silver. . Y#54.	90.00
Pr31	1957	103	100 Lire. Silver. . Y#55.	100
Pr32	1958	103	Lira. Silver. . Y#49.	40.00
Pr33	1958	103	2 Lire. Silver. . Y#50.	50.00
Pr34	1958	103	5 Lire. Silver. . Y#51.	60.00
Pr35	1958	103	10 Lire. Silver. . Y#52.	70.00
Pr36	1958	103	20 Lire. Silver. . Y-A52.	80.00
Pr37	1958	103	50 Lire. Silver. . Y#54.	90.00
Pr38	1958	103	100 Lire. Silver. . Y#55.	100
Pr39	1958	103	500 Lire. Silver. . Y#56.	125
Pr40	1959	103	Lira. Silver. . Y#58.	40.00
Pr41	1959	103	2 Lire. Silver. . Y#59.	50.00
Pr42	1959	103	5 Lire. Silver. . Y#60.	60.00
Pr43	1959	103	10 Lire. Silver. . Y#61.	70.00
Pr44	1959	103	20 Lire. Silver. . Y#62.	80.00
Pr45	1959	103	50 Lire. Silver. . Y#63.	90.00
Pr46	1959	103	100 Lire. Silver. . Y#64.	100
Pr47	1959	103	500 Lire. Silver. . Y#65.	125
Pr48	1960	103	Lira. Silver. . Y#58.	40.00
Pr49	1960	103	2 Lire. Silver. . Y#59.	50.00
Pr50	1960	103	5 Lire. Silver. . Y#60.	60.00
Pr51	1960	103	10 Lire. Silver. . Y#61.	70.00
Pr52	1960	103	20 Lire. Silver. . Y#62.	80.00
Pr53	1960	103	50 Lire. Silver. . Y#63.1.	90.00
Pr54	1960	103	100 Lire. Silver. . Y#64.1.	100
Pr55	1960	103	500 Lire. Silver. . Y#65.1.	125
Pr56	1961	103	Lira. Silver. . Y#58.	40.00
Pr57	1961	103	2 Lire. Silver. . Y#59.	50.00
Pr58	1961	103	5 Lire. Silver. . Y#60.	60.00
Pr59	1961	103	10 Lire. Silver. . Y#61.	70.00
Pr60	1961	103	20 Lire. Silver. . Y#62.	80.00
Pr61	1961	103	50 Lire. Silver. . Y#63.1.	90.00
Pr62	1961	103	100 Lire. Silver. . Y#64.1.	100
Pr63	1961	103	500 Lire. Silver. . Y#65.1.	125
Pr64	1962	103	Lira. Silver. . Y#58.	40.00
Pr65	1962	103	2 Lire. Silver. . Y#59.	50.00
Pr66	1962	103	5 Lire. Silver. . Y#60.	60.00
Pr67	1962	103	10 Lire. Silver. . Y#61.	70.00
Pr68	1962	103	20 Lire. Silver. . Y#62.	80.00
Pr69	1962	103	50 Lire. Silver. . Y#63.1.	90.00
Pr70	1962	103	100 Lire. Silver. . Y#64.1.	100
Pr71	1962	103	500 Lire. Silver. . Y#65.1.	125
Pr72	1962	103	Lira. Silver. . Y#67.	40.00
Pr73	1962	103	2 Lire. Silver. . Y#68.	50.00
Pr74	1962	103	5 Lire. Silver. . Y#69.	60.00
Pr75	1962	103	10 Lire. Silver. . Y#70.	70.00
Pr76	1962	103	20 Lire. Silver. . Y#71.	80.00
Pr77	1962	103	50 Lire. Silver. . Y#72.	90.00
Pr78	1962	103	100 Lire. Silver. . Y#73.	100
Pr79	1962	103	500 Lire. Silver. . Y#74.	125
Pr80	1963	103	Lira. Silver. . Y#76.	40.00
Pr81	1963	103	2 Lire. Silver. . Y#77.	50.00
Pr82	1963	103	5 Lire. Silver. . Y#78.	60.00
Pr83	1963	103	10 Lire. Silver. . Y#79.	70.00
Pr84	1963	103	20 Lire. Silver. . Y#80.	80.00
Pr85	1963	103	50 Lire. Silver. . Y#81.	90.00
Pr86	1963	103	100 Lire. Silver. . Y#82.	100
Pr87	1963	103	500 Lire. Silver. . Y#83.	125
Pr88	1964	103	Lira. Silver. . Y#76.	40.00
Pr89	1964	103	2 Lire. Silver. . Y#77.	50.00
Pr90	1964	103	5 Lire. Silver. . Y#78.	60.00
Pr91	1964	103	10 Lire. Silver. . Y#79.	70.00
Pr92	1964	103	20 Lire. Silver. . Y#80.	80.00
Pr93	1964	103	50 Lire. Silver. . Y#81.	90.00
Pr94	1964	103	100 Lire. Silver. . Y#82.	100
Pr95	1964	103	500 Lire. Silver. . Y#83.	125
Pr96	1965	103	Lira. Silver. . Y#76.	40.00
Pr97	1965	103	2 Lire. Silver. . Y#77.	50.00
Pr98	1965	103	5 Lire. Silver. . Y#78.	60.00
Pr99	1965	103	10 Lire. Silver. . Y#79.	70.00
Pr100	1965	103	20 Lire. Silver. . Y#80.	80.00
Pr101	1965	103	50 Lire. Silver. . Y#81.	90.00
Pr102	1965	103	100 Lire. Silver. . Y#82.	100
Pr103	1965	103	500 Lire. Silver. . Y#83.	125
Pr104	1966	103	Lira. Silver. . Y#84.	40.00
Pr105	1966	103	2 Lire. Silver. . Y#85.	50.00
Pr106	1966	103	5 Lire. Silver. . Y#86.	60.00
Pr107	1966	103	10 Lire. Silver. . Y#87.	70.00
Pr108	1966	103	20 Lire. Silver. . Y#88.	80.00
Pr109	1966	103	50 Lire. Silver. . Y#89.	90.00
Pr110	1966	103	100 Lire. Silver. . Y#90.	100
Pr111	1966	103	500 Lire. Silver. . Y#91.	125
Pr112	(1967)	103	Lira. Silver. . Y#92.	40.00
Pr113	(1967)	103	2 Lire. Silver. . Y#93.	50.00
Pr114	(1967)	103	5 Lire. Silver. . Y#94.	60.00
Pr115	(1967)	103	10 Lire. Silver. . Y#95.	70.00
Pr116	(1967)	103	20 Lire. Silver. . Y#96.	80.00
Pr117	1967	103	50 Lire. Silver. . Y#97.	90.00
Pr118	1967	103	100 Lire. Silver. . Y#98.	100
Pr119	1967	103	500 Lire. Silver. . Y#99.	125
Pr120	(1968)	103	Lira. Silver. . Y#100.	40.00
Pr121	(1968)	103	2 Lire. Silver. . Y#101.	50.00
Pr122	(1968)	103	5 Lire. Silver. . Y#102.	60.00
Pr123	(1968)	103	10 Lire. Silver. . Y#103.	70.00
Pr124	(1968)	103	20 Lire. Silver. . Y#104.	80.00
Pr125	(1968)	103	50 Lire. Silver. . Y#105.	90.00
Pr126	(1968)	103	100 Lire. Silver. . Y#106.	100
Pr127	(1968)	103	500 Lire. Silver. . Y#107.	125
Pr128	1969	103	Lira. Silver. . Y#108.	40.00
Pr129	1969	103	2 Lire. Silver. . Y#109.	50.00
Pr130	1969	103	5 Lire. Silver. . Y#110.	60.00
Pr131	1969	103	10 Lire. Silver. . Y#111.	70.00
Pr132	1969	103	20 Lire. Silver. . Y#112.	80.00
Pr133	1969	103	50 Lire. Silver. . Y#113.	90.00
Pr134	1969	103	100 Lire. Silver. . Y#114.	100
Pr135	1969	103	500 Lire. Silver. . Y#115.	125
Pr136	1970	103	Lira. Silver. . Y#116.	40.00
Pr137	1970	103	2 Lire. Silver. . Y#117.	50.00
Pr138	1970	103	5 Lire. Silver. . Y#118.	60.00
Pr139	1970	103	10 Lire. Silver. . Y#119.	70.00
Pr140	1970	103	20 Lire. Silver. . Y#120.	80.00
Pr141	1970	103	50 Lire. Silver. . Y#121.	90.00
Pr142	1970	103	100 Lire. Silver. . Y#122.	100
Pr143	1970	103	500 Lire. Silver. . Y#123.	125
Pr144	1971	103	Lira. Silver. . Y#116.	40.00
Pr145	1971	103	2 Lire. Silver. . Y#117.	50.00
Pr146	1971	103	5 Lire. Silver. . Y#118.	60.00
Pr147	1971	103	10 Lire. Silver. . Y#119.	70.00
Pr148	1971	103	20 Lire. Silver. . Y#120.	80.00
Pr149	1971	103	50 Lire. Silver. . Y#121.	90.00
Pr150	1971	103	100 Lire. Silver. . Y#122.	100
Pr151	1971	103	500 Lire. Silver. . Y#123.	120
Pr152	1972	103	Lira. Silver. . Y#116.	40.00
Pr153	1972	103	2 Lire. Silver. . Y#117.	50.00
Pr154	1972	103	5 Lire. Silver. . Y#118.	60.00
Pr155	1972	103	10 Lire. Silver. . Y#119.	70.00
Pr156	1972	103	20 Lire. Silver. . Y#120.	80.00
Pr157	1972	103	50 Lire. Silver. . Y#121.	90.00
Pr158	1972	103	100 Lire. Silver. . Y#122.	100
Pr159	1972	103	500 Lire. Silver. . Y#123.	125
Pr160	1973	103	Lira. Silver. . Y#116.	40.00
Pr161	1973	103	2 Lire. Silver. . Y#117.	50.00
Pr162	1973	103	5 Lire. Silver. . Y#118.	60.00
Pr163	1973	103	10 Lire. Silver. . Y#119.	70.00
Pr164	1973	103	20 Lire. Silver. . Y#120.	80.00
Pr165	1973	103	50 Lire. Silver. . Y#121.	90.00
Pr166	1973	103	100 Lire. Silver. . Y#122.	100
Pr167	1973	103	500 Lire. Silver. . Y#123.	125
Pr168	1974	103	Lira. Silver. . Y#116.	40.00
Pr169	1974	103	2 Lire. Silver. . Y#117.	50.00
Pr170	1974	103	5 Lire. Silver. . Y#118.	60.00

KM#	Date	Mintage	Identification	Mkt Val
Pr171	1974	103	10 Lire. Silver. . Y#119.	70.00
Pr172	1974	103	20 Lire. Silver. . Y#120.	80.00
Pr173	1974	103	50 Lire. Silver. . Y#121.	90.00
Pr174	1974	103	100 Lire. Silver. . Y#122.	100
Pr175	1974	103	500 Lire. Silver. . Y#123.	125
Pr176	1975	103	Lira. Silver. . Y#116.	40.00
Pr177	1975	103	2 Lire. Silver. . Y#117.	50.00
Pr178	1975	103	5 Lire. Silver. . Y#118.	60.00
Pr179	1975	103	10 Lire. Silver. . Y#119.	70.00
Pr180	1975	103	20 Lire. Silver. . Y#120.	80.00
Pr181	1975	103	50 Lire. Silver. . Y#121.	90.00
Pr182	1975	103	100 Lire. Silver. . Y#122.	100
Pr183	1975	103	500 Lire. Silver. . Y#123.	125
Pr184	1975	103	Lira. Silver. . Y#124.	40.00
Pr185	1975	103	2 Lire. Silver. . Y#125.	50.00
Pr186	1975	103	5 Lire. Silver. . Y#126.	60.00
Pr187	1975	103	10 Lire. Silver. . Y#127.	70.00
Pr188	1975	103	20 Lire. Silver. . Y#128.	80.00
Pr189	1975	103	50 Lire. Silver. . Y#129.	90.00
Pr190	1975	103	100 Lire. Silver. . Y#130.	100
Pr191	1975	103	500 Lire. Silver. . Y#131.	120

MINT SETS

KM#	Date	Mintage	Identification	Issue Price	Mkt Val
MS107	2001 (8)	26,000	Y#331-338	21.25	200
MS1	1929 (9)	10,000	Y#1-9	—	470
MS2	1929 (8)	10,000	Y#1-8	—	170
MS3	1930 (9)	2,621	Y#1-9	—	825
MS4	1930 (8)	50,000	Y#1-8	—	85.00
MS5	1931 (9)	3,343	Y#1-9	—	575
MS6	1931 (8)	50,000	Y#1-8	—	85.00
MS7	1932 (9)	5,073	Y#1-9	—	475
MS8	1932 (8)	50,000	Y#1-8	—	85.00
MS10	1933-34 (8)	50,000	Y#11-18	—	125
MS9	1933-34 (9)	23,235	Y#11-19	—	500
MS11	1934 (9)	2,533	Y#1-9	—	575
MS12	1934 (8)	30,000	Y#1-8	—	85.00
MS13	1935 (9)	2,105	Y#1-9	—	685
MS14	1935 (8)	9,000	Y#1-8	—	250
MS15	1936 (9)	8,239	Y#1-8, 10	—	350
MS16	1936 (8)	40,000	Y#1-8	—	85.00
MS17	1937 (9)	2,000	Y#1-8, 10	—	3,075
MS18	1937 (8)	20,000	Y#1-8	—	85.00
MS19	1938 (3)	—	Y#1-2, 10 Rare	—	—
MS20	1939 (9)	2,700	Y#22-30.1	—	435
MS21	1939 (8)	10,000	Y#22-29	—	110
MS22	1939 (2)	30,000	Y#20, 21	—	50.00
MS23	1940 (9)	2,000	Y#22, 23, 24a-27a, 28-30.1	—	470
MS24	1940 (8)	10,000	Y#22, 23, 24a-27a, 28-29	—	100
MS25	1941 (9)	2,000	Y#22, 23, 24a-27a, 28-30.2	—	580
MS26	1941 (8)	4,000	Y#22, 23, 24a-27a, 28-29	—	200
MS27	1942 (9)	2,000	Y#31-39	—	630
MS28	1942 (8)	4,000	Y#31-38	—	230
MSA29	1942 (4)	—	Y#33-36	—	—
MS29	1943 (9)	1,000	Y#31-39	—	820
MS30	1943 (8)	1,000	Y#31-38	—	320
MS31	1944 (9)	1,000	Y#31-39	—	820
MS32	1944 (8)	1,000	Y#31-38	—	320
MS33	1945 (9)	1,000	Y#31-39	—	820
MS34	1945 (8)	1,000	Y#31-38	—	320
MS35	1946 (9)	1,000	Y#31-39	—	820
MS36	1946 (8)	1,000	Y#31-38	—	320
MS37	1947 (5)	1,000	Y#39-43	—	530
MS38	1947 (4)	50,000	Y#40-43	—	28.00
MS39	1947 (2)	—	Y#42-43	—	16.00
MS40	1948 (5)	5,000	Y#39-43	—	280
MS41	1948 (4)	10,000	Y#40-43	—	28.00
MS42	1949 (5)	1,000	Y#39-43	—	535
MS43	1949 (4)	10,000	Y#40-43	—	35.00
MS44	1950 (5)	20,000	Y#44-48	—	265
MS45	1950 (4)	50,000	Y#44-47	—	23.00
MS46	1951 (5)	1,000	Y#49.1-53.1	—	500
MS47	1951 (4)	400,000	Y#49.1, 50, 51.1-52.1	—	5.00
MS54	1956 (7)	1,000	Y#49.2-55	—	500
MS48	1952 (5)	1,000	Y#49.1-52.1, 53.1	—	500
MS49	1952 (4)	400,000	Y#49.1-52.1	—	5.00
MS50	1953 (5)	1,000	Y#49.1-52.1, 53.1	—	500
MS51	1953 (4)	400,000	Y#49.1-52.1	—	5.00
MS52	1955 (7)	1,000	Y#49.1-55	—	550
MS53	1955 (6)	10,000	Y#49.1-52.1, 54.1, 55	—	18.00
MS55	1956 (6)	10,000	Y#49.2-52.2, 54.2, 55	—	18.00
MS56	1957 (8)	2,000	Y#49.1-A52, A53, 54.2, 55	—	310
MS57	1957 (6)	20,000	Y#49.1-52.2, 54.2, 55	—	12.00
MS58	1958 (8)	3,000	Y#49.1-52.2, 54.2-57	—	320
MS59	1958 (7)	20,000	Y#49.1-52.2, 54.2-56	—	35.00
MS60	1959 (9)	3,000	Y#58.1-64.1, 65-66	—	1,300
MS61	1959 (8)	25,000	Y#58.1-64.1, 65	—	85.00
MS62	1960 (8)	25,000	Y#58.1-59.1, 60.2-64.2, 65.1	—	85.00
MS63	1961 (8)	25,000	Y#58.2-62.2, 63.2-64.2, 65.1	—	60.00
MS64	1962 (8)	25,000	Y#58.2-64.2, 65.1	—	55.00
MS65	1962 (8)	50,000	Y#67-74	—	40.00
MS66	1963 (8)	60,000	Y#76.1-83.1	—	45.00
MS68	1964 (8)	60,000	Y#76.2-79.2, 80.1-81.1, 82.2-83.2	—	40.00
MS69	1965 (8)	60,000	Y#76.2-83.2	—	35.00
MS70	1966 (8)	90,000	Y#84-91	—	20.00
MS71	1967 (8)	100,000	Y#92-99	3.25	20.00
MS72	1968 (8)	100,000	Y#100-107	4.20	25.00
MS73	1969 (8)	100,000	Y#108-115	4.20	28.00
MS74	1970 (8)	100,000	Y#116-123	5.00	25.00
MS75	1971 (8)	110,000	Y#116-123	—	20.00
MS76	1972 (8)	110,000	Y#116-123	6.00	20.00
MS77	1973 (8)	120,000	Y#116-123	6.75	20.00
MS78	1974 (8)	120,000	Y#116-123	7.25	20.00
MS79	1975 (8)	132,000	Y#116-123	9.00	20.00
MS80	1975 (8)	170,000	Y#124-131	—	28.00
MSA80	1975 (5)	—	Y#126-130	—	7.50
MS81	1976 (8)	180,000	Y#116-123	—	20.00
MS82	1977 (7)	180,000	Y#116-120, 122, 132	—	20.00
MS83	1978 (7)	180,000	Y#133-139	—	20.00
MS84	1979 (6)	156,000	Y#143-148	—	30.00
MS85	1980 (6)	—	Y#143-148	18.00	25.00
MS86	1981 (6)	—	Y#155-160	—	25.00
MS87	1982 (7)	120,000	Y#161-167	—	25.00
MS88	1983 (7)	120,000	Y#170-176	—	35.00
MS93	1983/84 (2)	130,000	Y#168-169	—	40.00
MS89	1984 (7)	—	Y#177-183	—	35.00
MS90	1985 (7)	—	Y#185-191	—	45.00
MS91	1986 (7)	—	Y#192-198	23.50	45.00
MS92	1987 (7)	—	Y#199-205	27.00	45.00
MSA93	1987 (5)	—	Y#200-204	—	10.00
MS94	1988 (7)	—	Y#206-212	—	50.00
MS95	1989 (7)	—	Y#213-219	30.00	45.00
MS96	1990 (7)	—	Y#220-226	33.00	50.00
MS97	1991 (7)	—	Y#228-234	25.00	45.00
MS98	1992 (7)	—	Y#236-242	25.00	45.00
MS99	1993 (7)	—	Y#244-250	—	45.00
MS100	1994 (7)	—	Y#252-258	—	45.00
MS101	1995 (7)	—	Y#262-268	32.50	45.00
MS102	1996 (7)	—	Y#272-278	33.00	45.00
MS103	1997 (8)	—	Y#280-287	—	45.00
MS104	1998 (8)	—	Y#293-300	—	45.00
MS105	1999 (8)	—	Y#205-312	—	45.00
MS106	2000 (8)	—	Y#323-330	37.50	110

PROOF SETS

KM#	Date	Mintage	Identification	Issue Price	Mkt Val
PS1	1995 (2)	30,000	Y#260-261	75.00	100
PS2	1996 (2)	30,000	Y#270-271	75.00	140
PS4	1997 (2)	6,000	Y#288-289	547	625
PSA5	2000 (10)	30,000	Y#288, 289, 301, 302, 316, 317, 320, 321, 356, 357	—	1,800
PS3	1998 (2)	30,000	Y#290-291	—	140

PROVA SETS

KM#	Date	Mintage	Identification	Issue Price	Mkt Val
PrS1	1951 (4)	103	Pr1-Pr4	—	300
PrS2	1952 (4)	103	Pr5-Pr8	—	300
PrS3	1953 (4)	103	Pr9-Pr12	—	300
PrS4	1955 (6)	103	Pr13-Pr18	—	425
PrS5	1956 (6)	103	Pr19-Pr24	—	425
PrS6	1957 (7)	103	Pr25-31	—	425
PrS7	1958 (8)	103	Pr32-Pr39	—	600
PrS8	1959 (8)	103	Pr40-Pr47	—	600
PrS9	1960 (8)	103	Pr48-Pr55	—	600
PrS10	1961 (8)	103	Pr56-Pr63	—	600
PrS11	1962 (8)	103	Pr64-Pr71	—	600
PrS12	1962 (8)	103	Pr72-Pr79	—	600
PrS13	1963 (8)	103	Pr80-Pr87	—	600
PrS14	1964 (8)	103	Pr88-Pr95	—	600
PrS15	1965 (8)	103	Pr96-103	—	600
PrS16	1966 (8)	103	Pr104-Pr111	—	600
PrS17	1967 (8)	103	Pr112-Pr119	—	600
PrS18	1968 (8)	103	Pr120-Pr127	—	600
PrS19	1969 (8)	103	Pr128-Pr135	—	600
PrS20	1970 (8)	103	Pr136-Pr143	—	600
PrS21	1971 (8)	103	Pr144-Pr151	—	600
PrS22	1972 (8)	103	Pr152-Pr159	—	600
PrS23	1973 (8)	103	Pr160-Pr167	—	600
PrS24	1974 (8)	103	Pr168-Pr175	—	600
PrS25	1975 (8)	103	Pr176-Pr183	—	600
PrS26	1975 (8)	103	Pr184-Pr191	—	600

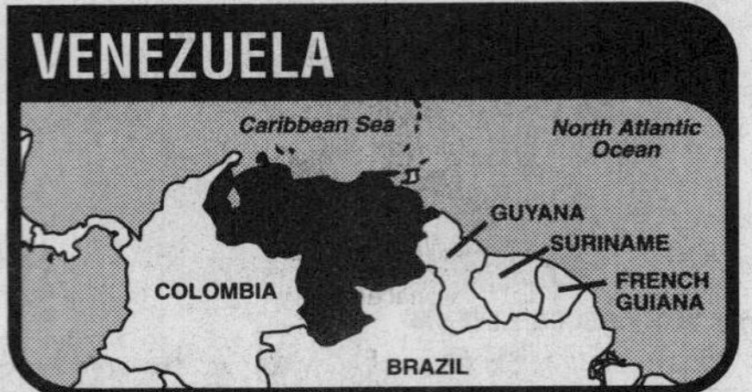

The Republic of Venezuela ("Little Venice"), located on the northern coast of South America between Colombia and Guyana, has an area of 352,145 sq. mi.(912,050 sq. km.) and a population of 20 million. Capital: Caracas. Petroleum and mining provide a significant portion of Venezuela's exports. Coffee, grown on 60,000 plantations, is the chief crop. Metalurgy, refining, oil, iron and steel production are the main employment industries.

Columbus discovered Venezuela on his third voyage in 1498. Initial exploration did not reveal Venezuela to be a land of great wealth. An active pearl trade operated on the offshore islands and slavers raided the interior in search of Indians to be sold into slavery, but no significant mainland settlements were made before 1567 when Caracas was founded. Venezuela, the home of Bolivar, was among the first South American colonies to rebel against Spain in 1810. The declaration of Independence of Venezuela was signed by seven provinces which are represented by the seven stars of the Venezuelan flag. Coinage of Caracas and Margarita use the seven stars in their designs. These original provinces were: Barcelona, Barinas, Caracas, Cumana, Margarita, Merida and Trujillo. The Provinces of Coro, Guyana and Maracaibo were added to Venezuela during the Independence War. Independence was attained in 1821 but not recognized by Spain until 1845. Together with Ecuador, Panama and Colombia, Venezuela was part of "Gran Colombia" until 1830, when it became a sovereign and independent state.

RULER

Republic, 1823-present

MINT MARKS

A - Paris
(a) - Paris, privy marks only
(aa) - Altena
(b) - Berlin
(bb) - Brussels
(cc) – Canada

(c) - Caracas
(d) - Denver
H, Heaton - Heaton, Birmingham
(l) - London
(m) - Madrid
(mm) - Mexico
(o) - Ontario
(p) - Philadelphia
(s) - San Francisco
(sc) - Schwerte - Vereinigte Deutsche Nickelwerke
(w) - Werdohl - Vereinigte Deutsche Metalwerke

MONETARY SYSTEM

100 Centimos = 1 Bolivar

REPUBLIC OF VENEZUELA

REFORM COINAGE

1896; 100 Centimos = 1 Bolivar

Y# 27 5 CENTIMOS

Copper-Nickel **Obv:** National arms, stars above **Obv. Legend:** ESTRADOS UNIDOS DE VENEZUELA **Rev:** Value within wreath

Date	Mintage	F	VF	XF	Unc	BU
1915(p)	2,000,000	1.00	4.00	50.00	150	300
1921(p)	2,000,000	0.50	4.00	70.00	200	300
1925(p)	2,000,000	0.30	1.00	6.00	15.00	40.00
1927(p)	2,000,000	0.30	1.00	6.00	15.00	40.00
1929(p)	2,000,000	0.25	1.00	6.00	15.00	40.00
1936(p)	5,000,000	0.15	0.50	4.00	10.00	20.00
1938(p)	6,000,000	0.10	0.20	3.00	8.00	20.00

Y# 29 5 CENTIMOS

Brass **Obv:** National arms, stars above **Rev:** Denomination within wreath

Date	Mintage	F	VF	XF	Unc	BU
1944(d)	4,000,000	0.50	1.00	4.50	20.00	60.00

Y# 29a 5 CENTIMOS

Copper-Nickel **Obv:** National arms, stars above **Rev:** Denomination within wreath

Date	Mintage	F	VF	XF	Unc	BU
1945(p)	12,000,000	0.10	0.20	0.50	4.00	6.00
1946(p)	12,000,000	0.10	0.20	0.50	4.00	6.00
1948(p)	18,000,000	0.10	0.20	0.50	3.00	5.00

Y# 38.1 5 CENTIMOS

Copper-Nickel **Obv:** National arms, stars above **Rev:** Denomination within wreath

Date	Mintage	F	VF	XF	Unc	BU
1958(p)	25,000,000	—	—	—	0.75	1.25

Y# 38.2 5 CENTIMOS

Copper-Nickel **Obv:** National arms, stars above **Rev:** Denomination within wreath

Date	Mintage	F	VF	XF	Unc	BU
1964(m)	40,000,000	—	—	—	0.50	1.00
1965(m)	60,000,000	—	—	—	0.50	1.00

Y# 38.3 5 CENTIMOS

Copper-Nickel **Obv:** National arms, stars above **Rev:** Denomination within wreath

Date	Mintage	F	VF	XF	Unc	BU
1971(o)	40,000,000	—	—	—	0.50	1.00

Y# 49 5 CENTIMOS

Copper Clad Steel **Obv:** National arms, stars above **Rev:** Denomination below spray

Date	Mintage	F	VF	XF	Unc	BU
1974(w)	200,000,000	—	—	—	0.15	2.00
1976(w)	200,000,000	—	—	—	0.15	2.00
1977(l)	600,000,000	—	—	—	0.15	1.00

Y# 49a 5 CENTIMOS

Nickel Clad Steel **Obv:** National arms, stars above **Rev:** Denomination below spray

Date	Mintage	F	VF	XF	Unc	BU
1983(w)	600,000,000	—	—	—	0.10	0.20

Y# 49b 5 CENTIMOS

Copper-Nickel Clad Steel **Obv:** National arms, stars above **Rev:** Denomination below spray

Date	Mintage	F	VF	XF	Unc	BU
1986(w)	500,000,000	—	—	—	0.10	0.20

Y# A40 10 CENTIMOS

Copper-Nickel **Obv:** National arms, stars above **Rev:** Denomination within wreath

Date	Mintage	F	VF	XF	Unc	BU
1971(o)	60,000,000	—	—	0.10	0.25	0.50

Y# 28 12-1/2 CENTIMOS

Copper-Nickel **Obv:** National arms, stars above **Obv. Legend:** ESTRADOS UNIDOS DE VENEZUELA **Rev:** Value within wreath **Note:** Varieties exist.

Date	Mintage	F	VF	XF	Unc	BU
1925(p)	800,000	2.50	6.50	45.00	200	400
1927(p)	800,000	1.00	2.00	12.00	75.00	150
1929(p)	800,000	0.15	0.50	5.00	55.00	100
1936(p)	1,200,000	0.15	0.30	2.00	25.00	50.00
1938(p)	1,600,000	0.15	0.30	1.00	18.00	40.00

Y# 30 12-1/2 CENTIMOS

Brass **Obv:** National arms, stars above **Rev:** Denomination within wreath

Date	Mintage	F	VF	XF	Unc	BU
1944(d)	800,000	2.50	4.50	9.00	60.00	150

Y# 30a 12-1/2 CENTIMOS

Copper-Nickel **Obv:** National arms, stars above **Rev:** Denomination within wreath

Date	Mintage	F	VF	XF	Unc	BU
1945(p)	11,200,000	0.10	0.20	0.35	9.00	15.00
1946(p)	9,200,000	0.10	0.20	0.35	12.00	20.00
1948(s)	6,000,000	0.10	0.20	0.35	8.00	15.00

Y# 39 12-1/2 CENTIMOS

Copper-Nickel **Obv:** National arms, stars above **Rev:** Denomination within wreath, knobbed 2

Date	Mintage	F	VF	XF	Unc	BU
1958(p)	10,000,000	—	—	0.20	2.00	4.00

Y# A39.1 12-1/2 CENTIMOS

Copper-Nickel **Obv:** National arms, flat stars **Rev:** Denomination within wreath, plain 2

Date	Mintage	F	VF	XF	Unc	BU
1969(m)	2,000,000	—	—	—	50.00	80.00

Y# A39.2 12-1/2 CENTIMOS

Copper-Nickel **Obv:** National arms, raised stars **Rev:** Denomination within wreath, outlined stem ends

Date	Mintage	F	VF	XF	Unc	BU
1969(m)	Inc. above	—	—	—	150	250

Y# A39.3 12-1/2 CENTIMOS

Copper-Nickel **Obv:** National arms, stars above **Rev:** Denomination within wreath, solid stem ends

Date	Mintage	F	VF	XF	Unc	BU
1969(m)	Inc. above	—	—	—	150	250

Note: 1969 dated strikes were not released into circulation

Y# 20 GR 1.250 (1/4 Bolivar)

1.2500 g., 0.8350 Silver .0336 oz. ASW **Obv:** National arms **Obv. Legend:** ESTRADOS UNIDOS DE VENEZUELA. **Rev:** Head left **Rev. Legend:** BOLIVAR LIBERTADOR **Rev. Designer:** Albert Barre

Date	Mintage	F	VF	XF	Unc	BU
1901(a)	393,000	7.00	25.00	55.00	300	600
1903(p)	400,000	6.00	20.00	50.00	200	375
1911(a)	600,000	2.50	5.00	12.00	75.00	125
1912(a)	800,000	3.00	6.00	15.00	100	200
1919(p)	400,000	2.50	5.00	12.00	75.00	200
1921(p) High 2	800,000	2.00	4.00	10.00	50.00	125
1921(p) Low 2	Inc. above	1.00	3.00	10.00	50.00	125
1924(p)	400,000	1.00	3.00	10.00	35.00	80.00
1929(p)	1,200,000	—	BV	1.00	6.00	15.00
1935(p)	3,400,000	—	BV	1.00	3.00	8.00
1936(p)	2,800,000	—	BV	1.00	3.00	8.00
1944(p)	1,800,000	—	BV	1.00	2.00	5.00
1945(p)	8,000,000	—	—	BV	1.50	2.50
1946(p)	8,000,000	—	—	BV	1.00	2.00
1948(s)	8,638,000	—	—	BV	1.00	2.00

Y# 35 25 CENTIMOS

1.2500 g., 0.8350 Silver .0336 oz. ASW **Obv:** National arms **Rev:** Head of Bolivar left **Rev. Designer:** Albert Barre

Date	Mintage	F	VF	XF	Unc	BU
1954(p)	36,000,000	—	—	BV	1.00	1.50

Y# 35a 25 CENTIMOS

1.2500 g., 0.8350 Silver .0336 oz. ASW **Obv:** National arms **Rev:** Head of Bolivar left

Date	Mintage	F	VF	XF	Unc	BU
1960(a)	48,000,000	—	—	BV	0.75	1.50

Y# 40 25 CENTIMOS

Nickel, 17 mm. **Obv:** National arms **Rev:** Head of Bolivar left **Rev. Designer:** Albert Barre

Date	Mintage	F	VF	XF	Unc	BU
1965(l)	240,000,000	—	—	0.10	0.35	1.00

Y# 50.1 25 CENTIMOS

1.7500 g., Nickel, 17 mm. **Obv:** National arms **Rev:** Head of Bolivar left **Rev. Designer:** Albert Barre **Note:** 1.18mm thick.

Date	Mintage	F	VF	XF	Unc	BU
1977(w)	240,000,000	—	—	0.10	0.25	0.50
1978	—	—	—	0.10	0.25	0.50

Y# 50.2 25 CENTIMOS

1.5000 g., Nickel, 17 mm. **Obv:** National arms **Rev:** Head of Bolivar left **Note:** Dies vary for each date; thin.

Date	Mintage	F	VF	XF	Unc	BU
1977(w)	Inc. above	—	—	0.10	0.25	0.50
1978(w)	200,000,000	—	—	0.10	0.25	0.50
1987	150,000,000	—	—	0.10	0.25	0.50

Y# 50a 25 CENTIMOS

1.5000 g., Nickel Clad Steel, 17 mm. **Obv:** National arms **Rev:** Head of Bolivar left **Note:** Varieties exist.

Date	Mintage	F	VF	XF	Unc	BU
1989(sc)	510,000,000	—	—	0.10	0.25	0.50
1990(mm)	400,000,000	—	—	0.10	0.25	0.50

Y# 21 GR 2.500 (1/2 Bolivar)

2.5000 g., 0.8350 Silver .0671 oz. ASW **Obv:** Arms within sprigs above banner, cornucopias above **Obv. Legend:** ESTRADOS UNIDOS DE VENEZUELA **Rev:** Head of Bolivar left **Rev. Legend:** BOLIVAR LIBERTADOR **Rev. Designer:** Albert Barre

Date	Mintage	F	VF	XF	Unc	BU
1901(a)	600,000	20.00	50.00	175	750	1,400

Date	Mintage	F	VF	XF	Unc	BU
Note: Privy mark placement varies with 1901						
1903(p)	200,000	75.00	200	600	2,000	3,250
1911(a)	300,000	30.00	60.00	200	600	1,200
Note: Privy mark placement varies with 1911						
1912(a)	1,920,000	5.00	15.00	50.00	300	600
1919(p)	400,000	6.00	20.00	80.00	400	1,000
1921(p) Normal date	600,000	2.50	7.00	16.00	100	250
1921(p) Narrow date	Inc. above	3.50	9.00	27.50	125	300
1921(p) Wide date	Inc. above	3.50	9.00	27.50	125	300
1924(p)	800,000	2.50	7.00	16.00	85.00	200
1929(p)	400,000	1.25	2.00	6.00	55.00	135
1935(p)	1,000,000	—	BV	1.25	12.00	30.00
1936(p)	600,000	BV	1.25	5.00	50.00	125

Y# 21a GR 2.500 (1/2 Bolivar)

2.5000 g., 0.8350 Silver .0671 oz. ASW **Obv:** National arms above ribbon, plants flank, cornucopias above **Rev:** Head of Bolivar left **Rev. Designer:** Albert Barre

Date	Mintage	F	VF	XF	Unc	BU
1944(d)	500,000	1.25	3.00	5.00	15.00	30.00
Note: Accent in Bolivar						
1944(d)	Inc. above	1.50	5.00	10.00	25.00	50.00
Note: Without accent in Bolivar						
1945(p)	4,000,000	—	BV	1.25	5.00	10.00
1946(p)	2,500,000	—	BV	1.25	5.00	10.00

Y# 36 50 CENTIMOS

2.5000 g., 0.8350 Silver .0671 oz. ASW, 18 mm. **Obv:** National arms **Rev:** Head of Bolivar left **Rev. Designer:** Albert Barre

Date	Mintage	F	VF	XF	Unc	BU
1954(p)	15,000,000	—	—	BV	3.00	5.00

Y# 36a 50 CENTIMOS

2.5000 g., 0.8350 Silver .0671 oz. ASW, 18 mm. **Obv:** National arms **Rev:** Head of Bolivar left **Rev. Designer:** Albert Barre

Date	Mintage	F	VF	XF	Unc	BU
1960(a)	20,000,000	—	—	BV	2.00	3.00

Y# 41 50 CENTIMOS

Nickel, 20 mm. **Obv:** National arms **Rev:** Head of Bolivar left **Rev. Designer:** Albert Barre

Date	Mintage	F	VF	XF	Unc	BU
1965(l)	180,000,000	—	0.10	0.15	0.35	1.00
1985(o)	50,000,000	—	0.10	0.15	0.35	1.00

Y# 41a 50 CENTIMOS

3.2000 g., Nickel Clad Steel, 20 mm. **Obv:** National arms **Rev:** Head of Bolivar left

Date	Mintage	F	VF	XF	Unc	BU
1988(w)	80,000,000	—	0.10	0.15	0.30	0.50
1989(w)	260,000,000	—	0.10	0.15	0.30	0.50
1990(l)	300,000,000	—	0.10	0.15	0.30	0.50
Note: Die varieties exist for 1990 dated strikes						

Y# 22 GRAM 5 (Bolivar)

5.0000 g., 0.8350 Silver .1342 oz. ASW **Obv:** Arms within sprigs above banner, cornucopias above **Obv. Legend:** ESTRADOS UNIDOS DE VENEZUELA. **Rev:** Head of Bolivar left **Rev. Legend:** BOLIVAR LIBERTADOR **Rev. Designer:** Albert Barre

Date	Mintage	F	VF	XF	Unc	BU
1901(a)	323,000	20.00	55.00	150	650	1,250
1903(p)	800,000	5.00	15.00	90.00	350	850
1911(a)	1,500,000	3.00	5.00	40.00	200	650
1912(a) Wide date	820,000	6.00	16.50	75.00	300	800
1912(a) Narrow date	Inc. above	6.00	16.50	75.00	300	800
1919(p)	1,000,000	2.25	3.00	12.00	45.00	110
1921(p)	1,000,000	2.25	3.00	12.00	40.00	100
1924(p)	1,500,000	BV	2.25	6.00	30.00	75.00
1926(p)	1,000,000	BV	2.25	6.00	30.00	75.00
1929(p)	2,500,000	—	BV	2.25	8.00	20.00
1935(p)	5,000,000	—	BV	2.25	5.00	12.50
1936(p)	5,000,000	—	BV	2.25	5.00	12.50

Y# 22a GRAM 5 (Bolivar)

5.0000 g., 0.8350 Silver .1342 oz. ASW **Obv:** National arms above ribbon, plants flank, cornucopias above **Rev:** Head of Bolivar left **Rev. Designer:** Albert Barre

Date	Mintage	F	VF	XF	Unc	BU
1945(p)	8,000,000	—	—	BV	3.50	5.00

Y# 37 BOLIVAR

5.0000 g., 0.8350 Silver .1342 oz. ASW **Obv:** National arms above ribbon, plants flank, cornucopias above **Rev:** Head of Bolivar left **Rev. Designer:** Albert Barre

Date	Mintage	F	VF	XF	Unc	BU
1954(p)	13,500,000	—	—	BV	2.50	4.00

Y# 37a BOLIVAR

5.0000 g., 0.8350 Silver .1342 oz. ASW **Obv:** National arms above ribbon, plants flank, cornucopias above **Rev:** Head of Bolivar left **Rev. Designer:** Albert Barre

Date	Mintage	F	VF	XF	Unc	BU
1960(a)	30,000,000	—	—	BV	2.25	4.00
Note: Thin letters						
1960(a)	Inc. above	—	—	BV	2.25	4.00
Note: Thick letters						
1965(l)	20,000,000	—	—	BV	2.25	3.00

Y# 42 BOLIVAR

Nickel, 23 mm. **Obv:** National arms above ribbon, plants flank, cornucopias above **Rev:** Head of Bolivar left **Rev. Designer:** Albert Barre

Date	Mintage	F	VF	XF	Unc	BU
1967(l)	180,000,000	—	0.10	0.15	0.75	1.00

Y# 52 BOLIVAR

Nickel, 23 mm. **Obv:** National arms above ribbon, plants flank, cornucopias above **Rev:** Head of Bolivar left **Rev. Designer:** Albert Barre **Note:** Dies vary for each date.

Date	Mintage	F	VF	XF	Unc	BU
1977(l)	200,000,000	—	0.10	0.15	0.65	1.00
1986(w)	200,000,000	—	0.10	0.15	0.50	1.00
1986(w) Prooflike	50,000,000	—	0.10	0.15	0.60	1.50

Y# 52a.2 BOLIVAR

4.2000 g., Nickel Clad Steel, 23 mm. **Obv:** National arms above ribbon, plants flank, cornucopias above **Rev:** Head of Bolivar left **Note:** Dies vary for each date. Obverse has large letters and date

Date	Mintage	F	VF	XF	Unc	BU
1989(sc)	600,000,000	—	0.10	0.15	0.45	0.60
1990(mm)	600,000,000	—	0.10	0.15	0.45	0.60

Y# 52a.1 BOLIVAR

4.2000 g., Nickel Clad Steel, 23 mm. **Obv:** National arms above ribbon, plants flank, cornucopias above **Rev:** Head of Bolivar left **Note:** Both sides of coin have small letters and date

Date	Mintage	F	VF	XF	Unc	BU
1989(w)	370,000,000	—	0.10	0.15	0.45	0.60

Y# 23 GRAM 10 (2 Bolivares)

10.0000 g., 0.8350 Silver .2685 oz. ASW **Obv:** Arms within sprigs above banner, cornucopias above **Obv. Legend:** ESTRADOS UNIDOS DE VENEZUELA. **Rev:** Head of Bolivar left **Rev. Legend:** BOLIVAR LIBERTADOR **Rev. Designer:** Albert Barre

Date	Mintage	F	VF	XF	Unc	BU
1902(p)	500,000	11.50	45.00	200	500	1,000
1903(p)	500,000	12.50	50.00	250	550	1,100
1904(a) Large 0, small 4	550,000	11.50	40.00	175	500	1,000
1904(a) Large 0, large 4	Inc. above	11.50	40.00	175	500	1,000
1904(a) Small 0, large 4	Inc. above	11.50	45.00	185	550	1,100
1904(a) Small 0, large slant 4	Inc. above	11.50	45.00	185	550	1,100
1904(a) Small 0, small 4	50,000	20.00	55.00	200	600	1,150
1905(a) Upright 5	750,000	4.50	16.50	100	400	800
1905(a) Slant 5	Inc. above	4.50	16.50	100	400	800
1911(a)	750,000	4.50	16.50	60.00	275	650
1912(a)	500,000	4.50	16.50	140	400	1,000
1913(a) Normal date	210,000	40.00	250	500	1,000	2,000
1913(a) Raised 3	Inc. above	40.00	250	500	1,000	2,000
1919(p)	1,000,000	BV	4.50	11.50	125	300
1922(p) Narrow date	1,000,000	BV	4.50	11.50	85.00	200
1922(p) Wide date	Inc. above	BV	4.50	11.50	85.00	200
1922(p) Low first 2	Inc. above	BV	4.50	11.50	85.00	200
1924(p)	1,250,000	BV	4.50	11.50	85.00	200
1926(p)	1,000,000	BV	4.50	11.50	85.00	200
1929(p)	1,500,000	—	BV	8.00	20.00	50.00
1930(p)	425,000	BV	7.00	25.00	130	300
1935(p)	3,000,000	—	BV	4.50	8.00	20.00
1936(p)	2,500,000	—	BV	4.50	8.00	20.00

Y# 23a GRAM 10 (2 Bolivares)

10.0000 g., 0.8350 Silver .2685 oz. ASW **Obv:** National arms above ribbon, plants flank, cornucopias above **Rev:** Head of Bolivar left **Rev. Designer:** Albert Barre

Date	Mintage	F	VF	XF	Unc	BU
1945(p)	3,000,000	—	—	BV	4.50	6.00

Y# A37 2 BOLIVARES

10.0000 g., 0.8350 Silver .2685 oz. ASW **Obv:** National arms above ribbon, plants flank, cornucopias above **Rev:** Head of Bolivar left **Rev. Designer:** Albert Barre

Date	Mintage	F	VF	XF	Unc	BU
1960(a)	4,000,000	—	—	BV	4.50	6.00
1965(l)	7,170,000	—	—	BV	4.50	6.00

Y# 43 2 BOLIVARES

Nickel, 27 mm. **Obv:** National arms above ribbon, plants flank, cornucopias above **Rev:** Head of Bolivar left **Rev. Designer:** Albert Barre **Note:** Dies vary for each date.

Date	Mintage	F	VF	XF	Unc	BU
1967(l)	50,000,000	—	—	0.25	0.50	1.50
1986(w)	50,000,000	—	—	0.25	0.50	1.50
Note: Die varieties exist for 1986 strikes						
1986(w) Prooflike	—	—	—	0.25	0.50	1.50
Note: Die varieties exist for 1986 strikes						
1988(c)	80,000,000	—	—	0.25	0.50	1.50

Y# 43a.1 2 BOLIVARES

7.5000 g., Nickel Clad Steel, 27 mm. **Obv:** Small letters in legend, raised motto in ribbon, lines beneath horse, "R" in 'Libertador' 2mm away from truncation **Rev:** Head of Bolivar left, small letters

Date	Mintage	F	VF	XF	Unc	BU
1989(sc)	200,000,000	—	—	0.20	0.75	1.50
1990(c)	400,000,000	—	—	0.20	0.75	1.50
Note: Two varieties of 1990 exist						

Y# 43a.2 2 BOLIVARES

7.5000 g., Nickel Clad Steel, 27 mm. **Obv:** Large letters in legend, no lines beneath horse, "R" in 'Libertador' touching truncation **Rev:** Head of Bolivar left, large letters

Date	Mintage	F	VF	XF	Unc	BU
1989(w)	100,000,000	—	—	0.20	0.75	1.50
1989(c)	95,000,000	—	—	0.20	0.75	1.50

Y# 24.2 GRAM 25 (5 Bolivares)

25.0000 g., 0.9000 Silver .7234 oz. ASW **Obv:** Date on ribbon right of arms 13 DE APRIL DE 1864, cornucopias above **Obv. Legend:** ESTRADOS UNIDOS DE VENEZUELA **Rev:** Head of Bolivar left **Rev. Legend:** BOLIVAR LIBERTADOR

Date	Mintage	F	VF	XF	Unc	BU
1901(a)	90,000	20.00	100	375	1,500	3,000
1902(p) Wide date	500,000	11.50	16.00	120	700	1,000
1902(p) Narrow date	Inc. above	11.50	16.00	120	700	1,000
1903(p)	200,000	11.50	16.00	120	700	1,400
1904(a)	200,000	11.50	16.00	150	1,000	3,000
1905(a)	300,000	11.50	16.00	120	650	1,250
1910(a) Oval 0	400,000	11.50	16.00	85.00	450	900
1910(a) Round 0	Inc. above	12.50	25.00	130	650	1,250
1911(a) Normal date	1,104,000	BV	13.50	45.00	225	500
1911(a) Wide date	Inc. above	BV	13.50	45.00	225	500
1911(a) Narrow date	Inc. above	BV	13.50	45.00	225	500
1912(a) Normal date	696,000	BV	13.50	45.00	225	500
1912(a) Wide date	Inc. above	BV	13.50	45.00	225	500
1912(a) Narrow date	Inc. above	BV	13.50	45.00	225	500
1919(p)	400,000	BV	13.50	30.00	175	350
1921(p) Wide date	500,000	BV	13.50	25.00	100	200
1921(p) Narrow date	Inc. above	BV	13.50	25.00	100	200
1924(p) Wide date	500,000	BV	13.50	25.00	100	200
1924(p) Narrow date	Inc. above	BV	137	25.00	100	200
1924(p) Low 9	Inc. above	BV	13.50	25.00	100	200
1926(p)	800,000	BV	12.50	22.50	80.00	150
1929(p) High 9	800,000	BV	12.50	22.00	60.00	120
1929(p) Low 9	Inc. above	BV	12.50	22.00	60.00	120
1935(p)	1,600,000	BV	11.50	16.50	38.00	60.00
1936(p) Normal date	2,000,000	BV	11.50	16.50	38.00	60.00
1936(p) High 3	Inc. above	BV	11.50	16.50	38.00	60.00
1936(p) Low 3	Inc. above	BV	11.50	16.50	38.00	60.00

Y# 44 5 BOLIVARES

Nickel, 31 mm. **Obv:** National arms above ribbon, plants flank, cornucopias above **Rev:** Head of Bolivar left **Rev. Designer:** Albert Barre

Date	Mintage	F	VF	XF	Unc	BU
1973(m)	20,000,000	—	0.45	0.75	1.75	10.00

Y# 53.1 5 BOLIVARES

Nickel, 31 mm. **Obv:** National arms above ribbon, plants flank, cornucopias above **Rev:** Head of Bolivar left **Rev. Designer:** Albert Barre

Date	Mintage	F	VF	XF	Unc	BU
1977(m)	60,000,000	—	—	0.50	1.50	2.00

Y# 53.2 5 BOLIVARES

Nickel **Obv:** National arms above ribbon, plants flank, cornucopias above, date and denomination below **Rev:** Head of Bolivar left

Date	Mintage	F	VF	XF	Unc	BU
1987(c)	25,000,000	—	—	0.50	1.50	2.00
1987(c) Prooflike	Inc. above	—	—	—	—	30.00
1988(w)	20,000,000	—	—	1.00	5.00	10.00

Y# 53a.1 5 BOLIVARES

13.3000 g., Nickel Clad Steel, 31 mm. **Obv:** National arms above ribbon, plants flank, cornucopias above, small letters **Rev:** Head of Bolivar left, large letters **Rev. Designer:** Albert Barre

Date	Mintage	F	VF	XF	Unc	BU
1989(w)	55,000,000	—	—	0.50	1.50	2.00
1989(w) Prooflike	26,000,000	—	—	1.00	2.00	3.00

Y# 53a.2 5 BOLIVARES

13.3000 g., Nickel Clad Steel, 31 mm. **Obv:** Large letters **Rev:** Small letters

Date	Mintage	F	VF	XF	Unc	BU
1989(sc)	100,000,000	—	—	0.50	1.50	3.00
1990(c)	200,000,000	—	—	0.50	1.50	3.00

Y# 53a.3 5 BOLIVARES

13.3000 g., Nickel Clad Steel, 31 mm. **Obv:** National arms above ribbon, plants flank, cornucopias above **Rev:** Head of Bolivar left **Rev. Designer:** Albert Barre **Note:** Large letters in legends.

Date	Mintage	F	VF	XF	Unc	BU
1990	—	—	—	0.65	1.75	3.00

Y# 31 GR 3.2258 (10 Bolivares)

3.2258 g., 0.9000 Gold .0933 oz. AGW **Obv:** National arms above ribbon, plants flank, cornucopias above **Rev:** Head of Bolivar right **Rev. Designer:** Albert Barre

Date	Mintage	F	VF	XF	Unc	BU
1930(p)	Est. 500,000	—	BV	65.00	80.00	100
Note: Only 10% of the total mintage was released; the balance remaining as part of the nation's gold reserve						

Y# 45 10 BOLIVARES

30.0000 g., 0.9000 Silver .8681 oz. ASW **Obv:** Arms within inset at left, inscription at right **Rev:** Head of Bolivar within inset at right, inscription at left **Rev. Designer:** Albert Barre **Edge Lettering:** CENTENARIO DE LA EFIGLE DEL LIBERTADOR EN EL MONEDA

Date	Mintage	F	VF	XF	Unc	BU
1973(o)	2,000,000	—	—	—	14.00	16.00
1973(o) Proof	200	Value: 400				

Y# 75 10 BOLIVARES

Nickel Clad Steel **Obv:** National arms **Rev:** Head of Bolivar left within 7-sided outline **Rev. Designer:** Albert Barre

Date	Mintage	F	VF	XF	Unc	BU
1998	—	—	—	—	0.25	0.50

Y# 80 10 BOLIVARES

2.3300 g., Nickel Clad Steel, 16.85 mm. **Obv:** National arms left of denomination **Rev:** Head of Bolivar left with new mint mark at left, 7-sided outline surrounds **Rev. Designer:** Albert Barre **Edge:** Reeded **Note:** Struck at Maracay Mint.

Date	Mintage	F	VF	XF	Unc	BU
2000	—	—	—	—	0.25	0.50

Y# 32 GR 6.4516 (20 Bolivares)

6.4516 g., 0.9000 Gold .1867 oz. AGW **Obv:** Arms within sprigs above banner, cornucopias above **Obv. Legend:** ESTRADOS UNIDOS DE VENEZUELA **Rev:** Head of Bolivar right **Rev. Legend:** BOLIVAR LIBERTADOR **Rev. Designer:** Albert Barre

Date	Mintage	F	VF	XF	Unc	BU
1904(a)	100,000	—	BV	130	140	150
1905(a)	100,000	—	BV	130	140	150
1910(a)	70,000	—	BV	130	145	160
Note: Die varieties exist in the placement of dot between date and Lei, Type 1 is evenly spaced, Type 2 had dot closer to L of Lei						
1911(a)	80,000	—	BV	130	140	150
Note: Die varieties exist in the placement of dot between date and Lei, Type 1 is evenly spaced, Type 2 had dot closer to L of Lei						
1912(a)	150,000	—	BV	130	140	150
Note: Die varieties exist in the placement of the torch privy mark in relation to bust truncation; Type 1 is well below truncation, Type 2 is slightly below truncation and Type 3 is in line with the truncation						

Y# 76 20 BOLIVARES

Nickel Clad Steel **Obv:** National arms **Rev:** Head of Bolivar left within 7-sided outline **Rev. Designer:** Albert Barre

Date	Mintage	F	VF	XF	Unc	BU
1998	—	—	—	—	0.25	0.50

Y# 76.1 20 BOLIVARES

4.3200 g., Nickel Clad Steel, 20 mm. **Obv:** National arms **Rev:** Head of Bolivar left within 7-sided outline **Edge:** Plain

Date	Mintage	F	VF	XF	Unc	BU
1999(c)	—	—	—	0.30	0.60	—

Y# 81 20 BOLIVARES

4.3200 g., Nickel Clad Steel, 20 mm. **Obv:** National arms left of denomination **Rev:** Head of Bolivar left, with new mint mark at left, 7-sided outline surrounds **Rev. Designer:** Albert Barre **Edge:** Plain **Note:** Struck at Maracay Mint.

Date	Mintage	F	VF	XF	Unc	BU
2000	—	—	—	—	0.25	0.50

Y# 46 25 BOLIVARES

28.2800 g., 0.9250 Silver .8411 oz. ASW **Subject:** Conservation **Obv:** National arms above ribbon, plants flank, cornucopias above **Rev:** Jaguar, denomination below

Date	Mintage	F	VF	XF	Unc	BU
1975(I)	38,000	—	—	—	22.50	30.00
1975(I) Proof	8,000,000	Value: 45.00				

Y# 47 50 BOLIVARES

35.0000 g., 0.9250 Silver 1.0409 oz. ASW **Subject:** Conservation **Obv:** National arms above ribbon, plants flank, cornucopias above **Rev:** Giant Armadillo

Date	Mintage	F	VF	XF	Unc	BU
1975(I)	39,000	—	—	—	25.00	35.00
1975(I) Proof	8,000,000	Value: 50.00				

Y# 66 50 BOLIVARES

31.1000 g., 0.9000 Silver .9000 oz. ASW **Subject:** 50th Anniversary of Central Bank **Obv:** Flag design with initials in circle at right **Rev:** Building facade

Date	Mintage	F	VF	XF	Unc	BU
1990(c) Proof	10,000	Value: 40.00				

Y# 67 50 BOLIVARES

15.5500 g., 0.9000 Gold .4500 oz. AGW **Subject:** 50th Anniversary of Central Bank **Obv:** Flag design with initials in circle at right **Rev:** Building facade

Date	Mintage	F	VF	XF	Unc	BU
1990(c) Proof	5,000	Value: 500				

Y# 77 50 BOLIVARES

Nickel Clad Steel **Obv:** National arms **Rev:** Head of Bolivar left within 7-sided outline **Rev. Designer:** Albert Barre

Date	Mintage	F	VF	XF	Unc	BU
1998	—	—	—	—	0.35	0.70

Y# 77 50 BOLIVARES

Nickel Clad Steel **Obv:** National arms **Rev:** Head of Bolivar left within 7-sided outline **Rev. Designer:** Albert Barre

Date	Mintage	F	VF	XF	Unc	BU
1998	—	—	—	—	0.35	0.70

Y# 77.1 50 BOLIVARES

6.6500 g., Nickel Clad Steel, 23 mm. **Obv:** National arms above ribbon, plants flank, cornucopias above **Rev:** Head of Bolivar left and mint mark, 7-sided outline surrounds **Edge:** Reeded

Date	Mintage	F	VF	XF	Unc	BU
1999(c)	—	—	—	0.40	0.80	—

Y# 82 50 BOLIVARES

6.6500 g., Nickel Clad Steel, 23 mm. **Obv:** National arms left of denomination **Rev:** Head of Bolivar left with new mint mark at left, 7-sided outline surrounds **Rev. Designer:** Albert Barre **Edge:** Reeded

Date	Mintage	F	VF	XF	Unc	BU
2000	—	—	—	—	0.30	0.80

Y# 55 75 BOLIVARES

17.0000 g., 0.9000 Silver .4920 oz. ASW **Subject:** 50th Anniversary - Sucre's Death **Obv:** Body on ground at right, mountains in background, horse at left **Rev:** Head of Bolivar 3/4 facing divides dates

Date	Mintage	F	VF	XF	Unc	BU
1980(I)	500,000	—	—	—	10.00	15.00
1980(I) Proof	200	Value: 550				

Y# 56 100 BOLIVARES

22.0000 g., 0.9000 Silver .6367 oz. ASW **Subject:** 150th Anniversary - Bolivar's Death **Obv:** Monument **Rev:** Bust of Bolivar facing divides dates

Date	Mintage	F	VF	XF	Unc	BU
1980(I)	500,000	—	—	—	12.50	25.00
1980(I) Proof	200	Value: 550				

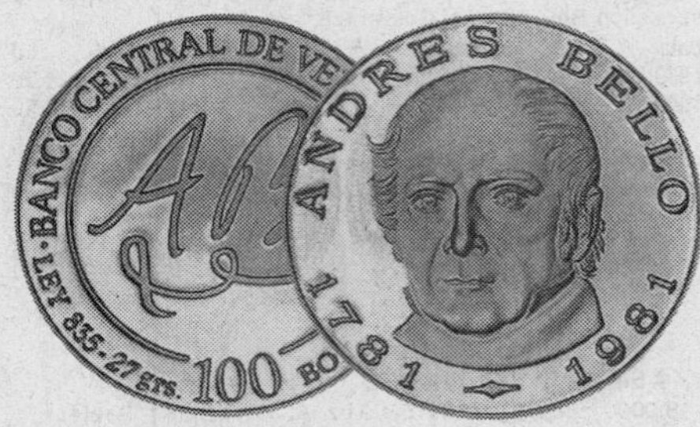

Y# 57 100 BOLIVARES

27.0000 g., 0.8350 Silver .7249 oz. ASW **Subject:** 200th Anniversary - Birth of Andres Bello **Obv:** Initials within circle **Rev:** Head of Bolivar facing, dates below

Date	Mintage	F	VF	XF	Unc	BU
ND(1981)(w)	200	—	—	—	400	—
ND(1981)(w) Proof	500,000	Value: 12.50				

Y# 58 100 BOLIVARES

31.0000 g., 0.9000 Silver .9000 oz. ASW **Subject:** 200th Anniversary - Birth of Simon Bolivar **Obv:** Building **Rev:** Bookshselves back of 3/4 figure looking left

Date	Mintage	F	VF	XF	Unc	BU
ND(1983)(w) Proof	300,000	Value: 18.00				

Y# 60 100 BOLIVARES

31.0000 g., 0.9000 Silver .9000 oz. ASW, 35 mm. **Subject:** 200th Anniversary - Birth of Jose M. Vargas **Obv:** Steepled building within circle **Rev:** Bust of Bolivar facing within circle

Date	Mintage	F	VF	XF	Unc	BU
ND(1986)(I)	500,000	—	—	—	14.50	16.50
ND(1986)(I) Proof	500	Value: 250				

Note; Beware of some altered circulation coins to look like proofs

Y# 78 100 BOLIVARES
Nickel Clad Steel **Obv:** National arms above ribbon, plants flank, cornucopias above **Rev:** Head of Bolivar left within 7-sided outline **Rev. Designer:** Albert Barre

Date	Mintage	F	VF	XF	Unc	BU
1998	—	—	—	—	0.50	1.00

Y# 78.1 100 BOLIVARES
6.8200 g., Nickel-Clad Steel, 25 mm. **Obv:** National arms above ribbon, plants flank, cornucopias above **Rev:** Head of Bolivar and mint mark, 7-sided outline surrounds **Edge:** Plain

Date	Mintage	F	VF	XF	Unc	BU
1999(c)	—	—	—	0.60	1.20	—

Y# 54 500 BOLIVARES
18.0000 g., 0.9000 Gold .5209 oz. AGW, 30 mm. **Subject:** Nationalization of Oil Industry **Obv:** Oil derricks within inset at left **Rev:** Head of Bolivar left within inset

Date	Mintage	F	VF	XF	Unc	BU
1975(c) Proof	100	Value: 13,000				

Y# 64 500 BOLIVARES
31.1000 g., 0.9000 Silver .9000 oz. ASW **Obv:** National arms above ribbon, plants flank, cornucopias above **Rev:** Head of Bolivar left, dates below

Date	Mintage	F	VF	XF	Unc	BU
1990(mm) Proof	30,000	Value: 25.00				

Y# 69 500 BOLIVARES
31.1000 g., 0.9000 Silver .9000 oz. ASW **Subject:** Battle of Matasiete **Obv:** National arms above ribbon, plants flank, cornucopias above **Rev:** Monument divides dates below mountains

Date	Mintage	F	VF	XF	Unc	BU
1992(w) Proof	10,000	Value: 25.00				

Y# 71 500 BOLIVARES
31.1000 g., 0.9000 Silver .9000 oz. ASW **Subject:** 50th Anniversary - United Nations **Obv:** National arms above ribbon, plants flank, cornucopias above **Rev:** UN logo within wreath

Date	Mintage	F	VF	XF	Unc	BU
1995(cc) Proof	10,000	Value: 25.00				

Y# 72 500 BOLIVARES
31.1000 g., 0.9000 Silver .9000 oz. ASW **Subject:** 200th Anniversary - Sucre's Birth **Obv:** National arms above ribbon, plants flank, cornucopias above **Rev:** Bust of Bolivar facing, dates below

Date	Mintage	F	VF	XF	Unc	BU
1995(cc) Proof	15,000	Value: 25.00				

Y# 74 500 BOLIVARES
31.1000 g., 0.9000 Silver .9000 oz. ASW **Subject:** Manuel Gual and Jose Maria Espana **Obv:** National arms above ribbon, plants flank, cornucopias above **Rev:** Two busts above dates

Date	Mintage	F	VF	XF	Unc	BU
1997A Proof	10,000	Value: 25.00				

Y# 79 500 BOLIVARES
Nickel Clad Steel, 28.4 mm. **Obv:** National arms above ribbon, plants flank, cornucopias above **Rev:** Head of Bolivar left within 7-sided outline **Rev. Designer:** Albert Barre

Date	Mintage	F	VF	XF	Unc	BU
1998	—	—	—	—	0.75	1.50

Y# 84 500 BOLIVARES
8.4000 g., Nickel Clad Steel, 28.35 mm. **Obv:** National arms above ribbon, plants flank, cornucopias above **Rev:** Head of Bolivar left with square mint mark, 7-sided outline surrounds **Edge:** Reeded and Plain sections

Date	Mintage	F	VF	XF	Unc	BU
1999	—	—	—	—	1.50	2.00

Y# 48.1 1000 BOLIVARES
33.4370 g., 0.9000 Gold .9676 oz. AGW, 34 mm. **Subject:** Conservation Series - Cock of the Rocks **Obv:** National arms above ribbon, plants flank, cornucopias above **Rev:** Bird on branch

Date	Mintage	F	VF	XF	Unc	BU
1975(I)	5,047	—	—	—	675	725
1975(I) Proof	483	Value: 1,250				

Y# 48.2 1000 BOLIVARES
33.4370 g., 0.9000 Gold .9676 oz. AGW, 34 mm. **Subject:** Conservation Series - Cock of the Rocks **Obv:** National arms above ribbon, plants flank, cornucopias above **Rev:** Bird on branch with smooth wings

Date	Mintage	F	VF	XF	Unc	BU
1975(I)	Inc. above	—	—	—	700	800

Y# 68 1100 BOLIVARES
27.0000 g., 0.9250 Silver .8029 oz. ASW **Subject:** Ibero - American Series **Obv:** Arms at center within legend, 13 shields surround **Rev:** Statue

Date	Mintage	F	VF	XF	Unc	BU
1991(mm) Proof	30,000	Value: 60.00				

Y# 59 3000 BOLIVARES
31.1000 g., 0.9000 Gold .9000 oz. AGW **Subject:** 200th Anniversary - Birth of Simon Bolivar **Obv:** Building **Rev:** Bookshelves back of 3/4 figure looking left

Date	Mintage	F	VF	XF	Unc	BU
ND(1983)(w) Proof	10,000	Value: 685				

Y# 62 5000 BOLIVARES
15.5500 g., 0.9000 Gold .4500 oz. AGW, 27 mm. **Obv:** National arms above ribbon, plants flank, cornucopias above **Rev:** Bust of Bolivar 3/4 left, dates below

Date	Mintage	F	VF	XF	Unc	BU
1988(cc) Proof	25,000	Value: 315				

Y# 63 5000 BOLIVARES
15.5500 g., 0.9000 Gold .4500 oz. AGW, 27 mm. **Obv:** National arms above ribbon, plants flank, cornucopias above **Rev:** Bust of Bolivar facing, dates below

Date	Mintage	F	VF	XF	Unc	BU
1988(cc) Proof	25,000	Value: 315				

Y# 65 5000 BOLIVARES
15.5500 g., 0.9000 Gold .4500 oz. AGW, 27 mm. **Obv:** National arms above ribbon, plants flank, cornucopias above **Rev:** Head of Bolivar left, dates below

Date	Mintage	F	VF	XF	Unc	BU
1990(mm) Proof	10,000	Value: 325				

Y# 73 5000 BOLIVARES
15.5500 g., 0.9000 Gold .4500 oz. AGW, 27 mm. **Subject:** 200th Anniversary - Sucre's Birth **Obv:** National arms above ribbon, plants flank, cornucopias above **Rev:** Bust of Bolivar looking left, dates below

Date	Mintage	F	VF	XF	Unc	BU
1995(cc) Proof	10,000	Value: 325				

Y# 61 10000 BOLIVARES
31.1000 g., 0.9000 Gold .9000 oz. AGW, 35 mm. **Obv:** National arms above ribbon, plants flank, cornucopias above **Rev:** Head of Bolivar right **Rev. Designer:** Albert Barre

Date	Mintage	F	VF	XF	Unc	BU
1987(c) Proof	50,000	Value: 635				

ESSAIS

KM#	Date	Mintage	Identification	Mkt Val
E26	1991(c)	—	1300 Bolivares. Copper. M1, thin planchet	—
E27	1991(c)	—	1300 Bolivares. Copper. M1, thick planchet.	—
E18	1991(c)	—	1300 Bolivares. 0.9000 Copper. M1, thick planchet.	—

PATTERNS

Including off metal strikes

KM#	Date	Mintage	Identification	Mkt Val
Pn46-47	1973(m)	—	5 Bolivares. Nickel.	700
Pn48	1977(w)	—	25 Centimos. Nickel.	100
Pn49	1977(m)	—	5 Bolivares. Nickel.	200
Pn50	1981(w)	—	100 Bolivares. Silver. Y57, with LEY.	400
Pn51	1990(c)	—	50 Bolivares. Lead.	500
Pn52	1990(c)	—	50 Bolivares. Silver.	600
Pn53	1990(c)	—	50 Bolivares. Gold. Medal rotation	650
Pn54	1990(c)	—	50 Bolivares. Gold. Coin rotation.	650
Pn55	1990(c)	—	50 Bolivares. Gold.	1,100
Pn56	1990	—	5000 Bolivares. Copper-Nickel. Y65.	2,000

TRIAL STRIKES

KM#	Date	Mintage	Identification	Mkt Val
TS9	1977	—	10 Bolivares. 0.9000 Silver. Uniface reverse.	1,000
TS10	1973(c)	—	10 Bolivares. Silver. 2 obverses.	400
TS11	1975(c)	—	500 Bolivares. Gold plated; Uniface obverse.	15,000
TS12	1975(c)	—	500 Bolivares. Gold plated; Uniface reverse.	15,000
TS13	1977(m)	—	5 Bolivares. Nickel. Uniface obverse.	200
TS14	1990(c)	—	50 Bolivares. Copper. Y66, uniface obverse.	600
TS15	1990(c)	—	50 Bolivares. Copper. Y66, uniface reverse.	600
TS16	1990(c)	—	50 Bolivares. Bronze. Y66, uniface obverse.	600
TS17	1990(c)	—	50 Bolivares. Bronze. Y66, uniface reverse.	600
TS18	1990(c)	—	50 Bolivares. Silver. Y66, uniface obverse.	1,000
TS19	1990(c)	—	50 Bolivares. Silver. Y#66. Uniface.	600
TS20	1990(d)	—	50 Bolivares. Copper. Y67, uniface obverse.	600
TS21	1990(c)	—	50 Bolivares. Copper. Y67, uniface reverse.	600

KM#	Date	Mintage	Identification	Mkt Val
TS22	1991	—	1100 Bolivares. Silver. Arms at center within legend, 13 shields surround. Y68, uniface obverse.	650

KM#	Date	Mintage	Identification	Mkt Val
TS23	ND (1991)	—	1100 Bolivares. Silver. Statue, two dates at right. Y68, uniface reverse.	650

KM#	Date	Mintage	Identification	Mkt Val
TS24	1991(c)	—	1300 Bolivares. Copper. Numbers on and below shield, text below. Y79, uniface obverse.	350

KM#	Date	Mintage	Identification	Mkt Val
TS25	1991(c)	—	1300 Bolivares. Copper. Two busts facing. Y79, uniface reverse.	350
TS26	1991(c)	—	1300 Bolivares. Silver. Y79, uniface obverse.	450
TS27	1991(c)	—	1300 Bolivares. Silver. Y79, uniface reverse.	450

PRIVATE PATTERNS

KM#	Date	Mintage	Identification	Mkt Val
PPn1	1930	—	5 Bolivares. 0.9000 Silver. Cornucopias flank shielded arms, ribbon below, date above. Bust facing. Gomez, Bayer Hauptmunzamt, incuse lettered inscription on edge.	7,000

Note: Prepared by Karl Goetz. Later strikes and uniface trial strikes with original dies in various metals exist, as do modern fabrications. Mulings with Goetz German patterns exist but are possible modern restrikes or reproductions, refer to Unusual World Coins for detailed listings

KM#	Date	Mintage	Identification	Mkt Val
PPn2	1973(c)	—	10 Bolivares. Silver. Arms within inset at left, legend and denomination at right. Head left within inset, name below, dates at left.	800
PPn3	1973(c)	—	10 Bolivares. Silver. Double obverse similar to KM45.	600

PRIVATE TRIAL STRIKES

KM#	Date	Mintage	Identification	Mkt Val
PTS1	1973	—	10 Bolivares. Gilt Copper center. Uniface obverse similar to KM45. (TS2)	300
PTS2	1973	—	10 Bolivares. Gilt Copper. Uniface reverse similar to KM45. (TS3)	500

LEPER COLONIES

CABO BLANCO

In the late 1600's the Hospital de Lazarinos was built in Hoyada, outside of Caracas for the care and confinement of those suffering from leprosy. Early in the 1900's this hospital was relocated to Maiquetia, also near Caracas and became known as Cabo Blanco. The hospital remained in use until the early 1970's and coins were struck in 1936 for patient use within the confines of this institution.

LEPROSARIUM COINAGE

KM# L11 0.05 BOLIVAR (5 Centimos)
Brass **Note:** Prev. KM#10.

Date	Mintage	VG	F	VF	XF	Unc
1936	—	3.00	6.00	10.00	20.00	—

KM# L12 0.12-1/2 BOLIVAR (12-1/2 Centimos)
Brass **Note:** Prev. KM#L11.

Date	Mintage	VG	F	VF	XF	Unc
1936	—	20.00	40.00	60.00	100	—

KM# L13 0.50 BOLIVAR (50 Centimos)
Brass **Note:** Prev. KM#L12.

Date	Mintage	VG	F	VF	XF	Unc
1936	—	30.00	50.00	90.00	120	—

KM# L14 BOLIVAR
Brass **Note:** Prev. KM#L13.

Date	Mintage	VG	F	VF	XF	Unc
1936	—	50.00	85.00	150	250	—

KM# L15 2 BOLIVARES
Brass **Note:** Prev. KM#L14.

Date	Mintage	VG	F	VF	XF	Unc
1936	—	60.00	100	165	270	—

KM# L16 5 BOLIVARES
Brass **Note:** Prev. KM#L15.

Date	Mintage	VG	F	VF	XF	Unc
1936	—	80.00	140	220	375	—

KM# L17 10 BOLIVARES
Brass **Note:** Prev. KM#L16.

Date	Mintage	VG	F	VF	XF	Unc
1936	—	120	200	320	500	—

KM# L18 20 BOLIVARES
Brass **Note:** Prev. KM#L17.

Date	Mintage	VG	F	VF	XF	Unc
1936	—	175	300	500	900	—

ISLA DE PROVIDENCIA

Between 1916 and 1939 the name of Burro Island was changed to Isla de Providencia and the name of the colony was redesignated to match this new title. One series of coins for colony commerce use only was issued in 1939 under the name Leproserias Nacionales Isla De Providencia.

LEPROSARIUM COINAGE

KM# L19 0.05 BOLIVAR (5 Centimos)
Brass **Note:** Prev. KM#L20.

Date	Mintage	VG	F	VF	XF	Unc
1939	—	2.00	4.00	8.00	16.00	—

KM# L20 0.12-1/2 BOLIVAR (12-1/2 Centimos)
Brass **Note:** Prev. KM#L21.

Date	Mintage	VG	F	VF	XF	Unc
1939	—	2.50	5.00	8.00	16.00	—

KM# L20a 0.12-1/2 BOLIVAR (12-1/2 Centimos)
Copper-Nickel **Note:** Prev. KM#L21a.

Date	Mintage	VG	F	VF	XF	Unc
1939 Rare	—	—	—	—	—	—

KM# L21 0.50 BOLIVAR (50 Centimos)
Brass **Note:** Prev. KM#L22.

Date	Mintage	VG	F	VF	XF	Unc
1939	—	20.00	40.00	75.00	125	—

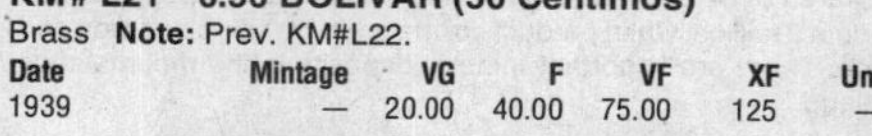

KM# L22 BOLIVAR
Brass **Note:** Prev. KM#L23.

Date	Mintage	VG	F	VF	XF	Unc
1939	—	25.00	50.00	90.00	150	—

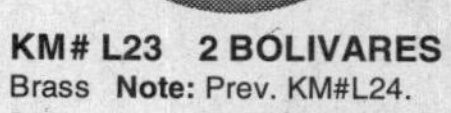

KM# L23 2 BOLIVARES
Brass **Note:** Prev. KM#L24.

Date	Mintage	VG	F	VF	XF	Unc
1939	—	30.00	60.00	110	185	—

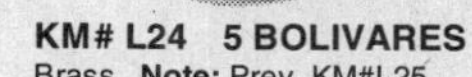

KM# L24 5 BOLIVARES
Brass **Note:** Prev. KM#L25.

Date	Mintage	VG	F	VF	XF	Unc
1939	—	40.00	85.00	165	275	—

KM# L25 10 BOLIVARES
Brass **Note:** Prev. KM#L26.

Date	Mintage	VG	F	VF	XF	Unc
1939	—	—	—	—	—	—

Note: Reported, not confirmed; According to records, coins with the 10 Bolivares denomination were authorized to be struck, but at present none are known to exist in the numismatic community

MARACAIBO LAZARETO NACIONAL

In 1826 Simon Bolivar authorized the establishment of Lazareto Maracaibo on Burro Island in Lake Maracaibo. Over time this became a large leper colony maintained by the Venezuelan Government, where hundreds of people suffering from Hansen's disease were cared for. To provide a monetary system and prevent regular coinage, handled by lepers, to re-circulate in the general population, the Venezuelan Government created a special currency. These coins had value only on the island until 30 years ago, when the illness was almost fully extinguished in South America and medical research revealed that little risk.was involved in handling these coins. The first issues under the name Lazareto Nacional Maracaibo were struck in the late 1880's and the final series was issued in 1916.

LEPROSARIUM COINAGE

KM# L10 5 CENTIMOS
Brass **Note:** Prev. KM#L8.

Date	Mintage	VG	F	VF	XF	Unc
1916	—	3.00	6.00	10.00	20.00	—

KM# L3 1/8 BOLIVAR
Brass **Note:** Prev. KM#L1.

Date	Mintage	VG	F	VF	XF	Unc
1913	—	3.50	7.00	12.00	25.00	—
1916	—	20.00	40.00	80.00	135	—

KM# L3a 1/8 BOLIVAR
Copper Nickel **Note:** Prev. KM#L1a.

Date	Mintage	VG	F	VF	XF	Unc
1913	—	7.00	15.00	25.00	50.00	—

KM# L4 1/2 BOLIVAR
Brass **Note:** Similar to 1/8 Bolivar KM#L5. Prev. KM#L2.

Date	Mintage	VG	F	VF	XF	Unc
1913	—	20.00	35.00	75.00	125	—
1916	—	35.00	65.00	140	250	—

KM# L5 BOLIVAR
Brass **Note:** Prev. KM#L3.

Date	Mintage	VG	F	VF	XF	Unc
1913	—	20.00	30.00	45.00	75.00	—
1916	—	25.00	40.00	55.00	90.00	—

KM# L6 2 BOLIVARES
Brass **Obv:** Similar to 20 Bolivares, KM#L9 **Note:** Prev. KM#L4.

Date	Mintage	VG	F	VF	XF	Unc
1913	—	25.00	40.00	60.00	100	—
1916	—	35.00	50.00	70.00	120	—

KM# L7 5 BOLIVARES
Brass **Note:** Similar to 1/8 Bolivar, KM#L3. Prev. KM#L5.

Date	Mintage	VG	F	VF	XF	Unc
1913	—	55.00	100	175	275	—
1916	—	85.00	120	200	350	—

KM# L8 10 BOLIVARES

Brass **Note:** Similar to 1/8 Bolivar, KM#L3. Prev. KM#L6.

Date	Mintage	VG	F	VF	XF	Unc
1913	—	60.00	120	200	350	—
1916	—	90.00	180	300	500	—

KM# L9 20 BOLIVARES

Brass **Rev:** Similar to 2 Bolivares, KM#L6 **Note:** Prev. KM#L7.

Date	Mintage	VG	F	VF	XF	Unc
1913	—	175	275	500	800	—
1916	—	250	350	600	1,000	—

VIET NAM

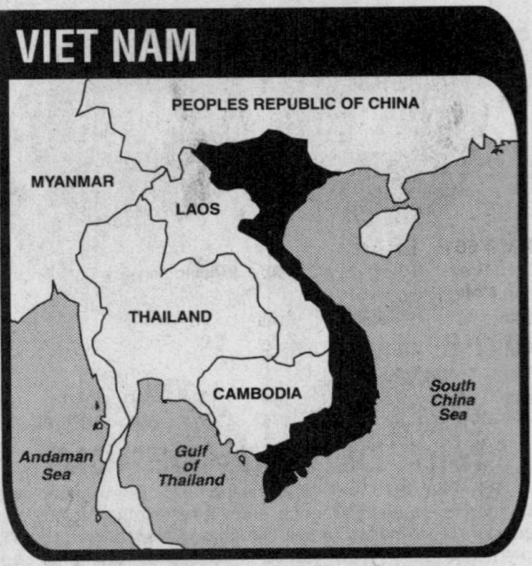

In 207 B.C. a Chinese general set up the Kingdom of Nam-Viet on the Red River. This kingdom was over-thrown by the Chinese under the Han Dynasty in 111 B.C., where upon the country became a Chinese province under the name of Giao-Chi, which was later changed to Annam or peaceful or pacified South. Chinese rule was maintained until 968, when the Vietnamese became independent until 1407 when China again invaded Viet Nam. The Chinese were driven out in 1428 and the country became independent and named Dai-Viet. Gia Long united the North and South as Dai Nam in 1802.

After the French conquered Dai Nam, they split the country into three parts. The South became the Colony of Cochin china; the North became the Protectorate of Tonkin; and the central became the Protectorate of Annam. The emperors were permitted to have their capital in Hue and to produce small quantities of their coins, presentation pieces, and bullion bars. Annam had an area of 57,840 sq. mi. (141,806 sq. km.) and a population of about 6 million. Chief products of the area are silk, cinnamon and rice. There are important mineral deposits in the mountainous inland.

EMPERORS

Thanh Thai, 1888-1907	成泰
Duy Tan, 1907-1916	維新
Khai Dinh, 1916-1925	啓定
Bao Dai, 1926-1945	保大

IDENTIFICATION

Khai 啓

寳 Bao

通 Thong

Dinh 定

CYCLICAL DATES

	庚	辛	壬	癸	甲	乙	丙	丁	戊	己
戌	1850 1910		1862 1922		1874 1934		1886 1946		1838 1898	
亥		1851 1911		1863 1923		1875 1935		1887 1947		1839 1899
子	1840 1900		1852 1912		1864 1924		1876 1936		1888 1948	
丑		1841 1901		1853 1913		1865 1925		1877 1937		1889 1949
寅	1830 1890		1842 1902		1854 1914		1866 1926		1878 1938	
卯		1831 1891		1843 1903		1855 1915		1867 1927		1879 1939
辰	1880 1940		1832 1892		1844 1904		1856 1916		1868 1928	
巳		1881 1941		1833 1893		1845 1905		1857 1917		1869 1929
午	1870 1930		1882 1942		1834 1894		1846 1906		1858 1918	
未		1871 1931		1883 1943		1835 1895		1847 1907		1859 1919
申	1860 1920		1872 1932		1884 1944		1836 1896		1848 1908	
酉		1861 1921		1873 1933		1885 1945		1837 1897		1849 1909

NOTE: This table has been adapted from *Chinese Bank Notes* by Ward Smith and Brian Matravers.

Cyclical dates consist of a pair of characters one of which indicates the animal associated with that year. Every 60 years, this pair of characters is repeated. The first character of a cyclical date corresponds to a character in the first row of the chart above. The second character is taken from the column at left. In this catalog where a cyclical date is used, the abbreviation CD appears before the A.D. date.

Annamese silver and gold coins were sometimes dated according to the year of the emperor's reign. In this case, simply add the year of reign to the year in which the reign would be 1849 (1847 plus 3 = 1850 -1 = 1849 or 1847 = 1; 1848 = 2; 1849 = 3). In this catalog the A.D. date appears in parenthesis followed by the year of reign.

NUMERALS

NUMBER	CONVENTIONAL	FORMAL	COMMERCIAL
1	一 元	壹 弌	〡
2	二	弍 貳	〢
3	三	叁 弎	〣
4	四	肆	〤
5	五	伍	〥
6	六	陸	〦
7	七	柒	〧
8	八	捌	〨
9	九	玖	〩
10	十	拾 什	十
20	十 二 or 廿	拾貳	〢十
25	五 十 二 or 五廿	伍拾貳	〢十〥
30	十 三 or 卅	拾叁	〣十
100	百 一	佰壹	〡百
1,000	千 一	仟壹	〡千
10,000	萬 一	萬壹	〡万
100,000	萬十 億一	萬拾 億壹	十万
1,000,000	萬百一	萬佰壹	〡百万

NOTE: This table has been adapted from *Chinese Bank Notes* by Ward Smith and Brian Matravers.

MONETARY SYSTEM

10 Dong (zinc) = 1 Dong (copper)
600 Dong (zinc) = 1 Quan (string of ¬¬cash)
Approx. 2600 Dong (zinc) = 1 Piastre

NOTE: Ratios between metals changed frequently, therefore the above is given as an approximate relationship.

SILVER and GOLD

2-1/2 Quan = 1 Lang
10 Tien (Mace) = 1 Lang (Tael)
14 to 17 Piastres (silver) = 1 Piastre (gold)
14 to 17 Lang (silver) = 1 Lang (gold)

The real currency of Dai Nam and An Nam consisted of copper and zinc coins similar to Chinese cash-style coins and were called sapeques and dongs by the French.

The smaller gold pieces saw a limited circulation, mainly among the local merchants and foreign traders. The larger gold pieces were used mainly for hoarding, while most of these were intended as rewards and gifts. Many of these gold pieces appear to have been struck from silver coin dies or vice-versa.

NOTE: Sch# are in reference to Albert Schroeder's *Annam, Etudes Numismatiques* or to the same numbering system used in *Gold and Silver Coins of Annam"*, by Bernard Permar and John Novak.

CHARACTER IDENTIFICATION

The Vietnamese used Chinese-style characters for official documents and coins and bars. Some were modified to their liking and will sometimes not match the Chinese character for the same word. The above identification and this table will translate most of the Vietnamese characters (Chinese-style) on their coins and bars described herein.

Chinese/French
Vietnamese/English

An Nam = name of the French protectorate

Dai Nam = name of the country under Gia Long's Nguyen dynasty

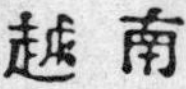

Viet Nam = name used briefly during Minh Mang's reign and became the modern name of the country

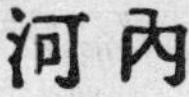

Ha Noi = city and province in north Dai NamTonkin

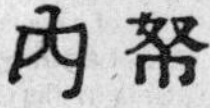

Noi Thang = court treasury in the capital of Hue

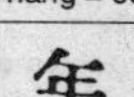

Nien = year

Tao = made

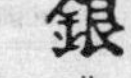

Ngan = silver

Kim = gold

Tien = a weight of about 3.78 grams

Lang = a weight of about 37.78 grams

Quan = a string of cash-style coins

Phan = a weight of about .38 grams

Van = cash-style coins

中平

Trung Binh = a name of weight standard

FRENCH PROTECTORATE OF ANNAM

CAST COINAGE

KM# 654 PHAN
Cast Copper Alloys **Ruler:** Khai Dinh **Obv. Inscription:** "Khai Dinh Thong Bao" **Note:** Prev. Y#4.

Date	Mintage	Good	VG	F	VF	XF
ND(1916-25)	—	5.50	9.00	15.00	25.00	—

KM# 661 PHAN
Cast Brass **Ruler:** Bao Dai **Obv. Inscription:** Bao-dai Thong bao **Note:** Prev. Y#6a.

Date	Mintage	Good	VG	F	VF	XF
ND(1926-45)	—	2.50	5.00	7.50	12.50	—

KM# 652 10 VAN
Cast Brass **Ruler:** Duy Tan **Obv. Inscription:** "Duy Tan Thong Bao" **Rev. Inscription:** "10 Van" **Note:** Prev. Y#3.

Date	Mintage	Good	VG	F	VF	XF
ND(1907-16)	—	0.50	0.75	1.25	2.50	—

KM# 664 10 VAN
Copper Alloys **Ruler:** Bao Dai **Obv. Inscription:** "Bao Dai Thong Bao" **Rev. Inscription:** "10 Van" **Note:** Prev. Y#7.

Date	Mintage	Good	VG	F	VF	XF
ND(1926-45)	—	2.00	3.50	7.50	12.50	—

X# 31 15 VAN
9.2200 g., Cast Copper, 33.1 mm. **Obv. Inscription:** Thanh Dinh Trung Bao **Rev:** Plain

Date	Mintage	F	VF	XF	Unc	BU
ND(1916-25)	—	7.50	12.50	—	—	—

MILLED COINAGE

Brass

KM# 656 PHAN
Brass **Ruler:** Khai Dinh **Obv:** Characters slightly different **Obv. Inscription:** "Khai Dinh Thong Bao" **Note:** Prev. Y#5.2.

Date	Mintage	Good	VG	F	VF	XF
ND(1916-25)	—	2.00	3.50	6.00	10.00	—

KM# 655 PHAN
Brass **Ruler:** Khai Dinh **Obv. Inscription:** "Khai Dinh Thong Bao" **Note:** Uniface. Prev. Y#5.1.

Date	Mintage	Good	VG	F	VF	XF
ND(1916-25)	—	1.75	2.75	4.50	7.50	—

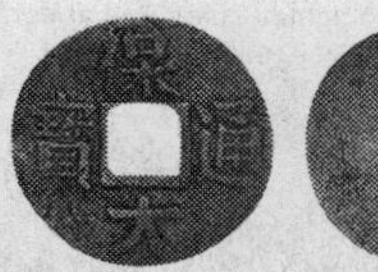

KM# 662 PHAN
Copper Alloys, 18 mm. **Ruler:** Bao Dai **Obv. Inscription:** "Bao Dai Thong Bao" **Note:** Prev. Y#6.

Date	Mintage	Good	VG	F	VF	XF
ND(1926-45)	—	2.50	5.00	7.50	12.50	—

BULLION SILVER BARS

All of the bars described here are inscribed with their weight, except the 10 Lang banana bars, and many contain a date or the name of the province in which they were made.

KM# 658 LANG
Silver **Ruler:** Khai Dinh **Note:** Date on edge. Weight unknown.

Date	Mintage	VG	F	VF	XF	Unc
CD1919	—	75.00	125	185	275	—

KM# 659 LANG
Silver **Ruler:** Khai Dinh **Note:** Date on edge. Weight unknown.

Date	Mintage	VG	F	VF	XF	Unc
CD1922	—	75.00	125	185	275	—

REBEL COMMUNIST STATE

MILLED COINAGE

KM# 1 20 XU
Aluminum **Ruler:** Bao Dai **Obv:** Star, date below **Obv. Legend:** VIET NAM DAN CHU CHONG HOA **Rev:** Denomination **Rev. Inscription:** 20 XU

Date	Mintage	F	VF	XF	Unc	BU
1945(v)	—	40.00	125	175	250	—

KM# 2.1 5 HAO
Aluminum **Obv:** Ceremonial pot **Obv. Legend:** VIET-NAM DAN-CHU CONG-HAO **Rev:** Value incused in star **Rev. Inscription:** 5 HAO

Date	Mintage	F	VF	XF	Unc	BU
1946(v)	—	4.00	10.00	20.00	60.00	—

Note: Commonly encountered with rotated dies

KM# 2.2 5 HAO
Aluminum **Obv:** Ceremonial pot **Obv. Legend:** VIET-NAM DAN-CHU CONG-HOA **Rev:** Value raised in star

Date	Mintage	F	VF	XF	Unc	BU
1946(v)	—	—	30.00	100	200	—

KM# 3 DONG
Aluminum **Obv:** Head right **Obv. Legend:** VIET-NAM DAN-CHU

CONG-HOA **Rev:** Value to right of spray **Rev. Inscription:** 1 DONG

Date	Mintage	F	VF	XF	Unc	BU
1946(v)	—	15.00	35.00	85.00	160	—

KM# 4 2 DONG

Bronze **Obv:** Bust of Ho Chi Minh 3/4 facing **Obv. Legend:** CHU TICH HO MIHN **Rev:** Value above and below in wreath, Nam II at bottom **Rev. Legend:** VIET-NAM DAN CHU CONG HOA **Rev. Inscription:** HAI DONG **Note:** Varieties exist.

Date	Mintage	F	VF	XF	Unc	BU
1946(v)	—	7.50	15.00	40.00	100	—

NORTH VIET NAM

INDEPENDENT COMMUNIST STATE

PRESENTATION COINAGE

KM# A5 10 VIET

4.1625 g., 0.9000 Gold 0.1205 oz. AGW, 17 mm. **Obv:** Head of Ho Chi Minh right **Obv. Legend:** "CHU-TICH HO-CHI-MINH" **Rev:** Denomination above grain sheaves **Rev. Legend:** "VIET-NAM DAN-CHU CONG-HOA" **Rev. Inscription:** 10 Viet

Date	Mintage	F	VF	XF	Unc	BU
1948(v)	—	—	—	250	350	400

KM# B5 20 VIET

8.3250 g., 0.9000 Gold 0.2409 oz. AGW, 21 mm. **Obv:** Head of Ho Chi Minh right **Obv. Legend:** "CHU-TICH HO-CHI-MINH" **Rev:** Denomination above grain sheaves **Rev. Legend:** "VIET-NAM DAN-CHU CONG-HOA" **Rev. Inscription:** "20 VIET"

Date	Mintage	F	VF	XF	Unc	BU
1948(v)	—	—	—	400	500	550

KM# C5 50 VIET

16.6500 g., 0.9000 Gold 0.4818 oz. AGW, 29 mm. **Obv:** Head of Ho Chi Minh right **Obv. Legend:** "CHU-TICH HO-CHI-MINH" **Rev:** Denomination above grain sheaves **Rev. Legend:** "VIET-NAM DAN-CHU CONG-HOA" **Rev. Inscription:** "50 VIET"

Date	Mintage	F	VF	XF	Unc	BU
1948(v)	—	—	—	600	700	750

REFORM COINAGE

KM# 5 XU

Aluminum **Obv:** Center hole within arms **Obv. Legend:** "NUOC VIET NAM DAN CHU CONG HOA" **Rev:** Center hole divides date and denomination **Rev. Legend:** "NGAN HANG QUOC GIA VIET NAM" **Rev. Inscription:** Value: "MOT XU"

Date	Mintage	F	VF	XF	Unc	BU
1958(s)	—	1.25	2.50	5.00	8.00	—

KM# 6 2 XU

Aluminum **Obv:** Center hole within arms **Obv. Legend:** "NUOC VIET NAM DAN CHU CONG HOA" **Rev:** Center hole divides denomination and date **Rev. Legend:** "NGAN HANG QUOC GIA VIET NAM" **Rev. Inscription:** Value: "HAI XU"

Date	Mintage	F	VF	XF	Unc	BU
1958(s)	—	1.50	3.00	6.00	10.00	—

KM# 7 5 XU

Aluminum **Obv:** Center hole within arms **Obv. Legend:** "NUOC VIET NAM DAN CHU CONG HOA" **Rev:** Center hole divides denomination and date **Rev. Legend:** "NGAN HANG QUOC GIA VIET NAM" **Rev. Inscription:** Value: "NAM XU"

Date	Mintage	F	VF	XF	Unc	BU
1958(s)	—	2.00	4.00	8.00	15.00	—

PATTERNS

Including off metal strikes

KM#	Date	Mintage	Identification	Mkt Val
Pn1	1946(v)	—	5 Dong. Bronze. VIET NAM DAN CHU CONG HOA.	—

SOCIALIST REPUBLIC

SOCIALIST REPUBLIC

STANDARD COINAGE

KM# 11 HAO

Aluminum **Obv:** Arms **Rev:** Spray divides denomination **Rev. Legend:** "NGAN HANG NHA NUOC VIET NAM" **Rev. Inscription:** "1 HAO"

Date	Mintage	F	VF	XF	Unc	BU
1976(s)	—	1.25	2.50	5.00	10.00	—

KM# 12 2 HAO

Aluminum **Obv:** Arms **Rev:** Spray divides denomination **Rev. Legend:** "NGAN HANG NHA HUOC VIET NAM" **Rev. Inscription:** "2 HOA"

Date	Mintage	F	VF	XF	Unc	BU
1976(s)	—	1.25	2.50	5.00	10.00	—

KM# 13 5 HAO

Aluminum **Obv:** Arms **Rev:** Denomination above ornament

Date	Mintage	F	VF	XF	Unc	BU
1976	—	1.50	3.00	6.00	12.00	—

KM# 14 DONG

Aluminum **Obv:** Arms **Rev:** Ornaments flank thick denomination **Rev. Legend:** "NGAN HANG NHA NUOC VIET NAM" **Rev. Inscription:** "1 DONG"

Date	Mintage	F	VF	XF	Unc	BU
1976(s)	—	4.00	8.00	16.00	35.00	—

KM# 36a 5 DONG

8.7700 g., 0.9000 Silver .2538 oz. ASW **Obv:** Arms **Obv. Legend:** "CONG HOA XA HOI CHU NGHIA VIET NAM" **Obv. Inscription:** "5 DONG" **Rev:** Mythological bird - Phoenix flying right **Rev. Inscription:** "CHIM PHUONG"

Date	Mintage	F	VF	XF	Unc	BU
1989(L) Proof	—	Value: 12.50				

KM# 36 5 DONG

Brass **Obv:** Arms **Obv. Legend:** "CONG HOA XA HOI CHU NGHIA VIET NAM" **Obv. Inscription:** "5 DONG" **Rev:** Mythological bird - Phoenix flying right **Rev. Legend:** "CHIM PHUONG" **Note:** KM#36 and 36a were minted in the Leningrad (St. Petersburg) Mint (L) as gifts to the Vietnamese government and were not circulated. KM#36a was available in boxed sets of three, with KM#38a and 40a, and KM#36 and 36a were also available as encapsulated individual pieces.

Date	Mintage	F	VF	XF	Unc	BU
1989(L) Proof	—	Value: 10.00				

KM# 15 10 DONG

Copper-Nickel **Subject:** Nature **Obv:** Arms **Obv. Legend:** "CONG HOA XA HOI CHU NGHIA VIET NAM" **Rev:** Water buffalo head left, "TRAU" below **Rev. Legend:** "BAO VE THIEN NHIEM"

Date	Mintage	F	VF	XF	Unc	BU
1986(h)	5,000	—	—	—	14.00	20.00

KM# 16 10 DONG

Copper-Nickel **Subject:** Nature **Obv:** Arms **Obv. Legend:** "CONG HOA XA HOI CHU NGHIA VIET NAM" **Rev:** Peacock head right, "CONG" below **Rev. Legend:** "BAO VE THIEN NHIEN"

Date	Mintage	F	VF	XF	Unc	BU
1986(h)	5,000	—	—	—	14.00	20.00

KM# 17 10 DONG

Copper-Nickel **Subject:** Nature **Obv:** Arms **Obv. Legend:** "CONG HOA XA HOI CHU NGHIA VIET NAM" **Rev:** Elephant head left, "VOI" below **Rev. Legend:** "BAO VE THIEM NHIEN"

Date	Mintage	F	VF	XF	Unc	BU
1986(h)	5,000	—	—	—	17.50	25.00

KM# 28 10 DONG

Copper-Nickel **Subject:** Wildlife Preservation **Obv:** Arms **Obv. Legend:** "CONG HOA XA HOI CHU NGHIA VIET NAM" **Rev:** Orangutan with logo **Rev. Legend:** "BAO VE THIEM NHIEN, DUOI UOI"

Date	Mintage	F	VF	XF	Unc	BU
1987(h)	22,000	—	—	—	20.00	25.00

KM# 37.1 10 DONG

11.3100 g., Copper-Nickel, 30 mm. **Obv:** Arms **Obv. Legend:**

"CONG HOA XA HOI CHU NGHIA VIET NAM" **Rev:** Dragon ship **Rev. Legend:** "THUYEN CO." **Edge:** Plain

Date	Mintage	F	VF	XF	Unc	BU
1988(h)	—	—	—	—	8.50	10.00

KM# 37.2 10 DONG

29.7500 g., Copper, 38 mm. **Obv:** State emblem **Rev:** Asian Dragon Ship **Edge:** Plain

Date	Mintage	F	VF	XF	Unc	BU
1988(h)	—	—	—	—	10.00	11.50

KM# 38 10 DONG

Brass **Obv:** Arms **Obv. Legend:** "CONG HOA XA HOI CHU NGHIA VIET NAM" **Rev:** One-pillar Pagoda above water and legend **Rev. Legend:** "CHUA MOT COT-HANOI" **Note:** KM#38 and 38a were minted in the Leningrad (St. Petersburg) Mint (L) as gifts to the Vietnamese government and were not circulated. KM#38a was available in boxed sets of three, with KM#36a and 40a, and KM#38 and 38a were also available as encapsulated individual pieces.

Date	Mintage	F	VF	XF	Unc	BU
1989(L) Proof	—	Value: 7.00				

KM# 27 10 DONG

Copper-Nickel **Subject:** Soccer - Italy **Obv:** Arms **Obv. Legend:** "CONG HOA XA HOI CHU NGHIA VIET NAM" **Rev:** Soccer player **Rev. Legend:** "GIAI BONGDA THE GIOI"

Date	Mintage	F	VF	XF	Unc	BU
1989(h)	—	—	—	—	10.00	12.00

KM# 38a 10 DONG

0.9000 Silver **Obv:** Arms **Obv. Legend:** "CONG HOA XA HOI CHU NGHIA VIET NAM" **Rev:** One-pillar Pagoda above water and legend **Rev. Legend:** "CHUA MOT COT-HANOI"

Date	Mintage	F	VF	XF	Unc	BU
1989(L) Proof	—	Value: 20.00				

KM# 33 10 DONG

Copper-Nickel **Obv:** Arms **Obv. Legend:** "CONG HOA XA HOI CHU NGHIA VIET NAM" **Rev:** Crested Gibbons **Rev. Legend:** "BAO VE THIEM NHIEN, DUOI UOI"

Date	Mintage	F	VF	XF	Unc	BU
1990(h)	20,000	—	—	—	35.00	50.00

KM# 39 10 DONG

Copper-Nickel **Obv:** Arms **Obv. Legend:** "CONG HOA XA HOI CHU NGHIA VIET NAM" **Rev:** Steam and sailship - Savannah **Rev. Legend:** "THUYEN CO SAVANNAH"

Date	Mintage	F	VF	XF	Unc	BU
1991(h)	—	—	—	—	8.50	10.00

KM# 46 10 DONG

Copper **Series:** World Cup Soccer **Obv:** Arms **Obv. Legend:** "CONG HOA XA HOI CHU NGHIA VIET NAM" **Rev:** Soccer player and U.S. Capitol **Rev. Legend:** "CUP BONG DA THE GIOI LAN THU XV, HOA KY"

Date	Mintage	F	VF	XF	Unc	BU
1992(h)	—	—	—	—	6.50	8.50

KM# 44 10 DONG

Copper-Nickel **Series:** Prehistoric Animals **Obv:** Arms **Obv. Legend:** "CONG HOA XA HOI CHU NGHIA VIET NAM" **Rev:** Diplodocus **Rev. Legend:** "DONG VAT CO DAI"

Date	Mintage	F	VF	XF	Unc	BU
1993(h)	—	—	—	—	22.00	30.00

KM# 49 10 DONG

Copper-Nickel **Subject:** World Food Summit **Obv:** Arms **Obv. Legend:** "CONG HOA XA HOI CHU NGHIA VIET NAM" **Rev:** Rice harvesting scene, logo above **Rev. Legend:** "MOI NGHI THUONG DINH THE GIOI VE LUOIN THUC"

Date	Mintage	F	VF	XF	Unc	BU
1996(h)	—	—	—	—	6.00	8.00

KM# 40a 20 DONG

0.9000 Silver **Obv:** Arms **Obv. Legend:** "CONG HOA XA HOI CHU NGHIA VIET NAM" **Rev:** Head left, dates at right **Rev. Legend:** "HO CHI MINH"

Date	Mintage	F	VF	XF	Unc	BU
1989(L) Proof	—	Value: 37.50				

KM# 40 20 DONG

Brass **Subject:** 100th Anniversary - Birth of Ho Chi Minh **Obv:** Arms **Obv. Legend:** "CONG HOA XA HOI CHU NGHIA VIET NAM" **Rev:** Head left, dates at right **Rev. Legend:** "HO CHI MINH" **Edge:** Nikolay Nosov **Note:** KM#40 and 40a were minted in the Leningrad (St. Petersburg) Mint (L) as gifts to the Vietnamese government and were not circulated. KM#40a was available in boxed sets of three, with KM#36a and 38a, and KM#40 and 40a were also available as encapsulated individual pieces.

Date	Mintage	F	VF	XF	Unc	BU
1989(L) Proof	—	Value: 14.50				

KM# 18 100 DONG

12.0000 g., 0.9990 Silver .3855 oz. ASW **Obv:** Arms **Obv. Legend:** "CONG HOA XA HOI CHU NGHIA VIET NAM" **Rev:** Junk under sail **Rev. Legend:** "VIETNAM, THUYEN BUOM"

Date	Mintage	F	VF	XF	Unc	BU
1986(h)	2,000	—	—	—	35.00	50.00

KM# 19 100 DONG

12.0000 g., 0.9990 Silver .3855 oz. ASW **Subject:** Wildlife **Obv:** Arms **Obv. Legend:** "CONG HOA XA HOI CHU NGHIA VIET NAM" **Rev:** Water buffalo right looking left **Rev. Legend:** "BAO VE THIEN KHIEN, TRAU"

Date	Mintage	F	VF	XF	Unc	BU
1986(h)	5,000	—	—	—	32.50	45.00

KM# 20 100 DONG

12.0000 g., 0.9990 Silver .3855 oz. ASW **Subject:** Wildlife **Obv:** Arms **Obv. Legend:** "CONG HOA XA HOI CHU NGHIA VIET NAM" **Rev:** Peacock left **Rev. Legend:** "BAO VE THIEN NHIEN, CONG"

Date	Mintage	F	VF	XF	Unc	BU
1986(h)	5,000	—	—	—	27.50	35.00

KM# 21 100 DONG

12.0000 g., 0.9990 Silver .3855 oz. ASW **Subject:** Wildlife **Obv:** Arms **Obv. Legend:** "CONG HOA XA HOI CHU NGHIA VIET NAM" **Rev:** Elephant walking right **Rev. Legend:** "BAO VI THIEN NHIEN, VOI"

Date	Mintage	F	VF	XF	Unc	BU
1986(h)	5,000	—	—	—	45.00	60.00

KM# 22 100 DONG

12.0000 g., 0.9990 Silver .3855 oz. ASW **Subject:** 100 Years of the Automobile **Obv:** Arms **Obv. Legend:** "CONG HOA XA HOI CHU NGHIA VIET NAM" **Rev:** Jaguar 3/4 left **Rev. Legend:** "100 NAN XE O TO A DOI, 1886-1986"

Date	Mintage	F	VF	XF	Unc	BU
1986(h)	2,000	—	—	—	35.00	50.00

KM# 23 100 DONG
6.0000 g., 0.9990 Silver .1927 oz. ASW **Series:** Calgary Olympics **Obv:** Arms **Obv. Legend:** "CONG HOA XA HOI CHU NGHIA VIET NAM" **Rev:** Skier **Rev. Legend:** "THE VAN HOI O-LIM-PIC MUA DONG XV, GAN-GA-RAY 1986"

Date	Mintage	F	VF	XF	Unc	BU
1986(h)	3,700	—	—	—	27.50	35.00

KM# 24 100 DONG
12.0000 g., 0.9990 Silver .3855 oz. ASW **Series:** Seoul Olympics **Obv:** Arms **Obv. Legend:** "CONG HOA XA HOI CHU NGHIA VIET NAM" **Rev:** Fencer **Rev. Legend:** "THE VAN HOI O LIM PIC MUA HE"

Date	Mintage	F	VF	XF	Unc	BU
1986(h)	10,000	—	—	—	10.00	12.00

KM# 29 100 DONG
12.0000 g., 0.9990 Silver .3855 oz. ASW **Subject:** Soccer - Mexico **Obv:** Arms **Obv. Legend:** "CONG HOA XA HOI CHU NGHIA VIET NAM" **Rev:** Soccer player **Rev. Legend:** "GIAI VO DICH BONG DA THE GIOI LAM THU XIII, ME HI CO"

Date	Mintage	F	VF	XF	Unc	BU
1986(h)	2,000	—	—	—	27.50	35.00

KM# 25.1 100 DONG
15.9900 g., 0.9800 Silver .5039 oz. ASW **Obv:** Arms **Obv. Legend:** "CONG HOA XA HOI CHU NGHIA VIET NAM" **Rev:** Suphanna hong (dragon ship) **Rev. Legend:** "THUYEN CO"

Date	Mintage	F	VF	XF	Unc	BU
1988(h)	3,000	—	—	—	20.00	22.50
1988(h) Proof	—	Value: 27.50				

KM# 25.2 100 DONG
15.9900 g., 0.9800 Silver .5039 oz. ASW **Obv:** Arms **Obv. Legend:** "CONG HOA XA HOI CHU NGHIA VIET NAM" **Rev:** Dragon ship **Rev. Legend:** "THUYEN CO"

Date	Mintage	F	VF	XF	Unc	BU
1988(h)	—	Value: 27.50				

KM# 26 100 DONG
12.0000 g., 0.9990 Silver .3855 oz. ASW **Subject:** Soccer - 1988 **Obv:** Arms **Obv. Legend:** "CONG HOA XA HOI CHU NGHIA VIET NAM" **Rev:** Soccer players **Rev. Legend:** "GIAI BONG DA CHAU AU, CONG HOA LIEN BANG DUCTHUYENCO."

Date	Mintage	F	VF	XF	Unc	BU
1988(h)	1,500	—	—	—	27.50	35.00

KM# 30 100 DONG
16.0000 g., 0.9990 Silver .5145 oz. ASW **Subject:** Soccer - Italy **Obv:** Arms **Obv. Legend:** "CONG HOA XA HOI CHU NGHIA VIET NAM" **Rev:** Soccer player **Rev. Legend:** "GIAI BONG DA THE GIOI, I-TA-LI-A"

Date	Mintage	F	VF	XF	Unc	BU
1989(h) Proof	10,000	Value: 28.50				

KM# 31 100 DONG
16.0000 g., 0.9990 Silver .5145 oz. ASW **Series:** Summer Olympics **Subject:** Rowing **Obv:** Arms **Obv. Legend:** "CONG HOA XA HOI CHU NGHIA VIET NAM" **Rev:** Six people rowing **Rev. Legend:** "THE VAN HOI LAN THU XXV, BARCELONA 1992"

Date	Mintage	F	VF	XF	Unc	BU
1989(h) Proof	10,000	Value: 25.00				

KM# 32 100 DONG
16.0000 g., 0.9990 Silver .5145 oz. ASW **Series:** Winter Olympics **Subject:** Hockey **Obv:** Arms **Obv. Legend:** "CONG HOA XA HOI CHU NGHIA VIET NAM" **Rev:** Hockey players **Rev. Legend:** "THE VAN HOI MUA DONG XVI, ALBERTVILLE 1992"

Date	Mintage	F	VF	XF	Unc	BU
1990(h) Proof	10,000	Value: 40.00				

KM# 34 100 DONG
12.0000 g., 0.9990 Silver .3858 oz. ASW **Subject:** Soccer **Obv:** Arms **Obv. Legend:** "CONG HOA XA HOI CHU NGHIA VIET NAM" **Rev:** Soccer players within design **Rev. Legend:** "CUP BONG DA THE FIOI LAN THU XV, HOA KY 1994"

Date	Mintage	F	VF	XF	Unc	BU
1991(h)	—	—	—	—	22.50	25.00

KM# 35 100 DONG
16.0000 g., 0.9990 Silver .5145 oz. ASW **Obv:** Arms **Obv. Legend:** "CONG HOA XA HOI CHU NGHIA VIET NAM" **Rev:** Steamship Savannah **Rev. Legend:** "THUYEN CO SAVANNAH"

Date	Mintage	F	VF	XF	Unc	BU
1991(h) Proof	—	Value: 35.00				

KM# 70 100 DONG
19.9000 g., 0.9990 Silver 0.6392 oz. ASW, 38.1 mm. **Obv:** Arms **Rev:** Soccer player with U.S. Capital building in background **Edge:** Reeded

Date	Mintage	F	VF	XF	Unc	BU
1992 Proof	—	Value: 25.00				

KM# 42 100 DONG
16.0000 g., 0.9990 Silver .5145 oz. ASW **Series:** Prehistoric Animals **Obv:** Arms **Obv. Legend:** "CONG HOA XA HOI CHU NGHIA VIET NAM" **Rev:** Rhamphorhynchus **Rev. Legend:** "DONG VAT CO DAI"

Date	Mintage	F	VF	XF	Unc	BU
1993(h) Proof	—	Value: 60.00				

KM# 43 100 DONG
16.0000 g., 0.9990 Silver .5145 oz. ASW **Obv:** Arms **Obv. Legend:** "CONG HOA XA HOI CHU NGHIA VIET NAM" **Rev:** Elephants **Rev. Legend:** "BAO VI THIEN NHIEN - VOI"

Date	Mintage	F	VF	XF	Unc	BU
1993(h) Proof	—	Value: 40.00				

KM# 45 100 DONG
16.0000 g., 0.9990 Silver .5145 oz. ASW **Series:** Prehistoric Animals **Obv:** Arms **Obv. Legend:** "CONG HOA XA HOI CHU NGHIA VIET NAM" **Rev:** Edaphosaurus **Rev. Legend:** "DONG VAT CO DAI"

Date	Mintage	F	VF	XF	Unc	BU
1994(h) Proof	—	Value: 50.00				

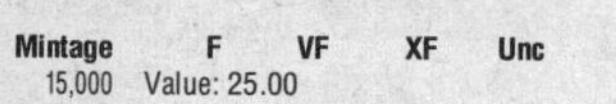

KM# 47 100 DONG
20.0000 g., 0.9990 Silver .6424 oz. ASW **Series:** Olympics **Obv:** Arms **Obv. Legend:** "CONG HOA XA HOI CHU NGHIA VIET NAM" **Rev:** Gymnast on pommel horse **Rev. Legend:** "TU ATEN DEN ATLANTA"

Date	Mintage	F	VF	XF	Unc	BU
1995(h) Proof	15,000	Value: 25.00				

KM# 48 100 DONG
20.0000 g., 0.9990 Silver And Enamel .6424 oz. **Obv:** Arms **Obv. Legend:** "CONG HOA XA HOI CHU NGHIA VIET NAM" **Rev:** Caracal **Rev. Legend:** "THU AN THIT/CARACAL CARACAL"

Date	Mintage	F	VF	XF	Unc	BU
1996(h) Proof	—	Value: 60.00				

KM# 50 100 DONG
20.0000 g., 0.9990 Silver And Enamel .6430 oz. **Subject:** World Food Summit **Obv:** Arms **Obv. Legend:** "CONG HOA XA HOI CHU NGHIA VIET NAM" **Rev:** Rice harvesting scene, logo above **Rev. Legend:** "HOI NGHI THUONG DINH THE GIOI VE LUONG THUC"

Date	Mintage	F	VF	XF	Unc	BU
1996(h) Proof	—	Value: 40.00				

KM# 60 100 DONG
16.0000 g., 0.9990 Silver 0.5139 oz. ASW, 38 mm. **Subject:** UNICEF **Obv:** Arms **Rev:** Child on water buffalo **Edge:** Reeded

Date	Mintage	F	VF	XF	Unc	BU
1997 Proof	25,000	Value: 20.00				

KM# 41 500 DONG
3.1030 g., 0.9990 Gold 0.0997 oz. AGW **Subject:** 100th Anniversary - Birth of Ho Chi Minh **Obv:** Arms **Obv. Legend:** "CONG HOA XA HOI CHU NGHIA VIET NAM" **Note:** KM#41 were minted at the Havana Mint (h) as "Gift Coins" to the Vietnamese people and were delivered encapsulated and in presentation boxes. This piece is cataloged as A24 and illustrated in Gunter Schon's World Coins Catalogue.

Date	Mintage	F	VF	XF	Unc	BU
1989(L)	—	—	—	—	350	500

KM# 54 5000 DONG
1.2441 g., 0.9999 Gold .0400 oz. AGW, 13.92 mm. **Subject:** Year of the Dragon **Obv:** Arms **Obv. Legend:** "CONG HOA XA HOI CHU NGHIA VIET NAM" **Rev:** Dragon with radiant sun **Rev. Legend:** "RONG VIET NAM" **Edge:** Reeded

Date	Mintage	F	VF	XF	Unc	BU
2000(S)	—	Value: 40.00				

KM# 51 10000 DONG
20.0000 g., 0.9250 Silver .5948 oz. ASW, 38.7 mm. **Subject:** Year of the Dragon **Obv:** Arms **Obv. Legend:** "CONG HOA XA HOI CHU NGHIA VIET NAM" **Rev:** Dragon with radiant sun **Edge:** Reeded

Date	Mintage	F	VF	XF	Unc	BU
2000(S) Proof	10,000	Value: 35.00				

KM# 52 10000 DONG
20.0000 g., 0.9250 Silver .5948 oz. ASW, 38.7 mm. **Subject:** Year of the Dragon **Obv:** Arms **Obv. Legend:** "CONG HOA XA HOI CHU NGHIA VIET NAM" **Rev:** Multicolor dragon **Rev. Legend:** "RONG VIET NAM" **Edge:** Reeded

Date	Mintage	F	VF	XF	Unc	BU
2000(S) Proof	10,000	Value: 35.00				

KM# 53 10000 DONG
20.0000 g., 0.9250 Silver .5948 oz. ASW, 38.7 mm. **Subject:** Year of the Dragon **Obv:** Arms **Obv. Legend:** "CONG HOA XA HOI CHU NGHIA VIET NAM" **Rev:** Two dragons **Edge:** Reeded

Date	Mintage	F	VF	XF	Unc	BU
2000(S) Proof	10,000	Value: 35.00				

KM# 55 20000 DONG
7.7749 g., 0.9999 Gold .2500 oz. AGW, 22 mm. **Subject:** Year of the Dragon **Obv:** Arms **Obv. Legend:** "CONG HOA XA HOI CHU NGHIA VIET NAM" **Rev:** Dragon and clouds **Rev. Legend:** "RONG VIET NAM" **Edge:** Reeded

Date	Mintage	F	VF	XF	Unc	BU
2000(S) Proof	1,800	Value: 225				

KM# 56 50000 DONG
15.5518 g., 0.9999 Gold .5000 oz. AGW, 27 mm. **Subject:** Year of the Dragon **Obv:** Arms **Obv. Legend:** "CONG HOA XA HOI CHU NGHIA VIET NAM" **Rev:** Dragon before radiant sun **Rev. Legend:** "RONG VIET NAM" **Edge:** Reeded

Date	Mintage	F	VF	XF	Unc	BU
2000(S) Proof	3,800	Value: 375				

PATTERNS

KM#	Date	Mintage	Identification	Mkt Val
Pn1	1976(s)	—	Hao. Silver. Arms. "NGAN HANG NHA NUOC VIET NAM". KM#11	—
Pn2	1976(s)	—	Dong. Silver. Arms. "NGAN HANG NHA NUOC VIET NAM". KM#14	—

PIEFORTS

KM#	Date	Mintage	Identification	Mkt Val
PE1	1990(h)	110	Dong. Silver. KM#32	150

MINT SETS

KM#	Date	Mintage	Identification	Issue Price	Mkt Val
MS1	1958-1976(s) (7)	—	KM#5-7, Democratic Republic; KM#11-14, Socialist Republic	—	85.00
MS2	1975/1976(s) (7)	—	KM#8-14 NOTE: Created and sold by the Bank for Foreign Trade of Viet Nam to tourists and collectors.	—	15.00

PROOF SETS

KM#	Date	Mintage	Identification	Issue Price	Mkt Val
PS1	1989(L) (3)	—	KM#36a, 38a, 40a	—	75.00
PS2	2000(S) (3)	2,000	KM#51-53	—	100
PS3	2000(S) (2)	800	KM#55-56	—	570

STATE OF SOUTH VIET NAM

DEMOCRATIC STATE

STANDARD COINAGE

KM# 1 10 SU
Aluminum **Obv:** Three conjoined busts left **Obv. Legend:** "QUOC-GIA VIET-NAM" **Rev:** Rice plant (oryza sativa - Gramineae) dividing value **Rev. Legend:** "VIET-NAM"

Date	Mintage	F	VF	XF	Unc	BU
1953(a)	20,000,000	0.50	1.00	2.00	4.00	—

KM# 2 20 SU
Aluminum **Obv:** Three conjoined busts left **Obv. Legend:** "QUOC-GIA VIET-NAM" **Rev:** Rice plant dividing value **Rev. Legend:** "VIET-NAM"

Date	Mintage	F	VF	XF	Unc	BU
1953(a)	15,000,000	0.40	0.75	1.50	3.00	—

KM# 3 50 XU
Aluminum **Obv:** Three busts; 3/4 left, facing and 3/4 right **Obv. Legend:** "QUOC-GIA VIET-NAM" **Rev:** Dragons flank denomination **Rev. Legend:** "VIET-NAM"

Date	Mintage	F	VF	XF	Unc	BU
1953(a)	15,000,000	3.00	6.00	12.00	25.00	—

REPUBLIC OF VIET NAM

STANDARD COINAGE

KM# 4 50 SU
Aluminum **Obv:** Bust of Ngo Dihn Diem left **Obv. Legend:** "VIET-NAM CONG-HOA" **Rev:** Bamboo plants divide denomination
Note: The 1960 50 Su coin was minted by the Paris Mint with the French spelling Su for Xu. The coin was restruck with the correct Xu, a new date of 1963, and is cataloged as KM#6.

Date	Mintage	F	VF	XF	Unc	BU
1960(a)	10,000,000	1.00	2.00	4.00	8.00	—
1960(a) Proof	—	Value: 80.00				

KM# 6 50 XU
Aluminum **Obv:** Bust of Ngo Dihn Diem left **Obv. Legend:** "VIET-NAM CONG-HOA" **Rev:** Bamboo plants divide denomination

Date	Mintage	F	VF	XF	Unc	BU
1963	20,000,000	0.40	0.80	1.50	4.00	—
1963 Proof	—	Value: 80.00				

KM# 5 DONG
Copper-Nickel, 22 mm. **Obv:** Bust of Ngo Dihn Diem left **Obv. Legend:** "VIET-NAM CONG-HAO" **Rev:** Bamboo plants divide denomination

Date	Mintage	F	VF	XF	Unc	BU
1960(a)	105,000,000	0.20	0.50	1.25	2.50	6.50
1960(a) Proof	—	Value: 80.00				

KM# 7 DONG
Copper-Nickel, 22.3 mm. **Obv:** Denomination **Obv. Legend:** "VIET-NAM CONG-HAO" **Rev:** Rice stalks

Date	Mintage	F	VF	XF	Unc	BU
1964	190,000,000	0.20	0.35	0.75	1.50	3.50
1964 Proof	—	—	—	—	—	—

KM# 7a DONG
Nickel-Clad Steel **Obv:** Denomination **Obv. Legend:** "VIET-NAM CONG-HAO" **Rev:** Rice stalks

Date	Mintage	F	VF	XF	Unc	BU
1971	—	0.10	0.15	0.35	1.00	3.00

KM# 12 DONG
Aluminum **Series:** F.A.O. **Obv:** Denomination **Obv. Legend:** "VIET-NAM CONG-HAO" **Rev:** Rice stalks **Rev. Legend:** "TANG-GIA SAN-NUAT LUONG-THUC"

Date	Mintage	F	VF	XF	Unc	BU
1971	30,000,000	0.25	0.50	1.00	2.50	5.50

KM# 9 5 DONG
Copper-Nickel **Obv:** Denomination **Obv. Legend:** "VIET-NAM CONG-HAO" **Rev:** Rice stalks **Rev. Legend:** "NGAN-HANG VIET-NAM CONG-HOA" **Shape:** Scalloped

Date	Mintage	F	VF	XF	Unc	BU
1966	100,000,000	0.25	0.50	1.00	2.00	4.00

KM# 9a 5 DONG
Nickel-Clad Steel **Obv:** Denomination **Obv. Legend:** "VIET-NAM CONG-HAO" **Rev:** Rice stalks **Rev. Legend:** "NGAN-HANG VIET-NAM CONG-HOA"

Date	Mintage	F	VF	XF	Unc	BU
1971	15,000,000	0.40	0.75	1.50	3.00	7.50

KM# 8 10 DONG
Copper-Nickel, 25.5 mm. **Obv:** Denomination **Obv. Legend:** "VIET-NAM CONG-HAO" **Rev:** Rice stalks

Date	Mintage	F	VF	XF	Unc	BU
1964	45,000,000	0.25	0.50	1.00	2.00	6.00

KM# 8a 10 DONG
Nickel-Clad Steel **Obv:** Denomination **Obv. Legend:** "VIET-NAM CONG-HAO" **Rev:** Rice stalks

Date	Mintage	F	VF	XF	Unc	BU
1968	30,000,000	0.25	0.50	1.00	2.00	6.00
1970	50,000,000	0.25	0.50	1.00	2.00	6.00

KM# 13 10 DONG
Brass-Clad Steel, 24 mm. **Series:** F.A.O. **Obv:** Denomination **Obv. Legend:** "VIET-NAM CONG-HAO, NGAN-HUAN QUOC-GIA VIET-NAM" **Rev:** Farmers in rice paddy **Rev. Legend:** "TANG-GIA SAM-XUAT NONG-PHAN"

Date	Mintage	F	VF	XF	Unc	BU
1974	30,000,000	0.25	0.50	1.00	2.00	4.00

KM# 10 20 DONG
Nickel-Clad Steel **Obv:** Denomination **Obv. Legend:** "VIET-NAM CONG-HAO"-**Rev:** Farmer in rice paddy **Rev. Legend:** "NGAN-HANG QUOC-GIA VIET-NAM" **Designer:** Lu'u Tri

Date	Mintage	F	VF	XF	Unc	BU
1968	—	0.75	1.50	3.00	6.00	10.00

KM# 11 20 DONG
Nickel-Clad Steel **Series:** F.A.O. **Obv:** Denomination **Obv. Legend:** "VIET-NAM CONG-HAO" **Rev:** Farmer in rice paddy **Rev. Legend:** "CHIEN-TICH THE-GIOI CHONG NAM DOI" **Shape:** 12-sided **Designer:** Lu'u Tri

Date	Mintage	F	VF	XF	Unc	BU
1968	500,000	1.00	2.00	4.00	8.00	12.00

KM# 14 50 DONG

Nickel Clad Steel **Series:** F.A.O. **Obv:** Denomination **Obv. Legend:** "VIET-NAM CONG-HAO, NGAN-HANG QUOC-GIA VIET-NAM" **Rev:** Farmers in rice paddy **Rev. Legend:** "TANG-GIA SAM-XUAT NONG-PHAN"

Date	Mintage	F	VF	XF	Unc	BU
1975	1,010,000	—	—	400	650	800

Note: It is reported that all but a few examples were disposed of as scrap metal

PEOPLE'S REVOLUTIONARY GOVERNMENT

STANDARD COINAGE

KM# A8 XU

Aluminum **Obv:** Star above center hole, spray below **Obv. Legend:** "NGAN HANG VIET NAM" **Rev:** 1 above center hole, MOT XU below, grain stalks flank

Date	Mintage	F	VF	XF	Unc	BU
ND(1975)	—	1.00	2.50	5.00	12.00	—

KM# A9 2 XU

Aluminum **Obv:** Wreath surrounds center hole, HAI XU below **Obv. Legend:** "NGAN HANG VIET NAM" **Rev:** Ornaments surround center hole, 2 above, XU below ornamentation

Date	Mintage	F	VF	XF	Unc	BU
1975	—	2.00	4.00	7.00	20.00	—

KM# A10 5 XU

Aluminum **Obv:** Denomination below center hole **Obv. Legend:** "NGAN HANG VIET NAM" **Rev:** "NAM XU" above, 5 below in stylized sprays

Date	Mintage	F	VF	XF	Unc	BU
ND(1975)	—	2.00	4.00	9.00	25.00	—

ESSAIS

Standard metals unless otherwise noted

KM#	Date	Mintage	Identification	Issue Price	Mkt Val
E1	1953	1,200	10 Su. Aluminum. KM#1	—	25.00
E2	1953(a)	1,200	20 Su. Aluminum. KM#2	—	30.00
E3	1953(a)	1,200	50 Su. Aluminum. KM#3	—	35.00

PATTERNS

Including off metal strikes

KM#	Date	Mintage	Identification	Mkt Val
Pn1	1963	—	50 Xu. Aluminum-Bronze.	400
Pn2	1963	—	50 Xu. Copper-Nickel.	400

PIEFORTS WITH ESSAI

Standard metals unless otherwise noted

KM#	Date	Mintage	Identification	Issue Price	Mkt Val
PE1	1953(a)	104	10 Su. Aluminum. KM#1	—	200
PE2	1953(a)	104	20 Su. Aluminum. KM#2	—	200
PE3	1953(a)	104	50 Xu. Aluminum. KM#3	—	300

WEST AFRICAN STATES

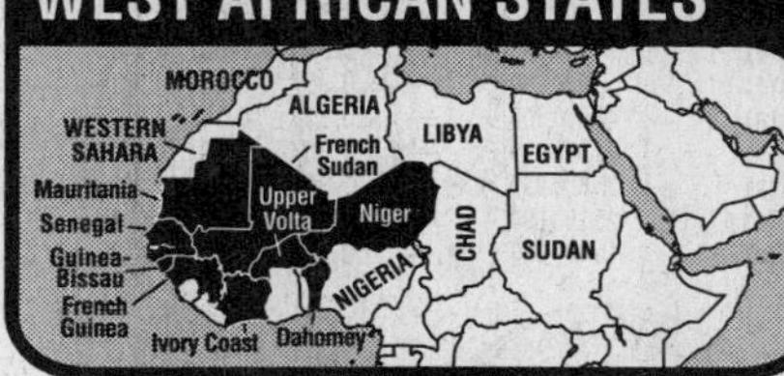

The West African States, a former federation of eight French colonial territories on the northwest coast of Africa, had area of 1,831,079 sq. mi. (4,742,495 sq. km.) and a population of about 17 million. Capital: Dakar. The constituent territories were Mauritania, Senegal, Dahomey, French Sudan, Ivory Coast, Upper Volta, Niger and French Guinea.

The members of the federation were overseas territories within the French Union until Sept. of 1958 when all but French Guinea approved the constitution of the Fifth French Republic, there by electing to become autonomous members of the new French Community. French Guinea voted to become the fully independent Republic of Guinea. The other seven attained independence in 1960. The French West Africa territories were provided with a common currency, a practice which was continued as the monetary union of the West African States which provides a common currency to the autonomous republics of Dahomey (now Benin), Senegal, Upper Volta (now Burkina Faso), Ivory Coast, Mali, Togo and Niger.

For earlier coinage refer to Togo, and French West Africa.

MINT MARKS

(a)- Paris, privy marks only

MONETARY SYSTEM

100 Centimes = 1 Franc

FEDERATION

STANDARD COINAGE

KM# 3.1 FRANC

Aluminum, 23 mm. **Obv:** Taku symbol divides denomination **Rev:** Gazelle head facing (gazella leptoceros - bovidae) **Designer:** G.B.L. Bazor

Date	Mintage	F	VF	XF	Unc	BU
1961(a)	3,000,000	—	0.15	0.30	0.60	0.85
1964(a)	10,500,000	—	0.15	0.30	0.60	0.85
1965(a)	6,000,000	—	0.15	0.30	0.60	0.85
1967(a)	2,500,000	—	0.15	0.30	0.60	0.85
1971(a)	8,000,000	—	0.15	0.30	0.60	0.85
1972(a)	4,000,000	—	0.15	0.30	0.60	0.85
1973(a)	4,500,000	—	0.15	0.30	0.60	0.85
1974(a)	4,500,000	—	0.15	0.30	0.60	0.85
1975(a)	18,000,000	—	0.15	0.30	0.60	0.85

KM# 3.2 FRANC

Aluminum, 23 mm. **Obv:** Taku symbol divides denomination **Rev:** Engraver general's name

Date	Mintage	F	VF	XF	Unc	BU
1962(a)	2,000,000	—	2.00	5.00	10.00	12.00
1963(a)	4,500,000	—	1.50	4.00	7.00	9.00

KM# 8 FRANC

Steel **Obv:** Taku symbol **Rev:** Value and date **Designer:** R. Joly

Date	Mintage	F	VF	XF	Unc	BU
1976(a)	8,000,000	—	—	0.10	0.35	0.60
1977(a)	14,700,000	—	—	0.10	0.35	0.60
1978(a)	21,800,000	—	—	0.10	0.35	0.60
1979(a)	16,600,000	—	—	0.10	0.35	0.60
1980(a)	13,000,000	—	—	0.10	0.35	0.60
1981(a)	2,000,000	—	—	0.10	0.35	0.60
1982(a)	6,000,000	—	—	0.10	0.35	0.60
1984(a)	33,400,000	—	—	0.10	0.35	0.60
1985(a)	26,900,000	—	—	—	—	—
1988(a)	—	—	—	0.10	0.35	0.60
1990(a)	10,000,000	—	—	0.10	0.35	0.60
1991(a)	3,500,000	—	—	0.10	0.35	0.60
1992(a)	6,000,000	—	—	0.10	0.35	0.60
1995(a)	3,000,000	—	—	0.10	0.35	0.60
1996(a)	3,000,000	—	—	0.10	0.35	0.60
1997(a)	1,500,000	—	—	0.10	0.35	0.60
1999(a)	1,000,000	—	—	0.10	0.35	0.60
2000(a)	—	—	—	0.10	0.35	0.60

KM# 2 5 FRANCS

Aluminum-Bronze **Obv:** Taku symbol divides denomination **Rev:** Gazelle head facing **Designer:** G.B.L. Bazor

Date	Mintage	F	VF	XF	Unc	BU
1960(a)	5,000,000	—	0.20	0.40	0.70	1.00

KM# 2a 5 FRANCS

Aluminum-Nickel-Bronze, 20 mm. **Obv:** Taku symbol divides value **Rev:** Gazelle head facing

Date	Mintage	F	VF	XF	Unc	BU
1965(a)	12,500,000	—	0.20	0.40	0.70	1.00
1967(a)	6,500,000	—	0.20	0.40	0.70	1.00
1968(a)	6,000,000	—	0.20	0.45	0.75	1.10
1969(a)	8,000,000	—	0.20	0.40	0.70	1.00
1970(a)	10,005,000	—	0.20	0.40	0.70	1.00
1971(a)	10,000,000	—	0.20	0.40	0.70	1.00
1972(a)	5,000,000	—	0.20	0.40	0.70	1.00
1973(a)	6,000,000	—	0.20	0.45	0.75	1.10
1974(a)	13,326,000	—	0.10	0.15	0.30	0.50
1975(a)	16,840,000	—	0.20	0.40	0.70	1.00
1976(a)	20,010,000	—	0.20	0.30	0.60	0.85
1977(a)	22,000,000	—	0.20	0.30	0.60	0.85
1978(a)	40,000,000	—	0.20	0.30	0.60	0.85
1979(a)	11,000,000	—	0.10	0.20	0.40	0.60
1980(a)	18,000,000	—	0.10	0.20	0.40	0.60
1981(a)	18,000,000	—	0.10	0.20	0.40	0.60
1982(a)	25,000,000	—	0.10	0.20	0.40	0.60
1984(a)	31,700,000	—	0.10	0.20	0.40	0.60
1985(a)	16,000,000	—	0.10	0.20	0.40	0.60
1986(a)	8,000,000	—	0.10	0.20	0.40	0.60
1987(a)	26,500,000	—	0.10	0.20	0.40	0.60
1989(a)	44,500,000	—	0.10	0.20	0.40	0.60
1990(a)	—	—	0.10	0.20	0.40	0.60
1991(a)	19,000,000	—	0.10	0.20	0.40	0.60
1992(a)	—	—	0.10	0.20	0.40	0.60
1993(a)	—	—	0.10	0.20	0.40	0.60
1994(a)	20,000,000	—	0.10	0.20	0.40	0.60
1995(a)	—	—	0.10	0.20	0.40	0.60
1996(a)	21,500,000	—	0.10	0.20	0.40	0.60
1997(a)	18,000,000	—	0.10	0.20	0.40	0.60
1999(a)	36,900,000	—	0.10	0.20	0.40	0.60
2000(a)	—	—	0.10	0.20	0.40	0.60

KM# 1 10 FRANCS

Aluminum-Bronze **Obv:** Taku symbol divides denomination **Rev. Designer:** Gazelle head facing **Designer:** G.B.L. Bazor

Date	Mintage	F	VF	XF	Unc	BU
1959(a)	10,000,000	—	0.15	0.30	0.60	0.85
1964(a)	10,000,000	—	0.20	0.40	0.70	1.00

KM# 1a 10 FRANCS

Aluminum-Nickel-Bronze **Obv:** Taku symbol divides denomination **Rev:** Gazelle head facing

Date	Mintage	F	VF	XF	Unc	BU
1966(a)	6,000,000	—	0.20	0.40	0.70	1.00
1967(a)	3,500,000	—	0.25	0.50	0.90	1.25
1968(a)	6,000,000	—	0.20	0.40	0.70	1.00
1969(a)	7,000,000	—	0.25	0.50	0.90	1.25
1970(a)	7,000,000	—	0.15	0.30	0.60	0.85
1971(a)	8,000,000	—	0.15	0.30	0.60	0.85
1972(a)	5,500,000	—	0.20	0.40	0.70	1.00
1973(a)	3,000,000	—	0.20	0.40	0.70	1.00
1974(a)	10,000,000	—	0.15	0.30	0.60	0.85
1975(a)	17,000,000	—	0.15	0.30	0.60	0.85
1976(a)	18,000,000	—	0.15	0.30	0.60	0.85
1977(a)	11,000,000	—	0.15	0.25	0.50	0.75
1978(a)	21,000,000	—	0.15	0.25	0.50	0.75
1979(a)	11,000,000	—	0.15	0.25	0.50	0.75
1980(a)	16,000,000	—	0.15	0.25	0.50	0.75
1981(a)	12,000,000	—	0.15	0.25	0.50	0.75

KM# 10 10 FRANCS

Brass **Series:** F.A.O. **Obv:** Taku symbol divides value **Rev:** People getting water **Designer:** R. Joly

Date	Mintage	F	VF	XF	Unc	BU
1981(a)	2,000,000	—	0.25	0.50	1.25	1.50

Date	Mintage	F	VF	XF	Unc	BU
1982(a)	23,000,000	—	0.25	0.50	1.25	1.50
1983(a)	6,000,000	—	0.25	0.50	1.25	1.50
1984(a)	10,000,000	—	0.25	0.50	1.25	1.50
1985(a)	5,000,000	—	0.25	0.50	1.25	1.50
1986(a)	7,500,000	—	0.25	0.50	1.25	1.50
1987(a)	28,000,000	—	0.25	0.50	1.25	1.50
1989(a)	40,500,000	—	0.25	0.50	1.25	1.50
1990(a)	18,000,000	—	0.25	0.50	1.25	1.50
1991(a)	18,000,000	—	0.25	0.50	1.25	1.50
1992(a)	5,000,000	—	0.25	0.50	1.25	1.50
1993(a)	4,400,000	—	0.25	0.50	1.25	1.50
1994(a)	19,900,000	—	0.25	0.50	1.25	1.50
1995(a)	3,700,000	—	0.25	0.50	1.25	1.50
1996(a)	33,300,000	—	0.25	0.50	1.25	1.50
1997(a)	38,200,000	—	0.25	0.50	1.25	1.50
1999(a)	33,000,000	—	0.25	0.50	1.25	1.50
2000(a)	6,500,000	—	0.25	0.50	1.25	1.50

KM# 5 25 FRANCS

Aluminum-Bronze, 27 mm. **Obv:** Taku divides denomination **Rev:** Gazelle head facing **Designer:** G.B.L. Bazor

Date	Mintage	F	VF	XF	Unc	BU
1970(a)	7,000,000	—	0.25	0.45	1.00	1.25
1971(a)	7,000,000	—	0.50	0.75	1.25	1.50
1972(a)	2,000,000	—	1.50	2.50	4.50	6.00
1975(a)	5,035,000	—	0.25	0.45	1.00	1.25
1976(a)	3,365,000	—	0.25	0.45	1.00	1.25
1977(a)	3,288,000	—	0.25	0.45	1.00	1.25
1978(a)	6,800,000	—	0.25	0.45	1.00	1.25
1979(a)	5,200,000	—	0.25	0.45	1.00	1.25

KM# 9 25 FRANCS

Aluminum-Bronze, 27 mm. **Series:** F.A.O. **Obv:** Taku symbol divides value **Rev:** Figure filling tube

Date	Mintage	F	VF	XF	Unc	BU
1980(a)	7,800,000	—	0.25	0.75	1.75	2.00
1981(a)	4,000,000	—	0.25	0.75	1.75	2.00
1982(a)	8,000,000	—	0.25	0.75	1.75	2.00
1984(a)	15,300,000	—	0.25	0.75	1.75	2.00
1985(a)	8,587,000	—	0.25	0.75	1.75	2.00
1987(a)	9,000,000	—	0.25	0.75	1.75	2.00
1989(a)	17,600,000	—	0.25	0.75	1.75	2.00
1990(a)	6,000,000	—	0.25	0.75	1.75	2.00
1991(a)	1,700,000	—	0.25	0.75	1.75	2.00
1992(a)	6,000,000	—	0.25	0.75	1.75	2.00
1994(a)	8,200,000	—	0.25	0.75	1.75	2.00
1995(a)	—	—	0.25	0.75	1.75	2.00
1996(a)	18,300,000	—	0.25	0.75	1.75	2.00
1997(a)	22,000,000	—	0.25	0.75	1.75	2.00
1999(a)	16,700,000	—	0.25	0.75	1.75	2.00
2000(a)	16,800,000	—	0.25	0.75	1.75	2.00

KM# 6 50 FRANCS

Copper-Nickel, 21.5 mm. **Series:** F.A.O. **Obv:** Taku symbol **Rev:** Value within mixed sprigs and nuts **Designer:** R. Joly

Date	Mintage	F	VF	XF	Unc	BU
1972(a)	20,000,000	—	0.35	0.50	1.25	1.50
1974(a)	3,000,000	—	0.50	0.75	1.50	1.75
1975(a)	9,000,000	—	0.25	0.40	1.00	1.25
1976(a)	6,002,000	—	0.35	0.50	1.25	1.50
1977(a)	4,832,000	—	0.35	0.50	1.25	1.50
1978(a)	7,200,000	—	0.35	0.50	1.25	1.50
1979(a)	4,200,000	—	0.35	0.50	1.25	1.50
1980(a)	7,200,000	—	0.35	0.50	1.25	1.50
1981(a)	6,000,000	—	0.35	0.50	1.25	1.50
1982(a)	12,000,000	—	0.35	0.50	1.25	1.50
1984(a)	25,500,000	—	0.35	0.50	1.25	1.50
1985(a)	4,120,000	—	0.35	0.50	1.25	1.50
1986(a)	—	—	0.35	0.50	1.25	1.50
1987(a)	10,000,000	—	0.35	0.50	1.25	1.50
1989(a)	17,000,000	—	0.35	0.50	1.25	1.50
1990(a)	7,500,000	—	0.35	0.50	1.25	1.50
1991(a)	5,600,000	—	0.35	0.50	1.25	1.50
1992(a)	7,000,000	—	0.35	0.50	1.25	1.50
1993(a)	2,800,000	—	0.35	0.50	1.25	1.50
1995(a)	40,000,000	—	0.35	0.50	1.25	1.50
1996(a)	20,500,000	—	0.35	0.50	1.25	1.50
1997(a)	25,800,000	—	0.35	0.50	1.25	1.50
1999(a)	25,200,000	—	0.35	0.50	1.25	1.50
2000(a)	14,400,000	—	0.35	0.50	1.25	1.50

KM# 4 100 FRANCS

Nickel, 26 mm. **Obv:** Taku symbol **Rev:** Value within flower wreath **Designer:** R. Joly

Date	Mintage	F	VF	XF	Unc	BU
1967(a)	—	—	0.75	1.00	2.50	3.00
1968(a)	25,000,000	—	0.75	1.00	2.50	3.00
1969(a)	25,000,000	—	0.75	1.00	2.50	3.00
1970(a)	4,510,000	—	0.80	1.50	3.50	5.00
1971(a)	12,000,000	—	0.50	0.75	1.85	2.25
1972(a)	5,000,000	—	0.60	0.85	2.00	2.50
1973(a)	5,000,000	—	0.60	0.85	2.00	2.50
1974(a)	8,500,000	—	0.60	0.75	1.85	2.25
1975(a)	16,000,000	—	0.60	0.75	1.85	2.25
1976(a)	11,575,000	—	0.60	0.75	1.85	2.25
1977(a)	6,200,000	—	0.60	0.75	1.85	2.25
1978(a)	12,000,000	—	0.60	0.75	1.85	2.25
1979(a)	12,400,000	—	0.60	0.85	2.00	2.50
1980(a)	13,000,000	—	0.60	0.75	2.00	2.50
1981(a)	8,000,000	—	0.60	0.75	2.00	2.50
1982(a)	18,000,000	—	0.60	0.75	2.00	2.50
1984(a)	2,500,000	—	0.65	0.85	2.25	2.75
1985(a)	1,460,000	—	0.65	0.85	2.25	2.75
1987(a)	9,000,000	—	0.65	0.85	2.25	2.75
1989(a)	16,500,000	—	0.65	0.85	2.25	2.75
1990(a)	6,500,000	—	0.65	0.85	2.25	2.75
1991(a)	1,000,000	—	0.65	0.85	2.25	2.75
1992(a)	4,000,000	—	0.65	0.85	2.25	2.75
1996(a)	24,000,000	—	0.65	0.85	2.25	2.75
1997(a)	69,000,000	—	0.65	0.85	2.25	2.75
2000(a)	1,800,000	—	0.60	0.85	2.25	2.75

KM# 13 250 FRANCS

Bi-Metallic Brass center in Copper-Nickel ring **Obv:** Map on globe, Taku symbol at top **Rev:** Stalks behind denomination, circle surrounds

Date	Mintage	F	VF	XF	Unc	BU
1992(a)	9,000,000	—	1.75	2.75	7.00	8.00
1993(a)	10,000,000	—	1.75	2.75	7.00	8.00
1996(a)	7,500,000	—	2.00	3.00	8.00	9.00

KM# 7 500 FRANCS

25.0000 g., 0.9000 Silver .7234 oz. ASW **Subject:** 10th Anniversary of Monetary Union **Obv:** Gold weight in the shape of a fish, "Taku", a symbol of prosperity **Rev:** Shields of seven states and script form circle around denomination and date **Designer:** R. Joly

Date	Mintage	F	VF	XF	Unc	BU
1972(a)	100,000	—	—	17.50	40.00	42.50
1972(a) Prooflike	2,000	—	—	—	—	75.00

KM# 11 5000 FRANCS

24.9500 g., 0.9000 Silver .7220 oz. ASW **Subject:** 20th Anniversary of Monetary Union **Obv:** Gold weight in the shape of a fish, "Taku", a symbol of prosperity **Rev:** Six interlaced birds symbolizing states **Designer:** R. Joly

Date	Mintage	F	VF	XF	Unc	BU
1982(a)	200,000	—	—	15.00	45.00	52.00

KM# 12 5000 FRANCS

14.4900 g., 0.9000 Gold .4193 oz. AGW **Subject:** 20th Anniversary of Monetary Union **Obv:** Gold weight in the shape of a fish, "Taku", a symbol of prosperity **Rev:** Six interlaced birds symbolizing states **Designer:** R. Joly

Date	Mintage	F	VF	XF	Unc	BU
1982(a)	—	—	—	—	400	485

ESSAIS

KM#	Date	Mintage	Identification	Issue Price	Mkt Val
E1	1959(a)	—	10 Francs. Aluminum-Bronze. KM1.	—	17.00
E2	1960(a)	—	5 Francs. Aluminum-Bronze. KM2.	—	15.00
E3	1961(a)	—	Franc. Aluminum. KM3.	—	15.00
E4	1967(a)	1,600	100 Francs. Nickel. KM4.	—	20.00
E4a	1967(a)	100	100 Francs. Silver. KM4.	—	110
E4b	1967(a)	21	100 Francs. Gold. KM4.	—	750
E5	1970(a)	1,450	25 Francs. Aluminum-Bronze. KM5.	—	17.00
E6	1972(a)	1,750	50 Francs. Copper-Nickel. KM6.	—	15.00
E6a	1972(a)	120	50 Francs. Silver. KM6.	—	80.00
E6b	1972(a)	17	50 Francs. Gold. KM6.	—	700
E7	1972(a)	1,300	500 Francs. Silver. KM7.	—	45.00
E8	1976(a)	1,900	Franc. Steel. KM8.	—	15.00

KM#	Date	Mintage	Identification	Issue Price	Mkt Val
E9	1980(a)	3,000	25 Francs. Aluminum-Bronze. Figure filling tube, date above. KM9.	—	15.00
E10	1980(a)	5	25 Francs. Gold.	—	1,800
E11	1980(a)	1,700	500 Francs.	—	40.00
E12	1981(a)	1,950	10 Francs. Brass. KM10.	—	12.00
E13	1982(a)	1,700	5000 Francs. Silver. KM11.	—	85.00
E14	1982(a)	12	5000 Francs. Gold. KM11.	—	1,500

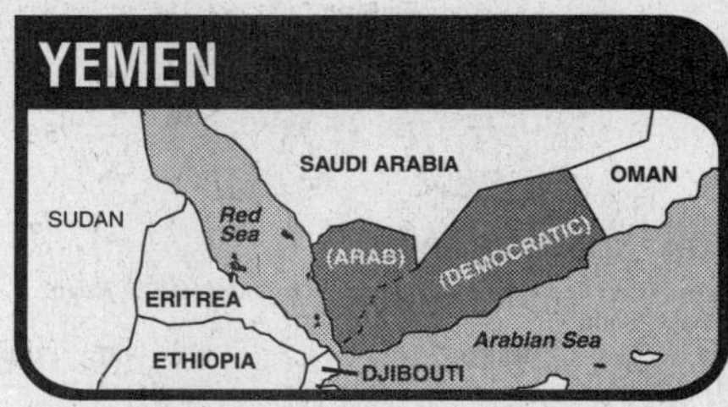

One of the oldest centers of civilization in the Middle East, Yemen was once part of the Minaean Kingdom and of the ancient Kingdom of Sheba, after which it was captured successively by Egyptians, Ethiopians and Romans. It was converted to Islam in 628 A.D. and administered as a caliphate until 1538, when it came under Ottoman occupation in 1849. The second Ottoman occupation which began in 1872 was maintained until 1918 when autonomy was achieved through revolution.

TITLE

المملكة المتوكلية اليمنية

al-Mamlaka(t) al-Mutawakkiliya(t) al-Yamaniya(t)

RULER

Ottoman, until 1625

QASIMID IMAMS

al-Mansur Muhammad bin Yahya,
(Imam Mansur) AH1307-1322/1890-1904AD
al Hadi al-Hasan bin Yahya
(Counter Imam, in Sa'da) AH1322/1904AD
al-Mutawakkil Yahya bin Muhammad
(Imam Yahya) AH1322-1367/1904-1948AD
al-Nasir Ahmad bin Yahya,
(Imam Ahmad) AH1367-1382/
1948-1962AD
al-Badr Muhammad bin Ahmad,
(Imam Badr) AH1382-1388/
1962-1968AD (mostly in exile)

MINT NAME

San'a

MONETARY SYSTEM

After Accession of Iman Yahya
AH1322/1904AD
1 Zalat = 1/160 Riyal
2 Zalat = 1 Halala = 1/80 Riyal
2 Halala = 1 Buqsha = 1/40 Riyal
40 Buqsha = 1 Riyal

NOTE:The Riyal was called an IMADI (RIYAL) during the reign of Imam Yahya "Imadi" honorific name for Yahyawi and an AHMADI (RIYAL) during the reign of Imam Ahmad. The 1 Zalat, Y#2.1, D1, A3, A4 and all Imam Yahya gold strikes except Y#F10, bear no indication of value. Many of the Mutawakkilite coins after AH1322/1904AD bear the denomination expressed as fraction of the Riyal as follows.

BRONZE and ALUMINUM

Thumn ushr = 1/80 Riyal = 1/2 Buqsha = 1 Halala
Rub ushr = 1/40 Riyal = 1 Buqsha
Nisf ushr = 1/20 Riyal = 2 Buqsha = 1/2 Bawlah
Nisf thumn = 1/16 Riyal = 2-1/2 Buqsha
Ushr = 1/10 Riyal = 4 Buqsha = 1 Bawlah
Thumn = 1/8 Riyal = 5 Buqsha
Rub = 1/4 Riyal = 10 Buqsha
Nisf = 1/2 Riyal = 20 Buqsha
1 Riyal (Imadi, Ahmadi) = 40 Buqsha

DATING

All coins of Imam Yahya have accession date AH1322 on obverse and actual date of issue on reverse. All coins of Imam Ahmad bear accession date AH1367 on obverse and actual date on reverse.

If not otherwise noted, all coins of Imam Yahya and Imam Ahad as well as the early issues of the Republic (Y#20 through Y#A25 and Y#32), were struck at the mint in Sana'a. The Sana'a Mint was essentially a medieval mint, using hand-cut dies and crudely machined blanks. There is a large amount of variation from one die to the next in arrangement of legends and ornaments, form of crescents, number of stars, size of the circle, etc., and literally hundreds of subtypes could be identified. Types are divided only when there are changes in the inscriptions, or major variations in the basic type, such as the presence or absence of "Rabb al-Alamin" in the legend or the position of the word *Sana* (= year) in relation to the year.

NOTE: All "ZALAT" coins are without mint name or denomination.

al-Mansur Muhammad bin Yahya (Imam Mansur)

AH1307-1322 / 1890-1904AD

Coins for this ruler were struck at Qaflat Idhar. Harf and Kabir strikes have similar inscriptions with varieties in position of date, legend arrangements and ornamentation. No indication of denomination on coins.

HAMMERED COINAGE

KM# 403 HARF

Bronze **Note:** Similar to 1 Kabir, KM#410.

Date	Mintage	Good	VG	F	VF	XF
AH1320	—	—	—	—	—	—

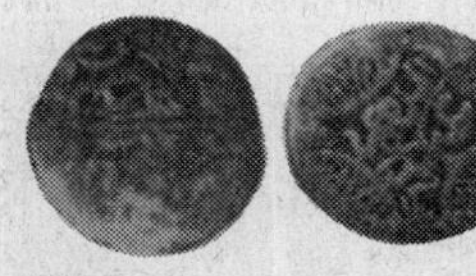

KM# 410 KABIR

Silver, 15-16 mm. **Obv:** Similar to KM#409 **Rev:** "Allah/Abd/" date, divided by ornament, wtih four circular segments **Note:** Weight varies: 0.60-1.00 gram. Size varies. Varieties with three and four stars on reverse exist. Varieties of planchet thickness exist.

Date	Mintage	Good	VG	F	VF	XF
AH1319	—	15.00	30.00	50.00	150	—
AH1320	—	15.00	30.00	50.00	150	—
AH1321	—	15.00	30.00	50.00	150	—

al Hadi al-Hasan

AH1322 / 1904AD

MILLED COINAGE

Y# C1 HALALA

1.9300 g., Bronze **Obv:** Al-Hasan/bin Yahya/Sana 1322 **Rev:** Al-Hadi/Li-din Allah

Date	Mintage	Good	VG	F	VF	XF
AH1322	—	—	—	—	—	—

al-Mutawakkil Yahya bin Muhammad (Imam Yahya)

AH1322-1367 / 1904-1948AD

MILLED COINAGE

Y# 1.1 ZALAT

Bronze **Obv:** Inscription in three lines above accession date AH1322 **Edge:** Plain **Note:** Weight varies: 0.90-1.60 grams. Obverse varieties with no stars or two stars. Reverse with eight stars. Size of inner circle varies, various planchet thicknesses.

Date	Mintage	Good	VG	F	VF	XF
AH1341	—	15.00	30.00	100	160	—
AH1342	—	5.00	12.00	30.00	50.00	—
AH1343	—	4.00	10.00	20.00	40.00	—
Note: 1343 also known with seven stars						
AH1344	—	5.00	12.00	30.00	50.00	—
Note: 1344 also exists with traces of reeded edges						
AH1345	—	10.00	25.00	75.00	125	—
AH1346	—	4.00	10.00	20.00	40.00	—

Y# 1.2 ZALAT

Bronze **Obv:** Inscription in two lines above accession date AH1322

Date	Mintage	Good	VG	F	VF	XF
AH1342	—	5.00	12.00	30.00	50.00	—

Note: Obverse varieties with 1, 2, and 4 stars, and reverse with 8, 11, 12, 13, 14, 15, 16, 17, 20, and 22 stars exist; Some specimens show traces of reeded edges; Various planchet thicknesses exist

Y# 1.4 ZALAT

Bronze **Obv:** Crescent below accession date AH1322

Date	Mintage	Good	VG	F	VF	XF
AH1342	—	300	425	650	1,000	—

Note: Varieties exist with 11, 14, 15, 16, and 17 stars on reverse and with 1, 2, and 4 stars on obverse; Various planchet thicknesses

Y# 1.7 ZALAT

Bronze **Obv:** Inscription in three lines above accession date AH1322 **Rev:** Date in margin at bottom

Date	Mintage	Good	VG	F	VF	XF
AH1342 Rare	—	—	—	—	—	—

Note: Obverse varieties with 1 and 2 stars, Reverse with 11 stars, various planchet thicknesses

Y# 1.8 ZALAT

Bronze **Obv:** Inscription in three lines above accession date AH1322

Date	Mintage	Good	VG	F	VF	XF
AH1344	—	—	—	—	—	—

Y# B1 ZALAT

Bronze **Obv:** Inscription in two lines above accession date AH1322 **Note:** Probably struck at Shaharah about 1925. Dies were reportedly prepared in Italy. For silver strikes, see Y#A4.

Date	Mintage	Good	VG	F	VF	XF
NDAH1322(ca.1925)	—	30.00	60.00	125	200	—
Note: This issue is believed to be a pattern						
ND(ca.1925)	—	30.00	60.00	125	200	—
Note: Possibly a pattern						

Y# D1 1/80 RIYAL (1/2 Buqsha)

Bronze **Obv:** Crescent below accession date AH1322 **Obv. Inscription:** Rabb al-Alamin **Rev:** Toughra **Note:** Without denomination or mint name.

Date	Mintage	Good	VG	F	VF	XF
ND(ca.1911) Rare; Accessional date only	—	—	—	—	—	—

Y# 2.1 1/80 RIYAL (1/2 Buqsha)

Bronze **Note:** Accession date AH1322 above crescent on obverse and within crescent on reverse.

Date	Mintage	Good	VG	F	VF	XF
ND(ca.1911)	—	12.50	25.00	50.00	85.00	—

Note: Probably struck at Shaharah

Y# 2.2 1/80 RIYAL (1/2 Buqsha)

Bronze **Obv:** Crescent below accession date AH1322 **Note:** Thin flan, 1.50-3.00 grams. The number and arrangement of stars and the size of the circle on the reverse vary as well as the exact arrangement of the legends which sometimes vary within each year. The reverse exists with 10, 12, 14, 20, 22, 24, 28, and 34 stars. Obverse varieties exist with 1, 2, 3 or 4 stars and without stars. Accession date: AH(1)322 or 1322. Struck at Shaharah.

Date	Mintage	Good	VG	F	VF	XF
AH1330	—	20.00	35.00	60.00	100	—

Date	Mintage	Good	VG	F	VF	XF
AH1331	—	20.00	35.00	75.00	150	—
AH1332	—	10.00	15.00	25.00	40.00	—
AH1333	—	10.00	15.00	25.00	40.00	—
AH1337	—	10.00	15.00	25.00	40.00	—
AH1338	—	10.00	15.00	25.00	40.00	—
AH1339	—	10.00	15.00	25.00	40.00	—

Y# 2.3 1/80 RIYAL (1/2 Buqsha)

Bronze **Rev:** "Duriba Bi Sana'a" added

Date	Mintage	Good	VG	F	VF	XF
AH1340	—	10.00	20.00	40.00	75.00	—
Note: AH1340 exists with 4 and 8 stars on reverse						
AH1341	—	10.00	20.00	40.00	75.00	—
Note: AH1341 exists with 4 stars on reverse						

Y# 2.4 1/80 RIYAL (1/2 Buqsha)

Bronze **Obv:** Without "Rabb al-Alamin" with crescent below accession date AH1322 **Note:** Weight and diameter varies.

Date	Mintage	Good	VG	F	VF	XF
AH1341	—	12.00	25.00	50.00	85.00	—
Note: AH1341 exists with 4 stars on reverse						
AH1342	—	12.00	25.00	50.00	85.00	—
Note: AH1342 coins exist with 4 and 6 stars on reverse						

Y# 2.5 1/80 RIYAL (1/2 Buqsha)

Bronze (Red To Yellow) **Obv:** Crescent below accession date AH1332 **Obv. Inscription:** Rabb al-alamin **Rev:** "Sana" above date **Note:** Number and arrangement of stars on reverse (4, 5, 6, 7, or 8) as well as the size of the inner circle vary. Varieties exist in the form of crescent and arrangement of legends and planchet thicknesses.

Date	Mintage	Good	VG	F	VF	XF
AH1339	—	7.00	12.00	25.00	40.00	—
AH1341	—	7.00	12.00	25.00	40.00	—
AH1342	—	2.00	5.00	12.00	20.00	—
AH1343	—	2.00	5.00	12.00	20.00	—
AH1344	—	2.00	5.00	12.00	20.00	—
AH1345	—	1.50	4.00	8.00	15.00	—
AH1346	—	1.50	3.00	6.00	12.00	—
Note: Some examples of AH1346 show the 6 re-engraved over low I						
AH1347	—	1.50	4.00	8.00	15.00	—
AH1348	—	1.50	4.00	8.00	15.00	—
AH1349	—	1.50	4.00	8.00	15.00	—
AH1350	—	1.50	4.00	8.00	15.00	—
AH135x	—	1.50	4.00	8.00	15.00	—
AH1351	—	2.00	6.00	12.00	20.00	—
AH1352	—	2.00	6.00	12.00	20.00	—
AH1353	—	2.00	6.00	12.00	20.00	—
AH1358	—	—	—	—	—	—
Note: Reported, not confirmed						
AH1359	—	2.50	6.00	12.00	20.00	—
AH1360	—	2.50	4.00	8.00	15.00	—
AH1361	—	4.00	8.00	15.00	25.00	—

Y# 2.6 1/80 RIYAL (1/2 Buqsha)

3.0000 g., Bronze **Rev:** "Sana" below date **Note:** Thin flan. Struck at Shaharah.

Date	Mintage	Good	VG	F	VF	XF
AH1333	—	80.00	100	200	300	—

Y# 2.7 1/80 RIYAL (1/2 Buqsha)

Bronze **Note:** Thick flan. Weight varies: 4-5.4 grams. Varieties with 10 and 14 stars on reverse. Obverse with 1, 2, 3, 4, or no stars. Varieties of legend distribution. Some coins occur with light silver wash. Struck at Shaharah.

Date	Mintage	Good	VG	F	VF	XF
AH1332	—	10.00	15.00	25.00	40.00	—
AH1333	—	10.00	15.00	25.00	40.00	—
AH1338	—	10.00	15.00	25.00	40.00	—

Y# 2.8 1/80 RIYAL (1/2 Buqsha)

Bronze **Note:** Mule, two obverses.

Date	Mintage	Good	VG	F	VF	XF
ND(ca.1911-21)	—	20.00	30.00	60.00	100	—

Y# A3 1/40 RIYAL (1 Buqsha)

Billon/Silver **Note:** Weight varies: 0.65-1.25 grams. Size varies: 15-16 mm. Accession date: AH1322.

Date	Mintage	VG	F	VF	XF	Unc
ND(ca.1911-21)	—	275	550	1,100	1,650	—

Date	Mintage	VG	F	VF	XF	Unc

Note: Minted at Qaflat Idhar, without mint name or denomination

Y# 3.1 1/40 RIYAL (1 Buqsha)

Bronze **Obv:** Without "Rabb al-Alamin", with crescent below accession date AH1322 **Rev:** "Sana" below date

Date	Mintage	VG	F	VF	XF	Unc
AH1341	—	10.00	20.00	40.00	80.00	—
Note: Varieties of borders, arrangement of legends, and thickness of planchets exist						

Y# 3.2 1/40 RIYAL (1 Buqsha)

Bronze (Red To Yellow) **Obv:** Crescent below accession date AH1322 **Obv. Inscription:** Rabb al-Alamin **Rev:** "Sana" above date, small "Sana'a" and three leaf ornaments plus star in border legend

Date	Mintage	VG	F	VF	XF	Unc
AH1342	—	4.00	10.00	20.00	60.00	—
Note: AH1342 exists with 4 leaf ornaments and without star in border legend						
AH13442		65.00	125	—	—	—
AH1343	—	4.00	10.00	20.00	60.00	—
AH1344	—	15.00	30.00	50.00	75.00	—

Y# 3.3 1/40 RIYAL (1 Buqsha)

Bronze (Red To Yellow) **Obv:** Crescent below accession date AH1322 **Rev:** Large "Sana'a" in legend **Note:** Varieties in arrangement of legends, ornaments, form of the crescent, and size of the circle on reverse exist; weight varies.

Date	Mintage	VG	F	VF	XF	Unc
AH1344	—	12.00	20.00	35.00	100	—
AH1345	—	12.00	20.00	35.00	100	—
AH1349	—	1.50	3.50	10.00	25.00	—
AH1353	—	—	—	—	—	—
Note: Reported, not confirmed						
AH1358	—	2.00	4.00	10.00	25.00	—
AH1359	—	2.00	4.00	10.00	25.00	—
AH1360	—	2.00	4.00	10.00	25.00	—
AH1361/0	—	10.00	20.00	50.00	75.00	—
AH1362/0	—	2.50	5.00	10.00	35.00	—
AH1362	—	1.50	3.50	10.00	30.00	—
AH1363	—	1.50	5.00	12.00	35.00	—
AH1364	—	1.50	5.00	12.00	35.00	—
AH1365/4	—	2.25	5.00	12.00	35.00	—
AH1365	—	2.50	5.00	12.00	35.00	—
AH1366	—	1.50	3.50	12.00	30.00	—
AH1366/x	—	2.50	5.00	12.00	35.00	—
AH1367	—	10.00	20.00	50.00	75.00	—

Y# A4 1/20 IMADI RIYAL

Silver **Obv:** Inscription in two lines above

Date	Mintage	VG	F	VF	XF	Unc
ND(1911-21)	—	60.00	120	250	400	—
Note: Dated accessionally on obverse without mint name or denomination; Probably struck at Shaharah about 1925; dies were reportedly prepared in Italy; Strikes in nickel reported; See Y#B1;This issue is believed to be a pattern						

Y# B4 1/20 IMADI RIYAL

Silver **Obv:** Crescent below accession date AH1322 **Rev:** Without "Sana"

Date	Mintage	VG	F	VF	XF	Unc
AH1337 Rare	—	—	—	—	—	—
Note: Three stars on reverse						

Y# 4.1 1/20 IMADI RIYAL

Silver **Obv:** Without "Rabb al-Alamin", with crescent below accession date AH1322 **Note:** Varieties in arrangement of legends, size of circle, and with 3 and 4 stars on reverse exist. Variety of Y#4 dated with 2 digits AH(13)22 of the accessional year are considered local contemporary counterfeits by leading authorities. They are reported having been produced by the Zaraing tribe at Bait Al-Faqih.

Date	Mintage	F	VF	XF	Unc
AH1337	—	40.00	80.00	150	250	—
AH1338 Rare	—	—	—	—	—	—
AH1339	—	40.00	80.00	150	250	—
Note: Some strikes show accessional year as 322 only						
AH1340	—	20.00	30.00	60.00	100	—
Note: Some strikes show accessional year as 322 only						
AH1342	—	5.00	12.00	30.00	60.00	—
AH1343	—	4.00	10.00	25.00	50.00	—
AH1344	—	4.00	10.00	25.00	50.00	—
AH1345/2	—	4.00	10.00	25.00	50.00	—
AH1345	—	4.00	10.00	25.00	50.00	—
AH1347	—	5.00	12.00	30.00	60.00	—
AH1348	—	4.00	10.00	25.00	50.00	—
AH1349	—	4.00	10.00	25.00	50.00	—
AH1350	—	4.00	12.00	30.00	60.00	—
AH1351	—	5.00	15.00	35.00	75.00	—
AH1352	—	4.00	12.00	30.00	60.00	—
AH1353	—	4.00	12.00	30.00	60.00	—
AH1358	—	3.00	8.00	20.00	40.00	—
AH1359	—	3.00	8.00	20.00	40.00	—
AH1362/58	—	5.00	15.00	30.00	60.00	—
AH1362/59	—	5.00	15.00	30.00	60.00	—
AH1363	—	4.00	10.00	30.00	60.00	—
AH1364/46	—	3.00	8.00	20.00	40.00	—
AH1364	—	3.00	8.00	20.00	40.00	—
AHx364	—	3.00	8.00	20.00	40.00	—
AH1365	—	3.00	10.00	25.00	50.00	—
AH1366/44	—	4.00	12.00	30.00	60.00	—
AH1366	—	4.00	12.00	30.00	60.00	—

Y# 4.4 1/20 IMADI RIYAL

Silver **Rev:** Border legend shifted to left **Note:** Accession date AH1322.

Date	Mintage	VG	F	VF	XF	Unc
AH1340 Rare	—	—	—	—	—	—
Note: Three stars on reverse						

Y# 4.2 1/20 IMADI RIYAL

Silver **Obv:** Crescent **Rev:** "Sana" below date, normal legend position **Note:** Four stars on reverse.

Date	Mintage	VG	F	VF	XF	Unc
AH1341	—	40.00	80.00	150	250	—
AHx341	—	40.00	80.00	150	250	—

Y# 5.1 1/10 IMADI RIYAL

Silver **Obv:** Crescent below accession date AH1322 **Obv. Inscription:** Rabb al-Alamin **Rev:** Without "Sana"

Date	Mintage	VG	F	VF	XF	Unc
AH1337	—	30.00	60.00	100	175	—
Note: Reverse varieties with 3, 4, and 5 stars. Size of circle and form of crescent varies						

Y# 5.2 1/10 IMADI RIYAL

Silver **Obv:** Without "Rabb al-Alamin", with crescent below accession date AH1322

Date	Mintage	VG	F	VF	XF	Unc
AH1339	—	20.00	40.00	75.00	150	—

Note: Some AH1339 strikes show accession date as 322

Date	Mintage	VG	F	VF	XF	Unc
AH1340	—	20.00	40.00	75.00	150	—

Note: AH1340 also exists with three stars, others with six stars on reverse

Date	Mintage	VG	F	VF	XF	Unc
AH1341	—	20.00	40.00	75.00	150	—
AH1348	—	100	150	350	500	—

Y# 5.3 1/10 IMADI RIYAL

Silver **Obv:** Crescent below accession date AH1322 **Rev:** "Sana" below date **Note:** Varieties with three and six stars on the reverse exist.

Date	Mintage	VG	F	VF	XF	Unc
AH1341	—	20.00	40.00	75.00	150	—
AH1342	—	20.00	40.00	75.00	150	—

Y# 5.5 1/10 IMADI RIYAL

Silver **Obv:** Without "Rabb al-Alamin" **Rev:** "Sana" above date **Note:** Form of crescent, size of circle on reverse, and arrangement of legends vary. Normal reverse contains 6 stars though varieties with 7, 8, 9, 10, and 12 stars on reverse exist. Some earlier dates show varying amounts of edge reeding.

Date	Mintage	VG	F	VF	XF	Unc
AH1342	—	4.00	10.00	25.00	50.00	—
AH1343	—	4.00	10.00	25.00	50.00	—
AH1344	—	3.00	8.00	20.00	40.00	—
AH1345	—	3.00	8.00	20.00	40.00	—
AH1347	—	3.00	8.00	20.00	40.00	—
AH1348	—	3.00	8.00	20.00	35.00	—
AH1349	—	3.00	6.00	15.00	30.00	—

Note: Reported, not confirmed

Date	Mintage	VG	F	VF	XF	Unc
AH1351	—	4.00	10.00	25.00	40.00	—
AH1352	—	4.00	10.00	25.00	40.00	—
AH1358/49	—	3.00	8.00	15.00	30.00	—
AH1358	—	3.00	8.00	15.00	30.00	—
AH1359/3	—	3.00	8.00	15.00	30.00	—
AH1359/49	—	3.00	8.00	15.00	30.00	—
AH1362/44	—	4.00	10.00	25.00	40.00	—
AH1362/59	—	4.00	10.00	25.00	40.00	—
AH1363	—	3.00	8.00	25.00	45.00	—
AH1364/43	—	3.00	8.00	20.00	40.00	—
AH1364/3	—	3.00	8.00	25.00	45.00	—
AH1364/52	—	3.00	8.00	25.00	45.00	—
AH1364	—	3.00	8.00	15.00	35.00	—
AH1365	—	3.00	8.00	15.00	35.00	—
AH1366/5	—	3.00	10.00	20.00	50.00	—
AH1366/5x	—	3.00	10.00	20.00	50.00	—

Y# 5.4 1/10 IMADI RIYAL

Silver **Obv:** Crescent below accession date AH1322 **Obv. Inscription:** Rabb al-Alamin **Rev:** "Sana" above date **Note:** Varieties with 8, 9, and 10 stars on reverse exist.

Date	Mintage	VG	F	VF	XF	Unc
AH1342	—	20.00	40.00	75.00	150	—

Y# 5.5 1/10 IMADI RIYAL

Silver **Obv:** Without "Rabb al-Alamin" **Rev:** "Sana" above date **Note:** Form of crescent, size of circle on reverse, and arrangement of legends vary. Normal reverse contains 6 stars though varieties with 7, 8, 9, 10, and 12 stars on reverse exist. Some earlier dates show varying amounts of edge reeding.

Y# 8 1/8 IMADI RIYAL

Silver **Obv:** One or no stars in crescent below accession date AH1322 **Rev:** "Thumn" in place of "Ushr" below date, 6 stars

Date	Mintage	VG	F	VF	XF	Unc
AH1339	—	325	550	1,100	1,650	—

Y# 6.1 1/4 IMADI RIYAL

Silver **Obv:** Without "Rabb al-Alamin", with crescent below accession date AH1322 **Rev:** "Sana" below date

Date	Mintage	VG	F	VF	XF	Unc
AH1341	—	20.00	45.00	75.00	150	—

Note: AH1341 with 4 stars on reverse

Date	Mintage	VG	F	VF	XF	Unc
AH1342	—	25.00	50.00	100	175	—

Note: AH1342 with 4 stars on reverse and 2 stars flanking date

Y# 6.2 1/4 IMADI RIYAL

Silver **Obv:** Crescent below accession date AH1322 **Obv. Inscription:** Rabb al-Alamin **Rev:** "Sana" above date, two stars and two ornaments in border

Date	Mintage	VG	F	VF	XF	Unc
AH1342	—	70.00	100	300	450	—

Y# 6.5 1/4 IMADI RIYAL

Silver **Obv:** Crescent below accession date AH1322 **Rev:** "Sana" below date, eight stars in border

Date	Mintage	VG	F	VF	XF	Unc
AH1342	—	100	150	300	500	—

Y# 6.6 1/4 IMADI RIYAL

Silver **Obv:** Crescent below accession date AH1322 **Rev:** "Sana" below date, one star in border

Date	Mintage	VG	F	VF	XF	Unc
AH1342	—	100	150	300	500	—

Note: Obverse varieties with one and two stars exist

Y# 10 1/4 IMADI RIYAL

Silver **Obv:** Crescent below accession date AH1322 **Rev:** Redesigned, date moved to margin **Edge:** Plain, traces of reeding to full reeding known **Note:** The size of the reverse inner circle varies, 12 to 16 crescents on obverse.

Date	Mintage	VG	F	VF	XF	Unc
AH1342	—	20.00	40.00	75.00	150	—
AH1343	—	20.00	60.00	100	175	—
AH1344	—	4.25	10.00	25.00	75.00	—
AH1345	—	4.25	10.00	25.00	60.00	—
AH1349	—	—	—	—	—	—

Note: Reported, not confirmed

Date	Mintage	VG	F	VF	XF	Unc
AH1351	—	20.00	30.00	50.00	100	—
AH1352	—	5.00	12.00	20.00	40.00	—
AH1358	—	3.50	5.50	15.00	35.00	—
AH1359	—	3.50	5.50	15.00	35.00	—
AH1363	—	3.50	8.00	20.00	40.00	—
AH1364/3	—	4.25	8.00	20.00	40.00	—
AH1364	—	3.50	5.00	20.00	40.00	—
AH1365/4	—	4.25	6.00	20.00	40.00	—
AH1365	—	3.50	5.00	20.00	40.00	—
AH1366	—	3.50	5.00	20.00	40.00	—

Y# 7 IMADI RIYAL

28.0700 g., Silver **Obv:** Double crescent below accession date AH1322 **Note:** Several die varieties exist, possibly struck over a number of years with frozen date AH1344. Edge varieties exist.

Date	Mintage	VG	F	VF	XF	Unc
AH1342	—	—	—	—	—	—

Note: Reported, not confirmed

Date	Mintage	VG	F	VF	XF	Unc
AH1344	—	7.00	12.00	18.00	28.00	40.00

Note: Copper trial strikes dated AH1344 reported

Date	Mintage	VG	F	VF	XF	Unc
AH1365 Two known	—	—	—	—	—	2,000

GOLD PRESENTATION COINAGE

All Imam Yahya gold strikes are considered presentation issues which were based on the gold standard of the Turkish Lira.

Y# A10 1/8 LIRA (1/40 Riyal)

0.9200 g., Gold **Note:** Accession date: AH1322.

Date	Mintage	VG	F	VF	XF	Unc
AH(13)44	—	—	—	—	1,350	—

Y# B10 1/4 LIRA (1/20 Riyal)

1.7000 g., Gold **Note:** Accession date: AH1322.

Date	Mintage	VG	F	VF	XF	Unc
AH(13)44	—	—	—	—	1,500	—

Y# C10 1/2 LIRA (1/10 Riyal)

3.3100 g., Gold **Note:** Accession date: AH1322.

Date	Mintage	VG	F	VF	XF	Unc
AH(13)44	—	—	—	—	1,650	—

Y# D10 LIRA (1/5 Riyal)

6.8000 g., Gold **Obv:** Crescent below accession date AH1322

Date	Mintage	VG	F	VF	XF	Unc
AH(13)44	—	—	—	—	2,000	—

Y# E10 2-1/2 LIRA (1/2 Riyal)

17.7000 g., Gold **Obv:** Crescent below accession date AH1322

Date	Mintage	VG	F	VF	XF	Unc
AH(13)44	—	—	—	—	3,500	—

Y# K10 2-1/2 LIRA (1/2 Riyal)

Gold **Note:** Weight varies: 17.44-17.82 grams. Accession date: AH1322.

Date	Mintage	VG	F	VF	XF	Unc
AH1352	—	—	—	—	2,500	—

Y# F10 5 LIRA (1 Riyal)

35.5000 g., Gold **Note:** Similar to 1 Imadi Riyal, Y#7.

Date	Mintage	VG	F	VF	XF	Unc
AH1344 Rare	—	—	—	—	—	—

Note: Dies of AH1344 Riyal silver and gold strikes are not identical

Y# P10 5 LIRA (1 Riyal)

34.2400 g., Gold **Note:** Thin planchet strike of 10 Lira (2 Riyal), Y#N10.

Date	Mintage	VG	F	VF	XF	Unc
AH1358 2 known	—	—	—	—	3,250	—

Y# M10 10 LIRA (2 Riyal)

69.8300 g., Gold **Obv:** Similar to Gold 2-1/2 Lira, Y#K10 **Note:** Accession date: AH1322.

Date	Mintage	VG	F	VF	XF	Unc
AH1352	—	—	—	—	6,500	—

Y# N10 10 LIRA (2 Riyal)

69.8300 g., Gold **Obv:** Crescent below accession date AH1322 **Rev:** Two crossed flags in center **Rev. Legend:** "Duriba bi-dar al-khilafa al-mutawakkiliya bi Sana'a 'asimat al-Yamam sana 1358"

Date	Mintage	VG	F	VF	XF	Unc
AH1358 4 known	—	—	—	—	5,500	—

al-Nasir Ahmad bin Yahya (Imam Ahmad)

AH1367-1382 / 1948-1962AD

MILLED COINAGE

Y# 11.1 1/80 RIYAL (1 Halala = 1/2 Buqsha)

Bronze (Red To Yellow) **Obv:** Crescent below accession date AH1367 which may vary as 1367/1267, 1367/1777, etc. **Rev:** "Sana" above date **Note:** There is a variation in the number of stars on reverse, as follows: AH1368 - 8 stars; AH1371-74 and some AH1381 (not overdate) - 7 stars; AH1375-81 including some AH1381, some AH1382, and all AH1381 overdates - 8 stars. Varieties of arrangement of legends, form of crescent, and size of circle on reverse exist. Some earlier dates exist on thinner planchets.

Date	Mintage	VG	F	VF	XF	Unc
AH1368	—	1.00	2.00	5.00	10.00	—
AH1371	—	0.30	1.00	3.00	8.00	—
AH1372	—	0.30	1.00	3.00	8.00	—
AH1373	—	0.30	0.60	1.00	3.00	—
AH1374	—	0.30	1.00	3.00	8.00	—
AH1275 Error for 1375	—	1.00	2.00	6.00	12.00	—
AH1375	—	—	—	—	—	—
AH1376	—	—	—	—	—	—
AH1376/86 Error	—	—	—	—	—	—
AH1278 Error for 1378	—	1.00	2.00	6.00	12.00	—
AH1378	—	—	—	—	—	—
AHx379	—	1.00	2.00	6.00	12.00	—
AH1379	—	0.50	1.00	2.50	5.00	—
AH1380/1	—	1.00	2.00	6.00	12.00	—
AH1380/79	—	0.50	1.00	2.50	5.00	—
AH1380/9	—	0.50	1.00	2.50	5.00	—
AH1380	—	0.50	1.00	2.50	5.00	—
AH1381/80/79	—	0.40	0.85	1.50	2.50	—
AH1381/79	—	0.40	0.85	1.50	2.50	—
AH1381	—	0.20	0.40	0.75	1.25	—
AH1382	—	5.00	10.00	15.00	20.00	—

Y# 11.2 1/80 RIYAL (1 Halala = 1/2 Buqsha)

Bronze **Rev:** Without "Sana"

Date	Mintage	VG	F	VF	XF	Unc
AH1373 Rare	—	—	—	—	—	—

Y# 11a 1/80 RIYAL (1 Halala = 1/2 Buqsha)

Aluminum **Obv:** Crescent below accession date AH1367 **Rev:** "Sana" above date **Note:** AH1374 and some AH1380 have 7 stars, the rest have 8 stars on reverse. Dies of 1/80 Riyal, Y#11.1, were used.

Date	Mintage	VG	F	VF	XF	Unc
AH1374	—	0.25	1.00	2.50	5.00	—
AH1375	—	0.75	2.50	5.50	10.00	—
AH1376	—	0.25	1.50	4.00	8.00	—
AH1377	—	0.75	2.50	5.50	10.00	—
AH1378	—	0.25	1.00	2.50	5.00	—
AH1378/6	—	0.25	1.00	2.50	5.00	—
AH1379/5	—	0.75	2.50	5.50	10.00	—
AH1379/8	—	0.75	2.50	5.50	10.00	—
AH1379	—	0.25	1.00	2.50	5.00	—
AH1380	—	0.25	1.00	2.50	5.00	—

Y# 11.3 1/80 RIYAL (1 Halala = 1/2 Buqsha)

Bronze **Obv:** Crescent below accession date AH1367 **Note:** Struck with dies of 1/4 Ahmadi Riyal, Y#15 on 1/80 Riyal planchet.

Date	Mintage	VG	F	VF	XF	Unc
AH(13)80 Rare	—	—	—	—	—	—

Y# 18 1/80 RIYAL (1 Halala = 1/2 Buqsha)

Aluminum **Note:** Accession date: AH1367.

Date	Mintage	VG	F	VF	XF	Unc
ND	—	0.15	0.25	0.50	1.00	—

Note: Struck privately in Lebanon in 1955 and 1956 and released into circulation in 1956

Y# 12.1 1/40 RIYAL (1 Buqsha)

Bronze (Red To Yellow) **Obv:** Crescent below accession date AH1367 **Rev:** "Sana" above date, large "Sana'a" in border legend **Note:** Some dates exist on thinner planchets and weight varies.

Date	Mintage	VG	F	VF	XF	Unc
AH1368	—	0.50	1.00	4.00	12.00	—
Note: AH1368 also exists with accession date 13776 (error) known						
AH1369	—	0.75	1.25	5.00	15.00	—
AH1370	—	0.35	0.75	3.00	6.00	—
AH1371	—	0.35	0.75	3.00	6.00	—
AH1372	—	0.35	0.75	2.00	4.00	—
AH1373/1	—	—	—	—	—	—
AH1373/2	—	0.85	1.80	3.00	6.00	—
AH1373	—	0.35	0.75	2.00	4.00	—
AH1374	—	0.35	0.75	2.00	4.00	—
AH1375/4	—	0.50	1.00	3.00	6.00	—
AH1377	—	—	—	—	—	—

Note: Reported, not confirmed

Y# 12.2 1/40 RIYAL (1 Buqsha)

Bronze (Red To Yellow) **Obv:** Crescent below accession date AH1367 **Rev:** Small "Sana'a" in legend **Note:** Varieties of arrangement of legends, form of crescent, and size of circle exist.

Date	Mintage	VG	F	VF	XF	Unc
AH1371	—	0.35	0.75	3.00	6.00	—
AH1374	—	0.35	0.75	2.00	4.00	—
AH1375	—	0.35	0.75	2.00	4.00	—
AH1376	—	0.50	1.00	5.00	12.00	—
Note: Exists with accession date 1376 instead of 1367 on obverse						
AH1377/6	—	0.85	1.75	4.00	8.00	—
Note: Exists with accession date 1376 instead of 1367 on obverse						
AH1377	—	0.85	1.75	5.00	10.00	—
AH1378/5	—	—	—	—	—	—
AH1379/7	—	0.85	1.75	4.00	8.00	—
AH1380/79	—	0.85	1.75	4.00	8.00	—
AH1380	—	10.00	20.00	50.00	75.00	—

Y# 12.3 1/40 RIYAL (1 Buqsha)

Bronze (Red To Yellow) **Obv:** Crescent below accession date AH1367 **Rev:** Large "Sana'a" in legend, without "Sana" above date

Date	Mintage	VG	F	VF	XF	Unc
AH1371	—	0.50	1.00	4.00	12.00	—

Y# 12a.1 1/40 RIYAL (1 Buqsha)

Aluminum **Obv:** Crescent below accession date AH1367 **Rev:** "Sana" above date, large "Sana'a" in border legend **Note:** Dies of 1/40 Riyal, Y#12.1, were used.

Date	Mintage	VG	F	VF	XF	Unc
AH1371	—	0.50	1.00	4.00	10.00	—
AH1373	—	0.50	1.00	4.00	10.00	—
AH1374	—	0.50	1.00	4.00	10.00	—
AH1375	—	0.50	1.00	4.00	10.00	—
AH1377	—	15.00	30.00	50.00	90.00	—

Y# 12a.2 1/40 RIYAL (1 Buqsha)

Aluminum **Obv:** Crescent below accession date AH1367 **Rev:** Small "Sana'a" in legend **Note:** Dies of 1/40 Riyal, Y#12.2, were used. AH1376 and AH1377 plain dates also exist with accession date AH1376 instead of AH1367 on obverse. Varieties exist.

Date	Mintage	VG	F	VF	XF	Unc
AH1375	—	0.50	1.00	4.00	10.00	—
AH1376	—	0.50	1.00	4.00	10.00	—
AH1377/6	—	10.00	20.00	40.00	75.00	—
AH1377	—	15.00	30.00	50.00	90.00	—

Y# 19 1/40 RIYAL (1 Buqsha)

Aluminum **Note:** Accession date: AH1367 at bottom.

Date	Mintage	VG	F	VF	XF	Unc
ND	—	0.25	0.45	0.65	1.00	2.50

Note: Struck privately in Lebanon in 1955 and 1956 and released into circulation in 1956

Y# 13 1/16 AHMADI RIYAL

Silver **Obv:** Crescent below accession date AH1367 **Obv. Inscription:** Amir al-Mu'minin **Shape:** 5-sided **Note:** Arrangement of legends and size of inner circle on reverse vary.

Date	Mintage	VG	F	VF	XF	Unc
AH1367	—	1.00	2.00	6.00	12.00	—

Date	Mintage	VG	F	VF	XF	Unc
AH1368	—	1.00	1.75	5.00	10.00	—
AH1371	—	1.00	1.75	5.00	10.00	—
AH1374	—	1.00	1.50	4.00	8.00	—

Y# 13.1 1/16 AHMADI RIYAL

Silver **Obv:** Crescent below accession date AH1367, 1/8 Ahmadi Riyal, Y#14 **Rev:** Y#13 **Shape:** 5-sided **Note:** Mule. Ends of crescents cut off on reverse.

Date	Mintage	VG	F	VF	XF	Unc
AH1374	—	20.00	40.00	100	150	—

Y# A14 1/10 AHMADI RIYAL

Silver **Obv:** Crescent below accession date AH1367

Date	Mintage	VG	F	VF	XF	Unc
AH1370	—	400	750	1,250	1,500	—

Y# 14a 1/8 AHMADI RIYAL

Silver **Shape:** Hexagonal

Date	Mintage	VG	F	VF	XF	Unc
AH1368	—	350	650	1,250	1,850	—

Y# 14 1/8 AHMADI RIYAL

Silver **Obv:** Crescent below accession date AH1367 **Note:** Pentagonal planchet. Arrangement of legends and size of inner circle on reverse vary.

Date	Mintage	VG	F	VF	XF	Unc
AH1367	—	4.00	8.00	15.00	30.00	—
AH1368	—	2.75	4.00	8.00	20.00	—
AH1370	—	2.75	4.00	8.00	20.00	—
AH1371	—	2.00	3.50	6.00	15.00	—
AH1372	—	2.00	2.75	4.00	10.00	—
AH1373	—	2.00	2.75	4.00	10.00	—
AH1374	—	2.00	3.00	5.00	15.00	—
AH1375/1	—	4.00	10.00	40.00	80.00	—
AH1379/x	—	2.00	3.00	5.00	15.00	—
AH1379/5	—	2.00	3.00	5.00	15.00	—
AH1379	—	2.00	3.50	6.00	15.00	—
AH1380	—	2.00	3.75	7.00	20.00	—

Y# 15 1/4 AHMADI RIYAL

Silver **Obv:** Crescent below accession date AH1367 **Edge:** Reeded **Note:** The size of inner circle as well as the arrangement of legends on reverse vary. All dates have only the final 2 digits on the coin.

Date	Mintage	VG	F	VF	XF	Unc
AH(13)67	—	3.75	5.50	7.50	15.00	—
AH(13)68	—	3.75	5.50	7.50	15.00	—
AH(13)70	—	3.25	4.50	6.00	12.00	—
AH(13)71/68	—	6.00	8.00	12.50	20.00	—
AH(13)71/0	—	4.50	6.50	9.00	15.00	—
AH(13)71	—	3.25	4.50	6.00	10.00	—
AH(13)72	—	3.25	4.50	6.00	10.00	—
AH(13)74	—	3.25	4.50	6.00	10.00	—
AH(13)75/3	—	4.50	6.50	9.00	15.00	—
AH(13)75	—	3.25	4.50	6.00	10.00	—
AH(13)77/5	—	4.50	6.50	9.00	15.00	—
AH(13)80	—	30.00	60.00	100	175	—

Y# 15a 1/4 AHMADI RIYAL

Copper

Date	Mintage	VG	F	VF	XF	Unc
AH(13)81d Rare	—	—	—	—	—	—

Note: This issue is considered a pattern

Y# 16.1 1/2 AHMADI RIYAL

Silver **Obv:** Double crescent below accession date AH1367 **Rev:** Full dates; denomination and mint name read inward

Date	Mintage	VG	F	VF	XF	Unc
AH1367	—	7.00	10.00	15.00	35.00	—
AH1368	—	7.00	10.00	15.00	35.00	—
AH1369	—	6.00	8.00	12.50	20.00	—
AH1370	—	8.00	12.50	20.00	40.00	—
AH1371	—	8.00	12.50	20.00	40.00	—
AH1372/68	—	7.00	10.00	15.00	30.00	—
AH1373	—	9.00	15.00	25.00	45.00	—
AH1375	—	—	—	—	—	—
Note: Reported, not confirmed						
AH(13)75	—	30.00	50.00	80.00	100	—
AH1377	—	—	—	—	—	—

Y# 16.2 1/2 AHMADI RIYAL

Silver **Obv:** Double crescent below accession date AH1367 **Rev:** Full dates; denomination and mint name read outward **Edge:** Reeded **Note:** Arrangement of legends and size of circle on reverse vary. These coins were struck over blanks punched from Maria Theresa Thalers. The outer rings are reported to have circulated as currency, but this is doubtful, as they are found only counterstamped "Void" in Arabic.

Date	Mintage	VG	F	VF	XF	Unc
AH1377	—	6.00	8.00	12.50	20.00	—
AH1378	—	7.00	10.00	15.00	25.00	—
AH1379	—	6.00	8.00	12.50	20.00	—
AH1380	—	17.50	30.00	40.00	75.00	—
AH1381	—	12.50	22.50	30.00	50.00	—
AH1382	—	8.00	12.50	25.00	40.00	—

Y# 16a 1/2 AHMADI RIYAL

Copper

Date	Mintage	VG	F	VF	XF	Unc
AH1381 Rare	—	—	—	—	—	—

Note: This issue is considered a pattern

Y# 17 AHMADI RIYAL

Silver, 39.5 mm. **Obv:** Double crescent below accession date AH1367 **Note:** These are usually found struck over Austrian Maria Theresa Talers and occasionally over other foreign crowns. All Y-17s have 1367 in the center obverse. The date for each piece is located in the lower left of the reverse. Varieties exist.

Date	Mintage	F	VF	XF	Unc
AH1367	—	20.00	30.00	45.00	80.00
AH1370	—	15.00	20.00	30.00	55.00
AH1371	—	15.00	20.00	30.00	55.00
AH1372/68	—	—	—	—	—
Note: Reported, not confirmed					
AH1373	—	12.50	15.00	22.50	35.00
Note: Most AH1373 Riyals appear to be weakly struck from recut AH1372 dies, and the dates are easily confused					
AH1374	—	13.50	16.50	25.00	45.00
AH1375	—	13.50	16.50	25.00	45.00
AH1377	—	13.50	16.50	25.00	45.00
Note: Reported, not confirmed					
AH1378	—	13.50	16.50	25.00	45.00
AH1380	—	13.50	16.50	25.00	45.00
AH1381	—	13.50	16.50	25.00	45.00

GOLD COINAGE

Imam Ahmad gold strikes were based on the gold standard of the Turkish Lira (7.2164 g gold). Strikes on the British Gold Standard can have an additional countermark of an Arabic 1, 2, or 4, probably indicating the equivalence to 1, 2, or 4 British Sovereigns.

Y# G15 GOLD 1/4 RIYAL (1 Lira - Sovereign)

Gold **Obv:** Crescent below accession date AH1367 **Note:** Weight varies: 6.30-8.90 grams. Dies of silver 1/4 Ahmadi riyal, (Y#15) were used.

Date	Mintage	F	VF	XF	Unc
AH(13)71	—	—	450	850	1,500
AH(13)75/3	—	—	450	850	1,500
AH(13)75	—	—	450	850	1,500
AH(13)77/5	—	—	450	850	1,500

Y# G16.1 GOLD 1/2 RIYAL (2-1/2 Lira - 2 Sovereigns)

Gold **Obv:** Double crescent below accession date AH1367 **Rev:** Full dates; denomination and mint name read inward **Note:** Weight varies: 15.57-17.99 grams.

Date	Mintage	F	VF	XF	Unc
AH1369 Rare	—	—	—	—	—
Note: Currently, one known					
AH1370	—	425	650	1,200	2,000
AH1371	—	425	650	1,200	2,000
AH1375	—	425	650	1,200	2,000
AH(13)75	—	425	650	1,200	2,000
AH1377	—	425	650	1,200	2,000

Y# G16.2 GOLD 1/2 RIYAL (2-1/2 Lira - 2 Sovereigns)

Gold **Obv:** Double crescent below accession date AH1367 **Rev:** Full date; denomination and mint name read outward **Note:** Dies of silver 1/2 Ahmadi Riyal, (Y#16) were used.

Date	Mintage	F	VF	XF	Unc
AH1377	—	425	650	1,200	2,000
AH1378	—	425	650	1,200	2,000
AH1379	—	425	650	1,200	2,000
AH1380	—	425	650	1,200	2,000
AH1381	—	425	650	1,200	2,000

Y# G17.1 GOLD RIYAL (5 Lira - 4 Sovereigns)

32.4860 g., 0.9000 Gold 0.94 oz. AGW, 40 mm. **Obv:** Double crescent below accession date AH1367 with incuse Arabic number four above sword handles **Rev:** Arabic legend and inscription

Date	Mintage	F	VF	XF	Unc
AH1371 Rare	—	—	—	—	—
AH1372 Rare	—	—	—	—	—

Y# G17.2 GOLD RIYAL (5 Lira - 4 Sovereigns)

32.4860 g., 0.9000 Gold, 40 mm. **Obv:** Double crescent below accession date AH1367 without incuse Arabic number four above sword handles **Rev:** Arabic legend and inscription **Note:** Weight varies: 30.46-39.06 grams. Dies of silver Ahmadi Riyal (Y#17) were used.

Date	Mintage	F	VF	XF	Unc
AH1373	—	—	750	1,000	1,800
AH1374	—	—	750	1,000	1,800
AH1375	—	—	750	1,000	1,800
AH1377	—	—	750	1,000	1,800
AH1378	—	—	750	1,000	1,800
AH1381	—	—	750	1,000	1,800

YEMEN ARAB REPUBLIC

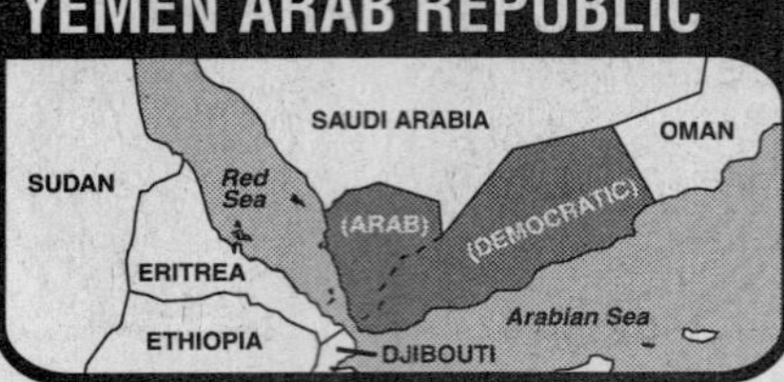

The northwestern region of present day Yemen was dominated by Ottoman Turks until 1918. Formal boundaries were established in 1934 and a Republic was formed in 1962 leading to an eight year civil war between royalist imam and new republican forces.

REPUBLIC

MILLED COINAGE

Y# 20 1/80 RIYAL (1/2 Buqsha)

Bronze **Obverse:** Denomination within circle **Reverse:** Hand holding torch within circle **Note:** Varieties exist.

Date	Mintage	F	VF	XF	Unc
AH1382	—	—	0.50	2.00	5.00

Y# 21.1 1/80 RIYAL (1/2 Buqsha)

Bronze **Obverse:** Denomination within circle **Reverse:** Full star between lines within circle

Date	Mintage	F	VF	XF	Unc
AH1382	—	—	2.00	6.00	15.00

Y# 21.2 1/80 RIYAL (1/2 Buqsha)

Bronze **Obverse:** Denomination within circle **Reverse:** Outlined star between lines within circle **Note:** Varieties exist.

Date	Mintage	F	VF	XF	Unc
AH13882 (sic)	—	—	—	—	—
AH1382	—	—	2.00	6.00	15.00

Y# 26 1/2 BUQSHA

Copper-Aluminum **Mint:** Cairo **Obverse:** Denomination within circle **Reverse:** Leafy branch within wreath **Note:** Varieties exist.

Date	Mintage	F	VF	XF	Unc
AH1382-1963	10,000,000	—	0.15	0.20	0.35

Y# 32 1/2 BUQSHA

Bronze **Obverse:** Denomination within circle **Reverse:** Full star between lines within circle **Note:** Varieties exist.

Date	Mintage	F	VF	XF	Unc
AH1382	—	—	3.00	5.00	9.00

Y# 22 1/40 RIYAL (1 Buqsha)

Brass Or Bronze **Obverse:** Denomination within circle **Reverse:** Hand holding torch within circle **Note:** Dated both sides; AH1382, AH1383 and AH1384/3 are dated AH1382 on obverse, actual date on reverse; AH1384 and AH1384/284 dated AH1384 on both sides. There are varieties of date size and design.

Date	Mintage	F	VF	XF	Unc
AH1382	—	—	0.75	1.00	2.25
AH1383/282	—	—	0.75	1.00	2.25
AH1383	—	—	1.50	2.25	6.00
AH1384/284	—	—	0.75	1.00	2.25
AH1384/3	—	—	0.75	1.00	2.25
AH1384	—	—	4.00	7.50	20.00

Y# 27 BUQSHA

Copper-Aluminum **Mint:** Cairo **Obverse:** Denomination within circle **Reverse:** Leafy branch within wreath

Date	Mintage	F	VF	XF	Unc
AH1382-1963	10,377,000	—	0.20	0.40	1.00

Y# 23.1 1/20 RIYAL (2 Buqsha)

0.7200 Silver **Obverse:** Denomination within circle **Reverse:** Three stones on top row of wall within circle **Note:** Thick variety, 1.10-1.60 grams

Date	Mintage	F	VF	XF	Unc
AH1382	—	20.00	35.00	60.00	125

Y# 23.2 1/20 RIYAL (2 Buqsha)

0.7200 Silver **Obverse:** Denomination within circle **Reverse:** Two stones on top row of wall within circle **Note:** Thin variety, 0.60-0.90 grams

Date	Mintage	F	VF	XF	Unc
AH1382	—	15.00	30.00	50.00	100

Y# A27 2 BUQSHA

Copper-Aluminum **Obverse:** Denomination within circle **Reverse:** Leafy branch within wreath

Date	Mintage	F	VF	XF	Unc
AH1382-1963	—	—	0.25	0.60	1.25

Y# 24.1 1/10 RIYAL (4 Buqsha)

0.7200 Silver **Reverse:** Three or four stones in top row of wall within circle **Note:** Thick variety, 2.40-3.00 grams

Date	Mintage	F	VF	XF	Unc
AH1382	—	5.00	15.00	25.00	50.00

Y# 24.2 1/10 RIYAL (4 Buqsha)

0.7200 Silver **Obverse:** Denomination within circle **Reverse:** Four stones in top row of wall within circle **Note:** Thin variety, 1.40-1.80 grams. Edge varieties, varying number of stones in wall, exist.

Date	Mintage	F	VF	XF	Unc
AH1382	—	—	2.50	6.00	15.00

Y# 28 5 BUQSHA

0.7200 Silver **Mint:** Cairo **Obverse:** Denomination within circle **Reverse:** Leafy branch within wreath, dates below

Date	Mintage	F	VF	XF	Unc
AH1382-1963	1,600,000	—	1.50	1.75	2.50

Y# 25.1 2/10 RIYAL (8 Buqsha)

0.7200 Silver **Obverse:** Denomination within circle **Reverse:** Tree and wall within circle **Note:** Thick variety, 5.80-6.50 grams.

Date	Mintage	F	VF	XF	Unc
AH1382	—	6.00	15.00	25.00	50.00

Y# 25.2 2/10 RIYAL (8 Buqsha)

0.7200 Silver **Obverse:** Denomination within circle **Reverse:** Tree and wall within circle **Note:** Thin variety, 4.90-5.10 grams.

Date	Mintage	F	VF	XF	Unc
AH1382	—	—	75.00	150	250

Y# A25.1 1/4 RIYAL (10 Buqsha)

0.7200 Silver **Obverse:** Denomination within circle **Reverse:** Tree and wall within circle **Note:** Thick variety, 6.00-7.30 grams.

Date	Mintage	F	VF	XF	Unc
AH1382	—	250	500	1,000	1,750

Y# A25.2 1/4 RIYAL (10 Buqsha)

0.7200 Silver **Obverse:** Denomination within circle **Reverse:** Tree and wall within circle **Note:** Thin variety, 4.00-4.60 grams. Overstrikes over earlier 1/4 Riyal coins exist.

Date	Mintage	F	VF	XF	Unc
AH1382	—	250	500	1,000	1,750

Y# 29 10 BUQSHA

5.0000 g., 0.7200 Silver .1157 oz. ASW **Obverse:** Denomination within circle **Reverse:** Leafy branch within wreath

Date	Mintage	F	VF	XF	Unc
AH1382-1963	1,024,000	—	2.50	3.00	5.00

Y# 30 20 BUQSHA

9.8500 g., 0.7200 Silver .2280 oz. ASW **Obverse:** Denomination within circle **Reverse:** Leafy branch within wreath

Date	Mintage	F	VF	XF	Unc
AH1382-1963	1,016,000	—	4.50	6.00	8.00

Y# 31 RIYAL

19.7500 g., 0.7200 Silver .4571 oz. ASW **Obverse:** Denomination within wreath **Reverse:** Leafy branch within wreath

Date	Mintage	F	VF	XF	Unc
AH1382-1963	4,614,000	—	7.50	9.00	13.50

DECIMAL COINAGE

100 Fils = 1 Riyal/Rial

Y# 33 FILS

Aluminum **Obverse:** National arms **Reverse:** Denomination within circle

Date	Mintage	F	VF	XF	Unc
AH1394-1974	Est. 1,000,000	—	3.00	5.00	10.00

Note: It is doubtful that the entire mintage was released for circulation

Date	Mintage	F	VF	XF	Unc
AH1394-1974 Proof	5,024	Value: 1.50			
AH1400-1980 Proof	10,000	Value: 1.50			

Y# 43 FILS

Aluminum **Series:** F.A.O. **Obverse:** National arms **Reverse:** Denomination within circle

Date	Mintage	F	VF	XF	Unc
AH1398-1978	7,050	—	—	1.25	3.00

Y# 34 5 FILS

2.7500 g., Brass, 21 mm. **Obverse:** National arms **Reverse:** Denomination within circle

Date	Mintage	F	VF	XF	Unc
AH1394-1974	10,000,000	—	0.50	1.00	2.50
AH1394-1974 Proof	—	Value: 2.50			
AH1400-1980 Proof	—	Value: 2.00			

Y# 38 5 FILS

2.7500 g., Brass, 21 mm. **Series:** F.A.O. **Obverse:** National arms **Reverse:** Denomination within circle

Date	Mintage	F	VF	XF	Unc
AH1394-1974	500,000	—	—	0.10	0.25

Y# 35 10 FILS

4.2500 g., Brass, 23 mm. **Obverse:** National arms **Reverse:** Denomination within circle

Date	Mintage	F	VF	XF	Unc
AH1394-1974	20,000,000	—	0.50	1.00	2.50
AH1394-1974 Proof	5,024	Value: 2.50			
AH1400-1980 Proof	10,000	Value: 2.00			

Y# 39 10 FILS

4.2500 g., Brass, 23 mm. **Series:** F.A.O. **Obverse:** National arms **Reverse:** Denomination within circle

Date	Mintage	F	VF	XF	Unc
AH1394-1974	200,000	—	—	0.10	0.25

Y# 36 25 FILS

3.0000 g., Copper-Nickel, 20 mm. **Obverse:** National arms **Reverse:** Denomination within circle

Date	Mintage	F	VF	XF	Unc
AH1394-1974	15,000,000	—	0.25	0.50	3.00
AH1394-1974 Proof	5,024	Value: 3.00			
AH1399-1979	11,000,000	—	0.25	0.50	2.00
AH1400-1980 Proof	10,000	Value: 2.25			

Y# 40 25 FILS

3.0000 g., Copper-Nickel, 20 mm. **Series:** F.A.O. **Obverse:** National arms **Reverse:** Denomination within circle

Date	Mintage	F	VF	XF	Unc
AH1394-1974	40,000	—	0.20	0.40	1.00

Y# 37 50 FILS

5.3000 g., Copper-Nickel, 24 mm. **Obverse:** National arms **Reverse:** Denomination within circle

Date	Mintage	F	VF	XF	Unc
AH1394-1974	10,000,000	—	0.35	0.75	2.50
AH1394-1974 Proof	5,024	Value: 3.50			
AH1399-1979	4,000,000	—	0.35	0.75	2.50
AH1400-1980 Proof	10,000	Value: 2.50			
AH1405-1985	—	—	0.35	0.75	2.50

Y# 41 50 FILS

5.3000 g., Copper-Nickel, 24 mm. **Series:** F.A.O. **Obverse:** National arms **Reverse:** Denomination within circle

Date	Mintage	F	VF	XF	Unc
AH1394-1974	25,000	—	0.25	0.50	1.25

KM# 1 RIYAL

12.0000 g., 0.9250 Silver .3569 oz. ASW **Subject:** Qadhi Mohammed Mahmud Azzubairi Memorial **Obverse:** National arms **Reverse:** Figure on camel right

Date	Mintage	F	VF	XF	Unc
1969 Proof	3,200	Value: 17.50			

KM# 1a RIYAL

20.4800 g., 0.9000 Gold .5926 oz. AGW **Subject:** Qadhi Mohammed Mahmud Azzubairi Memorial **Obverse:** National arms **Reverse:** Figure on camel right

Date	Mintage	F	VF	XF	Unc
1969 Proof	100	Value: 435			

Y# 42 RIYAL

8.0000 g., Copper-Nickel, 28 mm. **Obverse:** National arms **Reverse:** Denomination within circle

Date	Mintage	F	VF	XF	Unc
AH1396-1976	7,800,000	—	0.50	1.25	2.50
AH1400-1980 Proof	—	Value: 5.00			
AH1405-1985	—	—	0.50	1.25	2.50
AH1414-1993	—	—	0.50	1.25	2.50

Y# 44 RIYAL

8.0000 g., Copper-Nickel, 28 mm. **Series:** F.A.O. **Obverse:** National arms **Reverse:** Denomination within circle

Date	Mintage	F	VF	XF	Unc
AH1398-1978	7,050	—	—	2.00	5.00

KM# 2.1 2 RIYALS

25.0000 g., 0.9250 Silver .7435 oz. ASW **Subject:** Apollo II - Cape Kennedy **Obverse:** Eagle with shield on breast and flags on legs **Reverse:** Space shuttle and launch pad **Note:** Dotted border.

Date	Mintage	F	VF	XF	Unc
1969	7,583	—	—	—	25.00
1969 Proof	200	Value: 50.00			

KM# 2.2 2 RIYALS

25.0000 g., 0.9250 Silver .7435 oz. ASW **Obverse:** Eagle with shield on breast and flags on legs **Reverse:** Space shuttle and launch pad **Note:** Border of dots near rim.

Date	Mintage	F	VF	XF	Unc
1969 Proof; restrike	1,000	Value: 28.50			

KM# 3.1 2 RIYALS

25.0000 g., 0.9250 Silver .7435 oz. ASW **Subject:** Apollo II - Moon Landing **Obverse:** Eagle with shield on breast and flags on legs **Reverse:** Moon landing scene **Note:** Dotted border.

Date	Mintage	F	VF	XF	Unc
1969	7,583	—	—	—	25.00
1969 Proof	200	Value: 50.00			

KM# 3.2 2 RIYALS

25.0000 g., 0.9250 Silver .7435 oz. ASW **Obverse:** Eagle with shield on breast and flags on legs **Reverse:** Moon landing scene **Note:** Border of dots near rim.

Date	Mintage	F	VF	XF	Unc
1969 Proof; restrike	1,000	Value: 28.50			

KM# 4 2 RIYALS

25.0000 g., 0.9250 Silver .7435 oz. ASW **Subject:** Qadhi Mohammed Mahmud Azzubairi Memorial **Obverse:** National arms **Reverse:** Roaring lion's head 3/4 left

Date	Mintage	F	VF	XF	Unc
1969 Proof	4,200	Value: 40.00			

KM# 4a 2 RIYALS

42.2900 g., 0.9000 Gold 1.2238 oz. AGW **Subject:** Qadhi Mohammed Mahmud Azzubairi Memorial **Obverse:** National arms **Reverse:** Roaring lion's head 3/4 left

Date	Mintage	F	VF	XF	Unc
1969 Proof	100	Value: 1,000			

KM# 14 2-1/2 RIYALS

9.0000 g., 0.9250 Silver .2676 oz. ASW **Subject:** Oil Exploration **Obverse:** National arms **Reverse:** Oil derricks in field

Date	Mintage	F	VF	XF	Unc
AH1395-1975	Est. 205,000	—	—	—	15.00
AH1395-1975 Proof	Est. 5,000	Value: 35.00			

KM# 6 5 RIYALS/RIALS

4.9000 g., 0.9000 Gold .1418 oz. AGW **Subject:** Qadhi Mohammed Mahmud Azzubairi Memorial **Obverse:** Monument **Reverse:** Denomination within circle

Date	Mintage	F	VF	XF	Unc
1969 Proof	—	Value: 140			

KM# 15 5 RIYALS/RIALS

18.0000 g., 0.9250 Silver .5353 oz. ASW **Subject:** Mona Lisa **Reverse:** Mona Lisa within center box, chain with ornaments surrounds

Date	Mintage	F	VF	XF	Unc
AH1395-1975	235,000	—	—	—	20.00
AH1395-1975 Proof	5,000	Value: 50.00			

KM# 7 10 RIYALS/RIALS

9.8000 g., 0.9000 Gold .2836 oz. AGW **Subject:** Qadhi Mohammed Mahmud Azzubairi Memorial **Obverse:** National arms **Reverse:** Three leaping gazelles right

Date	Mintage	F	VF	XF	Unc
1969 Proof	—	Value: 225			

KM# 23 10 RIYALS/RIALS

12.0800 g., 0.9250 Silver .3569 oz. ASW **Obverse:** Camel with rider right **Reverse:** National arms **Note:** Mule.

Date	Mintage	F	VF	XF	Unc
1969 Proof	—	Value: 40.00			

KM# 16 10 RIYALS/RIALS

36.0000 g., 0.9250 Silver 1.0707 oz. ASW **Series:** Montreal Olympics **Obverse:** National arms **Reverse:** Olympic events surround central flame

Date	Mintage	F	VF	XF	Unc
AH1395-1975	8,000	—	—	—	90.00
AH1395-1975 Proof	4,000	Value: 140			

KM# 28 10 RIYALS/RIALS

35.9000 g., 0.9250 Silver 1.0676 oz. ASW, 45.6 mm. **Mint:** Numismatica Italiana **Subject:** Montreal Olympics **Obverse:** National arms **Reverse:** Olympic events surround central flame **Edge:** Plain

Date	Mintage	F	VF	XF	Unc
AH1395-1975 Proof	100	Value: 400			

KM# 17 15 RIALS

54.0000 g., 0.9250 Silver 1.6061 oz. ASW **Subject:** Jerusalem **Reverse:** Domed buildings

Date	Mintage	F	VF	XF	Unc
AH1395-1975	70,000	—	—	—	40.00
AH1395-1975 Proof	5,000	Value: 100			

KM# 8 20 RIYALS/RIALS

19.6000 g., 0.9000 Gold .5672 oz. AGW **Subject:** Apollo II - Moon Landing **Obverse:** Eagle with shield on breast and flags on legs **Reverse:** Shuttle above astronauts on moons surface

Date	Mintage	F	VF	XF	Unc
1969 Proof	—	Value: 420			

KM# 9 20 RIYALS/RIALS

19.6000 g., 0.9000 Gold .5672 oz. AGW **Subject:** Qadhi Mohammed Mahmud Azzubairi Memorial **Obverse:** National arms **Reverse:** Camel with rider right

Date	Mintage	F	VF	XF	Unc
1969 Proof	—	Value: 450			

KM# 18 20 RIYALS/RIALS

0.9000 Gold **Subject:** Albakiriah Mosque **Reverse:** Mosque within oval **Shape:** Octagon

Date	Mintage	F	VF	XF	Unc
AH1395-1975	—	—	—	—	265
AH1395-1975 Proof	3,500	Value: 285			

KM# 19 25 RIYALS/RIALS

0.9000 Gold **Subject:** Oil Exploration **Obverse:** National arms within rounded square **Reverse:** Oil derricks in field, rounded square surrounds

Date	Mintage	F	VF	XF	Unc
AH1395-1975	—	—	—	—	160
AH1395-1975 Proof	3,500	Value: 180			

Y# 46 25 RIYALS/RIALS

28.2800 g., 0.9250 Silver .8411 oz. ASW **Series:** International Year of the Disabled Person **Obverse:** National arms **Reverse:** Head right

Date	Mintage	F	VF	XF	Unc
AH1401-1981	10,000	—	—	—	32.50
AH1401-1981 Proof	Est. 10,000	Value: 50.00			

Y# 47 25 RIYALS/RIALS

28.2800 g., 0.9250 Silver .8411 oz. ASW **Subject:** 20th Anniversary of the Revolution

Date	Mintage	F	VF	XF	Unc
AH1402-1982 Proof	2,000	Value: 55.00			

Y# 45 25 RIYALS/RIALS

28.2500 g., 0.9250 Silver .8402 oz. ASW **Series:** International Year of the Child **Obverse:** National arms within wreath of leaves **Reverse:** Children dancing, logos flank

Date	Mintage	F	VF	XF	Unc
AH1403-1983 Proof	6,604	Value: 18.50			

Y# 49 25 RIYALS/RIALS

28.2500 g., 0.9250 Silver .8402 oz. ASW **Series:** Decade for Women **Obverse:** National arms within wreath of leaves **Reverse:** Three half-figures of women looking left, ankh on dove cutout at left

Date	Mintage	F	VF	XF	Unc
AH1405-1985 Proof	1,000	Value: 42.50			

KM# 10 30 RIYALS

29.4000 g., 0.9000 Gold .8508 oz. AGW **Subject:** Qadhi Mohammed Mahmud Azzubairi Memorial **Obverse:** National arms **Reverse:** Head 3/4 right

Date	Mintage	F	VF	XF	Unc
1969 Proof	—	Value: 635			

KM# 11 50 RIYALS/RIALS

49.9700 g., Silver **Subject:** Qadhi Mohammed Mahmud Azzubairi Memorial **Obverse:** National arms **Reverse:** Lion

Date	Mintage	F	VF	XF	Unc
1969 Proof; restrike	—	Value: 50.00			

KM# 11a 50 RIYALS/RIALS

49.0000 g., 0.9000 Gold 1.4180 oz. AGW **Subject:** Qadhi Mohammed Mahmud Azzubairi Memorial **Obverse:** National arms above dates and denomination

Date	Mintage	F	VF	XF	Unc
1969 Proof	—	Value: 1,100			

KM# 20 50 RIYALS/RIALS

9.1000 g., 0.9000 Gold .2633 oz. AGW **Subject:** Mona Lisa **Reverse:** Mona Lisa within box, chain with ornaments surrounds

Date	Mintage	F	VF	XF	Unc
AH1395-1975	—	—	—	—	250
AH1395-1975 Proof	3,500	Value: 350			

KM# 21 75 RIYALS

13.6500 g., 0.9000 Gold .3950 oz. AGW **Series:** Montreal Olympics **Obverse:** Arms **Reverse:** XXI Olympiad

Date	Mintage	F	VF	XF	Unc
AH1395-1975	—	—	—	—	300
AH1395-1975 Proof	3,500	Value: 375			

KM# 22 100 RIALS

18.2000 g., 0.9000 Gold .5266 oz. AGW **Obverse:** National arms **Reverse:** Domed buildings

Date	Mintage	F	VF	XF	Unc
AH1395-1975	—	—	—	—	400
AH1395-1975 Proof	3,500	Value: 450			

KM# 24 500 RIYALS/RIALS

15.9800 g., 0.9170 Gold .4711 oz. AGW **Series:** International Year of the Disabled Person **Obverse:** National arms **Reverse:** Head of Bolivar facing, tiny logos flank below

Date	Mintage	F	VF	XF	Unc
AH1401-1981	—	—	—	—	400
AH1401-1981 Proof	—	Value: 500			

Y# 48 500 RIYALS/RIALS

15.9000 g., 0.9170 Gold .4686 oz. AGW **Subject:** 20th Anniversary of the Revolution **Reverse:** Ship within small center circle, figures above, oil derrick at left, grain sprig at right, circle surrounds all

Date	Mintage	F	VF	XF	Unc
AH1402-1982 Proof	1,000	Value: 385			

ESSAIS

KM#	Date	Mintage	Identification	Mkt Val
E1	AH1385	500	Rial. 0.7200 Silver. .	27.50

PIEFORTS

KM#	Date	Mintage	Identification	Mkt Val
P1	AH1981	1,150	25 Riyals/Rials. Silver. . I.Y.D.P.; Y#46	115
P2	AH1981	—	500 Riyals/Rials. Gold. . I.Y.P.D.; KM#24	1,000
P3	AH1983	—	25 Riyals/Rials. 0.9250 Silver. 57.0000 g. Arms, legend, date. Children. I.Y.C.; Y#45	175

TRIAL STRIKES

KM#	Date	Mintage	Identification	Mkt Val
TS1	AH1975	—	100 Rials. Goldine. Uniface; national arms divide dates, denomination below.	—

MINT SETS

KM#	Date	Mintage	Identification	Issue Price	Mkt Val
MS1	1975 (4)	—	KM#14-17	50.00	175
MS2	1975 (5)	—	KM#18-22	360	1,130

PROOF SETS

KM#	Date	Mintage	Identification	Issue Price	Mkt Val
PS1	1969 (7)	2,000	KM#1, 4, 6, 7, 9-11	375	1,350
PS2	1969 (4)	1,500	KM#1-4	—	125
PS4	1969 (3)	—	KM#2, 3, 6	78.00	175
PS5	1974 (5)	5,024	Y#33-37	15.00	12.50
PS6	1975 (5)	3,500	KM#18-22	485	1,450
PS7	1975 (4)	5,000	KM#14-17	75.00	335
PS8	1980 (6)	10,000	Y#33-37, 42	31.00	16.00

YEMEN REPUBLIC

The Republic of Yemen, formerly Yemen Arab Republic and Peoples Democratic Republic of Yemen, is located on the southern coast of the Arabian Peninsula. It has an area of 205,020 sq. mi. (531,000 sq. km.) and a population of 12 million. Capital: San'a. The port of Aden is the main commercial center and the area's most valuable natural resource. Recent oil and gas finds and a developing petroleum industry have improved their economic prospects. Agriculture and local handicrafts are the main industries. Cotton, fish, coffee, rock salt and hides are exported.

On May 22, 1990, the Yemen Arab Republic (North Yemen) and Peoples Democratic Republic of Yemen (South Yemen) merged into a unified Republic of Yemen. Disagreements between the two former governments simmered until civil war erupted in 1994, with the northern forces of the old Yemen Arab Republic eventually prevailing.

TITLE

دار الخلافة

Dar al-Khilafa(t)

REPUBLIC

MILLED COINAGE

KM# 25 RIYAL

2.6500 g., Stainless Steel, 19.95 mm. **Obv:** Denomination within circle **Rev:** National arms **Shape:** 21-sided

Date	Mintage	F	VF	XF	Unc	BU
AH1414-1993	—	—	—	—	1.25	1.75

KM# 26 5 RIYALS

4.5000 g., Stainless Steel, 22.85 mm. **Obv:** Denomination within circle **Rev:** Building **Shape:** 21-sided

Date	Mintage	F	VF	XF	Unc	BU
AH1414-1993	—	—	—	—	1.75	2.25

KM# 27 10 RIYALS

6.0500 g., Stainless Steel, 26 mm. **Obv:** Denomination within circle **Rev:** Bridge at Shaharah

Date	Mintage	F	VF	XF	Unc	BU
AH1416-1995	—	—	—	—	2.75	3.50

YEMEN, DEMOCRATIC REPUBLIC

SAUDI ARABIA, OMAN, SUDAN, Red Sea, (ARAB), (DEMOCRATIC), ERITREA, Arabian Sea, ETHIOPIA, DJIBOUTI

The southeast region of present day Yemen was predominately controlled by the British since their occupation of Aden in 1839. Independence was declared November 30, 1967 after the collapse of the Federation of South Arabia and the withdrawal of the British.

TITLES

Al-Jumhuriya(t) al-Yamaniya(t)
ad-Dimiqratiya(t) ash-Sha'biya(t)

MONETARY SYSTEM

Falus, Fulus — Fals, Fils — Falsan, Filsan

1000 Fils = 1 Dinar

PEOPLES DEMOCRATIC REPUBLIC

DECIMAL COINAGE

KM# 3 2-1/2 FILS

0.6500 g., Aluminum, 17 mm. **Obv:** Denomination and dates **Rev:** Leafy plant

Date	Mintage	F	VF	XF	Unc	BU
AH1393-1973	20,000,000	—	0.25	0.65	1.50	2.50

KM# 2 5 FILS

1.3500 g., Bronze, 23.1 mm. **Obv:** 8-sided star design **Rev:** Crossed daggers

Date	Mintage	F	VF	XF	Unc	BU
1971	2,000,000	—	0.30	0.60	1.00	1.50

KM# 4 5 FILS

1.3500 g., Aluminum, 23.1 mm. **Obv:** Denomination and dates **Rev:** Spiny lobster

Date	Mintage	F	VF	XF	Unc	BU
AH1393-1973	20,000,000	—	0.15	0.30	1.00	1.50
AH1404-1984	—	—	0.15	0.30	1.00	1.50

KM# 9 10 FILS

2.2000 g., Aluminum, 25.6 mm. **Obv:** Monument **Rev:** Denomination within circle **Shape:** Scallop

Date	Mintage	F	VF	XF	Unc	BU
1981	—	—	0.35	0.75	2.00	3.00

KM# 5 25 FILS
4.5500 g., Copper-Nickel, 20 mm. **Obv:** 8-sided star design **Rev:** Dhow

Date	Mintage	F	VF	XF	Unc	BU
1976	2,000,000	—	0.25	0.50	1.25	2.25
1977	1,000,000	—	0.25	0.50	1.50	2.50
1979	—	—	0.25	0.50	1.50	2.50
1982	—	—	0.25	0.50	1.50	2.50
1984	—	—	0.25	0.50	1.75	2.75

KM# 6 50 FILS
9.1000 g., Copper-Nickel, 27.8 mm. **Obv:** 8-sided star design **Rev:** Dhow

Date	Mintage	F	VF	XF	Unc	BU
1976	2,000,000	—	0.35	0.75	2.50	3.50
1977	2,000,000	—	0.35	0.75	2.50	3.50
1979	—	—	0.35	0.75	2.50	3.50
1984	—	—	0.35	0.75	2.50	3.50

KM# 10 100 FILS
10.0000 g., Copper-Nickel, 23.1 mm. **Obv:** Monument **Rev:** Denomination within circle **Shape:** 8-sided

Date	Mintage	F	VF	XF	Unc	BU
1981	—	—	0.50	1.00	3.00	4.50

KM# 7 250 FILS
11.2000 g., Copper-Nickel, 31 mm. **Subject:** 10th Anniversary of Independence **Obv:** Monument **Rev:** Ship at sea with date below

Date	Mintage	F	VF	XF	Unc	BU
1977	30,000	2.50	5.00	10.00	25.00	—

KM# 11 250 FILS
11.2000 g., Copper-Nickel, 31 mm. **Obv:** Monument **Rev:** Denomination within circle

Date	Mintage	F	VF	XF	Unc	BU
1981	—	—	1.50	3.00	5.50	7.00

KM# 12 2 DINARS
28.2800 g., 0.9250 Silver .8411 oz. ASW **Subject:** International Year of Disabled Persons - Abdulla Baradoni **Obv:** Head right **Rev:** Triangular design within wreath divides date

Date	Mintage	F	VF	XF	Unc	BU
1981	10,000	—	—	—	47.50	50.00
1981 Proof	10,000	Value: 52.50				

KM# 8 5 DINARS
12.5000 g., 0.9250 Silver .3718 oz. ASW **Subject:** 10th Anniversary of Independence **Obv:** Monument **Rev:** Ship at sea with date below

Date	Mintage	F	VF	XF	Unc	BU
1977 Proof	6,000	Value: 60.00				

KM# 13 50 DINARS
15.9800 g., 0.9170 Gold .4712 oz. AGW **Series:** International Year of Disabled Persons **Obv:** National arms **Rev:** Triangular design within wreath divides date

Date	Mintage	F	VF	XF	Unc	BU
1981	2,100	—	—	—	500	550
1981 Proof	1,100	Value: 750				

PIEFORTS

KM#	Date	Mintage	Identification	Mkt Val
P1	1981	1,050	2 Dinars. Silver. KM#12.	200
P2	1981	500	50 Dinars. Gold. KM#13.	1,500

The Federal Republic of Yugoslavia, formerly the Socialist Federal Republic of Yugoslavia, a Balkan country located on the east shore of the Adriatic Sea, has an area of 39,450 sq. mi. (102,173 sq. km.) and a population of 10.5 million. Capital: Belgrade. The chief industries area agriculture, mining, manufacturing and tourism. Machinery, nonferrous metals, meat and fabrics are exported.

Yugoslavia was proclaimed on Dec. 1, 1918, after the union of the Kingdom of Serbia, Montenegro and the South Slav territories of Austria-Hungary; and changed its official name from the Kingdom of the Serbs, Croats and Slovenes to the Kingdom of Yugoslavia on Oct. 3, 1929.The republic was composed of six autonomous republics -Serbia, Croatia, Slovenia, Bosnia-Herzegovina, Macedonia and Montenegro - and two autonomous provinces within Serbia: Kosovo-Melohija and Vojvodina. The government of Yugoslavia attempted to remain neutral in World War II but, yielding to German pressure, aligned itself with the Axis powers in March of 1941; a few days later it was overthrown by revolutionary forces and its neutrality reasserted. The Nazis occupied the country on April 6, and throughout the remaining war years were resisted by a number of guerrilla armies, notably that of Marshal Josip Broz Tito. After the defeat of the Axis powers, a leftist coalition headed by Tito abolished the monarchy and, on Jan. 31, 1946, established a "People's Republic". The collapse of the Federal Republic during 1991-1992 has resulted in the autonomous republics of Croatia, Slovenia, Bosnia-Herzegovina and Macedonia declaring their respective independence. Bosnia-Herzegovina is under military contest with the Serbian, Croat and Muslim populace opposing each other. Besides the remainder of the older Serbian sectors, a Serbian enclave in Knin located in southern Croatia has emerged called REPUBLIKE SRPSKEKRAJINE or Serbian Republic - Krajina whose capital is Knin and has also declared its independence in1992 when the former Republics of Serbia and Montenegro became the Federal Republic of Yugoslavia.

The name Yugoslavia appears on the coinage in letters of the Cyrillic alphabet alone until formation of the Federated Peoples Republic of Yugoslavia in 1953, after which both the Cyrillic and Latin alphabets are employed. From 1965, the coin denomination appears in the 4 different languages of the federated republics in letters of both the Cyrillic and Latin alphabets.

DENOMINATIONS
Para ПАРА
Dinar, ДИНАР, Dinara ДИНАРА
Dinari ДИНАРИ, Dinarjev

RULERS
Petar I, 1918-1921
Alexander I, 1921-1934
Petar II, 1934-1945

MINT MARKS
(a) - Paris, privy marks only
(b) - Brussels
(k) - КОВНИЦА,...А.Д. = Kovnica, A.D. (Akcionarno Drustvo) Belgrade
(l) - London
(p) - Poissy (thunderbolt)
(v) – Vienna

MONETARY SYSTEM
100 Para = 1 Dinar

KINGDOM OF THE SERBS, CROATS AND SLOVENES

STANDARD COINAGE

KM# 1 5 PARA
Zinc, 18.8 mm. **Ruler:** Petar I **Obv:** Crowned and mantled arms

on shield **Obv. Designer:** Adolf Hoffmann **Rev:** Denomination above date **Rev. Designer:** Joseph Prinz **Edge:** Plain

Date	Mintage	F	VF	XF	Unc	BU
1920(v)	3,825,514	3.00	7.50	15.00	42.00	—

KM# 2 10 PARA
Zinc, 20.85 mm. **Ruler:** Petar I **Obv:** Crowned and mantled arms on shield **Obv. Designer:** Adolf Hoffmann **Rev:** Denomination above date **Rev. Designer:** Joseph Prinz **Edge:** Plain

Date	Mintage	F	VF	XF	Unc	BU
1920(v)	58,946,122	1.50	3.50	9.00	24.00	—

KM# 3 25 PARA
Nickel-Bronze, 24 mm. **Ruler:** Petar I **Obv:** Crowned and mantled arms on shield **Obv. Designer:** Adolf Hoffmann **Rev:** Denomination above date **Rev. Designer:** Joseph Prinz **Edge:** Plain

Date	Mintage	F	VF	XF	Unc	BU
1920(v)	48,173,138	1.50	3.50	9.50	25.00	—

KM# 4 50 PARA
Nickel-Bronze, 18 mm. **Ruler:** Alexander I **Obv:** Head left **Rev:** Denomination and date within crowned wreath **Edge:** Milled **Designer:** A. Patey **Note:** Mint mark: lightning bolt.

Date	Mintage	F	VF	XF	Unc	BU
1925(b)	24,500,000	0.50	1.00	2.00	7.00	—
1925(p)	25,000,000	0.50	1.50	3.00	8.00	—

KM# 5 DINAR
Nickel-Bronze, 23 mm. **Ruler:** Alexander I **Obv:** Head left **Rev:** Denomination and date within crowned wreath **Edge:** Milled **Designer:** A. Patey **Note:** Mint mark: lightning bolt.

Date	Mintage	F	VF	XF	Unc	BU
1925(b)	37,000,000	0.50	1.00	2.50	7.50	—
1925(p)	37,500,410	0.75	1.50	3.00	8.00	—

KM# 6 2 DINARA
Nickel-Bronze, 27 mm. **Ruler:** Alexander I **Obv:** Head left **Rev:** Denomination and date within crowned wreath **Edge:** Milled **Designer:** A. Patey **Note:** Mint mark: lightning bolt.

Date	Mintage	F	VF	XF	Unc	BU
1925(b)	29,500,000	1.00	2.00	5.00	13.00	—
1925(p)	25,004,177	1.00	2.50	5.50	15.00	—

KM# 7 20 DINARA
6.4516 g., 0.9000 Gold .1867 oz. AGW, 21 mm. **Ruler:** Alexander I **Obv:** Head left **Rev:** Denomination and date within crowned wreath **Edge:** Milled

Date	Mintage	F	VF	XF	Unc	BU
1925	1,000,000	135	150	185	250	—
1925 Proof	—	—	—	—	—	—

KINGDOM OF YUGOSLAVIA

STANDARD COINAGE

KM# 17 25 PARA
Bronze, 20 mm. **Ruler:** Petar II **Obv:** Center hole within crowned wreath **Rev:** Center hole divides denomination **Edge:** Plain **Note:** 4 mm hole in center of coin.

Date	Mintage	F	VF	XF	Unc	BU
1938	40,000,000	1.25	2.50	5.50	14.00	—
1938 Proof	—	—	—	—	—	—

KM# 18 50 PARA
Aluminum-Bronze, 18 mm. **Ruler:** Petar II **Obv:** Crown **Rev:** Denomination above date **Edge:** Plain

Date	Mintage	F	VF	XF	Unc	BU
1938	100,000,000	0.50	1.00	2.50	7.50	—

KM# 19 DINAR
Aluminum-Bronze, 21 mm. **Ruler:** Petar II **Obv:** Crown **Rev:** Denomination above date **Edge:** Plain

Date	Mintage	F	VF	XF	Unc	BU
1938	100,000,000	0.50	0.75	2.00	6.00	—
1938 Proof	—	—	—	—	—	—

KM# 20 2 DINARA
Aluminum-Bronze, 24.5 mm. **Ruler:** Petar II **Obv:** Crown **Rev:** Denomination above date, large numeral **Edge:** Plain

Date	Mintage	F	VF	XF	Unc	BU
1938	74,250,000	0.50	1.00	3.50	9.00	—
1938 Proof	—	—	—	—	—	—

KM# 21 2 DINARA
Aluminum-Bronze, 24.5 mm. **Ruler:** Petar II **Obv:** 12 mm crown **Rev:** Denomination above date, large numeral **Edge:** Plain

Date	Mintage	F	VF	XF	Unc	BU
1938	750,000	6.00	10.00	19.00	38.00	—
1938 Proof	—	—	—	—	—	—

KM# 10 10 DINARA
7.0000 g., 0.5000 Silver .1125 oz. ASW **Ruler:** Alexander I **Obv:** Head left **Rev:** Crowned double eagle with shield on breast **Edge:** Milled

Date	Mintage	F	VF	XF	Unc	BU
1931(l)	19,000,000	2.00	4.00	8.00	18.00	—
1931(l) Proof	—	—	—	—	—	—
1931(a)	4,000,000	3.50	7.00	15.00	32.00	—
1931(a) Proof	—	—	—	—	—	—

KM# 22 10 DINARA
Nickel, 23 mm. **Ruler:** Petar II **Obv:** Head right **Rev:** Denomination and date within crowned wreath **Edge:** Milled **Designer:** F. Dincic

Date	Mintage	F	VF	XF	Unc	BU
1938	25,000,000	0.50	1.00	2.00	4.50	—

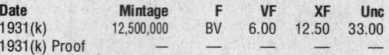

KM# 11 20 DINARA
14.0000 g., 0.5000 Silver .2250 oz. ASW, 31 mm. **Ruler:** Alexander I **Obv:** Head left **Rev:** Crowned double eagle with shield on breast **Edge:** Milled **Designer:** Percy Metcalfe

Date	Mintage	F	VF	XF	Unc	BU
1931(k)	12,500,000	BV	6.00	12.50	33.00	—
1931(k) Proof	—	—	—	—	—	—

KM# 23 20 DINARA
9.0000 g., 0.7500 Silver .217 oz. ASW **Ruler:** Petar II **Obv:** Head left **Rev:** Crowned double eagle with shield on breast **Edge Lettering:** BOG CUVA JUGOSLAVIJU ***

Date	Mintage	F	VF	XF	Unc	BU
1938	15,000,000	BV	3.50	6.00	12.50	—

KM# 16 50 DINARA
23.3300 g., 0.7500 Silver .5626 oz. ASW, 36 mm. **Ruler:** Alexander I **Obv:** Head left **Rev:** Crowned double eagle with shield on breast **Edge Lettering:** BOG CUVA JUGOSLAVIJU

Date	Mintage	F	VF	XF	Unc	BU
1932(k)	5,500,000	10.00	22.00	45.00	180	—
1932(l)	5,500,000	10.00	25.00	50.00	200	—
1932(l) Proof	—	Value: 2,200				

KM# 24 50 DINARA
15.0000 g., 0.7500 Silver .3617 oz. ASW, 31 mm. **Ruler:** Petar II **Obv:** Head right **Rev:** Crowned double eagle with shield on breast

Date	Mintage	F	VF	XF	Unc	BU
1938	10,000,000	BV	6.00	9.00	18.00	—

TRADE COINAGE

Trade-coinage countermarks were applied by the Yugoslav Control Office for Noble Metals to confirm gold purity. The initial countermark displayed a sword, but part way through the first production year, this was retired and the second countermark, showing an ear of corn, was used.

KM# 12.1 DUKAT
3.4900 g., 0.9860 Gold .1106 oz. AGW **Ruler:** Alexander I **Countermark:** Birds **Obv:** Head left, small legend with КОВНИЦ, А.Д. below head **Obv. Designer:** Richard Plecht **Rev:** Crowned double eagle with shield on breast **Rev. Designer:** Joseph Prinz **Edge:** Milled

Date	Mintage	F	VF	XF	Unc	BU
1931(k)	Est. 50,000	—	100	150	200	—
1932(k) Rare	Inc. below	—	—	—	—	—

Note: The 1932(k) examples with sword countermark are believed to be mint sports

KM# 12.2 DUKAT
3.4900 g., 0.9860 Gold .1106 oz. AGW **Ruler:** Alexander I **Countermark:** Ear of corn **Obv:** Head left **Rev:** Crowned double eagle with shield on breast **Note:** Forgeries bearing no countermark exist for 1932 and possibly other dates. Small legend on both sides

Date	Mintage	F	VF	XF	Unc	BU
1931(k)	Est. 150,000	—	90.00	140	185	—
1932(k)	Est. 70,000	—	95.00	145	195	—
1933(k)	Est. 40,000	—	135	185	300	—
1934(k)	Est. 2,000	—	500	850	1,250	—

KM# 12.3 DUKAT
3.4900 g., 0.9860 Gold .1106 oz. AGW **Ruler:** Alexander I **Countermark:** Sword **Obv:** Head left **Rev:** Crowned double eagle with shield on breast **Note:** Mule.

Date	Mintage	F	VF	XF	Unc	BU
1931(k)	—	—	—	3,000	5,000	—

KM# 13.1 DUKAT
3.4900 g., 0.9860 Gold .1106 oz. AGW **Ruler:** Alexander I **Obv:** Head left **Rev:** Crowned double eagle with shield on breast **Note:** Large legend on both sides.

Date	Mintage	F	VF	XF	Unc	BU
1931(k)	2,869	—	—	3,500	5,500	—

KM# 13.2 DUKAT
3.4900 g., 0.9860 Gold .1106 oz. AGW **Ruler:** Alexander I **Countermark:** Sword **Obv:** Head left **Rev:** Crowned double eagle with shield on breast **Note:** Large-letter varieties bear the Kovnica, A.D. mint mark but were actually struck in Vienna.

Date	Mintage	F	VF	XF	Unc	BU
1931(k)	Inc. above	—	—	4,000	6,500	—

KM# 14.2 4 DUKATA
13.9600 g., 0.9860 Gold .4425 oz. AGW **Ruler:** Alexander I **Countermark:** Ear of corn **Obv:** Conjoined busts of royal couple left **Rev:** Crowned double eagle with shield on breast

Date	Mintage	F	VF	XF	Unc	BU
1931(k)	Est. 15,000	—	450	750	950	—
1932(k)	Est. 10,000	—	400	725	1,000	—
1933(k)	Est. 2,000	—	1,000	1,600	2,500	—

KM# 14.1 4 DUKATA
13.9600 g., 0.9860 Gold .4425 oz. AGW **Ruler:** Alexander I **Countermark:** Sword **Obv:** Jugate busts of royal couple left **Obv. Designer:** Richard Placht **Rev:** Crowned double eagle with shield on breast **Rev. Designer:** Joseph Prinz **Edge:** Milled **Note:** Small legend on both sides. The 1932(k) examples with birds countermark are believed to be mint sports.

Date	Mintage	F	VF	XF	Unc	BU
1931(k)	Est. 10,000	—	450	750	950	—
1932(k) Rare	Inc. below	—	—	—	—	—

KM# 14.3 4 DUKATA
13.9600 g., 0.9860 Gold .4425 oz. AGW **Ruler:** Alexander I **Obv:** Jugate busts of royal couple left **Rev:** Crowned double eagle with shield on breast **Note:** Without countermark on either side. Only one genuine piece has been reported.

Date	Mintage	F	VF	XF	Unc	BU
1931(k) Rare	—	—	—	—	—	—

KM# A15.1 4 DUKATA
13.9600 g., 0.9860 Gold .4425 oz. AGW **Ruler:** Alexander I **Obv:** Conjoined busts of royal couple left **Rev:** Crowned double eagle with shield on breast **Note:** Large legend on both sides. Sword Countermark.

Date	Mintage	F	VF	XF	Unc	BU
1931(k) Rare	51	—	—	—	—	—

KM# A15.2 4 DUKATA
13.9600 g., 0.9860 Gold .4425 oz. AGW **Ruler:** Alexander I **Countermark:** Sword **Obv:** Conjoined busts of royal couple left, large legend **Rev:** Crowned double eagle with shield on breast, large legend **Note:** Large-letter varieties bear the Kovnica, A.D. mint mark but were actually struck in Vienna.

Date	Mintage	F	VF	XF	Unc	BU
1931(k)	Inc. above	—	—	—	—	—

POST WAR COINAGE

KM# 25 50 PARA
Zinc, 18 mm. **Obv:** State emblem, nine stars below **Rev:** Denomination surrounded by stars **Edge:** Milled

Date	Mintage	F	VF	XF	Unc	BU
1945	40,000,000	0.50	1.00	3.00	9.00	—

KM# 26 DINAR
Zinc, 20 mm. **Obv:** State emblem, nine stars below **Rev:** Stars surround denomination **Edge:** Milled

Date	Mintage	F	VF	XF	Unc	BU
1945	90,000,000	0.50	1.00	2.50	7.00	—

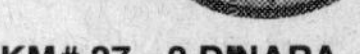

KM# 27 2 DINARA
Zinc, 22 mm. **Obv:** State emblem, nine stars below **Rev:** Stars surround denomination **Edge:** Milled

Date	Mintage	F	VF	XF	Unc	BU
1945	70,000,000	0.50	1.25	3.00	9.00	—

KM# 28 5 DINARA
Zinc, 26.5 mm. **Obv:** State emblem, nine stars below **Rev:** Stars surround denomination **Edge:** Milled

Date	Mintage	F	VF	XF	Unc	BU
1945	50,000,000	1.00	2.00	4.00	12.00	—

FEDERAL PEOPLE'S REPUBLIC

STANDARD COINAGE

KM# 29 50 PARA
Aluminum, 17.4 mm. **Obv:** State emblem **Rev:** Denomination divides date, seven stars above **Edge:** Plain

Date	Mintage	F	VF	XF	Unc	BU
1953	—	—	—	0.10	0.50	—

KM# 30 DINAR
Aluminum, 19.8 mm. **Obv:** State emblem **Rev:** Denomination divides date, seven stars above **Edge:** Plain

Date	Mintage	F	VF	XF	Unc	BU
1953	—	—	0.10	0.15	0.50	—

KM# 31 2 DINARA
Aluminum, 22.2 mm. **Obv:** State emblem **Rev:** Denomination divides date, seven stars above **Edge:** Plain

Date	Mintage	F	VF	XF	Unc	BU
1953	—	—	0.10	0.25	0.75	—

KM# 32 5 DINARA
Aluminum, 24.6 mm. **Obv:** State emblem **Rev:** Denomination divides date, seven stars above **Edge:** Plain

Date	Mintage	F	VF	XF	Unc	BU
1953	—	0.10	0.25	0.50	1.00	—

KM# 33 10 DINARA
Aluminum-Bronze, 21 mm. **Obv:** State emblem **Rev:** Hand holding grain stalks below head left **Edge:** Milled **Designer:** F. M. Dincic

Date	Mintage	F	VF	XF	Unc	BU
1955	—	0.15	0.30	0.75	1.50	—

KM# 34 20 DINARA

Aluminum-Bronze, 25.5 mm. **Obv:** State emblem **Rev:** Head at left looking right, cogwheel lower right **Edge:** Milled **Designer:** F. M. Dincic

Date	Mintage	F	VF	XF	Unc	BU
1955	—	0.25	0.50	1.00	2.00	—

KM# 35 50 DINARA

Aluminum-Bronze, 25.5 mm. **Obv:** State emblem **Rev:** Two jugate heads right, cogwheel below **Edge:** Milled **Designer:** F. M. Dincic

Date	Mintage	F	VF	XF	Unc	BU
1955	—	0.25	0.75	2.00	4.50	—

SOCIALIST FEDERAL REPUBLIC

STANDARD COINAGE

KM# 42 5 PARA

Copper-Zinc, 16 mm. **Obv:** State emblem **Rev:** Denomination above date within wreath, six stars above **Edge:** Milled

Date	Mintage	F	VF	XF	Unc	BU
1965	23,839,900	—	0.10	0.20	0.40	—

KM# 43 5 PARA

Copper-Zinc, 16 mm. **Obv:** State emblem **Rev:** Denomination divides date **Edge:** Milled

Date	Mintage	F	VF	XF	Unc	BU
1965	16,200,000	—	—	0.10	0.20	—
1973	36,384,000	—	—	0.10	0.15	—
1974	3,628,000	—	—	0.10	0.25	—
1975	20,272,000	—	—	0.10	0.15	—
1976	30,490,000	—	—	0.10	0.15	—
1977	10,270,000	—	—	0.10	0.15	—
1978	12,000,000	—	—	0.10	0.15	—
1979	20,414,000	—	—	0.10	0.15	—
1980	22,412,000	—	—	0.10	0.15	—
1981	630,000	—	0.10	0.25	0.50	—

KM# 44 10 PARA

Copper-Zinc, 21 mm. **Obv:** State emblem **Rev:** Denomination divides date **Edge:** Milled

Date	Mintage	F	VF	XF	Unc	BU
1965	15,400,000	—	—	0.10	0.20	—
1973	15,647,000	—	—	0.10	0.20	—
1974	60,139,000	—	—	0.10	0.20	—
1975	36,139,000	—	—	0.10	0.15	—
1976	36,111,000	—	—	0.10	0.15	—
1977	40,451,000	—	—	0.10	0.15	—
1978	50,129,000	—	—	0.10	0.15	—
Note: Two varieties of "7" exist						
1979	89,738,000	—	—	0.10	0.15	—
1980	90,111,000	—	—	0.10	0.15	—
1981	14,090,000	—	—	0.10	0.15	—

KM# 139 10 PARA

Copper-Zinc **Obv:** State emblem **Rev:** Denomination

Date	Mintage	F	VF	XF	Unc	BU
1990	174,028,000	—	—	0.10	0.15	—
1991	60,828,000	—	—	0.15	0.35	—

KM# 45 20 PARA

Copper-Zinc, 23.2 mm. **Obv:** State emblem **Rev:** Denomination divides date **Edge:** Milled **Note:** Thickness varies: 1.3-1.5 mm.

Date	Mintage	F	VF	XF	Unc	BU
1965	—	—	—	0.10	0.30	—
1973	30,448,000	—	—	0.10	0.30	—
1974	31,364,000	—	—	0.10	0.30	—
1975	44,683,000	—	—	0.10	0.30	—
1976	33,312,000	—	—	0.10	0.30	—
1977	40,782,000	—	—	0.10	0.30	—
1978	39,999,000	—	—	0.10	0.30	—
1979	49,121,000	—	—	0.10	0.30	—
1980	73,757,000	—	—	0.10	0.30	—
1981	96,144,000	—	—	0.10	0.30	—

KM# 140 20 PARA

Copper-Zinc **Obv:** State emblem **Rev:** Denomination above date

Date	Mintage	VG	F	VF	XF	Unc
1990	174,028,500	—	—	0.10	0.20	0.50
1991	60,828,000	—	—	0.10	0.20	0.50

KM# 84 25 PARA

Bronze, 17 mm. **Obv:** State emblem **Rev:** Denomination above date **Edge:** Plain

Date	Mintage	F	VF	XF	Unc	BU
1982	185,316,000	—	—	0.10	0.25	—
1983	65,290,000	—	—	0.15	0.30	—

KM# 46.1 50 PARA

Copper-Zinc, 25.5 mm. **Obv:** State emblem **Rev:** Denomination divides date **Edge:** Milled

Date	Mintage	F	VF	XF	Unc	BU
1965	—	—	0.10	0.20	0.65	—
1973	23,739,000	—	0.10	0.20	0.65	—
1974	33,000	1.00	1.50	2.50	5.00	—
1975	10,220,000	—	0.10	0.20	0.80	—
1976	8,438,000	—	0.10	0.20	1.00	—
1977	17,864,000	—	0.10	0.20	0.75	—
1978	40,177,000	—	0.10	0.20	0.65	—
Note: Two varieties of "7" exist						
1979	3,021,000	0.50	1.00	2.00	5.00	—

KM# 46.2 50 PARA

Copper-Zinc **Obv:** State emblem **Rev:** Denomination divides date

Date	Mintage	F	VF	XF	Unc	BU
1979	12,278,000	0.20	0.50	1.00	2.50	—
1980	24,974,000	—	0.10	0.20	0.65	—
1981	40,319,000	—	0.10	0.20	0.65	—

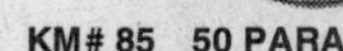

KM# 85 50 PARA

2.8500 g., Bronze, 19 mm. **Obv:** State emblem **Rev:** Denomination above date **Edge:** Plain

Date	Mintage	F	VF	XF	Unc	BU
1982	79,584,000	—	—	0.10	0.20	—
1983	72,100,000	—	—	0.10	0.20	—
1984	59,642,000	0.25	0.50	1.00	1.50	—

KM# 141 50 PARA

Copper-Zinc **Obv:** State emblem **Rev:** Denomination

Date	Mintage	F	VF	XF	Unc	BU
1990	137,873,000	—	—	0.10	0.20	—
1991	42,152,000	—	0.20	0.40	1.00	—

KM# 36 DINAR

Aluminum, 19.8 mm. **Obv:** State emblem **Rev:** Denomination divides date, seven stars above **Edge:** Plain

Date	Mintage	F	VF	XF	Unc	BU
1963	—	—	—	0.10	0.15	—

KM# 47 DINAR

Copper-Nickel, 21.8 mm. **Obv:** State emblem **Rev:** Denomination and date within wreath, six stars above **Edge:** Milled

Date	Mintage	F	VF	XF	Unc	BU
1965	75,822,000	0.10	0.15	0.30	0.60	—

KM# 48 DINAR

Copper-Nickel, 21.8 mm. **Obv:** State emblem **Rev:** Denomination above date within wreath, six stars above **Edge:** Milled

Date	Mintage	F	VF	XF	Unc	BU
1968	35,497,000	0.10	0.20	0.40	0.80	—

KM# 59 DINAR

Copper-Nickel-Zinc, 21.8 mm. **Obv:** State emblem **Rev:** Text surrounds denomination within wreath, six stars above **Edge:** Milled

Date	Mintage	F	VF	XF	Unc	BU
1973	18,974,000	—	0.10	0.15	0.40	—
1974	42,724,000	—	0.10	0.15	0.35	—
1975	30,260,000	—	0.10	0.15	0.35	—
1976	21,849,000	—	0.10	0.15	0.35	—
1977	30,468,000	—	0.10	0.15	0.35	—
Note: Two varieties of wreath						
1977 Proof	—	Value: 40.00				
1978	35,032,000	—	0.10	0.15	0.35	—
1979	39,844,000	—	0.10	0.15	0.35	—
1980	60,630,000	—	0.10	0.15	0.35	—
1981	56,650,000	—	0.10	0.15	0.35	—

KM# 61 DINAR

Copper-Nickel-Zinc, 21.8 mm. **Series:** F.A.O. **Obv:** State emblem **Rev:** Text surrounds denomination, stylized grain stalks at sides **Edge:** Milled

Date	Mintage	F	VF	XF	Unc	BU
1976	500,000	—	0.10	0.30	1.00	—

KM# 86 DINAR

3.6000 g., Nickel-Brass, 20 mm. **Obv:** State emblem **Rev:** Text surrounds denomination **Edge:** Milled

Date	Mintage	F	VF	XF	Unc	BU
1982	70,105,000	—	—	0.10	0.30	—
1983	114,180,000	—	—	0.10	0.20	—
1984	172,185,000	—	—	0.10	0.20	—
1985	64,436,000	—	—	0.10	0.25	—
1986	122,643,000	—	—	0.10	0.20	—

KM# 142 DINAR

Copper-Nickel-Zinc **Obv:** State emblem **Rev:** Text surrounds denomination **Edge:** Milled

Date	Mintage	F	VF	XF	Unc	BU
1990	172,105,000	—	—	0.10	0.25	—
1991	79,549,000	—	0.15	0.25	0.75	—

KM# 37 2 DINARA

Aluminum, 22.2 mm. **Obv:** State emblem **Rev:** Denomination divides date, seven stars above **Edge:** Plain

Date	Mintage	F	VF	XF	Unc	BU
1963	—	—	0.10	0.15	0.25	—

KM# 55 2 DINARA

Copper-Nickel-Zinc, 24.5 mm. **Series:** F.A.O. **Obv:** State emblem **Rev:** Text surrounds denomination, grain stalks at sides **Edge:** Milled

Date	Mintage	F	VF	XF	Unc	BU
1970	500,000	—	0.20	0.40	1.00	—

KM# 57 2 DINARA

Copper-Nickel-Zinc, 24.5 mm. **Obv:** State emblem **Rev:** Text encircles denomination, wreath surrounds, six stars above **Edge:** Milled

Date	Mintage	F	VF	XF	Unc	BU
1971	10,413,000	—	0.10	0.30	0.70	—
1972	18,446,000	—	0.10	0.20	0.50	—
1973	31,848,000	—	0.10	0.20	0.45	—
1974	10,989,000	—	0.10	0.20	0.50	—
1975	92,000	2.00	4.00	7.50	15.00	—
1976	6,092,000	—	0.10	0.20	0.50	—
1977	19,335,000	—	0.10	0.20	0.50	—
1978	13,035,000	—	0.10	0.20	0.50	—
1979	20,069,000	—	0.10	0.20	0.45	—
1980	36,088,000	—	0.10	0.20	0.45	—
1981	42,599,000	—	0.10	0.20	0.45	—

KM# 87 2 DINARA

4.4000 g., Nickel-Brass, 22 mm. **Obv:** State emblem **Rev:** Text surrounds denomination **Edge:** Milled

Date	Mintage	F	VF	XF	Unc	BU
1982	40,632,000	—	0.10	0.15	0.35	—
1983	35,468,000	—	0.10	0.15	0.35	—
1984	51,500,000	—	0.10	0.15	0.35	—
1985	81,100,000	—	0.10	0.15	0.35	—
1986	50,453,000	—	0.10	0.15	0.35	—

KM# 143 2 DINARA

Copper-Nickel-Zinc **Obv:** State emblem **Rev:** Text surrounds denomination

Date	Mintage	F	VF	XF	Unc	BU
1990	15,936,000	0.15	0.30	0.60	2.00	—
1991	32,836,000	—	0.20	0.40	1.00	—
1992	14,155,000	2.50	3.50	7.00	12.50	—

KM# 38 5 DINARA

Aluminum, 24.6 mm. **Obv:** State emblem **Rev:** Denomination divides date, seven stars above **Edge:** Plain

Date	Mintage	F	VF	XF	Unc	BU
1963	—	0.10	0.20	0.35	0.50	—

KM# 56 5 DINARA

Copper-Nickel-Zinc, 27.5 mm. **Series:** F.A.O. **Obv:** State emblem **Rev:** Text surrounds denomination, grain stalks at sides **Edge:** Milled

Date	Mintage	F	VF	XF	Unc	BU
1970	500,000	0.20	0.50	1.00	2.50	—

KM# 58 5 DINARA

Copper-Nickel-Zinc, 27.5 mm. **Obv:** State emblem **Rev:** Text encircles denomination, wreath surrounds, six stars above **Edge:** Milled **Note:** Regular issue.

Date	Mintage	F	VF	XF	Unc	BU
1971	10,224,000	0.20	0.40	0.60	1.00	—
Note: Two varieties of wreath						
1972	27,974,000	0.10	0.20	0.35	0.60	—
Note: Two varieties of 2 in date						
1973	12,705,000	0.20	0.40	0.60	1.00	—
1974	6,054,000	0.25	0.50	1.00	2.00	—
1975	13,533,000	0.10	0.20	0.35	0.60	—
1976	4,965,383	0.10	0.25	0.40	0.80	—
1977	922,000	0.30	0.60	1.20	2.50	—
1978	1,000,000	0.10	0.25	0.50	1.50	—
1979	3,000,000	0.10	0.25	0.40	0.80	—
1980	9,977,000	0.10	0.20	0.35	0.60	—
1981	15,450,000	0.10	0.20	0.35	0.60	—

KM# 60 5 DINARA

Copper-Nickel-Zinc, 27.5 mm. **Subject:** 30th Anniversary of Nazi Defeat **Obv:** State emblem **Rev:** Denomination, six stars

Date	Mintage	F	VF	XF	Unc	BU
1975	1,020,000	0.25	0.50	1.00	2.50	—

KM# 88 5 DINARA

5.5000 g., Nickel-Brass, 24 mm. **Obv:** State emblem **Rev:** Denomination **Edge:** Milled

Date	Mintage	F	VF	XF	Unc	BU
1982	40,956,000	—	0.10	0.15	0.50	—
1983	40,156,000	—	0.10	0.15	0.50	—
1984	33,023,000	—	0.10	0.15	0.50	—
1985	94,422,000	—	0.10	0.15	0.50	—
1986	37,199,000	—	0.10	0.15	0.50	—

KM# 144 5 DINARA

Copper-Nickel-Zinc **Obv:** State emblem **Rev:** Denomination

Date	Mintage	F	VF	XF	Unc	BU
1990	9,354,000	0.25	0.45	1.00	2.50	—
1991	113,420,000	—	0.25	0.50	1.25	—
1992	15,970,000	1.50	2.50	4.00	7.00	—

KM# 145 5 DINARA

Copper-Nickel-Zinc **Subject:** 1990 Chess Olympiad **Obv:** State emblem within flat bottom circle **Rev:** Logo

Date	Mintage	F	VF	XF	Unc	BU
1990 Proof	20,000	Value: 7.00				

KM# 39 10 DINARA

Aluminum-Bronze, 21 mm. **Obv:** State emblem **Rev:** Hand holding grain stalks below head left **Edge:** Milled **Designer:** F. Dincic

Date	Mintage	F	VF	XF	Unc	BU
1963	—	0.15	0.30	0.75	1.25	—

KM# 62 10 DINARA
Copper-Nickel, 30 mm. **Obv:** State emblem **Rev:** Text encircles denomination, wreath surrounds, six stars above **Edge:** Milled

Date	Mintage	F	VF	XF	Unc	BU
1976	10,549,500	0.30	0.60	0.75	1.25	—
1977	39,645,000	0.30	0.60	0.75	1.00	—
Note: Two varieties of wreath						
1978	29,834,000	0.30	0.60	0.75	1.00	—
1979	4,969,000	0.30	0.60	0.75	1.00	—
1980	10,139,000	0.30	0.60	0.75	1.00	—
1981	20,166,000	0.30	0.60	0.75	1.00	—

KM# 63 10 DINARA
Copper-Nickel-Zinc, 30 mm. **Series:** F.A.O. **Obv:** State emblem **Rev:** Text surrounds denomination, grain stalks at sides, six stars above

Date	Mintage	F	VF	XF	Unc	BU
1976	500,000	0.50	0.75	1.00	2.50	—

KM# 89 10 DINARA
5.2000 g., Copper-Nickel, 23 mm. **Obv:** State emblem **Rev:** Text surrounds denomination **Edge:** Milled

Date	Mintage	F	VF	XF	Unc	BU
1982	8,862,000	—	0.10	0.20	0.80	—
1983	42,400,000	—	0.10	0.20	0.75	—
1984	30,900,000	—	0.10	0.20	0.75	—
1985	31,647,000	—	0.10	0.20	0.75	—
1986	40,739,000	—	0.10	0.20	0.75	—
1987	104,988,000	—	0.10	0.20	0.75	—
1988	27,614,000	—	0.10	0.20	0.75	—

KM# 96 10 DINARA
Copper-Nickel, 30 mm. **Subject:** 40th Anniversary - Battle of Neretva River **Obv:** State emblem within flat bottomed circle **Rev:** Bridge over the River Neretva **Edge:** Milled

Date	Mintage	F	VF	XF	Unc	BU
ND(1983)	900,000	—	1.00	2.00	4.00	6.00
ND(1983) Proof	100,000	Value: 8.00				

KM# 97.1 10 DINARA
Copper-Nickel, 30 mm. **Subject:** 40th Anniversary - Battle of Sutjeska River **Obv:** State emblem within flat bottom circle **Rev:** Pathway divides monument **Edge:** Milled

Date	Mintage	F	VF	XF	Unc	BU
ND(1983)	900,000	—	1.00	1.50	3.00	5.00
ND(1983) Proof	100,000	Value: 7.50				

KM# 97.2 10 DINARA
Copper-Nickel **Subject:** 40th Anniversary - Battle of Sutjeska River **Obv:** State emblem within flat bottom circle **Rev:** Without pathway in front of monument

Date	Mintage	F	VF	XF	Unc	BU
ND(1983)	—	—	3.00	6.00	10.00	12.00

KM# 131 10 DINARA
Brass **Obv:** Text surrounds state emblem within square **Rev:** Denomination within square, text on four sides **Edge:** Plain

Date	Mintage	F	VF	XF	Unc	BU
1988	35,992,000	—	—	0.10	0.25	0.35
1989	75,000,000	—	—	0.10	0.25	0.35

KM# 40 20 DINARA
Aluminum-Bronze, 23.2 mm. **Obv:** State emblem **Rev:** Head at left looking right, cogwheel below **Edge:** Milled **Designer:** F. Dincic

Date	Mintage	F	VF	XF	Unc	BU
1963	—	0.50	1.00	1.75	3.50	—

KM# 49 20 DINARA
9.0000 g., 0.9250 Silver .2676 oz. ASW, 28 mm. **Subject:** 25th Anniversary of Republic **Obv:** State emblem within circle **Rev:** Head left **Edge:** Milled **Note:** Mint mark: NI (Numismatica Italiana, Milano, Italy).

Date	Mintage	VG	F	VF	XF	Unc
1968 Proof	100,000	Value: 25.00				
1968 NI Proof	Inc. above	Value: 25.00				

KM# 112 20 DINARA
Copper-Zinc-Nickel, 25 mm. **Obv:** State emblem **Rev:** Denomination **Edge:** Milled

Date	Mintage	F	VF	XF	Unc	BU
1985	5,000,000	—	0.10	0.15	0.50	—
1986	20,235,000	—	0.10	0.15	0.35	—
1987	39,514,000	—	0.10	0.15	0.35	—

KM# 132 20 DINARA
Brass **Obv:** Text surrounds state emblem within square **Rev:** Denomination within square, text on four sides **Edge:** Plain

Date	Mintage	F	VF	XF	Unc	BU
1988	29,775,000	—	—	0.10	0.25	0.35
1989	12,994,000	—	—	0.10	0.25	0.35

KM# 41 50 DINARA
Aluminum-Bronze, 25.5 mm. **Obv:** State emblem **Rev:** Conjoined heads looking right, cogwheel below **Edge:** Milled **Designer:** Dincic **Note:** Exists with filled letter in denomination. Two varieties of the letter "P" in ANHAPA.

Date	Mintage	F	VF	XF	Unc	BU
1963	—	1.00	2.50	6.00	16.00	—

KM# 50 50 DINARA
20.0000 g., 0.9250 Silver .5948 oz. ASW, 34 mm. **Subject:** 25th Anniversary of Republic **Obv:** State emblem within circle **Rev:** Head left within circle **Note:** Mint mark: NI.

Date	Mintage	F	VF	XF	Unc	BU
ND(1968) Proof	100,000	Value: 40.00				
ND(1968) NI Proof	Inc. above	Value: 40.00				

KM# 113 50 DINARA
Copper-Zinc-Nickel, 27 mm. **Obv:** State emblem **Rev:** Denomination **Edge:** Milled

Date	Mintage	F	VF	XF	Unc	BU
1985	25,488,000	—	0.10	0.25	0.75	—
1986	20,353,000	—	0.10	0.25	0.75	—
1987	21,792,000	—	0.10	0.25	0.75	—
1988	28,370,000	—	0.10	0.25	0.75	—

KM# 133 50 DINARA
Brass **Obv:** Text surrounds state emblem within square **Rev:** Denomination within square, text on four sides

Date	Mintage	F	VF	XF	Unc	BU
1988	46,973,000	—	—	0.10	0.25	0.35
1989	2,999,000	—	0.50	1.00	2.00	3.50
Note: Not issued						

KM# 51 100 DINARA
7.8200 g., 0.9000 Gold .2263 oz. AGW **Subject:** 25th Anniversary of Republic **Obv:** State emblem within circle **Rev:** Figures with arms raised, large rock in background

Date	Mintage	F	VF	XF	Unc	BU
ND(1968) Proof	10,000	Value: 165				
ND(1968) NI Proof	Inc. above	Value: 165				

KM# 65 100 DINARA
10.0000 g., 0.9250 Silver .2974 oz. ASW, 28 mm. **Subject:** 8th Mediterranean Games at Split **Obv:** Map of Split left of emblem **Rev:** Bust left **Designer:** Zlatara Majdanpek

Date	Mintage	F	VF	XF	Unc	BU
1978 Proof	71,000	Value: 22.50				

KM# 90 100 DINARA
13.0000 g., 0.9250 Silver .3867 oz. ASW, 30 mm. **Series:** 1984 Winter Olympics **Subject:** Ice Hockey **Obv:** Emblem and Olympic logo on separate shields within flat bottom circle **Rev:** Hockey players **Edge:** Milled **Designer:** Zlatara Majdanpek

Date	Mintage	F	VF	XF	Unc	BU
1982 Proof	110,000	Value: 10.00				

KM# 98 100 DINARA
13.0000 g., 0.9250 Silver .3867 oz. ASW, 30 mm. **Series:** 1984 Winter Olympics **Subject:** Figure Skating **Obv:** Emblem and Olympic logo on separate shields within flat bottom circle **Rev:** Figure skater **Designer:** Zlatara Majdanpek

Date	Mintage	VG	F	VF	XF	Unc
1983 Proof	110,000	Value: 10.00				

KM# 99 100 DINARA
13.0000 g., 0.9250 Silver .3867 oz. ASW, 30 mm. **Series:** 1984 Winter Olympics **Subject:** Bobsledding **Obv:** Emblem and Olympic logo on separate shields within flat bottom circle **Rev:** Bobsledders **Designer:** Zlatara Majdanpek

Date	Mintage	F	VF	XF	Unc	BU
1983 Proof	110,000	Value: 10.00				

KM# 105 100 DINARA
13.0000 g., 0.9250 Silver .3867 oz. ASW, 30 mm. **Series:** 1984 Winter Olympics **Subject:** Speed Skating **Obv:** Emblem and Olympic logo on separate shields within flat bottom circle **Rev:** Skater **Designer:** Zlatara Majdanpek

Date	Mintage	F	VF	XF	Unc	BU
1984 Proof	110,000	Value: 10.00				

KM# 106 100 DINARA
13.0000 g., 0.9250 Silver .3867 oz. ASW, 30 mm. **Series:** 1984 Winter Olympics **Subject:** Pairs Figure Skating **Obv:** Emblem and Olympic logo on separate shields within flat bottom circle **Rev:** Figure skaters **Designer:** Zlatara Majdanpek

Date	Mintage	F	VF	XF	Unc	BU
1984 Proof	110,000	Value: 10.00				

KM# 114 100 DINARA
Copper-Zinc-Nickel, 29 mm. **Obv:** State emblem **Rev:** Denomination **Edge:** Milled

Date	Mintage	F	VF	XF	Unc	BU
1985	18,684,000	—	0.25	0.65	1.50	—
1986	17,905,000	—	0.20	0.50	1.00	—
1987	94,069,000	—	—	0.40	0.80	—
1988	50,294,000	—	—	0.40	0.80	—

KM# 115 100 DINARA
Copper-Nickel-Zinc **Subject:** 40th Anniversary - Liberation From Fascism **Obv:** State emblem within flat bottom circle **Rev:** Head left within circle of design

Date	Mintage	F	VF	XF	Unc	BU
ND(1985) Proof	200,000	Value: 4.00				

KM# 127.1 100 DINARA
Copper-Nickel **Subject:** 200th Anniversary - Birth of Karajich **Obv:** State emblem **Rev:** Squared head right

Date	Mintage	F	VF	XF	Unc	BU
1987 Proof	Est. 200,000	Value: 4.00				

KM# 127.2 100 DINARA
Copper-Nickel **Subject:** 200th Anniversary - Birth of Karajich **Obv:** State emblem within flat bottom circle **Rev:** Squared head right

Date	Mintage	F	VF	XF	Unc	BU
1987 Proof	Inc. above	Value: 25.00				

KM# 134 100 DINARA
Brass **Obv:** Text surrounds state emblem within square **Rev:** Denomination within square, text on four sides

Date	Mintage	F	VF	XF	Unc	BU
1988	12,610,000	—	—	0.15	0.30	0.50
1989	124,260,000	—	—	0.15	0.30	0.50

KM# 146 100 DINARA
13.0000 g., 0.9250 Silver .3867 oz. ASW **Subject:** 1990 Chess Olympiad **Obv:** State emblem within flat bottom circle **Rev:** Petrovaradin clock tower, chessboard background

Date	Mintage	F	VF	XF	Unc	BU
1990 Proof	10,000	Value: 27.50				

KM# 66 150 DINARA
12.5000 g., 0.9250 Silver .3717 oz. ASW, 30 mm. **Subject:** 8th Mediterranean Games at Split **Obv:** State emblem above boats **Rev:** Head left **Designer:** Zlatara Majdanpek

Date	Mintage	F	VF	XF	Unc	BU
1978 Proof	70,000	Value: 22.50				

KM# 147 150 DINARA
17.0000 g., 0.9250 Silver .5056 oz. ASW **Subject:** 1990 Chess Olympiad **Obv:** State emblem within flat bottom circle **Rev:** Globe, chessboard design at right

Date	Mintage	F	VF	XF	Unc	BU
1990 Proof	10,000	Value: 37.50				

KM# 52 200 DINARA
15.6400 g., 0.9000 Gold .4526 oz. AGW, 30 mm. **Subject:** 25th Anniversary of Republic **Obv:** State emblem within circle **Rev:** Head left

Date	Mintage	F	VF	XF	Unc	BU
ND(1968) Proof	10,000	Value: 325				
ND(1968) NI Proof	Inc. above	Value: 325				

KM# 64 200 DINARA
15.0000 g., 0.7500 Silver .3617 oz. ASW **Subject:** Tito's 85th Birthday **Obv:** State emblem at left, dates at right, denomination below, fan background **Rev:** Head left

Date	Mintage	F	VF	XF	Unc	BU
1977 Proof	500,000	Value: 11.50				

KM# 64a 200 DINARA

0.6000 g., 0.7500 Silver .2701 oz. ASW **Subject:** Tito's 85th Birthday **Obv:** State emblem at left, dates at right, denomination below, fan background **Rev:** Head left **Note:** Edge varieties with inscription in Cyrillic, Western and alternating Cyrillic-Western exist.

Date	Mintage	F	VF	XF	Unc	BU
1977	300,000	—	—	—	8.00	10.00

KM# 67 200 DINARA

15.0000 g., 0.9250 Silver .4461 oz. ASW **Subject:** 8th Mediterranean Games at Split **Obv:** State emblem at left, ancient urn at right **Rev:** Head left **Designer:** Zlatara Majdanpek

Date	Mintage	F	VF	XF	Unc	BU
1978 Proof	58,000	Value: 25.00				

KM# 68 250 DINARA

17.5000 g., 0.9250 Silver .5204 oz. ASW, 34 mm. **Subject:** 8th Mediterranean Games at Split **Obv:** Basilica of St. Donat in Zadar **Rev:** Head left **Designer:** Zlatara Majdanpek

Date	Mintage	F	VF	XF	Unc	BU
1979 Proof	48,000	Value: 30.00				

KM# 91 250 DINARA

17.0000 g., 0.9250 Silver .5056 oz. ASW, 34 mm. **Series:** 1984 Winter Olympics **Obv:** Emblem and Olympic logo on separate shields within flat bottom circle **Rev:** Sarajevo view within circle **Designer:** Zlatara Majdanpek

Date	Mintage	F	VF	XF	Unc	BU
1982 Proof	110,000	Value: 11.50				

KM# 100 250 DINARA

17.0000 g., 0.9250 Silver .5056 oz. ASW, 34 mm. **Series:** 1984 Winter Olympics **Obv:** Emblem and Olympic logo on separate shields within flat bottom circle **Rev:** Artifact within circle **Designer:** Zlatara Majdanpek

Date	Mintage	F	VF	XF	Unc	BU
1983 Proof	110,000	Value: 11.50				

KM# 101 250 DINARA

17.0000 g., 0.9250 Silver .5056 oz. ASW, 34 mm. **Series:** 1984 Winter Olympics **Obv:** Emblem and Olympic logo on separate shields within flat bottom circle **Rev:** Radimlja tombs **Designer:** Zlatara Majdanpek

Date	Mintage	F	VF	XF	Unc	BU
1983 Proof	110,000	Value: 11.50				

KM# 107 250 DINARA

17.0000 g., 0.9250 Silver .5056 oz. ASW, 34 mm. **Series:** 1984 Winter Olympics **Obv:** Emblem and Olympic logo on separate shields within flat bottom circle **Rev:** Jajce village **Designer:** Zlatara Majdanpek

Date	Mintage	F	VF	XF	Unc	BU
1984 Proof	110,000	Value: 11.50				

KM# 108 250 DINARA

17.0000 g., 0.9250 Silver .5056 oz. ASW, 34 mm. **Series:** 1984 Winter Olympics **Obv:** Emblem and Olympic logo on separate shields within flat bottom circle **Rev:** Head of Tito left **Designer:** Zlatara Majdanpek

Date	Mintage	F	VF	XF	Unc	BU
1984 Proof	110,000	Value: 11.50				

KM# 69 300 DINARA

20.0000 g., 0.9250 Silver .5948 oz. ASW, 36 mm. **Subject:** Eighth Mediterranean Games at Split **Obv:** State emblem and date above church **Rev:** Bust left **Designer:** Zlatara Majdanpek

Date	Mintage	F	VF	XF	Unc	BU
1978 Proof	36,000	Value: 35.00				

KM# 70 350 DINARA

22.5000 g., 0.9250 Silver .6692 oz. ASW, 36 mm. **Subject:** 8th Mediterranean Games at Split **Obv:** Statue divides emblem and denomination **Rev:** Head left **Designer:** Zlatara Majdanpek

Date	Mintage	F	VF	XF	Unc	BU
1978 Proof	24,000	Value: 37.50				

KM# 71 400 DINARA

25.0000 g., 0.9250 Silver .7435 oz. ASW, 40 mm. **Subject:** 8th Mediterranean Games at Split **Obv:** State emblem above pillared building **Rev:** Head left **Designer:** Zlatara Majdanpek

Date	Mintage	F	VF	XF	Unc	BU
1978 Proof	24,000	Value: 37.50				

KM# 53 500 DINARA

39.1000 g., 0.9000 Gold 1.1315 oz. AGW, 45 mm. **Subject:** 25th Anniversary of Republic **Obv:** State emblem **Rev:** Figures with arms raised, large rock in background

Date	Mintage	F	VF	XF	Unc	BU
ND(1968) Proof	10,000	Value: 800				
ND(1968) NI Proof	Inc. above	Value: 800				

KM# 76 500 DINARA

8.0000 g., 0.9250 Silver .2379 oz. ASW, 27 mm. **Subject:** Vukovar Congress **Obv:** State emblem above city hall of Vukovar **Rev:** Bust 3/4 left

Date	Mintage	F	VF	XF	Unc	BU
1980 Proof	18,000	Value: 20.00				

KM# 80 500 DINARA

8.0000 g., 0.7500 Silver .1865 oz. ASW, 27 mm. **Subject:** World Table Tennis Championship Games **Obv:** State emblem above town Novi Sad **Rev:** Stylized flower

Date	Mintage	F	VF	XF	Unc	BU
1981 Proof	18,000	Value: 25.00				

KM# 92 500 DINARA
23.0000 g., 0.9250 Silver .6841 oz. ASW **Series:** 1984 Winter Olympics **Subject:** Downhill Skiing **Obv:** Emblem and Olympic logo on separate shields within flat bottom circle **Rev:** Skier **Designer:** Zlatara Majdanpek

Date	Mintage	F	VF	XF	Unc	BU
1982 Proof	110,000	Value: 13.50				

KM# 102 500 DINARA
23.0000 g., 0.9250 Silver .6841 oz. ASW, 38 mm. **Series:** 1984 Winter Olympics **Subject:** Ski Jumping **Obv:** Emblem and Olympic logo on separate shields within flat bottom circle **Rev:** Ski jumper right **Designer:** Zlatara Majdanpek

Date	Mintage	F	VF	XF	Unc	BU
1983 Proof	110,000	Value: 13.50				

KM# 103 500 DINARA
23.0000 g., 0.9250 Silver .6841 oz. ASW, 38 mm. **Series:** 1984 Winter Olympics **Subject:** Biathalon **Obv:** Emblem and Olympic logo on separate shields within flat bottom circle **Rev:** Bi-athletes **Designer:** Zlatara Majdanpek

Date	Mintage	F	VF	XF	Unc	BU
1983 Proof	110,000	Value: 13.50				

KM# 109 500 DINARA
23.0000 g., 0.9250 Silver .6841 oz. ASW, 38 mm. **Series:** 1984 Winter Olympics **Subject:** Cross-country Skiing **Obv:** Emblem and Olympic logo on separate shields within flat bottom circle **Rev:** Skier **Designer:** Zlatara Majdanpek

Date	Mintage	F	VF	XF	Unc	BU
1984 Proof	110,000	Value: 13.50				

KM# 110 500 DINARA
23.0000 g., 0.9250 Silver .6841 oz. ASW, 38 mm. **Series:** 1984 Winter Olympics **Subject:** Slalom Skiing **Obv:** Emblem and Olympic logo on separate shields within flat bottom circle **Rev:** Skier

Date	Mintage	F	VF	XF	Unc	BU
1984 Proof	110,000	Value: 13.50				

KM# 116 500 DINARA
13.0000 g., 0.9250 Silver .3867 oz. ASW **Subject:** Ski Jumping Championship **Obv:** Similar to 10,000 Dinara, KM#123 **Rev:** Herons

Date	Mintage	F	VF	XF	Unc	BU
1985 Proof	50,000	Value: 15.00				

KM# 54 1000 DINARA
78.2000 g., 0.9000 Gold 2.2630 oz. AGW, 55 mm. **Subject:** 25th Anniversary of Republic **Obv:** State emblem **Rev:** Bust of Tito left

Date	Mintage	F	VF	XF	Unc	BU
ND(1968) Proof	10,000	Value: 1,600				
ND(1968) NI Proof	Inc. above	Value: 1,600				

KM# 78 1000 DINARA
25.9000 g., 0.7500 Silver .6245 oz. ASW **Subject:** Tito's Death **Obv:** State emblem on map of Yugoslavia, globe background **Rev:** Bust 3/4 left **Designer:** Zlatara Majdanpek **Note:** Eyes with and without pupils.

Date	Mintage	F	VF	XF	Unc	BU
1980	800,000	—	—	—	25.00	27.50

KM# 77 1000 DINARA
14.0000 g., 0.9250 Silver .4164 oz. ASW, 30 mm. **Subject:** Vukovar Congress **Obv:** State emblem above city hall in Vukovar **Rev:** Bust 3/4 left

Date	Mintage	F	VF	XF	Unc	BU
1980 Proof	16,000	Value: 27.50				

KM# 78a 1000 DINARA
26.0000 g., 0.9250 Silver .7733 oz. ASW **Subject:** Tito's Death **Obv:** State emblem on map of Yugoslavia, globe background **Rev:** Bust 3/4 left

Date	Mintage	F	VF	XF	Unc	BU
1980 Proof	200,000	Value: 30.00				
1980 ZM Proof	Inc. above	Value: 30.00				

KM# 81 1000 DINARA
14.0000 g., 0.7500 Silver .4164 oz. ASW, 30 mm. **Subject:** World Table Tennis Championship Games **Obv:** State emblem above town Novi Sad **Rev:** Hand with racket hitting ball

Date	Mintage	F	VF	XF	Unc	BU
1981 Proof	16,000	Value: 27.50				

KM# 82 1000 DINARA
14.0000 g., 0.7500 Silver .4164 oz. ASW, 30 mm. **Subject:** 40th Anniversary of Uprising and Revolution **Obv:** State emblem **Rev:** Bust and dates left, stars in background

Date	Mintage	F	VF	XF	Unc	BU
1981 Proof	100,000	Value: 22.00				

KM# 93 1000 DINARA
18.0000 g., 0.9250 Silver .5354 oz. ASW **Subject:** International Canoeing Championships **Obv:** State emblem left of statue **Rev:** City views, bird on left

Date	Mintage	F	VF	XF	Unc	BU
1982 Proof	46,000	Value: 30.00				

KM# 117 1000 DINARA
23.0000 g., 0.9250 Silver .6841 oz. ASW, 38 mm. **Subject:** Ski Jumping Championship **Obv:** State emblem on shield within flat bottom circle, denomination below **Rev:** Bloudek

Date	Mintage	F	VF	XF	Unc	BU
1985 Proof	20,000	Value: 30.00				

KM# 118 1000 DINARA
23.0000 g., 0.9250 Silver .6841 oz. ASW, 38 mm. **Subject:** Ski Jumping Championship **Obv:** Similar to 10,000 Dinara, KM#123 **Rev:** Slovenian cradle

Date	Mintage	F	VF	XF	Unc	BU
1985 Proof	20,000	Value: 30.00				

KM# 119 1000 DINARA
6.0000 g., 0.9250 Silver .1784 oz. ASW **Subject:** Sinjska Alka **Obv:** State emblem at left of map outline **Rev:** Figures with pack horse

Date	Mintage	F	VF	XF	Unc	BU
ND(1985) Proof	60,000	Value: 15.00				

KM# 148 1000 DINARA
3.5000 g., 0.9000 Gold .1013 oz. AGW **Subject:** 1990 Chess Olympiad **Obv:** State emblem above denomination **Rev:** Logo

Date	Mintage	F	VF	XF	Unc	BU
1990 Proof	2,000	Value: 175				

KM# 72 1500 DINARA
8.8000 g., 0.9000 Gold .2546 oz. AGW, 24 mm. **Subject:** 8th Mediterranean Games at Split **Obv:** State emblem above rings **Rev:** Head left **Designer:** Zlatara Majdanpek

Date	Mintage	F	VF	XF	Unc	BU
1978 Proof	35,000	Value: 190				

KM# 79 1500 DINARA
22.0000 g., 0.9250 Silver .6542 oz. ASW, 34 mm. **Subject:** Vukovar Congress **Obv:** State emblem above city hall in Vukovar **Rev:** Bust 3/4 left

Date	Mintage	F	VF	XF	Unc	BU
1980 Proof	16,000	Value: 35.00				

KM# 83 1500 DINARA
22.0000 g., 0.7500 Silver .5329 oz. ASW, 34 mm. **Subject:** World Table Tennis Championship Games **Obv:** State emblem over town view **Rev:** Stylized design of city

Date	Mintage	F	VF	XF	Unc	BU
1981 Proof	16,000	Value: 35.00				

KM# 94 1500 DINARA
22.0000 g., 0.9250 Silver .6542 oz. ASW, 36 mm. **Subject:** International Canoeing Championships **Rev:** Tito **Designer:** Zlatara Majdanpek

Date	Mintage	F	VF	XF	Unc	BU
1982 Proof	36,000	Value: 32.50				

KM# 73 2000 DINARA
11.8000 g., 0.9000 Gold .3414 oz. AGW, 27 mm. **Subject:** 8th Mediterranean Games at Split **Obv:** State emblem above city view **Rev:** Head left **Designer:** Zlatara Majdanpek

Date	Mintage	F	VF	XF	Unc	BU
1978 Proof	35,000	Value: 250				

KM# 120 2000 DINARA
14.0000 g., 0.9250 Silver .4164 oz. ASW **Subject:** Sinska Alka **Obv:** State emblem left of map outline **Rev:** Three figures on horseback

Date	Mintage	F	VF	XF	Unc	BU
ND(1985) Proof	20,000	Value: 22.50				

KM# 74 2500 DINARA
14.7000 g., 0.9000 Gold .4254 oz. AGW **Subject:** 8th Mediterranean Games at Split **Obv:** State emblem above stadium **Rev:** Bust left

Date	Mintage	F	VF	XF	Unc	BU
1978 Proof	35,000	Value: 300				

KM# 121 3000 DINARA
26.0000 g., 0.9250 Silver .7733 oz. ASW **Subject:** Sinkska Alka **Obv:** State emblem left of map outline **Rev:** Armored figures

Date	Mintage	F	VF	XF	Unc	BU
ND(1985) Proof	20,000	Value: 35.00				

KM# 128 3000 DINARA
13.0000 g., 0.9250 Silver .3867 oz. ASW **Subject:** 200th Anniversary - Birth of Krajich **Obv:** State emblem on shield within flat bottom circle **Rev:** Squared head right

Date	Mintage	F	VF	XF	Unc	BU
1987 Proof	50,000	Value: 30.00				

KM# 75 5000 DINARA
29.5000 g., 0.9000 Gold .8536 oz. AGW, 38 mm. **Subject:** 8th Mediterranean Games at Split **Obv:** State emblem above palace of Diocletian in Split **Rev:** Bust left **Designer:** Zlatara Majdanpek

Date	Mintage	F	VF	XF	Unc	BU
1978 Proof	12,000	Value: 600				

KM# 95 5000 DINARA
8.0000 g., 0.9000 Gold .2315 oz. AGW, 24 mm. **Series:** 1984 Winter Olympics **Obv:** Emblem and Olympic logo on separate shields within flat bottom circle **Rev:** Olympic emblem within circle

Date	Mintage	F	VF	XF	Unc	BU
1982 Proof	55,000	Value: 165				

KM# 104 5000 DINARA
8.0000 g., 0.9000 Gold .2315 oz. AGW, 24 mm. **Series:** 1984 Winter Olympics **Obv:** Emblem and Olympic logo on separate shields within flat bottom circle **Rev:** Bust 3/4 left within circle

Date	Mintage	F	VF	XF	Unc	BU
1983 Proof	55,000	Value: 165				

KM# 111 5000 DINARA
8.0000 g., 0.9000 Gold .2315 oz. AGW, 24 mm. **Series:** 1984 Winter Olympics **Obv:** Emblem and Olympic logo on separate shields within flat bottom circle **Rev:** Olympic torch within circle

Date	Mintage	F	VF	XF	Unc	BU
1984 Proof	55,000	Value: 165				

KM# 122 5000 DINARA
23.5000 g., 0.9250 Silver .6989 oz. ASW **Subject:** 400th Anniversary - Liberation from Fascism **Note:** Similar to 100 Dinara, KM#115.

Date	Mintage	F	VF	XF	Unc	BU
1985 Proof	100,000	Value: 40.00				

KM# 129 5000 DINARA
17.0000 g., 0.9250 Silver .5056 oz. ASW **Subject:** 200th Anniversary - Birth of Karajich **Obv:** State emblem on shield within flat bottom circle **Rev:** Squared head right

Date	Mintage	F	VF	XF	Unc	BU
1987 Proof	Est. 50,000	Value: 35.00				

KM# 135 5000 DINARA
Copper-Zinc-Nickel **Subject:** Non-aligned Summit **Obv:** State emblem **Rev:** Symbols within circle

Date	Mintage	F	VF	XF	Unc	BU
ND(1989) Proof	50,000	Value: 4.50				

KM# 123 10000 DINARA
8.0000 g., 0.9000 Gold .2315 oz. AGW, 24 mm. **Subject:** World Ski Jumping Championship

Date	Mintage	F	VF	XF	Unc	BU
1985 Proof	10,000	Value: 175				

KM# 124 10000 DINARA
5.0000 g., 0.9000 Gold .1447 oz. AGW **Subject:** Sinjska Alka

Date	Mintage	F	VF	XF	Unc	BU
ND(1985) Proof	12,000	Value: 150				

KM# 125 20000 DINARA
8.0000 g., 0.9000 Gold .2315 oz. AGW **Subject:** Sinjska Alka

Date	Mintage	F	VF	XF	Unc	BU
ND(1985) Proof	8,000	Value: 250				

KM# 126 40000 DINARA
14.0000 g., 0.9000 Gold .4083 oz. AGW **Subject:** Sinjska Alka **Obv:** State emblem left of map outline **Rev:** Three figures on horseback

Date	Mintage	F	VF	XF	Unc	BU
ND(1985) Proof	5,000	Value: 475				

KM# 130 50000 DINARA
8.0000 g., 0.9000 Gold .2315 oz. AGW **Subject:** 200th Anniversary - Birth of Karajich **Obv:** State emblem on shield within flat bottom circle **Rev:** Squared head right

Date	Mintage	F	VF	XF	Unc	BU
1987 Proof	Est. 10,000	Value: 185				

KM# 136 50000 DINARA
13.0000 g., 0.9250 Silver .3867 oz. ASW **Subject:** Non-aligned Summit **Obv:** State emblem above denomination **Rev:** Statue left divides dates within circle

Date	Mintage	F	VF	XF	Unc	BU
ND(1989) Proof	15,000	Value: 25.00				

KM# 137 100000 DINARA
17.0000 g., 0.9250 Silver .5056 oz. ASW **Subject:** Non-aligned Summit **Obv:** State emblem above denomination **Rev:** Building above dates within circle

Date	Mintage	F	VF	XF	Unc	BU
ND(1989) Proof	10,000	Value: 35.00				

KM# 138 2000000 DINARA
8.0000 g., 0.9000 Gold .2315 oz. AGW **Subject:** Non-aligned Summit **Obv:** State emblem above denomination **Rev:** Symbols within circle

Date	Mintage	F	VF	XF	Unc	BU
ND(1989) Proof	5,000	Value: 240				

FEDERAL REPUBLIC

STANDARD COINAGE

KM# 161 PARA
Brass **Obv:** Monogram on shield **Rev:** Denomination and date

Date	Mintage	F	VF	XF	Unc	BU
1994	25,350,000	—	—	—	0.35	0.50

KM# 164.1 5 PARA
Brass **Obv:** Monogram on shield **Rev:** Denomination and date

Date	Mintage	F	VF	XF	Unc	BU
1994	30,408,000	—	—	—	0.50	0.65
1995	3,400,000	—	—	—	0.60	0.85

KM# 164.2 5 PARA
Brass, 17 mm. **Obv:** Monogram on shield **Rev:** Denomination and date **Note:** Reduced size.

Date	Mintage	F	VF	XF	Unc	BU
1996	9,951,000	—	—	—	0.50	0.70

KM# 162.1 10 PARA
Copper-Nickel-Zinc **Obv:** Monogram on shield **Rev:** Denomination and date

Date	Mintage	F	VF	XF	Unc	BU
1994	52,161,000	—	—	—	0.50	0.65

KM# 162.2 10 PARA
Brass **Obv:** Monogram on shield **Rev:** Denomination and date **Note:** Reduced size.

Date	Mintage	F	VF	XF	Unc	BU
1995	31,041,000	—	—	—	0.65	0.85

KM# 173 10 PARA
Brass **Obv:** National arms **Rev:** Denomination and date

Date	Mintage	F	VF	XF	Unc	BU
1996	18,129,000	—	—	—	0.50	0.65
1997	21,384,000	—	—	—	0.50	0.65
1998	5,153,000	—	—	—	0.50	0.70

KM# 163 50 PARA
Copper-Nickel-Zinc **Obv:** Monogram on shield **Rev:** Date and denomination

Date	Mintage	F	VF	XF	Unc	BU
1994	45,013,000	—	—	—	0.75	0.90

KM# 163a 50 PARA
Brass **Obv:** Monogram on shield **Rev:** Date and denomination

Date	Mintage	F	VF	XF	Unc	BU
1995	19,193,000	—	—	—	1.00	1.20

KM# 174 50 PARA
Brass **Obv:** National arms **Rev:** Date and denomination

Date	Mintage	F	VF	XF	Unc	BU
1996	3,520,000	—	—	—	1.00	1.25
1997	14,742,000	—	—	—	1.00	1.20
1998	20,050,000	—	—	—	1.00	1.20
1999	18,140,000	—	—	—	1.00	1.20

KM# 179 50 PARA
3.3000 g., Brass, 18 mm. **Obv:** Head 3/4 facing **Rev:** National arms above denomination **Edge:** Plain

Date	Mintage	F	VF	XF	Unc	BU
2000	23,821,000	—	—	—	0.25	0.45

KM# 165 NOVI DINAR
Copper-Nickel-Zinc **Obv:** Monogram on shield **Rev:** Date and denomination

Date	Mintage	F	VF	XF	Unc	BU
1994	47,755,000	—	—	—	1.00	1.20
1995	10,359,000	—	—	—	1.25	1.50

KM# 168 NOVI DINAR
Copper-Nickel-Zinc **Obv:** National arms **Rev:** Date and denomination **Note:** Reduced size.

Date	Mintage	F	VF	XF	Unc	BU
1996	80,122,000	—	—	—	1.00	1.20
1999	21,686,000	—	—	—	1.00	1.20

KM# 149 DINAR
Copper-Zinc **Obv:** Monogram on shield **Rev:** Date and denomination

Date	Mintage	F	VF	XF	Unc	BU
1992	49,269,000	—	0.10	0.30	0.60	0.75

KM# 154 DINAR
Copper-Zinc-Nickel **Obv:** Monogram on shield **Rev:** Date and denomination

Date	Mintage	F	VF	XF	Unc	BU
1993	20,249,000	—	0.10	0.20	0.50	0.65

KM# 160 DINAR
Copper-Zinc-Nickel **Obv:** Monogram on shield **Rev:** Date and denomination

Date	Mintage	F	VF	XF	Unc	BU
1994	10,747,000	—	—	—	1.00	1.20

KM# 180 DINAR
4.4000 g., Copper-Zinc-Nickel, 20 mm. **Obv:** National arms within circle **Rev:** Building **Edge:** Reeded

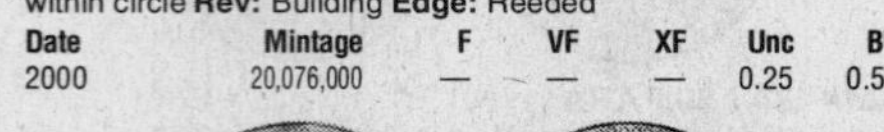

Date	Mintage	F	VF	XF	Unc	BU
2000	20,076,000	—	—	—	0.25	0.50

KM# 150 2 DINARA
Copper-Zinc **Obv:** Monogram on shield **Rev:** Large, thick denomination, date below

Date	Mintage	F	VF	XF	Unc	BU
1992	10,571,000	—	0.20	0.40	1.00	1.25

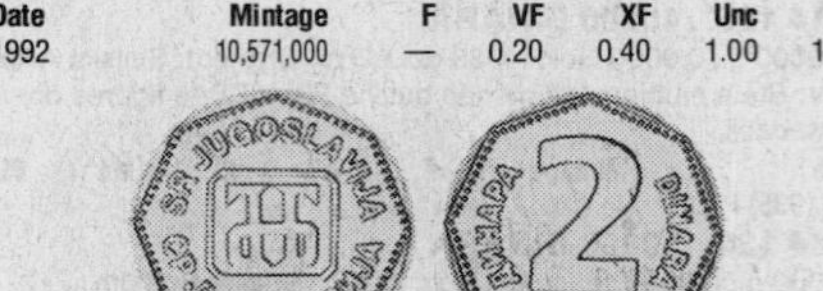

KM# 155 2 DINARA
Copper-Zinc-Nickel **Obv:** Monogram on shield **Rev:** Denomination and date

Date	Mintage	F	VF	XF	Unc	BU
1993	10,263,000	—	0.10	0.20	0.50	0.70

KM# 181 2 DINARA
5.2000 g., Copper-Nickel-Zinc, 21.9 mm. **Obv:** National arms within circle **Rev:** Church **Edge:** Reeded

Date	Mintage	F	VF	XF	Unc	BU
2000	10,071,000	—	—	—	0.25	0.50

KM# 151 5 DINARA
Copper-Zinc **Obv:** Monogram on shield **Rev:** Large, thick denomination, date below

Date	Mintage	F	VF	XF	Unc	BU
1992	26,658,000	—	0.15	0.30	0.75	0.90

KM# 156 5 DINARA
Copper-Zinc-Nickel **Obv:** Monogram on shield **Rev:** Denomination and date

Date	Mintage	F	VF	XF	Unc	BU
1993	10,135,000	—	0.10	0.20	0.50	0.65

KM# 182 5 DINARA
6.3000 g., Copper-Nickel-Zinc, 24 mm. **Obv:** National arms **Rev:** Domed building, denomination and date at left **Edge:** Reeded

Date	Mintage	F	VF	XF	Unc	BU
2000	32,762,500	—	—	—	1.25	1.50

KM# 152 10 DINARA
Copper-Zinc-Nickel **Obv:** Monogram on shield **Rev:** Large, thick denomination, date below

Date	Mintage	F	VF	XF	Unc	BU
1992	76,607,000	—	0.10	0.25	0.60	0.75

KM# 157 10 DINARA
Copper-Zinc-Nickel **Obv:** Monogram on shield **Rev:** Large denomination, date below

Date	Mintage	F	VF	XF	Unc	BU
1993	20,461,000	—	0.15	0.30	0.70	1.00

KM# 169 20 NOVIH DINARA
Copper-Zinc-Nickel **Subject:** Nikola Tesla **Obv:** National arms **Rev:** Head 3/4 left

Date	Mintage	F	VF	XF	Unc	BU
1996 Proof	9,743	Value: 12.50				

KM# 153 50 DINARA
Copper-Zinc-Nickel **Obv:** Monogram on shield **Rev:** Large, thick denomination, date below

Date	Mintage	F	VF	XF	Unc	BU
1992	50,571,000	—	0.25	0.50	1.00	1.25

KM# 158 50 DINARA
Copper-Zinc-Nickel **Obv:** Monogram on shield **Rev:** Large denomination, date below

Date	Mintage	F	VF	XF	Unc	BU
1993	10,823,000	—	0.20	0.40	0.80	1.00

KM# 159 100 DINARA
Brass **Obv:** Monogram on shield **Rev:** Denomination and date

Date	Mintage	F	VF	XF	Unc	BU
1993	14,294,500	—	0.25	0.50	1.00	1.25

KM# 166 150 NOVIH DINARA
7.8000 g., 0.9000 Gold .2257 oz. AGW **Subject:** 110th Anniversary - National Bank **Obv:** National arms, building at left **Rev:** Peace dove in flight

Date	Mintage	F	VF	XF	Unc	BU
ND(1995) Proof	100,000	Value: 180				

KM# 170 200 NOVIH DINARA
13.0000 g., 0.9250 Silver .3867 oz. ASW **Subject:** Nikola Tesla **Obv:** National arms **Rev:** Head 3/4 left

Date	Mintage	F	VF	XF	Unc	BU
1996 Proof	9,847	Value: 32.00				

KM# 171 300 NOVIH DINARA
26.0000 g., 0.9250 Silver .7734 oz. ASW **Subject:** Nikola Tesla **Obv:** National arms **Rev:** Head 3/4 left

Date	Mintage	F	VF	XF	Unc	BU
1996 Proof	9,034	Value: 45.00				

KM# 167 500 DINARA
Brass **Obv:** Monogram on shield **Rev:** Denomination and date **Note:** All but 1,000 reported melted. Not released for circulation.

Date	Mintage	F	VF	XF	Unc	BU
1993	—	—	—	—	6.50	7.00

KM# 175 600 NOVIH DINARA
3.4550 g., 0.9000 Gold .1 oz. AGW **Subject:** Chilander Monastery **Obv:** Monastery **Rev:** Portraits of SS Simon and Sava

Date	Mintage	F	VF	XF	Unc	BU
1998(1999)	10,000	—	—	—	—	125

KM# 172 1000 NOVIH DINARA
8.6400 g., 0.9000 Gold .25 oz. AGW **Subject:** Nikola Tesla **Obv:** National arms **Rev:** Head 3/4 left

Date	Mintage	F	VF	XF	Unc	BU
1996 Proof	4,617	Value: 250				

KM# 176 1500 NOVIH DINARA
8.6400 g., 0.9000 Gold .2500 oz. AGW **Subject:** Chilander Monastery **Obv:** Monastery **Rev:** Portraits of SS Simon and Sava

Date	Mintage	F	VF	XF	Unc	BU
1998(1999)	Est. 5,000	—	—	—	—	190

KM# 177 3000 NOVIH DINARA
17.2770 g., 0.9000 Gold .4999 oz. AGW **Subject:** Chilander Monastery **Obv:** Monastery **Rev:** Portraits of SS Simon and Sava

Date	Mintage	F	VF	XF	Unc	BU
1998 Proof	500	Value: 425				
1999 Proof	500	Value: 425				

KM# 178 6000 NOVIH DINARA
34.5550 g., 0.9000 Gold .9999 oz. AGW **Subject:** Chilander Monastery **Obv:** Monastery **Rev:** Portraits of SS Simon and Sava

Date	Mintage	F	VF	XF	Unc	BU
1998 Proof	500	Value: 750				
1999 Proof	500	Value: 750				

PATTERNS

Including off metal strikes

Patterns Pn1-Pn8 previously listed here are now listed under Serbia.

KM#	Date	Mintage	Identification	Mkt Val
Pn9	1925	—	50 Para. Nickel. KM4. By Pattey.	700
Pn9a	1925	1	50 Para. Silver. KM4. By Pattey.	500
Pn10	1925	—	Dinar. Nickel. KM5. By Pattey.	400
Pn10a	1925	—	Dinar. Copper. KM5. By Pattey.	400
PnA11	1925	—	Dinar. Aluminum. By Pattey.	400
Pn11	1925	—	Dinar. Nickel. KM5.	400
Pn12	1925	—	2 Dinara. Nickel-Bronze. KM6. ESSAI.	1,000
Pn12a	1925	—	2 Dinara. Copper-Nickel. KM6. ESSAI. 3 millimeters thick.	1,000
Pn13	1925	—	2 Dinara. Nickel. KM6.	600
Pn14	1925(a)	—	10 Dinara. Gold.	—
Pn15	1926(k)	—	Dukat. Gold.	—
Pn16	1926	—	4 Dukata. Silver. 39.5 mm. River scene.	—
Pn17	1926(k)	—	4 Dukata. Gold. River scene.	—
Pn19	1931	—	4 Dukata. Gold. 15.0000 g. ESSAI.	—
Pn20	ND	—	4 Dukata. Silver.	—
Pn21	1932	—	50 Dinara. Bronze. Milled edge.	400
Pn21a	1932	—	50 Dinara. Copper.	400
Pn22	1938	—	10 Dinara. Copper.	200
Pn23	1938	—	20 Dinara. Copper.	250
Pn24	1938	—	50 Dinara. Copper.	300
Pn25	1953	—	25 Para. Aluminum. Hole in center.	400
Pn26	1978	20	25 Para. Aluminum.	—
Pn27	1978	19	Dinar. Copper-Nickel.	—
Pn28	1978	15	10 Dinara. Copper-Nickel.	—

PIEFORTS

KM#	Date	Mintage	Identification	Mkt Val
P1	ND(1931-1934)	—	4 Dukata. Gold. 46.4500 g. Conjoined busts.	—

TRIAL STRIKES

KM#	Date	Mintage	Identification	Mkt Val
TS1	1931(a)	—	Dukat. Gold. Uniface. ESSAI Paris/1931.	—

KM#	Date	Mintage	Identification	Mkt Val
TS2	1931(a)	—	4 Dukata. Gold. Uniface. ESSAI Paris/1931.	—
TS3	1931	—	4 Dukata. Bronze. Uniface.	—
TS4	ND(1931)(k)	—	4 Dukata. 0.9167 Gold. 46.5000 g. Uniface obverse. KM#14 (hallmarked 22K on edge).	—
TS5	1931(k)	—	4 Dukata. Platinum. Uniface.	—
TS6	1931(k)	—	8 Dukata. Gold. Uniface.	—
TS7	1931	—	8 Dukata. 0.9000 Gold. 30.6180 g. Uniface. ESSAI/PARIS/1931.	—
TS8	1931	2	12 Dukata. 0.9000 Gold. Uniface. ESSAI/PARIS/1931. 45.875-46.45 grams.	—

MINT SETS

KM#	Date	Mintage	Identification	Issue Price	Mkt Val
MS1	1953/1955 (7)	—	KM29-35	—	5.00
MS10	1986 (7)	—	KM86-89, 112-114	—	3.00
MS11	1987 (4)	—	KM89, 112-114	—	3.00
MS12	1988 (7)	—	KM89, 113-114, 131-134	—	3.00
MS13	1989 (4)	—	KM131-134	—	6.50
MS14	1990 (6)	—	KM139-144	—	4.50
MS15	1991 (6)	—	KM139-144	—	4.00
MS16	1992 (2)	—	KM143-144	—	35.00
MS2	1963 (6)	—	KM36-41	—	8.00
MS3	1965 (5)	—	KM42, 44-47	—	4.00
MS4	1965 (5)	—	KM43-47	—	4.00
MS5	1982 (6)	—	KM84-89	—	3.00
MS6	1983 (6)	—	KM84-89	—	3.00
MS7	1983 (2)	—	KM96-97. Blue plastic wallet.	—	6.50
MS8	1984 (5)	—	KM85-89	—	3.00
MS9	1985 (7)	—	KM86-89, 112-114	—	3.00

PROOF SETS

KM#	Date	Mintage	Identification	Issue Price	Mkt Val
PS1	1968 (6)	10,000	KM49-54	—	2,150
PS2	1968 (4)	10,000	KM51-54	—	2,100
PS3	1968 (2)	10,000	KM49-50	15.00	75.00
PS4	1978 (7)	6,000	KM65-71	—	185
PS5	1978 (11)	12,000	KM65-75	—	1,310
PS6	1980 (3)	—	KM76-77, 79	—	85.00
PS7	1981 (3)	—	KM80-81, 83	—	95.00
PS8	1982 (3)	—	KM90-92	—	40.00
PS9	1982 (2)	—	KM93-94	—	60.00
PS10	1983 (3)	—	KM98, 100, 102	—	40.00
PS11	1983 (3)	—	KM99, 101, 103	—	40.00
PS12	1983 (2)	100,000	KM96-97	—	15.00
PS13	1984 (3)	—	KM105, 107, 109	—	40.00
PS14	1984 (3)	—	KM106, 108, 110	—	40.00
PS15	Mixed dates (3)	—	KM95, 104, 111	—	360
PS16	1985 (6)	—	KM119-121, 124-126	—	935
PS17	1985 (4)	—	KM116-118, 123	—	240
PS18	1985 (3)	—	KM116-118	—	75.00
PS19	1985 (3)	—	KM119-121	—	60.00
PS20	1987 (3)	—	KM128-130	—	245
PS21	1987 (2)	—	KM128-129	—	70.00
PS22	1989 (3)	—	KM136-138	—	300
PS23	1989 (2)	—	KM136-137	—	60.00
PS24	1990 (3)	—	KM146-148	—	255
PS25	1990 (2)	10,000	KM146-147	—	80.00
PS26	1998(1999) (4)	—	KM#175-178	—	1,400
PS27	1998-1999 (4)	—	KM#175-176 dated 1998; KM#177-178 dated 1999	—	1,400

ZAÏRE

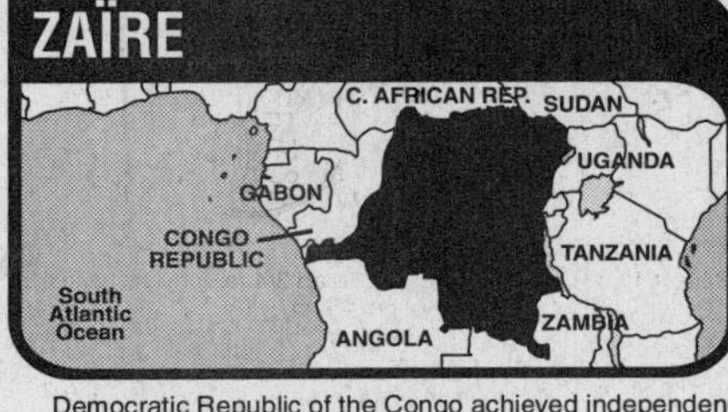

Democratic Republic of the Congo achieved independence on June 30, 1960. It followed the same monetary system as when under the Belgians. Monetary Reform of 1967 introduced new denominations and coins. The name of the country was changed to **Zaire** in 1971.

Under the command of Laurent Kabila, rebel forces overthrew ruler Sese Seko Mobutu in May of 1997. Self appointed President Kabila has officially renamed the country the Democratic Republic of Congo.

MONETARY SYSTEM
100 Makuta = 1 Zaire

1993 -
3,000,000 old Zaires = 1 Nouveau Zaire

REPUBLIC

DECIMAL COINAGE

KM# 12 5 MAKUTA
Copper-Nickel **Obv:** Denomination **Rev:** Mobuto bust left

Date	Mintage	F	VF	XF	Unc	BU
1977	8,000,000	—	0.50	1.00	3.50	—

KM# 7 10 MAKUTA
Copper-Nickel **Obv:** Mobuto bust 1/4 right **Rev:** Arms below denomination

Date	Mintage	F	VF	XF	Unc	BU
1973	5,000,000	—	2.25	4.00	8.00	—
1975	—	—	2.25	4.00	8.00	—
1976	—	—	2.50	4.50	9.00	—
1978	—	—	2.50	4.50	9.00	—

KM# 8 20 MAKUTA
Copper-Nickel **Obv:** Mobuto bust right **Rev:** Hand with torch

Date	Mintage	F	VF	XF	Unc	BU
1973	—	—	3.00	5.50	12.00	—
1976	—	—	3.50	6.50	14.00	—

KM# 13 ZAIRE
Brass **Obv:** Denomination **Rev:** Bust facing

Date	Mintage	F	VF	XF	Unc	BU
1987	—	—	0.50	1.00	2.00	—

KM# 9 2-1/2 ZAIRES
28.2800 g., 0.9250 Silver .8411 oz. ASW **Subject:** Conservation **Obv:** Mobuto bust 1/4 right **Rev:** Mountain gorillas

Date	Mintage	F	VF	XF	Unc	BU
1975	5,735	—	—	—	35.00	37.50
1975 Proof	6,629	Value: 45.00				

KM# 1 5 ZAIRES
27.8401 g., 0.9250 Silver .8280 oz. ASW **Obv:** Mobuto bust left **Rev:** Hotel Intercontinental

Date	Mintage	F	VF	XF	Unc	BU
1971 Proof	—	Value: 35.00				

KM# 10 5 ZAIRES
35.0000 g., 0.9250 Silver 1.0409 oz. ASW **Subject:** Conservation **Obv:** Mobuto bust 1/4 right **Rev:** Okapi right

Date	Mintage	F	VF	XF	Unc	BU
1975	5,734	—	—	—	35.00	37.50
1975 Proof	6,431	Value: 45.00				

KM# 14 5 ZAIRES
Brass, 24 mm. **Obv:** Denomination **Rev:** Mobuto bust facing

Date	Mintage	F	VF	XF	Unc	BU
1987	—	—	0.65	1.25	2.50	—

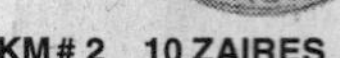

KM# 2 10 ZAIRES
9.9600 g., 0.9000 Gold .2882 oz. AGW **Obv:** Mobuto bust left **Rev:** Hotel Intercontinental

Date	Mintage	F	VF	XF	Unc	BU
1971 Proof	—	Value: 215				

KM# 3 10 ZAIRES
6.0400 g., 0.9990 Platinum .1940 oz. APW **Obv:** Mobuto bust left **Rev:** Hotel Intercontinental

Date	Mintage	F	VF	XF	Unc	BU
1971 Proof	—	Value: 265				

KM# 19 10 ZAIRES
Brass **Obv:** Denomination **Rev:** Mobuto bust facing

Date	Mintage	F	VF	XF	Unc	BU
1988	—	—	2.00	4.50	9.00	—

KM# 4 20 ZAIRES
20.9000 g., 0.9000 Gold .6048 oz. AGW **Obv:** Mobuto bust left **Rev:** Hotel Intercontinental

Date	Mintage	F	VF	XF	Unc	BU
1971 Proof	—	Value: 445				

KM# 5 20 ZAIRES
3.8900 g., 0.9990 Platinum .1250 oz. APW **Obv:** Mobuto bust left **Rev:** Hotel Intercontinental

Date	Mintage	F	VF	XF	Unc	BU
1971 Proof	—	Value: 170				

KM# 6 50 ZAIRES
46.9600 g., 0.9000 Gold 1.3590 oz. AGW **Obv:** Mobuto bust 3/4 left **Rev:** Hotel Intercontinental

Date	Mintage	F	VF	XF	Unc	BU
1971 Proof	—	Value: 1,000				

KM# 11 100 ZAIRES
33.4370 g., 0.9000 Gold .9676 oz. AGW **Subject:** Conservation **Obv:** Mobuto bust 1/4 right **Rev:** Leopard right

Date	Mintage	F	VF	XF	Unc	BU
1975	1,415	—	—	—	675	725
1975 Proof	279	Value: 850				

KM# 20 500 NOUVEAUX ZAIRES
20.0000 g., 0.5000 Silver .3215 oz. ASW **Subject:** Wildlife of Africa **Obv:** African map, arms at left **Rev:** Leopard on branch

Date	Mintage	F	VF	XF	Unc	BU
1996 Proof	10,000	Value: 35.00				

KM# 21 500 NOUVEAUX ZAIRES
20.0000 g., 0.5000 Silver .3215 oz. ASW **Subject:** Wildlife of Africa **Obv:** African map, arms at left **Rev:** Gorilla left

Date	Mintage	F	VF	XF	Unc	BU
1996 Proof	Est. 10,000	Value: 35.00				

KM# 22 500 NOUVEAUX ZAIRES
20.0000 g., 0.5000 Silver .3215 oz. ASW **Subject:** Wildlife of Africa **Obv:** African map, arms at left **Rev:** Two okapi

Date	Mintage	F	VF	XF	Unc	BU
1996 Proof	Est. 10,000	Value: 37.50				

KM# 23 1000 NOUVEAUX ZAIRES
29.6300 g., 0.9250 Silver .8811 oz. ASW **Subject:** Wildlife of Africa **Obv:** African map, arms at left **Rev:** Hippopotamus left

Date	Mintage	F	VF	XF	Unc	BU
1997 Proof	Est. 20,000	Value: 37.50				

KM# 24 1000 NOUVEAUX ZAIRES
30.0900 g., 0.9250 Silver .8948 oz. ASW **Subject:** Wildlife of Africa **Obv:** African map, arms at left **Rev:** Sailing ship "Portuguese Caravel"

Date	Mintage	F	VF	XF	Unc	BU
1997 Proof	Est. 20,000	Value: 42.50				

KM# 25 5000 NOUVEAUX ZAIRES
411.4224 g., 0.9990 Silver 13.2143 oz. ASW **Subject:** Wildlife of Africa **Obv:** African map, arms at left **Rev:** Leopard on branch **Edge:** Reeded

Date	Mintage	F	VF	XF	Unc	BU
1996 Proof	1,000	Value: 225				

KM# 26 10000 NOUVEAUX ZAIRES
822.8449 g., 0.9990 Silver 26.4286 oz. ASW **Subject:** Wildlife of Africa **Obv:** African map, arms at left **Rev:** Gorilla left **Edge:** Reeded

Date	Mintage	F	VF	XF	Unc	BU
1996 Proof	1,000	Value: 435				

PROOF SETS

KM#	Date	Mintage	Identification	Issue Price	Mkt Val
PS1	1971 (6)	—	KM1-6	—	1,775
PS2	1975 (2)	500	KM9-10	60.00	90.00

ZAMBIA

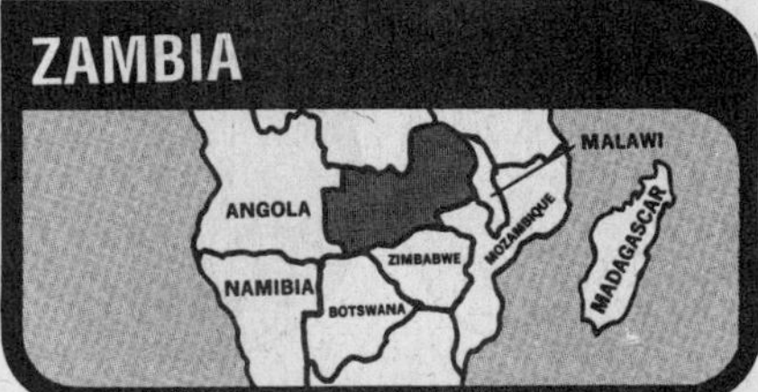

The Republic of Zambia (formerly Northern Rhodesia), a landlocked country in south-central Africa, has an area of 290,586 sq. mi. (752,610 sq. km.) and a population of*7.9 million. Capital: Lusaka. The economy of Zambia is based principally on copper, of which Zambia is the world's third largest producer. Copper, zinc, lead, cobalt and tobacco are exported.

The area that is now Zambia was brought within the British sphere of influence in 1888 by empire builder Cecil Rhodes, who obtained mining concessions in south-central Africa from indigenous chiefs. The territory was ruled by the British South Africa Company, which Rhodes established, until 1924 when its administration was transferred to the British government as a protectorate. In1953, Northern Rhodesia was joined with Nyasaland and the colony of Southern Rhodesia to form the Federation of Rhodesia and Nyasaland. Northern Rhodesia seceded from the Federation on Oct. 24, 1964, and became the independent Republic of Zambia. Zambia is a member of the Commonwealth of Nations. The president is Chief of State.

Zambia converted to a decimal coinage on January 16, 1969.

For earlier coinage refer to Rhodesia and Nyasaland.

RULERS
British, until 1964

MONETARY SYSTEM
12 Pence = 1 Shilling
20 Shillings = 1 Pound

REPUBLIC

STANDARD COINAGE

KM# 5 PENNY
Bronze **Obv:** Date below center hole **Rev:** Denomination below center hole

Date	Mintage	F	VF	XF	Unc	BU
1966	7,200,000	0.25	0.45	0.85	1.75	2.75
1966 Proof	60	—	—	—	—	—

KM# 1 6 PENCE
Copper-Nickel-Zinc **Obv:** National arms divide date **Rev:** Morning Glory (Ipomoea sp. convolvulaceae), denomination below

Date	Mintage	F	VF	XF	Unc	BU
1964	3,500,000	0.15	0.30	0.60	1.20	1.50
1964 Proof	5,000	Value: 1.75				

KM# 6 6 PENCE
Copper-Nickel-Zinc **Obv:** Head of K.D. Kaunda right, date below **Rev:** Morning glory, denomination below

Date	Mintage	F	VF	XF	Unc	BU
1966	7,200,000	0.25	0.50	1.00	2.00	2.50
1966 Proof	60	—	—	—	—	—

KM# 2 SHILLING
Copper-Nickel **Obv:** National arms divides date **Rev:** Crowned Hornbill, oribi and denomination

Date	Mintage	F	VF	XF	Unc	BU
1964	3,510,000	0.25	0.50	1.00	2.00	2.50
1964 Proof	5,000	Value: 3.50				

KM# 7 SHILLING
Copper-Nickel **Obv:** Head of K.D. Kaunda right, date below **Rev:** Crowned hornbill and denomination

Date	Mintage	F	VF	XF	Unc	BU
1966	5,000,000	0.35	0.75	1.50	3.25	4.00
1966 Proof	60	—	—	—	—	—

KM# 3 2 SHILLINGS
Copper-Nickel **Obv:** National arms divides date **Rev:** Bohor Reedbuck right and denomination

Date	Mintage	F	VF	XF	Unc	BU
1964	3,770,000	0.35	0.75	1.50	3.00	5.00
1964 Proof	5,000	Value: 6.00				

KM# 8 2 SHILLINGS
Copper-Nickel **Obv:** Head of K.D. Kaunda right, date below **Rev:** Bohor Reedbuck right and denomination

Date	Mintage	F	VF	XF	Unc	BU
1966	5,000,000	0.45	1.00	2.25	4.50	5.00
1966 Proof	60	—	—	—	—	—

KM# 4 5 SHILLINGS
Copper-Nickel, 38.8 mm. **Subject:** 1st Anniversary of Independence **Obv:** National arms with supporters, denomination below **Rev:** Head of K.D. Kaunda right, date below **Edge Lettering:** ONE ZAMBIA ONE NATION * 24.10.1964 * **Designer:** D.A.H. Byatt **Note:** Two edge ltter varieties.

Date	Mintage	F	VF	XF	Unc	BU
1965	10,000	—	2.50	3.50	6.50	8.00
1965 Proof	20,000	Value: 9.00				

DECIMAL COINAGE

100 Ngwee = 1 Kwacha

KM# 9 NGWEE
2.1000 g., Bronze, 17.5 mm. **Obv:** Head of K.D. Kaunda right, date below **Rev:** Aardvark left, denomination below

Date	Mintage	F	VF	XF	Unc	BU
1968	8,000,000	—	0.10	0.30	1.50	—
1968 Proof	4,000	Value: 1.50				
1969	16,000,000	—	0.10	0.20	1.00	—
1972	21,000,000	—	0.10	0.20	1.00	—

Date	Mintage	F	VF	XF	Unc	BU
1978	23,976,000	—	0.10	0.20	1.00	—
1978 Proof	24,000	Value: 1.50				

KM# 9a NGWEE

2.1000 g., Copper-Clad Steel, 17.5 mm. **Obv:** Head of K.D. Kaunda right, date below **Rev:** Aardvark left, denomination below

Date	Mintage	F	VF	XF	Unc	BU
1982	10,000,000	—	0.10	0.20	1.00	—
1983	60,000,000	—	0.10	0.20	1.00	—

KM# 10 2 NGWEE

4.2000 g., Bronze, 21 mm. **Obv:** Head of K.D. Kaunda right, date below **Rev:** Martial Eagle, denomination at right

Date	Mintage	F	VF	XF	Unc	BU
1968	19,000,000	—	0.10	0.20	1.00	1.50
1968 Proof	4,000	Value: 1.50				
1978	—	—	0.15	0.25	1.25	2.00
1978 Proof	24,000	Value: 2.00				

KM# 10a 2 NGWEE

Copper-Clad Steel, 21 mm. **Obv:** Head of K.D. Kaunda right, date below **Rev:** Martial Eagle, denomination at right

Date	Mintage	F	VF	XF	Unc	BU
1982	7,500,000	—	0.10	0.20	1.00	—
1983	60,000,000	—	0.10	0.15	0.75	—

KM# 11 5 NGWEE

2.8000 g., Copper-Nickel, 19.4 mm. **Obv:** Head of K.D. Kaunda right, date below **Rev:** Morning Glory, denomination below

Date	Mintage	F	VF	XF	Unc	BU
1968	12,000,000	—	0.20	0.30	0.60	—
1968 Proof	4,000	Value: 1.75				
1972	9,000,000	—	0.20	0.30	0.60	—
1978	1,976,000	—	0.20	0.30	0.60	—
1978 Proof	24,000	Value: 2.00				
1982	12,000,000	—	0.20	0.30	0.60	—
1987	10,000,000	—	0.20	0.30	0.60	—

KM# 12 10 NGWEE

5.6500 g., Copper-Nickel-Zinc, 23.6 mm. **Obv:** K.D. Kaunda head right **Rev:** Crowned Hornbill and denomination

Date	Mintage	F	VF	XF	Unc	BU
1968	1,000,000	—	0.40	0.85	1.75	—
1968 Proof	4,000	Value: 2.00				
1972	1,000,000	—	0.30	0.50	1.00	—
1978	1,976,000	—	0.30	0.50	1.00	—
1978 Proof	24,000	Value: 2.25				
1982	8,000,000	—	0.30	0.50	1.00	—
1983	2,500	—	0.30	0.50	1.00	—
1987	6,000,000	—	0.30	0.50	1.00	—

KM# 13 20 NGWEE

11.3000 g., Copper-Nickel, 28.5 mm. **Obv:** Head of K.D. Kaunda right, date below **Rev:** Bohur Reedbuck right and denomination

Date	Mintage	F	VF	XF	Unc	BU
1968	1,500,000	—	0.75	1.50	2.50	—
1968 Proof	4,000	Value: 2.75				
1972	7,500,000	—	0.50	1.00	2.00	—
1978 Proof	24,000	Value: 3.00				
1983	998,000	—	0.75	1.50	2.50	—
1987	—	—	0.50	1.00	2.00	—
1988	3,000,000	—	0.50	1.00	2.00	—

KM# 22 20 NGWEE

11.3000 g., Copper-Nickel, 28.5 mm. **Series:** F.A.O. - World Food Day **Obv:** Head of K.D. Kaunda right, date below **Rev:** Corn plant, date and denomination within inner circle

Date	Mintage	F	VF	XF	Unc	BU
1981	970,000	—	0.75	1.50	2.75	—

KM# 23 20 NGWEE

11.3000 g., Copper-Nickel, 28.5 mm. **Subject:** 20th Anniversary - Bank of Zambia **Obv:** Head of K.D. Kaunda right, date below **Rev:** Bank building divides dates, denomination above

Date	Mintage	F	VF	XF	Unc	BU
1985	—	—	0.50	1.00	1.50	—

KM# 23a 20 NGWEE

11.3100 g., 0.9250 Silver .3364 oz. ASW, 28.5 mm. **Subject:** 20th Anniversary - Bank of Zambia **Obv:** Head of K.D. Kaunda right, date below **Rev:** Bank building divides dates, denominaton above

Date	Mintage	F	VF	XF	Unc	BU
1985 Proof	—	Value: 6.00				

KM# 29 25 NGWEE

Nickel Plated Steel **Obv:** National arms with supporters, date below **Rev:** Crowned Hornbill and denomination

Date	Mintage	F	VF	XF	Unc	BU
1992	—	—	—	—	0.75	—

KM# 14 50 NGWEE

11.6000 g., Copper-Nickel, 30 mm. **Series:** F.A.O. **Obv:** Head of K.D. Kaunda right, date below **Rev:** Ear of corn divides denomination **Shape:** 12-sided

Date	Mintage	F	VF	XF	Unc	BU
ND(1969)	70,000	—	2.00	3.50	5.50	—

KM# 15 50 NGWEE

11.6000 g., Copper-Nickel, 30 mm. **Series:** F.A.O. **Obv:** Head of K.D. Kaunda right, date below **Rev:** Ear of corn divides denomination **Shape:** 12-sided

Date	Mintage	F	VF	XF	Unc	BU
1972	510,000	—	1.25	2.50	4.50	—

KM# 16 50 NGWEE

11.6000 g., Copper-Nickel, 30 mm. **Subject:** Second Republic, 13 December 1972 **Obv:** Head of K.D. Kaunda right, date below **Rev:** National arms with supporters, denomination below **Shape:** 12-sided

Date	Mintage	F	VF	XF	Unc	BU
1972	6,000,000	—	1.00	2.00	4.00	—
1972 Proof	2,000	Value: 7.00				
1978 Proof	24,000	Value: 5.00				
1983	998,000	—	1.00	2.00	4.00	—

KM# 24 50 NGWEE

11.6000 g., Copper-Nickel, 30 mm. **Subject:** 40th Anniversary of United Nations **Obv:** Head of K.D. Kaunda right, date below **Rev:** United Nations logo **Shape:** 12-sided

Date	Mintage	F	VF	XF	Unc	BU
1985	—	—	1.00	1.25	2.50	—

KM# 24a 50 NGWEE

11.6600 g., 0.9250 Silver .3468 oz. ASW **Subject:** 40th Anniversary of United Nations **Obv:** Head of K.D. Kaunda right, date below **Rev:** United Nations logo **Shape:** 12-sided

Date	Mintage	F	VF	XF	Unc	BU
1985 Proof	—	Value: 6.50				

KM# 30 50 NGWEE

Nickel Plated Steel **Obv:** National arms with supporters, date below **Rev:** Kafue Lechwe and denomination

Date	Mintage	F	VF	XF	Unc	BU
1992	—	—	—	—	1.50	—

KM# 17 KWACHA

Copper-Nickel **Subject:** 10th Anniversary of Independence **Obv:** Head of K.D. Kaunda right, date below **Rev:** National arms with supporters, denomination below

Date	Mintage	F	VF	XF	Unc	BU
ND(1974)	4,000	—	—	—	20.00	—
ND(1974) Proof	1,500	Value: 35.00				

KM# 26 KWACHA

Nickel-Brass **Obv:** Head of K.D. Kaunda right, date below **Rev:** Two falcons on branch divided by denomination

Date	Mintage	F	VF	XF	Unc	BU
1989	8,000,000	—	0.75	1.50	4.00	5.00

KM# 38 KWACHA

Brass **Obv:** National arms with supporters, date below **Rev:** Two falcons on branch divided by denomination

Date	Mintage	F	VF	XF	Unc	BU
1992	—	—	—	—	1.50	2.00

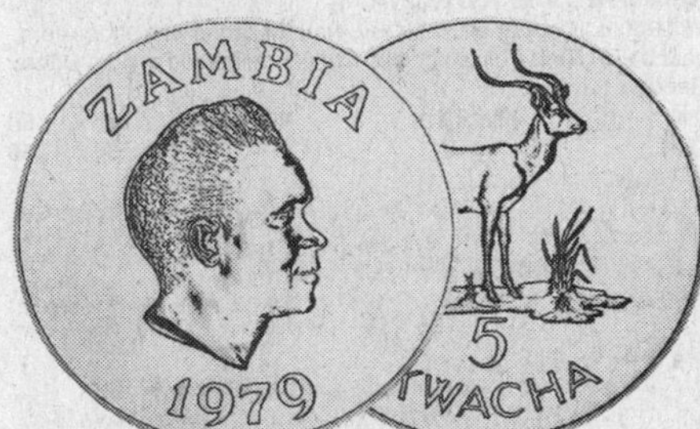

KM# 18 5 KWACHA

25.3100 g., 0.9250 Silver .7527 oz. ASW **Subject:** Conservation **Obv:** Head of K.D. Kaunda right, date below **Rev:** Kafue Lechwe right, denomination below

Date	Mintage	F	VF	XF	Unc	BU
1979	3,250	—	—	—	17.50	24.00

KM# 18a 5 KWACHA

28.2800 g., 0.9250 Silver .8411 oz. ASW **Subject:** Conservation **Obv:** Head of K.D. Kaunda right, date below **Rev:** Kafue Lechwe right, denomination below

Date	Mintage	F	VF	XF	Unc	BU
1979 Proof	3,407	Value: 27.50				

KM# 31 5 KWACHA

Brass **Obv:** National arms with supporters, date below **Rev:** Oryx right and denomination

Date	Mintage	F	VF	XF	Unc	BU
1992	—	—	—	—	2.00	2.50

KM# 19 10 KWACHA

31.6500 g., 0.9250 Silver .9398 oz. ASW **Subject:** Conservation **Obv:** Head of K.D. Kaunda right, date below **Rev:** Taita Falcon flying right, denomination below

Date	Mintage	F	VF	XF	Unc	BU
1979	3,250	—	—	—	20.00	22.50

KM# 19a 10 KWACHA

35.0000 g., 0.9250 Silver 1.0409 oz. ASW **Subject:** Conservation **Obv:** Head of K.D. Kaunda right, date below **Rev:** Taita Falcon flying right, denomination below

Date	Mintage	F	VF	XF	Unc	BU
1979 Proof	3,256	Value: 30.00				

KM# 21 10 KWACHA

27.2200 g., 0.9250 Silver .8095 oz. ASW **Series:** International Year of the Child **Obv:** Head of K.D. Kaunda right, date below **Rev:** 3 children on playground equipment

Date	Mintage	F	VF	XF	Unc	BU
1980 Proof	12,000	Value: 16.50				

KM# 25 10 KWACHA

27.2200 g., 0.9250 Silver .8095 oz. ASW **Series:** World Wildlife Fund **Obv:** Head of K.D. Kaunda right, date below **Rev:** White-winged Flufftail, denomination below

Date	Mintage	F	VF	XF	Unc	BU
1986 Proof	25,000	Value: 27.50				

KM# 27 10 KWACHA

27.2200 g., 0.9250 Silver .8095 oz. ASW **Subject:** 70th Anniversary - Save the Children Fund **Obv:** Head of K.D. Kaunda right, date below **Rev:** Child holding up corn cob, denomination below

Date	Mintage	F	VF	XF	Unc	BU
1989 Proof	Est. 20,000	Value: 22.50				

KM# 32 10 KWACHA

Brass **Obv:** National arms, date below **Rev:** Rhinoceros facing and denomination

Date	Mintage	F	VF	XF	Unc	BU
1992	—	—	—	—	2.50	3.00

KM# 39 10 KWACHA

20.0000 g., 0.9990 Silver .6430 oz. ASW **Subject:** World Cup Soccer **Obv:** National arms with supporters divide date, denomination below **Rev:** Player kicking ball; .999 in field

Date	Mintage	F	VF	XF	Unc	BU
1994 Proof	—	Value: 50.00				

KM# 119 10 KWACHA

27.3400 g., Copper-Nickel, 40.1 mm. **Subject:** UNICEF **Obv:** National arms with supporters divide date, denomination below **Rev:** Three boys playing soccer **Edge:** Reeded

Date	Mintage	F	VF	XF	Unc	BU
2000 Matte	—	—	—	—	9.00	10.00

KM# 119a 10 KWACHA

27.2200 g., 0.9250 Silver 0.8095 oz. ASW, 40.1 mm. **Subject:** UNICEF **Obv:** National arms with supporters divide date, denomination below **Rev:** Three boys playing soccer **Edge:** Reeded

Date	Mintage	F	VF	XF	Unc	BU
2000 Proof	25,000	Value: 17.50				

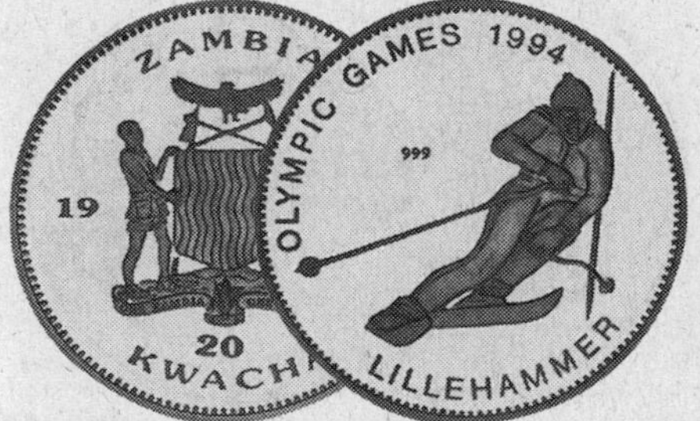

KM# 33 20 KWACHA

10.1700 g., 0.9990 Silver .3266 oz. ASW **Series:** 1994 Olympics **Obv:** National arms **Rev:** Slalom skier

Date	Mintage	F	VF	XF	Unc	BU
1994 Proof	25,000	Value: 22.50				

KM# 51 75 KWACHA

5.0000 g., 0.9990 Silver .1606 oz. ASW, 22 mm. **Subject:** Diana - The People's Princess **Obv:** National arms with supporters divide date **Rev:** Bust facing

Date	Mintage	F	VF	XF	Unc	BU
1997 Proof	—	Value: 12.50				

KM# 28 100 KWACHA
28.2800 g., 0.9250 Silver .8411 oz. ASW **Series:** Barcelona Summer Olympics **Subject:** Boxing **Obv:** National arms with supporters, date below **Rev:** 2 boxers in ring fighting, denomination above **Rev. Designer:** Willem Vis

Date	Mintage	F	VF	XF	Unc	BU
1992 Proof	Est. 50,000	Value: 27.50				

KM# 50 100 KWACHA
Copper-Nickel **Obv:** National arms with supporters **Rev:** Charging bull elephant, denomination at right

Date	Mintage	F	VF	XF	Unc	BU
1997	—	—	—	—	25.00	28.00

KM# 56 100 KWACHA
28.2800 g., 0.9990 Silver .9083 oz. ASW **Obv:** National arms with supporters, date below **Rev:** Crocodile, denomination at right

Date	Mintage	F	VF	XF	Unc	BU
1998 Proof	Est. 25,000	Value: 50.00				

KM# 56a 100 KWACHA
28.2800 g., Copper-Nickel **Obv:** National arms with supporters, date below **Rev:** Crocodile, denomination at right **Edge:** Reeded

Date	Mintage	F	VF	XF	Unc	BU
1998	Est. 100,000	—	—	—	15.00	17.50

KM# 57 100 KWACHA
28.2800 g., 0.9990 Silver .9083 oz. ASW **Obv:** National arms with supporters, date below **Rev:** Leopard on branch left, denomination below

Date	Mintage	F	VF	XF	Unc	BU
1998 Proof	Est. 25,000	Value: 60.00				

KM# 57a 100 KWACHA
28.2800 g., Copper-Nickel **Obv:** National arms with supporters, date below **Rev:** Leopard on branch left, denomination below **Edge:** Reeded

Date	Mintage	F	VF	XF	Unc	BU
1998	Est. 100,000	—	—	—	15.00	17.50

KM# 58 100 KWACHA
28.2800 g., 0.9990 Silver .9083 oz. ASW **Obv:** National arms with supporters, date below **Rev:** Black Rhinoceros running right, denomination above

Date	Mintage	F	VF	XF	Unc	BU
1998 Proof	Est. 25,000	Value: 60.00				

KM# 58a 100 KWACHA
28.2800 g., Copper-Nickel **Obv:** National arms with supporters, date below **Rev:** Rhinoceros running right, denomination above **Edge:** Reeded

Date	Mintage	F	VF	XF	Unc	BU
1998	Est. 100,000	—	—	—	15.00	17.50

KM# 59 100 KWACHA
28.2800 g., 0.9990 Silver .9083 oz. ASW **Obv:** National arms with supporters, date below **Rev:** Hippopotamus and calf, denomination above

Date	Mintage	F	VF	XF	Unc	BU
1998 Proof	Est. 25,000	Value: 60.00				

KM# 59a 100 KWACHA
28.2800 g., Copper-Nickel **Obv:** National arms with supporters, date below **Rev:** Hippopotamus and calf, denomination above **Edge:** Reeded

Date	Mintage	F	VF	XF	Unc	BU
1998	Est. 100,000	—	—	—	17.00	17.50

KM# 60 100 KWACHA
28.2800 g., 0.9990 Silver .9083 oz. ASW **Obv:** National arms with supporters, date below **Rev:** Antelopes jumping over denomination

Date	Mintage	F	VF	XF	Unc	BU
1998 Proof	Est. 25,000	Value: 55.00				

KM# 60a 100 KWACHA
28.2800 g., Copper-Nickel **Obv:** National arms with supporters, date below **Rev:** Antelopes jumping over denomination **Edge:** Reeded

Date	Mintage	F	VF	XF	Unc	BU
1998	Est. 100,000	—	—	—	15.00	17.50

KM# 61 100 KWACHA
28.2800 g., 0.9990 Silver .9083 oz. ASW **Obv:** National arms with supporters, date below **Rev:** Pelican on branch, denomination at right

Date	Mintage	F	VF	XF	Unc	BU
1998 Proof	Est. 25,000	Value: 60.00				

KM# 61a 100 KWACHA
28.2800 g., Copper-Nickel **Obv:** National arms with supporters, date below **Rev:** Pelican on branch, denomination at right **Edge:** Reeded

Date	Mintage	F	VF	XF	Unc	BU
1998	Est. 100,000	—	—	—	15.00	17.50

KM# 62 100 KWACHA
28.2800 g., 0.9990 Silver .9083 oz. ASW **Obv:** National arms with supporters, date below **Rev:** Storks left and right, denomination at right

Date	Mintage	F	VF	XF	Unc	BU
1998 Proof	Est. 25,000	Value: 50.00				

KM# 62a 100 KWACHA
28.2800 g., Copper-Nickel **Obv:** National arms with supporters, date below **Rev:** Storks left and right, denomination at right **Edge:** Reeded

Date	Mintage	F	VF	XF	Unc	BU
1998	Est. 100,000	—	—	—	15.00	17.50

KM# 63 100 KWACHA
28.2800 g., 0.9990 Silver .9083 oz. ASW **Obv:** National arms with supporters, date below **Rev:** Burchell's Zebra right, denomination at right

Date	Mintage	F	VF	XF	Unc	BU
1998 Proof	Est. 25,000	Value: 55.00				

KM# 63a 100 KWACHA
28.2800 g., Copper-Nickel **Obv:** National arms with supporters, date below **Rev:** Zebra right, denomination at right **Edge:** Reeded

Date	Mintage	F	VF	XF	Unc	BU
1998	Est. 100,000	—	—	—	15.00	17.50

KM# 64 100 KWACHA
28.2800 g., 0.9990 Silver .9083 oz. ASW **Obv:** National arms with supporters, date below **Rev:** Flamingos, denomination at left

Date	Mintage	F	VF	XF	Unc	BU
1998 Proof	Est. 25,000	Value: 50.00				

KM# 64a 100 KWACHA
28.2800 g., Copper-Nickel **Obv:** National arms with supporters, date below **Rev:** Flamingo, denomination at left **Edge:** Reeded

Date	Mintage	F	VF	XF	Unc	BU
1998	Est. 100,000	—	—	—	15.00	17.50

KM# 65 100 KWACHA
28.2800 g., 0.9990 Silver .9083 oz. ASW **Obv:** National arms with supporters, date below **Rev:** Giraffes, denomination at left

Date	Mintage	F	VF	XF	Unc	BU
1998 Proof	Est. 25,000	Value: 60.00				

KM# 65a 100 KWACHA
28.2800 g., Copper-Nickel **Obv:** National arms with supporters, date below **Rev:** Giraffes, denomination at left **Edge:** Reeded

Date	Mintage	F	VF	XF	Unc	BU
1998	Est. 100,000	—	—	—	15.00	17.50

KM# 66 100 KWACHA
28.2800 g., 0.9990 Silver .9083 oz. ASW **Obv:** National arms with supporters, date below **Rev:** Lion facing, denomination at left

Date	Mintage	F	VF	XF	Unc	BU
1998 Proof	Est. 25,000	Value: 60.00				

KM# 66a 100 KWACHA
28.2800 g., Copper-Nickel **Obv:** National arms with supporters, date below **Rev:** Lion facing, denomination at left **Edge:** Reeded

Date	Mintage	F	VF	XF	Unc	BU
1998	Est. 100,000	—	—	—	15.00	17.50

KM# 67 100 KWACHA
28.2800 g., 0.9990 Silver .9083 oz. ASW **Obv:** National arms with supporters, date below **Rev:** Two gazelles, denomination above

Date	Mintage	F	VF	XF	Unc	BU
1998 Proof	Est. 25,000	Value: 50.00				

KM# 67a 100 KWACHA
28.2800 g., Copper-Nickel **Obv:** National arms with supporters, date below **Rev:** Gazelle, denomination above **Edge:** Reeded

Date	Mintage	F	VF	XF	Unc	BU
1998	Est. 100,000	—	—	—	15.00	17.50

Note: Please note that the copper-nickel versions were offered to the market almost two months after the silver version

KM# 52 200 KWACHA
Copper-Nickel **Subject:** Diana - The People's Princess **Obv:** National arms with supporters divide date, denomination below **Rev:** Head facing

Date	Mintage	F	VF	XF	Unc	BU
1997 Proof	—	Value: 8.00				

KM# 52a 200 KWACHA
31.1300 g., 0.9990 Silver 0.9999 oz. ASW, 35 mm. **Obv:** National arms with supporters divide date, denomination below **Rev:** Head facing **Edge:** Partially reeded with metal content from 5-7 o'clock

Date	Mintage	F	VF	XF	Unc	BU
1997 Proof	197	Value: 55.00				

KM# 20 250 KWACHA
33.6300 g., 0.9000 Gold .9371 oz. AGW **Subject:** Conservation **Obv:** Head of K.D. Kaunda right, date below **Rev:** African wild dog right, denomination below

Date	Mintage	F	VF	XF	Unc	BU
1979	455	—	—	—	675	725
1979 Proof	245	Value: 850				

KM# 34 250 KWACHA
136.0800 g., 0.9250 Silver 4.0474 oz. ASW, 63 mm. **Obv:** National arms with supporters, date below **Rev:** African fish eagles, one on branch and one in flight, denomination below **Note:** Photo reduced.

Date	Mintage	F	VF	XF	Unc	BU
1993	400	—	—	—	—	125
1993 Proof	5,000	Value: 85.00				

KM# 35 250 KWACHA
136.0800 g., 0.9250 Silver 4.0474 oz. ASW, 63 mm. **Obv:** National arms with supporters, date below **Rev:** Saddle-billed stork drinking, denomination below **Note:** Photo reduced.

Date	Mintage	F	VF	XF	Unc	BU
1993	400	—	—	—	—	125
1993 Proof	5,000	Value: 85.00				

KM# 36 250 KWACHA
136.0800 g., 0.9250 Silver 4.0474 oz. ASW, 63 mm. **Obv:** National arms with supporters, date below **Rev:** Paradise Flycatchers on branch, denomination below **Note:** Photo reduced.

Date	Mintage	F	VF	XF	Unc	BU
1993	400	—	—	—	—	125
1993 Proof	5,000	Value: 85.00				

KM# 37 250 KWACHA
136.0800 g., 0.9250 Silver 4.0474 oz. ASW, 63 mm. **Obv:** National arms with supporters, date below **Rev:** Red-breasted Swallows facing each other on branches, denomination below **Note:** Photo reduced.

Date	Mintage	F	VF	XF	Unc	BU
1993	400	—	—	—	—	135
1993 Proof	5,000	Value: 90.00				

KM# 173 250 KWACHA
136.0800 g., 0.9250 Silver 4.0469 oz. ASW, 62.9 mm. **Subject:** Birds **Obv:** National arms with supporters, date below **Rev:** Two Lizard Buzzards, denomination below **Edge:** Reeded **Note:** Photo reduced.

Date	Mintage	F	VF	XF	Unc	BU
1994 Proof	—	Value: 100				

KM# 40 500 KWACHA
31.7730 g., 0.9990 Silver 1.025 oz. ASW **Subject:** Equality **Obv:** National arms with supporters divide date, denomination below **Rev:** Black and white face profiles

Date	Mintage	F	VF	XF	Unc	BU
1994 Proof	—	Value: 32.50				

KM# 41 500 KWACHA
31.7730 g., 0.9990 Silver 1.025 oz. ASW **Subject:** Freedom of Speech **Obv:** National arms with supporters divide date, denomination below **Rev:** Perched African Fish Eagle

Date	Mintage	F	VF	XF	Unc	BU
1994 Proof	—	Value: 45.00				

KM# 42 500 KWACHA
31.7730 g., 0.9990 Silver 1.025 oz. ASW **Subject:** Rights of Religion and Culture **Obv:** National arms with supporters divide date, denomination below **Rev:** Books, scroll, and mask

Date	Mintage	F	VF	XF	Unc	BU
1994 Proof	—	Value: 25.00				

KM# 43 500 KWACHA
31.7730 g., 0.9990 Silver 1.025 oz. ASW **Subject:** Rights of Association **Obv:** National arms with supporters divide date, denomination below **Rev:** Lion cub and lamb

Date	Mintage	F	VF	XF	Unc	BU
1994 Proof	—	Value: 47.50				

KM# 44 500 KWACHA
31.7730 g., 0.9990 Silver 1.025 oz. ASW **Subject:** Rights to Work **Obv:** National arms with supporters divide date, denomination below **Rev:** African Masked Weaver building nest

Date	Mintage	F	VF	XF	Unc	BU
1994 Proof	—	Value: 45.00				

KM# 45 500 KWACHA
31.7730 g., 0.9990 Silver 1.025 oz. ASW **Subject:** Rights to Health **Obv:** National arms with supporters divide date, denomination below **Rev:** Shaman and Caduceus

Date	Mintage	F	VF	XF	Unc	BU
1994 Proof	—	Value: 25.00				

KM# 46 500 KWACHA
31.7730 g., 0.9990 Silver 1.025 oz. ASW **Subject:** Rights of the Disabled **Obv:** National arms divide date, denomination below **Rev:** Three elephants

Date	Mintage	F	VF	XF	Unc	BU
1994 Proof	—	Value: 47.50				

KM# 47 500 KWACHA
31.7730 g., 0.9990 Silver 1.025 oz. ASW **Subject:** Rights to a Clean Environment **Obv:** National arms divide date, denomination below **Rev:** Two South African Shelducks

Date	Mintage	F	VF	XF	Unc	BU
1994 Proof	—	Value: 45.00				

KM# 48 500 KWACHA
31.7730 g., 0.9990 Silver 1.025 oz. ASW **Subject:** Children's Rights **Obv:** National arms divide date, denomination below **Rev:** Fawn

Date	Mintage	F	VF	XF	Unc	BU
1994 Proof	—	Value: 45.00				

KM# 49 500 KWACHA
31.7730 g., 0.9990 Silver 1.025 oz. ASW **Subject:** Women's Rights **Obv:** National arms divide date, denomination below **Rev:** Women with firewood

Date	Mintage	F	VF	XF	Unc	BU
1994 Proof	—	Value: 22.50				

KM# 136 500 KWACHA
223.0000 g., 0.9990 Silver 7.1624 oz. ASW, 75.15 mm. **Subject:** Equality **Obv:** National arms divide date, denomination below **Rev:** Black and white facial profiles **Edge:** Reeded **Note:** Photo reduced.

Date	Mintage	F	VF	XF	Unc	BU
1995 Proof	—	Value: 175				

KM# 53 500 KWACHA
31.1035 g., 0.9990 Silver 1.0000 oz. ASW **Subject:** Diana - The People's Princess **Obv:** National arms divide date, denomination below **Rev:** Diana facing

Date	Mintage	F	VF	XF	Unc	BU
1997 Proof	Est. 13,211	Value: 22.50				

KM# 109 1000 KWACHA
20.0000 g., 0.9250 Silver .5948 oz. ASW, 38.6 mm. **Series:** Sydney Olympics **Obv:** Crowned head right within circle, divides date above arms and denomination **Rev:** Discus thrower **Edge:** Plain

Date	Mintage	F	VF	XF	Unc	BU
1999 Proof	—	Value: 35.00				

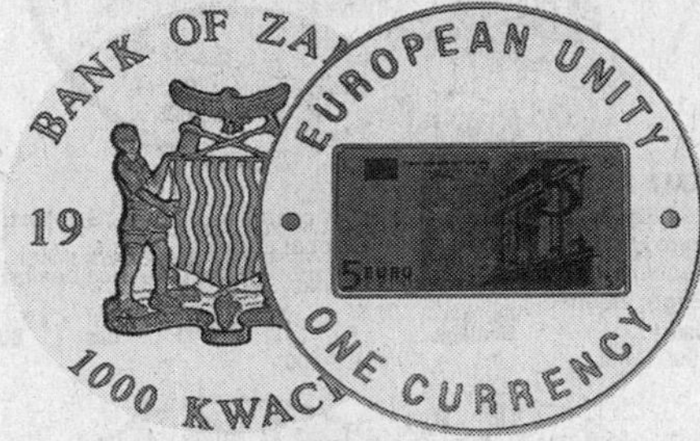

KM# 120 1000 KWACHA
28.5000 g., Silver-Plated Copper-Nickel, 38 mm. **Subject:** European Unity - One Currency **Obv:** National arms divide date, denomination below **Rev:** Multicolor 5 Euro note face design **Edge:** Reeded

Date	Mintage	F	VF	XF	Unc	BU
1999 Proof	—	Value: 20.00				

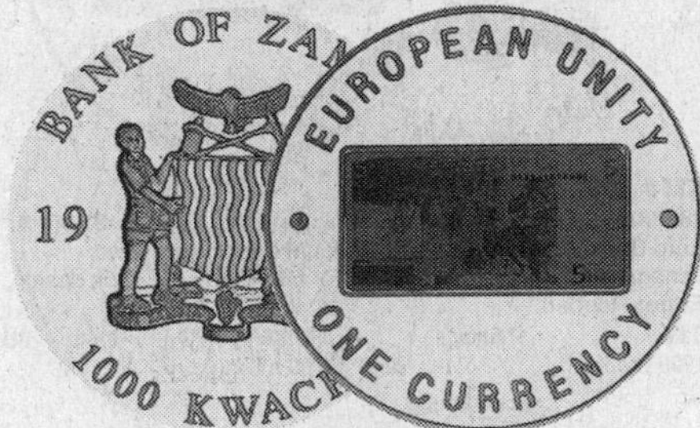

KM# 121 1000 KWACHA
28.5000 g., Silver-Plated Copper-Nickel, 38 mm. **Subject:** European Unity - One Currency **Obv:** National arms divide date, denomination below **Rev:** Multicolor 5 Euro note back design **Edge:** Reeded

Date	Mintage	F	VF	XF	Unc	BU
1999 Proof	—	Value: 20.00				

KM# 122 1000 KWACHA
28.5000 g., Silver-Plated Copper-Nickel, 38 mm. **Subject:** European Unity - One Currency **Obv:** National arms divide date, denomination below **Rev:** Multicolor 10 Euro note face design **Edge:** Reeded

Date	Mintage	F	VF	XF	Unc	BU
1999 Proof	—	Value: 20.00				

KM# 123 1000 KWACHA
28.5000 g., Silver-Plated Copper-Nickel, 38 mm. **Subject:** European Unity - One Currency **Obv:** National arms divide date, denomination below **Rev:** Multicolor 10 Euro note back design **Edge:** Reeded

Date	Mintage	F	VF	XF	Unc	BU
1999 Proof	—	Value: 20.00				

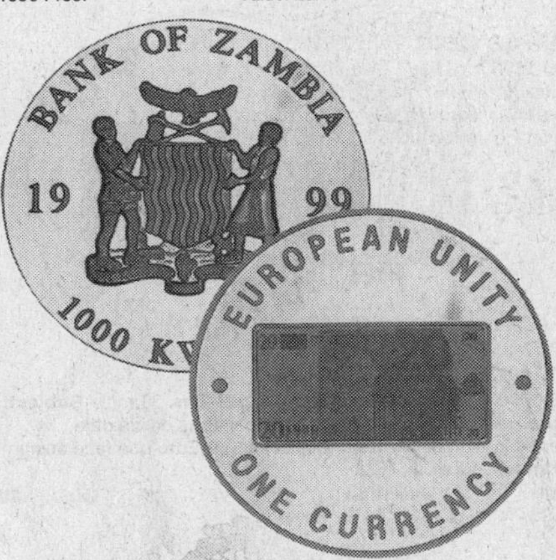

KM# 124 1000 KWACHA
28.5000 g., Silver-Plated Copper-Nickel, 38 mm. **Subject:** European Unity - One Currency **Obv:** National arms divide date, denomination below **Rev:** Multicolor 20 Euro note face design **Edge:** Reeded

Date	Mintage	F	VF	XF	Unc	BU
1999 Proof	—	Value: 20.00				

KM# 125 1000 KWACHA
28.5000 g., Silver-Plated Copper-Nickel, 38 mm. **Subject:** European Unity - One Currency **Obv:** National arms divide date, denomination below **Rev:** Multicolor 20 Euro note back design **Edge:** Reeded

Date	Mintage	F	VF	XF	Unc	BU
1999 Proof	—	Value: 20.00				

KM# 126 1000 KWACHA
28.5000 g., Silver-Plated Copper-Nickel, 38 mm. **Subject:** European Unity - One Currency **Obv:** National arms divide date, denomination below **Rev:** Multicolor 50 Euro note face design **Edge:** Reeded

Date	Mintage	F	VF	XF	Unc	BU
1999 Proof	—	Value: 20.00				

KM# 127 1000 KWACHA
28.5000 g., Silver-Plated Copper-Nickel, 38 mm. **Subject:** European Unity - One Currency **Obv:** National arms divide date, denomination below **Rev:** Multicolor 50 Euro note back design **Edge:** Reeded

Date	Mintage	F	VF	XF	Unc	BU
1999 Proof	—	Value: 20.00				

KM# 128 1000 KWACHA
28.5000 g., Silver Plated Copper-Nickel-Zinc, 38 mm. **Subject:** Euro Banknotes Series **Obv:** National arms divide date, denomination below **Rev:** Multicolor 100 Euro noe face design **Edge:** Reeded

Date	Mintage	F	VF	XF	Unc	BU
1999 Proof	—	Value: 20.00				

KM# 129 1000 KWACHA
28.5000 g., Silver Plated Copper-Nickel-Zinc, 38 mm. **Subject:** Euro Banknotes Series **Obv:** National arms divide date, denomination below **Rev:** Multicolor 100 Euro note back design **Edge:** Reeded

Date	Mintage	F	VF	XF	Unc	BU
1999 Proof	—	Value: 20.00				

KM# 130 1000 KWACHA
28.5000 g., Silver Plated Copper-Nickel-Zinc, 38 mm. **Subject:** Euro Banknotes Series **Obv:** National arms divide date, denomination below **Rev:** Multicolor 200 Euro note face design **Edge:** Reeded

Date	Mintage	F	VF	XF	Unc	BU
1999 Proof	—	Value: 20.00				

KM# 131 1000 KWACHA
28.5000 g., Silver Plated Copper-Nickel-Zinc, 38 mm. **Subject:** Euro Banknotes Series **Obv:** National arms divide date, denomination below **Rev:** Multicolor 200 Euro note back design **Edge:** Reeded

Date	Mintage	F	VF	XF	Unc	BU
1999 Proof	—	Value: 20.00				

KM# 132 1000 KWACHA
28.5000 g., Silver Plated Copper-Nickel-Zinc, 38 mm. **Subject:** Euro Banknotes Series **Obv:** National arms divide date, denomination below **Rev:** Multicolor 500 Euro note face design **Edge:** Reeded

Date	Mintage	F	VF	XF	Unc	BU
1999 Proof	—	Value: 20.00				

KM# 133 1000 KWACHA
28.5000 g., Silver Plated Copper-Nickel-Zinc, 38 mm. **Subject:** Euro Banknotes Series **Obv:** National arms divide date, denomination below **Rev:** Multicolor 500 Euro note back design **Edge:** Reeded

Date	Mintage	F	VF	XF	Unc	BU
1999 Proof	—	Value: 20.00				

KM# 176 1000 KWACHA
19.9200 g., 0.9250 Silver 0.5924 oz. ASW, 38.4 mm. **Obv:** British Queen Elizabeth II above Zambian arms **Rev:** 1st Man on the Moon **Edge:** Plain

Date	Mintage	F	VF	XF	Unc	BU
1999 Proof	—	Value: 40.00				

KM# 91 1000 KWACHA
28.7200 g., Copper-Nickel, 38 mm. **Subject:** European Unity **Obv:** National arms divide date, denomination below **Rev:** Multicolor 20 euro note **Edge:** Plain **Note:** Deleted per contributor

Date	Mintage	F	VF	XF	Unc	BU
1999	—	Value: 20.00				

KM# 74 1000 KWACHA
29.0000 g., Copper-Nickel, 40 mm. **Obv:** Crowned head right above arms with supporters divides date **Rev:** Dated calendar within circular design **Shape:** 7-sided

Date	Mintage	F	VF	XF	Unc	BU
2000 Proof	—	Value: 12.50				

KM# 75 1000 KWACHA
20.0000 g., Copper-Nickel, 48x30 mm. **Subject:** 100th Birthday - Queen Mother **Obv:** Head with tiara right divides date above arms **Rev:** Shaded bust facing **Edge:** Reeded **Shape:** Oval

Date	Mintage	F	VF	XF	Unc	BU
2000 Proof	—	Value: 13.50				

KM# 76 1000 KWACHA
20.0000 g., Copper-Nickel, 48x30 mm. **Subject:** 100th Birthday - Queen Mother **Obv:** Head with tiara right divides date above arms **Rev:** Black and white photo of Queen Mother seated on throne at 1937 coronation

Date	Mintage	F	VF	XF	Unc	BU
2000 Proof	50,000	Value: 13.50				

KM# 77 1000 KWACHA
20.0000 g., Copper-Nickel, 48x30 mm. **Subject:** 100th Birthday - Queen Mother **Obv:** Head with tiara right divides date above arms **Rev:** Black and white photo of Queen Mother as an elderly lady

Date	Mintage	F	VF	XF	Unc	BU
2000 Proof	50,000	Value: 13.50				

KM# 95 1000 KWACHA
Copper-Nickel, 48 x 30.1 mm. **Series:** 1,000 Years of Exploration **Obv:** Head with tiara right divides date above arms **Rev:** Multicolor portrait of Lief Ericksson and Viking ship **Edge:** Reeded

Date	Mintage	F	VF	XF	Unc	BU
2000 Proof	15,000	Value: 10.00				

KM# 96 1000 KWACHA
Copper-Nickel **Series:** 1,000 Years of Exploration **Obv:** Head with tiara right divides date above arms **Rev:** Multicolor portrait of Marco Polo and ship

Date	Mintage	F	VF	XF	Unc	BU
2000 Proof	15,000	Value: 10.00				

KM# 97 1000 KWACHA
Copper-Nickel **Series:** 1,000 Years of Exploration **Obv:** Head with tiara right divides date above arms **Rev:** Multicolor portrait of Columbus and ship

Date	Mintage	F	VF	XF	Unc	BU
2000 Proof	15,000	Value: 10.00				

KM# 98 1000 KWACHA
Copper-Nickel **Series:** 1,000 Years of Exploration **Obv:** Head with tiara right divides date above arms **Rev:** Multicolor portrait of Sir Francis Drake and ship

Date	Mintage	F	VF	XF	Unc	BU
2000 Proof	15,000	Value: 10.00				

KM# 99 1000 KWACHA
Copper-Nickel **Series:** 1,000 Years of Exploration **Obv:** Head with tiara right divides date above arms **Rev:** Multicolor portrait of Captain Cook and ship

Date	Mintage	F	VF	XF	Unc	BU
2000 Proof	15,000	Value: 10.00				

KM# 100 1000 KWACHA
Copper-Nickel **Series:** 1,000 Years of Exploration **Obv:** Head with tiara right divides date above arms **Rev:** Multicolor portrait of Amundsen and ship

Date	Mintage	F	VF	XF	Unc	BU
2000 Proof	15,000	Value: 10.00				

KM# 147 1000 KWACHA
28.9000 g., 0.9250 Silver 0.8595 oz. ASW, 40.3 mm. **Subject:** African Wildlife **Obv:** Head with tiara right divides date above arms **Rev:** Multicolor snarling leopard under protective acrylic, denomination below **Edge:** Reeded

Date	Mintage	F	VF	XF	Unc	BU
2000 Proof	—	Value: 50.00				

KM# 148 1000 KWACHA
28.9000 g., 0.9250 Silver 0.8595 oz. ASW, 40.3 mm. **Subject:** African Wildlife **Obv:** Head with white tiara right divides date above national arms **Rev:** Multicolor white stork under protective acrylic, denomination below **Edge:** Reeded

Date	Mintage	F	VF	XF	Unc	BU
2000 Proof	—	Value: 50.00				

KM# 149 1000 KWACHA
28.9000 g., 0.9250 Silver 0.8595 oz. ASW, 40.3 mm. **Subject:** African Wildlife **Obv:** Head with tiara right divides date above national arms **Rev:** Multicolor cheetah under protective acrylic, denomination below **Edge:** Reeded

Date	Mintage	F	VF	XF	Unc	BU
2000 Proof	—	Value: 50.00				

KM# 137 2000 KWACHA
22.5000 g., Copper-Nickel, 38 mm. **Subject:** World Cup Soccer **Obv:** National arms with supporters divide date, denomination below **Rev:** Player kicking ball **Edge:** Reeded

Date	Mintage	F	VF	XF	Unc	BU
1994 Proof	—	Value: 20.00				

KM# 138 2000 KWACHA
22.5000 g., Copper-Nickel, 38 mm. **Subject:** World Cup Soccer **Obv:** National arms with supporters divide date, denomination below **Rev:** Two players in action **Edge:** Reeded

Date	Mintage	F	VF	XF	Unc	BU
1994 Proof	—	Value: 20.00				

KM# 139 2000 KWACHA
22.5000 g., Copper-Nickel, 38 mm. **Subject:** World Cup Soccer **Obv:** National arms with supporters divide date, denomination below **Rev:** Three players and "Winner Brazil" **Edge:** Reeded

Date	Mintage	F	VF	XF	Unc	BU
1994 Proof	—	Value: 20.00				

KM# 152 2000 KWACHA
20.2200 g., 0.9999 Silver 0.65 oz. ASW, 38 mm. **Subject:** World History **Obv:** National arms with supporters divide date, denomination below **Rev:** Human figure study **Edge:** Reeded

Date	Mintage	F	VF	XF	Unc	BU
1997 Proof	—	Value: 35.00				

KM# 54 2000 KWACHA
3.1103 g., 0.9999 Gold .1000 oz. AGW **Subject:** Diana - The People's Princess **Obv:** National arms with supporters divide date, denomination below **Rev:** Head facing **Note:** Similar to 200 Kwacha, KM#52.

Date	Mintage	F	VF	XF	Unc	BU
1997 Proof	—	Value: 85.00				

KM# 68 2000 KWACHA
15.5518 g., 0.9990 Silver .5000 oz. ASW **Subject:** Taipai Subway **Obv:** National arms **Rev:** Train with inset diamond headlight **Note:** Struck at Singapore Mint.

Date	Mintage	F	VF	XF	Unc	BU
1998 Proof	9,999	Value: 40.00				

KM# 146 2000 KWACHA/100 GUILDERS
25.0000 g., 0.9990 Silver 0.803 oz. ASW, 38 mm. **Subject:** World Cup Soccer **Obv:** National arms with supporters divide date, denomination below **Rev:** Two soccer players of Suriname **Edge:** Reeded **Note:** Zambia/Suriname muled dies error. Obverse is Zambia and the reverse is Suriname.

Date	Mintage	F	VF	XF	Unc	BU
1994 Proof	—	Value: 100				

KM# 55 2500 KWACHA
155.5175 g., 0.9990 Silver 5.0000 oz. ASW **Subject:** Diana - The People's Princess **Obv:** National arms with supporters divide date, denomination below **Rev:** With sons, William and Harry

Date	Mintage	F	VF	XF	Unc	BU
1997 Proof	Est. 1,997	Value: 135				

KM# 107 2500 KWACHA
15.5535 g., 0.9250 Silver .4626 oz. ASW, 36 mm. **Series:** World Health Organization **Obv:** National arms with supporters divide date, denomination below **Rev:** Bust at left facing right, logo at right **Edge:** Reeded

Date	Mintage	F	VF	XF	Unc	BU
1998 Proof	—	Value: 30.00				

KM# 134 4000 KWACHA
31.1035 g., 0.9990 Silver 0.999 oz. ASW, 38.5 mm. **Subject:** Year of the Tiger **Obv:** National arms with supporters divide date, denomination below **Rev:** Gold bat disc mounted above tiger **Edge:** Reeded

Date	Mintage	F	VF	XF	Unc	BU
1997 Proof	—	Value: 125				

KM# 155 4000 KWACHA
30.3300 g., 0.9990 Silver 0.9742 oz. ASW, 38 mm. **Subject:** King of Peace - King Hussein of Jordan **Obv:** National arms with supporters divide date, denomination below **Rev:** Bust at left looking right, multicolor view of Petra at right **Edge:** Reeded

Date	Mintage	F	VF	XF	Unc	BU
1998 Proof	—	Value: 50.00				

KM# 69 4000 KWACHA
31.1035 g., 0.9990 Silver 1.0000 oz. ASW **Subject:** Taipai Subway **Obv:** National arms **Rev:** Train with inset diamond headlight **Note:** Struck at Singapore Mint.

Date	Mintage	F	VF	XF	Unc	BU
1998 Proof	9,999	Value: 60.00				

KM# 161 4000 KWACHA
28.9500 g., Copper-Nickel, 37.9 mm. **Subject:** Patrons of the Ocean **Obv:** National arms divide date above "999", denomination below **Rev:** Sea Turtle and fish **Edge:** Reeded

Date	Mintage	F	VF	XF	Unc	BU
1998 Proof	—	Value: 25.00				

KM# 162 4000 KWACHA
28.9500 g., Copper-Nickel, 37.9 mm. **Subject:** Patrons of the Ocean **Obv:** National arms divide date above "999", denomination below **Rev:** Sea horse and fish **Edge:** Reeded

Date	Mintage	F	VF	XF	Unc	BU
1998 Proof	—	Value: 25.00				

KM# 163 4000 KWACHA
28.9500 g., Copper-Nickel, 37.9 mm. **Subject:** Patrons of the Ocean **Obv:** National arms divide date above "999", denomination below **Rev:** Two dolphins **Edge:** Reeded

Date	Mintage	F	VF	XF	Unc	BU
1998 Proof	—	Value: 25.00				

KM# 164 4000 KWACHA
28.9500 g., Copper-Nickel, 37.9 mm. **Subject:** Patrons of the Ocean **Obv:** National arms divide date above "999", denomination below **Rev:** Coelacanth **Edge:** Reeded

Date	Mintage	F	VF	XF	Unc	BU
1998 Proof	—	Value: 25.00				

KM# 175 4000 KWACHA
23.0000 g., 0.9990 Silver 0.7387 oz. ASW, 40 mm. **Obv:** Head with tiara right divides date above arms **Rev:** Dated calendar **Shape:** Seven sided

Date	Mintage	F	VF	XF	Unc	BU
2000 Proof-like	—	—	—	—	—	50.00

KM# 158 4000 KWACHA
31.0000 g., 0.9990 Silver 0.9957 oz. ASW, 38.8 mm. **Subject:** African Wildlife **Obv:** Head with tiara right divides date above arms **Rev:** Leopard and two cubs, denomination below **Edge:** Reeded

Date	Mintage	F	VF	XF	Unc	BU
2000 Proof	—	Value: 40.00				

KM# 78 4000 KWACHA
20.0000 g., 0.9250 Silver .5948 oz. ASW, 48x30 mm. **Subject:** 100th Birthday - Queen Mother **Obv:** Head with tiara right divides

date above arms **Rev:** Black and white photo of the Queen Mother as a young lady **Edge:** Reeded **Shape:** Oval

Date	Mintage	F	VF	XF	Unc	BU
2000 Proof	25,000	Value: 40.00				

KM# 79 4000 KWACHA
20.0000 g., 0.9250 Silver .5948 oz. ASW, 48x30 mm. **Subject:** 100th Birthday - Queen Mother **Obv:** Head with tiara right divides date above arms **Rev:** Black and white photo of Queen Mother on throne at 1937 coronation **Shape:** Oval

Date	Mintage	F	VF	XF	Unc	BU
2000 Proof	25,000	Value: 40.00				

KM# 80 4000 KWACHA
20.0000 g., 0.9250 Silver .5948 oz. ASW, 48x30 mm. **Subject:** 100th Birthday - Queen Mother **Obv:** Head with tiara right divides date above arms **Rev:** Black and white photo of an elderly Queen Mother **Shape:** Oval

Date	Mintage	F	VF	XF	Unc	BU
2000 Proof	25,000	Value: 40.00				

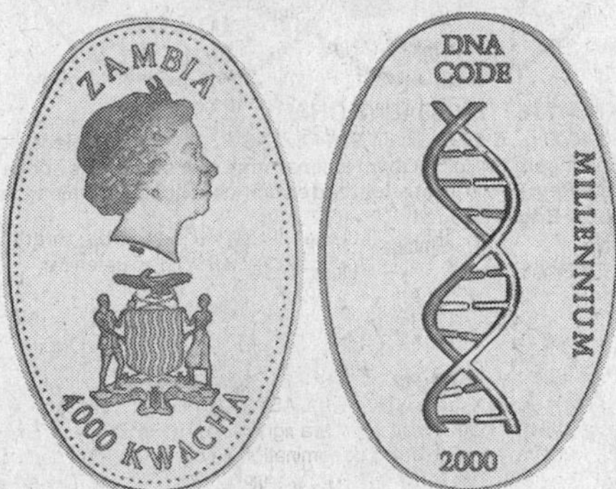

KM# 84 4000 KWACHA
20.0000 g., 0.9250 Silver .5948 oz. ASW, 30.1x48 mm. **Subject:** Millennium - DNA Code **Obv:** Head with tiara right above arms and denomination **Rev:** DNA chain, date below **Edge:** Reeded

Date	Mintage	F	VF	XF	Unc	BU
2000 Proof	—	Value: 32.50				

KM# 85 4000 KWACHA
25.1000 g., 0.9250 Silver .7465 oz. ASW, 37.9 mm. **Series:** Wildlife Protection **Obv:** Crowned head right below arms **Rev:** Lion head hologram **Edge:** Reeded **Note:** Lighter weight and smaller diameter than official specifications.

Date	Mintage	F	VF	XF	Unc	BU
2000 Proof	5,000	Value: 60.00				

KM# 101 4000 KWACHA
20.0000 g., 0.9250 Silver .5948 oz. ASW, 48x30.1 mm. **Series:** 1000 Years of Exploration **Obv:** Head with tiara right divides date above arms **Rev:** Multicolor portrait of Leif Eriksson and ship **Edge:** Reeded **Shape:** Oval

Date	Mintage	F	VF	XF	Unc	BU
2000 Proof	5,000	Value: 40.00				

KM# 102 4000 KWACHA
20.0000 g., 0.9250 Silver .5948 oz. ASW **Subject:** 1000 Years of Exploration **Obv:** Head with tiara right divides date above arms **Rev:** Multicolor portrait of Marco Polo and ship **Shape:** Oval

Date	Mintage	F	VF	XF	Unc	BU
2000 Proof	5,000	Value: 40.00				

KM# 103 4000 KWACHA
20.0000 g., 0.9250 Silver .5948 oz. ASW **Subject:** 1000 Years of Exploration **Obv:** Head with tiara right divides date above arms **Rev:** Multicolor portrait of Columbus and ship **Shape:** Oval

Date	Mintage	F	VF	XF	Unc	BU
2000 Proof	5,000	Value: 40.00				

KM# 104 4000 KWACHA
20.0000 g., 0.9250 Silver .5948 oz. ASW **Subject:** 1000 Years of Exploration **Obv:** Head with tiara right divides date above arms **Rev:** Multicolor portrait of Sir Francis Drake and ship

Date	Mintage	F	VF	XF	Unc	BU
2000 Proof	5,000	Value: 40.00				

KM# 105 4000 KWACHA
20.0000 g., 0.9250 Silver .5948 oz. ASW **Subject:** 1000 Years of Exploration **Obv:** Head with tiara right divides date above arms **Rev:** Multicolor portrait of Captain Cook and ship **Shape:** Oval

Date	Mintage	F	VF	XF	Unc	BU
2000 Proof	5,000	Value: 40.00				

KM# 106 4000 KWACHA
20.0000 g., 0.9250 Silver .5948 oz. ASW **Subject:** 1000 Years of Exploration **Obv:** Head with tiara right divides date above arms **Rev:** Multicolor portrait of Amundsen and ship **Shape:** Oval

Date	Mintage	F	VF	XF	Unc	BU
2000 Proof	5,000	Value: 40.00				

KM# 144 5000 KWACHA
Silver **Rev:** Lions, map, and arms

Date	Mintage	F	VF	XF	Unc	BU
1997 Proof	2,000	Value: 210				

KM# 177 5000 KWACHA
31.2000 g., 0.9990 Silver 1.0021 oz. ASW, 40 mm. **Obv:** National arms **Rev:** Asian General behind red flowers **Edge:** Reeded

Date	Mintage	F	VF	XF	Unc	BU
1997 Proof	—	Value: 50.00				

KM# 108 5000 KWACHA

31.2100 g., 0.9250 Silver .9282 oz. ASW, 40 mm. **Subject:** World Health Organization **Obv:** National arms with supporters divide date, denomination below **Rev:** Bust at left facing right, logo at right **Edge:** Reeded

Date	Mintage	F	VF	XF	Unc	BU
1998 Proof	—	Value: 40.00				

KM# 70 5000 KWACHA

7.7759 g., 0.9990 Gold .2500 oz. AGW **Subject:** Taipai Subway **Obv:** National arms **Rev:** Train with inset diamond headlight **Note:** Struck at Singapore Mint.

Date	Mintage	F	VF	XF	Unc	BU
1998 Proof	999	Value: 350				

KM# 157 5000 KWACHA

31.1600 g., 0.9990 Silver 1.0008 oz. ASW, 38.8 mm. **Subject:** African Wildlife **Obv:** National arms with supporters divide date, denomination below **Rev:** Lions' pride, denomination above **Edge:** Reeded

Date	Mintage	F	VF	XF	Unc	BU
1999 Proof	—	Value: 40.00				

KM# 73 5000 KWACHA

31.1346 g., 0.9990 Silver 1.0000 oz. ASW **Subject:** African Wildlife **Obv:** National arms with supporters divide date, denomination below **Rev:** Elephant and calf in water with metal content statement

Date	Mintage	F	VF	XF	Unc	BU
1999	—	—	—	—	24.00	—
1999 Matte	—	—	—	—	30.00	—

KM# 92 5000 KWACHA

31.2100 g., 0.9990 Silver 1.0024 oz. ASW, 38.7 mm. **Subject:** African Wildlife **Obv:** National arms with supporters, date below **Rev:** Elephant mother and calf right, denomination below **Edge:** Reeded

Date	Mintage	F	VF	XF	Unc	BU
1999 Proof	—	Value: 22.50				

KM# 150 5000 KWACHA

31.1035 g., 0.9999 Silver 0.9999 oz. ASW, 38 mm. **Subject:** Chinese Zodiac **Obv:** Dragon on Chinese map above national arms **Rev:** Cartoon rabbit within inner circle **Edge:** Reeded

Date	Mintage	F	VF	XF	Unc	BU
ND Proof	—	Value: 45.00				

KM# 151 5000 KWACHA

31.1035 g., 0.9999 Silver 0.9999 oz. ASW, 38 mm. **Subject:** Chinese Zodiac **Obv:** Dragon on Chinese map above national arms **Rev:** Cartoon bull within inner circle **Edge:** Reeded

Date	Mintage	F	VF	XF	Unc	BU
ND Proof	—	Value: 45.00				

KM# 81 5000 KWACHA

27.0000 g., 0.9990 Gold .8672 oz. AGW, 48x30 mm. **Subject:** 100th Birthday - Queen Mother **Obv:** Head with tiara right divides date above arms **Rev:** Black and white photo of the Queen Mother as a young lady **Edge:** Reeded **Shape:** Oval

Date	Mintage	F	VF	XF	Unc	BU
2000 Proof	100	Value: 700				

KM# 82 5000 KWACHA

27.0000 g., 0.9990 Gold .8672 oz. AGW, 48x30 mm. **Subject:** 100th Birthday - Queen Mother **Obv:** Head with tiara right divides date above arms **Rev:** Black ad white photo of Queen Mother on throne at 1937 coronation **Shape:** Oval

Date	Mintage	F	VF	XF	Unc	BU
2000 Proof	100	Value: 700				

KM# 83 5000 KWACHA

27.0000 g., 0.9990 Gold .8672 oz. AGW, 48x30 mm. **Subject:** 100th Birthday - Queen Mother **Obv:** Head with tiara right divides date above arms **Rev:** Black and white photo of an elderly Queen Mother **Shape:** Oval

Date	Mintage	F	VF	XF	Unc	BU
2000 Proof	100	Value: 700				

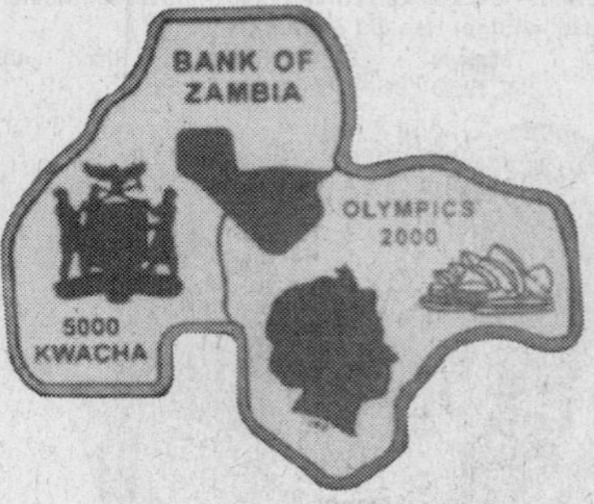

KM# 115 5000 KWACHA

31.3600 g., 0.9250 Silver .9326 oz. ASW, 48.7x41.75 mm. **Subject:** Olympics **Obv:** National arms at left, map above head right with tiara, at center, swimmer at right **Rev:** Runners and map **Edge:** Plain **Shape:** Irregular **Note:** Irregular shape.

Date	Mintage	F	VF	XF	Unc	BU
2000 Proof	—	Value: 55.00				

KM# 145 10000 KWACHA

Silver **Rev:** Kudu, map, and arms

Date	Mintage	F	VF	XF	Unc	BU
1997 Proof	2,000	Value: 360				

KM# 116 10000 KWACHA

30.4000 g., 0.9990 Silver .9764 oz. ASW, 34 mm. **Subject:** Endangered Wildlife **Obv:** National arms with supporters above date **Rev:** Bird in flight at left, bird on branch at right, denomination below **Edge:** Reeded

Date	Mintage	F	VF	XF	Unc	BU
1997 Proof	—	Value: 42.50				

KM# 86 10000 KWACHA

30.2800 g., 0.9990 Silver .9726 oz. ASW, 34 mm. **Series:** Endangered Wildlife **Obv:** National arms with supporters, date below **Rev:** Lion family, denomination below **Edge:** Reeded **Note:** 3.8mm thick.

Date	Mintage	F	VF	XF	Unc	BU
1997 Proof	—	Value: 40.00				

KM# 71 10000 KWACHA

15.5518 g., 0.9999 Gold .5000 oz. AGW **Subject:** Taipai Subway **Obv:** National arms **Rev:** Train with inset diamond headlight **Note:** Struck at Singapore Mint.

Date	Mintage	F	VF	XF	Unc	BU
1998 Proof	99	Value: 650				

KM# 93 20000 KWACHA
1000.0000 g., 0.9990 Silver 32.1186 oz. ASW, 101 mm. **Subject:** Ko-Imari VOC Plate **Obv:** Head with tiara right **Rev:** Multicolor plate design **Edge:** Reeded **Note:** Photo reduced. Struck on behalf of the Fiji International Mint.

Date	Mintage	F	VF	XF	Unc	BU
2000FIM Proof	500	Value: 700				

KM# 72 500000 KWACHA
155.5175 g., 0.9999 Gold 5.0000 oz. AGW **Subject:** Taipai Subway **Obv:** National arms **Rev:** Train with inset diamond headlight **Note:** Struck at Singapore Mint.

Date	Mintage	F	VF	XF	Unc	BU
1998 Proof	99	Value: 3,500				

PATTERNS

Including off metal strikes

KM#	Date	Mintage	Identification	Mkt Val
Pn1	1994	—	10 Kwacha. Copper-Nickel. KM#39	80.00
Pn2	1994	—	10 Kwacha. Silver. Similar to KM#39, .999 Cu Ni in field.	80.00
Pn3	1994	—	2000 Kwacha. Copper-Nickel. Similar to KM#39	—
Pn4	1998	—	1000 Kwacha. Copper-Nickel. 28.5000 g. 38.6 mm. National arms. Portrait and memorial. Reeded edge.	125
Pn5	1998	—	4000 Kwacha. 0.9990 Silver. 30.8300 g. 38 mm. National arms. Bust of Princess Diana in high collar 1/2 facing. Reeded edge.	225
Pn6	1998	—	1000 Kwacha. Copper-Nickel. 28.8500 g. 38 mm. National arms. Princess Diana in high collar. Reeded edge. Princess Diana in High collar. Proof.	125

PIEFORTS

KM#	Date	Mintage	Identification	Mkt Val
P1	1980	76	10 Kwacha. Silver. KM#21	100

TRIAL STRIKES

KM#	Date	Mintage	Identification	Mkt Val
TS1	1997	—	200 Kwacha. Gilt Bronze. 26.3000 g. 38.9 mm. National arms. "TRIAL STRIKE BRONZE". Reeded edge. Proof	—

KM#	Date	Mintage	Identification	Mkt Val
TS2	ND (1997)	—	200 Kwacha. Gilt Bronze. 26.2400 g. 38.9 mm. "TRIAL STRIKE BRONZE". Diana. Reeded edge. Proof	—

KM#	Date	Mintage	Identification	Mkt Val
TS3	1997	—	200 Kwacha. Copper-Nickel. 26.4100 g. 38.9 mm. National arms. "TRIAL STRIKE CUPRO-NICKLE". Reeded edge. Proof	—

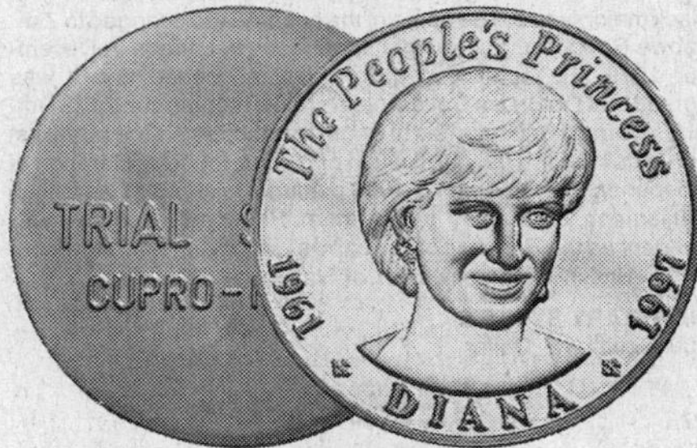

KM#	Date	Mintage	Identification	Mkt Val
TS4	ND (1997)	—	200 Kwacha. Copper-Nickel. 26.4600 g. 38.9 mm. "TRIAL STRIKE CUPRO-NICKLE". Diana. Reeded edge. Proof	—

KM#	Date	Mintage	Identification	Mkt Val
TS5	1997	—	200 Kwacha. 0.9990 Silver. 31.2500 g. 38.9 mm. National arms. "TRIAL STRIKE SILVER". Reeded edge. Proof	—

KM#	Date	Mintage	Identification	Mkt Val
TS6	ND (1997)	—	200 Kwacha. 0.9990 Silver. 31.2500 g. 38.9 mm. "TRIAL STRIKE SILVER". Diana. Reeded edge. Proof	—

MINT SETS

KM#	Date	Mintage	Identification	Issue Price	Mkt Val
MS1	1968 (5)	—	KM#9-13	2.00	7.00

PROOF SETS

KM#	Date	Mintage	Identification	Issue Price	Mkt Val
PS1	1964 (3)	5,000	KM#1-3	—	10.00
PS2	1965 (2)	100	KM#4 (2 pieces)	—	15.00
PS3	1966 (8)	30	KM#5-8, double sets	—	—
PS4	1968 (5)	4,000	KM#9-13	10.00	9.50
PS5	1978 (6)	20,000	KM#9-13, 16	21.00	16.50
PS6	1994 (10)	—	KM#40-49	300	285
PS7	1998 (12)	25,000	KM#56-67	672	685
PS8	2000 (3)	50,000	KM#75-77	—	45.00
PS9	2000 (3)	25,000	KM#78-80	—	120
PS10	2000 (4)	100	KM#81-83	—	2,025

ZANZIBAR

The British protectorate of Zanzibar and adjacent small islands, located in the Indian Ocean 22 miles (35 km.) off the coast of Tanganyika, comprised a portion of British East Africa. Zanzibar was also the name of a sultanate which included the Zanzibar and Kenya protectorates. Zanzibar has an area of 637 sq. mi. (1,651 sq. km.). Chief city: Zanzibar. The islands are noted for their cloves, of which Zanzibar is the world's foremost producer.

Zanzibar came under Portuguese control in 1503, was conquered by the Omani Arabs in 1698, became independent of Oman in 1860, and (with Pemba) came under British control in 1890. Britain granted the protectorate self-government in 1961, and independence within the British Commonwealth on Dec. 19, 1963. On April 26,1964, Tanganyika and Zanzibar (with Pemba) united to form the United Republic of Tanganyika and Zanzibar. The name of the country, which remained within the British Commonwealth was changed to Tanzania on Oct. 29,1964.

TITLE

زنجبار زنجبارا

Zanjibara

RULER

Sultan Ali Bin Hamud, 1902-1911AD

MONETARY SYSTEM

64 Pysa (Pice) = 1 Rupee
136 Pysa = 1 Ryal (to 1908)
100 Cents = 1 Rupee (to 1909)

BRITISH PROTECTORATE

DECIMAL COINAGE

100 Cents = 1 Rupee

KM# 8 CENT

Bronze **Ruler:** Sultan Ali Bin Hamud **Obv:** Inscription **Rev:** Palm tree divides value

Date	Mintage	F	VF	XF	Unc	BU
1908	1,000,000	75.00	150	300	450	—

KM# 9 10 CENTS

Bronze **Ruler:** Sultan Ali Bin Hamud **Obv:** Inscription **Rev:** Palm tree divides value

Date	Mintage	F	VF	XF	Unc	BU
1908	100,000	100	225	400	750	—

KM# 10 20 CENTS

Nickel **Ruler:** Sultan Ali Bin Hamud **Obv:** Inscription **Rev:** Palm tree divides value

Date	Mintage	F	VF	XF	Unc	BU
1908	100,000	150	300	500	950	—

ZIMBABWE

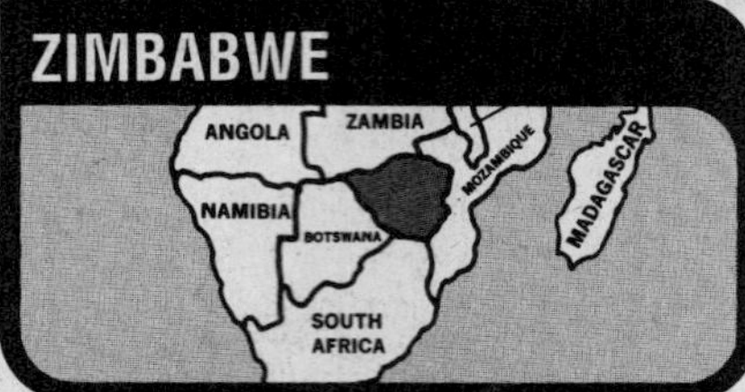

The Republic of Zimbabwe (formerly the Republic of Rhodesia or Southern Rhodesia), located in the east-central part of southern Africa, has an area of 150,804 sq. mi. (390,580sq. km.) and a population of *10.1 million. Capital: Harare (formerly Salisbury). The economy is based on agriculture and mining. Tobacco, sugar, asbestos, copper, chrome, ore and coal are exported.

The Rhodesian area contains extensive evidence of the habitat of paleolithic man and earlier civilizations, notably the world-famous ruins of Zimbabwe, a gold-trading center that flourished about the 14th or 15th century A.D. The Portuguese of the 16th century were the first Europeans to attempt to develop south-central Africa, but it re-mained for Cecil Rhodes and the British South Africa Co. to open the hinterlands. Rhodes obtained a concession for mineral rights from local chiefs in 1888 and administered his African empire (named Southern Rhodesia in 1895) through the British South Africa Co. until 1923, when the British government annexed the area after the white settlers voted for existence as a separate entity, rather than for incorporation into the Union of South Africa. From Sept. of 1953 through 1963 Southern Rhodesia was joined with the British Protectorates of Northern Rhodesia and Nyasaland into a multiracial federation, known as the Federation of Rhodesia and Nyasaland. When the federation was dissolved at the end of 1963, Northern Rhodesia and Nyasaland became the independent states of Zambia and Malawi.

Britain was prepared to grant independence to Southern Rhodesia but declined to do so when the politically dominant white Rhodesians refused to give assurances of representative government. On Nov. 11, 1965, following two years of unsuccessful negotiation with the British government, Prime Minister Ian Smith issued an unilateral declaration of independence. Britain responded with economic sanctions supported by the United Nations. After further futile attempts to effect an accommodation, the Rhodesian Parliament severed all ties with Britain and on March 2, 1970, established the Republic of Rhodesia.

On March 3, 1978, Prime Minister Ian Smith and three moderate black nationalist leaders signed an agreement providing for black majority rule. The name of the country was changed to Zimbabwe Rhodesia. Following a conference in London in December 1979, the opposition government conceded and it was agreed that the British Government should resume control. A British Governor soon returned to Southern Rhodesia. One of his first acts was to affirm the nullification of the purported declaration of independence. On April 18, 1980 pursuant to an act of the British Parliament, the colony of Southern Rhodesia became independent as the Republic of Zimbabwe, which remains a member of the British Commonwealth of Nations.

MONETARY SYSTEM

100 Cents = 1 Dollar

REPUBLIC

DECIMAL COINAGE

KM# 1 CENT

3.1000 g., Bronze, 18.45 mm. **Obv:** Bird statue above date **Rev:** Denomination within wreath **Designer:** Jeff Huntly

Date	Mintage	F	VF	XF	Unc	BU
1980	10,000,000	—	0.10	0.20	0.40	0.65
1980 Proof	15,000	Value: 1.50				
1982	—	—	0.10	0.20	0.40	0.65
1983	—	—	0.10	0.20	0.40	0.65
1986	—	—	0.10	0.20	0.40	0.65
1988	—	—	0.10	0.20	0.40	0.65

KM# 1a CENT

Bronze Plated Steel, 18.45 mm. **Obv:** Bird statue above date **Rev:** Denomination within wreath

Date	Mintage	F	VF	XF	Unc	BU
1989	—	—	0.10	0.20	0.50	0.75
1990	—	—	0.10	0.20	0.50	0.75
1991	—	—	0.10	0.20	0.50	0.75
1994	—	—	0.10	0.20	0.50	0.75
1995	—	—	0.10	0.20	0.50	0.75
1997	—	—	0.10	0.20	0.50	0.75
1997 Proof	5,500	Value: 1.00				
1999	—	—	0.10	0.20	0.50	0.75

KM# 2 5 CENTS

2.6000 g., Copper-Nickel, 17 mm. **Obv:** Bird statue above date **Rev:** Rabbit left, denomination above **Designer:** Jeff Huntly

Date	Mintage	F	VF	XF	Unc	BU
1980	—	—	0.15	0.30	1.00	1.25
1980 Proof	15,000	Value: 1.50				
1982	—	—	0.15	0.30	1.00	1.25
1983	—	—	0.15	0.30	1.00	1.25
1988	—	—	0.15	0.30	1.00	1.25
1989	—	—	0.15	0.30	1.00	1.25
1990	—	—	0.15	0.30	1.00	1.25
1991	—	—	0.15	0.30	1.00	1.25
1995	—	—	0.15	0.30	1.00	1.25
1996	—	—	0.15	0.30	1.00	1.25
1997	—	—	0.15	0.30	1.00	1.25
1997 Proof	Est. 5,500	Value: 2.00				
1999	—	—	0.15	0.30	1.00	1.25

KM# 3 10 CENTS

3.7800 g., Copper-Nickel, 20 mm. **Obv:** Bird statue above date **Rev:** Baobab tree, denomination at right **Designer:** Jeff Huntly

Date	Mintage	F	VF	XF	Unc	BU
1980	—	—	0.15	0.30	0.75	1.00
1980 Proof	15,000	Value: 2.00				
1983	—	—	0.15	0.30	0.75	1.00
1987	—	—	0.15	0.30	0.75	1.00
1988	—	—	0.15	0.30	0.75	1.00
1989	—	—	0.15	0.30	0.75	1.00
1991	—	—	0.15	0.30	0.75	1.00
1994	—	—	0.15	0.30	0.75	1.00
1997	—	—	0.15	0.30	0.75	1.00
1997 Proof	Est. 5,500	Value: 3.00				
1999	—	—	0.15	0.30	0.75	1.00

KM# 4 20 CENTS

5.7000 g., Copper-Nickel, 22.95 mm. **Obv:** Bird statue above date **Rev:** Bridge, denomination below **Edge:** Plain **Designer:** Jeff Huntly

Date	Mintage	F	VF	XF	Unc	BU
1980	—	—	0.25	0.50	1.50	1.75
1980 Proof	15,000	Value: 2.50				
1983	—	—	0.25	0.50	1.50	1.75
1987	—	—	0.20	0.40	1.25	1.50
1988	—	—	0.20	0.40	1.25	1.50
1989	—	—	0.20	0.40	1.25	1.50
1990	—	—	0.20	0.40	1.25	1.50
1991	—	—	0.20	0.40	1.25	1.50
1994	—	—	0.20	0.40	1.25	1.50
1996	—	—	0.20	0.40	1.25	1.50
1997	—	—	0.20	0.40	1.25	1.50
1997 Proof	Est. 5,500	Value: 4.00				

KM# 5 50 CENTS

7.5200 g., Copper-Nickel, 25.95 mm. **Obv:** Bird statue above date **Rev:** Radiant sun landscape, denomination above **Edge:** Plain **Designer:** Jeff Huntly

Date	Mintage	F	VF	XF	Unc	BU
1980	—	—	0.60	1.25	2.25	2.50
1980 Proof	15,000	Value: 4.50				
1988	—	—	0.40	1.00	1.75	2.00
1989	—	—	0.40	1.00	1.75	2.00
1990	—	—	0.40	1.00	1.75	2.00
1993	—	—	0.40	1.00	1.75	2.00
1995	—	—	0.40	1.00	1.75	2.00
1997	—	—	0.40	1.00	1.75	2.00
1997 Proof	Est. 5,500	Value: 8.00				

KM# 6 DOLLAR

10.0000 g., Copper-Nickel, 28.95 mm. **Obv:** Bird statue above date **Rev:** Ruins between trees, denomination above **Edge:** Reeded **Designer:** Jeff Huntly

Date	Mintage	F	VF	XF	Unc	BU
1980	—	—	1.00	1.50	3.00	3.50
1980 Proof	15,000	Value: 6.50				
1993	—	—	1.00	1.50	3.00	3.50
1997	—	—	1.00	1.50	3.00	3.50
1997 Proof	Est. 5,500	Value: 12.00				

KM# 12 2 DOLLARS

9.5200 g., Brass, 24.5 mm. **Obv:** Bird statue above date **Rev:** Pangolin below denomination **Edge:** Reeded **Designer:** Jeff Huntly

Date	Mintage	F	VF	XF	Unc	BU
1997	—	—	1.25	2.25	5.00	5.50
1997 Proof	Est. 5,500	Value: 20.00				

KM# 7 10 DOLLARS

31.1035 g., 0.9990 Silver 1.0000 oz. ASW **Series:** Wildlife Landmark **Obv:** Victoria Falls bridge **Rev:** Lions

Date	Mintage	F	VF	XF	Unc	BU
1996 Proof	5,000	Value: 55.00				

KM# 8 10 DOLLARS

31.1035 g., 0.9990 Silver 1.0000 oz. ASW **Series:** Wildlife Landmark **Obv:** Motopo Hills **Rev:** Cape buffalo

Date	Mintage	F	VF	XF	Unc	BU
1996 Proof	5,000	Value: 55.00				

KM# 9 10 DOLLARS

31.1035 g., 0.9990 Silver 1.0000 oz. ASW **Series:** Wildlife Landmark **Obv:** Zimbabwe Ruins **Rev:** Leopard in a tree

Date	Mintage	F	VF	XF	Unc	BU
1996 Proof	5,000	Value: 55.00				

KM# 10 10 DOLLARS

31.1035 g., 0.9990 Silver 1.0000 oz. ASW **Series:** Wildlife Landmark **Obv:** Kariba Dam **Rev:** Two elephants

Date	Mintage	F	VF	XF	Unc	BU
1996 Proof	5,000	Value: 55.00				

KM# 11 10 DOLLARS

31.1035 g., 0.9990 Silver 1.0000 oz. ASW **Series:** Wildlife Landmark **Obv:** Reserve bank building **Rev:** Rhinoceros

Date	Mintage	F	VF	XF	Unc	BU
1996 Proof	5,000	Value: 55.00				

PROOF SETS

KM#	Date	Mintage	Identification	Issue Price	Mkt Val
PS1	1980 (6)	15,000	KM#1-6	29.00	18.50
PS2	1997 (7)	5,500	KM#1a, 2-6, 12	45.00	50.00

INSTANT IDENTIFIER

Aachen (German States)

Albania

Austria

Baden (German States)

Brandenburg Ansbach (German States)

Finland

Jever (German States)

Frankfurt (German States)

Furstenberg (German States)

Geneva (Swiss Cantons)

German Empire (Yugoslavia)

Montenegro (German States)

Nürnberg (Italian States)

Milan

Prussia (German States)

Russia (Czarist) Russian Poland

Schwarzburg-Rudolstadt (German States)

Schwarzburg-Sondershausen (German States)

Serbia (Yugoslavia)

Teutonic Order (German States)

Genoa (Italian States)

Syrian Arab Republic

United Arab Republic (Egypt, Syria)

Arab Republic of Egypt Libya

Yemen Arab Republic

Bulgaria

Burma (Myanmar)

Ethiopia

Finland

Norway

Gorizia (Italian States)

Hannover (German States)

Hesse-Darmstadt (German States)

Hohenlohe-Neuenstein-Oehringen (German States)

Iran (Persia)

Morocco

Siberia

Tibet (China)

Nepal

Morocco (AH1371-1951AD)

Manchoukuo (Puppet State-China)

Japan

INSTANT IDENTIFIER

Hanau-Munzenberg (German States)

Nassau (German States)

Hesse-Cassel (German States)

Sri Lanka (Ceylon)

Tibet (China)

Utrecht (Netherlands)

Venice (Italian States)

Neuchatel (Swiss Cantons)

China (Empire-Provincial)

China (Empire-Provincial)

Japan

Japan

African States

Bretzenheim (German States)

Hall in Swabia (German States)

Greenland

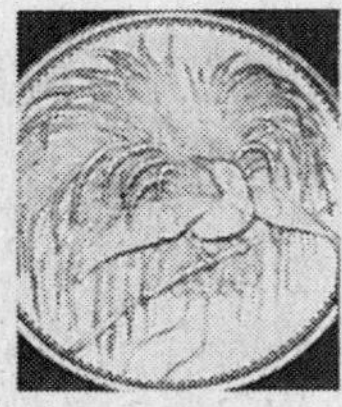
German New Guinea (Papua New Guinea)

Lithuania

Mongolia

Sudan

Algeria

Lowenstein-Wertheim (German States)

Maldive Islands

Afghanistan

Ireland

Israel

Lebanon

Papal States (Italian States)

Regensburg (German States)

Sweden

North Korea

CCCP-Russia

CCCP-Russia

Yugoslavia

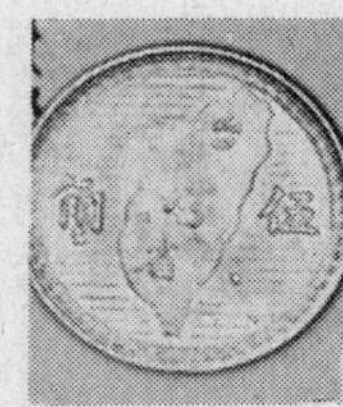
Taiwan (Rep. of China)

Mainz (German States)

Solms-Laubach (German States)

Ticino (Swiss Cantons)

Fugger (German States)

Naples & Sicily (Italian States)

Saxe-Saalfeld (German States)

Stolberg-Stolberg (German States)

INSTANT IDENTIFIER

French Colonial

French Colonial

French Colonial

Bangladesh

Isle of Man
Sicily

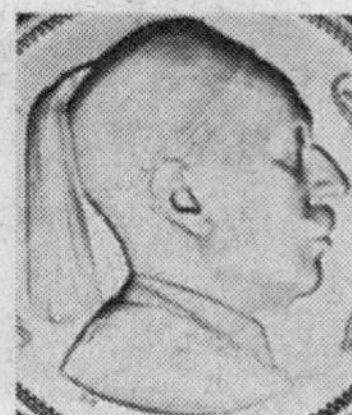
Libya

Anhalt-Bernburg
(German States)

Aargau
(Swiss Cantons)

Augsburg
(German States)

Basel
(Swiss Cantons)

Bavaria
(German States)

Brazil

Bremen
(German States)

Luzern
(Swiss Cantons)

Chur Pfalz
(German States)

Fulda
(German States)

Glarus
(Swiss Cantons)

Grand Duchy
of Warsaw
(Poland)

Graubunden
(Swiss Cantons)

Hamburg
(German States)

Lucca
(Italian States)

Hesse-Cassel
(German States)

Hesse-Homburg
(German States)

Hildesheim
(German States)

Hohenzollern-
Hechingen
(German States)

Hungary

Julich-Berg
(German States)

Gelderland
(Netherlands)

Lippe-Detmold
(German States)

Lübeck
(German States)

Mecklenburg-
Strelitz
(German States)

Oldenburg
(German States)

Passau
(German States)

Portugal

Vaud
(Swiss Cantons)

Anhalt
(Joint Coinage)
(German States)

Oldenburg
(German States)

Schwarzenberg
(German States)

Schaffhausen
(Swiss Cantons)

Paderborn
(German States)

Thurgau
(Swiss Cantons)

Westfrisia
(Netherlands)

INSTANT IDENTIFIER

Arenberg (German States)

Rhenish Confederation (German States)

Reuss-Greiz (German States)

Sardinia (Italian States)

Saxony (German States)

Schaumburg-Lippe (German States)

Schleswig-Holstein (German States)

St. Gall (Swiss Cantons)

Slovakia

Solothurn (Swiss Cantons)

Unterwalden (Nidwalden) (Swiss Cantons)

Württemberg (German States)

Würzburg (German States)

Zurich (Swiss Cantons)

Waldeck-Pyrmont (German States)

Iraq

Pakistan

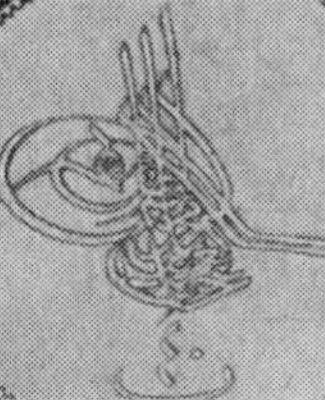
Turkey-Egypt Sudan, Algeria (Ottoman Empire)

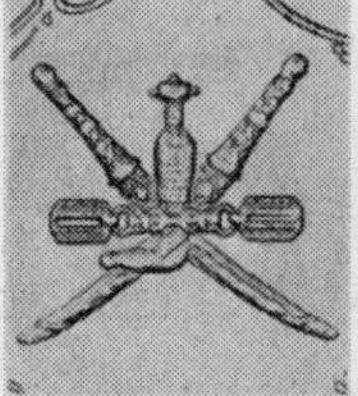
Muscat & Oman, Oman

Saudi Arabia

Tunisia

Wismar (German States)

Order of Malta

Bamberg (German States)

Brunswick-Wolfenbüttel (German States)

Brunswick-Lüneburg (German States

Erfurt Mainz (German States)

Hannover (German States)

Eichstätt (German States)

Greece

Serbia

Switzerland

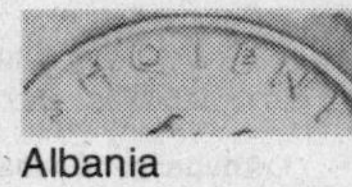
Albania

Thailand (Siam)

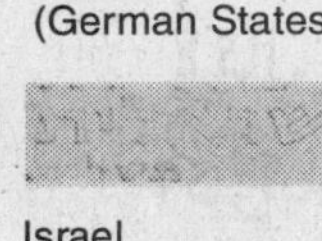
Israel

Japan (Dai Nippon)

South Korea

Sitten (Swiss Cantons)

Rostock (German States)

Saint Alban (German States)

English East India Co. (Sumatra)

China, Japan, Annam, Korea
(All Holed 'cash' coins look quite similar.)

Japan

Korea

ILLUSTRATED GUIDE TO EASTERN MINT NAMES

Compiled by Dr. N. Douglas Nicol, 2006

- **Abarquh** (Iran) — ابرقوه
- **‘Abdullahnagar** (Pihani) — عبدالله نگر
- **Abu Arish** (the Yemen) — ابو عريش
- **Abushahr** (Bushire - Iran) — ابو سهر
- **‘Adan** (Aden-the Yemen) — عدن
- **Adoni** (Imtiyazgarh-Mughal) — ادوني
- **Adrana** (see Edirne)
- **Advani** (Adoni - Mughal) — ادواني
- **Afghanistan** — افغانستان
- **Agra** (Mughal) — اگره
- **Ahmadabad** (Gujarat Sultanate, Mughal, Maratha, Bombay Presidency, Baroda) — احمداباد
- **Ahmadnagar** (Ahmadnagar Sultanate, Mughal) — احمدنگر
- **Ahmadnagar Farrukhabad** (state, Afghanistan) — احمدنگر فرخ اباد
- **Ahmadpur** (Bahawalpur, Afghanistan) — احمدپور
- **Ahmadshahi** (Qandahar - Afghanistan) — احمدشاهي
- **Ahsanabad** (Kulbarga - Mughal) — احسن اباد
- **Ajman** (United Arab Emirates) — عجمان
- **Ajmer** (Salimabad - Mughal, Maratha, Gwalior, Jodhpur) — اجمير
- **Ajmer Salimabad** (Mughal) — اجمير سليم اباد
- **Akalpurakh** (Kashmir, Sikh) — اكال پورخ
- **Akbarabad** (Agra - Mughal, Maratha, Bharatpur) — اكبراباد
- **Akbarnagar** (Rajmahal - Mughal) — اكبرنگر
- **Akbarpur** (Tanda - Mughal) — اكبرپور
- **Akbarpur Tanda** (Mughal) — اكبرپور تانده
- **Akhtarnagar** (Awadh - Mughal) — اخترنگر
- **‘Akka** (Ottoman Turkey) — عكّا عكّة
- **Aksu** (China - Sinkiang) — اقسو اقصو
- **al-Aliya** — العالية
- **‘Alamgirnagar** (Mughal, Koch) — عالمگيرنگر
- **‘Alamgirpur** (Bhilsa, Vidisha-Mughal, Gwalior) — عالم گيرپور
- **Amul** (Iran) — آمل
- **al-‘Arabiya as-Sa‘udiya** (Saudi Arabia) — العربية السعودية
- **al-‘Ara’ish** (Larache - Morocco) — العرائش
- **Algeria** (al-Jaza’ir) — الجزائر
- **‘Alinagar** (Calcutta - Mughal) — علي نگر
- **‘Alinagar Kalkatah** (Calcutta - Bengal Pres.) — علي نگر كلكته
- **Allahabad** (Mughal, Awadh) — الله اباد
- **Almora** (Gurkha)
- **Alwar** (Mughal) — الوار
- **Amaravati** (Hyderabad) — امراوتي
- **Amasya** (Amasia - Turkey) — اماسية
- **Amid** (Turkey) — آمد
- **Amritsar** (Ambratsar - Sikh) — امبرت سر امرت سر
- **Amirkot** (Umarkot - Mughal) — اميركوت
- **Anandgharh** (Anandpur - Mughal) — انندگهره
- **Andijan** (Andigan - Central Asia) — اندجان اندگان
- **Anhirwala Pattan** (Mughal) — انحيروالا پتن
- **Ankaland** (Bi-Ankaland - in England, Birmingham and London mints for Morocco) — انكلند بانكلند
- **Ankara** (Anguriya, Engüriye - Turkey) — انگورية انقرية انقرة
- **Anupnagar Shahabad** (Mughal) — انوپنگر شاه باد
- **Anwala** (Anola - Mughal, Rohilkhand, Afghanistan) — انوله
- **Aqsara** (Aqsaray, Aksara - the Yemen) — اقصرا اقصراي اكصرا
- **Ardabil** (Iran) — اردبيل
- **Ardanuç** (Turkey) — اردنوچ اردانيچ
- **Ardanush** (Iran) — اردنوش
- **Arjish** (Iran) — ارجيش
- **Arkat** (Arcot - Mughal, French India, Madras Presidency) — اركات
- **Asafabad** (Bareli - Mughal, Awadh) — اصف اباد
- **Asafabad Bareli** (Mughal, Awadh) — اصفاباد
- **Asafnagar** (Aklooj - Mughal, Rohilkhand, Awadh) — اصف نگر اصفنگر
- **Asfarayin** (Central Asia, Iran) — اسفراين
- **Asfi** (Safi - Morocco) — اسفي
- **Asir** (Asirgarh - Mughal) — اسير
- **Astarabad** (Central Asia, Iran) — استراباد
- **Atak** (Attock - Mughal, Afghanistan) — اتك
- **Atak Banaras** (Mughal) — اتك بنارس
- **Atcheh** (Sultanate, Netherlands East Indies) — اچه
- **Athani** (Maratha) — اثاني
- **Aurangabad** (Khujista Bunyad - Mughal, Hyderabad) — اورنگ اباد
- **Aurangnagar** (Mughal, Maratha) — اورنگ نگر
- **Ausa** (Mughal) — اوسا
- **Awadh** (Oudh, Khitta - Awadh state) — اوده
- **Awbah** (Central Asia) — اوبه
- **Ayasluk** (Ayasoluq, Ephesus - Turkey) — اياسلق اياثلق
- **Aydaj** (Iran) — ايدج
- **Azak** (Azow - Turkey) — آزاق آزق
- **A‘zamnagar** (Gokak - Mughal) — اعظم نگر
- **A‘zamnagar Bankapur** (Mughal) — اعظم نگر بنكاپور
- **A‘zamnagar Gokak** (Belgaum - Mughal, Kolhapur) — اعظم نگر گوكاك
- **‘Azimabad** (Patna - Mughal, Bengal Presidency) — عظيم اباد
- **Badakhshan** (Mughal, Central Asia, Afghanistan) — بدخشان
- **Bagalkot** (Maratha) — بگلكوت
- **Bagchih Serai** (Krim) — باغچه سراي
- **Baghdad** (Bagdad - Iraq) — بغداد
- **Bahadurgarh** (Mughal) — بهادرگره

Bahawalpur (Bahawalpur state, Afghanistan) بهاولپور

Bahraich (Mughal) بهرايچ بهريچ

Bahrain (al-Bahrayn) البحرين

Bairata (Mughal) بيراتة

Bakhar (Bakkar, Bakhar, Bhakhar, Bhakkar - Mughal, Sind, Afghanistan) بهكّر بهكهر

Baku (Bakuya - Iran) باكو باكويه

Balanagor Gadha (Mandla - Maratha) بالانگر گدها

Balapur (two places - one in Kandesh, one in Sira - Mughal) بالاپور

Balhari (Bellary - Mysore) بلهاري

Balikesir (Turkey) بالكسير

Balkh (Mughal, Central Asia, Afghanistan) بلخ

Balwantnagar (Jhansi - Mughal, Maratha, Gwalior) بلونت نگر

Banaras (Benares, Varanasi - Mughal, Bengal Presidency, Awadh) بنارس

Banda Malwari (Maratha) بنده ملواري

Bandar (Iran) بندر

Bandar Abbas (Iran) بندر عباس

Bandar Abu Shahr (Iran) بندر ابو شهر

Bandar Shahi (Mughal) بندرشاهي

Bandhu (Qila - Mughal) بندحو

Bangala (Mughal) بنگالة

Banjarmasin (Netherlands East Indies) بنجرمسن

Bankapur (Mughal) بنكپ بنكاپور

Baramati (Sultanate, Mughal) بارامتي برامتي

Bareli (Bareilly - Mughal, Rohilkhand, Awadh, Afghanistan) بريلي

Bariz (Paris, in Paris - Morocco) باريز بباريز

Baroda (Vadodara - Baroda state) بروده

Basoda (Gwalior) بسوده

al-Basra (Basra - Iraq) البصرة

Batan (Baltistan? - Ladakh) بتان

Bela (Las Bela state) بيله

Belgrad (Turkey) بنگالور

Bengalur (Bangalor - Mysore) بنگالور

Berar (Mughal) برار

Berlin (for Morocco) برلين

Bhakkar, Bhakhar (See Bakkar)

Bharatpur (Braj Indrapur) بهرت پور

Bhaunagar (Mughal) بهاونگر

Bhelah (See Bela) بهله

Bhilsa (Alamgirpur - Mughal) بهيلسة

Bhilwara (Mewar) بهيلوارا

Bhopal (Bhopal state) بهوپال

Bhuj (Kutch) بهوج

Bhujnagar (Bhuj - Kutch) بهوج نگر

Bidlis (Bitlis - Turkey) بدليس بتليس

Bidrur (Mughal) بدرور

Bihbihan (Behbehan - Iran) بهبهان

Bijapur (Bijapur Sultanate, Mughal) بيجاپور

Bikanir (Mughal, Bikanir state) بيكانير

Bindraban (Vrindavan - Mughal, Bindraban state) بندربن

Bisauli (Rohilkhand) بسولے بسولي

Biyar (Iran) بيار

Borujerd (Iran) بروجرد

Bosna (Sarajevo - Turkey) بوسنه

Bosna Saray (Sarajevo - Turkey) بوسنة سراي

Braj Indrapur (Bharatpur) برج اندرپور

Broach (Baroch, Bharoch - Mughal, Broach state, Gwalior) بروني

Brunei (Malaya) بروني

Bukhara (Central Asia) بخارا

Bukhara-yi Sharif (Central Asia) بخاراي شريف

Bundi (Bundi state) بوندي

Burhanabad (Mughal) برهان اباد

Burhanpur (Mughal, Maratha, Gwalior) برهانپور

Bursa (Brusa - Turkey) برسه بروسه

Bushanj (Iran) بوشنج

Bushire (see Abushahr)

Çaniçe (Chanicha - Turkey) چانيچه چاينيچه

Chakan (Maratha) چاكن

Champanir (Gujarat Sultanate) چانپانير

Chanda (Maratha) چانده

Chanderi (Gwalior) چنديري

Chandor (Maratha, Indore) چاندور

Chhachrauli (Kalsia) چحچرولي

Chhatarpur (Chhatarpur state) چترپور

Chikodi (Maratha) چكودي

Chinapattan (Madras - Mughal) چيناپتن

Chinchwar (Maratha) چنچور

Chitor (Akbarpur - Mughal) چيتور

Chunar (Mughal) چنار

Cuttack (see Katak)

Dadiyan (Iran) داديان

Dalipnagar (Datia) دليپ نگر

Damarvar (Mysore) دماروار

al-Damigh (the Yemen) الدامغ

Damla (Mughal) داملا

Darband (Derbent - Azerbaijan, Iran) دربند

Darfur (see al-Fashir)

Darur (Mughal) درور دارر

Daulatabad (Deogir - Mughal, Hyderabad) دولت اباد دولتاباد

Daulat Anjazanchiya (see Comoros) دولة انجزنچية

Daulatgarh (Rahatgarh - Bharatpur, Gwalior) دولت گره

Daulat Qatar (State of Qatar - Qatar) دولة قطر

Dawar (Iran) داور

al-Dawla al-Mughribiya (Empire of Morocco) الدولة المغربية

Dawlatabad (Iran) دولتاباد

Dawraq (Iran) دورق

Dehdasht (Iran) دهدشت

Dehli (Shahjahanabad - Mughal, Afghanistan) دهلي

Deli (Netherlands East Indies) دلي

Deogarh (Partabgarh) ديوگره

Deogir (Daulatabad - Mughal) ديوگير

Dera (Derah - Mughal, Sikh, Afghanistan) ديره

Derajat (Mughal, Sikh, Afghanistan) ديره جات

Dewal Bandar (Mughal) ديول بندر

Dezful (Iran) دزفول

Dhamar (the Yemen) ذمار ذمر

Dharwar (Mysore) دهاروار

Dholapur (Dholapur state) دهولپور دهولپور

Dicholi (Mughal, Maratha) ديچولي

Dilshadabad (Mughal, Narayanpett) دلشاداباد

Dimashq (Damascus - Syria) دمشق

Diyar Bakr (Turkey) جيبوتي

Djibouti (Jaibuti - French Somaliland) جيبوتي

Dogam (Dogaon - Mughal) دوگام

Dogaon (Mughal) دوگاون

Edirne (Adrianople - Turkey) ادرنه

Elichpur (Mughal, Hyderabad) ايلچپور

Erzurum (Theodosiopolis - Turkey) ارزروم

Faiz Hisar (Gooty - Mysore) فعز حصار

Farahabad (Iran) فرح اباد

Farkhanda Bunyad (Hyderabad - Mughal) فرخنده بنياد

Farrukhabad (Ahmadnagar - Mughal, Bengal Presidency) فرخ اباد

Farrukhi (Feroke - Mysore) فرخي

Farrukhnagar (Mughal) فرخ نگر

Farrukhyab Hisar (Chitradurga - Mysore) فرخياب حصار

Fas (Fez - Morocco) فاس

Fas al-Jadid (see al-Madina al-Bayda' - Morocco) فاش الجديد

al-Fashir (Darfur, Sudan) الفشير

Fathabad Dharur (Mughal) فبح اباد دهرور

Fathnagar (Aurangabad - Mughal) فتحنگر

Fathpur (Nusratabad, Sikri - Mughal) فتحپور

Fedala (Fadalat al-Muhammadiya - Morocco) فضالة

Fergana (Central Asia) فرغانة

Filastin (Palestine) فاسطين

Filibe (Philipopolis, Plovdiv - Turkey) فيليپ فلبه

Firozgarh (Yadgir - Mughal) فيروزگره

Firoznagar (Mughal, Hyderabad) فيروزنگر

al-Fujaira (United Arab Emirates) الفجيرة

Fuman (Iran) فومان

Gadraula (Mughal) گدرولة

Gadwal (Hyderabad) گدوال

Gajjikota (Mughal) گجيكوتا

Ganja (Ganjah, Genje - Elizabethpol, Kirovabad in Azerbaijan, Iran, Turkey) گنجه

Ganjikot (Genjikot - Mughal) گنجيكوت

Gargaon (Assam) گرگاو

Garha (Mughal) گارحة

Gelibolu (Gallipoli - Turkey) گليبولى

Ghazni (Afghanistan) غزني

al-Ghurfa (Hadhramaut) الغرفة

Gilan (Iran) گنلان

Gobindpur (Mughal) گوبندپور

Gohad (Mughal, Dholapur) گوهد

Gokak (Belgaum, 'Azamnagar - Mughal) گوكاك

Gokul (Bindraban) گوكل

Gokulgarh (Mughal) گوكل گره

Gorakpur (Muazzamabad - Mughal) گوركپور

Gözlü (see Shahr-Gözlü - Krim) گوزلو

Gulbarga (Kulbarga, Ahsanabad - Mughal) گلبرگة

Gulkanda (Golkona - Sultanate, Mughal) گلكندة

Gulshanabad (Nasik - Mughal, Maratha) گلشن اباد

Gümüsh-hane (Turkey) گمشخانه

Guti (Gooty - Mughal, Mysore) گوتي

Guzelhisar (Turkey) گوزلحصر

Gwaliar (Mughal, Gwalior state, Gwalior Fort) گواليار

Hafizabad (Mughal) هافظاباد

Haidarabad (Hyderabad, Haidrabad, Farkhanda Bunyad - Golkanda Sultanate, Mughal, Hyderabad state, Sind, Afghanistan) حيدراباد

Haidarnagar (Bednur, Nagar - Mysore) حيدرنگر

Hajipur (Mughal) حجيپور

Halab (Aleppo - Syria) بلب

Hamadan (Iran) همدان

Hansi (Qanauj - Mughal, Awadh) هانسي

al-Haramayn ash-Sharifayn (Mecca and Medina in Arabia - Ottoman Turkey) الشريفين الحرمين

al-Harar (Ethiopia) الهرر

Hardwar (Haridwar, Tirath - Mughal, Saharanpur) هاردوار

Harput, Harburt (see Khartapirt)

Harran (Turkey) حران

Hasanabad (Mughal) حسن اباد

Hathras (Mughal, Awadh) هاتهرس

Hathrasa (Hathras) هاتهرسا

Hawran (Horan - Syria) حوران

Hawta (the Yemen) حوطة

Hawz (Morocco) حوز

al-Hejaz (Saudi Arabia) الحجاز

Herat (Afghanistan, Central Asia, Iran) هراة هرات

al-Hilla (Hille - Iraq) الحلة

Hinganhat (Maratha) حنگنهات

Hisar (Mughal) حصار

Hisar (Central Asia) حصر

Hisar Firoza (Mughal) حصار فيروزة

al-Hisn (el-Hisin - Turkey) الحصن

Hizan (Khizan - Turkey) هزان خيزان

Hukeri (Mughal, Maratha) هوكري

Husaingarh (Mughal) حسين گره

Huwayza (Iran) حويزة

Ibb (the Yemen) ايب

Ilahabad (Allahabad) اله اباد

Ilahabas (Mughal) اله اباس

Ili (China - Sinkiang) الي

al-Imarat al-'Arabiya al-Muttahida (United Arab Emirates) امتيازگره

Imtiyazgarh (Adoni - Mughal) امتيازگره

Indore (Indore state) اندور

Inebolu (Turkey) اينه بولى

Inegöl (Turkey) اينه كول

Iran ايران

al-Iraq

Iravan (Eravan, Erewan, Revan – Iran, Yeravan – Armenia) ايروان

'Isagarh (Gwalior) عيسى گره

Isfahan (Iran) اصفهان

Islamabad (Mathura – Mughal, Bindraban اسلام اباد

Islam Bandar (Rajapur – Mughal) اسلام بندر

Islambul (Istanbul – Turkey) اسلامبول

Islamnagar (Navanagar – Mughal) اسلام نگر

Ismailgarh (Mughal) اسمعيل گره

Italian Somaliland (Somalia) الصومال الايطاليانية

Itawa (Mughal, Maratha, Rohilkhand, Awadh اتاوه اتاوا

Izmir (Turkey) ازمير ازمر

Jabbalpur (Mughal) جَبالپور

Ja'farabad urf Chandor (Indore) جعفراباد عرف چاندور

Jahangirnagar (Dacca - Mughal, Bengal Presidency) جهانگيرنگر

Jaipur (Sawai - Mughal) جي پور

Jaisalmir (Jaisalmir state) جيسلمير

Jalalnagar (Mughal) جلال نگر

Jalalpur (Mughal) جلالپور

Jalaun (Jalon - Maratha) جلون

Jalesar (Mughal) جليسار

Jallandar (Jullundur - Mughal) جالندر جلّندر

Jalnapur (Jalna - Mughal) جالنة پور

Jambusar (Baroda) جمبوسر

Jammu (Jamun - Kashmir) جمون

Jaora (Jaora state) جاوره

Jaunpur (Mughal) جونپور

Java (Netherlands East Indies) جاو جاوا

Jaytapur (Jaiyatpur - Mughal) جيت پور

Jaza'ir (Algiers) جزائر

Jaza'ir Gharb (Algiers) جزائر غرب

al-Jaza'ir-i Gharb (Algiers) الجزائر غرب

Jelu (Jelou - Iran) جلو

Jerba (Cerbe, Gabes - Tunis) جربة

Jering (Jaring, Jerin - Thailand) جريج جرين

Jhalawar (Jhalawar state) جهالاوار

Jinji (Nusratgarh - Mughal) جنجي

Jind (Jind state) جيند

Jodhpur (Mughal, Jodhpur state) جودهپور

Jordan (al-Urdunn) الاردن

al-Jumhuriya al-'Arabiya al-Muttahida (The United Arab Republic - Egypt, Syria and the Yemen) الجمهورية العربية المتحدة

al-Jumhuriya al-'Arabiya al-Suriya (The Arab Republic of Syria) الجمهورية العربية السورية

al-Jumhuriya al-'Arabiya al-Yamaniya (The Arab Republic of the Yemen) الجمهورية العربية اليمنية

al-Jumhuriya al-'Iraqiya (The Republic of Iraq) الجمهورية العراقية

al-Jumhuriya al-Libiya (The Republic of Libya) الجمهورية الليبية

al-Jumhuriya al-Lubnaniya (The Republic of Lebanon) الجمهورية اللبنانية

al-Jumhuriya as-Somal (The Republic of Somalia) الجمهورية الصومال

al-Jumhuriya as-Sudan (The Republic of the Sudan) الجمهورية السودان

al-Jumhuriya as-Sudan al-Dimuqratiya (The Democratic Republic of the Sudan) الجمهورية السودان الديمقراطية

al-Jumhuriya as-Suriiya (The Republic of Syria) الجمهورية السورية

al-Jumhuriya at-Tunisiya (The Republic of Tunisia) الجمهورية العراقية

al-Jumhuriya al-Yaman al-Dimuqratia al-Shu'ubiya (The Peoples' Democratic Republic of the Yemen) الجمهورية اليمن الديمقراطية الشعبية

Jumhuriyeti Turkiye (The Republic of Turkey) جمهوريتى توركيه

Junagarh (Junagadh - Mughal) جونة گره

al-Junub al-Arabi (South Arabia) الجنوب العربي

Kabul (Mughal, Afghanistan) كابل

Kaffa (Krim) كفّة

Kalanur (Mughal) كالانور

Kalat (Kalat state) قلات كلات

Kalian (Kalayani - Hyderabad) كليان

Kalikut (Calicut, Kozhikode - Mysore) كليكوت

Kalkatah (Calcutta, Alinagar - Mughal, Bengal Presidency) كلكته

Kalpi (Mughal, Maratha) كلپي

Kanauj (Qanauj - Mughal, Awadh) قنوج

Kanauj urf Shahgarh (Qanauj - Mughal, Awadh) قنوج عرف شاه گره

Kanbayat (Kambayat, Kanbat, Khambayat - Mughal, Cambay state) كمبايت كهنبايت كنبات كنبايت

Kandahar (see Qandahar)

Kangun (Hosakote - Mughal) كنگون

Kanji (Conjeeveram - Mughal) كنجي

Kankurti (Mughal, Maratha) كانكرتي

Kara Amid (Turkey) قره آمد

Karahisar (Qara-Hisar - Turkey) قراحصار قره حسار

Kararabad (Karad - Mughal) كراراباد

Karatova (Kratova - Turkey) قراطوه قراطوه

Karauli (Karauli state) كرولي

Karimabad (Mughal) كريم اباد

Karnatak (Carnatic - Mughal) كرناتك

Karpa (Kurpa - Mughal) كرپا

Kars (Qars - Turkey) قارص قارس

Kashan (Iran) كاشان

Kashgar (China - Sinkiang) كاشغر كشقر

Kashmir (Srinagar - Kashmir Sultanate, Mughal, Sikh, Afghanistan) كشمير

Kastamonu (Turkey) قسطموني

Katak (Cuttack - Mughal, Maratha) كتك

Katak Banaras (Mughal) كتك بنارس

Kawkaban (the Yemen) كوكبان

Kayeri (Turkey) قيصري قيسري

Kedah (Straits Settlements, Malaya) كداه

Kelantan (Straits Settlements, Malaya) كلنتن

Kemasin (Straits Settlements, Malaya) كماسن

Khairabad (Mughal) خيراباد

Khairnagar (Mughal) خيرنگر

Khairpur (Mughal, Sind) خيرپور

Khaliqabad (Dindigal - Mysore) خالق اباد

Khambayat (Kanbayat - Mughal) كمنبايت

Khanabad (Afghanistan) خان اباد

Khanja (Canca, Hanca - Turkey) خانجة خانجا

Khanpur (Bahawalpur) خانپور

Khartapirt (Harput, Harburt - Turkey) خرتبرت
خربت خربرت

Khizan (Turkey) خيزان

Khoqand (Central Asia) خوقند

Khotan (Khutan, China - Sinkiang) خوتن ختن

Khoy (Khoi, Khui - Iran) خوي

Khujista Bunyad (Aurangabad - Mughal, Hyderabad) خجسته بنياد

al-Khurfa (the Yemen) الخرفاة

Khurshid Sawad (Mysore) خورشيد سواد

Khwarizm (Central Asia) خوارزم

Kighi (Turkey) كيغي

Kirman (Kerman - Iran) كرمان

Kirmanshahan (Kermanshah - Iran) كرمانساهان

Kishangar (Kishangar state) كشنگره

Kishtwar (Mughal) كشتوار

Koçaniye (Kochana - Turkey) قوچانية

Koilkunda (Mughal) كويلكونده

Kolapur (Mughal, Kolhapur) كولاپور كلاپور

Konya (Turkey) قونية

Kora (Mughal, Maratha, Awadh) كورا

Kosantina (see Qusantinia)

Kosova (Kosovo - Turkey) قوصوه قوسوه

Kostantaniye (see Qustantaniya)

Kotah (Kotah state) كوته

Kotah urf Nandgaon كوته عرف نندگانو

Kubrus (Cyprus - Turkey) قبرص

Kuch Hijri (Kunch) كوچ حجري

Kuchaman (Mughal) كچامن

Kuche (China - Sinkiang) كوچا

Kufan (Kufin - Central Asia) كوفن كوفين

Kulbarga (see Gulbarga)

Kumber (Kumbar - see Maha Indrapur)

Kunar (Maratha) كنار

Kunch (Maratha) كونچ

Kurdasht (Azerbaijan) كرداشت كردشت

Kuwait (al-Kuwayt) الكويت

Ladakh (Ladakah - Kashmir, Afghanistan) لداكه لداخ

Lahej (the Yemen) لحج

Lahijan (Iran) لاهيجان

Lahore (Lahur - Mughal, Sikh, Afghanistan) لاهور

Lahri Bandar (Mughal) لهري بندر

Lar (Iran) لار

Larenda (Turkey) لارندة

Lashkar (Gwalior) لاشكار

Lebanon (Lubnan) لبنان

Legeh (Thailand) لغكه

Libya ليبيا

Lucknow (Lakhnau - Mughal, Awadh) لكهنو

Machhli Bandar (Masulipatam) مچهلي بندر

Machhlipatan (Masulipatam - Mughal, French India, Madras Pres.) مچهلي پتن

Madankot (Mughal) مدنكوت

al-Madina al-Bayda' (see Fas al-Jadid - Morocco) المدينة البيضاء

Madrid (for Morocco) مدريد

al-Maghrib (Morocco) المغرب

Maha Indrapur (Dig, Kumbar - Mughal, Bharatpur) مهه اندرپور

Mahle (Male - Maldive Islands) محلي

Mahmud Bandar (Porto Novo - Mughal) محمودبندر

Mahoba (Maratha) مهوبة

Mailapur (Madras - Mughal) ميلاپور

Makhsusabad (Murshidabad - Mughal) مخصوص اباد

Malharnagar (Indore, also for Maheshwar) ملهارنگر

Malher (Malhar, Mulher - Mughal) ملهر

Maliknagar (Mughal) ملك نگر

Malnapur (Mughal) مالناپور

Malpur (Mughal) مالپور

Maluka (Netherlands East Indies) ملوكة

al-Mamlaka al-'Arabiya as-Sa'udiya (The Kingdom of Saudi Arabia) المملكة العربية السعودية

al-Mamlaka al-Libiya (The Kingdom of Libya) المملكة الليبية

al-Mamlaka al-Maghribiya (The Kingdom of Morocco) المملكة المغربية

al-Mamlaka al-Misriya (The Kingdom of Egypt) المملكة المصرية

al-Mamlaka al-Mutawakkiliya al-Yamaniya (The Mutawakkilite Kingdom of the Yemen) المملكة المتوكلية اليمنية

al-Mamlaka al-Tunisiya (The Kingdom of Tunisia) المملكة التونسية

al-Mamlaka al-Urdunniya al-Hashimiya (The Hashimite Kingdom of Jordan) الاردنية الهاشمية

Manastir (Turkey) مناستر

Mandasor (Gwalior) منديسور

Mandla (Maratha) مندلا

Mandu (Mughal) مندو

Mangarh (Mughal) مانگره

Manghir (Monghyr - Bihar) مانگهير

Manikpur (Mughal) مانکپور

Maragha (Azerbaijan, Iran) مراغة

Marakesh (Marrakech - Morocco) مراكش

Mar'ash (Turkey) مرعش

Mardin (Turkey) ماردين

Marv (Central Asia, Iran) ماروار

Marwar (Jodhpur, Nagor, Pali, Sojat) ماروار

al-Mu'askar (Mascara - Algeria) المعسكر

Mashhad (Iran) مشهد

Mashhad Imam Rida (Iran) مشهد امام رضى

Mathura (Islamabad - Mughal, Bindraban) متهره

Mazandaran (Iran) مازندران

Mecca (Makkah - al-Hejaz) مكّة

Medea (Algeria) مدية

Meknes (Miknas - Morocco) مكناس

Menangkabau (Netherlands East Indies) منڤكابو

Merta (Mirath - Mughal, Jodhpur) ميرتا ميرتة

Misr (Egypt, Turkey) مصر

Modava (Moldava - Turkey) موداوه مداوه

Mombasa (Kenya) موداوه مداوه

Mosul (al-Mawsil - Iraq) موصل الموصل

Muazzamabad (Gorakpur - Mughal, Awadh) معظم اباد

Muhammadabad (Udaipur - Mughal) محمداباد

Muhammadabad Banaras (Mughal, Awadh, Bengal Presidency, fictitious for Lucknow) محمداباد بنارس

Muhammadabad urf Kalpi (Kalpi) محمداباد عرف كلپي

al-Muhammadiya (al-Masila - Morocco) المحمدية

al-Muhammadiya ash-Sharifa (Morocco) المحمدية الشريفة

Muhammadnagar Tandah (Awadh) محمدنگر تانده

Muhiabad Poona (Maratha) محيى اباد پونه

Mujahidabad (Mughal) مجاهداباد

Mujibalanagar (Rohilkhand) مجى بالانگر

al-Mukala (the Yemen) المكلا

Mukha (Mocca - the Yemen) مخا

Mukhtara (the Yemen) مختارة

Müküs (Turkey) مكس

Multan (Mughal, Sikh, Afghanistan) ملتان

Muminabad (Bindraban) مؤمن اباد

Munbai (Mumbai, Bombay - Mughal, Bombay Presidency) منبي

Mungir (Mughal) مهنگير

Muradabad (Mughal, Rohilkhand, Awadh, Afghanistan) مراداباد

Murshidabad (Makhsusabad - Mughal, French India, Bengal Pres.) مرشداباد

Murtazabad (Mughal) مرتضاباد

Muscat (Oman) مسقط

Mustafabad (Rampur - Rohilkhand) مصطفاباد

Muzaffargarh (Jhajjar - Mughal) مظفرگره

Mysore (Mahisur - Mysore state) مهيسور مهي سور

Nabha (Sirkar - Nabha state) سركار نابهه

Nagar (Ahmadnagar, Bednur - Maratha, Mysore) نگر

Nagar Ijri (Srinagar in Bundelkand) نگر يجري

Nagor (Mughal, Jodhpur) ناگور

Nagpur (Maratha) ناگپور

Nahan (Sirmur) ناهن

Nahtarnagar (Trichinopoly - Arcot) نهتر نگر

Najafgarh (Mughal, Rohilkhand) نجف گره

Najibabad (Mughal, Sikh, Rohilkhand, Awadh, Afghanistan) نجيب اباد نجيباباد

Nakhjuvan (Iran, Azerbaijan) نخجوان

Nandgaon (Nandgano - Kotah) نندگانو

Nandgaon urf Kotah نندگانو عرف كوته

Narnol (Mughal) نارنول

Narwar (Sipri - Mughal, Gwalior, Narwar state) نرور

Nasirabad (Sagar, Wanparti - Hyderabad) نصر اباد

Nasirabad (Dharwar - Mughal) نصيراباد

Nasiri (Iran) ناصري

Nasrullahnagar (Rohilkhand) نصرالله نگر

Nazarbar (Mysore) نظربار

Nejd (Saudi Arabia) نجد

Nigbolu (Turkey) نگبولو

Nihavand (Iran) نهاوند

Nimak (Sikh) نمك

Nimruz (Central Asia, Iran) نمرز نيمروز

Nipani (Maratha) نپني

Nisa (Iran) نسا

Nishapur (Naysabur - Iran) نيشاپور

Novabirda (Novoberda - Turkey) نوابرده

Novar (Turkey) نوار

Nukhwi (Iran, Azerbaijan) نخوي

Nusratabad (Dharwar, Nasratabad, Fathpur - Mughal) نصرت اباد

Nusratgarh (Jinji - Mughal) نصرت گره

Ohri (Okhri, Ochrida - Turkey) اوخري

Oman ('Uman) عمان

Omdurman (Umm Durman - the Sudan) ام درمان

Orchha (Orchha state) اورچهه

Ordu-Bagh (Iran) اوردوباغ

Ordu-yi Humayun (Turkey) اردو همايون

Orissa (Mughal) اوريسة

Pahang (Straits Settlements) فاحغ

Pakistan پاكستان

Palembang (Netherlands East Indies) فلمبغ

Palestine (see Filastin)

Pali (Jodhpur) پالي

Panahabad (Iran, Karabagh) پناه اباد

Panipat پاني پت
(Mughal)

Parenda پرينده پرنده
(Purenda - Mughal)

Parnala (Qila) پرنالا (قلع)
(Mughal)

Patan پتن
(Seringapatan - Mysore)

al-Patani الفطاني
(Patani - Thailand)

Pathankot پشنكوت

Patna پتنة
(Azimabad - Mughal, Bengal Presidency)

Pattan پتن
(Anhirwala - Mughal)

Pattan Deo پتن ديو
(Somnath – Mughal)

Perak فيرق
(Straits Settlements, Malaya)

Peshawar پشاور
(Mughal, Sikh, Afghanistan, Iran)

Petlad پتلاد
(Baroda)

Phonda پهونده
(Mughal)

Pondichery پرچري
(Pholcheri - French India)

Pondichery پرچري
(Porcheri - French India)

Poona پونه
(Punah, Pune, Muhiabad - Mughal, Maratha)

Pulu Malayu فولو ملايو
(IslandoftheMalays-Sumatra, Netherlands East Indies)

Pulu Penang فولو فنيغ
(Penang, Prince of Wales Island - Straits Settlements, Malaya)

Pulu Percha فولو فرج
(Island of Sumatra - Netherlands East Indies)

Punamali پونامالي
(Mughal)

Punch پونچ
(Mughal)

Purbandar پوربندر
(Porbandar - Mughal)

Qafsa قفصة
(Capsa - Tunis, Tunisia)

al-Qahira القاهرة
(Cairo - Egypt)

Qaiti القعياطي
(the Yemen)

Qamarnagar قمرنگر
(Karnul - Mughal)

Qanauj
(see Kanauj)

Qandahar قندهار
(Ahmadshahi - Mughal, Afghanistan, Iran)

Qarshi قرشي
(Central Asia)

Qasbah Panipat قصبة پاني پت
(Rohilkhand)

Qatar wa Dubai قطر و دبي
(Qatar and Dubai - Qatar)

Qazvin قزوين
(Iran)

Qubba قبة
(Azerbaijan)

Qumm قم
(Qomm - Iran)

Qunduz قندوز
(Central Asia)

Qusantinia قسنطينية قسطنطينة قسنطينة
(Qustantina, Qusantina - Constantine, Algiers)

Qustantaniya قسطنطنية
(Constantinople - Turkey)

Rabat رباط
(Morocco)

Rabat al-Fath رباط الفتح
(Rabat - Morocco)

Rada' راداء
(the Yemen)

Radhanpur رادهنپور
(Radhanpur state)

Rajapur راجاپور
(Islam Bandar - Mughal)

Rajgarh راج گره
(Alwar)

Ramhurmuz رامهرمز
(Iran)

Ra'nash رعنش
(Ramhurmuz - Iran)

Rangpur رنگپور
(Assam)

Ranthor رنتهور
(Ranthambhor - Mughal)

Ras al-Khaima رأس الخيمة
(United Arab Emirates)

Rasht رشت
(Resht - Iran)

Ratlam رتلام
(Ratlam state)

Ravishnagar Sagar روش نگر ساگر
(Garhakota - Gwalior)

Rehman رحمن
(Reman - Thailand)

Revan روان
(Iravan - Armenia)

Rewan ريوان
(Rewa)

Reza'iyeh رضائية
(Urumi - Iran)

Rikab ركاب
(Rekab - Afghanistan, Iran)

Rohtas رحتاس رهتاس
(Rohtak - Mughal)

Rudana ردانة
(Taroudant - Morocco)

Ruha الرها رها رهى
(al-Ruha - Turkey)

Sa'adnagar سعدنگر
(Aklaj - Mughal)

Sabzavar سبزوار
(Iran)

Sa'da صعدة
(the Yemen)

Sagar ساگر
(Maratha, Bengal Pres.)

Saharanpur سهارنپور
(Mughal)

Sahibabad Hansi صاحب اباد هنسي
(Hansi state)

Sahrind سرهند سهرند
(Sarhind - Mughal, Cis-Sutlej Patiala, Afghanistan)

Sailana سيلانه
(Sailana state)

Saimur سيمور
(Mughal)

al-Saiwi السيوي
(Sai, Saiburi, Teluban - Thailand)

Sakiz سكيز ساقز
(Saqyz, Scio - Turkey)

Sakkhar سكهر
(Mughal)

Sala سلا
(Sale - Morocco)

Salamabad سلام اباد
(Satyamangalam - Mysore)

Salimabad سليم اباد
(Ajmer - Mughal)

Samandra سمندره
(Turkey)

Samarqand سمرقند
(Central Asia)

San'a صنعاء
(the Yemen)

Sanbal سنبل
(Sambhal - Mughal)

Sanbhar سانبهر
(Sambhar - Mughal)

Sangamner سنگمنر
(Mughal)

Sangli سنگلي
(Maratha)

al-Saniya السنية
(Turkey)

Sarakhs سرخس
(Iran)

Sarangpur سارنگپور
(Mughal)

Saray سراي
(Turkey)

Sari ساري
(Iran)

Sari Pol سر پل
(Afghanistan)

Sarhind
(see Sahrind)

Sashti
(in Devanagari) (Maratha)

Satara ستارا
(Mughal)

Saudi Arabia العربية السعودية
(see al-Hejaz, Nejd)

Sawai Jaipur سواي جيپور
(Jaipur, fictitious for Karauli)

Sawai Madhopur سواي مادهوپور
(Jaipur, fictitious for Sikar)

Sawuj Balaq ساوج بلاق
(Iran)

Selam سيلم
(Selam state)

Selanghur
(Selangor - Straits Settlements, Malaya) سلاغور

Selanik
(Salonika - Turkey) سلانيك

Selefke
(Turkey) سلفكه

Semnan
(Simnan - Iran) سمنان

Serbernik
(Turkey) سربرنيك

Serez
(see Siroz - Turkey) سرز سريز

Seringapatan
(Mysore)

Shadiabad Urf Mandu
(Mughal) شادياباد ارف مندو

Shadman
(Central Asia) شادمان

Shadora
(Gwalior) شادهوره

Shahabad
(Awadh) شاه اباد قنوج شاهاباد

Shahabad Qanauj
(Mughal, Rohilkhand, Awadh) شاه اباد قنوج

Shahgarh Qanauj
(Mughal) شاه گره قنوج

Shahjahanabad
(Dehli - Mughal, Bhilwara, Bindraban, Chitor, Mathura, Shapura, Udaipur, also fictitious for Bagalkot, Jaisalmir, Satara-EIC) شاه جهان اباد

Shahr-Gözlü
(see Gözlü - Krim) شهرگوزلو

Shakola
(Mughal) شكولا

Shamakhi
(Shamakha, Shemakhi - Iran, Azerbaijan) شماخي شماخه

Sharakat Almaniya
(German East Africa Co.) شراكة المانيا

ash-Sharja
(Sharja - United Arab Emirates) الشارجة

Shekki
(Iran) شكّى

Sheopur
(Gwalior) شيوپور

Shergarh
(Shirgarh - Mughal) شيرگره

Sherkot
(Mughal) شيركوت

Sherpur
(Shirpur - Mughal) شيرپور

Shikarpur
(Sind) شكارپور

Shiraz
(Iran) شيراز

Shirvan
(Azerbaijan, Iran, Turkey) شيروان شروان

Sholapur
(Mughal) شولاپور

Shustar
(Iran) شوستر

Siak
(Netherlands East Indies) سيك

Sidrekipsi
(Turkey) بسدره قپسى

Siirt
(Sa'irt - Turkey) سعرت

Sijilmasa
(Sizilmassa - Morocco) سجلماسة

Sikakul
(Chicacole - Mughal) سيكاكل

Sikandarah
(Sikandra – Mughal) سكندره

Sind
(Mughal, Sind state, Afghanistan, Iran) سند

Singgora
(Thailand) سڠگورا

Sira
(Mughal) سيرة

Sironj
(Mughal, Indore, Tonk) سرونج

Siroz
(see Serez - Turkey) سيروز

Sistan
(Iran) سيستان

Sitamau
(Sitamo) سيتامو

Sitapur
(Mughal) سيتاپور

Sitpur
(Sidhpur in Gujarat? - Mughal) سيتپور

Sivas
(Siwas - Turkey) سيواس

Sofia
(Turkey) صوفية

Sojat
(Jodhpur) سوجت

al-Somal al-Italyaniya
(Italian Somaliland, Somalia) الصومال الايطاليانية

Srebernice
(Serbernichna - Turkey) سربرنيچه

Sri
(Amritsar) سري

Sri Akalpur
(Malkarian) سري اكلپور

Srinagar
(Mughal, Garhwal, Kashmir) سرينگر

Srinagar
(in Bundelkhand - Maratha) سرينگر

Sultanabad
(Iran) سلطاناباد

Sultanpur
(Mughal) سلطانپور

Sumenep
(Netherlands East Indies) سمنف

Surat
(Mughal, French India, Bombay Presidency, fictitious for Chand) سورت

Suriya
(Syria) سورية

al-Suwair/al-Suwaira
(Essaouir, Essaouira - Mogador, Morocco) السوير الصويرة

Tabaristan
(Iran) طبرستان

Tabriz
(Iran, Turkey) تبريز

Tadpatri
(Mughal) تدپتري

Ta'izz
(the Yemen) تعز

Tanah Malayu
(Land of the Malays - Sumatra, Malacca, Straits Settlements) تانة ملايو

Tana Ugi
(Land of the Bugis - Netherlands East Indies) تانة اغيسى

Tanda
(Akbarpur - Bengal Sultanate, Mughal, Awadh) تانده

Tanja
(Tangier - Morocco) طنجة

Tappal
(Mughal) تپّل

Taqidemt
(Algiers) تاقدمت

Tarablus
(Tripoli in Lebanon) طرابلس

Tarablus Gharb
(Tripoli West - in Libya) طرابلس غرب

Tarapatri
(Mughal) تراپتري

Tarim
(the Yemen) تريم

Tashkand
(Tashkent - Central Asia) تشكند

Tashqurghan
(Afghanistan) تاشقورغان

Tatta
(Tattah - Mughal, Sind, Afghanistan) تته

Tehran
(Iran) طهران

Tellicherry
(French India, Bombay Presidency) تلجري تالچري

Termez
(Central Asia) ترمذ

Tetuan
(Tetouan, Titwan - Morocco) تطوان

Tibet
(Mughal, Ladakh) تبت

Tiflis
(Georgia, Iran) تفليس

Tilimsan
(Tlemcen, Aghadir - Algiers) تلمسان

Tirat Hardwar
(Hardwar) تيرتهردوار

Tire
(Turkey) تيره

Tokat
(Tuqat - Turkey) توقاط توقات
دوقات طوقات

Tonk
(Tonk state) تونك

Toragal
(Mughal, Maratha) تورگل توراگال

Trabzon
(Trebizond - Turkey) طرابزون طرابزن

Trengganu
(Straits Settlements, Malaya) ترغگانو

Tunis
(Tunisia) تونس

Tuyserkan
(Iran) توي سركان

Udaipur
(Muhammadabad - Mughal) اوديپور اديپور

Udgir
(Mughal) ادگير

Ujjain
(Mughal, Gwalior) اجين

Ujjain Dar al-Fath (Gwalior) اجين دارالفتح

Ujjainpur (Mughal) اجين پور

Umarkot (Mughal) امركوت

Umm al-Qalwain (United Arab Emirates) ام القيوين

United Arab Emirates (see al-Imarat al-'Arabiya al-Muttahida)

Urdu (Camp mint - Mughal, Central Asia, Iran) اردو

Urdu Dar Rahi-i-Dakkin (Mughal) اردو دار راه دكين

Urdu Zafar Qirin (Mughal) اردو ظفر قرين

al-Urdunn (Jordan) الاردن

Urumchi (China - Sinkiang) ارومچي

اورومي ارومية

Urumi (Urumia, Urmia, Reza'iya - Iran) ارمية

Ushi (China - Sinkiang) اوش

Üsküp (Uskub, Skopje, Kosovo - Turkey) اسكوپ

Van (Wan - Turkey, Armenia) وان

Varne (Turkey) ورنه

al-Yaman (the Yemen) اليمن

Yarkand (China - Sinkiang) يارقند

Yarkhissarmaran (China - Sinkiang) ياركسارمرن

Yazd (Iran) يزد

Yenishehr (Larissa - Turkey) ينكى شهر

Za (Taorirt - Morocco) صا

Zabid (the Yemen) زبيد

Zafarabad (Bidar - Mughal, Gurramkonda - Mysore) ظفراباد

Zafarnagar (Fathabad - Mughal) ظفرنگر

Zafarpur (Mughal) ظفرپور

Zain-ul-Bilad (Ahmadabad - Mughal) زين البلاد

Zanjibar (Zanjibara - Zanzibar) زنجبار زنجبارا

Zebabad (Mughal, Sardhanah) زيب اباد

Zegam (Zigam - Iran) زگام

Zinjan (Zanjan - Iran) زنجان

al-Zuhra (the Yemen) الزهرة

MINT EPITHETS

Geographical Terms:

Baldat (City - Agra, Allahabad, Burhanpur, Bikanir, Patna, Sarhind, Ujjain) بلدات

Bandar (Port - Dewal, Hari, Surat, Machhlipatan) بندر

Dakhil (Breach, Entrance - Chitor) داخل

Dawla/Daula (State, State of) دولة

Hazrat (Royal Residence - Fas, Marakesh, Dehli) حضرة

Khitta (District - Awadh, Kalpi, Kashmir, Lakhnau) خطة

Negri (State of - Straits Settlements, Malaya, Netherlands East Indies, Thailand) نكري

Qasba (Town - Panipat, Sherkot) قصبة

Qila (Fort - Agra, Alwar, Bandhu, Gwalior, Punch) قلعة قلع

Qila Muqam (Fort Residence - Gwalior) قلعة مقام

Qita (District - Bareli) قطة

Sarkar (County - Lakhnau, Torgal) سركار

Shahr (City - Anhirwala Pattan) شهر

Suba (Province - Awadh) سوبة

Tirtha (Shrine - Hardwar) ترتة

Poetic Allusion:

Ashraf al-Bilad (Most Noble of Cities - Qandahar/Ahmadshahi) اشراف البلاد

Baldat-i-Fakhira (Splendid City - Burhanpur) بلدات فخيرة

Bandar-i-Mubarak (Blessed Port - Surat) بندر مبارك

Dar-ul-Aman (Abode of Security - Agra, Jammu, Multan, Sarhind) دار الامان

Dar-ul-Barakat (Abode of Blessings - Jodhpur, Nagor) دار البركات

Dar-ul-Fath (Seat of Conquest - Ujjain) دار الفتح

Dar-ul-Islam (Abode of Islam - Bahawalpur, Dogaon, Mandisor) دار الاسلام

Dar-ul-Jihad (Seat of Holy War - Hyderabad) دار الجهاد

Dar-ul-Khair (Abode of Beneficence - Ajmer) دار الخير

Dar-ul-Khilafa (Abode of the Caliphate - Agra, Ahmadabad, Akbarabad, Akbarpur Tanda, Awadh, Bahraich, Daulatabad, Dogaon, Gorakpur, Gwalior, Jaunpur, Kanauj, Lahore, Lakhnau, Malpur, Shahgarh, Shahjahanabad, Tehran, the Yemen) دار الخلافة

Dar-ul-Mansur (Abode of the Victorious - Ajmer, Jodhpur) دار المنصور

Dar-ul-Mulk (Seat of Kingship - Dehli, Fathpur, Kabul) دار الملك

Dar an-Nusrat (Abode of Succor - Herat) دار النصرات

Dar-ur-Riyasa (Seat of the Chief of State - Jaisalmir) دار الرياسة

Dar-us-Salam (Abode of Peace - Dogaon, Mandisor, Legeh) دار السلام

Dar-us-Saltana (Seat of the Sultanate - Ahmadabad, Burhanpur, Fathpur, Herat, Kabul, Kora, Lahore) دار السلطنة

Dar-ul-Surur (Abode of Happiness - Bahawalpur, Burhanpur, Saharanpur) دار السرور

Dar-uz-Zafar (Seat of Victory - Advani, Bijapur) دار الظفر

Dar-uz-Zarb (Seat of the Mint - Jaunpur, Kalpi, Patna) دار الضرب

Farkhanda Bunyad (Of Auspicious Foundation - Hyderabad) فرخنده بنياد

Hazrat (Venerable - Dehli) حضرت

Khujista Bunyad (Of Fortunate Foundation - Aurangabad) خجستة بنياد

Mustaqarr-ul-Khilafa (Residence of the Caliphate - Akbarabad, Ajmer) مستقر الخلافة

Mustaqarr-ul-Mulk (Abode of Kingship - Akbarabad, Azimabad) مستقر الملك

Sawai (One-fourth, i.e. "a notch better" - Jaipur) سواي

Umm al-Bilad (Mother of Cities - Balkh) ام البلاد

Zain-ul-Bilad (The Most-Beautiful of Cities – Ahmadabad) زين البلاد

BOCA RATON PUBLIC LIBRARY, FLORIDA
3 3656 0421693 0